D0924769

New American Standard Bible

Reference Edition

COLLINS WORLD

©THE LOCKMAN FOUNDATION
1960, 1962, 1963, 1968, 1971, 1972, 1973, 1975

A Corporation Not for Profit

La Habra, CA

Producers of Amplified Translations

All Rights Reserved

Printed in the United States of America

To Be Read

SCRIPTURAL PROMISE

"The grass withers, the flower fades, but the Word of our God stands forever." Isaiah 40:8

FOREWORD

The New American Standard Bible has been produced with the conviction that the words of Scripture as originally penned in the Hebrew and Greek were inspired by God. Since they are the eternal Word of God, the Holy Scriptures speak with fresh power to each generation, to give wisdom that leads to salvation, that men may serve God to the glory of Christ.

The Editorial Board had a two-fold purpose in making this translation: to adhere as closely as possible to the original languages of the Holy Scriptures, and to make the translation in a fluent and readable style according to current English usage.

THE FOURFOLD AIM

OF

THE LOCKMAN FOUNDATION

1. These publications shall be true to the original Hebrew and Greek.
2. They shall be grammatically correct.
3. They shall be understandable to the masses.
4. They shall give the Lord Jesus Christ His proper place, the place which the Word gives Him; therefore, no work will ever be personalized.

PRINCIPLES OF TRANSLATION

Greek Text: Consideration was given to the latest available manuscripts with a view to determining the best Greek text. In most instances the 23rd edition of the Nestle Greek New Testament was followed.

Modern English Usage: The attempt has been made to render the grammar and terminology in contemporary English. When it was felt that the word-for-word literalness was unacceptable to the modern reader, a change was made in the direction of a more current English idiom. In the instances where this has been done, the more literal rendering has been indicated in the notes.

Alternative Readings: In addition to the more literal renderings, notations have been made to include alternate translations, readings of variant manuscripts and explanatory equivalents of the text. Only such notations have been used as have been felt justified in assisting the reader's comprehension of the terms used by the original author.

Hebrew Text: In the present translation the latest edition of Rudolph Kittel's BIBLIA HEBRAICA has been employed together with the most recent light from lexicography, cognate languages, and the Dead Sea Scrolls.

Hebrew Tenses: Consecution of tenses in Hebrew remains a puzzling factor in translation. The translators have been guided by the requirements of a literal translation, the sequence of tenses, and the immediate and broad contexts.

Greek Tenses:

1. A careful distinction has been made in the treatment of the Greek aorist tense (usually translated as the English past, "He did") and the Greek imperfect tense (rendered either as English past progressive, "He was doing"; or, if inceptive, as "He *began* to do" or "He started to do"); or else if customary past, as "He used to do." "Began" is italicized if it renders an imperfect tense, in order to distinguish it from the Greek verb for "begin."

2. On the other hand, not all aorists have been rendered as English pasts ("He did"), for some of them are clearly to be rendered as English perfects ("He has done"), or even as past perfects ("He had done"), judging from the context in which

they occur. Such aorists have been rendered as perfects or past perfects in this translation.

3. As for the distinction between aorist and present imperatives, the translators have usually rendered these imperatives in the customary manner, rather than attempting any such fine distinction as, "Begin to do!" (for the aorist imperative), or, "Continually do!" (for the present imperative).
4. As for sequence of tenses, the translators took care to follow English rules rather than Greek in translating Greek presents, imperfects and aorists. Thus, where English says, "We knew that he was doing," Greek puts it, "We knew that he does"; similarly, "We knew that he had done," is the Greek, "We knew that he did." Likewise, the English, "When he had come, they met him," is represented in Greek by: "When he came, they met him." In all cases a consistent transfer has been made from the Greek tense in the subordinate clause to the appropriate tense in English.
5. In the rendering of negative questions introduced by the particle **mē** (which always expects the answer, "No") the wording has been altered from a mere, "Will he not do this?" to a more accurate, "He will not do this, will he?"

The Proper Name for God: To professing Christians, the name of God is most significant and understandably so. It is inconceivable to think of spiritual matters without a proper designation for the Supreme Deity. Thus the most common name for deity is God, a translation of the original Elohim. The normal word for Master is Lord, a rendering of Adonai. There is yet another name which is particularly assigned to God as His special or proper name, that is, the four letters YHWH. See Exodus 3 and Isaiah 42:8. This name has not been pronounced by the Jews because of reverence for the great sacredness of the divine name. Therefore, it was consistently pronounced and translated LORD. The only exception to this translation of YHWH is when it occurs in immediate proximity to the word Lord, that is, Adonai. In that case it is regularly translated GOD in order to avoid confusion.

It is known that for many years YHWH has been transliterated as Yahweh, however no complete certainty attaches to this pronunciation.

The Lockman Foundation

EXPLANATION OF GENERAL FORMAT

NOTES AND CROSS REFERENCES are placed in a column in the center of the page and listed under verse numbers to which they refer. Superior numbers refer to literal renderings, alternate translations, or explanations. Superior letters refer to cross references. Cross references in italics are parallel passages.

PARAGRAPHS are designated by bold face numbers or letters.

QUOTATION MARKS are used in the text in accordance with modern English usage.

"THOU, THY AND THEE" are changed to "you" except in the language of prayer when addressing Deity.

PERSONAL PRONOUNS are capitalized when pertaining to Deity.

ITALICS are used in the text to indicate words which are not found in the original Hebrew or Greek but implied by it. Italics are used in the marginal notes to signify alternate readings for the text.

SMALL CAPS in the New Testament are used in the text to indicate Old Testament quotes.

ASTERISK—In regard to the use in Greek of the historical present, the translators recognized that in some contexts the present tense seems more unexpected and unjustified to the English reader than a past tense would have been. But Greek authors frequently used the present tense for the sake of heightened vividness, thereby transporting their readers in imagination to the actual scene at the time of occurrence. However, the translators felt that it would be wise to change these historical presents to English past tenses. Therefore verbs marked with an asterisk (*) represent historical presents in the Greek which have been translated with an English past tense in order to conform to modern usage.

Abbreviations and Special Markings:

DSS = Dead Sea Scrolls.

Gk. = Septuagint (LXX) text.

Heb. = Hebrew text, usually Masoretic.

M.T. = Masoretic text.

Lit. = A literal translation.

Or = An alternate translation justified by the Hebrew or Greek.

[ ] = Brackets in the text are around words probably not in the original writings.

[?] = After some references indicates a similar name, place or thing not necessarily identical with that in the text.

f, ff = following verse or verses.

ms., mss. = manuscript, manuscripts.

BOOKS OF THE OLD TESTAMENT

	PAGE
Genesis	1
Exodus	53
Leviticus	97
Numbers	128
Deuteronomy	172
Joshua	210
Judges	236
Ruth	261
First Samuel	265
Second Samuel	298
First Kings	326
Second Kings	358
First Chronicles	389
Second Chronicles	419
Ezra	454
Nehemiah	464
Esther	479
Job	486
Psalms	520
Proverbs	607
Ecclesiastes	635
Song of Solomon	643
Isaiah	649
Jeremiah	714
Lamentations	780
Ezekiel	786
Daniel	839
Hosea	856
Joel	865
Amos	869
Obadiah	877
Jonah	878
Micah	880
Nahum	886
Habakkuk	888
Zephaniah	891
Haggai	894
Zechariah	896
Malachi	905

BOOKS OF THE NEW TESTMENT

PAGE

The Gospel:—
According to Matthew 911
According to Mark 946
According to Luke 968
According to John 1005
The Acts 1033
Romans 1069
First Corinthians 1083
Second Corinthians 1097
Galatians 1106
Ephesians 1111
Philippians 1116
Colossians 1119
First Thessalonians 1122
Second Thessalonians 1125
First Timothy 1127
Second Timothy 1131
Titus 1134
Philemon 1135
Hebrews 1136
James 1147
First Peter 1151
Second Peter 1155
First John 1158
Second John 1162
Third John 1162
Jude 1163
Revelation 1164

New

American Standard

Bible

Old Testament

GENESIS

The Creation

[a]IN the beginning [b]God [c]created the
heavens and the earth.
2 And the earth was [1a]formless
and void, and [b]darkness was over
the [2]surface of the deep; and [c]the
Spirit of God [d]was [3]moving over the
[2]surface of the waters.
3 Then [a]God said, "Let there be
light"; and there was light.
4 And God saw that the light was
[a]good; and God [b]separated the light
from the darkness.
5 And [a]God called the light day,
and the darkness He called night.
And [b]there was evening and there
was morning, one day.
6 Then God said, "Let there be an
[1a]expanse in the midst of the waters, and let it separate the waters
from the waters."
7 And God made the expanse,
and separated [a]the waters which
were below the expanse from the
waters [b]which were above the expanse; and it was so.
8 And God called the expanse
heaven. And there was evening and
there was morning, a second day.
9 Then God said, "[a]Let the waters
below the heavens be gathered into
one place, and let [b]the dry land appear"; and it was so.
10 And God called the dry land
earth, and the [a]gathering of the waters He called seas; and God saw
that it was good.
11 Then God said, "Let the earth
sprout [1a]vegetation, [2]plants yielding
seed, *and* fruit trees bearing fruit after [3]their kind, [4]with seed in them,
on the earth"; and it was so.
12 And the earth brought forth
vegetation, plants yielding seed after their kind, and trees bearing
fruit, with seed in them, after their
kind; and God saw that it was good.
13 And there was evening and
there was morning, a third day.
14 Then God said, "Let there be
[1a]lights in the [b]expanse of the heavens to separate the day from the
night, and let them be for [c]signs, and
for [d]seasons, and for days and years;
15 and let them be for lights in the
expanse of the heavens to give light
on the earth"; and it was so.
16 And God made the two great
lights, the [a]greater light [1]to govern
the day, and the lesser light [1]to govern the night; *He made* [b]the stars
also.
17 [a]And God placed them in the
expanse of the heavens to give light
on the earth,
18 and [1]to govern the day and the
night, and to separate the light from
the darkness; and God saw that it
was good.
19 And there was evening and
there was morning, a fourth day.
20 Then God said, "Let the waters
[1]teem with swarms of living creatures, and let birds fly above the
earth [2]in the open expanse of the
heavens."
21 And God created [a]the great sea
monsters, and every living creature
that moves, with which the waters
swarmed after their kind, and every
winged bird after its kind; and God
saw that it was good.
22 And God blessed them, saying,
"Be fruitful and multiply, and fill the
waters in the seas, and let birds multiply on the earth."
23 And there was evening and
there was morning, a fifth day.
24 [a]Then God said, "Let the earth
bring forth living creatures after
[1]their kind: cattle and creeping
things and beasts of the earth after
[1]their kind"; and it was so.
25 And God made the [a]beasts of
the earth after [1]their kind, and the
cattle after [1]their kind, and every
thing that creeps on the ground after its kind; and God saw that it was
good.
26 Then God said, "Let [a]Us make
[b]man in Our image, according to
Our likeness; and let them [c]rule over
the fish of the sea and over the birds
of the [1]sky and over the cattle and
over all the earth, and over every
creeping thing that creeps on the
earth."
27 And God created man [a]in His
own image, in the image of God He
created him; [b]male and female He
created them.
28 And God blessed them; and
God said to them, "[a]Be fruitful and
multiply, and fill the earth, and subdue it; and rule over the fish of the
sea and over the birds of the [1]sky,
and over every living thing that
[2]moves on the earth."
29 Then God said, "Behold, [a]I have
given you every plant yielding seed
that is on the [1]surface of all the
earth, and every tree [2]which has
fruit yielding seed; it shall be food
for you;
30 and [a]to every beast of the earth

1 [a]Ps. 102:25; Is. 40:21; John 1:1, 2 [b]Ps. 89:11; 90:2; Acts 17:24 [c]Is. 42:5; 45:18
2 [1]Or, *a waste and emptiness* [2]Lit., *face of* [3]Or, *hovering* [a]Jer. 4:23 [b]Job 38:9 [c]Ps. 104:30 [d]Deut. 32:11; Is. 31:5
3 [a]Ps. 33:6, 9; 2 Cor. 4:6
4 [a]Ps. 145:9, 10 [b]Is. 45:7
5 [a]Ps. 74:16 [b]Ps. 65:8
6 [1]Or, *firmament,* also vs. 7, 8, 14, 15, 17, 20 [a]Is. 40:22
7 [a]Job 38:8-11 [b]Ps. 148:4
9 [a]Ps. 104:6-9; Jer. 5:22; 2 Pet. 3:5 [b]Ps. 24:1, 2; 95:5
10 [a]Ps. 33:7; 95:5; 146:6
11 [1]Or, *grass* [2]Or, *herbs* [3]Lit., *its* [4]Lit., *in which is its seed* [a]Ps. 65:9-13; 104:14
14 [1]Or, *luminaries, light-bearers* [a]Ps. 74:16; 136:7 [b]Ps. 19:1; 150:1 [c]Jer. 10:2 [d]Ps. 104:19
16 [1]Lit., *for the dominion of* [a]Ps. 136:8, 9 [b]Job 38:7; Ps 8:3; Is. 40:26
17 [a]Jer. 33:20
18 [1]Lit., *for the dominion of*
20 [1]Or, *swarm* [2]Lit., *on the face of*
21 [a]Ps. 104:25-28
24 [1]Lit., *its* [a]Gen. 2:19
25 [1]Lit., *its* [a]Gen. 7:21, 22; Jer. 27:5
26 [1]Lit., *heavens* [a]Gen. 3:22; 11:7 [b]Gen. 5:1; 9:6 [c]Ps. 8:6-8
27 [a]1 Cor. 11:7 [b]Matt. 19:4; Mark 10:6
28 [1]Lit., *heavens* [2]Or, *creeps* [a]Gen. 9:1, 7; Ps. 127:3, 5
29 [1]Lit., *face of* [2]Lit., *in which is the fruit of a tree yielding seed* [a]Ps. 104:14; 136:25
30 [a]Ps. 145:15

and to every bird of the [1]sky and to every thing that [2]moves on the earth [3]which has life, *I have given* every green plant for food"; and it was so.
31 And God saw all that He had made, and behold, it was very [a]good. And there was evening and there was morning, the sixth day.

Chapter 2

The Creation of Man and Woman

THUS the heavens and the earth were completed, and all [a]their hosts.
2 And by [a]the seventh day God completed His work which He had done; and [b]He rested on the seventh day from all His work which He had done.
3 Then God blessed the seventh day and sanctified it, because in it He rested from all His work which God had created [1]and made.
4 [1a]This is the account of the heavens and the earth when they were created, in [b]the day that the LORD God made earth and heaven.
5 [a]Now no shrub of the field was yet in the earth, and no plant of the field had yet sprouted, [b]for the LORD God had not sent rain upon the earth; and there was no man to [1]cultivate the ground.
6 But a [1]mist used to rise from the earth and water the whole [2]surface of the ground.
7 [a]Then the LORD God formed man of dust from the ground, and breathed into his nostrils the breath of life; and [b]man became a living [1]being.
8 And the LORD God planted a [a]garden toward the east, in Eden; and there He placed the man whom He had formed.
9 [a]And out of the ground the LORD God caused to grow every tree that is pleasing to the sight and good for food; [b]the tree of life also in the midst of the garden, and the tree of the knowledge of good and evil.
10 Now a river [1]flowed out of Eden to water the garden; and from there it divided and became four [2]rivers.
11 The name of the first is Pishon; it [1]flows around the whole land of Havilah, where there is gold.
12 And the gold of that land is good; the bdellium and the onyx stone are there.
13 *And the* name of the second river is Gihon; it [1]flows around the whole land of Cush.
14 And the name of the third river is [1a]Tigris; it [2]flows east of Assyria. And the fourth [b]river is the [3]Euphrates.
15 Then the LORD God took the man and put him into the garden of Eden to cultivate it and keep it.
16 And the LORD God [a]commanded the man, saying, "From any tree of the garden you may eat freely;
17 but from the tree of the knowledge of good and evil you shall not [1]eat, for in the day that you eat from it [a]you shall surely die."
18 Then the LORD God said, "It is not good for the man to be alone; [a]I will make him a helper [1]suitable for him."
19 And [a]out of the ground the LORD God formed every beast of the field and every bird of the [1]sky, and brought *them* [b]to the man to see what he would call them; and whatever the man called a living creature, that was its name.
20 And the man gave names to all the cattle, and to the birds of the [1]sky, and to every beast of the field, but for [2]Adam there was not found [a]a helper [3]suitable for him.
21 So the LORD God caused a deep sleep to fall upon the man, and he slept; then He took one of his ribs, and closed up the flesh at that place.
22 And the LORD God [1]fashioned into a woman [a]the rib which He had taken from the man, and brought her to the man.
23 And the man said,
"[a]This is now bone of my bones,
And flesh of my flesh;
[1]She shall be called [2]Woman,
Because [1]she was taken out of [3]Man."
24 [a]For this cause a man shall leave his father and his mother, and shall cleave to his wife; and they shall become one flesh.
25 [a]And the man and his wife were both naked and were not ashamed.

Chapter 3

The Fall of Man

NOW [a]the serpent was more crafty than any beast of the field which the LORD God had made. And he said to the woman, "Indeed, has God said, 'You shall not eat from [1]any tree of the garden'?"
2 And the woman said to the serpent, "[a]From the fruit of the trees of the garden we may eat;
3 but from the fruit of the tree which is in the middle of the garden, God has said, 'You shall not eat from it or touch it, lest you die.'"
4 [a]And the serpent said to the woman, "You surely shall not die!

30 [1]Lit., *heavens* [2]Or, *creeps* [3]Lit., *in which is a living soul*
31 [a]Ps. 104:24, 28; 119:68
1 [a]Deut. 4:19; 17:3
2 [a]Ex. 20:8-11 [b]Heb. 4:4
3 [1]Lit., *to make*
4 [1]Lit., *These are the generations* [a]Job 38:4-11 [b]Gen. 1:3-31
5 [1]Lit., *work, serve* [a]Gen. 1:11 [b]Jer. 10:12, 13
6 [1]Or, *flow* [2]Lit., *face of*
7 [1]Lit., *soul* [a]Gen. 3:19 [b]1 Cor. 15:45
8 [a]Gen. 13:10; Is. 51:3; Ezek. 28:13
9 [a]Ezek. 47:12 [b]Gen. 3:22; Rev. 2:7; 22:2, 14
10 [1]Lit., *was going out* [2]Lit., *heads*
11 [1]Lit., *surrounds*
13 [1]Lit., *is the one surrounding*
14 [1]Heb., *Hiddekel* [2]Lit., *is the one going* [3]Heb., *Perath* [a]Dan. 10:4 [b]Gen. 15:18
16 [a]Gen. 3:2, 3
17 [1]Lit., *eat from it* [a]Deut. 30:15, 19, 20; Rom. 6:23; 1 Tim. 5:6; James 1:15
18 [1]Lit., *corresponding to* [a]1 Cor. 11:9
19 [1]Lit., *heavens* [a]Gen. 1:24 [b]Gen. 1:26
20 [1]Lit., *heavens* [2]Or, *man* [3]Lit., *corresponding to* [a]Gen. 2:18
22 [1]Lit., *built* [a]1 Cor. 11:8, 9
23 [1]Lit., *This one* [2]Heb., *Ishshah* [3]Heb., *Ish* [a]Eph. 5:28, 29
24 [a]Matt. 19:5; Mark 10:7, 8; 1 Cor. 6:16; Eph. 5:31
25 [a]Gen. 3:7, 10, 11
1 [1]Or, *every* [a]2 Cor. 11:3; Rev. 12:9; 20:2
2 [a]Gen. 2:16, 17
4 [a]John 8:44

5 "For God knows that in the day
you eat from it your eyes will be
opened, and [a]you will be like God,
knowing good and evil."
6 [a]When the woman saw that the
tree was good for food, and that it
was a delight to the eyes, and that
the tree was desirable to make *one*
wise, she took from its fruit and ate;
and she gave also to her husband
with her, and he ate.
7 Then the eyes of both of them
were opened, and they [a]knew that
they were naked; and they sewed fig
leaves together and made themselves [1]loin coverings.
8 And they heard the sound of
[a]the LORD God walking in the garden in the [1]cool of the day, [b]and the
man and his wife hid themselves
from the presence of the LORD God
among the trees of the garden.
9 Then the LORD God called to the
man, and said to him, "[a]Where are
you?"
10 And he said, "[a]I heard the
sound of Thee in the garden, and I
was afraid because I was naked; so
I hid myself."
11 And He said, "Who told you
that you were naked? Have you eat-
en from the tree of which I commanded you not to eat?"
12 [a]And the man said, "The
woman whom Thou gavest *to be*
with me, she gave me from the tree,
and I ate."
13 Then the LORD God said to the
woman, "What is this you have
done?" And the woman said, "[a]The
serpent deceived me, and I ate."
14 And the LORD God said to the
serpent,
"[a]Because you have done this,
Cursed are you more than all
cattle,
And more than every beast of
the field;
On your belly shall you go,
And [b]dust shall you eat
All the days of your life;
15 And I will put enmity
Between you and the woman,
And between your seed and
her seed;
[a]He shall [1]bruise you on the
head,
And you shall bruise him on
the heel."
16 To the woman He said,
"I will greatly multiply
Your pain [1]in childbirth,
[a]In pain you shall bring forth
children;
Yet your desire shall be for
your husband,

5 [a]Is. 14:14; Ezek. 28:2, 12-17

6 [a]1 Tim. 2:14; James 1:14, 15; 1 John 2:16

7 [1]Or, *girdles* [a]Is. 47:3; Lam. 1:8

8 [1]Lit., *wind, breeze* [a]Gen. 18:33; Lev. 26:12; Deut. 23:14 [b]Hos. 10:8; Rev. 6:15-17

9 [a]Gen. 4:9; 18:9

10 [a]Ex. 20:18, 19; Deut. 5:25

12 [a]Job 31:33; Prov. 28:13

13 [a]2 Cor. 11:3; 1 Tim. 2:14

14 [a]Deut. 28:15-20 [b]Is. 65:25; Mic. 7:17

15 [1]Or, *crush* [a]Rom. 16:20

16 [1]Lit., *and your pregnancy, conception* [a]1 Tim. 2:15 [b]1 Cor. 14:34

17 [1]Or, *sorrow* [a]Gen. 5:29; Rom. 8:20-22 [b]Job 5:7; 14:1

18 [1]Lit., *plant*

19 [a]Ps. 90:3; 104:29; Eccles. 12:7 [b]Gen. 2:7

20 [1]Lit., *Living or Life* [a]2 Cor. 11:3; 1 Tim. 2:13

22 [a]Gen. 1:26 [b]Gen. 2:9

24 [a]Ezek. 31:11 [b]Ex. 25:18-22; Ezek. 10:1-20 [c]Gen. 2:9

1 [1]Lit., *knew* [2]I.e., Gotten one [3]Or, *man, the LORD*

2 [a]Luke 11:50, 51 [b]Gen. 46:32; 47:3

3 [1]Lit., *at the end of days*

4 [a]Heb. 11:4 [b]1 Sam. 15:22

And [b]he shall rule over you."
17 Then to Adam He said, "Because you have listened to the voice
of your wife, and have eaten from
the tree about which I commanded
you, saying, 'You shall not eat from
it';
[a]Cursed is the ground because
of you;
[b]In [1]toil you shall eat of it
All the days of your life.
18 "Both thorns and thistles it
shall grow for you;
And you shall eat the [1]plants
of the field;
19 By the sweat of your face
You shall eat bread,
Till you [a]return to the ground,
Because [b]from it you were
taken;
For you are dust,
And to dust you shall return."
20 Now the man called his wife's
name [1a]Eve, because she was the
mother of all *the* living.
21 And the LORD God made garments of skin for Adam and his
wife, and clothed them.
22 Then the LORD God said, "Behold, the man has become like one
of [a]Us, knowing good and evil; and
now, lest he stretch out his hand,
and take also from [b]the tree of life,
and eat, and live forever"—
23 therefore the LORD God sent
him out from the garden of Eden, to
cultivate the ground from which he
was taken.
24 So [a]He drove the man out; and
at the east of the garden of Eden He
stationed the [b]cherubim, and the
flaming sword which turned every
direction, to guard the way to [c]the
tree of life.

CHAPTER 4

Cain and Abel

NOW the man [1]had relations with
his wife Eve, and she conceived and
gave birth to [2]Cain, and she said, "I
have gotten a [3]manchild with *the*
help of the LORD."
2 And again, she gave birth to his
brother Abel. And [a]Abel was [b]a
keeper of flocks, but Cain was a tiller of the ground.
3 So it came about [1]in the course
of time that Cain brought an offering to the LORD of the fruit of the
ground.
4 And [a]Abel, on his part also
brought of the firstlings of his flock
and of their fat portions. And [b]the
LORD had regard for Abel and for his
offering;

5 but [a]for Cain and for his offering He had no regard. So [b]Cain became very angry and his countenance fell.

6 Then the LORD said to Cain, "[a]Why are you angry? And why has your countenance fallen?

7 "[a]If you do well, [1]will not *your countenance* be lifted up? [b]And if you do not do well, sin is crouching at the door; and its desire is for you, [c]but you must master it."

8 And Cain [1]told Abel his brother. And it came about when they were in the field, that Cain rose up against Abel his brother and [a]killed him.

9 Then the LORD said to Cain, "[a]Where is Abel your brother?" And he said, "I do not know. Am I my brother's keeper?"

10 And He said, "What have you done? [a]The voice of your brother's blood is crying to Me from the ground.

11 "And now [a]you are cursed from the ground, which has opened its mouth to receive your brother's blood from your hand.

12 "[a]When you cultivate the ground, it shall no longer yield its strength to you; [b]you shall be a vagrant and a wanderer on the earth."

13 And Cain said to the LORD, "My punishment is too great to bear!

14 "Behold, Thou hast [a]driven me this day from the face of the ground; and from Thy face I shall be hidden, and [b]I shall be a vagrant and a wanderer on the earth, and it will come about that [c]whoever finds me will kill me."

15 [a]So the LORD said to him, "Therefore whoever kills Cain, vengeance will be taken on him [b]sevenfold." And the LORD [1]appointed a sign for Cain, lest anyone finding him should slay him.

16 Then Cain went out from the presence of the LORD, and [1]settled in the land of [2]Nod, east of Eden.

17 And Cain [1]had relations with his wife and she conceived, and gave birth to Enoch; and he built a city, and called the name of the city Enoch, after the name of his son.

18 Now to Enoch was born Irad; and Irad [1]became the father of Mehujael; and Mehujael [1]became the father of Methushael; and Methushael [1]became the father of Lamech.

19 And Lamech took to himself [a]two wives: the name of the one was Adah, and the name of the other, Zillah.

20 And Adah gave birth to Jabal; he was the father of those who dwell in tents and *have* livestock.

21 And his brother's name was Jubal; he was the father of all those who play the lyre and pipe.

22 As for Zillah, she also gave birth to Tubal-cain, the forger of all implements of bronze and iron; and the sister of Tubal-cain was Naamah.

23 And Lamech said to his wives,
"Adah and Zillah,
Listen to my voice,
You wives of Lamech,
Give heed to my speech,
[a]For I [1]have killed a man for wounding me;
And a boy for striking me;
24 If Cain is avenged [a]sevenfold,
Then Lamech seventy-sevenfold."

25 And [a]Adam [1]had relations with his wife again; and she gave birth to a son, and named him [2]Seth, for, *she said,* "God [3]has appointed me another [4]offspring in place of Abel; [b]for Cain killed him."

26 And to Seth, to him also [a]a son was born; and he called his name Enosh. Then *men* began [b]to call [1]upon the name of the LORD.

CHAPTER 5

Descendants of Adam

THIS is the book of the generations of Adam. In the day when God created man, He made him [a]in the likeness of God.

2 He created them [a]male and female, and He [b]blessed them and named them [1]Man in the day when they were created.

3 When Adam had lived one hundred and thirty years, he [1]became the father of *a son* in his own likeness, according to his image, and named him Seth.

4 Then the days of Adam after he became the father of Seth were eight hundred years, and he had *other* sons and daughters.

5 So all the days that Adam lived were nine hundred and thirty years, and he died.

6 And Seth lived one hundred and five years, and became the father of Enosh.

7 Then Seth lived eight hundred and seven years after he became the father of Enosh, and he had *other* sons and daughters.

8 So all the days of Seth were nine hundred and twelve years, and he died.

9 And Enosh lived ninety years, and became the father of Kenan.

---

5 [a]Num. 16:15; 1 Sam. 16:7 [b]Is. 3:9; Jude 11

6 [a]Jonah 4:4

7 [1]Or, *surely you will be accepted* [a]Jer. 3:12; Mic. 7:18 [b]Num. 32:23 [c]Job 11:14, 15; Rom. 6:12, 16

8 [1]Lit., *said to* [a]Matt. 23:35; 1 John 3:12

9 [a]Gen. 3:9

10 [a]Num. 35:33; Deut. 21:1-9; Heb. 12:24; Rev. 6:9, 10

11 [a]Gen. 3:14

12 [a]Deut. 28:15-24; Joel 1:10-20 [b]Lev. 26:17, 36

14 [a]Gen. 3:24; Jer. 52:3 [b]Deut. 28:64-67 [c]Num. 35:19

15 [1]Or, *set a mark on* [a]Rom. 2:4 [b]Gen. 4:24

16 [1]Lit., *dwelt* [2]I.e., Wandering

17 [1]Lit., *knew*

18 [1]Lit., *begot*

19 [a]Gen. 2:24

23 [1]Or, *kill* [a]Ex. 20:13; Lev. 19:18; Deut. 32:35; Ps. 94:1

24 [a]Gen. 4:15

25 [1]Lit., *knew* [2]Heb., *Sheth* [3]Heb., *shath* [4]Lit., *seed* [a]Gen. 5:3 [b]Gen. 4:8

26 [1]Or, *by* [a]Luke 3:38 [b]Gen. 12:8; 26:25

1 [a]Gen. 1:27

2 [1]Lit., *Adam* [a]Mark 10:6 [b]Gen. 1:28

3 [1]Lit., *begot,* and so throughout the chap.

10 Then Enosh lived eight hundred and fifteen years after he became the father of Kenan, and he had *other* sons and daughters.

11 So all the days of Enosh were nine hundred and five years, and he died.

12 And Kenan lived seventy years, and became the father of Mahalalel.

13 Then Kenan lived eight hundred and forty years after he became the father of Mahalalel, and he had *other* sons and daughters.

14 So all the days of Kenan were nine hundred and ten years, and he died.

15 And Mahalalel lived sixty-five years, and became the father of Jared.

16 Then Mahalalel lived eight hundred and thirty years after he became the father of Jared, and he had *other* sons and daughters.

17 So all the days of Mahalalel were eight hundred and ninety-five years, and he died.

18 And Jared lived one hundred and sixty-two years, and became the father of Enoch.

19 Then Jared lived eight hundred years after he became the father of Enoch, and he had *other* sons and daughters.

20 So all the days of Jared were nine hundred and sixty-two years, and he died.

21 And Enoch lived sixty-five years, and became the father of Methuselah.

22 Then Enoch [a]walked with God three hundred years after he became the father of Methuselah, and he had *other* sons and daughters.

23 So all the days of Enoch were three hundred and sixty-five years.

24 And Enoch walked with God; and he was not, for God [a]took him.

25 And Methuselah lived one hundred and eighty-seven years, and became the father of Lamech.

26 Then Methuselah lived seven hundred and eighty-two years after he became the father of Lamech, and he had *other* sons and daughters.

27 So all the days of Methuselah *were nine hundred and sixty-*nine years, and he died.

28 And Lamech lived one hundred and eighty-two years, and became the father of a son.

29 Now he called his name Noah, saying, "This one shall [1]give us rest from our work and from the toil of our hands *arising from* [a]the ground which the LORD has cursed."

30 Then Lamech lived five hundred and ninety-five years after he became the father of Noah, and he had *other* sons and daughters.

31 So all the days of Lamech were seven hundred and seventy-seven years, and he died.

32 And Noah was [a]five hundred years old, and Noah became the father of Shem, Ham, and Japheth.

CHAPTER 6

The Corruption of Mankind

NOW it came about, when men began to multiply on the face of the land, and daughters were born to them,

2 that the sons of God saw that the daughters of men were [1]beautiful; and they took wives for themselves, whomever they chose.

3 Then the LORD said, "[a]My Spirit shall not [1]strive with man forever, [2]because he also is flesh; [3]nevertheless his days shall be one hundred and twenty years."

4 The [a]Nephilim were on the earth in those days, and also afterward, when the sons of God came in to the daughters of men, and they bore *children* to them. Those were the mighty men who *were* of old, men of renown.

5 Then the LORD saw that the wickedness of man was great on the earth, and that [a]every intent of the thoughts of his heart was only evil continually.

6 And [a]the LORD was sorry that He had made man on the earth, and He was grieved [1]in His heart.

7 And the LORD said, "[a]I will blot out man whom I have created from the face of the land, from man to animals to creeping things and to birds of the [1]sky; for [b]I am sorry that I have made them."

8 But Noah [a]found favor in the eyes of the LORD.

9 These are *the records of* the generations of Noah. Noah was a [a]righteous man, [1b]blameless in his [2]time; Noah [c]walked with God.

10 And Noah [1]became the father of three sons: Shem, Ham, and Japheth.

11 Now the earth was [a]corrupt in the sight of God, and the earth was [b]filled with violence.

12 And God looked on the earth, and behold, it was corrupt; for [a]all flesh had corrupted their way upon the earth.

13 Then God said to Noah, "[a]The end of all flesh has come before Me; for the earth is filled with violence

22 [a]Gen. 6:9; 17:1; 24:40; 48:15

24 [a]2 Kin. 2:10; Ps. 49:15; 73:24; Heb. 11:5

29 [1]Lit., *comfort us in* [a]Gen. 3:17-19

32 [a]Gen. 7:6

2 [1]Lit., good

3 [1]Or, *rule in*, some ancient versions read, *abide in* [2]Or, *in his going astray he is flesh* [3]Or, *therefore* [a]1 Pet. 3:20

4 [a]Num. 13:33

5 [a]Gen. 8:21; Ps. 14:1-3

6 [1]Lit., *to* [a]Jer. 18:7-10

7 [1]Lit., *heavens* [a]Deut. 28:63; 29:20 [b]Amos 7:3, 6

8 [a]Ex. 33:17

9 [1]Lit., *complete, perfect;* or, *having integrity* [2]Lit., *generations* [a]Ps. 37:39 [b]Gen. 17:1; Deut. 18:13; Job 1:1 [c]Gen. 5:24

10 [1]Lit., *begot*

11 [a]Deut. 31:29; Judg. 2:19 [b]Ezek. 8:17

12 [a]Ps. 14:1-3

13 [a]Is. 34:1-4; Ezek. 7:2, 3

because of them; and behold, I am about to destroy them with the earth.

14 "Make for yourself an ark of gopher wood; you shall make the ark with rooms, and shall [1]cover it inside and out with pitch.

15 "And this is how you shall make it: the length of the ark three hundred [1]cubits, its breadth fifty [1]cubits, and its height thirty [1]cubits.

16 "You shall make a [1]window for the ark, and finish it to a cubit from [2]the top; and set the door of the ark in the side of it; you shall make it with lower, second, and third decks.

17 "And behold, I, even I am bringing the flood of water upon the earth, to destroy all flesh in which is the breath of life, from under heaven; everything that is on the earth shall perish.

18 "But I will establish [a]My covenant with you; and [b]you shall enter the ark—you and your sons and your wife, and your sons' wives with you.

19 "[a]And of every living thing of all flesh, you shall bring two of every *kind* into the ark, to keep *them* alive with you; they shall be male and female.

20 "[a]Of the birds after their kind, and of the animals after their kind, of every creeping thing of the ground after its kind, two of every *kind* shall come to you to keep *them* alive.

21 "And as for you, take for yourself some of all food which is edible, and gather *it* to yourself; and it shall be for food for you and for them."

22 [a]Thus Noah did; according to all that God had commanded him, so he did.

CHAPTER 7

The Flood

THEN the LORD said to Noah, "Enter the ark, you and all your household; for you *alone* I have seen *to be* [a]righteous before Me in this [1]time.

2 "You shall take [1]with you of every [a]clean animal [2]by sevens, a male and his female; and of the animals that are not clean two, a male and his female;

3 also of the birds of the [1]sky, [2]by sevens, male and female, to keep [3]offspring alive on the face of all the earth.

4 "For after [a]seven more days, I will send rain on the earth [b]forty days and forty nights; and I will blot out from the face of the land [c]every living thing that I have made."

5 [a]And Noah did according to all that the LORD had commanded him.

6 Now Noah was [a]six hundred years old when the flood of water [1]came upon the earth.

7 Then [a]Noah and his sons and his wife and his sons' wives with him entered the ark because of the water of the flood.

8 [a]Of clean animals and animals that are not clean and birds and everything that creeps on the ground,

9 there went into the ark to Noah [1]by twos, male and female, as God had commanded Noah.

10 And it came about after [a]the seven days, that the water of the flood [1]came upon the earth.

11 In the [a]six hundredth year of Noah's life, in the second month, on the seventeenth day of the month, on the same day all [b]the fountains of the great deep burst open, and the [1]floodgates of the sky were opened.

12 And [a]the rain [1]fell upon the earth for forty days and forty nights.

13 On the very same day [a]Noah and Shem and Ham and Japheth, the sons of Noah, and Noah's wife and the three wives of his sons with them, entered the ark,

14 they and every beast after its kind, and all the cattle after [1]their kind, and every creeping thing that creeps on the earth after its kind, and every bird after its kind, [2]all sorts of birds.

15 So they went into the ark to Noah, [a]by twos of all flesh in which was the breath of life.

16 And those that entered, male and female of all flesh, entered as God had commanded him; and the LORD closed *it* behind him.

17 Then the flood [1]came upon the earth for [a]forty days; and the water increased and lifted up the ark, so that it rose above the earth.

18 And the water prevailed and increased greatly upon the earth; and the ark [1]floated on the [2]surface of the water.

19 And the water prevailed more and more upon the earth, so that all the high mountains [1]everywhere under the heavens were covered.

20 The water prevailed fifteen [1]cubits higher, [a]and the mountains were covered.

21 [a]And all flesh that [1]moved on the earth perished, birds and cattle and beasts and every swarming thing that swarms upon the earth, and all mankind;

22 of all that was on the dry land, all in whose nostrils was the breath of the spirit of life, died.

14 [1]Or, *pitch*
15 [1]I.e., one cubit equals approx. 18 inches
16 [1]Or, *roof* [2]Lit., *above*
18 [a]Gen. 9:9-16; 17:7 [b]Gen. 7:7
19 [a]Gen. 7:2, 14, 15
20 [a]Gen. 7:3
22 [a]Gen. 7:5
1 [1]Lit., *generation* [a]Gen. 6:9
2 [1]Lit., *to* [2]Lit., *seven seven* [a]Lev. 11:1-31; Deut. 14:3-20
3 [1]Lit., *heavens* [2]Lit., *seven seven* [3]Lit., *seed*
4 [a]Gen. 7:10 [b]Gen. 7:12, 17 [c]Gen. 6:7, 13
5 [a]Gen. 6:22
6 [1]Lit., *was* [a]Gen. 5:32
7 [a]Gen. 6:18; 7:13
8 [a]Gen. 6:19, 20; 7:2, 3
9 [1]Lit., *two two*
10 [1]Lit., *were* [a]Gen. 7:4
11 [1]Or, *windows of the heavens* [a]Gen. 7:6 [b]Gen. 8:2
12 [1]Lit., *was* [a]Gen. 7:4, 17
13 [a]Gen. 6:18; 7:7
14 [1]Lit., *its* [2]Lit., *every bird, every wing*
15 [a]Gen. 6:19; 7:9
17 [1]Lit., *was* [a]Gen. 7:4
18 [1]Lit., *went* [2]Lit., *face*
19 [1]Lit., *which were under all the heavens*
20 [1]I.e., one cubit equals 18 inches [a]Gen. 8:4
21 [1]Or, *crept* [a]Gen. 6:7, 13, 17; 7:4

23 Thus He blotted out [1]every living thing that was upon the face of
the land, from man to animals to
creeping things and to birds of the
[2]sky, and they were blotted out
from the earth; and only [a]Noah was
left, together with those that were
with him in the ark.
24 [a]And the water prevailed upon
the earth one hundred and fifty
days.

Chapter 8

The Flood Subsides

BUT God remembered Noah and
all the beasts and all the cattle that
were with him in the ark; and [a]God
caused a wind to pass over the
earth, and the water subsided.
2 Also [a]the fountains of the deep
and the [1]floodgates of the [2]sky were
closed, and [b]the rain from the [2]sky
was restrained;
3 and the water receded steadily
from the earth, and at the end [a]of
one hundred and fifty days the water decreased.
4 And in the seventh month, on
the seventeenth day of the month,
[a]the ark rested upon the mountains
of Ararat.
5 And the water decreased steadily until the tenth month; in the
tenth month, on the first day of the
month, the tops of the mountains
became visible.
6 Then it came about at the end of
forty days, that Noah opened the
window of the ark which he had
made;
7 and he sent out a raven, and it
[1]flew here and there until the water
was dried up [2]from the earth.
8 Then he sent out a dove from
him, to see if the water was abated
from the face of the land;
9 but the dove found no resting
place for the sole of her foot, so she
returned to him into the ark; for the
water was on the [1]surface of all the
earth. Then he put out his hand and
took her, and brought her into the
ark to himself.
10 So he waited yet another seven
days; and again he sent out the dove
from the ark.
11 And the dove came to him
toward [1]evening; and behold, in her
[2]beak was a freshly picked olive
leaf. So Noah knew that the water
was abated from the earth.
12 Then he waited yet another
seven days, and sent out [a]the dove;
but she did not return to him again.
13 Now it came about in the [a]six
hundred and first year, in the first
month, on the first of the month, the
water was dried up [1]from the earth.
Then Noah removed the covering of
the ark, and looked, and behold, the
[2]surface of the ground was dried up.
14 And in the second month, on
the twenty-seventh day of the
month, the earth was dry.
15 Then God spoke to Noah, saying,
16 "Go out of the ark, you and your
wife and your sons and your sons'
wives with you.
17 "Bring out with you every living
thing of all flesh that is with you,
birds and animals and every creeping thing that creeps on the earth,
that they may [1a]breed abundantly
on the earth, and be fruitful and
multiply on the earth."
18 So Noah went out, and his sons
and his wife and his sons' wives
with him.
19 Every beast, every creeping
thing, and every bird, everything
that moves on the earth, went out
[1]by their families from the ark.
20 Then Noah built [a]an altar to the
LORD, and took of every [b]clean animal and of every clean bird and offered [c]burnt offerings on the altar.
21 And the LORD [a]smelled the
soothing aroma; and the LORD said
[1]to Himself, "I will never again
[b]curse the ground on account of
man, for [c]the [2]intent of man's heart
is evil from his youth; [d]and I will
never again [3]destroy every living
thing, as I have done.
22 "While the earth remains,
Seedtime and harvest,
And cold and heat,
And [a]summer and winter,
And day and night
Shall not cease."

Chapter 9

Covenant of the Rainbow

AND God blessed Noah and his
sons and said to them, "[a]Be fruitful
and multiply, and fill the earth.
2 "And the fear of you and the terror of you shall be on every beast of
the earth and on every bird of the
[1]sky; with everything that creeps on
the ground, and all the fish of the
sea, into your hand they are given.
3 "Every moving thing that is alive
shall be food for you; I give all to
you, [a]as *I gave* the green plant.
4 "Only you shall not eat flesh
with its life, *that is,* [a]its blood.

23 [1]Lit., *all existence* [2]Lit., *heavens* [a]Matt. 24:38, 39; Luke 17:26, 27; 1 Pet. 3:20; 2 Pet. 2:5
24 [a]Gen. 8:3
1 [a]Job 12:15; Ps. 29:10; Is. 44:27; Nah. 1:4
2 [1]Or, *windows of the heavens* [2]Lit., *heavens* [a]Gen. 7:11 [b]Gen. 7:4, 12
3 [a]Gen. 7:24
4 [a]Gen. 7:20
7 [1]Lit., *went out, going and returning* [2]Lit., *from upon*
9 [1]Lit., *face*
11 [1]Lit., *time of evening* [2]Lit., *mouth*
12 [a]Jer. 48:28
13 [1]Lit., *from upon* [2]Lit., *face* [a]Gen. 7:6
17 [1]Or, *swarm* [a]Gen. 1:22, 28
19 [1]Or, *according to their kind*
20 [a]Gen. 12:7, 8; 13:18; 22:9 [b]Gen. 7:2 [c]Gen. 22:2; Ex. 10:25
21 [1]Lit., *to His heart* [2]Or, *inclination* [3]Lit., *smite* [a]Ex. 29:18, 25 [b]Gen. 6:7, 13 [c]Gen. 6:5 [d]Gen. 9:11
22 [a]Ps. 74:17; Jer. 33:20, 25
1 [a]Gen. 1:28; 9:7
2 [1]Lit., *heavens*
3 [a]Gen. 1:29
4 [a]Lev. 17:10-16; Deut. 12:16, 23

5"And surely I will require [1a]your
lifeblood; [2b]from every beast I will
require it. And [2]from *every* man,
[2]from every man's brother I will require the life of man.
6 "[a]Whoever sheds man's blood,
By man his blood shall be
shed,
For in the image of God
He made man.
7 "And as for you, [a]be fruitful
and multiply;
[1]Populate the earth abundantly and multiply in it."
8 Then God spoke to Noah and to
his sons with him, saying,
9"Now behold, [a]I Myself do establish My covenant with you, and
with your [1]descendants after you;
10 and with every living creature
that is with you, the birds, the cattle,
and every beast of the earth with
you; of all that comes out of the ark,
even every beast of the earth.
11"And I establish My covenant
with you; and all flesh shall [a]never
again be cut off by the water of the
flood, [b]neither shall there again be a
flood to destroy the earth."
12 And God said, "This is [a]the sign
of the covenant which I am making
between Me and you and every living creature that is with you, for [1]all
successive generations;
13 I set My [a]bow in the cloud, and
it shall be for a sign of a covenant
between Me and the earth.
14"And it shall come about, when I
bring a cloud over the earth, that the
bow shall be seen in the cloud,
15 and [a]I will remember My covenant, which is between Me and you
and every living creature of all flesh;
and [b]never again shall the water become a flood to destroy all flesh.
16"When the bow is in the cloud,
then I will look upon it, to remember
the everlasting covenant between
God and every living creature of all
flesh that is on the earth."
17 And God said to Noah, "This is
the sign of the covenant which I
have established between Me and
all flesh that is on the earth."
18 Now the sons of Noah who
came out of the ark were Shem and
Ham and Japheth; and [a]Ham was
the father of Canaan.
19 These three *were* the sons of
Noah; and [a]from these the whole
earth was [1]populated.
20 Then Noah began [1]farming and
planted a vineyard.
21 And he drank of the wine and
became drunk, and uncovered himself inside his tent.
22 And [a]Ham, the father of Canaan, saw the nakedness of his father, and told his two brothers outside.
23 But Shem and Japheth took a
garment and laid it upon both their
shoulders and walked backward
and covered the nakedness of their
father; and their faces were [1]turned
away, so that they did not see their
father's nakedness.
24 When Noah awoke from his
wine, he knew what his youngest
son had done to him.
25 So he said,
"[a]Cursed be Canaan;
[1]A servant of servants
He shall be to his brothers."
26 He also said,
"[a]Blessed be the LORD,
The God of Shem;
And let Canaan be [1]his servant.
27 "[a]May God enlarge Japheth,
And let him dwell in the tents
of Shem;
And let Canaan be [1]his servant."
28 And Noah lived three hundred
and fifty years after the flood.
29 So all the days of Noah were
nine hundred and fifty years, and he
died.

CHAPTER 10

Descendants of Noah

NOW these are *the records of* the
generations of Shem, Ham, and Japheth, the sons of Noah; and sons
were born to them after the flood.
2 [a]The sons of Japheth *were* [b]Go-
mer and Magog and [c]Madai and [d]Ja-
van and Tubal and [e]Meshech and Tiras.
3 And the sons of Gomer *were*
[a]Ashkenaz and [b]Riphath and [c]To-
garmah.
4 And the sons of Javan *were*
Elishah and [a]Tarshish, Kittim and
[b]Dodanim.
5 From these the coastlands of
the nations [1]were separated into
their lands, every one according to
his language, according to their
families, into their nations.
6 [a]And the sons of Ham *were*
Cush and Mizraim and Put and Canaan.
7 And the sons of Cush *were* [a]Se-
ba and Havilah and Sabtah and
[b]Raamah and Sabteca; and the sons
of Raamah *were* [b]Sheba and [c]De-
dan.
8 Now Cush [1]became the father
of Nimrod; he [2]became a mighty one
on the earth.

5 [1]Lit., *your blood of your lives* [2]Lit., *from the hand of* [a]Ex. 20:13; 21:12 [b]Ex. 21:28, 29
6 [a]Num. 35:33
7 [1]Lit., *swarm in the earth* [a]Gen. 9:1
9 [1]Lit., *seed* [a]Gen. 6:18
11 [a]Gen. 8:21 [b]Is. 54:9
12 [1]Or, *everlasting generations* [a]Gen. 9:13, 17; 17:11
13 [a]Ezek. 1:28
15 [a]Deut. 7:9 [b]Gen. 9:11
18 [a]Gen. 9:25-27
19 [1]Lit., *scattered* [a]Gen. 9:1, 7; 10:32
20 [1]Lit., to be *a farmer*
22 [a]Hab. 2:15
23 [1]Lit., *backward*
25 [1]I.e., The lowest of servants [a]Deut. 27:16
26 [1]Or, *their* [a]Gen. 14:20; 24:27
27 [1]Or, *their* [a]Gen. 10:2-5; Is. 66:19
2 [a]1 Chr. 1:5-7 [b]Ezek. 38:2, 6 [c]2 Kin. 17:6 [d]Is. 66:19 [e]Ezek. 38:2
3 [a]Jer. 51:27 [b]1 Chr. 1:6, *Diphath* [c]Ezek. 27:14
4 [a]Ezek. 27:12, 25 [b]1 Chr. 1:7, *Rodanim*
5 [1]Or, *separated themselves*
6 [a]1 Chr. 1:8-10
7 [a]Is. 43:3 [b]Ezek. 27:22 [c]Ezek. 27:15, 20
8 [1]Lit., *begot* [2]Lit., *began to be*

9 He was a mighty hunter before
the LORD; therefore it is said, "Like
Nimrod a mighty hunter before the
LORD."
10 And the beginning of his kingdom was [1a]Babel and Erech and Ac-
cad and Calneh, in the land of [b]Shi-
nar.
11 From that land he went forth
[a]into Assyria, and built Nineveh and
Rehoboth-Ir and Calah,
12 and Resen between Nineveh
and Calah; that is the great city.
13 And Mizraim [1]became the father of [a]Ludim and Anamim and Le-
habim and Naphtuhim
14 and Pathrusim and Casluhim
(from which came the Philistines)
and Caphtorim.
15 And Canaan [1]became the father of [a]Sidon, his first-born, and
[b]Heth
16 and [a]the Jebusite and the Amorite and the Girgashite
17 and the Hivite and the Arkite
and the Sinite
18 and the Arvadite and the Zema-
rite and the Hamathite; and afterward the families of the Canaanite
were spread abroad.
19 And the territory of the Canaanite [1]extended from Sidon as
you go toward Gerar, as far as Gaza;
as you go toward [a]Sodom and Gomorrah and Admah and Zeboiim, as
far as Lasha.
20 These are the sons of Ham, according to their families, according
to their languages, by their lands, by
their nations.
21 And also to Shem, the father of
all the children of Eber, *and* the
[1]older brother of Japheth, children
were born.
22 [a]The sons of Shem *were* [b]Elam
and [c]Asshur and [d]Arpachshad and
[e]Lud and Aram.
23 And the sons of Aram *were* [a]Uz
and Hul and Gether and Mash.
24 And Arpachshad [1]became the
father of [a]Shelah; and Shelah [1]be-
came the father of Eber.
25 And two sons were born to
Eber; the name of the one *was* [1]Pe-
leg, for in his days the earth was divided; and his brother's name *was*
Joktan.
26 And Joktan [1]became the father
of Almodad and Sheleph and Hazar-
maveth and Jerah
27 and Hadoram and Uzal and
Diklah
28 and [1]Obal and Abimael and
Sheba
29 and Ophir and Havilah and Jobab; all these were the sons of Joktan.
30 Now their [1]settlement [2]ex-
tended from Mesha as you go
toward Sephar, the hill country of
the east.
31 These are the sons of Shem, according to their families, according
to their languages, by their lands,
according to their nations.
32 These are the families of the
sons of Noah, according to their genealogies, by their nations; and [a]out
of these the nations were separated
on the earth after the flood.

CHAPTER 11

Universal Language, Babel, Confusion

NOW the whole earth [1]used the
same language and [2]the same
words.
2 And it came about as they journeyed east, that they found a plain
in the land [a]of Shinar and [1]settled
there.
3 And they said to one another,
"Come, let us make bricks and burn
them thoroughly." And they used
brick for stone, and they used [a]tar
for mortar.
4 And they said, "Come, let us
build for ourselves a city, and a
tower whose top [a]*will reach* into
heaven, and let us make for ourselves [b]a name; lest we [c]be scattered abroad over the face of the
whole earth."
5 [a]And the LORD came down to
see the city and the tower which the
sons of men had built.
6 And the LORD said, "Behold,
they are one people, and they all
have [1a]the same language. And this
is what they began to do, and now
nothing which they purpose to do
will be [2]impossible for them.
7 "Come, [a]let Us go down and
there [b]confuse their [1]language, that
they may not understand one another's [1]speech."
8 So the LORD [a]scattered them
abroad from there over the face of
the whole earth; and they stopped
building the city.
9 Therefore its name was called
[1a]Babel, because there the LORD
confused the [2]language of the whole
earth; and from there the LORD scattered them abroad over the face of
the whole earth.

Descendants of Shem

10 [a]These are *the records of* the
generations of Shem. Shem was one
hundred years old, and [1]became the
father of Arpachshad two years after the flood;

10 [1]Or, *Babylon* [a]Gen. 11:9 [b]Gen. 11:2; 14:1

11 [a]Mic. 5:6

13 [1]Lit., *begot* [a]Jer. 46:9

15 [1]Lit., *begot* [a]1 Chr. 1:13; Jer. 47:4 [b]Gen. 23:3

16 [a]Gen. 15:19-21

19 [1]Lit., *was* [a]Gen. 14:2, 3

21 [1]Or, *the brother of Japheth the elder*

22 [a]1 Chr. 1:17 [b]Gen. 14:1, 9 [c]2 Kin. 15:29 [d]Gen. 11:10 [e]Is. 66:19

23 [a]Job 1:1; Jer. 25:20

24 [1]Lit., *begot* [a]Luke 3:35

25 [1]I.e., Division

26 [1]Lit., *begot*

28 [1]In 1 Chr. 1:22, *Ebal*

30 [1]Lit., *dwelling* [2]Lit., *was*

32 [a]Gen. 9:19

1 [1]Lit., *was one lip* [2]Or, *few;* or, *one* set of *words*

2 [1]Lit., *dwelt* [a]Gen. 10:10; 14:1

3 [a]Gen. 14:10

4 [a]Deut. 1:28; 9:1; Ps. 107:26 [b]Gen. 6:4; 2 Sam. 8:13 [c]Deut. 4:27

5 [a]Gen. 18:21; Ex. 3:8; 19:11, 18, 20

6 [1]Lit., *one lip* [2]Lit., *withheld from* [a]Gen. 11:1

7 [1]Lit., *lip* [a]Gen. 1:26 [b]Ex. 4:11; Is. 33:19

8 [a]Gen. 11:4

9 [1]Or, *Babylon;* cf. Heb., *balal,* confuse [2]Lit., *lip* [a]Gen. 10:10

10 [1]Lit., *begot,* and so throughout the chap. [a]Gen. 10:22-25

11 and Shem lived five hundred years after he became the father of Arpachshad, and he had *other* sons and daughters.

12 And Arpachshad lived thirty-five years, and became the father of Shelah;

13 and Arpachshad lived four hundred and three years after he became the father of Shelah, and he had *other* sons and daughters.

14 And Shelah lived thirty years, and became the father of Eber;

15 and Shelah lived four hundred and three years after he became the father of Eber, and he had *other* sons and daughters.

16 And Eber lived thirty-four years, and became the father of Peleg;

17 and Eber lived four hundred and thirty years after he became the father of Peleg, and he had *other* sons and daughters.

18 And Peleg lived thirty years, and became the father of Reu;

19 and Peleg lived two hundred and nine years after he became the father of Reu, and he had *other* sons and daughters.

20 And Reu lived thirty-two years, and became the father of Serug;

21 and Reu lived two hundred and seven years after he became the father of Serug, and he had *other* sons and daughters.

22 And Serug lived thirty years, and became the father of Nahor;

23 and Serug lived two hundred years after he became the father of Nahor, and he had *other* sons and daughters.

24 And Nahor lived twenty-nine years, and became the father of [a]Terah;

25 and Nahor lived one hundred and nineteen years after he became the father of Terah, and he had *other* sons and daughters.

26 And Terah lived seventy years, and became the father of Abram, Nahor and Haran.

27 Now these are *the records of* the generations of Terah. Terah became the father of Abram, Nahor and Haran; and [a]Haran became the father of Lot.

28 And Haran died [1]in the presence of his father Terah in the land of his birth, in [a]Ur of the Chaldeans.

29 And Abram and [a]Nahor took wives for themselves. The name of Abram's wife was [b]Sarai; and the name of Nahor's wife was [c]Milcah, the daughter of Haran, the father of Milcah [1]and Iscah.

30 And [a]Sarai was barren; she had no child.

31 And Terah took Abram his son, and Lot the son of Haran, his grandson, and Sarai his daughter-in-law, his son Abram's wife; and they went out [1]together from [a]Ur of the Chaldeans in order to enter the land of Canaan; and they went as far as Haran, and [2]settled there.

32 And the days of Terah were two hundred and five years; and Terah died in Haran.

Chapter 12

Abram Journeys to Egypt

NOW [a]the LORD said to Abram,
"[1]Go forth from your country,
And from your relatives
And from your father's house,
To the land which I will show you;
2 And [a]I will make you a great nation,
And [b]I will bless you,
And make your name great;
And so [1c]you shall be a blessing;
3 And [a]I will bless those who bless you,
And the one who [1]curses you I will [2]curse.
[b]And in you all the families of the earth shall be blessed."

4 So Abram went forth as the LORD had spoken to him; and [a]Lot went with him. Now Abram was seventy-five years old when he departed from Haran.

5 And Abram took Sarai his wife and Lot his nephew, and all their [a]possessions which they had accumulated, and [b]the [1]persons which they had acquired in Haran, and they [2]set out for the land of Canaan; [c]thus they came to the land of Canaan.

6 And Abram passed through the land as far as the site [a]of Shechem, to the [1]oak of Moreh. Now the Canaanite *was* then in the land.

7 And the LORD [a]appeared to Abram and said, "[b]To your [1]descendants I will give this land." So he built [c]an altar there to the LORD who had appeared to him.

8 Then he proceeded from there to the mountain on the east of Bethel, and pitched his tent, with [a]Bethel on the west and Ai on the east; and there he built an altar to the LORD and [b]called upon the name of the LORD.

9 And Abram journeyed on, continuing toward [a]the [1]Negev.

24 [a]Josh. 24:2
27 [a]Gen. 11:31; 12:4
28 [1]Or, *during the lifetime of* [a]Gen. 11:31
29 [1]Lit., *and the father of* [a]Gen. 24:10 [b]Gen. 20:12 [c]Gen. 22:20, 23; 24:15
30 [a]Gen. 16:1
31 [1]Lit., *with them* [2]Lit., *dwelt* [a]Gen. 15:7; Neh. 9:7
1 [1]Lit., *Go for yourself* [a]Acts 7:3; Heb. 11:8
2 [1]Lit., *be a blessing* [a]Gen. 17:4, 5; 18:18 [b]Gen. 22:17 [c]Zech. 8:13
3 [1]Or, *reviles* [2]Or, *bind under a curse* [a]Gen. 27:29 [b]Acts 3:25; Gal. 3:8
4 [a]Gen. 11:27, 31
5 [1]Lit., *souls* [2]Lit., *went forth to go to* [a]Gen. 13:6 [b]Gen. 14:14; Lev. 22:11 [c]Gen. 11:31
6 [1]Or, *terebinth* [a]Gen. 35:4; Deut. 11:30
7 [1]Lit., *seed* [a]Gen. 17:1; 18:1 [b]Gen. 13:15; 15:18; Gal. 3:16 [c]Gen. 13:18; 22:9
8 [a]Josh. 8:9, 12 [b]Gen. 4:26; 21:33
9 [1]I.e., South country [a]Gen. 13:1, 3; 20:1; 24:62

10 Now there was a famine in the
land; so Abram went down to Egypt
to sojourn there, for the famine was
severe in the land.
11 And it came about when he
[1]came near to Egypt, that he said to
Sarai his wife, "See now, I know
that you are a [2a]beautiful woman;
12 [a]and it will come about when
the Egyptians see you, that they will
say, 'This is his wife'; and they will
kill me, but they will let you live.
13 "Please say that you are [a]my sister so that it may go well with me
because of you, and that [1b]I may live
on account of you."
14 And it came about when Abram
came into Egypt, the Egyptians
[1]saw that the woman was very
beautiful.
15 And Pharaoh's officials saw her
and praised her to Pharaoh; and [a]the
woman was taken into Pharaoh's
house.
16 Therefore [a]he treated Abram
well for her sake; and [1b]gave him
sheep and oxen and donkeys and
male and female servants and female donkeys and camels.
17 But the LORD [a]struck Pharaoh
and his house with great plagues because of Sarai, Abram's wife.
18 Then Pharaoh called Abram
and said, "[a]What is this you have
done to me? Why did you not tell me
that she was your wife?
19 "Why did you say, 'She is my sister,' so that I took her for my wife?
Now then, [1]here is your wife, take
her and go."
20 And Pharaoh commanded *his*
men concerning him; and they [1]es-
corted him away, with his wife and
all that belonged to him.

CHAPTER 13

Abram and Lot

SO Abram went up from Egypt to
[a]the [1]Negev, he and his wife and all
that belonged to him; and Lot with
him.
2 Now Abram was very rich in
livestock, in silver and in gold.
3 And he went [1]on his journeys
from the [2]Negev as far as Bethel, to
the place where his tent had been at
the beginning, [a]between Bethel and
Ai,
4 to the place of the altar, which
he had made there formerly; and
there Abram called on the name of
the LORD.
5 Now [a]Lot, who went with A-
bram, also had flocks and herds and
tents.
6 And [a]the land could not [1]sus-
tain them [2]while dwelling together;
[b]for their possessions were so great
that they were not able [b]to remain
together.
7 [a]And there was strife between
the herdsmen of Abram's livestock
and the herdsmen of Lot's livestock.
Now [b]the Canaanite and the Perizzite were dwelling then in the land.
8 [a]Then Abram said to Lot,
"Please let there be no strife between you and me, nor between my
herdsmen and your herdsmen, for
we are brothers.
9 "Is not the whole land before
you? Please separate from me: if *to*
the left, then I will go to the right; or
if *to* the right, then I will go to the
left."
10 And Lot lifted up his eyes and
saw all the [1a]valley of the Jordan,
that it was well watered everywhere—*this was* before the LORD
destroyed Sodom and Gomorrah—
like [b]the garden of the LORD, [c]like
the land of Egypt as you go to [d]Zoar.
11 So Lot chose for himself all the
[1]valley of the Jordan; and Lot journeyed eastward. Thus they separated from each other.
12 Abram [1]settled in the land of
Canaan, while Lot [1]settled in [a]the
cities of the [2]valley, and moved his
tents as far as Sodom.
13 Now the men of Sodom were
wicked [1]exceedingly and [a]sinners
against the LORD.
14 And the LORD said to Abram,
after Lot had separated from him,
"[a]Now lift up your eyes and look
from the place where you are, northward and southward and eastward
and westward;
15 [a]for all the land which you see,
[b]I will give it to you and to your [1]de-
scendants forever.
16 "And I will make your [1]descen-
dants [a]as the dust of the earth; so
that if anyone can number the dust
of the earth, then your [1]descendants
can also be numbered.
17 "Arise, [a]walk about the land
through its length and breadth; for
[b]I will give it to you."
18 Then Abram moved his tent
and came and dwelt by the [1]oaks of
[a]Mamre, which are in Hebron, and
there he built [b]an altar to the LORD.

CHAPTER 14

War of the Kings

AND it came about in the days of
Amraphel king of [a]Shinar, Arioch
king of Ellasar, Chedorlaomer king
of [b]Elam, and Tidal king of [1]Goiim,

11 [1]Lit., *drew near to enter* [2]Lit., *woman of beautiful appearance* [a]Gen. 26:7; 29:17
12 [a]Gen. 20:11
13 [1]Lit., *my soul* [a]Gen. 20:2, 5, 12 [b]Jer. 38:17, 20
14 [1]Lit., *saw the woman that she was*
15 [a]Gen. 20:2
16 [1]Lit., *he had* [a]Gen. 20:14 [b]Gen. 13:2
17 [a]Ps. 105:14
18 [a]Gen. 20:9, 10
19 [1]Or, *behold*
20 [1]Lit., *sent*
1 [1]I.e., South country [a]Gen. 12:9
3 [1]Lit., *by his stages* [2]I.e., South country [a]Gen. 12:8
5 [a]Gen. 12:5
6 [1]Lit., *bear* [2]Lit., *to dwell* [a]Gen. 36:7 [b]Gen. 12:5, 16; 13:2
7 [a]Gen. 26:20 [b]Gen. 12:6; 15:19-21
8 [a]Prov. 15:18; 20:3
10 [1]Lit., *circle* [a]Gen. 19:17-29; Deut. 34:3 [b]Gen. 2:8 [c]Gen. 47:6 [d]Gen. 14:8; Deut. 34:3
11 [1]Lit., *circle*
12 [1]Lit., *dwelt* [2]Lit., *circle* [a]Gen. 14:2; 19:24, 25
13 [1]Lit., *wicked and sinners exceedingly* [a]Gen. 39:9; Num. 32:23; 2 Pet. 2:7, 8
14 [a]Deut. 3:27; 34:1-4
15 [1]Lit., *seed* [a]Gen. 12:7 [b]Gen. 13:17; 15:7, 8; 17:8
16 [1]Lit., *seed* [a]Gen. 16:10; 28:14; Num. 23:10
17 [a]Num. 13:17-24 [b]Gen. 13:15
18 [1]Or, *terebinths* [a]Gen. 14:13 [b]Gen. 8:20; 12:7, 8
1 [1]Or, *nations* [a]Gen. 10:10; 11:2 [b]Gen. 10:22; Dan. 8:2

2 *that* they made war with Bera king of Sodom, and with Birsha king of Gomorrah, Shinab king of [a]Admah, and Shemeber king of [b]Zeboiim, and the king of Bela (that is, [c]Zoar).

3 All these [1]came as allies to [a]the valley of Siddim (that is, [b]the Salt Sea).

4 Twelve years they had served Chedorlaomer, but the thirteenth year they rebelled.

5 And in the fourteenth year Chedorlaomer and the kings that were with him, came and [1]defeated the [a]Rephaim in [b]Ashteroth-karnaim and the Zuzim in Ham and the Emim in [2c]Shaveh-kiriathaim,

6 and the [a]Horites in their Mount Seir, as far as [b]El-paran, which is by the wilderness.

7 Then they turned back and came to En-mishpat (that is, [a]Kadesh), and [1]conquered all the country of the Amalekites, and also the Amorites, who lived in [b]Hazazon-tamar.

8 And the king of Sodom and the king of Gomorrah and the king of Admah and the king of Zeboiim and the king of Bela (that is, Zoar) came out; and they arrayed for battle against them in [a]the valley of Siddim,

9 against Chedorlaomer king of Elam and Tidal king of [1]Goiim and Amraphel king of Shinar and Arioch king of Ellasar—four kings against five.

10 Now the valley of Siddim was full of tar pits; and [a]the kings of Sodom and Gomorrah fled, and they fell into them. But those who survived fled to the hill country.

11 Then they took all the goods of Sodom and Gomorrah and all their food supply, and departed.

12 And they also took Lot, [a]Abram's nephew, and his possessions and departed, [b]for he was living in Sodom.

13 Then [1]a fugitive came and told Abram the [a]Hebrew. Now he was [2]living by the [3]oaks of [b]Mamre the Amorite, brother of Eshcol and brother of Aner, and these were [c]allies with Abram.

14 And when Abram heard that [a]his [1]relative had been taken captive, he [2]led out his trained men, [b]born in his house, three hundred and eighteen, and went in pursuit as far as [c]Dan.

15 And [a]he divided [1]his forces against them by night, he and his servants, and [2]defeated them, and pursued them as far as Hobah, which is [3]north of [b]Damascus.

16 And he brought back all the goods, and also brought back [a]his [1]relative Lot with his possessions, and also the women, and the people.

God's Promise to Abram

17 Then after his return from the [1]defeat of Chedorlaomer and the kings who were with him, [a]the king of Sodom went out to meet him at the valley of Shaveh (that is, [b]the King's Valley).

18 And [a]Melchizedek king of Salem brought out [b]bread and wine; now he was a [c]priest of [1]God Most High.

19 And he blessed him and said,
"Blessed be Abram of God Most High,
[1a]Possessor of heaven and earth;
20 And blessed be God Most High,
Who has delivered your enemies into your hand."
[a]And he gave him a tenth of all.

21 And the king of Sodom said to Abram, "Give the [1]people to me and take the goods for yourself."

22 And Abram said to the king of Sodom, "I have [1]sworn to the LORD [a]God Most High, [2]possessor of heaven and earth,

23 that [a]I will not take a thread or a sandal thong or anything that is yours, lest you should say, 'I have made Abram rich.'

24 "[1]I will take nothing except what the young men have eaten, and the share of the men who went with me, [a]Aner, Eshcol, and Mamre; let them take their share."

CHAPTER 15

Abram Promised a Son

AFTER these things [a]the word of the LORD came to Abram in a vision, saying,
"[b]Do not fear, Abram,
I am [c]a shield to you;
Your [d]reward shall be very great."

2 And Abram said, "O Lord [1]GOD, what wilt Thou give me, since I [2]am childless, and the [3]heir of my house is Eliezer of Damascus?"

3 And Abram said, "[1]Since Thou hast given no [2]offspring to me, [3]one [a]born in my house is my heir."

4 Then behold, the word of the LORD came to him, saying, "This

2 [a]Gen. 10:19 [b]Deut. 29:23 [c]Gen. 13:10
3 [1]Lit., *joined together* [a]Gen. 14:8, 10 [b]Deut. 3:17; Josh. 3:16
5 [1]Lit., *smote* [2]Or, *the plain of Kiriathaim* [a]Deut. 3:11, 13 [b]Deut. 1:4; Josh. 9:10 [c]Num. 32:37
6 [a]Gen. 36:20; Deut. 2:12, 22 [b]Gen. 21:21; Num. 10:12
7 [1]Lit., *smote* [a]Num. 13:26 [b]2 Chr. 20:2
8 [a]Gen. 14:3
9 [1]Or, *nations*
10 [a]Gen. 14:17, 21, 22
12 [a]Gen. 11:27 [b]Gen. 13:12
13 [1]Lit., *the* [2]Lit., *abiding* [3]Or, *terebinths* [a]Gen. 40:15; Ex. 3:18 [b]Gen. 13:18 [c]Gen. 21:27, 32
14 [1]Lit., *brother* [2]Or, *mustered* [a]Gen. 14:12 [b]Gen. 12:5; Eccles. 2:7 [c]1 Kin. 15:20
15 [1]Lit., *himself* [2]Lit., *smote* [3]Lit., *on the left* [a]Judg. 7:16 [b]Gen. 15:2
16 [1]Lit., *brother* [a]Gen. 14:12, 14
17 [1]Lit., *smiting* [a]Gen. 14:10 [b]2 Sam. 18:18
18 [1]Heb., *El Elyon*, also vs. 19, 20, 22 [a]Heb. 7:1 [b]Ps. 104:15 [c]Ps. 110:4; Heb. 5:6, 10
19 [1]Or, *Creator* [a]Gen. 14:22
20 [a]Heb. 7:4
21 [1]Lit., *soul*
22 [1]Lit., *lifted up my hand* [2]Or, *Creator* [a]Gen. 14:19
23 [a]2 Kin. 5:16
24 [1]Lit., *not to me except* [a]Gen. 14:13
1 [a]Gen. 15:4; 1 Sam. 15:10 [b]Gen. 21:17; 26:24 [c]Deut. 33:29 [d]Num. 18:20
2 [1]YHWH, usually rendered LORD [2]Lit., *go* [3]Lit., *son of acquisition*
3 [1]Lit., *Behold* [2]Lit., *seed* [3]Lit., *and behold, a son of* [a]Gen. 14:14

man will not be your heir; [a]but one
who shall come forth from your own
[1]body, he shall be your heir."
5 And He took him outside and
said, "Now look toward the heavens, and [a]count the stars, if you are
able to count them." And He said to
him, "[b]So shall your [1]descendants
be."
6 [a]Then he believed in the LORD;
and He reckoned it to him as righteousness.
7 And He said to him, "I am the
LORD who brought you out of [a]Ur of
the Chaldeans, to [b]give you this land
to [1]possess it."
8 And he said, "O Lord [1]GOD,
[a]how may I know that I shall [2]pos-
sess it?"
9 So He said to him, "[1]Bring Me a
three year old heifer, and a three
year old female goat, and a three
year old ram, and a turtledove, and
a young pigeon."
10 Then he [1]brought all these to
Him and [a]cut them [2]in two, and laid
each half opposite the other; but he
did not cut [b]the birds.
11 And the birds of prey came
down upon the carcasses, and A-
bram drove them away.
12 Now when the sun was going
down, [a]a deep sleep fell upon A-
bram; and behold, [1]terror *and* great
darkness fell upon him.
13 And God said to Abram,
"Know for certain that [a]your [1]de-
scendants will be strangers in a land
that is not theirs, [2]where [b]they will
be enslaved and oppressed [c]four
hundred years.
14 "But I will also judge the nation
whom they will serve; and afterward they will come out [a]with
[1]many possessions.
15 "And as for you, [a]you shall go to
your fathers in peace; you shall be
buried at a good old age.
16 "Then in [a]the fourth generation
they shall return here, for [b]the iniquity of the Amorite is not yet complete."
17 And it came about when the
sun had set, that it was very dark,
and behold, *there appeared* a smoking oven and a flaming torch which
[a]passed between these pieces.
18 On that day the LORD made a
covenant with Abram, saying,
"To your [1]descendants I have
given this land,
From [a]the river of Egypt as far
as the great river, the river
Euphrates:
19 [a]the Kenite and the Kenizzite
and the Kadmonite
20 and the Hittite and the Perizzite
and the Rephaim
21 and the Amorite and the Canaanite and the Girgashite and the
Jebusite."

CHAPTER 16

Sarai and Hagar

NOW [a]Sarai, Abram's wife had
borne him no *children*, and she had
[b]an Egyptian maid whose name was
Hagar.
2 So Sarai said to Abram, "Now
behold, the LORD has prevented me
from bearing *children*. [a]Please go in
to my maid; perhaps I shall [1]obtain
children through her." And Abram
listened to the voice of Sarai.
3 And after Abram had [1]lived
[a]ten years in the land of Canaan,
Abram's wife Sarai took Hagar the
Egyptian, her maid, and gave her to
her husband Abram as his wife.
4 And he went in to Hagar, and
she conceived; and when she saw
that she had conceived, her mistress
was despised in her sight.
5 And Sarai said to Abram,
"[a]May the wrong done me be upon
you. I gave my maid into your
[1]arms; but when she saw that she
had conceived, I was despised in her
[2]sight. [b]May the LORD judge between [3]you and me."
6 But Abram said to Sarai, "Behold, [a]your maid is in your [1]power;
do to her what is good in your
[2]sight." So Sarai treated her
harshly, and she fled from her presence.
7 Now [a]the angel of the LORD
found her by a spring of water in the
wilderness, by the spring on the way
to [b]Shur.
8 And he said, "Hagar, Sarai's
maid, [a]where have you come from
and where are you going?" And she
said, "I am fleeing from the presence of my mistress Sarai."
9 Then the angel of the LORD said
to her, "Return to your mistress,
and submit yourself [1]to her authority."
10 Moreover, the angel of the
LORD said to her, "[a]I will greatly
multiply your [1]descendants so that
[2]they shall be too many to count."
11 The angel of the LORD said to
her further,
"Behold, you are with child,
And you shall bear a son;
And you shall call his name
[1]Ishmael,
Because [a]the LORD [2]has given
heed to your affliction.

4 [1]Lit., *inward parts* [a]Gal. 4:28
5 [1]Lit., *seed* [a]Gen. 22:17; 26:4; Deut. 1:10 [b]Ex. 32:13; Rom. 4:18
6 [a]Rom. 4:3; Gal. 3:6; James 2:23
7 [1]Or, *inherit* [a]Gen. 11:31 [b]Gen. 13:15,17
8 [1]YHWH, usually rendered LORD [2]Or, *inherit* [a]Luke 1:18
9 [1]Lit., *Take*
10 [1]Lit., *took* [2]Lit., *in the midst* [a]Gen. 15:17 [b]Lev. 1:17
12 [1]Or, *a terror of great darkness* [a]Gen. 2:21; 28:11; Job 33:15
13 [1]Lit., *seed* [2]Lit., *and shall serve them; and they shall afflict them* [a]Acts 7:6, 17 [b]Deut. 5:15 [c]Ex. 12:40; Gal. 3:17
14 [1]Lit., *great* [a]Ex. 12:32-38
15 [a]Gen. 25:8; 47:30
16 [a]Gen. 15:13 [b]Lev. 18:24-28
17 [a]Jer. 34:18 19
18 [1]Lit., *seed* [a]Ex. 23:31; Num. 34:1-15; Deut. 1:7, 8
19 [a]Ex. 3:17; 23:28; Josh. 21:43; 24:11

1 [a]Gen. 11:30 [b]Gen. 12:16
2 [1]Lit., *be built from her* [a]Gen. 30:3, 4, 9, 10
3 [1]Lit., *dwelt* [a]Gen. 12:4
5 [1]Lit., *bosom* [2]Lit., *eyes* [3]Lit., *me and you* [a]Jer. 51:35 [b]Gen. 31:53
6 [1]Lit., *hand* [2]Lit., *eyes* [a]Gen. 16:9
7 [a]Gen. 21:17, 18; 22:11, 15; 31:11 [b]Gen. 20:1
8 [a]Gen. 3:9; 1 Kin. 19:9, 13
9 [1]Lit., *under her hands*
10 [1]Lit., *seed* [2]Or, *it shall not be counted for multitude* [a]Gen. 17:20
11 [1]I.e., God hears [2]Lit., *has heard* [a]Ex. 3:7, 9

12 "And he will be a [a]wild donkey
of a man,
His hand *will be* against everyone,
And everyone's hand *will be*
against him;
And he will [1]live [2b]to the east
of all his brothers."
13 Then she called the name of the
LORD who spoke to her, "[1a]Thou art
[2]a God who sees"; for she said,
"Have I even [3]remained alive here
after seeing Him?"
14 Therefore the well was called
[1]Beer-lahai-roi; behold, it is between [a]Kadesh and Bered.
15 So Hagar bore Abram a son;
and Abram called the name of his
son, whom Hagar bore, Ishmael.
16 And Abram was [a]eighty-six
years old when Hagar bore Ishmael
to [1]him.

CHAPTER 17

Abraham and the Covenant of Circumcision

NOW when Abram was ninety-
nine years old, [a]the LORD appeared
to Abram and said to him,
"I am [1]God [b]Almighty;
Walk before Me, and be
[2c]blameless.
2 "And I will [1]establish My [a]cov-
enant between Me and you,
And I will [b]multiply you exceedingly."
3 And Abram [a]fell on his face,
and God talked with him, saying,
4 "As for Me, behold, My covenant is with you,
And you shall be the father of
a [a]multitude of nations.
5 "No longer shall your name be
called [1]Abram,
But [a]your name shall be
[2]Abraham;
For [b]I will make you the father
of a multitude of nations.
6"And I will make you exceedingly fruitful, and I will make nations of you, and [a]kings shall come
forth from you.
7"And I will establish My covenant between Me and you and your
[1]descendants after you throughout
their generations for an [a]everlasting
covenant, [b]to be God to you and [c]to
your [1]descendants after you.
8"And [a]I will give to you and to
your [1]descendants after you, the
land of your sojournings, all the
land of Canaan, for an everlasting
possession; and I will be their God."
9 God said further to Abraham,
"Now as for you, [a]you shall keep My
covenant, you and your [1]descen-
dants after you throughout their
generations.
10"[a]This is My covenant, which
you shall keep, between Me and you
and your [1]descendants after you:
every male among you shall be circumcised.
11"And [a]you shall be circumcised
in the flesh of your foreskin; and it
shall be the sign of the covenant between Me and you.
12"And every male among you
who is [a]eight days old shall be circumcised throughout your generations, a *servant* who is born in the
house or who is bought with money
from any foreigner, who is not of
your [1]descendants.
13"A *servant* who is born in your
house or [a]who is bought with your
money shall surely be circumcised;
thus shall My covenant be in your
flesh for an everlasting covenant.
14"But an uncircumcised male
who is not circumcised in the flesh
of his foreskin, that person shall be
cut off from his people; he has broken My covenant."
15 Then God said to Abraham, "As
for Sarai your wife, you shall not
call her name Sarai, but [1]Sarah *shall
be* her name.
16"And I will bless her, and indeed
I will give you [a]a son by her. Then I
will bless her, and she shall be *a
mother of* nations; [b]kings of peoples
shall [1]come from her."
17 Then Abraham [a]fell on his face
and laughed, and said in his heart,
"Will a child be born to a man one
hundred years old? And will Sarah,
who is ninety years old, bear *a
child?*"
18 And Abraham said to God, "Oh
that Ishmael might live before
Thee!"
19 But God said, "No, but Sarah
your wife shall bear you [a]a son, and
you shall call his name [1]Isaac; and [b]I
will establish My covenant with him
for an everlasting covenant for his
[2]descendants after him.
20"And as for Ishmael, I have
heard you; behold, I will bless him,
and [a]will make him fruitful, and will
multiply him exceedingly. [b]He shall
[1]become the father of twelve
princes, and I will make him a great
nation.
21"But My covenant I will establish with [a]Isaac, whom Sarah will
bear to you at this season next
year."
22 And when He finished talking
with him, [a]God went up from Abraham.
23 Then Abraham took Ishmael

12 [1]Lit., *dwell* [2]Lit., *before the face of;* or, *in defiance of* [a]Job 24:5; 39:5-8 [b]Gen. 25:18
13 [1]Or, *Thou, God, dost see me* [2]Heb., *Elroi* [3]Lit., *seen here after the one who saw me* [a]Gen. 32:30
14 [1]I.e., The well of the living one who sees me [a]Gen. 14:7
16 [1]Lit., *Abram* [a]Gen. 12:4; 16:3
1 [1]Heb., *El Shaddai* [2]Lit., *complete, perfect;* or, *having integrity* [a]Gen. 12:7; 18:1 [b]Gen. 28:3; 35:11 [c]Gen. 6:9; Deut. 18:13
2 [1]Lit., *give* [a]Gen. 15:18 [b]Gen. 13:16; 15:5
3 [a]Gen. 17:17; 18:2
4 [a]Gen. 35:11; 48:19
5 [1]I.e., Exalted father [2]I.e., father of a multitude [a]Neh. 9:7 [b]Rom. 4:17
6 [a]Gen. 17:16; 35:11
7 [1]Lit., *seed* [a]Gen. 17:13, 19; Ps. 105:9, 10 [b]Lev. 11:45; 26:12, 45 [c]Gal. 3:16
8 [1]Lit., *seed* [a]Gen. 12:7; 13:15, 17
9 [1]Lit., *seed* [a]Ex. 19:5
10 [1]Lit., *seed* [a]John 7:22; Acts 7:8
11 [a]Ex. 12:48; Deut. 10:16
12 [1]Lit., *seed* [a]Lev. 12:3
13 [a]Ex. 12:44
15 [1]I.e., Princess
16 [1]Lit., *be* [a]Gen. 18:10 [b]Gen. 17:6; 36:31
17 [a]Gen. 17:3
19 [1]I.e., He laughs [2]Lit., *seed* [a]Gen. 17:16; 21:2 [b]Gen. 26:2-5
20 [1]Lit., *beget twelve princes* [a]Gen. 16:10 [b]Gen. 25:16
21 [a]Gen. 17:19; 18:10, 14
22 [a]Gen. 18:33; 35:13

his son, and all *the servants* who were [a]born in his house and all who were bought with his money, every male among the men of Abraham's household, and circumcised the flesh of their foreskin in the very same day, as God had said to him.

24 Now Abraham was ninety-nine years old when [a]he was circumcised in the flesh of his foreskin.

25 And [a]Ishmael his son was thirteen years old when he was circumcised in the flesh of his foreskin.

26 In the very same day Abraham was circumcised, and Ishmael his son.

27 And all the men of his household, who were born in the house or bought with money from a foreigner, were circumcised with him.

Chapter 18

Birth of Isaac Promised

Now [a]the Lord appeared to him by the [1b]oaks of Mamre, while he was sitting at the tent door in the heat of the day.

2 And when he lifted up his eyes and looked, behold, three [a]men were standing opposite him; and when he saw *them,* he ran from the tent door to meet them, and bowed himself to the earth,

3 and said, "[1]My lord, if now I have found favor in [2]your sight, please do not [3]pass [2]your servant by.

4 "Please let a little water be brought and [a]wash your feet, and [1]rest yourselves under the tree;

5 and [a]I will [1]bring a piece of bread, that you may [2]refresh yourselves; after that you may go on, since you have [3]visited your servant." And they said, "So do, as you have said."

6 So Abraham hurried into the tent to Sarah, and said, "[1]Quickly, prepare three [2]measures of fine flour, knead *it,* and make bread cakes."

7 Abraham also ran to the herd, and took a tender and [1]choice calf, and gave *it* to the servant; and he hurried to prepare it.

8 And he took curds and milk and the calf which he had prepared, and placed *it* before them; and he was standing by them under the tree [1]as they ate.

9 Then they said to him, "Where is Sarah your wife?" And he said, "Behold, in the tent."

10 And he said, "[a]I will surely return to you [1]at this time next year; and behold, Sarah your wife shall have a son." And Sarah was listening at the tent door, which was behind him.

11 Now [a]Abraham and Sarah were old, advanced in age; Sarah was past [1]childbearing.

12 And Sarah laughed [1]to herself, saying, "After I have become old, shall I have pleasure, my [a]lord being old also?"

13 And the Lord said to Abraham, "Why did Sarah laugh, saying, 'Shall I indeed [1]bear *a child,* when I am *so* old?'

14 "[a]Is anything too [1]difficult for the Lord? At the [b]appointed time I will return to you, [2]at this time next year, and Sarah shall have a son."

15 Sarah denied *it* however, saying, "I did not laugh"; for she was afraid. And He said, "No, but you did laugh."

16 Then [a]the men rose up from there, and looked down toward Sodom; and Abraham was walking with them to send them off.

17 And [a]the Lord said, "Shall I hide from Abraham what [b]I am about to do,

18 since Abraham will surely become a great and [1]mighty nation, and in him [a]all the nations of the earth will be blessed?

19 "For I have [1a]chosen him, in order that he may command his children and his household after him [b]to keep the way of the Lord by doing righteousness and justice; in order that the Lord may bring upon Abraham [c]what He has spoken about him."

20 And the Lord said, "[a]The outcry of Sodom and Gomorrah is indeed great, and their sin is exceedingly grave.

21 "[a]I will go down now, and see if they have done entirely according to its outcry, which has come to Me; and if not, I will know."

22 Then the [a]men turned away from there and went toward Sodom, while Abraham was still standing before [b]the Lord.

23 And Abraham came near and said, "[a]Wilt Thou indeed sweep away the righteous with the wicked?

24 "Suppose there are fifty righteous within the city; wilt Thou indeed sweep *it* away and not [1]spare the place for the sake of the fifty righteous who are in it?

25 "Far be it from Thee to do [1]such a thing, to slay the righteous with the wicked, so that [a]the righteous and the wicked are *treated* alike.

23 [a]Gen. 14:14
24 [a]Rom. 4:11
25 [a]Gen. 16:16
1 [1]Or, *terebinths* [a]Gen. 12:7; 17:1 [b]Gen. 13:18; 14:13
2 [a]Gen. 18:16, 22; 32:24; Josh. 5:13; Judg. 13:6-11
3 [1]Or, *O Lord* [2]Or, *Thy* [3]Lit., *pass away from your servant*
4 [1]Lit., *support* [a]Gen. 19:2; 24:32; 43:24
5 [1]Lit., *take* [2]Lit., *sustain your heart* [3]Lit., *come to* [a]Judg. 6:18, 19; 13:15, 16
6 [1]Lit., *Hasten three measures* [2]Heb., *seah;* i.e., one seah equals approximately eleven quarts
7 [1]Lit., *good*
8 [1]Lit., *and*
10 [1]Lit., *when the time revives* [a]Rom. 9:9
11 [1]Lit., *the manner of women* [a]Gen. 17:17
12 [1]Lit., *within* [a]1 Pet. 3:6
13 [1]Lit., *surely bear*
14 [1]Or, *wonderful* [2]Lit., *when the time revives* [a]Jer. 32:17, 27 [b]Gen. 17:21; 18:10
16 [a]Gen. 18:2, 22; 19:1
17 [a]Gen. 18:22, 26, 33 [b]Gen. 18:21; 19:24
18 [1]Or, *populous* [a]Gal. 3:8
19 [1]Lit., *known* [a]Neh. 9:7; Amos 3:2 [b]Gen. 17:9 [c]Gen. 12:2, 3
20 [a]Gen. 19:13; Ezek. 16:49, 50
21 [a]Gen. 11:5; Ex. 3:8
22 [a]Gen. 18:16; 19:1 [b]Gen. 18:17
23 [a]Ex. 23:7
24 [1]Or, *forgive*
25 [1]Lit., *after this manner* [a]Deut. 1:16, 17

Far be it from Thee! Shall not [b]the
Judge of all the earth [2]deal justly?"
26 So the LORD said, "If I find in
Sodom fifty righteous within the
city, then I will [1]spare the whole
place on their account."
27 And Abraham answered and
said, "Now behold, I have [1]ventured
to speak to the Lord, [a]although I am
but dust and ashes.
28 "Suppose the fifty righteous are
lacking five, wilt Thou destroy the
whole city because of five?" And He
said, "I will not destroy *it* if I find
forty-five there."
29 And he spoke to Him yet again
and said, "Suppose forty are found
there?" And He said, "I will not do *it*
on account of the forty."
30 Then he said, "[a]Oh may the
Lord not be angry, and I shall speak;
suppose thirty are found there?"
And He said, "I will not do *it* if I find
thirty there."
31 And he said, "Now behold, I
have [1]ventured to speak to the Lord;
suppose twenty are found there?"
And He said, "I will not destroy *it* on
account of the twenty."
32 Then he said, "Oh may the Lord
not be angry, and I shall speak only
this once; suppose ten are found
there?" And He said, "I will not destroy *it* on account of the ten."
33 And as soon as He had finished
speaking to Abraham [a]the LORD departed; and Abraham returned to
his place.

CHAPTER 19

The Doom of Sodom

NOW the [a]two angels came to
Sodom in the evening as Lot was
sitting in the gate of Sodom. When
[b]Lot saw *them,* he rose to meet them
and [1]bowed down *with his* face to
the ground.
2 And he said, "Now behold, my
lords, please turn aside into your
servant's house, and spend the
night, and wash your feet; then you
may rise early and go on your way."
They said however, "No, but we
shall spend the night in the square."
3 Yet he urged them strongly, so
they turned aside to him and entered his house; [a]and he prepared a
feast for them, and baked unleavened bread, and they ate.
4 Before they lay down, [a]the men
of the city, the men of Sodom, surrounded the house, both young and
old, all the people [1]from every quarter;
5 and they called to Lot and said
to him, "[a]Where are the men who
came to you tonight? Bring them out
to us that we may [1]have relations
with them."
6 But Lot went out to them at the
doorway, and shut the door behind
him,
7 and said, "Please, my brothers,
do not act wickedly.
8 "Now behold, [a]I have two
daughters who have not [1]had relations with man; please let me bring
them out to you, and do to them
[2]whatever you like; only do nothing
to these men, inasmuch as they
have come under the [3]shelter of my
roof."
9 But they said, "Stand aside."
Furthermore, they said, "This one
came in [1]as an alien, and already [a]he
is acting like a judge; now we will
treat you worse than them." So they
pressed hard against [2]Lot and came
near to break the door.
10 But [a]the men reached out their
[1]hands and brought Lot into the
house [2]with them, and shut the
door.
11 And [a]they [1]struck the men who
were at the doorway of the house
with blindness, both small and
great, so that they wearied *themselves trying* to find the doorway.
12 Then the men said to Lot,
"Whom else have you here? A son-
in-law, and your sons, and your
daughters, and whomever you have
in the city, bring *them* out of the
place;
13 for we are about to destroy this
place, because [a]their outcry has become so great before the LORD that
[b]the LORD has sent us to destroy it."
14 And Lot went out and spoke to
his sons-in-law, who [1]were to marry
his daughters, and said, "Up, get out
of this place, for the LORD will destroy the city." [a]But he appeared to
his sons-in-law [2]to be jesting.
15 And when morning dawned,
the angels urged Lot, saying, "Up,
take your wife and your two daughters, who are here, lest you be swept
away in the [1]punishment of the
city."
16 But he hesitated. So the men
[a]seized his hand and the hand of his
wife and the [1]hands of his daughters, [2]for the compassion of the
LORD *was* upon him; and they
brought him out, and put him outside the city.
17 And it came about when they
had brought them outside, that [1]one
said, "[a]Escape for your life! [b]Do not
look behind you, and do not stay
[2]anywhere in the [c]valley; escape to

25 [2]Lit., *do justice* [b]Deut. 32:4

26 [1]Or, *forgive*

27 [1]Lit., *undertaken* [a]Gen. 3:19; Job 30:19; 42:6

30 [a]Ex. 32:22

31 [1]Lit., *undertaken*

33 [a]Gen. 17:22; 35:13

1 [1]Lit., *bowed himself* [a]Gen. 18:22 [b]Gen. 18:2-5

3 [a]Gen. 18:6-8

4 [1]Or, *without exception;* lit., *from every end* [a]Gen. 13:13; 18:20

5 [1]I.e., have intercourse [a]Lev. 18:22; Judg. 19:22

8 [1]I.e., had intercourse [2]Lit., *as is good in your sight* [3]Lit., *shadow* [a]Judg. 19:24

9 [1]Lit., *to sojourn* [2]Lit., *the man, against Lot* [a]Ex. 2:14

10 [1]Lit., *hand* [2]Lit., *to* [a]Gen. 19:1

11 [1]Lit., *smote* [a]Deut. 28:28, 29; Acts 13:11

13 [a]Gen. 18:20 [b]Lev. 26:30-33; Deut. 4:26; 28:45

14 [1]Or, *had married;* lit., *were taking* [2]Lit., *like one who was jesting* [a]Jer. 43:1, 2

15 [1]Or, *iniquity*

16 [1]Lit., *hand* [2]Lit., *in* [a]Deut. 5:15; 6:21; 7:8

17 [1]Lit., *he* [2]Lit., *in all the circle* [a]Jer. 48:6 [b]Gen. 19:26 [c]Gen. 13:10

[d]the [3]mountains, lest you be swept
away."
18 But Lot said to them, "Oh no,
my lords!
19"Now behold, your servant has
found favor in your sight, and you
have magnified your lovingkindness, which you have shown me by
saving my life; but I cannot escape
to the [1]mountains, lest the disaster
overtake me and I die;
20 now behold, this town is near
enough to flee to, and it is small.
Please, let me escape there (is it not
small?) [1]that my life may be saved."
21 And he said to him, "Behold, I
grant you this [1]request also, not to
overthrow the town of which you
have spoken.
22"Hurry, escape there, for I cannot do anything until you arrive
there." Therefore the name of the
town was called [1]Zoar.
23 The sun had risen over the
earth when Lot came to Zoar.
24 Then the LORD [a]rained on Sodom and Gomorrah brimstone and
fire from the LORD out of heaven,
25 and [a]He overthrew those cities,
and all the [1]valley, and all the inhabitants of the cities, and what
grew on the ground.
26 But his wife, from behind him,
[a]looked *back;* and she became a pillar of salt.
27 Now Abraham arose early in
the morning *and went* to [a]the place
where he had stood before the LORD;
28 and he looked down toward
Sodom and Gomorrah, and toward
all the land of the [1]valley, and he
saw, and behold, [a]the smoke of the
land ascended like the smoke of a
[2]furnace.
29 Thus it came about, when God
destroyed the cities of the [1]valley,
that [a]God remembered Abraham,
and [b]sent Lot out of the midst of the
overthrow, when He overthrew the
cities in which Lot lived.

Lot is Debased

30 And Lot went up from Zoar,
and [1]stayed in the [2]mountains, and
his two daughters with him; for he
was afraid to [3]stay in Zoar; and he
[1]stayed in a cave, he and his two
daughters.
31 Then the first-born said to the
younger, "Our father is old, and
there is not a man [1]on earth to come
in to us after the manner of the
earth.
32"Come, let us make our father
drink wine, and let us lie with him,
that we may preserve [1]our family
through our father."
33 So they made their father drink
wine that night, and the first-born
went in and lay with her father; and
he did not know when she lay down
or when she arose.
34 And it came about on the morrow, that the first-born said to the
younger, "Behold, I lay last night
with my father; let us make him
drink wine tonight also; then you go
in and lie with him, that we may preserve [1]our family through our father."
35 So they made their father drink
wine that night also, and the younger arose and lay with him; and he
did not know when she lay down or
when she arose.
36 Thus both the daughters of Lot
were with child by their father.
37 And the first-born bore a son,
and called his name [a]Moab; he is the
father of the Moabites to this day.
38 And as for the younger, she also
bore a son, and called his name Ben-
ammi; he is the father of the [1]sons of
[a]Ammon to this day.

CHAPTER 20

Abraham's Treachery

NOW Abraham journeyed from
[a]there toward the land of [b]the [1]Neg-
ev, and [2]settled between Kadesh
and Shur; then he sojourned in [c]Ge-
rar.
2 And Abraham said of Sarah his
wife, "[a]She is my sister." So [b]A-
bimelech king of Gerar sent and
took Sarah.
3 [a]But God came to Abimelech in
a dream of the night, and said to
him, "Behold, you are a dead man
because of the woman whom you
have taken, for she is [1]married."
4 Now Abimelech had not come
near her; and he said, "Lord, wilt
Thou slay a nation, even *though*
[1]blameless?
5"Did he not himself say to me,
'She is my sister'? And she [a]herself
said, 'He is my brother.' In [b]the integrity of my heart and the innocence of my [1]hands I have done
this."
6 Then God said to him in the
dream, "Yes, I know that in the integrity of your heart you have done
this, and I also [1]kept you from sinning against Me; therefore I did not
let you touch her.
7"Now therefore restore the
man's wife, for [a]he is a prophet, and
he will pray for you, and you will
live. But if you do not restore *her,*
know that you shall surely die, you
and all who are yours."

17 [3]Lit., *mountain* [d]Gen. 14:10

19 [1]Lit., *mountain*

20 [1]Lit., *and my soul will live*

21 [1]Lit., *thing*

22 [1]I.e., Small

24 [a]Luke 17:29; Jude 7

25 [1]Lit., *circle* [a]Deut. 29:23; Is. 13:19; Lam. 4:6; 2 Pet. 2:6

26 [a]Gen. 19:17; Luke 17:32

27 [a]Gen. 18:22

28 [1]Lit., *circle* [2]Lit., *kiln* [a]Rev. 9:2

29 [1]Lit., *circle* [a]Deut. 7:8; 9:5, 27 [b]2 Pet. 2:7

30 [1]Lit., *dwelt* [2]Lit., *mountain* [3]Lit., *dwell*

31 [1]Or, *in the land*

32 [1]Lit., *seed from our father*

34 [1]Lit., *seed from our father*

37 [a]Deut. 2:9

38 [1]Heb., *Bene-Ammon* [a]Deut. 2:19

1 [1]I.e., South country [2]Lit., *dwelt* [a]Gen. 18:1 [b]Gen. 12:9 [c]Gen. 26:1, 6

2 [a]Gen. 12:13; 20:12 [b]Gen. 12:15

3 [1]Lit., *married to a husband* [a]Gen. 12:17, 18

4 [1]Lit., *righteous*

5 [1]Lit., *palms* [a]Gen. 20:13 [b]1 Kin. 9:4; Ps. 7:8; 26:6

6 [1]Lit., *restrained*

7 [a]1 Sam. 7:5; Job 42:8

8 So Abimelech arose early in the morning and called all his servants and told all these things in their hearing; and the men were greatly frightened.

9 [a]Then Abimelech called Abraham and said to him, "What have you done to us? And [1]how have I sinned against you, that you have brought on me and on my kingdom a great sin? You have done to me [2]things that ought not to be done."

10 And Abimelech said to Abraham, "What have you [1]encountered, that you have done this thing?"

11 And Abraham said, "Because I thought, surely there is no fear of God in this place; and [a]they will kill me because of my wife.

12 "Besides, she actually is my sister, the daughter of my father, but not the daughter of my mother, and she became my wife;

13 and it came about, when God caused me to wander from my father's house, that I said to her, 'This is [1]the kindness which you will show to me: [2]everywhere we go, [a]say of me, "He is my brother." ' "

14 [a]Abimelech then took sheep and oxen and male and female servants, and gave them to Abraham, and restored his wife Sarah to him.

15 And Abimelech said, "[a]Behold, my land is before you; [1]settle wherever [2]you please."

16 And to Sarah he said, "Behold, I have given your brother a thousand pieces of silver; behold, it is [1]your vindication before all who are with you, and before all men you are cleared."

17 And [a]Abraham prayed to God; and God healed Abimelech and his wife and his maids, so that they bore *children*.

18 [a]For the LORD had closed fast all the wombs of the household of Abimelech because of Sarah, Abraham's wife.

CHAPTER 21

Isaac Is Born

[a]THEN the LORD took note of Sarah as He had said, and the LORD did for Sarah as He had [1]promised.

2 [a]So Sarah conceived and bore a son to Abraham in his old age, at [b]the appointed time of which God had spoken to him.

3 And Abraham called the name of his son who was born to him, whom Sarah bore to him, [a]Isaac.

4 Then Abraham circumcised his son Isaac when he was [a]eight days old, as God had commanded him.

5 Now Abraham was [a]one hundred years old when his son Isaac was born to him.

6 And Sarah said, "God has made [a]laughter for me; everyone who hears will laugh [1]with me."

7 And she said, "[a]Who would have said to Abraham that Sarah would nurse children? Yet I have borne him a son in his old age."

8 And the child grew and was weaned, and Abraham made a great feast on the day that Isaac was weaned.

Sarah Turns against Hagar

9 Now Sarah saw [a]the son of Hagar the Egyptian, whom she had borne to Abraham, [1]mocking.

10 Therefore she said to Abraham, "[a]Drive out this maid and her son, for the son of this maid shall not be an heir with my son [1]Isaac."

11 [a]And the matter [1]distressed Abraham greatly because of his son.

12 But God said to Abraham, "[1]Do not be distressed because of the lad and your maid; whatever Sarah tells you, listen to her, for [a]through Isaac [2]your descendants shall be named.

13 "And of [a]the son of the maid I will make a nation also, because he is your [1]descendant."

14 So Abraham rose early in the morning, and took bread and a [1]skin of water, and gave *them* to Hagar, putting *them* on her shoulder, and *gave her* the boy, and sent her away. And she departed, and wandered about in the wilderness of Beersheba.

15 And the water in the skin was used up, and she [1]left the boy under one of the bushes.

16 Then she went and sat down opposite him, about a bowshot away, for she said, "Do not let me [1]see the boy die." And she sat opposite him, and [a]lifted up her voice and wept.

17 And God [a]heard the lad crying; and the angel of God called to Hagar from heaven, and said to her, "What is the matter with you, Hagar? [b]Do not fear, for God has heard the voice of the lad where he is.

18 "Arise, lift up the lad, and hold him by [1]the hand; [a]for I will make a great nation of him."

19 Then God opened her eyes and she saw [a]a well of water; and she went and filled the [1]skin with water, and gave the lad a drink.

9 [1]Lit., *what* [2]Lit., *deeds* [a]Gen. 12:18
10 [1]Lit., *seen*
11 [a]Gen. 12:12; 26:7
13 [1]Lit., *your* [2]Lit., *at every place where* [a]Gen. 20:5
14 [a]Gen. 12:16
15 [1]Lit., *dwell* [2]Lit., *it is good in your sight* [a]Gen. 34:10
16 [1]Lit., *for you a covering of the eyes*
17 [a]Num. 12:13; 21:7
18 [a]Gen. 12:17
1 [1]Lit., *spoken* [a]Gen. 17:16, 21; 18:10, 14
2 [a]Gal. 4:22; Heb. 11:11 [b]Gen. 17:21; 18:10, 14
3 [a]Gen. 17:19, 21
4 [a]Gen. 17:12; Acts 7:8
5 [a]Gen. 17:17
6 [1]Lit., *for* [a]Gen. 18:13; Is. 54:1
7 [a]Gen. 18:13
9 [1]Or, *playing* [a]Gen. 16:15
10 [1]Lit., *with Isaac* [a]Gal. 4:30
11 [1]Lit., *was very grievous in Abraham's sight* [a]Gen. 17:18
12 [1]Lit., *Do not let it be grievous in your sight* [2]Lit., *your seed will be called* [a]Rom. 9:7; Heb. 11:18
13 [1]Lit., *seed* [a]Gen. 16:10; 21:18; 25:12-18
14 [1]I.e., a skin used as a bottle
15 [1]Lit., *cast*
16 [1]Lit., *look upon the death of the child* [a]Jer. 6:26; Amos 8:10
17 [a]Ex. 3:7; Deut. 26:7; Ps. 6:8 [b]Gen. 26:24
18 [1]Lit., *your* [a]Gen. 16:10; 21:13; 25:12
19 [1]Note v. 14 [a]Gen. 16:7, 14

20 And [a]God was with the lad, and
he grew; and he [1]lived in the wilderness, and became an archer.
21 And [a]he [1]lived in the wilderness
of Paran; and his mother took a wife
for him from the land of Egypt.

Covenant with Abimelech

22 Now it came about at that time,
that [a]Abimelech and Phicol, the
commander of his army, spoke to
Abraham, saying, "[b]God is with you
in all that you do;
23 now therefore swear to me here
by God that you will not deal falsely
with me, or with my offspring, or
with my posterity; but according to
the kindness that I have shown to
you, you shall show to me, and to
the land in which you have sojourned."
24 And Abraham said, "I swear
it."
25 But Abraham [1]complained to
Abimelech because of the well of
water which the servants of Abimelech [a]had seized.
26 And Abimelech said, "I do not
know who has done this thing; neither did you tell me, nor did I hear of
it [1]until today."
27 And Abraham took sheep and
oxen, and gave them to Abimelech;
and [a]the two of them made a covenant.
28 Then Abraham set seven ewe
lambs of the flock by themselves.
29 And Abimelech said to Abraham, "What do these seven ewe
lambs mean, which you have set by
themselves?"
30 And he said, "You shall take
these seven ewe lambs from my
hand in order that it may be a witness to me, that I dug this well."
31 Therefore he called that place
[a]Beersheba; because there the two
of them took an oath.
32 So they made a covenant at
Beersheba; and Abimelech and Phicol, the commander of his army,
arose and returned to the land of the
Philistines.
33 And *Abraham* planted a tamarisk tree at Beersheba, and there [a]he
called on the name of the LORD, the
[b]Everlasting God.
34 And Abraham sojourned [a]in
the land of the Philistines for many
days.

CHAPTER 22

The Offering of Isaac

NOW it came about after these
things, that [a]God tested Abraham,
and said to him, "[b]Abraham!" And
he said, "Here I am."
2 And He said, "Take now [a]your
son, your only son, whom you love,
Isaac, and go to the land of [b]Moriah;
and offer him there as a [c]burnt offering on one of the mountains of
which I will tell you."
3 So Abraham rose early in the
morning and saddled his donkey,
and took two of his young men with
him and Isaac his son; and he split
wood for the burnt offering, and
arose and went to the place of which
God had told him.
4 On the third day Abraham
raised his eyes and saw the place
from a distance.
5 And Abraham said to his young
men, "Stay here with the donkey,
and I and the lad will go yonder; and
we will worship and return to you."
6 And Abraham took the wood of
the burnt offering and [a]laid it on
Isaac his son, and he took in his
hand the fire and the knife. So the
two of them walked on together.
7 And Isaac spoke to Abraham
his father and said, "My father!"
And he said, "Here I am, my son."
And he said, "Behold, the fire and
the wood, but where is the [a]lamb for
the burnt offering?"
8 And Abraham said, "God will
[1]provide for Himself the lamb for
the burnt offering, my son." So the
two of them walked on together.
9 Then they came to [a]the place of
which God had told him; and Abraham built [b]the altar there, and arranged the wood, and bound his son
Isaac, and [c]laid him on the altar on
top of the wood.
10 And Abraham stretched out his
hand, and took the knife to slay his
son.
11 But [a]the angel of the LORD
called to him from heaven, and said,
"Abraham, Abraham!" And he said,
"Here I am."
12 And he said, "Do not stretch
out your hand against the lad, and
do nothing to him; for now I know
that you [1]fear God, since you have
not withheld [a]your son, your only
son, from Me."
13 Then Abraham raised his eyes
and looked, and behold, behind *him*
a ram caught in the thicket by his
horns; and Abraham went and took
the ram, and offered him up for a
burnt offering in the place of his son.
14 And Abraham called the name
of that place [1]The LORD Will Provide, as it is said to this day, "In the
mount of the LORD [a]it will [2]be provided."
15 Then the angel of the LORD

20 [1]Lit., *dwelt* [a]Gen. 28:15; 39:2, 3, 21
21 [1]Lit., *dwelt* [a]Gen. 25:18
22 [a]Gen. 20:14; 26:26 [b]Gen. 26:28
25 [1]Lit., *reproved* [a]Gen. 26:15, 18, 20-22
26 [1]Lit., *except*
27 [a]Gen. 26:31
31 [a]Gen. 21:14; 26:33
33 [a]Gen. 12:8 [b]Ex. 15:18; Deut. 32:40; Ps. 90:2; Is. 40:28; Jer. 10:10
34 [a]Gen. 22:19
1 [a]Deut. 8:2, 16 [b]Gen. 22:11
2 [a]Gen. 22:12, 16; John 3:16; 1 John 4:9 [b]2 Chr. 3:1 [c]Gen. 8:20
6 [a]John 19:17
7 [a]Ex. 29:38-42; John 1:29, 36; Rev. 13:8
8 [1]Lit., *see*
9 [a]Gen. 22:2 [b]Gen. 12:7, 8; 13:18 [c]Heb. 11:17-19
11 [a]Gen. 16:7-11; 21:17, 18
12 [1]Or, *reverence;* lit., *a fearer of God* [a]Gen. 22:2, 16
14 [1]Heb., YHWH-*jireh* [2]Lit., *be seen* [a]Gen. 22:8

called to Abraham a second time from heaven,

16 and said, "[a]By Myself I have sworn, declares the LORD, because you have done this thing, and have not withheld your son, your only son,

17 indeed I will greatly bless you, and I will greatly multiply your [1]seed as the [a]stars of the heavens, and as [b]the sand which is on the seashore; and [c]your [1]seed shall possess the gate of [2]their enemies.

18 "And [a]in your [1]seed all the nations of the earth shall [2]be blessed, because you have [b]obeyed My voice."

19 [a]So Abraham returned to his young men, and they arose and went together to Beersheba; and Abraham lived at Beersheba.

20 Now it came about after these things, that it was told Abraham, saying, "Behold, [a]Milcah [1]also has borne children to your brother Nahor:

21 Uz his first-born and Buz his brother and Kemuel the father of Aram

22 and Chesed and Hazo and Pildash and Jidlaph and Bethuel."

23 And Bethuel [1]became the father of [a]Rebekah: these eight Milcah bore to Nahor, Abraham's brother.

24 And his concubine, whose name was Reumah, [1]also bore Tebah and Gaham and Tahash and Maacah.

CHAPTER 23

Death and Burial of Sarah

NOW [1]Sarah lived one hundred and twenty-seven years; *these were* the years of the life of Sarah.

2 And Sarah died in [a]Kiriath-arba (that is, Hebron) in the land of Canaan; and Abraham [1]went in to mourn for Sarah and to weep for her.

3 Then Abraham rose from before his dead, and spoke to the [a]sons of Heth, saying,

4 "I am [a]a stranger and a sojourner among you; give me a [1]burial site among you, that I may bury my dead out of my sight."

5 And the sons of Heth answered Abraham, saying to him,

6 "Hear us, my lord, you are a [1a]mighty prince among us; bury your dead in the choicest of our graves; none of us will refuse you his grave for burying your dead."

7 So Abraham rose and bowed to the people of the land, the sons of Heth.

8 And he spoke with them, saying, "If it is your [1]wish *for me* to bury my dead out of my sight, hear me, and approach [a]Ephron the son of Zohar for me,

9 that he may give me the cave of Machpelah which he owns, which is at the end of his field; for the full price let him give it to me in [1]your presence for a [2]burial site."

10 Now Ephron was sitting among the sons of Heth; and Ephron the Hittite answered Abraham in the hearing of the sons of Heth; *even* [a]of all who went in at the gate of his city, saying,

11 "No, my lord, hear me; I give you the field, and I give you the cave that is in it. In the presence of the sons of my people I give it to you; bury your dead."

12 And Abraham bowed before the people of the land.

13 And he spoke to Ephron in the hearing of the people of the land, saying, "If you will only please listen to me; I will give the price of the field, accept *it* from me, that I may bury my dead there."

14 Then Ephron answered Abraham, saying to him,

15 "My lord, listen to me; a piece of land worth four hundred [a]shekels of silver, what is that between me and you? So bury your dead."

16 And Abraham listened to Ephron; and Abraham [a]weighed out for Ephron the silver which he had named in the [1]hearing of the sons of Heth, four hundred shekels of silver, [2]commercial standard.

17 So [a]Ephron's field, which was in Machpelah, which faced Mamre, the field and cave which was in it, and all the trees which were in the field, that were [1]within all the confines of its border, [2]were deeded over

18 to Abraham for a possession [a]in the presence of the sons of Heth, before all who went in at the gate of his city.

19 And after this, Abraham buried Sarah his wife in the cave of the field at Machpelah facing Mamre (that is, Hebron) in the land of Canaan.

20 So the field, and the cave that is in it, [1]were deeded over to Abraham for a [2]burial site by the sons of Heth.

CHAPTER 24

A Bride for Isaac

NOW Abraham was old, advanced in age; and the LORD had [a]blessed Abraham in every way.

16 [a]Heb. 6:13, 14

17 [1]Or, *descendants* [2]Lit., *his* [a]Gen. 15:5; 26:4 [b]Gen. 32:12 [c]Gen. 24:60

18 [1]Or, *descendants* [2]Or, *bless themselves* [a]Acts 3:25; Gal. 3:8, 16 [b]Gen. 18:19

19 [a]Gen. 22:5

20 [1]Lit., *she also* [a]Gen. 11:29

23 [1]Lit., *begot* [a]Gen. 24:15

24 [1]Lit., *she also*

1 [1]Lit., *the life of Sarah was*

2 [1]Or, *proceeded* [a]Josh. 14:15; 15:13; 21:11

3 [a]Gen. 10:15; 15:20

4 [1]Lit., *possession of a grave* [a]Lev. 25:23; 1 Chr. 29:15; Ps. 39:12; Heb. 11:9, 13

6 [1]Lit., *prince of God* [a]Gen. 14:14; 20:7

8 [1]Lit., *soul* [a]Gen. 25:9

9 [1]Lit., *in the midst of you* [2]Lit., *possession of a burial place*

10 [a]Gen. 23:18; 34:20, 24; Ruth 4:1, 11

15 [a]Ex. 30:13

16 [1]Lit., *ears* [2]Lit., *current according to the merchant* [a]2 Sam. 14:26; Jer. 32:9; Zech. 11:12

17 [1]Lit., *in all its border around* [2]Or, *were ratified* [a]Gen. 25:9; 49:29, 30; 50:13

18 [a]Gen. 23:10

20 [1]Or, *were ratified* [2]Lit., *possession of a burial place*

1 [a]Gen. 24:35; 12:2

2 And Abraham said to his servant, the oldest of his household, who had charge of all that he owned, "[a]Please place your hand under my thigh,

3 and I will make you swear by the LORD, [a]the God of heaven and the God of earth, that you shall not take a wife for my son from the daughters of [b]the Canaanites, among whom I live,

4 but you shall go to [a]my country and to my relatives, and take a wife for my son Isaac."

5 And the servant said to him, "Suppose the woman will not be willing to follow me to this land; should I take your son back to the land from where you came?"

6 Then Abraham said to him, "[a]Beware lest you take my son back there!

7 "[a]The LORD, the God of heaven, who took me from my father's house and from the land of my birth, and who spoke to me, and who swore to me, saying, '[b]To your [1]descendants I will give this land', He will send [c]His angel before you, and you will take a wife for my son from there.

8 "But if the woman is not willing to follow you, then you will be free from this my oath; [a]only do not take my son back there."

9 So the servant [a]placed his hand under the thigh of Abraham his master, and swore to him concerning this matter.

10 Then the servant took ten camels from the camels of his master, and set out with a variety of [a]good things of his master's in his hand; and he arose, and went to [1]Mesopotamia, to [b]the city of Nahor.

11 And he made the camels kneel down outside the city by [a]the well of water at evening time, [b]the time when women go out to draw water.

12 And he said, "[a]O LORD, the God of my master Abraham, [b]please [1]grant me success today, and show lovingkindness to my master Abraham.

13 "Behold, [a]I am standing by the [1]spring, and the daughters of the men of the city are coming out to draw water;

14 now may it be that the girl to whom I say, 'Please let down your jar so that I may drink,' and [1]who answers, 'Drink, and I will water your camels also';—*may* she *be the one* whom Thou hast appointed for Thy servant Isaac; and by this I shall know that Thou hast shown lovingkindness to my master."

Rebekah Is Chosen

15 And it came about [a]before he had finished speaking, that behold, [b]Rebekah who was born to Bethuel the son of Milcah, the wife of Abraham's brother Nahor, came out with her jar on her shoulder.

16 And the girl was [a]very beautiful, a virgin, and no man had [1]had relations with her; and she went down to the spring and filled her jar, and came up.

17 Then the servant ran to meet her, and said, "Please let me drink a little water from your jar."

18 And [a]she said, "Drink, my lord"; and she quickly lowered her jar to her hand, and gave him a drink.

19 Now when she had finished giving him a drink, [a]she said, "I will draw also for your camels until they have finished drinking."

20 So she quickly emptied her jar into the trough, and ran back to the well to draw, and she drew for all his camels.

21 [a]Meanwhile, the man was gazing at her [1]in silence, to know whether the LORD had made his journey successful or not.

22 Then it came about, when the camels had finished drinking, that the man took a [a]gold ring weighing a half-shekel and two bracelets for her [1]wrists weighing ten shekels in gold,

23 and said, "Whose daughter are you? Please tell me, is there room for us to lodge in your father's house?"

24 And she said to him, "[a]I am the daughter of Bethuel, the son of Milcah, whom she bore to Nahor."

25 Again she said to him, "We have plenty of both straw and feed, and room to lodge in."

26 Then the man [a]bowed low and worshiped the LORD.

27 And he said, "[a]Blessed be the LORD, the God of my master Abraham, who has not forsaken His lovingkindness and His truth toward my master; as for me, [b]the LORD has guided me in the way to the house of my master's brothers."

28 Then [a]the girl ran and told her mother's household about these things.

29 Now Rebekah had a brother whose name was [a]Laban; and Laban ran outside to the man at the spring.

30 And it came about that when he saw the ring, and the bracelets on his sister's [1]wrists, and when he heard the words of Rebekah his sis-

2 [a]Gen. 47:29
3 [a]Gen. 14:19, 22 [b]Gen. 10:18, 19; 26:34, 35; 28:1, 2, 8
4 [a]Gen. 12:1; Heb. 11:15
6 [a]Gen. 24:8
7 [1]Lit., *seed* [a]Gen. 24:3 [b]Gen. 12:7; 13:15; 15:18 [c]Gen. 16:7; 21:17; 22:11; Ex. 23:20, 23
8 [a]Gen. 24:6
9 [a]Gen. 24:2
10 [1]Heb., *Aram-naharaim, Aram of the two rivers* [a]Gen. 24:22, 53 [b]Gen. 11:31, 32
11 [a]Gen. 24:42 [b]1 Sam. 9:11
12 [1]Lit., *cause to occur for me* [a]Gen. 24:27, 42, 48 [b]Gen. 27:20
13 [1]Lit., *fountain of water* [a]Gen. 24:43
14 [1]Lit., *she will say*
15 [a]Gen. 24:45 [b]Gen. 22:20, 23
16 [1]Lit., *known* [a]Gen. 12:11; 29:17
18 [a]Gen. 24:14, 46
19 [a]Gen. 24:14
21 [1]Lit., *keeping silent* [a]Gen. 24:12-14, 27, 52
22 [1]Lit., *hands* [a]Gen. 24:47
24 [a]Gen. 24:15
26 [a]Gen. 24:48, 52
27 [a]Gen. 24:12, 42, 48 [b]Gen. 24:21
28 [a]Gen. 29:12
29 [a]Gen. 29:13
30 [1]Lit., *hands*

ter, saying, "[2]This is what the man said to me," he went to the man; and behold, he was standing by the camels at the spring.

31 And he said, "[a]Come in, blessed of the LORD! Why do you stand outside since [b]I have prepared the house, and a place for the camels?"

32 So the man entered the house. Then [1]Laban unloaded the camels, and he gave straw and feed to the camels, and water to wash his feet and the feet of the men who were with him.

33 But when *food* was set before him to eat, he said, "I will not eat until I have told my business." And he said, "Speak on."

34 So he said, "I am [a]Abraham's servant.

35"And [a]the LORD has greatly blessed my master, so that he has become [1]rich; and He has given him [b]flocks and herds, and silver and gold, and servants and maids, and camels and donkeys.

36"[a]Now Sarah my master's wife bore a son to my master [1]in her old age; [b]and he has given him all that he has.

37"[a]And my master made me swear, saying, 'You shall not take a wife for my son from the daughters of the Canaanites, in whose land I [1]live;

38 but you shall go to my father's house, and to my relatives, and take a wife for my son.'

39"[a]And I said to my master, 'Suppose the woman does not follow me.'

40"And he said to me, '[a]The LORD, before whom I have walked, will send His angel with you to make your journey successful, and you will take a wife for my son from my relatives, and from my father's house;

41 [a]then you will be free from my oath, when you come to my relatives; and if they do not give her to you, you will be free from my oath.'

42"So [a]I came today to the spring, and said, 'O LORD, the God of my master Abraham, if now Thou wilt make my journey on which I go successful;

43 [a]behold, I am standing by the [1]spring, and may it be that the maiden who comes out to draw, and to whom I say, "[b]Please let me drink a little water from your jar";

44 and she will say to me, "You drink, and I will draw for your camels also"; let her be the woman whom the LORD has appointed for my master's son.'

45"Before I had finished [a]speaking in my heart, behold, [b]Rebekah came out with her jar on her shoulder, and went down to the spring and drew; and [c]I said to her, 'Please let me drink.'

46"And she quickly lowered her jar from her *shoulder*, and said, '[a]Drink, and I will water your camels also'; so I drank, and she watered the camels also.

47"[a]Then I asked her, and said, 'Whose daughter are you?' And she said, 'The daughter of Bethuel, Nahor's son, whom Milcah bore to him'; and I put the ring on her nose, and the bracelets on her [1]wrists.

48"And [a]I bowed low and worshiped the LORD, and blessed the LORD, the God of my master Abraham, [b]who had guided me in the right way to take the daughter of my master's [1]kinsman for his son.

49"So now if you are going to [1a]deal kindly and truly with my master, tell me; and if not, let me know, that I may turn to the right hand or the left."

50 Then Laban and Bethuel answered and said, "The matter comes from the LORD; [a]so we cannot speak to you bad or good.

51"Behold, Rebekah is before you, take *her* and go, and let her be the wife of your master's son, as the LORD has spoken."

52 And it came about when Abraham's servant heard their words, that he [a]bowed himself to the ground [1]before the LORD.

53 And the servant brought out [a]articles of silver and articles of gold, and garments, and gave them to Rebekah; he also gave precious things to her brother and to her mother.

54 Then he and the men who were with him ate and drank and spent the night. When they arose in the morning, he said, "[a]Send me away to my master."

55 But her brother and her mother said, "[a]Let the girl stay with us *a few* days, say ten; afterward she may go."

56 And he said to them, "Do not delay me, since the LORD has prospered my way. Send me away that I may go to my master."

57 And they said, "We will call the girl and [1]consult her wishes."

58 Then they called Rebekah and said to her, "Will you go with this man?" And she said, "I will go."

59 Thus they sent away their sister Rebekah and [a]her nurse with Abraham's servant and his men.

30 [2]Lit., *Thus the man*

31 [a]Gen. 29:14 [b]Gen. 18:3-5; 19:2, 3

32 [1]Lit., *he*

34 [a]Gen. 24:2

35 [1]Lit., *great* [a]Gen. 24:1 [b]Gen. 13:2

36 [1]Lit., *after she was old* [a]Gen. 21:1-7 [b]Gen. 25:5

37 [1]Lit., *dwell* [a]Gen. 24:2-4

39 [a]Gen. 24:5

40 [a]Gen. 24:7

41 [a]Gen. 24:8

42 [a]Gen. 24:11, 12

43 [1]Lit., *fountain of water* [a]Gen. 24:13 [b]Gen. 24:14

45 [a]1 Sam. 1:13 [b]Gen. 24:15 [c]Gen. 24:17

46 [a]Gen. 24:18

47 [1]Lit., *hands* [a]Gen. 24:23, 24

48 [1]Lit., *brother* [a]Gen. 24:26, 52 [b]Gen. 24:27

49 [1]Lit., *show lovingkindness and truth* [a]Gen. 47:29; Josh. 2:14

50 [a]Gen. 31:24, 29

52 [1]Lit., *to* [a]Gen. 24:26, 48

53 [a]Gen. 24:10, 22

54 [a]Gen. 24:56; 30:25

55 [a]Judg. 19:4

57 [1]Lit., *ask her mouth*

59 [a]Gen. 35:8

60 And they blessed Rebekah and
said to her,
"May you, our sister,
[a]Become thousands of ten
thousands,
And may [b]your [1]descendants
possess
The gate of those who hate
them."

Isaac Marries Rebekah

61 Then Rebekah arose with her
maids, and they mounted the camels and followed the man. So the
servant took Rebekah and departed.
62 Now Isaac had come from
going to [a]Beer-lahai-roi; for he [1]was
living in [2b]the Negev.
63 And Isaac went out [a]to [1]medi-
tate in the field toward evening; and
[b]he lifted up his eyes and looked,
and behold, camels were coming.
64 And Rebekah lifted up her eyes,
and when she saw Isaac she dismounted from the camel.
65 And she said to the servant,
"Who is that man walking in the
field to meet us?" And the servant
said, "He is my master." Then she
took her [1]veil and covered herself.
66 And the servant told Isaac all
the things that he had done.
67 Then Isaac brought her into his
mother Sarah's tent, and he took
Rebekah, and she became his wife;
and [a]he loved her; thus Isaac was
comforted after [b]his mother's death.

Chapter 25

Abraham's Death

Now Abraham took another wife,
[1]whose name was Keturah.
2 And [a]she bore to him Zimran
and Jokshan and Medan and Midian
and Ishbak and Shuah.
3 And Jokshan [1]became the father of Sheba and Dedan. And the
sons of Dedan were Asshurim and
Letushim and Leummim.
4 And the sons of Midian *were*
Ephah and Epher and Hanoch and
Abida and Eldaah. All these *were*
the sons of Keturah.
5 [a]Now Abraham gave all that he
had to Isaac;
6 but to the sons of [1]his concubines, Abraham gave gifts while he
was still living, and sent them away
from his son Isaac eastward, to the
land of the east.
7 And these are [1]all the years of
Abraham's life that he lived, [a]one
hundred and seventy-five years.
8 And Abraham breathed his last
and died [a]in a [1]ripe old age, an old
man and satisfied with *life;* and he
was [b]gathered to his people.
9 Then his sons Isaac and Ishmael buried him in [a]the cave of
Machpelah, in the field of Ephron
the son of Zohar the Hittite, facing
Mamre,
10 the field which Abraham purchased from the sons of Heth; there
Abraham was buried with Sarah his
wife.
11 And it came about after the
death of Abraham, that [a]God
blessed his son Isaac; and Isaac
[1]lived by [b]Beer-lahai-roi.

Descendants of Ishmael

12 Now these are *the records of*
the generations of [a]Ishmael, Abraham's son, whom Hagar the Egyptian, Sarah's maid, bore to Abraham;
13 and these are the names of [a]the
sons of Ishmael, by their names, [1]in
the order of their birth: Nebaioth,
the first-born of Ishmael, and Kedar
and Adbeel and Mibsam
14 and Mishma and Dumah and
Massa,
15 Hadad and Tema, Jetur, Naphish and Kedemah.
16 These are the sons of Ishmael
and these are their names, by their
villages, and by their camps;
[a]twelve princes according to their
[1]tribes.
17 And these are the years of the
life of Ishmael, [a]one hundred and
thirty-seven years; and he breathed
his last and died, and was [b]gathered
to his people.
18 And they [1]settled from Havilah
to [a]Shur which is [2]east of Egypt [3]as
one goes toward Assyria; [b]he [4]set-
tled in defiance of all his [5]relatives.

Isaac's Sons

19 Now these are *the records of*
the generations of Isaac, Abraham's
son: Abraham [1]became the father of
Isaac;
20 and Isaac was forty years old
when he took [a]Rebekah, the daughter of Bethuel the [1]Syrian of Paddan-aram, the sister of Laban the
[1]Syrian, to be his wife.
21 And Isaac prayed to the Lord
on behalf of his wife, because she
was barren; and [a]the Lord [1]an-
swered him and Rebekah his wife
conceived.
22 But the children struggled together within her; and she said, "If it
is so, why then am I *this way?*" So
she went to inquire of the Lord.
23 And the Lord said to her,

60 [1]Lit., *seed* [a]Gen. 17:16 [b]Gen. 22:17

62 [1]Lit., *was dwelling* [2]I.e., South country [a]Gen. 16:14; 25:11 [b]Gen. 20:1

63 [1]Or, *stroll,* meaning uncertain. [a]Ps. 119:15, 27, 48; 143:5; 145:5 [b]Gen. 18:2

65 [1]Or, *shawl*

67 [a]Gen. 29:18 [b]Gen. 23:1, 2; 25:20

1 [1]Lit., *and her name*

2 [a]1 Chr. 1:32, 33

3 [1]Lit., *begot*

5 [a]Gen. 24:35, 36

6[1]Lit., *concubines which belonged to Abraham*

7 [1]Lit., *the days of* [a]Gen. 12:4

8 [1]Lit., *good* [a]Gen. 15:15 [b]Gen. 25:17; 35:29; 49:29, 33

9 [a]Gen. 23:17, 18

11 [1]Lit., *dwelt* [a]Gen. 12:2, 3; 22:17; 26:3 [b]Gen. 24:62

12 [a]Gen. 16:15

13 [1]Lit., *in regard to their generations* [a]1 Chr. 1:29-31

16 [1]Or, *peoples* [a]Gen. 17:20

17 [a]Gen. 16:16 [b]Gen. 25:8

18 [1]Lit., *dwelt* [2]Lit., *before* [3]Lit., *as you go* [4]Lit., *fell over against* [5]Lit., *brothers* [a]Gen. 20:1 [b]Gen. 16:12

19 [1]Lit., *begot*

20 [1]Heb., *Aramean* [a]Gen. 24:15, 29

21 [1]Lit., *was entreated of him* [a]1 Sam. 1:17; Ps. 127:3

"[a]Two nations are in your womb;
[b]And two peoples shall be separated from your body;
And one people shall be stronger than the other;
And [c]the older shall serve the younger."

24 When her days to be delivered were fulfilled, behold, there were twins in her womb.

25 Now the first came forth red, all over like a hairy garment; and they named him Esau.

26 And afterward his brother came forth with [a]his hand holding on to Esau's heel, so his name was called [1]Jacob; and Isaac was [b]sixty years old when she gave birth to them.

27 When the boys grew up, Esau became a skillful hunter, a man of the field; but Jacob was a [1]peaceful man, [2]living in tents.

28 Now Isaac loved Esau, because [1]he had a taste for game; but Rebekah loved Jacob.

29 And when Jacob had cooked [a]stew, Esau came in from the field and he was [1]famished;

30 and Esau said to Jacob, "Please let me have a swallow of [1]that red stuff there, for I am [2]famished." Therefore his name was called [3]Edom.

31 But Jacob said, "[1]First sell me your [a]birthright."

32 And Esau said, "Behold, I am about to die; so of what *use* then is the birthright to me?"

33 And Jacob said, "[1]First swear to me"; so he swore to him, and [a]sold his birthright to Jacob.

34 Then Jacob gave Esau bread and lentil stew; and he ate and drank, and rose and went on his way. Thus Esau despised his birthright.

Chapter 26

Isaac Settles in Gerar

Now there was [a]a famine in the land, besides the previous famine that had occurred in the days of Abraham. So Isaac went to Gerar, to [b]Abimelech king of the Philistines.

2 And the Lord [a]appeared to him and said, "Do not go down to Egypt; [1b]stay in the land of which I shall tell you.

3 "Sojourn in this land and [a]I will be with you and bless you, for [b]to you and to your [1]descendants I will give all these lands, and I will establish [c]the oath which I swore to your father Abraham.

4 "And [a]I will multiply your [1]descendants as the stars of heaven, and will give your [1]descendants all these lands; and [b]by your [1]descendants all the nations of the earth [2]shall be blessed;

5 because Abraham [1]obeyed Me and kept My charge, My commandments, My statutes and My laws."

6 So Isaac [1]lived in Gerar.

7 When the men of the place asked about his wife, he said, "[a]She is my sister," for he was afraid to say, "my wife," *thinking*, "[1]the men of the place might kill me on account of Rebekah, for she is [b]beautiful."

8 And it came about, when he had been there a long time, that Abimelech king of the Philistines looked out through a window, and saw, and behold, Isaac was caressing his wife Rebekah.

9 Then Abimelech called Isaac and said, "Behold, certainly she is your wife! How then did you say, 'She is my sister'?" And Isaac said to him, "Because I said, 'Lest I die on account of her.' "

10 And [a]Abimelech said, "What is this you have done to us? One of the people might easily have lain with your wife, and you would have brought guilt upon us."

11 So Abimelech charged all the people, saying, "He who touches this man or his wife shall surely be put to death."

12 Now Isaac sowed in that land, and [1]reaped in the same year a hundredfold. And [a]the Lord blessed him,

13 and the man became rich, and continued to grow [1]richer until he became very [1]wealthy;

14 for [a]he had possessions of flocks [1]and herds and a great household, so that the Philistines envied him.

15 Now [a]all the wells which his father's servants had dug in the days of Abraham his father, the Philistines stopped up [1]by filling them with earth.

16 Then Abimelech said to Isaac, "Go away from us, for you are [1]too powerful for us."

17 And Isaac departed from there and camped in the valley of Gerar, and [1]settled there.

Quarrel over the Wells

18 Then Isaac dug again the wells of water which [1]had been dug in the days of his father Abraham, for the Philistines had stopped them up af-

23 [a]Gen. 17:4-6, 16; Num. 20:14; Deut. 2:4, 8 [b]Gen. 27:29 [c]Gen. 27:40; Mal. 1:2, 3; Rom. 9:12

26 [1]I.e., One who takes by the heel or supplants [a]Hos. 12:3 [b]Gen. 25:20

27 [1]Lit., *complete* [2]Lit., *dwelling*

28 [1]Lit., *game was in his mouth*

29 [1]Lit., *weary* [a]2 Kin. 4:38

30 [1]Lit., *the red, this red* [2]Lit., *weary* [3]Or, *Red*

31 [1]Lit., *Today* [a]Deut. 21:16, 17; 1 Chr. 5:1, 2

33 [1]Lit., *Today* [a]Heb. 12:16

1 [a]Gen. 12:10 [b]Gen. 20:1,2

2 [1]Lit., *dwell* [a]Gen. 12:7; 17:1; 18:1 [b]Gen. 12:1

3 [1]Lit., *seed* [a]Gen. 26:24; 28:15; 31:3 [b]Gen. 12:7; 13:15; 15:18 [c]Gen. 22:16-18

4 [1]Lit., *seed* [2]Or, *bless themselves* [a]Gen. 15:5; 22:17; Ex. 32:13 [b]Gen. 22:18; Gal. 3:8

5 [1]Lit., *hearkened to My voice*

6 [1]Lit., *dwelt*

7 [1]Lit., *lest . . . place* [a]Gen. 12:13; 20:2, 12 [b]Gen. 12:11; 29:17

10 [a]Gen. 20:9

12 [1]Lit., *found* [a]Gen. 26:3

13 [1]Lit., *great*

14 [1]Lit., *and possessions of herds* [a]Gen. 24:35; 25:5

15 [1]Lit., *and filled them* [a]Gen. 21:25, 30

16 [1]Lit., *much mightier than we*

17 [1]Lit., *dwelt*

18 [1]Lit., *they had dug*

ter the death of Abraham; and he
[2]gave them the same names which
his father had [3]given them.
19 But when Isaac's servants dug
in the valley and found there a well
of [1]flowing water,
20 the herdsmen of Gerar quarreled with the herdsmen of Isaac,
saying, "The water is ours!" So he
named the well [1]Esek, because they
contended with him.
21 Then they dug another well,
and they quarreled over it too, so he
named it [1]Sitnah.
22 And he moved away from there
and dug another well, and they did
not quarrel over it; so he named it
[1]Rehoboth, for he said, "[2a]At last
the LORD has made [3]room for us,
and we shall be fruitful in the land."
23 Then he went up from there to
[a]Beersheba.
24 And the LORD [a]appeared to him
the same night and said,
"[b]I am the God of your father
Abraham;
Do not fear, for I am with you.
I [c]will bless you, and multiply
your [1]descendants,
For the sake of My servant
Abraham."
25 So he built an [a]altar there, and
called upon the name of the LORD,
and pitched his tent there; and there
Isaac's servants dug a well.

Covenant with Abimelech

26 Then [a]Abimelech came to him
from Gerar [1]with his adviser Ahuz-
zath, and Phicol the commander of
his army.
27 And Isaac said to them, "Why
have you come to me, since you hate
me, and have sent me away from
you?"
28 And they said, "We see plainly
[a]that the LORD has been with you; so
we said, 'Let there now be an oath
between us, *even* between [1]you and
us, and let us make a covenant with
you,
29 that you will do us no harm,
just as we have not touched you
[1]and have done to you nothing but
good, and have sent you away in
peace. You are now the blessed of
the LORD.'"
30 Then he made them a feast, and
they ate and drank.
31 And in the morning they arose
early and [1a]exchanged oaths; then
Isaac sent them away and they departed from him in peace.
32 Now it came about on the same
day, that Isaac's servants came in
and told him about the well which

18 [2]Lit., *called their names as the names* [3]Lit., *called*
19 [1]Lit., *living*
20 [1]I.e., Contention
21 [1]I.e., Enmity
22 [1]I.e., broad places [2]Lit., *Truly now* [3]Or, *broad* [a]Ps. 4:1; Is. 54:2
23 [a]Gen. 22:19
24 [1]Lit., *seed* [a]Gen. 26:2 [b]Gen. 17:7, 8; 24:12; Ex. 3:6 [c]Gen. 22:17; 26:3
25 [a]Gen. 12:7, 8; 13:4
26 [1]Lit., *and his confidential friend* [a]Gen. 21:22
28 [1]Lit., *us and you* [a]Gen. 21:22, 23
29 [1]Lit., *and just as we*
31 [1]Lit., *swore one to another* [a]Gen. 21:31
33 [a]Gen. 21:31
34 [1]Lit., *took as wife* [a]Gen. 28:8; 36:2
35 [1]Lit., *were a bitterness of spirit to* [a]Gen. 27:46
1 [a]Gen. 48:10; 1 Sam. 3:2 [b]Gen. 25:25, 33, 34
2 [1]Lit., *he* [a]Gen. 47:29
3 [a]Gen. 25:28
4 [a]Gen. 27:19, 25, 31
6 [a]Gen. 25:28
8 [1]Lit., *my voice* [2]Lit., *according to what* [a]Gen. 27:13, 43
9 [1]Lit., *take* [2]Lit., *kids of goats*
11 [1]Lit., *said to* [a]Gen. 25:25
12 [1]Lit., *mocker* [a]Gen. 27:21, 22
13 [a]Gen. 27:8

they had dug, and said to him, "We
have found water."
33 So he called it [a]Shibah; therefore the name of the city is Beersheba to this day.
34 And when Esau was forty years
old [a]he [1]married Judith the daughter of Beeri the Hittite, and Basemath the daughter of Elon the Hittite;
35 and [a]they [1]brought grief to
Isaac and Rebekah.

CHAPTER 27

Jacob's Deception

NOW it came about, when Isaac
was old, and [a]his eyes were too dim
to see, that he called his [b]older son
Esau and said to him, "My son."
And he said to him, "Here I am."
2 [a]And [1]Isaac said, "Behold now,
I am old *and* I do not know the day
of my death.
3 "Now then, please take your
gear, your quiver and your bow, and
go out to the field and [a]hunt game
for me;
4 and prepare a savory dish for
me such as I love, and bring it to me
that I may eat, so that [a]my soul may
bless you before I die."
5 And Rebekah was listening
while Isaac spoke to his son Esau.
So when Esau went to the field to
hunt for game to bring *home,*
6 [a]Rebekah said to her son Jacob,
"Behold, I heard your father speak
to your brother Esau, saying,
7 'Bring me *some* game and prepare a savory dish for me, that I may
eat, and bless you in the presence of
the LORD before my death.'
8 "Now therefore, my son, [a]listen
to [1]me [2]as I command you.
9 "Go now to the flock and [1]bring
me two choice [2]kids from there, that
I may prepare them *as* a savory dish
for your father, such as he loves.
10 "Then you shall bring *it* to your
father, that he may eat, so that he
may bless you before his death."
11 And Jacob [1]answered his
mother Rebekah, "Behold, Esau my
brother is a [a]hairy man and I am a
smooth man.
12 "[a]Perhaps my father will feel
me, then I shall be as a [1]deceiver in
his sight; and I shall bring upon myself a curse and not a blessing."
13 But his mother said to him,
"Your curse be on me, my son; only
[a]obey my voice, and go, get *them* for
me."
14 So he went and got *them,* and
brought *them* to his mother; and his

mother made savory food such as
his father loved.
15 Then Rebekah took the [1]best
[a]garments of Esau her elder son,
which were with her in the house,
and put them on Jacob her younger
son.
16 And she put the skins of the
[1]kids on his hands and on the
smooth part of his neck.
17 She also gave the savory food
and the bread, which she had made,
[1]to her son Jacob.
18 Then he came to his father and
said, "My father." And he said,
"Here I am. Who are you, my son?"
19 And Jacob said to his father, "I
am Esau your first-born; I have done
as you told me. [a]Get up, please, sit
and eat of my game, that [1b]you may
bless me."
20 And Isaac said to his son, "How
is it that you have *it* so quickly, my
son?" And he said, "[a]Because the
LORD your God caused *it* to happen
to me."
21 Then Isaac said to Jacob,
"Please come close, that [a]I may feel
you, my son, whether you are really
my son Esau or not."
22 So Jacob came close to Isaac
his father, and he felt him and said,
"The voice is the voice of Jacob, but
the hands are the hands of Esau."
23 And he did not recognize him,
because his hands were [a]hairy like
his brother Esau's hands; so he
blessed him.
24 And he said, "Are you really my
son Esau?" And he said, "I am."
25 So he said, "Bring *it* to me, and
I will eat of my son's game, that [1a]I
may bless you." And he brought *it*
to him, and he ate; he also brought
him wine and he drank.
26 Then his father Isaac said to
him, "Please come close and kiss
me, my son."
27 So he came close and kissed
him; and when he smelled the smell
of his garments, he [a]blessed him and
said,

"See, [b]the smell of my son
Is like the smell of a field
[c]which the LORD has blessed;
28 Now may [a]God give you of the
dew of heaven,
And of the fatness of the earth,
And an abundance of grain
and new wine;
29 [a]May peoples serve you,
And nations bow down to you;
[b]Be master of your brothers,
[c]And may your mother's sons
bow down to you.
[d]Cursed be those who curse
you,
And blessed be those who
bless you."

The Stolen Blessing

30 Now it came about, as soon as
Isaac had finished blessing Jacob,
and Jacob had hardly gone out from
the presence of Isaac his father, that
Esau his brother came in from his
hunting.
31 Then he also made savory food,
and brought it to his father; and he
said to his father, "[a]Let my father
arise, and eat of his son's game, that
[1b]you may bless me."
32 And Isaac his father said to
him, "[a]Who are you?" And he said,
"I am your son, [b]your first-born,
Esau."
33 Then Isaac [1]trembled violently,
and said, "[a]Who was he then that
hunted game and brought *it* to me,
so that I ate of all *of it* before you
came, and blessed him? [b]Yes, and
he shall be blessed."
34 When Esau heard the words of
his father, [a]he cried out with an exceedingly great and bitter cry, and
said to his father, "Bless me, *even*
me also, O my father!"
35 And he said, "[a]Your brother
came deceitfully, and has taken
away your blessing."
36 Then he said, "[1]Is he not rightly
named [a]Jacob, for he has sup-
planted me these two times? He
took away my birthright, and behold, now he has taken away my
blessing." And he said, "Have you
not reserved a blessing for me?"
37 But Isaac answered and said to
Esau, "Behold, I have made him
[a]your master, and all his [1]relatives I
have given to him [2]as servants; and
with grain and new wine I have sus-
tained him. Now as for you then,
what can I do, my son?"
38 And Esau said to his father,
"Do you have only one blessing, my
father? Bless me, *even* me also, O
my father." So Esau lifted his voice
and [a]wept.
39 Then Isaac his father answered
and [a]said to him,

"Behold, [1b]away from the [2]fer-
tility of the earth shall be
your dwelling,
And [1]away from the dew of
heaven from above.
40 "And by your sword you shall
live,
And your brother [a]you shall
serve;
But it shall come about [b]when
you become restless,
That you shall [1]break his yoke
from your neck."

15 [1]Lit., *desirable;* or, *choice* [a]Gen. 27:27
16 [1]Lit., *kids of the goats*
17 [1]Lit., *into the hand of*
19 [1]Lit., *your soul* [a]Gen. 27:31 [b]Gen. 27:4
20 [a]Gen. 24:12
21 [a]Gen. 27:12
23 [a]Gen. 27:16
25 [1]Lit., *my soul* [a]Gen. 27:4
27 [a]Heb. 11:20 [b]Song of Sol. 4:11 [c]Ps. 65:10
28 [a]Gen. 27:39; Deut. 33:13, 28; Prov. 3:20; Zech. 8:12
29 [a]Gen. 25:23; Is. 45:14; 49:7, 23; 60:12, 14 [b]Gen. 9:26, 27; 27:37 [c]Gen. 37:7, 10 [d]Gen. 12:3; Num. 24:9
31 [1]Lit., *your soul* [a]Gen. 27:19 [b]Gen. 27:4
32 [a]Gen. 27:18 [b]Gen. 25:33, 34
33 [1]Lit., *trembled with a very great trembling* [a]Gen. 27:35 [b]Gen. 25:23
34 [a]Heb. 12:17
35 [a]Gen. 27:19
36 [1]Or, *Was he then named Jacob that he has...* [a]Gen. 25:26, 32-34
37 [1]Lit., *brothers* [2]Lit., *for* [a]Gen. 27:28, 29
38 [a]Heb. 12:17
39 [1]Or, *of* [2]Lit., *fatness* [a]Heb. 11:20 [b]Gen. 27:28; Deut. 33:13, 28
40 [1]Lit., *tear off* [a]Gen. 27:29 [b]2 Kin. 8:20-22

41 So Esau [a]bore a grudge against Jacob because of the blessing with which his father had blessed him; and Esau said [1]to himself, "The days of mourning for my father are near; then I will kill my brother Jacob."

42 Now when the words of her elder son Esau were reported to Rebekah, she sent and called her younger son Jacob, and said to him, "Behold your brother Esau is consoling himself concerning you, *by planning* to kill you.

43 "Now therefore, my son, [a]obey my voice, and arise, flee to Haran, to my brother [b]Laban!

44 "And stay with him [a]a few days, until your brother's fury [1]subsides,

45 until your brother's anger against you subsides, and he forgets [a]what you did to him. Then I shall send and get you from there. Why should I be bereaved of you both in one day?"

46 And Rebekah said to Isaac, "I am tired of [1]living because of [a]the daughters of Heth; if Jacob takes a wife from the daughters of Heth, like these, from the daughters of the land, what good will my life be to me?"

CHAPTER 28

Jacob Is Sent Away

So Isaac called Jacob and blessed him and charged him, and said to him, "[a]You shall not take a wife from the daughters of Canaan.

2 "Arise, go to Paddan-aram, to the house of [a]Bethuel your mother's father; and from there take to yourself a wife from the daughters of Laban your mother's brother.

3 "And may [1a]God Almighty [b]bless you and [c]make you fruitful and [d]multiply you, that you may become a [e]company of peoples.

4 "May He also give you the blessing of Abraham, to you and to your [1]descendants with you; that you may [a]possess the land of your sojournings, which God gave to Abraham."

5 Then [a]Isaac sent Jacob away, and he went to Paddan-aram to Laban, son of Bethuel the [1]Syrian, the brother of Rebekah, the mother of Jacob and Esau.

6 Now Esau saw that Isaac had blessed Jacob and sent him away to Paddan-aram, to take to himself a wife from there, *and that* when he blessed him he charged him, saying, "[a]You shall not take a wife from the daughters of Canaan,"

7 and that Jacob had obeyed his father and his mother and had gone to Paddan-aram.

8 So Esau saw that [a]the daughters of Canaan displeased [1]his father Isaac;

9 and Esau went to Ishmael, and [1]married, [a]besides the wives that he had, Mahalath the daughter of Ishmael, Abraham's son, the sister of Nebaioth.

Jacob's Dream

10 Then Jacob departed from [a]Beersheba and went toward [b]Haran.

11 And he [1]came to [2]a [a]certain place and spent the night there, because the sun had set; and he took one of the stones of the place and put it [3]under his head, and lay down in that place.

12 And [a]he had a dream, and behold, a ladder was set on the earth with its top reaching to heaven; and behold, [b]the angels of God were ascending and descending on it.

13 And behold, [a]the LORD stood [1]above it and said, "I am the LORD, [b]the God of your father Abraham and the God of Isaac; the land on which you lie, I will give it [c]to you and to [d]your [2]descendants.

14 "Your [1]descendants shall also be like [a]the dust of the earth, and you shall [2]spread out [b]to the west and to the east and to the north and to the south; and [c]in you and in your [1]descendants shall all the families of the earth be blessed.

15 "And behold, [a]I am with you, and [b]will keep you wherever you go, and [c]will bring you back to this land; for [d]I will not leave you until I have done what I have [1]promised you."

16 Then Jacob [a]awoke from his sleep and said, "[b]Surely the LORD is in this place, and I did not know it."

17 And he was afraid and said, "[a]How awesome is this place! This is none other than the house of God, and this is the gate of heaven."

18 So Jacob rose early in the morning, and took [a]the stone that he had put [1]under his head and set it up as a pillar, and poured oil on its top.

19 And he called the name of that place [1]Bethel; however, [2]previously the name of the city had been [a]Luz.

20 Then Jacob [a]made a vow, saying, "[b]If God will be with me and will keep me on this journey that I [1]take, and will give me [2]food to eat and garments to wear,

21 and I return to my father's house in [1]safety, then the LORD will be my God.

---

41 [1]Lit., *in his heart* [a]Gen. 32:3-11
43 [a]Gen. 27:8, 13 [b]Gen. 24:29
44 [1]Lit., *turns away* [a]Gen. 31:41
45 [a]Gen. 27:12, 19, 35
46 [1]Lit., *my life* [a]Gen. 26:34, 35
1 [a]Gen. 24:3, 4
2 [a]Gen. 25:20
3 [1]Heb., *El Shaddai* [a]Gen. 17:1; 35:11; 48:3 [b]Gen. 22:17 [c]Gen. 17:6, 20 [d]Gen. 17:2; 26:4, 24 [e]Gen. 35:11; 48:4
4 [1]Lit., *seed* [a]Gen. 15:7, 8
5 [1]Lit., *Aramean* [a]Gen. 27:43
6 [a]Gen. 28:1
8 [1]Lit., *in the eyes of his* [a]Gen. 26:34, 35; 27:46
9 [1]Lit., *took for his wife* [a]Gen. 26:34; 36:2
10 [a]Gen. 26:23 [b]Gen. 12:4, 5; 27:43
11 [1]Lit., *lighted on* [2]Lit., *the place* [3]Lit., *at his head-place* [a]Gen. 28:19
12 [a]Num. 12:6 [b]John 1:51
13 [1]Or, *beside him* [2]Lit., *seed* [a]Gen. 35:1; Amos 7:7 [b]Gen. 26:3, 24 [c]Gen. 13:15, 17; 26:3 [d]Gen. 12:7; 15:18
14 [1]Lit., *seed* [2]Lit., *break through* [a]Gen. 13:16; 22:17 [b]Gen. 13:14, 15 [c]Gen. 12:3; 18:18; 22:18; 26:4
15 [1]Lit., *spoken to* [a]Gen. 26:3 [b]Num. 6:24; Ps. 121:7, 8 [c]Gen. 48:21; Deut. 30:3 [d]Deut. 7:9; 31:6, 8
16 [a]1 Kin. 3:15; Jer. 31:26 [b]Ps. 139:7-12
17 [a]Ps. 68:35
18 [1]Lit., *at his head-place* [a]Gen. 28:11; 35:14
19 [1]I.e., the house of God [2]Lit., *at the first* [a]Gen. 35:6; 48:3
20 [1]Lit., *go* [2]Lit., *bread* [a]Gen. 31:13 [b]Gen. 28:15
21 [1]Lit., *peace*

22"And this stone, which I have set
up as a pillar, [a]will be God's house;
and [b]of all that Thou dost give me I
will surely give a tenth to Thee."

Chapter 29

Jacob Meets Rachel

THEN Jacob [1]went on his journey,
and came to the land of [a]the sons of
the east.
2 And he looked, and [1]saw [a]a well
in the field, and behold, three flocks
of sheep were lying there beside it,
for from that well they watered the
flocks. Now the stone on the mouth
of the well was large.
3 When all the flocks were gathered there, they would then roll the
stone from the mouth of the well,
and water the sheep, and put the
stone back in its place on the mouth
of the well.
4 And Jacob said to them, "My
brothers, where are you from?" And
they said, "We are from [a]Haran."
5 And he said to them, "Do you
know Laban the [a]son of Nahor?"
And they said, "We know *him*."
6 And he said to them, "Is it well
with him?" And they said, "It is
well, and behold, [a]Rachel his daughter is coming with the sheep."
7 And he said, "Behold, it is still
high day; it is not time for the livestock to be gathered. Water the
sheep, and go, pasture them."
8 But they said, "We cannot, until all the flocks are gathered, and
they roll the stone from the mouth
of the well; then we water the
sheep."
9 While he was still speaking
with them, Rachel came with her father's sheep, for she was a shep-
herdess.
10 And it came about, when Jacob
saw Rachel the daughter of Laban
his mother's brother, and the sheep
of Laban his mother's brother, that
Jacob went up, and rolled the stone
from the mouth of the well, and watered the flock of Laban his mother's brother.
11 Then Jacob kissed Rachel, and
lifted his voice and wept.
12 And Jacob told Rachel that he
was a [1a]relative of her father and
that he was Rebekah's son, and [b]she
ran and told her father.
13 So it came about, when [a]Laban
heard the news of Jacob his sister's
son, that he ran to meet him, and
[b]embraced him and kissed him, and
brought him to his house. Then he
related to Laban all these things.

14 And Laban said to him, "Surely
you are [a]my bone and my flesh."
And he stayed with him a month.
15 Then Laban said to Jacob, "Because you are my [1]relative, should
you therefore serve me for nothing?
Tell me, what shall [a]your wages
be?"
16 Now Laban had two daughters;
the name of the older was Leah, and
the name of the younger was Rachel.
17 And Leah's eyes were weak,
but Rachel was [a]beautiful of form
and [1]face.
18 Now Jacob [a]loved Rachel, so he
said, "[b]I will serve you seven years
for your younger daughter Rachel."
19 And Laban said, "It is better
that I give her to you than that I
should give her to another man; stay
with me."
20 So Jacob served seven years for
Rachel and they seemed to him but
a few days because of his love for
her.

Laban's Treachery

21 Then Jacob said to Laban,
"Give *me* my wife, for my [1]time is
completed, that I may go in to her."
22 And Laban gathered all the
men of the place, and made a feast.
23 Now it came about in the evening that he took his daughter Leah,
and brought her to him; and *Jacob*
went in to her.
24 Laban also gave his maid Zilpah to his daughter Leah as a maid.
25 So it came about in the morning
that, behold, it was Leah! And he
said to Laban, "[a]What is this you
have done to me? Was it not for Rachel that I served with you? Why
then have you [b]deceived me?"
26 But Laban said, "It is not [1]the
practice in our place, to [2]marry off
the younger before the first-born.
27"[a]Complete the bridal week of
this one, and we will give you the
other also for the service which
[b]you shall serve with me for another
seven years."
28 And Jacob did so and completed her week, and he gave him
his daughter Rachel as his wife.
29 Laban also gave his maid Bilhah to his daughter Rachel as her
maid.
30 So *Jacob* went in to Rachel
also, and indeed [a]he loved Rachel
more than Leah, and he served with
[1]Laban for another seven years.
31 Now the LORD saw that Leah
was [1]unloved, and He opened her
womb, but Rachel was barren.
32 And Leah conceived and bore a

22 [a]Gen. 35:7 [b]Deut. 14:22
1 [1]Lit., *lifted up his feet* [a]Judg. 6:3, 33
2 [1]Lit., *behold* [a]Gen. 24:10, 11; Ex. 2:15, 16
4 [a]Gen. 28:10
5 [a]Gen. 24:24, 29
6 [a]Ex. 2:16
12 [1]Lit., *brother* [a]Gen. 28:5 [b]Gen. 24:28
13 [a]Gen. 24:29-31 [b]Gen. 33:4
14 [a]Judg. 9:2
15 [1]Lit., *brother* [a]Gen. 31:41
17 [1]Lit., *beautiful of appearance* [a]Gen. 12:11, 14; 26:7
18 [a]Gen. 24:67 [b]Hos. 12:12
21 [1]Lit., *days*
25 [a]Gen. 12:18; 20:9; 26:10 [b]1 Sam. 28:12
26 [1]Lit., *done thus in* [2]Lit., *give*
27 [a]Judg. 14:12 [b]Gen. 31:41
30 [1]Lit., *him* [a]Gen. 29:17, 18
31 [1]Lit., *hated*

son and named him [1]Reuben, for she said, "Because the LORD has [2a]seen my affliction; surely now my husband will love me."

33 Then she conceived again and bore a son and said, "[a]Because the LORD has [1]heard that I am [2]unloved, He has therefore given me this *son* also." So she named him Simeon.

34 And she conceived again and bore a son and said, "Now this time my husband will become [1]attached to me, because I have borne him three sons." Therefore he was named [a]Levi.

35 And she conceived again and bore a son and said, "This time I will [1a]praise the LORD." Therefore she named him [2]Judah. Then she stopped bearing.

CHAPTER 30

The Sons of Jacob

NOW when Rachel saw that she bore Jacob no children, [1]she became jealous of her sister; and she said to Jacob, "[a]Give me children, or else I die."

2 Then Jacob's anger burned against Rachel, and he said, "Am I in the place of God, who has [a]withheld from you the fruit of the womb?"

3 And she said, "[a]Here is my maid Bilhah, go in to her, that she may bear on my knees, that [1]through her I too may have children."

4 So [a]she gave him her maid Bilhah as a wife, and Jacob went in to her.

5 And Bilhah conceived and bore a son.

6 Then Rachel said, "God has [1]vindicated me, and has indeed heard my voice and has given me a son." Therefore she named him [2]Dan.

7 And Rachel's maid Bilhah conceived again and bore Jacob a second son.

8 So Rachel said, "With [1]mighty wrestlings I have [2]wrestled with my sister, *and* I have indeed prevailed." And she named him Naphtali.

9 When Leah saw that she had stopped bearing, she took her maid Zilpah and gave her to Jacob as a wife.

10 And Leah's maid Zilpah bore Jacob a son.

11 Then Leah said, "[1]How fortunate!" So she named him [2]Gad.

12 And Leah's maid Zilpah bore Jacob a second son.

13 Then Leah said, "[1]Happy am I! For women will call me happy." So she named him [2]Asher.

14 Now in the days of wheat harvest Reuben went and found [a]mandrakes in the field, and brought them to his mother Leah. Then Rachel said to Leah, "Please give me some of your son's mandrakes."

15 But she said to her, "Is it a small matter for you to take my husband? And would you take my son's mandrakes also?" So Rachel said, "Therefore he may lie with you tonight in return for your son's mandrakes."

16 When Jacob came in from the field in the evening, then Leah went out to meet him and said, "You must come in to me, for I have surely hired you with my son's mandrakes." So he lay with her that night.

17 And God gave heed to Leah, and she conceived and bore Jacob a fifth son.

18 Then Leah said, "God has given me my [1]wages, because I gave my maid to my husband." So she named him Issachar.

19 And Leah conceived again and bore a sixth son to Jacob.

20 Then Leah said, "God has endowed me with a good gift; now my husband [1]will dwell with me, because I have borne him six sons." So she named him Zebulun.

21 And afterward she bore a daughter and named her Dinah.

22 Then [a]God remembered Rachel, and God gave heed to her and opened her womb.

23 So she conceived and bore a son and said, "God has taken away my reproach."

24 And she named him Joseph, saying, "[a]May the LORD [1]give me another son."

Jacob Prospers

25 Now it came about when Rachel had borne Joseph, that Jacob said to Laban, "[a]Send me away, that I may go to my own place and to my own country.

26 "Give *me* my wives and my children [a]for whom I have served you, and let me depart; for you yourself know my service which I have [1]rendered you."

27 But Laban said to him, "If now [1]it pleases you, *stay with me;* I have divined [a]that the LORD has blessed me on your account."

28 And he [1]continued, "[a]Name me your wages, and I will give it."

29 But he said to him, "You your-

32 [1]I.e., See, a son [2]Lit., *looked upon* [a]Gen. 16:11; 31:42
33 [1]Heb., *shama,* related to Simeon [2]Lit., *hated* [a]Deut. 21:15
34 [1]Heb., *lavah,* related to Levi [a]Gen. 49:5
35 [1]From Heb., *Jadah,* related to Judah [2]Heb., *Jehudah* [a]Gen. 49:8; Matt. 1:2
1 [1]Lit., *Rachel* [a]1 Sam. 1:5, 6
2 [a]Gen. 20:18; 29:31
3 [1]Lit., *from her I too may be built* [a]Gen. 16:2
4 [a]Gen. 16:3, 4
6 [1]Lit., *judged* [2]I.e., He judged
8 [1]Lit., *wrestlings of God* [2]From Heb., *niphtal,* related to Naphtali
11 [1]Lit., *"With fortune!"* Some versions read, *Fortune has come* [2]I.e., Fortune
13 [1]Lit., *"With my happiness!"* [2]I.e., Happy
14 [a]Song of Sol. 7:13
18 [1]Heb., *sachar,* related to Issachar
20 [1]Heb., *zabal,* related to Zebulun. Some translate *will honor*
22 [a]1 Sam. 1:19, 20
24 [1]Lit., *add to me;* Heb., *Joseph* [a]Gen. 35:17
25 [a]Gen. 24:54, 56
26 [1]Lit., *served* [a]Gen. 29:18, 27; Hos. 12:12
27 [1]Lit., *I have found favor in your eyes* [a]Gen. 39:5
28 [1]Lit., *said* [a]Gen. 29:15; 31:7, 41

self know how I have served you and how your cattle have [1]fared with me.

30"For you had little before [1]I came, and it has [2]increased to a multitude; and the LORD has blessed you [3]wherever I turned. But now, when shall I provide for my own household also?"

31 So he said, "What shall I give you?" And Jacob said, "You shall not give me anything. If you will do this *one* thing for me, I will again pasture *and* keep your flock:

32 let me pass through your entire flock today, removing from there every [a]speckled and spotted sheep, and every black one among the lambs, and the spotted and speckled among the goats; and *such* shall be my wages.

33"So my [1]honesty will answer for me later, when you come concerning my [2]wages. Every one that is not speckled and spotted among the goats and black among the lambs, *if found* with me, will be considered stolen."

34 And Laban said, "[1]Good, let it be according to your word."

35 So he removed on that day the striped and spotted male goats and all the speckled and spotted female goats, every one with white in it, and all the black ones among the sheep, and gave them into the [1]care of his sons.

36 And he put *a distance of* three days' journey between himself and Jacob, and Jacob fed the rest of Laban's flocks.

37 Then Jacob [1]took fresh rods of poplar and almond and plane trees, and peeled white stripes in them, exposing the white which *was* [2]in the rods.

38 And he set the rods which he had peeled in front of the flocks in the gutters, *even* in the watering troughs, where the flocks came to drink; and they [1]mated when they came to drink.

39 So the flocks [1]mated by the rods, and the flocks brought forth striped, speckled, and spotted.

40 And Jacob separated the lambs, and [1]made the flocks face toward the striped and all the black in the flock of Laban; and he put his own herds apart, and did not put them with Laban's flock.

41 Moreover, it came about whenever the [1]stronger of the flock [2]were mating, that Jacob would place the rods in the sight of the flock in the gutters, so that they might [3]mate by the rods;

42 but when the flock was feeble, he did not put *them* in; so the feebler were Laban's and the [1]stronger Jacob's.

43 So [a]the man [1]became exceedingly prosperous, and had large flocks and female and male servants and camels and donkeys.

CHAPTER 31

Jacob Leaves Secretly for Canaan

NOW [1]Jacob heard the words of Laban's sons, saying, "Jacob has taken away all that was our father's, and from what belonged to our father he has made all this [2]wealth."

2 And Jacob saw the [1]attitude of Laban, and behold, it was not *friendly* toward him as formerly.

3 Then the LORD said to Jacob, "Return to the land of your fathers and to your relatives, and [a]I will be with you."

4 So Jacob sent and called Rachel and Leah to his flock in the field,

5 and said to them, "I see your father's [1]attitude, that it is not *friendly* toward me as formerly, but [a]the God of my father has been with me.

6"And you know that I have served your father with all my strength.

7"Yet your father has [a]cheated me and [b]changed my wages ten times; however, [c]God did not allow him to hurt me.

8"If he spoke thus, 'The speckled shall be your wages,' then all the flock brought forth speckled; and if he spoke thus, 'The striped shall be your wages,' then all the flock brought forth striped.

9"Thus God has taken away your father's livestock and given *them* to me.

10"And it came about at the time when the flock were [1]mating that I lifted up my eyes and saw in a dream, and behold, the male goats which were [2]mating *were* striped, speckled and mottled.

11"Then [a]the angel of God said to me in the dream, 'Jacob,' and I said, 'Here I am.'

12"And he said, 'Lift up, now, your eyes and see *that* all the male goats which are [1]mating are striped, speckled, and mottled; for I have seen all that Laban has been doing to you.

13 'I am [a]the God *of* Bethel, where you [b]anointed a pillar, where you

---

29 [1]Lit., *been*

30 [1]Lit., *me* [2]Lit., *broken forth* [3]Lit., *at my foot*

32 [a]Gen. 31:8

33 [1]Lit., *righteousness* [2]Lit., *wages which are before you*

34 [1]Lit., *Behold, would that it might be*

35 [1]Lit., *hand*

37 [1]Lit., *took to himself* [2]Lit., *on*

38 [1]Or, *conceived*

39 [1]Or, *conceived*

40 [1]Lit., *set the faces of*

41 [1]Lit., *bound ones;* i.e., firm and compact [2]Or, *conceived* [3]Or, *conceive*

42 [1]Lit., *bound ones;* i.e., firm and compact

43 [1]Lit., *broke forth* [a]Gen. 12:16; 13:2; 24:35; 26:13, 14

1 [1]Lit., *he* [2]Lit., *glory*

2 [1]Lit., *face*

3 [a]Gen. 28:15

5 [1]Lit., *face* [a]Gen. 28:13, 15; 31:29, 42, 53

7 [a]Gen. 29:25 [b]Gen. 31:41 [c]Gen. 31:29

10 [1]Or, *conceiving* [2]Lit., *leaping upon the flock*

11 [a]Gen. 16:7-11; 22:11, 15; 31:13

12 [1]Lit., *leaping upon the flock*

13 [a]Gen. 28:13 [b]Gen. 28:18, 20

made a vow to Me; now arise, [1]leave
this land, and [c]return to the land of
your birth.' "
14 And Rachel and Leah answered
and said to him, "Do we still have
any portion or inheritance in our father's house?
15"Are we not reckoned by him as
foreigners? For [a]he has sold us, and
has also [1]entirely consumed [2]our
purchase price.
16"Surely all the wealth which
God has taken away from our father
belongs to us and our children; now
then, do whatever God has said to
you."
17 Then Jacob arose and put his
children and his wives upon camels;
18 and he drove away all his livestock and all his property which he
had gathered, his acquired livestock
which he had gathered in Paddan-
aram, [a]to go to the land of Canaan to
his father Isaac.
19 When Laban had gone to shear
his flock, then Rachel stole the
[1a]household idols that were her father's.
20 And Jacob [1]deceived Laban the
Syrian, by not telling him that he
was fleeing.
21 So he fled with all that he had;
and he arose and crossed the *Euphrates* River, and set his face
toward the hill country of [a]Gilead.

Laban Pursues Jacob

22 When it was told Laban on the
third day that Jacob had fled,
23 then he took his [1]kinsmen with
him, and pursued him *a distance of*
seven days' journey; and he overtook him in the hill country of Gilead.
24 And [a]God came to Laban the
[1]Syrian in a [b]dream of the night, and
said to him, "[2c]Be careful that you
do not speak to Jacob either good or
bad."
25 And Laban caught up with Jacob. Now Jacob had pitched his tent
in the hill country, and Laban with
his [1]kinsmen camped in the hill
country of Gilead.
26 Then Laban said to Jacob,
"What have you done [1]by deceiving
me and carrying away my daughters like captives of the sword?
27"Why did you flee secretly and
[1]deceive me, and did not tell me, so
that I might have sent you away
with joy and with songs, with [a]tim-
brel and with [b]lyre;
28 and did not allow me [a]to kiss
my sons and my daughters? Now
you have done foolishly.
29"It is in [1]my power to do you
harm, but [a]the God of your father
spoke to me last night, saying, '[2b]Be
careful not to speak either good or
bad to Jacob.'
30"And now you have indeed gone
away because you longed greatly
for your father's house; *but* why did
you steal [a]my gods?"
31 Then Jacob answered and said
to Laban, "Because I was afraid, for
I said, 'Lest you would take your
daughters from me by force.'
32"[a]The one with whom you find
your gods shall not live; in the presence of our [1]kinsmen [2]point out
what is yours [3]among my belong-
ings and take *it* for yourself." For
Jacob did not know that Rachel had
stolen them.
33 So Laban went into Jacob's
tent, and into Leah's tent, and into
the tent of the two maids, but he did
not find *them*. Then he went out of
Leah's tent and entered Rachel's
tent.
34 Now Rachel had taken the
[1]household idols and put them in the
camel's saddle, and she sat on them.
And Laban felt through all the tent,
but did not find *them*.
35 And she said to her father, "Let
not my lord be angry that I cannot
rise before you, for the manner of
women is upon me." So he
searched, but did not find the
[1]household idols.
36 Then Jacob became angry and
contended with Laban; and Jacob
answered and said to Laban, "What
is my transgression? What is my sin,
that you have hotly pursued me?
37"Though you have felt through
all my goods, what have you found
of all your household goods? Set *it*
here before my [1]kinsmen and your
[1]kinsmen, that they may decide between us two.
38"These twenty years I *have been*
with you; your ewes and your female goats have not miscarried, nor
have I eaten the rams of your flocks.
39"That which was torn *of beasts* I
did not bring to you; I bore the loss
of it myself. You required it of my
hand *whether* stolen by day or stolen by night.
40"*Thus* I was: by day the [1]heat
consumed me, and the frost by
night, and my sleep fled from my
eyes.
41"These twenty years I have been
in your house; [a]I served you fourteen years for your two daughters,
and six years for your flock, and you
[b]changed my wages ten times.

13 [1]Lit., *go out from* [c]Gen. 28:15

15 [1]I.e., enjoyed the benefit of [2]Lit., *our money* [a]Gen. 29:20, 23, 27

18 [a]Gen. 35:27-29

19 [1]Heb., *teraphim* [a]Gen. 31:30, 34; Judg. 17:5; 1 Sam. 19:13; Hos. 3:4

20 [1]Lit., *stole the heart of Laban the Aramean*

21 [a]Gen. 37:25

23 [1]Lit., *brothers*

24 [1]Lit., *Aramean* [2]Lit., *Take heed to yourself* [a]Gen. 31:29 [b]Gen. 20:3, 6; 31:11 [c]Gen. 31:7, 29

25 [1]Lit., *brothers*

26 [1]Lit., *and have stolen my heart*

27 [1]Lit., *steal me* [a]Ex. 15:20 [b]Gen. 4:21

28 [a]Gen. 31:55

29 [1]Lit., *the power of my hand* [2]Lit., *Take heed to yourself* [a]Gen. 31:5, 42, 53 [b]Gen. 31:24

30 [a]Gen. 31:19

32 [1]Lit., *brothers* [2]Lit., *recognize* [3]Lit., *with me* [a]Gen. 44:9

34 [1]Heb., *teraphim*

35 [1]Heb., *teraphim*

37 [1]Lit., *brothers*

40 [1]Or, *drought*

41 [a]Gen. 29:27, 30 [b]Gen. 31:7

42"If [a]the God of my father, the God of Abraham, and the fear of Isaac, had not been for me, surely now you would have sent me away empty-handed. [b]God has seen my affliction and the toil of my hands, so He [c]rendered judgment last night."

The Covenant of Mizpah

43 Then Laban answered and said to Jacob, "The daughters are my daughters, and the children are my children, and [a]the flocks are my flocks, and all that you see is mine. But what can I do this day to these my daughters or to their children whom they have borne?

44"So now come, let us [a]make a covenant, [1]you and I, and let it be a witness between [2]you and me."

45 Then Jacob took [a]a stone and set it up *as* a pillar.

46 And Jacob said to his [1]kinsmen, "Gather stones." So they took stones and made a heap, and they ate there by the heap.

47 Now Laban [a]called it [1]Jegar-sahadutha, but Jacob called it [2]Galeed.

48 And Laban said, "This heap is a witness between [1]you and me this day." Therefore it was named Galeed;

49 and [1a]Mizpah, for he said, "May the LORD watch between [2]you and me when we are [3]absent one from the other.

50"If you mistreat my daughters, or if you take wives besides my daughters, *although* no man is with us, see, [a]God is witness between [1]you and me."

51 And Laban said to Jacob, "Behold this heap and behold the pillar which I have set between [1]you and me.

52"This heap is a witness, and the pillar is a witness, that I will not pass by this heap to you for harm, and you will not pass by this heap and this pillar to me, for harm.

53"[a]The God of Abraham and the God of Nahor, the God of their father, judge between us." So Jacob swore by [b]the fear of his father Isaac.

54 [a]Then Jacob offered a sacrifice on the mountain, and called his [1]kinsmen to [2]the meal; and they ate [3]the meal and spent the night on the mountain.

55 [1]And early in the morning Laban arose, and [a]kissed his sons and his daughters and blessed them. Then Laban departed and returned to his place.

CHAPTER 32

Jacob's Fear of Esau

NOW as Jacob went on his way, [a]the angels of God met him.

2 And Jacob said when he saw them, "This is God's [1]camp." So he named that place [2a]Mahanaim.

3 Then Jacob [a]sent messengers before him to his brother Esau in the land of [b]Seir, the [1]country of [c]Edom.

4 He also commanded them saying, "Thus you shall say to my lord Esau: 'Thus says your servant Jacob, "I have sojourned with Laban, and [a]stayed until now;

5 and [a]I have oxen and donkeys *and* flocks and male and female servants; and I have sent to tell my lord, that I may find favor in your sight." ' "

6 And the messengers returned to Jacob, saying, "We came to your brother Esau, and furthermore he is coming to meet you, and four hundred men are with him."

7 Then Jacob was [a]greatly afraid and distressed; and he divided the people who were with him, and the flocks and the herds and the camels, into two companies;

8 for he said, "If Esau comes to the one company and [1]attacks it, then the company which is left will escape."

9 And Jacob said, "O [a]God of my father Abraham and God of my father Isaac, O LORD, who didst say to me, '[b]Return to your country and to your relatives, and I will [1]prosper you,'

10 [1]I am unworthy [a]of all the lovingkindness and of all the [2]faithfulness which Thou hast shown to Thy servant; for with my staff *only* I crossed this Jordan, and now I have become two companies.

11"Deliver me, I pray, [a]from the hand of my brother, from the hand of Esau; for I fear him, lest he come and [1]attack me, the mothers with the children.

12"For Thou didst say, '[a]I will surely [1]prosper you, and [b]make your [2]descendants as the sand of the sea, which cannot be numbered for multitude.' "

13 So he spent the night there. Then he [1]selected from what [2]he had with him a present for his brother Esau:

14 two hundred female goats and twenty male goats, two hundred ewes and twenty rams,

15 thirty milking camels and their colts, forty cows and ten bulls,

42 [a]Gen. 31:5, 29, 53 [b]Gen. 29:32 [c]Gen. 31:24, 29
43 [a]Gen. 31:1
44 [1]Lit., *I and you* [2]Lit., *me and you* [a]Gen. 21:27, 32
45 [a]Gen. 28:18; Josh. 24:26, 27
46 [1]Lit., *brothers*
47 [1]I.e., The heap of witness, in Aramaic [2]I.e., The heap of witness, in Hebrew [a]Josh. 22:34
48 [1]Lit., *me and you*
49 [1]Lit., *The Mizpah*, i.e., The watchtower [2]Lit., *me and you* [3]Lit., *hidden* [a]Judg. 11:29
50 [1]Lit., *me and you* [a]Jer. 29:23; 42:5
51 [1]Lit., *me and you*
53 [a]Gen. 28:13 [b]Gen. 31:42
54 [1]Lit., *brothers* [2]Lit., *eat bread* [3]Lit., *bread* [a]Ex. 18:12
55 [1]Chap. 32:1 in Hebrew [a]Gen. 31:28, 43
1 [a]2 Kin. 6:16, 17; Ps. 34:7
2 [1]Or, *company* [2]I.e., Two Camps, or, Two Companies [a]Josh. 21:38; 2 Sam. 2:8
3 [1]Lit., *field* [a]Gen. 27:41, 42; 32:7, 11 [b]Gen. 14:6 [c]Gen. 25:30; 36:8, 9
4 [a]Gen. 31:41
5 [a]Gen. 30:43
7 [a]Gen. 32:11
8 [1]Lit., *smites*
9 [1]Lit., *do good with you* [a]Gen. 31:42 [b]Gen. 28:15; 31:13
10 [1]Lit., *I am less than all* [2]Or, *truth* [a]Gen. 24:27
11 [1]Lit., *smite* [a]Gen. 27:41, 42; 33:4
12 [1]Lit., *do good with* [2]Lit., *seed* [a]Gen. 28:14 [b]Gen. 22:17
13 [1]Lit., *took* [2]Lit., *had come to his hand*

twenty female donkeys and ten
male donkeys.
16 And he delivered *them* into the
hand of his servants, every drove by
itself, and said to his servants, "Pass
on before me, and put a space between droves."
17 And he commanded the [1]one in
front, saying, "When my brother
Esau meets you and asks you, saying, 'To whom do you belong, and
where are you going, and to whom
do these *animals* in front of you belong?'
18 then you shall say, '*These* belong to your servant Jacob; it is a
present sent to my lord Esau. And
behold, he also is behind us.' "
19 Then he commanded also the
second and the third, and all those
who followed the droves, saying,
"After this manner you shall speak
to Esau when you find him;
20 and you shall say, 'Behold, your
servant Jacob also is behind us.' "
For he said, "I will appease him with
the present that goes before me.
Then afterward I will see his face;
perhaps he will accept me."
21 So the present passed on before
him, while he himself spent that
night in the camp.
22 Now he arose that same night
and took his two wives and his two
maids and his eleven children, and
crossed the ford of the [a]Jabbok.
23 And he took them and sent
them across the stream. And he sent
across whatever he had.

Jacob Wrestles with an Angel

24 Then Jacob was left alone, and
a man [a]wrestled with him until daybreak.
25 And when he saw that he had
not prevailed against him, he
touched the socket of his thigh; so
the socket of Jacob's thigh was dis-
located while he wrestled with him.
26 Then he said, "Let me go, for
the dawn is breaking." But he said,
"I will not let you go unless you
bless me."
27 So he said to him, "What is
your name?" And he said, "Jacob."
28 And [a]he said, "Your name shall
no longer be Jacob, but [1]Israel; for
you have striven with God and with
men and have prevailed."
29 Then [a]Jacob asked him and
said, "Please tell me your name."
But he said, "Why is it that you ask
my name?" And he blessed him
there.
30 So Jacob named the place [1]Pe-
niel, for *he said,* "[a]I have seen God
face to face, yet my [2]life has been
preserved."
31 Now the sun rose upon him just
as he crossed over [a]Penuel, and he
was limping on his thigh.
32 Therefore, to this day the sons
of Israel do not eat the sinew of the
hip which is on the socket of the
thigh, because he touched the
socket of Jacob's thigh in the sinew
of the hip.

Chapter 33

Jacob Meets Esau

THEN Jacob lifted his eyes and
looked, and behold, [a]Esau was coming, and four hundred men with
him. So he divided the children
[1]among Leah and Rachel and the
two maids.
2 And he put the maids and their
children [1]in front, and Leah and her
children [2]next, and Rachel and
Joseph [2]last.
3 But he himself passed on ahead
of them and bowed down to the
ground seven times, until he came
near to his brother.
4 Then Esau ran to meet him and
embraced him, and [a]fell on his neck
and kissed him, and they wept.
5 And he lifted his eyes and saw
the women and the children, and
said, "[1]Who are these with you?" So
he said, "[a]The children whom God
has graciously given your servant."
6 Then the maids came near
[1]with their children, and they
bowed down.
7 And Leah likewise came near
with her children, and they bowed
down; and afterward Joseph came
near with Rachel, and they bowed
down.
8 And he said, "What do you
mean by [a]all this company which I
have met?" And he said, "To find
favor in the sight of my lord."
9 But Esau said, "[a]I have plenty,
my brother; let what you have be
your own."
10 And Jacob said, "No, please, if
now I have found favor in your
sight, then take my present from my
hand, [1]for I see your face as one sees
the face of God, and you have received me favorably.
11 "Please take my [1]gift which has
been brought to you, [a]because God
has dealt graciously with me, and
because I have [2]plenty." Thus he
urged him and he took *it.*
12 Then [1]Esau said, "Let us take
our journey and go, and I will go
before you."

17 [1]Lit., *first*
22 [a]Deut. 3:16; Josh. 12:2
24 [a]Hos. 12:3, 4
28 [1]I.e., He who strives with God, or, God strives [a]Gen. 35:10; 1 Kin. 18:31
29 [a]Judg. 13:17, 18
30 [1]I.e., The face of God [2]Lit., *soul* [a]Gen. 16:13; Ex. 33:20; Num. 12:8; Judg. 6:22; 13:22
31 [a]Judg. 8:8
1 [1]Or, *to* [a]Gen. 32:6
2 [1]Lit., *first* [2]Lit., *behind*
4 [a]Gen. 45:14, 15
5 [1]Or, *"What relation are these to you?"* [a]Gen. 48:9
6 [1]Lit., *they and*
8 [a]Gen. 32:14-16
9 [a]Gen. 27:39, 40
10 [1]Lit., *for therefore I have seen your face like seeing God's face*
11 [1]Lit., *blessing* [2]Lit., *all* [a]Gen. 30:43
12 [1]Lit., *he*

13 But he said to him, "My lord
knows that the children are frail and
that the flocks and herds which are
nursing are [1]a care to me. And if
they are driven hard one day, all the
flocks will die.
14"Please let my lord pass on before his servant; and I will proceed
at my leisure, according to the pace
of the cattle that are before me and
according to the pace of the children, until I come to my lord at
[a]Seir."
15 And Esau said, "Please let me
leave with you some of the people
who are with me." But he said,
"[1]What need is there? Let me find
favor in the sight of my lord."
16 So Esau returned that day on
his way to Seir.
17 And Jacob journeyed to [1a]Suc-
coth; and built for himself a house,
and made booths for his livestock,
therefore the place is named Succoth.

Jacob Settles in Shechem

18 Now Jacob came safely to the
city of [a]Shechem, which is in the
land of Canaan, when he came from
[b]Paddan-aram, and camped before
the city.
19 And [a]he bought the piece of
land where he had pitched his tent
from the hand of the sons of Hamor,
Shechem's father, for one hundred
[1]pieces of money.
20 Then he erected there an altar,
and called it [1]El-Elohe-Israel.

CHAPTER 34

The Treachery of Jacob's Sons

NOW [a]Dinah the daughter of
Leah, whom she had borne to Jacob,
went out to [1]visit the daughters of
the land.
2 And when Shechem the son of
Hamor [a]the Hivite, the prince of the
land, saw her, he took her and lay
with her [1]by force.
3 And [1]he was deeply attracted
to Dinah the daughter of Jacob, and
he loved the girl and [2]spoke tenderly
to her.
4 So Shechem spoke to his father
Hamor, saying, "Get me this young
girl for a wife."
5 Now Jacob heard that he had
defiled Dinah his daughter; but his
sons were with his livestock in the
field, so Jacob kept silent until they
came in.
6 Then Hamor the father of Shechem went out to Jacob to speak
with him.
7 Now the sons of Jacob came in
from the field when they heard *it;*
and the men were grieved, and they
were very angry because he had
done a [1a]disgraceful thing in Israel
[2]by lying with Jacob's daughter, for
such a thing ought not to be done.
8 But Hamor spoke with them,
saying, "The soul of my son Shechem longs for your daughter;
please give her to him [1]in marriage.
9"And intermarry with us; give
your daughters to us, and take our
daughters for yourselves.
10"Thus you shall [1]live with us,
and [a]the land shall be *open* before
you; [1]live and trade in it, and acquire property in it."
11 Shechem also said to her father
and to her brothers, "If I find favor
in your sight, then I will give whatever you say to me.
12"Ask me ever so much bridal
payment and gift, and I will give according as you say to me; but give
me the girl [1]in marriage."
13 But Jacob's sons answered Shechem and his father Hamor, with
deceit, and spoke to them, because
he had defiled Dinah their sister.
14 And they said to them, "We
cannot do this thing, to give our sister to [a]one who is uncircumcised,
for that would be a disgrace to us.
15"Only on this *condition* will we
consent to you: if you will become
like us, in that every male of you be
circumcised,
16 then we will give our daughters
to you, and we will take your daughters for ourselves, and we will [1]live
with you and become one people.
17"But if you will not listen to us to
be circumcised, then we will take
our daughter and go."
18 Now their words seemed [1]rea-
sonable to Hamor and Shechem,
Hamor's son.
19 And the young man did not delay to do the thing, because he was
delighted with Jacob's daughter.
Now he was more respected than all
the household of his father.
20 So Hamor and his son Shechem
came to the gate of their city, and
spoke to the men of their city, saying,
21"These men are [1]friendly with
us; therefore let them [2]live in the
land and trade in it, for behold, the
land is [3]large enough for them. Let
us take their daughters [4]in marriage, and give our daughters to
them.
22"Only on this *condition* will the
men consent to us to [1]live with us, to
become one people: that every male

13 [1]Lit., *upon me*
14 [a]Gen. 32:3
15 [1]Lit., *"Why this?"*
17 [1]I.e., Booths [a]Judg. 8:5, 14; Ps. 60:6
18 [a]Gen. 12:6; Josh. 24:1; Judg. 9:1 [b]Gen. 25:20; 28:2
19 [1]Heb., *qesitah* [a]Josh. 24:32; John 4:5
20 [1]I.e., God, the God of Israel
1 [1]Lit., *see* [a]Gen. 30:21
2 [1]Lit., *and humbled her* [a]Gen. 34:30
3 [1]Lit., *his soul clung* [2]Lit., *spoke to the heart of the girl*
7 [1]Lit., *senseless* [2]Lit., *to lie* [a]Deut. 22:21; Judg. 20:6; 2 Sam. 13:12
8 [1]Lit., *for a wife*
10 [1]Lit., *dwell* [a]Gen. 13:9; 20:15
12 [1]Lit., *for a wife*
14 [a]Gen. 17:14
16 [1]Lit., *dwell*
18 [1]Lit., *good*
21 [1]Lit., *peaceful* [2]Lit., *dwell* [3]Lit., *wide of hands before them* [4]Lit., *to us for wives*
22 [1]Lit., *dwell*

among us be circumcised as they
are circumcised.
23 "Will not their livestock and
their property and all their animals
be ours? Only let us consent to
them, and they will [1]live with us."
24 And [a]all who went out of the
gate of his city listened to Hamor
and to his son Shechem, and every
male was circumcised, all who went
out of the gate of his city.
25 Now it came about on the third
day, when they were in pain, that
two of Jacob's sons, [a]Simeon and
Levi, Dinah's brothers, each took
his sword and came upon the city
unawares, and killed every male.
26 And they killed Hamor and his
son Shechem with the edge of the
sword, and took Dinah from Shechem's house, and went forth.
27 Jacob's sons came upon the
slain and looted the city, because
they had defiled their sister.
28 They took their flocks and their
herds and their donkeys, and that
which was in the city and that which
was in the field;
29 and they captured and looted
all their wealth and all their little
ones and their wives, even all that
was in the houses.
30 Then Jacob said to Simeon and
Levi, "You have brought trouble on
me, [a]by making me odious among
the inhabitants of the land, among
[b]the Canaanites and the Perizzites;
and [1c]my men being few in number,
they will gather together against me
and [2]attack me and I shall be destroyed, I and my household."
31 But they said, "Should he [1]treat
our sister as a harlot?"

Chapter 35

Jacob Moves to Bethel

THEN God said to Jacob, "Arise,
go up to [a]Bethel, and [1]live there; and
make an altar there to [b]God, who
appeared to you when you fled
[2]from your brother Esau."
2 So Jacob said to his household
and to all who were with him, "Put
away [a]the foreign gods which are
among you, and [b]purify yourselves,
and change your garments;
3 and let us arise and go up to
Bethel; and I will make [a]an altar
there to God, who answered me in
the day of my distress, and [b]has
been with me [1]wherever I have
gone."
4 So they gave to Jacob all the
foreign gods which [1]they had, and
the rings which were in their ears;
and Jacob hid them under the [2]oak
which was near Shechem.
5 As they journeyed, there was
[1a]a great terror upon the cities
which were around them, and they
did not pursue the sons of Jacob.
6 So Jacob came to [a]Luz (that is,
Bethel), which is in the land of Canaan, he and all the people who
were with him.
7 And [a]he built an altar there, and
called the place [1]El-bethel, because
there God had revealed Himself to
him, when he fled [2]from his brother.
8 Now [a]Deborah, Rebekah's
nurse, died, and she was buried below Bethel under the oak; it was
named [1]Allon-bacuth.

Jacob Is Named Israel

9 Then God appeared to Jacob
again when he came from Paddan-aram, and He [a]blessed him.
10 And [a]God said to him,
"Your name is Jacob;
[1]You shall no longer be called
Jacob,
But Israel shall be your name."
Thus He called [2]him Israel.
11 God also said to him,
"I am [1a]God Almighty;
[b]Be fruitful and multiply;
A nation and a [c]company of
nations shall [2]come from
you,
And [d]kings shall [2]come forth
from [3]you.
12 "And [a]the land which I gave to
Abraham and Isaac,
I will give it to you,
And I will give the land to your
[1]descendants after you."
13 Then [a]God went up from him in
the place where He had spoken with
him.
14 And Jacob set up [a]a pillar in the
place where He had spoken with
him, a pillar of stone, and he poured
out a [1]libation on it; he also poured
oil on it.
15 So Jacob named the place
where God had spoken with him,
[1]Bethel.
16 Then they journeyed from
Bethel; and when there was still
some distance to go to [a]Ephrath, Rachel began to give birth and she
[1]suffered severe labor.
17 And it came about when she
was in severe labor that the midwife
said to her, "Do not fear, for now
[a]you have *another* son."
18 And it came about as her soul
was departing (for she died), that
she named him [1]Ben-oni; but his father called him [2]Benjamin.
19 So [a]Rachel died and was buried

23 [1]Lit., *dwell*
24 [a]Gen. 23:10
25 [a]Gen. 49:5-7
30 [1]Lit., *I, few in number* [2]Lit., *smite*
[a]Ex. 5:21; 2 Sam. 10:6 [b]Gen. 13:7; 34:2 [c]Gen. 46:26, 27; 1 Chr. 16:19
31 [1]Or, *make*
1 [1]Lit., *dwell* [2]Lit., *from the face of*
[a]Gen. 28:19 [b]Gen. 28:13
2 [a]Gen. 31:19, 30 [b]Ex. 19:10, 14
3 [1]Lit., *in the way which*
[a]Gen. 28:20-22 [b]Gen. 28:15
4 [1]Lit., *in their hand* [2]Or, *terebinth*
5 [1]Or, *a terror of God*
[a]Ex. 15:16; Deut. 2:25
6 [a]Gen. 28:19; 48:3
7 [1]I.e., the God of Bethel [2]Lit., *from the face of*
[a]Gen. 35:3
8 [1]I.e., Oak of weeping
[a]Gen. 24:59
9 [a]Gen. 32:29
10 [1]Lit., *Your name* [2]Lit., *his name*
[a]Gen. 32:28
11 [1]Heb., *El Shaddai* [2]Or, *come into being* [3]Lit., *your loins*
[a]Gen. 17:1; 28:3 [b]Gen. 9:1, 7 [c]Gen. 48:4 [d]Gen. 17:6, 16; 36:31
12 [1]Lit., *seed*
[a]Gen. 13:15; 26:3; 28:13
13 [a]Gen. 17:22; 18:33
14 [1]Or, *drink offering*
[a]Gen. 28:18, 19; 31:45
15 [1]I.e., the house of God
16 [1]Lit., *had difficulty in her giving birth*
[a]Gen. 35:19; Ruth 4:11; Mic. 5:2
17 [a]Gen. 30:24
18 [1]I.e., the son of my sorrow [2]I.e., the son of the right hand
19 [a]Gen. 48:7

on the way to Ephrath (that is, Bethlehem).
20 And Jacob set up a pillar over
her grave; that is the [a]pillar of Rachel's grave to this day.
21 Then Israel journeyed on and
pitched his tent beyond the [1]tower
of [2]Eder.
22 And it came about while Israel
was dwelling in that land, that [a]Reu-
ben went and lay with Bilhah his father's concubine; and Israel heard *of*
it.

The Sons of Israel

Now there were twelve sons of Jacob—
23 [a]the sons of Leah: Reuben, Jacob's first-born, then Simeon and
Levi and Judah and Issachar and
Zebulun;
24 [a]the sons of Rachel: Joseph and
Benjamin;
25 and [a]the sons of Bilhah, Rachel's maid: Dan and Naphtali;
26 and [a]the sons of Zilpah, Leah's
maid: Gad and Asher. These are the
sons of Jacob who were born to him
in Paddan-aram.
27 And Jacob came to his father
Isaac at [a]Mamre of Kiriath-arba
(that is, Hebron), where Abraham
and Isaac had sojourned.
28 Now the days of Isaac were
[a]one hundred and eighty years.
29 And Isaac breathed his last and
died, and was [a]gathered to his people, an [b]old man [1]of ripe age; and his
sons Esau and Jacob buried him.

Chapter 36

Esau Moves

NOW these are *the records of* the
generations of [a]Esau (that is,
Edom).
2 Esau took [a]his wives from the
daughters of Canaan: Adah the
daughter of Elon the Hittite, and
Oholibamah the daughter of Anah
and the [b]granddaughter of Zibeon
the Hivite;
3 also Basemath, Ishmael's
daughter, the sister of Nebaioth.
4 And Adah bore Eliphaz to Esau,
and Basemath bore Reuel,
5 and Oholibamah bore Jeush
and Jalam and Korah. These are the
sons of Esau who were born to him
in the land of Canaan.
6 [a]Then Esau took his wives and
his sons and his daughters and all
[1]his household, and his livestock
and all his cattle and all his goods
which he had acquired in the land of
Canaan, and went to *another* land
away from his brother Jacob.

20 [a]1 Sam. 10:2

21 [1]Heb., *Migdal-eder* [2]Or, *flock*

22 [a]Gen. 49:4; 1 Chr. 5:1

23 [a]Gen. 29:31-35; 30:18-20

24 [a]Gen. 30:22-24; 35:18

25 [a]Gen. 30:5-8

26 [a]Gen. 30:10-13

27 [a]Gen. 18:1; 23:19

28 [a]Gen. 25:26

29 [1]Lit., *and satisfied with days* [a]Gen. 25:8 [b]Gen. 15:15

1 [a]Gen. 25:30

2 [a]Gen. 26:34; 28:9 [b]Gen. 36:24

6 [1]Lit., *the souls of his house* [a]Gen. 12:5

7 [1]Lit., *dwell* [a]Gen. 13:6

8 [a]Gen. 32:3 [b]Gen. 36:1, 19

9 [1]Lit., *Edom*

11 [1]In 1 Chr. 1:36, *Zephi*

14 [1]Gr., *son* [2]Lit., *and she*

16 [1]Lit., *of Eliphaz*

17 [1]Lit., *of Reuel*

18 [1]Lit., *of Oholibamah, Esau's wife*

20 [a]Gen. 14:6; Deut. 2:12, 22; 1 Chr. 1:38-42

21 [1]Lit., *of the Horites*

7 [a]For their property had become
too great for them to [1]live together,
and the land where they sojourned
could not sustain them because of
their livestock.
8 So Esau lived in the hill country
of [a]Seir; Esau is [b]Edom.
9 These then are *the records of*
the generations of Esau the father of
[1]the Edomites in the hill country of
Seir.

Descendants of Esau

10 These are the names of Esau's
sons: Eliphaz the son of Esau's wife
Adah, Reuel the son of Esau's wife
Basemath.
11 And the sons of Eliphaz were
Teman, Omar, [1]Zepho and Gatam
and Kenaz.
12 And Timna was a concubine of
Esau's son Eliphaz and she bore
Amalek to Eliphaz. These are the
sons of Esau's wife Adah.
13 And these are the sons of Reuel:
Nahath and Zerah, Shammah and
Mizzah. These were the sons of
Esau's wife Basemath.
14 And these were the sons of
Esau's wife Oholibamah, the daughter of Anah and the [1]granddaughter
of Zibeon: [2]she bore to Esau, Jeush
and Jalam and Korah.
15 These are the chiefs of the sons
of Esau. The sons of Eliphaz, the
first-born of Esau, are chief Teman,
chief Omar, chief Zepho, chief Kenaz,
16 chief Korah, chief Gatam, chief
Amalek. These are the chiefs [1]de-
scended from Eliphaz in the land of
Edom; these are the sons of Adah.
17 And these are the sons of Reuel,
Esau's son: chief Nahath, chief Zerah, chief Shammah, chief Mizzah.
These are the chiefs [1]descended
from Reuel in the land of Edom;
these are the sons of Esau's wife
Basemath.
18 And these are the sons of
Esau's wife Oholibamah: chief
Jeush, chief Jalam, chief Korah.
These are the chiefs [1]descended
from Esau's wife Oholibamah, the
daughter of Anah.
19 These are the sons of Esau (that
is, Edom), and these are their chiefs.
20 These are the sons of Seir [a]the
Horite, the inhabitants of the land:
Lotan and Shobal and Zibeon and
Anah,
21 and Dishon and Ezer and Dishan. These are the chiefs [1]de-
scended from the Horites, the sons
of Seir in the land of Edom.
22 And the sons of Lotan were

Hori and [1]Hemam; and Lotan's sister was Timna.
23 And these are the sons of Shobal: [1]Alvan and Manahath and Ebal,
[2]Shepho and Onam.
24 And these are the sons of
Zibeon: Aiah and Anah—he is the
Anah who found the hot springs in
the wilderness when he was pasturing the donkeys of his father Zibeon.
25 And these are the children of
Anah: Dishon, and Oholibamah, the
daughter of Anah.
26 And these are the sons of [1]Di-
shon: [2]Hemdan and Eshban and Ithran and Cheran.
27 These are the sons of Ezer: Bilhan and Zaavan and [1]Akan.
28 These are the sons of Dishan:
Uz and Aran.
29 These are the chiefs [1]descended
from the Horites: chief Lotan, chief
Shobal, chief Zibeon, chief Anah,
30 chief Dishon, chief Ezer, chief
Dishan. These are the chiefs [1]de-
scended from the Horites, according to their *various* chiefs in the land
of Seir.
31 Now these are the kings who
reigned in the land of Edom before
any [a]king reigned over the sons of
Israel.
32 [1]Bela the son of Beor reigned in
Edom, and the name of his city was
Dinhabah.
33 Then Bela died, and Jobab the
son of Zerah of Bozrah became king
in his place.
34 Then Jobab died, and Husham
of the land of the Temanites became
king in his place.
35 Then Husham died, and Hadad
the son of Bedad, who [1]defeated
Midian in the field of Moab, became
king in his place; and the name of
his city was Avith.
36 Then Hadad died, and Samlah
of Masrekah became king in his
place.
37 Then Samlah died, and Shaul of
Rehoboth on the *Euphrates* River
became king in his place.
38 Then Shaul died, and Baal-hanan the son of Achbor became king
in his place.
39 Then Baal-hanan the son of
Achbor died, and [1]Hadar became
king in his place; and the name of
his city was [2]Pau; and his wife's
name was Mehetabel, the daughter
of Matred, daughter of Mezahab.
40 Now these are the names of the
chiefs [1]descended from Esau, according to their families *and* their
localities, by their names: chief Timna, chief [2]Alvah, chief Jetheth,
41 chief Oholibamah, chief Elah,
chief Pinon,
42 chief Kenaz, chief Teman, chief
Mibzar,
43 chief Magdiel, chief Iram.
These are the chiefs of Edom (that
is, Esau, the father of the [1]Edom-
ites), according to their habitations
in the land of their possession.

Chapter 37

Joseph's Dream

NOW Jacob lived in [a]the land
[1]where his father had sojourned, in
the land of Canaan.
2 These are *the records of* the
generations of Jacob.
Joseph, when [a]seventeen years of
age, was pasturing the flock with his
brothers while he was *still* a youth,
along with [b]the sons of Bilhah and
the sons of Zilpah, his father's
wives. And Joseph brought back a
bad report about them to their father.
3 Now Israel loved Joseph more
than all his sons, because he was
[a]the son of his old age; and he made
him a [1b]varicolored tunic.
4 And his brothers saw that their
father loved him more than all his
brothers; and so they hated him and
could not speak to him [1]on friendly
terms.
5 Then Joseph [1a]had a dream,
and when he told it to his brothers,
they hated him even more.
6 And he said to them, "Please
listen to this dream which I have
[1]had;
7 for behold, we were binding
sheaves in the field, and lo, my sheaf
rose up and also stood erect; and behold, your sheaves gathered around
and [a]bowed down to my sheaf."
8 Then his brothers said to him,
"[a]Are you actually going to reign
over us? Or are you really going to
rule over us?" So they hated him
even more for his dreams and for his
words.
9 Now he [1]had still another
dream, and related it to his brothers,
and said, "Lo, I have [1]had still another dream; and behold, the sun
and the moon and eleven stars were
bowing down to me."
10 And he related *it* to his father
and to his brothers; and his father
rebuked him and said to him, "What
is this dream that you have [1]had?
Shall I and your mother and [a]your
brothers actually come to bow ourselves down before you to the
ground?"
11 And [a]his brothers were jealous

22 [1]In 1 Chr. 1:39, *Homam*
23 [1]In 1 Chr. 1:40, *Alian* [2]In 1 Chr. 1:40, *Shephi*
26 [1]Heb., *Dishan*, but cf. 1 Chr. 1:41 [2]In 1 Chr. 1:41, *Hamran*
27 [1]In 1 Chr. 1:42, *Jaakan*
29 [1]Lit., *of the Horites*
30 [1]Lit., *of the Horites*
31 [a]Gen. 17:6, 16; 35:11; 1 Chr. 1:43
32 [1]Lit., *And Bela*
35 [1]Or, *smote*
39 [1]In 1 Chr. 1:50, *Hadad* [2]In 1 Chr. 1:50, *Pai*
40 [1]Lit., *of Esau* [2]In 1 Chr. 1:51, *Aliah*
43 [1]Heb., *Edom*
1 [1]Lit., *of his father's sojournings* [a]Gen. 17:8; 28:4
2 [a]Gen. 41:46 [b]Gen. 35:25, 26
3 [1]Or, *full-length robe* [a]Gen. 44:20 [b]Gen. 37:23, 32
4 [1]Lit., *in peace*
5 [1]Lit., *dreamed* [a]Gen. 28:12; 31:10, 11, 24
6 [1]Lit., *dreamed*
7 [a]Gen. 42:6, 9; 43:26; 44:14
8 [a]Gen. 49:26; Deut. 33:16
9 [1]Lit., *dreamed*
10 [1]Lit., *dreamed* [a]Gen. 27:29
11 [a]Acts 7:9

of him, but his father kept the saying *in mind.*
12 Then his brothers went to pasture their father's flock in Shechem.
13 And Israel said to Joseph, "Are
not your brothers pasturing *the
flock* in [a]Shechem? Come, and I will
send you to them." And he said to
him, "[1]I will go."
14 Then he said to him, "Go now
and see about the welfare of your
brothers and the welfare of the
flock; and bring word back to me."
[a]So he sent him from the valley of
Hebron, and he came to Shechem.
15 And a man found him, and behold, he was wandering in the field;
and the man asked him, [1]"What are
you looking for?"
16 And he said, "I am looking for
my brothers; please tell me where
they are pasturing *the flock.*"
17 Then the man said, "They have
moved from here; for I heard *them*
say, 'Let us go to [a]Dothan.'" So
Joseph went after his brothers and
found them at Dothan.

The Plot against Joseph

18 [1]When they saw him from a
distance and before he came close
to them, they plotted against him to
put him to death.
19 And they said to one another,
"[1]Here comes this dreamer!
20 "Now then, come and let us kill
him and throw him into one of the
pits; and [a]we will say, 'A wild beast
devoured him.' Then let us see what
will become of his dreams!"
21 But [a]Reuben heard *this* and rescued him out of their hands and
said, "Let us not [1]take his life."
22 Reuben further said to them,
"Shed no blood. Throw him into this
pit that is in the wilderness, but do
not lay hands on him"—that he
might rescue him out of their hands,
to restore him to his father.
23 So it came about, when Joseph
[1]reached his brothers, that they
stripped Joseph of his [2]tunic, the
varicolored tunic that was on him;
24 and they took him and threw
him into the pit. Now the pit was
empty, without any water in it.
25 Then they sat down to eat [1]a
meal. And as they raised their eyes
and looked, behold, a caravan of
[a]Ishmaelites was coming from Gilead, with their camels bearing
[2][b]aromatic gum and [3][c]balm and
[4]myrrh, [5]on their way to bring *them*
down to Egypt.
26 And Judah said to his brothers,
"What profit is it for us to kill our
brother and [a]cover up his blood?
27 "[a]Come and let us sell him to the
Ishmaelites and not lay our hands
on him; for he is our brother, our
own flesh." And his brothers listened *to him.*
28 Then some [a]Midianite traders
passed by, so they pulled *him* up
and lifted Joseph out of the pit, and
[b]sold [1]him to the Ishmaelites for
twenty *shekels* of silver. Thus [c]they
brought Joseph into Egypt.
29 Now Reuben returned to the
pit, and behold, Joseph was not in
the pit; so he [a]tore his garments.
30 And he returned to his brothers
and said, "[a]The boy is not *there;* as
for me, where am I to go?"
31 So [a]they took Joseph's tunic,
and slaughtered a male goat, and
dipped the tunic in the blood;
32 and they sent the varicolored
tunic and brought it to their father
and said, "We found this; please
[1]examine *it* to *see* whether it is your
son's tunic or not."
33 Then he [1]examined it and said,
"It is my son's tunic. [a]A wild beast
has devoured him; Joseph has
surely been torn to pieces!"
34 So Jacob [a]tore his clothes, and
put sackcloth on his loins, and
mourned for his son many days.
35 Then all his sons and all his
daughters arose to comfort him, but
he refused to be comforted. And he
said, "Surely I will go down to [a]She-
ol in mourning for my son." So his
father wept for him.
36 Meanwhile, the [1]Midianites
[a]sold him in Egypt to Potiphar, Pharaoh's officer, the captain of the
bodyguard.

CHAPTER 38

Judah and Tamar

AND it came about at that time,
that Judah [1]departed from his
brothers, and [2]visited a certain
[a]Adullamite, whose name was Hirah.
2 And Judah saw there a daughter of a certain Canaanite whose
name was Shua; and he took her and
went in to her.
3 So she conceived and bore a
son and he named him [a]Er.
4 Then she conceived again and
bore a son and named him Onan.
5 And she bore still another son
and named him Shelah; and it was
at Chezib [1]that she bore him.
6 Now Judah took a wife for Er
his first-born, and her name *was* Tamar.
7 But [a]Er, Judah's first-born, was
evil in the sight of the LORD, so the
LORD took his life.

13 [1]Lit., *"Behold me."* [a]Gen. 33:18-20
14 [a]Gen. 35:27
15 [1]Lit., *saying, "What . . . ?"*
17 [a]2 Kin. 6:13
18 [1]Or, *And*
19 [1]Lit., *Behold, this master of dreams comes*
20 [a]Gen. 37:32
21 [1]Lit., *smite his soul* [a]Gen. 42:22
23 [1]Lit., *came to* [2]Or, *full-length robe*
25 [1]Lit., *bread* [2]Or, *ladanum spice* [3]Or, *mastic* [4]Or, *resinous bark* [5]Lit., *going* [a]Gen. 16:12; 37:28; 39:1 [b]Gen. 43:11 [c]Jer. 8:22; 46:11
26 [a]Gen. 37:20
27 [a]Gen. 42:21
28 [1]Lit., *Joseph* [a]Gen. 37:25; Judg. 6:1; 8:22, 24 [b]Gen. 45:4; Acts 7:9 [c]Gen. 39:1
29 [a]Gen. 37:34; 44:13
30 [a]Gen. 42:13, 36
31 [a]Gen. 37:3, 23
32 [1]Or, *recognize*
33 [1]Or, *recognized* [a]Gen. 37:20
34 [a]Gen. 37:29
35 [a]Gen. 25:8; 35:29; 37:33; 42:38; 44:29, 31
36 [1]Lit., *Medanites* [a]Gen. 39:1
1 [1]Lit., *went down* [2]Lit., *turned aside to* [a]Josh. 15:35; 1 Sam. 22:1
3 [a]Gen. 46:12; Num. 26:19
5 [1]Lit., *when*
7 [a]1 Chr. 2:3

8 Then Judah said to Onan, "[a]Go in to your brother's wife, and perform your duty as a brother-in-law to her, and raise up [1]offspring for your brother."

9 And Onan knew that the [1]offspring would not be his; so it came about that when he went in to his brother's wife, he [2]wasted his seed on the ground, in order not to give [1]offspring to his brother.

10 But what he did was displeasing in the sight of the LORD; so He took his life also.

11 Then Judah said to his daughter-in-law Tamar, "[a]Remain a widow in your father's house until my son Shelah grows up"; for he [1]thought, "[2]*I am afraid* that he too may die like his brothers." So Tamar went and lived in her father's house.

12 Now [1]after a considerable time Shua's daughter, the wife of Judah, died; and when [2]the time of mourning was ended, Judah went up to his sheepshearers at [a]Timnah, he and his friend Hirah the Adullamite.

13 And it was told to Tamar, "[1]Behold, your father-in-law is going up to Timnah to shear his sheep."

14 So she [1]removed her widow's garments and [a]covered *herself* with a [2]veil, and wrapped herself, and sat in the gateway of [b]Enaim, which is on the road to Timnah; for she saw that Shelah had grown up, and she had not been given to him as a wife.

15 When Judah saw her, he thought she *was* a harlot, for she had covered her face.

16 So he turned aside to her by the road, and said, "[1]Here now, let me come in to you"; for he did not know that she was his daughter-in-law. And she said, "What will you give me, that you may come in to me?"

17 He said, therefore, "I will send you a [1]kid from the flock." She said, moreover, "Will you give a pledge until you send *it?*"

18 And he said, "What pledge shall I give you?" And she said, "[a]Your seal and your cord, and your staff that is in your hand." So he gave *them* to her, and went in to her, and she conceived by him.

19 Then she arose and departed, and [1]removed her [2]veil and put on her widow's garments.

20 When Judah sent the [1]kid by his friend the Adullamite, to receive the pledge from the woman's hand, he did not find her.

21 And he asked the men of her place, saying, "Where is the temple prostitute who was by the road at Enaim?" But they said, "There has been no temple prostitute here."

22 So he returned to Judah, and said, "I did not find her; and furthermore, the men of the place said, 'There has been no temple prostitute here.' "

23 Then Judah said, "Let her [1]keep them, lest we become a laughingstock. [2]After all, I sent this kid, but you did not find her."

24 Now it was about three months later that Judah was informed, "[1]Your daughter-in-law Tamar has played the harlot, and behold, she is also with child by harlotry." Then Judah said, "Bring her out and [a]let her be burned!"

25 It was while she was being brought out that she sent to her father-in-law, saying, "I am with child by the man to whom these things belong." And she said, "Please examine and see, whose signet ring and cords and staff are these?"

26 And Judah recognized *them,* and said, "She is more righteous than I, inasmuch as I did not give her to my son Shelah." And he did not [1]have relations with her again.

27 And it came about at the time she was giving birth, that behold, there were [a]twins in her womb.

28 Moreover, it took place while she was giving birth, one put out a hand, and the midwife took and tied a scarlet *thread* on his hand, saying, "This one came out first."

29 But it came about as he drew back his hand, that behold, his brother came out. Then she said, "What a breach you have made for yourself!" So he was named [1a]Perez.

30 And afterward his brother came out who had the scarlet *thread* on his hand; and he was named [1a]Zerah.

CHAPTER 39

Joseph's Success in Egypt

NOW Joseph had been taken down to Egypt; and Potiphar, an Egyptian officer of Pharaoh, the captain of the bodyguard, bought him [1]from the [a]Ishmaelites, who had taken him down there.

2 And [a]the LORD was with Joseph, so he became a [1]successful man. And he was in the house of his master the Egyptian.

3 Now his master [a]saw that the LORD was with him and *how* the LORD [b]caused all that he did to prosper in his hand.

4 So Joseph found favor in his

---

8 [1]Lit., *seed* [a]Deut. 25:5, 6; Matt. 22:24

9 [1]Lit., *seed* [2]Lit., *spilled on the ground*

11 [1]Lit., *said* [2]Lit., *Lest he also die* [a]Ruth 1:12, 13

12 [1]Lit., *the days became many and* [2]Lit., *Judah was comforted, he* [a]Josh. 15:10, 57

13 [1]Lit., *saying, Behold*

14 [1]Lit., *removed from herself* [2]Or, *shawl* [a]Gen. 24:65 [b]Josh. 15:34

16 [1]Or, *Come, now . . .*

17 [1]Lit., *kid of goats*

18 [a]Gen. 41:42

19 [1]Lit., *removed from herself* [2]Or, *shawl*

20 [1]Lit., *kid of goats by the hand of*

23 [1]Lit., *take for herself* [2]Lit., *Behold*

24 [1]Lit., *saying, Your* [a]Lev. 21:9

26 [1]Lit., *know her yet again*

27 [a]Gen. 25:24-26

29 [1]I.e., A breach [a]Gen. 46:12; Ruth 4:12

30 [1]I.e., A dawning or brightness [a]1 Chr. 2:5

1 [1]Lit., *from the hand of* [a]Gen. 37:25, 28, 36; Ps. 105:17

2 [1]Or, *prosperous* [a]Gen. 39:3, 21, 23

3 [a]Gen. 21:22; 26:28 [b]Ps. 1:3

sight, and [1]became his personal servant; and he made him overseer
over his house, and [a]all that he
owned he put in his [2]charge.
5 And it came about that from
the time he made him overseer in
his house, and over all that he
owned, the LORD [a]blessed the Egyptian's house on account of Joseph;
thus [b]the LORD's blessing was upon
all that he owned, in the house and
in the field.
6 So he left everything he owned
in Joseph's [1]charge; and with him
there he did not [2]concern himself
with anything except the [3]food
which he [4]ate. Now Joseph was
[a]handsome in form and appearance.
7 And it came about after these
events [a]that his master's wife
[1]looked with desire at Joseph, and
she said, "Lie with me."
8 But [a]he refused and said to his
master's wife, "Behold, with me
here, my master [1]does not concern
himself with anything in the house,
and he has put all that he owns in
my [2]charge.
9 "[1a]There is no one greater in this
house than I, and he has withheld
nothing from me except you, because you are his wife. How then
could I do this great evil, and [b]sin
against God?"
10 And it came about as she spoke
to Joseph day after day, that he did
not listen to her to lie beside her, *or*
be with her.
11 Now it happened [1]one day that
he went into the house to do his
work, and none of the men of the
household was there inside.
12 And she caught him by his garment, saying, "Lie with me!" And he
left his garment in her hand and
fled, and went outside.
13 [1]When she saw that he had left
his garment in her hand, and had
fled outside,
14 she called to the men of her
household, and said to them, "See,
he has brought in a [1]Hebrew to us to
make sport of us; he came in to me
to lie with me, and I [2]screamed.
15 "And it came about when he
heard that I raised my voice and
[1]screamed, that he left his garment
beside me and fled, and went outside."
16 So she [1]left his garment beside
her until his master came home.
17 Then she spoke to him [1]with
these words, "[2]The Hebrew slave,
whom you brought to us, came in to
me to make sport of me;
18 and it happened as I raised my
voice and [1]screamed, that he left his
garment beside me and fled outside."

Joseph Imprisoned

19 Now it came about when his
master heard the words of his wife,
which she spoke to him, saying,
"[1]This is what your slave did to me,"
that his anger burned.
20 So Joseph's master took him
and [a]put him into the jail, the place
where the king's prisoners were
confined; and he was there in the
jail.
21 But [a]the LORD was with Joseph
and extended kindness to him, and
gave him favor in the sight of the
chief jailer.
22 And the chief jailer [a]committed
to Joseph's [1]charge all the prisoners
who were in the jail; so that whatever was done there, he was [2]re-
sponsible *for it.*
23 [a]The chief jailer did not supervise anything under [1]Joseph's
charge because [b]the LORD was with
him; and whatever he did, [c]the LORD
made to prosper.

CHAPTER 40

Joseph Interprets a Dream

THEN it came about after these
things [a]the cupbearer and the baker
for the king of Egypt offended their
lord, the king of Egypt.
2 And Pharaoh was furious with
his two officials, the chief cupbearer
and the chief baker.
3 So he put them in confinement
in the house of the [a]captain of the
bodyguard, in the jail, the *same*
place where Joseph was imprisoned.
4 And the captain of the bodyguard put Joseph in charge of them,
and he [1]took care of them; and they
were in confinement for [2]some time.
5 Then the cupbearer and the baker for the king of Egypt, who were
confined in jail, they both had a
dream the same night, each man
with his *own* dream *and* each dream
with its *own* interpretation.
6 [1]When Joseph came to them in
the morning and observed them,
[2]behold, they were dejected.
7 And he asked Pharaoh's officials who were with him in confinement in his master's house, "[1a]Why
are your faces so sad today?"
8 Then they said to him, "[a]We
have [1]had a dream and there is no
one to interpret it." Then Joseph
said to them, "[b]Do not interpreta-

4 [1]Or, *ministered to him* [2]Lit., *hand* [a]Gen. 39:8, 22
5 [a]Gen. 30:27 [b]Deut. 28:3, 4, 11
6 [1]Lit., *hand* [2]Lit., *know* [3]Lit., *bread* [4]Or, *used to eat* [a]Gen. 29:17
7 [1]Lit., *lifted up her eyes at* [a]Prov. 7:15-20
8 [1]Lit., *does not know what is in the house* [2]Lit., *hand* [a]Prov. 6:23, 24
9 [1]Or, *He is not greater* [a]Gen. 41:40 [b]Gen. 42:18; 2 Sam. 12:13
11 [1]Lit., *about this day*
13 [1]Lit., *And it came about when*
14 [1]Lit., *Hebrew man* [2]Lit., *called with a great voice.*
15 [1]Lit., *called out*
16 [1]Lit., *let . . . lie beside*
17 [1]Lit, *according to* [2]Lit., *saying, "The*
18 [1]Lit., *called out*
19 [1]Lit., *According to these things your slave*
20 [a]Ps. 105:18
21 [a]Gen. 39:2; Ps. 105:19; Acts 7:9
22 [1]Lit., *hand* [2]Lit., *the doer* [a]Gen. 39:4
23 [1]Lit., *his hand* [a]Gen. 39:3, 8 [b]Gen. 39:2 [c]Gen. 39:3
1 [a]Gen. 40:11, 13
3 [a]Gen. 39:1, 20
4 [1]Lit., *ministered to* [2]Lit., *days*
6 [1]Or, *And* [2]Lit., *and behold*
7 [1]Lit., *saying, Why* [a]Neh. 2:2
8 [1]Lit., *dreamed* [a]Gen. 41:15 [b]Gen. 41:16; Dan. 2:27, 28

tions belong to God? Tell *it* to me,
please."
9 So the chief cupbearer told his
dream to Joseph, and said to him,
"In my dream, [1]behold, *there was* a
vine in front of me;
10 and on the vine *were* three
branches. And as it was budding, its
blossoms came out, *and* its clusters
produced ripe grapes.
11"Now Pharaoh's cup was in my
hand; so I took the grapes and
squeezed them into Pharaoh's cup,
and I put the cup into Pharaoh's
[1]hand."
12 Then Joseph said to him, "This
is the interpretation of it: the three
branches are three days;
13 within three more days Pharaoh will [1]lift up your head and restore you to your [2]office; and you
will put Pharaoh's cup into his hand
according to your former custom
when you were his cupbearer.
14"Only [1]keep me in mind when it
goes well with you, and please do
me a kindness [2]by mentioning me to
Pharaoh, and get me out of this
house.
15"For [a]I was in fact kidnapped
from the land of the Hebrews, and
even here I have done nothing that
they should have put me into the
[1]dungeon."
16 When the chief baker saw that
he had interpreted favorably, he
said to Joseph, "I also *saw* in my
dream, and behold, *there were* three
baskets of white bread on my head;
17 and in the top basket *there were*
some of all [1]sorts of baked food for
Pharaoh, and the birds were eating
them out of the basket on my head."
18 Then Joseph answered and
said, "This is its interpretation: the
three baskets are three days;
19 within three more days Pharaoh will lift up your head from you
and will hang you on a tree; and the
birds will eat your flesh off you."
20 Thus it came about on the third
day, *which was* Pharaoh's birthday,
that he made a feast for all his servants; [a]and he lifted up the head of
the chief cupbearer and the head of
the chief baker among his servants.
21 And he restored the chief cupbearer to his [1]office, and [a]he put the
cup into Pharaoh's [2]hand;
22 but [a]he hanged the chief baker,
just as Joseph had interpreted to
them.
23 Yet the chief cupbearer did not
remember Joseph, but forgot him.

CHAPTER 41

Pharaoh's Dream

NOW it happened at the end of
two full years that Pharaoh had a
dream, and behold, he was standing
by the Nile.
2 And lo, from the Nile there
came up seven cows, sleek and [1]fat;
and they grazed in the [a]marsh grass.
3 Then behold, seven other cows
came up after them from the Nile,
ugly and [1]gaunt, and they stood by
the *other* cows on the bank of the
Nile.
4 And the ugly and [1]gaunt cows
ate up the seven sleek and fat cows.
Then Pharaoh awoke.
5 And he fell asleep and dreamed
a second time; and behold, seven
ears of grain came up on a single
stalk, plump and good.
6 Then behold, seven ears, thin
and scorched by the east wind,
sprouted up after them.
7 And the thin ears swallowed up
the seven plump and full ears. Then
Pharaoh awoke, and behold, *it was* a
dream.
8 Now it came about in the morning that [a]his spirit was troubled, so
he sent and called for all the [1b]magi-
cians of Egypt, and all its wise men.
And Pharaoh told them his [2]dreams,
but [c]there was no one who could interpret them to Pharaoh.
9 Then the chief cupbearer spoke
to Pharaoh, saying, "I would make
mention today of [a]my *own* [1]of-
fenses.
10"Pharaoh was furious with his
servants, and he put me in confinement in the house of the captain of
the bodyguard, *both* me and the
chief baker.
11"And we had a dream on [1]the
same night, [2]he and I; each of us
dreamed according to the interpretation of his *own* dream.
12"Now a Hebrew youth *was* with
us there, a servant of the captain of
the bodyguard, and we related *them*
to him, and he interpreted our
dreams for us. To each one he interpreted according to his *own* dream.
13"And it came about that just [a]as
he interpreted for us, so it happened; he restored me in my [1]office,
but he hanged him."

Joseph Interprets

14 [a]Then Pharaoh sent and called
for Joseph, and they [b]hurriedly
brought him out of the dungeon; and
when he had shaved himself and
changed his clothes, he came to
Pharaoh.

9 [1]Lit., *and behold*
11 [1]Lit., *palm*
13 [1]Or possibly, *forgive you* [2]Lit., *place*
14 [1]Lit., *remember me with yourself* [2]Lit., *and mention*
15 [1]Or, *pit* [a]Gen. 37:26-28
17 [1]Lit., *food for Pharaoh made by a baker*
20 [a]2 Kin. 25:27; Jer. 52:31
21 [1]Lit., *wine-pouring* [2]Lit., *palm* [a]Gen. 40:13
22 [a]Gen. 40:19
2 [1]Lit., *fat of flesh* [a]Job 8:11; Is. 19:6, 7
3 [1]Lit., *lean of flesh*
4 [1]Lit., *lean of flesh*
8 [1]Or, *soothsayer priests* [2]Lit., *dream* [a]Dan. 2:1, 3 [b]Ex. 7:11, 22 [c]Dan. 2:27; 4:7
9 [1]Or, *sins* [a]Gen. 40:23
11 [1]Lit., *one night* [2]Lit., *I and he*
13 [1]Lit., *place* [a]Gen. 40:21, 22
14 [a]Ps. 105:20 [b]Dan. 2:25

15 And Pharaoh said to Joseph, "I have had a dream, [a]but no one can interpret it; and I have heard [1]it said about you, that [2]when you hear a dream you can interpret it."

16 Joseph then answered Pharaoh, saying, "[1a]It is not in me; [b]God will [2]give Pharaoh a favorable answer."

17 So Pharaoh spoke to Joseph, "In my dream, behold, I was standing on the bank of the Nile;

18 and behold, seven cows, [1]fat and sleek came up out of the Nile; and they grazed in the marsh grass.

19 "And lo, seven other cows came up after them, poor and very ugly and [1]gaunt, such as I had never seen for [2]ugliness in all the land of Egypt;

20 and the lean and [1]ugly cows ate up the first seven fat cows.

21 "Yet when they had [1]devoured them, it could not be [2]detected that they had [1]devoured them; [3]for they were just as ugly as [4]before. Then I awoke.

22 "I saw also in my dream, and behold, seven ears, full and good, came up on a single stalk;

23 and lo, seven ears, withered, thin, *and* scorched by the east wind, sprouted up after them;

24 and the thin ears swallowed the seven good ears. Then I told it to the [1]magicians, but there was no one who could explain it to me."

25 Now Joseph said to Pharaoh, "Pharaoh's [1]dreams are one *and the same;* [a]God has told to Pharaoh what He is about to do.

26 "The seven good cows are seven years; and the seven good ears are seven years; the [1]dreams are one *and the same.*

27 "And the seven lean and ugly cows that came up after them are seven years, and the seven thin ears scorched by the east wind [a]shall be seven years of famine.

28 "[1]It is as I have spoken to Pharaoh: [a]God has shown to Pharaoh what He is about to do.

29 "Behold, [a]seven years of great abundance are coming in all the land of Egypt;

30 and after them [a]seven years of famine will [1]come, and all the abundance will be forgotten in the land of Egypt; and the famine will [2]ravage the land.

31 "So the abundance will be unknown in the land because of that subsequent famine; for it *will be* very severe.

32 "[a]Now as for the repeating of the dream to Pharaoh twice, *it means* that the matter is determined by God, and God will quickly bring it about.

33 "And now let Pharaoh look for a man [a]discerning and wise, and set him over the land of Egypt.

34 "Let Pharaoh take action to appoint overseers [1]in charge of the land, and let him exact a fifth *of the produce* of the land of Egypt in the seven years of abundance.

35 "Then [a]let them gather all the food of these good years that are coming, and store up the grain for food in the cities under Pharaoh's authority, and let them guard *it.*

36 "And let the food become as a reserve for the land for the seven years of famine which will occur in the land of Egypt, so that the land may not perish during the famine."

37 Now the [1]proposal seemed good [2]to Pharaoh and [2]to all his servants.

Joseph Is Made a Ruler of Egypt

38 Then Pharaoh said to his servants, "Can we find a man like this, [a]in whom is a divine spirit?"

39 So Pharaoh said to Joseph, "Since God has informed you of all this, [a]there is no one so discerning and wise as you are.

40 "[a]You shall be over my house, and according to your [1]command all my people shall [2]do homage; only in the throne I will be greater than you."

41 And Pharaoh said to Joseph, "See I have set you [a]over all the land of Egypt."

42 Then Pharaoh [a]took off his signet ring from his hand, and put it on Joseph's hand, and clothed him in garments of fine linen, and [b]put the gold necklace around his neck.

43 And he had him ride in [1]his second chariot; and they proclaimed before him, "[2]Bow the knee!" And he set him over all the land of Egypt.

44 Moreover, Pharaoh said to Joseph, "*Though* I am Pharaoh, yet [a]without [1]your permission no one shall raise his hand or foot in all the land of Egypt."

45 Then Pharaoh named Joseph [1]Zaphenath-paneah; and he gave him Asenath, the daughter of Potiphera priest of [2a]On, as his wife. And Joseph went forth over the land of Egypt.

46 Now Joseph was [a]thirty years old when he [1]stood before Pharaoh, king of Egypt. And Joseph went out from the presence of Pharaoh, and went through all the land of Egypt.

47 And during the seven years of

15 [1]Lit., *about you, saying* [2]Lit., *you hear a dream to interpret it* [a]Gen. 41:8
16 [1]Lit., *Apart from me* [2]Lit., *answer the peace of Pharaoh* [a]Dan. 2:30; Zech. 4:6; Acts 3:12; 2 Cor. 3:5 [b]Gen. 40:8; 41:25, 28, 32
18 [1]Lit., *fat of flesh*
19 [1]Lit., *lean of flesh* [2]Lit., *badness*
20 [1]Lit., *bad*
21 [1]Lit., *entered their inward parts* [2]Or, *known* [3]Lit., *and* [4]Lit., *in the beginning*
24 [1]Or, *soothsayer priests*
25 [1]Lit., *dream is* [a]Gen. 41:28, 32
26 [1]Lit., *dream is*
27 [a]2 Kin. 8:1
28 [1]Lit., *That is the thing which I spoke* [a]Gen. 41:25, 32
29 [a]Gen. 41:47
30 [1]Lit., *arise* [2]Lit., *destroy* [a]Gen. 41:54, 56; 47:13
32 [a]Gen. 41:25, 28
33 [a]Gen. 41:39
34 [1]Lit., *over*
35 [a]Gen. 41:48
37 [1]Lit., *word* [2]Lit., *in the sight of*
38 [a]Dan. 4:8, 9, 18; 5:11, 14
39 [a]Gen. 41:33
40 [1]Lit., *mouth* [2]Lit., *kiss* [a]Ps. 105:21, 22; Acts 7:10
41 [a]Gen. 42:6
42 [a]Esther 3:10 [b]Dan. 5:7, 16, 29
43 [1]Lit., *the second . . . which was his* [2]Heb., *Abreck: "Attention" or "make way"*
44 [1]Lit., *you no one* [a]Ps. 105:22
45 [1]Probably Egyptian for "God speaks; he lives" [2]Or, *Heliopolis* [a]Jer. 43:13; Ezek. 30:17
46 [1]Or, *entered the service of* [a]Gen. 37:2

plenty the land brought forth [1]abun-
dantly.
48 So he gathered all the food of
these seven years which occurred in
the land of Egypt, and placed the
food in the cities; he placed in every
city the food from its own surrounding fields.
49 Thus Joseph stored up grain [1]in
great abundance like the sand of the
sea, until he stopped [2]measuring *it*,
for it was [3]beyond measure.

The Sons of Joseph

50 Now before the year of famine
came, two sons were born to
Joseph, whom Asenath, the daughter of Potiphera priest of [1]On, bore
to him.
51 And Joseph named the first-
born [1]Manasseh, "For," *he said*,
"God has made me forget all my
trouble and all my father's household."
52 And he named the second [1]E-
phraim, "For," *he said*, "[a]God has
made me fruitful in the land of my
affliction."
53 When the seven years of plenty
which had been in the land of Egypt
came to an end,
54 and [a]the seven years of famine
began to come, just as Joseph had
said, then there was famine in all the
lands; but in all the land of Egypt
there was bread.
55 So when all the land of Egypt
was famished, the people cried out
to Pharaoh for bread; and Pharaoh
said to all the Egyptians, "Go to
Joseph; whatever he says to you,
you shall do."
56 When the famine was *spread*
over all the face of the earth, then
Joseph opened all [1]the storehouses,
and sold to the Egyptians; and the
famine was severe in the land of
Egypt.
57 And *the people of* all the earth
came to Egypt to buy grain from
Joseph, because the famine was severe in all the earth.

Chapter 42

Joseph's Brothers Sent to Egypt

Now [a]Jacob saw that there was
grain in Egypt, and Jacob said to his
sons, "Why are you staring at one
another?"
2 And he said, "Behold, I have
heard that there is grain in Egypt; go
down there and buy *some* for us
[1]from that place, [a]so that we may
live and not die."
3 Then ten brothers of Joseph
went down to buy grain from Egypt.
4 But Jacob did not send Joseph's
brother [a]Benjamin with his brothers, for he said, "[1]I am afraid that
harm may befall him."
5 So the sons of Israel came to
buy grain among those who were
coming, [a]for the famine was in the
land of Canaan *also*.
6 Now [a]Joseph was the ruler over
the land; he was the one who sold to
all the people of the land. And Joseph's brothers came and [b]bowed
down to him with *their* faces to the
ground.
7 When Joseph saw his brothers
he recognized them, but he disguised himself to them and [a]spoke
to them harshly. And he said to
them, "Where have you come
from?" And they said, "From the
land of Canaan, to buy food."
8 But Joseph had recognized his
brothers, although [a]they did not recognize him.
9 And Joseph [a]remembered the
dreams which he [1]had about them,
and said to them, "You are spies;
you have come to look at the [2]unde-
fended parts of our land."
10 Then they said to him, "No, [a]my
lord, but your servants have come to
buy food.
11 "We are all sons of one man; we
are [a]honest men, your servants are
not spies."
12 Yet he said to them, "No, but
you have come to look at the [1]unde-
fended parts of our land!"
13 But they said, "Your servants
are twelve brothers *in all*, the sons
of one man in the land of Canaan;
and behold, the youngest is with
[a]our father today, and [b]one is no
more."
14 And Joseph said to them, "It is
as I said [1]to you, you are spies;
15 by this you will be tested: by
the life of Pharaoh, you shall not go
from this place unless your youngest brother comes here!
16 "Send one of you that he may get
your brother, while you remain confined, that your words may be
tested, whether there is [a]truth in
you. But if not, by the life of Pharaoh, surely you are spies."
17 So he put them all together in
[a]prison for three days.
18 Now Joseph said to them on the
third day, "Do this and live, for [a]I
fear God:
19 if you are honest men, let one of
your brothers be confined in [1]your
prison; but as for *the rest of* you, go,
carry grain for the famine of your
households,
20 and [a]bring your youngest

47 [1]Lit., *by handfuls*
49 [1]Lit., *very much* [2]Lit., *numbering* [3]Or, *without number*
50 [1]Or, *Heliopolis*
51 [1]I.e., Making to forget
52 [1]I.e., Fruitfulness [a]Gen. 17:6; 28:3; 49:22
54 [a]Gen. 41:30; Ps. 105:16; Acts 7:11
56 [1]Lit., *that which was in them*
1 [a]Acts 7:12
2 [1]Lit., *from there* [a]Gen. 43:8
4 [1]Lit., *Lest harm* [a]Gen. 35:24
5 [a]Gen. 41:57; Acts 7:11
6 [a]Gen. 41:41, 55 [b]Gen. 37:8-10; 41:43
7 [a]Gen. 42:30
8 [a]Gen. 37:2; 41:46, 53
9 [1]Lit., *had dreamed* [2]Lit., *nakedness of the land* [a]Gen. 37:6-9
10 [a]Gen. 37:8
11 [a]Gen. 42:16, 19, 31, 34
12 [1]Lit., *nakedness of the land*
13 [a]Gen. 43:7 [b]Gen. 37:30; 42:32; 44:20
14 [1]Lit., *to you, saying*
16 [a]Gen. 42:11
17 [a]Gen. 40:4, 7
18 [a]Gen. 39:9
19 [1]Lit., *the house of your prison*
20 [a]Gen. 42:34

brother to me, so your words may
be verified, and you will not die."
And they did so.
21 Then they said to one another,
"[a]Truly we are guilty concerning
our brother, because we saw the distress of his soul when he pleaded
with us, yet we would not listen;
therefore this distress has come
upon us."
22 And Reuben answered them,
saying, "[a]Did I not tell [1]you, 'Do not
sin against the boy'; and you would
not listen? [2b]Now comes the reckoning for his blood."
23 They did not know, however,
that Joseph understood, for there
was an interpreter between them.
24 And he turned away from them
and [a]wept. But when he returned to
them and spoke to them, he [b]took
Simeon from them and bound him
before their eyes.
25 [a]Then Joseph gave orders to fill
their bags with grain and to restore
every man's money in his sack, and
to give them provisions for the journey. And thus it was done for them.
26 So they loaded their donkeys
with their grain, and departed from
there.
27 And as one *of them* opened his
sack to give his donkey fodder at the
lodging place, he saw his money;
and behold, it was in the mouth of
his sack.
28 Then he said to his brothers,
"My money has been returned, and
behold, it is even in my sack." And
their hearts [1]sank, and they *turned*
[2]trembling to one another, saying,
"[a]What is this that God has done to
us?"

Simeon Is Held Hostage

29 When they came to their father
Jacob in the land of Canaan, they
told him all that had happened to
them, saying,
30"The man, the lord of the land,
spoke harshly with us, and took us
for spies of the country.
31"But we said to him, 'We are
[a]honest men; we are not spies.
32 'We are twelve brothers, sons of
our father; one is no more, and the
youngest is with our father today in
the land of Canaan.'
33"And the man, the lord of the
land, said to us, 'By this I shall know
that you are honest men: leave one
of your brothers with me and take
grain for the famine of your households, and go.
34 'But bring your youngest
brother to me that I may know that

21 [a]Gen. 37:26-28; 45:3

22 [1]Lit., *you saying* [2]Lit., *And behold, his blood also is required* [a]Gen. 37:22 [b]Gen. 9:5-6

24 [a]Gen. 43:30; 45:14, 15 [b]Gen. 43:14, 23

25 [a]Gen. 44:1

28 [1]Lit., *went out* [2]Lit., *trembled* [a]Gen. 43:23

31 [a]Gen. 42:11

34 [1]Lit., *you are honest*

35 [a]Gen. 43:12, 15

37 [1]Lit., *hand*

38 [1]Lit., *he* [2]Lit., *on which you are going* [a]Gen. 37:35; 44:29, 31

1 [a]Gen. 41:56, 57

3 [1]Lit., *us, saying* [a]Gen. 43:5; 44:23

6 [1]Lit., *to tell*

7 [1]Lit., *told him according to these words* [a]Gen. 42:13; 43:27

8 [a]Gen. 42:2

9 [a]Gen. 42:37

you are not spies, but [1]honest men.
I will give your brother to you, and
you may trade in the land.'"
35 Now it came about as they were
emptying their sacks, that behold,
[a]every man's bundle of money *was*
in his sack; and when they and their
father saw their bundles of money,
they were dismayed.
36 And their father Jacob said to
them, "You have bereaved me of my
children: Joseph is no more, and
Simeon is no more, and you would
take Benjamin; all these things are
against me."
37 Then Reuben spoke to his father, saying, "You may put my two
sons to death if I do not bring him
back to you; put him in my [1]care,
and I will return him to you."
38 But [1]Jacob said, "My son shall
not go down with you; for his
brother is dead, and he alone is left.
If harm should befall him on the
journey [2]you are taking, then you
will [a]bring my gray hair down to
Sheol in sorrow."

CHAPTER 43

The Return to Egypt

[a]NOW the famine was severe in the
land.
2 So it came about when they had
finished eating the grain which they
had brought from Egypt, that their
father said to them, "Go back, buy
us a little food."
3 Judah spoke to him, however,
saying, "[a]The man solemnly warned
[1]us, 'You shall not see my face unless your brother is with you.'
4"If you send our brother with us,
we will go down and buy you food.
5"But if you do not send *him*, we
will not go down; for the man said to
us, 'You shall not see my face unless
your brother is with you.'"
6 Then Israel said, "Why did you
treat me so badly [1]by telling the
man whether you still had *another*
brother?"
7 But they said, "The man questioned particularly about us and our
relatives, saying, '[a]Is your father
still alive? Have you *another*
brother?' So we [1]answered his questions. Could we possibly know that
he would say, 'Bring your brother
down'?"
8 And Judah said to his father Israel, "Send the lad with me, and we
will arise and go, [a]that we may live
and not die, we as well as you and
our little ones.
9"[a]I myself will be surety for him;

[1]you may hold me responsible for
him. If I do not bring him *back* to
you and set him before you, then [2]let
me bear the blame before you forever.
10"For if we had not delayed,
surely by now we could have returned twice."
11 Then their father Israel said to
them, "If *it must be* so, then do this:
take some of the best products of
the land in your [1]bags, and carry
down to the man [a]as a present, a
little [2b]balm and a little honey, [3]aro-
matic gum and [4]myrrh, pistachio
nuts and almonds.
12"And take double *the* money in
your hand, and take back in your
hand [a]the money that was returned
in the mouth of your sacks; perhaps
it was a mistake.
13"Take your brother also, and
arise, return to the man;
14 and may [1a]God Almighty
[b]grant you compassion in the sight
of the man, that he may release to
you [c]your other brother and Benjamin. And as for me, [d]if I am bereaved of my children, I am bereaved."
15 So the men took [a]this present,
and they took double *the* money in
their hand, and Benjamin; then they
arose and went down to Egypt and
stood before Joseph.

Joseph Sees Benjamin

16 When Joseph saw Benjamin
with them, he said to his house
steward, "Bring the men into the
house, and slay *an animal* and make
ready; for the men are to dine with
me at noon."
17 So the man did as Joseph said,
and [1]brought the men to Joseph's
house.
18 Now the men were afraid, because they were brought to Joseph's
house; and they said, "*It is* because
of the money that was returned in
our sacks the first time that we are
being brought in, that he may [1]seek
occasion against us and fall upon us,
and take us for slaves with our donkeys."
19 So they came near to Joseph's
house steward, and spoke to him at
the entrance of the house,
20 and said, "Oh, my lord, we indeed came down the first time to
buy food,
21 and it came about when we
came to the lodging place, that we
opened our sacks, and behold, [a]each
man's money was in the mouth of
his sack, our money in [1]full. So [b]we
have brought it back in our hand.
22"We have also brought down
other money in our hand to buy
food; we do not know who put our
money in our sacks."
23 And he said, "[1]Be at ease, do
not be afraid. [a]Your God and the
God of your father has given you
treasure in your sacks; [2]I had your
money." Then [b]he brought Simeon
out to them.
24 Then the man brought the men
into Joseph's house and [a]gave them
water, and they washed their feet;
and he gave their donkeys fodder.
25 So they prepared [a]the present
[1]for Joseph's coming at noon; for
they had heard that they were to eat
[2]a meal there.
26 When Joseph came home, they
brought into the house to him the
present which was in their hand and
[a]bowed to the ground before him.
27 Then he asked them about their
welfare, and said, "[a]Is your old father well, of whom you spoke? Is he
still alive?"
28 And they said, "Your servant
our father is well; he is still alive."
[a]And they bowed down [1]in homage.
29 As he lifted his eyes and saw his
brother Benjamin, his mother's son,
he said, "Is this [a]your youngest
brother, of whom you spoke to me?"
And he said, "[b]May God be gracious
to you, my son."
30 And Joseph hurried *out* for [1]he
was deeply stirred over his brother,
and he sought *a place* to weep; and
he entered his chamber and [a]wept
there.
31 Then he washed his face, and
came out; and he [a]controlled himself and said, "[1]Serve the meal."
32 So they served him by himself,
and them by themselves, and the
Egyptians, who ate with him, by
themselves; because the Egyptians
could not eat bread with the Hebrews, for that is [1a]loathsome to the
Egyptians.
33 Now they [1]were seated before
him, [a]the first-born according to his
birthright and the youngest according to his youth, and the men looked
at one another in astonishment.
34 And he took portions to them
from [1]his own table; [a]but Benjamin's portion was five times as
much as any of theirs. So they
feasted and drank freely with him.

Chapter 44

The Brothers Are Brought Back

[a]THEN he commanded his house
steward, saying, "Fill the men's

9 [1]Lit., *from my hand you may require him* [2]Lit., *I shall have sinned before you all the days*

11 [1]Or, *vessels* [2]Or, *mastic* [3]Or, *ladanum spice* [4]Or, *resinous bark* [a]Gen. 43:25, 26 [b]Gen. 37:25

12 [a]Gen. 43:21, 22

14 [1]Heb., *El Shaddai* [a]Gen. 17:1; 28:3; 35:11 [b]Ps. 106:46 [c]Gen. 42:24 [d]Gen. 42:36

15 [a]Gen. 43:11

17 [1]Lit., *the man brought*

18 [1]Lit., *roll himself upon us*

21 [1]Lit., *its weight* [a]Gen. 42:35 [b]Gen. 43:12, 15

23 [1]Lit., *Peace be to you* [2]Lit., *your money had come to me* [a]Gen. 42:28 [b]Gen. 42:24

24 [a]Gen. 18:4; 19:2; 24:32

25 [1]Lit., *until* [2]Lit., *bread* [a]Gen. 43:11, 15

26 [a]Gen. 37:7, 10

27 [a]Gen. 43:7; 45:3

28 [1]Lit., *and prostrated themselves* [a]Gen. 37:7, 10

29 [a]Gen. 42:13 [b]Num. 6:25; Ps. 67:1

30 [1]Lit., *his compassion grew warm* [a]Gen. 42:24; 45:2, 14, 15; 46:29

31 [1]Lit., *"Set on bread."* [a]Gen. 45:1

32 [1]Lit., *an abomination* [a]Gen. 46:34

33 [1]Lit., *sat* [a]Gen. 42:7

34 [1]Lit., *his face* [a]Gen. 35:24

1 [a]Gen. 42:25

sacks with food, as much as they
can carry, and put each man's money in the mouth of his sack.
2"And put my cup, the silver cup,
in the mouth of the sack of the youngest, and his money for the grain."
And he did [1]as Joseph had told *him*.
3 [1]As soon as it was light, the
men were sent away, they with their
donkeys.
4 They had *just* gone out of [a]the
city, *and* were not far off, when
Joseph said to his house steward,
"Up, follow the men; and when you
overtake them, say to them, 'Why
have you repaid evil for good?
5 'Is not this the one from which
my lord drinks, and which he indeed
uses for [a]divination? You have done
wrong in doing this.' "
6 So he overtook them and spoke
these words to them.
7 And they said to him, "Why
does my lord speak such words as
these? Far be it from your servants
to do such a thing.
8"Behold, [a]the money which we
found in the mouth of our sacks we
have brought back to you from the
land of Canaan. How then could we
steal silver or gold from your lord's
house?
9"[a]With whomever of your servants it is found, let him die, and we
also will be my lord's [b]slaves."
10 So he said, "Now let it also be
according to your words; he with
whom it is found shall be my slave,
and *the rest of* you shall be innocent."
11 Then they hurried, each man
lowered his sack to the ground, and
each man opened his sack.
12 And he searched, beginning
with the oldest and ending with the
youngest, and [a]the cup was found in
Benjamin's sack.
13 Then they [a]tore their clothes,
and when each man loaded his donkey, they returned to [b]the city.
14 When Judah and his brothers
came to Joseph's house, he was still
there, and [a]they fell to the ground
before him.
15 And Joseph said to them,
"What is this deed that you have
done? Do you not know that such a
man as I can indeed practice [a]divi-
nation?"
16 So Judah said, "What can we
say to my lord? What can we speak?
And how can we justify ourselves?
God has found out the iniquity of
your servants; behold, we are my
lord's [a]slaves, both we and the one
in whose [1]possession the cup has
been found."
17 But he said, "Far be it from me
to do this. The man in whose [1]pos-
session the cup has been found, he
shall be my slave; but as for you, go
up in peace to your father."
18 Then Judah approached him,
and said, "Oh my lord, may your
servant please speak a word in my
lord's ears, and [1]do not be angry
with your servant; for [a]you are
equal to Pharaoh.
19"[a]My lord asked his servants,
saying, 'Have you a father or a
brother?'
20"And we said to my lord, 'We
have an old father and [a]a little child
of *his* old age. Now his brother [b]is
dead, so he alone is left of his
mother, and his father loves him.'
21"Then you said to your servants,
'Bring him down to me, that I may
set my eyes on him.'
22"But we said to my lord, 'The lad
cannot leave his father, for if he
should leave his father, his father
would die.'
23"You said to your servants, however, '[a]Unless your youngest
brother comes down with you, you
shall not see my face again.'
24"Thus it came about when we
went up to your servant my father,
we told him the words of my lord.
25"And our father said, 'Go back,
buy us a little food.'
26"But we said, 'We cannot go
down. If our youngest brother is
with us, then we will go down; for
we cannot see the man's face unless
our youngest brother is with us.'
27"And your servant my father
said to us, 'You know that my wife
bore me two sons;
28 and the one went out from me,
and [a]I said, "Surely he is torn in
pieces," and I have not seen him
since.
29 'And if you take this one also
from [1]me, and harm befalls him, you
will [a]bring my gray hair down to
Sheol in [2]sorrow.'
30"Now, therefore, when I come to
your servant my father, and the lad
is not with us, since [1a]his life is
bound up in the lad's life,
31 it will come about when he sees
that the lad is not *with us*, that he
will die. Thus your servants will
[a]bring the gray hair of your servant
our father down to Sheol in sorrow.
32"For your servant [a]became
surety for the lad to my father, saying, 'If I do not bring him *back* to
you, then [1]let me bear the blame before my father forever.'
33"Now, therefore, please let your

2 [1]Or, *according to the word*
3 [1]Lit., *The morning was light*
4 [a]Gen. 44:13
5 [a]Gen. 30:27; 44:15; Lev. 19:26; Deut. 18:10-14
8 [a]Gen. 43:21
9 [a]Gen. 31:32 [b]Gen. 44:16
12 [a]Gen. 44:2
13 [a]Gen. 37:29, 34 [b]Gen. 44:4
14 [a]Gen. 37:7, 10
15 [a]Gen. 44:5
16 [1]Lit., *hand* [a]Gen. 44:9
17 [1]Lit., *hand*
18 [1]Lit., *let not your anger burn against* [a]Gen. 37:7, 8; 41:40-44
19 [a]Gen. 43:7
20 [a]Gen. 43:8; 44:30 [b]Gen. 37:33; 42:13, 38
23 [a]Gen. 43:3
28 [a]Gen. 37:31-35
29 [1]Lit., *my face* [2]Lit., *evil* [a]Gen. 42:38; 44:31
30 [1]Lit., *his soul is bound with his soul* [a]1 Sam. 18:1
31 [a]Gen. 44:29
32 [1]Lit., *and I shall have sinned for all the days before my father* [a]Gen. 43:9

servant remain instead of the lad a
slave to my lord, and let the lad go
up with his brothers.
34 "For how shall I go up to my father if the lad is not with me, lest I
see the evil that would [1]overtake my
father?"

Chapter 45

Joseph Deals Kindly with His Brothers

THEN Joseph could not control
himself before all those who stood
by him, and he cried, "Have everyone go out from me." So there [1]was
no man with him [a]when Joseph
made himself known to his brothers.
2 And [a]he [1]wept so loudly that
the Egyptians heard *it*, and the
household of Pharaoh heard *of it*.
3 Then Joseph said to his brothers, "I am Joseph! [a]Is my father still
alive?" But his brothers could not
answer him, for [b]they were dismayed at his presence.
4 Then Joseph said to his brothers, "Please come [1]closer to me."
And they came [1]closer. And he said,
"I am your brother Joseph, whom
you sold into Egypt.
5 "And now do not be grieved or
angry [1]with yourselves, because
[a]you sold me here; for [b]God sent me
before you to preserve life.
6 "For the famine *has been* in the
land [a]these two years, and there are
still five years in which there will be
neither plowing nor harvesting.
7 "And [a]God sent me before you
to preserve for you a remnant in the
earth, and to keep you alive by a
great [1]deliverance.
8 "Now, therefore, it was not you
who sent me here, but God; and He
has made me a father to Pharaoh
and lord of all his household and
ruler over all the land of Egypt.
9 "Hurry and go up to my father,
and [a]say to him, 'Thus says your son
Joseph, "God has made me lord of
all Egypt; come down to me, do not
delay.
10 "And you shall [1]live in the land
of [a]Goshen, and you shall be near
me, you and your children and your
children's children and your flocks
and your herds and all that you
have.
11 "There I will also [a]provide for
you, for there are still five years of
famine *to come*, lest you and your
household and all that you have be
impoverished." '
12 "And behold, your eyes see, and
the eyes of my brother Benjamin
see, that it is my mouth which is
speaking to you.
13 "Now you must tell my father of
all my splendor in Egypt, and all
that you have seen; and you must
hurry and [a]bring my father down
here."
14 Then he fell on his brother Benjamin's neck and [a]wept; and Benjamin wept on his neck.
15 And he kissed all his brothers
and wept on them, and afterward
his brothers talked with him.
16 Now when [a]the [1]news was
heard in Pharaoh's house [2]that Joseph's brothers had come, it
[3]pleased Pharaoh and his servants.
17 Then Pharaoh said to Joseph,
"Say to your brothers, 'Do this: load
your beasts and [1]go to the land of
Canaan,
18 and take your father and your
households and come to me, and [a]I
will give you the [1]best of the land of
Egypt and you shall eat the fat of the
land.'
19 "Now you are ordered, 'Do this:
[1]take [a]wagons from the land of
Egypt for your little ones and for
your wives, and bring your father
and come.
20 'And do not [1]concern yourselves with your goods, for the [2]best
of all the land of Egypt is yours.' "
21 Then the sons of Israel did so;
and Joseph gave them [a]wagons according to the [1]command of Pharaoh, and gave them provisions for
the journey.
22 To [1]each of them he gave
[a]changes of garments, but to Benjamin he gave three hundred *pieces of*
silver and [b]five changes of garments.
23 And to his father he sent [1]as follows: ten donkeys loaded with the
[2]best things of Egypt, and ten female donkeys loaded with grain and
bread and sustenance for his father
[3]on the journey.
24 So he sent his brothers away,
and [1]as they departed, he said to
them, "Do not [2]quarrel on the journey."
25 Then they went up from Egypt,
and came to the land of Canaan to
their father Jacob.
26 And they told him, saying,
"Joseph is still alive, and indeed he
is ruler over all the land of Egypt."
But [1]he was stunned, for [a]he did not
believe them.
27 When they told him all the
words of Joseph that he had spoken
to them, and when he saw the [a]wag-
ons that Joseph had sent to carry

34 [1]Lit., *find*

1 [1]Lit., *stood* [a]Acts 7:13

2 [1]Lit., *gave forth his voice in weeping* [a]Gen. 45:14, 15; 46:29

3 [a]Gen. 43:27 [b]Gen. 37:20-28; 42:21, 22

4 [1]Lit., *near*

5 [1]Lit., *in your eyes* [a]Gen. 37:28; 44:20 [b]Gen. 45:7, 8; 50:20

6 [a]Gen. 37:2; 41:46, 53

7 [1]Lit., *escaped company* [a]Gen. 45:5

9 [a]Acts 7:14

10 [1]Lit., *dwell* [a]Gen. 46:28, 34

11 [a]Gen. 47:12

13 [a]Acts 7:14

14 [a]Gen. 45:2

16 [1]Lit., *voice* [2]Lit., *saying, "Joseph's brothers have come."* [3]Lit., *was good in the eyes of* [a]Acts 7:13

17 [1]Lit., *come, go*

18 [1]Lit., *good* [a]Gen. 27:28

19 [1]Lit., *take for yourselves* [a]Gen. 45:21, 27; 46:5; Num. 7:3-8

20 [1]Lit., *let your eye look with regret upon your vessels* [2]Lit., *good*

21 [1]Lit., *mouth* [a]Gen. 45:19

22 [1]Lit., *all of them he gave each man* [a]2 Kin. 5:5 [b]Gen. 43:34

23 [1]Lit., *like this* [2]Lit., *good* [3]Lit., *for*

24 [1]Lit., *they departed; and he said* [2]Lit., *be agitated*

26 [1]Lit., *his heart grew numb* [a]Gen. 37:31-35

27 [a]Gen. 45:19

him, the spirit of their father Jacob
revived.
28 Then Israel said, "It is enough;
my son Joseph is still alive. I will go
and see him before I die."

Chapter 46

Jacob Moves to Egypt

So Israel set out with all that he
had, and came to [a]Beersheba, and
offered sacrifices to the [b]God of his
father Isaac.
2 And [a]God spoke to Israel [1]in visions of the night and said, "[b]Jacob,
Jacob." And he said, "Here I am."
3 And He said, "[a]I am God, the
God of your father; do not be afraid
to go down to Egypt, for I will make
you a great nation there.
4 "[a]I will go down with you to
Egypt, and [b]I will also surely bring
you up again; and [c]Joseph will
[1]close your eyes."
5 Then Jacob arose from Beersheba; and the sons of Israel carried
their father Jacob and their little
ones and their wives, in the [a]wagons
which Pharaoh had sent to carry
him.
6 And they took their livestock
and their property, which they had
acquired in the land of Canaan, and
[a]came to Egypt, Jacob and all his
[1]descendants with him:
7 his sons and his grandsons with
him, his daughters and his grand-
daughters, and all his [1]descendants
he brought with him to Egypt.

Those Who Came to Egypt

8 Now these are the [a]names of
the sons of Israel, Jacob and his
sons, who went to Egypt: Reuben,
Jacob's first-born.
9 And the sons of Reuben: Hanoch and Pallu and Hezron and Carmi.
10 And the sons of Simeon: [1]Je-
muel and Jamin and Ohad and [2]Ja-
chin and [3]Zohar and Shaul the son
of a Canaanite woman.
11 And the sons of Levi: [1]Gershon,
Kohath, and Merari.
12 And the sons of Judah: Er and
Onan and Shelah and Perez and Zerah (but Er and Onan died in the
land of Canaan). And the sons of
Perez were Hezron and Hamul.
13 And the sons of Issachar: Tola
and [1]Puvvah and [2]Iob and Shimron.
14 And the sons of Zebulun: Sered
and Elon and Jahleel.
15 These are the sons of Leah,
whom she bore to Jacob in Paddan-
aram, with his daughter Dinah; [1]all
his sons and his daughters *numbered* thirty-three.
16 And the sons of Gad: [1]Ziphion
and Haggi, Shuni and [2]Ezbon, Eri
and [3]Arodi and Areli.
17 And the sons of Asher: Imnah
and Ishvah and Ishvi and Beriah and
their sister Serah. And the sons of
Beriah: Heber and Malchiel.
18 These are the sons of Zilpah,
whom Laban gave to his daughter
Leah; and she bore to Jacob these
sixteen persons.
19 The sons of Jacob's wife Rachel: Joseph and Benjamin.
20 Now to Joseph in the land of
Egypt were born Manasseh and E-
phraim, whom Asenath, the daughter of Potiphera, priest of On, bore
to him.
21 And the sons of Benjamin: Bela
and Becher and Ashbel, Gera and
Naaman, [1]Ehi and Rosh, [2]Muppim
and [3]Huppim and Ard.
22 These are the sons of Rachel,
who were born to Jacob; *there were*
fourteen persons in all.
23 And the sons of Dan: [1]Hushim.
24 And the sons of Naphtali: [1]Jah-
zeel and Guni and Jezer and [2]Shil-
lem.
25 These are the sons of Bilhah,
whom Laban gave to his daughter
Rachel, and she bore these to Jacob;
there were seven persons in all.
26 All the persons belonging to Jacob, who came to Egypt, [1]his direct
descendants, not including the
wives of Jacob's sons, *were* sixty-six
persons in all,
27 and the sons of Joseph, who
were born to him in Egypt were
[1]two; [a]all the persons of the house of
Jacob, who came to Egypt, *were*
seventy.
28 Now he sent Judah before him
to Joseph, to point out *the way* before him to [a]Goshen; and they came
into the land of Goshen.
29 And Joseph [1]prepared his
chariot and went up to Goshen to
meet his father Israel; as soon as he
appeared [2]before him, he fell on his
neck and [a]wept on his neck a long
time.
30 Then Israel said to Joseph,
"Now let me die, since I have seen
your face, that you are still alive."
31 And Joseph said to his brothers
and to his father's household, "[a]I
will go up and tell Pharaoh, and will
say to him, 'My brothers and my father's household, who *were* in the
land of Canaan, have come to me;
32 and the men are shepherds, for
they have been [1]keepers of livestock; and they have brought their

1 [a]Gen. 28:10 [b]Gen. 26:24; 28:13
2 [1]Lit., *in the visions* [a]Num. 12:6; Job 33:14, 15 [b]Gen. 22:11; 31:11
3 [a]Gen. 17:1; 28:13
4 [1]Lit., *put his hand on* [a]Gen. 28:15 [b]Gen. 50:24; Ex. 3:8 [c]Gen. 50:1
5 [a]Gen. 45:21
6 [1]Lit., *seed* [a]Acts 7:15
7 [1]Lit., *seed*
8 [a]Num. 26:5; 1 Chr. 2:1 ff.
10 [1]Num. 26:12; in 1 Chr. 4:24, *Nemuel* [2]In 1 Chr. 4:24, *Jarib* [3]In Num. 26:13; and 1 Chr. 4:24, *Zerah*
11 [1]In 1 Chr. 6:16, *Gershom*
13 [1]In Num. 26:23, *Puvah;* in 1 Chr. 7:1, *Puah;* [2]Num. 26:24; in 1 Chr. 7:1, *Jashub*
15 [1]Lit., *all the souls of*
16 [1]In Num. 26:15, *Zephon* [2]In Num. 26:16, *Ozni* [3]In Num. 26:17, *Arod*
21 [1]In Num. 26:38, *Ahiram* [2]In Num. 26:39, *Shephupham;* 1 Chr. 7:12, *Shuppim* [3]In Num. 26:39, *Hupham*
23 [1]In Num. 26:42, *Shuham*
24 [1]In 1 Chr. 7:13, *Jahziel* [2]In 1 Chr. 7:13, *Shallum*
26 [1]Lit., *who came out of his loins*
27 [1]Lit., *two souls* [a]Ex. 1:5; Deut. 10:22; Acts 7:14
28 [a]Gen. 45:10
29 [1]Lit., *tied, harnessed* [2]Lit., *to* [a]Gen. 45:14, 15
31 [a]Gen. 47:1
32 [1]Lit., *men*

flocks and their herds and all that they have.'

33 "And it shall come about when Pharaoh calls you and says, 'What is your occupation?'

34 that you shall say, 'Your servants have been [1]keepers of livestock from our youth even until now, both we [a]and our fathers,' that you may [2]live in the land of [b]Goshen; for every shepherd is [3]loathsome to the Egyptians."

Chapter 47

Jacob's Family Settles in Goshen

THEN Joseph went in and told Pharaoh, and said, "My father and my brothers and their flocks and their herds and all that they have, have come out of the land of Canaan; and behold, they are in the land of Goshen."

2 And he took five men from among his brothers, and presented them to Pharaoh.

3 Then Pharaoh said to his brothers, "What is your occupation?" So they said to Pharaoh, "Your servants are [a]shepherds, both we and our fathers."

4 And they said to Pharaoh, "We have come to sojourn in the land, for there is no pasture for your servants' flocks, for the famine is severe in the land of Canaan. Now, therefore, please let your servants [1]live in the land of Goshen."

5 Then Pharaoh said to [1]Joseph, "Your father and your brothers have come to you.

6 "The land of Egypt is [1]at your disposal; [2]settle your father and your brothers in [a]the best of the land, let them [3]live in the land of Goshen; and if you know any [b]capable men among them, then [4]put them in charge of my livestock."

7 Then Joseph brought his father Jacob and [1]presented him to Pharaoh; and Jacob [a]blessed Pharaoh.

8 And Pharaoh said to Jacob, "How many [1]years have you lived?"

9 So Jacob said to Pharaoh, "The [1]years of my sojourning are one hundred and [2]thirty; few and [3]unpleasant have been the [1]years of my life, nor have [a]they [4]attained the [1]years [5]that my fathers lived during the days of their sojourning."

10 And Jacob [a]blessed Pharaoh, and went out from [1]his presence.

11 So Joseph [1]settled his father and his brothers, and gave them a possession in the land of Egypt, in [a]the best of the land, in the land of Rameses, as Pharaoh had ordered.

12 And Joseph provided his father and his brothers and all his father's household with [1]food, according to their [a]little ones.

13 Now there was no [1]food in all the land, because the famine was very severe, so that the land of Egypt and the land of Canaan languished because of the famine.

14 And Joseph gathered all the money that was found in the land of Egypt and in the land of Canaan for the grain which they bought, and Joseph brought the money into Pharaoh's house.

15 And when the money was all spent in the land of Egypt and in the land of Canaan, all the Egyptians came to Joseph [1]and said, "Give us [2]food, for why should we die in your presence? For *our* money [3]is gone."

16 Then Joseph said, "Give up your livestock, and I will give you *food* for your livestock, since *your* money [1]is gone."

17 So they brought their livestock to Joseph, and Joseph gave them [1]food in exchange for the horses and the [2]flocks and the herds and the donkeys; and he [3]fed them with [1]food in exchange for all their livestock [4]that year.

18 And when that year was ended, they came to him the [1]next year and said to him, "We will not hide from my lord that our money is all spent, and the [2]cattle are my lord's. There is nothing left [3]for my lord except our bodies and our lands.

19 "Why should we die before your eyes, both we and our land? Buy us and our land for [1]food, and we and our land will be slaves to Pharaoh. So give us seed, that we may live and not die, and that the land may not be desolate."

Result of the Famine

20 So Joseph bought all the land of Egypt for Pharaoh, for [1]every Egyptian sold his field, because the famine was severe upon them. Thus the land became Pharaoh's.

21 And as for the people, he removed them to the cities from one end of Egypt's border to the other.

22 Only the land of the priests he did not buy, for the priests had an allotment from Pharaoh, and they [1]lived off the allotment which Pharaoh gave them. Therefore, they did not sell their land.

23 Then Joseph said to the people, "Behold, I have today bought you and your land for Pharaoh; now, *here* is seed for you, and you may sow the land.

34 [1]Lit., *men* [2]Lit., *dwell* [3]Lit., *an abomination* [a]Gen. 13:7, 8; 26:20; 37:2 [b]Gen. 45:10, 18; 47:6, 11; Ex. 3:22

3 [a]Gen. 46:34

4 [1]Lit., *dwell*

5 [1]Lit., *Joseph, saying*

6 [1]Lit., *before you* [2]Lit., *cause them to dwell* [3]Lit., *dwell* [4]Lit., *appoint them rulers* [a]Gen. 45:10, 18; 47:11 [b]Ex. 18:21, 25

7 [1]Lit., *set him before* [a]Gen. 47:10; 2 Sam. 14:22; 1 Kin. 8:66

8 [1]Lit., *are the days of the years of your life*

9 [1]Lit., *days of the years* [2]Lit., *thirty years* [3]Lit., *evil* [4]Lit., *reached* [5]Lit., *of the life of my fathers* [a]Gen. 25:7; 35:28

10 [1]Lit., *Pharaoh's* [a]Gen. 47:7

11 [1]Lit., *caused to dwell* [a]Gen. 47:6, 27

12 [1]Or, *bread* [a]Gen. 45:11

13 [1]Or, *bread*

15 [1]Lit., *saying* [2]Or, *bread* [3]Lit., *ceases*

16 [1]Lit., *ceases*

17 [1]Or, *bread* [2]Lit., *livestock of the flocks and livestock of the herds* [3]Lit., *led them as a shepherd* [4]Lit., *in that year*

18 [1]Lit., *second* [2]Lit., *livestock of the cattle* [3]Lit., *in the presence of*

19 [1]Or, *bread*

20 [1]Lit., *Egypt, every man*

22 [1]Lit., *ate their allotment*

24"And [1]at the harvest you shall
give a [a]fifth to Pharaoh, and four-
fifths shall be your own for seed of
the field and for your food and for
those of your households and as
food for your little ones."
25 So they said, "You have saved
our lives! Let us find favor in the
sight of my lord, and we will be Pharaoh's slaves."
26 And Joseph made it a statute
concerning the land of Egypt *valid*
to this day, that Pharaoh should
have the fifth; only the land of the
priests [1]did not become Pharaoh's.
27 Now Israel [1]lived in the land of
Egypt, in [2]Goshen, and they acquired [a]property in it and [b]were
fruitful and became very numerous.
28 And Jacob lived in the land of
Egypt [a]seventeen years; so the
[1]length of Jacob's life was one hundred and forty-seven years.
29 When [1]the time for Israel to die
drew near, he called his son Joseph
and said to him, "Please, if I have
found favor in your sight, [a]place
now your hand under my thigh and
[b]deal with me in kindness and
[2]faithfulness. Please do not bury me
in Egypt,
30 but when I lie down [a]with my
fathers, you shall carry me out of
Egypt and bury me in [b]their burial
place." And he said, "I will do as you
have said."
31 And he said, "[a]Swear to me."
So he swore to him. Then Israel
bowed *in worship* at the head of the
bed.

Chapter 48

Israel's Last Days

Now it came about after these
things that [1]Joseph was told, "Behold, your father is sick." So he took
his two sons [a]Manasseh and Ephraim with him.
2 When [1]it was told to Jacob,
"Behold, your son Joseph has come
to you," Israel [2]collected his
strength and sat [3]up in the bed.
3 Then Jacob said to Joseph,
"[1a]God Almighty appeared to me at
[b]Luz in the land of Canaan and
blessed me,
4 and He said to me, 'Behold, I
will make you fruitful and numerous, and I will make you a company
of peoples, and will give this land to
your [1]descendants after you for an
everlasting possession.'
5"And now your two sons, who
were born to you in the land of
Egypt before I came to you in Egypt,
are mine; [a]Ephraim and Manasseh
shall be mine, as [b]Reuben and Simeon are.
6"But your offspring that [1]have
been born after them shall be yours;
they shall be called by the [2]names of
their brothers in their inheritance.
7"Now as for me, when I came
from [a]Paddan, [b]Rachel died, [1]to my
sorrow, in the land of Canaan on the
journey, when there was still some
distance to go to Ephrath; and I buried her there on the way to Ephrath
(that is, Bethlehem)."
8 When Israel [a]saw Joseph's
sons, he said, "Who are these?"
9 And Joseph said to his father,
"[a]They are my sons, whom God has
given me here." So he said, "Bring
them to me, please, that I may bless
them."
10 Now [a]the eyes of Israel were so
dim from age *that* he could not see.
Then [1]Joseph brought them close to
him, and he kissed them and embraced them.
11 And Israel said to Joseph, "I
never [1]expected to see your face,
and behold, God has let me see your
[2]children as well."
12 Then Joseph [1]took them from
his knees, and bowed with [a]his face
to the ground.
13 And Joseph took them both, E-
phraim with his right hand toward
Israel's left, and Manasseh with his
left hand toward Israel's right, and
brought them close to him.
14 But Israel stretched out his
right hand and laid it on the head of
Ephraim, who was the younger, and
his left hand on Manasseh's head,
[1]crossing his hands, [2]although [a]Ma-
nasseh was the first-born.
15 And he blessed Joseph, and
said,

"[a]The God before whom my fathers Abraham and Isaac walked,
[b]The God who has been my shepherd [1]all my life to this day,
16 [a]The angel who has redeemed me from all evil,
Bless the lads;
And may my name [1]live on in them,
And the [2]names of my fathers Abraham and Isaac;
And [b]may they grow into a multitude in the midst of the earth."

17 When Joseph saw that his father laid his right hand on Ephraim's
head, it displeased him; and he
grasped his father's hand to remove

24 [1]Lit., *it shall come about . . . that you shall* [a]Gen. 41:34
26 [1]Lit., *alone did*
27 [1]Lit., *dwelt* [2]Lit., *in the land of Goshen* [a]Gen. 47:11 [b]Gen. 35:11; Ex. 1:7
28 [1]Lit., *the days of Jacob, the years of his life* [a]Gen. 47:9
29 [1]Lit., *the days of Israel to die drew near* [2]Lit., *truth* [a]Gen. 24:2 [b]Gen. 24:49
30 [a]Gen. 15:15; Deut. 31:16 [b]Gen. 23:17-20; 49:29-32
31 [a]Gen. 21:23, 24; 24:3; 31:53; 50:25
1 [1]Lit., *one said to Joseph* [a]Gen. 41:51, 52
2 [1]Lit., *one told Jacob and said* [2]Lit., *strengthened himself* [3]Lit., *upon the bed*
3 [1]Heb., *El Shaddai* [a]Gen. 35:9-12 [b]Gen. 28:19; 35:6
4 [1]Lit., *seed*
5 [a]Gen. 48:1 [b]1 Chr. 5:1, 2
6 [1]Lit., *you have begotten* [2]Lit., *name*
7 [1]Lit., *upon me* [a]Gen. 33:18 [b]Gen. 35:19, 20
8 [a]Gen. 48:10
9 [a]Gen. 33:5
10 [1]Lit., *he* [a]Gen. 27:1
11 [1]Lit., *meditated, judged* [2]Lit., *seed*
12 [1]Lit., *made them come out* [a]Gen. 42:6
14 [1]Or, *consciously directing* [2]Lit., *when* [a]Gen. 41:51, 52
15 [1]Lit., *from the continuance of me* [a]Gen. 17:1 [b]Gen. 49:24
16 [1]Lit., *be called* [2]Lit., *name* [a]Gen. 22:11, 15-18; 28:13-15; 31:11 [b]Gen. 28:14; 46:3

it from Ephraim's head to Manasseh's head.
18 And Joseph said to his father,
"Not so, my father, for this one is
the first-born. Place your right hand
on his head."
19 But his father refused and said,
"I know, my son, I know; he also
shall become a people and he also
shall be great. However, his younger brother shall be greater than he,
and [a]his [1]descendants shall become
a [2]multitude of nations."
20 And he blessed them that day,
saying,

"By you Israel shall pronounce
blessing, saying,
'May God make you like E-
phraim and Manasseh!' "

Thus he put Ephraim before Manasseh.
21 Then Israel said to Joseph, "Behold, I am about to die, but [a]God will
be with you, and [b]bring you back to
the land of your fathers.
22 "And I give you one [1]portion
more than your brothers, [a]which I
took from the hand of the Amorite
with my sword and my bow."

CHAPTER 49

Israel's Prophecy Concerning His Sons

THEN Jacob summoned his sons
and said, "Assemble yourselves that
I may tell you what shall befall you
[a]in the [1]days to come.

2 "Gather together and hear, O sons of Jacob;
And listen to Israel your father.

3 "Reuben, you are my first-born;
My might and [a]the beginning of my strength,
[1]Preeminent in dignity and [1]preeminent in power.
4 "[1]Uncontrolled as water, you shall not have preeminence,
[a]Because you went up to your father's bed;
Then you defiled *it*—he went up to my couch.

5 "[a]Simeon and Levi are brothers;
Their swords are implements of violence.
6 "[a]Let my soul not enter into their council;
Let not my glory be united with their assembly;
Because in their anger they slew [1]men,
And in their self-will they lamed [2]oxen.
7 "Cursed be their anger, for it is fierce;
And their wrath, for it is cruel.
[a]I will [1]disperse them in Jacob,
And scatter them in Israel.

8 "Judah, your brothers shall praise you;
Your hand shall be on the neck of your enemies;
[a]Your father's sons shall bow down to you.
9 "Judah is a [a]lion's whelp;
From the prey, my son, you have gone up.
He [1]couches, he lies down as a lion,
And as a [2]lion, who [3]dares rouse him up?
10 "[a]The scepter shall not depart from Judah,
Nor the ruler's staff from between his feet,
[1]Until Shiloh comes,
And [b]to him *shall be* the obedience of the peoples.
11 "[1a]He ties *his* foal to the vine,
And his donkey's colt to the choice vine;
[b]He washes his garments in wine,
And his robes in the blood of grapes.
12 "His eyes are [1]dull from wine,
And his teeth [2]white from milk.

13 "[a]Zebulun shall dwell at the seashore;
And he *shall be* [1]a haven for ships,
And his flank *shall be* toward Sidon.

14 "Issachar is [1]a strong donkey,
[a]Lying down between the [2]sheepfolds.
15 "When he saw that a resting place was good
And that the land was pleasant,
He bowed his shoulder to bear *burdens*,
And became a slave at forced labor.

16 "[a]Dan shall [b]judge his people,
As one of the tribes of Israel.
17 "Dan shall be a serpent in the way,
A horned snake in the path,
That bites the horse's heels,
So that his rider falls backward.
18 "[a]For Thy salvation I wait, O LORD.

19 [1]Lit., *seed* [2]Lit., *fulness* [a]Gen. 28:14; 46:3
21 [a]Gen. 26:3 [b]Gen. 28:15; 46:4; 50:24
22 [1]Or, *ridge;* lit., *shoulder;* Heb., *Shechem* [a]Josh. 24:32; John 4:5
1 [1]Lit., *end of the days* [a]Num. 24:14
3 [1]Lit., *preeminence* [a]Deut. 21:17; Ps. 78:51; 105:36
4 [1]Or, *Boiling over;* lit., *recklessness* [a]Gen. 35:22; Deut. 27:20
5 [a]Gen. 34:25-30
6 [1]Lit., *a man* [2]Lit., *an ox* [a]Ps. 64:2
7 [1]Lit., *divide* [a]Josh. 19:1, 9; 21:1-42
8 [a]Gen. 27:29; 1 Chr. 5:2
9 [1]Lit., *bows down* [2]Or, *lioness* [3]Lit., *shall* [a]Ezek. 19:5-7; Mic. 5:8
10 [1]Or, *Until he comes to Shiloh;* or *Until he comes to whom it belongs* [a]Num. 24:17; Ps. 60:7; 108:8 [b]Ps. 2:6-9; 72:8-11
11 [1]Lit., *Binding of* [a]Deut. 8:7, 8; 2 Kin. 18:32 [b]Is. 63:2
12 [1]Or, *darker than* [2]Or, *whiter than*
13 [1]Lit., *for a shore of ships* [a]Deut. 33:18, 19
14 [1]Lit., *a donkey of bone* [2]Or, *saddlebags* [a]Judg. 5:16; Ps. 68:13
16 [a]Deut. 33:22; Judg. 18:26, 27 [b]Gen. 30:6
18 [a]Ex. 15:2; Ps. 25:5; 40:1-3; 119:166, 174; Is. 25:9; Mic. 7:7

19 “[a]As for Gad, [1]raiders shall raid
him,
But he shall raid *at* their
[2]heels.

20 “[1][a]As for [b]Asher, his [2]food shall
be [3]rich,
And he shall yield royal dain-
ties.

21 “[a]Naphtali is a doe let loose,
He gives beautiful words.

22 “[a]Joseph is a fruitful [1]bough,
A fruitful [1]bough by a spring;
Its [2]branches run over a wall.
23 “The archers bitterly attacked
him,
And shot *at him* and harassed
him;
24 But his bow remained [1]firm,
And [2][a]his arms were agile,
From the hands of the [b]Mighty
One of Jacob
(From there is [c]the Shepherd,
[d]the Stone of Israel),
25 From [a]the God of your father
who helps you,
And [1][b]by the [2]Almighty who
blesses you
[c]*With* blessings of heaven
above,
Blessings of the deep that lies
beneath,
Blessings of the breasts and of
the womb.
26 “The blessings of your father
Have surpassed the blessings
of my ancestors
Up to the [1]utmost bound of
[a]the everlasting hills;
May they be on the head of
Joseph,
And on the crown of the head
of the one distinguished
among his brothers.

27 “Benjamin is a [1]ravenous wolf;
In the morning he devours the
prey,
And in the evening he divides
the spoil.”

28 All these are the twelve tribes
of Israel, and this is what their father said to them [1]when he blessed
them. He blessed them, every one
[2]with the blessing appropriate to
him.
29 Then he charged them and said
to them, “I am about to be [a]gathered
to my people; bury me with my fathers in the cave that is in [b]the field
of Ephron the Hittite,
30 in the cave that is in the field of
Machpelah, which is before Mamre,
in the land of Canaan, which Abraham bought along with the field

19 [1]Lit., *a raiding band* [2]Lit., *heel* [a]Deut. 33:20

20 [1]Lit., *From* [2]Or, *bread* [3]Lit., *fat* [a]Deut. 33:24, 25 [b]Gen. 30:13

21 [a]Deut. 33:23

22 [1]Lit., *son* [2]Lit., *daughters* [a]Deut. 33:13-17

24 [1]I.e., in an unyielding position [2]Lit., *the arms of his hands* [a]Ps. 18:34; 73:23; Is. 41:10 [b]Ps. 132:2, 5; Is. 1:24; 49:26 [c]Ps. 23:1; 80:1 [d]Ps. 118:22; Is. 28:16; 1 Pet. 2:6-8

25 [1]Or, *with* [2]Heb., *Shaddai* [a]Gen. 28:13; 32:9 [b]Gen. 28:3; 48:3 [c]Gen. 27:28

26 [1]Lit., *limit* or *desire* [a]Deut. 33:15, 16

27 [1]Lit., *a wolf that tears*

28 [1]Lit., *and* [2]Lit., *according to his blessing*

29 [a]Gen. 25:8 [b]Gen. 23:16-20

30 [1]Lit., *possession of a burial place*

31 [a]Gen. 25:9 [b]Gen. 23:19 [c]Gen. 35:29

33 [a]Gen. 25:8; Acts 7:15 [b]Gen. 49:29

2 [a]Gen. 50:26

3 [1]Lit., *fulfilled* [2]Or, *him* [3]Lit., *so are fulfilled the days of embalming* [a]Gen. 50:10; Num. 20:29; Deut. 34:8

4 [1]Lit., *weeping* [2]Lit., *In the ears of*

5 [a]Gen. 47:29-31

10 [1]Heb., *Goren ha-Atad* [2]Lit., *heavy* [3]Lit., *made a mourning for seven days*

from Ephron the Hittite for a [1]burial
site.
31 “There they buried [a]Abraham
and his wife [b]Sarah, there they buried [c]Isaac and his wife Rebekah, and
there I buried Leah—
32 the field and the cave that is in
it, purchased from the sons of
Heth.”
33 When Jacob finished charging
his sons, he drew his feet into the
bed and [a]breathed his last, and was
[b]gathered to his people.

Chapter 50

The Death of Israel

THEN Joseph fell on his father’s
face, and wept over him and kissed
him.
2 And Joseph commanded his
servants the physicians to embalm
his father. So the physicians [a]em-
balmed Israel.
3 Now forty days were [1]required
for [2]it, for [3]such is the period required for embalming. And the
Egyptians [a]wept for him seventy
days.
4 And when the days of [1]mourn-
ing for him were past, Joseph spoke
to the household of Pharaoh, saying,
“If now I have found favor in your
sight, please speak [2]to Pharaoh, saying,
5 ‘[a]My father made me swear,
saying, “Behold, I am about to die;
in my grave which I dug for myself
in the land of Canaan, there you
shall bury me.” Now therefore,
please let me go up and bury my
father; then I will return.’ ”
6 And Pharaoh said, “Go up and
bury your father, as he made you
swear.”
7 So Joseph went up to bury his
father, and with him went up all the
servants of Pharaoh, the elders of
his household and all the elders of
the land of Egypt,
8 and all the household of Joseph
and his brothers and his father’s
household; they left only their little
ones and their flocks and their herds
in the land of Goshen.
9 There also went up with him
both chariots and horsemen; and it
was a very great company.
10 When they came to the [1]thresh-
ing floor of Atad, which is beyond
the Jordan, they lamented there
with a very great and [2]sorrowful
lamentation; and he [3]observed
seven days mourning for his father.
11 Now when the inhabitants of

the land, the Canaanites, saw the mourning at [1]the threshing floor of Atad, they said, "This is a [2]grievous [3]mourning for the Egyptians." Therefore it was named [4]Abel-mizraim, which is beyond the Jordan.

Burial at Machpelah

12 And thus his sons did for him as he had charged them;

13 for his sons carried him to the land of Canaan, and buried him in [a]the cave of the field of Machpelah before Mamre, which Abraham had bought along with the field for a [1]burial site from Ephron the Hittite.

14 And after he had buried his father, Joseph returned to Egypt, he and his brothers, and all who had gone up with him to bury his father.

15 When Joseph's brothers saw that their father was dead, they said, "[a]What if Joseph should bear a grudge against us and pay us back in full for all the wrong which we did to him!"

16 So they [1]sent *a message* to Joseph, saying, "Your father charged before he died, saying,

17 'Thus you shall say to Joseph, "Please forgive, I beg you, the transgression of your brothers and their sin, for they did you wrong."' And now, please forgive the transgression of the servants of the God of your father." And Joseph wept when they spoke to him.

18 Then his brothers also came and [a]fell down before him and said, "Behold, we are your servants."

19 But Joseph said to them, "Do not be afraid, for am I in God's place?

20 "And as for you, [a]you meant evil against me, *but* God meant it for good in order to bring about [1]this present result, to preserve many people alive.

21 "So therefore, do not be afraid; [a]I will provide for you and your little ones." So he comforted them and spoke [1]kindly to them.

Death of Joseph

22 Now Joseph stayed in Egypt, he and his father's household, and Joseph lived one hundred and ten years.

23 And Joseph saw the third generation of Ephraim's sons; also the sons of Machir, the son of Manasseh, were born [a]on Joseph's knees.

24 And Joseph said to his brothers, "I am about to die, but [a]God will surely [1]take care of you, and bring you up from this land to the land which He [2]promised on oath to [b]Abraham, to [c]Isaac and [d]to Jacob."

25 Then Joseph made the sons of Israel swear, saying, "God will surely [1]take care of you, and [a]you shall carry my bones up from here."

26 So Joseph died at the age of one hundred and ten years; and [1]he was [a]embalmed and placed in a coffin in Egypt.

11 [1]Heb., *Goren ha-Atad* [2]Lit., *heavy* [3]Heb., *ebel* [4]I.e., the meadow (or mourning) of Egypt

13 [1]Lit., *possession of a burial place* [a]Gen. 23:16-20

15 [a]Gen. 37:28; 42:21, 22

16 [1]Lit., *commanded*

18 [a]Gen. 37:8-10; 41:43

20 [1]Lit., *as it is this day* [a]Gen. 37:26, 27; 45:5, 7

21 [1]Lit., *to their heart* [a]Gen. 45:11; 47:12

23 [a]Gen. 30:3

24 [1]Or, *visit* [2]Lit., *swore* [a]Gen. 48:21; Heb. 11:22 [b]Gen. 13:15, 17; 15:7, 8 [c]Gen. 26:3 [d]Gen. 28:13; 35:12

25 [1]Or, *visit* [a]Ex. 13:19; Josh. 24:32; Heb. 11:22

26 [1]Lit., *they embalmed him* [a]Gen. 50:2

EXODUS

Israel Multiplies in Egypt

NOW these are the [a]names of the sons of Israel who came to Egypt with Jacob; they came each one with his household:

2 Reuben, Simeon, Levi and Judah;

3 Issachar, Zebulun and Benjamin;

4 Dan and Naphtali, Gad and Asher.

5 And all the [1]persons who came from the loins of Jacob were [a]seventy [2]in number, but Joseph was *already* in Egypt.

6 And [a]Joseph died, and all his brothers and all that generation.

7 But the sons of Israel [a]were fruitful and [1]increased greatly, and multiplied, and became exceedingly [2]mighty, so that the land was filled with them.

8 Now a new [a]king arose over Egypt, who did not know Joseph.

9 And [a]he said to his people, "Behold, the people of the sons of Israel are more and mightier than we.

10 "Come, let us deal wisely with them, lest they multiply and [1]in the event of war, they also join themselves to those who hate us, and fight against us, and [2]depart from the land."

11 So they appointed [a]taskmasters over them to afflict them with [1]hard labor. And they built for Pharaoh [b]storage cities, Pithom and Raamses.

12 But the more they afflicted them, [a]the more they multiplied and the more they spread out, so that they were in dread of the sons of Israel.

13 And the Egyptians compelled

1 [a]Gen. 46:8-27

5 [1]Lit., *souls* [2]Lit., *as to souls* [a]Gen. 46:26, 27; Deut. 10:22

6 [a]Gen. 50:26

7 [1]Lit., *swarmed* [2]Or, *numerous* [a]Gen. 12:2; 28:3; 35:11; 46:3; 47:27; 48:4; Acts 7:17

8 [a]Acts 7:18, 19

9 [a]Ps. 105:24, 25

10 [1]Lit., *it came about when war befalls that* [2]Lit., *go up from*

11 [1]Lit., *their burdens* [a]Ex. 3:7; 5:6 [b]1 Kin. 9:19; 2 Chr. 8:4

12 [a]Ex. 1:7

the sons of Israel [a]to labor rigor-
ously;
14 and they made their lives bitter
with hard labor in mortar and bricks
and at *all kinds* of labor in the field,
all their labors which they rigor-
ously [1]imposed on them.
15 Then the king of Egypt spoke to
the Hebrew midwives, one of whom
[1]was named Shiphrah, and the other
[1]was named Puah;
16 and he said, "When you are
helping the Hebrew women to give
birth and see *them* upon the birth-
stool, [a]if it is a son, then you shall
put him to death; but if it is a daughter, then she shall live."
17 But the midwives [1a]feared God,
and did not do as the king of Egypt
had [2]commanded them, but let the
boys live.
18 So the king of Egypt called for
the midwives, and said to them,
"Why have you done this thing, and
let the boys live?"
19 And the midwives said to Pharaoh, "Because the Hebrew women
are not as the Egyptian women; for
they are vigorous, and they give
birth before the midwife [1]can get to
them."
20 So God was good to the midwives, and [a]the people multiplied,
and became very [1]mighty.
21 And it came about because the
midwives [1a]feared God, that He [2]es-
tablished [3]households for them.
22 Then Pharaoh commanded all
his people, saying, "[a]Every son who
is born [1]you are to cast into [b]the
Nile, and every daughter you are to
keep alive."

Chapter 2

The Birth of Moses

NOW a man from [a]the house of
Levi went and [1]married a daughter
of Levi.
2 And the woman conceived and
bore a son; and when she saw [1]that
he was [2a]beautiful, she hid him for
three months.
3 But when she could hide him no
longer, she got him a [1a]wicker [2]bas-
ket and covered it over with tar and
pitch. Then she put the child into it,
and set *it* among the [b]reeds by the
bank of the Nile.
4 And [a]his sister stood at a distance to [1]find out what would [2]hap-
pen to him.
5 Then the daughter of Pharaoh
came down [a]to bathe at the Nile,
with her maidens walking alongside
the Nile; and she saw the [1]basket
among the reeds and sent her maid,
and she brought it to *her.*
6 When she opened *it,* she [1]saw
the child, and behold, *the* [2]boy was
crying. And she had pity on him and
said, "This is one of the Hebrews'
children."
7 Then his sister said to Pharaoh's daughter, "Shall I go and call
[1]a nurse for you from the Hebrew
women, that she may nurse the
child for you?"
8 And Pharaoh's daughter said to
her, "Go *ahead.*" So the girl went
and called the child's mother.
9 Then Pharaoh's daughter said
to her, "Take this child away and
nurse him for me and I shall give
you your wages." So the woman
took the child and nursed him.
10 And the child grew, and she
brought him to Pharaoh's daughter,
and [a]he became her son. And she
named him [1]Moses, and said, "Because I [2]drew him out of the water."
11 Now it came about in those
days, [a]when Moses had grown up,
that he went out to his brethren and
looked on their [1b]hard labors; and
[c]he saw an Egyptian beating a Hebrew, one of his brethren.
12 So he [1]looked this way and
that, and when he saw there was no
one *around,* he [a]struck down the
Egyptian and hid him in the sand.
13 And he went out [a]the next day,
and behold, two Hebrews were
[1]fighting with each other; and he
said to the [2]offender, "Why are you
striking your companion?"
14 But he said, "[a]Who made you a
[1]prince or a judge over us? Are you
[2]intending to kill me, as you killed
the Egyptian?" Then Moses was
afraid, and said, "Surely the matter
has become known."

Moses Escapes to Midian

15 When Pharaoh heard of this
matter, he tried to kill Moses. But
[a]Moses fled from the presence of
Pharaoh and [1]settled in the land of
Midian; and he sat down [b]by a well.
16 Now [a]the priest of Midian had
seven daughters; and [b]they came to
draw water, and filled the troughs to
water their father's flock.
17 Then the shepherds came and
drove them away, but [a]Moses stood
up and helped them, and watered
their flock.
18 When they came to [a]Reuel their
father, he said, "Why have you
come *back* so soon today?"
19 So they said, "An Egyptian delivered us from the hand of the shepherds; and what is more, he even

13 [a]Gen. 15:13; Deut. 4:20
14 [1]Lit., *worked through them*
15 [1]Lit., *the name was*
16 [a]Acts 7:19
17 [1]Or, *revered* [2]Lit., *spoken to* [a]Ex. 1:21
19 [1]Lit., *comes to*
20 [1]Or, *numerous* [a]Ex. 1:12; Is. 3:10
21 [1]Or, *revered* [2]Lit., *made* [3]Or, *families* [a]Ex. 1:17
22 [1]Some versions insert, *to the Hebrews* [a]Acts 7:19 [b]Gen. 41:1
1 [1]Lit., *took* [a]Ex. 6:16, 18, 20
2 [1]Lit., *him that* [2]Lit., good [a]Acts 7:20; Heb. 11:23
3 [1]I.e., of papyrus reeds [2]Or, *chest* [a]Is. 18:2 [b]Is. 19:6
4 [1]Lit., *know* [2]Lit., *be done* [a]Ex. 15:20; Num. 26:59
5 [1]Or, *chest* [a]Ex. 7:15; 8:20
6 [1]Heb., *saw it, the child* [2]Or, *lad*
7 [1]Lit., *a woman giving suck*
10 [1]Heb., *Mosheh,* from *mashah* [2]Heb., *mashah* [a]Acts 7:21
11 [1]Lit., *burdens* [a]Acts 7:23; Heb. 11:24-26 [b]Ex. 1:11; 5:4, 5; 6:6, 7
12 [1]Lit., *turned* [a]Acts 7:24, 25
13 [1]Or, *quarreling* [2]Or, *the guilty one* [a]Acts 7:26-28
14 [1]Lit., *man, a prince* [2]Lit., *saying in your heart* [a]Gen. 19:9; Acts 7:27, 28
15 [1]Lit., *dwelt* [a]Acts 7:29 [b]Gen. 24:11; 29:2
16 [a]Ex. 3:1; 18:12 [b]Gen. 24:13, 19
17 [a]Gen. 29:3, 10
18 [a]Ex. 3:1; Num. 10:29

drew the water for us and watered
the flock."
20 And he said to his daughters,
"Where is he then? Why is it that
you have left the man behind? Invite
him [1]to have something to eat."
21 [a]And Moses was willing to
dwell with the man, and he gave his
daughter [b]Zipporah to Moses.
22 Then she gave birth to [a]a son,
and he named him [1]Gershom, for he
said, "I have been [b]a [2]sojourner in a
foreign land."
23 Now it came about in *the*
course of [a]those many days that the
king of Egypt died. And the sons of
Israel [b]sighed because of the bondage, and they cried out; and [c]their
cry for help because of *their* bondage rose up to God.
24 So God heard their groaning;
and God remembered [a]His covenant
with Abraham, Isaac, and Jacob.
25 And God saw the sons of Israel,
and God [1]took notice *of them.*

Chapter 3

The Burning Bush

Now Moses was pasturing the
flock of [a]Jethro his father-in-law,
the priest of Midian; and he led the
flock to the [1]west side of the wilderness, and came to [b]Horeb, the
[c]mountain of God.
2 And [a]the angel of the Lord appeared to him in a blazing fire from
the midst of a [b]bush; and he looked,
and behold, the bush was burning
with fire, yet the bush was not consumed.
3 So Moses said, "[1a]I must turn
aside now, and see this [2]marvelous
sight, why the bush is not burned
up."
4 When the Lord saw that he
turned aside to look, [a]God called to
him from the midst of the bush, and
said, "Moses, Moses!" And he said,
"Here I am."
5 Then He said, "Do not come
near here; [a]remove your sandals
from your feet, for the place on
which you are standing is holy
ground."
6 He said also, "[a]I am the God of
your father, the God of Abraham,
the God of Isaac, and the God of Jacob." [b]Then Moses hid his face, for
he was afraid to look at God.
7 And the Lord said, "I have
surely [a]seen the affliction of My people who are in Egypt, and have giv-
en heed to their cry because of their
taskmasters, for I am aware of their
sufferings.
8 "So I have come down [a]to deliver them from the [1]power of the
Egyptians, and to bring them up
from that land to a good and spacious land, to a land [b]flowing with
milk and honey, to the place of [c]the
Canaanite and the Hittite and the
Amorite and the Perizzite and the
Hivite and the Jebusite.
9 "And now, behold, [a]the cry of
the sons of Israel has come to Me;
furthermore, I have seen the oppression with which the Egyptians are
oppressing them.

The Mission of Moses

10 "Therefore, come now, and I will
send you to Pharaoh, [a]so that you
may bring My people, the sons of
Israel, out of Egypt."
11 But Moses said to God, "[a]Who
am I, that I should go to Pharaoh,
and that I should bring the sons of
Israel out of Egypt?"
12 And He said, "Certainly [a]I will
be with you, and this shall be the
sign to you that it is I who have sent
you: [b]when you have brought the
people out of Egypt, [c]you shall
[1]worship God at this mountain."
13 Then Moses said to God, "Behold, I am going to the sons of Israel,
and I shall say to them, 'The God of
your fathers has sent me to you.'
Now they may say to me, 'What is
His name?' What shall I say to
them?"
14 And God said to Moses, "[1a]I
AM WHO [1]I AM"; and He said,
"Thus you shall say to the sons of
Israel, '[1]I AM has sent me to you.' "
15 And God, furthermore, said to
Moses, "Thus you shall say to the
sons of Israel, '[a]The Lord, the God
of your fathers, the God of Abraham, the God of Isaac, and the God
of Jacob, has sent me to you.' This is
My name forever, and this is My
[b]memorial-name to all generations.
16 "Go and gather the elders of Israel together, and say to them, '[a]The
Lord, the God of your fathers, the
God of Abraham, Isaac and Jacob,
has appeared to me, saying, "[1]I am
indeed concerned about you and
what has been done to you in Egypt.
17 "So [a]I said, I will bring you up
out of the affliction of Egypt to the
land of [b]the Canaanite and the Hittite and the Amorite and the Perizzite and the Hivite and the Jebusite,
to a land [c]flowing with milk and
honey." '
18 "And [a]they will [1]pay heed to
what you say; and [b]you with the elders of Israel will come to the king
of Egypt, and you will say to him,

20 [1]Lit., *that he may eat bread*
21 [a]Acts 7:29 [b]Ex. 4:25; 18:2
22 [1]Cf. Heb. *ger sham, a stranger there* [2]Heb. *ger* [a]Ex. 4:20; 18:3, 4 [b]Gen. 23:4; Heb. 11:13, 14
23 [a]Acts 7:30 [b]Ex. 6:5, 9 [c]Ex. 3:7, 9; Deut. 26:7; James 5:4
24 [a]Gen. 22:16-18; 26:2-5; 28:13-15; Ps. 105:8, 42
25 [1]Lit., *knew them*
1 [1]Or, *rear part* [a]Ex. 2:18; 4:18; 18:12; Num. 10:29 [b]Ex. 3:12; 17:6; 33:6 [c]Ex. 4:27; 18:5; 24:13
2 [a]Gen. 22:11, 15; Ex. 3:4-11, 16 [b]Deut. 33:16; Mark 12:26; Luke 20:37; Acts 7:30
3 [1]Lit., *Let me turn* [2]Lit., *great* [a]Acts 7:31
4 [a]Ex. 4:5
5 [a]Josh. 5:15; Acts 7:33
6 [a]Matt. 22:31, 32; Mark 12:26; Luke 20:37 [b]Acts 7:32
7 [a]Ex. 2:25; Neh. 9:9; Is. 63:9; Acts 7:34
8 [1]Lit., *hand* [a]Gen. 15:13-16; 46:4; 50:24, 25 [b]Ex. 3:17; 13:5; Jer. 11:5 [c]Gen. 15:19-21; Josh. 24:11
9 [a]Ex. 2:23
10 [a]Gen. 15:13; Ex. 12:40, 41; Acts 7:6, 7
11 [a]Ex. 4:10; 6:12
12 [1]Or, *serve* [a]Gen. 31:3; Ex. 4:12, 15; 33:14-16; Josh. 1:5 [b]Ex. 19:1 [c]Ex. 19:2, 3
14 The name of God, *YHWH*, rendered Lord, derived from the verb *HAYAH, to be* [a]Ex. 6:3; John 8:58; Heb. 13:8; Rev. 1:8; 4:8
15 [a]Ex. 3:6, 13 [b]Ps. 30:4; 97:12; 102:12; 135:13; Hos. 12:5
16 [1]Lit., *Visiting I have visited* [a]Ex. 3:2
17 [a]Gen. 15:13-21; 46:4; 50:24, 25 [b]Josh. 24:11 [c]Ex. 3:8
18 [1]Lit., *hear your voice* [a]Ex. 4:31 [b]Ex. 5:1

'The LORD, the God of the Hebrews,
has met with us. So now, please, let
us go a [c]three days' journey into the
wilderness, that we may sacrifice to
the LORD our God.'
19"But I know that the king of
Egypt [a]will not permit you to go,
[b]except [1]under compulsion.
20"So I will stretch out [a]My hand,
and strike Egypt with all My [b]mira-
cles which I shall do in the midst of
it; and [c]after that he will let you go.
21"And I will grant this people [a]fa-
vor in the sight of the Egyptians;
and it shall be that when you go, you
will not go empty-handed.
22"But every woman [a]shall ask of
her neighbor and the woman who
lives in her house, articles of silver
and articles of gold, and clothing;
and you will put them on your sons
and daughters. Thus you will plunder the Egyptians."

CHAPTER 4

Moses Given Powers

THEN Moses answered and said,
"What if they will not believe me, or
[a]listen [1]to what I say? For they may
say, '[b]The LORD has not appeared to
you.' "
2 And the LORD said to him,
"What is that in your hand?" And he
said, "[a]A staff."
3 Then He said, "Throw it on the
ground." So he threw it on the
ground, and [a]it became a serpent;
and Moses fled from it.
4 But the LORD said to Moses,
"Stretch out your hand and grasp *it*
by its tail"—so he stretched out his
hand and caught it, and it became a
staff in his [1]hand—
5"that they may believe that the
LORD, the God of their fathers, the
God of Abraham, the God of Isaac,
and the God of Jacob, has appeared
to you."
6 And the LORD furthermore said
to him, "Now put your hand into
your bosom." So he put his hand
into his bosom, and when he took it
out, behold, his hand was [a]leprous
like snow.
7 Then He said, "Put your hand
into your bosom again." So he put
his hand into his bosom again; and
when he took it out of his bosom,
behold, [a]it was restored like *the rest
of* his flesh.
8"And it shall come about that if
they will not believe you or [1]heed
the [2]witness of the first sign, they
may believe the [2]witness of the last
sign.
9"But it shall be that if they will
not believe even these two signs or
heed what you say, then you shall
take some water from the Nile and
pour it on the dry ground; and the
water which you take from the Nile
[a]will become blood on the dry
ground."
10 Then Moses said to the LORD,
"Please, Lord, [a]I have never been
[1]eloquent, neither [2]recently nor in
time past, nor since Thou hast spoken to Thy servant; for I am [3]slow of
speech and [3]slow of tongue."
11 And the LORD said to him,
"Who has made man's mouth? Or
[a]who makes *him* dumb or deaf, or
seeing or blind? Is it not I, the LORD?
12"Now then go, and [a]I, even I, will
be with your mouth, and [b]teach you
what you are to say."
13 But he said, "Please, Lord, now
[1]send *the message* by whomever
Thou wilt."

Aaron to be Moses' Mouthpiece

14 Then the anger of the LORD
burned against Moses, and He said,
"Is there not your brother Aaron the
Levite? I know that he speaks [1]flu-
ently. And moreover, behold, [a]he is
coming out to meet you; when he
sees you, he will be glad in his heart.
15"And you are to speak to him
and [a]put the words in his mouth;
and I, even I, will be with your
mouth and his mouth, and I will
teach you what you are to do.
16"Moreover, [a]he shall speak for
you to the people; and it shall come
about that he shall be as a mouth for
you, and you shall be as God to him.
17"And you shall take in your hand
[a]this staff, [b]with which you shall
perform the signs."
18 Then Moses departed and returned to [1]Jethro [a]his father-in-law,
and said to him, "Please, let me go,
that I may return to my brethren
who are in Egypt, and see if they are
still alive." And Jethro said to
Moses, "Go in peace."
19 Now the LORD said to Moses in
Midian, "Go [1]back to Egypt, for [a]all
the men who were seeking your life
are dead."
20 So Moses took his wife and his
[a]sons and mounted them on a donkey, and he returned to the land of
Egypt. Moses also took the [b]staff of
God in his hand.
21 And the LORD said to Moses,
"When you go [1]back to Egypt see
that you perform before Pharaoh all
[a]the wonders which I have put in
your [2]power; but [b]I will harden his

18 [c]Ex. 5:3; 8:27
19 [1]Lit., *by a strong hand* [a]Ex. 5:2 [b]Ex. 6:1
20 [a]Ex. 6:1; 7:4, 5; 9:15; 13:3, 9, 14 [b]Ex. 15:11; Deut. 6:22; Neh. 9:10 [c]Ex. 11:1; 12:31-33
21 [a]Ex. 11:3; 12:36
22 [a]Ex. 11:2; 12:35
1 [1]Lit., *to my voice* [a]Ex. 3:18; 6:30 [b]Ex. 3:15, 16
2 [a]Ex. 4:17, 20
3 [a]Ex. 7:10-12
4 [1]Lit., *palm*
6 [a]Num. 12:10; 2 Kin. 5:27
7 [a]Num. 12:13-15; Deut. 32:39; 2 Kin. 5:14; Matt. 8:3; Luke 17:12-14
8 [1]Lit., *listen to* [2]Lit., *voice*
9 [a]Ex. 7:19, 20
10 [1]Lit., *a man of words* [2]Lit., *yesterday* [3]Lit., *heavy* [a]Ex. 3:11; 4:1; 6:12; Jer. 1:6
11 [a]Ps. 94:9; 146:8; Matt. 11:5; Luke 1:20, 64
12 [a]Ex. 4:15, 16; Deut. 18:18; Is. 50:4; Jer. 1:9 [b]Matt. 10:19, 20; Mark 13:11; Luke 12:11, 12; 21:14, 15
13 [1]Lit., *send by the hand which Thou sendest*
14 [1]Lit., *speaking he speaks* [a]Ex. 4:27
15 [a]Ex. 4:12, 30; Num. 23:5, 12, 16; Is. 51:16; 59:21; Jer. 1:9
16 [a]Ex. 7:1, 2
17 [a]Ex. 4:2, 20; 17:9 [b]Ex. 7:9-20; 14:16
18 [1]Heb., *Jether* [a]Ex. 2:21; 3:1
19 [1]Lit., *return* [a]Ex. 2:15, 23
20 [a]Ex. 18:3, 4; Acts 7:29 [b]Ex. 4:17; 17:9; Num. 20:8
21 [1]Lit., *to return* [2]Lit., *hand* [a]Ex. 11:9, 10 [b]Ex. 7:3, 13; 9:12, 35; 10:1, 20, 27; 14:4, 8; Deut. 2:30; John 12:40; Rom. 9:18

heart so that he will not let the people go.
22 "Then you shall say to Pharaoh, 'Thus says the LORD, "[a]Israel is My son, My first-born.
23 "So I said to you, '[a]Let My son go, that he may serve Me'; but you have refused to let him go. Behold, [b]I will kill your son, your first-born." ' "
24 Now it came about at the lodging place on the way that the LORD met him and [a]sought to put him to death.
25 Then Zipporah took [a]a flint and cut off her son's foreskin and [1]threw *it* at Moses' feet, and she said, "You are indeed a bridegroom of blood to me."
26 So He let him alone. At that time she said, "*You are* a bridegroom of blood"—[1]because of the circumcision.
27 [a]Now the LORD said to Aaron, "Go to meet Moses in the wilderness." So he went and met him at the mountain of God, and he kissed him.
28 And Moses told Aaron all the words of the LORD with which He had sent him, and all the signs that He had commanded him *to do*.
29 Then Moses and Aaron went and [a]assembled all the elders of the sons of Israel;
30 and [a]Aaron spoke all the words which the LORD had spoken to Moses. He then performed the [b]signs in the sight of the people.
31 So [a]the people believed; and when they heard that the LORD [1]was concerned about the sons of Israel and that He had seen their affliction, then [b]they bowed low and worshiped.

CHAPTER 5

Israel's Labor Increased

AND afterward Moses and Aaron came and said to Pharaoh, "[a]Thus says the LORD, the God of Israel, '[b]Let My people go that they may celebrate a feast to Me in the wilderness.' "
2 But Pharaoh said, "[a]Who is the LORD that I should obey His voice to let Israel go? I do not know the LORD, and besides, [b]I will not let Israel go."
3 Then they said, "[a]The God of the Hebrews has met with us. Please, let us go a three days' journey into the wilderness that we may sacrifice to the LORD our God, lest He fall upon us with pestilence or with the sword."
4 But the king of Egypt said to them, "Moses and Aaron, why do you [1]draw the people away from their [2]work? Get *back* to your [3][a]labors!"
5 Again Pharaoh said, "Look, [a]the people of the land are now many, and you would have them cease from their labors!"
6 So the same day Pharaoh commanded [a]the taskmasters over the people and their [b]foremen, saying,
7 "You are no longer to give the people straw to make brick as previously; let them go and gather straw for themselves.
8 "But the quota of bricks which they were making previously, you shall impose on them; you are not to reduce any of it. Because they are [a]lazy, therefore they cry out, '[1]Let us go and sacrifice to our God.'
9 "Let the labor be heavier on the men, and let them work at it that they may pay no attention to false words."
10 So [a]the taskmasters of the people and their foremen went out and spoke to the people, saying, "Thus says Pharaoh, 'I am not going to give you *any* straw.
11 'You go *and* get straw for yourselves wherever you can find *it;* but none of your labor will be reduced.' "
12 So the people scattered through all the land of Egypt to gather stubble for straw.
13 And the taskmasters pressed them, saying, "Complete your [1]work quota, [2]*your* daily amount, just as when [3]you had straw."
14 Moreover, [a]the foremen of the sons of Israel, whom Pharaoh's taskmasters had set over them, [b]were beaten [1]and were asked, "Why have you not completed your required amount either yesterday or today in making brick as previously?"
15 Then the foremen of the sons of Israel came and cried out to Pharaoh, saying, "Why do you deal this way with your servants?
16 "There is no straw given to your servants, yet they keep saying to us, 'Make bricks!' And behold, your servants are being beaten; but it is the fault of your *own* people."
17 But he said, "You are [a]lazy, *very* lazy; therefore you say, 'Let us go *and* sacrifice to the LORD.'
18 "So go now *and* work; for you shall be given no straw, yet you must deliver the quota of bricks."
19 And the foremen of the sons of Israel saw that they were in trouble

22 [a]Is. 63:16; 64:8; Jer. 31:9; Hos. 11:1
23 [a]Ex. 5:1; 6:11; 7:16 [b]Ex. 12:29
24 [a]Num. 22:22
25 [1]Lit., *made it touch at his feet* [a]Gen. 17:14; Josh. 5:2, 3
26 [1]Lit., *with reference to*
27 [a]Ex. 4:14
29 [a]Ex. 3:16
30 [a]Ex. 4:15, 16 [b]Ex. 4:1-9
31 [1]Lit., *had visited* [a]Ex. 3:18 [b]Ex. 12:27
1 [a]Ex. 3:18 [b]Ex. 4:23
2 [a]Job 21:15 [b]Ex. 3:19
3 [a]Ex. 3:18
4 [1]Lit., *loose* [2]Lit., *works* [3]Lit., *burdens* [a]Ex. 1:11; 2:11; 6:5-7
5 [a]Ex. 1:7, 9
6 [a]Ex. 1:11; 3:7; 5:10, 13, 14 [b]Ex. 5:10, 14, 15, 19
8 [1]Lit., *saying, 'Let* [a]Ex. 5:17
10 [a]Ex. 5:6
13 [1]Lit., *works* [2]Lit., *the matter of a day in its day* [3]Lit., *there was*
14 [1]Lit., *saying* [a]Ex. 5:6 [b]Is. 10:24
17 [a]Ex. 5:8

[1]because they were told, "You must
not reduce *your* daily amount of
bricks."
20 When they left Pharaoh's presence, they met Moses and Aaron as
they were waiting for them.
21 And [a]they said to them, "[b]May
the LORD look upon you and judge
you, for you have [c]made [1]us odious
in Pharaoh's sight and in the sight of
his servants, to put a sword in their
hand to kill us."
22 Then Moses returned to the
LORD and said, "[a]O LORD, why hast
Thou brought harm to this people?
Why didst Thou ever send me?
23"Ever since I came to Pharaoh to
speak in Thy name, he has done
harm to this people; [a]and Thou hast
not delivered Thy people at all."

CHAPTER 6

God Promises Action

THEN the LORD said to Moses,
"Now you shall see what I will do to
Pharaoh; for [1a]under compulsion he
shall let them go, and [1]under compulsion he shall drive them out of
his land."
2 God spoke further to Moses
and said to him, "I am [a]the LORD;
3 and I appeared to Abraham,
Isaac, and Jacob, as [1]God Almighty,
[a]but *by* My name, [2]LORD, I did not
make Myself known to them.
4"And I also established [a]My covenant with them, to give them the
land of Canaan, the land in which
they sojourned.
5"And furthermore I have [a]heard
the groaning of the sons of Israel,
because the Egyptians are holding
them in bondage; and I have remembered My covenant.
6"Say, therefore, to the sons of Israel, '[a]I am the LORD, and [b]I will
bring you out from under the burdens of the Egyptians, and I will deliver you from their bondage. I will
also redeem you with [c]an outstretched arm and with great judgments.
7 'Then I will take you [a]for My
people, and I will be [2]your God; and
[b]you shall know that I am the LORD
your God, who brought you out
from under the burdens of the Egyptians.
8 'And I will bring you to the land
which [a]I [1]swore to give to Abraham,
Isaac, and Jacob, and [b]I will give it
to you *for* a possession; [c]I am the
LORD.' "
9 So Moses spoke thus to the
sons of Israel, but they did not listen
to Moses on [a]account of *their* despondency and cruel bondage.
10 Now the LORD spoke to Moses,
saying,
11"[a]Go, [1]tell Pharaoh king of
Egypt [2]to let the sons of Israel go
out of his land."
12 But Moses spoke before the
LORD, saying, "Behold, the sons of
Israel have not listened to me; [a]how
then will Pharaoh listen to me, for I
am unskilled in speech?"
13 Then the LORD spoke to Moses
and to Aaron, and gave them a
charge to the sons of Israel and to
Pharaoh king of Egypt, to bring the
sons of Israel out of the land of
Egypt.

The Heads of Israel

14 These are the heads of their fathers' households. [a]The sons of Reuben, Israel's first-born: Hanoch and
Pallu, Hezron and Carmi; these are
the families of Reuben.
15 And the sons of Simeon: Jemuel and Jamin and Ohad and Jachin and Zohar and Shaul the son of
a Canaanite woman; these are the
families of Simeon.
16 And these are the names of [a]the
sons of Levi according to their generations: Gershon and Kohath and
Merari; and the [1]length of Levi's life
was one hundred and thirty-seven
years.
17 [a]The sons of Gershon: Libni and
Shimei, according to their families.
18 And [a]the sons of Kohath: Amram and Izhar and Hebron and Uzziel; and the [1]length of Kohath's life
was one hundred and thirty-three
years.
19 And the sons of Merari: Mahli
and Mushi. These are the families of
the Levites according to their generations.
20 And [a]Amram [1]married his father's sister Jochebed, and she bore
him Aaron and Moses; and the
[2]length of Amram's life was one
hundred and thirty-seven years.
21 And [a]the sons of Izhar: Korah
and Nepheg and Zichri.
22 [a]And the sons of Uzziel: Mishael and [1]Elzaphan and Sithri.
23 And Aaron married Elisheba,
the daughter of [a]Amminadab, the
sister of [b]Nahshon, and she bore
him [c]Nadab and Abihu, Eleazar and
Ithamar.
24 And the [a]sons of Korah: Assir
and Elkanah and [1]Abiasaph; these
are the families of the Korahites.
25 And Aaron's son [a]Eleazar married one of the daughters of Putiel,
and she bore him [b]Phinehas. These

19 [1]Lit., *saying*
21 [1]Lit., *our savor to stink* [a]Ex. 14:11; 15:24; 16:2 [b]Gen. 16:5; 31:53 [c]Gen. 34:30; 1 Sam. 27:12
22 [a]Num. 11:11; Jer. 4:10
23 [a]Ex. 3:8
1 [1]Lit., *by a strong hand* [a]Ex. 3:19, 20; 7:4, 5; 12:31, 33, 39; 13:3
2 [a]Ex. 3:14, 15
3 [1]Heb., *El Shaddai* [2]YHWH, usually rendered LORD [a]Ps. 68:4; 83:18; Is. 52:6; Jer. 16:21; Ezek. 37:6, 13
4 [a]Gen. 12:7; 15:18; 26:3, 4; 28:4, 13
5 [a]Ex. 2:24
6 [a]Ex. 13:3, 14; 20:2; Deut. 6:12 [b]Ex. 12:51; 16:6; 18:1 [c]Deut. 4:34; 5:15; 26:8
7 [a]Deut. 4:20 [b]Ex. 16:12; Is. 41:20; 49:23, 26; 60:16
8 [1]Lit., *lifted up My hand* [a]Gen. 15:18; Num. 14:30; Neh. 9:15; Ezek. 20:5, 6 [b]Josh. 24:13; Ps. 136:21, 22 [c]Ex. 6:6
9 [a]Ex. 2:23
11 [1]Lit., *speak to* [2]Lit., *that he let* [a]Ex. 4:22, 23
12 [a]Ex. 4:1, 10; 6:30
14 [a]Gen. 46:9; Num. 26:5-11
16 [1]Lit., *years* [a]Gen. 46:11; Num. 3:17; 1 Chr. 6:1
17 [a]Num. 3:18-20; 1 Chr. 6:17
18 [1]Lit., *years* [a]Num. 3:19
20 [1]Lit., *took to him to wife,* also vs. 23, 25 [2]Lit., *years* [a]Ex. 2:1, 2; Num. 26:59
21 [a]Num. 16:1; 1 Chr. 6:37, 38
22 [1]In Num. 3:30, *Elizaphan* [a]Lev. 10:4; Num. 3:30
23 [a]Ruth 4:19, 20; 1 Chr. 2:10 [b]Num. 1:7; 2:3 [c]Lev. 10:1; Num. 3:2
24 [1]In 1 Chr. 6:23 and 9:19, *Ebiasaph* [a]1 Chr. 6:22, 23
25 [a]Josh. 24:33 [b]Num. 25:7, 11; Ps. 106:30

are the heads of the fathers' *households* of the Levites according to their families.

26 It was *the same* Aaron and Moses to whom the LORD said, "[a]Bring out the sons of Israel from the land of Egypt according to their hosts."

27 They were the ones [a]who spoke to Pharaoh king of Egypt [1]about bringing out the sons of Israel from Egypt; it was *the same* Moses and Aaron.

28 Now it came about on the day when the LORD spoke to Moses in the land of Egypt,

29 that the LORD spoke to Moses, saying, "[a]I am the LORD; [b]speak to Pharaoh king of Egypt all that I speak to you."

30 But Moses said before the LORD, "Behold, I am [1a]unskilled in speech; how then will Pharaoh listen to me?"

CHAPTER 7

"I Will Stretch Out My Hand"

THEN the LORD said to Moses, "[a]See, I make you *as* God to Pharaoh, and your brother Aaron shall be your prophet.

2 "You shall speak all that I command you, and your brother Aaron shall speak to Pharaoh that he let the sons of Israel go out of his land.

3 "But [a]I will harden Pharaoh's heart that I may multiply My signs and My wonders in the land of Egypt.

4 "When [a]Pharaoh will not listen to you, then I will lay My hand on Egypt, and [b]bring out My hosts, My people the sons of Israel, from the land of Egypt by [c]great judgments.

5 "And [a]the Egyptians shall know that I am the LORD, when I stretch out My hand on Egypt and bring out the sons of Israel from their midst."

6 So Moses and Aaron did *it;* [a]as the LORD commanded them, thus they did.

7 And Moses was [a]eighty years old and Aaron [1]eighty-three, when they spoke to Pharaoh.

Aaron's Rod Becomes a Serpent

8 Now the LORD spoke to Moses and Aaron, saying,

9 "When Pharaoh speaks to you, saying, '[1a]Work a miracle,' then you shall say to Aaron, 'Take your staff and throw *it* down before Pharaoh, *that* it may become a serpent.' "

10 So Moses and Aaron came to Pharaoh, and thus they did just as the LORD had commanded; and Aaron threw his staff down before Pharaoh and [1]his servants, and it [a]became a serpent.

11 Then Pharaoh also called for *the* wise men and *the* sorcerers, and they also, the [1a]magicians of Egypt, [b]did [2]the same with their secret arts.

12 For each one threw down his staff and they turned into serpents. But Aaron's staff swallowed up their staffs.

13 Yet Pharaoh's heart was [1]hardened, and [a]he did not listen to them, as the LORD had said.

Water Is Turned to Blood

14 Then the LORD said to Moses, "Pharaoh's heart is [1]stubborn; he refuses to let the people go.

15 "Go to Pharaoh in the morning [1]as [a]he is going out to the water, and station yourself to meet him on the bank of the Nile; and you shall take in your hand [b]the staff that was turned into a serpent.

16 "[a]And you will say to him, 'The LORD, the God of the Hebrews, sent me to you, saying, "[b]Let My people go, that they may serve Me in the wilderness. But behold, you have not listened until now."

17 'Thus says the LORD, "[a]By this you shall know that I am the LORD: behold, I will strike [1]the water that is in the Nile with the staff that is in my hand, and [b]it shall be turned to blood.

18 "And [a]the fish that are in the Nile will die, and the Nile will [1]become foul; and the Egyptians will [2b]find difficulty in drinking water from the Nile." ' "

19 Then the LORD said to Moses, "Say to Aaron, 'Take your staff and [a]stretch out your hand over the waters of Egypt, over their rivers, over their [1]streams, and over their pools, and over all their reservoirs of water, that they may become blood; and there shall be blood throughout all the land of Egypt, both in *vessels of* wood and in *vessels of* stone.' "

20 So Moses and Aaron did even as the LORD had commanded. And he lifted up [1]the staff and struck the water that *was* in the Nile, in the sight of Pharaoh and in the sight of his servants, and [a]all the water that *was* in the Nile was turned to blood.

21 And the fish that *were* in the Nile died, and the Nile [1]became foul, so that the Egyptians could not drink water from the Nile. And the blood was through all the land of Egypt.

---

26 [a]Ex. 6:13
27 [1]Lit., *to bring out* [a]Ex. 5:1
29 [a]Ex. 6:2, 6, 8 [b]Ex. 6:11; 7:2
30 [1]Lit., *uncircumcised of lips* [a]Ex. 4:10; 6:12
1 [a]Ex. 4:16
2 [a]Ex. 4:15
3 [a]Ex. 4:21
4 [a]Ex. 3:19, 20; 11:9 [b]Ex. 12:51; 13:3, 9 [c]Ex. 6:6
5 [a]Ex. 7:17; 8:19; 10:7
6 [a]Gen. 6:22; 7:5; Ex. 7:2
7 [1]Lit., *83 years old* [a]Deut. 34:7; Acts 7:23, 30
9 [1]Lit., *Show a wonder for yourselves* [a]Is. 7:11; John 2:18
10 [1]Lit., *before his* [a]Ex. 4:3; 7:9
11 [1]Or, *soothsayer priests* [2]Lit., *thus* [a]Gen. 41:8 [b]Ex. 7:22; 8:7, 18; 2 Tim. 3:9
13 [1]Lit., *strong* [a]Ex. 7:4; 8:15
14 [1]Or, *hard;* lit., *heavy*
15 [1]Lit., *behold* [a]Ex. 2:5; 8:20 [b]Ex. 4:2, 3; 7:10
16 [a]Ex. 3:13, 18; 4:22; 5:1 [b]Ex. 4:23; 5:1, 3
17 [1]Lit., *upon the waters* [a]Ex. 5:2; 7:5; 10:2 [b]Ex. 4:9; 7:20; Rev. 11:6; 16:4, 6
18 [1]I.e., have a bad smell [2]Or, *be weary of* [a]Ex. 7:21 [b]Ex. 7:21, 24
19 [1]Or, *canals* [a]Ex. 8:5, 6, 16; 9:22; 10:12, 21; 14:21, 26
20 [1]Lit., *with the staff* [a]Ps. 78:44; 105:29
21 [1]I.e., had a bad smell

22 [a]But the [1]magicians of Egypt did [2]the same with their secret arts; and Pharaoh's heart was [3]hardened, and he did not listen to them, as the LORD had said.

23 Then Pharaoh turned and went into his house [1]with no concern even for this.

24 So all the Egyptians dug around the Nile for water to drink, for they could not drink of the water of the Nile.

25 And seven days [1]passed after the LORD had struck the Nile.

CHAPTER 8

Frogs over the Land

1 THEN the LORD said to Moses, "Go to Pharaoh and say to him, 'Thus says the LORD, "[a]Let My people go, that they may serve Me.

2 "But if you refuse to let *them* go, behold, I will smite your whole territory with frogs.

3 "And the Nile will swarm with frogs, which will come up and go into your house and into your bedroom and on your bed, and into the houses of your servants and on your people, and into your ovens and into your kneading bowls.

4 "So the frogs will come up on you and your people and all your servants." ' "

5 [1]Then the LORD said to Moses, "Say to Aaron, '[a]Stretch out your hand with your staff over the rivers, over the [2]streams and over the pools, and make frogs come up on the land of Egypt.' "

6 So Aaron stretched out his hand over the waters of Egypt, and the [1a]frogs came up and covered the land of Egypt.

7 [a]And the [1]magicians did [2]the same with their secret arts, [3]making frogs come up on the land of Egypt.

8 Then Pharaoh [a]called for Moses and Aaron and said, "[b]Entreat the LORD that He remove the frogs from me and from my people; and [c]I will let the people go, that they may sacrifice to the LORD."

9 And Moses said to Pharaoh, "[1]The honor is yours to tell me: when shall I entreat for you and your servants and your people, that the frogs be [2]destroyed from you and your houses, *that* they may be left only in the Nile?"

10 Then he said, "Tomorrow." So he said, "*May it be* according to your word, that you may know that there is [a]no one like the LORD our God.

11 "And the [a]frogs will depart from you and your houses and your servants and your people; they will be left only in the Nile."

12 Then Moses and Aaron went out from Pharaoh, and [a]Moses cried to the LORD concerning the frogs which He had [1]inflicted upon Pharaoh.

13 And the LORD did according to the word of Moses, and the frogs died out of the houses, the courts, and the fields.

14 So they piled them in heaps, and the land [1]became foul.

15 But when Pharaoh saw that there was relief, he [1]hardened his heart and [a]did not listen to them, as the LORD had said.

The Plague of Insects

16 Then the LORD said to Moses, "Say to Aaron, 'Stretch out your staff and strike the dust of the earth, that it may become [1]gnats through all the land of Egypt.' "

17 And they did so; and Aaron stretched out his hand with his staff, and struck the dust of the earth, and there were [1]gnats on man and beast. All the dust of the earth became [1a]gnats through all the land of Egypt.

18 And the [1]magicians tried with their secret arts to bring forth [2]gnats, but [a]they could not; so there were [2]gnats on man and beast.

19 Then the [1]magicians said to Pharaoh, "[a]This is the finger of God." But Pharaoh's heart was [2]hardened, and he did not listen to them, as the LORD had said.

20 Now the LORD said to Moses, "[a]Rise early in the morning and present yourself before Pharaoh, [1]as [b]he comes out to the water, and say to him, 'Thus says the LORD, "[c]Let My people go, that they may serve Me.

21 "For if you will not let My people go, behold, I will send swarms of insects on you and on your servants and on your people and into your houses; and the houses of the Egyptians shall be full of swarms of insects, and also the ground on which they *dwell*.

22 "[a]But on that day I will set apart the land of Goshen, where My people are [1]living, so that no swarms of insects will be there, in order that you may know that [2b]I, the LORD, am in the midst of the land.

23 "And I will [1]put a division between My people and your people. Tomorrow this sign shall occur." ' "

24 Then the LORD did so. And

22 [1]Or, *soothsayer priests* [2]Lit., *thus* [3]Lit., *strong* [a]Ex. 7:11; 8:7

23 [1]Lit., *and he did not set his heart even to this*

25 [1]Lit., *were fulfilled*

1 [1]Chap. 7:26 in Heb. [a]Ex. 3:18; 4:23; 5:1, 3

5 [1]Chap. 8:1 in Heb. [2]Or, *canals* [a]Ex. 7:19

6 [1]Lit., *frog* [a]Ps. 78:45; 105:30

7 [1]Or, *soothsayer priests* [2]Lit., *thus* [3]Lit., *and made* [a]Ex. 7:11, 22

8 [a]Ex. 8:25; 9:27; 10:16 [b]Ex. 8:28 [c]Ex. 8:15, 29

9 [1]Lit., *Glory over me* [2]Lit., *cut off*

10 [a]Ex. 9:14; Deut. 4:35, 39; 33:26; Ps. 86:8; Is. 46:9; Jer. 10:6, 7

11 [a]Ex. 8:13

12 [1]Lit., *placed* [a]Ex. 8:30; 9:33; 10:18

14 [1]I.e., had a bad smell

15 [1]Lit., *made heavy* [a]Ex. 7:4

16 [1]Or, *lice*

17 [1]Or, *lice* [a]Ps. 105:31

18 [1]Or, *soothsayer priests* [2]Or, *lice* [a]Ex. 7:11, 12; 8:7; 9:11

19 [1]Or, *soothsayer priests* [2]Lit., *strong* [a]Ex. 7:5; 10:7

20 [1]Lit., *behold* [a]Ex. 9:13 [b]Ex. 2:5; 7:15 [c]Ex. 3:18; 4:23; 5:1, 3

22 [1]Lit., *standing* [2]Or, *I am the LORD in the midst of the earth* [a]Ex. 9:4, 6, 24; 10:23; 11:7 [b]Ex. 9:29; 19:5; 20:11

23 [1]Lit., *set a ransom*

there came [1]great swarms of insects
into the house of Pharaoh and the
houses of his servants and the land
was [a]laid waste because of the
swarms of insects in all the land of
Egypt.
25 And Pharaoh [a]called for Moses
and Aaron and said, "[b]Go, sacrifice
to your God within the land."
26 But Moses said, "It is not right
to do so, for we shall sacrifice to the
LORD our God [1]what is an abomination to the Egyptians. If we sacrifice
[1]what is an abomination to the
Egyptians before their eyes, will
they not then stone us?
27"We must go a [a]three days' journey into the wilderness and sacrifice
to the LORD our God as He [1]com-
mands us."
28 And Pharaoh said, "[a]I will let
you go, that you may sacrifice to the
LORD your God in the wilderness;
only you shall not go very far away.
[b]Make supplication for me."
29 Then Moses said, "Behold, I am
going out from you, and I shall make
supplication to the LORD that the
swarms of insects may depart from
Pharaoh, from his servants, and
from his people tomorrow; only do
not let Pharaoh [a]deal deceitfully
again in not letting the people go to
sacrifice to the LORD."
30 So Moses went out from Pharaoh and made supplication to the
LORD.
31 And the LORD did [1]as Moses
asked, and removed the swarms of
insects from Pharaoh, from his servants and from his people; not one
remained.
32 But Pharaoh [1]hardened his
heart this time also, and [a]he did not
let the people go.

CHAPTER 9

Egyptian Cattle Die

THEN the LORD said to Moses,
"Go to Pharaoh and speak to him,
'Thus says the LORD, the God of the
Hebrews, "[a]Let My people go, that
they may serve Me.
2"For if you refuse to let *them* go,
and [1]continue to hold them,
3 behold, the hand of the LORD
[1]will come *with* a very severe pestilence on your livestock which are in
the field, on the horses, on the donkeys, on the camels, on the herds,
and on the flocks.
4"[a]But the LORD will make a distinction between the livestock of Israel and the livestock of Egypt, so
that [b]nothing will die of all that belongs to the sons of Israel." ' "
5 And the LORD set a definite
time, saying, "Tomorrow the LORD
will do this thing in the land."
6 So the LORD did this thing on
the morrow, and [a]all the livestock of
Egypt died; [b]but of the livestock of
the sons of Israel, not one died.
7 And Pharaoh sent, and behold,
there was not even one of the livestock of Israel dead. But the heart of
Pharaoh was [1]hardened, and he did
not let the people go.

The Plague of Boils

8 Then the LORD said to Moses
and Aaron, "Take for yourselves
handfuls of soot from a kiln, and let
Moses throw it toward the sky in the
sight of Pharaoh.
9"And it will become fine dust
over all the land of Egypt, and will
become boils breaking out with
[a]sores on man and beast through all
the land of Egypt."
10 So they took soot from a kiln,
and stood before Pharaoh; and
Moses threw it toward the sky, and
it became boils breaking out with
sores on man and beast.
11 [a]And the magicians could not
stand before Moses because of the
boils, for the boils were on the [1]ma-
gicians [2]as well as on all the Egyptians.
12 And [a]the LORD [1]hardened Pharaoh's heart, and he did not listen to
them, just as the LORD had spoken
to Moses.
13 Then the LORD said to Moses,
"[a]Rise up early in the morning and
stand before Pharaoh and say to
him, 'Thus says the LORD, the God of
the Hebrews, "[b]Let My people go,
that they may serve Me.
14"For this time I will send all My
plagues [1]on you and your servants
and your people, so that you may
know that there is [a]no one like Me in
all the earth.
15"For *if by* now I had put forth My
hand and struck you and your people with pestilence, you would then
have been cut off from the earth.
16"But, indeed, [a]for this cause I
have allowed you to [1]remain, in order to show you My power, and in
order to proclaim My name through
all the earth.
17"Still you exalt yourself against
My people [1]by not letting them go.

The Plague of Hail

18"Behold, about this time tomorrow, [a]I will [1]send a very heavy hail,
such as has not been *seen* in Egypt
from the day it was founded [2]until
now.

24 [1]Lit., *heavy* [a]Ps. 78:45; 105:31

25 [a]Ex. 8:8; 9:27; 10:16 [b]Ex. 9:28; 10:8, 24; 12:31

26 [1]Lit., *the abomination of Egypt*

27 [1]Lit., *says to us* [a]Ex. 3:18; 5:3

28 [a]Ex. 8:8, 15, 29, 32 [b]Ex. 8:8

29 [a]Ex. 8:8, 15

31 [1]Lit., *according to the word of Moses*

32 [1]Lit., *made heavy* [a]Ex. 4:21; 8:8, 15

1 [a]Ex. 4:23; 8:1

2 [1]Lit., *still hold*

3 [1]Lit., *will be*

4 [a]Ex. 8:22 [b]Ex. 9:6

6 [a]Ex. 9:19, 20, 25 [b]Ex. 9:4

7 [1]Lit., *heavy* [a]Ex. 7:14; 8:32

9 [a]Rev. 16:2

11 [1]Or, *soothsayer priests* [2]Lit., *and on all* [a]Ex. 8:18

12 [1]Lit., *made strong* [a]Ex. 4:21

13 [a]Ex. 8:20 [b]Ex. 4:23

14 [1]Lit., *to your heart* [a]Ex. 8:10

16 [1]Lit., *stand* [a]Rom. 9:17

17 [1]Lit., *so as not to let*

18 [1]Lit., *cause to rain* [2]Lit., *and until now* [a]Ex. 9:23, 24

19“Now therefore send, bring
[a]your livestock and whatever you
have in the field to safety. [b]Every
man and beast that is found in the
field and is not brought home, when
the hail comes down on them, will
die.” ’ ”
20 [a]The one among the servants of
Pharaoh who [1]feared the word of
the LORD made his servants and his
livestock flee into the houses;
21 but he who [1]paid no regard to
the word of the LORD [2]left his servants and his livestock in the field.
22 Now the LORD said to Moses,
“Stretch out your hand toward the
sky, that [1a]hail may fall on all the
land of Egypt, on man and on beast
and on every plant of the field,
throughout the land of Egypt.”
23 And Moses stretched out his
staff toward the sky, and the LORD
[1]sent [2]thunder and hail, and fire ran
down to the earth. And [a]the LORD
rained hail on the land of Egypt.
24 So there was hail, and fire
[1]flashing continually in the midst of
the hail, very severe, such as had not
been in all the land of Egypt since it
became a nation.
25 And [a]the hail struck all that
was in the field through all the land
of Egypt, both man and beast; the
hail also struck every plant of the
field and shattered every tree of the
field.
26 [a]Only in the land of Goshen,
where the sons of Israel *were*, there
was no hail.
27 Then Pharaoh [1a]sent for Moses
and Aaron, and said to them, “[b]I
have sinned this time; the LORD is
the righteous one, and I and my people are the wicked ones.
28“[a]Make supplication to the
LORD, for there has been enough of
God’s [1]thunder and hail; and [b]I will
let you go, and you shall stay no
longer.”
29 And Moses said to him, “As
soon as I go out of the city, I will
spread out my [1]hands to the LORD;
the [2]thunder will cease, and there
will be hail no longer, that you may
know that [a]the earth is the LORD’s.
30“[a]But as for you and your servants, I know that you do not yet
[1]fear [2]the LORD God.”
31 (Now the flax and the barley
were [1]ruined, for the barley was in
the ear and the flax was in bud.
32 But the wheat and the spelt
were not [1]ruined, for they *ripen*
late.)
33 So Moses went out of the city
from Pharaoh, and spread out his
[1]hands to the LORD; and the [2]thun-
der and the hail ceased, and rain [3]no
longer poured on the earth.
34 But when Pharaoh saw that the
rain and the hail and the [1]thunder
had ceased, he sinned again and
[2]hardened his heart, he and his servants.
35 And Pharaoh’s heart was
[1]hardened, and he did not let the
sons of Israel go, just as the [a]LORD
had spoken through Moses.

CHAPTER 10

The Plague of Locusts

THEN the LORD said to Moses,
“Go to Pharaoh, for [a]I have [1]hard-
ened his heart and the heart of his
servants, that I may [2]perform these
signs of Mine [3]among them,
2 and [a]that you may tell in the
[1]hearing of your son, and of your
grandson, how I made a mockery of
the Egyptians, and how I [2]per-
formed My signs among them; [b]that
you may know that I am the LORD.”
3 And Moses and Aaron went to
Pharaoh and said to him, “Thus says
the LORD, the God of the Hebrews,
‘How long will you refuse to humble
yourself before Me? [a]Let My people
go, that they may serve Me.
4 ‘For if you refuse to let My people go, behold, tomorrow I will bring
locusts into your territory.
5 ‘And they shall cover the surface of the land, so that no one shall
be able to see the land. They shall
also eat the rest of what has escaped—what is left to you from the
hail—and they shall eat every tree
which sprouts for you out of the
field.
6 ‘Then your houses shall be
filled, and the houses of all your servants and the houses of all the Egyptians, *something* which neither your
fathers nor your grandfathers have
seen, from the day that they [1]came
upon the earth until this day.’ ” And
he turned and went out from Pharaoh.
7 And [a]Pharaoh’s servants said
to him, “How long will this man be
a snare to us? Let the men go, that
they may serve the LORD their God.
Do you not [1]realize that Egypt is destroyed?”
8 So Moses and Aaron [a]were
brought back to Pharaoh, and he
said to them, “[b]Go, serve the LORD
your God! [1]Who are the ones that
are going?”
9 And Moses said, “[a]We shall go
with our young and our old; with our

19 [a]Ex. 9:6 [b]Ex. 9:25

20 [1]Or, *revered* [a]Prov. 13:13

21 [1]Lit., *did not set his heart to* [2]Lit., *then left*

22 [1]Lit., *there may be hail* [a]Rev. 16:21

23 [1]Lit., *gave* [2]Lit., *sounds* [a]Gen. 19:24; Josh. 10:11; Is. 30:30; Ezek. 38:22; Rev. 8:7

24 [1]Lit., *taking hold of itself*

25 [a]Ex. 9:19; Ps. 78:47, 48; 105:32

26 [a]Ex. 8:22

27 [1]Lit., *sent and called* [a]Ex. 8:8 [b]Ex. 10:16, 17; 2 Chr. 12:6; Ps. 129:4

28 [1]Lit., *sounds* [a]Ex. 8:8 [b]Ex. 8:25; 10:8, 24

29 [1]Lit., *palms* [2]Lit., *sounds* [a]Ex. 8:22; 19:5; 20:11; Ps. 24:1

30 [1]Or, *reverence* [2]Lit., *before the LORD* [a]Ex. 8:29

31 [1]Lit., *smitten*

32 [1]Lit., *smitten*

33 [1]Lit., *palms* [2]Lit., *sounds* [3]Lit., *was not poured*

34 [1]Lit., *sounds* [2]Lit., *made heavy*

35 [1]Lit., *strong* [a]Ex. 4:21

1 [1]Lit., *made heavy* [2]Lit., *put* [3]Lit., *in his midst* [a]Ex. 4:21; 7:13

2 [1]Lit., *ears* [2]Lit., *put* [a]Ex. 12:26, 27; 13:8, 14, 15; Deut. 4:9; Ps. 44:1 [b]Ex. 7:5, 17

3 [a]Ex. 4:23

6 [1]Lit., *were*

7 [1]Lit., *know* [a]Ex. 7:5; 8:19; 12:33

8 [1]Lit., *Who and who are* [a]Ex. 8:8 [b]Ex. 8:25

9 [a]Ex. 12:37, 38

sons and our daughters, [b]with our
flocks and our herds we will go, for
we [1]must hold a feast to the LORD."
10 Then he said to them, "Thus
may the LORD be with you, [1]if ever I
let you and your little ones go! Take
heed, for evil is [2]in your mind.
11 "Not so! Go now, the men
among you, and serve the LORD, for
[1]that is what you desire." So [a]they
were driven out from Pharaoh's
presence.
12 Then the LORD said to Moses,
"[a]Stretch out your hand over the
land of Egypt for the locusts, that
they may come up on the land of
Egypt, and eat every plant of the
land, *even* all that the hail has left."
13 So Moses stretched out his staff
over the land of Egypt, and the LORD
directed an east wind on the land all
that day and all that night; and when
it was morning, the east wind
[1]brought the [a]locusts.
14 And [a]the locusts came up over
all the land of Egypt and settled in
all the territory of Egypt; *they were*
very [1]numerous. There had never
been so *many* [2]locusts, nor would
there be so *many* [3]again.
15 For they covered the surface of
the whole land, so that the land was
darkened; and they [a]ate every plant
of the land and all the fruit of the
trees that the hail had left. Thus
nothing green was left on tree or
plant of the field through all the land
of Egypt.
16 Then Pharaoh hurriedly [a]called
for Moses and Aaron, and he said,
"[b]I have sinned against the LORD
your God and against you.
17 "Now therefore, please forgive
my sin only this once, and [a]make
supplication to the LORD your God,
that He would only remove this
death from me."
18 And he went out from Pharaoh
and made supplication to the LORD.
19 So the LORD shifted *the wind* to
a very strong west wind which took
up the locusts and drove them into
the [1]Red Sea; not one locust was left
in all the territory of Egypt.
20 But [a]the LORD [1]hardened Pharaoh's heart, and he did not let the
sons of Israel go.

Darkness over the Land

21 Then the LORD said to Moses,
"Stretch out your hand toward the
sky, that there may be darkness
over the land of Egypt, even a darkness [a]which may be felt."
22 So Moses stretched out his
hand toward the sky, and there was
[a]thick darkness in all the land of
Egypt for three days.
23 They did not see one another,
nor did anyone rise from his place
for three days, [a]but all the sons of
Israel had light in their dwellings.
24 Then Pharaoh [a]called to Moses,
and said, "Go, serve the LORD; only
let your flocks and your herds be detained. Even your little ones may go
with you."
25 But Moses said, "You must also
[1]let us have sacrifices and burnt offerings, that we may [2]sacrifice *them*
to the LORD our God.
26 "[a]Therefore, our livestock, too,
will go with us; not a hoof will be left
behind, for we shall take some of
them to serve the LORD our God.
And until we arrive there, we ourselves do not know with what we
shall serve the LORD."
27 But [a]the LORD [1]hardened Pharaoh's heart, and he was not willing
to let them go.
28 Then Pharaoh said to him,
"[a]Get away from me! [1]Beware, do
not see my face again, for in the day
you see my face you shall die!"
29 And Moses said, "You are right;
[a]I shall never see your face again!"

CHAPTER 11

The Last Plague

NOW the LORD said to Moses,
"One more plague I will bring on
Pharaoh and on Egypt; [a]after that he
will let you go from here. When he
lets you go, he will surely drive you
out from here completely.
2 "Speak now in the [1]hearing of
the people that [a]each man ask from
his neighbor and each woman from
her neighbor for articles of silver
and articles of gold."
3 [a]And the LORD gave the people
favor in the sight of the Egyptians.
[b]Furthermore, the man Moses *him-*
self was [1]greatly esteemed in the
land of Egypt, *both* in the sight of
Pharaoh's servants and in the sight
of the people.
4 And Moses said, "Thus says the
LORD, 'About [a]midnight I am going
out into the midst of Egypt,
5 and [a]all the first-born in the
land of Egypt shall die, from the
first-born of the Pharaoh who sits on
his throne, even to the first-born of
the slave girl who is behind the millstones; all the first-born of the cattle
as well.
6 'Moreover, there shall be [a]a
great cry in all the land of Egypt,

9 [1]Lit., *have a feast* [b]Ex. 5:1; 10:26
10 [1]Lit., *when I* [2]Lit., *before your face*
11 [1]Lit., *you desire it* [a]Ex. 10:28
13 [1]Lit., *carried* [a]Ps. 78:46; 105:34
14 [1]Lit., *heavy* [2]Lit., *locusts like them before them* [3]Lit., *after them* [a]Joel 1:4, 7; 2:1-11
15 [a]Ex. 10:5
16 [a]Ex. 8:8 [b]Ex. 9:27
17 [a]Ex. 8:8, 28
19 [1]Lit., *Sea of Reeds*
20 [1]Lit., *made strong* [a]Ex. 4:21; 11:10
21 [a]Deut. 28:29
22 [a]Ps. 105:28
23 [a]Ex. 8:22
24 [a]Ex. 8:8, 25
25 [1]Lit., *give into our hand* [2]Lit., *make*
26 [a]Ex. 10:9
27 [1]Lit., *made strong* [a]Ex. 10:20
28 [1]Lit., *Take heed to yourself* [a]Ex. 10:11
29 [a]Ex. 11:8; Heb. 11:27
1 [a]Ex. 12:31, 33, 39
2 [1]Lit., *ears* [a]Ex. 3:22; 12:35, 36
3 [1]Lit., *very great* [a]Ex. 3:21; 12:36 [b]Deut. 34:10-12
4 [a]Ex. 12:29
5 [a]Ex. 12:12, 29; Ps. 78:51; 105:36; 135:8; 136:10
6 [a]Ex. 12:30

such as there has not been *before*
and such as shall never be again.
7 '[a]But against any of the sons of
Israel a dog shall not *even* [1]bark,
whether against man or beast, that
you may [2]understand how the LORD
makes a distinction between Egypt
and Israel.'
8"And [a]all these your servants
will come down to me and bow
themselves [1]before me, saying, 'Go
out, you and all the people who [2]fol-
low you,' and after that I will go
out." [b]And he went out from Pharaoh in hot anger.
9 Then the LORD said to Moses,
"[a]Pharaoh will not listen to you, so
that My wonders will be multiplied
in the land of Egypt."
10 And [a]Moses and Aaron performed all these wonders before
Pharaoh; yet the LORD [1]hardened
Pharaoh's heart, and he did not let
the sons of Israel go out of his land.

CHAPTER 12

The Passover Lamb

NOW the LORD said to Moses and
Aaron in the land of [1]Egypt,
2"[a]This month shall be the beginning of months for you; it is to be the
first month of the year to you.
3"Speak to all the congregation of
Israel, saying, 'On the tenth of this
month they are each one to take a
[1]lamb for themselves, according to
their fathers' households, a [1]lamb
for [2]each household.
4 'Now if the household is too
small for a [1]lamb, then he and his
neighbor nearest to his house are to
take one according to the [2]number
of persons *in them;* according to
[3]what each man should eat, you are
to [4]divide the lamb.
5 'Your [1]lamb shall be [a]an unblemished male a year old; you may
take it from the sheep or from the
goats.
6 'And [1]you shall keep it until the
[a]fourteenth day of the same month,
then the whole assembly of the congregation of Israel is to kill it [2b]at
twilight.
7 '[a]Moreover, they shall take
some of the blood and put it on the
two doorposts and on the lintel [1]of
the houses in which they eat it.
8 'And they shall eat the flesh
[a]that *same* night, [b]roasted with fire,
and they shall eat it with [c]unleav-
ened bread [1d]and bitter herbs.
9 'Do not eat any of it raw or
boiled at all with water, but rather
[a]roasted with fire, *both* its head and
its legs along with [b]its entrails.
10 '[a]And you shall not leave any of
it over until morning, but whatever
is left of it until morning, you shall
burn with fire.
11 'Now you shall eat it in this
manner: *with* your loins girded,
your sandals on your feet, and your
staff in your hand; and you shall eat
it in haste—it is [a]the LORD's Passover.
12 'For I will go through the land of
Egypt on that night, and will strike
down all the first-born in the land of
Egypt, both man and beast; and
[a]against all the gods of Egypt I will
execute judgments—I am the LORD.
13 'And the blood shall be a sign
for you on the houses where you
[1]live; and when I see the blood I will
pass over you, and no plague will
befall you [2]to destroy *you* when I
strike the land of Egypt.

Feast of Unleavened Bread

14 'Now [a]this day will be [b]a memorial to you, and you shall celebrate it
as a feast to the LORD; throughout
your generations you are to celebrate it *as* [c]a [1]permanent ordinance.
15 '[a]Seven days you shall eat unleavened bread, but on the first day
you shall [1]remove leaven from your
houses; for whoever eats anything
leavened from the first day until the
seventh day, [b]that [2]person shall be
cut off from Israel.
16 'And [a]on the first day you shall
have a holy assembly, and *another*
holy assembly on the seventh day;
no work at all shall be done on them,
except what must be eaten [1]by every person, that alone may be [2]pre-
pared by you.
17 'You shall also observe the
Feast of Unleavened Bread, for on
this [a]very day I brought your hosts
out of the land of Egypt; therefore
you shall observe this day throughout your generations as [b]a [1]perma-
nent ordinance.
18 '[a]In the first *month,* on the fourteenth day of the month at evening,
you shall eat unleavened bread, until the twenty-first day of the month
at evening.
19 '[a]Seven days there shall be no
leaven found in your houses; for
whoever eats what is leavened, that
[1]person shall be cut off from the
congregation of Israel, whether *he is*
an alien or a native of the land.
20 'You shall not eat anything leavened; in all your dwellings you shall
eat unleavened bread.' "
21 Then [a]Moses called for all the
elders of Israel, and said to them,

7 [1]Lit., *sharpen his tongue* [2]Lit., *know* [a]Ex. 8:22
8 [1]Lit., *to* [2]Lit., *are at your feet* [a]Ex. 12:31-33 [b]Heb. 11:27
9 [a]Ex. 7:4
10 [1]Lit., *made strong* [a]Ex. 4:21; 10:20, 27
1 [1]Lit., *Egypt, saying*
2 [a]Ex. 13:4; 23:15; 34:18; Deut. 16:1
3 [1]Or, *kid* [2]Lit., *the*
4 [1]Or, *kid* [2]Or, *amount* [3]Lit., *each man's eating* [4]Lit., *compute for*
5 [1]Or, *kid* [a]Lev. 22:18-20
6 [1]Lit., *it shall be to you for a guarding* [2]Lit., *between the two evenings* [a]Ex. 12:14, 17; Lev. 23:5; Num. 9:1-3, 11 [b]Deut. 16:4, 6
7 [1]Lit., *upon* [a]Ex. 12:22
8 [1]Lit., *in addition to* [a]Ex. 34:25; Num. 9:12 [b]Deut. 16:7 [c]Deut. 16:3, 4 [d]Num. 9:11
9 [a]Ex. 12:8 [b]Ex. 29:13, 17, 22
10 [a]Ex. 16:19; 23:18; 34:25
11 [a]Ex. 12:13, 21, 27, 43
12 [a]Num. 33:4
13 [1]Lit., *are* [2]Lit., *for destruction*
14 [1]Or, *eternal* [a]Ex. 12:6 [b]Ex. 13:9 [c]Ex. 12:17, 24; 13:10
15 [1]Lit., *cause to cease* [2]Lit., *soul* [a]Ex. 23:15; 34:18; Deut. 16:3 [b]Ex. 12:19
16 [1]Lit., *pertaining to* [2]Lit., *done* [a]Lev. 23:7, 8
17 [1]Or, *eternal* [a]Ex. 12:41 [b]Ex. 12:14; 13:3, 10
18 [a]Ex. 12:2; Lev. 23:5-8; Num. 28:16-25
19 [1]Lit., *soul* [a]Ex. 12:15
21 [a]Heb. 11:28

“[1]Go and take for yourselves [2]lambs
according to your families, and slay
[b]the Passover *lamb*.
22“[a]And you shall take a bunch of
hyssop and dip it in the blood which
is in the basin, and [1]apply some of
the blood that is in the basin to the
lintel and the two doorposts; and
none of you shall go outside the
door of his house until morning.

A Memorial of Redemption

23“For [a]the LORD will pass through
to smite the Egyptians; and when
He sees the blood on the lintel and
on the two doorposts, the LORD will
pass over the door and will not allow the destroyer to come in to your
houses to smite *you*.
24“And [a]you shall observe this
event as an ordinance for you and
your children forever.
25“And it will come about when
you enter the land which the LORD
will give you, as He has [1]promised,
that you shall observe this [2]rite.
26“[a]And it will come about when
your children will say to you,
‘[1]What does this rite mean to you?’
27 that you shall say, ‘It is a Passover sacrifice to [a]the LORD [1]who
passed over the houses of the sons
of Israel in Egypt when He smote
the Egyptians, but [2]spared our
homes.’ ” [b]And the people bowed
low and worshiped.
28 Then the sons of Israel went
and did *so;* just as the LORD had
commanded Moses and Aaron, so
they did.
29 Now it came about at [a]midnight
that the LORD struck all [b]the first-
born in the land of Egypt, from the
first-born of Pharaoh who sat on his
throne to the first-born of the captive who was in the dungeon, and all
the first-born of [c]cattle.
30 And Pharaoh arose in the night,
he and all his servants and all the
Egyptians; and there was [a]a great
cry in Egypt, for there was no home
where there was not someone dead.
31 Then [a]he called for Moses and
Aaron at night and said, “Rise up,
[b]get out from among my people,
both you and the sons of Israel; and
go, [1]worship the LORD, as you have
said.
32“Take [a]both your flocks and
your herds, as you have said, and go,
and bless me also.”

Exodus of Israel

33 And [a]the Egyptians urged the
people, to send them out of the land
in haste, for they said, “We shall all
be dead.”
34 So the people took [a]their dough
before it was leavened, *with* their
kneading bowls bound up in the
clothes on their shoulders.
35 [a]Now the sons of Israel had
done according to the word of
Moses, for they had requested from
the Egyptians articles of silver and
articles of gold, and clothing;
36 and the LORD had given the
people favor in the sight of the
Egyptians, so that they let them
have their request. Thus they [a]plun-
dered the Egyptians.
37 Now the sons of Israel journeyed from [a]Rameses to Succoth,
about [b]six hundred thousand men
on foot, aside from children.
38 And a [a]mixed multitude also
went up with them, [1]along with
flocks and herds, a [b]very large number of livestock.
39 And they baked the dough
which they had brought out of
Egypt into cakes of unleavened
bread. For it had not become leavened, since they were [a]driven out of
Egypt and could not delay, nor had
they [1]prepared any provisions for
themselves.
40 Now the time [1]that the sons of
Israel lived in Egypt was [a]four hundred and thirty years.
41 And it came about at the end of
four hundred and thirty years, [1]to
[a]the very day, that [b]all the hosts of
the LORD went out from the land of
Egypt.

Ordinance of the Passover

42 [a]It is a night [1]to be observed for
the LORD for having brought them
out from the land of Egypt; this
night is for the LORD, [1]to be observed [2]by all the sons of Israel
throughout their generations.
43 And the LORD said to Moses
and Aaron, “This is the ordinance of
[a]the Passover: no [1b]foreigner is to
eat of it;
44 but every man's [a]slave purchased with money, after you have
circumcised him, then he may eat of
it.
45“A sojourner or a hired servant
shall not eat of it.
46“It is to be eaten in a single
house; you are not to bring forth any
of the flesh outside of the house,
[a]nor are you to break any bone of it.
47“[a]All the congregation of Israel
are to [1]celebrate this.
48“But if a [1]stranger sojourns with
you, and [2]celebrates the Passover to
the LORD, let all his males be circumcised, and then let him come
near to [3]celebrate it; and he shall be

21 [1]Lit., *Draw out* [2]Lit., *sheep* [b]Ex. 12:11
22 [1]Lit., *cause to touch* [a]Ex. 12:7
23 [a]Ex. 11:4; 12:12, 13
24 [a]Ex. 12:14, 17; 13:5, 10
25 [1]Lit., *spoken* [2]Lit., *service*
26 [1]Lit., *What is this service to you?* [a]Ex. 10:2; 13:14, 15; Josh. 4:6
27 [1]Lit., *because He* [2]Lit., *delivered* [a]Ex. 12:11 [b]Ex. 4:31
29 [a]Ex. 11:4, 5 [b]Ex. 4:23; Ps. 78:51; 105:36 [c]Ex. 9:6
30 [a]Ex. 11:6
31 [1]Or, *serve* [a]Ex. 8:8 [b]Ex. 8:25
32 [a]Ex. 10:9, 26
33 [a]Ex. 10:7; 11:1; 12:39; Ps. 105:38
34 [a]Ex. 12:39
35 [a]Ex. 3:21, 22; 11:2, 3; Ps. 105:37
36 [a]Ex. 3:22
37 [a]Num. 33:3, 4 [b]Ex. 38:26; Num. 1:46; 2:32; 11:21; 26:51
38 [1]Lit., *and* [a]Num. 11:4 [b]Ex. 17:3; Num. 20:19; 32:1; Deut. 3:19
39 [1]Lit., *made* [a]Ex. 11:1; 12:31-33
40 [1]Or, *of the sons of Israel who dwelt* [a]Gen. 15:13, 16; Acts 7:6; Gal. 3:17
41 [1]Lit., *that it happened on this very day* [a]Ex. 12:17 [b]Ex. 3:8, 10; 6:6
42 [1]Or, *of vigil* [2]Lit., *to the sons* [a]Ex. 13:10; 34:18; Deut. 16:1
43 [1]Lit., *son of a stranger* [a]Ex. 12:11 [b]Ex. 12:48
44 [a]Gen. 17:12, 13; Lev. 22:11
46 [a]Num. 9:12; John 19:33, 36
47 [1]Lit., *do* [a]Num. 9:13, 14
48 [1]Lit., *sojourner* [2]Lit., *does* [3]Lit., *do*

like a native of the land. But no uncircumcised person may eat of it.
49"[1][a]The same law shall [2]apply to
the native as to the [3]stranger who
sojourns among you."
50 Then all the sons of Israel did
so; they did just as the LORD had
commanded Moses and Aaron.
51 And it came about on that same
day that [a]the LORD brought the sons
of Israel out of the land of Egypt [1]by
their hosts.

CHAPTER 13

Consecration of the First-born

THEN the LORD spoke to Moses,
saying,
2"[a]Sanctify to Me every first-
born, the first [1]offspring of every
womb among the sons of Israel,
both of man and beast; it belongs to
Me."
3 And Moses said to the people,
"Remember this day in which you
went out from Egypt, from the
house of [1]slavery; for [a]by [2]a powerful hand the LORD brought you out
from this place. [b]And nothing leavened shall be eaten.
4"On this day in the [a]month of
Abib, you are about to go forth.
5"And it shall be when the LORD
[a]brings you to the land of the Canaanite, the Hittite, the Amorite, the
Hivite and the Jebusite, which He
swore to your fathers to give you, a
land flowing with milk and honey,
[b]that you shall [1]observe this rite in
this month.
6"For [a]seven days you shall eat
unleavened bread, and on the seventh day there shall be a feast to the
LORD.
7"Unleavened bread shall be eat-
en throughout the seven days; and
nothing leavened shall be seen
[1]among you, nor shall any leaven be
seen [1]among you in all your borders.
8"[a]And you shall tell your son on
that day, saying, 'It is because of
what the LORD did for me when I
came out of Egypt.'
9"And [a]it shall [1]serve as a sign to
you on your hand, and as a reminder
[2]on your forehead, that the law of
the LORD may be in your mouth; for
with [b]a powerful hand the LORD
brought you out of Egypt.
10"Therefore, you shall [a]keep this
ordinance at its appointed time
from [1]year to year.
11"Now it shall come about when
[a]the LORD brings you to the land of
the Canaanite, as He swore to you
and to your fathers, and gives it to
you,
12 that [a]you shall [1]devote to the
LORD the first [2]offspring of every
womb, and [3]the first offspring of every beast that you own; the males
belong to the LORD.
13"But [a]every first [1]offspring of a
donkey you shall redeem with a
lamb, but if you do not redeem *it,*
then you shall break its neck; and
every first-born of man among your
sons you shall redeem.
14"[a]And it shall be when your son
asks you in time to come, saying,
'What is this?' then you shall say to
him, '[b]With a [1]powerful hand the
LORD brought us out of Egypt, from
the house of [2]slavery.
15 'And it came about, when Pharaoh was stubborn about letting us
go, that the LORD killed every first-
born in the land of Egypt, both the
first-born of man and the first-born
of beast. Therefore, I sacrifice to the
LORD the males, the first [1]offspring
of every womb, but every first-born
of my sons I redeem.'
16"So [a]it shall [1]serve as a sign on
your hand, and as [2]phylacteries [3]on
your forehead, for with a [4]powerful
hand the LORD brought us out of
Egypt."

God Leads the People

17 Now it came about when Pharaoh had let the people go, that God
did not lead them by the way of the
land of the Philistines, even though
it was near; for God said, "[a]Lest the
people change their minds when
they see war, and they return to
Egypt."
18 Hence God led the people
around by the way of the wilderness
to the [1]Red Sea; and the sons of Israel went up [a]in martial array from
the land of Egypt.
19 And Moses took [a]the bones of
Joseph with him, for he had made
the sons of Israel solemnly swear,
saying, "God shall surely [1]take care
of you; and you shall carry my bones
from here with you."
20 Then they set out from [a]Suc-
coth and camped in Etham on the
edge of the wilderness.
21 And [a]the LORD was going before them in a pillar of cloud by day
to lead them on the way, and in a
pillar of fire by night to give them
light, that they might [1]travel by day
and by night.
22 [1]He did not take away the pillar
of cloud by day, nor the pillar of fire
by night, from before the people.

49 [1]Lit., *One law* [2]Lit., *be* [3]Lit., *sojourner* [a]Lev. 24:22; Num. 15:15, 16, 29
51 [1]Lit., *according to* [a]Ex. 12:41
2 [1]Lit., *opening* [a]Ex. 13:12, 13, 15; 22:29; Luke 2:23
3 [1]Lit., *slaves* [2]Lit., *strength of hand* [a]Ex. 3:20; 6:1 [b]Ex. 12:19
4 [a]Ex. 12:22
5 [1]Lit., *serve this service* [a]Ex. 3:8, 17; Josh. 24:11 [b]Ex. 12:25
6 [a]Ex. 12:15-20
7 [1]Lit., *to*
8 [a]Ex. 10:2; 13:14
9 [1]Lit., *be for* [2]Lit., *between your eyes* [a]Ex. 12:14; 13:16; Deut. 6:8; 11:18 [b]Ex. 13:3
10 [1]Lit., *days to days* [a]Ex. 12:24, 25; 13:5
11 [a]Ex. 13:5
12 [1]Lit., *cause to pass over* [2]Lit., *opening* [3]Lit., *every issue the offspring of a beast* [a]Ex. 13:1, 2
13 [1]Lit., *opening* [a]Ex. 34:20
14 [1]Lit., *strength of hand* [2]Lit., *slaves* [a]Ex. 10:2; 12:26, 27; 13:8; Deut. 6:20 [b]Ex. 13:3, 9
15 [1]Lit., *opening*
16 [1]Lit., *be for* [2]Or, *frontlet-bands* [3]Lit., *between your eyes* [4]Lit., *strength of hand* [a]Ex. 13:9
17 [a]Ex. 14:11, 12; Num. 14:1-4; Deut. 17:16
18 [1]Lit., *Sea of Reeds* [a]Josh. 1:14; 4:12, 13
19 [1]Lit., *visit* [a]Gen. 50:24, 25; Josh. 24:32; Acts 7:15, 16
20 [a]Ex. 12:37; Num. 33:6
21 [1]Lit., *go* [a]Ex. 14:19, 24; 33:9, 10; Ps. 78:14; 99:7; 105:39; 1 Cor. 10:1
22 [1]Or, *the pillar of cloud by day and the pillar of fire by night did not depart*

CHAPTER 14

Pharaoh in Pursuit

NOW the LORD spoke to Moses, saying,

2 "Tell the sons of Israel to turn back and camp before [a]Pi-hahiroth, between Migdol and the sea; you shall camp in front of Baal-zephon, opposite it, by the sea.

3 "For Pharaoh will say of the sons of Israel, 'They are wandering aimlessly in the land; the wilderness has shut them in.'

4 "Thus [a]I will [1]harden Pharaoh's heart, and [b]he will chase after them; and I will be honored through Pharaoh and all his army, and [c]the Egyptians will know that I am the LORD." And they did so.

5 When the king of Egypt was told that the people had fled, [1]Pharaoh and his servants had a change of heart toward the people, and they said, "What is this we have done, that we have let Israel go from serving us?"

6 So he made his chariot ready and took his people with him;

7 and he took six hundred select chariots, and all the *other* chariots of Egypt with officers over all of them.

8 And [a]the LORD [1]hardened the heart of Pharaoh, king of Egypt, and he chased after the sons of Israel as the sons of Israel were going out [2b]boldly.

9 Then the Egyptians chased after them *with* all the horses *and* chariots of Pharaoh, his horsemen and his army, and they overtook them camping by the sea, [a]beside Pi-hahiroth, in front of Baal-zephon.

10 And as Pharaoh drew near, the sons of Israel [1]looked, and behold, the Egyptians were marching after them, and they became very frightened; [a]so the sons of Israel cried out to the LORD.

11 Then [a]they said to Moses, "Is it because there were no graves in Egypt that you have taken us away to die in the wilderness? Why have you dealt with us in this way, [1]bringing us out of Egypt?

12 "Is this not the word that we spoke to you in Egypt, saying, '[1]Leave us alone that we may serve the Egyptians'? For it would have been better for us to serve the Egyptians than to die in the wilderness."

The Sea Is Divided

13 But Moses said to the people, "[a]Do not fear! [1]Stand by and see [b]the salvation of the LORD which He will accomplish for you today; for the Egyptians whom you have seen today, you will never see them again forever.

14 "[a]The LORD will fight for you while [b]you keep silent."

15 Then the LORD said to Moses, "Why are you crying out to me? Tell the sons of Israel to go forward.

16 "And as for you, lift up [a]your staff and stretch out your hand over the sea and divide it, and the sons of Israel shall [1]go through the midst of the sea on dry land.

17 "And as for Me, behold, [a]I will [1]harden the hearts of the Egyptians so that they will go in after them; and I will be honored through Pharaoh and all his army, through his chariots and his horsemen.

18 "[a]Then the Egyptians will know that I am the LORD, when I am honored through Pharaoh, through his chariots and his horsemen."

19 And [a]the angel of God, who had been going before the camp of Israel, moved and went behind them; and the pillar of cloud moved from before them and stood behind them.

20 So it came between the camp of Egypt and the camp of Israel; and there was the cloud [1]along with the darkness, yet it gave light at night. Thus the one did not come near the other all night.

21 [a]Then Moses stretched out his hand over the sea; and the LORD [1]swept the sea *back* by a strong east wind all night, and turned the sea into [b]dry land, so [c]the waters were divided.

22 [a]And the sons of Israel [1]went through the midst of the sea on the dry land, and [b]the waters *were like* a wall to them on their right hand and on their left.

23 Then [a]the Egyptians took up the pursuit, and all Pharaoh's horses, his chariots and his horsemen went in after them into the midst of the sea.

24 And it came about at the morning watch, that [a]the LORD looked down on the [1]army of the Egyptians [2]through the pillar of fire and cloud and brought the [1]army of the Egyptians into confusion.

25 And He [1]caused their chariot wheels to swerve, and He made them drive with difficulty; so the Egyptians said, "Let [2]us flee from Israel, [a]for the LORD is fighting for them against the Egyptians."

26 Then the LORD said to Moses, "[a]Stretch out your hand over the sea

2 [a]Num. 33:7

4 [1]Lit., *make strong* [a]Ex. 4:21; 14:17 [b]Ex. 14:17, 23 [c]Ex. 7:5; 14:25

5 [1]Lit., *the heart of Pharaoh . . . was changed*

8 [1]Lit., *made strong* [2]Lit., *with a high hand* [a]Ex. 14:4 [b]Num. 33:3; Acts 13:17

9 [a]Ex. 14:2

10 [1]Lit., *lifted up their eyes* [a]Neh. 9:9

11 [1]Lit., *so as to bring* [a]Ex. 5:21; 15:24; 16:2; Ps. 106:7, 8

12 [1]Lit., *Cease from us*

13 [1]Or, *Take your stand* [a]Gen. 15:1; 46:3; Ex. 20:20 [b]Ex. 14:30; 15:2

14 [a]Ex. 15:3; Deut. 1:30; 3:22 [b]Is. 30:15

16 [1]Lit., *enter the* [a]Ex. 4:17, 20; 17:5, 6; Num. 20:8, 9, 11; Is. 10:26

17 [1]Lit., *make strong* [a]Ex. 14:4

18 [a]Ex. 14:25

19 [a]Ex. 13:21, 22

20 [1]Lit., *and the darkness*

21 [1]Lit., *caused to go* [a]Ex. 7:19; 14:16 [b]Ps. 106:9; 136:13, 14 [c]Ps. 78:13; 114:3, 5; Is. 63:12, 13

22 [1]Lit., *entered the* [a]Josh. 3:17; 4:22; Neh. 9:11; Heb. 11:29 [b]Ex. 14:29; 15:8

23 [a]Ex. 14:4, 17

24 [1]Lit., *camp* [2]Or, *in* [a]Ex. 13:21

25 [1]Or, *removed* [2]Lit., *me* [a]Ex. 14:4, 18

26 [a]Ex. 14:16

so that the waters may come back
over the Egyptians, over their chariots and their horsemen."
27 So Moses stretched out his
hand over the sea, and the sea returned to its normal state at daybreak, while the Egyptians were
fleeing [1]right into it; then the LORD
[2a]overthrew the Egyptians in the
midst of the sea.
28 And the waters returned and
covered the chariots and the horsemen, [1]even Pharaoh's entire army
that had gone into the sea after
them; [a]not even one of them remained.
29 But the sons of Israel walked on
[a]dry land through the midst of the
sea, and the waters *were like* a wall
to them on their right hand and on
their left.
30 [a]Thus the LORD saved Israel
that day from the hand of the Egyptians, and Israel saw the Egyptians
dead on the seashore.
31 And when Israel saw the great
[1]power which the LORD had [2]used
against the Egyptians, the people
[3]feared the LORD, and [a]they believed
in the LORD and in His servant
Moses.

CHAPTER 15

The Song of Moses and Israel

[a]

THEN Moses and the sons of Israel
sang this song to the LORD, [1]and
said,
"[2b]I will sing to the LORD, for
He [3]is highly exalted;
[c]The horse and its rider He has
hurled into the sea.
2 "[1a]The LORD is my strength and
song,
And He has become my salvation;
[b]This is my God, and I will
praise Him;
[c]My father's God, and I will
extol Him.
3 "[a]The LORD is a warrior;
[1b]The LORD is His name.
4 "[a]Pharaoh's chariots and his
army He has cast into the
sea;
And the choicest of his officers
are [1]drowned in the [2]Red
Sea.
5 "The deeps cover them;
[a]They went down into the
depths like a stone.
6 "[a]Thy right hand, O LORD, is
majestic in power,
[b]Thy right hand, O LORD, shatters the enemy.
7 "And in the greatness of Thine
[1]excellence Thou [a]dost overthrow those who rise up
against Thee;
[b]Thou dost send forth Thy
burning anger, *and* it consumes them as chaff.
8 "[a]And at the blast of Thy nostrils the waters were piled
up,
[b]The flowing waters stood up
like a heap;
The deeps were congealed in
the heart of the sea.
9 "[a]The enemy said, 'I will pursue, I will overtake, I will divide the spoil;
My [1]desire shall be [2]gratified
against them;
I will draw out my sword, my
hand shall [3]destroy them.'
10 "[a]Thou didst blow with Thy
wind, the sea covered them;
[b]They sank like lead in the
[1]mighty waters.
11 "[a]Who is like Thee among the
gods, O LORD?
Who is like Thee, [b]majestic in
holiness,
[c]Awesome in praises, [d]work-
ing wonders?
12 "[a]Thou didst stretch out Thy
right hand,
The earth swallowed them.
13 "In Thy lovingkindness Thou
hast [a]led the people whom
Thou hast [b]redeemed;
In Thy strength Thou hast
guided *them* [c]to Thy holy
habitation.
14 "[a]The peoples have heard, they
tremble;
Anguish has gripped the inhabitants of Philistia.
15 "Then the [a]chiefs of Edom were
dismayed;
[b]The leaders of Moab, trembling grips them;
[c]All the inhabitants of Canaan
have melted away.
16 "[a]Terror and dread fall upon
them;
[b]By the greatness of Thine arm
they are motionless as stone;
Until Thy people pass over, O
LORD,
Until the people pass over
whom Thou [c]hast purchased.
17 "[a]Thou wilt bring them and
[b]plant them in [c]the mountain
of Thine inheritance,
[d]The place, O LORD, which
Thou hast made for Thy
dwelling,

27 [1]Lit., *to meet it* [2]Lit., *shook off* [a]Ex. 15:1, 7
28 [1]Lit., *in respect to* [a]Ps. 78:53; 106:11
29 [a]Ex. 14:22; Ps. 66:6; Is. 11:15
30 [a]Ex. 14:13; Ps. 106:8, 10, 21, 22; Is. 63:8, 11
31 [1]Lit., *hand* [2]Lit., *done* [3]Or, *revered* [a]Ps. 106:12
1 [1]Lit., *and said, saying* [2]Or, *"Let me sing* [3]Or, *triumphed gloriously* [a]Ps. 106:12; Rev. 15:3 [b]Is. 12:5; 42:10-12 [c]Jer. 51:21
2 [1]Heb., *YAH* [a]Is. 12:2 [b]Ps. 48:14 [c]Ex. 3:6, 15, 16
3 [1]YHWH, usually rendered LORD [a]Ex. 14:14 [b]Ex. 3:15; 6:2, 7, 8; Ps. 24:8
4 [1]Lit., *sunk* [2]Lit., *Sea of Reeds* [a]Ex. 14:6, 7, 17, 28
5 [a]Ex. 14:10; Neh. 9:11
6 [a]Ex. 3:20; 6:1 [b]Ps. 118:15, 16
7 [1]Or, *exaltation* [a]Ex. 14:27 [b]Ps. 78:49, 50
8 [a]Ex. 14:22, 29 [b]Ps. 78:13
9 [1]Lit., *soul* [2]Lit., *be filled with them* [3]Or, *dispossess, bring to ruin* [a]Ex. 14:5, 8, 9
10 [1]Or, *majestic* [a]Ex. 14:27, 28 [b]Ex. 15:5
11 [a]Ex. 8:10; 9:14; Deut. 3:24; Ps. 71:19; Mic. 7:18 [b]Is. 6:3; Rev. 4:8 [c]Ps. 22:23 [d]Ps. 72:18; 136:4
12 [a]Ex. 15:6
13 [a]Neh. 9:12; Ps. 77:20 [b]Ex. 15:16; Ps. 77:15 [c]Ex. 15:17; Ps. 78:54
14 [a]Deut. 2:25; Hab. 3:7
15 [a]Gen. 36:15 [b]Num. 22:3, 4; Ps. 114:5, 7 [c]Josh. 2:9, 11, 24
16 [a]Ex. 23:27 [b]Ex. 15:5, 6 [c]Ex. 15:13; Ps. 74:2
17 [a]Ex. 23:20; 32:34 [b]Ps. 44:2; 80:8, 15 [c]Ps. 2:6; 78:54, 68 [d]Ps. 68:16; 76:2; 132:13, 14

[e]The sanctuary, O LORD, which Thy hands have established.
18 "[a]The LORD shall reign forever and ever."

19 [a]For the horses of Pharaoh with his chariots and his horsemen went into the sea, and the LORD brought back the waters of the sea on them; but the sons of Israel walked on [b]dry land through the midst of the sea.

20 And [a]Miriam the prophetess, Aaron's sister, took the [b]timbrel in her hand, and all the women went out after her with timbrels and with [1c]dancing.

21 And Miriam answered them,
"[a]Sing to the LORD, for He [1]is highly exalted;
The horse and his rider He has hurled into the sea."

The LORD Provides Water

22 [a]Then Moses [1]led Israel from the [2]Red Sea, and they went out into [b]the wilderness of [c]Shur; and they went three days in the wilderness and found no water.

23 And when they came to [a]Marah, they could not drink the waters [1]of Marah, for they were [2]bitter; therefore it was named [3]Marah.

24 So the people [a]grumbled at Moses, saying, "What shall we drink?"

25 Then he [a]cried out to the LORD, and the LORD showed him [b]a tree; and he threw *it* into the waters, and the waters became sweet. There He made for them a statute and regulation, and there He [c]tested them.

26 And He said, "[a]If you will give earnest heed to the voice of the LORD your God, and do what is right in His sight, and give ear [b]to His commandments, and keep all His statutes, [c]I will put none of the diseases on you which I have put on the Egyptians; for I, [d]the LORD, am your healer."

27 Then they came to [a]Elim where there *were* twelve springs of water and seventy date palms, and they camped there beside the waters.

CHAPTER 16

The LORD Provides Manna

THEN they set out from Elim, and all the congregation of the sons of Israel came to the wilderness of [a]Sin, which is between Elim and Sinai, on [b]the fifteenth day of the second month after their departure from the land of Egypt.

2 And the whole congregation of the sons of Israel [a]grumbled against Moses and Aaron in the wilderness.

3 And the sons of Israel said to them, "[a]Would that we had died by the LORD's hand in the land of Egypt, [b]when we sat by the pots of [1]meat, when we ate bread to the full; for you have brought us out into this wilderness to kill this whole assembly with hunger."

4 Then the LORD said to Moses, "Behold, [a]I will rain bread from heaven for you; and the people shall go out and gather a day's portion every day, that I may [b]test them, whether or not they will walk in My [1]instruction.

5 "And it will come about [a]on the sixth day, when they prepare what they bring in, it will be twice as much as they gather daily."

6 So Moses and Aaron said to all the sons of Israel, "At evening [1]you will know that the LORD has brought you out of the land of Egypt;

7 and in the morning [1]you will see [a]the glory of the LORD, for [b]He hears your grumblings against the LORD; and [c]what are we, that you grumble against us?"

The LORD Provides Meat

8 And Moses said, "*This will happen* when the LORD gives you [1]meat to eat in the evening, and bread to the full in the morning; for the LORD hears your grumblings which you grumble against Him. And what are we? Your grumblings are not against us but against the LORD."

9 Then Moses said to Aaron, "Say to all the congregation of the sons of Israel, '[a]Come near before the LORD, for He has heard your grumblings.' "

10 And it came about as Aaron spoke to the whole congregation of the sons of Israel, that they [1]looked toward the wilderness, and behold, [a]the glory of the LORD appeared in the cloud.

11 And the LORD spoke to Moses, saying,

12 "I have heard the grumblings of the sons of Israel; speak to them, saying, '[1]At twilight you shall eat [2]meat, and in the morning you shall be filled with bread; and you shall know that I am the LORD your God.' "

13 So it came about at evening that [a]the quails came up and covered the camp, and in the morning there was a layer of dew around the camp.

---

17 [e]Ps. 78:69
18 [a]Ps. 10:16; 29:10
19 [a]Ex. 14:23, 28 [b]Ex. 14:22, 29
20 [1]Lit., *dances* [a]Ex. 2:4; 6:20; Num. 26:59 [b]Ps. 81:2; 149:3 [c]Ps. 30:11; 150:4
21 [1]Or, *has triumphed gloriously* [a]Ex. 15:1
22 [1]Lit., *caused Israel to journey* [2]Lit., *Sea of Reeds* [a]Ps. 77:20; 78:52, 53 [b]Num. 33:8 [c]Gen. 16:7; 20:1
23 [1]Lit., *from* [2]Heb., *Marim* [3]I.e., Bitterness [a]Num. 33:8
24 [a]Ex. 14:11; Ps. 106:13
25 [a]Ex. 14:10 [b]Ezek. 47:7, 8 [c]Ex. 16:4
26 [a]Ex. 19:5, 6 [b]Ex. 20:2-17 [c]Deut. 7:15; 28:58, 60 [d]Deut. 32:39; Ps. 103:3
27 [a]Num. 33:9
1 [a]Num. 33:10, 11 [b]Ex. 12:6, 51; 19:1
2 [a]Ex. 14:11; 1 Cor. 10:10
3 [1]Or, *flesh* [a]Ex. 17:3; Num. 14:2, 3; 20:3 [b]Num. 11:4, 5
4 [1]Or, *law* [a]John 6:31; Neh. 9:15; Ps. 78:23-25; 105:40; 1 Cor. 10:3 [b]Ex. 15:25; Deut. 8:2, 16
5 [a]Ex. 16:22
6 [1]Lit., *and you*
7 [1]Lit., *and you* [a]Ex. 16:12 [b]Num. 14:27; 17:5 [c]Num. 16:11
8 [1]Or, *flesh*
9 [a]Num. 16:16
10 [1]Lit., *turned* [a]Ex. 16:7; Num. 16:19
12 [1]Lit., *Between the two evenings* [2]Or, *flesh*
13 [a]Num. 11:31; Ps. 78:27-29; 105:40

14 [a]When the layer of dew [1]evap-
orated, behold, on the [2]surface of
the wilderness [b]there was a fine
flake-like thing, fine as the hoarfrost
on the ground.
15 When the sons of Israel saw *it*,
they said to one another, "[1]What is
it?" For they did not know what it
was. And Moses said to them, "[a]It is
the bread which the LORD has given
you to eat.
16"This is [1]what the LORD has
commanded, 'Gather of it every
man [2]as much as he should eat; you
shall take [3]an omer apiece according to the number of persons each of
you has in his tent.' "
17 And the sons of Israel did so,
and *some* gathered much and *some*
little.
18 When they measured it with an
omer, [a]he who had gathered much
had no excess, and he who had gathered little had no lack; every man
gathered [1]as much as he should eat.
19 And Moses said to them, "[a]Let
no man leave any of it until morning."
20 But they did not listen to
Moses, and some left part of it until
morning, and it bred worms and became foul; and Moses was angry
with them.
21 And they gathered it morning
by morning, every man [1]as much as
he should eat; but when the sun
grew hot, it would melt.

The Sabbath Observed

22 [a]Now it came about on the
sixth day they gathered twice as
much bread, two omers for each
one. When all the [b]leaders of the
congregation came and told Moses,
23 then he said to them, "This is
what the LORD [1]meant: [a]Tomorrow
is a sabbath observance, a holy sabbath to the LORD. Bake what you
will bake and boil what you will boil,
and [b]all that is left over [2]put aside to
be kept until morning."
24 So they [1]put it aside until morning, as Moses had ordered, and [a]it
did not become foul, nor was there
any worm in it.
25 And Moses said, "Eat it today,
for today is a sabbath to the LORD;
today you will not find it in the field.
26"Six days you shall gather it, but
on the seventh day, *the* sabbath,
there will be [1]none."
27 And it came about on the seventh day that some of the people
went out to gather, but they found
none.
28 Then the LORD said to Moses,
"[a]How long do you refuse to keep
My commandments and My [1]in-
structions?
29"See, [1]the LORD has given you
the sabbath, therefore He gives you
bread for two days on the sixth day.
Remain every man in his place; let
no man go out of his place on the
seventh day."
30 So the people rested on the seventh day.
31 And the house of [a]Israel named
it [1]manna, and it was like [b]coriander
seed, white; and its taste was like
wafers with honey.
32 Then Moses said, "This is [1]what
the LORD has commanded, 'Let an
omerful of it be kept throughout
your generations, that they may see
the bread that I fed you in the wilderness, when I brought you out of
the land of Egypt.' "
33 And Moses said to Aaron,
"[a]Take a jar and put an omerful of
manna in it, and place it before the
LORD, to be kept throughout your
generations."
34 As the LORD commanded
Moses, so Aaron placed it before
[a]the Testimony, to be kept.
35 [a]And the sons of Israel ate the
manna forty years, until they came
to an inhabited land; they ate the
manna until they came to the border
of the land of Canaan.
36 (Now an omer is a tenth of an
ephah.)

CHAPTER 17

Water in the Rock

THEN all the congregation of the
sons of Israel journeyed by [1]stages
from the wilderness of [a]Sin, according to the [2]command of the LORD,
and camped at [b]Rephidim, and
there was no water for the people to
drink.
2 Therefore the people [a]quar-
reled with Moses and said, "Give us
water that we may drink." And
Moses said to them, "[b]Why do you
quarrel with me? Why do you test
the LORD?"
3 But the people thirsted there
for water; and [1]they grumbled
against Moses and said, "[a]Why,
now, have you brought us up from
Egypt, to kill [2]us and [3]our children
and [3b]our livestock with thirst?"
4 So Moses cried out to the LORD,
saying, "What shall I do to this people? A [a]little more and they will
stone me."
5 Then the LORD said to Moses,
"Pass before the people and take

14 [1]Lit., *had gone up* [2]Lit., *face of* [a]Num. 11:7-9 [b]Ex. 16:31

15 [1]Heb., *Man hu*, cf. v. 31 [a]Ex. 16:4

16 [1]Lit., *the thing which* [2]Lit., *according to his eating* [3]Lit., *an omer for a head*

18 [1]Lit., *according to his eating* [a]2 Cor. 8:15

19 [a]Ex. 12:10; 16:23; 23:18

21 [1]Lit., *according to his eating*

22 [a]Ex. 16:5 [b]Ex. 34:31

23 [1]Lit., *spoke* [2]Lit., *lay up for you* [a]Ex. 20:8; 23:12; Neh. 9:13, 14 [b]Ex. 16:19

24 [1]Lit., *laid it up* [a]Ex. 16:20

26 [1]Lit., *none on it*

28 [1]Or, *laws* [a]Ps. 78:10

29 [1]Lit., *for the LORD*

31 [1]Heb., *man*, cf. v. 15 [a]Num. 11:7-9; Deut. 8:3, 16 [b]Ex. 16:14

32 [1]Lit., *the thing which*

33 [a]Heb. 9:4; Rev. 2:17

34 [a]Ex. 25:16; 27:21

35 [a]Josh. 5:12; Neh. 9:20, 21

1 [1]Lit., *their journeyings* [2]Lit., *mouth* [a]Ex. 16:1 [b]Ex. 19:2; Num. 33:14

2 [a]Ex. 14:11; Num. 20:2, 3, 13 [b]Ex. 16:8

3 [1]Lit., *the people* [2]Lit., *me* [3]Lit., *my* [a]Ex. 16:3 [b]Ex. 12:38

4 [a]Num. 14:10; 1 Sam. 30:6

with you some of [a]the elders of Israel; and take in your hand your
staff with which [b]you struck the
Nile, and go.
6 "Behold, I will stand before you
there on the rock at [a]Horeb; and
[b]you shall strike the rock, and water
will come out of it, that the people
may drink." And Moses did so in the
sight of the elders of Israel.
7 And he named the place [1a]Mas-
sah and [2b]Meribah because of the
quarrel of the sons of Israel, and because they [c]tested the LORD, saying,
"Is the LORD among us, or not?"

Amalek Fought

8 Then [a]Amalek came and fought
against Israel at [b]Rephidim.
9 So Moses said to [a]Joshua,
"Choose men for us, and go out,
fight against Amalek. Tomorrow I
will station myself on the top of the
hill with [b]the staff of God in my
hand."
10 And Joshua did as Moses [1]told
him, [2]and fought against Amalek;
and Moses, Aaron, and [a]Hur went
up to the top of the hill.
11 So it came about when Moses
held his hand up, that Israel prevailed, and when he let his hand
[1]down, Amalek prevailed.
12 But Moses' hands were heavy.
Then they took a stone and put it
under him, and he sat on it; and Aaron and Hur [a]supported his hands,
one on one side and one on the other. Thus his hands were steady until
the sun set.
13 So Joshua [1]overwhelmed Amalek and his people with the edge of
the sword.
14 Then the LORD said to Moses,
"[a]Write this in [1]a book as a memorial, and [2]recite it to Joshua, [3]that [b]I
will utterly blot out the memory of
Amalek from under heaven."
15 And Moses built an [a]altar, and
named it [b]The LORD is My Banner;
16 and he said, "[a]The LORD has
sworn; the LORD will have war
against Amalek from generation to
generation."

CHAPTER 18

Jethro, Moses' Father-in-law

NOW [a]Jethro, the priest of Midian,
Moses' father-in-law, heard of all
that God had done for Moses and for
Israel His people, how the LORD had
brought Israel out of Egypt.
2 And Jethro, Moses' father-in-
law, took Moses' wife [a]Zipporah, after he had sent her away,
3 and her [a]two sons, of whom
[1]one was named Gershom, for he
said, "I have been [b]a [2]sojourner in a
foreign land."
4 And [1]the other was named [2]Eli-
ezer, for *he said*, "[a]The God of my
father was my help, and delivered
me from the sword of Pharaoh."
5 Then Jethro, Moses' father-in-
law, came with his sons and his wife
to Moses [1]in the wilderness where
he was camped, at [a]the mount of
God.
6 And he [1]sent word to Moses, "I,
your father-in-law Jethro, am coming to you with your wife and her
two sons with her."
7 Then Moses went out to meet
his father-in-law, and [a]he bowed
down and [b]kissed him; and they
asked [c]each other of their welfare,
and went into the tent.
8 And Moses told his father-in-
law all that the LORD had done to
Pharaoh and to the Egyptians [a]for
Israel's sake, all the [b]hardship that
had befallen them on the journey,
and *how* [c]the LORD had delivered
them.
9 And Jethro rejoiced over all
[a]the goodness which the LORD had
done to Israel, [1]in delivering [2]them
from the hand of the Egyptians.
10 So Jethro said, "[a]Blessed be the
LORD who delivered you from the
hand of the Egyptians and from the
hand of Pharaoh, *and* who delivered
the people from under the hand of
the Egyptians.
11 "Now I know that [a]the LORD is
greater than all the gods; [1]indeed, it
was proven when they dealt proudly
against [2]the people."
12 [a]Then Jethro, Moses' father-in-
law, took a burnt offering and sacrifices for God, and Aaron came with
all the elders of Israel to eat [1]a meal
with Moses' father-in-law before
God.
13 And it came about the next day
that Moses sat to judge the people,
and the people stood about Moses
from the morning until the evening.
14 Now when Moses' father-in-
law saw all that he was doing for the
people, he said, "What is this thing
that you are doing for the people?
Why do you alone sit *as judge* and
all the people stand about you from
morning until evening?"
15 And Moses said to his father-in-
law, "Because the people come to
me [a]to inquire of God.
16 "When they have a [1]dispute, it
comes to me, and I judge between a
man and his neighbor, and make

5 [a]Ex. 3:16, 18 [b]Ex. 7:20
6 [a]Ex. 3:1 [b]Deut. 8:15; Neh. 9:15; Ps. 78:15; 105:41; 1 Cor. 10:4
7 [1]I.e., Test [2]I.e., Quarrel [a]Deut. 6:16; 9:22; Ps. 95:8 [b]Num. 20:13, 24; 27:14; Ps. 81:7 [c]Num. 14:22; Deut. 33:8
8 [a]Num. 24:20; Deut. 25:17-19 [b]Ex. 17:1
9 [a]Ex. 24:13 [b]Ex. 4:20
10 [1]Lit., *said to* [2]Lit., *to fight* [a]Ex. 24:14; 31:2
11 [1]Lit., *rest*
12 [a]Is. 35:3
13 [1]Lit., *weakened*
14 [1]Lit., *the book* [2]Lit., *place it in the ears of* [3]Or, *for* [a]Ex. 24:4; 34:27; Num. 33:2 [b]Deut. 25:19
15 [a]Ex. 24:4 [b]Gen. 22:14
16 [a]Gen. 22:16
1 [a]Ex. 2:16, 18; 3:1
2 [a]Ex. 2:21; 4:25
3 [1]Lit., *the name of the one was* [2]Heb., *ger* [a]Ex. 2:22; 4:20; Acts 7:29 [b]Ex. 2:22
4 [1]Lit., *the name of the other was* [2]Heb., *Eliezer;* i.e., My God is help [a]Gen. 49:25
5 [1]Lit., *unto* [a]Ex. 3:1, 12; 4:27; 24:13
6 [1]Lit., *said*
7 [a]Gen. 43:26, 28 [b]Ex. 4:27 [c]Gen. 43:27
8 [a]Ex. 4:23; 7:4, 5 [b]Num. 20:14; Neh. 9:32 [c]Ex. 15:6, 16
9 [1]Lit., *in that He had delivered* [2]Lit., *him* [a]Is. 63:7-14
10 [a]1 Kin. 8:56; Ps. 68:19, 20
11 [1]Lit., *indeed, in the thing in which they* [2]Lit., *them* [a]Ex. 12:12; 15:11
12 [1]Lit., *bread* [a]Gen. 31:54; Ex. 24:5
15 [a]Num. 9:6, 8; 27:5; Deut. 17:8-13
16 [1]Lit., *matter*

known the statutes of God and His laws."

Jethro Counsels Moses

17 And Moses' father-in-law said to him, "The thing that you are doing is not good.

18"[a]You will surely wear out, both yourself and [1]these people who are with you, for the [2]task is too heavy for you; you cannot do it alone.

19"Now listen to [1]me: I shall give you counsel, and God be with you. [2]You be the people's representative before God, and you bring the [3]disputes to God,

20 [a]then teach them the statutes and the laws, and make known to them the way in which they are to walk, and the work they are to do.

21"Furthermore, you shall [1]select out of all the people [a]able men who fear God, men of truth, those who hate dishonest gain; and you shall place *these* over them, *as* leaders of thousands, [2]of hundreds, [2]of fifties and [2]of tens.

22"And let them judge the people at all times; and let it be [a]that every major [1]dispute they will bring to you, but every minor [1]dispute they themselves will judge. So it will be easier for you, and they will bear *the burden* with you.

23"If you do this thing and God so commands you, then you will be able to [1]endure, and all [2]these people also will go to [3]their place in peace."

24 So Moses listened [1]to his father-in-law, and did all that he had said.

25 And Moses chose [a]able men out of all Israel, and made them heads over the people, leaders of thousands, [1]of hundreds, [1]of fifties and [1]of tens.

26 And they judged the people at all times; [a]the difficult [1]dispute they would bring to Moses, but every minor [1]dispute they themselves would judge.

27 Then Moses [1a]bade his father-in-law farewell, and he went his way into his own land.

Chapter 19

Moses on Sinai

[a]IN the third month after the sons of Israel had gone out of the land of Egypt, [1]on that very day they came into the wilderness of [b]Sinai.

2 When they set out from [a]Rephidim, they came to the wilderness of Sinai, and camped in the wilderness; and there Israel camped in front of [b]the mountain.

3 And Moses went up to God, and the LORD called to him from the mountain, saying, "Thus you shall say to the house of Jacob and tell the sons of Israel:

4 'You yourselves have seen what I did to the Egyptians, and *how* I bore you on [a]eagles' wings, and brought you to Myself.

5 'Now then, [a]if you will indeed obey My voice and [b]keep My covenant, then you shall be [c]My [1]own possession among all the peoples, for [d]all the earth is Mine;

6 and you shall be to Me [a]a kingdom of priests and [b]a holy nation.' These are the words that you shall speak to the sons of Israel."

7 [a]So Moses came and called the elders of the people, and set before them all these words which the LORD had commanded him.

8 [a]And all the people answered together and said, "All that the LORD has spoken we will do!" And Moses brought back the words of the people to the LORD.

9 And the LORD said to Moses, "Behold, I shall come to you in [a]a thick cloud, in order that the people may hear when I speak with you, and may also believe in you forever." Then Moses told the words of the people to the LORD.

10 The LORD also said to Moses, "Go to the people and consecrate them today and tomorrow, and let them [a]wash their garments;

11 and let them be ready for the third day, for on [a]the third day the LORD will come down on Mount Sinai in the sight of all the people.

12"And you shall set bounds for the people all around, saying, '[1]Beware that you do not go up on the mountain or touch the border of it; whoever touches the mountain shall surely be put to death.

13 'No hand shall touch him, but [a]he shall surely be stoned or [1]shot through; whether beast or man, he shall not live.' When the ram's horn sounds a long blast, they shall come up to [b]the mountain."

14 So Moses went down from the mountain to the people and consecrated the people, and they washed their garments.

15 And he said to the people, "Be ready for the third day; do not go near a woman."

16 [a]So it came about on the third day, when it was morning, that there were [1]thunder and lightning flashes and a thick cloud upon the

18 [1]Lit., *this* [2]Lit., *matter* [a]Num. 11:14, 17; Deut. 1:12

19 [1]Lit., *my voice* [2]Lit., *You be for the people in front of God* [3]Lit., *matters*

20 [a]Deut. 1:18

21 [1]Lit., *see* [2]Lit., *leaders of* [a]Ex. 18:25; Deut. 1:13, 15; Ps. 15:1-5

22 [1]Lit., *matter* [a]Deut. 1:17, 18

23 [1]Lit., *stand* [2]Lit., *this* [3]Lit., *his*

24 [1]Lit., *to the voice of*

25 [1]Lit., *leaders of* [a]Ex. 18:21

26 [1]Lit., *matter* [a]Ex. 18:22

27 [1]Lit., *sent off his father-in-law* [a]Num. 10:29, 30

1 [1]Lit., *on this day* [a]Ex. 12:6, 51; 16:1 [b]Deut. 1:6; 4:10, 15; 5:2

2 [a]Ex. 17:1; Num. 33:15 [b]Ex. 18:5

4 [a]Deut. 32:11

5 [1]Or, *special treasure* [a]Ex. 15:26 [b]Ps. 78:10 [c]Deut. 7:6; 14:2 [d]Ex. 9:29

6 [a]1 Pet. 2:5, 9; Rev. 1:6; 5:10 [b]Deut. 14:21; 26:19

7 [a]Ex. 4:29, 30

8 [a]Ex. 4:31; 24:3, 7; Deut. 5:27

9 [a]Ex. 19:16; 24:15, 16; Ps. 99:7

10 [a]Gen. 35:2; Num. 8:7; 19:19; Rev. 22:14

11 [a]Ex. 19:16

12 [1]Lit., *Take heed to yourselves*

13 [1]I.e., with arrows [a]Heb. 12:20 [b]Ex. 19:17

16 [1]Lit., *sounds* [a]Heb. 12:18, 19

mountain and a very loud trumpet
sound, so that all the people who
were in the camp trembled.
17 And Moses brought the people
out of the camp to meet God, and
they stood at the [1]foot of the mountain.

The LORD *Visits Sinai*

18 [a]Now Mount Sinai *was* all in
smoke because the LORD descended
upon it [b]in fire; and its smoke ascended like [c]the smoke of a furnace,
and [d]the whole mountain [1]quaked
violently.
19 When the sound of the trumpet
grew louder and louder, Moses
spoke and God answered him with
[1]thunder.
20 [a]And the LORD came down on
Mount Sinai, to the top of the mountain; and the LORD called Moses to
the top of the mountain, and Moses
went up.
21 Then the LORD spoke to Moses,
"Go down, [1]warn the people, lest
[a]they break through to the LORD to
gaze, and many of them [2]perish.
22"And also let the [a]priests who
come near to the LORD consecrate
themselves, lest the LORD break out
against them."
23 And Moses said to the LORD,
"The people cannot come up to
Mount Sinai, for Thou didst warn
us, saying, '[a]Set bounds about the
mountain and consecrate it.' "
24 Then the LORD said to him,
"[1]Go down and come up *again,* [a]you
and Aaron with you; but do not let
the [b]priests and the people break
through to come up to the LORD, lest
He break forth upon them."
25 So Moses went down to the
people and told them.

CHAPTER 20

The Ten Commandments

THEN God spoke all these words,
saying,
2"I am the LORD your God, [a]who
brought you out of the land of
Egypt, out of the house of [1]slavery.
3"You shall have no other [a]gods
[1]before Me.
4"[a]You shall not make for yourself [1]an idol, or any likeness of what
is in heaven above or on the earth
beneath or in the water under the
earth.
5"[a]You shall not worship them or
serve them; for I, the LORD your
God, am a [b]jealous God, [c]visiting
the iniquity of the fathers on the
children, on the third and the fourth
generations of those who hate Me,
6 but showing lovingkindness to
[a]thousands, to those who love Me
and keep My commandments.
7"[a]You shall not take the name of
the LORD your God in vain, for the
LORD will not [1]leave him unpunished who takes His name in vain.
8"Remember [a]the sabbath day, to
keep it holy.
9"Six days you shall labor and [a]do
all your work,
10 but the seventh day is a sabbath
of the LORD your God; *in it* you shall
not do any work, you or your son or
your daughter, your male or your female servant or your cattle or your
sojourner who [1]stays with you.
11"[a]For in six days the LORD made
the heavens and the earth, the sea
and all that is in them, and rested on
the seventh day; therefore the LORD
blessed the sabbath day and made it
holy.
12"[a]Honor your father and your
mother, that your [b]days may be prolonged in the land which the LORD
your God gives you.
13"[a]You shall not murder.
14"[a]You shall not commit adultery.
15"[a]You shall not steal.
16"[a]You shall not bear false witness against your [b]neighbor.
17"[a]You shall not covet your
neighbor's house; you shall not covet your neighbor's wife or his male
servant or his female servant or his
ox or his donkey or anything that
belongs to your neighbor."
18 [a]And all the people perceived
the [1]thunder and the lightning
flashes and the sound of the trumpet
and the mountain smoking; and
when the people saw *it,* they trembled and stood at a distance.
19 [a]Then they said to Moses,
"Speak [1]to us yourself and we will
listen; but let not God speak [1]to us,
lest we die."
20 And Moses said to the people,
"[a]Do not be afraid; for God has
come in order [b]to test you, and in
order that [c]the fear of Him may [1]re-
main with you, so that you may not
sin."
21 So the people stood at a distance, while Moses approached [a]the
thick cloud where God *was.*
22 Then the LORD said to Moses,
"Thus you shall say to the sons of
Israel, 'You yourselves have seen
that [a]I have spoken [1]to you from
heaven.
23 '[a]You shall not make *other gods*
besides Me; [b]gods of silver or gods
of gold, you shall not make for yourselves.

17 [1]Lit., *lower part*
18 [1]Or, *trembled* [a]Ps. 104:32; 144:5 [b]Deut. 5:4; Heb. 12:18 [c]Gen. 19:28 [d]Ps. 68:7, 8
19 [1]Or, *a voice;* lit., *a sound*
20 [a]Neh. 9:13
21 [1]Lit., *testify to* [2]Lit., *fall* [a]Ex. 3:5; 1 Sam. 6:19
22 [a]Ex. 19:24; 24:5; Lev. 10:3; 21:6-8
23 [a]Ex. 19:12
24 [1]Lit., *Go, descend* [a]Ex. 24:1, 9, 12 [b]Ex. 19:22
2 [1]Lit., *slaves* [a]Ex. 15:13, 16; Deut. 5:6; 7:8
3 [1]Or, *besides Me* [a]Ex. 15:11; 20:23
4 [1]Or, *a graven image* [a]Lev. 26:1; Deut. 4:15-19; 27:15
5 [a]Ex. 23:24 [b]Ex. 34:14; Deut. 4:24 [c]Ex. 34:6, 7; Deut. 5:9, 10
6 [a]Deut. 7:9
7 [1]Or, *hold him guiltless* [a]Lev. 19:12; Deut. 6:13; 10:20
8 [a]Ex. 23:12; 31:15
9 [a]Ex. 34:21; 35:2, 3
10 [1]Lit., *is in your gates*
11 [a]Gen. 2:2, 3; Ex. 31:17
12 [a]Lev. 19:3; Matt. 15:4; 19:19; Eph. 6:2 [b]Deut. 5:16, 33; 6:2; 11:8
13 [a]Ex. 21:12; Matt. 19:18; Rom. 13:9
14 [a]Lev. 20:10; Matt. 19:18; Rom. 13:9
15 [a]Ex. 21:16; Lev. 19:11, 13; Matt. 19:18; Rom. 13:9
16 [a]Ex. 23:1, 7; Matt. 19:18 [b]Lev. 19:18
17 [a]Rom. 7:7
18 [1]Lit., *sounds* [a]Ex. 19:16, 18
19 [1]Lit., *with* [a]Deut. 5:5, 23-27; Heb. 12:19
20 [1]Lit., *be before* [a]Ex. 14:13 [b]Ex. 15:25 [c]Deut. 4:10
21 [a]Ex. 19:16; Deut. 5:22
22 [1]Lit., *with* [a]Deut. 4:36; 5:24
23 [a]Ex. 20:3 [b]Ex. 32:1, 2, 4; Deut. 29:17

24 'You shall make [a]an altar of earth for Me, and you shall sacrifice on it your [b]burnt offerings and your [c]peace offerings, your sheep and your oxen; in every place [d]where I cause My name to be remembered, I will come to you and bless you.

25 'And if you make an altar of stone for Me, you shall not build it of [a]cut stones, for if you wield your tool on it, you will profane it.

26 'And you shall not go up by steps to My altar, that [a]your nakedness may not be exposed on it.'

Chapter 21

Ordinances for the People

"Now these are the ordinances which you are to set before them.

2"If you buy [a]a Hebrew slave, he shall serve for six years; but on the seventh he shall go out as a free man without payment.

3"If he comes [1]alone, he shall go out [1]alone; if he is the husband of a wife, then his wife shall go out with him.

4"If his master gives him a wife, and she bears him sons or daughters, the wife and her children shall belong to her master, and he shall go out [1]alone.

5"But if the slave plainly says, 'I love my master, my wife and my children; I will not go out as a free man,'

6 then his master shall bring him to [1a]God, then he shall bring him to the door or the doorpost. And his master shall pierce his ear with an awl; and he shall serve him permanently.

7"[a]And if a man sells his daughter as a female slave, she is not to [1]go free [b]as the male slaves [1]do.

8"If she is [1]displeasing in the eyes of her master [2]who designated her for himself, then he shall let her be redeemed. He does not have authority to sell her to a foreign people because of his [3]unfairness to her.

9"And if he designates her for his son, he shall deal with her according to the custom of daughters.

10"If he takes to himself another woman, he may not reduce her [1]food, her clothing, or [a]her conjugal rights.

11"And if he will not do these three *things* for her, then she shall go out for nothing, without *payment of* money.

Personal Injuries

12"[a]He who strikes a man so that he dies shall surely be put to death.

13"[a]But [1]if he did not lie in wait *for him*, but God let *him* fall into his hand, then I will appoint you a place to which he may flee.

14"[a]If, however, a man acts presumptuously toward his neighbor, so as to kill him craftily, you are to take him *even* from My altar, that he may die.

15"And he who strikes his father or his mother shall surely be put to death.

16"[a]And he who [1]kidnaps a man, whether he sells him or he is found in his [2]possession, shall surely be put to death.

17"[a]And he who curses his father or his mother shall surely be put to death.

18"And if men have a quarrel and one strikes the other with a stone or with *his* fist, and he does not die but [1]remains in bed;

19 if he gets up and walks around outside on his staff, then he who struck him shall go unpunished; he shall only pay for his [1]loss of time, and [2]shall take care of him until he is completely healed.

20"And if a man strikes his male or female slave with a rod and he dies [1]at his hand, he shall [2]be punished.

21"If, however, he [1]survives a day or two, no vengeance shall be taken; [a]for he is his [2]property.

22"And *if* men struggle with each other and strike a woman with child so that [1]she has a miscarriage, yet there is no *further* injury, he shall surely be fined as the woman's husband [2]may demand of him; and he shall pay [3]as the judges *decide.*

23"But if there is *any further* injury, [a]then you shall appoint *as a penalty* life for life,

24 [a]eye for eye, tooth for tooth, hand for hand, foot for foot,

25 burn for burn, wound for wound, [1]bruise for bruise.

26"And if a man strikes the eye of his male or female slave, and destroys it, he shall let him go free on account of his eye.

27"And if he [1]knocks out a tooth of his male or female slave, he shall let him go free on account of his tooth.

28"And if an ox gores a man or a woman [1]to death, [a]the ox shall surely be stoned and its flesh shall not be eaten; but the owner of the ox shall go unpunished.

29"If, however, an ox was previously in the habit of goring, and its owner has been warned, yet he does not confine it, and it kills a man or a woman, the ox shall be stoned and its owner also shall be put to death.

20:24 [a]Ex. 20:25; 27:1-8 [b]Ex. 10:25; 18:12 [c]Ex. 24:5 [d]Deut. 12:5; 26:2
25 [a]Deut. 27:5, 6
26 [a]Ex. 28:42, 43
21:2 [a]Lev. 25:39-43; Deut. 15:12-18
3 [1]Lit., *by himself*
4 [1]Lit., *by himself*
6 [1]Or, *the judges who acted in God's name* [a]Ex. 22:8, 9, 28
7 [1]Lit., *go out* [a]Neh. 5:5 [b]Ex. 21:2, 3
8 [1]Lit., *bad* [2]Another reading is, *so that he did not designate her* [3]Lit., *dealing treacherously*
10 [1]Lit., *flesh* [a]1 Cor. 7:3, 5
12 [a]Gen. 9:6; Lev. 24:17
13 [1]Lit., *he who* [a]Num. 35:10-34; Deut. 19:1-13; Josh. 20:1-9
14 [a]1 Kin. 2:28-34
16 [1]Lit., *steals* [2]Lit., *hand* [a]Deut. 24:7
17 [a]Lev. 20:9; Matt. 15:4; Mark 7:10
18 [1]Lit., *lies*
19 [1]Lit., *his sitting* [2]Lit., *healing, he shall cause to be healed*
20 [1]Lit., *under* [2]Lit., *suffer vengeance*
21 [1]Lit., *stands* [2]Lit., *money* [a]Lev. 25:44-46
22 [1]Lit., *her children come out* [2]Lit., *lays on him* [3]Lit., *by arbitration*
23 [a]Lev. 24:19; Deut. 19:21
24 [a]Lev. 24:20; Matt. 5:38
25 [1]Lit., *welt*
27 [1]Lit., *causes to fall*
28 [1]Lit., *so that he dies* [a]Gen. 9:5

30“If a ransom is [1]demanded of
him, then he shall give for the redemption of his life whatever is [1]de-
manded of him.
31“Whether it gores a son or [1]a
daughter, it shall be done to him according to [2]the same rule.
32“If the ox gores a male or female
slave, the [1]owner shall give his *or*
her master [a]thirty shekels of silver,
and the ox shall be stoned.
33“And if a man opens a pit, or
[1]digs a pit and does not cover it
over, and an ox or a donkey falls
into it,
34 the owner of the pit shall make
restitution; he shall [1]give money to
its owner, and the dead *animal* shall
become his.
35“And if one man’s ox hurts another’s so that it dies, then they shall
sell the live ox and divide its price
equally; and also they shall divide
the dead *ox.*
36“Or *if* it is known that the ox was
previously in the habit of goring, yet
its owner has not confined it, he
shall surely pay ox for ox, and the
dead *animal* shall become his.

CHAPTER 22

Property Rights

“[1]IF a man steals an ox or a sheep,
and slaughters it or sells it, he shall
pay five oxen for the ox and [a]four
sheep for the sheep.
2“[1]If the thief is [2]caught while
breaking in, and is struck so that he
dies, there will be no bloodguiltiness
on his account.
3“*But* if the sun has risen on him,
there will be [1]bloodguiltiness on his
account. He shall surely make restitution; if he owns nothing, then he
shall be sold for his theft.
4“If what he stole is actually
found alive in his [1]possession,
whether an ox or a donkey or a
sheep, he shall pay double.
5“If a man lets a field or vineyard
be grazed *bare* and lets his animal
loose so that it grazes in another
man’s field, he shall make restitution from the best of his own field
and the best of his own vineyard.
6“If a fire breaks out and spreads
to thorn bushes, so that stacked
grain or the standing grain or the
field *itself* is consumed, he who
started the fire shall surely make
restitution.
7“[a]If a man gives his neighbor
money or goods to keep *for him,* and
it is stolen from the man’s house, if
the thief is [1]caught, he shall pay
double.
8“If the thief is not [1]caught, then
the owner of the house shall [2]appear
before [3a]the judges, *to* determine
whether he [4]laid his hands on his
neighbor’s property.
9“For every [1]breach of trust,
whether it is for ox, for donkey, for
sheep, for clothing, *or* for any lost
thing about which one says, ‘This is
it,’ the [2]case of both parties shall
come before [3a]the judges; he whom
[3]the judges condemn shall pay double to his neighbor.
10“If a man gives his neighbor a
donkey, an ox, a sheep, or any animal to keep *for him,* and it dies or is
hurt or is driven away while no one
is looking,
11 an oath before the LORD shall
be made by the two of them, [1]that
he has not [2]laid hands on his neighbor’s property; and its owner shall
accept *it,* and he shall not make restitution.
12“But if it is actually stolen from
him, he shall make restitution to its
owner.
13“If it is all torn to pieces, let him
bring it as evidence; he shall not
make restitution for what has been
torn to pieces.
14“And if a man [1]borrows *any-*
thing from his neighbor, and it is injured or dies while its owner is not
with it, he shall make full restitution.
15“If its owner is with it, he shall
not make restitution; if it is hired, it
came for its hire.

Sundry Laws

16“[a]And if a man seduces a virgin
who is not engaged, and lies with
her, he must pay a dowry for her *to*
be his wife.
17“If her father absolutely refuses
to give her to him, he shall [1]pay
money equal to the dowry for virgins.
18“You shall not allow a [a]sorceress
to live.
19“[a]Whoever lies with an animal
shall surely be put to death.
20“[a]He who sacrifices to [1]any god,
other than to the LORD alone, shall
be [2b]utterly destroyed.
21“And you shall not wrong [a]a
stranger or oppress him, for you
were strangers in the land of Egypt.
22“[a]You shall not afflict any widow
or orphan.
23“If you afflict him at all, *and* [a]if
he does cry out to Me, [b]I will surely
hear his cry;
24 and My anger will be kindled,
and I will kill you with the sword;

30 [1]Lit., *laid on him*
31 [1]Lit., *gores a daughter* [2]Lit., *this judgment*
32 [1]Lit., *he* [a]Zech. 11:12; Matt. 26:15
33 [1]Lit., *if a man digs*
34 [1]Lit., *give back*
1 [1]Ch. 21:37 in Heb. [a]2 Sam. 12:6; Luke 19:8
2 [1]Ch. 22:1 in Heb. [2]Lit., *found*
3 [1]I.e., if he is killed
4 [1]Lit., *hand*
7 [1]Lit., *found* [a]Lev. 6:1-7
8 [1]Lit., *found* [2]Lit., *approach to* [3]Or, *God* [4]Lit., *stretched his hand* [a]Ex. 21:6; 22:9, 28; Deut. 17:8, 9; 19:17
9 [1]Or, *matter of transgression* [2]Lit., *matter* [3]Or, *God* [a]Ex. 22:8, 28
11 [1]Lit., *whether* [2]Lit., *stretched his hand*
14 [1]Lit., *asks*
16 [a]Deut. 22:28, 29
17 [1]Lit., *weigh out silver*
18 [a]Lev. 20:27; Deut. 18:10; Jer. 27:9, 10
19 [a]Lev. 18:23; 20:15, 16; Deut. 27:21
20 [1]Lit., *the gods* [2]Lit., *put under the ban* [a]Ex. 32:8; 34:15; Lev. 17:7
21 [a]Lev. 19:33, 34; Deut. 1:16; 27:19
22 [a]Deut. 24:17, 18; Prov. 23:10, 11; Jer. 7:6, 7; 23:3
23 [a]Deut. 15:9; Luke 18:7 [b]Deut. 10:18; Ps. 10:14, 17, 18; 68:5

[a]and your wives shall become widows and your children fatherless.
25"[a]If you lend money to My people, to the poor [1]among you, you are
not to [2]act as a creditor to him; you
shall not [3]charge him [b]interest.
26"If you ever take your neighbor's
cloak as a pledge, you are to return
it to him before the sun sets,
27 for that is his only covering; it is
his cloak for his body. What else
shall he sleep in? And it shall come
about that [a]when he cries out to Me,
I will hear *him*, for I am gracious.
28"You shall not [1a]curse God, [b]nor
curse a ruler of your people.
29"[a]You shall not delay *the offering from* [1]your harvest and your vintage. [b]The first-born of your sons
you shall give to Me.
30"You shall do the same with
your oxen *and* with your sheep. It
shall be with its mother seven days;
[a]on the eighth day you shall give it
to Me.
31"[a]And you shall be holy men to
Me, therefore [b]you shall not eat *any*
flesh torn to pieces in the field; you
shall throw it to the dogs.

Chapter 23

Sundry Laws

"[a]YOU shall not carry a false rumor; do not join your hand with a
wicked man to be a [b]malicious witness.
2"You shall not follow [1]a multitude in doing evil, nor shall you [2]tes-
tify in a dispute so as to turn aside
after [1]a multitude in order to [a]per-
vert *justice;*
3 [a]nor shall you [1]be partial to a
poor man in his dispute.
4"[a]If you meet your enemy's ox or
his donkey wandering away, you
shall surely return it to him.
5"If you see the donkey of one
who hates you lying *helpless* under
its load, you shall refrain from leaving it to him, you shall surely release
it with him.
6"[a]You shall not pervert the justice *due* to your needy *brother* in his
dispute.
7"[a]Keep far from a false charge,
and do not [b]kill the innocent or the
righteous, for [c]I will not acquit the
guilty.
8"[a]And you shall not take a bribe,
for a bribe blinds the clear-sighted
and [1]subverts the cause of the just.
9"[a]And you shall not oppress a
[1]stranger, since you yourselves
know the [2]feelings of a [1]stranger,
for you *also* were [1]strangers in the
land of Egypt.

The Sabbath and Land

10"[a]And you shall sow your land
for six years and gather in its yield,
11 but *on* the seventh year you
shall let it rest and lie fallow, so that
the needy of your people may eat;
and whatever they leave the beast
of the field may eat. You are to do
the same with your vineyard *and*
your olive *grove.*
12"[a]Six days you are to do your
work, but on the seventh day you
shall cease *from labor* in order that
your ox and your donkey may rest,
and the son of your female slave, as
well as [1]your stranger, may refresh
themselves.
13"Now [a]concerning everything
which I have said to you, be on your
guard; and [b]do not mention the
name of other gods, nor let *them* be
heard [1]from your mouth.

Three National Feasts

14"[a]Three times a year you shall
celebrate a feast to Me.
15"You shall observe the Feast of
Unleavened Bread; for seven days
you are to eat unleavened bread, as
I commanded you, at the appointed
time in the [a]month Abib, for in it
you came out of Egypt. And [1b]none
shall appear before Me empty-
handed.
16"Also *you shall observe* [a]the
Feast of the Harvest *of* the first
fruits of your labors *from* what you
sow in the field; also the Feast of the
Ingathering at the end of the year
when you gather in *the fruit of* your
labors from the field.
17"[a]Three times a year all your
males shall appear before the Lord
[1]God.
18"[a]You shall not offer the blood of
My sacrifice with leavened bread;
[b]nor is the fat of My [1]feast to remain
overnight until morning.
19"You shall bring [a]the choice first
fruits of your soil into the house of
the Lord your God. [b]You are not to
boil a kid in the milk of its mother.

Conquest of the Land

20"Behold, I am going to send [a]an
angel before you to guard you along
the way, and [b]to bring you into the
place which I have prepared.
21"Be on your guard before him
and obey his voice; [a]do not be rebellious toward him, for he will not pardon your transgression, since [b]My
name is in him.
22"But if you will truly obey his
voice and do all that I say, then [a]I
will be an enemy to your enemies

24 [a]Ps. 109:2, 9
25 [1]Lit., *with* [2]Lit., *be* [3]Lit., *lay upon* [a]Lev. 25:35-37 [b]Deut. 23:19, 20
27 [a]Ex. 22:23
28 [1]Or, *revile* [a]Lev. 24:15, 16 [b]Acts 23:5
29 [1]Lit., *your fulness and your tears* [a]Ex. 23:16, 19; Deut. 26:2-11 [b]Ex. 13:2
30 [a]Gen. 17:12
31 [a]Ex. 19:6; Lev. 11:44 [b]Lev. 7:24; 17:15
1 [a]Ex. 20:16 [b]Deut. 19:16-21; Ps. 35:11
2 [1]Lit., *many men* [2]Or, *answer* [a]Deut. 16:19
3 [1]Lit., *honor* [a]Ex. 23:6; Lev. 19:15; Deut. 1:17
4 [a]Deut. 22:1-4
6 [a]Ex. 23:2, 3
7 [a]Ex. 20:16; Ps. 119:29 [b]Ex. 20:13; Deut. 27:25 [c]Ex. 34:7; Deut. 25:1; Rom. 1:18
8 [1]Or, *distorts the words* [a]Deut. 10:17; 16:19; Prov. 17:23; Is. 5:22, 23
9 [1]Or, *sojourner(s)* [2]Lit., *soul* [a]Ex. 22:21
10 [a]Ex. 23:29; Lev. 25:1-7
12 [1]Lit., *the sojourner* [a]Ex. 20:8-11; 31:15; 35:2, 3
13 [1]Lit., *on* [a]Deut. 4:9, 23 [b]Josh. 23:7; Ps. 16:4
14 [a]Ex. 34:22-24; Deut. 16:16
15 [1]Lit., *they . . . not* [a]Ex. 12:2; 13:4 [b]Ex. 22:29; 34:20
16 [a]Ex. 34:22
17 [1]YHWH usually rendered Lord [a]Ex. 23:14
18 [1]Or, *festival* [a]Ex. 34:25; Lev. 2:11 [b]Ex. 12:10; Lev. 7:15
19 [a]Ex. 22:29; 34:26 [b]Deut. 14:21
20 [a]Ex. 3:2; 14:19; 23:23; 32:34; 33:2 [b]Ex. 15:16, 17
21 [a]Deut. 9:7 [b]Ex. 3:14; 6:3; 34:5-7
22 [a]Gen. 12:3; Num. 24:9; Deut. 30:7

and an adversary to your adversaries.

23“[a]For My angel will go before you and bring you in to *the* land of the Amorites, the Hittites, the Perizzites, the Canaanites, the Hivites and the Jebusites; and I will completely destroy them.

24“[a]You shall not worship their gods, nor serve them, nor do according to their deeds; [b]but you shall utterly overthrow them, and break their [c]*sacred* pillars in pieces.

25“[a]But you shall serve the LORD your God, [1]and He will bless your bread and your water; and [b]I will remove sickness from your midst.

26“There shall be no one miscarrying or [a]barren in your land; [b]I will fulfill the number of your days.

27“I will [a]send My terror ahead of you, and throw into confusion all the people among whom you come, and I will make all your enemies turn *their* backs to you.

28“And I will send [a]hornets ahead of you, that they may [b]drive out the Hivites, the Canaanites, and the Hittites before you.

29“I will not drive them out before you in a single year, that the land may not become desolate, and the beasts of the field become too numerous for you.

30“I will drive them out before you [a]little by little, until you become fruitful and take possession of the land.

31“[a]And I will fix your boundary from the [1]Red Sea to the sea of the Philistines, and from the wilderness to the River *Euphrates;* [b]for I will deliver the inhabitants of the land into your hand, and [c]you will drive them out before you.

32“[a]You shall [1]make no covenant with them [b]or with their gods.

33“[a]They shall not live in your land, lest they make you sin against Me; for *if* you serve their gods, it will surely be a snare to you.”

CHAPTER 24

People Affirm Their Covenant with God

THEN He said to Moses, “[a]Come up to the LORD, you and Aaron, [b]Nadab and Abihu and seventy of the elders of Israel, and you shall worship at a distance.

2“Moses alone, however, shall come near to the LORD, but they shall not come near, nor shall the people come up with him.”

3 Then Moses came and recounted to the people all the words of the LORD and all the [1]ordinances; and all the people answered with one voice, and said, “[a]All the words which the LORD has spoken we will do!”

4 And [a]Moses wrote down all the words of the LORD. Then he arose early in the morning, and built an [b]altar [1]at the foot of the mountain with twelve pillars for the twelve tribes of Israel.

5 And he sent young men of the sons of Israel, [a]and they offered burnt offerings and sacrificed young bulls as peace offerings to the LORD.

6 And [a]Moses took half of the blood and put *it* in basins, and the *other* half of the blood he sprinkled on the altar.

7 Then he took [a]the book of the covenant and read *it* in the hearing of the people; and they said, “[b]All that the LORD has spoken we will do, and we will be obedient!”

8 So [a]Moses took the blood and sprinkled *it* on the people, and said, “Behold, [b]the blood of the covenant, which the LORD has [1]made with you [2]in accordance with all these words.”

9 Then Moses went up [1]with Aaron, [a]Nadab and Abihu, and seventy of the elders of Israel,

10 and [a]they saw the God of Israel; and under His feet [1b]there appeared to be a pavement of sapphire, [2]as clear as the sky itself.

11 Yet He did not stretch out His hand against the nobles of the sons of Israel; and [a]they beheld God, and they ate and drank.

12 Now the LORD said to Moses, “Come up to Me on the mountain and [1]remain there, and [a]I will give you the stone tablets [2]with the law and the commandment which I have written for their instruction.”

13 So Moses arose [1]with [a]Joshua his [2]servant, and Moses went up to [b]the mountain of God.

14 But to the elders he said, “[a]Wait here for us until we return to you. And behold, [b]Aaron and Hur are with you; whoever [1]has a legal matter, let him approach them.”

15 Then Moses went up to the mountain, and [a]the cloud covered the mountain.

16 And the glory of the LORD [1]rested on Mount Sinai, and the cloud covered it for six days; and on the seventh day He [a]called to Moses from the midst of the cloud.

17 [a]And to the eyes of the sons of Israel the appearance of the glory of the LORD was like a [b]consuming fire on the mountain top.

---

23 [a]Josh. 24:11
24 [a]Ex. 20:5; 23:13, 33 [b]Num. 33:52; Deut. 7:5; 12:3; 2 Kin. 18:4 [c]Ex. 34:13; Lev. 26:1; 2 Kin. 3:2
25 [1]Or, *that He may bless* [a]Lev. 26:3-13; Deut. 28:1-14 [b]Ex. 15:26; Deut. 7:15
26 [a]Deut. 7:14 [b]Deut. 4:40; Job 5:26
27 [a]Ex. 15:16 [b]Deut. 7:23
28 [a]Deut. 7:20; Josh. 24:12 [b]Ex. 33:2; 34:11
30 [a]Deut. 7:22
31 [1]Lit., *Sea of Reeds* [a]Gen. 15:18; Deut. 1:7, 8 [b]Deut. 2:36; Josh. 21:44 [c]Josh. 24:12, 18
32 [1]Lit., *cut* [a]Ex. 34:12; Deut. 7:2 [b]Ex. 23:13, 24
33 [a]Deut. 7:1-5, 16
1 [a]Ex. 19:24 [b]Ex. 6:23; Lev. 10:1, 2
3 [1]Or, *judgments* [a]Ex. 19:8; 24:7
4 [1]Lit., *under* [a]Ex. 17:14; 34:27 [b]Ex. 17:15
5 [a]Ex. 18:12
6 [a]Ps. 99:6
7 [a]Ex. 24:4 [b]Ex. 24:3
8 [1]Lit., *cut* [2]Lit., *on all* [a]Heb. 9:19, 20 [b]Zech. 9:11; Matt. 26:28; Luke 22:20; 1 Cor. 11:25
9 [1]Lit., *and* [a]Ex. 24:1
10 [1]Lit., *like a pavement* [2]Lit., *and as* [a]Ex. 24:11; Num. 12:8; Is. 6:5; John 1:18; 6:46 [b]Ezek. 1:26; Matt. 17:2; Rev. 4:3
11 [a]Ex. 24:10
12 [1]Lit., *be* [2]Lit., *and* [a]Ex. 31:18
13 [1]Lit., *and* [2]Or, *minister* [a]Ex. 17:9-14; 33:11 [b]Ex. 3:1
14 [1]Lit., *is a master of matters* [a]Gen. 22:5 [b]Ex. 17:10, 12
15 [a]Ex. 19:9
16 [1]Lit., *dwelt* [a]Ps. 99:7
17 [a]Ex. 3:2; Ezek. 1:28 [b]Deut. 4:24; 9:3; Heb. 12:29

18 And Moses entered the midst of the cloud [1]as he went up to the mountain; and Moses was on the mountain [a]forty days and forty nights.

CHAPTER 25

Offerings for the Sanctuary

THEN the LORD spoke to Moses, saying,
2 "[a]Tell the sons of Israel to [1]raise a [2]contribution for Me; [b]from every man whose heart moves him you shall [1]raise My [2]contribution.
3 "And this is the [1]contribution which you are to [2]raise from them: gold, silver and bronze,
4 [1]blue, purple and scarlet *material,* fine linen, goat *hair,*
5 rams' skins dyed red, porpoise skins, acacia wood,
6 oil for lighting, spices for the anointing oil and for the fragrant incense,
7 onyx stones and setting stones, for the ephod and for the [1]breastpiece.
8 "And let them construct a sanctuary for Me, [a]that I may dwell among them.
9 "[a]According to all that I am going to show you, *as* the pattern of the tabernacle and the pattern of all its furniture, just so you shall construct *it.*

Ark of the Covenant

10 "[a]And they shall construct an ark of acacia wood two and a half [1]cubits [2]long, and one and a half cubits [3]wide, and one and a half cubits [4]high.
11 "And you shall [a]overlay it with pure gold, inside and out you shall overlay it, and you shall make a gold molding [1]around it.
12 "And you shall cast four gold rings for it, and [1]fasten them on its four feet, and two rings shall be on one side of it and two rings on the other side of it.
13 "And you shall make poles of acacia wood and overlay them with gold.
14 "And you shall put the poles into the rings on the sides of the ark, to carry the ark with them.
15 "The poles shall [1]remain in the rings of the ark; they shall not be removed from it.
16 "And you shall [a]put into the ark the testimony which I shall give you.
17 "And you shall make a [1]mercy seat of pure gold, two and a half [2]cubits [3]long and one and a half cubits [4]wide.
18 "And you shall make two cherubim of gold, make them of hammered work [1]at the two ends of the mercy seat.
19 "And make one cherub [1]at one end and one cherub [1]at the other end; you shall make the cherubim *of one piece* with the mercy seat at its two ends.
20 "And [a]the cherubim shall have *their* wings spread upward, covering the mercy seat with their wings and [1]facing one another; the faces of the cherubim are to be *turned* toward the mercy seat.
21 "And you shall put the mercy seat [1]on top of the ark, and in the ark you shall put the testimony which I shall give to you.
22 "And [a]there I will meet with you, and from above the mercy seat, from between the two cherubim which are upon the ark of the testimony, I will speak to you about all that I will give you in commandment for the sons of Israel.

The Table of Showbread

23 "[a]And you shall make a table of acacia wood, two cubits [1]long and one cubit [2]wide and one and a half cubits [3]high.
24 "And you shall overlay it with pure gold and make a gold [a]border around it.
25 "And you shall make for it a rim of a handbreadth around *it;* and you shall make a gold border for the rim around it.
26 "And you shall make four gold rings for it and put rings on the four corners which are on its four feet.
27 "The rings shall be close to the rim as holders for the poles to carry the table.
28 "And you shall make the poles of acacia wood and overlay them with gold, so that with them the table may be carried.
29 "And you shall make its [1]dishes and its pans and its jars and its [2]bowls, with which to pour libations; you shall make them of pure gold.
30 "And you shall set [a]the bread of the [1]Presence on the table before Me [2]at all times.

The Golden Lampstand

31 "[a]Then you shall make a lampstand of pure gold. The lampstand *and* its base and its shaft are to be made of hammered work; its cups, its [1]bulbs and its flowers shall be *of one piece* with it.

---

18 [1]Lit., *and* [a]Ex. 34:28; Deut. 9:9; 10:10
2 [1]Lit., *take* [2]Or, *heave offering* [a]Ex. 35:4-9 [b]Ex. 35:5, 21; 2 Cor. 8:11, 12
3 [1]Or, *heave offering* [2]Lit., *take*
4 [1]Or, *violet*
7 [1]Or, *pouch*
8 [a]Ex. 29:45, 46; Num. 5:3; Deut. 12:11; Rev. 21:3
9 [a]Ex. 25:40; 26:30; Acts 7:44; Heb. 8:2, 5
10 [1]A cubit was about 18 in. [2]Lit., *its length* [3]Lit., *its width* [4]Lit., *its height* [a]Ex. 37:1-9
11 [1]Lit., *on it round about* [a]Heb. 9:4
12 [1]Or, *put*
15 [1]Lit., *be*
16 [a]Heb. 9:4
17 [1]Lit., *propitiatory;* and so through v. 22 [2]I.e., one cubit equals approximately 18 inches [3]Lit., *its length* [4]Lit., *its width*
18 [1]Lit., *from*
19 [1]Lit., *from*
20 [1]Lit., *their faces to* [a]1 Kin. 8:7; Heb. 9:5
21 [1]Lit., *above, upon*
22 [a]Ex. 29:42, 43; 30:6, 36
23 [1]Lit., *its length* [2]Lit., *its width* [3]Lit., *its height* [a]Ex. 37:10-16
24 [a]Ex. 25:11
29 [1]Or, *platters* [2]Lit., *libation bowls*
30 [1]Lit., *Face* [2]Or, *continually* [a]Ex. 39:36; 40:23; Lev. 24:5-9
31 [1]Or, *calyx* [a]Ex. 37:17-24

32"And six branches shall go out from its sides; three branches of the lampstand from its one side, and three branches of the lampstand from its [1]other side.

33"Three cups *shall be* shaped like almond *blossoms* in the one branch, a [1]bulb and a flower, and three cups shaped like almond *blossoms* in the [2]other branch, a [1]bulb and a flower—so for six branches going out from the lampstand;

34 and in the lampstand four cups shaped like almond *blossoms,* its [1]bulbs and its flowers.

35"And a [1]bulb shall be under the *first* pair of branches *coming* out of it, and a [1]bulb under the *second* pair of branches *coming* out of it, and a [1]bulb under the *third* pair of branches *coming* out of it, for the six branches coming out of the lampstand.

36"Their [1]bulbs and their branches *shall be of one piece* with it; all of it shall be one piece of hammered work of pure gold.

37"Then you shall make its lamps seven *in number;* and they shall [1]mount its lamps so as to shed light on the space in front of it.

38"And its snuffers and [1]their trays *shall be* of pure gold.

39"It shall be made from a talent of pure gold, with all these utensils.

40"And [a]see that you make *them* [b]after the pattern for them, which was shown to you on the mountain.

CHAPTER 26

Curtains of Linen

"[a]MOREOVER you shall make the tabernacle with ten curtains of fine twisted linen and [1]blue and purple and scarlet *material;* you shall make them with cherubim, the work of a skillful workman.

2"The length of each curtain shall be twenty-eight [1]cubits, and the width of each curtain four [1]cubits; all the curtains shall have [2]the same measurements.

3"Five curtains shall be [1]joined to one another; and *the other* five curtains *shall be* [1]joined to one another.

4"And you shall make loops of [1]blue on the edge of the [2]outermost curtain in the *first* set, and likewise you shall make *them* on the edge of the curtain that is outermost in the second [3]set.

5"You shall make fifty loops in the one curtain, and you shall make fifty loops on the [1]edge of the curtain that is in the second [2]set; the loops shall be opposite each other.

6"And you shall make fifty clasps of gold, and [1]join the curtains to one another with the clasps, that the [2]tabernacle may be a unit.

Curtains of Goats' Hair

7"Then you shall make curtains of goats' *hair* for a tent over the tabernacle; you shall make eleven curtains in all.

8"The length of each curtain *shall be* thirty [1]cubits, and the width of each curtain four cubits; the eleven curtains shall have [2]the same measurements.

9"And you shall [1]join five curtains by themselves, and the *other* six curtains by themselves, and you shall double over the sixth curtain [2]at the front of the tent.

10"And you shall make fifty loops on the edge of the [1]curtain that is outermost in the *first* [2]set, and fifty loops on the edge of the curtain *that is outermost in* the second [2]set.

11"And you shall make fifty clasps of [1]bronze, and you shall put the clasps into the loops and [2]join the tent together, that it may be [3]a unit.

12"And the [1]overlapping part that is left over in the curtains of the tent, the half curtain that is left over, shall lap over the back of the tabernacle.

13"And the cubit on one side and the cubit on the other, of what is left over in the length of the curtains of the tent, shall lap over the sides of the tabernacle on one side and on the other, to cover it.

14"And you shall make a covering for the tent of rams' skins [1]dyed red, and a covering of porpoise skins above.

Boards and Sockets

15"Then you shall make [a]the boards for the tabernacle of acacia wood, standing upright.

16"Ten cubits *shall be* the length of [1]each board, and one and a half cubits the width of each board.

17"There *shall be* two tenons for each board, [1]fitted to one another; thus you shall do for all the boards of the tabernacle.

18"And you shall make the boards for the tabernacle: twenty boards [1]for the south side.

19"And you shall make forty [1]sockets of silver under the twenty boards, two [1]sockets under one board for its two tenons and two [1]sockets under another board for its two tenons;

20 and for the second side of the tabernacle, on the north side, twenty boards,

32 [1]Lit., *second*
33 [1]Or, *calyx* [2]Lit., *one branch*
34 [1]Or, *calyxes*
35 [1]Or, *calyx*
36 [1]Or, *calyxes*
37 [1]Lit., *raise up*
38 [1]Lit., *its snuff dishes*
40 [a]Heb. 8:5 [b]Ex. 25:9
1 [1]Or, *violet* [a]Ex. 36:8-19
2 [1]I.e., One cubit equals approximately 18 inches [2]Lit., *one measure*
3 [1]Or, *coupled*
4 [1]Or, *violet* [2]Lit., *one curtain from the end in the coupling* [3]Lit., *coupling*
5 [1]Lit., *end* [2]Lit., *coupling*
6 [1]Or, *couple* [2]Or, *dwelling place,* and so throughout the chap.
8 [1]I.e., one cubit equals approximately 18 inches [2]Lit., *one measure*
9 [1]Or, *couple* [2]Lit., *toward the front of the face of the tent*
10 [1]Lit., *one curtain* [2]Lit., *coupling*
11 [1]Or, *copper* [2]Or, *couple* [3]Lit., *one*
12 [1]Lit., *excess*
14 [1]Or, *tanned*
15 [a]Ex. 36:20-34
16 [1]Lit., *the*
17 [1]Lit., *bound*
18 [1]Lit., *toward the side of the Negev to the south*
19 [1]Or, *bases*

21 and their forty [1]sockets of silver; two [1]sockets under one board and two [1]sockets under another board.

22 "And for the [1]rear of the tabernacle, to the west, you shall make six boards.

23 "And you shall make two boards for the corners of the tabernacle at the [1]rear.

24 "And they shall be double beneath, and together they shall be complete [1]to its top [2]to the first ring; thus it shall be with both of them: they shall form the two corners.

25 "And there shall be eight boards with their [1]sockets of silver, sixteen [1]sockets; two [1]sockets under one board and two [1]sockets under another board.

26 "Then you shall make bars of acacia wood, five for the boards of one side of the tabernacle,

27 and five bars for the boards of the [1]other side of the tabernacle, and five bars for the boards of the side of the tabernacle for the [2]rear *side* to the west.

28 "And the middle bar in the [1]center of the boards shall pass through from end to end.

29 "And you shall overlay the boards with gold and make their rings of gold *as* holders for the bars; and you shall overlay the bars with gold.

30 "Then you shall erect the tabernacle [a]according to its plan which you have been shown in the mountain.

The Veil and Screen

31 "And you shall make [a]a veil of [1]blue and purple and scarlet *material* and fine twisted linen; it shall be made with cherubim, the work of a skillful workman.

32 "And you shall [1]hang it on four pillars of acacia overlaid with gold, their hooks *also being of* gold, on four [2]sockets of silver.

33 "And you shall [1]hang up the veil under the clasps, and shall bring in the ark of the testimony there within the veil; and the veil shall [2]serve for you as a partition between the holy place and the holy of holies.

34 "And you shall put the mercy seat on the ark of the testimony in the holy of holies.

35 "And you shall set the table outside the veil, and the lampstand opposite the table on the side of the tabernacle toward the south; and you shall put the table on the north side.

21 [1]Or, *bases*
22 [1]Lit., *extreme parts*
23 [1]Lit., *extreme parts*
24 [1]Or, *at its head* [2]Or, *with reference to*
25 [1]Or, *bases*
27 [1]Lit., *second* [2]Lit., *extreme parts*
28 [1]Lit., *midst*
30 [a]Ex. 25:9
31 [1]Or, *violet* [a]Ex. 36:35, 36; Matt. 27:51; Heb. 9:3
32 [1]Lit., *put* [2]Or, *bases*
33 [1]Lit., *put* [2]Lit., *separate for you between*
36 [1]Or, *violet* [2]Lit., *variegator;* i.e., a weaver in colors
37 [1]Or, *bases* [2]Or, *copper*
1 [1]I.e., one cubit equals approximately 18 inches [a]Ex. 38:1-7
2 [1]Or, *copper,* and so for *bronze* throughout the chap.
4 [1]Lit., *on*
9 [1]Or, *dwelling place* [2]Lit., *For the side of the Negev to the south* [a]Ex. 38:9-20
10 [1]Or, *bases* [2]Or, *fillets, rings*
11 [1]Or, *bases*
12 [1]Or, *bases*

36 "And you shall make a screen for the doorway of the tent of [1]blue and purple and scarlet *material* and fine twisted linen, the work of a [2]weaver.

37 "And you shall make five pillars of acacia for the screen, and overlay them with gold, their hooks *also being of* gold; and you shall cast five [1]sockets of [2]bronze for them.

Chapter 27

The Bronze Altar

"AND you shall make [a]the altar of acacia wood, five [1]cubits long and five cubits wide; the altar shall be square, and its height shall be three cubits.

2 "And you shall make its horns on its four corners; its horns shall be of one piece with it, and you shall overlay it with [1]bronze.

3 "And you shall make its pails for removing its ashes, and its shovels and its basins and its forks and its firepans; you shall make all its utensils of bronze.

4 "And you shall make for it a grating of network of bronze, and on the net you shall make four bronze rings [1]at its four corners.

5 "And you shall put it beneath, under the ledge of the altar, that the net may reach halfway up the altar.

6 "And you shall make poles for the altar, poles of acacia wood, and overlay them with bronze.

7 "And its poles shall be inserted into the rings, so that the poles shall be on the two sides of the altar when it is carried.

8 "You shall make it hollow with planks; as it was shown to you in the mountain, so they shall make *it*.

Court of the Tabernacle

9 "And you shall make [a]the court of the [1]tabernacle. [2]On the south side *there shall be* hangings for the court of fine twisted linen one hundred cubits long for one side;

10 and its pillars *shall be* twenty, with their twenty [1]sockets of bronze; the hooks of the pillars and their [2]bands *shall be* of silver.

11 "And likewise for the north side in length *there shall be* hangings one hundred *cubits* long, and its twenty pillars with their twenty [1]sockets of bronze; the hooks of the pillars and their bands *shall be* of silver.

12 "And *for* the width of the court on the west side *shall be* hangings of fifty cubits *with* their ten pillars and their ten [1]sockets.

13"And the width of the court on the [1]east side *shall be* fifty cubits.

14"The hangings for the *one* [1]side *of the gate shall be* fifteen cubits *with* their three pillars and their three [2]sockets.

15"And for the [1]other [2]side *shall be* hangings of fifteen cubits *with* their three pillars and their three [3]sockets.

16"And for the gate of the court there *shall be* a screen of twenty cubits, of [1]blue and purple and scarlet *material* and fine twisted linen, the work of a [2]weaver, *with* their four pillars and their four [3]sockets.

17"All the pillars around the court shall be furnished with silver bands *with* their hooks of silver and their [1]sockets of bronze.

18"The length of the court *shall be* one hundred cubits, and the width fifty throughout, and the height five cubits of fine twisted linen, and their [1]sockets of bronze.

19"All the utensils of the tabernacle *used* in all its service, and all its pegs, and all the pegs of the court, *shall be* of bronze.

20"And you shall charge the sons of Israel, that they bring you [a]clear oil of beaten olives for the [1]light, to make a lamp [2]burn continually.

21"In the [a]tent of meeting, outside the veil which is before the testimony, Aaron and his sons shall keep it in order from evening to morning before the LORD; *it shall be* a perpetual statute throughout their generations [1]for the sons of Israel.

CHAPTER 28

Garments of the Priests

"THEN [a]bring near to yourself Aaron your brother, and his sons with him, from among the sons of Israel, to minister as priest to Me—Aaron, [b]Nadab and Abihu, Eleazar and Ithamar, Aaron's sons.

2"And you shall make holy garments for Aaron your brother, for glory and for beauty.

3"And you shall speak to all the [1]skillful persons whom I have endowed with [2]the spirit of wisdom, that they make Aaron's garments to consecrate him, that he may minister as priest to Me.

4"And these are the garments which they shall make: a [1]breastpiece and an ephod and a robe and a tunic of checkered work, a turban and a sash, and they shall make holy garments for Aaron your brother and his sons, that he may minister as priest to Me.

5"And they shall take [a]the gold and the [1]blue and the purple and the scarlet *material* and the fine linen.

6"They shall also make [a]the ephod of gold, of [1]blue and purple *and* scarlet *material* and fine twisted linen, the work of the skillful workman.

7"It shall have two shoulder pieces joined to its two ends, that it may be joined.

8"And the skillfully woven band, which is on it, shall be like its workmanship, [1]of the same material: of gold, of [2]blue and purple and scarlet *material* and fine twisted linen.

9"And you shall take two onyx stones and engrave on them the names of the sons of Israel,

10 six of their names on the one stone, and the names of the remaining six on the [1]other stone, according to their birth.

11"[1]As a jeweler engraves a signet, you shall engrave the two stones according to the names of the sons of Israel; you shall [2]set them in filigree *settings* of gold.

12"And you shall put the two stones on the shoulder pieces of the ephod, *as* stones of memorial for the sons of Israel, and Aaron shall bear their names before the LORD on his two shoulders for a memorial.

13"[a]And you shall make filigree *settings* of gold,

14 and two chains of pure gold; you shall make them of twisted cordage work, and you shall put the corded chains on the filigree *settings*.

15"And you shall make a [1]breastpiece of judgment, the work of a skillful workman; like the work of the ephod you shall make it: of gold, of [2]blue and purple and scarlet *material* and fine twisted linen you shall make it.

16"It shall be square *and* folded double, a span [1]in length and a span [1]in width.

17"And you shall [1]mount on it four rows of stones; the first row *shall be* a row of ruby, topaz and emerald;

18 and the second row a turquoise, a sapphire and a diamond;

19 and the third row a jacinth, an agate and an amethyst;

20 and the fourth row a beryl and an onyx and a jasper; they shall be [1]set in gold filigree.

21"And the stones shall be according to the names of the sons of Israel: twelve, according to their names; they shall be *like* the engravings of a seal, each according to his name for the twelve tribes.

13 [1]Lit., *east side eastward*

14 [1]Lit., *shoulder* [2]Or, *bases*

15 [1]Lit., *second* [2]Lit., *shoulder* [3]Or, *bases*

16 [1]Or, *violet* [2]Lit., *variegator;* i.e., a weaver in colors [3]Or, *bases*

17 [1]Or, *bases*

18 [1]Or, *bases*

20 [1]Or, *luminary* [2]Lit., *ascend* [a]Ex. 35:8, 28; Lev. 24:1-4

21 [1]Lit., *from* [a]Ex. 25:22; 29:42; 30:36

1 [a]Ps. 99:6; Heb. 5:4 [b]Ex. 24:1, 9

3 [1]Lit., *wise of heart* [2]I.e., artistic skill

4 [1]Or, *pouch*

5 [1]Or, *violet* [a]Ex. 25:3

6 [1]Or, *violet* [a]Ex. 39:2-7

8 [1]Lit., *from it* [2]Or, *violet*

10 [1]Lit., *second*

11 [1]Lit., *A work of a lapidary, engravings of a seal* [2]Lit., *make them to be surrounded*

13 [a]Ex. 39:16-18

15 [1]Or, *pouch* [2]Or, *violet*

16 [1]Lit., *its*

17 [1]Lit., *fill in a setting of stones, four rows of stones*

20 [1]Lit., *inwoven with gold in their settings*

22“And you shall make on the
[1]breastpiece chains of twisted cordage work in pure gold.
23“And you shall make on the
breastpiece two rings of gold, and
shall put the two rings on the two
ends of the breastpiece.
24“And you shall put the two cords
of gold on the two rings at the ends
of the breastpiece.
25“And you shall put the *other* two
ends of the two cords on the two
filigree *settings,* and put them on the
shoulder pieces of the ephod, at the
front of it.
26“And you shall make two rings
of gold and shall place them on the
two ends of the breastpiece, on the
edge of it, which is toward the inner
side of the ephod.
27“And you shall make two rings
of gold and put them on the bottom
of the two shoulder pieces of the e-
phod, on the front of it close to the
place where it is joined, above the
skillfully woven band of the ephod.
28“And they shall bind the breastpiece by its rings to the rings of the
ephod with a [1]blue cord, that it may
be on the skillfully woven band of
the ephod, and that the breastpiece
may not come loose from the ephod.
29“And Aaron shall carry the
names of the sons of Israel in the
breastpiece of judgment over his
heart when he enters the holy place,
for a memorial before the LORD continually.
30“And you shall put in the breastpiece of judgment the [1]Urim and the
Thummim, and they shall be over
Aaron’s heart when he goes in before the LORD; and Aaron shall carry
the judgment of the sons of Israel
over his heart before the LORD continually.
31“[a]And you shall make the robe
of the ephod all of [1]blue.
32“And there shall be an opening
[1]at its top in the middle of it; around
its opening there shall be a binding
of woven work, as *it were* the opening of a coat of mail, that it may not
be torn.
33“And you shall make on its hem
pomegranates of blue and purple
and scarlet *material,* all around on
its hem, and bells of gold between
them all around:
34 a golden bell and a pomegranate, a golden bell and a pomegranate, all around on the hem of the
robe.
35“And it shall be on Aaron [1]when
he ministers; and [2]its tinkling may
be heard when he enters and [3]leaves
the holy place before the LORD, that
he may not die.
36“You shall also make [a]a plate of
pure gold and shall engrave on it,
like the engravings of a seal, ‘Holy
to the LORD.’
37“And you shall [1]fasten it on a
[2]blue cord, and it shall be on the turban; it shall be at the front of the
turban.
38“And it shall be on Aaron’s forehead, and Aaron shall [1]take away
[a]the iniquity of the holy things
which the sons of Israel consecrate,
with regard to all their holy gifts;
and it shall always be on his forehead, that they may be accepted before the LORD.
39“And you shall weave [a]the tunic
of checkered work of fine linen, and
shall make a turban of fine linen,
and you shall make a sash, the work
of a [1]weaver.
40“And for Aaron’s sons you shall
make tunics; you shall also make
sashes for them, and you shall make
[1a]caps for them, for glory and for
beauty.
41“And you shall put them on Aaron your brother and on his sons with
him; and you shall anoint them and
[1]ordain them and consecrate them,
that they may serve Me as priests.
42“And you shall make for them
[a]linen breeches to cover *their* bare
flesh; they shall [1]reach from the
loins even to the thighs.
43“And they shall be on Aaron and
on his sons when they enter the tent
of meeting, or [a]when they approach
the altar to minister in the holy
place, so that they do not incur
[1]guilt and die. It *shall be* a statute
forever to him and to his [2]descen-
dants after him.

CHAPTER 29

Consecration of the Priests

“[a]NOW this is [1]what you shall do
to them to consecrate them to minister as priests to Me: take one
young bull and two rams without
blemish,
2 and [a]unleavened bread and unleavened cakes mixed with oil, and
unleavened wafers [1]spread with oil;
you shall make them of fine wheat
flour.
3“And you shall put them in one
basket, and present them in the basket along with the bull and the two
rams.
4“Then you shall bring Aaron and
his sons to the doorway of the tent

22 [1]Or, *pouch,* and so through v. 30
28 [1]Or, *violet*
30 [1]I.e., Lights and the Perfections
31 [1]Or, *violet* [a]Ex. 39:22-26
32 [1]Or, *for his head*
35 [1]Lit., *for ministering* [2]Lit., *its sound* [3]Lit., *comes out* from
36 [a]Ex. 39:30, 31
37 [1]Lit., *place* [2]Or, *violet*
38 [1]Or, *bear* [a]Lev. 10:17; 22:16; Num.18:1
39 [1]Lit., *variegator;* i.e., a weaver in colors [a]Ex. 39:27-29
40 [1]Lit., *headgear* [a]Ex. 29:9; 39:28; Lev.8:13
41 [1]Lit., *fill their hand*
42 [1]Lit., *be* [a]Ex. 39:28
43 [1]Or, *iniquity* [2]Lit., *seed* [a]Ex. 20:26
1 [1]Lit., *the thing which* [a]Lev. 8:1-34
2 [1]Or, *anointed* [a]Lev. 6:19-23

of meeting, and wash them with water.
5"And you shall take the garments, and put on Aaron the [a]tunic
and [b]the robe of the ephod and [c]the
ephod and [d]the [1]breastpiece, and
gird him with the skillfully [e]woven
band of the ephod;
6 and you shall set the [a]turban on
his head, and put [b]the holy crown on
the turban.
7"Then you shall take [a]the anointing oil, and pour it on his head and
anoint him.
8"And you shall bring his sons
and put [a]tunics on them.
9"And you shall gird them with
[a]sashes, Aaron and his sons, and
bind [1]caps on them, and they shall
have [b]the priesthood by a perpetual
statute. So you shall [2]ordain Aaron
and his sons.

The Sacrifices

10"Then you shall bring the bull
before the tent of meeting, and Aaron and his sons shall lay their hands
on the head of the bull.
11"And you shall slaughter the bull
before the LORD at the doorway of
the tent of meeting.
12"And you shall take some of the
blood of the bull and put *it* on the
horns of the altar with your finger;
and you shall pour out all the blood
at the base of the altar.
13"And you shall take all the fat
that covers the entrails and the
[1]lobe of the liver, and the two kidneys and the fat that is on them, and
offer them up in smoke on the altar.
14"But the flesh of the bull and its
hide and its refuse, you shall burn
with fire outside the camp; it is a sin
offering.
15"You shall also take the one ram,
and Aaron and his sons shall lay
their hands on the head of the ram;
16 and you shall slaughter the ram
and shall take its blood and sprinkle
it around on the altar.
17"Then you shall cut the ram into
its pieces, and wash its entrails and
its legs, and put *them* [1]with its
pieces and [2]its head.
18"And you shall offer up in smoke
the whole ram on the altar; it is a
burnt offering to the LORD: it is a
soothing aroma, an offering by fire
to the LORD.
19"Then you shall take the [1]other
ram, and Aaron and his sons shall
lay their hands on the head of the
ram.
20"And you shall slaughter the
ram, and take some of its blood and
put *it* on the lobe of Aaron's right
ear and on the lobes of his sons'
right ears and on the thumbs of their
right hands and on the big toes of
their right feet, and sprinkle the *rest*
of the blood around on the altar.
21"Then you shall take some of the
blood that is on the altar and some
of the anointing oil, and sprinkle *it*
on Aaron and on his garments, and
on his sons and on his sons' garments with him; so he and his garments shall be consecrated, as well
as his sons and his sons' garments
with him.
22"You shall also take the fat from
the ram and the fat tail, and the fat
that covers the entrails and the
[1]lobe of the liver, and the two kidneys and the fat that is on them and
the right thigh (for it is a ram of [2]or-
dination),
23 and one cake of bread and one
cake of bread *mixed with* oil and
one wafer from the basket of unleavened bread which is *set* before
the LORD;
24 and you shall put [1]all these [2]in
the [3]hands of Aaron and [2]in the
[3]hands of his sons, and shall wave
them as a wave offering before the
LORD.
25"And you shall take them from
their hands, and offer them up in
smoke on the altar on the burnt offering for a soothing aroma before
the LORD; it is an offering by fire to
the LORD.
26"Then you shall take [a]the breast
of Aaron's ram of [1]ordination, and
wave it as a wave offering before the
LORD; and it shall be your portion.
27"And you shall consecrate the
breast of the wave offering and the
thigh of the heave offering which
was waved and which was [1]offered
from the ram of [2]ordination, from
the one which was for Aaron and
from the one which was for his sons.
28"And it shall be for Aaron and
his sons as *their* portion forever
from the sons of Israel, for it is a
heave offering; and it shall be a
heave offering from the sons of Israel from the sacrifices of their
peace offerings, *even* their heave offering to the LORD.
29"And the holy garments of Aaron shall be for his sons after him,
[1]that in them they may be anointed
and ordained.
30"For seven days the one of his
sons who is priest in his stead shall
put them on when he enters the tent
of meeting to minister in the holy
place.

5 [1]Or, *pouch* [a]Ex. 28:39 [b]Ex. 28:31 [c]Ex. 28:6 [d]Ex. 28:15 [e]Ex. 28:8

6 [a]Ex. 28:4, 39 [b]Ex. 28:36, 37; Lev. 8:9

7 [a]Ps. 133:2

8 [a]Ex. 28:39, 40

9 [1]Lit., *headgear* [2]Lit., *fill the hand of* [a]Ex. 28:40 [b]Ex. 40:15; Num. 3:10; 18:7; 25:13; Deut. 18:5

13 [1]Or, *appendage on*

17 [1]Lit., *on* [2]Lit., *on its*

19 [1]Lit., *second*

22 [1]Or, *appendage on* [2]Lit., *filling*

24 [1]Lit., *the whole* [2]Lit., *on* [3]Lit., *palms*

26 [1]Lit., *filling* [a]Lev. 7:31-34

27 [1]Lit., *heaved or lifted up* [2]Lit., *filling*

29 [1]Lit., *for anointing in them and filling their hand in them*

Food of the Priests

31"And you shall take the ram of
[1]ordination and boil its flesh in a
holy place.
32"And Aaron and his sons shall
eat the flesh of the ram, and the
bread that is in the basket, at the
doorway of the tent of meeting.
33"Thus they shall eat [1]those
things by which atonement was
made [2]at their ordination *and* consecration; but a [3a]layman shall not
eat *them*, because they are holy.
34"And [a]if any of the flesh of [1]ordi-
nation or any of the bread remains
until morning, then you shall burn
the remainder with fire; it shall not
be eaten, because it is holy.
35"And thus you shall do to Aaron
and to his sons, according to all that
I have commanded you; you shall
[1]ordain them through [a]seven days.
36"And each day you shall offer a
bull as a sin offering for atonement,
and you shall [1]purify the altar when
you make atonement [2]for it; and you
shall anoint it to consecrate it.
37"For seven days you shall make
atonement [1]for the altar and consecrate it; then the altar shall be most
holy, *and* whatever touches the altar shall be holy.
38"Now [a]this is what you shall offer on the altar: two one year old
lambs each day, continuously.
39"The one lamb you shall offer in
the morning, and the [1]other lamb
you shall offer at [2]twilight;
40 and there *shall be* one-tenth *of
an ephah* of fine flour mixed with
one-fourth of a hin of beaten oil, and
one-fourth of a hin of wine for a libation with one lamb.
41"And the [1]other lamb you shall
offer at [2]twilight, and shall offer
with it [3]the same grain offering as
the morning and [4]the same libation,
for a soothing aroma, an offering by
fire to the LORD.
42"It shall be a continual burnt offering throughout your generations
at the doorway of the tent of meeting before the LORD, where I will
meet with you, to speak to you
there.
43"And I will meet there with the
sons of Israel, and it shall be consecrated by My glory.
44"And I will consecrate the tent
of meeting and the altar; I will also
consecrate Aaron and his sons to
minister as priests to Me.
45"And [a]I will dwell among the
sons of Israel and will be their God.
46"And they shall know that I am
the LORD their God who brought
them out of the land of Egypt, that I
might dwell among them; I am the
LORD their God.

CHAPTER 30

The Altar of Incense

"MOREOVER, you shall make
[a]an altar as a place for burning incense; you shall make it of acacia
wood.
2"Its length *shall be* a [1]cubit, and
its width a cubit, it shall be square,
and its height *shall be* two cubits; its
horns *shall be* [2]of one piece with it.
3"And you shall overlay it with
pure gold, its top and its [1]sides all
around, and its horns; and you shall
make a gold molding all around for
it.
4"And you shall make two gold
rings for it under its molding; you
shall make *them* on its two sides—
on [1]opposite sides—and [2]they shall
be holders for poles with which to
carry it.
5"And you shall make the poles of
acacia wood and overlay them with
gold.
6"And you shall put [1]this altar in
front of the veil that is [2]near the ark
of the testimony, in front of the
[3]mercy seat that is over *the ark of*
the testimony, where I will meet
with you.
7"And Aaron shall burn fragrant
incense on it; he shall burn it every
morning when he trims the lamps.
8"And when Aaron [1]trims the
lamps at [2]twilight, he shall burn incense. *There shall be* perpetual incense before the LORD throughout
your generations.
9"You shall not offer any strange
incense on [1]this altar, or burnt offering or meal offering; and you shall
not pour out a libation on it.
10"And Aaron shall make atonement on its horns once a year; he
shall make atonement on it with the
blood of the sin offering of atonement once a year throughout your
generations. It is most holy to the
LORD."
11 The LORD also spoke to Moses,
saying,
12"When you take [a]a [1]census of
the sons of Israel [2]to number them,
then each one of them shall give a
ransom for [3]himself to the LORD,
when you [4]number them, that there
may be no plague among them
when you [4]number them.
13"This is what everyone who [1]is
numbered shall give: half a shekel
according to the shekel of the sanc-

31 [1]Lit., *filling*

33 [1]Lit., *them* [2]Lit., *to fill their hand to sanctify them* [3]Lit., *stranger* [a]Lev. 22:10, 13

34 [1]Lit., *filling* [a]Ex. 12:10; 23:18; 34:25

35 [1]Lit., *fill their hand* [a]Lev. 8:33

36 [1]Or, *offer a sin offering on the altar* [2]Lit., *upon*

37 [1]Lit., *upon*

38 [a]Num. 28:3-31; 29:6-38

39 [1]Lit., *second* [2]Lit., *between the two evenings*

41 [1]Lit., *second* [2]Lit., *between the two evenings* [3]Lit., *according to the grain offering of the morning* [4]Lit., *according to its*

45 [a]Ex. 25:8; Num. 5:3; Deut. 12:11

1 [a]Ex. 37:25-29

2 [1]I.e., a cubit equals approx. 18 inches [2]Lit., *from itself*

3 [1]Lit., *walls*

4 [1]Lit., *its two* [2]Lit., *it*

6 [1]Lit., *it* [2]Lit., *upon, or over* [3]Lit., *propitiatory*

8 [1]Lit., *causes to ascend* [2]Lit., *between the two evenings*

9 [1]Lit., *it*

12 [1]Lit., *sum* [2]Lit., *for their being mustered* [3]Lit., *his soul* [4]Lit., *muster* [a]Ex. 38:25, 26; Num. 1:2; 26:2

13 [1]Lit., *passes over to those who are mustered*

tuary (the shekel is twenty gerahs), half a shekel as a [2]contribution to the LORD.

14 "Everyone who [1]is numbered, from twenty years old and over, shall give the [2]contribution to the LORD.

15 "The rich shall not pay more, and the poor shall not pay less than the half shekel, when you give the [1]contribution to the LORD to make atonement for [2]yourselves.

16 "And you shall take the atonement money from the sons of Israel, and shall give it for the service of the tent of meeting, that it may be a memorial for the sons of Israel before the LORD, to make atonement for [1]yourselves."

17 And the LORD spoke to Moses, saying,

18 "You shall also make [a]a laver of [1]bronze, with its base of bronze, for washing; and you shall put it between the tent of meeting and the altar, and you shall put water in it.

19 "And Aaron and his sons shall wash their hands and their feet from it;

20 when they enter the tent of meeting, they shall wash with water, that they may not die; or when they approach the altar to minister, by offering up in smoke a fire *sacrifice* to the LORD.

21 "So they shall wash their hands and their feet, that they may not die; and it shall be a perpetual statute for them, for [1]Aaron and his [2]descendants throughout their generations."

The Anointing Oil

22 Moreover, the LORD spoke to Moses, saying,

23 "Take also for yourself the finest of spices: of flowing myrrh five hundred *shekels*, and of fragrant cinnamon half as much, two hundred and fifty, and of fragrant cane two hundred and fifty,

24 and of cassia five hundred, according to the shekel of the sanctuary, and of olive oil a hin.

25 "And you shall make [1]of these a holy anointing oil, a perfume mixture, the work of a perfumer; it shall be [a]a holy anointing oil.

26 "And with it you shall anoint the tent of meeting and the ark of the testimony,

27 and the table and all its utensils, and the lampstand and its utensils, and the altar of incense,

28 and the altar of burnt offering and all its utensils, and the laver and its stand.

29 "You shall also consecrate them, that they may be most holy; whatever touches them shall be holy.

30 "And you shall anoint Aaron and his sons, and consecrate them, that they may minister as priests to Me.

31 "And you shall speak to the sons of Israel, saying, 'This shall be a holy anointing oil to Me throughout your generations.

32 'It shall not be poured on [1]anyone's body, nor shall you make *any* like it, in [2]the same proportions; it is holy, *and* it shall be holy to you.

33 'Whoever shall mix *any* like it, or whoever puts any of it on a [1]layman, [2]shall be cut off from his people.' "

The Incense

34 Then the LORD said to Moses, "Take for yourself spices, stacte and onycha and galbanum, spices with pure frankincense; there shall be an equal part of each.

35 "And with it you shall make incense, a perfume, the work of a perfumer, salted, pure, *and* holy.

36 "And you shall beat some of it very fine, and put part of it before the testimony in the tent of meeting, where I shall meet with you; it shall be most holy to you.

37 "And the incense which you shall make, you shall not make in [1]the same proportions for yourselves, it shall be holy to you for the LORD.

38 "Whoever shall make *any* like it, to [1]use as perfume, [2]shall be cut off from his people."

CHAPTER 31

The Skilled Craftsmen

[a]NOW the LORD spoke to Moses, saying,

2 "See, I have called by name Bezalel, the son of Uri, the son of Hur, of the tribe of Judah.

3 "And I have filled him with the Spirit of God in wisdom, in understanding, in knowledge, and in all *kinds of* [1]craftsmanship,

4 to [1]make artistic designs for work in gold, in silver, and in [2]bronze,

5 and in the cutting of stones [1]for settings, and in the carving of wood, that he may work in all *kinds of* [2]craftsmanship.

6 "And behold, I Myself have [1]appointed with him Oholiab, the son of Ahisamach, of the tribe of Dan; and in the hearts of all who are [2]skillful I have put [3]skill, that they may

13 [2]Lit., *heave offering*

14 [1]Note 1, v. 13 [2]Lit., *heave offering of the LORD*

15 [1]Lit., *heave offering of the LORD* [2]Lit., *your souls*

16 [1]Lit., *your souls*

18 [1]Or, *copper* [a]Ex. 38:8

21 [1]Lit., *him* [2]Lit., *seed*

25 [1]Lit., *it* [a]Ex. 37:29; 40:9; Lev. 8:10

32 [1]Lit., *the flesh of man* [2]Lit., *its proportion*

33 [1]Lit., *stranger* [2]Lit., *even he shall*

37 [1]Lit., *its proportion*

38 [1]Lit., *smell of it* [2]Lit., *even he shall*

1 [a]Ex. 35:30-36:1

3 [1]Or, *workmanship*

4 [1]Lit., *devise devices* [2]Or, *copper*

5 [1]Lit., *to fill in (for a setting)* [2]Or, *workmanship*

6 [1]Lit., *given* [2]Lit., *wise of heart* [3]Lit., *wisdom*

make all that I have commanded
you:
7 the tent of meeting, and the ark
of testimony, and the [1]mercy seat
upon it, and all the furniture of the
tent,
8 the table also and its [1]utensils,
and the [a]pure *gold* lampstand with
all its [1]utensils, and the altar of incense,
9 the altar of burnt offering also
with all its [1]utensils, and the laver
and its stand,
10 the [1]woven garments as well,
and the holy garments for Aaron the
priest, and the garments of his sons,
with which to [2]carry on their priesthood;
11 the anointing oil also, and the
fragrant incense for the holy place,
they are to make *them* according to
all that I have commanded you."

The Sign of the Sabbath

12 And the LORD spoke to Moses,
saying,
13"But as for you, speak to the
sons of Israel, saying, '[a]You shall
surely observe My sabbaths; for *this*
is [b]a sign between Me and you
throughout your generations, that
you may know that I am the LORD
who sanctifies you.
14 'Therefore you are to observe
the sabbath, for it is holy to you.
[a]Everyone who profanes it shall
surely be put to death; for whoever
does any work on it, that person
shall be cut off from among his people.
15 'For six days work may be done,
but on the seventh day there is a
[a]sabbath of complete rest, holy to
the LORD; [b]whoever does any work
on the sabbath day shall surely be
put to death.
16 'So the sons of Israel shall observe the sabbath, to [1]celebrate the
sabbath throughout their generations as a perpetual covenant.'
17"[a]It is a sign between Me and the
sons of Israel forever; [b]for in six
days the LORD made heaven and
earth, but on the seventh day He
ceased *from labor,* and was refreshed."
18 And when He had finished
speaking with him upon Mount Sinai, He gave Moses [a]the two tablets
of the testimony, tablets of stone,
[b]written by the finger of God.

CHAPTER 32

The Golden Calf

NOW when the people saw that
Moses [a]delayed to come down from
the mountain, the people assembled
about Aaron, and said to him,
"Come, [b]make us [1]a god who will go
before us; as for [c]this Moses, the
man who brought us up from the
land of Egypt, we do not know what
has become of him."
2 And Aaron said to them, "[a]Tear
off the gold rings which are in the
ears of your wives, your sons, and
your daughters, and bring *them* to
me."
3 Then all the people tore off the
gold rings which were in their ears,
and brought *them* to Aaron.
4 And he took *this* from their
hand, and fashioned it with a grav-
ing tool, and made it into a [a]molten
calf; and they said, "[1]This is your
god, O Israel, who brought you up
from the land of Egypt."
5 Now when Aaron saw *this,* he
built an altar before it; and Aaron
made a proclamation and said, "Tomorrow *shall be* a feast to the
LORD."
6 So the next day they rose early
and [a]offered burnt offerings, and
brought peace offerings; and [b]the
people sat down to eat and to drink,
and rose up [c]to play.
7 Then the LORD spoke to Moses,
"Go [1]down at once, for your people,
whom [a]you brought up from the
land of Egypt, have corrupted *themselves.*
8"They have quickly turned aside
from the way which I commanded
them. They have made for themselves a molten calf, and have worshiped it, and [a]have sacrificed to it,
and said, '[1]This is your god, O Israel,
who brought you up from the land
of Egypt!' "
9 [a]And the LORD said to Moses, "I
have seen this people, and behold,
they are [1b]an obstinate people.
10"Now then [a]let Me alone, that
My anger may burn against them,
and that I may destroy them; and I
will make of you a great nation."

Moses' Entreaty

11 Then [a]Moses entreated the
LORD his God, and said, "O LORD,
why doth Thine anger burn against
Thy people whom Thou hast
brought out from the land of Egypt
with great power and with a mighty
hand?
12"Why should [a]the Egyptians
speak, saying, 'With evil *intent* He
brought them out to kill them in the
mountains and to destroy them
from the face of the earth'? Turn
from Thy burning anger and change

7 [1]Lit., *propitiatory*
8 [1]Or, *vessels* [a]Lev. 24:4
9 [1]Or, *vessels*
10 [1]Or, *service garments* [2]Lit., *minister as priests*
13 [a]Ex. 20:8 [b]Ex. 31:17; Ezek. 20:12, 20
14 [a]Ex. 31:15; 35:2; Num. 15:32, 35, John 7:23
15 [a]Ex. 16:23; 35:2, 3 [b]Ex. 31:14
16 [1]Lit., *do*
17 [a]Ex. 31:13 [b]Gen. 2:2, 3; Ex. 20:11
18 [a]Ex. 24:12 [b]Ex. 32:15, 16; 34:1, 28
1 [1]Or, *gods* [a]Ex. 24:18; Deut. 9:11, 12 [b]Acts 7:40 [c]Ex. 14:11
2 [a]Ex. 35:22
4 [1]Or, *"These are your gods* [a]Deut. 9:16; Acts 7:41
6 [a]Acts 7:41 [b]1 Cor. 10:7 [c]Ex. 32:17-19; Num. 25:2
7 [1]Lit., *go down* [a]Ex.32:4, 11; Deut. 9:12
8 [1]Or, *These are your gods* [a]Ex. 22:20; 34:15; Deut. 32:17
9 [1]Or, *a stiff-necked* [a]Num. 14:11-20 [b]Ex. 33:3, 5; 34:9; Acts 7:51
10 [a]Deut. 9:14
11 [a]Deut. 9:18
12 [a]Deut. 9:28; Josh. 7:9

Thy mind about *doing* harm to Thy
people.
13"Remember Abraham, Isaac,
and Israel, Thy servants to whom
Thou didst [a]swear by Thyself, and
didst say to them, 'I will multiply
your [1]descendants [b]as the stars of
the heavens, and [c]call this land of
which I have spoken I will give to
your [1]descendants, and they shall
inherit *it* forever.' "
14 [a]So the LORD changed His mind
about the harm which He said He
would do to His people.
15 [a]Then Moses turned and went
down from the mountain with the
two tablets of the testimony in his
hand, [b]tablets which were written
on both [1]sides; they were written on
one *side* and the other.
16 And the tablets were God's
work, and the writing was God's
writing engraved on the tablets.
17 Now when Joshua heard the
sound of the people [1]as they
shouted, he said to Moses, "There is
a sound of war in the camp."
18 But he said,
"It is not the sound of the cry of
triumph,
Nor is it the sound of the cry of
defeat;
But the sound of singing I
hear."

Moses' Anger

19 And it came about, as soon as
[1]Moses came near the camp, that he
saw the calf and *the* [a]dancing; and
Moses' anger burned, and [b]he threw
the tablets from his hands and shattered them [2]at the foot of the mountain.
20 [a]And he took the calf which
they had made and burned *it* with
fire, and ground it to powder, and
scattered it over the surface of the
water, and made the sons of Israel
drink *it.*
21 Then Moses said to Aaron,
"What did this people do to you,
that you have brought *such* great sin
upon them?"
22 And Aaron said, "Do not let the
anger of my lord burn; you know the
people yourself, [a]that they are
[1]prone to evil.
23"For [a]they said to me, 'Make [1]a
god for us who will go before us; for
this Moses, the man who brought us
up from the land of Egypt, we do not
know what has become of him.'
24"And I said to them, 'Whoever
has any gold, let them tear it off.' So
they gave *it* to me, and [a]I threw it
into the fire, and out came this calf."
25 Now when Moses saw that the
people were [1]out of control—for
[a]Aaron had let them [2]get out of control to be a derision among [3]their
enemies—
26 then Moses stood in the gate of
the camp, and said, "Whoever is for
the LORD, *come* to me!" And all the
sons of Levi gathered together to
him.
27 And he said to them, "Thus
says the LORD, the God of Israel,
'Every man *of you* put his sword
upon his thigh, and go back and
forth from gate to gate in the camp,
and kill every man his brother, and
every man his friend, and every man
his [1]neighbor.' "
28 So [a]the sons of Levi did [1]as
Moses instructed, and about three
thousand men of the people fell that
day.
29 Then Moses said, "[1]Dedicate
yourselves today to the LORD—for
every man has been against his son
and against his brother—in order
that He may bestow a blessing upon
you today."
30 And it came about on the next
day that Moses said to the people,
"You yourselves have [1]committed a
great sin; and now I am going up to
the LORD, perhaps I can make atonement for your sin."
31 Then Moses returned to the
LORD, and said, "Alas, this people
has [1]committed a great sin, and they
have made [2]a [a]god of gold for themselves.
32"But now, if Thou wilt, forgive
their sin—and if not, please blot me
out from Thy [a]book which Thou
hast written!"
33 And the LORD said to Moses,
"Whoever has sinned against Me, [a]I
will blot him out of My book.
34"But go now, lead the people
[a]where I told you. Behold, [b]My angel shall go before you; nevertheless
in the day when I [1]punish, [c]I will
[2]punish them for their sin."
35 [a]Then the LORD smote the people, because of what [b]they did with
the calf which Aaron had made.

CHAPTER 33

The Journey Resumed

THEN the LORD spoke to Moses,
"Depart, go up from here, you and
the people whom you have brought
up from the land of Egypt, to the
land of which [a]I swore to Abraham,
Isaac, and Jacob, saying, 'To your
[1]descendants I will give it.'
2"And I will send [a]an angel before
you and [b]I will drive out the Canaanite, the Amorite, the Hittite, the

13 [1]Lit., *seed* [a]Gen. 22:16-18 [b]Gen. 15:5; 26:4 [c]Ex. 13:5, 11; 33:1
14 [a]Ps. 106:45
15 [1]Lit., *their sides* [a]Deut. 9:15 [b]Ex. 31:18
17 [1]Lit., *in its shouting*
19 [1]Lit., *he* [2]Lit., *beneath* [a]Ex. 32:6 [b]Deut. 9:17
20 [a]Deut. 9:21
22 [1]Lit., *in evil* [a]Deut. 9:24
23 [1]Or, *gods* [a]Ex. 32:1-4
24 [a]Ex. 32:4
25 [1]Lit., *let loose* [2]Lit., *go loose* [3]Lit., *those who rise against them* [a]1 Kin. 12:28-30; 14:16
27 [1]Or, *kin*
28 [1]Lit., *according to Moses' word* [a]Num. 25:7-13; Deut. 33:9
29 [1]Lit., *"Fill your hand*
30 [1]Lit., *sinned*
31 [1]Lit., *sinned* [2]Or, *gods* [a]Ex. 20:23
32 [a]Ps. 69:28; Is. 4:3; Dan. 12:1; Mal. 3:16, 17
33 [a]Ex. 17:14; Deut. 29:20; Ps. 9:5
34 [1]Lit., *visit* [2]Lit., *visit their sin upon them* [a]Ex. 3:17 [b]Ex. 23:20 [c]Ps. 99:8
35 [a]Ex. 32:28 [b]Ex. 32:4, 24
1 [1]Lit., *seed* [a]Ex. 32:13
2 [a]Ex. 32:34 [b]Ex. 23:27-31

Perizzite, the Hivite and the Jebusite.
3"*Go up* to a land [a]flowing with
milk and honey; for I will not go up
in your midst, because you are [1b]an
obstinate people, lest [c]I destroy you
on the way."
4 When the people heard this
[1]sad word, [a]they went into mourning, and none of them put on his ornaments.
5 For the LORD had said to Moses,
"Say to the sons of Israel, 'You are
[1a]an obstinate people; should I go up
in your midst for one moment, I
would destroy you. Now therefore
put off your ornaments from you,
that I may know what I will do with
you.'"
6 So the sons of Israel stripped
themselves of their ornaments from
Mount Horeb *onward.*
7 Now Moses used to take [a]the
tent and pitch it outside the camp, a
good distance from the camp, and
he called it the tent of meeting. And
it came about, that everyone who
sought the LORD would go out to the
tent of meeting which was outside
the camp.
8 And it came about, whenever
Moses went out to the tent, that all
the people would arise and stand,
each at the entrance of his tent, and
gaze after Moses until he entered
the tent.
9 And it came about, whenever
Moses entered the tent, [a]the pillar of
cloud would descend and stand at
the entrance of the tent; [b]and [1]the
LORD would speak with Moses.
10 When all the people saw the pillar of cloud standing at the entrance
of the tent, all the people would
arise and worship, each at the entrance of his tent.
11 Thus [a]the LORD used to speak to
Moses face to face, just as a man
speaks to his friend. When [1]Moses
returned to the camp, his servant
Joshua, the son of Nun, a young
man, would not depart from the
tent.

Moses Intercedes

12 Then Moses said to the LORD,
"See, Thou dost say to me, '[a]Bring
up this people!' But Thou Thyself
hast not let me know [b]whom Thou
wilt send with me. [c]Moreover, Thou
hast said, 'I have known you by
name, and you have also found favor in My sight.'
13"Now therefore, I pray Thee, if I
have found favor in Thy sight, let me
know [a]Thy ways, that I may know
Thee, so that I may find favor in Thy

3 [1]Lit., *a stiff-necked* [a]Ex. 3:8, 17 [b]Ex. 32:9; 33:5 [c]Ex. 32:10
4 [1]Lit., *evil* [a]Num. 14:39
5 [1]Lit., *a stiff-necked* [a]Ex. 33:3
7 [a]Ex. 18:7, 12-16
9 [1]Lit., *He* [a]Ex. 13:21 [b]Ps. 99:7
11 [1]Lit., *he* [a]Num. 12:8; Deut. 34:10
12 [a]Ex. 3:10; 32:34 [b]Ex. 33:2 [c]Ex. 33:17
13 [a]Ps. 25:4; 51:13 [b]Ex. 3:7, 10; 5:1; 32:12, 14
14 [a]Deut. 4:37; Is. 63:9 [b]Deut. 12:10; 25:19; Josh. 22:4
15 [a]Ps. 80:3, 7, 19
16 [1]Lit., *ground* [a]Lev. 20:24, 26
17 [a]Ex. 33:12
18 [1]Lit., *he* [a]Ex. 33:20-23
19 [a]Ex. 34:6, 7 [b]Rom. 9:15
20 [a]Is. 6:5
21 [1]Lit., *with* [a]Ps. 18:2, 46; 27:5; 61:2; 62:7
22 [a]Is. 49:2; 51:16
1 [a]Ex. 24:12; 31:18
2 [1]Or, *place yourself before* [a]Ex. 19:11, 18, 20
3 [1]Lit., *on all* [a]Ex. 19:12, 13
4 [a]Ex. 34:1

sight. [b]Consider too, that this nation
is Thy people."
14 And He said, "[a]My presence
shall go *with you,* and [b]I will give
you rest."
15 Then he said to Him, "[a]If Thy
presence does not go *with us,* do not
lead us up from here.
16"For how then can it be known
that I have found favor in Thy sight,
I and Thy people? Is it not by Thy
going with us, so that [a]we, I and Thy
people, may be distinguished from
all the *other* people who are upon
the face of the [1]earth?"
17 And the LORD said to Moses, "I
will also do this thing of which you
have spoken; [a]for you have found
favor in My sight, and I have known
you by name."
18 [a]Then [1]Moses said, "I pray
Thee, show me Thy glory!"
19 And He said, "[a]I Myself will
make all My goodness pass before
you, and will proclaim the name of
the LORD before you; and [b]I will be
gracious to whom I will be gracious,
and will show compassion on whom
I will show compassion."
20 But He said, "You cannot see
My face, [a]for no man can see Me
and live!"
21 Then the LORD said, "Behold,
there is a place [1]by Me, and [a]you
shall stand *there* on the rock;
22 and it will come about, while
My glory is passing by, that I will
put you in the cleft of the rock and
[a]cover you with My hand until I
have passed by.
23"Then I will take My hand away
and you shall see My back, but My
face shall not be seen."

CHAPTER 34

The Two Tablets Replaced

NOW the LORD said to Moses,
"Cut out for yourself [a]two stone
tablets like the former ones, and I
will write on the tablets the words
that were on the former tablets
which you shattered.
2"So be ready by morning, and
come up in the morning to [a]Mount
Sinai, and [1]present yourself there to
Me on the top of the mountain.
3"And [a]no man is to come up with
you, nor let any man be seen [1]any-
where on the mountain; even the
flocks and the herds may not graze
in front of that mountain."
4 So he cut out [a]two stone tablets
like the former ones, and Moses
rose up early in the morning and
went up to Mount Sinai, as the LORD

had commanded him, and he took two stone tablets in his hand.

5 And [a]the LORD descended in the cloud and stood there with him as [1]he called upon the name of the LORD.

6 Then the LORD passed by in front of him and proclaimed, "The LORD, the LORD God, [a]compassionate and gracious, slow to anger, and abounding in lovingkindness and [1]truth;

7 who [a]keeps lovingkindness for thousands, who forgives iniquity, transgression and sin; yet He [b]will by no means leave *the guilty* unpunished, visiting the iniquity of fathers on the children and on the grandchildren to the third and fourth generations."

8 And Moses made haste [1]to bow low toward the earth and worship.

9 And he said, "[a]If now I have found favor in Thy sight, O LORD, I pray, [b]let the LORD go along in our midst, even though [1c]the people are so obstinate; and do Thou [d]pardon our iniquity and our sin, and [e]take us as Thine own [2]possession."

The Covenant Renewed

10 Then [1]God said, "Behold, [a]I am going to make a covenant. Before all your people [b]I will perform miracles which have not been [2]produced in all the earth, nor among any of the nations; and all the people [3]among whom you live will see the working of the LORD, for it is a fearful thing that I am going to perform with you.

11 "[1]Be sure to observe what I am commanding you this day: behold, [a]I am going to drive out the Amorite before you, and the Canaanite, the Hittite, the Perizzite, the Hivite and the Jebusite.

12 "[a]Watch yourself that you make no covenant with the inhabitants of the land into which you are going, lest it become a snare in your midst.

13 "[a]But *rather,* you are to tear down their altars and smash their *sacred* pillars and cut down their [1b]Asherim

14 —for [a]you shall not worship any other god, for the LORD, whose name is Jealous, is a jealous God—

15 lest you make a covenant with the inhabitants of the land and they play the harlot with their gods, and [a]sacrifice to their gods, and someone [b]invite you [1]to eat of his sacrifice;

16 and [a]you take some of his daughters for your sons, and his daughters play the harlot with their gods, and cause your sons *also* to play the harlot with their gods.

17 "[a]You shall make for yourself no molten gods.

18 "You shall observe [a]the Feast of Unleavened Bread. For [b]seven days you are to eat unleavened bread, [1]as I commanded you, at the appointed time in the [c]month of Abib, for in the month of Abib you came out of Egypt.

19 "[a]The [1]first offspring from every womb belongs to Me, and all your male livestock, the [1]first offspring from [2]cattle and sheep.

20 "[a]And you shall redeem with a lamb the [1]first offspring from a donkey; and if you do not redeem *it,* then you shall break its neck. You shall redeem [b]all the first-born of your sons. And [2c]none shall appear before Me empty-handed.

21 "You shall work [a]six days, but on the seventh day you shall rest; *even* during plowing time and harvest you shall rest.

22 "And you shall celebrate [a]the Feast of Weeks, *that is,* the first fruits of the wheat harvest, and the Feast of Ingathering at the turn of the year.

23 "[a]Three times a year all your males are to appear before the Lord [1]GOD, the God of Israel.

24 "For I will [1]drive out nations before you and enlarge your borders, and no man shall covet your land when you go up three times a year to appear before the LORD your God.

25 "[a]You shall not [1]offer the blood of My sacrifice with leavened bread, [b]nor is the sacrifice of the Feast of the Passover to [2]be left over until morning.

26 "You shall bring [a]the very first of the first fruits of your soil into the house of the LORD your God. You shall not boil a kid in its mother's milk."

27 Then the LORD said to Moses, "[a]Write [1]down these words, [b]for in accordance with these words I have made a covenant with you and with Israel."

28 So he was there with the LORD [a]forty days and forty nights; he did not eat bread or drink water. And [b]he wrote on the tablets the words of the covenant, [c]the Ten [1]Commandments.

Moses' Face Shines

29 And it came about when Moses was coming down from Mount Sinai (and the two tablets of the testimony *were* in Moses' hand as he was coming down from the moun-

5 [1]Or, *he called out with the name of the LORD* [a]Ex. 19:9; 33:9
6 [1]Or, *faithfulness* [a]Num. 14:18; Deut. 4:31; Neh. 9:17; Ps. 86:15; 103:8; 145:8
7 [a]Ex. 20:5, 6 [b]Ex. 23:7
8 [1]Lit., *and bowed*
9 [1]Lit., *it is a people stiff-necked* [2]Or, *inheritance* [a]Ex. 33:13 [b]Ex. 33:12 [c]Ex. 32:9 [d]Ex. 34:7 [e]Deut. 4:20; 9:26, 29; 32:9; Ps. 33:12
10 [1]Lit., He *said* [2]Lit., *created* [3]Lit., *in whose midst you are* [a]Ex. 34:27, 28 [b]Ps. 72:18; 136:4
11 [1]Lit., *Observe for yourself* [a]Ex. 33:2
12 [a]Ex. 23:32, 33
13 [1]I.e., wooden symbols of a female deity [a]Ex. 23:24 [b]Judg. 6:25, 26
14 [a]Ex. 20:3, 5; Deut. 4:24
15 [1]Lit., *and you eat* [a]Ex. 22:20; 32:8 [b]Num. 25:1, 2; Deut. 32:37, 38
16 [a]Deut. 7:3; Josh. 23:12, 13
17 [a]Ex. 20:23
18 [1]Or, *which* [a]Ex. 12:17 [b]Ex. 12:15, 16 [c]Ex. 12:2; 13:4
19 [1]Lit., *Every* [2]Or, *oxen* [a]Ex. 13:2
20 [1]Lit., *first opening of* [2]Lit., *they shall not* [a]Ex. 13:13 [b]Ex. 13:15; Num. 3:45 [c]Ex. 22:29
21 [a]Ex. 31:15; 35:2
22 [a]Ex. 23:16; Lev. 23:15
23 [1]YHWH, usually rendered LORD [a]Ex. 23:14-17
24 [1]Or, *dispossess*
25 [1]Lit., *slaughter* [2]Lit., *remain overnight* [a]Ex. 23:18 [b]Ex. 12:10
26 [a]Ex. 23:19
27 [1]Lit., *for yourself* [a]Ex. 17:14; 24:4 [b]Ex. 34:10
28 [1]Lit., *Words* [a]Ex. 24:18 [b]Ex. 31:18; 34:1 [c]Deut. 4:13; 10:4

tain), that Moses did not know that the skin of his face shone because of his speaking with Him.

30 So when Aaron and all the sons of Israel saw Moses, behold, the skin of his face shone, and [a]they were afraid to come near him.

31 Then Moses called to them, and Aaron and all [a]the rulers in the congregation returned to him; and Moses spoke to them.

32 And afterward all the sons of Israel came near, and he commanded them *to do* everything that the LORD had spoken [1]to him on Mount Sinai.

33 When Moses had finished speaking with them, [a]he put a veil over his face.

34 But whenever Moses went in before the LORD to speak with Him, [a]he would take off the veil until he came out; and whenever he came out and spoke to the sons of Israel what he had been commanded,

35 the sons of Israel would see the face of Moses, that the skin of Moses' face shone. So Moses would replace the veil over his face until he went in to speak with Him.

CHAPTER 35

The Sabbath Emphasized

THEN Moses assembled all the congregation of the sons of Israel, and said to them, "These are the things that the LORD has commanded *you* to [1]do.

2 "[a]For six days work may be done, but on the seventh day you shall have a holy *day,* [b]a sabbath of complete rest to the LORD; [c]whoever does any work on it shall be put to death.

3 "[a]You shall not kindle a fire in any of your dwellings on the sabbath day."

4 And Moses spoke to all the congregation of the sons of Israel, saying, "This is the thing which the LORD has commanded, saying,

5 '[a]Take from among you a [1]contribution to the LORD; whoever is of a willing heart, let him bring it as the LORD's [1]contribution: gold, silver, and [2]bronze,

6 and [1]blue, purple and scarlet *material,* fine linen, goats' *hair,*

7 and rams' skins [1]dyed red, and porpoise skins, and acacia wood,

8 and oil for lighting, and spices for the anointing oil, and for the fragrant incense,

9 and onyx stones and setting stones, for the ephod and for the [1]breastpiece.

Tabernacle Workmen

10 'And let every skillful man among you come, and make all that the LORD has commanded:

11 the [1]tabernacle, its tent and its covering, its hooks and its boards, its bars, its pillars, and its [2]sockets;

12 the ark and its poles, the [1]mercy seat, and the curtain of the screen;

13 the table and its poles, and all its [1]utensils, and the [a]bread of the [2]Presence;

14 the lampstand also for the light and its utensils and its lamps and the oil for the light;

15 and the altar of incense and its poles, and the anointing oil and the fragrant incense, and the screen for the doorway at the [1]entrance of the tabernacle;

16 the altar of burnt offering with its [1]bronze grating, its poles, and all its [2]utensils, the [3]basin and its stand;

17 the hangings of the court, its pillars and its [1]sockets, and the screen for the gate of the court;

18 the pegs of the tabernacle and the pegs of the court and their cords;

19 the [1a]woven garments, for ministering in the holy place, the holy garments for Aaron the priest, and the garments of his sons, to minister as priests.' "

Gifts Received

20 Then all the congregation of the sons of Israel departed from Moses' presence.

21 And [a]everyone whose heart [1]stirred him and everyone whose spirit [2]moved him came *and* brought the LORD's [3]contribution for the work of the tent of meeting and for all its service and for the holy garments.

22 Then all [1]whose hearts moved them, both men and women, came *and* brought brooches and [2]earrings and signet rings and bracelets, all articles of gold; so *did* every man who [3]presented an offering of gold to the LORD.

23 And every man, [1]who had in his possession [2]blue and purple and scarlet *material* and fine linen and goats' *hair* and rams' skins [3]dyed red and porpoise skins, brought them.

24 Everyone who could make a [1]contribution of silver and [2]bronze brought the LORD's [1]contribution; and every man, [3]who had in his possession acacia wood for any work of the service, brought it.

30 [a]2 Cor. 3:7
31 [a]Ex. 16:22
32 [1]Lit., *with*
33 [a]2 Cor. 3:13
34 [a]2 Cor. 3:16
1 [1]Lit., *do them.*
2 [a]Ex. 31:15 [b]Ex. 16:23 [c]Num. 15:32-36
3 [a]Ex. 12:16
5 [1]Or, *heave offering* [2]Or, *copper* [a]Ex. 25:1-9
6 [1]Or, *violet*
7 [1]Or, *tanned*
9 [1]Or, pouch
11 [1]Lit., *dwelling place* [2]Or, *bases*
12 [1]Lit., *propitiatory*
13 [1]Or, *vessels* [2]Lit., *Face* [a]Ex. 25:30
15 [1]Or, *doorway*
16 [1]Or, *copper* [2]Or, *vessels* [3]Or, *laver*
17 [1]Or, *bases*
19 [1]Or, *service garments* [a]Ex. 31:10
21 [1]Lit., *lifted up* [2]Or, *made him willing* [3]Or, *heave offering* [a]Ex. 25:2
22 [1]Or, *who were willing-hearted* [2]Or, *nose rings* [3]Lit., *waved a wave offering*
23 [1]Lit., *with whom was found* [2]Or, *violet* [3]Or, *tanned*
24 [1]Or, *heave offering* [2]Or, *copper* [3]Lit., *with whom was found*

25 And all the [1]skilled women
spun with their hands, and brought
what they had spun, *in* [2]blue and
purple *and* scarlet *material* and *in*
fine linen.
26 And all the women whose heart
[1]stirred with a skill spun the goats'
hair.
27 And the rulers brought the
onyx stones and the stones for setting for the ephod and for the
[1]breastpiece;
28 and the spice and the oil for the
light and for the anointing oil and
for the fragrant incense.
29 The [1]Israelites, all the men and
women, whose heart [2]moved them
to bring *material* for all the work,
which the LORD had commanded
through Moses to be done, brought
a freewill offering to the LORD.
30 [a]Then Moses said to the sons of
Israel, "See, the LORD has called by
name Bezalel the son of Uri, the son
of Hur, of the tribe of Judah.
31 "And He has filled him with the
Spirit of God, in wisdom, in understanding and in knowledge and in all
[1]craftsmanship;
32 [1]to make designs for working in
gold and in silver and in [2]bronze,
33 and in the cutting of stones for
settings, and in the carving of wood,
so as to perform in every inventive
work.
34 "He also has put in his heart to
teach, both he and Oholiab, the son
of Ahisamach, of the tribe of Dan.
35 "He has filled them with [1]skill to
perform every work of an engraver
and of a designer and of an embroi-
derer, in [2]blue and in purple *and* in
scarlet *material,* and in fine linen,
and of a weaver, as performers of
every work and makers of designs.

CHAPTER 36

The Tabernacle Underwritten

"NOW Bezalel and Oholiab, and
every [1]skillful person in whom the
LORD has put [2]skill and understanding to know how to perform all the
work [3]in the construction of the
sanctuary, shall perform in accordance with all that the LORD has commanded."
2 Then Moses called Bezalel and
Oholiab and every [1]skillful person in
[2]whom the LORD had put [3]skill, everyone whose heart stirred him, to
come to the work to perform it.
3 And they received from Moses
all the [1]contributions which the
sons of Israel had brought [2]to perform the work [3]in the construction
of the sanctuary. And they still *con-*
tinued bringing to him freewill offerings every morning.
4 And all the [1]skillful men who
were performing all the work of the
sanctuary came, each from [2]the
work which [3]he was performing,
5 and they said to [1]Moses, "[a]The
people are bringing much more than
enough for the [2]construction work
which the LORD commanded *us* to
[3]perform."
6 So Moses issued a command,
and a [1]proclamation was circulated
throughout the camp, saying, "Let
neither man nor woman any longer
perform work for the [2]contributions
of the sanctuary." Thus the people
were restrained from bringing *any*
more.
7 [a]For the [1]material they had was
sufficient and more than enough for
all the work, to perform it.

Construction Proceeds

8 [a]And all the [1]skillful men
among those who were performing
the work made the [2]tabernacle with
ten curtains; of fine twisted linen
and [3]blue and purple and scarlet
material, with cherubim, the work
of a skillful workman, [4]Bezalel
made them.
9 The length of each curtain was
twenty-eight [1]cubits, and the width
of each curtain four [1]cubits; all the
curtains had [2]the same measurements.
10 And he [1]joined five curtains to
one another, and *the other* five curtains he [1]joined to one another.
11 And he made loops of [1]blue on
the edge of the [2]outermost curtain
in the first [3]set; he did likewise on
the edge of the curtain that was
[2]outermost in the second [3]set.
12 He made fifty loops in the one
curtain and he made fifty loops on
the [1]edge of the curtain that was in
the second [2]set; the loops were opposite each other.
13 And he made fifty clasps of
gold, and [1]joined the curtains to one
another with the clasps, so the tabernacle was [2]a unit.
14 Then he made curtains of goats'
hair for a tent over the tabernacle;
he made eleven curtains [1]in all.
15 The length of each curtain was
thirty cubits, and four cubits the
width of each curtain; the eleven
curtains had [1]the same measurements.
16 And he [1]joined five curtains by
themselves, and *the other* six curtains by themselves.
17 Moreover, he made fifty loops
on the edge of the curtain that was

25 [1]Lit., *women wise of heart* [2]Or, *violet*
26 [1]Lit., *lifted them up in wisdom*
27 [1]Or, *pouch*
29 [1]Lit., *sons of Israel* [2]Lit., *made them willing*
30 [a]Ex. 31:1-6
31 [1]Or, *work*
32 [1]Lit., *devise devices* [2]Or, *copper*
35 [1]Lit., *wisdom of heart* [2]Or, *violet*
1 [1]Lit., *man wise of heart* [2]Lit., *wisdom* [3]Or, *connected with the service of;* lit., *of the service of*
2 [1]Lit., *man wise of heart* [2]Lit., *whose heart* [3]Lit., *wisdom*
3 [1]Lit., *lifted offering* [2]Lit., *to perform it for the work* [3]Lit., *of the service of*
4 [1]Lit., *wise* [2]Lit., *his* [3]Lit., *they were*
5 [1]Lit., *Moses, saying,* [2]Lit., *service for the work* [3]Lit., *perform it* [a]2 Chr. 24:14; 31:6-10
6 [1]Lit., *voice* [2]Lit., *heave offering*
7 [1]Lit., *work* [a]1 Kin. 8:64
8 [1]Lit., *wise of heart* [2]Lit., *dwelling place* [3]Or, *violet* [4]Lit., *he* [a]Ex. 26:1-14
9 [1]I.e., one cubit equals approximately 18 inches. [2]Lit., *one measure*
10 [1]Or, *coupled*
11 [1]Or, *violet* [2]Lit., *one curtain from the end in the coupling* [3]Lit., *coupling*
12 [1]Lit., *end* [2]Lit., *coupling*
13 [1]Or, *coupled* [2]Lit., *one*
14 [1]Lit., *them*
15 [1]Lit., *one measure*
16 [1]Or, *coupled*

outermost in the *first* [1]set, and he made fifty loops on the edge of the curtain *that was outermost in* the second [1]set.

18 And he made fifty clasps of [1]bronze to [2]join the tent together, that it might be [3]a unit.

19 And he made a covering for the tent of rams' skins [1]dyed red, and a covering of porpoise skins above.

20 [a]Then he made the boards for the tabernacle of acacia wood, standing upright.

21 Ten cubits was the length of [1]each board, and one and a half cubits the width of each board.

22 There were two tenons for each board, [1]fitted to one another; thus he did for all the boards of the tabernacle.

23 And he made the boards for the tabernacle: twenty boards [1]for the south side;

24 and he made forty [1]sockets of silver under the twenty boards; two [1]sockets under one board for its two tenons and two [1]sockets under another board for its two tenons.

25 Then for the second side of the tabernacle, on the north side, he made twenty boards,

26 and their forty [1]sockets of silver; two [1]sockets under one board and two [1]sockets under another board.

27 And for the [1]rear of the tabernacle, to the west, he made six boards.

28 And he made two boards for the corners of the [1]tabernacle at the [2]rear.

29 And they were double beneath, and together they were complete to its [1]top [2]to the first ring; thus he did with both of them for the two corners.

30 And there were eight boards with their [1]sockets of silver, sixteen [1]sockets, [2]two under every board.

31 Then he made bars of acacia wood, five for the boards of one side of the tabernacle,

32 and five bars for the boards of the [1]other side of the tabernacle, and five bars for the boards of the tabernacle for the [2]rear *side* to the west.

33 And he made the middle bar to pass through in the [1]center of the boards from end to end.

34 And he overlaid the boards with gold and made their rings of gold *as* holders for the bars, and overlaid the bars with gold.

35 [a]Moreover, he made the veil of [1]blue and purple and scarlet *material,* and fine twisted linen; he made it with cherubim, the work of a skillful workman.

36 And he made four pillars of acacia for it, and overlaid them with gold, with their hooks of gold; and he cast four [1]sockets of silver for them.

37 And he made a screen for the doorway of the tent, of [1]blue and purple and scarlet *material,* and fine twisted linen, the work of a [2]weaver;

38 and *he made* its five pillars with their hooks, and he overlaid their tops and their [1]bands with gold; but their five [2]sockets were of [3]bronze.

Chapter 37

Construction Continues

[a]NOW Bezalel made the ark of acacia wood; its length was two and a half [1]cubits, and its width one and a half cubits, and its height one and a half cubits;

2 and he overlaid it with pure gold inside and out, and made a gold molding for it all around.

3 And he cast four rings of gold for it on its four feet; even two rings on one side of it, and two rings on the [1]other side of it.

4 And he made poles of acacia wood and overlaid them with gold.

5 And he put the poles into the rings on the sides of the ark, to carry [1]it.

6 And he made a [1]mercy seat of pure gold, two and a half cubits [2]long, and one and a half cubits [3]wide.

7 And he made two cherubim of gold; he made them of hammered work, [1]at the two ends of the mercy seat;

8 one cherub [1]at the one end, and one cherub [1]at the other end; he made the cherubim *of one piece* with the mercy seat [1]at the two ends.

9 And the cherubim had *their* wings spread upward, covering the [1]mercy seat with their wings, with their faces toward each other; the faces of the cherubim were toward the mercy seat.

10 [a]Then he made the table of acacia wood, two [1]cubits [2]long and a cubit [3]wide and one and a half cubits [4]high.

11 And he overlaid it with pure gold, and made a gold molding for it all around.

12 And he made a rim for it of a handbreadth all around, and made a gold molding for its rim all around.

17 [1]Lit., *coupling*
18 [1]Or, *copper* [2]Or, *couple* [3]Lit., *one*
19 [1]Or, *tanned*
20 [a]Ex 26:15-29
21 [1]Lit., *the*
22 [1]Lit., *bound*
23 [1]Lit., *toward the side of Negev to the south*
24 [1]Or, *bases*
26 [1]Or, *bases*
27 [1]Lit., *extreme parts*
28 [1]Lit., *dwelling place* [2]Lit., *extreme parts*
29 [1]Or, *head* [2]Or, *with reference to*
30 [1]Or, *bases* [2]Lit., *two sockets*
32 [1]Or, *second* [2]Lit., *extreme parts*
33 [1]Lit., *midst*
35 [1]Or, *violet* [a]Ex. 26:31-37
36 [1]Or, *bases*
37 [1]Or, *violet* [2]Lit., *variegator;* i.e., a weaver in colors
38 [1]Or, *fillets, rings* [2]Or, *bases* [3]Or, *copper*
1 [1]I.e., one cubit equals approximately 18 inches [a]Ex. 25:10-20
3 [1]Lit., *second*
5 [1]Lit., *the ark*
6 [1]Lit., *propitiatory* [2]Lit., *its length* [3]Lit., *its width*
7 [1]Lit., *from*
8 [1]Lit., *from*
9 [1]Lit., *propitiatory*
10 [1]I.e., one cubit equals approximately 18 inches [2]Lit., *its length* [3]Lit., *its width* [4]Lit., *its height* [a]Ex. 25:23-29

13 And he cast four gold rings for it and put the rings on the four corners that were on its four feet.

14 Close by the rim were the rings, the holders for the poles to carry the table.

15 And he made the poles of acacia wood and overlaid them with gold, to carry the table.

16 And he made the utensils which were on the table, its [1]dishes and its pans and its [2]bowls and its jars, with which to pour out libations, of pure gold.

17 [a]Then he made the lampstand of pure gold. He made the lampstand of hammered work, its base and its shaft; its cups, its [1]bulbs and its flowers were *of one piece* with it.

18 And there were six branches going out of its sides; three branches of the lampstand from the one side of it, and three branches of the lampstand from the [1]other side of it;

19 three cups shaped like almond *blossoms,* a [1]bulb and a flower in one branch, and three cups shaped like almond *blossoms,* a [1]bulb and a flower in the other branch—so for the six branches going out of the lampstand.

20 And in the lampstand *there were* four cups shaped like almond *blossoms,* its [1]bulbs and its flowers;

21 and a [1]bulb was under the *first* pair of branches *coming* out of it, and a [1]bulb under the *second* pair of branches *coming* out of it, and a [1]bulb under the *third* pair of branches *coming* out of it, for the six branches coming out of the lampstand.

22 Their [1]bulbs and their branches were *of one piece* with it; the whole of it *was* a single hammered work of pure gold.

23 And he made its seven lamps with its snuffers and its [1]trays of pure gold.

24 He made it and all its utensils from a talent of pure gold.

25 [a]Then he made the altar of incense of acacia wood: a cubit [1]long and a cubit [2]wide, square, and two cubits [3]high; its horns were *of one piece* with it.

26 And he overlaid it with pure gold, its top and its [1]sides all around, and its horns; and he made a gold molding for it all around.

27 And he made two golden rings for it under its molding, on its two sides—on opposite sides—as holders for poles with which to carry it.

28 And he made the poles of acacia wood and overlaid them with gold.

29 [a]And he made the holy anointing oil and the pure, fragrant incense of spices, the work of a perfumer.

Chapter 38

The Tabernacle Completed

[a]THEN he made the altar of burnt offering of acacia wood, five [1]cubits [2]long, and five cubits [3]wide, square, and three cubits [4]high.

2 And he made its horns on its four corners, its horns [1]being *of one piece* with it, and he overlaid it with [2]bronze.

3 And he made all the utensils of the altar, the pails and the shovels and the basins, the flesh hooks and the firepans; he made all its utensils of bronze.

4 And he made for the altar a grating of bronze network beneath, under its ledge, reaching halfway up.

5 And he cast four rings on the four ends of the bronze grating *as* holders for the poles.

6 And he made the poles of acacia wood and overlaid them with bronze.

7 And he inserted the poles into the rings on the sides of the altar, with which to carry it. He made it hollow with planks.

8 [a]Moreover, he made the laver of bronze with its base of bronze, [1]from the mirrors of the serving women who served at the doorway of the tent of meeting.

9 [a]Then he made the court: for the [1]south side the hangings of the court were of fine twisted linen, one hundred cubits;

10 their twenty pillars, and their twenty [1]sockets, *made* of bronze; the hooks of the pillars and their [2]bands *were* of silver.

11 And for the north side *there were* one hundred cubits; their twenty pillars and their twenty [1]sockets *were* of bronze, the hooks of the pillars and their [2]bands *were* of silver.

12 And for the west side *there were* hangings of fifty cubits *with* their ten pillars and their ten [1]sockets; the hooks of the pillars and their [2]bands *were* of silver.

13 And for the [1]east side fifty cubits.

14 The hangings for the *one* [1]side *of the gate were* fifteen cubits, *with* their three pillars and their three [2]sockets,

---

16 [1]Or, *platters* [2]Lit., *libation bowls*

17 [1]Or, *calyxes* [a]Ex. 25:31-39

18 [1]Lit., *second*

19 [1]Or, *calyx*

20 [1]Or, *calyxes*

21 [1]Or, *calyx*

22 [1]Or, *calyxes*

23 [1]Lit., *snuff dishes*

25 [1]Lit., *its length* [2]Lit., *its width* [3]Lit., *its height* [a]Ex. 30:1-5

26 [1]Lit., *walls*

29 [a]Ex. 30:23-25, 34, 35

1 [1]I.e., one cubit equals approximately 18 inches [2]Lit., *its length* [3]Lit., *its width* [4]Lit., *its height* [a]Ex. 27:1-8

2 [1]Lit., *were* [2]Or, *copper*, and so for *bronze* throughout the chap.

8 [1]Lit., *with* [a]Ex. 30:18

9 [1]Lit., *to the side of the Negev, to the south* [a]Ex. 27:9-19

10 [1]Or, *bases* [2]Or, *fillets, rings*

11 [1]Or, *bases* [2]Or, *fillets, rings*

12 [1]Or, *bases* [2]Or, *fillets, rings*

13 [1]Lit., *east side, eastward*

14 [1]Lit., *shoulder* [2]Or, *bases*

15 and so for the [1]other [2]side. [3]On
both sides of the gate of the court
were hangings of fifteen cubits, *with*
their three pillars and their three
[4]sockets.
16 All the hangings of the court all
around *were* of fine twisted linen.
17 And the [1]sockets for the pillars
were of [2]bronze, the hooks of the
pillars and their [3]bands, of silver;
and the overlaying of their tops, of
silver, and all the pillars of the court
were furnished with silver [3]bands.
18 And the screen of the gate of
the court was the work of the
[1]weaver, of [2]blue and purple and
scarlet *material,* and fine twisted
linen. And the length was twenty
cubits and the [3]height was five cubits, corresponding to the hangings
of the court.
19 And their four pillars and their
four [1]sockets *were* of bronze; their
hooks *were* of silver, and the overlaying of their tops and their [2]bands
were of silver.
20 And all the pegs of the [1]taber-
nacle and of the court all around
were of bronze.

The Cost of the Tabernacle

21 [1]This is the number of *the
things for* the [2]tabernacle, the [2]tab-
ernacle of the testimony, as they
were [3]numbered according to the
[4]command of Moses, for the service
of the Levites, by the hand of Ithamar, the son of Aaron the priest.
22 Now Bezalel, the son of Uri the
son of Hur, of the tribe of Judah,
made all that the LORD had commanded Moses.
23 And with him was Oholiab, the
son of Ahisamach, of the tribe of
Dan, an engraver and a skillful
workman and a [1]weaver in [2]blue
and in purple and in scarlet *material,* and fine linen.
24 All the gold that was used for
the work, in all the work of the sanctuary, even the gold of the wave offering, was 29 talents and 730 shekels, according to the shekel of the
sanctuary.
25 [a]And the silver of those of the
congregation who were [1]numbered
was 100 talents and 1,775 shekels,
according to the shekel of the sanctuary;
26 a beka a head (*that is,* half a
shekel according to the shekel of the
sanctuary), for each one who passed
over to those who were [1]numbered,
from twenty years old and upward,
for [a]603,550 men.
27 And the hundred talents of silver were for casting the [1]sockets of
the sanctuary and the [1]sockets of
the veil; one hundred [1]sockets for
the hundred talents, a talent for a
[1]socket.
28 And of the 1,775 *shekels,* he
made hooks for the pillars and overlaid their tops and made [1]bands for
them.
29 And the bronze of the wave offering was 70 talents, and 2,400
shekels.
30 And with it he made the [1]sock-
ets to the doorway of the tent of
meeting, and the bronze altar and
its bronze grating, and all the utensils of the altar,
31 and the [1]sockets of the court all
around and the [1]sockets of the gate
of the court, and all the pegs of the
[2]tabernacle and all the pegs of the
court all around.

CHAPTER 39

The Priestly Garments

MOREOVER, from the [1]blue and
purple and scarlet *material,* they
made finely woven garments for
ministering in the holy place, [2]as
well as the holy garments which
were for Aaron, just as the LORD had
commanded Moses.
2 [a]And he made the ephod of
gold, *and* of [1]blue and purple and
scarlet *material,* and fine twisted
linen.
3 Then they hammered out gold
sheets and cut *them* into threads [1]to
be woven in *with* the [2]blue and the
purple and the scarlet *material,* and
the fine linen, the work of a skillful
workman.
4 They made attaching shoulder
pieces for [1]the ephod; it was attached at its two *upper* ends.
5 And the skillfully woven band
which was on it was like its workmanship, [1]of the same material: of
gold *and* of [2]blue and purple and
scarlet *material,* and fine twisted
linen, just as the LORD had commanded Moses.
6 And they made the onyx
stones, set in gold filigree *settings;*
they were engraved *like* the engravings of a signet, according to the
names of the sons of Israel.
7 And he placed them on the
shoulder pieces of the ephod, *as* memorial stones for the sons of Israel,
just as the LORD had commanded
Moses.
8 [a]And he made the breastpiece,
the work of a skillful workman, like
the workmanship of the ephod: of

---

15 [1]Lit., *second* [2]Lit., *shoulder* [3]Lit., *On this side and on that side* [4]Or, *bases*
17 [1]Or, *bases* [2]Or, *copper* [3]Or, *fillets, rings*
18 [1]Lit., *variegator;* i.e., a weaver in colors [2]Or, *violet* [3]Lit., *height in width*
19 [1]Or, *bases* [2]Or, *fillets, rings*
20 [1]Lit., *dwelling place*
21 [1]Lit., *These are the appointed things of the tabernacle* [2]Lit., *dwelling place* [3]Lit., *appointed* [4]Lit., *mouth*
23 [1]Lit., *variegator;* i.e., a weaver in colors [2]Or, *violet*
25 [1]Lit., *mustered* [a]Ex. 30:11-16
26 [1]Lit., *mustered* [a]Ex. 12:37; Num. 1:46; 26:51
27 [1]Or, *bases*
28 [1]Or, *fillets, rings*
30 [1]Or, *bases*
31 [1]Or, *bases* [2]Lit., *dwelling place*
1 [1]Or, *violet* [2]Lit., *and they made*
2 [1]Or, *violet* [a]Ex. 28:6-12
3 [1]Lit., *to work* [2]Or, *violet*
4 [1]Lit., *it*
5 [1]Lit., *from it* [2]Or, *violet*
8 [a]Ex. 28:15-28

gold *and* of [1]blue and purple and
scarlet *material* and fine twisted lin-
en.
9 It was square; they made the
breastpiece folded double, a span
[1]long and a span [2]wide when folded
double.
10 And they [1]mounted four rows
of stones on it. The first row *was* a
row of ruby, topaz, and emerald;
11 and the second row, a turquoise, a sapphire and a diamond;
12 and the third row, a jacinth, an
agate, and an amethyst;
13 and the fourth row, a beryl, an
onyx, and a jasper. They were set in
gold filigree *settings* when they
were [1]mounted.
14 And the stones were corresponding to the names of the sons of
Israel; they were twelve, corresponding to their names, *engraved*
with the engravings of a signet, each
with its name for the twelve tribes.
15 And they made on the breastpiece chains like cords, of twisted
cordage work in pure gold.
16 And they made two gold filigree *settings* and two gold rings, and
put the two rings on the two ends of
the breastpiece.
17 Then they put the two gold
cords in the two rings at the ends of
the breastpiece.
18 And they put the *other* two
ends of the two cords on the two
filigree *settings*, and put them on the
shoulder pieces of the ephod at the
front of it.
19 And they made two gold rings
and placed *them* on the two ends of
the breastpiece, on its inner edge
which was next to the ephod.
20 Furthermore, they made two
gold rings and placed them on the
bottom of the two shoulder pieces of
the ephod, on the front of it, close to
the place where it joined, above the
woven band of the ephod.
21 And they bound the breastpiece
by its rings to the rings of the ephod
with a [1]blue cord, that it might be on
the woven band of the ephod, and
that the breastpiece might not come
loose from the ephod, just as the
LORD had commanded Moses.
22 [a]Then he made the robe of the
ephod of woven work, all of [1]blue;
23 [a]and the opening of the robe
was *at the top* in the center, as the
opening of a coat of mail, with a
binding all around its opening, that
it might not be torn.
24 And they made pomegranates
of [1]blue and purple and scarlet *ma-*
terial and twisted *linen* on the hem
of the robe.
25 They also made bells of pure
gold, and put the bells between the
pomegranates all around on the
hem of the [1]robe,
26 [1]alternating a bell and a pomegranate all around on the hem of the
robe, for the service, just as the
LORD had commanded Moses.
27 [a]And they made the tunics of
finely woven linen for Aaron and his
sons,
28 and the turban of fine linen, and
the decorated [1]caps of fine linen,
and the linen breeches of fine
twisted linen,
29 and the sash of fine twisted lin-
en, and [1]blue and purple and scarlet
material, the work of the [2]weaver,
just as the LORD had commanded
Moses.
30 [a]And they made the plate of the
holy crown of pure gold, and [1]in-
scribed it like the engravings of a
signet, "Holy to the LORD."
31 And they [1]fastened a [2]blue cord
to it, to [1]fasten it on the turban
above, just as the LORD had commanded Moses.
32 Thus all the work of the [1]taber-
nacle of the tent of meeting was
completed; and the sons of Israel
did according to all that the LORD
had commanded Moses; so they did.
33 And they brought the tabernacle to Moses, the tent and all its [1]fur-
nishings: its clasps, its boards, its
bars, and its pillars and its [2]sockets;
34 and the covering of rams' skins
[1]dyed red, and the covering of porpoise skins, and the screening veil;
35 the ark of the testimony and its
poles and the [1]mercy seat;
36 the table, all its utensils, and
the bread of the [1]Presence;
37 the pure *gold* lampstand, [1]with
its arrangement of lamps and all its
utensils, and the oil for the light;
38 and the gold altar, and the
anointing oil and the fragrant incense, and the veil for the doorway
of the tent;
39 the [1]bronze altar and its
[1]bronze grating, its poles and all its
utensils, the laver and its stand;
40 the hangings for the court, its
pillars and its [1]sockets, and the
screen for the gate of the court, its
cords and its pegs and all the [2]equip-
ment for the service of the tabernacle, for the tent of meeting;
41 the woven garments for ministering in the holy place and the holy
garments for Aaron the priest and
the garments of his sons, to minister
as priests.
42 So the sons of Israel did all the

8 [1]Or, *violet*
9 [1]Lit., *its length* [2]Lit., *its width*
10 [1]Lit., *filled*
13 [1]Lit., *filled*
21 [1]Or, *violet*
22 [1]Or, *violet* [a]Ex. 28:31-34
24 [1]Or, *violet*
25 [1]Lit., *robe, between the pomegranates*
26 [1]Lit., *a bell and a pomegranate, a bell . . .*
27 [a]Ex. 28:39, 40, 42
28 [1]Lit., *headgear*
29 [1]Or, *violet* [2]Lit., *variegator;* i.e., a weaver in colors
30 [1]Lit., *wrote on it a writing* [a]Ex. 28:36, 37
31 [1]Lit., *put* [2]Or, *violet*
32 [1]Lit., *dwelling place*
33 [1]Or, *utensils* [2]Or, *bases*
34 [1]Or, *tanned*
35 [1]Lit., *propitiatory*
36 [1]Lit., *Face*
37 [1]Lit., *its lamps, the lamps set in order*
39 [1]Or, *copper*
40 [1]Or, *bases* [2]Or, *utensils*

work according to all that the LORD had commanded Moses.

43 And Moses [1]examined all the work and behold, they had done it; just as the LORD had commanded, this they had done. So Moses blessed them.

CHAPTER 40

The Tabernacle Erected

THEN the LORD spoke to Moses, saying,

2 "[a]On the first day of the first month you shall set up the [1]tabernacle of the tent of meeting.

3 "And you shall place the ark of the testimony there, and you shall screen the ark with the veil.

4 "And you shall bring in the table and [1]arrange what belongs on it; and you shall bring in the lampstand and [2]mount its lamps.

5 "Moreover, you shall set the gold altar of incense before the ark of the testimony, and set up the veil for the doorway to the tabernacle.

6 "And you shall set the altar of burnt offering in front of the doorway of the tabernacle of the tent of meeting.

7 "And you shall set the laver between the tent of meeting and the altar, and put water [1]in it.

8 "And you shall set up the court all around and [1]hang up the veil for the gateway of the court.

9 "Then you shall take the anointing oil and anoint the tabernacle and all that is in it, and shall consecrate it and all its [1]furnishings; and it shall be holy.

10 "And you shall anoint the altar of burnt offering and all its utensils, and consecrate the altar; and the altar shall be most holy.

11 "And you shall anoint the laver and its stand, and consecrate it.

12 "Then you shall bring Aaron and his sons to the doorway of the tent of meeting and wash them with water.

13 "And you shall put the holy garments on Aaron and anoint him and consecrate him, that he may minister as a priest to Me.

14 "And you shall bring his sons and put tunics on them;

15 and you shall anoint them even as you have anointed their father, that they may minister as priests to Me; and their anointing shall [1]qualify them for a [a]perpetual priesthood throughout their generations."

16 Thus Moses did; according to all that the LORD had commanded him, so he did.

17 Now it came about [a]in the first month [1]of the second year, on the first day of the month, that the [2]tabernacle was erected.

18 And Moses erected the tabernacle and [1]laid its [2]sockets, and set up its boards, and [1]inserted its bars and erected its pillars.

19 And he spread the tent over the tabernacle and put the covering of the tent [1]on top of it, just as the LORD had commanded Moses.

20 Then he took [a]the testimony and put *it* into the ark, and [1]attached the poles to the ark, and put the [2]mercy seat [3]on top of the ark.

21 And he brought the ark into the tabernacle, and set up a veil for the screen, and screened off the ark of the testimony, just as the LORD had commanded Moses.

22 Then he put the table in the tent of meeting, on the north side of the tabernacle, outside the veil.

23 And he set the arrangement of [a]bread in order on it before the LORD, just as the LORD had commanded Moses.

24 Then he placed the lampstand in the tent of meeting, opposite the table, on the south side of the tabernacle.

25 And he lighted the lamps before the LORD, just as the LORD had commanded Moses.

26 Then he placed the gold altar in the tent of meeting in front of the veil;

27 and he burned fragrant incense on it, just as the LORD had commanded Moses.

28 Then he set up the [1]veil for the doorway of the tabernacle.

29 And he set the altar of burnt offering *before* the doorway of the tabernacle of the tent of meeting, and offered on it the burnt offering and the meal offering, just as the LORD had commanded Moses.

30 And he placed the laver between the tent of meeting and the altar, and put water in it for washing.

31 [a]And from it Moses and Aaron and his sons washed their hands and their feet.

32 When they entered the tent of meeting, and when they approached the altar, they washed, just as the LORD had commanded Moses.

33 And he erected the court all around the [1]tabernacle and the altar, and [2]hung up the veil for the gateway of the court. Thus Moses finished the work.

---

43 [1]Lit., *saw*

2 [1]Lit., *dwelling place* [a]Ex. 19:1; 40:17; Num. 1:1

4 [1]Lit., *arrange its arrangement* [2]Or, *light*

7 [1]Lit., *there*

8 [1]Lit., *put the screen*

9 [1]Or, *utensils*

15 [1]Lit., *be for them* [a]Ex. 29:9

17 [1]Lit., *in* [2]Lit., *dwelling place* [a]Ex. 40:2

18 [1]Lit., *put* [2]Or, *bases*

19 [1]Lit., *over it above*

20 [1]Lit., *set* [2]Lit., *propitiatory* [3]Lit., *over the ark above* [a]Deut. 10:5; 1 Kin. 8:9; 2 Chr. 5:10; Heb. 9:4

23 [a]Ex. 25:30; Lev. 24:5, 6

28 [1]Or, *screen*

31 [a]Ex. 30:19, 20

33 [1]Or, *dwelling place* [2]Lit., *put the screen*

The Glory of the LORD

34 [a]Then the cloud covered the tent of meeting, and the glory of the LORD filled the tabernacle.

35 And Moses was not able to enter the tent of meeting because the cloud had settled on it, and the glory of the LORD filled the tabernacle.

36 And throughout all their journeys whenever the cloud was taken up from over the tabernacle, the sons of Israel would set out;

37 but if the cloud was not taken up, then they did not set out until the day when it was taken up.

38 For throughout all their journeys, the cloud of the LORD was on the tabernacle by day, and there was fire in it by night, in the sight of all the house of Israel.

34 [a]Num. 9:15-23

LEVITICUS

The Law of Burnt Offerings

THEN [a]the LORD called to Moses and spoke to him from the tent of meeting, saying,

2 "Speak to the sons of Israel and say to them, 'When any man of you brings an [1a]offering to the LORD, you shall bring your [1]offering of animals from [b]the herd or the flock.

3 'If his offering is a [a]burnt offering from the herd, he shall offer it a male [b]without defect; he shall offer it [c]at the doorway of the tent of meeting, that he may be accepted before the LORD.

4 '[a]And he shall lay his hand on the head of the burnt offering, that it may be accepted for him to make [b]atonement on his behalf.

5 'And [a]he shall slay the [1]young bull before the LORD; and Aaron's sons, the priests, shall offer up [b]the blood and [c]sprinkle the blood around on the altar that is at the doorway of the tent of meeting.

6 '[a]He shall then skin the burnt offering and cut it into its pieces.

7 '[a]And the sons of Aaron the priest shall put fire on the altar and arrange wood on the fire.

8 'Then Aaron's sons, the priests, shall arrange the pieces, the head, and the [a]suet over the wood which is on the fire that is on the altar.

9 'Its entrails, however, and its legs he shall wash with water. And [a]the priest shall offer up in smoke all of it on the altar for a burnt offering, an offering by fire of [b]a soothing aroma to the LORD.

10 'But if his offering is from the flock, of the sheep or of the goats, for a burnt offering, he shall offer it a male without defect.

11 'And he shall slay it on the side of the altar [a]northward before the LORD, and Aaron's sons, the priests, shall sprinkle its blood around on the altar.

12 'He shall then cut it into its pieces with its head and its [a]suet, and the priest shall arrange them on the wood which is on the fire that is on the altar.

13 'The entrails, however, and the legs he shall wash with water. And [a]the priest shall offer all of it, and offer it up in smoke on the altar; it is a burnt offering, an offering by fire of a soothing aroma to the LORD.

14 'But if his offering to the LORD is a burnt offering of birds, then he shall bring his offering from the [a]turtledoves or from young pigeons.

15 'And the priest shall bring it to the altar and wring off its head, and offer it up in smoke on the altar; and its blood is to be drained out [a]on the side of the altar.

16 'He shall also take away its crop with its feathers, and cast it beside the altar eastward, to the place of the [1]ashes.

17 'Then [a]he shall tear it by its wings, *but* shall not sever *it*. And the priest shall offer it up in smoke on the altar on the wood which is on the fire; it is a burnt offering, an offering by fire of a soothing aroma to the LORD.

CHAPTER 2

The Law of Grain Offerings

'NOW when anyone presents a [a]grain offering as an offering to the LORD, his offering shall be of fine flour, and he shall pour oil on it and put frankincense on it.

2 'He shall then bring it to Aaron's sons, the priests; and shall take from it [a]his handful of its fine flour and of its oil with all of its frankincense. And the priest shall offer *it* up in smoke *as* its [b]memorial portion on the altar, an offering by fire of a soothing aroma to the LORD.

3 'And [a]the remainder of the grain offering belongs to [b]Aaron and his

1 [a]Num. 7:89; Ex. 25:22

2 [1]Heb., *qorban* [a]Mark 7:11 [b]Lev. 22:19

3 [a]Lev. 6:8-13 [b]Lev. 22:20-24; Deut. 15:21; 17:1 [c]Lev. 17:8, 9; Deut. 12:6, 11

4 [a]Ex. 29:10, 15, 19 [b]Lev. 4:20, 26, 31; 2 Chr. 29:23, 24

5 [1]Or, *one of the herd;* lit., *son of the herd* [a]Ex. 29:11, 16, 20 [b]Lev. 17:11 [c]Lev. 1:11; 3:2, 8, 13

6 [a]Lev. 7:8

7 [a]Lev. 6:8-13

8 [a]Lev. 3:3, 4

9 [a]Num. 15:8-10; 28:12, 14 [b]Gen. 8:21; Ex. 29:18, 25; Eph. 5:2

11 [a]Lev. 1:5

12 [a]Lev. 3:3, 4

13 [a]Num. 15:4-7; 28:12-14

14 [a]Gen. 15:9

15 [a]Lev. 5:9

16 [1]Or, *fat ashes*

17 [a]Gen. 15:10; Lev. 5:8

1 [a]Lev. 6:14-18

2 [a]Lev. 5:12; 6:15 [b]Lev. 2:9, 16; 5:12

3 [a]Lev. 6:16 [b]Lev. 10:12, 13

sons: a thing most holy, of the offerings to the LORD by fire.
4 'Now when you bring an offering of a grain offering baked in an
oven, *it shall be* unleavened cakes of
fine flour mixed with oil, or unleavened wafers [1]spread with oil.
5 'And if your offering is a grain
offering *made* on the griddle, *it
shall be* of fine flour, unleavened,
mixed with oil;
6 you shall break it into bits, and
pour oil on it; it is a grain offering.
7 'Now if your offering is a grain
offering *made* in a [1]pan, it shall be
made of fine flour with oil.
8 'When you bring in the grain offering which is made of these things
to the LORD, it shall be presented to
the priest and he shall bring it to the
altar.
9 'The priest then shall take up
from the grain offering [a]its memorial portion, and shall offer *it* up in
smoke on the altar *as* an offering by
fire of a soothing aroma to the LORD.
10 'And [a]the remainder of the grain
offering belongs to Aaron and his
sons: a thing most holy, of the offerings to the LORD by fire.
11 '[a]No grain offering, which you
bring to the LORD, shall be made
with leaven, for you shall not offer
[1]up in smoke any leaven or any honey as an offering by fire to the LORD.
12 '[a]As an offering of first fruits,
you shall bring them to the LORD,
but they shall not ascend for a
soothing aroma on the altar.
13 'Every grain offering of yours,
moreover, you shall season with
salt, so that [a]the salt of the covenant
of your God shall not be lacking
from your grain offering; with all
your offerings you shall offer salt.
14 'Also if you bring a grain offering of early ripened things to the
LORD, you shall bring [a]fresh heads
of grain roasted in the fire, grits of
new growth, for the grain offering of
your early ripened things.
15 'You shall then put oil on it and
lay incense on it; it is a grain offering.
16 'And the priest shall offer up in
smoke [a]its memorial portion, part of
its grits and its oil with all its incense as an offering by fire to the
LORD.

CHAPTER 3

The Law of Peace Offerings

'NOW if this offering is a [a]sacri-
fice of peace offerings, if he is going
to offer out of the herd, whether
male or female, he shall offer it
[b]without defect before the LORD.
2 '[a]And he shall lay his hand on
the head of his offering and [b]slay it
at the doorway of the tent of meeting, and Aaron's sons, the priests,
shall sprinkle the blood around on
the altar.
3 'And from the sacrifice of the
peace offerings, he shall present an
offering by fire to the LORD, the fat
that covers the entrails and all the
fat that is on the entrails,
4 and the two kidneys with the
fat that is on them, which is on the
loins, and the [1]lobe of the liver,
which he shall remove with the kidneys.
5 'Then [a]Aaron's sons shall offer
it up in smoke on the altar [b]on the
burnt offering, which is on the wood
that is on the fire; [c]it is an offering by
fire of a soothing aroma to the LORD.
6 'But if his offering for a sacrifice
of peace offerings to the LORD is
from the flock, he shall offer it, male
or female, [a]without defect.
7 'If he is going to offer [a]a lamb
for his offering, then he shall offer it
[b]before the LORD,
8 and [a]he shall lay his hand on the
head of his offering, and [b]slay it before the tent of meeting; and Aaron's sons shall [c]sprinkle its blood
around on the altar.
9 'And from the sacrifice of peace
offerings he shall bring as an offering by fire to the LORD, its fat, [1]the
entire fat tail which he shall remove
close to the backbone, and the fat
that covers the entrails and all the
fat that is on the entrails,
10 and the two kidneys with the
fat that is on them, which is on the
loins, and the [1]lobe of the liver,
which he shall remove [a]with the kidneys.
11 'Then the priest shall offer *it* up
in smoke [a]on the altar, *as* [b]food, an
offering by fire to the LORD.
12 'Moreover, if his offering is [a]a
goat, then he shall offer it before the
LORD,
13 and he shall lay his hand on its
head and slay it before the tent of
meeting; and the sons of Aaron shall
sprinkle its blood around on the altar.
14 'And from it he shall present his
offering as an offering by fire to the
LORD, the fat that covers the entrails and all the fat that is on the
entrails,
15 and the two kidneys with the
fat that is on them, which is on the
loins, and the [1]lobe of the liver,

4 [1]Lit., *anointed*
7 [1]Lit., *lidded cooking pan*
9 [a]Lev. 2:2
10 [a]Lev. 2:3
11 [1]Lit., *up from it* [a]Ex. 23:18; 34:25; Lev. 6:16, 17
12 [a]Lev. 7:13; 23:17, 18
13 [a]Num. 18:19; 2 Chr. 13:5; Ezek. 43:24
14 [a]Lev. 23:14
16 [a]Lev. 2:2
1 [a]Lev. 7:11-34 [b]Lev. 22:21
2 [a]Lev. 1:4 [b]Ex. 29:11, 16, 20
4 [1]Or, *appendage on*
5 [a]Lev. 7:28-34 [b]Ex. 29:38, 42; Num. 28:3-10 [c]Num. 15:8-10; 28:12-14
6 [a]Lev. 3:1
7 [a]Num. 15:4, 5; 28:5-7 [b]Lev. 17:8, 9
8 [a]Lev. 1:4 [b]Lev. 3:2 [c]Lev. 1:5
9 [1]Lit., *the fat tail, entire*
10 [1]Or, *appendage on* [a]Lev. 3:4
11 [a]Lev. 3:5 [b]Lev. 3:16; 21:6, 8, 17
12 [a]Num. 15:6-11
15 [1]Or, *appendage on*

which he shall remove [a]with the kidneys.
16 'And the priest shall offer them
up in smoke on the altar *as* food, an
offering by fire for a soothing aroma; [a]all fat is the LORD's.
17 'It is a perpetual statute
throughout your generations in all
your dwellings: you shall not eat
any fat [a]or any blood.' "

CHAPTER 4

The Law of Sin Offerings

THEN the LORD spoke to Moses,
saying,
2 "Speak to the sons of Israel, saying, 'If a person sins [a]unintention-
ally in any of the [1]things which the
LORD has commanded not to be
done, and commits any of them,
3 [a]if the anointed priest sins so as
to bring guilt on the people, then let
him offer to the LORD a [1]bull without
defect as a sin offering for the sin he
has [2]committed.
4 'And he shall bring the bull to
the doorway of the tent of meeting
before the LORD, and [a]he shall lay
his hand on the head of the bull, and
slay the bull before the LORD.
5 'Then the [a]anointed priest is to
take some of the blood of the bull
and bring it to the tent of meeting,
6 and the priest shall dip his finger in the blood, and sprinkle some
of the blood seven times before the
LORD, in front of [a]the veil of the
sanctuary.
7 'The priest shall also put some
of the blood on the horns of [a]the altar of fragrant incense which is before the LORD in the tent of meeting;
and all the blood of the bull he shall
pour out at the base of the altar of
burnt offering which is at the doorway of the tent of meeting.
8 '[a]And he shall remove from it all
the fat of the bull of the sin offering:
the fat that covers the entrails, and
all the fat which is on the entrails,
9 and the two kidneys with the
fat that is on them, which is on the
loins, and the [1]lobe of the liver,
which he shall remove [a]with the kidneys
10 (just as it is removed from the
ox of the sacrifice of peace offerings), and the priest is to offer them
up in smoke on the altar of burnt
offering.
11 'But the hide of the bull and all
its flesh with its head and its legs
and its entrails and its refuse,
12 [1]that is, all *the rest of* the bull,
he is to bring out to [a]a clean place
outside the camp where the [2]ashes
are poured out, and burn it on wood
with fire; where the [2]ashes are
poured out it shall be burned.
13 '[a]Now if the whole congregation
of Israel commits error, and the
matter [1]escapes the notice of the assembly, and they commit any of the
[2]things which the LORD has commanded not to be done, and they become guilty;
14 [a]when the sin [1]which they have
[2]committed becomes known, then
the assembly shall offer [b]a [3]bull of
the herd for a sin offering, and bring
it before the tent of meeting.
15 'Then [a]the elders of the congregation shall lay their hands on the
head of the bull before the LORD,
and the bull shall be slain [b]before
the LORD.
16 'Then the anointed priest is to
bring some of the blood of the bull
to the tent of meeting;
17 and [a]the priest shall dip his finger in the blood, and sprinkle *it*
seven times before the LORD, in
front of the veil.
18 'And he shall put some of the
blood on the horns of [a]the altar
which is before the LORD [1]in the tent
of meeting; and all the blood he shall
pour out at the base of the altar of
burnt offering which is at the doorway of the tent of meeting.
19 '[a]And he shall remove all its fat
from it and offer it up in smoke on
the altar.
20 'He shall also do with the bull
just as he did with [a]the bull of the
sin offering; thus he shall do with it.
So the priest shall make atonement
for them, and they shall be forgiven.
21 'Then he is to bring out the bull
to *a place* outside the camp, and
burn it as he burned the first bull; it
is [a]the sin offering for the assembly.
22 'When [a]a leader [b]sins and unintentionally does any one of all the
[1]things which the LORD God has
commanded not to be done, and he
becomes guilty,
23 [1a]if his sin [2]which he has committed is made known to him, he
shall bring for his offering a [3b]goat,
[c]a male without defect.
24 'And he shall lay his hand on the
head of the male goat, and slay it in
the place where [1]they slay the burnt
offering before the LORD; it is a sin
offering.
25 'Then the priest is to take some
of the blood of the sin offering with
his finger, and put it on [a]the horns of
the altar of burnt offering; and *the*
rest of its blood he shall pour out at

15 [a]Lev. 3:4
16 [a]Lev. 7:23-25
17 [a]Lev. 17:10-16
2 [1]Lit., *commands of the LORD which are not to be done* [a]Lev. 4:22, 27; 5:15-18; 22:14
3 [1]Or, *bull of the herd* [2]Lit., *sinned* [a]Lev. 4:14, 23, 28
4 [a]Lev. 1:4
5 [a]Lev. 4:3
6 [a]Ex. 40:21, 26
7 [a]Lev. 4:18, 25, 30, 34
8 [a]Lev. 3:3, 4
9 [1]Or, *appendage on* [a]Lev. 3:4
12 [1]Lit., *and* [2]Or, *fat ashes are* [a]Lev. 6:10, 11
13 [1]Lit., *is hidden from the eyes of* [2]Lit., *commands of the LORD which are not to be done* [a]Num. 15:24-26
14 [1]Lit., *concerning which* [2]Lit., *sinned* [3]Or, *bull of the herd;* lit., *son of the herd* [a]Lev. 4:3 [b]Lev. 4:3, 23, 28
15 [a]Lev. 8:14, 18, 22; Num. 8:10, 12 [b]Lev. 1:3
17 [a]Lev. 4:6
18 [1]Lit., *which is in* [a]Lev. 4:7, 25, 30, 34
19 [a]Lev. 4:8
20 [a]Lev. 4:8, 21
21 [a]Lev. 4:13; 16:15-17; Num. 15:24-26
22 [1]Lit., *commands of the LORD which are not to be done* [a]Num. 31:13; 32:2 [b]Lev. 4:2
23 [1]Lit., *or* [2]Lit., *in which he has sinned* [3]Lit., *buck of the goats* [a]Lev. 4:3 [b]Lev. 4:3, 14, 28 [c]Lev. 4:28
24 [1]Lit., *one slays*
25 [a]Lev. 4:7, 18, 30, 34

the base of the altar of burnt offering.
26 '[a]And all its fat he shall offer up
in smoke on the altar as *in the case*
of the fat of the sacrifice of peace
offerings. Thus the priest shall make
atonement for him in regard to his
sin, and he shall be forgiven.
27 'Now if [1]anyone of [2]the common
people sins [a]unintentionally in
doing any of the [3]things which the
LORD has commanded not to be
done, and becomes guilty,
28 [1][a]if his sin, which he has [2]com-
mitted is made known to him, then
he shall bring for his offering a
[3][b]goat, a [c]female without defect, for
his sin which he has [2]committed.
29 'And [a]he shall lay his hand on
the head of the sin offering, and
[b]slay the sin offering at the place of
the burnt offering.
30 'And the priest shall take some
of its blood with his finger and put it
on the horns of [a]the altar of burnt
offering; and [b]all *the rest of* its blood
he shall pour out at the base of the
altar.
31 '[a]Then he shall remove all its
fat, just as the fat was removed
from the sacrifice of peace offerings;
and the priest shall offer it up in
smoke on the altar for a soothing
aroma to the LORD. Thus the priest
shall make atonement for him, [1]and
he shall be forgiven.
32 'But if he brings [a]a lamb as his
offering for a sin offering, he shall
bring it, a female without defect.
33 'And [a]he shall lay his hand on
the head of the sin offering, and slay
it for a sin offering [b]in the place
where [1]they slay the burnt offering.
34 'And the priest is to take some
of the blood of the sin offering with
his finger and put it on the horns of
[a]the altar of burnt offering; and [b]all
the rest of its blood he shall pour out
at the base of the altar.
35 'Then he shall remove [a]all its
fat, just as the fat of the lamb is removed from the sacrifice of the
peace offerings, and the priest shall
offer them up in smoke on the altar,
on the offerings by fire to the LORD.
Thus the priest shall make atonement for him in regard to his sin
which he has [1]committed, and he
shall be forgiven.

CHAPTER 5

The Law of Guilt Offerings

'NOW if a person sins, after he
hears a [1]public [a]adjuration *to tes-*
tify, when he is a witness, whether
he has seen or *otherwise* known, if
he does not tell *it*, then he will bear
his [2]guilt.
2 'Or if a person touches [a]any unclean thing, whether a carcass of an
unclean beast, or the carcass of unclean cattle, or a carcass of unclean
swarming things, though it is hidden from him, and he is unclean,
then he will be guilty.
3 'Or if he touches human uncleanness, of whatever *sort* his uncleanness *may* be with which he becomes unclean, and it is hidden
from him, and then he comes to
know *it*, he will be guilty.
4 'Or if a person swears thoughtlessly with his lips to do evil or to do
good, in whatever matter a man
may speak thoughtlessly with an
oath, and it is hidden from him, and
then he comes to know *it*, he will be
guilty in one of these.
5 'So it shall be when he becomes
guilty in one of these, that he shall
[a]confess that in which he has
sinned.
6 'He shall also bring his guilt offering to the LORD for his sin which
he has [1]committed, [a]a female from
the flock, a lamb or a [2]goat as a sin
offering. So the priest shall make
atonement on his behalf for his sin.
7 'But if [1]he cannot afford a lamb,
then he shall bring to the LORD his
guilt offering for that in which he
has sinned, two turtledoves or two
young pigeons, [a]one for a sin offering and the other for a burnt offering.
8 'And he shall bring them to the
priest, who shall offer first that
which is for the sin offering and
shall nip its head at the front of its
neck, but he [a]shall not sever *it*.
9 'He shall also sprinkle some of
the blood of the sin offering [a]on the
side of the altar, while the rest of the
blood shall be drained out [b]at the
base of the altar: it is a sin offering.
10 'The second he shall then prepare as a burnt offering [a]according
to the ordinance. So the priest shall
make atonement on his behalf for
his sin which he has [1]committed,
and it shall be forgiven him.
11 'But [a]if his [1]means are insufficient for two turtledoves or two
young pigeons, then for his offering
for that which he has sinned, he
shall bring the tenth of an [2]ephah of
fine flour for a sin offering; [b]he shall
not put oil on it or place incense on
it, for it is a sin offering.
12 'And he shall bring it to the
priest, and the priest shall take his
handful of it as its memorial portion

26 [a]Lev. 4:19

27 [1]Lit., *one soul* [2]Lit., *the people of the land* [3]Lit., *commands of the* LORD *which are not to be done* [a]Lev. 4:2

28 [1]Lit., *or* [2]Lit., *sinned* [3]Or, *female goat* [a]Lev. 4:3 [b]Lev. 4:3, 14, 23, 32 [c]Lev. 4:23

29 [a]Lev. 1:4 [b]Lev. 1:5, 11

30 [a]Lev. 4:7, 18, 25, 34 [b]Lev. 4:7

31 [1]Or, *so that he may be* [a]Lev. 4:8

32 [a]Lev. 4:28

33 [1]Lit., *one slays* [a]Lev. 1:4, 5 [b]Lev. 4:29

34 [a]Lev. 4:7, 18, 25, 30 [b]Lev. 4:7

35 [1]Lit., *sinned* [a]Lev. 4:31

1 [1]Lit., *voice of an oath* [2]Or, *iniquity* [a]Prov. 29:24; Jer. 23:10

2 [a]Lev. 11:8, 11, 24-39; Num. 19:11-16; Deut. 14:8

5 [a]Lev. 16:21; 26:40; Num. 5:7; Prov. 28:13

6 [1]Lit., *sinned* [2]Lit., *female goat* [a]Lev. 4:28, 32

7 [1]Lit., *his hand does not reach enough for* [a]Lev. 12:6, 8; 14:22, 30, 31

8 [a]Lev. 1:17

9 [a]Lev. 1:15 [b]Lev. 4:7

10 [1]Lit., *sinned* [a]Lev. 1:14-17

11 [1]Lit., *hand does not reach* [2]I.e., approx. one bushel [a]Lev. 14:21-32; 27:8 [b]Lev. 2:1, 2

and offer *it* up in smoke on the altar, [1]with the offerings of the LORD by fire: it is a sin offering.

13 'So the priest shall make atonement for him concerning his sin which he has [1]committed from [a]one of these, and it shall be forgiven him; then [b]*the rest* shall become the priest's, like the grain offering.' "

14 Then the LORD spoke to Moses, saying,

15 "[a]If a person acts unfaithfully and sins [b]unintentionally against the LORD's holy things, then he shall bring his [c]guilt offering to the LORD: [d]a ram without defect from the flock, according to your valuation in silver by shekels, in *terms of* the [e]shekel of the sanctuary, for a guilt offering.

16 "[a]And he shall make restitution for that which he has sinned against the holy thing, and shall add to it a fifth part of it, and give it to the priest. [b]The priest shall then make atonement for him with the ram of the guilt offering, and it shall be forgiven him.

17 "Now if a person sins and does any of the things [1]which the LORD has commanded not to be done, [a]though he was unaware, still he is guilty, and shall bear his punishment.

18 "He is then to bring to the priest [a]a ram without defect from the flock, according to your valuation, for a guilt offering. So the priest shall make atonement for him concerning his error in which he sinned [b]unintentionally and did not know *it*, and it shall be forgiven him.

19 "It is a guilt offering; he was certainly guilty before the LORD."

CHAPTER 6

Guilt Offering

1 THEN the LORD spoke to Moses, saying,

2 "[a]When a person sins and acts unfaithfully against the LORD, and deceives his companion in regard to a deposit or a security entrusted *to him*, or through robbery, or *if* he has extorted from his companion,

3 or has found what was lost and lied about it and sworn falsely, so that he sins in regard to any one of the things a man may do;

4 then it shall be, when he sins and becomes guilty, that he shall restore what he took by robbery, or what he got by extortion, or the deposit which was [1]entrusted to him, or the lost thing which he found,

5 or anything about which he swore falsely; [a]he shall make restitution for it [1]in full, and add to it one-fifth more. [b]He shall give it to the one to whom it belongs on the day *he presents* his guilt offering.

6 "Then he shall bring to the priest his guilt offering to the LORD, [a]a ram without defect from the flock, according to your valuation, for a guilt offering,

7 and [a]the priest shall make atonement for him before the LORD; and he shall be forgiven for any one of the things which he may have done to incur guilt."

The Priest's Part in the Offerings

8 [1]Then the LORD spoke to Moses, saying,

9 "Command Aaron and his sons, saying, 'This is [a]the law for the burnt offering: the burnt offering itself *shall remain* on the hearth on the altar all night until the morning, and [b]the fire on the altar is to be kept burning on it.

10 'And the priest is to put on [a]his linen robe, and he shall put on undergarments next to his flesh; and he shall take up the [1]ashes *to* which the fire [2]reduces the burnt offering on the altar, and place them beside the altar.

11 'Then he shall take off his garments and put on other garments, and carry the [1]ashes outside the camp to a clean place.

12 'And the fire on the altar shall be kept burning on it. It shall not go out, but the priest shall burn wood on it every morning; and he shall lay out the burnt offering on it, and offer up in smoke the fat portions of the peace offerings [a]on it.

13 'Fire shall be kept burning continually on the altar; it is not to go out.

14 'Now this is the law of the grain offering: the sons of Aaron shall present it before the LORD in front of the altar.

15 '[a]Then one *of them* shall lift up from it a handful of the fine flour of the grain offering, [1]with its oil and all the incense that is on the grain offering, and he shall offer *it* up in smoke on the altar, a soothing aroma, as its memorial offering to the LORD.

16 '[a]And what is left of it Aaron and his sons are to eat. It shall be eaten as unleavened cakes in a holy place; they are to eat it in the court of the tent of meeting.

17 '[a]It shall not be baked with leaven. I have given it as their share

---

12 [1]Lit., *upon*

13 [1]Lit., *sinned* [a]Lev. 5:4-5 [b]Lev. 2:3

15 [a]Num. 5:5-8 [b]Lev. 4:2; 22:14 [c]Lev. 7:1-10 [d]Lev. 6:6 [e]Ex. 30:13

16 [a]Lev. 6:5; 22:14; Num. 5:7, 8 [b]Lev. 7:2-7

17 [1]Lit., *the commands of the* LORD *which are* [a]Lev. 4:2; 5:19

18 [a]Lev. 5:15 [b]Lev. 5:17

1 [1]In Heb. text, 5:20

2 [a]Ex. 22:7-15

4 [1]Or, *deposited with*

5 [1]Lit., *in its sum* [a]Lev. 5:16 [b]Num. 5:8

6 [a]Lev. 5:15

7 [a]Lev. 7:2-5

8 [1]In Heb. text, 6:1

9 [a]Ex. 29:38-42; Num. 28:3-10 [b]Lev. 6:12, 13

10 [1]Or, *fat ashes* [2]Lit., *consumes* [a]Ex. 28:39, 42; 39:27, 28

11 [1]Or, *fat ashes*

12 [a]Lev. 3:5

15 [1]Lit., *and some of* [a]Lev. 2:2

16 [a]Lev. 2:3; 10:12-14

17 [a]Lev. 2:11

from My offerings by fire; [b]it is most
holy, like the sin offering and [c]the
guilt offering.
18 '[a]Every male among the sons of
Aaron may eat it; it is a permanent
ordinance throughout your generations, from the offerings by fire to
the LORD. [b]Whoever touches them
shall become consecrated.' "
19 Then the LORD spoke to Moses,
saying,
20"This is the offering which Aaron and his sons are to present to the
LORD on the day when he is
anointed; the tenth of an ephah of
fine flour as [a]a [1]regular grain offering, half of it in the morning and half
of it in the evening.
21"It shall be prepared with oil on
a [a]griddle. When it is *well* stirred,
you shall bring it. You shall present
the grain offering in baked pieces as
a soothing aroma to the LORD.
22"And the anointed priest who
will be in his place [1]among his sons
shall [2]offer it. By a permanent ordinance it shall be entirely offered up
in smoke to the LORD.
23"So every grain offering of the
priest shall be burned entirely. It
shall not be eaten."
24 Then the LORD spoke to Moses,
saying,
25"Speak to Aaron and to his sons,
saying, 'This is the law of the sin
offering: [a]in the place where the
burnt offering is slain the sin offering shall be slain before the LORD; it
is most holy.
26 '[a]The priest who offers it for sin
shall eat it. It shall be eaten in a holy
place, in the court of the tent of
meeting.
27 '[a]Anyone who touches its flesh
shall become consecrated; and
when any of its blood [1]splashes on a
garment, in a holy place you shall
wash what was splashed on.
28 'Also [a]the earthenware vessel in
which it was boiled shall be broken;
and if it was boiled in a bronze vessel, then it shall be scoured and
rinsed in water.
29 '[a]Every male among the priests
may eat of it; it is most holy.
30 'But no sin offering [a]of which
any of the blood is brought into the
tent of meeting to make atonement
[b]in the holy place shall be eaten; [c]it
shall be burned with fire.

CHAPTER 7

The Priest's Part in the Offerings

'NOW this is the law of the [a]guilt
offering; it is most holy.
2 'In [a]the place where they slay
the burnt offering they are to slay
the guilt offering, and he shall sprinkle its blood around on the altar.
3 'Then he shall offer from it all its
fat: the [a]fat tail and the fat that covers the entrails,
4 and the two kidneys with the
fat that is on them, which is on the
loins, and the lobe on the liver he
shall remove [a]with the kidneys.
5 'And the priest shall offer them
up in smoke on the altar as an offering by fire to the LORD; it is a guilt
offering.
6 '[a]Every male among the priests
may eat of it. It shall be eaten in a
holy place; it is most holy.
7 '[a]The guilt offering is like the sin
offering, there is one law for them;
the [b]priest who makes atonement
with it [1]shall have it.
8 'Also the priest who presents
any man's burnt offering, [1]that
priest shall have for himself the skin
of the burnt offering which he has
presented.
9 'Likewise, every grain offering
that is baked in the oven, and everything prepared in a [1]pan or on a
[a]griddle, [2]shall belong to the priest
who presents it.
10 'And every grain offering mixed
with oil, or dry, shall [1]belong to all
the sons of Aaron, [2]to all alike.
11 'Now this is the law of the sacrifice of peace offerings which shall
be presented to the LORD.
12 'If he offers it by way of [a]thanks-
giving, then along with the sacrifice
of thanksgiving he shall offer unleavened cakes mixed with oil, and
unleavened wafers [1]spread with oil,
and cakes *of well* stirred fine flour
mixed with oil.
13 'With the sacrifice of his peace
offerings for thanksgiving, he shall
present his offering with cakes of
[a]leavened bread.
14 'And of [1]this he shall present
one of every offering as a [2]contribu-
tion to the LORD; it shall [3]belong to
the priest who sprinkles the blood of
the peace offerings.
15 '[a]Now *as for* the flesh of the sacrifice of his thanksgiving peace offerings, it shall be eaten on the day
of his offering; he shall not leave any
of it over until morning.
16 'But if the sacrifice of his offering is a [a]votive or a freewill offering,
it shall be eaten on the day that he
offers his sacrifice; and on the [1]next
day what is left of it may be eaten;
17 [a]but what is left over from the
flesh of the sacrifice on the third day
shall be burned with fire.

17 [b]Lev. 6:26, 29, 30 [c]Lev. 7:7; 10:16-18
18 [a]Lev. 6:29; 1 Cor. 9:13 [b]Lev. 6:27
20 [1]Lit., *grain offering continually* [a]Num. 4:16
21 [a]Lev. 2:5
22 [1]Lit., *from among* [2]Lit., *do*
25 [a]Lev. 1:11
26 [a]Lev. 6:29
27 [1]Lit., *one sprinkles* [a]Lev. 7:19
28 [a]Lev. 11:33; 15:12
29 [a]Lev. 6:18
30 [a]Lev. 4:1-21 [b]Lev. 4:7, 18 [c]Lev. 4:11, 12, 21
1 [a]Lev. 5:14-6:7
2 [a]Lev. 1:11
3 [a]Lev. 3:9
4 [a]Lev. 3:4
6 [a]Lev. 6:18, 29
7 [1]Lit., *it shall be for him* [a]Lev. 6:30 [b]1 Cor. 9:13; 10:18
8 [1]Lit., *for the priest, it shall be for him*
9 [1]Lit., *lidded cooking pan* [2]Lit., *for the priest, it shall be for him* [a]Lev. 2:5
10 [1]Lit., *be* [2]Lit., *a man as his brother*
12 [1]Or, *anointed* [a]Lev. 7:15
13 [a]Lev. 2:12; 23:17, 18
14 [1]Lit., *it* [2]Or, *heave offering* [3]Lit., *be for*
15 [a]Lev. 22:29, 30
16 [1]Lit., *morrow and what* [a]Lev. 19:5-8
17 [a]Ex. 12:10

18 'So if any of the flesh of the sacrifice of his peace offerings should
ever be eaten on the third day, he
who offers it shall not be accepted,
and it shall not be reckoned to his
benefit. It shall be an offensive
thing, and the person who eats of it
shall bear his *own* iniquity.
19 'Also the flesh that touches anything unclean shall not be eaten; it
shall be burned with fire. [1]As for
other flesh, anyone who is clean
may eat *such* flesh.
20 '[a]But the person who eats the
flesh of the sacrifice of peace offerings which belong to the LORD, [1]in
his uncleanness, that person shall be
cut off from his people.
21 '[a]And when anyone touches
anything unclean, whether human
uncleanness, or an unclean animal,
or any unclean [1]detestable thing,
and eats of the flesh of the sacrifice
of peace offerings which belong to
the LORD, that person shall be cut off
from his people.' "
22 Then the LORD spoke to Moses,
saying,
23 "Speak to the sons of Israel, saying, 'You shall not eat [a]any fat *from*
an ox, a sheep, or a goat.
24 'Also the fat of *an animal* which
dies, and the fat of an animal [a]torn
by beasts, may be put to any other
use, but you must certainly not eat
it.
25 'For whoever eats the fat of the
animal from which [1]an offering by
fire is offered to the LORD, even the
person who eats shall be cut off
from his people.
26 '[a]And you are not to eat any
blood, either of bird or animal, in
any of your dwellings.
27 'Any person who eats any
blood, even that person shall be cut
off from his people.' "
28 Then the LORD spoke to Moses,
saying,
29 "Speak to the sons of Israel, saying, 'He who offers the sacrifice of
his peace offerings to the LORD shall
bring his offering to the LORD from
the sacrifice of his peace offerings.
30 'His own hands are to bring offerings by fire to the LORD. He shall
bring the fat with the breast, that
the breast may be [1]presented as a
wave offering before the LORD.
31 'And the priest shall offer up the
fat in smoke on the altar; but [a]the
breast shall belong to Aaron and his
sons.
32 'And you shall give the right
thigh to the priest as a [1]contribution
from the sacrifices of your peace offerings.
33 'The one among the sons of Aaron who offers the blood of the peace
offerings and the fat, the right thigh
shall be his as *his* portion.
34 'For I have taken the breast of
the wave offering and the thigh of
the [1]contribution from the sons of
Israel from the sacrifices of their
peace offerings, and have given
them to Aaron the priest and to his
sons as *their* due forever from the
sons of Israel.
35 'This is [1]that which is consecrated to Aaron and [1]that [a]which is
consecrated to his sons from the offerings by fire to the LORD, in that
day when he presented them to
serve as priests to the LORD.
36 '[1]These the LORD had commanded to be given them from the
sons of Israel in the day that He
anointed them. It is *their* due forever throughout their generations.' "
37 This is the law of the burnt offering, the grain offering and the sin
offering and the guilt offering and
[a]the ordination offering and the sacrifice of peace offerings,
38 [a]which the LORD commanded
Moses at Mount Sinai in the day
that He commanded the sons of Israel to [1]present their offerings to the
LORD in the wilderness of Sinai.

CHAPTER 8

The Consecration of Aaron and His Sons

THEN the LORD spoke to Moses,
saying,
2 "[a]Take Aaron and his sons with
him, and the [b]garments and [c]the
anointing oil and the bull of the sin
offering, and the two rams and the
basket of unleavened bread;
3 and assemble all the congregation to the doorway of the tent of
meeting."
4 So Moses did just as the LORD
commanded him. When the congregation was assembled to the doorway of the tent of meeting,
5 Moses said to the congregation,
"This is the thing which the LORD
has commanded to do."
6 Then [a]Moses had Aaron and his
sons come near, and washed them
with water.
7 And he put the tunic on him and
girded him with the sash, and
clothed him with the robe, and put
the ephod on him; and he girded him
with the artistic band of the ephod,
[1]with which he tied *it* to him.

19 [1]Lit., *And the flesh*
20 [1]Lit., *and his uncleanness is on him* [a]Lev. 22:3-7; Num. 19:13
21 [1]Some mss. read, *swarming thing* [a]Lev. 5:2, 3
23 [a]Lev. 3:17
24 [a]Ex. 22:31; Lev. 17:15; 22:8
25 [1]Lit., *he offers an offering by fire*
26 [a]Lev. 17:10-16
30 [1]Lit., *waved*
31 [a]Num. 18:11; Deut. 18:3
32 [1]Or, *heave offering*
34 [1]Or, *heave offering*
35 [1]Lit., *the anointed portion of* [a]Num. 18:8
36 [1]Lit., *which*
37 [a]Ex. 29:22-34; Lev. 8:22-23
38 [1]Or, *offer* [a]Lev. 1:1; 26:46; 27:34; Deut. 4:5
2 [a]Ex. 28:1 [b]Lev. 6:10 [c]Ex. 30:25
6 [a]Ex. 29:4-6
7 [1]Lit., *and with it*

8 He then placed the [1]breastpiece
on him, and in the [1]breastpiece he
put [2a]the Urim and the Thummim.
9 He also placed the turban on his
head, and on the turban, at its front,
he placed [a]the golden plate, the holy
crown, just as the LORD had commanded Moses.
10 Moses then took [a]the anointing
oil and anointed the [1]tabernacle and
all that was in it, and consecrated
them.
11 And he sprinkled some of it on
the altar seven times and anointed
the altar and all its utensils, and the
basin and its stand, to [a]consecrate
them.
12 Then he poured some of the [a]a-
nointing oil on Aaron's head and
anointed him, to consecrate him.
13 [a]Next Moses had Aaron's sons
come near and clothed them with
tunics, and girded them with sashes,
and bound [1]caps on them, just as
the LORD had commanded Moses.
14 Then he brought [a]the bull of the
sin offering, and Aaron and his sons
laid their hands on the head of the
bull of the sin offering.
15 Next [1]Moses slaughtered *it* and
took the blood and with his finger
[a]put *some of it* around on the horns
of the altar, and purified the altar.
Then he poured out *the rest of* the
blood at the base of the altar and
consecrated it, to make atonement
for it.
16 He also took all the fat that was
on the entrails and the [1]lobe of the
liver, and the two kidneys and their
fat; and Moses offered it up in
smoke on the altar.
17 [a]But the bull and its hide and its
flesh and its refuse, he burned in the
fire outside the camp, just as the
LORD had commanded Moses.
18 Then he presented [a]the ram of
the burnt offering, and Aaron and
his sons laid their hands on the head
of the ram.
19 And [1]Moses slaughtered *it* and
sprinkled the blood around on the
altar.
20 When he had cut the ram into
its pieces, Moses [a]offered up the
head and the pieces and the suet in
smoke.
21 After he had washed the entrails and the legs with water,
Moses offered up the whole ram in
smoke on the altar. It was a burnt
offering for a soothing aroma; it was
an offering by fire to the LORD, just
as the LORD had commanded Moses.
22 Then he presented the second
ram, [a]the ram of [1]ordination; and
Aaron and his sons laid their hands
on the head of the ram.
23 And [1]Moses slaughtered *it* and
took some of its blood and [a]put it on
the lobe of Aaron's right ear, and on
the thumb of his right hand, and on
the big toe of his right foot.
24 He also had Aaron's sons come
near; and Moses put some of the
blood on the lobe of their right ear,
and on the thumb of their right
hand, and on the big toe of their
right foot. Moses then sprinkled *the
rest of* the blood around on the altar.
25 And he took the fat, and the fat
tail, and all the fat that was on the
entrails, and the [1]lobe of the liver
and the two kidneys and their fat
and the right thigh.
26 And from the basket of unleavened bread that was before the
LORD, he took one unleavened cake
and one cake of bread *mixed with*
oil and one wafer, and placed *them*
on the portions of fat and on the
right thigh.
27 He then put all *these* on the
hands of Aaron and on the hands of
his sons, and presented them as a
wave offering before the LORD.
28 Then Moses took them from
their hands and offered them up in
smoke on the altar with the burnt
offering. They were an ordination
offering for a soothing aroma; it was
an offering by fire to the LORD.
29 Moses also took [a]the breast and
presented it for a wave offering before the LORD; it was [b]Moses' portion of the ram of ordination, just as
the LORD had commanded Moses.
30 So Moses took some of the
anointing oil and some of the blood
which was on the altar, and sprinkled it on Aaron, on his garments,
on his sons, and on the garments of
his sons with him; and he consecrated Aaron, his garments, and his
sons, and the garments of his sons
with him.
31 Then Moses said to Aaron and
to his sons, "[a]Boil the flesh at the
doorway of the tent of meeting, and
eat it there together with the bread
which is in the basket of the ordination offering, just as I commanded,
[b]saying, 'Aaron and his sons shall
eat it.'
32 "And the remainder of the flesh
and of the bread you shall burn in
the fire.
33 "[a]And you shall not go outside
the doorway of the tent of meeting
for seven days, until the day that the
period of your ordination is fulfilled;
for he will [1]ordain you through
seven days.

8 [1]Lit., *pouch* [2]I.e., the Lights and Perfections [a]Ex. 28:30
9 [a]Ex. 28:36
10 [1]Or, *dwelling place* [a]Lev. 8:2
11 [a]Ex. 29:36, 37; 30:29
12 [a]Ex. 30:30
13 [1]Lit., *headgear* [a]Ex. 29:8, 9
14 [a]Ex. 29:10
15 [1]Lit., *he slaughtered it and Moses took* [a]Lev. 4:7
16 [1]Or, *appendage on*
17 [a]Lev. 4:11, 12
18 [a]Lev. 8:2
19 [1]Lit., *he slaughtered it and Moses sprinkled*
20 [a]Lev. 1:8
22 [1]Lit., *filling*, and so throughout the chap. [a]Lev. 8:2
23 [1]Lit., *he slaughtered it and Moses took* [a]Ex. 29:20, 21
25 [1]Or, *appendage on*
29 [a]Lev. 7:31-34 [b]Ps. 99:6
31 [a]Ex. 29:31 [b]Ex. 29:32
33 [1]Lit., *fill your hands* [a]Ex. 29:35

34 "The LORD has commanded to do as has been done this day, to make atonement on your behalf.

35 "At the doorway of the tent of meeting, moreover, you shall remain day and night for seven days, and keep the charge of the LORD, that you may not die, for so I have been commanded."

36 Thus Aaron and his sons did all the things which the LORD had commanded through Moses.

CHAPTER 9

Aaron Offers Sacrifices

NOW it came about on the eighth day that Moses called Aaron and his sons and the elders of Israel;

2 and he said to Aaron, "Take for yourself a calf, a bull, for a sin offering and a ram for a burnt offering, *both* without defect, and offer *them* before the LORD.

3 "Then to the sons of Israel you shall speak, saying, 'Take a male goat for a sin offering, and a calf and a lamb, both one year old, without defect, for a burnt offering,

4 and an ox and a ram for peace offerings, to sacrifice before the LORD, and a grain offering mixed with oil; for today the LORD shall appear to you.'"

5 So they took what Moses had commanded to the front of the tent of meeting, and the whole congregation came near and stood before the LORD.

6 And Moses said, "This is the thing which the LORD has commanded you to do, that [a]the glory of the LORD may appear to you."

7 Moses then said to Aaron, "Come near to the altar and [1]offer your sin offering and your burnt offering, that you may make atonement for yourself and for the people; then make the offering [2]for the people, that you may make atonement for them, just as the LORD has commanded."

8 [a]So Aaron came near to the altar and slaughtered the calf of the sin offering which was for himself.

9 [a]And Aaron's sons presented the blood to him; and he dipped his finger in the blood, and put *some* on the horns of the altar, and poured out *the rest of* the blood at the base of the altar.

10 The fat and the kidneys and the [1]lobe of the liver of the sin offering, he then offered up in smoke on the altar just as the LORD had commanded Moses.

11 The flesh and the skin, however, he burned with fire outside the camp.

12 Then he slaughtered the burnt offering; and Aaron's sons handed the blood to him and he sprinkled it around on the altar.

13 And they handed the burnt offering to him in [1]pieces with the head, and he offered *them* up in smoke on the altar.

14 He also washed the entrails and the legs, and offered *them* up in smoke with the burnt offering on the altar.

15 Then he presented the people's offering, and took the [a]goat of the sin offering which was for the people, and slaughtered it and offered it for sin, like the first.

16 He also presented the burnt offering, and [1]offered it according to [a]the ordinance.

17 Next he presented [a]the grain offering, and filled his [1]hand with some of it and offered *it* up in smoke on the altar, [b]besides the burnt offering of the morning.

18 Then [a]he slaughtered the ox and the ram, the sacrifice of peace offerings which was for the people; and Aaron's sons handed the blood to him and he sprinkled it around on the altar.

19 As for the portions of fat from the ox and from the ram, the fat tail, and the *fat* [a]covering, and the kidneys and the [1]lobe of the liver,

20 they now placed the portions of fat on the breasts; and he offered [1]them up in smoke on the altar.

21 But [a]the breasts and the right thigh Aaron [1]presented as a wave offering before the LORD, just as Moses had commanded.

22 Then Aaron lifted up his hands toward the people and blessed them, and he stepped down after making the sin offering and the burnt offering and the peace offerings.

23 And Moses and Aaron went into the tent of meeting. When they came out and blessed the people, [a]the glory of the LORD appeared to all the people.

24 [a]Then fire came out from before the LORD and consumed the burnt offering and the portions of fat on the altar; and when all the people saw *it*, they shouted and fell on their faces.

CHAPTER 10

The Sin of Nadab and Abihu

NOW [a]Nadab and Abihu, the sons of Aaron, took their respective [b]fire-

6 [a]Lev. 8:23
7 [1]Lit., *make* [2]Lit., *of*
8 [a]Lev. 4:1-12
9 [a]Lev. 9:12, 18
10 [1]Or, *appendage on*
13 [1]Lit., *its pieces*
15 [a]Lev. 4:27-31
16 [1]Lit., *made* [a]Lev. 1:1-13
17 [1]Lit., *palm* [a]Lev. 2:1-3 [b]Lev. 3:5
18 [a]Lev. 3:1-11
19 [1]Or, *appendage on* [a]Lev. 3:9
20 [1]Lit., *the portions of fat*
21 [1]Lit., *waved* [a]Lev. 7:30-34
23 [a]Lev. 9:6
24 [a]1 Kin. 18:38
1 [a]Ex. 24:1, 9; Num. 3:2 [b]Lev. 16:12

pans, and after putting fire in them,
placed incense on it and offered
strange fire before the LORD, which
He had not commanded them.
2 [a]And fire came out from the
presence of the LORD and consumed
them, and they died before the
LORD.
3 Then Moses said to Aaron, "It is
what the LORD spoke, saying,

'By those who [a]come near Me I
[1b]will be treated as holy,
And before all the people I will
[c]be honored.' "

So Aaron, therefore, kept silent.
4 Moses called also to [a]Mishael
and Elzaphan, the sons of Aaron's
uncle Uzziel, and said to them,
"Come forward, carry your [1]rela-
tives away from the front of the
sanctuary to the outside of the
camp."
5 So they came forward and carried them still in their [a]tunics to the
outside of the camp, as Moses had
said.
6 Then Moses said to Aaron and
to his sons Eleazar and Ithamar,
"[a]Do not [1]uncover your heads nor
tear your clothes, so that you may
not die, and that He may not [b]be-
come wrathful against all the congregation. But your [2]kinsmen, the
whole house of Israel, shall bewail
the burning which the LORD has
[3]brought about.
7"You shall not even go out from
the doorway of the tent of meeting,
lest you die; for [a]the LORD's anointing oil is upon you." So they did according to the word of Moses.
8 The Lord then spoke to Aaron,
saying,
9"[a]Do not drink wine or strong
drink, neither you nor your sons
with you, when you come into the
tent of meeting, so that you may not
die—it is a perpetual statute
throughout your generations—
10 and [a]so as to make a distinction
between the holy and the profane,
and between the unclean and the
clean,
11 and [a]so as to teach the sons of
Israel all the statutes which the
LORD has spoken to them through
Moses."
12 Then Moses spoke to Aaron,
and to his surviving sons, [a]Eleazar
and Ithamar, "[b]Take the grain offering that is left over from the LORD's
offerings by fire and eat it unleavened beside the altar, for it is most
holy.
13"You shall eat it, moreover, in a
holy place, because it is your due
and your sons' due out of the LORD's
offerings by fire; for thus I have
been commanded.
14"[a]The breast of the wave offering, however, and the thigh of the
offering you may eat in a clean
place, you and your sons and your
daughters with you; for they have
been given as your due and your
sons' due out of the sacrifices of the
peace offerings of the sons of Israel.
15"[a]The thigh offered by lifting up
and the breast offered by waving,
they shall bring along with the offerings by fire of the portions of fat, to
present as a wave offering before
the LORD; so it shall be a thing perpetually due you and your sons with
you, just as the LORD has commanded."
16 But Moses searched carefully
for the [a]goat of the sin offering, and
behold, it had been burned up! So he
was angry with Aaron's surviving
sons Eleazar and Ithamar, saying,
17"Why [a]did you not eat the sin
offering at the holy place? For it is
most holy, and [1]He gave it to you to
bear away [b]the guilt of the congregation, to make atonement for them
before the LORD.
18"Behold, [a]since its blood had not
been brought inside, into the sanctuary, you should certainly have
[b]eaten it in the sanctuary, just as I
commanded."
19 But Aaron spoke to Moses, "Behold, this very day they presented
their sin offering and their burnt offering before the LORD. When
[1]things like these happened to me, if
I had eaten a sin offering today,
would it have been good in the sight
of the LORD?"
20 And when Moses heard *that*, it
seemed good in his sight.

CHAPTER 11

Laws about Animals for Food

THE LORD spoke again to Moses
and to Aaron, saying to them,
2"Speak to the sons of Israel, saying, '[a]These are the creatures which
you may eat from all the animals
that are on the earth.
3 'Whatever divides a hoof, thus
making split hoofs, *and* chews the
cud, among the animals, that you
may eat.
4 'Nevertheless, [a]you are not to
eat of these, among those which
chew the cud, or among those which
divide the hoof: the camel, for
though it chews cud, it does not divide the hoof, it is unclean to you.
5 'Likewise, the rock badger, for

2 [a]Num. 3:4; 26:61

3 [1]Or, *will show Myself holy* [a]Lev. 21:6 [b]Ex. 30:30; Ezek. 38:16 [c]Ex. 14:4, 17

4 [1]Lit., *brothers* [a]Ex. 6:18, 22

5 [a]Ex. 29:5; Lev. 8:13

6 [1]Lit., *unbind* [2]Lit., *brothers* [3]Lit., *burned* [a]Lev. 21:1-5, 10-12 [b]Num. 1:53; 16:22, 46; 18:5; Josh. 7:1; 22:18, 20; 2 Sam. 24:1

7 [a]Lev. 21:12

9 [a]Ezek. 44:21

10 [a]Lev. 11:47; 20:25; Ezek. 22:26

11 [a]Deut. 17:10, 11; 33:10

12 [a]Ex. 6:23; Num. 3:2 [b]Lev. 6:14-18

14 [a]Lev. 7:30-34

15 [a]Lev. 7:34

16 [a]Lev. 9:3, 15

17 [1]Or, *was given* [a]Lev. 6:24-30 [b]Ex. 28:38; Lev. 22:16; Num. 18:1

18 [a]Lev. 6:30 [b]Lev. 6:26

19 [1]Cf. vs. 1-4

2 [a]Deut. 14:3-21

4 [a]Acts 10:14

though it chews cud, it does not divide the hoof, it is unclean to you;
6 the [1]rabbit also, for though it
chews cud, it does not divide the
hoof, it is unclean to you;
7 and the pig, for though it divides the hoof, thus making a split
hoof, it does not chew cud, it is unclean to you.
8 'You shall not eat of their flesh
nor touch their carcasses; they are
unclean to you.
9 'These you may eat, whatever is
in the water: all that have fins and
scales, those in the water, in the
seas or in the rivers, you may eat.
10 'But whatever is in the seas and
in the rivers, that do not have fins
and scales among all the teeming
life of the water, and among all the
living creatures that are in the water, they are detestable things to
you,
11 and they shall be [1]abhorrent to
you; you may not eat of their flesh,
and their carcasses you shall detest.
12 'Whatever in the water does not
have fins and scales is [1]abhorrent to
you.

Avoid the Unclean

13 'These, moreover, you shall detest among the birds; they are [1]ab-
horrent, not to be eaten: the [2]eagle
and the vulture and the [3]buzzard,
14 and the kite and the falcon in its
kind,
15 every raven in its kind,
16 and the ostrich and the owl and
the sea gull and the hawk in its kind,
17 and the little owl and the cormorant and the [1]great owl,
18 and the white owl and the [1]peli-
can and the carrion vulture,
19 and the stork, the heron in its
kinds, and the hoopoe, and the bat.
20 'All the [1]winged insects that
walk on *all* fours are detestable to
you.
21 'Yet these you may eat among
all the [1]winged insects which walk
on *all* fours: those which have above
their feet jointed legs with which to
jump on the earth.
22 'These of them you may eat: the
locust in its kinds, and the devastat-
ing locust in its kinds, and the
cricket in its kinds, and the grasshopper in its kinds.
23 'But all other [1]winged insects
which are four-footed are detestable
to you.
24 'By these, moreover, you will be
made unclean: whoever touches
their carcasses becomes unclean
until evening,
25 and [a]whoever picks up any of
their carcasses shall wash his
clothes and be unclean until evening.
26 'Concerning all the animals
which divide the hoof, but do not
make a split *hoof*, or which do not
chew cud, they are unclean to you:
whoever touches them becomes unclean.
27 'Also whatever walks on its
paws, among all the creatures that
walk on *all* fours, are unclean to
you; whoever touches their carcasses becomes unclean until evening,
28 and the one who picks up their
carcasses shall wash his clothes and
be unclean until evening; they are
unclean to you.
29 'Now these are to you the unclean among the swarming things
which swarm on the earth: the mole,
and the mouse, and the [1]great lizard
in its kinds,
30 and the gecko, and the [1]croco-
dile, and the lizard, and the [2]sand
reptile, and the chameleon.
31 'These are to you the unclean
among all the swarming things;
whoever touches them when they
are dead becomes unclean until evening.
32 'Also anything on which one of
them may fall when they are dead,
becomes unclean, including any
wooden article, or clothing, or a
skin, or a sack—any article [1]of
which use is made —it shall be put
in the water and be unclean until
evening, then it becomes clean.
33 'As for any [a]earthenware vessel
into which one of them may fall,
whatever is in it becomes unclean
and you shall break [1]the vessel.
34 'Any of the [1]food which may be
eaten, on which water comes, shall
become unclean; and any [1]liquid
which may be drunk in every vessel
shall become unclean.
35 'Everything, moreover, on
which part of their carcass may fall
becomes unclean; an oven or a
[1]stove shall be smashed; they are
unclean and shall continue as unclean to you.
36 'Nevertheless a spring or a cistern [1]collecting water shall be clean,
though the one who touches their
carcass shall be unclean.
37 'And if a part of their carcass
falls on any seed for sowing which is
to be sown, it is clean.
38 'Though if water is put on the
seed, and a part of their carcass falls
on it, it is unclean to you.
39 'Also if one of the animals dies
which you have for food, the one

6 [1]Or, *hare*
11 [1]Lit., *detestable things*
12 [1]Lit., *detestable things*
13 [1]Lit., *a detestable thing* [2]Or, *vulture* [3]Or, *black vulture*
17 [1]Specifically, *great horned owl*
18 [1]Or, *owl;* or, *jackdaw*
20 [1]Lit., *swarming things with wings*
21 [1]Note v. 20
23 [1]Note v. 20
25 [a]Lev. 11:40
29 [1]Or, *thorn-tailed lizard*
30 [1]Or, *lizard* [2]Species as yet undefined
32 [1]Lit., *with which work is done*
33 [1]Lit., *it* [a]Lev. 6:28; 15:12
34 [1]I.e., if touched by a carcass; cf. 29-32
35 [1]Lit., *hearth for supporting (two) pots*
36 [1]Lit., *of a gathering of*

who touches its carcass becomes
unclean until evening.
40 '[a]He too, who eats some of its
carcass shall wash his clothes and
be unclean until evening; and the
one who picks up its carcass shall
wash his clothes and be unclean until evening.
41 '[a]Now every swarming thing
that swarms on the earth is detestable, not to be eaten.
42 'Whatever crawls on its belly,
and whatever walks on *all* fours,
whatever has many feet, in respect
to every swarming thing that
swarms on the earth, you shall not
eat them, for they are detestable.
43 '[a]Do not render [1]yourselves detestable through any of the swarming things that swarm; and you shall
not make yourselves unclean with
them so that you become unclean.
44 'For [a]I am the LORD your God.
Consecrate yourselves therefore,
and [b]be holy; for I am holy. And you
shall not make yourselves unclean
with any of the swarming things
that swarm on the earth.
45 '[a]For I am the LORD, who
brought you up from the land of
Egypt, to be your God; thus you
shall be holy for I am holy.' "
46 This is the law regarding the
animal, and the bird, and every living thing that moves in the waters,
and everything that swarms on the
earth,
47 [a]to make a distinction between
the unclean and the clean, and between the edible creature and the
creature which is not to be eaten.

CHAPTER 12

Laws of Motherhood

THEN the LORD spoke to Moses,
saying,
2 "Speak to the sons of Israel, saying, 'When a woman [1]gives birth
and bears a male *child*, then she
shall be unclean for seven days, [a]as
in the days of [2]her menstruation she
shall be unclean.
3 'And on [a]the eighth day the flesh
of his foreskin shall be circumcised.
4 'Then she shall remain in the
blood of *her* purification for thirty-
three days; she shall not touch any
consecrated thing, nor enter the
sanctuary, until the days of her purification are completed.
5 'But if she bears a female *child*,
then she shall be unclean for two
weeks, as in her [1]menstruation; and
she shall remain in the blood of *her*
purification for sixty-six days.
6 'And [a]when the days of her purification are completed, for a son or
for a daughter, she shall bring to the
priest at the doorway of the tent of
meeting, a one year old lamb for a
burnt offering, and a young pigeon
or a turtledove [b]for a sin offering.
7 'Then he shall offer it before the
LORD and make atonement for her;
and she shall be cleansed from the
[1]flow of her blood. This is the law for
her who bears *a child, whether* a
male or a female.
8 'But if [1]she cannot afford a
lamb, then she shall take [a]two turtledoves or two young pigeons, [b]the
one for a burnt offering and the other for a sin offering; and the priest
shall make atonement for her, and
she shall be clean.' "

CHAPTER 13

The Test for Leprosy

THEN the LORD spoke to Moses
and to Aaron, saying,
2 "When a man has on the skin of
his [1]body a swelling or a scab or a
bright spot, and it becomes [2]an infection of leprosy on the skin of his
[1]body, [a]then he shall be brought to
Aaron the priest, or to one of his
sons the priests.
3 "And the priest shall look at the
mark on the skin of the [1]body, and if
the hair in the infection has turned
white and the infection appears to
be deeper than the skin of his [1]body,
it is an infection of leprosy; when
the priest has looked at him, he shall
pronounce him unclean.
4 "But if the bright spot is white
on the skin of his [1]body, and [2]it does
not appear to be deeper than the
skin, and the hair on it has not
turned white, then the priest shall
[3]isolate *him who has* the infection
for seven days.
5 "And the priest shall look at him
on the seventh day, and if in his eyes
the infection [1]has not changed, *and*
the infection has not spread on the
skin, then the priest shall [2]isolate
him for seven more days.
6 "And the priest shall look at him
again on the seventh day; and if the
infection has faded, and the mark
has not spread on the skin, then the
priest shall pronounce him clean; it
is *only* a scab. And he shall wash his
clothes and be clean.
7 "But if the scab spreads farther
on the skin, after he has shown himself to the priest for his cleansing, he
shall appear again to the priest.
8 "And the priest shall look, and if

40 [a]Lev. 17:15; 22:8
41 [a]Lev. 11:29
43 [1]Lit., *your souls* [a]Lev. 20:25
44 [a]Ex. 6:7; 16:12; 23:25 [b]1 Pet. 1:16
45 [a]Lev. 22:33; 25:38; 26:45
47 [a]Lev. 10:10
2 [1]Lit., *produces seed* [2]Lit., *the impurity of her sickness* [a]Lev. 15:19; 18:19
3 [a]Gen. 17:12
5 [1]Lit., *impurity*
6 [a]Luke 2:22 [b]Lev. 5:7
7 [1]Lit., *fountain*
8 [1]Lit., *her hand does not find a sufficiency of a lamb* [a]Luke 2:22-24 [b]Lev.5:7
2 [1]Lit., *flesh* [2]Lit., *a mark, stroke* and so throughout the chap. [a]Deut. 24:8
3 [1]Lit., *flesh*
4 [1]Lit., *flesh* [2]Lit., *the appearance of it is not deeper* [3]Lit., *shut up*
5 [1]Lit., *has stood* [2]Lit., *shut up*

the scab has spread on the skin, then the priest shall pronounce him unclean; it is leprosy.

9"When the infection of leprosy is on a man, then he shall be brought to the priest.

10"The priest shall then look, and if there is a [a]white swelling in the skin, and it has turned the hair white, and there is quick raw flesh in the swelling,

11 it is [1]a chronic leprosy on the skin of his [2]body, and the priest shall pronounce him unclean; he shall not [3]isolate him, for he is unclean.

12"And if the leprosy breaks out farther on the skin, and the leprosy covers all the skin of *him who has* the infection from his head even to his feet, [1]as far as the priest can see,

13 then the priest shall look, and behold, *if* the leprosy has covered all his [1]body, he shall pronounce clean *him who has* the infection; it has all turned white *and* he is clean.

14"But whenever raw flesh appears on him, he shall be unclean.

15"And the priest shall look at the raw flesh, and he shall pronounce him unclean; the raw flesh is unclean, it is leprosy.

16"Or if the raw flesh turns again and is changed to white, then he shall come to the priest,

17 and the priest shall look at him, and behold, *if* the infection has turned to white, then the priest shall pronounce clean *him who has* the infection; he is clean.

18"And when the [1]body has a boil on its skin, and it is healed,

19 and in the place of the boil there is a white swelling or a reddish-white, bright spot, then it shall be shown to the priest;

20 and the priest shall look, and behold, *if* [1]it appears to be lower than the skin, and the hair on it has turned white, then the priest shall pronounce him unclean; it is the infection of leprosy, it has broken out in the boil.

21"But if the priest looks at it, and behold, there are no white hairs in it and it is not lower than the skin and is faded, then the priest shall [1]isolate him for seven days;

22 and if it spreads farther on the skin, then the priest shall pronounce him unclean; it is an infection.

23"But if the bright spot remains in its place, and does not spread, it is *only* the scar of the boil; and the priest shall pronounce him clean.

24"Or if the [1]body sustains in its skin a burn by fire, and the raw *flesh* of the burn becomes a bright spot, reddish-white, or white,

25 then the priest shall look at it. And if the hair in the bright spot has turned white, and it appears to be deeper than the skin, it is leprosy; it has broken out in the burn. Therefore, the priest shall pronounce him unclean; it is an infection of leprosy.

26"But if the priest looks at it, and indeed, there is no white hair in the bright spot, and it is no [1]deeper than the skin, but is dim, then the priest shall [2]isolate him for seven days;

27 and the priest shall look at him on the seventh day. If it spreads farther in the skin, then the priest shall pronounce him unclean; it is an infection of leprosy.

28"But if the bright spot remains in its place, and has not spread in the skin, but is dim, it is the swelling from the burn; and the priest shall pronounce him clean, for it is *only* the scar of the burn.

29"Now if a man or woman has an infection on the head or on the beard,

30 then the priest shall look at the infection, and if it appears to be deeper than the skin, and there is thin yellowish hair in it, then the priest shall pronounce him unclean; it is a scale, it is leprosy of the head or of the beard.

31"But if the priest looks at the infection of the scale, and indeed, it appears to be no deeper than the skin, and there is no black hair in it, then the priest shall [1]isolate *the person* with the scaly infection for seven days.

32"And on the seventh day the priest shall look at the infection, and if the scale has not spread, and no yellowish hair has [1]grown in it, and the appearance of the scale is no deeper than the skin,

33 then he shall shave himself, but he shall not shave the scale; and the priest shall [1]isolate *the person* with the scale seven more days.

34"Then on the seventh day the priest shall look at the scale, and if the scale has not spread in the skin, and it appears to be no deeper than the skin, the priest shall pronounce him clean; and he shall wash his clothes and be clean.

35"But if the scale spreads farther in the skin after his cleansing,

36 then the priest shall look at him, and if the scale has spread in the skin, the priest need not seek for the yellowish hair; he is unclean.

37"If in his sight the scale has remained, however, and black hair

10 [a]Num. 12:10; 2 Kin. 5:27; 2 Chr. 26:19, 20

11 [1]Lit., *an old* [2]Lit., *flesh* [3]Lit., *shut up*

12 [1]Lit., *with regard to the whole sight of the priest's eyes*

13 [1]Lit., *flesh*

18 [1]Lit., *flesh*

20 [1]Lit., *the appearance of it is lower*

21 [1]Lit., *shut up*

24 [1]Lit., *flesh*

26 [1]Lit., *lower* [2]Lit., *shut up*

31 [1]Lit., *shut up*

32 [1]Lit., *been*

33 [1]Lit., *shut up*

has grown in it, the scale has healed, he is clean; and the priest shall pronounce him clean.

38"And when a man or a woman has bright spots on the skin of the [1]body, *even* white bright spots,

39 then the priest shall look, and if the bright spots on the skin of their [1]bodies are a faint white, it is [2]eczema that has broken out on the skin; he is clean.

40"Now if a [1]man loses the hair of his head, he is bald; he is clean.

41 "And if his head becomes bald at the [1]front and sides, he is bald on the forehead; he is clean.

42"But if on the bald head or the bald forehead, there occurs a reddish-white infection, it is leprosy breaking out on his bald head or on his bald forehead.

43"Then the priest shall look at him; and if the swelling of the infection is reddish-white on his bald head or on his bald forehead, like the appearance of leprosy in the skin of the [1]body,

44 he is a leprous man, he is unclean. The priest shall surely pronounce him unclean; his infection is on his head.

45"As for the leper who has the infection, his clothes shall be torn, and [a]the hair of his head shall be [1]uncovered, and he shall [b]cover his mustache and cry, '[c]Unclean! Unclean!'

46"He shall remain unclean all the days during which he has the infection; he is unclean. He shall live alone; his dwelling shall be [a]outside the camp.

47"When a garment has a [1]mark of leprosy in it, whether it is a wool garment or a linen garment,

48 whether in [1]warp or woof, of linen or of wool, whether in leather or in any article made of leather,

49 if the mark is greenish or reddish in the garment or in the leather, or in the [1]warp or in the woof, or in any article of leather, it is a leprous mark and shall be shown to the priest.

50"Then the priest shall look at the mark, and shall [1]quarantine the article with the mark for seven days.

51"He shall then look at the mark on the seventh day; if the mark has spread in the garment, whether in the warp or in the woof, or in the leather, whatever the purpose for which the leather is used, the mark is a [1]leprous malignancy, it is unclean.

52"So he shall burn the garment, whether the warp or the woof, in wool or in linen, or any article of leather in which the mark occurs, for it is a [1]leprous malignancy; it shall be burned in the fire.

53"But if the priest shall look, and indeed, the mark has not spread in the garment, either in the warp or in the woof, or in any article of leather,

54 then the priest shall order them to wash the thing in which the mark occurs, and he shall [1]quarantine it for seven more days.

55"After the article with the mark has been washed, the priest shall again look, and if the mark has not changed its appearance, even though the mark has not spread, it is unclean; you shall burn it in the fire, [1]whether an eating away has produced bareness on the top or on the front of it.

56"Then if the priest shall look, and if the mark has faded after it has been washed, then he shall tear it out of the garment or out of the leather, whether from the warp or from the woof;

57 and if it appears again in the garment, whether in the warp or in the woof, or in any article of leather, it is an outbreak; the article with the mark shall be burned in the fire.

58"And the garment, whether the warp or the woof, or any article of leather from which the mark has departed when you washed it, it shall then be washed a second time and shall be clean."

59 This is the law for the mark of leprosy in a garment of wool or linen, whether in the warp or in the woof, or in any article of leather, for pronouncing it clean or unclean.

Chapter 14

Law of Cleansing a Leper

THEN the LORD spoke to Moses, saying,

2 "This shall be the law of the leper in the day of his cleansing. [a]Now he shall be brought to the priest,

3 and the priest shall go [a]out to the outside of the camp. Thus the priest shall look, and if the [1]infection of leprosy has been healed in the leper,

4 then the priest shall give orders to take two live clean birds and [a]cedar wood and a [1]scarlet string and hyssop for the one who is to be cleansed.

5"The priest shall also give orders to slay the one bird in an earthenware vessel over [1]running water.

6"*As for* the live bird, he shall

38 [1]Lit., *flesh*

39 [1]Lit., *flesh* [2]Lit., *tetter*

40 [1]Lit., *man's head becomes bald*

41 [1]Lit., *border of his face*

43 [1]Lit., *flesh*

45 [1]Or, *disheveled* [a]Lev. 10:6 [b]Ezek. 24:17, 22; Mic. 3:7 [c]Lam. 4:15

46 [a]Num. 5:1-4; 12:14

47 [1]Lit., *infection*, and so throughout the chap.

48 [1]Or, *weaving or texture*

49 [1]Or, *weaving or texture*

50 [1]Lit., *shut up*

51 [1]Lit., *malignant leprosy*

52 [1]Lit., *malignant leprosy*

54 [1]Lit., *shut up*

55 [1]Lit., *it is*

2 [a]Matt. 8:4; Mark 1:44; Luke 5:14; 17:14

3 [1]Lit., *mark, stroke*, and so throughout the chap. [a]Lev. 13:46

4 [1]Lit., *scarlet color and* [a]Lev. 14:6, 49, 51, 52; Num. 19:6

5 [1]Lit., *living*

take it, together with [a]the cedar wood and the [1]scarlet string and the [b]hyssop, and shall dip them and the live bird in the blood of the bird that was slain over the [2]running water.

7 "He shall then sprinkle seven times the one who is to be cleansed from the leprosy, and shall pronounce him clean, and shall let the live bird go free over the open field.

8 "[a]The one to be cleansed shall then wash his clothes and shave off all his hair, and bathe in water and [b]be clean. Now afterward, he may enter the camp, but he shall stay outside his tent for seven days.

9 "And it will be on the seventh day that he shall shave off all his hair: he shall shave his head and his beard and his eyebrows, even all his hair. He shall then wash his clothes and bathe his [1]body in water and [a]be clean.

10 "Now on the eighth day he is to take two male lambs without defect, and a yearling ewe lamb without defect, and three-tenths *of an* [1]*ephah* of fine flour mixed with oil for a grain offering, and one [2a]log of oil;

11 and the priest who pronounces him clean shall present the man to be cleansed and the [1]aforesaid before the LORD at the doorway of the tent of meeting.

12 "Then the priest shall take the one male lamb and bring it for a [a]guilt offering, with the [1b]log of oil, and present them as a wave offering before the LORD.

13 "Next he shall slaughter the male lamb in [a]the place where they slaughter the sin offering and the burnt offering, at the place of the sanctuary—for the guilt offering, [b]like the sin offering, belongs to the priest; it is most holy.

14 "The priest shall then take some of the blood of the [a]guilt offering, and the priest shall put *it* on [b]the lobe of the right ear of the one to be cleansed, and on the thumb of his right hand, and on the big toe of his right foot.

15 "The priest shall also take some of the [1a]log of oil, and pour *it* into his left palm;

16 the priest shall then dip his right-hand finger into the oil that is in his left palm, and with his finger sprinkle some of the oil seven times before the LORD.

17 "And of the remaining oil which is in his palm, the priest shall put some on the right ear lobe of the one to be cleansed, and on the thumb of his right hand, and on the big toe of his right foot, on the blood of the guilt offering;

18 while the rest of the oil that is in the priest's palm, he shall put on the head of the one to be cleansed. So the priest shall make atonement on his behalf before the LORD.

19 "The priest shall next offer the [a]sin offering and make atonement for the one to be cleansed from his uncleanness. Then afterward, he shall slaughter the burnt offering.

20 "And the priest shall offer up the burnt offering and the grain offering on the altar. Thus the priest shall make atonement for him, and [a]he shall be clean.

21 "[a]But if he is poor, and his [1]means are insufficient, then he is to take one male lamb for a [b]guilt offering as a wave offering to make atonement for him, and one-tenth *of an* [2]*ephah* of fine flour mixed with oil for a grain offering, and a [3c]log of oil,

22 and two turtledoves or two young pigeons which [1]are within his means, [a]the one shall be a [b]sin offering and the other a burnt offering.

23 "[a]Then the eighth day he shall bring them for his cleansing to the priest, at the doorway of the tent of meeting, before the LORD.

24 "And the priest shall take the lamb of the guilt offering, and [a]the [1]log of oil, and the priest shall offer them for a wave offering before the LORD.

25 "Next he shall slaughter the lamb of the guilt offering; and the priest is to take some of the blood of the guilt offering and put *it* on [a]the lobe of the right ear of the one to be cleansed and on the thumb of his right hand, and on the big toe of his right foot.

26 "The priest shall also pour some of the oil into his left palm;

27 and with his right-hand finger the priest shall sprinkle some of the oil that is in his left palm seven times before the LORD.

28 "The priest shall then put some of the oil that is in his palm on the lobe of the right ear of the one to be cleansed, and on the thumb of his right hand, and on the big toe of his right foot, on the place of the blood of the guilt offering.

29 "Moreover, the rest of the oil that is in the priest's palm he shall put on the head of the one to be cleansed, to make atonement on his behalf before the LORD.

30 "He shall then offer one of the turtledoves or young pigeons, [1]which are within his means.

6 [1]Lit., *scarlet color and* [2]Lit., *living* [a]Lev. 14:4 [b]Ps. 51:7

8 [a]Num. 8:7 [b]Lev. 14:9, 20

9 [1]Lit., *flesh* [a]Lev. 14:8, 20

10 [1]I.e., Approx. one bushel [2]Approx. one pint [a]Lev. 14:12, 15, 21, 24

11 [1]Lit., *them*

12 [1]Approx. one pint [a]Lev. 14:19 [b]Lev. 14:10

13 [a]Lev. 1:11 [b]Lev. 6:24-30

14 [a]Lev. 14:19 [b]Lev. 8:23, 24

15 [1]Approx. one pint [a]Lev. 14:10

19 [a]Lev. 14:12

20 [a]Lev. 14:8, 9

21 [1]Lit., *hand is not reaching* [2]I.e., Approx. one bushel [3]Approx. one pint [a]Lev. 5:11; 27:8 [b]Lev. 14:22 [c]Lev. 14:10

22 [1]Lit., *his hand reaches* [a]Lev. 5:7 [b]Lev. 14:21, 24, 25

23 [a]Lev. 14:10, 11

24 [1]Approx. one pint [a]Lev. 14:10

25 [a]Lev. 14:14

30 [1]Lit., *from those which his hand can reach*

31 "*He shall offer* what [1]he can afford, [a]the one for a sin offering, and
the other for a burnt offering, together with the grain offering. So
the priest shall make atonement before the LORD on behalf of the one to
be cleansed.
32 "This is the law *for him* in whom
there is an infection of leprosy,
whose [1]means are limited for his
cleansing."

Cleansing a Leprous House

33 The LORD further spoke to
Moses and to Aaron, saying,
34 "When you enter the land of Canaan, which I give you for a possession, and I put a mark of leprosy on
a house in the land of your possession,
35 then the one who owns the
house shall come and tell the priest,
saying, '*Something* like [a]a mark *of*
leprosy has become visible to me in
the house.'
36 "The priest shall then order that
they empty the house before the
priest goes in to look at the mark, so
that everything in the house need
not become unclean; and afterward
the priest shall go in to look at the
house.
37 "So he shall look at the mark,
and if the mark on the walls of the
house has greenish or reddish de-
pressions, and appears deeper than
the [1]surface;
38 then the priest shall come out of
the house, to the [1]doorway, and
[2]quarantine the house for seven
days.
39 "And the priest shall return on
the seventh day and [1]make an inspection. If the mark has indeed
spread in the walls of the house,
40 then the priest shall order them
to tear out the stones with the mark
in them and throw them away [1]at an
unclean place outside the city.
41 "And he shall have the house
scraped all around [1]inside, and they
shall dump the plaster that they
scrape off at an unclean place outside the city.
42 "Then they shall take other
stones and replace *those* stones; and
he shall take other plaster and re-
plaster the house.
43 "If, however, the mark breaks
out again in the house, after he has
torn out the stones and scraped the
house, and after it has been replastered,
44 then the priest shall come in
and [1]make an inspection. If he sees
that the mark has indeed spread in
the house, it is a malignant mark in
the house; it is unclean.
45 "He shall therefore tear down
the house, its stones, and its timbers, and all the plaster of the house,
and he shall take *them* outside the
city to an [a]unclean place.
46 "Moreover, whoever goes into
the house during the time that he
has [1]quarantined it, becomes unclean until evening.
47 "Likewise, whoever lies down in
the house shall wash his clothes,
and whoever eats in the house shall
wash his clothes.
48 "If, on the other hand, the priest
comes in and [1]makes an inspection,
and the mark has not indeed spread
in the house after the house has
been replastered, then the priest
shall pronounce the house clean because the mark has [2]not reappeared.
49 "To cleanse the house then, he
shall take [a]two birds and cedar
wood and a [1]scarlet string and hyssop,
50 and he shall slaughter the one
bird in an earthenware vessel over
[1]running water.
51 "Then he shall take the cedar
wood and the hyssop and the [1]scar-
let string, with the live bird, and dip
them in the blood of the slain bird,
as well as in the [2]running water, and
sprinkle the house seven times.
52 "He shall thus cleanse the house
with the blood of the bird and with
the [1]running water, along with the
live bird and with the cedar wood
and with the hyssop and with the
[2]scarlet string.
53 "However, he shall let the live
bird go free outside the city into the
open field. So he shall make atonement for the house, and it shall be
clean."
54 This is the law for any mark of
leprosy—even for a scale,
55 and for the leprous garment or
house,
56 and for a swelling, and for a
scab, and for a bright spot—
57 to teach [1]when they are unclean, and [1]when they are clean.
This is the law of leprosy.

CHAPTER 15

Cleansing Unhealthiness

THE LORD also spoke to Moses and
to Aaron, saying,
2 "Speak to the sons of Israel, and
say to them, '[a]When any man has a
discharge from his [1]body, [2]his discharge is unclean.
3 'This, moreover, shall be his uncleanness in his discharge: it is his

31 [1]Lit., *his hand can reach* [a]Lev. 5:7
32 [1]Lit., *hand does not reach*
35 [a]Ps. 91:10
37 [1]Lit., *wall*
38 [1]Lit., *doorway of the house* [2]Lit., *shut up*
39 [1]Lit., *look*
40 [1]Lit., *to*
41 [1]Lit., *from the house around*
44 [1]Lit., *look*
45 [a]Lev. 14:41
46 [1]Lit., *shut up*
48 [1]Lit., *looks* [2]Lit., *healed*
49 [1]Lit., *scarlet color* [a]Lev. 14:4
50 [1]Lit., *living*
51 [1]Lit., *scarlet color* [2]Lit., *living*
52 [1]Lit., *living* [2]Lit., *scarlet color*
57 [1]Lit., *in the day of*
2 [1]Lit., *flesh,* and so throughout the chap. [2]Or, *by his discharge, he is unclean* [a]Lev. 22:4; Num. 5:2; 2 Sam. 3:29

uncleanness whether his body al-
lows its discharge to flow, or
whether his body obstructs its discharge.
4 'Every bed on which the person
with the discharge lies becomes unclean, and everything on which he
sits becomes unclean.
5 'Anyone, moreover, who
touches his bed shall wash his
clothes and bathe in water and be
unclean until evening;
6 and whoever sits on the thing
on which the man with the discharge has been sitting, shall wash
his clothes and bathe in water and
be unclean until evening.
7 'Also whoever touches the [1]per-
son with the discharge shall wash
his clothes and bathe in water and
be unclean until evening.
8 'Or if the man with the discharge spits on one who is clean, he
too shall wash his clothes and bathe
in water and be unclean until evening.
9 'And every saddle on which the
person with the discharge rides becomes unclean.
10 'Whoever then touches any of
the things which were under him
shall be unclean until evening, and
he who carries them shall wash his
clothes and bathe in water and be
unclean until evening.
11 'Likewise, whomever the one
with the discharge touches without
having rinsed his hands in water
shall wash his clothes and bathe in
water and be unclean until evening.
12 'However, an [a]earthenware vessel which the person with the discharge touches shall be broken, and
every wooden vessel shall be rinsed
in water.
13 'Now when the man with the
discharge becomes cleansed from
his discharge, then he shall count off
for himself seven days for his
cleansing; he shall then wash his
clothes and bathe his body in [1]run-
ning water and shall become clean.
14 'Then on the eighth day he shall
take for himself two turtledoves or
two young pigeons, and come before the LORD to the doorway of the
tent of meeting, and give them to
the priest;
15 and the priest shall offer them,
[a]one for a sin offering, and the other
for a burnt offering. So the priest
shall make atonement on his behalf
before the LORD because of his discharge.
16 '[a]Now if a [1]man has a seminal
emission, he shall bathe all his body
in water and be unclean until evening.
17 'As for any garment or any
leather on which there is seminal
emission, it shall be washed with
water and be unclean until evening.
18 'If a man lies with a woman *so
that* there is a seminal emission,
they shall both bathe in water and
be [a]unclean until evening.
19 'When a woman has a discharge, *if* her discharge in her body
is blood, she shall continue in her
menstrual impurity for seven days;
and whoever touches her shall be
unclean until evening.
20 'Everything also on which she
lies during her menstruation impurity shall be unclean, and everything
on which she sits shall be unclean.
21 'And anyone who touches her
bed shall wash his clothes and bathe
in water and be unclean until evening.
22 'And whoever touches any thing
on which she sits shall wash his
clothes and bathe in water and be
unclean until evening.
23 'Whether it be on the bed or on
the thing on which she is sitting,
when he touches it, he shall be unclean until evening.
24 '[a]And if a man actually lies with
her, so that her menstrual impurity
is on him, he shall be unclean seven
days, and every bed on which he lies
shall be unclean.
25 '[a]Now if a woman has a discharge of her blood many days, not
at the period of her menstrual impurity, or if she has a discharge beyond
[1]that period, all the days of her impure discharge she shall continue as
though [2]in her menstrual impurity;
she is unclean.
26 'Any bed on which she lies all
the days of her discharge shall be to
her like [1]her bed at menstruation;
and every thing on which she sits
shall be unclean, like [2]her uncleanness at that time.
27 'Likewise, whoever touches
them shall be unclean and shall
wash his clothes and bathe in water
and be unclean until evening.
28 'When she becomes clean from
her discharge, she shall count off for
herself seven days; and afterward
she shall be clean.
29 'Then on the eighth day she
shall take for herself two turtledoves or two young pigeons, and
bring them in to the priest, to the
doorway of the tent of meeting.
30 'And the priest shall offer the
[a]one for a sin offering and the other
for a burnt offering. So the priest

7 [1]Lit., *flesh*
12 [a]Lev. 6:28; 11:33
13 [1]Lit., *living*
15 [a]Lev. 5:7
16 [1]Lit., *man's, goes out from him* [a]Lev. 22:4; Deut. 23:10, 11
18 [a]1 Sam. 21:4
24 [a]Lev. 18:19; 20:18
25 [1]Lit., *her menstrual impurity* [2]Lit., *in the days of* [a]Matt. 9:20; Mark 5:25; Luke 8:43
26 [1]Lit., *the bed of her menstrual impurity* [2]Lit., *the uncleanness of her menstrual impurity*
30 [a]Lev. 5:7

shall make atonement on her behalf before the LORD because of her impure discharge.'

31"Thus you shall keep the sons of Israel separated from their uncleanness, lest they die in their uncleanness by their [a]defiling My [1]tabernacle that is among them."

32 This is the law for the one with a discharge, and for the man [1]who has a seminal emission so that he is unclean by it,

33 and for the woman who is ill because of menstrual impurity, and for the one who has a discharge, whether a male or a female, or a man who lies with an unclean woman.

CHAPTER 16

Law of Atonement

NOW the LORD spoke to Moses after [a]the death of the two sons of Aaron, when they had approached the presence of the LORD and died.

2 And the LORD said to Moses, "Tell your brother Aaron that he shall not enter [a]at any time into the holy place inside the veil, before the [1]mercy seat which is on the ark, lest he die; for [b]I will appear in the cloud over the [1]mercy seat.

3"Aaron shall enter the holy place with this: with a [1]bull for a [a]sin offering and a ram for a burnt offering.

4"He shall put on the [a]holy linen tunic, and the linen undergarments shall be next to his [1]body, and he shall be girded with the linen sash, and attired with the linen turban (these are holy garments). Then he shall [b]bathe his [1]body in water and put them on.

5"And he shall take from the congregation of the sons of Israel [a]two male goats for a sin offering and one ram for a burnt offering.

6"Then [a]Aaron shall offer the bull for the sin offering which is for himself, that he may make atonement for himself and for his household.

7"And he shall take the two goats and present them before the LORD at the doorway of the tent of meeting.

8"And Aaron shall cast lots for the two goats, one lot for the LORD and the other lot for the [1]scapegoat.

9"Then Aaron shall offer the goat on which the lot for the LORD fell, and make it a sin offering.

10"But the goat on which the lot for the [1]scapegoat fell, shall be presented alive before the LORD, to make atonement upon it, to send it into the wilderness as the [1]scapegoat.

11"Then Aaron shall offer the bull of the sin offering [a]which is for himself, and make atonement for himself and [b]for his household, and he shall slaughter the bull of the sin offering which is for himself.

12"And he shall take a [a]firepan full of coals of fire from upon the altar before the LORD, and [1]two handfuls of finely ground [b]sweet incense, and bring *it* inside the veil.

13"And he shall put the incense on the fire before the LORD, that the cloud of incense may cover the [1]mercy seat that is on *the ark of* the testimony, [a]lest he die.

14"Moreover, [a]he shall take some of the blood of the bull and sprinkle *it* [b]with his finger on the [1]mercy seat on the east *side*; also in front of the [1]mercy seat he shall sprinkle some of the blood with his finger seven times.

15"Then he shall slaughter the goat of the sin offering [a]which is for the people, and bring its blood inside the veil, and do with its blood as he did with the blood of the bull, and sprinkle it on the [1]mercy seat and in front of the [1]mercy seat.

16"And [a]he shall make atonement for the holy place, because of the impurities of the sons of Israel, and because of their transgressions, in regard to all their sins; and thus he shall do for the tent of meeting which abides with them in the midst of their impurities.

17"When he goes in to make atonement in the holy place, no one shall be in the tent of meeting until he comes out, that he may make atonement for himself and for his household and for all the assembly of Israel.

18"Then he shall go out to the altar that is before the LORD and make atonement for it, and shall take some of the blood of the bull and of the blood of the goat, and [a]put it on the horns of the altar on all sides.

19"And [a]with his finger he shall sprinkle some of the blood on it seven times, and cleanse it, and from the impurities of the sons of Israel consecrate it.

20"When he finishes atoning for the holy place, and the tent of meeting and the altar, he shall offer the live goat.

21"Then Aaron shall lay both of his hands on the head of the live goat, and [a]confess over it all the iniquities of the sons of Israel, and all their transgressions [1]in regard to all their

31 [1]Or, *dwelling place* [a]Lev. 20:3; Num. 19:13, 20; Ezek. 36:17

32 [1]Lit., *whose seminal emission goes out from him*

1 [a]Lev. 10:1, 2

2 [1]Lit., *propitiatory* [a]Ex. 30:10; Heb. 9:7, 25 [b]Ex. 25:21, 22

3 [1]Or, *bull of the herd* [a]Lev. 4:1-12; 16:6

4 [1]Lit., *flesh* [a]Ex. 28:39, 42 [b]Lev. 16:24

5 [a]Lev. 4:13-21

6 [a]Heb. 5:3

8 [1]Lit., *goat of removal,* or else a name: *Azazel*

10 [1]Lit., *goat of removal,* or else a name: *Azazel*

11 [a]Heb. 7:27; 9:7 [b]Lev. 16:33

12 [1]Lit., *the filling of the hollow of his hands* [a]Lev. 10:1 [b]Ex. 30:34-38

13 [1]Lit., *propitiatory* [a]Ex. 28:43; Lev. 22:9; Num. 4:15, 20

14 [1]Lit., *propitiatory* [a]Heb. 9:25 [b]Lev. 4:6, 17

15 [1]Lit., *propitiatory* [a]Heb. 7:27; 9:7

16 [a]Ex. 29:36, 37; 30:10; Heb. 2:17

18 [a]Lev. 4:25; Ezek. 43:20, 22

19 [a]Lev. 16:14

21 [1]Lit., *in addition to* [a]Lev. 5:5

sins; and he shall lay them on the
head of the goat and send *it* away
into the wilderness by the hand of a
man who *stands* in readiness.
22"And the goat shall bear on itself
all their iniquities to a solitary land;
and he shall release the goat in the
wilderness.
23"Then Aaron shall come into the
tent of meeting, and take off [a]the
linen garments which he put on
when he went into the holy place,
and shall leave them there.
24"And [a]he shall bathe his [1]body
with water in a holy place and put
on [b]his clothes, and come forth and
offer his burnt offering and the
burnt offering of the people, and
make atonement for himself and for
the people.
25"Then he shall offer up in smoke
the fat of the sin offering on the altar.
26"And the one who released the
goat as the [1]scapegoat [a]shall wash
his clothes and bathe his [2]body with
water; then afterward he shall come
into the camp.
27"But the bull of the sin offering
and the goat of the sin offering,
[a]whose blood was brought in to
make atonement in the holy place,
shall be taken outside the camp, and
they shall burn their hides, their
flesh, and their refuse in the fire.
28"Then the [a]one who burns them
shall wash his clothes and bathe his
body with water, then afterward he
shall come into the camp.

An Annual Atonement

29"And *this* shall be a permanent
statute for you: [a]in the seventh
month, on the tenth day of the
month, you shall humble your souls,
and not [b]do any work, whether the
native, or the alien who sojourns
among you;
30 for it is on this day that [1]atone-
ment shall be made for you to
cleanse you; you shall be clean from
all your sins before the LORD.
31"It is to be a sabbath of solemn
rest for you, that you may [a]humble
your souls; it is a permanent statute.
32"So the priest who is anointed
and [1]ordained to serve as priest in
his father's place shall make atonement: he shall thus put on [a]the linen
garments, the holy garments,
33 and make atonement for the
holy sanctuary; and he shall make
atonement for the tent of meeting
and for the altar. He shall also make
atonement for [a]the priests and for
all the people of the assembly.
34"Now you shall have this as a
permanent statute, to [a]make atonement for the sons of Israel for all
their sins once every year." And just
as the LORD had commanded Moses,
so he did.

CHAPTER 17

Blood for Atonement

THEN the LORD spoke to Moses,
saying,
2"Speak to Aaron and to his sons,
and to all the sons of Israel, and say
to them, 'This is what the LORD has
commanded, saying,
3"Any man from the house of Israel who slaughters an ox, or a
lamb, or a goat in the camp, or who
slaughters it outside the camp,
4 and [a]has not brought it to the
doorway of the tent of meeting to
present *it* as an offering to the LORD
before the [1]tabernacle of the LORD,
bloodguiltiness is to be reckoned to
that man. He has shed blood and
that man shall be cut off from
among his people.
5"[1]The reason is so that the sons
of Israel may bring their sacrifices
which they were sacrificing in the
open field, that they may bring them
in to the LORD, at the doorway of the
tent of meeting to the priest, and
sacrifice them as sacrifices of peace
offerings to the LORD.
6"And the priest shall sprinkle
the blood on the altar of the LORD at
the doorway of the tent of meeting,
and offer up the fat in smoke as a
soothing aroma to the LORD.
7"And [a]they shall no longer sacrifice their sacrifices to the [1]goat demons with which they play the harlot. This shall be a permanent
statute to them throughout their
generations." '
8"Then you shall say to them,
'Any man from the house of Israel,
or from the aliens who sojourn
among them, who offers a burnt offering or sacrifice,
9 and [a]does not bring it to the
doorway of the tent of meeting to
[1]offer it to the LORD, that man also
shall be cut off from his people.
10 '[a]And any man from the house
of Israel, or from the aliens who sojourn among them, who eats any
blood, [b]I will set My face against
that person who eats blood, and will
cut him off from among his people.
11 'For [a]the [1]life of the flesh is in
the blood, and I have given it to you
on the altar to make atonement for
your souls; for it is the blood by reason of the [1]life that makes atonement.'

23 [a]Lev. 16:4
24 [1]Lit., *flesh* [a]Lev. 16:4 [b]Ex. 28:40, 41
26 [1]Lit., *goat of removal,* or else a name: *Azazel* [2]Lit., *flesh* [a]Lev. 11:25, 40
27 [a]Heb. 13:11
28 [a]Num. 19:8
29 [a]Lev. 23:27 [b]Ex. 31:14, 15
30 [1]Lit., *he shall make*
31 [a]Lev. 23:32; Ezra 8:21; Is. 58:3, 5; Dan. 10:12
32 [1]Lit., *whose hand is filled* [a]Lev. 16:4
33 [a]Lev. 16:11
34 [a]Heb. 9:7
4 [1]Lit., *dwelling place* [a]Deut. 12:5-21
5 [1]Lit., *In order that*
7 [1]Or, *goat-idols* [a]Ex. 22:20; 32:8; 34:15; Deut. 32:17; 2 Chr. 11:15
9 [1]Lit., *do* [a]Ex. 20:24; Lev. 17:4
10 [a]Lev. 3:17; 7:26, 27; Deut. 12:16, 23-25 [b]Lev. 20:3, 6
11 [1]Lit., *soul* [a]Gen. 9:4; Lev. 17:14

12"Therefore I said to the sons of
Israel, 'No person among you may
eat blood, nor may any alien who
sojourns among you eat blood.'
13"So when any man from the sons
of Israel, or from the aliens who sojourn among them, [1]in hunting
catches a beast or a bird which may
be eaten, [a]he shall pour out its blood
and cover it with earth.
14"[a]For *as for the* [1]life of all flesh,
its blood is *identified* with its [1]life.
Therefore I said to the sons of Israel,
'You are not to eat the blood of any
flesh, for the [1]life of all flesh is its
blood; whoever eats it shall be cut
off.'
15"[a]And when any person eats *an
animal* which dies, or is torn *by
beasts*, whether he is a native or an
alien, he shall wash his clothes and
bathe in water, and remain unclean
until evening; then he will become
clean.
16"But if he does not wash *them* or
bathe his body, then he shall bear
his [1]guilt."

CHAPTER 18

Laws on Immoral Relations

THEN the LORD spoke to Moses,
saying,
2"Speak to the sons of Israel and
say to them, '[a]I am the LORD your
God.
3 'You shall not do [1]what is [a]done
in the land of Egypt where you lived,
nor are you to do [1]what is [b]done in
the land of Canaan where I am
bringing you; you shall not walk in
their statutes.
4 'You are to perform My judgments and keep My statutes, [1]to live
in accord with them; [a]I am the LORD
your God.
5 'So you shall keep My statutes
and My judgments, [a]by which a
man may live if he does them; I am
the LORD.
6 'None of you shall approach any
blood relative [1]of his to uncover nakedness; I am the LORD.
7 '[a]You shall not uncover the nakedness of your father, that is, the
nakedness of your mother. She is
your mother; you are not to uncover
her nakedness.
8 'You shall not uncover the nakedness of your father's wife; it is
your father's nakedness.
9 '[a]The nakedness of your sister,
either your father's daughter or
your mother's daughter, whether
born at home or born outside, their
nakedness you shall not uncover.
10 'The nakedness of your son's
daughter or your daughter's daughter, their nakedness you shall not
uncover; for [1]their nakedness is
yours.
11 'The nakedness of your father's
wife's daughter, [1]born to your father, she is your sister, you shall not
uncover her nakedness.
12 '[a]You shall not uncover the nakedness of your father's sister; she
is your father's blood relative.
13 'You shall not uncover the nakedness of your mother's sister, for
she is your mother's blood relative.
14 '[a]You shall not uncover the nakedness of your father's brother;
you shall not approach his wife, she
is your aunt.
15 '[a]You shall not uncover the nakedness of your daughter-in-law;
she is your son's wife, you shall not
uncover her nakedness.
16 '[a]You shall not uncover the nakedness of your brother's wife; it is
your brother's nakedness.
17 '[a]You shall not uncover the nakedness of a woman and of her
daughter, nor shall you take her
son's daughter or her daughter's
daughter, to uncover her nakedness;
they are blood relatives. It is [1]lewd-
ness.
18 'And you shall not [1]marry a
woman in addition to [2]her sister [3]as
a rival while she is alive, to uncover
her nakedness.
19 '[a]Also you shall not approach a
woman to uncover her nakedness
during her [b]menstrual impurity.
20 '[a]And you shall not have intercourse with your neighbor's wife, to
be defiled with her.
21 'Neither shall you give any of
your offspring [a]to [1]offer them to
Molech, nor shall you [b]profane the
name of your God; I am the LORD.
22 '[a]You shall not lie with a male as
[1]one lies with a female; it is an
abomination.
23 '[a]Also you shall not have intercourse with any animal to be defiled
with it, nor shall any woman stand
before an animal to [1]mate with it; it
is a perversion.
24 'Do not defile yourselves by any
of these things; for by all these [a]the
nations which I am casting out before you have become defiled.
25 'For the land has become defiled, [a]therefore I have visited its
[1]punishment upon it, so the land
[b]has spewed out its inhabitants.
26 'But as for you, you are to keep
My statutes and My judgments, and
shall not do any of these abomina-

13 [1]Lit., *who in hunting* [a]Deut. 12:16
14 [1]Lit., *soul* [a]Lev. 17:11
15 [a]Ex. 22:31; Lev. 7:24; 22:8
16 [1]Or, *iniquity*
2 [a]Lev. 11:44
3 [1]Lit., *according to the deed of* [a]Ezek. 20:7, 8 [b]Lev. 18:24-30; 20:23
4 [1]Lit., *to walk in them* [a]Lev. 18:2
5 [a]Ezek. 20:11; Luke 10:28; Rom. 10:5; Gal. 3:12
6 [1]Lit., *of his flesh*
7 [a]Lev. 20:11; Deut. 27:20; Ezek. 22:10
9 [a]Lev. 18:11; 20:17; Deut. 27:22
10 [1]Lit., *they are your nakedness*
11 [1]Lit., *begotten of*
12 [a]Lev. 20:19
14 [a]Lev. 20:20
15 [a]Lev. 20:12
16 [a]Lev. 20:21
17 [1]Or, *wickedness* [a]Lev. 20:14
18 [1]Lit., *take a wife* [2]Or, *another* [3]Lit., *to be*
19 [a]Lev. 15:24; 20:18 [b]Lev. 12:2
20 [a]Lev. 20:10
21 [1]Lit., *cause to pass over* [a]Lev. 20:2-5; Deut. 12:31 [b]Lev. 19:12; 20:3; 21:6
22 [1]Lit., *those who* [a]Lev. 20:13; Deut. 23:18
23 [1]Or, *lie* [a]Ex. 22:19; Lev. 20:15, 16; Deut. 27:21
24 [a]Lev. 18:3
25 [1]Lit., *iniquity* [a]Lev. 20:23; Deut. 9:5; 18:12 [b]Lev. 18:28; 20:22

tions, *neither* the native, nor the alien who sojourns among you;

27 (for the men of the land who have been before you have done all these abominations, and the land has become defiled);

28 so that the land may not spew you out, should you defile it, as it has spewed out the nation which has been before you.

29 'For whoever does any of these abominations, [1]those persons who do *so* shall be cut off from among their people.

30 'Thus you are to keep [a]My charge, that you do not practice any of the abominable customs which have been practiced before you, so as not to defile yourselves with them; [b]I am the LORD your God.' "

CHAPTER 19

Idolatry Forbidden

THEN the LORD spoke to Moses, saying,

2 "Speak to all the congregation of the sons of Israel and say to them, '[a]You shall be holy, for I the LORD your God am holy.

3 'Every one of you shall reverence his mother and his father, and you shall keep [a]My sabbaths; [b]I am the LORD your God.

4 'Do not turn to [a]idols or make for yourselves molten [b]gods; I am the LORD your God.

5 'Now when you offer a sacrifice of peace offerings to the LORD, you shall offer it so that you may be accepted.

6 'It shall be eaten the same day you offer *it*, and the next day; but what remains until the third day shall be burned with fire.

7 'So if it is eaten at all on the third day, it is an offense; it will not be accepted.

8 'And everyone who eats it will bear his iniquity, for he has profaned the holy thing of the LORD; and that person shall be cut off from his people.

Sundry Laws

9 '[a]Now when you reap the harvest of your land, you shall not reap to the very corners of your field, neither shall you gather the gleanings of your harvest.

10 'Nor shall you glean your vineyard, nor shall you gather the fallen fruit of your vineyard; you shall leave them for the needy and for the stranger. I am the LORD your God.

11 '[a]You shall not steal, nor deal falsely, nor lie to one another.

12 '[a]And you shall not swear falsely by My name, so as to [b]profane the name of your God; I am the LORD.

13 '[a]You shall not oppress your neighbor, nor rob *him*. [b]The wages of a hired man are not to remain with you all night until morning.

14 'You shall not curse a deaf man, nor [a]place a stumbling block before the blind, but you shall revere your God; I am the LORD.

15 '[a]You shall do no injustice in judgment; you shall not be partial to the poor nor defer to the great, but you are to judge your neighbor fairly.

16 'You shall not go about as [a]a slanderer among your people, and you are not to [1]act against the [2b]life of your neighbor; I am the LORD.

17 'You [a]shall not hate your [1]fellow-countryman in your heart; you [b]may surely reprove your neighbor, but shall not incur sin because of him.

18 '[a]You shall not take vengeance, [b]nor bear any grudge against the sons of your people, but [c]you shall love your neighbor as yourself; I am the LORD.

19 'You are to keep My statutes. You shall not breed together two kinds of your cattle; [a]you shall not sow your field with two kinds of seed, nor wear a garment upon you of two kinds of material mixed together.

20 '[a]Now if a man lies carnally with a woman who is a slave acquired for *another* man, but who has in no way been redeemed, nor given her freedom, there shall be punishment; they shall not, *however*, be put to death, because she was not free.

21 'And he shall bring his guilt offering to the LORD to the doorway of the tent of meeting, [a]a ram for a guilt offering.

22 'The priest shall also make atonement for him with the ram of the guilt offering before the LORD for his sin which he has committed, and the sin which he has committed shall be forgiven him.

23 'And when you enter the land and plant all kinds of trees for food, then you shall count their fruit as [1]forbidden. Three years it shall be [1]forbidden to you; *it* shall not be eaten.

24 'But in the fourth year all its fruit shall be holy, an offering of praise to the LORD.

25 'And in the fifth year you are to eat of its fruit, that its yield may in-

29 [1]Or, *and the*
30 [a]Lev. 22:9; Deut. 11:1 [b]Lev. 18:2
2 [a]I Pet. 1:16
3 [a]Ex. 20:8 [b]Lev. 11:44
4 [a]Lev. 26:1; Ps. 96:5; 115:4-7 [b]Ex. 20:23; 34:17
9 [a]Lev. 23:22; Deut. 24:20-22
11 [a]Ex. 20:15, 16
12 [a]Ex. 20:7 [b]Lev. 18:21
13 [a]Ex. 22:7-15, 21-27 [b]Deut. 24:15
14 [a]Deut. 27:18
15 [a]Ex. 23:3, 6; Deut. 1:17; 10:17
16 [1]Lit., *stand* [2]Lit., *blood* [a]Ps. 15:3; Jer. 6:28; 9:4; Ezek. 22:9 [b]Ex. 23:7; Deut. 27:25
17 [1]Lit., *brother* [a]I John 2:9, 11; 3:15 [b]Matt. 18:15; Luke 17:3
18 [a]Deut. 32:35; Rom. 12:19; Heb. 10:30 [b]Ps. 103:9 [c]Matt. 19:19; Mark 12:31; Luke 10:27; Rom. 13:9
19 [a]Deut. 22:9, 11
20 [a]Deut. 22:23-27
21 [a]Lev. 6:1-7
23 [1]Lit., *uncircumcised*

crease for you; I am the LORD your
God.
26 'You shall not eat *anything*
[a]with the blood, nor practice [b]divi-
nation or soothsaying.
27 '[a]You shall not round off the
side-growth of your heads, nor
harm the edges of your beard.
28 'You shall not make any cuts in
your [1]body for the [2]dead, nor make
any tattoo marks on yourselves: I
am the LORD.
29 '[a]Do not [1]profane your daughter
by making her a harlot, so that the
land may not fall to harlotry, and the
land become full of lewdness.
30 'You shall [a]keep My sabbaths
and [b]revere My sanctuary; I am the
LORD.
31 'Do not turn to [1a]mediums or
spiritists; do not seek them out to be
defiled by them. I am the LORD your
God.
32 '[a]You shall rise up before the
grayheaded, and honor the [1]aged,
and you shall revere your God; I am
the LORD.
33 '[a]When a stranger resides with
you in your land, you shall not do
him wrong.
34 'The stranger who resides with
you shall be to you as the native
among you, and [a]you shall love him
as yourself; for you were aliens in
the land of Egypt: I am the LORD
your God.
35 '[a]You shall do no wrong in judgment, in measurement of weight, or
capacity.
36 'You shall have just balances,
just weights, a just [1]ephah, and a
just [2]hin: I am the LORD your God,
who brought you out from the land
of Egypt.
37 'You shall thus observe all My
statutes, and all My ordinances, and
do them: I am the LORD.' "

CHAPTER 20

On Human Sacrifice and Immoralities

THEN the LORD spoke to Moses,
saying,
2 "You shall also say to the sons of
Israel, 'Any man from the sons of
Israel or from the aliens sojourning
in Israel, [a]who gives any of his [1]off-
spring to Molech, shall surely be put
to death; [b]the people of the land
shall stone him with stones.
3 'I will also set My face against
that man and will cut him off from
among his people, because he has
given some of his [1]offspring to Molech, [a]so as to defile My sanctuary
and [b]to profane My holy name.
4 'If the people of the land, however, [1]should ever disregard that
man when he gives any of his [2]off-
spring to Molech, so as not to put
him to death,
5 then I Myself will set My face
against that man and against his
family; and I will cut off from among
their people both him and all those
who play the harlot after him, by
playing the harlot after Molech.
6 'As for the person who turns to
[1a]mediums and to spiritists, to play
the harlot after them, I will also set
My face against that person and will
cut him off from among his people.
7 'You shall consecrate yourselves therefore and [a]be holy, for I
am the LORD your God.
8 'And you shall keep My statutes
and practice them; I am the LORD
who sanctifies you.
9 '[a]If *there is* anyone who curses
his father or his mother, he shall
surely be put to death; he has cursed
his father or his mother, his bloodguiltiness is upon him.
10 '[a]If *there is* a man who commits
adultery with another man's wife,
one who commits adultery with his
friend's wife, the adulterer and the
adulteress shall surely be put to
death.
11 '[a]If *there is* a man who lies with
his father's wife, he has uncovered
his father's nakedness; both of them
shall surely be put to death, their
bloodguiltiness is upon them.
12 '[a]If *there is* a man who lies with
his daughter-in-law, both of them
shall surely be put to death; they
have committed [1]incest, their
bloodguiltiness is upon them.
13 '[a]If *there is* a man who lies with
a male as those who lie with a
woman, both of them have committed a detestable act; they shall
surely be put to death. Their bloodguiltiness is upon them.
14 '[a]If *there is* a man who [1]marries
a woman and her mother, it is immorality; both he and they shall be
burned with fire, that there may be
no immorality in your midst.
15 '[a]If *there is* a man who lies with
an animal, he shall surely be put to
death; you shall also kill the animal.
16 'If *there is* a woman who approaches any animal to [1]mate with
it, you shall kill the woman and the
animal; they shall surely be put to
death. Their bloodguiltiness is upon
them.
17 '[a]If *there is* a man who takes his
sister, his father's daughter or his
mother's daughter, so that he sees
her nakedness and she sees his nakedness, it is a disgrace; and they

26 [a]Lev. 17:10 [b]Deut. 18:10
27 [a]Lev. 21:5
28 [1]Lit., *flesh* [2]Lit., *soul*
29 [1]Or, *degrade* [a]Lev. 21:9; Deut. 22:21; 23:17, 18
30 [a]Lev. 19:3 [b]Lev. 26:2
31 [1]Or, *ghosts or spirits* [a]Lev. 20:6, 27; Deut. 18:11
32 [1]Lit., *face of the aged* [a]Lam. 5:12
33 [a]Ex. 22:21
34 [a]Lev. 19:18
35 [a]Deut. 25:13-16
36 [1]Approx. one bushel [2]Approx. one gallon
2 [1]Lit., *seed* [a]Lev. 18:21 [b]Lev. 20:27; 24:14-23; Num. 15:35, 36; Deut. 21:21
3 [1]Lit., *seed* [a]Lev. 15:31 [b]Lev. 18:21
4 [1]Lit., *hiding they hide their eyes from* [2]Lit., *seed*
6 [1]Or, *ghosts and spirits* [a]Lev. 19:31
7 [a]1 Pet. 1:16
9 [a]Ex. 21:17; Deut. 27:16
10 [a]Ex. 20:14; Lev. 18:20; Deut. 5:18
11 [a]Lev. 18:7, 8
12 [1]Lit., *confusion;* i.e., a violation of divine order [a]Lev. 18:15
13 [a]Lev. 18:22
14 [1]Lit., *takes* [a]Deut. 27:23
15 [a]Lev. 18:23
16 [1]Lit., *lie*
17 [a]Lev. 18:9

shall be cut off in the sight of the
sons of their people. He has uncovered his sister's nakedness; he bears
his guilt.
18 '[a]If *there is* a man who lies with
a [1]menstruous woman and uncovers her nakedness, he has laid bare
her flow, and she has [2]exposed the
flow of her blood; thus both of them
shall be cut off from among their
people.
19 '[a]You shall also not uncover the
nakedness of your mother's sister or
of your father's sister, for such a one
has made naked his [1]blood relative;
they shall bear their guilt.
20 '[a]If *there is* a man who lies with
his uncle's wife he has uncovered
his uncle's nakedness; they shall
bear their sin. They shall die childless.
21 '[a]If *there is* a man who takes his
brother's wife, it is [1]abhorrent; he
has uncovered his brother's nakedness. They shall be childless.
22 'You are therefore to keep all
My statutes and all My ordinances
and do them, so that the land to
which I am bringing you to [1]live will
not [a]spew you out.
23 'Moreover, you shall not [1]follow
[a]the customs of the nation which I
shall drive out before you, for they
did all these things, and [b]therefore I
have abhorred them.
24 'Hence I have said to you, "[a]You
are to possess their land, and I Myself will give it to you to possess it,
a land flowing with milk and honey." I am the LORD your God, who
has [b]separated you from the peoples.
25 '[a]You are therefore to make a
distinction between the clean animal and the unclean, and between
the unclean bird and the clean; and
you shall not make [1]yourselves detestable by animal or by bird or by
anything [2]that creeps on the
ground, which I have separated for
you as unclean.
26 'Thus you are to be holy to Me,
for I the LORD am holy; and I [a]have
set you apart from the peoples to be
Mine.
27 'Now a man or a woman [a]who is
a medium or a [1]spiritist shall surely
be put to death. They shall be stoned
with stones, their bloodguiltiness is
upon them.' "

CHAPTER 21

Regulations Concerning Priests

THEN the LORD said to Moses,
"Speak to the priests, the sons of
Aaron, and say to them, '[a]No one
shall defile himself for a *dead* person among his people,
2 [a]except for his relatives who
are nearest to him, his mother and
his father and his son and his daughter and his brother,
3 also for his virgin sister, who is
near to him [1]because she has had no
husband; for her he may defile himself.
4 'He shall not defile himself as a
[1]relative by marriage among his
people, and so profane himself.
5 '[a]They shall not make any baldness on their heads, [b]nor shave off
the edges of their beards, [c]nor make
any cuts in their flesh.
6 'They shall be holy to their God
and [a]not profane the name of their
God, for they present the offerings
by fire [1]to the LORD, [b]the bread of
their God; so they shall be holy.
7 '[a]They shall not take a woman
who is profaned by harlotry, nor
shall they take a woman divorced
from her husband; for he is holy to
his God.
8 'You shall consecrate him,
therefore, for he offers [a]the bread of
your God; he shall be holy to you;
for I the LORD, who sanctifies you,
am holy.
9 '[a]Also the daughter of any
priest, if she profanes herself by
harlotry, she profanes her father;
she shall be burned with fire.
10 'And the priest who is the highest among his brothers, on whose
head the anointing oil has been
poured, and [1]who has been consecrated to wear the garments, [a]shall
not [2]uncover his head, nor tear his
clothes;
11 [a]nor shall he approach any
dead person, nor defile himself *even*
for his father or his mother;
12 [a]nor shall he go out of the sanctuary, nor profane the sanctuary of
his God; for [b]the consecration of the
anointing oil of his God is on him: I
am the LORD.
13 'And he shall take a wife in her
virginity.
14 '[a]A widow, or a divorced
woman, or one who is profaned by
harlotry, these he may not take; but
rather he is to [1]marry a virgin of his
own people;
15 that he may not profane his
[1]offspring among his people: for I
am the LORD who sanctifies him.' "
16 Then the LORD spoke to Moses,
saying,
17 "Speak to Aaron, saying, 'No
man of your [1]offspring throughout
their generations who has a defect

18 [1]Lit., *sick* [2]Or, *uncovered* [a]Lev. 15:24; 18:19
19 [1]Lit., *flesh* [a]Lev. 18:12, 13
20 [a]Lev. 18:14
21 [1]Or, *an impure deed* [a]Lev. 18:16
22 [1]Lit., *dwell in it* [a]Lev. 18:28
23 [1]Lit., *walk in the statutes* [a]Lev. 18:3 [b]Lev. 18:25
24 [a]Ex. 13:5; 33:3 [b]Ex. 33:16; Lev. 20:26
25 [1]Lit., *your souls* [2]Lit., *with which the ground creeps* [a]Lev. 10:10; 11:1-47; Deut. 14:3-21
26 [a]Lev. 20:24
27 [1]Lit., *spiritist among them* [a]Lev. 19:31
1 [a]Lev. 19:28; Ezek. 44:25
2 [a]Lev. 21:11
3 [1]Or, *whom no man has had*
4 [1]Lit., *husband among*
5 [a]Deut. 14:1; Ezek. 44:20 [b]Lev. 19:27 [c]Deut. 14:1
6 [1]Lit., *of* [a]Lev. 18:21 [b]Lev. 3:11
7 [a]Lev. 21:13, 14
8 [a]Lev. 21:6
9 [a]Lev. 19:29
10 [1]Lit., *whose hand has been filled* [2]Lit., *unbind* [a]Lev. 10:6, 7
11 [a]Lev. 19:28
12 [a]Lev. 10:7 [b]Ex. 29:6, 7
14 [1]Lit., *take as wife* [a]Lev. 21:7; Ezek. 44:22
15 [1]Lit., *seed*
17 [1]Lit., *seed*

shall approach to offer the [a]bread of
his God.
18 '[a]For no one who has a defect
shall approach: a blind man, or a
lame man, or he who has a [1a]dis-
figured *face*, or any deformed *limb*,
19 or a man who has a broken foot
or broken hand,
20 or a hunchback or a dwarf, or
one who has a [1]defect in his eye or
eczema or scabs or [a]crushed testicles.
21 'No man among the [1]descen-
dants of Aaron the priest, who has a
defect, is to come near to offer the
LORD's offerings by fire; *since* he has
a defect, he shall not come near to
offer [a]the bread of his God.
22 'He may eat [a]the bread of his
God, *both* of the most holy and of
the holy,
23 only he shall not go in to the veil
or come near the altar because he
has a defect, that he may not profane My sanctuaries. For I am the
LORD who sanctifies them.' "
24 So Moses spoke to Aaron and
to his sons and to all the sons of Israel.

CHAPTER 22

Sundry Rules for Priests

THEN the LORD spoke to Moses,
saying,
2"Tell Aaron and his sons to be
careful with the holy *gifts* of the
sons of Israel, which they dedicate
to Me, so as not to profane My holy
name; I am the LORD.
3"Say to them, '[a]If any man
among all your [1]descendants
throughout your generations approaches the holy *gifts* which the
sons of Israel dedicate to the LORD,
while he has an uncleanness, that
person shall be cut off from before
Me. I am the LORD.
4 '[a]No man, of the [1]descendants
of Aaron, who is a leper or who has
a discharge, may eat of the holy *gifts*
until he is clean. [b]And if one touches
anything made unclean by a corpse
or if [c]a man has a seminal emission,
5 or [a]if a man touches any teeming things, by which he is made unclean, or any man by whom he is
made unclean, whatever his uncleanness;
6 a [1]person who touches any
such shall be unclean until evening,
and shall not eat of the holy *gifts*,
unless he has bathed his [2]body in
water.
7 'But when the sun sets, he shall
be clean, and afterward he shall eat
of the holy *gifts*, for it is his [1]food.
8 'He shall not eat [a]*an animal*
which dies or is torn *by beasts*, becoming unclean by it; I am the LORD.
9 'They shall therefore keep [a]My
charge, so that [b]they may not bear
sin because of it, and die thereby because they profane it; I am the LORD
who sanctifies them.
10 '[a]No [1]layman, however, is to eat
the holy *gift*; a sojourner with the
priest or a hired man shall not eat of
the holy *gift*.
11 '[a]But if a priest buys a [1]slave as
his property with his money, [2]that
one may eat of it, and those who are
born in his house may eat of his
[3]food.
12 'And if a priest's daughter is
married to a [1]layman, she shall not
eat of the [2]offering of the *gifts*.
13 'But if a priest's daughter becomes a widow or divorced, and has
no child and returns to her father's
house as in her youth, she shall eat
of her father's [1]food; [a]but no [2]lay-
man shall eat of it.
14 '[a]But if a man eats a holy *gift*
unintentionally, then he shall add to
it a fifth of it and shall give the holy
gift to the priest.
15 'And they shall not profane the
holy *gifts* of the sons of Israel which
they offer to the LORD,
16 and *so* cause them [a]to bear
[1]punishment for guilt by eating their
holy *gifts*; for I am the LORD who
sanctifies them.' "

Flawless Animals for Sacrifice

17 Then the LORD spoke to Moses,
saying,
18"Speak to Aaron and to his sons
and to all the sons of Israel, and say
to them, 'When any man of the
house of Israel or of the aliens in
Israel, who presents his offering,
whether it is any of their [1]votive or
any of their freewill offerings, which
they present to the LORD for a burnt
offering,
19 [a]for you to be accepted, *it must
be* a male without defect from the
cattle, the sheep, or the goats.
20 'Whatever has a defect, you
shall not offer, for it will not be accepted for you.
21 'And when a man offers a sacrifice of peace offerings to the LORD to
[1]fulfill a special vow, or for a freewill offering, of the herd or of the
flock, it must be perfect to be accepted; there shall be no defect in it.
22 'Those *that are* blind or frac-
tured or maimed or having a running sore or eczema or scabs, you
shall not offer to the LORD, nor make

17 [a]Lev. 21:6
18 [1]Lit., *slit* [a]Lev. 22:19-25
20 [1]Lit., *obscurity* [a]Deut. 23:1; Is. 56:3-5
21 [1]Lit., *seed* [a]Lev. 21:6
22 [a]1 Cor. 9:13
3 [1]Lit., *seed* [a]Lev. 7:20, 21; Num. 19:13
4 [1]Lit., *seed* [a]Lev. 14:1-32 [b]Lev. 11:24-28, 39, 40 [c]Lev. 15:16, 17
5 [a]Lev. 11:24-28
6 [1]Lit., *soul* [2]Lit., *flesh*
7 [1]Lit., *bread*
8 [a]Lev. 7:24; 11:39, 40; 17:15
9 [a]Lev. 18:30 [b]Lev. 22:16
10 [1]Lit., *stranger* [a]Ex. 29:33; Lev. 22:13
11 [1]Lit., *soul* [2]Lit., *he may* [3]Lit., *bread* [a]Gen. 17:13; Ex. 12:44
12 [1]Lit., *stranger* [2]Lit., *heave offering*
13 [1]Lit., *bread* [2]Lit., *stranger* [a]Lev. 22:10
14 [a]Lev. 5:15, 16
16 [1]Or, *iniquity requiring a guilt offering* [a]Lev. 22:9; 10:17
18 [1]Lit., *vows*
19 [a]Lev. 21:18-21; Deut. 15:21
21 [1]Or, *make a special votive offering*

of them an offering by fire on the altar to the LORD.

23 'In respect to an ox or a lamb which has an [1]overgrown or stunted *member*, you may present it for a freewill offering, but for a vow it shall not be accepted.

24 'Also [a]anything *with its testicles* bruised or crushed or torn or cut, you shall not offer to the Lord, or [1]sacrifice in your land,

25 nor shall you accept any such from the hand of a foreigner for offering [a]as the [1]food of your God; for their corruption is in them, they have a defect, they shall not be accepted for you.' "

26 Then the LORD spoke to Moses, saying,

27"When an ox or a sheep or a goat is born, it shall [1]remain [a]seven days [2]with its mother, and from the eighth day on it shall be accepted as a sacrifice of an offering by fire to the LORD.

28"[a]But, *whether* it is an ox or a sheep, you shall not kill *both* it and its young in one day.

29"And when you sacrifice [a]a sacrifice of thanksgiving to the LORD, you shall sacrifice it so that you may be accepted.

30"It shall be eaten on the same day, you shall leave none of it until morning: I am the LORD.

31"So you shall keep My commandments, and do them: I am the LORD.

32"And you shall not profane My holy name, but I will be sanctified among the sons of Israel: I am the LORD who sanctifies you,

33 [a]who brought you out from the land of Egypt, to be your God: I am the LORD."

CHAPTER 23

Laws of Religious Festivals

THE LORD spoke again to Moses, saying,

2"Speak to the sons of Israel, and say to them, '[a]The LORD's appointed times which you shall [b]proclaim as holy convocations—My appointed times are these:

3 '[a]For six days work may be done; but on the seventh day there is a sabbath of complete rest, a holy convocation. You shall not do any work; it is a sabbath to the LORD in all your dwellings.

4 'These are the [a]appointed times of the LORD, holy convocations which you shall proclaim at the times appointed for them.

5 '[a]In the first month, on the fourteenth day of the month [1]at twilight is the LORD's Passover.

6 'Then on the fifteenth day of the same month there is the Feast of Unleavened Bread to the LORD; for seven days you shall eat unleavened bread.

7 'On the first day you shall have a holy convocation; you shall [a]not do any laborious work.

8 'But for seven days you shall present an offering by fire to the LORD. On the seventh day is a holy convocation; you shall not do any laborious work.' "

9 Then the LORD spoke to Moses, saying,

10"Speak to the sons of Israel, and say to them, 'When you enter the land which I am going to give to you and [a]reap its harvest, then you shall bring in the sheaf of the first fruits of your harvest to the priest.

11 'And he shall wave the sheaf before the LORD for you to be accepted; on the day after the sabbath the priest shall wave it.

12 'Now on the day when you wave the sheaf, you shall offer a male lamb one year old without defect for a burnt offering to the LORD.

13 'Its [a]grain offering shall then be two-tenths *of an ephah* of fine flour mixed with oil, an offering by fire to the LORD *for* a soothing aroma, with its libation, a fourth of a [1]hin of wine.

14 'Until this same day, until you have brought in the offering of your God, [a]you shall eat neither bread nor roasted grain nor new growth. It is to be a perpetual statute throughout your generations in all your dwelling places.

15 '[a]You shall also count for yourselves from the day after the sabbath, from the day when you brought in the sheaf of the wave offering; there shall be seven complete sabbaths.

16 'You shall count fifty days to the day after the seventh sabbath; then you shall present a [a]new grain offering to the LORD.

17 'You shall bring in from your dwelling places two *loaves* of bread for a wave offering, made of two-tenths *of an* [1]*ephah*; they shall be of a fine flour, baked [a]with leaven as first fruits to the LORD.

18 'Along with the bread, you shall present seven one year old male lambs without defect, and a bull of the herd, and two rams; they are to be a burnt offering to the LORD, with

23 [1]Or, *deformed*

24 [1]Lit., *do* [a]Lev. 21:20

25 [1]Lit., *bread* [a]Lev. 21:22

27 [1]Lit., *be* [2]Lit., *under* [a]Ex. 22:30

28 [a]Deut. 22:6, 7

29 [a]Lev. 7:12

33 [a]Lev. 11:45

2 [a]Lev. 23:4, 37, 44; Num. 29:39 [b]Lev. 23:21

3 [a]Lev. 19:3; Ex. 31:13-17; 35:2, 3

4 [a]Lev. 23:2

5 [1]Lit., *between the two evenings* [a]Ex. 12:18, 19; Num. 28:16-25

7 [a]Lev. 23:8, 21, 25, 35, 36

10 [a]Ex. 23:19; 34:26

13 [1]Approx. one gallon [a]Lev. 6:20

14 [a]Ex. 34:26; Num. 15:20, 21

15 [a]Num. 28:26-31; Deut. 16:9-12

16 [a]Num. 28:26

17 [1]I.e., Approx. one bushel [a]Lev. 2:12; 7:13

their grain offering and their libations, an offering by fire of a soothing aroma to the LORD.

19 'You shall also offer [a]one male goat for a sin offering and two male lambs one year old for a sacrifice of peace offerings.

20 'The priest shall then wave them with the bread of the first fruits for a wave offering with two lambs before the LORD; they are to be holy to the LORD for the priest.

21 'On this same day you shall [a]make a proclamation as well; you are to have a holy convocation. You shall do no laborious [b]work. It is to be a perpetual statute in all your dwelling places throughout your generations.

22 '[a]When you reap the harvest of your land, moreover, you shall not reap to the very corners of your field, nor gather the gleaning of your harvest; you are to leave them for the needy and the alien. I am the LORD your God.' "

23 Again the LORD spoke to Moses, saying,

24 "Speak to the sons of Israel, saying, '[a]In the seventh month on the first of the month, you shall have a [1]rest, a [b]reminder by blowing *of trumpets*, a holy convocation.

25 'You shall [a]not do any laborious work, but you shall present an offering by fire to the LORD.' "

The Day of Atonement

26 And the LORD spoke to Moses, saying,

27 "On exactly [a]the tenth day of this seventh month is [b]the day of atonement; it shall be a holy convocation for you, and you shall humble your souls and present an offering by fire to the LORD.

28 "Neither shall you do any work on this same day, for it is a [a]day of atonement, [b]to make atonement on your behalf before the LORD your God.

29 "If there is any [1]person who will not humble himself on this same day, he shall be cut off from his people.

30 "As for any person who does any work on this same day, that person I will destroy from among his people.

31 "You shall do no work at all. It is to be a perpetual statute throughout your generations in all your dwelling places.

32 "It is to be a sabbath of complete rest to you, and you shall humble your souls; on the ninth of the month at evening, from evening until evening you shall keep your sabbath."

33 Again the LORD spoke to Moses, saying,

34 "Speak to the sons of Israel, saying, 'On [a]the fifteenth of this seventh month is the Feast [b]of Booths for seven days to the LORD.

35 'On the first day is a holy convocation; you shall do [a]no laborious work of any kind.

36 '[a]For seven days you shall present an offering by fire to the LORD. On [b]the eighth day you shall have a holy convocation and present an offering by fire to the LORD; it is an assembly. You shall do no laborious work.

37 'These are [a]the appointed times of the LORD which you shall proclaim as holy convocations, to present offerings by fire to the LORD—burnt offerings and grain offerings, sacrifices and libations, [b]*each* day's matter on its own day—

38 besides *those of* the sabbaths of the LORD, and besides your gifts, and besides all your [1]votive and freewill offerings, which you give to the LORD.

39 'On exactly the fifteenth day of the seventh month, when you have gathered in the crops of the land, you shall celebrate the feast of the LORD for seven days, with a [1]rest on the first day and a [1]rest on the eighth day.

40 'Now on the first day you shall take for yourselves the [1]foliage of beautiful trees, palm branches and boughs of leafy trees and willows of the brook; and you shall rejoice before the LORD your God for seven days.

41 'You shall thus celebrate it *as* a feast to the LORD for seven days in the year. It *shall be* a perpetual statute throughout your generations; you shall celebrate it in the seventh month.

42 'You shall [1]live [a]in booths for seven days; all the native-born in Israel shall [1]live in booths,

43 so that your generations may know that I had the sons of Israel live in booths when I brought them out from the land of Egypt. I am the LORD your God.' "

44 So Moses declared to the sons of Israel [a]the appointed times of the LORD.

19 [a]Num. 28:30

21 [a]Lev. 23:2, 4 [b]Lev. 23:7

22 [a]Lev. 19:9

24 [1]Lit., *sabbath rest* [a]Num. 29:1 [b]Num. 10:9, 10

25 [a]Lev. 23:21

27 [a]Lev. 16:29; 25:9; Num. 29:7 [b]Lev. 23:28

28 [a]Lev. 23:27 [b]Lev. 16:34

29 [1]Lit., *soul*

34 [a]Num. 29:12 [b]Lev. 23:42, 43; Deut. 16:13, 16

35 [a]Lev. 23:25

36 [a]Num. 29:12-34 [b]Num. 29:35-38

37 [a]Lev. 23:2 [b]Num. 28:1-29, 38

38 [1]Lit., *vows, and besides all your*

39 [1]Lit., *sabbath rest*

40 [1]Lit., *products, fruit*

42 [1]Lit., *dwell* [a]Lev. 23:34

44 [a]Lev. 23:37

Chapter 24

The Lamb and the Bread of the Sanctuary

THEN the LORD spoke to Moses, saying,

2 "Command the sons of Israel that they bring to you [a]clear oil from beaten olives for the [1]light, to make a lamp [2]burn continually.

3 "Outside the veil of testimony in the tent of meeting, Aaron shall keep it in order from evening to morning before the LORD continually; *it shall be* a perpetual statute throughout your generations.

4 "He shall keep the lamps in order on the [a]pure *gold* lampstand before the LORD continually.

5 "[a]Then you shall take fine flour and bake twelve cakes with it; two-tenths *of an ephah* shall be *in* each cake.

6 "And you shall set them *in* two rows, six *to* a row, on the [a]pure *gold* table before the LORD.

7 "And you shall put pure frankincense on each row, that it may be [a]a memorial portion for the bread, *even* an offering by fire to the LORD.

8 "[a]Every sabbath day he shall set it in order before the LORD [b]continually; it is an everlasting covenant [1]for the sons of Israel.

9 "[a]And it shall be for Aaron and his sons, and they shall eat it in a holy place; for it is most holy to him from the LORD's offerings by fire, *his* portion forever."

10 Now the son of an Israelite woman, whose father was an Egyptian, went out among the sons of Israel; and the Israelite woman's son and a man of Israel struggled with each other in the camp.

11 And the son of the Israelite woman blasphemed the [a]Name and cursed. So they brought him to Moses. (Now his mother's name was Shelomith, the daughter of Dibri, of the tribe of Dan.)

12 And they put him in [1]custody [2]so that [a]the command of the LORD might be made clear to them.

13 Then the LORD spoke to Moses, saying,

14 "Bring the one who has cursed outside the camp, and let all who heard him [a]lay their hands on his head; then [b]let all the congregation stone him.

15 "And you shall speak to the sons of Israel, saying, '[a]If anyone curses his God, then he shall bear his sin.

16 'Moreover, the one who blasphemes the name of the LORD shall surely be put to death; all the congregation shall certainly stone him. The alien as well as the native, when he blasphemes the Name, shall be put to death.

"An Eye for an Eye"

17 '[a]And if a man [1]takes the life of any human being, he shall surely be put to death.

18 'And [a]the one who [1]takes the life of an animal shall make it good, life for life.

19 'And if a man [1]injures his neighbor, just as he has done, so it shall be done to him:

20 [a]fracture for fracture, [b]eye for eye, tooth for tooth; just as he has [1]injured a man, so it shall be [2]inflicted on him.

21 '[a]Thus the one who [1]kills an animal shall make it good, but the one who [1]kills a man shall be put to death.

22 'There shall be [a]one [1]standard for you; it shall be for the stranger as well as the native, for I am the LORD your God.' "

23 Then Moses spoke to the sons of Israel, and they brought the one who had cursed outside the camp and stoned him with stones. Thus the sons of Israel did, just as the LORD had commanded Moses.

Chapter 25

The Sabbatic Year and Year of Jubilee

THE LORD then spoke to Moses [1]at Mount Sinai, saying,

2 "Speak to the sons of Israel, and say to them, 'When you come into the land which I shall give you, then the land shall have a sabbath to the LORD.

3 '[a]Six years you shall sow your field, and six years you shall prune your vineyard and gather in its crop,

4 but during [a]the seventh year the land shall have a sabbath rest, a sabbath to the LORD; you shall not sow your field nor prune your vineyard.

5 'Your harvest's [1]aftergrowth you shall not reap, and your grapes of untrimmed vines you shall not gather; the land shall have a sabbatical year.

6 '[a]And all of you shall have the sabbath *products* of the land for food; yourself, and your male and female slaves, and your hired man and your foreign resident, th who live as aliens with you.

7 'Even your cattle and

2 [1]Or, *luminary* [2]Lit., *ascend* [a]Ex. 27:20, 21
4 [a]Ex. 25:31; 31:8; 37:17
5 [a]Ex. 25:30; 39:36; 40:23
6 [a]Ex. 25:24
7 [a]Lev. 2:2, 9, 16
8 [1]Lit., *from* [a]Matt. 12:5 [b]Ex. 25:30; Num. 4:7
9 [a]Matt. 12:4; Mark 2:26; Luke 6:4
11 [a]Ex. 3:15; 22:28
12 [1]Or, *prison* [2]Lit., *to declare distinctly to them according to the mouth of the LORD* [a]Ex. 18:15
14 [a]Deut. 13:9; 17:7 [b]Lev. 20:2, 27; Deut. 21:21
15 [a]Ex. 22:28
17 [1]Lit., *smites* [a]Ex. 21:12; Num. 35:30, 31; Deut. 27:24
18 [1]Lit., *smites* [a]Lev. 24:21
19 [1]Lit., *gives a blemish*
20 [1]Lit., *given a blemish* [2]Lit., *given* [a]Ex. 21:23; Deut. 19:21 [b]Matt. 5:38
21 [1]Lit., *smites* [a]Lev. 24:17
22 [1]Lit., *judgment* [a]Ex. 12:49; Num. 9:14; 15:15, 16, 29
1 [1]Or, *on*
3 [a]Ex. 23:10, 11
4 [a]Lev. 25:20
5 [1]Lit., *growth from spilled kernels*
6 [a]Lev. 25:20, 21

mals that are in your land shall have all its crops to eat.

8 'You are also to count off seven sabbaths of years for yourself, seven times seven years, so that you have the time of the seven sabbaths of years, *namely*, forty-nine years.

9 'You shall then sound a ram's horn abroad on [a]the tenth day of the seventh month; on the day of atonement you shall sound a horn all through your land.

10 'You shall thus consecrate the fiftieth year and proclaim [1]a release through the land to all its inhabitants. It shall be a jubilee for you, [2]and [a]each of you shall return to his own property, [2]and each of you shall return to his family.

11 'You shall have the fiftieth year as a jubilee; you shall not sow, nor reap its aftergrowth, nor gather in *from* its untrimmed vines.

12 'For it is a jubilee; it shall be holy to you. You shall eat its crops out of the field.

13 '[a]On this year of jubilee each of you shall return to his own property.

14 'If you make a sale, moreover, to your friend, or buy from your friend's hand, [a]you shall not wrong one another.

15 'Corresponding to the number of years after the jubilee, you shall buy from your [1]friend; he is to sell to you according to the number of years of crops.

16 '[a]In proportion to the [1]extent of the years you shall increase its price, and in proportion to the fewness of the years, you shall diminish its price; for *it is* a number of crops he is selling to you.

17 'So [a]you shall not wrong one another, but you shall [1]fear your God; for I am the LORD your God.

18 'You shall thus observe My statutes, and keep My judgments, so as to carry them out, that [a]you may live securely on the land.

19 'Then the land will yield its produce, so that you can eat your fill and live securely on it.

20 'But if you say, "[a]What are we going to eat on the seventh year [1]if we do not sow or gather in our crops?"

21 then I will so order My blessing for you in the sixth year that it will bring forth the crop for three years.

22 'When you are sowing the eighth year, you can still eat [a]old things from the crop, eating *the old* until the ninth year when its crop comes in.

The Law of Redemption

23 'The land, moreover, shall not be sold permanently, for [a]the land is Mine; for [b]you are *but* aliens and sojourners with Me.

24 'Thus for every [1]piece of your property, you are to provide for the redemption of the land.

25 '[a]If a [1]fellow-countryman of yours becomes so poor he has to sell part of his property, then his nearest kinsman is to come and buy back what his [1]relative has sold.

26 'Or in case a man has no kinsman, but so [1]recovers his means as to find sufficient for its redemption,

27 [a]then he shall calculate the years since its sale and refund the balance to the man to whom he sold it, and so return to his property.

28 'But if [1]he has not found sufficient means to get it back for himself, then what he has sold shall remain in the hands of its purchaser until the year of jubilee; but at the jubilee it shall [2]revert, that [a]he may return to his property.

29 'Likewise, if a man sells a dwelling house in a walled city, then his redemption right remains valid until a full year from its sale; his right of redemption lasts a full year.

30 'But if it is not bought back for him within the space of a full year, then the house that is in the walled city passes permanently to its purchaser throughout his generations; it does not [1]revert in the jubilee.

31 'The houses of the villages, however, which have no surrounding wall shall be considered [1]as open fields; they have redemption rights and [2]revert in the jubilee.

32 'As for [a]cities of the Levites, the Levites have a permanent right of redemption for the houses of the cities which are their possession.

33 'What, therefore, [1]belongs to the Levites may be redeemed and a house sale [2]in the city of this possession [3]reverts in the jubilee, for the houses of the Levites are their possession among the sons of Israel.

34 '[a]But pasture fields of their cities shall not be sold, for that is their perpetual possession.

Of Poor Countrymen

35 '[a]Now in case a [1]countryman of yours becomes poor and his [2]means with regard to you falter, then you are to sustain him, like a stranger or a sojourner, that he may live with you.

36 '[a]Do not take [1]usurious interest from him, but revere your God, that

9 [a]Lev. 23:27

10 [1]Or, *liberty* [2]Or, *when* [a]Lev. 25:13, 28, 54

13 [a]Lev. 25:10

14 [a]Lev. 25:17

15 [1]Lit., *friend's hands*

16 [1]Lit., *multiplied* [a]Lev. 25:27, 51, 52

17 [1]Or, *reverence* [a]Lev. 25:14

18 [a]Lev. 26:4, 5

20 [1]Or, *behold* [a]Lev. 25:4

22 [a]Lev. 26:10

23 [a]Ex. 19:5 [b]Gen. 23:4; 1 Chr. 29:15; Ps. 39:12; Heb. 11:13; 1 Pet. 2:11

24 [1]Lit., *land*

25 [1]Lit., *brother* [a]Ruth 2:20; 4:4, 6

26 [1]Lit., *his hand reaches*

27 [a]Lev. 25:16

28 [1]Lit., *his hand has not found sufficient to* [2]Lit., *go out* [a]Lev. 25:10, 13

30 [1]Lit., *go out*

31 [1]Lit., *according to* [2]Lit., *go out*

32 [a]Num. 35:1-8

33 [1]Lit., *is from* [2]Lit., *and* [3]Lit., *goes out*

34 [a]Num. 35:2-5

35 [1]Lit., *brother* [2]Lit., *hand* [a]Deut. 15:7-11; 24:14, 15

36 [1]Lit., *interest and usury* [a]Ex. 22:25; Deut. 23:19, 20

your [2]countryman may live with you.

37 'You shall not give him your silver at interest, nor your food for gain.

38 '[a]I am the LORD your God, who brought you out of the land of Egypt to give you the land of Canaan *and* [b]to be your God.

39 '[a]And if a [1]countryman of yours becomes so poor with regard to you that he sells himself to you, you shall not subject him to a slave's service.

40 'He shall be with you as a hired man, as [a]if he were a sojourner with you, until the year of jubilee.

41 'He shall then go out from you, he and his sons with him, and shall go back to his family, that he may return to the property of his forefathers.

42 'For they are My servants whom I brought out from the land of Egypt; they are not to be sold *in* a slave sale.

43 '[a]You shall not rule over him with severity, but are to revere your God.

44 'As for your male and female slaves whom you may have—you may acquire male and female slaves from the pagan nations that are around you.

45 'Then, too, *it is* out of the sons of the sojourners who live as aliens among you that you may gain acquisition, and out of their families who are with you, whom they will have [1]produced in your land; they also may become your possession.

46 'You may even bequeath them to your sons after you, to receive as a possession; you can use them as permanent slaves. [a]But in respect to your [1]countrymen, the sons of Israel, you shall not rule with severity over one another.

Of Redeeming a Poor Man

47 'Now if the [1]means of a stranger or of a sojourner with you becomes sufficient, and a [2]countryman of yours becomes so poor with regard to him as to sell himself to a stranger who is sojourning with you, or to the descendants of a stranger's family,

48 then he shall have redemption right after he has been sold. One of his brothers may redeem him,

49 or his uncle, or his uncle's son, may redeem him, or one of his blood relatives from his family may redeem him; or [1a]if he prospers, he may redeem himself.

50 'He then with his purchaser shall calculate from the year when he sold himself to him up to the year of jubilee; and the price of his sale shall correspond to the number of years. *It is* like the days of a hired man *that* he shall be with him.

51 'If there are still many years, [a]he shall refund part of his purchase price in proportion to them for his own redemption;

52 and if few years remain until the year of jubilee, he shall so calculate with him. In proportion to his years he is to refund *the amount for* his redemption.

53 'Like a man hired year by year he shall be with him; [a]he shall not rule over him with severity in your sight.

54 'Even if he is not redeemed by [1]these *means*, [a]he shall still go out in the year of jubilee, he and his sons with him.

55 'For the sons of Israel are My servants; they are My servants whom I brought out from the land of Egypt. I am the LORD your God.

CHAPTER 26

Blessings of Obedience

'YOU shall not make for yourselves [1a]idols, nor shall you set up for yourselves [b]an image or [c]a *sacred* pillar, nor shall you place a [d]figured stone in your land to bow down [2]to it; for I am the LORD your God.

2 '[a]You shall keep My sabbaths and reverence My sanctuary; I am the LORD.

3 '[a]If you walk in My statutes and keep My commandments so as to carry them out,

4 then I shall give you rains in their season, so that the land will yield its produce and the trees of the field will bear their fruit.

5 '[a]Indeed, your threshing will last for you until grape gathering, and grape gathering will last until sowing time. You will thus eat your [1]food to the full and [b]live securely in your land.

6 '[a]I shall also grant peace in the land, so that [b]you may lie down with no one making *you* tremble. [c]I shall also eliminate harmful beasts from the land, and [d]no sword will pass through your land.

7 'But you will chase your enemies, and they will fall before you by the sword;

8 [a]five of you will chase a hundred, and a hundred of you will chase ten thousand, and your en-

36 [2]Lit., *brother*

38 [a]Lev. 11:45 [b]Gen. 17:7

39 [1]Lit., *brother* [a]Ex. 21:2-6; Deut. 15:12-18

40 [a]Ex. 21:2

43 [a]Ex. 1:13, 14; Lev. 25:46, 53; Ezek. 34:4

45 [1]Lit., *begotten*

46 [1]Lit., *brothers* [a]Lev. 25:43

47 [1]Lit., *hand . . . reaches* [2]Lit., *brother*

49 [1]Lit., *his hand has reached* [a]Lev. 25:26, 27

51 [a]Lev. 25:16

53 [a]Lev. 25:43

54 [1]Or, *these years* [a]Lev. 25:10, 13, 28

1 [1]Or, *graven images* [2]Lit., *over* [a]Lev. 19:4 [b]Ex. 20:4 [c]Ex. 23:24 [d]Num. 33:52

2 [a]Lev. 19:30

3 [a]Deut. 7:12-26; 28:1-14

5 [1]Lit., *bread* [a]Amos 9:13 [b]Lev. 25:18, 19

6 [a]Ps. 29:11; 85:8; 147:14 [b]Zeph. 3:13 [c]Lev. 26:22 [d]Lev. 26:25

8 [a]Deut. 32:30

emies will fall before you by the
sword.
9 'So I will turn toward you and
[a]make you fruitful and multiply you,
and I will [b]confirm My covenant
with you.
10 '[a]And you will eat the old supply
and clear out the old because of the
new.
11 '[a]Moreover, I will make My
[1]dwelling among you, and My soul
will not [2]reject you.
12 '[a]I will also walk among you and
be your God, and you shall be My
people.
13 '[a]I am the LORD your God, who
brought you out of the land of Egypt
so that *you* should not be their
slaves, and [b]I broke the bars of your
yoke and made you walk erect.

Penalties of Disobedience

14 '[a]But if you do not obey Me and
do not carry out all these commandments,
15 if, instead, you reject My statutes, and if [a]your soul abhors My
ordinances so as not to carry out all
My commandments, *and* so [b]break
My covenant,
16 I, in turn, will do this to you: I
will appoint over you a [a]sudden terror, consumption and fever that
shall waste away the eyes and cause
the [b]soul to pine away; also, [c]you
shall sow your seed uselessly, for
your enemies shall eat it up.
17 'And I will set My face against
you so that you shall be struck down
before your enemies; and [a]those
who hate you shall rule over you,
and [b]you shall flee when no one is
pursuing you.
18 'If also after these things, you do
not obey Me, then I will punish you
[a]seven times more for your sins.
19 'And I will also [a]break down
your pride of power; I will also make
your sky like iron and your earth
like bronze.
20 'And [a]your strength shall be
spent uselessly, for your land shall
not yield its produce and the trees of
the land shall not yield their fruit.
21 'If then, you [1a]act with hostility
against Me and are unwilling to
obey Me, I will increase the plague
on you [b]seven times according to
your sins.
22 'And I will let loose among you
the beasts of the field, which shall
bereave you of your children and
destroy your cattle and reduce your
number so that your roads lie deserted.
23 '[a]And if by these things you are
not turned to Me, but act with hos-

9 [a]Gen. 17:6; 22:17; 48:4 [b]Gen. 17:7
10 [a]Lev. 25:22
11 [1]Or, *tabernacle* [2]Lit., *abhor* [a]Ex. 25:8; 29:45, 46
12 [a]Gen. 3:8; Deut. 23:14; 2 Cor. 6:16
13 [a]Ex. 20:2 [b]Ezek. 34:27
14 [a]Deut. 28:15-68; Josh. 23:15
15 [a]Lev. 26:11 [b]Lev. 26:9
16 [a]Ps. 78:33 [b]Ezek. 24:23; 33:10 [c]Judg. 6:3-6
17 [a]Ps. 106:41 [b]Lev. 26:36, 37; Ps. 53:5; Prov. 28:1
18 [a]Lev. 26:21, 24, 28
19 [a]Is. 28:1-3; Ezek. 24:21
20 [a]Is. 17:10, 11; Jer. 12:13
21 [1]Lit., *walk*, and so throughout the chap. [a]Lev. 26:23, 27, 40 [b]Lev. 26:18
23 [a]Lev. 26:21
24 [a]Lev. 26:28, 41 [b]Lev. 26:21
25 [a]Jer. 50:28; 51:11 [b]Num. 14:12
26 [1]Lit., *by weight* [a]Is. 3:1; Ezek. 4:16, 17; 5:16
28 [a]Lev. 26:24, 41
30 [1]Lit., *corpses* [a]2 Kin. 23:20; Ezek. 6:3, 6; Amos 7:9 [b]2 Chr. 34:4, 7; Is. 27:9
31 [1]Lit., *give desolation to* [a]Jer. 44:2, 6, 22 [b]Is. 63:18; Lam. 2:7 [c]Amos 5:21
32 [a]Jer. 12:11; 33:10 [b]Jer. 18:16; 19:8
33 [a]Ps. 44:11; 106:27; Jer. 31:10; Ezek. 12:15
34 [1]Lit., *satisfy* [a]Lev. 26:43; 2 Chr. 36:21
36 [1]Lit., *the flight of the sword* [a]Is. 30:17; Lam. 1:3, 6; 4:19
37 [1]Lit., *you will stand* [a]Jer. 6:21; Nah. 3:3

tility against Me,
24 then I will [a]act with hostility
against you; and I, even I, will strike
you [b]seven times for your sins.
25 'I will also bring upon you a
sword which will execute [a]ven-
geance for the covenant; and when
you gather together into your cities,
I will send [b]pestilence among you,
so that you shall be delivered into
enemy hands.
26 '[a]When I break your staff of
bread, ten women will bake your
bread in one oven, and they will
bring back your bread [1]in rationed
amounts, so that you will eat and
not be satisfied.
27 'Yet if in spite of this, you do not
obey Me, but act with hostility
against Me,
28 then [a]I will act with wrathful
hostility against you; and I, even I,
will punish you seven times for your
sins.
29 'Further, you shall eat the flesh
of your sons and the flesh of your
daughters you shall eat.
30 'I then [a]will destroy your high
places, and cut down your [b]incense
altars, and heap your [1]remains on
the [1]remains of your idols; for My
soul shall abhor you.
31 'I will [1]lay [a]waste your cities as
well, and will make your [b]sanctu-
aries desolate; and I will not [c]smell
your soothing aromas.
32 'And I will make [a]the land desolate [b]so that your enemies who settle in it shall be appalled over it.
33 'You, however, I [a]will scatter
among the nations and will draw out
a sword after you, as your land becomes desolate and your cities become waste.
34 '[a]Then the land will [1]enjoy its
sabbaths all the days of the desolation, while you are in your enemies'
land; then the land will rest and [1]en-
joy its sabbaths.
35 'All the days of *its* desolation it
will observe the rest which it did not
observe on your sabbaths, while you
were living on it.
36 'As for those of you who may be
left, I will also bring [a]weakness into
their hearts in the lands of their enemies. And the sound of a driven
leaf will chase them and even when
no one is pursuing, they will flee [1]as
though from the sword, and they
will fall.
37 '[a]They will therefore stumble
over each other as if *running* from
the sword, although no one is pursuing; and you will have *no strength*
[1]to stand up before your enemies.

38 'But [a]you will perish among the nations, and your enemies' land will consume you.

39 '[a]So those of you who may be left will rot away because of their iniquity in the lands of your enemies; and also because of the iniquities of their forefathers they will rot away with them.

40 '[a]If they confess their iniquity and the iniquity of their forefathers, in their unfaithfulness which they committed against Me, and also in their acting with hostility against Me—

41 I also was acting with hostility against them, to bring them into the land of their enemies—[a]or if their uncircumcised heart becomes humbled so that [b]they then make amends for their iniquity,

42 then I will remember [a]My covenant with Jacob, and I will remember also My covenant [b]with Isaac, and [c]My covenant with Abraham as well, and I will remember the land.

43 '[a]For the land shall be abandoned by them, and shall make up for its sabbaths while it is made desolate without them. They, meanwhile, shall be making amends for their iniquity, [1]because they rejected My ordinances and their [b]soul abhorred My statutes.

44 'Yet in spite of this, when they are in the land of their enemies, I will not reject them, nor will I [a]so [b]abhor them as to destroy them, [c]breaking My covenant with them; for I am the LORD their God.

45 'But I will remember for them the [a]covenant with their ancestors, whom I brought out of the land of Egypt in the sight of the nations, that [b]I might be their God. I am the LORD.' "

46 [a]These are the statutes and ordinances and laws which the LORD established between Himself and the sons of Israel [1]through Moses at Mount Sinai.

CHAPTER 27

Rules Concerning Valuations

AGAIN, the LORD spoke to Moses, saying,

2 "Speak to the sons of Israel, and say to them, 'When a man makes a difficult vow, he *shall be valued* according to your valuation of persons belonging to the LORD.

3 'If your valuation is of the male from twenty years even to sixty years old, then your valuation shall be fifty shekels of silver, after [a]the shekel of the sanctuary.

4 'Or if it is a female, then your valuation shall be thirty shekels.

5 'And if it be from five years even to twenty years old then your valuation for the male shall be twenty shekels, and for the female ten shekels.

6 'But if *they are* from a month even up to five years old, then your valuation shall be [a]five shekels of silver for the male, and for the female your valuation shall be three shekels of silver.

7 'And if *they are* from sixty years old and upward, if it is a male, then your valuation shall be fifteen shekels, and for the female ten shekels.

8 'But if he is poorer than your valuation, then he shall be placed before the priest, and the priest shall value him; [a]according to [1]the means of the one who vowed, the priest shall value him.

9 'Now if it is an animal of the kind which [1]men can present as an offering to the LORD, any such that one gives to the LORD shall be holy.

10 '[a]He shall not replace it or exchange it, a good for a bad, or a bad for a good; or if he does exchange animal for animal, then both it and its substitute shall become holy.

11 'If, however, it is any unclean animal of the kind which [1]men do not present as an offering to the LORD, then he shall place the animal before the priest.

12 'And the priest shall value it [1]as either good or bad; as you, the priest, value it, so it shall be.

13 'But if he should ever *wish to* redeem it, then he shall add one-fifth of it to your valuation.

14 'Now if a man consecrates his house as holy to the LORD, then the priest shall value it [1]as either good or bad; as the priest values it, so it shall stand.

15 'Yet if the one who consecrates it should *wish to* redeem his house, then he shall add one-fifth of your valuation price to it, so that it may be his.

16 'Again, if a man consecrates to the LORD part of the fields of his own property, then your valuation shall be [1]proportionate to the seed needed for it: a homer of barley seed at fifty shekels of silver.

17 'If he consecrates his field as of the year of jubilee, according to your valuation it shall stand.

18 'If he consecrates his field after the jubilee, however, then the priest shall calculate the price for [1]him [2]proportionate to the years that are left until the year of jubilee; and it

38 [a]Deut. 4:26
39 [a]Ezek. 4:17; 33:10
40 [a]Jer. 3:12-15; 14:20; Hos. 5:15
41 [a]Jer. 4:4; 9:25, 26; Ezek. 44:9 [b]Ezek. 20:43
42 [a]Gen. 28:13-15; 35:11, 12 [b]Gen. 26:2-5 [c]Gen. 22:15-18
43 [1]Lit., *because and by the cause* [a]Lev. 26:34 [b]Lev. 26:11
44 [a]Deut. 4:31; Jer. 30:11 [b]Lev. 26:11 [c]Jer. 33:20-26
45 [a]Ex. 6:6-8 [b]Gen. 17:7
46 [1]Lit., *by the hand of* [a]Lev. 7:38; 27:34; Deut. 4:5; 29:1
3 [a]Ex. 30:13; Lev. 27:25
6 [a]Num. 18:16
8 [1]Lit., *what the hand reaches* [a]Lev. 5:11; 14:21-24
9 [1]Lit., *they*
10 [a]Lev. 27:33
11 [1]Lit., *they*
12 [1]Lit., *between*
14 [1]Lit., *between good*
16 [1]Lit., *according to its seed*
18 [1]Or, *it* [2]Lit., *according to the years*

shall be deducted from your valuation.

19 'And if the one who consecrates it should ever wish to redeem the field, then he shall add one-fifth of your valuation price to it, so that it may pass to him.

20 'Yet if he will not redeem the field, [1]but has sold the field to another man, it may no longer be redeemed;

21 and when it [1]reverts in the jubilee, the field shall be holy to the LORD, like a field [2]set apart; it shall be for the priest as his [3]property.

22 'Or if he consecrates to the LORD a field which he has bought, which is not a part of the field of his own [1]property,

23 then the priest shall calculate for [1]him the amount of your valuation up to the year of jubilee; and he shall on that day give your valuation as holy to the LORD.

24 'In the year of jubilee the field shall return to the one from whom he bought it, to whom the possession of the land belongs.

25 'Every valuation of yours, moreover, shall be after [a]the shekel of the sanctuary. The shekel shall be twenty gerahs.

26 '[a]However, a first-born among animals, which as a first-born belongs to the LORD, no man may consecrate it; whether ox or sheep, it is the LORD's.

27 'But if *it is* among the unclean animals, then he shall [1]redeem it according to your valuation, and add to it one-fifth of it; and if it is not redeemed, then it shall be sold according to your valuation.

28 'Nevertheless, any [a]proscribed thing which a man [1]sets apart to the LORD out of all that he has, of man or animal or of the fields of his own property, shall not be sold or redeemed. Every proscribed thing is most holy to the LORD.

29 'No proscribed *person* who may have been [1]set apart among men shall be ransomed; he shall surely be put to death.

30 'Thus all the tithe of the land, of the seed of the land or of the fruit of the tree, is the LORD's; it is holy to the LORD.

31 'If, therefore, a man wishes to redeem part of his tithe, he shall add to it one-fifth of it.

32 'And for every tenth part of herd or flock, whatever passes under the rod, the tenth one shall be holy to the LORD.

33 '[a]He is not to be concerned whether *it is* good or bad, nor shall he exchange it; or if he does exchange it, then both it and its substitute shall become holy. It shall not be redeemed.' "

34 [a]These are the commandments which the LORD commanded Moses for the sons of Israel at Mount Sinai.

20 [1]Or, *if he*
21 [1]Lit., *goes out* [2]Or, *devoted, banned* [3]Lit., *possession*
22 [1]Lit., *possession*
23 [1]Or, *it*
25 [a]Lev. 27:3
26 [a]Ex. 13:2
27 [1]Or, *ransom*
28 [1]Or, *puts under bans* [a]Num. 18:14; Josh. 6:17-19
29 [1]Or, *put under the ban*
33 [a]Lev. 27:10
34 [a]Lev. 26:46; Deut. 4:5

NUMBERS

The Census of Israel's Warriors

THEN the LORD spoke to Moses in the wilderness of Sinai, in the tent of meeting, on [a]the first of the second month, in the second year after they had come out of the land of Egypt, saying,

2 "[a]Take a [1]census of all the congregation of the sons of Israel, by their families, by their fathers' households, according to the number of names, every male, head by head

3 from [a]twenty years old and upward, whoever *is able to* go out to war in Israel, you and Aaron shall [1]number them by their armies.

4 "With you, moreover, there shall be a man of each tribe, [a]each one head of his father's household.

5 "These then are the names of the men who shall stand with you: of Reuben, Elizur the son of Shedeur;

6 of Simeon, Shelumiel the son of Zurishaddai;

7 of Judah, Nahshon the son of Amminadab;

8 of Issachar, Nethanel the son of Zuar;

9 of Zebulun, Eliab the son of Helon;

10 of the sons of Joseph: of Ephraim, Elishama the son of Ammihud; of Manasseh, Gamaliel the son of Pedahzur;

11 of Benjamin, Abidan the son of Gideoni;

12 of Dan, Ahiezer the son of Ammishaddai;

13 of Asher, Pagiel the son of Ochran;

14 of Gad, Eliasaph the son of Deuel;

15 of Naphtali, Ahira the son of Enan.

16 "These are they who were [a]called of the congregation, the

1 [a]Ex. 40:2, 17
2 [1]Lit., *sum* [a]Ex. 12:37; 38:25, 26; Num. 26:2
3 [1]Lit., *muster,* and so throughout the chap. [a]Ex. 30:14; 38:26
4 [a]Ex. 18:21, 24; Num. 1:16; Deut. 1:15
16 [a]Num. 16:2; 26:9

leaders of their fathers' tribes; they
were the heads of [1]divisions of Israel."
17 So Moses and Aaron took these
men who had been designated by
name,
18 and they assembled all the congregation together on the [a]first of
the second month. Then they registered by ancestry in their families,
by their fathers' households, according to the number of names,
from twenty years old and upward,
head by head,
19 just as the LORD had commanded Moses. So he numbered
them in the wilderness of Sinai.
20 [a]Now the sons of Reuben, Israel's first-born, their genealogical
registration by their families, by
their fathers' households, according
to the number of names, head by
head, every male from twenty years
old and upward, whoever *was able
to* go out to war,
21 their numbered men, of the
tribe of Reuben, *were* 46,500.
22 [a]Of the sons of Simeon, their
genealogical registration by their
families, by their fathers' households, their numbered men, according to the number of names, head by
head, every male from twenty years
old and upward, whoever *was able
to* go out to war,
23 their numbered men, of the
tribe of Simeon, *were* 59,300.
24 [a]Of the sons of Gad, their genealogical registration by their families, by their fathers' households,
according to the number of names,
from twenty years old and upward,
whoever *was able to* go out to war,
25 their numbered men, of the
tribe of Gad, *were* 45,650.
26 [a]Of the sons of Judah, their genealogical registration by their families, by their fathers' households,
according to the number of names,
from twenty years old and upward,
whoever *was able to* go out to war,
27 their numbered men, of the
tribe of Judah, *were* 74,600.
28 [a]Of the sons of Issachar, their
genealogical registration by their
families, by their fathers' households, according to the number of
names, from twenty years old and
upward, whoever *was able to* go out
to war,
29 their numbered men, of the
tribe of Issachar, *were* 54,400.
30 [a]Of the sons of Zebulun, their
genealogical registration by their
families, by their fathers' households, according to the number of
names, from twenty years old and

16 [1]Lit., *thousands,* or, *clans*
18 [a]Num. 1:1
20 [a]Num. 26:5-11
22 [a]Num. 26:12-14
24 [a]Num. 26:15-18
26 [a]Num. 26:19-22
28 [a]Num. 26:23-25
30 [a]Num. 26:26, 27
32 [a]Num. 26:35-37
34 [a]Num. 26:28-34
36 [a]Num. 26:38-41
38 [a]Num. 26:42, 43
40 [a]Num. 26:44-47
42 [a]Num. 26:48-50

upward, whoever *was able to* go out
to war,
31 their numbered men, of the
tribe of Zebulun, *were* 57,400.
32 [a]Of the sons of Joseph, *namely,*
of the sons of Ephraim, their genealogical registration by their families,
by their fathers' households, according to the number of names,
from twenty years old and upward,
whoever *was able to* go out to war,
33 their numbered men, of the
tribe of Ephraim, *were* 40,500.
34 [a]Of the sons of Manasseh, their
genealogical registration by their
families, by their fathers' households, according to the number of
names, from twenty years old and
upward, whoever *was able to* go out
to war,
35 their numbered men, of the
tribe of Manasseh, *were* 32,200.
36 [a]Of the sons of Benjamin, their
genealogical registration by their
families, by their fathers' households, according to the number of
names, from twenty years old and
upward, whoever *was able to* go out
to war,
37 their numbered men, of the
tribe of Benjamin, *were* 35,400.
38 [a]Of the sons of Dan, their genealogical registration by their families, by their fathers' households,
according to the number of names,
from twenty years old and upward,
whoever *was able to* go out to war,
39 their numbered men, of the
tribe of Dan, *were* 62,700.
40 [a]Of the sons of Asher, their genealogical registration by their families, by their fathers' households,
according to the number of names,
from twenty years old and upward,
whoever *was able to* go out to war,
41 their numbered men, of the
tribe of Asher, *were* 41,500.
42 [a]Of the sons of Naphtali, their
genealogical registration by their
families, by their fathers' households, according to the number of
names, from twenty years old and
upward, whoever *was able to* go out
to war,
43 their numbered men, of the
tribe of Naphtali, *were* 53,400.
44 These are the ones who were
numbered, whom Moses and Aaron
numbered, with the leaders of Israel, twelve men, each of whom was
of his father's household.
45 So all the numbered men of the
sons of Israel by their fathers'
households, from twenty years old
and upward, whoever *was able to*
go out to war in Israel,

46 even all the numbered men
were [a]603,550.

Levites Exempted

47 [a]The Levites, however, were
not numbered among them by their
fathers' tribe.
48 For the LORD had spoken to
Moses, saying,
49"Only the tribe of Levi you shall
not number, nor shall you take their
[1]census among the sons of Israel.
50"But you shall [a]appoint the Levites over the [1]tabernacle of the testimony, and over all its furnishings
and over all that belongs to it. They
shall carry the tabernacle and all its
furnishings, and they shall take care
of it; they shall also camp around
the [1]tabernacle.
51"[a]So when the tabernacle is to
set out, the Levites shall take it
down; and when the tabernacle encamps, the Levites shall set it up.
But [b]the [1]layman who comes near
shall be put to death.
52"[a]And the sons of Israel shall
camp, each man by his own camp,
and each man by his own standard,
according to their armies.
53"[a]But the Levites shall camp
around the tabernacle of the testimony, that there may be no wrath
on the congregation of the sons of
Israel. So the Levites shall keep
charge of the tabernacle of the testimony."
54 Thus the sons of Israel did; according to all which the LORD had
commanded Moses, so they did.

CHAPTER 2

Arrangement of the Camps

NOW the LORD spoke to Moses
and to Aaron, saying,
2"[a]The sons of Israel shall camp,
each by his own standard, with the
[1]banners of their fathers' households; they shall camp around the
tent of meeting [2]at a distance.
3"Now those who camp on the
east side toward the sunrise *shall be*
of the standard of the camp of Judah, by their armies, and the leader
of the sons of Judah: [a]Nahshon the
son of Amminadab,
4 and his army, even their [1]num-
bered men, 74,600.
5"And those who camp next to
him *shall be* the tribe of Issachar,
and the leader of the sons of Issachar: [a]Nethanel the son of Zuar,
6 and his army, even their numbered men, 54,400.
7"Then *comes* the tribe of Zebulun, and the leader of the sons of
Zebulun: [a]Eliab the son of Helon,
8 and his army, even his numbered men, 57,400.
9"The total of the numbered men
of the camp of Judah: 186,400, by
their armies. They shall set out first.
10"On the south side *shall be* the
standard of the camp of Reuben by
their armies, and the leader of the
sons of Reuben: [a]Elizur the son of
Shedeur,
11 and his army, even their numbered men, 46,500.
12"And those who camp next to
him *shall be* the tribe of Simeon, and
the leader of the sons of Simeon:
[a]Shelumiel the son of Zurishaddai,
13 and his army, even their numbered men, 59,300.
14"Then *comes* the tribe of Gad,
and the leader of the sons of Gad:
Eliasaph the son of [1a]Deuel,
15 and his army, even their numbered men, 45,650.
16"The total of the numbered men
of the camp of Reuben: 151,450 by
their armies. And they shall set out
second.
17"[a]Then the tent of meeting shall
set out *with* the camp of the Levites
in the midst of the camps; just as
they camp, so they shall set out, every man in his place, by their standards.
18"On the west side *shall be* the
standard of the camp of Ephraim by
their armies, and the leader of the
sons of Ephraim *shall be* [a]Elishama
the son of Ammihud,
19 and his army, even their numbered men, 40,500.
20"And next to him *shall be* the
tribe of Manasseh, and the leader of
the sons of Manasseh: [a]Gamaliel the
son of Pedahzur,
21 and his army, even their numbered men, 32,200.
22"Then *comes* the tribe of Benjamin, and the leader of the sons of
Benjamin: [a]Abidan the son of Gideoni,
23 and his army, even their numbered men, 35,400.
24"The total of the numbered men
of the camp of Ephraim: 108,100, by
their armies. And they shall set out
third.
25"On the north side *shall be* the
standard of the camp of Dan by
their armies, and the leader of the
sons of Dan: [a]Ahiezer the son of
Ammishaddai,
26 and his army, even their numbered men, 62,700.
27"And those who camp next to
him *shall be* the tribe of Asher, and
the leader of the sons of Asher: [a]Pa-
giel the son of Ochran,

46 [a]Ex. 12:37; 38:26; Num. 2:32; 26:51
47 [a]Num. 2:33; 3:14-39; 4:49; 26:57-64
49 [1]Lit., *sum*
50 [1]Lit., *dwelling place,* and so throughout the chap. [a]Num. 3:25-37
51 [1]Lit., *stranger* [a]Num. 4:1-33 [b]Num. 3:10, 38; 4:15, 19, 20
52 [a]Num. 2:2
53 [a]Num. 3:23, 29, 35
2 [1]Lit., *signs* [2]Or, *facing it* [a]Num. 1:52
3 [a]Num. 1:7
4 [1]Lit., *mustered,* and so throughout the chap.
5 [a]Num. 1:8
7 [a]Num. 1:9
10 [a]Num. 1:5
12 [a]Num. 1:6
14 [1]Many mss. read, *Reuel* [a]Num. 1:14
17 [a]Num. 1:53
18 [a]Num. 1:10
20 [a]Num. 1:10
22 [a]Num. 1:11
25 [a]Num. 1:12
27 [a]Num. 1:13

28 and his army, even their numbered men, 41,500.

29 "Then *comes* the tribe of Naphtali, and the leader of the sons of Naphtali: [a]Ahira the son of Enan,

30 and his army, even their numbered men, 53,400.

31 "The total of the numbered men of the camp of Dan, *was* 157,600. They shall set out last by their standards."

32 These are the numbered men of the sons of Israel by their fathers' households; the total of the numbered men of the camps by their armies, [a]603,550.

33 [a]The Levites, however, were not numbered among the sons of Israel, just as the LORD had commanded Moses.

34 Thus the sons of Israel did; according to all that the LORD commanded Moses, so they camped by their standards, and so they set out, every one by his family, according to his father's household.

CHAPTER 3

Levites to Be Priesthood

[a]NOW these are *the records of* the generations of Aaron and Moses at the time when the LORD spoke with Moses on Mount Sinai.

2 [a]These then are the names of the sons of Aaron: Nadab the first-born, and Abihu, Eleazar and Ithamar.

3 These are the names of the sons of Aaron, the anointed priests, whom he [1]ordained to serve as priests.

4 [a]But Nadab and Abihu died before the LORD when they offered strange fire before the LORD in the wilderness of Sinai; and they had no children. So Eleazar and Ithamar served as priests [1]in the lifetime of their father Aaron.

5 Then the LORD spoke to Moses, saying,

6 "[a]Bring the tribe of Levi near and set them before Aaron the priest, that they may serve him.

7 "And they shall perform the duties for [1]him and for the whole congregation before the tent of meeting, to do the service of the tabernacle.

8 "They shall also keep all the furnishings of the tent of meeting, along with the duties of the sons of Israel, to do the service of the tabernacle.

9 "You shall thus [a]give the Levites to Aaron and to his sons; they are wholly given to him from among the sons of Israel.

10 "So you shall appoint Aaron and his sons that [a]they may keep their priesthood, but [b]the [1]layman who comes near shall be put to death."

11 Again the LORD spoke to Moses, saying,

12 "Now, behold, I [a]have taken the Levites from among the sons of Israel instead of every [b]first-born, the first issue of the womb among the sons of Israel. So the Levites shall be Mine.

13 "For all the first-born are Mine; on the day that I struck down all the first-born in the land of Egypt, I sanctified to Myself all the first-born in Israel, from man to beast. They shall be Mine; I am the LORD."

14 Then the LORD spoke to Moses in the wilderness of Sinai, saying,

15 "[1a]Number the sons of Levi by their fathers' households, by their families; every male from a month old and upward you shall number."

16 So Moses numbered them according to the [1]word of the LORD, just as he had been commanded.

17 [a]These then are the sons of Levi by their names: Gershon and Kohath and Merari.

18 And these are the names of the sons of Gershon by their families: Libni and Shimei;

19 and the sons of Kohath by their families: Amram and Izhar, Hebron and Uzziel;

20 and the sons of Merari by their families: Mahli and Mushi. These are the families of the Levites according to their fathers' households.

21 Of Gershon *was* the family of the Libnites and the family of the Shimeites; these *were* the families of the Gershonites.

22 Their numbered men, in the numbering of every male from a month old and upward, *even* their numbered men *were* 7,500.

23 The families of the Gershonites were to camp behind the [1]tabernacle westward,

24 and the leader of the fathers' households of the Gershonites *was* Eliasaph the son of Lael.

Duties of the Priests

25 Now the duties of the sons of Gershon in the tent of meeting *involved* the tabernacle and the tent, its covering, and the screen for the doorway of the tent of meeting,

26 and the hangings of the court, and the screen for the doorway of the court, which is around the taber-

29 [a]Num. 1:15
32 [a]Num. 1:46
33 [a]Num. 1:47
1 [a]Ex. 6:20-27
2 [a]Num. 26:60
3 [1]Lit., *filled their hand*
4 [1]Lit., *before the face* [a]Lev. 10:1, 2; Num. 26:61
6 [a]Num. 8:6-22; 18:1-7; Deut. 10:8
7 [1]Lit., *him and the duties of the whole congregation*
9 [a]Num. 18:6
10 [1]Lit., *stranger* [a]Ex. 29:9 [b]Num. 1:51
12 [a]Num. 3:45; 8:14 [b]Ex. 13:2
15 [1]Lit., *muster*, and so throughout the chap. [a]Num. 1:47
16 [1]Lit., *mouth*
17 [a]Ex. 6:16-22
23 [1]Lit., *dwelling place*, and so throughout the chap.

nacle and the altar, and its cords, according to all the service [1]concerning them.

27 And of Kohath *was* the family of the Amramites and the family of the Izharites and the family of the Hebronites and the family of the Uzzielites; these were the families of the Kohathites.

28 In the numbering of every male from a month old and upward, *there were* 8,600, performing the duties of the sanctuary.

29 The families of the sons of Kohath were to camp on the southward side of the tabernacle,

30 and the leader of the fathers' households of the Kohathite families was Elizaphan the son of Uzziel.

31 Now their duties *involved* the ark, the table, the lampstand, the altars, and the utensils of the sanctuary with which they minister, and the screen, and all the service [1]concerning them;

32 and Eleazar the son of Aaron the priest *was* the chief of the leaders of Levi, *and had* the oversight of those who perform the duties of the sanctuary.

33 Of Merari *was* the family of the Mahlites and the family of the Mushites; these *were* the families of Merari.

34 Their numbered men in the numbering of every male from a month old and upward, *were* 6,200.

35 And the leader of the fathers' households of the families of Merari *was* Zuriel the son of Abihail. They *were* to camp on the northward side of the tabernacle.

36 Now the appointed duties of the sons of Merari *involved* the frames of the tabernacle, its bars, its pillars, its sockets, all its equipment, and the service concerning them,

37 and the pillars around the court with their sockets and their pegs and their cords.

38 Now those who were to camp before the tabernacle eastward, before the tent of meeting toward the sunrise, are Moses and Aaron and his sons, performing the duties of the sanctuary for the obligation of the sons of Israel; but [a]the [1]layman coming near was to be put to death.

39 All the numbered men of the Levites, whom Moses and Aaron numbered at the [1]command of the LORD by their families, every male from a month old and upward, *were* [a]22,000.

First-born Redeemed

40 Then the LORD said to Moses, "Number every first-born male of the sons of Israel from a month old and upward, and [1]make a list of their names.

41 "And you shall take the Levites for Me, I am the LORD, instead of all the first-born among the sons of Israel, and the cattle of the Levites instead of all the first-born among the cattle of the sons of Israel."

42 So Moses numbered all the first-born among the sons of Israel, just as the LORD had commanded him;

43 and all the first-born males by the number of names from a month old and upward, for their numbered men were [a]22,273.

44 Then the LORD spoke to Moses, saying,

45 "[a]Take the Levites instead of all the first-born among the sons of Israel and the cattle of the Levites. And the Levites shall be Mine; I am the LORD.

46 "[a]And for the ransom of the 273 of the first-born of the sons of Israel who are in excess beyond the Levites,

47 you shall take five shekels apiece, per head; you shall take *them* in [a]terms of the shekel of the sanctuary (the shekel is twenty [1]gerahs),

48 and give the money, the ransom of those who are in excess among them, to Aaron and to his sons."

49 So Moses took the ransom money from those who were in excess, beyond those ransomed by the Levites;

50 from the first-born of the sons of Israel he took the money in terms of the shekel of the sanctuary, 1,365.

51 Then Moses gave the ransom money to Aaron and to his sons, at the [1]command of the LORD, just as the LORD had commanded Moses.

CHAPTER 4

Duties of the Kohathites

THEN the LORD spoke to Moses and to Aaron, saying,

2 "Take [1]a census of the [2]descendants of Kohath from among the sons of Levi, by their families, by their fathers' households,

3 from [a]thirty years and upward, even to fifty years old, all who enter the service to do the work in the tent of meeting.

4 "This is the work of the [1]descendants of Kohath in the tent of meet-

26 [1]Lit., *of it*

31 [1]Lit., *of it*

38 [1]Lit., *stranger* [a]Num. 1:51

39 [1]Lit., *word* [a]Num. 3:43; 4:48; 26:62

40 [1]Lit., *take the number*

43 [a]Num. 3:39

45 [a]Num. 3:12

46 [a]Ex. 13:13, 15; Num. 18:15, 16

47 [1]I.e., A gerah equals approx. one-fortieth ounce [a]Ex. 30:13

51 [1]Lit., *mouth*

2 [1]Lit., *the sum* [2]Lit., *sons*

3 [a]Num. 4:23, 30, 35; 8:24

4 [1]Lit., *sons*

ing, *concerning* the most holy things.

5"When the camp sets out, Aaron and his sons shall go in and they shall take down [a]the veil of the screen and cover the ark of the testimony with it;

6 and they shall lay a [a]covering of porpoise skin on it, and shall spread over *it* a cloth of pure [1]blue, and shall insert its poles.

7"Over the table of the bread of the Presence they shall also spread a cloth of [1]blue and put on it the dishes and the spoons and the sacrificial bowls and the jars for the libation, and [a]the continual bread shall be on it.

8"And they shall spread over them a cloth of scarlet *material,* and cover the same with a covering of porpoise skin, and they shall insert its poles.

9"Then they shall take a [1]blue cloth and cover the lampstand for the light, along with its lamps and its snuffers, and its [2]trays and all its oil vessels, by which they serve it;

10 and they shall put it and all its utensils in a covering of porpoise skin, and shall put it on the carrying bars.

11"And over the golden altar they shall spread a [1]blue cloth and cover it with a covering of porpoise skin, and shall insert its poles;

12 and they shall take all the utensils of service, with which they serve in the sanctuary, and put them in a [1]blue cloth and cover them with a covering of porpoise skin, and put them on the carrying bars.

13"Then they shall take away the [1]ashes from the [a]altar, and spread a purple cloth over it.

14"They shall also put on it all its utensils by which they serve in connection with it: the firepans, the forks and shovels and the basins, all the utensils of the altar; and they shall spread a cover of porpoise skin over it and insert its poles.

15"And when Aaron and his sons have finished covering the holy *objects* and all the furnishings of the sanctuary, when the camp is to set out, after that the sons of Kohath shall come to carry *them,* so that they may not touch the holy *objects* [a]and die. These are the [1]things in the tent of meeting which the sons of Kohath are to carry.

16"And the responsibility of Eleazar the son of Aaron the priest is [a]the oil for the light and the [b]fragrant incense and [c]the continual grain offering and [d]the anointing oil—the responsibility of all the [1]tabernacle and of all that is in it, with the sanctuary and its furnishings."

17 Then the LORD spoke to Moses and to Aaron, saying,

18"Do not let the tribe of the families of the Kohathites be cut off from among the Levites.

19"But do this to them that they may live and [a]not die when they approach the most holy *objects:* Aaron and his sons shall go in and assign each of them to his work and to his load;

20 but they shall not go in to see the holy *objects* even for a moment, lest they die."

Duties of the Gershonites

21 Then the LORD spoke to Moses, saying,

22"Take [1]a census of the sons of Gershon [2]also, by their fathers' households, by their families;

23 from [a]thirty years and upward to fifty years old, you shall [1]number them; all who enter to perform the service to do the work in the tent of meeting.

24"This is the service of the families of the Gershonites, in serving and in carrying:

25 they shall carry the curtains of the tabernacle and the tent of meeting *with* its covering and [a]the covering of porpoise skin that is on top of it, and the screen for the doorway of the tent of meeting,

26 and the hangings of the court, and the screen for the doorway of the gate of the court which is around the tabernacle and the altar, and their cords and all the equipment for their service; and all that is to be done, [1]they shall perform.

27"All the service of the sons of the Gershonites, in all their loads and in all their work, shall be *performed* at the [1]command of Aaron and his sons; and you shall assign to them as a duty all their loads.

28"This is the service of the families of the sons of the Gershonites in the tent of meeting, and their duties *shall be* [1]under the direction of Ithamar the son of Aaron the priest.

Duties of the Merarites

29"*As for* the sons of Merari, you shall number them by their families, by their fathers' households;

30 from [a]thirty years and upward even to fifty years old, you shall number them, everyone who enters the service to do the work of the tent of meeting.

5 [a]Ex. 40:5

6 [1]Or, *violet* [a]Num. 4:25

7 [1]Or, *violet* [a]Ex. 25:30; Lev. 24:5-9

9 [1]Or, *violet* [2]Lit., *snuff dishes*

11 [1]Or, *violet*

12 [1]Or, *violet*

13 [1]Or, *fat ashes;* i.e., soaked with fat [a]Ex. 27:1-8

15 [1]Lit., *burden . . . of the sons* [a]Num. 1:51; 4:19, 20; 2 Sam. 6:6, 7

16 [1]Lit., *dwelling place,* and so throughout the chap. [a]Lev. 24:1-3 [b]Ex. 30:34-38 [c]Lev. 6:20 [d]Ex. 30:22-33

19 [a]Num. 4:15

22 [1]Lit., *the sum* [2]Lit., *also them*

23 [1]Lit., *muster,* and so throughout the chap. [a]Num. 4:3

25 [a]Ex. 26:14; Num. 4:6

26 [1]Lit., *so they shall serve*

27 [1]Lit., *mouth*

28 [1]Lit., *in the hand*

30 [a]Num. 4:3

31"Now this is the duty of their
loads, for all their service in the tent
of meeting: the boards of the tabernacle and its bars and its pillars and
its [1]sockets,
32 and the pillars around the court
and their [1]sockets and their pegs
and their cords, with all their equipment and with all their service; and
you shall assign *each man* by name
the items [2]he is to carry.
33"This is the service of the families of the sons of Merari, according
to all their service in the tent of
meeting, [1]under the direction of
Ithamar the son of Aaron the
priest."
34 So Moses and Aaron and the
leaders of the congregation numbered the sons of the Kohathites by
their families, and by their fathers'
households,
35 from thirty years and upward
even to fifty years old, everyone
who entered the service for work in
the tent of meeting.
36 And their numbered men by
their families were 2,750.
37 These are the numbered men of
the Kohathite families, everyone
who was serving in the tent of meeting, whom Moses and Aaron numbered according to the [1]command-
ment of the LORD [2]through Moses.
38 And the numbered men of the
sons of Gershon by their families,
and by their fathers' households,
39 from thirty years and upward
even to fifty years old, everyone
who entered the service for work in
the tent of meeting.
40 And their numbered men by
their families, by their fathers'
households, were 2,630.
41 These are the numbered men of
the families of the sons of Gershon,
everyone who was serving in the
tent of meeting, whom Moses and
Aaron numbered according to the
[1]commandment of the LORD.
42 And the numbered men of the
families of the sons of Merari by
their families, by their fathers'
households,
43 from thirty years and upward
even to fifty years old, everyone
who entered the service for work in
the tent of meeting.
44 And their numbered men by
their families were 3,200.
45 These are the numbered men of
the families of the sons of Merari,
whom Moses and Aaron numbered
according to the [1]commandment of
the LORD [2]through Moses.
46 All the numbered men of the
Levites, whom Moses and Aaron
and the leaders of Israel numbered,
by their families and by their fathers' households,
47 from thirty years and upward
even to fifty years old, everyone
who could enter to do the work of
service and the work of carrying in
the tent of meeting.
48 And their numbered men were
[a]8,580.
49 According to the [1]command-
ment of the LORD [2]through Moses,
they [a]were numbered, everyone by
his serving or carrying; thus these
were his numbered men, just as the
LORD had commanded Moses.

CHAPTER 5

On Defilement

[a]THEN the LORD spoke to Moses,
saying,
2"Command the sons of Israel
that they send away from the camp
every leper and everyone having a
discharge and everyone who is [a]un-
clean because of a *dead* person.
3"You shall send away both male
and female; you shall send them
outside the camp so that they will
not defile their camp where I dwell
[a]in their midst."
4 And the sons of Israel did so
and sent them outside the camp;
just as the LORD had spoken to
Moses, thus the sons of Israel did.
5 Then the LORD spoke to Moses,
saying,
6"Speak to the sons of Israel,
'[a]When a man or woman commits
any of the sins of mankind, acting
unfaithfully against the LORD, and
that person is guilty,
7 then [1]he shall [a]confess [2]his sins
which [3]he has committed, and he
shall make restitution in full for his
wrong, and add to it one-fifth of it,
and give *it* to him whom he has
wronged.
8 'But if the man has no [1]relative
to whom restitution may be made
for the wrong, the restitution which
is made for the wrong *must go* to the
LORD for the priest, besides the ram
of atonement, by which atonement
is made for him.
9 '[a]Also every [1]contribution pertaining to all the holy *gifts* of the
sons of Israel, which they offer to
the priest, shall be his.
10 'So every man's holy *gifts* shall
be his; whatever any man gives to
the priest, it becomes his.' "

The Adultery Test

11 Then the LORD spoke to Moses,
saying,

31 [1]Or, *bases*
32 [1]Or *bases* [2]Lit., *of the duty of their loads.*
33 [1]Lit., *in the hand*
37 [1]Lit., *mouth* [2]Lit., *by the hand of*
41 [1]Lit., *mouth*
45 [1]Lit., *mouth* [2]Lit., *by the hand of*
48 [a]Num. 3:39
49 [1]Lit., *mouth* [2]Lit., *by the hand of* [a]Num. 1:47
1 [a]Lev. 13:46; Num. 12:15
2 [a]Num. 19:11
3 [a]Lev. 26:12; Num. 35:34
6 [a]Lev. 5:14-6:7
7 [1]Lit., *they* [2]Lit., *their* [3]Lit., *they have* [a]Lev. 5:5
8 [1]Lit., *redeemer*
9 [1]Lit., *heave offering* [a]Lev. 7:32, 34; 10:14, 15

12 "Speak to the sons of Israel, and
say to them, 'If any man's wife [a]goes
astray and is unfaithful to him,
13 and a man has intercourse with
her and it is hidden from the eyes of
her husband and she is [1]undetected,
although she has defiled herself, and
there is no witness against her and
she has not been caught in the act,
14 [1]if a spirit of jealousy comes
over him and he is jealous of his
wife when she has defiled herself, or
if a spirit of jealousy comes over
him and he is jealous of his wife
when she has not defiled herself,
15 the man shall then bring his
wife to the priest, and shall bring *as*
[1]an offering for her one-tenth of an
[2]ephah of barley meal; he shall not
pour oil on it, nor put frankincense
on it, for it is a grain offering of jealousy, a grain offering of memorial,
[a]a reminder of iniquity.
16 'Then the priest shall bring her
near and have her stand before the
LORD,
17 and the priest shall take holy
water in an earthenware vessel; and
[1]he shall take some of the dust that
is on the floor of the tabernacle and
put *it* into the water.
18 'The priest shall then have the
woman stand before the LORD and
let *the hair of* the woman's head go
loose, and place the grain offering of
memorial [1]in her hands, which is the
grain offering of jealousy, and in the
hand of the priest is to be the water
of bitterness that brings a curse.
19 'And the priest shall have her
take an oath and shall say to the
woman, "If no man has lain with
you and if you have not [a]gone astray
into uncleanness, *being* under *the
authority of* your husband, be [1]im-
mune to this water of bitterness that
brings a curse;
20 if you, however, have [a]gone
astray, *being* under *the authority of*
your husband, and if you have defiled yourself and a man other than
your husband has had intercourse
with you,"
21 then the priest shall have the
woman swear with the oath of the
curse, and the priest shall say to the
woman, "The LORD make you a
curse and an oath among your people by the LORD's making your thigh
[1]waste away and your abdomen
swell;
22 and this water that brings a
curse shall go into your [1]stomach,
and make your abdomen swell and
your thigh [2]waste away." And the
woman shall say, "Amen. Amen."
23 'The priest shall then write
these curses on a scroll, and he shall
[1]wash them off into the water of bitterness.
24 'Then he shall make the woman
drink the water of bitterness that
brings a curse, so that the water
which brings a curse will go into her
[1]and *cause* bitterness.
25 'And the priest shall take the
grain offering of jealousy from the
woman's hand, and he shall wave
the grain offering before the LORD
and bring it to the altar;
26 and the priest shall take a handful of the grain offering as its memorial offering and offer *it* up in smoke
on the altar, and afterward he shall
make the woman drink the water.
27 'When he has made her drink
the water, then it shall come about,
if she has defiled herself and has
been unfaithful to her husband, that
the water which brings a curse shall
go into her [1]and *cause* bitterness,
and her abdomen will swell and her
thigh will [2]waste away, and the
woman will become [a]a curse among
her people.
28 'But if the woman has not defiled herself and is clean, she will
then be free and conceive [1]children.
29 'This is the law of jealousy:
when a wife, *being* under *the authority of* her husband, [a]goes astray
and defiles herself,
30 or when a spirit of jealousy
comes over a man and he is jealous
of his wife, he shall then make the
woman stand before the LORD, and
the priest shall apply all this law to
her.
31 'Moreover, the man shall be free
from [1]guilt, but that woman shall
bear her [1]guilt.' "

CHAPTER 6

Law of the Nazirites

AGAIN the LORD spoke to Moses,
saying,
2 "Speak to the sons of Israel, and
say to them, 'When a man or woman
makes a [1]special vow, the vow of [a]a
[2]Nazirite, to [3]dedicate himself to the
LORD,
3 he shall abstain from wine and
strong drink; he shall drink no vinegar, whether made from wine or
strong drink, neither shall he drink
any grape juice, nor eat fresh or
dried grapes.
4 'All the days of his [1]separation
he shall not eat anything that is produced by the grape vine, from *the*
seeds even to *the* skin.
5 'All the days of his vow of separation [a]no razor shall pass over his

12 [a]Num. 5:19, 20, 29
13 [1]Lit., *concealed*
14 [1]Lit., *and*
15 [1]Lit., *her* [2]I.e., approx. one bushel [a]Ezek. 29:16
17 [1]Lit., *the priest*
18 [1]Lit., *on her palms*
19 [1]Lit., *free from* [a]Num. 5:12
20 [a]Num. 5:12
21 [1]Lit., *fall*
22 [1]Or, *inward parts* [2]Lit., *fall*
23 [1]Lit., *wipe*
24 [1]Lit., *to*
27 [1]Lit., *to* [2]Lit., *fall* [a]Jer. 29:18; 42:18; 44:12
28 [1]Lit., *seed*
29 [a]Num. 5:12
31 [1]Or, *iniquity*
2 [1]Or, *difficult* [2]I.e., one separated [3]Or, *live as a Nazirite* [a]Judg. 13:5; 16:17; Amos 2:11, 12
4 [1]Or, *living as a Nazirite*, and so through v. 21
5 [a]1 Sam. 1:11

head. He shall be holy until the days
are fulfilled for which he separated
himself to the LORD; he shall let the
locks of hair on his head grow long.
6 '[a]All the days of his separation
to the LORD he shall not go near to a
dead person.
7 'He shall not make himself unclean for his father or for his
mother, for his brother or for his sister, when they die, because his separation to God is on his head.
8 'All the days of his separation he
is holy to the LORD.
9 'But if a man dies very suddenly
beside him and he defiles his dedicated head *of hair,* then [a]he shall
shave his head on the day when he
becomes clean; [b]he shall shave it on
the seventh day.
10 'Then on the eighth day he shall
bring two turtledoves or two young
pigeons to the priest, to the doorway
of the tent of meeting.
11 'And the priest shall offer [a]one
for a sin offering and *the* other for a
burnt offering, and make atonement
for him [1]concerning his sin because
of the *dead* person. And that same
day he shall consecrate his head,
12 and shall dedicate to the LORD
his days [1]as a [2]Nazirite, and shall
bring a male lamb a year old for a
guilt offering; but the former days
shall be void because his separation
was defiled.
13 'Now this is the law of the Nazirite when the days of his separation
are fulfilled, he shall bring [1]the offering to the doorway of the tent of
meeting.
14 'And he shall present his offering to the LORD: one male lamb a
year old without defect for a burnt
offering and one [a]ewe-lamb a year
old without defect for a sin offering
and one ram without defect for a
peace offering,
15 and a basket of unleavened
cakes of fine flour mixed with oil
and unleavened wafers spread with
oil, along with [a]their grain offering
and their libations.
16 'Then the priest shall present
them before the LORD and shall offer
his sin offering and his burnt offering.
17 'He shall also offer the ram for a
sacrifice of peace offerings to the
LORD, together with the basket of
unleavened cakes; the priest shall
likewise offer its grain offering and
its libation.
18 '[a]The Nazirite shall then shave
his dedicated head *of hair* at the
doorway of the tent of meeting, and
take the dedicated hair of his head
and put *it* on the fire which is under
the sacrifice of peace offerings.
19 '[a]And the priest shall take the
ram's shoulder *when it has been*
boiled, and one unleavened cake out
of the basket, and one unleavened
wafer, and shall put *them* on the
[1]hands of the Nazirite after he has
shaved his [2]dedicated *hair.*
20 'Then the priest shall wave them
for a wave offering before the LORD.
It is holy for the priest, together
with the breast offered by waving
and the thigh offered by lifting up;
and afterward the Nazirite may
drink wine.'
21 "This is the law of the Nazirite
who vows his offering to the LORD
according to his separation, in addition to what *else* [1]he can afford; according to his vow which he takes,
so he shall do according to the law
of his separation."

Aaron's Benediction

22 Then the LORD spoke to Moses,
saying,
23 "Speak to Aaron and to his sons,
saying, 'Thus [a]you shall bless the
sons of Israel. You shall say to them:
24 The LORD [a]bless you, and
[b]keep you;
25 The LORD [a]make His face
shine on you,
And [b]be gracious to you;
26 The LORD [a]lift up His countenance on you,
And [b]give you peace.'
27 "So they shall [1a]invoke My name
on the sons of Israel, and I then will
bless them."

CHAPTER 7

Offerings of the Leaders

NOW it came about on [a]the day
that Moses had finished setting up
the tabernacle, he [b]anointed it and
consecrated it with all its furnishings and the altar and all its utensils,
he anointed them and consecrated
them also.
2 Then [a]the leaders of Israel, the
heads of their fathers' households,
made an offering (they were the
leaders of the tribes; they were the
ones who [1]were over the [2]numbered
men).
3 When they brought their offering before the Lord, six [a]covered
carts and twelve oxen, a cart for *every* two of the leaders and an ox for
each one, then they presented them
before the tabernacle.
4 Then the LORD spoke to Moses,
saying,

6 [a]Lev. 21:1-3; Num. 19:11-22
9 [a]Lev. 14:8, 9 [b]Num. 6:18
11 [1]Lit., *because of that which he sinned* [a]Lev. 5:7
12 [1]Or, *of dedication* [2]I.e., one separated
13 [1]Lit., *it*
14 [a]Lev. 14:10; Num. 15:27
15 [a]Num 15:1-7
18 [a]Num. 6:9
19 [1]Lit., *palms* [2]Or, *separated* [a]Lev. 7:28-34
21 [1]Lit., *his hand can reach*
23 [a]1 Chr. 23:13
24 [a]Deut. 28:3-6; Ps. 28:9 [b]1 Sam. 2:9; Ps. 17:8
25 [a]Ps. 80:3, 7, 19 [b]Ps. 86:16
26 [a]Ps. 4:6; 44:3 [b]Ps. 29:11; 37:11, 37
27 [1]Lit., *put* [a]2 Sam. 7:23
1 [a]Ex. 40:17 [b]Ex. 40:9-11; Num. 7:10, 84, 88
2 [1]Lit., *stood* [2]Lit., *mustered* [a]Num. 1:5-16
3 [a]Is. 66:20

5 "Accept *these things* from them,
that they may be [1]used in the service of the tent of meeting, and you
shall give them to the Levites, *to*
each man according to his service."
6 So Moses took the carts and the
oxen, and gave them to the Levites.
7 Two carts and four oxen he
gave to the sons of Gershon, according to [a]their service,
8 and four carts and eight oxen
he gave to the sons of Merari, according to [a]their service, under the
[1]direction of Ithamar the son of Aaron the priest.
9 But he did not give *any* to the
sons of Kohath because theirs *was*
[a]the service of the holy *objects,*
which they carried on the shoulder.
10 And the leaders offered the
dedication *offering* [1]for the altar
[2]when [a]it was anointed, so the leaders offered their offering before the
altar.
11 Then the LORD said to Moses,
"Let them present their offering,
one leader each day, for the dedication of the altar."
12 Now the one who presented his
offering on the first day *was* Nahshon the son of Amminadab, of the
tribe of Judah;
13 and his offering *was* one silver
[1a]dish whose weight *was* one hundred and thirty *shekels,* one silver
bowl of seventy shekels, [b]according
to [2]the shekel of the sanctuary, both
of them full of fine flour mixed with
oil for a grain offering;
14 one gold pan of ten *shekels,* full
of incense;
15 one [1]bull, one ram, one male
lamb one year old, for a burnt offering;
16 one male goat for a sin offering;
17 and for the sacrifice of peace offerings, two oxen, five rams, five
male goats, five male lambs one
year old. This *was* the offering of
Nahshon the son of Amminadab.
18 On the second day Nethanel the
son of Zuar, leader of Issachar, presented *an offering;*
19 he presented as his offering one
silver dish whose weight *was* one
hundred and thirty *shekels,* one silver bowl of seventy shekels, according to the shekel of the sanctuary,
both of them full of fine flour mixed
with oil for a grain offering;
20 one gold pan of ten *shekels,* full
of incense;
21 one bull, one ram, one male
lamb one year old, for a burnt offering;
22 one male goat for a sin offering;
23 and for the sacrifice of peace offerings, two oxen, five rams, five
male goats, five male lambs one
year old. This *was* the offering of
Nethanel the son of Zuar.
24 On the third day *it was* Eliab
the son of Helon, leader of the sons
of Zebulun;
25 his offering *was* one silver dish
whose weight *was* one hundred and
thirty *shekels,* one silver bowl of
seventy shekels, according to the
shekel of the sanctuary, both of
them full of fine flour mixed with oil
for a grain offering;
26 one gold pan of ten *shekels,* full
of incense;
27 one young bull, one ram, one
male lamb one year old, for a burnt
offering;
28 one male goat for a sin offering;
29 and for the sacrifice of peace offerings, two oxen, five rams, five
male goats, five male lambs one
year old. This *was* the offering of
Eliab the son of Helon.
30 On the fourth day *it was* Elizur
the son of Shedeur, leader of the
sons of Reuben;
31 his offering *was* one silver dish
whose weight *was* one hundred and
thirty *shekels,* one silver bowl of
seventv shekels, according to the
shekel of the sanctuary, both of
them full of fine flour mixed with oil
for a grain offering;
32 one gold pan of ten *shekels,* full
of incense;
33 one bull, one ram, one male
lamb one year old, for a burnt offering;
34 one male goat for a sin offering;
35 and for the sacrifice of peace offerings, two oxen, five rams, five
male goats, five male lambs one
year old. This *was* the offering of
Elizur the son of Shedeur.
36 On the fifth day *it was* Shelumiel the son of Zurishaddai, leader of
the children of Simeon;
37 his offering *was* one silver dish
whose weight *was* one hundred and
thirty *shekels,* one silver bowl of
seventy shekels, according to the
shekel of the sanctuary, both of
them full of fine flour mixed with oil
for a grain offering;
38 one gold pan of ten *shekels,* full
of incense;
39 one bull, one ram, one male
lamb one year old, for a burnt offering;
40 one male goat for a sin offering;
41 and for the sacrifice of peace offerings, two oxen, five rams, five
male goats, five male lambs one
year old. This *was* the offering of
Shelumiel the son of Zurishaddai.

5 [1]Lit., *for serving*

7 [a]Num. 4:24-26

8 [1]Lit., *hand* [a]Num. 4:31, 32

9 [a]Num. 4:5-15

10 [1]Lit., *of* [2]Lit., *in the day that* [a]Num. 7:1; 2 Chr. 7:9

13 [1]Or, *platter,* and so through v. 85 [2]I.e., approx. one-half ounce, and so through v. 86 [a]Ex. 25:29; 37:16 [b]Num. 3:47

15 [1]Or, *bull of the herd,* and so through v. 81

42 On the sixth day *it was* Eliasaph the son of Deuel, leader of the
sons of Gad;
43 his offering *was* one silver dish
whose weight *was* one hundred and
thirty *shekels,* one silver bowl of
seventy shekels, according to the
shekel of the sanctuary, both of
them full of fine flour mixed with oil
for a grain offering;
44 one gold pan of ten *shekels,* full
of incense;
45 one bull, one ram, one male
lamb one year old, for a burnt offering;
46 one male goat for a sin offering;
47 and for the sacrifice of peace offerings, two oxen, five rams, five
male goats, five male lambs one
year old. This *was* the offering of
Eliasaph the son of Deuel.
48 On the seventh day *it was* Elishama the son of Ammihud, leader of
the sons of Ephraim;
49 his offering *was* one silver dish
whose weight *was* one hundred and
thirty *shekels,* one silver bowl of
seventy shekels, according to the
shekel of the sanctuary, both of
them full of fine flour mixed with oil
for a grain offering;
50 one gold pan of ten *shekels,* full
of incense;
51 one bull, one ram, one male
lamb one year old, for a burnt offering;
52 one male goat for a sin offering;
53 and for the sacrifice of peace offerings, two oxen, five rams, five
male goats, five male lambs one
year old. This *was* the offering of
Elishama the son of Ammihud.
54 On the eighth day *it was* Gamaliel the son of Pedahzur, leader of
the sons of Manasseh;
55 his offering *was* one silver dish
whose weight *was* one hundred and
thirty *shekels,* one silver bowl of
seventy shekels, according to the
shekel of the sanctuary, both of
them full of fine flour mixed with oil
for a grain offering;
56 one gold pan of ten *shekels,* full
of incense;
57 one bull, one ram, one male
lamb one year old, for a burnt offering;
58 one male goat for a sin offering;
59 and for the sacrifice of peace offerings, two oxen, five rams, five
male goats, five male lambs one
year old. This *was* the offering of
Gamaliel the son of Pedahzur.
60 On the ninth day *it was* Abidan
the son of Gideoni, leader of the
sons of Benjamin;
61 his offering *was* one silver dish
whose weight *was* one hundred and
thirty *shekels,* one silver bowl of
seventy shekels, according to the
shekel of the sanctuary, both of
them full of fine flour mixed with oil
for a grain offering;
62 one gold pan of ten *shekels,* full
of incense;
63 one bull, one ram, one male
lamb one year old, for a burnt offering;
64 one male goat for a sin offering;
65 and for the sacrifice of peace offerings, two oxen, five rams, five
male goats, five male lambs one
year old. This *was* the offering of
Abidan the son of Gideoni.
66 On the tenth day *it was* Ahiezer
the son of Ammishaddai, leader of
the sons of Dan;
67 his offering *was* one silver dish
whose weight *was* one hundred and
thirty *shekels,* one silver bowl of
seventy shekels, according to the
shekel of the sanctuary, both of
them full of fine flour mixed with oil
for a grain offering;
68 one gold pan of ten *shekels,* full
of incense;
69 one bull, one ram, one male
lamb one year old, for a burnt offering;
70 one male goat for a sin offering;
71 and for the sacrifice of peace offerings, two oxen, five rams, five
male goats, five male lambs one
year old. This *was* the offering of
Ahiezer the son of Ammishaddai.
72 On the eleventh day *it was* Pagiel the son of Ochran, leader of the
sons of Asher;
73 his offering *was* one silver dish
whose weight *was* one hundred and
thirty *shekels,* one silver bowl of
seventy shekels, according to the
shekel of the sanctuary, both of
them full of fine flour mixed with oil
for a grain offering;
74 one gold pan of ten *shekels,* full
of incense;
75 one bull, one ram, one male
lamb one year old, for a burnt offering;
76 one male goat for a sin offering;
77 and for the sacrifice of peace offerings, two oxen, five rams, five
male goats, five male lambs one
year old. This *was* the offering of Pagiel the son of Ochran.
78 On the twelfth day *it was* Ahira
the son of Enan, leader of the sons of
Naphtali;
79 his offering *was* one silver dish
whose weight *was* one hundred and
thirty *shekels,* one silver bowl of
seventy shekels, according to the
shekel of the sanctuary, both of

them full of fine flour mixed with oil
for a grain offering;
80 one gold pan of ten *shekels*, full
of incense;
81 one bull, one ram, one male
lamb one year old, for a burnt offering;
82 one male goat for a sin offering;
83 and for the sacrifice of peace offerings, two oxen, five rams, five
male goats, five male lambs one
year old. This *was* the offering of
Ahira the son of Enan.
84 This *was* [a]the dedication *offer-*
ing [1]for the altar from the leaders of
Israel [2]when [b]it was anointed:
twelve silver dishes, twelve silver
bowls, twelve gold pans,
85 each silver dish *weighing* one
hundred and thirty *shekels* and each
bowl seventy; all the silver of the
utensils *was* 2,400 *shekels*, according to the shekel of the sanctuary;
86 the twelve gold pans, full of incense, *weighing* ten *shekels* apiece,
according to the shekel of the sanctuary, all the gold of the pans 120
shekels;
87 all the oxen for the burnt offering twelve bulls, *all* the rams
twelve, the male lambs one year old
with their grain offering twelve, and
the male goats for a sin offering
twelve;
88 and all the oxen for the sacrifice
of peace offerings 24 bulls, *all* the
rams 60, the male goats 60, the male
lambs one year old 60. [a]This *was* the
dedication *offering* for the altar after it was anointed.
89 Now when [a]Moses went into
the tent of meeting to speak with
Him, he heard the voice speaking to
him from above [b]the [1]mercy seat
that was on the ark of the testimony,
from [c]between the two cherubim, so
He spoke to him.

CHAPTER 8

The Seven Lamps

THEN the LORD spoke to Moses,
saying,
2 "Speak to Aaron and say to him,
'When you [1]mount the lamps, the
seven lamps will [a]give light in the
front of the lampstand.' "
3 Aaron therefore did so; he
[1]mounted its lamps at the front of
the lampstand, just as the LORD had
commanded Moses.
4 [a]Now this was the workmanship of the lampstand, hammered
work of gold; from its base to its
flowers, it was hammered work;
[b]according to the pattern which the
LORD had showed Moses, so he
made the lampstand.

Cleansing the Levites

5 Again the LORD spoke to
Moses, saying,
6 "Take the Levites from among
the sons of Israel and cleanse them.
7 "And thus you shall do to them,
for their [1]cleansing: *sprinkle* [2]puri-
fying [a]water on them, and let them
[3][b]use a razor over their whole
[4]body, and [c]wash their clothes, and
they shall be clean.
8 "Then let them take a [1]bull with
[a]its grain offering, fine flour mixed
with oil; and a second [1]bull you shall
take for a sin offering.
9 "So you shall present the Levites
before the tent of meeting. You shall
also assemble the whole congregation of the sons of Israel,
10 and present the Levites before
the LORD; and the sons of Israel shall
lay their hands on the Levites.
11 "Aaron then shall [1]present the
Levites before the LORD as a [a]wave
offering from the sons of Israel, that
they may [2]qualify to perform the
service of the LORD.
12 "Now the Levites shall lay their
hands on the heads of the bulls; then
offer the one for a sin offering and
the other for a burnt offering to the
LORD, to make atonement for the
Levites.
13 "And you shall have the Levites
stand before Aaron and before his
sons so as to present them as a wave
offering to the LORD.
14 "Thus you shall separate the Levites from among the sons of Israel,
and [a]the Levites shall be Mine.
15 "Then after that the Levites may
go in to serve the tent of meeting.
But you shall cleanse them and
present them as a wave offering;
16 for they are [a]wholly given to
Me from among the sons of Israel. I
have taken them for Myself [b]instead
of every first issue of the womb, the
first-born of all the sons of Israel.
17 "For every first-born among the
sons of Israel is Mine, among the
men and among the animals; on the
day that I struck down all the first-
born in the land of Egypt I sanctified
them for Myself.
18 "But I have taken the Levites instead of every first-born among the
sons of Israel.
19 "And I have given the Levites as
[1]a gift to Aaron and to his sons from
among the sons of Israel, to perform
the service of the sons of Israel at
the tent of meeting, and to make
atonement on behalf of the sons of

84 [1]Lit., *of* [2]Lit., *in the day that* [a]Num. 7:10 [b]Num. 7:1
88 [a]Num. 7:1, 10
89 [1]Lit., *propitiatory* [a]Ex. 40:34, 35 [b]Ex. 25:21, 22 [c]Ps. 80:1; 99:1
2 [1]Lit., *raise up* [a]Ex. 25:37; Lev. 24:2, 4
3 [1]Lit., *raised up*
4 [a]Ex. 25:31-40 [b]Ex. 25:9, 40; 26:30
7 [1]Lit., *this their cleansing* [2]Lit., *water of sin* [3]Lit., *cause to pass* [4]Lit., *flesh* [a]Num. 19:9, 13, 20 [b]Lev. 14:8, 9 [c]Num. 8:21
8 [1]Or, *bull of the herd* [a]Num. 15:8-10
11 [1]Lit., *wave,* and so throughout the chap. [2]Lit., *be able* [a]Lev. 7:30, 34
14 [a]Num. 3:12
16 [a]Num. 3:9 [b]Ex. 13:2
19 [1]Lit., *given ones*

Israel, that there may be no [a]plague
among the sons of Israel by [2]their
coming near to the sanctuary."
20 Thus did Moses and Aaron and
all the congregation of the sons of
Israel to the Levites; according to all
that the LORD had commanded
Moses concerning the Levites, so
the sons of Israel did to them.
21 [a]The Levites, too, purified
themselves from sin and washed
their clothes; and Aaron presented
them as a wave offering before the
LORD. Aaron also made atonement
for them to cleanse them.
22 Then after that the Levites
went in to perform their service in
the tent of meeting before Aaron
and before his sons; just as the LORD
had commanded Moses concerning
the Levites, so they did to them.

Retirement

23 Now the LORD spoke to Moses,
saying,
24"This is what *applies* to the Levites: from [a]twenty-five years old
and upward [1]they shall enter to perform service in the work of the tent
of meeting.
25"But at the age of fifty years they
shall [1]retire from service in the
work and not work any more.
26"They may, however, [1]assist
their brothers in the tent of meeting,
to keep an obligation; but they
themselves shall do no work. Thus
you shall deal with the Levites concerning their obligations."

CHAPTER 9

The Passover

THUS the LORD spoke to Moses in
the wilderness of Sinai, in [a]the first
month of the second year after they
had come out of the land of Egypt,
saying,
2"Now, let the sons of Israel observe the Passover at [a]its appointed
time.
3"On the fourteenth day of this
month, [1]at twilight, you shall observe it at its appointed time; you
shall observe it according to all its
statutes and according to all its ordinances."
4 So Moses [1]told the sons of Israel to observe the Passover.
5 And they observed the Passover in the first *month*, on the fourteenth day of the month, at twilight,
in the wilderness of Sinai; according
to all that the LORD had commanded
Moses, so the sons of Israel did.
6 But there were *some* men who
were [a]unclean because of *the* [1]dead
person, so that they could not observe Passover on that day; so they
came before Moses and Aaron on
that day.
7 And those men said to him.
"*Though* we are unclean because of
the [1]dead person, why are we restrained from presenting the offering of the LORD at its appointed time
among the sons of Israel?"
8 Moses therefore said to them,
"[1a]Wait, and I will listen to what the
LORD will command concerning
you."
9 Then the LORD spoke to Moses,
saying,
10"Speak to the sons of Israel, saying, 'If any one of you or of your
generations becomes unclean because of a *dead* [1]person, or is on a
distant journey, he may, however,
observe the Passover to the LORD.
11 'In the second month on the
fourteenth day at twilight, they shall
observe it; they shall eat it with unleavened bread and bitter herbs.
12 'They shall leave none of it until
morning, [a]nor break a bone of it; according to all the statute of the Passover they shall observe it.
13 '[a]But the man who is clean and
is not on a journey, and yet [1]ne-
glects to observe the Passover, that
[2]person shall then be cut off from
his people, for he did not present the
offering of the LORD at its appointed
time. That man shall bear his sin.
14 '[a]And if an alien sojourns
among you and [1]observes the Passover to the LORD, according to the
statute of the Passover and according to its ordinance, so he shall do;
you shall have [b]one statute, both for
the alien and for the native of the
land.'"

The Cloud on the Tabernacle

15 Now on [a]the day that the tabernacle was erected [b]the cloud covered the tabernacle, the [c]tent of the
testimony, and [d]in the evening it
was like the appearance of fire over
the tabernacle, until morning.
16 So it was continuously; the
cloud would cover it *by day*, and the
appearance of fire by night.
17 [a]And whenever the cloud was
lifted from over the tent, afterward
the sons of Israel would then set out;
and in the place where the cloud settled down, there the sons of Israel
would camp.
18 At the [1]command of the LORD
the sons of Israel would set out, and
at the [1]command of the LORD they
would camp; as long as the cloud

19 [2]Lit., *the sons of Israel's* [a]Num. 1:53
21 [a]Num. 8:7
24 [1]Lit., *he* [a]Num. 4:3
25 [1]Lit., *return*
26 [1]Lit., *serve*
1 [a]Ex. 40:2, 17; Num. 1:1
2 [a]Ex. 12:6
3 [1]Lit., *between the two evenings*, and so throughout the chap.
4 [1]Lit., *spoke to*
6 [1]Lit., *soul of man* [a]Num. 19:11-22
7 [1]Lit., *soul of man*
8 [1]Lit., *Stand* [a]Ex. 18:15
10 [1]Lit., *soul*
12 [a]Ex. 12:46; John 19:36
13 [1]Or, *ceases* [2]Lit., *soul* [a]Ex. 12:47
14 [1]Or, *would observe* [a]Ex. 12:48 [b]Ex. 12:49; Lev. 24:22; Num. 15:15, 16, 29
15 [a]Ex 40:1, 17 [b]Ex. 40:34 [c]Num. 17:7 [d]Ex. 13:21, 22
17 [a]Ex. 40:36-38; Num. 10:11, 12
18 [1]Lit., *mouth*

settled over the tabernacle, they remained camped.
19 Even when the cloud lingered
over the tabernacle for many days,
[1]the sons of Israel would keep the
LORD's charge and not set out.
20 If [1]sometimes the cloud remained a few days over the tabernacle, according to the [2]command of
the LORD they remained camped.
Then according to the [2]command of
the LORD they set out.
21 If [1]sometimes the cloud [2]re-
mained from evening until morning,
when the cloud was lifted in the
morning, they would move out; or *if
it remained* in the daytime and at
night, whenever the cloud was
lifted, they would set out.
22 Whether it was two days or a
month or a year that the cloud lingered over the tabernacle, staying
above it, the sons of Israel remained
camped and did not set out; but
when it was lifted, they did set out.
23 At the [1]command of the LORD
they camped, and at the [1]command
of the LORD they set out; they kept
the LORD's charge, according to the
[1]command of the LORD through
Moses.

CHAPTER 10

The Silver Trumpets

THE LORD spoke further to Moses,
saying,
2 "Make yourself two trumpets of
silver, of hammered work you shall
make them; and you shall use them
for summoning the congregation
and for having the camps set out.
3 "And when both are blown, all
the congregation shall gather themselves to you at the doorway of the
tent of meeting.
4 "Yet if *only* one is blown, then
the leaders, the heads of the [1]divi-
sions of Israel, shall assemble before you.
5 "But when you blow an alarm,
the camps that are pitched [a]on the
east side shall set out.
6 "And when you blow an alarm
the second time, the camps that are
pitched on [a]the south side shall set
out; an alarm is to be blown for
them to set out.
7 "When convening the assembly,
however, you shall blow without
sounding an alarm.
8 "[a]The priestly sons of Aaron,
moreover, shall blow the trumpets;
and [1]this shall be for you a perpetual
statute throughout your generations.

19 [1]Lit., *and the*

20 [1]Lit., *it was that* [2]Lit., *mouth*

21 [1]Lit., *it was that* [2]Lit., *was*

23 [1]Lit., *mouth*

4 [1]Lit., *thousands*, or, *clans*

5 [a]Num. 10:14

6 [a]Num. 10:18

8 [1]Lit., *it* [a]Num. 31:6

10 [1]Or, *times* [a]Ps. 81:3-5

11 [1]Lit., *dwelling place* and so throughout the chap. [a]Ex. 40:17

13 [1]Lit., *mouth* [a]Deut. 1:6

14 [a]Num. 2:3-9

17 [a]Num. 4:21-32

18 [a]Num. 2:10-16

21 [a]Num. 4:4-20 [b]Num. 10:17

22 [a]Num. 2:18-24

9 "And when you go to war in your
land against the adversary who attacks you, then you shall sound an
alarm with the trumpets, that you
may be remembered before the
LORD your God, and be saved from
your enemies.
10 "Also in the day of your gladness
and in your appointed [1]feasts, and
on the first *days* of your months,
[a]you shall blow the trumpets over
your burnt offerings, and over the
sacrifices of your peace offerings;
and they shall be as a reminder of
you before your God. I am the LORD
your God."

The Tribes Leave Sinai

11 Now it came about in [a]the second year, in the second month, on
the twentieth of the month, that the
cloud was lifted from over the [1]tab-
ernacle of the testimony;
12 and the sons of Israel set out on
their journeys from the wilderness
of Sinai. Then the cloud settled
down in the wilderness of Paran.
13 [a]So they moved out for the first
time according to the [1]command-
ment of the LORD through Moses.
14 And the standard of the camp
of the sons of Judah, according to
their armies, [a]set out first, with Nahshon the son of Amminadab, over
its army,
15 and Nethanel the son of Zuar,
over the tribal army of the sons of
Issachar;
16 and Eliab the son of Helon over
the tribal army of the sons of Zebulun.
17 [a]Then the tabernacle was taken
down; and the sons of Gershon and
the sons of Merari, who were carrying the tabernacle, set out.
18 Next [a]the standard of the camp
of Reuben, according to their
armies, set out with Elizur the son of
Shedeur, over its army,
19 and Shelumiel the son of Zurishaddai over the tribal army of the
sons of Simeon,
20 and Eliasaph the son of Deuel
was over the tribal army of the sons
of Gad.
21 [a]Then the Kohathites set out,
carrying the holy *objects;* and [b]the
tabernacle was set up before their
arrival.
22 [a]Next the standard of the camp
of the sons of Ephraim, according to
their armies, was set out, with Elishama the son of Ammihud over its
army,
23 and Gamaliel the son of Pedahzur over the tribal army of the sons
of Manasseh;

24 and Abidan the son of Gideoni
over the tribal army of the sons of
Benjamin.
25 [a]Then the standard of the camp
of the sons of Dan, according to
their armies, *which formed* the [b]rear
guard for all the camps, set out, with
Ahiezer the son of Ammishaddai
over its army,
26 and Pagiel the son of Ochran
over the tribal army of the sons of
Asher;
27 and Ahira the son of Enan over
the tribal army of the sons of Naphtali.
28 [1]This was the order of march of
the sons of Israel by their armies as
they set out.
29 Then Moses said to [a]Hobab the
son of [b]Reuel the Midianite, Moses'
father-in-law, "We are setting out to
the place of which the LORD said, '[c]I
will give it to you'; [d]come with us
and we will do you good, for the
LORD [e]has [1]promised good concerning Israel."
30 But he said to him, "[a]I will not
come, but rather will go to my *own*
land and relatives."
31 Then he said, "Please do not
leave us, inasmuch as you know
where we should camp in the wilderness, and you will be as eyes for
us.
32 "So it will be, if you go with us,
it will come about that [1a]whatever
good the LORD [2]does for us, [b]we will
[3]do for you."
33 [a]Thus they set out from the
mount of the LORD three days' journey, with [b]the ark of the covenant of
the LORD journeying in front of
them for the [1]three days, to seek out
[c]a resting place for them.
34 [a]And the cloud of the LORD was
over them by day, when they set out
from the camp.
35 Then it came about when the
ark set out that Moses said,

"[a]Rise up, O LORD!
And let Thine enemies be scattered,
And let those [b]who hate Thee
flee [1]before Thee."

36 And when it came to rest, he
said,

"[a]Return Thou, O LORD
To the myriad [b]thousands of
Israel."

CHAPTER 11

The People Complain

NOW the people became like
[a]those who complain of adversity
[b]in the hearing of the LORD; and
when the LORD heard *it,* His anger
was kindled, and the fire of the LORD
burned among them and consumed
some of the outskirts of the camp.
2 [a]The people therefore cried out
to Moses, and Moses prayed to the
LORD, and the fire [1]died out.
3 So the name of that place was
called [1a]Taberah, because the fire of
the LORD burned among them.
4 And the [a]rabble who were
among them [1]had greedy desires;
and also the sons of Israel wept
again and said, "[b]Who will give us
[2]meat to eat?
5 "[a]We remember the fish which
we used to eat free in Egypt, the cu-
cumbers and the melons and the
leeks and the onions and the garlic,
6 but now [a]our [1]appetite is gone.
There is nothing at all [2]to look at
except this manna."
7 [a]Now the manna was like cori-
ander seed, and its appearance like
that of bdellium.
8 The people would go about and
gather *it* and grind *it* [1]between two
millstones or beat *it* in the mortar,
and boil *it* in the pot and make cakes
with it; and its taste was as the taste
of [2]cakes baked with oil.
9 [a]And when the dew fell on the
camp at night, the manna would fall
[1]with it.

The Complaint of Moses

10 Now Moses heard the people
weeping throughout their families,
each man at the doorway of his tent;
and the anger of the LORD was kindled greatly, and [1]Moses was displeased.
11 [a]So Moses said to the LORD,
"Why hast Thou [1]been so hard on
Thy servant? And why have I not
found favor in Thy sight, that Thou
hast laid the burden of all this people on me?
12 "Was it I who conceived all this
people? Was it I who brought them
forth, that Thou shouldest say to
me, 'Carry them in your bosom as a
[1a]nurse carries a nursing infant, to
the land which [b]Thou didst swear to
their fathers'?
13 "Where am I to get meat to give
to [a]all this people? For they weep
before me, saying, 'Give us meat
that we may eat!'
14 "[a]I alone am not able to carry all
this people, because it is too [1]bur-
densome for me.
15 "[a]So if Thou art going to deal
thus with me, please kill me at once,
if I have found favor in Thy sight,
and do not let me see my wretched-
ness."

25 [a]Num. 2:25-31 [b]Josh. 6:9, 13
28 [1]Lit., *These are the settings out of the sons*
29 [1]Lit., *spoken* [a]Judg. 4:11 [b]Ex. 2:18; 3:1; 18:12 [c]Gen. 12:7; Ex. 6:4-8 [d]Ps. 95:1-7; 100:1-5 [e]Deut. 4:40; 30:5
30 [a]Judg. 1:16; Matt. 21:28, 29
32 [1]Lit., *that good which* [2]Lit., *does good* [3]Lit., *do good* [a]Ps. 22:27-31; 67:5-7 [b]Lev. 19:34; Deut. 10:18
33 [1]Lit., *three days' journey* [a]Num. 10:11 [b]Deut. 1:33 [c]Is. 11:10
34 [a]Num. 9:15-23
35 [1]Or, *from Thy presence* [a]Ps. 68:1, 2; Is. 17:12-14 [b]Deut. 7:10; 32:41
36 [a]Is. 63:17 [b]Deut. 1:10
1 [a]Num. 14:2; 16:11; 17:5 [b]Num. 11:18; 14:28
2 [1]Lit., *sank down* [a]Num. 12:11, 13; 21:7
3 [1]I.e., Burning [a]Deut. 9:22
4 [1]Lit., *desired a desire* [2]Lit., *flesh,* and so throughout the chap. [a]Ex. 12:38; 1 Cor. 10:6 [b]Ps. 78:20
5 [a]Ex. 16:3
6 [1]Lit., *soul is dried up* [2]Lit., *for our eyes* [a]Num. 21:5
7 [a]Ex. 16:31
8 [1]Lit., *with* [2]Lit., *juice of oil*
9 [1]Lit., *on* [a]Ex. 16:13, 14
10 [1]Lit., it was *evil in Moses' sight*
11 [1]Lit., *dealt ill with* [a]Ex. 5:22
12 [1]Or, *foster-father* [a]2 Kin. 10:1, 5; Is. 49:23 [b]Gen. 24:7; Ex. 13:5, 11; 33:1
13 [a]Num. 11:21, 22; John 6:5-9
14 [1]Lit., *heavy* [a]Ex. 18:18; Deut. 1:12
15 [a]Ex. 32:32

Seventy Elders to Assist

16 The LORD therefore said to
Moses, "Gather for Me seventy men
from the elders of Israel, [a]whom you
know to be the elders of the people
and their officers and bring them to
the tent of meeting, and let them
take their stand there with you.
17 "[a]Then I will come down and
speak with you there, and I will take
of the Spirit who is upon you, and
will put *Him* upon them; and they
shall bear the burden of the people
with you, so that you shall not bear
it all alone.
18 "And say to the people, '[a]Conse-
crate yourselves for tomorrow, and
you shall eat meat; for you have
wept [b]in the ears of the LORD, saying, "Oh that someone would give
us meat to eat! For we were well-off
in Egypt." Therefore the LORD will
give you meat and you shall eat.
19 'You shall eat, not one day, nor
two days, nor five days, nor ten
days, nor twenty days,
20 [1]but a whole month, until it
comes out of your nostrils and becomes loathsome to you; because
[a]you have rejected the LORD who is
among you and have wept before
Him, saying, "Why did we ever
leave Egypt?" ' "
21 But Moses said, "The people,
among whom I am, are 600,000 on
foot; yet Thou hast said, 'I will give
them meat in order that they may
eat for a whole month.'
22 "Should flocks and herds be
slaughtered for them, to be sufficient for them? Or should all the fish
of the sea be gathered together for
them, to be sufficient for them?"
23 And the LORD said to Moses, "Is
[a]the LORD's [1]power limited? Now
you shall see whether My word will
[2]come true for you or not."
24 So Moses went out and [a]told
the people the words of the LORD.
Also, he gathered seventy men of
the elders of the people, and stationed them around the tent.
25 [a]Then the LORD came down in
the cloud and spoke to him; and He
took of the Spirit who was upon him
and placed *Him* upon the seventy
elders. And it came about that when
the Spirit rested upon them, they
prophesied. But they did not do *it*
again.
26 But two men had remained in
the camp; the name of one was Eldad and the name of the [1]other Medad. And [a]the Spirit rested upon
them (now they were among those
who had been registered, but had
not gone out to the tent), and they
prophesied in the camp.
27 So a young man ran and told
Moses and said, "Eldad and Medad
are prophesying in the camp."
28 Then [a]Joshua the son of Nun,
the attendant of Moses from his
youth, answered and said, "[b]Moses,
my lord, restrain them."
29 But Moses said to him, "Are
you jealous for my sake? Would that
all the LORD's people were prophets,
that the LORD would put His Spirit
upon them!"
30 Then Moses [1]returned to the
camp, *both* he and the elders of Israel.

The Quail and the Plague

31 [a]Now there went forth a wind
from the LORD, and it brought quail
from the sea, and let *them* fall beside the camp, about a day's journey
on this side and a day's journey on
the other side, all around the camp,
and [1]about two [2]cubits *deep* on the
surface of the ground.
32 And the people [1]spent all day
and all night and all the next day,
and gathered the quail (he who
gathered least gathered ten [2]ho-
mers) and they spread *them* out for
themselves all around the camp.
33 [a]While the meat was still between their teeth, before it was
chewed, the anger of the LORD was
kindled against the people, and the
LORD struck the people with a very
severe plague.
34 So the name of that place was
called [1a]Kibroth-hattaavah, because
there they buried the people who
had been greedy.
35 From Kibroth-hattaavah the
people set out for Hazeroth, and
they [1]remained at Hazeroth.

CHAPTER 12

The Murmuring of Miriam and Aaron

THEN Miriam and Aaron spoke
against Moses because of the Cushite woman whom he had married
(for he had married a [a]Cushite
woman);
2 [a]and they said, "Has the LORD
indeed spoken only through Moses?
Has He not spoken through us as
well?" And the LORD heard it.
3 (Now the man Moses was [a]very
humble, more than any man who
was on the face of the earth.)
4 And suddenly the LORD said to
Moses and Aaron and to Miriam,
"You three come out to the tent of
meeting." So the three of them
came out.
5 [a]Then the LORD came down in a

16 [a]Ex. 18:25
17 [a]Num. 11:25
18 [a]Ex. 19:10, 22 [b]Num. 11:1
20 [1]Lit., *until* [a]Josh. 24:27; 1 Sam. 10:19
23 [1]Lit., *hand short* [2]Lit., *befall you* [a]Is. 50:2; 59:1
24 [a]Num. 11:16
25 [a]Num. 11:17; 12:5
26 [1]Lit., *second* [a]Num. 24:2; 1 Sam. 10:6; 2 Chr. 15:1; Neh. 9:30
28 [a]Ex. 33:11; Josh. 1:1 [b]Mark 9:38-40
30 [1]Lit., *removed himself*
31 [1]Or, from *about two cubits above* [2]I.e., one cubit equals 18 inches [a]Ex. 16:13; Ps. 78:26-28; 105:40
32 [1]Lit., *rose* [2]I.e., one homer equals about 11 bushels
33 [a]Ps. 78:29-31; 106:15
34 [1]I.e., The graves of greediness [a]Deut. 9:22
35 [1]Lit., *were*
1 [a]Ex. 2:21
2 [a]Num. 16:3
3 [a]Matt. 11:29
5 [a]Ex. 19:9; 34:5

pillar of cloud and stood at the doorway of the tent, and He called [1]Aaron and Miriam. When they had both come forward,

6 He said,
"Hear now My words:
If there is a prophet among you,
I, the LORD, shall make Myself known to him in a [a]vision.
I shall speak with him in a [b]dream.
7 "Not so, with [a]My servant Moses,
[b]He is faithful in all My household;
8 [a]With him I speak mouth to mouth,
Even openly, and not in dark sayings,
And he beholds [b]the form of the LORD.
Why then were you not afraid
To speak against My servant, against Moses?"

9 So the anger of the LORD burned against them and [a]He departed.

10 But when the cloud had withdrawn from over the tent, behold, [a]Miriam *was* leprous, as [b]*white as* snow. As Aaron turned toward Miriam, behold, she *was* leprous.

11 Then Aaron said to Moses, "Oh, my lord, I beg you, [a]do not account *this* sin to us, in which we have acted foolishly and in which we have sinned.

12 "Oh do not let her be like one dead, whose flesh is half eaten away when he comes from his mother's womb!"

13 And Moses cried out to the LORD, saying, "Oh God, [a]heal her, I pray!"

14 But the LORD said to Moses, "If her father had but [a]spit in her face, would she not bear her shame for seven days? Let her be shut up for seven days [b]outside the camp, and afterward she may be received again."

15 So Miriam was shut up outside the camp for seven days, and the people did not move on until Miriam was received again.

16 Afterward, however, the people moved out from Hazeroth and camped in the wilderness of Paran.

CHAPTER 13

Spies View the Land

THEN [a]the LORD spoke to Moses saying,

2 "Send out for yourself men so that they may spy out the land of Canaan, which I am going to give to the sons of Israel; you shall send a man from each of their fathers' tribes, every one a leader among them."

3 So Moses sent them from the wilderness of Paran at the [1]command of the LORD, all of them men who were heads of the sons of Israel.

4 These then *were* their names: from the tribe of Reuben, Shammua the son of Zaccur;

5 from the tribe of Simeon, Shaphat the son of Hori;

6 from the tribe of Judah, Caleb the son of Jephunneh;

7 from the tribe of Issachar, Igal the son of Joseph;

8 from the tribe of Ephraim, [a]Hoshea the son of Nun;

9 from the tribe of Benjamin, Palti the son of Raphu;

10 from the tribe of Zebulun, Gaddiel the son of Sodi;

11 from the tribe of Joseph, from the tribe of Manasseh, Gaddi the son of Susi;

12 from the tribe of Dan, Ammiel the son of Gemalli;

13 from the tribe of Asher, Sethur the son of Michael;

14 from the tribe of Naphtali, Nahbi the son of Vophsi;

15 from the tribe of Gad, Geuel the son of Machi.

16 These are the names of the men whom Moses sent to spy out the land; but Moses called [a]Hoshea the son of Nun, Joshua.

17 When Moses sent them to spy out the land of Canaan, he said to them, "Go up [1]there into [a]the [2]Negev; then go up into the hill country.

18 "And see what the land is like, and whether the people who live in it are strong *or* weak, whether they are few or many.

19 "And how is the land in which they live, is it good or bad? And how are the cities in which they live, are *they* [1]like *open* camps or with fortifications?

20 "And [a]how is the land, is it fat or lean? Are there trees in it or not? [1]Make an [b]effort then to get some of the fruit of the land." Now the time was the time of the first ripe grapes.

21 So they went up and spied out the land from [a]the wilderness of Zin as far as Rehob, [1b]at Lebo-hamath.

22 When they had gone up into [a]the Negev, [1]they came to Hebron where [b]Ahiman, Sheshai and Talmai, the [2]descendants of [c]Anak were. (Now Hebron was built seven years before [d]Zoan in Egypt.)

5 [1]Or, *"Aaron and Miriam!"*

6 [a]Gen. 46:2; 1 Sam. 3:15 [b]Gen. 31:11; 1 Kin. 3:5, 15

7 [a]Josh. 1:1 [b]Heb. 3:2, 5

8 [a]Deut. 34:10; Hos. 12:13 [b]Ex. 20:4; 24:10, 11; Deut. 5:8; Ps. 17:15

9 [a]Gen. 17:22; 18:33

10 [a]Deut. 24:9 [b]Ex. 4:6; 2 Kin. 5:27

11 [a]2 Sam. 19:19; 24:10

13 [a]Ps. 30:2; 41:4; Is. 30:26; Jer. 17:14

14 [a]Deut. 25:9; Job 17:6; 30:10; Is. 50:6 [b]Num. 5:1-4

1 [a]Deut. 1:22, 23

3 [1]Lit., *mouth*

8 [a]Num. 13:16; Deut. 32:44

16 [a]Num. 13:8; Deut. 32:44

17 [1]Lit., *here* [2]I.e., South country, and so throughout the chap. [a]Gen. 12:9; 13:1, 3

19 [1]Lit., *in*

20 [1]Lit., *Use your strength* [a]Deut. 1:24, 25 [b]Deut. 31:6, 23

21 [1]Or, *to the entrance of Hamath* [a]Num. 20:1; 27:14; 33:36 [b]Josh. 13:5

22 [1]Lit., Most mss. read, *one came* [2]Lit., *children* [a]Num. 13:17 [b]Josh. 15:14 [c]Num. 13:28, 33 [d]Ps. 78:12, 43

23 Then they came to the [1]valley
of [2a]Eshcol and from there cut down
a branch with a single cluster of
grapes; and they carried it on a pole
between two *men,* with some of the
pomegranates and the figs.
24 That place was called the valley
of [1]Eshcol, because of the cluster
which the sons of Israel cut down
from there.

The Spies' Reports

25 When they returned from spying out the land, at the end of forty
days,
26 they proceeded to come to
Moses and Aaron and to all the congregation of the sons of Israel [1]in
the wilderness of Paran, at [a]Kadesh;
and they brought back word to them
and to all the congregation and
showed them the fruit of the land.
27 Thus they told him, and said,
"We went in to the land where you
sent us; and [a]it certainly does flow
with milk and honey, and [b]this is its
fruit.
28 "Nevertheless, the people who
live in the land are strong, and the
cities are fortified *and* very large;
and moreover, we saw [a]the [1]descen-
dants of Anak there.
29 "Amalek is living in the land of
[a]the Negev and the Hittites and the
Jebusites and [b]the Amorites are living in the hill country, and [c]the Canaanites are living by the sea and by
the side of the Jordan."
30 Then Caleb quieted the people
[1]before Moses, and said, "We
should by all means go up and take
possession of it, for we shall surely
overcome it."
31 But the men who had gone up
with him said, "[a]We are not able to
go up against the people, for they
are too strong for us."
32 So they gave out to the sons of
Israel [a]a bad report of the land
which they had spied out, saying,
"The land through which we have
gone, in spying it out, is [b]a land that
devours its [1]inhabitants; and [c]all the
people whom we saw in it are men
of *great* size.
33 "There also we saw the [a]Nephi-
lim (the sons of Anak are part of the
Nephilim); and [b]we became like
grasshoppers in our own sight, and
so we were in their sight."

CHAPTER 14

The People Rebel

THEN all the congregation [1]lifted
up their voices and cried, and the
people wept [2]that night.
2 And all the sons of Israel
[a]grumbled against Moses and Aaron; and the whole congregation said
to them, "[b]Would that we had died
in the land of Egypt! Or would that
we had died in this wilderness!
3 "And why is the LORD bringing
us into this land, [a]to fall by the
sword? [b]Our wives and our little
ones will become plunder; would it
not be better for us to return to
Egypt?"
4 So they said to one another,
"Let us appoint a leader and return
to Egypt."
5 [a]Then Moses and Aaron fell on
their faces in the presence of all the
assembly of the congregation of the
sons of Israel.
6 And Joshua the son of Nun and
Caleb the son of Jephunneh, of
those who had spied out the land,
tore their clothes;
7 and they spoke to all the congregation of the sons of Israel, saying, "[a]The land which we passed
through to spy out is an exceedingly
good land.
8 "[a]If the LORD is pleased with us,
then He will bring us into this land,
and give it to us—[b]a land which
flows with milk and honey.
9 "Only [a]do not rebel against the
LORD; and do not [b]fear the people of
the land, for they shall be our [1]prey.
Their [2]protection has been removed
from them, and the LORD is with us;
do not fear them."
10 [a]But all the congregation said
to stone them with stones. Then [b]the
glory of the LORD appeared in the
tent of meeting to all the sons of Israel.

Moses Pleads for the People

11 [a]And the LORD said to Moses,
"How long will this people spurn
Me? And how long will [b]they not believe in Me, despite all the signs
which I have performed in their
midst?
12 "I will smite them with [1a]pestil-
ence and dispossess them, and I
[b]will make you into a nation greater
and mightier than they."
13 [a]But Moses said to the LORD,
"Then the Egyptians will hear of it,
for by Thy strength Thou didst bring
up this people from their midst,
14 and they will tell *it* to the inhabitants of this land. They have
heard that Thou, O LORD, art in the
midst of this people, for [a]Thou, O
LORD, art seen eye to eye, while Thy
cloud stands over them; and Thou
dost go before them in a pillar of

23 [1]Or, *wadi* [2]I.e., Cluster [a]Gen. 14:13; Num. 13:24; 32:9; Deut. 1:24
24 [1]I.e., Cluster
26 [1]Lit., *to* [a]Num. 20:1, 14; 32:8
27 [a]Ex. 3:8, 17; 13:5 [b]Deut. 1:25
28 [1]Lit., *born ones* [a]Num. 13:33
29 [a]Num. 13:17; 14:25, 45 [b]Josh. 10:6 [c]Num. 14:43, 45
30 [1]Lit., *toward*
31 [a]Deut. 1:28; 9:1-3
32 [1]Or, *settlers* [a]Num. 14:36, 37; Ps. 106:24 [b]Ezek. 36:13, 14 [c]Amos 2:9
33 [a]Gen. 6:4 [b]Deut. 1:28; 9:2; Josh. 11:21
1 [1]Lit., *lifted and gave their voice* [2]Lit., *in that*
2 [a]Num. 11:1 [b]Num. 11:5; 16:13; 20:3, 4; 21:5
3 [a]Ex. 5:21; 16:3 [b]Num. 14:31; Deut. 1:39
5 [a]Num. 16:4
7 [a]Num. 13:27; Deut. 1:25
8 [a]Deut. 10:15 [b]Ex. 3:8; Num. 13:27
9 [1]Lit., *food* [2]Lit., *shadow* [a]Deut. 1:26; 9:23, 24 [b]Deut. 1:21, 29
10 [a]Ex. 17:4 [b]Ex. 16:10; Lev. 9:23
11 [a]Ex. 32:9-13 [b]Ps. 106:24
12 [1]Lit., *the pestilence* [a]Lev. 26:25; Deut. 28:21 [b]Ex. 32:10
13 [a]Ps. 106:23
14 [a]Ex. 13:21; Deut. 5:4

cloud by day and in a pillar of fire by
night.
15"Now if Thou dost slay this people as one man, [a]then the nations
who have heard of Thy fame will
[1]say,
16 'Because the LORD could not
bring this people into the land which
He promised them by oath, therefore He slaughtered them in the wilderness.'
17"But now, I pray, let the power
of the Lord be great, just as Thou
hast [1]declared,
18 '[a]The LORD is slow to anger and
abundant in lovingkindness, forgiving iniquity and transgression; but
He will by no means clear *the guilty,*
visiting the iniquity of the fathers on
the children [1]to the third and the
fourth *generations.'*
19"[a]Pardon, I pray, the iniquity of
this people according to the greatness of Thy lovingkindness, just as
Thou also hast forgiven this people,
from Egypt even until now."

The LORD Pardons and Rebukes

20 So the LORD said, "[a]I have pardoned *them* according to your word;
21 but indeed, [a]as I live, [1b]all the
earth will be filled with the glory of
the LORD.
22"Surely [a]all the men who have
seen My glory and My signs, which
I performed in Egypt and in the wilderness, yet have put Me to the test
these [b]ten times and have not listened to My voice,
23 [a]shall by no means see the land
which I swore to their fathers, nor
shall any of those who spurned Me
see it.
24"But My servant Caleb, [a]be-
cause he has had a different spirit
and has followed Me fully, [1b]I will
bring into the land [2]which he entered, and his [3]descendants shall
take possession of it.
25"[a]Now the Amalekites and the
Canaanites live in the valleys; turn
tomorrow and set out to the wilderness by the way of the [1]Red Sea."
26 And the LORD spoke to Moses
and Aaron, saying,
27"How long *shall I bear* with this
evil congregation who are [a]grum-
bling against Me? I have heard the
complaints of the sons of Israel,
which they are [1]making against Me.
28"Say to them, '[a]As I live,' says
the LORD, 'just as [b]you have spoken
in My hearing, so I will surely do to
you;
29 your corpses shall fall in this
wilderness, even all [a]your [1]num-
bered men, according to your complete number from twenty years old
and upward, who have grumbled
against Me.
30 'Surely you shall not come into
the land in which I [1]swore to settle
you, [a]except Caleb the son of Jephunneh and Joshua the son of Nun.
31 '[a]Your children, however,
whom you said would become a
prey—I will bring them in, and they
shall know the land which you have
rejected.
32 '[a]But as for you, your corpses
shall fall in this wilderness.
33 'And your sons shall be shepherds for [a]forty years in the wilderness, and they shall [1]suffer *for* your
[2]unfaithfulness, until your corpses
[3]lie in the wilderness.
34 'According to the number of
days which you spied out the land,
forty days, for every day you shall
bear your [1]guilt a year, *even* forty
years, and you shall know My opposition.
35 'I, the LORD, have spoken, surely
this I will do to all this evil congregation who are gathered together
against Me. In this wilderness they
shall be destroyed, and there they
shall die.' "
36 [a]As for the men whom Moses
sent to spy out the land and who
returned and made all the congregation grumble against him by bringing out a bad report concerning the
land,
37 even those men who brought
out the very bad report of the land
died by a [a]plague before the LORD.
38 But Joshua the son of Nun and
Caleb the son of Jephunneh remained alive out of those men who
went to spy out the land.

Israel Repulsed

39 And when Moses spoke [a]these
words to all the sons of Israel, [b]the
people mourned greatly.
40 In the morning, however, they
rose up early and went up to the
[1]ridge of the hill country, saying,
"[a]Here we are; [2]we have indeed
sinned, but we will go up to the
place which the LORD has promised."
41 But Moses said, "Why then are
you transgressing the [1]command-
ment of the LORD, when it will not
succeed?
42"Do not go up, lest you be struck
down before your enemies, for the
LORD is not among you.
43"For the Amalekites and the Canaanites will be there in front of
you, and you will fall by the sword,
inasmuch as you have turned back

15 [1]Lit., *speak, saying* [a]Ex. 32:12
17 [1]Lit., *spoken, saying*
18 [1]Lit., *on* [a]Ex. 34:6, 7
19 [a]Ex. 32:32; 34:9
20 [a]Mic. 7:18-20
21 [1]Lit., *and all* [a]Num. 14:28; Deut. 32:40; Is. 49:18 [b]Is. 6:3; Hab. 2:14
22 [a]1 Cor. 10:5 [b]Ex. 5:21; 14:11; 15:24; 16:2; 17:2, 3; 32:1; Num. 11:1, 4; 12:1; 14:2
23 [a]Num. 26:65; 32:11
24 [1]Lit., *him I* [2]Lit., *where* [3]Lit., *seed* [a]Num. 14:7-9 [b]Num. 26:65; 32:12; Deut. 1:36; Josh. 14:6-15
25 [1]Lit., *Sea of Reeds* [a]Num. 13:29
27 [1]Lit., *complaining* [a]Num. 11:1
28 [a]Num. 14:21 [b]Num. 14:2; Deut. 2:14, 15; Heb. 3:17
29 [1]Lit., *mustered* [a]Num. 1:45, 46
30 [1]Lit., *raised My hand* [a]Num. 14:24
31 [a]Num. 14:3
32 [a]Num. 26:64, 65; 32:13; 1 Cor. 10:5
33 [1]Lit., *bear* [2]Lit., *fornications* [3]Lit., *are finished* [a]Deut. 2:7; 8:2, 4; 29:5
34 [1]Or, *iniquities*
36 [a]Num. 13:4-16, 32
37 [a]Num. 16:49
39 [a]Num. 14:28-35 [b]Ex. 33:4
40 [1]Or, *top of the mountain* [2]Or, *and we will go up . . . for we have sinned* [a]Deut. 1:41-44
41 [1]Lit., *mouth*

from following the LORD. And the LORD will not be with you."

44 But they went up heedlessly to the [1]ridge of the hill country; neither [a]the ark of the covenant of the LORD nor Moses left the camp.

45 Then the Amalekites and the Canaanites who lived in that hill country came down, and struck them and beat them down as far as [a]Hormah.

CHAPTER 15

Laws for Canaan

NOW the LORD spoke to Moses, saying,

2 "Speak to the sons of Israel, and say to them, 'When you enter the land [1]where you are to live, which I am giving you,

3 then make an offering by fire to the LORD, a burnt offering or a sacrifice to [1]fulfill a special vow, or as a freewill offering or in your [a]appointed times, to make a soothing aroma to the LORD, from the herd or from the flock.

4 '[a]And the one who presents his offering shall present to the LORD a grain offering of one-tenth *of an ephah* of fine flour mixed with one-fourth of a [1]hin of oil,

5 and you shall prepare wine for the libation, one-fourth of a hin, with the burnt offering or for the sacrifice, for [a]each lamb.

6 'Or for a ram you shall prepare as a grain offering two-tenths *of an ephah* of fine flour mixed with one-third of a hin of oil;

7 and for the libation you shall offer one-third of a hin of wine as a soothing aroma to the LORD.

8 'And when you prepare [a]a bull as a burnt offering or a sacrifice, to [1]fulfill a special vow, or for peace offerings to the LORD,

9 then you shall offer with the bull a grain offering of three-tenths *of an ephah* of fine flour mixed with one-half a hin of oil;

10 and you shall offer as the libation one-half a hin of wine as an offering by fire, as a soothing aroma to the LORD.

11 'Thus it shall be done for each ox, or for each ram, or for each of the male lambs, or of the goats.

12 'According to the number that you prepare, so you shall do for everyone according to their number.

13 'All who are native shall do these things in this manner, in presenting an offering by fire, as a soothing aroma to the LORD.

Law of the Sojourner

14 'And if an alien sojourns with you, or one who may be among you throughout your generations, and he *wishes to* make an offering by fire, as a soothing aroma to the LORD, just as you do, so he shall do.

15 '*As for* the assembly, there shall be [a]one statute for you and for the alien who sojourns *with you*, a perpetual statute throughout your generations; as you are, so shall the alien be before the LORD.

16 'There is to be one law and one ordinance for you and for the alien who sojourns with you.' "

17 Then the LORD spoke to Moses, saying,

18 "Speak to the sons of Israel, and say to them, 'When you enter the land where I bring you,

19 then it shall be, that when you eat of the [1]food of the land, you shall lift up an [2]offering to the LORD.

20 '[a]Of the first of your [1]dough you shall lift up a cake as an [2]offering; as [b]the [2]offering of the threshing floor, so you shall lift it up.

21 'From the first of your [1]dough you shall give to the LORD an [2]offering throughout your generations.

22 'But when you unwittingly fail and do not observe all these commandments, which the LORD has spoken to Moses,

23 *even* all that the LORD has commanded you [1]through Moses, from the day when the LORD gave commandment and onward throughout your generations,

24 then it shall be, if it is done [a]unintentionally, [1]without the knowledge of the congregation, that all the congregation shall offer one bull for a burnt offering, as a soothing aroma to the LORD, [b]with its grain offering, and its libation, according to the ordinance, and one male goat for a sin offering.

25 'Then the priest shall make atonement for all the congregation of the sons of Israel, and they shall be forgiven; for it was an error, and they have brought their offering, an offering by fire to the LORD, and their sin offering before the LORD, for their error.

26 'So all the congregation of the sons of Israel will be forgiven, with the alien who sojourns among them, for *it happened* to all the people through [a]error.

27 'Also if one person sins unintentionally, then he shall offer a one year old female goat for a sin offering.

44 [1]Or, *top of the mountain* [a]Num. 31:6

45 [a]Num. 21:3

2 [1]Lit., *of your dwellings*

3 [1]Or, *make a special votive offering* [a]Lev. 23:1-44

4 [1]I.e., approx. one gallon, and so through v. 10 [a]Num. 28:1-29, 40

5 [a]Lev. 1:10; 3:6; Num. 15:11

8 [1]Or, *make a special votive offering* [a]Lev. 1:3; 3:1

15 [a]Num. 9:14; 15:29

19 [1]Lit., *bread* [2]Or, *heave offering*

20 [1]Or, *coarse meal* [2]Or, *heave offering* [a]Ex. 34:26; Lev. 23:14 [b]Deut. 14:22, 23; 16:13

21 [1]Or, *coarse meal* [2]Or, *offering lifted up*

23 [1]Lit., *by the hand of*

24 [1]Lit., *from the eyes of the congregation* [a]Lev. 4:2, 22, 27; 5:15, 18 [b]Num. 15:8-10

26 [a]Num. 15:24

28 'And the priest shall make atonement before the LORD for the person who goes astray when he sins unintentionally, making atonement for him [1]that he may be forgiven.

29 'You shall have one law for him who does *anything* unintentionally, for him who is native among the sons of Israel and for the alien who sojourns among them.

30 'But the person who does *anything* [a]defiantly, whether he is native or an alien, that one is blaspheming the LORD; and that person shall be cut off from among his people.

31 'Because he has despised the word of the LORD and has broken His commandment, that person shall be completely cut off; his [1]guilt *shall be* on him.' "

Sabbath-breaking Punished

32 Now while the sons of Israel were in the wilderness, they found a man [a]gathering wood on the sabbath day.

33 And those who found him gathering wood brought him to Moses and Aaron, and to all the congregation;

34 and they put him in [1]custody [a]because it had not been [2]declared what should be done to him.

35 Then the LORD said to Moses, "The man shall surely be put to death; [a]all the congregation shall stone him with stones outside the camp."

36 So all the congregation brought him outside the camp, and stoned him [1]to death with stones, just as the LORD had commanded Moses.

37 The LORD also spoke to Moses, saying,

38 "Speak to the sons of Israel, and tell them that they shall make for themselves [a]tassels on the corners of their garments throughout their generations, and that they shall put on the tassel of each corner a cord of blue.

39 "And it shall be a tassel for you [1]to look at and [a]remember all the commandments of the LORD, so as to do them and not [2]follow after your own heart and your own eyes, after which you played the harlot,

40 in order that you may remember to do all My commandments, and be holy to your God.

41 "I am the LORD your God who brought you out from the land of Egypt to be your God; I am the LORD your God."

28 [1]Or, *and he shall*

30 [a]Num. 14:40-44; Deut. 1:43; 17:12, 13

31 [1]Or, *iniquity*

32 [a]Ex. 31:14, 15; 35:2, 3

34 [1]Or, *prison* [2]Lit., *declared distinctly* [a]Num. 9:8

35 [a]Lev. 20:2, 27; 24:14-23; Deut. 21:21

36 [1]Lit., *with stones and he died*

38 [a]Deut. 22:12; Matt. 23:5

39 [1]Lit., *and you shall look at it* [2]Lit., *seek* [a]Deut. 4:23; 6:12; 8:11, 14, 19

1 [a]Ex. 6:21; Jude 11 [b]Num. 26:9; Deut. 11:6

2 [1]Lit., *and men from* [2]Lit., *called ones of* [a]Num. 1:16; 26:9

3 [1]Lit., *It is much for you* [a]Num. 12:2; Ps. 106:16 [b]Num. 16:7 [c]Num. 5:3

4 [a]Num. 14:5

5 [a]Lev. 10:3; Ps. 65:4 [b]Num. 17:5, 8

6 [1]Lit., *his*

7 [1]Lit., *It is much for you* [a]Num. 16:3

9 [1]Or, *too little for you* [a]Num. 3:6, 9

10 [a]Num. 3:10; 18:1-7

11 [1]Lit., *what* [a]Ex. 16:7 [b]1 Cor. 10:10

12 [1]Lit., *to call*

13 [1]Lit., *a little thing* [a]Ex. 16:3; Num. 11:4-6 [b]Num. 14:2, 3

CHAPTER 16

Korah's Rebellion

NOW [a]Korah the son of Izhar, the son of Kohath, the son of Levi, with [b]Dathan and Abiram, the sons of Eliab, and On the son of Peleth, sons of Reuben, took *action,*

2 and they rose up before Moses, [1]together with some of the sons of Israel, two hundred and fifty leaders of the congregation, [2][a]chosen in the assembly, men of renown.

3 And they assembled together [a]against Moses and Aaron, and said to them, "[1][b]You have gone far enough, for all the congregation are holy, every one of them, and [c]the LORD is in their midst; so why do you exalt yourselves above the assembly of the LORD?"

4 When Moses heard *this,* [a]he fell on his face;

5 and he spoke to Korah and all his company, saying, "Tomorrow morning the LORD will show who is His, and [a]who is holy, and will bring *him* near to Himself; even [b]the one whom He will choose, He will bring near to Himself.

6 "Do this: take censers for yourselves, Korah and all [1]your company,

7 and put fire in them, and lay incense upon them in the presence of the LORD tomorrow; and the man whom the LORD chooses *shall be* the one who is holy. [1][a]You have gone far enough, you sons of Levi!"

8 Then Moses said to Korah, "Hear now, you sons of Levi,

9 is it [1]not enough for you that the God of Israel has separated you from the *rest of* the congregation of Israel, [a]to bring you near to Himself, to do the service of the tabernacle of the LORD, and to stand before the congregation to minister to them;

10 and that He has brought you near, *Korah,* and all your brothers, sons of Levi, with you? And are you [a]seeking for the priesthood also?

11 "Therefore you and all your company are gathered together [a]against the LORD; but as for Aaron, [1]who is he that [b]you grumble against him?"

12 Then Moses sent [1]a summons to Dathan and Abiram, the sons of Eliab; but they said, "We will not come up.

13 "Is it [1]not enough that you have brought us up out of a [a]land flowing with milk and honey [b]to have us die in the wilderness, but you would also lord it over us?

14“Indeed, you have not brought
us [a]into a land flowing with milk and
honey, nor have you given us an inheritance of [b]fields and vineyards.
Would you [1c]put out the eyes of
[2]these men? We will not come up!”
15 Then Moses became very angry
and said to the LORD, “[a]Do not regard their offering! [b]I have not taken
a single donkey from them, nor have
I done harm to any of them.”
16 And Moses said to Korah, “You
and all your company be present before the LORD tomorrow, both you
and they along with Aaron.
17“And each of you take his firepan and put incense on [1]it, and each
of you bring his censer before the
LORD, two hundred and fifty firepans; also you and Aaron *shall* each
bring his firepan.”
18 So they each took his *own* censer and put fire on [1]it, and laid incense on [1]it; and they stood at the
doorway of the tent of meeting, with
Moses and Aaron.
19 Thus Korah assembled all the
congregation against them at the
doorway of the tent of meeting. And
[a]the glory of the LORD appeared to
all the congregation.
20 Then the LORD spoke to Moses
and Aaron, saying,
21“[a]Separate yourselves from
among this congregation, [b]that I
may consume them instantly.”
22 But they fell on their faces, and
said, “O God, [a]Thou God of the spirits of all flesh, [b]when one man sins,
wilt Thou be angry with the entire
congregation?”
23 Then the LORD spoke to Moses,
saying,
24“Speak to the congregation, saying, ‘[a]Get back from around the
dwellings of Korah, Dathan and
Abiram.’ ”
25 Then Moses arose and went to
Dathan and Abiram, with the elders
of Israel following him,
26 and he spoke to the congregation, saying, “Depart now from the
tents of these wicked men, and
touch nothing that belongs to them,
[a]lest you be swept away in all their
sin.”
27 So they got back from around
the dwellings of Korah, Dathan and
Abiram; and Dathan and Abiram
came out *and* stood at the doorway
of their tents, along with their wives
and [a]their sons and their little ones.
28 And Moses said, “By this you
shall know that [a]the LORD has sent
me to do all these deeds; for [1]this is
not my doing.
29“If these men die [1]the death of
all men, or [2]if they suffer the fate of
all men, *then* the LORD has not sent
me.
30“But if the LORD [1]brings about
an entirely new thing and the
ground opens its mouth and swallows them up with all that is theirs,
and they descend alive into [2]Sheol,
then you will understand that these
men have spurned the LORD.”
31 Then it came about as he finished speaking all these words, that
the ground that was under them
split open;
32 and [a]the earth opened its
mouth and swallowed them up, and
their households, and [b]all the men
who belonged to Korah, with *their*
possessions.
33 So they and all that belonged to
them went down alive to [1]Sheol;
and the earth closed over them, and
they perished from the midst of the
assembly.
34 And all Israel who *were* around
them fled at their [1]outcry, for they
said, “[2]The earth may swallow us
up!”
35 [a]Fire also came forth from the
LORD and consumed the [b]two hundred and fifty men who were offering the incense.
36 [1]Then the LORD spoke to
Moses, saying,
37“Say to Eleazar, the son of Aaron the priest, that he shall take up
the censers out of the midst of the
[1]blaze, for they are holy; and you
scatter the [2]burning coals abroad.
38“As for the censers of these
[1]men who have sinned at the cost of
their lives, let them be made into
hammered sheets for a plating of
the altar, since they did present
them before the LORD and they are
holy; and they shall be for a sign to
the sons of Israel.”
39 So Eleazar the priest took the
bronze censers which the men who
were burned had offered; and they
hammered them out as a plating for
the altar,
40 as a [1]reminder to the sons of
Israel that [a]no [2]layman who is not of
the [3]descendants of Aaron should
come near [b]to burn incense before
the LORD; that he might not become
like Korah and his company—just
as the LORD had spoken to him
[4]through Moses.

Murmuring and Plague

41 But on the next day all the congregation of the sons of Israel
[a]grumbled against Moses and Aaron, saying, “You are the ones who

14 [1]Lit., *bore out* [2]Lit., *those* [a]Num. 13:27; 14:8 [b]Ex. 22:5; 23:11; Num. 20:5 [c]Judg. 16:21; 1 Sam. 11:2

15 [a]Gen. 4:4, 5 [b]1 Sam. 12:3

17 [1]Lit., *them*

18 [1]Lit., *them*

19 [a]Num. 14:10; 16:42; 20:6

21 [a]Num. 16:45 [b]Ex. 32:10, 12

22 [a]Num. 27:16 [b]Gen. 18:23-32; Lev. 4:3

24 [a]Num. 16:45

26 [a]Gen. 19:15, 17

27 [a]Num. 26:11

28 [1]Lit., *not from my heart* [a]Ex. 3:12-15; 4:12, 15

29 [1]Lit., *like the death* [2]Lit., *the visitation of all men be visited upon them*

30 [1]Lit., *creates a new creation* [2]I.e., the nether world

32 [a]Num. 26:10; Deut. 11:6; Ps. 106:17 [b]Num. 26:11

33 [1]I.e., the nether world

34 [1]Or, *voice* [2]Lit., *Lest the earth*

35 [a]Num. 11:1-3; 26:10 [b]Num. 16:2

36 [1]Chap. 17:1 in Heb.

37 [1]Or, *place of burning* [2]Lit., *the fire*

38 [1]Lit., *sinners against their lives*

40 [1]Or, *memorial* [2]Lit., *stranger* [3]Lit., *seed* [4]Lit., *by the hand of* [a]Num. 1:51 [b]Ex. 30:7-10

41 [a]Num. 16:3

have caused the death of the LORD's people."

42 It came about, however, when the congregation had assembled against Moses and Aaron, that they turned toward the tent of meeting, and behold, the cloud covered it and [a]the glory of the LORD appeared.

43 Then Moses and Aaron came to the front of the tent of meeting,

44 and the LORD spoke to Moses, saying,

45 "[1][a]Get away from among this congregation, that I may consume them instantly." Then they fell on their faces.

46 And Moses said to Aaron, "Take your censer and put in it fire from the altar, and lay incense *on it;* then bring it quickly to the congregation and [a]make atonement for them, for [b]wrath has gone forth from the LORD, the plague has begun!"

47 Then Aaron took *it* as Moses had spoken, and ran into the midst of the assembly, for behold, the plague had begun among the people. [a]So he put *on* the incense and made atonement for the people.

48 And he took his stand between the dead and the living, so that the plague was checked.

49 [a]But those who died by the plague were 14,700, besides those who [b]died on account of Korah.

50 Then Aaron returned to Moses at the doorway of the tent of meeting, for the plague had been checked.

CHAPTER 17

1 *Aaron's Rod Buds*

THEN the LORD spoke to Moses, saying,

2 "Speak to the sons of Israel, and get from them a rod for each father's household: twelve rods, from all their leaders according to their fathers' households. You shall write each name on his rod,

3 and write Aaron's name on the rod of Levi; for there is one rod for the head *of each* of their fathers' households.

4 "You shall then deposit them in the tent of meeting in front of [a]the testimony, where I meet with you.

5 "And it will come about that the rod of [a]the man whom I choose will sprout. Thus I shall lessen from upon Myself the grumblings of the sons of Israel, who are grumbling against you."

6 Moses therefore spoke to the sons of Israel, and all their leaders gave him a rod apiece, for each leader according to their fathers' households, twelve rods, with the rod of Aaron among their rods.

7 So Moses deposited the rods before the LORD in [a]the tent of the testimony.

8 Now it came about on the next day that Moses went into the tent of the testimony; and behold, [a]the rod of Aaron for the house of Levi had sprouted and put forth buds and produced blossoms, and it bore ripe almonds.

9 Moses then brought out all the rods from the presence of the LORD to all the sons of Israel; and they looked, and each man took his rod.

10 But the LORD said to Moses, "Put back the rod of Aaron [a]before the testimony [1]to be kept as a sign against the [2][b]rebels, that you may put an end to their grumblings against Me, so that they should not die."

11 Thus Moses did; just as the LORD had commanded him, so he did.

12 Then the sons of Israel spoke to Moses, saying, "[a]Behold, we perish, we are dying, we are all dying!

13 "[a]Everyone who comes near, who comes near to the tabernacle of the LORD, must die. Are we to perish completely?"

CHAPTER 18

Duties of Levites

SO the LORD said to Aaron, "You and your sons and your father's household with you shall [a]bear the guilt [1]in connection with the sanctuary; and you and your sons with you shall bear the guilt [2]in connection with your priesthood.

2 "But bring with you also your brothers, the tribe of Levi, the tribe of your father, that they may be [a]joined with you and serve you, while you and your sons with you are before the tent of the testimony.

3 "And they shall thus attend to your obligation and the obligation of all the tent, but [a]they shall not come near to the furnishings of the sanctuary and [b]the altar, lest both they and you die.

4 "And they shall be joined with you and attend to the obligations of the tent of meeting, for all the service of the tent; but an [1]outsider may not come near you.

5 "So you shall attend to the obligations of the sanctuary and the ob-

---

42 [a]Num. 16:19
45 [1]Or, *Arise* [a]Num. 16:21, 24
46 [a]Num. 25:13; Is. 6:6, 7 [b]Num. 18:5; Deut. 9:22
47 [a]Num. 25:7, 8, 13
49 [a]Num. 25:9 [b]Num. 16:32, 35
1 [1]In Heb., chap. 17:16
4 [a]Ex. 25:16, 21, 22; Num. 17:7
5 [a]Num. 16:5
7 [a]Num. 1:50, 53; 9:15
8 [a]Heb. 9:4
10 [1]Lit., *for preserving* [2]Lit., *sons of rebellion* [a]Num. 17:4 [b]Deut. 9:7, 24
12 [a]Is. 6:5
13 [a]Num. 1:51
1 [1]Lit., *of the sanctuary* [2]Lit., *of your priesthood* [a]Ex. 28:38; Lev. 10:17; 22:16
2 [a]Num. 3:5-10
3 [a]Num. 4:15-20 [b]Num. 1:51; 18:7
4 [1]Lit., *stranger*

ligations of the altar, [a]that there may no longer be wrath on the sons of Israel.

6"And behold, I Myself have taken your [1]fellow-Levites from among the sons of Israel; they are [a]a gift to you, [2]dedicated to the LORD, to perform the service for the tent of meeting.

7"But you and your sons with you shall [a]attend to your priesthood for everything concerning the altar and inside the veil, and you are to perform service. I am giving you the priesthood as [b]a [1]bestowed service, but [c]the [2]outsider who comes near shall be put to death."

The Priests' Portion

8 Then the LORD spoke to Aaron, "Now behold, I Myself have given you charge of My [1a]offerings, even all the holy gifts of the sons of Israel, I have given them to you as a portion, and to your sons as a perpetual allotment.

9"This shall be yours from the most holy *gifts, reserved* from the fire; every offering of theirs, even [a]every grain offering and every [b]sin offering and every guilt offering, which they shall render to Me, shall be most holy for you and for your sons.

10"As the most holy *gifts* you shall eat it; every male shall eat it. It shall be holy to you.

11"This also is yours, [a]the offering of their gift, even all the wave offerings of the sons of Israel; I have [b]given them to you and to your sons and daughters with you, as a perpetual allotment. Everyone of your household who is clean may eat it.

12"[a]All the [1]best of the fresh oil and all the [1]best of the fresh wine and of the grain, the first fruits of those which they give to the LORD, I give them to you.

13"[a]The first ripe fruits of all that is in their land, which they bring to the LORD, shall be yours; everyone of your household who is clean may eat it.

14"[a]Every devoted thing in Israel shall be yours.

15"[1a]Every first issue of the womb of all flesh, whether man or animal, which they offer to the LORD, shall be yours; nevertheless the first-born of man you shall surely redeem, and the first-born of unclean animals you shall redeem.

16"And as to their redemption price, from a month old you shall redeem them, by your valuation, five [1]shekels in silver, according to

5 [a]Num. 16:46

6 [1]Lit., *brethren the* [2]Lit., *given* [a]Num. 3:9

7 [1]Lit., *service of gift* [2]Lit., *stranger* [a]Ex. 29:9 [b]Num. 18:20; Deut. 18:2; Matt. 10:8; 1 Pet. 5:2, 3 [c]Num. 1:51

8 [1]Lit., *heave offerings,* and so throughout the chap. [a]Lev. 7:28-34

9 [a]Lev. 2:1-16 [b]Lev. 6:30

11 [a]Num. 18:1; Deut. 18:3 [b]Lev. 22:1-16

12 [1]Lit., *fat* [a]Deut. 18:4; 32:14; Ps. 81:16; 147:14

13 [a]Ex. 22:29; 23:19; 34:26

14 [a]Lev. 27:1-33

15 [1]Lit., *Everything that opens* [a]Ex. 13:13, 15; Num. 3:46

16 [1]A shekel equals approx. one-half ounce.

18 [1]Lit., *flesh*

19 [1]Lit., *seed* [a]Num. 18:11 [b]2 Chr. 13:5

20 [a]Deut. 10:9; 12:12; 14:27, 29 [b]Deut. 18:2; Josh. 13:33; Ezek. 44:28

21 [a]Lev. 27:30-33

22 [a]Num. 1:51

23 [a]Num. 18:1 [b]Num. 18:20

26 [a]Num. 18:21 [b]Neh. 10:38

the [1]shekel of the sanctuary, which is twenty gerahs.

17"But the first-born of an ox or the first-born of a sheep or the first-born of a goat, you shall not redeem; they are holy. You shall sprinkle their blood on the altar and shall offer up their fat in smoke *as* an offering by fire, for a soothing aroma to the LORD.

18"And their [1]meat shall be yours; it shall be yours like the breast of a wave offering and like the right thigh.

19"[a]All the offerings of the holy *gifts,* which the sons of Israel offer to the LORD, I have given to you and your sons and your daughters with you, as a perpetual allotment. It is [b]an everlasting covenant of salt before the LORD to you and your [1]descendants with you."

20 Then the LORD said to Aaron, "[a]You shall have no inheritance in their land, nor own any portion among them; [b]I am your portion and your inheritance among the sons of Israel.

21"And to the sons of Levi, behold, I have given all the [a]tithe in Israel for an inheritance, in return for their service which they perform, the service of the tent of meeting.

22"And [a]the sons of Israel shall not come near the tent of meeting again, lest they bear sin and die.

23"Only the Levites shall perform the service of the tent of meeting, and they shall [a]bear their iniquity; it shall be a perpetual statute throughout your generations, and among the sons of Israel [b]they shall have no inheritance.

24"For the tithe of the sons of Israel, which they offer as an offering to the LORD, I have given to the Levites for an inheritance; therefore I have said concerning them, 'They shall have no inheritance among the sons of Israel.' "

25 Then the LORD spoke to Moses, saying,

26"Moreover, you shall speak to the Levites and say to them, 'When you take from the sons of Israel [a]the tithe which I have given you from them for your inheritance, then you shall present an offering from it to the LORD, a [b]tithe of the tithe.

27 'And your offering shall be reckoned to you as the grain from the threshing floor or the full produce from the wine vat.

28 'So you shall also present an offering to the LORD from your tithes, which you receive from the sons of

Israel; and from it you shall give the
LORD's offering to Aaron the priest.
29 'Out of all your gifts you shall
present every offering due to the
LORD, from all the [1]best of them,
[2]the sacred part from them.'
30"And you shall say to them,
'When you have [1]offered from it the
best of it, then *the rest* shall be reckoned to the Levites as the product of
the threshing floor, and as the product of the wine vat.
31 'And you may eat it anywhere,
you and your households, for it is
your compensation in return for
your service in the tent of meeting.
32 'And you shall bear no sin by
reason of it, when you have [1]offered
the [2]best of it. But you shall not
[a]profane the sacred gifts of the sons
of Israel, lest you die.' "

CHAPTER 19

Ordinance of the Red Heifer

THEN the LORD spoke to Moses
and Aaron, saying,
2"This is the statute of the law
which the LORD has commanded,
saying, 'Speak to the sons of Israel
that they bring you an [a]unblemished
red heifer in which is no defect, *and*
[b]on which a yoke has never [1]been
placed.
3 'And you shall give it to [a]Eleazar
the priest, and it shall [b]be brought
outside the camp and be slaughtered in his presence.
4 'Next Eleazar the priest shall
take some of its blood with his finger, and [a]sprinkle some of its blood
toward the front of the tent of meeting seven times.
5 'Then the heifer shall be burned
in his sight; its hide and its flesh and
its blood, with its refuse, shall be
burned.
6 'And the priest shall take [a]cedar
wood and hyssop and scarlet *material,* and cast it into the midst of the
[1]burning heifer.
7 'The priest [a]shall then wash his
clothes and bathe his [1]body in water, and afterward come into the
camp, but the priest shall be unclean until evening.
8 'The one who burns it shall also
wash his clothes in water and bathe
his [1]body in water, and shall be unclean until evening.
9 'Now a man who is clean shall
gather up the ashes of the heifer and
deposit them outside the camp in a
clean place, and [1]the congregation
of the sons of Israel shall keep it as
[a]water to remove impurity; it is [2]pu-
rification from sin.
10 'And the one who gathers the
ashes of the heifer [a]shall wash his
clothes and be unclean until evening; and it shall be a perpetual statute to the sons of Israel and to the
alien who sojourns among them.
11 '[a]The one who touches the
corpse of any [1]person shall be unclean for seven days.
12 'That one shall [a]purify himself
from uncleanness with [1]the water
on the third day and on the seventh
day, *and then* he shall be clean; but
if he does not purify himself on the
third day and on the seventh day, he
shall not be clean.
13 '[a]Anyone who touches a corpse,
the [1]body of a man who has died,
and does not purify himself, [b]defiles
the [2]tabernacle of the LORD; and
that person shall be cut off from Israel. Because the water for impurity
was not [3c]sprinkled on him, he shall
be unclean; his uncleanness is still
on him.
14 'This is the law when a man dies
in a tent: everyone who comes into
the tent and everyone who is in the
tent shall be unclean for seven days.
15 'And every open vessel, which
has no covering [1]tied down on it,
shall be unclean.
16 '[a]Also, anyone who in the open
field touches one who has been slain
with a sword or who has died *naturally,* or a human bone or a grave,
shall be unclean for seven days.
17 'Then for the unclean *person*
they shall take some of the [1]ashes of
the [2]burnt [3a]purification from sin
and [4]flowing water shall be [5]added
to them in a vessel.
18 'And a clean person shall take
hyssop and dip *it* in the water, and
sprinkle *it* on the tent and on all the
furnishings and on the persons who
were there, and on the one who
touched the bone or the one slain or
the one dying *naturally* or the
grave.
19 'Then the clean *person* [a]shall
sprinkle on the unclean on the third
day and on the seventh day; and on
the seventh day he shall purify him
from uncleanness, and he shall
wash his clothes and bathe *himself*
in water and shall be clean by evening.
20 'But the man who is unclean and
does not purify himself from uncleanness, that person shall be cut
off from the midst of the assembly,
because he has [a]defiled the sanctuary of the LORD; the water for impurity has not been sprinkled on him,
he is unclean.
21 'So it shall be a perpetual stat-

29 [1]Lit., *fat* [2]Lit., *its*

30 [1]Lit., *lifted*

32 [1]Lit., *lifted* [2]Lit., *fat* [a]Lev. 22:15, 16

2 [1]Lit., *come up* [a]Lev. 22:20-25 [b]Deut. 21:3

3 [a]Num. 3:4 [b]Lev. 4:11, 12, 21; Num. 19:9

4 [a]Lev. 4:6, 17

6 [1]Lit., *burning of the heifer* [a]Lev. 14:4

7 [1]Lit., *flesh* [a]Lev. 16:26, 28; 22:6

8 [1]Lit., *flesh*

9 [1]Lit., *it shall be to the congregation . . . Israel, for a guarding as water of impurity* [2]Or, *sin offering* [a]Num. 8:7

10 [a]Num. 19:7

11 [1]Lit., *soul of man* [a]Lev. 21:1, 11; Num. 5:2; 6:6; Acts 21:26, 27

12 [1]Lit., *it* [a]Num. 19:19

13 [1]Lit., *soul* [2]Lit., *dwelling place* [3]Or, *thrown* [a]Lev. 7:20, 21; 22:3-7 [b]Lev. 15:31; 20:3; Num. 19:20 [c]Num. 19:19

15 [1]Lit., *cord*

16 [a]Num. 31:19

17 [1]Lit., *dust* [2]Lit., *burning of the* [3]Or, *sin offering* [4]Lit., *living* [5]Lit., *put* [a]Num. 19:9

19 [a]Ezek. 36:25; Heb. 10:22

20 [a]Num. 19:13

ute for them. And he [a]who sprinkles
the water for impurity shall wash
his clothes, and he who touches the
water for impurity shall be unclean
until evening.
22 '[a]Furthermore, anything that
the unclean *person* touches shall be
unclean; and the person who
touches *it* shall be unclean until evening.' "

Chapter 20

Death of Miriam

THEN the sons of Israel, the whole
congregation, came to the [a]wilder-
ness of Zin in the first month; and
the people stayed at Kadesh. Now
Miriam died there and was buried
there.
2 [a]And there was no water for the
congregation; and they assembled
themselves against Moses and Aaron.
3 [a]The people thus contended
with Moses and spoke, saying, "[b]If
only we had perished [c]when our
brothers perished before the LORD!
4 "Why then have you brought the
LORD's assembly into this wilderness, for us and our beasts to die
[1]here?
5 "And why have you made us
come up from Egypt, to bring us in
to this wretched place? [a]It is not a
place of [1]grain or figs or vines or
pomegranates, nor is there water to
drink."
6 Then Moses and Aaron came in
from the presence of the assembly
to the doorway of the tent of meeting, and fell on their faces. Then the
glory of the LORD appeared to them;
7 and the LORD spoke to Moses,
saying,

The Water of Meribah

8 "Take [a]the rod; and you and
your brother Aaron assemble the
congregation and speak to the rock
before their eyes, that it may yield
its water. You shall thus bring forth
water for them out of the rock and
let the congregation and their beasts
drink."
9 So Moses took the rod from before the LORD, just as He had commanded him;
10 and Moses and Aaron gathered
the assembly before the rock. And
he said to them, "Listen now, you
rebels; shall we bring forth water for
you out of this rock?"
11 Then Moses lifted up his hand
and struck the rock twice with his
rod; and [a]water came forth abun-

21 [a]Num. 19:7
22 [a]Lev. 5:2, 3; 7:21; 22:5, 6
1 [a]Num. 13:21; 27:14; 33:36
2 [a]Ex. 17:1
3 [a]Ex. 17:2 [b]Num. 14:2, 3 [c]Num. 16:31-35
4 [1]Lit., *there*
5 [1]Lit., *seed* [a]Num. 16:14
8 [a]Ex. 4:17, 20; 17:5, 6
11 [a]Ps. 78:16; Is. 48:21; 1 Cor. 10:4
12 [a]Num. 20:24; 27:14; Deut. 1:37; 3:26, 27
13 [1]I.e., Contention [2]Or, *where* [a]Ex. 17:7
14 [a]Gen. 36:31-39; Deut. 2:4 [b]Josh. 2:9, 10; 9:9, 10, 24
16 [a]Ex. 14:19
18 [1]Lit., *me* [a]Num. 24:18
19 [1]Lit., *give* [2]Or, *no great thing* [a]Ex. 12:38
20 [1]Lit., *people*
21 [a]Judg. 11:17 [b]Deut. 2:8
22 [a]Num. 20:1, 14
23 [a]Num. 33:37
24 [a]Gen. 25:8 [b]Num. 20:5, 10

dantly, and the congregation and
their beasts drank.
12 But the LORD said to Moses and
Aaron, "[a]Because you have not believed Me, to treat Me as holy in the
sight of the sons of Israel, therefore
you shall not bring this assembly
into the land which I have given
them."
13 Those *were* the waters of
[1a]Meribah, [2]because the sons of Israel contended with the LORD, and
He proved Himself holy among
them.
14 From Kadesh Moses then sent
messengers to [a]the king of Edom:
"Thus your brother Israel has said,
'You [b]know all the hardship that has
befallen us;
15 that our fathers went down to
Egypt, and we stayed in Egypt a
long time, and the Egyptians treated
us and our fathers badly.
16 'But when we cried out to the
LORD, He heard our voice and sent
[a]an angel and brought us out from
Egypt; now behold, we are at Kadesh, a town on the edge of your
territory.
17 'Please let us pass through your
land. We shall not pass through field
or through vineyard; we shall not
even drink water from a well. We
shall go along the king's highway,
not turning to the right or left, until
we pass through your territory.' "
18 [a]Edom, however, said to him,
"You shall not pass through [1]us, lest
I come out with the sword against
you."
19 Again, the sons of Israel said to
him, "We shall go up by the highway, and if I and [a]my livestock do
drink any of your water, then I will
[1]pay its price. Let me only pass
through on my feet, [2]nothing *else*."
20 But he said, "You shall not pass
through." And Edom came out
against him with a heavy [1]force, and
with a strong hand.
21 [a]Thus Edom refused to allow Israel to pass through his territory;
[b]so Israel turned away from him.
22 Now when they set out from
[a]Kadesh, the sons of Israel, the
whole congregation, came to Mount
Hor.
23 Then the LORD spoke to Moses
and Aaron at [a]Mount Hor by the
border of the land of Edom, saying,

The Death of Aaron

24 "Aaron shall be [a]gathered to his
people; for he shall not enter the
land which I have given to the sons
of Israel, because [b]you rebelled

against My [1]command at the waters
of Meribah.
25"Take Aaron and his son [a]Elea-
zar, and bring them up to Mount
Hor;
26 and strip Aaron of his garments
and put them on his son Eleazar. So
Aaron will be [a]gathered *to his people,* and will die there."
27 So Moses did just as the LORD
had commanded, and they went up
to Mount Hor in the sight of all the
congregation.
28 And after Moses had stripped
Aaron of his garments and put them
on his son Eleazar, [a]Aaron died
there on the mountain top. Then
Moses and Eleazar came down from
the mountain.
29 And when all the congregation
saw that Aaron had died, all the
house of Israel wept for Aaron
thirty days.

CHAPTER 21

Arad Conquered

WHEN the Canaanite, the king of
[a]Arad, who lived in the [1]Negev,
heard that Israel was coming by the
way of [2]Atharim; then he fought
against Israel, and took some of
them captive.
2 So Israel made a vow to the
LORD, and said, "If Thou wilt indeed
deliver this people into my hand,
then I will [1]utterly destroy their
cities."
3 And the LORD heard the voice
of Israel, and delivered up the Canaanites; then they [1]utterly destroyed them and their cities. Thus
the name of the place was called
[2a]Hormah.
4 Then they set out from Mount
Hor by the way of the [1]Red Sea, to
[a]go around the land of Edom; and
the [2]people became impatient because of the journey.
5 And the people spoke against
God and Moses, "[a]Why have you
brought us up out of Egypt to die in
the wilderness? For there is no [1]food
and no water, and [2b]we loathe this
miserable food."

The Bronze Serpent

6 [a]And the LORD sent fiery serpents among the people and [b]they
bit the people, so that [c]many people
of Israel died.
7 [a]So the people came to Moses
and said, "We have sinned, because
we have spoken against the LORD
and you; intercede with the LORD,
that He may remove the serpents
from us." And Moses interceded for
the people.
8 Then the LORD said to Moses,
"[1]Make a [a]fiery *serpent,* and set it on
a standard; and it shall come about,
that everyone who is bitten, when
he looks at it, he shall live."
9 And Moses made a [a]bronze serpent and set it on the standard; and
it came about, that if a serpent bit
any man, when he looked to the
bronze serpent, he lived.
10 [a]Now the sons of Israel moved
out and camped in Oboth.
11 And they journeyed from
Oboth, and camped at Iyeabarim, in
the wilderness which is opposite
Moab, to the [1]east.
12 [a]From there they set out and
camped in [1]Wadi Zered.
13 From there they journeyed and
camped on the other side of the Arnon, which is in the wilderness that
comes out of the border of the Amorites, for the Arnon is the border of
Moab, between Moab and the Amorites.
14 Therefore it is said in the Book
of the Wars of the LORD,
"Waheb in Suphah,
And the wadis of the Arnon,
15 And the slope of the wadis
That extends to the site of [a]Ar,
And leans to the border of
Moab."
16 [a]And from there *they continued*
to [1]Beer, that is the well where the
LORD said to Moses, "Assemble the
people, that I may give them water."
17 Then Israel sang this song:
"Spring up, O well! Sing to it!
18 "The well, which the leaders
sank,
Which the nobles of the people
dug,
With the scepter *and* with
their staffs."
And from the wilderness *they continued* to Mattanah,
19 and from Mattanah to Nahaliel,
and from Nahaliel to Bamoth,
20 and from Bamoth to the valley
that is in the land of Moab, at the top
of Pisgah which overlooks the
[1]wasteland.

Two Victories

21 [a]Then Israel sent messengers to
Sihon, king of the Amorites, saying,
22"[a]Let me pass through your
land. We will not turn off into field
or vineyard; we will not drink water
from wells. We will go by the king's
highway until we have passed
through your border."
23 [a]But Sihon would not permit Israel to pass through his border. So

24 [1]Lit., *mouth*
25 [a]Num. 3:4
26 [a]Num. 20:24
28 [a]Num. 33:38; Deut. 10:6; 32:50
1 [1]I.e., South country [2]Or, *the spies* [a]Num. 33:40; Josh. 12:14; Judg. 1:16
2 [1]Lit., *devote to destruction*
3 [1]Lit., *devoted to destruction* [2]I.e., A devoted thing; or, Destruction [a]Num. 14:45
4 [1]Lit., *Sea of Reeds* [2]Lit., *soul of the people was short* [a]Deut. 2:8
5 [1]Lit., *bread* [2]Lit., *our soul* [a]Num. 14:2, 3 [b]Num. 11:6
6 [a]Deut. 8:15 [b]Jer. 8:17 [c]1 Cor. 10:9
7 [a]Num. 11:2
8 [1]Lit., *Make for yourself* [a]Is. 14:29; 30:6; John 3:14
9 [a]2 Kin. 18:4; John 3:14, 15
10 [a]Num. 33:43, 44
11 [1]Lit., *sunrise*
12 [1]I.e., a dry ravine except during rainy season [a]Num. 33:45
15 [a]Num. 21:28; Deut. 2:9, 18, 29
16 [1]I.e., A well [a]Num. 33:46-49
20 [1]Or, *Jeshimon*
21 [a]Deut. 2:26-37
22 [a]Num. 20:16, 17
23 [a]Num. 20:21

Sihon gathered all his people and went out against Israel in the wilderness, and came to [b]Jahaz and fought against Israel.

24 Then Israel [1]struck him with the edge of the sword, and took possession of his land from the Arnon to the Jabbok, as far as the sons of Ammon; for the [a]border of the sons of Ammon *was* [2]Jazer.

25 And Israel took all these cities and [a]Israel lived in all the cities of the Amorites, in Heshbon, and in all her [1]villages.

26 For Heshbon was the city of Sihon, king of the Amorites, who had fought against the former king of Moab and had taken all his land out of his hand, as far as the Arnon.

27 Therefore those who use proverbs say,

"Come to Heshbon! Let it be built!
So let the city of Sihon be established.

28 "[a]For a fire went forth from Heshbon,
A flame from the town of Sihon;
It devoured [b]Ar of Moab,
The [1c]dominant [2]heights of the Arnon.

29 "[a]Woe to you, O Moab!
You are ruined, O people of [b]Chemosh!
[c]He has given his sons as fugitives,
[d]And his daughters into captivity,
To an Amorite king, Sihon.

30 "But we have cast them down,
Heshbon is ruined as far as [a]Dibon,
Then we have laid waste even to Nophah,
Which *reaches* to Medeba."

31 Thus Israel lived in the land of the Amorites.

32 And Moses sent to spy out [a]Jazer, and they captured its villages and dispossessed the Amorites who *were* there.

33 [a]Then they turned and went up by the way of Bashan, and Og the king of Bashan went out [1]with all his people, for battle at Edrei.

34 But the LORD said to Moses, "Do not fear him, for I have given him into your hand, and all his people and his land; and you shall do to him as you did to Sihon, king of the Amorites, who lived at Heshbon."

35 So they [1]killed him and his sons and all his people, until there was no remnant left him; and they possessed his land.

23 [b]Deut. 2:32

24 [1]Lit., *smote,* so with Gk. and Latin [2]M.T. reads *strong* [a]Deut. 2:37

25 [1]Lit., *daughters* [a]Amos 2:10

28 [1]Lit., *lords of the* [2]Or, *Bamoth* [a]Jer. 48:45 [b]Num. 21:15 [c]Num. 22:41; Is. 15:2; 16:12

29 [a]Jer. 48:46 [b]Judg. 11:24; 1 Kin. 11:33; 2 Kin. 23:13 [c]Is. 15:5 [d]Is. 16:2

30 [a]Num. 32:3, 34

32 [a]Num. 32:1, 3, 35

33 [1]Lit., *he and* [a]Deut. 3:1-7

35 [1]Lit., *smote*

1 [a]Num. 33:48, 49

3 [a]Ex. 15:15

4 [1]Lit., *assembly* [a]Num. 25:15-18; 31:1-3

5 [1]I.e., Euphrates [a]Josh. 24:9 [b]Num. 23:7; Deut. 23:4

6 [1]Or, *numerous* [2]Lit., *smite* [a]Num. 22:17; 23:7, 8 [b]Num. 22:12; 24:9

7 [1]Lit., *spoke* [a]Num. 23:23; 24:1; Josh. 13:22

12 [a]Num. 23:8; 24:9

CHAPTER 22

Balak Sends for Balaam

[a]THEN the sons of Israel journeyed, and camped in the plains of Moab beyond the Jordan *opposite* Jericho.

2 Now Balak the son of Zippor saw all that Israel had done to the Amorites.

3 [a]So Moab was in great fear because of the people, for they were numerous; and Moab was in dread of the sons of Israel.

4 And Moab said to the elders of [a]Midian, "Now this [1]horde will lick up all that is around us, as the ox licks up the grass of the field." And Balak the son of Zippor was king of Moab at that time.

5 [a]So he sent messengers to Balaam the son of Beor, at [b]Pethor, which is near the [1]River, *in* the land of the sons of his people, to call him, saying, "Behold, a people came out of Egypt; behold, they cover the surface of the land, and they are living opposite me.

6 "[a]Now, therefore, please come, [b]curse this people for me since they are too [1]mighty for me; perhaps I may be able to [2]defeat them and drive them out of the land. For I know that he whom you bless is blessed, and he whom you curse is cursed."

7 So the elders of Moab and the elders of Midian departed with the *fees for* [a]divination in their hand; and they came to Balaam and [1]repeated Balak's words to him.

8 And he said to them, "Spend the night here, and I will bring word back to you as the LORD may speak to me." And the leaders of Moab stayed with Balaam.

9 Then God came to Balaam and said, "Who are these men with you?"

10 And Balaam said to God, "Balak the son of Zippor, king of Moab, has sent *word* to me,

11 'Behold, there is a people who came out of Egypt and they cover the surface of the land; now come, curse them for me; perhaps I may be able to fight against them, and drive them out.' "

12 And God said to Balaam, "Do not go with them; [a]you shall not curse the people; for they are blessed."

13 So Balaam arose in the morning and said to Balak's leaders, "Go back to your land, for the LORD has refused to let me go with you."

14 And the leaders of Moab arose and went to Balak, and said, "Balaam refused to come with us."

15 Then Balak again sent leaders, more numerous and more distinguished than [1]the former.

16 And they came to Balaam and said to him, "Thus says Balak the son of Zippor, 'Let nothing, I beg you, hinder you from coming to me;

17 for I will indeed honor you richly, and I will do whatever you say to me. [a]Please come then, curse this people for me.' "

18 And Balaam answered and said to the servants of Balak, "[a]Though Balak were to give me his house full of silver and gold, I could not do anything, either small or great, contrary to the [1]command of the LORD my God.

19 "And now please, you also stay here tonight, and I will find out what else the LORD will speak to me."

20 And God came to Balaam at night and said to him, "If the men have come to call you, rise up *and* go with them; but [a]only the word which I speak to you shall you do."

21 [a]So Balaam arose in the morning, and saddled his donkey, and went with the leaders of Moab.

The Angel and Balaam

22 But God was angry because he was going, and the angel of the LORD took his stand in the way as an adversary against him. Now he was riding on his donkey and his two servants were with him.

23 When the donkey saw the angel of the LORD standing in the way with his drawn sword in his hand, the donkey turned off from the way and went into the field; but Balaam struck the donkey to turn her back into the way.

24 Then the angel of the LORD stood in a narrow path of the vineyards, *with* a wall on this side and a wall on that side.

25 When the donkey saw the angel of the LORD, she pressed herself to the wall and pressed Balaam's foot against the wall, so he struck her again.

26 And the angel of the LORD went further, and stood in a narrow place where there was no way to turn to the right hand or the left.

27 When the donkey saw the angel of the LORD, she lay down under Balaam; so Balaam was angry and struck the donkey with his stick.

28 And [a]the LORD opened the mouth of the donkey, and she said to Balaam, "What have I done to you, that you have struck me these three times?"

29 Then Balaam said to the donkey, "Because you have made a mockery of me! If there had been a sword in my hand, I would have killed you by now."

30 And the donkey said to Balaam, "Am I not your donkey on which you have ridden all your life to this day? Have I ever been accustomed to do so to you?" And he said, "No."

31 Then the LORD opened the eyes of Balaam, and he saw [a]the angel of the LORD standing in the way with his drawn sword in his hand; and he bowed [1]all the way to the ground.

32 And the angel of the LORD said to him, "Why have you struck your donkey these three times? Behold, I have come out as an adversary, because your way was [1]contrary to me.

33 "But the donkey saw me and turned aside from me these three times. If she had not turned aside from me, I would surely have killed you just now, and let her live."

34 And Balaam said to the angel of the LORD, "[a]I have sinned, for I did not know that you were standing in the way against me. Now then, if it is displeasing to you, I will turn back."

35 But the angel of the LORD said to Balaam, "Go with the men, but [a]you shall speak only the word which I shall [1]tell you." So Balaam went along with the leaders of Balak.

36 When Balak heard that Balaam was coming, he went out to meet him at the city of Moab, which is on the Arnon border, [1]at the extreme end of the border.

37 Then Balak said to Balaam, "Did I not urgently send to you to call you? Why did you not come to me? Am I really unable to honor you?"

38 So Balaam said to Balak, "Behold, I have come now to you! [a]Am I able to speak anything at all? The word that God puts in my mouth, that I shall speak."

39 And Balaam went with Balak, and they came to Kiriath-huzoth.

40 And Balak sacrificed oxen and sheep, and sent *some* to Balaam and the leaders who were with him.

41 Then it came about in the morning that Balak took Balaam, and brought him up to [1a]the high places of Baal; and he saw from there [2a][b]portion of the people.

15 [1]Lit., *these*
17 [a]Num. 22:6
18 [1]Lit., *mouth* [a]Num. 22:38; 24:13
20 [a]Num. 22:35; 23:5, 12, 16, 26; 24:13
21 [a]2 Pet. 2:15
28 [a]2 Pet. 2:16
31 [1]Lit., *and prostrated himself to his face* [a]Josh. 5:13-15
32 [1]Lit., *reckless*
34 [a]Num. 14:40
35 [1]Or, *speak to* [a]Num. 22:20
36 [1]Lit., *which is at*
38 [a]Num. 22:18
41 [1]Or, *Bamoth-baal* [2]Lit., *the end of the camp* [a]Num. 21:28 [b]Num. 23:13

Chapter 23

The Prophecies of Balaam

THEN Balaam said to Balak,
"Build seven altars for me here, and
prepare seven bulls and seven rams
for me here."
2 And Balak did just as Balaam
had spoken, and Balak and Balaam
offered up a bull and a ram on each
altar.
3 Then Balaam said to Balak,
"Stand beside your burnt offering,
and I will go; perhaps the LORD will
come to me, and whatever He
shows me I will tell you." So he
went to a bare hill.
4 Now God met Balaam, and he
said to Him, "I have set up the seven
altars, and I have offered up a bull
and a ram on each altar."
5 Then the LORD [a]put a word in
Balaam's mouth and said, "Return
to Balak, and you shall speak thus."
6 So he returned to him, and behold, he was standing beside his
burnt offering, he and all the leaders
of Moab.
7 And he took up his [1]discourse
and said,

"From [a]Aram Balak has brought me,
Moab's king from the mountains of the East,
'[b]Come curse Jacob for me,
And come, denounce Israel!'

8 "[a]How shall I curse, whom God has not cursed?
And how can I denounce, whom the LORD has not denounced?

9 "As I see him from the top of the rocks,
And I look at him from the hills;
[a]Behold, a people *who* dwells apart,
And shall not be reckoned among the nations.

10 "[a]Who can count the dust of Jacob,
Or number the fourth part of Israel?
[b]Let [1]me die the death of the upright,
[c]And let my end be like his!"

11 Then Balak said to Balaam,
"What have you done to me? I took
you to curse my enemies, but behold, you have actually blessed
them!"
12 And he answered and said,
"Must I not be careful to speak
[a]what the LORD puts in my mouth?"
13 Then Balak said to him, "Please
come with me to another place from
where you may see them, although
you will only see the extreme end of
them, and will not see all of them;
and curse them for me from there."
14 So he took him to the field of
Zophim, to the top of Pisgah, and
built seven altars and offered a bull
and a ram on *each* altar.
15 And he said to Balak, "Stand
here beside your burnt offering,
while I myself meet *the LORD* yonder."
16 Then the LORD met Balaam and
[a]put a word in his mouth and said,
"Return to Balak, and thus you shall
speak."
17 And he came to him, and behold, he was standing beside his
burnt offering, and the leaders of
Moab with him. And Balak said to
him, "What has the LORD spoken?"
18 Then he took up his [1]discourse
and said,

"Arise, O Balak, and hear;
Give ear to me, O son of Zippor!

19 "[a]God is not a man, that He should lie,
Nor a son of man, that He should repent;
[b]Has He said, and will He not do it?
Or has He spoken, and will He not make it good?

20 "Behold, I have received *a command* to bless;
When He has blessed, then [a]I cannot revoke it.

21 "[a]He has not observed [1]misfortune in Jacob;
[b]Nor has He seen trouble in Israel;
[c]The LORD his God is with him,
[d]And the shout of a king is among them.

22 "[a]God brings them out of Egypt,
He is for them like the horns of the wild ox.

23 "[a]For there is no omen against Jacob,
Nor is there any divination against Israel;
At the proper time it shall be said to Jacob
And to Israel, what God has done.

24 "[a]Behold, a people rises like a lioness,
And as a lion it lifts itself;
It shall not lie down until it devours the prey,
And drinks the blood of the slain."

25 Then Balak said to Balaam, "Do
not curse them at all nor bless them
at all!"

5 [a]Num. 22:20
7 [1]Lit., *parable* [a]Num. 22:5; Deut. 23:4 [b]Num. 22:6
8 [a]Num. 22:12
9 [a]Deut. 32:8; 33:28
10 [1]Lit., *my soul* [a]Gen. 13:16; 28:14 [b]Is. 57:1 [c]Ps. 37:37
12 [a]Num. 22:20
16 [a]Num. 22:20
18 [1]Lit., *parable*
19 [a]1 Sam. 15:29 [b]Is. 40:8; 55:11
20 [a]Is. 43:13
21 [1]Or, *iniquity* [a]Num. 14:18, 19, 34; Ps. 32:2, 5 [b]Deut. 9:24; 32:5; Jer. 50:20 [c]Ex. 3:12; Deut. 31:23 [d]Deut. 33:5; Ps. 89:15-18
22 [a]Num. 24:8
23 [a]Num. 22:7; 24:1; Josh. 13:22
24 [a]Gen. 49:9; Nah. 2:11, 12

26 But Balaam answered and said
to Balak, "Did I not tell you,
'[1a]Whatever the LORD speaks, that I
must do'?"
27 Then Balak said to Balaam,
"Please come, I will take you to another place; perhaps it will be
[1]agreeable with God that you curse
them for me from there."
28 So Balak took Balaam to the
top of Peor which overlooks the
[1]wasteland.
29 And Balaam said to Balak,
"Build seven altars for me here and
prepare seven bulls and seven rams
for me here."
30 And Balak did just as Balaam
had said, and offered up a bull and a
ram on *each* altar.

CHAPTER 24

The Prophecy from Peor

WHEN Balaam saw that it
[1]pleased the LORD to bless Israel, he
did not go as at other times to [2]seek
[a]omens but he set his face toward
the [b]wilderness.
2 And Balaam lifted up his eyes
and saw Israel [1]camping tribe by
tribe; and [a]the Spirit of God came
upon him.
3 And he took up his [1]discourse
and said,

"[a]The oracle of Balaam the son of Beor,
And the oracle of the man whose eye is opened;
4 The oracle of him who [a]hears the [1]words of God,
Who sees the [b]vision of [2]the Almighty,
Falling down, yet having his eyes uncovered,
5 How fair are your tents, O Jacob,
Your dwellings, O Israel!
6 "Like [1]valleys that stretch out,
Like gardens beside the river,
Like [a]aloes planted by the LORD,
Like [b]cedars beside the waters.
7 "Water shall flow from his buckets,
And his seed *shall be* by many waters,
And his king shall be higher than [a]Agag,
[b]And his kingdom shall be exalted.
8 "[a]God brings him out of Egypt,
He is for him like the horns of the wild ox.
[b]He shall devour the nations *who are* his adversaries,
And shall crush their bones in pieces,
And shatter *them* with his [c]arrows.
9 "[a]He [1]couches, he lies down as a lion,
And as a [2]lion, who [3]dares rouse him?
[b]Blessed is everyone who blesses you,
And cursed is everyone who curses you."

10 Then Balak's anger burned
against Balaam, and he struck his
[1]hands together; and Balak said to
Balaam, "I called you to curse my
enemies, but behold, you have persisted in blessing them these three
times!
11 "Therefore, [1]flee to your place
now. I said I would honor you
greatly, but behold, the LORD has
held you back from honor."
12 And Balaam said to Balak,
"[a]Did I not tell your messengers
whom you had sent to me, saying,
13 'Though Balak were to give me
his house full of silver and gold, I
could not do anything contrary to
the [1]command of the LORD, either
good or bad, [a]of my own [2]accord.
[b]What the LORD speaks, that I will
speak'?
14 "And now behold, [a]I am going to
my people; come, *and* I will advise
you what this people will do to your
people in the [1]days to come."
15 And he took up his discourse
and said,

"[a]The oracle of Balaam the son of Beor,
And the oracle of the man whose eye is opened,
16 The oracle of him who hears the [1]words of God,
And knows the knowledge of the [2]Most High,
Who sees the vision of [3]the Almighty,
Falling down, yet having his eyes uncovered.
17 "I see him, but not now;
I behold him, but not near;
A star shall come forth from Jacob,
[a]And a scepter shall rise from Israel,
[b]And shall crush through the [1]forehead of Moab,
And [2]tear down all the sons of [3]Sheth.
18 "[a]And Edom shall be a possession,
[b]Seir, its enemies, also shall be a possession,
While Israel performs valiantly.

26 [1]Lit., *saying, 'Whatever* [a]Num. 22:18

27 [1]Lit., *right in the sight of God*

28 [1]Or, *Jeshimon*

1 [1]Lit., *was good in the eyes of* [2]Lit., *encounter* [a]Num. 22:7; 23:23 [b]Num. 23:28

2 [1]Lit., *dwelling* [a]Num. 11:26

3 [1]Lit., *parable,* and so throughout the chap. [a]Num. 24:15, 16

4 [1]Lit., *sayings* [2]Heb., *Shaddai* [a]Num. 22:20 [b]Gen. 15:1; Num. 12:6

6 [1]Or possibly, *palm trees* [a]Ps. 45:8 [b]Ps. 1:3

7 [a]Num. 24:20; 1 Sam. 15:8 [b]Ps. 145:11-13

8 [a]Num. 23:22 [b]Num. 23:24; Ps. 2:9 [c]Ps. 45:5

9 [1]Lit., *bows down* [2]Or, *lioness* [3]Lit., *shall* [a]Gen. 49:9; Num. 23:24 [b]Gen. 12:3; 27:29

10 [1]Lit., *palms*

11 [1]Lit., *flee for yourself*

12 [a]Num. 22:18

13 [1]Lit., *mouth* [2]Lit., *heart* [a]Num. 16:28 [b]Num. 22:20

14 [1]Lit., *end of the days* [a]Num. 31:8, 16; Josh. 13:22

15 [a]Num. 24:3, 4

16 [1]Lit., *sayings* [2]Heb., *Elyon* [3]Heb., *Shaddai*

17 [1]Lit., *corners* [2]Another reading is, *the crown of the head of* [3]I.e., Tumult [a]Gen. 49:10 [b]Num. 21:29; Is. 15:1-16:14

18 [a]Gen. 27:29 [b]Gen. 32:3

19 "[a]One from Jacob shall have dominion,
And shall destroy the remnant from the city."
20 And he looked at Amalek and
took up his discourse and said,
"Amalek was the first of the nations,
[a]But his end *shall be* [1]destruction."
21 And he looked at the [a]Kenite,
and took up his discourse and said,
"Your dwelling place is enduring,
And your nest is set in the cliff.
22 "Nevertheless Kain shall be consumed,
How long shall [a]Asshur [1]keep you captive?"
23 And he took up his discourse
and said,
"Alas, who can live except God has ordained it?
24 "But ships *shall come* from the coast of [a]Kittim,
And they shall afflict Asshur and shall afflict [b]Eber;
[c]So they also *shall come* to destruction."
25 Then Balaam arose and de-
parted and returned to [a]his place,
and Balak also went his way.

CHAPTER 25

The Sin of Peor

WHILE Israel remained at [a]Shit-
tim, the people began [b]to play the
harlot with the daughters of Moab.
2 For [a]they invited the people to
the sacrifices of their gods, and the
people ate and bowed down to their
gods.
3 So [a]Israel joined themselves to
[1]Baal of Peor, and the LORD was angry against Israel.
4 And the LORD said to Moses,
"Take all the leaders of the people
and execute them [1]in broad daylight
before the LORD, so that the fierce
anger of the LORD may turn away
from Israel."
5 So Moses said to the judges of
Israel, "Each of you slay his men
who have joined themselves to
[1]Baal of Peor."
6 Then behold, one of the sons of
Israel came and brought to his [1]rela-
tives a [a]Midianite woman, in the
sight of Moses and in the sight of all
the congregation of the sons of Israel, while they were weeping at the
doorway of the tent of meeting.
7 [a]When Phinehas the son of Eleazar, the son of Aaron the priest,
saw it, he arose from the midst of
the congregation, and took a spear
in his hand;
8 and he went after the man of
Israel into the [1]tent, and pierced
both of them through, the man of
Israel and the woman, through the
[2]body. So the plague on the sons of
Israel was checked.
9 [a]And those who died by the
plague were 24,000.

The Zeal of Phinehas

10 Then the LORD spoke to Moses,
saying,
11 "Phinehas the son of Eleazar, the
son of Aaron the priest, has turned
away My wrath from the sons of Israel, in that he was jealous with My
jealousy among them, so that I did
not destroy the sons of Israel in My
jealousy.
12 "Therefore say, '[a]Behold, I give
him My [b]covenant of peace;
13 and it shall be for him and his
[1]descendants after him, a covenant
of a [a]perpetual priesthood, because
he was jealous for his God, and
[b]made atonement for the sons of Israel.' "
14 Now the name of the [1]slain man
of Israel who was [1]slain with the
Midianite woman, was Zimri the
son of Salu, a leader of a father's
household among the Simeonites.
15 And the name of the Midianite
woman who was [1]slain was [a]Cozbi
the daughter of [b]Zur, [2]who was
head of the people of a father's
household in Midian.
16 Then the LORD spoke to Moses,
saying,
17 "[a]Be hostile to the Midianites
and strike them;
18 for they have been hostile to
you with their tricks, with which
they have deceived you in the affair
of Peor, and in the affair of Cozbi,
the daughter of the leader of Midian,
their sister who was slain on the day
of the plague because of Peor."

CHAPTER 26

1 *Census of a New Generation*

THEN it came about after the
[a]plague, [2]that the LORD spoke to
Moses and to Eleazar the son of
Aaron the priest, saying,
2 "[a]Take a [1]census of all the congregation of the sons of Israel from
twenty years old and upward, by
their fathers' households, whoever
is able to go out to war in Israel."
3 So Moses and Eleazar the priest
spoke with them in the plains of
Moab by the Jordan at Jericho, saying,

19 [a]Amos 9:11, 12
20 [1]Lit., *to destroying* [a]Num. 24:24
21 [a]Gen. 15:19
22 [1]Lit., *take* [a]Gen. 10:21, 22
24 [a]Gen. 10:4; Ezek. 27:6 [b]Gen. 10:21 [c]Num. 24:20
25 [a]Num. 24:14
1 [a]Num. 33:49; Josh. 2:1 [b]Num. 31:16; 1 Cor. 10:8; Rev. 2:14
2 [a]Ex. 34:15; Deut. 32:38
3 [1]Or, *Baal-peor* [a]Ps. 106:28, 29; Hos. 9:10
4 [1]Lit., *in front of the sun*
5 [1]Or, *Baal-peor*
6 [1]Lit., *brothers* [a]Num. 22:4
7 [a]Num. 16:46-48; Ps. 106:30
8 [1]Or, *inner rooms* [2]Or, *belly*
9 [a]Num. 14:37; 16:48-50; 31:16
12 [a]Ps. 106:31 [b]Is. 54:10; Ezek. 34:25; 37:26
13 [1]Lit., *seed* [a]Ex. 29:9 [b]Num. 16:46
14 [1]Lit., *smitten*
15 [1]Lit., *smitten* [2]Lit., *he* [a]Num. 25:18 [b]Num. 31:8
17 [a]Num. 25:1; 31:1-3
1 [1]In Heb. 25:19 [2]In Heb. 26:1 [a]Num. 25:9
2 [1]Lit., *sum* [a]Ex. 30:11-16; 38:25, 26; Num. 1:2

4 "*Take a census of the people*
from twenty years old and upward,
as the LORD has commanded
Moses."
Now the sons of Israel who came
out of the land of Egypt *were:*
5 Reuben, Israel's first-born, the
sons of Reuben: *of* Hanoch, the family of the Hanochites; of Pallu, the
family of the Palluites;
6 of Hezron, the family of the
Hezronites; of Carmi, the family of
the Carmites.
7 These are the families of the
Reubenites, and those who were
numbered of them were [a]43,730.
8 And the son of Pallu: Eliab.
9 And the sons of Eliab: Nemuel
and Dathan and Abiram. These are
the Dathan and Abiram who were
[a]called by the congregation, who
contended against Moses and
against Aaron in the company of
Korah, when they contended
against the LORD,
10 and [a]the earth opened its
mouth and swallowed them up
along with Korah, when that company died, [b]when the fire devoured
250 men, so that they became a
[1]warning.
11 [a]The sons of Korah, however,
did not die.
12 The sons of Simeon according
to their families: of [1]Nemuel, the
family of the Nemuelites; of Jamin,
the family of the Jaminites; of [2]Ja-
chin, the family of the Jachinites;
13 of [1]Zerah, the family of the Zerahites; of Shaul, the family of the
Shaulites.
14 These are the families of the
Simeonites, [a]22,200.
15 The sons of Gad according to
their families: of [1]Zephon, the family of the Zephonites; of Haggi, the
family of the Haggites; of Shuni, the
family of the Shunites;
16 of [1]Ozni, the family of the Oz-
nites; of Eri, the family of the Erites;
17 of [1]Arod, the family of the Aro-
dites; of Areli, the family of the Are-
lites.
18 These are the families of the
sons of Gad according to those who
were numbered of them, [a]40,500.
19 The sons of Judah *were* Er and
Onan, but Er and Onan died in the
land of Canaan.
20 And the sons of Judah according to their families were: of Shelah,
the family of the Shelanites; of Perez, the family of the Perezites; of Zerah, the family of the Zerahites.
21 And the sons of Perez were: of
Hezron, the family of the Hezronites; of Hamul, the family of the Ha-
mulites.
22 These are the families of Judah
according to those who were numbered of them, [a]76,500.
23 The sons of Issachar according
to their families: *of* Tola, the family
of the Tolaites; of Puvah, the family
of the Punites;
24 of [1]Jashub, the family of the
Jashubites; of Shimron, the family
of the Shimronites.
25 These are the families of Issachar according to those who were
numbered of them, [a]64,300.
26 The sons of Zebulun according
to their families: of Sered, the family of the Seredites; of Elon, the family of the Elonites; of Jahleel, the
family of the Jahleelites.
27 These are the families of the
Zebulunites according to those who
were numbered of them, [a]60,500.
28 The sons of Joseph according to
their families: Manasseh and Ephraim.
29 The sons of Manasseh: of Machir, the family of the Machirites;
and Machir [1]became the father of
Gilead: of Gilead, the family of the
Gileadites.
30 These are the sons of Gilead: *of*
[1]Iezer, the family of the Iezerites; of
Helek, the family of the Helekites;
31 and *of* Asriel, the family of the
Asrielites; and *of* Shechem, the family of the Shechemites;
32 and *of* Shemida, the family of
the Shemidaites; and *of* Hepher, the
family of the Hepherites.
33 Now Zelophehad the son of Hepher had no sons, but only daughters; and [a]the names of the daughters of Zelophehad were Mahlah,
Noah, Hoglah, Milcah and Tirzah.
34 These are the families of Manasseh; and those who were numbered of them were [a]52,700.
35 These are the sons of Ephraim
according to their families: of
Shuthelah, the family of the Shuthe-
laites; of [1]Becher, the family of the
Becherites; of Tahan, the family of
the Tahanites.
36 And these are the sons of
Shuthelah: of Eran, the family of the
Eranites.
37 These are the families of the
sons of Ephraim according to those
who were numbered of them,
[a]32,500. These are the sons of
Joseph according to their families.
38 The sons of Benjamin according to their families: of Bela, the
family of the Belaites; of Ashbel, the
family of the Ashbelites; of [1]Ahi-
ram, the family of the Ahiramites;

7 [a]Num. 1:21
9 [a]Num. 1:16; 16:2
10 [1]Lit., *sign* [a]Num. 16:32 [b]Num. 16:35, 38
11 [a]Num. 16:27, 33; Deut. 24:16
12 [1]In Gen. 46:10; Ex. 6:15, *Jemuel* [2]In 1 Chr. 4:24, *Jarib*
13 [1]In Gen. 46:10, *Zohar*
14 [a]Num. 1:23
15 [1]In Gen. 46:16, *Ziphion*
16 [1]In Gen. 46:16, *Ezbon*
17 [1]In Gen. 46:16, *Arodi*
18 [a]Num. 1:25
22 [a]Num. 1:27
24 [1]In Gen. 46:13, *Iob*
25 [a]Num. 1:29
27 [a]Num. 1:31
29 [1]Lit., *begot*
30 [1]In. Josh. 17:2, *Abiezer* cf. Judg. 6:11, 24, 34
33 [a]Num. 27:1
34 [a]Num. 1:35
35 [1]In 1 Chr. 7:20, *Bered*
37 [a]Num. 1:33
38 [1]In Gen. 46:21, *Ehi*; in 1 Chr. 8:1, *Aharah*

39 of [1]Shephupham, the family of
the Shuphamites; of [2]Hupham, the
family of the Huphamites.
40 And the sons of Bela were [1]Ard
and Naaman: *of Ard,* the family of
the Ardites; of Naaman, the family
of the Naamites.
41 These are the sons of Benjamin
according to their families; and
those who were numbered of them
were [a]45,600.
42 These are the sons of Dan according to their families: of [1]Shu-
ham, the family of the Shuhamites.
These are the families of Dan according to their families.
43 All the families of the Shuhamites, according to those who were
numbered of them, were [a]64,400.
44 The sons of Asher according to
their families: of Imnah, the family
of the Imnites; of Ishvi, the family of
the Ishvites; of Beriah, the family of
the Beriites.
45 Of the sons of Beriah: of Heber,
the family of the Heberites; of Malchiel, the family of the Malchielites.
46 And the name of the daughter
of Asher *was* Serah.
47 These are the families of the
sons of Asher according to those
who were numbered of them,
[a]53,400.
48 The sons of Naphtali according
to their families: of Jahzeel, the family of the Jahzeelites; of Guni, the
family of the Gunites;
49 of Jezer, the family of the Jeze-
rites; of Shillem, the family of the
Shillemites.
50 These are the families of Naphtali according to their families; and
those who were numbered of them
were [a]45,400.
51 These are those who were numbered of the sons of Israel, [a]601,730.
52 Then the LORD spoke to Moses,
saying,
53 "[1]Among these the land shall be
divided for an inheritance according
to the number of names.
54 "[a]To the larger *group* you shall
increase their inheritance, and to
the smaller *group* you shall diminish
their inheritance; each shall be giv-
en their inheritance according to
those who were numbered of them.
55 "But the land shall be [a]divided
by lot. They shall [1]receive their inheritance according to the names of
the tribes of their fathers.
56 "According to the selection by
lot, their inheritance shall be divided between the larger and the
smaller *groups.*"
57 And these are those who were
numbered of the Levites according
to their families: of Gershon, the
family of the Gershonites; of Kohath, the family of the Kohathites;
of Merari, the family of the Merarites.
58 These are the families of Levi:
the family of the Libnites, the family
of the Hebronites, the family of the
Mahlites, the family of the Mushites, the family of the Korahites.
[a]And Kohath [1]became the father of
Amram.
59 And the name of Amram's wife
was Jochebed, the daughter of Levi,
who was born to Levi in Egypt; and
she bore to Amram: Aaron and
Moses and their sister Miriam.
60 [a]And to Aaron were born Nadab and Abihu, Eleazar and Ithamar.
61 [a]But Nadab and Abihu died
when they offered strange fire before the LORD.
62 And those who were numbered
of them were [a]23,000, every male
from a month old and upward, for
[b]they were not numbered among
the sons of Israel [c]since no inheritance was given to them among the
sons of Israel.
63 These are those who were numbered by Moses and Eleazar the
priest, who numbered the sons of Israel in the plains of Moab by the Jordan at Jericho.
64 [a]But among these there was not
a man of those who were numbered
by Moses and Aaron the priest, who
numbered the sons of Israel in the
wilderness of Sinai.
65 For the LORD had said [1]of them,
"They shall surely die in the wilderness." And not a man was left of
them, except Caleb the son of Jephunneh, and Joshua the son of
Nun.

CHAPTER 27

A Law of Inheritance

THEN [a]the daughters of Zelophehad, the son of Hepher, the son of
Gilead, the son of Machir, the son of
Manasseh, of the families of Manasseh the son of Joseph, came near;
and these are [b]the names of his
daughters: Mahlah, Noah and Hoglah and Milcah and Tirzah.
2 And they stood before Moses
and before Eleazar the priest and
before the leaders and all the congregation, at the doorway of the tent
of meeting, saying,
3 "Our father died in the wilderness, yet he was not among the company of those who gathered them-

39 [1]In Gen. 46:21, *Muppim;* in 1 Chr. 7:12, *Shuppim* [2]In Gen. 46:21, *Muppim* and *Huppim*
40 [1]In 1 Chr. 8:3, *Addar*
41 [a]Num. 1:37
42 [1]In Gen. 46:23, *Hushim*
43 [a]Num. 1:39
47 [a]Num. 1:41
50 [a]Num. 1:43
51 [a]Ex. 12:37; 38:26; Num. 1:46; 11:21
53 [1]Lit., *To*
54 [a]Num. 33:54
55 [1]Lit., *inherit according to* [a]Num. 33:54; 34:13
58 [1]Lit., *begot* [a]Ex. 6:20
60 [a]Num. 3:2
61 [a]Lev. 10:1, 2; Num. 3:4
62 [a]Num. 3:39 [b]Num. 1:47 [c]Num. 18:23, 24
64 [a]Num. 14:29-35; Deut. 2:14-16; Heb. 3:17
65 [1]Or, *too*
1 [a]Num. 26:33; 36:1 [b]Num. 26:33

selves together against the LORD in
the company of Korah; but [a]he died
in his own sin, and [b]he had no sons.
4 "Why should the name of our father be withdrawn from among his
family because he had no son? Give
us a possession among our father's
brothers."
5 [a]And Moses brought their case
before the LORD.
6 Then the LORD spoke to Moses,
saying,
7 "[a]The daughters of Zelophehad
are right in *their* statements. You
shall surely give them a hereditary
possession among their father's
brothers, and you shall transfer the
inheritance of their father to them.
8 "Further, you shall speak to the
sons of Israel, saying, 'If a man dies
and has no son, then you shall transfer his inheritance to his daughter.
9 'And if he has no daughter, then
you shall give his inheritance to his
brothers.
10 'And if he has no brothers, then
you shall give his inheritance to his
father's brothers.
11 'And if his father has no brothers, then you shall give his inheritance to his nearest relative in his
own family, and he shall possess it;
and it shall be a statutory ordinance
to the sons of Israel, just as the LORD
commanded Moses.' "
12 [a]Then the LORD said to Moses,
"Go up to this [b]mountain of Abarim,
and see the land which I have given
to the sons of Israel.
13 "And when you have seen it, you
too [a]shall be gathered to your people, as Aaron your brother [1]was;
14 for in the wilderness of Zin,
during the strife of the congregation, [a]you rebelled against My [1]com-
mand [2]to treat Me as holy before
their eyes at the water." (These are
the waters of Meribah of Kadesh in
the wilderness of Zin.)

Joshua to Succeed Moses

15 Then Moses spoke to the LORD,
saying,
16 "[a]May the LORD, the God of the
spirits of all flesh, appoint a man
over the congregation,
17 who will go out [1]and come in
before them, and who will lead them
out and [2]bring them in, that the congregation of the LORD may not be
like sheep which have no shepherd."
18 So the LORD said to Moses,
"[1]Take Joshua the son of Nun, a
man [a]in whom is the Spirit, and [b]lay
your hand on him;
19 and have him stand before Eleazar the priest and before all the
congregation; and [a]commission him
in their sight.
20 "And you shall put some of your
[1]authority on him, in order that all
the congregation of the sons of Israel may obey *him*.
21 "Moreover, he shall stand before
Eleazar the priest, who shall inquire
for him [a]by the judgment of the
Urim before the LORD. At his [1]com-
mand they shall go out and at his
[1]command they shall come in, *both*
he and the sons of Israel with him,
even all the congregation."
22 And Moses did just as the LORD
commanded him; and he took
Joshua and set him before Eleazar
the priest, and before all the congregation.
23 Then he laid his hands on him
and commissioned him, just as the
LORD had spoken [1]through Moses.

CHAPTER 28

Laws for Offerings

THEN the LORD spoke to Moses,
saying,
2 "Command the sons of Israel
and say to them, 'You shall [1]be careful to present My offering, My [a]food
for My offerings by fire, of a soothing aroma to Me, at their appointed
time.'
3 "[a]And you shall say to them,
'This is the offering by fire which
you shall offer to the LORD; two
male lambs one year old without defect *as* a continual burnt offering every day.
4 'You shall offer the one lamb in
the morning, and the other lamb you
shall offer [1]at twilight.
5 'Also a tenth of an ephah of fine
flour for a grain offering, mixed with
a fourth of a hin of beaten oil.
6 'It is a continual burnt offering
which was ordained in Mount Sinai
as a soothing aroma, an offering by
fire to the LORD.
7 'Then the libation with it *shall*
be a fourth of a hin for each lamb, in
the holy place you shall pour out a
libation of strong drink to the LORD.
8 'And the other lamb you shall
offer [1]at twilight; as the grain offering of the morning and as its libation, you shall offer it, an offering by
fire, a soothing aroma to the LORD.
9 'Then on the sabbath day two
male lambs one year old without defect, and two-tenths *of an* [1]*ephah* of
fine flour mixed with oil as a grain
offering, and its libation.
10 'The burnt offering of every sab-

3 [a]Num. 26:64, 65 [b]Num. 26:33
5 [a]Num. 9:8; 27:21
7 [a]Num. 36:2; Josh. 17:4
12 [a]Deut. 32:48-52 [b]Num. 33:47, 48
13 [1]Lit., *was gathered* [a]Num. 31:2
14 [1]Lit., *mouth* [2]Lit., *for My sanctity* [a]Num. 20:12
16 [a]Num. 16:22
17 [1]Lit., *before them and who will* [2]Lit., *who will bring*
18 [1]Lit., *Take for yourself* [a]Num. 11:25-29; Deut. 34:9 [b]Num. 27:23
19 [a]Deut. 3:28; 31:3, 7, 8, 23
20 [1]Lit., *majesty*
21 [1]Lit., *mouth* [a]1 Sam. 28:6
23 [1]Lit., *by the hand of*
2 [1]Lit., *watch* [a]Lev. 3:11
3 [a]Ex. 29:38-42
4 [1]Lit., *between the two evenings*
8 [1]Lit., *between the two evenings*
9 [1]I.e., Approx. one bushel

bath is in addition to the [a]continual burnt offering and its libation.

11 'Then [a]at the beginning of each of your months you shall present a burnt offering to the LORD; two [1]bulls and one ram, seven male lambs one year old without defect,

12 [a]and three-tenths *of an* [1]*ephah* of fine flour for a grain offering, mixed with oil, for each bull; and two-tenths of fine flour for a grain offering, mixed with oil, for the one ram;

13 and a tenth *of an* [1]*ephah* of fine flour mixed with oil for a grain offering for each lamb, for a burnt offering of a soothing aroma, an offering by fire to the LORD.

14 'And their libations shall be half a hin of wine for a bull and a third of a hin for the ram and a fourth of a hin for a lamb; this is the burnt offering of each month throughout the months of the year.

15 'And one male goat for a sin offering to the LORD; it shall be offered with its libation in addition to the [a]continual burnt offering.

16 '[a]Then on the fourteenth day of the first month shall be the LORD's Passover.

17 'And on the fifteenth day of this month *shall be* a feast, unleavened bread *shall be* eaten for seven days.

18 'On the first day *shall be* a holy convocation; you shall do no laborious work.

19 'And you shall present an offering by fire, a burnt offering to the LORD: two [1]bulls and one ram and seven male lambs one year old, having them without defect.

20 'And for their grain offering, you shall offer fine flour mixed with oil; three-tenths *of an* [1]*ephah* for a bull and two-tenths for the ram.

21 'A tenth *of an* [1]*ephah* you shall offer for [2]each of the seven lambs,

22 and one male goat for a sin offering, to make atonement for you.

23 'You shall present these besides [a]the burnt offering of the morning, which is for a continual burnt offering.

24 'After this manner you shall present daily, for seven days, [a]the food of the offering by fire, of a soothing aroma to the LORD; it shall be presented with its libation in addition to the [b]continual burnt offering.

25 'And on the seventh day you shall have a holy convocation; [a]you shall do no laborious work.

26 'Also on [a]the day of the first fruits, when you present a new grain offering to the LORD in your *Feast of* Weeks, you shall have a holy convocation; [b]you shall do no laborious work.

27 'And you shall offer a burnt offering for a soothing aroma to the LORD, two young bulls, one ram, seven male lambs one year old,

28 and their grain offering, fine flour mixed with oil, three-tenths *of an* [1]*ephah* for each bull, two-tenths for the one ram,

29 a tenth for [1]each of the seven lambs,

30 one male goat to make atonement for you.

31 '[a]Besides the continual burnt offering and its grain offering, you shall present *them* with their libations. They shall be [1]without defect.

CHAPTER 29

Offerings of the Seventh Month

'[a]NOW in the seventh month, on the first day of the month, you shall also have a holy convocation; [b]you shall do no laborious work. It will be to you a day for blowing trumpets.

2 'And you shall offer a burnt offering as a soothing aroma to the LORD: one [1]bull, one ram, *and* seven male lambs one year old without defect;

3 also their grain offering, fine flour mixed with oil, three-tenths *of an* [1]*ephah* for the bull, two-tenths for the ram,

4 and one-tenth for [1]each of the seven lambs.

5 'And *offer* one male goat for a sin offering, to make atonement for you,

6 [a]besides the burnt offering of the new moon, and its grain offering, and the [b]continual burnt offering and its grain offering, and their libations, according to their ordinance, for a soothing aroma, an offering by fire to the LORD.

7 'Then on [a]the tenth day of this seventh month you shall have a holy convocation, and you shall humble yourselves; you shall not do any work.

8 'And you shall present a burnt offering to the LORD *as* a soothing aroma: one bull, one ram, seven male lambs one year old, having them without defect;

9 and their grain offering, fine flour mixed with oil, three-tenths *of an* [1]*ephah* for the bull, two-tenths for the one ram,

10 a tenth for each of the seven lambs;

11 one male goat for a sin offering,

---

10 [a]Num. 28:3

11 [1]Lit., *bulls of the herd* [a]Num. 10:10; Ezek. 46:6, 7

12 [1]I.e., Approx. one bushel [a]Num. 15:4-12

13 [1]I.e., Approx. one bushel

15 [a]Num. 28:3

16 [a]Ex. 12:14-20; Lev. 23:5-8; Deut. 16:1-8

19 [1]Or, *bulls of the herd*

20 [1]I.e., Approx. one bushel

21 [1]I.e., Approx. one bushel [2]Lit., *each lamb*

23 [a]Num. 28:3

24 [a]Lev. 3:11 [b]Num. 28:3

25 [a]Num. 28:18

26 [a]Ex. 23:16; 34:22; Lev. 23:15-21; Deut. 16:9-12 [b]Num. 28:18

28 [1]I.e., Approx. one bushel

29 [1]Lit., *each lamb*

31 [1]Lit., *without defect to you* [a]Num. 28:3

1 [a]Ex. 23:16; 34:22; Lev. 23:23-25 [b]Num. 28:26

2 [1]Or, *bull of a herd*, and so throughout the chap.

3 [1]I.e., Approx. one bushel

4 [1]Lit., *each lamb*, and so throughout the chap.

6 [a]Num. 28:27 [b]Num. 28:3

7 [a]Lev. 16:29-34; 23:26-32

9 [1]I.e., Approx. one bushel

besides the sin offering of atonement and [a]the continual burnt offering and its grain offering, and their libations.

12 'Then on [a]the fifteenth day of the seventh month you shall have a holy convocation; you [b]shall do no laborious work, and you shall observe a feast to the LORD for seven days.

13 'And you shall present a burnt offering, an offering by fire as a soothing aroma to the LORD: thirteen bulls, two rams, fourteen male lambs one year old, which are without defect,

14 and their grain offering, fine flour mixed with oil, three-tenths *of an* [1]*ephah* for [2]each of the thirteen bulls, two-tenths for [3]each of the two rams,

15 and a tenth for each of the fourteen lambs;

16 and one male goat for a sin offering, [a]besides the continual burnt offering, its grain offering and its libation.

17 'Then on [a]the second day: twelve bulls, two rams, fourteen male lambs one year old without defect;

18 and their grain offering and their libations for the bulls, for the rams and for the lambs, by their number according to the ordinance;

19 and one male goat for a sin offering, [a]besides the continual burnt offering and its grain offering, and their libations.

20 'Then on the third day: eleven bulls, two rams, fourteen male lambs one year old without defect;

21 and their grain offering and their libations for the bulls, for the rams and for the lambs, their number according to the ordinance;

22 and one male goat for a sin offering, besides the continual burnt offering and its grain offering and its libation.

23 'Then on the fourth day: ten bulls, two rams, fourteen male lambs one year old without defect;

24 their grain offering and their libations for the bulls, for the rams and for the lambs, by their number according to the ordinance;

25 and one male goat for a sin offering, besides the continual burnt offering, its grain offering and its libation.

26 'Then on the fifth day: nine bulls, two rams, fourteen male lambs one year old without defect;

27 and their grain offering and their libations for the bulls, for the rams and for the lambs, by their number according to the ordinance;

28 and one male goat for a sin offering, besides the continual burnt offering and its grain offering and its libation.

29 'Then on the sixth day: eight bulls, two rams, fourteen male lambs one year old without defect;

30 and their grain offering and their libations for the bulls, for the rams and for the lambs, by their number according to the ordinance;

31 and one male goat for a sin offering, besides the continual burnt offering, its grain offering and its libations.

32 'Then on the seventh day: seven bulls, two rams, fourteen male lambs one year old without defect;

33 and their grain offering and their libations for the bulls, for the rams and for the lambs, by their number according to the ordinance;

34 and one male goat for a sin offering, besides the continual burnt offering, its grain offering and its libation.

35 '[a]On the eighth day you shall have a solemn assembly; you shall do no laborious work.

36 'But you shall present a burnt offering, an offering by fire, as a soothing aroma to the LORD: one bull, one ram, seven male lambs one year old without defect;

37 their grain offering and their libations for the bull, for the ram and for the lambs, by their number according to the ordinance;

38 and one male goat for a sin offering, besides the continual burnt offering and its grain offering and its libation.

39 'You shall present these to the LORD at your [a]appointed times, besides your [1]votive offerings and your freewill offerings, for your burnt offerings and for your grain offerings and for your libations and for your peace offerings.' "

40 [1]And Moses spoke to the sons of Israel in accordance with all that the LORD had commanded Moses.

CHAPTER 30

The Law of Vows

THEN Moses spoke to the heads of the tribes of the sons of Israel, saying, "This is the word which the LORD has commanded.

2 "[a]If a man makes a vow to the LORD, or takes an oath to bind himself with a binding obligation, he shall not violate his word; he shall

11 [a]Num. 28:3
12 [a]Lev. 23:33-35 [b]Num. 29:1
14 [1]I.e., Approx. one bushel [2]Lit., *each bull* [3]Lit., *each ram*
16 [a]Num. 28:3
17 [a]Lev. 23:36
19 [a]Num. 28:8
35 [a]Lev. 23:36
39 [1]Lit., *vows* [a]Lev. 23:2
40 [1]Chap. 30:1 in Heb.
2 [a]Deut. 23:21-23; Matt. 5:33

do according to all that proceeds out
of his mouth.
3"Also if a woman makes a vow
to the LORD, and binds herself by an
obligation in her father's house in
her youth,
4 and her father hears her vow
and her obligation by which she has
bound herself, and her father [1]says
nothing to her, then all her vows
shall stand, and every obligation by
which she has bound herself shall
stand.
5"But if her father should forbid
her on the day he hears *of it,* none of
her vows or her obligations by
which she has bound herself shall
stand; and the LORD will forgive her
because her father had forbidden
her.
6"However, if she should [1]marry
while [2]under her vows or the rash
statement of her lips by which she
has bound herself,
7 and her husband hears of it and
says nothing to her on the day he
hears *it,* then her vows shall stand
and her obligations by which she
has bound herself shall stand.
8"But if on the day her husband
hears *of it,* he forbids her, then he
shall annul her vow which [1]she is
under and the rash statement of her
lips by which she has bound herself;
and the LORD will forgive her.
9"But the vow of a widow or of a
divorced woman, everything by
which she has bound herself, shall
stand against her.
10"However, if she vowed in her
husband's house, or bound herself
by an obligation with an oath,
11 and her husband heard *it,* but
said nothing to her *and* did not forbid her, then all her vows shall
stand, and every obligation by
which she bound herself shall stand.
12"But if her husband indeed annuls them on the day he hears *them,*
then whatever proceeds out of her
lips concerning her vows or concerning the obligation of herself,
shall not stand; her husband has annulled them, and the LORD will forgive her.
13"Every vow and every binding
oath to humble herself, her husband
may confirm it or her husband may
annul it.
14"But if her husband indeed says
nothing to her from day to day, then
he confirms all her vows or all her
obligations which are on her; he has
confirmed them, because he said
nothing to her on the day he heard
them.
15"But if he indeed annuls them af-

4 [1]Lit., *is silent to her,* and so throughout the chap.

6 [1]Lit., *be to a husband* [2]Lit., *her vows are on her*

8 [1]Lit., *is on her*

2 [a]Num. 25:1, 16, 17 [b]Num. 20:24, 26; 27:13

3 [1]Lit., *be* [a]Lev. 26:25

5 [1]Lit., *delivered*

6 [a]Num. 14:44 [b]Num. 10:8, 9

8 [a]Josh. 13:21 [b]Num. 25:15 [c]Num. 31:16; Josh. 13:22

ter he has heard them, then he shall
bear her guilt."
16 These are the statutes which
the LORD commanded Moses, *as* between a man and his wife, *and as*
between a father and his daughter,
while she is in her youth in her father's house.

CHAPTER 31

The Slaughter of Midian

THEN the LORD spoke to Moses,
saying,
2"[a]Take full vengeance for the
sons of Israel on the Midianites; afterward you will be [b]gathered to
your people."
3 And Moses spoke to the people,
saying, "Arm men from among you
for the war, that they may [1]go
against Midian, to execute [a]the
LORD's vengeance on Midian.
4"A thousand from each tribe of
all the tribes of Israel you shall send
to the war."
5 So there were [1]furnished from
the thousands of Israel, a thousand
from each tribe, twelve thousand
armed for war.
6 And Moses sent them, a thousand from each tribe, to the war,
and Phinehas the son of Eleazar the
priest, to the war with them, [a]and
the holy vessels and [b]the trumpets
for the alarm in his hand.
7 So they made war against Midian, just as the LORD had commanded Moses, and they killed every male.
8 And they killed the kings of
Midian along with the *rest of* their
slain: [a]Evi and Rekem and [b]Zur and
Hur and Reba, the five kings of Midian; [c]they also killed Balaam the son
of Beor with the sword.
9 And the sons of Israel captured
the women of Midian and their little
ones; and all their cattle and all their
flocks and all their goods, they plundered.
10 Then they burned all their cities
where they lived and all their camps
with fire.
11 And they took all the spoil and
all the prey, both of man and of
beast.
12 And they brought the captives
and the prey and the spoil to Moses,
and to Eleazar the priest and to the
congregation of the sons of Israel, to
the camp at the plains of Moab,
which are by the Jordan opposite
Jericho.
13 And Moses and Eleazar the
priest and all the leaders of the con-

gregation went out to meet them outside the camp.

14 And Moses was angry with the officers of the army, the captains of thousands and the captains of hundreds, who had come from service in the war.

15 And Moses said to them, "Have you [1]spared all the women?

16 "[a]Behold, these [1]caused the sons of Israel, through the [2]counsel of [b]Balaam, to [3]trespass against the LORD in the matter of Peor, so the plague was among the congregation of the LORD.

17 "[a]Now therefore kill every male among the little ones, and kill every woman who has known man [1]intimately.

18 "But all the [1]girls who have not known man [2]intimately, [3]spare for yourselves.

19 "[a]And you, camp outside the camp seven days; whoever has killed any person, and whoever has touched any slain, purify yourselves, you and your captives, on the third day and on the seventh day.

20 "And you shall purify for yourselves every garment and every article of [1]leather and all the work of goats' *hair,* and all articles of wood."

21 Then Eleazar the priest said to the men of war who had gone to battle, "This is the statute of the law which the LORD has commanded Moses:

22 only the gold and the silver, the bronze, the iron, the tin and the lead,

23 everything that can stand the fire, you shall pass through the fire, and it shall be clean, but it shall be purified with water for impurity. But whatever cannot stand the fire you shall pass through the water.

24 "And you shall wash your clothes on the seventh day and be clean, and afterward you may enter the camp."

Division of the Booty

25 Then the LORD spoke to Moses, saying,

26 "You and Eleazar the priest and the heads of the fathers' *households* of the congregation, take a count of the booty [1]that was captured, both of man and of animal;

27 and divide the booty between the warriors who went out to battle and all the congregation.

28 "[a]And levy a tax for the LORD from the men of war who went out to battle, one [1]in five hundred of the

15 [1]Lit., *let . . . live*

16 [1]Lit., *were to* [2]Lit., *word* [3]Possibly, *defect from the Lord* [a]Num. 25:1-9 [b]Num. 31:8

17 [1]Lit., *by lying with a man* [a]Deut. 7:2; 20:16-18

18 [1]Lit., *female children* [2]Lit., *by lying with a man* [3]Lit., *keep alive*

19 [a]Num. 19:11-22

20 [1]Or, *skin*

26 [1]Lit., *of captives*

28 [1]Lit., *soul from* [a]Num. 18:21-30

29 [1]Lit., *heave offering,* and so throughout the chap.

32 [1]Lit., *people*

35 [1]Lit., *by lying with man*

42 [1]Or, *divided*

persons and of the cattle and of the donkeys and of the sheep;

29 take it from their half and give it to Eleazar the priest, as an [1]offering to the LORD.

30 "And from the sons of Israel's half, you shall take one drawn out of every fifty of the persons, of the cattle, of the donkeys and of the sheep, from all the animals, and give them to the Levites who keep charge of the tabernacle of the LORD."

31 And Moses and Eleazar the priest did just as the LORD had commanded Moses.

32 Now the booty that remained from the spoil which the [1]men of war had plundered was 675,000 sheep,

33 and 72,000 cattle,

34 and 61,000 donkeys,

35 and of human beings, of the women who had not known man [1]intimately, all the persons were 32,000.

36 And the half, the portion of those who went out to war, was *as follows:* the number of sheep was 337,500,

37 and the LORD's levy of the sheep was 675,

38 and the cattle were 36,000, from which the LORD's levy was 72.

39 And the donkeys were 30,500, from which the LORD's levy was 61.

40 And the human beings were 16,000, from whom the LORD's levy was 32 persons.

41 And Moses gave the levy *which was* the LORD's offering to Eleazar the priest, just as the LORD had commanded Moses.

42 As for the sons of Israel's half, which Moses [1]separated from the men who had gone to war—

43 now the congregation's half was 337,500 sheep,

44 and 36,000 cattle,

45 and 30,500 donkeys,

46 and the human beings were 16,000—

47 and from the sons of Israel's half, Moses took one drawn out of every fifty, both of man and of animals, and gave them to the Levites, who kept charge of the tabernacle of the LORD, just as the LORD had commanded Moses.

48 Then the officers who were over the thousands of the army, the captains of thousands and the captains of hundreds, approached Moses;

49 and they said to Moses, "Your servants have taken a census of men of war who are in our charge, and no man of us is missing.

50 "So we have brought as an offer-

ing to the LORD what each man found, articles of gold, armlets and bracelets, signet rings, earrings and necklaces, to make atonement for ourselves before the LORD."

51 And Moses and Eleazar the priest took the gold from them, all kinds of wrought articles.

52 And all the gold of the offering which they offered up to the LORD, from the captains of thousands and the captains of hundreds, was 16,750 shekels.

53 [a]The men of war had taken booty, every man for himself.

54 So Moses and Eleazar the priest took the gold from the captains of thousands and of hundreds, and brought it to the tent of meeting as a memorial for the sons of Israel before the LORD.

CHAPTER 32

Reuben and Gad Settle in Gilead

NOW the sons of Reuben and the sons of Gad had an [a]exceedingly large number of livestock. So when they saw the land of [b]Jazer and the land of Gilead, that [1]it was indeed a place suitable for livestock,

2 the sons of Gad and the sons of Reuben came and spoke to Moses and to Eleazar the priest and to the leaders of the congregation, saying,

3 "[a]Ataroth, Dibon, Jazer, Nimrah, Heshbon, Elealeh, Sebam, Nebo and Beon,

4 the land which the LORD [1]conquered before the congregation of Israel, is a land for livestock; and your servants have livestock."

5 And they said, "If we have found favor in your sight, let this land be given to your servants as a possession; do not take us across the Jordan."

6 But Moses said to the sons of Gad and to the sons of Reuben, "Shall your brothers go to war while you yourselves sit here?

7 "[a]Now why [1]are you discouraging the sons of Israel from crossing over into the land which the LORD has given them?

8 "[1]This is what your fathers did when I sent them from [a]Kadesh-barnea to see the land.

9 "For when they went up to the [1]valley of Eshcol and saw the land, they [2]discouraged the sons of Israel so that they did not go into the land which the LORD had given them.

10 "So the LORD's anger burned in that day, and He swore, saying,

11 '[a]None of the men who came up from Egypt, from twenty years old and upward, shall see the land which I swore to Abraham, to Isaac and to Jacob; for they did not follow Me fully,

12 except Caleb the son of Jephunneh the Kenizzite and Joshua the son of Nun, for they have followed the LORD fully.'

13 "[a]So the LORD's anger burned against Israel, and He made them wander in the wilderness forty years, until the entire generation of those who had done evil in the sight of the LORD was destroyed.

14 "Now behold, you have risen up in your fathers' place, a brood of sinful men, to add still more to the burning anger of the LORD against Israel.

15 "For if you turn away from following Him, He will once more abandon them in the wilderness; and you will destroy all these people."

16 Then they came near to him and said, "We will build here sheepfolds for our livestock and cities for our little ones;

17 [a]but we ourselves will be armed ready *to go* before the sons of Israel, until we have brought them to their place, while our little ones live in the fortified cities because of the inhabitants of the land.

18 "[a]We will not return to our homes until every one of the sons of Israel has possessed his inheritance.

19 "For we will not have an inheritance with them on the other side of the Jordan and beyond, because our inheritance has fallen to us on this side of Jordan toward the east."

20 [a]So Moses said to them, "If you will do [1]this, if you will arm yourselves before the LORD for the war,

21 and all of you armed men cross over the Jordan before the LORD until He has driven His enemies out from before Him,

22 [a]and the land is subdued before the LORD, then afterward you shall return and be free of obligation toward the LORD and toward Israel, and this land shall be yours for a possession before the LORD.

23 "But if you will not do so, behold, you have sinned against the LORD, and be sure your sin will find you out.

24 "Build yourselves cities for your little ones, and sheepfolds for your sheep; and [a]do [1]what you have promised."

25 And the sons of Gad and the sons of Reuben spoke to Moses, say-

53 [a]Num. 31:32

1 [1]Lit., *behold, the place, a place for* [a]Ex. 12:38 [b]Num. 21:32

3 [a]Num. 32:34-38

4 [1]Lit., *smote*

7 [1]Lit., *restraining the heart* [a]Num. 13:27-14:4

8 [1]Lit., *Thus your fathers* [a]Num. 13:3, 26; Deut. 1:19-25

9 [1]Or, *wadi* [2]Lit., *restrained the heart*

11 [a]Num. 14:28-30

13 [a]Num. 14:33-35

17 [a]Josh. 4:12, 13

18 [a]Josh. 22:1-4

20 [1]Lit., *this thing* [a]Deut. 3:18

22 [a]Deut. 3:20

24 [1]Lit., *that which has come out of your mouth* [a]Num. 30:2

ing, "Your servants will do just as my lord commands.

26 "Our little ones, our wives, our livestock and all our cattle shall [1]remain there in the cities of Gilead;

27 while your servants, everyone who is armed for war, will cross over in the presence of the LORD to battle, just as my lord says."

28 So Moses gave command concerning them to Eleazar the priest, and to Joshua the son of Nun, and to the heads of the fathers' *households* of the tribes of the sons of Israel.

29 And Moses said to them, "If the sons of Gad and the sons of Reuben, everyone who is armed for battle, will cross with you over the Jordan in the presence of the LORD, and the land will be subdued before you, then you shall give them the land of Gilead for a possession;

30 but if they will not cross over with you armed, they shall have possessions among you in the land of Canaan."

31 And the sons of Gad and the sons of Reuben answered, saying, "As the LORD has said to your servants, so we will do.

32 "We ourselves will cross over armed in the presence of the LORD into the land of Canaan, and the possession of our inheritance *shall remain* with us across the Jordan."

33 [a]So Moses gave to them, to the sons of Gad and to the sons of Reuben and to the half-tribe of Joseph's son Manasseh, the kingdom of Sihon, king of the Amorites and the kingdom of Og, the king of Bashan, the land with its cities with *their* [1]territories, the cities of the surrounding land.

34 And the sons of Gad built Dibon and Ataroth and Aroer,

35 and Atroth-shophan and Jazer and Jogbehah,

36 and Beth-nimrah and Beth-haran as fortified cities, and sheepfolds for sheep.

37 And the sons of Reuben built Heshbon and Elealeh and Kiriathaim,

38 and Nebo and Baal-meon—*their* names being changed—and Sibmah, and they gave *other* names to the cities which they built.

39 And the sons of Machir the son of Manasseh went to Gilead and took it, and dispossessed the Amorites who were in it.

40 So Moses gave Gilead to Machir the son of Manasseh, and he lived in it.

41 And Jair the son of Manasseh went and took its [1]towns, and called them [2a]Havvoth-jair.

42 And Nobah went and took Kenath and its villages, and called it Nobah after his own name.

CHAPTER 33

Review of the Journey from Egypt to Jordan

THESE are the journeys of the sons of Israel, by which they came out from the land of Egypt by their armies, under [a]the [1]leadership of Moses and Aaron.

2 And Moses recorded their starting places according to their journeys by the [1]command of the LORD, and these are their journeys according to their starting places.

3 [a]And they journeyed from Rameses in the first month, on the fifteenth day of the first month; on the [1]next day after the Passover the sons of Israel [b]started out [2]boldly in the sight of all the Egyptians,

4 while the Egyptians were burying all their first-born whom the LORD had struck down among them. The LORD had also executed judgments [a]on their gods.

5 Then the sons of Israel journeyed from Rameses, and camped in Succoth.

6 [a]And they journeyed from Succoth, and camped in Etham, which is on the edge of the wilderness.

7 [a]And they journeyed from Etham, and turned back to Pi-hahiroth, which faces Baal-zephon; and they camped before Migdol.

8 [a]And they journeyed [1]from before Hahiroth, and passed through the midst of the sea into the wilderness; and [b]they went three days' journey in the wilderness of Etham, and camped at Marah.

9 [a]And they journeyed from Marah, and came to Elim; and in Elim there were twelve springs of water and seventy palm trees; and they camped there.

10 And they journeyed from Elim, and camped by the [1]Red Sea.

11 And they journeyed from the [1]Red Sea, and camped in [a]the wilderness of Sin.

12 And they journeyed from the wilderness of Sin, and camped at Dophkah.

13 And they journeyed from Dophkah, and camped at Alush.

14 And they journeyed from Alush, and camped [a]at Rephidim; now it was there that the people had no water to drink.

15 And they journeyed from

---

26 [1]Lit., *be*

33 [1]Lit., *borders* [a]Deut. 3:8-17; Josh. 12:1-6

41 [1]Lit., *tent villages* [2]I.e., the towns of Jair [a]Deut. 3:14; Judg. 10:4

1 [1]Lit., *hand* [a]Ps. 77:20; 105:26; Mic. 6:4

2 [1]Lit., *mouth*

3 [1]Lit., *morrow* [2]Lit., *with a high hand* [a]Ex. 12:37 [b]Ex. 14:8

4 [a]Ex. 12:12

6 [a]Ex. 13:20

7 [a]Ex. 14:1, 2

8 [1]Many mss. read, *from Pi-hahiroth* [a]Ex. 14:22 [b]Ex. 15:22

9 [a]Ex. 15:27

10 [1]Lit., *Sea of Reeds*

11 [1]Lit., *Sea of Reeds* [a]Ex. 16:1

14 [a]Ex. 17:1

Rephidim, and camped in [a]the wilderness of Sinai.
16 And they journeyed from the
wilderness of Sinai, and camped at
[a]Kibroth-hattaavah.
17 And they journeyed from Kibroth-hattaavah, and camped at [a]Ha-
zeroth.
18 And they journeyed from Hazeroth, and camped at Rithmah.
19 And they journeyed from Rithmah, and camped at Rimmon-perez.
20 And they journeyed from Rimmon-perez, and camped at Libnah.
21 And they journeyed from Libnah, and camped at Rissah.
22 And they journeyed from Rissah, and camped in Kehelathah.
23 And they journeyed from Kehelathah, and camped at Mount Shepher.
24 And they journeyed from
Mount Shepher, and camped at Ha-
radah.
25 And they journeyed from Hara-
dah, and camped at Makheloth.
26 And they journeyed from Makheloth, and camped at Tahath.
27 And they journeyed from Tahath, and camped at Terah.
28 And they journeyed from Terah, and camped at Mithkah.
29 And they journeyed from Mithkah, and camped at Hashmonah.
30 And they journeyed from Hashmonah, and camped at [a]Moseroth.
31 And they journeyed from Mo-
seroth, and camped at Bene-jaakan.
32 And they journeyed from Bene-
jaakan, and camped at Hor-haggid-
gad.
33 And they journeyed from Hor-
haggidgad, and camped at [a]Jotba-
thah.
34 And they journeyed from Jotbathah, and camped at Abronah.
35 And they journeyed from Abronah, and camped at [a]Ezion-geber.
36 And they journeyed from
Ezion-geber, and camped in the wilderness of [a]Zin, that is, Kadesh.
37 And they journeyed from Kadesh, and camped at [a]Mount Hor,
[b]at the edge of the land of Edom.
38 [a]Then Aaron the priest went up
to Mount Hor at the [1]command of
the LORD, and died there, in the fortieth year after the sons of Israel had
come from the land of Egypt on the
first *day* in the fifth month.
39 And Aaron was one hundred
twenty-three years old when he died
on Mount Hor.
40 Now the Canaanite, the king of
[a]Arad [1]who lived in the [2]Negev in
the land of Canaan, heard of the
coming of the sons of Israel.
41 Then they journeyed from
Mount Hor, and camped at Zalmo-
nah.
42 And they journeyed from Zal-
monah, and camped at Punon.
43 And they journeyed from Punon, and camped at [a]Oboth.
44 And they journeyed from
Oboth, and camped at Iye-abarim,
at the border of Moab.
45 And they journeyed from Iyim,
and camped at Dibon-gad.
46 And they journeyed from Dibon-gad, and camped at Almon-dib-
lathaim.
47 And they journeyed from Al-
mon-diblathaim, and camped in the
mountains of [a]Abarim, before Nebo.
48 And they journeyed from the
mountains of Abarim, and [a]camped
in the plains of Moab by the Jordan
opposite Jericho.
49 And they camped by the Jordan, from Beth-jeshimoth as far as
[a]Abel-shittim in the plains of Moab.

Law of Possessing the Land

50 Then the LORD spoke to Moses
in the plains of Moab by the Jordan
opposite Jericho, saying,
51 "Speak to the sons of Israel and
say to them, 'When you cross over
the Jordan into the land of Canaan,
52 then you shall drive out all the
inhabitants of the land from before
you, and [a]destroy all their figured
stones, and destroy all their molten
images and demolish all their high
places;
53 [a]and you shall take possession
of the land and live in it, for I have
given the land to you to possess it.
54 '[a]And you shall inherit the land
by lot according to your families; to
the larger you shall give more inheritance, and to the smaller you
shall give less inheritance. Wherever the lot falls to anyone, that
shall be his. You shall inherit according to the tribes of your fathers.
55 'But if you do not drive out the
inhabitants of the land from before
you, then it shall come about that
those whom you let remain of them
will become [a]as pricks in your eyes
and as thorns in your sides, and they
shall trouble you in the land in
which you live.
56 'And it shall come about that as
I plan to do to them, so I will do to
you.' "

CHAPTER 34

Instruction for Apportioning Canaan

THEN the LORD spoke to Moses,
saying,

15 [a]Ex. 19:1
16 [a]Num. 11:34
17 [a]Num. 11:35
30 [a]Deut. 10:6
33 [a]Deut. 10:7
35 [a]Deut. 2:8
36 [a]Num. 20:1
37 [a]Num. 20:22 [b]Num. 20:16
38 [1]Lit., *mouth* [a]Num. 20:28
40 [1]Lit., *and he* [2]I.e., South country [a]Num. 21:1
43 [a]Num. 21:10, 11
47 [a]Num. 27:12
48 [a]Num. 22:1
49 [a]Num. 25:1
52 [a]Ex. 23:24; Lev. 26:1; Deut. 7:5; 12:3, 30; Ps. 106:34
53 [a]Deut. 11:31; 17:14; Josh. 21:43
54 [a]Num. 26:53-56
55 [a]Josh. 23:13

2 "Command the sons of Israel and say to them, 'When you enter the land of Canaan, this is the land that shall fall to you as an inheritance, *even the* land of Canaan according to its borders.

3 '[a]Your southern [1]sector shall [2]extend from the wilderness of Zin along the side of Edom, and your southern border shall [2]extend from the end of the Salt Sea [b]eastward.

4 'Then your border shall turn *direction* from the south to the ascent of Akrabbim, and [1]continue to Zin, and its [2]termination shall be to the south of Kadesh-barnea; and it shall [3]reach Hazaraddar, and [1]continue to Azmon.

5 'And the border shall turn *direction* from Azmon to the brook of Egypt, and its termination shall be at [a]the sea.

6 'As for the western border, you shall have the Great Sea, that is, *its* [1]coastline; this shall be your west border.

7 '[a]And this shall be your north border: you shall draw your *border* line from the Great Sea to Mount Hor.

8 'You shall draw a line from Mount Hor to [a]the [1]Lebo-hamath, and the termination of the border shall be at Zedad;

9 and the border shall proceed to Ziphron, and its termination shall be at Hazar-enan. This shall be your north border.

10 'For your eastern border you shall also draw a line from Hazar-enan to Shepham,

11 and the border shall go down from Shepham to [a]Riblah on the east side of Ain; and the border shall go down and reach to the [1]slope on the east side of the sea of [b]Chinnereth.

12 'And the border shall go down to the Jordan and its termination shall be at the Salt Sea. This shall be your land according to its borders all around.' "

13 So Moses commanded the sons of Israel, saying, "[a]This is the land that you are to apportion by lot among you as a possession, which the LORD has commanded to give to the nine and a half tribes.

14 "[a]For the tribe of the sons of Reuben have received *theirs* according to their fathers' households, and the tribe of the sons of Gad according to their fathers' households, and the half-tribe of Manasseh have received their possession.

15 "The two and a half tribes have received their possession across the Jordan opposite Jericho, eastward toward the sunrising."

16 Then the LORD spoke to Moses, saying,

17 "[a]These are the names of the men who shall apportion the land to you for inheritance: Eleazar the priest and Joshua the son of Nun.

18 "And you shall take one leader of every tribe to apportion the land for inheritance.

19 "And these are the names of the men: of the tribe of Judah, Caleb the son of Jephunneh.

20 "And of the tribe of the sons of Simeon, Samuel the son of Ammihud.

21 "Of the tribe of Benjamin, Elidad the son of Chislon.

22 "And of the tribe of the sons of Dan a leader, Bukki the son of Jogli.

23 "Of the sons of Joseph: of the tribe of the sons of Manasseh a leader, Hanniel the son of Ephod.

24 "And of the tribe of the sons of Ephraim a leader, Kemuel the son of Shiphtan.

25 "And of the tribe of the sons of Zebulun a leader, Elizaphan the son of Parnach.

26 "And of the tribe of the sons of Issachar a leader, Paltiel the son of Azzan.

27 "And of the tribe of the sons of Asher a leader, Ahihud the son of Shelomi.

28 "And of the tribe of the sons of Naphtali a leader, Pedahel the son of Ammihud."

29 These are those whom the LORD commanded to apportion the inheritance to the sons of Israel in the land of Canaan.

CHAPTER 35

Cities for the Levites

[a]NOW the LORD spoke to Moses in the plains of Moab by the Jordan opposite Jericho, saying,

2 "Command the sons of Israel that they give to the Levites from the inheritance of their possession, cities to live in; and you shall give to the Levites pasture lands around the cities.

3 "And the cities shall be theirs to live in; and their pasture lands shall be for their cattle and for their herds and for all their beasts.

4 "And the pasture lands of the cities which you shall give to the Levites *shall extend* from the wall of the city [1]outward a thousand cubits around.

5 "You shall also measure outside

3 [1]Lit., *side* [2]Lit., *be* [a]Josh. 15:1-3 [b]Josh. 15:5

4 [1]Lit., *pass along* [2]Lit., *goings out*, and so throughout the chap. [3]Lit., *go forth to*

5 [a]Josh. 15:4

6 [1]Lit., *border*

7 [a]Ezek. 47:15-17

8 [1]Or, *entrance of Hamath* [a]Josh. 13:5

11 [1]Lit., *shoulder* [a]2 Kin. 23:33 [b]Deut. 3:17; Josh. 13:27

13 [a]Gen. 15:18; Deut. 11:24

14 [a]Num. 32:33

17 [a]Josh. 14:1, 2

1 [a]Lev. 25:32-34

4 [1]Lit., *and outward*

the city on the east side two thousand cubits, and on the south side two thousand cubits, and on the west side two thousand cubits, and on the north side two thousand cubits, with the city in the center. This shall become theirs as pasture lands for the cities.

Cities of Refuge

6 "And the cities which you shall give to the Levites *shall be* the [a]six cities of refuge, which you shall give for the manslayer to flee to; and in addition to them you shall give forty-two cities.

7 "All the cities which you shall give to the Levites *shall be* forty-eight cities, [1]together with their pasture lands.

8 "[a]As for the cities which you shall give from the possession of the sons of Israel, you shall take more from the larger and you shall take less from the smaller; each shall give some of his cities to the Levites in proportion to his possession which he inherits."

9 Then the LORD spoke to Moses, saying,

10 "Speak to the sons of Israel and say to them, 'When you cross the Jordan into the land of Canaan,

11 [a]then you shall select for yourselves cities to be your cities of refuge, that the manslayer who has [1]killed any person [b]unintentionally may flee there.

12 'And the cities shall be to you as a refuge from the avenger, so that the manslayer may not die until he stands before the congregation for [1]trial.

13 'And the cities which you are to give shall be your six cities of refuge.

14 'You shall give three cities across the Jordan and three cities [1]in the land of Canaan; they are to be cities of refuge.

15 'These six cities shall be for refuge for the sons of Israel, and for the alien and for the sojourner among them; that anyone who [1]kills a person [a]unintentionally may flee there.

16 '[a]But if he struck him down with an iron object, so that he died, he is a murderer; the murderer shall surely be put to death.

17 'And if he struck him down with a stone in the hand, by which he may die, and *as a result* he died, he is a murderer; the murderer [a]shall surely be put to death.

18 'Or if he struck him with a wooden object in the hand, by which he may die, and *as a result* he died, he is a murderer; the murderer shall surely be put to death.

19 'The blood avenger himself shall put the murderer to death; he shall put him to death when he meets him.

20 'And if he pushed him of hatred, or threw something at him lying in wait and *as a result* he died,

21 or if he struck him down with his hand in enmity, and *as a result* he died, the one who struck him shall surely be put to death, he is a murderer; the blood avenger shall put the murderer to death when he meets him.

22 '[a]But if he pushed him suddenly without enmity, or threw something at him without lying in wait,

23 or with any [1]deadly object of stone, and without seeing it dropped on him so that he died, while he was not his enemy nor seeking his injury,

24 then the congregation shall judge between the slayer and the blood avenger according to these ordinances.

25 'And the congregation shall deliver the manslayer from the hand of the blood avenger, and the congregation shall restore him to his city of refuge to which he fled; and he shall live in it until the death of the high priest who was anointed with the holy oil.

26 'But if the manslayer shall at any time go beyond the border of his city of refuge to which he may flee,

27 and the blood avenger finds him outside the border of his city of refuge, and the blood avenger kills the manslayer, he shall not be guilty of blood

28 because he should have remained in his city of refuge until the death of the high priest. But after the death of the high priest the manslayer shall return to the land of his possession.

29 'And these things shall be for a statutory ordinance to you throughout your generations in all your dwellings.

30 '[a]If anyone kills a person, the murderer shall be put to death at the [1]evidence of witnesses, but [b]no person shall be put to death on the testimony of one witness.

31 'Moreover, you shall not take ransom for the life of a murderer who is guilty of death, but he shall surely be put to death.

32 'And you shall not take ransom for him who has fled to his city of refuge, that he may return to live in

6 [a]Josh. 20:7-9

7 [1]Lit., *them*

8 [a]Lev. 25:32-34; Num. 26:54; 33:54; Josh. 21:1-42

11 [1]Lit., *smote* [a]Deut. 19:1-13 [b]Ex. 21:13; Lev. 4:2, 22; Num. 35:22

12 [1]Lit., *judgment*

14 [1]Lit., *you shall give in*

15 [1]Lit., *smites* [a]Num. 35:11

16 [a]Ex. 21:12, 14; Lev. 24:17

17 [a]Num. 35:31

22 [a]Num. 35:11

23 [1]Lit., *by which he may die*

30 [1]Lit., *mouth* [a]Num. 35:16 [b]Deut. 17:6; 19:15; Matt. 18:16; John 7:51; 8:17, 18

the land [1]before the death of the priest.

33 '[a]So you shall not pollute the land in which you are; for blood pollutes the land and no expiation can be made for the land for the blood that is shed on it, except [b]by the blood of him who shed it.

34 'And you shall not [a]defile the land in which you live, in the midst of which [b]I dwell; for I the LORD am dwelling in the midst of the sons of Israel.' "

CHAPTER 36

[a] *Inheritance by Marriage*

AND the heads of the fathers' *households* of the family of the sons of Gilead, the son of Machir, the son of Manasseh, of the families of the sons of Joseph, came near and spoke before Moses and before the leaders, the heads of the fathers' *households* of the sons of Israel,

2 and they said, "The LORD commanded my lord to give the land by lot to the sons of Israel as an inheritance, and my lord [a]was commanded by the LORD to give the inheritance of Zelophehad our brother to his daughters.

3 "But if they [1]marry one of the sons of the *other* tribes of the sons of Israel, their inheritance will be withdrawn from the inheritance of our fathers and will be added to the inheritance of the tribe to which they belong; thus it will be withdrawn from our allotted inheritance.

4 "And when the [a]jubilee of the sons of Israel [1]comes, then their inheritance will be added to the inheritance of the tribe to which they belong; so their inheritance will be withdrawn from the inheritance of the tribe of our fathers."

5 Then Moses commanded the sons of Israel according to the [1]word of the LORD, saying, "The tribe of the sons of Joseph are right in *their* statements.

6 "This is [1]what the LORD has commanded concerning the daughters of Zelophehad, saying, 'Let them marry [2]whom they wish; only they must marry within the family of the tribe of their father.'

7 "Thus no inheritance of the sons of Israel shall [1]be transferred from tribe to tribe, for the sons of Israel shall each [2]hold to the inheritance of the tribe of his fathers.

8 "[a]And every daughter who comes into possession of an inheritance of any tribe of the sons of Israel, shall be wife to one of the family of the tribe of her father, so that the sons of Israel each may possess the inheritance of his fathers.

9 "Thus no inheritance shall [1]be transferred from one tribe to another tribe, for the tribes of the sons of Israel shall each [2]hold to his own inheritance."

10 Just as the LORD had commanded Moses, so the daughters of Zelophehad did:

11 [a]Mahlah, Tirzah, Hoglah, Milcah and Noah, the daughters of Zelophehad married their uncles' sons.

12 They married *those* from the families of the sons of Manasseh the son of Joseph, and their inheritance [1]remained with the tribe of the family of their father.

13 [a]These are the commandments and the ordinances which the LORD commanded to the sons of Israel through Moses in the plains of Moab by the Jordan *opposite* Jericho.

32 [1]Or, *until*
33 [a]Deut. 21:7, 8; Ps. 106:38 [b]Gen. 9:6
34 [a]Lev. 18:24, 25 [b]Num. 5:3
1 [a]Num. 27:1
2 [a]Num. 27:5, 6
3 [1]Lit., *become wives to,* in this chap.
4 [1]Lit., *shall be* [a]Lev. 25:10
5 [1]Lit., *mouth*
6 [1]Lit., *the thing which* [2]Lit., *to the good one in their eyes*
7 [1]Lit., *turn about* [2]Lit., *cleave*
8 [a]1 Chr. 23:22
9 [1]Lit., *turn about* [2]Lit., *cleave*
11 [a]Num. 26:33
12 [1]Lit., *was*
13 [a]Lev. 26:46

DEUTERONOMY

Israel's History after the Exodus

THESE are the words which Moses spoke to all Israel [a]across the Jordan in the wilderness, in the [b]Arabah opposite [1]Suph, between Paran and Tophel and Laban and Hazeroth and Dizahab.

2 It is eleven days' *journey* from [a]Horeb by the way of Mount [b]Seir to [c]Kadesh-barnea.

3 And it came about in the [a]fortieth year, on the first day of the eleventh month, that Moses spoke to the children of Israel, [b]according to all that the LORD had commanded him *to give* to them,

4 after he had [1a]defeated Sihon the king of the Amorites, who lived in Heshbon, and Og the king of Bashan, who lived in Ashtaroth and Edrei.

5 Across the Jordan in the land of Moab, Moses undertook to expound this law, saying,

6 "The LORD our God [a]spoke to us at Horeb, saying, 'You have [1]stayed long enough at this mountain.

7 'Turn and set your journey, and go to [a]the hill country of the Amor-

1 [1]Perhaps Red Sea [a]Deut. 4:46 [b]Deut. 2:8
2 [a]Ex. 3:1; 17:6 [b]Gen. 32:3 [c]Num. 32:8
3 [a]Num. 33:38 [b]Deut. 4:1, 2
4 [1]Lit., *smitten* [a]Num. 21:24, 25
6 [1]Lit., *dwelt* [a]Num. 10:11-13
7 [a]Gen. 15:18; Deut. 11:24; Josh. 10:40

ites, and to all their neighbors in the
Arabah, in the hill country and in
the lowland and in [b]the [1]Negev and
by the seacoast, the land of the Canaanites, and Lebanon, as far as the
great river, the river Euphrates.
8 'See, I have placed the land before you; go in and possess the land
which the LORD [a]swore to give to
your fathers, to Abraham, to Isaac,
and to Jacob, to them and their [1]de-
scendants after them.'
9"And I spoke to you at that time,
saying, '[a]I am not able to bear *the
burden* of you alone.
10 'The LORD your God has [a]multi-
plied you, and behold, you are this
day as the stars of heaven for multitude.
11 'May the LORD, the God of your
fathers, increase you a thousand-
fold more than you are, and bless
you, just as He has [1]promised you!
12 'How can I alone bear the load
and burden of you and your strife?
13 '[1a]Choose wise and discerning
and experienced men from your
tribes, and I will appoint them as
your heads.'
14"And you answered me and said,
'The thing which you have said to do
is good.'
15"So I took the heads of your
tribes, wise and experienced men,
and [1]appointed them heads over
you, leaders of thousands, and [2]of
hundreds, [2]of fifties and [2]of tens,
and officers for your tribes.
16"Then I charged your judges at
that time, saying, 'Hear *the cases*
between your [1]fellow-countrymen,
and judge righteously between a
man and his [2]fellow-countryman, or
the alien who is with him.
17 '[a]You shall not show partiality
in judgment; you shall hear the
small and the great alike. You shall
not fear [1]man, for the judgment is
God's. And [b]the case that is too hard
for you, you shall bring to me, and I
will hear it.'
18"[a]And I commanded you at that
time all the things that you should
do.
19"Then we set out from [a]Horeb,
and went through all that [b]great and
terrible wilderness which you saw,
on the way to the [c]hill country of the
Amorites, just as the LORD our God
had commanded us; and we came to
[d]Kadesh-barnea.
20"And I said to you, 'You have
come to the hill country of the Amorites which the LORD our God is
about to give us.
21 'See, the LORD your God has
placed the land before you; go up,
take possession, as the LORD, the
God of your fathers, has spoken to
you. Do not fear or be dismayed.'
22"[a]Then all of you approached me
and said, 'Let us send men before us,
that they may search out the land
for us, and bring back to us word of
the way by which we should go up,
and the cities which we shall enter.'
23"And the thing pleased me and I
took twelve of your men, one man
for each tribe.
24"And [a]they turned and went up
into the hill country, and came to
the valley of Eshcol, and spied it out.
25"Then they took *some* of the
fruit of the land in their hands and
brought it down to us; and they
brought us back a report and said,
'It is a good land which the LORD our
God is about to give us.'
26"[a]Yet you were not willing to go
up, but rebelled against the [1]com-
mand of the LORD your God;
27 and [a]you grumbled in your
tents and said, 'Because the LORD
hates us, He has brought us out of
the land of Egypt to deliver us into
the hand of the Amorites to destroy
us.
28 'Where can we go up? Our
brethren have made our hearts melt,
saying, "The people are bigger and
taller than we; the cities are large
and fortified to heaven. And besides, we saw [a]the sons of the Anakim there." '
29"Then I said to you, 'Do not be
shocked, nor fear them.
30 'The LORD your God who goes
before you will [a]Himself fight on
your behalf, [1]just as He did for you
in Egypt before your eyes,
31 and in the wilderness where
you saw how [a]the LORD your God
carried you, just as a man carries his
son, in all the way which you have
walked, until you came to this
place.'
32"But [1]for all this, you did not
trust the LORD your God,
33 [a]who goes before you on *your*
way, to seek out a place for you to
encamp, in fire by night and cloud
by day, to show you the way in
which you should go.
34"Then the LORD heard the sound
of your words, and He was angry
and [a]took an oath, saying,
35 'Not one of these men, this evil
generation, shall see the good land
which I swore to give your fathers,
36 except Caleb the son of Jephunneh; he shall see it, and [a]to him and
to his sons I will give the land on
which he has set foot, because he
has followed the LORD fully.'

7 [1]I.e., South country [b]Gen. 12:9
8 [1]Lit., *seed* [a]Gen. 26:3; Ex. 33:1; Num. 14:23; 32:11
9 [a]Ex. 18:18, 24
10 [a]Gen. 15:5; 22:17; Deut. 10:22; 26:5
11 [1]Lit., *spoken to*
13 [1]Lit., *Give for yourselves* [a]Ex. 18:21
15 [1]Lit., *gave* [2]Lit., *leaders of*
16 [1]Lit., *brothers* [2]Lit., *brother*
17 [1]Lit., *because of man* [a]Deut. 10:17; 16:19; 24:17 [b]Ex. 18:19, 23
18 [a]Ex. 18:20
19 [a]Deut. 1:2 [b]Deut. 2:7; 8:15; 32:10 [c]Deut. 1:7 [d]Deut. 1:2
22 [a]Num. 13:1-3
24 [a]Num. 13:21-25
26 [1]Lit., *mouth* [a]Num. 14:1-4
27 [a]Ps. 106:25
28 [a]Num. 13:28, 33; Deut. 9:2
30 [1]Lit., *according to all that* [a]Ex. 14:14; Deut. 3:22; 20:4
31 [a]Acts 13:18
32 [1]Lit., *in this matter*
33 [a]Num. 9:15-23
34 [a]Num. 14:28-30
36 [a]Num. 14:24; Josh. 14:9

37“[a]The LORD was angry with me also on your account, saying, ‘[b]Not even you shall enter there.

38 ‘Joshua the son of Nun, who stands before you, [a]he shall enter there; encourage him, for [b]he shall cause Israel to inherit it.

39 ‘Moreover, [a]your little ones who you said would become a prey, and your sons, who this day have no knowledge of good or evil, shall enter there, and I will give it to them, and they shall possess it.

40 ‘But as for you, [a]turn around and set out for the wilderness by the way to the [1]Red Sea.’

41“[a]Then you answered and said to me, ‘We have sinned against the LORD; we will indeed go up and fight, just as the LORD our God commanded us.’ And every man of you girded on his weapons of war, and regarded it as easy to go up into the hill country.

42“[a]And the LORD said to me, ‘Say to them, “Do not go up, nor fight, for I am not among you; lest you be [1]defeated before your enemies.” ’

43“So I spoke to you, but you would not listen. Instead [a]you rebelled against the [1]command of the LORD, and acted presumptuously and went up into the hill country.

44“[a]And the Amorites who [1]lived in that hill country came out against you, and chased you as bees do, and crushed you from Seir to Hormah.

45“Then you returned and wept before the LORD; but the LORD did not listen to your voice, nor give ear to you.

46“So you remained in Kadesh [a]many days, [1]the days that you spent *there*.

CHAPTER 2

Wanderings in the Wilderness

“[a]THEN we turned and set out for the wilderness by the way to the [1]Red Sea, as the LORD spoke to me, and circled [b]Mount Seir for many days.

2“And the LORD spoke to me, saying,

3 ‘You have circled this mountain long enough. Now turn north,

4 [a]and command the people, saying, “You will pass through the territory of your brothers the sons of Esau who live in Seir; and [b]they will be afraid of you. So be very careful;

5 do not [1]provoke them, for I will not give you any of their land, even *as little as* a [2]footstep because I have given Mount Seir to Esau as a possession.

6“You shall buy food from them with money so that you may eat, and you shall also purchase water from them with money so that you may drink.

7“For the LORD your God has blessed you in all [1]that you have done; He has known your [2]wanderings through this [a]great wilderness. These [b]forty years the LORD your God has been with you; you have not lacked a thing.” ’

8“So we passed beyond our brothers the sons of Esau, who live in Seir, away from the [a]Arabah road, away from Elath and from Ezion-geber. And we turned and passed through by the way of the wilderness of Moab.

9“Then the LORD said to me, ‘Do not harass Moab, nor provoke them to war, for I will not give you any of [1]their land as a possession, because I have given [a]Ar to [b]the sons of Lot as a possession.

10 (The Emim lived there formerly, a people as great, numerous, and tall as the Anakim.

11 Like the Anakim, they are also regarded as [a]Rephaim, but the Moabites call them Emim.

12 [a]The Horites formerly lived in Seir, but the sons of Esau dispossessed them and destroyed them from before them and settled in their place, [b]just as Israel did to the land of [1]their possession which the LORD gave to them.)

13 ‘Now arise and cross over the [1]brook Zered yourselves.’ So we crossed over the [1]brook Zered.

14“Now the [1]time that it took for us to come from Kadesh-barnea, until we crossed over the [2]brook Zered, was [a]thirty-eight years; until [b]all the generation of the men of war perished from within the camp, as the LORD had sworn to them.

15“[a]Moreover the hand of the LORD was against them, to destroy them from within the camp, until they all perished.

16“So it came about when [a]all the men of war had finally perished from among the people,

17 that the LORD spoke to me, saying,

18 ‘You shall cross over [a]Ar, the border of Moab, today.

19 ‘And when you come opposite the sons of Ammon, do not harass them nor provoke them, for I will not give you any of the land of the sons of Ammon as a possession, be-

---

37 [a]Num. 20:12 [b]Num. 27:13, 18

38 [a]Num. 14:20 [b]Num. 34:17; Deut. 3:28; 31:7; Josh. 11:23

39 [a]Num. 14:3, 31

40 [1]Or, *Sea of Reeds* [a]Num. 14:25

41 [a]Num. 14:40

42 [1]Lit., *smitten* [a]Num. 14:41-43

43 [1]Lit., *mouth* [a]Num. 14:40

44 [1]Lit., *dwelt* [a]Num. 14:45

46 [1]Lit., *as the days* [a]Deut. 2:7, 14

1 [1]Or, *Sea of Reeds* [a]Num. 21:4 [b]Deut. 1:2

4 [a]Num. 20:14-21 [b]Ex. 15:15

5 [1]Or, *engage in strife with* [2]Lit., *treading of a sole of a foot*

7 [1]Lit., *the work of your hand* [2]Lit., *goings* [a]Deut. 1:19 [b]Num. 14:33, 34; 32:13; Deut. 2:14

8 [a]Deut. 1:1

9 [1]Lit., *his* [a]Num. 21:15, 28; Deut. 2:18, 29 [b]Gen. 19:36, 37

11 [a]Gen. 14:5; Deut. 2:20

12 [1]Lit., *his* [a]Deut. 2:22 [b]Num. 21:25, 35

13 [1]Or, *wadi*

14 [1]Lit., *days in which we went* [2]Or, *wadi* [a]Deut. 2:7 [b]Num. 14:29-35; 26:64, 65; Ps. 106:26; 1 Cor. 10:5

15 [a]Jude 5

16 [a]Deut. 2:14

18 [a]Deut. 2:9

cause I have given it to [a]the sons of
Lot as a possession.'
20 (It is also regarded as the land
of the [a]Rephaim, *for* Rephaim formerly lived in it, but the Ammonites
call them Zamzummin,
21 a people as great, numerous,
and tall as the Anakim, but the LORD
destroyed them before them. And
they dispossessed them and settled
in their place,
22 just as He did for the sons of
Esau, who live in Seir, when He destroyed [a]the Horites from before
them; and they dispossessed them,
and settled in their place even to this
day.
23 And the [a]Avvim, who lived in
villages as far as Gaza, the [1b]Caph-
torim who came from [2c]Caphtor,
destroyed them and lived in their
place.)
24 'Arise, set out, and pass through
the [1]valley of Arnon. Look! I have
given Sihon the Amorite, king of
Heshbon, and his land into your
hand; begin to take possession and
contend with him in battle.
25 'This day I will begin to put [a]the
dread and fear of you [1]upon the peoples [2]everywhere under the heavens, who, when they hear the report
of you, [b]shall tremble and be in anguish because of you.'
26 "[a]So I sent messengers from the
wilderness of Kedemoth to Sihon
king of Heshbon with words of
peace, saying,
27 'Let me pass through your land,
I will [1]travel only on the highway; I
will not turn aside to the right or to
the left.
28 'You will sell me food for money
so that I may eat, and give me water
for money so that I may drink, only
let me pass through on [1]foot,
29 just as the sons of Esau who
live in Seir and the Moabites who
live in [a]Ar did for me, until I cross
over the Jordan into the land which
the LORD our God is giving to us.'
30 "But Sihon king of Heshbon was
not willing for us to pass [1]through
his land; for the LORD your God
hardened his spirit and made his
heart obstinate, in order to deliver
him into your hand, as *he is* today.
31 "And the LORD said to me, 'See,
I have begun to deliver Sihon and
his land [1]over to you. Begin to [2]oc-
cupy, that you may possess his
land.'
32 "Then Sihon [1]with all his people
came out to meet us in battle at Jahaz.
33 "And the LORD our God delivered him [1]over to us; and we [2]de-
feated him with his sons and all his
people.
34 "So we captured all his cities at
that time, and [1a]utterly destroyed
[2]the men, women and children of
every city. We left no survivor.
35 "We took [a]only the animals as
our booty and the spoil of the cities
which we had captured.
36 "From [a]Aroer which is on the
edge of the [1]valley of Arnon and
from the city which is in the [1]valley,
even to Gilead, there was no city
that was too high for us; the LORD
our God delivered all [2]over to us.
37 "[a]Only you did not go near to the
land of the sons of Ammon, all along
the [1]river Jabbok and the cities of
the hill country, and wherever the
LORD our God had commanded us.

CHAPTER 3

Conquests Recounted

"[a]THEN we turned and went up
the road to Bashan, and Og, king of
Bashan, [1]with all his people came
out to meet us in battle at Edrei.
2 "But the LORD said to me, 'Do
not fear him, for I have delivered
him and all his people and his land
into your hand; and you shall do to
him just as you did to Sihon king of
the Amorites, who lived at Heshbon.'
3 "So the LORD our God delivered
Og also, king of Bashan, with all his
people into our hand, and we smote
[1]them until no survivor was [2]left.
4 "And we captured all his cities at
that time; there was not a city which
we did not take from them: sixty
cities, all the region of [a]Argob, the
kingdom of Og in Bashan.
5 "All these were cities fortified
with high walls, gates and bars, besides a great many [1]unwalled
towns.
6 "And we [1]utterly destroyed
them, as we did to Sihon king of
Heshbon, [2a]utterly destroying [3]the
men, women and children of every
city.
7 "[a]But all the animals and the
spoil of the cities we took as our
booty.
8 "[a]Thus we took the land at that
time from the hand of the two kings
of the Amorites who were beyond
the Jordan, from the [1]valley of Arnon to Mount Hermon
9 (Sidonians [a]call Hermon [b]Siri-
on, and the Amorites call it Senir):
10 all the cities of the tableland
and all Gilead and all Bashan, as far
as Salecah and Edrei, cities of the
kingdom of Og in Bashan.

19 [a]Deut. 2:9
20 [a]Deut. 2:11
22 [a]Deut. 2:12
23 [1]I.e., Philistines [2]I.e., Crete [a]Josh. 13:3 [b]Gen. 10:14; 1 Chr. 1:12 [c]Jer. 47:4; Amos 9:7
24 [1]Or, *wadi*
25 [1]Lit., *in front of* [2]Lit., *under all the heavens* [a]Ex. 23:27; Deut. 11:25; Josh. 2:9 [b]Ex. 15:14-16
26 [a]Num. 21:21-32
27 [1]Lit., *go by the way*
28 [1]Lit., *my feet*
29 [a]Deut. 2:9
30 [1]Lit., *by him*
31 [1]Lit., *before you* [2]Lit., *possess*
32 [1]Lit., *he and*
33 [1]Lit., *before us* [2]Lit., *smote*
34 [1]Or, *put under the ban* [2]Lit., *every city of man...* [a]Deut. 3:6
35 [a]Deut. 3:7
36 [1]Or, *wadi* [2]Lit., *before us* [a]Deut. 3:12; 4:48
37 [1]Or, *wadi* [a]Deut. 2:19
1 [1]Lit., *he and* [a]Num. 21:33-35
3 [1]Lit., *him* [2]Lit., *left to him*
4 [a]Deut. 2:13, 14; 1 Kin. 4:13
5 [1]Or, *rural*
6 [1]Or, *put them under the ban* [2]Or, *putting under the ban* [3]Lit., *every city of men...* [a]Deut. 2:34
7 [a]Deut. 2:35
8 [1]Or, *wadi* [a]Num. 32:33; Josh. 12:1-7; 13:8-12
9 [a]Deut. 4:48; Josh. 11:17; Ps. 42:6; 133:3 [b]Ps. 29:6

11 (For only Og king of Bashan was left of the remnant of the [a]Rephaim. Behold, his [1]bedstead was an iron [1]bedstead; it is in [b]Rabbah of the sons of Ammon. Its length was nine cubits and its width four cubits [2]by ordinary cubit.)

12"So we took possession of this land at that time. From [a]Aroer, which is by the [1]valley of Arnon, and half the hill country of [b]Gilead and its cities, I gave to the Reubenites and to the Gadites.

13"And the rest of Gilead, and all Bashan, the kingdom of Og, I gave to the half-tribe of Manasseh, all the region of Argob (concerning all Bashan, it is called the land of Rephaim.

14 [a]Jair the son of Manasseh took all the region of Argob as far as the border of the Geshurites and the Maacathites, and called [1]it, *that is,* Bashan, after his own name, [2]Havvoth-jair, *as it is* to this day.)

15"[a]And to Machir I gave Gilead.

16"And to the Reubenites and to the Gadites, I gave from Gilead even as far as the [1]valley of Arnon, the middle of the [1]valley [2]as *a* border and as far as the [1]river Jabbok, the border of the sons of Ammon;

17 the Arabah also, with the Jordan [1]as *a* border, from [2a]Chinnereth even as far as the sea of the Arabah, the Salt Sea, [3]at the foot of the slopes of Pisgah on the east.

18"Then I commanded you at that time, saying, 'The LORD your God has given you this land to possess it; [a]all you valiant men shall cross over armed before your brothers, the sons of Israel.

19 'But your wives and your little ones and your livestock (I know that you have [a]much livestock), shall remain in your cities which I have given you,

20 until the LORD gives rest to your fellow-countrymen as to you, and they also possess the land which the LORD your God will give them beyond the Jordan. [a]Then you may return every man to his possession, which I have given you.'

21"And I commanded Joshua at that time, saying, 'Your eyes have seen all that the LORD your God has done to these two kings; so the LORD shall do to all the kingdoms into which you are about to cross.

22 'Do not fear them, for the LORD your God [a]is the one fighting for you.'

23"I also pleaded with the LORD at that time, saying,

24 'O Lord [1]GOD, Thou hast begun to show Thy servant Thy greatness and Thy strong hand; for what god is there in heaven or on earth who can do such works and mighty acts as Thine?

25 'Let me, I pray, cross over and see the fair land that is beyond the Jordan, [1]that good hill country and Lebanon.'

26"But [a]the LORD was angry with me on your account, and would not listen to me; and the LORD said to me, '[1]Enough! Speak to Me no more of this matter.

27 'Go up to the top of [a]Pisgah and lift up your eyes to the west and north and south and east, and see *it* with your eyes, [b]for you shall not cross over this Jordan.

28 '[a]But charge Joshua and encourage him and strengthen him; [b]for he shall go across [1]at the head of this people, and he shall give them as an inheritance the land which you will see.'

29"So we remained in the valley opposite [a]Beth-peor.

CHAPTER 4

Israel Urged to Obey God's Law

"AND now, O Israel, listen to the statutes and the judgments which [a]I am teaching you to perform, in order that [b]you may live and go in and take possession of the land which the LORD, the God of your fathers, is giving you.

2"[a]You shall not add to the word which [b]I am commanding you, nor take away from it, that you may keep the commandments of the LORD your God which I command you.

3"[a]Your eyes have seen what the LORD has done in the case of Baal-peor, for all the men who followed Baal-peor, the LORD your God has destroyed [1]them from among you.

4"But you who held fast to the LORD your God are alive today, every one of you.

5"See, I have taught you statutes and judgments [a]just as the LORD my God commanded me, that you should do thus in the land where you are entering to possess it.

6"So keep and do *them,* [a]for that is your wisdom and your understanding in the sight of the peoples who will hear all these statutes and say, 'Surely this great nation is a wise and understanding people.'

7"For what great nation is there that has a god [a]so near to it as is the LORD our God [b]whenever we call on Him?

---

11 [1]Or, *couch* [2]Lit., *by a man's forearm* [a]Deut. 2:11, 20 [b]2 Sam. 11:1; 12:26; Jer. 49:2

12 [1]Or, *wadi* [a]Deut. 2:36 [b]Num. 32:32-38; Josh. 13:8-13

14 [1]Lit., *them* [2]I.e., the towns of Jair [a]Num. 32:41; 1 Chr. 2:22

15 [a]Num. 32:40

16 [1]Or, *wadi* [2]Lit., *and*

17 [1]Lit., *under* [2]I.e., The Sea of Galilee [3]Lit., *under* [a]Num. 34:11; Josh. 13:27

18 [a]Num. 32:20; Josh. 4:12, 13

19 [a]Ex. 12:38

20 [a]Josh. 22:4

22 [a]Deut. 1:30

24 [1]YHWH, usually rendered LORD

25 [1]Lit., *this*

26 [1]Lit., *Enough for you* [a]Deut. 1:37

27 [a]Num. 23:14; 27:12 [b]Deut. 1:37

28 [1]Lit., *before this people* [a]Num. 27:18; Deut. 31:3, 7, 8, 23 [b]Deut. 1:38

29 [a]Num. 25:1-3; Deut. 4:46; 34:6

1 [a]Deut. 1:3 [b]Deut. 5:33; 8:1; 16:20; 30:16, 19

2 [a]Deut. 12:32 [b]Deut. 4:5, 14, 40

3 [1]Lit., *him* [a]Num. 25:1-9

5 [a]Lev. 26:46; 27:34

6 [a]Deut. 30:19, 20; 32:46, 47

7 [a]Ps. 148:14 [b]Ps. 34:18; 85:9

8 "Or what great nation is there that has [a]statutes and judgments as righteous as this whole law which I am setting before you today?

9 "Only [a]give heed to yourself and keep your soul diligently, lest you forget the things which your eyes have seen, and lest they depart from your heart [b]all the days of your life; but [c]make them known to your sons and your grandsons.

10 "*Remember* the day you stood before the LORD your God at Horeb, when the LORD said to me, 'Assemble the people to Me, that I may let them hear My words [a]so they may learn to [1]fear Me all the days they live on the earth, and that they may [b]teach their children.'

11 "And you came near and stood at the foot of the mountain, [a]and the mountain burned with fire to the *very* heart of the heavens: darkness, cloud and thick gloom.

12 "Then the LORD spoke to you from the midst of the fire; you heard the sound of words, but you saw no form—only a voice.

13 "So He declared to you His covenant which He commanded you to perform, *that is,* [a]the ten [1]commandments; and [b]He wrote them on two tablets of stone.

14 "And the LORD commanded me at that time to teach you statutes and judgments, that you might perform them in the land where you are going over to possess it.

15 "So watch yourselves carefully, since you did not see any form on the day the LORD spoke to you at Horeb from the midst of the fire,

16 lest you [a]act corruptly and [b]make a graven image for yourselves in the form of any figure, the likeness of male or female,

17 the likeness of any animal that is on the earth, the likeness of any winged bird that flies in the sky,

18 the likeness of anything that creeps on the ground, the likeness of any fish that is in the water below the earth.

19 "And *beware,* lest you lift up your eyes to heaven and see the sun and the moon and the stars, all the host of heaven, [a]and be drawn away and worship them and serve them, those which the LORD your God has allotted to all the peoples under the whole heaven.

20 "But the LORD has taken you and brought you out of [a]the iron furnace, from Egypt, to be a people for His own possession, as today.

21 "[a]Now the LORD was angry with me on your account, and swore that I should not cross the Jordan, and that I should not enter the good land which the LORD your God is giving you as an inheritance.

22 "For [a]I shall die in this land, I shall not cross the Jordan, but you shall cross and take possession of this good land.

23 "So watch yourselves, [a]lest you forget the covenant of the LORD your God, which He made with you, and [b]make for yourselves a graven image in the form of anything *against* which the LORD your God has commanded you.

24 "For the LORD your God is a [a]consuming fire, a [b]jealous God.

25 "When you [1]become the father of children and children's children and have remained long in the land, and [a]act corruptly, and [b]make an [2]idol in the form of anything, and do that which is evil in the sight of the LORD your God *so as* to provoke Him to anger,

26 I [a]call heaven and earth to witness against you today, that you shall [b]surely perish quickly from the land where you are going over the Jordan to possess it. You shall not [1]live long on it, but shall be utterly destroyed.

27 "And the LORD will [a]scatter you among the peoples, and you shall be left few in number among the nations, where the LORD shall drive you.

28 "And there you will serve gods, the work of man's hands, [a]wood and stone, [b]which neither see nor hear nor eat nor smell.

29 "[a]But from there you will seek the LORD your God, and you will find *Him* if you search for Him [b]with all your heart and all your soul.

30 "When you [a]are in distress and all these things have come upon you, in the latter days, you will return to the LORD your God and listen to His voice.

31 "For the LORD your God is a [a]compassionate God; [b]He will not fail you nor [c]destroy you nor [d]forget the covenant with your fathers which He swore to them.

32 "Indeed, [a]ask now concerning the former days which were before you, since the [b]day that God created [1]man on the earth, and *inquire* [c]from one end of the heavens to the other. Has *anything* been done like this great thing, or has *anything* been heard like it?

33 "[a]Has *any* people heard the voice of God speaking from the midst of the fire, as you have heard *it,* and survived?

8 [a]Ps. 89:14; 97:2; 119:144, 160, 172

9 [a]Deut. 4:23; 6:12; 8:11, 14, 19 [b]Deut. 6:2; 12:1; 16:3 [c]Deut. 4:10; 6:7, 20-25; 11:19; 32:46

10 [1]Or, *reverence* [a]Deut. 14:23; 17:19; 31:12, 13 [b]Deut. 4:9

11 [a]Ex. 19:18; Heb. 12:18, 19

13 [1]Lit., *words* [a]Ex. 34:28; Deut. 10:4 [b]Ex. 31:18; 34:1, 28

16 [a]Deut. 4:25; 9:12; 31:29 [b]Deut. 5:8, 9

19 [a]Deut. 13:5, 10

20 [a]1 Kin. 8:51; Jer. 11:4

21 [a]Deut. 1:37

22 [a]Num. 27:13, 14

23 [a]Deut. 4:9 [b]Deut. 4:16

24 [a]Ex. 24:17; Deut. 9:3; Heb. 12:29 [b]Deut. 5:9; 6:15

25 [1]Lit., *beget* [2]Or, *a graven image* [a]Deut. 4:16 [b]Deut. 4:23

26 [1]Lit., *prolong your days* [a]Deut. 30:19; 31:28; 32:1 [b]Deut. 7:4; 8:19, 20

27 [a]Deut. 28:64; 29:28

28 [a]Deut. 28:36, 64; 29:17 [b]Ps. 115:4-8

29 [a]Deut. 30:1-3, 10 [b]Deut. 6:5; 10:12

30 [a]Ps. 18:6; 59:16; 107:6, 13

31 [a]Ex. 34:6 [b]Deut. 31:6, 8; Josh. 1:5; 1 Chr. 28:20; Heb. 13:5 [c]Jer. 30:11 [d]Lev. 26:45

32 [1]Or, *Adam* [a]Deut. 32:7 [b]Gen. 1:27; Is. 45:12 [c]Deut. 28:64

33 [a]Ex. 20:22; Deut. 5:24, 26

34 "[a]Or has a god tried to go to take for himself a nation from within *another* nation [b]by trials, by signs and wonders and by war and [c]by a mighty hand and by an outstretched arm and by great terrors, [1]as the LORD your God did for you in Egypt before your eyes?

35 "To you it was shown that you might know that the LORD, He is God; [a]there is no other besides Him.

36 "[a]Out of the heavens He let you hear His voice to discipline you; and on earth He let you see His great fire, and you heard His words from the midst of the fire.

37 "[1a]Because He loved your fathers, therefore He chose [2]their descendants after them. And He [3b]personally brought you from Egypt by His great power,

38 driving out from before you nations greater and mightier than you, to bring you in *and* [a]to give you their land for an inheritance, as it is today.

39 "Know therefore today, and take it to your heart, that the LORD, He is God in heaven above and on the earth below; [a]there is no other.

40 "[a]So you shall keep His statutes and His commandments which I am [1]giving you today, that [b]it may go well with you and with your children after you, and [c]that you may [2]live long on the land which the LORD your God is giving you for all time."

41 [a]Then Moses set apart three cities across the Jordan to the [1]east,

42 that a manslayer might flee there, who unintentionally slew his neighbor without having enmity toward him in time past; and by fleeing to one of these cities he might live:

43 Bezer in the wilderness on the plateau for the Reubenites, and Ramoth in Gilead for the Gadites, and Golan in Bashan for the Manassites.

44 Now this is the law which Moses set before the sons of Israel;

45 these are the testimonies and the statutes and the ordinances which Moses spoke to the sons of Israel, when they came out from Egypt,

46 across the Jordan, in the valley [a]opposite Beth-peor, in the land of [b]Sihon king of the Amorites who lived at Heshbon, whom Moses and the sons of Israel [1]defeated when they came out from Egypt.

47 And they took possession of his land and the land of Og king of Bashan, the two kings of the Amorites, *who were* across the Jordan to the [1]east,

48 from [a]Aroer, which is on the edge of the [1]valley of Arnon, even as far as [b]Mount Sion (that is, Hermon),

49 with all the Arabah across the Jordan to the east, even as far as the sea of the Arabah, [1]at the foot of the slopes of Pisgah.

CHAPTER 5

The Ten Commandments Repeated

THEN Moses summoned all Israel, and said to them, "Hear, O Israel, the statutes and the ordinances which I am speaking today in your [1]hearing, that you may learn them and observe [2]them carefully.

2 "The LORD our God made [a]a covenant with us at Horeb.

3 "[a]The LORD did not make this covenant with our fathers, but with us, *with* all those of [1]us alive here today.

4 "The LORD spoke to you [a]face to face at the mountain [b]from the midst of the fire,

5 *while* I was standing between the LORD and you at that time, to declare to you the word of the LORD; [a]for you were afraid because of the fire and did not go up the mountain. [1]He said,

6 '[a]I am the LORD your God, who brought you out of the land of Egypt, out of the house of [1]slavery.

7 'You shall have no other gods [1]before Me.

8 'You shall not make for yourself [1]an idol, *or* any likeness *of* what is in heaven above [2]or on the earth beneath [2]or in the water under the earth.

9 'You shall not worship them or serve them; for I, the LORD your God, am a jealous God, visiting the iniquity of the fathers on the children, and on the third and the fourth *generations* of those who hate Me,

10 but showing lovingkindness to thousands, to those who love Me and keep My commandments.

11 '[a]You shall not take the name of the LORD your God in vain, for the LORD will not [1]leave him unpunished who takes His name in vain.

12 'Observe the sabbath day to keep it holy, as the LORD your God commanded you.

13 'Six days you shall labor and do all your work,

14 but the seventh day is a sabbath of the LORD your God; *in it* you shall not do any work, you or your son or your daughter or your male servant

---

34 [1]Lit., *according to all that* [a]Deut. 33:29; Ex. 14:30 [b]Deut. 7:19 [c]Deut. 5:15; 6:21; Ps. 136:12

35 [a]Deut. 4:39; Ex. 8:10; 9:14; Mark 12:32

36 [a]Deut. 4:33; 8:5; Neh. 9:13; Heb. 12:25

37 [1]Lit., *And instead, because* [2]Lit., *his seed* [3]Lit., *with His presence* [a]Deut. 7:7, 8; 10:15; 33:3 [b]Ex. 33:14; Is. 63:9

38 [a]Num. 32:4; 34:14, 15

39 [a]Deut. 4:35

40 [1]Lit., *commanding* [2]Lit., *prolong your days* [a]Deut. 4:2; Ps. 105:45 [b]Deut. 5:16, 29, 33 [c]Ex. 23:26; Deut. 32:47

41 [1]Lit., *sunrise* [a]Num. 35:6; Deut. 19:2-13; Josh. 20:7-9

46 [1]Lit., *smote* [a]Deut. 3:29 [b]Num. 21:21-25

47 [1]Lit., *sunrise*

48 [1]Or, *wadi* [a]Deut. 2:36 [b]Deut. 3:9

49 [1]Lit., *under*

1 [1]Lit., *ears* [2]Lit., *to do them*

2 [a]Ex. 19:5; Mal. 4:4

3 [1]Lit., *us ourselves* [a]Num. 26:63-65

4 [a]Num. 14:14 [b]Deut. 4:33

5 [1]Lit., *saying* [a]Ex. 19:16, 21-24

6 [1]Lit., *slaves* [a]Ex. 20:2-17

7 [1]Or, *besides*

8 [1]Or, *a graven image* [2]Lit., *or what is*

11 [1]Or, *hold him guiltless* [a]Deut. 6:13; 10:20

or your female servant or your ox or your donkey or any of your cattle or your sojourner who [1]stays with you, so that your male and your female servant may rest as well as you.

15 '[a]And you shall remember that you were a slave in the land of Egypt, and the LORD your God brought you out of there by a mighty hand and by an outstretched arm; therefore the LORD your God commanded you to observe the sabbath day.

16 'Honor your father and your mother, as the LORD your God has commanded you, that your days may be prolonged, and that it may go well with you on the land which the LORD your God gives you.

17 'You shall not murder.

18 'You shall not commit adultery.

19 'You shall not steal.

20 'You shall not bear false witness against your neighbor.

21 '[a]You shall not covet your neighbor's wife, and you shall not desire your neighbor's house, his field or his manservant, his ox or his donkey or anything that belongs to your neighbor.'

Moses Interceded

22"These words the LORD spoke to all your assembly at the mountain from the midst of the fire, *of* the cloud and *of* the thick gloom, with a great voice, and He added no more. And [a]He wrote them on two tablets of stone and gave them to me.

23"And it came about, when you heard the voice from the midst of the darkness, while the mountain was burning with fire, that you came near to me, all the heads of your tribes and your elders.

24"And you said, 'Behold, the LORD our God has shown us His glory and His greatness, and we have heard His voice from the midst of the fire; we have seen today that God speaks with man, yet he lives.

25 '[a]Now then why should we die? For this great fire will consume us; if we hear the voice of the LORD our God any longer, then we shall die.

26 'For who is there of all flesh, who has heard the voice of the living God speaking from the midst of the fire, as we *have*, and lived?

27 '[1]Go near and hear all that the LORD our God says; then speak to us all that the LORD our God will speak to you, and we will hear and do *it*.'

28"And the LORD heard the voice of your words when you spoke to me, [a]and the LORD said to me, 'I have heard the voice of the words of this people which they have spoken to you. They have done well in all that they have spoken.

29 '[a]Oh that they had such a heart in them, that they would fear Me, and keep all My commandments always, that [b]it may be well with them and with their sons forever!

30 'Go, say to them, "Return to your tents."

31 '[a]But as for you, stand here by Me, that I may speak to you all the commandments and the statutes and the judgments which you shall teach them, that they may observe *them* in the land which I give them to possess.'

32"So you shall observe to do just as the LORD your God has commanded you; [a]you shall not turn aside to the right or to the left.

33"You shall walk in all the way which the LORD your God has commanded you, [a]that you may live, and that it may be well with you, and that you may prolong *your* days in the land which you shall possess.

CHAPTER 6

Obey God and Prosper

"NOW this is the commandment, the statutes and the judgments which the LORD your God has commanded *me* to teach you, that you might do *them* in the land where you are going over to possess it,

2 so that you and your son and your grandson might [a]fear the LORD your God, to keep all His statutes and His commandments, which I command you, [b]all the days of your life, and that your days may be prolonged.

3"O Israel, you should listen and [1]be careful to do *it*, that [a]it may be well with you and that you may multiply greatly, just as the LORD, the God of your fathers, has promised you, *in* [b]a land flowing with milk and honey.

4"[a]Hear, O Israel! The LORD is our God, the [b]LORD is one!

5"And you shall love the LORD your God with all your heart and with all your soul and with all your might.

6"And these words, which I am commanding you today, shall be on your heart;

7 and [a]you shall teach them diligently to your sons and shall talk of them when you sit in your house and when you walk by the way and when you lie down and when you rise up.

14 [1]Lit., *is in your gates*
15 [a]Ex. 20:11
21 [a]Rom. 7:7; 13:9
22 [a]Ex. 31:18; Deut. 4:13
25 [a]Ex. 20:18, 19; Deut. 18:16
27 [1]Lit., *Go yourself*
28 [a]Deut. 18:17
29 [a]Ps. 81:13; Is. 48:18 [b]Deut. 5:16, 33
31 [a]Ex. 24:12
32 [a]Deut. 17:20; 28:14; Josh. 1:7; 23:6
33 [a]Deut. 4:1, 40
2 [a]Deut. 10:12 [b]Deut. 4:9
3 [1]Lit., *keep* [a]Deut. 5:33 [b]Ex. 3:8, 17
4 [a]Matt. 22:37; Mark 12:29, 30; Luke 10:27 [b]Deut. 4:35, 39
7 [a]Deut. 4:9

8"[a]And you shall bind them as a
sign on your hand and they shall be
as [1]frontals [2]on your forehead.
9"[a]And you shall write them on
the doorposts of your house and on
your gates.
10"Then it shall come about when
the LORD your God brings you into
the land which He swore to your fathers, Abraham, Isaac and Jacob, to
give you, [a]great and splendid cities
which you did not build,
11 and houses full of all good
things which you did not fill, and
hewn cisterns which you did not
dig, vineyards and olive trees which
you did not plant, and [a]you shall eat
and be satisfied,
12 then watch yourself, lest [a]you
forget the LORD who brought you
from the land of Egypt, out of the
house of [1]slavery.
13"[a]You shall [1]fear *only* the LORD
your God; and you shall [2]worship
Him, and [b]swear by His name.
14"You shall not follow other gods,
any of the gods of the peoples who
surround you,
15 for the LORD your God in the
midst of you is a [a]jealous God; otherwise the anger of the LORD your
God will be kindled against you, and
He will [1]wipe you off the face of the
earth.
16"[a]You shall not put the LORD
your God to the test, [b]as you tested
Him at Massah.
17"[a]You should diligently keep the
commandments of the LORD your
God, and His testimonies and His
statutes which He has commanded
you.
18"And you shall do what is right
and good in the sight of the LORD,
that [a]it may be well with you and
that you may go in and possess the
good land which the LORD swore to
give your fathers,
19 by driving out all your enemies
from before you, as the LORD has
spoken.
20"[a]When your son asks you in
time to come, saying, 'What *do* the
testimonies and the statutes and the
judgments *mean* which the LORD
commanded you?'
21 then you shall say to your son,
'We were slaves to Pharaoh in
Egypt; and the LORD brought us
from Egypt with a mighty hand.
22 'Moreover, the LORD showed
great and distressing signs and wonders before our eyes against Egypt,
Pharaoh and all his household;
23 and He brought us out from
there in order to bring us in, to give
us the land which He had sworn to
our fathers.'
24"So the LORD commanded us to
observe all these statutes, [a]to fear
the LORD our God for our good always and for our survival, as *it is*
today.
25"And [a]it will be righteousness
for us if we [1]are careful to observe
all this commandment before the
LORD our God, just as He commanded us.

CHAPTER 7

Warnings

"[a]WHEN the LORD your God
shall bring you into the land where
you are entering to possess it, and
shall clear away many nations before you, the Hittites and the Girgashites and the Amorites and the Canaanites and the Perizzites and the
Hivites and the Jebusites, [b]seven
nations greater and stronger than
you,
2 and when the LORD your God
shall deliver them before you, and
you shall [1]defeat them, [a]then you
shall [2]utterly destroy them. [b]You
shall make no covenant with them
[c]and show no favor to them.
3"Furthermore, [a]you shall not intermarry with them; you shall not
give your [1]daughters to [2]their sons,
nor shall you take [3]their daughters
for your [4]sons.
4"For [1]they will turn your [2]sons
away from [3]following Me to serve
other gods; then the anger of the
LORD will be kindled against you,
and [a]He will quickly destroy you.
5"But thus you shall do to them:
[a]you shall tear down their altars,
and smash their *sacred* pillars, and
hew down their [1]Asherim, and burn
their graven images with fire.
6"For you are [a]a holy people to
the LORD your God; the LORD your
God has chosen you to be [b]a people
for His [1]own possession out of all
the peoples who are on the face of
the [2]earth.
7"[a]The LORD did not set His love
on you nor choose you because you
were more in number than any of
the peoples, for you were the fewest
of all peoples,
8 but because the LORD loved you
and kept the oath which He swore to
your forefathers, the LORD brought
you out by a mighty hand, and redeemed you from the house of [1]slav-
ery, from the hand of Pharaoh king
of Egypt.
9"Know therefore that the LORD
your God, [a]He is God, the faithful

---

8 [1]Or, *frontlet bands* [2]Lit., *between your eyes* [a]Ex. 12:14; 13:9, 16; Deut. 11:18

9 [a]Deut. 11:20

10 [a]Deut. 9:1; 19:1; Josh. 24:13

11 [a]Deut. 8:10; 11:15; 14:29

12 [1]Lit., *slaves* [a]Deut. 4:9

13 [1]Or, *reverence* [2]Or, *serve* [a]Matt. 4:10; Luke 4:8 [b]Deut. 5:11; 10:20

15 [1]Lit., *destroy* [a]Deut. 4:24; 5:9

16 [a]Matt. 4:7; Luke 4:12 [b]Ex. 17:7

17 [a]Deut. 11:22

18 [a]Deut. 4:40

20 [a]Ex. 13:8, 14

24 [a]Deut. 10:12

25 [1]Lit., *keep* [a]Deut. 24:13

1 [a]Deut. 20:16-18 [b]Acts 13:19

2 [1]Lit., *smite* [2]Lit., *surely devote* [a]Num. 31:17 [b]Ex. 23:32 [c]Deut. 7:16; 13:8

3 [1]Lit., *daughter* [2]Lit., *his son* [3]Lit., *his daughter* [4]Lit., *son* [a]Ex. 34:15, 16

4 [1]Lit., *he* [2]Lit., *son* [3]Lit., *after* [a]Deut. 4:26

5 [1]I.e., wooden symbols of a female deity [a]Ex. 23:24; 34:13; Deut. 12:3

6 [1]Or, *special treasure* [2]Lit., *ground* [a]Ex. 19:6; Deut. 14:2, 21 [b]Ex. 19:5; Deut. 14:2; 26:18

7 [a]Deut. 4:37

8 [1]Lit., *slaves*

9 [a]Deut. 4:35, 39

God, who keeps [1]His covenant and [1]His lovingkindness to a thousandth generation with those who [b]love Him and keep His commandments;

10 but repays those who hate Him to [1]their faces, to destroy [2]them; He will not delay [3]with him who hates Him, He will repay him to his face.

11 "Therefore, you shall keep the commandment and the statutes and the judgments which I am commanding you today, to do them.

Promises of God

12 "[a]Then it shall come about, because you listen to these judgments and keep and do them, that the LORD your God will keep with you [1]His covenant and [1]His lovingkindness which He swore to your forefathers.

13 "And He will love you and bless you and [a]multiply you; He will also bless the fruit of your womb and the fruit of your ground, your grain and your new wine and your oil, the increase of your herd and the young of your flock, [1]in the land which He swore to your forefathers to give you.

14 "You shall be blessed above all peoples; there shall be no male or female [a]barren among you or among your cattle.

15 "And [a]the LORD will remove from you all sickness; and He will not put on you any of the harmful diseases of Egypt which you have known, but He will lay them on all who hate you.

16 "And you shall consume all the peoples whom the LORD your God will deliver to you; [a]your eye shall not pity them, neither shall you serve their gods, for that *would be* [b]a snare to you.

17 "If you should say in your heart, 'These nations are greater than I; how can I dispossess them?'

18 you shall not be afraid of them; you shall well remember what the LORD your God did to Pharaoh and to all Egypt:

19 [a]the great trials which your eyes saw and the signs and the wonders and the mighty hand and the outstretched arm by which the LORD your God brought you out. So shall the LORD your God do to all the peoples of whom you are afraid.

20 "Moreover, the LORD your God will send [a]the hornet against them, until those who are left and hide themselves from you perish.

21 "You shall not dread [1]them, for [a]the LORD your God is in your midst, a great and awesome God.

22 "[a]And the LORD your God will clear away these nations before you little by little; you will not be able to put an end to them quickly, lest the [1]wild beasts grow too numerous for you.

23 "[a]But the LORD your God shall deliver them before you, and will [1]throw them into great confusion until they are destroyed.

24 "[a]And He will deliver their kings into your hand so that you shall make their name perish from under heaven; [b]no man will be able to stand before you until you have destroyed them.

25 "[a]The graven images of their gods you are to burn with fire; you shall not covet the silver or the gold that is on them, nor take it for yourselves, lest you be snared by it, for it is an abomination to the LORD your God.

26 "And you shall not bring an abomination into your house, and become a [1]devoted thing like it; you shall utterly detest it and you shall utterly abhor it, for it is a [1]devoted thing.

CHAPTER 8

God's Gracious Dealings

"ALL the commandments that I am commanding you today you shall be careful to do, that you [a]may live and multiply, and go in and possess the land which the LORD swore *to give* to your forefathers.

2 "[a]And you shall remember all the way which the LORD your God has led you in the wilderness these forty years, that He might humble you, [b]testing you, to know what was in your heart, whether you would keep His commandments or not.

3 "And He humbled you and let you be hungry, and fed you with manna which you did not know, nor did your fathers know, that He might make you [1]understand that [a]man does not live by bread alone, but man lives by everything that proceeds out of the mouth of the LORD.

4 "[a]Your clothing did not wear out on you, nor did your foot swell these forty years.

5 "[a]Thus you are to know in your heart that the LORD your God was disciplining you just as a man disciplines his son.

6 "Therefore, you shall keep the commandments of the LORD your God, to walk in His ways and to [1]fear Him.

9 [1]Lit., *the* [b]Deut. 5:10

10 [1]Lit., *his face* [2]Lit., *him* [3]Lit., *to*

12 [1]Lit., *the* [a]Lev. 26:3-13; Deut. 28:1-14

13 [1]Lit., *on* [a]Lev. 26:9; Deut. 13:17; 30:5

14 [a]Ex. 23:26

15 [a]Ex. 15:26

16 [a]Deut. 7:2 [b]Ex. 23:33

19 [a]Deut. 4:34

20 [a]Ex. 23:28; Josh. 24:12

21 [1]Lit., *from before them* [a]Ex. 29:45

22 [1]Lit., *beasts of the field* [a]Ex. 23:29, 30

23 [1]Lit., *confuse them with* [a]Ex. 23:27; Josh. 10:10

24 [a]Josh. 6:2; 10:23 [b]Deut. 11:25; Josh. 1:5; 10:8; 23:9

25 [a]Deut. 7:2

26 [1]Or, *banned*

1 [a]Deut. 4:1

2 [a]Deut. 8:16 [b]Ex. 15:25; 20:20

3 [1]Lit., *know* [a]Matt. 4:4; Luke 4:4

4 [a]Deut. 29:5; Neh. 9:21

5 [a]Deut. 4:36; Prov. 3:12; Heb. 12:6

6 [1]Or, *reverence*

7"For [a]the LORD your God is
bringing you into a good land, a land
of brooks of water, of fountains and
springs, flowing forth in valleys and
hills;
8 a land of wheat and barley, of
vines and fig trees and pomegranates, a land of olive oil and honey;
9 a land where you shall eat food
without scarcity, in which you shall
not lack anything; a land whose
stones are iron, and out of whose
hills you can dig copper.
10"When [a]you have eaten and are
satisfied, you shall bless the LORD
your God for the good land which
He has given you.
11"[1]Beware lest you [a]forget the
LORD your God by not keeping His
commandments and His ordinances
and His statutes which I am commanding you today;
12 lest, when you have eaten and
are satisfied, and have built good
houses and lived *in them,*
13 and when your herds and your
flocks multiply, and your silver and
gold multiply, and all that you have
multiplies,
14 then your heart becomes
[1]proud, and you [a]forget the LORD
your God who brought you out from
the land of Egypt, out of the house
of [2]slavery.
15"He led you through [a]the great
and terrible wilderness, *with its*
[b]fiery serpents and scorpions and
thirsty ground where there was no
water; He [c]brought water for you
out of the rock of flint.
16"In the wilderness He fed you
manna [a]which your fathers did not
know, that He might humble you
and that He might [b]test you, to do
good for you [1]in the end.
17"Otherwise, you may say in your
heart, 'My power and the strength
of my hand made me this wealth.'
18"But you shall remember the
LORD your God, for [a]it is He who is
giving you power to make wealth,
that He may confirm His covenant
which He swore to your fathers, as
it is this day.
19"And it shall come about if you
ever forget the LORD your God, and
go after other gods and serve them
and worship them, [a]I testify against
you today that you shall surely perish.
20"Like the nations that the LORD
makes to perish before you, so you
shall perish; because you would not
listen to the voice of the LORD your
God.

7 [a]Deut. 11:9-12; Jer. 2:7
10 [a]Deut. 6:11
11 [1]Lit., *take heed to yourself* [a]Deut. 4:9
14 [1]Lit., *lifted up* [2]Lit., *slaves* [a]Deut. 8:11
15 [a]Deut. 1:19 [b]Num. 21:6 [c]Ex. 17:6; Num. 20:11; Deut. 32.13, Ps. 78:15; 114:8
16 [1]Lit., *at your end* [a]Ex. 16:15 [b]Deut. 8:2
18 [a]Prov. 10:22; Hos. 2:8
19 [a]Deut. 4:26; 30:18
1 [1]Lit., *and fortified*
2 [a]Num. 13:22, 28, 33; Josh. 11:21, 22
3 [a]Deut. 4:24
4 [1]Lit., *you saying,* [a]Deut. 7:24; 31:27 [b]Lev. 18:3, 24-30; Deut. 12:31; 18:9-14
5 [1]Lit., *word*
6 [1]Or, *stiff-necked* [a]Deut. 9:13; 10:16; 31:27
7 [a]Num. 14:22
8 [a]Ex. 32:7-10
9 [a]Ex. 24:18; Deut. 8:3; 9:18
10 [a]Deut. 4:13

CHAPTER 9

Israel Provoked God

"HEAR, O Israel! You are crossing over the Jordan today to go in to
dispossess nations greater and
mightier than you, great cities
[1]fortified to heaven,
2 a people great and tall, the sons
of the Anakim, whom you know and
of whom you have heard *it said,*
'[a]Who can stand before the sons of
Anak?'
3"Know therefore today that it is
the LORD your God who is crossing
over before you as [a]a consuming
fire. He will destroy them and He
will subdue them before you, so that
you may drive them out and destroy
them quickly, just as the LORD has
spoken to you.
4"Do not say in your heart when
the LORD your God has driven them
out before [1]you, '[a]Because of my
righteousness the LORD has brought
me in to possess this land,' but *it is*
[b]because of the wickedness of these
nations *that* the LORD is dispossessing them before you.
5"It is not for your righteousness
or for the uprightness of your heart
that you are going to possess their
land, but *it is* because of the wickedness of these nations *that* the LORD
your God is driving them out before
you, in order to confirm the [1]oath
which the LORD swore to your fathers, to Abraham, Isaac and Jacob.
6"Know, then, *it is* not because of
your righteousness *that* the LORD
your God is giving you this good
land to possess, for you are [a]a [1]stub-
born people.
7"Remember, do not forget how
you provoked the LORD your God to
wrath in the wilderness; [a]from the
day that you left the land of Egypt
until you arrived at this place, you
have been rebellious against the
LORD.
8"Even [a]at Horeb you provoked
the LORD to wrath, and the LORD
was so angry with you that He
would have destroyed you.
9"When I went up to the mountain to receive the tablets of stone,
the tablets of the covenant which
the LORD had made with you, then I
remained on the mountain forty
days and nights; [a]I neither ate bread
nor drank water.
10"And the LORD gave me the two
tablets of stone [a]written by the finger of God; and on them *were* all the
words which the LORD had spoken
with you at the mountain from the

midst of the fire on the day of the
assembly.
11"And it came about [a]at the end
of forty days and nights that the
LORD gave me the two tablets of
stone, the tablets of the covenant.
12"[a]Then the LORD said to me,
'Arise, go down from here quickly,
for your people whom you brought
out of Egypt have acted corruptly.
They have quickly turned aside
from the way which I commanded
them; they have made a molten
image for themselves.'
13"The LORD spoke further to me,
saying, 'I have seen this people, and
indeed, it is a [1]stubborn people.
14 '[a]Let Me alone, that I may destroy them and blot out their name
from under heaven; and I will make
of you a nation mightier and greater
than they.'
15"[a]So I turned and came down
from the mountain while the mountain was burning with fire, and the
two tablets of the covenant were in
my two hands.
16"And I saw that you had indeed
sinned against the LORD your God.
You had made for yourselves a molten calf; you had turned aside
quickly from the way which the
LORD had commanded you.
17"And I took hold of the two tablets and threw them from my hands,
and smashed them before your
eyes.
18"[a]And I fell down before the
LORD, [b]as at the first, forty days and
nights; [c]I neither ate bread nor
drank water, [d]because of all your sin
which you had committed in doing
what was evil in the sight of the
LORD to provoke Him to anger.
19"For [a]I was afraid of the anger
and hot displeasure with which the
LORD was wrathful against you in
order to destroy you, [b]but the LORD
listened to me that time also.
20"And the LORD was angry
enough with Aaron to destroy him;
so I also prayed for Aaron at the
same time.
21"[a]And I took your [1]sinful *thing*,
the calf which you had made, and
burned it with fire and crushed it,
grinding it very small until it was as
fine as dust; and I threw its dust into
the brook that came down from the
mountain.
22"Again at [a]Taberah and at [b]Mas-
sah and at [c]Kibroth-hattaavah you
provoked the LORD to wrath.
23"And when the LORD sent you
from Kadesh-barnea, saying, 'Go up
and possess the land which I have
given you,' then you rebelled

11 [a]Deut. 9:9
12 [a]Ex. 32:7, 8
13 [1]Or, *stiff-necked*
14 [a]Ex. 32:10
15 [a]Ex. 32:15-19
18 [a]Ex. 34:28 [b]Deut. 10:10 [c]Deut. 9:9 [d]Ex. 34:9
19 [a]Heb. 12:21 [b]Ex. 34:10
21 [1]Lit., *sin* [a]Ex. 32:20
22 [a]Num. 11:3 [b]Ex. 17:7 [c]Num. 11:34
23 [1]Lit., *mouth*
24 [a]Deut. 9:7
25 [1]Lit., *fell down* [a]Deut. 9:18
26 [a]Ex. 32:11-13
28 [1]Lit., *spoken to*
29 [a]Ps. 106:40 [b]Deut. 4:34
1 [a]Ex. 34:1 [b]Ex. 25:10
2 [a]Deut. 4:13 [b]Ex. 25:16
3 [a]Ex. 37:1-9 [b]Ex. 34:4
4 [1]Lit., *Words* [a]Ex. 34:28; Deut. 4:13
5 [a]Ex. 40:20
6 [1]Or, *the wells of the sons of Jaakan* [a]Num. 33:30, 31 [b]Num. 20:25-28

against the [1]command of the LORD
your God; you neither believed Him
nor listened to His voice.
24"[a]You have been rebellious
against the LORD from the day I
knew you.
25"[a]So I fell down before the LORD
the forty days and nights, which I
[1]did because the LORD had said He
would destroy you.
26"[a]And I prayed to the LORD, and
said, 'Oh Lord GOD do not destroy
Thy people, even Thine inheritance,
whom Thou hast redeemed through
Thy greatness, whom Thou hast
brought out of Egypt with a mighty
hand.
27 'Remember Thy servants, Abraham, Isaac, and Jacob; do not look
at the stubbornness of this people or
at their wickedness or their sin.
28 'Otherwise the land from which
Thou didst bring us may say, "Because the LORD was not able to
bring them into the land which He
had [1]promised them and because
He hated them He has brought them
out to slay them in the wilderness."
29 'Yet they are Thy people, even
[a]Thine inheritance, whom Thou hast
brought out by Thy [b]great power
and Thine outstretched arm.'

CHAPTER 10

The Tablets Rewritten

"AT that time the LORD said to
me, '[a]Cut out for yourself two tablets of stone like the former ones,
and come up to Me on the mountain,
and [b]make an ark of wood for yourself.
2 'And [a]I will write on the tablets
the words that were on the former
tablets which you shattered, and
[b]you shall put them in the ark.'
3"So [a]I made an ark of acacia
wood and [b]cut out two tablets of
stone like the former ones, and went
up on the mountain with the two
tablets in my hand.
4"And He wrote on the tablets,
like the former writing, [a]the Ten
[1]Commandments which the LORD
had spoken to you on the mountain
from the midst of the fire on the day
of the assembly; and the LORD gave
them to me.
5"Then I turned and came down
from the mountain, and [a]put the
tablets in the ark which I had made;
and there they are, as the LORD commanded me."
6 (Now the sons of Israel set out
from [1]Beeroth [a]Bene-jaakan to Mo-
serah. [b]There Aaron died and there

he was buried and Eleazar his son
ministered as priest in his place.
7 [a]From there they set out to
Gudgodah; and from Gudgodah to
Jotbathah, a land of brooks of water.
8 [a]At that time the LORD set apart
the tribe of Levi to carry the ark of
the covenant of the LORD, to stand
before the LORD [b]to serve Him and
to bless in His name until this day.
9 [a]Therefore, Levi does not have
a portion or inheritance with his
brothers; the LORD is his inheritance, just as the LORD your God
spoke to him.)
10"[a]I, moreover, stayed on the
mountain forty days and forty
nights like the first time, and the
LORD listened to me that time also;
the LORD was not willing to destroy
you.
11"Then the LORD said to me,
'Arise, proceed on your journey
ahead of the people, that they may
go in and possess the land which I
swore to their fathers to give them.'
12"[a]And now, Israel, what does the
LORD your God require from you,
but to [1]fear the LORD your God, to
walk in all His ways and [b]love Him,
and to serve the LORD your God with
[c]all your heart and with all your
soul,
13 *and* to keep the LORD's commandments and His statutes which
I am commanding you today for
your good?
14"Behold, [a]to the LORD your God
belong heaven and the [1]highest
heavens, the earth and all that is in
it.
15"[a]Yet on your fathers did the
LORD set His affection to love them,
and He chose their [1]descendants after them, *even* you above all peoples, as *it is* this day.
16"[a]Circumcise then [1]your heart,
and [b]stiffen your neck no more.
17"[a]For the LORD your God is the
God of gods and the Lord of lords,
the great, the mighty, and the awesome God [b]who does not show partiality, nor [c]take a bribe.
18"He executes justice for [a]the orphan and the widow, and shows His
love for the alien by giving him food
and clothing.
19"[a]So show your love for the
alien, for you were aliens in the land
of Egypt.
20"You shall fear the LORD your
God; you shall serve Him and [a]cling
to Him, and [b]you shall swear by His
name.
21"He is [a]your praise and He is
your God, who has done these great
and awesome things for you which
your eyes have seen.
22"[a]Your fathers went down to
Egypt seventy persons in *all*, [b]and
now the LORD your God has made
you as numerous as the stars of
heaven.

CHAPTER 11

Rewards of Obedience

"YOU shall therefore [a]love the
LORD your God, and always [b]keep
His charge, His statutes, His ordinances, and His commandments.
2"And know this day [a]that I *am*
not *speaking* with your sons who
have not known and who have not
seen the [1]discipline of the LORD your
God—His greatness, His mighty
hand, and His outstretched arm,
3 and His signs and His works
which He did in the midst of Egypt
to Pharaoh the king of Egypt and to
all his land;
4 and what He did to Egypt's
army, to its horses and its chariots,
[a]when He made the water of the
[1]Red Sea to [2]engulf them while they
were pursuing you, and the LORD
[3]completely destroyed them;
5 and what He did to you in the
wilderness until you came to this
place;
6 and [a]what He did to Dathan and
Abiram, the sons of Eliab, the son of
Reuben, when the earth opened its
mouth and swallowed them, their
households, their tents, and [b]every
living thing that [1]followed them,
among Israel—
7 but your own eyes have seen all
the great work of the LORD which
He did.
8"You shall therefore keep every
commandment which I am commanding you today, [a]so that you
may be strong and go in and possess
the land into which you are about to
cross to possess it;
9 [a]so that you may prolong *your*
days on the land which the LORD
swore to your fathers to give to
them and to their [1]descendants, a
land flowing with milk and honey.
10"For the land, into which you are
entering to possess it, is not like the
land of Egypt from which you came,
where you used to sow your seed
and water it with your [1]foot like a
vegetable garden.
11"But the land into which you are
about to cross to possess it, a land of
hills and valleys, drinks water from
the rain of heaven,
12 a land for which the LORD your
God cares; the eyes of the LORD your

7 [a]Num. 33:33, 34
8 [a]Num. 3:6; 18:1-7; Deut. 31:9 [b]Deut. 17:12; 18:5; 21:5
9 [a]Num. 18:20, 24
10 [a]Deut. 9:18
12 [1]Or, *reverence* [a]Mic. 6:8 [b]Deut. 6:5 [c]Deut. 4:29
14 [1]Lit., *heaven of heavens* [a]1 Kin. 8:27; Neh. 9:6; Ps. 68:33; 115:16
15 [1]Lit., *seed* [a]Deut. 4:37
16 [1]Lit., *the foreskin of your heart* [a]Jer. 4:4 [b]Deut. 9:6
17 [a]Josh. 22:22; Ps. 136:2 [b]Deut. 1:17 [c]Deut. 16:19
18 [a]Ex. 22:22-24; Ps. 68:5
19 [a]Lev. 19:34; Ezek. 47:22, 23
20 [a]Deut. 11:22; 13:4 [b]Deut. 5:11; 6:13
21 [a]Ps. 109:1; 148:14
22 [a]Gen. 46:27 [b]Deut. 1:10
1 [a]Deut. 6:5; 10:12 [b]Lev. 18:30; 22:9
2 [1]Or, *instruction* [a]Deut. 4:34
4 [1]Lit., *Sea of Reeds* [2]Lit., *flow over their faces* [3]Lit., *to this day* [a]Ex. 14:28; Deut. 1:40; 2:1
6 [1]Lit., *was at their feet* [a]Num. 16:31-33 [b]Num. 26:10, 11
8 [a]Deut. 31:6, 7, 23
9 [1]Lit., *seed* [a]Deut. 4:40; 5:33; 6:2
10 [1]I.e., probably a treadmill

God are always on it, from the [1]beginning even to the end of the year.

13"And it shall come about, if you listen obediently to my commandments which I am commanding you today, [a]to love the LORD your God and to serve Him [b]with all your heart and all your soul,

14 that '[1a]I will give the rain for your land in its season, the [2]early and [3]late rain, that you may gather in your grain and your new wine and your oil.

15 'And I will give grass in your fields for your cattle, and [a]you shall eat and be satisfied.'

16"[1]Beware, lest your hearts be deceived and you turn away and serve other gods and worship them.

17"Or the anger of the LORD will be kindled against you, and He will shut up the heavens [a]so that there will be no rain and the ground will not yield its fruit; and [b]you will perish quickly from the good land which the LORD is giving you.

18"[a]You shall therefore [1]impress these words of mine on your heart and on your soul; and you shall bind them as a sign on your hand, and they shall be as [2]frontals [3]on your forehead.

19"[a]And you shall teach them to your sons, talking of them when you sit in your house and when you walk along the road and when you lie down and when you rise up.

20"[a]And you shall write them on the doorposts of your house and on your gates,

21 so that your days and the days of your sons may be multiplied on the land which the LORD swore to your fathers to give them, as [1]long as the heavens *remain* above the earth.

22"For if you are [a]careful to keep all this commandment which I am commanding you, to do it, [b]to love the LORD your God, to walk in all His ways and [c]hold fast to Him;

23 then the LORD will drive out all these nations from before you, and you will dispossess nations greater and mightier than you.

24"[a]Every place on which the sole of your foot shall tread shall be yours; [b]your border shall be from the wilderness to Lebanon, *and* from the river, the river Euphrates, as far as [1]the Western Sea.

25"[a]There shall no man be able to stand before you; the LORD your God shall lay the dread of you and the fear of you on all the land on which you set foot, as He has spoken to you.

26"[a]See, I am setting before you today a blessing and a curse:

27 the blessing, if you listen to the commandments of the LORD your God, which I am commanding you today;

28 and the curse, if you do not listen to the commandments of the LORD your God, but turn aside from the way which I am commanding you today, [1]by following other gods which you have not known.

29"And it shall come about, when the LORD your God brings you into the land where you are entering to possess it, [a]that you shall place the blessing on Mount Gerizim and the curse on Mount Ebal.

30"Are they not across the Jordan, west of the way toward the sunset, in the land of the Canaanites who live in the Arabah, opposite [a]Gilgal, beside [b]the [1]oaks of Moreh?

31"For you are about to cross the Jordan to go in to possess the land which the LORD your God is giving you, and [a]you shall possess it and live in it,

32 and you shall be careful to do all the statutes and the judgments which I am setting before you today.

CHAPTER 12

Laws of the Sanctuary

"THESE are the statutes and the judgments which you shall carefully observe in the land which the LORD, the God of your fathers, has given you to possess [1a]as long as you live on the [2]earth.

2"You shall utterly destroy all the places where the nations whom you shall dispossess serve their gods, on the high mountains and on the hills and under every green tree.

3"And [a]you shall tear down their altars and smash their *sacred* pillars and burn their [1]Asherim with fire, and you shall cut down the engraved images of their gods, and you shall obliterate their name from that place.

4"You shall not act like this toward the *LORD* your God.

5"[a]But you shall seek *the LORD* at the place which the LORD your God shall choose from all your tribes, to establish His name there for His dwelling, and there you shall come.

6"And there you shall bring your burnt offerings, your sacrifices, your tithes, the [1]contribution of your hand, your votive offerings, your freewill offerings, and the firstborn of your herd and of your flock.

12 [1]Lit., *beginning of the year*

13 [a]Deut. 11:1 [b]Deut. 4:29

14 [1]Some ancient versions read *He* [2]I.e., autumn [3]I.e., spring [a]Deut. 28:12

15 [a]Deut. 6:11

16 [1]Lit., *Watch yourselves*

17 [a]Deut. 28:24 [b]Deut. 4:26

18 [1]Lit., *put* [2]Lit., *frontlet bands* [3]Lit., *between your eyes* [a]Ex. 12:14; 13:9, 16; Deut. 6:8

19 [a]Deut. 4:9, 10; 6:7

20 [a]Deut. 6:9

21 [1]Lit., *the days of the heavens*

22 [a]Deut. 6:17 [b]Deut. 11:1 [c]Deut. 10:20

24 [1]I.e., the Mediterranean [a]Josh. 1:3 [b]Gen. 15:18; Ex. 23:31; Deut. 1:7, 8

25 [a]Ex. 23:27; Deut. 7:24

26 [a]Deut. 30:1, 19

28 [1]Lit., *to follow*

29 [a]Deut. 27:12; Josh. 8:33

30 [1]Lit., *terebinths* [a]Josh. 4:19 [b]Gen. 12:6

31 [a]Deut. 17:14; Josh. 21:43

1 [1]Lit., *all the days* [2]Lit., *ground* [a]Deut. 4:9

3 [1]I.e., wooden symbols of a female deity [a]Deut. 7:5

5 [a]Ex. 20:24; Deut. 12:11, 13

6 [1]Or, *heave offering*

7"There also you and your households shall eat before the LORD your
God, and [a]rejoice in all [1]your undertakings in which the LORD your God
has blessed you.
8"You shall not do at all what we
are doing here today, every man
doing whatever is right in his own
eyes;
9 for you have not as yet come to
[a]the resting place and the [b]inheri-
tance which the LORD your God is
giving you.
10"When you cross the Jordan and
live in the land which the LORD your
God is giving you to inherit, and [a]He
gives you rest from all your enemies
around *you* so that you live in security,
11 [a]then it shall come about that
the place in which the LORD your
God shall choose for His name to
dwell, there you shall bring all that I
command you: your burnt offerings
and your sacrifices, your tithes and
the [1]contribution of your hand, and
all your choice votive offerings
which you will vow to the LORD.
12"And you shall [a]rejoice before
the LORD your God, you and your
sons and daughters, your male and
female servants, and the [b]Levite
who is within your gates, since [c]he
has no portion or inheritance with
you.
13"[a]Be careful that you do not offer your burnt offerings in every *cultic* place you see,
14 but in the place which the LORD
chooses in one of your tribes, there
you shall offer your burnt offerings,
and there you shall do all that I command you.
15"[a]However, you may slaughter
and eat meat within any of your
gates, [1]whatever you desire, according to the blessing of the LORD your
God which He has given you; the
unclean and the clean may eat of it,
as of [b]the gazelle and the deer.
16"[a]Only you shall not eat the
blood; [b]you are to pour it out on the
ground like water.
17"[a]You are not allowed to eat
within your gates the tithe of your
grain, or new wine, or oil, or the
first-born of your herd or flock, or
any of your votive offerings which
you vow, or your freewill offerings,
or the [1]contribution of your hand.
18"But you shall eat them before
the LORD your God in [a]the place
which the LORD your God will
choose, you and your son and
daughter, and your male and female
servants, and the [b]Levite who is
within your gates; and you shall [c]re-
joice before the LORD your God in all
[1]your undertakings.
19"Be careful that you do not forsake the Levite [1]as long as you live
in your land.
20"When the LORD your God extends your border as He has promised you, and you say, 'I will eat
meat,' because [1]you desire to eat
meat, *then* you may eat meat,
[2]whatever you desire.
21"If the place which the LORD
your God chooses to put His name is
too far from you, then you may
slaughter of your herd and flock
which the LORD has given you, as I
have commanded you; and you may
eat within your gates [1]whatever you
desire.
22"Just as a gazelle or a deer is eat-
en, so you shall eat it; the unclean
and the clean alike may eat of it.
23"Only be sure [a]not to eat the
blood, for the blood is the [1]life, and
you shall not eat the [1]life with the
flesh.
24"You shall not eat it; you shall
pour it out on the ground like water.
25"You shall not eat it, in order
that [a]it may be well with you and
your sons after you, for you will be
doing what is right in the sight of the
LORD.
26"[a]Only your holy things which
you may have and your votive offerings, you shall take and go to the
place which the LORD chooses.
27"And you shall offer your burnt
offerings, the flesh and the blood, on
the altar of the LORD your God; and
the blood of your sacrifices shall be
poured out on the altar of the LORD
your God, and [a]you shall eat the
flesh.
28"Be careful to listen to all these
words which I command you, in order that [a]it may be well with you
and your sons after you forever, for
you will be doing what is good and
right in the sight of the LORD your
God.
29"When the LORD your God cuts
off before you the nations which you
are going in to dispossess, and you
dispossess them and dwell in their
land,
30 beware that you are not ensnared [1]to follow them, after they
are destroyed before you, and that
you do not inquire after their gods,
saying, 'How do these nations serve
their gods, that I also may do likewise?'
31"[a]You shall not behave thus
toward the LORD your God, for every abominable act which the LORD
hates they have done for their gods;

7 [1]Lit., *the putting forth of your hand* [a]Deut. 12:12, 18; 14:26; 28:47
9 [a]Deut. 3:20; 25:19; 95:11 [b]Deut. 4:21
10 [a]Josh. 11:23
11 [1]Or, *heave offering* [a]Deut. 12:5
12 [a]Deut. 12:7 [b]Deut. 12:18, 19; 26:11-13 [c]Deut. 10:9
13 [a]Deut. 12:5, 11
15 [1]Lit., *in every desire of your soul* [a]Deut. 12:20-23 [b]Deut. 12:22; 14:5
16 [a]Lev. 17:10-12 [b]Deut. 15:23
17 [1]Lit., *heave offering* [a]Deut. 12:26
18 [1]Lit., *the putting forth of your hand* [a]Deut. 12:5 [b]Deut. 12:12 [c]Deut. 12:7
19 [1]Lit., *all your days upon your land*
20 [1]Lit., *your soul* [2]Lit., *every desire of your soul*
21 [1]Lit., *in every desire of your soul*
23 [1]Lit., *soul* [a]Deut. 12:16
25 [a]Deut. 4:40
26 [a]Deut. 12:17
27 [a]Lev. 3:1-17
28 [a]Deut. 4:40
30 [1]Lit., *after them*
31 [a]Deut. 9:5

for [b]they even burn their sons and daughters in the fire to their gods.

32“[1a]Whatever I command you, you shall be careful to do; you shall not add to nor take away from it.

Chapter 13

Shun Idolatry

“[1a]If a prophet or a dreamer of dreams arises among you and gives you a sign or a wonder,

2 and the sign or the wonder comes true, concerning which he spoke to you, saying, ‘[a]Let us go after other gods (whom you have not known) and let us serve them,’

3 you shall not listen to the words of that prophet or that dreamer of dreams; for the LORD your God is [a]testing you to find out if [b]you love the LORD your God with all your heart and with all your soul.

4“You shall follow the LORD your God and fear Him; and you shall keep His commandments, listen to His voice, serve Him, and [a]cling to Him.

5“But that prophet or that dreamer of dreams shall be [a]put to death, because he has [1]counseled [2]rebellion against the LORD your God who brought you from the land of Egypt and redeemed you from the house of [3]slavery, [b]to seduce you from the way in which the LORD your God commanded you to walk. So you shall purge the evil from among you.

6“[a]If your brother, your mother’s son, or your son or daughter, or the wife [1]you cherish, or your friend who is as your own soul, entice you secretly, saying, ‘[b]Let us go and serve other gods’ (whom neither you nor your fathers have known,

7 of the gods of the peoples who are around you, near you or far from you, from one end of the earth to the other end),

8 you shall not yield to him or listen to him; [a]and your eye shall not pity him, nor shall you spare or conceal him.

9“[a]But you shall surely kill him; [b]your hand shall be first against him to put him to death, and afterwards the hand of all the people.

10“So you shall stone him [1]to death because he has sought [a]to seduce you from the LORD your God who brought you out from the land of Egypt, out of the house of [2]slavery.

11“Then all Israel will hear and be afraid, and will never again do such a wicked thing among you.

12“If you hear in one of your cities, which the LORD your God is giving you to live in, *anyone* saying *that*

13 some worthless men have gone out from among you and have seduced the inhabitants of their city, saying, ‘[a]Let us go and serve other gods’ (whom you have not known),

14 then you shall investigate and search out and inquire thoroughly. And if it is true and the matter established that this abomination has been done among you,

15 [a]you shall surely strike the inhabitants of that city with the edge of the sword, [1]utterly destroying it and all that is in it and its cattle with the edge of the sword.

16“[a]Then you shall gather all its booty into the middle of its open square and burn the city and all its booty with fire as a whole burnt offering to the LORD your God; and it shall be a [1]ruin forever. It shall never be rebuilt.

17“And nothing from that which is put under the ban shall cling to your hand, in order that the LORD may turn from [a]His burning anger and [b]show mercy to you, and have compassion on you and [c]make you increase, just as He has sworn to your fathers,

18 [1]if you will listen to the voice of the LORD your God, [2]keeping all His commandments which I am commanding you today, [3]and doing what is right in the sight of the LORD your God.

Chapter 14

Clean and Unclean Animals

“You are the sons of the LORD your God; [a]you shall not cut yourselves nor [1]shave your forehead for the sake of the dead.

2“For you are [a]a holy people to the LORD your God; and the LORD has chosen you to be a people for His [1]own possession out of all the peoples who are on the face of the earth.

3“You shall not eat any detestable thing.

4“[a]These are the animals which you may eat: the ox, the sheep, the goat,

5 [1]the deer, the gazelle, the roebuck, the wild goat, the ibex, the antelope and the mountain sheep.

6“And any animal that divides the hoof and has the hoof split in [1]two *and* [2]chews the cud, among the animals, that you may eat.

7“Nevertheless, you are not to eat

31 [b]Lev. 18:21; Deut. 18:10; Ps. 106:37

32 [1]Lit., *All the thing that* [a]Deut. 4:2

1 [1]In Heb., 13:2 [a]Matt. 24:24; Mark 13:22

2 [a]Deut. 13:6, 13

3 [a]Ex. 20:20 Deut. 8:2, 16 [b]Deut. 6:5

4 [a]Deut. 10:20

5 [1]Lit., *spoken* [2]Lit., *turning aside* [3]Lit., *slaves* [a]Deut. 13:9, 15; 17:5 [b]Deut. 4:19; 13:10

6 [1]Lit., *of your bosom* [a]Deut. 17:2-7; 29:18 [b]Deut. 13:2

8 [a]Deut. 7:2

9 [a]Deut. 13:5 [b]Lev. 24:14; Deut. 17:7

10 [1]Lit., *with stones so that he dies* [2]Lit., *slaves* [a]Deut. 13:5

13 [a]Deut. 13:2

15 [1]Or, *putting it under the ban* [a]Deut. 13:5

16 [1]Lit., *mound* [a]Deut. 7:25, 26

17 [a]Ex. 32:12; Num. 25:4 [b]Deut. 30:3 [c]Deut. 7:13

18 [1]Or, *for* [2]Lit., *to keep* [3]Lit., *to do*

1 [1]Lit., *make a baldness between your eyes* [a]Lev. 21:5

2 [1]Or, *special treasure* [a]Deut. 7:6

4 [a]Lev. 11:1-45; Acts 10:14

5 [1]Exact identification of these animals is uncertain

6 [1]Lit., *two hoofs* [2]Lit., *brings up*

of these among those which [1]chew
the cud, or among those that divide
the hoof in [2]two: the camel and the
[3]rabbit and the rock-badger, for
though they [1]chew the cud, they do
not divide the hoof; they are unclean
for you.
8"And the pig, because it divides
the hoof but *does* not *chew* the cud,
it is unclean for you. You shall not
eat any of their flesh nor touch their
carcasses.
9"These you may eat of all that
are in water: anything that has fins
and scales you may eat,
10 but anything that does not have
fins and scales you shall not eat; it is
unclean for you.
11"You may eat any clean bird.
12"But these are the ones which
you shall not eat: the [1]eagle and the
vulture and the [2]buzzard,
13 and the red kite, the falcon, and
the kite in their kinds,
14 and every raven in its kind,
15 and the ostrich, the owl, the sea
gull, and the hawk in their kinds,
16 the little owl, the [1]great owl, the
white owl,
17 the pelican, the carrion vulture,
the cormorant,
18 the stork, and the heron in their
kinds, and the hoopoe and the bat.
19"And all the [1]teeming life with
wings are unclean to you; they shall
not be eaten.
20"You may eat any clean bird.
21"You shall not eat anything
which dies *of itself.* You may give it
to the alien who is in your [1]town, so
that he may eat it, or you may sell it
to a foreigner, for you are [a]a holy
people to the LORD your God. [b]You
shall not boil a kid in its mother's
milk.
22"You shall surely tithe all the
produce from [1]what you sow, which
comes out of the field every year.
23"And you shall eat in the presence of the LORD your God, [a]at the
place where He chooses to establish
His name, the tithe of your grain,
your new wine, your oil, and the
first-born of your herd and your
flock, in order that you may [b]learn
to fear the LORD your God always.
24"And if the [1]distance is so great
for you that you are not able to
[2]bring *the tithe,* since the place
where the LORD your God chooses
[a]to set His name is too far away
from you when the LORD your God
blesses you,
25 then you shall [1]exchange *it* for
money, and bind the money in your
hand and go to the place which the
LORD your God chooses.
26"And you may spend the money
for whatever your [1]heart desires, for
oxen, or sheep, or wine, or strong
drink, or whatever your [1]heart [2]de-
sires; and [a]there you shall eat in the
presence of the LORD your God and
rejoice, you and your household.
27"Also you shall not neglect [a]the
Levite who is in your [1]town, [b]for he
has no portion or inheritance among
you.
28"[a]At the end of every third year
you shall bring out all the tithe of
your produce in that year, and shall
deposit *it* in your [1]town.
29"And the Levite, [a]because he has
no portion or inheritance among
you, and [b]the alien, the [1]orphan and
the widow who are in your [2]town,
shall come and [c]eat and be satisfied,
in order that the LORD your God
may bless you in all the work of
your hand which you do.

CHAPTER 15

The Sabbatic Year

"[a]AT the end of *every* seven years
you shall [1]grant a remission *of*
debts.
2"And this is the manner of remission: every creditor shall release
what he has loaned to his neighbor;
he shall not exact it of his neighbor
and his brother, because the LORD's
remission has been proclaimed.
3"From a foreigner you may
exact *it,* but your hand shall release
whatever of yours is with your
brother.
4"However, there shall be no poor
among you, since the LORD will
surely bless you in the land which
the LORD your God is giving you as
an inheritance to possess,
5 if only you listen obediently to
the voice of the LORD your God, to
observe carefully all this commandment which I am commanding you
today.
6"[a]For the LORD your God shall
bless you as He has promised you,
and you will lend to many nations,
but you will not borrow; and you
will rule over many nations, but
they will not rule over you.
7"If there is [a]a poor man with
you, one of your brothers, in any of
your [1]towns in your land which the
LORD your God is giving you, you
shall not harden your heart, nor
close your hand from your poor
brother;
8 but you shall freely open your
hand to him, and shall generously
lend him sufficient for his need *in*
whatever he lacks.

7 [1]Lit., *brings up* [2]Lit., *a cleaving* [3]Or, *hare*

12 [1]Or, *vulture* [2]Or, *black vulture*

16 [1]Or, *great horned owl*

19 [1]I.e., flying insects

21 [1]Lit., *gates* [a]Deut. 14:2 [b]Ex. 23:19; 34:26

22 [1]Lit., *your seed*

23 [a]Deut. 12:5 [b]Deut. 4:10

24 [1]Lit., *way* [2]Lit., *carry it* [a]Deut. 12:5

25 [1]Lit., *give in money*

26 [1]Lit., *soul* [2]Lit., *asks of you* [a]Deut. 12:7

27 [1]Lit., *gates* [a]Deut. 12:12 [b]Deut. 10:9

28 [1]Lit., *gates* [a]Deut. 26:12

29 [1]Or, *fatherless* [2]Lit., *gates* [a]Deut. 10:9 [b]Deut. 16:11, 14; 24:19-21; 26:12 [c]Deut. 6:11

1 [1]Lit., *make a release* [a]Deut. 31:10

6 [a]Deut. 28:12, 13

7 [1]Lit., *gates* [a]Deut. 15:11

9"Beware, lest there is a base [1]thought in your heart, saying, '[a]The seventh year, the year of remission, is near,' and your eye is hostile toward your poor brother, and you give him nothing; then he [b]may cry to the LORD against you, and it will be a sin in you.

10"You shall generously give to him, and your heart shall not be grieved when you give to him, because for this thing the LORD your God will bless you in all your work and in all [1]your undertakings.

11"[a]For the poor will never cease *to be* [1]in the land; therefore I command you, saying, 'You shall freely open your hand to your brother, to your needy and poor in your land.'

12"[a]If your [1]kinsman, a Hebrew man or woman, is sold to you, then he shall serve you six years, but in the seventh year you shall set him [2]free.

13"And when you set him [1]free, you shall not send him away emptyhanded.

14"You shall furnish him liberally from your flock and from your threshing floor and from your wine vat; you shall give to him as the LORD your God has blessed you.

15"And you shall remember that you were a slave in the land of Egypt, and the LORD your God redeemed you; therefore I command you [1]this today.

16"And it shall come about if he says to you, 'I will not go out from you,' because he loves you and your household, since he fares well with you;

17 then you shall take an awl and pierce it through his ear into the door, and he shall be your servant forever. And also you shall do likewise to your maidservant.

18"It shall not seem hard to you when you set him [1]free, for he has given you six years *with* [2]double the service of a hired man; so the LORD your God will bless you in whatever you do.

19"[a]You shall consecrate to the LORD your God all the first-born males that are born of your herd and of your flock; you shall not work with the first-born of your herd, nor shear the first-born of your flock.

20"[a]You and your household shall eat it every year before the LORD your God in the place which the LORD chooses.

21"[a]But if it has any [1]defect, *such as* lameness or blindness, *or* any serious [1]defect, you shall not sacrifice it to the LORD your God.

22"You shall eat it within your gates; the unclean and the clean alike *may eat it,* as [a]a gazelle or a deer.

23"Only you shall not eat its blood; you are to pour it out on the ground like water.

CHAPTER 16

The Feasts of Passover, of Weeks, and of Booths

"OBSERVE [a]the month of Abib and [1]celebrate the Passover to the LORD your God, for in the month of Abib the LORD your God brought you out of Egypt by night.

2"And you shall sacrifice the Passover to the LORD your God from the flock and the herd, in the place where the LORD chooses to establish His name.

3"[a]You shall not eat leavened bread with it; seven days you shall eat with it unleavened bread, the bread of affliction (for you came out of the land of Egypt in haste), in order that you may remember [b]all the days of your life the day when you came out of the land of Egypt.

4"For seven days no leaven shall be seen with you in all your territory, and none of the flesh which you sacrifice on the evening of the first day shall remain overnight until morning.

5"You are not allowed to sacrifice the Passover in any of your [1]towns which the LORD your God is giving you;

6 but [a]at the place where the LORD your God chooses to establish His name, you shall sacrifice the Passover in the evening at sunset, at the time that you came out of Egypt.

7"And you shall cook and eat *it* in the place which the LORD your God chooses. And in the morning you are to return to your tents.

8"Six days you shall eat unleavened bread, and on the seventh day there shall be [a]a solemn assembly to the LORD your God; you shall do no work *on it.*

9"[a]You shall count seven weeks for yourself; you shall begin to count seven weeks from the time you begin to put the sickle to the standing grain.

10"Then you shall [1]celebrate the Feast of Weeks to the LORD your God with a tribute of a freewill offering of your hand, which you shall give just as the LORD your God blesses you;

15:9 [1]Lit., *word* [a]Deut. 15:1 [b]Ex. 22:23; Deut. 24:15

10 [1]Lit., *the putting forth of your hand*

11 [1]Lit., *in the midst of* [a]Matt. 26:11; Mark 14:7; John 12:8

12 [1]Lit., *brother* [2]Lit., *free from you* [a]Ex. 21:2-6; Lev. 25:39-43

13 [1]Lit., *free from you*

15 [1]Lit., *this thing*

18 [1]Lit., *free from you* [2]Lit., *double the amount*

19 [a]Ex. 13:2

20 [a]Lev. 7:15-18

21 [1]Lit., *blemish* [a]Lev. 22:19-25

22 [a]Deut. 12:15, 16

16:1 [1]Lit., *perform* [a]Ex. 12:2

3 [a]Ex. 12:8, 15 [b]Deut. 4:9

5 [1]Lit., *gates*

6 [a]Deut. 12:5

8 [a]Lev. 23:36

9 [a]Ex. 23:16; 34:22; Lev. 23:15; Num. 28:26

10 [1]Lit., *perform*

11 and you shall [a]rejoice before
the LORD your God, you and your
son and your daughter and your
male and female servants and [b]the
Levite who is in your [1]town, and
[c]the stranger and the [2]orphan and
the widow who are in your midst, in
the place where the LORD your God
chooses to establish His name.
12"And you shall remember that
you were a slave in Egypt, and you
shall be careful to observe these
statutes.
13"[a]You shall [1]celebrate the Feast
of Booths seven days after you have
gathered in from your threshing
floor and your wine vat;
14 and you shall [a]rejoice in your
feast, you and your son and your
daughter and your male and female
servants and the Levite and the
stranger and the [1]orphan and the
widow who are in your [2]towns.
15"Seven days you shall celebrate
a feast to the LORD your God in the
place which the LORD chooses, because the LORD your God will bless
you in all your produce and in all the
work of your hands, so that you
shall be altogether joyful.
16"[a]Three times in a year all your
males shall appear before the LORD
your God in the place which He
chooses, at the Feast of Unleavened
Bread and at the Feast of Weeks and
at the Feast of Booths, and [b]they
shall not appear before the LORD
empty-handed.
17"Every man [1]shall give as he is
able, according to the blessing of the
LORD your God which He has given
you.
18"You shall appoint for yourself
judges and officers in all your
[1]towns which the LORD your God is
giving you, according to your tribes,
and they shall judge the people with
righteous judgment.
19"[a]You shall not distort justice;
you shall not [1]be partial, and you
shall not take a bribe, for a bribe
blinds the eyes of the wise and perverts the words of the righteous.
20"Justice, *and only* justice, you
shall pursue, that [a]you may live and
possess the land which the LORD
your God is giving you.
21"[a]You shall not plant for yourself an [1]Asherah of any kind of tree
beside the altar of the LORD your
God, which you shall make for yourself.
22"Neither shall you set up for
yourself a *sacred* pillar which the
LORD your God hates.

11 [1]Lit., *gates* [2]Or, *fatherless* [a]Deut. 12:7 [b]Deut. 12:12 [c]Deut. 14:29

13 [1]Lit., *perform* [a]Lev. 23:34-43

14 [1]Or, *fatherless* [2]Lit., *gates* [a]Deut. 16:11

16 [a]Ex. 23:14-17; 34:23, 24 [b]Ex. 22:29; 34:20

17 [1]Lit., *according to the gift of his hand,*

18 [1]Lit., *gates*

19 [1]Lit., *regard persons* [a]Deut. 1:17; 10:17

20 [a]Deut. 4:1

21 [1]I.e., wooden symbols of a female deity [a]Deut. 7:5

1 [1]Lit., *evil thing* [a]Deut. 15:21

2 [1]Lit., *gates* [a]Deut. 13:6-11

5 [1]Lit., *death with stones*

6 [1]Lit., *mouth* [a]Num. 35:30; Deut. 19:15

7 [a]Lev. 24:14; Deut. 13:9

8 [1]Lit., *blood to blood* [2]Lit., *judgment to judgment* [3]Lit., *stroke to stroke* [4]Lit., *gates* [a]Deut. 12:5

9 [a]Deut. 19:17

10 [1]Lit., *mouth*

11 [1]Lit., *mouth* [a]Deut. 25:1

CHAPTER 17

Administration of Justice

"[a]YOU shall not sacrifice to the
LORD your God an ox or a sheep
which has a blemish or any [1]defect,
for that is a detestable thing to the
LORD your God.
2"[a]If there is found in your midst,
in any of your [1]towns, which the
LORD your God is giving you, a man
or a woman who does what is evil in
the sight of the LORD your God, by
transgressing His covenant,
3 and has gone and served other
gods and worshiped them, or the
sun or the moon or any of the heavenly host, which I have not commanded,
4 and if it is told you and you
have heard of it, then you shall inquire thoroughly. And behold, if it is
true and the thing certain that this
detestable thing has been done in Israel,
5 then you shall bring out that
man or that woman who has done
this evil deed, to your gates, *that is,*
the man or the woman, and you
shall stone them to [1]death.
6"[a]On the [1]evidence of two witnesses or three witnesses, he who is
to die shall be put to death; he shall
not be put to death on the [1]evidence
of one witness.
7"[a]The hand of the witnesses
shall be first against him to put him
to death, and afterward the hand of
all the people. So you shall purge the
evil from your midst.
8"If any case is too difficult for
you to decide, between [1]one kind of
homicide or another, between [2]one
kind of lawsuit or another, and between [3]one kind of assault or another, being cases of dispute in your
[4]courts, then you shall arise and go
up to [a]the place which the LORD
your God chooses.
9"So you shall come to [a]the Levitical priest or the judge who is *in office* in those days, and you shall inquire *of them,* and they will declare
to you the verdict in the case.
10"And you shall do according to
the [1]terms of the verdict which they
declare to you from that place
which the LORD chooses; and you
shall be careful to observe according to all that they teach you.
11"[a]According to the [1]terms of the
law which they teach you, and according to the verdict which they
tell you, you shall do; you shall not
turn aside from the word which they

declare to you, to the right or the
left.
12"And the man who acts [a]pre-
sumptuously by not listening to the
priest who stands there to serve the
LORD your God, nor to the judge,
that man shall die; thus you shall
purge the evil from Israel.
13"Then all the people will hear
and be afraid, and will not act [a]pre-
sumptuously again.
14"When you enter the land which
the LORD your God gives you, and
you [a]possess it and live in it, and you
say, '[b]I will set a king over me like
all the nations who are around me,'
15 you shall surely set a king over
you whom the LORD your God
chooses, *one* from among your
[1]countrymen you shall set as king
over yourselves; you may not put a
foreigner over yourselves who is not
your [1]countryman.
16"[a]Moreover, he shall not multiply horses for himself, nor shall he
[b]cause the people to return to Egypt
to multiply horses, since the LORD
has said to you, 'You shall never
again return that way.'
17"[a]Neither shall he multiply
wives for himself, [1]lest his heart
turn away; nor shall he greatly increase silver and gold for himself.
18"Now it shall come about when
he sits on the throne of his kingdom,
he shall write for himself a copy of
this law on a scroll [1a]in the presence
of the Levitical priests.
19"And it shall be with him, and he
shall read it [a]all the days of his life,
that he may learn to fear the LORD
his God, [1]by carefully observing all
the words of this law and these statutes,
20 that his heart may not be lifted
up above his [1]countrymen [a]and that
he may not turn aside from the commandment, to the right or the left; in
order that he and his sons may continue long in his kingdom in the
midst of Israel.

CHAPTER 18

Portion of the Levites

"[a]THE Levitical priests, the whole
tribe of Levi, shall have no portion
or inheritance with Israel; they shall
eat the LORD's offerings by fire and
His [1]portion.
2"And they shall have no inheritance among their [1]countrymen; the
LORD is their inheritance, as He
[2]promised them.
3"[a]Now this shall be the priests'
due from the people, from those
who offer a sacrifice, either an ox or
a sheep, of which they shall give to
the priest the shoulder and the two
cheeks and the stomach.
4"You shall give him the first
fruits of your grain, your new wine,
and your oil, and the first shearing
of your sheep.
5"[a]For the LORD your God has
chosen him and his sons from all
your tribes, to stand [1]and serve in
the name of the LORD forever.
6"Now if a Levite comes from any
of your [1]towns throughout Israel
where he resides, and comes [2]when-
ever he desires to the place which
the LORD chooses,
7 then he shall serve in the name
of the LORD his God, like all his fellow Levites who stand there before
the LORD.
8"[a]They shall eat [1]equal portions,
except *what they receive* from the
sale of their fathers' *estates.*

Spiritism Forbidden

9"When you enter the land which
the LORD your God gives you, you
shall not learn to [1a]imitate the detestable things of those nations.
10"There shall not be found among
you anyone [a]who makes his son or
his daughter pass through the fire,
one who uses divination, one [b]who
practices witchcraft, or one who interprets omens, or a sorcerer,
11 or one who casts a spell, or a
medium, or a spiritist, or one who
calls up the dead.
12"For whoever does these things
is detestable to the LORD; and because of these detestable things the
LORD your God will drive them out
before you.
13"[a]You shall be [1]blameless before
the LORD your God.
14"For those nations, which you
shall dispossess, listen to those who
practice witchcraft and to diviners,
but as for you, the LORD your God
has not allowed you *to do* so.
15"[a]The LORD your God will raise
up for you a prophet like me from
among you, from your [1]country-
men, you shall listen to him.
16"This is [a]according to all that
you asked of the LORD your God in
Horeb on the day of the assembly,
saying, 'Let me not hear again the
voice of the LORD my God, let me
not see this great fire any more, lest
I die.'
17"[a]And the LORD said to me,
'They have [1]spoken well.
18 'I will raise up a prophet from
among their [1]countrymen like you,
and I will put My words in his

12 [a]Deut. 1:43; 17:13; 18:20

13 [a]Deut. 17:12

14 [a]Deut. 11:31; Josh. 21:43 [b]1 Sam. 8:5, 19, 20

15 [1]Lit., *brother(s)*

16 [a]1 Kin. 4:26; 10:26-29 [b]Is. 31:1; Ezek. 17:15

17 [1]Lit., *nor* [a]2 Sam. 5:13; 12:11; 1 Kin. 11:3, 4

18 [1]Lit., *from before* [a]Deut. 31:24-26

19 [1]Lit., *to keep to do them* [a]Deut. 4:9, 10

20 [1]Lit., *brothers* [a]Deut. 5:32

1 [1]Or, *inheritance* [a]Deut. 10:9; 1 Cor. 9:13

2 [1]Lit., *brothers* [2]Lit., *spoke to*

3 [a]Lev. 7:32-34; Num. 18:11, 12

5 [1]Lit., *to* [a]Ex. 29:9

6 [1]Lit., *gates* [2]Lit., *with all the desire of his soul*

8 [1]Lit., *portion like portion* [a]Lev. 27:30-33; Num. 18:21-24

9 [1]Lit., *do according to* [a]Deut. 9:5

10 [a]Deut. 12:31 [b]Ex. 22:18; Lev. 19:26, 31; 20:6; Jer. 27:9, 10; Mal. 3:5

13 [1]Lit., *complete, perfect;* or, *having integrity* [a]Gen. 6:9; 17:1; Matt. 5:48

15 [1]Lit., *brothers* [a]John 1:21, 25; Acts 3:22; 7:37

16 [a]Ex. 20:18, 19; Deut. 5:23-27

17 [1]Lit., *done well what they have spoken* [a]Deut. 5:28

18 [1]Lit., *brothers*

mouth, and he shall speak to them
all that I command him.
19 '[a]And it shall come about that
whoever will not listen to My words
which he shall speak in My name, I
Myself will require *it* of him.
20 'But the prophet who shall
speak a word [a]presumptuously in
My name which I have not commanded him to speak, or [b]which he
shall speak in the name of other
gods, [1]that prophet shall die.'
21 "And [1]you may say in your
heart, 'How shall we know the word
which the LORD has not spoken?'
22 "When a prophet speaks in the
name of the LORD, if the thing does
not come about or come true, that is
the thing which the LORD has not
spoken. The prophet has spoken it
[a]presumptuously; you shall not be
afraid of him.

CHAPTER 19

Cities of Refuge

"[a]WHEN the LORD your God cuts
off the nations, whose land the LORD
your God gives you, and you dispossess them and settle in their cities
and in their houses,
2 [a]you shall set aside three cities
for yourself in the midst of your
land, which the LORD your God
gives you to [1]possess.
3 "You shall prepare the [1]roads
for yourself, and divide into three
parts the territory of your land,
which the LORD your God will give
you as a possession, [2]so that any
manslayer may flee there.
4 "[a]Now this is the case of the
manslayer who may flee there and
live: when he [1]kills his friend [2]unin-
tentionally, [3]not hating him previously—
5 as when *a man* goes into the
forest with his friend to cut wood,
and his hand [1]swings the axe to cut
down the tree, and the iron *head*
slips off the [2]handle and [3]strikes his
friend so that he dies—he may flee
to one of these cities and live;
6 lest the avenger of blood pursue
the manslayer [1]in the heat of his anger, and overtake him, because the
way is long, and [2]take his life,
though he was not deserving of
death, since he had not hated him
previously.
7 "Therefore, I command you,
saying, 'You shall set aside three
cities for yourself.'
8 "And if the LORD your God en-

19 [a]Acts 3:23; Heb. 12:25

20 [1]Lit., *and that* [a]Deut. 17:12 [b]Deut. 13:1, 2

21 [1]Lit., *if you say*

22 [a]Deut. 18:20

1 [a]Deut. 6:10, 11

2 [1]Lit., *possess it* [a]Deut. 4:41

3 [1]Lit., *road* [2]Lit., *and it shall be for every manslayer to flee there*

4 [1]Lit., *smites* [2]Lit., *without knowledge* [3]Lit., *and he was not hating him previously* [a]Num. 35:9-34

5 [1]Lit., *is thrust with* [2]Lit., wood [3]Lit., *finds*

6 [1]Lit., *while his heart is hot* [2]Lit., *smite him in the soul*

8 [1]Lit., *spoke*

9 [1]Lit., *keep . . . to do it* [a]Deut. 6:5

10 [a]Num. 35:33; Deut. 21:1-9

11 [1]Lit., *him in the soul*

13 [1]Lit., *Your eye* [a]Deut. 7:2

14 [1]Lit., *possess it* [a]Deut. 27:17

15 [1]Lit., *in any sin, which he sins* [2]Lit., *mouth of two witnesses, or by the mouth of three* [a]Num. 35:30; Deut. 17:6; Matt. 18:16; 2 Cor. 13:1

16 [1]Lit., *testify against* [2]Lit., *turning aside* [a]Ex. 23:1

17 [a]Deut. 17:9

18 [1]Lit., *testified against* [a]Deut. 25:1

21 [1]Lit., *your eye* [a]Deut. 19:13 [b]Ex. 21:23; Lev. 24:20 [c]Matt. 5:38

larges your territory, just as He has
sworn to your fathers, and gives you
all the land which He [1]promised to
give your fathers—
9 if you [1]carefully observe all this
commandment, which I command
you today, [a]to love the LORD your
God, and to walk in His ways always—then you shall add three
more cities for yourself, besides
these three.
10 "So innocent blood will not be
shed in the midst of your land which
the LORD your God gives you as an
inheritance, and [a]bloodguiltiness be
on you.
11 "But if there is a man who hates
his neighbor and lies in wait for him
and rises up against him and strikes
[1]him so that he dies, and he flees to
one of these cities,
12 then the elders of his city shall
send and take him from there and
deliver him into the hand of the
avenger of blood, that he may die.
13 "[1a]You shall not pity him, but
you shall purge the blood of the innocent from Israel, that it may go
well with you.

Laws of Landmark and Testimony

14 "[a]You shall not move your
neighbor's boundary mark, which
the ancestors have set, in your inheritance which you shall inherit in
the land that the LORD your God
gives you to [1]possess.
15 "[a]A single witness shall not rise
up against a man on account of any
iniquity or any sin [1]which he has
committed; on the [2]evidence of two
or three witnesses a matter shall be
confirmed.
16 "[a]If a malicious witness rises up
against a man to [1]accuse him of
[2]wrongdoing,
17 then both the men who have the
dispute shall stand [a]before the
LORD, before the priests and the
judges who will be *in office* in those
days.
18 "And the judges [a]shall investigate thoroughly; and if the witness
is a false witness *and* he has [1]ac-
cused his brother falsely,
19 then you shall do to him just as
he had intended to do to his brother.
Thus you shall purge the evil from
among you.
20 "And the rest will hear and be
afraid, and will never again do such
an evil thing among you.
21 "Thus [1a]you shall not show pity:
[b]life for life, [c]eye for eye, tooth for
tooth, hand for hand, foot for foot.

Chapter 20

Laws of Warfare

"WHEN you go out to battle against your enemies and see horses and chariots *and* people more numerous than you, [a]do not be afraid of them; for the LORD your God, who brought you up from the land of Egypt, is with you.

2"Now it shall come about that when you are approaching the battle, the priest shall come near and speak to the people.

3"And he shall say to them, 'Hear, O Israel, you are approaching the battle against your enemies today. Do not be fainthearted. [a]Do not be afraid, or panic, or tremble before them,

4 for the LORD your God [a]is the one who goes with you, to fight for you against your enemies, to save you.'

5"The officers also shall speak to the people, saying, 'Who is the man that has built a new house and has not dedicated it? Let him depart and return to his house, lest he die in the battle and another man dedicate it.

6 'And who is the man that has planted a vineyard and has not [1]begun to use its fruit? Let him depart and return to his house, lest he die in the battle and another man [1]begin to use its fruit.

7 '[a]And who is the man that is engaged to a woman and has not [1]married her? Let him depart and return to his house, lest he die in the battle and another man [2]marry her.'

8"Then the officers shall speak further to the people, and they shall say, '[a]Who is the man that is afraid and fainthearted? Let him depart and return to his house, so that [1]he might not make his brothers' hearts melt like his heart.'

9"And it shall come about that when the officers have finished speaking to the people, they shall appoint commanders of armies at the head of the people.

10"When you approach a city to fight against it, you shall [1]offer it terms of peace.

11"And it shall come about, if it [1]agrees to make peace with you and opens to you, then it shall be that all the people who are found in it shall become your forced labor and shall serve you.

12"However, if it does not make peace with you, but makes war against you, then you shall besiege it.

13"When the LORD your God gives it into your hand, you shall strike all the [1]men in it with the edge of the sword.

14"Only the women and the children and the animals and all that is in the city, all its spoil, you shall take as booty for yourself; and you shall [1]use the spoil of your enemies which the LORD your God has given you.

15"Thus you shall do to all the cities that are very far from you, which are not of the cities of these nations [1]nearby.

16"[a]Only in the cities of these peoples that the LORD your God is giving you as an inheritance, you shall not leave alive anything that breathes.

17"But you shall [1]utterly destroy them, the Hittite and the Amorite, the Canaanite and the Perizzite, the Hivite and the Jebusite, as the LORD your God has commanded you,

18 in order that they may not teach you to do [a]according to all their detestable things which they have done for their gods, so that you would sin against the LORD your God.

19"When you besiege a city a long time, to make war against it in order to capture it, you shall not destroy its trees by swinging an axe against them; for you may eat from them, and you shall not cut them down. [1]For is the tree of the field a man, that it should [2]be besieged by you?

20"Only the trees which you know [1]are not fruit trees you shall destroy and cut down, that you may construct siegeworks against the city that is making war with you until it falls.

Chapter 21

Expiation of a Crime

"IF a slain person is found lying in the open country in the land which the LORD your God gives you to [1]possess, *and* it is not known who has struck him,

2 then your elders and your judges shall go out and measure *the distance* to the cities which are around the slain one.

3"And it shall be that the city which is nearest to the slain man, that is, the elders of that city, shall take a heifer of the herd, which has not been worked and which has not pulled in a yoke;

4 and the elders of that city shall bring the heifer down to a valley with running water, which has not

---

1 [a]Deut. 3:22; 7:18; 31:6, 8

3 [a]Deut. 20:1; Josh. 23:10

4 [a]Deut. 1:30

6 [1]Lit., *treat(ed) it as common*

7 [1]Lit., *taken* [2]Lit., *take* [a]Deut. 24:5

8 [1]So with Gk. and other ancient versions. [a]Judg. 7:3

10 [1]Lit., *call to it for peace*

11 [1]Lit., *answers peace*

13 [1]Lit., *males*

14 [1]Lit., *eat*

15 [1]Lit., *here*

16 [a]Ex. 23:31-33; Deut. 7:1-5

17 [1]Or, *put them under the ban*

18 [a]Deut. 9:5

19 [1]Read as interrogative with ancient versions [2]Lit., *come before you in the siege*

20 [1]Lit., *they are not trees for food*

1 [1]Lit., *possess it*

been plowed or sown, and shall break the heifer's neck there in the valley.

5"Then [a]the priests, the sons of Levi, shall come near, for the LORD your God has chosen them to serve Him and to bless in the name of the LORD; and every dispute and every [1]assault [2]shall be settled by them.

6"And all the elders of that city [1]which is nearest to the slain man shall wash their hands over the heifer whose neck was broken in the valley;

7 and they shall answer and say, 'Our hands have not shed this blood, nor did our eyes see *it*.

8 '[1]Forgive Thy people Israel whom Thou hast redeemed, O LORD, and do not place the guilt of [a]innocent blood in the midst of Thy people Israel.' And the bloodguiltiness shall be [2]forgiven them.

9"[a]So you shall remove the guilt of innocent blood from your midst, when you do what is right in the eyes of the LORD.

Domestic Relations

10"When you go out to battle against your enemies, and the LORD your God delivers them into your hands, and you take them away captive,

11 and see among the captives a beautiful woman, and have a desire for her and would take her as a wife for yourself,

12 then you shall bring her home to your house, and she shall [a]shave her head and [1]trim her nails.

13"She shall also [1]remove the clothes of her captivity and shall remain in your house, and mourn her father and mother a full month; and after that you may go in to her and be her husband and she shall be your wife.

14"And it shall be, if you are not pleased with her, then you shall let her go [1]wherever she wishes; but you shall certainly not sell her for money, you shall not [2]mistreat her, because you have humbled her.

15"If a man has two wives, the one loved and the other [1]unloved, and *both* the loved and the [1]unloved have borne him sons, if the first-born son belongs to the [1]unloved,

16 then it shall be in the day he [1]wills what he has to his sons, he cannot make the son of the loved the first-born before the son of the [2]unloved, who is the first-born.

17"But he shall acknowledge the first-born, the son of the [1]unloved, by giving him a double portion of all that [2]he has, for he is the [a]beginning of his strength; to him belongs the right of the first-born.

18"If any man has a stubborn and rebellious son who will not obey his father or his mother, and when they chastise him, he will not even listen to them,

19 then his father and mother shall seize him, and bring him out to the elders of his city [1]at the gateway of his home town.

20"And they shall say to the elders of his city, 'This son of ours is stubborn and rebellious, he will not obey us, he is a glutton and a drunkard.'

21"[a]Then all the men of his city shall stone him to death; so you shall remove the evil from your midst, and all Israel shall hear *of it* and fear.

22"And if a man has committed a sin [a]worthy of death, and he is put to death, and you hang him on a tree,

23 [a]his corpse shall not hang all night on the tree, but you shall surely bury him on the same day (for [b]he who is hanged is [1]accursed of God), so that you do not defile your land which the LORD your God gives you as an inheritance.

CHAPTER 22

Sundry Laws

"[a]YOU shall not see your [1]countryman's ox or his sheep straying away, and [2]pay no attention to them; you shall certainly bring them back to your countryman.

2"And if your countryman is not near you, or if you do not know him, then you shall bring it home to your house, and it shall remain with you until your countryman looks for it; then you shall restore it to him.

3"And thus you shall do with his donkey, and you shall do the same with his garment, and you shall do likewise with anything lost by your countryman, which he has lost and you have found. You are not allowed to [1]neglect *them*.

4"You shall not see your countryman's donkey or his ox fallen down on the way, and [1]pay no attention to them; you shall certainly help him to raise *them* up.

5"A woman shall not wear man's clothing, nor shall a man put on a woman's clothing; for whoever does these things is an abomination to the LORD your God.

6"If you happen to come upon a bird's nest along the way, in any tree or on the ground, with young ones or eggs, and the mother sitting on

5 [1]Lit., *stroke* [2]Lit., *shall be according to their mouth* [a]Deut. 17:9-11; 19:17

6 [1]Lit., *who are*

8 [1]Lit., *Cover over, atone for* [2]Lit., *covered over, atoned for* [a]Num. 35:33, 34

9 [a]Deut. 19:13

12 [1]Lit., *do* [a]Lev. 14:8, 9; Num. 6:9

13 [1]Lit., *remove from her*

14 [1]Lit., *according to her soul* [2]Or, *enslave*

15 [1]Lit., *hated*

16 [1]Lit., *makes to inherit* [2]Lit., *hated*

17 [1]Lit., *hated* [2]Lit., *is found with him* [a]Gen. 49:3

19 [1]Lit., *and to the gate of his place*

21 [a]Lev. 20:2, 27; 24:14-23; Num. 15:25, 36

22 [a]Matt. 26:66; Mark 14:64

23 [1]Lit., *the curse of God* [a]Josh. 8:29; 10:26, 27; John 19:31 [b]Gal. 3:13

1 [1]Lit., *brother;* so through v. 4 [2]Lit., *hide yourself from them* [a]Ex. 23:4, 5

3 [1]Lit., *hide yourself*

4 [1]Lit., *hide yourself from them*

the young or on the eggs, [a]you shall not take the mother with the young;

7 you shall certainly let the mother go, but the young you may take for yourself, [a]in order that it may be well with you, and that you may prolong your days.

8"When you build a new house, you shall make a parapet for your roof, that you may not bring bloodguilt on your house if anyone falls from it.

9"[a]You shall not sow your vineyard with two kinds of seed, lest [1]all the produce of the seed which you have sown, and the increase of the vineyard become defiled.

10"You shall not plow with an ox and a donkey together.

11"[a]You shall not wear a material mixed of wool and linen together.

12"[a]You shall make yourself tassels on the four corners of your garment with which you cover yourself.

Laws on Morality

13"[a]If any man takes a wife and goes in to her and *then* [1]turns against her,

14 and charges her with shameful deeds and [1]publicly defames her, and says, 'I took this woman, *but* when I came near her, I did not find her a virgin,'

15 then the girl's father and her mother shall take and bring out the *evidence* of the girl's virginity to the elders of the city at the gate.

16"And the girl's father shall say to the elders, 'I gave my daughter to this man for a wife, but he [1]turned against her;

17 and behold, he has charged her with shameful deeds, saying, "I did not find your daughter a virgin." But [1]this is the *evidence* of my daughter's virginity.' And they shall spread the garment before the elders of the city.

18"So the elders of that city shall take the man and chastise him,

19 and they shall fine him a hundred *shekels* of silver and give it to the girl's father, because he [1]publicly defamed a virgin of Israel. And she shall remain his wife; he cannot [2]divorce her all his days.

20"But if this [1]charge is true, that the girl was not found a virgin,

21 then they shall bring out the girl to the doorway of her father's house, and the men of her city shall stone her [1]to death because she has [a]committed an act of folly in Israel, by playing the harlot in her father's house; thus you shall purge the evil from among you.

22"[a]If a man is found lying with a married woman, then both of them shall die, the man who lay with the woman, and the woman; thus you shall purge the evil from Israel.

23"[a]If there is a girl who is a virgin engaged to a man, and *another* man finds her in the city and lies with her,

24 then you shall bring them both out to the gate of that city and you shall stone them [1]to death; the girl, because she did not cry out in the city, and the man, because he has violated his neighbor's wife. Thus you shall purge the evil from among you.

25"But if in the field the man finds the girl who is engaged, and the man forces her and lies with her, then only the man who lies with her shall die.

26"But you shall do nothing to the girl; there is no sin in the girl worthy of death, for just as a man rises against his neighbor and murders him, so is this case.

27"When he found her in the field, the engaged girl cried out, but there was no one to save her.

28"[a]If a man finds a girl who is a virgin, who is not engaged, and seizes her and lies with her and they are discovered,

29 then the man who lay with her shall give to the girl's father fifty *shekels* of silver, and she shall become his wife because he has violated her; he cannot divorce her all his days.

30"[1a]A man shall not take his father's wife so that he shall not uncover his father's skirt.

CHAPTER 23

Persons Excluded from the Assembly

"[a]NO one who is [1]emasculated, or has his male organ cut off, shall enter the assembly of the LORD.

2"No one of illegitimate birth shall enter the assembly of the LORD; none of his *descendants,* even to the tenth generation, shall enter the assembly of the LORD.

3"No Ammonite or Moabite shall enter the assembly of the LORD; none of their *descendants,* even to the tenth generation, shall ever enter the assembly of the LORD,

4 because they did not meet you with [1]food and water on the way when you came out of Egypt, and because they hired against you [a]Ba-

6 [a]Lev. 22:28
7 [a]Deut. 4:40
9 [1]Lit., *the fulness, seed* [a]Lev. 19:19
11 [a]Lev. 19:19
12 [a]Num. 15:37-41; Matt. 23:5
13 [1]Lit., *hates her* [a]Deut. 24:1
14 [1]Lit., *causes an evil name to go out against her*
16 [1]Lit., *hated her*
17 [1]Lit., *these are*
19 [1]Lit., *caused an evil name to go out against a virgin* [2]Lit., *send her away*
20 [1]Lit., *matter*
21 [1]Lit., *with stones so that she dies* [a]Lev. 19:29; 21:9; Deut. 23:17, 18
22 [a]Lev. 20:10; Ezek. 16:38; John 8:5
23 [a]Lev. 19:20-22
24 [1]Lit., *with stones so that they die*
28 [a]Ex. 22:16
30 [1]Ch. 23:1 in Heb. [a]Deut. 27:20
1 [1]Lit., *wounded by crushing* of testicles [a]Lev. 21:20; 22:24
4 [1]Lit., *bread* [a]Num. 22:5; 23:7; 2 Pet. 2:15; Jude 11

laam the son of Beor from Pethor of [2]Mesopotamia, to curse you.

5"Nevertheless, the LORD your God was not willing to listen to Balaam, but the LORD your God turned the curse into a blessing for you because the LORD your God [a]loves you.

6"You shall never seek their peace or their prosperity all your days.

7"You shall not detest an Edomite, for he is your brother; you shall not detest an Egyptian, because you were an alien in his land.

8"The sons of the third generation who are born to them may enter the assembly of the LORD.

9"When you go out as an [1]army against your enemies, then you shall keep yourself from every evil thing.

10"[a]If there is among you any man who is unclean because of a nocturnal emission, then he must go outside the camp; he may not [1]reenter the camp.

11"But it shall be when evening approaches, he shall bathe himself with water, and at sundown he may [1]reenter the camp.

12"You shall also have a place outside the camp and go out there,

13 and you shall have a [1]spade among your tools, and it shall be when you sit down outside, you shall dig with it and shall turn [2]to cover up your excrement.

14"Since [a]the LORD your God walks in the midst of your camp to deliver you and to [1]defeat your enemies before you, therefore your camp must be holy; and He must not see [2]anything indecent among you [3]lest He turn away from you.

15"You shall not hand over to his master a slave who has [1]escaped from his master to you.

16"He shall live with you in your midst, in the place which he shall choose in one of your [1]towns where it pleases him; you shall not mistreat him.

17"[a]None of the daughters of Israel shall be a cult prostitute, nor shall any of the sons of Israel be a cult prostitute.

18"You shall not bring the hire of a harlot or the wages of a [1a]dog into the house of the LORD your God for any votive offering, for both of these are an abomination to the LORD your God.

19"[a]You shall not charge interest to your [1]countrymen: interest on money, food, *or* anything that may be loaned at interest.

4 [2]Heb. *Aram-naharaim*

5 [a]Deut. 4:37

9 [1]Or, *camp*

10 [1]Lit., *come to the midst of* [a]Lev. 15:16

11 [1]Lit., *come to the midst of*

13 [1]Lit., *peg* [2]Lit., *and*

14 [1]Lit., *give up* [2]Lit., *nakedness of anything* [3]Lit., *and* [a]Lev. 26:12

15 [1]Lit., *delivered himself*

16 [1]Lit., *gates*

17 [a]Deut. 22:21

18 [1]I.e., male prostitute, sodomite [a]Lev. 18:22; 20:13

19 [1]Lit., *brothers* [a]Ex. 22:25; Lev. 25:35-37

20 [1]Lit., *brother* [2]Lit., *the putting forth of your hand* [3]Lit., *possess it* [a]Deut. 28:12

21 [1]Lit., *for* [a]Num. 30:1, 2; Matt. 5:33

23 [1]Lit., *spoken with your mouth*

24 [1]Lit., *according to your satisfaction of your soul* [2]Or, *vessel*

25 [a]Matt. 12:1; Mark 2:23; Luke 6:1

1 [1]Lit., *if* [a]Num. 5:12, 28 Deut. 22:13-21 [b]Matt. 5:31; 19:7-9; Mark 10:4, 5

3 [1]Lit., *hates her*

5 [a]Deut. 20:7

20"[a]You may charge interest to a foreigner, but to your [1]countryman you shall not charge interest, so that the LORD your God may bless you in all [2]that you undertake in the land which you are about to enter to [3]possess.

21"[a]When you make a vow to the LORD your God, you shall not delay to pay it, for it would be sin in you, [1]and the LORD your God will surely require it of you.

22"However, if you refrain from vowing, it would not be sin in you.

23"You shall be careful to perform what goes out from your lips, just as you have voluntarily vowed to the LORD your God, what you have [1]promised.

24"When you enter your neighbor's vineyard, then you may eat grapes [1]until you are fully satisfied, but you shall not put any in your [2]basket.

25"[a]When you enter your neighbor's standing grain, then you may pluck the heads with your hand, but you shall not wield a sickle in your neighbor's standing grain.

CHAPTER 24

Law of Divorce

"WHEN a man takes a wife and marries her, and it happens [1]that she finds no favor in his eyes because he has found some [a]indecency in her, and [b]he writes her a certificate of divorce and puts *it* in her hand and sends her out from his house,

2 and she leaves his house and goes and becomes another man's *wife*,

3 and if the latter husband [1]turns against her and writes her a certificate of divorce and puts *it* in her hand and sends her out of his house, or if the latter husband dies who took her to be his wife,

4 *then* her former husband who sent her away is not allowed to take her again to be his wife, since she has been defiled; for that is an abomination before the LORD, and you shall not bring sin on the land which the LORD your God gives you as an inheritance.

5"[a]When a man takes a new wife, he shall not go out with the army, nor be charged with any duty; he shall be free at home one year and shall give happiness to his wife whom he has taken.

Sundry Laws

6"No one shall take a handmill or an upper millstone in pledge, for he would be taking a life in pledge.

7"[a]If a man is [1]caught kidnapping any of his [2]countrymen of the sons of Israel, and he deals with him violently, or sells him, then that thief shall die; so you shall purge the evil from among you.

8"[a]Be careful against [1]an infection of leprosy, that you diligently observe and do according to all that the Levitical priests shall teach you; as I have commanded them, so you shall be careful to do.

9"Remember what the LORD your God did [a]to Miriam on the way as you came out of Egypt.

10"[a]When you make your neighbor a loan of any sort, you shall not enter his house to take his pledge.

11"You shall remain outside, and the man to whom you make the loan shall bring the pledge out to you.

12"And if he is a poor man, you shall not sleep with his pledge.

13"When the sun goes down you shall surely return the pledge to him, that he may sleep in his cloak and bless you; and [a]it will be righteousness for you before the LORD your God.

14"[a]You shall not oppress a hired servant *who is* poor and needy, whether *he is* one of your [1]countrymen or one of your aliens who is in your land in your [2]towns.

15"[a]You shall give him his wages on his day [1]before the sun sets, for he is poor and sets his [2]heart on it; so that [b]he may not cry against you to the LORD and it become sin in you.

16"[a]Fathers shall not be put to death [1]for *their* sons, nor shall sons be put to death [1]for *their* fathers; everyone shall be put to death for his own sin.

17"[a]You shall not pervert the justice [1]due an alien *or* an [2]orphan, nor take a widow's garment in pledge.

18"But you shall remember that you were a slave in Egypt, and that the LORD your God redeemed you from there; therefore I am commanding you to do this thing.

19"[a]When you reap your harvest in your field and have forgotten a sheaf in the field, you shall not go back to get it; it shall be [b]for the alien, for the [1]orphan, and for the widow, in order that the LORD your God may bless you in all the work of your hands.

20"[a]When you beat your olive tree, you shall not go over the boughs [1]again; it shall be [b]for the alien, for the [2]orphan, and for the widow.

21"When you gather the grapes of your vineyard, you shall not [1]go over it again; it shall be for the alien, for the [2]orphan, and for the widow.

22"And you shall remember that you were a slave in the land of Egypt; therefore I am commanding you to do this thing.

CHAPTER 25

Sundry Laws

"[a]IF there is a dispute between men and they go to [1]court, and [2]the judges decide their case, [b]and they justify the righteous and condemn the wicked,

2 then it shall be if the wicked man [1]deserves to be beaten, the judge shall then make him lie down and be beaten in his presence with the number of stripes according to his [2]guilt.

3"[a]He may beat him forty times *but* no more, lest he beat him with many more stripes than these, and your brother be degraded in your eyes.

4"[a]You shall not muzzle the ox while he is threshing.

5"When brothers live together and one of them dies and has no son, the wife of the deceased shall not be *married* outside *the family* to a strange man. [a]Her husband's brother shall go in to her and take her to himself as wife and perform the duty of a husband's brother to her.

6"And it shall be that the firstborn whom she bears shall [1]assume the name of his dead brother, that [a]his name may not be blotted out from Israel.

7"[a]But if the man does not desire to take his brother's wife, then his brother's wife shall go up to the gate to the elders and say, 'My husband's brother refuses to establish a name for his brother in Israel; he is not willing to perform the duty of a husband's brother to me.'

8"Then the elders of his city shall summon him and speak to him. And *if* he persists and says, 'I do not desire to take her,'

9 [a]then his brother's wife shall come to him in the sight of the elders, and pull his sandal off his foot and [b]spit in his face; and she shall [1]declare, 'Thus it is done to the man

---

7 [1]Lit., *found stealing* [2]Lit., *brothers* [a]Ex. 21:16

8 [1]Lit., *a mark or stroke* [a]Lev. 13:1-14, 57

9 [a]Num. 12:10

10 [a]Ex. 22:26, 27

13 [a]Deut. 6:25

14 [1]Lit., *brothers* [2]Lit., *gates* [a]Lev. 25:35-43; Deut. 15:7-18; 1 Tim. 5:18

15 [1]Lit., *that the sun shall not go down on it* [2]Lit., *soul* [a]Lev. 19:13; James 5:4 [b]Ex. 22:23; Deut. 15:9

16 [1]Or, *with* [a]2 Kin. 14:6; 2 Chr. 25:4; Jer. 31:29, 30; Ezek. 18:20

17 [1]Lit., *of* [2]Or, *fatherless* [a]Deut. 1:17; 10:17; 16:19

19 [1]Or, *fatherless* [a]Lev. 19:9, 10; 23:22 [b]Deut. 14:29

20 [1]Lit., *after yourself* [2]Or, *fatherless* [a]Lev. 19:10 [b]Deut. 24:19

21 [1]Lit., *glean it after yourself* [2]Or, *fatherless*

1 [1]Lit., *the judgment* [2]Lit., *they judge them* [a]Deut. 17:8-13; 19:17 [b]Deut. 1:16, 17

2 [1]Lit., *is a son of beating* [2]Or, *wickedness*

3 [a]2 Cor. 11:24

4 [a]1 Cor. 9:9; 1 Tim. 5:18

5 [a]Matt. 22:24; Mark 12:19; Luke 20:28

6 [1]Lit., *stand on* [a]Ruth 4:5, 10

7 [a]Ruth 4:1, 2

9 [1]Lit., *answer and say* [a]Ruth 4:7, 8 [b]Num. 12:14

who does not build up his brother's house.'

10"And in Israel his name shall be called, 'The house of him whose sandal is removed.'

11"If *two* men, a man and his [1]countryman, are struggling together, and the wife of one comes near to deliver her husband from the hand of the one who is striking him, and puts out her hand and seizes his genitals,

12 then you shall cut off her [1]hand; [2a]you shall not show pity.

13"[a]You shall not have in your bag [1]differing weights, a large and a small.

14"You shall not have in your house [1]differing measures, a large and a small.

15"You shall have a full and just weight; you shall have a full and just [1]measure, that your days may be prolonged in the [2]land which the LORD your God gives you.

16"For everyone who does these things, everyone who acts unjustly is an abomination to the LORD your God.

17"[a]Remember what Amalek did to you along the way when you came out from Egypt,

18 how he met you along the way and attacked among you all the stragglers at your rear when you were faint and weary; and he did not [1]fear God.

19"Therefore it shall come about when the LORD your God has given you [a]rest from all your surrounding enemies, in the land which the LORD your God gives you as an inheritance to [1]possess, you shall blot out the memory of Amalek from under heaven; you must not forget.

CHAPTER 26

Offering First Fruits

"THEN it shall be, when you enter the land which the LORD your God gives you as an inheritance, and you possess it and live in it,

2 that you shall take some of [a]the first of all the produce of the ground which you shall bring in from your land that the LORD your God gives you, and you shall put *it* in a basket and go to the place where the LORD your God chooses to establish His name.

3"And you shall go to the priest who is in office at that time, and say to him, 'I declare this day to the LORD [1]my God that I have entered the land which the LORD swore to our fathers to give us.'

4"Then the priest shall take the basket from your hand and set it down before the altar of the LORD your God.

5"And you shall answer and say before the LORD your God, '[a]My father was a [1]wandering Aramean, and he went down to Egypt and [2]sojourned there, [b]few in number; but there he became a [c]great, mighty and populous nation.

6 'And the Egyptians treated us harshly and afflicted us, and imposed hard labor on us.

7 'Then we cried to the LORD, the God of our fathers, and the LORD heard our voice and saw our affliction and our toil and our oppression;

8 [a]and the LORD brought us out of Egypt with a mighty hand and an outstretched arm and with great terror and with signs and wonders;

9 and He has brought us to this place, and has given us this land, [a]a land flowing with milk and honey.

10 'And now behold, I have brought the first of the produce of the ground which Thou, O LORD hast given me.' And you shall set it down before the LORD your God, and worship before the LORD your God;

11 and you and [a]the Levite and the alien who is among you shall [b]rejoice in all the good which the LORD your God has given you and your household.

12"[a]When you have finished [1]paying all the tithe of your increase in the third year, the year of tithing, then you shall give it to the Levite, to the stranger, to the [2]orphan and to the widow, that they may eat in your [3]towns, and be satisfied.

13"And you shall say before the LORD your God, 'I have removed the sacred *portion* from *my* house, and also have given it to the Levite and the alien, the [1]orphan and the widow, according to all Thy commandments which Thou hast commanded me; I have not transgressed or forgotten any of Thy commandments.

14 'I have not eaten of it [1]while mourning, nor have I removed any of it while I was unclean, nor offered any of it to the dead. I have listened to the voice of the LORD my God; I have done according to all that Thou hast commanded me.

15 'Look down from Thy holy habitation, from heaven, and bless Thy people Israel, and the ground which Thou hast given us, [a]a land flowing

11 [1]Lit., *brother*
12 [1]Lit., *palm* [2]Lit., *your eye* [a]Deut. 7:2
13 [1]Lit., *a stone and a stone* [a]Lev. 19:35-37
14 [1]Lit., *an ephah and an ephah*
15 [1]Lit., *ephah* [2]Lit., *ground*
17 [a]Ex. 17:8-16
18 [1]Or, *reverence*
19 [1]Lit., *possess it* [a]Deut. 12:9
2 [a]Ex. 22:29; 23:16, 19
3 [1]So with Gk; Heb., *your*
5 [1]Or, *perishing* [2]Or, *lived as an alien* [a]Gen. 25:30; 31:40-42; 43:1-14 [b]Gen. 46:27 [c]Deut. 1:10; 10:22
8 [a]Deut. 4:34
9 [a]Ex. 3:8, 17
11 [a]Deut. 12:12 [b]Deut. 12:7
12 [1]Lit., *tithing* [2]Or, *fatherless* [3]Lit., *gates* [a]Deut. 14:28, 29; Heb. 7:5, 9, 10
13 [1]Or, *fatherless*
14 [1]Lit., *while in my*
15 [a]Deut. 26:9

with milk and honey, as Thou didst
swear to our fathers.'
16"This day the LORD your God
commands you to do these statutes
and ordinances. You shall therefore
be careful to do them [a]with all your
heart and with all your soul.
17"You have today declared the
LORD to be your God, and [1]that you
would walk in His ways and keep
His statutes, His commandments
and His ordinances, and listen to His
voice.
18"And the LORD has today declared you to be [a]His people, a treasured possession, as He promised
you, and [1]that you should keep all
His commandments;
19 and [1]that He shall [a]set you high
above all nations which He has
made, for praise, fame, and honor;
and that you shall be [b]a consecrated
people to the LORD your God, as He
has spoken."

CHAPTER 27

The Curses of Mount Ebal

THEN Moses and the elders of Israel charged the people, saying,
"Keep all the commandments
which I command you today.
2"[a]So it shall be on the day when
you shall cross the Jordan to the
land which the LORD your God gives
you, that you shall set up for yourself large stones, and coat them with
lime
3 and write on them all the words
of this law, when you cross over, in
order that you may enter the land
which the LORD your God gives you,
[a]a land flowing with milk and honey, as the LORD, the God of your fathers, [1]promised you.
4"So it shall be when you cross
the Jordan, you shall set up on
Mount Ebal, these stones, [1]as I am
commanding you today, and you
shall coat them with lime.
5"Moreover, you shall build there
an altar to the LORD your God, an
altar of stones; you shall not [1]wield
an iron *tool* on them.
6"You shall build the altar of the
LORD your God of [1]uncut stones;
and you shall offer on it burnt offerings to the LORD your God;
7 and you shall sacrifice peace offerings and eat there, and you shall
[a]rejoice before the LORD your God.
8"And you shall write on the
[1]stones all the words of this law
very distinctly."
9 Then Moses and the Levitical

16 [a]Deut. 4:29
17 [1]Lit., *to walk in*
18 [1]Lit., *to keep all*
[a]Deut. 7:6
19 [1]Lit., *to set you*
[a]Deut. 28:1, 13
[b]Deut. 7:6
2 [a]Josh. 8:30-32
3 [1]Lit., *spoke to*
[a]Deut. 26:9
4 [1]Lit., *which*
5 [1]Lit., *lift up*
6 [1]Lit., *whole*
7 [a]Deut. 26:11
8 [1]I.e., stones coated with lime, cf. v. 4
10 [1]Lit., *listen to the voice of*
12 [a]Josh. 8:33-35
15 [1]Or, *a graven image*
[a]Ex. 20:4, 23; 34:17
16 [a]Ex. 21:17; Lev. 20:9; Ezek. 22:7
17 [a]Deut. 19:14
18 [a]Lev. 19:14
19 [1]Or, *fatherless*
[a]Deut. 24:17
20 [a]Lev. 18:8; 20:11; Deut. 22:30
21 [a]Ex. 22:19; Lev. 18:23
22 [a]Lev. 18:9; 20:17
23 [a]Lev. 20:14
24 [a]Ex. 21:12; Lev. 24:17; Num. 35:30, 31
25 [a]Ex. 23:7
26 [a]Gal. 3:10

priests spoke to all Israel, saying,
"Be silent and listen, O Israel! This
day you have become a people for
the LORD your God.
10"You shall therefore [1]obey the
LORD your God, and do His commandments and His statutes which
I command you today."
11 Moses also charged the people
on that day, saying,
12"When you cross the Jordan,
these shall stand on Mount Gerizim
to bless the people: [a]Simeon, Levi,
Judah, Issachar, Joseph, and Benjamin.
13"And for the curse, these shall
stand on Mount Ebal: Reuben, Gad,
Asher, Zebulun, Dan, and Naphtali.
14"The Levites shall then answer
and say to all the men of Israel with
a loud voice,
15 'Cursed is the man who makes
[1][a]an idol or a molten image, an
abomination to the LORD, the work
of the hands of the craftsman, and
sets *it* up in secret.' And all the people shall answer and say, 'Amen.'
16 '[a]Cursed is he who dishonors his
father or mother.' And all the people
shall say, 'Amen.'
17 '[a]Cursed is he who moves his
neighbor's boundary mark.' And all
the people shall say, 'Amen.'
18 '[a]Cursed is he who misleads a
blind *person* on the road.' And all
the people shall say, 'Amen.'
19 '[a]Cursed is he who distorts the
justice due an alien, [1]orphan, and
widow.' And all the people shall say,
'Amen.'
20 '[a]Cursed is he who lies with his
father's wife, because he has uncovered his father's skirt.' And all the
people shall say, 'Amen.'
21 '[a]Cursed is he who lies with any
animal.' And all the people shall say,
'Amen.'
22 '[a]Cursed is he who lies with his
sister, the daughter of his father or
of his mother.' And all the people
shall say, 'Amen.'
23 '[a]Cursed is he who lies with his
mother-in-law.' And all the people
shall say, 'Amen.'
24 '[a]Cursed is he who strikes his
neighbor in secret.' And all the people shall say, 'Amen.'
25 '[a]Cursed is he who accepts a
bribe to strike down an innocent
person.' And all the people shall say,
'Amen.'
26 '[a]Cursed is he who does not confirm the words of this law by doing
them.' And all the people shall say,
'Amen.'

CHAPTER 28

Blessings at Gerizim

“[a]NOW it shall be, if you will diligently [1]obey the LORD your God, being careful to do all His commandments which I command you today, the LORD your God [b]will set you high above all the nations of the earth.

2“And all these blessings shall come upon you and overtake you, if you will [1]obey the LORD your God.

3“Blessed *shall* you *be* in the city, and blessed *shall* you *be* in the [1]country.

4“Blessed *shall be* the [1]offspring of your [2]body and the [1]produce of your ground and the [1]offspring of your beasts, the increase of your herd and the young of your flock.

5“Blessed *shall be* your basket and your kneading bowl.

6“Blessed *shall* you *be* when you come in, and blessed *shall* you *be* when you go out.

7“The LORD will cause your enemies who rise up against you to be [1]defeated before you; they shall come out against you one way and shall flee before you seven ways.

8“The LORD will command the blessing upon you in your barns and in all that you put your hand to, and He will bless you in the land which the LORD your God gives you.

9“The LORD will establish you as a holy people to Himself, as He swore to you, if you will keep the commandments of the LORD your God, and walk in His ways.

10“So all the peoples of the earth shall see that [1]you are called by the name of the LORD; and they shall be afraid of you.

11“[a]And the LORD will make you abound in prosperity, in the [1]offspring of your [2]body and in the [1]offspring of your beast and in the [1]produce of your ground, in the land which the LORD swore to your fathers to give you.

12“The LORD will open for you His good storehouse, the heavens, to give rain to your land in its season and to bless all the work of your hand; and [a]you shall lend to many nations, but you shall not borrow.

13“[a]And the LORD shall make you the head and not the tail, and you only shall be above, and you shall not be underneath, if you will listen to the commandments of the LORD your God, which I charge you today, to [1]observe *them* carefully,

14 and [a]do not turn aside from any of the words which I command you today, to the right or to the left, to go after other gods to serve them.

Consequences of Disobedience

15“[a]But it shall come about, if you will not [1]obey the LORD your God, to observe to do all His commandments and His statutes with which I charge you today, that all these curses shall come upon you and overtake you.

16“[a]Cursed *shall* you *be* in the city, and cursed *shall* you *be* in the [1]country.

17“[a]Cursed *shall be* your basket and your kneading bowl.

18“[a]Cursed *shall be* the [1]offspring of your [2]body and the [1]produce of your ground, the increase of your herd and the young of your flock.

19“[a]Cursed *shall* you *be* when you come in, and cursed *shall* you *be* when you go out.

20“[a]The LORD will send upon you curses, confusion, and rebuke, in all [1]you undertake to do, until you are destroyed and until [b]you perish quickly, on account of the evil of your deeds, because you have forsaken Me.

21“[a]The LORD will make the pestilence cling to you until He has consumed you from the land, where you are entering to possess it.

22“The LORD will smite you with consumption and with fever and with inflammation and with fiery heat and with [1]the sword and [a]with blight and with mildew, and they shall pursue you until [b]you perish.

23“And [1]the heaven which is over your head shall be bronze, and the earth which is under you, iron.

24“[a]The LORD will make the rain of your land powder and dust; from heaven it shall come down on you until you are destroyed.

25“[a]The LORD will cause you to be [1]defeated before your enemies; you shall go out one way against them, but you shall flee seven ways before them, and you shall [b]be *an example of* terror to all the kingdoms of the earth.

26“[a]And your carcasses shall be food to all birds of the sky and to the beasts of the earth, and there shall be no one to frighten *them* away.

27“[a]The LORD will smite you with the boils of Egypt and with tumors and with the scab and with the itch, from which you cannot be healed.

28“The LORD will smite you with madness and with blindness and with bewilderment of heart;

29 and you shall [1a]grope at noon,

1 [1]Lit., *listen to the voice of* [a]Ex. 23:22-27; Lev. 26:3-13; Deut. 7:12-26 [b]Deut. 28:13; 26:19

2 [1]Lit., *listen to the voice of*

3 [1]Or, *field*

4 [1]Lit., *fruit* [2]Lit., *womb*

7 [1]Lit., *smitten*

10 [1]Lit., *the name of the LORD is called upon you*

11 [1]Lit., *fruit* [2]Or, *womb* [a]Deut. 28:4

12 [a]Deut. 23:20

13 [1]Lit., *keep and do* [a]Deut. 28:1, 44

14 [a]Deut. 5:32

15 [1]Lit., *listen to the voice of* [a]Lev. 26:14-43; Josh. 23:15

16 [1]Or, *field* [a]Deut. 28:3

17 [a]Deut. 28:5

18 [1]Lit., *fruit* [2]Or, *womb* [a]Deut. 28:4

19 [a]Deut. 28:6

20 [1]Lit., *the putting forth of your hand which you do* [a]Deut. 28:8 [b]Deut. 4:26

21 [a]Lev. 26:25; Num. 14:12

22 [1]Another reading is, *drought* [a]Amos 4:9 [b]Deut. 4:29

23 [1]Lit., *your*

24 [a]Deut. 11:17; 28:12

25 [1]Lit., *smitten* [a]Deut. 28:7 [b]2 Chr. 29:8; Jer. 15:4

26 [a]Jer. 7:33; 16:4; 19:7; 34:20

27 [a]Deut. 28:60, 61; 7:15

29 [1]Lit., *be groping* [a]Ex. 10:21

as the blind man gropes in darkness,
and you shall not prosper in your
ways; but you shall only be oppressed and robbed continually,
with none to save you.
30"You shall betroth a wife, but
another man shall violate her; [a]you
shall build a house, but you shall not
live in it; you shall plant a vineyard,
but you shall not [1]use its fruit.
31"Your ox shall be slaughtered
before your eyes, but you shall not
eat of it; your donkey shall be torn
away from you, and shall not be restored to you; your sheep shall be
given to your enemies, and you shall
have none to save you.
32"[a]Your sons and your daughters
shall be given to another people,
while your eyes shall look on and
yearn for them continually; but
there shall be nothing [1]you can do.
33"A people whom you do not
know shall eat up the produce of
your ground and all your labors, and
you shall never be anything but oppressed and crushed continually.
34"And you shall be driven mad by
the sight of [1]what you see.
35"[a]The LORD will strike you on
the knees and legs with sore boils,
from which you cannot be healed,
from the sole of your foot to the
crown of your head.
36"[a]The LORD will bring you and
your king, whom you shall set over
you, to a nation which neither you
nor your fathers have known, and
there you shall serve other gods,
[b]wood and stone.
37"And [a]you shall become a horror, a proverb, and a taunt among all
the people where the LORD will
drive you.
38"[a]You shall bring out much seed
to the field but you shall gather in
little, for [b]the locust shall consume
it.
39"[a]You shall plant and cultivate
vineyards, but you shall neither
drink of the wine nor gather *the
grapes,* for the worm shall devour
them.
40"[a]You shall have olive trees
throughout your territory but you
shall not anoint yourself with the
oil, for your olives shall drop off.
41"[a]You shall [1]have sons and
daughters but they shall not be
yours, for they shall go into captivity.
42"[a]The cricket shall possess all
your trees and the produce of your
ground.
43"[a]The alien who is among you
shall rise above you higher and
higher, but you shall go down lower
and lower.
44"[a]He shall lend to you, but you
shall not lend to him; [b]he shall be the
head, and you shall be the tail.
45"So all these curses shall come
on you and pursue you and overtake
you [a]until you are destroyed, because you would not [1]obey the LORD
your God by keeping His commandments and His statutes which He
commanded you.
46"And they shall become a sign
and a wonder on you and your [1]de-
scendants forever.
47"[a]Because you did not serve the
LORD your God with joy and a glad
heart, for the abundance of all
things;
48 therefore you shall serve your
enemies whom the LORD shall send
against you, [a]in hunger, in thirst, in
nakedness, and in the lack of all
things; and He [b]will put an iron yoke
on your neck until He has destroyed
you.
49"[a]The LORD will bring a nation
against you from afar, from the end
of the earth, as the eagle swoops
down, a nation whose language you
shall not understand,
50 a nation of fierce countenance
who shall have no respect for the
old, nor show favor to the young.
51"Moreover, it shall eat the [1]off-
spring of your herd and the produce
of your ground until you are destroyed, who also leaves you no
grain, new wine, or oil, nor the increase of your herd or the young of
your flock until they have caused
you to perish.
52"[a]And it shall besiege you in all
your [1]towns until your high and
fortified walls in which you trusted
come down throughout your land,
and it shall besiege you in all your
[1]towns throughout your land which
the LORD your God has given you.
53"[a]Then you shall eat the [1]off-
spring of your own body, the flesh of
your sons and of your daughters
whom the LORD your God has given
you, during the siege and the distress by which your enemy shall
[2]oppress you.
54"The man who is [1]refined and
very delicate among you [2]shall be
hostile toward his brother and
toward the wife [3]he cherishes and
toward the rest of his children who
remain,
55 so that he will not give *even* one
of them any of the flesh of his children which he shall eat, since he has
nothing *else* left, during the siege
and the distress by which your ene-

30 [1]Lit., *begin it* [a]Amos 5:11
32 [1]Lit., *in the power of your hand* [a]Deut. 28:41
34 [1]Lit., *your eyes which you*
35 [a]Deut. 28:27
36 [a]2 Kin. 17:4, 6; 24:12, 14; 25:7, 11 [b]Deut. 4:28
37 [a]Jer. 19:8; 29:18
38 [a]Is. 5:10; Mic. 6:15 [b]Joel 1:4
39 [a]Is. 5:10; 17:10, 11
40 [a]Jer. 11:16; Mic. 6:15
41 [1]Lit., *beget* [a]Deut. 28:32
42 [a]Deut. 28:38
43 [a]Deut. 28:13
44 [a]Deut. 28:12 [b]Deut. 28:13
45 [1]Lit., *listen to the voice of* [a]Deut. 4:25, 26
46 [1]Lit., *seed*
47 [a]Deut. 12:7
48 [a]Lam. 4:4-6 [b]Jer. 28:13, 14
49 [a]Is. 5:26-30; 7:18-20
51 [1]Lit., *fruit*
52 [1]Lit., *gates* [a]Jer. 10:17, 18; Zeph. 1:15, 16
53 [1]Lit., *fruit* [2]Or, *distress* [a]Lev. 26:29; Jer. 19:9; Lam. 2:20
54 [1]Lit., *tender* [2]Lit., *his eye shall be evil toward* [3]Lit., *of his bosom*

my shall [1]oppress you in all your [2]towns.

56"[a]The [1]refined and delicate woman among you, who would not venture to set the sole of her foot on the ground for delicateness and [2]refinement, [3]shall be hostile toward the husband [4]she cherishes and toward her son and daughter,

57 and toward her afterbirth which issues from between her [1]legs and toward her children whom she bears; for she shall eat them secretly for lack of anything *else,* during the siege and the distress by which your enemy shall [2]oppress you in your [3]towns.

58"If you are not careful to observe all the words of this law which are written in this book, to [1]fear this honored and awesome name, [2]the LORD your God,

59 then the LORD will bring extraordinary plagues on you and [1]your descendants, even [2]severe and lasting plagues, and miserable and chronic sicknesses.

60"[a]And He will bring back on you all the diseases of Egypt of which you were afraid, and they shall cling to you.

61"Also every sickness and every plague which, not written in the book of this law, the LORD will bring on you [a]until you are destroyed.

62"Then you shall be left few in number, [a]whereas you were as the stars of heaven for multitude, because you did not [1]obey the LORD your God.

63"And it shall come about that as the LORD delighted over you to prosper you, and multiply you, so the LORD will delight over you to make you perish and destroy you; and you shall be [a]torn from the land where you are entering to possess it.

64"Moreover, the LORD will [a]scatter you among all peoples, from one end of the earth to the other end of the earth; and there you shall [b]serve other gods, wood and stone, which you or your fathers have not known.

65"And [a]among those nations you shall find no rest, and there shall be no resting place for the sole of your foot; but there the LORD will give you a trembling heart, failing of eyes, and despair of soul.

66"So your life shall [1]hang in doubt before you; and you shall be in dread night and day, and shall have no assurance of your life.

67"In the morning you shall say, 'Would that it were evening!' And at evening you shall say, 'Would that it were morning!' because of the dread of your heart which you dread, and for the sight of your eyes which you shall see.

68"And the LORD will bring you back to Egypt in ships, by the way about which [a]I spoke to you, 'You will never see it again!' And there you shall offer yourselves for sale to your enemies as male and female slaves, but there will be no buyer."

55 [1]Or, *distress* [2]Lit., *gates*
56 [1]Lit., *tender* [2]Lit., *tenderness* [3]Lit., *her eye shall be evil toward* [4]Lit., *of her bosom* [a]Lam. 4:10
57 [1]Lit., *feet* [2]Or, *distress* [3]Lit., *gates*
58 [1]Or, *reverence* [2]YHWH, or Yahweh
59 [1]Lit., *plague on your seed* [2]Lit., *great*
60 [a]Deut. 28:27
61 [a]Deut. 4:25, 26
62 [1]Lit., *listen to the voice of* [a]Deut. 1:10
63 [a]Jer. 12:14; 45:4
64 [a]Deut. 4:27 [b]Deut. 4:28; 29:26; 32:17
65 [a]Lam. 1:3
66 [1]Lit., *be hung for you in front;*
68 [a]Ex. 13:14
1 [1]Chap. 28:69 in Heb. [a]Lev. 26:46; 27:34 [b]Deut. 5:2, 3
2 [1]Chap. 29:1 in Heb.
4 [a]Rom. 11:8; Is. 6:9, 10; Acts 28:26, 27
5 [a]Deut. 8:4
6 [a]Deut. 8:3
7 [1]Lit., *came to* [2]Lit., *smote* [a]Num. 21:21-24, 33, 35; Deut. 2:26-3:17
8 [a]Num. 32:32; Deut. 3:12, 13
9 [a]Deut. 4:6 [b]Josh. 1:7
11 [a]Josh. 9:21, 23, 27

CHAPTER 29

The Covenant in Moab

[1][a]THESE are the words of the covenant which the LORD commanded Moses to make with the sons of Israel in the land of Moab, besides the [b]covenant which He had made with them at Horeb.

2 [1]And Moses summoned all Israel and said to them, "You have seen all that the LORD did before your eyes in the land of Egypt to Pharaoh and all his servants and all his land;

3 the great trials which your eyes have seen, those great signs and wonders.

4"Yet to this day [a]the LORD has not given you a heart to know, nor eyes to see, nor ears to hear.

5"And I have led you forty years in the wilderness; [a]your clothes have not worn out on you, and your sandal has not worn out on your foot.

6"[a]You have not eaten bread, nor have you drunk wine or strong drink, in order that you might know that I am the LORD your God.

7"[a]When you [1]reached this place, Sihon the king of Heshbon and Og the king of Bashan came out to meet us for battle, but we [2]defeated them;

8 and we took their land and [a]gave it as an inheritance to the Reubenites, the Gadites, and the half-tribe of the Manassites.

9"[a]So keep the words of this covenant to do them, [b]that you may prosper in all that you do.

10"You stand today, all of you, before the LORD your God: your chiefs, your tribes, your elders and your officers, *even* all the men of Israel,

11 your little ones, your wives, and the alien who is within your camps, from [a]the one who chops your wood to the one who draws your water,

12 that you may enter into the covenant with the LORD your God, and into His oath which the LORD your God is making with you today,

13 in order that He may establish

you today as His people and that
[a]He may be your God, just as He
spoke to you and as He swore to
your fathers, to Abraham, Isaac,
and Jacob.
14"Now not with you alone am I
making this covenant and this oath,
15 but both with those who stand
here with us today in the presence
of the LORD our God and with those
who are not with us here today
16 (for you know how we lived in
the land of Egypt, and how we came
through the midst of the nations
through which you passed.
17"Moreover, you have seen their
abominations and their idols *of*
[a]wood, stone, silver, and gold,
which *they had* with them);
18 [a]lest there shall be among you a
man or woman, or family or tribe,
whose heart turns away today from
the LORD our God, to go and serve
the gods of those nations; lest there
shall be among you [b]a root bearing
poisonous fruit and wormwood.
19"And it shall be when he hears
the words of this curse, that he will
[1]boast, saying, 'I have peace though
I walk in the stubbornness of my
heart in order [2]to destroy the watered *land* with the dry.'
20"The LORD shall never be willing
to forgive him, but rather the anger
of the LORD and His jealousy will
[1a]burn against that man, and every
curse which is written in this book
will [2]rest on him, and the LORD will
[b]blot out his name from under
heaven.
21"Then the LORD will single him
out for [1]adversity from all the tribes
of Israel, according to all the curses
of the covenant [a]which are written
in this book of the law.
22"Now the generation to come,
your sons who rise up after you and
[a]the foreigner who comes from a
distant land, when they see the
plagues of the land and the diseases
with which the LORD has [1]afflicted
it, will say,
23 'All its land is [a]brimstone and
salt, [b]a burning waste, [1]unsown and
unproductive, and no grass grows in
it, like the overthrow of Sodom and
Gomorrah, Admah and Zeboiim,
which the LORD overthrew in His
anger and in His wrath.'
24"And all the nations shall say,
'Why has the LORD done thus to this
land? Why this great [1]outburst of
anger?'
25"Then *men* shall say, '[a]Because
they forsook the covenant of the
LORD, the God of their fathers,
which He made with them when He
brought them out of the land of
Egypt.
26 'And they went and served other gods and worshiped them, gods
whom they have not known and
whom He had not [1]allotted to them.
27 'Therefore, the anger of the
LORD burned against that land, to
bring upon it every curse which is
written in this book;
28 and [a]the LORD uprooted them
from their land in anger and in fury
and in great wrath, and cast them
into another land, as *it is* this day.'
29"The secret things belong to the
LORD our God, but the things revealed belong to us and to our sons
forever, that we may observe all the
words of this law.

CHAPTER 30

Restoration Promised

"SO it shall become when all of
these things have come upon you,
[a]the blessing and the curse which I
have set before you, and you [1]call
them to mind [b]in all nations where
the LORD your God has banished
you,
2 and you [a]return to the LORD
your God and [1]obey Him [b]with all
your heart and soul according to all
that I command you today, you and
your sons,
3 then the LORD your God will
[a]restore [1]you from captivity, and
have compassion on you, and will
gather you again from all the peoples where the LORD your God has
[b]scattered you.
4"If your outcasts are at the ends
of the [1]earth, [a]from there the LORD
your God will gather you, and from
there He will [2]bring you back.
5"And [a]the LORD your God will
bring you into the land which your
fathers possessed, and you shall
possess it; and He will prosper you
and [b]multiply you more than your
fathers.
6"Moreover the LORD your God
will circumcise your heart and the
heart of your [1]descendants, [a]to love
the LORD your God with all your
heart and with all your soul, in order
that you may live.
7"[a]And the LORD your God will
[1]inflict all these curses on your enemies and on those who hate you,
who persecuted you.
8"And you shall again [1]obey the
LORD, and observe all His commandments which I command you
today.

13 [a]Gen. 17:7; Ex. 6:7
17 [a]Ex. 20:23; Deut. 4:28; 28:36
18 [a]Deut. 13:6 [b]Deut. 32:32; Heb. 12:15
19 [1]Lit., *bless himself in his heart* [2]I.e., to destroy everything
20 [1]Lit., *smoke* [2]Lit., *lie down* [a]Ps. 74:1; 80:4 [b]Ex. 32:33; Deut. 9:14; 2 Kin. 14:27
21 [1]Lit., *evil* [a]Deut. 30:10
22 [1]Lit., *made it sick* [a]Jer. 19:8; 49:17; 50:13
23 [1]Lit., *it is not sown and does not cause to sprout* [a]Gen. 19:24; Is. 34:9 [b]Is. 1:7; 64:11
24 [1]Lit., *heat*
25 [a]2 Kin. 17:9-23; 2 Chr. 36:13-21
26 [1]Lit., *portioned*
28 [a]Ezek. 19:12, 13
1 [1]Lit., *cause them to return to your heart* [a]Deut. 11:26; 30:15, 19 [b]Lev. 26:40-45; Deut. 28:64; 29:28
2 [1]Lit., *listen to His voice* [a]Deut. 4:29, 30 [b]Deut. 4:29
3 [1]Lit., *your captivity* [a]Gen. 28:15; 48:21 [b]Deut. 4:27
4 [1]Lit., *sky* [2]Lit., *take you* [a]Neh. 1:9; Is. 43:6; 48:20; 62:11
5 [a]Jer. 29:14; 30:3 [b]Deut. 7:13; 13:17
6 [1]Lit., *seed* [a]Deut. 6:5
7 [1]Lit., *put* [a]Deut. 7:15
8 [1]Lit., *listen to the voice of*

9"[a]Then the LORD your God will [1]prosper you abundantly in all the work of your hand, in the [2]offspring of your [3]body and in the [2]offspring of your cattle and in the [2]produce of your ground, for the LORD will again rejoice over you for good, just as He rejoiced over your fathers;

10 [1]if you [2]obey the LORD your God to keep His commandments and His statutes which [a]are written in this book of the law, [1]if you turn to the LORD your God [b]with all your heart and soul.

11"For this commandment which I command you today is not too difficult for you, nor is it [1]out of reach.

12"It is not in heaven, [1]that you should say, '[a]Who will go up to heaven for us to get it for us and make us hear it, that we may observe it?'

13"Nor is it beyond the sea, [1]that you should say, 'Who will cross the sea for us to get it for us and make us hear it, that we may observe it?'

14"But the word is very near you, in your mouth and in your heart, that you may observe it.

Choose Life

15"See, I have set before you today life and [1]prosperity, and death and [2]adversity;

16 in that I command you today [a]to love the LORD your God, to walk in His ways and to keep His commandments and His statutes and His judgments, that you [b]may live and multiply, and that the LORD your God may bless you in the land where you are entering to possess it.

17"But if your heart turns away and you will not obey, but are drawn away and worship other gods and serve them,

18 I declare to you today that [a]you shall surely perish. You shall not prolong *your* days in the land where you are crossing the Jordan to enter [1]and possess it.

19"[a]I call heaven and earth to witness against you today, that I have set before you life and death, [b]the blessing and the curse. So choose life in order that you may live, you and your [1]descendants,

20 [a]by loving the LORD your God, by obeying His voice, and [b]by holding fast to Him; [c]for [1]this is your life and the length of your days, [2]that you may live in the land which the LORD swore to your fathers, to Abraham, Isaac, and Jacob, to give them."

CHAPTER 31

Moses' Last Counsel

SO Moses went and spoke these words to all Israel.

2 And he said to them, "I am [a]a hundred and twenty years old today; I am no longer able to come and go, and the LORD has said to me, '[b]You shall not cross this Jordan.'

3"It is the LORD your God who will cross ahead of you; He will destroy these nations before you, and you shall dispossess them. [a]Joshua is the one who will cross ahead of you, just as the LORD has spoken.

4"And the LORD will do to them just as He did to Sihon and Og, the kings of the Amorites, and to their land, when He destroyed them.

5"And the LORD will deliver them up before you, and you shall do to them according to all the commandments which I have commanded you.

6"Be strong and courageous, [a]do not be afraid or tremble at them, for the LORD your God is the one who goes with you. [b]He will not fail you or forsake you."

7 Then Moses called to Joshua and said to him in the sight of all Israel, "[a]Be strong and courageous, for you shall go with this people into the land which the LORD has sworn to their fathers to give them, and you shall give it to them as an inheritance.

8"And the LORD is the one who goes ahead of you; He will be with you. [a]He will not fail you or forsake you. Do not fear, or be dismayed."

9 So Moses wrote this law and gave it to the priests, the sons of Levi [a]who carried the ark of the covenant of the LORD, and to all the elders of Israel.

10 Then Moses commanded them, saying, "At the end of *every* seven years, at the time of [a]the year of remission of debts, at the Feast of Booths,

11 when all Israel comes to appear before the LORD your God at [a]the place which He will choose, you shall read this law in front of all Israel in their hearing.

12"Assemble the people, the men and the women and children and [1]the alien who is in your [2]town, in order that they may hear and [a]learn and fear the LORD your God, and be careful to observe all the words of this law.

13"And their children, who have

9 [1]Lit., *make you have excess for good* [2]Lit., *fruit* [3]Lit., *womb* [a]Jer. 31:27, 28

10 [1]Or, *for you will* [2]Lit., *listen to the voice of* [a]Deut. 29:21 [b]Deut. 4:29

11 [1]Lit., *far off*

12 [1]Lit., *to say* [a]Rom. 10:6-8

13 [1]Lit., *to say*

15 [1]Lit., *good* [2]Lit., *evil*

16 [a]Deut. 6:5 [b]Deut. 4:1; 30:19

18 [1]Lit., *to* [a]Deut. 4:26

19 [1]Lit., *seed* [a]Deut. 4:26 [b]Deut. 30:1

20 [1]Lit., *that* [2]Lit., *to dwell* [a]Deut. 6:5 [b]Deut. 10:20 [c]Deut. 4:1; 32:47

2 [a]Deut. 34:7 [b]Deut. 1:37

3 [a]Num. 27:18

6 [a]Deut. 20:1 [b]Heb. 13:5

7 [a]Deut. 1:38; 3:28

8 [a]Deut. 31:6

9 [a]Num. 4:5, 6, 15; Deut. 10:8; 31:25, 26

10 [a]Deut. 15:1, 2

11 [a]Deut. 12:5

12 [1]Lit., *your alien* [2]Lit., *gates* [a]Deut. 4:10

not known, will hear and learn to fear the LORD your God, as long as you live on the land [1]which you are about to cross the Jordan to [2]possess."

Israel Will Fall Away

14 Then the LORD said to Moses, "Behold, [1a]the time for you to die is near; call Joshua, and present yourselves at the tent of meeting, that I may commission him." [b]So Moses and Joshua went and presented themselves at the tent of meeting.

15 [a]And the LORD appeared in the tent in a pillar of cloud, and the pillar of cloud stood at the doorway of the tent.

16 And the LORD said to Moses, "Behold, [a]you are about to lie down with your fathers; and [b]this people will arise and play the harlot with the strange gods of the land, into the midst of which they are going, and [c]will forsake Me and break My covenant which I have made with them.

17 "[a]Then My anger will be kindled against them in that day, and I will forsake them and hide My face from them, and they shall be consumed, and many evils and troubles shall come upon them; so that they will say in that day, 'Is it not because our God is not among us that these evils have come upon us?'

18 "But I will surely hide My face in that day because of all the evil which they will do, for they will turn to other gods.

19 "Now therefore [a]write this song for yourselves, and teach it to the sons of Israel; put it [1]on their lips, in order that this song may be a witness for Me against the sons of Israel.

20 "[a]For when I bring them into the land flowing with milk and honey, which I swore to their fathers, and they have eaten and are satisfied and [b]become [1]prosperous, then they will turn to other gods and serve them, and spurn Me and break My covenant.

21 "Then it shall come about, [a]when many evils and troubles have come upon them, that this song will testify before them as a witness (for it shall not be forgotten from the [1]lips of their descendants); for I know their intent which they are [2]developing today, before I have brought them into the land which I swore."

22 [a]So Moses wrote this song the same day, and taught it to the sons of Israel.

Joshua Is Commissioned

23 [a]Then He commissioned Joshua the son of Nun, and said, "Be strong and courageous, for you shall bring the sons of Israel into the land which I swore to them, and [b]I will be with you."

24 And it came about, when Moses finished writing the words of this law in a book until they were complete,

25 that Moses commanded the Levites [a]who carried the ark of the covenant of the LORD, saying,

26 "Take this book of the law and place it beside the ark of the covenant of the LORD your God, that it may [1]remain there as a witness against you.

27 "For I know [a]your rebellion and [b]your [1]stubbornness; behold, while I am still alive with you today, you have been rebellious against the LORD; how much more, then, after my death?

28 "Assemble to me all the elders of your tribes and your officers, that I may speak these words in their hearing and [a]call the heavens and the earth to witness against them.

29 "For I know that after my death you will act corruptly and turn from the way which I have commanded you; and evil will befall you in the latter days, for you will do that which is evil in the sight of the LORD, provoking Him to anger with the work of your hands."

30 Then Moses spoke in the hearing of all the assembly of Israel the words of this song, until they were complete:

CHAPTER 32

The Song of Moses

"[a]GIVE ear, oh heavens, and let me speak;
And let the earth hear the words of my mouth.
2 "[a]Let my teaching drop as the rain,
My speech distill as the dew,
As the droplets on the fresh grass
And as the showers on the herb.
3 "[a]For I proclaim the name of the LORD;
[b]Ascribe greatness to our God!
4 "[a]The Rock! His work is perfect,
[b]For all His ways are [1]just;
[c]A God of faithfulness and without injustice,
Righteous and upright is He.

13 [1]Lit., *where* [2]Lit., *possess it*
14 [1]Lit., *your days to die are* [a]Num. 27:12, 13; Deut. 4:22; 32:50 [b]Ex. 33:9-11
15 [a]Ex. 33:9
16 [a]Gen. 15:15 [b]Deut. 4:25-28; Judg. 2:11, 12 [c]Judg. 10:6
17 [a]Judg. 2:14; 6:13
19 [1]Lit., *in their mouths* [a]Deut. 31:22
20 [1]Lit., *fat* [a]Deut. 6:10-12; 8:10, 19; 11:16, 17 [b]Deut. 32:15-17
21 [1]Lit., *mouth of its seed* [2]Lit., *making* [a]Lev. 26:41; Deut. 4:30
22 [a]Deut. 31:19
23 [a]Deut. 31:7 [b]Ex. 3:12
25 [a]Deut. 31:9
26 [1]Lit., *be*
27 [1]Lit., *stiff neck* [a]Deut. 9:7 [b]Deut. 9:6, 13
28 [a]Deut. 4:26
1 [a]Deut. 4:26; Is. 1:2
2 [a]Is. 55:10, 11
3 [a]Ex. 33:19; 34:5, 6 [b]Deut. 3:24; 5:24
4 [1]Or, *judgment* [a]Deut. 32:15, 18, 30 [b]Gen. 18:25 [c]Deut. 7:9

5"[1][a]They have acted corruptly toward Him,
They are not His children, because of their defect;
[b]*But are* a perverse and crooked generation.
6"Do you thus repay the LORD,
[a]O foolish and unwise people?
[b]Is not He your Father who has bought you?
[c]He has made you and established you.
7"Remember the days of old,
Consider the years of all generations.
[a]Ask your father, and he will inform you,
Your elders, and they will tell you.
8"When the Most High gave the nations their inheritance,
When He separated the sons of [1]man,
He set the boundaries of the peoples
[a]According to the number of the sons of Israel.
9"[a]For the LORD's portion is His people;
Jacob is the allotment of His inheritance.
10"[a]He found him in a desert land,
And in the howling waste of a wilderness;
He encircled him, He cared for him,
He guarded him as [b]the pupil of His eye.
11"[a]Like an eagle that stirs up its nest,
That hovers over its young,
[b]He spread His wings and caught them,
He carried them on His pinions.
12"[a]The LORD alone guided him,
[b]And there was no foreign god with him.
13"[a]He made him ride on the high places of the earth,
And he ate the produce of the field;
[b]And He made him suck honey from the rock,
And oil from the flinty rock,
14 Curds of cows, and milk of the flock,
With fat of lambs,
And rams, the breed of Bashan, and goats,
[a]With the finest of the wheat—
And of the blood of grapes you drank wine.

15"[a]But [1]Jeshurun grew fat and kicked—
You are grown fat, thick, and sleek—

5 [1]Lit., *It has* [a]Deut. 4:25; 31:29 [b]Matt. 17:17

6 [a]Deut. 32:28 [b]Deut. 1:31 [c]Deut. 32:15

7 [a]Ex. 12:26; Ps. 78:5-8

8 [1]Or, *Adam* [a]Num. 23:9; Deut. 33:28

9 [a]1 Kin. 8:51, 53; Jer. 10:16

10 [a]Deut. 1:19 [b]Ps. 17:8; Zech. 2:8

11 [a]Ex. 19:4; Deut. 33:12 [b]Ps. 18:10-18

12 [a]Deut. 4:35, 39 [b]Deut. 32:39; Is. 43:12

13 [a]Is. 58:14 [b]Deut. 8:8; Ps. 81:16

14 [a]Ps. 81:16; 147:14

15 [1]I.e., Israel [a]Deut. 31:20 [b]Judg. 10:6 [c]Deut. 32:6 [d]Deut. 32:4

16 [a]Ps. 78:58 [b]Ps. 106:29

17 [a]Lev. 17:7; 1 Cor. 10:20 [b]Deut. 28:64 [c]Judg. 5:8

18 [a]Deut. 32:4 [b]Ps. 106:21

19 [a]Lev. 26:30; Ps. 106:40 [b]Jer. 44:21-23

20 [a]Deut. 31:29 [b]Deut. 32:5 [c]Deut. 9:23

21 [1]Lit., *vanities* [a]Deut. 32:16 [b]Deut. 32:17; 1 Kin. 16:13, 26 [c]Rom. 10:19

22 [1]I.e., the nether world [a]Num. 16:33-35; Ps. 18:7, 8 [b]Lev. 26:20

23 [a]Deut. 29:21 [b]Ps. 18:14; 45:5

24 [1]Lit., *burning heat* [a]Deut. 28:22, 48 [b]Ps. 91:6 [c]Lev. 26:22 [d]Amos 5:18, 19

25 [a]Lam. 1:20; Ezek. 7:15 [b]2 Chr. 36:17; Lam. 2:21

[b]Then he forsook God [c]who made him,
And scorned [d]the Rock of his salvation.
16"[a]They made Him jealous with strange *gods;*
[b]With abominations they provoked Him to anger.
17"[a]They sacrificed to demons *who were* not God,
[b]*To gods* whom they have not known,
[c]New *gods* who came lately,
Whom your fathers did not dread.
18"You neglected [a]the Rock who begot you,
[b]And forgot the God who gave you birth.

19"[a]And the LORD saw *this,* and spurned *them*
[b]Because of the provocation of His sons and daughters.
20"Then He said, 'I will hide My face from them,
[a]I will see what their end *shall be;*
[b]For they are a perverse generation,
[c]Sons in whom is no faithfulness.
21 '[a]They have made Me jealous with *what* is not God;
They have provoked Me to anger with their [1][b]idols.
[c]So I will make them jealous with *those who* are not a people;
I will provoke them to anger with a foolish nation,
22 [a]For a fire is kindled in My anger,
And burns to the lowest part of [1]Sheol,
[b]And consumes the earth with its yield,
And sets on fire the foundations of the mountains.

23 '[a]I will heap misfortunes on them;
[b]I will use My arrows on them.
24 '[a]*They shall be* wasted by famine, and consumed by [1]plague
[b]And bitter destruction;
[c]And the teeth of beasts I will send upon them,
[d]With the venom of crawling things of the dust.
25 '[a]Outside the sword shall bereave,
And inside terror—
[b]Both young man and virgin,
The nursling with the man of gray hair.

26 'I would have said, "[a]I will cut them to pieces,
[b]I will remove the memory of them from men,"
27 [a]Had I not feared the provocation by the enemy,
Lest their adversaries should misjudge,
Lest they should say, "[b]Our hand is [1]triumphant,
And the LORD has not done all this." '

28 "[a]For they are a nation [1]lacking in counsel,
And there is no understanding in them.
29 "[a]Would that they were wise, that they understood this,
[b]That they would discern their [1]future!
30 "[a]How could one chase a thousand,
And two put ten thousand to flight,
Unless their [b]Rock had sold them,
And the LORD had given them up?
31 "Indeed their rock is not like our Rock,
[a]Even our enemies [1]themselves judge this.
32 "For their vine is from the vine of Sodom,
And from the fields of Gomorrah;
Their grapes are grapes of [a]poison,
Their clusters, bitter.
33 "Their wine is the venom of [1]serpents,
And the [2]deadly poison of cobras.

34 '[a]Is it not laid up in store with Me,
Sealed up in My treasuries?
35 '[a]Vengeance is Mine, and retribution,
[b]In due time their foot will slip;
[c]For the day of their calamity is near,
And the impending things are hastening upon them.'
36 "[a]For the LORD will vindicate His people,
[b]And will have compassion on His servants;
When He sees that *their* [1]strength is gone,
And there is none *remaining,* bond or free.
37 "And He will say, '[a]Where are their gods,
The rock in which they sought refuge?

26 [a]Deut. 4:27; 28:64 [b]Deut. 9:14
27 [1]Lit., *high* [a]Deut. 9:26 [b]Num. 15:30
28 [1]Lit., *perishing* [a]Deut. 32:6
29 [1]Or, *latter end* [a]Deut. 5:29 [b]Deut. 31:29
30 [a]Lev. 26:7, 8 [b]Deut. 32:4
31 [1]Lit., *are judges* [a]Ex. 14:25
32 [a]Deut. 29:18
33 [1]Lit., *dragons* [2]Lit., *cruel*
34 [a]Jer. 44:21
35 [a]Rom. 12:19 [b]Jer. 23:12 [c]Ezek. 7:5-10
36 [1]Lit., *hand* [a]Heb. 10:30 [b]Lev. 26:43-45; Deut. 30:1-3
37 [a]Jer. 2:28
38 [a]Num. 25:1, 2 [b]Jer. 11:12
39 [a]Is. 41:4; 43:10 [b]Deut. 32:12 [c]1 Sam. 2:6 [d]Ps. 51:8 [e]Ps. 50:22
40 [a]Ezek. 20:5, 6
41 [1]Or, *lightning* [a]Is. 34:6-8 [b]Jer. 50:28-32
42 [1]Lit., *head* [a]Deut. 32:23 [b]Jer. 12:12; 46:10, 14
43 [a]Rom. 15:10 [b]2 Kin. 9:7 [c]Is. 1:24, 25 [d]Ps. 65:3; 79:9
44 [1]Lit., *Hoshea* [a]Num. 13:8, 16
46 [1]Lit., *to do* [a]Ezek. 40:4; 44:5 [b]Deut. 4:9
47 [1]Lit., *where* [2]Lit., *possess it* [a]Deut. 8:3; 30:20 [b]Deut. 4:40; 33:25
49 [1]Lit., *which is opposite* [a]Num. 27:12-14; Deut. 3:27

38 '[a]Who ate the fat of their sacrifices,
And drank the wine of their libation?
[b]Let them rise up and help you,
Let them be your hiding place!
39 '[a]See now that I, I am He,
[b]And there is no god besides Me;
[c]It is I who put to death and give life.
[d]I have wounded, and it is I who heal;
[e]And there is no one who can deliver from My hand.
40 'Indeed, [a]I lift up My hand to heaven,
And say, as I live forever,
41 [a]If I sharpen My [1]flashing sword,
And My hand takes hold on justice,
[b]I will render vengeance on My adversaries,
And I will repay those who hate Me.
42 '[a]I will make My arrows drunk with blood,
[b]And My sword shall devour flesh,
With the blood of the slain and the captives,
From the long-haired [1]leaders of the enemy.'
43 "[a]Rejoice, O nations, *with* His people;
[b]For He will avenge the blood of His servants,
[c]And will render vengeance on His adversaries,
[d]And will atone for His land *and* His people."
44 Then Moses came and spoke all
the words of this song in the hearing
of the people, he, with [1a]Joshua the
son of Nun.
45 When Moses had finished
speaking all these words to all Israel,
46 he said to them, "[a]Take to your
heart all the words with which I am
warning you today, which you shall
command [b]your sons to observe
[1]carefully, *even* all the words of this
law.
47 "For it is not an idle word for
you; indeed [a]it is your life. And [b]by
this word you shall prolong your
days in the land, [1]which you are
about to cross the Jordan to [2]possess."
48 And the LORD spoke to Moses
that very same day, saying,
49 "[a]Go up to this mountain of the
Abarim, Mount Nebo, which is in
the land of Moab [1]opposite Jericho,
and look at the land of Canaan,

which I am giving to the sons of Israel for a possession.

50 "Then die on the mountain where you ascend, and be [a]gathered to your people, as Aaron your brother died on Mount Hor and was gathered to his people,

51 [a]because you broke faith with Me in the midst of the sons of Israel at the waters of Meribah-kadesh, in the [b]wilderness of Zin, because you did not treat Me as holy in the midst of the sons of Israel.

52 "[a]For you shall see the land at a distance, but [b]you shall not go there, into the land which I am giving the sons of Israel."

CHAPTER 33

The Blessing of Moses

NOW this is the blessing with which Moses [a]the man of God blessed the sons of Israel before his death.

2 And he said,
"[a]The LORD came from Sinai,
[b]And [1]dawned on them from Seir;
[c]He shone forth from Mount Paran,
And He came from [d]the [2]midst of ten thousand holy ones;
[e]At His right hand there was [3]flashing lightning for them.
3 "[a]Indeed, He loves [1]the people;
[b]All [2]Thy holy ones are in Thy hand,
[c]And they [3]followed in Thy steps;
Everyone receives of Thy words.
4 "[a]Moses charged us with a law,
[b]A possession for the assembly of Jacob.
5 "[a]And He was king in Jeshurun,
When the heads of the people were gathered,
The tribes of Israel together.

6 "[a]May Reuben live and not die,
Nor his men be few."

7 [a]And this regarding Judah; so he said,
"Hear, O LORD, the voice of Judah,
And bring him to his people.
With his hands he contended for [1]them;
And mayest Thou be a help against his adversaries."

8 And of Levi he said,
"*Let* Thy [a]Thummim and Thy Urim *belong* to [1]Thy [b]godly man,
[c]Whom Thou didst prove at Massah,
With whom Thou didst contend at the waters of Meribah;
9 [a]Who said of his father and his mother,
'I did not consider them';
And he did not acknowledge his brothers,
Nor did he regard his own sons,
For they observed Thy word,
And kept Thy covenant.
10 "[a]They shall teach Thine ordinances to Jacob,
And Thy law to Israel.
[b]They shall put incense [1]before Thee,
And whole burnt offerings on Thine altar.
11 "O LORD, bless his substance,
And accept the work of his hands;
Shatter the loins of those who rise up against him,
And those who hate him, so that they may not rise *again.*"

12 Of Benjamin he said,
"[a]May the beloved of the LORD dwell in security by Him,
[b]Who shields him all the day,
[c]And he dwells between His shoulders."

13 And of Joseph he said,
"[a]Blessed of the LORD *be* his land,
With the choice things of heaven, with the dew,
And from the deep lying beneath,
14 And with the choice yield of the sun,
And with the choice produce of the months.
15 "And with the [1]best things of the ancient mountains,
And with the choice things of the everlasting hills,
16 And with the choice things of the earth and its fulness,
And the favor [a]of Him who dwelt in the bush.
Let it come to the head of Joseph,
And to the crown of the head of the one distinguished among his brothers.
17 "As the first-born of his ox, majesty is his,
And his horns are the horns of [a]the wild ox;
With them he shall [b]push the peoples,

50 [a]Gen. 25:8
51 [a]Num. 20:12 [b]Num. 27:14
52 [a]Deut. 34:1-3 [b]Deut. 1:37; 3:27
1 [a]Josh. 14:6
2 [1]Lit., *rose to* [2]Lit., *myriads of holiness* [3]Or, *a fiery law* [a]Ex. 19:18, 20; Ps. 68:8, 17 [b]Judg. 5:4 [c]Num. 10:12; Hab. 3:3 [d]Dan. 7:10 [e]Ex. 23:20-22
3 [1]Lit., *peoples* [2]Lit., *His* [3]Or, *lie down at Thy feet* [a]Deut. 4:37 [b]Deut. 7:6; 14:2 [c]Deut. 6:1-9
4 [a]Deut. 4:2 [b]Deut. 8:3; Ps. 119:111
5 [a]Num. 23:21
6 [a]Gen. 49:3, 4
7 [1]Lit., *him* [a]Gen. 49:8-12
8 [1]Lit., *him* [a]Lev. 8:8 [b]Ps. 106:16 [c]Ex. 17:7; Num. 20:13, 24; Deut. 6:16
9 [a]Ex. 32:27-29
10 [1]Lit., *in Thy nostrils* [a]Lev. 10-11; Deut. 31:9-13 [b]Lev. 16:12, 13
12 [a]Deut. 4:37; 12:10 [b]Deut. 32:11 [c]Ex. 28:12
13 [a]Gen. 27:27, 28; 49:22-26
15 [1]Or, *chief*
16 [a]Ex. 2:2-6
17 [a]Num. 23:22 [b]Ps. 44:5

All [1]at once, *to* the ends of the
earth.
And those are the ten thousands of Ephraim,
And those are the thousands
of Manasseh."

18 [a]And of Zebulun he said,
"Rejoice, Zebulun, in your
going forth,
And, Issachar, in your tents.
19 "[a]They shall call peoples *to* the
mountain;
There they shall offer righteous [b]sacrifices;
For they shall [1]draw out [c]the
abundance of the seas,
And the hidden treasures of
the sand."

20 [a]And of Gad he said,
"Blessed is the one who en-
larges Gad;
He lies down [b]as a [1]lion,
And tears the arm, also the
crown of the head.
21 "[a]Then he [1]provided the first
part for himself,
[b]For there the ruler's portion
was [2]reserved;
[c]And he came *with* the leaders
of the people;
[d]He executed the justice of the
LORD,
And His ordinances with Israel."

22 [a]And of Dan he said,
"Dan is [b]a lion's whelp,
That leaps forth from Ba-
shan."

23 And of Naphtali he said,
"[a]O Naphtali, satisfied with favor,
And full of the blessing of the
LORD,
Take possession of the sea and
the south."

24 [a]And of Asher he said,
"More blessed than sons is
Asher;
May he be favored by his
brothers,
[b]And may he dip his foot in oil.
25 "[a]Your locks shall be iron and
bronze,
[b]And according to your days,
so shall your leisurely walk
be.

26 "[a]There is none like the God of
[1]Jeshurun,
[b]Who rides the heavens [2]to
your help,
And through the skies in His
majesty.
27 "[a]The eternal God is a [1]dwell-
ing place,
[b]And underneath are the everlasting arms;
[c]And He drove out the enemy
from before you,
[d]And said, 'Destroy!'
28 "[a]So Israel dwells in security,
[b]The fountain of Jacob se-
cluded,
[c]In a land of grain and new
wine;
[d]His heavens also drop down
dew.
29 "[a]Blessed are you, O Israel;
[b]Who is like you, a people
saved by the LORD,
[c]Who is the shield of your
help,
[d]And the sword of your majesty!
[e]So your enemies shall cringe
before you,
[f]And you shall tread upon
their high places."

CHAPTER 34

The Death of Moses

[a]NOW Moses went up from the
plains of Moab to Mount Nebo, to
the top of Pisgah, which is opposite
Jericho. And the LORD [b]showed him
all the land, Gilead as far as Dan,
2 and all Naphtali and the land of
Ephraim and Manasseh, and all the
land of Judah as far as the [1]Western
Sea,
3 and the [1]Negev and the plain in
the valley of Jericho, the city of
palm trees, as far as Zoar.
4 Then the LORD said to him,
"This is the land which [a]I swore to
Abraham, Isaac, and Jacob, saying,
'I will give it to your [1]descendants';
I have let you see *it* with your eyes,
but you shall not go over there."
5 So Moses [a]the servant of the
LORD [b]died there in the land of
Moab, according to the [1]word of the
LORD.
6 And He buried him in the valley
in the land of Moab, [a]opposite Beth-
peor; but no man knows his burial
place to this day.
7 Although Moses was [a]one hundred and twenty years old when he
died, his eye was not dim, nor his
vigor abated.
8 So the sons of Israel wept for
Moses in the plains of Moab [a]thirty
days; then the days of weeping *and*
mourning for Moses came to an end.
9 Now Joshua the son of Nun was
[a]filled with the spirit of wisdom, for

17 [1]Or, *together*
18 [a]Gen. 49:13-15
19 [1]Lit., *suck* [a]Ex. 15:17; Ps. 2:6; Is. 2:3 [b]Ps. 4:5; 51:19 [c]Is. 60:5
20 [1]Or, *lioness* [a]Gen. 49:19 [b]Gen. 49:9
21 [1]Lit., *saw* [2]Or, *covered up* [a]Num. 32:1-5 [b]Num. 34:14 [c]Josh. 4:12 [d]Josh. 22:1-3
22 [a]Gen. 49:16 [b]Ezek. 19:2, 3
23 [a]Gen. 49:21
24 [a]Gen. 49:20 [b]Job 29:6
25 [a]Ps. 147:13 [b]Deut. 4:40; 32:47
26 [1]I.e., Israel [2]Lit., *in* [a]Deut. 4:35 [b]Deut. 10:14; Ps. 68:33, 34
27 [1]Or, *refuge* [a]Ps. 90:1, 2 [b]Gen. 49:24 [c]Ex. 34:11; Josh. 24:18 [d]Deut. 7:2
28 [a]Deut. 33:12 [b]Num. 23:9, Deut. 32:8 [c]Gen. 27:28, 37 [d]Deut. 33:13
29 [a]Ps. 1:1; 32:1, 2 [b]Deut. 4:32 [c]Gen. 15:1; Ps. 33:20; 115:9-11 [d]Ps. 68:34 [e]Ps. 66:3 [f]Num. 33:52; Deut. 32:13
1 [a]Deut. 32:49 [b]Deut. 32:52
2 [1]I.e., Mediterranean Sea
3 [1]I.e., South country
4 [1]Lit., *seed* [a]Gen. 12:7; 26:3; 28:13
5 [1]Lit., *mouth* [a]Num. 12:7 [b]Deut. 32:50
6 [a]Deut. 3:29; 4:46
7 [a]Deut. 31:2
8 [a]Deut. 1:3; Josh. 4:19
9 [a]Num. 27:18, 23

Moses had laid his hands on him; and the sons of Israel listened to him and did as the LORD had commanded Moses.

10 Since then no prophet has risen in Israel like Moses, whom [a]the LORD knew face to face,

11 for all the signs and wonders which the LORD sent him to perform in the land of Egypt against Pharaoh, all his servants, and all his land,

12 and for all the mighty [1]power and for all the great terror which Moses performed in the sight of all Israel.

10 [a]Num. 12:8
12 [1]Lit., *hand*

THE BOOK OF JOSHUA

God's charge to Joshua

1 NOW it came about after the death of Moses the servant of the LORD that the LORD spoke to Joshua the son of Nun, Moses' [1]servant, saying,

2 "Moses [a]My servant is dead; now therefore arise, [b]cross this Jordan, you and all this people, to the land which I am giving to them, to the sons of Israel.

3 "[a]Every place on which the sole of your foot treads, I have given it to you, just as I spoke to Moses.

4 "From the wilderness and this Lebanon, even as far as the great river, the river Euphrates, all the land of the Hittites, and as far as the Great Sea toward the setting of the sun, will be your territory.

5 "[a]No man will *be able to* stand before you all the days of your life. Just as I have been with Moses, I will be with you; [b]I will not fail you or forsake you.

6 "Be strong and courageous, for you shall give this people possession of the land which I swore to their fathers to give them.

7 "[a]Only be strong and very courageous; [1]be careful to do according to all the law which Moses My servant commanded you; do not turn from it to the right or to the left, so that you may [2]have success wherever you go.

8 "[a]This book of the law shall not depart from your mouth, but you shall meditate on it day and night, so that you may [1]be careful to do according to all that is written in it; [b]for then you will make your way prosperous, and then you will [2]have success.

9 "Have I not commanded you? [a]Be strong and courageous! Do not tremble or be dismayed, [b]for the LORD your God is with you wherever you go."

1 [1]Or, *minister*
2 [a]Num. 12:7; Deut. 34:5 [b]Deut. 11:24; Josh. 1:11
3 [a]Deut. 11:24
5 [a]Deut. 7:24; Heb. 13:5 [b]Deut. 31:6, 7
7 [1]Lit., *observe* [2]Or, *act wisely* [a]Deut. 5:32
8 [1]Lit., *observe* [2]Or, *act wisely* [a]Deut. 31:24; Josh. 8:34 [b]Deut. 29:9; Ps. 1:1-3
9 [a]Josh. 1:7 [b]Deut. 31:8
11 [a]Josh. 3:2
12 [1]Lit., *said, saying* [a]Num. 32:20-22
13 [a]Deut. 3:18-20
15 [1]Lit., *the land of your possession* [2]Lit., *it* [a]Josh. 22:4 [b]Josh. 1:1
17 [a]Josh. 1:5, 9
18 [1]Lit., *mouth*

Joshua Assumes Command

10 Then Joshua commanded the officers of the people, saying,

11 "Pass through the midst of the camp and command the people, saying, 'Prepare provisions for yourselves, for within [a]three days you are to cross this Jordan, to go in to possess the land which the LORD your God is giving you, to possess it.' "

12 [a]And to the Reubenites and to the Gadites and to the half-tribe of Manasseh, Joshua [1]said,

13 "Remember the word which Moses the servant of the LORD commanded you, saying, '[a]The LORD your God gives you rest, and will give you this land.'

14 "Your wives, your little ones, and your cattle shall remain in the land which Moses gave you beyond the Jordan, but you shall cross before your brothers in battle array, all your valiant warriors, and shall help them,

15 until the LORD gives your brothers rest, as *He gives* you, and they also possess the land which the LORD your God is giving them. [a]Then you shall return to [1]your own land, and possess [2]that which Moses [b]the servant of the LORD gave you beyond the Jordan toward the sunrise."

16 And they answered Joshua, saying, "All that you have commanded us we will do, and wherever you send us we will go.

17 "Just as we obeyed Moses in all things, so we will obey you; [a]only may the LORD your God be with you, as He was with Moses.

18 "Anyone who rebels against your [1]command and does not obey your words in all that you command him, shall be put to death; only be strong and courageous."

CHAPTER 2

Rahab Shelters Spies

THEN Joshua the son of Nun sent
two men as spies secretly from
[a]Shittim, saying, "Go, view the land,
especially Jericho." So they went
and came into the house of [b]a harlot
whose name was Rahab, and
[1]lodged there.
2 And it was told the king of Jericho, saying, "Behold, men from the
sons of Israel have come here tonight to search out the land."
3 And the king of Jericho sent
word to Rahab, saying, "Bring out
the men who have come to you, who
have entered your house, for they
have come to search out all the
land."
4 But the woman had taken the
two men and hidden them, and she
said, "Yes, the men came to me, but
I did not know where they were
from.
5 "And it came about when *it was*
time to shut the gate, at dark, that
the men went out; I do not know
where the men went. Pursue them
quickly, for you will overtake
them."
6 [a]But she had brought them up
to the roof and hidden them in the
stalks of flax which she had laid in
order on the roof.
7 So the men pursued them on
the road to the Jordan to the fords;
and as soon as those who were pursuing them had gone out, they shut
the gate.
8 Now before they lay down, [1]she
came up to them on the roof,
9 and said to the men, "[a]I know
that the LORD has given you the
land, and that the [b]terror of you has
fallen on us, and that all the inhabitants of the land have [1]melted away
before you.
10 "[a]For we have heard how the
LORD dried up the water of the [1]Red
Sea before you when you came out
of Egypt, and what you did to the
two kings of the Amorites who were
beyond the Jordan, to Sihon and Og,
whom you [2]utterly destroyed.
11 "And when we heard *it,* our
hearts melted and no [1]courage remained in any man any longer because of you; for the LORD your God,
He is God in heaven above and on
earth beneath.
12 "Now therefore, please swear to
me by the LORD, since I have dealt
kindly with you, that you also will
deal kindly with my father's household, and give me a [a]pledge of
[1]truth,
13 and [1]spare my father and my
mother and my brothers and my sisters, with all who belong to them,
and deliver our [2]lives from death."
14 So the men said to her, "Our
[1]life [2]for yours if you do not tell this
business of ours; and it shall come
about when the LORD gives us the
land that we will [a]deal kindly and
[3]faithfully with you."

The Promise to Rahab

15 Then she let them down by a
rope through the window, for her
house was on the city wall, so that
she was living on the wall.
16 And she said to them, "[a]Go to
the hill country, lest the pursuers
happen upon you, and hide yourselves there for three days, until the
pursuers return. Then afterward
you may go on your way."
17 And the men said to her, "[a]We
shall be free from this oath [1]to you
which you have made us swear,
18 [1]unless, when we come into the
land, you tie this cord of scarlet
thread in the window through which
you let us down, and [a]gather to
yourself into the house your father
and your mother and your brothers
and all your father's household.
19 "And it shall come about that
anyone who goes out of the doors of
your house into the street, his blood
shall be on his own head, and we
shall be free; but anyone who is with
you in the house, his blood *shall be*
on our head, if a hand is *laid* on him.
20 "But if you tell this business of
ours, then we shall be free from the
oath which you have made us
swear."
21 And she said, "According to
your words, so be it." So she sent
them away, and they departed; and
she tied the scarlet cord in the window.
22 And they departed and came to
the hill country, and remained there
for three days until the pursuers returned. Now the pursuers had
sought *them* [1]all along the road, but
had not found *them.*
23 Then the two men returned and
came down from the hill country
and crossed over and came to
Joshua the son of Nun, and they related to him all that had happened to
them.
24 And they said to Joshua,
"Surely the LORD has given all the
land into our hands, and [a]all the inhabitants of the land, moreover,
have [1]melted away before us."

1 [1]Lit., *lay down* [a]Num. 25:1; Josh. 3:1 [b]Heb. 11:31; James 2:25
6 [a]James 2:25
8 [1]Lit., *then she*
9 [1]Or, *become demoralized* [a]Num. 20:24; Josh. 9:9, 10, 24 [b]Ex. 23:27; Deut. 2:25
10 [1]Lit., *Sea of Reeds* [2]Or, *put under the ban* [a]Num. 23:22
11 [1]Lit., *spirit arose*
12 [1]Or, *faithfulness* [a]Josh. 2:18
13 [1]Lit., *let live* [2]Lit., *souls*
14 [1]Lit., *soul* [2]Lit., *instead of you to die* [3]Or, *truly* [a]Gen. 24:49
16 [a]James 2:25
17 [1]Lit., *of yours* [a]Gen. 24:8
18 [1]Lit., *behold* [a]Josh. 2:12
22 [1]Lit., *through all the road*
24 [1]Or, *become demoralized* [a]Josh. 2:9

CHAPTER 3

Israel Crosses the Jordan

THEN Joshua rose early in the
morning; and he and all the sons of
Israel set out from [a]Shittim and
came to the Jordan, and they lodged
there before they crossed.
2 And it came about [a]at the end
of three days that the officers went
through the midst of the camp;
3 and they commanded the people, saying, "When you see the [a]ark
of the covenant of the LORD your
God with the Levitical priests carrying it, then you shall set out from
your place and go after it.
4"However, there shall be between you and it a distance of about
2,000 [1]cubits by measure. Do not
come near it, that you may know the
way by which you shall go, for you
have not passed this way before."
5 Then Joshua said to the people,
"[a]Consecrate yourselves, for tomorrow the LORD will do wonders
among you."
6 And Joshua spoke to the
priests, saying, "Take up the ark of
the covenant and cross over ahead
of the people." So they took up the
ark of the covenant and went ahead
of the people.
7 Now the LORD said to Joshua,
"This day I will begin to [a]exalt you
in the sight of all Israel, that they
may know that just as I have been
with Moses, I will be with you.
8"You shall, moreover, command
the priests who are carrying the ark
of the covenant, saying, 'When you
come to the edge of the waters of
the Jordan, you shall stand *still* in
the Jordan.' "
9 Then Joshua said to the sons of
Israel, "Come here, and hear the
words of the LORD your God."
10 And Joshua said, "By this you
shall know that the living God is
among you, and that He will assuredly dispossess from before you
the Canaanite, the Hittite, the Hivite, the Perizzite, the Girgashite,
the Amorite, and the Jebusite.
11"Behold, the ark of the covenant
of the Lord of all the earth is crossing over ahead of you into the Jordan.
12"[a]Now then, take for yourselves
twelve men from the tribes of Israel,
one man for each tribe.
13"And it shall come about when
the soles of the feet of the priests
who carry the ark of the LORD, the
Lord of all the earth, shall rest in the
waters of the Jordan, the waters of
the Jordan shall be cut off, *and* the
waters which are [1]flowing down
from above [2]shall [a]stand in one
heap."
14 So it came about when the people set out from their tents to cross
the Jordan with the priests carrying
the ark of the covenant before the
people,
15 and when those who carried the
ark came into the Jordan, and the
feet of the priests carrying the ark
were dipped in the edge of the water
(for the Jordan overflows all its
banks all the days of harvest),
16 [a]that the waters which were
[1]flowing down from above stood
and rose up in [b]one heap, a great
distance away at Adam, the city
that is beside Zarethan; and those
which were [1]flowing down toward
the sea of the [c]Arabah, the Salt Sea,
were completely cut off. So the people crossed opposite Jericho.
17 And the priests who carried the
ark of the covenant of the LORD
stood firm [a]on dry ground in the
middle of the Jordan while all Israel
crossed on dry ground, until all the
nation had finished crossing the Jordan.

CHAPTER 4

Memorial Stones from Jordan

NOW it came about when all the
nation had finished crossing the Jordan, that the LORD spoke to Joshua,
saying,
2"[a]Take for yourselves twelve
men from the people, one man from
each tribe,
3 and command them, saying,
'Take up for yourselves twelve
stones from here out of the middle
of the Jordan, from the place where
the priests' feet are standing firm,
and carry them over with you, and
lay them down in [a]the lodging place
where you will lodge tonight.' "
4 So Joshua called the twelve
men whom he had appointed from
the sons of Israel, one man from
each tribe;
5 and Joshua said to them,
"[1]Cross again to the ark of the LORD
your God into the middle of the Jordan, and each of you take up a stone
on his shoulder, according to the
number of the tribes of the sons of
Israel.
6"[1]Let this be a sign among you,
so that [a]when your children ask [2]lat-
er, saying, 'What do these stones
mean to you?'
7 then you shall say to them, 'Be-

---

1 [a]Josh. 2:1
2 [a]Josh. 1:11
3 [a]Deut. 31:9
4 [1]I.e., one cubit equals approximately 18 inches
5 [a]Ex. 19:10, 11; Josh. 7:13
7 [a]Josh. 4:14
12 [a]Josh. 4:2
13 [1]Lit., *going* [2]Lit., *and they shall* [a]Ex. 15:8
16 [1]Lit., *going* [a]Ps. 66:6; 74:15; 114:3, 5 [b]Josh. 3:13 [c]Deut. 1:1
17 [a]Ex. 14:21, 22, 29
2 [a]Josh. 3:12
3 [a]Josh. 4:20
5 [1]Lit., *Cross before the ark*
6 [1]Lit., *That this may be* [2]Lit., *tomorrow* [a]Ex. 12:26; 13:4; Josh. 4:21

cause the waters of the Jordan were
cut off before the ark of the covenant of the LORD; when it crossed
the Jordan, the waters of the Jordan
were cut off.' So these stones shall
become a memorial to the sons of
Israel forever."
8 And thus the sons of Israel did,
as Joshua commanded, and took up
twelve stones from the middle of the
Jordan, just as the LORD spoke to
Joshua, according to the number of
the tribes of the sons of Israel; and
they carried them over with them to
[a]the lodging place, and put them
down there.
9 Then Joshua set up twelve
stones in the middle of the Jordan at
the place where the feet of the
priests who carried the ark of the
covenant were standing, and they
are there to this day.
10 For the priests who carried the
ark were standing in the middle of
the Jordan until everything was
completed that the LORD had commanded Joshua to speak to the people, according to all that Moses had
commanded Joshua. And the people
hurried and crossed;
11 and it came about when all the
people had finished crossing, that
the ark of the LORD and the priests
crossed before the people.
12 [a]And the sons of Reuben and
the sons of Gad and the half-tribe of
Manasseh crossed over in battle array before the sons of Israel, just as
Moses had spoken to them;
13 about 40,000, equipped for war,
crossed for battle before the LORD to
the desert plains of Jericho.
14 [a]On that day the LORD exalted
Joshua in the sight of all Israel; so
that they [1]revered him, just as they
had [1]revered Moses all the days of
his life.
15 Now the LORD said to [1]Joshua,
16 "Command the priests who carry the ark of the testimony that they
come up from the Jordan."
17 So Joshua commanded the
priests, saying, "Come up from the
Jordan."
18 And it came about when the
priests who carried the ark of the
covenant of the LORD had come up
from the middle of the Jordan, and
the soles of the priests' feet were
[1]lifted up to the dry ground, that the
waters of the Jordan returned to
their place, and went over all its
banks as before.
19 Now the people came up from
the Jordan on the [a]tenth of the first
month and camped at Gilgal on the
eastern edge of Jericho.
20 [a]And [1]those twelve stones
which they had taken from the Jordan, Joshua set up [b]at Gilgal.
21 And he said to the sons of [1]Is-
rael, "When your children ask their
fathers in time to come, saying,
'What are these stones?'
22 then you shall inform your children, saying, 'Israel crossed this
Jordan on [a]dry ground.'
23 "For the LORD your God dried up
the waters of the Jordan before you
until you had crossed, just as the
LORD your God had done to the [1]Red
Sea, which He dried up before us
until we had crossed;
24 that all the peoples of the earth
may know that the hand of the LORD
is mighty, so that you may [1]fear the
LORD your God [2]forever."

CHAPTER 5

Israel is Circumcised

NOW it came about when all the
kings of the Amorites who *were* beyond the Jordan to the west, and all
the kings of the Canaanites [a]who
were by the sea, [b]heard how the
LORD had dried up the waters of the
Jordan before the sons of Israel until
[1]they had crossed, that their hearts
melted, and there was no spirit in
them any longer, because of the
sons of Israel.
2 At that time the LORD said to
Joshua, "Make for yourself flint
[a]knives and circumcise again the
sons of Israel the second time."
3 So Joshua made himself flint
knives and circumcised the sons of
Israel at [1]Gibeath-haaraloth.
4 And this is the reason why
Joshua circumcised them: [a]all the
people who came out of Egypt who
were males, all the men of war, died
in the wilderness along the way, after they came out of Egypt.
5 For all the people who came out
were circumcised, but all the people
who were born in the wilderness
along the way as they came out of
Egypt had not been circumcised.
6 For the sons of Israel walked
[a]forty years in the wilderness, until
all the nation, *that is,* the men of war
who came out of Egypt, [1]perished
because they did not listen to the
voice of the LORD, [b]to whom the
LORD had sworn that He would not
let them see the land which the
LORD had sworn to their fathers to
give us, a land flowing with milk and
honey.

8 [a]Josh. 4:20
12 [a]Num. 32:17
14 [1]Or, *feared* [a]Josh. 3:7
15 [1]Lit., *Joshua, saying*
18 [1]Lit., *drawn out*
19 [a]Deut. 1:3
20 [1]Lit., *these* [a]Josh. 4:8 [b]Josh. 4:3, 8
21 [1]Lit., *Israel, saying,*
22 [a]Josh. 3:17
23 [1]Lit., *Sea of Reeds*
24 [1]Or, *reverence* [2]Lit., *all the days*
1 [1]Other mss. read, *we* [a]Num. 13:29 [b]Josh. 2:10, 11
2 [a]Ex. 4:25
3 [1]I.e., the hill of the foreskins
4 [a]Deut. 2:14
6 [1]Lit., *were finished* [a]Deut. 2:7, 14 [b]Num. 14:29-35; 26:63-65

7 And their children whom He raised up in their place, Joshua [1]circumcised; for they were uncircumcised, because they had not circumcised them along the way.

8 Now it came about when they had finished circumcising all the nation, that they remained in their places in the camp until they were [1]healed.

9 Then the LORD said to Joshua, "Today I have rolled away [a]the reproach of Egypt from you." So the name of that place is called [1]Gilgal to this day.

10 While the sons of Israel camped at Gilgal, [a]they observed the Passover on the evening of the [b]fourteenth day of the month on the desert plains of Jericho.

11 And on the [1]day after the Passover, on [2]that very day, they ate some of the produce of the land, unleavened cakes and parched grain.

12 And [a]the manna ceased on the [1]day after they had eaten some of the produce of the land, so that the sons of Israel no longer had manna, but they ate some of the yield of the land of Canaan during that year.

13 Now it came about when Joshua was by Jericho, that he lifted up his eyes and looked, and behold, [a]a man was standing opposite him with his sword drawn in his hand, and Joshua went to him and said to him, "Are you for us or for our adversaries?"

14 And he said, "No, rather I indeed come now *as* captain of the host of the LORD." And Joshua fell on his face to the earth, and bowed down, and said to him, "What has my lord to say to his servant?"

15 And the captain of the LORD's host said to Joshua, "[a]Remove your sandals from your feet, for the place where you are standing is holy." And Joshua did so.

CHAPTER 6

The Conquest of Jericho

NOW Jericho was tightly shut because of the sons of Israel; no one went out and no one came in.

2 And the LORD said to Joshua, "See, I have given Jericho into your hand, with [a]its king *and* the valiant warriors.

3 "And you shall march around the city, all the men of war circling the city once. You shall do so for six days.

4 "Also seven priests shall carry seven [a]trumpets of rams' horns before the ark; then on the seventh day you shall march around the city seven times, and the priests shall blow the trumpets.

5 "And it shall be that when they make a long blast with the ram's horn, and when you hear the sound of the trumpet, all the people shall shout with a great shout; and the wall of the city will fall down [1]flat, and the people will go up every man straight [2]ahead."

6 So Joshua the son of Nun called the priests and said to them, "Take up the ark of the covenant, and let seven priests carry seven trumpets of rams' horns before the ark of the LORD."

7 Then [1]he said to the people, "Go forward, and march around the city, and let the armed men go on before the ark of the LORD."

8 And it was *so*, that when Joshua had spoken to the people, the seven priests carrying the seven trumpets of rams' horns before the LORD went forward and blew the trumpets; and the ark of the covenant of the LORD followed them.

9 And the armed men went before the priests who blew the trumpets, and [a]the rear guard came after the ark, while they continued to blow the trumpets.

10 But Joshua commanded the people, saying, "You shall not shout nor let your voice be heard, nor let a word proceed out of your mouth, until the day I tell you, 'Shout!' Then you shall shout!"

11 So he had the ark of the LORD [1]taken around the city, circling *it* once; then they came into the camp and spent the night in the camp.

12 Now Joshua rose early in the morning, and the priests took up the ark of the LORD.

13 And [a]the seven priests carrying the seven trumpets of rams' horns before the ark of the LORD went on continually, and blew the trumpets; and the armed men went before them, and [b]the rear guard came after the ark of the LORD, while they continued to blow the trumpets.

14 Thus the second day they marched around the city once and returned to the camp; they did so for six days.

15 Then it came about on the seventh day that they rose early at the dawning of the day and marched around the city in the same manner seven times; only on that day they marched around the city seven times.

7 [1]Lit., *circumcised them*
8 [1]Lit., *revived*
9 [1]I.e., Rolling [a]Zeph. 2:8
10 [a]Ex. 12:18 [b]Josh. 4:19
11 [1]Lit., *morrow* [2]Lit., *this*
12 [1]Lit., *morrow* [a]Ex. 16:35
13 [a]Gen. 18:1, 2; 32:24, 30; Num. 22:31
15 [a]Ex. 3:5
2 [a]Deut. 7:24
4 [a]Lev. 25:9
5 [1]Lit., *in its place* [2]Lit., *before himself*
7 [1]Or, *they*
9 [a]Josh. 6:13; Is. 52:12
11 [1]Lit., *to go around*
13 [a]Josh. 6:4 [b]Josh. 6:9

16 And it came about at the seventh time, when the priests blew the trumpets, Joshua said to the people, "Shout! For the LORD has given you the city.

17"And the city shall be [a]under the ban, it and all that is in it belongs to the LORD; only Rahab the harlot [1]and all who are with her in the house shall live, because she hid the messengers whom we sent.

18"But as for you, only keep yourselves from the things under the ban, lest you [1]covet *them* and take some of the things under the ban, [a]so you would make the camp of Israel accursed and bring trouble on it.

19"[a]But all the silver and gold and articles of bronze and iron are holy to the LORD; they shall go into the treasury of the LORD."

20 So the people shouted, and [1]*priests* blew the trumpets; and it came about, when the people heard the sound of the trumpet, that the people shouted with a great shout and the [a]wall fell down [2]flat, so that the people went up into the city, every man straight [3]ahead, and they took the city.

21 [a]And they [1]utterly destroyed everything in the city, both man and woman, young and old, and ox and sheep and donkey, with the edge of the sword.

22 And Joshua said to the two men who had spied out the land, "[a]Go into the harlot's house and bring the woman and all she has out of there, as you have sworn to her."

23 So the young men who were spies went in and [a]brought out Rahab and her father and her mother and her brothers and all she had; they also brought out all her relatives, and placed them outside the camp of Israel.

24 [a]And they burned the city with fire, and all that was in it. Only the silver and gold and articles of bronze and iron, they put into the treasury of the [1]house of the LORD.

25 [a]However, Rahab the harlot and her father's household and all she had, Joshua [1]spared; and she has lived in the midst of Israel to this day, for [b]she hid the messengers whom Joshua sent to spy out Jericho.

26 Then Joshua made them take an oath at that time, saying, "[a]Cursed before the LORD is the man who rises up and builds this city Jericho; with *the loss of* his first-born he shall lay its foundation, and with *the loss of* his youngest son he shall set up its gates."

27 So the LORD was with Joshua, and his fame was in all the land.

CHAPTER 7

Israel Is Defeated at Ai

[a]BUT the sons of Israel acted unfaithfully in regard to the things under the ban, for Achan, the son of Carmi, the son of Zabdi, the son of Zerah, from the tribe of Judah, took some of the things under the ban, therefore the anger of the LORD burned against the sons of Israel.

2 Now Joshua sent men from Jericho to Ai, which is near [a]Beth-aven, east of Bethel, and said to them, "[1]Go up and spy out the land." So the men went up and spied out Ai.

3 And they returned to Joshua and said to him, "Do not let all the people go up; *only* about two or three thousand men need go up [1]to Ai; do not make all the people toil up there, for they are few."

4 So about three thousand men from the people went up there, but they fled [1]from the men of Ai.

5 And the men of Ai struck down about thirty-six of their men, and pursued them [1]*from* the gate as far as Shebarim, and struck them down on the descent, so the hearts of the people melted and became as water.

6 Then Joshua [a]tore his clothes and fell to the earth on his face before the ark of the LORD until the evening, *both* he and the elders of Israel; and [b]they put dust on their heads.

7 And Joshua said, "Alas, O Lord [1]GOD, why didst Thou ever bring this people over the Jordan, *only* to deliver us into the hand of the Amorites, to destroy us? If only we had been willing [2]to dwell beyond the Jordan!

8"Oh Lord, what can I say since Israel has turned *their* [1]back before their enemies?

9"[a]For the Canaanites and all the inhabitants of the land will hear of it, and they will surround us and cut off our name from the earth. And what wilt Thou do for Thy great name?"

10 So the LORD said to Joshua, "Rise up! Why is it that you have fallen on your face?

11"Israel has sinned, and [a]they have also transgressed My covenant which I commanded them. And they

17 [1]Lit., *she and all* [a]Lev. 27:28; Deut. 20:17

18 [1]Lit., *devote* [a]Josh. 7:1

19 [a]Num. 31:11, 12, 21-23

20 [1]Or, *they* [2]Lit., *in its place* [3]Lit., *before himself* [a]Heb. 11:30

21 [1]Or, *put under the ban* [a]Deut. 20:16

22 [a]Josh. 2:12-19

23 [a]Heb. 11:31

24 [1]I.e., tabernacle [a]Deut. 20:16-18

25 [1]Lit., *let live* [a]Heb. 11:31 [b]Josh. 2:6

26 [a]1 Kin. 16:34

1 [a]Josh. 6:17-19

2 [1]Lit., *saying,* "Go [a]Josh. 18:12; 1 Sam. 13:5; 14:23

3 [1]Lit., *and smite*

4 [1]Lit., *before*

5 [1]Lit., *before*

6 [a]Job 2:12; 42:6 [b]Lam. 2:10; Rev. 18:19

7 [1]Lit., YHWH, usually rendered LORD [2]Lit., *and had dwelt*

8 [1]Lit., *neck*

9 [a]Ex. 32:12; Deut. 9:28

11 [a]Josh. 6:18, 19

have even taken some of the things
under the ban and have both stolen
and deceived. Moreover, they have
also put *them* among their own
things.
12"Therefore the sons of Israel
cannot stand before their enemies;
they turn *their* [1]backs before their
enemies, for they have become accursed. I will not be with you any
more unless you destroy the things
under the ban from your midst.
13"Rise up! [a]Consecrate the people
and say, 'Consecrate yourselves for
tomorrow, for thus the LORD, the
God of Israel, has said, "[b]There are
things under the ban in your midst,
O Israel. You cannot stand before
your enemies until you have removed the things under the ban
from your midst."
14 'In the morning then you shall
come near by your tribes. And it
shall be that the tribe which the
LORD takes *by lot* shall come near by
families, and the family which the
LORD takes shall come near by
households, and the household
which the LORD takes shall come
near man by man.
15 'And it shall be that the one who
is taken with the things under the
ban shall be burned with fire, he and
all that belongs to him, because he
has transgressed the covenant of
the LORD, and because he has committed a disgraceful thing in Israel.' "

The Sin of Achan

16 So Joshua arose early in the
morning and brought Israel near by
[1]tribes, and the tribe of Judah was
taken.
17 And he brought the family of
Judah near, and he took the family
of the Zerahites; and he brought the
family of the Zerahites near man by
man, and Zabdi was taken.
18 And he brought his household
near man by man; and Achan, son of
Carmi, son of Zabdi, son of Zerah,
from the tribe of Judah, was taken.
19 Then Joshua said to Achan,
"My son, I implore you, give glory to
the LORD, the God of Israel, and give
praise to Him; and tell me now what
you have done. Do not hide it from
me."
20 So Achan answered Joshua and
said, "Truly, I have sinned against
the LORD, the God of Israel, and
[1]this is what I did;
21 when I saw among the spoil a
beautiful mantle from Shinar and
two hundred shekels of silver and a
bar of gold fifty shekels in weight,
then I coveted them and took them;
and behold, they are concealed in
the earth inside my tent with the silver underneath it."
22 So Joshua sent messengers,
and they ran to the tent; and behold,
it was concealed in his tent with the
silver underneath it.
23 And they took them from inside
the tent and brought them to Joshua
and to all the sons of Israel, and they
poured them out before the LORD.
24 Then Joshua and all Israel with
him, took Achan the son of Zerah,
the silver, the mantle, the bar of
gold, his sons, his daughters, his
[1]oxen, his donkeys, his sheep, his
tent and all that belonged to him;
and they brought them up to [a]the
valley of [2]Achor.
25 And Joshua said, "Why have
you [a]troubled us? The LORD will
trouble you this day." And all Israel
stoned [1]them with stones; and they
burned them with fire [2]after they
had stoned them with stones.
26 And they raised over him a
great heap of stones that stands to
this day, and the LORD turned from
the fierceness of His anger. Therefore the name of that place has been
called [a]the valley of [1]Achor to this
day.

CHAPTER 8

The Conquest of Ai

NOW the LORD said to Joshua,
"[a]Do not fear or be dismayed. Take
all the people of war with you and
arise, go up to Ai; see, [b]I have given
into your hand the king of Ai, his
people, his city, and his land.
2"And you shall do to Ai and its
king just as you did to Jericho and
its king; you shall take [a]only its spoil
and its cattle as plunder for yourselves. [1]Set an ambush for the city
behind it."
3 So Joshua rose with all the people of war to go up to Ai; and Joshua
chose 30,000 men, valiant warriors,
and sent them out at night.
4 And he commanded them, saying, "See, you are going to ambush
the city from behind [1]it. Do not go
very far from the city, but all of you
be ready.
5"Then I and all the people who
are with me will approach the city.
And it will come about when they
come out to meet us as at the first,
that we will flee before them.
6"And they will come out after us
until we have drawn them away
from the city, for they will say,

12 [1]Lit., *necks*
13 [a]Josh. 3:5 [b]Josh. 6:18
16 [1]Lit., *its tribes*
20 [1]Lit., *thus and thus I did*
24 [1]Or, *cattle* [2]I.e., Trouble [a]Josh. 15:7
25 [1]Lit., *him* [2]Lit., *and they stoned* [a]Josh. 6:18
26 [1]I.e., Trouble [a]Is. 65:10; Hos. 2:15
1 [a]Josh. 1:9; 10:8 [b]Josh. 6:2
2 [1]Lit., *Set for yourself* [a]Deut. 20:14; Josh. 8:27
4 [1]Lit., *the city*

'*They* are fleeing before us as at the
first.' So we will flee before them.
7"And you shall rise from *your*
ambush and take possession of the
city, for the LORD your God will deliver it into your hand.
8"Then it will be when you have
seized the city, that you shall set the
city on fire. You shall do *it* [a]accord-
ing to the word of the LORD. See, I
have commanded you."
9 So Joshua sent them away, and
they went to the place of ambush
and remained between Bethel and
Ai, on the west side of Ai; but
Joshua spent that night among the
people.
10 Now Joshua rose early in the
morning and mustered the people,
and he went up with the elders of
Israel before the people to Ai.
11 Then all the people of war who
were with him went up and drew
near and arrived in front of the city,
and camped on the north side of Ai.
Now *there was* a valley between
him and Ai.
12 And he took about 5,000 men
and set them in ambush between
Bethel and Ai, on the west side of
the [1]city.
13 So they stationed the people, all
the army that was on the north side
of the city, and its rear guard on the
west side of the city, and Joshua
spent that night in the midst of the
valley.
14 And it came about when the
king of Ai saw *it*, that the men of the
city hurried and rose up early and
went out to meet Israel in battle, he
and all his people at the appointed
place before the [a]desert plain. But
he did not know that *there was* an
ambush against him behind the city.
15 And Joshua and all Israel pretended to be beaten before them,
and fled by the way of the wilderness.
16 And all the people who were in
the city were called together to pursue them, and they pursued Joshua,
and were drawn away from the city.
17 So not a man was left in Ai or
Bethel who had not gone out after
Israel, and they left the city [1]un-
guarded and pursued Israel.
18 Then the LORD said to Joshua,
"[a]Stretch out the javelin that is in
your hand toward Ai, for I will give
it into your hand." So Joshua
stretched out the javelin that was in
his hand toward the city.
19 And the *men in* ambush rose
quickly from their place, and when
he had stretched out his hand, they
ran and entered the city and captured it; and they quickly set the city
on fire.
20 When the men of Ai turned
[1]back and looked, behold, the
smoke of the city ascended to the
sky, and they had no place to flee
this way or that, for the people who
had been fleeing to the wilderness
turned against the pursuers.
21 When Joshua and all Israel saw
that the *men in* ambush had captured the city and that the smoke of
the city ascended, they turned back
and [1]slew the men of Ai.
22 And [1]the others came out from
the city to encounter them, so that
they were *trapped* in the midst of
Israel, [2]some on this side and some
on that side; and they [3]slew them
[a]until no one was left [4]of those who
survived or escaped.
23 But they took alive the king of
Ai and brought him to Joshua.
24 Now it came about when Israel
had finished killing all the inhabitants of Ai in the field in the wilderness where they pursued them, and
all of them were fallen by the edge
of the sword until they were destroyed, then all Israel returned to
Ai and struck it with the edge of the
sword.
25 [a]And all who fell that day, both
men and women, were 12,000—all
the [1]people of Ai.
26 For Joshua did not withdraw
his hand with which [a]he stretched
out the javelin until he had [1]utterly
destroyed all the inhabitants of Ai.
27 [a]Israel took only the cattle and
the spoil of that city as plunder for
themselves, according to the word
of the LORD which He had commanded Joshua.
28 So Joshua burned Ai and made
it a heap forever, a desolation until
this day.
29 [a]And he hanged the king of Ai
on a tree until evening; and at sunset
Joshua gave command and they
took his body down from the tree,
and threw it at the entrance of the
city gate, and raised over it a great
heap of stones *that stands* to this
day.
30 Then Joshua built an altar to
the LORD, the God of Israel, in
[a]Mount Ebal,
31 just as Moses the servant of the
LORD had commanded the sons of
Israel, as it is written in the book of
the law of Moses, [a]an altar of uncut
stones, on which no man had
wielded an iron *tool;* and they offered burnt offerings on it to the
LORD, and sacrificed peace offerings.

8 [a]Deut. 20:16-18; Josh. 8:2
12 [1]I.e., Ai
14 [a]Josh. 3:16
17 [1]Lit., *open*
18 [a]Ex. 14:16; 17:9-13; Josh. 8:26
20 [1]Lit., *behind them*
21 [1]Lit., *smote*
22 [1]Lit., *these came* [2]Lit., *these . . . those* [3]Lit., *smote* [4]Lit., *for it* [a]Josh. 8:8
25 [1]Lit., *men* [a]Deut. 20:16-18
26 [1]Or, *put under the ban* [a]Ex. 17:11, 12
27 [a]Josh. 8:2
29 [a]Deut. 21:22, 23
30 [a]Deut. 27:2-8
31 [a]Ex. 20:25

32 And he wrote there on the stones a copy of the law of Moses, which [1]he had written, in the presence of the sons of Israel.

33 [a]And all Israel with their elders and officers and their judges were standing on both sides of the ark before the Levitical priests who carried the ark of the covenant of the LORD, the stranger as well as the native. Half of them *stood* in front of Mount Gerizim and half of them in front of Mount Ebal, just as Moses the servant of the LORD had given command at first to bless the people of Israel.

34 Then afterward he read all the words of the law, the blessing and the curse, according to all that is written in [a]the book of the law.

35 There was not a word of all that Moses had commanded which Joshua did not read before all the assembly of Israel with the women and the little ones and the strangers who were [1]living among them.

CHAPTER 9

Guile of the Gibeonites

NOW it came about when [a]all the kings who were beyond the Jordan, in the hill country and in the lowland and on all the coast of the Great Sea toward Lebanon, the Hittite and the Amorite, the Canaanite, the Perizzite, the Hivite and the Jebusite, heard of it,

2 that they gathered themselves together with [1]one accord to fight with Joshua and with Israel.

3 When the inhabitants of [a]Gibeon heard what Joshua had done to Jericho and to Ai,

4 they also acted craftily and [1]set out as envoys, and took worn-out sacks on their donkeys, and wineskins, worn-out and torn and [2]mended,

5 and worn-out and patched sandals on their feet, and worn-out clothes on themselves; and all the bread of their provision was dry *and* had become crumbled.

6 And they went to Joshua to the camp at Gilgal, and said to him and to the men of Israel, "We have come from a far country; now therefore, make a covenant with us."

7 And the men of Israel said to the [a]Hivites, "Perhaps you are living [1]within our land; [b]how then shall we make a covenant with you?"

8 But they said to Joshua, "We are your servants." Then Joshua said to them, "Who are you, and where do you come from?"

9 And they said to him, "Your servants have come from [a]a very far country because of the [1]fame of the LORD your God; for [b]we have heard the report of Him and all that He did in Egypt,

10 and all that He did to the two kings of the Amorites who were beyond the Jordan, to Sihon king of Heshbon and to Og king of Bashan who was at Ashtaroth.

11 "So our elders and all the inhabitants of our country spoke to us, saying, 'Take provisions in your hand for the journey, and go to meet them and say to them, "We are your servants; now then, make a covenant with us." '

12 "This our bread *was* warm *when* we took it for our provisions out of our houses on the day that we left to come to you; but now behold, it is dry and has become crumbled.

13 "And these wineskins which we filled were new, and behold, they are torn; and these our clothes and our sandals are worn out because of the very long journey."

14 So the men of Israel took some of their provisions, and [a]did not ask for the [1]counsel of the LORD.

15 [a]And Joshua made peace with them and made a covenant with them, to let them live; and the leaders of the congregation swore *an oath* to them.

16 And it came about at the end of three days after they had made a covenant with them, that they heard that they were neighbors and that they were living [1]within their land.

17 Then the sons of Israel set out and came to their cities on the third day. Now their cities *were* Gibeon and Chephirah and Beeroth and Kiriath-jearim.

18 And the sons of Israel did not strike them because the leaders of the congregation had sworn to them by the LORD the God of Israel. And the whole congregation grumbled against the leaders.

19 But all the leaders said to the whole congregation, "We have sworn to them by the LORD, the God of Israel, and now we cannot touch them.

20 "This we will do to them, even let them live, lest wrath be upon us for the oath which we swore to them."

21 And the leaders said to them, "Let them live." So they became hewers of wood and drawers of wa-

32 [1]I.e., Moses
33 [a]Deut. 27:11-14
34 [a]Josh. 1:8
35 [1]Lit., *walking*
1 [a]Num. 13:29; Josh. 3:10
2 [1]Lit., *one mouth*
3 [a]Josh. 9:17, 22; 10:2; 21:17
4 [1]Lit., *went and traveled as envoys* [2]Lit., *tied up*
7 [1]Lit., *among us* [a]Josh. 9:2; 11:19 [b]Ex. 23:32
9 [1]Or, *name* [a]Josh. 9:16, 17 [b]Josh. 2:9; 9:24
14 [1]Lit., *mouth* [a]Num. 27:21
15 [a]Ex. 23:32
16 [1]Lit., *among them*

ter for the whole congregation, just
as the leaders had spoken to them.
22 Then Joshua called for them
and spoke to them, saying, "Why
have you deceived us, saying, 'We
are very far from you,' [a]when you
are living [1]within our land?
23"Now therefore, you are cursed,
and [1]you shall never cease being
slaves, both hewers of wood and
drawers of water for the house of
my God."
24 So they answered Joshua and
said, "[a]Because it was certainly told
your servants that the LORD your
God had commanded His servant
Moses to give you all the land, and
to destroy all the inhabitants of the
land before you; therefore we feared
greatly for our lives because of you,
and have done this thing.
25"And now behold, we are in your
hands; do as it seems good and right
in your sight to do to us."
26 Thus he did to them, and delivered them from the hands of the
sons of Israel, and they did not kill
them.
27 But Joshua made them that day
hewers of wood and drawers of water for the congregation and for the
altar of the LORD, to this day, [a]in the
place which He would choose.

CHAPTER 10

Five Kings Attack Gibeon

NOW it came about when Adoni-
zedek king of Jerusalem heard that
Joshua had captured Ai, and had
[1]utterly destroyed it (just as he had
done to Jericho and its king, so he
had done to Ai and its king), and
that the inhabitants of Gibeon had
made peace with Israel and were
[2]within their land,
2 that [1]he feared greatly, because
Gibeon *was* a great city, like one of
the royal cities, and because it was
greater than Ai, and all its men *were*
mighty.
3 Therefore Adoni-zedek of Jerusalem sent *word* [a]to Hoham king of
Hebron and to Piram king of Jarmuth and to Japhia king of Lachish
and to Debir king of Eglon, saying,
4"Come up to me and help me,
and let us [1]attack Gibeon, for it has
made peace with Joshua and with
the sons of Israel."
5 So the five kings of [a]the Amorites, the king of Jerusalem, the king
of Hebron, the king of Jarmuth, the
king of Lachish, *and* the king of Eglon, gathered together and went up,
they with all their armies, and
camped by Gibeon and fought
against it.
6 Then the men of Gibeon sent
word to Joshua to the camp at Gilgal, saying, "Do not [1]abandon your
servants; come up to us quickly and
save us and help us, for all the kings
of the Amorites that live in the hill
country have assembled against
us."
7 So Joshua went up from Gilgal,
he and all the people of war with
him and all the valiant warriors.
8 And the LORD said to Joshua,
"[a]Do not fear them, for I have given
them into your hands; not [1]one of
them shall stand before you."
9 So Joshua came upon them
suddenly [1]by marching all night
from Gilgal.
10 [a]And the LORD confounded
them before Israel, and He [1]slew
them with a great slaughter at Gibeon, and pursued them by the way
of the ascent of Beth-horon, and
struck them as far as Azekah and
Makkedah.
11 And it came about as they fled
from before Israel, *while* they were
at the descent of Beth-horon, that
the LORD threw large stones from
heaven on them as far as Azekah,
and they died; *there were* more who
died [1]from the hailstones than those
whom the sons of Israel killed with
the sword.
12 Then Joshua spoke to the LORD
in the day when the LORD delivered
up the Amorites before the sons of
Israel, and he said in the sight of
Israel,

"O sun, stand still at Gibeon,
And O moon in the valley of
Aijalon."
13 [a]So the sun stood still, and the
moon stopped,
Until the nation avenged
themselves of their enemies.

Is it not written in the book of [b]Ja-
shar? And [c]the sun stopped in the
middle of the sky, and did not hasten to go *down* for about a whole
day.
14 And there was no day like that
before it or after it, when the LORD
listened to the voice of a man; for
[a]the LORD fought for Israel.
15 Then Joshua and all Israel with
him returned to the camp to Gilgal.

Victory at Makkedah

16 Now these [a]five kings had fled
and hidden themselves in the cave
at Makkedah.
17 And it was told Joshua, saying,

22 [1]Lit., *among us* [a]Josh. 9:17
23 [1]Lit., *a servant shall not be cut off from you*
24 [a]Josh. 9:9
27 [a]Deut. 12:5
1 [1]Or, *put under the ban* [2]Lit., *among them*
2 [1]Lit., *they*
3 [a]Josh. 10:23
4 [1]Lit., *smite*
5 [a]Num. 13:29
6 [1]Lit., *slacken your hands from*
8 [1]Lit., *a man* [a]Josh. 1:5, 9
9 [1]Lit., *he went up*
10 [1]Lit., *struck* [a]Deut. 7:23
11 [1]Lit., *with*
13 [a]Hab. 3:11 [b]2 Sam. 1:18 [c]Is. 38:8
14 [a]Ex. 14:14; Deut. 1:30; Josh. 10:42
16 [a]Josh. 10:5

"The five kings have been found
hidden in the cave at Makkedah."
18 And Joshua said, "Roll large
stones against the mouth of the
cave, and assign men by it to guard
them,
19 but do not stay *there* yourselves; pursue your enemies and [1]at-
tack them in the rear. Do not allow
them to enter their cities, for the
LORD your God has delivered them
into your hand."
20 And it came about when Joshua
and the sons of Israel had finished
[1]slaying them with a very great
slaughter, [a]until they were destroyed, and the survivors *who* remained of them [2]had entered the
fortified cities,
21 that all the people returned to
the camp to Joshua at Makkedah in
peace. No one [1]uttered a word
against any of the sons of Israel.
22 Then Joshua said, "Open the
mouth of the cave and bring these
five kings out to me from the cave."
23 And they did so, and [a]brought
these five kings out to him from the
cave: the king of Jerusalem, the king
of Hebron, the king of Jarmuth, the
king of Lachish, *and* the king of Eglon.
24 And it came about when they
brought these kings out to Joshua,
that Joshua called for all the men of
Israel, and said to the chiefs of the
men of war who had gone with him,
"Come near, put your feet on the
necks of these kings." So they came
near and put their feet on their
necks.
25 Joshua then said to them, "[a]Do
not fear or be dismayed! Be strong
and courageous, for thus the LORD
will do to all your enemies with
whom you fight."
26 So afterward Joshua struck
them and put them to death, and he
[a]hanged them on five trees; and they
hung on the trees until evening.
27 And it came about at [1]sunset
that Joshua commanded, and [a]they
took them down from the trees and
threw them into the cave where
they had hidden themselves, and
put large stones over the mouth of
the cave, to this very day.
28 Now Joshua captured Makkedah on that day, and struck it and its
king with the edge of the sword; [a]he
[1]utterly destroyed [2]it and every
[3]person who was in it. He left no
survivor. Thus he did to the king of
Makkedah [b]just as he had done to
the king of Jericho.

Joshua's Conquest of Southern Palestine

29 Then Joshua and all Israel with
him passed on from Makkedah to
Libnah, and fought against Libnah.
30 And the LORD gave it also with
its king into the hands of Israel, and
he struck it and every person who
was in it with the edge of the sword.
He left no survivor in it. Thus he did
to its king just as he had done to the
king of Jericho.
31 And Joshua and all Israel with
him passed on from Libnah to Lachish, and they camped by it and
fought against it.
32 And the LORD gave Lachish into
the hands of Israel; and he captured
it on the second day, and struck it
and every person who *was* in it with
the edge of the sword, according to
all that he had done to Libnah.
33 Then Horam king of Gezer
came up to help Lachish, and
Joshua [1]defeated him and his people
until he had left him no survivor.
34 And Joshua and all Israel with
him passed on from Lachish to Eglon, and they camped by it and
fought against it.
35 And they captured it on that
day and struck it with the edge of
the sword; and he [1]utterly destroyed
that day every person who *was* in it,
according to all that he had done to
Lachish.
36 Then Joshua and all Israel with
him went up from Eglon to Hebron,
and they fought against it.
37 And they captured it and struck
it and its king and all its cities and
all the persons who *were* in it with
the edge of the sword. He left no
survivor, according to all that he
had done to Eglon. And he [1]utterly
destroyed it and every person who
was in it.
38 Then Joshua and all Israel with
him returned to Debir, and they
fought against it.
39 And he captured it and its king
and all its cities, and they struck
them with the edge of the sword,
and [1]utterly destroyed every person
who was in it. He left no survivor.
Just as he had done to Hebron, so he
did to Debir and its king, as he had
also done to Libnah and its king.
40 Thus Joshua struck all the land,
[a]the hill country and the [1]Negev and
the lowland and the slopes and [b]all
their kings. He left no survivor, but
[c]he [2]utterly destroyed all who
breathed, just as the LORD, the God
of Israel, had commanded.
41 And Joshua struck them from

19 [1]Lit., *smite their tail*
20 [1]Lit., *striking* [2]Lit., *and had* [a]Deut. 20:16
21 [1]Lit., *sharpened his tongue*
23 [a]Deut. 7:24
25 [a]Josh. 10:8
26 [a]Josh. 8:29
27 [1]Lit., *the time of the going of the sun* [a]Deut. 21:22, 23
28 [1]Or, *put under the ban* [2]Some mss. read *them* [3]Lit., *soul,* and so throughout the chap. [a]Deut. 20:16 [b]Josh. 6:21
33 [1]Lit., *smote*
35 [1]Or, *put under the ban*
37 [1]Or, *put it under the ban*
39 [1]Or, *put it under the ban*
40 [1]I.e., South country [2]Or, *put it under the ban* [a]Deut. 1:7 [b]Deut. 7:24 [c]Deut. 20:16

Kadesh-barnea even as far as Gaza, and all the country of [a]Goshen even as far as Gibeon.

42 And Joshua captured all these kings and their lands at one time, because the LORD, the God of Israel, [a]fought for Israel.

43 So Joshua and all Israel with him returned to the camp at Gilgal.

CHAPTER 11

Northern Palestine Taken

THEN it came about, when Jabin king of [a]Hazor heard *of it,* that he sent to Jobab king of Madon and to the king of Shimron and to the king of Achshaph,

2 and to the kings who were of the north in the hill country, and in the [a]Arabah—south of [1]Chinneroth and in the lowland and on the [2]heights of Dor on the west—

3 to the Canaanite on the east and on the west, and the Amorite and the Hittite and the Perizzite and the Jebusite in the hill country, and the Hivite [1]at the foot of Hermon in the land of Mizpeh.

4 And they came out, they and all their armies with them, *as* many people *as* [a]the sand that is on the seashore, with very many horses and chariots.

5 So all of these kings having agreed to meet, came and encamped together at the waters of Merom, to fight against Israel.

6 Then the LORD said to Joshua, "[a]Do not be afraid because of them, for tomorrow at this time I will deliver all of them slain before Israel; you shall [b]hamstring their horses and burn their chariots with fire."

7 So Joshua and all the people of war with him came upon them suddenly by the waters of Merom, and attacked them.

8 And the LORD delivered them into the hand of Israel, so that they [1]defeated them, and pursued them as far as great Sidon and [a]Misrephoth-maim and the valley of [b]Mizpeh to the east; and they struck them until no survivor was left to them.

9 And Joshua did to them as the LORD had told him; he [a]hamstrung their horses, and burned their chariots with fire.

10 Then Joshua turned back at that time, and captured [a]Hazor and struck its king with the sword; for Hazor formerly was the head of all these kingdoms.

11 [a]And they struck every person who was in it with the edge of the sword, [1]utterly destroying *them;* there was no one left who breathed. And he burned Hazor with fire.

12 And Joshua captured all the cities of these kings, and all their kings, and he struck them with the edge of the sword, *and* utterly destroyed them; just as Moses the servant of the LORD had commanded.

13 However, Israel did not burn any cities that stood on their mounds, except Hazor alone, *which* Joshua burned.

14 [a]And all the spoil of these cities and the cattle, the sons of Israel took as their plunder; but they struck every man with the edge of the sword, until they had destroyed them. They left no one who breathed.

15 Just as the LORD had commanded Moses his servant, so Moses commanded Joshua, and so Joshua did; he left nothing undone of all that the LORD had commanded Moses.

16 Thus Joshua took all that land: [a]the hill country and all the [1]Negev, all that land of Goshen, the lowland, [b]the Arabah, the hill country of Israel and its lowland

17 from [a]Mount Halak, that rises toward Seir, even as far as Baal-gad in the valley of Lebanon [1]at the foot of Mount Hermon. And he captured [b]all their kings and struck them down and put them to death.

18 Joshua waged war a long time with all these kings.

19 There was not a city which made peace with the sons of Israel except [a]the Hivites living in Gibeon; they took them all in battle.

20 [a]For it was of the LORD to [1]harden their hearts, to meet Israel in battle in order that he might utterly destroy them, that they might [2]receive no mercy, but that he might destroy them, just as the LORD had commanded Moses.

21 Then Joshua came at that time and cut off [a]the Anakim from the hill country, from Hebron, from Debir, from Anab and from all the hill country of Judah and from all the hill country of Israel. Joshua utterly destroyed them with their cities.

22 There were no Anakim left in the land of the sons of Israel; only in Gaza, in Gath, and in Ashdod some remained.

23 So Joshua took the whole land, according to all that the LORD had spoken to Moses, and [a]Joshua gave

41 [a]Josh. 11:16; 15:51
42 [a]Josh. 10:14
1 [a]Josh 11:10
2 [1]I.e., Sea of Galilee [2]Or, *Naphoth-dor* [a]Josh. 12:3-13:27
3 [1]Lit., *under*
4 [a]Judg. 7:12
6 [a]Josh. 10:8 [b]2 Sam. 8:4
8 [1]Lit., *smote* [a]Josh. 13:6 [b]Josh. 11:3
9 [a]Josh. 11:6
10 [a]Josh. 11:1
11 [1]Or, *putting them under the ban.* So throughout the chapter [a]Deut. 20:16
14 [a]Num. 31:11, 12
16 [1]I.e., South country [a]Josh. 10:40, 41 [b]Josh. 11:2
17 [1]Lit., *under* [a]Josh. 12:7 [b]Deut. 7:24
19 [a]Josh. 9:3, 7
20 [1]Lit., *make strong* [2]Lit., *have* [a]Ex. 14:17
21 [a]Num. 13:33; Deut. 9:2
23 [a]Deut. 1:38

it for an inheritance to Israel according to their divisions by their tribes. [b]Thus the land had rest from war.

Chapter 12

Kings Defeated by Israel

[a]Now these are the kings of the land whom the sons of Israel [1]defeated, and whose land they possessed beyond the Jordan toward the sunrise, from the valley of the Arnon as far as Mount Hermon, and all the Arabah to the east:

2 Sihon king of the Amorites, who lived in Heshbon, *and* ruled from Aroer, which is on the edge of the valley of the Arnon, both [a]the middle of the valley and half of Gilead, even as far as the brook Jabbok, the border of the sons of Ammon;

3 and the [a]Arabah as far as the Sea of [1]Chinneroth toward the east, and as far as the sea of the Arabah, *even* the Salt Sea, eastward [2]toward [b]Beth-jeshimoth, and on the south, [3]at the foot of the slopes of Pisgah;

4 and the territory of Og king of Bashan, one of [a]the remnant of Rephaim, who lived at Ashtaroth and at Edrei,

5 and ruled over Mount Hermon and Salecah and all Bashan, as far as the border of the Geshurites and the Maacathites, and half of Gilead, *as far as* the border of Sihon king of Heshbon.

6 Moses the servant of the LORD and the sons of Israel [1]defeated them; and Moses the servant of the LORD gave it to the Reubenites and the Gadites, and the half-tribe of Manasseh as a possession.

7 Now these are the kings of the land whom Joshua and the sons of Israel [1]defeated beyond the Jordan toward the west, from Baal-gad in the valley of Lebanon even as far as [a]Mount Halak, which rises toward Seir; and Joshua gave it to the tribes of Israel as a possession according to their divisions,

8 [a]in the hill country, in the lowland, in the Arabah, on the slopes, and in the wilderness, and in the [1]Negev; the Hittite, the Amorite and the Canaanite, the Perizzite, the Hivite and the Jebusite:

9 the king of Jericho, one; the king of Ai, which is beside Bethel, one;

10 the king of Jerusalem, one; the king of Hebron, one;

11 the king of Jarmuth, one; the king of Lachish, one;

12 the king of Eglon, one; the king of Gezer, one;

13 the king of Debir, one; the king of Geder, one;

14 the king of Hormah, one; the king of [a]Arad, one;

15 the king of Libnah, one; the king of Adullam, one;

16 the king of Makkedah, one; the king of Bethel, one;

17 the king of Tappuah, one; the king of Hepher, one;

18 the king of Aphek, one; the king of Lasharon, one;

19 the king of Madon, one; the king of Hazor, one;

20 the king of Shimron-meron, one; the king of Achshaph, one;

21 the king of Taanach, one; the king of Megiddo, one;

22 the king of Kedesh, one; the king of Jokneam in Carmel, one;

23 the king of Dor in the [1]heights of Dor, one; the king of Goiim in Gilgal, one;

24 the king of Tirzah, one: [a]in all, thirty-one kings.

Chapter 13

Canaan Divided Among the Tribes

[a]Now Joshua was old *and* advanced in years when the LORD said to him, "You are old *and* advanced in years, and very much of the land remains to be possessed.

2 "This is the land that remains: all the regions *of* the Philistines and all *those of* the Geshurites;

3 from the Shihor which is [1]east of Egypt, even as far as the border of Ekron to the north (it is counted as Canaanite); the five lords of the Philistines: the Gazite, the Ashdodite, the Ashkelonite, the Gittite, the Ekronite; and the Avvite

4 [1]to the south, all the land of the Canaanite, and Mearah that belongs to the Sidonians, as far as Aphek, to the border of the Amorite;

5 and the land of the Gebalite, and all of Lebanon, toward the [1]east, from Baal-gad below Mount Hermon as far as [2]Lebo-hamath.

6 "All the inhabitants of the hill country from Lebanon as far as [a]Misrephoth-maim, all the Sidonians, I will [1]drive them out from before the sons of Israel; only allot it to Israel for an inheritance as I have commanded you.

7 "Now therefore apportion this land for an inheritance to the nine tribes, and the half-tribe of Manasseh."

23 [b]Deut. 12:9, 10; 25:19; Heb. 4:8

1 [1]Lit., *smote* [a]Num. 32:33; Deut. 3:8-17

2 [a]Deut. 2:36

3 [1]I.e., Galilee [2]Lit., *the way of* [3]Lit., *under* [a]Josh. 11:2 [b]Josh. 13:20

4 [a]Deut. 3:11

6 [1]Lit., *smote*

7 [1]Lit., *smote* [a]Josh. 11:17

8 [1]I.e., South country [a]Josh. 11:16

14 [a]Num. 21:1

23 [1]Or, *Naphath-dor*

24 [a]Deut. 7:24

1 [a]Josh. 14:10

3 [1]Lit., *on the face of*

4 [1]Or, *from the Teman*

5 [1]Lit., *sunrise* [2]Or, *the entrance of Hamath*

6 [1]Or, *dispossess* [a]Josh. 11:8

8 With [1]the other half-tribe, the
Reubenites and the Gadites received their inheritance which
Moses gave them [a]beyond the Jordan to the east, just as Moses the
servant of the LORD gave to them;
9 from Aroer, which is on the
edge of the valley of the Arnon, with
the city which is in the middle of the
valley, and all the plain of Medeba,
as far as Dibon;
10 and all the cities of Sihon king
of the Amorites, who reigned in
Heshbon, as far as the border of the
sons of Ammon;
11 and Gilead, and the [1]territory of
the Geshurites and Maacathites,
and all Mount Hermon, and all Bashan as far as Salecah;
12 all the kingdom of Og in Bashan, who reigned in Ashtaroth and
in Edrei (he alone was left of the
remnant of the Rephaim); for Moses
struck them and dispossessed them.
13 But the sons of Israel did not
dispossess the Geshurites or the
Maacathites; for Geshur and Maa-
cath live among Israel until this day.
14 [a]Only to the tribe of Levi he did
not give an inheritance; the offerings by fire to the LORD, the God of
Israel, are [1]their inheritance, as He
spoke to him.
15 So Moses gave *an inheritance*
to the tribe of the sons of Reuben
according to their families.
16 And their [1]territory was from
[a]Aroer, which is on the edge of the
valley of the Arnon, with the city
which is in the middle of the valley
and all the plain by Medeba;
17 Heshbon, and all its cities
which are on the plain: Dibon and
Bamoth-baal and Beth-baal-meon,
18 and Jahaz and Kedemoth and
Mephaath,
19 and Kiriathaim and Sibmah
and Zereth-shahar on the hill of the
valley,
20 and Beth-peor and the slopes of
Pisgah and Beth-jeshimoth,
21 even all the cities of the plain
and all the kingdom of Sihon king of
the Amorites who reigned in Heshbon, whom Moses struck with the
chiefs of Midian, [a]Evi and Rekem
and Zur and Hur and Reba, the
princes of Sihon, who lived in the
land.
22 The sons of Israel also killed
[a]Balaam the son of Beor, the diviner, with the sword among *the rest of*
their slain.
23 And the border of the sons of
Reuben was the [1]Jordan. This was
the inheritance of the sons of Reuben according to their families, the
cities and their villages.
24 Moses also gave *an inheritance*
to the tribe of Gad, to the sons of
Gad, according to their families.
25 And their territory was Jazer,
and all the cities of Gilead, and half
the land of the sons of Ammon, as
far as Aroer which is before Rabbah;
26 and from Heshbon as far as Ra-
math-mizpeh and Betonim, and
from Mahanaim as far as the border
of [1]Debir;
27 and in the valley, Beth-haram
and Beth-nimrah and Succoth and
Zaphon, the rest of the kingdom of
Sihon king of Heshbon, with the
Jordan [1]as a border, as far as the
lower end of the Sea of [2a]Chinnereth
beyond the Jordan to the east.
28 This is the inheritance of the
sons of Gad according to their families, the cities and their villages.
29 Moses also gave *an inheritance*
to the half-tribe of Manasseh; and it
was for the half-tribe of the sons of
Manasseh according to their families.
30 And their territory was from
Mahanaim, all Bashan, all the kingdom of Og king of Bashan, and all
[a]the [1]towns of Jair, which are in Bashan, sixty cities;
31 also half of Gilead, with Ashtaroth and Edrei, the cities of the kingdom of Og in Bashan, *were* for the
sons of Machir the son of Manasseh,
for half of the sons of Machir according to their families.
32 These are *the territories* which
Moses apportioned for an inheritance in the plains of Moab, beyond
the Jordan at Jericho to the east.
33 [a]But to the tribe of Levi, Moses
did not give an inheritance; the
LORD, the God of Israel, is their inheritance, as He had [1]promised to
them.

CHAPTER 14

Caleb's Request

NOW these are *the territories*
which the sons of Israel inherited in
the land of Canaan, which [a]Eleazar
the priest, and Joshua the son of
Nun, and the heads of the [1]house-
holds of the tribes of the sons of Israel apportioned to them for an inheritance,
2 by the lot of their inheritance,
as the LORD commanded [1]through
Moses, for the nine tribes and the
half-tribe.

8 [1]Lit., *it, the* [a]Josh. 12:1-6
11 [1]Or, *border*
14 [1]Lit., *his* [a]Deut. 18:1, 2
16 [1]Or, *border* [a]Josh. 13:9
21 [a]Num. 31:8
22 [a]Num. 31:8
23 [1]Lit., *Jordan and border*
26 [1]Or, *Lidebir*
27 [1]Lit., *and border* [2]I.e., Galilee [a]Num. 34:11; Deut. 3:17
30 [1]Lit., *tent villages* [a]Num. 32:41
33 [1]Lit., *spoken to* [a]Josh. 13:14
1 [1]Lit., *fathers'* [a]Num. 34:16-29
2 [1]Lit., *by the hand of*

3 [a]For Moses had given the inheritance of the two tribes and the half-tribe beyond the Jordan; [b]but he did not give an inheritance to the Levites among them.

4 For the sons of Joseph were two tribes, Manasseh and Ephraim, and they did not give a portion to the Levites in the land, except cities to live in, with their pasture lands for their livestock and for their property.

5 Thus the sons of Israel did just as the LORD had commanded Moses, and they divided the land.

6 Then the sons of Judah drew near to Joshua in Gilgal, and [a]Caleb the son of Jephunneh the Kenizzite said to him, "You know the word which the LORD spoke to Moses the man of God concerning [1]you and me in Kadesh-barnea.

7"I was forty years old when Moses the servant of the LORD sent me from Kadesh-barnea to spy out the land, and I brought word back to him as *it was* in my heart.

8"Nevertheless my brethren who went up with me made the heart of the people [1]melt with fear; but I followed the LORD my God fully.

9"[a]So Moses swore on that day, saying, 'Surely the land on which your foot has trodden shall be an inheritance to you and to your children forever, because you have followed the LORD my God fully.'

10"And now behold, the LORD has let me live, just as He spoke, these forty-five years, from the time that the LORD spoke this word to Moses, when Israel walked in the wilderness; and now behold, I am eighty-five years old today.

11"I am still as strong today as I was in the day Moses sent me; as my strength was then, so my strength is now, for war and for going out and coming in.

12"Now then, give me this hill country about which the LORD spoke on that day, for you heard on that day that [a]Anakim *were* there, with great fortified cities; perhaps the LORD will be with me, and I shall [1]drive them out as the LORD has spoken."

13 So Joshua blessed him, and gave Hebron to Caleb the son of Jephunneh for an inheritance.

14 Therefore, Hebron became the inheritance of Caleb the son of Jephunneh the Kenizzite until this day, because he followed the LORD God of Israel fully.

15 Now the name of Hebron was formerly [1]Kiriath-arba; *for Arba* was the greatest man among the Anakim. [a]Then the land had rest from war.

CHAPTER 15

Territory of Judah

[a]NOW the lot for the tribe of the sons of Judah according to their families [1]reached the [b]border of Edom, southward to the wilderness of [c]Zin at the extreme south.

2 And their south border was from the lower end of the Salt Sea, from the bay that turns to the south.

3 Then it proceeded southward to the ascent of Akrabbim and continued to Zin, then went up by the south of Kadesh-barnea and continued to Hezron, and went up to Addar and turned about to Karka.

4 And it continued to Azmon and proceeded to the [1]brook of Egypt; and the [2]border ended at the sea. This shall be your south border.

5 [a]And the east border *was* the Salt Sea, as far as the [1]mouth of the Jordan. [b]And the border of the north side was from the bay of the sea at the [1]mouth of the Jordan.

6 Then the border went up to Beth-hoglah, and continued on the north of Beth-arabah, and the border went up to the stone of Bohan the son of Reuben.

7 And the border went up to Debir from [a]the valley of Achor, and turned northward toward Gilgal which is opposite the ascent of Adummim, which is on the south of the valley; and the border continued to the waters of En-shemesh, and [1]it ended at En-rogel.

8 Then the border went up the valley of Ben-hinnom to the slope of the [a]Jebusite on the south (that is, Jerusalem); and the border went up to the top of the mountain which is before the valley of Hinnom to the west, which is at the end of the valley Rephaim toward the north.

9 And from the top of the mountain the border curved to the spring of the waters of Nephtoah and proceeded to the cities of Mount Ephron, then the border curved to Baalah (that is, Kiriath-jearim).

10 And the border turned about from Baalah westward to Mount Seir, and continued to the slope of Mount Jearim on the north (that is, Chesalon), and went down to Beth-shemesh and continued through Timnah.

11 And the border proceeded to the side of Ekron northward. Then

3 [a]Num. 32:33 [b]Josh. 13:14
6 [1]Lit., *me and concerning you* [a]Num. 13:6, 30; 14:6, 24, 30
8 [1]Lit., *become demoralized*
9 [a]Deut. 1:36
12 [1]Or, *dispossess* [a]Num. 13:33
15 [1]I.e., the city of Arba [a]Josh. 11:23
1 [1]Lit., *was to* [a]Num. 34:3, 4 [b]Num. 20:16 [c]Deut. 32:51
4 [1]Or, *wadi* [2]Lit., *goings out of the border were*
5 [1]Lit., *end* [a]Num. 34:3 [b]Josh. 18:15-19
7 [1]Lit., *the goings out of it were* [a]Deut. 7:24
8 [a]Josh. 15:63

the border curved to Shikkeron and
continued to Mount Baalah and proceeded to Jabneel, and the [1]border
ended at the sea.
12 And the west border *was* at the
Great Sea, even *its* [1]coastline. This
is the border around the sons of Judah according to their families.
13 [a]Now he gave to Caleb the son
of Jephunneh a portion [b]among the
sons of Judah, according to the
[1]command of the LORD to Joshua,
namely, [2]Kiriath-arba, *Arba being*
the father of Anak (that is, Hebron).
14 And [a]Caleb [1]drove out from
there the three sons of Anak: Sheshai and Ahiman and Talmai, the
children of Anak.
15 Then he went up from there
against the inhabitants of Debir;
now the name of Debir formerly
was Kiriath-sepher.
16 And Caleb said, "The one who
[1]attacks Kiriath-sepher and captures it, [2]I will give him Achsah my
daughter as a wife."
17 [a]And Othniel the son of Kenaz,
the brother of Caleb, captured it; so
he gave him Achsah his daughter as
a wife.
18 And it came about that when
she came *to him,* she persuaded him
to ask her father for a field. So she
alighted from the donkey, and Caleb
said to her, "What do you want?"
19 Then she said, "Give me a
blessing; since you have given me
the land of the [1]Negev, give me also
springs of water." So he gave her
the upper springs and the lower
springs.
20 This is the inheritance of the
tribe of the sons of Judah according
to their families.
21 Now the cities at the extremity
of the tribe of the sons of Judah
toward the border of Edom in the
south were Kabzeel and [a]Eder and
Jagur,
22 and Kinah and Dimonah and
Adadah,
23 and Kedesh and Hazor and Ith-
nan,
24 Ziph and Telem and Bealoth,
25 and Hazor-hadattah and Keri-
oth-hezron (that is, Hazor),
26 Amam and Shema and Moladah,
27 and Hazar-gaddah and Hesh-
mon and Beth-pelet,
28 and Hazar-shual and [a]Beershe-
ba and Biziothiah,
29 Baalah and Iim and Ezem,
30 and Eltolad and Chesil and Hormah,
31 and [a]Ziklag and Madmannah
and Sansannah,
32 and Lebaoth and Shilhim and
Ain and Rimmon; in all, twenty-nine
cities with their villages.
33 In the lowland: [a]Eshtaol and
Zorah and Ashnah,
34 and Zanoah and En-gannim,
Tappuah and Enam,
35 Jarmuth and [a]Adullam, Socoh
and Azekah,
36 and Shaaraim and Adithaim
and Gederah and Gederothaim;
fourteen cities with their villages.
37 Zenan and Hadashah and Mig-
dal-gad,
38 and Dilean and Mizpeh and
Joktheel,
39 [a]Lachish and Bozkath and Eglon,
40 and Cabbon and Lahmas and
Chitlish,
41 and Gederoth, Beth-dagon and
Naamah and Makkedah; sixteen
cities with their villages.
42 Libnah and Ether and Ashan,
43 and Iphtah and Ashnah and Ne-
zib,
44 and Keilah and Achzib and
Mareshah; nine cities with their villages.
45 Ekron, with its towns and its
villages;
46 from Ekron even to the sea, all
that were by the [1]side of Ashdod,
with their villages.
47 Ashdod, its towns and its villages; Gaza, its towns and its villages; as far as [a]the [1]brook of Egypt
and the Great Sea, even *its* [2]coast-
line.
48 And in the hill country: Shamir
and Jattir and Socoh,
49 and Dannah and Kiriath-san-
nah (that is, Debir),
50 and Anab and Eshtemoh and
Anim,
51 and Goshen and Holon and Gi-
loh; eleven cities with their villages.
52 Arab and Dumah and Eshan,
53 and Janum and Beth-tappuah
and Aphekah,
54 and Humtah and Kiriath-arba
(that is, Hebron), and Zior; nine
cities with their villages.
55 Maon, Carmel and Ziph and
Juttah,
56 and Jezreel and Jokdeam and
Zanoah,
57 Kain, Gibeah and Timnah; ten
cities with their villages.
58 Halhul, Beth-zur and Gedor,
59 and Maarath and Beth-anoth
and Eltekon; six cities with their villages.
60 Kiriath-baal (that is, Kiriath-
jearim), and Rabbah; two cities with
their villages.

11 [1]Lit., *goings out . . . were*
12 [1]Lit., *border*
13 [1]Lit., *mouth* [2]I.e., the city of Arba [a]Josh. 14:13-15 [b]Num. 13:6
14 [1]Or, *dispossessed* [a]Num. 13:33; Deut.9:2; Josh. 11:21, 22
16 [1]Lit., *smites* [2]Lit., *and I*
17 [a]Judg. 1:13; 3:9
19 [1]I.e., South country
21 [a]Gen. 35:21
28 [a]Gen. 21:31
31 [a]1 Sam. 27:6; 30:1
33 [a]Judg. 13:25; 16:31
35 [a]1 Sam. 22:1
39 [a]Josh. 10:3; 2 Kin. 14:19
46 [1]Lit., *hand*
47 [1]Or, *wadi* [2]Lit., *border* [a]Josh. 13:3

61 In the wilderness: Beth-arabah, Middin and Secacah,

62 and Nibshan and the City of Salt and Engedi; six cities with their villages.

63 Now as for the [a]Jebusites, the inhabitants of Jerusalem, the sons of Judah could not [1]drive them out; so the Jebusites live with the sons of Judah at Jerusalem until this day.

CHAPTER 16

Territory of Ephraim

THEN the lot for the sons of Joseph went from the Jordan at Jericho to the waters of Jericho on the east into [a]the wilderness, going up from Jericho through the hill country to Bethel.

2 And it went from Bethel to Luz, and continued to the border of the Archites at Ataroth.

3 And it went down westward to the territory of the Japhletites, as far as the territory of lower [a]Beth-horon even to [b]Gezer, and [1]it ended at the sea.

4 And the sons of Joseph, Manasseh and Ephraim, received their inheritance.

5 Now *this* was the territory of the sons of Ephraim according to their families: the border of their inheritance eastward was [a]Ataroth-addar, as far as upper Beth-horon.

6 Then the border went westward at [a]Michmethath on the north, and the border turned about eastward to Taanath-shiloh, and continued *beyond* it to the east of Janoah.

7 And it went down from Janoah to Ataroth and to [a]Naarah, then reached Jericho and came out at the Jordan.

8 From [a]Tappuah the border continued westward to the [1]brook of Kanah, and [2]it ended at the sea. This is the inheritance of the tribe of the sons of Ephraim according to their families,

9 *together* with the cities which were set apart for the sons of Ephraim in the midst of the inheritance of the sons of Manasseh, all the cities with their villages.

10 [a]But they did not [1]drive out the Canaanites who lived in Gezer, so [b]the Canaanites live in the midst of Ephraim to this day, and they became forced laborers.

CHAPTER 17

Territory of Manasseh

NOW *this* was the lot for the tribe of Manasseh, for he was the firstborn of Joseph. To Machir the firstborn of Manasseh, the father of Gilead, [1]was allotted Gilead and Bashan, because he was a man of war.

2 So *the lot* was *made* for the rest of the sons of Manasseh according to their families: for the sons of Abiezer and for the sons of Helek and for the sons of Asriel and for the sons of Shechem and for the sons of Hepher and for the sons of Shemida; these *were* the male *descendants* of Manasseh the son of Joseph according to their families.

3 [a]However, Zelophehad, the son of Hepher, the son of Gilead, the son of Machir, the son of Manasseh, had no sons, only daughters; and these are the names of his daughters: Mahlah and Noah, Hoglah, Milcah and Tirzah.

4 And they came near before Eleazar the priest and before Joshua the son of Nun and before the leaders, saying, "The LORD commanded Moses to give us an inheritance among our brothers." So [a]according to the [1]command of the LORD he gave them an inheritance among their father's brothers.

5 Thus there fell ten portions to Manasseh, besides the land of Gilead and Bashan, which is beyond the Jordan,

6 because the daughters of Manasseh received an inheritance among his sons. And the [a]land of Gilead belonged to the rest of the sons of Manasseh.

7 And the border of Manasseh [1]ran from Asher to Michmethath which was east of Shechem; then the border went [2]southward to the inhabitants of En-tappuah.

8 The land of Tappuah belonged to Manasseh, but Tappuah on the border of Manasseh *belonged* to the sons of Ephraim.

9 And the border went down to the [1]brook of Kanah, southward of the [1]brook (these cities *belonged* to Ephraim among the cities of Manasseh), and the border of Manasseh *was* on the north side of the [1]brook, and [2]it ended at the sea.

10 The south side *belonged* to Ephraim and the north side to Manasseh, and the sea was [1]their border; and they reached to Asher on the north and to Issachar on the east.

11 And in Issachar and in Asher, [a]Manasseh had Beth-shean and its towns and Ibleam and its towns, and the inhabitants of Dor and its towns, and the inhabitants of Endor and its towns, and the inhabitants of Taanach and its towns, and

63 [1]Or, *dispossess them* [a]Judg. 1:21; 2 Sam. 5:6

1 [a]Josh. 8:15; 18:12

3 [1]Lit., *goings out of it were* [a]Josh. 18:13; 1 Kin. 9:17 [b]Josh. 10:33

5 [a]Josh. 18:13

6 [a]Josh. 17:7

7 [a]1 Chr. 7:28

8 [1]Or, *wadi* [2]Lit., *goings out of it were* [a]Josh. 17:8

10 [1]Or, *dispossess* [a]Judg. 1:29; 1 Kin. 9:16 [b]Josh. 17:12, 13

1 [1]Lit., *and there was to him*

3 [a]Num. 26:33; 27:1-7

4 [1]Lit., *mouth* [a]Num. 27:5-7

6 [a]Josh. 13:30, 31

7 [1]Lit., *was* [2]Lit., *to the right hand*

9 [1]Or, *wadi* [2]Lit., *goings out of it were*

10 [1]Lit., *its*

11 [a]1 Chr. 7:29

the inhabitants of Megiddo and its
towns, the third is [b]Napheth.
12 [a]But the sons of Manasseh
could not take possession of these
cities, because the Canaanites persisted in living in that land.
13 And it came about when the
sons of Israel became strong, [a]they
put the Canaanites to forced labor,
but they did not [1]drive them out
completely.
14 Then the sons [a]of Joseph spoke
to Joshua, saying, "Why have you
given me only one lot and one portion for an inheritance, since I am a
numerous people whom the LORD
has thus far blessed?"
15 And Joshua said to them, "If
you are a numerous people, go [1]up
to the forest and [2]clear a place for
yourself there in the land of the Perizzites and of the Rephaim, since the
hill country of Ephraim is too narrow for you."
16 And the sons of Joseph said,
"The hill country is not enough for
us, and all the Canaanites who live
in the valley land have [a]chariots of
iron, both those who are in Beth-
shean and its towns, and those who
are in the valley of Jezreel."
17 And Joshua spoke to the house
of Joseph, to Ephraim and Manasseh, saying, "You are a numerous
people and have great power; you
shall not have one lot *only*,
18 but the hill country shall be
yours. For though it is a forest, you
shall [1]clear it, and to its [2]farthest
borders it shall be yours; for you
shall [3]drive out the Canaanites,
even though they have [a]chariots of
iron *and* though they are strong."

CHAPTER 18

Rest of the Land Divided

THEN the whole congregation of
the sons of Israel assembled themselves at [a]Shiloh, and set up the tent
of meeting there; and the land was
subdued before them.
2 And there remained among the
sons of Israel seven tribes who had
not divided their inheritance.
3 So Joshua said to the sons of
Israel, "How long will you put off
entering to take possession of the
land which the LORD, the God of
your fathers, has given you?
4 "Provide for yourselves three
men from [1]each tribe that I may
send them, and that they may arise
and walk through the land and write
a description of it according to their
inheritance; then they shall [2]return
to me.
5 "And they shall divide it into
seven portions; Judah shall stay in
its territory on the south, and the
house of Joseph shall stay in their
territory on the north.
6 "And you shall describe the land
in seven divisions, and bring *the description* here to me. And I will cast
lots for you here before the LORD
our God.
7 "For [a]the Levites have no portion among you, because the priesthood of the LORD is [1]their inheritance. Gad and Reuben and the half-
tribe of Manasseh also have received their inheritance eastward
beyond the Jordan, which Moses
the servant of the LORD gave them."
8 Then the men arose and went,
and Joshua commanded those who
went to describe the land, saying,
"Go and walk through the land and
describe it, and return to me; then I
will cast lots for you here before the
LORD in [a]Shiloh."
9 So the men went and passed
through the land, and described it
by cities in seven divisions in a
book; and they came to Joshua to
the camp at Shiloh.
10 [a]And Joshua cast lots for them
in Shiloh before the LORD, and there
Joshua divided the land to the sons
of Israel according to their divisions.

The Territory of Benjamin

11 Now the lot of the tribe of the
sons of Benjamin came up according to their families, and the territory of their lot [1]lay between the
sons of Judah and the sons of
Joseph.
12 And their border on the north
side was from the Jordan, then the
border went up to the side of Jericho
on the north, and went up through
the hill country westward; and [1]it
ended at the wilderness of Beth-
aven.
13 And from there the border continued to Luz, to the side of Luz
(that is, Bethel) southward; and the
border went down to Ataroth-ad-
dar, near the hill which *lies* on the
south of lower Beth-horon.
14 And the border extended *from
there,* and turned round on the west
side southward, from the hill which
lies before Beth-horon southward;
and [1]it ended at Kiriath-baal (that is,
Kiriath-jearim), a city of the sons of
Judah. This *was* the west side.

11 [b]Josh. 11:2; 12:23
12 [a]Judg. 1:27
13 [1]Or, *dispossess* [a]Josh. 16:10
14 [a]Num. 13:8
15 [1]Lit., *up for yourself* [2]Lit., *cut down*
16 [a]Josh. 17:18; Judg. 1:19; 4:3, 13
18 [1]Lit., *cut down* [2]Lit., *goings out* [3]Or, *dispossess* [a]Josh. 17:16
1 [a]Judg. 21:19; Jer. 7:12; 26:6, 9
4 [1]Lit., *the* [2]Lit., *come*
7 [1]Lit., *his* [a]Num. 18:7, 20; Josh. 13:33
8 [a]Josh. 18:1
10 [a]Num. 34:16-29; Josh. 19:51
11 [1]Lit., *went out*
12 [1]Lit., *goings out of it were*
14 [1]Lit., *goings out of it were*

15 [a]Then the south side *was* from
the edge of Kiriath-jearim, and the
border went westward and went to
the fountain of the waters of Nephtoah.
16 And the border went down to
the edge of the hill which is in the
valley of Ben-hinnom, which is in
the vale of Rephaim northward; and
it went down to the valley of Hinnom, to the slope of the Jebusite
southward, and went down to En-
rogel.
17 And it extended northward and
went to En-shemesh and went to
Geliloth, which is opposite the ascent of Adummim, and it went
down to the stone of Bohan the son
of Reuben.
18 And it continued to the side in
front of the Arabah northward, and
went down to the Arabah.
19 And the border continued to
the side of Beth-hoglah northward;
and the [1]border ended at the north
bay of the Salt Sea, at the south end
of the Jordan. This *was* the south
border.
20 Moreover, the Jordan was its
border on the east side. This *was* the
inheritance of the sons of Benjamin,
according to their families *and* according to its borders all around.
21 Now the cities of the tribe of the
sons of Benjamin according to their
families were Jericho and Beth-hoglah and Emek-keziz,
22 and Beth-arabah and Zemaraim and Bethel,
23 and Avvim and Parah and Ophrah,
24 and Chephar-ammoni and Oph-
ni and Geba; twelve cities with their
villages.
25 Gibeon and Ramah and Beeroth,
26 and Mizpeh and Chephirah and
Mozah,
27 and Rekem and Irpeel and
Taralah,
28 and Zelah, Haeleph and the
Jebusite (that is, Jerusalem), Gibeah, Kiriath; fourteen cities with
their villages. This is the inheritance
of the sons of Benjamin according
to their families.

CHAPTER 19

Territory of Simeon

THEN the second lot [1]fell to Simeon, to the tribe of the sons of Simeon
according to their families, and their
inheritance was in the midst of the
inheritance of the sons of Judah.
2 So they had as their inheritance
Beersheba and [1]Sheba and Moladah,
3 and Hazar-shual and Balah and
Ezem,
4 and Eltolad and Bethul and
Hormah,
5 and Ziklag and Beth-marcaboth and Hazar-susah,
6 and Beth-lebaoth and Sharuhen, thirteen cities with their villages;
7 Ain, Rimmon and Ether and A-
shan, four cities with their villages;
8 and all the villages which *were*
around these cities as far as Baal-
ath-beer, Ramah of the [1]Negev. This
was the inheritance of the tribe of
the sons of Simeon according to
their families.
9 The inheritance of the sons of
Simeon *was taken* from the portion
of the sons of Judah, for the share of
the sons of Judah was too large for
them; so the sons of Simeon received *an* inheritance in the midst of
[1]Judah's inheritance.

Territory of Zebulun

10 Now the third lot came up for
the sons of Zebulun according to
their families. And the territory of
their inheritance was as far as Sarid.
11 Then their border went up to
the west and to Maralah, it then
[1]touched Dabbesheth, and reached
to the [2]brook that is before Jokneam.
12 Then it turned from Sarid to the
east toward the sunrise as far as the
border of Chisloth-tabor, and it proceeded to Daberath and [1]up to Japhia.
13 And from there it continued
eastward toward the sunrise to
Gath-hepher, to Eth-kazin, and it
proceeded to Rimmon [1]which
stretches to Neah.
14 And the border circled around
it on the north to Hannathon, and [1]it
ended at the valley of Iphtahel.
15 *Included* also *were* Kattah and
Nahalal and Shimron and Idalah
and Bethlehem; twelve cities with
their villages.
16 This *was* the inheritance of the
sons of Zebulun according to their
families, these cities with their villages.

Territory of Issachar

17 The fourth lot [1]fell to Issachar,
to the sons of Issachar according to
their families.
18 And their territory was to Jezreel and *included* Chesulloth and
Shunem,

15 [a]Josh. 15:5-9
19 [1]Lit., *goings out of the border were*
1 [1]Lit., *came out*
2 [1]Or, *Shema*, cf. Josh. 15:26
8 [1]I.e., South country
9 [1]Lit., *their*
11 [1]Or, *reached to* [2]Or, *wadi*
12 [1]Lit., *went up*
13 [1]Or, *and is marked off*
14 [1]Lit., *goings out of it were*
17 [1]Lit., *came out*

19 and Hapharaim and Shion and Anaharath,

20 and Rabbith and Kishion and Ebez,

21 and Remeth and En-gannim and En-haddah and Beth-pazzez.

22 And the border reached to Tabor and Shahazumah and Beth-shemesh, and [1]their border ended at the Jordan; sixteen cities with their villages.

23 This *was* the inheritance of the tribe of the sons of Issachar according to their families, the cities with their villages.

Territory of Asher

24 Now the fifth lot [1]fell to the tribe of the sons of Asher according to their families.

25 And their territory was Helkath and Hali and Beten and Achshaph,

26 and Allammelech and Amad and Mishal; and it reached to Carmel on the west and to Shihor-libnath.

27 And it turned toward the [1]east to Beth-dagon, and reached to Zebulun, and to the valley of Iphtahel northward to Beth-emek and Neiel; then it proceeded on [2]north to Cabul,

28 and Ebron and Rehob and Hammon and Kanah, as far as Great Sidon.

29 And the border turned to Ramah, and to the fortified city of Tyre; then the border turned to Hosah, and [1]it ended at the sea by the region of Achzib.

30 *Included* also *were* Ummah, and Aphek and Rehob; twenty-two cities with their villages.

31 This *was* the inheritance of the tribe of the sons of Asher according to their families, these cities with their villages.

Territory of Naphtali

32 The sixth lot [1]fell to the sons of Naphtali; to the sons of Naphtali according to their families.

33 And their border was from Heleph, from the oak in Zaanannim and Adami-nekeb and Jabneel, as far as Lakkum; and [1]it ended at the Jordan.

34 Then the border turned westward to Aznoth-tabor, and proceeded from there to Hukkok; and it reached to Zebulun on the south and [1]touched Asher on the west, and to Judah at the Jordan toward the [2]east.

35 And the fortified cities *were* Ziddim, Zer and Hammath, Rakkath and Chinnereth,

36 and Adamah and Ramah and Hazor,

37 and Kedesh and Edrei and En-hazor,

38 and Yiron and Migdal-el, Horem and Beth-anath and Beth-shemesh; nineteen cities with their villages.

39 This *was* the inheritance of the tribe of the sons of Naphtali according to their families, the cities with their villages.

Territory of Dan

40 The seventh lot [1]fell to the tribe of the sons of Dan according to their families.

41 And the territory of their inheritance was Zorah and Eshtaol and Irshemesh,

42 and Shaalabbin and Aijalon and Ithlah,

43 and Elon and Timnah and Ekron,

44 and Eltekeh and Gibbethon and Baalath,

45 and Jehud and Bene-berak and Gath-rimmon,

46 and Me-jarkon and Rakkon, with the territory over against [1]Joppa.

47 And the territory of the sons of Dan proceeded [1]beyond them; for the sons of Dan went up and fought with Leshem and captured it. Then they struck it with the edge of the sword and possessed it and [2]settled in it; and they called Leshem Dan after the name of Dan their father.

48 This *was* the inheritance of the tribe of the sons of Dan according to their families, these cities with their villages.

49 When they finished apportioning the land for inheritance by its borders, the sons of Israel gave an inheritance in their midst to Joshua the son of Nun.

50 In accordance with the [1]command of the LORD they gave him the city for which he asked, [a]Timnath-serah in the hill country of Ephraim. So he built the city and [2]settled in it.

51 [a]These are the inheritances which Eleazar the priest and Joshua the son of Nun and the heads of the [1]households of the tribes of the sons of Israel distributed by lot in Shiloh before the LORD, at the doorway of the tent of meeting. So they finished dividing the land.

CHAPTER 20

Six Cities of Refuge

THEN the LORD spoke to Joshua, saying,

22 [1]Lit., *goings out of their border were*
24 [1]Lit., *came out*
27 [1]Lit., *sunrise* [2]Lit., *from the left hand*
29 [1]Lit., *goings out of it were*
32 [1]Lit., *came out*
33 [1]Lit., *goings out of it were*
34 [1]Or, *reached to* [2]Lit., *sunrise*
40 [1]Lit., *came out*
46 [1]Heb., *Japho*
47 [1]Lit., *from* [2]Lit., *dwelt*
50 [1]Lit., *mouth* [2]Lit., *dwelt* [a]Num. 13:8; Josh. 24:30
51 [1]Lit., *fathers* [a]Josh. 18:10

2 "Speak to the sons of Israel, saying, '[1]Designate [a]the cities of refuge, of which I spoke to you [2]through Moses,

3 that the manslayer who [1]kills any person unintentionally, without premeditation, may flee there, and they shall become your refuge from the avenger of blood.

4 'And he shall flee to one of these cities, and shall stand at the entrance of the gate of the city and state his case in the hearing of the elders of that city; and they shall [1]take him into the city to them and give him a place, so that he may dwell among them.

5 'Now if the avenger of blood pursues him, then they shall not deliver the manslayer into his hand, because he struck his neighbor without premeditation and did not hate him beforehand.

6 'And he shall dwell in that city until he stands before the congregation for judgment, until the death of the one who is high priest in those days. Then the manslayer shall [1]return to his own city and to his own house, to the city from which he fled.' "

7 So they [1]set apart [a]Kedesh in [2]Galilee in the hill country of Naphtali and Shechem in the hill country of Ephraim, and Kiriath-arba (that is, Hebron) in [b]the hill country of Judah.

8 And beyond the Jordan east of Jericho, they [1]designated Bezer in the wilderness on the plain from the tribe of Reuben, and Ramoth in Gilead from the tribe of Gad, and Golan in Bashan from the tribe of Manasseh.

9 These were the appointed cities for all the sons of Israel and for the stranger who sojourns among them, that whoever [1]kills any person unintentionally may flee there, and not die by the hand of the avenger of blood until he stands before the congregation.

Chapter 21

Forty-eight Cities of the Levites

THEN the heads of [1]households [a]of the Levites approached Eleazar the priest and Joshua the son of Nun and the heads of [1]households of the tribes of the sons of Israel.

2 And they spoke to them at Shiloh in the land of Canaan, saying, "[a]The LORD commanded [1]through Moses to give us cities to live in, with their pasture lands for our cattle."

2 [1]Lit., *set for yourselves* [2]Lit., *by the hand of* [a]Num. 35:6-34; Deut. 4:41; 19:2
3 [1]Lit., *smites*
4 [1]Lit., *gather*
6 [1]Lit., *return and come*
7 [1]Lit., *sanctified* [2]Heb. *Galil* [a]Josh. 21:32; 1 Chr. 6:76 [b]Josh. 21:11; Luke 1:39
8 [1]Lit., *set*
9 [1]Lit., *smites*
1 [1]Lit., *fathers* [a]Num. 35:1-8
2 [1]Lit., *by the hand of* [a]Num. 35:2
3 [1]Lit., *mouth*
4 [1]Lit., *had*
5 [1]Lit., *had*
6 [1]Lit., *had*
7 [1]Lit., *had*
8 [1]Lit., *by the hand of*

3 So the sons of Israel gave the Levites from their inheritance these cities with their pasture lands, according to the [1]command of the LORD.

4 Then the lot came out for the families of the Kohathites. And the sons of Aaron the priest, who were of the Levites, [1]received thirteen cities by lot from the tribe of Judah and from the tribe of the Simeonites and from the tribe of Benjamin.

5 And the rest of the sons of Kohath [1]received ten cities by lot from the families of the tribe of Ephraim and from the tribe of Dan and from the half-tribe of Manasseh.

6 And the sons of Gershon [1]received thirteen cities by lot from the families of the tribe of Issachar and from the tribe of Asher and from the tribe of Naphtali and from the half-tribe of Manasseh in Bashan.

7 The sons of Merari according to their families [1]received twelve cities from the tribe of Reuben and from the tribe of Gad and from the tribe of Zebulun.

8 Now the sons of Israel gave by lot to the Levites these cities with their pasture lands, as the LORD had commanded [1]through Moses.

9 And they gave these cities which are *here* mentioned by name from the tribe of the sons of Judah and from the tribe of the sons of Simeon;

10 and they were for the sons of Aaron, one of the families of the Kohathites, of the sons of Levi, for the lot was theirs first.

11 Thus they gave them Kiriath-arba, *Arba being* the father of Anak (that is, Hebron), in the hill country of Judah, with its surrounding pasture lands.

12 But the fields of the city and its villages, they gave to Caleb the son of Jephunneh as his possession.

13 So to the sons of Aaron the priest they gave Hebron, the city of refuge for the manslayer, with its pasture lands, and Libnah with its pasture lands,

14 and Jattir with its pasture lands and Eshtemoa with its pasture lands,

15 and Holon with its pasture lands and Debir with its pasture lands,

16 and Ain with its pasture lands and Juttah with its pasture lands *and* Beth-shemesh with its pasture lands; nine cities from these two tribes.

17 And from the tribe of Benja-

min, Gibeon with its pasture lands, Geba with its pasture lands,

18 Anathoth with its pasture lands and Almon with its pasture lands; four cities.

19 All the cities of the sons of Aaron, the priests, were thirteen cities with their pasture lands.

20 Then the cities from the tribe of Ephraim were allotted to the families of the sons of Kohath, the Levites, *even to* the rest of the sons of Kohath.

21 And they gave them Shechem, the city of refuge for the manslayer, with its pasture lands, in the hill country of Ephraim, and Gezer with its pasture lands,

22 and Kibzaim with its pasture lands and Beth-horon with its pasture lands; four cities.

23 And from the tribe of Dan, Elteke with its pasture lands, Gibbethon with its pasture lands,

24 Aijalon with its pasture lands, Gath-rimmon with its pasture lands; four cities.

25 And from the half-tribe of Manasseh, *they allotted* Taanach with its pasture lands and Gath-rimmon with its pasture lands; two cities.

26 All the cities with their pasture lands for the families of the rest of the sons of Kohath were ten.

27 And to the sons of Gershon, one of the families of the Levites, from the half-tribe of Manasseh, *they gave* Golan in Bashan, the city of refuge for the manslayer, with its pasture lands, and Be-eshterah with its pasture lands; two cities.

28 And from the tribe of Issachar, *they gave* Kishion with its pasture lands, Daberath with its pasture lands,

29 Jarmuth with its pasture lands, En-gannim with its pasture lands; four cities.

30 And from the tribe of Asher, *they gave* Mishal with its pasture lands, Abdon with its pasture lands,

31 Helkath with its pasture lands and Rehob with its pasture lands; four cities.

32 And from the tribe of Naphtali, *they gave* Kedesh in Galilee, the city of refuge for the manslayer, with its pasture lands and Hammoth-dor with its pasture lands and Kartan with its pasture lands; three cities.

33 All the cities of the Gershonites according to their families were thirteen cities with their pasture lands.

34 And to the families of the sons of Merari, the rest of the Levites, *they gave* from the tribe of Zebulun, Jokneam with its pasture lands and Kartah with its pasture lands.

35 Dimnah with its pasture lands, Nahalal with its pasture lands; four cities.

36 And from the tribe of Reuben, *they gave* Bezer with its pasture lands and Jahaz with its pasture lands,

37 Kedemoth with its pasture lands and Mephaath with its pasture lands; four cities.

38 And from the tribe of Gad, *they gave* Ramoth in Gilead, the city of refuge for the manslayer, with its pasture lands and Mahanaim with its pasture lands,

39 Heshbon with its pasture lands, Jazer with its pasture lands; four cities in all.

40 All *these were* the cities of the sons of Merari according to their families, the rest of the families of the Levites; and their lot was twelve cities.

41 [a]All the cities of the Levites in the midst of the possession of the sons of Israel were forty-eight cities with their pasture lands.

42 These cities each had its surrounding pasture lands; thus *it was* with all these cities.

43 [a]So the LORD gave Israel all the land which He had sworn to give to their fathers, and [b]they possessed it and lived in it.

44 And the LORD [a]gave them rest on every side, according to all that He had sworn to their fathers, and [b]no one of all their enemies stood before them; [c]the LORD gave all their enemies into their hand.

45 [a]Not [1]one of the good [2]promises which the LORD had [3]made to the house of Israel failed; all came to pass.

CHAPTER 22

Tribes beyond Jordan Return

[a]THEN Joshua summoned the Reubenites and the Gadites and the half-tribe of Manasseh,

2 and said to them, "You have kept all that Moses the servant of the LORD commanded you, [a]and have listened to my voice in all that I commanded you.

3 "You have not forsaken your brothers these many days to this day, but have kept the charge of the commandment of the LORD your God.

4 "[a]And now the LORD your God has given rest to your brothers, as He spoke to them; therefore turn

41 [a]Num. 35:7

43 [a]Deut. 34:4 [b]Num. 33:53; Deut. 11:31; 17:14

44 [a]Josh. 1:13; 23:1 [b]Deut. 7:24 [c]Ex. 23:31

45 [1]Lit., *a word* [2]Lit., *words* [3]Lit., *spoken* [a]Josh. 23:14; 1 Kin. 8:56

1 [a]Num. 32:20-22

2 [a]Josh. 1:12-18

4 [a]Num. 32:18; Deut. 3:20

now and go to your tents, to the land of your possession, which Moses the servant of the LORD gave you beyond the Jordan.

5 "[a]Only be very careful to observe the commandment and the law which Moses the servant of the LORD commanded you, to love the LORD your God and walk in all His ways and keep His commandments and hold fast to Him and serve Him [b]with all your heart and with all your soul."

6 So Joshua blessed them and sent them away, and they went to their tents.

7 [a]Now to the one half-tribe of Manasseh Moses had given *a possession* in Bashan, [b]but to the other half Joshua gave *a possession* among their brothers westward beyond the Jordan. So when Joshua sent them away to their tents, he blessed them,

8 and said to [1]them, "Return to your tents with great riches and with very much livestock, with silver, gold, bronze, iron, and with very many clothes; divide the spoil of your enemies with your brothers."

9 And the sons of Reuben and the sons of Gad and the half-tribe of Manasseh returned *home* and departed from the sons of Israel at Shiloh which is in the land of Canaan, to go to the land of Gilead, to the land of their possession which they had possessed, according to the [1]command of the LORD [2]through Moses.

The Offensive Altar

10 And when they came to the region of the Jordan which is in the land of Canaan, the sons of Reuben and the sons of Gad and the half-tribe of Manasseh built an altar there by the Jordan, a large altar in appearance.

11 And the sons of Israel heard *it* [1]said, "Behold, the sons of Reuben and the sons of Gad and the half-tribe of Manasseh have built [a]an altar at the [2]frontier of the land of Canaan, in the region of the Jordan, on the side *belonging to* the sons of Israel."

12 And when the sons of Israel heard *of it,* the whole congregation of the sons of Israel gathered themselves at [a]Shiloh, to go up against them in war.

13 Then the sons of Israel sent to the sons of Reuben and to the sons of Gad and to the half-tribe of Manasseh, into the land of Gilead, [a]Phinehas the son of Eleazar the priest,

14 and with him ten chiefs, one chief for each father's household from each of the tribes of Israel; and each one of them *was* the head of his father's household among the [1]thousands of Israel.

15 And they came to the sons of Reuben and to the sons of Gad and to the half-tribe of Manasseh, to the land of Gilead, and they spoke with them saying,

16 "Thus says the whole congregation of the LORD, 'What is this unfaithful act which you have committed against the God of Israel, turning away from following the LORD this day, by building yourselves [a]an altar, to rebel against the LORD this day?

17 'Is not [a]the [1]iniquity of Peor enough for us, from which we have not cleansed ourselves to this day, although a plague came on the congregation of the LORD,

18 that you must turn away this day from following the LORD? And it will come about if you rebel against the LORD today, that He will be angry with the whole congregation of Israel tomorrow.

19 'If, however, the land of your possession is unclean, then [1]cross into the land of the possession of the LORD, where the LORD's [a]tabernacle [2]stands, and take possession among us. Only do not rebel against the LORD, or rebel against us by building an altar for yourselves, besides the altar of the LORD our God.

20 'Did not [a]Achan the son of Zerah act unfaithfully in the things under the ban, and wrath fall on all the congregation of Israel? And that man did not perish alone in his iniquity.' "

21 Then the sons of Reuben and the sons of Gad and the half-tribe of Manasseh answered, and spoke to the heads of the [1]families of Israel.

22 "The Mighty One, God, the LORD, the Mighty One, God, the LORD! He knows, and may Israel itself know. If *it was* in rebellion, or if in an unfaithful act against the LORD do not Thou save us this day!

23 "If we have built us an altar to turn away from following the LORD, or [a]if to offer a burnt offering or grain offering on it, or if to offer sacrifices of peace offerings on it, may the LORD Himself require it.

24 "But truly we have done this out of concern, [1]for a reason, saying, 'In time to come your sons may say to

5 [a]Deut. 5:10 [b]Deut. 4:29
7 [a]Num. 32:33 [b]Josh. 17:1-13
8 [1]Lit., *them, saying, "Return*
9 [1]Lit., *mouth* [2]Lit., *by the hand of*
11 [1]Lit., *saying* [2]Lit., *front* [a]Deut. 12:5; Josh. 22:19
12 [a]Josh. 18:1
13 [a]Num. 25:7, 11; 31:6
14 [1]Or, *families*
16 [a]Josh. 22:11
17 [1]Lit., *the iniquity . . . little for us* [a]Num. 25:1-9
19 [1]Lit., *cross for yourselves* [2]Lit., *abides* [a]Josh. 22:11
20 [a]Josh. 7:1-26
21 [1]Lit., *thousands*
23 [a]Deut. 12:11
24 [1]Lit., *from*

our [2]sons, "What have you to do
with the LORD, the God of Israel?
25"For the LORD has made the Jordan a border between us and you,
you sons of Reuben and sons of Gad;
you have no portion in the LORD."
So your sons may make our sons
stop fearing the LORD.'
26"Therefore we said, 'Let us
[1]build an altar, not for burnt offering
or for sacrifice;
27 rather it shall be a witness between us and you and between our
generations after us, that we are to
perform the service of the LORD before Him with our burnt offerings,
and with our sacrifices and with our
peace offerings, that your sons may
not say to our sons in time to come,
"You have no portion in the LORD." '
28"Therefore we said, 'It shall also
come about if they say *this* to us or
to our generations in time to come,
then we shall say, "See the copy of
the altar of the LORD which our fathers made, not for burnt offering or
for sacrifice; rather it is a witness
between us and you." '
29"Far be it from us that we should
rebel against the LORD and turn
away from following the LORD this
day, by building an altar for burnt
offering, for grain offering or for
sacrifice, besides the altar of the
LORD our God which is before His
[1]tabernacle."
30 So when Phinehas the priest
and the leaders of the congregation,
even the heads of the [1]families of
Israel who *were* with him, heard the
words which the sons of Reuben
and the sons of Gad and the sons of
Manasseh spoke, it pleased them.
31 And Phinehas the son of Eleazar the priest said to the sons of
Reuben and to the sons of Gad and
to the sons of Manasseh, "Today we
know that the LORD is in our midst,
because you have not committed
this unfaithful act against the LORD;
now you have delivered the sons of
Israel from the hand of the LORD."
32 Then Phinehas the son of Eleazar the priest and the leaders returned from the sons of Reuben and
from the sons of Gad, from the land
of Gilead, to the land of Canaan, to
the sons of Israel, and brought back
word to them.
33 And the word pleased the sons
of Israel, and the sons of Israel
blessed God; and they did not speak
of going up against them in war, to
destroy the land in which the sons of
Reuben and the sons of Gad were
living.
34 And the sons of Reuben and the
sons of Gad [a]called the altar *Wit-*
ness; "For," *they said,* "it is a witness between us that the LORD is
God."

CHAPTER 23

Joshua's Farewell Address

NOW it came about after many
days, when the LORD had given [a]rest
to Israel from all their enemies [1]on
every side, and Joshua was old, advanced in years,
2 [a]that Joshua called for all Israel, for their elders and their heads
and their judges and their officers,
and said to them, "I am old, advanced in years.
3"And you have seen all that the
LORD your God has done to all these
nations because of you, for [a]the
LORD your God is He who has been
fighting for you.
4"See, [a]I have apportioned to you
these nations which remain as an inheritance for your tribes, with all
the nations which I have cut off,
from the Jordan even to the Great
Sea toward the setting of the sun.
5"And the LORD your God, He
shall thrust them out from before
you and [1]drive them from before
you; and [a]you shall possess their
land, just as the LORD your God
[2]promised you.
6"[a]Be very firm, then, to keep and
do [b]all that is written in the book of
the law of Moses, so that you may
not turn aside from it to the right
hand or to the left,
7 in order that you may not [1]asso-
ciate with these nations, these
which remain among you, [a]or mention the name of their gods, or
[b]make *anyone* swear *by them,* or
[c]serve them, or bow down to them.
8"But you are to cling to the LORD
your God, as you have done to this
day.
9"[a]For the LORD has [1]driven out
great and strong nations from before you; and as for you, [b]no man
has stood before you to this day.
10"[a]One of your men puts to flight
a thousand, for the LORD your God is
[b]He who fights for you, just as He
[1]promised you.
11"So take diligent heed to yourselves to love the LORD your God.
12"For if you ever go back and
[a]cling to the rest of these nations,
these which remain among you, and
[b]intermarry with them, so that you
[1]associate with them and they with
you,
13 know with certainty that the

24 [2]Lit., *sons, saying*
26 [1]Lit., *prepare to build for ourselves*
29 [1]Lit., *dwelling place*
30 [1]Lit., *thousands*
34 [a]Gen. 31:47-49
1 [1]Lit., *from round about* [a]Josh. 21:44
2 [a]Josh. 24:1
3 [a]Deut. 1:30
4 [a]Ex. 23:30
5 [1]Or, *dispossess* [2]Lit., *spoke to* [a]Num. 33:53
6 [a]Deut. 5:32 [b]Josh. 1:7
7 [1]Lit., *go among* [a]Ex. 23:13; Ps. 16:4 [b]Deut. 6:13; 10:20 [c]Ex. 20:5
9 [1]Or, *dispossessed* [a]Ex. 23:23, 30 [b]Deut. 7:24
10 [1]Lit., *spoke to* [a]Lev. 26:8; Deut. 28:7 [b]Josh. 23:3
12 [1]Lit., *go among* [a]Ex. 34:15, 16; Ps. 106:34, 35 [b]Deut. 7:3, 4; Ezra 9:2; Neh. 13:25

LORD your God will not continue to
[1]drive these nations out from before
you; but they [a]shall be a snare and a
trap to you, and a whip on your
sides and thorns in your eyes, until
you perish from off this good land
which the LORD your God has given
you.
14"Now behold, today [a]I am going
the way of all the earth, and you
know in all your hearts and in all
your souls [b]that not one word of all
the good words which the LORD
your God spoke concerning you has
failed; all have [1]been fulfilled for
you, not [2]one of them has failed.
15"And it shall come about that
just as all the good words which the
LORD your God spoke to you have
come upon you, [a]so the LORD will
bring upon you all the threats, until
He has destroyed you from off this
good land which the LORD your God
has given you.
16"[a]When you transgress the covenant of the LORD your God, which
He commanded you, and go and
serve other gods, and bow down to
them, then the anger of the LORD
will burn against you, and you shall
perish quickly from off the good
land which He has given you."

CHAPTER 24

Joshua Reviews Israel's History

[a]THEN Joshua gathered all the
tribes of Israel to Shechem, and
called for the elders of Israel and for
their heads and their judges and
their officers; and they presented
themselves before God.
2 And Joshua said to all the people, "Thus says the LORD, the God of
Israel, 'From ancient times your fathers lived beyond the [1]River,
namely, [a]Terah, the father of Abraham and the father of Nahor, and
they served other gods.
3 '[a]Then I took your father Abraham from beyond the [1]River, and
led him through all the land of Canaan, and [b]multiplied his [2]descen-
dants and gave him [c]Isaac.
4 'And to Isaac I gave [a]Jacob and
Esau, and to Esau [b]I gave Mount
Seir, to possess it; but [c]Jacob and
his sons went down to Egypt.
5 'Then [a]I sent Moses and Aaron,
and I plagued Egypt [1]by what I did
in its midst; and afterward I brought
you out.
6 'And I brought your fathers out
of Egypt, and [a]you came to the sea;
and Egypt pursued your fathers
with chariots and horsemen to the
[1]Red Sea.
7 'But when they cried out to the
LORD, He put darkness between you
and the Egyptians, and brought the
sea upon them and covered them;
and your own eyes saw what I did in
Egypt. And [a]you lived in the wilderness for a long time.
8 'Then [a]I brought you into the
land of the Amorites who lived beyond the Jordan, and they fought
with you; and I gave them into your
hand, and you took possession of
their land when I destroyed them
before you.
9 'Then [a]Balak the son of Zippor,
king of Moab, arose and fought
against Israel, and he sent and summoned Balaam the son of Beor to
curse you.
10 'But I was not willing to listen to
Balaam. So he had to bless you, and
I delivered you from his hand.
11 'And [a]you crossed the Jordan
and came to Jericho; and the citizens of Jericho fought against you,
and [b]the Amorite and the Perizzite
and the Canaanite and the Hittite
and the Girgashite, the Hivite and
the Jebusite. Thus [c]I gave them into
your hand.
12 'Then I [a]sent the hornet before
you and it [1]drove out the two kings
of the Amorites from before you,
[b]*but* not by your sword or your bow.
13 '[a]And I gave you a land on
which you had not labored, and
cities which you had not built, and
you have lived in them; you are eating of vineyards and oliveyards
which you did not plant.'

"We Will Serve the LORD"

14"[a]Now, therefore, [1]fear the LORD
and serve Him in sincerity and
[2]truth; and put away the gods which
your fathers served beyond the
[3]River and in Egypt, and serve the
LORD.
15"And if it is disagreeable in your
sight to serve the LORD, choose for
yourselves today whom you will
serve: whether the gods which your
fathers served which were beyond
the River, or the gods of the Amorites in whose land you are living;
but as for me and my house, we will
serve the LORD."
16 And the people answered and
said, "Far be it from us that we
should forsake the LORD to serve
other gods;
17 for the LORD our God is He who
brought us and our fathers up out of
the land of Egypt, from the house of

13 [1]Or, *dispossess* [a]Ex. 23:33; 34:12; Deut. 7:16

14 [1]Lit., *come* [2]Lit., *one word* [a]1 Kin. 2:2 [b]Josh. 21:45

15 [a]Lev. 26:14-33; Deut. 28:15

16 [a]Deut. 4:25, 26

1 [a]Josh. 23:2

2 [1]I.e., Euphrates [a]Gen. 11:27-32

3 [1]I.e., Euphrates [2]Lit., *seed* [a]Gen. 12:1; 24:7 [b]Gen. 15:5 [c]Gen. 21:3

4 [a]Gen. 25:25, 26 [b]Deut. 2:5 [c]Gen. 46:6, 7

5 [1]Lit., *according to* [a]Ex. 4:14-17

6 [1]Lit., *Sea of Reeds* [a]Ex. 14:2-31

7 [a]Deut. 1:46; 2:14

8 [a]Num. 21:21-35

9 [a]Num. 22:2

11 [a]Josh. 3:16, 17 [b]Ex. 23:23, 28; Deut. 7:1 [c]Ex. 23:31

12 [1]Lit., *drove them out* [a]Ex. 23:28; Deut. 7:20 [b]Ps. 44:3

13 [a]Deut. 6:10, 11

14 [1]Or, *reverence* [2]Or, *faithfulness* [3]I.e., Euphrates [a]Deut. 10:12; 18:13; 1 Sam. 12:24

[1]bondage, and who did these great
signs in our sight and preserved us
through all the way in which we
went and among all the peoples
through whose midst we passed.
18"And the LORD drove out from
before us all the peoples, even the
Amorites who lived in the land. We
also will serve the LORD, for He is
our God."
19 Then Joshua said to the people,
"You will not be able to serve the
LORD, [a]for He is a holy God. He is [b]a
jealous God; [c]He will not forgive
your transgression or your sins.
20"[a]If you forsake the LORD and
serve foreign gods, then He will turn
and do you harm and consume you
after He has done good to you."
21 And the people said to Joshua,
"No, but we will serve the LORD."
22 And Joshua said to the people,
"You are witnesses against yourselves that you have chosen for
yourselves the LORD, to serve Him."
And they said, "We are witnesses."
23"Now therefore, put away the
foreign gods which are in your
midst, and [a]incline your hearts to
the LORD, the God of Israel."
24 [a]And the people said to Joshua,
"We will serve the LORD our God
and we will [1]obey His voice."
25 [a]So Joshua made a covenant
with the people that day, and made
for them a statute and an ordinance
in Shechem.
26 And Joshua wrote these words
in the book of the law of God; and he
took a large stone and set it up there
under the oak that was by the sanctuary of the LORD.
27 And Joshua said to all the people, "Behold, [a]this stone shall be for
a witness against us, for it has heard
all the words of the LORD which He
spoke [1]to us; thus it shall be for a
witness against you, lest you deny
your God."
28 Then Joshua dismissed the people, each to his inheritance.

Joshua's Death and Burial

29 And it came about after these
things that Joshua the son of Nun,
the servant of the LORD, died, being
one hundred and ten years old.
30 And they buried him in the territory of his inheritance in [a]Tim-
nath-serah, which is in the hill country of Ephraim, on the north of
Mount Gaash.
31 And Israel served the LORD all
the days of Joshua and all the days
of the elders who [1]survived Joshua,
and had known all the deeds of the
LORD which He had done for Israel.
32 [a]Now they buried the bones of
Joseph, which the sons of Israel
brought up from Egypt, at Shechem,
in the piece of ground [b]which Jacob
had bought from the sons of Hamor
the father of Shechem for one hundred [1]pieces of money; and they became the inheritance of Joseph's
sons.
33 And Eleazar the son of Aaron
died; and they buried him [1]at Gibeah of [a]Phinehas his son, which was
given him in the hill country of
Ephraim.

17 [1]Lit., *bondmen*
19 [a]Lev. 19:2; 20:7, 26 [b]Ex. 20:5; 34:14 [c]Ex. 23:21
20 [a]Deut. 4:25, 26
23 [a]1 Kin. 8:57, 58; Ps. 119:36; 141:4
24 [1]Lit., *listen to* [a]Ex. 19:8; 24:3, 7; Deut. 5:27
25 [a]Ex. 24:8
27 [1]Lit., *with* [a]Josh. 22:27, 34
30 [a]Josh. 19:50
31 [1]Lit., *prolonged days after*
32 [1]Heb. *qesitah* [a]Gen. 50:24, 25; Ex. 13:19; Acts 7:15, 16 [b]Gen. 33:19
33 [1]Or, *on the hill* [a]Josh. 22:13

THE BOOK OF JUDGES

Jerusalem Is Captured

NOW it came about after the
death of Joshua that the sons of Israel [a]inquired of the LORD, saying,
"Who shall go up first for us
[b]against the Canaanites, to fight
against them?"
2 And the LORD said, "Judah
shall go up; behold, I have given the
land into his hand."
3 Then Judah said to Simeon his
brother, "Come up with me into [1]the
territory allotted me, that we may
fight against the Canaanites; and [2]I
in turn will go with you into [3]the
territory allotted you."
4 And Judah went up, and the
LORD gave the Canaanites and the
Perizzites into their hands; and they
[1]defeated ten thousand men at Bezek.
5 And they found Adoni-bezek in
Bezek and fought against him and
they [1]defeated the Canaanites and
the Perizzites.
6 But Adoni-bezek fled; and they
pursued him and caught him and
cut off his [1]thumbs and big toes.
7 And Adoni-bezek said, "Seventy kings with their thumbs and
their big toes cut off used to gather
up *scraps* under my table; as I have
done, so God has repaid me." So
they brought him to Jerusalem and
he died there.
8 Then the sons of Judah fought
against [a]Jerusalem and captured it
and struck it with the edge of the
sword and set the city on fire.
9 And afterward the sons of Judah went down to fight against the
Canaanites living in the hill country
and in the [1]Negev and in the lowland.
10 [a]So Judah went against the Canaanites who lived in Hebron (now
the name of Hebron formerly *was*
Kiriath-arba); and they struck Sheshai and Ahiman and Talmai.

Capture of Other Cities

11 Then from there he went
against the inhabitants of Debir
(now the name of Debir formerly
was Kiriath-sepher).
12 And Caleb said, "The one who
attacks Kiriath-sepher and captures
it, I will even give him my daughter
Achsah for a wife."
13 And [a]Othniel the son of Kenaz,
Caleb's younger brother, captured
it; so he gave him his daughter Achsah for a wife.
14 Then it came about when she
came *to him,* that she persuaded
him to ask her father for a field.
Then she alighted from [1]her donkey,
and Caleb said to her, "What [2]do
you want?"
15 And she said to him, "Give me a
blessing, since you have given me
the land of the [1]Negev, give me also
springs of water." So Caleb gave her
the upper springs and the lower
springs.
16 And the [1]descendants of [a]the
Kenite, Moses' father-in-law, went
up from the [b]city of palms with the
sons of Judah, to the wilderness of
Judah which is in the south of [c]A-
rad; and they went and lived with
the people.
17 Then Judah went with Simeon
his brother, and they struck the Canaanites living in Zephath, and utterly destroyed it. So the name of
the city was called [a]Hormah.
18 And Judah took Gaza with its
territory and Ashkelon with its territory and Ekron with its territory.
19 Now the LORD was with Judah,
and they took possession of the hill
country; but they could not [1]drive
out the inhabitants of the valley because they had [a]iron chariots.
20 Then they gave Hebron to Caleb, [a]as Moses had [1]promised; and
he drove out from there [b]the three
sons of Anak.
21 [a]But the sons of Benjamin did
not drive out the Jebusites who
lived in Jerusalem; so the Jebusites
have lived with the sons of Benjamin in Jerusalem to this day.
22 Likewise the house of Joseph
went up against Bethel, and the
LORD was with them.
23 And the house of Joseph spied
out Bethel ([a]now the name of the
city was formerly Luz).
24 And the spies saw a man coming out of the city, and they said to
him, "Please show us the entrance
to the city and we will treat you
kindly."
25 So he showed them the entrance to the city, and they struck
the city with the edge of the sword,
[a]but they let the man and all his
family go free.
26 And the man went into the land
of the Hittites and built a city and

1 [a]Num. 27:21 [b]Judg. 1:27; 2:21-23; 3:1-6
3 [1]Lit., *my lot* [2]Lit., *I, even I* [3]Lit., *your lot*
4 [1]Lit., *smote them*
5 [1]Lit., *smote*
6 [1]Lit., *thumbs of his hands and his feet*
8 [a]Josh. 15:63; Judg. 1:21
9 [1]I.e., South country
10 [a]Josh. 15:13-19
13 [a]Judg. 3:9
14 [1]Lit., *the* [2]Lit., *for yourself*
15 [1]I.e., South country
16 [1]Lit., *sons* [a]Num. 10:20-32; Judg. 4:11 [b]Deut. 34:3; Judg. 3:13 [c]Num. 21:1
17 [a]Num. 21:3
19 [1]Or, *dispossess* [a]Josh. 17:16; Judg. 4:3, 13
20 [1]Lit., *spoken* [a]Josh. 14:9 [b]Josh. 15:14; Judg. 1:10
21 [a]Josh. 15:63; Judg. 1:8
23 [a]Gen. 28:19
25 [a]Josh. 6:25

named it Luz [1]which is its name to this day.

Places Not Conquered

27 [a]But Manasseh did not take possession of Beth-shean and its villages, or Taanach and its villages, or the inhabitants of Dor and its villages, or the inhabitants of Ibleam and its villages, or the inhabitants of Megiddo and its villages; so [b]the Canaanites persisted in living in that land.

28 And it came about when Israel became strong, that they put the Canaanites to forced labor, but they did not drive them out completely.

29 [a]Neither did Ephraim drive out the Canaanites who were living in Gezer; so the Canaanites lived in Gezer among them.

30 Zebulun did not drive out the inhabitants of Kitron, or the inhabitants of Nahalol; so the Canaanites lived among them and became subject to forced labor.

31 Asher did not drive out the inhabitants of Acco, or the inhabitants of Sidon, or of Ahlab, or of Achzib, or of Helbah, or of Aphik, or of Rehob.

32 So the Asherites lived among the Canaanites, the inhabitants of the land; for they did not drive them out.

33 Naphtali did not drive out the inhabitants of Beth-shemesh, or the inhabitants of Beth-anath, but lived among the Canaanites, the inhabitants of the land; and the inhabitants of Beth-shemesh and Beth-anath became forced labor for them.

34 Then the Amorites [1]forced the sons of Dan into the hill country, for they did not allow them to come down to the valley;

35 yet the Amorites persisted in [1]living in Mount Heres, in Aijalon and in Shaalbim; but when the [2]power of the house of Joseph [3]grew strong, they became forced labor.

36 And the border of the Amorites ran from the [a]ascent of Akrabbim, from Sela and upward.

Chapter 2

Israel Rebuked

Now [a]the angel of the Lord came up from Gilgal to [b]Bochim. And he said, "[c]I brought you up out of Egypt and led you into the land which I have sworn to your fathers; and I said, '[d]I will never break My covenant with you,

2 and as for you, [a]you shall make no covenant with the inhabitants of this land; [b]you shall tear down their altars.' But you have not [1]obeyed Me; what is this you have done?

3 "Therefore [a]I also said, 'I will not drive them out before you; but they shall [1]become [b]*as thorns* in your sides, and their gods shall be a snare to you.' "

4 And it came about when the angel of the Lord spoke these words to all the sons of Israel, that the people lifted up their voices and wept.

5 So they named that place [1]Bochim; and there they sacrificed to the Lord.

Joshua Dies

6 [a]When Joshua had dismissed the people, the sons of Israel went each to his inheritance to possess the land.

7 And the people served the Lord all the days of Joshua, and all the days of the elders who [1]survived Joshua, who had seen all the great work of the Lord which He had done for Israel.

8 Then Joshua the son of Nun, the servant of the Lord, died at the age of one hundred and ten.

9 And they buried him in the territory of his inheritance in Timnath-heres, in the hill country of Ephraim, north of Mount Gaash.

10 And all that generation also were gathered to their fathers; and there arose another generation after them who did not know the Lord, nor yet the work which He had done for Israel.

Israel Serves Baals

11 Then the sons of Israel did [a]evil in the sight of the Lord, and [1]served the [b]Baals,

12 and [a]they forsook the Lord, the God of their fathers, who had brought them out of the land of Egypt, and followed other gods from *among* the gods of the peoples who were around them, and bowed themselves down to them; thus they provoked the Lord to anger.

13 So they forsook the Lord and [a]served Baal and the Ashtaroth.

14 [a]And the anger of the Lord burned against Israel, and He gave them into the hands of plunderers who plundered them; and [b]He sold them into the hands of their enemies around *them,* so that they could no longer stand before their enemies.

15 Wherever they went, the hand of the Lord was against them for evil, as the Lord had spoken and as

---

26 [1]Lit., *it*

27 [a]Josh. 17:12 [b]Judg. 1:1

29 [a]Josh. 16:10

34 [1]Lit., *pressed*

35 [1]Lit., *dwelling* [2]Lit., *hand* [3]Lit., *was heavy*

36 [a]Josh. 15:3

1 [a]Judg. 6:11; 13:2-21 [b]Judg. 2:5 [c]Ex. 20:2 [d]Gen. 17:7, 8; Lev. 26:42, 44; Deut. 7:9

2 [1]Lit., *listened to My voice* [a]Ex. 23:32 [b]Ex. 34:12, 13

3 [1]Some ancient mss. read *be adversaries, and* [a]Josh. 23:13 [b]Num. 33:55

5 [1]I.e., Weepers

6 [a]Josh. 24:28-31

7 [1]Lit., *prolonged days after*

11 [1]Or, *worshiped* [a]Judg. 3:7, 12; 4:1; 6:1 [b]Judg. 6:25; 8:33; 10:6

12 [a]Deut. 31:16

13 [a]Judg. 10:6

14 [a]Deut. 31:17; Ps. 106:40-42 [b]Deut. 28:25; 32:30

the LORD had sworn to them, so that
they were severely distressed.
16 [a]Then the LORD raised up
judges [1]who delivered them from
the hands of those who plundered
them.
17 And yet they did not listen to
their judges, for they played the harlot after other gods and bowed
themselves down to them. They
turned aside quickly from the way
[a]in which their fathers had walked
in obeying the commandments of
the LORD; they did not do as *their
fathers.*
18 And when the LORD raised up
judges for them, the LORD was with
the judge and delivered them from
the hand of their enemies all the
days of the judge; for the LORD was
moved to pity by their groaning because of those who oppressed and
afflicted them.
19 But it came about when the
judge died, that they would turn
back and act more corruptly than
their fathers, in following other
gods to serve them and bow down to
them; they did not abandon their
practices or their stubborn ways.
20 [a]So the anger of the LORD
burned against Israel, and He said,
"Because this nation has transgressed My covenant which I commanded their fathers, and has not
listened to My voice,
21 [a]I also will no longer drive out
before them any of the nations
which Joshua left when he died,
22 in order to test Israel by them,
whether they will keep the way of
the LORD to walk in it as their fathers [1]did, or not."
23 So the LORD allowed those nations to remain, not driving them
out quickly; and He did not give
them into the hand of Joshua.

CHAPTER 3

Idolatry Leads to Servitude

[a]NOW these are the nations which
the LORD left, to test Israel by them
(*that is*, all who had not [1]experi-
enced any of the wars of Canaan;
2 only in order that the generations of the sons of Israel might [1]be
taught war, [2]those who had not [3]ex-
perienced it formerly).
3 *These nations are*: the five lords
of the Philistines and all the Canaanites and the Sidonians and [a]the
Hivites who lived in Mount Lebanon, from Mount Baal-hermon as
far as [1]Lebo-hamath.
4 And they were for [1a]testing Israel, to find out if they would [2]obey
the commandments of the LORD,
which He had commanded their fathers [3]through Moses.
5 And the sons of Israel lived
among the Canaanites, the Hittites,
the Amorites, the Perizzites, the Hivites, and the Jebusites;
6 and [a]they took their daughters
for themselves as wives, and gave
their own daughters to their sons,
and served their gods.
7 And the sons of Israel did [a]what
was evil in the sight of the LORD, and
[b]forgot the LORD their God, and
[c]served the Baals and the [1]Ashe-
roth.
8 Then the anger of the LORD was
kindled against Israel, so that He
sold them into the hands of Cushan-
rishathaim king of [1]Mesopotamia;
and the sons of Israel served Cushan-rishathaim eight years.

The First Judge Delivers Israel

9 And when the sons of Israel
cried to the LORD, the LORD raised
up a deliverer for the sons of Israel
to deliver them, [a]Othniel the son of
Kenaz, Caleb's younger brother.
10 And [a]the Spirit of the LORD
came upon him, and he judged Israel. When he went out to war, the
LORD gave Cushan-rishathaim king
of [1]Mesopotamia into his hand, so
that [2]he prevailed over Cushan-rishathaim.
11 Then the land had rest forty
years. And Othniel the son of Kenaz
died.
12 Now the sons of Israel again
[a]did evil in the sight of the LORD. So
[b]the LORD strengthened Eglon the
king of Moab against Israel, because
they had done evil in the sight of the
LORD.
13 And he gathered to himself the
sons of Ammon and Amalek; and he
went and [1]defeated Israel, and they
possessed [a]the city of the palm
trees.
14 And the sons of Israel served
Eglon the king of Moab eighteen
years.

Ehud Delivers from Moab

15 But when the sons of Israel
cried to the LORD, the LORD raised
up a deliverer for them, Ehud the
son of Gera, the Benjamite, a left-
handed man. And the sons of Israel
sent tribute by [1]him to Eglon the
king of Moab.
16 And Ehud made himself a
sword which had two edges, a cubit

16 [1]Lit., *and they* [a]Ps. 106:43-45
17 [a]Judg. 2:7
20 [a]Judg. 2:14
21 [a]Josh. 23:4, 5, 13
22 [1]Lit., *kept*
1 [1]Lit., *known* [a]Judg. 1:1
2 [1]Lit., *know, to teach them* [2]Lit., *only* [3]Lit., *known*
3 [1]Or, *the entrance of Hamath* [a]Josh. 9:3, 7; 11:19
4 [1]Lit., *testing by them* [2]Lit., *hear* [3]Lit., *by the hand of* [a]Deut. 8:2
6 [a]Ex. 34:15, 16; Deut. 7:3, 4; Josh. 23:12
7 [1]I.e., wooden symbol of a female deity [a]Judg. 2:11 [b]Deut. 4:9 [c]Judg. 2:13
8 [1]Heb., *Aram-naharaim*
9 [a]Judg. 1:13
10 [1]Heb., *Aram* [2]Lit., *his hand was strong* [a]Num. 11:25-29; 24:2
12 [a]Judg. 2:11 [b]Judg. 2:14
13 [1]Lit., *smote* [a]Deut. 34:3; Judg. 1:16
15 [1]Lit., *his hand*

in length; and he bound it on his right thigh under his cloak.

17 And he presented the tribute to Eglon king of Moab. Now Eglon was a very fat man.

18 And it came about when he had finished presenting the tribute, that he sent away the people who had carried the tribute.

19 But he himself turned back from the idols which were at Gilgal, and said, "I have a secret message for you, O king." And he said, "Keep silence." And all who attended him left him.

20 And Ehud came to him while he was sitting alone in his cool roof chamber. And Ehud said, "I have a message from God for you." And he arose from his seat.

21 And Ehud stretched out his left hand, took the sword from his right thigh and thrust it into his belly.

22 The handle also went in after the blade, and the fat closed over the blade, for he did not draw the sword out of his belly; and the refuse came out.

23 Then Ehud went out into the vestibule and shut the doors of the roof chamber behind him, and locked *them*.

24 When he had gone out, his servants came and looked, and behold, the doors of the roof chamber were locked; and they said, "[a]He is only [1]relieving himself in the cool room."

25 And they waited [a]until they [1]became anxious; but behold, he did not open the doors of the roof chamber. Therefore they took the key and opened them, and behold, their master had fallen to the [2]floor dead.

26 Now Ehud escaped while they were delaying, and he passed by the idols and escaped to Seirah.

27 And it came about when he had arrived, that he blew the horn in the hill country of Ephraim; and the sons of Israel went down with him from the hill country, and he *was* in front of them.

28 And he said to them, "Pursue *them*, for the LORD has given your enemies the Moabites into your hands." So they went down after him and seized [a]the fords of the Jordan opposite Moab, and did not allow anyone to cross.

29 And they struck down at that time about ten thousand Moabites, all robust and valiant men; and no one escaped.

30 So Moab was subdued that day under the hand of Israel. And the land was undisturbed for eighty years.

Shamgar Delivers from Philistines

31 And after him came [a]Shamgar the son of Anath, who struck down six hundred Philistines with an oxgoad; and he also saved Israel.

CHAPTER 4

Deborah and Barak Deliver from Canaanites

THEN the sons of Israel again did evil in the sight of the LORD, after Ehud died.

2 And the LORD sold them into the hand of [a]Jabin king of Canaan, who reigned in Hazor; and the commander of his army was Sisera, who lived in [b]Harosheth-hagoyim.

3 And the sons of Israel cried to the LORD; for he had [a]nine hundred iron chariots, and he oppressed the sons of Israel severely for twenty years.

4 Now Deborah, a [1]prophetess, the wife of Lappidoth, was judging Israel at that time.

5 And she used to [1]sit under the palm tree of Deborah between Ramah and Bethel in the hill country of Ephraim; and the sons of Israel came up to her for judgment.

6 Now she sent and summoned [a]Barak the son of Abinoam from Kedesh-naphtali, and said to him, "[1]Behold, the LORD, the God of Israel, has commanded, 'Go and march to Mount Tabor, and take with you ten thousand men from the sons of Naphtali and from the sons of Zebulun.

7 'And I will draw out to you Sisera, the commander of Jabin's army, with his chariots and his [1]many *troops* to the river Kishon; and [a]I will give him into your hand.' "

8 Then Barak said to her, "If you will go with me, then I will go; but if you will not go with me, I will not go."

9 And she said, "I will surely go with you; nevertheless, the honor shall not be yours on the journey that you are about to take, [a]for the LORD will sell Sisera into the hands of a woman." Then Deborah arose and went with Barak to Kedesh.

10 And Barak called [a]Zebulun and Naphtali together to Kedesh, and ten thousand men went up [1b]with him; Deborah also went up with him.

11 Now Heber [a]the Kenite had separated himself from the Kenites, from the sons of Hobab the father-in-law of Moses, and had pitched his

24 [1]Lit., *covering his feet* [a]1 Sam. 24:3

25 [1]Lit., *were ashamed* [2]Lit., *earth* [a]2 Kin. 2:17; 8:11

28 [a]Judg. 7:24; 12:5

31 [a]Judg. 5:6

2 [a]Josh. 11:1, 10 [b]Judg. 4:13, 16

3 [a]Judg. 1:19

4 [1]Lit., *woman prophetess*

5 [1]Or, *live*

6 [1]Or, *"Has not . . . commanded . . . ?* [a]Heb. 11:32

7 [1]Lit., *multitude* [a]Ps. 83:9

9 [a]Judg. 4:21

10 [1]Lit., *at his feet* [a]Judg. 5:18 [b]Judg. 4:14; 5:15; 8:5

11 [a]Judg. 1:16

tent as far away as the [1]oak in [b]Zaanannim, which is near Kedesh.

12 Then they told Sisera that Barak the son of Abinoam had gone up to Mount Tabor.

13 And Sisera called together all his chariots, [a]nine hundred iron chariots, and all the people who *were* with him, from [b]Harosheth-hagoyim to the river Kishon.

14 And Deborah said to Barak, "Arise! For this is the day in which the LORD has given Sisera into your hands; [1]behold, the LORD has gone out before you." So Barak went down from Mount Tabor with ten thousand men following him.

15 [a]And the LORD [1]routed Sisera and all *his* chariots and all *his* army, with the edge of the sword before Barak; and Sisera alighted from *his* chariot and fled away on foot.

16 But Barak pursued the chariots and the army as far as Harosheth-hagoyim, and all the army of Sisera fell by the edge of the sword; [a]not even one was left.

17 Now Sisera fled away on foot to the tent of Jael the wife of Heber the Kenite, for *there was* peace between Jabin the king of Hazor and the house of Heber the Kenite.

18 And Jael went out to meet Sisera, and said to him, "Turn aside, my master, turn aside to me! Do not be afraid." And he turned aside to her into the tent, and she covered him with a [1]rug.

19 [a]And he said to her, "Please give me a little water to drink, for I am thirsty." So she opened a [1]bottle of milk and gave him a drink; then she covered him.

20 And he said to her, "Stand in the doorway of the tent, and it shall be if anyone comes and inquires of you, and says, 'Is there anyone here?' that you shall say, 'No.' "

21 But Jael, Heber's wife, took a tent peg and [1]seized a hammer in her hand, and went secretly to him and drove the peg into his temple, and it went through into the ground; for he was sound asleep and exhausted. So he died.

22 And behold, as Barak pursued Sisera, Jael came out to meet him and said to him, "Come, and I will show you the man whom you are seeking." And he entered [1]with her, and behold Sisera was lying dead with the tent peg in his temple.

23 So God subdued on that day Jabin the king of Canaan before the sons of Israel.

24 And the hand of the sons of Israel pressed heavier and heavier upon Jabin the king of Canaan, until they had [1]destroyed Jabin the king of Canaan.

CHAPTER 5

The Song of Deborah and Barak

[a]THEN Deborah and Barak the son of Abinoam sang on that day, saying,

2 "[a]That [1]the leaders led in Israel,
That [b]the people volunteered,
Bless the LORD!
3 "Hear, O kings; give ear, O rulers!
[a]I—to the LORD, I will sing,
I will sing praise to the LORD, the God of Israel.
4 "[a]LORD, when Thou didst go out from Seir,
When Thou didst march from the field of Edom,
[b]The earth quaked, the heavens also dripped,
Even the clouds dripped water.
5 "[a]The mountains [1]quaked at the presence of the LORD,
[b]This Sinai, at the presence of the LORD, the God of Israel.

6 "In the days of [a]Shamgar the son of Anath,
In the days of [b]Jael, the highways [1]were deserted,
And travelers [2]went by [3]roundabout ways.
7 "The peasantry ceased, they ceased in Israel,
Until I, Deborah, arose,
Until I arose, a mother in Israel.
8 "[a]New gods were chosen;
[b]Then war *was* in the gates.
Not a shield or a spear was seen
Among forty thousand in Israel.
9 "My heart *goes out* to [a]the commanders of Israel,
The volunteers among the people;
Bless the LORD!
10 "[a]You who ride on [1]white donkeys,
You who sit on *rich* carpets,
And you who travel on the road—[2]sing!
11 "At the sound of those who divide *flocks* among [a]the watering places,
There they shall recount [b]the righteous deeds of the LORD,
The righteous deeds for His [1]*peasantry* in Israel.
Then the people of the LORD went down [c]to the gates.

11 [1]Or, *terebinth* [b]Josh. 19:33
13 [a]Judg. 4:3 [b]Judg. 4:2
14 [1]Or, *has not the LORD gone...?*
15 [1]Lit., *confused* [a]Deut. 7:23; Josh. 10:10
16 [a]Ex. 14:28; Ps. 83:9
18 [1]Or, *blanket*
19 [1]I.e., skin container [a]Judg. 5:24-27
21 [1]Lit., *placed*
22 [1]Lit., *to*
24 [1]Lit., *cut off*
1 [a]Ex. 15:1
2 [1]Or, *locks hung loose in* [a]Judg. 5:9 [b]Ps. 110:3
3 [a]Ps. 27:6
4 [a]Deut. 33:2; Ps. 68:7; Hab. 3:3 [b]Ps. 68:8, 9
5 [1]Lit., *flowed* [a]Ex. 19:18 [b]Ps. 68:8
6 [1]Lit., *had ceased* [2]Lit., *walked* [3]Lit., *twisted* [a]Judg. 3:31 [b]Judg. 4:17
8 [a]Deut. 32:17 [b]Judg. 5:11
9 [a]Judg. 5:2
10 [1]Or, *tawny* [2]Or, *declare it* [a]Judg. 10:4; 12:14
11 [1]Or, *rural dwellers* [a]Gen. 24:11; 29:2, 3 [b]1 Sam. 12:7; Mic. 6:5 [c]Judg. 5:8

12 "[a]Awake, awake, Deborah;
Awake, awake, [1]sing a song!
Arise, Barak, and [b]take away
your captives, O son of Abinoam.
13 "Then survivors came down to
the nobles;
The people of [a]the LORD came
down to me as warriors.
14 "From Ephraim those whose
root is [a]in Amalek *came
down,*
Following you, Benjamin,
with your peoples;
From Machir commanders
came down,
And from Zebulun those who
wield the staff of [1]office.
15 "And the [1]princes of Issachar
were with Deborah;
As *was* Issachar, so *was* Barak;
Into the valley they rushed [a]at
his [2]heels;
[b]Among the divisions of Reuben
There were great resolves of
heart.
16 "Why did you sit among [a]the
[1]sheepfolds,
To hear the piping for the
flocks?
Among the divisions of Reuben
There were great searchings of
heart.
17 "[a]Gilead [1]remained across the
Jordan;
And why did Dan stay in
ships?
Asher sat at the seashore,
And [1]remained by its landings.
18 "[a]Zebulun *was* a people who
despised their lives *even* to
death,
And Naphtali also, on the high
places of the field.

19 "[a]The kings came *and* fought;
Then fought the kings of Canaan
[b]At Taanach near the waters
of Megiddo;
[c]They took no plunder in silver.
20 "[a]The stars fought from
heaven,
From their courses they
fought against Sisera.
21 "The torrent of Kishon swept
them away,
The ancient torrent, the torrent Kishon.
[a]O my soul, march on with
strength.

22 "[a]Then the horses' hoofs beat
From the dashing, the dashing
of his [1]valiant steeds.
23 'Curse Meroz,' said the angel
of the LORD,
'Utterly curse its inhabitants;
[a]Because they did not come to
the help of the LORD,
To the help of the LORD
against the warriors.'

24 "[a]Most blessed of women is
Jael,
The wife of Heber the Kenite;
Most blessed is she of women
in the tent.
25 "He asked for water *and* she
gave him milk;
In a magnificent bowl she
brought him curds.
26 "She reached out her hand for
the tent peg,
And her right hand for the
workmen's hammer.
Then she struck Sisera, she
smashed his head;
And she shattered and pierced
his temple.
27 "Between her feet he bowed, he
fell, he lay;
Between her feet he bowed, he
fell;
Where he bowed, there he fell
[1]dead.

28 "[a]Out of the window she looked
and lamented,
The mother of Sisera through
the [1]lattice,
'Why does his chariot delay in
coming?
Why do the [2]hoofbeats of his
chariots tarry?'
29 "Her wise princesses would answer her,
Indeed she repeats her words
to herself,
30 '[a]Are they not finding, are they
not dividing the spoil?
A maiden, two maidens for every warrior;
To Sisera a spoil of dyed work,
A spoil of dyed work embroidered,
Dyed work of double embroi-
dery on the [1]neck of the
spoiler?'
31 "[a]Thus let all Thine enemies
perish, O LORD;
[b]But let those who love Him be
like the rising of the sun in its
might."
And the land was undisturbed for
forty years.

12 [1]Or, *utter* [a]Ps. 57:8 [b]Ps. 68:18; Eph. 4:8
13 [a]Judg. 5:23; Ps. 18:9
14 [1]Lit., *the scribe* [a]Judg. 12:15
15 [1]So with ancient versions, Heb., *My princes* [2]Lit., *feet* [a]Judg. 5:10 [b]Is. 15:6-9
16 [1]Or, *saddlebags* [a]Num. 32:1, 2, 24, 36
17 [1]Or, *dwelt* [a]Josh. 22:9
18 [a]Judg. 4:6, 10
19 [a]Josh. 11:1, 2; Judg. 4:13 [b]Judg. 1:27 [c]Judg. 5:30
20 [a]Josh. 10:12-14
21 [a]Ex. 15:2; Ps. 44:5
22 [1]Lit., *mighty ones* [a]Job 39:19-25
23 [a]Judg. 5:13
24 [a]Judg. 4:19-21
27 [1]Lit., *devastated*
28 [1]Or, *window* [2]Lit., *steps* [a]Prov. 7:6
30 [1]Lit., *necks of the spoil* [a]Ex. 15:9
31 [a]Ps. 68:2; 92:9 [b]Ps. 19:4-6; 89:36, 37

Chapter 6

Israel Oppressed by Midian

THEN the sons of Israel [a]did what was evil in the sight of the LORD; and the LORD gave them into the hands of [b]Midian seven years.

2 And the [1]power of Midian prevailed against Israel. Because of Midian the sons of Israel made for themselves the dens which were in the mountains and the caves and the strongholds.

3 For it was when Israel had sown, that the Midianites would come up with the Amalekites and the sons of the east and [1]go against them.

4 So they would camp against them and [a]destroy the produce of the earth [1]as far as Gaza, and [b]leave no sustenance in Israel as well as no sheep, ox, or donkey.

5 For they would come up with their livestock and their tents, they would come in [a]like locusts for number, both they and their camels were innumerable; and they came into the land to devastate it.

6 So Israel was brought [a]very low because of Midian, and the sons of Israel cried to the LORD.

7 Now it came about when the sons of Israel cried to the LORD on account of Midian,

8 that the LORD sent a prophet to the sons of Israel, and [a]he said to them, "Thus says the LORD, the God of Israel, 'It was I who brought you up from Egypt, and brought you out from the house of [1]slavery.

9 'And I delivered you from the hands of the Egyptians and from the hands of all your oppressors, and dispossessed them before you and gave you their land,

10 and I said to you, "I am the LORD your God; you shall not fear the gods of the Amorites in whose land you live. But you have not [1]obeyed Me." ' "

Gideon Is Visited

11 Then [a]the angel of the LORD came and sat under the [1]oak that was in Ophrah, which belonged to Joash the [b]Abiezrite as his son [c]Gideon was beating out wheat in the wine press in order to save *it* from the Midianites.

12 And the angel of the LORD appeared to him and said to him, "The LORD is with you, O valiant warrior."

13 Then Gideon said to him, "Oh my lord, if the LORD is with us, why then has all this happened to us? And where are all His miracles which our fathers told us about, saying, 'Did not the LORD bring us up from Egypt?' But [a]now the LORD has abandoned us and given us into the hand of Midian."

14 And the LORD [1]looked at him and said, "Go in this your strength and deliver Israel from the hand of Midian. Have I not sent you?"

15 [a]And he said to Him, "O Lord, [1]how shall I deliver Israel? Behold, my family is the least in [b]Manasseh, and I am the youngest in my father's house."

16 [a]But the LORD said to him, "Surely I will be with you, and you shall [1]defeat Midian as one man."

17 So [1]Gideon said to Him, "If now I have found favor in Thy sight, then show me [a]a sign that it is Thou who speakest with me.

18 "Please do not depart from here, until I come *back* to Thee, and bring out my offering and lay it before Thee." And He said, "I will remain until you return."

19 Then Gideon went in and [a]prepared a kid and unleavened bread from an [1]ephah of flour; he put the meat in a basket [2]and the broth in a pot, and brought *them* out to him under the [3]oak, and presented *them*.

20 And the angel of God said to him, "Take the meat and the unleavened bread and lay them on this rock, and pour out the broth." And he did so.

21 Then the angel of the LORD put out the end of the staff that was in his hand and touched the meat and the unleavened bread; and [a]fire sprang up from the rock and consumed the meat and the unleavened bread. Then the angel of the LORD [1]vanished from his sight.

22 [a]When Gideon saw that he was the angel of the LORD, [1]he said, "Alas, O Lord [2]GOD! For now I have seen the angel of the LORD face to face."

23 And the LORD said to him, "Peace to you, do not fear; you shall not die."

24 Then Gideon built an altar there to the LORD and named it [1]The LORD is Peace. To this day it is still in Ophrah of the Abiezrites.

25 Now the same night it came about that the LORD said to him, "Take your father's bull [1]and a second bull seven years old, and pull down the altar of Baal which belongs to your father, and cut down the [2a]Asherah that is beside it;

26 and build an altar to the LORD your God on the top of this strong-

1 [a]Judg. 2:11 [b]Num. 22:4; 25:15-18; 31:1-3
2 [1]Lit., *hand*
3 [1]Lit., *go up*
4 [1]Lit., *until your coming* [a]Lev. 26:16 [b]Deut. 28:31
5 [a]Judg. 7:12; 8:10
6 [a]Deut. 28:43
8 [1]Lit., *slaves* [a]Judg. 2:1, 2
10 [1]Lit., *listened to my voice*
11 [1]Or, *terebinth* [a]Judg. 2:1; 6:14; 13:3 [b]Josh. 17:2; Judg. 6:15 [c]Heb. 11:32
13 [a]Judg. 6:1; Ps. 44:9
14 [1]Or, *turned toward*
15 [1]Lit., *with what* [a]Ex. 3:11 [b]Judg. 6:11
16 [1]Lit., *smite* [a]Ex. 3:12; Josh. 1:5
17 [1]Lit., *he* [a]Josh. 6:37; Is. 38:7, 8
19 [1]I.e., approx. one bushel [2]Lit., *and he put* [3]Or, *terebinth* [a]Gen. 10:6-8
21 [1]Or, departed [a]Lev. 9:24
22 [1]Lit., *Gideon* [2]YHWH, usually rendered LORD [a]Gen. 32:30; Ex. 33:20; Judg. 13:21, 22
24 [1]Heb., *Yahweh-shalom*
25 [1]Or, *even* [2]I.e., wooden symbol of a female deity. Also vs. 26, 28, 30 [a]Ex. 34:13

hold in an orderly manner, and take
a second bull and offer a burnt offering with the wood of the Asherah
which you shall cut down."
27 Then Gideon took ten men of
his servants and did as the LORD had
spoken to him; and it came about,
because he was too afraid of his father's household and the men of the
city to do it by day, that he did it by
night.

The Altar of Baal Destroyed

28 When the men of the city arose
early in the morning, behold, the altar of Baal was torn down, and the
Asherah which was beside it was
cut down, and the second bull was
offered on the altar which had been
built.
29 And they said to one another,
"Who did this thing?" And when
they searched about and inquired,
they said, "Gideon the son of Joash
did this thing."
30 Then the men of the city said to
Joash, "Bring out your son, that he
may die, for he has torn down the
altar of Baal, and indeed, he has cut
down the Asherah which was beside
it."
31 But Joash said to all who stood
against him, "Will you contend for
Baal, or will you deliver him? Whoever will [1]plead for him shall be put
to death by morning. If he is a god,
let him contend for himself, because
someone has torn down his altar."
32 Therefore on that day he named
him [a]Jerubbaal, that is to say, "Let
Baal contend against him," because
he had torn down his altar.
33 Then all the Midianites and the
Amalekites and the sons of the east
assembled themselves; and they
crossed over and camped in [a]the
valley of Jezreel.
34 So [a]the Spirit of the LORD
[1]came upon Gideon; and he [b]blew a
trumpet, and the Abiezerites were
called together to follow him.
35 And he sent messengers
throughout Manasseh, and they also
were called together to follow him;
and he sent messengers to Asher,
[a]Zebulun, and Naphtali, and [b]they
came up to meet them.

Sign of the Fleece

36 Then Gideon said to God, "[a]If
Thou wilt deliver Israel [1]through
me, as Thou hast spoken,
37 behold, I will put a fleece of
wool on the threshing floor. If there
is dew on the fleece only, and it is
dry on all the ground, then I will
know that Thou wilt deliver Israel
[1]through me, as Thou hast spoken."
38 And it was so. When he arose
early the next morning and
squeezed the fleece, he drained the
dew from the fleece, a bowl full of
water.
39 Then Gideon said to God, "[a]Do
not let Thine anger burn against me
that I may speak once more; please
let me make a test once more with
the fleece, let it now be dry only on
the fleece, and let there be dew on
all the ground."
40 And God did so that night; for it
was dry only on the fleece, and dew
was on all the ground.

CHAPTER 7

Gideon's 300 Chosen Men

THEN [a]Jerubbaal (that is, Gideon)
and all the people who were with
him, rose early and camped beside
[1]the spring [b]of Harod; and the camp
of Midian was on the north side of
[2]them by the hill of [c]Moreh in the
valley.
2 And the LORD said to Gideon,
"The people who are with you are
too many for Me to give Midian into
their hands, [a]lest Israel [1]become
boastful, saying, 'My own [2]power
has delivered me.'
3 "Now therefore [1]come, proclaim
in the hearing of the people, saying,
'[a]Whoever is afraid and trembling,
let him return and depart from
Mount Gilead.'" So 22,000 people
returned, but 10,000 remained.
4 [a]Then the LORD said to Gideon,
"The people are still too many; bring
them down to the water and I will
test them for you there. Therefore it
shall be that he of whom I say to
you, 'This one shall go with you,' he
shall go with you; but everyone of
whom I say to you, 'This one shall
not go with you,' he shall not go."
5 So he brought the people down
to the water. And the LORD said to
Gideon, "You shall separate everyone who laps the water with his
tongue, as a dog laps, as well as everyone who kneels to drink."
6 Now the number of those who
lapped, putting their hand to their
mouth, was 300 men; but all the rest
of the people kneeled to drink water.
7 And the LORD said to Gideon, "I
will deliver you with the 300 men
who lapped and will give the Midianites into your hands; so let all the
other people go, each man to his
[1]home."

31 [1]Or, *contend*
32 [a]Judg. 7:1
33 [a]Josh. 17:16
34 [1]Lit., *clothed* [a]Judg. 3:10 [b]Judg. 3:27
35 [a]Judg. 4:6, 10; 5:18 [b]Judg. 7:3
36 [1]Lit., *by my hand* [a]Judg. 6:14, 16, 17
37 [1]Lit., *by my hand*
39 [a]Gen. 18:32
1 [1]Or, *En-Harod* [2]Lit., *him* [a]Judg. 6:32 [b]Judg. 7:3 [c]Gen. 12:6; Deut. 11:30
2 [1]Lit., *glorify itself against me* [2]Lit., *hand* [a]Deut. 8:17, 18
3 [1]Or, *please* [a]Deut. 20:8
4 [a]1 Sam. 14:6
7 [1]Lit., *place*

8 So [1]the 300 men took the people's provisions and their trumpets
into their hands. And [2]Gideon sent
all the *other* men of Israel, each to
his tent, but retained the 300 men;
and the camp of Midian was below
him in the valley.
9 Now the same night it came
about that the LORD said to him,
"Arise, go down against the camp,
[a]for I have given it into your hands.
10"But if you are afraid to go
down, go with Purah your servant
down to the camp,
11 and you will hear what they
say; and [a]afterward your hands will
be strengthened that you may go
down against the camp." So he went
with Purah his servant down to the
[1]outposts of the army that was in
the camp.
12 Now the Midianites and the
Amalekites and all the sons of the
east were lying in the valley [a]as numerous as locusts; and their camels
were without number, [b]as numerous as the sand on the seashore.
13 When Gideon came, behold, a
man was relating a dream to his
friend. And he said, "Behold, I [1]had
a dream; [2]a loaf of barley bread was
tumbling into the camp of Midian,
and it came to the tent and struck it
so that it fell, and turned it [3]upside
down so that the tent lay flat."
14 And his friend answered and
said, "This is nothing less than the
sword of Gideon the son of Joash, a
man of Israel; God has given Midian
and all the camp [a]into his hand."
15 And it came about when Gideon heard the account of the dream
and its interpretation, that he
bowed in worship. He returned to
the camp of Israel and said, "Arise,
for the LORD has given the camp of
Midian into your hands."
16 And he divided the 300 men
into three [1]companies, and he put
trumpets and empty pitchers into
the hands of all of them, with
torches inside the pitchers.
17 And he said to them, "Look at
me, and do likewise. And behold,
when I come to the outskirts of the
camp, [1]do as I do.
18"When I and all who are with me
blow the trumpet, then you also
blow the trumpets all around the
camp, and say, 'For the LORD and
for Gideon.' "

Confusion of the Enemy

19 So Gideon and the hundred
men who were with him came to the
outskirts of the camp at the beginning of the middle watch, when they
had just posted the watch; and they
blew the trumpets and smashed the
pitchers that were in their hands.
20 When the three [1]companies
blew the trumpets and broke the
pitchers, they held the torches in
their left hands and the trumpets in
their right hands for blowing, and
cried, "A sword for the LORD and for
Gideon!"
21 And each stood in his place
around the camp; and all the [1]army
ran, crying out as they fled.
22 And when they blew 300 trumpets, the [a]LORD set the sword of one
against another even throughout
the whole [1]army; and the [1]army fled
as far as Beth-shittah toward Zere-
rah, as far as the edge of [b]Abel-me-
holah, by Tabbath.
23 And the men of Israel were
summoned from [a]Naphtali and
Asher and all Manasseh, and they
pursued Midian.
24 And Gideon sent messengers
throughout all the hill country of E-
phraim, saying, "Come down
[1]against Midian and [a]take the waters before them, as far as Beth-bar-
ah and the Jordan." So all the men
of Ephraim were summoned, and
they took the waters as far as Beth-
barah and the Jordan.
25 And [a]they captured the two
leaders of Midian, Oreb and Zeeb,
and they killed Oreb at the rock of
Oreb, and they killed Zeeb at the
wine press of Zeeb, while they pursued Midian; and they brought the
heads of Oreb and Zeeb to Gideon
[b]from across the Jordan.

CHAPTER 8

Zeba and Zalmunna Routed

THEN the men of Ephraim said to
him, "[a]What is this thing you have
done to us, not calling us when you
went to fight against Midian?" And
they contended with him vigorously.
2 But he said to them, "What
have I done now in comparison with
you? Is not the gleaning *of the
grapes* of Ephraim better than the
vintage of Abiezer?
3"God has given the leaders of
Midian, Oreb and Zeeb into your
hands; and what was I able to do in
comparison with you?" Then their
[1]anger toward him subsided when
he said [2]that.
4 Then Gideon and the 300 men
who were with him came [a]to the
Jordan *and* crossed over, weary yet
pursuing.

8 [1]Lit., *they* [2]Lit., *he*
9 [a]Josh. 2:24; 10:8; 11:6
11 [1]Lit., *extremity of the battle array* [a]Judg. 7:15
12 [a]Judg. 6:5; 8:10 [b]Josh. 11:4
13 [1]Lit., *dreamed* [2]Lit., *and behold, a loaf* [3]Lit., *upwards*
14 [a]Josh. 2:9
16 [1]Lit., *heads*
17 [1]Lit., *it shall come about that just as I do, so you shall do.*
20 [1]Lit., *heads*
21 [1]Or, *camp*
22 [1]Or, *camp* [a]1 Sam. 14:20 [b]1 Kin. 4:12; 19:16
23 [a]Judg. 6:35
24 [1]Lit., *to meet* [a]Judg. 3:28
25 [a]Ps. 83:11; Is. 10:26 [b]Judg. 8:4
1 [a]Judg. 12:1
3 [1]Lit., *spirit* [2]Lit., *this thing*
4 [a]Judg. 7:25

5 And he said to the men of [a]Succoth, "Please give loaves of bread to the people who are following me, for they are weary, and I am pursuing Zebah and Zalmunna, the kings of Midian."

6 And the leaders of Succoth said, "[1a]Are the hands of Zebah and Zalmunna already in your hands, that we should give bread to your army?"

7 And Gideon said, "[1]All right, [a]when the LORD has given Zebah and Zalmunna into my hand, then I will [2]thrash your [3]bodies with the thorns of the wilderness and with briers."

8 And he went up from there to [a]Penuel, and spoke similarly to them; and the men of Penuel answered him just as the men of Succoth had answered.

9 So he spoke also to the men of Penuel, saying, "When I return safely, [a]I will tear down this tower."

10 Now Zebah and Zalmunna were in Karkor, and their [1]armies with them, about 15,000 men, all who were left of the entire [2]army of the sons of the east; [a]for the fallen were 120,000 [3]swordsmen.

11 And Gideon went up by the way of those who lived in tents on the east of Nobah and Jogbehah, and [1]attacked the camp, when the camp was [2]unsuspecting.

12 When Zebah and Zalmunna fled, he pursued them and captured the two kings of Midian, Zebah and Zalmunna, and routed the whole [1]army.

13 Then Gideon the son of Joash returned from the battle [1]by the ascent of Heres.

14 And he captured a youth [1]from Succoth and questioned him. Then *the youth* wrote down for him the princes of Succoth and its elders, seventy-seven men.

15 And he came to the men of Succoth and said, "Behold Zebah and Zalmunna, concerning whom you taunted me, saying, '[1a]Are the hands of Zebah and Zalmunna already in your hand, that we should give bread to your men who are weary?' "

16 And he took the elders of the city, and thorns of the wilderness and briers, and he [1]disciplined the men of Succoth with them.

17 [a]And he tore down the tower of Penuel and killed the men of the city.

18 Then he said to Zebah and Zalmunna, "What kind of men *were* they whom you killed at Tabor?" And they said, "They were like you, each one [1]resembling the son of a king."

19 And he said, "They *were* my brothers, the sons of my mother. *As* the LORD lives, if only you had let them live, I would not kill you."

20 So he said to Jether his firstborn, "Rise, kill them." But the youth did not draw his sword, for he was afraid, because he was still a youth.

21 Then Zebah and Zalmunna said, "Rise up yourself, and fall on us; for as the man, so is his strength." [a]So Gideon arose and killed Zebah and Zalmunna, and [b]took the crescent ornaments which were on their camels' necks.

22 Then the men of Israel said to Gideon, "Rule over us, both you and your son, also your son's son, for you have delivered us from the hand of Midian."

23 But Gideon said to them, "I will not rule over you, nor shall my son rule over you; the LORD shall rule over you."

24 Yet Gideon said to them, "I would [1]request of you, that each of you give me [2]an earring from his spoil." (For they had gold earrings, because they were Ishmaelites.)

25 And they said, "We will surely give *them.*" So they spread out a garment, and every one of them threw an earring there from his spoil.

26 And the weight of the gold earrings that he requested was 1,700 *shekels* of gold, besides the crescent ornaments and the pendants and the purple robes which *were* on the kings of Midian, and besides the neck bands that *were* on their camels' necks.

27 And Gideon made it into [a]an ephod, and placed it in his city, Ophrah, and all Israel played the harlot with it there, so that it became a snare to Gideon and his household.

Forty Years of Peace

28 So Midian was subdued before the sons of Israel, and they did not lift up their heads any more. And the land was undisturbed for forty years in the days of Gideon.

29 Then [a]Jerubbaal the son of Joash went and lived in his own house.

30 Now Gideon had [a]seventy sons who [1]were his direct descendants, for he had many wives.

31 And his concubine who was in Shechem also bore him a son, and he [1]named him Abimelech.

5 [a]Gen. 33:17

6 [1]Lit., *Is the palm* [a]Judg. 8:15

7 [1]Lit., *For thus* [2]Or, *trample* [3]Lit., *flesh* [a]Judg. 7:15

8 [a]Gen. 32:30, 31

9 [a]Judg. 8:17

10 [1]Or, *camps* [2]Or, *camp* [3]Lit., *men who drew sword* [a]Judg. 6:5; 7:12; Ps. 83:9; Is. 9:4

11 [1]Lit., *smote* [2]Or, *secure*

12 [1]Or, *camp*

13 [1]Or, *from*

14 [1]Lit., *of the men of*

15 [1]Lit., *Is the palm* [a]Judg. 8:6

16 [1]Lit., *made the men . . . to know*

17 [a]Judg. 8:9

18 [1]Lit., *like the form of the sons*

21 [a]Ex. 28:6-35; Judg. 17:5; 18:14-20 [b]Judg. 8:26

24 [1]Lit., *request a request* [2]Or, *a nose ring*

27 [a]Ex. 28:6-35; Judg. 17:5; 18:14-20

29 [a]Judg. 7:1

30 [1]Lit., *came from his loins* [a]Judg. 9:2, 5

31 [1]Lit., *appointed his name*

32 And Gideon the son of Joash died at a ripe old age and was buried in the tomb of his father Joash, in Ophrah of the Abiezrites.

33 Then it came about, as soon as Gideon was dead, [a]that the sons of Israel again played the harlot with the Baals, and made [b]Baal-berith their god.

34 Thus the sons of Israel [a]did not remember the LORD their God, who had delivered them from the hands of all their enemies on every side;

35 nor did they show kindness to the household of Jerubbaal (*that is,* Gideon), in accord with all the good that he had done to Israel.

CHAPTER 9

Abimelech's Conspiracy

AND [a]Abimelech the son of Jerubbaal went to Shechem to his mother's [1]relatives, and spoke to them and to the whole clan of the household of his mother's father, saying,

2"Speak, now, in the hearing of all the leaders of Shechem, 'Which is better for you, that [a]seventy men, all the sons of Jerubbaal, rule over you, or that one man rule over you?' Also, remember that I am [b]your bone and your flesh."

3 And his mother's [1]relatives spoke all these words on his behalf in the hearing of all the leaders of Shechem; and [2]they were inclined to follow Abimelech, for they said, "He is our [3]relative."

4 And they gave him seventy *pieces* of silver from the house of [a]Baal-berith with which Abimelech hired worthless and reckless fellows, and they followed him.

5 Then he went to his father's house at Ophrah, and killed his brothers the sons of Jerubbaal, [a]seventy men, on one stone. But Jotham the youngest son of Jerubbaal was left, for he hid himself.

6 And all the men of Shechem and all [1]Beth-millo assembled together, and they went and made Abimelech king, by the [2]oak of the pillar which was in Shechem.

7 Now when they told Jotham, he went and stood on the top of [a]Mount Gerizim, and lifted his voice and called out. Thus he said to them, "Listen to me, O men of Shechem, that God may listen to you.

8"Once the trees went forth to anoint a king over them, and they said to the olive tree, 'Reign over us!'

9"But the olive tree said to them, 'Shall I leave my fatness with [1]which God and men are honored, and go to wave over the trees?'

10"Then the trees said to the fig tree, 'You come, reign over us!'

11"But the fig tree said to them, 'Shall I leave my sweetness and my good [1]fruit, and go to wave over the trees?'

12"Then the trees said to the vine, 'You come, reign over us!'

13"But the vine said to them, 'Shall I leave my new wine, which cheers God and men, and go to wave over the trees?'

14"Finally all the trees said to the bramble, 'You come, reign over us!'

15"And the bramble said to the trees, 'If in [1]truth you are anointing me as king over you, come and take refuge in my shade; but if not, may fire come out from the bramble and consume the cedars of Lebanon.'

16"Now therefore, if you have dealt in [1]truth and integrity in making Abimelech king, and if you have dealt well with [a]Jerubbaal and his house, and [2]have dealt with him [3]as he deserved—

17 for my father fought for you and [1]risked his life and delivered you from the hand of Midian;

18 but you have risen against my father's house today and have killed [a]his sons, seventy men, on one stone, and have made Abimelech, [b]the son of his maidservant, king over the men of Shechem, because he is your [1]relative—

19 if then you have dealt in [1]truth and integrity with Jerubbaal and his house this day, rejoice in Abimelech, and let him also rejoice in you.

20"But if not, let fire come out from Abimelech and consume the men of Shechem and [1]Beth-millo; and let fire come out from the men of Shechem and from [1]Beth-millo, and consume Abimelech."

21 Then Jotham escaped and fled, and went to Beer and remained there because of Abimelech his brother.

Shechem and Abimelech Fall

22 Now Abimelech ruled over Israel three years.

23 [a]Then God sent an evil spirit between Abimelech and the men of Shechem; and the men of Shechem dealt treacherously with Abimelech,

24 [a]in order that the violence [1]done to the seventy sons of Jerubbaal might come, and [b]their blood might be laid on Abimelech their brother, who killed them, and on the

33 [a]Judg. 2:11, 12 [b]Judg. 9:4, 27, 46
34 [a]Deut. 4:9; Judg. 3:7
1 [1]Lit., *brothers* [a]Judg. 8:31, 35
2 [a]Judg. 8:30 [b]Gen. 29:14
3 [1]Lit., *brothers* [2]Lit., *their hearts inclined after* [3]Lit., *brother*
4 [a]Judg. 8:33
5 [a]Judg. 9:2
6 [1]Or, *the house of Millo* [2]Or, *terebinth*
7 [a]Deut. 11:29, 30
9 [1]Lit., *which by me*
11 [1]Or, *produce*
15 [1]Or, *sincerity*
16 [1]Or, *sincerity* [2]Lit., *if you have* [3]Lit., *according to the dealing of his hands* [a]Judg. 8:35
17 [1]Lit., *cast his soul in front*
18 [1]Lit., *brother* [a]Judg. 9:5 [b]Judg. 8:31
19 [1]Or, *sincerity*
20 [1]Or, *the house of Millo*
23 [a]1 Sam. 16:14
24 [1]Lit., *of the seventy* [a]Deut. 27:25; Judg. 9:56, 57 [b]Num. 35:33

men of Shechem, who strengthened
his hands to kill his brothers.
25 And the men of Shechem set
[1]men in ambush against him on the
tops of the mountains, and they
robbed all who might pass by them
along the road; and it was told to
Abimelech.
26 Now Gaal the son of Ebed came
with his [1]relatives, and crossed over
into Shechem; and the men of Shechem put their trust in him.
27 And they went out into the field
and gathered *the grapes of* their
vineyards and trod *them,* and held a
[1]festival; and they went into the
house of [a]their god, and ate and
drank and cursed Abimelech.
28 Then Gaal the son of Ebed said,
"Who is Abimelech, and who is Shechem, that we should serve him? Is
he not the son of Jerubbaal, and *is*
Zebul *not* his [1]lieutenant? Serve the
men of Hamor the father of Shechem; but why should we serve
him?
29"[1][a]Would, therefore, that this
people were under my authority!
Then I would remove Abimelech."
And he said to Abimelech, "Increase your army, and come out."
30 And when Zebul the ruler of the
city heard the words of Gaal the son
of Ebed, his anger burned.
31 And he sent messengers to
Abimelech [1]deceitfully, saying, "Behold, Gaal the son of Ebed and his
[2]relatives have come to Shechem;
and behold, they are [3]stirring up the
city against you.
32"Now therefore, arise by night,
you and the people who are with
you, and lie in wait in the field.
33"And it shall come about in the
morning, as soon as the sun is up,
that you shall rise early and rush
upon the city; and behold, when he
and the people who are with him
come out against you, you shall [a]do
to them [1]whatever you can."
34 So Abimelech and all the people who *were* with him arose by
night and lay in wait against Shechem in four [1]companies.
35 Now Gaal the son of Ebed went
out and stood in the entrance of the
city gate; and Abimelech and the
people who *were* with him arose
from the ambush.
36 And when Gaal saw the people,
he said to Zebul, "[1]Look, people are
coming down from the tops of the
mountains." But Zebul said to him,
"You are seeing the shadow of the
mountains as *if they were* men."
37 And Gaal spoke again and said,
"Behold, people are coming down
from [a]the [1]highest part of the land,
and one [2]company comes by the
way of [3]the diviners' [4]oak."
38 Then Zebul said to him,
"Where is your [1]boasting now with
which you said, 'Who is Abimelech
that we should serve him?' Is this
not the people whom you despised?
Go out now and fight with them!"
39 So Gaal went out before the
leaders of Shechem and fought with
Abimelech.
40 And Abimelech chased him,
and he fled before him; and many
fell wounded up to the entrance of
the gate.
41 Then Abimelech remained at
Arumah, but Zebul drove out Gaal
and his [1]relatives so that they could
not remain in Shechem.
42 Now it came about the next
day, that the people went out to the
field, and it was told to Abimelech.
43 So he took [1]his people and divided them into three [2]companies,
and lay in wait in the field; when he
looked and [3]saw the people coming
out from the city, he arose against
them and [4]slew them.
44 Then Abimelech and the [1]com-
pany who was with him dashed forward and stood in the entrance of
the city gate; the other two [2]compa-
nies then dashed against all who
were in the field and [3]slew them.
45 And Abimelech fought against
the city all that day, and he captured
the city and killed the people who
were in it; then he razed the city and
sowed it with salt.
46 When all the leaders of the
tower of Shechem heard of *it,* they
entered the inner chamber of the
[1]temple of [a]El-berith.
47 And it was told Abimelech that
all the leaders of the tower of Shechem were gathered together.
48 So Abimelech went up to
Mount [a]Zalmon, he and all the people who *were* with him; and Abimelech took [1]an axe in his hand and
cut down a branch from the trees,
and lifted it and laid *it* on his shoulder. Then he said to the people who
were with him, "What you have
seen me do, hurry *and* do [2]like-
wise."
49 And all the people also cut
down each one his branch and followed Abimelech, and put *them* on
the inner chamber and set the inner
chamber on fire over those *inside,*
so that all the men of the tower of
Shechem also died, about a thousand men and women.
50 Then Abimelech went to The-

25 [1]Lit., *liers-in-wait for*
26 [1]Lit., *brothers*
27 [1]Lit., *rejoicing* [a]Judg. 8:33; 9:46
28 [1]Lit., *overseer*
29 [1]Lit., *And who will give this people into my hand* [a]2 Sam. 15:4
31 [1]Or, *in Tormah* [2]Lit., *brothers* [3]Lit., *besieging*
33 [1]Lit., *as your hand can find* [a]1 Sam. 10:7
34 [1]Lit., *heads*
36 [1]Lit., *Behold*
37 [1]Or, *center* [2]Lit., *head* [3]Heb., *Elommeonenim* [4]Or, *terebinth* [a]Ezek. 38:12
38 [1]Lit., *mouth*
41 [1]Lit., *brothers*
43 [1]Lit., *the* [2]Lit., *heads* [3]Lit., *behold* [4]Lit., *smote*
44 [1]Singular with Gk; Heb. plural, *heads* [2]Lit., *heads* [3]Lit., *smote*
46 [1]Lit., *house* [a]Judg. 8:33
48 [1]Lit., *the axes* [2]Lit., *like me* [a]Ps. 68:14

bez, and he camped against Thebez and captured it.

51 But there was a strong tower in the center of the city, and all the men and women with all the leaders of the city fled there and shut themselves in; and they went up on the roof of the tower.

52 So Abimelech came to the tower and fought against it, and approached the entrance of the tower to burn it with fire.

53 But [a]a certain woman threw an upper millstone on Abimelech's head, crushing his skull.

54 Then he called quickly to the young man, his armor bearer, and said to him, "Draw your sword and kill me, lest it be said of me, 'A woman slew him.' " So [1]the young man pierced him through, and he died.

55 And when the men of Israel saw that Abimelech was dead, each departed to his [1]home.

56 Thus God repaid the wickedness of Abimelech, which he had done to his father, in killing his seventy brothers.

57 Also God returned all the wickedness of the men of Shechem on their heads, and the curse of Jotham the son of Jerubbaal came [1]upon them.

Chapter 10

Oppression of Philistines and Ammonites

Now after Abimelech died, Tola the son of Puah, the son of Dodo, a man of Issachar, arose to save Israel; and he lived in Shamir in the hill country of Ephraim.

2 And he judged Israel twenty-three years. Then he died and was buried in Shamir.

3 And after him, Jair the Gileadite arose, and judged Israel twenty-two years.

4 And he had thirty sons who rode on thirty donkeys, and they had thirty cities [1]in the land of Gilead [a]that are called [2]Havvoth-jair to this day.

5 And Jair died and was buried in Kamon.

6 Then the sons of Israel again did evil in the sight of the LORD, [a]served the Baals and the Ashtaroth, the gods of [1]Syria, the gods of Sidon, the gods of Moab, [b]the gods of the sons of Ammon, and the gods of the Philistines; thus [c]they forsook the LORD and did not serve Him.

7 And the anger of the LORD burned against Israel, and He sold them into the hands of the Philistines, and into the hands of the sons of Ammon.

8 And they [1]afflicted and crushed the sons of Israel [2]that year; for eighteen years they *afflicted* all the sons of Israel who were beyond the Jordan [3]in Gilead in the land of the Amorites.

9 And the sons of Ammon crossed the Jordan to fight also against Judah, Benjamin, and the house of Ephraim, so that Israel was greatly distressed.

10 Then the sons of Israel cried out to the LORD, saying, "We have sinned against Thee, for indeed, we have forsaken our God and served the Baals."

11 And the LORD said to the sons of Israel, "*Did I* not *deliver you* from the Egyptians, the Amorites, the sons of Ammon, and the Philistines?

12 "Also when the Sidonians, the Amalekites and the Maonites oppressed you, you cried out to Me, and I delivered you from their hands.

13 "Yet you have forsaken Me and served other gods; therefore I will deliver you no more.

14 "[a]Go and cry out to the gods which you have chosen; let them deliver you in the time of your distress."

15 And the sons of Israel said to the LORD, "We have sinned, do to us whatever seems good to Thee; only please deliver us this day."

16 [a]So they put away the foreign gods from among them, and served the LORD; and [1b]He could bear the misery of Israel no longer.

17 Then the sons of Ammon were summoned, and they camped in Gilead. And the sons of Israel gathered together, and camped in [a]Mizpah.

18 And the people, the leaders of Gilead, said to one another, "Who is the man who will begin to fight against the sons of Ammon? He shall become head over all the inhabitants of Gilead."

Chapter 11

Jephthah the Ninth Judge

Now [a]Jephthah the Gileadite was a [1]valiant warrior, but he was the son of a harlot. And Gilead [2]was the father of Jephthah.

2 And Gilead's wife bore him sons; and when his wife's sons grew up, they drove Jephthah out and said to him, "You shall not have an

53 [a]2 Sam. 11:21
54 [1]Lit., *his*
55 [1]Lit., *place*
57 [1]Lit., *to*
4 [1]Lit., *which are in* [2]I.e., the towns of Jair [a]Num. 32:41
6 [1]Heb., *Aram* [a]Judg. 2:13 [b]Judg. 11:24 [c]Deut. 31:16, 17; 32:15
8 [1]Lit., *shattered* [2]Lit., *in that* [3]Lit., *which is in*
14 [a]Deut. 32:37
16 [1]Lit., *His soul was short with the misery* [a]Josh. 24:23 [b]Deut. 32:36
17 [a]Judg. 11:29
1 [1]Or, *mighty man of valor* [2]Lit., *begat* [a]Heb. 11:32

inheritance in our father's house, for
you are the son of another woman."
3 So Jephthah fled from his
brothers and lived in the land of
[a]Tob; and worthless fellows gathered themselves [1]about Jephthah,
and they went out with him.
4 And it came about after a while
that [a]the sons of Ammon fought
against Israel.
5 And it happened when the sons
of Ammon fought against Israel that
the elders of Gilead went to get
Jephthah from the land of Tob;
6 and they said to Jephthah,
"Come and be our chief that we may
fight against the sons of Ammon."
7 Then Jephthah said to the elders of Gilead, "Did you not hate me
and drive me from my father's
house? So why have you come to me
now when you are in trouble?"
8 And the elders of Gilead said to
Jephthah, "For this reason we have
now returned to you, that you may
go with us and fight with the sons of
Ammon and [a]become head over all
the inhabitants of Gilead."
9 So Jephthah said to the elders
of Gilead, "If you take me back to
fight against the sons of Ammon
and the LORD gives them up [1]to me,
will I become your head?"
10 And the elders of Gilead said to
Jephthah, "[a]The LORD is [1]witness
between us; surely we will do [2]as
you have said."
11 Then Jephthah went with the
elders of Gilead, and the people
made him head and chief over them;
and Jephthah spoke all his words
before the LORD at [a]Mizpah.
12 Now Jephthah sent messengers
to the king of the sons of Ammon,
saying, "What is between you and
me, that you have come to me to
fight against my land?"
13 And the king of the sons of Ammon said to the messengers of Jephthah, "Because Israel took away my
land when they came up from
Egypt, from the Arnon as far as the
Jabbok and the Jordan; therefore,
return them peaceably now."
14 But Jephthah sent messengers
again to the king of the sons of Ammon,
15 and they said to him, "Thus
says Jephthah, 'Israel did not take
away the land of Moab, nor the land
of the sons of Ammon.
16 'For when they came up from
Egypt, and Israel went through the
wilderness to the [1]Red Sea and
[a]came to Kadesh,
17 then Israel sent messengers to
the king of Edom, saying, "Please
let us pass through your land," but
the king of Edom would not listen.
[a]And they also sent to the king of
Moab, but he would not consent. So
Israel remained at Kadesh.
18 'Then they went through the
wilderness and [a]around the land of
Edom and the land of Moab, and
came to the east side of the land of
Moab, and they camped beyond the
Arnon; but they [b]did not enter the
territory of Moab, for the Arnon *was*
the border of Moab.
19 'And Israel sent [a]messengers to
Sihon king of the Amorites, the king
of Heshbon, and Israel said to him,
"Please let us pass through your
land to our place."
20 'But Sihon did not trust Israel to
pass through his territory; so Sihon
gathered all his people and camped
in Jahaz, and fought with Israel.
21 'And the LORD, the God of Israel, gave Sihon and all his people
into the hand of Israel, and they [1]de-
feated them; so Israel possessed all
the land of the Amorites, the inhabitants of that country.
22 '[a]So they possessed all the territory of the Amorites, from the Arnon as far as the Jabbok, and from
the wilderness as far as the Jordan.
23 'Since now the LORD, the God of
Israel, drove out the Amorites from
before His people Israel, are you
then to possess it?
24 'Do you not possess what [a]Che-
mosh your god gives you to possess? So whatever the LORD our God
has driven out before us, we will
possess it.
25 'And now are you any better
than [a]Balak the son of Zippor, king
of Moab? Did he ever strive with Israel, or did he ever fight against
them?
26 '[a]While Israel lived in Heshbon
and its villages, and in Aroer and its
villages, and in all the cities that are
on the banks of the Arnon, three
hundred years, why did you not recover them within that time?
27 'I therefore have not sinned
against you, but you are doing me
wrong by making war against me;
[a]may the LORD, the Judge, judge today between the sons of Israel and
the sons of Ammon.'"
28 But the king of the sons of Ammon [1]disregarded the message
which Jephthah sent him.

Jephthah's Tragic Vow

29 Now [a]the Spirit of the LORD
came upon Jephthah, so that he
passed through Gilead and Manas-

3 [1]Lit., *to* [a]2 Sam. 10:6, 8
4 [a]Judg. 10:9, 17
8 [a]Judg. 10:18
9 [1]Lit., *before*
10 [1]Lit., *hearer* [2]Lit., *according to your word* [a]Gen. 31:50
11 [a]Judg. 11:29
16 [1]Lit., *Sea of Reeds* [a]Num. 20:1, 4-21
17 [a]Josh. 24:9
18 [a]Num. 21:4; Deut. 2:8 [b]Deut. 2:9, 18, 19
19 [a]Num. 21:21-32; Deut. 2:26-36
21 [1]Lit., *smote*
22 [a]Deut. 2:37
24 [a]Num. 21:29; 1 Kin. 11:7
25 [a]Num. 22:2; Josh. 24:9; Mic. 6:5
26 [a]Num. 21:25, 26; Deut. 2:36
27 [a]Gen. 16:5; 18:25; 31:53; 1 Sam. 24:12, 15
28 [1]Lit., *did not listen to the words*
29 [a]Judg. 3:10

seh, then he passed through Mizpah of Gilead, and from Mizpah of Gilead he went on to the sons of Ammon.

30 And Jephthah made a vow to the LORD and said, "If Thou wilt indeed give the sons of Ammon into my hand,

31 then it shall be that whatever comes out of the doors of my house to meet me when I return in peace from the sons of Ammon, it shall be the LORD'S, and I will offer it up as a burnt offering."

32 So Jephthah crossed over to the sons of Ammon to fight against them; and the LORD gave them into his hand.

33 And he struck them with a very great slaughter from Aroer to the entrance of [a]Minnith, twenty cities, and as far as Abel-keramin. So the sons of Ammon were subdued before the sons of Israel.

34 When Jephthah came to his house at [a]Mizpah, behold, his daughter was coming out to meet him [b]with tambourines and with dancing. Now she was his one *and* only child; besides her he had neither son nor daughter.

35 And it came about when he saw her, that he tore his clothes and said, "Alas, my daughter! You have brought me very low, and you are among those who trouble me; for I have [1]given my word to the LORD, and [a]I cannot take *it* back."

36 So she said to him, "My father, you have [1]given your word to the LORD; do to me [2]as you have said, since the LORD has avenged you of your enemies, the sons of Ammon."

37 And she said to her father, "Let this thing be done for me; let me alone two months, that I may [1]go to the mountains and weep because of my virginity, I and my companions."

38 Then he said, "Go." So he sent her away for two months; and she left with her companions, and wept on the mountains because of her virginity.

39 And it came about at the end of two months that she returned to her father, who did to her according to the vow which he had made; and she [1]had no relations with a man. Thus it became a custom in Israel,

40 that the daughters of Israel went yearly to [1]commemorate the daughter of Jephthah the Gileadite four days in the year.

CHAPTER 12

Jephthah and His Successors

THEN the men of Ephraim were summoned, and they crossed [1]to Zaphon and [a]said to Jephthah, "Why did you cross over to fight against the sons of Ammon without calling us to go with you? We will burn your house down on you."

2 And Jephthah said to them, "I and my people were at great strife with the sons of Ammon; when I called you, you did not deliver me from their hand.

3 "And when I saw that you would not deliver *me,* I [1a]took my life in my hands and crossed over against the sons of Ammon, and the LORD gave them into my hand. Why then have you come up to me this day, to fight against me?"

4 Then Jephthah gathered all the men of Gilead and fought Ephraim; and the men of Gilead [1]defeated Ephraim, because they said, "You are fugitives of Ephraim, O Gileadites, in the midst of Ephraim *and* in the midst of Manasseh."

5 And the Gileadites [a]captured the fords of the Jordan opposite Ephraim. And it happened when *any of* the fugitives of Ephraim said, "Let me cross over," the men of Gilead would say to him, "Are you an Ephraimite?" If he said, "No,"

6 then they would say to him, "Say now 'Shibboleth.' " But he said "Sibboleth," for he could not [1]pronounce it correctly. Then they seized him and slew him at the fords of the Jordan. Thus there fell at that time 42,000 of Ephraim.

7 And Jephthah judged Israel six years. Then Jephthah the Gileadite died and was buried in *one of* the cities of Gilead.

8 Now Ibzan of Bethlehem judged Israel after him.

9 And he had thirty sons, and thirty daughters *whom* he [1]gave in marriage outside *the family,* and he brought in thirty daughters from outside for his sons. And he judged Israel seven years.

10 Then Ibzan died and was buried in Bethlehem.

11 Now Elon the Zebulunite judged Israel after him; and he judged Israel ten years.

12 Then Elon the Zebulunite died and was buried at Aijalon in the land of Zebulun.

13 Now Abdon the son of Hillel the Pirathonite judged Israel after him.

---

33 [a]Ezek. 27:15

34 [a]Judg. 10:17; 11:11 [b]Ex. 15:20; 1 Sam. 18:6; Jer. 31:4

35 [1]Lit., *opened my mouth* [a]Num. 30:2; Eccles. 5:4, 5

36 [1]Lit., *opened your mouth* [2]Lit., *according to what has proceeded from your mouth*

37 [1]Lit., *go and go down on*

39 [1]Lit., *knew no man*

40 [1]Lit., *recount:* ancient versions, *lament*

1 [1]Or, *northward* [a]Judg. 8:1

3 [1]Lit., *put my soul in my palm* [a]1 Sam. 19:5; 28:21; Job 13:14

4 [1]Lit., *smote*

5 [a]Judg. 3:28

6 [1]Lit., *speak so*

9 [1]Lit., *sent outside*

14 And he had forty sons and thirty grandsons who rode on seventy donkeys; and he judged Israel eight years.
15 Then Abdon the son of Hillel the Pirathonite died and was buried at Pirathon in the land of Ephraim, in the hill country of the Amalekites.

Chapter 13

Philistines Oppress Again

NOW the sons of Israel [a]again did evil in the sight of the LORD, so that the LORD gave them into the hands of the Philistines forty years.
2 And there was a certain man of [a]Zorah, of the family of the Danites, whose name was Manoah; and his wife was barren and had borne no *children.*
3 [a]Then the angel of the LORD appeared to the woman, and said to her, "Behold now, you are barren and have borne no *children,* but you shall conceive and give birth to a son.
4 "Now therefore, be careful not to drink wine or strong drink, nor eat any unclean thing.
5 "[a]For behold, you shall conceive and give birth to a son, and no razor shall come upon his head, for the boy shall be a [b]Nazirite to God from the womb; and he shall begin to deliver Israel from the hands of the Philistines."
6 Then the woman came and told her husband, saying, "[a]A man of God came to me and his appearance was like the appearance of the angel of God, very awesome. And I did not ask him where he *came* from, nor did he tell me his name.
7 "But he said to me, 'Behold, you shall conceive and give birth to a son, and now you shall not drink wine or strong drink nor eat any unclean thing, for the boy shall be a Nazirite to God from the womb to the day of his death.' "
8 Then Manoah entreated the LORD and said, "O Lord, please let [a]the man of God whom Thou hast sent come to us again that he may teach us what to do for the boy who is to be born."
9 And God listened to the voice of Manoah; and [a]the angel of God came again to the woman as she was sitting in the field, but Manoah her husband was not with her.
10 So the woman ran quickly and told her [1]husband, "Behold, [a]the man who [2]came the *other* day has appeared to me."
11 Then Manoah arose and followed his wife, and when he came to the man he said to him, "Are you [a]the man who spoke to the woman?" And he said, "I am."
12 And Manoah said, "Now when your words come *to pass,* what shall be the boy's mode of life and his vocation?"
13 So [a]the angel of the LORD said to Manoah, "[b]Let the woman pay attention [1]to all that I said.
14 "She should not eat anything that comes from the [a]vine nor drink wine or strong drink, nor eat any unclean thing; let her observe all that I commanded."
15 Then Manoah said to [a]the angel of the LORD, "Please let us detain you so that we may prepare a kid for you."
16 And the angel of the LORD said to Manoah, "Though you detain me, [a]I will not eat your [1]food, but if you prepare a burnt offering, *then* offer it to the LORD." For Manoah did not know that he was the angel of the LORD.
17 And Manoah said to the angel of the LORD, "[a]What is your name, so that when your words come *to pass,* we may honor you?"
18 But the angel of the LORD said to him, "Why do you ask my name, seeing it is [1a]wonderful?"
19 So [a]Manoah took the kid with the grain offering and offered it on the rock to the LORD, and He performed wonders while Manoah and his wife looked on.
20 For it came about when the flame went up from the altar toward heaven, that the angel of the LORD ascended in the flame of the altar. When Manoah and his wife saw *this,* they fell on their faces to the ground.
21 Now the angel of the LORD appeared no more to Manoah or his wife. [a]Then Manoah knew that he was the angel of the LORD.
22 So Manoah said to his wife, "[a]We shall surely die, for we have seen God."
23 But his wife said to him, "If the LORD had desired to kill us, He would not have accepted a burnt offering and a grain offering from our hands, nor would He have shown us all these things, nor would He have let us hear *things* like this at this time."
24 Then the woman gave birth to a son and named him Samson; and the child grew up and the LORD blessed him.

1 [a]Judg. 2:11
2 [a]Josh. 19:41
3 [a]Judg. 6:11, 14; 12:6, 8, 10, 11; Luke 1:11-13
5 [a]Luke 1:15 [b]Num. 6:2
6 [a]Judg. 6:11; 13:8, 10, 11
8 [a]Judg. 13:3, 7
9 [a]Judg. 13:8
10 [1]Lit., *husband, and said to him* [2]Lit., *came to me* [a]Judg. 13:9
11 [a]Judg. 13:8
13 [1]Lit., *from* [a]Judg. 13:11 [b]Judg. 13:4
14 [a]Num. 6:4
15 [a]Judg. 13:3
16 [1]Lit., *bread* [a]Judg. 6:20
17 [a]Gen. 32:29
18 [1]I.e., incomprehensible [a]Is. 9:6
19 [a]Judg. 6:20, 21
21 [a]Judg. 13:16
22 [a]Judg. 6:22

25 And [a]the Spirit of the LORD began to stir him in [1b]Mahaneh-dan, between Zorah and Eshtaol.

CHAPTER 14

Samson's Marriage

THEN Samson went down to Timnah and saw a woman in Timnah, *one* of the daughters of the Philistines.

2 So he came [1]back and told his father and [2]mother, "I saw a woman in Timnah, *one* of the daughters of the Philistines; now therefore, get her for me as a wife."

3 Then his father and his mother said to him, "Is there no woman among the daughters of your [1]relatives, or among all [2]our people, that you go to take a wife from the uncircumcised Philistines?" But Samson said to his father, "Get her for me, for she [3]looks good to me."

4 However, his father and mother did not know that it was of the LORD, [a]for He was seeking an occasion against the Philistines. Now at that time the Philistines were ruling over Israel.

5 Then Samson went down to Timnah with his father and mother, and came as far as the vineyards of Timnah; and behold, a young lion *came* roaring toward him.

6 And [a]the Spirit of the LORD [1]came upon him mightily, so that [b]he tore him as one tears a kid though he had nothing in his hand; but he did not tell his father or mother what he had done.

7 So he went down and talked to the woman; and she [1]looked good to Samson.

8 When he returned later to take her, he turned aside to look at the carcass of the lion; and behold, a swarm of bees and honey were in the body of the lion.

9 So he scraped [1]the honey into his [2]hands and went on, eating as he went. When he came to his father and mother, he gave *some* to them and they ate *it;* but he did not tell them that he had scraped the honey out of the body of the lion.

10 Then his father went down to the woman; and Samson made a feast there, for the young men customarily did this.

11 And it came about when they saw him that they brought thirty companions to be with him.

Samson's Riddle

12 Then Samson said to them, "Let me now [a]propound a riddle to you; if you will indeed tell it to me within the [b]seven days of the feast, and find it out, then I will give you thirty linen wraps and thirty changes of clothes.

13 "But if you are unable to tell me, then you shall give me thirty linen wraps and thirty changes of clothes." And they said to him, "Propound your riddle, that we may hear it."

14 So he said to them,

"Out of the eater came something to eat,
And out of the strong came something sweet."

But they could not tell the riddle in three days.

15 Then it came about on the [1]fourth day that they said to Samson's wife, "Entice your husband, that he may tell us the riddle, lest we burn you and your father's house with fire. Have you invited us to impoverish us? Is this not *so?*"

16 And Samson's wife wept before him and said, "You only hate me, and you do not love me; you have propounded a riddle to the sons of my people, and have not told *it* to me." And he said to her, "Behold, I have not told *it* to my father or mother; so should I tell you?"

17 However she wept before him seven days while their feast lasted. And it came about on the seventh day that he told her because she pressed him so hard. She then told the riddle to the sons of her people.

18 So the men of the city said to him on the seventh day before the sun went down,

"What is sweeter than honey?
And what is stronger than a lion?"

And he said to them,

"If you had not plowed with my heifer,
You would not have found out my riddle."

19 Then [a]the Spirit of the LORD [1]came upon him mightily, and he went down to Ashkelon and killed thirty of them and took their spoil, and gave the changes *of clothes* to those who told the riddle. And his anger burned, and he went up to his father's house.

20 But Samson's wife was *given* to his companion who had been his [1]friend.

25 [1]I.e., the camp of Dan [a]Judg. 3:10 [b]Judg. 18:11, 12
2 [1]Lit., *up* [2]Lit., *mother, saying,*
3 [1]Lit., *brothers* [2]Lit., *my* [3]Lit., *is right in my eyes*
4 [a]Josh. 11:20
6 [1]Lit., *rushed upon* [a]Judg. 3:10 [b]1 Sam. 17:34-36
7 [1]Lit., *was right in Samson's eyes*
9 [1]Lit., *it* [2]Lit., *palms*
12 [a]Ezek. 17:2 [b]Gen. 29:27
15 [1]So with some ancient versions. Heb., *seventh*
19 [1]Lit., *rushed upon* [a]Judg. 3:10
20 [1]Or, *best man*

Chapter 15

Samson Burns Philistine Crops

BUT after a while, in the time of wheat harvest, it came about that Samson visited his wife [a]with a young goat, and said, "I will go in to my wife in *her* room." But her father did not let him enter.

2 And her father said, "I really thought that you hated her intensely; so I gave her to your companion. Is not her younger sister [1]more beautiful than she? Please let her be yours [2]instead."

3 Samson then said to them, "This time I shall be blameless in regard to the Philistines when I do them harm."

4 And Samson went and caught three hundred foxes, and took torches, and turned *the foxes* tail to tail, and put one torch in the middle between two tails.

5 When he had set fire to the torches, he released [1]the foxes into the standing grain of the Philistines, thus burning up both the shocks and the standing grain, along with the vineyards *and* groves.

6 Then the Philistines said, "Who did this?" And they said, "Samson, the son-in-law of the Timnite, because [1]he took his wife and gave her to his companion." So the Philistines came up and [a]burned her and her father with fire.

7 And Samson said to them, "Since you act like this, I will surely take revenge on you, but after that I will quit."

8 And he struck them [1]ruthlessly with a great slaughter; and he went down and lived in the cleft of the rock of Etam.

9 Then the Philistines went up and camped in Judah, and spread out in Lehi.

10 And the men of Judah said, "Why have you come up against us?" And they said, "We have come up to bind Samson in order to do to him as he did to us."

11 Then 3,000 men of Judah went down to the cleft of the rock of Etam and said to Samson, "Do you not know [a]that the Philistines are rulers over us? What then is this that you have done to us?" And he said to them, "As they did to me, so I have done to them."

12 And they said to him, "We have come down to bind you so that we may give you into the hands of the Philistines." And Samson said to them, "Swear to me that you will not [1]kill me."

13 So they said to [1]him, "No, but we will bind you fast and give you into their hands; yet surely we will not kill you." Then they bound him with two new ropes and brought him up from the rock.

14 When he came to Lehi, the Philistines shouted as they met him. And [a]the Spirit of the LORD [1]came upon him mightily so that the ropes that were on his arms were as flax that is burned with fire, and his bonds [2]dropped from his hands.

15 And he found a fresh jawbone of a donkey, so he [1]reached out and took it and [2]killed a thousand men with it.

16 Then Samson said,

"With the jawbone of a donkey,
[1]Heaps upon heaps,
With the jawbone of a donkey
I have [2]killed a thousand men."

17 And it came about when he had finished speaking, that he threw the jawbone from his hand; and he named that place [1]Ramath-lehi.

18 Then he became very thirsty, and he [a]called to the LORD and said, "Thou hast given this great deliverance by the hand of Thy servant, and now [1]shall I die of thirst [2]and fall into the hands of the uncircumcised?"

19 But God split the hollow place that is in Lehi so that water came out of it. When he drank, his [1]strength returned and he revived. Therefore, he named it [2]En-hakkore, which is in Lehi to this day.

20 So [a]he judged Israel twenty years in [b]the days of the Philistines.

Chapter 16

Samson's Weakness

NOW Samson went to [a]Gaza and saw a harlot there, and went in to her.

2 *When it was told* to the Gazites, saying, "Samson has come here," they surrounded *the place* and lay in wait for him all night at the gate of the city. And they kept silent all night, saying, "*Let us wait* until the morning light, then we will kill him."

3 Now Samson lay until midnight, and at midnight he arose and took hold of the doors of the city gate and the two posts and pulled them up along with the bars; then he put them on his shoulders and car-

1 [a]Gen. 38:17
2 [1]Lit., *better* [2]Lit., *instead of her*
5 [1]Lit., *them*
6 [1]I.e., the Timnite [a]Judg. 14:15
8 [1]Lit., *leg on thigh*
11 [a]Judg. 13:1; 14:4
12 [1]Lit., *fall upon me yourselves*
13 [1]Lit., *him, saying*
14 [1]Lit., *rushed upon* [2]Lit., *were melted* [a]Judg. 14:19; 1 Sam. 11:6
15 [1]Lit., *stretched out his hand* [2]Lit., *smote*
16 [1]Lit., *Heap, two heaps;* Heb. is same root as donkey [2]Lit., *smitten*
17 [1]I.e., The high place of the jawbone
18 [1]Or, *I shall . . . circumcised* [2]Or, *or* [a]Judg. 16:28
19 [1]Lit., *spirit* [2]I.e., the spring of him who called
20 [a]Heb. 11:32 [b]Judg. 13:1; 16:31
1 [a]Josh. 15:47

ried them up to the top of the mountain which is opposite Hebron.

4 After this it came about that he loved a woman in the valley of Sorek, whose name was Delilah.

5 And the [a]lords of the Philistines came up to her, and said to her, "[b]Entice him, and see where his great strength *lies* and [1]how we may overpower him that we may bind him to afflict him. Then we will each give you eleven hundred *pieces* of silver."

6 So Delilah said to Samson, "Please tell me where your great strength is and [1]how you may be bound to afflict you."

7 And Samson said to her, "If they bind me with seven fresh cords that have not been dried, then I shall become weak and be like any *other* man."

8 Then the lords of the Philistines brought up to her seven fresh cords that had not been dried, and she bound him with them.

9 Now she had *men* lying in wait in an inner room. And she said to him, "The Philistines are upon you, Samson!" But he snapped the cords as a string of tow snaps when it [1]touches fire. So his strength was not discovered.

10 Then Delilah said to Samson, "Behold, you have deceived me and told me lies; now please tell me, [1]how you may be bound."

11 And he said to her, "If they bind me tightly with new ropes [1]which have not been used, then I shall become weak and be like any *other* man."

12 So Delilah took new ropes and bound him with them and said to him, "The Philistines are upon you, Samson!" For the *men* were lying in wait in the inner room. But he snapped [1]the ropes from his arms like a thread.

13 Then Delilah said to Samson, "Up to now you have deceived me and told me lies; tell me [1]how you may be bound." And he said to her, "If you weave the seven locks of my [2]hair with the web [3][and fasten it with a pin, then I shall become weak and be like any other man."

14 So while he slept, Delilah took the seven locks of his [1]hair and wove them into the web.] And she fastened *it* with the pin, and said to him, "The Philistines are upon you, Samson!" But he awoke from his sleep and pulled out the pin of the loom and the web.

15 Then she said to him, "[a]How can you say, 'I love you,' when your heart is not with me? You have deceived me these three times and have not told me where your great strength is."

16 And it came about when she pressed him daily with her words and urged him, that his soul was [1]annoyed to death.

17 So he told her all *that was* in his heart and said to her, "A razor has never come on my head, for I have been a [a]Nazirite to God from my mother's womb. If I am shaved, then my strength will leave me and I shall become weak and be like any *other* man."

Delilah Extracts His Secret

18 When Delilah saw that he had told her all *that was* in his heart, she sent and called the lords of the Philistines, saying, "Come up once more, for he has told me all *that is* in his heart." Then the lords of the Philistines came up to her, and brought the money in their hands.

19 And she made him sleep on her knees, and called for a man and had him shave off the seven locks of his [1]hair. Then she began to afflict him, and his strength left him.

20 And she said, "The Philistines are upon you, Samson!" And he awoke from his sleep and said, "I will go out as at other times and shake myself free." But he did not know that the LORD had departed from him.

21 Then the Philistines seized him and gouged out his eyes; and they brought him down to Gaza and bound him with bronze chains, and he was a grinder in the prison.

22 However, the hair of his head began to grow again after it was shaved off.

23 Now the lords of the Philistines assembled to offer a great sacrifice to [a]Dagon their god, and to rejoice, for they said,

"Our god has given Samson our
enemy into our hands."

24 When the people saw him, they praised their god, for they said,

"Our god has given our enemy
into our hands,
Even the destroyer of our
country,
Who has slain many of us."

25 It so happened when [1]they were in high spirits, that they said, "Call for Samson, that he may amuse us." So they called for Samson from the prison, and he [2]entertained them. And they made him stand between the pillars.

26 Then Samson said to the boy

5 [1]Lit., *by what* [a]Josh. 13:3 [b]Judg. 14:15
6 [1]Lit., *by what*
9 [1]Lit., *smells*
10 [1]Lit., *by what*
11 [1]Lit., *with which work has not been done*
12 [1]Lit., *them*
13 [1]Lit., *by what* [2]Lit., *head* [3]The passage in brackets is found in Gk. but not in any Heb. mss.
14 [1]Lit., *head*
15 [a]Judg. 14:16
16 [1]Lit., *impatient to the point of*
17 [a]Num. 6:5; Judg. 13:5
19 [1]Lit., *head*
23 [a]1 Sam. 5:2
25 [1]Lit., *their heart was pleasant* [2]Lit., *made sport before them*

who was holding his hand, "Let me feel the pillars on which the house rests, that I may lean against them."

27 Now the house was full of men and women, and all the lords of the Philistines were there. And about 3,000 men and women were on the roof looking on while Samson was amusing *them.*

Samson Is Avenged

28 [a]Then Samson called to the LORD and said, "O Lord [1]GOD, please remember me and please strengthen me just this time, O God, that I may at once be avenged of the Philistines for my two eyes."

29 And Samson grasped the two middle pillars on which the house rested, and braced himself against them, the one with his right hand and the other with his left.

30 And Samson said, "Let me die with the Philistines!" And he bent with [1]all his might so that the house fell on the lords and all the people who were in it. So the dead whom he killed at his death were more than those whom he killed in his life.

31 Then his brothers and all his father's household came down, took him, brought him up, and buried him between Zorah and Eshtaol in the tomb of Manoah his father. [a]Thus he had judged Israel twenty years.

CHAPTER 17

Micah's Idolatry

NOW there was a man of the hill country of Ephraim whose name was Micah.

2 And he said to his mother, "The eleven hundred *pieces* of silver which were taken from you, about which you uttered a curse [1]in my hearing, behold, the silver is with me; I took it." And his mother said, "Blessed be my son by the LORD."

3 He then returned the eleven hundred *pieces* of silver to his mother, and his mother said, "I wholly dedicate the silver from my hand to the LORD for my son [a]to make a graven image and a molten image; now therefore, I will return [1]them to you."

4 So when he returned the silver to his mother, his mother took two hundred *pieces* of silver and gave them to the silversmith who made [1]them into a graven image and a molten image, and [2]they were in the house of Micah.

5 And the man Micah had a [1]shrine and he made an [a]ephod and [2b]household idols and [3]consecrated one of his sons, [c]that he might become his priest.

6 In those days [a]there was no king in Israel; [b]every man did what was right in his own eyes.

7 Now there was a young man from [a]Bethlehem in Judah, of the family of Judah, who was a Levite; and he was [1]staying there.

8 Then the man departed from the city, from Bethlehem in Judah, to [1]stay wherever he might find *a place;* and as he made his journey, he came to the [a]hill country of Ephraim to the house of Micah.

9 And Micah said to him, "Where do you come from?" And he said to him, "I am a Levite from Bethlehem in Judah, and I am going to [1]stay wherever I may find *a place.*"

10 Micah then said to him, "Dwell with me and be [a]a father and a priest to me, and I will give you ten *pieces* of silver a year, a suit of clothes, and your maintenance." So the Levite went *in.*

11 And the Levite agreed to live with the man; and the young man became to him like one of his sons.

12 So Micah [1]consecrated the Levite, and the young man [a]became his priest and [2]lived in the house of Micah.

13 Then Micah said, "Now I know that the LORD will prosper me, seeing I have a Levite as priest."

CHAPTER 18

Danites Seek Territory

[a]IN those days there was no king of Israel; and [b]in those days the tribe of the Danites was seeking an inheritance for themselves to live in, for until that day [1]an inheritance had not [2]been allotted to them as a possession among the tribes of Israel.

2 So the sons of Dan sent from their family five men out of their whole number, [1]valiant men from [a]Zorah and Eshtaol, to spy out the land and to search it; and they said to them, "Go, search the land." And they came to [b]the hill country of Ephraim, to the house of Micah, and lodged there.

3 When they were near the house of Micah, they recognized the voice of the young man, the Levite; and they turned aside there, and said to him, "Who brought you here? And what are you doing in this *place?* And what do you have here?"

4 And he said to them, "Thus and so has Micah done to me, and he has

---

28 [1]YHWH, usually rendered LORD [a]Judg. 15:18

30 [1]Lit., *strength*

31 [a]Judg. 15:20

2 [1]Lit., *and also spoke it in my ears*

3 [1]Lit., *it* [a]Ex. 20:4, 23; 34:17

4 [1]Lit., *it* [2]Lit., *it was*

5 [1]Lit., *house of gods* [2]Heb., *teraphim* [3]Lit., *filled the hand of* [a]Judg. 18:24 [b]Judg. 8:27; 18:14 [c]Gen. 31:19

6 [a]Judg. 18:1; 19:1 [b]Deut. 12:8

7 [1]Or, *sojourning* [a]Judg. 19:1; Ruth 1:1, 2; Mic. 5:2; Matt. 2:1

8 [1]Or, *sojourn* [a]Josh. 24:33

9 [1]Or, *sojourn*

10 [a]Judg. 18:19

12 [1]Lit., *filled the hand of* [2]Lit., *was* [a]Num. 16:10; 18:1-7

1 [1]Lit., *it* [2]Lit., *fallen* [a]Judg. 17:6; 19:1 [b]Josh. 19:40-48

2 [1]Lit., *men, sons of valor* [a]Judg. 13:25 [b]Judg. 17:1

hired me, and [a]I have become his priest."

5 And they said to him, "Inquire of God, please, that we may know whether our way on which we are going will be prosperous."

6 And the priest said to them, "Go in peace; your way in which you are going [1]has the LORD's approval."

7 Then the five men departed and came to [a]Laish and saw the people who were in it living in security, after the manner of the Sidonians, quiet and secure; for there was no [1]ruler humiliating *them* for anything in the land, and they were far from the Sidonians and had no dealings with anyone.

8 When they came back to their brothers at Zorah and Eshtaol, their brothers said to them, "What *do* you *report?*"

9 And they said, "Arise, and let us go up against them; for we have seen the land, and behold, it is very good. And will you [1]sit still? Do not delay to go, to enter, to possess the land.

10"When you enter, you shall come to a secure people with a spacious land; for God has given it into your hand, a place where there is no lack of anything that is on the earth."

11 Then from the family of the Danites, from Zorah and from Eshtaol, six hundred men armed with weapons of war set out.

12 And they went up and camped at Kiriath-jearim in Judah. Therefore they called that place [1a]Mahaneh-dan to this day; behold, it is [2]west of Kiriath-jearim.

13 And they passed from there to the hill country of Ephraim and came to the house of Micah.

Danites Take Micah's Idols

14 Then the five men who went to spy out the country of Laish answered and said to their kinsmen, "Do you know that there are in these houses [a]an ephod and [1]household idols and a graven image and a molten image? Now therefore, consider what you should do."

15 And they turned aside there and came to the house of the young man, the Levite, to the house of Micah, and asked him of his welfare.

16 And the six hundred men armed with their weapons of war, who were of the sons of Dan, stood by the entrance of the gate.

17 Now the five men who went to spy out the land went up *and* entered there, *and* took the graven image and the ephod and [1]household idols and the molten image, while the priest stood by the entrance of the gate with the six hundred men armed with weapons of war.

18 And when these went into Micah's house and took the graven image, the ephod and [1]household idols and the molten image, the priest said to them, "What are you doing?"

19 And they said to him, "Be silent, put your hand over your mouth and come with us, and be to us [a]a father and a priest. Is it better for you to be a priest to the house of one man, or to be priest to a tribe and a family in Israel?"

20 And the priest's heart was glad, and he took the ephod and [1]household idols and the graven image, and went among the people.

21 Then they turned and departed, and put the little ones and the livestock and the valuables in front of them.

22 When they had gone some distance from the house of Micah, the men who *were* in the houses near Micah's house assembled and overtook the sons of Dan.

23 And they cried to the sons of Dan, who turned [1]around and said to Micah, "What is *the matter* with you, that you have assembled together?"

24 And he said, "You have taken away my gods which I made, and the priest, and have gone away, and what do I have besides? So how can you say to me, 'What is *the matter* with you?' "

25 And the sons of Dan said to him, "Do not let your voice be heard among us, lest [1]fierce men fall upon you and you [2]lose your life, with the lives of your household."

26 So the sons of Dan went on their way; and when Micah saw that they were too strong for him, he turned and went back to his house.

27 Then they took what Micah had made and the priest who had belonged to him, and came to [a]Laish, to a people quiet and secure, and struck them with the edge of the sword; and they burned the city with fire.

28 And there was no one to deliver *them,* because it was far from Sidon and they had no dealings with anyone, and it was in the valley which is near [a]Beth-rehob. And they rebuilt the city and lived in it.

29 And they called the name of the

4 [a]Judg. 17:12

6 [1]Lit., *is before the LORD*

7 [1]Lit., *a possessor of restraint* [a]Josh. 19:47; Judg. 18:29

9 [1]Lit., *be*

12 [1]I.e., the camp of Dan [2]Lit., *behind* [a]Judg. 13:25

14 [1]Heb., *teraphim* [a]Judg. 17:5

17 [1]Heb., *teraphim*

18 [1]Heb., *teraphim*

19 [a]Judg. 17:10

20 [1]Heb., *teraphim*

23 [1]Lit., *their faces*

25 [1]Lit., *bitter of soul* [2]Lit., *gather*

27 [a]Josh. 19:47; Judg. 18:7

28 [a]2 Sam. 10:6

city Dan, after the name of Dan their
father who was born in Israel; however, the name of the city formerly
was Laish.
30 And the sons of Dan set up for
themselves [a]the graven image; and
Jonathan, the son of [b]Gershom, the
son of [1]Manasseh, [c]he and his sons
were priests to the tribe of the Danites until the day of the captivity of
the land.
31 So they set up for themselves
Micah's graven image which he had
made, all the time that the house of
God was at Shiloh.

Chapter 19

A Levite's Concubine Degraded

NOW it came about in those days,
when [a]there was no king in Israel,
that there was a certain Levite
[1]staying in the remote part of the
hill country of Ephraim, who took a
concubine for himself from Bethlehem in Judah.
2 But his concubine played the
harlot against him, and she went
away from him to her father's house
in Bethlehem in Judah, and was
there for a period of four months.
3 Then her husband arose and
went after her to [a]speak [1]tenderly to
her in order to bring her back, [2]tak-
ing with him his servant and a pair
of donkeys. So she brought him into
her father's house, and when the
girl's father saw him, he was glad to
meet him.
4 And his father-in-law, the girl's
father, detained him; and he remained with him three days. So they
ate and drank and lodged there.
5 Now it came about on the
fourth day that they got up early in
the morning, and he [1]prepared to
go; and the girl's father said to his
son-in-law, "[a]Sustain [2]yourself with
a piece of bread, and afterward you
may go."
6 So both of them sat down and
ate and drank together; and the
girl's father said to the man, "Please
be willing to spend the night, and
[a]let your heart be merry."
7 Then the man arose to go, but
his father-in-law urged him so that
he spent the night there again.
8 And on the fifth day he arose to
go early in the morning, and the
girl's father said, "Please sustain
[1]yourself, and wait until [2]after-
noon"; so both of them ate.
9 When the man arose to go
along with his concubine and servant, his father-in-law, the girl's father, said to him, "Behold now, the
day has drawn [1]to a close; please
spend the night. Lo, the day is [2]com-
ing to an end; spend the night here
that your heart may be merry. Then
tomorrow you may arise early for
your journey so that you may go
[3]home."
10 But the man was not willing to
spend the night, so he arose and departed and came to *a place* opposite
[a]Jebus (that is, Jerusalem). And
there were with him a pair of saddled donkeys; his concubine also
was with him.
11 When they *were* near Jebus, the
day was almost gone; and [a]the servant said to his master, "Please
come, and let us turn aside into this
city of the Jebusites and spend the
night in it."
12 However, his master said to
him, "We will not turn aside into the
city of foreigners who are not of the
sons of Israel; but we will go on as
far as Gibeah."
13 And he said to his servant,
"Come and let us approach one of
these places; and we will spend the
night in Gibeah or Ramah."
14 So they passed along and went
their way, and the sun set on them
near Gibeah which belongs to Benjamin.
15 And they turned aside there in
order to enter *and* lodge in Gibeah.
When [1]they entered, [1]they sat down
in the open square of the city, for no
one took them into *his* house to
spend the night.
16 Then behold, an old man was
coming out of the field from his
work at evening. Now the man was
from [a]the hill country of Ephraim,
and he was [1]staying in Gibeah, but
the men of the place [b]were Benjamites.
17 And he lifted up his eyes and
saw the traveler in the open square
of the city; and the old man said,
"Where are you going, and where
do you come from?"
18 And he said to him, "We are
passing from Bethlehem in Judah to
the remote part of the hill country of
Ephraim, *for* I am from there, and I
went to Bethlehem in Judah. But I
am *now* going to [1]my house, and no
man will take me into his house.
19 "Yet there is both straw and fodder for our donkeys, and also bread
and wine for me, [1]your maidservant, and [a]the young man who is
with your servants; there is no lack
of anything."
20 And the old man said, "Peace to
you. Only let me *take care of* all

30 [1]Some ancient versions read, *Moses* [a]Judg. 17:3, 5 [b]Ex. 2:22; 18:3 [c]Judg. 17:3, 5

1 [1]Or, sojourning [a]Judg. 18:1

3 [1]Lit., *to her heart* [2]Lit., *and* [a]Gen. 34:3; 50:21

5 [1]Lit., *arose* [2]Lit., *your heart* [a]Gen. 18:5; Judg. 19:8

6 [a]Judg. 16:25; 19:9, 22; Ruth 3:7; 1 Kin. 21:7; Esth. 1:10

8 [1]Lit., *your heart* [2]Lit., *the day declines*

9 [1]Lit., *toward evening* [2]Lit., *declining* [3]Lit., *to your tent*

10 [a]1 Chr. 11:4, 5

11 [a]Judg. 19:19

15 [1]So with Gk.; M.T., *he*

16 [1]Or, *sojourning* [a]Judg. 19:1 [b]Judg. 19:14

18 [1]Heb., *the house of the Lord,* cf. v. 29

19 [1]I.e., my concubine [a]Judg. 19:11

your needs; however, do not spend
the night in the open square."
21 [a]So he took him into his house
and gave the donkeys fodder, and
they washed their feet and ate and
drank.
22 While they were [1]making merry, behold, [a]the men of the city, certain [2b]worthless fellows, surrounded the house, pounding the
door; and they spoke to the owner of
the house, the old man, saying,
"Bring out the man who came into
your house that we may have [3]rela-
tions with him."
23 Then the man, the owner of the
house, went out to them and said to
them, "No, my fellows, please do
not act so wickedly; since this man
has come into my house, [a]do not
commit this act of folly.
24"[a]Here is my virgin daughter
and his concubine. Please let me
bring them out that you may ravish
them and do to them [1]whatever you
wish. But do not commit such an act
of folly against this man."
25 But the men would not listen to
him, so the man seized his concubine and brought *her* out to them.
And they raped her and abused her
all night until morning, then let her
go at the approach of dawn.
26 [1]As the day began to dawn, the
woman came and fell down at the
doorway of the man's house where
her master was, until *full* daylight.
27 When her master arose in the
morning and opened the doors of
the house and went out to go on his
way, then behold, his concubine
was lying at the doorway of the
house, with her hands on the threshold.
28 And he said to her, "Get up and
let us go," [a]but there was no answer.
Then he placed her on the donkey;
and the man arose and went to his
[1]home.
29 When he entered his house, he
took a knife and laid hold of his concubine and [a]cut her in twelve pieces,
limb by limb, and sent her throughout the territory of Israel.
30 And it came about that all who
saw *it* said, "Nothing like this has
ever happened or been seen from
the day when the sons of Israel
came up from the land of Egypt to
this day. Consider it, take counsel
and speak up!"

CHAPTER 20

Resolve to Punish the Guilty

THEN all the sons of Israel from
Dan to Beersheba, including the
land of Gilead, came out, and the
congregation assembled as one man
to the LORD at [a]Mizpah.
2 And the [1]chiefs of all the people, *even* of all the tribes of Israel,
took their stand in the assembly of
the people of God, 400,000 foot [2]sol-
diers who drew the sword.
3 (Now the sons of Benjamin
heard that the sons of Israel had
gone up to Mizpah.) And the sons of
Israel said, "Tell *us*, how did this
wickedness take place?"
4 So the Levite, the husband of
the woman who was murdered, answered and said, "I came with my
concubine to spend the night at Gibeah which belongs to Benjamin.
5"But the men of Gibeah rose up
against me and surrounded the
house at night because of me. They
intended to kill me; instead, they
ravished my concubine so that she
died.
6"And I took hold of my concubine and cut her in pieces and sent
her throughout the land of Israel's
inheritance; for they have committed a lewd and disgraceful act in Israel.
7"Behold, all you sons of Israel,
give your advice and counsel here."
8 Then all the people arose as one
man, saying, "Not one of us will go
to his tent, nor will any of us return
to his house.
9"But now this is the thing which
we will do to Gibeah; *we will go up*
against it by lot.
10"And we will take 10 men out of
100 throughout the tribes of Israel,
and 100 out of 1,000, and 1,000 out
of 10,000 to [1]supply food for the
people, that when they come to
[2]Gibeah of Benjamin, they may
[3]punish *them* for all the disgraceful
acts that they have committed in Israel."
11 Thus all the men of Israel were
gathered against the city, united as
one man.
12 Then the tribes of Israel sent
men through the entire [1]tribe of
Benjamin, saying, "What is this
wickedness that has taken place
among you?
13"Now then, deliver up the men,
the [1a]worthless fellows in Gibeah,
that we may put them to death and
remove *this* wickedness from Israel." But the sons of Benjamin
would not listen to the voice of their
brothers, the sons of Israel.
14 And the sons of Benjamin gathered from the cities to Gibeah, to go
out to battle against the sons of Israel.

21 [a]Gen. 24:32, 33
22 [1]Lit., *making their hearts merry* [2]Lit., *sons of Belial* [3]Lit., *intercourse* [a]Gen. 19:4, 5; Ezek. 16:46-48 [b]Deut. 13:13; 1 Sam. 2:12; 1 Kin. 21:10; 2 Cor. 6:15
23 [a]Gen. 34:7; Deut. 22:21; Judg. 20:6; 2 Sam. 13:12
24 [1]Lit., *the good in your eyes* [a]Gen. 19:8
26 [1]Lit., *At the turning of the morning*
28 [1]Lit., *place* [a]Judg. 20:5
29 [a]1 Sam. 11:12
1 [a]1 Sam. 7:5
2 [1]Lit., *cornerstones* [2]Lit., *men*
10 [1]Lit., *take* [2]Heb., *Geba* [3]Lit., *do*
12 [1]Lit., *tribes*
13 [1]Lit., *sons of Belial* [a]2 Cor. 6:15

15 And from the cities on that day
the sons of Benjamin were [1]num-
bered, [a]26,000 men who draw the
sword, besides the inhabitants of
Gibeah who were [1]numbered, 700
choice men.
16 Out of all these people 700
choice men were left-handed; each
one could sling a stone at a hair and
not miss.
17 Then the men of Israel besides
Benjamin were [1]numbered, 400,000
men who draw the sword; all these
were men of war.

Civil War, Benjamin Defeated

18 Now the sons of Israel arose,
went up to Bethel, and [a]inquired of
God, and said, "Who shall go up
first for us to battle against the sons
of Benjamin?" Then the LORD said,
"Judah *shall go up* first."
19 So the sons of Israel arose in
the morning and camped against
Gibeah.
20 And the men of Israel went out
to battle against Benjamin, and the
men of Israel arrayed for battle
against them at Gibeah.
21 Then the sons of Benjamin
came out of Gibeah and [1a]felled to
the ground on that day 22,000 men
of Israel.
22 But the people, the men of Israel, encouraged themselves and arrayed for battle again in the place
where they had arrayed themselves
the first day.
23 [a]And the sons of Israel went up
and wept before the LORD until evening, and [b]inquired of the LORD, saying, "Shall we again draw near for
battle against the sons of my
brother Benjamin?" And the LORD
said, "Go up against him."
24 Then the sons of Israel [1]came
against the sons of Benjamin the
second day.
25 And Benjamin went out
[1]against them from Gibeah the second day and [2a]felled to the ground
again 18,000 men of the sons of Israel; all these drew the sword.
26 Then [a]all the sons of Israel and
all the people went up and came to
Bethel and wept; thus they remained there before the LORD and
fasted that day until evening. And
they offered burnt offerings and
peace offerings before the LORD.
27 And the sons of Israel [a]inquired
of the LORD (for the ark of the covenant of God *was* there in those
days,
28 and Phinehas the son of Eleazar, Aaron's son, stood before it to
minister in those days), saying,
"Shall I yet again go out to battle
against the sons of my brother Benjamin, or shall I cease?" And the
LORD said, "Go up, [a]for tomorrow I
will deliver them into your hand."
29 [a]So Israel set men in ambush
around Gibeah.
30 And the sons of Israel went up
against the sons of Benjamin on the
third day and arrayed themselves
against Gibeah, as at other times.
31 [a]And the sons of Benjamin
went out [1]against the people and
were drawn away from the city, and
they began to strike [2]and kill some
of the people, as at other times, on
the highways, one of which goes up
to Bethel and the other to Gibeah,
and in the field, about thirty men of
Israel.
32 And the sons of Benjamin said,
"They are struck down before us, as
at the first." But the sons of Israel
said, "Let us flee that we may draw
them away from the city to the highways."
33 Then all the men of Israel arose
from their place and arrayed themselves at Baal-tamar; [a]and the men
of Israel in ambush broke out of
their place, even out of Maareh-
geba.
34 When ten thousand choice men
from all Israel came against Gibeah,
the battle became [1]fierce; but [2]Ben-
jamin did not know that [3]disaster
was [4]close to them.
35 And the LORD struck Benjamin
before Israel, so that the sons of Israel destroyed 25,100 men of Benjamin that day, all [1]who draw the
sword.
36 So the sons of Benjamin saw
that they were [1]defeated. When the
men of Israel gave [2]ground to Benjamin because they relied on the
men in ambush whom they had set
against Gibeah,
37 the men in ambush hurried and
rushed against Gibeah; the men in
ambush also deployed and struck all
the city with the edge of the sword.
38 Now the appointed sign between the men of Israel and the men
in ambush was [a]that they should
make a great cloud of smoke rise
from the city.
39 Then the men of Israel turned in
the battle, and Benjamin began to
strike [1]and kill about thirty men of
Israel, [a]for they said, "Surely they
are [2]defeated before us, as in the
first battle."
40 But when the cloud began to
rise from the city in a column of
smoke, Benjamin looked behind

15 [1]Or, *mustered* [a]Num. 1:36, 37; 2:23; 26:41
17 [1]Or, *mustered*
18 [a]Num. 27:21; Judg. 20:23, 27
21 [1]Lit., *destroyed* [a]Judg. 20:25
23 [a]Josh. 7:6, 7 [b]Judg. 20:18
24 [1]Lit., *approached*
25 [1]Lit., *to meet* [2]Lit., *destroyed*
26 [a]Judg. 20:23; 21:2
27 [a]Judg. 20:18
28 [a]Judg. 7:9
29 [a]Josh. 8:4
31 [1]Lit., *to meet* [2]Lit., *slain ones* [a]Josh. 8:16
33 [a]Josh. 8:19
34 [1]Lit., *heavy* [2]Lit., *they* [3]Lit., *evil* [4]Lit., *touching*
35 [1]Lit., *these*
36 [1]Lit., *smitten* [2]Lit., *place*
38 [a]Josh. 8:20
39 [1]Lit., *slain ones* [2]Lit., *smitten* [a]Judg. 20:32

them; and behold, the whole city
was going up *in smoke* to heaven.
41 Then the men of Israel turned,
and the men of Benjamin were terrified; for they saw that [1]disaster was
[2]close to them.
42 Therefore, they turned their
backs before the men of Israel [a]to-
ward the direction of the wilderness, but the battle overtook them
while those who came out of the
cities destroyed them in the midst of
them.
43 They surrounded Benjamin,
pursued them without rest *and* trod
them down opposite Gibeah toward
the [1]east.
44 Thus 18,000 men of Benjamin
fell; all these were valiant warriors.
45 [1]The rest turned and fled
toward the wilderness to the rock of
[a]Rimmon, but they [2]caught 5,000 of
them on the highways and overtook
them [3]at Gidom and [4]killed 2,000 of
them.
46 So all of Benjamin who fell that
day were 25,000 men who draw the
sword; all these were valiant warriors.
47 But 600 men turned and fled
toward the wilderness to the rock of
Rimmon, and they remained at the
rock of Rimmon four months.
48 The men of Israel then turned
back against the sons of Benjamin
and struck them with the edge of the
sword, both the entire city with the
cattle and all that they found; they
also set on fire all the cities which
they found.

CHAPTER 21

Mourning Lost Tribe

NOW the men of Israel [a]had sworn
in Mizpah, saying, "None of us shall
give his daughter to Benjamin [1]in
marriage."
2 [a]So the people came to Bethel
and sat there before God until evening, and lifted up their voices and
wept [1]bitterly.
3 And they said, "Why, O LORD,
God of Israel, has this come about in
Israel, so that one tribe should be
missing today in Israel?"
4 And it came about the next day
that the people arose early and built
[a]an altar there, and offered burnt offerings and peace offerings.
5 Then the sons of Israel said,
"Who is there among all the tribes
of Israel who did not come up in the
assembly to the LORD?" For [1]they
had taken a great oath concerning
him who did not come up to the
LORD at Mizpah, saying, "He shall
surely be put to death."
6 And the sons of Israel were
sorry for their brother Benjamin
and said, "One tribe is cut off from
Israel today.
7 "What shall we do for wives for
those who are left, since we have
[a]sworn by the LORD not to give them
any of our daughters in marriage?"

Provision for Their Survival

8 And they said, "What one is
there of the tribes of Israel who did
not come up to the LORD at Mizpah?" And behold, no one had come
to the camp from Jabesh-gilead to
the assembly.
9 For when the people were
[1]numbered, behold, not one of the
inhabitants of Jabesh-gilead was
there.
10 And the congregation sent
12,000 of the valiant warriors there,
and commanded them, saying, "Go
and [a]strike the inhabitants of Jabesh-gilead with the edge of the
sword, with the women and the little ones.
11 "And this is the thing that you
shall do: you shall utterly destroy
every man and every woman who
has [1]lain with a man."
12 And they found among the inhabitants of Jabesh-gilead 400
young virgins who had not known a
man by lying with [1]him; and they
brought them to the camp at Shiloh,
which is in the land of Canaan.
13 Then the whole congregation
sent *word* and spoke to the sons of
Benjamin who were at the rock of
Rimmon, and [a]proclaimed peace to
them.
14 And Benjamin returned at that
time, and they gave them the
women whom they had kept alive
from the women of Jabesh-gilead;
yet they [1]were not enough for them.
15 And the people were sorry for
Benjamin because the LORD had
made a breach in the tribes of Israel.
16 Then the elders of the congregation said, "What shall we do for
wives for those who are left, since
the women are destroyed out of
Benjamin?"
17 And they said, "*There must be*
an inheritance for the survivors of
Benjamin, that a tribe may not be
blotted out from Israel.
18 "But we cannot give them wives
of our daughters." For the sons of
Israel [a]had sworn, saying, "Cursed
is he who gives a wife to Benjamin."
19 So they said, "Behold, there is a
feast of the LORD from year to year

41 [1]Lit., *evil* [2]Lit., *touching*
42 [a]Josh. 8:15, 24
43 [1]Lit., *sunrise*
45 [1]So with Gk.; Heb., *And they* [2]Lit., *gleaned* [3]Lit., *as far as* [4]Lit., *smote* [a]Judg. 21:13
1 [1]Lit., *for a wife* [a]Judg. 21:7, 18
2 [1]Lit., *with great weeping* [a]Judg. 20:26
4 [a]Deut. 12:5 2 Sam. 24:25
5 [1]Lit., *there was a great oath*
7 [a]Judg. 21:1
9 [1]Or, *mustered*
10 [a]Num. 31:17
11 [1]Lit., *known lying with*
12 [1]Lit., *a male*
13 [a]Deut. 20:10
14 [1]Lit., *did not find so*
18 [a]Judg. 21:1

in [a]Shiloh, which is on the north side of Bethel, on the east side of the highway that goes up from Bethel to Shechem, and on the south side of Lebonah."

20 And they commanded the sons of Benjamin, saying, "Go and lie in wait in the vineyards,

21 and watch; and behold, if the daughters of Shiloh come out to [1][a]take part in the dances, then you shall come out of the vineyards and each of you shall catch his wife from the daughters of Shiloh, and go to the land of Benjamin.

22 "And it shall come about, when their fathers or their brothers come to complain to us, that we shall say to them, 'Give them to us voluntarily, because we did not take for each man of Benjamin [1]a wife in battle, [2]nor did you give *them* to them, [a]*else* you would now be guilty.'"

23 And the sons of Benjamin did so, and took wives according to their number from those who danced, whom they carried away. And they went and returned to their inheritance, and [a]rebuilt the cities and lived in them.

24 And the sons of Israel departed from there at that time, every man to his tribe and family, and each one of them went out from there to his inheritance.

25 [a]In those days there was no king in Israel; everyone did what was right in his own eyes.

19 [a]Josh. 18:1; Judg. 18:31; 1 Sam. 1:3
21 [1]Lit., *dance* [a]Ex. 15:20; Judg. 11:34
22 [1]Lit., *his* [2]Lit., *because* [a]Judg. 21:1, 18
23 [a]Judg. 20:48
25 [a]Judg. 17:6; 18:1; 19:1

THE BOOK OF RUTH

Naomi Widowed

NOW it came about in the days [a]when the judges [1]governed, that there was a famine in the land. And a certain man of Bethlehem in Judah went to sojourn in the land of Moab [2]with his wife and his two sons.

2 And the name of the man *was* Elimelech, and the name of his wife, Naomi; and the names of his two sons *were* Mahlon and Chilion, Ephrathites of Bethlehem in Judah. Now they entered the land of Moab and remained there.

3 Then Elimelech, Naomi's husband, died; and she was left with her two sons.

4 And they took for themselves Moabite women *as* wives; the name of the one was Orpah and the name of the other Ruth. And they lived there about ten years.

5 Then [1]both Mahlon and Chilion also died; and the woman was bereft of her two children and her husband.

6 Then she arose with her daughters-in-law that she might return from the land of Moab, for she had heard in the land of Moab that the LORD had [a]visited His people in giving them food.

7 So she departed from the place where she was, and her two daughters-in-law with her; and they went on the way to return to the land of Judah.

8 And Naomi said to her two daughters-in-law, "Go, return each of you to her mother's house. May the LORD deal kindly with you as you have dealt with the dead and with me.

9 "May the LORD grant that you may find rest, each in the house of her husband." Then she kissed them, and they lifted up their voices and wept.

10 And they said to her, "*No,* but we will surely return with you to your people."

11 But Naomi said, "Return, my daughters. Why should you go with me? Have I yet sons in my womb, that they may be your husbands?

12 "Return, my daughters! Go, for I am too old to have a husband. If I said I have hope, if I should even have a husband tonight and also bear sons,

13 would you therefore wait until they were grown? Would you therefore refrain from marrying? No, my daughters; for it is [1]harder for me than for you, for the hand of the LORD has gone forth against me."

Ruth's Loyalty

14 And they lifted up their voices and wept again; and Orpah kissed her mother-in-law, but Ruth clung to her.

15 Then she said, "Behold, your sister-in-law has gone back to her people and her gods; return after your sister-in-law."

16 But Ruth said, "Do not urge me to leave you *or* turn back from following you; for where you go, I will go, and where you lodge, I will lodge. Your people *shall be* my people, and your God, my God.

1 [1]Or, *judged* [2]Lit., *he, and* [a]Judg. 2:16-18
5 [1]Lit., *both of them*
6 [a]Ex. 4:31
13 [1]Lit., *more bitter*

17"Where you die, I will die, and there I will be buried. Thus may the LORD do to me, and worse, if *anything but* death parts you and me."

18 When she saw that she was determined to go with her, she [1]said no more to her.

19 So they both went until they came to Bethlehem. And it came about when they had come to Bethlehem, that all the city was stirred because of them, and [1]the women said, "Is this Naomi?"

20 And she said to them, "Do not call me [1]Naomi; call me [2]Mara, for [3a]the Almighty has dealt very bitterly with me.

21"I went out full, but the LORD has brought me back empty. Why do you call me Naomi, since the LORD has witnessed against me and [1]the Almighty has afflicted me?"

22 So Naomi returned, and with her Ruth the Moabitess, her daughter-in-law, who returned from the land of Moab. And they came to Bethlehem at [a]the beginning of barley harvest.

CHAPTER 2

Ruth Gleans in Boaz' Field

NOW Naomi had [1]a kinsman of her husband, a [2]man of great wealth, of the family of [a]Elimelech, whose name was Boaz.

2 And Ruth the Moabitess said to Naomi, "Please let me go to the field and [a]glean among the ears of grain after one in whose sight I may find favor." And she said to her, "Go, my daughter."

3 So she departed and went and gleaned in the field after the reapers; and [1]she happened to come to the portion of the field belonging to Boaz, who was of the family of Elimelech.

4 Now behold, Boaz came from Bethlehem and said to the reapers, "May the LORD be with you." And they said to him, "May the LORD bless you."

5 Then Boaz said to his servant who was [1]in charge of the reapers, "Whose young woman is this?"

6 And the servant [1]in charge of the reapers answered and said, "She is the young Moabite woman who returned with Naomi from the land of Moab.

7"And she said, 'Please let me glean and gather after the reapers among the sheaves.' Thus she came and has remained from the morning until now; she has been sitting in the house for a little while."

8 Then Boaz said to Ruth, "[1]Listen carefully, my daughter. Do not go to glean in another field; furthermore, do not go on from this one, but stay here with my maids.

9"Let your eyes be on the field which they reap, and go after them. Indeed, I have commanded the servants not to touch you. When you are thirsty, go to the [1]water jars and drink from what the servants draw."

10 Then she fell on her face, bowing to the ground and said to him, "Why have I found favor in your sight that you should take notice of me, since I am a foreigner?"

11 And Boaz answered and said to her, "All that you have done for your mother-in-law after the death of your husband has been fully reported to me, and how you left your father and your mother and the land of your birth, and came to a people that you did not previously know.

12"May the LORD reward your work, and your wages be full from the LORD, the God of Israel, [a]under whose wings you have come to seek refuge."

13 Then she said, "I have found favor in your sight, my lord, for you have comforted me and indeed have spoken [1]kindly to your maidservant, though I am not like one of your maidservants."

14 And at mealtime Boaz said to her, "[1]Come here, that you may eat of the bread and dip your piece of bread in the vinegar." So she sat beside the reapers; and he [2]served her roasted grain, and she ate and was satisfied [a]and had some left.

15 When she rose to glean, Boaz commanded his servants, saying, "Let her glean even among the sheaves, and do not insult her.

16"And also you shall purposely pull out for her *some grain* from the bundles and leave *it* that she may glean, and do not rebuke her."

17 So she gleaned in the field until evening. Then she beat out what she had gleaned, and it was about an ephah of barley.

18 And she took *it* up and went into the city, and her mother-in-law saw what she had gleaned. She also took *it* out and [a]gave [1]Naomi what she had left after [2]she was satisfied.

19 Her mother-in-law then said to her, "Where did you glean today and where did you work? May he who took notice of you be blessed." So she told her mother-in-law with

18 [1]Lit., *ceased to speak*
19 [1]Lit., *they*
20 [1]I.e., Pleasant [2]I.e., Bitter [3]Heb., *Shaddai* [a]Ex. 6:3; Job 6:4
21 [1]Heb., *Shaddai*
22 [a]Ex. 9:31; Lev. 23:10, 11
1 [1]Or, *an acquaintance* [2]Or, *mighty, valiant man* [a]Ruth 1:2
2 [a]Lev. 19:9, 10; 23:22; Ruth 2:7
3 [1]Lit., *her chance chanced upon*
5 [1]Lit., *who was appointed over*
6 [1]Lit., *who was appointed over*
8 [1]Lit., *Have you not heard*
9 [1]Lit., *vessels*
12 [a]Ruth 1:16
13 [1]Lit., *to the heart of your*
14 [1]Lit., *Draw near* [2]Lit., *held out to* [a]Ruth 2:18
18 [1]Lit., *her* [2]Lit., *her satiety* [a]Ruth 2:14

whom she had worked and said,
"The name of the man with whom I
worked today is Boaz."
20 And Naomi said to her daughter-in-law, "May he be blessed of
the LORD who has not withdrawn
his kindness to the living and to the
dead." Again Naomi said to her,
"The man is [1]our relative, he is one
of our [2]closest relatives."
21 Then Ruth the Moabitess said,
"[1]Furthermore, he said to me, 'You
should stay close to my servants until they have finished all my harvest.' "
22 And Naomi said to Ruth her
daughter-in-law, "It is good, my
daughter, that you go out with his
maids, lest *others* fall upon you in
another field."
23 So she stayed close by the
maids of Boaz in order to glean until
[a]the end of the barley harvest and
the wheat harvest. And she lived
with her mother-in-law.

CHAPTER 3

Boaz Will Redeem Ruth

THEN Naomi her mother-in-law
said to her, "My daughter, shall I not
seek [1]security for you, that it may
be well with you?
2"And now is not Boaz [a]our [1]kins-
man, with whose maids you were?
Behold, he winnows barley at the
threshing floor tonight.
3"Wash yourself therefore, and
anoint yourself and put on your *best*
clothes, and go down to the threshing floor; *but* do not make yourself
known to the man until he has finished eating and drinking.
4"And it shall be when he lies
down, that you shall [1]notice the
place where he lies, and you shall go
and uncover his feet and lie down;
then he will tell you what you shall
do."
5 And she said to her, "All that
you say I will do."
6 So she went down to the
threshing floor and did according to
all that her mother-in-law had commanded her.
7 When Boaz had eaten and
drunk and his heart was merry, he
went to lie down at the end of the
heap of grain; and she came secretly, and uncovered his feet and
lay down.
8 And it happened in the middle
of the night that the man was startled and [1]bent forward; and behold,
a woman was lying at his feet.
9 And he said, "Who are you?"
And she answered, "I am Ruth your
maid. So spread your covering over
your maid, for you are a [1]close relative."
10 Then he said, "May you be
blessed of the LORD, my daughter.
You have shown your last kindness
to be better than the first by not
going after young men, whether
poor or rich.
11"And now, my daughter, do not
fear. I will do for you whatever you
[1]ask, for all my people in the [2]city
know that you are [a]a woman of excellence.
12"And now it is true I am a [1]close
relative; however, there is a [1]rela-
tive closer than I.
13"Remain this night, and when
morning comes, if he will [1]redeem
you, good; let him redeem you. But
if he does not wish to [1]redeem you,
then I will redeem you, as the LORD
lives. Lie down until morning."
14 So she lay at his feet until
morning and rose before one could
recognize another; and he said, "Let
it not be known that the woman
came to the threshing floor."
15 Again he said, "Give me the
cloak that is on you and hold it." So
she held it, and he measured six
measures of barley and laid *it* on
her. Then [1]she went into the city.
16 And when she came to her
mother-in-law, she said, "[1]How did
it go, my daughter?" And she told
her all that the man had done for
her.
17 And she said, "These six *measures* of barley he gave to me, for he
said, 'Do not go to your mother-in-
law empty-handed.' "
18 Then she said, "Wait, my
daughter, until you know how the
matter [1]turns out; for the man will
not rest until he has [2]settled it today."

CHAPTER 4

The Marriage of Ruth

NOW Boaz went up to the gate
and sat down there, and behold, [a]the
[1]close relative of whom Boaz spoke
was passing by, so he said, "Turn
aside, [2]friend, sit down here." And
he turned aside and sat down.
2 And he took ten men of the elders of the city and said, "Sit down
here." So they sat down.
3 Then he said to the [1]closest
relative, "Naomi, who has come
back from the land of Moab, has to
sell the piece of land [a]which belonged to our brother Elimelech.

20 [1]Lit., *near to us* [2]Lit., *redeemers*
21 [1]Lit., *Also that*
23 [a]Deut. 16:9
1 [1]Lit., *rest*
2 [1]Or, *acquaintance* [a]Deut. 25:5-10
4 [1]Lit., *know*
8 [1]Lit., *twisted himself*
9 [1]Or, *redeemer*
11 [1]Lit., *say* [2]Lit., *gate* [a]Prov. 31:10
12 [1]Or, *redeemer*
13 [1]Or, *act as close relative to*
15 [1]So with many mss.; M.T., *he*
16 [1]Lit., *Who are you?*
18 [1]Lit., *falls* [2]Lit., *finish the matter*
1 [1]Or, *redeemer* [2]Lit., *a certain one* [a]Ruth 3:12
3 [1]Lit., *redeemer* [a]Lev. 25:25

4 "So I thought to [1]inform you,
saying, 'Buy *it* before those who are
sitting *here,* and before the elders of
my people. If you will redeem *it,* redeem *it;* but if [2]not, tell me that I
may know; for there is no one but
you to redeem *it,* and I am after
you.'" And he said, "I will redeem
it."
5 Then Boaz said, "On the day
you buy the field from the hand of
Naomi, you must also acquire Ruth
the Moabitess, the widow of the deceased, in order to raise up the name
of the deceased on his inheritance."
6 And [a]the [1]closest relative said,
"I cannot redeem it for myself, lest I
[2]jeopardize my own inheritance.
Redeem *it* for yourself; you *may
have* my right of redemption, for I
cannot redeem *it.*"
7 Now this was [a]*the custom* in
former times in Israel concerning
the redemption and the exchange *of
land* to confirm any matter: a man
removed his sandal and gave it to
another; and this was the *manner of*
attestation in Israel.
8 So the [1]closest relative said to
Boaz, "Buy *it* for yourself." And he
removed his sandal.
9 Then Boaz said to the elders
and all the people, "You are witnesses today that I have bought
from the hand of Naomi all that belonged to Elimelech and all that belonged to Chilion and Mahlon.
10"Moreover, I have acquired
Ruth the Moabitess, the widow of
Mahlon, to be my wife in order to
raise up the name of the deceased
on his inheritance, so that the name
of the deceased may not be cut off
from his brothers or from the [1]court
of his *birth* place; you are witnesses
today."
11 And all the people who were in
the [1]court, and the elders, said, "*We
are* witnesses. May the LORD make
the woman who is coming into your
home [a]like Rachel and Leah, both of
whom built the house of Israel; and
may you achieve [2]wealth in Ephrathah and [3]become famous in Bethlehem.
12"Moreover, may your house be
like the house of [a]Perez whom Tamar bore to Judah, through the [1]off-
spring which the LORD shall give
you by this young woman."
13 So Boaz took Ruth, and she became his wife, and he went in to her.
And the LORD [1]enabled her to conceive, and she gave birth to a son.
14 Then the women said to Naomi,
"Blessed is the LORD who has not
left you without a [1]redeemer today,
and may his name [2]become famous
in Israel.
15"May he also be to you a restorer
of life and a sustainer of your old
age; for your daughter-in-law, who
loves you [1a]and is better to you than
seven sons, has given birth to him."

The Line of David Began Here

16 Then Naomi took the child [1]and
laid him in her lap, and became his
nurse.
17 And the neighbor women gave
him a name, saying, "A son has been
born to Naomi!" So they named him
Obed. He is the father of Jesse, the
father of David.
18 Now these are the generations
of Perez: [a]to Perez [1]was born Hezron,
19 and to Hezron was born Ram,
and to Ram, Amminadab,
20 and to Amminadab was born
Nahshon, and to Nahshon, Salmon,
21 and to Salmon was born Boaz,
and to Boaz, Obed,
22 and to Obed was born Jesse,
and to Jesse, David.

4 [1]Lit., *uncover your ear* [2]Lit., *no one will redeem*

6 [1]Lit., *redeemer* [2]Lit., *ruin* [a]Lev. 25:25

7 [a]Deut. 25:8-10

8 [1]Lit., *redeemer*

10 [1]Lit., *gate*

11 [1]Lit., *gate* [2]Or, *power* [3]Lit., *call the name in* [a]Gen. 29:25-30

12 [1]Lit., *seed* [a]Gen. 38:29; 46:12; Ruth 4:18

13 [1]Lit., *gave her conception*

14 [1]Or, *closest relative* [2]Lit., *be called in*

15 [1]Lit., *who* [a]Ruth 1:16, 17; 2:11, 12

16 [1]I.e., as her own

18 [1]Lit., *begot* and so through v. 22 [a]Matt. 1:4-6

THE FIRST BOOK OF SAMUEL

Elkanah and His Wives

NOW there was a certain man
from [a]Ramathaim-zophim from the
[b]hill country of Ephraim, and his
name was [c]Elkanah the son of Jeroham, the son of Elihu, the son of
Tohu, the son of Zuph, an Ephraimite.
2 And he had [a]two wives: the
name of one was [b]Hannah and the
name of the other Peninnah; and
Peninnah had children, but Hannah
had no children.
3 Now this man would go up
from his city [a]yearly [b]to worship
and to sacrifice to the LORD of hosts
in [c]Shiloh. And the two sons of Eli,
Hophni and Phinehas were priests
to the LORD there.
4 And when the day came that Elkanah sacrificed, he [a]would give
portions to Peninnah his wife and to
all her sons and her daughters;
5 but to Hannah he would give [a]a
double portion, for he loved Hannah, [b]but the LORD had closed her
womb.
6 Her rival, however, [a]would provoke her bitterly to irritate her, because the LORD had closed her
womb.
7 And it happened year after
year, as often as she went up to the
house of the LORD, she would provoke her, so she wept and would not
eat.
8 Then Elkanah her husband said
to her, "Hannah, why do you weep
and why do you not eat and why is
your heart sad? [a]Am I not better to
you than ten sons?"
9 Then Hannah rose after eating
and drinking in Shiloh. Now Eli the
priest was sitting on the seat by the
doorpost of [a]the temple of the LORD.
10 And she, [1]greatly distressed,
prayed to the LORD and wept bitterly.
11 And she [a]made a vow and said,
"O LORD of hosts, if Thou wilt indeed [b]look on the affliction of Thy
maidservant and remember me, and
not forget Thy maidservant, but wilt
give Thy maidservant a [1]son, then I
will give him to the LORD all the
days of his life, and [c]a razor shall
never come on his head."
12 Now it came about, as she [1]con-
tinued praying before the LORD, that
Eli was watching her mouth.
13 As for Hannah, [a]she was speaking in her heart, only her lips were
moving, but her voice was not
heard. So Eli thought she was
drunk.
14 Then Eli said to her, "[a]How
long will you make yourself drunk?
Put away your wine from you."
15 But Hannah answered and said,
"No, my lord, I am a woman [1]op-
pressed in spirit; I have drunk neither wine nor strong drink, but I
[a]have poured out my soul before the
LORD.
16 "Do not [1]consider your maidservant as a worthless woman; for I
have spoken until now [a]out of my
great concern and [2]provocation."
17 Then Eli answered and said,
"[a]Go in peace; and may the God of
Israel [b]grant your petition that you
have asked of Him."
18 And she said, "[a]Let your maidservant find favor in your sight." So
the woman went her way and ate,
and [b]her face was no longer *sad*.

Samuel Is Born to Hannah

19 Then they arose early in the
morning and worshiped before the
LORD, and returned again to their
house in [a]Ramah. And Elkanah [1]had
relations with Hannah his wife, and
[b]the LORD remembered her.
20 And it came about [1]in due time,
after Hannah had conceived, that
she gave birth to a son; and she
named him Samuel, *saying,* "[a]Be-
cause I have asked him of the
LORD."
21 Then the man Elkanah [a]went
up with all his household to offer to
the LORD the yearly sacrifice and
pay his vow.
22 But Hannah did not go up, for
she said to her husband, "*I will not
go up* until the child is weaned; then
I will [a]bring him, that he may appear
before the LORD and [b]stay there forever."
23 And [a]Elkanah her husband said
to her, "Do what seems best [1]to you.
Remain until you have weaned him;
only [b]may the LORD confirm His
word." So the woman remained and
nursed her son until she weaned
him.
24 Now when she had weaned
him, [a]she took him up with her, with
a three-year-old bull and one ephah
of flour and a jug of wine, and

1 [a]1 Sam. 1:19 [b]Josh. 17:17, 18 [c]1 Chr. 6:22-28, 33-38
2 [a]Deut. 21:15-17 [b]Luke 2:36
3 [a]Ex. 34:23; 1 Sam. 1:21; Luke 2:41 [b]Deut. 12:5-7 [c]Josh. 18:1
4 [a]Deut. 12:17, 18
5 [a]Gen. 43:34 [b]Gen. 16:1; 30:1
6 [a]Job 24:21
8 [a]Ruth 4:15
9 [a]1 Sam. 3:3
10 [1]Lit., *bitter of soul*
11 [1]Lit., *seed of men* [a]Num. 30:6-11 [b]Gen. 29:32 [c]Num. 6:5; Judg. 13:5; Luke 1:15
12 [1]Lit., *multiplied*
13 [a]Gen. 24:42-45
14 [a]Acts 2:4, 13
15 [1]Lit., *severe* [a]Ps. 62:8
16 [1]Lit., *give* [2]Lit., *my provocation* [a]Luke 6:45
17 [a]1 Sam. 25:35; 2 Kin. 5:19; Mark 5:34 [b]Ps. 20:3-5
18 [a]Ruth 2:13 [b]Rom. 15:13
19 [1]Lit., *knew* [a]1 Sam. 1:1; 2:11 [b]Gen. 21:1; 30:22
20 [1]Lit., *at the circuit of the days* [a]Gen. 41:51, 52; Ex. 2:10, 22; Matt. 1:21
21 [a]Deut. 12:11; 1 Sam. 1:3
22 [a]Luke 2:22 [b]1 Sam. 1:11, 28
23 [1]Lit., *in your eyes* [a]Num. 30:10, 11 [b]1 Sam. 1:17
24 [a]Num. 15:9, 10; Deut. 12:5, 6

brought him to [b]the house of the
LORD in Shiloh, although the child
was young.
25 Then [a]they slaughtered the
bull, and [b]brought the boy to Eli.
26 And she said, "Oh, my lord! [a]As
your soul lives, my lord, I am the
woman who stood here beside you,
praying to the LORD.
27 "[a]For this boy I prayed, and the
LORD has given me my petition
which I asked of Him.
28 "[a]So I have also [1]dedicated him
to the LORD; as long as he lives he is
[1]dedicated to the LORD." And he
worshiped the LORD there.

CHAPTER 2

Hannah's Song of Thanksgiving

THEN Hannah [a]prayed and said,
"My heart exults in the LORD;
[b]My [1]horn is exalted in the LORD,
My mouth [2]speaks boldly against my enemies,
Because [c]I rejoice in Thy salvation.
2 "[a]There is no one holy like the LORD,
Indeed, [b]there is no one besides Thee,
[c]Nor is there any rock like our God.
3 "[1]Boast no more so very proudly,
[a]Do not let arrogance come out of your mouth;
[b]For the LORD is a God of knowledge,
[c]And with Him actions are weighed.
4 "[a]The bows of the mighty are shattered,
[b]But the feeble gird on strength.
5 "Those who were full hire themselves out for bread,
But those who were hungry cease *to hunger*.
[a]Even the barren gives birth to seven,
But [b]she who has many children languishes.
6 "[a]The LORD kills and makes alive;
[b]He brings down to [1]Sheol and raises up.
7 "[a]The LORD makes poor and rich;
[b]He brings low, He also exalts.
8 "[a]He raises the poor from the dust,
[b]He lifts the needy from the ash heap
[c]To make them sit with nobles,
And inherit a seat of honor;
[d]For the pillars of the earth are the LORD's,
And He set the world on them.
9 "[a]He keeps the feet of His godly ones,
[b]But the wicked ones are silenced in darkness;
[c]For not by might shall a man prevail.
10 "[a]Those who contend with the LORD will be shattered;
[b]Against them He will thunder in the heavens,
[c]The LORD will judge the ends of the earth;
[d]And He will give strength to His king,
[e]And will exalt the [1]horn of His anointed."
11 Then Elkanah went to his home
at [a]Ramah. [b]But the boy ministered
to the LORD before Eli the priest.

The Sin of Eli's Sons

12 Now the sons of Eli were
[1a]worthless men; they did not know
the LORD
13 [a]and the custom of the priests
with the people. When any man was
offering a sacrifice, the priest's servant would come while the meat
was boiling, with a three-pronged
fork in his hand.
14 Then he would thrust it into the
pan, or kettle, or caldron, or pot; all
that the fork brought up the priest
would take for himself. Thus they
did in Shiloh to all the Israelites who
came there.
15 Also, before [a]they burned the
fat, the priest's servant would come
and say to the man who was sacrificing, "Give the priest meat for
roasting, as he will not take boiled
meat from you, only raw."
16 And if the man said to him,
"They must surely [1]burn the fat
[2]first, and then take as much as [3]you
desire," then he would say, "No, but
you shall give *it to me* now; and if
not, I will take it by force."
17 Thus the sin of the young men
was very great before the LORD, for
the men [a]despised the offering of
the LORD.

Samuel before the LORD as a Boy

18 Now [a]Samuel was ministering
before the LORD, *as* a boy [1b]wearing
a linen ephod.
19 And his mother would make
him a little [a]robe and bring it to him
from year to year when she would
come up with her husband to offer
[b]the yearly sacrifice.
20 Then Eli would [a]bless Elkanah

24 [b]Josh. 18:1; 1 Sam. 4:3, 4
25 [a]Lev. 1:5 [b]Luke 2:22
26 [a]2 Kin. 2:2
27 [a]1 Sam. 1:11
28 [1]Lit., *lent* [a]1 Sam. 1:11, 22
1 [1]I.e., strength [2]Lit., *is enlarged* [a]1 Sam. 2:1-10; Ps. 72:20; Hab. 3:1; Luke 1:46-55 [b]Deut. 33:17; Job 16:15; Ps. 89:17 [c]Is. 12:2
2 [a]Ex. 15:11 [b]2 Sam. 22:32 [c]Deut. 32:30, 31
3 [1]Lit., *Talk much* [a]Prov. 8:13 [b]1 Sam. 16:7; 1 Kin. 8:39 [c]Prov. 16:2; 24:12
4 [a]Ps. 37:15; 46:9 [b]Ps. 18:39; Heb. 11:32-34
5 [a]Ruth 4:15; Ps. 113:9 [b]Jer. 15:9
6 [1]I.e., the nether world [a]Deut. 32:39; 2 Kin. 5:7; Rev. 1:18 [b]Is. 26:19
7 [a]Deut. 8:17, 18 [b]Job 5:11; James 4:10
8 [a]Job 42:10-12; Ps. 75:7 [b]2 Sam. 7:8; Dan. 2:48; James 2:5 [c]Job 36:7 [d]Job 38:4-6; Ps. 75:3
9 [a]Ps. 91:11, 12; 1 Pet. 1:5 [b]Matt. 8:12 [c]Ps. 33:16, 17
10 [1]I.e., strength [a]Ex. 15:6; Ps. 2:9 [b]1 Sam. 7:10; Ps. 18:13, 14 [c]Ps. 96:13; 98:9; Matt. 25:31, 32 [d]Ps. 21:1, 7 [e]Ps. 89:24
11 [a]1 Sam. 1:1, 19 [b]1 Sam. 1:28; 2:18
12 [1]Lit., *sons of Belial* [a]Jer. 2:8; 9:3, 6
13 [a]Lev. 7:29-34
15 [a]Lev. 3:3-5
16 [1]Lit., *offer up in smoke* [2]Lit., *like the day* [3]Lit., *your soul*
17 [a]Mal. 2:7-9
18 [1]Lit., *girded with* [a]1 Sam. 2:11; 3:1 [b]1 Sam. 22:18
19 [a]Ex. 28:31 [b]1 Sam. 1:3, 21
20 [a]Luke 2:34

and his wife and say, "May the LORD
give you [1]children from this woman
in place of [2]the one she [b]dedicated
to the LORD." And they went to their
own [3]home.
21 And [a]the LORD visited Hannah;
and she conceived and gave birth to
three sons and two daughters. And
[b]the boy Samuel grew before the
LORD.

Eli Rebukes His Sons

22 Now Eli was very old; and he
heard [a]all that his sons were doing
to all Israel, and how they lay with
[b]the women who served at the doorway of the tent of meeting.
23 And he said to them, "Why do
you do such things, the evil things
that I hear from all these people?
24 "No, my sons; for the report is
not good [a]which I hear [1]the LORD's
people circulating.
25 "If one man sins against another,
[a]God will mediate for him; but [b]if a
man sins against the LORD, who can
intercede for him?" But they would
not listen to the voice of their father,
for the [c]LORD desired to put them to
death.
26 Now the boy [a]Samuel [1]was
growing in stature and in favor both
with the LORD and with men.
27 Then [a]a man of God came to Eli
and said to him, "Thus says the
LORD, '[b]Did I *not* indeed reveal Myself to the house of your father when
they were in Egypt *in bondage* to
Pharaoh's house?
28 'And [a]did I *not* choose them
from all the tribes of Israel to be My
priests, to go up to My altar, to burn
incense, to carry an ephod before
Me; and did I *not* give to the house
of your father all the fire *offerings* of
the sons of Israel?
29 'Why do you [a]kick at My sacrifice and at My offering [b]which I
have commanded *in My* [c]dwelling,
and [d]honor your sons above Me, by
making yourselves fat with the
[1]choicest of every offering of My
people Israel?'
30 "Therefore the LORD God of Israel declares, '[a]I did indeed say that
your house and the house of your
father should walk before Me forever'; but now the LORD declares,
'Far be it from Me—for [b]those who
honor Me I will honor, and those
[c]who despise Me will be lightly esteemed.
31 'Behold, [a]the days are coming
when I will break your [1]strength
and the [1]strength of your father's
house so that there will not be an old
man in your house.
32 'And you will see [a]the distress of
My dwelling, in *spite of* all that [1]I do
good for Israel; and an [b]old man will
not be in your house forever.
33 'Yet I will not cut off every man
of yours from My altar [1]that your
eyes may fail *from weeping* and
your soul grieve, and all the increase
of your house will die [2]in the prime
of life.
34 'And this will be [a]the sign to you
which shall come concerning your
two sons, Hophni and Phinehas: [b]on
the same day both of them shall die.
35 'But [a]I will raise up for Myself a
faithful priest who will do according
to what is in My heart and in My
soul; and [b]I will build him an enduring house, and he will walk before
[c]My anointed always.
36 'And it shall come about that everyone who is left in your house
shall come and bow down to him for
a [1]piece of silver or a loaf of bread,
and say, "Please [2]assign me to one
of the priest's offices so that I may
eat a piece of bread." ' "

CHAPTER 3

The Prophetic Call to Samuel

NOW [a]the boy Samuel was ministering to the LORD before Eli. And
[b]word from the LORD was rare in
those days, [1]visions were infre-
quent.
2 And it happened at that time as
Eli was lying down in his place (now
[a]his eyesight had begun to grow dim
and he could not see well),
3 and [a]the lamp of God had not
yet gone out, and Samuel was lying
down in the temple of the LORD
where the ark of God *was*,
4 that the LORD called Samuel;
and he said, "[a]Here I am."
5 Then he ran to Eli and said,
"Here I am, for you called me." But
he said, "I did not call, lie down
again." So he went and lay down.
6 And the LORD called yet again,
"Samuel!" So Samuel arose and
went to Eli, and said, "Here I am, for
you called me." But he [1]answered,
"I did not call, my son, lie down
again."
7 [a]Now Samuel did not yet know
the LORD, nor had the word of the
LORD yet been revealed to him.
8 So the LORD called Samuel
again for the third time. And he
arose and went to Eli, and said,
"Here I am, for you called me."
Then Eli discerned that the LORD
was calling the boy.

20 [1]Lit., *seed* [2]Lit., *the one asked for which was lent* [3]Lit., *place* [b]1 Sam. 1:11, 27, 28
21 [a]Gen. 21:1 [b]1 Sam. 2:26; 3:19-21; Luke 2:40
22 [a]1 Sam. 2:13-17 [b]Ex. 38:8
24 [1]Or, *making the LORD's people transgress* [a]1 Kin. 15:26
25 [a]Deut. 1:17 [b]Num. 15:30; 1 Sam. 3:14; Heb. 10:26, 27 [c]Ex. 4:21; Josh. 11:20
26 [1]Lit., *was going on both great and good* [a]1 Sam. 2:21; Luke 2:52
27 [a]Deut. 33:1; Judg. 13:6 [b]Ex. 4:14-16; 12:1, 43
28 [a]Ex. 28:1-4; 30:7, 8; Lev. 8:7, 8
29 [1]Or, *first* [a]1 Sam. 2:13-17 [b]Deut. 12:5-9 [c]Ps. 26:8 [d]Matt. 10:37
30 [a]Ex. 29:9; Num. 25:13 [b]Ps. 50:23 [c]Mal. 2:9
31 [1]Or, *arm* [a]1 Sam. 4:11-18; 22:17-20
32 [1]Lit., *he* [a]1 Kin. 2:26, 27 [b]Zech. 8:4
33 [1]Lit., *to waste away your eyes and to grieve your soul* [2]Lit., *as men*
34 [a]1 Sam. 10:7-9; 1 Kin. 13:3 [b]1 Sam. 4:11, 17
35 [a]1 Sam. 3:1; 7:9; 9:12, 13 [b]1 Sam. 8:3-5; 1 Kin. 11:38 [c]1 Sam. 10:9, 10; 12:3; 16:13
36 [1]Or, *payment* [2]Lit., *attach*
1 [1]Lit., *no vision spread abroad* [a]1 Sam. 2:11, 18 [b]Ps. 74:9; Ezek. 7:26; Amos 8:11, 12
2 [a]1 Sam. 4:15
3 [a]Ex. 25:31-37; Lev. 24:3
4 [a]Is. 6:8
6 [1]Lit., *said*
7 [a]1 Cor. 13:11

9 And Eli said to Samuel, "Go lie down, and it shall be if He calls you, that you shall say, 'Speak, LORD, for Thy servant is listening.'" So Samuel went and lay down in his place.

10 Then the LORD came and stood and called as at other times, "Samuel! Samuel!" And Samuel said, "Speak, for Thy servant is listening."

11 And the LORD said to Samuel, "Behold, [a]I am about to do a thing in Israel at which both ears of everyone who hears it will tingle.

12 "In that day [a]I will carry out against Eli all that I have spoken concerning his house, from beginning to end.

13 "For [a]I have told him that I am about to judge his house forever for [b]the iniquity which he knew, because [c]his sons brought a curse on themselves and [d]he did not rebuke them.

14 "And therefore I have sworn to the house of Eli that [a]the iniquity of Eli's house shall not be atoned for by sacrifice or offering forever."

15 So Samuel lay down until morning. Then he [a]opened the doors of the house of the LORD. But Samuel was afraid to tell [b]the vision to Eli.

16 Then Eli called Samuel and said, "Samuel, my son." And he said, "Here I am."

17 And he said, "What is the word that He spoke to you? Please do not hide it from me. [a]May God do so to you, and more also, if you hide anything from me of all the words that He spoke to you."

18 So Samuel told him everything and hid nothing from him. And he said, "[a]It is the LORD; let Him do what seems good to Him."

19 Thus [a]Samuel grew and [b]the LORD was with him and [c]let none of his words [1]fail.

20 And all Israel [a]from Dan even to Beersheba knew that Samuel was confirmed as a prophet of the LORD.

21 And the LORD appeared again at Shiloh, [a]because the LORD revealed Himself to Samuel at Shiloh by the word of the LORD.

CHAPTER 4

Philistines Take the Ark in Victory

THUS the word of Samuel came to all Israel. Now Israel went out to meet the Philistines in battle and camped beside [a]Ebenezer while the Philistines camped in [b]Aphek.

2 And the Philistines drew up in battle array to meet Israel. When the battle spread, Israel was [1]defeated before the Philistines who killed about four thousand men on the battlefield.

3 When the people came into the camp, the elders of Israel said, "[a]Why has the LORD defeated us today before the Philistines? [b]Let us take to ourselves from Shiloh the ark of the covenant of the LORD, that [1]it may come among us and deliver us from the power of our enemies."

4 So the people sent to Shiloh, and from there they carried the ark of the covenant of the LORD of hosts [a]who sits *above* the cherubim; and the two sons of Eli, Hophni and Phinehas, *were* there with the ark of the covenant of God.

5 And it happened as the ark of the covenant of the LORD came into the camp, that [a]all Israel shouted with a great shout, so that the earth resounded.

6 And when the Philistines heard the noise of the shout, they said, "What *does* the noise of this great shout in the camp of the Hebrews *mean?*" Then they understood that the ark of the LORD had come into the camp.

7 And the Philistines were afraid, for they said, "God has come into the camp." And they said, "[a]Woe to us! For nothing like this has happened before.

8 "Woe to us! Who shall deliver us from the hand of these mighty gods? These are the gods who smote the Egyptians with all *kinds of* plagues in the wilderness.

9 "[a]Take courage and be men, O Philistines, lest you become slaves to the Hebrews, [b]as they have been slaves to you; therefore, be men and fight."

10 So the Philistines fought and [a]Israel was [1]defeated, and [b]every man fled to his tent, and the slaughter was very great; for there fell of Israel thirty thousand foot soldiers.

11 And the ark of God was taken; and [a]the two sons of Eli, Hophni and Phinehas, died.

12 Now a man of Benjamin ran from the battle line and came to Shiloh the same day with [a]his clothes torn and [1]dust on his head.

13 When he came, behold, [a]Eli was sitting on *his* seat [1]by the road eagerly watching, because his heart was trembling for the ark of God. So the man came to tell *it* in the city, and all the city cried out.

14 When Eli heard the noise of the outcry, he said, "What *does* the

11 [a]2 Kin. 21:12; Jer. 19:3
12 [a]1 Sam. 2:27-36
13 [a]1 Sam. 2:29-31 [b]1 Sam. 2:22 [c]1 Sam. 2:12, 17, 22 [d]Deut. 17:12; 21:18
14 [a]Lev. 15:31; Is. 22:14
15 [a]1 Chr. 15:23 [b]1 Sam. 3:10
17 [a]2 Sam. 3:35
18 [a]Ex. 34:5-7; Lev. 10:3; Job 2:10; Is. 39:8
19 [1]Lit., *fall to the ground* [a]1 Sam. 2:21 [b]Gen. 21:22; 28:15 [c]1 Sam. 9:6
20 [a]Judg. 20:1
21 [a]1 Sam. 3:10
1 [a]1 Sam. 7:12 [b]Josh. 12:18; 1 Sam. 29:1
2 [1]Lit., *smitten*
3 [1]Or, *he* [a]Josh. 7:7, 8 [b]Num. 10:35; Josh. 6:6
4 [a]2 Sam. 6:2
5 [a]Josh. 6:5, 20
7 [a]Ex. 15:14
9 [a]1 Cor. 16:13 [b]Judg. 13:1; 1 Sam. 14:21
10 [1]Lit., *smitten* [a]Deut. 28:15, 25; 1 Sam. 4:2 [b]2 Sam. 18:17; 2 Kin. 14:12
11 [a]1 Sam. 2:34; Ps. 78:56-64
12 [1]Lit., *ground* [a]Josh. 7:6; 2 Sam. 1:2; Neh. 9:1
13 [1]Gk. version reads, *beside the gate watching the road;* see v. 18 [a]1 Sam. 1:9; 4:18

noise of this commotion *mean?*"
Then the man came hurriedly and
told Eli.
15 Now Eli was ninety-eight years
old, and [a]his eyes were set so that he
could not see.
16 And the man said to Eli, "I am
the one who came from the battle
line. Indeed, I escaped from the battle line today." And he said, "[a]How
did things go, my son?"
17 Then the one who brought the
news answered and said, "Israel has
fled before the Philistines and there
has also been a great slaughter
among the people, and your two
sons also, Hophni and Phinehas, are
dead, and the ark of God has been
taken."
18 And it came about when he
mentioned the ark of God that [1a]Eli
fell off the seat backward beside the
gate, and his neck was broken and
he died, for [2]he was old and heavy.
Thus he judged Israel forty years.
19 Now his daughter-in-law,
Phinehas' wife, was pregnant and
about to give birth; and when she
heard the news that the ark of God
was taken and that her father-in-law
and her husband had died, she
kneeled down and gave birth, for
her pains came upon her.
20 And about the time of her death
the women who stood by her said to
her, "[a]Do not be afraid, for you have
given birth to a son." But she did not
answer or pay attention.
21 And she called the boy [1]Icha-
bod, saying, "[a]The glory has departed from Israel," because [b]the
ark of God was taken and because
of her father-in-law and her husband.
22 And she said, "The glory has
departed from Israel, for the ark of
God was taken."

CHAPTER 5

Capture of the Ark Provokes God

NOW the Philistines took the ark
of God and [a]brought it from Eben-
ezer to [b]Ashdod.
2 Then the Philistines took the
ark of God and brought it to [a]the
house of Dagon, and set it by Dagon.
3 When the Ashdodites arose
early the next morning, behold, [a]Da-
gon had fallen on his face to the
ground before the ark of the LORD.
So they took Dagon and [b]set him in
his place again.
4 But when they arose early the
next morning, behold, Dagon had
fallen on his face to the ground before the ark of the LORD. And the
head of Dagon and both the palms
of his hands *were* cut off on the
threshold; [1]only the trunk of Dagon
was left to him.
5 Therefore neither the priests of
Dagon nor all who enter Dagon's
house tread on the threshold of Dagon in Ashdod to this day.
6 Now [a]the hand of the LORD was
heavy on the Ashdodites, and [b]He
ravaged them and smote them with
[c]tumors, both Ashdod and its territories.
7 When the men of Ashdod saw
that it was so, they said, "The ark of
the God of Israel must not remain
with us, for His hand is severe on us
and on Dagon our god."
8 So they sent and [a]gathered all
the lords of the Philistines to them
and said, "What shall we do with
the ark of the God of Israel?" And
they said, "Let the ark of the God of
Israel be brought around to Gath."
And they brought the ark of the God
of Israel *around.*
9 And it came about that after
they had brought it around, [a]the
hand of the LORD was against the
city with very great confusion; and
He smote the men of the city, both
young and old, so that [b]tumors
broke out on them.
10 So they sent the ark of God to
Ekron. And it happened as the ark of
God came to Ekron that the Ekron-
ites cried out, saying, "They have
brought the ark of the God of Israel
around to [1]us, to kill [1]us and [2]our
people."
11 They [a]sent therefore and gathered all the lords of the Philistines
and said, "Send away the ark of the
God of Israel, and let it return to its
own place, that it may not kill [1]us
and [2]our people." For there was a
deadly confusion throughout the
city; [b]the hand of God was very
heavy there.
12 And the men who did not die
were smitten with tumors and [a]the
cry of the city went up to heaven.

CHAPTER 6

The Ark Returned to Israel

NOW the ark of the LORD had been
in the [1]country of the Philistines
seven months.
2 And [a]the Philistines called for
the priests and the diviners, saying,
"What shall we do with the ark of
the LORD? Tell us [1]how we shall
send it to its place."
3 And they said, "If you send

15 [a]1 Kin. 14:4
16 [a]2 Sam. 1:4
18 [1]Lit., *he* [2]Lit., *the man* [a]1 Sam. 4:13
20 [a]Gen. 35:16-19
21 [1]I.e., No glory [a]Ps. 26:8; Jer. 2:11 [b]1 Sam. 4:11
1 [a]1 Sam. 4:1; 7:12 [b]Josh. 13:3
2 [a]Judg. 16:23-30; 1 Chr. 10:8-10
3 [a]Is. 19:1; 46:1, 2 [b]Is. 46:7
4 [1]So with ancient versions; Heb., *only Dagon.*
6 [a]Ex. 9:3; 1 Sam. 5:7, 11 [b]1 Sam. 6:5 [c]Deut. 28:27; Ps. 78:66
8 [a]1 Sam. 5:11; 29:6-11
9 [a]1 Sam. 5:11; 7:13 [b]1 Sam. 5:6
10 [1]Lit., *me* [2]Lit., *my*
11 [1]Lit., *me* [2]Lit., *my* [a]1 Sam. 5:8 [b]1 Sam. 5:6, 9
12 [a]Ex. 12:30
1 [1]Lit., *field*
2 [1]Or, *with what* [a]Gen. 41:8; Ex. 7:11; Is. 2:6

away the ark of the God of Israel, [a]do not send it empty; but you shall surely [b]return to Him a guilt offering. Then you shall be healed and it shall be known to you why His hand is not removed from you."

4 Then they said, "What shall be the guilt offering which we shall return to Him?" And they said, "Five golden [a]tumors and five golden mice [b]*according to* the number of the lords of the Philistines, for one plague was on all of [1]you and on your lords.

5 "So you shall make likenesses of your tumors and likenesses of your mice that ravage the land, and [a]you shall give glory to the God of Israel; perhaps [b]He will ease His hand from you, [c]your gods, and your land.

6 "Why then do you harden your hearts [a]as the Egyptians and Pharaoh hardened their hearts? When He had severely dealt with them, [b]did they not allow [1]the people to go, and they departed?

7 "Now therefore take and [a]prepare a new cart and two milch cows on which there [b]has never been a yoke; and hitch the cows to the cart and take their calves home, away from them.

8 "And take the ark of the LORD and place it on the cart; and put [a]the articles of gold which you return to Him as [b]a guilt offering in a box by its side. Then send it away that it may go.

9 "And watch, if it goes up by the way of its own territory to [a]Beth-shemesh, then He has done us this great evil. But if not, then [b]we shall know that it was not His hand that struck us; it happened to us by chance."

10 Then the men did so, and took two milch cows and hitched them to the cart, and shut up their calves at home.

11 And they put the ark of the LORD on the cart, and the box with the golden mice and the likenesses of their tumors.

12 And the cows took the straight way in the [1]direction of [a]Beth-shemesh; they went along [b]the highway, lowing as they went, and did not turn aside to the right or to the left. And the lords of the Philistines followed them to the border of Beth-shemesh.

13 Now *the people of* Beth-shemesh were reaping their wheat harvest in the valley, and they raised their eyes and saw the ark and were glad to see *it*.

14 And the cart came into the field of Joshua the Beth-shemite and stood there where there *was* a large stone; and they split the wood of the cart and [a]offered the cows as a burnt offering to the LORD.

15 And [a]the Levites took down the ark of the LORD and the box that was with it, in which were the articles of gold, and put them on the large stone; and the men of Beth-shemesh offered burnt offerings and sacrificed sacrifices that day to the LORD.

16 And when the five lords of the Philistines saw it, they returned to Ekron that day.

17 And [a]these are the golden tumors which the Philistines returned for a guilt offering to the LORD: one for Ashdod, one for Gaza, one for Ashkelon, one for Gath, one for Ekron;

18 and the golden mice, *according* to the number of all the cities of the Philistines belonging to the five lords, [a]both of fortified cities and of country villages. [b]The large [1]stone on which they set the ark of the LORD *is a witness* to this day in the field of Joshua the Beth-shemite.

19 And [a]He struck down some of the men of Beth-shemesh because they had looked into the ark of the LORD. He struck down of all the people, 50,070 men, and the people mourned because the LORD had struck the people with a great slaughter.

20 And the men of Beth-shemesh said, "[a]Who is able to stand before the LORD, this holy God? And to whom shall He go up from us?"

21 So they sent messengers to the inhabitants of [a]Kiriath-jearim, saying, "The Philistines have brought back the ark of the LORD; come down and take it up to you."

CHAPTER 7

Deliverance from the Philistines

AND the men of Kiriath-jearim came and took the ark of the LORD and [a]brought it into the house of Abinadab on the hill, and consecrated Eleazar his son to keep the ark of the LORD.

2 And it came about from the day that the ark remained at Kiriath-jearim that the time was long, for it was twenty years; and all the house of Israel lamented after the LORD.

3 Then Samuel spoke to all the house of Israel, saying, "[a]If you return to the LORD with all your heart, [b]remove the foreign gods and the

3 [a]Ex. 23:15; Deut. 16:16 [b]Lev. 5:15, 16

4 [1]Lit., *them* [a]1 Sam. 5:6, 9, 12; 6:17 [b]Judg. 3:3; 1 Sam. 6:17, 18

5 [a]Josh. 7:19; Is. 42:12 [b]1 Sam. 5:6, 11 [c]1 Sam. 5:3, 4, 7

6 [1]Lit., *them* [a]Ex. 8:15, 32; 9:34 [b]Ex. 12:31

7 [a]2 Sam. 6:3 [b]Num. 19:2; Deut. 21:3, 4

8 [a]1 Sam. 6:4, 5 [b]1 Sam. 6:3

9 [a]Josh. 15:10; 21:16 [b]1 Sam. 6:3

12 [1]Lit., *way* [a]1 Sam. 6:9 [b]Num. 20:19

14 [a]2 Sam. 24:22; 2 Kin. 19:21

15 [a]Ex. 4:14; Josh. 3:3

17 [a]1 Sam. 6:4

18 [1]So some mss. and versions. Heb., *Abel* [a]Deut. 3:5 [b]1 Sam. 14:15

19 [a]Num. 4:5, 15, 20; 2 Sam. 6:7

20 [a]Lev. 11:44, 45; 2 Sam. 6:9

21 [a]Josh. 9:17; 15:9, 60

1 [a]2 Sam. 6:3, 4

3 [a]Joel 2:12-14 [b]Josh. 24:14, 23; Judg. 10:16

[c]Ashtaroth from among you and
[d]direct your hearts to the LORD and
[e]serve Him alone; and He will deliver you from the hand of the Philistines."
4 So the sons of Israel removed
the Baals and the Ashtaroth and
served the LORD alone.
5 Then Samuel said, "Gather all
Israel to [a]Mizpah, and [b]I will pray to
the LORD for you."
6 And they gathered to Mizpah,
and drew water and [a]poured it out
before the LORD, and [b]fasted on that
day, and said there, "[c]We have
sinned against the LORD." And Samuel judged the sons of Israel at Mizpah.
7 Now when the Philistines heard
that the sons of Israel had gathered
to Mizpah, the lords of the Philistines went up against Israel. And
when the sons of Israel heard it,
[a]they were afraid of the Philistines.
8 Then the sons of Israel said to
Samuel, "[a]Do not cease to cry to the
LORD our God for us, that He may
save us from the hand of the Philistines."
9 And Samuel took [a]a suckling
lamb and offered it for a whole
burnt offering to the LORD; and
Samuel cried to the LORD for Israel
and [b]the LORD answered him.
10 Now Samuel was offering up
the burnt offering, and the Philistines drew near to battle against Israel. But [a]the LORD thundered with a
great [1]thunder on that day against
the Philistines and [b]confused them,
so that they were [2]routed before Israel.
11 And the men of Israel went out
of Mizpah and pursued the Philistines, and struck them down as far
as below Bethcar.
12 Then Samuel [a]took a stone and
set it between Mizpah and Shen,
and named it [1]Ebenezer, saying,
"Thus far the LORD has helped us."
13 [a]So the Philistines were subdued and [b]they did not come any
more within the border of Israel.
And the hand of the LORD was
against the Philistines all the days of
Samuel.
14 And the cities which the Philistines had taken from Israel were restored to Israel, from Ekron even to
Gath; and Israel delivered their territory from the hand of the Philistines. So there was peace between
Israel and [a]the Amorites.

Samuel's Ministry

15 Now Samuel [a]judged Israel all
the days of his life.

3 [c]Judg. 2:13; 1 Sam. 31:10 [d]Deut. 13:4; 2 Chr. 19:3 [e]Deut. 6:13; Matt. 4:10
5 [a]Judg. 20:1 [b]1 Sam. 8:6; 12:17-19
6 [a]1 Sam. 1:15; Ps. 62:8; Lam. 2:19 [b]Lev. 16:29; Neh. 9:1 [c]Judg. 10:10
7 [a]1 Sam. 13:6; 17:11
8 [a]1 Sam. 12:19-24; Is. 37:4
9 [a]Lev. 22:27 [b]Ps. 99:6; Jer. 15:1
10 [1]Lit., *voice* [2]Lit., *smitten* [a]1 Sam. 2:10; 2 Sam. 22:14, 15; Ps. 29:3, 4 [b]Josh. 10:10; Ps. 18:14
12 [1]I.e., The stone of help [a]Gen. 35:14; Josh. 4:9; 24:26
13 [a]Judg. 13:1-15 [b]1 Sam. 13:5
14 [a]Num. 13:29; Josh. 10:5-10
15 [a]1 Sam. 7:6; 12:11
16 [a]Gen. 28:19; 35:6 [b]Josh. 5:9, 10 [c]1 Sam. 7:5
17 [a]1 Sam. 1:1, 19; 2:11
1 [a]Deut. 16:18, 19
2 [a]Gen. 22:19; 1 Kin. 19:3; Amos 5:5
3 [a]Ex. 23:6, 8; Deut. 16:19
4 [a]1 Sam. 7:17
5 [a]Deut. 17:14, 15
6 [1]Or, *evil* [a]1 Sam. 12:17 [b]1 Sam. 15:11
7 [a]Ex. 16:8; 1 Sam. 10:19
9 [1]Lit., *testify to* [2]Lit., *custom* [a]Ezek. 3:18 [b]1 Sam. 8:11-18; 10:25
10 [a]1 Sam. 8:4
11 [1]Lit., *custom* [a]Deut. 17:14-20; 1 Sam. 10:25 [b]1 Sam. 14:52 [c]2 Sam. 15:1
12 [a]Num. 31:14; 1 Sam. 22:7

16 And he used to go annually on
circuit to [a]Bethel and [b]Gilgal and
[c]Mizpah, and he judged Israel in all
these places.
17 Then his return *was* to [a]Ramah,
for his house *was* there, and there he
judged Israel; and he built there an
altar to the LORD.

CHAPTER 8

Israel Demands a King

AND it came about when Samuel
was old that [a]he appointed his sons
judges over Israel.
2 Now the name of his first-born
was Joel, and the name of his second, Abijah; *they* were judging in
[a]Beersheba.
3 His sons, however, did not walk
in his ways, but turned aside after
dishonest gain and [a]took bribes and
perverted justice.
4 Then all the elders of Israel
gathered together and came to Samuel at [a]Ramah;
5 and they said to him, "Behold,
you have grown old, and your sons
do not walk in your ways. Now [a]ap-
point a king for us to judge us like all
the nations."
6 But the thing was [1a]displeasing
in the sight of Samuel when they
said, "Give us a king to judge us."
And [b]Samuel prayed to the LORD.
7 And the LORD said to Samuel,
"Listen to the voice of the people in
regard to all that they say to you, for
[a]they have not rejected you, but
they have rejected Me from being
king over them.
8"Like all the deeds which they
have done since the day that I
brought them up from Egypt even to
this day—in that they have forsaken
Me and served other gods—so they
are doing to you also.
9"Now then, listen to their voice;
[a]however, you shall solemnly [1]warn
them and tell them of [b]the [2]proce-
dure of the king who will reign over
them."

Warning Concerning a King

10 So Samuel spoke all the words
of the LORD to [a]the people who had
asked of him a king.
11 And he said, "[a]This will be the
[1]procedure of the king who will
reign over you: [b]he will take your
sons and place *them* for himself in
his chariots and among his horsemen and [c]they will run before his
chariots.
12"And [a]he will appoint for himself commanders of thousands and

of fifties, and *some* to [1]do his plowing and to reap his harvest and to
make his weapons of war and equipment for his chariots.
13"He will also take your daughters for perfumers and cooks and
bakers.
14"And [a]he will take the best of
your fields and your vineyards and
your olive groves, and give *them* to
his servants.
15"And he will take a tenth of your
seed and of your vineyards, and give
to his officers and to his servants.
16"He will also take your male servants and your female servants and
your best young men and your donkeys, and [1]use *them* for his work.
17"He will take a tenth of your
flocks, and you yourselves will become his servants.
18"Then [a]you will cry out in that
day because of your king whom you
have chosen for yourselves, but [b]the
LORD will not answer you in that
day."
19 Nevertheless, the people refused to listen to the voice of Samuel, and they said, "No, but there
shall be a king over us,
20 [a]that we also may be like all the
nations, that our king may judge us
and go out before us and fight our
battles."
21 Now after Samuel had heard all
the words of the people, [a]he repeated them in the LORD's hearing.
22 And the LORD said to Samuel,
"[a]Listen to their voice, and [1]appoint
them a king." So Samuel said to the
men of Israel, "Go every man to his
city."

CHAPTER 9

Saul's Search

NOW there was a man of Benjamin whose name was [a]Kish the son
of Abiel, the son of Zeror, the son of
Becorath, the son of Aphiah, the son
of a Benjamite, a mighty man of
[1]valor.
2 And he had a son whose name
was Saul, a [a]choice and handsome
man, and there was not a more
handsome person than he among
the sons of Israel; [b]from his shoulders and up he was taller than any of
the people.
3 Now the donkeys of Kish,
Saul's father, were lost. So Kish said
to his son Saul, "Take now with you
one of the servants, and arise, go
search for the donkeys."
4 And he passed through [a]the hill
country of Ephraim and passed
through the land of [b]Shalishah, but
they did not find *them.* Then they
passed through the land of [c]Shaa-
lim, but *they were* not *there.* Then he
passed through the land of the Benjamites, but they did not find *them.*
5 When they came to the land of
[a]Zuph, Saul said to his servant who
was with him, "Come, and let us return, [b]lest my father cease *to be concerned* about the donkeys and become anxious for us."
6 And he said to him, "Behold
now, there is [a]a man of God in this
city, and the man is held in honor;
[b]all that he says surely comes true.
Now let us go there, [c]perhaps he can
tell us about our journey on which
we have set out."
7 Then Saul said to his servant,
"But behold, if we go, what shall we
bring the man? For the bread is gone
from our sack and there is [a]no present to bring to the man of God.
What do we have?"
8 And the servant answered Saul
again and said, "Behold, I have in
my hand a fourth of a shekel of silver; I will give *it* to the man of God
and he will [a]tell us our way."
9 (Formerly in Israel, when a
man went to inquire of God, he used
to say, "Come, and let us go to the
seer"; for *he who is called* a prophet
now was formerly called [a]a seer.)
10 Then Saul said to his servant,
"Well said; come, let us go." So they
went to the city where the man of
God was.
11 As they went up the slope to the
city, [a]they found young women
going out to draw water, and said to
them, "Is the seer here?"
12 And they answered them and
said, "He is; [1]see, *he is* ahead of you.
Hurry now, for he has come into the
city today, for [a]the people have a
sacrifice on [b]the high place today.
13"As soon as you enter the city
you will find him before he goes up
to the high place to eat, for the people will not eat until he comes, because [a]he must bless the sacrifice;
afterward those who are invited will
eat. Now therefore go up for you
will find him at once."
14 So they went up to the city. As
they came into the city, behold,
Samuel was coming out toward
them to go up to the high place.

God's Choice for King

15 Now a day before Saul's coming, [a]the LORD had [1]revealed *this* to
Samuel saying,
16"About this time tomorrow I will
send you a man from the land of

---

12 [1]Lit., *plow his plowing*
14 [a]1 Kin. 21:7; Ezek. 46:18
16 [1]Lit., *make*
18 [a]Is. 8:21 [b]Prov. 1:25-28; Mic. 3:4
20 [a]1 Sam. 8:5
21 [a]Judg. 11:11
22 [1]Lit., *cause a king to reign for them* [a]1 Sam. 8:7
1 [1]Or, *wealth,* or, *influence* [a]1 Sam. 14:51; 1 Chr. 9:36-39
2 [a]1 Sam. 10:24 [b]1 Sam. 10:23
4 [a]Josh. 24:33 [b]2 Kin. 4:42 [c]Josh. 19:42
5 [a]1 Sam. 1:1 [b]1 Sam. 10:2
6 [a]Deut. 33:1; 2 Kin. 5:8 [b]2 Sam. 3:19 [c]Gen. 24:42
7 [a]1 Kin. 14:3; 2 Kin. 5:15; 8:8, 9; Ezek. 13:19
8 [a]1 Sam. 9:6
9 [a]2 Sam. 24:11; 1 Chr. 9:22; 26:28; Is. 30:10
11 [a]Gen. 24:15; 29:9; Ex. 2:16
12 [1]Or, *behold* [a]Num. 28:11-15 [b]1 Sam. 7:17; 10:5
13 [a]Luke 9:16; John 6:11
15 [1]Lit., *uncovered the ear* [a]1 Sam. 15:1; Acts 13:21

Benjamin, and [a]you shall anoint him
to be prince over My people Israel;
and he shall deliver My people from
the hand of the Philistines. For [b]I
have regarded My people, because
their cry has come to Me."
17 When Samuel saw Saul, the
LORD [1]said to him, "[a]Behold, the
man of whom I spoke to you! This
one shall rule over My people."
18 Then Saul approached Samuel
in the gate, and said, "Please tell me
where the seer's house is."
19 And Samuel answered Saul and
said, "I am the seer. Go up before
me to the high place, for you shall
eat with me today; and in the morning I will let you go, and will tell you
all that is on your mind.
20 "And [a]as for your donkeys
which were lost three days ago, do
not set your mind on them, for they
have been found. And [b]for whom is
all that is desirable in Israel? Is it not
for you and for all your father's
household?"
21 And Saul answered and said,
"[a]Am I not a Benjamite, of [b]the
smallest of the tribes of Israel, and
my family the least of all the families of the [1]tribe of Benjamin? Why
then do you speak to me in this
way?"
22 Then Samuel took Saul and his
servant and brought them into the
hall, and gave them a place at the
head of those who were invited,
who were about thirty men.
23 And Samuel said to the cook,
"[1]Bring the portion that I gave you,
concerning which I said to you, 'Set
it [2]aside.' "
24 Then the cook [a]took up the leg
with what was on it and set *it* before
Saul. And *Samuel* said, "Here is
what has been reserved! Set *it* before you *and* eat, because it has
been kept for you until the appointed time, [1]since I said I have invited the people." So Saul ate with
Samuel that day.
25 When they came down from
the high place into the city, *Samuel*
spoke with Saul [a]on the roof.[1]
26 And they arose early; and it
came about at daybreak that Samuel called to Saul on the roof, saying, "Get up, that I may send you
away." So Saul arose, and both he
and Samuel went out into the street.
27 As they were going down to the
edge of the city, Samuel said to
Saul, "Say to the servant that he
might go ahead of us and pass on,
but you remain standing now, that I
may proclaim the word of God to
you."

CHAPTER 10

Saul among Prophets

THEN [a]Samuel took the flask of
oil, poured it on his head, [b]kissed
him and said, "Has not [c]the LORD
anointed you a ruler over [d]His inheritance?
2 "When you go from me today,
then you will find two men close to
[a]Rachel's tomb in the territory of
Benjamin at Zelzah; and they will
say to you, '[b]The donkeys which you
went to look for have been found.
Now behold, your father has
[1]ceased to be concerned about the
donkeys and is anxious for you, saying, "What shall I do about my
son?" '
3 "Then you will go on further
from there, and you will come as far
as the [1a]oak of Tabor, and there
three men going up [b]to God at
Bethel will meet you, one carrying
three kids, another carrying three
loaves of bread, and another carrying a jug of wine;
4 and they will greet you and give
you two *loaves* of bread, which you
will accept from their hand.
5 "Afterward you will come to
[1a]the hill of God where the Philistine
garrison is; and it shall be as soon as
you have come there to the city, that
you will meet [b]a group of prophets
coming down from the high place
with harp, tambourine, flute, and a
lyre before them, and [c]they will be
prophesying.
6 "Then [a]the Spirit of the LORD
will come upon you mightily, and
[b]you shall prophesy with them and
be changed into another man.
7 "And it shall be when these signs
come to you, [a]do for yourself what
[1]the occasion requires; for [b]God is
with you.
8 "And [a]you shall go down before
me to Gilgal; and behold, I will come
down to you to offer burnt offerings
and [b]sacrifice peace offerings. [c]You
shall wait seven days until I come to
you and show you what you should
do."
9 Then it happened when he
turned his back to leave Samuel,
God [a]changed [1]his heart; and all
those signs came about on that day.
10 [a]When they came to [1]the hill
there, behold, a group of prophets
met him; and the Spirit of God came
upon him mightily, so that he prophesied among them.
11 And it came about, when all
who knew him previously saw that
he prophesied now with the proph-

16 [a]1 Sam. 10:1 [b]Ex. 3:7, 9

17 [1]Lit., *answered* [a]1 Sam. 16:12

20 [a]1 Sam. 9:3 [b]1 Sam. 8:5; 12:13

21 [1]So some ancient versions; Heb., *tribes* [a]1 Sam. 15:17 [b]Judg. 20:46-48

23 [1]Lit., *Give* [2]Lit., *with you*

24 [1]Lit., *saying* [a]Ex. 29:22, 27; Lev. 7:32, 33; Num. 18:18

25 [1]Gk. adds, *and they spread a bed for Saul on the roof and he slept.* [a]Deut. 22:8; Acts 10:9

1 [a]Ex. 30:23-33; 1 Sam. 16:13; 2 Kin. 9:3, 6 [b]Ps. 2:12 [c]1 Sam. 10:9, 10; 16:13; 26:9; 2 Sam. 1:14 [d]Deut. 32:9; Ps. 78:71

2 [1]Lit., *abandoned the matter of* [a]Gen. 35:16-20; 48:7 [b]1 Sam. 9:3-5

3 [1]Or, *terebinth* [a]Gen. 35:8 [b]Gen. 28:16, 22; 35:1, 3, 7

5 [1]Or, *Gibeath-haelohim* [a]1 Sam. 13:2, 3 [b]1 Sam. 19:20; 2 Kin. 2:3, 5, 15 [c]2 Kin. 3:15; 1 Chr. 25:1-6

6 [a]Num. 11:25, 29; Judg. 14:6 [b]1 Sam. 10:10; 19:23, 24

7 [1]Lit., *your hand finds* [a]Eccles. 9:10 [b]Josh. 1:5

8 [a]1 Sam. 13:8 [b]1 Sam. 11:15 [c]1 Sam. 13:8

9 [1]Lit., *for him another heart* [a]1 Sam. 10:6

10 [1]Or, *Gibeath* [a]1 Sam. 10:5, 6

ets, that the people said to one another, "What has happened to the
son of Kish? [a]Is Saul also among the
prophets?"
12 And a man there answered and
said, "Now, who is their father?"
Therefore it became a proverb: "Is
Saul also among the prophets?"
13 When he had finished prophesying, he came to the high place.
14 Now [a]Saul's uncle said to him
and his servant, "Where did you
go?" And he said, "[b]To look for the
donkeys. When we saw that they
could not be found, we went to Samuel."
15 And Saul's uncle said, "Please
tell me what Samuel said to you."
16 So Saul said to his uncle, "[a]He
told us plainly that the donkeys had
been found." But he did not tell him
about the matter of the kingdom
which Samuel had mentioned.

Saul Publicly Chosen King

17 Thereafter Samuel called the
people together to the LORD [a]at Mizpah;
18 and he said to the sons of Israel,
"[a]Thus says the LORD, the God of
Israel, 'I brought Israel up from
Egypt, and I delivered you from the
hand of the Egyptians, and from the
[1]power of all the kingdoms that
were oppressing you.'
19 "But you [a]today rejected your
God, who delivers you from all your
calamities and your distresses; yet
you have said, '[1]No, but set a king
over us!' Now therefore [b]present
yourselves before the LORD by your
tribes and by your clans."
20 Thus Samuel brought all the
tribes of Israel near, and the tribe of
Benjamin was taken by lot.
21 Then he brought the tribe of
Benjamin near by its families, and
the Matrite family was taken. And
Saul the son of Kish was taken; but
when they looked for him, he could
not be found.
22 Therefore [a]they inquired further of the LORD, "Has the man
come here yet?" So the LORD said,
"Behold, he is hiding himself by the
baggage."
23 So they ran and took him from
there, and when he stood among the
people, [a]he was taller than any of
the people from his shoulders upward.
24 And Samuel said to all the people, "Do you see him [a]whom the
LORD has chosen? Surely there is no
one like him among all the people."
So all the people shouted and said,
"[1b]Long live the king!"
25 Then Samuel told the people
[a]the ordinances of the kingdom, and
wrote *them* in the book and [b]placed
it before the LORD. And Samuel sent
all the people away, each one to his
house.
26 And Saul also went [a]to his
house at Gibeah; and the valiant
men whose hearts God had touched
went with him.
27 But certain [1]worthless men
said, "How can this one deliver us?"
And they despised him and [a]did not
bring him any present. But he kept
silent.

CHAPTER 11

Saul Defeats the Ammonites

NOW [a]Nahash the Ammonite
came up and [1]besieged [b]Jabesh-gil-
ead; and all the men of Jabesh said
to Nahash, "Make [c]a covenant with
us and we will serve you."
2 But Nahash the Ammonite said
to them, "I will make *it* with you on
this condition, [a]that I will gouge out
the right eye of every one of you,
thus I will make it [b]a reproach on all
Israel."
3 And [a]the elders of Jabesh said
to him, "Let us alone for seven days,
that we may send messengers
throughout the territory of Israel.
Then, if there is no one to deliver us,
we will come out to you."
4 Then the messengers came [a]to
Gibeah of Saul and spoke these
words in the hearing of the people,
and all the people [b]lifted up their
voices and wept.
5 Now behold, Saul was coming
from the field [a]behind the oxen; and
[1]he said, "What is *the matter* with
the people that they weep?" So they
related to him the words of the men
of Jabesh.
6 Then [a]the Spirit of God came
upon Saul mightily when he heard
these words, and [1]he became very
angry.
7 And he took a yoke of oxen and
[a]cut them in pieces, and sent *them*
throughout the territory of Israel by
the hand of messengers, saying,
"[b]Whoever does not come out after
Saul and after Samuel, so shall it be
done to his oxen." Then the dread of
the LORD fell on the people, and they
came out [c]as one man.
8 And he [1]numbered them in [a]Be-
zek; and the sons of Israel were
[b]300,000, and the men of Judah
30,000.

11 [a]1 Sam. 19:24; Amos 7:14, 15; Matt. 13:54-57
14 [a]1 Sam. 14:50 [b]1 Sam. 9:4-6
16 [a]1 Sam. 9:20
17 [a]1 Sam. 7:5
18 [1]Lit., *hand* [a]Judg. 6:8, 9
19 [1]So with several mss. and versions; M.T. *to Him* [a]1 Sam. 8:6, 7 [b]Josh. 7:14-17; 24:1; Prov. 16:33
22 [a]Ex. 28:30; Num 27:21; 1 Sam. 23:2, 4, 9-11
23 [a]1 Sam. 9:2
24 [1]Lit., *May the king live* [a]Deut. 17:15; 2 Sam. 21:6 [b]1 Kin. 1:25, 34, 39
25 [a]Deut. 17:14-20; 1 Sam. 8:11-18 [b]Deut. 31:26
26 [a]1 Sam. 11:4; 15:34
27 [1]Lit., *sons of Belial*, cf. 2 Cor. 6:15 [a]1 Kin. 10:25; 2 Chr. 17:5
1 [1]Lit., *camped against* [a]1 Sam. 12:12 [b]Judg. 21:8; 1 Sam. 31:11 [c]1 Kin. 20:34; Ezek. 17:13
2 [a]Num. 16:14 [b]1 Sam. 17:26; Ps. 44:13
3 [a]1 Sam. 8:4
4 [a]1 Sam. 10:26; 15:34 [b]Gen. 27:38; Judg. 2:4; 1 Sam. 30:4
5 [1]Lit., *Saul* [a]1 Kin. 19:19
6 [1]Lit., *his anger burned exceedingly* [a]Judg. 3:10; 6:34; 13:25; 14:6; 1 Sam. 10:10; 16:13
7 [a]Judg. 19:29 [b]Judg. 21:5, 8, 10 [c]Judg. 20:1
8 [1]Lit., *mustered* [a]Judg. 1:5 [b]Judg. 20:2

9 And they said to the messengers who had come, "Thus you shall
say to the men of Jabesh-gilead, 'Tomorrow, by the time the sun is hot,
you shall have deliverance.' " So the
messengers went and told the men
of Jabesh; and they were glad.
10 Then the men of Jabesh said,
"[a]Tomorrow we will come out to
you, and you may do to us whatever
seems good [1]to you."
11 And it happened the next morning that Saul put the people [a]in three
companies; and they came into the
midst of the camp at the morning
watch, and struck down the Ammonites until the heat of the day.
And it came about that those who
survived were scattered, so that no
two of them were left together.
12 Then the people said to Samuel,
"[a]Who is he that said, 'Shall Saul
reign over us?' [1b]Bring the men, that
we may put them to death."
13 But Saul said, "[a]Not a man shall
be put to death this day, for today
[b]the LORD has accomplished deliverance in Israel."
14 Then Samuel said to the people,
"Come and let us go to [a]Gilgal and
[b]renew the kingdom there."
15 So all the people went to Gilgal,
and there they made Saul king [a]be-
fore the LORD in Gilgal. There they
also [b]offered sacrifices of peace offerings before the LORD; and there
Saul and all the men of Israel rejoiced greatly.

CHAPTER 12

Samuel Addresses Israel

THEN Samuel said to all Israel,
"Behold, [a]I have listened to your
voice in all that you said to me, and
I [b]have [1]appointed a king over you.
2 "And now, [a]here is the king
walking before you, but [b]I am old
and gray, and behold [c]my sons are
with you. And [d]I have walked before
you from my youth even to this day.
3 "Here I am; bear witness against
me before the LORD and [a]His
anointed. [b]Whose ox have I taken,
or whose donkey have I taken, or
whom have I defrauded? Whom
have I oppressed, or [c]from whose
hand have I taken a bribe to blind
my eyes with it? I will restore *it* to
you."
4 And they said, "You have not
defrauded us, or oppressed us, or
taken anything from any man's
hand."
5 And he said to them, "The LORD
is witness against you, and His
anointed is witness this day that
[a]you have found nothing [b]in my
hand." And they said, "*He is* witness."
6 Then Samuel said to the people,
"It is the LORD who [1a]appointed
Moses and Aaron and who brought
your fathers up from the land of
Egypt.
7 "So now, take your stand, [a]that I
may plead with you before the LORD
concerning all the righteous acts of
the LORD which He did for you and
your fathers.
8 "When Jacob went into Egypt
and [a]your fathers cried out to the
LORD, then [b]the LORD sent Moses
and Aaron [1c]who brought your fathers out of Egypt and settled them
in this place.
9 "But [a]they forgot the LORD their
God, so [b]He sold them into the hand
of Sisera, captain of the army of Hazor, and [c]into the hand of the Philistines and [d]into the hand of the king
of Moab, and they fought against
them.
10 "And [a]they cried out to the LORD
and said, 'We have sinned because
we have forsaken the LORD and
have served [b]the Baals and the Ashtaroth; but [c]now deliver us from the
hands of our enemies, and we will
serve Thee.'
11 "Then the LORD sent [a]Jerubbaal
and [1b]Bedan and Jephthah and
Samuel, and delivered you from the
hands of your enemies all around, so
that you lived in security.

The King Confirmed

12 "When you saw [a]that Nahash
the king of the sons of Ammon came
against you, you said to me, '[b]No,
but a king shall reign over us,' [c]al-
though the LORD your God *was* your
king.
13 "Now therefore, [a]here is the king
whom you have chosen, [b]whom you
have asked for, and behold, the
LORD has set a king over you.
14 "[a]If you will fear the LORD and
serve Him, and listen to His voice
and not rebel against the [1]command
of the LORD, then both you and also
the king who reigns over you will
follow the LORD your God.
15 "And [a]if you will not listen to the
voice of the LORD, but rebel against
the [1]command of the LORD, then
[b]the hand of the LORD will be
against you, [c]*as it was* against your
fathers.
16 "Even now, [a]take your stand and
see this great thing which the LORD
will do before your eyes.

10 [1]Lit., *in your sight* [a]1 Sam. 11:3
11 [a]Judg. 7:16
12 [1]Lit., *Give* [a]1 Sam. 10:27 [b]Luke 19:27
13 [a]1 Sam. 10:27; 2 Sam. 19:22 [b]Ex. 14:13; 1 Sam. 19:5
14 [a]1 Sam. 7:16; 10:8 [b]1 Sam. 10:25
15 [a]1 Sam. 10:17 [b]1 Sam. 10:8
1 [1]Lit., *made* [a]1 Sam. 8:7, 9, 22 [b]1 Sam. 10:24; 11:14, 15
2 [a]1 Sam. 8:20 [b]1 Sam. 8:1, 5 [c]1 Sam. 8:3, 5 [d]1 Sam. 3:10, 19, 20
3 [a]1 Sam. 10:1; 24:6; 2 Sam. 1:14 [b]Ex. 20:17; Num. 16:15; Acts 20:33 [c]Ex. 23:8; Deut. 16:19
5 [a]Acts 23:9; 24:20 [b]Ex. 22:4
6 [1]Lit., *made* [a]Ex. 6:26
7 [a]Ezek. 20:35; Mic. 6:1-5
8 [1]Lit., *and they brought* [a]Ex. 2:23-25 [b]Ex. 3:10; 4:14-16 [c]1 Sam. 10:18
9 [a]Deut. 32:18; Judg. 3:7 [b]Judg. 4:2 [c]Judg. 3:31; 10:7; 13:1 [d]Judg. 3:12-30
10 [a]Judg. 10:10 [b]Judg. 2:13; 3:7 [c]Judg. 10:15, 16
11 [1]Gk. and Syr. read *Barak* [a]Judg. 6:31, 32 [b]Judg. 4:6; 11:1
12 [a]1 Sam. 11:1, 2 [b]1 Sam. 8:6, 19 [c]Judg. 8:23; 1 Sam. 8:7
13 [a]1 Sam. 10:24 [b]1 Sam. 8:5; 12:17, 19; Hos. 13:11
14 [1]Lit., *mouth* [a]Josh. 24:14
15 [1]Lit., *mouth* [a]Josh. 24:20; Is. 1:20 [b]1 Sam. 5:9 [c]1 Sam. 12:9
16 [a]Ex. 14:13, 31

17"[a]Is it not the wheat harvest today? [b]I will call to the LORD, that He
may send [1]thunder and rain. Then
you will know and see that [c]your
wickedness is great which you have
done in the sight of the LORD by asking for yourselves a king."
18 So Samuel called to the LORD,
and the LORD sent [1]thunder and rain
that day; and [a]all the people greatly
feared the LORD and Samuel.
19 Then all the people said to Samuel, "[a]Pray for your servants to the
LORD your God, so that we may not
die, for we have added to all our sins
[b]*this* evil by asking for ourselves a
king."
20 And Samuel said to the people,
"Do not fear. You have committed
all this evil, yet [a]do not turn aside
from following the LORD, but serve
the LORD with all your heart.
21"And you must not turn aside,
for *then you would go* after [a]futile
things which can not profit or deliver, because they are futile.
22"For [a]the LORD will not abandon
His people [b]on account of His great
name, because the LORD [c]has been
pleased to make you a people for
Himself.
23"Moreover, as for me, [a]far be it
from me that I should sin against the
LORD by ceasing to pray for you; but
[b]I will instruct you in the good and
right way.
24"[a]Only [1]fear the LORD and serve
Him in truth with all your heart; for
consider [b]what great things He has
done for you.
25"[a]But if you still do wickedly,
[b]both you and your king [c]shall be
swept away."

CHAPTER 13

War with the Philistines

SAUL was *forty* years old when he
began to reign, and he reigned
thirty-two years over Israel.
2 Now Saul chose for himself
3,000 men of Israel, of which 2,000
were with Saul in [a]Michmash and in
the hill country of Bethel, while
1,000 were with Jonathan at [b]Gibe-
ah of Benjamin. But he sent away
the rest of the people, each to his
tent.
3 And Jonathan smote [a]the garrison of the Philistines that was in
[b]Geba, and the Philistines heard of
it. Then Saul [c]blew the trumpet
throughout the land, saying, "Let
the Hebrews hear."
4 And all Israel heard [1]the news
that Saul had smitten the garrison
of the Philistines, and also that Israel [a]had become odious to the Philistines. The people were then summoned [2]to Saul at Gilgal.
5 Now the Philistines assembled
to fight with Israel, 30,000 chariots
and 6,000 horsemen, and [a]people
like the sand which is on the seashore in abundance; and they came
up and camped in Michmash, east of
[b]Beth-aven.
6 When the men of Israel saw
that they were in a strait (for the
people were hard-pressed), then
[a]the people hid themselves in caves,
in thickets, in cliffs, in cellars, and in
pits.
7 Also *some of* the Hebrews
crossed the Jordan into the land of
[a]Gad and Gilead. But as for Saul, he
was still in Gilgal, and all the people
followed him trembling.
8 Now [a]he waited seven days, according to the appointed time [1]set
by Samuel, but Samuel did not
come to Gilgal; and the people were
scattering from him.
9 So Saul said, "Bring to me the
burnt offering and the peace offerings." And [a]he offered the burnt offering.
10 And it came about as soon as he
finished offering the burnt offering,
that behold, Samuel came; and
[a]Saul went out to meet him *and* to
[1]greet him.

Saul Assumes Priestly Office

11 But Samuel said, "What have
you done?" And Saul said, "Because
I saw that the people were scattering from me, and that you did not
come within the appointed days,
and that [a]the Philistines were as-
sembling at Michmash,
12 therefore I said, 'Now the Philistines will come down against me
at Gilgal, and I have not asked the
favor of the LORD.' So I forced myself and offered the burnt offering."
13 And Samuel said to Saul, "[a]You
have acted foolishly; [b]you have not
kept the commandment of the LORD
your God, which He commanded
you, for now the LORD would have
established your kingdom [1]over Israel [c]forever.
14"But [a]now your kingdom shall
not endure. [b]The LORD has sought
out for Himself a man after His own
heart, and the LORD has appointed
him as ruler over His people, because you have not kept what the
LORD commanded you."
15 Then Samuel arose and went up
from Gilgal to [a]Gibeah of Benjamin.
And Saul [1]numbered the people

17 [1]Lit., *sounds* [a]Prov. 26:1 [b]1 Sam. 7:9, 10 [c]1 Sam. 8:7
18 [1]Lit., *sounds* [a]Ex. 14:31
19 [a]Ex. 9:28; 1 Sam. 12:23; Jer. 15:1 [b]1 Sam. 12:17, 20
20 [a]Deut. 11:16
21 [a]Is. 41:29; Hab. 2:18
22 [a]Deut. 31:6; 1 Kin. 6:13 [b]Ex. 32:12; Num. 14:13 [c]Deut. 7:6-11; 1 Pet. 2:9
23 [a]Rom. 1:9; Col. 1:9; 1 Thess. 3:10; 2 Tim. 1:3 [b]1 Kin. 8:36; Prov. 4:11
24 [1]Or, *reverence* [a]Eccles. 12:13 [b]Deut. 10:21
25 [a]Is. 1:20; 3:11 [b]Josh. 24:20 [c]1 Sam. 31:1-5; Hos. 10:3
2 [a]1 Sam. 13:5; 14:31 [b]1 Sam. 10:26
3 [a]1 Sam. 10:5 [b]1 Sam. 13:16; 14:5 [c]Judg. 3:27; 6:34
4 [1]Lit., *saying* [2]Lit., *after* [a]Gen. 34:30; Ex. 5:21; 2 Sam. 10:6
5 [a]Josh. 11:4 [b]1 Sam. 14:23
6 [a]Judg. 6:2
7 [a]Num. 32:33
8 [1]Lit., *which* [a]1 Sam. 10:8
9 [a]2 Sam. 24:25; 1 Kin. 3:4
10 [1]Lit., *bless* [a]1 Sam. 15:13
11 [a]1 Sam. 2:5, 16, 23
13 [1]Lit., *to* [a]2 Chr. 16:9 [b]1 Sam. 15:22, 28 [c]1 Sam. 1:22
14 [a]1 Sam. 15:28 [b]Acts 13:22
15 [1]Lit., *mustered* [a]1 Sam. 13:2

who were present with him, [b]about
six hundred men.
16 Now Saul and his son Jonathan
and the people who were present
with them were staying in [a]Geba of
Benjamin while the Philistines
camped at Michmash.
17 And [a]the [1]raiders came from
the camp of the Philistines in three
[2]companies: one [3]company turned
[4]toward [b]Ophrah, to the land of
Shual,
18 and another [1]company turned
[2]toward [a]Beth-horon, and another
[1]company turned [2]toward the border which overlooks the valley of
[b]Zeboim toward the wilderness.
19 Now [a]no blacksmith could be
found in all the land of Israel, for the
Philistines said, "Lest the Hebrews
make [1]swords or spears."
20 So all Israel went down to the
Philistines, each to sharpen his
plowshare, his mattock, his axe, and
his hoe.
21 And the charge was [1]two-thirds
of a shekel for the plowshares, the
mattocks, the forks, and the axes,
and to fix the hoes.
22 So it came about on the day of
battle that [a]neither sword nor spear
was found in the hands of any of the
people who *were* with Saul and
Jonathan, but they were found with
Saul and his son Jonathan.
23 And [a]the garrison of the Philistines went out to [b]the pass of Michmash.

Chapter 14

Jonathan's Victory

Now the day came that Jonathan,
the son of Saul, said to the young
man who was carrying his armor,
"Come and let us cross over to the
Philistines' garrison that is on yonder side." But he did not tell his father.
2 And Saul was staying in the
outskirts of [a]Gibeah under the
pomegranate tree which is in [b]Mig-
ron. And the people who *were* with
him *were* [c]about six hundred men,
3 and [a]Ahijah, the son of Ahitub,
[b]Ichabod's brother, the son of
Phinehas, the son of Eli, the priest of
the LORD at [c]Shiloh, [d]was [1]wearing
an ephod. And the people did not
know that Jonathan had gone.
4 And [a]between the passes by
which Jonathan sought to cross
over to the Philistines' garrison,
there was a sharp crag on the one
side, and a sharp crag on the other
side, and the name of the one was
Bozez, and the name of the other
Seneh.
5 The one crag rose on the north
opposite Michmash, and the other
on the south opposite Geba.
6 Then Jonathan said to the
young man who was carrying his armor, "Come and let us cross over to
the garrison of [a]these uncircumcised; perhaps the LORD will work
for us, for [b]the LORD is not restrained to save by many or by
few."
7 And his armor bearer said to
him, "Do all that is in your heart;
turn yourself, *and* here I am with
you according to your [1]desire."
8 Then Jonathan said, "[a]Behold,
we will cross over to the men and
reveal ourselves to them.
9 "If they [1]say to us, 'Wait until we
come to you'; then we will stand in
our place and not go up to them.
10 "But if they [1]say, 'Come up to
us,' then we will go up, for the LORD
has given them into our hands; and
[a]this shall be the sign to us."
11 And when both of them revealed themselves to the garrison of
the Philistines, the Philistines said,
"Behold, [a]Hebrews are coming out
of the holes where they have hidden
themselves."
12 So the men of the garrison
[1]hailed Jonathan and his armor
bearer and said, "Come up to us and
[a]we will tell you something." And
Jonathan said to his armor bearer,
"Come up after me, for [b]the LORD
has given them into the hands of Israel."
13 Then Jonathan climbed up on
his hands and feet, with his armor
bearer behind him; and they fell before Jonathan, and his armor bearer
put some to death after him.
14 And that first slaughter which
Jonathan and his armor bearer
made was about twenty men within
about half a furrow in an acre of
land.
15 And there was a trembling in
the camp, in the field, and among all
the people. Even the garrison and
[a]the raiders trembled, and [b]the
earth quaked so [c]that it became a
[1]great trembling.
16 Now Saul's watchmen in Gibeah of Benjamin looked, and behold,
the multitude melted away; and
they went here and *there.*
17 And Saul said to the people
who *were* with him, "[1]Number now
and see who has gone from us." And
when they had [1]numbered, behold,
Jonathan and his armor bearer were
not *there.*

15 [b]1 Sam. 13:2, 6, 7; 14:2
16 [a]1 Sam. 13:2, 3
17 [1]Lit., *destroyers* [2]Lit., *heads* [3]Lit., *head* [4]Lit., *toward the direction of* [a]1 Sam. 14:15 [b]Josh. 18:23
18 [1]Lit., *head* [2]Lit., *the direction of* [a]Josh. 18:13, 14 [b]Neh. 11:34
19 [1]Lit., *sword or spear* [a]Judg. 5:8; 2 Kin. 24:14
21 [1]Heb., *a pim*
22 [a]Judg. 5:8
23 [a]1 Sam. 14:1; 2 Sam. 23:14 [b]1 Sam. 14:4, 5; Is. 10:28
2 [a]1 Sam. 13:15, 16 [b]Is. 10:28 [c]1 Sam. 13:15
3 [1]Lit., *carrying* [a]1 Sam. 22:9-12, 20 [b]1 Sam. 4:21 [c]1 Sam. 1:3 [d]1 Sam. 2:28
4 [a]1 Sam. 13:23
6 [a]1 Sam. 17:26, 36; Jer. 9:25, 26 [b]Judg. 7:4, 7; 1 Sam. 17:46, 47; Heb. 11:34
7 [1]Lit., *heart*
8 [a]Judg. 7:9-14
9 [1]Lit., *say thus*
10 [1]Lit., *say thus* [a]Gen. 24:14; Judg. 6:36
11 [a]1 Sam. 13:6; 14:22
12 [1]Lit., *answered* [a]Judg. 8:16; 1 Sam. 17:43, 44 [b]2 Sam. 5:24
15 [1]Lit., *trembling of God* [a]1 Sam. 13:17, 18 [b]1 Sam. 7:10 [c]2 Kin. 7:6
17 [1]Lit., *muster(ed)*

18 Then Saul said to Ahijah, "[a]Bring the ark of God here." For the ark of God was at that time [1]with the sons of Israel.

19 And it happened [a]while Saul talked to the priest, that the commotion in the camp of the Philistines continued and increased; so Saul said to the priest, "Withdraw your hand."

20 Then Saul and all the people who *were* with him rallied and came to the battle; and behold, [a]every man's sword was against his fellow, *and there was* very great confusion.

21 Now the Hebrews *who* were with the Philistines previously, who went up with them all around in the camp, even [a]they also *turned* to be with the Israelites who *were* with Saul and Jonathan.

22 When all the [a]men of Israel who had hidden themselves in the hill country of Ephraim heard that the Philistines had fled, even they also pursued them closely in the battle.

23 So [a]the LORD delivered Israel that day, and the battle [1]spread beyond [b]Beth-aven.

Saul's Foolish Order

24 Now the men of Israel were hard-pressed on that day, for Saul had [a]put the people under oath, saying, "Cursed be the man who eats food [1]before evening, and until I have avenged myself on my enemies." So none of the people tasted food.

25 And all *the people of* the land entered the forest, and there was honey on the ground.

26 When the people entered the forest, behold, [a]*there was* a flow of honey; but no man put his hand to his mouth, for the people feared the oath.

27 But Jonathan had not heard when his father put the people under oath; therefore, [a]he put out the end of the staff that *was* in his hand and dipped it in the honeycomb, and put his hand to his mouth, and [b]his eyes brightened.

28 Then one of the people answered and said, "Your father strictly put the people under oath, saying, 'Cursed be the man who eats food today.' " And the people were weary.

29 Then Jonathan said, "[a]My father has troubled the land. See now, how my eyes have brightened because I tasted a little of this honey.

30 "How much more, if only the people had eaten freely today of the spoil of their enemies which they found! For now the slaughter among the Philistines has not been great."

31 And they struck among the Philistines that day from [a]Michmash to [b]Aijalon. And the people were very weary.

32 And [a]the people [1]rushed greedily upon the spoil, and took sheep and oxen and calves, and slew *them* on the ground; and the people ate *them* [b]with the blood.

33 Then they told Saul, saying, "Behold, the people are sinning against the LORD by eating with the blood." And he said, "You have acted treacherously; roll a great stone to me today."

34 And Saul said, "Disperse yourselves among the people and say to them, 'Each one of you bring me his ox or his sheep, and slaughter *it* here and eat; and do not sin against the LORD by eating with the blood.' " So all the people that night brought each one his ox [1]with him, and slaughtered *it* there.

35 And [a]Saul built an altar to the LORD; it was the first altar that he built to the LORD.

36 Then Saul said, "Let us go down after the Philistines by night and take spoil among them until the morning light, and let us not leave a man of them." And they said, "Do whatever seems good [1]to you." So [a]the priest said, "Let us draw near to God here."

37 And [a]Saul inquired of God, "Shall I go down after the Philistines? Wilt Thou give them into the hand of Israel?" But [b]He did not answer him on that day.

38 And Saul said, "[a]Draw near here, all you [1]chiefs of the people, and investigate and see how this sin has happened today.

39 "For [a]as the LORD lives, who delivers Israel, though it is in Jonathan my son, he shall surely die." But not one of all the people answered him.

40 Then he said to all Israel, "You shall be on one side and I and Jonathan my son will be on the other side." And the people said to Saul, "Do what seems good [1]to you."

41 Therefore, Saul said to the LORD, the God of Israel, "[a]Give a perfect *lot*." And Jonathan and Saul were taken, but the people escaped.

42 And Saul said, "Cast *lots* between me and Jonathan my son." And Jonathan was taken.

43 Then Saul said to Jonathan, "[a]Tell me what you have done." So Jonathan told him and said, "[b]I indeed tasted a little honey with the

18 [1]Lit., *and* [a]1 Sam. 23:9; 30:7
19 [a]Num. 27:21
20 [a]Judg. 7:22; 2 Chr. 20:23
21 [a]1 Sam. 29:4
22 [a]1 Sam. 13:6
23 [1]Lit., *passed over* [a]Ex. 14:30; 2 Chr. 32:22 [b]1 Sam. 13:5
24 [1]Lit., *until* [a]Josh. 6:26
26 [a]Matt. 3:4
27 [a]1 Sam. 14:43 [b]1 Sam. 30:12
29 [a]Josh. 7:25; 1 Kin. 18:18
31 [a]1 Sam. 14:5 [b]Josh. 10:12
32 [1]Lit., *did with regard to the spoil* [a]1 Sam. 15:19 [b]Gen. 9:4; Lev. 17:10-14; Acts 15:20
34 [1]Lit., *in his hand*
35 [a]1 Sam. 7:12, 17
36 [1]Lit., *in your eyes* [a]1 Sam. 14:3, 18, 19
37 [a]1 Sam. 10:22 [b]1 Sam. 28:6
38 [1]Lit., *corners* [a]Josh. 7:11, 12; 1 Sam. 10:19, 20
39 [a]1 Sam. 14:24, 44
40 [1]Lit., *in your eyes*
41 [a]Acts 1:24
43 [a]Josh. 7:19 [b]1 Sam. 14:27

end of the staff that was in my hand.
Here I am, I must die!"
44 And Saul said, "[a]May God do
[1]this *to me* and more also, for [b]you
shall surely die, Jonathan."
45 But the people said to Saul,
"Must Jonathan die, who has
[1]brought about this great deliverance in Israel? Far from it! As the
LORD lives, [a]there shall not one hair
of his head fall to the ground, for he
has worked with God this day." So
the people [2]rescued Jonathan and
he did not die.
46 Then Saul went up from [1]pur-
suing the Philistines, and the Philistines went to their own place.

Constant Warfare

47 Now when Saul had taken the
kingdom over Israel, he fought
against all his enemies on every
side, against Moab, [a]the sons of Ammon, Edom, [b]the kings of Zobah,
and [c]the Philistines; and wherever
he turned, he [1]inflicted punishment.
48 And he acted valiantly and
[1a]defeated the Amalekites, and delivered Israel from the hands of
[2]those who plundered them.
49 Now [a]the sons of Saul were
Jonathan and Ishvi and Malchi-
shua; and the names of his two
daughters *were these:* the name of
the first-born [b]Merab and the name
of the younger [c]Michal.
50 And the name of Saul's wife
was Ahinoam the daughter of
Ahimaaz. And [a]the name of the captain of his army was Abner the son
of Ner, Saul's uncle.
51 [a]And Kish *was* the father of
Saul, and Ner the father of Abner
was the son of Abiel.
52 Now the war against the Philistines was severe all the days of Saul;
and when Saul saw any mighty man
or any valiant man, he [1a]attached
him to [2]his staff.

CHAPTER 15

Saul's Disobedience

THEN Samuel said to Saul, "[a]The
LORD sent me to anoint you as king
over His people, over Israel; now
therefore listen to the [1]words of the
LORD.
2 "Thus says the LORD of hosts, 'I
will [1]punish Amalek [a]*for* what he
did to Israel, how he set himself
against him on the way while he was
coming up from Egypt.
3 'Now go and strike Amalek and
[a]utterly destroy all that he has, and
do not spare him; but [b]put to death
both man and woman, child and infant, ox and sheep, camel and donkey.' "
4 Then Saul summoned the people and [1]numbered them in [a]Telaim,
200,000 foot soldiers and 10,000
men of Judah.
5 And Saul came to the city of
Amalek, and set an ambush in the
valley.
6 And Saul said to [a]the Kenites,
"Go, depart, go down from among
the Amalekites, lest I destroy you
with them; for [b]you showed kindness to all the sons of Israel when
they came up from Egypt." So the
Kenites departed from among the
Amalekites.
7 So [a]Saul [1]defeated the Amalekites, from [b]Havilah as you go to
[c]Shur, which is [2]east of Egypt.
8 And he captured [a]Agag the
king of the Amalekites alive, and
[b]utterly destroyed all the people
with the edge of the sword.
9 But Saul and the people [a]spared
Agag and the best of the sheep, the
oxen, the fatlings, the lambs, and all
that was good, and were not willing
to destroy them utterly; but everything despised and worthless, that
they utterly destroyed.

Samuel Rebukes Saul

10 Then the word of the LORD
came to Samuel, saying,
11 "[a]I regret that I have made Saul
king, for [b]he has turned back from
[1]following Me, and has not carried
out My commands." And Samuel
was distressed and [c]cried out to the
LORD all night.
12 And Samuel rose early in the
morning to meet Saul; and it was
told Samuel, saying, "Saul came to
[a]Carmel, and behold, he set up a
monument for himself, then turned
and proceeded on [1]down to [b]Gil-
gal."
13 And Samuel came to Saul, and
Saul said to him, "[a]Blessed are you
of the LORD! I have carried out the
command of the LORD."
14 But Samuel said, "[a]What then
is this [1]bleating of the sheep in my
ears, and the [1]lowing of the oxen
which I hear?"
15 And Saul said, "They have
brought them from the Amalekites,
for [a]the people spared the best of
the sheep and oxen, to sacrifice to
the LORD your God; but the rest we
have utterly destroyed."
16 Then Samuel said to Saul,
"Wait, and let me tell you what the
LORD said to me last night." And he
said to him, "Speak!"

44 [1]Lit., *thus*
[a]1 Sam. 25:22
[b]1 Sam. 14:39
45 [1]Lit., *worked*
[2]Lit., *ransomed*
[a]2 Sam. 14:11;
1 Kin. 1:52;
Acts 27:34
46 [1]Lit., *after*
47 [1]Or, *condemned*
[a]1 Sam. 11:1-13
[b]2 Sam. 8:3-10
[c]1 Sam. 14:52
48 [1]Lit., *smote*
[2]Lit., *its plunderers*
[a]1 Sam. 15:3, 7
49 [a]1 Sam. 31:2;
1 Chr. 10:2
[b]1 Sam. 18:17-19
[c]1 Sam. 18:20, 27;
19:12;
2 Sam. 6:20-23
50 [a]2 Sam. 2:8
51 [a]1 Sam. 9:1, 21
52 [1]Lit., *gathered* [2]Lit., *himself*
[a]1 Sam. 8:11
1 [1]Lit., *sound of the words*
[a]1 Sam. 9:16
2 [1]Or, *visit*
[a]Ex. 17:8-16;
Num. 24:20;
Deut. 25:17-19
3 [a]Num. 24:20;
Deut. 20:16-18;
Josh. 6:17-21
[b]1 Sam. 22:19
4 [1]Lit., *mustered*
[a]Josh. 15:24
6 [a]Judg. 1:16;
4:11 [b]Ex. 18:9, 10,
19; Num. 10:29-32
7 [1]Lit., *smote*
[2]Lit., *before*
[a]1 Sam. 14:48
[b]Gen. 16:7; 25:17,
18 [c]Ex. 15:22;
1 Sam. 27:8
8 [a]Num. 24:7;
Esth. 3:1
[b]1 Sam. 27:8;
30:1; 2 Sam. 8:12
9 [a]1 Sam. 15:3,
15, 19
11 [1]Lit., *after*
[a]Gen. 6:6, 7;
Ex. 32:14;
2 Sam. 24:16
[b]1 Kin. 9:6, 7
[c]Ex. 32:11-13;
Luke 6:12
12 [1]Lit., *and went down*
[a]Josh. 15:55;
1 Sam 25:2
[b]1 Sam. 13:13, 14
13 [a]Gen. 14:19;
2 Sam. 2:5
14 [1]Lit., *sound*
[a]Ex. 32:21-24
15 [a]Gen. 3:12,
13; Ex. 32:22, 23;
1 Sam. 15:9, 21

17 And Samuel said, "Is it not true, [a]though you were little in your own eyes, you were *made* the head of the tribes of Israel? And the LORD anointed you king over Israel,

18 and the LORD sent you on a [1]mission, and said, '[a]Go and utterly destroy the sinners, the Amalekites, and fight against them until they are exterminated.'

19"Why then did you not obey the voice of the LORD, [a]but rushed upon the spoil and did what was evil in the sight of the LORD?"

20 Then Saul said to Samuel, "[a]I did obey the voice of the LORD, and went on the [1]mission on which the LORD sent me, and have brought back Agag the king of Amalek, and have utterly destroyed the Amalekites.

21"But [a]the people took *some* of the spoil, sheep and oxen, the choicest of the things devoted to destruction, to sacrifice to the LORD your God at Gilgal."

22 And Samuel said,
"[a]Has the LORD as much delight in burnt offerings and sacrifices
As in obeying the voice of the LORD?
Behold, [b]to obey is better than sacrifice,
And to heed than the fat of rams.

23 "For rebellion is as the sin of [a]divination,
And insubordination is as [b]iniquity and idolatry.
Because you have rejected the word of the LORD,
[c]He has also rejected you from *being* king."

24 Then Saul said to Samuel, "[a]I have sinned; [b]I have indeed transgressed the [1]command of the LORD and your words, because I feared the people and listened to their voice.

25"Now therefore, [a]please pardon my sin and return with me, that I may worship the LORD."

26 But Samuel said to Saul, "I will not return with you; for [a]you have rejected the word of the LORD, and the LORD has rejected you from being king over Israel."

27 And as Samuel turned to go, [a]*Saul* seized the edge of his robe, and it tore.

28 So Samuel said to him, "[a]The LORD has torn the kingdom of Israel from you today, and has given it to your neighbor who is better than you.

29"And also the [1a]Glory of Israel [b]will not lie or change His mind; for He is not a man that He should change His mind."

30 Then he said, "I have sinned; [a]*but* please honor me now before the elders of my people and before Israel, and go back with me, [b]that I may worship the LORD your God."

31 So Samuel went back following Saul, and Saul worshiped the LORD.

32 Then Samuel said, "Bring me Agag, the king of the Amalekites." And Agag came to him [1]cheerfully. And Agag said, "Surely the bitterness of death is past."

33 But Samuel said, "[a]As your sword has made women childless, so shall your mother be childless among women." And Samuel hewed Agag to pieces before the LORD at Gilgal.

34 Then Samuel went to [a]Ramah, but Saul went up to his house at [b]Gibeah of Saul.

35 And [a]Samuel did not see Saul again until the day of his death; for Samuel [b]grieved over Saul. And the LORD regretted that He had made Saul king over Israel.

CHAPTER 16

Samuel Goes to Bethlehem

NOW the LORD said to Samuel, "[a]How long will you grieve over Saul, since [b]I have rejected him from being king over Israel? [c]Fill your horn with oil, and go; I will send you to [d]Jesse the Bethlehemite, for I have selected a king for Myself among his sons."

2 But Samuel said, "How can I go? When Saul hears *of it,* he will kill me." And the LORD said, "[a]Take a heifer with you, and say, 'I have come to sacrifice to the LORD.'

3"And you shall invite Jesse to the sacrifice, and [a]I will show you what you shall do; and [b]you shall anoint for Me the one whom I [1]designate to you."

4 So Samuel did what the LORD said, and came to [a]Bethlehem. And the elders of the city came trembling to meet him and said, "[b]Do you come in peace?"

5 And he said, "In peace; I have come to sacrifice to the LORD. [a]Consecrate yourselves and come with me to the sacrifice." He also consecrated Jesse and his sons, and invited them to the sacrifice.

6 Then it came about when they entered, that he looked at [a]Eliab and thought, "Surely the LORD's anointed is before Him."

---

17 [a]1 Sam. 9:21; 10:22
18 [1]Lit., *way* [a]1 Sam. 15:3
19 [a]1 Sam. 14:32
20 [1]Lit., *way* [a]1 Sam. 15:13
21 [a]Ex. 32:22, 23; 1 Sam. 15:15
22 [a]Ps. 40:6-8; 51:16, 17; Is. 1:11-15; Mic. 6:6-8 [b]Jer. 7:22, 23; Hos. 6:6; Mark 12:33
23 [a]Deut. 18:10 [b]Gen. 31:19, 34 [c]1 Sam. 13:14
24 [1]Lit., *mouth* [a]Num. 22:34; 2 Sam. 12:13; Ps. 51:4 [b]Prov. 29:25; Is. 51:12, 13
25 [a]Ex. 10:17
26 [a]1 Sam. 13:14; 16:1
27 [a]1 Kin. 11:30, 31
28 [a]1 Sam. 28:17, 18
29 [1]Or, *Eminence* [a]1 Chr. 29:11; Ps. 18:1, 2 [b]Num. 23:19; Ezek. 24:14
30 [a]John 12:43 [b]Is. 29:13
32 [1]Or, *in bonds*
33 [a]Gen. 9:6; Judg. 1:7; Matt. 7:2
34 [a]1 Sam. 7:17 [b]1 Sam. 11:4
35 [a]1 Sam. 19:24 [b]1 Sam. 16:1
1 [a]1 Sam. 15:35 [b]1 Sam. 13:13, 14; 15:23 [c]1 Sam. 9:16; 10:1; 2 Kin. 9:1 [d]Ruth 4:18-22
2 [a]1 Sam. 20:29
3 [1]Lit., *say to you* [a]Ex. 4:15; Acts 9:6 [b]Deut. 17:14, 15; 1 Sam. 9:16
4 [a]Gen. 48:7; Luke 2:4 [b]1 Kin. 2:13; 2 Kin. 9:22; 1 Chr. 12:17, 18
5 [a]Gen. 35:2; Ex. 19:10
6 [a]1 Sam. 17:13

7 But the LORD said to Samuel,
"Do not look at his appearance or at
the height of his stature, because I
have rejected him; for [1]God *sees* not
as man sees, for man looks at the
outward appearance, [a]but the LORD
looks at the heart."
8 Then Jesse called [a]Abinadab,
and made him pass before Samuel.
And he said, "Neither has the LORD
chosen this one."
9 Next Jesse made [a]Shammah
pass by. And he said, "Neither has
the LORD chosen this one."
10 Thus Jesse made seven of his
sons pass before Samuel. But Samuel said to Jesse, "The LORD has not
chosen these."
11 And Samuel said to Jesse, "Are
these all the children?" And he said,
"[a]There remains yet the youngest,
and behold, he is tending the
sheep." Then Samuel said to Jesse,
"Send and [1]bring him; for we will
not sit down until he comes here."

David Anointed

12 So he sent and brought him in.
Now he was ruddy, with [a]beautiful
eyes and a handsome appearance.
And the LORD said, "[b]Arise, anoint
him; for this is he."
13 Then Samuel took the horn of
oil and [a]anointed him in the midst of
his brothers; and [b]the Spirit of the
LORD came mightily upon David
from that day forward. And Samuel
arose and went to Ramah.
14 [a]Now the Spirit of the LORD departed from Saul, and [b]an evil spirit
from the LORD terrorized him.
15 Saul's servants then said to
him, "Behold now, an evil spirit
from God is terrorizing you.
16"Let our lord now command
your servants who are before you.
Let them seek a man who is a skillful player on the harp; and it shall
come about when the evil spirit
from God is on you, that [a]he shall
play *the harp* with his hand, and you
will be well."
17 So Saul said to his servants,
"Provide for me now a man who can
play well, and bring *him* to me."
18 Then one of the young men answered and said, "Behold, I have
seen a son of Jesse the Bethlehemite
who is a skillful musician, [a]a mighty
man of valor, a warrior, one prudent
in speech, and a handsome man; and
[b]the LORD is with him."
19 So Saul sent messengers to
Jesse, and said, "Send me your son
David who is with the flock."
20 And Jesse [a]took a donkey
loaded with bread and a jug of wine
and a young goat, and sent *them* to
Saul by David his son.
21 Then David came to Saul and
[1a]attended him, and [2]Saul loved him
greatly; and he became his armor
bearer.
22 And Saul sent to Jesse, saying,
"Let David now stand before me; for
he has found favor in my sight."
23 So it came about whenever [a]the
evil spirit from God came to Saul,
David would take the harp and play
it with his hand; and Saul would be
refreshed and be well, and the evil
spirit would depart from him.

CHAPTER 17

Goliath's Challenge

NOW [a]the Philistines gathered
their armies for battle; and they
were gathered at Socoh which belongs to Judah, and they camped between [b]Socoh and [c]Azekah, in
[d]Ephes-dammim.
2 And Saul and the men of Israel
were gathered, and camped in [a]the
valley of Elah, and drew up in battle
array to encounter the Philistines.
3 And the Philistines stood on the
mountain on one side while Israel
stood on the mountain on the other
side, with the valley between them.
4 Then a champion came out
from the armies of the Philistines
named [a]Goliath, from [b]Gath, whose
height was six [1]cubits and a span.
5 And *he had* a bronze helmet on
his head, and he was clothed with
scale armor [1]which weighed five
thousand shekels of bronze.
6 *He* also *had* bronze [1]greaves on
his legs and a [a]bronze javelin *slung*
between his shoulders.
7 And [a]the shaft of his spear was
like a weaver's beam, and the head
of his spear *weighed* six hundred
shekels of iron; [b]his shield-carrier
also walked before him.
8 And he stood and shouted to
the ranks of Israel, and said to them,
"Why do you come out to draw up
in battle array? Am I not the Philistine and you [a]servants of Saul?
Choose a man for yourselves and let
him come down to me.
9"[a]If he is able to fight with me
and [1]kill me, then we will become
your servants; but if I prevail
against him and [1]kill him, then you
shall become our servants and serve
us."
10 Again the Philistine said, "[a]I
defy the ranks of Israel this day;
give me a man that we may fight
together."

16:7 [1]So with Gk.; Heb., *He sees not what man sees* [a]1 Sam.2:3; 1 Kin. 8:39; 1 Chr. 28:9; Luke 16:15
8 [a]1 Sam. 17:13
9 [a]1 Sam. 17:13
11 [1]Lit., *take* [a]1 Sam. 17:12; 2 Sam. 13:3
12 [a]Gen. 39:6; Ex. 2:2; Acts 7:20 [b]1 Sam. 9:17
13 [a]1 Sam. 10:1 [b]1 Sam. 10:6, 9, 10
14 [a]1 Sam. 11:6; 18:12; 28:15 [b]1 Sam. 16:15, 16; 18:10; 19:9; 1 Kin. 22:19-22
16 [a]1 Sam. 18:10; 19:9; 2 Kin. 3:15
18 [a]1 Sam. 17:32-36 [b]1 Sam. 3:19
20 [a]1 Sam. 10:4, 27; Prov. 18:16
21 [1]Lit., *stood before him* [2]Lit., *he* [a]Gen. 41:46; Prov. 22:29
23 [a]1 Sam. 16:14-16

17:1 [a]1 Sam. 13:5 [b]2 Chr. 28:18 [c]Josh. 10:10 [d]1 Chr. 11:13
2 [a]1 Sam. 21:9
4 [1]One cubit equals approx. 18 inches [a]2 Sam. 21:19 [b]Josh. 11:21, 22
5 [1]Lit., *and the weight of the armor* was
6 [1]Or, *shin guards* [a]1 Sam. 17:45
7 [a]2 Sam. 21:19; 1 Chr. 11:23 [b]1 Sam. 17:41
8 [a]1 Sam. 8:17
9 [1]Lit., *smite* [a]2 Sam. 2:12-16
10 [a]1 Sam. 17:26, 36, 45

11 When Saul and all Israel heard
these words of the Philistine, they
were dismayed and greatly afraid.
12 Now David was [a]the son of [1]the
[b]Ephrathite of Bethlehem in Judah,
whose name was Jesse, and [c]he had
eight sons. And [2]Jesse was old in the
days of Saul, advanced *in years*
among men.
13 And the three older sons of
Jesse had [1]gone after Saul to the
battle. And [a]the names of his three
sons who went to the battle were
Eliab the first-born, and the second
to him Abinadab, and the third
Shammah.
14 And [a]David was the youngest.
Now the three oldest followed Saul,
15 [a]but David went back and forth
from Saul to tend his father's flock
at Bethlehem.
16 And the Philistine came [1]for-
ward morning and evening for forty
days, and took his stand.
17 Then Jesse said to David his
son, "[a]Take now for your brothers
an ephah of this roasted grain and
these ten loaves, and run to the
camp to your brothers.
18"[a]Bring also these ten cuts of
cheese to the commander of *their*
thousand, [b]and look into the welfare
of your brothers, and bring back
[1]news of them.
19"For Saul and they and all the
men of Israel are in the valley of
Elah, fighting with the Philistines."

David Accepts the Challenge

20 So David arose early in the
morning and left the flock with a
keeper and took *the supplies* and
went as Jesse had commanded him.
And he came to the [a]circle of the
camp while the army was going out
in battle array shouting the war cry.
21 And Israel and the Philistines
drew up in battle array, army
against army.
22 Then David left his [a]baggage in
the [1]care of the baggage keeper, and
ran to the battle line and entered in
order to greet his brothers.
23 As he was talking with them,
behold, the champion, the Philistine
from Gath named Goliath, was coming up from the army of the Philistines, and he spoke [a]these same
words; and David heard *them*.
24 When all the men of Israel saw
the man, they fled from him and
were greatly afraid.
25 And the men of Israel said,
"Have you seen this man who is
coming up? Surely he is coming up
to defy Israel. And it will be that the
king will enrich the man who kills
him with great riches and [a]will give
him his daughter [b]and make his father's house [1]free in Israel."
26 Then David spoke to the men
who were standing by him, saying,
"What will be done for the man who
kills this Philistine, and takes away
[a]the reproach from Israel? For who
is this [b]uncircumcised Philistine,
that he should [c]taunt the armies of
[d]the living God?"
27 And the people [1]answered him
in accord with this word, saying,
"[a]Thus it will be done for the man
who kills him."
28 Now Eliab his oldest brother
heard when he spoke to the men;
and [a]Eliab's anger burned against
David and he said, "Why have you
come down? And with whom have
you left those few sheep in the wilderness? I know your insolence and
the wickedness of your heart; for
you have come down in order to see
the battle."
29 But David said, "What have I
done now? [a]Was it not just a [1]ques-
tion?"
30 Then he turned [1]away from him
to another and [a]said the same thing;
and the people answered the same
thing as [2]before.

David Kills Goliath

31 When the words which David
spoke were heard, they told *them*
[1]to Saul, and he sent for him.
32 And David said to Saul, "[a]Let
no man's heart fail on account of
him; [b]your servant will go and fight
with this Philistine."
33 Then Saul said to David, "You
are not able to go against this Philistine to fight with him; for you are
but a youth while he has been a warrior from his youth."
34 But David said to Saul, "Your
servant was tending his father's
sheep. When a lion or a bear came
and took a lamb from the flock,
35 I went out after him and [1]at-
tacked him, and [a]rescued *it* from his
mouth; and when he rose up against
me, I seized *him* by his beard and
[1]struck him and killed him.
36"Your servant has [1]killed both
the lion and the bear; and this uncircumcised Philistine will be like one
of them, since he has taunted the
armies of the living God."
37 And David said, "[a]The LORD
who delivered me from the paw of
the lion and from the paw of the
bear, He will deliver me from the
hand of this Philistine." And Saul

12 [1]Lit., *this* [2]Lit., *the man* [a]Ruth 4:22; 1 Sam. 16:18 [b]Gen. 35:19 [c]1 Sam. 16:10, 11; 1 Chr. 2:13-15
13 [1]Lit., *gone; they went* [a]1 Sam. 16:6, 8, 9
14 [a]1 Sam. 16:11
15 [a]1 Sam. 16:21-23
16 [1]Lit., *near*
17 [a]1 Sam. 25:18
18 [1]Lit., *their pledge* [a]1 Sam. 16:20 [b]Gen. 37:13, 14
20 [a]1 Sam. 26:5, 7
22 [1]Lit., *hand* [a]Judg. 18:21; Is. 10:28
23 [a]1 Sam. 17:8-10
25 [1]I.e., free from taxes and public service [a]Josh. 15:16 [b]1 Sam. 8:11
26 [a]1 Sam. 11:2 [b]1 Sam. 14:6; 17:36; Jer. 9:25, 26 [c]1 Sam. 17:10 [d]Deut. 5:26; 2 Kin. 19:4
27 [1]Lit., *said to* [a]1 Sam. 17:25
28 [a]Gen. 37:4, 8-36
29 [1]Lit., *word* [a]1 Sam. 17:17
30 [1]Lit., *from beside him* [2]Lit., *the former word* [a]1 Sam. 17:26, 27
31 [1]Lit., *before*
32 [a]Deut. 20:1-4 [b]1 Sam. 16:18
35 [1]Lit., *smote* [a]Amos 3:12
36 [1]Lit., *smitten*
37 [a]2 Tim. 4:17

said to David, "[b]Go, and may the LORD be with you."

38 Then Saul clothed David with his garments and put a bronze helmet on his head, and he clothed him with armor.

39 And David girded his sword over his armor and tried to walk, for he had not tested *them*. So David said to Saul, "I cannot go with these, for I have not tested *them*." And David took them [1]off.

40 And he took his stick in his hand and chose for himself five smooth stones from the brook, and put them in the shepherd's bag which he had, even in *his* pouch, and [a]his sling was in his hand; and he approached the Philistine.

41 Then the Philistine came on and approached David, with the shield-bearer in front of him.

42 When the Philistine looked and saw David, [a]he disdained him; for he was *but* a youth, and [b]ruddy, with a handsome appearance.

43 And the Philistine said to David, "[a]Am I a dog, that you come to me with sticks?" And [b]the Philistine cursed David by his gods.

44 The Philistine also said to David, "Come to me, and I will give your flesh [a]to the birds of the sky and the beasts of the field."

45 Then David said to the Philistine, "You come to me with a sword, a spear, and a javelin, [a]but I come to you in the name of the LORD of hosts, the God of the armies of Israel, whom you have taunted.

46 "This day the LORD will deliver you up into my hands, and I will strike you down and remove your head from you. And I will give the dead bodies of the army of the Philistines this day to the birds of the sky and the wild beasts of the earth, [a]that all the earth may know that there is a God in Israel,

47 and that all this assembly may know that [a]the LORD does not deliver by sword or by spear; for the battle is the LORD's and He will give you into our hands."

48 Then it happened when the Philistine rose and came and drew near to meet David, that [a]David ran quickly toward the battle line to meet the Philistine.

49 And David put his hand into his bag and took from it a stone and slung *it*, and struck the Philistine on his forehead. And the stone sank into his forehead, so that he fell on his face to the ground.

50 Thus David prevailed over the Philistine with a sling and a stone, and he struck the Philistine and killed him; but there was no sword in David's hand.

51 Then David ran and stood over the Philistine and [a]took his sword and drew it out of its sheath and killed him, and cut off his head with it. [b]When the Philistines saw that their champion was dead, they fled.

52 And the men of Israel and Judah arose and shouted and pursued the Philistines as far as [1]the entrance to the valley, and to the gates of [a]Ekron. And the slain Philistines [2]lay along the way to [b]Shaaraim, even to Gath and Ekron.

53 And the sons of Israel returned from chasing the Philistines and plundered their camps.

54 Then David took the Philistine's head and brought it to Jerusalem, but he put his weapons in his tent.

55 Now when Saul saw David going out against the Philistine, he said to Abner the commander of the army, "Abner, whose son is [a]this young man?" And Abner said, "By your life, O king, I do not know."

56 And the king said, "You inquire whose son the youth is."

57 So when David returned from killing the Philistine, Abner took him and [a]brought him before Saul with the Philistine's head in his hand.

58 And Saul said to him, "Whose son are you, young man?" And David answered, "[a]*I am* the son of your servant Jesse the Bethlehemite."

CHAPTER 18

Jonathan and David

NOW it came about when he had finished speaking to Saul, that [a]the soul of Jonathan was knit to the soul of David, and [b]Jonathan loved him as himself.

2 And Saul took him that day and [a]did not let him return to his father's house.

3 Then [a]Jonathan made a covenant [1]with David because he loved him as himself.

4 And [a]Jonathan stripped himself of the robe that was on him and gave it to David, with his armor, including his sword and his bow and his belt.

5 So David went out wherever Saul sent him, *and* [1]prospered; and Saul set him over the men of war. And it was pleasing in the sight of all the people and also in the sight of Saul's servants.

---

37 [b]1 Sam. 20:13
39 [1]Lit., *off from himself*
40 [a]Judg. 20:16
42 [a]Prov. 16:18 [b]1 Sam. 16:12
43 [a]1 Sam. 24:14; 2 Sam. 3:8 [b]1 Kin. 20:10
44 [a]1 Sam. 17:46
45 [a]2 Chr. 32:8; Ps. 124:8; Heb. 11:34
46 [a]1 Kin. 18:36; 2 Kin. 19:19; Is. 37:20
47 [a]1 Sam. 14:6; 2 Chr. 14:11; 20:15; Ps. 44:6
48 [a]Ps. 27:3
51 [a]1 Sam. 21:9; 2 Sam. 23:21 [b]Heb. 11:34
52 [1]Lit., *your coming* [2]Lit., *fell* [a]Josh. 15:11 [b]Josh. 15:36
55 [a]1 Sam. 16:12, 21, 22
57 [a]1 Sam. 17:54
58 [a]1 Sam. 17:12
1 [a]Gen. 44:30 [b]Deut. 13:6; 1 Sam. 20:17; 2 Sam. 1:26
2 [a]1 Sam. 17:15
3 [1]Lit., *and* [a]1 Sam. 20:8-17
4 [a]Gen. 41:42; 1 Sam. 17:38; Esth. 6:8
5 [1]Or, *acted wisely*

6 And it happened as they were coming, when David returned from killing the Philistine, that [a]the women came out of all the cities of Israel, singing and dancing, to meet King Saul, with tambourines, with joy and with [1]musical instruments.
7 And the women [a]sang as they [1]played, and said,

"[b]Saul has slain his thousands,
[c]And David his ten thousands."

8 Then Saul became very angry, for this saying [1]displeased him; and he said, "They have ascribed to David ten thousands, but to me they have ascribed thousands. Now [a]what more can he have but the kingdom?"
9 And Saul looked at David with suspicion from that day on.

Saul Turns against David

10 Now it came about on the next day that [a]an evil spirit from God came mightily upon Saul, and [b]he raved in the midst of the house, while David was playing *the harp* with his hand, [1c]as usual; and [2d]a spear *was* in Saul's hand.
11 And [a]Saul hurled the spear for he thought, "I will [1]pin David to the wall." But David [2]escaped from his presence twice.
12 Now [a]Saul was afraid of David, [b]for the LORD was with him but [c]had departed from Saul.
13 Therefore Saul removed him from [1]his presence, and appointed him as his commander of a thousand; and [a]he went out and came in before the people.
14 And David was [1]prospering in all his ways for [a]the LORD *was* with him.
15 When Saul saw that he was [1]prospering greatly, he dreaded him.
16 But [a]all Israel and Judah loved David, and he went out and came in before them.
17 Then Saul said to David, "[a]Here is my older daughter Merab; I will give her to you as a wife, only be a valiant man for me and fight [b]the LORD's battles." For Saul thought, "My hand shall not be against him, but [c]let the hand of the Philistines be against him."
18 But David said to Saul, "[a]Who am I, and what is my life *or* my father's family in Israel, that I should be the king's son-in-law?"
19 So it came about at the time when Merab, Saul's daughter, should have been given to David, that she was given to [a]Adriel [b]the Meholathite for a wife.

David Marries Saul's Daughter

20 Now [a]Michal, Saul's daughter, loved David. When they told Saul, the thing was agreeable [1]to him.
21 And Saul thought, "I will give her to him that she may become a snare to him, and [a]that the hand of the Philistines may be against him." Therefore Saul said to David, "[b]For a second time you may be my son-in-law today."
22 Then Saul commanded his servants, "Speak to David secretly, saying, 'Behold, the king delights in you, and all his servants love you; now therefore, become the king's son-in-law.' "
23 So Saul's servants spoke these words [1]to David. But David said, "Is it trivial in your sight to become the king's son-in-law, [a]since I am a poor man and lightly esteemed?"
24 And the servants of Saul reported to him [1]according to these words *which* David spoke.
25 Saul then said, "Thus you shall say to David, 'The king does not desire any [a]dowry except a hundred foreskins of the Philistines, [b]to take vengeance on the king's enemies.' " Now [c]Saul planned to make David fall by the hand of the Philistines.
26 When his servants told David these words, [1]it pleased David to become the king's son-in-law. [2a]Before the days had expired
27 David rose up and went, [a]he and his men, and struck down two hundred men among the Philistines. Then [b]David brought their foreskins, and they gave them in full number to the king, that he might become the king's son-in-law. So Saul gave him Michal his daughter for a wife.
28 When Saul saw and knew that the LORD was with David, and *that* Michal, Saul's daughter, loved him,
29 then Saul was even more afraid of David. Thus Saul was David's enemy continually.
30 Then the commanders of the Philistines went out *to battle*, and it happened as often as they went out, that David [a]behaved himself more wisely than all the servants of Saul. So his name was highly esteemed.

CHAPTER 19

David Protected from Saul

NOW Saul told Jonathan his son and all his servants [a]to put David to

6 [1]I.e., triangles, or, three-stringed instruments [a]Ex. 15:20, 21; Judg. 11:34; Ps. 68:25; 149:3
7 [1]Or, *danced* [a]Ex. 15:21; 1 Sam. 21:11; 29:5 [b]1 Sam. 21:11 [c]2 Sam. 18:3
8 [1]Lit., *was evil in his eyes* [a]1 Sam. 15:28
10 [1]Lit., *day by day* [2]Lit., *the* [a]1 Sam. 16:14 [b]1 Sam. 19:23, 24 [c]1 Sam. 16:23 [d]1 Sam. 19:9
11 [1]Lit., *strike David and the wall* [2]Lit., *turned about* [a]1 Sam. 19:10; 20:33
12 [a]1 Sam. 18:15, 29 [b]1 Sam. 16:13, 18 [c]1 Sam. 16:14; 28:15
13 [1]Lit., *with him* [a]1 Sam. 18:16; 2 Sam. 5:2
14 [1]Or, *acting wisely* [a]1 Sam. 16:18
15 [1]Or, *acting very wisely*
16 [a]1 Sam. 18:5
17 [a]1 Sam. 17:25 [b]Num. 21:14; 1 Sam. 17:36, 47; 25:28 [c]1 Sam. 18:21, 25
18 [a]1 Sam. 9:21; 18:23; 2 Sam. 7:18
19 [a]2 Sam. 21:8 [b]Judg. 7:22; 1 Kin. 19:16
20 [1]Lit., *in his sight* [a]1 Sam. 18:28
21 [a]1 Sam. 18:17 [b]1 Sam. 18:26
23 [1]Lit., *in the ears of* [a]Gen. 29:20; 34:12
24 [1]Lit., *by saying according*
25 [a]Ex. 22:17 [b]1 Sam. 14:24 [c]1 Sam. 18:17
26 [1]Lit., *it was agreeable in the sight of* [2]Lit., *And the days had not expired* [a]1 Sam. 18:21
27 [a]1 Sam. 18:17 [b]2 Sam. 3:14
30 [a]1 Sam. 18:5
1 [a]1 Sam. 18:8, 9

death. But [b]Jonathan, Saul's son,
greatly delighted in David.
2 So Jonathan told David, saying
"Saul my father is seeking to put
you to death. Now therefore, please
be on guard in the morning, and stay
in a secret place and hide yourself.
3"And I will go out and stand beside my father in the field where you
are, and I will speak with my father
about you; [a]if I [1]find out anything,
then I shall tell you."
4 Then Jonathan [a]spoke well of
David to Saul his father, and said to
him, "[b]Do not let the king sin
against his servant David, since he
has not sinned against you, and
since his deeds *have been* very
[1]beneficial to you.
5"For [a]he took his life in his hand
and struck the Philistine, and [b]the
LORD brought about a great deliverance for all Israel; you saw *it* and
rejoiced. [c]Why then will you sin
against innocent blood, by putting
David to death without a cause?"
6 And Saul listened to the voice
of Jonathan, and Saul vowed, "As
the LORD lives, he shall not be put to
death."
7 Then Jonathan called David,
and Jonathan told him all these
words. And Jonathan brought David to Saul, and he was in his presence as [a]formerly.
8 When there was war again, David went out and fought with the
Philistines, and [1]defeated them with
great slaughter, so that they fled before him.
9 Now there was [a]an evil spirit
from the LORD on Saul as he was
sitting in his house [b]with his spear in
his hand, [c]and David was playing
the harp with *his* hand.
10 [a]And Saul tried to [1]pin David to
the wall with the spear, but he
slipped away out of Saul's presence,
so that he struck the spear into the
wall. And David fled and escaped
that night.
11 Then [a]Saul sent messengers to
David's house to watch him, in order to put him to death in the morning. But Michal, David's wife, told
him, saying, "If you do not save
your life tonight, tomorrow you will
be put to death."
12 [a]So Michal let David down
through a window, and he went out
and fled and escaped.
13 And Michal took [a]the [1]house-
hold idol and laid *it* on the bed, and
put a quilt of goats' *hair* at its head,
and covered *it* with clothes.
14 When Saul sent messengers to
take David, she said, "[a]He is sick."

15 Then Saul sent messengers to
see David, saying, "Bring him up to
me on [1]his bed, that I may put him
to death."
16 When the messengers entered,
behold, the [1]household idol *was* on
the bed with the quilt of goats' *hair*
at its head.
17 So Saul said to Michal, "Why
have you deceived me like this and
let my enemy go, so that he has escaped?" And Michal said to Saul,
"He said to me, 'Let me go! Why
should I put you to death?' "
18 Now David fled and escaped
and came [a]to Samuel at Ramah, and
told him all that Saul had done to
him. And he and Samuel went and
stayed in [b]Naioth.
19 And it was told Saul, saying,
"Behold, David is at Naioth in Ramah."
20 Then [a]Saul sent messengers to
take David, but when they saw [b]the
company of the prophets prophesying, with Samuel standing *and* pre-
siding over them, the Spirit of God
came upon the messengers of Saul;
and [c]they also prophesied.
21 And when it was told Saul, he
sent other messengers, and they
also prophesied. So Saul sent messengers again the third time, and
they also prophesied.
22 Then he himself went to Ramah, and came as far as the large
well that is in Secu; and he asked
and said, "Where are Samuel and
David?" And *someone* said, "Behold, they are at Naioth in Ramah."
23 And he [1]proceeded there to
Naioth in Ramah; and [a]the Spirit of
God came upon him also, so that he
went along prophesying continually
until he came to Naioth in Ramah.
24 And he also stripped off his
clothes, and he too prophesied before Samuel and [1]lay down [2a]naked
all that day and all that night. Therefore they say, "[b]Is Saul also among
the prophets?"

CHAPTER 20

David and Jonathan Covenant

THEN David fled from Naioth in
Ramah, and came and [a]said [1]to
Jonathan, "What have I done? What
is my iniquity? And what is my sin
before your father, that he is seeking my life?"
2 And he said to him, "Far from
it, you shall not die. Behold, my father does nothing either great or
small [1]without disclosing it to me.

1 [b]1 Sam. 18:1-3
3 [1]Lit. *see* [a]1 Sam. 20:9, 13
4 [1]Lit., *good* [a]1 Sam. 20:32 [b]Gen. 42:22
5 [a]1 Sam. 17:49, 50 [b]1 Sam. 11:13 [c]Deut. 19:10-13; Ps. 94:21
7 [a]1 Sam. 16:21; 18:2, 10, 13
8 [1]Lit., *smote*
9 [a]1 Sam. 16:14; 18:10, 11 [b]1 Sam. 18:10 [c]1 Sam. 16:16
10 [1]Lit., *strike David and the wall* [a]1 Sam. 18:11; 20:33
11 [a]Judg. 16:2; Ps. 59:title
12 [a]Josh. 2:15; 2 Cor. 11:33
13 [1]Heb., *teraphim* [a]Gen. 31:19; Judg. 18:14, 17
14 [a]Josh. 2:5
15 [1]Lit., *the*
16 [1]Heb., *teraphim*
18 [a]1 Sam. 7:17 [b]2 Kin. 6:1, 2
20 [a]1 Sam. 19:11, 14 [b]1 Sam. 10:5, 6, 10 [c]Num. 11:25
23 [1]Lit., *went* [a]1 Sam. 10:10
24 [1]Lit., *fell* [2]I.e., without outward garments [a]Is. 20:2 [b]1 Sam. 10:10-12
1 [1]Lit., *before* [a]1 Sam. 24:9
2 [1]Lit., *and he does not uncover my ear*

So why should my father hide this thing from me? It is not so!"

3 Yet David [a]vowed again, [1]saying, "Your father knows well that I have found favor in your sight, and he has said, 'Do not let Jonathan know this, lest he be grieved.' But truly [b]as the LORD lives and as your soul lives, there is [2]hardly a step between me and death."

4 Then Jonathan said to David, "Whatever [1]you say, I will do for you."

5 So David said to Jonathan, "Behold, tomorrow is [a]the new moon, and I ought [b]to sit down to eat with the king. But let me go, [c]that I may hide myself in the field until the third evening.

6 "If your father misses me at all, then say, 'David earnestly asked *leave* of me to run to [a]Bethlehem his city, because it is [b]the yearly sacrifice there for the whole family.'

7 "If he [1]says, 'It is good,' your servant *shall be* safe; but if he is very angry, know that he has decided on evil.

8 "Therefore deal kindly with your servant, for [a]you have brought your servant into a covenant of the LORD with you. But [b]if there is iniquity in me, put me to death yourself; for why then should you bring me to your father?"

9 And Jonathan said, "Far be it from you! For if I should indeed learn that evil has been decided by my father to come upon you, then would I not tell you about it?"

10 Then David said to Jonathan, "Who will tell me [1]if your father answers you harshly?"

11 And Jonathan said to David, "Come, and let us go out into the field." So both of them went out to the field.

12 Then Jonathan said to David, "The LORD, the God of Israel, *be witness*! When I have sounded out my father about this time tomorrow, *or* the third day, behold, if there is good *feeling* toward David, shall I not then send to you and [1]make it known to you?

13 "If it please my father to do you harm, [a]may the LORD do so to Jonathan and more also, if I do not [1]make it known to you and send you away, that you may go in safety. And [b]may the LORD be with you as He has been with my father.

14 "And if I am still alive, will you not show me the lovingkindness of the LORD, that I may not die?

15 "And [a]you shall not cut off your lovingkindness from my house forever, not even when the LORD cuts off every one of the enemies of David from the face of the earth."

16 So Jonathan made a *covenant* with the house of David, *saying*, "[a]May the LORD require *it* at the hands of David's enemies."

17 And Jonathan made David vow again because of his love for him, because [a]he loved him as he loved his own life.

18 Then Jonathan said to him, "[a]Tomorrow is the new moon, and you will be missed because your seat will be empty.

19 "When you have stayed for three days, you shall go down quickly and come to the place where you hid yourself on that eventful day, and you shall remain by the stone Ezel.

20 "And I will shoot three arrows to the side, as though I shot at a target.

21 "And behold, I will send the lad, *saying*, 'Go, find the arrows.' If I specifically say to the lad, 'Behold, the arrows are on this side of you, get them,' then come; for there is safety for you and [1]no harm, as the LORD lives.

22 "But if I [1]say to the youth, '[a]Behold, the arrows are beyond you,' go, for the LORD has sent you away.

23 "[a]As for the [1]agreement of which you and I have spoken, behold, [b]the LORD is between you and me forever."

24 So David hid in the field; and when the new moon came, the king sat down to eat food.

25 And the king sat on his seat as usual, the seat by the wall; then Jonathan rose up and Abner sat down by Saul's side, but [a]David's place was empty.

26 Nevertheless Saul did not speak anything that day, for he thought, "It is an accident, [a]he is not clean, surely *he is* not clean."

27 And it came about the next day, the second *day* of the new moon, that David's place was empty; so Saul said to Jonathan his son, "Why has the son of Jesse not come to the meal, either yesterday or today?"

28 Jonathan then answered Saul, "[a]David earnestly asked leave of me *to go* to Bethlehem,

29 for he said, 'Please [1]let me go, since our family has a sacrifice in the city, and my brother has commanded me to attend. And now, if I have found favor in your sight, please let me get away that I may see my brothers.' For this reason he has not come to the king's table."

3 [1]Lit., *and said* [2]Lit., *about* [a]Deut. 6:13 [b]1 Sam. 25:26; 2 Kin. 2:6

4 [1]Lit., *your soul says*

5 [a]Num. 10:10; 28:11-15; Amos 8:5 [b]1 Sam. 20:24, 27 [c]1 Sam. 19:2

6 [a]1 Sam. 17:58 [b]Deut. 12:5

7 [1]Lit., *says thus*

8 [a]1 Sam. 18:3; 23:18 [b]2 Sam. 14:32

10 [1]Lit., *or what*

12 [1]Lit., *uncover your ear*

13 [1]Lit., *uncover your ear* [a]Ruth 1:17; 1 Sam. 3:17 [b]1 Sam. 18:12

15 [a]2 Sam. 9:1

16 [a]Deut. 23:21

17 [a]1 Sam. 18:1

18 [a]1 Sam. 20:5, 25

21 [1]Lit., *there is nothing*

22 [1]Lit., *say thus* [a]1 Sam. 20:37

23 [1]Lit., *word* [a]1 Sam. 20:14, 15 [b]Gen. 31:49, 53

25 [a]1 Sam. 20:18

26 [a]Lev. 7:20, 21; 1 Sam. 16:5

28 [a]1 Sam. 20:6

29 [1]Lit., *send me away*

Saul Is Angry with Jonathan

30 Then Saul's anger burned against Jonathan and he said to him, "You son of a perverse, rebellious woman! Do I not know that you are choosing the son of Jesse to your own shame and to the shame of your mother's nakedness?

31 "For [1]as long as the son of Jesse lives on the earth, neither you nor your kingdom will be established. Therefore now, send and bring him to me, for [a]he [2]must surely die."

32 But Jonathan answered Saul his father and said to him, "[a]Why should he be put to death? What has he done?"

33 Then [a]Saul hurled his spear at him to strike him down; [b]so Jonathan knew that his father had decided to put David to death.

34 Then Jonathan arose from the table in fierce anger, and did not eat food on the second day of the new moon, for he was grieved over David because his father had dishonored him.

35 Now it came about in the morning that Jonathan went out into the field for the appointment with David, and a little lad *was* with him.

36 And he said to his lad, "[a]Run, find now the arrows which I am about to shoot." As the lad was running, he shot [1]an arrow past him.

37 When the lad reached the place of the arrow which Jonathan had shot, Jonathan called after the lad, and said, "[a]Is not the arrow beyond you?"

38 And Jonathan called after the lad, "Hurry, be quick, do not stay!" And Jonathan's lad picked up the arrow and came to his master.

39 But the lad was not aware of anything; only Jonathan and David knew about the matter.

40 Then Jonathan gave his weapons to his lad and said to him, "Go, bring *them* to the city."

41 When the lad was gone, David rose from the south side and fell on his face to the ground, and [a]bowed three times. And they kissed each other and wept together, but [b]David more.

42 And Jonathan said to David, "[a]Go in safety, inasmuch as we have sworn to each other in the name of the LORD, saying, '[b]The LORD will be between me and you, and between my [1]descendants and your [1]descendants forever.' " [2]Then he rose and departed, while Jonathan went into the city.

CHAPTER 21

David Takes Consecrated Bread

THEN David came to [a]Nob to [b]Ahimelech the priest; and [c]Ahimelech came trembling to meet David, and said to him, "Why are you alone and no one with you?"

2 And David said to Ahimelech the priest, "The king has commissioned me with a matter, and has said to me, 'Let no one know anything about the matter on which I am sending you and with which I have commissioned you; and I have [1]directed the young men to a certain place.'

3 "Now therefore, what [1]do you have on hand? Give [2]me five loaves of bread, or whatever can be found."

4 And the priest answered David and said, "There is no ordinary bread [1]on hand, but there is [a]consecrated bread; if only the young men have kept themselves from women."

5 And David answered the priest and said to him, "[a]Surely women have been kept from us as previously when I set out and the vessels of the young men were holy, though it was an ordinary journey; how much more then today will [1]their vessels *be holy*?"

6 So [a]the priest gave him consecrated *bread*; for there was no bread there but the bread of the Presence which was removed from before the LORD, in order to put hot bread *in its place* when it was taken away.

7 Now one of the servants of Saul was there that day, detained before the LORD; and his name was [a]Doeg the Edomite, the [b]chief of Saul's shepherds.

8 And David said to Ahimelech, "Now is there not a spear or a sword [1]on hand? For I brought neither my sword nor my weapons [2]with me, because the king's matter was urgent."

9 Then the priest said, "[a]The sword of Goliath the Philistine, whom you [1]killed [b]in the valley of Elah, behold, it is wrapped in a cloth behind the ephod; if you would take it for yourself, take *it*. For there is no other except it here." And David said, "There is none like it; give it to me."

10 Then David arose and fled that day from Saul, and went to [a]Achish king of Gath.

11 But the [a]servants of Achish said to him, "Is this not David the king of

31 [1]Lit., *all the days which* [2]Lit., *is a son of death* [a]2 Sam. 12:5
32 [a]1 Sam. 19:5
33 [a]1 Sam. 18:11; 19:10 [b]1 Sam. 20:7
36 [1]Lit., *the* [a]1 Sam. 20:20, 21
37 [a]1 Sam. 20:22
41 [a]Gen. 42:6 [b]1 Sam. 18:3
42 [1]Lit., *seed* [2]Chap. 21:1 in Heb. [a]1 Sam. 20:22 [b]1 Sam. 20:15, 16, 23
1 [a]1 Sam. 22:19 [b]1 Sam. 14:3; Mark 2:26 [c]1 Sam. 16:4
2 [1]Lit., *caused to know*
3 [1]Lit., *is under your hand?* [2]Lit., *in my hand*
4 [1]Lit., *under my hand* [a]Lev. 24:5-9; Matt. 12:4
5 [1]Lit., *it be holy in the vessel* [a]Ex. 19:14, 15
6 [a]Matt. 12:3, 4; Mark 2:25
7 [a]1 Sam. 14:47; 22:9; Ps. 52: title [b]1 Chr. 27:29, 31
8 [1]Lit., *under your hand* [2]Lit., *in my hand*
9 [1]Lit., *smote* [a]1 Sam. 17:54 [b]1 Sam. 17:2
10 [a]Ps. 34:title
11 [a]Ps. 56:title

the land? [b]Did they not sing of this one as they danced, saying,

'Saul has slain his thousands,
And David his ten thousands'?"

12 And David [a]took these words [1]to heart, and greatly feared Achish king of Gath.

13 So he [a]disguised his sanity before them, and acted insanely in their hands, and scribbled on the doors of the gate, and let his saliva run down into his beard.

14 Then Achish said to his servants, "Behold, you see the man behaving as a madman. Why do you bring him to me?

15 "Do I lack madmen, that you have brought this one to act the madman in my presence? Shall this one come into my house?"

Chapter 22

The Priests Slain at Nob

So David departed from there and [a]escaped to [b]the cave of Adullam; and when his brothers and all his father's household heard *of it*, they went down there to him.

2 And everyone who was in distress, and everyone who [1]was in debt, and everyone who was [2]discontented, gathered to him; and he became captain over them. Now there were [a]about four hundred men with him.

3 And David went from there to Mizpah of Moab; and he said to the king of Moab, "Please let my father and my mother come *and stay* with you until I know what God will do for me."

4 Then he left them with the king of Moab; and they stayed with him all the time that David was in the stronghold.

5 And [a]the prophet Gad said to David, "Do not stay in the stronghold; depart, and go into the land of Judah." So David departed and went into the forest of Hereth.

6 Then Saul heard that David and the men who were with him had been discovered. Now [a]Saul was sitting in Gibeah, under the tamarisk tree on the height with his spear in his hand, and all his servants were standing around him.

7 And Saul said to his servants who stood around him, "Hear now, O Benjamites! Will the son of Jesse also give to all of you fields and vineyards? [a]Will he make you all commanders of thousands and commanders of hundreds?

8 "For all of you have conspired against me so that there is no one who [1]discloses to me [a]when my son makes *a covenant* with the son of Jesse, and there is none of you [b]who is sorry for me or [1]discloses to me that my son has stirred up my servant against me to lie in ambush, as *it is* this day."

9 Then [a]Doeg the Edomite, who was [1]standing by the servants of Saul, answered and said, "[b]I saw the son of Jesse coming to Nob, to [c]Ahimelech the son of Ahitub.

10 "And [a]he inquired of the LORD for him, [b]gave him provisions, and [c]gave him the sword of Goliath the Philistine."

11 Then the king sent someone to summon Ahimelech the priest, the son of Ahitub, and all his father's household, the priests who were in Nob; and all of them came to the king.

12 And Saul said, "Listen now, son of Ahitub." And he [1]answered, "Here I am, my lord."

13 Saul then said to him, "Why have you and the son of Jesse conspired against me, in that you have given him bread and a sword and have inquired of God for him, that he should rise up against me [a]by lying in ambush as *it is* this day?"

14 [a]Then Ahimelech answered the king and said, "And who among all your servants is as faithful as David, even the king's son-in-law, who [1]is captain over your guard, and is honored in your house?

15 "Did I *just* begin [a]to inquire of God for him today? Far be it from me! Do not let the king impute anything to his servant *or* to any of the household of my father, for your servant knows nothing [1]at all of this whole affair."

16 But the king said, "You shall surely die, Ahimelech, you and all your father's household!"

17 And [a]the king said to the [1]guards who were attending him, "Turn around and put the priests of the LORD to death, because their hand also is with David and because they knew that he was fleeing and did not [2]reveal it to me." But the servants of the king were not willing to put forth their hands to [3]attack the priests of the LORD.

18 Then the king said to Doeg, "You turn around and [1]attack the priests." And Doeg the Edomite turned around and [2]attacked the priests, and [a]he killed that day eighty-five men [b]who wore the linen ephod.

---

11 [b]1 Sam. 18:7; 29:5
12 [1]Lit., *in his* [a]Luke 2:19
13 [a]Ps. 34:title
1 [a]Ps. 57:title; 142:title [b]Josh. 12:15; 15:35; 2 Sam. 23:13
2 [1]Lit., *had a creditor* [2]Lit., *bitter of soul* [a]1 Sam. 23:13; 25:13
5 [a]2 Sam. 24:11; 1 Chr. 29:29; 2 Chr. 29:25
6 [a]Judg. 4:5; 1 Sam. 14:2
7 [a]1 Sam. 8:14; 1 Chr. 12:16-18
8 [1]Lit., *uncovers my ear* [a]1 Sam. 18:3; 20:16 [b]1 Sam. 23:21
9 [1]Or, *set over* [a]Ps. 52:title [b]1 Sam. 21:1 [c]1 Sam. 14:3; 21:1
10 [a]1 Sam. 10:22 [b]1 Sam. 21:6, 9 [c]1 Sam. 21:9
12 [1]Lit., *said*
13 [a]1 Sam. 22:8
14 [1]So with Gk., Heb., *turns aside to* [a]1 Sam. 19:4, 5; 20:32
15 [1]Lit., *small or great* [a]2 Sam. 5:19, 23
17 [1]Lit., *runners* [2]Lit., *uncover my ear* [3]Lit., *fall upon* [a]2 Kin. 10:25; 2 Chr. 12:10
18 [1]Lit., *smite* [2]Lit., *smote* [a]1 Sam. 2:31 [b]1 Sam. 2:18

19 And [a]he struck Nob the city of
the priests with the edge of the
sword, both men and women, children and infants; also oxen, donkeys, and sheep, *he struck* with the
edge of the sword.
20 But [a]one son of Ahimelech the
son of Ahitub, named Abiathar, [b]es-
caped and fled after David.
21 And Abiathar told David that
Saul had killed the priests of the
LORD.
22 Then David said to Abiathar, "I
knew on that day, when [a]Doeg the
Edomite was there, that he would
surely tell Saul. I have brought
about *the death* of every person in
your father's household.
23"Stay with me, do not be afraid,
for [a]he who seeks my life seeks your
life; for you are [1]safe with me."

CHAPTER 23

David Delivers Keilah

THEN they told David, saying,
"Behold, the Philistines are fighting
against [a]Keilah, and are plundering
the threshing floors."
2 So David [a]inquired of the LORD,
saying, "Shall I go and [1]attack these
Philistines?" And the LORD said to
David, "Go and [1]attack the Philistines, and deliver Keilah."
3 But David's men said to him,
"Behold, we are afraid here in Judah. How much more then if we go
to Keilah against the ranks of the
Philistines?"
4 Then David inquired of the
LORD once more. And the LORD answered him and said, "Arise, go
down to Keilah, for [a]I will give the
Philistines into your hand."
5 So David and his men went to
Keilah and fought with the Philistines; and he led away their livestock and struck them with a great
slaughter. Thus David delivered the
inhabitants of Keilah.
6 Now it came about, when Abiathar the son of Ahimelech [a]fled to
David at Keilah, *that* he came down
with an ephod in his hand.
7 When it was told Saul that David had come to Keilah, Saul said,
"God has [1]delivered him into my
hand, for he shut himself in by entering a city with double gates and
bars."
8 So Saul summoned all the people for war, to go down to Keilah to
besiege David and his men.
9 Now David knew that Saul was
plotting evil against him; so he said
to [a]Abiathar the priest, "[b]Bring the
ephod here."
10 Then David said, "O LORD God
of Israel, Thy servant has heard for
certain that Saul is seeking to come
to Keilah to destroy the city on my
account.
11"Will the men of Keilah surrender me into his hand? Will Saul
come down just as Thy servant has
heard? O LORD God of Israel, I pray,
tell Thy servant." And the LORD
said, "He will come down."
12 Then David said, "Will the men
of Keilah surrender me and my men
into the hand of Saul?" And the
LORD said, "[a]They will surrender
you."
13 Then David and his men, [a]about
six hundred, arose and departed
from Keilah, and they went [b]wher-
ever they could go. When it was told
Saul that David had escaped from
Keilah, he [1]gave up the pursuit.
14 And David stayed in the wilderness in the strongholds, and remained in the hill country in the wilderness of [a]Ziph. And Saul sought
him every day, but [b]God did not deliver him into his hand.

Saul Pursues David

15 Now David [1]became aware that
Saul had come out to seek his life
while David was in the wilderness
of Ziph at Horesh.
16 And Jonathan, Saul's son, arose
and went to David at Horesh, and
[1a]encouraged him in God.
17 Thus he said to him, "Do not be
afraid, because the hand of Saul my
father shall not find you, and you
will be king over Israel and I will be
next to you; and [a]Saul my father
knows that also."
18 So [a]the two of them made a
covenant before the LORD; and David stayed at Horesh while Jonathan
went to his house.
19 Then [a]Ziphites came up to Saul
at Gibeah, saying, "Is David not hiding with us in the strongholds at Horesh, on [b]the hill of Hachilah, which
is on the [1]south of [2]Jeshimon?
20"Now then, O king, come down
according to all the desire of your
soul to [1]do so; and [a]our part *shall be*
to surrender him into the king's
hand."
21 And Saul said, "May you be
blessed of the LORD; [a]for you have
had compassion on me.
22"Go now, make more sure, and
investigate and see his place where
his [1]haunt is, *and* who has seen him
there; for I am told that he is very
cunning.
23"So look, and learn about all the

19 [a]1 Sam. 15:3
20 [a]1 Sam. 23:9; 30:7; 2 Sam. 2:1; 1 Kin. 2:26, 27 [b]1 Sam. 2:33
22 [a]1 Sam. 21:7
23 [1]Lit., *a charge* [a]1 Kin. 2:26
1 [a]Josh. 15:44; Neh. 3:17, 18
2 [1]Lit., *smite* [a]1 Sam. 23:4, 6, 9-12; 2 Sam. 5:19, 23
4 [a]Josh. 8:7; Judg. 7:7
6 [a]1 Sam. 22:20
7 [1]Lit., *alienated*
9 [a]1 Sam. 22:20 [b]1 Sam. 23:6; 30:7
12 [a]Judg. 15:10-13; 1 Sam. 23:20
13 [1]Lit., *ceased going out* [a]1 Sam. 22:2; 25:13 [b]2 Sam. 15:20
14 [a]Josh. 15:55; 2 Chr. 11:8 [b]Ps. 32:7
15 [1]Lit., *saw*
16 [1]Lit., *strengthened his hand* [a]1 Sam. 30:6; Neh. 2:18
17 [a]1 Sam. 20:31; 24:20
18 [a]1 Sam. 18:3; 20:12-17; 2 Sam. 9:1
19 [1]Lit., *right side* [2]Or, *the desert* [a]1 Sam. 26:1; Ps. 51:title [b]1 Sam. 26:3
20 [1]Lit., *come down* [a]1 Sam. 23:12
21 [a]1 Sam. 22:8
22 [1]Lit., *foot*

hiding places where he hides himself, and return to me with certainty, and I will go with you; and it
shall come about if he is in the land
that I will search him out among all
the thousands of Judah."
24 Then they arose and went to
Ziph before Saul. Now David and
his men were in the wilderness of
[a]Maon, in the Arabah to the [1]south
of [2]Jeshimon.
25 When Saul and his men went to
seek *him*, they told David, and he
came down to the rock and stayed in
the wilderness of Maon. And when
Saul heard *it*, he pursued David in
the wilderness of Maon.
26 And Saul went on one side of
the mountain, and David and his
men on the other side of the mountain; and David was hurrying to get
away from Saul, for Saul and his
men [a]were surrounding David and
his men to seize them.
27 But a messenger came to Saul,
saying, "Hurry and come, for the
Philistines have made a raid on the
land."
28 So Saul returned from pursuing
David, and went to meet the Philistines; therefore they called that
place [1]the Rock of Escape.
29 [1]And David went up from there
and stayed in the strongholds of
[a]Engedi.

CHAPTER 24

David Spares Saul's Life

NOW it came about [a]when Saul
returned from pursuing the Philistines, [b]he was told, saying, "Behold,
David is in the wilderness of En-
gedi."
2 Then [a]Saul took three thousand
chosen men from all Israel, and
went to seek David and his men in
front of the Rocks of the Wild
Goats.
3 And he came to the sheepfolds
on the way, where there *was* a cave;
and Saul [a]went in to [1]relieve himself. Now [b]David and his men were
sitting in the inner recesses of the
cave.
4 And the men of David said to
him, "Behold, [a]*this is* the day of
which the LORD said to you, 'Behold;
I am about to give your enemy into
your hand, and you shall do to him
as it seems good [1]to you.'" Then
David arose and cut off the edge of
Saul's robe secretly.
5 And it came about afterward
that [a]David's [1]conscience bothered
him because he had cut off the edge
of Saul's *robe*.
6 So he said to his men, "[a]Far be
it from me because of the LORD that
I should do this thing to my lord, the
LORD's anointed, to stretch out my
hand against him, since he is the
LORD's anointed."
7 And David [1]persuaded his men
with *these* words and did not allow
them to rise up against Saul. And
Saul arose, [2]left the cave, and went
on *his* way.
8 Now afterward David arose
and went out of the cave and called
after Saul, saying, "My lord the
king!" And when Saul looked behind him, [a]David bowed with his
face to the ground and prostrated
himself.
9 And David said to Saul, "Why
do you listen to the words of men,
saying, 'Behold, David seeks [1]to
harm you'?
10 "[a]Behold, this day your eyes
have seen that the LORD had given
you today into my hand in the cave,
and [b]some said to kill you, but *my
eye* had pity on you; and I said, 'I will
not stretch out my hand against my
lord, for he is the LORD's anointed.'
11 "Now, [a]my father, see! Indeed,
see the edge of your robe in my
hand! For in that I cut off the edge of
your robe and did not kill you, know
and perceive that there is no evil or
[1]rebellion in my hands, and I have
not sinned against you, though you
[b]are lying in wait for my life to take
it.
12 "[a]May the LORD judge between
[1]you and me, and may the LORD
avenge me on you; but my hand
shall not be against you.
13 "As the proverb of the ancients
says, '[a]Out of the wicked comes
forth wickedness'; but my hand
shall not be against you.
14 "After whom has the king of Israel come out? Whom are you pursuing? A dead dog, [a]a single flea?
15 "[a]The LORD therefore be judge
and decide between [1]you and me;
and may He see and [b]plead my
cause, and [2]deliver me from your
hand."
16 Now it came about when David
had finished speaking these words
to Saul, that Saul said, "[a]Is this your
voice, my son David?" Then Saul
lifted up his voice and wept.
17 [a]And he said to David, "You are
more righteous than I; for [b]you have
dealt well with me, while I have
dealt wickedly with you.
18 "And you have declared today
that you have done good to me, that

24 [1]Lit., *right side* [2]Or, *the desert* [a]Josh. 15:55; 1 Sam. 25:2
26 [a]Ps. 17:9
28 [1]Heb., *Sela-hammahlekoth*
29 [1]Chap. 24:1 in Heb. [a]Josh. 15:62; 2 Chr. 20:2
1 [a]1 Sam. 23:28, 29 [b]1 Sam. 23:19
2 [a]1 Sam. 26:2
3 [1]Lit., *cover his feet* [a]Judg. 3:24 [b]Ps. 57:title; 142:title
4 [1]Lit., *in your sight* [a]1 Sam. 23:17; 25:28-30
5 [1]Lit., *heart struck* [a]2 Sam. 24:10
6 [a]1 Sam. 26:11
7 [1]Lit., *tore apart* [2]Lit., *from*
8 [a]1 Sam. 25:23, 24; 1 Kin. 1:31
9 [1]Lit., *your hurt*
10 [a]Ps. 7:3, 4 [b]1 Sam. 24:4
11 [1]Lit., *transgression* [a]2 Kin. 5:13 [b]1 Sam. 23:14, 23; 26:20
12 [1]Lit., *me and you* [a]Gen. 31:53; Judg. 11:27; 1 Sam. 26:10, 23
13 [a]Matt. 7:16-20
14 [a]1 Sam. 26:20
15 [1]Lit., *me and you* [2]Lit., *vindicate* [a]1 Sam. 24:12 [b]Ps. 35:1
16 [a]1 Sam. 26:17
17 [a]1 Sam. 26:21 [b]Matt. 5:44

[a]the LORD delivered me into your
hand and *yet* you did not kill me.
19 "For if a man [a]finds his enemy,
will he let him go away [1]safely? May
the LORD therefore reward you with
good in return for what you have
done to me this day.
20 "And now, behold, [a]I know that
you shall surely be king, and that
[b]the kingdom of Israel shall be established in your hand.
21 "So now [a]swear to me by the
LORD that you will not cut off my
[1]descendants after me, and that you
will not destroy my name from my
father's household."
22 And David swore to Saul. And
Saul went to his home, but David
and his men went up to [a]the stronghold.

CHAPTER 25

Samuel's Death

[a]THEN Samuel died; and all Israel
gathered together and [b]mourned for
him, and [c]buried him at his house in
Ramah. And David arose and went
down to the [d]wilderness of Paran.

Nabal and Abigail

2 Now *there was* a man in [a]Maon
whose business was in [b]Carmel; and
the man was [c]very [1]rich, and he had
three thousand sheep and a thousand goats. And it came about while
[d]he was shearing his sheep in Carmel
3 (now the man's name was Nabal, and his wife's name was Abigail. And the woman was [1]intelli-
gent and beautiful in appearance,
but the man was harsh and evil in
his dealings, and he was [a]a Caleb-
ite),
4 that David heard in the wilderness that Nabal was shearing his
sheep.
5 So David sent ten young men,
and David said to the young men,
"Go up to Carmel, [1]visit Nabal and
greet him in my name;
6 and thus you shall say, '[1]Have a
long life, [a]peace be to you, and
peace be to your house, and peace
be to all that you have.
7 'And now I have heard [a]that you
have shearers; now your shepherds
have been with us and we have not
insulted them, [b]nor have they
missed anything all the days they
were in Carmel.
8 'Ask your young men and they
will tell you. Therefore let *my* young
men find favor in your eyes, for we
have come on [a]a [1]festive day. Please
give whatever you find at hand to
your servants and to your son David.'"
9 When David's young men
came, they spoke to Nabal according to all these words in David's
name; then they waited.
10 But Nabal answered David's
servants, and said, "[a]Who is David?
And who is the son of Jesse? There
are many servants today who are
each breaking away from his master.
11 "Shall I then take my bread and
my water and my meat that I have
slaughtered for my shearers, and
give it to men [1]whose origin I do not
know?"
12 So David's young men retraced
their way and went back; and they
came and told him according to all
these words.
13 And David said to his men,
"Each *of you* gird on his sword." So
each man girded on his sword. And
David also girded on his sword, and
about [a]four hundred men went up
behind David while two hundred
[b]stayed with the baggage.
14 But one of the young men told
Abigail, Nabal's wife, saying, "Behold, David sent messengers from
the wilderness to [1a]greet our master, and he scorned them.
15 "Yet the men were very good to
us, and we were not [a]insulted, nor
did we miss anything [1]as long as we
went about with them, while we
were in the fields.
16 "[a]They were a wall to us both by
night and by day, all the time we
were with them tending the sheep.
17 "Now therefore know and [1]con-
sider what you should do, for evil is
plotted against our master and
against all his household; and he is
such a [2]worthless man that no one
can speak to him."

Abigail Intercedes

18 Then Abigail hurried and [a]took
two hundred *loaves* of bread and
two jugs of wine and five sheep already prepared and five measures of
roasted grain and a hundred clusters of raisins and two hundred
cakes of figs, and loaded *them* on
donkeys.
19 And she said to her young men,
"[a]Go on before me; behold, I am
coming after you." But she did not
tell her husband Nabal.
20 And it came about as she was
riding on her donkey and coming
down by the hidden part of the
mountain, that behold, David and

18 [a]1 Sam. 26:23
19 [1]Lit., *on a good road* [a]1 Sam. 23:17
20 [a]1 Sam. 23:17 [b]1 Sam. 13:14
21 [1]Lit., *seed* [a]Gen. 21:23; 1 Sam. 20:14-17; 2 Sam. 21:6-8
22 [a]1 Sam. 23:29
1 [a]1 Sam. 28:3 [b]Deut. 34:8 [c]2 Kin. 21:18; 2 Chr. 33:20 [d]Gen. 21:21; Num. 10:12; 13:3
2 [1]Lit., *great* [a]1 Sam. 23:24 [b]Josh. 15:55 [c]2 Sam. 19:32 [d]2 Sam. 13:23
3 [1]Lit., *of good understanding* [a]Josh. 15:13; 1 Sam. 30:14
5 [1]Lit., *go into*
6 [1]Lit., *To life* [a]1 Chr. 12:18
7 [a]2 Sam. 13:23, 24 [b]1 Sam. 15:21
8 [1]Lit., *good* [a]Neh. 8:10-12
10 [a]Judg. 9:28
11 [1]Lit., *from where they are*
13 [a]1 Sam. 23:13 [b]1 Sam. 30:24
14 [1]Lit., *bless* [a]1 Sam. 13:10; 15:13
15 [1]Lit., *all the days* [a]1 Sam. 25:7, 21
16 [a]Ex. 14:22
17 [1]Lit., *see* [2]Lit., *son of Belial*
18 [a]2 Sam. 16:1; 1 Chr. 12:40
19 [a]Gen. 32:16, 20

his men were coming down toward
her; so she met them.
21 Now David had said, “Surely in
vain I have guarded all that this *man*
has in the wilderness, so that nothing was missed of all that belonged
to him; and he has returned me evil
for good.
22“[a]May God do so to the enemies
of David, and more also, [b]if by
morning I leave *as much as* one
[1]male of any who belong to him.”
23 When Abigail saw David, she
hurried and dismounted from her
donkey, and fell on her face before
David, [a]and bowed herself to the
ground.
24 And she fell at his feet and said,
“On me [1]alone, my lord, be the
blame. And please let your maidservant speak [2]to you, and listen to the
words of your maidservant.
25“Please do not let my lord [1]pay
attention to this [2]worthless man,
Nabal, for as his name is, so is he.
[3]Nabal is his name and folly is with
him; but I your maidservant did not
see the young men of my lord whom
you sent.
26“Now therefore, my lord, as the
LORD lives, and as your soul lives,
since the LORD has restrained you
from [1]shedding blood, and [a]from
[2]avenging yourself by your own
hand, now then [b]let your enemies,
and those who seek evil against my
lord, be as Nabal.
27“And now let [a]this [1]gift which
your maidservant has brought to
my lord be given to the young men
who [2]accompany my lord.
28“Please forgive [a]the transgression of your maidservant; for [b]the
LORD will certainly make for my
lord an enduring house, because my
lord is [c]fighting the battles of the
LORD, and [d]evil shall not be found in
you all your days.
29“And should anyone rise up to
pursue you and to seek your [1]life,
then the [1]life of my lord shall be
bound in the bundle of the living
with the LORD your God; but the
[1]lives of your enemies [a]He will sling
out [2]as from the hollow of a sling.
30“And it shall come about when
the LORD shall do for my lord according to all the good that He has
spoken concerning you, and [a]shall
appoint you ruler over Israel,
31 that this will not [1]cause grief or
a troubled heart to my lord, both by
having shed blood without cause
and by my lord having [2]avenged
himself. [a]When the LORD shall deal
well with my lord, then remember
your maidservant.”

32 Then David said to Abigail,
“[a]Blessed be the LORD God of Israel,
who sent you this day to meet me,
33 and blessed be your discernment, and blessed be you, [a]who
have kept me this day from
[1]bloodshed, and from [2]avenging
myself by my own hand.
34“Nevertheless, as the LORD God
of Israel lives, [a]who has restrained
me from harming you, unless you
had come quickly to meet me,
surely there would not have been
left to Nabal until the morning light
as much as one [1]male.”
35 So David received from her
hand what she had brought him, and
he said to her, “[a]Go up to your house
in peace. See, I have listened to [1]you
and [2b]granted your request.”
36 Then Abigail came to Nabal,
and behold, he was holding [a]a feast
in his house, like the feast of a king.
And Nabal’s heart was merry within
him, for he was very drunk; so [b]she
did not tell him anything [1]at all until
the morning light.
37 But it came about in the morning, when the wine had gone out of
Nabal, that his wife told him these
things, and his heart died within him
so that he became *as* a stone.
38 And about ten days later, it
happened that [a]the LORD struck Nabal, and he died.

David Marries Abigail

39 When David heard that Nabal
was dead, he said, “Blessed be the
LORD, who has [a]pleaded the cause of
my reproach from the hand of Nabal, and [b]has kept back His servant
from evil. [c]The LORD has also returned the evildoing of Nabal on his
own head.” Then David sent [1d]a proposal to Abigail, to take her as his
wife.
40 When the servants of David
came to Abigail at Carmel, they
spoke to her, saying, “David has
sent us to you, to take you as his
wife.”
41 And she arose [a]and bowed with
her face to the ground and said, “Behold, your maidservant is a maid [b]to
wash the feet of my lord’s servants.”
42 Then [a]Abigail quickly arose,
and rode on a donkey, with her five
maidens who [1]attended her; and she
followed the messengers of David,
and became his wife.
43 David had also taken Ahinoam
of [a]Jezreel, and they both became
his wives.
44 Now Saul had given [a]Michal his

22 [1]Lit., *who urinates against the wall* [a]1 Sam. 3:17; 20:13 [b]1 Kin. 14:10
23 [a]1 Sam. 20:41
24 [1]Lit., *even me* [2]Lit., *in your ears*
25 [1]Lit., *set his heart to* [2]Lit., *man of Belial* [3]I.e., Fool
26 [1]Lit., *coming in with blood* [2]Lit., *saving* [a]Heb. 10:30 [b]2 Sam. 18:32
27 [1]Lit., *blessing* [2]Lit., *walk at the feet of* [a]Gen. 33:11; 1 Sam. 30:26
28 [a]1 Sam. 25:24 [b]1 Sam. 22:14; 2 Sam. 7:16 [c]1 Sam. 18:17 [d]1 Sam. 24:11; Ps. 7:3
29 [1]Lit., *soul* [2]Lit., *in the midst* [a]Jer. 10:18
30 [a]1 Sam. 13:14
31 [1]Lit., *become staggering to you or a stumbling of the heart* [2]Lit., *saved* [a]Gen. 40:14; 1 Sam. 25:30
32 [a]Ex. 18:10
33 [1]Lit., *coming in with blood* [2]Lit., *saving* [a]1 Sam. 25:26
34 [1]Lit., *who urinates against the wall* [a]1 Sam. 25:26
35 [1]Lit., *your voice* [2]Lit., *lifted up your face* [a]1 Sam. 20:42; 2 Kin. 5:19 [b]Gen. 19:21
36 [1]Lit., *small or large* [a]2 Sam. 13:23 [b]1 Sam. 25:19
38 [a]1 Sam. 26:10
39 [1]Lit., *and spoke* [a]1 Sam. 24:15 [b]1 Sam. 26:34 [c]2 Sam. 3:28, 29 [d]Song of Sol. 8:8
41 [a]1 Sam. 25:23 [b]Mark 1:7
42 [1]Lit., *walked at her feet* [a]Gen. 24:61-67
43 [a]Josh. 15:56
44 [a]1 Sam. 18:27; 2 Sam. 3:14

daughter, David's wife, to Palti the
son of Laish, who was from [b]Gallim.

Chapter 26

David Again Spares Saul

THEN the Ziphites came to Saul at
Gibeah, saying, "[a]Is not David hiding on the hill of Hachilah, *which is*
before [1]Jeshimon?"
2 So Saul arose and went down to
the wilderness of Ziph, having with
him [a]three thousand chosen men of
Israel, to search for David in the wilderness of Ziph.
3 And Saul camped in the hill of
Hachilah, which is before [1]Jeshi-
mon, [a]beside the road, and David
was staying in the wilderness.
When [b]he saw that Saul came after
him into the wilderness,
4 David sent out spies, and he
knew that Saul was definitely coming.
5 David then arose and came to
the place where Saul had camped.
And David saw the place where
Saul lay, and [a]Abner the son of Ner,
the commander of his army; and
Saul was lying in the circle of the
camp, and the people were camped
around him.
6 Then David answered and said
to Ahimelech [a]the Hittite and to [b]A-
bishai the son of Zeruiah, Joab's
brother, saying, "Who [c]will go
down with me to Saul in the camp?"
And Abishai said, "I will go down
with you."
7 So David and Abishai came to
the people by night, and behold,
Saul lay sleeping inside the circle of
the camp, with his spear stuck in the
ground at his head; and Abner and
the people were lying around him.
8 Then Abishai said to David,
"Today God has delivered your enemy into your hand; now therefore,
please let me strike him with the
spear [1]to the ground with one
stroke, and I will not [2]strike him the
second time."
9 But David said to Abishai, "Do
not destroy him, for [a]who can
stretch out his hand against the
LORD's anointed and be without
guilt?"
10 David also said, "As the LORD
lives, [a]surely the LORD will strike
him, or [b]his day will come that he
dies, or [c]he will go down into battle
and perish.
11 "[a]The LORD forbid that I should
stretch out my hand against the
LORD's anointed; but now please
take the spear that is at his head and
the jug of water, and let us go."
12 So David took the spear and the
jug of water from *beside* Saul's
head, and they went away, but no
one saw or knew *it*, nor did any
awake, for they were all asleep, because [a]a sound sleep from the LORD
had fallen on them.
13 Then David crossed over to the
other side, and stood on top of the
mountain at a distance *with* a large
area between them.
14 And David called to the people
and to Abner the son of Ner, saying,
"Will you not answer, Abner?" Then
Abner answered and said, "Who are
you who calls to the king?"
15 So David said to Abner, "Are
you not a man? And who is like you
in Israel? Why then have you not
guarded your lord the king? For one
of the people came to destroy the
king your lord.
16 "This thing that you have done is
not good. As the LORD lives, *all* of
you [1][a]must surely die, because you
did not guard your lord, the LORD's
anointed. And now, see where the
king's spear is, and the jug of water
that was at his head."
17 Then Saul recognized David's
voice and said, "[a]Is this your voice,
my son David?" And David said, "It
is my voice, my lord the king."
18 He also said, "[a]Why then is my
lord pursuing his servant? For what
have I done? Or what evil is in my
hand?
19 "Now therefore, please let my
lord the king listen to the words of
his servant. If [a]the LORD has stirred
you up against me, [b]let Him [1]accept
an offering; but [c]if it is [2]men, cursed
are they before the LORD, for [d]they
have driven me out today that I
should have no attachment with the
inheritance of the LORD, saying, 'Go,
serve other gods.'
20 "Now then, do not let my blood
fall to the ground away from the
presence of the LORD; for the king of
Israel has come out to search for [a]a
single flea, just as one hunts a partridge in the mountains."
21 Then Saul said, "[a]I have sinned.
Return, my son David, for I will not
harm you again because my life was
precious in your sight this day. Behold, I have played the fool and have
committed a serious error."
22 And David answered and said,
"Behold the spear of the king! Now
let one of the young men come over
and take it.
23 "And [a]the LORD will repay each
man *for* his righteousness and his
faithfulness; for the LORD delivered
you into *my* hand today, but [b]I re-

---

44 [b]Is. 10:31

1 [1]Or, *the desert* [a]1 Sam. 23:19; Ps. 54:title

2 [a]1 Sam. 13:2; 24:2

3 [1]Or, *the desert* [a]1 Sam. 24:3 [b]1 Sam. 23:15

5 [a]1 Sam. 14:50, 51; 17:55

6 [a]Gen. 23:3; 26:34; Josh. 3:10; 1 Kin. 10:29; 2 Kin. 7:6 [b]1 Chr. 2:15, 16 [c]Judg. 7:10, 11

8 [1]Lit., *even into* [2]Lit., *repeat with respect to him*

9 [a]1 Sam. 24:6, 7; 2 Sam. 1:14, 16

10 [a]1 Sam. 25:26, 38 [b]Deut. 31:14 [c]1 Sam. 31:6

11 [a]1 Sam. 24:6, 12

12 [a]Gen. 2:21; 15:12

16 [1]Lit., *are surely sons of death* [a]1 Sam. 20:31

17 [a]1 Sam. 24:16

18 [a]1 Sam. 24:9, 11-14

19 [1]Lit., *smell* [2]Lit., *sons of men* [a]2 Sam. 16:11 [b]Gen. 8:21 [c]1 Sam. 24:9 [d]Josh. 22:25-27

20 [a]1 Sam. 24:14

21 [a]1 Sam. 15:24, 30; 24:17

23 [a]1 Sam. 24:19 [b]1 Sam. 24:12

fused to stretch out my hand against the LORD's anointed.

24 "Now behold, as your life was [a]highly valued in my sight this day, so may my life be highly valued in the sight of the LORD, and may He [b]deliver me from all distress."

25 Then Saul said to David, "[a]Blessed are you, my son David; you will both accomplish much and surely prevail." So [b]David went on his way, and Saul returned to his place.

CHAPTER 27

David Flees to the Philistines

THEN David said [1]to himself, "Now I will perish one day by the hand of Saul. [a]There is nothing better for me than [2]to escape into the land of the Philistines. Saul then will despair of searching for me any more in all the territory of Israel, and I will escape from his hand."

2 So David arose and crossed over, he and [a]the six hundred men who were with him, to [b]Achish the son of Maoch, king of Gath.

3 And David lived with Achish at Gath, he and his men, [a]each with his household, *even* David with [b]his two wives, Ahinoam the Jezreelitess, and Abigail the Carmelitess, Nabal's [1]widow.

4 Now it was told Saul that David had fled to Gath, so he no longer searched for him.

5 Then David said to Achish, "If now I have found favor in your sight, let them give me a place in one of the cities in the country, that I may live there; for why should your servant live in the royal city with you?"

6 So Achish gave him Ziklag that day; therefore [a]Ziklag has belonged to the kings of Judah to this day.

7 And the number of days that David lived in the country of the Philistines was [a]a year and four months.

8 Now David and his men went up and raided [a]the Geshurites and the Girzites and [b]the Amalekites; for they were the inhabitants of the land from ancient times, as you come to [c]Shur even as far as the land of Egypt.

9 And David [1]attacked the land and did not leave a man or a woman alive, and he [a]took away the sheep, the cattle, the donkeys, the camels, and the clothing. Then he returned and came to Achish.

10 Now Achish said, "Where have you [a]made a raid today?" And David said, "Against the [1]Negev of Judah and against the [1]Negev of [b]the Jerahmeelites and against the [1]Negev of [c]the Kenites."

11 And David did not leave a man or a woman alive, to bring to Gath, saying, "Lest they should tell about us, saying, 'So has David done and so *has been* his practice all the time he has lived in the country of the Philistines.' "

12 So Achish believed David, saying, "He has surely made himself odious among his people Israel; therefore he will become my servant forever."

CHAPTER 28

Saul and the Spirit Medium

NOW it came about in those days that [a]the Philistines gathered their armed camps for war, to fight against Israel. And Achish said to David, "Know assuredly that you will go out with me in the camp, you and your men."

2 And David said to Achish, "Very well, you shall know what your servant can do." So Achish said to David, "Very well, I will make you [1]my bodyguard [a]for life."

3 Now [a]Samuel was dead, and all Israel had lamented him and buried him [b]in Ramah his own city. And Saul had removed from the land those who [c]were mediums and spiritists.

4 So the Philistines gathered together and came and camped [a]in Shunem; and Saul gathered all Israel together and they camped in [b]Gilboa.

5 When Saul saw the camp of the Philistines, he was afraid and his heart trembled greatly.

6 [a]When Saul inquired of the LORD, [b]the LORD did not answer him, either by [c]dreams or by [d]Urim or by prophets.

7 Then Saul said to his servants, "Seek for me a woman who is a medium, that I may go to her and inquire of her." And his servants said to him, "Behold, [a]there is a woman who is a medium at [b]En-dor."

8 Then Saul [a]disguised himself by putting on other clothes, and went, he and two men with him, and they came to the woman by night; and he said, "[b]Conjure up for me, please, and [c]bring up for me whom I shall [1]name to you."

9 But the woman said to him, "Behold, you know [a]what Saul has done, how he has cut off those who are mediums and spiritists from the

24 [a]1 Sam. 18:30 [b]Ps. 54:7
25 [a]1 Sam. 24:19 [b]1 Sam. 24:22
1 [1]Lit., *in his heart* [2]Lit., *that I should surely escape* [a]1 Sam. 26:19
2 [a]1 Sam. 25:13 [b]1 Sam. 21:10; 1 Kin. 2:39
3 [1]Lit., *wife* [a]1 Sam. 30:3; 2 Sam. 2:3 [b]1 Sam. 25:42, 43
6 [a]Josh. 15:31; 19:5; Neh. 11:28
7 [a]1 Sam. 29:3
8 [a]Josh. 13:2, 13 [b]Ex. 17:8; 1 Sam. 15:7, 8 [c]Ex. 15:22
9 [1]Lit., *smote* [a]1 Sam. 15:3; Job 1:3
10 [1]I.e., South country [a]1 Sam. 23:27 [b]1 Sam. 30:29; 1 Chr. 2:9, 25 [c]Judg. 1:16; 4:11
1 [a]1 Sam. 29:1
2 [1]Lit., *keeper of my head* [a]1 Sam. 1:22, 28
3 [a]1 Sam. 25:1 [b]1 Sam. 7:17 [c]Lev. 19:31; Deut. 18:10; 1 Sam. 15:23
4 [a]1 Kin. 1:3; 2 Kin. 4:8 [b]1 Sam. 31:1
6 [a]1 Chr. 10:13, 14 [b]Prov. 1:24-31 [c]Num. 12:6; Joel 2:28 [d]Ex. 28:30; 2 Sam. 8:17
7 [a]Acts 16:16 [b]Josh. 17:1; Ps. 83:10
8 [1]Lit., *say* [a]2 Chr. 18:29; 35:22 [b]Is. 8:19 [c]Deut. 18:10, 11
9 [a]1 Sam. 28:3

land. Why are you then laying a
snare for my life to bring about my
death?"
10 And Saul vowed to her by the
LORD, saying, "As the LORD lives,
there shall no punishment come
upon you for this thing."
11 Then the woman said, "Whom
shall I bring up for you?" And he
said, "Bring up Samuel for me."
12 When the woman saw Samuel,
she cried out with a loud voice; and
the woman spoke to Saul, saying,
"Why have you deceived me? For
you are Saul."
13 And the king said to her, "Do
not be afraid; but what do you see?"
And the woman said to Saul, "I see
a [1]divine being coming up out of the
earth."
14 And he said to her, "What is his
form?" And she said, "An old man is
coming up, and [a]he is wrapped with
a robe." And Saul knew that it was
Samuel, and [b]he bowed with his
face to the ground and did homage.
15 Then Samuel said to Saul,
"Why have you disturbed me by
bringing me up?" And Saul answered, "I am greatly distressed; for
the Philistines are waging war
against me, and [a]God has departed
from me and [b]answers me no more,
either through prophets or by
dreams; therefore I have called you,
that you may make known to me
what I should do."
16 And Samuel said, "Why then
do you ask me, since the LORD has
departed from you and has become
your adversary?
17"And the LORD has done [1]ac-
cordingly [a]as He spoke through me;
for the LORD has torn the kingdom
out of your hand and given it to your
neighbor, to David.
18"As [a]you did not [1]obey the LORD
and did not execute His fierce wrath
on Amalek, so the LORD has done
this thing to you this day.
19"Moreover the LORD will also
give over Israel along with you into
the hands of the Philistines, therefore tomorrow [a]you and your sons
will be with me. Indeed the LORD
will give over the army of Israel into
the hands of the Philistines!"
20 Then Saul immediately fell full
length upon the ground and was
very afraid because of the words of
Samuel; also there was no strength
in him, for he had eaten no [1]food all
day and all night.
21 And the woman came to Saul
and saw that he was terrified, and
said to him, "Behold, your maidservant has [1]obeyed you, and [a]I have

13 [1]Or, *god*
14 [a]1 Sam. 15:27 [b]1 Sam. 24:8
15 [a]1 Sam. 16:13, 14; 18:12 [b]1 Sam. 28:6
17 [1]Lit., *for himself* [a]1 Sam. 15:28
18 [1]Lit., *listen to the voice of* [a]1 Sam. 15:9, 20, 26
19 [a]1 Sam. 31:2; Job 3:17-19
20 [1]Lit., *bread*
21 [1]Lit., *listened to your voice* [2]Lit., *put* [a]1 Sam. 19:5
23 [1]Lit., *their voices* [a]2 Kin. 5:13 [b]Esth. 1:6; Ezek. 23:41
24 [a]Gen. 18:6, 7
1 [a]1 Sam. 28:1, 2 [b]Josh. 12:18; 1 Sam. 4:1 [c]1 Kin. 18:19; 21:1; 2 Kin. 9:30
2 [a]1 Sam. 28:1, 2
3 [1]Lit., *fell* [a]1 Sam. 27:7 [b]1 Sam. 27:1-6; 1 Chr. 12:19, 20
4 [1]Lit., *those* [a]1 Sam. 27:6 [b]1 Sam. 14:21
5 [a]1 Sam. 18:7; 21:11

[2]taken my life in my hand, and have
listened to your words which you
spoke to me.
22"So now also, please listen to the
voice of your maidservant, and let
me set a piece of bread before you
that *you may* eat and have strength
when you go on *your* way."
23 But he refused and said, "I will
not eat." [a]However, his servants together with the woman urged him,
and he listened to [1]them. So he
arose from the ground and sat on
[b]the bed.
24 And the woman had a fattened
calf in the house, and [a]she quickly
slaughtered it; and she took flour,
kneaded it, and baked unleavened
bread from it.
25 And she brought *it* before Saul
and his servants, and they ate. Then
they arose and went away that
night.

CHAPTER 29

The Philistines Mistrust David

NOW [a]the Philistines gathered together all their armies to [b]Aphek,
while the Israelites were camping
by the spring which is in [c]Jezreel.
2 And the lords of the Philistines
were proceeding on by hundreds
and by thousands, and [a]David and
his men were proceeding on in the
rear with Achish.
3 Then the commanders of the
Philistines said, "What *are* these
Hebrews *doing here*?" And Achish
said to the commanders of the Philistines, "Is this not David, the servant of Saul the king of Israel, [a]who
has been with me these days, or
rather these years, and [b]I have
found no fault in him from the day
he [1]deserted *to me* to this day?"
4 But the commanders of the Philistines were angry with him, and
the commanders of the Philistines
said to him, "Make the man go back,
that he may return [a]to his place
where you have assigned him, and
do not let him go down to battle
with us, [b]lest in the battle he become an adversary to us. For with
what could this *man* make himself
acceptable to his lord? *Would it* not
be with the heads of [1]these men?
5"Is this not David, [a]of whom
they sing in the dances, saying,
'Saul has slain his thousands,
And David his ten thou-
sands'?"
6 Then Achish called David and
said to him, "*As* the LORD lives, you
have been upright, and your going
out and your coming in with me in

the army are pleasing in my sight; [a]for I have not found evil in you from the day of your coming to me to this day. Nevertheless, you are not pleasing in the sight of the lords.

7 "Now therefore return, and go in peace, that you may not displease the lords of the Philistines."

8 And David said to Achish, "[a]But what have I done? And what have you found in your servant from the day when I came before you to this day, that I may not go and fight against the enemies of my lord the king?"

9 But Achish answered and said to David, "I know that you are pleasing in my sight, [a]like an angel of God; nevertheless [b]the commanders of the Philistines have said, 'He must not go up with us to the battle.'

10 "Now then arise early in the morning [a]with the servants of your lord who have come with you, and as soon as you have arisen early in the morning and have light, depart."

11 So David arose early, he and his men, to depart in the morning, to return to the land of the Philistines. And the Philistines went up to Jezreel.

CHAPTER 30

David's Victory Over the Amalekites

THEN it happened when David and his men came to [a]Ziklag on the third day, that [b]the Amalekites had made a raid on the [1]Negev and on [c]Ziklag, and had [2]overthrown Ziklag and burned it with fire;

2 and they took captive the women *and all* who were in it, both small and great, [1a]without killing anyone, and carried *them* off and went their way.

3 And when David and his men came to the city, behold, it was burned with fire, and their wives and their sons and their daughters had been taken captive.

4 Then David and the people who were with him lifted their voices and wept until there was no strength in them to weep.

5 Now [a]David's two wives had been taken captive, Ahinoam the Jezreelitess and Abigail the [1]widow of Nabal the Carmelite.

6 Moreover David was greatly distressed because [a]the people spoke of stoning him, for all the people were [1]embittered, each one because of his sons and his daughters. But [b]David strengthened himself in the LORD his God.

7 Then [a]David said to Abiathar the priest, the son of Ahimelech, "Please bring me the ephod." So Abiathar brought the ephod to David.

8 And [a]David inquired of the LORD, saying, "[b]Shall I pursue this band? Shall I overtake them?" And He said to him, "Pursue, for you shall surely overtake them, [c]and you shall surely rescue *all*."

9 So David went, [a]he and the six hundred men who were with him, and came to the brook Besor, *where* those left behind remained.

10 But David pursued, he and four hundred men, for [a]two hundred who were too exhausted to cross the brook Besor, remained *behind*.

11 Now they found an Egyptian in the field and brought him to David, and gave him bread and he ate, and they provided him water to drink.

12 And they gave him a piece of fig cake and two clusters of raisins, and he ate; [a]then his spirit [1]revived. For he had not eaten bread or drunk water for three days and three nights.

13 And David said to him, "To whom do you belong? And where are you from?" And he said, "I am a young man of Egypt, a servant of an Amalekite; and my master left me behind when I fell sick three days ago.

14 "We made a raid on [a]the [1]Negev of the Cherethites, and on that which belongs to Judah, and on [b]the [1]Negev of Caleb, and [c]we burned Ziklag with fire."

15 Then David said to him, "Will you bring me down to this band?" And he said, "Swear to me by God that you will not kill me or deliver me into the hands of my master, and I will bring you down to this band."

16 And when he had brought him down, behold, they were [1]spread over all the land, eating and drinking and [2]dancing because of [a]all the great spoil that they had taken from the land of the Philistines and from the land of Judah.

17 And David [1]slaughtered them [a]from the twilight [2]until the evening of [3]the next day; and not a man of them escaped, except four hundred young men who rode on [b]camels and fled.

18 So David recovered all that the Amalekites had taken, and [1]rescued his two wives.

19 But nothing of theirs was missing, whether small or great, sons or daughters, spoil or anything that they had taken for themselves; [a]David brought *it* all back.

6 [a]1 Sam. 27:8-12; 29:3
8 [a]1 Sam. 27:10-12
9 [a]2 Sam. 14:17, 20; 19:27 [b]1 Sam. 29:4
10 [a]1 Chr. 12:19, 22
1 [1]I.e., South country [2]Lit., *smote* [a]1 Sam. 29:4, 11 [b]1 Sam. 15:7; 27:8-10 [c]1 Sam. 27:6, 8
2 [1]Lit., *they did not kill* [a]1 Sam. 27:11
5 [1]Lit., *wife* [a]1 Sam. 25:42, 43
6 [1]Lit., *bitter in soul* [a]Ex. 17:4 [b]1 Sam. 23:16; Ps. 18:2; 27:14
7 [a]1 Sam. 23:9
8 [a]1 Sam. 23:2, 4 [b]Ex. 15:9 [c]1 Sam. 30:18
9 [a]1 Sam. 27:2
10 [a]1 Sam. 30:9, 21
12 [1]Lit., *returned to him* [a]Judg. 15:19
14 [1]I.e., South country [a]1 Sam. 1:16; 2 Sam. 8:18; Ezek. 25:16 [b]Josh. 14:13; 21:11, 12 [c]1 Sam. 30:1
16 [1]Lit., *left* [2]Lit., *keeping a pilgrim-feast* [a]1 Sam. 30:14
17 [1]Lit., *smote* [2]Lit., *even until* [3]Lit., *their* [a]1 Sam. 11:11 [b]Judg. 7:12; 1 Sam. 15:3
18 [1]Lit., *David rescued*
19 [a]1 Sam. 30:8

20 So David had [1]captured all the
sheep and the cattle *which the people* drove ahead of [2]the *other* livestock, and they said, "[a]This is David's spoil."

The Spoils Are Divided

21 When [a]David came to the two
hundred men who were too exhausted to follow David, who had
also been left at the brook Besor,
and they went out to meet David
and to meet the people who were
with him, then David approached
the people and greeted them.
22 Then all the wicked and worthless men among those who went
with David answered and said, "Because they did not go with [1]us, we
will not give them any of the spoil
that we have recovered, except to
every man his wife and his children,
that they may lead *them* away and
depart."
23 Then David said, "You must
not do so, my brothers, with what
the LORD has given us, who has kept
us and delivered into our hand the
band that came against us.
24"And who will listen to you in
this matter? For [a]as his share is who
goes down to the battle, so shall his
share be who stays by the baggage;
they shall share alike."
25 And so it has been from that
day forward, that he made it a statute and an ordinance for Israel to
this day.
26 Now when David came to Ziklag, he sent *some* of the spoil to the
elders of Judah, to his friends, saying, "Behold, [a]a [1]gift for you from
the spoil of [b]the enemies of the
LORD:
27 to those who were in [a]Bethel,
and to those who were in [b]Ramoth
of the [1]Negev, and to those who
were in [c]Jattir,
28 and to those who were in [a]Aro-
er, and to those who were in [b]Siph-
moth, and to those who were in
[c]Eshtemoa,
29 and to those who were in Racal,
and to those who were in the cities
of [a]the Jerahmeelites, and to those
who were in the cities of [b]the Kenites,
30 and to those who were in [a]Hor-
mah, and to those who were in [b]Bor-
ashan, and to those who were in A-
thach,
31 and to those who were in [a]He-
bron, and to all the places where David himself and his men were accustomed to [b]go."

CHAPTER 31

Saul and His Sons Slain

[a]NOW the Philistines were fighting
against Israel, and the men of Israel
fled from before the Philistines and
fell slain [b]on Mount Gilboa.
2 And the Philistines overtook
Saul and his sons; and the Philistines [1]killed Jonathan and Abinadab
and Malchi-shua the sons of Saul.
3 And [a]the battle went heavily
against Saul, and the archers [1]hit
him; and he was badly wounded by
the archers.
4 [a]Then Saul said to his armor
bearer, "Draw your sword and
pierce me through with it, lest
[b]these uncircumcised come and
pierce me through and make sport
of me." But his armor bearer would
not, for he was greatly afraid. [c]So
Saul took his sword and fell on it.
5 And when his armor bearer saw
that Saul was dead, he also fell on
his sword and died with him.
6 Thus Saul died with his three
sons, his armor bearer, and all his
men on that day together.
7 And when the men of Israel
who were on the other side of the
valley, with those who were beyond
the Jordan, saw that the men of Israel had fled and that Saul and his
sons were dead, they abandoned the
cities and fled; then the Philistines
came and lived in them.
8 And it came about on the [1]next
day when the Philistines came to
strip the slain, that they found Saul
and his three sons fallen on Mount
Gilboa.
9 And they cut off his head, and
stripped off his weapons, and sent
them [1]throughout the land of the
Philistines, [a]to carry the good news
[b]to the house of their idols and to
the people.
10 And they put his weapons in
the [1]temple of [a]Ashtaroth, and [b]they
fastened his body to the wall of
[c]Bethshan.
11 Now when [a]the inhabitants of
Jabesh-gilead heard [1]what the Philistines had done to Saul,
12 [a]all the valiant men rose and
walked all night, and took the body
of Saul and the bodies of his sons
from the wall of Bethshan, and they
came to Jabesh, and [b]burned them
there.
13 And they took their bones and
[a]buried them under [b]the tamarisk
tree at Jabesh, and [c]fasted seven
days.

20 [1]Lit., *taken* [2]Lit., *those livestock* [a]1 Sam. 30:26-31
21 [a]1 Sam. 30:10
22 [1]Lit., *me*
24 [a]Num. 31:27; Josh. 22:8
26 [1]Lit., *blessing* [a]1 Sam. 25:27 [b]1 Sam. 18:17; 25:28
27 [1]I.e., South country [a]Josh. 15:30; 19:4 [b]Josh. 19:8 [c]Josh. 15:48; 21:14
28 [a]1 Chr. 11:44 [b]1 Chr. 27:27 [c]Josh. 15:50
29 [a]1 Sam. 27:10 [b]1 Sam. 15:6
30 [a]Josh. 12:14; 15:30; 19:4 [b]Josh. 15:42; 19:7
31 [a]Num. 13:22; Josh. 14:13-15; 21:11-13 [b]1 Sam. 23:22
1 [a]1 Chr. 10:1-12 [b]1 Sam. 28:4
2 [1]Lit., *smote*
3 [1]Lit., *found* [a]2 Sam. 1:6
4 [a]Judg. 9:54 [b]Judg. 14:3 [c]2 Sam. 1:6, 10
8 [1]Lit., *morrow*
9 [1]Lit., *to . . . around* [a]2 Sam. 1:20 [b]Judg. 16:23, 24
10 [1]Lit., *house* [a]Judg. 2:13; 1 Sam. 7:3 [b]1 Sam. 31:12; 2 Sam. 21:14 [c]Josh. 17:11
11 [1]Lit., *about him what* [a]1 Sam. 11:1-13
12 [a]2 Sam. 2:4-7 [b]2 Chr. 16:14
13 [a]2 Sam. 21:12-14 [b]1 Sam. 22:6 [c]2 Sam. 1:12

THE SECOND BOOK OF SAMUEL

David Learns of Saul's Death

NOW it came about after [a]the
death of Saul, when David had returned from [b]the slaughter of the
Amalekites, that David remained
two days in Ziklag.
2 And it happened on the third
day, that behold, [a]a man came out of
the camp from Saul, [b]with his
clothes torn and [1]dust on his head.
And it came about when he came to
David that [c]he fell to the ground and
prostrated himself.
3 Then David said to him, "From
where do you come?" And he said to
him, "I have escaped from the camp
of Israel."
4 And David said to him, "[a]How
did things go? Please tell me." And
he said, "The people have fled from
the battle, and also many of the people have fallen and are dead; and
Saul and Jonathan his son are dead
also."
5 So David said to the young man
who told him, "How do you know
that Saul and his son Jonathan are
dead?"
6 And the young man who told
him said, "By chance I happened to
be on [a]Mount Gilboa, and behold,
[b]Saul was leaning on his spear. And
behold, the chariots and the horsemen pursued him closely.
7 "And when he looked behind
him, he saw me and called to me.
And I said, 'Here I am.'
8 "And he said to me, 'Who are
you?' And I [1]answered him, '[a]I am
an Amalekite.'
9 "Then he said to me, 'Please
stand beside me and kill me; for agony has seized me because my [1]life
still lingers in me.'
10 "So I stood beside him [a]and
killed him, because I knew that he
could not live after he had fallen.
And [b]I took the crown which *was* on
his head and the bracelet which *was*
on his arm, and I have brought them
here to my lord."
11 Then [a]David took hold of his
clothes and tore them, and *so* also
did all the men who *were* with him.
12 And they mourned and wept
and [a]fasted until evening for Saul
and his son Jonathan and for the
people of the LORD and the house of
Israel, because they had fallen by
the sword.
13 And David said to the young
man who told him, "Where are you
from?" And he [1]answered, "[a]I am
the son of an alien, an Amalekite."
14 Then David said to him, "How
is it you were not afraid [a]to stretch
out your hand to destroy the LORD's
anointed?"
15 And David called one of the
young men and said, "Go, [1]cut him
down." [a]So he struck him and he
died.
16 And David said to him, "[a]Your
blood is on your head, for [b]your
mouth has testified against you,
saying, 'I have killed the LORD's
anointed.' "

David's Dirge for Saul and Jonathan

17 Then [a]David chanted with this
lament over Saul and Jonathan his
son
18 and he told *them* to teach the
sons of Judah *the song of* the bow;
behold, it is written in [a]the book of
Jashar.
19 "[1]Your beauty, O Israel, is slain
on your high places!
[a]How have the mighty fallen!
20 "[a]Tell *it* not in Gath,
Proclaim it not in the streets of
Ashkelon;
Lest [b]the daughters of the Philistines rejoice,
Lest the daughters of [c]the uncircumcised exult.
21 "[a]O mountains of Gilboa,
[b]Let not dew or rain be on you,
nor fields of offerings;
For there the shield of the
mighty was defiled,
The shield of Saul, not [c]anoint-
ed with oil.
22 "[a]From the blood of the slain,
from the fat of the mighty,
[b]The bow of Jonathan did not
turn back,
And the sword of Saul did not
return empty.
23 "Saul and Jonathan, beloved
and pleasant in their life,
And in their death they were
not parted;
[a]They were swifter than eagles,
[b]They were stronger than
lions.
24 "O daughters of Israel, weep
over Saul,
Who clothed you luxuriously
in scarlet,

1 [a]1 Sam. 31:6 [b]1 Sam. 30:1, 17, 26
2 [1]Lit., *ground* [a]2 Sam. 4:10 [b]1 Sam. 4:12 [c]1 Sam. 25:23
4 [a]1 Sam. 4:16
6 [a]1 Sam. 28:4; 31:6 [b]1 Sam. 31:2-4
8 [1]Lit., *said to* [a]1 Sam. 15:3; 30:1, 13, 17
9 [1]Lit., *whole life is still in me*
10 [a]Judg. 9:54 [b]2 Kin. 11:12
11 [a]Gen. 37:29, 34
12 [a]2 Sam. 3:35
13 [1]Lit., *said* [a]2 Sam. 1:8
14 [a]1 Sam. 24:6; 26:9, 11, 16
15 [1]Lit., *fall upon him* [a]2 Sam. 4:10, 12
16 [a]2 Sam. 3:28, 29 [b]2 Sam. 1:10; Luke 19:22
17 [a]2 Chr. 35:25
18 [a]Josh. 10:13
19 [1]Lit., *The* [a]2 Sam. 1:25, 27
20 [a]1 Sam. 31:8-13; Mic. 1:10 [b]Ex. 15:20, 21; 1 Sam. 18:6 [c]1 Sam. 14:6
21 [a]1 Sam. 31:1 [b]Ezek. 31:15 [c]Is. 21:5
22 [a]Deut. 32:42; Is. 34:6 [b]1 Sam. 18:4
23 [a]Jer. 4:13 [b]Judg. 14:18

Who put ornaments of gold on
your apparel.
25 "[a]How have the mighty fallen
in the midst of the battle!
Jonathan is slain on your high
places.
26 "I am distressed for you, my
brother Jonathan;
You have been very pleasant
to me.
[a]Your love to me was more
wonderful
Than the love of women.
27 "[a]How have the mighty fallen,
And [b]the weapons of war perished!"

Chapter 2

David Made King Over Judah

THEN it came about afterwards
that [a]David inquired of the LORD,
saying, "Shall I go up to one of the
cities of Judah?" And the LORD said
to him, "Go up." So David said,
"Where shall I go up?" And He said,
"[b]To Hebron."
2 So David went up there, and
[a]his two wives also, Ahinoam the
Jezreelitess and Abigail the [1]widow
of Nabal the Carmelite.
3 And [a]David brought up his men
who *were* with him, each with his
household; and they lived in the
cities of Hebron.
4 Then the men of Judah came
and there [a]anointed David king over
the house of Judah.
And they told David, saying, "It
was [b]the men of Jabesh-gilead who
buried Saul."
5 And David sent messengers to
the men of Jabesh-gilead, and said
to them, "[a]May you be blessed of
the LORD because you have [1]shown
this kindness to Saul your lord, and
have buried him.
6 "And now [a]may the LORD [1]show
lovingkindness and truth to you;
and I also will [1]show this goodness
to you, because you have done this
thing.
7 "Now therefore let your hands
be strong, and be [1]valiant; for Saul
your lord is dead, and also the house
of Judah has anointed me king over
them."

Ish-bosheth Made King Over Israel

8 But [a]Abner the son of Ner, commander of Saul's army, had taken
[1]Ish-bosheth the son of Saul, and
brought him over to [b]Mahanaim.
9 And he made him king over
[a]Gilead, over the [b]Ashurites, over
[c]Jezreel, over Ephraim, and over
Benjamin, even over all Israel.
10 Ish-bosheth, Saul's son, was
forty years old when he became
king over Israel, and he was king for
two years. The house of Judah, however, followed David.
11 And [a]the [1]time that David was
king in Hebron over the house of Judah was seven years and six
months.

Civil War

12 Now Abner the son of Ner,
went out from Mahanaim to [a]Gibe-
on with the servants of Ish-bosheth
the son of Saul.
13 And [a]Joab the son of Zeruiah
and the servants of David went out
and met [1]them by the pool of Gibeon; and they sat down, [2]one on the
one side of the pool and [2]the other
on the other side of the pool.
14 Then Abner said to Joab, "Now
let the young men arise and [1a]hold a
contest before us." And Joab said,
"Let them arise."
15 So they arose and went over by
count, twelve for Benjamin and Ish-
bosheth the son of Saul, and twelve
of the servants of David.
16 And each one of them seized
his [1]opponent by the head, and
thrust his sword in his [2]opponent's
side; so they fell down together.
Therefore that place was called
[3]Helkath-hazzurim, which is in Gibeon.
17 And that day the battle was
very severe, and [a]Abner and the
men of Israel were beaten before the
servants of David.
18 Now [a]the three sons of Zeruiah
were there, Joab and Abishai and
Asahel; and Asahel *was* [b]as [1]swift-
footed as one of the gazelles which
is in the field.
19 And Asahel pursued Abner and
did not [1]turn to the right or to the
left from following Abner.
20 Then Abner looked behind him
and said, "Is that you, Asahel?" And
he answered, "It is I."
21 So Abner said to him, "[1]Turn to
your right or to your left, and take
hold of one of the young men for
yourself, and take for yourself his
spoil." But Asahel was not willing to
turn aside from following him.
22 And Abner repeated again to
Asahel, "Turn [1]aside from following
me. Why should I strike you to the
ground? [a]How then could I lift up
my face to your brother Joab?"
23 However, he refused to turn
aside; therefore Abner struck him in

25 [a]2 Sam. 1:19, 27
26 [a]1 Sam. 18:1-4
27 [a]2 Sam. 1:19, 25 [b]Is. 13:5
1 [a]1 Sam. 23:2, 4, 9-12 [b]Josh. 14:13; 1 Sam. 30:31
2 [1]Lit., *wife* [a]1 Sam. 25:42, 43
3 [a]1 Sam. 30:9; 1 Chr. 12:1
4 [a]1 Sam. 16:13; 2 Sam. 5:3, 5 [b]1 Sam. 31:11-13
5 [1]Lit., *done* [a]1 Sam. 23:21
6 [1]Lit., *do* [a]Ex. 34:6
7 [1]Lit., *sons of valor*
8 [1]I.e., Man of shame; cf. 1 Chr. 8:33, *Eshbaal* [a]1 Sam. 14:50 [b]Gen. 32:2, 10; 2 Sam. 17:24
9 [a]Josh. 22:9 [b]Judg. 1:32 [c]1 Sam. 29:1
11 [1]Lit., *number of days* [a]2 Sam. 5:5
12 [a]Josh. 10:12; 18:25
13 [1]Lit., *them together* [2]Lit., *these* [a]2 Sam. 8:16; 1 Chr. 2:16; 11:6
14 [1]Lit., *make sport* [a]2 Sam. 2:16, 17
16 [1]Lit., *fellow* [2]Lit., *fellow's* [3]I.e., The field of sword-edges
17 [a]2 Sam. 3:1
18 [1]Lit., *light in his feet* [a]1 Chr. 2:16 [b]1 Chr. 12:8; Hab. 3:19
19 [1]Lit., *turn to go to*
21 [1]Lit., *Turn for yourself*
22 [1]Lit., *aside for yourself* [a]2 Sam. 3:27

the belly [a]with the butt end of the spear, so that the spear came out at his back. And he fell there and died on the spot. And it came about that all who came to the place where [b]Asahel had fallen and died, stood still.

24 But Joab and Abishai pursued Abner, and when the sun was going down, they came to the hill of Ammah, which is in front of Giah by the way of the wilderness of Gibeon.

25 And the sons of Benjamin gathered together behind Abner and became one band, and they stood on the top of a certain hill.

26 Then Abner called to Joab and said, "Shall the sword devour forever? Do you not know that it will be bitter in the end? How long will you [1]refrain from telling the people to turn back from following their brothers?"

27 And Joab said, "As God lives, [a]if you had not spoken, surely then the people would have gone away in the morning, each from following his brother."

28 So Joab blew the trumpet; and all the people halted and pursued Israel no longer, [a]nor did they continue to fight any more.

29 Abner and his men then went through the Arabah all that night; so they crossed the Jordan, walked all morning, and came to [a]Mahanaim.

30 Then Joab returned from following Abner; when he had gathered all the people together, [1]nineteen of David's servants besides Asahel were missing.

31 But the servants of David had struck down many of Benjamin and Abner's men, *so that* three hundred and sixty men died.

32 And they took up Asahel and buried him in his father's tomb which was in Bethlehem. Then Joab and his men went all night until the day [1]dawned at Hebron.

Chapter 3

The House of David Strengthened

NOW [a]there was a long war between the house of Saul and the house of David; and David grew steadily stronger, but the house of Saul grew weaker continually.

2 [a]Sons were born to David at Hebron: his first-born was Amnon, by [b]Ahinoam the Jezreelitess;

3 and his second, Chileab, by Abigail the [1]widow of Nabal the Carmelite; and the third, Absalom the son of [a]Maacah, the daughter of Talmai, [b]king of Geshur;

4 and the fourth, [a]Adonijah the son of Haggith; and the fifth, Shephatiah the son of Abital;

5 and the sixth, Ithream, by David's wife Eglah. These were born to David at Hebron.

Abner Joins David

6 And it came about while there was war between the house of Saul and the house of David that Abner was making himself strong in the house of Saul.

7 Now Saul had a concubine whose name was [a]Rizpah, the daughter of Aiah; and [1]Ish-bosheth said to Abner, "Why have you gone in to my father's concubine?"

8 Then Abner was very angry over the words of Ish-bosheth and said, "[a]Am I a dog's head that belongs to Judah? Today I show kindness to the house of Saul your father, to his brothers and to his friends, and have not delivered you into the hands of David; and yet today you charge me with a guilt concerning the woman.

9 "[a]May God do so to Abner, and more also, if [b]as the LORD has sworn to David, I do not accomplish this for him,

10 to transfer the kingdom from the house of Saul, and to establish the throne of David over Israel and over Judah, [a]from Dan even to Beersheba."

11 And he could no longer answer Abner a word, because he was afraid of him.

12 Then Abner sent messengers to David in his place, saying, "Whose is the land? Make your covenant with me, and behold, my hand shall be with you to bring all Israel over to you."

13 And he said, "Good! I will make a covenant with you, but I demand one thing of you, [1]namely, [a]you shall not see my face unless you [b]first bring Michal, Saul's daughter, when you come to see [2]me."

14 So David sent messengers to Ish-bosheth, Saul's son, saying, "Give me my wife Michal, to whom I was betrothed [a]for a hundred foreskins of the Philistines."

15 And Ish-bosheth sent and took her from *her* husband, from [1a]Paltiel the son of Laish.

16 But her husband went with her, weeping as he went, and followed her as far as [a]Bahurim. Then Abner said to him, "Go, return." So he returned.

23 [a]1 Sam. 26:7 [b]2 Sam. 20:12
26 [1]Lit., *not tell the people*
27 [a]2 Sam. 2:14
28 [a]2 Sam. 3:1
29 [a]2 Sam. 2:8
30 [1]Lit., *nineteen men*
32 [1]Lit., *lighted on them*
1 [a]1 Kin. 14:30
2 [a]1 Chr. 3:1-3 [b]1 Sam. 25:42, 43
3 [1]Lit., *wife* [a]1 Sam. 27:8 [b]2 Sam. 14:32; 15:8
4 [a]1 Kin. 1:5
7 [1]So some ancient mss. and versions; M.T., *he* [a]2 Sam. 21:8-11
8 [a]1 Sam. 24:14; 2 Sam. 9:8
9 [a]1 Kin. 19:2 [b]1 Sam. 15:28; 25:28-31
10 [a]1 Sam. 3:20
13 [1]Lit., *saying* [2]Lit., *my face* [a]Gen. 43:3 [b]1 Sam. 18:20; 19:11
14 [a]1 Sam. 18:25, 27
15 [1]I.e., Palti [a]1 Sam. 25:44
16 [a]2 Sam. 16:5

17 Now Abner had [1]consultation
with [a]the elders of Israel, saying, "In
times past you were seeking for David to be king over you.
18"Now then, do *it*! For the LORD
has spoken of David, saying, '[a]By
the hand of My servant David [1]I will
save My people Israel from the hand
of the Philistines and from the hand
of all their enemies.' "
19 And Abner also spoke in the
hearing of Benjamin; and in addition Abner went to speak in the
hearing of David in Hebron all that
seemed good to Israel and to [a]the
whole house of Benjamin.
20 Then Abner and twenty men
with him came to David at Hebron.
And David made a feast for Abner
and the men who were with him.
21 And Abner said to David, "Let
me arise and go, and [a]gather all Israel to my lord the king that they
may make a covenant with you, and
that [b]you may be king over all that
your soul desires." So David sent
Abner away, and he went in peace.
22 And behold, [a]the servants of
David and Joab came from a raid
and brought much spoil with them;
but Abner was not with David in
Hebron, for he had sent him away,
and he had gone in peace.
23 When Joab and all the army
that was with him arrived, they told
Joab, saying, "Abner the son of Ner
came to the king, and he has sent
him away, and he has gone in
peace."
24 Then Joab came to the king and
said, "What have you done? Behold,
Abner came to you; why then have
you sent him away and he is already
gone?
25"You know Abner the son of
Ner, that he came to deceive you
and to learn of [a]your going out and
coming in, and to find out all that
you are doing."

Joab Murders Abner

26 When Joab came out from David, he sent messengers after Abner,
and they brought him back from the
well of Sirah; but David did not
know *it*.
27 So when Abner returned to Hebron, Joab took him aside into the
middle of the gate to speak with him
privately, and there [a]he struck him
in the belly so that he died on account of the blood of Asahel his
brother.
28 And afterward when David
heard it, he said, "I and my kingdom
are innocent before the LORD forever of the blood of Abner the son of
Ner.
29"[a]May it [1]fall on the head of Joab
and on all his father's house; and
may there not fail from the house of
Joab [b]one who has a discharge, or
who is a leper, or who takes hold of
a distaff, or who falls by the sword,
or who lacks bread."
30 So Joab and Abishai his brother
killed Abner [a]because he had put
their brother Asahel to death in the
battle at Gibeon.

David Mourns Abner

31 Then David said to Joab and to
all the people who were with him,
"[a]Tear your clothes and gird on
sackcloth and lament before Abner." And King David walked behind the bier.
32 Thus they buried Abner in Hebron; and the king lifted up his voice
and wept at the grave of Abner, and
all the people wept.
33 And [a]the king chanted a *lament*
for Abner and said,
"Should Abner die as a fool
dies?
34 "Your hands were not bound,
nor your feet put in fetters;
As one falls before the
[1]wicked, you have fallen."
And all the people wept again over
him.
35 Then all the people came [a]to
[1]persuade David to eat bread while
it was still day; but David vowed,
saying, "[b]May God do so to me, and
more also, if I taste bread or anything else [c]before the sun goes
down."
36 Now all the people took note *of
it*, and it [1]pleased them, just as everything the king did [2]pleased all
the people.
37 So all the people and all Israel
understood that day that it had not
been *the will* of the king to put Abner the son of Ner to death.
38 Then the king said to his servants, "Do you not know that a
prince and a great man has fallen
this day in Israel?
39"And I am [a]weak today, though
anointed king; and these men [b]the
sons of Zeruiah are too difficult for
me. [c]May the LORD repay the
evildoer according to his evil."

CHAPTER 4

Ish-bosheth Murdered

NOW when [1]Ish-bosheth, Saul's
son, heard that [a]Abner had died in
Hebron, [2b]he lost courage, and all
Israel was disturbed.

17 [1]Lit., *a word* [a]1 Sam. 8:4
18 [1]So many ancient mss. and versions; M.T., *he* [a]1 Sam. 9:16; 15:28
19 [a]1 Sam. 10:20, 21
21 [a]2 Sam. 3:10, 12 [b]1 Kin. 11:37
22 [a]1 Sam. 27:8
25 [a]Deut. 28:6; 1 Sam. 29:6
27 [a]2 Sam. 2:23; 20:9, 10; 1 Kin. 2:5
29 [1]Lit., *whirl* [a]Deut. 21:6-9; 1 Kin. 2:31-33 [b]Lev. 13:46
30 [a]2 Sam. 2:23
31 [a]Gen. 37:34; Judg. 11:35
33 [a]2 Sam. 1:17; 2 Chr. 35:25
34 [1]Lit., *sons of wickedness*
35 [1]Lit., *cause* [a]2 Sam. 12:17 [b]1 Sam. 3:17 [c]2 Sam. 1:12
36 [1]Lit., *was good in their eyes* [2]Lit., *was good in the eyes of all*
39 [a]1 Chr. 29:1; 2 Chr. 13:7 [b]2 Sam. 19:5-7 [c]1 Kin. 2:32-34
1 [1]So some ancient mss.; M.T., *he* [2]Lit., *his hands dropped* [a]2 Sam. 3:27 [b]Ezra 4:4

2 And Saul's son *had* two men
who were commanders of bands:
the name of the one was Baanah and
the name of the other Rechab, sons
of Rimmon the Beerothite, of the
sons of Benjamin (for [a]Beeroth is
also considered [b]*part* of Benjamin,
3 and the Beerothites fled to [a]Git-
taim, and have been aliens there until this day).
4 Now [a]Jonathan, Saul's son, had
a son crippled in his feet. He was
five years old when the [b]report of
Saul and Jonathan came from Jezreel, and his nurse took him up and
fled. And it happened that in her
hurry to flee, he fell and became
lame. And his name was [1c]Mephibo-
sheth.
5 So the sons of Rimmon the Beerothite, Rechab and Baanah, departed and came [a]to the house of
Ish-bosheth in the heat of the day
while he was taking his midday rest.
6 [1]And they came to the middle
of the house as [2]if to get wheat, and
[a]they struck him in the belly; and
Rechab and Baanah his brother escaped.
7 Now when they came into the
house, as he was lying on his bed in
his bedroom, they struck him and
killed him and beheaded him. And
they took his head and [1a]traveled by
way of the Arabah all night.
8 Then they brought the head of
Ish-bosheth to David at Hebron, and
said to the king, "Behold, the head
of Ish-bosheth, [a]the son of Saul,
your enemy, who sought your life;
thus the LORD has given my lord the
king vengeance this day on Saul and
his [1]descendants."
9 And David answered Rechab
and Baanah his brother, sons of
Rimmon the Beerothite, and said to
them, "As the LORD lives, [a]who has
redeemed my life from all distress,
10 [a]when one told me, saying, 'Behold, Saul is dead,' and [1]thought he
was bringing good news, I seized
him and killed him in Ziklag, which
was the reward I gave him for *his*
news.
11"How much more, when wicked
men have killed a righteous man in
his own house on his bed, shall I not
now [a]require his blood from your
hand, and [1]destroy you from the
earth?"
12 Then [a]David commanded the
young men, and they killed them
and cut off their hands and feet, and
hung them up beside the pool in Hebron. But they took the head of Ish-
bosheth [b]and buried it in the grave
of Abner in Hebron.

2 [a]Josh. 9:17 [b]Josh. 18:25
3 [a]Neh. 11:33
4 [1]I.e., Merib-baal [a]2 Sam. 9:3, 6 [b]1 Sam. 31:1-4 [c]1 Chr. 8:34; 9:40
5 [a]2 Sam. 2:8
6 [1]Lit., *And here* [2]Lit., *takers of wheat* [a]2 Sam. 2:23
7 [1]Lit., *went* [a]2 Sam. 2:29
8 [1]Lit., *seed* [a]1 Sam. 24:4; 25:29
9 [a]1 Kin. 1:29
10 [1]Lit., *he was as a bearer of good news in his own eyes* [a]2 Sam. 1:2, 4, 15
11 [1]Lit., *burn* [a]Gen. 9:5; Ps. 9:12
12 [a]2 Sam. 1:15 [b]2 Sam. 3:32

1 [1]Lit., *said, saying* [a]1 Chr. 11:1-3 [b]2 Sam. 19:13
2 [a]1 Sam. 18:5, 13, 16 [b]Gen. 49:24; 2 Sam. 7:7 [c]1 Sam. 25:30
3 [a]2 Sam. 3:21 [b]1 Sam. 16:13; 2 Sam. 2:4
4 [a]Gen. 41:46; Num. 4:3; Luke 3:23 [b]1 Kin. 2:11; 1 Chr. 26:31
5 [a]2 Sam. 2:11
6 [1]Lit., *David, saying* [2]Lit., *saying* [a]1 Chr. 11:4-9 [b]Josh. 15:63; 18:28; Judg. 1:21
7 [a]2 Sam. 6:12, 16; 1 Kin. 2:10; 9:24
9 [1]I.e., Citadel [a]2 Sam. 5:7 [b]1 Kin. 9:15, 24
10 [a]2 Sam. 3:1
11 [a]1 Chr. 14:1; 1 Kin. 5:2, 10, 18 [b]Ps. 30:title
13 [a]Deut. 17:17; 1 Chr. 3:9

CHAPTER 5

David King Over All Israel

[a]
THEN all the tribes of Israel came
to David at Hebron and [1]said, "Behold, we are [b]your bone and your
flesh.
2"Previously, when Saul was king
over us, [a]you were the one who led
Israel out and in. And the LORD said
to you, '[b]You will shepherd My people Israel, and you will be [c]a ruler
over Israel.' "
3 So all the elders of Israel came
to the king at Hebron, and King David [a]made a covenant with them before the LORD at Hebron; then [b]they
anointed David king over Israel.
4 David was [a]thirty years old
when he became king, *and* [b]he
reigned forty years.
5 At Hebron [a]he reigned over Judah seven years and six months,
and in Jerusalem he reigned thirty-
three years over all Israel and Judah.
6 [a]Now the king and his men
went to [b]Jerusalem against the
Jebusites, the inhabitants of the
land, and they said to [1]David, "You
shall not come in here, but the blind
and lame shall turn you away";
[2]thinking, "David cannot enter
here."
7 Nevertheless, David captured
the stronghold of Zion, that is [a]the
city of David.
8 And David said on that day,
"Whoever would strike the Jebusites, let him reach the lame and the
blind, who are hated by David's
soul, through the water tunnel."
Therefore they say, "The blind or
the lame shall not come into the
house."
9 So David lived in the stronghold, and called it [a]the city of David.
And David built all around from
[1b]Millo and inward.
10 And [a]David became greater
and greater, for the LORD God of
hosts was with him.
11 [a]Then Hiram king of Tyre sent
messengers to David with cedar
trees and carpenters and stonema-
sons; and [b]they built a house for David.
12 And David realized that the
LORD had established him as king
over Israel, and that He had exalted
his kingdom for the sake of His people Israel.
13 Meanwhile [a]David took more
concubines and wives from Jerusalem, after he came from Hebron;

and more sons and daughters were born to David.

14 Now [a]these are the names of those who were born to him in Jerusalem: Shammua, Shobab, Nathan, Solomon,

15 Ibhar, Elishua, Nepheg, Japhia,

16 Elishama, Eliada and Eliphelet.

War with the Philistines

17 When the Philistines heard that they had anointed David king over Israel, [a]all the Philistines went up to seek out David; and when David heard *of it,* he went down to the [b]stronghold.

18 Now the Philistines came and spread themselves out in [a]the valley of Rephaim.

19 Then [a]David inquired of the LORD, saying, "Shall I go up against the Philistines? Wilt Thou give them into my hand?" And [b]the LORD said to David, "Go up, for I will certainly give the Philistines into your hand."

20 So David came to [a]Baal-perazim, and [1]defeated them there; and he said, "The LORD has broken through my enemies before me like the break-through of waters." Therefore he named that place [2]Baal-perazim.

21 And they abandoned their idols there, so [a]David and his men carried them away.

22 Now [a]the Philistines came up once again and spread themselves out in the valley of Rephaim.

23 And when [a]David inquired of the LORD, He said, "You shall not go *directly* up; circle around behind them and come at them in front of the [1]balsam trees.

24 "And it shall be, when [a]you hear the sound of marching in the tops of the [1]balsam trees, then you shall act promptly, for then [b]the LORD will have gone out before you to strike the army of the Philistines."

25 Then David did so, just as the LORD had commanded him, and struck down the Philistines from [a]Geba until you come to [b]Gezer.

CHAPTER 6

Peril in Moving the Ark

[a]NOW David again gathered all the chosen men of Israel, thirty thousand.

2 And David arose and went with all the people who were with him to [a]Baale-judah, to bring up from there the ark of God which is called by the [b]Name, the very name of the LORD of hosts who [c]is [1]enthroned *above* the cherubim.

3 And they [1]placed the ark of God on [a]a new cart that they might bring it from the house of Abinadab which was on the hill; and Uzzah and Ahio, the sons of Abinadab, were leading the new cart.

4 So [a]they brought it with the ark of God from the house of Abinadab, which was on the hill; and Ahio was walking ahead of the ark.

5 Meanwhile, David and all the house of Israel [a]were celebrating before the LORD [b]with all kinds of *instruments made* of [1]fir wood, and with lyres, harps, tambourines, castanets and cymbals.

6 But when they came to the threshing floor of [a]Nacon, Uzzah [b]reached out toward the ark of God and took hold of it, for the oxen nearly upset *it.*

7 And the anger of the LORD burned against Uzzah, and [a]God struck him down there for [1]his irreverence; and he died there by the ark of God.

8 And David became angry because [1]of the LORD's outburst against Uzzah, and that place is called [2]Perez-uzzah to this day.

9 So David was afraid of the LORD that day; and he said, "How can the ark of the LORD come to me?"

10 And David was unwilling to move the ark of the LORD into the city of David with him; but David took it aside to the house of [a]Obed-edom the Gittite.

11 Thus the ark of the LORD remained in the house of Obed-edom the Gittite three months, and the LORD blessed Obed-edom and all his household.

The Ark Is Brought to Jerusalem

12 Now it was told King David, saying, "The LORD has blessed the house of Obed-edom and all that belongs to him, on account of the ark of God." [a]And David went and brought up the ark of God from the house of Obed-edom into [b]the city of David with gladness.

13 And so it was, that when the bearers of the ark of the LORD had gone six paces, he sacrificed an ox and a fatling.

14 And [a]David was dancing before the LORD with all *his* might, and David was [1b]wearing a linen ephod.

15 So David and all the house of Israel were bringing up the ark of the LORD with shouting and the sound of the trumpet.

14 [a]1 Chr. 3:5-8

17 [a]1 Sam. 29:1 [b]2 Sam. 23:14; 1 Chr. 11:16

18 [a]Gen. 14:5; Josh. 15:8; 17:15; 18:16

19 [a]1 Sam. 23:2 [b]1 Sam. 2:1

20 [1]Lit., *David smote* [2]I.e., The master of breakthrough [a]Is. 28:21

21 [a]1 Chr. 14:12

22 [a]2 Sam. 5:18

23 [1]Or, *baka-shrubs* [a]2 Sam. 5:19

24 [1]Or, *baka-shrubs* [a]2 Kin. 7:6 [b]Judg. 4:14

25 [a]Is. 28:21 [b]Josh. 12:12; 21:21

1 [a]1 Chr. 13:5-14

2 [1]Lit., *sitting* [a]Josh. 15:9, 10; 1 Sam. 7:1 [b]Lev. 24:16 [c]Ex. 25:22

3 [1]Lit., *caused to ride* [a]1 Sam. 6:7

4 [a]1 Sam. 7:1

5 [1]Or, *cypress* [a]1 Sam. 18:6, 7 [b]1 Chr. 13:7, 8

6 [a]1 Chr. 13:9 [b]Num. 4:15, 19, 20

7 [1]Lit., *the* [a]1 Sam. 6:19

8 [1]Lit., *the LORD broke through a break-through* [2]I.e., The break-through of Uzzah

10 [a]1 Chr. 26:4-8

12 [a]1 Chr. 15:25-16:3 [b]1 Kin. 8:1

14 [1]Lit., *girded with* [a]Ex. 15:20, 21; Judg. 11:34 [b]Ex. 19:6; 1 Sam. 2:18, 28

16 Then it happened *as* the ark of
the LORD came into the city of David
that [a]Michal the daughter of Saul
looked out of the window and saw
King David leaping and dancing before the LORD; and she despised him
in her heart.
17 So they brought in the ark of
the LORD and set it [a]in its place inside the tent which David had
pitched for it; and [b]David offered
burnt offerings and peace offerings
before the LORD.
18 And when David had finished
offering the burnt offering and the
peace offering, [a]he blessed the people in the name of the LORD of hosts.
19 Further, he distributed to all the
people, to all the multitude of Israel,
both to men and women, a cake of
bread and one of dates and one of
raisins to each one. Then all the people departed each to his house.
20 But when David returned to
bless his household, Michal the
daughter of Saul came out to meet
David and said, "How the king of
Israel distinguished himself today!
[1a]He uncovered himself today in the
eyes of his servants' maids as one of
the foolish ones shamelessly uncovers himself!"
21 So David said to Michal, "[a]*It
was* before the LORD, who chose me
above your father and above all his
house, to appoint me ruler over the
people of the LORD, over Israel;
therefore I will celebrate before the
LORD.
22"And I will be more lightly esteemed than this and will be humble
in my own eyes, but with the maids
of whom you have spoken, with
them I will be distinguished."
23 And Michal the daughter of
Saul had no child to the day of her
death.

CHAPTER 7

David Plans to Build a Temple

[a]NOW it came about when the king
lived in his house, and the LORD had
given him rest on every side from all
his enemies,
2 that the king said to [a]Nathan
the prophet, "See now, I dwell in [b]a
house of cedar, but the ark of God
[c]dwells within tent curtains."
3 And Nathan said to the king,
"[a]Go, do all that is in your mind, for
the LORD is with you."
4 But it came about in the same
night that the word of the LORD
came to Nathan, saying,
5"Go and say to My servant David, 'Thus says the LORD, "[a]Are you
the one who should build Me a
house to dwell in?
6"For [a]I have not dwelt in a house
since the day I brought up the sons
of Israel from Egypt, even to this
day; but I have been moving about
[b]in a tent, even in a [1]tabernacle.
7"[a]Wherever I have gone with all
the sons of Israel, did I speak a word
with one of the tribes of Israel,
[b]which I commanded to shepherd
My people Israel, saying, 'Why have
you not built Me a house of cedar?' " '

God's Covenant with David

8"Now therefore, thus you shall
say to My servant David, 'Thus says
the LORD of hosts, "[a]I took you from
the pasture, from following the
sheep, [b]that you should be ruler
over My people Israel.
9"And [a]I have been with you
wherever you have gone and [b]have
cut off all your enemies from before
you; and I will make you a great
name, like the names of the great
men who are on the earth.
10"I will also appoint a place for
My people Israel and [a]will plant
them, that they may live in their
own place and not be disturbed
again, [b]nor will the [1]wicked afflict
them any more as formerly,
11 even [a]from the day that I commanded judges to be over My people Israel; and [b]I will give you rest
from all your enemies. The LORD
also declares to you that [c]the LORD
will make a house for you.
12"[a]When your days are complete
and you lie down with your fathers,
I will raise up your [1]descendant after you, who will come forth from
[2]you, and I will establish his kingdom.
13"[a]He shall build a house for My
name, and [b]I will establish the
throne of his kingdom forever.
14"[a]I will be a father to him and he
will be a son to Me; [b]when he commits iniquity, I will correct him with
the rod of men and the strokes of the
sons of men,
15 but My lovingkindness shall
not depart from him, [a]as I took *it*
away from Saul, whom I removed
from before you.
16"And [a]your house and your kingdom shall endure before [1]Me forever; your throne shall be established forever." ' "
17 In accordance with all these
words and all this vision, so Nathan
spoke to David.

16 [a]2 Sam. 3:14
17 [a]1 Chr. 15:1; 2 Chr. 1:4 [b]1 Kin. 8:62-65
18 [a]1 Kin. 8:14, 15
20 [1]Lit., *who* [a]2 Sam. 6:14, 16
21 [a]1 Sam. 13:14; 15:28
1 [a]1 Chr. 17:1-27
2 [a]2 Sam. 6:17; 12:1; 1 Kin. 1:22; 1 Chr. 29:29; 2 Chr. 9:29 [b]2 Sam. 5:11 [c]Ex. 26:1
3 [a]1 Kin. 8:17, 18
5 [a]1 Kin. 5:3, 4; 8:19
6 [1]Lit., *dwelling place* [a]Josh. 18:1; 1 Kin. 8:16 [b]Ex. 40:18, 34
7 [a]Lev. 26:11, 12 [b]2 Sam. 5:2
8 [a]1 Sam. 16:11, 12; Ps. 78:70, 71 [b]1 Sam. 6:21
9 [a]1 Sam. 5:10 [b]Ps. 18:37-42
10 [1]Lit., *sons of wickedness* [a]Ex. 15:17; Is. 5:2, 7 [b]Ps. 89:22, 23; Is. 60:18
11 [a]Judg. 2:14-16; 1 Sam. 12:9-11 [b]2 Sam. 7:1 [c]1 Sam. 7:27; 25:28
12 [1]Lit., *seed* [2]Lit., *your bowels* [a]1 Kin. 2:1
13 [a]1 Kin. 6:12; 8:19 [b]Is. 9:7; 49:8
14 [a]Ps. 89:26, 27; Heb. 1:5 [b]1 Kin. 11:34; Ps. 89:30-33
15 [a]1 Sam. 15:23; 16:14
16 [1]So with Gk. and some ancient mss.; M.T., *you* [a]2 Sam. 7:13; Ps. 89:36, 37

David's Prayer

18 Then David the king went in and sat before the LORD, and he said, "[a]Who am I, O Lord [1]GOD, and what is my house, that Thou hast brought me this far?

19 "And yet this was insignificant in Thine eyes, O Lord GOD, [a]for Thou hast spoken also of the house of Thy servant concerning the distant future. And [b]this is the [1]custom of man, O Lord GOD.

20 "And again what more can David say to Thee? For [a]Thou knowest Thy servant, O Lord GOD!

21 "[a]For the sake of Thy word, and according to Thine own heart, Thou hast done all this greatness to let Thy servant know.

22 "For this reason [a]Thou art great, O Lord GOD; for [b]there is none like Thee, and there is no God besides Thee, [c]according to all that we have heard with our ears.

23 "And [a]what one nation on the earth is like Thy people Israel, whom God went to redeem for Himself as a people and to make a name for Himself, and [b]to do a great thing for Thee and awesome things for Thy land, before [c]Thy people whom [d]Thou hast redeemed for Thyself from Egypt, *from* nations and their gods?

24 "For [a]Thou hast established for Thyself Thy people Israel as Thine own people forever, and [b]Thou, O LORD, hast become their God.

25 "Now therefore, O LORD God, the word that Thou hast spoken concerning Thy servant and his house, confirm *it* forever, and do as Thou hast spoken,

26 [a]that Thy name may be magnified forever, by saying, 'The LORD of hosts is God over Israel'; and may the house of Thy servant David be established before Thee.

27 "For Thou, O LORD of hosts, the God of Israel, hast [1]made a revelation to Thy servant, saying, '[a]I will build you a house'; therefore Thy servant has found [2]courage to pray this prayer to Thee.

28 "And now, O Lord GOD, Thou art God, and [a]Thy words are truth, and Thou hast [1]promised this good thing to Thy servant.

29 "Now therefore may it please Thee to bless the house of Thy servant, that it may continue forever before Thee. For Thou, O Lord GOD, hast spoken; and [a]with Thy blessing may the house of Thy servant be blessed forever."

18 [1]YHWH, usually rendered LORD and so throughout the chap. [a]Ex. 3:11; 1 Sam. 18:18
19 [1]Or, *law* [a]2 Sam. 7:11-16; 1 Chr. 17:17 [b]Is. 55:8, 9
20 [a]1 Sam. 16:7; John 21:17
21 [a]1 Chr. 17:19
22 [a]Deut. 3:24; Ps. 48:1; 86:10 [b]Ex. 15:11; 1 Sam. 2:2 [c]Ex. 10:2; Ps. 44:1
23 [a]Deut. 4:32-38 [b]Deut. 10:21 [c]Deut. 15:15 [d]Deut. 9:26
24 [a]Deut. 32:6 [b]Gen. 17:7, 8; Ex. 6:7
26 [a]Ps. 72:18, 19
27 [1]Lit., *uncovered the ear of* [2]Lit., *his heart* [a]2 Sam. 7:13
28 [1]Or, *spoken* [a]Ex. 34:6; John 17:17
29 [a]Num. 6:24
1 [1]Lit., *smote* [2]Lit., *the bridle of the mother city* [a]1 Chr. 18
2 [a]Num. 24:17 [b]1 Sam. 22:3, 4 [c]1 Kin. 4:21; 2 Kin. 3:4 [d]2 Kin. 17:3
3 [1]Lit., *hand* [2]I.e., Euphrates [a]2 Kin. 10:16, 19; 1 Sam. 14:47 [b]2 Kin. 10:15-19
4 [a]Josh. 11:6, 9
5 [1]Heb., *Aram* [2]Lit., *smote* [a]1 Kin. 11:23-25; 15:18
6 [a]2 Sam. 8:2 [b]2 Sam. 3:18
7 [1]Lit., *on*
8 [1]Or, *Tibhath,* 1 Chr. 18:8 [a]Ezek. 47:16
9 [1]Lit., *smitten* [a]1 Kin. 8:65; 2 Chr. 8:4
10 [1]In 1 Chr. 18:10, *Hadoram* [2]Lit., *ask him of his welfare* [3]Lit., *smitten* [4]Lit., *was a man of wars* [5]Lit., *there were in his hand*
11 [a]1 Kin. 7:51
12 [1]Or, *Edom* [a]2 Sam. 8:2 [b]2 Sam. 10:14 [c]2 Sam. 5:17-25 [d]1 Sam. 27:8; 30:17-20
13 [1]Lit., *smiting* [2]Or, *Edom* [a]2 Sam. 7:9 [b]2 Kin. 14:7

CHAPTER 8

David's Triumphs

[a]NOW after this it came about that David [1]defeated the Philistines and subdued them; and David took [2]control of the chief city from the hand of the Philistines.

2 And [a]he defeated [b]Moab, and measured them with the line, making them lie down on the ground; and he measured two lines to put to death and one full line to keep alive. And [c]the Moabites became servants to David, [d]bringing tribute.

3 Then David defeated [a]Hadadezer, the son of Rehob king of Zobah, as [b]he went to restore his [1]rule at the [2]River.

4 And David captured from him 1,700 horsemen and 20,000 foot soldiers; and David [a]hamstrung the chariot horses, but reserved *enough* of them for 100 chariots.

5 And when [1a]the Syrians of Damascus came to help Hadadezer, king of Zobah, David [2]killed 22,000 men of [1]the Syrians.

6 Then David put garrisons in Syria of Damascus, and [a]the Syrians became servants to David, bringing tribute. And [b]the LORD helped David wherever he went.

7 And David took the shields of gold which were [1]carried by the servants of Hadadezer, and brought them to Jerusalem.

8 And from [1]Betah and from [a]Berothai, cities of Hadadezer, King David took a very large amount of bronze.

9 Now when Toi king of [a]Hamath heard that David had [1]defeated all the army of Hadadezer,

10 Toi sent [1]Joram his son to King David to [2]greet him and bless him, because he had fought against Hadadezer and [3]defeated him; for Hadadezer [4]had been at war with Toi. And [5]*Joram* brought with him articles of silver, of gold and of bronze.

11 King David also dedicated [a]these to the LORD, with the silver and gold that he had dedicated from all the nations which he had subdued:

12 from [1]Syria and [a]Moab and [b]the sons of Ammon and [c]the Philistines and [d]Amalek, and from the spoil of Hadadezer, son of Rehob, king of Zobah.

13 So [a]David made a name *for himself* when he returned from [1]killing 18,000 [2]Syrians in [b]the Valley of Salt.

14 And he put garrisons in Edom.

In all Edom he put garrisons, and
[a]all the Edomites became servants
to David. And [b]the LORD helped David wherever he went.
15 So David reigned over all Israel;
and David [1]administered justice
and righteousness for all his people.
16 And Joab the son of Zeruiah
was over the army, and [a]Jehosha-
phat the son of Ahilud *was* [b]record-
er.
17 And [a]Zadok the son of Ahitub
and Ahimelech the son of Abiathar
were [b]priests, and Seraiah *was* [c]sec-
retary.
18 And [a]Benaiah the son of Jehoiada [1]was over the [b]Cherethites
and the Pelethites; and David's sons
were [2c]chief ministers.

CHAPTER 9

David's Kindness to Mephibosheth

THEN David said, "Is there yet
[1]anyone left of the house of Saul,
[a]that I may show him kindness for
Jonathan's sake?"
2 Now there was a servant of the
house of Saul whose name was
Ziba, and they called him to David;
and the king said to him, "Are you
[a]Ziba?" And he said, "*I am* your servant."
3 And the king said, "Is there not
yet anyone of the house of Saul to
whom I may show the [a]kindness of
God?" And Ziba said to the king,
"[b]There is still a son of Jonathan
who is crippled in both feet."
4 So the king said to him, "Where
is he?" And Ziba said to the king,
"Behold, he is [a]in the house of Machir the son of Ammiel in Lo-debar."
5 Then King David sent and
brought him from the house of Machir the son of Ammiel, from Lo-debar.
6 And [a]Mephibosheth, the son of
Jonathan the son of Saul, came to
David and [b]fell on his face and prostrated himself. And David said,
"Mephibosheth." And he said,
"Here is your servant!"
7 And David said to him, "Do not
fear, for [a]I will surely show kindness
to you for the sake of your father
Jonathan, and [b]will restore to you
all the [1]land of your [2]grandfather
Saul; and [c]you shall [3]eat at my table
regularly."
8 Again he prostrated himself
and said, "What is your servant,
that you should regard [a]a dead dog
like me?"
9 Then the king called Saul's servant Ziba, and said to him, "[a]All
that belonged to Saul and to all his
house I have given to your master's
[1]grandson.
10 "And you and your sons and
your servants shall cultivate the
land for him, and you shall bring in
the produce so that your master's
grandson may have food; nevertheless [a]Mephibosheth your master's
grandson [b]shall [1]eat at my table
regularly." Now Ziba had fifteen
sons and twenty servants.
11 Then Ziba said to the king, "According to all that my lord the king
commands his servant so your servant will do." So Mephibosheth ate
at [1]David's table as one of the king's
sons.
12 And Mephibosheth had a young
son whose name was [a]Mica. And all
who lived in the house of Ziba were
servants to Mephibosheth.
13 So Mephibosheth lived in Jerusalem, for [a]he ate at the king's table
regularly. Now [b]he was lame in both
feet.

CHAPTER 10

Ammon and Syria Defeated

[a]NOW it happened afterwards that
[b]the king of the Ammonites died,
and Hanun his son became king in
his place.
2 Then David said, "I will show
kindness to Hanun the son of [a]Na-
hash, just as his father showed kindness to me." So David sent [1]some of
his servants to console him concerning his father. But when David's servants came to the land of the Ammonites,
3 the princes of the Ammonites
said to Hanun their lord, "[1]Do you
think that David is honoring your
father because he has sent consolers
to you? [a]Has David not sent his servants to you in order to search the
city, to spy it out and overthrow it?"
4 So Hanun took David's servants and [a]shaved off half of their
beards, and [b]cut off their garments
in the middle as far as their hips, and
sent them away.
5 When they told *it* to David, he
sent to meet them, for the men were
greatly humiliated. And the king
said, "[1]Stay at Jericho until your
beards grow, and then return."
6 Now when the sons of Ammon
saw that [a]they had become odious
to David, the sons of Ammon sent
and [b]hired [1]the Syrians of [c]Beth-re-
hob and [1]the [d]Syrians of Zobah,
20,000 foot soldiers, and the king of

14 [a]Gen. 27:37-40; Num. 24:17, 18 [b]2 Sam. 8:6
15 [1]Lit., *was doing*
16 [a]1 Kin. 4:3 [b]2 Kin. 18:18, 37
17 [a]1 Chr. 6:4-8 [b]1 Chr. 16:39, 40 [c]2 Kin. 18:18
18 [1]Lit., *and the Cherethites* [2]Lit., *priests* [a]1 Kin. 4:4 [b]1 Sam. 30:14; 2 Sam. 15:18; 20:7, 23; 1 Kin. 1:38, 44 [c]1 Chr. 18:17
1 [1]Lit., *he who is* [a]1 Sam. 20:14-17, 42
2 [a]2 Sam. 16:1-4; 19:17, 29
3 [a]1 Sam. 20:14 [b]2 Sam. 4:4
4 [a]1 Sam. 17:27-29
6 [a]2 Sam. 16:4; 19:24-30 [b]1 Sam. 25:23
7 [1]Lit., *field* [2]Lit., *father* [3]Lit., *eat bread* [a]2 Sam. 9:1, 3 [b]2 Sam. 12:8 [c]2 Sam. 19:28; 1 Kin. 2:7; 2 Kin. 25:29
8 [a]2 Sam. 16:9
9 [1]Lit., *son* [a]2 Sam. 16:4; 19:29
10 [1]Lit., *eat bread* [a]2 Sam. 9:7, 11, 13 [b]2 Sam. 19:28; 1 Kin. 2:7
11 [1]Lit., *my*
12 [a]1 Chr. 8:34
13 [a]2 Sam. 9:7, 11 [b]2 Sam. 9:3
1 [a]1 Chr. 19:1-19 [b]1 Sam. 11:1
2 [1]Lit., *by the hand of* [a]1 Sam. 11:1
3 [1]Lit., *"In your eyes is David honoring* [a]Gen. 42:9, 16
4 [a]Is. 15:2; Jer. 41:5 [b]Is. 20:4
5 [1]Lit., *Return to*
6 [1]Heb., *Aram* (vs. 6-19) [a]Gen. 34:30; 1 Sam. 27:12 [b]2 Sam. 8:3, 5; 2 Kin. 7:6 [c]Gen. 36:37; Judg. 18:28 [d]2 Sam. 8:3

[e]Maacah with 1,000 men, and the
men of Tob with 12,000 men.
7 When David heard *of it,* he sent
Joab and all the army, the mighty
men.
8 And the sons of Ammon came
out and drew up in battle array [a]at
the entrance of the [1]city, while the
Syrians of Zobah and of Rehob and
the men of [b]Tob and Maacah *were*
by themselves [c]in the field.
9 Now when Joab saw that [1]the
battle was set against him in front
and in the rear, he selected from all
the choice men of Israel, and arrayed *them* against the Syrians.
10 But the remainder of the people
he placed in the hand of Abishai his
brother, and he arrayed *them*
against the sons of Ammon.
11 And he said, "If the Syrians are
too strong for me, then you shall
help me, but if the sons of Ammon
are too strong for you, then I will
come to help you.
12"[a]Be strong, and [b]let us show
ourselves courageous for the sake of
our people and for the cities of our
God; and [c]may the LORD do what is
good in His sight."
13 So Joab and the people who
were with him drew near to the battle against the Syrians, and [a]they
fled before him.
14 When the sons of Ammon saw
that the Syrians fled, they *also* fled
before Abishai and entered the city.
[a]Then Joab returned from *fighting*
against the sons of Ammon and
came to Jerusalem.
15 When the Syrians saw that they
had been [1]defeated by Israel, they
gathered themselves together.
16 [a]And Hadadezer sent and
brought out the Syrians who were
beyond the [1]River, and they came to
Helam; and [b]Shobach the commander of the army of Hadadezer
[2]led them.
17 Now when it was told David, he
gathered all Israel together and
crossed the Jordan, and came to Helam. And the Syrians arrayed themselves to meet David and fought
against him.
18 But the Syrians fled before Israel, and David killed [a]700 charioteers of the Syrians and 40,000
horsemen and struck down Sho-
bach the commander of their army,
and he died there.
19 When all the kings, servants of
Hadadezer, saw that they were [1]de-
feated by Israel, [a]they made peace
with Israel and served them. So the
Syrians feared to help the sons of
Ammon any more.

CHAPTER 11

Bathsheba, David's Great Sin

[a]
THEN it happened [1b]in the spring,
at the time when kings go out *to battle,* that David sent Joab and his servants with him and all Israel, and
they destroyed the sons of Ammon
and [c]besieged Rabbah. But David
stayed at Jerusalem.
2 Now when evening came [a]Da-
vid arose from his bed and walked
around on [b]the roof of the king's
house, and from the roof he saw a
woman bathing; and the woman
was very beautiful in appearance.
3 So David sent and inquired
about the woman. And one said, "Is
this not [a]Bathsheba, the daughter of
Eliam, the wife of [b]Uriah the Hittite?"
4 And David sent messengers
and took her, and when she came to
him, [a]he lay with her; [b]and when she
had purified herself from her uncleanness, she returned to her
house.
5 And the woman conceived; and
she sent and told David, and said,
"[a]I am pregnant."
6 Then David sent to Joab, *saying,* "Send me Uriah the Hittite." So
Joab sent Uriah to David.
7 When Uriah came to him, [a]Da-
vid asked concerning the welfare of
Joab and [1]the people and the state
of the war.
8 Then David said to Uriah, "Go
down to your house, and [a]wash your
feet." And Uriah went out of the
king's house, and [b]a present from
the king [1]was sent out after him.
9 But Uriah slept [a]at the door of
the king's house with all the servants of his lord, and did not go
down to his house.
10 Now when they told David,
saying, "Uriah did not go down to
his house," David said to Uriah,
"Have you not come from a journey? Why did you not go down to
your house?"
11 And Uriah said to David, "[a]The
ark and Israel and Judah are staying
in [1]temporary shelters, and my lord
Joab and [b]the servants of my lord
are camping in the open field. Shall
I then go to my house to eat and to
drink and to lie with my wife? [c]By
your life and the life of your soul, I
will not do this thing."
12 Then David said to Uriah, "Stay
here today also, and tomorrow I will
let you go." So Uriah remained in
Jerusalem that day and the [1]next.
13 Now David called him, and he

6 [e]Deut. 3:14
8 [1]Lit., *gate* [a]1 Chr. 19:9 [b]Judg. 11:3, 5 [c]Josh. 13:9, 16
9 [1]Lit., *the faces of the battle were against*
12 [a]Deut. 31:6; Josh. 1:6 [b]1 Cor. 16:13 [c]1 Sam. 3:18
13 [a]1 Kin. 20:13-21
14 [a]2 Sam. 11:1
15 [1]Lit., *smitten before*
16 [1]I.e., Euphrates [2]Lit., *before* [a]2 Sam. 8:3-8 [b]1 Chr. 19:16
18 [a]1 Chr. 19:18
19 [1]Lit., *smitten before* [a]2 Sam. 8:6
1 [1]Lit., *at the return of the year* [a]1 Chr. 20:1 [b]2 Sam. 10:14; 1 Kin. 20:22, 26 [c]2 Sam. 12:26-28; Jer. 49:2, 3; Amos 1:14
2 [a]2 Sam. 4:5, 7 [b]Deut. 22:8; 1 Sam. 9:25; Matt. 24:17; Acts 10:9
3 [a]1 Chr. 3:5 [b]2 Sam. 23:39
4 [a]Ps. 51:title; James 1:14, 15 [b]Lev. 12:2-5; 15:19-28; 18:19
5 [a]Lev. 20:10; Deut. 22:22
7 [1]Lit., *welfare of* [a]Gen. 37:14; 1 Sam. 17:22
8 [1]Lit., *went out* [a]Gen. 43:24; Luke 7:44 [b]Gen. 43:34
9 [a]1 Kin. 14:27, 28
11 [1]Or, *booths* [a]2 Sam. 7:2, 6 [b]2 Sam. 20:6 [c]2 Sam. 4:9; 14:19
12 [1]Lit., *morrow*

ate and drank before him, and he made him drunk; and in the evening he went out to lie on his bed [a]with his lord's servants, but he did not go down to his house.

14 Now it came about in the morning that David [a]wrote a letter to Joab, and sent *it* by the hand of Uriah.

15 And he had written in the letter, saying, "[1]Place Uriah in the front line of the [2]fiercest battle and withdraw from him, [a]so that he may be struck down and die."

16 So it was as Joab kept watch on the city, that he put Uriah at the place where he knew there *were* valiant men.

17 And the men of the city went out and fought against Joab, and some of the people among David's servants fell; and [a]Uriah the Hittite also died.

18 Then Joab sent and reported to David all the events of the war.

19 And he charged the messenger, saying, "When you have finished telling all the events of the war to the king,

20 and if it happens that the king's wrath rises and he says to you, 'Why did you go so near to the city to fight? Did you not know that they would shoot from the wall?

21 'Who [a]struck down Abimelech the son of Jerubbesheth? Did not a woman throw an upper millstone on him from the wall so that he died at Thebez? Why did you go so near the wall?'—then you shall say, 'Your servant Uriah the Hittite is dead also.' "

22 So the messenger departed and came and reported to David all that Joab had sent him *to tell.*

23 And the messenger said to David, "The men prevailed against us and came out against us in the field, but we [1]pressed them as far as the entrance of the gate.

24 "Moreover, the archers shot at your servants from the wall; so some of the king's servants are dead, and your servant Uriah the Hittite is also dead."

25 Then David said to the messenger, "Thus you shall say to Joab, 'Do not let this thing [1]displease you, for the sword devours one as well as another; make your battle against the city stronger and overthrow it;' and *so* encourage him."

26 Now when the wife of Uriah heard that Uriah her husband was dead, [a]she mourned for her husband.

27 When the *time of* mourning was over, David sent and [1]brought her to his house and [a]she became his wife; then she bore him a son. But [b]the thing that David had done was evil in the sight of the LORD.

CHAPTER 12

Nathan Rebukes David

THEN the LORD sent [a]Nathan to David. And [b]he came to him, and [1c]said,

"There were two men in one city, the one rich and the other poor.

2 "The rich man had a great many flocks and herds.

3 "But the poor man had nothing except [a]one little ewe lamb
Which he bought and nourished;
And it grew up together with him and his children.
It would eat of his [1]bread and drink of his cup and lie in his bosom,
And was like a daughter to him.

4 "Now a traveler came to the rich man,
And he [1]was unwilling to take from his own flock or his own herd,
To prepare for the wayfarer who had come to him;
Rather he took the poor man's ewe lamb and prepared it for the man who had come to him."

5 [a]Then David's anger burned greatly against the man, and he said to Nathan, "As the LORD lives, surely the man who has done this [1b]deserves to die.

6 "And he must make restitution for the lamb [a]fourfold, because he did this thing and had no compassion."

7 Nathan then said to David, "[a]You are the man! Thus says the LORD God of Israel, '[b]It is I who anointed you king over Israel and it is I who delivered you from the hand of Saul.

8 'I also gave you [a]your master's house and your master's wives into your [1]care, and I gave you the house of Israel and Judah; and if *that had been* too little, I would have added to you many more things like these!

9 'Why [a]have you despised the word of the LORD by doing evil in His sight? [b]You have struck down Uriah the Hittite with the sword, [c]have taken his wife to be your wife,

13 [a]2 Sam. 11:9
14 [a]1 Kin. 21:8-10
15 [1]Lit., *Give* [2]Lit., *strong* [a]2 Sam. 12:9
17 [a]2 Sam. 11:21
21 [a]Judg. 9:50-54
23 [1]Lit., *were upon*
25 [1]Lit., *be evil in your sight*
26 [a]Gen. 50:10; Deut. 34:8; 1 Sam. 31:13
27 [1]Lit., *gathered* [a]2 Sam. 12:9 [b]Ps. 51:4, 5
1 [1]Lit., *said to him* [a]2 Sam. 7:2, 4, 17 [b]Ps. 51:title [c]2 Sam. 14:4-7; 1 Kin. 20:35-41
3 [1]Lit., *morsel* [a]2 Sam. 11:3
4 [1]Lit., *spared*
5 [1]Lit., *is a son of death* [a]1 Kin. 20:39, 40 [b]1 Sam. 26:16
6 [a]Ex. 22:1
7 [a]1 Kin. 20:42 [b]1 Sam. 16:13
8 [1]Lit., *bosom* [a]2 Sam. 9:7
9 [a]1 Sam. 15:23, 26 [b]2 Sam. 11:14-17, 27 [c]2 Sam. 11:27

and have killed him with the sword
of the sons of Ammon.
10 'Now therefore, [a]the sword shall
never depart from your house, because you have despised Me and
have taken the wife of Uriah the Hittite to be your wife.'
11 "Thus says the LORD, 'Behold, I
will raise up evil against you from
your own household; [a]I will even
take your wives before your eyes,
and give *them* to your companion,
and he shall lie with your wives in
[1]broad daylight.
12 'Indeed [a]you did it secretly, but
[b]I will do this thing before all Israel,
and [1]under the sun.' "
13 Then David said to Nathan, "[a]I
have sinned against the LORD." And
Nathan said to David, "The LORD
also has [1b]taken away your sin; you
shall not die.
14 "However, because by this deed
you have [a]given occasion to the enemies of the LORD to blaspheme, the
child also that is born to you shall
surely die."
15 So Nathan went to his house.

Loss of a Child

Then [a]the LORD struck the child
that Uriah's [1]widow bore to David,
so that he was *very* sick.
16 David therefore inquired of
God for the child; and David fasted
and went and [a]lay all night on the
ground.
17 And [a]the elders of his household stood beside him in order to
raise him up from the ground, but he
was unwilling and would not eat
food with them.
18 Then it happened on the seventh day that the child died. And the
servants of David were afraid to tell
him that the child was dead, for they
said, "Behold, while the child was
still alive, we spoke to him and he
did not listen to our voice. How then
can we tell him that the child is
dead, since he might do *himself*
harm!"
19 But when David saw that his
servants were whispering together,
David perceived that the child was
dead; so David said to his servants,
"Is the child dead?" And they said,
"He is dead."
20 So David arose from the
ground, [a]washed, anointed *himself,*
and changed his clothes; and he
came into the house of the LORD and
worshiped. Then he came to his own
house, and when he requested, they
set food before him and he ate.
21 Then his servants said to him,
"What is this thing that you have
done? [1]While the child was alive,
you fasted and wept; but when the
child died, you arose and ate food."
22 And he said, "While the child
was *still* alive, [a]I fasted and wept;
for I said, '[b]Who knows, the LORD
may be gracious to me, that the
child may live.'
23 "But now he has died; why
should I fast? Can I bring him back
again? [a]I shall go to him, but [b]he will
not return to me."

Solomon Born

24 Then David comforted his wife
Bathsheba, and went in to her and
lay with her; and she gave birth to a
son, and [1a]he named him Solomon.
Now the LORD loved him
25 and sent *word* through Nathan
the prophet, and he named him
[1]Jedidiah for the LORD's sake.

War Again

26 [a]Now Joab fought against Rabbah of the sons of Ammon, and captured the royal city.
27 And Joab sent messengers to
David and said, "I have fought
against Rabbah, I have even captured the city of waters.
28 "Now therefore gather the rest
of the people together and camp
against the city and capture it, lest I
capture the city myself and it be
named after me."
29 So David gathered all the people and went to Rabbah, fought
against it, and captured it.
30 Then he took the crown of
[1]their king from his head; and its
weight *was* a talent of gold, and *in it*
[2]*was* a precious stone; and it was
placed on David's head. And he
brought out the spoil of the city in
great amounts.
31 He also brought out the people
who were in it, and [1a]set *them* under
saws, sharp iron instruments, and
iron axes, and made them pass
through the brickkiln. And thus he
did to all the cities of the sons of
Ammon. Then David and all the
people returned *to* Jerusalem.

CHAPTER 13

Amnon and Tamar

NOW it was after this that [a]Absa-
lom the son of David had a beautiful
sister whose name was [b]Tamar, and
[c]Amnon the son of David loved her.
2 And Amnon was so frustrated
because of his sister Tamar that he
made himself ill, for she was a virgin, and it seemed [1]hard to Amnon
to do anything to her.

10 [a]2 Sam. 13:28; 18:14; 1 Kin. 2:25
11 [1]Lit., *the sight of this sun* [a]2 Sam. 16:21, 22
12 [1]Lit., *before* [a]2 Sam. 11:4-15 [b]2 Sam. 16:22
13 [1]Lit., *caused your sin to pass away* [a]1 Sam. 15:24, 30; 2 Sam. 24:10; Luke 18:13 [b]Lev. 20:10; 24:17; Prov. 28:13; Mic. 7:18
14 [a]Is. 52:5; Rom. 2:24
15 [1]Lit., *wife* [a]1 Sam. 25:38
16 [a]2 Sam. 13:31; Neh. 1:4
17 [a]Gen. 24:2
20 [a]Matt. 6:17
21 [1]Lit., *On account of*
22 [a]Is. 38:1-3 [b]Jon. 3:9
23 [a]Gen. 37:35 [b]Job 7:8-10
24 [1]Some mss. read, *she* [a]1 Chr. 22:9
25 [1]I.e., Beloved of the LORD
26 [a]1 Chr. 20:1-3
30 [1]Or, *Malcam;* Zeph. 1:5 [2]Or, *were precious stones*
31 [1]Cf. 1 Chr. 20:3 [a]Heb. 11:37
1 [a]2 Sam. 3:2, 3; 1 Chr. 3:2 [b]1 Chr. 3:9 [c]2 Sam. 3:2
2 [1]Lit., *hard in Amnon's eyes*

3 But Amnon had a friend whose name was Jonadab, the son of [a]Shimeah, David's brother; and Jonadab was a very shrewd man.

4 And he said to him, "O son of the king, why are you so depressed morning after morning? Will you not tell me?" Then Amnon said to him, "I am in love with Tamar, the sister of my brother Absalom."

5 Jonadab then said to him, "Lie down on your bed and pretend to be ill; when your father comes [a]to see you, say to him, 'Please let my sister Tamar come and give me *some* food to eat, and let her prepare the food in my sight, that I may see *it* and eat from her hand.' "

6 So Amnon lay down and pretended to be ill; when the king came to see him, Amnon said to the king, "Please let my sister Tamar come and [a]make me a couple of cakes in my sight, that I may eat from her hand."

7 Then David sent to the house for Tamar, saying, "Go now to your brother Amnon's house, and prepare food for him."

8 So Tamar went to her brother Amnon's house, and he was lying down. And she took dough, kneaded *it,* made cakes in his sight, and baked the cakes.

9 And she took the pan and [1]dished *them* out before him, but he refused to eat. And Amnon said, "[a]Have everyone go out from me." So everyone went out from him.

10 Then Amnon said to Tamar, "Bring the food into the [1]bedroom, that I may eat from your hand." So Tamar took the cakes which she had made and brought them into the bedroom to her brother Amnon.

11 When she brought *them* to him to eat, he took hold of her and said to her, "Come, lie with me, my sister."

12 But she answered him, "No, my brother, do not violate me, for [a]such a thing is not done in Israel; do not do this [b]disgraceful thing!

13 "As for me, where could I [1]get rid of my reproach? And as for you, you will be like one of the [2]fools in Israel. Now therefore, please speak to the king, for [a]he will not withhold me from you."

14 However, he would not listen to [1]her; since he was stronger than she, he violated her and lay with her.

15 Then Amnon hated her with a very great hatred; for the hatred with which he hated her was greater than the love with which he had loved her. And Amnon said to her, "Get up, go away!"

16 But she said to him, "No, because this wrong in sending me away is greater than the other that you have done to me!" Yet he would not listen to her.

17 Then he called his young man who attended him and said, "Now throw this woman out of my *presence,* and lock the door behind her."

18 Now she had on [a]a [1]long-sleeved garment; for in this manner the virgin daughters of the king dressed themselves in robes. Then his attendant took her out and locked the door behind her.

19 And [a]Tamar put [1]ashes on her head, and [b]tore her [2]long-sleeved garment which *was* on her; and [c]she put her hand on her head and went away, crying aloud as she went.

20 Then Absalom her brother said to her, "Has Amnon your brother been with you? But now keep silent, my sister, he is your brother; do not take this matter to heart." So Tamar remained and was desolate [a]in her brother Absalom's house.

21 Now when King David heard of all these matters, he was very angry.

22 But Absalom did not speak to Amnon [a]either good or bad; for Absalom hated Amnon because he had violated his sister Tamar.

23 Now it came about after two full years that Absalom [a]had sheepshearers in Baal-hazor, which is near Ephraim, and Absalom invited all the king's sons.

Absalom Avenges Tamar

24 And Absalom came to the king and said, "Behold now, your servant has sheepshearers; please let the king and his servants go with your servant."

25 But the king said to Absalom, "No, my son, we should not all go, lest we be burdensome to you." Although he [1]urged him, he would not go, but blessed him.

26 Then [a]Absalom said, "If not, please let my brother Amnon go with us." And the king said to him, "Why should he go with you?"

27 But when Absalom [1]urged him, he let Amnon and all the king's sons go with him.

28 And Absalom commanded his servants, saying, "See now, [a]when Amnon's heart is merry with wine, and when I say to you, 'Strike Amnon,' then put him to death. Do not fear; have not I myself commanded you? Be courageous and be [1]valiant."

3 [a]1 Sam. 16:9
5 [a]2 Kin. 8:29
6 [a]Gen. 18:6
9 [1]Lit., *poured* [a]Gen. 45:1
10 [1]Or, *inner room*
12 [a]Lev. 20:17 [b]Judg. 19:23; 20:6
13 [1]Lit., *cause to go* [2]Or, *disgraceful ones* [a]Gen. 20:12
14 [1]Lit., *her voice*
18 [1]Lit., *a varicolored tunic* [a]Gen. 37:3, 23; Judg. 5:30
19 [1]Or, *dust* [2]Lit., *varicolored tunic* [a]1 Sam. 4:12; Esth. 4:1; Jer. 2:37 [b]Gen. 37:29; 2 Sam. 1:11 [c]Jer. 2:37
20 [a]2 Sam. 14:24
22 [a]Gen. 31:24
23 [a]1 Sam. 25:7
25 [1]Lit., *broke through*
26 [a]2 Sam. 3:27; 11:13-15
27 [1]Lit., *broke through*
28 [1]Lit., *sons of valor* [a]Judg. 19:6, 9, 22; 1 Sam. 25:36-38

29 And the servants of Absalom
did to Amnon just as Absalom had
commanded. Then all the king's
sons arose and each mounted [a]his
mule and fled.
30 Now it was while they were on
the way that the report came to David, saying, "Absalom has struck
down all the king's sons, and not
one of them is left."
31 Then the king arose, [a]tore his
clothes and [b]lay on the ground; and
all his servants were standing by
with clothes torn.
32 And [a]Jonadab, the son of Shim-
eah, David's brother, [1]responded,
"Do not let my lord [2]suppose they
have put to death all the young men,
the king's sons, for Amnon alone is
dead; because by the [3]intent of Absalom this has been determined
since the day that he violated his sister Tamar.
33 "Now therefore, do not let my
lord the king [a]take the report to
[1]heart, namely, 'all the king's sons
are dead', for only Amnon is dead."
34 Now [a]Absalom had fled. And
[b]the young man who was the watchman raised his eyes and looked, and
behold, many people were coming
from the road behind him by the
side of the mountain.
35 And Jonadab said to the king,
"Behold, the king's sons have come;
according to your servant's word, so
it happened."
36 And it came about as soon as he
had finished speaking, that behold,
the king's sons came and lifted their
voices and wept; and also the king
and all his servants wept [1]very bitterly.
37 Now [a]Absalom fled and went to
[b]Talmai the son of Ammihud, the
king of [c]Geshur. And *David*
mourned for his son every day.
38 [a]So Absalom had fled and gone
to Geshur, and was there three
years.
39 And *the heart of* King David
longed to go out to Absalom; for [a]he
was comforted concerning Amnon,
since he was dead.

CHAPTER 14

The Woman of Tekoa

NOW Joab the son of Zeruiah perceived that [a]the king's heart *was* inclined toward Absalom.
2 So Joab sent to [a]Tekoa and
[1]brought a wise woman from there
and said to her, "Please [b]pretend to
be a mourner, and put on mourning
garments now, and [c]do not anoint
yourself with oil, but like a woman
who has been mourning for the dead
many days;
3 then go to the king and speak to
him in this manner." So Joab put
[a]the words in her mouth.
4 Now when the woman of Tekoa
[1]spoke to the king, she fell on her
face to the ground and [a]prostrated
herself and said, "[b]Help, O king."
5 And the king said to her, "What
is your trouble?" And she [1]an-
swered, "[a]Truly I am a widow, for
my husband is dead.
6 "And your maidservant had two
sons, but the two of them struggled
together in the field, and there was
no [1]one to separate them, so one
struck the other and killed him.
7 "Now behold, [a]the whole family
has risen against your maidservant,
and they say, 'Hand over the one
who struck his brother, that we may
put him to death for the life of his
brother whom he killed, [b]and destroy the heir also.' Thus they will
extinguish my coal which is left, so
as to [1]leave my husband neither
name nor remnant on the face of the
earth."
8 Then the king said to the
woman, "Go to your house, and I
will give orders concerning you."
9 And the woman of Tekoa said
to the king, "O my lord, the king,
[a]the iniquity is on me and my father's house, but [b]the king and his
throne are guiltless."
10 So the king said, "Whoever
speaks to you, bring him to me, and
he will not touch you any more."
11 Then she said, "Please let the
king remember the LORD your God,
[a]*so that* the avenger of blood may
not continue to destroy, lest they destroy my son." And he said, "[b]As
the LORD lives, not one hair of your
son shall fall to the ground."
12 Then the woman said, "Please
let your maidservant speak a word
to my lord the king." And he said,
"Speak."
13 And the woman said, "[a]Why
then have you planned such a thing
against the people of God? For in
speaking this word the king is as
one who is guilty, *in that* the king
does not bring back [b]his banished
one.
14 "For [a]we shall surely die and are
[b]like water spilled on the ground
which cannot be gathered up again.
Yet God does not take away life, but
plans [1]ways so that [c]the banished
one may not be cast out from him.
15 "Now [1]the reason I have come to
speak this word to my lord the king

---

29 [a]2 Sam. 18:9; 1 Kin. 1:33, 38
31 [a]2 Sam. 1:11 [b]2 Sam. 12:16
32 [1]Lit., *answered and said* [2]Lit., *say* [3]Lit., *mouth* [a]2 Sam. 13:3-5
33 [1]Lit., *his heart* [a]2 Sam. 19:19
34 [a]2 Sam. 13:37, 38 [b]2 Sam. 18:24
36 [1]Lit., *with a very great weeping*
37 [a]2 Sam. 13:34 [b]2 Sam. 3:3 [c]2 Sam. 14:23, 32
38 [a]2 Sam. 13:34
39 [a]2 Sam. 12:19-23
1 [a]2 Sam. 13:39
2 [1]Lit., *took* [a]2 Sam. 23:26; 2 Chr. 11:6; Amos 1:1 [b]1 Kin. 20:35-43 [c]2 Sam. 12:20
3 [a]2 Sam. 14:19
4 [1]Many mss. and ancient versions read, *came* [a]1 Sam. 25:23 [b]2 Kin. 6:26-28
5 [1]Lit., *said* [a]2 Sam. 12:1-7; 14:5-21
6 [1]Lit., *deliverer between*
7 [1]Lit., *set* [a]Num. 35:19; Deut. 19:12, 13 [b]Matt. 21:38
9 [a]Gen. 43:9; 1 Sam. 25:24 [b]1 Kin. 2:33
11 [a]Num. 35:19, 21; Deut. 19:4-10 [b]1 Sam. 14:45; 1 Kin. 1:52; Matt. 10:30
13 [a]2 Sam. 12:7; 1 Kin. 20:40-42 [b]2 Sam. 13:37, 38
14 [1]Lit., *devices* [a]Job 30:23; 34:15; Heb. 9:27 [b]Ps. 58:7 [c]Num. 35:15, 25, 28
15 [1]Lit., *that*

is because the people have made me afraid; so your maidservant said, 'Let me now speak to the king, perhaps the king will perform the [2]request of his maidservant.

16 'For the king will hear [1]and deliver his maidservant from the [2]hand of the man who would destroy [3]both me and my son from [a]the inheritance of God.'

17 "Then your maidservant said, 'Please let the word of my lord the king be [1]comforting, for as [a]the angel of God, so is my lord the king to discern good and evil. And may the LORD your God be with you.' "

18 Then the king answered and said to the woman, "Please do not hide anything from me that I am about to ask you." And the woman said, "Let my lord the king please speak."

19 So the king said, "Is the hand of Joab with you in all this?" And the woman answered and said, "As your soul lives, my lord the king, no one can turn to the right or to the left from anything that my lord the king has spoken. Indeed, it was [a]your servant Joab who commanded me, and it was he who put all these words in the mouth of your maidservant;

20 in order to change the appearance of things your servant Joab has done this thing. But my lord is wise, [a]like the wisdom of the angel of God, to know all that is in the earth."

Absalom Is Recalled

21 Then the king said to Joab, "Behold now, [a]I will surely do this thing; go therefore, bring back the young man Absalom."

22 And Joab fell on his face to the ground, prostrated himself and blessed the king; then Joab said, "Today your servant knows that I have found favor in your sight, O my lord, the king, in that the king has performed the [1]request of his servant."

23 So Joab arose and went to [a]Geshur, and brought Absalom to Jerusalem.

24 However the king said, "Let him turn to [a]his own house, and let him not see my face." So Absalom turned to his own house and did not see the king's face.

25 Now in all Israel was no one as handsome as Absalom, so highly praised; [a]from the sole of his foot to the crown of his head there was no defect in him.

26 And when he [a]cut the hair of his head (and it was at the end of every year that he cut *it*, for it was heavy on him so he cut it), he weighed the hair of his head at 200 shekels by the king's weight.

27 And [a]to Absalom there were born three sons, and one daughter whose name was [b]Tamar; she was a woman of beautiful appearance.

28 Now Absalom lived two full years in Jerusalem, [a]and did not see the king's face.

29 Then Absalom sent for Joab, to send him to the king, but he would not come to him. So he sent again a second time, but he would not come.

30 Therefore he said to his servants, "See, [a]Joab's [1]field is next to mine, and he has barley there; go and set it on fire." So Absalom's servants set the [1]field on fire.

31 Then Joab arose, came to Absalom at his house and said to him, "Why have your servants set my [1]field on fire?"

32 And Absalom [1]answered Joab, "Behold, I sent for you, saying, 'Come here, that I may send you to the king, to say, "Why have I come from Geshur? It would be better for me still to be there." ' Now therefore let me see the king's face; [a]and if there is iniquity in me, let him put me to death."

33 So when Joab came to the king and told him, he called for Absalom. Thus he came to the king and prostrated himself on his face to the ground before the king, and [a]the king kissed Absalom.

CHAPTER 15

Absalom's Conspiracy

NOW it came about after this that [a]Absalom provided for himself a chariot and horses, and fifty men as runners before him.

2 And Absalom used to rise early and [a]stand beside the way to the gate; and it happened that when any man had a suit to come to the king for judgment, Absalom would call to him and say, "From what city are you?" And he would say, "Your servant is from one of the tribes of Israel."

3 Then Absalom would say to him, "See, your [1]claims are good and right, but no man listens to you on the part of the king."

4 Moreover, Absalom would say, "[a]Oh that one would appoint me judge in the land, then every man

15 [2]Lit., *word*
16 [1]Lit., *to* [2]Lit., *palm* [3]Lit., *together* [a]Deut. 32:9; 1 Sam. 26:19
17 [1]Lit., *for rest* [a]1 Sam. 29:9; 2 Sam. 14:20; 19:27
19 [a]2 Sam. 14:3
20 [a]2 Sam. 14:17; 19:27
21 [a]2 Sam. 14:11
22 [1]Lit., *word*
23 [a]2 Sam. 13:37, 38
24 [a]2 Sam. 13:20
25 [a]Deut. 28:35; Job 2:7; Is. 1:6
26 [a]Ezek. 44:20
27 [a]2 Sam. 18:18 [b]2 Sam. 13:1
28 [a]2 Sam. 14:24
30 [1]Lit., *portion* [a]Judg. 15:3-5
31 [1]Lit., *portion*
32 [1]Lit., *said to* [a]1 Sam. 20:8
33 [a]Gen. 33:4; Luke 15:20
1 [a]1 Kin. 1:5
2 [a]Ruth 4:1; 2 Sam. 19:8
3 [1]Lit., *words*
4 [a]Judg. 9:1-5, 29

who has any suit or cause could
come to me, and I would give him
justice."
5 And it happened that when a
man came near to prostrate himself
before him, he would put out his
hand and take hold of him and [a]kiss
him.
6 And in this manner Absalom
dealt with all Israel who came to the
king for judgment; so Absalom stole
away the hearts of the men of Israel.
7 Now it came about at the end of
[1]forty years that Absalom said to
the king, "Please let me go and pay
my vow which I have vowed to the
LORD, in [a]Hebron.
8"For your servant [a]vowed a vow
while I was living at Geshur in [1]Syr-
ia, saying, '[b]If the LORD shall indeed
bring me back to Jerusalem, then I
will serve the LORD.' "
9 And the king said to him, "Go in
peace." So he arose and went to Hebron.
10 But Absalom sent spies
throughout all the tribes of Israel,
saying, "As soon as you hear the
sound of the trumpet, then you shall
say, '[a]Absalom is king in Hebron.' "
11 Then two hundred men went
with Absalom from Jerusalem,
[a]who were invited and [b]went [1]inno-
cently, and they did not know anything.
12 And Absalom sent for [a]Ahitho-
phel the Gilonite, David's counselor,
from his city [b]Giloh, while he was
offering the sacrifices. And the conspiracy was strong, for [c]the people
increased continually with Absalom.

David Flees Jerusalem

13 Then a messenger came to David, saying, "[a]The hearts of the men
of Israel are [1]with Absalom."
14 And David said to all his servants who were with him at Jerusalem, "[a]Arise and let us flee, for *otherwise* none of us shall escape from
Absalom. Go in haste, lest he overtake us quickly and bring down calamity on us and strike the city with
the edge of the sword."
15 Then the king's servants said to
the king, "Behold, your servants *are
ready to do* whatever my lord the
king chooses."
16 So the king went out and all his
household [1]with him. But [a]the king
left ten concubines to keep the
house.
17 And the king went out and all
the people [1]with him, and they
stopped at the last house.
18 Now all his servants passed on
beside him, [a]all the Cherethites, all
the Pelethites, and all the Gittites,
[b]six hundred men who had come
[1]with him from Gath, passed on before the king.
19 Then the king said to [a]Ittai the
Gittite, "Why will you also go with
us? Return and remain with the
king, for you are a foreigner and
also an exile; *return* to your own
place.
20"You came *only* yesterday, and
shall I today make you wander with
us, while [a]I go where I will? Return
and take back your brothers; [b]mer-
cy and [1]truth be with you."
21 But Ittai answered the king and
said, "[a]As the LORD lives, and as my
lord the king lives, surely wherever
my lord the king may be, whether
for death or for life, there also your
servant will be."
22 Therefore David said to Ittai,
"Go and pass over." So Ittai the Gittite passed over with all his men and
all the little ones who *were* with
him.
23 While all the country was
weeping with a loud voice, all the
people passed over. The king also
passed over [a]the brook Kidron, and
all the people passed over toward
[b]the way of the wilderness.
24 Now behold, [a]Zadok also *came*,
and all the Levites with him [b]carry-
ing the ark of the covenant of God.
And they set down the ark of God,
and [c]Abiathar came up until all the
people had finished passing from
the city.
25 And the king said to Zadok,
"Return the ark of God to the city. If
I find favor in the sight of the LORD,
then [a]He will bring me back again,
and show me both it and [b]His habitation.
26"But if He should say thus, '[a]I
have no delight in you,' behold, here
I am, [b]let Him do to me as seems
good [1]to Him."
27 The king said also to Zadok the
priest, "Are you *not* [a]a seer? Return
to the city in peace and your [b]two
sons with you, your son Ahimaaz
and Jonathan the son of Abiathar.
28"See, I am going to wait [a]at the
fords of the wilderness until word
comes from you to inform me."
29 Therefore Zadok and Abiathar
returned the ark of God to Jerusalem and remained there.
30 And David went up the ascent
of the *Mount of* Olives, and wept as
he went, and [a]his head was covered
and he walked [b]barefoot. Then all
the people who were with him each

5 [a]2 Sam. 14:33; 20:9
7 [1]Some ancient versions render *four* [a]2 Sam. 3:2, 3
8 [1]Heb., *Aram* [a]2 Sam. 13:37, 38 [b]Gen. 28:20, 21
10 [a]1 Kin. 1:34; 2 Kin. 9:13
11 [1]Lit., *in their integrity* [a]1 Sam. 9:13 [b]1 Sam. 22:15
12 [a]2 Sam. 15:31 [b]Josh. 15:51 [c]Ps. 3:1
13 [1]Lit., *after* [a]Judg. 9:3; 2 Sam. 15:6
14 [a]2 Sam. 12:11; Ps. 3:title
16 [1]Lit., *at his feet* [a]2 Sam. 16:21, 22
17 [1]Lit., *at his feet*
18 [1]Lit., *at his feet* [a]2 Sam. 8:18 [b]1 Sam. 23:13; 25:13; 30:1, 9
19 [a]2 Sam. 18:2
20 [1]Or, *faithfulness* [a]1 Sam. 23:13 [b]2 Sam. 2:6
21 [a]Ruth 1:16, 17
23 [a]1 Kin. 15:13; 2 Chr. 29:16 [b]2 Sam. 15:28; 16:2
24 [a]2 Sam. 8:17; 20:25 [b]Num. 4:15; 1 Sam. 4:4, 5 [c]1 Sam. 22:20
25 [a]Ps. 43:3 [b]Ex. 15:13; Jer. 25:30
26 [1]Lit., *in His sight* [a]2 Sam. 11:27; 1 Chr. 21:7 [b]1 Sam. 3:18
27 [a]1 Sam. 9:6-9 [b]2 Sam. 17:17
28 [a]Josh. 5:10; 2 Sam. 17:16
30 [a]Esth. 6:12; Ezek. 24:17, 23 [b]Is. 20:2-4

covered his head and went up weeping as they went.
31 Now someone told David, saying, "[a]Ahithophel is among the conspirators with Absalom." And David said, "O LORD, I pray, [b]make the
counsel of Ahithophel foolishness."
32 It happened as David was coming to the summit, where God was
worshiped, that behold, Hushai the
[a]Archite met him with his [1]coat
torn, and [2]dust on his head.
33 And David said to him, "If you
pass over with me, then you will be
[a]a burden to me.
34"But if you return to the city, and
[a]say to Absalom, 'I will be your servant, O king; as I have been your
father's servant in time past, so I
will now be your servant,' then you
can thwart the counsel of Ahithophel for me.
35"And are not Zadok and Abiathar the priests with you there? So
it shall be that [a]whatever you hear
from the king's house, you shall report to Zadok and Abiathar the
priests.
36"Behold [a]their two sons are with
them there, Ahimaaz, Zadok's son
and Jonathan, Abiathar's son; and
[b]by them you shall send me everything that you hear."
37 So Hushai, [a]David's friend,
came into the city, and [b]Absalom
came into Jerusalem.

CHAPTER 16

Ziba, a False Servant

NOW when David had passed [a]a
little beyond the summit, behold,
[b]Ziba the servant of Mephibosheth
met him [c]with a couple of saddled
donkeys, and on them *were* two
hundred loaves of bread, a hundred
clusters of raisins, a hundred summer fruits, and a jug of wine.
2 And the king said to Ziba,
"Why do you have these?" And Ziba
said, "[a]The donkeys are for the
king's household to ride, and the
bread and summer fruit for the
young men to eat, and the wine, [b]for
whoever is faint in the wilderness to
drink."
3 Then the king said, "And where
is [a]your master's son?" And [b]Ziba
said to the king, "Behold, he is staying in Jerusalem, for he said, 'Today
the house of Israel will restore the
kingdom of my father to me.' "
4 So the king said to Ziba, "Behold, all that belongs to Mephibosheth is yours." And Ziba said, "I
prostrate myself; let me find favor in
your sight, O my lord, the king!"

David Is Cursed

5 When King David came to [a]Ba-
hurim, behold, there came out from
there a man of the family of the
house of Saul [b]whose name was
Shimei, the son of Gera; he came out
[c]cursing continually as he came.
6 And he threw stones at David
and at all the servants of King David; and all the people and all the
mighty men were at his right hand
and at his left.
7 And thus Shimei said when he
cursed, "Get out, get out, [a]you man
of bloodshed, and worthless fellow!
8"[a]The LORD has returned upon
you all the bloodshed of the house of
Saul, in whose place you have
reigned; and the LORD has given the
kingdom into the hand of your son
Absalom. And behold, you are
taken in your own evil, for you are a
man of bloodshed!"
9 Then [a]Abishai the son of
Zeruiah said to the king, "Why
should [b]this dead dog [c]curse my
lord the king? Let me go over now,
and [1]cut off his head."
10 But the king said, "[a]What have
I to do with you, O sons of Zeruiah?
[b]If he curses, and if the LORD has
told him, 'Curse David,' [c]then who
shall say, 'Why have you done so?' "
11 Then David said to Abishai and
to all his servants, "Behold, [a]my son
who came out from [1]me seeks my
life; how much more now this Benjamite? Let him alone and let him
curse, [b]for the LORD has told him.
12"Perhaps the LORD will look on
my affliction and [1a]return good to
me instead of his cursing this day."
13 So David and his men went on
the way; and Shimei went along on
the hillside parallel with him and as
he went he cursed, and cast stones
and threw dust at him.
14 And the king and all the people
who were with him arrived weary
and he refreshed himself there.

Absalom Enters Jerusalem

15 [a]Then Absalom and all the people, the men of Israel, entered Jerusalem, and Ahithophel with him.
16 Now it came about when [a]Hu-
shai the Archite, David's friend,
came to Absalom, that [b]Hushai said
to Absalom, "[c]*Long* live the king!
Long live the king!"
17 And Absalom said to Hushai,
"Is this your [1]loyalty to your friend?
[a]Why did you not go with your
friend?"
18 Then Hushai said to Absalom,
"No! For whom the LORD, this people, and all the men of Israel have

31 [a]2 Sam. 15:12 [b]2 Sam. 16:23; 17:14, 23
32 [1]Or., *tunic* [2]Lit., *ground* [a]Josh. 16:2
33 [a]2 Sam. 19:35
34 [a]2 Sam. 16:19
35 [a]2 Sam. 17:15, 16
36 [a]2 Sam. 15:27 [b]2 Sam. 17:17
37 [a]2 Sam. 16:16; 1 Chr. 27:33 [b]2 Sam. 16:15
1 [a]2 Sam. 15:32 [b]2 Sam. 9:2-13 [c]1 Sam. 25:18
2 [a]Judg. 10:4 [b]2 Sam. 17:29
3 [a]2 Sam. 9:9, 10 [b]2 Sam. 19:26, 27
5 [a]2 Sam. 3:16; 17:18 [b]2 Sam. 19:16-23; 1 Kin. 2:8, 9, 44 [c]Ex. 22:28; 1 Sam. 17:43
7 [a]2 Sam. 12:9
8 [a]2 Sam. 21:1-9
9 [1]Lit., *take off* [a]1 Sam. 26:8; 2 Sam. 19:21; Luke 9:54 [b]2 Sam. 9:8 [c]Ex. 22:28
10 [a]2 Sam. 3:39; 19:22 [b]John 18:11 [c]Rom. 9:20
11 [1]Lit., *my body* [a]2 Sam. 12:11 [b]Gen. 45:5; 1 Sam. 26:19
12 [1]Lit., *the LORD will return* [a]Deut. 23:5; Rom. 8:28
15 [a]2 Sam. 15:12, 37
16 [a]2 Sam. 15:37 [b]2 Sam. 15:34 [c]1 Sam. 10:24; 2 Kin. 11:12
17 [1]Or, *kindness* [a]2 Sam. 19:25

chosen, his will I be, and with him I
will remain.
19"And besides, [a]whom should I
serve? *Should I* not *serve* in the presence of his son? As I have served in
your father's presence, so I will be in
your presence."
20 Then Absalom said to Ahithophel, "Give your advice. What shall
we do?"
21 And Ahithophel said to Absalom, "[a]Go in to your father's concubines, whom he has left to keep the
house; then all Israel will hear that
you have made yourself odious
to your father. The hands of all
who are with you will also be
strengthened."
22 So they pitched a tent for Absalom on the roof, [a]and Absalom went
in to his father's concubines [b]in the
sight of all Israel.
23 And [a]the advice of Ahithophel,
which he [1]gave in those days, *was* as
if one inquired of the word of God;
[b]so was all the advice of Ahithophel
regarded by both David and Absalom.

CHAPTER 17

Hushai's Counsel

FURTHERMORE, Ahithophel said
to Absalom, "Please let me choose
12,000 men that I may arise and pursue David tonight.
2"And [a]I will come upon him
while he is weary and [1]exhausted
and will terrify him so that all the
people who are with him will flee.
Then [b]I will strike down the king
alone,
3 and I will bring back all the people to you. [1]The return of everyone
depends on the man you seek; *then*
all the people shall be at peace."
4 So the [1]plan pleased Absalom
and all the elders of Israel.
5 Then Absalom said, "Now call
[a]Hushai the Archite also, and let us
hear what [1]he has to say."
6 When Hushai had come to Absalom, Absalom said to [1]him,
"Ahithophel has spoken [2]thus. Shall
we [3]carry out his plan? If not, you
speak."
7 So Hushai said to Absalom,
"[a]This time the advice that Ahithophel has [1]given is not good."
8 Moreover, Hushai said, "You
know your father and his men, that
they are mighty men and they are
[1]fierce, [a]like a bear robbed of her
cubs in the field. And your father is
an [2]expert in warfare, and will not
spend the night with the people.
9"Behold, he has now hidden
himself in one of the [1]caves or in
another place; and it will be [2]when
he falls on them at the first attack,
that whoever hears *it* will say,
'There has been a slaughter among
the people who follow Absalom.'
10"And even the one who is valiant, whose heart is like the heart of
a lion, [a]will completely [1]lose heart;
for all Israel knows that your father
is a mighty man and those who are
with him are valiant men.
11"But I counsel that all Israel be
surely gathered to you, [a]from Dan
even to Beersheba, [b]as the sand that
is by the sea in abundance, and that
[1]you personally go into battle.
12"So we shall come to him in one
of the places where he can be found,
and we will [1]fall on him [a]as the dew
falls on the ground; and of him and
of all the men who are with him, not
even one will be left.
13"And if he withdraws into a city,
then all Israel shall bring ropes to
that city, and we will [a]drag it into
the [1]valley until not even a small
stone is found there."
14 Then Absalom and all the men
of Israel said, "The counsel of Hushai the Archite is better than the
counsel of Ahithophel." For [a]the
LORD had ordained to thwart the
good counsel of Ahithophel, in order
that the LORD might bring calamity
on Absalom.

Hushai's Warning Saves David

15 Then [a]Hushai said to Zadok
and to Abiathar the priests, "[1]This is
what Ahithophel counseled Absalom and the elders of Israel, and
[1]this is what I have counseled.
16"Now therefore send quickly
and tell David, saying, '[a]Do not
spend the night at the fords of the
wilderness, but by all means cross
over, lest the king and all the people
who are with him be [1]destroyed."
17 [a]Now Jonathan and Ahimaaz
were staying at [b]En-rogel, and a
maidservant would go and tell
them, and they would go and tell
King David, for they could not be
seen entering the city.
18 But a lad did see them, and told
Absalom; so the two of them departed quickly and came to the
house of a man [a]in Bahurim, who
had a well in his courtyard, and they
went down [1]into it.
19 And [a]the woman [1]took a covering and spread it over the well's
mouth and scattered grain on it, so
that nothing was known.

19 [a]2 Sam. 15:34
21 [a]2 Sam. 15:16
22 [a]2 Sam. 15:16; 20:3 [b]2 Sam. 12:11, 12
23 [1]Lit., *advised* [a]2 Sam. 17:14, 23 [b]2 Sam. 15:12
2 [1]Lit., *slack of hands* [a]2 Sam. 16:14 [b]1 Kin. 22:31
3 [1]Lit., *Like the return of the whole is the man whom you seek*
4 [1]Lit., *word was pleasing in the sight of*
5 [1]Lit., *is in his mouth—even he* [a]2 Sam. 15:32-34
6 [1]Lit., *him, saying* [2]Lit., *according to this word* [3]Lit., *do his word*
7 [1]Lit., *advised* [a]2 Sam. 16:21
8 [1]Lit., *bitter of soul* [2]Lit., *man of war* [a]Hos. 13:8
9 [1]Lit., *pits* [2]Lit., *according to a falling among them*
10 [1]Lit., *melt* [a]Josh. 2:9-11
11 [1]Lit., *your face go* [a]1 Sam. 3:20 [b]Gen. 22:17; 1 Sam. 13:5
12 [1]Lit., *settle down* [a]Ps. 110:3; Mic. 5:7
13 [1]Or, *wadi* [a]Mic. 1:6
14 [a]2 Sam. 15:31, 34
15 [1]Lit., *Thus and thus* [a]2 Sam. 15:35, 36
16 [1]Lit., *swallowed up* [a]2 Sam. 15:28
17 [a]2 Sam. 15:27, 36 [b]Josh. 15:7; 18:16
18 [1]Lit., *there* [a]2 Sam. 3:16; 16:5
19 [1]Lit., *took and spread the covering* [a]Josh. 2:4-6

20 Then Absalom's servants came to the woman at the house and said, "Where are Ahimaaz and Jonathan?" And [a]the woman said to them, "They have crossed the brook of water." And when they searched and could not find *them,* they returned to Jerusalem.

21 And it came about after they had departed that they came up out of the well and went and told King David; and they said to David, "[a]Arise and cross over the water quickly for thus Ahithophel has counseled against you."

22 Then David and all the people who *were* with him arose and crossed the Jordan; and by [1]dawn not even one remained who had not crossed the Jordan.

23 Now when Ahithophel saw that his counsel was not [1]followed, he [2]saddled *his* donkey and arose and went to his home, to [a]his city, and [3b]set his house in order, and [c]strangled himself; thus he died and was buried in the grave of his father.

24 Then David came to [a]Mahanaim. And Absalom crossed the Jordan, he and all the men of Israel with him.

25 And Absalom set [a]Amasa over the army in place of Joab. Now Amasa was the son of a man whose name was [1]Jithra the Israelite, who went in to Abigail the daughter of [b]Nahash, sister of Zeruiah, Joab's mother.

26 And Israel and Absalom camped in the land of Gilead.

27 Now when David had come to Mahanaim, [a]Shobi the son of Nahash from [b]Rabbah of the sons of Ammon, [c]Machir the son of Ammiel from Lo-debar, and [d]Barzillai the Gileadite from Rogelim,

28 brought beds, basins, pottery, wheat, barley, flour, parched *grain,* beans, lentils, parched *seeds,*

29 honey, curds, sheep, and cheese of the herd, for David and for the people who *were* with him, to eat; for they said, "The people are hungry and weary and thirsty [a]in the wilderness."

Chapter 18

Absalom Slain

THEN David [1]numbered the people who were with him and [a]set over them commanders of thousands and commanders of hundreds.

2 And David sent the people out, [a]one third under the [1]command of Joab, one third under the [1]command of Abishai the son of Zeruiah, Joab's brother, and one third under the [1]command of [b]Ittai the Gittite. And the king said to the people, "I myself will surely go out with you also."

3 But the people said, "[a]You should not go out; for if we indeed flee, they will not care about us, even if half of us die, they will not care about us. But [1]you are worth ten thousand of us; therefore now it is better that you *be ready* to help us from the city."

4 Then the king said to them, "Whatever seems best to you I will do." So [a]the king stood beside the gate, and all the people went out by hundreds and thousands.

5 And the king charged Joab and Abishai and Ittai, saying, "*Deal* gently for my sake with the young man Absalom." And [a]all the people heard when the king charged all the commanders concerning Absalom.

6 Then the people went out into the field against Israel, and the battle took place in [a]the forest of Ephraim.

7 And the people of Israel were [1]defeated there before the servants of David, and the slaughter there that day was great, 20,000 men.

8 For the battle there was spread over the whole countryside, and the forest devoured more people that day than the sword devoured.

9 Now Absalom happened to meet the servants of David. For Absalom was riding on *his* mule, and the mule went under the thick branches of a great oak. And [a]his head caught fast in the oak, so he was [1]left hanging between heaven and earth, while the mule that was under him kept going.

10 When a certain man saw *it,* he told Joab and said, "Behold, I saw Absalom hanging in an oak."

11 Then Joab said to the man who had told him, "Now behold, you saw *him!* Why then did you not strike him there to the ground? And I would have given you ten *pieces* of silver and a belt."

12 And the man said to Joab, "Even if I should receive a thousand *pieces of* silver in my hand, I would not put out my hand against the king's son; for [a]in our hearing the king charged you and Abishai and Ittai, saying, '[1]Protect for me the young man Absalom!'

13 "Otherwise, if I had dealt treacherously against his life (and [a]there is nothing hidden from the king), then you yourself would have stood aloof."

20 [a]Lev. 19:11; Josh. 2:3-5; 1 Sam. 19:12-17

21 [a]2 Sam. 17:15, 16

22 [1]Lit., *the light of the morning*

23 [1]Lit., *done* [2]Lit., *bound* [3]Lit., *gave charge to* [a]2 Sam. 15:12 [b]2 Kin. 20:1 [c]Matt. 27:5

24 [a]Gen. 32:2, 10; 2 Sam. 2:8

25 [1]I.e., Jether the Ishmaelite, cf. 1 Chr. 2:17 [a]2 Sam. 19:13; 20:9-12; 1 Kin. 2:5, 32 [b]1 Chr. 2:13, 16

27 [a]1 Sam. 11:1; 2 Sam. 10:1, 2 [b]2 Sam. 12:26, 29 [c]2 Sam. 9:4 [d]2 Sam. 19:31-40; 1 Kin. 2:7

29 [a]2 Sam. 16:2, 14

1 [1]Lit., *mustered* [a]Ex. 18:25; Num. 31:14; 1 Sam. 22:7

2 [1]Lit., *hand* [a]Judg. 7:16; 1 Sam. 11:11 [b]2 Sam. 15:19-22

3 [1]So with some ancient versions; M.T., *for now there are ten thousand like us* [a]2 Sam. 21:17

4 [a]2 Sam. 18:24

5 [a]2 Sam. 18:12

6 [a]Josh. 17:15, 18; 2 Sam. 17:26

7 [1]Lit., *smitten*

9 [1]Lit., *placed* [a]2 Sam. 14:26

12 [1]So with some mss. and the ancient versions; M.T., *Take care whoever* you are *of* [a]2 Sam. 18:5

13 [a]2 Sam. 14:19, 20

14 Then Joab said, "I will not [1]waste time here with you." [a]So he took three spears in his hand and thrust them through the heart of Absalom while he was yet alive in the [2]midst of the oak.

15 And ten young men who carried Joab's armor gathered around and struck Absalom and killed him.

16 Then [a]Joab blew the trumpet, and the people returned from pursuing Israel, for Joab restrained the people.

17 And they took Absalom and cast him into [1]a deep pit in the forest and [a]erected over him a very great heap of stones. And [b]all Israel fled, each to his tent.

18 Now Absalom in his lifetime had taken and [a]set up for himself a pillar which is in [b]the King's Valley, for he said, "[c]I have no son [1]to preserve my name." So he named the pillar after his own name, and it is called Absalom's monument to this day.

David is Grief-stricken

19 Then [a]Ahimaaz the son of Zadok said, "Please let me run and bring the king news [b]that the LORD has [1]freed him from the hand of his enemies."

20 But Joab said to him, "You are not the man to carry news this day, but you shall carry news another day; however, you shall carry no news today because the king's son is dead."

21 Then Joab said to the Cushite, "Go, tell the king what you have seen." So the Cushite bowed to Joab and ran.

22 Now Ahimaaz the son of Zadok said once more to Joab, "But whatever happens, please let me also run after the Cushite." And Joab said, "Why would you run, my son, since [a]you will have no reward for going?"

23 "But whatever happens," *he said*, "I will run." So he said to him, "Run." Then Ahimaaz ran by way of the plain and passed up the Cushite.

24 Now [a]David was sitting between the two gates; and [b]the watchman went up to the roof of the gate by the wall, and raised his eyes and looked, and behold, a man running by himself.

25 And the watchman called and told the king. And the king said, "If he is by himself there is good news in his mouth." And he came nearer and nearer.

26 Then the watchman saw another man running; and the watchman called to the gatekeeper and said, "Behold, *another* man running by himself." And the king said, "This one also is bringing good news."

27 And the watchman said, "I [1]think the running of the first one [a]is like the running of Ahimaaz the son of Zadok." And the king said, "[b]This is a good man and comes with good news."

28 And Ahimaaz called and said to the king, "[1]All is well." And [a]he prostrated himself before the king with his face to the ground. And he said, "[b]Blessed is the LORD your God, who has delivered up the men who lifted their hands against my lord the king."

29 And the king said, "[a]Is it well with the young man Absalom?" And Ahimaaz answered, "When Joab sent the king's servant, and your servant, I saw a great tumult, but [b]I did not know what *it was*."

30 Then the king said, "Turn aside and stand here." So he turned aside and stood still.

31 And behold, the Cushite arrived, and the Cushite said, "Let my lord the king receive good news, for [a]the LORD has [1]freed you this day from the hand of all those who rose up against you."

32 Then the king said to the Cushite, "[a]Is it well with the young man Absalom?" And the Cushite answered, "[b]Let the enemies of my lord the king, and all who rise up against you for evil, be as that young man!"

33 [1]And the king was deeply moved and went up to the chamber over the gate and wept. And thus he said as he walked, "[a]O my son Absalom, my son, my son Absalom! [b]Would I had died instead of you, O Absalom, my son, my son!"

CHAPTER 19

Joab Reproves David's Lament

THEN it was told Joab, "Behold, [a]the king is weeping and mourns for Absalom."

2 And the [1]victory that day was turned to mourning for all the people, for the people heard *it* said that day, "The king is grieved for his son."

3 So the people went by stealth into the city that day, as people who are humiliated steal away when they flee in battle.

4 And the king [a]covered his face and [1]cried out with a loud voice, "[b]O

14 [1]Lit., *tarry thus* [2]Lit., *heart* [a]2 Sam. 14:30
16 [a]2 Sam. 2:28; 20:22
17 [1]Lit., *the great* [a]Deut. 21:20, 21; Josh. 7:26; 8:29 [b]2 Sam. 19:8; 20:1, 22
18 [1]Lit., *for the sake of remembering* [a]1 Sam. 15:12 [b]Gen. 14:17 [c]2 Sam. 14:27
19 [1]Lit., *vindicated* [a]2 Sam. 15:36 [b]2 Sam. 18:31
22 [a]2 Sam. 18:29
24 [a]2 Sam. 19:8 [b]2 Sam. 13:34; 2 Kin. 9:17
27 [1]Lit., *see* [a]2 Kin. 9:20 [b]1 Kin. 1:42
28 [1]Heb., *"Peace."* [a]1 Sam. 25:23; 2 Sam. 14:4 [b]1 Sam. 17:46
29 [a]2 Sam. 20:9; 2 Kin. 4:26 [b]2 Sam. 18:22
31 [1]Lit., *vindicated* [a]Judg. 5:31; 2 Sam. 18:19
32 [a]2 Sam. 18:29 [b]1 Sam. 25:26
33 [1]Ch. 19:1 in Heb. [a]2 Sam. 19:4 [b]Ex. 32:32; Rom. 9:3
1 [a]2 Sam. 18:5, 14
2 [1]Lit., *salvation*
4 [1]Lit., *the king cried* [a]2 Sam. 15:30 [b]2 Sam. 18:33

my son Absalom, O Absalom, my son, my son!"

5 Then Joab came into the house to the king and said, "Today you have covered with shame the faces of all your servants, who today have saved your life and the lives of your sons and daughters, the lives of your wives, and the lives of your concubines,

6 by loving those who hate you, and by hating those who love you. For you have shown today that [1]princes and servants are nothing to you; for I know this day that if Absalom were alive and all of us were dead today, then [2]you would be pleased.

7 "Now therefore arise, go out and speak [1]kindly to your servants, for I swear by the LORD, if you do not go out, surely not a man will pass the night with you, and this will be worse for you than all the evil that has come upon you from your youth until now."

David Restored as King

8 So the king arose and sat in the gate. When they told all the people, saying, "Behold, the king is [a]sitting in the gate," then all the people came before the king.

Now [b]Israel had fled, each to his tent.

9 And all the people were quarreling throughout all the tribes of Israel, saying, "[a]The king delivered us from the [1]hand of our enemies and [b]saved us from the [1]hand of the Philistines, but now [c]he has fled out of the land from Absalom.

10 "However, Absalom, whom we anointed over us, has died in battle. Now then, why are you silent about bringing the king back?"

11 Then [a]King David sent to Zadok and Abiathar the priests, saying, "Speak to the elders of Judah, saying, 'Why are you the last to bring the king back to his house, since the word of all Israel has come to the king, *even* to his house?

12 'You are my brothers; [a]you are my bone and my flesh. Why then should you be the last to bring back the king?'

13 "And [a]say to Amasa, 'Are you not my bone and my flesh? [b]May God do so to me, and more also, if you will not be [c]commander of the army before me continually [d]in place of Joab.' "

14 Thus he turned the hearts of all the men of Judah [a]as one man, so that they sent *word* to the king, *saying*, "Return, you and all your servants."

15 The king then returned and came as far as the Jordan. And Judah came to [a]Gilgal in order to go to meet the king, to bring the king across the Jordan.

16 Then [a]Shimei the son of Gera, the Benjamite who was from Bahurim, hurried and came down with the men of Judah to meet King David.

17 And there were a thousand men of Benjamin with him, with [a]Ziba the servant of the house of Saul, and his fifteen sons and his twenty servants with him; and they rushed to the Jordan before the king.

18 Then they kept crossing the ford to bring over the king's household, and to do what was good in his sight. And Shimei the son of Gera fell down before the king as he was about to cross the Jordan.

19 So he said to the king, "[a]Let not my lord consider me guilty, nor remember what your servant did wrong on the day when my lord the king came out from Jerusalem, so that the king should [1]take *it* to heart.

20 "For your servant knows that I have sinned; therefore behold, I have come today, [a]the first of all the house of Joseph to go down to meet my lord the king."

21 But Abishai the son of Zeruiah answered and said, "[a]Should not Shimei be put to death for this, [b]because he cursed the LORD's anointed?"

22 David then said, "[a]What have I to do with you, O sons of Zeruiah, that you should this day be an adversary to me? [b]Should any man be put to death in Israel today? For do I not know that I am king over Israel today?"

23 And the king said to Shimei, "[a]You shall not die." Thus the king swore to him.

24 Then [a]Mephibosheth the [1]son of Saul came down to meet the king; and [b]he had neither [2]cared for his feet, nor [2]trimmed his mustache, nor [c]washed his clothes, from the day the king departed until the day he came *home* in peace.

25 And it was when he came from Jerusalem to meet the king, that the king said to him, "[a]Why did you not go with me, Mephibosheth?"

26 So he answered, "O my lord, the king, my servant deceived me; for your servant said, 'I will saddle a donkey for myself that I may ride on

6 [1]Or, *commanders* [2]Lit., *it would be right in your eyes*
7 [1]Lit., *to the heart*
8 [a]2 Sam. 15:2; 18:24 [b]2 Sam. 18:17
9 [1]Lit., *palm* [a]2 Sam. 8:1-14 [b]2 Sam. 5:20; 8:1 [c]2 Sam. 15:14
11 [a]2 Sam. 15:29
12 [a]2 Sam. 5:1
13 [a]2 Sam. 17:25 [b]1 Kin. 19:2 [c]2 Sam. 8:16 [d]2 Sam. 3:27-39; 19:5-7
14 [a]Judg. 20:1
15 [a]Josh. 5:9; 1 Sam. 11:14, 15
16 [a]2 Sam. 16:5-13; 1 Kin. 2:8
17 [a]2 Sam.16:1-4; 19:26, 27
19 [1]Lit., *set* [a]1 Sam. 22:15; 2 Sam. 16:6-8
20 [a]2 Sam. 16:5
21 [a]2 Sam. 16:7, 8 [b]Ex. 22:28
22 [a]2 Sam. 3:39; 16:9, 10 [b]1 Sam. 11:13
23 [a]1 Kin. 2:8
24 [1]I.e., grandson [2]Lit., *done* [a]2 Sam. 9:6-10 [b]2 Sam. 12:20 [c]Ex. 19:10
25 [a]2 Sam. 16:17

it and go with the king,' [a]because
your servant is lame.
27"Moreover, [a]he has slandered
your servant to my lord the king; but
my lord the king is [b]like the angel of
God, therefore do what is good in
your sight.
28"For [a]all my father's household
was nothing but dead men before
my lord the king; [b]yet you set your
servant among those who ate at
your own table. What right do I
have yet that I should [1]complain any
more to the king?"
29 So the king said to him, "Why
do you still speak of your affairs? I
have [1]decided, 'You and Ziba shall
divide the land.' "
30 And Mephibosheth said to the
king, "Let him even take it all, since
my lord the king has come safely to
his own house."
31 Now [a]Barzillai the Gileadite
had come down from Rogelim; and
he went on to the Jordan with the
king to [1]escort him over the Jordan.
32 Now Barzillai was very old,
being eighty years old; and he had
[1]sustained the king while he stayed
at Mahanaim, for he was a very
great man.
33 And the king said to Barzillai,
"You cross over with me and I will
[1]sustain you in Jerusalem with me."
34 But Barzillai said to the king,
"[a]How long [1]have I yet to live, that
I should go up with the king to Jerusalem?
35"I am [1]now [a]eighty years old.
Can I distinguish between good and
bad? Or can your servant taste what
I eat or what I drink? Or can I hear
any more [b]the voice of singing men
and women? [c]Why then should your
servant be an added burden to my
lord the king?
36"Your servant would merely
cross over the Jordan with the king.
Why should the king compensate
me *with* this reward?
37"Please let your servant return,
that I may die in my own city near
the grave of my father and my
mother. However, here is your servant [a]Chimham, let him cross over
with my lord the king, and do for
him what is good in your sight."
38 And the king answered, "Chimham shall cross over with me, and I
will do for him what is good in your
sight; and whatever you [1]require of
me, I will do for you."
39 All the people crossed over the
Jordan and the king crossed too.
The king then [a]kissed Barzillai and
blessed him, and he returned to his
place.

40 Now the king went on to Gilgal,
and Chimham went on with him;
and all the people of Judah and also
[a]half the people of Israel [1]accompa-
nied the king.
41 And behold, all the men of Israel came to the king and said to the
king, "[a]Why had our brothers [b]the
men of Judah stolen you away, and
brought the king and his household
and all David's men with him over
the Jordan?"
42 Then all the men of Judah answered the men of Israel, "Because
[a]the king is a close relative to [1]us.
Why then [2]are you angry about this
matter? Have we eaten at all at the
king's *expense*, or has [3]anything
been taken for us?"
43 But the men of Israel answered
the men of Judah and said, "[1a]We
have ten parts in the king, therefore
[1]we also have more *claim* on David
than you. Why then did you treat us
with contempt? Was it not [1]our advice first to bring back [1]our king?"
Yet the words of the men of Judah
were harsher than the words of the
men of Israel.

Chapter 20

Sheba's Revolt

NOW a worthless fellow happened
to be [a]there whose name was Sheba,
the son of [b]Bichri, a Benjamite; and
he blew the trumpet and said,
"[c]We have no portion in David,
Nor do we have inheritance in
[d]the son of Jesse;
[e]Every man to his tents, O Israel!"
2 So all the men of Israel [1]with-
drew from following David, *and* followed Sheba the son of Bichri; but
the men of Judah [2]remained steadfast to their king, from the Jordan
even to Jerusalem.
3 Then David came to his house
at Jerusalem, and [a]the king took the
ten women, the concubines whom
he had left to keep the house, and
placed them under guard and provided them with sustenance, but did
not go in to them. So they were shut
up until the day of their death, living
as widows.
4 Then the king said to [a]Amasa,
"Call out the men of Judah for me
within three days, and be present
here yourself."
5 So Amasa went to call out *the
men of* Judah, but he [a]delayed
longer than the set time which he
had appointed him.
6 And David said to [a]Abishai,
"Now Sheba the son of Bichri will

26 [a]2 Sam. 9:3
27 [a]2 Sam. 16:3, 4 [b]2 Sam. 14:17, 20
28 [1]Lit., *cry out* [a]2 Sam. 21:6-9 [b]2 Sam. 9:7, 10, 13
29 [1]Lit., *said*
31 [1]Lit., *send* [a]2 Sam. 17:27-29; 1 Kin. 2:7
32 [1]Or, *provided food for*
33 [1]Or, *provide food for*
34 [1]Lit., *are the days of the years of my life* [a]Gen. 47:8
35 [1]Lit., *today* [a]Ps. 90:10 [b]Eccl. 2:8; Is. 5:11, 12 [c]2 Sam. 15:33
37 [a]2 Sam. 19:40; 1 Kin. 2:7; Jer. 41:17
38 [1]Lit., *choose*
39 [a]Gen. 31:55; Ruth 1:14; 2 Sam. 14:33
40 [1]Lit., *crossed over with* [a]2 Sam. 19:9, 10
41 [a]Judg. 8:1; 12:1 [b]2 Sam. 19:11, 12
42 [1]Lit., *me* [2]Lit., *is it hot to you* [3]Or, *a gift* [a]2 Sam. 19:12
43 [1]Singular in Heb. [a]2 Sam. 5:1; 1 Kin. 11:30, 31
1 [a]2 Sam. 16:7 [b]Gen. 46:21 [c]2 Sam. 19:43; 1 Kin. 12:16 [d]1 Sam. 22:7-9 [e]1 Sam. 13:2; 2 Sam. 18:17; 2 Chr. 10:16
2 [1]Lit., *went up* [2]Lit., *clung to*
3 [a]2 Sam. 15:16; 16:21, 22
4 [a]2 Sam. 17:25; 19:13
5 [a]1 Sam. 13:8
6 [a]2 Sam. 21:17

do us more harm than Absalom;
[b]take your lord's servants and pursue him, lest he find for himself
fortified cities and escape from our
sight."
7 So Joab's men went out after
him, [a]along with the Cherethites
and the Pelethites and [b]all the
mighty men; and they went out
from Jerusalem to pursue Sheba the
son of Bichri.
8 When they were at the large
stone which is in [a]Gibeon, Amasa
came [1]to meet them. Now Joab was
[2]dressed in his military attire, and
over it was a belt with a sword in its
sheath fastened at his waist; and as
he went forward, it fell out.
9 And Joab said to Amasa, "Is it
well with you, my brother?" And
[a]Joab took Amasa by the beard with
his right hand to kiss him.

Amasa Murdered

10 But Amasa was not on guard
against the sword which was in
Joab's hand so [a]he struck him in the
belly with it and poured out his inward parts on the ground, and did
not *strike* him again; and he died.
Then Joab and Abishai his brother
pursued Sheba the son of Bichri.
11 Now there stood by him one of
Joab's young men, and said, "Whoever favors Joab and whoever is for
David, [a]*let him* follow Joab."
12 But Amasa lay wallowing in *his*
blood in the middle of the highway.
And when the man saw that all the
people stood still, he [1]removed
Amasa from the highway into the
field and threw a garment over him
when he saw that everyone who
came by him stood still.

Revolt Put Down

13 As soon as he was removed
from the highway, all the men
passed on after Joab to pursue Sheba the son of Bichri.
14 Now he went through all the
tribes of Israel to Abel even to Beth-
maacah and all the [a]Berites; and
they were gathered together and
also went after him.
15 And they came and besieged
him in [a]Abel Beth-maacah, and
[b]they [1]cast up a mound against the
city, and it stood by the rampart;
and all the people who were with
Joab were wreaking destruction in
order to topple the wall.
16 Then [a]a wise woman called
from the city, "Hear, hear! Please
tell Joab, 'Come here that I may
speak with you.'"
17 So he approached her, and the

6 [b]2 Sam. 11:11; 1 Kin. 1:33
7 [a]2 Sam. 8:18; 1 Kin. 1:38 [b]2 Sam. 15:18
8 [1]Lit., *before* [2]Lit., *girded with military garment as clothing* [a]2 Sam. 2:13; 3:30
9 [a]Matt. 26:49
10 [a]2 Sam. 2:23; 3:27; 1 Kin. 2:5
11 [a]2 Sam. 20:13
12 [1]Lit., *caused to turn*
14 [a]Num. 21:16
15 [1]Lit., *poured out* [a]1 Kin. 15:20; 2 Kin. 15:29 [b]2 Kin. 19:32; Ezek. 4:2
16 [a]2 Sam. 14:2
19 [a]Deut. 20:10 [b]1 Sam. 26:19; 2 Sam. 14:16; 21:3
21 [a]Josh. 24:33 [b]2 Sam. 20:2
22 [a]2 Sam. 21:16; Eccles. 9:13-16 [b]2 Sam. 20:1
23 [a]2 Sam. 8:16-18; 1 Kin. 4:3-6
26 [a]2 Sam. 23:38
1 [a]Gen. 12:10; 26:1; 42:5 [b]Num. 27:21
2 [1]Lit., *had sworn to* [2]Lit., *smite* [a]Josh. 9:3, 15-20 [b]Ex. 34:11-16; Deut. 7:2; 1 Sam. 28:3

woman said, "Are you Joab?" And
he answered, "I am." Then she said
to him, "Listen to the words of your
maidservant." And he answered, "I
am listening."
18 Then she spoke, saying, "Formerly they used to say, 'They will
surely ask *advice* at Abel,' and thus
they ended *the dispute*.
19 "I am of those who are peace-
able *and* faithful in Israel. [a]You are
seeking to destroy a city even a
mother in Israel. Why would you
swallow up [b]the inheritance of the
LORD?"
20 And Joab answered and said,
"Far be it, far be it from me that I
should swallow up or destroy!
21 "Such is not the case. But a man
from [a]the hill country of Ephraim,
[b]Sheba the son of Bichri by name,
has lifted up his hand against King
David. Only hand him over, and I
will depart from the city." And the
woman said to Joab, "Behold, his
head will be thrown to you over the
wall."
22 Then the woman [a]wisely came
to all the people. And they cut off
the head of Sheba the son of Bichri
and threw it to Joab. So [b]he blew the
trumpet, and they were dispersed
from the city, each to his tent. Joab
also returned to the king at Jerusalem.
23 [a]Now Joab was over the whole
army of Israel, and Benaiah the son
of Jehoiada was over the Cherethites and the Pelethites;
24 and Adoram was over the
forced labor, and Jehoshaphat the
son of Ahilud was the recorder;
25 and Sheva was scribe, and Zadok and Abiathar were priests;
26 and [a]Ira the Jairite was also a
priest to David.

CHAPTER 21

Gibeonite Revenge

NOW there was [a]a famine in the
days of David for three years, year
after year; and [b]David sought the
presence of the LORD. And the LORD
said, "It is for Saul and his bloody
house, because he put the Gibeonites to death."
2 So the king called the Gibeonites and spoke to them (now the
Gibeonites were not of the sons of
Israel but of the remnant of the Amorites, and [a]the sons of Israel [1]made
a covenant with them, but Saul had
sought to [2]kill them [b]in his zeal for
the sons of Israel and Judah).

3 Thus David said to the Gibeonites, "What should I do for you? And
how can I make atonement [a]that
you may bless the inheritance of the
LORD?"
4 Then the Gibeonites said to
him, "[a]We have no *concern* of silver
or gold with Saul or his house, nor is
it for us to put any man to death in
Israel." And he said, "I will do for
you whatever you say."
5 So they said to the king, "[a]The
man who consumed us, and who
planned [1]to exterminate us from remaining within any border of Israel,
6 let seven men from his sons be
given to us, and we will [1]hang them
[a]before the LORD in Gibeah of Saul,
[b]the chosen of the LORD." And the
king said, "I will give *them*."
7 But the king spared [a]Mephibo-
sheth, the son of Jonathan the son of
Saul, [b]because of the oath of the
LORD which was between them, between David and Saul's son Jonathan.
8 So the king took the two sons of
[a]Rizpah the daughter of Aiah, Ar-
moni and Mephibosheth whom she
had born to Saul, and the five sons
of [1]Merab the daughter of Saul,
whom she had born to Adriel the
son of Barzillai the [b]Meholathite.
9 Then he gave them into the
hands of the Gibeonites, and they
[1]hanged them in the mountain before the LORD, so that the seven of
them fell together; and they were
put to death in the first days of harvest at [a]the beginning of barley harvest.
10 [a]And Rizpah the daughter of
Aiah took sackcloth and spread it
for herself on the rock, from the beginning of harvest until [1]it rained on
them from the sky; and [b]she [2]al-
lowed neither the birds of the sky to
rest on them by day nor the beasts
of the field by night.
11 When it was told David what
Rizpah the daughter of Aiah, the
concubine of Saul, had done,
12 then David went and took [a]the
bones of Saul and the bones of Jonathan his son from the men of Jabesh-gilead, who had stolen them
from the open square of [b]Bethshan,
[c]where the Philistines had hanged
them on the day [d]the Philistines
struck down Saul in Gilboa.
13 And he brought up the bones of
Saul and the bones of Jonathan his
son from there, and they gathered
the bones of those who had been
[1]hanged.
14 And they buried the bones of
Saul and Jonathan his son in the
country of Benjamin in [a]Zela, in the
grave of Kish his father; thus they
did all that the king commanded,
and after that [b]God was moved by
entreaty for the land.
15 Now when [a]the Philistines were
at war again with Israel, David went
down and his servants with him;
and as they fought against the Philistines, David became weary.
16 Then Ishbi-benob, who was
[a]among the descendants of the
[1]giant, the weight of whose spear
was three hundred *shekels* of
bronze in weight, [2]was girded with a
new *sword*, and he [3]intended to kill
David.
17 But [a]Abishai the son of Zeruiah
helped him, and struck the Philistine and killed him. Then the men of
David swore to him, saying, "[b]You
shall not go out again with us to battle, that you may not extinguish [c]the
lamp of Israel."
18 [a]Now it came about after this
that there was war again with the
Philistines at Gob; then [b]Sibbecai
the Hushathite struck down Saph,
who was among the descendants of
the [1]giant.
19 And there was war with the
Philistines again at Gob, and Elhanan the son of Jaare-oregim the
Bethlehemite [1]killed [2]Goliath the
Gittite, [a]the shaft of whose spear
was like a weaver's beam.
20 And there was war at Gath
again, where there was a man of
great stature who had six fingers on
each hand and six toes on each foot,
twenty-four in number; and he also
had been born [a]to the [1]giant.
21 And when he defied Israel,
Jonathan the son of Shimei, David's
brother, struck him down.
22 [a]These four were born to the
[1]giant in Gath, and they fell by the
hand of David and by the hand of his
servants.

CHAPTER 22

David's Psalm of Deliverance

[a]AND David spoke [b]the words of
this song to the LORD in the day that
the LORD delivered him from the
[1]hand of all his enemies and from
the [1]hand of Saul.
2 And he said,
"[a]The LORD is my [1]rock and my
fortress and my deliverer;
3 [1a]My God, my rock, in whom I
take refuge;
My [b]shield and [c]the horn of
my salvation, my stronghold
and [d]my refuge;

3 [a]1 Sam. 26:19; 2 Sam. 20:19
4 [a]Num. 35:31, 32
5 [1]Lit., *against us that we should be exterminated* [a]2 Sam. 21:1
6 [1]Lit., *expose them* [a]Num. 25:4 [b]1 Sam. 10:24
7 [a]2 Sam. 4:4; 9:10 [b]1 Sam. 18:3; 20:12-17; 23:18
8 [1]So Gk. and Heb. mss. [a]2 Sam. 3:7 [b]1 Kin. 19:16
9 [1]Lit., *exposed them* [a]Ex. 9:31, 32
10 [1]Lit., *water was poured* [2]Lit., *gave* [a]Deut. 21:23 [b]1 Sam. 17:44, 46
12 [a]1 Sam. 31:11-13 [b]Josh. 17:11 [c]1 Sam. 31:10 [d]1 Sam. 31:4
13 [1]Lit., *exposed*
14 [a]Josh. 18:28 [b]Josh. 7:26; 2 Sam. 24:25
15 [a]2 Sam. 5:17-25
16 [1]Heb., *Raphah* [2]Lit., *and he was* [3]Lit., *said* [a]Num. 13:22, 28; Josh. 15:14; 2 Sam. 21:18-22
17 [a]2 Sam. 20:6-10 [b]2 Sam. 18:3 [c]2 Sam. 22:29; 1 Kin. 11:36
18 [1]Heb., *Raphah* [a]1 Chr. 20:4-8 [b]1 Chr. 11:29; 27:11
19 [1]Lit., *smote* [2]In 1 Chr. 20:5, *Lahmi, the brother of Goliath* [a]1 Sam. 17:7
20 [1]Heb., *Raphah* [a]2 Sam. 21:16, 18
22 [1]Heb., *Raphah* [a]1 Chr. 20:8
1 [1]Lit., *palm* [a]Ps. 18:2-50 [b]Ex. 15:1; Deut. 31:30
2 [1]Lit., *crag* [a]1 Sam. 23:25; 24:2; Ps. 31:3; 71:3
3 [1]Lit., *God of my rock* [a]Deut. 32:4, 37; 1 Sam. 2:2 [b]Gen. 15:1; Deut. 33:29 [c]Deut. 33:17; Luke 1:69 [d]Ps. 9:9

My savior, Thou dost save me from violence.
4 "I call upon the LORD, [a]who is worthy to be praised;
And I am saved from my enemies.
5 "For [a]the waves of death encompassed me;
[b]The torrents of [1]destruction [2]overwhelmed me;
6 [a]The cords of [1]Sheol surrounded me;
The snares of death confronted me.
7 "[a]In my distress I called upon the LORD,
Yes, I [1]cried to my God;
And from His temple He heard my voice,
And my cry for help *came* into His ears.
8 "Then [a]the earth shook and quaked,
[b]The foundations of heaven were trembling
And were shaken, because He was angry.
9 "[a]Smoke went up [1]out of His nostrils,
And fire from His mouth devoured;
[b]Coals were kindled by it.
10 "He bowed the heavens also, and came down
With [a]thick darkness under His feet.
11 "[a]And He rode on a cherub and flew;
And He [1]appeared on [b]the wings of the wind.
12 "[a]And He made darkness [1]canopies around Him,
A mass of waters, thick clouds of the sky.
13 "From the brightness before Him
[a]Coals of fire were kindled.
14 "[a]The LORD thundered from heaven,
And the Most High uttered His voice.
15 "[a]And He sent out arrows, and scattered them,
Lightning, and [1]routed them.
16 "Then the channels of the sea appeared,
The foundations of the world were [1]laid bare,
By the rebuke of the LORD,
[a]At the blast of the breath of His nostrils.
17 "[a]He sent from on high, He took me;
[b]He drew me out of many waters.
18 "He delivered me from my strong enemy,
From those who hated me, for they were too strong for me.
19 "They confronted me in the day of my calamity,
[a]But the LORD was my support.
20 "[a]He also brought me forth into a broad place;
He rescued me, [b]because He delighted in me.
21 "[a]The LORD has rewarded me according to my righteousness;
[b]According to the cleanness of my hands He has recompensed me.
22 "[a]For I have kept the ways of the LORD,
And have not acted wickedly against my God.
23 "[a]For all His ordinances *were* before me;
And *as for* His statutes, I did not depart from [1]them.
24 "[a]I was also [1]blameless toward Him,
And I kept myself from my iniquity.
25 "[a]Therefore the LORD has recompensed me according to my righteousness,
According to my cleanness before His eyes.
26 "[a]With the [1]kind Thou dost show Thyself [1]kind,
With the blameless Thou dost show Thyself blameless;
27 [a]With the pure Thou dost show Thyself pure,
[b]And with the perverted Thou dost show Thyself [1]astute.
28 "[a]And Thou dost save an afflicted people;
[b]But Thine eyes are on the haughty *whom* Thou dost abase.
29 "[a]For Thou art my lamp, O LORD;
And the LORD illumines my darkness.
30 "[a]For by Thee I can [1]run upon a troop;
By my God I can leap over a wall.
31 "[a]As for God, His way is blameless;
[b]The word of the LORD is tested;
[c]He is a shield to all who take refuge in Him.
32 "[a]For who is God, besides the LORD?
[b]And who is a rock, besides our God?

4 [a]Ps. 48:1; 96:4
5 [1]Heb., *Belial* [2]Or, *terrified* [a]Ps. 93:4; Jon. 2:3 [b]Ps. 69:14, 15
6 [1]I.e., the nether world [a]Ps. 116:3
7 [1]Or, *called* [a]Ps. 116:4; 120:1
8 [a]Judg. 5:4; Ps. 97:4 [b]Job 26:11
9 [1]Or, *in His wrath* [a]Heb. 12:29 [b]2 Sam. 22:13
10 [a]Ex. 19:16; 1 Kin. 8:12; Ps. 97:2; Nah. 1:3
11 [1]Many mss. read, *sped* [a]2 Sam. 6:2 [b]Ps. 104:3
12 [1]Or, *pavilions* [a]Job 36:29
13 [a]2 Sam. 22:9
14 [a]Job 37:2-5; Ps. 29:3
15 [1]Lit., *confused* [a]Deut. 32:23; Josh. 10:10; 1 Sam. 7:10
16 [1]Or, *uncovered* [a]Ex. 15:8; Nah. 1:4
17 [a]Ps. 144:7 [b]Ex. 2:10
19 [a]Ps. 23:4
20 [a]Ps. 31:8; 118:5 [b]2 Sam. 15:26
21 [a]1 Sam. 26:23; 1 Kin. 8:32 [b]Ps. 24:4
22 [a]Gen. 18:19; Ps. 128:1; Prov. 8:32
23 [1]Lit., *it* [a]Deut. 6:6-9; Ps. 119:30, 102
24 [1]Lit., *complete* or *having integrity* [a]Gen. 6:9; 7:1; Eph. 1:4; Col. 1:21, 22
25 [a]2 Sam. 22:21
26 [1]Or, *loyal* [a]Matt. 5:7
27 [1]Lit., *twisted* [a]Matt. 5:8; 1 John 3:3 [b]Lev. 26:23, 24; Rom. 1:28
28 [a]Ex. 3:7, 8; Ps. 72:12, 13 [b]Is. 2:11; 5:15
29 [a]2 Sam. 21:17; 1 Kin. 11:36; Ps. 27:1
30 [1]Or, *crush a troop* [a]2 Sam. 5:6-8
31 [a]Deut. 32:4; Matt. 5:48 [b]Ps. 12:6; 119:140; Prov. 30:5 [c]2 Sam. 22:3; Ps. 84:9
32 [a]1 Sam. 2:2 [b]2 Sam. 22:2

33 "[a]God is my strong fortress;
And He [1]sets the [2]blameless in [3]His way.
34 "[a]He makes [1]my feet like hinds' *feet*,
[b]And sets me on my high places.
35 "[a]He trains my hands for battle,
[b]So that my arms can bend a bow of bronze.
36 "Thou hast also given me [a]the shield of Thy salvation,
And Thy [1]help makes me great.
37 "[a]Thou dost enlarge my steps under me,
And my [1]feet have not slipped.
38 "I pursued my enemies and [a]destroyed them,
And I did not turn back until they were consumed.
39 "And I have devoured them and shattered them, so that they did not rise;
And [a]they fell under my feet.
40 "For Thou hast girded me with strength for battle;
Thou hast [1]subdued under me [a]those who rose up against me.
41 "Thou hast also [a]made my enemies turn *their* backs to me,
And I [1]destroyed those who hated me.
42 "[a]They looked, but there was none to save;
[b]*Even* to the LORD, but He did not answer them.
43 "[a]Then I pulverized them as the dust of the earth,
[b]I crushed *and* stamped them as the mire of the streets.
44 "[a]Thou hast also delivered me from the contentions of my people;
[b]Thou hast kept me as head of the nations;
[c]A people whom I have not known serve me.
45 "[a]Foreigners pretend obedience to me;
As soon as they hear, they obey me.
46 "Foreigners [1]lose heart,
[a]And [2]come trembling out of their [3]fortresses.
47 "The LORD lives, and blessed be my rock;
And exalted be [1][a]God, the rock of my salvation,
48 [a]The God who executes vengeance for me,
[b]And brings down peoples under me,
49 Who also brings me out from my enemies;
Thou dost even lift me above [a]those who rise up against me;
[b]Thou dost rescue me from the violent man.
50 "[a]Therefore I will give thanks to Thee, O LORD, among the nations,
And I will sing praises to Thy name.
51 "[a]*He* is a tower of [1]deliverance to His king,
And [b]shows lovingkindness to His anointed,
[c]To David and his [2]descendants forever."

CHAPTER 23

David's Last Song

NOW these are the last words of David.
David the son of Jesse declares,
[a]And the man who was raised on high declares,
[b]The anointed of the God of Jacob,
And the sweet psalmist of Israel,
2 "[a]The Spirit of the LORD spoke by me,
And His word was on my tongue.
3 "The God of Israel said,
[a]The Rock of Israel spoke to me,
'[b]He who rules over men righteously,
[c]Who rules in the fear of God,
4 [a]Is as the light of the morning *when* the sun rises,
A morning without clouds,
When the tender grass *springs* out of the earth,
Through sunshine after rain.'
5 "Truly is not my house so with God?
For [a]He has made an everlasting covenant with me,
Ordered in all things, and secured;
For all my salvation and all *my* desire,
Will He not indeed make *it* grow?
6 "[a]But the worthless, every one of them will be thrust away like thorns,
Because they cannot be taken in hand;
7 But the man who touches them

33 [1]Or, *sets free* [2]Lit., *complete* or *having integrity* [3]Another reading is, *my* [a]2 Sam. 22:2; Ps. 31:3, 4
34 [1]Another reading is, *His* [a]2 Sam. 2:18; Heb. 3:19 [b]Deut. 32:13
35 [a]Ps. 144:1 [b]Job 20:24
36 [1]Lit., *answering* [a]Eph. 6:16, 17
37 [1]Lit., *ankles* [a]2 Sam. 22:20; Prov. 4:12
38 [a]Ex. 15:9
39 [a]Mal. 4:3
40 [1]Lit., *caused to bow down* [a]Ps. 44:5
41 [1]Or, *silenced* [a]Ex. 23:27; Josh. 10:24
42 [a]Is. 17:7, 8 [b]1 Sam. 28:6; Is. 1:15
43 [a]2 Kin. 13:7 [b]Is. 10:6; Mic. 7:10
44 [a]2 Sam. 3:1; 19:9, 14 [b]2 Sam. 8:1-14 [c]Is. 55:5
45 [a]Ps. 66:3; 81:15
46 [1]Lit., *languish* [2]Lit., *gird themselves* [3]Lit., *fastnesses* [a]1 Sam. 14:11; Mic. 7:17
47 [1]Lit., *the God of the rock* [a]2 Sam. 22:3; Ps. 89:26
48 [a]1 Sam. 24:12; 25:39; 2 Sam. 4:8; Ps. 94:1 [b]Ps. 144:2
49 [a]Ps. 44:5 [b]Ps. 140:1, 4, 11
50 [a]Rom. 15:9
51 [1]I.e., victories; lit., *salvation* [2]Lit., *seed* [a]Ps. 144:10 [b]Ps. 89:24 [c]2 Sam. 7:12-16
1 [a]2 Sam. 7:8, 9; Ps. 78:70, 71 [b]1 Sam. 16:12, 13; Ps. 89:20
2 [a]Matt. 22:43; 2 Pet. 1:21
3 [a]2 Chr. 22:2, 3, 32 [b]Ps. 72:1-3; Is. 11:1-5 [c]2 Chr. 19:7, 9
4 [a]Judg. 5:31; Ps. 72:6
5 [a]2 Sam. 7:12; Ps. 89:29; Is. 55:3
6 [a]Matt. 13:41

Must be [1]armed with iron and
the shaft of a spear,
And [a]they will be completely
burned with fire in *their*
[2]place."

His Mighty Men

8 [a]These are the names of the mighty men whom David had: Josheb-basshebeth a Tahchemonite, chief of the [1]captains, he was called Adino the Eznite, because of eight hundred slain *by him* at one time;

9 and after him was Eleazar the son of [a]Dodo the [b]Ahohite, one of the three mighty men with David when they [1]defied the Philistines who were gathered there to battle and the men of Israel had [2]withdrawn.

10 [a]He arose and struck the Philistines until his hand was weary and [1]clung to the sword, and [b]the LORD brought about a great [2]victory that day; and the people returned after him only to strip *the slain*.

11 Now after him was Shammah the son of Agee a [a]Hararite. And the Philistines were gathered [1]into a troop, where there was a plot of ground full of lentils, and the people fled from the Philistines.

12 But he took his stand in the midst of the plot, defended it and struck the Philistines; and [a]the LORD brought about a great [1]victory.

13 Then three of the thirty chief men went down and came to David in the harvest time to the [a]cave of Adullam, while the troop of the Philistines was camping in [b]the valley of Rephaim.

14 And David was then [a]in the stronghold, while the garrison of the Philistines was then in Bethlehem.

15 And David had a craving and said, "Oh that someone would give me water to drink from the well of Bethlehem which is by the gate!"

16 So the three mighty men broke through the camp of the Philistines, and drew water from the well of Bethlehem which was by the gate, and took *it* and brought *it* to David. Nevertheless he would not drink it, but [a]poured it out to the LORD;

17 and he said, "Be it far from me, O LORD, that I should do this. [a]*Shall I drink* the blood of the men who went in *jeopardy* of their lives?" Therefore he would not drink it. These things the three mighty men did.

18 And [a]Abishai, the brother of Joab, the son of Zeruiah, was [b]chief of the [1]thirty. And he swung his spear against three hundred [2]and killed *them*, and had a name as well as the three.

19 He was most honored of the thirty, therefore he became their commander; however, he did not attain to the three.

20 Then [a]Benaiah the son of Jehoiada, the son of a valiant man of [b]Kabzeel, who had done mighty deeds, [1]killed the [2]two *sons of* Ariel of Moab. He also went down and killed a lion in the middle of a pit on a snowy day.

21 And he [1]killed an Egyptian, [2]an impressive man. Now the Egyptian *had* a spear in his hand, but he went down to him with a club and snatched the spear from the Egyptian's hand, and killed him with his own spear.

22 These *things* [a]Benaiah the son of Jehoiada did, and had a name as well as the three mighty men.

23 He was honored among the thirty, but he did not attain to the three. And David appointed him over his guard.

24 [a]Asahel the brother of Joab was among the thirty; Elhanan the son of Dodo of Bethlehem,

25 [a]Shammah the [b]Harodite, Elika the Harodite,

26 Helez the Paltite, Ira the son of Ikkesh the [a]Tekoite,

27 Abiezer the [a]Anathothite, Mebunnai the Hushathite,

28 Zalmon the Ahohite, Maharai the [a]Netophathite,

29 [a]Heleb the son of Baanah the Netophathite, Ittai the son of Ribai of [b]Gibeah of the sons of Benjamin,

30 Benaiah a [a]Pirathonite, Hiddai of the brooks of [b]Gaash,

31 Abi-albon the Arbathite, Azmaveth the [a]Barhumite,

32 Eliahba the [a]Shaalbonite, the sons of Jashen, Jonathan,

33 [a]Shammah the Hararite, Ahiam the son of Sharar the Ararite,

34 Eliphelet the son of Ahasbai, the son of [a]the Maacathite, [b]Eliam the son of [c]Ahithophel the Gilonite,

35 [a]Hezro the [b]Carmelite, Paarai the Arbite,

36 Igal the son of Nathan of [a]Zobah, Bani the Gadite,

37 Zelek the Ammonite, Naharai the [a]Beerothite, armor bearers of Joab the son of Zeruiah,

38 [a]Ira the [b]Ithrite, Gareb the Ithrite,

39 [a]Uriah the Hittite; thirty-seven in all.

7 [1]Lit., *filled* [2]Lit., *sitting* [a]Matt. 3:10; 13:30; Heb. 6:8
8 [1]Or, *three* [a]1 Chr. 11:11-47
9 [1]Lit., *reproached* [2]Lit., *gone up* [a]1 Chr. 27:4 [b]1 Chr. 8:4
10 [1]Lit., *his hand clung* [2]Lit., *salvation* [a]1 Chr. 11:13 [b]1 Sam. 11:13; 19:5
11 [1]Possibly, at Lehi [a]2 Sam. 23:33
12 [1]Lit., *salvation* [a]2 Sam. 23:10
13 [a]1 Sam. 22:1 [b]2 Sam. 5:18
14 [a]1 Sam. 22:4, 5
16 [a]Gen. 35:14
17 [a]Lev. 17:10
18 [1]So two Heb. mss. and Syriac; M.T. *three* [2]Lit., *slain ones* [a]2 Sam. 10:10, 14; 18:2 [b]1 Chr. 11:20, 21
20 [1]Lit., *smote* [2]Or, *two lion-like heroes* [a]2 Sam. 8:18, 20, 23 [b]Josh. 15:21
21 [1]Lit., *smote* [2]Lit., *a man of appearance*
22 [a]2 Sam. 23:20
24 [a]2 Sam. 2:18; 1 Chr. 27:7
25 [a]1 Chr. 11:27; [b]Judg. 7:1
26 [a]2 Sam. 14:2
27 [a]Josh. 21:18
28 [a]2 Kin. 25:23
29 [a]1 Chr. 11:30 [b]Josh. 18:28
30 [a]Judg. 12:13, 15 [b]Josh. 24:30
31 [a]2 Sam. 3:16
32 [a]Josh. 19:42
33 [a]2 Sam. 23:11
34 [a]2 Sam. 10:6, 8; 20:14 [b]2 Sam. 11:3 [c]2 Sam. 15:12
35 [a]1 Chr. 11:37 [b]Josh. 15:55
36 [a]2 Sam. 8:3
37 [a]2 Sam. 4:2
38 [a]2 Sam. 20:26 [b]1 Chr. 2:53
39 [a]2 Sam. 11:3, 6

CHAPTER 24

The Census Taken

[a]NOW [b]again the anger of the LORD
burned against Israel, and it incited
David against them to say, "[c]Go,
number Israel and Judah."
2 And the king said to Joab the
commander of the army who was
with him, "Go about now through
all the tribes of Israel, [a]from Dan to
Beersheba, and [1]register the people,
that I may know the number of the
people."
3 But Joab said to the king,
"[a]Now may the LORD your God add
to the people a hundred times as
many as they are, while the eyes of
my lord the king *still* see; but why
does my lord the king delight in this
thing?"
4 Nevertheless, the king's word
prevailed against Joab and against
the commanders of the army. So
Joab and the commanders of the
army went out from the presence of
the king, to [1]register the people of
Israel.
5 And they crossed the Jordan
and camped in [a]Aroer, on the right
side of the city that is in the middle
of the valley of Gad, and toward [b]Ja-
zer.
6 Then they came to Gilead and
to [1]the land of Tahtim-hodshi, and
they came to Dan-jaan and around
to [a]Sidon,
7 and came to the [a]fortress of
Tyre and to all the cities of the [b]Hi-
vites and of the Canaanites, and
they went out to the south of Judah,
to [c]Beersheba.
8 So when they had gone about
through the whole land, they came
to Jerusalem at the end of nine
months and twenty days.
9 And Joab gave [a]the number of
the [1]registration of the people to the
king; and there were in Israel [b]eight
hundred thousand valiant men who
drew the sword, and the men of Judah were five hundred thousand
men.
10 Now [a]David's heart [1]troubled
him after he had numbered the people. So David said to the LORD, "[b]I
have sinned greatly in what I have
done. But now, O LORD, please [2]take
away the iniquity of Thy servant, for
[c]I have acted very foolishly."
11 When David arose in the morning, the word of the LORD came to
[a]the prophet Gad, David's [b]seer,
saying,
12 "Go and speak to David, 'Thus
the LORD says, "I am offering you
three things; choose for yourself one
of them, which I may do to you." ' "
13 So Gad came to David and told
him, and said to him, "Shall [a]seven
years of famine come to you in your
land? Or will you flee three months
before your foes while they pursue
you? Or shall there be three days'
pestilence in your land? Now consider and see what answer I shall
return to Him who sent me."
14 Then David said to Gad, "I am
in great distress. Let us now fall into
the hand of the LORD [a]for His mercies are great, but do not let me fall
into the hand of man."

Pestilence Sent

15 So [a]the LORD [1]sent a pestilence
upon Israel from the morning until
the appointed time; and seventy
thousand men of the people [b]from
Dan to Beersheba died.
16 [a]When the angel stretched out
his hand toward Jerusalem to destroy it, [b]the LORD relented from the
calamity, and said to the angel who
destroyed the people, "It is enough!
Now relax your hand!" And the angel of the LORD was by the threshing
floor of Araunah the Jebusite.
17 Then David spoke to the LORD
when he saw the angel who was
striking down the people, and said,
"Behold, [a]it is I who have sinned,
and it is I who have done wrong; but
[b]these sheep, what have they done?
Please let Thy hand be against me
and against my father's house."

David Builds an Altar

18 So Gad came to David that day
and said to him, "Go up, erect an
altar to the LORD on the threshing
floor of [a]Araunah the Jebusite."
19 And David went up according
to the word of Gad, just as the LORD
had commanded.
20 And Araunah looked down and
saw the king and his servants crossing over toward him; and Araunah
went out and bowed his face to the
ground before the king.
21 Then Araunah said, "Why has
my lord the king come to his servant?" And David said, "To buy the
threshing floor from you, in order to
build an altar to the LORD, [a]that the
plague may be held back from the
people."
22 And Araunah said to David,
"Let my lord the king take and offer
up what is good in his sight. Look,
[a]the oxen for the burnt offering, the
threshing sledges and the yokes of
the oxen for the wood.

1 [a]1 Chr. 21:1 [b]2 Sam. 21:1, 2 [c]1 Chr. 27:23, 24
2 [1]Lit., *muster* [a]Judg. 20:1; 2 Sam. 3:10
3 [a]Deut. 1:11
4 [1]Lit., *muster*
5 [a]Deut. 2:36; Josh. 13:9, 16 [b]Num. 21:32; 32:35
6 [1]Or, *Kadesh in the land of the Hittite* [a]Josh. 19:28; Judg. 1:31
7 [a]Josh. 19:29 [b]Josh. 11:3; Judg. 3:3 [c]Gen. 21:22-33
9 [1]Lit., *muster* [a]Num. 1:44-46 [b]1 Chr. 21:5
10 [1]Lit., *smote* [2]Lit., *cause to pass away* [a]1 Sam. 24:5 [b]2 Sam. 12:13 [c]1 Sam. 13:13; 2 Chr. 16:9
11 [a]1 Sam. 22:5; 1 Chr. 29:29 [b]1 Sam. 9:9
13 [a]1 Chr. 21:12; Ezek. 14:21
14 [a]Ps. 51:1; 130:4, 7
15 [1]Lit., *gave* [a]1 Chr. 21:14; 27:24 [b]2 Sam. 24:2
16 [a]Ex. 12:23; 2 Kin. 19:35; Acts 12:23 [b]Ex. 32:14; 1 Sam. 15:11
17 [a]2 Sam. 24:10 [b]2 Sam. 7:8; Ps. 74:1
18 [a]2 Chr. 3:1
21 [a]Num. 16:44-50
22 [a]1 Sam. 6:14; 1 Kin. 19:21

23“[a]Everything, O king, Araunah gives to the king.” And Araunah said to the king, “May the LORD your God [b]accept you.”

24 However, the king said to Araunah. “No, but I will surely buy *it* from you for a price, for [a]I will not offer burnt offerings to the LORD my God [1]which cost me nothing.” So [b]David bought the threshing floor and the oxen for fifty shekels of silver.

25 And David built there an altar to the LORD, and offered burnt offerings and peace offerings. [a]Thus the LORD was moved by entreaty for the land, and the plague was held back from Israel.

23 [a]Gen. 23:8-16 [b]Ezek. 20:40, 41
24 [1]Lit., *gratuitously* [a]Mal. 1:13, 14 [b]1 Chr. 21:24, 25
25 [a]2 Sam. 21:14

THE FIRST BOOK OF THE KINGS

David in Old Age

NOW King David was old, advanced in age; and they covered him with clothes, but he could not keep warm.

2 So his servants said to him, “Let them seek a young virgin for my lord the king, and let her [1]attend the king and become his nurse; and let her lie in your bosom, that my lord the king may keep warm.”

3 So they searched for a beautiful girl throughout all the territory of Israel, and found Abishag the [a]Shunammite, and brought her to the king.

4 And the girl was very beautiful; and she became the king’s nurse and served him, but the king did not [1]cohabit with her.

5 Now [a]Adonijah the son of Haggith exalted himself, saying, “I will be king.” So [b]he prepared for himself chariots and horsemen with fifty men to run before him.

6 And his father had never [1]crossed him at any time by asking, “Why have you done so?” And he was also a very handsome man; and [2a]he was born after Absalom.

7 And [1]he had conferred with [a]Joab the son of Zeruiah and with [b]Abiathar the priest; and following Adonijah they helped him.

8 But [a]Zadok the priest, [b]Benaiah the son of Jehoiada, [c]Nathan the prophet, Shimei, Rei, and [d]the mighty men who belonged to David, were not with Adonijah.

9 And Adonijah sacrificed sheep and oxen and fatlings by the [1]stone of Zoheleth, which is beside [a]En-rogel; and he invited all his brothers, the king’s sons, and all the men of Judah, the king’s servants.

10 But he did not invite Nathan the prophet, Benaiah, the mighty men, and [a]Solomon his brother.

Nathan and Bathsheba

11 Then Nathan spoke to Bathsheba the mother of Solomon, saying, “Have you not heard that Adonijah the son of Haggith has become king, and David our lord does not know *it?*

12“So now come, please let me give you counsel and save your life and the life of your son Solomon.

13“Go [1]at once to King David and say to him, ‘Have you not, my lord, O king, sworn to your maidservant, saying, “[a]Surely Solomon your son shall be king after me, and he shall sit on my throne”? Why then has Adonijah become king?’

14“Behold, while you are still there speaking with the king, I will come in after you and confirm your words.”

15 So Bathsheba went in to the king in the bedroom. Now [a]the king was very old, and Abishag the Shunammite was ministering to the king.

16 Then Bathsheba bowed and prostrated herself [1]before the king. And the king said, “What [2]do you wish?”

17 And she said to him, “My lord, you swore to your maidservant by the LORD your God, *saying,* ‘[a]Surely your son Solomon shall be king after me and he shall sit on my throne.’

18“And now, behold, Adonijah is king; and now, my lord the king, you do not know *it.*

19“And [a]he has sacrificed oxen and fatlings and sheep in abundance, and has invited all the sons of the king and Abiathar the priest and Joab the commander of the army; but he has not invited Solomon your servant.

20“And as for you now, my lord the king, the eyes of all Israel are on you, to tell them who shall sit on the throne of my lord the king after him.

21“Otherwise it will come about, [a]as soon as my lord the king sleeps with his fathers, that I and my son

2 [1]Lit., *stand before*
3 [a]Josh. 19:18; 1 Sam. 28:4
4 [1]Lit., *know her*
5 [a]2 Sam. 3:4 [b]2 Sam. 15:1
6 [1]Lit., *pained him* [2]Lit., *she gave him birth* [a]2 Sam. 3:3, 4
7 [1]Lit., *his words were* [a]1 Chr. 11:6 [b]1 Sam. 22:20, 23
8 [a]2 Sam. 20:25; 1 Chr. 16:39 [b]2 Sam. 8:18 [c]2 Sam. 12:1 [d]2 Sam. 23:8-39
9 [1]Or, *Gliding* or *Serpent Stone* [a]Josh. 15:7; 18:16; 2 Sam. 17:17
10 [a]2 Sam. 12:24
13 [1]Lit., *and enter* [a]1 Kin. 1:30; 1 Chr. 22:9-13
15 [a]1 Kin. 1:1
16 [1]Lit., *to* [2]Lit., *to you*
17 [a]1 Kin. 1:13
19 [a]1 Kin. 1:9
21 [a]Deut. 31:16; 2 Sam. 7:12; 1 Kin. 2:10

Solomon will be considered [1]offend-
ers."
22 And behold, while she was still
speaking with the king, Nathan the
prophet came in.
23 And they told the king, saying,
"Here is Nathan the prophet." And
when he came in before the king, he
prostrated himself [1]before the king
with his face to the ground.
24 Then Nathan said, "My lord the
king, have you said, 'Adonijah shall
be king after me, and he shall sit on
my throne'?
25"[a]For he has gone down today
and has sacrificed oxen and fatlings
and sheep in abundance, and has invited all the king's sons and the
commanders of the army and Abiathar the priest, and behold, they
are eating and drinking before him;
and they say, '[b]*Long* live King Adonijah!'
26"[a]But me, *even* me your servant,
and Zadok the priest and Benaiah
the son of Jehoiada and your servant Solomon, he has not invited.
27"Has this thing been done by my
lord the king, and you have not
shown to your [1]servants who should
sit on the throne of my lord the king
after him?"
28 Then King David answered and
said, "Call Bathsheba to me." And
she came into the king's presence
and stood before the king.
29 And the king vowed and said,
"[a]As the LORD lives, who has redeemed my life from all distress,
30 surely as [a]I vowed to you by the
LORD the God of Israel, saying,
'Your son Solomon shall be king after me, and he shall sit on my throne
in my place'; I will indeed do so this
day."
31 Then Bathsheba bowed with
her face to the ground, and prostrated herself [1]before the king and
said, "[a]May my lord King David live
forever."
32 Then King David said, "Call to
me [a]Zadok the priest, Nathan the
prophet, and Benaiah the son of Jehoiada." And they came into the
king's presence.
33 And the king said to them,
"Take with you [a]the servants of
your lord, and have my son Solomon ride on my own mule, and
bring him down to [b]Gihon.
34"And let Zadok the priest and
Nathan the prophet [a]anoint him
there as king over Israel, and [b]blow
the trumpet and say, '[c]*Long* live
King Solomon!'
35"Then you shall come up after
him, and he shall come and sit on
my throne and be king in my place;
for I have appointed him to be ruler
over Israel and Judah."
36 And Benaiah the son of Jehoiada answered the king and said,
"Amen! Thus may the LORD, the
God of my lord the king, say.
37"[a]As the LORD has been with my
lord the king, so may He be with
Solomon, and [b]make his throne
greater than the throne of my lord
King David!"

Solomon Anointed King

38 So [a]Zadok the priest, Nathan
the prophet, Benaiah the son of Jehoiada, [b]the Cherethites, and the
Pelethites went down and had Solomon ride on King David's mule, and
brought him to [c]Gihon.
39 Zadok the priest then [a]took the
horn of oil from the tent and [b]a-
nointed Solomon. Then they [c]blew
the trumpet, and all the people said,
"Long live King Solomon!"
40 And all the people went up after
him, and the people [1]were playing
on flutes and rejoicing with great
joy, so that the earth [2]shook at their
noise.
41 Now Adonijah and all the
guests who were with him heard *it,*
as they finished eating. When Joab
heard the sound of the trumpet, he
said, "Why [1]is the city making such
an uproar?"
42 While he was still speaking, behold, [a]Jonathan the son of Abiathar
the priest came. Then Adonijah
said, "Come in, for [b]you are a valiant man and bring good news."
43 But Jonathan answered and
said to Adonijah, "No! Our lord
King David has made Solomon king.
44"The king has also sent with him
Zadok the priest, Nathan the
prophet, Benaiah the son of Jehoiada, the Cherethites, and the Pelethites; and they have made him
ride on the king's mule.
45"And Zadok the priest and Nathan the prophet have anointed him
king in Gihon, and they have come
up from there rejoicing, [a]so that the
city is in an uproar. This is the noise
which you have heard.
46"Besides, [a]Solomon has even
taken his seat on the throne of the
kingdom.
47"And moreover, the king's servants came to bless our lord King
David, saying, 'May [a]your God
make the name of Solomon better
than your name and his throne
greater than your throne!' And [b]the
king bowed himself on the bed.

21 [1]Lit., *sinners*
23 [1]Lit., *to*
25 [a]1 Kin. 1:9 [b]1 Sam. 10:24
26 [a]1 Kin. 1:8, 10
27 [1]Some mss. read *servant*
29 [a]2 Sam. 4:9
30 [a]1 Kin. 1:13, 17
31 [1]Lit., *to* [a]Dan. 2:4; 3:9
32 [a]1 Kin. 1:8
33 [a]2 Sam. 20:6, 7 [b]2 Chr. 32:30; 33:14
34 [a]1 Sam. 10:1; 16:3, 12 [b]2 Sam. 15:10 [c]1 Kin. 1:25
37 [a]Josh. 1:5, 17; 1 Sam. 20:13 [b]1 Kin. 1:47
38 [a]1 Kin. 1:8 [b]2 Sam. 8:18 [c]1 Kin. 1:33
39 [a]Ex. 30:23-32; 1 Chr. 16:39; Ps. 89:20 [b]1 Chr. 29:22 [c]1 Kin. 1:34
40 [1]Lit., *fluting* [2]Lit., *was split*
41 [1]Lit., *is the sound of the city an uproar*
42 [a]2 Sam. 15:27, 36; 17:17 [b]2 Sam. 18:27
45 [a]1 Kin. 1:40
46 [a]1 Chr. 29:23
47 [a]1 Kin. 1:37 [b]Gen. 47:31

48 “The king has also said thus,
‘Blessed be the LORD, the God of Israel, who [a]has granted one to sit on
my throne today while my own eyes
see *it*.’ ”
49 Then all the guests of Adonijah
were terrified; and they arose and
each went on his way.
50 And Adonijah was afraid of
Solomon, and he arose, went and
[a]took hold of the horns of the altar.
51 Now it was told Solomon, saying, “Behold, Adonijah is afraid of
King Solomon, for behold, he has
taken hold of the horns of the altar,
saying, ‘Let King Solomon swear to
me today that he will not put his
servant to death with the sword.’ ”
52 And Solomon said, “If he will
be a worthy man, [a]not one of his
hairs will fall to the ground; but if
wickedness is found in him, he will
die.”
53 So King Solomon sent, and they
brought him down from the altar.
And he came and prostrated himself
[1]before King Solomon, and Solomon said to him, “Go to your
house.”

CHAPTER 2

David’s Charge to Solomon

AS David’s [1a]time to die drew near,
he charged Solomon his son, saying,
2 “[a]I am going the way of all the
earth. [b]Be strong, therefore, and
[1]show yourself a man.
3 “And keep the charge of the
LORD your God, to walk in His ways,
to keep His statutes, His commandments, His ordinances, and His testimonies, [a]according to what is written in the law of Moses, that [b]you
may succeed in all that you do and
wherever you turn,
4 so that [a]the LORD may carry out
His promise which He spoke concerning me, saying, [b]‘If your sons
are careful of their way, [c]to walk before Me in [1]truth with all their heart
and with all their soul, [2d]you shall
not lack a man on the throne of Israel.’
5 “Now you also know what Joab
the [a]son of Zeruiah did to me, what
he did to the two commanders of the
armies of Israel, to [b]Abner the son
of Ner, and to [c]Amasa the son of
Jether, whom he killed; he also
[1]shed the blood of war in peace. And
he put the blood of war on his belt
[2]about his waist, and on his sandals
[3]on his feet.
6 “[a]So act according to your wisdom, and do not let his gray hair go
down to [1]Sheol in peace.

48 [a]2 Sam. 7:12; 1 Kin. 3:6
50 [a]Ex. 27:2; 30:10; 1 Kin. 2:28
52 [a]1 Sam. 14:45; 2 Sam. 14:11
53 [1]Lit., *to*
1 [1]Lit., *days* [a]Gen. 47:29; Deut. 31:14
2 [1]Lit., *become a man* [a]Josh. 23:14 [b]Deut. 31:7, 23; Josh. 1:6, 7
3 [a]Deut. 17:18-20 [b]1 Chr. 22:12, 13
4 [1]Or, *faithfulness* [2]Lit., *there shall not be cast off to you a man from before Me* [a]2 Sam. 7:25 [b]Ps. 132:12 [c]2 Kin. 20:3 [d]2 Sam. 7:12, 13; 1 Kin. 8:25; 9:5
5 [1]Lit., *made* [2]Lit., *that was about* [3]Lit., *that were on* [a]2 Sam. 2:13, 18 [b]2 Sam. 3:27; 1 Kin. 2:32 [c]2 Sam. 20:10
6 [1]I.e., the nether world [a]1 Kin. 2:9
7 [1]Lit., *came near to* [a]2 Sam. 19:31-38 [b]2 Sam. 9:7, 10 [c]2 Sam. 17:27-29
8 [1]Or, *grievous* [a]2 Sam. 16:5-8 [b]2 Sam. 19:18-23
9 [1]I.e., the nether world [a]1 Kin. 2:6
10 [a]Acts 2:29; 13:36 [b]2 Sam. 5:7; 1 Kin. 3:1
11 [a]2 Sam. 5:4, 5; 1 Chr. 29:26, 27 [b]2 Sam. 5:5
12 [a]1 Chr. 29:23; 2 Chr. 1:1
13 [a]1 Sam. 16:4
15 [1]Lit., *set their faces on me* [a]2 Sam. 3:3, 4; 1 Kin. 2:22 [b]1 Kin. 1:5-25 [c]1 Kin. 1:38-50 [d]1 Chr. 22:9, 10; 28:5-7
16 [1]Lit., *turn away my face*
17 [1]Lit., *turn away your face* [a]2 Sam. 12:8; 1 Kin. 1:3, 4
19 [a]1 Kin. 15:13

7 “[a]But show kindness to the sons
of Barzillai the Gileadite, and [b]let
them be among those who eat at
your table; [c]for they [1]assisted me
when I fled from Absalom your
brother.
8 “And behold, [a]there is with you
Shimei the son of Gera the Benjamite, of Bahurim; now it was he who
cursed me with a [1]violent curse on
the day I went to Mahanaim. But
when [b]he came down to me at the
Jordan, I swore to him by the LORD,
saying, ‘I will not put you to death
with the sword.’
9 “Now therefore, do not let him
go unpunished, [a]for you are a wise
man; and you will know what you
ought to do to him, and you will
bring his gray hair down to [1]Sheol
with blood.”

Death of David

10 Then [a]David slept with his fathers and was buried in [b]the city of
David.
11 And [a]the days that David
reigned over Israel *were* forty years:
[b]seven years he reigned in Hebron,
and thirty-three years he reigned in
Jerusalem.
12 And [a]Solomon sat on the
throne of David his father, and his
kingdom was firmly established.
13 Now Adonijah the son of Haggith came to Bathsheba the mother
of Solomon. And she said, “Do you
[a]come peacefully?” And he said,
“Peacefully.”
14 Then he said, “I have something *to say* to you.” And she said,
“Speak.”
15 So he said, “You know that [a]the
kingdom was mine and [b]that all Israel [1]expected me to be king; [c]how-
ever, the kingdom has turned about
and become my brother’s, [d]for it
was his from the LORD.
16 “And now I am making one request of you; do not [1]refuse me.”
And she said to him, “Speak.”
17 Then he said, “Please speak to
Solomon the king, for he will not
[1]refuse you, that [a]he may give me
Abishag the Shunammite as a
wife.”
18 And Bathsheba said, “Very
well; I will speak to the king for
you.”

Adonijah Executed

19 So Bathsheba went to King
Solomon to speak to him for Adonijah. And the king arose to meet her,
bowed before her, and sat on his
throne; then he [a]had a throne set for

the king's mother, and [b]she sat on his right.

20 Then she said, "I am making one small request of you; [a]do not [1]refuse me." And the king said to her, "Ask, my mother, for I will not [2]refuse you."

21 So she said, "[a]Let Abishag the Shunammite be given to Adonijah your brother as a wife."

22 And King Solomon answered and said to his mother, "And why are you asking Abishag the Shunammite for Adonijah? [a]Ask for him also the kingdom—[b]for he is my older brother—even for him, for [c]Abiathar the priest, and for Joab the son of Zeruiah!"

23 Then King Solomon swore by the LORD, saying, "May God do so to me and more also, if Adonijah has [a]not spoken this word against his own [1]life.

24 "Now therefore as the LORD lives, who has established me and set me on the throne of David my father, and [a]who has made me a house as He promised, surely Adonijah will be put to death today."

25 So King Solomon [a]sent Benaiah the son of Jehoiada; and he fell upon him so that he died.

26 Then to Abiathar the priest the king said, "[a]Go to Anathoth to your own field, [b]for you [1]deserve to die; but I will not put you to death at this time, because [c]you carried the ark of the Lord [2]GOD before my father David, and because [d]you were afflicted in everything with which my father was afflicted."

27 So Solomon dismissed Abiathar from being priest to the LORD, in order to fulfill [a]the word of the LORD, which He had spoken concerning the house of Eli in Shiloh.

Joab Executed

28 Now the news came to Joab, [a]for Joab had followed Adonijah, [b]although he had not followed Absalom. And Joab fled to the tent of the LORD and [c]took hold of the horns of the altar.

29 And it was told King Solomon that Joab had fled to the tent of the LORD, and behold, he is beside the altar. Then Solomon [a]sent Benaiah the son of Jehoiada, saying, "Go, fall upon him."

30 So Benaiah came to the tent of the LORD, and said to him, "Thus the king has said, 'Come out.' " But he said, "No, for I will die here." And Benaiah brought the king word again, saying, "Thus spoke Joab, and thus he answered me."

31 And the king said to him, "[a]Do as he has spoken and fall upon him and bury him, [b]that you may remove from me and from my father's house the blood which Joab shed without cause.

32 "And [a]the LORD will return his blood on his own head, [b]because he fell upon two men more righteous and better than he and killed them with the sword, while my father David did not know *it:* [c]Abner the son of Ner, commander of the army of Israel, and [d]Amasa the son of Jether, commander of the army of Judah.

33 "[a]So shall their blood return on the head of Joab and on the head of his [1]descendants forever; but to David and his [1]descendants and his house and his throne, may there be peace from the LORD forever."

34 Then [a]Benaiah the son of Jehoiada went up and fell upon him and put him to death, and he was buried at his own house in the wilderness.

35 And [a]the king appointed Benaiah the son of Jehoiada over the army in his place, and the king appointed [b]Zadok the priest [c]in the place of Abiathar.

Shimei Executed

36 Now the king sent and called for [a]Shimei and said to him, "Build for yourself a house in Jerusalem and live there, and do not go out from there to any place.

37 "For it will happen on the day you go out and [a]cross over the [1]brook Kidron, you will know for certain that you shall surely die; [b]your blood shall be on your own head."

38 Shimei then said to the king, "The word is good. As my lord the king has said, so your servant will do." So Shimei lived in Jerusalem many days.

39 But it came about at the end of three years, that two of the servants of Shimei ran away [a]to Achish son of Maacah, king of Gath. And they told Shimei, saying, "Behold, your servants are in Gath."

40 Then Shimei arose and saddled his donkey, and went to Gath to Achish to look for his servants. And Shimei went and brought his servants from Gath.

41 And it was told Solomon that Shimei had gone from Jerusalem to Gath, and had returned.

42 So the king sent and called for Shimei and said to him, "Did I not make you swear by the LORD and

19 [b]Ps. 45:9
20 [1]Lit., *turn away my face* [2]Lit., *turn away your face* [a]1 Kin. 2:16
21 [a]1 Kin. 1:3, 4
22 [a]2 Sam. 12:8 [b]1 Kin. 1:6; 2:15; 1 Chr. 3:2, 5 [c]1 Kin. 1:7
23 [1]Lit., *soul* [a]Ruth 1:17
24 [a]2 Sam. 7:11, 13; 1 Chr. 22:10
25 [a]2 Sam. 8:18
26 [1]Lit., *are a man of death* [2]YHWH, usually rendered LORD [a]Josh. 21:18; Jer. 1:1 [b]1 Sam. 26:16 [c]1 Sam. 23:6; 2 Sam. 15:24-29 [d]1 Sam. 22:20-23; 23:8, 9
27 [a]1 Sam. 2:27-36
28 [a]1 Kin. 1:7 [b]2 Sam. 17:25; 18:2 [c]1 Kin. 1:50
29 [a]1 Kin. 2:25
31 [a]Ex. 21:14 [b]Num. 35:33; Deut. 19:13
32 [a]Gen. 9:6; Judg. 9:24, 57 [b]2 Chr. 21:13, 14 [c]2 Sam. 3:27 [d]2 Sam. 20:9, 10
33 [1]Lit., *seed* [a]2 Sam. 3:29
34 [a]1 Kin. 2:25
35 [a]1 Kin. 4:4 [b]1 Chr. 29:22 [c]1 Kin. 2:27
36 [a]1 Kin. 2:8
37 [1]Or, *wadi* [a]2 Sam. 15:23 [b]2 Sam. 1:16
39 [a]1 Sam. 27:2

solemnly warn you, saying, 'You
will know for certain that on the day
you depart and go anywhere, you
shall surely die'? And you said to
me, 'The word which I have heard is
good.'
43"Why then have you not kept the
oath of the LORD, and the command
which I [1]have laid on you?"
44 The king also said to Shimei,
"[a]You know all the evil which [1]you
acknowledge in your heart, which
you did to my father David; therefore [b]the LORD shall return your evil
on your own head.
45"But King Solomon shall be
blessed, and [a]the throne of David
shall be established before the LORD
forever."
46 [a]So the king commanded Benaiah the son of Jehoiada, and he went
out and fell upon him so that he
died. [b]Thus the kingdom was established in the hands of Solomon.

CHAPTER 3

Solomon's Rule Consolidated

THEN [a]Solomon [1]formed a marriage alliance with Pharaoh king of
Egypt, and took Pharaoh's daughter
[b]and brought her to the city of David, [c]until he had finished building
his own house and the house of the
LORD and [d]the wall around Jerusalem.
2 [a]The people were still sacrificing on the high places, because
there was no house built for the
name of the LORD until those days.
3 Now [a]Solomon loved the LORD,
[b]walking in the statutes of his father
David, except he sacrificed and
burned incense on the high places.
4 [a]And the king went to [b]Gibeon
to sacrifice there, [c]for that was the
great high place; Solomon offered a
thousand burnt offerings on that altar.
5 [a]In Gibeon the LORD appeared
to Solomon [b]in a dream at night; and
God said, "Ask what *you wish* me to
give you."

Solomon's Prayer

6 Then Solomon said, "[a]Thou
hast shown great lovingkindness to
Thy servant David my father, [b]ac-
cording as he walked before Thee in
[1]truth and righteousness and uprightness of heart toward Thee; and
[c]Thou hast [2]reserved for him this
great lovingkindness, that Thou
hast given him a son to sit on his
throne, as *it is* this day.
7"And now, O LORD my God,
[a]Thou hast made Thy servant king
in place of my father David, yet [b]I
am but a little child; [c]I do not know
how to go out or come in.
8"And [a]Thy servant is in the
midst of Thy people which Thou
hast chosen, [b]a great people who
cannot be numbered or counted for
multitude.
9"So [a]give Thy servant an [1]under-
standing heart to judge Thy people
[b]to discern between good and evil.
For who is able to judge this [2]great
people of Thine?"

God's Answer

10 And [1]it was pleasing in the
sight of the Lord that Solomon had
asked this thing.
11 And God said to him, "Because
you have asked this thing and have
not asked for yourself [1]long life, nor
have asked riches for yourself, nor
have you asked for the life of your
enemies, but have asked for yourself [2]discernment to understand justice,
12 behold, [a]I have done according
to your words. Behold, [b]I have given
you a wise and discerning heart, so
that there has been no one like you
before you, nor shall one like you
arise after you.
13"[a]And I have also given you
what you have not asked, both
riches and honor, so that there will
not be any among the kings like you
all your days.
14"And [a]if you walk in My ways,
keeping My statutes and commandments, as your father David walked,
then I will prolong your days."
15 Then [a]Solomon awoke, and behold, it was a dream. And he came
to Jerusalem and stood before the
ark of the covenant of the Lord, and
offered burnt offerings and made
peace offerings, and [b]made a feast
for all his servants.

Solomon Wisely Judges

16 Then two women who were
harlots came to the king and [a]stood
before him.
17 And the one woman said, "Oh,
my lord, [1]this woman and I live in
the same house; and I gave birth to
a child while she *was* in the house.
18"And it happened on the third
day after I gave birth, that this
woman also gave birth to a child,
and we were together. There was no
stranger with us in the house, only
the two of us in the house.
19"And this woman's son died in
the night, because she lay on it.
20"So she arose in the middle of

43 [1]Lit., *commanded*
44 [1]Lit., *your heart acknowledges* [a]2 Sam. 16:5-13 [b]1 Sam. 25:39; 2 Kin. 11:1, 12-16
45 [a]2 Sam. 7:13
46 [a]1 Kin. 2:25, 34 [b]1 Kin. 2:12; 2 Chr. 1:1
1 [1]Lit., *made himself a son-in-law of Pharaoh* [a]1 Kin. 7:8; 9:16, 24; 2 Chr. 8:11 [b]1 Kin. 9:24 [c]1 Kin. 7:1; 9:10 [d]1 Kin. 9:15
2 [a]Lev. 17:3-5; Deut. 12:13, 14
3 [a]Deut. 6:5; Ps. 31:23 [b]1 Kin. 2:3; 9:4; 11:4, 6, 38
4 [a]2 Chr. 1:3 [b]Josh. 18:21-25 [c]1 Chr. 16:39; 21:29
5 [a]1 Kin. 9:2; 11:9 [b]Num. 12:6; Matt. 1:20
6 [1]Or, *faithfulness* [2]Lit., *kept* [a]2 Sam. 7:8-17 [b]1 Kin. 9:4 [c]1 Kin. 1:48
7 [a]1 Chr. 22:9-13 [b]1 Chr. 29:1; Jer. 1:6, 7 [c]Num. 27:17
8 [a]Ex. 19:6; Deut. 7:6 [b]Gen. 15:5; 22:17
9 [1]Lit., *hearing* [2]Lit., *heavy* [a]Ps. 72:1, 2; Prov. 2:3-9; James 1:5 [b]2 Sam. 14:17
10 [1]Lit., *the thing*
11 [1]Lit., *many days* [2]Lit., *hearing*
12 [a]1 John 5:14, 15 [b]1 Kin. 4:29-31; 5:12
13 [a]1 Kin. 4:21-24; 10:23, 27
14 [a]1 Kin. 3:6
15 [a]Gen. 41:7 [b]1 King. 8:65
16 [a]Num. 27:2
17 [1]Lit., *I and this woman*

the night and took my son from beside me while your maidservant
slept, and laid him in her bosom,
and laid her dead son in my bosom.
21 "And when I rose in the morning
to nurse my son, behold, he was
dead; but when I looked at him carefully in the morning, behold, he was
not my son, whom I had borne."
22 Then the other woman said,
"No! For the living one is my son,
and the dead one is your son." But
[1]the first woman said, "No! For the
dead one is your son, and the living
one is my son." Thus they spoke before the king.
23 Then the king said, "[1]The one
says, 'This is my son who is living,
and your son is the dead one'; and
[1]the other says, 'No! For your son is
the dead one, and my son is the living one.'"
24 And the king said, "Get me a
sword." So they brought a sword
before the king.
25 And the king said, "Divide the
living child in two, and give half to
the one and half to the other."
26 Then the woman whose child
was the living one spoke to the king,
for [1a]she was deeply stirred over her
son and said, "Oh, my lord, give her
the living child, and by no means kill
him." But the other said, "He shall
be neither mine nor yours; divide
him!"
27 Then the king answered and
said, "Give the first woman the living child, and by no means kill him.
She is his mother."
28 When all Israel heard of the
judgment which the king had
[1]handed down, they feared the king;
for [a]they saw that the wisdom of
God was in him to [2]administer justice.

Chapter 4

Solomon's Officials

Now King Solomon was king
over all Israel.
2 And these were his officials:
Azariah the son of Zadok *was* [a]the
priest;
3 Elihoreph and Ahijah, the sons
of Shisha *were* secretaries; Jehoshaphat the son of Ahilud *was* the recorder;
4 and Benaiah the son of Jehoiada *was* over the army; and Zadok and Abiathar *were* priests;
5 and Azariah the son of Nathan
was over [a]the deputies; and Zabud
the son of Nathan, a priest, *was* the
king's friend;
6 and Ahishar was over the
household; and Adoniram the son of
Abda *was* over the men subject to
forced labor.
7 And Solomon had twelve deputies over all Israel, who [1]provided
for the king and his household; each
man had to [2]provide for a month in
the year.
8 And these are their names: Ben-
hur, in the [a]hill country of Ephraim;
9 Ben-deker in Makaz and [a]Sha-
albim and [b]Beth-shemesh and Elon-
beth-hanan;
10 Ben-hesed, in Arubboth ([a]So-
coh *was* his and all the land of [b]He-
pher);
11 Ben-abinadab, *in* all [1]the
[a]height of Dor (Taphath the daughter of Solomon was his wife);
12 Baana the son of Ahilud, *in*
[a]Taanach and Megiddo, and all
[b]Beth-shean which is beside [c]Zare-
than below Jezreel, from Beth-
shean to [d]Abel-meholah as far as
the other side of [e]Jokmeam;
13 Ben-geber, in [a]Ramoth-gilead
([b]the towns of Jair, the son of Manasseh, which are in Gilead were
his: [c]the region of Argob, which is in
Bashan, sixty great cities with walls
and bronze bars *were* his);
14 Ahinadab the son of Iddo, *in*
[a]Mahanaim;
15 [a]Ahimaaz, in Naphtali (he also
married Basemath the daughter of
Solomon);
16 Baana the son of [a]Hushai, in
Asher and [1]Bealoth;
17 Jehoshaphat the son of Paruah,
in Issachar;
18 [a]Shimei the son of Ela, in Benjamin;
19 Geber the son of Uri, in the land
of Gilead, [a]the country of Sihon king
of the Amorites and of Og king of
Bashan; and *he was* the only deputy
who *was* in the land.

Solomon's Power, Wealth and Wisdom

20 [a]Judah and Israel *were* as numerous as the sand that is on the
[1]seashore in abundance; *they* were
eating and drinking and rejoicing.
21 [1a]Now Solomon ruled over all
the kingdoms [b]from the [2]River *to*
the land of the Philistines and to the
border of Egypt; [c]*they* brought tribute and served Solomon all the days
of his life.
22 And Solomon's [1]provision for
one day was thirty [2]kors of fine flour
and sixty [2]kors of meal,
23 ten fat oxen, twenty [1]pasture-
fed oxen, a hundred sheep besides
deer, gazelles, roebucks, and fattened fowl.

22 [1]Lit., *this one was saying*
23 [1]Lit., *this one*
26 [1]Lit., *her compassion grew warm* [a]Gen. 43:30; Jer. 31:20
28 [1]Lit., *judged* [2]Lit., *do* [a]1 Kin. 3:9, 11, 12
2 [a]1 Chr. 6:10
5 [a]1 Kin. 4:7
7 [1]Lit., *nourished* [2]Lit., *nourish*
8 [a]Josh. 24:33
9 [a]Judg. 1:35 [b]Josh. 21:16
10 [a]Josh. 15:35 [b]Josh. 12:17
11 [1]Or, *Naphoth-dor* [a]Josh. 11:1, 2
12 [a]Judg. 5:19 [b]Josh. 17:11 [c]Josh. 3:16 [d]1 Kin. 19:16 [e]1 Chr. 6:68
13 [a]1 Kin. 22:3-15 [b]Num. 32:41 [c]Deut. 3:4
14 [a]Josh. 13:26
15 [a]2 Sam. 15:27
16 [1]Or, *in Aloth* [a]2 Sam. 15:32
18 [a]1 Kin. 1:8
19 [a]Deut. 3:8-10
20 [1]Lit., *sea* [a]Gen. 32:12; 1 Kin. 3:8
21 [1]Ch. 5:1 in Heb. [2]I.e., Euphrates [a]2 Chr. 9:26 [b]Gen. 15:18 [c]2 Sam. 8:2, 6
22 [1]Lit., *bread* [2]I.e., 1 kor equals approx. 10 bu.
23 [1]Lit., *oxen of the pasture*

24 For he had dominion over everything [1]west of the [2]River, from
Tiphsah even to [a]Gaza, [b]over all the
kings [1]west of the [2]River; and [c]he
had peace on all sides around about
him.
25 [a]So Judah and Israel lived in
safety, every man under his vine
and his fig tree, [b]from Dan even to
Beersheba, all the days of Solomon.
26 [a]And Solomon had [1]40,000
stalls of horses for his chariots, and
12,000 horsemen.
27 And those deputies [1]provided
for King Solomon and all who came
to King Solomon's table, each in his
month; they left nothing lacking.
28 They also brought barley and
straw for the horses and [a]swift
steeds to the place where it should
be, each according to his charge.
29 Now [a]God gave Solomon wisdom and very great discernment
and breadth of [1]mind, [b]like the sand
that is on the seashore.
30 And Solomon's wisdom surpassed the wisdom of all [a]the sons
of the east and [b]all the wisdom of
Egypt.
31 For [a]he was wiser than all men,
than [b]Ethan the Ezrahite, Heman,
[c]Calcol and Darda, the sons of Ma-
hol; and his [1]fame was *known* in all
the surrounding nations.
32 [a]He also spoke 3,000 proverbs,
and his songs were 1,005.
33 And he spoke of trees, from the
cedar that is in Lebanon even to the
hyssop that grows on the wall; he
spoke also of animals and birds and
creeping things and fish.
34 And [1]men [a]came from all peoples to hear the wisdom of Solomon,
from all the kings of the earth who
had heard of his wisdom.

Chapter 5

Alliance with King Hiram

1a
NOW Hiram king of Tyre sent his
servants to Solomon, when he heard
that they had anointed him king in
place of his father, for [b]Hiram had
[2]always been a friend of David.
2 Then Solomon sent *word* to Hiram, saying,
3"You know that [a]David my father was unable to build a house for
the name of the LORD his God because of the wars which surrounded
him, until the LORD put them under
the soles of his feet.
4"But now [a]the LORD my God has
given me rest on every side; there is
neither adversary nor [1]misfortune.
5"And behold, [a]I [1]intend to build
a house for the name of the LORD my
God, as the LORD spoke to David my
father, saying, 'Your son, whom I
will set on your throne in your place,
he will build the house for My
name.'
6"Now therefore, command that
they cut for me cedars from Lebanon, and my servants will be with
your servants; and I will give you
wages for your servants according
to all that you say, for you know that
there is no one among us who
knows how to cut timber like the
Sidonians."
7 And it came about when Hiram
heard the words of Solomon, that he
rejoiced greatly and said, "Blessed
be the LORD today, who has given to
David a wise son over this great
people."
8 So Hiram sent *word* to Solomon, saying, "I have heard *the message* which you have sent me; I will
do [1]what you desire concerning the
cedar and cypress timber.
9"My servants will bring *them*
down from Lebanon to the sea; and
I will make them into rafts *to go* by
sea [a]to the place where you [1]direct
me, and I will have them broken up
there, and you shall carry *them*
away. Then [b]you shall accomplish
my desire by giving food to my
household."
10 So [1]Hiram [2]gave Solomon [3]as
much as he desired of the cedar and
cypress timber.
11 Solomon then gave Hiram
20,000 [1]kors of wheat as food for his
household, and twenty [1]kors of
beaten oil; thus Solomon would give
Hiram year by year.
12 And [a]the LORD gave wisdom to
Solomon, just as He [1]promised him;
and there was peace between Hiram
and Solomon, and the two of them
made a covenant.

Conscription of Laborers

13 Now [a]King Solomon [1]levied
forced laborers from all Israel; and
the forced laborers [2]numbered
30,000 men.
14 And he sent them to Lebanon,
10,000 a month in relays; they were
in Lebanon a month *and* two
months at home. And [a]Adoniram
was over the forced laborers.
15 Now [a]Solomon had 70,000
[1]transporters, and 80,000 hewers *of
stone* in the mountains,
16 [a]besides Solomon's 3,300 chief
deputies who *were* over the [1]project
and who ruled over the people who
were doing the work.

24 [1]Lit., *beyond* [2]I.e., Euphrates [a]Judg. 1:18 [b]Ps. 72:11 [c]1 Chr. 22:9
25 [a]Jer. 23:6; Mic. 4:4; Zech. 3:10 [b]1 Sam. 3:20
26 [1]One ms. reads *4000*, cf. 2 Chr. 9:25 [a]1 Kin. 10:26
27 [1]Or, *nourished*
28 [a]Esth. 8:10, 14; Mic. 1:13
29 [1]Lit., *heart* [a]1 Kin. 3:12 [b]1 Kin. 4:20
30 [a]Gen. 29:1; Judg. 6:33 [b]Is. 19:11; Acts 7:22
31 [1]Lit., *name* [a]1 Kin. 3:12 [b]1 Chr. 15:19; Ps. 89: title [c]1 Chr. 2:6
32 [a]Prov. 1:1; Eccles. 12:9; Song of Sol. 1:1
34 [1]Lit., *they* [a]1 Kin. 10:1; 2 Chr. 9:23
1 [1]Ch. 5:15 in Heb. [2]Lit., *all the day* [a]2 Chr. 2:3 [b]2 Sam. 5:11; 1 Chr. 14:1
3 [a]1 Chr. 28:2, 3
4 [1]Lit., *evil occurrence* [a]1 Kin. 4:24; 1 Chr. 22:9
5 [1]Lit., *say* [a]2 Sam. 7:12, 13; 1 Chr. 17:12; 22:10; 28:6
8 [1]Lit., *all your pleasure*
9 [1]Lit., *send* [a]2 Chr. 2:16 [b]Ezra 3:7; Ezek. 27:17
10 [1]Heb., *Hirom* [2]Lit., *was giving* [3]Lit., *all his desire*
11 [1]I.e., 1 kor equals approx. 10 bu.
12 [1]Lit., *spoke to* [a]1 Kin. 3:12
13 [1]Lit., *raised up* [2]Lit., *was* [a]1 Kin. 4:6; 9:15
14 [a]1 Kin. 4:6
15 [1]Or, *burden bearers* [a]1 Kin. 9:20-22; 2 Chr. 2:17, 18
16 [1]Lit., *work* [a]1 Kin. 9:23

17 Then [a]the king commanded, and they quarried great stones, costly stones, to lay the foundation of the house with cut stones.

18 So Solomon's builders and [1]Hiram's builders and [a]the Gebalites [2]cut them, and prepared the timbers and the stones to build the house.

Chapter 6

The Building of the Temple

[a]NOW it came about in the four hundred and eightieth year after the sons of Israel came out of the land of Egypt, in the fourth year of Solomon's reign over Israel, in the month of Ziv which is the second month, that he [1]began to build the house of the LORD.

2 As for the house which King Solomon built for the LORD, its length *was* sixty [1]cubits and its width twenty *cubits* and its height thirty cubits.

3 And the porch in front of the nave of the house *was* twenty cubits [1]in length, [2]corresponding to the width of the house, *and* its [3]depth along the front of the house *was* ten cubits.

4 Also for the house [a]he made windows with *artistic* frames.

5 And [a]against the wall of the house he built stories encompassing the walls of the house around both the nave and the [b]inner sanctuary; thus he made [c]side chambers all around.

6 The lowest story *was* five cubits wide, and the middle *was* six cubits wide, and the third *was* seven cubits wide; for on the outside he [1]made offsets *in the wall* of the house all around in order that *the beams* should not [2]be inserted in the walls of the house.

7 And [a]the house, while it was being built, was built of stone [1]prepared at the quarry, and there was neither hammer nor axe nor any iron tool heard in the house while it was being built.

8 The doorway for the [1]lowest side chamber *was* on the right side of the house; and they would go up by winding stairs to the middle *story,* and from the middle to the third.

9 So [a]he built the house and finished it; and he covered the house with beams and [1]planks of cedar.

10 He also built the stories against the whole house, each five [1]cubits high; and they [2]were fastened to the house with timbers of cedar.

11 Now the word of the LORD came to Solomon saying,

12 "*Concerning* this house which you are building, [a]if you will walk in My statutes and execute My ordinances and keep all My commandments by walking in them, then I will carry out My word with you which I spoke to David your father.

13 "And [a]I will dwell among the sons of Israel, and [b]will not forsake My people Israel."

14 [a]So Solomon built the house and finished it.

15 Then he built the walls of the house on the inside with boards of cedar; from the floor of the house to the [1]ceiling he overlaid *the walls* on the inside with wood, and [a]he overlaid the floor of the house with boards of cypress.

16 [a]And he built twenty cubits on the rear part of the house with boards of cedar from the floor to the [1]ceiling; he built *them* for it on the inside as an inner sanctuary, *even* as [b]the most holy place.

17 And the house, that is, the nave in front of *the inner sanctuary,* was forty [1]cubits *long.*

18 And there was cedar on the house within, carved *in the shape* of [a]gourds and open flowers; all was cedar, there was no stone seen.

19 Then he prepared an inner sanctuary within the house in order to place there the ark of the covenant of the LORD.

20 And [1]the inner sanctuary *was* twenty cubits in length, twenty cubits in width, and twenty cubits in height, and he overlaid it with pure gold. He also overlaid the altar with cedar.

21 So Solomon overlaid the inside of the house with pure gold. And he drew chains of gold across the front of the inner sanctuary; and he overlaid it with gold.

22 And he overlaid the whole house with gold, until all the house was finished. Also [a]the whole altar which was by the inner sanctuary he overlaid with gold.

23 [a]Also in the inner sanctuary [b]he made two cherubim of olive wood, each ten cubits high.

24 And five cubits *was* the one wing of the cherub and five cubits the other wing of the cherub; from the end of one wing to the end of the other wing *were* ten cubits.

25 And the other cherub *was* ten cubits; both the cherubim were of

17 [a]1 Kin. 6:7; 1 Chr. 22:2

18 [1]Heb., *Hirom's* [2]Or, *chiseled* [a]Josh. 13:5; Ezek. 27:9

1 [1]Lit., *built* [a]2 Chr. 3:1, 2

2 [1]I.e., One cubit equals approx. 18 inches

3 [1]Lit., *in its length* [2]Lit., *on the face of* [3]Lit., *width*

4 [a]Ezek. 40:16; 41:16

5 [a]Ezek. 41:6 [b]1 Kin. 6:16, 19, 20 [c]Ezek. 41:5, 6

6 [1]Lit., *gave* [2]Lit., *take hold*

7 [1]Lit., *finished* [a]Ex. 20:25; Deut. 27:5, 6

8 [1]So with Gk. & versions; M.T., *middle*

9 [1]Lit., *rows* [a]1 Kin. 6:14, 38

10 [1]I.e., One cubit equals approx. 18 inches [2]Lit., *took hold*

12 [a]2 Sam. 7:5-16; 1 Kin. 9:4

13 [a]Ex. 25:8 [b]Deut. 31:6; Josh. 1:5

14 [a]1 Kin. 6:9, 38

15 [1]Lit., *walls of ceiling* [a]1 Kin. 7:7

16 [1]Lit., *walls* [a]2 Chr. 3:8 [b]Ex. 26:33, 34; 1 Kin. 8:6

17 [1]One cubit equals approx. 18 in.

18 [a]1 Kin. 7:24

20 [1]Lit., *before*

22 [a]Ex. 30:1, 3, 6

23 [a]2 Chr. 3:10-12 [b]Ex. 37:7-9

the same measure and the same
form.
26 The height of the one cherub
was ten cubits, and so *was* the other
cherub.
27 And he placed the cherubim in
the midst of the inner house, and
[a]the wings of the cherubim were
spread out, so that the wing of the
one was touching the *one* wall, and
the wing of the other cherub was
touching the other wall. So their
wings were touching each other in
the center of the house.
28 He also overlaid the cherubim
with gold.
29 Then he carved all the walls of
the house round about with carved
engravings of cherubim, palm trees,
and open flowers, inner and outer
sanctuaries.
30 And he overlaid the floor of the
house with gold, inner and outer
sanctuaries.
31 And for the entrance of the inner sanctuary he made doors of olive wood, the lintel *and* five-sided
doorposts.
32 So *he made* two doors of olive
wood, and he carved on them carv-
ings of cherubim, palm trees, and
open flowers, and overlaid them
with gold; and he spread the gold on
the cherubim and on the palm trees.
33 So also he made for the entrance of the nave four-sided doorposts of olive wood
34 and [a]two doors of cypress
wood; the two leaves of the one door
turned on pivots, and the two
[1]leaves of the other door turned on
pivots.
35 And he carved *on it* cherubim,
palm trees, and open flowers; and he
overlaid *them* with gold evenly applied on the engraved work.
36 And [a]he built the inner court
with three rows of cut stone and a
row of cedar beams.
37 [a]In the fourth year the foundation of the house of the LORD was
laid, in the month of Ziv.
38 And in the eleventh year, in the
month of Bul, which is the eighth
month, the house was finished
throughout all its parts and according to all its plans. So he was seven
years in building it.

CHAPTER 7

Solomon's Palace

NOW [a]Solomon was building his
own house thirteen years, and he
finished all his house.
2 And [a]he built the house of the
forest of Lebanon; its length was
100 [1]cubits and its width 50 cubits
and its height 30 cubits, on four
rows of cedar pillars with cedar
beams on the pillars.
3 And it was paneled with cedar
above the side chambers which
were on the 45 pillars, 15 in each
row.
4 And *there were artistic window*
frames in three rows, and window
was opposite window in three
ranks.
5 And all the doorways and doorposts had squared *artistic* frames,
and window was opposite window
in three ranks.
6 Then he made [a]the hall of pillars; its length was 50 cubits and its
width 30 cubits, and a porch *was* in
front of them and pillars and a
[b]threshold in front of them.
7 And he made the hall of the
throne where he was to judge, the
hall of judgment, and [a]it was paneled with cedar from floor to floor.
8 And his house where he was to
live, the other court inward from the
hall, was of the same workmanship.
[a]He also made a house like this hall
for Pharaoh's daughter, [b]whom
Solomon had married.
9 All these were of costly stones,
of stone cut according to measure,
sawed with saws, inside and outside; even from the foundation to
the coping, and so on the outside to
the great court.
10 And the foundation was of
costly stones, *even* large stones,
stones of ten cubits and stones of
eight cubits.
11 And above were costly stones,
stone cut according to measure, and
cedar.
12 So [a]the great court all around
had three rows of cut stone and a
row of cedar beams even as the inner court of the house of the LORD,
and [b]the porch of the house.

Hiram's Work in the Temple

13 Now [a]King Solomon sent and
brought Hiram from Tyre.
14 [a]He was a widow's son from the
tribe of Naphtali, and his father was
a man of Tyre, a worker in bronze;
and [b]he was filled with wisdom and
understanding and skill for doing
any work in bronze. So he came to
King Solomon and [c]performed all
his work.
15 And he fashioned [a]the two pillars of bronze, [b]eighteen cubits was
the height of one pillar, and a line of
twelve cubits [1]measured the circumference of both.
16 He also made two capitals of

27 [a]Ex. 25:20; 37:9; 1 Kin. 8:7
34 [1]So with Gk.; M.T., *curtains* [a]Ezek. 41:23-25
36 [a]1 Kin. 7:12; Jer. 36:10
37 [a]1 Kin. 6:1
1 [a]1 Kin. 3:1; 9:10; 2 Chr. 8:1
2 [1]I.e., One cubit equals approx. 18 inches [a]1 Kin. 10:17, 21; 2 Chr. 9:16
6 [a]1 Kin. 7:12 [b]Ezek. 41:25, 26
7 [a]1 Kin. 6:15, 16
8 [a]1 Kin. 9:24; 2 Chr. 8:11 [b]1 Kin. 3:1
12 [a]1 Kin. 6:36 [b]1 Kin. 7:6
13 [a]2 Chr. 2:13, 14
14 [a]2 Chr. 2:14 [b]Ex. 31:3-5; 35:31 [c]2 Chr. 4:11-16
15 [1]Lit., *went around the other pillar* [a]2 Kin. 25:17 [b]1 Kin. 7:41

molten bronze to set on the tops of the pillars; the height of the one capital was five [1]cubits and the height of the other capital was five cubits.

17 *There were* nets of network and twisted threads of chainwork for the capitals which were on the top of the pillars; seven for the one capital and seven for the other capital.

18 So he made the pillars, and two rows around on the one network to cover the capitals which were on the top of the pomegranates; and so he did for the other capital.

19 And the capitals which *were* on the top of the pillars in the porch were of lily design, four cubits.

20 And *there were* capitals also on the two pillars, close to the [1]rounded projection which was beside the network; and [a]the pomegranates *numbered* two hundred in rows around [2]both capitals.

21 [a]Thus he set up the pillars at the porch of the nave; and he set up the right pillar and named it [1]Jachin, and he set up the left pillar and named it [2]Boaz.

22 And on the top of the pillars was lily design. So the work of the pillars was finished.

23 [a]Now he made the sea of [b]cast *metal* ten cubits from brim to brim, circular in form, and its height was five cubits, and [1]thirty cubits in circumference.

24 And under its brim [a]gourds went around encircling it ten to a cubit, completely surrounding the sea; the gourds were in two rows, cast [1]with the rest.

25 [a]It stood on twelve oxen, three facing north, three facing west, three facing south, and three facing east; and the sea *was set* on top of them, and all their rear parts *turned* inward.

26 And it was a handbreadth thick, and its brim was made like the brim of a cup, *as* a lily blossom; it could hold two thousand baths.

27 Then [a]he made the ten stands of bronze; the length of each stand was four cubits and its width four cubits and its height three cubits.

28 And this was the design of the stands: they had borders, even borders between the [1]frames,

29 and on the borders which were between the [1]frames *were* lions, oxen and cherubim; and on the [1]frames there *was* a pedestal above, and beneath the lions and oxen *were* wreaths of hanging work.

30 Now each stand had four bronze wheels with bronze axles, and its four feet had supports; beneath the basin *were* cast supports with wreaths at each side.

31 And its opening inside the crown at the top *was* a cubit, and its opening *was* round like the design of a pedestal, a cubit and a half; and also on its opening *there were* engravings, and their borders were square, not round.

32 And the four wheels *were* underneath the borders, and the axles of the wheels *were* on the stand. And the height of a wheel *was* a cubit and a half.

33 And the workmanship of the wheels *was* like the workmanship of a chariot wheel. Their axles, their rims, their spokes, and their hubs *were* all cast.

34 Now *there were* four supports at the four corners of each stand; its supports *were* part of the stand itself.

35 And on the top of the stand *there was* a circular form half a [1]cubit high, and on the top of the stand its [2]stays and its borders *were* part of it.

36 And he engraved on the plates of its stays and on its borders, cherubim, lions and palm trees, according to the clear space on each, with wreaths *all* around.

37 [a]He made the ten stands like this: all of them had one casting, one measure and one form.

38 [a]And he made ten basins of bronze, one basin held forty baths; each basin *was* four cubits, *and* on each of the ten stands *was* one basin.

39 Then he set the stands, five on the right side of the house and five on the left side of the house; and he set the sea of cast metal on the right side of the house eastward toward the south.

40 Now Hiram made the basins and the shovels and the bowls. So Hiram finished doing all the work which he performed for King Solomon *in* the house of the LORD:

41 the two pillars and the two bowls of the capitals which *were* on the top of the [a]two pillars, and the two networks to cover the two bowls of the capitals which *were* on the top of the pillars;

42 and the [a]four hundred pomegranates for the two networks, two rows of pomegranates for each network to cover the two bowls of the capitals which *were* on the tops of the pillars;

43 and the ten stands with the ten basins on the stands;

16 [1]I.e., Approx. 18 inches

20 [1]Lit., *belly* [2]Lit., *on the other capital* [a]1 Kin. 7:42; 2 Chr. 3:16

21 [1]I.e., He shall establish [2]I.e., In it is strength [a]2 Chr. 3:17

23 [1]Lit., *a line of 30 cubits went around it* [a]2 Chr. 4:2 [b]2 Kin. 16:17; 25:13

24 [1]Lit., *in its casting* [a]1 Kin. 6:18

25 [a]Jer. 52:20

27 [a]1 Kin. 7:38; 2 Kin. 25:13; 2 Chr. 4:14

28 [1]Or, *crossbars*

29 [1]Or, *crossbars*

35 [1]I.e., Approx. 18 inches [2]Lit., *hands*

37 [a]2 Chr. 4:14

38 [a]2 Chr. 4:6

41 [a]1 Kin. 7:17, 18

42 [a]1 Kin. 7:20

44 and [a]the one sea and the twelve
oxen under the sea;
45 and the pails and the shovels
and the bowls; even all these utensils which Hiram made for King
Solomon *in* the house of the LORD
were of polished bronze.
46 [a]In the plain of the Jordan the
king cast them, in the clay ground
between [b]Succoth and [c]Zarethan.
47 And Solomon left all the utensils *unweighed*, because *they were*
too many; [a]the weight of the bronze
could not be ascertained.
48 And Solomon made all the furniture which *was in* the house of the
LORD: [a]the golden altar and the
golden table on which *was* the bread
of the Presence;
49 and the lampstands, five on the
right side and five on the left, in
front of the inner sanctuary, of pure
gold; and [a]the flowers and the lamps
and the tongs, of gold;
50 and the cups and the snuffers
and the bowls and the spoons and
the [a]firepans, of pure gold; and the
hinges both for the doors of the inner house, the most holy place, *and*
for the doors of the house, *that is*, of
the nave, of gold.
51 [a]Thus all the work that King
Solomon performed *in* the house of
the LORD was finished. And [b]Solo-
mon brought in the things dedicated
by his father David, the silver and
the gold and the utensils, *and* he *put*
them in the treasuries of the house
of the LORD.

CHAPTER 8

The Ark Brought into the Temple

[a]THEN Solomon assembled the elders of Israel and all [b]the heads of
the tribes, the leaders of the fathers'
households of the sons of Israel, to
King Solomon in Jerusalem, [c]to
bring up the ark of the covenant of
the LORD from [d]the city of David,
which is Zion.
2 And all the men of Israel assembled themselves to King Solomon at [a]the feast, in the month Eth-
anim, which is the seventh month.
3 Then all the elders of Israel
came, and [a]the priests took up the
ark.
4 And they brought up the ark of
the LORD and [a]the tent of meeting
and all the holy utensils, which were
in the tent, and the priests and the
Levites brought them up.
5 And King Solomon and all the
congregation of Israel, who were assembled to him, [a]were with him before the ark, sacrificing [1]so many
sheep and oxen they could not be
counted or numbered.
6 Then [a]the priests brought the
ark of the covenant of the LORD [b]to
its place, into the inner sanctuary of
the house, to the most holy place,
[c]under the wings of the cherubim.
7 For the cherubim spread *their*
wings over the place of the ark, and
the cherubim made a covering over
the ark and its poles from above.
8 But [a]the poles were so long that
the ends of the poles could be seen
from the holy place before the inner
sanctuary, but they could not be
seen outside; they are there to this
day.
9 [a]There was nothing in the ark
except the two tablets of stone
which Moses put there at Horeb,
where [b]the LORD made a covenant
with the sons of Israel, when they
came out of the land of Egypt.
10 And it came about when the
priests came from the holy place,
that [a]the cloud filled the house of
the LORD,
11 so that the priests could not
stand to minister because of the
cloud, for the glory of the LORD filled
the house of the LORD.

Solomon Addresses the People

12 [a]Then Solomon said, "The
LORD has said that [b]He would dwell
in the thick cloud.
13 "[a]I have surely built Thee a lofty house,
[b]A place for Thy dwelling forever."
14 Then the king [1]faced about and
[a]blessed all the assembly of Israel,
while all the assembly of Israel was
standing.
15 And he said, "[a]Blessed be the
LORD, the God of Israel, [b]who spoke
with His mouth to my father David
and has fulfilled *it* with His hand,
saying,
16 '[a]Since the day that I brought
My people Israel from Egypt, I did
not choose a city out of all the tribes
of Israel *in which* to build a house
that [b]My name might be there, but [c]I
chose David to be over My people
Israel.'
17 "[a]Now it was [1]in the heart of my
father David to build a house for the
name of the LORD, the God of Israel.
18 "But the LORD said to my father
David, 'Because it was [1]in your
heart to build a house for My name,
you did well that it was [1]in your
heart.
19 '[a]Nevertheless you shall not
build the house, but your son who

44 [a]1 Kin. 7:23, 25
46 [a]2 Chr. 4:17 [b]Josh. 13:27 [c]Josh. 3:16
47 [a]1 Chr. 22:3, 14
48 [a]Ex. 37:10-29; 2 Chr. 4:8
49 [a]Ex. 25:31-38
50 [a]Ex. 27:3; 2 Kin. 25:15
51 [a]2 Chr. 5:1 [b]2 Sam. 8:11; 2 Chr. 5:1
1 [a]2 Chr. 5:2-10 [b]Num. 1:4; 7:2 [c]2 Sam. 6:17 [d]2 Sam. 5:7
2 [a]Lev. 23:34; 1 Kin. 8:65; 2 Chr. 7:8-10
3 [a]Num. 7:9
4 [a]1 Kin. 3:4; 2 Chr. 1:3
5 [1]Lit., *sheep, numbered for multitude* [a]2 Sam. 6:13; 2 Chr. 1:6
6 [a]1 Kin. 8:3 [b]1 Kin. 6:19 [c]1 Kin. 6:27
8 [a]Ex. 25:13-15; 37:4, 5
9 [a]Ex. 25:16, 21; Deut. 10:2-5; Heb. 9:4 [b]Ex. 24:7, 8; Deut. 4:13
10 [a]Ex. 40:34, 35; 2 Chr. 7:1, 2
12 [a]2 Chr. 6:1 [b]Ps. 97:2
13 [a]2 Sam. 7:13 [b]Ex. 15:17
14 [1]Lit., *turned his face about* [a]2 Sam. 6:18; 1 Kin. 8:55
15 [a]1 Chr. 29:10, 20; Neh. 9:5 [b]2 Sam. 7:12, 13; 1 Chr. 22:10
16 [a]2 Sam. 7:4, 5 [b]Deut. 12:5, 11 [c]1 Sam. 16:1; 2 Sam. 7:8
17 [1]Lit., *with* [a]2 Sam. 7:2, 3; 1 Chr. 17:1, 2
18 [1]Lit., *with*
19 [a]2 Sam. 7:5, 12, 13; 1 Kin. 5:3, 5; 1 Chr. 22:8-10

[1]shall be born to you, he shall build
the house for My name.'
20"Now the LORD has fulfilled His
word which He spoke; for [a]I have
risen in place of my father David
and sit on the throne of Israel, as the
LORD [1]promised, and have built the
house for the name of the LORD, the
God of Israel.
21"And there I have set a place for
the ark, [a]in which is the covenant of
the LORD, which He made with our
fathers when He brought them from
the land of Egypt."

The Prayer of Dedication

22 Then [a]Solomon stood before
the altar of the LORD in the presence
of all the assembly of Israel and
[b]spread out his hands toward
heaven.
23 And he said, "O LORD, the God
of Israel, [a]there is no God like Thee
in heaven above or on earth beneath, [b]who art keeping covenant
and showing lovingkindness to Thy
servants who walk before Thee with
all their heart,
24 who hast kept with Thy servant, my father David, that which
Thou hast [1]promised him; indeed,
Thou hast spoken with Thy mouth
and hast fulfilled it with Thy hand as
it is this day.
25"Now therefore, O LORD, the
God of Israel, keep with Thy servant
David my father that which Thou
hast [1]promised him, saying, '[2][a]You
shall not lack a man to sit on the
throne of Israel, if only your sons
take heed to their way to walk before Me as you have walked.'
26"Now therefore, O God of Israel,
let Thy word, I pray Thee, be confirmed [a]which Thou hast spoken to
Thy servant, my father David.
27"But will God indeed dwell on
the earth? Behold, [a]heaven and the
[1]highest heaven cannot contain
Thee, how much less this house
which I have built!
28"Yet have regard to the prayer of
Thy servant and to his supplication,
O LORD my God, to listen to the cry
and to the prayer which Thy servant
prays before Thee today;
29 [a]that Thine eyes may be open
toward this house night and day,
toward the place of which Thou hast
said, 'My name shall be there,' to
listen to the prayer which Thy servant shall pray toward this place.
30"And listen to the supplication
of Thy servant and of Thy people
Israel, [a]when they pray toward this
place; hear Thou in heaven Thy
dwelling place; hear and forgive.

31"[a]If a man sins against his neighbor and is made to take an oath, and
he comes *and* takes an oath before
Thine altar in this house,
32 then hear Thou in heaven and
act and judge Thy servants, [a]con-
demning the wicked by bringing his
way on his own head and justifying
the righteous by giving him according to his righteousness.
33"[a]When Thy people Israel are
[1]defeated before an enemy, because
they have sinned against Thee, [b]if
they turn to Thee again and confess
Thy name and pray and make supplication to Thee in this house,
34 then hear Thou in heaven, and
forgive the sin of Thy people Israel,
and bring them back to the land
which Thou didst give to their fathers.
35"[a]When the heavens are shut up
and there is no rain, because they
have sinned against Thee, and they
pray toward this place and confess
Thy name and turn from their sin
when Thou dost afflict them,
36 then hear Thou in heaven and
forgive the sin of Thy servants and
of Thy people Israel, [a]indeed, teach
them the good way in which they
should walk. And [b]send rain on Thy
land, which Thou hast given Thy
people for an inheritance.
37"[a]If there is famine in the land, if
there is pestilence, if there is blight
or mildew, locust *or* grasshopper, if
their enemy besieges them in the
land of their [1]cities, whatever
plague, whatever sickness there is,
38 whatever prayer or supplication is made by any man *or* by all
Thy people Israel, [1]each knowing
the [2]affliction of his own heart, and
spreading his [3]hands toward this
house;
39 then hear Thou in heaven Thy
dwelling place, and forgive and act
and render to each according to all
his ways, [a]whose heart Thou knowest, for [b]Thou alone dost know the
hearts of all the sons of men,
40 that they may [1]fear Thee all the
days that they live [2]in the land
which Thou hast given to our fathers.
41"Also concerning the foreigner
who is not of Thy people Israel,
when he comes from a far country
for Thy name's sake
42 (for they will hear of Thy great
name [a]and Thy mighty hand, and of
Thine outstretched arm); when he
comes and prays toward this house,
43 hear Thou in heaven Thy dwelling place, and do according to all for
which the foreigner calls to Thee, in

19 [1]Lit., *is to come forth from your loins*

20 [1]Lit., *spoke* [a]1 Chr. 28:5, 6

21 [a]1 Kin. 8:9

22 [a]1 Kin. 8:54 [b]Ex. 9:33; Ezra 9:5

23 [a]1 Sam. 2:2; 2 Sam. 7:22 [b]Deut. 7:9; Neh. 1:5; 9:32

24 [1]Lit., *spoken to*

25 [1]Lit., *spoken to* [2]Lit., *There shall not be cut off to you a man from before Me.* [a]1 Kin. 2:4

26 [a]2 Sam. 7:25

27 [1]Lit., *heaven of heavens* [a]Ps. 139:7-16; Is. 66:1; Jer. 23:24; Acts 7:49

29 [a]2 Chr. 7:15; Neh. 1:6

30 [a]Dan. 6:10

31 [a]Ex. 22:8-11

32 [a]Deut. 25:1

33 [1]Lit., *smitten* [a]Lev. 26:17, 25; Deut. 28:25, 48 [b]Lev. 26:40-42

35 [a]Lev. 26:19; Deut. 11:16, 17; 2 Sam. 24:10-13

36 [a]1 Sam. 12:23; Ps. 27:11 [b]1 Kin. 18:1, 41-45; Jer. 14:22

37 [1]Lit., *gates* [a]Lev. 26:16, 25, 26; Deut. 28:21-23, 38-42

38 [1]Lit., *who shall know each* [2]Lit., *plague* [3]Lit., *palms*

39 [a]1 Sam. 2:3; 16:7 [b]1 Chr. 28:9; Jer. 17:10; John 2:24, 25

40 [1]Or, *revere* [2]Lit., *on the face of the land*

42 [a]Ex. 13:3; Deut. 3:24

order [a]that all the peoples of the earth may know Thy name, to [1]fear Thee, as *do* Thy people Israel, and that they may know that [2]this house which I have built is called by Thy name.

44"When Thy people go out to battle against [1]their enemy, by whatever way Thou shalt send them, and [a]they pray to the LORD [2]toward the city which Thou hast chosen and the house which I have built for Thy name,

45 then hear in heaven their prayer and their supplication, and maintain their [1]cause.

46"When they sin against Thee (for [a]there is no man who does not sin) and Thou art angry with them and dost deliver them to an enemy, so that [1]they take them away captive [b]to the land of the enemy, far off or near,

47 [a]if they [1]take thought in the land where they have been taken captive, and repent and make supplication to Thee in the land of those who have taken them captive, saying, '[b]We have sinned and have committed iniquity, we have acted wickedly,'

48 [a]if they return to Thee with all their heart and with all their soul in the land of their enemies who have taken them captive, and [b]pray to Thee toward their land which Thou hast given to their fathers, the city which Thou hast chosen, and the house which I have built for Thy name,

49 then hear their prayer and their supplication in heaven Thy dwelling place, and maintain their [1]cause,

50 and forgive Thy people who have sinned against Thee and all their transgressions which they have transgressed against Thee, and [a]make them *objects of* compassion before those who have taken them captive, that they may have compassion on them

51 ([a]for they are Thy people and Thine inheritance which Thou hast brought forth from Egypt, [b]from the midst of the iron furnace),

52 [a]that Thine eyes may be open to the supplication of Thy servant and to the supplication of Thy people Israel, to listen to them whenever they call to Thee.

53"For Thou hast separated them from all the peoples of the earth as Thine inheritance, [a]as Thou didst speak through Moses Thy servant, when Thou didst bring our fathers forth from Egypt, O Lord [1]GOD."

43 [1]Or, *reverence* [2]Lit., *Thy name is called upon this house which I have built* [a]Josh. 4:23; 1 Sam. 17:46
44 [1]Lit., *his* [2]Lit., *in the way of* [a]2 Chr. 14:11, 12
45 [1]Lit., *right* or *justice*
46 [1]Lit., *their captors take them captive* [a]Ps. 130:3, 4; Prov. 20:9; 1 John 1:8-10 [b]Lev. 26:34-39; 2 Kin. 17:6, 18; 25:21
47 [1]Lit., *return to their heart* [a]Lev. 26:40-42; Neh. 9:2 [b]Ezra 9:6, 7; Neh. 1:6
48 [a]Deut. 4:29; 1 Sam. 7:3, 4; Neh. 1:9 [b]Dan. 6:10; Jon. 2:4
49 [1]Lit., *judgment*
50 [a]2 Chr. 30:9; Acts 7:10
51 [a]Ex. 32:11, 12; Deut. 9:26-29 [b]Deut. 4:20; Jer. 11:4
52 [a]1 Kin. 8:29
53 [1]YHWH, usually rendered LORD [a]Ex. 19:5, 6; Deut. 9:26-29
54 [1]Lit., *palms* [a]2 Chr. 7:1 [b]2 Chr. 6:13
55 [a]Num. 6:23-26; 1 Kin. 8:14
56 [1]Lit., *spoke* [2]Lit., *fallen* [3]Lit., *word* [a]Josh. 21:45; 23:14, 15
57 [a]Josh. 1:5; 1 Sam. 12:22; Rom. 8:31; Heb. 13:5
58 [a]Ps. 119:36; Jer. 31:33
59 [1]Lit., *judgment*
60 [a]1 Kin. 8:43 [b]1 Kin. 18:39; Jer. 10:10-12
61 [1]Lit., *complete with* [a]Deut. 18:13; 2 Kin. 20:3
62 [a]2 Chr. 7:4-10 [b]2 Sam. 6:17-19; Ezra 6:16, 17
63 [a]Ezra 6:15-18; Neh. 12:27
64 [1]Lit., *made* [a]2 Chr. 4:1
65 [a]Lev. 23:34-42; 1 Kin. 8:2 [b]Num. 34:8; Josh. 13:5 [c]Gen. 15:18; Ex. 23:31; Josh. 13:3

Solomon's Benediction

54 [a]And it came about that when Solomon had finished praying this entire prayer and supplication to the LORD, [b]he arose from before the altar of the LORD, from kneeling on his knees with his [1]hands spread toward heaven.

55 And he stood and [a]blessed all the assembly of Israel with a loud voice, saying,

56"Blessed be the LORD, who has given rest to His people Israel, according to all that He [1]promised; [a]not one word has [2]failed of all His good [3]promise, which He [1]promised through Moses His servant.

57"May the LORD our God be with us, as He was with our fathers; [a]may He not leave us or forsake us,

58 that [a]He may incline our hearts to Himself, to walk in all His ways and to keep His commandments and His statutes and His ordinances, which He commanded our fathers.

59"And may these words of mine, with which I have made supplication before the LORD, be near to the LORD our God day and night, that He may maintain the [1]cause of His servant and the [1]cause of His people Israel, as each day requires,

60 so [a]that all the peoples of the earth may know that [b]the LORD is God; there is no one else.

61"[a]Let your heart therefore be [1]wholly devoted to the LORD our God, to walk in His statutes and to keep His commandments, as at this day."

Dedicatory Sacrifices

62 [a]Now the king and all Israel with him [b]offered sacrifice before the LORD.

63 And Solomon offered for the sacrifice of peace offerings, which he offered to the LORD, 22,000 oxen and 120,000 sheep. [a]So the king and all the sons of Israel dedicated the house of the LORD.

64 On the same day the king consecrated the middle of the court that *was* before the house of the LORD, because there he [1]offered the burnt offering and the grain offering and the fat of the peace offerings; for [a]the bronze altar that *was* before the LORD *was* too small to hold the burnt offering and the grain offering and the fat of the peace offerings.

65 So [a]Solomon observed the feast at that time, and all Israel with him, a great assembly [b]from the entrance of Hamath [c]to the brook of Egypt, before the LORD our God, for seven

days and seven *more* days, *even*
fourteen days.
66 On the eighth day he sent the
people away and they blessed the
king. Then they went to their tents
joyful and glad of heart for all the
goodness that the LORD had [1]shown
to David His servant and to Israel
His people.

CHAPTER 9

God's Promise and Warning

[a]NOW it came about when Solomon had finished building the house
of the LORD, and [b]the king's house,
and [c]all [1]that Solomon desired to do,
2 that [a]the LORD appeared to
Solomon a second time, as He had
appeared to him at Gibeon.
3 And the LORD said to him, "I
have heard your prayer and your
supplication, which you have made
before Me; I have consecrated this
house which you have built [a]by putting My name there forever, and
[b]My eyes and My heart will be there
perpetually.
4 "And as for you, [a]if you will walk
before Me as your father David
walked, in integrity of heart and uprightness, doing according to all
that I have commanded you *and* will
keep My statutes and My ordinances,
5 then [a]I will establish the throne
of your kingdom over Israel forever,
just as I [1]promised to your father
David, saying, '[2]You shall not lack a
man on the throne of Israel.'
6 "[a]But if you or your sons shall
indeed turn away from following
Me, and shall not keep My commandments and My statutes which I
have set before you and shall go and
serve other gods and worship them,
7 [a]then I will cut off Israel from
the land which I have given them,
and [b]the house which I have consecrated for My name, I will [1]cast out
of My sight. So [c]Israel will become a
proverb and a byword among all
peoples.
8 "And this house will become [1]a
heap of ruins; everyone who passes
by will be astonished and hiss and
say, '[a]Why has the LORD done thus
to this land and to this house?'
9 "And they will say, '[a]Because
they forsook the LORD their God,
who brought their fathers out of the
land of Egypt, and adopted other
gods and worshiped them and
served them, therefore the LORD
has brought all this adversity on
them.' "

66 [1]Lit., *done*
1 [1]Lit., *Solomon's desire which he was pleased to do* [a]2 Chr. 7:11 [b]1 Kin. 7:1, 2 [c]2 Chr. 8:6
2 [a]1 Kin. 3:5; 11:9
3 [a]1 Kin. 8:29 [b]Deut. 11:12; 2 Chr. 6:40
4 [a]1 Kin. 3:14; 11:4, 6, 8
5 [1]Lit., *spoke* [2]Lit., *There shall not be cut off to you a man* [a]2 Sam. 7:12, 16; 1 Kin. 2:4; 6:12
6 [a]2 Sam. 7:14-16; 1 Chr. 28:9
7 [1]Lit., *send* [a]Lev. 18:24-29; Deut. 4:26; 2 Kin. 17:23 [b]Jer. 7:4-14 [c]Deut. 28:37; Jer. 24:9
8 [1]Heb., *high* [a]Deut. 29:24-26; Jer. 22:8, 9, 28
9 [a]Deut. 29:25-28; Jer. 2:10-13
10 [a]2 Chr. 8:1 [b]1 Kin. 6:37, 38; 7:1; 9:1
12 [1]Lit., *were not right in his sight*
13 [1]Lit., *he called them* [2]I.e., As good as nothing [a]Josh. 19:27
14 [a]1 Kin. 9:11
15 [1]I.e., citadel [a]2 Sam. 5:9; 1 Kin. 9:24 [b]Josh. 11:1 [c]Josh. 17:11
16 [a]Josh. 16:10 [b]1 Kin. 3:1; 7:8
17 [a]Josh. 10:10
19 [1]Lit., *the* [2]Lit., *the desire of Solomon which he desired to build in Jerusalem* [3]Lit., *of* [a]1 Kin. 10:26; 2 Chr. 1:14 [b]1 Kin. 4:26 [c]1 Kin. 9:1
21 [a]Judg. 1:21-29; 3:1 [b]Josh. 15:63; 17:12, 13 [c]Judg. 1:28, 35 [d]Gen. 9:25, 26; Ezra 2:55, 58
22 [a]Lev. 25:39
23 [1]Or, *officers of the deputies* [a]2 Chr. 8:10 [b]1 Kin. 5:16
24 [a]1 Kin. 3:1; 7:8

Cities Given to Hiram

10 [a]And it came about [b]at the end
of twenty years in which Solomon
had built the two houses, the house
of the LORD and the king's house
11 (Hiram king of Tyre had supplied Solomon with cedar and cypress timber and gold according to
all his desire), then King Solomon
gave Hiram twenty cities in the land
of Galilee.
12 So Hiram came out from Tyre
to see the cities which Solomon had
given him, and they [1]did not please
him.
13 And he said, "What are these
cities which you have given me, my
brother?" So [1]they were called the
land of [2a]Cabul to this day.
14 [a]And Hiram sent to the king
120 talents of gold.
15 Now this is the account of the
forced labor which King Solomon
levied to build the house of the
LORD, his own house, the [1a]Millo,
the wall of Jerusalem, [b]Hazor, [c]Me-
giddo, and Gezer.
16 *For* Pharaoh king of Egypt had
gone up and captured Gezer, and
burned it with fire, and killed the
[a]Canaanites who lived in the city,
and had [b]given it *as* a dowry to his
daughter, Solomon's wife.
17 So Solomon rebuilt Gezer and
the lower [a]Beth-horon
18 and Baalath and Tamar in the
wilderness, in the land *of Judah,*
19 and all the storage cities which
Solomon had, even [a]the cities for
[1]his chariots and the cities for [1b]his
horsemen, and [2c]all that it pleased
Solomon to build in Jerusalem, in
Lebanon, and in all the land [3]under
his rule.
20 *As for* all the people who were
left of the Amorites, the Hittites, the
Perizzites, the Hivites and the Jebusites, who were not of the sons of
Israel,
21 [a]their descendants who were
left after them in the land [b]whom
the sons of Israel were unable to destroy utterly, [c]from them Solomon
levied [d]forced laborers, even to this
day.
22 But Solomon did not make
slaves [a]of the sons of Israel; for they
were men of war, his servants, his
princes, his captains, his chariot
commanders, and his horsemen.
23 These *were* the [1]chief officers
who were over Solomon's work,
[a]five hundred and fifty, [b]who ruled
over the people doing the work.
24 As soon as [a]Pharaoh's daughter
came up from the city of David to

her house which *Solomon* had built
for her, [b]then he built the Millo.
25 Now [a]three times in a year
Solomon offered burnt offerings and
peace offerings on the altar which
he built to the LORD, burning incense with them *on the altar* which
was before the LORD. So he finished
the house.
26 [a]King Solomon also built a fleet
of ships in [b]Ezion-geber, which is
near Eloth on the shore of the [1]Red
Sea, in the land of Edom.
27 [a]And Hiram sent his servants
with the fleet, sailors who knew the
sea, along with the servants of Solomon.
28 And they went to [a]Ophir, and
took four hundred and twenty talents of gold from there, and brought
it to King Solomon.

CHAPTER 10

The Queen of Sheba

[a]NOW when the [b]queen of [c]Sheba
heard about the fame of Solomon
concerning the name of the LORD,
she came [d]to test him with difficult
questions.
2 So she came to Jerusalem with
a very large retinue, with camels
[a]carrying spices and very much gold
and precious stones. When she
came to Solomon, she spoke with
him about all that was in her heart.
3 And Solomon [1]answered all her
questions; nothing was hidden from
the king which he did not [2]explain to
her.
4 When the queen of Sheba perceived all the wisdom of Solomon,
the house that he had built,
5 the food of his table, the seating
of his servants, the attendance of his
waiters and their attire, his cupbear-
ers, and [1a]his stairway by which he
went up to the house of the LORD,
there was no more spirit in her.
6 Then she said to the king, "It
was a true report which I heard in
my own land about your words and
your wisdom.
7"Nevertheless I did not believe
the [1]reports, until I came and my
eyes had seen it. And behold, the
half was not told me. You exceed *in*
wisdom and prosperity the report
which I heard.
8"How blessed are your men,
how blessed are these your servants
who stand before you continually
and hear your wisdom.
9"[a]Blessed be the LORD your God
who delighted in you to set you on
the throne of Israel; [b]because the
LORD loved Israel forever, therefore
He made you king, [c]to do justice and
righteousness."
10 And [a]she gave the king a hundred and twenty talents of gold, and
a very great *amount* of spices and
precious stones. Never again did
such abundance of spices come in as
that which the queen of Sheba gave
King Solomon.
11 [a]And also the ships of Hiram,
which brought gold from Ophir,
brought in from Ophir a very great
number of almug trees and precious
stones.
12 And the king made of the almug
trees supports for the house of the
LORD and for the king's house, also
lyres and harps for the singers; such
almug trees have not come in *again*,
nor have they been seen to this day.
13 And King Solomon gave to the
queen of Sheba all her desire which
she requested, besides what he gave
her according to [1]his royal bounty.
Then she turned and went to her
own land [2]together with her servants.

Wealth, Splendor and Wisdom

14 [a]Now the weight of gold which
came in to Solomon in one year *was*
666 talents of gold,
15 besides *that* from the traders
and the [1]wares of the merchants
and all the kings of the [2]Arabs and
the governors of the country.
16 And [a]King Solomon made 200
large shields of beaten gold, [1]using
600 *shekels of* gold on each large
shield.
17 And *he made* 300 shields of
beaten gold, [1]using three minas of
gold on each shield, and [a]the king
put them in the house of the forest
of Lebanon.
18 Moreover, the king made a
great throne of [a]ivory and overlaid it
with refined gold.
19 There *were* six steps to the
throne and a round top to the throne
at its rear, and [1]arms [2]on each side
of the seat, and two lions standing
beside the [1]arms.
20 And twelve lions were standing
there on the six steps on the one side
and on the other; nothing like *it* was
made for any other kingdom.
21 And all King Solomon's drinking vessels *were* of gold, and all the
vessels of the house of the forest of
Lebanon *were* of pure gold. None
was of silver; it was not considered
[1]valuable in the days of Solomon.
22 For [a]the king had at sea the
ships of Tarshish with the ships of
Hiram; once every three years the

24 [b]1 Kin. 9:15; 11:27; 2 Chr. 32:5
25 [a]Ex. 23:14-17; Deut. 16:16
26 [1]Or, *Sea of Reeds* [a]1 Kin. 22:48 [b]Num. 33:35; Deut. 2:8
27 [a]1 Kin. 5:6, 9; 10:11
28 [a]1 Chr. 29:4
1 [a]2 Chr. 9:1 [b]Matt. 12:42 [c]Gen. 10:7, 28; Ps. 72:10, 15 [d]Judg. 14:12-14; Ps. 49:4
2 [a]1 Kin. 10:10
3 [1]Lit., *told her all her words* [2]Lit., *tell her*
5 [1]Or, *his burnt offering which he offered* [a]1 Chr. 26:16
7 [1]Lit., *words*
9 [a]1 Kin. 5:7 [b]1 Chr. 17:22; 2 Chr. 2:11 [c]2 Sam. 8:15; 23:3
10 [a]1 Kin. 10:2
11 [a]1 Kin. 9:27, 28
13 [1]Lit., *the hand of King Solomon* [2]Lit., *she and*
14 [a]2 Chr. 9:13-28
15 [1]Or, *traffic* [2]Cf. 2 Chr. 9:14
16 [1]Lit., *he brought up* [a]1 Kin. 14:26-28; 2 Chr. 12:9, 10
17 [1]Lit., *he brought up* [a]1 Kin. 7:2
18 [a]1 Kin. 10:22; Ps. 45:8
19 [1]Lit., *hands* [2]Lit., *on this side and on this at the place of the seat*
21 [1]Lit., *anything*
22 [a]1 Kin. 9:26-28; 22:48

ships of Tarshish came bringing gold and silver, ivory and apes and peacocks.

23 [a]So King Solomon became greater than all the kings of the earth in riches and in wisdom.

24 And all the earth was seeking the presence of Solomon, [a]to hear his wisdom which God had put in his heart.

25 And they brought every man his gift, articles of silver and gold, garments, weapons, spices, horses, and mules, so much year by year.

26 [a]Now Solomon gathered chariots and horsemen; and he had 1,400 chariots and 12,000 horsemen, and he [1]stationed them in the [b]chariot cities and with the king in Jerusalem.

27 [a]And the king made silver *as common* as stones in Jerusalem, and he made cedars as plentiful as sycamore trees that are in the [1]lowland.

28 [a]Also Solomon's import of horses was from Egypt and Kue, and the king's merchants procured *them* from Kue for a price.

29 And a chariot [1]was imported from Egypt for 600 *shekels* of silver, and a horse for 150; and [2]by the same means they exported them [a]to all the kings of the Hittites and to the kings of [3]Syria.

Chapter 11

Solomon Turns from God

NOW [a]King Solomon loved many foreign women along with the daughter of Pharaoh: Moabite, Ammonite, Edomite, Sidonian, and Hittite women,

2 from the nations concerning which the LORD had said to the sons of Israel, "[a]You shall not [1]associate with them, neither shall they [1]associate with you, for they will surely turn your heart away after their gods." Solomon held fast to these in love.

3 [a]And he had seven hundred wives, princesses, and three hundred concubines, and his wives turned his heart away.

4 For it came about when Solomon was old, his wives turned his heart away after other gods; and [a]his heart was not [1]wholly devoted to the LORD his God, as the heart of David his father *had been.*

5 For Solomon went after [a]Ashtoreth the goddess of the Sidonians and after [b]Milcom the detestable idol of the Ammonites.

6 And Solomon did what was evil in the sight of the LORD, and did not follow the LORD fully, as David his father *had done.*

7 Then Solomon built a high place for [a]Chemosh the detestable idol of Moab, on the mountain which is [1]east of Jerusalem, and for [b]Molech the detestable idol of the sons of Ammon.

8 Thus also he did for all his foreign wives, who burned incense and sacrificed to their gods.

9 Now the LORD was angry with Solomon [a]because his heart was turned away from the LORD, the God of Israel, [b]who had appeared to him twice,

10 and [a]had commanded him concerning this thing, that he should not go after other gods; but he did not observe what the LORD had commanded.

11 So the LORD said to Solomon, "Because [1]you have done this, and you have not kept My covenant and My statutes, which I have commanded you, [a]I will surely tear the kingdom from you, and will give it to your servant.

12 "Nevertheless I will not do it in your days for the sake of your father David, *but* I will tear it out of the hand of your son.

13 "However, [a]I will not tear away all the kingdom, but [b]I will give one tribe to your son for the sake of My servant David and [c]for the sake of Jerusalem which I have chosen."

God Raises Adversaries

14 Then the LORD raised up an adversary to Solomon, Hadad the Edomite; he was of the [1]royal line in Edom.

15 For it came about, [a]when David was in Edom, and Joab the commander of the army had gone up to bury the slain, and had struck down every male in Edom

16 (for Joab and all Israel stayed there six months, until he had cut off every male in Edom),

17 that Hadad fled [1]to Egypt, he and certain Edomites of his father's servants with him, while Hadad *was* a young boy.

18 And they arose from Midian and came to [a]Paran; and they took men with them from Paran and came to Egypt, to Pharaoh king of Egypt, who gave him a house and assigned him food and gave him land.

23 [a]1 Kin. 3:12, 13; 4:30
24 [a]1 Kin. 3:9, 12, 28
26 [1]So with ancient versions, cf. 2 Chr. 9:25; Heb., *led* [a]1 Kin. 4:26; 2 Chr. 1:14-17; 9:25 [b]1 Kin. 9:19
27 [1]Or, *shephelah* [a]2 Chr. 1:15
28 [a]2 Chr. 1:16; 9:28
29 [1]Lit., *came up and went out from* [2]Lit., *in like manner by their hand* [3]Heb., *Aram* [a]2 Kin. 7:6, 7
1 [a]Deut. 17:17; Neh. 13:23-27
2 [1]Lit., *go among* [a]Ex. 23:31-33; 34:12-16
3 [a]2 Sam. 3:2-5; 5:13-16
4 [1]Lit., *complete with* [a]1 Kin. 9:4
5 [a]Judg. 2:13; 10:6; 1 Sam. 7:3, 4 [b]1 Kin. 11:7
7 [1]Lit., *before* [a]Num. 21:29; Judg. 11:24; 2 Kin. 23:13 [b]Lev. 20:2-5; 2 Kin. 23:10; Acts 7:3
9 [a]1 Kin. 11:2, 4 [b]1 Kin. 3:5; 9:2
10 [a]1 Kin. 6:12; 9:6, 7
11 [1]Lit., *this is with you* [a]1 Sam. 2:30; 1 Kin. 11:29-31; 12:15, 16, 20
13 [a]2 Sam. 7:15; 1 Chr. 17:13 [b]1 Kin. 11:32, 36; 12:20 [c]1 Kin. 8:29
14 [1]Lit., *king's seed*
15 [a]2 Sam. 8:14; 1 Chr. 18:12, 13
17 [1]Lit., *to go into*
18 [a]Num. 10:12; Deut. 1:1

19 Now Hadad found great favor [1]before Pharaoh, so that he gave him in marriage the sister of his own wife, the sister of Tahpenes the queen.

20 And the sister of Tahpenes bore his son Genubath, whom Tahpenes weaned in Pharaoh's house; and Genubath was in Pharaoh's house among the sons of Pharaoh.

21 But [a]when Hadad heard in Egypt that David slept with his fathers, and that Joab the commander of the army was dead, Hadad said to Pharaoh, "Send me away, that I may go to my own country."

22 Then Pharaoh said to him, "But what have you lacked with me, that behold, you are seeking to go to your own country?" And he answered, "Nothing; nevertheless you must surely [1]let me go."

23 [a]God also raised up *another* adversary to him, Rezon the son of Eliada, who had fled from his lord [b]Hadadezer king of Zobah.

24 And he gathered men to himself and became leader of a marauding band, [a]after David slew them of *Zobah;* and they went to Damascus and stayed [1]there, and reigned in Damascus.

25 So he was an adversary to Israel all the days of Solomon, along with the evil that Hadad *did;* and he abhorred Israel and reigned over [1]Syria.

26 Then [a]Jeroboam the son of Nebat, an Ephraimite of Zeredah, Solomon's servant, whose mother's name was Zeruah, a widow, [b]also [1]rebelled against the king.

27 Now this was the reason why he [1]rebelled against the king: [a]Solomon built the [2]Millo, *and* closed up the breach of the city of his father David.

28 Now the man Jeroboam was a valiant warrior, and when [a]Solomon saw that the young man was [1]industrious, he appointed him over all the [2]forced labor of the house of Joseph.

29 And it came about at that time, when Jeroboam went out of Jerusalem, that [a]the prophet Ahijah the Shilonite found him on the road. Now [1]Ahijah had clothed himself with a new cloak; and both of them were alone in the field.

30 Then [a]Ahijah took hold of the new cloak which was on him, and tore it into twelve pieces.

31 And he said to Jeroboam, "Take for yourself ten pieces; for thus says the LORD, the God of Israel, 'Behold, [a]I will tear the kingdom out of the hand of Solomon and give you ten tribes

32 ([a]but he will have one tribe, for the sake of My servant David and for the sake of Jerusalem, [b]the city which I have chosen from all the tribes of Israel),

33 because they have forsaken Me, and [a]have worshiped Ashtoreth the goddess of the Sidonians, Chemosh the god of Moab, and Milcom the god of the sons of Ammon; and they have not walked in My ways, doing what is right in My sight and *observing* My statutes and My ordinances, as his father David *did.*

34 'Nevertheless I will not take the whole kingdom out of his hand, but I will make him [1]ruler all the days of his life, for the sake of My servant David whom I chose, who observed My commandments and My statutes;

35 but [a]I will take the kingdom from his son's hand and give it to you, *even* ten tribes.

36 'But [a]to his son I will give one tribe, [b]that My servant David may have a lamp always before Me in Jerusalem, [c]the city where I have chosen for Myself to put My name.

37 'And I will take you, and you shall reign over whatever [1]you desire, and you shall be king over Israel.

38 'Then it will be, that if you listen to all that I command you and walk in My ways, and do what is right in My sight by observing My statutes and My commandments, as My servant David did, then [a]I will be with you and [b]build you an enduring house as I built for David, and I will give Israel to you.

39 'Thus I will afflict the [1]descendants of David for this, but not always.'"

40 Solomon sought therefore to put Jeroboam to death; but Jeroboam arose and fled to Egypt to [a]Shishak king of Egypt, and he was in Egypt until the death of Solomon.

The Death of Solomon

41 [a]Now the rest of the acts of Solomon and whatever he did, and his wisdom, are they not written in the book of the acts of Solomon?

42 Thus the time that Solomon reigned in Jerusalem over all Israel was forty years.

43 And Solomon [a]slept with his fathers and was buried in the city of his father David, and his son [b]Rehoboam reigned in his place.

19 [1]Lit., *in the sight of*
21 [a]1 Kin. 2:10
22 [1]Lit., *send me away*
23 [a]1 Kin. 11:14 [b]2 Sam. 8:3; 10:16
24 [1]Lit., *in it* [a]2 Sam. 10:8, 18
25 [1]Heb., *Aram*
26 [1]Lit., *lifted up a hand* [a]1 Kin. 11:11, 28; 12:2, 20; 2 Chr. 13:6 [b]2 Sam. 20:21
27 [1]Lit., *lifted up a hand* [2]I.e., citadel [a]1 Kin. 9:15, 24
28 [1]Lit., *a doer of work* [2]Lit., *burden* [a]Prov. 22:29
29 [1]Lit., *he* [a]1 Kin. 12:15; 14:2; 2 Chr. 9:29
30 [a]1 Sam. 15:27, 28
31 [a]1 Kin. 11:11, 12
32 [a]1 Kin. 11:13; 12:21 [b]1 Kin. 11:13; 14:21
33 [a]1 Kin. 11:5-8
34 [1]Or, *prince*
35 [a]1 Kin. 11:12; 12:16, 17
36 [a]1 Kin. 11:13 [b]1 Kin. 15:4; 2 Kin. 8:19 [c]1 Kin. 11:13
37 [1]Lit., *your soul desires*
38 [a]Deut. 31:8; Josh. 1:5 [b]2 Sam. 7:11, 27
39 [1]Lit., *seed*
40 [a]1 Kin. 14:25; 2 Chr. 12:2-9
41 [a]2 Chr. 9:29
43 [a]1 Kin. 2:10 [b]1 Kin. 14:21

Chapter 12

King Rehoboam Acts Foolishly

[a]THEN Rehoboam went to Shechem, for all Israel had come to
[b]Shechem to make him king.
2 Now it came about [a]when Jeroboam the son of Nebat heard *of it*
(for he was yet in Egypt, where he
had fled from the presence of King
Solomon while [1]he was living in
Egypt,
3 they sent and called him), that
Jeroboam and all the assembly of
Israel came and spoke to Rehoboam, saying,
4 "[a]Your father made our yoke
hard; therefore lighten the hard service of your father and his heavy
yoke which he put on us, and we will
serve you."
5 Then he said to them, "[a]Depart
[1]for three days, then return to me."
So the people departed.
6 And King Rehoboam [a]consult-
ed with the elders who had [1]served
his father Solomon while he was
still alive, saying, "How do you
counsel *me* to answer this people?"
7 Then they spoke to him, saying,
"If you will be a servant to this people today, will serve them, [1]grant
them their petition, and speak good
words to them, then they will be
your servants forever."
8 But he forsook the counsel of
the elders which they had given
him, and consulted with the young
men who grew up with him [1]and
served him.
9 So he said to them, "What
counsel do you give that we may answer this people who have spoken
to me, saying, 'Lighten the yoke
which your father put on us'?"
10 And the young men who grew
up with him spoke to him, saying,
"Thus you shall say to this people
who spoke to you, saying, 'Your father made our yoke heavy, now you
make it lighter for us!' But you shall
speak to them, 'My little finger is
thicker than my father's loins!
11 'Whereas my father loaded you
with a heavy yoke, I will add to your
yoke; my father disciplined you
with whips, but I will discipline you
with scorpions.'"
12 Then Jeroboam and all the people came to Rehoboam on the third
day as the king had [1]directed, saying, "[a]Return to me on the third
day."
13 And the king answered the people harshly, for he forsook the advice of the elders which they had
[1]given him,
14 and he spoke to them according
to the advice of the young men, saying, "[a]My father made your yoke
heavy, but I will add to your yoke;
my father disciplined you with
whips, but I will discipline you with
scorpions."
15 So the king did not listen to the
people; [a]for it was a turn *of events*
from the LORD, [b]that He might establish His word, which the LORD
spoke through Ahijah the Shilonite
to Jeroboam the son of Nebat.

The Kingdom Divided. Jeroboam Rules Israel

16 When all Israel *saw* that the
king did not listen to them, the people answered the king, saying,
"What portion do we have in
David?
We have no inheritance in the
son of Jesse;
[a]To your tents, O Israel!
Now look after your own
house, David!"
So Israel departed to their tents.
17 But [a]as for the sons of Israel
who lived in the cities of Judah, Rehoboam reigned over them.
18 Then King Rehoboam sent
[a]Adoram, who was over the forced
labor, and all Israel stoned him [1]to
death. And King Rehoboam made
haste to mount his chariot to flee to
Jerusalem.
19 [a]So Israel has been in rebellion
against the house of David to this
day.
20 And it came about when all Israel heard that Jeroboam had returned, that they sent and called
him to the assembly and made him
king over all Israel. [a]None but the
tribe of Judah followed the house of
David.
21 [a]Now when Rehoboam had
come to Jerusalem, he assembled all
the house of Judah and the tribe of
Benjamin, 180,000 chosen men who
were warriors, to fight against the
house of Israel to restore the kingdom to Rehoboam the son of Solomon.
22 But the word of God came to
[a]Shemaiah the man of God, saying,
23 "Speak to Rehoboam the son of
Solomon, king of Judah, and to all
the house of Judah and Benjamin
and to the [a]rest of the people, saying,
24 'Thus says the LORD, "You must
not go up and fight against your
[1]relatives the sons of Israel; return
every man to his house, [a]for this

1 [a]2 Chr. 10:1 [b]Judg. 9:6
2 [1]Lit., *Jeroboam* [a]1 Kin. 11:26, 40
4 [a]1 Sam. 8:11-18; 1 Kin. 4:7, 22-25; 9:15
5 [1]Lit., *yet three* [a]1 Kin. 12:12
6 [1]Lit., *stood before* [a]1 Kin. 4:1-6
7 [1]Lit., *answer them*
8 [1]Lit., *who stood before*
12 [1]Lit., *spoken* [a]1 Kin. 12:5
13 [1]Lit., *advised*
14 [a]Ex. 1:13, 14; 5:5-9, 16-18
15 [a]Deut. 2:30; Judg. 14:4; 1 Kin. 12:24 [b]1 Kin. 11:11, 31
16 [a]2 Sam. 20:1
17 [a]1 Kin. 11:13, 36
18 [1]Lit., *with stones that he died* [a]2 Sam. 20:24; 1 Kin. 4:6; 5:14
19 [a]2 Kin. 17:21
20 [a]1 Kin. 11:13, 32, 36
21 [a]2 Chr. 11:1
22 [a]2 Chr. 12:5-7
23 [a]1 Kin. 12:17
24 [1]Lit., *brothers* [a]1 Kin. 12:15

thing has come from Me." ' " So they listened to the word of the LORD, and returned and went *their way* according to the word of the LORD.

Jeroboam's Idolatry

25 Then [a]Jeroboam built Shechem in the hill country of Ephraim, and lived [1]there. And he went out from there and built [b]Penuel.

26 And Jeroboam said in his heart, "Now the kingdom will return to the house of David.

27"[a]If this people go up to offer sacrifices in the house of the LORD at Jerusalem, then the heart of this people will return to their lord, *even* to Rehoboam king of Judah; and they will kill me and return to Rehoboam king of Judah."

28 So the king [1]consulted, and [a]made two golden [b]calves, and he said to them, "It is too much for you to go up to Jerusalem; [c]behold your gods, O Israel, that brought you up from the land of Egypt."

29 And he set [a]one in [b]Bethel, and the other he put in [c]Dan.

30 Now [a]this thing became a sin, for the people went *to worship* before the one as far as Dan.

31 And [a]he made houses on high places, and [b]made priests from among [1]all the people who were not of the sons of Levi.

32 And Jeroboam [1]instituted a feast in the eighth month on the fifteenth day of the month, [a]like the feast which is in Judah, and he [2]went up to the altar; thus he did in Bethel, sacrificing to the calves which he had made. And he stationed in Bethel [b]the priests of the high places which he had made.

33 Then he [1]went up to the altar which he had made in Bethel on the fifteenth day in the eighth month, even in the month which he had [2]devised [3]in his own heart; and he [2]instituted a feast for the sons of Israel, and [1]went up to the altar [a]to burn [4]incense.

CHAPTER 13

Jeroboam Warned, Stricken

NOW behold, there came [a]a man of God from Judah to Bethel by the word of the LORD, while Jeroboam was standing by the altar [b]to burn incense.

2 And [a]he cried against the altar by the word of the LORD, and said, "O altar, altar, thus says the LORD, 'Behold, a son shall be born to the house of David, [b]Josiah by name; and on you he shall sacrifice the priests of the high places who burn incense on you, and human bones shall be burned on you.' "

3 Then he gave a [1]sign the same day, saying, "[a]This is the [1]sign which the LORD has spoken, 'Behold, the altar shall be split apart and the [2]ashes which are on it shall be poured out.' "

4 Now it came about when the king heard the saying of the man of God, which he cried against the altar in Bethel, that Jeroboam stretched out his hand from the altar, saying, "Seize him." But his hand which he stretched out against him dried up, so that he could not draw it back to himself.

5 The altar also was split apart and the [1]ashes were poured out from the altar, according to the [2]sign which the man of God had given by the word of the LORD.

6 And the king answered and said to the man of God, "Please [1a]entreat the LORD your God, and pray for me, that my hand may be restored to me." So [b]the man of God [2]entreated the LORD, and the king's hand was restored to him, and it became as it was before.

7 Then the king said to the man of God, "Come home with me and refresh yourself, and [a]I will give you a reward."

8 But the man of God said to the king, "[a]If you were to give me half your house I would not go with you, nor would I eat bread or drink water in this place.

9"For so [1]it was commanded me by the word of the LORD, saying, 'You shall eat no bread, nor drink water, nor return by the way which you came.' "

10 So he went another way, and did not return by the way which he came to Bethel.

The Disobedient Prophet

11 Now an old prophet [a]was living in Bethel; and his [1]sons came and told him all the deeds which the man of God had done that day in Bethel; the words which he had spoken to the king, these also they related to their father.

12 And their father said to them, "[1]Which way did he go?" Now his sons [2]had seen the way which the man of God who came from Judah had gone.

13 Then he said to his sons, "Saddle the donkey for me." So they saddled the donkey for him and he rode away on it.

25 [1]Lit., *in it* [a]Judg. 9:45-49 [b]Gen. 32:30, 31; Judg. 8:8, 17

27 [a]Deut. 12:5-7, 14

28 [1]Lit., *took counsel* [a]2 Kin. 10:29; 17:16; Hos. 8:4-7 [b]Hos. 10:5 [c]Ex. 32:4, 8

29 [a]Hos. 10:5 [b]Gen. 28:19 [c]Judg. 18:26-31

30 [a]1 Kin. 13:34; 2 Kin. 17:21

31 [1]Or, *extremities of* [a]1 Kin. 13:32 [b]1 Kin. 13:33; 2 Kin. 17:32; 2 Chr. 13:9

32 [1]Lit., *made* [2]Or, *offered upon* [a]Lev. 23:33, 34; Num. 29:12 [b]Amos 7:10-13

33 [1]Or, *offered upon* [2]Lit., *made* [3]Lit., *from* [4]Or, *sacrifices* [a]1 Kin. 13:1

1 [a]1 Kin. 12:22; 2 Kin. 23:17 [b]1 Kin. 12:33

2 [a]1 Kin. 13:32 [b]2 Kin. 23:15, 16

3 [1]Lit., *wonder* [2]Lit., *ashes of fat* [a]Ex. 4:1-5; Judg. 6:17

5 [1]Lit., *ashes of fat* [2]Lit., *wonder*

6 [1]Lit., *soften the face of* [2]Lit., *softened the face of* [a]Ex. 8:8, 28; 9:28; Acts 8:24 [b]Luke 6:27, 28

7 [a]1 Sam. 9:7, 8; 2 Kin. 5:15

8 [a]Num. 22:18; 24:13; 1 Kin. 13:16, 17

9 [1]Lit., *he commanded me*

11 [1]Lit., *son* [a]1 Kin. 13:25; 2 Kin. 23:18

12 [1]Lit., *Where is the way he went* [2]Some ancient versions read *showed him*

14 So he went after the man of
God and found him sitting under [1]an
oak; and he said to him, "Are you
the man of God who came from Judah?" And he said, "I am."
15 Then he said to him, "Come
home with me and eat bread."
16 And he said, "[a]I cannot return
with you, nor go with you, nor will I
eat bread or drink water with you in
this place.
17"For a command *came* to me [a]by
the word of the LORD, 'You shall eat
no bread, nor drink water there; do
not return by going the way which
you came.'"
18 And he said to him, "I also am a
prophet like you, and an angel spoke
to me by the word of the LORD, saying, 'Bring him back with you to
your house, that he may eat bread
and drink water.'" *But* he lied to
him.
19 So he went back with him, and
ate bread in his house and drank water.
20 Now it came about, as they
were sitting down at the table, that
the word of the LORD came to the
prophet who had brought him back;
21 and he cried to the man of God
who came from Judah, saying,
"Thus says the LORD, 'Because you
have [1]disobeyed the [2]command of
the LORD, and have not observed the
commandment which the LORD
your God commanded you,
22 but have returned and eaten
bread and drunk water in the place
of which He said to you, "Eat no
bread and drink no water"; your
body shall not come to the grave of
your fathers.'"
23 And it came about after he had
eaten bread and after he had drunk,
that he saddled the donkey for him,
for the prophet whom he had
brought back.
24 Now when he had gone, [a]a lion
met him on the way and killed him,
and his body was thrown on the
road, with the donkey standing beside it; the lion also was standing
beside the body.
25 And behold, men passed by and
saw the body thrown on the road,
and the lion standing beside the
body; so they came and told *it* in the
city where [a]the old prophet lived.
26 Now when the prophet who
brought him back from the way
heard *it*, he said, "It is the man of
God, who [1]disobeyed the [2]command
of the LORD; therefore the LORD has
given him to the lion, which has torn
him and killed him, according to the
word of the LORD which He spoke to
him."
27 Then he spoke to his sons, saying, "Saddle the donkey for me."
And they saddled *it*.
28 And he went and found his
body thrown on the road with the
donkey and the lion standing beside
the body; the lion had not eaten the
body nor torn the donkey.
29 So the prophet took up the
body of the man of God and laid it
on the donkey, and brought it back
and he came to the city of the old
prophet to mourn and to bury him.
30 And he laid his body in his own
grave, and they mourned over him,
saying, "Alas, my brother!"
31 And it came about after he had
buried him, that he spoke to his
sons, saying, "When I die, bury me
in the grave in which the man of
God is buried; [a]lay my bones beside
his bones.
32"[a]For the thing shall surely come
to pass which he cried by the word
of the LORD against the altar in
Bethel and [b]against all the houses of
the high places which are in the
cities of [c]Samaria."
33 After this event Jeroboam did
not return from his evil way, but
again he made priests of the high
places from among [1]all the people;
[a]any who would, he ordained, to be
priests of the high places.
34 [a]And [1]this event became sin to
the house of Jeroboam, [b]even to blot
it out and destroy *it* from off the
face of the earth.

CHAPTER 14

Ahijah Prophesies against the King

AT that time Abijah the son of
Jeroboam became sick.
2 And Jeroboam said to his wife,
"Arise now, and [a]disguise yourself
so that they may not know that you
are the wife of Jeroboam, and go to
[b]Shiloh; behold, Ahijah the prophet
is there, who [c]spoke concerning me
that I would be king over this people.
3"[a]And take ten loaves with you,
some cakes and a jar of honey, and
go to him. He will tell you what will
happen to the boy."
4 And Jeroboam's wife did so,
and arose and went to [a]Shiloh, and
came to the house of [b]Ahijah. Now
Ahijah could not see, [c]for his eyes
were [1]dim because of his age.
5 Now the LORD had said to Ahijah, "Behold, the wife of Jeroboam
is coming to [1]inquire of you con-

14 [1]Or, *a terebinth*
16 [a]1 Kin. 13:8, 9
17 [a]1 Kin. 20:35
21 [1]Lit., *rebelled against* [2]Lit., *mouth*
24 [a]1 Kin. 20:36
25 [a]1 Kin. 13:11
26 [1]Lit., *rebelled against* [2]Lit., *mouth*
31 [a]2 Kin. 23:17, 18
32 [a]1 Kin. 13:2 [b]1 Kin. 12:31 [c]1 Kin. 16:24
33 [1]Or, *extremities of* [a]Judg. 17:5
34 [1]Lit., *by this thing he became* [a]1 Kin. 12:30; 2 Kin. 17:21 [b]1 Kin. 14:10; 15:29, 30
2 [a]1 Sam. 28:8; 2 Sam. 14:2; 2 Chr. 18:29 [b]Josh. 18:1 [c]1 Kin. 11:29-31
3 [a]1 Sam. 9:7, 8; 1 Kin. 13:7; 2 Kin. 4:42
4 [1]Lit., *set* [a]1 Kin. 14:2 [b]1 Kin. 11:29 [c]1 Sam. 3:2; 4:15
5 [1]Lit., *seek a word from*

cerning her son, for he is sick. You
shall say thus and thus to her, for it
will be when she arrives that [a]she
will pretend to be another woman."
6 And it came about when Ahijah
heard the sound of her feet coming
in the doorway, that he said, "Come
in, wife of Jeroboam, why do you
pretend to be another woman? For I
am sent to you *with* a harsh *message.*
7 "Go, say to Jeroboam, 'Thus
says the LORD God of Israel, "[a]Be-
cause I exalted you from among the
people and made you leader over
My people Israel,
8 and tore the kingdom away
from the house of David and gave it
to you—[a]yet you have not been like
My servant David, who kept My
commandments and who followed
Me with all his heart, [b]to do only
that which was right in My sight;
9 you also have done more evil
than all who were before you, and
[a]have gone and made for yourself
other gods and [b]molten images to
provoke Me to anger, and [c]have cast
Me behind your back—
10 therefore behold, I am bringing
calamity on the house of Jeroboam,
and [a]will cut off from Jeroboam [1]ev-
ery male person, [b]both bond and
free in Israel, and I [c]will make a
clean sweep of the house of Jeroboam, as one sweeps away dung until it is all gone.
11 "[a]Anyone belonging to Jeroboam who dies in the city the dogs
will eat. And he who dies in the field
the birds of the heavens will eat; for
the LORD has spoken *it.*"'
12 "Now you arise, go to your
house. [a]When your feet enter the
city the child will die.
13 "And all Israel shall mourn for
him and bury him, for [1]he alone of
Jeroboam's *family* shall come to the
grave, because in him something
good was found toward the LORD
God of Israel in the house of Jeroboam.
14 "Moreover, [a]the LORD will raise
up for Himself a king over Israel
who shall cut off the house of Jeroboam this day [1]and from now on.
15 "For the LORD will strike Israel,
as a reed is shaken in the water; and
[a]He will uproot Israel from [b]this
good land which He gave to their
fathers, and [c]will scatter them beyond the *Euphrates* River, [d]because
they have made their [1]Asherim, provoking the LORD to anger.
16 "And He will give up Israel [a]on
account of the sins of Jeroboam,
which he [1]committed and with
which he made Israel to sin."
17 Then Jeroboam's wife arose
and departed and came to [a]Tirzah.
[b]As she was entering the threshold
of the house, the child died.
18 [a]And all Israel buried him and
mourned for him, according to the
word of the LORD which He spoke
through His servant Ahijah the
prophet.
19 Now the rest of the acts of Jeroboam, [a]how he made war and how
he reigned, behold, they are written
in the Book of the Chronicles of the
Kings of Israel.
20 And the time that Jeroboam
reigned *was* twenty-two years; and
he slept with his fathers, and Nadab
his son reigned in his place.

Rehoboam Misleads Judah

21 [a]Now Rehoboam the son of
Solomon reigned in Judah. Rehoboam was forty-one years old when he
became king, and he reigned seventeen years in Jerusalem, [b]the city
which the LORD had chosen from all
the tribes of Israel to put His name
there. And his mother's name was
Naamah the Ammonitess.
22 [a]And Judah did evil in the sight
of the LORD, and they provoked Him
to jealousy more than all that their
fathers had done, with [1]the sins
which they [2]committed.
23 For they also built for themselves [a]high places and *sacred* [b]pil-
lars and [1c]Asherim on every high
hill and [d]beneath every luxuriant
tree.
24 And there were also [a]male cult
prostitutes in the land. They did according to all the abominations of
the nations which the LORD dispossessed before the sons of Israel.
25 [a]Now it came about in the fifth
year of King Rehoboam, that Shishak the king of Egypt came up
against Jerusalem.
26 And he took away the treasures
of the house of the LORD and the
treasures of the king's house, and
[a]he took everything, [1b]even taking
all the shields of gold which Solomon had made.
27 So King Rehoboam made
shields of bronze in their place, and
[a]committed them to the [1]care of the
commanders of the [2]guard who
guarded the doorway of the king's
house.
28 Then it happened as often as
the king entered the house of the
LORD, that the [1]guards would carry
them and would bring them back
into the [1]guards' room.

5 [a]2 Sam. 14:2

7 [a]1 Kin. 11:28-31; 16:2

8 [a]1 Kin. 11:33, 38 [b]1 Kin. 15:5

9 [a]1 Kin. 12:28; 2 Chr. 11:15 [b]Ex. 34:17 [c]Ps. 50:17; Ezek. 23:35

10 [1]Lit., *him who urinates against the wall* [a]1 Kin. 21:21; 2 Kin. 9:8 [b]Deut. 32:36; 2 Kin. 14:26 [c]1 Kin. 15:29

11 [a]1 Kin. 16:4; 21:24

12 [a]1 Kin. 14:17

13 [1]Lit., *the one*

14 [1]Lit., *and what even now?* [a]1 Kin. 15:27-29

15 [1]I.e., wooden symbols of a female deity [a]Deut. 29:28; 2 Kin. 17:6 [b]Josh. 23:15, 16 [c]2 Kin. 15:29 [d]Ex. 34:13, 14; Deut. 12:3, 4

16 [1]Lit., *sinned* [a]1 Kin. 12:30; 13:34

17 [a]1 Kin. 15:21, 33; 16:6-9, 15, 23 [b]1 Kin. 14:12

18 [a]1 Kin. 14:13

19 [a]1 Kin. 14:30; 2 Chr. 13:2-20

21 [a]2 Chr. 12:13 [b]1 Kin. 11:32, 36

22 [1]Lit., *their* [2]Lit., *sinned* [a]2 Chr. 12:1, 14

23 [1]I.e., wooden symbols of a female deity [a]Deut. 12:2 [b]Deut. 16:22 [c]1 Kin. 14:15 [d]2 Kin. 17:10; Is. 57:5; Jer. 2:20

24 [a]Deut. 23:17

25 [a]2 Chr. 12:2, 9-11

26 [1]Lit., *and he took away* [a]1 Kin. 15:18 [b]1 Kin. 10:17

27 [1]Lit., *hand* [2]Lit., *runner* [a]1 Sam. 8:11; 22:17

28 [1]Lit., *runners*

29 [a]Now the rest of the acts of Rehoboam and all that he did, are they
not written in the Book of the
Chronicles of the Kings of Judah?
30 [a]And there was war between
Rehoboam and Jeroboam continually.
31 And Rehoboam slept with his
fathers, and was buried with his fathers in the city of David; and [a]his
mother's name was Naamah the
Ammonitess. And Abijam his son
became king in his place.

Chapter 15

Abijam Reigns over Judah

[a]
Now in the eighteenth year of
King Jeroboam, the son of Nebat,
Abijam became king over Judah.
2 He reigned three years in Jerusalem; and his mother's name was
[1]Maacah the daughter of [2]Abisha-
lom.
3 And he walked in all the sins of
his father which he had committed
before him; and [a]his heart was not
[1]wholly devoted to the Lord his
God, like the heart of his father David.
4 But for David's sake the Lord
his God gave him a [a]lamp in Jerusalem, to raise up his son after him
and to establish Jerusalem;
5 [a]because David did what was
right in the sight of the Lord, and
had not turned aside from any thing
that He commanded him all the
days of his life, [b]except in the case
of Uriah the Hittite.
6 [a]And there was war between
Rehoboam and Jeroboam all the
days of his life.
7 Now [a]the rest of the acts of Abijam and all that he did, are they not
written in the Book of the Chronicles of the Kings of Judah? [b]And
there was war between Abijam and
Jeroboam.

Asa Succeeds Abijam

8 [a]And Abijam slept with his fathers and they buried him in the city
of David; and Asa his son became
king in his place.
9 So in the twentieth year of Jeroboam the king of Israel, Asa began
to reign as king of Judah.
10 And he reigned forty-one years
in Jerusalem; and [a]his mother's
name was Maacah the daughter of
Abishalom.
11 And [a]Asa did what was right in
the sight of the Lord, like David his
father.
12 [a]He also put away the male cult
prostitutes from the land, and [b]re-
moved all the idols which his fathers
had made.
13 [a]And [1]he also removed Maacah
his mother from *being* queen
mother, because she had made a
horrid image [2]as an Asherah; and
Asa cut down her horrid image and
[b]burned *it* at the brook Kidron.
14 [a]But the high places were not
taken away; nevertheless [b]the heart
of Asa was [1]wholly devoted to the
Lord all his days.
15 And [a]he brought into the house
of the Lord the dedicated things of
his father and his own dedicated
things: silver and gold and utensils.
16 [a]Now there was war between
Asa and Baasha king of Israel all
their days.
17 [a]And Baasha king of Israel
went up against Judah and [1b]forti-
fied Ramah [c]in order to prevent *anyone* from going out or coming in to
Asa king of Judah.
18 Then [a]Asa took all the silver
and the gold which were left in the
treasuries of the house of the Lord
and the treasuries of the king's
house, and delivered them into the
hand of his servants. And [b]King Asa
sent them to Ben-hadad the son of
Tabrimmon, the son of Hezion, king
of [1]Syria, who lived in [c]Damascus,
saying,
19 "Let there be a [a]treaty between
[1]you and me, *as* between my father
and your father. Behold, I have sent
you a present of silver and gold; go,
break your treaty with Baasha king
of Israel so that he will withdraw
from me."
20 So Ben-hadad listened to King
Asa and sent the commanders of his
armies against the cities of Israel,
and [1]conquered [a]Ijon, [b]Dan, [c]Abel-
beth-maacah and all [d]Chinneroth,
besides all the land of Naphtali.
21 And it came about when Ba-
asha heard *of it* that [a]he ceased [1]for-
tifying Ramah, and remained in
[b]Tirzah.
22 Then King Asa made a proclamation to all Judah—none was
exempt—and they carried away the
stones of Ramah and its timber with
which Baasha had built. And King
Asa built with them [a]Geba of Benjamin and Mizpah.

Jehoshaphat Succeeds Asa

23 [a]Now the rest of all the acts of
Asa and all his might and all that he
did and the cities which he built, are
they not written in the Book of the
Chronicles of the Kings of Judah?
But in the time of his old age he was
diseased in his feet.

29 [a]2 Chr. 12:15, 16
30 [a]1 Kin. 12:21-24; 15:6
31 [a]1 Kin. 14:21
1 [a]2 Chr. 13:1
2 [1]Or, *Micaiah, the daughter of Uriel;* cf. 2 Chr. 13:2 [2]Or, *Absalom;* cf. 2 Chr. 11:20
3 [1]Lit., *complete with* [a]1 Kin. 11:4
4 [a]2 Sam. 21:17; 1 Kin. 11:36
5 [a]1 Kin. 9:4; 14:8 [b]2 Sam. 11:4, 15-17; 12:9, 10
6 [a]1 Kin. 14:30
7 [a]2 Chr. 13:2, 21, 22 [b]2 Chr. 13:3-20
8 [a]2 Chr. 14:1
10 [a]1 Kin. 15:2
11 [a]2 Chr. 14:2
12 [a]Deut. 23:17; 1 Kin. 14:24; 22:46 [b]1 Kin. 11:7, 8; 14:23; 2 Chr. 14:2-5
13 [1]Lit., *also Maacah his mother and he removed her* [2]Or, *for Asherah* [a]2 Chr. 15:16-18 [b]Ex. 32:20
14 [1]Lit., *complete with* [a]1 Kin. 22:43; 2 Kin. 12:3 [b]1 Kin. 8:61; 15:3
15 [a]1 Kin. 7:51
16 [a]1 Kin. 15:32
17 [1]Lit., *built* [a]2 Chr. 16:1-6 [b]1 Kin. 15:21, 22 [c]1 Kin. 12:26-29
18 [1]Heb., *Aram* [a]1 Kin. 14:26; 15:15 [b]2 Kin. 12:17, 18 [c]Gen. 14:15; 1 Kin. 11:23, 24
19 [1]Lit., *me and you* [a]2 Chr. 16:7
20 [1]Lit., *smote* [a]2 Kin. 15:29 [b]1 Kin. 12:29 [c]2 Kin. 15:29 [d]Josh. 11:2; 12:3
21 [1]Lit., *building* [a]1 Kin. 15:17 [b]1 Kin. 14:17; 16:15-18
22 [a]Josh. 18:24; 21:17
23 [a]2 Chr. 16:11-14

24 And Asa slept with his fathers
and was buried with his fathers in
the city of David his father; and [a]Je-
hoshaphat his son reigned in his
place.

Nadab, then Baasha, Rules over Israel

25 Now [a]Nadab the son of Jeroboam became king over Israel in the
second year of Asa king of Judah,
and he reigned over Israel two
years.
26 And he did evil in the sight of
the LORD, and [a]walked in the way of
his father and [b]in his sin which he
made Israel sin.
27 Then [a]Baasha the son of Ahijah
of the house of Issachar conspired
against him, and Baasha struck him
down at [b]Gibbethon, which belonged to the Philistines, while Nadab and all Israel were laying siege
to Gibbethon.
28 So Baasha killed him in the
third year of Asa king of Judah, and
reigned in his place.
29 And it came about, as soon as
he was king, he struck down all the
household of Jeroboam. He did not
leave to Jeroboam [1]any persons
alive, until he had destroyed them,
[a]according to the word of the LORD,
which He spoke by His servant Ahijah the Shilonite,
30 *and* because of the sins of Jeroboam which he sinned, and [a]which
he made Israel sin, because of his
provocation with which he provoked the LORD God of Israel to anger.
31 [a]Now the rest of the acts of Nadab and all that he did, are they not
written in the Book of the Chronicles of the Kings of Israel?

War with Judah

32 [a]And there was war between
Asa and Baasha king of Israel all
their days.
33 In the third year of Asa king of
Judah, Baasha the son of Ahijah became king over all Israel at Tirzah,
and reigned twenty-four years.
34 And he did evil in the sight of
the LORD, and [a]walked in the way of
Jeroboam and in his sin which he
made Israel sin.

CHAPTER 16

Prophecy against Baasha

NOW the word of the LORD came
to [a]Jehu the son of [b]Hanani against
Baasha, saying,
2"Inasmuch as I [a]exalted you
from the dust and made you leader
over My people Israel, and [b]you
have walked in the way of Jeroboam
and have made My people Israel sin,
provoking Me to anger with their
sins,
3 behold, [a]I will consume [b]Baa-
sha and his house, and [c]I will make
your house like the house of Jeroboam the son of Nebat.
4"[a]Anyone of Baasha who dies in
the city the dogs shall eat, and anyone of his who dies in the field the
birds of the heavens will eat."
5 [a]Now the rest of the acts of Baasha and what he did and his might,
are they not written in the Book of
the Chronicles of the Kings of Israel?

The Israelite Kings

6 And Baasha slept with his fathers and was buried in [a]Tirzah, and
Elah his son became king in his
place.
7 Moreover, the word of the LORD
through [a]the prophet Jehu the son
of Hanani also came against Baasha
and his household, both because of
all the evil which he did in the sight
of the LORD, provoking Him to anger with the work of his hands, in
being like the house of Jeroboam,
and because [b]he struck [1]it.
8 In the twenty-sixth year of Asa
king of Judah, Elah the son of Baasha became king over Israel at Tirzah, *and reigned* two years.
9 And his servant [a]Zimri, commander of half his chariots, conspired against him. Now he *was* at
Tirzah drinking himself drunk in the
house of Arza, [b]who *was* over the
household at Tirzah.
10 Then Zimri went in and struck
him and put him to death, in the
twenty-seventh year of Asa king of
Judah, and became king in his place.
11 And it came about, when he became king, as soon as he sat on his
throne, that [a]he [1]killed all the household of Baasha; he did not leave [2]a
single male, neither of his [3]relatives
nor of his friends.
12 Thus Zimri destroyed all the
household of Baasha, [a]according to
the word of the LORD, which He
spoke against Baasha through [b]Jehu
the prophet,
13 for all the sins of Baasha and
the sins of Elah his son, which they
sinned and which they made Israel
sin, [a]provoking the LORD God of Israel to anger with their [1]idols.
14 [a]Now the rest of the acts of
Elah and all that he did, are they not
written in the Book of the Chronicles of the Kings of Israel?
15 In the twenty-seventh year of

---

24 [a]1 Kin. 22:41-44; 2 Chr. 17:1
25 [a]1 Kin. 14:20
26 [a]1 Kin. 12:28-33; 13:33, 34 [b]1 Kin. 14:16; 15:30, 34
27 [a]1 Kin. 14:14 [b]Josh. 19:44; 21:23
29 [1]Lit., *any breath* [a]1 Kin. 14:9-16
30 [a]1 Kin. 15:26
31 [a]1 Kin. 14:19
32 [a]1 Kin. 15:16
34 [a]1 Kin. 15:26
1 [a]1 Kin. 16:7; 2 Chr. 19:2; 20:34 [b]2 Chr. 16:7-10
2 [a]1 Kin. 14:7 [b]1 Kin. 15:34
3 [a]1 Kin. 14:10; 21:21 [b]1 Kin. 16:11 [c]1 Kin. 15:29
4 [a]1 Kin. 14:11; 21:24
5 [a]1 Kin. 14:19; 15:31
6 [a]1 Kin. 14:17; 15:21
7 [1]Or, *him* [a]1 Kin. 16:1 [b]1 Kin. 14:14; 15:27, 29
9 [a]2 Kin. 9:30-33 [b]Gen. 24:2; 39:4; 1 Kin. 18:3
11 [1]Lit., *smote* [2]Lit., *him who urinates against the wall* [3]Lit., *redeemers* [a]1 Kin. 15:29; 16:3
12 [a]1 Kin. 16:3 [b]2 Chr. 19:2; 20:34
13 [1]Lit., *vanities* [a]Deut. 32:21; 1 Kin. 15:30
14 [a]1 Kin. 16:5

Asa king of Judah, Zimri reigned seven days at Tirzah. Now the people were camped against [a]Gibbethon, which belonged to the Philistines.

16 And the people who were camped heard [1]it said, "Zimri has conspired and has also struck down the king." Therefore all Israel made Omri, the commander of the army, king over Israel that day in the camp.

17 Then Omri and all Israel with him went up from Gibbethon, and they besieged Tirzah.

18 And it came about, when Zimri saw that the city was taken, that he went into the citadel of the king's house and burned the king's house over him with fire, and [a]died,

19 because of his sins which he sinned, doing evil in the sight of the LORD, [a]walking in the way of Jeroboam, and in his sin which he did, making Israel sin.

20 [a]Now the rest of the acts of Zimri and his conspiracy which he [1]carried out, are they not written in the Book of the Chronicles of the Kings of Israel?

21 Then the people of Israel were divided into two parts: half of the people followed Tibni the son of Ginath, to make him king; the *other* half followed Omri.

22 But the people who followed Omri prevailed over the people who followed Tibni the son of Ginath. And Tibni died and Omri became king.

23 In the thirty-first year of Asa king of Judah, Omri became king over Israel, and reigned twelve years; he reigned six years at [a]Tirzah.

24 And he bought the hill [1]Samaria from Shemer for two talents of silver; and he built on the hill, and named the city which he built [1a]Samaria, after the name of Shemer, the owner of the hill.

25 And [a]Omri did evil in the sight of the LORD, and [b]acted more wickedly than all who *were* before him.

26 For he [a]walked in all the way of Jeroboam the son of Nebat and in his sins which he made Israel sin, provoking the LORD God of Israel with their [1]idols.

27 Now the rest of the acts of Omri which he did and his might which he [1]showed, are they not written in the Book of the Chronicles of the Kings of Israel?

28 So Omri slept with his fathers, and was buried in Samaria; and Ahab his son became king in his place.

29 Now Ahab the son of Omri became king over Israel in the thirty-eighth year of Asa king of Judah, and Ahab the son of Omri reigned over Israel in Samaria twenty-two years.

30 And Ahab the son of Omri did evil in the sight of the LORD [a]more than all who were before him.

31 And it came about, as though it had been a trivial thing for him to walk in the sins of Jeroboam the son of Nebat, that [a]he married Jezebel the daughter of Ethbaal king of the [b]Sidonians, and went to serve Baal and worshiped him.

32 So he erected an altar for Baal in [a]the house of Baal, which he built in Samaria.

33 And Ahab also made [a]the [1]Asherah. Thus [b]Ahab did more to provoke the LORD God of Israel than all the kings of Israel who were before him.

34 [a]In his days Hiel the Bethelite built Jericho; he laid its foundations with the *loss of* Abiram his firstborn, and set up its gates with the *loss of* his youngest son Segub, according to the word of the LORD, which He spoke by Joshua the son of Nun.

CHAPTER 17

Elijah Predicts Drought

NOW Elijah the Tishbite, who was of [1a]the settlers of Gilead, said to Ahab, "[b]As the LORD, the God of Israel lives, before whom I stand, surely [c]there shall be neither dew nor rain these years, except by my word."

2 And the word of the LORD came to him, saying,

3 "Go away from here and turn eastward, and hide yourself by the brook Cherith, which is [1]east of the Jordan.

4 "And it shall be that you shall drink of the brook, and [a]I have commanded the ravens to provide for you there."

5 So he went and did according to the word of the LORD, for he went and lived by the brook Cherith, which is [1]east of the Jordan.

6 And the ravens brought him bread and meat in the morning and bread and meat in the evening, and he would drink from the brook.

7 And it happened after a while, that the brook dried up, because there was no rain in the land.

15 [a]1 Kin. 15:27
16 [1]Lit., *saying*
18 [a]1 Sam. 31:4, 5; 2 Sam. 17:23
19 [a]1 Kin. 12:28; 14:16; 15:26
20 [1]Lit., *conspired* [a]1 Kin. 16:5, 14, 27
23 [a]1 Kin. 15:21
24 [1]Heb., *Shomeron* [a]1 Kin. 16:28, 29, 32
25 [a]Mic. 6:16 [b]1 Kin. 14:9; 16:30-33
26 [1]Lit., *vanities* [a]1 Kin. 16:19
27 [1]Lit., *did*
30 [a]1 Kin. 14:9; 16:25
31 [a]Deut. 7:1-5 [b]1 Kin. 11:1-5; 2 Kin. 10:18; 17:16
32 [a]2 Kin. 10:21, 26, 27
33 [1]I.e., wooden symbol of a female deity [a]2 Kin. 13:6 [b]1 Kin. 14:9; 16:29, 30
34 [a]Josh. 6:26
1 [1]Or, *Tishbe in Gilead* [a]Judg. 12:4 [b]1 Kin. 18:10; 22:14; 2 Kin. 5:20 [c]1 Kin. 18:1; Luke 4:25; James 5:17
3 [1]Lit., *before*
4 [a]1 Kin. 16:9
5 [1]Lit., *before*

8 Then the word of the LORD came to him, saying,

9 "Arise, go to [a]Zarephath, which belongs to Sidon, and stay there; behold, [b]I have commanded a widow there to provide for you."

10 So he arose and went to Zarephath, and when he came to the gate of the city, behold, a widow was there gathering sticks; and [a]he called to her and said, "Please get me a little water in a [1]jar, that I may drink."

11 And as she was going to get *it*, he called to her and said, "Please bring me a piece of bread in your hand."

12 But she said, "[a]As the LORD your God lives, I have no [1b]bread, only a handful of flour in the [2]bowl and a little oil in the jar; and behold, I am gathering [3]a few sticks that I may go in and prepare for me and my son, that we may eat it and die."

13 Then Elijah said to her, "Do not fear; go, do as you have said, but make me a little bread cake from [1]it first, and bring *it* out to me, and afterward you may make *one* for yourself and for your son.

14 "For thus says the LORD God of Israel, 'The [1]bowl of flour shall not be exhausted, nor shall the jar of oil [2]be empty, until the day that the LORD sends rain on the face of the earth.' "

15 So she went and did according to the word of Elijah, and she and he and her household ate for *many* days.

16 The [1]bowl of flour was not exhausted nor did the jar of oil [2]become empty, according to the word of the LORD which He spoke through Elijah.

Elijah Raises Widow's Son

17 Now it came about after these things, that the son of the woman, the mistress of the house, became sick; and his sickness was so severe, that there was no breath left in him.

18 So she said to Elijah, "[a]What do I have to do with you, O [b]man of God? [1]You have come to me to bring my iniquity to remembrance, and to put my son to death!"

19 And he said to her, "Give me your son." Then he took him from her bosom and carried him up to the upper room where he was living, and laid him on his own bed.

20 And he called to the LORD and said, "O LORD my God, hast Thou also brought calamity to the widow with whom I am [1]staying, by causing her son to die?"

21 [a]Then he stretched himself upon the child three times, and called to the LORD, and said, "O LORD my God, I pray Thee, let this child's life return [1]to him."

22 And the LORD heard the voice of Elijah, [a]and the life of the child returned [1]to him and he revived.

23 And Elijah took the child, and brought him down from the upper room into the house and gave him to his mother; and Elijah said, "See, your son is alive."

24 Then the woman said to Elijah, "[a]Now I know that you are a man of God, and that the word of the LORD in your mouth is truth."

CHAPTER 18

Obadiah Meets Elijah

NOW it came about [a]*after* many days, that the word of the LORD came to Elijah in the third year, saying, "Go, show yourself to Ahab, and I will send rain on the face of the earth."

2 So Elijah went to show himself to Ahab. Now the famine *was* severe in Samaria.

3 And Ahab called Obadiah [a]who *was* over the household. (Now Obadiah [1]feared the LORD greatly;

4 for it came about, [a]when Jezebel [1]destroyed the prophets of the LORD, that Obadiah took a hundred prophets and hid them by fifties in a cave, and provided them with bread and water.)

5 Then Ahab said to Obadiah, "Go through the land to all the springs of water and to all the valleys; perhaps we will find grass and keep the horses and mules alive, and not [1]have to kill some of the cattle."

6 So they divided the land between them to [1]survey it; Ahab went one way by himself and Obadiah went another way by himself.

7 Now as Obadiah was on the way, behold, Elijah [1]met him, [a]and he recognized him and fell on his face and said, "Is this you, Elijah my master?"

8 And he said to him, "It is I. Go, say to your master, 'Behold, Elijah *is here.*' "

9 And he said, "What [1]sin have I committed, that you are giving your servant into the hand of Ahab, to put me to death?

10 "[a]As the LORD your God lives, there is no nation or kingdom where my master has not sent to search for you; and when they said, 'He is not

9 [a]Obad. 20; Luke 4:26 [b]1 Kin. 17:4
10 [1]Or, *vessel* [a]Gen. 24:17; John 4:7
12 [1]Lit., *cake* [2]Lit., *pitcher* [3]Lit., *two* [a]1 Kin. 17:1 [b]2 Kin. 4:2-7
13 [1]Lit., *there*
14 [1]Lit., *pitcher* [2]Lit., *lack*
16 [1]Lit., *pitcher* [2]Lit., *lack*
18 [1]Or, *Have you come ... death?* [a]2 Sam. 16:10; 2 Kin. 3:13; John 2:4 [b]1 Kin. 12:22
20 [1]Lit., *sojourning*
21 [1]Lit., *upon his inward part* [a]2 Kin. 4:34, 35; Acts 20:10
22 [1]Lit., *upon his inward part* [a]Heb. 11:35
24 [a]John 2:11; 3:2
1 [a]1 Kin. 17:1
3 [1]Or, *revered* [a]1 Kin. 16:9
4 [1]Lit., *cut off* [a]1 Kin. 17:13
5 [1]Lit., *cut off*
6 [1]Lit., *pass through*
7 [1]Lit., *to meet* [a]2 Kin. 1:6-8
9 [1]Lit., *have I sinned*
10 [a]1 Kin. 17:1

here', he made the kingdom or nation swear that they could not find
you.
11"And now you are saying, 'Go,
say to your master, "Behold, Elijah
is here." '
12"And it will come about when I
leave you [a]that the Spirit of the
LORD will carry you where I do not
know; so when I come and tell Ahab
and he cannot find you, he will kill
me, although *I* your servant have
[1]feared the LORD from my youth.
13"[a]Has it not been told to my
master what I did when Jezebel
killed the prophets of the LORD, that
I hid [1]a hundred prophets of the
LORD by fifties in a cave, and provided them with bread and water?
14"And now you are saying, 'Go,
say to your master, "Behold, Elijah
is here" '; he will then kill me."
15 And Elijah said, "[a]As the LORD
of hosts lives, before whom I stand,
I will surely show myself to him today."
16 So Obadiah went to meet Ahab,
and told him; and Ahab went to
meet Elijah.
17 And it came about, when Ahab
saw Elijah that [a]Ahab said to him,
"Is this you, you troubler of Israel?"
18 And he said, "I have not troubled Israel, but you and your father's house *have*, because [a]you
have forsaken the commandments
of the LORD, and [b]you have followed
the Baals.
19"Now then send *and* gather to
me all Israel at [a]Mount Carmel, [b]*together* with 450 prophets of Baal and
400 prophets of [c]the Asherah, who
eat at Jezebel's table."

God or Baal on Mount Carmel

20 So Ahab sent *a message* among
all the sons of Israel, and brought
the prophets together at Mount Carmel.
21 And Elijah came near to all the
people and said, "[a]How long *will*
you [1]hesitate between two opinions? [b]If the LORD is God, follow
Him; but if Baal, follow him." But
the people did not answer him a
word.
22 Then Elijah said to the people,
"I [a]alone am left a prophet of the
LORD, but Baal's prophets are [b]450
men.
23"Now let them give us two oxen;
and let them choose one ox for
themselves and cut it up, and place
it on the wood, but put no fire *under
it*; and I will prepare the other ox,
and lay it on the wood, and I will not
put a fire *under it*.
24"Then you call on the name of
your god, and I will call on the name
of the LORD, and [a]the God who answers by fire, He is God." And all
the people answered and said,
"[1]That is a good idea."
25 So Elijah said to the prophets of
Baal, "Choose one ox for yourselves
and prepare it first for you are
many, and call on the name of your
god, but put no fire *under it*."
26 Then they took the ox which
[1]was given them and they prepared
it and called on the name of Baal
from morning until noon saying, "O
Baal, answer us." But there was no
voice and no one answered. And
they [2]leaped about the altar which
[3]they made.
27 And it came about at noon, that
Elijah mocked them and said, "Call
out with a loud voice, for he is a god;
either he is occupied or gone aside,
or is on a journey, or perhaps he is
asleep and needs to be awakened."
28 So they cried with a loud voice
and [a]cut themselves according to
their custom with swords and
lances until the blood gushed out on
them.
29 And it came about when mid-
day was past, that they [1]raved [a]until
the time of the offering of the *evening* sacrifice; but there was no
voice, no one answered, and no [2]one
paid attention.
30 Then Elijah said to all the people, "Come near to me." So all the
people came near to him. And [a]he
repaired the altar of the LORD which
had been torn down.
31 And Elijah took twelve stones
according to the number of the
tribes of the sons of Jacob, to whom
the word of the LORD had come, saying, "[a]Israel shall be your name."
32 So with the stones he built an
altar in the name of the LORD, and he
made a trench around the altar,
large enough to hold two [1]measures
of seed.
33 [a]Then he arranged the wood
and cut the ox in pieces and laid *it*
on the wood. And he said, "Fill four
pitchers with water and pour *it* on
the burnt offering and on the wood."
34 And he said, "Do it a second
time," and they did it a second time.
And he said, "Do it a third time,"
and they did it a third time.
35 And the water flowed around
the altar, and he also filled the
trench with water.
36 Then it came about [a]at the time
of the offering of the *evening* sacrifice, that Elijah the prophet came

12 [1]Or, *revered* [a]2 Kin. 2:16; Ezek. 3:12, 14; Acts 8:39
13 [1]Lit., *a hundred men of the prophets* [a]1 Kin. 18:4
15 [a]1 Kin. 17:1
17 [a]Josh. 7:25; 1 Kin. 21:20
18 [a]1 Kin. 9:9; 2 Chr. 15:2 [b]1 Kin. 16:31; 21:25, 26
19 [a]Josh. 19:26; 2 Kin. 2:25 [b]1 Kin. 18:22 [c]1 Kin. 16:33
21 [1]Lit., *on the two divided opinions* [a]2 Kin. 17:41; Matt. 6:24 [b]Josh. 24:15
22 [a]1 Kin. 19:10, 14 [b]1 Kin. 18:19
24 [1]Lit., *The matter is good* [a]1 Kin. 18:38
26 [1]Lit., *he gave* [2]Lit., *limped*, i.e., a type of ceremonial dance [3]So some mss. and the ancient versions, M.T., *he*
28 [a]Lev. 19:28; Deut. 14:1; Mic. 6:7
29 [1]Lit., *prophesied* [2]Lit., *attentiveness* [a]Ex. 29:39, 41
30 [a]1 Kin. 19:10, 14; 2 Chr. 33:16
31 [a]Gen. 32:28; 35:10; 2 Kin. 17:34
32 [1]Heb., *seahs;* one seah equals approx. 11 qts.
33 [a]Gen. 22:9; Lev. 1:7, 8
36 [a]1 Kin. 18:29

near and said, "[b]O LORD, the God of
Abraham, Isaac and Israel, today let
it be known that Thou art God in
Israel, and that I am Thy servant,
and [c]that I have done all these
things at Thy word.

Elijah's Prayer

37"Answer me, O LORD, answer
me, that this people may know that
Thou, O LORD, art God, and *that*
Thou hast turned their heart back
again."
38 Then the [a]fire of the LORD fell,
and consumed the burnt offering
and the wood and the stones and the
dust, and licked up the water that
was in the trench.
39 And when all the people saw it,
they fell on their faces; and they
said, "[a]The LORD, He is God; the
LORD, He is God."
40 Then Elijah said to them,
"Seize the prophets of Baal; do not
let one of them escape." So they
seized them; and Elijah brought
them down to [a]the brook Kishon,
[b]and slew them there.
41 Now Elijah said to Ahab, "Go
up, eat and drink; for there is the
sound of the roar of a *heavy*
shower."
42 So Ahab went up to eat and
drink. But Elijah went up to the top
of [a]Carmel; and he crouched down
on the earth, and put his face between his knees.
43 And he said to his servant, "Go
up now, look toward the sea." So he
went up and looked and said,
"There is nothing." And he said,
"Go back" seven times.
44 And it came about at the seventh *time,* that he said, "Behold, [a]a
cloud as small as a man's hand is
coming up from the sea." And he
said, "Go up, say to Ahab, '[1]Prepare
your chariot and go down, so that
the *heavy* shower does not stop
you.' "
45 So it came about in a little
while, that the sky grew black with
clouds and wind, and there was a
heavy shower. And Ahab rode and
went to [a]Jezreel.
46 Then [a]the hand of the LORD was
on Elijah, and [b]he girded up his loins
and [1]outran Ahab to Jezreel.

CHAPTER 19

Elijah Flees from Jezebel

NOW Ahab told Jezebel all that
Elijah had done, and [1a]how he had
killed all the prophets with the
sword.
2 Then Jezebel sent a messenger
to Elijah, saying, "[a]So may the gods
do to me and even more, if I do not
make your [1]life as the [1]life of one of
them by tomorrow about this time."
3 And he [1]was afraid and arose
and ran for his [2]life and came to
[a]Beersheba, which belongs to Judah, and left his servant there.
4 But he himself went a day's
journey into the wilderness, and
came and sat down under a [1]juniper
tree; and [a]he requested for himself
that he might die, and said, "It is
enough; now, O LORD, take my [2]life,
for I am not better than my fathers."
5 And he lay down and slept under a [1]juniper tree; and behold,
there was [a]an angel touching him,
and he said to him, "Arise, eat."
6 Then he looked and behold,
there was at his head a bread cake
baked on hot stones, and a jar of
water. So he ate and drank and lay
down again.
7 And the angel of the LORD came
again a second time and touched
him and said, "Arise, eat, because
the journey is too great for you."
8 So he arose and ate and drank,
and went in the strength of that food
[a]forty days and forty nights to [b]Ho-
reb, the mountain of God.

Elijah at Horeb

9 Then he came there to a cave,
and lodged there; and behold, [a]the
word of the LORD *came* to him, and
He said to him, "What are you doing
here, Elijah?"
10 And he said, "[a]I have been very
zealous for the LORD, the God of
hosts; for the sons of Israel have forsaken Thy covenant, [b]torn down
Thine altars and killed Thy prophets
with the sword. And I alone am left;
and they seek my life, to take it
away."
11 So He said, "[a]Go forth, and
stand on the mountain before the
LORD." And behold, the LORD was
passing by! And a great and strong
wind was rending the mountains
and breaking in pieces the rocks before the LORD; *but* the LORD *was* not
in the wind. And after the wind an
earthquake, *but* the LORD *was* not in
the earthquake.
12 And after the earthquake a fire,
but the LORD *was* not in the fire; and
after the fire [a]a sound of a gentle
blowing.
13 And it came about when Elijah
heard *it,* that [a]he wrapped his face
in his mantle, and went out and
stood in the entrance of the cave.
And behold, [b]a voice *came* to him

36 [b]Ex. 3:6; 4:5 [c]Num. 16:28-32
38 [a]Gen. 15:17; Lev. 10:1, 2; 2 Kin. 1:12; Job 1:16
39 [a]1 Kin. 18:21, 24
40 [a]Judg. 4:7; 5:21 [b]Deut. 13:5; 18:20; 2 Kin. 10:24, 25
42 [a]1 Kin. 18:19, 20
44 [1]Lit., *Tie, harness* [a]Luke 12:54
45 [a]Josh. 17:16; Judg. 6:33
46 [1]Lit., *ran before* [a]2 Kin. 3:15; Is. 8:11 [b]2 Kin. 4:29; Jer. 1:17; 1 Pet. 1:13
1 [1]Lit., *all about how* [a]1 Kin. 18:40
2 [1]Lit., *soul* [a]1 Kin. 20:10; 2 Kin. 6:31
3 [1]Reading of many mss.; Heb. text may read, *saw* [2]Lit., *soul* [a]Gen. 21:31
4 [1]Or, *broom-tree* [2]Lit., *soul* [a]Num. 11:15; Jer. 20:14-18; Jon. 4:3, 8
5 [1]Or, *broom-tree* [a]Gen. 28:11-15
8 [a]Ex. 24:18; 34:28; Deut. 9:9-11, 18; Matt. 4:2 [b]Ex. 3:1; 4:27
9 [a]Ex. 33:21, 22
10 [a]Ex. 20:5; 34:14 [b]Rom. 11:4
11 [a]Ex. 19:20; 24:12, 18
12 [a]Job 4:16; Zech. 4:6
13 [a]Ex. 3:6 [b]1 Kin. 19:9

and said, "What are you doing here,
Elijah?"
14 Then he said, "[a]I have been
very zealous for the LORD, the God
of hosts; for the sons of Israel have
forsaken Thy covenant, torn down
Thine altars and killed Thy prophets
with the sword. And I alone am left;
and they seek my life, to take it
away."
15 And the LORD said to him, "Go,
return on your way to the wilderness of Damascus, and when you
have arrived, [a]you shall anoint Hazael king over [1]Syria;
16 and [a]Jehu the son of Nimshi
you shall anoint king over Israel;
and [b]Elisha the son of Shaphat of
Abel-meholah you shall anoint as
prophet in your place.
17 "And it shall come about, the
[a]one who escapes from the sword of
Hazael, Jehu [b]shall put to death, and
the one who escapes from the sword
of Jehu, Elisha shall put to death.
18 "[a]Yet I will leave 7,000 in Israel,
all the knees that have not bowed to
Baal and every mouth that has not
[b]kissed him."
19 So he departed from there and
found Elisha the son of Shaphat,
while he was plowing with twelve
pairs *of oxen* before him, and he
with the twelfth. And Elijah passed
over to him and threw [a]his mantle
on him.
20 And he left the oxen and ran
after Elijah and said, "Please [a]let me
kiss my father and my mother, then
I will follow you." And he said to
him, "Go back again, for what have
I done to you?"
21 So he returned from following
him, and took the pair of oxen and
sacrificed them and [a]boiled their
flesh with the implements of the
oxen, and gave *it* to the people and
they ate. Then he arose and followed Elijah and [b]ministered to
him.

CHAPTER 20

War with Syria

NOW [a]Ben-hadad king of Syria
gathered all his army, [b]and there
were thirty-two kings with him, and
horses and chariots. And he went up
and [c]besieged Samaria, and fought
against it.
2 Then he sent messengers to the
city to Ahab king of Israel, and said
to him, "Thus says Ben-hadad,
3 'Your silver and your gold are
mine; your most beautiful wives and
children are also mine.'"
4 And the king of Israel answered
and said, "It is according to your
word, my lord, O king; I am yours,
and all that I have."
5 Then the messengers returned
and said, "Thus says [1]Ben-hadad,
'Surely, I sent to you saying, "You
shall give me your silver and your
gold and your wives and your children,"
6 but about this time tomorrow I
will send my servants to you, and
they will search your house and the
houses of your servants; and it shall
come about, [1]whatever is desirable
in your eyes, they will [2]take in their
hand and carry away.'"
7 Then the king of Israel called all
the elders of the land and said,
"Please observe and [a]see how this
man is looking for trouble; for he
sent to me for my wives and my
children and my silver and my gold,
and I did not refuse him."
8 And all the elders and all the
people said to him, "Do not listen or
consent."
9 So he said to the messengers of
Ben-hadad, "Tell my lord the king,
'All that you sent for to your servant
at the first I will do, but this thing I
cannot do.'" And the messengers
departed and brought him word
again.
10 And Ben-hadad sent to him and
said, "May [a]the gods do so to me
and more also, if the dust of Samaria shall suffice for handfuls for
all the people who [1]follow me."
11 Then the king of Israel answered and said, "Tell *him*, '[a]Let not
him who girds on *his armor* boast
like him who takes *it* off.'"
12 And it came about when Ben-
hadad heard this message, as [a]he
was drinking [1]with the kings in the
[2]temporary shelters, that he said to
his servants, "Station *yourselves*."
So they stationed *themselves*
against the city.

Ahab Victorious

13 Now behold, a prophet approached Ahab king of Israel and
said, "Thus says the LORD, 'Have
you seen all this great multitude?
Behold, [a]I will deliver them into
your hand today, and [b]you shall
know that I am the LORD.'"
14 And Ahab said, "By whom?" So
he said, "Thus says the LORD, 'By
the young men of the rulers of the
provinces.'" Then he said, "Who
shall [1]begin the battle?" And he [2]an-
swered, "You."
15 Then he mustered the young
men of the rulers of the provinces,
and there were 232; and after them

14 [a]1 Kin. 19:10
15 [1]Heb., *Aram* [a]2 Kin. 8:8-15
16 [a]2 Kin. 9:1-10 [b]1 Kin. 19:19-21; 2 Kin. 2:9, 15
17 [a]2 Kin. 8:12; 13:3, 22 [b]2 Kin. 9:14-10:25
18 [a]Rom. 11:4 [b]Hos. 13:2
19 [a]1 Sam. 28:14; 2 Kin. 2:8, 13, 14
20 [a]Matt. 8:21, 22; Luke 9:61, 62; Acts 20:37
21 [a]2 Sam. 24:22 [b]1 Kin. 18:43; 2 Kin. 2:3
1 [a]1 Kin. 15:18, 20; 2 Kin. 6:24 [b]1 Kin. 22:31 [c]1 Kin. 16:24; 2 Kin. 6:24-29
5 [1]Lit., *Ben-hadad, saying*
6 [1]Lit., *all the desire of your eyes* [2]Lit., *put*
7 [a]2 Kin. 5:7
10 [1]Lit., *are at my feet* [a]1 Kin. 19:2; 2 Kin. 6:31
11 [a]Prov. 27:1
12 [1]Lit., *he and* [2]Or, *booths* [a]1 Kin. 16:9
13 [a]1 Kin. 20:28 [b]1 Kin. 18:36
14 [1]Lit., *bind* [2]Lit., *said*

he mustered all the people, *even* all
the sons of Israel, 7,000.
16 And they went out at noon,
while [a]Ben-hadad was drinking
himself drunk in the [1]temporary
shelters [2]with the thirty-two kings
who helped him.
17 And the young men of the rulers of the provinces went out first;
and Ben-hadad sent out and they
told him, saying, "Men have come
out from Samaria."
18 [a]Then he said, "If they have
come out for peace, take them alive;
or if they have come out for war,
take them alive."
19 So these went out from the city,
the young men of the rulers of the
provinces, and the army which followed them.
20 And they [1]killed each his man;
and the Syrians fled, and Israel pursued them, and Ben-hadad king of
Syria escaped on a horse with
horsemen.
21 And the king of Israel went out
and [1]struck the horses and chariots,
and [1]killed the Syrians with a great
slaughter.
22 Then [a]the prophet came near to
the king of Israel, and said to him,
"Go, strengthen yourself and observe and see what you have to do;
for [b]at the turn of the year the king
of Syria will come up against you."
23 Now the servants of the king of
Syria said to him, "[a]Their gods are
gods of the mountains, therefore
they were stronger than we; but
rather let us fight against them in
the plain, *and* surely we shall be
stronger than they.
24 "And do this thing: remove the
kings, each from his place, and put
captains in their place,
25 and [1]muster an army like the
army that you have lost, horse for
horse, and chariot for chariot. Then
we will fight against them in the
plain, and surely we shall be stronger than they." And he listened to
their voice and did so.

Another Syrian War

26 So it came about [a]at the turn of
the year, that Ben-hadad mustered
the Syrians and went up to [b]Aphek
to fight against Israel.
27 And the sons of Israel were
mustered and were provisioned and
went to meet them; and the sons of
Israel camped before them like two
little flocks of goats, [a]but the Syrians filled the country.
28 Then [a]a man of God came near
and spoke to the king of Israel and
said, "Thus says the LORD, 'Because
the Syrians have said, "[b]The LORD is
a god of *the* mountains, but He is not
a god of *the* valleys"; therefore I
[c]will give all this great multitude
into your hand, and you shall know
that I am the LORD.'"
29 So they camped one over
against the other seven days. And it
came about that on the seventh day,
the battle was joined, and the sons
of Israel [1]killed *of* the Syrians
100,000 foot soldiers in one day.
30 But the rest fled to [a]Aphek into
the city, and the wall fell on 27,000
men who were left. And Ben-hadad
fled and came into the city [b]into an
inner chamber.
31 And [a]his servants said to him,
"Behold now, we have heard that
the kings of the house of Israel are
merciful kings, please let us [b]put
sackcloth on our loins and ropes on
our heads, and go out to the king of
Israel; perhaps he will save your
[1]life."
32 So [a]they girded sackcloth on
their loins and *put* ropes on their
heads, and came to the king of Israel
and said, "[b]Your servant Ben-hadad
says, 'Please let me live.'" And he
said, "Is he still alive? He is my
brother."
33 Now the men [1]took this as an
omen, and quickly [2]catching his
word said, "Your brother Ben-hadad." Then he said, "Go, bring him."
Then Ben-hadad came out to him,
and he [3]took him up into the chariot.
34 And *Ben-hadad* said to him,
"[a]The cities which my father took
from your father I will restore, and
you shall make streets for yourself
in Damascus, as my father made in
Samaria." *Ahab said,* "And I will let
you go with this covenant." So he
made a covenant with him and let
him go.
35 Now a certain man of [a]the sons
of the prophets said to [1]another [b]by
the word of the LORD, "Please strike
me." But the man refused to strike
him.
36 Then he said to him, "Because
you have not listened to the voice of
the LORD, behold, as soon as you
have departed from me, [a]a lion will
[1]kill you." And as soon as he had
departed from him a lion found him,
and [2]killed him.
37 Then he found another man and
said, "Please [1]strike me." And the
man [2]struck him, [3]wounding him.
38 So the prophet departed and
waited for the king by the way, and
[a]disguised himself with a bandage
over his eyes.

16 [1]Or, *booths* [2]Lit., *he and the 32 kings* [a]1 Kin. 20:12
18 [a]2 Kin. 14:8-12
20 [1]Lit., *smote*
21 [1]Lit., *smote*
22 [a]1 Kin. 20:13 [b]2 Sam. 11:1; 1 Kin. 20:26
23 [a]1 Kin. 14:23
25 [1]Lit., *number*
26 [a]1 Kin. 20:22 [b]2 Kin. 13:17
27 [a]Judg. 6:3-5; 1 Sam. 13:5-8
28 [a]1 Kin. 17:18 [b]1 Kin. 20:23 [c]1 Kin. 20:13
29 [1]Lit., *smote*
30 [a]1 Kin. 20:26 [b]1 Kin. 22:25; 2 Chr. 18:24
31 [1]Lit., *soul* [a]1 Kin. 20:23-26 [b]Gen. 37:34; 2 Sam. 3:31
32 [a]1 Kin. 20:31 [b]1 Kin. 20:3-6
33 [1]Lit., *divined* [2]Lit., *caught from him* [3]Lit., *caused him to come up*
34 [a]1 Kin. 15:20
35 [1]Lit., *his neighbor* [a]2 Kin. 2:3-7 [b]1 Kin. 13:17, 18
36 [1]Lit., *smite* [2]Lit., *smote* [a]1 Kin. 13:24
37 [1]Lit., *smite* [2]Lit., *smote* [3]Lit., *striking and wounding*
38 [a]1 Kin. 14:2

39 And as the king passed by, he cried to the king and said, "Your servant went out into the midst of the battle; and behold, a man turned aside and brought a man to me and said, 'Guard this man; if for any reason he is missing, [a]then your life shall be for his life, or else you shall pay a talent of silver.'

40 "And while your servant was busy here and there, he was gone." And the king of Israel said to him, "So shall your judgment be; you yourself have decided *it*."

41 Then he hastily took the bandage away from his eyes, and the king of Israel recognized him that he was of the prophets.

42 And he said to him, "Thus says the LORD, 'Because you have let go out of *your* hand the man whom I had devoted to destruction, therefore [a]your [1]life shall go for his [1]life, and your people for his people.' "

43 So [a]the king of Israel went to his house sullen and vexed, and came to Samaria.

CHAPTER 21

Ahab Covets Naboth's Vineyard

NOW it came about after these things, that Naboth the Jezreelite had a vineyard which *was* in [a]Jezreel beside the palace of Ahab king of Samaria.

2 And Ahab spoke to Naboth, saying, "[a]Give me your vineyard, that I may have it for a vegetable garden because it is close beside my house, and I will give you a better vineyard than it in its place; if [1]you like, I will give you the price of [2]it in money."

3 But Naboth said to Ahab, "The LORD forbid me [a]that I should give you the inheritance of my fathers."

4 [a]So Ahab came into his house sullen and vexed because of the word which Naboth the Jezreelite had spoken to him; for he said, "I will not give you the inheritance of my fathers." And he lay down on his bed and turned away his face and ate no [1]food.

5 But Jezebel his wife came to him and said to him, "How is it that your spirit is so sullen that you are not eating [1]food?"

6 So he said to her, "Because I spoke to Naboth the Jezreelite, and said to him, 'Give me your vineyard for money; or else, if it pleases you, I will give you a vineyard in its place.' But he said, 'I will not give you my vineyard.' "

7 And Jezebel his wife said to him, "[a]Do you now [1]reign over Israel? Arise, eat bread, and let your heart be joyful; I will give you the vineyard of Naboth the Jezreelite."

8 [a]So she wrote letters in Ahab's name and sealed them with his seal, and sent letters to [b]the elders and to the nobles who were living with Naboth in his city.

9 Now she wrote in the letters, saying, "Proclaim a fast, and seat Naboth at the head of the people;

10 and seat two worthless men before him, and let them testify against him, saying, 'You cursed God and the king.' Then take him out and stone him [1]to death."

Jezebel's Plot

11 So the men of his city, the elders and the nobles who lived in his city, did as Jezebel had sent *word* to them, just as it was written in the letters which she had sent them.

12 They proclaimed a fast and seated Naboth at the head of the people.

13 Then the two worthless men came in and sat before him; and the worthless men testified against him, even against Naboth, before the people, saying, "Naboth cursed God and the king." [a]So they took him outside the city and stoned him [1]to death with stones.

14 Then they sent *word* to Jezebel, saying, "Naboth has been stoned, and is dead."

15 And it came about when Jezebel heard that Naboth had been stoned and was dead, that Jezebel said to Ahab, "Arise, take possession of the vineyard of Naboth, the Jezreelite, which he refused to give you for money; for Naboth is not alive, but dead."

16 And it came about when Ahab heard that Naboth was dead, that Ahab arose to go down to the vineyard of Naboth the Jezreelite, to take possession of it.

17 Then the word of the LORD came to Elijah the Tishbite, saying,

18 "Arise, go down to meet Ahab king of Israel, [a]who is in Samaria; behold, he is in the vineyard of Naboth where he has gone down to take possession of it.

19 "And you shall speak to him, saying, 'Thus says the LORD, "Have you murdered, and also taken possession?" ' And you shall speak to him, saying, 'Thus says the LORD, "[a]In the place where the dogs licked up the blood of Naboth the dogs

39 [a]2 Kin. 10:24
42 [1]Lit., *soul* [a]1 Kin. 20:39
43 [a]1 Kin. 21:4
1 [a]1 Kin. 18:45, 46
2 [1]Lit., *it is good in your eyes* [2]Lit., *this* [a]1 Sam. 8:14
3 [a]Lev. 25:23; Num. 36:7; Ezek. 46:18
4 [1]Lit., *bread* [a]1 Kin. 20:43
5 [1]Lit., *bread*
7 [1]Lit., *exercise kingship* [a]1 Sam. 8:14
8 [a]Esth. 3:12; 8:8, 10 [b]1 Kin. 20:7
10 [1]Lit., *so that he dies*
13 [1]Lit., *with stones so that he died* [a]2 Kin. 9:26
18 [a]1 Kin. 10:29
19 [a]1 Kin. 22:38; 2 Kin. 9:26

shall lick up your blood, even
yours." ' "
20 And Ahab said to Elijah,
"[a]Have you found me, O my enemy?" And he [1]answered, "I have
found *you,* [b]because you have sold
yourself to do evil in the sight of the
LORD.
21"Behold, I will bring evil upon
you, and [a]will utterly sweep you
away, and will cut off from Ahab
every male, both bond and free in
Israel;
22 and [a]I will make your house
[b]like the house of Jeroboam the son
of Nebat, and like the house of Baasha the son of Ahijah, because of
the provocation with which you
have provoked *Me* to anger, and *be-*
cause you [c]have made Israel sin.
23"And of Jezebel also has the
LORD spoken, saying, '[a]The dogs
shall eat Jezebel [b]in the [1]district of
Jezreel.'
24"[a]The one belonging to Ahab,
who dies in the city, the dogs shall
eat, and the one who dies in the field
the birds of heaven shall eat."
25 [a]Surely there was no one like
Ahab who sold himself to do evil in
the sight of the LORD, [1]because Jezebel his wife incited him.
26 And [a]he acted very abominably
in following idols, [b]according to all
that the Amorites had done, whom
the LORD cast out before the sons of
Israel.
27 And it came about when Ahab
heard these words, that [a]he tore his
clothes and put [1]on sackcloth and
fasted, and he lay in sackcloth and
went about [2]despondently.
28 Then the word of the LORD
came to Elijah the Tishbite, saying,
29"Do you see how Ahab has humbled himself before Me? Because he
has humbled himself before Me, I
will not bring the evil in his days,
but I will bring the evil upon his
house [a]in his son's days."

CHAPTER 22

Ahab's Third Campaign against Syria

AND [1]three years passed without
war between Syria and Israel.
2 [a]And it came about in the third
year, that [b]Jehoshaphat the king of
Judah came down to the king of Israel.
3 Now the king of Israel said to
his servants, "Do you know that
[a]Ramoth-gilead belongs to us, and
we [1]are still doing nothing to take it
out of the hand of the king of Syria?"
4 And he said to Jehoshaphat,
"Will you go with me to battle at
Ramoth-gilead?" And Jehoshaphat
said to the king of Israel, "[a]I am as
you are, my people as your people,
my horses as your horses."
5 Moreover, Jehoshaphat said to
the king of Israel, "Please inquire
[1]first for the word of the LORD."
6 Then [a]the king of Israel gathered the prophets together, about
four hundred men, and said to them,
"Shall I go against Ramoth-gilead to
battle or shall I refrain?" And they
said, "Go up, for the Lord will give *it*
into the hand of the king."
7 But [a]Jehoshaphat said, "Is
there not yet a prophet of the LORD
here, that we may inquire of him?"
8 And the king of Israel said to
Jehoshaphat, "There is yet one man
by whom we may inquire of the
LORD, but I hate him, because he
does not prophesy good concerning
me, but evil. *He is* Micaiah son of
Imlah." But Jehoshaphat said, "Let
not the king say so."
9 Then the king of Israel called an
officer and said, "[1]Bring quickly Micaiah son of Imlah."
10 Now the king of Israel and Jehoshaphat king of Judah were sitting each on his throne, arrayed in
their robes, at the threshing floor at
the entrance of the gate of Samaria;
and [a]all the prophets were prophesying before them.
11 Then Zedekiah the son of Chenaanah made [a]horns of iron for himself and said, "Thus says the LORD,
'[b]With these you shall gore the Syrians until they are consumed.' "
12 And all the prophets were
prophesying thus, saying, "Go up to
Ramoth-gilead and prosper, for the
LORD will give *it* into the hand of the
king."

Micaiah Predicts Defeat

13 Then the messenger who went
to summon Micaiah spoke to him
saying, "Behold now, the words of
the prophets are uniformly favorable to the king. Please let your
word be like the word of one of
them, and speak favorably."
14 But Micaiah said, "[a]As the
LORD lives, what [b]the LORD says to
me, that I will speak."
15 When he came to the king, the
king said to him, "Micaiah, shall we
go to Ramoth-gilead to battle, or
shall we refrain?" And he [1]an-
swered him, "[a]Go up and succeed,
and the LORD will give *it* into the
hand of the king."
16 Then the king said to him,

20 [1]Lit., *said* [a]1 Kin. 18:17 [b]1 Kin. 21:25
21 [a]1 Kin. 14:10; 2 Kin. 9:8
22 [a]1 Kin. 15:29 [b]1 Kin. 16:3, 11 [c]1 Kin. 12:30; 13:34; 14:16
23 [1]Lit., *portion;* some mss. read, *rampart* [a]2 Kin. 9:10, 30-37 [b]2 Sam. 20:15
24 [a]1 Kin. 14:11; 16:4
25 [1]Or, *whom Jezebel his wife incited* [a]1 Kin. 16:30-33; 21:20
26 [a]1 Kin. 15:12; 2 Kin. 17:12 [b]Gen. 15:16; Lev. 18:25-30
27 [1]Lit., *sackcloth on his flesh* [2]Or, *softly* [a]2 Sam. 3:31; 2 Kin. 6:30
29 [a]2 Kin. 9:25-37
1 [1]Lit., *they sat for three years*
2 [a]2 Chr. 18:2 [b]1 Kin. 15:24
3 [1]Lit., *are silent so as not* [a]Deut. 4:43; Josh. 21:38; 1 Kin. 4:13
4 [a]2 Kin. 3:7
5 [1]Lit., *as the day*
6 [a]1 Kin. 18:19
7 [a]2 Kin. 3:11
9 [1]Lit., *Hasten Micaiah*
10 [a]1 Kin. 22:6
11 [a]Zech. 1:18-21 [b]Deut. 33:17
14 [a]1 Kin. 18:10, 15 [b]Num. 22:18; 24:13
15 [1]Lit., *said to* [a]1 Kin. 22:12

"How many times must I adjure you
to speak to me nothing but the truth
in the name of the LORD?"
17 So he said,
"I saw all Israel
Scattered on the mountains,
[a]Like sheep which have no
shepherd.
And the LORD said, 'These
have no master.
Let each of them return to his
house in peace.' "
18 Then the king of Israel said to
Jehoshaphat, "[a]Did I not tell you
that he would not prophesy good
concerning me, but evil?"
19 And [1]Micaiah said, "Therefore,
hear the word of the LORD. [a]I saw
the LORD sitting on His throne, and
[b]all the host of heaven standing by
Him on His right and on His left.
20 "And the LORD said, 'Who will
entice Ahab to go up and fall at Ramoth-gilead?' And one said this
while another said that.
21 "Then a spirit came forward and
stood before the LORD and said, 'I
will entice him.'
22 "And the LORD said to him,
'How?' And he said, 'I will go out
and [a]be a deceiving spirit in the
mouth of all his prophets.' Then He
said, 'You are to entice *him* and also
prevail. Go and do so.'
23 "Now therefore, behold, the
LORD has put a deceiving spirit in
the mouth of all these your prophets; and the LORD has proclaimed disaster against you."
24 Then [a]Zedekiah the son of Chenaanah came near and struck Micaiah on the cheek and said, "How did
the Spirit of the LORD pass from me
to speak to you?"
25 And Micaiah said, "Behold, you
shall see on that day when you [a]en-
ter an inner room to hide yourself."
26 Then the king of Israel said,
"Take Micaiah and return him to
Amon the governor of the city and
to Joash the king's son;
27 and say, 'Thus says the king,
"[a]Put this man in prison, and feed
him [1]sparingly with bread and water until I return safely." ' "
28 And Micaiah said, "[a]If you indeed return safely the LORD has not
spoken by me." And he said, "[b]Lis-
ten, all you people."

Defeat and Death of Ahab

29 So [a]the king of Israel and Jehoshaphat king of Judah went up
against Ramoth-gilead.
30 And the king of Israel said to
Jehoshaphat, "[a]I will disguise myself and go into the battle, but you
put on your robes." So the king of
Israel disguised himself and went
into the battle.
31 Now [a]the king of Syria had
commanded the thirty-two captains
of his chariots, saying, "Do not fight
with small or great, but with the
king of Israel alone."
32 So it came about, when the captains of the chariots saw Jehoshaphat, that they said, "Surely it is the
king of Israel," and they turned
aside to fight against him, and Jehoshaphat cried out.
33 Then it happened, when the
captains of the chariots saw that it
was not the king of Israel, that they
turned back from pursuing him.
34 Now a certain man drew his
bow at random and struck the king
of Israel [1]in a joint of the armor. So
he said to the driver of his chariot,
"Turn [2]around, and take me out of
the [3]fight; [a]for I am severely
wounded."
35 And the battle [1]raged that day,
and the king was propped up in his
chariot in front of the Syrians, and
died at evening, and the blood from
the wound ran into the bottom of
the chariot.
36 [a]Then a cry passed throughout
the army close to sunset, saying,
"Every man to his city and every
man to his [1]country."
37 So the king died and was
brought to Samaria, and they buried
the king in Samaria.
38 And they washed the chariot by
the pool of Samaria, and the dogs
licked up his blood (now the harlots
bathed themselves *there*), [a]accord-
ing to the word of the LORD which
He spoke.
39 Now the rest of the acts of
Ahab and all that he did and [a]the
ivory house which he built and all
the cities which he built, are they
not written in the Book of the
Chronicles of the Kings of Israel?
40 So Ahab slept with his fathers,
and Ahaziah his son became king in
his place.

The New Rulers

41 [a]Now Jehoshaphat the son of
Asa became king over Judah in the
fourth year of Ahab king of Israel.
42 Jehoshaphat was thirty-five
years old when he became king, and
he reigned twenty-five years in Jerusalem. And his mother's name
was Azubah the daughter of Shilhi.
43 [a]And he walked in all the way
of Asa his father; he did not turn
aside from it, doing right in the sight
of the LORD. [b]However, the high

17 [a]Num. 27:17; 1 Kin. 22:34-36
18 [a]1 Kin. 22:8
19 [1]Lit., *he* [a]Is. 6:1; Ezek. 1:26-28; Dan. 7:9, 10 [b]Job 1:6; 2:1; Dan. 7:10
22 [a]Judg. 9:23; 1 Sam. 16:14; 18:10; 19:9
24 [a]1 Kin. 22:11; Matt. 5:39; Acts 23:2, 3
25 [a]1 Kin. 20:30
27 [1]Lit., *with bread of affliction and water of affliction* [a]2 Chr. 16:10; 18:25-27
28 [a]Deut. 18:22 [b]Mic. 1:2
29 [a]1 Kin. 22:3, 4
30 [a]2 Chr. 35:22
31 [a]1 Kin. 20:1, 16, 24; 2 Chr. 18:30
34 [1]Lit., *between the scale armor and the breastplate* [2]Lit., *your hand* [3]Lit., *camp* [a]2 Chr. 35:23
35 [1]Lit., *went up*
36 [1]Lit., *land* [a]2 Kin. 14:12
38 [a]1 Kin. 21:19
39 [a]Amos 3:15
41 [a]2 Chr. 20:31
43 [a]2 Chr. 17:3 [b]1 Kin. 15:14; 2 Kin. 12:3

places were not taken away; the people still sacrificed and burnt incense on the high places.

44 [a]Jehoshaphat also made peace with the king of Israel.

45 Now the rest of the acts of Jehoshaphat, and his might which he showed and how he warred, are they not written [a]in the Book of the Chronicles of the Kings of Judah?

46 And the remnant of [a]the sodomites who remained in the days of his father Asa, he [1]expelled from the land.

47 Now [a]there was no king in Edom; a deputy was king.

48 Jehoshaphat made [a]ships of Tarshish to go to [b]Ophir for gold, but they did not go for the ships were broken at [c]Ezion-geber.

49 Then Ahaziah the son of Ahab said to Jehoshaphat, "Let my servants go with your servants in the ships." But Jehoshaphat was not willing.

50 [a]And Jehoshaphat slept with his fathers and was buried with his fathers in the city of his father David, and Jehoram his son became king in his place.

51 Ahaziah the son of Ahab [a]became king over Israel in Samaria in the seventeenth year of Jehoshaphat king of Judah, and he reigned two years over Israel.

52 And he did evil in the sight of the LORD and [a]walked in the way of his father and in the way of his mother and in the way of Jeroboam the son of Nebat, who caused Israel to sin.

53 [a]So he served Baal and worshiped him and provoked the LORD God of Israel to anger according to all that his father had done.

44 [a]1 Kin. 22:2; 2 Kin. 8:18; 2 Chr. 19:2
45 [a]2 Chr. 20:34
46 [1]Lit., *consumed* [a]Gen. 19:5; Deut. 23:17; 1 Kin. 14:24; 15:12
47 [a]2 Sam. 8:14; 2 Kin. 3:9
48 [a]1 Kin. 10:22 [b]1 Kin. 9:28 [c]1 Kin. 9:26
50 [a]2 Chr. 21:1
51 [a]1 Kin. 22:40
52 [a]1 Kin. 15:26; 21:25
53 [a]1 Kin. 16:30-32

THE SECOND BOOK OF THE KINGS

Ahaziah's Messengers Meet Elijah

NOW [a]Moab rebelled against Israel after the death of Ahab.

2 And Ahaziah fell through the lattice in his upper chamber which *was* in Samaria, and became ill. So he sent messengers and said to them, "Go, [a]inquire of Baal-zebub, the god of Ekron, [b]whether I shall recover from this sickness."

3 But the angel of the LORD said to [a]Elijah the Tishbite, "Arise, go up to meet the messengers of the king of Samaria and say to them, 'Is it because there is no God in Israel *that* you are going to inquire of [b]Baal-zebub, the god of Ekron?'

4 "Now therefore thus says the LORD, '[1a]You shall not come down from the bed where you have gone up, but you shall surely die.' " Then Elijah departed.

5 When the messengers returned to him he said to them, "[1]Why have you returned?"

6 And they said to him, "A man came up to meet us and said to us, 'Go, return to the king who sent you and say to him, "Thus says the LORD, 'Is it because there is no God in Israel *that* you are sending [a]to inquire of Baal-zebub, the god of Ekron? Therefore [1]you shall not come down from the bed where you have gone up, but shall surely die.' " ' "

7 And he said to them, "What kind of man was he who came up to meet you and spoke these words to you?"

8 And they [1]answered him, "[a]*He was* a hairy man with a leather girdle [2]bound about his loins." And he said, "It is Elijah the Tishbite."

9 Then *the king* sent to him a captain of fifty with his fifty. And he went up to him, and behold, he was sitting on the top of the hill. And he said to him, "O man of God, the king says, 'Come down.' "

10 And Elijah answered and said to the captain of fifty, "If I am a man of God, [a]let fire come down from heaven and consume you and your fifty." [b]Then fire came down from heaven and consumed him and his fifty.

11 So he again sent to him another captain of fifty with his fifty. And he answered and said to him, "O man of God, thus says the king, 'Come down quickly.' "

12 And Elijah answered and said to them, "If I am a man of God, let fire come down from heaven and consume you and your fifty." Then the fire of God came down from heaven and consumed him and his fifty.

13 So he again sent the captain of a third fifty with his fifty. When the third captain of fifty went up, he came and bowed down on his knees before Elijah, and begged him and said to him, "O man of God, please let my life and the lives of these fifty

1 [a]2 Sam. 8:2; 2 Kin. 3:5
2 [a]2 Kin. 1:3, 6, 16; Matt. 10:25; Mark 3:22 [b]2 Kin. 8:7-10
3 [a]1 Kin. 17:1; 21:17 [b]2 Kin. 1:2
4 [1]Lit., *The bed where you went up, you shall not come down from it* [a]2 Kin. 1:6, 16
5 [1]Lit., *What is this that you have returned?*
6 [1]See v. 4, note 1 [a]2 Kin. 1:2
8 [1]Lit., *said* [2]Or, *girt* [a]Zech. 13:4; Matt. 3:4; Mark 1:6
10 [a]1 Kin. 18:36-38; Luke 9:54 [b]Job 1:16

servants of yours be precious in
your sight.
14"Behold fire came down from
heaven, and consumed the first two
captains of fifty with their fifties;
but now let my [1]life be precious in
your sight."
15 And [a]the angel of the LORD said
to Elijah, "Go down with him; do
not be afraid of him." So he arose
and went down with him to the king.
16 Then he said to him, "Thus says
the LORD, 'Because you have sent
messengers [a]to inquire of Baal-zebub, the god of Ekron—is it because
there is no God in Israel to inquire of
His word?—therefore [1]you shall not
come down from the bed where you
have gone up, but shall surely die.' "

Jehoram Reigns over Israel

17 So Ahaziah died according to
the word of the LORD which Elijah
had spoken. And because he had no
son, Jehoram became king in his
place [a]in the second year of Jehoram the son of Jehoshaphat, king of
Judah.
18 Now the rest of the acts of Ahaziah which he did, are they not written in the Book of the Chronicles of
the Kings of Israel?

CHAPTER 2

Elijah Taken to Heaven

AND it came about when the LORD
was about to [a]take up Elijah by a
[1]whirlwind to heaven, that Elijah
went with [b]Elisha from [c]Gilgal.
2 And Elijah said to Elisha,
"[a]Stay here please, for the LORD has
sent me as far as [b]Bethel." But Elisha said, "[c]As the LORD lives and as
you yourself live, I will not leave
you." So they went down to Bethel.
3 Then [a]the sons of the prophets
who *were at* Bethel came out to Elisha and said to him, "Do you know
that the LORD will take away your
master from over [1]you today?" And
he said, "Yes, I know; be still."
4 And Elijah said to him, "Elisha,
please [a]stay here, for the LORD has
sent me to [b]Jericho." But he said,
"[c]As the LORD lives, and as you
yourself live, I will not leave you."
So they came to Jericho.
5 And [a]the sons of the prophets
who *were* at Jericho approached Elisha and said to him, "[b]Do you know
that the LORD will take away your
master from over [1]you today?" And
he [2]answered, "Yes, I know; be
still."
6 Then Elijah said to him, "Please
[a]stay here, for the LORD has sent me
to [b]the Jordan." And he said, "As
the LORD lives, and as you yourself
live, I will not leave you." So the two
of them went on.
7 Now [a]fifty men of the sons of
the prophets went and stood opposite *them* at a distance, while the
two of them stood by the Jordan.
8 And Elijah [a]took his mantle and
folded it together and [b]struck the
waters, and they were divided here
and there, so that the two of them
crossed over on dry ground.
9 Now it came about when they
had crossed over, that Elijah said to
Elisha, "Ask what I shall do for you
before I am taken from you." And
Elisha said, "Please, let a double
portion of your spirit be upon me."
10 And he said, "You have asked a
hard thing. *Nevertheless,* if you see
me when I am taken from you, it
shall be so for you; but if not, it shall
not be *so.*"
11 Then it came about as they
were going along and talking, that
behold, *there appeared* [a]a chariot of
fire and horses of fire which separated the two of them. And Elijah
went up by a [1]whirlwind to heaven.
12 And Elisha saw *it* and cried out,
"[a]My father, my father, the [1]chari-
ots of Israel and its horsemen!" And
he saw him no more. Then [b]he took
hold of his own clothes and tore
them in two pieces.
13 He also took up the mantle of
Elijah that fell from him, and returned and stood by the bank of the
Jordan.
14 And he took the mantle of Elijah that fell from him, and struck
the waters and said, "Where is the
LORD, the God of Elijah?" And when
he also had [a]struck the waters, they
were divided here and there; and
Elisha crossed over.

Elisha Succeeds Elijah

15 Now when [a]the sons of the
prophets who *were* at Jericho opposite *him* saw him, they said, "The
spirit of Elijah rests on Elisha." And
they came to meet him and bowed
themselves to the ground before
him.
16 And they said to him, "Behold
now, there are with your servants
fifty strong men, please let them go
and search for your master; [1]per-
haps [a]the Spirit of the LORD has
taken him up and cast him on some
mountain or into some valley." And
he said, "You shall not send."
17 But when [a]they urged him until
he was ashamed, he said, "Send."
They sent therefore fifty men; and

14 [1]Lit., *soul*
15 [a]2 Kin. 1:3
16 [1]See v. 4, note 1 [a]2 Kin. 1:3
17 [a]2 Kin. 3:1; 8:16
1 [1]Or, *windstorm* [a]Gen. 5:24; Heb. 11:5 [b]1 Kin. 19:16-21 [c]Josh. 4:19
2 [a]Ruth 1:15 [b]1 Kin. 12:28, 29 [c]1 Sam. 1:26; 2 Kin. 4:6
3 [1]Lit., *your head* [a]2 Kin. 4:1, 38; 5:22
4 [a]2 Kin. 2:2 [b]Josh. 6:26 [c]2 Kin. 2:2
5 [1]Lit., *your head* [2]Lit., *said* [a]2 Kin. 2:3 [b]2 Kin. 2:3
6 [a]2 Kin. 2:2 [b]Josh. 3:8, 15-17
7 [a]2 Kin. 2:15, 16
8 [a]1 Kin. 19:13, 19 [b]Ex. 14:21, 22; 2 Kin. 2:14
11 [1]Or, *windstorm* [a]2 Kin. 6:17
12 [1]Lit., *chariot* [a]2 Kin. 13:14 [b]Gen. 37:34; Job 1:20
14 [a]2 Kin. 2:8
15 [a]2 Kin. 2:7
16 [1]Lit., *lest* [a]1 Kin. 18:12; Acts 8:39
17 [a]2 Kin. 8:11

they searched three days, but did
not find him.
18 And they returned to him while
he was staying at Jericho; and he
said to them, "Did I not say to you,
'Do not go'?"
19 Then the men of the city said to
Elisha, "Behold now, the situation
of this city is pleasant, as my lord
sees; but the water is bad, and the
land [1]is unfruitful."
20 And he said, "Bring me a new
jar, and put salt [1]in it." So they
brought *it* to him.
21 And he went out to the spring
of water, and [a]threw salt [1]in it and
said, "Thus says the LORD, 'I have
[2]purified these waters; there shall
not be from there death or [3]unfruit-
fulness any longer.'"
22 So the waters have been [1]puri-
fied to this day, according to the
word of Elisha which he spoke.
23 Then he went up from there to
Bethel; and as he was going up by
the way, young lads came out from
the city and mocked him and said to
him, "Go up, you baldhead; go up,
you baldhead!"
24 When he looked behind him
and saw them, he [a]cursed them in
the name of the LORD. Then two female bears came out of the woods
and tore up forty-two lads of [1]their
number.
25 And he went from there to
[a]Mount Carmel, and from there he
returned to Samaria.

CHAPTER 3

Jehoram Meets Moab Rebellion

NOW Jehoram the son of Ahab became king over Israel at Samaria [a]in
the eighteenth year of Jehoshaphat
king of Judah, and reigned twelve
years.
2 And he did evil in the sight of
the LORD, though not like his father
and his mother; for [a]he put away the
sacred pillar of Baal [b]which his father had made.
3 Nevertheless, [a]he clung to the
sins of Jeroboam the son of Nebat,
[b]which he made Israel sin; he did
not depart from them.
4 Now Mesha king of Moab was a
sheep breeder, and [a]used to pay the
king of Israel 100,000 lambs and the
wool of 100,000 rams.
5 But it came about, [a]when Ahab
died, the king of Moab rebelled
against the king of Israel.
6 And King Jehoram went out of
Samaria [1]at that time and mustered
all Israel.

19 [1]Lit., *causes barrenness*
20 [1]Lit., *there*
21 [1]Lit., *there* [2]Lit., *healed* [3]Lit., *barrenness* [a]Ex. 15:25, 26; 2 Kin. 4:41; 6:6
22 [1]Lit., *healed*
24 [1]Lit., *them* [a]Neh. 13:25-27
25 [a]1 Kin. 18:19, 20; 2 Kin. 4:25
1 [a]2 Kin. 1:17
2 [a]Ex. 23:24; 2 Kin. 10:18, 26-28 [b]1 Kin. 16:31, 32
3 [a]1 Kin. 12:28-32 [b]1 Kin. 14:9, 16
4 [a]2 Sam. 8:2; Is. 16:1, 2
5 [a]2 Kin. 1:1
6 [1]Lit., *in that day*
7 [a]1 Kin. 22:4
8 [1]Lit., *said*
9 [a]2 Kin. 3:1 [b]2 Kin. 3:7 [c]1 Kin. 22:47
11 [a]1 Kin. 22:7 [b]2 Kin. 2:25 [c]1 Kin. 19:21; John 13:4, 5, 13, 14
13 [a]Ezek. 14:3-5 [b]1 Kin. 18:19; 22:6-11, 22-25
14 [a]1 Kin. 17:1; 2 Kin. 5:16
15 [a]1 Sam. 16:23; 1 Chr. 25:1 [b]1 Kin. 18:46; Ezek. 1:3
19 [a]2 Kin. 3:25

7 Then he went and sent *word* to
Jehoshaphat the king of Judah, saying, "The king of Moab has rebelled
against me. Will you go with me to
fight against Moab?" And he said, "I
will go up; [a]I am as you are, my people as your people, my horses as
your horses."
8 And he said, "Which way shall
we go up?" And he [1]answered, "The
way of the wilderness of Edom."
9 So [a]the king of Israel went with
[b]the king of Judah and [c]the king of
Edom; and they made a circuit of
seven days' journey, and there was
no water for the army or for the cattle that followed them.
10 Then the king of Israel said,
"Alas! For the LORD has called these
three kings to give them into the
hand of Moab."
11 But Jehoshaphat said, "[a]Is
there not a prophet of the LORD
here, that we may inquire of the
LORD by him?" And one of the king
of Israel's servants answered and
said, "[b]Elisha the son of Shaphat is
here, [c]who used to pour water on
the hands of Elijah."
12 And Jehoshaphat said, "The
word of the LORD is with him." So
the king of Israel and Jehoshaphat
and the king of Edom went down to
him.
13 Now [a]Elisha said to the king of
Israel, "What do I have to do with
you? [b]Go to the prophets of your father and to the prophets of your
mother." And the king of Israel said
to him, "No, for the LORD has called
these three kings *together* to give
them into the hand of Moab."
14 And Elisha said, "[a]As the LORD
of hosts lives, before whom I stand,
were it not that I regard the presence of Jehoshaphat the king of Judah, I would not look at you nor see
you.
15"But now [a]bring me a minstrel."
And it came about, when the minstrel played, that [b]the hand of the
LORD came upon him.
16 And he said, "Thus says the
LORD, 'Make this valley full of
trenches.'
17"For thus says the LORD, 'You
shall not see wind nor shall you see
rain; yet that valley shall be filled
with water, so that you shall drink,
both you and your cattle and your
beasts.
18 'And this is but a slight thing in
the sight of the LORD; He shall also
give the Moabites into your hand.
19 '[a]Then you shall strike every
fortified city and every choice city,
and fell every good tree and stop all

springs of water, and mar every
good piece of land with stones.' "
20 And it happened in the morning
[a]about the time of offering the sacrifice, that behold, water came by the
way of Edom, and the country was
filled with water.
21 Now all the Moabites heard
that the kings had come up to fight
against them. And all who were able
to [1]put on armor and older were
summoned, and stood on the border.
22 And they rose early in the
morning, and the sun shone on the
water, and the Moabites saw the
water opposite *them* as red as blood.
23 Then they said, "This is blood;
the kings have surely fought together, and they have slain one another. Now therefore, Moab, to the
spoil!"
24 But when they came to the
camp of Israel, the Israelites arose
and struck the Moabites, so that
they fled before them; and they
went forward [1]into the land,
[2]slaughtering the Moabites.
25 [a]Thus they destroyed the cities;
and each one threw a stone on every
piece of good land and filled it. So
they stopped all the springs of water
and felled all the good trees, until in
[b]Kir-hareseth *only* they left its
stones; however, the slingers went
about *it* and struck it.
26 When the king of Moab saw
that the battle was too fierce for
him, he took with him 700 men who
drew swords, to break through to
the king of Edom; but they could
not.
27 Then he took his oldest son who
was to reign in his place, and [a]of-
fered him as a burnt offering on the
wall. And there came great wrath
against Israel, and they departed
from him and returned to their own
land.

Chapter 4

The Widow's Oil

NOW a certain woman of the
wives of [a]the sons of the prophets
cried out to [1]Elisha, "Your servant
my husband is dead, and you know
that your servant feared the LORD;
and [b]the creditor has come to take
my two children to be his slaves."
2 And Elisha said to her, "What
shall I do for you? Tell me, what do
you have in the house?" And she
said, "Your maidservant has nothing in the house except a jar of oil."
3 Then he said, "Go, borrow vessels at large for yourself from all

20 [a]Ex. 29:39, 40

21 [1]Lit., *gird themselves with a belt*

24 [1]Lit., *into it* [2]Lit., *smiting*

25 [a]2 Kin. 3:19 [b]Is. 16:7; Jer. 48:31, 36

27 [a]Amos 2:1; Mic. 6:7

1 [1]Lit., *Elisha, saying* [a]2 Kin. 2:3 [b]Lev. 25:39-41, 48; 1 Sam. 22:2; Neh. 5:2-5

7 [a]1 Kin. 12:22

8 [1]Lit., *great* [2]Lit., *bread* [a]Josh. 19:18 [b]2 Sam. 19:32

9 [a]2 Kin. 4:7

11 [1]Lit., *Now a day came that* [2]Lit., *lay there*

12 [a]2 Kin. 4:29-31; 5:20-27; 8:4, 5

13 [1]Lit., *fearful* [2]Lit., *fear* [3]Lit., *said*

14 [1]Lit., *said*

16 [1]Lit., *when the time revives* [a]Gen. 18:14 [b]2 Kin. 4:28

17 [1]Lit., *when the time revived*

your neighbors, *even* empty vessels;
do not get a few.
4 "And you shall go in and shut the
door behind you and your sons, and
pour out into all these vessels; and
you shall set aside what is full."
5 So she went from him and shut
the door behind her and her sons;
they were bringing *the vessels* to her
and she poured.
6 And it came about when the
vessels were full, that she said to her
son, "Bring me another vessel." And
he said to her, "There is not one vessel more." And the oil stopped.
7 Then she came and told [a]the
man of God. And he said, "Go, sell
the oil and pay your debt, and you
and your sons can live on the rest."

The Shunammite Woman

8 Now there came a day when
Elisha passed over to [a]Shunem,
where there was a [1b]prominent
woman, and she persuaded him to
eat [2]food. And so it was, as often as
he passed by, he turned in there to
eat [2]food.
9 And she said to her husband,
"Behold now, I perceive that this is
a holy [a]man of God passing by us
continually.
10 "Please, let us make a little
walled upper chamber and let us set
a bed for him there, and a table and
a chair and a lampstand; and it shall
be, when he comes to us, *that* he can
turn in there."
11 [1]One day he came there and
turned in to the upper chamber and
[2]rested.
12 Then he said to [a]Gehazi his servant, "Call this Shunammite." And
when he had called her, she stood
before him.
13 And he said to him, "Say now
to her, 'Behold, you have been [1]care-
ful for us with all this [2]care; what
can I do for you? Would you be spoken for to the king or to the captain
of the army?' " And she [3]answered,
"I live among my own people."
14 So he said, "What then is to be
done for her?" And Gehazi [1]an-
swered, "Truly she has no son and
her husband is old."
15 And he said, "Call her." When
he had called her, she stood in the
doorway.
16 Then he said, "[a]At this season
[1]next year you shall embrace a son."
And she said, "No, my lord, O man
of God, [b]do not lie to your maidservant."
17 And the woman conceived and
bore a son at that season [1]the next
year, as Elisha had said to her.

The Shunammite's Son

18 When the child was grown, the day came that he went out to his father to the reapers.

19 And he said to his father, "My head, my head." And he said to his servant, "Carry him to his mother."

20 When he had taken him and brought him to his mother, he sat on her [1]lap until noon, and *then* died.

21 And she went up and [a]laid him on the bed of [b]the man of God, and shut *the door* behind him, and went out.

22 Then she called to her husband and said, "Please send me one of the servants and one of the donkeys, that I may run to the man of God and return."

23 And he said, "Why will you go to him today? It is neither [a]new moon nor sabbath." And she said, "*It will be* well."

24 Then she saddled a donkey and said to her servant, "Drive and go forward; do not slow down [1]the pace for me unless I tell you."

25 So she went and came to the man of God to [a]Mount Carmel. And it came about when the man of God saw her at a distance, that he said to Gehazi his servant, "Behold, [1]yonder is the Shunammite.

26 "Please run now to meet her and say to her, 'Is it well with you? Is it well with your husband? Is it well with the child?'" And she [1]answered, "It is well."

27 When she came to the man of God [a]to the hill, she caught hold of his feet. And Gehazi came near to push her away; but the man of God said, "Let her alone, for her soul is [1]troubled within her; and the LORD has hid it from me and has not told me."

28 Then she said, "Did I ask for a son from my lord? Did I not say, '[a]Do not deceive me'?"

29 Then he said to Gehazi, "[a]Gird up your loins and [b]take my staff in your hand, and go your way; if you meet any man, do not [c]salute him, and if anyone salutes you, do not answer him; and [d]lay my staff on the lad's face."

30 And the mother of the lad said, "[a]As the LORD lives and as you yourself live, I will not leave you." And he arose and followed her.

31 Then Gehazi passed on before them and laid the staff on the lad's face, but there was neither sound nor [1]response. So he returned to meet him and told [2]him, "The lad has not awakened."

32 When Elisha came into the house, behold the lad was dead and laid on his bed.

33 So he entered and [a]shut the door behind them both, and prayed to the LORD.

34 And [a]he went up and lay on the child, and put his mouth on his mouth and his eyes on his eyes and his hands on his hands, and he stretched himself on him; and the flesh of the child became warm.

35 Then he returned and walked in the house once back and forth, and went up and stretched himself on him; and the lad sneezed seven times and the lad opened his eyes.

36 And he called Gehazi and said, "Call this Shunammite." So he called her. And when she came in to him, he said, "Take up your son."

37 Then she went in and fell at his feet and bowed herself to the ground, and [a]she took up her son and went out.

The Poisonous Stew

38 When Elisha returned to [a]Gilgal, *there was* [b]a famine in the land. [1]As [c]the sons of the prophets [d]were sitting before him, he said to his servant, "[e]Put on the large pot and boil stew for the sons of the prophets."

39 Then one went out into the field to gather herbs, and found a wild vine and gathered from it his lap full of wild gourds, and came and sliced them into the pot of stew, for they did not know *what they were.*

40 So they poured *it* out for the men to eat. And it came about as they were eating of the stew, that they cried out and said, "O man of God, there is death in the pot." And they were unable to eat.

41 But he said, "Now bring meal." [a]And he threw it into the pot, and he said, "Pour *it* out for the people that they may eat." Then there was no harm in the pot.

42 Now a man came from Baal-shalishah, and brought the man of God bread of the first fruits, twenty loaves of barley and fresh ears of grain in his sack. And he said, "[a]Give *them* to the people that they may eat."

43 And his attendant said, "What, shall I set this before a hundred men?" But he said, "Give *them* to the people that they may eat, for thus says the LORD, 'They shall eat and have *some* left over.'"

44 So he set *it* before them, and they ate and had *some* left over, according to the word of the LORD.

20 [1]Lit., *knees*
21 [a]2 Kin. 4:32 [b]2 Kin. 4:7
23 [a]Num. 10:10; 28:11; 1 Chr. 23:31
24 [1]Lit., *riding*
25 [1]Lit., *this Shunammite* [a]2 Kin. 2:25
26 [1]Lit., *said*
27 [1]Lit., *bitter* [a]2 Kin. 4:25
28 [a]2 Kin. 4:16
29 [a]1 Kin. 18:46; 2 Kin. 9:1 [b]Ex. 4:17; 2 Kin. 2:14 [c]Luke 10:4 [d]Ex. 7:19, 20; 14:16
30 [a]2 Kin. 2:2, 4
31 [1]Lit., *attentiveness* [2]Lit., *him, saying*
33 [a]2 Kin. 4:4; Matt. 6:6; Luke 8:51
34 [a]1 Kin. 17:21-23
37 [a]Heb. 11:35
38 [1]Lit., *And* [a]2 Kin. 2:1 [b]2 Kin. 8:1 [c]2 Kin. 2:3 [d]Luke 10:39; Acts 22:3 [e]Ezek. 11:3, 7, 11; 24:3
41 [a]Ex. 15:25; 2 Kin. 2:21
42 [a]Matt. 14:16-21; 15:32-38

CHAPTER 5

Naaman Is Healed

NOW [a]Naaman, captain of the
army of the king of Syria, was a
great man [1]with his master, and
highly respected, because by him
the LORD had given victory to Syria.
The man was also a valiant warrior,
but he was a leper.
2 Now the Syrians had gone out
[a]in bands, and had taken captive a
little girl from the land of Israel; and
she [1]waited on Naaman's wife.
3 And she said to her mistress, "I
wish that my master were [1]with the
prophet who is in Samaria! Then he
would cure him of his leprosy."
4 And [1]Naaman went in and told
his master, saying, "Thus and thus
spoke the girl who is from the land
of Israel."
5 Then the king of Syria said, "Go
[1]now, and I will send a letter to the
king of Israel." And he departed and
[a]took with him ten talents of silver
and six thousand *shekels* of gold and
ten [b]changes of clothes.
6 And he brought the letter to the
king of Israel, saying, "And now as
this letter comes to you, behold, I
have sent Naaman my servant to
you, that you may cure him of his
leprosy."
7 And it came about when the
king of Israel read the letter, that
[a]he tore his clothes and said, "[b]Am I
God, to kill and to make alive, that
this man is sending *word* to me to
cure a man of his leprosy? But [c]con-
sider now, and see how he is seeking
[1]a quarrel against me."
8 And it happened when Elisha
[a]the man of God heard that the king
of Israel had torn his clothes, that he
sent *word* to the king, saying, "Why
have you torn your clothes? Now let
him come to me, and he shall know
that there is a prophet in Israel."
9 So Naaman came with his
horses and his chariots, and stood at
the doorway of the house of Elisha.
10 And Elisha sent a messenger to
him, saying, "[a]Go and wash in the
Jordan seven times, and your flesh
shall be restored to you and *you
shall* be clean."
11 But Naaman was furious and
went away and said, "Behold, I
[1]thought, 'He will surely come out
to me, and stand and call on the
name of the LORD his God, and wave
his hand over the place, and cure the
leper.'
12 "Are not [1]Abanah and Pharpar,
the rivers of Damascus, better than
all the waters of Israel? Could I not
wash in them and be clean?" So he
turned and went away in a rage.
13 [a]Then his servants came near
and spoke to him and said, "[b]My father, had the prophet told you *to do
some* great thing, would you not
have done *it*? How much more *then*,
when he says to you, 'Wash, and be
clean'?"
14 So he went down and dipped
himself seven times in the Jordan,
according to the word of the man of
God; and [a]his flesh was restored like
the flesh of a little child, and [b]he was
clean.

Gehazi's Greed

15 When he returned to the man of
God [1]with all his company, and
came and stood before him, he said,
"Behold now, [a]I know that there is
no God in all the earth, but in Israel;
so please [b]take a [2]present from your
servant now."
16 But he said, "[a]As the LORD
lives, before whom I stand, [b]I will
take nothing." And he urged him to
take *it*, but he refused.
17 And Naaman said, "If not,
please let your servant at least be
given two mules' load of [a]earth; for
your servant will no more offer
burnt offering nor will he sacrifice to
other gods, but to the LORD.
18 "In this matter may the LORD
pardon your servant: when my master goes into the house of [a]Rimmon
to worship there, and [b]he leans on
my hand and I bow myself in the
house of Rimmon, when I bow myself in the house of Rimmon, the
LORD pardon your servant in this
matter."
19 And he said to him, "[a]Go in
peace." So he departed from him
some distance.
20 But [a]Gehazi, the servant of Elisha the man of God, [1]thought, "Behold, my master has spared this
Naaman the Syrian, [2]by not receiving from his hands what he brought.
[b]As the LORD lives, I will run after
him and take something from him."
21 So Gehazi pursued Naaman.
When Naaman saw one running after him, he came down from the
chariot to meet him and said, "Is all
well?"
22 And he said, "[a]All is well. My
master has sent me, saying, 'Behold,
just now two young men of the sons
of the prophets have come to me
from [b]the hill country of Ephraim.
Please give them a talent of silver
and [c]two changes of clothes.' "

1 [1]Lit., *before* [a]Luke 4:27
2 [1]Lit., *was before* [a]2 Kin. 6:23; 13:20
3 [1]Lit., *before*
4 [1]Lit., *he*
5 [1]Lit., *enter* [a]1 Sam. 9:7; 2 Kin. 4:42 [b]Judg. 14:12; 2 Kin. 5:22, 23
7 [1]Lit., *an occasion* [a]Gen. 37:29 [b]Gen. 30:2; 1 Sam. 2:6 [c]1 Kin. 20:7; Luke 11:54
8 [a]1 Kin. 12:22
10 [a]John 9:7
11 [1]Lit., *said*
12 [1]Another reading is *Amanah*
13 [a]1 Sam. 28:23 [b]2 Kin. 2:12; 6:21; 8:9
14 [a]2 Kin. 5:10; Job 33:25 [b]Luke 4:27; 5:13
15 [1]Lit., *he and* [2]Lit., *blessing* [a]Josh. 2:9-16; 1 Sam. 17:46, 47; 2 Kin. 5:8 [b]1 Sam. 25:27
16 [a]2 Kin. 3:14 [b]Gen. 14:22, 23; 2 Kin. 20:26
17 [a]Ex. 20:24
18 [a]1 Kin. 15:18 [b]2 Kin. 7:2, 17
19 [a]Ex. 4:18; 1 Sam. 1:17; Mark 5:34
20 [1]Lit., *said* [2]Lit., *from* [a]2 Kin. 4:12, 31, 36 [b]Ex. 20:7; 2 Kin. 6:31
22 [a]2 Kin. 4:26 [b]Josh. 24:33 [c]2 Kin. 5:5

23 And Naaman said, "[a]Be pleased
to take two talents." And he urged
him, and bound two talents of silver
in two bags with two changes of
clothes, and gave them to two of his
servants; and they carried *them* before him.
24 When he came to the [1]hill, he
took them from their hand and [a]de-
posited them in the house, and he
sent the men away, and they departed.
25 But he went in and stood before
his master. And Elisha said to him,
"Where have you been, Gehazi?"
And he said, "[a]Your servant went
nowhere."
26 Then he said to him, "Did not
my heart go *with you*, when the man
turned from his chariot to meet you?
[a]Is it a time to receive money and to
receive clothes and oliveyards and
vineyards and sheep and oxen and
male and female servants?
27"Therefore, the leprosy of Naaman shall cleave to you and to your
[1]descendants forever." So he went
out from his presence [a]a leper *as
white* as snow.

Chapter 6

The Axe Head Recovered

Now [a]the sons of the prophets
said to Elisha, "Behold now, the
place before you where we are living is too limited for us.
2"Please let us go to the Jordan,
and each of us take from there a
beam, and let us make a place there
for ourselves where we may live."
So he said, "Go."
3 Then one said, "Please be willing to go with your servants." And
he [1]answered, "I shall go."
4 So he went with them; and
when they came to the Jordan, they
cut down trees.
5 But as one was felling a beam,
[1]the axe head fell into the water; and
he cried out and said, "Alas, my
master! For it was borrowed."
6 Then the man of God said,
"Where did it fall?" And when he
showed him the place, [a]he cut off a
stick, and threw *it* in there, and
made the iron float.
7 And he said, "Take it up for
yourself." So he put out his hand
and took it.

The Syrians Plot to Capture Elisha

8 Now the king of Syria was warring against Israel; and he [1]coun-
seled with his servants saying, "In
such and such a place shall be my
camp."
9 And [a]the man of God sent *word*
to the king of Israel saying, "Beware
that you do not pass this place, for
the Syrians are coming down
there."
10 And the king of Israel sent to
the place about which the man of
God had told him; thus he warned
him, so that he guarded himself
there, [1]more than once or twice.
11 Now the heart of the king of
Syria was enraged over this thing;
and he called his servants and said
to them, "Will you tell me which of
us is for the king of Israel?"
12 And one of his servants said,
"No, my lord, O king; but Elisha, the
prophet who is in Israel, tells the
king of Israel the words that you
speak in your bedroom."
13 So he said, "Go and see where
he is, that I may send and take him."
And it was told him, saying, "Behold, he is in [a]Dothan."
14 And he sent horses and chariots
and a great army there, and they
came by night and surrounded the
city.
15 Now when the attendant of the
man of God had risen early and gone
out, behold, an army with horses
and chariots was circling the city.
And his servant said to him, "Alas,
my master! [1]What shall we do?"
16 So he [1]answered, "[a]Do not fear,
for [b]those who are with us are more
than those who are with them."
17 Then Elisha prayed and said,
"[a]O LORD, I pray, open his eyes that
he may see." And the LORD opened
the servant's eyes, and he saw; and
behold, the mountain was full of
[b]horses and chariots of fire all
around Elisha.
18 And when they came down to
him, Elisha prayed to the LORD and
said, "Strike this [1]people with blindness, I pray." So He [a]struck them
with blindness according to the
word of Elisha.
19 Then Elisha said to them, "This
is not the way, nor is this the city;
follow me and I will bring you to the
man whom you seek." And he
brought them to Samaria.
20 And it came about when they
had come into Samaria, that Elisha
said, "O [a]LORD, open the eyes of
these *men*, that they may see." So
the LORD opened their eyes, and
they saw; and behold, they were in
the midst of Samaria.
21 Then the king of Israel when he
saw them, said to Elisha, "[a]My father, shall I [1]kill them? Shall I [1]kill
them?"

23 [a]2 Kin. 6:3
24 [1]Lit., *Ophel* [a]Josh. 7:1, 11, 12, 21; 1 Kin. 21:16
25 [a]2 Kin. 5:22
26 [a]2 Kin. 5:16
27 [1]Lit., *seed* [a]Ex. 4:6; Num. 12:10
1 [a]2 Kin. 2:3
3 [1]Lit., *said*
5 [1]Lit., *as for the iron, it fell*
6 [a]Ex. 15:25; 2 Kin. 2:21; 4:41
8 [1]Lit., *took counsel*
9 [a]2 Kin. 4:1, 7; 6:12
10 [1]Lit., *not once or twice*
13 [a]Gen. 37:17
15 [1]Lit., *How*
16 [1]Lit., *said* [a]Ex. 14:13 [b]2 Chr. 32:7, 8; Rom. 8:31
17 [a]2 Kin. 6:20 [b]2 Kin. 2:11; Ps. 68:17; Zech. 6:1-7
18 [1]Lit., *nation* [a]Gen. 19:11
20 [a]2 Kin. 6:17
21 [1]Lit., *smite* [a]2 Kin. 2:12; 5:13; 8:9

22 And he [1]answered, "You shall
not [2]kill *them.* Would you [2a]kill
those you have taken captive with
your sword and with your bow? [b]Set
bread and water before them, that
they may eat and drink and go to
their master."
23 So he prepared a great feast for
them; and when they had eaten and
drunk he sent them away, and they
went to their master. And [a]the marauding bands of Syria did not come
again into the land of Israel.

The Siege of Samaria—Cannibalism

24 Now it came about after this,
that [a]Ben-hadad king of Syria gathered all his army and went up and
besieged Samaria.
25 And there was a great famine in
Samaria; and behold, they besieged
it, until a donkey's head was sold for
eighty *shekels* of silver, and a fourth
of a [1]kab of dove's dung for five
shekels of silver.
26 And as the king of Israel was
passing by on the wall a woman
cried out to him, saying, "Help, my
lord, O king!"
27 And he said, "[1]If the LORD does
not help you, from where shall I
help you? From the threshing floor,
or from the wine press?"
28 And the king said to her, "What
[1]is the matter with you?" And she
[2]answered, "This woman said to
me, 'Give your son that we may eat
him today, and we will eat my son
tomorrow.'
29"[a]So we boiled my son and ate
him; and I said to her on the next
day, 'Give your son, that we may eat
him'; but she has hidden her son."
30 And it came about when the
king heard the words of the woman,
that [a]he tore his clothes—now he
was passing by on the wall—and the
people looked, and behold, he had
sackcloth [1]beneath on his [2]body.
31 Then he said, "May [a]God do so
to me and more also, if the head of
Elisha the son of Shaphat [1]remains
on him today."
32 Now Elisha was sitting in his
house, and [a]the elders were sitting
with him. And *the king* sent a man
from his presence; but before the
messenger came to him, he said to
the elders, "Do you [b]see how this
son of a murderer has sent to take
away my head? Look, when the
messenger comes, shut the door and
[1]hold the door shut against him. Is
not the sound of his master's feet
behind him?"
33 And while he was still talking
with them, behold, the messenger
came down to him, and he said,
"[a]Behold, this evil is from the LORD;
why should I wait for the LORD any
longer?"

CHAPTER 7

Elisha Promises Food

THEN Elisha said, "Listen to the
word of the LORD; thus says the
LORD, '[a]Tomorrow about this time a
[1]measure of fine flour shall be *sold*
for a shekel, and two measures of
barley for a shekel, in the gate of
Samaria.'"
2 And [a]the royal officer on whose
hand the king was leaning answered
the man of God and said, "Behold,
[b]if the LORD should make windows
in heaven, could this thing be?"
Then he said, "Behold you shall see
it with your own eyes, but you shall
not eat [1]of it."

Four Lepers Relate Syrians' Flight

3 Now there were four [a]leprous
men at the entrance of the gate; and
they said to one another, "Why do
we sit here until we die?
4"If we say, 'We will enter the
city,' then the famine is in the city
and we shall die there; and if we sit
here, we die also. Now therefore
come, and let us [1]go over to [a] the
camp of the Syrians. If they spare
us, we shall live; and if they kill us,
we shall but die."
5 And they arose at twilight to go
to the camp of the Syrians; when
they came to the outskirts of the
camp of the Syrians, behold, there
was no one there.
6 For [a]the Lord had caused the
army of the Syrians to hear a sound
of chariots and a sound of horses,
even the sound of a great army, so
that they said to one another, "Behold, the king of Israel has hired
against us [b]the kings of the Hittites
and [c]the kings of the Egyptians, to
come upon us."
7 Therefore they arose and fled in
the twilight, and left their tents and
their horses and their donkeys, even
the camp just as it was, and fled for
their life.
8 When these lepers came to the
outskirts of the camp, they entered
one tent and ate and drank, and
[a]carried from there silver and gold
and clothes, and went and hid *them*;
and they returned and entered another tent and carried from there
also, and went and hid *them.*
9 Then they said to one another,
"We are not doing right. This day is
a day of good news, but we are

22 [1]Lit., *said* [2]Lit., *smite* [a]Deut. 20:11-16; 2 Chr. 28:8-15 [b]Rom. 12:20

23 [a]2 Kin. 5:2; 24:2

24 [a]1 Kin. 20:1

25 [1]I.e., one kab equals approx. 1 pint

27 [1]Lit., *No, let the LORD help you*

28 [1]Lit., *to you* [2]Lit., *said*

29 [a]Lev. 26:27-29; Deut. 28:52, 53, 57; Lam. 4:10

30 [1]Lit., *within* [2]Lit., *flesh* [a]1 Kin. 21:27

31 [1]Lit., *stands* [a]Ruth 1:17; 1 Kin. 19:2

32 [1]Lit., *press him with the door* [a]Ezek. 8:1; 14:1; 20:1 [b]1 Kin. 18:4, 13, 14; 21:10, 13

33 [a]Is. 8:21; Jer. 2:25

1 [1]Heb., *seah* [a]2 Kin. 7:18

2 [1]Lit., *from there* [a]2 Kin. 5:18; 7:17, 19 [b]Gen. 7:11; Mal. 3:10

3 [a]Lev. 13:45, 46; Num. 5:2-4; 12:10-14

4 [1]Lit., *fall* [a]2 Kin. 6:24

6 [a]2 Sam. 5:24 [b]1 Kin. 10:29 [c]2 Chr. 12:2, 3; Is. 31:1; 36:9

8 [a]Josh. 7:21

keeping silent; if we wait until morning light, punishment will [1]overtake us. Now therefore come, let us go and [a]tell the king's household."

10 So they came and called to the gatekeepers of the city, and they told them, saying, "We came to the camp of the Syrians, and behold, there was no one there, nor the voice of man, only the horses tied and the donkeys tied, and the tents just as they were."

11 And the gatekeepers called, and told *it* within the king's household.

12 Then the king arose in the night and said to his servants, "I will now tell you what the Syrians have done to us. They know that [a]we are hungry; therefore they have gone from the camp [b]to hide themselves in the field, saying, 'When they come out of the city, we shall capture them alive and get into the city.' "

13 And one of his servants answered and said, "Please, let some *men* take five of the horses which remain, which are left [1]in the city. Behold, they *will be in any case* like all the multitude of Israel who are left in it; behold, they *will be in any case* like all the multitude of Israel who have already perished, so let us send and see."

14 They took therefore two chariots with horses, and the king sent after the army of the Syrians, saying, "Go and see."

The Promise Fulfilled

15 And they went after them to the Jordan, and behold, all the way was full of clothes and equipment, which the Syrians had thrown away in their haste. Then the messengers returned and told the king.

16 So the people went out and plundered the camp of the Syrians. Then a [1]measure of fine flour *was sold* for a shekel and two [1]measures of barley for a shekel, [a]according to the word of the LORD.

17 Now the king appointed [a]the royal officer on whose hand he leaned [1]to have charge of the gate; but the people trampled on him at the gate, and he died just as the man of God had said, [b]who spoke when the king came down to him.

18 And it came about just as the man of God had spoken to the king, saying, "Two [1]measures of barley for a shekel and a [1]measure of fine flour for a shekel, shall be *sold* tomorrow about this time at the gate of Samaria."

19 Then the royal officer answered the man of God and said, "Now behold, [a]if the LORD should make windows in heaven, could such a thing be?" And he said, "Behold, you shall see it with your own eyes, but you shall not eat [1]of it."

20 And so it happened to him, for the people trampled on him at the gate, and he died.

CHAPTER 8

Jehoram Restores the Shunammite's Land

NOW [a]Elisha spoke to the woman whose son he had restored to life, saying, "Arise and go [1]with your household, and sojourn wherever you can sojourn; for the [b]LORD has called for a famine, and [c]it shall even come on the land for seven years."

2 So the woman arose and did according to the word of the man of God, and she went with her household and sojourned in the land of the Philistines seven years.

3 And it came about at the end of seven years, that the woman returned from the land of the Philistines; and she went out to [1]appeal to the king for her house and for her field.

4 Now the king was talking with [a]Gehazi, the servant of the man of God, saying, "Please relate to me all the great things that Elisha has done."

5 And it came about, as he was relating to the king how he had restored to life the one who was dead, that behold, the woman whose son he had restored to life, [1]appealed to the king for her house and for her field. And Gehazi said, "My lord, O king, this is the woman and this is her son, whom Elisha restored to life."

6 When the king asked the woman, she related *it* to him. So the king appointed for her a certain officer, saying, "Restore all that was hers and all the produce of the field from the day that she left the land even until now."

Elisha Predicts Evil from Hazael

7 Then Elisha came to [a]Damascus. Now [b]Ben-hadad king of Syria was sick, and it was told him, saying, "[c]The man of God has come here."

8 And the king said to [a]Hazael, "[b]Take a gift in your hand and go to meet the man of God, and [c]inquire

9 [1]Lit., *find* [a]2 Kin. 6:30

12 [a]2 Kin. 6:25-29 [b]Josh. 8:4-12

13 [1]Lit., *in it*

16 [1]Heb., *seah;* i.e., one seah equals approx. 11 quarts [a]2 Kin. 7:1

17 [1]Lit., *over the gate* [a]2 Kin. 7:2 [b]2 Kin. 6:32

18 [1]Heb., *seah;* i.e., one seah equals approx. 11 quarts

19 [1]Lit., *from there* [a]2 Kin. 7:2

1 [1]Lit., *you and your* [a]2 Kin. 4:18, 31-35; [b]Ps. 105:16; Hag. 1:11 [c]Gen. 41:27, 54

3 [1]Lit., *cry out*

4 [a]2 Kin. 4:12; 5:20-27

5 [1]Lit., *cried out*

7 [a]1 Kin. 11:24 [b]2 Kin. 6:24 [c]2 Kin. 5:20

8 [a]1 Kin. 19:15, 17 [b]1 Kin. 14:3 [c]2 Kin. 1:2

of the LORD by him, saying, 'Will I recover from this sickness?' "

9 So Hazael went to meet him and took a gift in his hand, even every kind of good thing of Damascus, forty camels' loads; and he came and stood before him and said, "[a]Your son Ben-hadad king of Syria has sent me to you, saying, 'Will I recover from this sickness?' "

10 Then Elisha said to him, "[a]Go, say to him, 'You shall surely recover,' but the [b]LORD has shown me that he will certainly die."

11 And he [1]fixed his gaze steadily *on him* [a]until he was ashamed, and the man of God wept.

12 And Hazael said, "Why does my lord weep?" Then he [1]answered, "Because [a]I know the evil that you will do to the sons of Israel: their strongholds you will set on fire, and their young men you will kill with the sword, and their little ones you [b]will dash in pieces, and their women with child you will rip up."

13 Then Hazael said, "But what is your servant, [a]*who is but* a dog, that he should do this great thing?" And Elisha [1]answered, "[b]The Lord has shown me that you will be king over Syria."

14 So he departed from Elisha and returned to his master, who said to him, "What did Elisha say to you?" And he [1]answered, "He told me that [a]you would surely recover."

15 And it came about on the morrow, that he took the cover and dipped it in water and spread it on his face, [a]so that he died. And Hazael became king in his place.

Another Jehoram Reigns in Judah

16 Now in the fifth year of [a]Joram the son of Ahab king of Israel, Jehoshaphat being then the king of Judah, Jehoram the son of Jehoshaphat king of Judah became king.

17 He was [a]thirty-two years old when he became king, and he reigned eight years in Jerusalem.

18 And he walked in the way of the kings of Israel, just as the house of Ahab had done, for [a]the daughter of Ahab became his wife; and he did evil in the sight of the LORD.

19 However, the LORD was not willing to destroy Judah, for the sake of David His servant, [a]since He had [1]promised him to give a [2]lamp to him through his sons always.

20 In his days [a]Edom revolted from under the hand of Judah, and made a king over themselves.

21 Then Joram crossed over to Zair, and all his chariots with him. And it came about that he arose by night and struck the Edomites who had surrounded him and the captains of the chariots; [a]but *his* [1]army fled to their tents.

22 [a]So Edom revolted [1]against Judah to this day. Then [b]Libnah revolted at the same time.

23 And the rest of the acts of Joram and all that he did, are they not written in the Book of the Chronicles of the Kings of Judah?

Ahaziah Succeeds Jehoram in Judah

24 So Joram slept with his fathers, and [a]was buried with his fathers in the city of David; and [b]Ahaziah his son became king in his place.

25 [a]In the twelfth year of Joram the son of Ahab king of Israel, Ahaziah the son of Jehoram king of Judah began to reign.

26 Ahaziah *was* twenty-two years old when he became king, and he reigned one year in Jerusalem. And his mother's name *was* Athaliah the granddaughter of Omri king of Israel.

27 And he walked in the way of the house of Ahab, and did evil in the sight of the LORD, like the house of Ahab *had done,* because he was a son-in-law of the house of Ahab.

28 Then he went with Joram the son of Ahab to war against [a]Hazael king of Syria at [b]Ramoth-gilead, and the Syrians [1]wounded Joram.

29 So [a]King Joram returned to be healed in Jezreel of the wounds which the Syrians had [1]inflicted on him at [b]Ramah, when he fought against Hazael king of Syria. Then [c]Ahaziah the son of Jehoram king of Judah went down to see Joram the son of Ahab in Jezreel because he was sick.

CHAPTER 9

Jehu Reigns over Israel

NOW Elisha the prophet called one of [a]the sons of the prophets, and said to him, "[b]Gird up your loins, and [c]take this flask of oil in your hand, and go to [d]Ramoth-gilead.

2 "When you arrive there, [1]search out [a]Jehu the son of Jehoshaphat the son of Nimshi, and go in and [2b]bid him arise from among his brothers, and bring him to an inner room.

3 "Then take the flask of oil and pour it on his head and say, 'Thus says the LORD, "[a]I have anointed you king over Israel." ' Then open the door and flee and do not wait."

9 [a]2 Kin. 5:13
10 [a]2 Kin. 8:14 [b]2 Kin. 8:15
11 [1]Lit., *made his face stand fast and he set* [a]2 Kin. 2:17
12 [1]Lit., *said* [a]2 Kin. 10:32, 33; 12:17; 13:3, 7 [b]2 Kin. 15:16; Nah. 3:10
13 [1]Lit., *said* [a]1 Sam. 17:43; 2 Sam. 9:8 [b]1 Kin. 19:15
14 [1]Lit., *said* [a]2 Kin. 8:10
15 [a]2 Kin. 8:10
16 [a]2 Kin. 1:17; 3:1
17 [a]2 Chr. 21:5-10
18 [a]2 Kin. 8:27
19 [1]Lit., *said* [2]I.e., descendant on the throne [a]2 Sam. 7:12-15; 1 Kin. 11:36
20 [a]1 Kin. 22:47; 2 Kin. 3:9, 26, 27; 8:22
21 [1]Lit., *the people* [a]2 Sam. 18:17; 19:8
22 [1]Lit., *from under the hand of* [a]Gen. 27:40 [b]Josh. 21:13; 2 Kin. 19:8
24 [a]2 Chr. 21:20 [b]2 Chr. 21:1, 7
25 [a]2 Chr. 22:1-6
28 [1]Lit., *smote* [a]2 Kin. 8:15 [b]1 Kin. 22:3, 29
29 [1]Lit., *struck* [a]2 Kin. 9:15 [b]2 Kin. 8:28; 2 Chr. 22:5, 6 [c]2 Kin. 9:16
1 [a]2 Kin. 2:3 [b]2 Kin. 4:29 [c]1 Sam. 10:1; 16:1; 1 Kin. 1:39 [d]2 Kin. 8:28, 29
2 [1]Lit., *and look there for* [2]Lit., *cause him to* [a]1 Kin. 19:16, 17; 2 Kin. 9:14, 20 [b]2 Kin. 9:5, 11
3 [a]2 Chr. 22:7

4 So [a]the young man, the servant
of the prophet, went to Ramoth-gilead.
5 When he came, behold, the captains of the army were sitting, and
he said, "I have a word for you, O
captain." And Jehu said, "[1]For
which *one* of us?" And he said, "For
you, O captain."
6 And he arose and went into the
house, and he poured the oil on his
head and said to him, "Thus says the
LORD, the God of Israel, '[a]I have
anointed you king over the people of
the LORD, *even* over Israel.
7 'And you shall strike the house
of Ahab your master, [a]that I may
avenge [b]the blood of My servants
the prophets, and the blood of all the
servants of the LORD, [c]at the hand of
Jezebel.
8 'For the whole house of Ahab
shall perish, and [a]I will cut off from
Ahab [b]every male person [c]both
bond and free in Israel.
9 'And [a]I will make the house of
Ahab like the house of Jeroboam the
son of Nebat, and [b]like the house of
Baasha the son of Ahijah.
10 'And [a]the dogs shall eat Jezebel
in the territory of Jezreel, and none
shall bury *her.*' " Then he opened
the door and fled.
11 Now Jehu came out to the servants of his master, and one said to
him, "[a]Is all well? Why did this
[b]mad fellow come to you?" And he
said to them, "You know very well
the man and his talk."
12 And they said, "It is a lie, tell us
now." And he said, "Thus and thus
he said to me, 'Thus says the LORD,
"I have anointed you king over Israel." ' "
13 Then [a]they hurried and each
man took his garment and placed it
under him on the bare steps, and
[b]blew the trumpet, saying, "Jehu is
king!"

Jehoram (Joram) Is Assassinated

14 So Jehu the son of Jehoshaphat
the son of Nimshi conspired against
Joram. [a]Now Joram [1]with all Israel
was [2]defending Ramoth-gilead
against Hazael king of Syria,
15 but [a]King [1]Joram had returned
to Jezreel to be healed of the
wounds which the Syrians had [2]in-
flicted on him when he fought with
Hazael king of Syria. So Jehu said,
"If this is your mind, *then* let no one
escape *or* [3]leave the city to go tell *it*
in Jezreel."
16 Then Jehu rode in a chariot and
went to Jezreel, for Joram was lying
there. [a]And Ahaziah king of Judah
had come down to see Joram.
17 Now the watchman was standing on the tower in Jezreel and he
saw the [1]company of Jehu as he
came, and said, "I see a [1]company."
And Joram said, "Take a horseman
and send him to meet them and let
him say, 'Is it peace?' "
18 So a horseman went to meet
him and said, "Thus says the king,
'Is it peace?' " And Jehu said,
"[a]What have you to do with peace?
Turn behind me." And the watchman [1]reported, "The messenger
came to them, but he did not return."
19 Then he sent out a second
horseman, who came to them and
said, "Thus says the king, 'Is it
peace?' " And Jehu [1]answered,
"What have you to do with peace?
Turn behind me."
20 And the watchman [1]reported,
"He came even to them, and he did
not return; and [a]the driving is like
the driving of [b]Jehu the son of Nimshi, for he drives furiously."
21 Then [1]Joram said, "[2]Get
ready." And they made his chariot
ready. [a]And [1]Joram king of Israel
and Ahaziah king of Judah went
out, each in his chariot, and they
went out to meet Jehu and found
him in the [3b]property of Naboth the
Jezreelite.
22 And it came about, when [1]Jo-
ram saw Jehu, that he said, "Is it
peace, Jehu?" And he [2]answered,
"What peace, [a]so long as the harlotries of your mother Jezebel and her
witchcrafts are so many?"
23 So [1]Joram [2]reined about and
fled and said to Ahaziah, "[a]*There is*
treachery, O Ahaziah!"
24 And [a]Jehu [1]drew his bow with
his full strength and [2]shot [3]Joram
between his arms; and the arrow
went [4]through his heart, and he
sank in his chariot.
25 Then *Jehu* said to Bidkar his officer, "Take *him* up and [a]cast him
into the [1]property of the field of Naboth the Jezreelite, for I remember
when [2]you and I were riding together after Ahab his father, that
the [b]LORD laid this [c]oracle against
him:
26 'Surely [a]I have seen yesterday
the blood of Naboth and the blood of
his sons,' says the LORD, 'and [b]I will
repay you in this [1]property,' says
the LORD. Now then, take and cast
him into the [1]property, according to
the word of the LORD."

4 [a]2 Kin. 9:1
5 [1]Lit., *To whom of us all?*
6 [a]2 Kin. 9:3
7 [a]Deut. 32:35, 43 [b]1 Kin. 18:4; 21:15, 21, 25 [c]2 Kin. 9:32-37
8 [a]1 Kin. 21:21; 2 Kin. 10:17 [b]1 Sam. 25:22 [c]Deut. 32:36; 2 Kin. 14:26
9 [a]1 Kin. 14:10, 11; 15:29 [b]1 Kin. 16:3-5, 11, 12
10 [a]1 Kin. 21:23; 2 Kin. 9:35, 36
11 [a]2 Kin. 9:17, 19, 22 [b]Jer. 29:26; Hos. 9:7; Mark 3:21
13 [a]Matt. 21:7, 8; Mark 11:7, 8 [b]2 Sam. 15:10; 1 Kin. 1:34, 39
14 [1]Lit., *he and* [2]Lit., *keeping* [a]1 Kin. 22:3; 2 Kin. 8:28
15 [1]Heb., *Jehoram* [2]Lit., *struck* [3]Lit., *go out from* [a]2 Kin. 8:29
16 [a]2 Kin. 8:29
17 [1]Lit., *multitude*
18 [1]Lit., *told, saying* [a]2 Kin. 9:19, 22
19 [1]Lit., *said*
20 [1]Lit., *told, saying* [a]2 Sam. 18:27 [b]1 Kin. 19:17
21 [1]Heb., *Jehoram* [2]Lit., *Yoke the chariot* [3]Lit., *portion* [a]2 Chr. 22:7 [b]1 Kin. 21:1-7, 15-19; 2 Kin. 9:26
22 [1]Heb., *Jehoram* [2]Lit., *said* [a]1 Kin. 16:30-33; 18:19; 2 Chr. 21:13
23 [1]Heb., *Jehoram* [2]Lit., *turned his hands* [a]2 Kin. 11:14
24 [1]Lit., *filled his hand with the bow* [2]Lit., *smote* [3]Heb., *Jehoram* [4]Lit., *out at* [a]1 Kin. 22:34
25 [1]Lit., *portion* [2]Lit., *I and you* [a]1 Kin. 21:1 [b]1 Kin. 21:19, 24-29 [c]Is. 13:1
26 [1]Lit., *portion* [a]1 Kin. 21:13 [b]2 Kin. 9:21, 25

Jehu Assassinates Ahaziah

27 [a]When Ahaziah the king of Judah saw *this,* he fled by the way of
the garden house. And Jehu pursued
him and said, "[1]Shoot him too, in
the chariot." *So they shot him* at the
ascent of Gur, which is at [b]Ibleam.
But he fled to Megiddo and died
there.
28 [a]Then his servants carried him
in a chariot to Jerusalem, and buried
him in his grave with his fathers in
the city of David.
29 Now in [a]the eleventh year of Joram, the son of Ahab, Ahaziah became king over Judah.
30 When Jehu came to Jezreel,
Jezebel heard *of it,* and [a]she painted
her eyes and adorned her head, and
looked out the window.
31 And as Jehu entered the gate,
she said, "[a]Is it [1]well, Zimri, [2]your
master's murderer?"
32 Then he lifted up his face to the
window and said, "Who is on my
side? Who?" And two or three officials looked down at him.

Jezebel Is Slain

33 And he said, "Throw her
down." So they threw her down,
and some of her blood was sprinkled on the wall and on the horses,
and he trampled her under foot.
34 When he came in, he ate and
drank; and he said, "See now to
[a]this cursed woman and bury her,
for [b]she is a king's daughter."
35 And they went to bury her, but
they found no more of her than the
skull and the feet and the palms of
her hands.
36 Therefore they returned and
told him. And he said, "This is the
word of the LORD, which He spoke
by His servant Elijah the Tishbite,
saying, '[a]In the [1]property of Jezreel
the dogs shall eat the flesh of Jezebel;
37 and [a]the corpse of Jezebel shall
be as dung on the face of the field in
the [1]property of Jezreel, so they
cannot say, "This is Jezebel." ' "

CHAPTER 10

Judgment upon Ahab's House

NOW Ahab had seventy sons in
[a]Samaria. And Jehu wrote letters
and sent *them* to Samaria, to the rulers of Jezreel, the elders, and to the
guardians of *the children of* Ahab,
saying,
2 "And now, when this letter
comes to you, since your master's
sons are with you, [1]as well as the
chariots and horses and a fortified
city and the weapons,
3 select the best and [1]fittest of
your master's sons, and set *him* on
his father's throne, and fight for
your master's house."
4 But they feared greatly and
said, "Behold, the two kings did not
stand before him; how then can we
stand?"
5 And the one who *was* over the
household, and he who *was* over the
city, the elders, and the guardians of
the children, sent *word* to Jehu, saying, "[a]We are your servants, all that
you say to us we will do, we will not
make any man king; do what is good
in your sight."
6 Then he wrote a letter to them a
second time saying, "If you are on
my side, and you will listen to my
voice, take the heads of the men,
your master's sons, and come to me
at Jezreel tomorrow about this
time." Now the king's sons, seventy
persons, *were* with the great men of
the city, *who* were rearing them.
7 And it came about when the letter came to them, that they took the
king's sons, and [a]slaughtered *them,*
seventy persons, and put their
heads in baskets, and sent *them* to
him at Jezreel.
8 When the messenger came and
told him, saying, "They have
brought the heads of the king's
sons," he said, "Put them in two
heaps at the entrance of the gate until morning."
9 Now it came about in the morning, that he went out and stood, and
said to all the people, "You are [1]in-
nocent; behold, [a]I conspired against
my master and killed him, but [b]who
[2]killed all these?
10 "Know then that [a]there shall fall
to the earth nothing of the word of
the LORD, which the LORD spoke
concerning the house of Ahab, for
the LORD has done [b]what He spoke
[1]through His servant Elijah."
11 So Jehu [1]killed all who remained of the house of Ahab in Jezreel, and all his great men and his
acquaintances and his priests, until
he left him without a survivor.
12 Then he arose and departed,
and went to Samaria. On the way
while he was at [1]Beth-eked of the
shepherds,
13 [a]Jehu [1]met the [2]relatives of A-
haziah king of Judah and said,
"Who are you?" And they [3]an-
swered, "We are the [2]relatives of A-
haziah; and we have come down [4]to
greet the sons of the king and the
sons of the queen mother."

27 [1]Lit., *smite* [a]2 Chr. 22:7, 9 [b]Josh. 17:11; Judg. 1:27
28 [a]2 Kin. 23:30
29 [a]2 Kin. 8:25
30 [a]Jer. 4:30; Ezek. 23:40
31 [1]Lit., *peace* [2]Lit., *his* [a]1 Kin. 16:9-20; 2 Kin. 9:18-22
34 [a]1 Kin. 21:25 [b]1 Kin. 16:31
36 [1]Lit., *portion* [a]1 Kin. 21:23
37 [1]Lit., *portion* [a]Jer. 8:1-3
1 [a]1 Kin. 16:24-29
2 [1]Lit., *and with you the*
3 [1]Lit., *most upright*
5 [a]Josh. 9:8, 11; 1 Kin. 20:4, 32; 2 Kin. 18:14
7 [a]Judg. 9:5; 2 Kin. 11:1
9 [1]Lit., *just* [2]Lit., *smote* [a]2 Kin. 9:14-24 [b]2 Kin. 10:6
10 [1]Lit., *by the hand of* [a]2 Kin. 9:7-10 [b]1 Kin. 21:19-29
11 [1]Lit., *smote*
12 [1]I.e., House of binding
13 [1]Lit., *found* [2]Lit., *brothers* [3]Lit., *said* [4]Lit., *about the welfare of* [a]2 Kin. 8:24, 29; 2 Chr. 21:17; 22:8

14 And he said, "Take them alive."
So they took them alive, and killed
them at the pit of Beth-eked, forty-
two men; and he left none of them.
15 Now when he had departed
from there, he [1]met [a]Jehonadab the
son of [b]Rechab *coming* to meet him;
and he [2]greeted him and said to him,
"Is your heart right, as my heart is
with your heart?" And Jehonadab
[3]answered, "It is." *Jehu said,* "If it
is, [c]give *me* your hand." And he
gave him his hand, and he took him
up to him into the chariot.
16 And he said, "Come with me
and [a]see my zeal for the LORD." So
[1]he made him ride in his chariot.
17 And when he came to Samaria,
[a]he [1]killed all who remained to
Ahab in Samaria, until he had destroyed him, [b]according to the word
of the LORD, which He spoke to Elijah.

Jehu Destroys Baal Worshipers

18 Then Jehu gathered all the people and said to them, "[a]Ahab served
Baal a little; Jehu will serve him
much.
19 "And now, [a]summon all the
prophets of Baal, all his worshipers
and all his priests; let no one be
missing, for I have a great sacrifice
for Baal; whoever is missing shall
not live." But Jehu did it in [1]cun-
ning, in order that he might destroy
the worshipers of Baal.
20 And Jehu said, "[a]Sanctify a solemn assembly for Baal." And [b]they
proclaimed *it.*
21 Then Jehu sent [1]throughout Israel and all the worshipers of Baal
came, so that there was not a man
left who did not come. And when
they went into [a]the house of Baal,
the house of Baal was filled from
one end to the other.
22 And he said to the one who *was*
[1]in charge of the wardrobe, "Bring
out garments for all the worshipers
of Baal." So he brought out garments for them.
23 And Jehu went into the house
of Baal with Jehonadab the son of
Rechab; and he said to the worshipers of Baal, "Search and see that
there may be here with you none of
the servants of the LORD, but only
the worshipers of Baal."
24 Then they went in to offer sacrifices and burnt offerings. Now Jehu
had stationed for himself eighty
men outside, and he had said, "[a]The
one who permits any of the men
whom I bring into your hands to escape, [1]shall give up his life in exchange."

15 [1]Lit., *found* [2]Lit., *blessed* [3]Lit., *said* [a]Jer. 35:6-19 [b]1 Chr. 2:55 [c]Ezra 10:19; Ezek. 17:18

16 [1]Lit., *they* [a]1 Kin. 19:10

17 [1]Lit., *smote* [a]2 Kin. 9:8 [b]2 Kin. 10:10

18 [a]1 Kin. 16:31, 32

19 [1]Lit., *insidiousness* [a]1 Kin. 18:19; 22:6

20 [a]Joel 1:14 [b]Ex. 32:4-6

21 [1]Lit., *in all* [a]1 Kin. 16:32; 2 Kin. 11:18

22 [1]Lit., *over the*

24 [1]Lit., *his soul for his soul* [a]1 Kin. 20:30-42

25 [1]Lit., *runners* [2]Lit., *smite* [3]Lit., *smote* [4]Lit., *city* [a]1 Sam. 22:17 [b]1 Kin. 18:40

26 [a]1 Kin. 14:23; 2 Kin. 3:2

27 [a]Ezra 6:11; Dan. 2:5; 3:29

29 [a]1 Kin. 12:28-30; 13:33, 34 [b]1 Kin. 12:29

30 [a]2 Kin. 15:12

31 [1]Lit., *did not watch* [a]2 Kin. 10:29

32 [1]Lit., *in* [2]Lit., *smote* [a]2 Kin. 13:25; 14:25 [b]1 Kin. 19:17; 2 Kin. 8:12; 13:22

33 [a]Deut. 2:36 [b]Amos 1:3-5

36 [1]Lit., *days*

1 [a]2 Chr. 22:10-12

25 Then it came about, as soon as
he had finished offering the burnt
offering, that Jehu said to the
[1a]guard and to the royal officers,
"[b]Go in, [2]kill them; let none come
out." And they [3]killed them with the
edge of the sword; and the [1]guard
and the royal officers threw *them*
out, and went to the [4]inner room of
the house of Baal.
26 And they brought out the *sacred* [a]pillars of the house of Baal,
and burned them.
27 They also broke down the *sacred* pillar of Baal and broke down
the house of Baal, and [a]made it a
latrine to this day.
28 Thus Jehu eradicated Baal out
of Israel.
29 However, [a]*as for* the sins of
Jeroboam the son of Nebat, which
he made Israel sin, from these Jehu
did not depart, *even* the [b]golden
calves that *were* at Bethel and that
were at Dan.
30 And the LORD said to Jehu, "Because you have done well in executing what is right in My eyes, *and*
have done to the house of Ahab according to all that *was* in My heart,
[a]your sons of the fourth generation
shall sit on the throne of Israel."
31 But Jehu [1]was not careful to
walk in the law of the LORD, the God
of Israel, with all his heart; [a]he did
not depart from the sins of Jeroboam, which he made Israel sin.
32 In those days the [a]LORD began
to cut off *portions* [1]from Israel; and
[b]Hazael [2]defeated them throughout
the territory of Israel:
33 from the Jordan eastward, all
the land of Gilead, the Gadites and
the Reubenites and the Manassites,
from [a]Aroer, which is by the valley
of the Arnon, even [b]Gilead and Bashan.

Jehoahaz Succeeds Jehu

34 Now the rest of the acts of Jehu
and all that he did and all his might,
are they not written in the Book of
the Chronicles of the Kings of Israel?
35 And Jehu slept with his fathers,
and they buried him in Samaria.
And Jehoahaz his son became king
in his place.
36 Now the [1]time which Jehu
reigned over Israel in Samaria *was*
twenty-eight years.

CHAPTER 11

Athaliah Queen of Judah

[a]WHEN Athaliah the mother of A-
haziah saw that her son was dead,

she rose and destroyed all the royal [1]offspring.

2 But Jehosheba, the daughter of King Joram, sister of Ahaziah, [a]took Joash the son of Ahaziah and stole him from among the king's sons who were being put to death, and placed him and his nurse in the bedroom. So they hid him from Athaliah, and he was not put to death.

3 So he was hidden with her in the house of the LORD six years, while Athaliah was reigning over the land.

4 [a]Now in the seventh year Jehoiada sent and brought the captains of hundreds of [b]the Carites and of the [1]guard, and brought them to him in the house of the LORD. Then he made a covenant with them and put them under oath in the house of the LORD, and showed them the king's son.

5 And he commanded them, saying, "This is the thing that you shall do: [a]one third of you, who come in on the sabbath and keep watch over the king's house

6 (one third also *shall be* at the gate Sur, and one third at the gate behind the [1]guards), [2]shall keep watch over the house for defense.

7 "And two parts of you, *even* all who go out on the sabbath, shall also keep watch over the house of the LORD for the king.

8 "Then you shall surround the king, each with his weapons in his hand; and whoever comes within the ranks shall be put to death. And [a]be with the king when he goes out and when he comes in."

9 So the captains of hundreds did according to all that Jehoiada the priest commanded. And each one of them took his men who were to come in on the sabbath, with those who were to go out on the sabbath, and came to Jehoiada the priest.

10 And [a]the priest gave to the captains of hundreds the spears and shields that had been King David's, which *were* in the house of the LORD.

11 And the [1]guards stood each with his weapons in his hand, from the right [2]side of the house to the left [2]side of the house, by the altar and by the house, around the king.

12 Then he brought the king's son out and [a]put the crown on him, and *gave him* [b]the testimony; and they made him king and anointed him, and they clapped their hands and said, "[c]Long live the king!"

13 When Athaliah heard the noise of the guard *and of* the people, she came to the people in the house of the LORD.

14 And she looked and behold, the king was standing [a]by the pillar, according to the custom, with the captains and the [1]trumpeters beside the king; and [b]all the people of the land rejoiced and blew trumpets. Then Athaliah [c]tore her clothes and cried, "[d]Treason! Treason!"

15 And Jehoiada the priest commanded the captains of hundreds who were appointed over the army, and said to them, "Bring her out [1]between the ranks, and whoever follows her put to death with the sword." For the priest said, "Let her not be put to death in the house of the LORD."

16 So they [1]seized her, and when she arrived at the horses' entrance of the king's house, she was put to death there.

17 Then [a]Jehoiada made a covenant between the LORD and the king and the people, that they should be the LORD's people, also [b]between the king and the people.

18 And all the people of the land went to [a]the house of Baal, and tore it down; [b]his altars and his images they broke in pieces thoroughly, and [c]killed Mattan the priest of Baal before the altars. And the priest appointed [1]officers over the house of the LORD.

19 And he took the captains of hundreds and the [a]Carites and the [1]guards and all the people of the land; and they brought the king down from the house of the LORD, and came by the way of [b]the gate of the [1]guards to the king's house. And he sat on the throne of the kings.

20 So all the people of the land rejoiced and the city was quiet. For they had put Athaliah to death with the sword at the king's house.

21 [1a]Jehoash was seven years old when he became king.

CHAPTER 12

Joash (Jehoash) Reigns over Judah

IN the seventh year of Jehu, Jehoash became king, and he reigned forty years in Jerusalem; and his mother's name was Zibiah of Beersheba.

2 And Jehoash did right in the sight of the LORD all his days in which Jehoiada the priest instructed him.

3 Only [a]the high places were not taken away; the people still sacrificed and burned incense on the high places.

1 [1]Lit., *seed*

2 [a]2 Kin. 11:21; 12:1

4 [1]Lit., *runners* [a]2 Chr. 23:1-21 [b]2 Sam. 20:23; 2 Kin. 11:19

5 [a]1 Chr. 9:25

6 [1]Lit., *runners* [2]Lit., *and shall*

8 [a]Num. 27:16, 17

10 [a]2 Sam. 8:7; 1 Chr. 18:7

11 [1]Lit., *runners* [2]Lit., *shoulder*

12 [a]2 Sam. 1:10 [b]Ex. 25:16; 31:18 [c]1 Sam. 10:24

14 [1]Lit., *trumpets* [a]2 Kin. 23:3; 2 Chr. 34:31 [b]1 Kin. 1:39, 40 [c]Gen. 37:29; 44:13 [d]2 Kin. 9:23

15 [1]Lit., *from within*

16 [1]Lit., *placed hands to her*

17 [a]Josh. 24:25; 2 Chr. 15:12-14; 34:31 [b]1 Sam. 10:25; 2 Sam. 5:3

18 [1]Lit., *offices* [a]2 Kin. 10:26, 27 [b]Deut. 12:2, 3 [c]1 Kin. 18:40

19 [1]Lit., *runners* [a]2 Kin. 11:4 [b]2 Kin. 11:6

21 [1]Ch. 12:1 in Heb. [a]2 Chr. 24:1-14

3 [a]2 Kin. 14:4; 15:35

The Temple to be Repaired

4 Then Jehoash said to the
priests, "All the money of the sacred
things [a]which is brought into the
house of the LORD, in current money, *both* [b]the money of each man's
assessment *and* all the money
[1]which any man's heart prompts
him to bring into the house of the
LORD,
5 let the priests take it for themselves, each from his acquaintance;
and they shall repair the [1]damages
of the house wherever any damage
may be found.
6 But it came about that in the
twenty-third year of King Jehoash
the priests had not repaired the
damages of the house.
7 Then King Jehoash called for
Jehoiada the priest, and for the *other* priests and said to them, "Why do
you not repair the damages of the
house? Now therefore take no *more*
money from your acquaintances,
but pay it for the damages of the
house."
8 So the priests agreed that they
should take no *more* money from
the people, nor repair the damages
of the house.
9 But [a]Jehoiada the priest took a
chest and bored a hole in its lid, and
put it beside the altar, on the right
side as one comes into the house of
the LORD; and the priests who
guarded the threshold put in it all
the money which was brought into
the house of the LORD.
10 And when they saw that there
was much money in the chest, [a]the
king's scribe and the high priest
came up and tied *it* in bags and
counted the money which was
found in the house of the LORD.
11 And they gave the money
which was weighed out into the
hands of those who did the work,
who had the oversight of the house
of the LORD; and they [1]paid it out to
the carpenters and the builders,
who worked on the house of the
LORD;
12 and [a]to the masons and the
stonecutters, and for buying timber
and hewn stone to repair the damages to the house of the LORD, and
for all that was [1]laid out for the
house to repair it.
13 But [a]there were not made for
the house of the LORD [b]silver cups,
snuffers, bowls, trumpets, any vessels of gold, or vessels of silver from
the money which was brought into
the house of the LORD;
14 for they gave that to those who
did the work, and with it they repaired the house of the LORD.
15 Moreover, [a]they did not require
an accounting from the men into
whose hand they gave the money to
pay to those who did the work, for
they dealt faithfully.
16 The [a]money from the guilt offerings and [b]the money from the sin
offerings, was not brought into the
house of the LORD; [c]it was for the
priests.
17 Then [a]Hazael king of Syria
went up and fought against Gath
and captured it, and [b]Hazael set his
face to go up to Jerusalem.
18 And [a]Jehoash king of Judah
took all the sacred things that Jehoshaphat and Jehoram and Ahaziah, his fathers, kings of Judah, had
dedicated, and [b]his own sacred
things and all the gold that was
found among the treasuries of the
house of the LORD and of the king's
house, and sent *them* to Hazael king
of Syria. Then he went away from
Jerusalem.

Joash (Jehoash) Succeeded by Amaziah in Judah

19 Now the rest of the acts of
Joash and all that he did, are they
not written in the Book of the
Chronicles of the Kings of Judah?
20 [a]And his servants arose and
made a conspiracy, and [b]struck
down Joash at [c]the house of Millo *as
he was* going down to Silla.
21 For Jozacar the son of Shimeath, and Jehozabad the son of
[a]Shomer, his servants, struck *him*,
and he died; and they buried him
with his fathers in the city of David,
and [b]Amaziah his son became king
in his place.

CHAPTER 13

Kings of Israel: Jehoahaz and Jehoash

IN the twenty-third year of Joash
the son of Ahaziah, king of Judah,
Jehoahaz the son of Jehu became
king over Israel at Samaria, *and he
reigned* seventeen years.
2 And he did evil in the sight of
the LORD, and followed the sins of
Jeroboam the son of Nebat, [a]with
which he made Israel sin; he did not
turn from them.
3 [a]So the anger of the LORD was
kindled against Israel, and He gave
them continually into the hand of
[b]Hazael king of Syria, and into the
hand of [c]Ben-hadad the son of Hazael.
4 Then [a]Jehoahaz entreated the

4 [1]Lit., *which it comes into . . . to bring* [a]2 Kin. 22:4 [b]Ex. 35:5, 22, 29; 1 Chr. 29:3-9

5 [1]Lit., *breaches* and so through v.12

9 [a]Mark 12:41; Luke 21:1

10 [a]2 Sam. 8:17; 2 Kin. 19:2; 22:3, 4, 12

11 [1]Lit., *brought*

12 [1]Lit., *went out* [a]2 Kin. 22:5, 6

13 [a]2 Chr. 24:14 [b]1 Kin. 7:48, 50

15 [a]2 Kin. 22:7

16 [a]Lev. 5:15-18 [b]Lev. 4:24, 29 [c]Lev. 7:7; Num. 18:19

17 [a]1 Kin. 19:17; 2 Kin. 8:12; 10:32, 33 [b]2 Chr. 24:23, 24

18 [a]1 Kin. 14:26; 15:18; 2 Kin. 16:8; 18:15, 16 [b]2 Kin. 12:4

20 [a]2 Chr. 24:25-27 [b]2 Kin. 14:5 [c]Judg. 9:6; 2 Sam. 5:9; 1 Kin. 11:27

21 [a]2 Chr. 24:26 [b]2 Kin. 14:1

2 [a]1 Kin. 12:26-33

3 [a]Judg. 2:14 [b]2 Kin. 12:17 [c]2 Kin. 13:24, 25

4 [a]Num. 21:7-9

favor of the LORD, and the LORD listened to him; for [b]He saw the oppression of Israel, how the king of
Syria oppressed them.
5 And the LORD gave Israel a
[1a]deliverer, so that they [2]escaped
from under the hand of the Syrians;
and the sons of Israel lived in their
tents as formerly.
6 Nevertheless they did not turn
away from the sins of the house of
Jeroboam, [a]with which he made Israel sin, but walked in [1]them; and
[b]the Asherah also remained standing in Samaria.
7 For he left to Jehoahaz of the
[1]army not more than fifty horsemen
and ten chariots and 10,000 footmen, for the king of Syria had destroyed them and [a]made them like
the dust at threshing.
8 Now the rest of the acts of Jehoahaz, and all that he did and his
might, are they not written in the
Book of the Chronicles of the Kings
of Israel?
9 And Jehoahaz slept with his fathers, and they buried him in Samaria; and Joash his son became
king in his place.
10 In the thirty-seventh year of
Joash king of Judah, Jehoash the
son of Jehoahaz, became king over
Israel in Samaria, *and reigned* sixteen years.
11 And he did evil in the sight of
the LORD; he did not turn away from
all the sins of Jeroboam the son of
Nebat, with which he made Israel
sin, but he walked in [1]them.
12 [a]Now the rest of the acts of
Joash and all that he did and his
might with which he fought against
Amaziah king of Judah, are they not
written in the Book of the Chronicles of the Kings of Israel?
13 So Joash slept with his fathers,
and Jeroboam sat on his throne; and
Joash was buried in Samaria with
the kings of Israel.

Death of Elisha

14 When Elisha [1]became sick with
the illness of which he was to die,
Joash the king of Israel came down
to him and wept over [2]him and said,
"[a]My father, my father, the chariots
of Israel and its horsemen!"
15 And Elisha said to him, "Take a
bow and arrows." So he [1]took a bow
and arrows.
16 Then he said to the king of Israel, "Put your hand on the bow."
And he put his hand *on it,* then Elisha laid his hands on the king's
hands.

4 [b]Ex. 3:7, 9; 2 Kin. 14:26
5 [1]Or, *savior* [2]Lit., *went out* [a]2 Kin. 13:25; 14:25, 27; Neh. 9:27
6 [1]Lit., *it* [a]2 Kin. 13:2 [b]1 Kin. 16:33
7 [1]Lit., *people* [a]Amos 1:3
11 [1]Lit., *it*
12 [a]2 Kin. 13:14-19; 14:8-15
14 [1]Lit., *was sick with his sickness* [2]Lit., *his face* [a]2 Kin. 2:12
15 [1]Lit., *took to himself*
17 [1]Lit., *smite* [2]Lit., *made an end of* [a]1 Kin. 20:26
18 [1]Lit., *stood*
19 [1]Lit., *made an end of* [a]2 Kin. 5:20 [b]2 Kin. 13:25
20 [a]2 Kin. 3:7; 24:2
22 [a]2 Kin. 8:12, 13
23 [a]2 Kin. 14:27 [b]1 Kin. 8:28 [c]Gen. 13:16, 17; 17:2-5
25 [1]Lit., *smote* [a]2 Kin. 10:32, 33; 14:25 [b]2 Kin. 13:18, 19
1 [a]2 Chr. 25:1 [b]2 Kin. 13:10

17 And he said, "Open the window
toward the east," and he opened *it.*
Then Elisha said, "Shoot!" And he
shot. And he said, "The LORD's arrow of victory, even the arrow of
victory over Syria; for you shall [1]de-
feat the Syrians at [a]Aphek until you
have [2]destroyed *them.*"
18 Then he said, "Take the arrows," and he took them. And he
said to the king of Israel, "Strike the
ground," and he struck *it* three
times and [1]stopped.
19 So [a]the man of God was angry
with him and said, "You should
have struck five or six times, then
you would have struck Syria until
you would have [1]destroyed *it.* But
now you shall strike Syria [b]*only*
three times."
20 And Elisha died, and they buried him. Now [a]the bands of the Moabites would invade the land in the
spring of the year.
21 And as they were burying a
man, behold, they saw a marauding
band; and they cast the man into the
grave of Elisha. And when the man
touched the bones of Elisha he revived and stood up on his feet.
22 Now [a]Hazael king of Syria had
oppressed Israel all the days of Jehoahaz.
23 But the [a]LORD was gracious to
them and [b]had compassion on them
and turned to them because of [c]His
covenant with Abraham, Isaac, and
Jacob, and would not destroy them
or cast them from His presence until
now.
24 When Hazael king of Syria
died, Ben-hadad his son became
king in his place.
25 Then [a]Jehoash the son of Jehoahaz took again from the hand of
Ben-hadad the son of Hazael the
cities which he had taken in war
from the hand of Jehoahaz his father. [b]Three times Joash [1]defeated
him and recovered the cities of Israel.

CHAPTER 14

Amaziah Reigns over Judah

[a]IN the second year of Joash son of
Joahaz king of Israel, [b]Amaziah the
son of Joash king of Judah became
king.
2 He was twenty-five years old
when he became king, and he
reigned twenty-nine years in Jerusalem. And his mother's name was
Jehoaddin of Jerusalem.
3 And he did right in the sight of
the LORD, yet not like David his fa-

ther; he did according to all that Joash his father had done.

4 Only [a]the high places were not taken away; [b]the people still sacrificed and burned incense on the high places.

5 Now it came about, as soon as the kingdom was firmly in his hand, that he [1a]killed his servants who had slain the king his father.

6 But the sons of the [1]slayers he did not put to death, according to what is written in the book of the law of Moses, as the LORD commanded, saying, "[a]The fathers shall not be put to death for the sons, nor the sons be put to death for the fathers; but [b]each shall be put to death for his own sin."

7 [a]He [1]killed *of* Edom in [b]the Valley of Salt 10,000 and took [c]Sela by war, and named it [d]Joktheel to this day.

8 [a]Then Amaziah sent messengers to Jehoash, the son of Jehoahaz son of Jehu, king of Israel, saying, "[b]Come, let us face each other."

9 And Jehoash king of Israel sent to Amaziah king of Judah, saying, "[a]The thorn bush which was in Lebanon sent to the cedar which was in Lebanon, saying, 'Give your daughter to my son in marriage.' But there passed by a wild beast that was in Lebanon, and trampled the thorn bush.

10 "[a]You have indeed [1]defeated Edom, and [b]your heart has [2]become proud. Enjoy your glory and stay at home; for why should you provoke trouble so that you, even you, should fall, and Judah with you?"

11 But Amaziah would not listen. So Jehoash king of Israel went up; [a]and he and Amaziah king of Judah faced each other at [b]Beth-shemesh, which belongs to Judah.

12 And Judah was defeated [1]by Israel, and [a]they fled each to his tent.

13 Then Jehoash king of Israel captured Amaziah king of Judah, the son of Jehoash the son of Ahaziah, at Beth-shemesh, and came to Jerusalem and tore down the wall of Jerusalem from [a]the Gate of Ephraim to [b]the Corner Gate, 400 [1]cubits.

14 And [a]he took all the gold and silver and all the utensils which were found in the house of the LORD, and in the treasuries of the king's house, the hostages also, and returned to Samaria.

Jeroboam II Succeeds Jehoash in Israel

15 [a]Now the rest of the acts of Jehoash which he did, and his might and how he fought with Amaziah king of Judah, are they not written in the Book of the Chronicles of the Kings of Israel?

16 So Jehoash slept with his fathers and was buried in Samaria with the kings of Israel; and Jeroboam his son became king in his place.

Azariah (Uzziah) Succeeds Amaziah in Judah

17 [a]And Amaziah the son of Joash king of Judah lived fifteen years after the death of Jehoash son of Jehoahaz king of Israel.

18 Now the rest of the acts of Amaziah, are they not written in the Book of the Chronicles of the Kings of Judah?

19 And they conspired against him in Jerusalem, and he fled to [a]Lachish; but they sent after him to Lachish and killed him there.

20 Then they brought him on horses and he was buried at Jerusalem with his fathers in the city of David.

21 And all the people of Judah took [1]Azariah, who *was* sixteen years old, and made him king in the place of his father Amaziah.

22 [a]He built Elath and restored it to Judah, after the king slept with his fathers.

23 In the fifteenth year of Amaziah the son of Joash king of Judah, Jeroboam the son of Joash king of Israel became king in Samaria, *and reigned* forty-one years.

24 And he did evil in the sight of the LORD; he did not depart from all the sins of Jeroboam the son of Nebat, which he made Israel sin.

25 [a]He restored the border of Israel from [b]the entrance of Hamath as far as [c]the Sea of the Arabah, according to the word of the LORD, the God of Israel, which He spoke [1]through His servant [d]Jonah the son of Amittai, the prophet, who was of [e]Gath-hepher.

26 For the [a]LORD saw the affliction of Israel, *which was* very bitter; for [b]there was neither bond nor free, nor was there any helper for Israel.

27 And the [a]LORD did not say that He would blot out the name of Israel from under heaven, but He saved them by the hand of Jeroboam the son of Joash.

Zechariah Reigns over Israel

28 Now the rest of the acts of Jeroboam and all that he did and his might, how he fought and how he recovered for Israel, [a]Damascus and [b]Hamath, *which had belonged* to Ju-

4 [a]2 Kin. 12:3 [b]2 Kin. 16:4

5 [1]Lit., *smote* [a]2 Kin. 12:20

6 [1]Lit., *smiters* [a]Deut. 24:16 [b]Jer. 31:30; Ezek. 18:4, 20

7 [1]Lit., *smote* [a]2 Chr. 25:11 [b]2 Sam. 8:13; 1 Chr. 18:12 [c]Is. 16:1 [d]Josh. 15:38

8 [a]2 Chr. 25:17-24 [b]2 Sam. 2:14-17

9 [a]Judg. 9:8-15

10 [1]Lit., *smitten* [2]Lit., *lifted you up* [a]2 Kin. 14:7 [b]Deut. 8:14; 2 Chr. 26:16

11 [a]2 Kin. 23:29 [b]Josh. 19:38

12 [1]Lit., *before* [a]2 Sam. 18:17

13 [1]One cubit equals approx. 18 in. [a]Neh. 8:16; 12:39 [b]2 Chr. 25:23

14 [a]1 Kin. 14:26; 2 Kin. 12:18

15 [a]2 Kin. 13:12, 13

17 [a]2 Chr. 25:25-28

19 [a]Josh. 10:31; 2 Kin. 18:14, 17

21 [1]In 2 Chr. 26:1, *Uzziah*

22 [a]1 Kin. 9:26; 2 Kin. 16:6; 2 Chr. 8:17

25 [1]Lit., *by* [a]2 Kin. 10:32; 13:25 [b]1 Kin. 8:65 [c]Deut. 3:17 [d]Jon. 1:1; Matt. 12:39, 40 [e]Josh. 19:13

26 [a]2 Kin. 13:4 [b]Deut. 32:36

27 [a]2 Kin. 13:23

28 [a]1 Kin. 11:24 [b]2 Chr. 8:3

dah, are they not written in the Book of the Chronicles of the Kings of Israel?

29 And Jeroboam slept with his fathers, even with the kings of Israel, and Zechariah his son became king in his place.

Chapter 15

Series of Kings: Azariah (Uzziah) over Judah

[a]IN the twenty-seventh year of Jeroboam king of Israel, Azariah son of Amaziah king of Judah became king.

2 He was [a]sixteen years old when he became king, and he reigned fifty-two years in Jerusalem; and his mother's name was [1]Jecoliah of Jerusalem.

3 And he did right in the sight of the LORD, according to all that his father Amaziah had done.

4 Only [a]the high places were not taken away; the people still sacrificed and burned incense on the high places.

5 [a]And the LORD struck the king, so that he was a leper to the day of his death. And he [b]lived in a separate house, [1]while Jotham the king's son was over the household, judging the people of the land.

6 Now the rest of the acts of Azariah and all that he did, are they not written in the Book of the Chronicles of the Kings of Judah?

7 And Azariah slept with his fathers, and they buried him with his fathers in the city of David, and Jotham his son became king in his place.

Zechariah over Israel

8 [a]In the thirty-eighth year of Azariah king of Judah, Zechariah the son of Jeroboam became king over Israel in Samaria *for* six months.

9 And he did evil in the sight of the LORD, as his fathers had done; he did not depart from the sins of Jeroboam the son of Nebat, which he made Israel sin.

10 Then Shallum the son of Jabesh conspired against him and [a]struck him before the people and [1]killed him, and reigned in his place.

11 Now the rest of the acts of Zechariah, behold they are written in the Book of the Chronicles of the Kings of Israel.

12 This is [a]the word of the LORD which He spoke to Jehu, saying, "Your sons to the fourth generation shall sit on the throne of Israel." And so it was.

13 Shallum son of Jabesh became king in the [a]thirty-ninth year of Uzziah king of Judah, and he reigned one month in [b]Samaria.

14 Then Menahem son of Gadi went up from [a]Tirzah and came to Samaria, and struck Shallum son of Jabesh in Samaria, and killed him and became king in his place.

15 Now the rest of the acts of Shallum and his conspiracy which he made, behold they are written in the Book of the Chronicles of the Kings of Israel.

16 Then Menahem struck Tiphsah and all who were in it and its borders from Tirzah, because they did not open *to him,* therefore he struck *it;* and he ripped up [a]all its women who were with child.

Menahem over Israel

17 In the [a]thirty-ninth year of Azariah king of Judah, Menahem son of Gadi became king over Israel *and reigned* ten years in Samaria.

18 And he did evil in the sight of the LORD; he did not depart all his days from the sins of Jeroboam the son of Nebat, which he made Israel sin.

19 [a]Pul, king of Assyria, came against the land, and Menahem gave Pul a thousand talents of silver so that his hand might be with him to strengthen the kingdom [1]under his rule.

20 Then Menahem exacted the money from Israel, even from all the mighty men of wealth, from each man fifty shekels of silver to pay the king of Assyria. So the king of Assyria returned and did not remain there in the land.

21 Now the rest of the acts of Menahem and all that he did, are they not written in the Book of the Chronicles of the Kings of Israel?

22 And Menahem slept with his fathers, and Pekahiah his son became king in his place.

Pekahiah over Israel

23 In [a]the fiftieth year of Azariah king of Judah, Pekahiah son of Menahem became king over Israel in Samaria, *and reigned* two years.

24 And he did evil in the sight of the LORD; he did not depart from the sins of Jeroboam son of Nebat, which he made Israel sin.

25 Then Pekah son of Remaliah, his officer, conspired against him and struck him in Samaria, in [a]the castle of the king's house with Ar-

1 [a]2 Kin. 14:17
2 [1]In 2 Chr. 26:3, *Jechiliah* [a]2 Chr. 26:3, 4
4 [a]2 Kin. 12:3
5 [1]Lit., *and* [a]2 Chr. 26:21-23 [b]Lev. 13:46; Num. 12:14
8 [a]2 Kin. 15:1
10 [1]Lit., *smote* [a]Amos 7:9
12 [a]2 Kin. 10:30
13 [a]2 Kin. 15:1, 8 [b]1 Kin. 16:24
14 [a]1 Kin. 14:17
16 [a]2 Kin. 8:12
17 [a]2 Kin. 15:1, 8, 13
19 [1]Lit., *in his hand* [a]1 Chr. 5:25, 26
23 [a]2 Kin. 15:1, 8, 13, 17
25 [a]1 Kin. 16:18

gob and Arieh; and with him were
fifty men of the Gileadites, and he
killed him and became king in his
place.
26 Now the rest of the acts of
Pekahiah and all that he did, behold
they are written in the Book of the
Chronicles of the Kings of Israel.

Pekah over Israel

27 In [a]the fifty-second year of Azariah king of Judah, Pekah son of
Remaliah became king over Israel in
Samaria, *and reigned* twenty years.
28 And he did evil in the sight of
the LORD; he did not depart from the
sins of Jeroboam son of Nebat,
which he made Israel sin.
29 In the days of Pekah king of Israel, [a]Tiglath-pileser king of Assyria
came and [1]captured Ijon and Abel-
beth-maacah and Janoah and Kedesh and Hazor and Gilead and
Galilee, all the land of Naphtali; and
[b]he carried them captive to Assyria.
30 And Hoshea the son of Elah
made a conspiracy against Pekah
the son of Remaliah, and struck him
and put him to death and became
king in his place, in the twentieth
year of Jotham the son of Uzziah.
31 Now the rest of the acts of Pekah and all that he did, behold, they
are written in the Book of the
Chronicles of the Kings of Israel.

Jothan over Judah

32 In the second year of Pekah the
son of Remaliah king of Israel, Jotham the son of Uzziah king of Judah became king.
33 [a]He was twenty-five years old
when he became king, and he
reigned sixteen years in Jerusalem;
and his mother's name *was* Jerusha
the daughter of Zadok.
34 And [a]he did what was right in
the sight of the LORD; he did according to all that his father Uzziah had
done.
35 Only [a]the high places were not
taken away; the people still sacrificed and burned incense on the high
places. [b]He built the upper gate of
the house of the LORD.
36 Now the rest of the acts of Jotham and all that he did, are they not
written in the Book of the Chronicles of the Kings of Judah?
37 In those days [a]the LORD began
to send Rezin king of Syria and Pekah the son of Remaliah against Judah.
38 And Jotham slept with his fathers, and he was buried with his
fathers in the city of David his fa-

27 [a]2 Kin. 15:23
29 [1]Lit., *took* [a]2 Kin. 15:19 [b]2 Kin. 17:6
33 [a]2 Chr. 27:1
34 [a]2 Kin. 15:3, 4; 2 Chr. 26:4, 5
35 [a]2 Kin. 12:3 [b]2 Chr. 23:20; 27:3
37 [a]2 Kin. 16:5; Is. 7:1
2 [a]2 Chr. 28:1-4
3 [1]Or, *dispossessed* [a]Lev. 18:21; 2 Kin. 17:17; 21:6 [b]Deut. 12:31; 2 Kin. 21:2, 11
4 [a]Deut. 12:2; 2 Kin. 14:4
5 [1]Lit., *fight* [a]2 Kin. 15:37; Is. 7:1 [b]2 Chr. 28:5, 6
6 [1]Lit., *Eloth* [2]So with some ancient versions; Heb., *Edomites* [a]2 Kin. 14:22; 2 Chr. 26:2
7 [1]Lit., *palm* [a]2 Chr. 28:16 [b]2 Kin. 15:29
8 [a]2 Kin. 12:17, 18; 18:15
9 [a]2 Chr. 28:21 [b]Amos 1:3-5 [c]Is. 22:6; Amos 9:7
10 [1]Lit., *likeness* [a]2 Kin. 15:29 [b]Is. 8:2

ther; and Ahaz his son became king
in his place.

CHAPTER 16

Ahaz Reigns over Judah

IN the seventeenth year of Pekah
the son of Remaliah, Ahaz the son of
Jotham, king of Judah, became
king.
2 [a]Ahaz *was* twenty years old
when he became king, and he
reigned sixteen years in Jerusalem;
and he did not do what was right in
the sight of the LORD his God, as his
father David *had done.*
3 But he walked in the way of the
kings of Israel, [a]and even made his
son pass through the fire, [b]accord-
ing to the abominations of the nations whom the LORD had [1]driven
out from before the sons of Israel.
4 And he [a]sacrificed and burned
incense on the high places and on
the hills and under every green tree.
5 Then [a]Rezin king of Syria and
Pekah son of Remaliah, king of Israel, came up to Jerusalem to *wage*
war; and they besieged Ahaz, [b]but
could not [1]overcome him.
6 At that time Rezin king of Syria
recovered [a]Elath for Syria, and
cleared the Judeans out of [1]Elath
entirely; and the [2]Syrians came to
Elath, and have lived there to this
day.

Ahaz Seeks Help of Syria

7 [a]So Ahaz sent messengers to
[b]Tiglath-pileser king of Assyria,
saying, "I am your servant and your
son; come up and deliver me from
the [1]hand of the king of Syria, and
from the [1]hand of the king of Israel,
who are rising up against me."
8 And [a]Ahaz took the silver and
gold that was found in the house of
the LORD and in the treasuries of the
king's house, and sent a present to
the king of Assyria.
9 [a]So the king of Assyria listened
to him; and the king of Assyria went
up against Damascus and [b]captured
it, and carried *the people of* it away
into exile to [c]Kir, and put Rezin to
death.

Damascus Falls

10 Now King Ahaz went to Damascus to meet [a]Tiglath-pileser
king of Assyria, and saw the altar
which *was* at Damascus; and King
Ahaz sent to [b]Urijah the priest the
[1]pattern of the altar and its model,
according to all its workmanship.
11 So Urijah the priest built an altar; according to all that King Ahaz

had sent from Damascus, thus Urijah the priest made *it*, [1]before the
coming of King Ahaz from Damascus.
12 And when the king came from
Damascus, the king saw the altar;
then the king approached the altar
and [1]went up to it,
13 and [1]burned his burnt offering
and his meal offering, and poured
his libation and sprinkled the blood
of his peace offerings on the altar.
14 And [a]the bronze altar, which
was before the LORD, [1]he brought
from the front of the house, from
between [b]*his* altar and the house of
the LORD, and he put it on the north
side of *his* altar.
15 Then King Ahaz [1]commanded
Urijah the priest, saying, "Upon the
great altar [2]burn [a]the morning burnt
offering and the evening meal offering and the king's burnt offering and
his meal offering, with the burnt offering of all the people of the land
and their meal offering and their libations; and sprinkle on it all the
blood of the burnt offering and all
the blood of the sacrifice. But [b]the
bronze altar shall be for me to inquire *by*."
16 So Urijah the priest did according to all that King Ahaz commanded.
17 Then King Ahaz [a]cut off the
borders of the stands, and removed
the laver from them; he also [b]took
down the sea from the bronze oxen
which were under it, and put it on a
pavement of stone.
18 And the covered way for the
sabbath which they had built in the
house, and the outer entry of the
king, he removed from the house of
the LORD because of the king of Assyria.

Hezekiah Reigns over Judah

19 Now the rest of the acts of Ahaz
which he did, are they not written
[a]in the Book of the Chronicles of the
Kings of Judah?
20 So Ahaz slept with his fathers,
and [a]was buried with his fathers in
the city of David; and his son Hezekiah reigned in his place.

CHAPTER 17

Hoshea Reigns over Israel

IN the twelfth year of Ahaz king of
Judah, [a]Hoshea the son of Elah became king over Israel in Samaria,
and reigned nine years.
2 And he did evil in the sight of
the LORD, only not as the kings of

11 [1]Lit., *until*

12 [1]Or, *offered on it*

13 [1]Lit., *offered in smoke*

14 [1]Lit., *he also* [a]Ex. 40:6, 29 [b]2 Kin. 16:11

15 [1]Lit., *commanded him, Urijah* [2]Lit., *offer in smoke* [a]Ex. 29:39-41 [b]2 Kin. 16:14

17 [a]1 Kin. 7:27, 28, 38 [b]1 Kin. 7:23, 25

19 [a]2 Chr. 28:26

20 [a]2 Chr. 28:27

1 [a]2 Kin. 15:30

3 [a]Hos. 10:14 [b]2 Kin. 18:9-12

5 [a]Hos. 13:16

6 [1]Cf. 1 Chr. 5:26 [a]Hos. 13:16 [b]Deut. 28:64; 29:27, 28 [c]2 Kin. 18:11; 1 Chr. 5:26 [d]Is. 37:12 [e]Is. 13:17; 21:2

7 [1]Lit., *revered,* and so throughout the chap. [a]Josh. 23:16 [b]Ex. 14:15-30 [c]Judg. 6:10

8 [1]Lit., *statutes* [2]Lit., *made* [a]Lev. 18:3; Deut. 18:9 [b]2 Kin. 16:3; 17:19

9 [1]Or, *uttered words which* [a]2 Kin. 18:8

10 [1]I.e., wooden symbols of a female deity [a]Ex. 34:12-14 [b]1 Kin. 14:23; Mic. 5:14

12 [a]Ex. 20:4

13 [a]Neh. 9:29, 30 [b]2 Kin. 17:23 [c]1 Sam. 9:9 [d]Jer. 7:3-7; 18:11; Ezek. 18:31

Israel who were before him.
3 [a]Shalmaneser king of Assyria
came up [b]against him, and Hoshea
became his servant and paid him
tribute.
4 But the king of Assyria found
conspiracy in Hoshea, who had sent
messengers to So king of Egypt and
had offered no tribute to the king of
Assyria, as *he had done* year by
year; so the king of Assyria shut him
up and bound him in prison.
5 Then the king of Assyria invaded the whole land and went up
to Samaria and [a]besieged it three
years.

Israel Captive

6 In the ninth year of Hoshea,
[a]the king of Assyria captured Samaria and [b]carried Israel away into
exile to Assyria, and [c]settled them
in Halah and [1]Habor, *on* the river of
[d]Gozan, and [e]in the cities of the
Medes.

Why Israel Fell

7 Now [a]this came about, because
the sons of Israel had sinned against
the LORD their God, [b]who had
brought them up from the land of
Egypt from under the hand of Pharaoh, king of Egypt, [c]and they had
[1]feared other gods
8 and [a]walked in the [1]customs of
the nations whom the LORD had
driven out before the sons of Israel,
and *in the customs* [b]of the kings of
Israel which they had [2]introduced.
9 And the sons of Israel [1]did
things secretly which were not
right, against the LORD their God.
Moreover, they built for themselves
high places in all their towns, from
[a]watchtower to fortified city.
10 And [a]they set for themselves
sacred pillars and [1b]Asherim on every high hill and under every green
tree,
11 and there they burned incense
on all the high places as the nations
did which the LORD had carried
away to exile before them; and they
did evil things provoking the LORD.
12 And they served idols, [a]con-
cerning which the LORD had said to
them, "You shall not do this thing."
13 Yet the [a]LORD warned Israel
and Judah, [b]through all His prophets *and* [c]every seer, saying, "[d]Turn
from your evil ways and keep My
commandments, My statutes according to all the law which I commanded your fathers, and which I
sent to you through My servants the
prophets."

14 However, they did not listen,
but [a]stiffened their neck [1]like their
fathers, who did not believe in the
LORD their God.
15 And [a]they rejected His statutes
and [b]His covenant which He made
with their fathers, and His warnings
with which He warned them. And
[c]they followed vanity and [d]became
vain, and *went* after the nations
which surrounded them, concerning
which the [e]LORD had commanded
them not to do like them.
16 And they forsook all the commandments of the LORD their God
and made for themselves molten
images, *even* [a]two calves, and
[b]made an [1]Asherah and [c]worshiped
all the host of heaven and [d]served
Baal.
17 Then [a]they made their sons and
their daughters pass through the
fire, and [b]practiced divination and
enchantments, and [c]sold themselves to do evil in the sight of the
LORD, provoking Him.
18 So the LORD was very angry
with Israel, and [a]removed them
from His [1]sight; [b]none was left except the tribe of Judah.
19 Also [a]Judah did not keep the
commandments of the LORD their
God, but [b]walked in the [1]customs
[2]which Israel had [3]introduced.
20 And the LORD rejected all the
[1]descendants of Israel and afflicted
them and [a]gave them into the hand
of plunderers, until He had cast
them [2]out of His sight.
21 When [a]He had torn Israel from
the house of David, [b]they made
Jeroboam the son of Nebat king.
Then [c]Jeroboam drove Israel away
from following the LORD, and made
them [1]commit a great sin.
22 And the sons of Israel walked in
all the sins of Jeroboam which he
did; they did not depart from them,
23 [a]until the LORD removed Israel
from His sight, [b]as He spoke
through all His servants the prophets. [c]So Israel was carried away into
exile from their own land to Assyria
until this day.

Cities of Israel Filled with Strangers

24 [a]And the king of Assyria
brought *men* from Babylon and
from Cuthah and from [b]Avva and
from [c]Hamath and Sephar-vaim,
and settled *them* in the cities of Samaria in place of the sons of Israel.
So they possessed Samaria and
lived in its cities.
25 And it came about at the beginning of their living there, that they
did not fear the LORD; therefore the
LORD sent lions among them which
killed some of them.
26 So they spoke to the king of Assyria, saying, "The nations whom
you have carried away into exile in
the cities of Samaria do not know
the custom of the god of the land; so
he has sent lions among them, and
behold, they kill them because they
do not know the custom of the god
of the land."
27 Then the king of Assyria commanded, saying, "Take there one of
the priests whom you carried away
into [1]exile, and let [2]him go and live
there; and let him teach them the
custom of the god of the land."
28 So one of the priests whom they
had carried away into exile from Samaria came and lived at Bethel, and
taught them how they should fear
the LORD.
29 But every nation still made
gods of its own and put them [a]in the
houses of the high places which the
people of Samaria had made, every
nation in their cities in which they
lived.
30 And [a]the men of Babylon made
Succoth-benoth, the men of Cuth
made Nergal, the men of Hamath
made Ashima,
31 and the Avvites made Nibhaz
and Tartak; and [a]the Sepharvites
burned their children in the fire to
[b]Adrammelech and Anammelech
the gods of [c]Sepharvaim.
32 [a]They also feared the LORD and
[1b]appointed from among themselves priests of the high places,
who acted for them in the houses of
the high places.
33 They feared the LORD and
served their own gods according to
the custom of the nations from
among whom they had been carried
away into exile.
34 To this day they do according to
the earlier customs: they do not fear
the LORD, nor do they [1]follow their
statutes or their ordinances or the
law, or the commandments which
the LORD commanded the sons of
Jacob, [a]whom He named Israel;
35 with whom the LORD made a
covenant and commanded them,
saying, "[a]You shall not fear other
gods, nor [b]bow down yourselves to
them nor serve them nor sacrifice to
them.
36"But the LORD, [a]who brought
you up from the land of Egypt with
great power and with [b]an outstretched arm, [c]Him you shall fear,
and to Him you shall bow yourselves down, and to Him you shall
sacrifice.

14 [1]Lit., *like the neck of* [a]Ex. 32:9; 33:3; Acts 7:51

15 [a]Jer. 8:9 [b]Ex. 24:6-8; Deut. 29:25 [c]Deut. 32:21 [d]Jer. 2:5; Rom. 1:21-23 [e]Deut. 12:30, 31

16 [1]I.e, a wooden symbol of a female deity [a]1 Kin. 12:28 [b]1 Kin. 14:15, 23 [c]Deut. 4:15, 19 2 Kin. 21:3 [d]1 Kin. 16:31

17 [a]2 Kin. 16:3 [b]Lev. 19:26; Deut. 18:10-12 [c]1 Kin. 21:20

18 [1]Lit., *face* [a]2 Kin. 17:6 [b]1 Kin. 11:13, 32, 36

19 [1]Lit., *statutes* [2]Lit., *of Israel which they* [3]Lit., *made* [a]1 Kin. 14:22, 23 [b]2 Kin. 16:3

20 [1]Lit., *seed* [2]Lit., *from His face* [a]2 Kin. 15:29

21 [1]Lit., *sin* [a]1 Kin. 11:11, 31 [b]1 Kin. 12:20 [c]1 Kin. 12:28-33

23 [a]2 Kin. 17:6 [b]2 Kin. 17:13 [c]2 Kin. 17:6

24 [a]Ezra 4:2, 10 [b]2 Kin. 18:34 [c]1 Kin. 8:65

27 [1]Lit., *exile from there* [2]Lit., *them*

29 [a]1 Kin. 12:31; 13:32

30 [a]2 Kin. 17:24

31 [a]2 Kin. 17:17 [b]2 Kin. 19:37 [c]2 Kin. 17:24

32 [1]Lit., *made for themselves from among* [a]Zeph. 1:5 [b]1 Kin. 12:31

34 [1]Lit., *do according to* [a]Gen. 32:28; 35:10

35 [a]Judg. 6:10 [b]Ex. 20:5

36 [a]Ex. 14:15-30 [b]Ex. 6:6; 9:15 [c]Lev. 19:32; Deut. 6:13

37"And the statutes and the ordinances and the law and the commandment, which He wrote for you,
[a]you shall observe to do forever; and
you shall not fear other gods.
38"And the covenant that I have
made with you, [a]you shall not forget, nor shall you fear other gods.
39"But the LORD your God you
shall fear; and He will deliver you
from the hand of all your enemies."
40 However, they did not listen,
but they did according to their earlier custom.
41 [a]So while these nations feared
the LORD, they also served their
[1]idols; their children likewise and
their grandchildren, as their fathers
did, so they do to this day.

CHAPTER 18

Hezekiah Reigns over Judah

NOW it came about [a]in the third
year of Hoshea, the son of Elah king
of Israel, that [b]Hezekiah the son of
Ahaz king of Judah became king.
2 He was [a]twenty-five years old
when he became king, and he
reigned twenty-nine years in Jerusalem; and his mother's name was
Abi the daughter of Zechariah.
3 [a]And he did right in the sight of
the LORD, according to all that his
father David had done.
4 [a]He removed the high places
and broke down the *sacred* pillars
and cut down the [1]Asherah. He also
broke in pieces [b]the bronze serpent
that Moses had made, for until those
days the sons of Israel burned incense to it; and it was called [2]Ne-
hushtan.
5 [a]He trusted in the LORD, the
God of Israel; [b]so that after him
there was none like him among all
the kings of Judah, nor *among those*
who were before him.
6 For he clung to the LORD; he did
not depart from following Him, but
kept His commandments, which the
LORD had commanded Moses.

Hezekiah Victorious

7 [a]And the LORD was with him;
wherever he went he prospered.
And [b]he rebelled against the king of
Assyria and did not serve him.
8 [a]He [1]defeated the Philistines as
far as Gaza and its territory, from
[b]watchtower to fortified city.
9 Now it came about in the fourth
year of King Hezekiah, which was
the seventh year of Hoshea son of
Elah king of Israel, that [a]Shalmane-
ser king of Assyria came up against
Samaria and besieged it.
10 And at the end of three years
they captured it; in the sixth year of
Hezekiah, which was the ninth year
of Hoshea king of Israel, Samaria
was captured.
11 Then the king of Assyria carried Israel away into exile to Assyria, and put them in Halah and on
the Habor, the river of Gozan, and in
the cities of the Medes,
12 because they did not obey the
voice of the LORD their God, but
transgressed His covenant, even all
that Moses the servant of the LORD
commanded; they would neither listen, nor do *it*.

Invasion of Judah

13 [a]Now in the fourteenth year of
King Hezekiah, Sennacherib king of
Assyria came up against all the
fortified cities of Judah and seized
them.
14 Then Hezekiah king of Judah
sent to the king of Assyria at Lachish, saying, "[a]I have done wrong.
[1]Withdraw from me; whatever you
[2]impose on me I will bear." So the
king of Assyria [3]required of Hezekiah king of Judah three hundred
talents of silver and thirty talents of
gold.
15 And [a]Hezekiah gave *him* all the
silver which was found in the house
of the LORD, and in the treasuries of
the king's house.
16 At that time Hezekiah cut off
the gold from the doors of the temple of the LORD, and *from* the doorposts which Hezekiah king of Judah
had overlaid, and gave it to the king
of Assyria.
17 Then the king of Assyria sent
[a]Tartan and Rab-saris and Rabshakeh from Lachish to King Hezekiah
with a large army to Jerusalem. So
they went up and came to Jerusalem. And when they went up, they
came and stood by the [b]conduit of
the upper pool, which is on the highway of the [1]fuller's field.
18 When they called to the king,
[a]Eliakim the son of Hilkiah, who
was over the household, and [b]Sheb-
nah the scribe and Joah the son of
Asaph the recorder, came out to
them.
19 Then Rabshakeh said to them,
"Say now to Hezekiah, 'Thus says
the great king, the king of Assyria,
"What is this confidence that you
[1]have?
20"You say (but *they are* [1]only
empty words), '*I have* counsel and
strength for the war.' Now on whom
do you rely, [a]that you have rebelled
against me?

37 [a]Deut. 5:32
38 [a]Deut. 4:23; 6:12
41 [1]Or, *graven images* [a]Zeph. 1:5; Matt. 6:24
1 [a]2 Kin. 16:2; 17:1 [b]2 Chr. 28:27
2 [a]2 Chr. 29:1, 2
3 [a]2 Kin. 20:3; 2 Chr. 31:20
4 [1]I.e., a wooden symbol of a female deity [2]I.e., a piece of bronze [a]2 Kin. 18:22; 2 Chr. 31:1 [b]Num. 21:8, 9
5 [a]2 Kin. 19:10 [b]2 Kin. 23:25
7 [a]Gen. 39:2, 3; 1 Sam. 18:14 [b]2 Kin. 16:7
8 [1]Lit., *smote* [a]2 Chr. 28:18; Is. 14:29 [b]2 Kin. 17:9
9 [a]2 Kin. 17:3-7
13 [a]2 Chr. 32:1; Is. 36:1-39:8
14 [1]Lit., *Return* [2]Lit., *give* [3]Lit., *put on* [a]2 Kin. 18:7
15 [a]1 Kin. 15:18, 19; 2 Kin. 12:18; 16:8
17 [1]I.e., launderer's [a]Is. 20:1 [b]2 Kin. 20:20; Is. 7:3
18 [a]2 Kin. 19:2; Is. 22:20 [b]Is. 22:15
19 [1]Lit., *trust*
20 [1]Lit., *a word of the lips* [a]2 Kin. 18:7

21"Now behold, you [1][a]rely on the
staff of this crushed reed, *even* on
Egypt; on which if a man leans, it
will go into his [2]hand and pierce it.
So is Pharaoh king of Egypt to all
who rely on him.
22"But if you say to me, 'We trust
in the LORD our God,' is it not He
whose high places and [a]whose altars Hezekiah has taken away, and
has said to Judah and to Jerusalem,
'You shall worship before this altar
in Jerusalem'?
23"Now therefore, [1]come, make a
bargain with my master the king of
Assyria, and I will give you two
thousand horses, if you are able on
your part to set riders on them.
24"How then can you [1]repulse one
[2]official of the least of my master's
servants, and [3]rely on Egypt for
chariots and for horsemen?
25"Have I now come up [1]without
the LORD's approval against this
place to destroy it? The LORD said to
me, 'Go up against this land and destroy it.' " ' "
26 Then Eliakim the son of Hilkiah
and Shebnah and Joah, said to Rabshakeh, "Speak now to your servants in Aramaic, for we [1]under-
stand *it;* and do not speak with us in
[2][a]Judean, in the hearing of the people who are on the wall."
27 But Rabshakeh said to them,
"Has my master sent me only to
your master and to you to speak
these words, *and* not to the men
who sit on the wall, *doomed* to eat
their own dung and drink their own
urine with you?"
28 Then Rabshakeh stood and
cried with a loud voice in Judean,
[1]saying, "Hear the word of the great
king, the king of Assyria.
29"Thus says the king, 'Do not let
Hezekiah deceive you, for he will
not be able to deliver you from [1]my
hand;
30 nor let Hezekiah make you
trust in the LORD, saying, "The LORD
will surely deliver us, and this city
shall not be given into the hand of
the king of Assyria."
31 'Do not listen to Hezekiah, for
thus says the king of Assyria,
"[1]Make your peace with me and
come out to me, and eat [a]each of his
vine and each of his fig tree and
drink each of the waters of his own
cistern,
32 until I come and take you away
[a]to a land like your own land, a land
of grain and new wine, a land of
bread and vineyards, a land of olive
trees and honey, that you may live

21 [1]Lit., *rely for yourself* [2]Lit., *palm* [a]Is. 30:2, 3, 7; Ezek. 29:6, 7

22 [a]2 Kin. 18:4; 2 Chr. 31:1

23 [1]Lit., *please exchange pledges*

24 [1]Lit., *turn away the face of* [2]Or, *governor* [3]Lit., *rely for yourself*

25 [1]Lit., *without the LORD*

26 [1]Lit., *hear* [2]I.e., Hebrew [a]Ezra 4:7; Dan. 2:4

28 [1]Lit., *and spoke, saying,*

29 [1]Heb., *his*

31 [1]Lit., *Make with me a blessing* [a]1 Kin. 4:20, 25

32 [a]Deut. 8:7-9; 11:12

33 [a]2 Kin. 19:12; Is. 10:10, 11

34 [a]2 Kin. 19:13 [b]Is. 10:9 [c]2 Kin. 17:24

35 [1]Lit., *who have*

37 [a]2 Kin. 18:26 [b]2 Kin. 6:30

1 [a]2 Chr. 32:20-22; Is. 37:1-38 [b]2 Kin. 18:37 [c]1 Kin. 21:27

2 [a]2 Sam. 3:31 [b]Is. 1:1; 2:1

4 [a]Josh. 14:12; 2 Sam. 16:12 [b]2 Kin. 18:35 [c]Is. 1:9

6 [a]2 Kin. 18:17 [b]2 Kin. 18:22-25; 30:35

7 [a]2 Kin. 7:6 [b]2 Kin. 19:37

and not die." But do not listen to
Hezekiah, when he misleads you,
saying, "The LORD will deliver us."
33 '[a]Has any one of the gods of the
nations delivered his land from the
hand of the king of Assyria?
34 '[a]Where are the gods of Hamath
and [b]Arpad? Where are the gods of
Sepharvaim, Hena and [c]Ivvah?
Have they delivered Samaria from
my hand?
35 'Who among all the gods of the
lands [1]have delivered their land
from my hand, that the LORD should
deliver Jerusalem from my hand?' "
36 But the people were silent and
answered him not a word, for the
king's commandment was, "Do not
answer him."
37 Then [a]Eliakim the son of Hilkiah, who was over the household,
and Shebna the scribe and Joah the
son of Asaph, the recorder, came to
Hezekiah [b]with their clothes torn
and told him the words of Rabshakeh.

CHAPTER 19

Isaiah Encourages Hezekiah

[a]AND when King Hezekiah heard
it, he [b]tore his clothes, [c]covered
himself with sackcloth and entered
the house of the LORD.
2 Then he sent Eliakim who was
over the household with Shebna the
scribe and the elders of the priests,
[a]covered with sackcloth, to [b]Isaiah
the prophet the son of Amoz.
3 And they said to him, "Thus
says Hezekiah, 'This day is a day of
distress, rebuke, and rejection; for
children have come to birth, and
there is no strength to *deliver.*
4 '[a]Perhaps the LORD your God
will hear all the words of Rabshakeh, whom his master the king of
Assyria has sent [b]to reproach the
living God, and will rebuke the
words which the LORD your God has
heard. Therefore, offer a prayer for
[c]the remnant that is left.' "
5 So the servants of King Hezekiah came to Isaiah.
6 And Isaiah said to them, "Thus
you shall say to your master, 'Thus
says the LORD, "Do not be afraid because of the words that you have
heard, with which the [a]servants of
the king of Assyria [b]have blasphemed Me.
7"Behold, I will put a spirit in him
so that [a]he shall hear a rumor and
return to his own land. And [b]I will
make him fall by the sword in his
own land." ' "

Sennacherib Defies God

8 Then Rabshakeh returned and
found the king of Assyria fighting
against [a]Libnah, for he had heard
that [1]the king had left [b]Lachish.
9 When he heard *them* say concerning Tirhakah king of [1]Cush,
"Behold, he has come out to fight
against you," he sent messengers
again to Hezekiah saying,
10 "Thus you shall say to Hezekiah
king of [1]Judah, 'Do not [a]let your
God in whom you trust deceive you
saying, "[b]Jerusalem shall not be giv-
en into the hand of the king of Assyria."
11 'Behold, you have heard what
the kings of Assyria have done to all
the lands, destroying them completely. So will you be [1]spared?
12 '[a]Did the gods of [1]those nations
which my fathers destroyed deliver
them, *even* [b]Gozan and [c]Haran and
Rezeph and [d]the sons of Eden who
were in Telassar?
13 '[a]Where is the king of Hamath,
the king of Arpad, the king of the
city of Sepharvaim, and *of* Hena and
Ivvah?' "

Hezekiah's Prayer

14 Then [a]Hezekiah took the [1]letter
from the hand of the messengers
and read it, and he went up to the
house of the LORD and [2]spread it out
before the LORD.
15 And Hezekiah prayed before
the LORD and said, "O LORD, the
God of Israel, [a]who art [1]enthroned
above the cherubim, [b]Thou art the
God, Thou alone, of all the kingdoms of the earth. Thou hast made
heaven and earth.
16 "[a]Incline Thine ear, O LORD, and
hear; [b]open Thine eyes, O LORD, and
see; and listen to the words of Sennacherib, which he has sent [c]to reproach the living God.
17 "Truly, O LORD, the kings of Assyria have devastated the nations
and their lands
18 and have cast their gods into
the fire, [a]for they were not gods but
the work of men's hands, wood and
stone. So they have destroyed them.
19 "And now, O LORD our God, I
pray, deliver us from his hand [a]that
all the kingdoms of the earth may
know that Thou alone, O [b]LORD, art
God."

God's Answer through Isaiah

20 Then Isaiah the son of Amoz
sent to Hezekiah saying, "Thus says
the LORD, the God of Israel, 'Because you have prayed to Me about
Sennacherib king of Assyria, [a]I have
heard *you*.'
21 "This is the word that the LORD
has spoken against him:
'She has despised you and
mocked you,
[a]The virgin daughter of Zion;
She [b]has shaken *her* head behind you,
The daughter of Jerusalem!
22 'Whom have you [a]reproached
and [b]blasphemed?
And against whom have you
raised *your* voice,
And [1]haughtily lifted up your
eyes?
Against the [c]Holy One of Israel!
23 '[a]Through your messengers
you have reproached the
Lord,
And you have said, "With my
many chariots
I came up to the heights of the
mountains,
To the remotest parts of Lebanon;
And I [1]cut down its tall cedars
and its choice cypresses.
And I [1]entered its farthest
lodging place, its [b]thickest
forest.
24 "I dug *wells* and drank foreign
waters,
And with the sole of my feet I
[1a]dried up
All the rivers of [2]Egypt."

25 '[a]Have you not heard?
Long ago I did it;
From ancient times I planned
it.
[b]Now I have brought it to pass,
That you should turn fortified
cities into ruinous heaps.
26 "Therefore their inhabitants
were short of strength,
They were dismayed and put
to shame;
They were [a]as the vegetation
of the field and as the green
herb,
As grass on the housetops is
scorched before it is grown
up.
27 "But I know your sitting down,
And your going out and your
coming in,
And your raging against Me.
28 'Because of your raging
against Me,
And because your [1]arrogance
has come up to My ears,
Therefore I [a]will put My hook
in your nose,
And My bridle in your lips,

8 [1]Lit., *he* [a]Josh. 10:29 [b]2 Kin. 18:14

9 [1]Or, *Ethiopia*

10 [1]Lit., *Judah, saying,* [a]2 Kin. 18:5 [b]2 Kin. 18:30

11 [1]Lit., *delivered*

12 [1]Lit., *the* [a]2 Kin. 18:33 [b]2 Kin. 17:6 [c]Gen. 11:31 [d]Is. 37:12

13 [a]2 Kin. 18:34

14 [1]Lit., *letters . . . read them* [2]Lit., *Hezekiah spread* [a]Is. 37:14

15 [1]Lit., *seated* [a]Is. 37:14 [b]2 Kin. 5:15

16 [a]Ps. 31:2; Is. 37:17 [b]1 Kin. 8:29; 2 Chr. 6:40 [c]2 Kin. 19:4

18 [a]Is. 44:9-20; Acts 17:29

19 [a]1 Kin. 8:42, 43 [b]2 Kin. 19:15

20 [a]2 Kin. 20:5

21 [a]Jer. 14:17; Lam. 2:13 [b]Ps. 109:25; Matt. 27:39

22 [1]Lit., *on high* [a]2 Kin. 19:4 [b]2 Kin. 19:6 [c]Is. 5:24; 30:11-15

23 [1]So with some ancient versions, M.T., *will cut. . .will enter* [a]2 Kin. 18:17 [b]2 Chr. 26:10; Is. 10:18

24 [1]So with some ancient versions, M.T., *will dry up* [2]Lit., *the besieged place* [a]Is. 19:6

25 [a]Is. 45:7 [b]Is. 10:5

26 [a]Ps. 129:6

28 [1]Lit., *complacency* [a]Ezek. 19:9; 29:4

And [b]I will turn you back by
the way which you came.
29 'Then this shall be [a]the sign for
you: [1]you shall eat this year what
grows of itself, in the second year
what springs from the same, and in
the third year sow, reap, plant vineyards, and eat their fruit.
30 '[a]And the surviving remnant of
the house of Judah shall again take
root downward and bear fruit upward.
31 'For out of Jerusalem shall go
forth a remnant, and [a]out of Mount
Zion [1]survivors. [b]The zeal of [2]the
LORD shall perform this.
32 'Therefore thus says the LORD
concerning the king of Assyria,
"[a]He shall not come to this city or
shoot an arrow there; neither shall
he come before it with a shield, nor
throw up a mound against it.
33 "[a]By the way that he came, by
the same he shall return, and he
shall not come to this city," ' declares the LORD.
34 '[a]For I will defend this city to
save it for My own sake and [b]for My
servant David's sake.' "
35 [a]Then it happened that night
that [b]the angel of the LORD went
out, and struck 185,000 in the camp
of the Assyrians; and when [1]men
rose early in the morning, behold, all
of them were [2]dead.
36 So [a]Sennacherib king of Assyria departed and returned *home,*
and lived at [b]Nineveh.
37 And it came about as he was
worshiping in the house of Nisroch
his god, that [1a]Adrammelech and
Sharezer killed him with the sword;
and they escaped into [b]the land of
Ararat. And [c]Esarhaddon his son
became king in his place.

CHAPTER 20

Hezekiah's Illness and Recovery

[a]IN those days Hezekiah became
[1]mortally ill. And Isaiah the prophet
the son of Amoz came to him and
said to him, "Thus says the LORD,
'[b]Set your house in order, for you
shall die and not live.' "
2 Then he turned his face to the
wall, and prayed to the LORD, saying,
3 "[a]Remember now, O LORD, I beseech Thee, [b]how I have walked before Thee in truth and with a whole
heart, and have done what is good in
Thy sight." And [c]Hezekiah wept
[1]bitterly.
4 And it came about before Isaiah
had gone out of the middle court,
that the word of the LORD came to
him, saying,
5 "Return and say to [a]Hezekiah
the leader of My people, 'Thus says
the LORD, the God of your father David, "[b]I have heard your prayer, [c]I
have seen your tears; behold, I will
heal you. On the third day you shall
go up to the house of the LORD.
6 "And I will add fifteen years to
your [1]life, and I will deliver you and
this city from the hand of the king of
Assyria; and [a]I will defend this city
for My own sake and for My servant
David's sake." ' "
7 Then Isaiah said, "Take a cake
of figs." And they took and laid *it* on
the boil, and he recovered.
8 Now Hezekiah said to Isaiah,
"What will be the sign that the LORD
will heal me, and that I shall go up to
the house of the LORD the third
day?"
9 And Isaiah said, "This shall be
the sign to you from the LORD, that
the LORD will do the thing that He
has spoken: shall the shadow go forward ten steps or go back ten
steps?"
10 So Hezekiah [1]answered, "It is
easy for the shadow to decline ten
steps; no, but let the shadow turn
backward ten steps."
11 And Isaiah the prophet cried to
the LORD, and [a]He brought the
shadow on the [1]stairway back ten
steps by which it had gone down on
the [1]stairway of Ahaz.

Hezekiah Shows Babylon His Treasures

12 [a]At that time [1]Berodach-bala-
dan a son of Baladan, king of Babylon, sent letters and a present to
Hezekiah, for he heard that Hezekiah had been sick.
13 And Hezekiah listened to them,
and showed them [a]all his treasure
house, the silver and the gold and
the spices and the precious oil and
the house of his armor and all that
was found in his treasuries. There
was nothing in his house, nor in all
his dominion, that Hezekiah did not
show them.
14 Then Isaiah the prophet came
to King Hezekiah and said to him,
"What did these men say, and from
where have they come to you?" And
Hezekiah said, "They have come
from a far country, from Babylon."
15 And he said, "What have they
seen in your house?" So Hezekiah
[1]answered, "They have seen all that
is in my house; there is nothing
among my treasuries that I have not
shown them."

28 [b]2 Kin. 19:33, 36

29 [1]Lit., *eating* [a]Ex. 3:12; 2 Kin. 20:8, 9

30 [a]2 Kin. 19:4; 2 Chr. 32:22, 23

31 [1]Lit., *those who escape* [2]Some ancient mss. read, *the* LORD *of hosts* [a]Is. 10:20 [b]Is. 9:7

32 [a]Is. 8:7-10

33 [a]2 Kin. 19:28

34 [a]2 Kin. 20:6; Is. 31:5 [b]1 Kin. 11:12, 13

35 [1]Lit., *they* [2]Lit., *dead bodies* [a]2 Chr. 32:21 [b]2 Sam. 24:16

36 [a]2 Kin. 19:7, 28, 33 [b]Jon. 1:2

37 [1]Some ancient mss. read, *Adrammelech and Sharezer his sons smote him* [a]2 Kin. 19:17, 31 [b]Gen. 8:4; Jer. 51:27 [c]Ezra 4:2

1 [1]Lit., *sick to the point of death* [a]2 Chr. 32:24; Is. 38:1-22 [b]2 Sam. 17:23

3 [1]Lit., *great weeping* [a]Neh. 5:19; 13:14, 22, 31 [b]2 Kin. 18:3-6 [c]2 Sam. 12:21, 22

5 [a]1 Sam. 9:16; 10:1 [b]2 Kin. 19:20 [c]Ps. 39:12

6 [1]Lit., *days* [a]2 Kin. 19:34

10 [1]Lit., *said*

11 [1]Lit., *steps* [a]Josh. 10:12-14

12 [1]Many mss. and ancient versions read, *Merodach-baladan;* cf. Is. 39:1 [a]2 Chr. 32:31; Is. 39:1-8

13 [a]2 Chr. 32:27

15 [1]Lit., *said*

16 Then Isaiah said to Hezekiah, "Hear the word of the LORD.

17 'Behold, the days are coming when [a]all that is in your house, and all that your fathers have laid up in store to this day shall be carried to Babylon; nothing shall be left,' says the LORD.

18 'And some [a]of your sons who shall issue from you, whom you shall beget, shall be taken away; and they shall become [b]officials in the palace of the king of Babylon.' "

19 Then Hezekiah said to Isaiah, "The word of the LORD which you have spoken is [a]good." For he [1]thought, "Is it not so, if there shall be peace and truth in my days?"

20 [a]Now the rest of the acts of Hezekiah and all his might, and how he made the pool and the conduit, and brought water into the city, are they not written in the Book of the Chronicles of the Kings of Judah?

21 [a]So Hezekiah slept with his fathers, and Manasseh his son became king in his place.

CHAPTER 21

Manasseh Succeeds Hezekiah

[a]MANASSEH was twelve years old when he became king, and he reigned fifty-five years in Jerusalem; and his mother's name was Hephzibah.

2 And he did evil in the sight of the LORD, [a]according to the abominations of the nations whom the LORD dispossessed before the sons of Israel.

3 For [a]he rebuilt the high places which Hezekiah his father had destroyed; and [b]he erected altars for Baal and made an [1]Asherah, as Ahab king of Israel had done, and [c]worshiped all the host of heaven and served them.

4 And [a]he built altars in the house of the LORD, of which the LORD had said, "[b]In Jerusalem I will put My name."

5 For he built altars for [a]all the host of heaven in [b]the two courts of the house of the LORD.

6 And [a]he made his son pass through the fire, [b]practiced witchcraft and used divination, and dealt with mediums and spiritists. He did much evil in the sight of the LORD provoking *Him to anger.*

7 Then [a]he set the carved image of Asherah that he had made, in the house of which the LORD said to David and to his son Solomon, "[b]In this house and in Jerusalem, which I have chosen from all the tribes of Israel, I will put My name forever.

8 "And I [a]will not make the feet of Israel wander any more from the land which I gave their fathers, if only they will observe to do according to all that I have commanded them, and according to all the law that My servant Moses commanded them."

9 But they did not listen, and Manasseh seduced them to do evil more than the nations whom the LORD destroyed before the sons of Israel.

The King's Idolatries Rebuked

10 Now the LORD spoke through His servants the prophets, saying,

11 "[a]Because Manasseh king of Judah has done these abominations, [b]having done wickedly more than all the Amorites did who *were* before him, and [c]has also made Judah sin [d]with his idols;

12 therefore thus says the LORD, the God of Israel, 'Behold, I am bringing *such* calamity on Jerusalem and Judah, that whoever hears of it, [a]both his ears shall tingle.

13 '[a]And I will stretch over Jerusalem the line of Samaria and the plummet of the house of Ahab, and I will wipe Jerusalem as one wipes a dish, wiping it and turning it upside down.

14 'And I will abandon the remnant of My inheritance and deliver them into the hand of their enemies, and they shall become as plunder and spoil to all their enemies;

15 because they have done evil in My sight, and have been provoking Me to anger, since the day their fathers came from Egypt, even to this day.' "

16 [a]Moreover, Manasseh shed very much innocent blood until he had filled Jerusalem from one end to another; besides his sin [b]with which he made Judah sin, in doing evil in the sight of the LORD.

17 [a]Now the rest of the acts of Manasseh and all that he did and his sin which he [1]committed, are they not written in the Book of the Chronicles of the Kings of Judah?

18 [a]And Manasseh slept with his fathers and was buried in the garden of his own house, [b]in the garden of Uzza, and Amon his son became king in his place.

Amon Succeeds Manasseh

19 Amon was twenty-two years old when he became king, and he reigned two years in Jerusalem; and

---

17 [a]2 Kin. 24:13; 25:13-15; Jer. 52:17-19

18 [a]2 Kin. 24:12; 2 Chr. 33:11 [b]Dan. 1:3-7

19 [1]Lit., *said* [a]1 Sam. 3:18

20 [a]2 Chr. 32:32

21 [a]2 Chr. 32:33

1 [a]2 Chr. 33:1-9

2 [a]2 Kin. 16:3

3 [1]I.e., a wooden symbol of a female deity [a]2 Kin. 18:4 [b]1 Kin. 16:31-33 [c]Deut. 17:2-5; 2 Kin. 17:16; 23:5

4 [a]2 Kin. 16:10-16 [b]1 Kin. 8:29

5 [a]2 Kin. 23:4, 5 [b]1 Kin. 7:12; 2 Kin. 23:12

6 [a]Lev. 18:21; 2 Kin. 16:3; 17:17 [b]Lev. 19:26, 31; Deut. 18:10-14

7 [a]Deut. 16:21; 2 Kin. 23:6 [b]1 Kin. 8:29; 9:3

8 [a]2 Sam. 7:10; 2 Kin. 18:11, 12

11 [a]2 Kin. 21:2; 24:3, 4 [b]Gen. 15:16; 1 Kin. 21:26 [c]2 Kin. 21:16 [d]2 Kin. 21:21

12 [a]1 Sam. 3:11; Jer. 19:3

13 [a]Is. 34:11; Amos 7:7, 8

16 [a]2 Kin. 24:4 [b]2 Kin. 21:11

17 [1]Lit., *sinned* [a]2 Chr. 33:11-19

18 [a]2 Chr. 33:20 [b]2 Kin. 21:26

his mother's name *was* Meshulle-
meth the daughter of Haruz of Jot-
bah.
20 And he did evil in the sight of
the LORD, [a]as Manasseh his father
had done.
21 For he walked in all the way
that his father had walked, and
served the idols that his father had
served and worshiped them.
22 So [a]he forsook the LORD, the
God of his fathers, and did not walk
in the way of the LORD.
23 And [a]the servants of Amon
conspired against him and killed the
king in his own house.
24 Then [a]the people of the land
[1]killed all those who had conspired
against King Amon, and the people
of the land made Josiah his son king
in his place.
25 Now the rest of the acts of
Amon which he did, are they not
written in the Book of the Chronicles of the Kings of Judah?
26 And he was buried in his grave
[a]in the garden of Uzza, and Josiah
his son became king in his place.

CHAPTER 22

Josiah Succeeds Amon

[a]JOSIAH was eight years old when
he became king, and he reigned
thirty-one years in Jerusalem; and
his mother's name *was* Jedidah the
daughter of Adaiah of [b]Bozkath.
2 And he did right in the sight of
the LORD and walked in all the way
of his father David, nor did he [a]turn
aside to the right or to the left.
3 Now it came about in the eighteenth year of King Josiah that the
king sent Shaphan, the son of Azaliah the son of Meshullam the scribe,
to the house of the LORD saying,
4"[a]Go up to Hilkiah the high
priest that he may [1]count the money
brought in to the house of the LORD
which the doorkeepers have gathered from the people.
5"[a]And let them deliver it into the
hand of the workmen who have the
oversight of the house of the LORD,
and let them give it to the workmen
who are in the house of the LORD to
repair the [1]damages of the house,
6 to the carpenters and the builders and the masons and for buying
timber and hewn stone to repair the
house.
7"Only [a]no accounting shall be
made with them for the money delivered into their hands, for they
deal faithfully."

The Lost Book

8 Then Hilkiah the high priest
said to Shaphan the scribe, "[a]I have
found the book of the law in the
house of the LORD." And Hilkiah
gave the book to Shaphan who read
it.
9 And Shaphan the scribe came
to the king and brought back word
to the king and said, "Your servants
have emptied out the money that
was found in the house, and have
delivered it into the hand of the
workmen who have the oversight of
the house of the LORD."
10 Moreover, Shaphan the scribe
told the king saying, "Hilkiah the
priest has given me a book." And
Shaphan read it in the presence of
the king.
11 And it came about when the
king heard the words of the book of
the law, that [a]he tore his clothes.
12 Then the king commanded Hilkiah the priest, [a]Ahikam the son of
Shaphan, [1b]Achbor the son of Micaiah, Shaphan the scribe, and Asaiah
the king's servant saying,
13"Go, inquire of the LORD for me
and the people and all Judah concerning the words of this book that
has been found, for [a]great is the
wrath of the LORD that burns
against us, because our fathers have
not listened to the words of this
book, to do according to all that is
written concerning us."

Huldah Predicts

14 So Hilkiah the priest, Ahikam,
Achbor, Shaphan, and Asaiah went
to Huldah the prophetess, the wife
of Shallum the son of [1a]Tikvah, the
son of Harhas, keeper of the wardrobe (now she lived in Jerusalem in
the [b]Second Quarter); and they
spoke to her.
15 And she said to them, "Thus
says the LORD God of Israel, 'Tell the
man who sent you to me,
16 thus says the LORD, "Behold, I
bring evil on this place and on its
inhabitants, *even* all the words of
the book which the king of Judah
has read.
17"[a]Because they have forsaken
Me and have burned incense to other gods that they might provoke Me
to anger with all the work of their
hands, therefore My wrath burns
against this place, and it shall not be
quenched." '
18"But to the king of Judah who
sent you to inquire of the LORD thus
shall you say to him, 'Thus says the

20 [a]2 Kin. 21:2-6, 11, 16
22 [a]2 Kin. 22:17; 1 Chr. 28:9
23 [a]2 Kin. 12:20; 14:19
24 [1]Lit., *smote* [a]2 Kin. 14:5
26 [a]2 Kin. 21:18
1 [a]2 Chr. 34:1 [b]Josh. 15:39
2 [a]Deut. 5:32; Josh. 1:7
4 [1]Or, *total* [a]2 Kin. 12:4, 9, 10
5 [1]Lit., *breach* [a]2 Kin. 12:11-14
7 [a]2 Kin. 12:15
8 [a]Deut. 31:24-26; 2 Chr. 34:14, 15
11 [a]Gen. 37:34; Josh. 7:6
12 [1]In 2 Chr. 34:20, *Abdon, son of Micah* [a]2 Kin. 25:22; Jer. 26:24 [b]2 Chr. 34:20
13 [a]Deut. 29:23-28; 31:17, 18
14 [1]In 2 Chr. 34:22, *Tokhath, son of Hasrah* [a]2 Chr. 34:22 [b]Zeph. 1:10
17 [a]Deut. 29:25, 26; 2 Kin. 21:22

LORD God of Israel, "*Regarding* the
words which you have heard,
19 [a]because your heart was tender
and [b]you humbled yourself before
the LORD when you heard what I
spoke against this place and against
its inhabitants that they should become [c]a desolation and a [d]curse,
and you have [e]torn your clothes and
wept before Me, I truly have heard
you," declares the LORD.
20"Therefore, behold, I will gather
you to your fathers, and [a]you shall
be gathered to your grave in peace,
neither shall your eyes see all the
evil which I will bring on this
place."' " So they brought back
word to the king.

CHAPTER 23

Josiah's Covenant

[a]THEN the king sent, and they
gathered to him all the elders of Judah and of Jerusalem.
2 And the king went up to the
house of the LORD and all the men of
Judah and all the inhabitants of Jerusalem with him, and the priests
and the prophets and all the people,
both small and great; and [a]he read in
their hearing all the words of the
book of the covenant, [b]which was
found in the house of the LORD.
3 And [a]the king stood by the pillar and made a covenant before the
LORD, [b]to walk after the LORD, and
to keep His commandments and His
testimonies and His statutes with all
his heart and all *his* soul, to carry
out the words of this covenant that
were written in this book. And all
the people [1]entered into the covenant.

Reforms under Josiah

4 Then the king commanded Hilkiah the high priest and [a]the priests
of the second order and the [1]door-
keepers, [b]to bring out of the temple
of the LORD all the vessels that were
made for Baal, for [2]Asherah, and for
all the host of heaven; and [c]he
burned them outside Jerusalem in
the fields of the Kidron, and carried
their ashes to Bethel.
5 And he did away with the idolatrous priests whom the kings of Judah had appointed to burn incense
in the high places in the cities of Judah and in the surrounding area of
Jerusalem, also those who burned
incense to Baal, to the sun and to the
moon and to the constellations and
to all the host of heaven.
6 And he brought out the Asherah from the house of the LORD outside Jerusalem to the brook Kidron,
and burned it at the brook Kidron,
and [a]ground *it* to dust, and [b]threw
its dust on the graves of the [1]com-
mon people.
7 He also broke down the houses
of the [a]*male* cult prostitutes which
were in the house of the LORD,
where [b]the women were weaving
[1]hangings for the Asherah.
8 Then he brought all the priests
from the cities of Judah, and defiled
the high places where the priests
had burned incense, from [a]Geba to
Beersheba; and he broke down the
high places of the gates which *were*
at the entrance of the gate of Joshua
the governor of the city, which *were*
on one's left at the city gate.
9 Nevertheless [a]the priests of the
high places did not go up to the altar
of the LORD in Jerusalem, but they
ate unleavened bread among their
brothers.
10 [a]He also defiled [1]Topheth,
which is in the valley of the son of
Hinnom, [b]that no man might make
his son or his daughter pass through
the fire for [c]Molech.
11 And he did away with the
horses which the kings of Judah had
given to the sun, at the entrance of
the house of the LORD, by the chamber of Nathan-melech the official,
which *was* in the precincts; and he
burned the chariots of the sun with
fire.
12 And [a]the altars which *were* on
the roof, the upper chamber of
Ahaz, which the kings of Judah had
made, and [b]the altars which Manasseh had made in the two courts of
the house of the LORD, the king
broke down; and he [1]ran from there,
and [c]threw their dust into the brook
Kidron.
13 And the high places which *were*
before Jerusalem, which *were* on
the right of [a]the mount of destruction which Solomon the king of Israel had built for [b]Ashtoreth the
abomination of the Sidonians, and
for [c]Chemosh the abomination of
Moab, and for Milcom the abomination of the sons of Ammon, the king
defiled.
14 And [a]he broke in pieces the *sacred* pillars and cut down the Asherim and [b]filled their places with human bones.
15 Furthermore, [a]the altar that
was at Bethel *and* the [b]high place
which Jeroboam the son of Nebat,
who made Israel sin, had made,
even that altar and the high place he
broke down. Then he [1c]demolished

19 [a]1 Sam. 24:5; Ps. 51:17 [b]Ex. 10:3; 1 Kin. 21:29 [c]Lev. 26:31 [d]Jer. 26:6 [e]2 Kin. 22:11

20 [a]2 Kin. 23:30

1 [a]2 Chr. 34:29-32

2 [a]Deut. 31:10-13 [b]2 Kin. 22:8

3 [1]Lit., *took a stand in* [a]2 Kin. 11:14, 17 [b]Deut. 13:4

4 [1]Lit., *keepers of the threshold* [2]I.e., A wooden symbol of a female deity, and so throughout the chap. [a]2 Kin. 25:18; Jer. 52:24 [b]2 Kin. 21:37 [c]2 Kin. 23:15

6 [1]Lit., *sons of the people* [a]2 Kin. 23:15 [b]2 Chr. 34:4

7 [1]Or, *tents;* lit., *houses* [a]1 Kin. 14:24; 15:12 [b]Ex. 35:25, 26; Ezek. 16:16

8 [a]Josh. 21:17; 1 Kin. 15:22

9 [a]Ezek. 44:10-14

10 [1]I.e., place of burning [a]Is. 30:33; Jer. 7:31, 32 [b]Lev. 18:21 [c]1 Kin. 11:7

12 [1]Or, *smashed them there* [a]Jer. 19:13; Zeph. 1:5 [b]2 Kin. 21:5 [c]2 Kin. 23:4, 6

13 [a]1 Kin. 11:7 [b]1 Kin. 11:5 [c]Num. 21:29

14 [a]Deut. 7:5, 25 [b]2 Kin. 23:16

15 [1]So the Gk.; Heb., *burned the high place* [a]1 Kin. 13:1 [b]1 Kin. 12:28-33 [c]2 Kin. 23:6

its stones, ground them to dust, and burned the Asherah.

16 Now when Josiah turned, he saw the graves that *were* there on the mountain, and he sent and took the bones from the graves and burned *them* on the altar and defiled it [a]according to the word of the LORD which the man of God proclaimed, who proclaimed these things.

17 Then he said, "What is this monument that I see?" And the men of the city told him, "[a]It is the grave of the man of God who came from Judah and proclaimed these things which you have done against the altar of Bethel."

18 And he said, "Let him alone; let no one disturb his bones." So they [1]left his bones undisturbed [a]with the bones of the prophet who came from Samaria.

19 And Josiah also removed all the houses of the high places which *were* [a]in the cities of Samaria, which the kings of Israel had made provoking [1]the LORD; and he did to them [2]just as he had done in Bethel.

20 And all the priests of the high places who *were* there [a]he slaughtered on the altars and burned human bones on them; then he returned to Jerusalem.

Passover Reinstituted

21 Then the king commanded all the people saying, "[a]Celebrate the Passover to the LORD your God [b]as it is written in this book of the covenant."

22 [a]Surely such a Passover had not been celebrated from the days of the judges who judged Israel, nor in all the days of the kings of Israel and of the kings of Judah.

23 But in the eighteenth year of King Josiah, this Passover was observed to the LORD in Jerusalem.

24 Moreover, Josiah [1]removed [a]the mediums and the spiritists and the [b]teraphim and [c]the idols and all the abominations that were seen in the land of Judah and in Jerusalem, [d]that he might [2]confirm the words of the law which were written [e]in the book that Hilkiah the priest found in the house of the LORD.

25 And before him there was no king [a]like him who turned to the LORD with all his heart and with all his soul and with all his might, according to all the law of Moses; nor did any like him arise after him.

26 However, the LORD did not turn from the fierceness of His great wrath with which His anger burned against Judah, [a]because of all the provocations with which Manasseh had provoked Him.

27 And the LORD said, "I will remove Judah also from My sight, [a]as I have removed Israel. And [b]I will cast off Jerusalem, this city which I have chosen, and the [1]temple of which I said, 'My name shall be there.' "

Jehoahaz Succeeds Josiah

28 Now the rest of the acts of Josiah and all that he did, are they not written in the Book of the Chronicles of the Kings of Judah?

29 [a]In his days [b]Pharaoh Neco king of Egypt went up to the king of Assyria to the river Euphrates. And King Josiah went to meet him, and when *Pharaoh Neco* saw him he killed him at [c]Megiddo.

30 And [a]his servants drove [1]his body in a chariot from Megiddo, and brought him to Jerusalem and buried him in his own tomb. [b]Then the people of the land took Jehoahaz the son of Josiah and anointed him and made him king in place of his father.

31 [a]Jehoahaz was twenty-three years old when he became king, and he reigned three months in Jerusalem; and his mother's name was [b]Hamutal the daughter of Jeremiah of Libnah.

32 And he did evil in the sight of the LORD, [a]according to all that his fathers had done.

33 And [a]Pharaoh Neco imprisoned him at [b]Riblah in the land of [c]Hamath, that he might not reign in Jerusalem; and he imposed on the land a fine of one hundred talents of silver and a talent of gold.

Jehoiakim Made King by Pharaoh

34 And Pharaoh Neco made [a]Eliakim the son of Josiah king in the place of Josiah his father, and [b]changed his name to Jehoiakim. But he took Jehoahaz away and [1c]brought *him* to Egypt, and he died there.

35 So Jehoiakim [a]gave the silver and gold to Pharaoh, but he taxed the land in order to give the money at the [1]command of Pharaoh. He exacted the silver and gold from the people of the land, each according to his valuation, to give it to Pharaoh Neco.

36 [a]Jehoiakim was twenty-five years old when he became king, and he reigned eleven years in Jerusalem; and his mother's name *was* Zebidah the daughter of Pedaiah of Rumah.

16 [a]1 Kin. 13:2

17 [a]1 Kin. 13:1, 30, 31

18 [1]Lit., *let his bones escape with* [a]1 Kin. 13:11, 31

19 [1]So with ancient versions. [2]Lit., *according to all the acts* [a]2 Chr. 34:6, 7

20 [a]2 Kin. 10:25; 11:18

21 [a]2 Chr. 35:1-17 [b]Num. 9:2-4; Deut. 16:2-8

22 [a]2 Chr. 35:18, 19

24 [1]Lit., *consumed* [2]Or, *perform* [a]Lev. 19:31; 2 Kin. 21:6 [b]Gen. 31:19 [c]2 Kin. 21:11, 21 [d]Deut. 18:10-22 [e]2 Kin. 22:8

25 [a]2 Kin. 18:5

26 [a]2 Kin. 21:11-13; Jer. 15:4

27 [1]Lit., *house* [a]2 Kin. 18:11 [b]2 Kin. 21:13, 14

29 [a]2 Chr. 35:20-24 [b]Jer. 46:2 [c]Judg. 5:19

30 [1]Lit., *him, dead* [a]2 Kin. 9:28 [b]2 Chr. 36:1-4

31 [a]1 Chr. 3:15; Jer. 22:11 [b]2 Kin. 24:18

32 [a]2 Kin. 21:2-7

33 [a]2 Kin. 23:29 [b]2 Kin. 25:6 [c]1 Kin. 8:65

34 [1]So with Gk.; Heb., *he came*, cf. 2 Chr. 36:4 [a]1 Chr. 3:15 [b]2 Kin. 24:17 [c]Jer. 22:11, 12; Ezek. 19:3, 4

35 [1]Lit., *mouth* [a]2 Kin. 23:33

36 [a]2 Chr. 36:5

37 And he did evil in the sight of
the LORD, [a]according to all that his
fathers had done.

CHAPTER 24

Babylon Controls Jehoiakim

[a]IN his days Nebuchadnezzar king
of Babylon came up, and Jehoiakim
became his servant *for* three years;
then he turned and rebelled against
him.
2 And the LORD sent against him
[a]bands of Chaldeans, [b]bands of Syrians, [c]bands of Moabites, and bands
of Ammonites. So He sent them
against Judah to destroy it, [d]accord-
ing to the word of the LORD, which
He had spoken through His servants
the prophets.
3 [a]Surely at the [1]command of the
LORD it came upon Judah, to remove
them from His sight [b]because of the
sins of Manasseh, according to all
that he had done,
4 and [a]also for the innocent blood
which he shed, for he filled Jerusalem with innocent blood; and the
LORD would not forgive.
5 Now the rest of the acts of Jehoiakim and all that he did, are they
not written in the Book of the
Chronicles of the Kings of Judah?

Jehoiachin Reigns

6 So [a]Jehoiakim slept with his fathers, and Jehoiachin his son became king in his place.
7 And [a]the king of Egypt did not
come out of his land again, [b]for the
king of Babylon had taken all that
belonged to the king of Egypt from
[c]the brook of Egypt to the river Euphrates.
8 [a]Jehoiachin was [b]eighteen
years old when he became king, and
he reigned three months in Jerusalem; and his mother's name *was* Ne-
hushta the daughter of Elnathan of
Jerusalem.
9 And he did evil in the sight of
the LORD, [a]according to all that his
father had done.

Deportation to Babylon

10 At that time the servants of
Nebuchadnezzar king of Babylon
went up to Jerusalem, and the city
came under siege.
11 And Nebuchadnezzar the king
of Babylon came to the city, while
his servants were besieging it.
12 And [a]Jehoiachin the king of Judah went out to the king of Babylon,
he and his mother and his servants
and his captains and his officials. So
[b]the king of Babylon took him captive in the eighth year of his reign.
13 And [a]he carried out from there
all the treasures of the house of the
LORD, and the treasures of the king's
house, and [b]cut in pieces all the vessels of gold [c]which Solomon king of
Israel had made in the temple of the
LORD, just as the LORD had said.
14 Then [a]he led away into exile all
Jerusalem and all the captains and
all the mighty men of valor, [b]ten
thousand captives, and [c]all the
craftsmen and the smiths. None remained [d]except the poorest people
of the land.
15 So [a]he led Jehoiachin away into
exile to Babylon; also the king's
mother and the king's wives and his
officials and the leading men of the
land, he led away into exile from Jerusalem to Babylon.
16 And all the men of valor, [a]seven
thousand, and the craftsmen and
the smiths, one thousand, all strong
and fit for war, and these the king of
Babylon brought into exile to Babylon.

Zedekiah Made King

17 [a]Then the king of Babylon
made [1]his uncle Mattaniah, king in
his place, and changed his name to
Zedekiah.
18 [a]Zedekiah was twenty-one
years old when he became king, and
he reigned eleven years in Jerusalem; and his mother's name *was*
[b]Hamutal the daughter of Jeremiah
of Libnah.
19 And he did evil in the sight of
the LORD, [a]according to all that Jehoiakim had done.
20 For through the anger of the
LORD *this* came about in Jerusalem
and Judah until He cast them out
from His presence. And [a]Zedekiah
rebelled against the king of Babylon.

CHAPTER 25

Nebuchadnezzar Besieges Jerusalem

[a]NOW it came about in the ninth
year of his reign, on the tenth day of
the tenth month, that [b]Nebuchad-
nezzar king of Babylon came, he
and all his army, against Jerusalem,
camped against it, [c]and built a siege
wall all around [1]it.
2 So the city was under siege until the eleventh year of King Zedekiah.
3 On the ninth day of the *fourth*
month [a]the famine was so severe in

37 [a]2 Kin. 23:32
1 [a]2 Chr. 36:6; Jer. 25:1
2 [a]Jer. 35:11 [b]2 Kin. 6:23 [c]2 Kin. 13:20 [d]2 Kin. 23:27
3 [1]Lit., *mouth* [a]2 Kin. 18:25 [b]2 Kin. 23:26
4 [a]2 Kin. 21:16
6 [a]Jer. 22:18, 19
7 [a]Jer. 37:5-7 [b]Jer. 46:2 [c]Gen. 15:18
8 [a]1 Chr. 3:16 [b]2 Chr. 36:9
9 [a]2 Kin. 21:2-7
12 [a]Jer. 24:1; 29:1, 2 [b]2 Chr. 36:10
13 [a]2 Kin. 20:17; Is. 39:6 [b]2 Kin. 25:13-15 [c]1 Kin. 7:48-50
14 [a]Jer. 24:1 [b]2 Kin. 24:16; Jer. 52:28 [c]Jer. 24:1; 29:2 [d]2 Kin. 25:12
15 [a]2 Chr. 36:10; Jer. 22:24-28
16 [a]2 Kin. 24:14
17 [1]I.e., Jehoiachin's uncle [a]2 Chr. 36:10-13
18 [a]Jer. 52:1 [b]2 Kin. 23:31
19 [a]2 Kin. 23:37
20 [a]2 Chr. 36:13
1 [1]Lit., *against it* [a]2 Chr. 36:17-20; Jer. 39:1-7 [b]Jer. 34:1, 2; Ezek. 24:2 [c]Ezek. 21:22
3 [a]2 Kin. 6:24, 25; Lam. 4:9, 10

the city that there was no food for the people of the land.

4 Then the city was broken into, and all the men of war fled by night by way of the gate between the two walls beside [a]the king's garden, though the Chaldeans were all around the city. And [1]they went by way of the Arabah.

5 But the army of the Chaldeans pursued the king and overtook him in the plains of Jericho and all his army was scattered from him.

6 Then [a]they captured the king and [b]brought him to the king of Babylon at [c]Riblah, and [1]he passed sentence on him.

7 And [a]they slaughtered the sons of Zedekiah before his eyes, then [b]put out the eyes of Zedekiah and bound him with bronze fetters and brought him to Babylon.

Jerusalem Burned and Plundered

8 [a]Now on the seventh day of the [b]fifth month, which was the nineteenth year of King Nebuchadnezzar, king of Babylon, Nebuzaradan the captain of the guard, a servant of the king of Babylon, came to Jerusalem.

9 And [a]he burned the house of the LORD, [b]the king's house, and all the houses of Jerusalem; even every great house he burned with fire.

10 So all the army of the Chaldeans who *were with* the captain of the guard [a]broke down the walls around Jerusalem.

11 Then [a]the rest of the people who were left in the city and the deserters who had deserted to the king of Babylon and the rest of the multitude, Nebuzaradan the captain of the guard carried away into exile.

12 But the captain of the guard left some of [a]the poorest of the land to be vinedressers and plowmen.

13 [a]Now the bronze pillars which were in the house of the LORD, and the stands and the bronze sea which were in the house of the LORD, the Chaldeans broke in pieces and carried the [1]bronze to Babylon.

14 [a]And they took away the pots, the shovels, the snuffers, the spoons, and all the bronze vessels which were used in *temple* service.

15 The captain of the guard also took away the firepans and the basins, what was fine gold and what was fine silver.

16 The two pillars, the one sea, and the stands which Solomon had made for the house of the LORD—[a]the bronze of all these vessels was beyond weight.

17 [a]The height of the one pillar was eighteen [1]cubits, and a bronze capital was on it; the height of the capital was three [1]cubits, with a network and pomegranates on the capital all around, all of bronze. And the second pillar was like these with network.

18 Then the captain of the guard took [a]Seraiah the chief priest and [b]Zephaniah the second priest, with the three [1]officers of the temple.

19 And from the city he took one official who was overseer of the men of war, and [a]five [1]of the king's advisers who were found in the city; and the [2]scribe of the captain of the army, who mustered the people of the land; and sixty men of the people of the land who were found in the city.

20 And Nebuzaradan the captain of the guard took them and brought them to the king of Babylon at [a]Riblah.

21 Then the king of Babylon struck them down and put them to death at Riblah in the land of Hamath. [a]So Judah was led away into exile from its land.

Gedaliah Made Governor

22 Now *as for* the people who were left in the land of Judah, whom Nebuchadnezzar king of Babylon had left, he appointed [a]Gedaliah the son of Ahikam, the son of Shaphan over them.

23 [a]When all the captains of the forces, they and *their* men, heard that the king of Babylon had appointed Gedaliah *governor,* they came to Gedaliah to [b]Mizpah, namely, Ishmael the son of Nethaniah, and Johanan the son of Kareah, and Seraiah the son of Tanhumeth the Netophathite, and Jaazaniah the son of the Maacathite, they and their men.

24 And Gedaliah swore to them and their men and said to them, "Do not be afraid of the servants of the Chaldeans; live in the land and serve the king of Babylon, and it will be well with you."

25 [a]But it came about in the seventh month, that Ishmael the son of Nethaniah, the son of Elishama, of the royal [1]family, came [2]with ten men and struck Gedaliah down so that he died along with the Jews and the Chaldeans who were with him at Mizpah.

26 [a]Then all the people, both small and great, and the captains of the forces arose and went to Egypt; for they were afraid of the Chaldeans.

4 [1]So some ancient mss. and versions. M.T., *he* [a]Neh. 3:15

6 [1]Lit., *they spoke judgment with him* [a]Jer. 34:21, 22 [b]Jer. 32:4 [c]2 Kin. 23:33

7 [a]Jer. 39:6, 7 [b]Ezek. 12:13

8 [a]Jer. 52:12 [b]Jer. 39:8-12

9 [a]2 Chr. 36:19; Ps. 74:3-7 [b]Amos 2:5

10 [a]2 Kin. 14:13; Neh. 1:3

11 [a]2 Chr. 36:20

12 [a]2 Kin. 24:14; Jer. 40:7

13 [1]Lit., *bronze of them* [a]2 Chr. 36:18

14 [a]1 Kin. 7:47-50

16 [a]1 Kin. 7:47

17 [1]I.e., one cubit equals approx. 18 in. [a]1 Kin. 7:15-22

18 [1]Lit., *keepers of the door* [a]1 Chr. 6:14; Ezra 7:1 [b]Jer. 21:1; 29:25, 29

19 [1]Lit., *men of those seeing the king's face* [2]Or, *scribe, a captain* [a]Esth. 1:14

20 [a]2 Kin. 23:33

21 [a]Deut. 28:64; 2 Kin. 23:27

22 [a]Jer. 39:14

23 [a]Jer. 40:7-9 [b]Josh. 18:26

25 [1]Lit., *seed* [2]Lit., *and ten men with him* [a]Jer. 41:1, 2

26 [a]Jer. 43:4-7

27 [a]Now it came about in the
thirty-seventh year of [b]the exile of
Jehoiachin king of Judah, in the
twelfth month, on the twenty-seventh *day* of the month, that Evil-me-
rodach king of Babylon, in the year
that he became king, [1c]released Jehoiachin king of Judah from prison;
28 and he spoke kindly to him and
set his throne above the throne of
the kings who *were* with him in
Babylon.
29 And Jehoiachin changed his
prison clothes, and [1a]had his meals
in the king's presence regularly all
the days of his life;
30 and for his [a]allowance, a regular allowance was given him by the
king, a portion for each day, all the
days of his life.

27 [1]Lit., *lifted up the head of* [a]Jer. 52:31-34 [b]2 Kin. 24:12, 15 [c]Gen. 40:13, 20

29 [1]Lit., *ate bread* [a]2 Sam. 9:7

30 [a]Neh. 11:23; 12:47

THE FIRST BOOK OF THE CHRONICLES

Genealogy from Adam

[a]ADAM, Seth, Enosh,
2 Kenan, Mahalalel, Jared,
3 Enoch, Methuselah, Lamech,
4 Noah, Shem, Ham and Japheth.
5 [a]The sons of Japheth *were* Gomer, Magog, Madai, Javan, Tubal,
Meshech, and Tiras.
6 And the sons of Gomer *were*
Ashkenaz, [1]Diphath, and Togar-
mah.
7 And the sons of Javan *were*
Elishah, Tarshish, Kittim, and [1]Rod-
anim.
8 The sons of Ham *were* Cush,
Mizraim, Put, and Canaan.
9 And the sons of Cush *were*
Seba, Havilah, Sabta, Raama, and
Sabteca; and the sons of Raamah
were Sheba and Dedan.
10 And Cush [1]became the father
of Nimrod; he began to be a mighty
one in the earth.
11 [a]And Mizraim became the father of the people of Lud, Anam, Le-
hab, Naphtuh,
12 Pathrus, Casluh, from which
the [1]Philistines came, and Caphtor.
13 And Canaan became the father
of Sidon, his first-born, Heth,
14 and the Jebusites, the Amorites, the Girgashites,
15 the Hivites, the Arkites, the Si-
nites,
16 the Arvadites, the Zemarites,
and the Hamathites.
17 [a]The sons of Shem *were* Elam,
Asshur, Arpachshad, Lud, Aram,
Uz, Hul, Gether, and [1]Meshech.
18 And Arpachshad became the
father of Shelah and Shelah became
the father of Eber.
19 And two sons were born to
Eber, the name of the one was Peleg,
for in his days the earth was divided,
and his brother's name was Joktan.
20 And Joktan became the father
of Almodad, Sheleph, Hazarma-
veth, Jerah,
21 Hadoram, Uzal, Diklah,
22 [1]Ebal, Abimael, Sheba,
23 Ophir, Havilah, and Jobab; all
these *were* the sons of Joktan.
24 [a]Shem, Arpachshad, Shelah,
25 Eber, Peleg, Reu,
26 Serug, Nahor, Terah,

Descendants of Abraham

27 Abram, that is Abraham.
28 The sons of Abraham *were*
Isaac and Ishmael.
29 [a]These are their genealogies:
the first-born of Ishmael *was* Nebaioth, then Kedar, Adbeel, Mibsam,
30 Mishma, Dumah, Massa, Hadad, Tema,
31 Jetur, Naphish and Kedemah;
these *were* the sons of Ishmael.
32 [a]And the sons of Keturah,
Abraham's concubine, *whom* she
bore, *were* Zimran, Jokshan, Medan, Midian, Ishbak, and Shuah.
And the sons of Jokshan *were* Sheba
and Dedan.
33 And the sons of Midian *were*
Ephah, Epher, Hanoch, Abida, and
Eldaah. All these were the sons of
Keturah.
34 And [a]Abraham became the father of Isaac. The sons of Isaac *were*
[b]Esau and Israel.
35 [a]The sons of Esau *were* Eliphaz,
Reuel, Jeush, Jalam, and Korah.
36 The sons of Eliphaz *were* Teman, Omar, [1]Zephi, Gatam, Kenaz,
Timna, and Amalek.
37 The sons of Reuel *were* Nahath,
Zerah, Shammah, and Mizzah.
38 [a]And the sons of Seir *were* Lotan, Shobal, Zibeon, Anah, Dishon,
Ezer, and Dishan.
39 And the sons of Lotan *were*
Hori and [1]Homam; and Lotan's sister *was* Timna.
40 The sons of Shobal *were* [1]Alian,
Manahath, Ebal, [2]Shephi, and

1 [a]Gen. 4:25-5:32

5 [a]Gen. 10:2-4

6 [1]In Gen. 10:3, *Riphath*

7 [1]In Gen. 10:4, *Dodanim*

10 [1]Lit., *begot*, and so throughout the chap.

11 [a]Gen. 10:13-18

12 [1]Or, *people of Pelisht*

17 [1]In Gen. 10:23, *Mash* [a]Gen. 10:22-29

22 [1]In Gen. 10:28, *Obal*

24 [a]Gen. 11:10-26; Luke 3:34-36

29 [a]Gen. 25:13-16

32 [a]Gen. 25:1-4

34 [a]1 Chr. 1:28 [b]Gen. 25:25, 26; 32:28

35 [a]Gen. 36:4-10

36 [1]In Gen. 36:11, *Zepho*

38 [a]Gen. 36:20-28

39 [1]In Gen. 36:22, *Hemam*

40 [1]In Gen. 36:23, *Alvan* [2]In Gen. 36:23, *Shepho*

Onam. And the sons of Zibeon *were* Aiah and Anah.

41 The [1]son of Anah *was* Dishon. And the sons of Dishon *were* [2]Hamran, Eshban, Ithran, and Cheran.

42 The sons of Ezer *were* Bilhan, Zaavan and [1]Jaakan. The sons of Dishan *were* Uz and Aran.

43 [a]Now these are the kings who reigned in the land of Edom before any king of the sons of Israel reigned. Bela *was* the son of Beor, and the name of his city was Dinhabah.

44 When Bela died, Jobab the son of Zerah of [a]Bozrah became king in his place.

45 When Jobab died, Husham of the land of [a]the Temanites became king in his place.

46 When Husham died, Hadad the son of Bedad, who [1]defeated Midian in the field of Moab, became king in his place; and the name of his city *was* Avith.

47 When Hadad died, Samlah of Masrekah became king in his place.

48 When Samlah died, Shaul of Rehoboth by the River became king in his place.

49 When Shaul died, Baal-hanan the son of Achbor became king in his place.

50 When Baal-hanan died, [1]Hadad became king in his place; and the name of his city was [2]Pai, and his wife's name was Mehetabel, the daughter of Matred, the daughter of Mezahab.

51 Then Hadad died. Now the chiefs of Edom were: chief Timna, chief [1]Aliah, chief Jetheth,

52 chief Oholibamah, chief Elah, chief Pinon,

53 chief Kenaz, chief Teman, chief Mibzar,

54 chief Magdiel, chief Iram. These *were* the chiefs of Edom.

CHAPTER 2

Genealogy: Twelve Sons of Jacob (Israel)

[a]THESE are the sons of Israel: Reuben, Simeon, Levi, Judah, Issachar, Zebulun,

2 Dan, Joseph, Benjamin, Naphtali, Gad, and Asher.

3 [a]The sons of Judah *were* Er, Onan, and Shelah; *these* three were born to him by Bath-shua the Canaanitess. And Er, Judah's first-born, was wicked in the sight of the LORD, so He put him to death.

4 And [a]Tamar his daughter-in-law bore him Perez and Zerah. Judah had five sons in all.

5 The sons of Perez *were* Hezron and Hamul.

6 And the sons of Zerah *were* [1]Zimri, Ethan, Heman, Calcol, and [2]Dara; five of them in all.

7 And the [1]son of Carmi *was* [2]Achar, the troubler of Israel, who violated the ban.

8 And the [1]son of Ethan *was* Azariah.

9 Now the sons of Hezron, who were born to him *were* Jerahmeel, Ram, and Chelubai.

10 And Ram [1]became the father of Amminadab, and Amminadab became the father of Nahshon, leader of the sons of Judah;

11 Nahshon became the father of Salma, Salma became the father of Boaz,

Genealogy of David

12 Boaz became the father of Obed, and Obed became the father of Jesse;

13 and Jesse became the father of Eliab his first-born, then Abinadab the second, Shimea the third,

14 Nethanel the fourth, Raddai the fifth,

15 Ozem the sixth, David the seventh;

16 and their sisters *were* Zeruiah and Abigail. And the three sons of Zeruiah *were* [1]Abshai, Joab, and Asahel.

17 And Abigail bore Amasa, and the father of Amasa was Jether the Ishmaelite.

18 Now Caleb the son of Hezron had sons by Azubah *his* wife, and by Jerioth; and these were her sons: Jesher, Shobab, and Ardon.

19 When Azubah died, Caleb married Ephrath, who bore him Hur.

20 And Hur became the father of Uri, and Uri became the father of Bezalel.

21 Afterward Hezron went in to the daughter of Machir the father of Gilead, whom he married when he was sixty years old; and she bore him Segub.

22 And Segub became the father of Jair, who had twenty-three cities in the land of Gilead.

23 But Geshur and Aram took [1]the towns of Jair from them, with Kenath and its villages, *even* sixty cities. All these were the sons of Machir, the father of Gilead.

24 And after the death of Hezron in Caleb-ephrathah, Abijah, Hezron's wife, bore him Ashhur the father of Tekoa.

25 Now the sons of Jerahmeel the first-born of Hezron *were* Ram the

---

41 [1]Lit., *sons* [2]In Gen. 36:26, *Hemdan*

42 [1]Or, *and Akan*

43 [a]Gen. 36:31-43

44 [a]Is. 34:6

45 [a]Job 2:11

46 [1]Lit., *smote*

50 [1]In Gen. 36:39, *Hadar* [2]In Gen. 36:39, *Pau*

51 [1]In Gen. 36:40, *Alvah*

1 [a]Gen. 35:22-26; 46:8-25

3 [a]Gen. 38:2-10

4 [a]Gen. 38:13-30

6 [1]In Josh. 7:1, *Zabdi* [2]In 1 Kin. 4:31, *Darda*

7 [1]Lit., *sons* [2]In Josh. 7:18, *Achan*

8 [1]Lit., *sons*

10 [1]Lit., *begot*, and so throughout the chap.

16 [1]In 2 Sam. 2:18, *Abishai*

23 [1]Or, *Havvoth-jair*

first-born, then Bunah, Oren, Ozem,
and Ahijah.
26 And Jerahmeel had another
wife, whose name was Atarah; she
was the mother of Onam.
27 And the sons of Ram, the first-
born of Jerahmeel, were Maaz, Jamin, and Eker.
28 And the sons of Onam were
Shammai and Jada. And the sons of
Shammai *were* Nadab and Abishur.
29 And the name of Abishur's wife
was Abihail, and she bore him Ah-
ban and Molid.
30 And the sons of Nadab *were*
Seled and Appaim, and Seled died
without sons.
31 And the [1]son of Appaim *was*
Ishi. And the [1]son of Ishi *was* Sheshan. And the [1]son of Sheshan *was*
Ahlai.
32 And the sons of Jada the
brother of Shammai *were* Jether
and Jonathan, and Jether died without sons.
33 And the sons of Jonathan *were*
Peleth and Zaza. These were the
sons of Jerahmeel.
34 Now Sheshan had no sons, only
daughters. And Sheshan had an
Egyptian servant whose name was
Jarha.
35 And Sheshan gave his daughter
to Jarha his servant in marriage, and
she bore him Attai.
36 And Attai became the father of
Nathan, and Nathan became the father of Zabad,
37 and Zabad became the father of
Ephlal, and Ephlal became the father of Obed,
38 and Obed became the father of
Jehu, and Jehu became the father of
Azariah,
39 and Azariah became the father
of Helez, and Helez became the father of Eleasah,
40 and Eleasah became the father
of Sismai, and Sismai became the
father of Shallum,
41 and Shallum became the father
of Jekamiah, and Jekamiah became
the father of Elishama.
42 Now the sons of Caleb, the
brother of Jerahmeel, *were* Mesha
his first-born, who was the father of
Ziph; and [1]his son was Mareshah,
the father of Hebron.
43 And the sons of Hebron *were*
Korah and Tappuah and Rekem and
Shema.
44 And Shema became the father
of Raham, the father of Jorkeam;
and Rekem became the father of
Shammai.
45 And the son of Shammai was
Maon, and Maon *was* the father of
Bethzur.
46 And Ephah, Caleb's concubine,
bore Haran, Moza, and Gazez; and
Haran became the father of Gazez.
47 And the sons of Jahdai *were*
Regem, Jotham, Geshan, Pelet, E-
phah, and Shaaph.
48 Maacah, Caleb's concubine,
bore Sheber and Tirhanah.
49 She also bore Shaaph the father
of Madmannah, Sheva the father of
Machbena and the father of Gibea;
and the daughter of Caleb *was* Achsah.
50 These were the sons of Caleb.
The [1]sons of Hur, the first-born of
Ephrathah, *were* Shobal the father
of Kiriath-jearim,
51 Salma the father of Bethlehem
and Hareph the father of Beth-ga-
der.
52 And Shobal the father of Kiriath-jearim had sons: Haroeh, half
of the Manahathites,
53 and the families of Kiriath-jearim: the Ithrites, the Puthites, the
Shumathites, and the Mishraites;
from these came the Zorathites and
the Eshtaolites.
54 The sons of Salma *were* Bethlehem and the Netophathites, Atroth-
beth-joab and half of the Manahathites, the Zorites.
55 And the families of scribes who
lived at Jabez *were* the Tirathites,
the Shimeathites, *and* the Sucath-
ites. Those are the Kenites who
came from Hammath, the father of
the house of Rechab.

Chapter 3

Family of David

[a]NOW these were the sons of David
who were born to him in Hebron:
the first-born *was* Amnon, by
Ahinoam the Jezreelitess: the second *was* Daniel, by Abigail the Carmelitess;
2 the third *was* Absalom the son
of Maacah, the daughter of Talmai
king of Geshur; the fourth *was* Adonijah the son of Haggith;
3 the fifth *was* Shephatiah, by
Abital; the sixth *was* Ithream, by his
wife Eglah.
4 Six were born to him in Hebron,
and [a]there he reigned seven years
and six months. And in Jerusalem
he reigned thirty-three years.
5 [a]And these were born to him in
Jerusalem: Shimea, Shobab, Nathan, and [b]Solomon, four, by [c]Bath-
shua the daughter of Ammiel;
6 and Ibhar, Elishama, Eliphelet,

31 [1]Lit., *sons*
42 [1]Lit., *the sons of*
50 [1]Lit., *son*
1 [a]2 Sam. 3:2-5
4 [a]2 Sam. 2:11; 5:4, 5
5 [a]2 Sam. 5:14-16; 1 Chr. 14:4-7 [b]2 Sam. 12:24, 25 [c]2 Sam. 11:3

7 Nogah, Nepheg, and Japhia,
8 Elishama, Eliada, and Eliphelet,
nine.
9 All *these were* the sons of David, besides the sons of the concubines; and [a]Tamar *was* their sister.
10 Now Solomon's son *was* Rehoboam, Abijah *was* his son, Asa his
son, Jehoshaphat his son,
11 Joram his son, Ahaziah his son,
Joash his son,
12 Amaziah his son, Azariah his
son, Jotham his son,
13 Ahaz his son, Hezekiah his son,
Manasseh his son,
14 Amon his son, Josiah his son.
15 And the sons of Josiah *were* Johanan the first-born, and the second
was Jehoiakim, the third Zedekiah,
the fourth Shallum.
16 And the sons of Jehoiakim *were*
Jeconiah his son, Zedekiah his son.
17 And the sons of Jeconiah, the
prisoner, *were* Shealtiel his son,
18 and Malchiram, Pedaiah, She-
nazzar, Jekamiah, Hoshama, and
Nedabiah.
19 And the sons of Pedaiah *were*
Zerubbabel and Shimei. And the
[1]sons of Zerubbabel *were* Meshullam and Hananiah, and Shelomith
was their sister;
20 and Hashubah, Ohel, Berechiah, Hasadiah, and Jushab-hesed,
five.
21 And the [1]sons of Hananiah
were Pelatiah and Jeshaiah, the sons
of Rephaiah, the sons of Arnan, the
sons of Obadiah, the sons of Shecaniah.
22 And the [1]son of Shecaniah *was*
Shemaiah, and the sons of Shemaiah *were* Hattush, Igal, Bariah, Neariah, and Shaphat, six.
23 And the [1]sons of Neariah *were*
Elioenai, Hizkiah, and Azrikam,
three.
24 And the sons of Elioenai *were*
Hodaviah, Eliashib, Pelaiah, Akkub,
Johanan, Delaiah, and Anani, seven.

CHAPTER 4

Line of Hur, Asher

[a]THE sons of Judah *were* Perez,
Hezron, Carmi, Hur, and Shobal.
2 And Reaiah the son of Shobal
[1]became the father of Jahath, and
Jahath became the father of Ahu-
mai and Lahad. These *were* the families of the Zorathites.
3 And these *were* the [1]sons of
Etam: Jezreel, Ishma, and Idbash;
and the name of their sister *was*
Hazzelelponi.
4 And Penuel *was* the father of
Gedor, and Ezer the father of Hu-
shah. These *were* the sons of Hur,
the first-born of Ephrathah, the father of Bethlehem.
5 And Ashhur, the father of Tekoa, had two wives, Helah and
Naarah.
6 And Naarah bore him Ahuz-
zam, Hepher, Temeni, and Haa-
hashtari. These were the sons of
Naarah.
7 And the sons of Helah *were* Ze-
reth, [1]Izhar and Ethnan.
8 And Koz became the father of
Anub and Zobebah, and the families
of Aharhel the son of Harum.
9 And Jabez was more honorable
than his brothers, and his mother
named him Jabez saying, "Because
I bore *him* with pain."
10 Now Jabez called on the God of
Israel, saying, "Oh that Thou
wouldst bless me indeed, and enlarge my border, and that Thy hand
might be with me, and that Thou
wouldst keep *me* from harm, that *it*
may not pain me!" And God granted
him what he requested.
11 And Chelub the brother of Shu-
hah became the father of Mehir,
who was the father of Eshton.
12 And Eshton became the father
of Beth-rapha and Paseah, and Te-
hinnah the father of [1]Ir-nahash.
These are the men of Recah.
13 Now the sons of Kenaz *were*
Othniel and Seraiah. And the [1]son of
Othniel *was* Hathath.
14 And Meonothai became the father of Ophrah, and Seraiah became
the father of Joab the father of [1]Ge-
harashim, for they were craftsmen.
15 And the sons of Caleb the son
of Jephunneh *were* Iru, Elah and
Naam; and the [1]son of Elah *was* [2]Ke-
naz.
16 And the sons of Jehallelel *were*
Ziph and Ziphah, Tiria and Asarel.
17 And the [1]sons of Ezrah *were* Jether, Mered, Epher, and Jalon.
([2]And these are the sons of Bithia
the daughter of Pharaoh, whom
Mered took) and she conceived and
bore Miriam, Shammai, and Ishbah
the father of Eshtemoa.
18 And his Jewish wife bore Jered
the father of Gedor, and Heber the
father of Soco, and Jekuthiel the father of Zanoah.
19 And the sons of the wife of Hodiah, the sister of Naham, *were* the
[1]fathers of Keilah the Garmite and
Eshtemoa the Maacathite.
20 And the sons of Shimon *were*
Amnon and Rinnah, Benhanan and
Tilon. And the sons of Ishi *were* Zo-
heth and Ben-zoheth.

9 [a]2 Sam. 13:1
19 [1]Lit., *son*
21 [1]Lit., *son*
22 [1]Lit., *sons*
23 [1]Lit., *son*
1 [a]1 Chr. 2:3
2 [1]Lit., *begot,* and so throughout the chap.
3 [1]So with some ancient versions, Heb., *father*
7 [1]Another reading is *Zohar*
12 [1]Or, *the city of Nahash*
13 [1]Lit., *sons*
14 [1]Or, *valley of craftsmen*
15 [1]Lit., *sons* [2]Lit., *and Kenaz*
17 [1]Lit., *son* [2]In the Heb. the words in ( ) are at the end of verse 18
19 [1]Lit., *father*

21 The sons of Shelah the son of
Judah *were* Er the father of Lecah
and Laadah the father of Mareshah,
and the families of the house of the
linen workers at Beth-ashbea;
22 and Jokim, the men of Cozeba,
Joash, Saraph, who ruled in Moab,
and Jaashubi-lehem. And the [1]rec-
ords are ancient.
23 These were the potters and the
inhabitants of Netaim and Gederah;
they lived there with the king for his
work.

Descendants of Simeon

24 The sons of Simeon *were* [1]Nem-
uel and Jamin, [2]Jarib, [3]Zerah, Shaul;
25 Shallum his son, Mibsam his
son, Mishma his son.
26 And the sons of Mishma *were*
Hammuel his son, Zaccur his son,
Shimei his son.
27 Now Shimei had sixteen sons
and six daughters; but his brothers
did not have many sons, nor did all
their family multiply like the sons of
Judah.
28 And they lived at Beersheba,
Moladah, and Hazar-shual,
29 at Bilhah, Ezem, Tolad,
30 Bethuel, Hormah, Ziklag,
31 Beth-marcaboth, Hazar-susim,
Beth-biri, and Shaaraim. These *were*
their cities until the reign of David.
32 And their villages *were* Etam,
Ain, Rimmon, Tochen, and Ashan,
five cities;
33 and all their villages that *were*
around the same cities as far as
[1]Baal. These *were* their settlements,
and they have their genealogy.
34 And Meshobab and Jamlech
and Joshah the son of Amaziah,
35 and Joel and Jehu the son of
Joshibiah, the son of Seraiah, the
son of Asiel,
36 and Elioenai, Jaakobah, Jesho-
haiah, Asaiah, Adiel, Jesimiel, Benaiah,
37 Ziza the son of Shiphi, the son
of Allon, the son of Jedaiah, the son
of Shimri, the son of Shemaiah;
38 these mentioned by name *were*
leaders in their families; and their
fathers' houses increased greatly.
39 And they went to the entrance
of Gedor, even to the east side of the
valley, to seek pasture for their
flocks.
40 And they found rich and good
pasture, and [a]the land was broad
and quiet and peaceful; for those
who lived there formerly *were* Ham-
ites.
41 And [a]these, recorded by name,
came in the days of Hezekiah king
of Judah, and [1]attacked their tents,
and the Meunites who were found
there, and destroyed them utterly to
this day, and lived in their place; because there was pasture for their
flocks.
42 And from them, from the sons
of Simeon, five hundred men went
to [a]Mount Seir, with Pelatiah, Neariah, Rephaiah, and Uzziel, the sons
of Ishi, as their leaders.
43 And [a]they [1]destroyed the remnant of the Amalekites who escaped, and have lived there to this
day.

Chapter 5

Genealogy from Reuben

NOW the sons of Reuben the first-
born of Israel (for [a]he was the first-
born, but because [b]he defiled his father's bed, [c]his birthright was given
to the sons of Joseph the son of Israel; so that he is not enrolled in the
genealogy according to the birthright.
2 [a]Though Judah prevailed over
his brothers, and [b]from him *came*
the leader, yet the birthright belonged to Joseph),
3 [a]the sons of Reuben the first-
born of Israel *were* Hanoch and
Pallu, Hezron and Carmi.
4 The sons of Joel *were* Shemaiah
his son, Gog his son, [a]Shimei his
son,
5 Micah his son, Reaiah his son,
Baal his son,
6 Beerah his son, whom [1]Tilgath-
pilneser king of Assyria carried
away into exile; he was leader of the
Reubenites.
7 And his [1]kinsmen by their families, [a]in the genealogy of their generations, *were* Jeiel the chief, then
Zechariah
8 and Bela the son of Azaz, the
son of Shema, the son of Joel, who
lived in [a]Aroer, even to Nebo and
Baal-meon.
9 And to the east he settled as far
as the entrance of the wilderness
from the river Euphrates, [a]because
their cattle had increased in the land
of Gilead.
10 And in the days of Saul [a]they
made war with the Hagrites, who
fell by their hand, so that they [1]oc-
cupied their tents throughout [2]all
the land east of Gilead.
11 Now the sons of Gad lived opposite them in the land of Bashan as
far as [a]Salecah.
12 Joel *was* the chief, and Sha-
pham the second, then Janai and
Shaphat in Bashan.

22 [1]Lit., *words*

24 [1]In Num. 26:12, *Jemuel* [2]In Num. 26:12, *Jachin* [3]In Gen. 46:10; Ex. 6:15, *Zohar*

33 [1]In Josh. 19:8, *Baalath*

40 [a]Judg. 18:7-10

41 [1]Lit., *smote* [a]1 Chr. 4:33-38

42 [a]Gen. 36:8, 9

43 [1]Lit., *smote* [a]1 Sam. 15:7, 8; 30:17

1 [a]Gen. 29:32; 1 Chr. 2:1 [b]Gen. 35:22; 49:4 [c]Gen. 48:15-22

2 [a]Gen. 49:8-10 [b]Mic. 5:2; Matt. 2:6

3 [a]Num. 26:5-9

4 [a]1 Chr. 5:8

6 [1]In 2 Kin. 15:29, *Tiglath-pileser*

7 [1]Lit., *brothers* [a]1 Chr. 5:17

8 [a]Num. 32:34; Josh. 12:2

9 [a]Josh. 22:8, 9

10 [1]Lit., *dwelt in* [2]Lit., *all the face of the east* [a]1 Chr. 5:18-21

11 [a]Deut. 3:10

13 And their [1]kinsmen of their fathers' households *were* Michael, Meshullam, Sheba, Jorai, Jacan, Zia, and Eber, seven.

14 These *were* the sons of Abihail, the son of Huri, the son of Jaroah, the son of Gilead, the son of Michael, the son of Jeshishai, the son of Jahdo, the son of Buz;

15 Ahi the son of Abdiel, the son of Guni, *was* head of their fathers' households.

16 And they lived in Gilead, in Bashan and in its towns, and in all the pasture lands of [a]Sharon, as far as their [1]borders.

17 All of these were enrolled in the genealogies in the days of [a]Jotham king of Judah and in the days of [b]Jeroboam king of Israel.

18 The sons of Reuben and the Gadites and the half-tribe of Manasseh, *consisting* of valiant men, men who bore shield and sword and shot with bow, and *were* skillful in battle, *were* 44,760, who [a]went to war.

19 And they made war against [a]the Hagrites, [b]Jetur, Naphish, and Nodab.

20 And they were helped against them, and the Hagrites and all who *were* with them were given into their hand; for [a]they cried out to God in the battle, and He was entreated for them, because [b]they trusted in Him.

21 And they took away their cattle: their 50,000 camels, 250,000 sheep, 2,000 donkeys, and 100,000 [1]men.

22 For many fell slain, because [a]the war *was* of God. And [b]they settled in their place until the [c]exile.

23 Now the sons of the half-tribe of Manasseh lived in the land; from Bashan to Baal-hermon and [a]Senir and Mount Hermon they were numerous.

24 And these were the heads of their fathers' households, even Epher, Ishi, Eliel, Azriel, Jeremiah, Hodaviah, and Jahdiel, mighty men of valor, famous men, heads of their fathers' households.

25 But they acted treacherously against the God of their fathers, and [a]played the harlot [b]after the gods of the peoples of the land, whom God had destroyed before them.

26 So the God of Israel stirred up the spirit of [a]Pul, king of Assyria, even the spirit of [1]Tilgath-pilneser king of Assyria, and he carried them away into exile, namely the Reubenites, the Gadites, and the half-tribe of Manasseh, and brought them to Halah, Habor, Hara, and to the river of Gozan, to this day.

Chapter 6

Genealogy: The Priestly Line

1a THE sons of Levi *were* [2]Gershon, Kohath and Merari.

2 And the sons of Kohath *were* Amram, Izhar, Hebron, and Uzziel.

3 And the children of Amram *were* Aaron, Moses, and Miriam. And the sons of Aaron *were* Nadab, Abihu, Eleazar, and Ithamar.

4 Eleazar [1]became the father of Phinehas, *and* Phinehas became the father of Abishua,

5 and Abishua became the father of Bukki, and Bukki became the father of Uzzi,

6 and Uzzi became the father of Zerahiah, and Zerahiah became the father of Meraioth,

7 Meraioth became the father of Amariah, and Amariah became the father of Ahitub,

8 and Ahitub became the father of Zadok, and Zadok became the father of Ahimaaz,

9 and Ahimaaz became the father of Azariah, and Azariah became the father of Johanan,

10 and Johanan became the father of Azariah (it was he who served as the priest in the house which Solomon built in Jerusalem),

11 and Azariah became the father of Amariah, and Amariah became the father of Ahitub,

12 and Ahitub became the father of Zadok, and Zadok became the father of [1]Shallum,

13 and Shallum became the father of Hilkiah, and Hilkiah became the father of Azariah,

14 and Azariah became the father of Seraiah, and Seraiah became the father of Jehozadak;

15 and Jehozadak went *along* when the LORD carried Judah and Jerusalem away into exile [1]by Nebuchadnezzar.

16 [1]The sons of Levi *were* [2]Gershom, Kohath, and Merari.

17 And these are the names of the sons of Gershom: Libni and Shimei.

18 And the sons of Kohath *were* Amram, Izhar, Hebron, and Uzziel.

19 The sons of Merari *were* Mahli and Mushi. And these are the families of the Levites according to their fathers' *households*.

20 Of Gershom: Libni his son, Jahath his son, Zimmah his son,

21 Joah his son, Iddo his son, Zerah his son, Jeatherai his son.

---

13 [1]Lit., *brother*

16 [1]Lit., *goings out* [a]1 Chr. 27:29

17 [a]2 Kin. 15:5, 32 [b]2 Kin. 14:16, 28

18 [a]Num. 1:3

19 [a]1 Chr. 5:10 [b]1 Chr. 1:31

20 [a]2 Chr. 14:11-13 [b]Ps. 9:10; 20:7, 8

21 [1]Lit., *souls of men*

22 [a]Josh. 23:10; 2 Chr. 32:8 [b]1 Chr. 4:41 [c]2 Kin. 15:29; 17:6

23 [a]Deut. 3:9

25 [a]Ex. 34:15 [b]2 Kin. 17:7

26 [1]In 2 Kin. 15:29, *Tiglath-pileser* [a]2 Kin. 15:19, 29; 2 Chr. 28:20

1 [1]Ch. 5:27 in Heb. [2]In v. 16, *Gershom* [a]Ex. 6:16-25

4 [1]Lit., *begot* and so throughout the chap.

12 [1]In ch. 9:11, *Meshullam*

15 [1]Lit., *by the hand of*

16 [1]Ch. 6:1 in Heb. [2]In v. 1, *Gershon*

22 The sons of Kohath *were* Amminadab his son, Korah his son, Assir his son,
23 Elkanah his son, Ebiasaph his
son, and Assir his son,
24 Tahath his son, Uriel his son,
Uzziah his son, and Shaul his son.
25 And the sons of Elkanah *were*
Amasai and Ahimoth.
26 *As for* Elkanah, the sons of Elkanah *were* Zophai his son and Nahath his son,
27 Eliab his son, Jeroham his son,
Elkanah his son.
28 And the sons of Samuel *were*
[1]Joel, the first-born and Abijah, the
second.
29 The sons of Merari *were* Mahli,
Libni his son, Shimei his son, Uzzah
his son,
30 Shimea his son, Haggiah his
son, Asaiah his son.
31 [a]Now these are those whom
David appointed over the service of
song in the house of the LORD, [b]after
the ark rested *there.*
32 And they ministered with song
before the tabernacle of the tent of
meeting, until Solomon had built
the house of the LORD in Jerusalem;
and they [1]served in their office according to their order.
33 And these are those who
[1]served with their sons. From the
sons of the Kohathites *were* Heman
the singer, the son of Joel, the son of
Samuel,
34 the son of Elkanah, the son of
Jeroham, the son of Eliel, the son of
Toah,
35 the son of Zuph, the son of Elkanah, the son of Mahath, the son of
Amasai,
36 the son of Elkanah, the son of
Joel, the son of Azariah, the son of
Zephaniah,
37 the son of Tahath, the son of
Assir, the son of Ebiasaph, the son
of Korah,
38 the son of Izhar, the son of Kohath, the son of Levi, the son of Israel.
39 And *Heman's* brother Asaph
stood at his right hand, even Asaph
the son of Berechiah, the son of
Shimea,
40 the son of Michael, the son of
Baaseiah, the son of Malchijah,
41 the son of Ethni, the son of Zerah, the son of Adaiah,
42 the son of Ethan, the son of
Zimmah, the son of Shimei,
43 the son of Jahath, the son of
Gershom, the son of Levi.
44 And on the left hand *were* their
[1]kinsmen the sons of Merari: Ethan
the son of Kishi, the son of Abdi, the
son of Malluch,
45 the son of Hashabiah, the son of
Amaziah, the son of Hilkiah,
46 the son of Amzi, the son of
Bani, the son of Shemer,
47 the son of Mahli, the son of Mushi, the son of Merari, the son of
Levi.
48 And their [1]kinsmen the Levites
were [2]appointed for all the service
of the tabernacle of the house of
God.
49 But Aaron and his sons [1a]of-
fered on the altar of burnt offering
and [b]on the altar of incense, for all
the work of the most holy place, and
[c]to make atonement for Israel, according to all that Moses the servant
of God had commanded.
50 [a]And these are the sons of Aaron: Eleazar his son, Phinehas his
son, Abishua his son,
51 Bukki his son, Uzzi his son,
Zerahiah his son,
52 Meraioth his son, Amariah his
son, Ahitub his son,
53 Zadok his son, Ahimaaz his
son.
54 Now these are their settlements
according to their camps within
their borders. To the sons of Aaron
of the families of the Kohathites (for
theirs was the [a]*first* lot),
55 to them they gave [a]Hebron in
the land of Judah, and its pasture
lands around it;
56 [a]but the fields of the city and its
villages, they gave to Caleb the son
of Jephunneh.
57 And [a]to the sons of Aaron they
gave the *following* cities of refuge:
Hebron, Libnah also with its pasture
lands, Jatir, Eshtemoa with its pasture lands,
58 [1]Hilen with its pasture lands,
Debir with its pasture lands,
59 [1]Ashan with its pasture lands,
and Beth-shemesh with its pasture
lands;
60 and from the tribe of Benjamin:
Geba with its pasture lands, [1]Alle-
meth with its pasture lands, and
Anathoth with its pasture lands. All
their cities throughout their families
were thirteen cities.
61 [a]Then to the rest of the sons of
Kohath *were given* by lot, from the
family of the tribe, from the half-
tribe, the half of Manasseh, ten
cities.
62 And to the sons of Gershom, according to their families, *were given*
from the tribe of Issachar and from
the tribe of Asher, the tribe of Naphtali, and the tribe of Manasseh, thirteen cities in Bashan.

28 [1]Cf. v. 33 and 1 Sam. 8:2
31 [a]1 Chr. 15:16-22, 27; 16:4-6 [b]2 Sam. 6:17; 1 Chr. 15:25-16:1
32 [1]Lit., *stood over*
33 [1]Lit., *stood*
44 [1]Lit., *brothers*
48 [1]Lit., *brothers* [2]Lit., *given*
49 [1]Lit., *offered up in smoke* [a]Ex. 27:1-8 [b]Ex. 30:1-7 [c]Ex. 30:10-16
50 [a]1 Chr. 6:4-8
54 [a]Josh. 21:4,10
55 [a]Josh. 14:13
56 [a]Josh. 15:13
57 [a]Josh. 21:13, 19
58 [1]In Josh. 21:15, *Holon*
59 [1]In Josh. 21:16, *Ain*
60 [1]In Josh. 21:18, *Almon*
61 [a]Josh. 21:5; 1 Chr. 6:66-70

63 [a]To the sons of Merari *were giv-*
en by lot, according to their families, from the tribe of Reuben, the
tribe of Gad, and the tribe of Zebulun, twelve cities.
64 [a]So the sons of Israel gave to
the Levites the cities with their pasture lands.
65 And they gave by lot from the
tribe of the sons of Judah, the tribe
of the sons of Simeon, and the tribe
of the sons of Benjamin, [a]these
cities which are mentioned by
name.
66 [a]Now some of the families of
the sons of Kohath had cities of
their territory from the tribe of E-
phraim.
67 And they gave to them the *fol-*
lowing cities of refuge: Shechem in
the hill country of Ephraim with its
pasture lands, Gezer also with its
pasture lands,
68 Jokmeam with its pasture
lands, Beth-horon with its pasture
lands,
69 Aijalon with its pasture lands,
and Gath-rimmon with its pasture
lands;
70 and from the half-tribe of Manasseh: Aner with its pasture lands
and Bileam with its pasture lands,
for the rest of the family of the sons
of Kohath.
71 To the sons of Gershom *were*
given, from the family of the half-
tribe of Manasseh: Golan in Bashan
with its pasture lands and Ashtaroth
with its pasture lands;
72 and from the tribe of Issachar:
Kedesh with its pasture lands, Daberath with its pasture lands,
73 and Ramoth with its pasture
lands, Anem with its pasture lands;
74 and from the tribe of Asher:
Mashal with its pasture lands, Abdon with its pasture lands,
75 Hukok with its pasture lands,
and Rehob with its pasture lands;
76 and from the tribe of Naphtali:
Kedesh in Galilee with its pasture
lands, Hammon with its pasture
lands, and Kiriathaim with its pasture lands.
77 To the rest of *the Levites,* the
sons of Merari, *were given,* from the
tribe of Zebulun: Rimmono with its
pasture lands, Tabor with its pasture lands;
78 and beyond the Jordan at Jericho, on the east side of the Jordan,
were given them, from the tribe of
Reuben: Bezer in the wilderness
with its pasture lands, Jahzah with
its pasture lands,
79 Kedemoth with its pasture
lands, and Mephaath with its pasture lands;
80 and from the tribe of Gad: Ramoth in Gilead with its pasture
lands, Mahanaim with its pasture
lands,
81 Heshbon with its pasture lands,
and Jazer with its pasture lands.

Chapter 7

Genealogy from Issachar

NOW the sons of Issachar *were*
four: Tola, [1]Puah, [2]Jashub, and
Shimron.
2 And the sons of Tola *were* Uzzi,
Rephaiah, Jeriel, Jahmai, Ibsam,
and Samuel, heads of their fathers'
households. *The sons* of Tola *were*
mighty men of valor in their generations; [a]their number in the days of
David was 22,600.
3 And the [1]son of Uzzi *was* Izrahiah. And the sons of Izrahiah *were*
Michael, Obadiah, Joel, Isshiah; all
five of them *were* chief men.
4 And with them by their generations according to their fathers'
households were 36,000 [1]troops of
the army for war, for they had many
wives and sons.
5 And their [1]relatives among all
the families of Issachar *were* mighty
men of valor, enrolled by genealogy,
in all 87,000.

Descendants of Benjamin

6 [a]*The sons of* Benjamin *were*
three: Bela and Becher and Jediael.
7 And the sons of Bela were five:
Ezbon, Uzzi, Uzziel, Jerimoth, and
Iri. They *were* heads of fathers'
households, mighty men of valor,
and were 22,034 enrolled by genealogy.
8 And the sons of Becher *were*
Zemirah, Joash, Eliezer, Elioenai,
Omri, Jeremoth, Abijah, Anathoth,
and Alemeth. All these *were* the
sons of Becher.
9 And they were enrolled by genealogy, according to their generations, heads of their fathers' households, 20,200 mighty men of valor.
10 And the [1]son of Jediael *was* Bilhan. And the sons of Bilhan *were*
Jeush, Benjamin, Ehud, Chenaanah,
Zethan, Tarshish, and Ahishahar.
11 All these *were* sons of Jediael,
according to the heads of their fathers' households, 17,200 mighty
men of valor, who were [1]ready to go
out with the army to war.
12 And [1]Shuppim and [2]Huppim
were the sons of [3]Ir; Hushim *was* the
[4]son of [5]Aher.

63 [a]Josh. 21:7, 34-40
64 [a]Josh. 21:3, 41, 42
65 [a]1 Chr. 6:57-60
66 [a]Josh. 21:20-26
1 [1]In Gen. 46:13, *Puvah* [2]In Gen. 46:13, *Iob*
2 [a]2 Sam. 24:1-9
3 [1]Lit., *sons*
4 [1]Or, *bands*
5 [1]Lit., *brothers,* and so throughout the chap.
6 [a]1 Chr. 8:1-40
10 [1]Lit., *sons*
11 [1]Lit., *going out*
12 [1]In Num. 26:39, *Shephupham* [2]In Num. 26:39, *Hupham* [3]In v. 7, *Iri* [4]Lit., *sons* [5]In Num. 26:38, *Ahiram*

Sons of Naphtali

13 The sons of Naphtali *were* [1]Jah-
ziel, Guni, Jezer, and [2]Shallum, the
sons of Bilhah.

Descendants of Manasseh

14 The sons of Manasseh *were*
Asriel, whom his Aramaean concubine bore; she bore Machir the father of Gilead.
15 And Machir took a wife for
Huppim and Shuppim, [1]whose sister's name was Maacah. And the
name of the second was Zelophehad, and Zelophehad had daughters.
16 And Maacah the wife of Machir
bore a son, and she named him Pe-
resh; and the name of his brother
was Sheresh, and his sons *were*
Ulam and Rakem.
17 And the [1]son of Ulam *was* Be-
dan. These *were* the sons of Gilead
the son of Machir, the son of Manasseh.
18 And his sister Hammolecheth
bore Ishhod and [1]Abiezer and Mahlah.
19 And the sons of Shemida were
Ahian and Shechem and Likhi and
Aniam.

Descendants of Ephraim

20 And [a]the sons of Ephraim *were*
Shuthelah and Bered his son, Tahath his son, Eleadah his son, Tahath his son,
21 Zabad his son, Shuthelah his
son, and Ezer and Elead whom the
men of Gath who were born in the
land killed because they came down
to take their livestock.
22 And their father Ephraim
mourned many days, and his relatives came to comfort him.
23 Then he went in to his wife, and
she conceived and bore a son, and
he named him [1]Beriah, because misfortune had come upon his house.
24 And his daughter was Sheerah,
[a]who built lower and upper Beth-
horon, also Uzzen-sheerah.
25 And Rephah was his son *along*
with Resheph, Telah his son, Tahan
his son,
26 Ladan his son, Ammihud his
son, Elishama his son,
27 [1]Non his son, and [a]Joshua his
son.
28 And [a]their possessions and settlements *were* Bethel with its towns,
and to the east [1]Naaran, and to the
west Gezer with its towns, and Shechem with its towns as far as [2]Ay-
yah with its towns,
29 and along the borders of the
sons of Manasseh, Beth-shean with
its towns, Taanach with its towns,
Megiddo with its towns, Dor with its
towns. In these lived the sons of
Joseph the son of Israel.

Descendants of Asher

30 [a]The sons of Asher *were* Imnah,
Ishvah, and Ishvi, Beriah, and Serah
their sister.
31 And the sons of Beriah *were*
Heber and Malchiel, who was the
father of Birzaith.
32 And Heber [1]became the father
of Japhlet, [2]Shomer, and Hotham,
and Shua their sister.
33 And the sons of Japhlet *were*
Pasach, Bimhal, and Ashvath. These
were the sons of Japhlet.
34 And the sons of [1]Shemer *were*
Ahi and Rohgah, Jehubbah and
Aram.
35 And the [1]sons of his brother
Helem *were* Zophah, Imna, Shelesh,
and Amal.
36 The sons of Zophah *were* Suah,
Harnepher, Shual, Beri, and Imrah,
37 Bezer, Hod, Shamma, Shilshah,
Ithran, and Beera.
38 And the sons of Jether *were* Jephunneh, Pispa, and Ara.
39 And the sons of Ulla *were* Arah,
Hanniel, and Rizia.
40 All these *were* the sons of
Asher, heads of the fathers' houses,
choice and mighty men of valor,
heads of the princes. And the number of them enrolled by genealogy
for service in war was 26,000 men.

Chapter 8

Genealogy from Benjamin

AND [a]Benjamin [1]became the father of Bela his first-born, Ashbel
the second, [b]Aharah the third,
2 Nohah the fourth, and Rapha
the fifth.
3 And Bela had sons: [1]Addar,
Gera, Abihud,
4 Abishua, Naaman, Ahoah,
5 Gera, Shephuphan, and Huram.
6 And these are the sons of Ehud:
these are the heads of fathers'
households of the inhabitants of
Geba, and they carried them into
exile to Manahath,
7 namely, Naaman, Ahijah, and
Gera—he carried them into exile;
and he became the father of Uzza
and Ahihud.
8 And Shaharaim became the father of children in the [1]country of
Moab, after he had [2]sent away Hushim and Baara his wives.
9 And by Hodesh his wife he became the father of Jobab, Zibia, Mesha, Malcam,

13 [1]In Gen. 46:24, *Jahzeel* [2]In Gen. 46:24; Num. 26:49, *Shillem*
15 [1]Lit., *and his*
17 [1]Lit., *sons*
18 [1]In Num. 26:30, *Iezer*
20 [a]Num. 26:35, 36
23 [1]I.e., on misfortune
24 [a]Josh. 16:3, 5
27 [1]In Ex. 33:11, *Nun* [a]Ex. 17:9-14; 24:13
28 [1]In Josh. 16:7, *Naarah* [2]Many mss. read, *Azzah* [a]Josh. 16:2
30 [a]Gen. 46:17; Num. 26:44-46
32 [1]Lit., *begot* [2]In v. 34, *Shemer*
34 [1]In v. 32, *Shomer*
35 [1]Lit., *son*
1 [1]Lit., *begot*, and so throughout the chap. [a]Gen. 46:21; 1 Chr. 7:6-12 [b]1 Chr. 7:12
3 [1]In Gen. 46:21; Num. 26:40, *Ard*
8 [1]Lit., *field* [2]Lit., *sent them away*

10 Jeuz, Sachia, Mirmah. These
were his sons, heads of fathers'
households.
11 And by Hushim he became the
father of Abitub and Elpaal.
12 And the sons of Elpaal *were*
Eber, Misham, and Shemed, who
built Ono and Lod, with its towns;
13 and Beriah and Shema, who
were heads of fathers' *households* of
the inhabitants of Aijalon, who put
to flight the inhabitants of Gath;
14 and [1]Ahio, Shashak, and Jeremoth.
15 And Zebadiah, Arad, Eder,
16 Michael, Ishpah, and Joha *were*
the sons of Beriah.
17 And Zebadiah, Meshullam,
Hizki, Heber,
18 Ishmerai, Izliah, and Jobab
were the sons of Elpaal.
19 And Jakim, Zichri, Zabdi,
20 Elienai, Zillethai, Eliel,
21 Adaiah, Beraiah, and Shimrath
were the sons of [1]Shimei.
22 And Ishpan, Eber, Eliel,
23 Abdon, Zichri, Hanan,
24 Hananiah, Elam, Anthothijah,
25 Iphdeiah, and Penuel *were* the
sons of Shashak.
26 And Shamsherai, Shehariah,
Athaliah,
27 Jaareshiah, Elijah, and Zichri
were the sons of Jeroham.
28 These were heads of the fathers' *households* according to their
generations, chief men, [1]who lived
in Jerusalem.
29 [a]Now in Gibeon, *Jeiel,* the father of Gibeon lived, and his wife's
name was Maacah;
30 and his first-born son *was* Abdon, then Zur, Kish, Baal, Nadab,
31 Gedor, Ahio, and [1]Zecher.
32 And Mikloth became the father
of [1]Shimeah. And they also lived
with their [2]relatives in Jerusalem
opposite their *other* [2]relatives.

Genealogy from King Saul

33 [a]And Ner became the father of
Kish, and Kish became the father of
Saul, and Saul became the father of
Jonathan, Malchi-shua, [1]Abinadab,
and [2]Eshbaal.
34 And the son of Jonathan *was*
[1]Merib-baal, and Merib-baal became the father of Micah.
35 And the sons of Micah *were* Pi-
thon, Melech, [1]Tarea, and Ahaz.
36 And Ahaz became the father of
[1]Jehoaddah, and Jehoaddah became the father of Alemeth, Azmaveth, and Zimri; and Zimri became
the father of Moza.
37 And Moza became the father of
Binea; [1]Raphah *was* his son, Eleasah
his son, Azel his son.
38 And Azel had six sons, and
these *were* their names: Azrikam,
Bocheru, Ishmael, Sheariah, Obadiah and Hanan. All these *were* the
sons of Azel.
39 And the sons of Eshek his
brother *were* Ulam his first-born,
Jeush the second, and Eliphelet the
third.
40 And the sons of Ulam were
mighty men of valor, archers, and
had many sons and grandsons, 150
of them. All these *were* of the sons
of Benjamin.

Chapter 9

People of Jerusalem

So all Israel was enrolled by genealogies; and behold, they are written
in the Book of the Kings of Israel.
And [a]Judah was carried away into
exile to Babylon for their unfaithfulness.
2 [a]Now the first who lived in their
possessions in their cities *were* Israel, the priests, the Levites and [b]the
[1]temple servants.
3 And some of the sons of Judah,
of the sons of Benjamin, and of the
sons of Ephraim and Manasseh
lived in Jerusalem:
4 Uthai the son of Ammihud, the
son of Omri, the son of Imri, the son
of Bani, from the sons of Perez the
son of Judah.
5 And from the Shilonites *were*
Asaiah the first-born and his sons.
6 And from the sons of Zerah
were Jeuel and their [1]relatives, 690
of them.
7 And from the sons of Benjamin
were Sallu the son of Meshullam,
the son of Hodaviah, the son of Hassenuah,
8 and Ibneiah the son of Jeroham,
and Elah the son of Uzzi, the son of
Michri, and Meshullam the son of
Shephatiah, the son of Reuel, the
son of Ibnijah;
9 and their relatives according to
their generations, [a]956. All these
were heads of fathers' *households*
according to their fathers' houses.
10 [a]And from the priests *were*
Jedaiah, Jehoiarib, Jachin,
11 and [1]Azariah the son of Hilkiah,
the son of Meshullam, the son of Zadok, the son of Meraioth, the son of
Ahitub, [a]the chief officer of the
house of God;
12 and Adaiah the son of Jeroham,
the son of Pashhur, the son of Malchijah, and Maasai the son of Adiel,
the son of Jahzerah, the son of Me-

14 [1]Or, *his brothers*
21 [1]In v. 13, *Shema*
28 [1]Lit., *these*
29 [a]1 Chr. 9:35-38
31 [1]In ch. 9:37, *Zechariah*
32 [1]In ch. 9:38, *Shimeam* [2]Lit., *brothers*
33 [1]1 Sam. 14:49, *Ishvi* [2]In 2 Sam. 2:8, *Ish-bosheth* [a]1 Chr. 9:39-44
34 [1]In 2 Sam. 4:4, *Mephibosheth*
35 [1]In 9:41, *Tahrea*
36 [1]In 9:42, *Jarah*
37 [1]In 9:43, *Rephaiah*
1 [a]1 Chr. 5:25, 26
2 [1]Heb., *Nethinim* [a]Neh. 11:3-22 [b]Ezra 2:43, 58; 8:20
6 [1]Lit., *brothers,* and so throughout the chap.
9 [a]Neh. 11:8
10 [a]Neh. 11:10-14
11 [1]In Neh. 11:11, *Seraiah* [a]Jer. 20:1

shullam, the son of Meshillemith,
the son of Immer;
13 and their relatives, heads of
their fathers' households, 1,760 very
able men for the work of the service
of the house of God.
14 [a]And of the Levites *were*
Shemaiah the son of Hasshub, the
son of Azrikam, the son of Hashabiah, of the sons of Merari;
15 and Bakbakkar, Heresh and
Galal and Mattaniah the son of
Mica, the son of [1]Zichri, the son of
Asaph,
16 and [1]Obadiah the son of
[2]Shemaiah, the son of Galal, the son
of Jeduthun, and Berechiah the son
of Asa, the son of Elkanah, who
lived in the villages of the Netophathites.
17 Now the gatekeepers *were*
[1]Shallum and Akkub and Talmon
and Ahiman and their relatives
(Shallum the chief
18 *being stationed* until now at
[a]the king's gate to the east). These
were the gatekeepers for the camp
of the sons of Levi.
19 And Shallum the son of Kore,
the son of Ebiasaph, the son of Korah, and his relatives, of his father's
house, the Korahites, *were* over the
work of the service, keepers of the
thresholds of the tent; and their fathers had been over the camp of the
LORD, keepers of the entrance.
20 And [a]Phinehas the son of Eleazar was ruler over them previously,
and the LORD was with him.
21 [a]Zechariah the son of Meshelemiah was gatekeeper of the entrance of the tent of meeting.
22 All these who were chosen to
be gatekeepers in the thresholds
were 212. These were enrolled by
genealogy in their villages, [a]whom
David and Samuel the seer appointed [b]in their office of trust.
23 So they and their sons [1]had
charge of the gates of the house of
the LORD, *even* the house of the tent,
as guards.
24 The gatekeepers were [1]on the
four sides, to the east, west, north,
and south.
25 And their relatives [a]in their villages [b]*were* to come in every seven
days from time to time *to be* with
[1]them;
26 for the four chief gatekeepers
who *were* Levites, were in an office
of trust, and were over the chambers and over the treasuries in the
house of God.
27 And they spent the night
around the house of God, [a]because
the watch was [1]committed to them;
and they *were* [2]in charge of opening
it morning by morning.
28 Now some of them [1]had charge
of the utensils of service, for [2]they
counted them when they brought
them in and when they took them
out.
29 Some of them also were appointed over the furniture and over
all the utensils of the sanctuary and
[a]over the fine flour and the wine and
the oil and the frankincense and the
spices.
30 And some of [a]the sons of the
priests prepared the mixing of the
spices.
31 And Mattithiah, one of the Levites, who was the first-born of
Shallum the Korahite, had [a]the [1]re-
sponsibility over the things which
were baked in pans.
32 And some of their relatives of
the sons of the Kohathites [a]*were*
over the showbread to prepare it every sabbath.
33 Now these are [a]the singers,
heads of fathers' *households* of the
Levites, *who lived* in the chambers
of the temple free *from other service;* for [1]they were engaged [b]in
their work day and night.
34 These were heads of fathers'
households of the Levites according
to their generations, chief men,
[1]who lived in Jerusalem.

Ancestry and Descendants of Saul

35 [a]And in Gibeon Jeiel the father
of Gibeon lived, and his wife's name
was Maacah,
36 and his first-born son *was* Abdon, then Zur, Kish, Baal, Ner, Nadab,
37 Gedor, Ahio, Zechariah, and
Mikloth.
38 And Mikloth became the father
of Shimeam. And they also lived
with their relatives in Jerusalem opposite their *other* relatives.
39 [a]And Ner became the father of
Kish, and Kish became the father of
Saul, and Saul became the father of
Jonathan, Malchi-shua, Abinadab,
and Eshbaal.
40 And the son of Jonathan *was*
Merib-baal; and Merib-baal became
the father of Micah.
41 And the sons of Micah *were* Pi-
thon, Melech, Tahrea, [a]*and Ahaz.*
42 And Ahaz became the father of
Jarah, and Jarah became the father
of Alemeth, Azmaveth, and Zimri;
and Zimri became the father of
Moza,
43 and Moza became the father of
Binea and Rephaiah his son, Eleasah
his son, Azel his son.

14 [a]Neh. 11:15-19
15 [1]In Neh. 11:17, *Zabdi*
16 [1]In Neh. 11:17, *Abda* [2]In Neh. 11:17, *Shammua*
17 [1]In v. 21, *Meshelemiah;* 26:14, *Shelemiah;* Neh. 12:25, *Meshullam*
18 [a]Ezek. 46:1, 2
20 [a]Num. 25:7-13
21 [a]1 Chr. 26:2, 14
22 [a]1 Chr. 26:1 [b]2 Chr. 31:15, 18
23 [1]Lit., were *over the gates*
24 [1]Lit., *to the four winds*
25 [1]Lit., *these* [a]1 Chr. 10:16 [b]2 Kin. 11:5, 7; 2 Chr. 23:8
27 [1]Lit., *on them* [2]Lit., *over the opening* [a]1 Chr. 23:30-32
28 [1]Lit., *were over the* [2]Lit., *by count they brought them in and by count they took them out*
29 [a]1 Chr. 23:29
30 [a]Ex. 30:23-25
31 [1]Lit., *office of trust* [a]1 Chr. 9:22
32 [a]Lev. 24:5-8
33 [1]Lit., *over them in the work* [a]1 Chr. 6:31-47; 25:1 [b]Ps. 134:1
34 [1]Lit., *these*
35 [a]1 Chr. 8:29-32
39 [a]1 Chr. 8:33-38
41 [a]1 Chr. 8:35-37

44 And Azel had six sons whose names are these: Azrikam, Bocheru and Ishmael and Sheariah and Obadiah and Hanan. These were the sons of Azel.

Chapter 10

Defeat and Death of Saul and His Sons

[a]NOW the Philistines fought against Israel; and the men of Israel fled before the Philistines, and fell slain on Mount Gilboa.

2 And the Philistines closely pursued Saul and his sons, and the Philistines struck down Jonathan, [1][a]Abinadab and Malchi-shua, the sons of Saul.

3 And the battle became heavy against Saul, and the archers [1]overtook him; and he was wounded by the archers.

4 Then Saul said to his armor bearer, "Draw your sword and thrust me through with it, lest these uncircumcised come and abuse me." But his armor bearer would not, for he was greatly afraid. Therefore Saul took his sword and fell on it.

5 And when his armor bearer saw that Saul was dead, he likewise fell on his sword and died.

6 Thus Saul died with his three sons, and all *those* of his house died together.

7 When all the men of Israel who were in the valley saw that they had fled, and that Saul and his sons were dead, they forsook their cities and fled; and the Philistines came and lived in them.

8 And it came about the next day, when the Philistines came to strip the slain, that they found Saul and his sons fallen on Mount Gilboa.

9 So they stripped him and took his head and his armor and sent *messengers* around the land of the Philistines, to carry the good news to their idols and to the people.

10 And they put his armor in the house of their gods and fastened his head in the house of Dagon.

Jabesh-gilead's Tribute to Saul

11 When all Jabesh-gilead heard all that the Philistines had done to Saul,

12 all the valiant men arose and took away the body of Saul and the bodies of his sons, and brought them to Jabesh and buried their bones under the oak in Jabesh, and fasted seven days.

1 [a]1 Sam. 31:1-13

2 [1]In 1 Sam. 14:49, *Ishvi* [a]1 Sam. 31:4

3 [1]Lit., *found him*

13 [a]1 Sam. 13:13, 14; 15:23 [b]1 Sam. 28:7

14 [a]1 Sam. 15:28; 1 Chr. 12:23

1 [1]Lit., *saying* [a]2 Sam. 5:1, 3, 6-10

2 [a]2 Sam. 5:2; 7:7

3 [a]1 Sam. 16:1, 3, 12, 13

4 [a]Josh. 15:8, 63; Judg. 1:21

6 [a]2 Sam. 8:16

8 [1]Or, *fortified* [2]I.e., citadel [3]Lit., *revived*

9 [a]2 Sam. 3:1

10 [a]2 Sam. 23:8-39 [b]1 Chr. 11:3

13 [a]So Saul died for his trespass which he committed against the LORD, because of the word of the LORD which he did not keep; and also [b]because he asked counsel of a medium, making inquiry *of it*,

14 and did not inquire of the LORD. Therefore He killed him, and [a]turned the kingdom to David the son of Jesse.

Chapter 11

David Made King over All Israel

[a]THEN all Israel gathered to David at Hebron [1]and said, "Behold, we are your bone and your flesh.

2 "In times past, even when Saul was king, you *were* the one who led out and brought in Israel; and the LORD your God said to you, '[a]You shall shepherd My people Israel, and you shall be prince over My people Israel.' "

3 So all the elders of Israel came to the king at Hebron, and David made a covenant with them in Hebron before the LORD; and they anointed David king over Israel, [a]according to the word of the LORD through Samuel.

Jerusalem, Capital City

4 Then David and all Israel went to Jerusalem ([a]that is, Jebus); and the Jebusites, the inhabitants of the land, *were* there.

5 And the inhabitants of Jebus said to David, "You shall not enter here." Nevertheless David captured the stronghold of Zion (that is, the city of David).

6 Now David had said, "Whoever strikes down a Jebusite first shall be chief and commander." [a]And Joab the son of Zeruiah went up first, so he became chief.

7 Then David dwelt in the stronghold; therefore it was called the city of David.

8 And he [1]built the city all around, from the [2]Millo even to the surrounding area; and Joab [3]repaired the rest of the city.

9 And [a]David became greater and greater, for the LORD of hosts *was* with him.

David's Mighty Men

10 [a]Now these are the heads of the mighty men whom David had, who gave him strong support in his kingdom, together with all Israel, to make him king, [b]according to the word of the LORD concerning Israel.

11 And these *constitute* the list of

the mighty men whom David had:
[a]Jashobeam, the son of a Hachmon-
ite, [b]the chief of the thirty; he lifted
up his spear against three hundred
[1]whom he killed at one time.
12 And after him was Eleazar the
son of [a]Dodo, the Ahohite, who *was*
[1]one of the three mighty men.
13 He was with David at [1]Pasdam-
mim [a]when the Philistines were
gathered together there to battle,
and there was a plot of ground full
of barley; and the people fled before
the Philistines.
14 And they took their stand in the
midst of the plot, and defended it,
and struck down the Philistines; and
the LORD saved them by a great [1]vic-
tory.
15 Now three of the thirty chief
men went down to the rock to David, into the cave of Adullam, while
[a]the army of the Philistines was
camping in the valley of Rephaim.
16 And David was then in the
stronghold, while [a]the garrison of
the Philistines *was* then in Bethlehem.
17 And David had a craving and
said, "Oh that someone would give
me water to drink from the well of
Bethlehem, which is by the gate!"
18 So the three broke through the
camp of the Philistines, and drew
water from the well of Bethlehem
which *was* by the gate, and took *it*
and brought *it* to David; nevertheless David would not drink it, but
poured it out to the LORD;
19 and he said, "Be it far from me
before my God that I should do this.
Shall I drink the blood of these men
who went [1]at the risk of their lives?
For at the risk of their lives they
brought it." Therefore he would not
drink it. These things the three
mighty men did.
20 As for [1]Abshai the brother of
Joab, he was chief of the [2]thirty, and
he swung his spear against three
hundred [3]and killed them; and he
had a name as well as the [2]thirty.
21 Of the three in the second *rank*
he was the most honored, and became their commander; however,
he did not attain to the *first* three.
22 [a]Benaiah the son of Jehoiada,
the son of a valiant man of Kabzeel,
mighty in deeds, struck down the
[1]two *sons of* Ariel of Moab. He also
went down and [2]killed a lion inside a
pit on a snowy day.
23 And he [1]killed an Egyptian, a
man of *great* stature five [2]cubits tall.
Now in the Egyptian's hand *was* [a]a
spear like a weaver's beam, but he
went down to him with a club and
snatched the spear from the Egyptian's hand, and [1]killed him with his
own spear.
24 These *things* Benaiah the son of
Jehoiada did, and had a name as
well as the three mighty men.
25 Behold, he was honored among
the thirty, but he did not attain to
the three; and David appointed him
over his guard.
26 Now the mighty men of the
armies *were* Asahel the brother of
Joab, Elhanan the son of Dodo of
Bethlehem,
27 [1]Shammoth the Harorite, Helez
the [2]Pelonite,
28 Ira the son of Ikkesh the Tekoite, Abiezer the Anathothite,
29 [1]Sibbecai the Hushathite, [2]Ilai
the Ahohite,
30 Maharai the Netophathite,
[1]Heled the son of Baanah the Netophathite,
31 Ithai the son of Ribai of Gibeah
of the sons of Benjamin, Benaiah the
Pirathonite,
32 [1]Hurai of the brooks of Gaash,
[2]Abiel the Arbathite,
33 Azmaveth the Baharumite,
Eliahba the Shaalbonite,
34 the sons of [1]Hashem the Gizon-
ite, Jonathan the son of Shagee the
Hararite,
35 Ahiam the son of [1]Sacar the
Hararite, [2]Eliphal the son of Ur,
36 Hepher the Mecherathite, Ahijah the Pelonite,
37 Hezro the Carmelite, [1]Naarai
the son of Ezbai,
38 Joel the brother of Nathan,
Mibhar the son of Hagri,
39 Zelek the Ammonite, Naharai
the Berothite, the armor bearer of
Joab the son of Zeruiah,
40 Ira the Ithrite, Gareb the Ithrite,
41 Uriah the Hittite, Zabad the son
of Ahlai,
42 Adina the son of Shiza the Reu-
benite, a chief of the Reubenites,
and thirty with him,
43 Hanan the son of Maacah and
Joshaphat the Mithnite,
44 Uzzia the Ashterathite, Shama
and Jeiel the sons of Hotham the
Aroerite,
45 Jediael the son of Shimri and
Joha his brother, the Tizite,
46 Eliel the Mahavite and Jeribai
and Joshaviah, the sons of Elnaam,
and Ithmah the Moabite,
47 Eliel and Obed and Jaasiel the
Mezobaite.

11 [1]Lit., *slain ones* [a]2 Sam. 23:8 [b]1 Chr. 12:18

12 [1]Lit., *among* [a]1 Chr. 27:4

13 [1]In 1 Sam. 17:1, *Ephesdammim* [a]2 Sam. 23:11, 12

14 [1]Or, *salvation*

15 [a]1 Chr. 14:9

16 [a]1 Sam. 10:5

19 [1]Lit., *with their souls*

20 [1]In 2 Sam. 23:18, *Abishai* [2]So Syriac; M.T., *three* [3]Lit., *slain ones*

22 [1]Or, *two lion-like heroes of* [2]Lit., *smote* [a]2 Sam. 8:18

23 [1]Lit., *smote* [2]One cubit equals approx. 18 in. [a]1 Sam. 17:7

27 [1]In 2 Sam. 23:25, *Shammah the Harodite* [2]In 2 Sam. 23:26, *Paltite*

29 [1]In 2 Sam. 23:27, *Mebunnai* [2]In 2 Sam. 23:28, *Zalmon*

30 [1]In 2 Sam. 23:29, *Heleb*

32 [1]In 2 Sam. 23:30, *Hiddai* [2]In 2 Sam. 23:31, *Abialbon*

34 [1]In 2 Sam. 23:32, *Jashen*

35 [1]In 2 Sam. 23:33, *Sharar* [2]In 2 Sam. 23:34, *Eliphelet the son of Ahasbai*

37 [1]In 2 Sam. 23:35, *Paarai the Arbite*

Chapter 12

David's Supporters in Ziklag

[a]NOW these are the ones who came to David at Ziklag, while he was still restricted because of Saul the son of Kish; and they were among the mighty men who helped *him* in war.

2 They were equipped with bows, [a]using both the right hand and the left *to sling* stones and *to shoot* arrows from the bow; [b]*they were* Saul's kinsmen from Benjamin.

3 The chief was Ahiezer, then Joash, the sons of Shemaah the Gibeathite; and Jeziel and Pelet, the sons of Azmaveth, and Beracah and Jehu the Anathothite,

4 and Ishmaiah the Gibeonite, a mighty man among the thirty, and over the thirty. [1]Then Jeremiah, Jahaziel, Johanan, Jozabad the Gederathite,

5 Eluzai, Jerimoth, Bealiah, Shemariah, Shephatiah the Haruphite,

6 Elkanah, Isshiah, Azarel, Joezer, Jashobeam, the Korahites,

7 and Joelah and Zebadiah, the sons of Jeroham of Gedor.

8 And from the Gadites there [1]came over to David in the stronghold in the wilderness, mighty men of valor, men trained for war, who could handle shield and spear, and whose faces were like the faces of lions, and [a]*they were* as swift as the gazelles on the mountains.

9 Ezer *was* the first, Obadiah the second, Eliab the third,

10 Mishmannah the fourth, Jeremiah the fifth,

11 Attai the sixth, Eliel the seventh,

12 Johanan the eighth, Elzabad the ninth,

13 Jeremiah the tenth, Machbannai the eleventh.

14 These of the sons of Gad were [1]captains of the army; [a]he who was least was equal to a hundred and the greatest to a thousand.

15 [a]These are the ones who crossed the Jordan in the first month when it was overflowing all its banks and they put to flight all those in the valleys, both to the east and to the west.

16 Then some of the sons of Benjamin and Judah came to the stronghold to David.

17 And David went out to meet them, and answered and said to them, "If you come peacefully to me to help me, my heart shall be united with you; but if to betray me to my adversaries, since there is no [1]wrong in my hands, may the God of our fathers look on *it* and decide."

18 Then [a]the Spirit [1]came upon [b]Amasai, who was the chief of the thirty, *and he said,*

"*We* are yours, O David,
And with you, O son of Jesse!
[c]Peace, peace to you,
And peace to him who helps
you;
Indeed, your God helps you!"

Then David received them and made them [2]captains of the band.

19 [a]From Manasseh also some defected to David, when he was about to go to battle with the Philistines against Saul. But they did not help them, for the lords of the Philistines after consultation sent him away, saying, "At *the cost of* our heads he may defect to his master Saul."

20 As he went to Ziklag, there defected to him from Manasseh: Adnah, Jozabad, Jediael, Michael, Jozabad, Elihu, and Zillethai, [1]captains of thousands who belonged to Manasseh.

21 And they helped David against [a]the band of raiders, for they were all mighty men of valor, and were captains in the army.

22 For day by day *men* came to David to help him, until there was a great army [a]like the army of God.

Supporters Gathered at Hebron

23 Now these are the numbers of the [1]divisions equipped for war, [a]who came to David at Hebron, [b]to turn the kingdom of Saul to him, [c]according to the [2]word of the LORD.

24 The sons of Judah who bore shield and spear *were* 6,800, equipped for war.

25 Of the sons of Simeon, mighty men of valor for war, 7,100.

26 Of the sons of Levi 4,600.

27 Now Jehoiada was the leader of *the house of* Aaron, and with him were 3,700,

28 also [a]Zadok, a young man mighty of valor, and of his father's house twenty-two captains.

29 And of the sons of Benjamin, [a]Saul's kinsmen, 3,000; for until now [b]the greatest part of them had kept their allegiance to the house of Saul.

30 And of the sons of Ephraim 20,800, mighty men of valor, famous men in their fathers' households.

31 And of the half-tribe of Manasseh 18,000, who were designated by name to come and make David king.

1 [a]1 Sam. 27:2-6
2 [a]Judg. 3:15; 20:16 [b]1 Chr. 12:29
4 [1]In Heb. the beginning of v. 5, making 41 vs. in chap.
8 [1]Lit., *separated themselves* [a]2 Sam. 2:18
14 [1]Or, *chiefs* [a]Deut. 32:30
15 [a]Josh. 3:15; 4:18
17 [1]Lit., *violence*
18 [1]Lit., *clothed* [2]Or, *chiefs* [a]Judg. 3:10; 6:34 [b]1 Chr. 2:17 [c]1 Sam. 25:5, 6
19 [a]1 Sam. 29:2-9
20 [1]Or, *chiefs*
21 [a]1 Sam. 30:1
22 [a]Gen. 32:2; Josh. 5:13-15
23 [1]Lit., *heads* [2]Lit., *mouth* [a]2 Sam. 2:3, 4 [b]1 Chr. 10:14 [c]1 Chr. 11:10
28 [a]2 Sam. 8:17; 1 Chr. 6:8, 53
29 [a]1 Chr. 12:2 [b]2 Sam. 2:8, 9

32 And of the sons of Issachar,
[a]men who understood the times,
with knowledge of what Israel
should do, their chiefs were two
hundred; and all their kinsmen were
at their command.
33 Of Zebulun, there were 50,000
who went out in the army, who
could draw up in battle formation
with all kinds of weapons of war
and helped *David* [1]with [a]an undivid-
ed heart.
34 And of Naphtali *there were*
1,000 captains, and with them
37,000 with shield and spear.
35 And of the Danites who could
draw up in battle formation, *there*
were 28,600.
36 And of Asher *there were* 40,000
who went out in the army to draw
up in battle formation.
37 And from the other side of the
Jordan, of the Reubenites and the
Gadites and of the half-tribe of Manasseh, *there were* 120,000 with all
kinds of weapons of war for the battle.
38 All these, being men of war,
who could draw up in battle formation, came to Hebron with [a]a perfect
heart, to make David king over all
Israel; and all the rest also of Israel
were of one mind to make David
king.
39 And they were there with David three days, eating and drinking;
for their kinsmen had prepared for
them.
40 Moreover those who were near
to them, *even* as far as Issachar and
Zebulun and Naphtali, [a]brought
food on donkeys, camels, mules,
and on oxen, great quantities of
flour cakes, fig cakes and bunches of
raisins, wine, oil, oxen and sheep.
There was joy indeed in Israel.

CHAPTER 13

Peril in Transporting the Ark

THEN David consulted with the
captains of the thousands and the
hundreds, even with every leader.
2 And David said to all the assembly of Israel, "If it seems good to
you, and if it is from the LORD our
God, let us send everywhere to our
kinsmen who remain in all the land
of Israel, also to the priests and Levites who are with them in their
cities with pasture lands, that they
may meet with us;
3 and let us bring back the ark of
our God to us, [a]for we did not seek it
in the days of Saul."
4 Then all the assembly said that
they would do so, for the thing was
right in the eyes of all the people.
5 [a]So David assembled all Israel
together, from the Shihor of Egypt
even to the entrance of Hamath, [b]to
bring the ark of God from Kiriath-
jearim.
6 [a]And David and all Israel went
up to [b]Baalah, *that is,* to Kiriath-
jearim, which belongs to Judah, to
bring up from there the ark of God,
the LORD [c]who is enthroned *above*
the cherubim, where His name is
called.
7 And they [1]carried the ark of
God on a new cart from [a]the house
of Abinadab, and Uzza and Ahio
drove the cart.
8 And David and all Israel were
celebrating before God with all *their*
might, [a]even with songs and with
lyres, harps, tambourines, cymbals,
and with trumpets.
9 When they came to [a]the threshing floor of Chidon, Uzza put out his
hand to hold the ark, because the
oxen nearly upset *it.*
10 And the anger of the LORD
burned against Uzza, so He struck
him down [a]because he put out his
hand to the ark; [b]and he died there
before God.
11 Then David became angry because [1]of the LORD's outburst
against Uzza; and he called that
place [2]Perez-uzza to this day.
12 And David was afraid of God
that day, saying, "How can I bring
the ark of God *home* to me?"
13 So David did not take the ark
with him to the city of David, but
took it aside [a]to the house of Obed-
edom the Gittite.
14 Thus the ark of God remained
with the family of Obed-edom in his
house three months; and [a]the LORD
blessed the family of Obed-edom
with all that he had.

CHAPTER 14

David's Family Enlarged

[a]NOW Hiram king of Tyre sent
messengers to David with cedar
trees, masons, and carpenters, to
build a house for him.
2 And David realized that the
LORD had established him as king
over Israel, *and* that his kingdom
was highly exalted, for the sake of
His people Israel.
3 Then David took more wives at
Jerusalem, and David [1]became the
father of more sons and daughters.
4 [a]And these are the names of the
children [1]born *to him* in Jerusalem:

32 [a]Esth. 1:13
33 [1]Lit., *not of double heart* [a]Ps. 12:2
38 [a]2 Sam. 5:1-3; 1 Chr. 12:33
40 [a]1 Sam. 25:18
3 [a]1 Sam. 7:1, 2
5 [a]2 Sam. 6:1; 1 Kin. 8:65; 1 Chr. 15:3 [b]1 Sam. 6:21; 7:1
6 [a]2 Sam. 6:2-11 [b]Josh. 15:9 [c]2 Kin. 19:15
7 [1]Lit., *caused to ride* [a]1 Sam. 7:1
8 [a]1 Chr. 15:16
9 [a]2 Sam. 6:6
10 [a]1 Chr. 15:13, 15 [b]Lev. 10:2
11 [1]Lit., *the LORD had broken through a break-through* [2]I.e., the break-through of Uzza
13 [a]2 Chr. 25
14 [a]1 Chr. 26:4, 5
1 [a]2 Sam. 5:11
3 [1]Lit., *begot*
4 [1]Lit., *were to* [a]1 Chr. 3:5-8

Shammua, Shobab, Nathan, Solomon,
5 Ibhar, Elishua, Elpelet,
6 Nogah, Nepheg, Japhia,
7 Elishama, Beeliada and Eliphelet.

Philistines Defeated

8 When the Philistines heard that
David had been anointed king over
all Israel, all the Philistines went up
in search of David; and David heard
of it and went out against them.
9 Now the Philistines had come
and [a]made a raid in the valley of
Rephaim.
10 And David inquired of God,
saying, "Shall I go up against the
Philistines? And wilt Thou give
them into my hand?" Then the LORD
said to him, "Go up, for I will give
them into your hand."
11 So they came up to Baal-pera-
zim, and David [1]defeated them
there; and David said, "God has broken through my enemies by my
hand, like the break-through of waters." Therefore they named that
place [2]Baal-perazim.
12 And they abandoned their gods
there; so David gave the order and
they were burned with fire.
13 And the Philistines made [a]yet
another raid in the valley.
14 And David inquired again of
God, and God said to him, "You
shall not go up after them; circle
around [1]behind them, and come at
them in front of the [2]balsam trees.
15 "And it shall be when you hear
the sound of marching in the tops of
the balsam trees, then you shall go
out to battle, for God will have gone
out before you to strike the army of
the Philistines."
16 And David did just as God had
commanded him, and they struck
down the army of the Philistines
from [1]Gibeon even as far as Gezer.
17 Then the fame of David went
out into all the lands; and [a]the LORD
brought the fear of him on all the
nations.

CHAPTER 15

Plans to Move the Ark to Jerusalem

NOW *David* built houses for himself in the city of David; and he prepared a place for the ark of God, and
[a]pitched a tent for it.
2 Then David said, "[a]No one is to
carry the ark of God but the Levites;
for the LORD chose them to carry the
ark of God, and to minister to Him
forever."
3 And [a]David assembled all Israel at Jerusalem, to bring up the
ark of the LORD [b]to its place, which
he had prepared for it.
4 And David gathered together
the sons of Aaron, and [a]the Levites;
5 of the sons of Kohath, Uriel the
chief, and 120 of his [1]relatives;
6 of the sons of Merari, Asaiah
the chief, and 220 of his relatives;
7 of the sons of Gershom, Joel the
chief, and 130 of his relatives;
8 of the sons of Elizaphan,
Shemaiah the chief, and 200 of his
relatives;
9 of the sons of Hebron, Eliel the
chief, and 80 of his relatives;
10 of the sons of Uzziel, Amminadab the chief, and 112 of his relatives.
11 Then David called for [a]Zadok
and [b]Abiathar the priests, and for
the Levites, for Uriel, Asaiah, Joel,
Shemaiah, Eliel, and Amminadab,
12 and said to them, "You are the
heads of the fathers' *households* of
the Levites; [a]consecrate yourselves
both you and your relatives, that
you may bring up the ark of the
LORD God of Israel, [b]to *the place*
that I have prepared for it.
13 "[a]Because you did not *carry it* at
the first, the LORD our God made an
outburst on us, for we did not seek
Him according to the ordinance."
14 [a]So the priests and the Levites
consecrated themselves to bring up
the ark of the LORD God of Israel.
15 And the sons of [a]the Levites
carried the ark of God on their
shoulders, with the poles thereon as
Moses had commanded according
to the word of the LORD.
16 Then David spoke to the chiefs
of the Levites [a]to appoint their relatives the singers, with instruments
of music, harps, lyres, loud-sounding cymbals, to raise sounds of joy.
17 So [a]the Levites appointed Heman the son of Joel, and from his
relatives, Asaph the son of Berechiah; and from the sons of Merari their
relatives, Ethan the son of Kusha-
iah,
18 and with them their relatives of
the second rank, Zechariah, [1]Ben,
Jaaziel, Shemiramoth, Jehiel, Unni,
Eliab, Benaiah, Maaseiah, Mattithiah, Eliphelehu, Mikneiah, Obed-
edom, and Jeiel, the gatekeepers.
19 So the singers, Heman, Asaph,
and Ethan *were appointed* to sound
aloud cymbals of bronze;
20 and Zechariah, Aziel, Shemiramoth, Jehiel, Unni, Eliab, Maaseiah, and Benaiah, with [1]harps *tuned*
to [a]alamoth;

---

9 [a]1 Chr. 11:15; 15:13
11 [1]Lit., *smote* [2]I.e., the master of break-through
13 [a]1 Chr. 15:9
14 [1]Lit., *from upon* [2]Or, *baka shrubs*
16 [1]In 2 Sam. 5:25, *Geba*
17 [a]Ex. 15:14-16; Deut. 2:25
1 [a]1 Chr. 15:3; 16:1; 17:1-5
2 [a]Num. 4:15
3 [a]1 Kin. 8:1; 1 Chr. 13:5 [b]2 Sam. 6:12, 17; 1 Chr. 15:1, 12
4 [a]1 Chr. 6:16-30; 12:26-28
5 [1]Lit., *brothers*, i.e., fellow tribesmen, and so throughout the chap.
11 [a]1 Chr. 12:28 [b]1 Sam. 22:20-23; 1 Kin. 2:26, 35
12 [a]Ex. 19:14, 15; 2 Chr. 35:6 [b]1 Chr. 15:1, 3
13 [a]2 Sam. 6:3; 1 Chr. 13:7
14 [a]1 Chr. 15:12
15 [a]Ex. 25:14; Num. 4:5
16 [a]1 Chr. 13:8; 25:1
17 [a]1 Chr. 25:1
18 [1]Omitted in Gk. and many mss.
20 [1]Or, *harps of maiden-like tone* [a]Ps. 46:title

21 and Mattithiah, Eliphelehu,
Mikneiah, Obed-edom, Jeiel, and
Azaziah, to lead with [1]lyres tuned to
[a]the sheminith.
22 And Chenaniah, chief of the Levites, was *in charge of* the singing;
he gave instruction in singing because he was skillful.
23 And Berechiah and Elkanah
were gatekeepers for the ark.
24 And Shebaniah, Joshaphat, Nethanel, Amasai, Zechariah, Benaiah,
and Eliezer, the priests, [a]blew the
trumpets before the ark of God.
Obed-edom and Jehiah also *were*
gatekeepers for the ark.
25 [a]So *it was* David, with the elders of Israel and the captains over
thousands, who went to bring up the
ark of the covenant of the LORD
from [b]the house of Obed-edom with
joy.
26 And it came about because God
was helping the Levites who were
carrying the ark of the covenant of
the LORD, that they sacrificed [a]sev-
en bulls and seven rams.
27 Now David was clothed with a
robe of fine linen with all the Levites
who were carrying the ark, and the
singers and Chenaniah the leader of
the singing *with* the singers. David
also wore an ephod of linen.
28 Thus all Israel brought up the
ark of the covenant of the LORD with
shouting, and with sound of the
horn, with trumpets, with loud-
sounding cymbals, with harps and
lyres.
29 And it happened when the ark
of the covenant of the LORD came to
the city of David, that Michal the
daughter of Saul looked out of the
window, and saw King David leaping and making merry; and she despised him in her heart.

CHAPTER 16

A Tent for the Ark

AND they brought in the ark of
God and [a]placed it inside the tent
which David had pitched for it, and
they offered burnt offerings and
peace offerings before God.
2 When David had finished offering the burnt offering and the peace
offerings, he blessed the people in
the name of the LORD.
3 And he distributed to every one
of Israel, both man and woman, to
every one a loaf of bread and a portion *of meat* and a raisin cake.
4 And he appointed some of the
Levites *as* ministers before the ark
of the LORD, even to celebrate and to
thank and praise the LORD God of
Israel:
5 Asaph the chief, and second to
him Zechariah, *then* [1]Jeiel, Shemiramoth, Jehiel, Mattithiah, Eliab, Benaiah, Obed-edom, and Jeiel, with
musical instruments, harps, lyres;
also Asaph *played* loud-sounding
cymbals,
6 and Benaiah and Jahaziel the
priests *blew* trumpets continually
before the ark of the covenant of
God.
7 Then on that day David [a]first
assigned [1]Asaph and his [2]relatives
to give thanks to the LORD.

Psalm of Thanksgiving

8 [a]Oh give thanks to the LORD, call upon His name;
[b]Make known His deeds among the peoples.
9 Sing to Him, sing praises to Him;
[1]Speak of all His [2]wonders.
10 [1]Glory in His holy name;
Let the heart of those who seek the LORD be glad.
11 [a]Seek the LORD and His strength;
Seek His face continually.
12 [a]Remember His wonderful deeds which He has done,
[b]His marvels and the judgments from His mouth,
13 O seed of Israel His servant,
Sons of Jacob, His chosen ones!
14 He is the LORD our God;
[a]His judgments are in all the earth.
15 Remember His covenant forever,
The word which He commanded to a thousand generations,
16 [a]*The covenant* which He made with Abraham,
And His oath to Isaac.
17 [a]He also confirmed it to Jacob for a statute,
To Israel as an everlasting covenant,
18 Saying, "[a]To you I will give the land of Canaan,
As the portion of your inheritance."
19 [a]When they were only a few in number,
Very few, and strangers in it,
20 And they wandered about from nation to nation,
And from *one* kingdom to another people,
21 He permitted no man to oppress them,

21 [1]Or, *octave harps* [a]Ps. 6:title
24 [a]1 Chr. 15:28; 16:6
25 [a]2 Sam. 6:12, 15 [b]1 Chr. 13:13
26 [a]Num. 23:1-4, 29
1 [a]1 Chr. 15:1
5 [1]Or, *Jaaziel,* 1 Chr. 15:18
7 [1]Lit., *by the hand of Asaph* [2]Lit., *brothers* [a]2 Sam. 22:1; 23:1
8 [a]Ps. 105:1-15 [b]1 Kin. 8:43; 2 Kin. 19.19
9 [1]Or, *Meditate on* [2]I.e., wonderful acts
10 [1]Or, *Boast*
11 [a]Ps. 24:6
12 [a]Ps. 103:2 [b]Ps. 78:43-68
14 [a]Ps. 48:10
16 [a]Gen. 17:2; 22:16-18; 26:3
17 [a]Gen. 35:11, 12
18 [a]Gen. 13:15
19 [a]Gen. 34:30; Deut. 7:7

And [a]He reproved kings for their sakes, *saying,*
22 "Do not touch My anointed ones,
And [a]do My prophets no harm."
23 [a]Sing to the LORD, all the earth;
Proclaim good tidings of His salvation from day to day.
24 Tell of His glory among the nations,
His wonderful deeds among all the peoples.
25 For [a]great is the LORD, and greatly to be praised;
He also is [b]to be feared above all gods.
26 For all the gods of the peoples are [1a]idols,
[b]But the LORD made the heavens.
27 Splendor and majesty are before Him,
Strength and joy are in His place.
28 Ascribe to the LORD, O families of the peoples,
Ascribe to the LORD glory and strength.
29 Ascribe to the LORD the glory due His name;
Bring an [1]offering, and come before Him;
[a]Worship the LORD in [2]holy array.
30 Tremble before Him, all the earth;
Indeed, the world is firmly established, it will not be moved.
31 [a]Let the heavens be glad, and let the earth rejoice;
And let them say among the nations, "[b]The LORD reigns."
32 [a]Let the sea [1]roar, and [2]all it contains;
Let the field exult, and all that is in it.
33 Then the trees of the forest will sing for joy before the LORD;
For He is coming to judge the earth.
34 [a]O give thanks to the LORD, for *He is* good;
For His lovingkindness is everlasting.
35 [a]Then say, "Save us, O God of our salvation,
And gather us and deliver us from the nations,
To give thanks to Thy holy name,
And [1]glory in Thy praise."
36 [a]Blessed be the LORD, the God of Israel,
From everlasting even to everlasting.
Then all the people [b]said, "Amen," and praised the LORD.

Worship Before the Ark

37 So he left Asaph and his [1]relatives there [a]before the ark of the covenant of the LORD, to minister before the ark continually, [b]as every day's work required;
38 and [a]Obed-edom with [1]his 68 relatives; Obed-edom, also the son of Jeduthun, and [b]Hosah as gatekeepers.
39 And *he left* [a]Zadok the priest and his [1]relatives the priests [b]before the [2]tabernacle of the LORD in the high place which *was* at Gibeon,
40 to offer burnt offerings to the LORD on the altar of burnt offering continually morning and evening, [a]even according to all that is written in the law of the LORD, which He commanded Israel.
41 And with them *were* [a]Heman and Jeduthun, and [b]the rest who were chosen, who were designated by name, to [c]give thanks to the LORD, because His lovingkindness is everlasting.
42 And with them *were* Heman and Jeduthun *with* trumpets and cymbals for those who should sound aloud, and *with* instruments *for* [a]the songs of God, and the sons of Jeduthun for the gate.
43 Then all the people departed each to his house, and David returned to bless his household.

CHAPTER 17

God's Covenant with David

[a]AND it came about, when David dwelt in his house, that David said to Nathan the prophet, "Behold, I am dwelling in a house of cedar, but the ark of the covenant of the LORD is under curtains."
2 Then Nathan said to David, "Do all that is in your heart, for God is with you."
3 And it came about the same night, that the word of God came to Nathan, saying,
4 "Go and tell David My servant, 'Thus says the LORD, [a]"You shall not build a house for Me to dwell in;
5 for I have not dwelt in a house since the day that I brought up Israel to this day, [a]but I have [1]gone from tent to tent and from *one* dwelling place *to another.*
6 "In all places where I have walked with all Israel, have I spoken

21 [a]Gen. 12:17; 20:3; Ex. 7:15-18
22 [a]Gen. 20:7
23 [a]Ps. 96:1-13
25 [a]Ps. 144:3-6 [b]Ps. 89:7
26 [1]Or, *non-existent things* [a]Lev. 19:4 [b]Ps. 102:25
29 [1]Or, *grain offering* [2]Or, *the splendor of holiness* [a]Ps. 29:2
31 [a]Is. 44:23; 49:13 [b]Ps. 93:1; 96:10
32 [1]Or, *thunder* [2]Lit., *its fulness* [a]Ps. 98:7
34 [a]Ps. 106:1; 136:1
35 [1]Lit., *boast* [a]Ps. 106:47, 48
36 [a]1 Kin. 8:15, 56; Ps. 72:18 [b]Deut. 27:15; Neh. 8:6
37 [1]Lit., *brothers* [a]1 Chr. 16:4, 5 [b]2 Chr. 8:14; Ezra 3:4
38 [1]Lit., *their brothers, 68* [a]1 Chr. 13:14 [b]1 Chr. 26:10
39 [1]Lit., *brothers* [2]Lit., *dwelling place* [a]1 Chr. 15:11 [b]1 Kin. 3:4
40 [a]Ex. 29:38-42; Num. 28:3, 4
41 [a]1 Chr. 6:33 [b]1 Chr. 25:1-6 [c]2 Chr. 5:13
42 [a]1 Chr. 25:7; 2 Chr. 7:6; 29:27
1 [a]2 Sam. 7:1-29
4 [a]1 Chr. 28:2, 3
5 [1]Lit., *been* [a]Ex. 40:2, 3; 2 Sam. 7:6

a word [a]with any of the judges of
Israel, whom I commanded to shepherd My people, saying, 'Why have
you not built for Me a house of cedar?' " '
7"Now, therefore, thus shall you
say to My servant David, 'Thus says
the LORD of hosts, "I took you from
the pasture, from following the
sheep, that you should be leader
over My people Israel.
8"And I have been with you wherever you have gone, and have cut off
all your enemies from before you;
and I will make you a name like the
name of the great ones who are in
the earth.
9"And I will appoint a place for
My people Israel, and will plant
them, that they may dwell in their
own place and be moved no more;
neither shall the [1]wicked waste
them any more as formerly,
10 even from the day that I commanded judges *to be* over My people Israel. And I will subdue all your
enemies. Moreover, I tell you that
the LORD will build a house for you.
11"And it shall come about when
your days are fulfilled that you must
go *to be* with your fathers, that I will
set up *one of* your [1]descendants after you, who shall be of your sons;
and I will establish his kingdom.
12"He shall build for Me a house,
and I will establish his throne forever.
13"[a]I will be his father, and he shall
be My son; and I will not take My
lovingkindness away from him, [b]as I
took it from him who was before
you.
14"But I will settle him in My
house and in My kingdom forever,
and his throne shall be established
forever." ' "
15 According to all these words
and according to all this vision, so
Nathan spoke to David.

David's Prayer in Response

16 Then David the king went in
and sat before the LORD and said,
"Who am I, O LORD God, and what
is my house that Thou hast brought
me this far?
17"And this was a small thing in
Thine eyes, O God; but Thou hast
spoken of Thy servant's house for a
great while to come, and hast regarded me according to the standard of a man of high degree, O
LORD God.
18"What more can David still *say*
to Thee concerning the honor *bestowed* on Thy servant? For Thou
knowest Thy servant.

6 [a]2 Sam. 7:7
9 [1]Lit., *sons of wickedness*
11 [1]Lit., *seed*
13 [a]Heb. 1:5 [b]1 Chr. 10:14
19 [a]2 Sam. 7:21; Is. 37:35
22 [a]Ex. 19:5, 6
26 [1]Lit., *said*
27 [1]Lit., *be*
1 [1]Lit., *smote* and so in vs. 1-3 [a]2 Sam. 8:1-18
3 [1]Lit., *hand*

19"O LORD, [a]for Thy servant's
sake, and according to Thine own
heart, Thou hast wrought all this
greatness, to make known all these
great things.
20"O LORD, there is none like Thee,
neither is there any God besides
Thee, according to all that we have
heard with our ears.
21"And what one nation in the
earth is like Thy people Israel,
whom God went to redeem for Himself *as* a people, to make Thee a
name by great and terrible things, in
driving out nations from before Thy
people, whom Thou didst redeem
out of Egypt?
22"[a]For Thy people Israel Thou
didst make Thine own people forever, and Thou, O LORD, didst become their God.
23"And now, O LORD, let the word
that Thou hast spoken concerning
Thy servant and concerning his
house, be established forever, and
do as Thou hast spoken.
24"And let Thy name be established and magnified forever, saying, 'The LORD of hosts is the God of
Israel, *even* a God to Israel; and the
house of David Thy servant is established before Thee.'
25"For Thou, O my God, hast revealed to Thy servant that Thou wilt
build for him a house; therefore Thy
servant hath found *courage* to pray
before Thee.
26"And now, O LORD, Thou art
God, and hast [1]promised this good
thing to Thy servant.
27"And now it hath pleased Thee
to bless the house of Thy servant,
that it may [1]continue forever before
Thee; for Thou, O LORD, hast
blessed, and it is blessed forever."

CHAPTER 18

David's Kingdom Strengthened

NOW after this [a]it came about that
David [1]defeated the Philistines and
subdued them and took Gath and its
towns from the hand of the Philistines.
2 And he defeated Moab, and the
Moabites became servants to David,
bringing tribute.
3 David also defeated Hadadezer
king of Zobah *as far as* Hamath, as
he went to establish his [1]rule to the
Euphrates River.
4 And David took from him 1,000
chariots and 7,000 horsemen and
20,000 foot soldiers, and David ham-
strung all the chariot horses, but re-

served *enough* of them for 100
chariots.
5 When [1]the Syrians of [2]Damas-
cus came to help Hadadezer king [a]of
Zobah, David [3]killed 22,000 men of
[1]the Syrians.
6 Then David put *garrisons* in
[1]Syria of [2]Damascus; and [1]the Syrians became servants to David,
bringing tribute. And the LORD
helped David wherever he went.
7 And David took the shields of
gold which were [1]carried by the servants of Hadadezer, and brought
them to Jerusalem.
8 Also from Tibhath and from
Cun, cities of Hadadezer, David
took a very large amount of bronze,
with which Solomon made the
bronze sea and the pillars and the
bronze utensils.
9 Now when [1]Tou king of Hamath heard that David had [2]de-
feated all the army of Hadadezer
king of Zobah,
10 he sent [1]Hadoram his son to
King David, to [2]greet him and to
bless him, because he had fought
against Hadadezer and had [3]de-
feated him; for Hadadezer had been
at war with Tou. And *Hadoram*
brought all kinds of articles of gold
and silver and bronze.
11 King David also dedicated
these to the LORD with the silver and
the gold which he had carried away
from all the nations: from Edom,
Moab, the sons of Ammon, the Philistines, and from Amalek.
12 Moreover Abishai the son of
Zeruiah [1]defeated 18,000 Edomites
in the Valley of Salt.
13 Then he put garrisons in Edom,
and all the Edomites became servants to David. And the LORD
helped David wherever he went.
14 So David reigned over all Israel;
and he [1]administered justice and
righteousness for all his people.
15 And [a]Joab the son of Zeruiah
was over the army, and Jehoshaphat the son of Ahilud *was* recorder;
16 and Zadok the son of Ahitub
and Abimelech the son of Abiathar
were priests, and Shavsha *was* sec-
retary;
17 and Benaiah the son of Jehoiada *was* over the Cherethites and
the Pelethites, and the sons of David
were chiefs at the king's side.

CHAPTER 19

David's Messengers Abused

[a]NOW it came about after this, that
Nahash the king of the sons of Ammon died, and his son became king
in his place.
2 Then David said, "I will show
kindness to Hanun the son of Nahash, because his father showed
kindness to me." So David sent
messengers to console him concerning his father. And David's servants
came into the land of the sons of
Ammon to Hanun, to console him.
3 But the princes of the sons of
Ammon said to Hanun, "[1]Do you
think that David is honoring your
father, in that he has sent comforters to you? Have not his servants
come to you to search and to overthrow and to spy out the land?"
4 So Hanun took David's servants and shaved them, and cut off
their garments in the middle as far
as their hips, and sent them away.
5 Then *certain persons* went and
told David about the men. And he
sent to meet them, for the men were
greatly humiliated. And the king
said, "[1]Stay at Jericho until your
beards grow, and *then* return."
6 When the sons of Ammon saw
that they had made themselves odious to David, Hanun and the sons of
Ammon sent 1,000 talents of silver
to hire for themselves chariots and
horsemen from Mesopotamia, from
Aram-maacah, and [a]from Zobah.
7 So they hired for themselves
32,000 chariots, and the king of
Maacah and his people, who came
and camped before [a]Medeba. And
the sons of Ammon gathered together from their cities and came to
battle.
8 When David heard *of it,* he sent
Joab and all the army, the mighty
men.
9 And the sons of Ammon came
out and drew up in battle array at
the entrance of the city, and the
kings who had come were by themselves in the field.

Ammon and Syria Defeated

10 Now when Joab saw that the
[1]battle was set against him in front
and in the rear, he selected from all
the choice men of Israel and they
arrayed themselves against the Syrians.
11 But the remainder of the people
he placed in the hand of [1]Abshai his
brother; and they arrayed themselves against the sons of Ammon.
12 And he said, "If the Syrians are
too strong for me, then you shall
help me; but if the sons of Ammon
are too strong for you, then I will
help you.
13 "Be strong, and let us show our-

18:5 [1]Heb., *Aram* [2]Heb., *Darmeseq* [3]Lit., *smote* [a]1 Chr. 19:6
6 [1]Heb., *Aram* [2]Heb., *Darmeseq*
7 [1]Lit., *on*
9 [1]In 2 Sam. 8:10, *Toi* [2]Lit., *smitten*
10 [1]In 2 Sam. 8:10, *Joram* [2]Lit., *ask him of his welfare* [3]Lit., *smitten*
12 [1]Lit., *smote*
14 [1]Lit., *was doing*
15 [a]1 Chr. 11:6
19:1 [a]2 Sam. 10:1-19
3 [1]Lit., *In your eyes is David honoring your father because*
5 [1]Lit., *Return to*
6 [a]1 Chr. 18:5, 9
7 [a]Num. 21:30; Josh. 13:9, 16
10 [1]Lit., *the face of the battle*
11 [1]In 2 Sam. 10:10, *Abishai*

selves courageous for the sake of
our people and for the cities of our
God; and may the LORD do what is
good in His sight."
14 So Joab and the people who
were with him drew near to the battle against the Syrians, and they fled
before him.
15 When the sons of Ammon saw
that the Syrians fled, they also fled
before Abshai his brother, and entered the city. Then Joab came to
Jerusalem.
16 When the Syrians saw that they
had been [1]defeated by Israel, they
sent messengers, and brought out
the Syrians who were beyond the
[2]River, with Shophach the commander of the army of Hadadezer
[3]leading them.
17 When it was told David, he
gathered all Israel together and
crossed the Jordan, and came upon
them and drew up in formation
against them. And when David
drew up in battle array against the
Syrians, they fought against him.
18 And the Syrians fled before Israel, and David killed of the Syrians
7,000 charioteers and 40,000 foot
soldiers, and put to death Shophach
the commander of the army.
19 So when the servants of Hadadezer saw that they were [1]defeated
by Israel, they made peace with David and served him. Thus the Syrians were not willing to help the
sons of Ammon any more.

CHAPTER 20

War with Philistine Giants

[a]THEN it happened [1]in the spring,
at the time when kings go out *to battle,* that Joab led out the army and
ravaged the land of the sons of Ammon, and came and besieged Rabbah. But David stayed at Jerusalem.
And [b]Joab struck Rabbah and overthrew it.
2 [a]And David took the crown of
[1]their king from his head, and he
found it to weigh a talent of gold,
and there was a precious stone in it;
and it was placed on David's head.
And he brought out the spoil of the
city, a very great amount.
3 And he brought out the people
who *were* in it, [a]and cut *them* with
saws and with sharp instruments
and with axes. And thus David did
to all the cities of the sons of Ammon. Then David and all the people
returned *to* Jerusalem.
4 [a]Now it came about after this,
that war [1]broke out at [2]Gezer with
the Philistines; then Sibbecai the
Hushathite [3]killed Sippai, one of the
descendants of the [4]giants, and they
were subdued.
5 And there was war with the
Philistines again, and Elhanan the
son of [a]Jair [1]killed Lahmi the
brother of Goliath the Gittite, the
[b]shaft of whose spear *was* like a
weaver's beam.
6 And again there was war at
Gath, where there was a man of
great stature who had twenty-four
fingers and toes, six *fingers on each
hand* and six *toes on each foot;* and
he also was descended from the giants.
7 And when he taunted Israel,
Jonathan the son of Shimea, David's
brother, [1]killed him.
8 These were descended from the
giants in Gath, and they fell by the
hand of David and by the hand of his
servants.

CHAPTER 21

Census Brings Pestilence

[a]THEN Satan stood up against Israel and moved David to number Israel.
2 So David said to Joab and to the
princes of the people, "[a]Go, number
Israel from Beersheba even to Dan,
and bring me *word* that I may know
their number."
3 And Joab said, "[a]May the LORD
add to His people a hundred times
as many as they are! But, my lord
the king, are they not all my lord's
servants? Why does my lord seek
this thing? Why should he be a
cause of guilt to Israel?"
4 Nevertheless, the king's word
prevailed against Joab. Therefore,
Joab departed and went throughout
all Israel, and came to Jerusalem.
5 And Joab gave the [1]number of
the [2]census of all the people to David. And [a]all Israel *were* 1,100,000
men who drew the sword; and Judah *was* 470,000 men who drew the
sword.
6 [a]But he did not [1]number Levi
and Benjamin among them, for the
king's [2]command was abhorrent to
Joab.
7 And [1]God was displeased with
this thing, so He struck Israel.
8 And David said to God, "I have
sinned greatly, in that I have done
this thing. [a]But now, please take
away the iniquity of Thy servant, for
I have done very foolishly."
9 And the LORD spoke to [a]Gad,
David's [b]seer, saying,

16 [1]Lit., *smitten before* [2]I.e., Euphrates [3]Lit., *before*
19 [1]Lit., *smitten before*
1 [1]Lit., *at the return of the year* [a]2 Sam. 11:1 [b]2 Sam. 12:26
2 [1]In Zeph. 1:5, *Malcam* [a]2 Sam. 12:30, 31
3 [a]2 Sam. 12:31
4 [1]Lit., *stood up* [2]In 2 Sam. 21:18, *Gob* [3]Lit., *smote* [4]Heb., *Raphah,* and so in vs. 6, 8 [a]2 Sam. 21:18-22
5 [1]Lit., *smote* [a]2 Sam. 21:19 [b]1 Sam. 17:7; 1 Chr. 11:23
7 [1]Lit., *smote*
1 [a]2 Sam. 24:1-25
2 [a]1 Chr. 27:23, 24
3 [a]Deut. 1:11
5 [1]Lit., *muster* [2]Lit., *numbering* [a]2 Sam. 24:9
6 [1]Lit., *muster* [2]Lit., *word* [a]1 Chr. 27:24
7 [1]Lit., *it was evil in the sight of God*
8 [a]2 Sam. 12:13
9 [a]2 Sam. 24:11; 1 Chr. 29:29 [b]1 Sam. 9:9

10 "Go and speak to David, saying, 'Thus says the LORD, "I [1]offer you three things; choose for yourself one of them, that I may do *it* to you." ' "

11 So Gad came to David and said to him, "Thus says the LORD, 'Take for yourself

12 [a]either three years of famine, or three months to be swept away before your foes, while the sword of your enemies overtakes *you,* or else three days of the sword of the LORD, even pestilence in the land, and the angel of the LORD destroying throughout all the territory of Israel.' Now, therefore, consider what answer I shall return to Him who sent me."

13 And David said to Gad, "I am in great distress; please let me fall into the hand of the LORD, [a]for His mercies are very great. But do not let me fall into the hand of man."

14 [a]So the LORD [1]sent a pestilence on Israel; 70,000 men of Israel fell.

15 And God sent an angel to Jerusalem to destroy it; but as he was about to destroy *it,* the LORD saw and [a]was sorry over the calamity, and said to the destroying angel, "It is enough; now relax your hand." And the angel of the LORD was standing by the threshing floor of [1]Ornan the Jebusite.

16 Then David lifted up his eyes and saw the angel of the LORD standing between earth and heaven, with his drawn sword in his hand stretched out over Jerusalem. Then David and the elders, [a]covered with sackcloth, fell on their faces.

17 And David said to God, "Is it not I who [1]commanded to count the people? Indeed, I am the one who has sinned and done very wickedly, [a]but these sheep, what have they done? O LORD my God, please let Thy hand be against me and my father's household, but not against Thy people that they should be plagued."

David's Altar

18 [a]Then the angel of the LORD [1]commanded Gad to say to David, that David should go up and build an altar to the LORD on the threshing floor of Ornan the Jebusite.

19 So David went up at the word of Gad, which he spoke in the name of the LORD.

20 Now Ornan turned back and saw the angel, and his four sons *who were* with him hid themselves. And Ornan was threshing wheat.

21 And as David came to Ornan, Ornan looked and saw David, and went out from the threshing floor, and prostrated himself [1]before David with his face to the ground.

22 Then David said to Ornan, "Give me the [1]site of *this* threshing floor, that I may build on it an altar to the LORD; for the full price you shall give it to me, that the plague may be restrained from the people."

23 And Ornan said to David, "Take *it* for yourself; and let my lord the king do what is good in his sight. See, I will give the oxen for burnt offerings and the threshing sledges for wood and the wheat for the grain offering; I will give *it* all."

24 But King David said to Ornan, "No, but I will surely buy *it* for the full price; for I will not take what is yours for the LORD, or offer a burnt offering [1]which costs me nothing."

25 So [a]David gave Ornan 600 shekels of gold by weight for the [1]site.

26 Then David built an altar to the LORD there, and offered burnt offerings and peace offerings. And he called to the LORD and [a]He answered him with fire from heaven on the altar of burnt offering.

27 And the LORD commanded the angel, and he put his sword back in its sheath.

28 At that time, when David saw that the LORD had answered him on the threshing floor of Ornan the Jebusite, he offered sacrifice there.

29 [a]For the tabernacle of the LORD, which Moses had made in the wilderness, and the altar of burnt offering *were* in the high place at Gibeon at that time.

30 But David could not go before it to inquire of God, for he was terrified by the sword of the angel of the LORD.

CHAPTER 22

David Prepares for Temple Building

THEN David said, "[a]This is the house of the LORD God, and this is the altar of burnt offering for Israel."

2 So David [1]gave orders to gather [a]the foreigners who were in the land of Israel, and [b]he set stonecutters to hew out stones to build the house of God.

3 And David [a]prepared large quantities of iron [1]to make the nails for the doors of the gates and for the clamps, and more [b]bronze than could be weighed;

4 and timbers of cedar logs beyond number, for [a]the Sidonians

---

10 [1]Lit., *stretch out to*
12 [a]2 Sam. 24:13
13 [a]Ps. 51:1; 130:4, 7
14 [1]Lit., *gave* [a]1 Chr. 27:24
15 [1]In 2 Sam. 24:16, *Araunah* [a]Ex. 32:14; 1 Sam. 15:11; Jon. 3:10
16 [a]1 Kin. 21:27
17 [1]Lit., *said* [a]2 Sam. 7:8; Ps. 74:1
18 [1]Lit., *said* [a]2 Chr. 3:1
21 [1]Lit., *to*
22 [1]Lit., *place*
24 [1]Lit., *gratuitously*
25 [1]Lit., *place* [a]2 Sam. 24:24
26 [a]Lev. 9:24; Judg. 6:21
29 [a]1 Kin. 3:4; 1 Chr. 16:39
1 [a]1 Chr. 21:18-28; 2 Chr. 3:1
2 [1]Lit., *said to* [a]1 Kin. 9:20, 21; 2 Chr. 2:17 [b]1 Kin. 5:17, 18
3 [1]Lit., *for* [a]1 Chr. 29:27 [b]1 Chr. 22:14
4 [a]1 Kin. 5:6-10

and Tyrians brought large quantities of cedar timber to David.

5 And David said, "My son [a]Solomon is young and inexperienced, and the house that is to be built for the LORD shall be exceedingly magnificent, famous and glorious throughout all lands. Therefore I will make preparation for it." So David made ample preparations before his death.

Solomon Charged with the Task

6 Then he called for his son Solomon, and charged him to build a house for the LORD God of Israel.

7 And David said to Solomon, "[a]My son, [1]I had intended to build a house to the name of the LORD my God.

8"But the word of the LORD came to me, saying, '[a]You have shed much blood, and have [1]waged great wars; you shall not build a house to My name, because you have shed *so* much blood on the earth before Me.

9 'Behold, a son shall be born to you, who shall be a man of rest; and [a]I will give him rest from all his enemies on every side; for [b]his name shall be [1]Solomon, and I will give peace and quiet to Israel in his days.

10 '[a]He shall build a house for My name, and he shall be My son, and I will be his father; and I will establish the throne of his kingdom over Israel forever.'

11"Now, my son, [a]the LORD be with you that you may be successful, and build the house of the LORD your God just as He has spoken concerning you.

12"[a]Only the LORD give you discretion and understanding, and give you charge over Israel, so that you may keep the law of the LORD your God.

13"[a]Then you shall prosper, if you are careful to observe the statutes and the ordinances which the LORD commanded Moses concerning Israel. [b]Be strong and courageous, do not fear nor be dismayed.

14"Now behold, [1]with great pains I have prepared for the house of the LORD [a]100,000 talents of gold and 1,000,000 talents of silver, and [b]bronze and iron beyond weight, for [2]they are in great quantity; also timber and stone I have prepared, and you may add to them.

15"Moreover, there are many workmen with you, stonecutters and masons of stone and carpenters, and all men who are skillful in every kind of work.

16"Of the gold, the silver and the bronze and the iron, there is no limit. Arise and work, and may [a]the LORD be with you."

17 [a]David also commanded all the leaders of Israel to help his son Solomon, *saying,*

18"Is not the LORD your God with you? And [a]has He not given you rest on every side? For He has given the inhabitants of the land into my hand, and the land is subdued before the LORD and before His people.

19"Now [a]set your heart and your soul to seek the LORD your God; arise, therefore, and build the sanctuary of the LORD God, [b]so that you may bring the ark of the covenant of the LORD, and the holy vessels of God into the house that is to be built [c]for the name of the LORD."

CHAPTER 23

Solomon Reigns

[a]NOW when David [1]reached old age, [b]he made his son Solomon king over Israel.

2 And he gathered together all the leaders of Israel with the priests and the Levites.

Offices of the Levites

3 And [a]the Levites were numbered from thirty years old and upward, and [b]their number by [1]census of men was 38,000.

4 Of these, 24,000 were [a]to oversee the work of the house of the LORD; and 6,000 *were* [b]officers and judges,

5 and 4,000 *were* gatekeepers, and [a]4,000 *were* praising the LORD with the instruments which [1]David made for giving praise.

6 And David divided them into divisions [a]according to the sons of Levi: Gershon, Kohath, and Merari.

Gershonites

7 Of the Gershonites *were* [1]Ladan and Shimei.

8 The sons of Ladan *were* Jehiel the first and Zetham and Joel, three.

9 The sons of Shimei *were* Shelomoth and Haziel and Haran, three. These were the heads of the fathers' *households* of Ladan.

10 And the sons of Shimei *were* Jahath, [1]Zina, Jeush, and Beriah. These four *were* the sons of Shimei.

11 And Jahath was the first, and Zizah the second; but Jeush and Beriah did not have many sons, so they became a father's household, one [1]class.

5 [a]1 Kin. 3:7; 1 Chr. 29:1
7 [1]Lit., *as for me, it was in my heart* [a]2 Sam. 7:2, 3; 1 Chr. 17:1
8 [1]Lit., *made* [a]1 Chr. 28:3
9 [1]I.e., Peaceful [a]1 Kin. 4:20, 25 [b]2 Sam. 12:24, 25
10 [a]2 Sam. 7:13, 14; 1 Chr. 17:12
11 [a]1 Chr. 22:16
12 [a]1 Kin. 3:9-12; 2 Chr. 1:10
13 [a]1 Chr. 28:7 [b]Josh. 1:6-9
14 [1]Lit., *in my affliction* [2]Lit., *it is* [a]1 Chr. 29:4 [b]1 Chr. 22:3
16 [a]1 Chr. 22:11
17 [a]1 Chr. 28:1-6
18 [a]1 Chr. 22:9; 23:25
19 [a]1 Chr. 28:9 [b]1 Kin. 8:6, 21; 2 Chr. 5:7 [c]1 Chr. 22:7
1 [1]Lit., *became old and sated with days* [a]1 Chr. 29:28 [b]1 Chr. 28:5; 29:22
3 [1]Lit., *their heads* [a]Num. 4:3-49 [b]Num. 4:48; 1 Chr. 23:24
4 [a]Ezra 3:8, 9 [b]1 Chr. 26:29
5 [1]Lit., *I made* [a]1 Chr. 15:16
6 [a]1 Chr. 6:1
7 [1]In Ex. 6:17, *Libni*
10 [1]In v. 11, *Zizah*
11 [1]Lit., *mustering*

Kohathites

12 The sons of Kohath were four:
Amram, Izhar, Hebron and Uzziel.
13 [a]The sons of Amram were Aaron and Moses. And [b]Aaron was set
apart to sanctify him as most holy,
he and his sons forever, [c]to burn incense before the LORD, to minister
to Him and to bless in His name forever.
14 But *as for* [a]Moses the man of
God, his sons were named among
the tribe of Levi.
15 The sons of Moses *were* Gershom and Eliezer.
16 The [1]son of Gershom *was* [2]She-
buel the chief.
17 And the [1]son of Eliezer was Re
habiah the chief; and Eliezer had no
other sons, but the sons of Rehabiah
were very many.
18 The [1]son of Izhar was [2]Shelo-
mith the chief.
19 The sons of Hebron *were* Jeriah
the first, Amariah the second, Jahaziel the third and Jekameam the
fourth.
20 The sons of Uzziel *were* Micah
the first and Isshiah the second.

Merarites

21 The sons of Merari were Mahli
and Mushi. The sons of Mahli *were*
Eleazar and Kish.
22 And Eleazar died and had no
sons, but daughters only, so their
brothers, the sons of Kish, took
them *as wives*.
23 The sons of Mushi *were* three:
Mahli, Eder, and Jeremoth.

Duties Revised

24 [a]These were the sons of Levi according to their fathers' households,
even the heads of the fathers' *households* of those of them who were
[1]counted, in the number of names
by their [2]census, doing the work for
the service of the house of the LORD,
[b]from twenty years old and upward.
25 For David said, "The LORD God
of Israel [a]has given rest to His people, and He dwells in Jerusalem forever.
26"And also, [a]the Levites will no
longer need to carry the tabernacle
and all its utensils for its service."
27 For by the last words of David
the sons of Levi *were* numbered,
from twenty years old and upward.
28 For their office is [1]to assist the
sons of Aaron with the service of the
house of the LORD, in the courts and
in the chambers and in the purifying
of all holy things, even the work of
the service of the house of God,
29 [a]and with the showbread, and
[b]the fine flour for a grain offering,
and unleavened wafers, or [c]what is
baked in the pan, or [d]what is well-
mixed, and [e]all measures of volume
and size.
30 And they are to stand every
morning to thank and to praise the
LORD, and likewise at evening,
31 and to offer all burnt offerings
to the LORD, [a]on the sabbaths, the
new moons and [b]the fixed festivals
in the number *set* by the ordinance
concerning them, continually before
the LORD.
32 Thus [a]they are to keep charge
of the tent of meeting, and charge of
the holy place, and [b]charge of the
sons of Aaron their [1]relatives, for
the service of the house of the LORD.

CHAPTER 24

Divisions of Levites

NOW the divisions of the [1]descen-
dants of Aaron *were these*. [a]The
sons of Aaron *were* Nadab, Abihu,
Eleazar, and Ithamar.
2 [a]But Nadab and Abihu died before their father and had no [1]sons.
So Eleazar and Ithamar served as
priests.
3 And David, with [a]Zadok of the
sons of Eleazar and Ahimelech of
the sons of Ithamar, divided them
according to their offices [1]for their
ministry.
4 Since more chief men were
found from the [1]descendants of Eleazar than the [1]descendants of Ithamar, they divided them thus: *there
were* sixteen heads of fathers'
households of the [1]descendants of
Eleazar, and eight of the [1]descen-
dants of Ithamar according to their
fathers' households.
5 [a]Thus they were divided by lot,
the one as the other; for they were
officers of the sanctuary and officers
of God, both from the [1]descendants
of Eleazar and the [1]descendants of
Ithamar.
6 And Shemaiah, the son of Nethanel the scribe, from the Levites,
recorded them in the presence of the
king, the princes, Zadok the priest,
[a]Ahimelech the son of Abiathar, and
the heads of the fathers' *households*
of the priests and of the Levites; one
fathers' household taken for Eleazar
and one taken for Ithamar.
7 Now the first lot came out for
Jehoiarib, the second for Jedaiah,
8 the third for Harim, the fourth
for Seorim,
9 the fifth for Malchijah, the sixth
for Mijamin,

13 [a]Ex. 6:20 [b]Ex. 28:1 [c]Ex. 30:6-10
14 [a]Deut. 33:1; Ps. 90: title
16 [1]Lit., *sons* [2]In ch. 24:20, *Shubael*
17 [1]Lit., *sons . . . were*
18 [1]Lit., *sons* [2]In ch. 24:22, *Shelomoth*
24 [1]Lit., *mustered* [2]Lit., *heads* [a]Num. 10:17, 21 [b]1 Chr. 23:3
25 [a]1 Chr. 22:18
26 [a]Num. 4:5, 15; 7:9
28 [1]Lit., *at the hand of*
29 [a]Lev. 24:5-9 [b]Lev. 6:20 [c]1 Chr. 9:31 [d]Lev. 6:21 [e]Lev. 19:35, 36
31 [a]Is. 1:13, 14 [b]Lev. 23:2-4
32 [1]Lit., *brothers* [a]Num. 1:53; 1 Chr. 9:27 [b]Num. 3:6-9, 38
1 [1]Lit., *sons* [a]Ex. 6:23
2 [1]Or, *children* [a]Lev. 10:2
3 [1]Lit., *in their service* [a]1 Chr. 3:31; 6:8
4 [1]Lit., *sons*
5 [1]Lit., *sons* [a]1 Chr. 24:31
6 [a]1 Chr. 18:16

10 the seventh for Hakkoz, the
eighth for [a]Abijah,
11 the ninth for Jeshua, the tenth
for Shecaniah,
12 the eleventh for Eliashib, the
twelfth for Jakim,
13 the thirteenth for Huppah, the
fourteenth for Jeshebeab,
14 the fifteenth for Bilgah, the sixteenth for Immer,
15 the seventeenth for Hezir, the
eighteenth for Happizzez,
16 the nineteenth for Pethahiah,
the twentieth for Jehezkel,
17 the twenty-first for Jachin, the
twenty-second for Gamul,
18 the twenty-third for Delaiah,
the twenty-fourth for Maaziah.
19 [a]These were their offices for
their ministry, when *they* came in to
the house of the LORD according to
the ordinance *given* to them through
Aaron their father, just as the LORD
God of Israel had commanded him.
20 Now for the rest of the sons of
Levi: of the sons of Amram, [1]Shu-
bael; of the sons of Shubael, Jehdeiah.
21 Of Rehabiah: of the sons of Rehabiah, Isshiah the first.
22 Of the Izharites, [1]Shelomoth; of
the sons of Shelomoth, Jahath.
23 And the sons [a]*of Hebron:* Jeriah
the first, Amariah the second, Jahaziel the third, Jekameam the fourth.
24 *Of* the sons of Uzziel, Micah; of
the sons of Micah, Shamir.
25 The brother of Micah, Isshiah;
of the sons of Isshiah, Zechariah.
26 The sons of Merari, Mahli and
Mushi; the sons of Jaaziah, Beno.
27 The sons of Merari: by Jaaziah
were Beno, Shoham, Zaccur, and
Ibri.
28 By Mahli: Eleazar, who had no
sons.
29 By Kish: the sons of Kish, Jerahmeel.
30 And the sons of Mushi: Mahli,
Eder, and Jerimoth. These *were* the
sons of the Levites according to
their fathers' households.
31 [a]These also cast lots just as
their [1]relatives the sons of Aaron in
the presence of David the king, [b]Za-
dok, Ahimelech, and the heads of
the fathers' *households* of the
priests and of the Levites—the head
of fathers' *households* as well as
those of his younger brother.

CHAPTER 25

Number and Services of Musicians

MOREOVER, David and the commanders of the army set apart for
the service *some* of the sons of [a]A-
saph and of Heman and of Jeduthun, who *were* to [b]prophesy with
lyres, [c]harps, and cymbals; and the
number of [1]those who performed
their service was:
2 of the sons of Asaph: Zaccur,
Joseph, Nethaniah, and [1]Asharelah;
the sons of Asaph *were* under the
[2]direction of Asaph, who prophesied under the [2]direction of the
king.
3 [a]Of Jeduthun, the sons of Jeduthun: Gedaliah, [1]Zeri, Jeshaiah,
[2]Shimei, Hashabiah, and Mattithiah, six, under the [3]direction of their
father Jeduthun with the harp, who
prophesied in giving thanks and
praising the LORD.
4 Of Heman, the sons of Heman:
Bukkiah, Mattaniah, [1]Uzziel, [2]She-
buel and Jerimoth, Hananiah, Hanani, Eliathah, Giddalti and Ro-
mamti-ezer, Joshbekashah, Mallothi, Hothir, Mahazioth.
5 All these *were* the sons of Heman [a]the king's seer to [1]exalt him
according to the words of God, for
God gave fourteen sons and three
daughters to Heman.
6 All these were under the [1]direc-
tion of their father to sing in the
house of the LORD, [a]with cymbals,
harps and lyres, for the service of
the house of God. [b]Asaph, Jeduthun
and Heman *were* under the [1]direc-
tion of the king.
7 And their number who were
trained in singing to the LORD, with
their [1]relatives, all who were skillful, *was* [a]288.

Divisions of Musicians

8 And [a]they cast lots for their duties, all alike, the small as well as the
great, the teacher *as well* as the pupil.
9 Now the first lot came out for
Asaph to Joseph, the second for
Gedaliah, he with his relatives and
sons *were* twelve;
10 the third to Zaccur, his sons
and his relatives, twelve;
11 the fourth to Izri, his sons and
his relatives, twelve;
12 the fifth to Nethaniah, his sons
and his relatives, twelve;
13 the sixth to Bukkiah, his sons
and his relatives, twelve;
14 the seventh to Jesharelah, his
sons and his relatives, twelve;
15 the eighth to Jeshaiah, his sons
and his relatives, twelve;
16 the ninth to Mattaniah, his sons
and his relatives, twelve;
17 the tenth to Shimei, his sons
and his relatives, twelve;

10 [a]Neh. 12:4; Luke 1:5
19 [a]1 Chr. 9:25
20 [1]In 23:16, *Shebuel*
22 [1]In 23:18, *Shelomith*
23 [a]1 Chr. 23:19
31 [1]Lit., *brothers* [a]1 Chr. 24:5, 6 [b]1 Chr. 24:6
1 [1]Lit., *workmen according to their service* [a]1 Chr. 6:33, 39 [b]2 Kin. 3:15 [c]1 Chr. 15:16
2 [1]In v. 14, *Jesharelah* [2]Lit., *hand*(s)
3 [1]In v. 11, *Izri* [2]So with mss. and ancient versions, cf. v. 17 [3]Lit., *hands* [a]1 Chr. 16:41, 42
4 [1]In v. 18, *Azarel* [2]In v. 20, *Shubael*
5 [1]Lit., *lift up the horn* [a]2 Sam. 24:11; 1 Chr. 21:9
6 [1]Lit., *hands* [a]1 Chr. 15:16 [b]1 Chr. 15:19
7 [1]Lit., *brothers,* and so throughout the chap. [a]1 Chr. 23:5
8 [a]1 Chr. 26:13

18 the eleventh to Azarel, his sons
and his relatives, twelve;
19 the twelfth to Hashabiah, his
sons and his relatives, twelve;
20 for the thirteenth, Shubael, his
sons and his relatives, twelve;
21 for the fourteenth, Mattithiah,
his sons and his relatives, twelve;
22 for the fifteenth to Jeremoth,
his sons and his relatives, twelve;
23 for the sixteenth to Hananiah,
his sons and his relatives, twelve;
24 for the seventeenth to Joshbekashah, his sons and his relatives,
twelve;
25 for the eighteenth to Hanani,
his sons and his relatives, twelve;
26 for the nineteenth to Mallothi,
his sons and his relatives, twelve;
27 for the twentieth to Eliathah,
his sons and his relatives, twelve;
28 for the twenty-first to Hothir,
his sons and his relatives, twelve;
29 for the twenty-second to Giddalti, his sons and his relatives,
twelve;
30 for the twenty-third to Mahazioth, his sons and his relatives,
twelve;
31 for the twenty-fourth to Ro-
mamti-ezer, his sons and his relatives, twelve.

Chapter 26

Divisions of the Gatekeepers

FOR the divisions of the gatekeepers *there were* of the Korahites,
[1]Meshelemiah the son of Kore, of
the sons of [2]Asaph.
2 And Meshelemiah had sons:
Zechariah the first-born, Jediael the
second, Zebadiah the third, Jathniel
the fourth,
3 Elam the fifth, Johanan the
sixth, Eliehoenai the seventh.
4 And Obed-edom had sons:
Shemaiah the first-born, Jehozabad
the second, Joah the third, Sacar the
fourth, Nethanel the fifth,
5 Ammiel the sixth, Issachar the
seventh, *and* Peullethai the eighth;
God had indeed blessed him.
6 Also to his son Shemaiah sons
were born who ruled over the house
of their father, for they were mighty
men of valor.
7 The sons of Shemaiah *were*
Othni, Rephael, Obed, and Elzabad,
whose brothers, Elihu and Semachi-
ah, were valiant men.
8 All these *were* of the sons of
Obed-edom; they and their sons and
their [1]relatives *were* able men with
strength for the service, 62 from
Obed-edom.

1 [1]In v. 14, *Shelemiah* [2]In 9:19, *Ebiasaph*

8 [1]Lit., *brothers*, and so throughout the chap.

10 [a]1 Chr. 16:38

13 [a]1 Chr. 24:5, 31; 25:8

18 [1]Possibly *court* or *colonnade* [a]2 Kin. 23:11

20 [1]So Gk.; Heb., *As for the Levites, Ahijah had* [2]Lit., *were over* [a]1 Chr. 26:22, 24, 26; 28:12; Ezra 2:69

22 [1]Lit., *were over*

26 [1]Lit., *were over* [a]2 Sam. 8:11

9 And Meshelemiah had sons and
relatives, 18 valiant men.
10 Also [a]Hosah, *one* of the sons of
Merari had sons: Shimri the first (although he was not the first-born, his
father made him first),
11 Hilkiah the second, Tebaliah
the third, Zechariah the fourth; all
the sons and relatives of Hosah *were*
13.
12 To these divisions of the gatekeepers, the chief men, *were* given
duties like their relatives to minister
in the house of the LORD.
13 [a]And they cast lots, the small
and the great alike, according to
their fathers' households, for every
gate.
14 And the lot to the east fell to
Shelemiah. Then they cast lots *for*
his son Zechariah, a counselor with
insight, and his lot came out to the
north.
15 For Obed-edom *it fell* to the
south, and to his sons went the
storehouse.
16 For Shuppim and Hosah *it was*
to the west, by the gate of Shalle-
cheth, on the ascending highway.
Guard corresponded to guard.
17 On the east there were six Levites, on the north four daily, on the
south four daily, and at the storehouse two by two.
18 At the [1][a]Parbar on the west
there were four at the highway and
two at the Parbar.
19 These were the divisions of the
gatekeepers of the sons of Korah
and of the sons of Merari.

Keepers of the Treasure

20 [1]And the Levites, their relatives, [2]had [a]charge of the treasures
of the house of God, and of the treasures of the dedicated gifts.
21 The sons of Ladan, the sons of
the Gershonites belonging to Ladan,
namely, the Jehielites, *were* the
heads of the fathers' *households,* belonging to Ladan the Gershonite.
22 The sons of Jehieli, Zetham and
Joel his brother, [1]had charge of the
treasures of the house of the LORD.
23 As for the Amramites, the Izharites, the Hebronites, and the Uzzielites,
24 Shebuel the son of Gershom,
the son of Moses, was officer over
the treasures.
25 And his relatives by Eliezer
were Rehabiah his son, Jeshaiah his
son, Joram his son, Zichri his son,
and Shelomoth his son.
26 This Shelomoth and his relatives [1]had charge of all the treasures
of the dedicated gifts, [a]which King

David and the heads of the fathers' *households,* the commanders of thousands and hundreds, and commanders of the army, had dedicated.

27 They dedicated [1]part of the spoil won in battles to repair the house of the LORD.

28 And all that Samuel the seer had dedicated and Saul the son of Kish, Abner the son of Ner and Joab the son of Zeruiah, every one who had dedicated *any thing, all of this* was [1]in the care of [2]Shelomoth and his relatives.

Outside Duties

29 As for the Izharites, Chenaniah and his sons [a]were *assigned* to outside duties for Israel, as [b]officers and judges.

30 As for the Hebronites, [a]Hashabiah and his relatives, 1,700 capable men, had charge of the affairs of Israel [1]west of the Jordan, for all the work of the LORD and the service of the king.

31 As for the Hebronites, [a]Jerijah the chief [1](these Hebronites were investigated according to their genealogies and fathers' *households,* in the fortieth year of David's reign, and men of outstanding capability were found among them at [b]Jazer of Gilead)

32 and his relatives, capable men, *were* 2,700 in number, heads of fathers' *households.* And King David made them overseers of the Reubenites, the Gadites and the half-tribe of the Manassites [a]concerning [1]all the affairs of God and of the king.

CHAPTER 27

Commanders of the Army

NOW *this is* the enumeration of the sons of Israel, the heads of fathers' *households,* the commanders of thousands and of hundreds, and their officers who served the king in all the affairs of the divisions which came in and went out month by month throughout all the months of the year, each division *numbering* 24,000.

2 Jashobeam the son of Zabdiel [1a]had charge of the first division for the first month; and in his division *were* 24,000.

3 *He was* from the sons of Perez, *and was* chief of all the commanders of the army for the first month.

4 Dodai the Ahohite and his division had charge of the division for the second month, Mikloth *being* the chief officer; and in his division *were* 24,000.

5 The third commander of the army for the third month *was* Benaiah, the son of Jehoiada the priest, *as* chief; and in his division *were* 24,000.

6 This Benaiah *was* the mighty man of the thirty, and had charge of thirty; and over his division was Ammizabad his son.

7 The fourth for the fourth month *was* Asahel the brother of Joab, and Zebadiah his son after him; and in his division *were* 24,000.

8 The fifth for the fifth month *was* the commander Shamhuth the Izrahite; and in his division *were* 24,000.

9 The sixth for the sixth month *was* Ira the son of Ikkesh the Tekoite; and in his division *were* 24,000.

10 The seventh for the seventh month *was* Helez the Pelonite of the sons of Ephraim; and in his division *were* 24,000.

11 The eighth for the eighth month *was* Sibbecai the Hushathite of the Zerahites; and in his division *were* 24,000.

12 The ninth for the ninth month *was* Abiezer the Anathothite of the Benjamites; and in his division *were* 24,000.

13 The tenth for the tenth month *was* Maharai the Netophathite of the Zerahites; and in his division *were* 24,000.

14 The eleventh for the eleventh month *was* Benaiah the Pirathonite of the sons of Ephraim; and in his division *were* 24,000.

15 The twelfth for the twelfth month *was* Heldai the Netophathite of Othniel; and in his division *were* 24,000.

Chief Officers of the Tribes

16 Now in charge of the tribes of Israel: chief officer for the Reubenites was Eliezer the son of Zichri; for the Simeonites, Shephatiah the son of Maacah;

17 for Levi, Hashabiah the son of Kemuel; for Aaron, Zadok;

18 for Judah, Elihu, *one* of David's brothers; for Issachar, Omri the son of Michael;

19 for Zebulun, Ishmaiah the son of Obadiah; for Naphtali, Jeremoth the son of Azriel;

20 for the sons of Ephraim, Hoshea the son of Azaziah; for the half-tribe of Manasseh, Joel the son of Pedaiah;

21 for the half-tribe of Manasseh

27 [1]Heb., *from the battles and from the spoil*

28 [1]Lit., *under the hand* [2]Heb., *Shelomith*

29 [a]Neh. 11:16 [b]1 Chr. 23:4

30 [1]Lit., *beyond the Jordan westward* [a]1 Chr. 27:17

31 [1]Heb., *according to the Hebronites . . . father's households* [a]1 Chr. 23:19 [b]1 Chr. 6:81

32 [1]Lit., *every matter of God and matter of the king.* [a]2 Chr. 19:11

2 [1]Lit., *was over,* and so throughout the chap. [a]2 Sam. 23:8-30; 1 Chr. 11:11-31

in Gilead, Iddo the son of Zechariah;
for Benjamin, Jaasiel the son of Abner;
22 for Dan, Azarel the son of Jeroham. [a]These *were* the princes of the
tribes of Israel.
23 But David did not [1]count those
twenty years of age and under, [a]be-
cause the LORD had said He would
multiply Israel [b]as the stars of
heaven.
24 Joab the son of Zeruiah had begun to count *them,* but did not finish; and because of [a]this, wrath
came upon Israel, and the number
was not included in the account of
the chronicles of King David.

Various Overseers

25 Now Azmaveth the son of Adiel
had charge of the king's storehouses. And Jonathan the son of Uzziah had charge of the storehouses
in the country, in the cities, in the
villages, and in the towers.
26 And Ezri the son of Chelub had
charge of the [1]agricultural workers
who tilled the soil.
27 And Shimei the Ramathite had
charge of the vineyards; and Zabdi
the Shiphmite had charge of the
[1]produce of the vineyards *stored* in
the wine cellars.
28 And Baal-hanan the Gederite
had charge of the olive and [a]syca-
more trees in the [1]shephelah; and
Joash had charge of the stores of oil.
29 And Shitrai the Sharonite had
charge of the cattle which were
grazing in [a]Sharon; and Shaphat the
son of Adlai had charge of the cattle
in the valleys.
30 And Obil the Ishmaelite had
charge of the camels; and Jehdeiah
the Meronothite had charge of the
donkeys.
31 And Jaziz the [a]Hagrite had
charge of the flocks. All these were
[1]overseers of the property which belonged to King David.

Counselors

32 Also Jonathan, David's uncle,
was a counselor, a man of understanding, and a scribe; and Jehiel
the son of Hachmoni [1]tutored the
king's sons.
33 And [a]Ahithophel was counselor
to the king; and [b]Hushai the Archite
was the king's friend.
34 And Jehoiada the son of [a]Bena-
iah, and [b]Abiathar [1]succeeded
Ahithophel; and Joab was the [c]com-
mander of the king's army.

22 [a]1 Chr. 28:1

23 [1]Lit., *take their number from* [a]1 Chr. 21:2-5 [b]Gen. 15:5

24 [a]2 Sam. 24:12-15; 1 Chr. 21:1-7

26 [1]Lit., *doers of the work of the field for the tilling of...*

27 [1]Lit., *what was in the vineyards of the storehouses of wine*

28 [1]Or, *lowlands* [a]1 Kin. 10:27; 2 Chr. 1:15

29 [a]1 Chr. 5:16

31 [1]Or, *rulers* [a]1 Chr. 5:10

32 [1]Lit., was *with*

33 [a]2 Sam. 15:12 [b]2 Sam. 15:32, 37

34 [1]Lit., *after* [a]1 Chr. 27:5 [b]1 Kin. 1:7 [c]1 Chr. 11:6

1 [a]1 Chr. 23:2; 27:1-31 [b]1 Chr. 11:10-47

2 [1]Lit., *in my heart* [2]Lit., *house of rest* [a]1 Chr. 17:1, 2 [b]Ps. 132:7; Is. 66:1

3 [a]1 Chr. 22:8

4 [a]1 Sam. 16:6-13 [b]1 Chr. 17:23, 27 [c]Gen. 49:8-10; 1 Chr. 5:2 [d]1 Sam. 16:1

5 [a]1 Chr. 3:1-9; 14:3-7 [b]1 Chr. 22:9, 10

6 [a]2 Sam. 7:13, 14

7 [1]Lit., *at this day* [a]1 Chr. 22:13

9 [1]Or, *the same* [2]Lit., *soul* [a]1 Kin. 8:61; 1 Chr. 29:17-19 [b]1 Sam. 16:7 [c]2 Chr. 15:2; Jer. 29:13

CHAPTER 28

David's Address About the Temple

NOW [a]David assembled at Jerusalem all the officials of Israel, the
princes of the tribes, and the commanders of the divisions that served
the king, and the commanders of
thousands, and the commanders of
hundreds, and the overseers of all
the property and livestock belonging to the king and his sons, with the
officials and [b]the mighty men, even
all the valiant men.
2 Then King David rose to his
feet and said, "Listen to me, my
brethren and my people; I [a]*had* [1]in-
tended to build a [2]permanent home
for the ark of the covenant of the
LORD and for [b]the footstool of our
God. So I had made preparations to
build *it.*
3 "But God said to me, '[a]You shall
not build a house for My name because you are a man of war and
have shed blood.'
4 "Yet, the LORD, the God of Israel, [a]chose me from all the house of
my father to be king over Israel [b]for-
ever. For [c]He has chosen Judah to
be a leader; and [d]in the house of Judah, my father's house, and among
the sons of my father He took pleasure in me to make *me* king over all
Israel.
5 "And [a]of all my sons (for the
LORD has given me many sons), [b]He
has chosen my son Solomon to sit
on the throne of the kingdom of the
LORD over Israel.
6 "And He said to me, 'Your son
[a]Solomon is the one who shall build
My house and My courts; for I have
chosen him to be a son to Me, and I
will be a father to him.
7 'And I will establish his kingdom forever, [a]if he resolutely performs My commandments and My
ordinances, as [1]is done now.'
8 "So now, in the sight of all Israel,
the assembly of the LORD, and in the
hearing of our God, observe and
seek after all the commandments of
the LORD your God in order that you
may possess the good land and bequeath *it* to your sons after you forever.
9 "As for you, my son Solomon,
know the God of your father, and
[a]serve Him with [1]a whole heart and
a willing [2]mind; [b]for the LORD
searches all hearts, and understands
every intent of the thoughts. [c]If you
seek Him, He will let you find Him;
but if you forsake Him, He will reject you forever.

10"Consider now, for the LORD has
chosen you to build a house for the
sanctuary; [a]be courageous and act."
11 Then David gave to his son
Solomon [a]the plan of [b]the porch *of*
the temple, its buildings, its storehouses, its upper rooms, its inner
rooms, and [c]the room for the mercy
seat;
12 and the plan of all that he had in
[1]mind, for the courts of the house of
the LORD, and for all the surrounding rooms, for [a]the storehouses of
the house of God, and for the storehouses of the dedicated things;
13 also for [a]the divisions of the
priests and [b]the Levites and for all
the work of the service of the house
of the LORD and for all the utensils
of service in the house of the LORD;
14 for the golden *utensils,* the
weight of gold for all utensils for every kind of service; for the silver
utensils, the weight *of silver* for all
utensils for every kind of service;
15 and the weight *of gold* for the
[a]golden lampstands and their
golden lamps, with the weight of
each lampstand and its lamps; and
the weight of silver for the silver
lampstands, with the weight of each
lampstand and its lamps according
to the use of each lampstand;
16 and the gold by weight for the
tables of showbread, for each table;
and silver for the silver tables;
17 and the forks, the basins, and
the pitchers of pure gold; and for the
golden bowls with the weight for
each bowl; and for the silver bowls
with the weight for each bowl;
18 and for [a]the altar of incense refined gold by weight; and gold for
the model of the chariot, *even* [b]the
cherubim, that spread out *their*
wings, and covered the ark of the
covenant of the LORD.
19"All *this,*" *said David,* "the LORD
made me understand in writing by
His hand upon me, [a]all the [1]details
of this pattern."
20 Then David said to his son Solomon, "[a]Be strong and courageous,
and act; do not fear nor be dismayed, for the LORD God, my God,
is with you. [b]He will not fail you nor
forsake you until all the work for the
service of the house of the LORD is
finished.
21"Now behold, [a]*there are* the divisions of the priests and the Levites
for all the service of the house of
God, and [b]every willing man of any
skill will be with you in all the work
for all kinds of service. The officials
also and all the people will be entirely at your command."

CHAPTER 29

Offerings for the Temple

THEN King David said to the entire assembly, "My son Solomon,
whom alone God has chosen, [a]is still
young and inexperienced and the
work is great; for [b]the [1]temple is not
for man, but for the LORD God.
2"Now [a]with all my ability I have
provided for the house of my God
the gold for the *things of* gold, and
the silver for the *things of* silver, and
the bronze for the *things of* bronze,
the iron for the *things of* iron, and
wood for the *things of* wood, onyx
stones and inlaid *stones,* stones of
antimony, and stones of various colors, and all kinds of precious stones,
and alabaster in abundance.
3"And moreover, in my delight in
the house of my God, the treasure I
have of gold and silver, I give to the
house of my God, over and above all
that I have already provided for the
holy [1]temple,
4 *namely,* [a]3,000 talents of gold,
of [b]the gold of Ophir, and 7,000 talents of refined silver, to overlay the
walls of the [1]buildings;
5 of gold for the *things of* gold,
and of silver for the *things of* silver,
that is, for all the work [1]done by the
craftsmen. Who then is willing [2]to
consecrate himself this day to the
LORD?"
6 Then [a]the rulers of the fathers'
households, and the princes of the
tribes of Israel, and the commanders of thousands and of hundreds,
with [b]the overseers over the king's
work, offered willingly;
7 and for the service for the
house of God they gave 5,000 talents
and 10,000 [a]darics of gold, and
10,000 talents of silver, and 18,000
talents of brass, and 100,000 talents
of iron.
8 And [1]whoever possessed *pre-*
cious stones gave them to the treasury of the house of the LORD, [2]in
care of [a]Jehiel the Gershonite.
9 Then the people rejoiced because they had offered so willingly,
for they made their offering to the
LORD [a]with a whole heart, and King
David also rejoiced greatly.

David's Prayer

10 So David blessed the LORD in
the sight of all the assembly; and
David said, "Blessed art Thou, O

10 [a]1 Chr. 22:13
11 [a]Ex. 25:40; 1 Chr. 28:12, 19 [b]1 Kin. 6:3 [c]Ex. 25:17-22
12 [1]Lit., *the spirit with him* [a]1 Chr. 26:20, 28
13 [a]1 Chr. 24:1 [b]1 Chr. 23:6
15 [a]Ex. 25:31-39
18 [a]Ex. 30:1-10 [b]Ex. 25:18-22
19 [1]Lit., *works* [a]1 Chr. 28:11, 12
20 [a]1 Chr. 22:13 [b]Josh. 1:5; Heb. 13:5
21 [a]1 Chr. 28:13 [b]Ex. 35:25-35; 36:1, 2
1 [1]Lit., *palace* [a]1 Chr. 22:5 [b]1 Chr. 29:19
2 [a]1 Chr. 22:3-5
3 [1]Lit., *house*
4 [1]Lit., *houses* [a]1 Chr. 22:14 [b]1 Kin. 9:28
5 [1]Lit., *by the hand of the craftsmen* [2]Lit., *to fill his hand*
6 [a]1 Chr. 27:1; 28:1 [b]1 Chr. 27:25-31
7 [a]Ezra 2:69; Neh. 7:70
8 [1]Lit., *those with whom were found* [2]Lit., *under the hand of* [a]1 Chr. 23:8
9 [a]1 Kin. 8:61; 2 Cor. 9:7

LORD God of Israel our father, forever and ever.
11 "[a]Thine, O LORD, is the greatness
and the power and the glory and the
victory and the majesty, indeed everything that is in the heavens and
the earth; Thine is the dominion, O
LORD, and Thou dost exalt Thyself
as head over all.
12 "[a]Both riches and honor *come*
from Thee, and Thou dost rule over
all, and [b]in Thy hand is power and
might; and it lies in Thy hand to
make great, and to strengthen everyone.
13 "Now therefore, our God, we
thank Thee, and praise Thy glorious
name.
14 "But who am I and who are my
people that we should [1]be able to
offer as generously as this? For all
things come from Thee, and from
Thy hand we have given Thee.
15 "For [a]we are sojourners before
Thee, and tenants, as all our fathers
were; [b]our days on the earth are like
a shadow, and there is no hope.
16 "O LORD our God, all this abundance that we have provided to
build Thee a house for Thy holy
name, it is from Thy hand, and all is
Thine.
17 "Since I know, O my God, that
[a]Thou triest the heart and [b]delight-
est in uprightness, I, in the integrity
of my heart, have willingly offered
all these *things;* so now with joy I
have seen Thy people, who are present here, make *their* offerings willingly to Thee.
18 "O LORD, the God of Abraham,
Isaac, and Israel, our fathers, preserve this forever in the [1]intentions
of the heart of Thy people, and direct their heart to Thee;
19 "and [a]give to my son Solomon a
perfect heart to keep Thy commandments, Thy testimonies, and
Thy statutes, and to do *them* all, and
[b]to build the [1]temple, for which I
have made provision."
20 Then David said to all the assembly, "Now bless the LORD your
God." And [a]all the assembly blessed
the LORD, the God of their fathers,
and [b]bowed low and did homage to
the LORD and to the king.

Sacrifices

21 And on the next day [a]they
[1]made sacrifices to the LORD and offered burnt offerings to the LORD,
1,000 bulls, 1,000 rams *and* 1,000
lambs, with their libations and sacrifices in abundance for all Israel.
22 So they ate and drank that day
before the LORD with great gladness.

Solomon Again Made King

And they made Solomon the son
of David king [a]a second time, and
they [b]anointed *him* as ruler for the
LORD and Zadok as priest.
23 Then Solomon sat on the throne
of the LORD as king instead of David
his father; and he prospered, and all
Israel obeyed him.
24 And all the officials, the mighty
men, and also all the sons of King
David [1]pledged allegiance to King
Solomon.
25 And [a]the LORD highly exalted
Solomon in the sight of all Israel,
and [b]bestowed on him royal majesty which had not been on any king
before him in Israel.
26 Now [a]David the son of Jesse
reigned over all Israel.
27 [a]And the period which he
reigned over Israel *was* forty years;
he reigned in Hebron seven years
and [1]in Jerusalem thirty-three
years.

Death of David

28 Then he died in [a]a [1]ripe old age,
[b]full of days, riches and honor; and
his son Solomon reigned in his
place.
29 Now the acts of King David,
from first to last, are written in the
chronicles of [a]Samuel the seer, in
the chronicles of [b]Nathan the
prophet, and in the chronicles of
[c]Gad the seer,
30 with all his reign, his power,
and [a]the circumstances which came
on him, on Israel, and on all the
kingdoms of the lands.

11 [a]Rev. 5:13
12 [a]2 Chr. 1:12 [b]2 Chr. 20:6
14 [1]Lit., *retain strength*
15 [a]Lev. 25:23 [b]Job 14:2, 10-12
17 [a]1 Chr. 28:9 [b]Ps. 15:2
18 [1]Lit., *intent of the thoughts of the heart*
19 [1]Lit., *palace* [a]1 Chr. 28:9; Ps. 72:1 [b]1 Chr. 29:1, 2
20 [a]Josh. 22:33 [b]Ex. 4:31
21 [1]Lit., *sacrificed* [a]1 Kin. 8:62, 63
22 [a]1 Chr. 23:1 [b]1 Kin. 1:33-39
24 [1]Lit., *put a hand under Solomon*
25 [a]2 Chr. 1:1 [b]1 Kin. 3:13; 2 Chr. 1:12
26 [a]1 Chr. 18:14
27 [1]Lit., *he reigned in* [a]2 Sam. 5:4, 5; 1 Kin. 2:11
28 [1]Lit., *good* [a]Gen. 15:15; Acts 13:36 [b]1 Chr. 23:1
29 [a]1 Sam. 9:9 [b]2 Sam. 7:2-4; 12:1-7 [c]1 Sam. 22:5
30 [a]Dan. 4:23, 25

THE SECOND BOOK OF THE CHRONICLES

Solomon Worships at Gibeon

NOW [a]Solomon the son of David established himself securely over his kingdom, and the LORD his God *was* with him and [b]exalted him greatly.

2 And Solomon spoke to all Israel, [a]to the commanders of thousands and of hundreds and to the judges and to every leader in all Israel, the heads of the fathers' *households.*

3 Then Solomon, and all the assembly with him, went to [a]the high place which was at Gibeon; [b]for God's tent of meeting was there, which Moses the servant of the LORD had made in the wilderness.

4 However, David had brought up [a]the ark of God from Kiriath-jearim [1]to the place he had prepared for it; for he had pitched a tent for it in Jerusalem.

5 Now [a]the bronze altar, which Bezalel the son of Uri, the son of Hur, had made, [1]was there before the tabernacle of the LORD, and Solomon and the assembly sought it out.

6 And Solomon went up there before the LORD to the bronze altar which *was* at the tent of meeting, and [a]offered a thousand burnt offerings on it.

7 [a]In that night God appeared to Solomon and said to him, "Ask what I shall give you."

Solomon's Prayer for Wisdom

8 And Solomon said to God, "Thou hast dealt with my father David with great lovingkindness, and [a]hast made me king in his place.

9 "Now, O LORD God, [a]Thy [1]promise to my father David is fulfilled; for Thou hast made me king over [b]a people as numerous as the dust of the earth.

10 "Give me now wisdom and knowledge, [a]that I may go out and come in before this people; for who can rule this great people of Thine?"

11 And God said to Solomon, "Because [1]you had this in mind, and did not ask for riches, wealth, or honor, or the life of those who hate you, nor have you even asked for long life, but you have asked for yourself wisdom and knowledge, that you may rule My people, over whom I have made you king,

12 wisdom and knowledge have been granted to you. And [a]I will give you riches and wealth and honor, [1]such as none of the kings who were before you has possessed, nor those who will [2]come after you."

13 [a]So Solomon went [1]from the high place which was at Gibeon, from the tent of meeting, to Jerusalem, and he reigned over Israel.

Solomon's Wealth

14 [a]And Solomon amassed chariots and horsemen. [b]He had 1,400 chariots, and 12,000 horsemen, and he stationed them in [c]the chariot cities and with the king at Jerusalem.

15 And the king made silver and gold as plentiful in Jerusalem as stones, and he made cedars as plentiful as sycamores in the [1]lowland.

16 And Solomon's horses were imported from Egypt and from Kue; the king's traders procured them from Kue for a price.

17 And they [1]imported chariots from Egypt for 600 *shekels* of silver apiece, and horses for 150 apiece, and [2]by the same means they [3]exported them to all the kings of the Hittites and the kings of Aram.

CHAPTER 2

Solomon Will Build a Temple and Palace

[1a]

NOW Solomon [2]decided to build a house for the name of the LORD, and a [3]royal palace for himself.

2 [1]So [a]Solomon [2]assigned 70,000 men to carry loads, and 80,000 men to quarry *stone* in the mountains, and 3,600 to supervise them.

3 [a]Then Solomon sent *word* to [1]Huram the king of Tyre, saying, "[b]As you dealt with David my father, and sent him cedars to build him a house to dwell in, so do for me.

4 "Behold, I am about to build a house for the name of the LORD my God, dedicating it to Him, [a]to burn fragrant incense before Him, and *to set out* [b]the showbread continually, and to offer [c]burnt offerings morning and evening, [d]on sabbaths and on new moons and on the appointed feasts of the LORD our God, this *being required* forever in Israel.

---

1 [a]1 Kin. 2:12, 46 [b]1 Chr. 29:25

2 [a]1 Chr. 28:1

3 [a]1 Kin. 3:4 [b]Ex. 36:8

4 [1]Lit., *where David had prepared for it* [a]1 Chr. 15:25-28

5 [1]Lit., *he put* [a]Ex. 31:9; 38:1-7

6 [a]1 Kin. 3:4

7 [a]1 Kin. 3:5-14

8 [a]1 Chr. 28:5

9 [1]Lit., *word* [a]2 Sam. 7:12-16 [b]Gen. 13:16; 22:17

10 [a]2 Sam. 5:2

11 [1]Lit., *this was in your heart*

12 [1]Lit., *which was not so to the kings who were before you* [2]Lit., *be* [a]1 Chr. 29:25; 2 Chr. 9:22

13 [1]Lit., *to* [a]2 Chr. 1:3

14 [a]1 Kin. 10:26-29 [b]1 Kin. 4:26 [c]1 Kin. 9:19

15 [1]Or, *shephelah*

17 [1]Lit., *brought up and brought out* [2]Lit., *and in like manner by their hand* [3]Lit., *brought out*

1 [1]Ch. 1:18 in Heb. [2]Lit., *said* [3]Lit., *house for his royalty* [a]1 Kin. 5:5

2 [1]Ch. 2:1 in Heb. [2]Lit., *numbered* [a]1 Kin. 5:15, 16; 2 Chr. 2:18

3 [1]In 1 Kin. 5:18, *Hiram* [a]1 Kin. 5:2-11 [b]1 Chr. 14:1

4 [a]Ex. 30:7 [b]Ex. 25:30 [c]Ex. 29:38-42 [d]Num. 28:9, 10

5"And the house which I am
about to build *will be* great; for
[a]greater is our God than all the gods.
6"But [a]who is able to build a
house for Him, for the heavens and
the highest heavens cannot contain
Him? So who am I, that I should
build a house for Him, except to
[1]burn *incense* before Him?
7"And now [a]send me a skilled
man to work in gold, silver, brass
and iron, and in purple, crimson and
violet *fabrics,* and who knows how
to make engravings, to *work* with
the skilled men [1b]whom I have in
Judah and Jerusalem, whom David
my father provided.
8"Send me also cedar, cypress
and algum timber from Lebanon,
for I know that your servants know
how to cut timber of Lebanon; and
indeed, [a]my servants *will work* with
your servants,
9 to prepare timber in abundance
for me, for the house which I am
about to build *will be* great and
wonderful.
10"Now behold, I will give to your
servants, the woodsmen who cut
the timber, 20,000 [1]kors of crushed
wheat, and 20,000 [1]kors of barley,
and 20,000 baths of wine, and 20,000
baths of oil."

Huram to Assist

11 Then Huram, king of Tyre, [1]an-
swered in a letter sent to Solomon:
"[a]Because the LORD loves His people, He has made you king over
them."
12 Then Huram [1]continued,
"Blessed be [a]the LORD, the God of
Israel, who has made heaven and
earth, who has given King David a
wise son, [2]endowed with discretion
and understanding, [b]who will build
a house for the LORD and a [3]royal
palace for himself.
13"And now I am sending a skilled
man, [1]endowed with understanding,
Huram-abi,
14 [a]the son of a [1]Danite woman
and [2]a Tyrian father, who knows
how to work in gold, silver, bronze,
iron, stone and wood, *and* in purple,
violet, linen and crimson fabrics,
and *who knows how* to make all
kinds of engravings and to [3]execute
any design which may be assigned
to him, *to work* with your skilled
men, and with [4]those of my lord David your father.
15"Now then, let my lord send to
his servants wheat and barley, oil
and wine, of [a]which he has spoken.
16"And [a]we will cut whatever timber you need from Lebanon, and
bring it to you on rafts by sea to
Joppa, so that you may carry it up to
Jerusalem."
17 And Solomon numbered all the
aliens who *were* in the land of Israel,
[a]following the [1]census which his father David had [2]taken; and 153,600
were found.
18 [a]And he appointed 70,000 of
them to carry loads, and 80,000 to
quarry *stones* in the mountains, and
3,600 supervisors to make the people work.

CHAPTER 3

The Temple Construction in Jerusalem

[a]THEN Solomon began to build the
house of the LORD in Jerusalem on
Mount Moriah, where *the LORD* had
appeared to his father David, at the
place that David had prepared, [b]on
the threshing floor of Ornan the
Jebusite.
2 And he began to build on the
second *day* in the second month [1]of
the fourth year of his reign.

Dimensions and Materials of the Temple

3 Now these are the [1]foundations
which Solomon laid for building the
house of God. The length in [2]cubits,
according to the old standard *was*
sixty cubits, and the width twenty
cubits.
4 And the porch which was in
front of the house [1]was as long as
the width of the house, twenty cubits, and the height 120; and inside
he overlaid it with pure gold.
5 And he overlaid [a]the [1]main
room with cypress wood and overlaid it with fine gold, and [2]orna-
mented it with palm trees and
chains.
6 Further, he [1]adorned the house
with precious stones; and the gold
was gold from [2]Parvaim.
7 [a]He also overlaid the house
with gold—the beams, the thresholds, and its walls, and its doors; and
he [b]carved cherubim on the walls.
8 Now he made [a]the [1]room of the
holy of holies: its length, across the
width of the house, *was* twenty cubits, and its width *was* twenty cubits; and he overlaid it with fine
gold, *amounting* to 600 talents.
9 And the weight of the nails was
fifty shekels of gold. He also overlaid [a]the upper rooms with gold.
10 [a]Then he made two [1]sculptured
cherubim in the room of the holy of
holies and overlaid them with gold.

5 [a]Ex. 15:11; 1 Chr. 16:25
6 [1]Lit., *offer up in smoke* [a]1 Kin. 8:27; 2 Chr. 6:18
7 [1]Lit., *who are with me* [a]Ex. 31:3-5; 2 Chr. 2:13, 14 [b]1 Chr. 22:15
8 [a]2 Chr. 9:10, 11
10 [1]A kor equals approx. 10 bu.
11 [1]Lit., *said . . . and he sent* [a]1 Kin. 10:9; 2 Chr. 9:8
12 [1]Lit., *said* [2]Lit., *knowing discretion* [3]Lit., *house for his royalty* [a]Ps. 33:6; 102:25 [b]2 Chr. 2:1
13 [1]Lit., *knowing understanding*
14 [1]Lit., *a woman of the daughters of Dan* [2]Lit., *whose father is a Tyrean man* [3]Lit., *devise any device* [4]Lit., *skilled men* [a]1 Kin. 7:14
15 [a]2 Chr. 2:10
16 [a]1 Kin. 5:8, 9
17 [1]Lit., *numbering* [2]Lit., *numbered of them* [a]1 Chr. 22:2
18 [a]2 Chr. 2:2
1 [a]1 Kin. 6:1 [b]1 Chr. 21:18
2 [1]Lit., *in*
3 [1]Lit., *founding of Solomon to build* [2]I.e., One cubit equals approx. 18 inches
4 [1]1 Kin. 6:3
5 [1]Lit., *great house* [2]Lit., *put on it palm trees* [a]1 Kin. 6:17
6 [1]Lit., *overlaid . . . for beauty* [2]Or, *country of gold*
7 [a]1 Kin. 6:20-22 [b]1 Kin. 6:29-35
8 [1]Lit., *house* [a]Ex. 26:33; 1 Kin. 6:16
9 [a]1 Chr. 28:11
10 [1]Lit., *cherubim of sculptured work* [a]1 Kin. 6:23-28

11 And the wingspan of the cherubim *was* twenty cubits; the wing of one, of five cubits, touched the wall of the house, and *its* other wing, of five cubits, touched the wing of the other cherub.

12 And the wing of the other cherub, of five cubits, touched the wall of the house; and *its* other wing of five cubits, was attached to the wing of the [1]first cherub.

13 The wings of these cherubim extended twenty cubits, and they stood on their feet [1]facing the *main* room.

14 [a]And he made the veil of violet, purple, crimson and fine linen, and he worked cherubim on it.

15 [a]He also made two pillars for the front of the house, thirty-five cubits [1]high, and the capital on the top of each *was* five cubits.

16 And he made chains in the inner sanctuary, and placed *them* on the tops of the pillars; and he made one hundred pomegranates and placed *them* on the chains.

17 [a]And he erected the pillars in front of the temple, one on the right and the other on the left, and named the one on the right Jachin and the one on the left Boaz.

Chapter 4

Furnishings of the Temple

THEN [a]he made a bronze altar, twenty cubits in length and twenty cubits in width and ten cubits in height.

2 [a]Also he made the cast *metal* sea, ten cubits from brim to brim, circular in form, and its height *was* five cubits and [1]its circumference thirty cubits.

3 Now figures like oxen *were* under it *and* all around it, ten cubits, entirely encircling the sea. The oxen *were* in two rows, cast [1]in one piece.

4 It stood on twelve oxen, three facing the north, three facing west, three facing south, and three facing east; and the sea *was set* on top of them, and all their hindquarters turned inwards.

5 And it was a handbreadth thick, and its brim was made like the brim of a cup, *like* a lily blossom; it [a]could hold 3,000 baths.

6 [a]He also made ten basins in which to wash, and he set five on the right side and five on the left, [1]to rinse things for the burnt offering; but the sea *was* for the priests to wash in.

7 Then [a]he made the ten golden lampstands in the way prescribed for them, and he set them in the temple, five on the right side and five on the left.

8 He also made [a]ten tables and placed them in the temple, five on the right side and five on the left. And he made one hundred golden bowls.

9 Then he made [a]the court of the priests and [b]the great court and doors for the court, and overlaid their doors with bronze.

10 And [a]he set the sea on the right [1]side *of the house* toward the southeast.

11 [a]Huram also made the pails, the shovels, and the bowls. So Huram finished doing the work which he performed for King Solomon in the house of God:

12 the two pillars, the bowls and the two capitals on top of the pillars, and the two networks to cover the two bowls of the capitals which were on top of the pillars,

13 and [a]the four hundred pomegranates for the two networks, two rows of pomegranates for each network to cover the two bowls of the capitals which were on the pillars.

14 [a]He also made the stands and he made the basins on the stands,

15 *and* the one sea with the twelve oxen under it.

16 And the pails, the shovels, the forks, and all its utensils, [a]Huram-abi made of polished bronze for King Solomon for the house of the LORD.

17 On the plain of the Jordan the king cast them, in the clay ground between Succoth and Zeredah.

18 [a]Thus Solomon made all these utensils in great quantities, for the weight of the bronze could not be found out.

19 Solomon also made all the things that *were* in the house of God: even the golden altar, [a]the tables with the bread of the Presence on them,

20 the lampstands with their lamps of pure gold, [a]to burn in front of the inner sanctuary in the way prescribed;

21 the flowers, the lamps, and the tongs of gold, of purest gold;

22 and the snuffers, the bowls, the spoons, and the firepans of pure gold; and the entrance of the house, its inner doors for the holy of holies, and the doors of the house, *that is,* of the nave, of gold.

12 [1]Lit., *other*
13 [1]Lit., *and their faces to*
14 [a]Ex. 26:31
15 [1]Lit., *long* [a]1 Kin. 7:15-20
17 [a]1 Kin. 7:21
1 [a]Ex. 27:1, 2; 2 Kin. 16:14
2 [1]Lit., *a line of 30 cubits encircling it round about* [a]1 Kin. 7:23-26
3 [1]Lit., *in its casting*
5 [a]1 Kin. 7:26
6 [1]Lit., *in which to* [a]1 Kin. 7:38, 40
7 [a]1 Kin. 7:49
8 [a]1 Kin. 7:48
9 [a]1 Kin. 6:36 [b]2 Kin. 21:5
10 [1]Lit., *shoulder* [a]1 Kin. 7:39
11 [a]1 Kin. 7:40-51
13 [a]1 Kin. 7:20
14 [a]1 Kin. 7:27-43
16 [a]1 Kin. 7:14; 2 Chr. 2:13
18 [a]1 Kin. 7:47
19 [a]2 Chr. 4:8
20 [a]Ex. 25:31-37; 2 Chr. 5:7

Chapter 5

The Ark Is Brought into the Temple

THUS all the work that Solomon performed for the house of the LORD was finished. And Solomon brought in the [1]things that David his father had dedicated, even the silver and the gold and all the utensils, *and* put *them* in the treasuries of the house of God.

2 [a]Then Solomon assembled to Jerusalem the elders of Israel and all the heads of the tribes, the leaders of the fathers' *households* of the sons of Israel, to bring up the ark of the covenant of the LORD out [b]of the city of David, which is Zion.

3 And all the men of Israel assembled themselves to the king at the feast, that is *in* the seventh month.

4 Then all the elders of Israel came, and [a]the Levites took up the ark.

5 And they brought up the ark and the tent of meeting and all the holy utensils which *were* in the tent; the Levitical priests brought them up.

6 And King Solomon and all the congregation of Israel who were assembled with him before the ark were sacrificing [1]so many sheep and oxen, that they could not be counted or numbered.

7 Then the priests brought the ark of the covenant of the LORD to its place, into the inner sanctuary of the house, to the holy of holies, under the wings of the cherubim.

8 For the cherubim spread their wings over the place of the ark, so that the cherubim made a covering over the ark and its [1]poles.

9 And the poles were so long that [a]the ends of the poles of the ark could be seen in front of the inner sanctuary, but they could not be seen outside; and [1]they are there to this day.

10 [a]There was nothing in the ark except the two tablets which Moses put *there* at Horeb, where the LORD made a covenant with the sons of Israel, when they came out of Egypt.

The Glory of God Fills the Temple

11 And when the priests came forth from the holy place (for all the priests who were present had sanctified themselves, without regard [a]to divisions),

12 and all the Levitical singers, [a]Asaph, Heman, Jeduthun, and their sons and kinsmen, clothed in fine linen, [b]with cymbals, harps, and lyres, standing east of the altar, and with them one hundred and twenty priests [c]blowing trumpets

13 in unison when the trumpeters and the singers were to make themselves heard with one voice to praise and to glorify the LORD, and when they lifted up their voice [a]accompanied by trumpets and cymbals and instruments of music, and when they praised the LORD *saying*, "[b]*He* indeed is good for His lovingkindness is everlasting," then the house, the house of the LORD, was filled with a cloud,

14 so that the priests could not stand to minister because of the cloud, for [a]the glory of the LORD filled the house of God.

Chapter 6

Solomon's Dedication

[a]THEN Solomon said,

"The LORD has said that He
would dwell in the thick
cloud.

2 "I have built Thee a lofty house,
And a place for Thy dwelling
forever."

3 Then the king [1]faced about and blessed all the assembly of Israel, while all the assembly of Israel was standing.

4 And he said, "Blessed be the LORD, the God of Israel, who spoke with His mouth to my father David and has fulfilled *it* with His hands, saying,

5 'Since the day that I brought My people from the land of Egypt, I did not choose a city out of all the tribes of Israel *in which* to build a house that My name might be there, nor did I choose any man for a leader over My people Israel;

6 but [a]I have chosen Jerusalem that My name might be there, and I [b]have chosen David to be over My people Israel.'

7 "[a]Now it was [1]in the heart of my father David to build a house for the name of the LORD, the God of Israel.

8 "But the LORD said to my father David, 'Because it was [1]in your heart to build a house for My name, you did well that it was [1]in your heart.

9 'Nevertheless you shall not build the house, but your son who [1]shall be born to you, he shall build the house for My name.'

10 "Now the LORD has fulfilled His word which He spoke; for I have risen in the place of my father David

---

Ch. 5: 1 [1]Lit., *dedicated things of David,*
2 [a]1 Kin. 8:1-9 [b]2 Chr. 1:4
4 [a]2 Chr. 5:7
6 [1]Lit., *sheep... numbered for multitude*
8 [1]Lit., *poles above*
9 [1]Lit., *it is* [a]1 Kin. 8:8, 9
10 [a]Deut. 10:2-5; Heb. 9:4
11 [a]1 Chr. 24:1-5
12 [a]1 Chr. 25:1-4 [b]1 Chr. 13:8; 15:16, 24 [c]2 Chr. 7:6
13 [a]1 Chr. 16:42 [b]1 Chr. 16:34; 2 Chr. 7:3
14 [a]1 Kin. 8:11

Ch. 6: 1 [a]1 Kin. 8:12-50
3 [1]Lit., *turned his face about*
6 [a]2 Chr. 12:13 [b]1 Chr. 28:4
7 [1]Lit., *with* [a]1 Kin. 5:3
8 [1]Lit., *with*
9 [1]Lit., *is to come forth from your loins*

and sit on the throne of Israel, as the
LORD [1]promised, and have built the
house for the name of the LORD, the
God of Israel.
11 "And there I have set the ark, [a]in
which is the covenant of the LORD,
which He made with the sons of Israel."

Solomon's Prayer of Dedication

12 Then he stood before the altar
of the LORD in the presence of all the
assembly of Israel and spread out
his hands.
13 [a]Now Solomon had made a
bronze platform, five cubits long,
five cubits wide, and three cubits
high, and had set it in the midst of
the court; and he stood on it, [b]knelt
on his knees in the presence of all
the assembly of Israel, and spread
out his hands toward heaven.
14 And he said, "O LORD, the God
of Israel, [a]there is no god like Thee
in heaven or on earth, [b]keeping covenant and showing lovingkindness
to Thy servants who walk before
Thee with all their heart;
15 [a]who has kept with Thy servant
David, my father, that which Thou
hast [1]promised him; indeed, Thou
hast spoken with Thy mouth, and
hast fulfilled it with Thy hand, as it
is this day.
16 "Now therefore, O LORD, the
God of Israel, keep with Thy servant
David, my father, that which Thou
hast [1]promised him, saying, '[2a]You
shall not lack a man to sit on the
throne of Israel, if only your sons
take heed to their way, to walk in
My law as you have walked before
Me.'
17 "Now therefore, O LORD, the
God of Israel, let Thy word be confirmed which Thou hast spoken to
Thy servant David.
18 "But will God indeed dwell with
mankind on the earth? Behold,
[a]heaven and the [1]highest heaven
cannot contain Thee; how much less
this house which I have built.
19 "Yet have regard to the prayer of
Thy servant and to his supplication,
O LORD my God, to listen to the cry
and to the prayer which Thy servant
prays before Thee;
20 that Thine eyes may be open
toward this house day and night,
toward the place of which Thou hast
said that *Thou wouldst* put Thy
name there, to listen to the prayer
which Thy servant shall pray
toward this place.
21 "And listen to the supplications
of Thy servant and of Thy people
Israel, when they pray toward this
place; hear Thou from Thy dwelling
place, from heaven; [a]hear Thou and
forgive.
22 "If a man sins against his neighbor, and is made to take an oath, and
he comes *and* takes an oath before
Thine altar in this house;
23 then hear Thou from heaven
and act and judge Thy servants,
[1]punishing the wicked by bringing
his way on his own head and justifying the righteous by giving him according to his righteousness.
24 "And if Thy people Israel [1]are
defeated before an enemy, because
they have sinned against Thee, and
they return *to Thee* and confess Thy
name, and pray and make supplication before Thee in this house;
25 then hear Thou from heaven
and forgive the sin of Thy people Israel, and bring them back to the
land which Thou hast given to them
and to their fathers.
26 "When the heavens are shut up
and there is no rain because they
have sinned against Thee, and they
pray toward this place and confess
Thy name, and turn from their sin
when Thou dost afflict them;
27 then hear Thou in heaven and
forgive the sin of Thy servants and
Thy people Israel, indeed, teach
them the good way in which they
should walk. And send rain on Thy
land, which Thou hast given to Thy
people for an inheritance.
28 "If there is famine in the land, if
there is pestilence, if there is blight
or mildew, if there is locust or grasshopper, if their enemies besiege
them in the land of their [1]cities,
whatever plague or whatever sickness *there is*,
29 whatever prayer or supplication is made by any man or by all
Thy people Israel, [1]each knowing
his own affliction and his own pain,
and spreading his hands toward this
house,
30 then hear Thou from heaven
Thy dwelling place, and forgive, and
render to each according to all his
ways, whose heart Thou knowest
[a]for Thou alone dost know the
hearts of the sons of men,
31 that they may [1]fear Thee, to
walk in Thy ways [2]as long as they
live in the land which Thou hast giv-
en to our fathers.
32 "Also concerning the foreigner
who is not from Thy people Israel,
when he comes from a far country
for Thy great name's sake and Thy
mighty hand and Thine outstretched arm, when they come and
pray toward this house,

10 [1]Lit., *spoke*
11 [a]2 Chr. 5:7, 10
13 [a]Neh. 8:4 [b]1 Kin. 8:54
14 [a]Ex. 15:11; Deut. 3:24 [b]Deut. 7:9
15 [1]Lit., *spoken to* [a]1 Chr. 22:9, 10
16 [1]Lit., *spoken to* [2]Lit., *there shall not be cut off to you a man from before Me* [a]1 Kin. 2:4; 2 Chr. 7:18
18 [1]Lit., *heaven of heavens* [a]2 Chr. 2:6
21 [a]Mic. 7:18
23 [1]Lit., *returning*
24 [1]Lit., *smitten*
28 [1]Lit., *gates*
29 [1]Lit., *whoever shall know*
30 [a]1 Sam. 16:7; 1 Chr. 28:9
31 [1]Or, *reverence* [2]Lit., *all the days that they live on the face of the land*

33 then hear Thou from heaven,
from Thy dwelling place, and do according to all for which the foreigner calls to Thee, in order that all
the peoples of the earth may know
Thy name, and [1]fear Thee, as *do* Thy
people Israel, and that they may
know that [2]this house which I have
built is [a]called by Thy name.
34 "When Thy people go out to battle against their enemies, by whatever way Thou shalt send them, and
they pray to Thee toward this city
which Thou hast chosen, and the
house which I have built for Thy
name,
35 then hear Thou from heaven
their prayer and their supplication,
and maintain their cause.
36 "When they sin against Thee
([a]for there is no man who does not
sin) and Thou art angry with them
and dost deliver them to an enemy,
so that [1]they take them away captive to a land far off or near,
37 if they [1]take thought in the land
where they are taken captive, and
repent and make supplication to
Thee in the land of their captivity,
saying, 'We have sinned, we have
committed iniquity, and have acted
wickedly';
38 if they return to Thee with all
their heart and with all their soul in
the land of their captivity, where
they have been taken captive, and
pray toward their land which Thou
hast given to their fathers, and the
city which Thou hast chosen, and
toward the house which I have built
for Thy name,
39 then hear from heaven, from
Thy dwelling place, their prayer and
supplications, and maintain their
cause, and forgive Thy people who
have sinned against Thee.
40 "Now, O my God, I pray Thee,
[a]let Thine eyes be open, and [b]Thine
ears attentive to the prayer *offered*
in this place.
41 "[a]Now therefore arise, O LORD
God, to Thy resting place, Thou and
the ark of Thy might; let Thy priests,
O LORD God, be clothed with salvation, and let Thy godly ones rejoice
in what is good.
42 "O LORD God, do not turn away
the face of Thine anointed; remember *Thy* lovingkindness to Thy servant David."

CHAPTER 7

The Shekinah Glory

[a]NOW when Solomon had finished
praying, [b]fire came down from
heaven and consumed the burnt offering and the sacrifices; and the
glory of the LORD filled the house.
2 And the priests could not enter
into the house of the LORD, because
the glory of the LORD filled the
LORD's house.
3 And all the sons of Israel, seeing the fire come down and the glory
of the LORD upon the house, bowed
down on the pavement with their
faces to the ground, and they worshiped and gave praise to the LORD,
saying, "[a]Truly He is good, truly His
lovingkindness is everlasting."

Sacrifices Offered

4 [a]Then the king and all the people offered sacrifice before the
LORD.
5 And King Solomon offered a
sacrifice of 22,000 oxen, and 120,000
sheep. Thus the king and all the people dedicated the house of God.
6 And the priests stood at their
posts and [a]the Levites, with the instruments of music to the LORD,
which King David had made for giving praise to the LORD—"for His
lovingkindness is everlasting"—
whenever [1]he gave praise by their
[2]means, while [b]the priests on the
other side blew trumpets; and all Israel was standing.
7 [a]Then Solomon consecrated
the middle of the court that *was* before the house of the LORD, for there
he offered the burnt offerings and
the fat of the peace offerings, because the bronze altar which Solomon had made was not able to contain the burnt offering, the grain
offering, and the fat.

The Feast of Dedication

8 So Solomon observed the feast
at that time for seven days, and all
Israel with him, a very great assembly, *who came* [a]from the entrance of
Hamath to the brook of Egypt.
9 And on the eighth day they held
[a]a solemn assembly, for the dedication of the altar they observed seven
days, and the feast seven days.
10 Then on the twenty-third day of
the seventh month he sent the people to their tents, rejoicing and happy of heart because of the goodness
that the LORD had shown to David
and to Solomon and to His people
Israel.

God's Promise and Warning

11 [a]Thus Solomon finished the
house of the LORD and the king's
palace, and successfully completed
all that [1]he had planned on doing in

---

33 [1]Or, *reverence* [2]Lit., *Thy name is called upon this house* [a]2 Chr. 7:14
36 [1]Lit., *their captors take them captive* [a]Job 15:14-16; James 3:2; 1 John 1:8-10
37 [1]Lit., *return to their heart*
40 [a]2 Chr. 7:15; Neh. 1:6, 11 [b]Ps. 17:1
41 [a]Ps. 132:8, 9
1 [a]1 Kin. 8:54 [b]1 Kin. 18:24, 38
3 [a]2 Chr. 5:13; 20:21
4 [a]1 Kin. 8:62, 63
6 [1]Lit., *David* [2]Lit., *hand* [a]1 Chr. 15:16-21 [b]2 Chr. 5:12
7 [a]1 Kin. 8:64-66
8 [a]1 Kin. 8:65
9 [a]Lev. 23:36
11 [1]Lit., *came upon the heart of Solomon to do* [a]1 Kin. 9:1-9

the house of the LORD and in his palace.
12 Then the LORD appeared to
Solomon at night and said to him, "I
have heard your prayer, and [a]have
chosen this place for Myself as a
house of sacrifice.
13"[a]If I shut up the heavens so that
there is no rain, or if I command the
locust to devour the land, or if I send
pestilence among My people,
14 [a]and My people [1]who are called
by My name humble themselves
and pray, and seek My face and turn
from their wicked ways, then I will
hear from heaven, will forgive their
sin, and will heal their land.
15"[a]Now My eyes shall be open
and My ears attentive to the [1]prayer
offered in this place.
16"For [a]now I have chosen and
consecrated this house that My
name may be there forever, and My
eyes and My heart will be there perpetually.
17"And as for you, if you walk before Me as your father David
walked even to do according to all
that I have commanded you and will
keep My statutes and My ordinances,
18 then I will establish your royal
throne as I covenanted with your father David, saying, '[1a]You shall not
lack a man *to be* ruler in Israel.'
19"[a]But if you turn away and forsake My statutes and My commandments which I have set before you
and shall go and serve other gods
and worship them,
20 [a]then I will uproot you from My
land which I have given [1]you, and
this house which I have consecrated
for My name I will cast out of My
sight, and I will make it [b]a proverb
and a byword among all peoples.
21"As for this house, which was
exalted, everyone who passes by it
will be astonished and say, '[a]Why
has the LORD done thus to this land
and to this house?'
22"And they will say, 'Because
they forsook the LORD, the God of
their fathers, who brought them
from the land of Egypt, and they
adopted other gods and worshiped
them and served them, therefore He
has brought all this adversity on
them.'"

CHAPTER 8

Solomon's Activities and Accomplishments

[a]
NOW it came about at the end of
the twenty years in which Solomon
had built the house of the LORD and
his own house
2 that he built the cities which
Huram had given to [1]him, and settled the sons of Israel there.
3 Then Solomon went to Ha-
math-zobah and captured it.
4 And he built Tadmor in the wilderness and all the storage cities
which he had built in Hamath.
5 He also built upper [a]Beth-horon
and lower Beth-horon, [b]fortified
cities *with* walls, gates, and bars;
6 and Baalath and all the storage
cities that Solomon had, and all the
cities for [1]his chariots and cities for
[1]his horsemen, and all that it
pleased Solomon to build in Jerusalem, in Lebanon, and in all the land
[2]under his rule.
7 [a]All of the people who were left
of the Hittites, the Amorites, the Perizzites, the Hivites, and the Jebusites, who were not of Israel,
8 namely, from their descendants
who were left after them in the land
whom the sons of Israel had not destroyed, [a]them Solomon raised as
forced laborers to this day.
9 But Solomon did not make
slaves for his work from the sons of
Israel; they were men of war, his
chief captains, and commanders of
his chariots and his horsemen.
10 And these were the chief [1]offi-
cers of King Solomon, two hundred
and fifty who ruled over the people.
11 [a]Then Solomon brought Pharaoh's daughter up from the city of
David to the house which he had
built for her; for he said, "My wife
shall not dwell in the house of David
king of Israel, because [1]the places
are holy where the ark of the LORD
has entered."
12 Then Solomon offered burnt offerings to the LORD on [a]the altar of
the LORD which he had built before
the porch;
13 and [a]*did* so according to the
daily rule, offering *them* up [b]accord-
ing to the commandment of Moses,
for the sabbaths, the new moons,
and the [c]three annual feasts—the
Feast of Unleavened Bread, the
Feast of Weeks, and the Feast of
Booths.
14 Now according to the ordinance of his father David, he appointed [a]the divisions of the priests
for their service, and [b]the Levites
for their duties of praise and ministering before the priests according
to the daily rule, and [c]the gatekeepers by their divisions at every gate;
for [d]David the man of God had so
commanded.

12 [a]Deut. 12:5, 11
13 [a]2 Chr. 6:26-28
14 [1]Lit., *over whom My name is called* [a]2 Chr. 6:37-39
15 [1]Lit., *prayer of this place* [a]2 Chr. 6:20, 40
16 [a]2 Chr. 7:12
18 [1]Lit., *there shall not be cut off to you a man* [a]2 Chr. 6:16
19 [a]Lev. 26:14, 33; Deut. 28:15
20 [1]Ancient versions, Heb. read, *them* [a]Deut. 29:28; 1 Kin. 14:15 [b]Deut. 28:37
21 [a]Deut. 29:24, 25
1 [a]1 Kin. 9:1-28
2 [1]Lit., *Solomon*
5 [a]1 Chr. 7:24 [b]2 Chr. 14:7
6 [1]Lit., *the* [2]Lit., *of*
7 [a]Gen. 15:18-21
8 [a]1 Kin. 4:6; 9:21
10 [1]Or, *deputies*
11 [1]Lit., *they are* [a]1 Kin. 3:1; 7:8
12 [a]2 Chr. 4:1
13 [a]Ex. 29:38-42 [b]Num. 28:3 [c]Ex. 23:14-17
14 [a]1 Chr. 24:1 [b]1 Chr. 25:1 [c]1 Chr. 26:1 [d]Neh. 12:24, 36

15 And they did not depart from
the commandment of the king to the
priests and Levites in any manner or
concerning the storehouses.
16 Thus all the work of Solomon
was carried out [1]from the day of the
foundation of the house of the LORD,
and until it was finished. So the
house of the LORD was completed.
17 Then Solomon went to [a]Ezion-
geber and to [b]Eloth on the seashore
in the land of Edom.
18 And Huram by his servants
sent him ships and servants who
knew the sea; and they went with
Solomon's servants to Ophir, and
[a]took from there four hundred and
fifty talents of gold, and brought
them to King Solomon.

CHAPTER 9

Visit of the Queen of Sheba

[a]NOW when the queen of Sheba
heard of the fame of Solomon, she
came to Jerusalem to test Solomon
with difficult questions. She had a
very large retinue, with camels carrying spices, and a large amount of
gold and precious stones; and when
she came to Solomon, she spoke
with him about all that was on her
heart.
2 And Solomon [1]answered all her
questions; nothing was hidden from
Solomon which he did not [2]explain
to her.
3 And when the queen of Sheba
had seen the wisdom of Solomon,
the house which he had built,
4 the food at his table, the seating
of his servants, the attendance of his
ministers and their attire, his cup-
bearers and their attire, and [1]his
stairway by which he went up to the
house of the LORD, she was breath-
less.
5 Then she said to the king, "It
was a true report which I heard in
my own land about your words and
your wisdom.
6"Nevertheless I did not believe
their reports until I came and my
eyes had seen it. And behold, the
half of the greatness of your wisdom
was not told me. You surpass the
report that I heard.
7"How [1]blessed are your men,
how [1]blessed are these your servants who stand before you continually and hear your wisdom.
8"Blessed be the LORD your God
who delighted in you, [a]setting you
on His throne as king for the LORD
your God; [b]because your God loved
Israel establishing them forever,
therefore He made you king over
them, to do justice and righteousness."
9 Then she gave the king one
hundred and twenty talents of gold,
and a very great *amount of* spices
and precious stones; there had never been spice like that which the
queen of Sheba gave to King Solomon.
10 And the servants of Huram and
the servants of Solomon [a]who
brought gold from Ophir, also
brought algum trees and precious
stones.
11 And from the algum the king
made steps for the house of the
LORD and for the king's palace, and
lyres and harps for the singers; and
none like that was seen before in the
land of Judah.
12 And King Solomon gave to the
queen of Sheba all her desire which
she requested besides *a return for*
what she had brought to the king.
Then she turned and went to her
own land with her servants.

Solomon's Wealth and Power

13 [a]Now the weight of gold which
came to Solomon in one year was
666 talents of gold,
14 besides that which the traders
and merchants brought; and all the
kings of Arabia and the governors of
the country brought gold and silver
to Solomon.
15 And King Solomon made 200
large shields of beaten gold, [1]using
600 *shekels of* beaten gold on each
large shield.
16 And *he made* 300 shields of
beaten gold, [1]using three hundred
shekels of gold on each shield, and
the king put them in the house of the
forest of Lebanon.
17 Moreover, the king made a
great throne of ivory and overlaid it
with pure gold.
18 And *there were* six steps to the
throne and a footstool in gold attached to the throne, and [1]arms [2]on
each side of the seat, and two lions
standing beside the [1]arms.
19 And twelve lions were standing
there on the six steps on the one side
and on the other; nothing like *it* was
made for any *other* kingdom.
20 And all King Solomon's drinking vessels *were* of gold, and all the
vessels of the house of the forest of
Lebanon *were* of pure gold; silver
was not considered [1]valuable in the
days of Solomon.
21 [a]For the king had ships which
went to Tarshish with the servants
of Huram; once every three years

16 [1]So ancient versions; M.T., *as far as*
17 [a]1 Kin. 9:26 [b]2 Kin. 14:22
18 [a]2 Chr. 9:10, 13
1 [a]1 Kin. 10:1-13; Matt. 12:42; Luke 11:31
2 [1]Lit., *told her all her words* [2]Lit., *tell*
4 [1]Or, *his burnt offering which he offered*
7 [1]Or, *happy*
8 [a]1 Chr. 28:5; 29:23 [b]Deut. 7:8; 2 Chr. 2:11
10 [a]2 Chr. 8:18
13 [a]1 Kin. 10:14-28
15 [1]Lit., *he brought up*
16 [1]Lit., *he brought up*
18 [1]Lit., *hands* [2]Lit., *on this side and on this at the place of the seat*
20 [1]Lit., *anything*
21 [a]2 Chr. 20:36, 37

the ships of Tarshish came bringing
gold and silver, ivory and apes and
peacocks.
22 [a]So King Solomon became
greater than all the kings of the
earth in riches and wisdom.
23 And all the kings of the earth
were seeking the presence of Solomon, to hear his wisdom which God
had put in his heart.
24 And they brought every man
his gift, articles of silver and gold,
garments, weapons, spices, horses,
and mules, so much year by year.
25 Now Solomon had [a]4,000 stalls
for horses and chariots and 12,000
horsemen, and he stationed them in
the chariot cities and with the king
in Jerusalem.
26 [a]And he was the ruler over all
the kings from the Euphrates River
even to the land of the Philistines,
and as far as the border of Egypt.
27 [a]And the king made silver *as
common* as stones in Jerusalem,
and he made cedars as plentiful as
sycamore trees that are in the [1]low-
land.
28 [a]And they were bringing horses
for Solomon from Egypt and from
all countries.
29 [a]Now the rest of the acts of
Solomon, from first to last, [b]are they
not written in the [1]records of Nathan the prophet, and in the prophecy of Ahijah the Shilonite, and in
the visions of [2]Iddo the seer concerning Jeroboam the son of Nebat?
30 And Solomon reigned forty
years in Jerusalem over all Israel.

Death of Solomon

31 And Solomon slept with his fathers and was buried in [a]the city of
his father David; and his son Rehoboam reigned in his place.

Chapter 10

Rehoboam's Reign of Folly

[a]THEN Rehoboam went to Shechem, for all Israel had come to Shechem to make him king.
2 And it came about when Jeroboam the son of Nebat heard *of it*
(for [a]he was in Egypt where he had
fled from the presence of King Solomon), that Jeroboam returned from
Egypt.
3 So they sent and summoned
him. When Jeroboam and all Israel
came, they spoke to Rehoboam,
saying,
4"Your father made our yoke
hard; now therefore lighten the hard
service of your father and his heavy
yoke which he put on us, and we will
serve you."
5 And he said to them, "Return to
me again in three days." So the people departed.
6 Then King Rehoboam consulted with the elders who had
[1]served his father Solomon while he
was still alive, saying, "How do you
counsel *me* to answer this people?"
7 And they spoke to him, saying,
"If you will be kind to this people
and please them and speak good
words to them, then they will be
your servants forever."
8 But he forsook the counsel of
the elders which they had given
him, and consulted with the young
men who grew up with him [1]and
served him.
9 So he said to them, "What
counsel do you give that we may answer this people, who have spoken
to me, saying, 'Lighten the yoke
which your father put on us'? "
10 And the young men who grew
up with him spoke to him, saying,
"Thus you shall say to the people
who spoke to you, saying, 'Your father made our yoke heavy, but you
make it lighter for us.' Thus you
shall say to them, 'My little finger is
thicker than my father's loins!
11 'Whereas my father loaded you
with a heavy yoke, I will add to your
yoke; my father disciplined you
with whips, but I *will discipline you*
with scorpions.' "
12 So Jeroboam and all the people
came to Rehoboam on the third day
as the king had [1]directed, saying,
"Return to me on the third day."
13 And the king answered them
harshly, and King Rehoboam forsook the counsel of the elders.
14 And he spoke to them according to the advice of the young men,
saying, "[1]My father made your yoke
heavy, but I will add to it; my father
disciplined you with whips, but I
will discipline you with scorpions."
15 So the king did not listen to the
people, [a]for it was a turn *of events*
from God [b]that the LORD might establish His word, which He spoke
through Ahijah the Shilonite to
Jeroboam the son of Nebat.
16 And when all Israel *saw* that
the king did not listen to them the
people answered the king, saying,
"[a]What portion do we have in David? *We have* no inheritance in the
son of Jesse.

> Every man to your tents, O Is-
> rael;
> Now look after your own
> house, David."

22 [a]1 Kin. 3:13; 2 Chr. 1:12
25 [a]Deut. 17:16; 1 Kin. 4:26; 10:26; 2 Chr. 1:14
26 [a]1 Kin. 4:21, 24
27 [1]Or, *shephelah* [a]2 Chr. 1:15-17
28 [a]2 Chr. 1:16
29 [1]Lit., *words* [2]Heb., *Jedo* [a]1 Kin. 11:41-43 [b]1 Chr. 29:29
31 [a]1 Kin. 2:10
1 [a]1 Kin. 12:1-20
2 [a]1 Kin. 11:40
6 [1]Lit., *stood before*
8 [1]Lit., *who stood before*
12 [1]Lit., *spoken*
14 [1]Many mss. read, *I have made*
15 [a]2 Chr. 25:16-20 [b]1 Kin. 11:29-39
16 [a]2 Sam. 20:1

[b]So all Israel departed to their tents.
17 But as for the sons of Israel who
lived in the cities of Judah, Rehoboam reigned over them.
18 Then King Rehoboam sent [a]Ha-
doram, who was over the forced labor, and the sons of Israel stoned
him [1]to death. And King Rehoboam
made haste to mount his chariot to
flee to Jerusalem.
19 So Israel has been in rebellion
against the house of David to this
day.

Chapter 11

Rehoboam Reigns Over Judah and Builds Cities

[a]NOW when Rehoboam had come
to Jerusalem, he assembled the
house of Judah and Benjamin,
180,000 chosen men who were warriors, to fight against Israel to restore the kingdom to Rehoboam.
2 But the word of the LORD came
to [a]Shemaiah the man of God, saying,
3 "Speak to Rehoboam the son of
Solomon, king of Judah, and to all
Israel in Judah and Benjamin, saying,
4 'Thus says the LORD, "You shall
not go up or fight against [a]your
[1]relatives; return every man to his
house, [b]for this thing is from
Me."'" So they listened to the
words of the LORD and returned
from going against Jeroboam.
5 Rehoboam lived in Jerusalem
and [a]built cities for defense in Judah.
6 Thus he built Bethlehem, Etam,
Tekoa,
7 Beth-zur, Soco, Adullam,
8 Gath, Mareshah, Ziph,
9 Adoraim, Lachish, Azekah,
10 Zorah, Aijalon, and Hebron,
which are fortified cities in Judah
and in Benjamin.
11 He also strengthened the fortresses and put officers in them and
stores of food, oil and wine.
12 And *he put* shields and spears
in every city and strengthened them
greatly. So he held Judah and Benjamin.
13 Moreover, the priests and the
Levites who were in all Israel stood
with him from all their districts.

Jeroboam Appoints False Priests

14 For [a]the Levites left their pasture lands and their property and
came to Judah and Jerusalem, for
[b]Jeroboam and his sons had excluded them from serving as priests
to the LORD.
15 And [a]he set up priests of his
own for the high places, for the sa-
tyrs, and for the calves which he had
made.
16 And [a]those from all the tribes of
Israel who set their hearts on seeking the LORD God of Israel, [1]fol-
lowed them to Jerusalem to sacrifice to the LORD God of their fathers.
17 [a]And they strengthened the
kingdom of Judah and supported
Rehoboam the son of Solomon for
three years, for they walked in the
way of David and Solomon for three
years.

Rehoboam's Family

18 Then Rehoboam took as a wife
Mahalath the daughter of Jerimoth
the son of David *and of* Abihail the
daughter of [a]Eliab the son of Jesse,
19 and she bore him sons: Jeush,
Shemariah, and Zaham.
20 And after her he took Maacah
the daughter of Absalom, and she
bore him Abijah, Attai, Ziza, and
Shelomith.
21 And Rehoboam loved Maacah
the daughter of Absalom more than
all his *other* wives and concubines.
For [a]he had taken eighteen wives
and sixty concubines and fathered
twenty-eight sons and sixty daughters.
22 And [a]Rehoboam appointed
Abijah the son of Maacah as head
and leader among his brothers, for
he *intended* to make him king.
23 And he acted wisely and distributed [1]some of his sons through
all the territories of Judah and Benjamin to all the fortified cities, and
he gave them food in abundance.
And he sought many wives *for
them.*

Chapter 12

Shishak of Egypt Invades Judah

IT took place [a]when the kingdom of
Rehoboam was established and
strong that [b]he and all Israel with
him forsook the law of the LORD.
2 [a]And it came about in King
Rehoboam's fifth year, because they
had been unfaithful to the LORD,
that [b]Shishak king of Egypt came up
against Jerusalem
3 with 1,200 chariots and 60,000
horsemen. And the people who
came with him from Egypt were
without number: [a]the Lubim, the
Sukkiim, and the Ethiopians.

16 [b]2 Chr. 10:19
18 [1]Lit., *with stones that he died* [a]1 Kin. 4:6; 5:14
1 [a]1 Kin. 12:21-24
2 [a]2 Chr. 12:5-7, 15
4 [1]Lit., *brothers* [a]2 Chr. 28:8-11 [b]2 Chr. 10:15
5 [a]2 Chr. 8:2-6; 11:23
14 [a]Num. 35:2-5 [b]1 Kin. 12:28-33; 2 Chr. 13:9
15 [a]1 Kin. 12:31; 13:33
16 [1]Lit., *came after* [a]2 Chr. 15:9
17 [a]2 Chr. 12:1
18 [a]1 Sam. 16:6
21 [a]Deut. 17:17
22 [a]Deut. 21:15-17
23 [1]Lit., *from all*
1 [a]2 Chr. 11:17; 12:13 [b]2 Chr. 26:13-16
2 [a]1 Kin. 14:25 [b]1 Kin. 11:40
3 [a]2 Chr. 16:8; Nah. 3:9

4 And he captured [a]the fortified cities of Judah and came as far as Jerusalem.

5 Then [a]Shemaiah the prophet came to Rehoboam and the princes of Judah who had gathered at Jerusalem because of Shishak, and he said to them, "Thus says the LORD, '[b]You have forsaken Me, so I also have forsaken you [1]to Shishak.' "

6 So the princes of Israel and the king humbled themselves and said, "The [a]LORD is righteous."

7 And when the LORD saw that they humbled themselves, the word of the LORD came to Shemaiah, saying, "[a]They have humbled themselves so I will not destroy them, but I will grant them some *measure* of deliverance, and [b]My wrath shall not be poured out on Jerusalem by means of Shishak.

8"But they will become his slaves so [a]that they may learn *the difference between* My service and the service of the kingdoms of the countries."

Plunder Impoverishes Judah

9 [a]So Shishak king of Egypt came up against Jerusalem, and took the treasures of the house of the LORD and the treasures of the king's palace. He took everything; [b]he even took the golden shields which Solomon had made.

10 Then King Rehoboam made shields of bronze in their place, and committed them to the [1]care of the commanders of the [2]guard who guarded the door of the king's house.

11 And it happened as often as the king entered the house of the LORD, the [1]guards came and carried them and *then* brought them back into the [1]guards' room.

12 And [a]when he humbled himself, the anger of the LORD turned away from him, so as not to destroy *him* completely; and also conditions [b]were good in Judah.

13 [a]So King Rehoboam strengthened himself in Jerusalem, and reigned. Now Rehoboam was forty-one years old when he began to reign, and he reigned seventeen years in Jerusalem, the city which the LORD had chosen from all the tribes of Israel, to put His name there. And his mother's name was Naamah the Ammonitess.

14 And he did evil [a]because he did not set his heart to seek the LORD.

15 [a]Now the acts of Rehoboam, from first to last, are they not written in the [1]records of [b]Shemaiah the prophet and of [c]Iddo the seer, according to genealogical enrollment? And *there were* wars between Rehoboam and Jeroboam continually.

16 And Rehoboam slept with his fathers, and was buried in the city of David; and his son [a]Abijah became king in his place.

CHAPTER 13

Abijah Succeeds Rehoboam

[a]IN the eighteenth year of King Jeroboam Abijah became king over Judah.

2 He reigned three years in Jerusalem; and his mother's name was [a]Micaiah the daughter of Uriel of Gibeah. [b]And there was war between Abijah and Jeroboam.

3 And Abijah began the battle with an army of valiant warriors, 400,000 chosen men, while Jeroboam drew up in battle formation against him with 800,000 chosen men *who were* valiant warriors.

Civil War

4 Then Abijah stood on Mount [a]Zemaraim, which is in the hill country of Ephraim, and said, "Listen to me, Jeroboam and all Israel:

5"Do you not know that [a]the LORD God of Israel gave the rule over Israel forever to David [1]and his sons by [b]a covenant of salt?

6"Yet [a]Jeroboam the son of Nebat, the servant of Solomon the son of David, rose up and rebelled against his [1]master,

7 and worthless men gathered about him, scoundrels, who proved too strong for Rehoboam, the son of Solomon, when [1a]he was young and timid and could not hold his own against them.

8"So now you intend to resist the kingdom of the LORD [1]through the sons of David, [2]being a great multitude and *having* with you [a]the golden calves which Jeroboam made for gods for you.

9"[a]Have you not driven out the priests of the LORD, the sons of Aaron and the Levites, and made for yourselves priests like the peoples of *other* lands? Whoever comes [b]to consecrate himself with a young bull and seven rams, even he may become a priest of *what are* [c]no gods.

10"But as for us, the LORD is our God, and we have not forsaken Him; and the sons of Aaron are ministering to the LORD as priests, and the Levites [1]attend to their work.

---

4 [a]2 Chr. 11:5-12
5 [1]Lit., *in the hand of* [a]2 Chr. 11:2 [b]Deut. 28:15; 2 Chr. 15:2
6 [a]Ex. 9:27; Dan. 9:14
7 [a]1 Kin. 21:29 [b]2 Chr. 34:25-27; Ps. 78:38
8 [a]Deut. 28:47, 48
9 [a]1 Kin. 14:26-28 [b]2 Chr. 9:15, 16
10 [1]Lit., *hands* [2]Lit., *runners*
11 [1]Lit., *runners*
12 [a]2 Chr. 12:6, 7 [b]2 Chr. 19:3
13 [a]1 Kin. 14:21
14 [a]2 Chr. 19:3
15 [1]Lit., *words* [a]1 Kin. 14:29 [b]2 Chr. 12:5 [c]2 Chr. 9:29
16 [a]2 Chr. 11:20
1 [a]1 Kin. 15:1, 2
2 [a]2 Chr. 11:20 [b]1 Kin. 15:7
4 [a]Josh. 18:22
5 [1]Lit., *to him and to his sons* [a]2 Sam. 7:12-16 [b]Lev. 2:13; Num. 18:19
6 [1]Or, *lord* [a]1 Kin. 11:26
7 [1]Lit., *Rehoboam* [a]2 Chr. 12:13
8 [1]Lit., *in the hands of* [2]Lit., *and you are a* [a]1 Kin. 12:28; 2 Chr. 11:15
9 [a]2 Chr. 11:14 [b]Ex. 29:29-33 [c]Jer. 2:11; 5:7
10 [1]Lit., *in the work*

11 "And every morning [a]they [1]burn
to the LORD burnt offerings and fragrant incense, and [b]the showbread
is *set* on the clean table, and the
golden lampstand with its lamps is
ready to light every evening; for we
keep the charge of the LORD our
God, but you have forsaken Him.
12 "Now behold, God is with us at
our head and [a]His priests with the
signal trumpets to sound the alarm
against you. O sons of Israel, do not
fight against the LORD God of your
fathers, for you will not succeed."
13 But Jeroboam [a]had set an ambush to come from the rear, so that
Israel was in front of Judah, and the
ambush was behind them.
14 When Judah turned around, behold, [1]they were attacked both front
and rear; so [a]they cried to the LORD,
and the priests blew the trumpets.
15 Then the men of Judah raised a
war cry, and when the men of Judah
raised the war cry, then it was that
God [1a]routed Jeroboam and all Israel before Abijah and Judah.
16 And when the sons of Israel fled
before Judah, [a]God gave them into
their hand.
17 And Abijah and his people defeated them with a great slaughter,
so that 500,000 chosen men of Israel
fell slain.
18 Thus the sons of Israel were
subdued at that time, and the sons
of Judah [1]conquered [a]because they
trusted in the LORD, the God of their
fathers.
19 And Abijah pursued Jeroboam,
and captured from him *several*
cities, Bethel with its villages, Jeshanah with its villages, and [1]Ephron
with its villages.

Death of Jeroboam

20 And Jeroboam did not again recover strength in the days of Abijah;
and the [a]LORD struck him and [b]he
died.
21 But Abijah became powerful,
and took fourteen wives to himself;
and became the father of twenty-
two sons and sixteen daughters.
22 Now the rest of the acts of Abijah, and his ways and his words are
written in [a]the [1]treatise of [b]the
prophet Iddo.

CHAPTER 14

Asa Succeeds Abijah in Judah

1a
SO Abijah slept with his fathers,
and they buried him in the city of
David, and his son Asa became king
in his place. The land was undisturbed for ten years during his days.
2 [1]And Asa did good and right in
the sight of the LORD his God,
3 for he removed [a]the foreign altars and [b]high places, tore down the
sacred pillars, cut down the [1c]A-
sherim,
4 and commanded Judah to seek
the LORD God of their fathers and to
observe the law and the commandment.
5 He also removed the high
places and the [a]incense altars from
all the cities of Judah. And the kingdom was undisturbed under him.
6 And [a]he built fortified cities in
Judah, since the land was undisturbed, and [1]there was no one at
war with him during those years,
[b]because the LORD had given him
rest.
7 For he said to Judah, "[a]Let us
build these cities and surround *them*
with walls and towers, gates and
bars. The land is still [1]ours, because
we have sought the LORD our God;
we have sought Him, and He has
given us rest on every side." So they
built and prospered.
8 Now Asa had an army of
[a]300,000 from Judah, bearing large
shields and spears, and 280,000
from Benjamin, bearing shields and
wielding bows; all of them were valiant warriors.
9 Now Zerah the Ethiopian
[a]came out against them with an
army of a million men and 300 chariots, and he came to [b]Mareshah.
10 So Asa went out [1]to meet him,
and they drew up in battle formation in the valley of Zephathah at
Mareshah.
11 Then Asa [a]called to the LORD
his God, and said, "Lord, there is no
one besides Thee to help *in the bat-*
tle between the powerful and those
who have no strength; so help us, O
LORD our God, [b]for we trust in Thee,
and in Thy name have come against
this multitude. O LORD, Thou art our
God; let not man prevail against
Thee."
12 So [a]the LORD [1]routed the Ethiopians before Asa and before Judah,
and the Ethiopians fled.
13 And Asa and the people who
were with him pursued them as far
as [a]Gerar; and so many Ethiopians
fell that [1]they could not recover, for
they were shattered before the
LORD, and before His army. And
they carried away very much plunder.
14 And they [1]destroyed all the
cities around Gerar, [a]for the dread

11 [1]Lit., *offer up in smoke* [a]Ex. 29:38; 2 Chr. 2:4 [b]Ex. 25:30-39; Lev. 24:5-9

12 [a]Num. 10:8, 9

13 [a]Josh. 8:4-9

14 [1]Lit., *the battle was before and behind them* [a]2 Chr. 14:11

15 [1]Lit., *smote* [a]2 Chr. 14:12

16 [a]2 Chr. 16:8

18 [1]Lit., *were strong* [a]2 Chr. 14:11

19 [1]Another reading is, *Ephrain*

20 [a]1 Sam. 25:38 [b]1 Kin. 14:20

22 [1]Heb., *midrash* [a]2 Chr. 24:27 [b]2 Chr. 9:29

1 [1]Ch. 13:23 in Heb. [a]1 Kin. 15:8

2 [1]Ch. 14:1 in Heb.

3 [1]I.e., wooden symbols of a female deity [a]Deut. 7:5 [b]1 Kin. 15:12-14 [c]Ex. 34:13

5 [a]2 Chr. 34:4, 7

6 [1]Lit., *there was not with him war* [a]2 Chr. 11:5 [b]2 Chr. 15:15

7 [1]Lit., *before us* [a]2 Chr. 8:5

8 [a]2 Chr. 13:3

9 [a]2 Chr. 12:2, 3; 16:8 [b]2 Chr. 11:8

10 [1]Lit., *before him*

11 [a]2 Chr. 13:14 [b]2 Chr. 13:18

12 [1]Lit., *struck* [a]2 Chr. 13:15

13 [1]Or, *there was none left alive* [a]Gen. 10:19

14 [1]Lit., *smote* [a]2 Chr. 17:10

of the LORD had fallen on them; and
they despoiled all the cities, for
there was much plunder in them.
15 They also struck down [1]those
who owned livestock, and they carried away large numbers of sheep
and camels. Then they returned to
Jerusalem.

CHAPTER 15

The Prophet Azariah Warns Asa

NOW [a]the Spirit of God came on
Azariah the son of Oded,
2 and he went out [1]to meet Asa
and said to him, "Listen to me, Asa,
and all Judah and Benjamin: [a]the
LORD is with you when you are with
Him. And [b]if you seek Him, He will
let you find Him; but if you forsake
Him, He will forsake you.
3 "And [a]for many days Israel was
without the true God and without [b]a
teaching priest and without law.
4 "But [a]in their distress they
turned to the LORD God of Israel,
and they sought Him, and He let
them find Him.
5 "[a]And in those times there was
no peace to him who went out or to
him who came in, for many disturbances [1]afflicted all the inhabitants
of the lands.
6 "And nation was crushed by nation, and city by city, for God troubled them with every kind of distress.
7 "But you, [a]be strong and do not
[1]lose courage, for there is reward
for your work."

Asa's Reforms

8 Now when Asa heard these
words and the [1]prophecy which
Azariah the son of Oded the prophet
spoke, he took courage and removed the abominable idols from
all the land of Judah and Benjamin
and from [a]the cities which he had
captured in the hill country of E-
phraim. [b]He then restored the altar
of the LORD which was in front of
the porch of the LORD.
9 And he gathered all Judah and
Benjamin and those from Ephraim,
Manasseh, and Simeon [a]who resided with them, for many defected
to him from Israel when they saw
that the LORD his God was with him.
10 So they assembled at Jerusalem in the third month of the fifteenth year of Asa's reign.
11 And [a]they sacrificed to the
LORD that day 700 oxen and 7,000
sheep from the spoil they had
brought.
12 And [a]they entered into the covenant to seek the LORD God of their
fathers with all their heart and soul;
13 and whoever would not seek
the LORD God of Israel [a]should be
put to death, whether small or great,
man or woman.
14 Moreover, they made an oath to
the LORD with a loud voice, with
shouting, with trumpets, and with
horns.
15 And all Judah rejoiced concerning the oath, for they had sworn
with their whole heart and had
sought Him [1]earnestly, and He let
them find Him. So [a]the LORD gave
them rest on every side.
16 [a]And he also removed Maacah,
the mother of King Asa, from the
position of queen mother, because
she had made a horrid image [1]as [b]an
Asherah, and [c]Asa cut down her
horrid image, crushed *it* and burned
it at the brook Kidron.
17 But the high places were not removed from Israel; nevertheless
Asa's heart was blameless all his
days.
18 And he brought into the house
of God the dedicated things of his
father and his own dedicated things:
silver and gold and utensils.
19 And there was no more war until the thirty-fifth year of Asa's
reign.

CHAPTER 16

[a] *Asa Wars against Baasha*

IN the thirty-sixth year of Asa's
reign Baasha king of Israel came up
against Judah and [1]fortified Ramah
in order to prevent *anyone* from
going out or coming in to Asa king
of Judah.
2 Then Asa brought out silver
and gold from the treasuries of the
house of the LORD and the king's
house, and sent them to Ben-hadad
king of [1]Syria, who lived in Damascus, saying,
3 "*Let there be* a treaty between
[1]you and me, *as* between my father
and your father. Behold, I have sent
you silver and gold; go, break your
treaty with Baasha king of Israel so
that he will withdraw from me."
4 So Ben-hadad listened to King
Asa and sent the commanders of his
armies against the cities of Israel,
and they [1]conquered Ijon, Dan,
Abel-maim, and all [a]the [2]store cities
of Naphtali.
5 And it came about when Ba-
asha heard *of it* that he ceased [1]for-
tifying Ramah and stopped his
work.

15 [1]Lit., *tents of livestock*

1 [a]2 Chr. 20:14; 24:20

2 [1]Lit., *before Asa* [a]2 Chr. 20:17 [b]2 Chr. 15:4, 15

3 [a]1 Kin. 12:28-33 [b]Lev. 10:8-11; 2 Chr. 17:9

4 [a]Deut. 4:29

5 [1]Lit., *were on* [a]Judg. 5:6

7 [1]Lit., *let your hands drop* [a]Josh. 1:7, 9

8 [1]With several ancient versions; Heb., *the prophecy, Oded the prophet* [a]2 Chr. 13:19 [b]2 Chr. 4:1; 8:12

9 [a]2 Chr. 11:16

11 [a]2 Chr. 14:13-15

12 [a]2 Chr. 23:16

13 [a]Ex. 22:20; Deut. 13:6-9

15 [1]Lit., *with their whole desire* [a]2 Chr. 14:7

16 [1]Or, for *Asherah* [a]1 Kin. 15:13-15 [b]Ex. 34:13 [c]2 Chr. 14:2-5

1 [1]Lit., *built* [a]1 Kin. 15:17-22

2 [1]Heb., *Aram*

3 [1]Lit., *me and you*

4 [1]Lit., *smote* [2]Lit., *storage places of the cities* [a]Ex. 1:11

5 [1]Lit., *building*

6 Then King Asa brought all Judah, and they carried away the
stones of Ramah and its timber with
which Baasha had been building,
and with them he [1]fortified Geba
and Mizpah.

Asa Imprisons the Prophet

7 At that time [a]Hanani the seer
came to Asa king of Judah and said
to him, "[b]Because you have relied
on the king of [1]Syria and have not
relied on the LORD your God, therefore the army of the king of [1]Syria
has escaped out of your hand.
8"Were not [a]the Ethiopians and
the Lubim [b]an immense army with
very many chariots and horsemen?
Yet, [c]because you relied on the
LORD, He delivered them into your
hand.
9"For [a]the eyes of the LORD move
to and fro throughout the earth that
He may strongly support those
[b]whose heart is completely His. You
have acted foolishly in this. Indeed,
from now on you will surely have
wars."
10 Then Asa was angry with the
seer and put him in [1]prison, for he
was enraged at him for this. And
Asa oppressed some of the people at
the same time.
11 [a]And now, the acts of Asa from
first to last, behold, they are written
in the Book of the Kings of Judah
and Israel.
12 And in the thirty-ninth year of
his reign Asa became diseased in his
feet. His disease was severe, yet
even in his disease he did not seek
the LORD but the physicians.
13 So Asa slept with his fathers,
[1]having died in the forty-first year of
his reign.
14 And they buried him in his own
tomb which he had cut out for himself in the city of David, and they
laid him in the resting place which
he had filled [a]with spices of various
kinds blended by the perfumers' art;
and [b]they made a very great fire for
him.

CHAPTER 17

Jehoshaphat Succeeds Asa

[a]JEHOSHAPHAT his son then became king in his place, and made his
position over Israel firm.
2 He placed troops in all [a]the
fortified cities of Judah, and set garrisons in the land of Judah, and in
the cities of Ephraim [b]which Asa his
father had captured.

His Good Reign

3 And the LORD was with Jehoshaphat because he [1]followed the
example of his father David's earlier
days and did not seek the Baals,
4 but sought the God of his father, [1]followed His commandments,
[a]and did not act as Israel did.
5 So the LORD established the
kingdom in his [1]control, and all Judah brought tribute to Jehoshaphat,
and [a]he had great riches and honor.
6 And [1]he took great pride in the
ways of the LORD and again [a]re-
moved the high places and the A-
sherim from Judah.
7 Then in the third year of his
reign he sent his officials, Ben-hail,
Obadiah, Zechariah, Nethanel, and
Micaiah, [a]to teach in the cities of Judah;
8 and with them [a]the Levites,
Shemaiah, Nethaniah, Zebadiah,
Asahel, Shemiramoth, Jehonathan,
Adonijah, Tobijah, and Tobadoni-
jah, the Levites; and with them
Elishama and Jehoram, the priests.
9 And they taught in Judah, *having* [a]the book of the law of the LORD
with them; and they went throughout all the cities of Judah and taught
among the people.
10 Now [a]the dread of the LORD
was on all the kingdoms of the lands
which *were* around Judah, so that
they did not make war against Jehoshaphat.
11 And [a]some of the Philistines
brought gifts and silver as tribute to
Jehoshaphat; the Arabians also
brought him flocks, 7,700 rams and
7,700 male goats.
12 So Jehoshaphat grew greater
and greater, and he built fortresses
and store cities in Judah.
13 And he had large supplies in the
cities of Judah, and warriors, valiant
men, in Jerusalem.
14 And this was their muster according to their fathers' households:
of Judah, commanders of thousands, Adnah *was* the commander,
and with him 300,000 valiant warriors;
15 and next to him *was* Johanan
the commander, and with him
280,000;
16 and next to him Amasiah the
son of Zichri, [a]who volunteered for
the LORD, and with him 200,000 valiant warriors;
17 and of Benjamin, Eliada a valiant warrior, and with him 200,000
armed with bow and shield;
18 and next to him Jehozabad, and
with him 180,000 equipped for war.

6 [1]Lit., *built*
7 [1]Heb., *Aram* [a]1 Kin. 16:1; 2 Chr. 19:2 [b]2 Chr. 14:11; 32:7, 8
8 [a]2 Chr. 14:9 [b]2 Chr. 12:3 [c]2 Chr. 13:16, 18
9 [a]Prov. 15:3; Zech. 4:10 [b]2 Chr. 15:17
10 [1]Lit., *house of the stocks*
11 [a]1 Kin. 15:23, 24
13 [1]Lit., *and*
14 [a]Gen. 50:2; John 12:7; 19:39, 40 [b]2 Chr. 21:19
1 [a]1 Kin. 15:24
2 [a]2 Chr. 11:5 [b]2 Chr. 15:8
3 [1]Lit., *walked in the earlier ways of his father*
4 [1]Lit., *walked in* [a]1 Kin. 12:28
5 [1]Lit., *hand* [a]2 Chr. 18:1
6 [1]Lit., *his heart was high* [a]2 Chr. 15:17
7 [a]2 Chr. 15:3; 35:3
8 [a]2 Chr. 19:8
9 [a]Deut. 6:4-9
10 [a]2 Chr. 14:14
11 [a]2 Chr. 9:14; 26:8
16 [a]Judg. 5:2, 9; 1 Chr. 29:9

19 These are they who served the king, apart from [a]those whom the king put in the fortified cities through all Judah.

Chapter 18

Jehoshaphat Allies with Ahab

Now [a]Jehoshaphat had great riches and honor; and he allied himself by marriage with Ahab.

2 [a]And some years later he went down to *visit* Ahab at Samaria. And Ahab slaughtered many sheep and oxen for him and the people who were with him, and induced him to go up against Ramoth-gilead.

3 And Ahab king of Israel said to Jehoshaphat king of Judah, "Will you go with me *against* Ramoth-gilead?" And he said to him, "I am as you are, and my people as your people, and *we will be* with you in the battle."

4 Moreover, Jehoshaphat said to the king of Israel, "Please inquire [1]first for the word of the Lord."

5 Then the king of Israel assembled the prophets, four hundred men, and said to them, "Shall we go against Ramoth-gilead to battle, or shall I refrain?" And they said, "Go up, for God will give *it* into the hand of the king."

6 But Jehoshaphat said, "Is there not yet a prophet of the LORD here that we may inquire of him?"

7 And the king of Israel said to Jehoshaphat, "There is yet one man by whom we may inquire of the LORD, but I hate him, for he never prophesies good concerning me but always evil. He is Micaiah, son of Imla." But Jehoshaphat said, "Let not the king say so."

Ahab's False Prophets Assure Victory

8 Then the king of Israel called an officer and said, "[1]Bring quickly Micaiah, Imla's son."

9 Now the king of Israel and Jehoshaphat the king of Judah were sitting each on his throne, arrayed in *their* robes, and *they* were sitting [a]at the threshing floor at the entrance of the gate of Samaria; and all the prophets were prophesying before them.

10 And Zedekiah the son of Chenaanah made horns of iron for himself and said, "Thus says the LORD, 'With these you shall gore the Syrians, until they are consumed.' "

11 And all the prophets were prophesying thus, saying, "Go up to Ramoth-gilead and succeed, for the LORD will give *it* into the hand of the king."

Micaiah Brings Word from God

12 Then the messenger who went to summon Micaiah spoke to him saying, "Behold, the words of the prophets are uniformly favorable to the king. So please let your word be like one of them and speak favorably."

13 But Micaiah said, "As the LORD lives, [a]what my God says, that I will speak."

14 And when he came to the king, the king said to him, "Micaiah, shall we go to Ramoth-gilead to battle, or shall I refrain?" He said, "Go up and succeed, for they will be given into your hand."

15 Then the king said to him, "How many times must I adjure you to speak to me nothing but the truth in the name of the LORD?"

16 So he said,
"I saw all Israel
Scattered on the mountains,
[a]Like sheep which have no shepherd;
And the LORD said,
'These have no master.
Let each of them return to his house in peace.' "

17 Then the king of Israel said to Jehoshaphat, "Did I not tell you that he would not prophesy good concerning me, but evil?"

18 And Micaiah said, "Therefore, hear the word of the LORD. [a]I saw the LORD sitting on His throne, and all the host of heaven standing on His right and on His left.

19 "And the LORD said, 'Who will entice Ahab king of Israel to go up and fall at Ramoth-gilead?' And one said this while another said that.

20 "Then a spirit came forward and stood before the LORD and said, 'I will entice him.' And the LORD said to him, 'How?'

21 "And he said, 'I will go and be a deceiving spirit in the mouth of all his prophets.' Then He said, 'You are to entice *him* and prevail also. Go and do so.'

22 "Now therefore, the LORD has put a deceiving spirit in the mouth of these your prophets; for the LORD has proclaimed disaster against you."

23 Then Zedekiah the son of Chenaanah came near and struck Micaiah on the cheek and said, "[1]How did the Spirit of the LORD pass from me to speak to you?"

24 And Micaiah said, "Behold, you

19 [a]2 Chr. 17:2
1 [a]2 Chr. 17:5
2 [a]1 Kin. 22:2-35
4 [1]Lit., *as the day*
8 [1]Lit., *Hasten*
9 [a]Ruth 4:1
13 [a]Num. 22:18-20, 35
16 [a]Num. 27:17; Ezek. 35:5-8; Matt. 9:36
18 [a]Is. 6:1-5; Dan. 7:9, 10
23 [1]Lit., *Which way*

shall see on that day, when you enter an inner room to hide yourself."
25 Then the king of Israel said,
"[a]Take Micaiah and return him to
Amon [b]the governor of the city, and
to Joash the king's son;
26 and say, 'Thus says the king,
"[a]Put this *man* in prison, and feed
him [1]sparingly with bread and water until I return safely."'"
27 And Micaiah said, "If you indeed return safely, the LORD has not
spoken by me." And he said, "[a]Lis-
ten, all you people."

Ahab's Defeat and Death

28 So the king of Israel and Jehoshaphat king of Judah went up
against Ramoth-gilead.
29 And the king of Israel said to
Jehoshaphat, "I will disguise myself
and go into battle, but you put on
your robes." So the king of Israel
disguised himself, and they went
into battle.
30 Now the king of Syria had commanded the captains of his chariots,
saying, "Do not fight with small or
great, but with the king of Israel
alone."
31 So it came about when the captains of the chariots saw Jehoshaphat, that they said, "It is the king of
Israel," and they turned aside to
fight against him. But Jehoshaphat
[a]cried out, and the LORD helped him,
and God diverted them from him.
32 Then it happened when the captains of the chariots saw that it was
not the king of Israel, that they
turned back from pursuing him.
33 And a certain man drew his
bow at random and struck the king
of Israel [1]in a joint of the armor. So
he said to the driver of the chariot,
"Turn [2]around, and take me out
of the [3]fight; for I am severely
wounded."
34 And the battle raged that day,
and the king of Israel propped himself up in his chariot in front of the
Syrians until the evening; and at
sunset he died.

CHAPTER 19

Jehu Rebukes Jehoshaphat

THEN Jehoshaphat the king of Judah returned in safety to his house
in Jerusalem.
2 And [a]Jehu the son of Hanani
the seer went out to meet him and
said to King Jehoshaphat, "[b]Should
you help the wicked and love those
who hate the LORD and [1c]so *bring*
wrath on yourself from the LORD?
3 "But [1a]there is *some* good in you,
for [b]you have removed the [2]Ashe-
roth from the land and you [c]have set
your heart to seek God."
4 So Jehoshaphat lived in Jerusalem and went out again among the
people from Beersheba to the hill
country of Ephraim and [a]brought
them back to the LORD, the God of
their fathers.

Reforms Instituted

5 And he appointed [a]judges in
the land in all the fortified cities of
Judah, city by city.
6 And he said to the judges,
"Consider what you are doing, for
[a]you do not judge for man but for
the LORD who is with you [1]when you
render judgment.
7 "Now then let the fear of the
LORD be upon you; [1]be very careful
what you do, for [2]the LORD our God
will [a]have no part in unrighteousness, [b]or partiality, or the taking of a
bribe."
8 And in Jerusalem also Jehoshaphat appointed some [a]of the Levites
and priests, and some of the heads
of the fathers' *households* of Israel,
for the judgment of the LORD and to
judge [1]disputes among the inhabitants of Jerusalem.
9 Then he charged them saying,
"Thus you shall do in the fear of the
LORD, faithfully and wholeheart-
edly.
10 "[a]And whenever any dispute
comes to you from your brethren
who live in their cities, between
blood and blood, between law and
commandment, statutes and ordinances, you shall warn them that
they may not be guilty before the
LORD, and [b]wrath may *not* come on
you and your brethren. Thus you
shall do and you will not be guilty.
11 "And behold, Amariah the chief
priest will be over you in [1a]all that
pertains to the LORD; and Zebadiah
the son of Ishmael, the ruler of the
house of Judah, in [1]all that pertains
to the king. Also the Levites shall be
officers before you. [2b]Act resolutely,
and the LORD be with the upright."

CHAPTER 20

Judah Invaded

NOW it came about after this that
the sons of Moab and the sons of
Ammon, together with some of the
[1]Meunites, came to make war
against Jehoshaphat.
2 Then some came and reported
to Jehoshaphat, saying, "A great
multitude is coming against you

25 [a]2 Chr. 18:8 [b]2 Chr. 34:8

26 [1]Lit., *with bread of affliction and water of affliction* [a]2 Chr. 16:10

27 [a]Mic. 1:2

31 [a]2 Chr. 13:14, 15

33 [1]Lit., *between the scale armor and the breastplate* [2]Lit., *your hand* [3]Lit., *camp*

2 [1]Lit., *by this* [a]1 Kin. 16:1; 2 Chr. 20:34 [b]2 Chr. 18:1, 3 [c]2 Chr. 24:18

3 [1]Lit., *good things are found* [2]I.e., wooden pillars [a]2 Chr. 12:12 [b]2 Chr. 17:6 [c]2 Chr. 12:14

4 [a]2 Chr. 15:8-13

5 [a]Deut. 16:18-20

6 [1]Lit., *in the word of judgment* [a]Lev. 19:15; Deut. 1:17

7 [1]Lit., *be careful and do* [2]Lit., *there is not with the LORD God* [a]Gen. 18:25; Deut. 32:4 [b]Deut. 10:17, 18

8 [1]So the versions. Heb. reads *disputes. And they returned to Jerusalem.* Or, *And they lived in Jerusalem* [a]2 Chr. 17:8, 9

10 [a]Deut. 17:8 [b]2 Chr. 19:2

11 [1]Lit., *every matter of* [2]Lit., *Be strong and do* [a]2 Chr. 19:8 [b]1 Chr. 28:20

1 [1]So with Gk., Heb., *Ammonites,* 1 Chr. 4:41; 2 Chr. 26:7

from beyond the sea, out of [1]Syria and behold, they are in [a]Hazazon-tamar (that is Engedi)."

3 And Jehoshaphat was afraid and [1a]turned his attention to seek the LORD; and [b]proclaimed a fast throughout all Judah.

4 So Judah gathered together to seek help from the LORD; they even came from all the cities of Judah to seek the LORD.

5 Then Jehoshaphat stood in the assembly of Judah and Jerusalem, in the house of the LORD before the new court,

Jehoshaphat's Prayer

6 and he said, "O LORD, the God of our fathers, [a]art Thou not God in the heavens? And [b]art Thou not ruler over all the kingdoms of the nations? Power and might are in Thy hand so that no one can stand against Thee.

7 "Didst Thou not, O our God, drive out the inhabitants of this land before Thy people Israel, and [a]give it to the descendants of Abraham Thy friend forever?

8 "And they lived in it, and have built Thee a sanctuary there for Thy name, saying,

9 '[a]Should evil come upon us, the sword, *or* judgment, or pestilence, or famine, we will stand before this house and before Thee (for [b]Thy name is in this house) and cry to Thee in our distress, and Thou wilt hear and deliver *us.*'

10 "And now behold, [a]the sons of Ammon and Moab and Mount Seir, [b]whom Thou didst not let Israel invade when they came out of the land of Egypt (they turned aside from them and did not destroy them),

11 behold *how* they are rewarding us, by coming to drive us out from Thy possession which Thou hast given us as an inheritance.

12 "O our God, [a]wilt Thou not judge them? For we are powerless before this great multitude who are coming against us; nor do we know what to do, but [b]our eyes are on Thee."

13 And all Judah was standing before the LORD, with their infants, their wives, and their children.

Jahaziel Answers the Prayer

14 Then in the midst of the assembly the Spirit of the LORD [a]came upon Jahaziel the son of Zechariah, the son of Benaiah, the son of Jeiel, the son of Mattaniah, the Levite of the sons of Asaph;

15 and he said, "Listen, all Judah and the inhabitants of Jerusalem and King Jehoshaphat: thus says the LORD to you, '[a]Do not fear or be dismayed because of this great multitude, for [b]the battle is not yours but God's.

16 'Tomorrow go down against them. Behold, they will come up by the ascent of Ziz, and you will find them at the end of the valley in front of the wilderness of Jeruel.

17 'You *need* not fight in this *battle;* station yourselves, [a]stand and see the salvation of the LORD on your behalf, O Judah and Jerusalem.' Do not fear or be dismayed; tomorrow go out to face them, [b]for the LORD is with you."

18 And Jehoshaphat bowed his head with *his* face to the ground, and all Judah and the inhabitants of Jerusalem fell down before the LORD, worshiping the LORD.

19 And the Levites, from the sons [a]of the Kohathites and of the sons of the Korahites, stood up to praise the LORD God of Israel, with a very loud voice.

Enemies Destroy Selves

20 And they rose early in the morning and went out to the wilderness of Tekoa; and when they went out, Jehoshaphat stood and said, "Listen to me, O Judah and inhabitants of Jerusalem, [a]put your trust in the LORD your God, and you will be established. Put your trust in His prophets and succeed."

21 And when he had consulted with the people, he appointed those who sang to the LORD and those who [a]praised *Him* in holy attire, as they went out before the army and said, "[b]Give thanks to the LORD, for His lovingkindness is everlasting."

22 And when they began singing and praising, the LORD [a]set ambushes against the sons of [b]Ammon, Moab, and Mount Seir, who had come against Judah; so they were [1]routed.

23 For the sons of Ammon and Moab rose up against the inhabitants of Mount Seir destroying *them* completely, and when they had finished with the inhabitants of Seir, [a]they helped to destroy one another.

24 When Judah came to the lookout of the wilderness, they looked toward the multitude; and behold, they *were* corpses lying on the ground, and no one had escaped.

25 And when Jehoshaphat and his people came to take their spoil, they found much among them, *including*

2 [1]Another reading is *Edom* [a]Gen. 14:7

3 [1]Lit., *set his face* [a]2 Chr. 19:3 [b]1 Sam. 7:6; Ezra 8:21

6 [a]Deut. 4:39 [b]1 Chr. 29:11

7 [a]Is. 41:8

9 [a]2 Chr. 6:28-30 [b]2 Chr. 6:20

10 [a]2 Chr. 20:1, 22 [b]Num. 20:17-21

12 [a]Judg. 11:27 [b]Ps. 25:15; 121:1, 2

14 [a]2 Chr. 15:1; 24:20

15 [a]Ex. 14:13; 2 Chr. 32:7, 8 [b]1 Sam. 17:47

17 [a]Ex. 14:13 [b]2 Chr. 15:2

19 [a]2 Chr. 7:3

20 [a]Is. 7:9

21 [a]1 Chr. 16:29; Ps. 29:2 [b]1 Chr. 16:34

22 [1]Lit., *struck down* [a]2 Chr. 13:13 [b]2 Chr. 20:10

23 [a]Judg. 7:22; 1 Sam. 14:20

goods, [1]garments, and valuable things which they took for themselves, more than they could carry. And they were three days taking the spoil because there was so much.

Triumphant Return to Jerusalem

26 Then on the fourth day they assembled in the valley of Beracah, for there they blessed the LORD. Therefore they have named that place "The Valley of [1]Beracah" until today.

27 And every man of Judah and Jerusalem returned with Jehoshaphat at their head, returning to Jerusalem with joy, for the LORD had made them to rejoice over their enemies.

28 And they came to Jerusalem with harps, lyres, and trumpets to the house of the LORD.

29 And [a]the dread of God was on all the kingdoms of the lands when they heard that the LORD had fought against the enemies of Israel.

30 So the kingdom of Jehoshaphat was at peace, [a]for his God gave him rest on all sides.

31 [a]Now Jehoshaphat reigned over Judah. He *was* thirty-five years old when he became king, and he reigned in Jerusalem twenty-five years. And his mother's name *was* Azubah the daughter of Shilhi.

32 And he walked in the way of his father Asa and did not depart from it, doing right in the sight of the LORD.

33 [a]The high places, however, were not removed; [b]the people had not yet directed their hearts to the God of their fathers.

34 Now the rest of the acts of Jehoshaphat, first [1]to last, behold, they are written in the annals of [a]Jehu the son of Hanani, [b]which is [2]recorded in the Book of the Kings of Israel.

Alliance Displeases God

35 [a]And after this Jehoshaphat king of Judah allied himself with Ahaziah king of Israel. He acted wickedly [1]in so doing.

36 So he allied himself with him to make ships to go [a]to Tarshish, and they made the ships in Ezion-geber.

37 Then Eliezer the son of Dodavahu of Mareshah prophesied against Jehoshaphat saying, "Because you have allied yourself with Ahaziah, the LORD has destroyed your works." So the ships were broken and could not go to Tarshish.

25 [1]So several ancient mss.; others read, *corpses*

26 [1]I.e., Blessing

29 [a]2 Chr. 14:6, 7; 15:15

30 [a]1 Kin. 22:41-43

31 [a]2 Chr. 17:6

33 [a]2 Chr. 17:6 [b]2 Chr. 19:3

34 [1]Lit., *and* [2]Lit., *taken up* [a]2 Chr. 19:2 [b]1 Kin. 16:1, 7

35 [1]Lit., *to do* [a]1 Kin. 22:48, 49

36 [a]2 Chr. 9:21

1 [a]1 Kin. 22:50

2 [a]2 Chr. 12:6; 23:2

3 [a]2 Chr. 11:5

4 [1]Lit., *risen up* [2]Lit., *strong*

5 [a]2 Kin. 8:17-22

6 [a]1 Kin. 12:28-30 [b]2 Chr. 18:1

7 [a]2 Sam. 7:12-17; 1 Kin. 11:13

8 [1]Lit., *from under the hand of* [a]2 Chr. 20:22, 23; 21:10

10 [1]Lit., *from under the hand of* [2]Lit., *from under his hand*

11 [a]1 Kin. 11:7 [b]Lev. 20:5

12 [a]2 Chr. 17:3, 4

CHAPTER 21

Jehoram Succeeds Jehoshaphat in Judah

[a]THEN Jehoshaphat slept with his fathers and was buried with his fathers in the city of David, and Jehoram his son became king in his place.

2 And he had brothers, the sons of Jehoshaphat: Azariah, Jehiel, Zechariah, Azariah, Michael, and Shephatiah. All these *were* the sons of Jehoshaphat king [a]of Israel.

3 And their father gave them many gifts of silver, gold and precious things, [a]with fortified cities in Judah, but he gave the kingdom to Jehoram because he was the firstborn.

4 Now when Jehoram had [1]taken over the kingdom of his father and made himself [2]secure, he killed all his brothers with the sword, and some of the rulers of Israel also.

5 [a]Jehoram *was* thirty-two years old when he became king, and he reigned eight years in Jerusalem.

6 [a]And he walked in the way of the kings of Israel, just as the house of Ahab did ([b]for Ahab's daughter was his wife), and he did evil in the sight of the LORD.

7 Yet the LORD was not willing to destroy the house of David because of the covenant which he had made with David, [a]and since He had promised to give a lamp to him and his sons forever.

Revolt against Judah

8 In his days [a]Edom revolted [1]against the rule of Judah, and set up a king over themselves.

9 Then Jehoram crossed over with his commanders and all his chariots with him. And it came about that he arose by night and struck down the Edomites who were surrounding him and the commanders of the chariots.

10 So Edom revolted [1]against Judah to this day. Then Libnah revolted at the same time [2]against his rule, because he had forsaken the LORD God of his fathers.

11 Moreover, [a]he made high places in the mountains of Judah, and caused the inhabitants of Jerusalem [b]to play the harlot and led Judah astray.

12 Then a letter came to him from Elijah the prophet saying, "Thus says the LORD God of your father David, 'Because [a]you have not walked in the ways of Jehoshaphat

your father [b]and the ways of Asa
king of Judah,
13 but [a]have walked in the way of
the kings of Israel, and have caused
Judah and the inhabitants of Israel
to play the harlot [b]as the house of
Ahab played the harlot, and you
[c]have also killed your brothers,
[1]your own family, who were better
than you,
14 behold, the LORD is going to
strike your people, your sons, your
wives, and all your possessions with
a great [1]calamity;
15 and [a]you [1]will suffer severe
sickness, a disease of your bowels,
until your bowels come out because
of the sickness, day by day.' "
16 Then [a]the LORD stirred up
against Jehoram the spirit of the
Philistines and [b]the Arabs who [1]bor-
dered the Ethiopians;
17 and they came against Judah
and invaded it, and carried away all
the possessions found in the king's
house together with his sons and his
wives, so that no son was left to him
except [1a]Jehoahaz, the youngest of
his sons.
18 So after all this the LORD smote
him [a]in his bowels with an incurable
sickness.
19 Now it came about in the
course of time, at the end of two
years, that his bowels came out because of his sickness and he died in
great pain. And his people made no
fire for him like [a]the fire for his fathers.
20 He was thirty-two years old
when he became king, and he
reigned in Jerusalem eight years;
and he departed [1a]with no one's regret, and they buried him in the city
of David, [b]but not in the tombs of
the kings.

CHAPTER 22

Ahaziah Succeeds Jehoram in Judah

[a]THEN the inhabitants of Jerusalem made [1]Ahaziah, his youngest
son, king in his place, for the band of
men who came with [b]the Arabs to
the camp had slain all the older
sons. So Ahaziah the son of Jehoram king of Judah began to reign.
2 Ahaziah *was* [1]twenty-two
years old when he became king, and
he reigned one year in Jerusalem.
And his mother's name was [a]Atha-
liah, the [2]granddaughter of Omri.
3 He also walked in the ways of
the house of Ahab, for his mother
was his counselor to do wickedly.
4 And he did evil in the sight of
the LORD like the house of Ahab, for
they were his counselors after the
death of his father, to his destruction.

Ahaziah Allies with Jehoram of Israel

5 He also walked according to
their counsel, and went with Jehoram the son of Ahab king of Israel to
wage war against Hazael king of
Syria at Ramoth-gilead. But the
[1]Syrians [2]wounded [3]Joram.
6 So he returned to be healed in
Jezreel of the wounds [1]which they
had inflicted on him at Ramah,
when he fought against Hazael king
of Syria. And [2]Ahaziah, the son of
Jehoram king of Judah, went down
to see Jehoram the son of Ahab in
Jezreel, because he was sick.
7 Now [a]the destruction of Ahaziah was from God, in that [1]he went to
Joram. For when he came, [b]he went
out with Jehoram against Jehu the
son of Nimshi, [c]whom the LORD had
anointed to cut off the house of
Ahab.

Jehu Murders Princes of Judah

8 [a]And it came about when Jehu
was executing judgment on the
house of Ahab, he found the princes
of Judah and the sons of Ahaziah's
brothers, ministering to Ahaziah,
and slew them.
9 [a]He also sought Ahaziah, and
they caught him while he was hiding
in Samaria; they brought him to
Jehu, put him to death, [b]and buried
him. For they said, "He is the son of
Jehoshaphat, [c]who sought the LORD
with all his heart." So there was no
one of the house of Ahaziah to retain the power of the kingdom.
10 [a]Now when Athaliah the
mother of Ahaziah saw that her son
was dead, she rose and [1]destroyed
all the royal [2]offspring of the house
of Judah.
11 But Jehoshabeath the king's
daughter took Joash the son of Ahaziah, and stole him from among the
king's sons who were being put to
death, and placed him and his nurse
in the bedroom. So Jehoshabeath,
the daughter of King Jehoram, the
wife of Jehoiada the priest (for she
was the sister of Ahaziah), hid him
from Athaliah so that she would not
put him to death.
12 And he was hidden with them
in the house of God six years while
Athaliah reigned over the land.

12 [b]2 Chr. 14:2-5

13 [1]Lit., *your father's house* [a]2 Chr. 21:6 [b]1 Kin. 16:31-33 [c]2 Chr. 21:4

14 [1]Lit., *blow*

15 [1]Lit., *in many sicknesses* [a]2 Chr. 21:18, 19

16 [1]Lit., *were at the hand of* [a]2 Chr. 33:11 [b]2 Chr. 17:11; 22:1

17 [1]In 2 Chr. 22:1, *Ahaziah* [a]2 Chr. 25:23

18 [a]2 Chr. 21:15

19 [a]2 Chr. 16:14

20 [1]Lit., *without desire* [a]Jer. 22:18, 28 [b]2 Chr. 24:25; 28:27

1 [1]In 2 Chr. 21:17, *Jehoahaz* [a]2 Kin. 8:24-29 [b]2 Chr. 21:16

2 [1]So some versions and 2 Kin. 8:26; Heb., *42 years* [2]Lit., *daughter* [a]2 Chr. 21:6

5 [1]So with 2 Kin. 8:28; Heb., *archers* [2]Lit., *smote* [3]I.e., Jehoram

6 [1]Lit., *with which . . . smitten* [2]So with 2 Kin. 8:29; Heb., *Azariah*

7 [1]Lit., *to go* [a]2 Chr. 10:15 [b]2 Kin. 9:21 [c]2 Kin. 9:6, 7

8 [a]2 Kin. 10:11-14

9 [a]2 Kin. 9:27 [b]2 Kin. 9:28 [c]2 Chr. 17:4

10 [1]So with 2 Kin. 11:1; Heb., *said* [2]Lit., *seed* [a]2 Kin. 11:1-3

Chapter 23

Jehoiada Sets Joash on the Throne of Judah

[a]NOW in the seventh year Jehoiada
strengthened himself, and took captains of hundreds: Azariah the son
of Jeroham, Ishmael the son of Johanan, Azariah the son of Obed,
Maaseiah the son of Adaiah, and
Elishaphat the son of Zichri, *and
they entered* into a covenant with
him.
2 And they went throughout Judah and gathered the Levites from
all the cities of Judah, and the heads
of the fathers' *households* of [a]Israel,
and they came to Jerusalem.
3 Then all the assembly made a
covenant with the king in the house
of God. And [1]Jehoiada said to them,
"Behold, the king's son shall reign,
[a]as the LORD has spoken concerning
the sons of David.
4 "This is the thing which you
shall do: one third of you, of the
priests and Levites [a]who come in on
the sabbath, *shall be* gatekeepers,
5 and one third *shall be* at the
king's house, and a third at the Gate
of the Foundation; and all the people
shall be in the courts of the house of
the LORD.
6 "But let no one enter the house
of the LORD except the priests and
[a]the ministering Levites; they may
enter, for they are holy. And let all
the people keep the charge of the
LORD.
7 "And the Levites will surround
the king, each man with his weapons in his hand; and whoever enters
the house, let him be killed. Thus be
with the king when he comes in and
when he goes out."
8 So the Levites and all Judah did
according to all that Jehoiada the
priest commanded. And each one of
them took his men who were to
come in on the sabbath, with those
who were to go out on the sabbath,
for Jehoiada the priest did not dismiss *any of* [a]the divisions.
9 Then Jehoiada the priest gave
to the captains of hundreds the
spears and the large and small
shields which had been King David's, which *were* in the house of
God.
10 And he stationed all the people,
each man with his weapon in his
hand, from the right [1]side of the
house to the left [1]side of the house,
by the altar and by the house,
around the king.
11 Then they brought out the
king's son and put the crown on
him, and *gave him* [a]the testimony,
and made him king. And Jehoiada
and his sons anointed him and said,
"[b]*Long* live the king!"

Athaliah Murdered

12 When Athaliah heard the noise
of the people running and praising
the king, she came into the house of
the LORD to the people.
13 And she looked, and behold, the
king was standing by his pillar at the
entrance, and the captains and the
[1]trumpeters *were* beside the king.
And all the people of the land rejoiced and blew trumpets, the singers with *their* musical instruments
[2]leading the praise. Then Athaliah
tore her clothes and said, "Treason!
Treason!"
14 And Jehoiada the priest
brought out the captains of hundreds who were appointed over the
army, and said to them, "Bring her
out [1]between the ranks; and whoever follows her, put to death with
the sword." For the priest said, "Let
her not be put to death in the house
of the LORD."
15 So they [1]seized her, and when
she arrived at [a]the entrance of the
Horse Gate of the king's house, they
[b]put her to death there.

Reforms Carried Out

16 Then Jehoiada made a covenant between himself and all the
people and the king, that they
should be the LORD's people.
17 And all the people went to the
house of Baal, and tore it down, and
they broke in pieces his altars and
his images, and [a]killed Mattan the
priest of Baal before the altars.
18 Moreover, Jehoiada placed the
offices of the house of the LORD under the [1]authority of [a]the Levitical
priests, [b]whom David had assigned
over the house of the LORD, to offer
the burnt offerings of the LORD, as it
is written in the law of Moses—
[c]with rejoicing and singing according to the [2]order of David.
19 And he stationed [a]the gatekeepers of the house of the LORD, so
that no one should enter *who was* in
any way unclean.
20 And he took the captains of
hundreds, the nobles, the rulers of
the people, and all the people of the
land, and brought the king down
from the house of the LORD, and
came through the upper gate to the
king's house. And they placed the
king upon the royal throne.
21 So all of the people of the land

1 [a]2 Kin. 11:4-20
2 [a]2 Chr. 11:13-17; 21:2
3 [1]Lit., *he* [a]2 Chr. 21:7
4 [a]1 Chr. 9:25
6 [a]1 Chr. 23:28-32
8 [a]1 Chr. 24:1
10 [1]Lit., *shoulder*
11 [a]Ex. 25:16, 21 [b]1 Sam. 10:24
13 [1]Lit., *trumpets* [2]Lit., *and leading for praising*
14 [1]Lit., *from within*
15 [1]Lit., *placed hands to her* [a]Neh. 3:28; Jer. 31:40 [b]2 Chr. 22:10
17 [a]Deut. 13:6-9; 1 Kin. 18:40
18 [1]Lit., *hand* [2]Lit., *hands of* [a]1 Chr. 23:6, 25-31; 2 Chr. 5:5 [b]1 Chr. 9:22 [c]2 Kin. 11:21; 12:1-15
19 [a]2 Chr. 26:4, 5

rejoiced and the city was quiet. For they had put Athaliah to death with the sword.

CHAPTER 24

Young Joash Influenced by Jehoiada

[a]JOASH *was* seven years old when he became king, and he reigned forty years in Jerusalem; his mother's name *was* Zibiah from Beer-sheba.

2 And [a]Joash did what was right in the sight of the LORD all the days of Jehoiada the priest.

3 And Jehoiada took two wives for him, and he became the father of sons and daughters.

Faithless Priests

4 Now it came about after this that Joash [1]decided [a]to restore the house of the LORD.

5 And he gathered the priests and Levites, and said to them, "Go out to the cities of Judah, and collect money from all [a]Israel to [1]repair the house of your God [2]annually, and you shall do the matter quickly." But the Levites did not act quickly.

6 So the king summoned Jehoiada the chief *priest* and said to him, "Why have you not required the Levites to bring in from Judah and from Jerusalem [a]the levy *fixed by* Moses the servant of the LORD on the congregation of Israel [b]for the tent of the testimony?"

7 For [a]the sons of the wicked Athaliah had broken into the house of God and even [1]used the holy things of the house of the LORD for the Baals.

Temple Repaired

8 So the king commanded, and they made a chest and set it outside by the gate of the house of the LORD.

9 And [a]they made a proclamation in Judah and Jerusalem to bring to the LORD [b]the levy *fixed by* Moses the servant of God on Israel in the wilderness.

10 And all the officers and all the people rejoiced and brought in their levies and [1]dropped *them* into the chest until they had finished.

11 And it came about whenever the chest was brought in to the king's officer by the Levites, and when they saw that there was much money, then the king's scribe and the chief priest's officer would come, empty the chest, take it, and return it to its place. Thus they did daily and collected much money.

12 And the king and Jehoiada gave it to those who did the work of the service of the house of the LORD; and they hired masons and carpenters to restore the house of the LORD, and also workers in iron and bronze to [1]repair the house of the LORD.

13 So the workmen labored, and the repair work progressed in their hands, and they [1]restored the house of God [2]according to its specifications, and strengthened it.

14 And when they had finished, they brought the rest of the money before the king and Jehoiada; and it was made into utensils for the house of the LORD, utensils for the service and the burnt offering, and pans and utensils of gold and silver. And they offered burnt offerings in the house of the LORD continually all the days of Jehoiada.

15 Now when Jehoiada [1]reached a ripe old age he died; he was one hundred and thirty years old at his death.

16 And they buried him [a]in the city of David among the kings, because he had done well in [b]Israel and [1]to God and His house.

17 But after the death of Jehoiada the officials of Judah came and bowed down to the king, and the king listened to them.

18 And [a]they abandoned the house of the LORD, the God of their fathers, and [b]served the [1]Asherim and the idols; so [c]wrath came upon Judah and Jerusalem for this their guilt.

19 Yet [a]He sent prophets to them to bring them back to the LORD; though they testified against them, they would not listen.

Joash Murders Son of Jehoiada

20 [a]Then the Spirit of God [1]came on Zechariah the son of Jehoiada the priest; and he stood above the people and said to them, "Thus God has said, 'Why do you transgress the commandments of the LORD and do not prosper? [b]Because you have forsaken the LORD, He has also forsaken you.' "

21 So [a]they conspired against him and at the command of the king they stoned him [1]to death in the court of the house of the LORD.

22 Thus Joash the king did not remember the kindness which his father Jehoiada had shown him, but he murdered his son. And as he died he said, "May [a]the LORD see and [1]avenge!"

1 [a]2 Kin. 11:21; 12:1-15

2 [a]2 Chr. 26:4, 5

4 [1]Lit., *was with a heart* [a]2 Chr. 24:7

5 [1]Lit., *to strengthen* [2]Lit., *from year to year* [a]2 Chr. 21:2

6 [a]Ex. 30:12-16 [b]Num. 1:50

7 [1]Lit., *made* [a]2 Chr. 21:17

9 [a]2 Chr. 36:22 [b]2 Chr. 24:6

10 [1]Lit., *threw*

12 [1]Lit., *to strengthen*

13 [1]Lit., *set up* [2]Lit., *upon its proportion*

15 [1]Lit., *became old and satisfied with days*

16 [1]Lit., *with* [a]2 Chr. 21:20 [b]2 Chr. 21:2

18 [1]I.e., wooden symbols of a female deity [a]2 Chr. 24:4 [b]Ex. 34:12-14 [c]Josh. 22:20

19 [a]Jer. 7:25

20 [1]Lit., *clothed* [a]2 Chr. 20:14 [b]Num. 14:41

21 [1]Lit., *with stones* [a]2 Chr. 15:2

22 [1]Lit., *seek,* or *require* [a]Neh. 9:26; Matt. 23:34, 35

Syria Invades and Defeats Judah

23 Now it came about at the turn
of the year that [a]the army of the Syrians came up against him; and they
came to Judah and Jerusalem, destroyed all the officials of the people
from among the people, and sent all
their spoil to the king of Damascus.
24 Indeed the army of the Syrians
came with a small number of men;
yet [a]the LORD delivered a very great
army into their hands, [b]because
they had forsaken the LORD, the God
of their fathers. Thus they executed
judgment on Joash.
25 [a]And when they had departed
from him (for they left him very
sick), his own servants conspired
against him because of the blood of
the [1]son of Jehoiada the priest, and
murdered him on his bed. So he
died, and they buried him in the city
of David, but they did not bury him
in the tombs of the kings.
26 Now these are those who conspired against him: Zabad the son of
Shimeath the Ammonitess, and Jehozabad the son of Shimrith the
Moabitess.
27 As to his sons and the many
[1]oracles against him and [a]the [2]re-
building of the house of God, behold, they are written in the [3b]trea-
tise of the Book of the Kings. Then
Amaziah his son became king in his
place.

CHAPTER 25

Amaziah Succeeds Joash in Judah

[a]AMAZIAH was twenty-five years
old when he became king, and he
reigned twenty-nine years in Jerusalem. And his mother's name was
Jehoaddan of Jerusalem.
2 And he did right in the sight of
the LORD, [a]yet not with a whole
heart.
3 Now it came about as soon as
the kingdom was [1]firmly in his
grasp, that he killed his servants
who had slain his father the king.
4 However, he did not put their
children to death, but *did* as it is
written in the law in the book of
Moses, which the LORD commanded, saying, "[a]Fathers shall not
be put to death for sons, nor sons be
put to death for fathers, but each
shall be put to death for his own
sin."

Amaziah Defeats Edomites

5 Moreover, Amaziah assembled
Judah and appointed them according to *their* fathers' households under commanders of thousands and
commanders of hundreds throughout Judah and Benjamin; and he
[1]took a census of those [a]from
twenty years old and upward, and
found them to be [b]300,000 choice
men, *able* to go to war *and* handle
spear and shield.
6 He hired also 100,000 valiant
warriors out of Israel for one hundred talents of silver.
7 But [a]a man of God came to him
saying, "O king, do not let the army
of Israel go with you, for the LORD is
not with Israel *nor with* any of the
sons of Ephraim.
8 "But if you do go, do *it*, be strong
for the battle; *yet* God will [1]bring
you down before the enemy, [a]for
God has power to help and to [1]bring
down."
9 And Amaziah said to the man
of God, "But what *shall we* do for
the hundred talents which I have
given to the troops of Israel?" And
the man of God answered, "The
LORD has much more to give you
than this."
10 Then Amaziah [1]dismissed
them, the troops which came to him
from Ephraim, to go home; so their
anger burned against Judah and
they returned [2]home in fierce anger.
11 Now Amaziah strengthened
himself, and led his people forth,
and went to [a]the Valley of Salt, and
struck down 10,000 of the sons of
Seir.
12 The sons of Judah also captured 10,000 alive and brought them
to the top of the cliff, and threw
them down from the top of the cliff
so that they were all dashed to
pieces.
13 But the [1]troops whom Amaziah
sent back from going with him to
battle, raided the cities of Judah,
[a]from Samaria to Beth-horon, and
struck down 3,000 of them, and
plundered much spoil.

Amaziah Rebuked for Idolatry

14 Now it came about after Amaziah came from slaughtering the
Edomites that [a]he brought the gods
of the sons of Seir, set them up as
his gods, bowed down before them,
and burned incense to them.
15 Then the anger of the LORD
burned against Amaziah, and He
sent him a prophet who said to him,
"Why have you sought the gods of
the people [a]who have not delivered
their own people from your hand?"
16 And it came about as he was
talking with him that [1]the king said

23 [a]Gen. 9:5
24 [a]2 Kin. 12:17 [b]2 Chr. 16:7, 8
25 [1]So some ancient versions; Heb., *sons* [a]2 Kin. 12:20, 21
27 [1]Or, *burdens upon* [2]Lit., *founding* [3]Heb., *midrash* [a]2 Chr. 24:12 [b]2 Chr. 13:22
1 [a]2 Kin. 14:1-6
2 [a]2 Chr. 25:14
3 [1]Lit., *firm upon him*
4 [a]Deut. 24:16
5 [1]Lit., *mustered* [a]Num. 1:3 [b]2 Chr. 26:13
7 [a]2 Kin. 4:9
8 [1]Lit., *cause to stumble* [a]2 Chr. 14:11; 20:6
10 [1]Lit., *separated* [2]Lit., *to their own place*
11 [a]2 Kin. 14:7
13 [1]Lit., *sons of the troops* [a]2 Chr. 19:4
14 [a]2 Chr. 28:23
15 [a]2 Chr. 25:11, 12
16 [1]Lit., *he*

to him, "Have we appointed you a royal counselor? Stop! Why should you be struck down?" Then the prophet stopped and said, "I know that God has planned to destroy you, because you have done this, and have not listened to my counsel."

Amaziah Defeated by Joash of Israel

17 [a]Then Amaziah king of Judah took counsel and sent to Joash the son of Jehoahaz the son of Jehu, the king of Israel, saying, "Come, let us face each other."

18 And Joash the king of Israel sent to Amaziah king of Judah, saying, "[a]The thorn bush which was in Lebanon sent to the cedar which was in Lebanon, saying, 'Give your daughter to my son in marriage.' But there passed by a wild beast that was in Lebanon, and trampled the thorn bush.

19 "You said, 'Behold, you have [1]defeated Edom.' And [a]your heart has [2]become proud in boasting. Now stay at home; for why should you provoke trouble that you, even you, should fall and Judah with you?"

20 But Amaziah would not listen, for it was from God, that He might deliver them into the hand *of Joash* because they had sought the gods of Edom.

21 So Joash king of Israel went up, and he and Amaziah king of Judah faced each other at Beth-shemesh, which belonged to Judah.

22 And Judah was defeated [1]by Israel, and they fled each to his tent.

23 Then Joash king of Israel captured Amaziah king of Judah, the son of Joash the son of [a]Jehoahaz, at Beth-shemesh, and brought him to Jerusalem, and tore down the wall of Jerusalem from the Gate of Ephraim to the Corner Gate, 400 [1]cubits.

24 And *he took* all the gold and silver, and all the utensils which were found in the house of God with [a]Obed-edom, and the treasures of the king's house, the hostages also, and returned to Samaria.

25 [a]And Amaziah, the son of Joash king of Judah, lived fifteen years after the death of Joash, son of Jehoahaz, king of Israel.

26 Now the rest of the acts of Amaziah, from first to last, behold, are they not written in the Book of the Kings of Judah and Israel?

27 And from the time that Amaziah turned away from following the LORD they conspired against him in Jerusalem, and he fled to Lachish; but they sent after him to Lachish and killed him there.

28 Then they brought him on horses and buried him with his fathers in the city of Judah.

Chapter 26

Uzziah Succeeds Amaziah in Judah

AND all the people of Judah took [1]Uzziah, who *was* sixteen years old, and made him king in the place of his father Amaziah.

2 He built Eloth and restored it to Judah after the king slept with his fathers.

3 Uzziah was [a]sixteen years old when he became king, and he reigned fifty-two years in Jerusalem; and his mother's name was [1]Jechiliah of Jerusalem.

4 And he did right in the sight of the LORD according to all that his father Amaziah had done.

5 And [a]he continued to seek God in the days of Zechariah, [b]who had understanding [1]through the vision of God; and [2][c]as long as he sought the LORD, God prospered him.

Uzziah Succeeds in War

6 Now he went out and [a]warred against the Philistines, and broke down the wall of Gath and the wall of Jabneh and the wall of Ashdod; and he built cities in *the area of* Ashdod and among the Philistines.

7 And [a]God helped him against the Philistines, and against the Arabians who lived in Gur-baal, and the Meunites.

8 [a]The Ammonites also gave tribute to Uzziah, and his [1]fame extended to the border of Egypt, for he became very strong.

9 Moreover, Uzziah built towers in Jerusalem at [a]the Corner Gate and at the [b]Valley Gate and at the corner buttress and fortified them.

10 And he built towers in the wilderness and [a]hewed many cisterns, for he had much livestock, both in the [1]lowland and in the plain. *He also had* plowmen and vinedressers in the hill country and the fertile fields, for he loved the soil.

11 Moreover, Uzziah had an army ready for battle, which [1]entered combat by divisions, according to the number of their muster, [2]prepared by Jeiel the scribe and Maaseiah the official, under the direction of Hananiah, one of the king's officers.

12 The total number of the heads

---

17 [a]2 Kin. 14:8-14
18 [a]Judg. 9:8-15
19 [1]Lit., *smitten* [2]Lit., *lifted you up to boast* [a]2 Chr. 26:16; 32:25
22 [1]Lit., *before*
23 [1]One cubit equals approximately 18 inches [a]2 Chr. 21:17; 22:1
24 [a]1 Chr. 26:15
25 [a]2 Kin. 14:17-22
1 [1]In 2 Kin. 14:20, *Azariah*
3 [1]In 2 Kin. 15:2, *Jecoliah* [a]2 Kin. 15:2, 3
5 [1]Many mss. read *in the fear of God* [2]Lit., *in the days of his seeking* [a]2 Chr. 24:2 [b]Dan. 1:17 [c]2 Chr. 15:2
6 [a]Is. 14:29
7 [a]2 Chr. 21:16
8 [1]Lit., *name went to the entering of Egypt* [a]2 Chr. 17:11
9 [a]2 Chr. 25:23 [b]Neh. 2:13, 15; 3:13
10 [1]Or, *shephelah* [a]Gen. 26:18-21
11 [1]Lit., *goes out to* [2]Lit., *by the hand of*

of the [1]*households,* of valiant warriors, was 2,600.
13 And under their direction was
an [1]elite army of [a]307,500, who
could wage war with great power,
to help the king against the enemy.
14 Moreover, Uzziah prepared
[1]for all the army shields, spears, hel-
mets, body armor, bows and sling
stones.
15 And in Jerusalem he made en-
gines *of war* invented by skillful
men to be on the towers and on the
corners, for the purpose of shooting
arrows and great stones. Hence his
[1]fame spread afar, for he was mar-
velously helped until he *was* strong.

Pride Is Uzziah's Undoing

16 But [a]when he became strong,
his heart was so [1]proud that he
acted corruptly, and he was unfaithful to the LORD his God, for [b]he entered the temple of the LORD to burn
incense on the altar of incense.
17 Then [a]Azariah the priest entered after him and with him eighty
priests of the LORD, valiant men.
18 And [a]they opposed Uzziah the
king and said to him, "[b]It is not for
you, Uzziah, to burn incense to the
LORD, [c]but for the priests, the sons
of Aaron who are consecrated to
burn incense. Get out of the sanctuary, for you have been unfaithful,
and will have no honor from the
LORD God."
19 But Uzziah, with a censer in his
hand for burning incense, was enraged; and while he was enraged
with the priests, [a]the leprosy broke
out on his forehead before the
priests in the house of the LORD, beside the altar of incense.
20 And Azariah the chief priest
and all the priests looked at him,
and behold, he *was* leprous on his
forehead; and they hurried him out
of there, and he himself also hastened to get out because the LORD
had smitten him.
21 [a]And King Uzziah was a leper
to the day of his death; and he lived
in [b]a separate house, being a leper,
for he was cut off from the house of
the LORD. And Jotham his son *was*
over the king's house judging the
people of the land.
22 Now the rest of the acts of Uzziah, first to last, the prophet [a]Isa-
iah, the son of Amoz, has written.
23 So Uzziah slept with his fathers, and they buried him with his
fathers [a]in the field of the grave
which belonged to the kings, for
they said, "He is a leper." And Jotham his son became king in his
place.

12 [1]Lit., *fathers' houses;* i.e., clans
13 [1]Lit., *powerful* [a]2 Chr. 25:5
14 [1]Lit., *for them, for all*
15 [1]Lit., *name*
16 [1]Lit., *lifted up* [a]Deut. 32:15; 2 Chr. 25:19 [b]1 Kin. 13:1-4
17 [a]1 Chr. 6:10
18 [a]2 Chr. 19:2 [b]Num. 16:39, 40 [c]Ex. 30:7, 8
19 [a]2 Kin. 5:25-27
21 [a]2 Kin. 15:5-7 [b]Lev. 13:46
22 [a]Is. 1:1
23 [a]2 Chr. 21:20; 28:27
1 [a]2 Kin. 15:33-35
2 [a]2 Chr. 26:16
3 [a]2 Chr. 33:14; Neh. 3:26
4 [a]2 Chr. 11:5
5 [1]A kor equals approx. 10 bu.
6 [a]2 Chr. 26:5
7 [a]2 Kin. 15:36
8 [a]2 Chr. 27:1
1 [a]2 Kin. 16:2-4 [b]2 Chr. 27:2
2 [a]2 Chr. 22:3 [b]Ex. 34:17
3 [a]Josh. 15:8 [b]Lev. 18:21; 2 Chr. 33:6 [c]2 Chr. 33:2

CHAPTER 27

Jotham Succeeds Uzziah in Judah

[a]JOTHAM was twenty-five years old
when he became king, and he
reigned sixteen years in Jerusalem.
And his mother's name was Jeru-
shah the daughter of Zadok.
2 And he did right in the sight of
the LORD, according to all that his
father Uzziah had done; [a]however
he did not enter the temple of the
LORD. But the people continued acting corruptly.
3 He built the upper gate of the
house of the LORD, and he built extensively the wall of [a]Ophel.
4 Moreover, he built [a]cities in the
hill country of Judah, and he built
fortresses and towers on the
wooded *hills.*
5 He fought also with the king of
the Ammonites and prevailed over
them so that the Ammonites gave
him during that year one hundred
talents of silver, ten thousand [1]kors
of wheat and ten thousand of barley.
The Ammonites also paid him this
amount in the second and in the
third year.
6 [a]So Jotham became mighty because he ordered his ways before
the LORD his God.
7 [a]Now the rest of the acts of Jotham, even all his wars and his acts,
behold, they are written in the Book
of the Kings of Israel and Judah.
8 He was [a]twenty-five years old
when he became king, and he
reigned sixteen years in Jerusalem.
9 And Jotham slept with his fathers, and they buried him in the
city of David; and Ahaz his son became king in his place.

CHAPTER 28

Ahaz Succeeds Jotham in Judah

[a]AHAZ *was* twenty years old when
he became king, and he reigned sixteen years in Jerusalem; and [b]he did
not do right in the sight of the LORD
as David his father *had done.*
2 [a]But he walked in the ways of
the kings of Israel; he also [b]made
molten images for the Baals.
3 Moreover, [a]he burned incense
in the valley of Ben-hinnom, and
[b]burned his sons in fire, [c]according
to the abominations of the nations
whom the LORD had driven out before the sons of Israel.

4 And he sacrificed and [a]burned
incense on the high places, on the
hills, and under every green tree.

Judah Is Invaded

5 Wherefore, [a]the LORD his God
delivered him into the hand of the
king of Syria; and they [1]defeated
him and carried away from him a
great number of captives, and
brought *them* to Damascus. And he
was also delivered into the hand of
the king of Israel, who [2]inflicted him
with heavy casualties.
6 For [a]Pekah the son of Remaliah
slew in Judah 120,000 in one day, all
valiant men, because they had forsaken the LORD God of their fathers.
7 And Zichri, a mighty man of E-
phraim, slew Maaseiah the king's
son, and Azrikam the ruler of the
house and Elkanah the second to the
king.
8 And [a]the sons of Israel carried
away captive of [b]their brethren
200,000 women, sons, and daughters; and [1]took also a great deal of
spoil from them, and they brought
the spoil to Samaria.
9 But a prophet of the LORD was
there, whose name *was* Oded; and
[a]he went out to meet the army
which came to Samaria and said to
them, "Behold, because the LORD,
the God of your fathers, [b]was angry
with Judah, He has delivered them
into your hand, and you have slain
them in a rage [c]*which* has even
reached heaven.
10"And now you are proposing to
subjugate for yourselves the people
of Judah and Jerusalem for male
and female slaves. Surely, *do* you
not *have* transgressions of your own
against the LORD your God?
11"Now therefore, listen to me and
return the captives [a]whom you captured from your brothers, for the
burning anger of the LORD is against
you."
12 Then some of the heads of the
sons of Ephraim—Azariah the son
of Johanan, Berechiah the son of
Meshillemoth, Jehizkiah the son of
Shallum, and Amasa the son of Had-
lai—arose against those who were
coming from the battle,
13 and said to them, "You must
not bring the captives in here, for
you are proposing *to bring* upon us
guilt against the LORD adding to our
sins and our guilt; for our guilt is
great so that *His* burning anger is
against Israel."
14 So the armed men left the captives and the spoil before the officers and all the assembly.
15 Then [a]the men who were designated by name arose, took the captives, and they clothed all their
naked ones from the spoil; and they
gave them clothes and sandals, fed
them and [b]gave them drink,
anointed them *with oil,* led all their
feeble ones on donkeys, and
brought them to Jericho, [c]the city of
palm trees, to their brothers; then
they returned to Samaria.

Compromise with Assyria

16 [a]At that time King Ahaz sent to
the [1]kings of Assyria for help.
17 [a]For again the Edomites had
come and attacked Judah, and carried away captives.
18 [a]The Philistines also had invaded the cities of the [1]lowland and
of the Negev of Judah, and had
taken Beth-shemesh, Aijalon, Gederoth, and Soco with its villages,
Timnah with its villages, and Gimzo
with its villages, and they settled
there.
19 For the LORD humbled Judah
because of Ahaz king of [a]Israel, for
he had brought about a lack of restraint in Judah and was very unfaithful to the LORD.
20 So [a]Tilgath-pilneser king of Assyria came against him and afflicted
him instead of strengthening him.
21 [a]And Ahaz took a portion out of
the house of the LORD and out of the
palace of the king and of the
princes, and gave *it* to the king of
Assyria; but it did not help him.
22 Now in the time of his distress
this same King Ahaz became yet
more unfaithful to the LORD.
23 [a]For he sacrificed to the gods of
Damascus which had [1]defeated
him, and said, "[b]Because the gods of
the kings of Syria helped them, I will
sacrifice to them that they may help
me." But they became the [2]downfall
of him and all Israel.
24 Moreover, when Ahaz gathered
together the utensils of the house of
God, he [a]cut the utensils of the
house of God in pieces; and he
[b]closed the doors of the house of the
LORD, and [c]made altars for himself
in every corner of Jerusalem.
25 And in every city of Judah he
made high places to burn incense to
other gods, and provoked the LORD,
the God of his fathers, to anger.
26 [a]Now the rest of his acts and all
his ways, from first to last, behold,
they are written in the Book of the
Kings of Judah and Israel.
27 So Ahaz slept with his fathers,
and they buried him in the city, in

4 [a]2 Chr. 28:25

5 [1]Lit., *smote* [2]Lit., *smote him with a great smiting* [a]2 Chr. 24:24

6 [a]2 Kin. 16:5

8 [1]Lit., *plundered* [a]Deut. 28:25, 41 [b]2 Chr. 11:4

9 [a]2 Chr. 25:15 [b]Is. 47:6 [c]Ezra 9:6; Rev. 18:5

11 [a]2 Chr. 28:8

15 [a]2 Chr. 28:12 [b]2 Kin. 6:22; Prov. 25:21, 22 [c]Deut. 34:3

16 [1]Ancient versions read *king* [a]2 Kin. 16:7

17 [a]Obad. 10, 14

18 [1]Or, *shephelah* [a]Ezek. 16:57

19 [a]2 Chr. 21:2

20 [a]1 Chr. 5:26

21 [a]2 Kin. 16:8, 9

23 [1]Lit., *smitten* [2]Lit., *stumbling* [a]2 Chr. 25:14 [b]Jer. 44:17, 18

24 [a]2 Kin. 16:17 [b]2 Chr. 29:7 [c]2 Chr. 30:14; 33:3-5

26 [a]2 Kin. 16:19, 20

Jerusalem, [a]for they did not bring
him into the tombs of the kings of
[b]Israel; and Hezekiah his son
reigned in his place.

CHAPTER 29

Hezekiah Succeeds Ahaz in Judah

[a]HEZEKIAH became king *when he*
was twenty-five years old; and he
reigned twenty-nine years in Jerusalem. And his mother's name *was*
Abijah, the daughter of Zechariah.
2 And [a]he did right in the sight of
the LORD, according to all that his
father David had done.
3 In the first year of his reign, in
the first month, he [a]opened the
doors of the house of the LORD and
repaired them.
4 And he brought in the priests
and the Levites, and gathered them
into the square on the east.

Reforms Begun

5 Then he said to them, "Listen to
me, O Levites. [a]Consecrate yourselves now, and consecrate the
house of the LORD, the God of your
fathers, and carry the uncleanness
out from the holy place.
6"For our fathers have been unfaithful and have done evil in the
sight of the LORD our God, and have
forsaken Him and [a]turned their
faces away from the dwelling place
of the LORD, and have [1]turned *their*
backs.
7"They have also shut the doors
of the porch and put out the lamps,
and have not burned incense or offered burnt offerings in the holy
place to the God of Israel.
8"Therefore [a]the wrath of the
LORD was against Judah and Jerusalem, and [b]He has made them an [c]ob-
ject of terror, of horror, and of [d]hiss-
ing, as you see with your own eyes.
9"For behold, [a]our fathers have
fallen by the sword, and our sons
and our daughters and our wives are
in captivity for this.
10"Now it is in my heart [a]to make
a covenant with the LORD God of
Israel, that His burning anger may
turn away from us.
11"My sons, do not be negligent
now, for [a]the LORD has chosen you
to stand before Him, to minister to
Him, and to be His ministers and
burn incense."
12 Then the Levites arose: [a]Ma-
hath, the son of Amasai and Joel the
son of Azariah, from the sons of [b]the
Kohathites; and from the sons of
Merari, Kish the son of Abdi and
Azariah the son of Jehallelel; and
from the Gershonites, Joah the son
of Zimmah and Eden the son of
Joah;
13 and from the sons of Elizaphan,
Shimri and [1]Jeiel; and from the sons
of Asaph, Zechariah and Mattaniah;
14 and from the sons of Heman,
[1]Jehiel and Shimei; and from the
sons of Jeduthun, Shemaiah and Uzziel.
15 And they assembled their
brothers, [a]consecrated themselves,
and went in [b]to cleanse the house of
the LORD, according to the commandment of the king [c]by the words
of the LORD.
16 So the priests went in to the inner part of the house of the LORD to
cleanse *it*, and every unclean thing
which they found in the temple of
the LORD they brought out to the
court of the house of the LORD. Then
the Levites received *it* to carry out
to [a]the Kidron [1]valley.
17 Now they began [1]the consecration [a]on the first *day* of the first
month, and on the eighth day of the
month they entered the porch of the
LORD. Then they consecrated the
house of the LORD in eight days, and
finished on the sixteenth day of the
first month.
18 Then they went in to King Hezekiah and said, "We have cleansed
the whole house of the LORD, the altar of burnt offering with all of its
utensils, and the table of showbread
with all of its utensils.
19"Moreover, [a]all the utensils
which King Ahaz had discarded
during his reign in his unfaithfulness, we have prepared and consecrated; and behold, they are before
the altar of the LORD."

Hezekiah Restores Temple Worship

20 Then King Hezekiah arose early and assembled the princes of the
city and went up to the house of the
LORD.
21 And they brought seven bulls,
seven rams, seven lambs, and seven
male goats [a]for a sin offering for the
kingdom, the sanctuary, and Judah.
And he ordered the priests, the sons
of Aaron, to offer *them* on the altar
of the LORD.
22 So they slaughtered the bulls,
and the priests took the blood and
sprinkled it on the altar. They also
slaughtered the rams and sprinkled
the blood on the altar; they slaughtered the lambs also and [a]sprinkled
the blood on the altar.
23 Then they brought the male

27 [a]2 Chr. 24:25 [b]2 Chr. 21:2
1 [a]2 Kin. 18:1-3
2 [a]2 Chr. 28:1; 34:2
3 [a]2 Chr. 28:24; 29:7
5 [a]2 Chr. 29:15, 34; 35:6
6 [1]Lit., *given* [a]Ezek. 8:16
8 [a]2 Chr. 24:15 [b]2 Chr. 28:5 [c]Deut. 28:25 [d]Jer. 25:9, 18
9 [a]2 Chr. 28:5-8, 17
10 [a]2 Chr. 23:16
11 [a]Num. 3:6; 8:6
12 [a]2 Chr. 31:13 [b]Num. 3:19, 20
13 [1]Or, *Jeuel*
14 [1]Or, *Jehuel*, 1 Chr. 15:18, 20
15 [a]2 Chr. 29:5 [b]1 Chr. 23:28 [c]2 Chr. 30:12
16 [1]Or, *wadi* [a]2 Chr. 15:16
17 [1]Lit., *to consecrate* [a]2 Chr. 29:3
19 [a]2 Chr. 28:24
21 [a]Lev. 4:3-14
22 [a]Lev. 4:18

goats of the sin offering before the
king and the assembly, and [a]they
laid their hands on them.
24 And the priests slaughtered
them and purged the altar with their
blood [a]to atone for all Israel, for the
king ordered the burnt offering and
the sin offering for all Israel.
25 [a]He then stationed the Levites
in the house of the LORD with cymbals, with harps, and with lyres, [b]ac-
cording to the command of David
and of [c]Gad the king's seer, and of
[d]Nathan the prophet; for the command was from the LORD through
His prophets.
26 And the Levites stood with [a]the
musical instruments of David, and
[b]the priests with the trumpets.
27 Then Hezekiah gave the order
to offer the burnt offering on the altar. When the burnt offering began,
[a]the song to the LORD also began
with the trumpets, [1]*accompanied*
by the instruments of David, king of
Israel.
28 While the whole assembly worshiped, the singers also sang and the
trumpets sounded; all this *continued* until the burnt offering was finished.
29 Now at the completion of the
burnt offerings, [a]the king and all
who were present with him bowed
down and worshiped.
30 Moreover, King Hezekiah and
the officials ordered the Levites to
sing praises to the LORD with the
words of David and Asaph the seer.
So they sang praises with joy, and
bowed down and worshiped.
31 Then Hezekiah answered and
said, "[a]Now *that* you have [1]conse-
crated yourselves to the LORD, come
near and bring sacrifices and thank
offerings to the house of the LORD."
And the assembly brought sacrifices and thank offerings, and [b]all
those who [2]were willing *brought*
burnt offerings.
32 And the number of the burnt offerings which the assembly brought
was 70 bulls, 100 rams, and 200
lambs: all these were for a burnt offering to the LORD.
33 And the consecrated things
were 600 bulls and 3,000 sheep.
34 But the priests were too few, so
that they were unable to skin all the
burnt offerings; [a]therefore their
brothers the Levites helped them
until the work was completed, and
until the *other* priests had consecrated themselves. For [b]the Levites
were [1]more conscientious to consecrate themselves than the priests.
35 And there *were* also [1a]many

23 [a]Lev. 4:15
24 [a]Lev. 4:26
25 [a]1 Chr. 25:6 [b]2 Chr. 8:14 [c]2 Sam. 24:11 [d]2 Sam. 7:2
26 [a]1 Chr. 23:5 [b]2 Chr. 5:12
27 [1]Lit., *and according to the authority of the instruments* [a]2 Chr. 23:18
29 [a]2 Chr. 20:18
31 [1]Lit., *filled your hands* [2]Lit., *willing of heart* [a]2 Chr. 13:9 [b]Ex. 35:5, 22
34 [1]Lit., *upright of heart* [a]2 Chr. 35:11 [b]2 Chr. 30:3
35 [1]Lit., *the burnt offerings to an abundance* [a]2 Chr. 29:32 [b]Lev. 3:16 [c]Num. 15:5-10
1 [1]Lit., *do*, so in vs. 2, 3, 5, 13, 21, 23
2 [a]Num. 9:10, 11; 2 Chr. 30:13, 15
3 [a]2 Chr. 29:17, 34
4 [1]Lit., *in the sight of all*
5 [1]Lit., *voice* [2]Lit., *written* [a]Judg. 20:1
6 [1]Lit., *runners* [2]Lit., *palm* [a]Esth. 8:14; Job 9:25; Jer. 51:31 [b]2 Chr. 28:20
7 [a]Ezek. 20:13 [b]2 Chr. 29:8
8 [1]Lit., *give a hand* [a]Ex. 32:9 [b]2 Chr. 29:10
9 [a]Deut. 30:2 [b]Ex. 34:6, 7; Mic. 7:18

burnt offerings with [b]the fat of the
peace offerings and with [c]the libations for the burnt offerings. Thus
the service of the house of the LORD
was established *again*.
36 Then Hezekiah and all the people rejoiced over what God had prepared for the people, because the
thing came about suddenly.

CHAPTER 30

All Israel Invited to the Passover

NOW Hezekiah sent to all Israel
and Judah and wrote letters also to
Ephraim and Manasseh, that they
should come to the house of the
LORD at Jerusalem to [1]celebrate the
Passover to the LORD God of Israel.
2 For the king and his princes and
all the assembly in Jerusalem had
decided [a]to celebrate the Passover
in the second month,
3 since they could not celebrate it
[a]at that time, because the priests
had not consecrated themselves in
sufficient numbers, nor had the people been gathered to Jerusalem.
4 Thus the thing was right in the
sight of the king and [1]all the assembly.
5 So they established a decree to
circulate a [1]proclamation throughout all Israel [a]from Beersheba even
to Dan, that they should come to
celebrate the Passover to the LORD
God of Israel at Jerusalem. For they
had not celebrated *it* in great numbers as it was [2]prescribed.
6 And [a]the [1]couriers went
throughout all Israel and Judah with
the letters from the hand of the king
and his princes, even according to
the command of the king, saying,
"O sons of Israel, return to the LORD
God of Abraham, Isaac, and Israel,
that He may return to those of you
who escaped *and* are left from [b]the
[2]hand of the kings of Assyria.
7 "[a]And do not be like your fathers
and your brothers, who were unfaithful to the LORD God of their fathers, so that [b]He made them a horror, as you see.
8 "Now do not [a]stiffen your neck
like your fathers, but [1]yield to the
LORD and enter His sanctuary which
He has consecrated forever, and
serve the LORD your God, [b]that His
burning anger may turn away from
you.
9 "For [a]if you return to the LORD,
your brothers and your sons *will
find* compassion before those who
led them captive, and will return to
this land. [b]For the LORD your God is

gracious and compassionate, and
will not turn *His* face away from you
if you return to Him."
10 So the [1]couriers passed from
city to city through the country of
Ephraim and Manasseh, and as far
as Zebulun, but [a]they laughed them
to scorn, and mocked them.
11 Nevertheless [a]some men of
Asher, Manasseh, and Zebulun
humbled themselves and came to
Jerusalem.
12 The hand of God was also on
Judah to give them one heart to do
what the king and the princes commanded by the word of the LORD.

Passover Reinstituted

13 Now many people were gathered at Jerusalem to celebrate the
Feast of Unleavened Bread [a]in the
second month, a very large assembly.
14 And they arose and removed
the altars which *were* in Jerusalem;
they also [a]removed all the incense
altars and [b]cast *them* into the brook
Kidron.
15 Then [a]they slaughtered the
Passover *lambs* on the fourteenth of
the second month. And [b]the priests
and Levites were ashamed of themselves and consecrated themselves,
and brought burnt offerings to the
house of the LORD.
16 And [a]they stood at their stations after their custom, according
to the law of Moses the man of God;
the priests sprinkled the blood
which they received from the hand
of the Levites.
17 For *there were* many in the assembly who had not consecrated
themselves; therefore, [a]the Levites
were over the slaughter of the Passover *lambs* for every one who *was*
unclean, in order to consecrate *them*
to the LORD.
18 For a multitude of the people,
[a]*even* many from Ephraim and Manasseh, Issachar and Zebulun, had
not purified themselves, [b]yet they
ate the Passover [c]otherwise than
[1]prescribed. For Hezekiah prayed
for them, saying, "May the good
LORD pardon
19 [a]everyone who prepares his
heart to seek God, the LORD God of
his fathers, though not according to
the purification *rules* of the sanctuary."
20 So the LORD heard Hezekiah
and healed the people.
21 And the sons of Israel present
in Jerusalem [a]celebrated the Feast
of Unleavened Bread *for* seven days
with great joy, and the Levites and

10 [1]Lit., *runners* [a]2 Chr. 36:16
11 [a]2 Chr. 30:18, 21, 25
13 [a]2 Chr. 30:2
14 [a]2 Chr. 28:24 [b]2 Chr. 29:16
15 [a]2 Chr. 30:2, 3 [b]2 Chr. 29:34
16 [a]2 Chr. 35:10, 15
17 [a]2 Chr. 29:34
18 [1]Lit., *written* [a]2 Chr. 30:11, 25 [b]Num. 9:10 [c]Ex. 12:43-49
19 [a]2 Chr. 19:3
21 [a]Ex. 12:15; 13:6
22 [1]Lit., *to the heart of* [a]2 Chr. 32:6 [b]Ezra 10:11
23 [a]1 Kin. 8:65
24 [a]2 Chr. 35:7, 8 [b]2 Chr. 29:34; 30:3
25 [a]2 Chr. 30:11, 18
26 [a]2 Chr. 7:8-10
27 [a]2 Chr. 23:18 [b]Num. 6:23 [c]Deut. 26:15; Ps. 68:5
1 [1]I.e., wooden symbols of a female deity [2]Lit., *even to completion* [a]2 Kin. 18:4
2 [a]1 Chr. 24:1 [b]1 Chr. 23:28-31
3 [a]2 Chr. 35:7

the priests praised the LORD day after day with loud instruments to the
LORD.
22 Then Hezekiah [a]spoke [1]encour-
agingly to all the Levites who
showed good insight *in the things* of
the LORD. So they ate for the appointed seven days, sacrificing
peace offerings and [b]giving thanks
to the LORD God of their fathers.
23 Then the whole assembly [a]de-
cided to celebrate *the feast* another
seven days, so they celebrated the
seven days with joy.
24 For [a]Hezekiah king of Judah
had contributed to the assembly
1,000 bulls and 7,000 sheep, and the
princes had contributed to the assembly 1,000 bulls and 10,000
sheep; and [b]a large number of
priests consecrated themselves.
25 And all the assembly of Judah
rejoiced, with the priests and the Levites, and [a]all the assembly that
came from Israel, both the sojourners who came from the land of Israel
and those living in Judah.
26 So there was great joy in Jerusalem, because there was nothing
like this in Jerusalem [a]since the
days of Solomon the son of David,
king of Israel.
27 Then [a]the Levitical priests
arose and [b]blessed the people; and
their voice was heard and their
prayer came to [c]His holy dwelling
place, to heaven.

CHAPTER 31

Idols Are Destroyed

NOW when all this was finished,
all Israel who were present went out
to the cities of Judah, [a]broke the pillars in pieces, cut down the [1]Ashe-
rim, and pulled down the high
places and the altars throughout all
Judah and Benjamin, as well as in
Ephraim and Manasseh, [2]until they
had destroyed them all. Then all the
sons of Israel returned to their
cities, each to his possession.
2 And Hezekiah appointed [a]the
divisions of the priests and the Levites by their divisions, each according to his service, *both* the priests
and the Levites, [b]for burnt offerings
and for peace offerings, to minister
and to give thanks and to praise in
the gates of the camp of the LORD.

Reforms Continued

3 *He* also *appointed* [a]the king's
portion of his goods for the burnt
offerings, *namely,* for the morning
and evening burnt offerings, and the

burnt offerings for the sabbaths and
for the new moons and for the fixed
festivals, [b]as it is written in the law
of the LORD.
4 Also he [1]commanded the people who lived in Jerusalem to give
[a]the portion due to the priests and
the Levites, that they might devote
themselves to the law of the LORD.
5 And as soon as the [1]order
spread, the sons of Israel provided
in abundance the first fruits of grain,
new wine, oil, honey, and of all the
produce of the field; and they
brought in abundantly [a]the tithe of
all.
6 And the sons of Israel and Judah who lived in the cities of Judah,
also brought in the tithe of oxen and
sheep, and [a]the tithe of [1]sacred gifts
which were consecrated to the LORD
their God, and placed *them* in heaps.
7 In the third month they began
to [1]make the heaps, and finished
them by the seventh month.
8 And when Hezekiah and the
rulers came and saw the heaps, they
blessed the LORD and His people Israel.
9 Then Hezekiah questioned the
priests and the Levites concerning
the heaps.
10 And Azariah the chief priest [a]of
the house of Zadok said to [1]him,
"[b]Since the contributions began to
be brought into the house of the
LORD, we have had enough to eat
with plenty left over, for the LORD
has blessed His people, and this
great quantity is left over."
11 Then Hezekiah commanded
them to prepare [a]rooms in the house
of the LORD, and they prepared
them.
12 And they faithfully brought in
the contributions and the tithes and
the consecrated things; and Conaniah the Levite *was* the officer in
charge [a]of them and his brother
Shimei *was* second.
13 And Jehiel, Azaziah, Nahath,
Asahel, Jerimoth, Jozabad, Eliel, Is-
machiah, Mahath, and Benaiah *were*
overseers [1]under the authority of
Conaniah and Shimei his brother by
the appointment of King Hezekiah,
and [a]Azariah *was* the *chief* officer of
the house of God.
14 And Kore the son of Imnah the
Levite, the keeper of the eastern
gate, was over the freewill offerings
of God, to apportion the contributions for the LORD and the most holy
things.
15 And [1]under his authority *were*
[a]Eden, Miniamin, Jeshua, Shemaiah, Amariah, and Shecaniah in [b]the

3 [b]Num. 28:1-29, 40

4 [1]Lit., *said to* [a]Num. 18:8

5 [1]Lit., *word* [a]Neh. 13:12

6 [1]Lit., *consecrated things* [a]Lev. 27:30; Deut. 14:28

7 [1]Lit., *found*

10 [1]Lit., *him, and he said* [a]1 Chr. 6:8, 9 [b]Mal. 3:10

11 [a]1 Kin. 6:5, 8

12 [a]2 Chr. 35:9

13 [1]Lit., *from the hand of* [a]2 Chr. 31:10

15 [1]Lit., *under his hand* [a]2 Chr. 29:12 [b]Josh. 21:9-19 [c]1 Chr. 9:22

16 [1]Heb., *three,* cf. 1 Chr. 23:3 [a]Ezra 3:4

17 [a]1 Chr. 23:24

18 [1]Lit., *with all* [2]Lit., *in their faithfulness*

19 [a]Lev. 25:34; Num. 35:2-5 [b]2 Chr. 31:12-15

20 [a]2 Kin. 20:3; 22:2

1 [1]Lit., *things and this faithfulness* [2]Lit., *said* [a]2 Kin. 18:13-19, 37; Is. 36:1-37:38

2 [1]Lit., *his face for war against*

4 [1]Lit., *in the midst of the land* [a]2 Kin. 20:20 [b]2 Chr. 32:30

5 [a]2 Chr. 25:23

cities of the priests, to distribute
[c]faithfully *their portions* to their
brothers by divisions, whether great
or small,
16 without regard to their genealogical enrollment, to the males
from [1]thirty years old and upward—everyone who entered the
house of the LORD [a]for his daily obligations—for their work in their
duties according to their divisions;
17 as well as the priests who were
enrolled genealogically according to
their fathers' households, and the
Levites [a]from twenty years old and
upwards, by their duties *and* their
divisions.
18 And the genealogical enrollment *included* [1]all their little children, their wives, their sons, and
their daughters, for the whole assembly, for they consecrated themselves [2]faithfully in holiness.
19 Also for the sons of Aaron the
priests *who were* in [a]the pasture
lands of their cities, or in each and
every city, [b]*there were* men who
were designated by name to distribute portions to every male among
the priests and to everyone genealogically enrolled among the Levites.
20 And thus Hezekiah did
throughout all Judah; and [a]he did
what *was* good, right, and true before the LORD his God.
21 And every work which he began in the service of the house of
God in law and in commandment,
seeking his God, he did with all his
heart and prospered.

CHAPTER 32

Sennacharib Invades Judah

[a]AFTER these [1]acts of faithfulness
Sennacherib king of Assyria came
and invaded Judah and besieged the
fortified cities, and [2]thought to
break into them for himself.
2 Now when Hezekiah saw that
Sennacherib had come, and that [1]he
intended to make war on Jerusalem,
3 he decided with his officers and
his warriors to cut off the *supply of*
water from the springs which *were*
outside the city, and they helped
him.
4 So many people assembled
[a]and stopped up all the springs and
[b]the stream which flowed [1]through
the region, saying, "Why should the
kings of Assyria come and find
abundant water?"
5 And he took courage and [a]re-
built all the wall that had been bro-

ken down, and [1]erected towers on it,
and *built* [b]another outside wall, and
strengthened [c]Millo *in* the city of
David, and made weapons and
shields in great number.
6 And he appointed military officers over the people, and gathered
them to him in the square at the city
gate, and [a]spoke [1]encouragingly to
them, saying,
7 "[a]Be strong and courageous, do
not fear or be dismayed because of
the king of Assyria, nor because of
all the multitude which is with him;
[b]for the one with us is greater than
the one with him.
8 "With him is *only* [a]an arm of
flesh, but [b]with us is the LORD our
God to help us and to fight our battles." And the people relied on the
words of Hezekiah king of Judah.

Sennacharib Undermines Hezekiah

9 After this Sennacherib king of
Assyria sent his servants to Jerusalem while he *was* [1]besieging Lachish with all his forces with him,
against Hezekiah king of Judah and
against all Judah who *were* at Jerusalem, saying,
10 "Thus says Sennacherib king of
Assyria, 'On what are you trusting
that you are remaining in Jerusalem
under siege?
11 'Is not Hezekiah misleading you
to give yourselves over to die by
hunger and by thirst, saying, "The
LORD our God will deliver us from
the [1]hand of the king of Assyria"?
12 '[a]Has not the same Hezekiah
taken away His high places and His
altars, and said to Judah and [1]Jeru-
salem, "You shall worship before
one altar, and on it you shall [2]burn
incense"?
13 'Do you not know what I and my
fathers have done to all the peoples
of the lands? Were the gods of the
nations of the lands able at all to
deliver their land from my hand?
14 '[a]Who *was there* among all the
gods of those nations which my fathers utterly destroyed who could
deliver his people out of my hand,
that your God should be able to deliver you from my hand?
15 'Now therefore, do not let Hezekiah deceive you or mislead you
like this, and do not believe him, for
no god of any nation or kingdom
was able to deliver his people from
my hand or from the hand of my
fathers. How much less shall your
God deliver you from my hand?' "
16 And his servants spoke further
against the LORD God and against
His servant Hezekiah.
17 He also wrote letters to insult
the LORD God of Israel, and to speak
against Him, saying, "[a]As the gods
of the nations of the lands [1]have not
delivered their people from my
hand, so the God of Hezekiah shall
not deliver His people from my
hand."
18 And they called this out with a
loud voice in the language of Judah
to the people of Jerusalem who
were on the wall, to frighten and terrify them, so that they might take
the city.
19 And they spoke [1]of the God of
Jerusalem as of the gods of the peoples of the earth, the work of men's
hands.

Hezekiah's Prayer Is Answered

20 But King Hezekiah and Isaiah
the prophet, the son of Amoz,
prayed about this and cried out to
heaven.
21 And the LORD sent an angel
who destroyed every mighty warrior, commander and officer in the
camp of the king of Assyria. So he
returned [1]in shame to his own land.
And when he had entered the temple of his god, some of his own children killed him there with the
sword.
22 So the LORD saved Hezekiah
and the inhabitants of Jerusalem
from the hand of Sennacherib the
king of Assyria, and from the hand
of all *others*, and [1]guided them on
every side.
23 And [a]many were bringing gifts
to the LORD at Jerusalem and choice
presents to Hezekiah king of Judah,
so that he was exalted in the sight of
all nations thereafter.
24 [a]In those days Hezekiah became [1]mortally ill; and he prayed to
the LORD, and [2]the LORD spoke to
him and gave him a sign.
25 But Hezekiah gave no return
for the benefit [1]he received, [a]be-
cause his heart was [2]proud; [b]there-
fore wrath came on him and on Judah and Jerusalem.
26 However, [a]Hezekiah [1]humbled
the pride of his heart, both he and
the inhabitants of Jerusalem, so that
the wrath of the LORD did not come
on them in the days of Hezekiah.
27 Now Hezekiah had immense
riches and honor; and he made for
himself treasuries for silver, gold,
precious stones, spices, shields and
all kinds of valuable articles,
28 storehouses also for the produce of grain, wine and oil, pens for

5 [1]Lit., *raised on the towers* [b]2 Kin. 25:4 [c]1 Kin. 9:24

6 [1]Lit., *upon their hearts* [a]2 Chr. 30:22

7 [a]1 Chr. 22:13 [b]2 Kin. 6:16

8 [a]Jer. 17:5 [b]2 Chr. 20:17

9 [1]Lit., *against*

11 [1]Lit., *palm*

12 [1]Lit., *Jerusalem, saying,* [2]Lit., *offer up in smoke* [a]2 Chr. 31:1

14 [a]Is. 10:9-11

17 [1]Lit., *who have* [a]2 Chr. 32:14

19 [1]Lit., *to*

21 [1]Lit., *in shame of face*

22 [1]Another reading is *gave them rest*

23 [a]2 Sam. 8:10

24 [1]Lit., *sick to the point of death* [2]Lit., *He* [a]2 Kin. 20:1-11; Is. 38:1-8

25 [1]Lit., *to him* [2]Lit., *high* [a]2 Chr. 26:16; 32:31 [b]2 Chr. 24:18

26 [1]Lit., *humbled himself in* [a]Jer. 26:18, 19

all kinds of cattle and [1]sheepfolds for the flocks.

29 And he made cities for himself, and acquired flocks and herds in abundance; for God had given him very great [1]wealth.

30 It was Hezekiah who [a]stopped the upper outlet of the waters of [b]Gihon and directed them to the west side of the city of David. And Hezekiah prospered in all that he did.

31 And even *in the matter of* [a]the envoys of the rulers of Babylon, who sent to him to inquire of [b]the wonder that had happened in the land, God left him *alone only* [c]to test him, that He might know all that was in his heart.

32 Now the rest of the acts of Hezekiah and his deeds of devotion, behold, they are written in the vision of Isaiah the prophet, the son of Amoz, in the Book of the Kings of Judah and Israel.

33 So Hezekiah slept with his fathers, and they buried him in the [1]upper section of the tombs of the sons of David; and all Judah and the inhabitants of Jerusalem honored him at his death. And his son Manasseh became king in his place.

Chapter 33

Manasseh Succeeds Hezekiah in Judah

[a]MANASSEH was twelve years old when he became king, and he reigned fifty-five years in Jerusalem.

2 And he did evil in the sight of the LORD [a]according to the abominations of the nations whom the LORD dispossessed before the sons of Israel.

3 For [a]he rebuilt the high places which Hezekiah his father had broken down; [b]he also erected altars for the Baals and made [1]Asherim, and worshiped all the host of heaven and served them.

4 And [a]he built altars in the house of the LORD of which the LORD had said, "My name shall be [b]in Jerusalem forever."

5 For he built altars for all the host of heaven in [a]the two courts of the house of the LORD.

6 And [a]he made his sons pass through the fire in the valley of Ben-hinnom; and he practiced witchcraft, used divination, practiced sorcery, and [b]dealt with mediums and spiritists. He did much evil in the

28 [1]So ancient versions; Heb., *flocks for the sheepfolds*

29 [1]Lit., *possessions, property*

30 [a]2 Kin. 20:20 [b]1 Kin. 1:33

31 [a]2 Kin. 20:12; Is. 39:1 [b]2 Chr. 32:24; Is. 38:7, 8 [c]Deut. 8:16

33 [1]Or, *ascent to*

1 [a]2 Kin. 21:1-9

2 [a]2 Chr. 28:3

3 [1]I.e., wooden symbols of a female deity [a]2 Chr. 31:1 [b]Deut. 16:21; 2 Kin. 23:5, 6

4 [a]2 Chr. 28:24 [b]2 Chr. 7:16

5 [a]2 Chr. 4:9

6 [a]2 Chr. 28:3 [b]Lev. 19:31; 20:27

7 [a]2 Chr. 33:15 [b]2 Chr. 33:4

8 [a]2 Sam. 7:10

11 [1]I.e., thongs put through the nose [a]Deut. 28:36 [b]2 Chr. 36:6

12 [a]2 Chr. 32:26

13 [a]1 Chr. 20; Ezra 8:23 [b]Dan. 4:32

14 [a]1 Kin. 1:33 [b]Neh. 3:3 [c]2 Chr. 27:3

15 [a]2 Chr. 33:3-7

17 [a]2 Chr. 32:12

sight of the LORD, provoking Him *to anger.*

7 Then he put [a]the carved image of the idol which he had made in the house of God, of which God had said to David and to Solomon his son, "[b]In this house and in Jerusalem, which I have chosen from all the tribes of Israel, I will put My name forever;

8 and I will not again remove the foot of Israel from the land [a]which I have appointed for your fathers, if only they will observe to do all that I have commanded them according to all the law, the statutes, and the ordinances *given* through Moses."

9 Thus Manasseh misled Judah and the inhabitants of Jerusalem to do more evil than the nations whom the LORD destroyed before the sons of Israel.

Manasseh's Idolatry Rebuked

10 And the LORD spoke to Manasseh and his people, but they paid no attention.

11 [a]Therefore the LORD brought the commanders of the army of the king of Assyria against them, and they captured Manasseh with [1]hooks, [b]bound him with bronze *chains,* and took him to Babylon.

12 And when he was in distress, he entreated the LORD his God and [a]humbled himself greatly before the God of his fathers.

13 When he prayed to Him, [a]He was moved by his entreaty and heard his supplication, and brought him again to Jerusalem to his kingdom. Then Manasseh [b]knew that the LORD *was* God.

14 Now after this he built the outer wall of the city of David on the west side of [a]Gihon, in the valley, even to the entrance of the [b]Fish Gate; and he encircled the [c]Ophel *with it* and made it very high. Then he put army commanders in all the fortified cities of Judah.

15 He also [a]removed the foreign gods and the idol from the house of the LORD, as well as all the altars which he had built on the mountain of the house of the LORD and in Jerusalem, and he threw *them* outside the city.

16 And he set up the altar of the LORD and sacrificed peace offerings and thank offerings on it; and he ordered Judah to serve the LORD God of Israel.

17 Nevertheless [a]the people still sacrificed in the high places, *although* only to the LORD their God.

18 Now the rest of the acts of Ma-

nasseh even [a]his prayer to his God,
and the words of [b]the seers who
spoke to him in the name of the
LORD God of Israel, behold, they are
among the records of the kings of
[c]Israel.
19 His prayer also and [a]*how God*
was entreated by him, and all his
sin, his unfaithfulness, and [b]the
sites on which he built high places
and erected the Asherim and the
carved images, before he humbled
himself, behold, they are written in
the records of the [1]Hozai.
20 So Manasseh slept with his fathers, and they buried him in his
own house. And Amon his son became king in his place.

Amon Becomes King in Judah

21 [a]Amon *was* twenty-two years
old when he became king, and he
reigned two years in Jerusalem.
22 And he did evil in the sight of
the LORD as Manasseh his father
[a]had done, and Amon sacrificed to
all [b]the carved images which his father Manasseh had made, and he
served them.
23 Moreover, he did not humble
himself before the LORD [a]as his father Manasseh had [1]done, but
Amon multiplied guilt.
24 Finally [a]his servants conspired
against him and put him to death in
his own house.
25 But the people of the land
[1]killed all the conspirators against
King Amon, and the people of the
land made Josiah his son king in his
place.

CHAPTER 34

Josiah Succeeds Amon in Judah

[a]JOSIAH *was* eight years old when
he became king, and he reigned
thirty-one years in Jerusalem.
2 And [a]he did right in the sight of
the LORD, and walked in the ways of
his father David and did not turn
aside to the right or to the left.
3 For in the eighth year of his
reign while he was still a youth, he
began to seek the God of his father
David; and in the twelfth year he began [a]to purge Judah and Jerusalem
of the high places, the Asherim, the
carved images, and the molten images.
4 And they tore down the altars
of the Baals in his presence, and [a]the
incense altars that were high above
them he chopped down; also the A-
sherim, the carved images, and the
molten images he broke in pieces
and [b]ground to powder and scattered *it* on the graves of those who
had sacrificed to them.
5 Then [a]he burned the bones of
the priests on their altars, and
purged Judah and Jerusalem.
6 And [a]in the cities of Manasseh,
Ephraim, Simeon even as far as
Naphtali, in their surrounding ruins,
7 he also tore down the altars and
[a]beat the Asherim and the carved
images into powder, and chopped
down all the incense altars throughout the land of Israel. Then he returned to Jerusalem.

Josiah Repairs the Temple

8 [a]Now in the eighteenth year of
his reign, when he had purged the
land and the house, he sent Shaphan
the son of Azaliah, and Maaseiah
[b]an official of the city, and Joah the
son of Joahaz the recorder, to repair
the house of the LORD his God.
9 And they came to [a]Hilkiah the
high priest and delivered the money
that was brought into the house of
God, which the Levites, the [1]door-
keepers, had collected [2]from [b]Ma-
nasseh and Ephraim, and from all
the remnant of Israel, and from all
Judah and Benjamin and the inhabitants of Jerusalem.
10 Then they gave *it* into the hands
of the workmen who had the oversight of the house of the LORD, and
the workmen who were working in
the house of the LORD [1]used it to
restore and repair the house.
11 They in turn gave *it* to the carpenters and to the builders to buy
quarried stone and timber for cou-
plings and to make beams for the
houses [a]which the kings of Judah
had let go to ruin.
12 And the men did the work faithfully with foremen over them to supervise: Jahath and Obadiah, the
Levites of the sons of Merari, Zechariah and Meshullam of the sons of
the Kohathites, and [a]the Levites, all
who were skillful with musical instruments.
13 *They were* also over [a]the burden bearers, and supervised all the
workmen from job to job; and *some*
of the Levites *were* scribes and officials and gatekeepers.

Hilkiah Discovers Lost Book of the Law

14 When they were bringing out
the money which had been brought
into the house of the LORD, [a]Hilkiah
the priest found the book of the law
of the LORD *given* by Moses.
15 And Hilkiah responded and

18 [a]2 Chr. 33:12, 13 [b]2 Chr. 33:10 [c]2 Chr. 21:2
19 [1]Gk. reads *seers* [a]2 Chr. 33:13 [b]2 Chr. 33:3
21 [a]2 Kin. 21:19-24
22 [a]2 Chr. 33:2-7 [b]2 Chr. 34:3, 4
23 [1]Lit., *humbled himself* [a]2 Chr. 33:12, 19
24 [a]2 Chr. 25:27
25 [1]Lit., *smote*
1 [a]2 Kin. 22:1, 2
2 [a]2 Chr. 29:2
3 [a]2 Chr. 33:22
4 [a]2 Kin. 23:4, 5, 11 [b]Ex. 32:20
5 [a]2 Kin. 23:20
6 [a]2 Kin. 23:15, 19
7 [a]2 Chr. 31:1
8 [a]2 Kin. 22:3-20 [b]2 Chr. 18:25
9 [1]Lit., *guardians of the threshold* [2]Lit., *from the hand of* [a]2 Chr. 35:8 [b]2 Chr. 30:10, 18
10 [1]Lit., *gave*
11 [a]2 Chr. 33:4-7
12 [a]1 Chr. 25:1
13 [a]2 Chr. 8:10; Neh. 4:10
14 [a]2 Chr. 34:9

said to Shaphan the scribe, "I have
found the book of the law in the
house of the LORD." And Hilkiah
gave the book to Shaphan.
16 Then Shaphan brought the
book to the king and [1]reported further word to the king, saying, "Everything that was [2]entrusted to your
servants they are doing.
17 "They have also emptied out the
money which was found in the
house of the LORD, and have delivered it into the hands of the supervisors and the workmen."
18 Moreover, Shaphan the scribe
told the king saying, "Hilkiah the
priest gave me a book." And Shaphan read from it in the presence of
the king.
19 And it came about when the
king heard the words of the law that
[a]he tore his clothes.
20 Then the king commanded Hilkiah, Ahikam the son of Shaphan,
[1]Abdon the son of Micah, Shaphan
the scribe, and Asaiah the king's
servant, saying,
21 "Go, inquire of the LORD for me
and for those who are left in Israel
and in Judah, concerning the words
of the book which has been found;
for [a]great is the wrath of the LORD
which is poured out on us because
our fathers have not observed the
word of the LORD, to do according to
all that is written in this book."

Huldah, the Prophetess, Speaks

22 So Hilkiah and *those* whom the
king [1]had told went to Huldah the
prophetess, the wife of Shallum the
son of [2]Tokhath, the son of Hasrah,
the keeper of the wardrobe (now
she lived in Jerusalem in the Second
Quarter); and they spoke to her regarding this.
23 And she said to them, "Thus
says the LORD, the God of Israel,
'Tell the man who sent you to Me,
24 thus says the LORD, "Behold, [a]I
am bringing evil on this place and
on its inhabitants, *even* all [b]the
curses written in the book which
they have read in the presence of the
king of Judah.
25 "[a]Because they have forsaken
Me and have burned incense to other gods, that they might provoke Me
to anger with all the works of their
hands, therefore My wrath will be
poured out on this place, and it shall
not be quenched." '
26 "But to the king of Judah who
sent you to inquire of the LORD, thus
you will say to him, 'Thus says the
LORD God of Israel *regarding* the
words which you have heard,

16 [1]Lit., *returned* [2]Lit., *given into the hand of*
19 [a]Josh. 7:6
20 [1]In 2 Kin. 22:12, *Achbor, son of Micaiah*
21 [a]2 Chr. 29:8
22 [1]So with Gk. [2]In 2 Kin. 22:14 *Tikvah, son of Harhas*
24 [a]2 Chr. 36:14-20 [b]Deut. 28:15-68
25 [a]2 Chr. 33:3
27 [1]Cf. 2 Kin. 22:19 [a]2 Chr. 12:7; 32:26
29 [a]2 Kin. 23:1-3
30 [a]Neh. 8:1-3
31 [1]So with some versions, cf. 2 Kin. 23:3 [a]2 Kin. 11:14; 2 Chr. 30:16 [b]2 Chr. 23:16; 29:10
33 [1]Lit., *days* [a]2 Chr. 34:3-7
1 [a]2 Kin. 23:21 [b]Ex. 12:6; Num. 9:3
2 [a]2 Chr. 29:11
3 [a]2 Chr. 17:8, 9; Neh. 8:7

27 "[a]Because your heart was tender
and you humbled yourself before
God, when you heard [1]His words
against this place and against its inhabitants, and *because* you humbled yourself before Me, tore your
clothes, and wept before Me, I truly
have heard you," declares the LORD.
28 "Behold, I will gather you to
your fathers and you shall be gathered to your grave in peace, so your
eyes shall not see all the evil which
I will bring on this place and on its
inhabitants." ' " And they brought
back word to the king.
29 [a]Then the king sent and gathered all the elders of Judah and Jerusalem.
30 And the king went up to the
house of the LORD and [a]all the men
of Judah, the inhabitants of Jerusalem, the priests, the Levites, and all
the people, from the greatest to the
least; and he read in their hearing all
the words of the book of the covenant which was found in the house
of the LORD.

Josiah's Good Reign

31 Then the king [a]stood in his
[1]place and [b]made a covenant before
the LORD to walk after the LORD, and
to keep His commandments and His
testimonies and His statutes with all
his heart and with all his soul, to
perform the words of the covenant
written in this book.
32 Moreover, he made all who
were present in Jerusalem and Benjamin to stand *with him.* So the inhabitants of Jerusalem did according to the covenant of God, the God
of their fathers.
33 And Josiah [a]removed all the
abominations from all the lands belonging to the sons of Israel, and
made all who were present in Israel
to serve the LORD their God.
Throughout his [1]lifetime they did
not turn from following the LORD
God of their fathers.

CHAPTER 35

The Passover Observed Again

THEN Josiah [a]celebrated the Passover to the LORD in Jerusalem, and
[b]they slaughtered the Passover *animals* on the fourteenth *day* of the
first month.
2 And he set the priests in their
offices and [a]encouraged them in the
service of the house of the LORD.
3 He also said to [a]the Levites who
taught all Israel *and* who were holy
to the LORD, "Put the holy ark in the

house which Solomon the son of David king of Israel built; [b]it will be a burden on *your* shoulders no longer. Now serve the LORD your God and His people Israel.

4 "And [a]prepare *yourselves* by your fathers' households in your divisions, according to the writing of David king of Israel and [b]according to the writing of his son Solomon.

5 "Moreover, [a]stand in the holy place according to the sections of the fathers' households of your brethren the [1]lay people, and according to the Levites, by division of a father's household.

6 "Now [a]slaughter the Passover *animals,* [b]sanctify yourselves, and prepare for your brethren to do according to the word of the LORD by Moses."

7 And Josiah contributed to the lay people, to all who were present, flocks of lambs and kids, all for the Passover offerings, numbering 30,000 plus 3,000 bulls; these were from the king's possessions.

8 His officers also contributed a freewill offering to the people, the priests, and the Levites. Hilkiah and Zechariah and Jehiel, [a]the officials of the house of God, gave to the priests for the Passover offerings 2,600 *from the flocks* and 300 bulls.

9 [a]Conaniah also, and Shemaiah and Nethanel, his brothers, and Hashabiah and Jeiel and Jozabad, the officers of the Levites, contributed to the Levites for the Passover offerings 5,000 *from the flocks* and 500 bulls.

10 So the service was prepared, and [a]the priests stood at their stations and the Levites by their divisions according to the king's command.

11 And [1a]they slaughtered the Passover *animals,* and while [b]the priests sprinkled [2]the blood *received* from their hand, [c]the Levites skinned them.

12 Then they removed the burnt offerings that *they* might give them to the sections of the fathers' households of the lay people to present to the LORD, as it is written in the book of Moses. They did this also with the bulls.

13 So [a]they roasted the Passover *animals* on the fire according to the ordinance, and they boiled [b]the holy things in pots, in kettles, in pans, and carried *them* speedily to all the lay people.

14 And afterwards they prepared for themselves and for the priests, because the priests, the sons of Aaron, *were* offering the burnt offerings and the fat until night; therefore the Levites prepared for themselves and for the priests, the sons of Aaron.

15 The singers, the sons of Asaph, *were* also at their stations [a]according to the command of David, Asaph, Heman, and Jeduthun the king's seer; and [b]the gatekeepers at each gate did not have to depart from their service, because the Levites their brethren prepared for them.

16 So all the service of the LORD was prepared on that day to celebrate the Passover, and to offer burnt offerings on the altar of the LORD according to the command of King Josiah.

17 Thus the sons of Israel who were present celebrated the Passover at that time, and [a]the Feast of Unleavened Bread seven days.

18 And [a]there had not been celebrated a Passover like it in Israel since the days of Samuel the prophet; nor had any of the kings of Israel celebrated such a Passover as Josiah did with the priests, the Levites, all Judah and Israel who were present, and the inhabitants of Jerusalem.

19 In the eighteenth year of Josiah's reign this Passover was celebrated.

Josiah Dies in Battle

20 [a]After all this, when Josiah had set the [1]temple in order, Neco king of Egypt came up to make war at [b]Carchemish on the Euphrates, and Josiah went out to engage him.

21 But [1]Neco sent messengers to him, saying, "[a]What have we to do with each other, O King of Judah? *I am* not *coming* against you today but against the house with which I am at war, and God has ordered me to hurry. Stop for your own sake *from interfering with* God who is with me, that He may not destroy you."

22 However, Josiah would not turn [1]away from him, but [a]disguised himself in order to make war with him; nor did he listen to the words of Neco [b]from the mouth of God, but came to make war on the plain of [c]Megiddo.

23 And the archers shot King Josiah, and the king said to his servants, "Take me away, for I am badly wounded."

24 So his servants took him out of the chariot and carried him in the second chariot which he had, and

3 [b]1 Chr. 23:26

4 [a]1 Chr. 9:10-13 [b]2 Chr. 8:14

5 [1]Lit., *sons of the people,* and so throughout the chap. [a]Ezra 6:18

6 [a]2 Chr. 35:1 [b]2 Chr. 29:5

8 [a]2 Chr. 31:13

9 [a]2 Chr. 31:12

10 [a]2 Chr. 35:5

11 [1]I.e., the Levites [2]So with the Gk. [a]2 Chr. 35:1, 6 [b]2 Chr. 29:22 [c]2 Chr. 29:34

13 [a]Ex. 12:8, 9 [b]Lev. 6:25

15 [a]1 Chr. 25:1 [b]1 Chr. 26:12-19

17 [a]2 Chr. 30:21

18 [a]2 Kin. 23:21; 2 Chr. 30:5

20 [1]Lit., *house* [a]2 Kin. 23:29, 30 [b]Is. 10:9; Jer. 46:2

21 [1]Lit., *he* [a]2 Chr. 25:19

22 [1]Lit., *his face* [a]2 Chr. 18:29 [b]2 Chr. 35:21 [c]Judg. 5:19

brought him to Jerusalem [1]where he
died and was buried in the tombs of
his fathers. [a]And all Judah and Jerusalem mourned for Josiah.
25 Then [a]Jeremiah chanted a lament for Josiah. And all the male
and female singers speak about Josiah in their lamentations to this
day. And they made them an ordinance in Israel; behold, they are also
written in the Lamentations.
26 Now the rest of the acts of Josiah and his deeds of devotion as
written in the law of the LORD,
27 and his acts, first to last, behold, they are written in the Book of
the Kings of Israel and Judah.

CHAPTER 36

Jehoahaz, Jehoiakim, then Jehoiachin Rule

[a]THEN the people of the land took
[1b]Joahaz the son of Josiah, and
made him king in place of his father
in Jerusalem.
2 Joahaz was twenty-three years
old when he became king, and he
reigned three months in Jerusalem.
3 Then the king of Egypt deposed
him at Jerusalem, and imposed on
the land a fine of one hundred talents of silver and one talent of gold.
4 And the king of Egypt made
Eliakim his brother king over Judah
and Jerusalem, and changed his
name to Jehoiakim. But [a]Neco took
Joahaz his brother and brought him
to Egypt.
5 [a]Jehoiakim was twenty-five
years old when he became king, and
he reigned eleven years in Jerusalem; and he did evil in the sight of
the LORD his God.
6 Nebuchadnezzar king of Babylon came up [a]against him and
[b]bound him with bronze *chains* [c]to
take him to Babylon.
7 [a]Nebuchadnezzar also brought
some of the articles of the house of
the LORD to Babylon and put them in
his temple at Babylon.
8 [a]Now the rest of the acts of Jehoiakim and [1]the abominations
which he did, and what was found
against him, behold, they are written in the Book of the Kings of Israel
and Judah. And Jehoiachin his son
became king in his place.
9 [a]Jehoiachin was eight years old
when he became king, and he
reigned three months and ten days
in Jerusalem, and he did evil in the
sight of the LORD.

24 [1]Lit., *and* [a]Lam. 4:20; Zech. 12:11
25 [a]Jer. 22:10
1 [1]I.e., short form of Jehoahaz [a]2 Kin. 23:30-34 [b]Jer. 22:11
4 [a]Jer. 22:10-12
5 [a]2 Kin. 23:36, 37; Jer. 22:13-19
6 [a]2 Kin. 24:1 [b]2 Chr. 33:11 [c]Jer. 22:19, 20
7 [a]2 Kin. 24:13
8 [1]Lit., *his* [a]2 Kin. 24:5
9 [a]2 Kin. 24:8-17
10 [a]2 Sam. 11:1 [b]Jer. 37:1
11 [a]2 Kin. 24:18-20; Jer. 52:1
12 [1]Lit., *from the mouth of the* LORD [a]2 Chr. 33:23 [b]Jer. 21:3-7
13 [a]Jer. 52:3; Ezek. 17:15 [b]2 Chr. 30:8
15 [a]Jer. 7:13; 25:3
16 [a]2 Chr. 30:10; Jer. 5:12, 13 [b]Prov. 1:24-32 [c]Ezra 5:12
17 [a]2 Kin. 25:1-7
18 [a]2 Chr. 36:7, 10
19 [a]2 Kin. 25:9; Jer. 52:13
20 [a]2 Kin. 25:11 [b]Jer. 27:7
21 [a]Jer. 29:10 [b]Lev. 26:33

Captivity in Babylon Begun

10 And [a]at the turn of the year
King Nebuchadnezzar sent and
brought him to Babylon with the
valuable articles of the house of the
LORD, and he made his kinsman
[b]Zedekiah king over Judah and Jerusalem.

Zedekiah Rules in Judah

11 [a]Zedekiah was twenty-one
years old when he became king, and
he reigned eleven years in Jerusalem.
12 And he did evil in the sight of
the LORD his God; [a]he did not humble himself [b]before Jeremiah the
prophet [1]who spoke for the LORD.
13 And [a]he also rebelled against
King Nebuchadnezzar who had
made him swear *allegiance* by God.
But [b]he stiffened his neck and hardened his heart against turning to the
LORD God of Israel.
14 Furthermore, all the officials of
the priests and the people were very
unfaithful *following* all the abominations of the nations; and they defiled the house of the LORD which He
had sanctified in Jerusalem.
15 And the LORD, the God of their
fathers, [a]sent *word* to them again
and again by His messengers, because He had compassion on His
people and on His dwelling place;
16 but they *continually* [a]mocked
the messengers of God, [b]despised
His words and scoffed at His prophets, [c]until the wrath of the LORD
arose against His people, until there
was no remedy.
17 [a]Therefore He brought up
against them the king of the Chaldeans who slew their young men with
the sword in the house of their sanctuary, and had no compassion on
young man or virgin, old man or in-
firm; He gave *them* all into his hand.
18 And [a]all the articles of the
house of God, great and small, and
the treasures of the house of the
LORD, and the treasures of the king
and of his officers, he brought *them*
all to Babylon.
19 Then [a]they burned the house of
God, and broke down the wall of Jerusalem and burned all its fortified
buildings with fire, and destroyed
all its valuable articles.
20 And those who had escaped
from the sword he [a]carried away to
Babylon; and [b]they were servants to
him and to his sons until the rule of
the kingdom of Persia,
21 [a]to fulfill the word of the LORD
by the mouth of Jeremiah, until [b]the

land had enjoyed its sabbaths. [c]All
the days of its desolation it kept sabbath [1]until seventy years were complete.

Cyrus Permits Return

22 [a]Now in the first year of Cyrus
king of Persia—in order to fulfill the
word of the LORD [b]by the mouth of
Jeremiah—the LORD [c]stirred up the
spirit of Cyrus king of Persia, so that
he sent a proclamation throughout
his kingdom, and also *put it* in writing, saying,
23 "Thus says Cyrus king of Persia,
'The LORD, the God of heaven, has
given me all the kingdoms of the
earth, and He has appointed me to
build Him a house in Jerusalem,
which is in Judah. Whoever there is
among you of all His people, may
the LORD his God be with him, and
let him go up!' "

21 [1]Lit., *to fulfill seventy years* [c]Lev. 25:4
22 [a]Ezra 1:1-3 [b]Jer. 25:12; 29:10 [c]Is. 44:28

THE BOOK OF EZRA

Cyrus' Proclamation

[a]NOW in the first year of Cyrus
king of Persia, in order to fulfill the
word of the LORD by the mouth of
Jeremiah, the LORD stirred up the
spirit of Cyrus king of Persia, so that
he [b]sent a proclamation throughout
all his kingdom, and also *put it* in
writing, saying,
2 "Thus says Cyrus king of Persia,
'The LORD, the God of heaven, has
given me all the kingdoms of the
earth, and [a]He has appointed me to
build Him a house in Jerusalem,
which is in Judah.
3 'Whoever there is among you of
all His people, may his God be with
him! Let him go up to Jerusalem
which is in Judah, and rebuild the
house of the LORD, the God of Israel;
[a]He is the God who is in Jerusalem.
4 'And every survivor, at whatever place he may [1]live, let the men
of [2]that place support him with silver and gold, with goods and cattle,
together with a freewill offering for
the house of God which is in Jerusalem.' "

Holy Vessels Restored

5 Then the heads of fathers'
households of Judah and Benjamin
and the priests and the Levites
arose, [a]even everyone whose spirit
God had stirred to go up and rebuild
the house of the LORD which is in
Jerusalem.
6 And all those about them [1a]en-
couraged them with articles of silver, with gold, with goods, with cattle, and with valuables, aside from
all that was given as a freewill offering.
7 [a]Also King Cyrus brought out
the articles of the house of the LORD,
[b]which Nebuchadnezzar had carried away from Jerusalem and put
in the house of his gods;
8 and Cyrus, king of Persia, had
them brought out by the hand of
Mithredath the treasurer, and he
counted them out to [a]Sheshbazzar,
the prince of Judah.
9 Now this *was* their number: [a]30
gold dishes, 1,000 silver dishes, 29
[1]duplicates;
10 30 gold bowls, 410 silver bowls
of a second *kind, and* 1,000 other
articles.
11 All the articles of gold and silver *numbered* 5,400. Sheshbazzar
brought them all up with the exiles
who went up from Babylon to Jerusalem.

CHAPTER 2

Number of Those Returning

[a]NOW these are the [1]people of the
province who came up out of the
captivity of the exiles whom Nebuchadnezzar the king of Babylon had
carried away to Babylon, and returned to Jerusalem and Judah,
each to his city.
2 [1]These came with Zerubbabel,
Jeshua, Nehemiah, [2]Seraiah, [3]Reel-
aiah, Mordecai, Bilshan, [4]Mispar,
Bigvai, [5]Rehum, and Baanah.
The number of the men of the people of Israel:
3 the sons of Parosh, 2,172;
4 the sons of Shephatiah, 372;
5 the sons of Arah, 775;
6 the sons of Pahath-moab of the
sons of Jeshua *and* Joab, 2,812;
7 the sons of Elam, 1,254;
8 the sons of Zattu, 945;
9 the sons of Zaccai, 760;
10 the sons of [1]Bani, 642;
11 the sons of Bebai, 623;
12 the sons of Azgad, 1,222;

1 [a]2 Chr. 36:22 [b]Ezra 5:13
2 [a]Is. 44:28; 45:1, 12, 13
3 [a]Dan. 6:26
4 [1]Or, *reside as an alien* [2]Lit., *his*
5 [a]Ezra 1:1
6 [1]Lit., *strengthened their hands* [a]Neh. 6:22; Is. 35:3
7 [a]Ezra 5:14; 6:5 [b]2 Chr. 36:7
8 [a]Ezra 5:14
9 [1]Heb. obscure, other possible meanings are *knives, censers* [a]Ezra 8:27
1 [1]Lit., *sons* [a]Neh. 7:6-73
2 [1]Lit., *who* [2]In Neh. 7:7, *Azariah* [3]In Neh. 7:7, *Raamiah* [4]In Neh. 7:7, *Mispereth* [5]In Neh. 7:7, *Nehum*
10 [1]In Neh. 7:15, *Binnui*

13 the sons of Adonikam, 666;
14 the sons of Bigvai, 2,056;
15 the sons of Adin, 454;
16 the sons of Ater of Hezekiah,
98;
17 the sons of Bezai, 323;
18 the sons of [1]Jorah, 112;
19 the sons of Hashum, 223;
20 the sons of [1]Gibbar, 95;
21 the [1]men of Bethlehem, 123;
22 the men of Netophah, 56;
23 the men of Anathoth, 128;
24 the sons of [1]Azmaveth, 42;
25 the sons of [1]Kiriath-arim,
Chephirah, and Beeroth, 743;
26 the sons of Ramah and Geba,
621;
27 the men of Michmas, 122;
28 the men of Bethel and Ai, 223;
29 the sons of Nebo, 52;
30 the sons of Magbish, 156;
31 the sons of the other Elam,
1,254;
32 the sons of Harim, 320;
33 the sons of Lod, Hadid, and
Ono, 725;
34 the [1]men of Jericho, 345;
35 the sons of Senaah, 3,630.

Priests Returning

36 [a]The priests: the sons of Jedaiah of the house of Jeshua, 973;
37 the sons of Immer, 1,052;
38 [a]the sons of Pashhur, 1,247;
39 the sons of Harim, 1,017.

Levites Returning

40 The Levites: the sons of Jeshua
and Kadmiel, of the sons of [1]Hoda-
viah, 74.
41 The singers: the sons of Asaph,
128.
42 The sons of the gatekeepers:
the sons of Shallum, the sons of
Ater, the sons of Talmon, the sons of
Akkub, the sons of Hatita, the sons
of Shobai, in all 139.
43 The temple servants: the sons
of Ziha, the sons of Hasupha, the
sons of Tabbaoth,
44 the sons of Keros, the sons of
[1]Siaha, the sons of Padon,
45 the sons of Lebanah, the sons of
Hagabah, the sons of Akkub,
46 the sons of Hagab, the sons of
Shalmai, the sons of Hanan,
47 the sons of Giddel, the sons of
Gahar, the sons of Reaiah,
48 the sons of Rezin, the sons of
Nekoda, the sons of Gazzam,
49 the sons of Uzza, the sons of
Paseah, the sons of Besai,
50 the sons of Asnah, the sons of
Meunim, the sons of [1]Nephisim,
51 the sons of Bakbuk, the sons of
Hakupha, the sons of Harhur,
52 the sons of [1]Bazluth, the sons of
Mehida, the sons of Harsha,
53 the sons of Barkos, the sons of
Sisera, the sons of Temah,
54 the sons of Neziah, the sons of
Hatipha.
55 The sons of Solomon's servants: the sons of Sotai, the sons of
[1]Hassophereth, the sons of [2]Peruda,
56 the sons of Jaalah, the sons of
Darkon, the sons of Giddel,
57 the sons of Shephatiah, the
sons of Hattil, the sons of Poche-
reth-hazzebaim, the sons of [1]Ami.
58 All the temple servants, and the
sons of Solomon's servants, were
392.
59 Now these are those who came
up from Tel-melah, Tel-harsha,
Cherub, [1]Addan, *and* Immer, but
they were not able to [2]give evidence
of their fathers' households, and
their [3]descendants, whether they
were of Israel:
60 the sons of Delaiah, the sons of
Tobiah, the sons of Nekoda, 652.

Priests Removed

61 And of the sons of the priests:
the sons of [1]Habaiah, the sons of
Hakkoz, the sons of [a]Barzillai, who
took a wife from the daughters of
Barzillai the Gileadite, and he was
called by their name.
62 These searched *among* their ancestral registration, but they could
not be located; [a]therefore they were
considered unclean and *were excluded* from the priesthood.
63 And the [1]governor said to them
[a]that they should not eat from the
most holy things until a priest stood
up with [b]Urim and Thummim.
64 The whole assembly [1]num-
bered 42,360,
65 besides their male and female
servants, [1]who numbered 7,337; and
they had 200 [a]singing men and
women.
66 Their horses were 736; their
mules, 245;
67 their camels, 435; *their* donkeys, 6,720.
68 And some of the heads of fathers' *households,* when they arrived at the house of the LORD which
is in Jerusalem, offered willingly for
the house of God to [1]restore it on its
foundation.
69 According to their ability they
gave [a]to the treasury for the work
61,000 gold drachmas, and 5,000 silver minas, and 100 priestly [1]gar-
ments.
70 Now the priests and the Levites, some of the people, the singers, the gatekeepers, and the temple

18 [1]In Neh. 7:24, *Hariph*
20 [1]In Neh. 7:25, *Gibeon*
21 [1]Lit., *sons*
24 [1]In Neh. 7:28, *Beth-azmaveth*
25 [1]In Neh. 7:29, *Kiriath-jearim*
34 [1]Lit., *sons*
36 [a]1 Chr. 24:7-18
38 [a]1 Chr. 9:12
40 [1]In Ezra 3:9, *Judah;* In Neh. 7:43, *Hodevah*
44 [1]In Neh. 7:47, *Sia*
50 [1]In Neh. 7:52, *Nephushesim*
52 [1]In Neh. 7:54, *Bazlith*
55 [1]In Neh. 7:57, *Sophereth* [2]In Neh. 7:57 *Perida*
57 [1]In Neh. 7:59, *Amon*
59 [1]In Neh. 7:61, *Addon* [2]Lit., *tell* [3]Lit., *seed*
61 [1]In Neh. 7:63, *Hobaiah* [a]2 Sam. 17:27
62 [a]Num. 16:39, 40
63 [1]Heb., *Tirshatha,* a Persian title [a]Lev. 2:3, 10 [b]Ex. 28:30
64 [1]Lit., *together was*
65 [1]Lit., *they were* [a]2 Chr. 35:25
68 [1]Lit., *establish*
69 [1]Or, *tunics* [a]Ezra 8:25-34

servants lived in their cities, and all Israel in their cities.

CHAPTER 3

Altar and Sacrifices Restored

[a]NOW when the seventh month came, and the sons of Israel *were* in the cities, the people gathered together as one man to Jerusalem.

2 Then [a]Jeshua the son of Jozadak and his brothers the priests, and [b]Zerubbabel the son [c]of Shealtiel, and his brothers arose and built the altar of the God of Israel, to offer burnt offerings on it, [d]as it is written in the law of Moses, the man of God.

3 So they set up the altar on its foundation, for [1a]they were terrified because of the peoples of the lands; and they [b]offered burnt offerings on it to the LORD, burnt offerings morning and evening.

4 [a]And they celebrated the Feast of [1]Booths, [b]as it is written, and *offered* [2]the fixed number of burnt offerings daily, [c]according to the ordinance, as each day required;

5 and afterward *there was* a continual burnt offering, also [a]for the new moons and [b]for all the fixed festivals of the LORD that were consecrated, and from every one who offered a freewill offering to the LORD.

6 From the first day of the seventh month they began to offer burnt offerings to the LORD, but the foundation of the temple of the LORD had not been laid.

7 Then they gave money to the masons and carpenters, and [a]food, drink, and oil to the Sidonians and to the Tyrians, [b]to bring cedar wood from Lebanon to the sea at Joppa, [c]according to the permission they had [1]from Cyrus king of Persia.

Temple Restoration Begun

8 Now in the second year of their coming to the house of God at Jerusalem in the second month, [a]Zerubbabel the son of Shealtiel and Jeshua the son of Jozadak and the rest of their brothers the priests and the Levites, and all who came from the captivity to Jerusalem, began *the work* and [b]appointed the Levites from twenty years and older to oversee the work of the house of the LORD.

9 Then Jeshua *with* his sons and brothers stood united *with* Kadmiel and his sons, the sons of [1]Judah *and* the sons of Henadad *with* their sons and brothers the Levites, to oversee the workmen in the temple of God.

10 Now when the builders had laid the foundation of the temple of the LORD, [1]the priests stood in their apparel with trumpets, and the Levites, the sons of Asaph, with cymbals, to praise the LORD [a]according to the [2]directions of King David of Israel.

11 And [a]they sang, praising and giving thanks to the LORD, *saying*, "[b]For He is good, for His lovingkindness is upon Israel forever." And all the people shouted with a great shout when they praised the LORD because the foundation of the house of the LORD was laid.

12 Yet many of the priests and Levites and heads of fathers' *households*, [a]the old men who had seen the first [1]temple, wept with a loud voice when the foundation of this house was laid before their eyes, while many shouted aloud for joy;

13 so that the people could not distinguish the sound of the shout of joy from the sound of the weeping of the people, for the people shouted with a loud shout, and the sound was heard far away.

CHAPTER 4

Adversaries Hinder the Work

NOW when [a]the enemies of Judah and Benjamin heard that [b]the people of the exile were building a temple to the LORD God of Israel,

2 they approached Zerubbabel and the heads of fathers' *households*, and said to them, "Let us build with you, for we, like you, seek your God; [a]and we have been sacrificing to Him since the days of [b]Esarhaddon king of Assyria, who brought us up here."

3 But Zerubbabel and Jeshua and the rest of the heads of fathers' *households* of Israel said to them, "[a]You have nothing in common with us in building a house to our God; but we ourselves will together build to the LORD God of Israel, [b]as King Cyrus, the king of Persia has commanded us."

4 Then [a]the people of the land [1]discouraged the people of Judah, and frightened them from building,

5 and hired counselors against them to frustrate their counsel all the days of Cyrus king of Persia, even until the reign of Darius king of Persia.

6 Now in the reign of [1a]Ahasuerus, in the beginning of his reign, they wrote an accusation against the inhabitants of Judah and Jerusalem.

1 [a]Neh. 7:73; 8:1

2 [a]Neh. 12:1, 8 [b]Ezra 2:2 [c]1 Chr. 3:17 [d]Deut. 12:5, 6

3 [1]Lit., *terror* was *upon them* [a]Ezra 4:4 [b]Num. 28:2

4 [1]Or, *Tabernacles* [2]Lit., *by number* [a]Neh. 8:14 [b]Ex. 23:16 [c]Num. 29:12

5 [a]Num. 28:11 [b]Num. 29:39

7 [1]Lit., *of* [a]2 Chr. 2:10 [b]2 Chr. 2:16 [c]Ezra 1:2; 6:3

8 [a]Ezra 3:2; 4:3 [b]1 Chr. 23:4, 24

9 [1]In Ezra 2:40, *Hodaviah*

10 [1]So with the Gk. and some mss., M.T., *they set the priests* [2]Lit., *hands* [a]1 Chr. 6:31; 25:1

11 [a]Neh. 12:24, 40 [b]1 Chr. 16:34

12 [1]Lit., *house* [a]Hag. 2:3

1 [a]Ezra 4:7-10 [b]Ezra 1:11

2 [a]2 Kin. 17:32 [b]2 Kin. 19:37

3 [a]Neh. 2:20 [b]Ezra 1:1, 2

4 [1]Lit., *weakened the hands of* [a]Ezra 3:3

6 [1]Or, *Xerxes*, Heb., *Ahashverosh* [a]Esth. 1:1; Dan. 9:1

7 And in the days of [1]Artaxerxes,
Bishlam, Mithredath, Tabeel, and
the rest of his colleagues, wrote to
Artaxerxes king of Persia; and the
[2]text of the letter was written in
Aramaic and translated [a]*from* Aramaic.

The Letter to King Artaxerxes

8 [1]Rehum the commander and
Shimshai the scribe wrote a letter
against Jerusalem to King Artaxerxes, as follows—
9 then *wrote* Rehum the commander and Shimshai the scribe and
[a]the rest of their colleagues, the
judges and [b]the lesser governors,
the officials, the secretaries, the men
of Erech, the Babylonians, the men
of Susa, that is, the Elamites,
10 and the rest of the nations
which the great and honorable [1]Os-
nappar deported and settled in the
city of Samaria, and in the rest of
the region beyond the [2]River. [a]And
now
11 this is the copy of the letter
which they sent to him: "To King
Artaxerxes: Your servants, the men
in the region beyond the River, and
now
12 let it be known to the king, that
the Jews who came up from you
have come to us at Jerusalem; they
are rebuilding [a]the rebellious and
evil city, and [b]are finishing the walls
and repairing the foundations.
13 "Now let it be known to the king,
that if that city is rebuilt and the
walls are finished, [a]they will not pay
tribute, custom, or toll, and it will
damage the revenue of the kings.
14 "Now because we [1]are in the service of the palace, and it is not fitting for us to see the king's dishonor, therefore we have sent and
informed the king,
15 so that a search may be made in
the record books of your fathers.
And you will discover in the record
books, and learn that that city is a
rebellious city and damaging to
kings and provinces, and that they
have incited revolt within it in past
days; therefore that city was laid
waste.
16 "We inform the king that, if that
city is rebuilt and the walls finished,
as a result you will have no possession in *the province* beyond the
River."

The King Replies and Work Stops

17 *Then* the king sent an answer to
Rehum the commander, to Shimshai the scribe, and to the rest of
their colleagues who live in Samaria
and in the rest of *the provinces* beyond the River: "Peace. And now
18 the document which you sent to
us has been [1a]translated and read
before me.
19 "And a decree has been [1]issued
by me, and a search has been made
and it has been discovered that that
city has risen up against the kings in
past days, that rebellion and revolt
have been perpetrated in it,
20 [a]that mighty kings have [1]ruled
over Jerusalem, governing all *the
provinces* beyond the River, and
that [b]tribute, custom, and toll were
paid to them.
21 "So, now issue a decree to make
these men stop *work,* that the city
may not be rebuilt until a decree is
issued by me.
22 "And beware of being negligent
in carrying out this *matter;* why
should damage increase to the detri-
ment of the kings?"
23 Then as soon as the copy of
King Artaxerxes' document was
read before Rehum and Shimshai
the scribe and their colleagues, they
went in haste to Jerusalem to the
Jews and stopped them by force of
arms.
24 Then work on the house of God
in Jerusalem ceased, and it was
stopped until the second year of the
reign of Darius king of Persia.

CHAPTER 5

Temple Work Resumed

WHEN the prophets, [a]Haggai the
prophet and [b]Zechariah the son of
Iddo, prophesied to the Jews who
were in Judah and Jerusalem, in the
name of the God of Israel, who was
over them,
2 then [a]Zerubbabel the son of
Shealtiel and Jeshua the son of Jozadak arose and began to rebuild the
house of God which is in Jerusalem;
and [b]the prophets of God were with
them supporting them.
3 At that time [a]Tattenai, the governor of *the province* beyond the
[1]River, and Shethar-bozenai and
their colleagues came to them and
spoke to them thus, "[b]Who issued
you a decree to rebuild this [2]temple
and to finish this structure?"
4 [a]Then we told them accordingly what the names of the men
were who were reconstructing this
building.
5 But [a]the eye of their God was
on the elders of the Jews, and they
did not stop them until a report
should come to Darius, and then a

7 [1]Heb., *Artahshashta* [2]Lit., *written* [a]2 Kin. 18:26; Dan. 2:4
8 [1]Ch. 4:8-6:18 is in Aramaic
9 [a]2 Kin. 17:24 [b]Ezra 5:6; 6:6
10 [1]I.e., probably Ashurbanipal [2]I.e., Euphrates River and so throughout the chap. [a]Ezra 4:11, 17; 7:12
12 [a]2 Chr. 36:13 [b]Ezra 5:3, 9
13 [a]Ezra 4:20
14 [1]Lit., *eat the salt*
18 [1]Lit., *plainly read before* [a]Neh. 8:8
19 [1]Lit., *put forth*
20 [1]Lit., *been* [a]1 Kin. 4:21; 1 Chr. 18:3 [b]Ezra 4:13; 7:24
1 [a]Hag. 1:1 [b]Zech. 1:1
2 [a]Ezra 3:2 [b]Ezra 6:14; Hag. 2:4; Zech. 3:1
3 [1]I.e., Euphrates River, and so throughout the chap. [2]Lit., *house,* and so throughout the chap. [a]Ezra 6:6, 13 [b]Ezra 1:3; 5:9
4 [a]Ezra 5:10
5 [a]Ezra 7:6, 28

written reply be returned concerning it.

Adversaries Write to Darius

6 *This is* the copy of the letter
which [a]Tattenai, the governor of *the*
province beyond the River, and Shethar-bozenai and his colleagues [b]the
officials, who were beyond the
River, sent to Darius the king.
7 They sent a report to him in
which it was written thus: "To Darius the king, all peace.
8 "Let it be known to the king, that
we have gone to the province of Judah, to the house of the great God,
which is being built with huge
stones, and [1]beams are being laid in
the walls; and this work is going on
with great care and is succeeding in
their hands.
9 "Then we asked those elders and
said to them thus, 'Who issued you
a decree to rebuild this temple and
to finish this structure?'
10 "We also asked them their
names so as to inform you, and that
we might write down the names of
the men who were at their head.
11 "And thus they [1]answered us,
saying, 'We are the servants of the
God of heaven and earth and are rebuilding the temple that was built
many years ago, [a]which a great king
of Israel built and finished.
12 'But [a]because our fathers had
provoked the God of heaven to
wrath, He gave them into the hand
of Nebuchadnezzar king of Babylon, the Chaldean, *who* destroyed
this temple and deported the people
to Babylon.
13 'However, [a]in the first year of
Cyrus king of Babylon, King Cyrus
issued a decree to rebuild this house
of God.
14 'And also [a]the gold and silver
utensils of the house of God which
Nebuchadnezzar had taken from
the temple [1]in Jerusalem, and
brought them to the temple of Babylon, these King Cyrus took from the
temple of Babylon, and they were
given to one [b]whose name was
Sheshbazzar, whom he had appointed governor.
15 'And he said to him, "Take these
utensils, go *and* deposit them in the
temple [1]in Jerusalem, and let the
house of God be rebuilt in its place."
16 'Then that Sheshbazzar came
and [a]laid the foundations of the
house of God [1]in Jerusalem; and
from then until now it has been under construction, and it is [b]not *yet*
completed.'
17 "And now, if it pleases the king
[a]let a search be conducted in the
king's treasure house, which is there
in Babylon, if it be that a decree was
issued by King Cyrus to rebuild this
house of God at Jerusalem; and let
the king send to us his decision concerning this *matter*."

CHAPTER 6

Darius Finds Cyrus' Decree

THEN King Darius issued a decree, and [a]search was made in the
[1]archives, where the treasures were
stored in Babylon.
2 And in [1]Ecbatana in the fortress, which is [a]in the province of
Media, a scroll was found and there
was written in it as follows: "Memo-
randum—
3 "[a]In the first year of King Cyrus,
Cyrus the king issued a decree:
'*Concerning* the house of God at Jerusalem, let the temple, the place
where sacrifices are offered, be rebuilt and let its foundations be [1]re-
tained, its height being 60 cubits and
its width 60 cubits;
4 [a]with three layers of huge
stones, and [1]one layer of timbers.
And let the cost be paid from the
[2]royal treasury.
5 'And also let [a]the gold and silver
utensils of the temple of God, which
Nebuchadnezzar took from the temple in Jerusalem and brought to
Babylon, be returned and [1]brought
to their places in the temple in Jerusalem; and you shall put *them* in the
house of God.'
6 "Now therefore, [a]Tattenai, governor of *the province* beyond the
[1]River, Shethar-bozenai, and [2]your
colleagues, the officials of *the prov-*
inces beyond the [1]River, [3]keep away
from there.
7 "Leave this work on the house of
God alone; let the governor of the
Jews and the elders of the Jews rebuild this house of God on its site.
8 "Moreover, [a]I issue a decree
concerning what you are to do for
these elders of Judah in the rebuilding of this house of God: the full cost
is to be paid to these people from the
royal treasury out of the taxes of *the*
provinces beyond the River, and
that without delay.
9 "And whatever is needed, both
young bulls, rams, and lambs for a
burnt offering to the God of heaven,
and wheat, salt, wine, and anointing
oil, as the priests in Jerusalem request, *it* is to be given to them daily
without fail,
10 that they may offer [1]acceptable

5:6 [a]Ezra 5:3 [b]Ezra 4:9
5:8 [1]Lit., *timber is*
5:11 [1]Lit., *returned us the word* [a]1 Kin. 6:1, 38
5:12 [a]2 Chr. 36:16, 17
5:13 [a]Ezra 1:1
5:14 [1]Lit., *that was in* [a]Ezra 1:7; 6:5; Dan. 5:2 [b]Ezra 1:8; 5:16
5:15 [1]Lit., *that is in*
5:16 [1]Lit., *that is in* [a]Ezra 3:8, 10 [b]Ezra 6:15
5:17 [a]Ezra 6:1, 2
6:1 [1]Lit., *house of the books* [a]Ezra 5:17
6:2 [1]Aramaic, *Achmetha* [a]2 Kin. 17:6
6:3 [1]Or, *fixed, laid* [a]Ezra 1:1; 5:13
6:4 [1]So Gk.; Aramaic, *a layer of new timber* [2]Lit., *king's house* [a]1 Kin. 6:36
6:5 [1]Lit., *go* [a]Ezra 1:7; 5:14
6:6 [1]I.e., Euphrates River, and so throughout the chap. [2]Aram., *their* [3]Lit., *be distant* [a]Ezra 6:13
6:8 [a]Ezra 6:4; 7:14-22
6:10 [1]Lit., *pleasing or sweet-smelling sacrifices*

sacrifices to the God of heaven and
[a]pray for the life of the king and his
sons.
11"And I issued a decree that [a]any
man who violates this edict, a timber shall be drawn from his house
and he shall be impaled on it and
[b]his house shall be made a refuse
heap on account of this.
12"And may the God who [a]has
caused His name to dwell there
overthrow any king or people who
[1]attempts to change *it,* so as to destroy this house of God in Jerusalem. I, Darius, have issued *this* decree, let *it* be carried out with all
diligence!"

The Temple Completed and Dedicated

13 Then [a]Tattenai, the governor of
the province beyond the River, Shethar-bozenai, and their colleagues
carried out *the decree* with all diligence, just as King Darius had sent.
14 And [a]the elders of the Jews
[1]were successful in building
through the prophesying of Haggai
the prophet and Zechariah the son
of Iddo. And [2]they finished building
according to the command of the
God of Israel and the decree [b]of Cyrus, [c]Darius, and [d]Artaxerxes king
of Persia.
15 And this temple was completed
[1]on the third day of the [a]month
Adar; it was the sixth year of the
reign of King Darius.
16 And the sons of Israel, the
priests, the Levites, and the rest of
the [1]exiles, [a]celebrated the dedication of this house of God with joy.
17 And they offered for the dedication of this temple of God 100 bulls,
200 rams, 400 lambs, and as a sin
offering for all Israel [a]12 male goats,
corresponding to the number of the
tribes of Israel.
18 Then they appointed the priests
to [a]their divisions and the Levites in
[b]their orders for the service of God
[1]in Jerusalem, [c]as it is written in the
book of Moses.

The Passover Observed

19 And [a]the exiles observed the
Passover on [b]the fourteenth of the
first month.
20 [a]For the priests and the Levites
had purified themselves together;
all of them were pure. Then [b]they
slaughtered the Passover *lamb* for
all the exiles, both for their brothers
the priests and for themselves.
21 And the sons of Israel who returned from exile and [a]all those who
had separated themselves from [b]the
impurity of the nations of the land to
join them, to seek the LORD God of
Israel, ate *the Passover.*
22 And [a]they observed the Feast
of Unleavened Bread seven days
with joy, for the LORD had caused
them to rejoice, and [b]had turned the
heart of [c]the king of Assyria toward
them to [1]encourage them in the
work of the house of God, the God
of Israel.

CHAPTER 7

Ezra Journeys from Babylon to Jerusalem

[a]NOW after these things, in the
reign of [b]Artaxerxes king of Persia,
there went up Ezra son of Seraiah,
son of Azariah, son of Hilkiah,
2 son of Shallum, son of Zadok,
son of Ahitub,
3 son of Amariah, son of Azariah,
son of Meraioth,
4 son of Zerahiah, son of Uzzi,
son of Bukki,
5 son of Abishua, son of Phinehas, son of Eleazar, son of Aaron the
chief priest.
6 This Ezra went up from Babylon, and he was a [a]scribe skilled in
the law of Moses, which the LORD
God of Israel had given; and the
king granted him all [1]he requested
[b]because the hand of the LORD his
God *was* upon him.
7 And [a]some of the sons of Israel
and some of the priests, the Levites,
the singers, the gatekeepers, and the
temple servants went up to Jerusalem in the seventh year of King Artaxerxes.
8 And he came to Jerusalem in
the fifth month, which was in the
seventh year of the king.
9 For on the first of the first
month [1]he began to go up from
Babylon; and on the first of the fifth
month he came to Jerusalem, [a]be-
cause the good hand of his God *was*
upon him.
10 For Ezra had set his heart to
[1]study the law of the LORD, and to
practice *it,* and [a]to teach *His* statutes and ordinances in Israel.

King's Decree on Behalf of Ezra

11 Now this is the copy of the decree which King Artaxerxes gave to
Ezra the priest, the scribe, [1]learned
in the words of the commandments
of the LORD and His statutes to Israel:
12"[1]Artaxerxes, [a]king of kings, to
Ezra the priest, the scribe of the law
of the God of heaven, perfect *peace.*
And now

10 [a]Ezra 7:23
11 [a]Ezra 7:26 [b]Dan. 2:5; 3:29
12 [1]Lit., *sends his hand* [a]Deut. 12:5, 11
13 [a]Ezra 6:6
14 [1]Lit., *were building and succeeding* [2]Lit., *built and finished* [a]Ezra 5:1, 2 [b]Ezra 1:1 [c]Ezra 6:12 [d]Ezra 7:1
15 [1]Lit., *until* [a]Esth. 3:7
16 [1]Lit., *sons of the captivity* [a]2 Chr. 7:5
17 [a]Ezra 8:35
18 [1]Lit., *which is in* [a]2 Chr. 35:5 [b]1 Chr. 23:6 [c]Num. 3:6; 8:9
19 [a]Ezra 1:11 [b]Ex. 12:6
20 [a]2 Chr. 29:34; 30:15 [b]2 Chr. 35:11
21 [a]Neh. 9:2; 10:28 [b]Ezra 9:11
22 [1]Lit., *strengthen their hands* [a]Ex. 12:15 [b]Ezra 7:27 [c]Ezra 1:1; 6:1
1 [a]1 Chr. 6:4-14 [b]Ezra 7:12, 21; Neh. 2:1
6 [1]Lit., *his request* [a]Ezra 7:11, 12, 21 [b]Ezra 7:9, 28
7 [a]Ezra 8:1-20
9 [1]Lit., *was the foundation* [a]Ezra 7:6
10 [1]Lit., *seek* [a]Ezra 7:25; Neh. 8:1
11 [1]Lit., *the scribe of*
12 [1]Ch. 7:12-26 is in Aramaic [a]Ezek. 26:7; Dan. 2:37

13 [a]I have issued a decree that any
of the people of Israel and their
priests and the Levites in my kingdom who are willing to go to Jerusalem, may go with you.
14 "Forasmuch as you are sent [1]by
the king and his [a]seven counselors
to inquire concerning Judah and Jerusalem according to the law of
your God which is in your hand,
15 and to bring the silver and gold,
which the king and his counselors
have freely offered to the God of Israel, [a]whose dwelling is in Jerusalem,
16 with [a]all the silver and gold
which you shall find in the whole
province of Babylon, along [b]with
the freewill offering of the people
and of the priests, who offered willingly for the house of their God
which is in Jerusalem;
17 with this money, therefore, you
shall diligently buy bulls, rams, and
lambs, [a]with their grain offerings
and their libations and [b]offer them
on the altar of the house of your God
which is in Jerusalem.
18 "And whatever seems good to
you and to your brothers to do with
the rest of the silver and gold, you
may do according to the will of your
God.
19 "Also the utensils which are giv-
en to you for the service of the house
of your God, deliver in full before
the God of Jerusalem.
20 "And the rest of the needs for
the house of your God, for which
you may have occasion to provide,
[a]provide *for it* from the royal treasury.
21 "And I, even I King Artaxerxes,
issue a decree to all the treasurers
who are *in the provinces* beyond the
[1]River, that whatever Ezra the
priest, [a]the scribe of the law of the
God of heaven, may require of you,
it shall be done diligently,
22 *even* up to 100 talents of silver,
100 [1]kors of wheat, 100 baths of
wine, 100 baths of oil, and salt [2]as
needed.
23 "Whatever is [1]commanded by
the God of heaven, let it be done
with zeal for the house of the God of
heaven, [a]lest there be wrath against
the kingdom of the king and his
sons.
24 "We also inform you that [a]it is
not allowed to [1]impose tax, tribute
or toll [b]*on* any of the priests, Levites, singers, doorkeepers, Nethinim, or servants of this house of
God.
25 "And you, Ezra, according to the
wisdom of your God which is in
your hand, [a]appoint magistrates
and judges that they may judge all
the people who are in *the province*
beyond the River, *even* all those
who know the laws of your God; and
you may [b]teach anyone who is ignorant *of them.*
26 "And [a]whoever will not observe
the law of your God and the law of
the king, let judgment be executed
upon him strictly, whether for death
or for [1]banishment or for confisca-
tion of goods or for imprisonment."

The King's Kindness

27 Blessed be the LORD, the God of
our fathers, [a]who has put *such a
thing* as this in the king's heart, to
adorn the house of the LORD which
is in Jerusalem,
28 and [a]has extended lovingkindness to me before the king and his
counselors and before all the king's
mighty princes. Thus I was
strengthened according to the hand
of the LORD my God upon me, and I
gathered [1]leading men from Israel
to go up with me.

CHAPTER 8

People Who Went with Ezra

NOW these are the heads of their
fathers' *households* and the genealogical enrollment of those who
went up with me from Babylon in
the reign of King Artaxerxes:
2 of the sons of Phinehas, Gershom; of the sons of Ithamar, Daniel; of the sons of David, Hattush;
3 of the sons of Shecaniah *who
was* of the sons of Parosh, Zechariah and with him 150 males *who
were in* the genealogical list;
4 of the sons of Pahath-moab,
Eliehoenai the son of Zerahiah and
200 males with him;
5 of the sons of Shecaniah, the
son of Jahaziel and 300 males with
him;
6 and of the sons of Adin, Ebed
the son of Jonathan and 50 males
with him;
7 and of the sons of Elam, Jeshaiah the son of Athaliah and 70 males
with him;
8 and of the sons of Shephatiah,
Zebadiah the son of Michael and 80
males with him;
9 of the sons of Joab, Obadiah the
son of Jehiel and 218 males with
him;
10 and of the sons of Shelomith,
the son of Josiphiah and 160 males
with him;
11 and of the sons of Bebai, Zecha-

13 [a]Ezra 6:1
14 [1]Lit., *from before* [a]Ezra 7:15, 28; 8:25
15 [a]Ezra 6:12
16 [a]Ezra 8:25 [b]Ezra 1:4, 6
17 [a]Num. 15:4-13 [b]Deut. 12:5-11
20 [a]Ezra 6:4
21 [1]Euphrates River and so throughout the chap. [a]Ezra 7:6
22 [1]One kor equals approx. ten bushels [2]Lit., *without prescription*
23 [1]Lit., *from the decree of* [a]Ezra 6:10
24 [1]Lit., *throw on them* [a]Ezra 4:13, 20 [b]Ezra 7:7
25 [a]Ex. 18:21; Deut. 16:18 [b]Ezra 7:10
26 [1]Lit., *rooting out* [a]Ezra 6:11, 12
27 [a]Ezra 6:22
28 [1]Lit., *heads* [a]Ezra 9:9

riah the son of Bebai and 28 males
with him;
12 and of the sons of Azgad, Johanan the son of Hakkatan and 110
males with him;
13 and of the sons of Adonikam,
the last ones, these being their
names, Eliphelet, Jeuel, and Shemaiah and 60 males with them;
14 and of the sons of Bigvai, Uthai
and [1]Zabbud and 70 males with
[2]them.

Ezra Sends for Levites

15 Now I assembled them at [a]the
river that runs to Ahava, where we
camped for three days; and when I
observed the people and the priests,
I [b]did not find any Levites there.
16 So I sent for Eliezer, Ariel,
Shemaiah, Elnathan, Jarib, Elnathan, Nathan, Zechariah, and Meshullam, [1]leading men, and for Joiarib and Elnathan, teachers.
17 And I sent them to Iddo the
[1]leading man at the place Casiphia;
and I [2]told them what to say to [3]Iddo
and his brothers, [a]the temple servants at the place Casiphia, *that is,*
to bring ministers to us for the
house of our God.
18 And [a]according to the good
hand of our God upon us they
brought us a man of insight of the
sons of Mahli, the son of Levi, the
son of Israel, namely Sherebiah, and
his sons and brothers, 18 men;
19 and Hashabiah and [1]Jeshaiah
of the sons of Merari, with his brothers and their sons, 20 men;
20 and 220 of [a]the temple servants, whom David and the princes
had given for the service of the Levites, all of them designated by
name.

Protection of God Invoked

21 Then I proclaimed [a]a fast there
at [b]the river of Ahava, that we might
humble ourselves before our God to
seek from Him a [1]safe journey for
us, our little ones, and all our possessions.
22 For I was ashamed to request
from the king troops and horsemen
to [1]protect us from the enemy on the
way, because we had said to the
king, "[a]The hand of our God is [2]fa-
vorably disposed to all those who
seek Him, but [b]His power and His
anger are against all those who forsake Him."
23 So we fasted and sought our
God concerning this *matter,* and He
[1]listened to our entreaty.
24 Then I set apart twelve of the
leading priests, [a]Sherebiah, Hashabiah, and with them ten of their
brothers;
25 and I [a]weighed out to them [b]the
silver, the gold, and the utensils, the
offering for the house of our God
which the king and [c]his counselors
and his princes, and all Israel present *there,* had offered.
26 [a]Thus I weighed into their
hands 650 talents of silver, and silver utensils *worth* 100 talents, *and*
gold talents,
27 and 20 gold bowls, *worth* 1,000
darics; and two utensils of fine shiny
bronze, precious as gold.
28 Then I said to them, "[a]You are
holy to the LORD, and the [b]utensils
are holy; and the silver and the gold
are a freewill offering to the LORD
God of your fathers.
29 "Watch and keep *them* [a]until
you weigh *them* before the leading
priests, the Levites, and the heads of
the fathers' *households* of Israel at
Jerusalem, *in* the chambers of the
house of the LORD."
30 So the priests and the Levites
[a]accepted the weighed out silver
and gold and the utensils, to bring
them to Jerusalem to the house of
our God.
31 Then we journeyed from [a]the
river Ahava on [b]the twelfth of the
first month to go to Jerusalem; and
[c]the hand of our God was over us,
and He delivered us from the hand
of the enemy and the ambushes by
the way.
32 [a]Thus we came to Jerusalem
and remained there three days.

Treasure Placed in the Temple

33 And on the fourth day the silver
and the gold and the utensils [a]were
weighed out in the house of our God
into the hand of [b]Meremoth the son
of Uriah the priest, and with him
was Eleazar the son of Phinehas;
and with them *were* the Levites,
Jozabad the son of Jeshua and Noadiah the son of Binnui.
34 Everything *was* numbered and
weighed, and all the weight was recorded at that time.
35 [a]The exiles who had come from
the captivity offered burnt offerings
to the God of Israel: [b]12 bulls for all
Israel, 96 rams, 77 lambs, 12 male
goats for a sin offering, all as a burnt
offering to the LORD.
36 Then [a]they delivered the king's
edicts to [b]the king's satraps, and to
the governors *in the provinces* beyond the [1]River, and they supported
the people and the house of God.

14 [1]Or, *Zakkur* [2]Or, *him*
15 [a]Ezra 8:21, 31 [b]Ezra 7:7; 8:2
16 [1]Lit., *heads*
17 [1]Lit., *head* [2]Lit., *put words in their mouth to say* [3]So Gk.; Heb., *Iddo his brother* [a]Ezra 2:43
18 [a]Ezra 7:6
19 [1]So Gk.; Heb., *with him Jeshaiah*
20 [a]Ezra 2:43; 7:7
21 [1]Lit., *straight way* [a]1 Sam. 7:6; 2 Chr. 20:3 [b]Ezra 8:15, 31
22 [1]Lit., *help* [2]Lit., *upon all . . . for good* [a]Ezra 7:6, 9, 28 [b]Josh. 22:16
23 [1]Lit., *was entreated by us*
24 [a]Ezra 8:18, 19
25 [a]Ezra 8:33 [b]Ezra 7:15, 16 [c]Ezra 7:14
26 [a]Ezra 1:9-11
28 [a]Lev. 21:6-8 [b]Lev. 22:2, 3
29 [a]Ezra 8:33, 34
30 [a]Ezra 1:9
31 [a]Ezra 8:15, 21 [b]Ezra 7:9 [c]Ezra 8:22
32 [a]Neh. 2:11
33 [a]Ezra 8:30 [b]Neh. 3:4, 21
35 [a]Ezra 2:1 [b]Ezra 6:17
36 [1]I.e. Euphrates River [a]Ezra 7:21-24 [b]Ezra 4:7; 5:6

Chapter 9

Mixed Marriages

NOW when these things had been completed, the princes approached me, saying, "The people of Israel and the priests and the Levites have not [a]separated themselves from the peoples of the lands, [b]according to their abominations, *those* of the Canaanites, the Hittites, the Perizzites, the Jebusites, the Ammonites, the Moabites, the Egyptians, and the Amorites.

2"For [a]they have taken some of their daughters *as wives* for themselves and for their sons, so that [b]the holy [1]race has [c]intermingled with the peoples of the lands; indeed, the hands of the princes and the rulers have been foremost in this unfaithfulness."

3 And when I heard about this matter, I [a]tore my garment and my robe, and pulled some of the hair from my head and my beard, and [b]sat down appalled.

4 Then [a]everyone who trembled at the words of the God of Israel on account of the unfaithfulness of the exiles gathered to me, and I sat appalled until [b]the evening offering.

Prayer of Confession

5 But at the evening offering I arose from my [1]humiliation, even with my garment and my robe torn, and I fell on my knees and [a]stretched out my [2]hands to the LORD my God;

6 and I said, "O my God, I am ashamed and embarrassed to lift up my face to Thee, my God, for our iniquities have [1]risen above our heads, and our [a]guilt has grown even to the heavens.

7"[a]Since the days of our fathers to this day we *have been* in great guilt, and on account of our iniquities we, our kings *and* our priests have been given into the hand of the kings of the lands, to the sword, to captivity, and to plunder and to [1b]open shame, as *it is* this day.

8"But now for a brief moment grace has been *shown* from the LORD our God, [a]to leave us an escaped remnant and to give us a [b]peg in His holy place, that our God may enlighten our eyes and grant us a little reviving in our bondage.

9"[a]For we are slaves; yet in our bondage, our God has not forsaken us, but [b]has extended lovingkindness to us in the sight of the kings of Persia, to give us reviving to raise up the house of our God, to restore its ruins, and to give us a wall in Judah and Jerusalem.

10"And now, our God, what shall we say after this? For we have forsaken Thy commandments,

11 which Thou hast commanded by Thy servants the prophets, saying, 'The land which you are entering to take possession of it is an unclean land with the uncleanness of the peoples of the lands, with their abominations which have filled it from end to end and [a]with their impurity.

12 'So now do not [a]give your daughters to their sons nor take their daughters to your sons, and never seek their peace or their prosperity, that you may be strong and eat the good *things* of the land and [b]leave *it* as an inheritance to your sons forever.'

13"And after all that has come upon us for our evil deeds and [a]our great guilt, since Thou our God hast requited *us* less than our iniquities *deserve,* and hast given us [b]an escaped remnant as this,

14 [a]shall we again break Thy commandments and intermarry with the peoples who commit these abominations? [b]Wouldst Thou not be angry with us [1]to the point of destruction, until there is no remnant nor any who escape?

15"O LORD God of Israel, [a]Thou art righteous, for we have been left an escaped remnant, as *it is* this day; behold, we are before Thee in [b]our guilt, for [c]no one can stand before Thee because of this."

Chapter 10

Reconciliation with God

NOW [a]while Ezra was praying and making confession, weeping and prostrating himself [b]before the house of God, a very large assembly, men, women, and children, gathered to him from Israel; for the people wept bitterly.

2 And Shecaniah the son of Jehiel, one of the sons of Elam, answered and said to Ezra, "[a]We have been unfaithful to our God, and have [1]married foreign women from the peoples of the land; yet now there is hope for Israel in spite of this.

3"So now [a]let us make a covenant with our God to put away all the wives and [1b]their children, according to the counsel of [2]my lord and of [c]those who tremble at the com-

1 [a]Ezra 6:21; Neh. 9:2 [b]Lev. 18:24-30

2 [1]Lit., *seed* [a]Ezra 10:2, 18 [b]Ex. 22:31 [c]Neh. 13:3

3 [a]2 Kin. 18:37 [b]Neh. 1:4

4 [a]Ezra 10:3 [b]Ex. 29:39

5 [1]Or, *fasting* [2]Lit., *palms* [a]Ex. 9:29

6 [1]Lit., *multiplied over the head* [a]2 Chr. 28:9; Ezra 9:13, 15; Rev. 18:5

7 [1]Lit., *shame of faces* [a]2 Chr. 29:6 [b]Dan. 9:7

8 [a]Ezra 9:13-15 [b]Is. 22:23

9 [a]Neh. 9:36 [b]Ezra 7:28

11 [a]Ezra 6:21

12 [a]Ezra 9:2 [b]Prov. 13:22

13 [a]Ezra 9:6, 7 [b]Ezra 9:8

14 [1]Lit., *to destroy* [a]Ezra 9:2 [b]Deut. 9:8, 14

15 [a]Neh. 9:33; Dan. 9:7 [b]Ezra 9:6 [c]Job 9:2

1 [a]Dan. 9:4, 20 [b]2 Chr. 20:9

2 [1]Lit., *given dwelling to* [a]Ezra 9:2

3 [1]Lit., *that which is born of them* [2]Or, *the Lord* [a]2 Chr. 34:31 [b]Ezra 10:44 [c]Ezra 9:4

mandment of our God; and let it be
done [d]according to the law.
4 "Arise! For *this* matter is [1]your
responsibility, but we will be with
you; [a]be courageous and act."
5 Then Ezra rose and [a]made the
leading priests, the Levites, and all
Israel, take oath that they would do
according to this [1]proposal; so they
took the oath.
6 Then Ezra [a]rose from before
the house of God and went into the
chamber of Jehohanan the son of
Eliashib. Although he went there,
[b]he did not eat bread, nor drink water, for he was mourning over the
unfaithfulness of the exiles.
7 And they made a proclamation
throughout Judah and Jerusalem to
all the exiles, that they should assemble at Jerusalem,
8 and that whoever would not
come within three days, according
to the counsel of the leaders and the
elders, all his possessions should be
forfeited and he himself excluded
from the assembly of the exiles.
9 So all the men of Judah and
Benjamin assembled at Jerusalem
within the three days. It was the
ninth month on the twentieth of the
month, and all the people sat in the
open square *before* the house of
God, [a]trembling because of this
matter and the heavy rain.
10 Then Ezra the priest stood up
and said to them, "You have been
unfaithful and have married foreign
wives adding to the guilt of Israel.
11 "Now, therefore, [a]make confession to the LORD God of your fathers, and do His will; and [b]separate
yourselves from the peoples of the
land and from the foreign wives."
12 Then all the assembly answered and said with a loud voice,
"That's right! As you have said, so it
is [1]our duty to *do.*
13 "But there are many people, it is
the rainy season, and we are not
able to stand in the open. Nor can
the task be done in one or two days,
for we have transgressed greatly in
this matter.
14 "Let our leaders [1]represent the
whole assembly and let all those in
our cities who have married foreign
wives come at appointed times, together with the elders and judges of
each city, until the [a]fierce anger of
our God on account of this matter is
turned away from us."
15 Only Jonathan the son of Asahel and Jahzeiah the son of Tikvah
[1]opposed this, with Meshullam and
Shabbethai the Levite supporting
them.

16 But the exiles did so. And Ezra
the priest [1]selected men *who were*
heads of fathers' *households* for
each of their father's *households,* all
of them by name. So they [2]convened
on the first day of the tenth month to
investigate the matter.
17 And they finished *investigating*
all the men who had married foreign
wives by the first of the first month.

List of Offenders

18 And among the sons of the
priests who had married foreign
wives were found of the sons of
Jeshua the son of Jozadak, and his
brothers: Maaseiah, Eliezer, Jarib,
and Gedaliah.
19 And they [1a]pledged to put away
their wives, and being guilty, [b]*they
offered* a ram of the flock for their
offense.
20 And of the sons of Immer *there
were* Hanani and Zebadiah;
21 and of the sons of Harim: Maaseiah, Elijah, Shemaiah, Jehiel, and
Uzziah;
22 and of the sons of Pashhur: Elioenai, Maaseiah, Ishmael, Nethanel,
Jozabad, and Elasah.
23 And of Levites *there were* Jozabad, Shimei, Kelaiah (that is, Kelita), Pethahiah, Judah, and Eliezer.
24 And of the singers *there was*
Eliashib; and of the gatekeepers:
Shallum, Telem, and Uri.
25 And of Israel, of the sons of Parosh *there were* Ramiah, Izziah,
Malchijah, Mijamin, Eleazar, Malchijah, and Benaiah;
26 and of the sons of Elam: Mattaniah, Zechariah, Jehiel, Abdi, Jeremoth, and Elijah;
27 and of the sons of Zattu: Elioenai, Eliashib, Mattaniah, Jeremoth,
Zabad, and Aziza;
28 and of the sons of Bebai: Jehohanan, Hananiah, Zabbai, *and* Ath-
lai;
29 and of the sons of Bani: Meshullam, Malluch, and Adaiah, Jashub,
Sheal, *and* Jeremoth;
30 and of the sons of Pahath-
moab: Adna, Chelal, Benaiah, Maaseiah, Mattaniah, Bezalel, Binnui,
and Manasseh;
31 and *of* the sons of Harim: Eliezer, Isshijah, Malchijah, Shemaiah,
Shimeon,
32 Benjamin, Malluch, *and* Shemariah;
33 of the sons of Hashum: Mattenai, Mattattah, Zabad, Eliphelet,
Jeremai, Manasseh, *and* Shimei;
34 of the sons of Bani: Maadai,
Amram, Uel,

3 [d]Deut. 7:2, 3

4 [1]Lit., *upon you*
[a]1 Chr. 28:10

5 [1]Lit., *word, thing*
[a]Neh. 5:12; 13:25

6 [a]Ezra 10:1
[b]Deut. 9:18

9 [a]Ezra 9:4; 10:3

11 [a]Lev. 26:40
[b]Ezra 10:3

12 [1]Lit., *upon us*

14 [1]Lit., *stand for*
[a]2 Chr. 29:10; 30:8

15 [1]Lit., *stood against*

16 [1]Heb. reads, *there were set apart Ezra the priest, men. . .*
[2]Lit., *sat*

19 [1]Lit., *gave their hand*
[a]2 Kin. 10:15
[b]Lev. 5:15; 6:6

35 Benaiah, Bedeiah, Cheluhi,
36 Vaniah, Meremoth, Eliashib,
37 Mattaniah, Mattenai, Jaasu,
38 Bani, Binnui, Shimei,
39 Shelemiah, Nathan, Adaiah,
40 Machnadebai, Shashai, Sharai,
41 Azarel, Shelemiah, Shemariah,
42 Shallum, Amariah, *and* Joseph.
43 Of the sons of Nebo *there were*
Jeiel, Mattithiah, Zabad, Zebina,
Jaddai, Joel, *and* Benaiah.
44 All these had married foreign
wives, and [a]some of them had wives
by whom they had children.

44 [a]Ezra 10:3

THE BOOK OF NEHEMIAH

Nehemiah's Grief for the Exiles

THE words of [a]Nehemiah the son
of Hacaliah.
Now it happened in [b]the month
Chislev, [c]*in* the twentieth year,
while I was in [d]Susa the [1]capitol,
2 that [a]Hanani, one of my brothers, and [1]some men from Judah
came; and I asked them concerning
the Jews who had escaped *and* had
survived the captivity, and about Jerusalem.
3 And they said to me, "The remnant there in the [a]province who survived the captivity are in great distress and [b]reproach, and [c]the wall of
Jerusalem is broken down and [d]its
gates are burned with fire."
4 Now it came about when I
heard these words, [a]I sat down and
wept and mourned for days; and I
was fasting and praying before [b]the
God of heaven.
5 And I said, "I beseech Thee, O
LORD God of heaven, [a]the great and
awesome God, who preserves the
covenant and lovingkindness for
those who love Him and keep His
commandments,
6 [a]let Thine ear now be attentive
and Thine eyes open to hear the
prayer of Thy servant which I am
praying before Thee now, day and
night, on behalf of the sons of Israel
Thy servants, [b]confessing the sins of
the sons of Israel which we have
sinned against Thee; [c]I and my father's house have sinned.
7"[a]We have acted very corruptly
against Thee and have not kept the
commandments, nor the statutes,
nor the ordinances [b]which Thou
didst command Thy servant Moses.
8"Remember the word which
Thou didst command Thy servant
Moses, saying, '[a]If you are unfaithful I will scatter you among the peoples;
9 [a]but if you return to Me and
keep My commandments and do
them, though those of you who have
been scattered were in the most remote part of the heavens, I [b]will
gather them from there and will
bring them [c]to the place where I
have chosen to cause My name to
dwell.'
10"And [a]they are Thy servants and
Thy people whom Thou didst redeem by Thy great power and by
Thy strong hand.
11"O Lord, I beseech Thee, [a]may
Thine ear be attentive to the prayer
of Thy servant and the prayer of Thy
servants who delight to [1]revere Thy
name, and make Thy servant successful today, and grant him compassion before this man."
Now I was the [b]cupbearer to the
king.

CHAPTER 2

Nehemiah's Prayer Answered

AND it came about in the month
Nisan, [a]in the twentieth year of King
[b]Artaxerxes, that wine *was* before
him, and [c]I took up the wine and
gave it to the king. Now I had not
been sad in his presence.
2 So the king said to me, "Why is
your face sad though you are not
sick? [a]This is nothing but sadness of
heart." Then I was very much
afraid.
3 And I said to the king, "[a]Let the
king live forever. Why should my
face not be sad [b]when the city, the
place of my fathers' tombs, lies
desolate and its gates have been
consumed by fire?"
4 Then the king said to me,
"What would you request?" [a]So I
prayed to the God of heaven.
5 And I said to the king, "If it
please the king, and if your servant
has found favor before you, send me
to Judah, to the city of my fathers'
tombs, that I may rebuild it."
6 Then the king said to me, the
queen sitting beside him, "How long
will your journey be, and when will
you return?" So it pleased the king
to send me, and [a]I gave him a definite time.
7 And I said to the king, "If it

1 [1]Or, *palace or citadel* [a]Neh. 10:1 [b]Zech. 7:1 [c]Neh. 2:1 [d]Esth. 1:2; Dan. 8:2
2 [1]Lit., *he and some* [a]Neh. 7:2
3 [a]Neh. 7:6 [b]Neh. 2:17 [c]Neh. 2:17 [d]Neh. 2:3
4 [a]Ezra 9:3; 10:1 [b]Neh. 2:4
5 [a]Neh. 4:14; 9:32
6 [a]Dan. 9:17 [b]Ezra 10:1; Dan. 9:20 [c]2 Chr. 29:6
7 [a]Dan. 9:5 [b]Deut. 28:14
8 [a]Lev. 26:33
9 [a]Deut. 30:2, 3 [b]Deut. 30:4 [c]Deut. 12:5
10 [a]Ex. 32:11; Deut. 9:29
11 [1]Or, *fear* [a]Neh. 1:6 [b]Gen. 40:21; Neh. 2:1
1 [a]Neh. 1:1 [b]Ezra 7:1 [c]Neh. 1:11
2 [a]Prov. 15:13
3 [a]Dan. 2:4 [b]Neh. 1:3
4 [a]Neh. 1:4
6 [a]Neh. 5:14; 13:6

please the king, let letters be given me [a]for the governors *of the provinces* beyond the River, that they may allow me to pass through until I come to Judah,

8 and a letter to Asaph the keeper of the king's [a]forest, that he may give me timber to make beams for the gates of [b]the fortress which is by the [1]temple, for the wall of the city, and for the house to which I will go." And the king granted *them* to me because [c]the good hand of my God *was* on me.

9 Then I came to [a]the governors *of the provinces* beyond the River and gave them the king's letters. Now [b]the king had sent with me officers of the army and horsemen.

10 And when [a]Sanballat the Horonite and Tobiah the Ammonite [1]official heard *about it,* it was very displeasing to them that someone had come to seek the welfare of the sons of Israel.

Nehemiah Inspects Jerusalem's Walls

11 So I came to Jerusalem and was there three days.

12 And I arose in the night, I and a few men with me. I did not tell any one what my God was putting into my [1]mind to do for Jerusalem and there was no animal with me except the animal on which I was riding.

13 So I went out at night by [a]the Valley Gate in the direction of the Dragon's Well and *on* to the [1]Refuse Gate, inspecting the walls of Jerusalem [b]which were broken down and its [c]gates which were consumed by fire.

14 Then I passed on to [a]the Fountain Gate and [b]the King's Pool, but there was no place for [1]my mount to pass.

15 So I went up at night by the ravine and inspected the wall. Then I entered the Valley Gate again and returned.

16 And the officials did not know where I had gone or what I had done; nor had I as yet told the Jews, the priests, the nobles, the officials, or the rest who did the work.

17 Then I said to them, "You see the bad situation we are in, that [a]Jerusalem is desolate and its gates burned by fire. Come, let us rebuild the wall of Jerusalem that we may no longer be a reproach."

18 And I told them how the hand of my God had been favorable to me, and also about the king's words which he had spoken to me. Then they said, "Let us arise and build." [a]So they put their hands to the good *work.*

19 But when Sanballat the Horonite, and Tobiah the Ammonite [1]official, and [a]Geshem the Arab heard *it,* [b]they mocked us and despised us and said, "What is this thing you are doing? [c]Are you rebelling against the king?"

20 So I answered them and said to them, "[a]The God of heaven will give us success; therefore we His servants will arise and build, but you have no portion, right, or memorial in Jerusalem."

Chapter 3

Builders of the Walls

THEN [a]Eliashib the high priest arose with his brothers the priests and built [b]the Sheep Gate; they consecrated it and [c]hung its doors. They consecrated [1]the wall to [d]the Tower of the Hundred *and* [e]the Tower of Hananel.

2 And next to him [a]the men of Jericho built, and next to [1]them Zaccur the son of Imri built.

3 Now the sons of Hassenaah built [a]the Fish Gate; they laid its beams and hung its doors with its bolts and bars.

4 And next to them Meremoth the son of Uriah, the son of Hakkoz made repairs. And next to him Meshullam the son of Berechiah the son of Meshezabel made repairs. And next to [1]him Zadok the son of Baana also made repairs.

5 Moreover, next to [1]him the Tekoites made repairs, but their nobles did not [2]support the work of their masters.

6 And Joiada the son of Paseah and Meshullam the son of Besodeiah repaired [a]the Old Gate; they laid its beams and hung its doors, with its bolts and its bars.

7 Next to them Melatiah the Gibeonite and Jadon the Meronothite, the men of Gibeon and of Mizpah, [1]also [a]made repairs for the official seat of the governor *of the province* beyond the River.

8 Next to him Uzziel the son of Harhaiah of the [a]goldsmiths made repairs. And next to him Hananiah, one of the perfumers, made repairs, and they restored Jerusalem as far as [b]the Broad Wall.

9 And next to them Rephaiah the son of Hur, [a]the official of half the district of Jerusalem, made repairs.

10 Next to them Jedaiah the son of Harumaph made repairs opposite

7 [a]Ezra 7:21; 8:36
8 [1]Lit., *house* [a]Eccles. 2:5, 6 [b]Neh. 7:2 [c]Ezra 7:6; Neh. 2:18
9 [a]Neh. 2:7 [b]Ezra 8:22
10 [1]Lit., *servant* [a]Neh. 2:19; 4:1
12 [1]Lit., *heart*
13 [1]Lit., *Gate of Ash-heaps* [a]Neh. 3:13 [b]Neh. 1:3 [c]Neh. 2:3, 17
14 [1]Lit., *the animal under me* [a]Neh. 3:15 [b]2 Kin. 20:20
17 [a]Neh. 1:3
18 [a]2 Sam. 2:7
19 [1]Lit., *servant* [a]Neh. 6:6 [b]Neh. 4:1 [c]Neh. 6:6
20 [a]Neh. 2:4
1 [1]Lit., *it* [a]Neh. 3:20; 13:28 [b]Neh. 3:32; 12:39 [c]Neh. 6:1; 7:1 [d]Neh. 12:39 [e]Jer. 31:38
2 [1]Lit., *him* [a]Neh. 7:36
3 [a]Neh. 12:39
4 [1]Lit., *them*
5 [1]Lit., *them* [2]Lit., *bring their neck to*
6 [a]Neh. 12:39
7 [1]Or, *which was under the jurisdiction of the* governor of the province *beyond the River, also made repairs* [a]Neh. 2:7
8 [a]Neh. 31:32 [b]Neh. 12:38
9 [a]Neh. 3:12, 17

his house. And next to him Hattush the son of Hashabneiah made repairs.

11 Malchijah the son of Harim and Hasshub the son of Pahath-moab repaired another section and [a]the Tower of Furnaces.

12 And next to him Shallum the son of Hallohesh, [a]the official of half the district of Jerusalem, made repairs, he and his daughters.

13 Hanun and the inhabitants of Zanoah repaired [a]the Valley Gate. They built it and hung its doors with its bolts and its bars, and a thousand cubits of the wall to the [1]Refuse Gate.

14 And Malchijah the son of Rechab, the official of the district of [a]Beth-haccherem repaired the [1b]Refuse Gate. He built it and hung its doors with its bolts and its bars.

15 Shallum the son of Col-hozeh, the official of the district of Mizpah, repaired [a]the Fountain Gate. He built it, covered it, and hung its doors with its bolts and its bars, and the wall of the Pool of Shelah at [b]the king's garden as far as [c]the steps that descend from the city of David.

16 After him Nehemiah the son of Azbuk, [a]official of half the district of Beth-zur, made repairs as far as *a point* opposite the tombs of David, and as far as [b]the Artificial Pool and the House of the Mighty Men.

17 After him the Levites carried out repairs *under* Rehum the son of Bani. Next to him Hashabiah, the official of half the district of Keilah, carried out repairs for his district.

18 After him their brothers carried out repairs *under* Bavvai the son of Henadad, official of *the other* half of the district of Keilah.

19 And next to him Ezer the son of Jeshua, [a]the official of Mizpah, repaired [1]another section, in front of the ascent of the armory [b]at the Angle.

20 After him Baruch the son of Zabbai zealously repaired another section, from the Angle to the doorway of the house of [a]Eliashib the high priest.

21 After him Meremoth the son of Uriah, the son of Hakkoz repaired another section, from the doorway of Eliashib's house even as far as the end of [1]his house.

22 And after him the priests, [a]the men of the [1]valley, carried out repairs.

23 After [1]them Benjamin and Hasshub carried out repairs in front of their house. After [1]them Azariah the son of Maaseiah, son of Ananiah carried out repairs beside his house.

24 After him Binnui the son of Henadad repaired another section, from the house of Azariah as far as [a]the Angle and as far as the corner.

25 Palal the son of Uzai *made repairs* in front of the Angle and the tower projecting from the upper house of the king, which is by [a]the court of the guard. After him Pedaiah the son of Parosh *made repairs.*

26 And [a]the temple servants living in [b]Ophel *made repairs* as far as the front of [c]the Water Gate toward the east and the projecting tower.

27 After him [a]the Tekoites repaired another section in front of the great projecting tower and as far as the wall of Ophel.

28 Above [a]the Horse Gate the priests carried out repairs, each in front of his house.

29 After [1]them Zadok the son of Immer carried out repairs in front of his house. And after him Shemaiah the son of Shecaniah, the keeper of the East Gate, carried out repairs.

30 After him Hananiah the son of Shelemiah, and Hanun the sixth son of Zalaph, repaired another section. After him Meshullam the son of Berechiah carried out repairs in front of [a]his own [1]quarters.

31 After him Malchijah [1]one of [a]the goldsmiths, carried out repairs as far as the house of the temple servants and of the merchants, in front of the [2]Inspection Gate and as far as the upper room of the corner.

32 And between the upper room of the corner and [a]the Sheep Gate the goldsmiths and the merchants carried out repairs.

Chapter 4

Work Is Ridiculed

1 Now it came about that when [a]Sanballat heard that we were rebuilding the wall, he became furious and very angry and mocked the Jews.

2 And he spoke in the presence of his brothers and [a]the [1]wealthy *men* of Samaria and said, "What are these feeble Jews doing? Are they going to restore *it* for themselves? Can they offer sacrifices? Can they finish in a day? Can they revive the stones from the [2b]dusty rubble even the burned ones?"

3 Now Tobiah the Ammonite *was* near him and he said, "Even what they are building—[a]if a fox should [1]jump on *it,* he would break their stone wall down!"

---

11 [a]Neh. 12:38
12 [a]Neh. 3:9
13 [1]Lit., *Gate of Ash-heaps* [a]Neh. 2:13
14 [1]Lit., *Gate of Ash-heaps* [a]Jer. 6:1 [b]Neh. 2:13
15 [a]Neh. 2:17 [b]2 Kin. 25:4 [c]Neh. 12:37
16 [a]Neh. 3:9, 12, 17 [b]2 Kin. 20:20; Is. 7:3
19 [1]Lit., *a second measure,* so in vs. 20, 21, 24, 30. [a]Neh. 3:15 [b]2 Chr. 26:9
20 [a]Neh. 3:1
21 [1]Lit., *Eliashib's*
22 [1]Lit., *circle;* i.e., lower Jordan valley [a]Neh. 12:28
23 [1]Lit., *him*
24 [a]Neh. 3:19
25 [a]Jer. 32:2
26 [a]Neh. 7:46 [b]Neh. 11:21 [c]Neh. 8:1
27 [a]Neh. 3:5
28 [a]2 Kin. 11:16; 2 Chr. 23:15; Jer. 31:40
29 [1]Lit., *him*
30 [1]Or, *cell* [a]Neh. 13:7
31 [1]Lit., *son of* [2]Or, *Mustering* [a]Neh. 3:8, 32
32 [a]Neh. 3:1
1 [1]Ch. 3:33 in Heb. [a]Neh. 2:10
2 [1]Or, *army* [2]Lit., *heaps of dust* [a]Ezra 4:9, 10 [b]Neh. 4:10
3 [1]Lit., *go up* [a]Lam. 5:18

4 [a]Hear, O our God, how we are
despised! [b]Return their reproach on
their own heads and give them up
for plunder in a land of captivity.
5 Do not [1a]forgive their iniquity
and let not their sin be blotted out
before Thee, for they have [2]demor-
alized the builders.
6 So we built the wall and the
whole wall was joined together to
half its *height*, for the people had a
[1]mind to work.
7 [1]Now it came about when Sanballat, Tobiah, the Arabs, the Ammonites, and the Ashdodites heard
that the [2]repair of the walls of Jerusalem went on, *and* that the
breaches began to be closed, they
were very angry.
8 And all of them conspired together to come *and* fight against Jerusalem and to cause a disturbance
in it.

Discouragement Overcome

9 But we prayed to our God, and
because of them we [a]set up a guard
against them day and night.
10 Thus [1]in Judah it was said,
"The strength of the burden
bearers is failing,
Yet there is much [2]rubbish;
And we ourselves are unable
To rebuild the wall."
11 And our enemies said, "They
will not know or see until we come
among them, kill them, and put a
stop to the work."
12 And it came about when the
Jews who lived near them came and
told us ten times, "[1]They will come
up against us from every place
where you may turn,"
13 then I stationed *men* in the lowest parts of the space behind the
wall, the [1]exposed places, and I [a]sta-
tioned the people in families with
their swords, spears, and bows.
14 When I *saw their fear*, I rose
and spoke to the nobles, the officials, and the rest of the people:
"[a]Do not be afraid of them; remember the Lord who is great and awesome, and [b]fight for your brothers,
your sons, your daughters, your
wives, and your houses."
15 And it happened when our enemies heard that it was known to us,
and that [a]God had frustrated their
plan, then all of us returned to the
wall, each one to his work.
16 And it came about from that
day on, that half of my servants carried on the work while half of them
held the spears, the shields, the
bows, and the breastplates; and the

4 [a]Ps. 123:3, 4 [b]Ps. 79:12
5 [1]Lit., *cover* [2]Lit., *offended against* [a]Ps. 69:27, 28; Jer. 18:23
6 [1]Lit., *heart*
7 [1]Ch. 4:1 in Heb. [2]Lit., *healing*
9 [a]Neh. 4:11
10 [1]Lit., *Judah said* [2]Lit., *dust*
12 [1]Gk., Heb. omits *they . . . up*
13 [1]Lit., *bare* [a]Neh. 4:17, 18
14 [a]Num. 14:9; Deut. 1:29, 30 [b]2 Sam. 10:12
15 [a]2 Sam. 17:14
18 [1]Lit., *he who sounded the trumpet*
20 [1]Lit., *assemble yourselves* [a]Ex. 14:14; Deut. 1:30
21 [1]Lit., *rising of the dawn* [2]Lit., *came out*
1 [a]Lev. 25:35; Deut. 15:7
4 [a]Ezra 4:13; 7:24
5 [1]Lit., *there is not the power in our hands* [a]Gen. 37:27 [b]Lev. 25:39

captains *were* behind the whole
house of Judah.
17 Those who were rebuilding the
wall and those who carried burdens
took *their* load with one hand doing
the work and the other holding a
weapon.
18 As for the builders, each *wore*
his sword girded at his side as he
built, while [1]the trumpeter *stood*
near me.
19 And I said to the nobles, the officials, and the rest of the people,
"The work is great and extensive,
and we are separated on the wall far
from one another.
20"At whatever place you hear the
sound of the trumpet, [1]rally to us
there. [a]Our God will fight for us."
21 So we carried on the work with
half of them holding spears from
[1]dawn until the stars [2]appeared.
22 At that time I also said to the
people, "Let each man with his servant spend the night within Jerusalem so that they may be a guard for
us by night and a laborer by day."
23 So neither I, my brothers, my
servants, nor the men of the guard
who followed me, none of us removed our clothes, each *took* his
weapon *even to* the water.

Chapter 5

Usury Abolished

Now [a]there was a great outcry of
the people and of their wives
against their Jewish brothers.
2 For there were those who said,
"We, our sons and our daughters,
are many; therefore let us get grain
that we may eat and live."
3 And there were others who
said, "We are mortgaging our fields,
our vineyards, and our houses that
we might get grain because of the
famine."
4 Also there were those who said,
"We have borrowed money [a]for the
king's tax *on* our fields and our vineyards.
5"And now [a]our flesh is like the
flesh of our brothers, our children
like their children. Yet behold, [b]we
are forcing our sons and our daughters to be slaves, and some of our
daughters are forced into bondage
already, and [1]we are helpless because our fields and vineyards belong to others."
6 Then I was very angry when I
had heard their outcry and these
words.
7 And I consulted with myself,
and contended with the nobles and

the rulers and said to them, "[a]You are exacting usury, each from his brother!" Therefore, I held a great assembly against them.

8 And I said to them, "We according to our ability [a]have [1]redeemed our Jewish brothers who were sold to the nations; now would you even sell your brothers that they may be sold to us?" Then they were silent and could not find a word *to say.*

9 Again I said, "The thing which you are doing is not good; should you not walk in the fear of our God because of [a]the reproach of the nations, our enemies?

10 "And likewise I, my brothers and my servants, are lending them money and grain. Please, let us leave off this usury.

11 "Please, give back to them this very day their fields, their vineyards, their olive groves, and their houses, also the hundredth *part* of the money and of the grain, the new wine, and the oil that you are exacting from them."

12 Then they said, "We [a]will give *it* back and [b]will require nothing from them; we will do exactly as you say." So I called the priests and [c]took an oath from them that they would do according to this [1]promise.

13 I [a]also shook out the [1]front of my garment and said, "Thus may God shake out every man from his house and from his possessions who does not fulfill this [2]promise; even thus may he be shaken out and emptied." And [b]all the assembly said, "Amen!" And they praised the LORD. Then the people did according to this [2]promise.

Nehemiah's Example

14 Moreover, from the day that I was appointed to be their governor in the land of Judah, from [a]the twentieth year to the [b]thirty-second year of King Artaxerxes, *for* twelve years, neither [c]I nor my [1]kinsmen have eaten the governor's food *allowance.*

15 But the former governors who were before me [1]laid burdens on the people and took from them bread and wine besides forty shekels of silver; even their servants domineered the people. But I did not do so [a]because of the fear of God.

16 And I also [1]applied myself to the work on this wall; we did not buy any land, and all my servants were gathered there for the work.

17 Moreover, [a]*there were* at my table one hundred and fifty Jews and officials, besides those who came to us from the nations that were around us.

18 Now [a]that which was prepared for each day was one ox *and* six choice sheep, also birds were prepared for me; and once in ten days all sorts of wine *were furnished* in abundance. Yet for all this [b]I did not demand the governor's food *allowance,* because the servitude was heavy on this people.

19 [a]Remember me, O my God, for good, *according to* all that I have done for this people.

CHAPTER 6

The Enemy's Plot

NOW it came about when it was reported to Sanballat, Tobiah, to Geshem the Arab, and to the rest of our enemies that I had rebuilt the wall, and *that* no breach remained in it [a]although at that time I had not set up the doors in the gates,

2 that Sanballat and Geshem sent *a message* to me, saying, "Come, let us meet together at [1]Chephirim in the plain of [a]Ono." But they were planning to [2]harm me.

3 So I sent messengers to them, saying, "I am doing a great work and I cannot come down. Why should the work stop while I leave it and come down to you?"

4 And they sent *messages* to me four times in this manner, and I answered them in the same way.

5 Then Sanballat sent his servant to me in the same manner a fifth time with an open letter in his hand.

6 In it was written, "It is reported among the nations, and [1]Gashmu says, that [a]you and the Jews are planning to rebel; therefore you are rebuilding the wall. And you are to be their king, according to these reports.

7 "And you have also appointed prophets to proclaim in Jerusalem concerning [1]you, 'A king is in Judah!' And now it will be reported to the king according to these reports. So come now, let us take counsel together."

8 Then I sent *a message* to him saying, "Such things as you are saying have not been done, but you are inventing them [1]in your own mind."

9 For all of them were *trying* to frighten us, [1]thinking, "[2]They will become discouraged with the work and it will not be done." But now, O *God,* strengthen my hands.

---

7 [a]Ex. 22:25; Lev. 25:36
8 [1]Lit., *bought* [a]Lev. 25:48
9 [a]Neh. 4:4
12 [1]Lit., *word* [a]2 Chr. 28:15 [b]Neh. 10:31 [c]Ezra 10:5
13 [1]Lit., *bosom* [2]Lit., *word* [a]Acts 18:6 [b]Neh. 8:6
14 [1]Lit., *brothers* [a]Neh. 1:1 [b]Neh. 13:6 [c]Ezra 4:13, 14
15 [1]Lit., *made heavy* [a]Neh. 5:9
16 [1]Or, *held fast*
17 [a]1 Kin. 18:19
18 [a]1 Kin. 4:22, 23 [b]2 Thess. 3:8
19 [a]Neh. 13:14, 22, 31
1 [a]Neh. 3:1, 3
2 [1]Another reading is, *one of the villages* [2]Lit., *do evil to me* [a]1 Chr. 8:12
6 [1]In v. 1 and elsewhere *Geshem* [a]Neh. 2:19
7 [1]Lit., *you, saying*
8 [1]Lit., *from your heart*
9 [1]Lit., *saying,* [2]Lit., *Their hands will drop from*

10 And when I entered the house of Shemaiah the son of Delaiah, son of Mehetabel, [a]who was [1]confined at home, he said, "Let us meet together in the house of God, within the temple, and let us close the doors of the temple, for they are coming to kill you, and they are coming to kill you at night."

11 But I said, "Should a man like me flee? And could one such as I go into the temple [1]to save his life? I will not go in."

12 Then I perceived [1]that surely God had not sent him, but he uttered *his* prophecy against me because Tobiah and Sanballat had hired him.

13 He was hired for this reason, [a]that I might become frightened and act accordingly and sin, so that they might have an evil report in order that they could reproach me.

14 [a]Remember, O my God, Tobiah and Sanballat according to these works of theirs, and also Noadiah [b]the prophetess and the rest of the prophets who were *trying* to frighten me.

The Wall Is Finished

15 So [a]the wall was completed on the twenty-fifth of *the month* Elul, in fifty-two days.

16 And it came about [a]when all our enemies heard *of it*, and all the nations surrounding us saw *it*, they [1]lost their confidence; for [b]they recognized that this work had been accomplished [2]with the help of our God.

17 Also in those days many letters went from the nobles of Judah to Tobiah, and Tobiah's *letters* came to them.

18 For many in Judah were bound by oath to him because he was the son-in-law of Shecaniah the son of Arah, and his son Jehohanan had married the daughter of Meshullam the son of Berechiah.

19 Moreover, they were speaking about his good deeds in my presence and reported my words to him. Then Tobiah sent letters to frighten me.

Chapter 7

Census of First Returned Exiles

Now it came about when [a]the wall was rebuilt and I had set up the doors, and the gatekeepers and the singers and the Levites were appointed,

2 that I put [a]Hanani my brother, and [b]Hananiah the commander of [c]the fortress, in charge of Jerusalem, for he was [d]a faithful man and feared God more than many.

3 Then I said to them, "Do not let the gates of Jerusalem be opened until the sun is hot, and while they are standing *guard*, let them shut and bolt the doors. Also appoint guards from the inhabitants of Jerusalem, each at his post, and each in front of his own house."

4 Now the city was large and spacious but the people in it were few and the houses were not built.

5 Then my God put it into my heart to assemble the nobles, the officials, and the people to be enrolled by genealogies. Then I found the book of the genealogy of those who came up first [1]in which I found the following record:

6 [a]These are the people of the province who came up from the captivity of the exiles whom Nebuchadnezzar the king of Babylon had carried away, and who returned to Jerusalem and Judah, each to his city,

7 who came with Zerubbabel, Jeshua, Nehemiah, [1]Azariah, [2]Raamiah, Nahamani, Mordecai, Bilshan, [3]Mispereth, Bigvai, [4]Nehum, Baanah.

The number of men of the people of Israel:

8 the sons of Parosh, 2,172;
9 the sons of Shephatiah, 372;
10 the sons of Arah, 652;
11 the sons of Pahath-moab of the sons of Jeshua and Joab, 2,818;
12 the sons of Elam, 1,254;
13 the sons of Zattu, 845;
14 the sons of Zaccai, 760;
15 the sons of [1]Binnui, 648;
16 the sons of Bebai, 628;
17 the sons of Azgad, 2,322;
18 the sons of Adonikam, 667;
19 the sons of Bigvai, 2,067;
20 the sons of Adin, 655;
21 the sons of Ater, of Hezekiah, 98;
22 the sons of Hashum, 328;
23 the sons of Bezai, 324;
24 the sons of [1]Hariph, 112;
25 the sons of [1]Gibeon, 95;
26 the men of Bethlehem and Netophah, 188;
27 the men of Anathoth, 128;
28 the men of [1]Beth-azmaveth, 42;
29 the men of [1]Kiriath-jearim, Chephirah, and Beeroth, 743;
30 the men of Ramah and Geba, 621;
31 the men of Michmas, 122;
32 the men of Bethel and Ai, 123;
33 the men of the other Nebo, 52;

10 [1]Lit., *shut up* [a]Jer. 36:5
11 [1]Lit., *and live*
12 [1]Lit., *and behold God*
13 [a]Neh. 6:6
14 [a]Neh. 13:29 [b]Ezek. 13:17
15 [a]Neh. 4:1, 2
16 [1]Lit., *fell exceedingly in their own eyes* [2]Lit., *from our God* [a]Neh. 2:10; 4:1, 7 [b]Ex. 14:25
1 [a]Neh. 6:1, 15
2 [a]Neh. 1:2 [b]Neh. 10:23 [c]Neh. 2:8 [d]Neh. 13:13
5 [1]Lit., *and I found written in it*
6 [a]Ezra 2:1-70
7 [1]In Ezra 2:2, *Seraiah* [2]In Ezra 2:2, *Reelaiah* [3]In Ezra 2:2, *Mispar* [4]In Ezra 2:2, *Rehum*
15 [1]In Ezra 2:10, *Bani*
24 [1]In Ezra 2:18, *Jorah*
25 [1]In Ezra 2:20, *Gibbar*
28 [1]In Ezra 2:24, *Azmareth*
29 [1]In Ezra 2:25, *Kiriath-arim*

34 the sons of the other Elam,
1,254;
35 the sons of Harim, 320;
36 the [1]men of Jericho, 345;
37 the sons of Lod, Hadid, and
Ono, 721;
38 the sons of Senaah, 3,930.
39 The priests: the sons of Jedaiah
of the house of Jeshua, 973;
40 the sons of Immer, 1,052;
41 the sons of Pashhur, 1,247;
42 the sons of Harim, 1,017.
43 The Levites: the sons of Jeshua,
of Kadmiel, of the sons of [1]Hode-
vah, 74.
44 The singers: the sons of Asaph,
148.
45 The gatekeepers: the sons of
Shallum, the sons of Ater, the sons
of Talmon, the sons of Akkub, the
sons of Hatita, the sons of Shobai,
138.
46 The temple servants: the sons
of Ziha, the sons of Hasupha, the
sons of Tabbaoth,
47 the sons of Keros, the sons of
[1]Sia, the sons of Padon,
48 the sons of Lebana, the sons of
Hagaba, the sons of Shalmai,
49 the sons of Hanan, the sons of
Giddel, the sons of Gahar,
50 the sons of Reaiah, the sons of
Rezin, the sons of Nekoda,
51 the sons of Gazzam, the sons of
Uzza, the sons of Paseah,
52 the sons of Besai, the sons of
Meunim, the sons of [1]Nephushesim,
53 the sons of Bakbuk, the sons of
Hakupha, the sons of Harhur,
54 the sons of [1]Bazlith, the sons of
Mehida, the sons of Harsha,
55 the sons of Barkos, the sons of
Sisera, the sons of Temah,
56 the sons of Neziah, the sons of
Hatipha.
57 The sons of Solomon's servants: the sons of Sotai, the sons of
[1]Sophereth, the sons of [2]Perida,
58 the sons of Jaala, the sons of
Darkon, the sons of Giddel,
59 the sons of Shephatiah, the
sons of Hattil, the sons of Poche-
reth-hazzebaim, the sons of [1]Amon.
60 All the temple servants and the
sons of Solomon's servants *were*
392.
61 And these *were* they who came
up from Tel-melah, Tel-harsha,
Cherub, Addon, and Immer; but
they could not show their fathers'
houses or their [1]descendants,
whether they were of Israel:
62 the sons of Delaiah, the sons of
Tobiah, the sons of Nekoda, 642.
63 And of the priests: the sons of
Hobaiah, the sons of Hakkoz, the
sons of Barzillai, who took a wife of
the daughters of Barzillai, the Gileadite, and was named after them.
64 These searched *among* their ancestral registration, but it could not
be located; therefore they were considered unclean *and excluded* from
the priesthood.
65 And [a]the [1]governor said to
them that they should not eat from
the most holy things until a priest
arose with Urim and Thummim.

Total of People and Gifts

66 The whole assembly together
was 42,360,
67 besides their male and their female servants, [1]of whom *there were*
7,337; and they had 245 male and
female singers.
68 [1]Their horses were 736; their
mules, 245;
69 *their* camels, 435; *their* donkeys, 6,720.
70 And some from among the
heads of fathers' *households* gave to
the work. The [1a]governor gave to
the treasury 1,000 gold drachmas,
50 basins, 530 priests' garments.
71 And some of the heads of fathers' *households* gave into the treasury of the work 20,000 gold drachmas, and 2,200 silver minas.
72 And that which the rest of the
people gave was 20,000 gold drachmas and 2,000 silver minas, and 67
priests' garments.
73 Now the priests, the Levites,
the gatekeepers, the singers, some
of the people, the temple servants,
and all Israel, lived in their cities.
[a]**A**nd when the seventh month
came, the sons of Israel *were* in their
cities.

CHAPTER 8

Ezra Reads the Law

AND all the people gathered as one
man at the square which was in
front of [a]the Water Gate, and they
[1]asked [b]Ezra the scribe to bring [c]the
book of the law of Moses which the
LORD had [2]given to Israel.
2 Then [a]Ezra the priest brought
the law before the assembly of men,
women, and all who *could* listen
with understanding, on [b]the first
day of the seventh month.
3 And he read from it before the
square which was in front of [a]the
Water Gate from [1]early morning until midday, in the presence of men
and women, those who could understand; and all the people were attentive to the book of the law.
4 And Ezra the scribe stood at a

36 [1]Lit., *sons*
43 [1]In Ezra 2:40, *Hodaviah*
47 [1]In Ezra 2:44, *Siaha*
52 [1]In Ezra 2:50, *Nephisim*
54 [1]In Ezra 2:52, *Bazluth*
57 [1]In Ezra 2:55, *Hassophereth* [2]In Ezra 2:55, *Peruda*
59 [1]In Ezra 2:57, *Ami*
61 [1]Lit., *seed*
65 [1]Heb. *Tirshathah*, a Persian title [a]Neh. 8:9; 10:1
67 [1]Lit., *these*
68 [1]So with some ancient mss. and Gk.; Ezra 2:66
70 [1]Heb. *Tirshathah*, a Persian title [a]Neh. 7:65; 8:9
73 [a]Ezra 3:1
1 [1]Lit., *said to* [2]Lit., *commanded* [a]Neh. 3:26 [b]Ezra 7:6 [c]2 Chr. 34:15
2 [a]Deut. 31:9-11; Neh. 8:9 [b]Lev. 23:24
3 [1]Lit., *the light* [a]Neh. 8:1

wooden podium which they had
made for the purpose. And beside
him stood Mattithiah, Shema,
Anaiah, Uriah, Hilkiah, and Maaseiah on his right hand; and Pedaiah,
Mishael, Malchijah, Hashum, Hash-
baddanah, Zechariah, *and* Meshullam on his left hand.
5 And Ezra opened [a]the book in
the sight of all the people for he was
standing above all the people; and
when he opened it, all the people
stood up.
6 Then Ezra blessed the LORD the
great God. And all the people answered, "[a]Amen, Amen!" [b]while
lifting up their hands; then [c]they
bowed low and worshiped the LORD
with *their* faces to the ground.
7 Also Jeshua, Bani, Sherebiah,
Jamin, Akkub, Shabbethai, Hodiah,
Maaseiah, Kelita, Azariah, Jozabad,
Hanan, Pelaiah, and the Levites, explained the law to the people while
the people *remained* in their place.
8 And they read from the book,
from the law of God, [1]translating to
give the sense so that they understood the reading.

"This Day Is Holy"

9 Then Nehemiah, who was the
[1a]governor, and Ezra [b]the priest *and*
scribe, and the Levites who taught
the people said to all the people,
"[c]This day is holy to the LORD your
God; do not [d]mourn or weep." For
all the people were weeping when
they heard the words of the law.
10 Then he said to them, "Go, eat
of the fat, drink of the sweet, and
[a]send portions to him who has nothing prepared; for this day is holy to
our Lord. Do not be grieved, for the
joy of the LORD is your strength."
11 So the Levites calmed all the
people, saying, "Be still, for the day
is holy, do not be grieved."
12 And all the people went away
to eat, to drink, [a]to send portions
and to [1]celebrate a great festival,
[b]because they understood the
words which had been made known
to them.

Feast of Booths Restored

13 Then on the second day the
heads of fathers' *households* of all
the people, the priests, and the Levites were gathered to Ezra the
scribe that they might gain insight
into the words of the law.
14 And they found written in the
law how the LORD had commanded
through Moses that the sons of Israel [a]should live in booths during
the feast of the seventh month.
15 [1a]So they proclaimed and circulated a proclamation in all their
cities and [b]in Jerusalem, saying,
"[c]Go out to the hills, and bring olive
branches, and [2]wild olive branches,
myrtle branches, palm branches,
and branches of *other* leafy trees, to
make booths, as it is written."
16 So the people went out and
brought *them* and made booths for
themselves, each [a]on his roof, and in
their courts, and in the courts of the
house of God, and in the square at
[b]the Water Gate, and in the square
at [c]the Gate of Ephraim.
17 And the entire assembly of
those who had returned from the
captivity made booths and lived in
[1]them. The sons of Israel [a]had indeed not done so from the days of
Joshua the son of Nun to that day.
And [b]there was great rejoicing.
18 And [a]he read from the book of
the law of God daily, from the first
day to the last day. And they [b]cele-
brated the feast seven days, and on
[c]the eighth day *there was* a solemn
assembly according to the ordinance.

CHAPTER 9

The People Confess Their Sin

NOW on the twenty-fourth day of
[a]this month the sons of Israel assembled [b]with fasting, in sackcloth,
and with [c]dirt upon them.
2 And the [1]descendants of Israel
separated themselves from all foreigners, and stood and confessed
their sins and the iniquities of their
fathers.
3 While [a]they stood in their
place, they read from the book of
the law of the LORD their God for a
fourth of the day; and for *another*
fourth they confessed and worshiped the LORD their God.
4 [a]Now on the Levites' platform
stood Jeshua, Bani, Kadmiel,
Shebaniah, Bunni, Sherebiah, Bani,
and Chenani, and cried with a loud
voice to the LORD their God.
5 Then the Levites, Jeshua, Kadmiel, Bani, Hashabneiah, Sherebiah,
Hodiah, Shebaniah, *and* Pethahiah,
said, "Arise, bless the LORD your
God forever and ever!
O may Thy glorious name be
blessed
And exalted above all blessing
and praise!
6"[a]Thou alone art the LORD.
[b]Thou hast made the heavens,
The heaven of heavens with all
their host,

---

5 [a]Neh. 8:3
6 [a]Neh. 5:13 [b]Gen. 14:22 [c]Ex. 4:31
8 [1]Or, *explaining*
9 [1]Heb., *Tirshatha,* a Persian title [a]Neh. 7:65, 70 [b]Neh. 12:26 [c]Neh. 8:2 [d]Deut. 12:7, 12
10 [a]Deut. 26:11-13
12 [1]Lit., *make a great rejoicing* [a]Neh. 8:10 [b]Neh. 8:7, 8
14 [a]Lev. 23:34, 40, 42
15 [1]Lit., *And that they will cause to be heard* [2]Heb., *oil tree,* species unknown [a]Lev. 23:4 [b]Deut. 16:16 [c]Lev. 23:40
16 [a]Jer. 32:29 [b]Neh. 8:1 [c]2 Kin. 14:13; Neh. 12:39
17 [1]Lit., *the booths* [a]2 Chr. 7:8; 8:13 [b]2 Chr. 30:21
18 [a]Deut. 31:11 [b]Lev. 23:36 [c]Num. 29:35
1 [a]Neh. 8:2 [b]Ezra 8:23 [c]1 Sam. 4:12
2 [1]Lit., *seed*
3 [a]Neh. 8:4
4 [a]Neh. 8:7
6 [a]Deut. 6:4; 2 Kin. 19:15 [b]Gen. 1:1

The earth and all that is on it,
The seas and all that is in them.
[c]Thou dost give life to all of them
And the heavenly host bows down before Thee.
7 "Thou art the LORD God,
[a]Who chose Abram
And brought him out from [b]Ur of the Chaldees,
And [c]gave him the name Abraham.
8 "And Thou didst find [a]his heart faithful before Thee,
And didst make a covenant with him
To give *him* the land of the Canaanite,
Of the Hittite and the Amorite,
Of the Perizzite, the Jebusite, and the Girgashite—
To give *it* to his [1]descendants.
And Thou [b]hast fulfilled Thy promise,
For Thou art righteous.

9 "[a]Thou didst see the affliction of our fathers in Egypt,
And didst [b]hear their cry by the [1]Red Sea.
10 "Then Thou didst perform signs and wonders against Pharaoh,
Against all his servants and all the people of his land;
For Thou didst know that [a]they acted arrogantly toward them,
And [b]didst make a name for Thyself as *it is* this day.
11 "And [a]Thou didst divide the sea before them,
So they passed through the midst of the sea on dry ground;
And [b]their pursuers Thou didst hurl into the depths,
Like a stone into [1]raging waters.
12 "And with a pillar of cloud [a]Thou didst lead them by day,
And with a pillar of fire by night
To light for them the way
In which they were to go.
13 "Then [a]Thou didst come down on Mount Sinai,
And didst [b]speak with them from heaven;
Thou didst give to them [c]just ordinances and true laws,
Good statutes and commandments.
14 "So Thou didst make known to them [a]Thy holy sabbath,
And didst lay down for them commandments, statutes, and law,
Through Thy servant Moses.
15 "Thou didst [a]provide bread from heaven for them for their hunger,
Thou didst [b]bring forth water from a rock for them for their thirst,
And Thou didst [c]tell them to enter in order to possess
The land which Thou didst [1]swear to give them.

16 "But they, our fathers, [a]acted arrogantly;
They [1b]became stubborn and would not listen to Thy commandments.
17 "And they refused to listen,
And [a]did not remember Thy wondrous deeds which Thou hadst performed among them;
So they became stubborn and [b]appointed a leader to return to their slavery [1]in Egypt.
But Thou art a God [c]of forgiveness,
Gracious and compassionate,
Slow to anger, and abounding in lovingkindness;
And Thou didst not forsake them.
18 "Even when they [a]made for themselves
A calf of molten metal
And said, 'This is your God
Who brought you up from Egypt,'
And committed great [1]blasphemies,
19 [a]Thou, in Thy great compassion,
Didst not forsake them in the wilderness;
[b]The pillar of cloud did not leave them by day,
To guide them on their way,
Nor the pillar of fire by night, to light for them the way in which they were to go.
20 "And [a]Thou didst give Thy good Spirit to instruct them,
Thy manna Thou didst not withhold from their mouth,
And Thou didst give them water for their thirst.
21 "Indeed, [a]forty years Thou didst provide for them in the wilderness *and* they were not in want,
Their clothes did not wear out, nor did their feet swell.
22 "Thou didst also give them kingdoms and peoples,

6 [c]Col. 1:17
7 [a]Gen. 12:1 [b]Gen. 11:31 [c]Gen. 17:5
8 [1]Lit., *seed* [a]Gen. 15:6, 18-21 [b]Josh. 21:43-45
9 [1]Or, *Sea of Reeds* [a]Ex. 3:7 [b]Ex. 7:8-14, 31; 14:10-12
10 [a]Ex. 5:2 [b]Ex. 9:16
11 [1]Lit., *strong, mighty* [a]Ex. 14:21 [b]Ex. 15:1, 5, 10
12 [a]Ex. 13:21, 22
13 [a]Ex. 19:11, 18-20 [b]Ex. 20:1 [c]Ps. 19:7-9
14 [a]Ex. 16:23; 20:8
15 [1]Lit., *lift up Thy hand* [a]Ex. 16:4, 14, 15 [b]Ex. 17:6; Num. 20:7-13 [c]Deut. 1:8
16 [1]Lit., *stiffened their neck;* so also v. 17. [a]Neh. 9:10 [b]Deut. 31:27; Neh. 9:29
17 [1]So Gk. and some Heb. mss.; Heb. reads, *in their rebellion* [a]Ps. 78:11, 42-55 [b]Num. 14:4 [c]Ex. 34:6, 7
18 [1]Lit., *acts of contempt* [a]Ex. 32:4-8, 31
19 [a]Neh. 9:27, 31 [b]Neh. 9:12
20 [a]Num. 11:17; Neh. 9:30; Is. 63:11-14
21 [a]Deut. 2:7

And Thou didst allot *them* to
them as a [1]boundary.
[a]And they took possession of
the land of Sihon [2]the king of
Heshbon,
And the land of Og the king of
Bashan.
23 "And Thou didst make their sons
numerous as [a]the stars of
heaven,
And Thou didst bring them into
the land
Which Thou hadst told their fathers to enter and possess.
24 "[a]So their sons entered and possessed the land.
And [b]Thou didst subdue before
them the inhabitants of the
land, the Canaanites,
And Thou didst give them into
their hand, with their kings,
and the peoples of the land,
To do with them [1]as they desired.
25 "And [a]they captured fortified
cities and a [1b]fertile land.
They took possession of
[c]houses full of every good
thing,
Hewn cisterns, vineyards, olive
groves,
Fruit trees in abundance.
So they ate, were filled, and
[d]grew fat,
And [e]reveled in Thy great goodness.

26 "[a]But they became disobedient
and rebelled against Thee,
And [b]cast Thy law behind their
backs
And [c]killed Thy prophets who
had [d]admonished them
So that they might return to
Thee,
And [e]they committed great
[1]blasphemies.
27 "Therefore Thou didst [a]deliver
them into the hand of their
oppressors who oppressed
them,
But when they cried to Thee [b]in
the time of their distress,
Thou didst hear from heaven,
and according to Thy great
compassion
Thou didst [c]give them deliver-
ers who delivered them from
the hand of their oppressors.
28 "But [a]as soon as they had rest,
they did evil again before
Thee;
Therefore Thou didst abandon
them to the hand of their enemies, so that they ruled over
them.
When they cried again to Thee,
Thou didst hear from heaven,
And [b]many times Thou didst
rescue them according to
Thy compassion,
29 And [a]admonished them in order to turn them back to Thy
law.
Yet [b]they acted arrogantly and
did not listen to Thy commandments but sinned
against Thine ordinances,
By [c]which if a man observes
them he shall live.
And they [1d]turned a stubborn
shoulder and stiffened their
neck, and would not listen.
30 "[a]However, Thou didst bear
with them for many years,
And [b]admonished them by
[c]Thy Spirit through Thy
prophets,
Yet they would not give ear.
Therefore Thou didst give them
into the hand of the peoples
of the lands.
31 "Nevertheless, in Thy great
compassion Thou [a]didst not
make an end of them or forsake them,
For Thou art [b]a gracious and
compassionate God.

32 "Now therefore, our God, [a]the
great, the mighty, and the
awesome God, who dost
keep covenant and loving-
kindness,
Do not let all the hardship seem
insignificant before Thee,
Which has come upon us, our
kings, our princes, our
priests, our prophets, our fathers, and on all Thy people,
[b]From the days of the kings of
Assyria to this day.
33 "However, [a]Thou art just in all
that has come upon us;
For Thou hast dealt faithfully,
but we have acted wickedly.
34 "For our kings, our leaders, our
priests, and our fathers have
not kept Thy law
Or paid attention to Thy commandments and Thine [1]ad-
monitions with which Thou
hast [2]admonished them.
35 "But [a]they, in their own kingdom,
[b]With Thy great goodness
which Thou didst give them,
With the broad and rich land
which Thou didst set before
them,
Did not serve Thee or turn from
their evil deeds.

22 [1]Lit., *side, corner* [2]So the Gk. and the Latin. Heb. reads, *and the land of the king of Heshbon* [a]Num. 21:21-35

23 [a]Gen. 15:5

24 [1]Lit., *according to their desire* [a]Josh. 21:43 [b]Josh. 18:1

25 [1]Lit., *fat* [a]Deut. 3:5 [b]Num. 13:20 [c]Deut. 6:11 [d]Deut. 32:15 [e]1 Kin. 8:66

26 [1]Lit., *acts of contempt* [a]Judg. 2:11 [b]1 Kin. 14:9 [c]2 Chr. 36:16 [d]Neh. 9:30 [e]Neh. 9:18

27 [a]Judg. 2:14 [b]Deut. 4:29 [c]Judg. 2:16

28 [a]Judg. 3:11 [b]Ps. 106:43

29 [1]Lit., *gave* [a]Neh. 9:26, 30 [b]Neh. 9:10, 16 [c]Lev. 18:5 [d]Zech. 7:11

30 [a]Ps. 95:10; Acts 13:18 [b]Neh. 9:26, 29 [c]Neh. 9:20

31 [a]Jer. 4:27 [b]Neh. 9:17

32 [a]Neh. 1:5 [b]2 Kin. 15:19

33 [a]Gen. 18:25; Jer. 12:1

34 [1]Lit., *testimonies* [2]Or, *witnessed*

35 [a]Deut. 28:47 [b]Neh. 9:25

36"Behold, [a]we are slaves today,
And as to the land which Thou
didst give to our fathers to
eat of its fruit and its bounty,
Behold, we are slaves on it.
37"And [a]its abundant produce is
for the kings
Whom Thou hast set over us
because of our sins;
They also rule over our bodies
And over our cattle as they
please,
So we are in great distress.

A Covenant Results

38"[1]Now because of all this
[a]We are making an agreement
in writing;
And on the [b]sealed document
are the names of our leaders,
our Levites *and* our priests."

CHAPTER 10

Signers of the Document

1
NOW on the [a]sealed document
were the names of: Nehemiah the
[2]governor, the son of Hacaliah, and
Zedekiah,
2 Seraiah, Azariah, Jeremiah,
3 Pashhur, Amariah, Malchijah,
4 Hattush, Shebaniah, Malluch,
5 Harim, Meremoth, Obadiah,
6 Daniel, Ginnethon, Baruch,
7 Meshullam, Abijah, Mijamin,
8 Maaziah, Bilgai, Shemaiah.
These *were* the priests.
9 And the Levites: Jeshua the son
of Azaniah, Binnui of the sons of
Henadad, Kadmiel;
10 also their brothers Shebaniah,
Hodiah, Kelita, Pelaiah, Hanan,
11 Mica, Rehob, Hashabiah,
12 Zaccur, Sherebiah, Shebaniah,
13 Hodiah, Bani, Beninu.
14 The leaders of the people: Parosh, Pahath-moab, Elam, Zattu,
Bani,
15 Bunni, Azgad, Bebai,
16 Adonijah, Bigvai, Adin,
17 Ater, Hezekiah, Azzur,
18 Hodiah, Hashum, Bezai,
19 Hariph, Anathoth, Nebai,
20 Magpiash, Meshullam, Hezir,
21 Meshezabel, Zadok, Jaddua,
22 Pelatiah, Hanan, Anaiah,
23 Hoshea, Hananiah, Hasshub,
24 Hallohesh, Pilha, Shobek,
25 Rehum, Hashabnah, Maaseiah,
26 Ahiah, Hanan, Anan,
27 Malluch, Harim, Baanah.

Obligations of the Document

28 Now [a]the rest of the people, the
priests, the Levites, the gatekeepers, the singers, the temple servants,
and [b]all those who had separated
themselves from the peoples of the
lands to the law of God, their wives,
their sons and their daughters, all
those who had knowledge and understanding,
29 are joining with their [1]kinsmen,
their nobles, and are [2a]taking on
themselves a curse and an oath to
walk in God's law, which was given
through Moses, God's servant, and
to keep and to observe all the commandments of [3]GOD our Lord, and
His ordinances and His statutes;
30 and [a]that we will not give our
daughters to the peoples of the land
or take their daughters for our sons.
31 As [a]for the peoples of the land
who bring wares or any grain on the
sabbath day to sell, we will not buy
from them on the sabbath or a holy
day; and we will forego *the crops* the
[b]seventh year and the [c]exaction of
every debt.
32 We also [1]placed ourselves under obligation to contribute yearly
[a]one third of a shekel for the service
of the house of our God:
33 for the showbread, for the continual grain offering, for the continual burnt offering, the sabbaths, the
new moon, for the appointed times,
for the holy things and for the sin
offerings to make atonement for Israel, and all the work of the house of
our God.
34 Likewise [a]we cast lots [b]for the
supply of wood *among* the priests,
the Levites, and the people in order
that they might bring it to the house
of our God, according to our fathers'
households, at fixed times annually,
to burn on the altar of the LORD our
God as it is written in the law;
35 and in order that they might
bring the first fruits of our ground
and [a]the first fruits of all the fruit of
every tree to the house of the LORD
annually,
36 and bring to the house of our
God the first-born of our sons and of
our cattle, and the first-born of our
herds and our flocks [a]as it is written
in the law, for the priests who are
ministering in the house of our God.
37 [a]We will also bring the first of
our [1]dough, our contributions, the
fruit of every tree, the new wine and
the oil [b]to the priests at the chambers of the house of our God, and
the [c]tithe of our ground to the Levites, for the Levites are they who
receive the tithes in all the rural
towns.
38 And [a]the priest, the son of Aaron, shall be with the Levites when
the Levites receive tithes, and the

36 [a]Deut. 28:48
37 [a]Deut. 28:33
38 [1]Ch. 10:1 in Heb. [a]Neh. 10:29 [b]Neh. 10:1
1 [1]Ch. 10:2 in Heb. [2]Heb., *Tirshatha,* a Persian title [a]Neh. 9:38
28 [a]Ezra 2:36-58 [b]Neh. 9:2
29 [1]Lit., *brothers* [2]Lit., *entering into a* [3]YHWH, usually renderd LORD [a]Neh. 5:12
30 [a]Ex. 34:16; Deut. 7:3
31 [a]Neh. 13:15-22 [b]Ex. 23:10, 11 [c]Deut. 15:1, 2
32 [1]Lit., *imposed commandments on us* [a]Ex. 30:11-16; Matt. 17:24
34 [a]Neh. 11:1 [b]Neh. 13:31
35 [a]Ex. 23:19
36 [a]Ex. 13:2
37 [1]Or, *coarse meal* [a]Lev. 23:17 [b]Neh. 13:5, 9 [c]Lev. 27:30
38 [a]Num. 18:26

Levites shall bring up the tenth of
the tithes to the house of our God, to
the chambers of [b]the storehouse.
39 For the sons of Israel and the
sons of Levi shall bring the [a]contri-
bution of the grain, the new wine
and the oil, to the chambers; there
are the utensils of the sanctuary, the
priests who are ministering, the
gatekeepers, and the singers. Thus
[b]we will not [1]neglect the house of
our God.

CHAPTER 11

Time Passes
Heads of Provinces

NOW [a]the leaders of the people
lived in Jerusalem, but the rest of
the people [b]cast lots to bring one out
of ten to live in Jerusalem, [c]the holy
city, while nine-tenths *remained* in
the *other* cities.
2 And the people blessed all the
men who volunteered to live in Jerusalem.
3 [a]Now these are the heads of the
provinces who lived in Jerusalem,
but in the cities of Judah [b]each lived
on his own property in their cities—
the [1]Israelites, the priests, the Levites, the [2c]temple servants and the
[3d]descendants of Solomon's servants.
4 And some of the sons of Judah
and some of the sons of Benjamin
lived in Jerusalem. From the sons of
Judah: Athaiah the son of Uzziah,
the son of Zechariah, the son of
Amariah, the son of Shephatiah, the
son of Mahalalel, of the sons of Perez;
5 and Maaseiah the son of Baruch, the son of Col-hozeh, the son of
Hazaiah, the son of Adaiah, the son
of Joiarib, the son of Zechariah, the
son of the Shilonite.
6 All the sons of Perez who lived
in Jerusalem were 468 able men.
7 Now these are the sons of Benjamin: Sallu the son of Meshullam,
the son of Joed, the son of Pedaiah,
the son of Kolaiah, the son of Maaseiah, the son of Ithiel, the son of
Jeshaiah;
8 and after him Gabbai *and* Sallai, 928.
9 And Joel the son of Zichri was
their overseer, and Judah the son of
Hassenuah was second [1]in command of the city.
10 From the priests: Jedaiah the
son of Joiarib, Jachin,
11 Seraiah the son of Hilkiah, the
son of Meshullam, the son of Zadok,
the son of Meraioth, the son of Ahitub, the leader of the house of God,
12 and their [1]kinsmen who performed the work of the [2]temple,
822; and Adaiah the son of Jeroham,
the son of Pelaliah, the son of Amzi,
the son of Zechariah, the son of
Pashhur, the son of Malchijah,
13 and his kinsmen, heads of fathers' *households,* 242; and Amash-
sai the son of Azarel, the son of Ah-
zai, the son of Meshillemoth, the son
of Immer,
14 and their brothers, valiant warriors, 128. And their overseer was
Zabdiel, the son of [1]Haggedolim.
15 Now from the Levites: Shemaiah the son of Hasshub, the son of
Azrikam, the son of Hashabiah, the
son of Bunni;
16 and Shabbethai and Jozabad,
from the [1]leaders of the Levites,
who [2]were in charge of [a]the outside
work of the house of God;
17 and Mattaniah the son of Mica,
the son of [1]Zabdi, the son of Asaph,
who was the [2]leader in beginning
the thanksgiving at prayer, and Bakbukiah, the second among his brethren; and [3]Abda the son of [4]Sham-
mua, the son of Galal, the son of
Jeduthun.
18 All the Levites in [a]the holy city
were 284.
19 Also the gatekeepers, Akkub,
Talmon, and their brethren, who
kept watch at the gates, *were* 172.

Outside Jerusalem

20 And the rest of Israel, of the
priests, *and* of the Levites, *were* in
all the cities of Judah, each [a]on his
own inheritance.
21 But [a]the temple servants were
living in Ophel, and Ziha and Gishpa
were [1]in charge of the temple servants.
22 Now [a]the overseer of the Levites in Jerusalem was Uzzi the son
of Bani, the son of Hashabiah, the
son of Mattaniah, the son of Mica,
from the sons of Asaph, who were
the singers for the [1]service of the
house of God.
23 [a]For *there was* a commandment from the king concerning
them and a firm regulation for the
song leaders [b]day by day.
24 And Pethahiah the son of Meshezabel, of the sons of Zerah the
son of Judah, was the king's [1]repre-
sentative in all matters concerning
the people.
25 Now as for the villages with
their fields, some of the sons of Judah lived in [a]Kiriath-arba and its
[1]towns, in [b]Dibon and its [1]towns,
and in Jekabzeel and its villages,

38 [b]Neh. 13:12, 13
39 [1]Lit., *forsake* [a]Deut. 12:6 [b]Neh. 13:10, 11
1 [a]Neh. 7:4 [b]Neh. 10:34 [c]Neh. 11:18; Is. 48:2
3 [1]Lit., *Israel* [2]Heb., *Nethinim* [3]Lit., *sons* [a]1 Chr. 9:2-34 [b]Neh. 11:20 [c]Ezra 2:43 [d]Neh. 7:57
9 [1]Lit., *over*
12 [1]Lit., *brothers,* and so through the chap. [2]Lit., *house*
14 [1]Or, *the great ones*
16 [1]Lit., *heads* [2]Lit., *over* [a]1 Chr. 26:29
17 [1]In 1 Chr. 9:15, *Zichri* [2]Lit., *head* [3]In 1 Chr. 9:16, *Obadiah* [4]In 1 Chr. 9:16, *Shemaiah*
18 [a]Neh. 11:1
20 [a]Neh. 11:3
21 [1]Lit., *over* [a]2 Chr. 27:3; Neh. 3:26
22 [1]Or, *work* [a]Neh. 11:9, 14
23 [a]Ezra 6:8; 7:20 [b]Neh. 12:47
24 [1]Lit., *hand*
25 [1]Lit., *daughters,* and so throughout the chap. [a]Josh. 14:15 [b]Josh. 13:9, 17

26 and in Jeshua, in Moladah and
Beth-pelet,
27 and in Hazar-shual, in Beersheba and its towns,
28 and in Ziklag, in Meconah and
in its towns,
29 and in En-rimmon, in Zorah
and in Jarmuth,
30 Zanoah, Adullam, and their villages, Lachish and its fields, Azekah
and its towns. So they encamped
from Beersheba as far as the valley
of Hinnom.
31 The sons of Benjamin also *lived*
from Geba *onward,* at Michmash
and Aija, at Bethel and its towns,
32 at Anathoth, Nob, Ananiah,
33 Hazor, Ramah, Gittaim,
34 Hadid, Zeboim, Neballat,
35 Lod and Ono, the valley of
craftsmen.
36 And from the Levites, *some* divisions in Judah belonged to Benjamin.

CHAPTER 12

Priests and Levites Who Returned to Jerusalem with Zerubbabel

NOW these are [a]the priests and
the Levites who came up with Zerubbabel the son of Shealtiel, and
Jeshua: Seraiah, Jeremiah, Ezra,
2 Amariah, Malluch, Hattush,
3 Shecaniah, Rehum, Meremoth,
4 Iddo, Ginnethoi, Abijah,
5 Mijamin, Maadiah, Bilgah,
6 Shemaiah and Joiarib, Jedaiah,
7 Sallu, Amok, Hilkiah, and Jedaiah. These were the heads of the
priests and their [1]kinsmen in the
days of Jeshua.
8 And the Levites *were* Jeshua,
Binnui, Kadmiel, Sherebiah, Judah,
and Mattaniah *who was* [1]in charge
of the songs of thanksgiving, he and
his brothers.
9 Also Bakbukiah and Unni, their
brothers, stood opposite them [a]in
their service divisions.
10 And Jeshua [1]became the father
of Joiakim, and Joiakim [1]became
the father of Eliashib, and Eliashib
[1]became the father of Joiada,
11 and Joiada became the father of
Jonathan, and Jonathan became the
father of Jaddua.
12 Now in the days of Joiakim the
priests, the heads of fathers' *households* were: of Seraiah, Meraiah; of
Jeremiah, Hananiah;
13 of Ezra, Meshullam; of Amariah, Jehohanan;
14 of [1]Malluchi, Jonathan; of
Shebaniah, Joseph;
15 of Harim, Adna; of Meraioth,
Helkai;
16 of Iddo, Zechariah; of Ginnethon, Meshullam;
17 of Abijah, Zichri; of Miniamin,
of Moadiah, Piltai;
18 of Bilgah, Shammua; of Shemaiah, Jehonathan;
19 of Joiarib, Mattenai; of Jedaiah,
Uzzi;
20 of Sallai, Kallai; of Amok, Eber;
21 of Hilkiah, Hashabiah; of Jedaiah, Nethanel.

The Chief Levites

22 As for the Levites, the heads of
fathers' *households* were registered
in the days of Eliashib, Joiada, and
Johanan, and Jaddua; so *were* the
priests in the reign of Darius the
Persian.
23 The sons of Levi, the heads of
fathers' *households,* were registered
in the Book of the Chronicles up to
the days of Johanan the son of Eliashib.
24 And the heads of the Levites
were Hashabiah, Sherebiah, and
Jeshua the son of Kadmiel, with
their brothers opposite them, [a]to
praise *and* give thanks, [1]as prescribed by David the man of God,
[b]division corresponding to division.
25 Mattaniah, and Bakbukiah,
Obadiah, Meshullam, Talmon, *and*
Akkub were gatekeepers keeping
watch at [a]the storehouses of the
gates.
26 These *served* in the days of
Joiakim the son of Jeshua, the son of
Jozadak, and in the days of [a]Nehe-
miah the governor and of Ezra the
priest *and* scribe.

Dedication of the Wall

27 Now at the dedication of the
wall of Jerusalem they sought out
the Levites from all their places, to
bring them to Jerusalem so that
they might celebrate the dedication
with gladness, with hymns of
thanksgiving and with songs [a]*to the
accompaniment* of cymbals, harps,
and lyres.
28 So the sons of the singers were
assembled from the district around
Jerusalem, and from [a]the villages of
the Netophathites,
29 from Beth-gilgal, and from
their fields in Geba and Azmaveth,
for the singers had built themselves
villages around Jerusalem.
30 And the priests and the Levites
[a]purified themselves; they also purified the people, the gates, and the
wall.

1 [a]Ezra 2:1; 7:7
7 [1]Lit., *brothers*
8 [1]Lit., *over*
9 [a]Neh. 12:24
10 [1]Lit., *begot* and so in vs. 11, 12
14 [1]In Neh. 12:2, *Malluch*
24 [1]Lit., *in the commandment of* [a]Neh. 11:17 [b]Neh. 12:9
25 [a]1 Chr. 26:15
26 [a]Neh. 8:9
27 [a]1 Chr. 15:16, 28
28 [a]1 Chr. 9:16
30 [a]Neh. 13:22, 30

Procedures for the Temple

31 Then I had the leaders of Judah
come up on top of the wall, and I
appointed two great [1]choirs, [2][a]the
first proceeding to the right on top
of the wall toward [b]the Refuse Gate.
32 Hoshaiah and half of the leaders of Judah followed them,
33 with Azariah, Ezra, Meshullam,
34 Judah, Benjamin, Shemaiah,
Jeremiah,
35 and some of the sons of the
priests with trumpets; *and* Zechariah the son of Jonathan, the son of
Shemaiah, the son of Mattaniah, the
son of Micaiah, the son of Zaccur,
the son of Asaph,
36 and his [1]kinsmen, Shemaiah,
Azarel, Milalai, Gilalai, Maai, Nethanel, Judah *and* Hanani, [a]with the
musical instruments of David the
man of God. And Ezra the scribe
went before them.
37 And at [a]the Fountain Gate they
went directly up [b]the steps of the
city of David by the stairway of the
wall above the house of David to
[c]the Water Gate on the east.
38 [a]The second [1]choir proceeded
to the [2]left, while I followed them
with half of the people on the wall,
[b]above the Tower of Furnaces, to
[c]the Broad Wall,
39 and above [a]the Gate of Ephraim, by [b]the Old Gate, by the [c]Fish
Gate, [d]the Tower of Hananel, and
the Tower of the Hundred, as far as
the Sheep Gate, and they stopped at
[e]the Gate of the Guard.
40 Then the two choirs took their
stand in the house of God. So did I
and half of the officials with me;
41 and the priests, Eliakim, Maaseiah, Miniamin, Micaiah, Elioenai,
Zechariah, and Hananiah, with the
trumpets;
42 and Maaseiah, Shemaiah, Eleazar, Uzzi, Jehohanan, Malchijah,
Elam, and Ezer. And the singers
[1]sang, with Jezrahiah *their* leader,
43 and on that day they offered
great sacrifices and rejoiced because God had given them great joy,
even the women and children rejoiced, so that the joy of Jerusalem
was heard from afar.
44 On that day [a]men were also appointed over the chambers for the
stores, the contributions, the first
fruits, and the tithes, to gather into
them from the fields of the cities the
portions required by the law for the
priests and Levites; for Judah rejoiced over the priests and Levites
who [1]served.

31 [1]Lit., *thanksgiving choirs* [2]Heb. reads *and processions to the right* . . . cf. v. 38 [a]Neh. 12:38 [b]Neh. 2:13

36 [1]Lit., *brothers* [a]Neh. 12:24

37 [a]Neh. 2:14 [b]Neh. 3:15 [c]Neh. 3:26

38 [1]Lit., *thanksgiving choir* [2]Lit., *front* [a]Neh. 12:31 [b]Neh. 3:11 [c]Neh. 3:8

39 [a]Neh. 8:16 [b]Neh. 3:6 [c]Neh. 3:3 [d]Neh. 3:1 [e]Neh. 3:25

42 [1]Lit., *caused their voices to be heard*

44 [1]Lit., *stood* cf. 2 Chr. 29:11 [a]Neh. 13:5, 12, 13

45 [1]Lit., *service* [a]1 Chr. 25:1; 26:1

46 [1]Lit., *heads,* cf. 1 Chr. 9:33 [a]2 Chr. 29:30

47 [a]Neh. 11:23 [b]Num. 18:21

1 [a]Neh. 9:3 [b]Deut. 23:3-5; Neh. 13:23

2 [a]Num. 22:3-11

3 [a]Neh. 9:2

4 [1]Lit., *close to* [a]Ex. 12:38 [b]Neh. 2:10

5 [1]Or, *chamber* [2]Lit., *heave offerings* [a]Neh. 2:10; 6:1, 17, 18

6 [a]Neh. 5:14 [b]Ezra 6:22

7 [1]Or, *understood* [2]Or, *chamber,* and so in vs. 8, 9 [a]Neh. 13:5

45 For they performed the [1]wor-
ship of their God and the service of
purification, together with the singers and the gatekeepers [a]in accordance with the command of David
and of his son Solomon.
46 For in the days of David and [a]A-
saph, in ancient times, *there were*
[1]leaders of the singers, songs of
praise and hymns of thanksgiving to
God.
47 And so all Israel in the days of
Zerubbabel and Nehemiah gave the
portions due the singers and the
gatekeepers [a]as each day required,
and [b]set apart the consecrated *portion* for the Levites, and the Levites
set apart the consecrated *portion*
for the sons of Aaron.

Chapter 13

Foreigners Excluded

On that day [a]they read aloud from
the book of Moses in the hearing of
the people; and there was found
written in it that [b]no Ammonite or
Moabite should ever enter the assembly of God,
2 because they did not meet the
sons of Israel with bread and water,
but [a]hired Balaam against them to
curse them. However, our God
turned the curse into a blessing.
3 So it came about, that when
they heard the law, [a]they excluded
all foreigners from Israel.

Tobiah Expelled and the Temple Cleansed

4 Now prior to this, Eliashib the
priest, [a]who was appointed over the
chambers of the house of our God,
being [1]related to [b]Tobiah,
5 had prepared a large [1]room for
him, where formerly they put the
grain offerings, the frankincense,
the utensils, and the tithes of grain,
wine and oil [a]prescribed for the Levites, the singers and the gatekeepers, and the [2]contributions for the
priests.
6 But during all this *time* I was
not in Jerusalem, for in [a]the thirty-
second year of [b]Artaxerxes king of
Babylon I had gone to the king. After some time, however, I asked
leave from the king,
7 and I came to Jerusalem and
[1]learned about the evil that Eliashib
had done for Tobiah, [a]by preparing
a [2]room for him in the courts of the
house of God.
8 And it was very displeasing to
me, so I threw all of Tobiah's household goods out of the room.

9 Then I gave an order and [a]they
cleansed the rooms; and I returned
there the utensils of the house of
God with the grain offerings and the
frankincense.

Tithes Restored

10 I also [1]discovered that [a]the portions of the Levites had not been
given *them,* so that the Levites and
the singers who performed the service had [2]gone away, [b]each to his
own field.
11 So I [1a]reprimanded the officials
and said, "[b]Why is the house of God
forsaken?" Then I gathered them together and restored them to their
posts.
12 All Judah then brought [a]the
tithe of the grain, wine, and oil into
the storehouses.
13 And in charge of the storehouses I appointed Shelemiah the
priest, Zadok the scribe, and Pedaiah of the Levites, and in addition to
them was Hanan the son of Zaccur,
the son of Mattaniah; for [a]they were
considered reliable, and it was
[1]their task to distribute to their
[2]kinsmen.
14 [a]Remember me for this, O my
God, and do not blot out my loyal
deeds which I have performed for
the house of my God and its services.

Sabbath Restored

15 In those days I saw in Judah
some who were treading wine
presses [a]on the sabbath, and bringing in sacks of grain and loading
them on donkeys, as well as wine,
grapes, figs, and all kinds of loads,
[b]and they brought *them* into Jerusalem on the sabbath day. So [c]I admonished *them* on the day they sold
food.
16 Also men of Tyre were living
[1]there *who* imported fish and all
kinds of merchandise, and sold
them to the sons of Judah on the
sabbath, even in Jerusalem.
17 Then [a]I [1]reprimanded the
nobles of Judah and said to them,
"What is this evil thing you are
doing, [2]by profaning the sabbath
day?
18 "[a]Did not your fathers do the
same so that our God brought on us,
and on this city, all this trouble? Yet
you are adding to the wrath on Israel by profaning the sabbath."
19 [a]And it came about that just as
it grew dark at the gates of Jerusalem before the sabbath, I commanded that the doors should be
shut [1]and that they should not open
them until after the sabbath. Then I
stationed some of my servants at
the gates *that* no load should enter
on the sabbath day.
20 Once or twice the traders and
merchants of every kind of merchandise spent the night outside Jerusalem.
21 Then [a]I [1]warned them and said
to them, "Why do you spend the
night in front of the wall? If you do
so again, I will [2]use force against
you." From that time on they did not
come on the sabbath.
22 And I commanded the Levites
that [a]they should purify themselves
and come as gatekeepers to sanctify
the sabbath day. *For* this also [b]re-
member me, O my God, and have
compassion on me according to the
greatness of Thy lovingkindness.

Mixed Marriages Forbidden

23 In those days I also saw that the
Jews had [1a]married women from
[b]Ashdod, [c]Ammon, *and* Moab.
24 As for their children, half spoke
in the language of Ashdod, and none
of them was able to speak the language of Judah, but [1]the language of
his own people.
25 So [a]I contended with them and
cursed them and [b]struck some of
them and pulled out their hair, and
[c]made them swear by God, "You
shall not give your daughters to
their sons, nor take of their daughters for your sons or for yourselves.
26 "[a]Did not Solomon king of Israel
sin regarding these things? [b]Yet
among the many nations there was
no king like him, and he was loved
by his God, and God made him king
over all Israel; nevertheless the foreign women caused even him to sin.
27 "[1]Do we then hear about you
that you have committed all this
great evil [a]by acting unfaithfully
against our God by [2]marrying foreign women?"
28 Even one of the sons of Joiada,
the son of Eliashib the high priest,
was a son-in-law of [a]Sanballat the
Horonite, so I drove him away from
me.
29 [a]Remember them, O my God,
[1]because they have defiled the
priesthood and the [b]covenant of the
priesthood and the Levites.
30 [a]Thus I purified them from everything foreign and appointed duties for the priests and the Levites,
each in his task,
31 and *I arranged* [a]for the supply
of wood at appointed times and for
the first fruits. [b]Remember me, O
my God, for good.

9 [a]2 Chr. 29:5, 15, 16

10 [1]Or, *knew* [2]Lit., *fled* [a]Neh. 10:37 [b]Neh. 12:28, 29

11 [1]Or, *contended with* [a]Neh. 13:17, 25 [b]Neh. 10:39

12 [a]Neh. 10:37; 12:44

13 [1]Lit., *on them to* [2]Lit., *brothers* [a]Neh. 7:2

14 [a]Neh. 5:19; 13:22, 31

15 [a]Ex. 20:8; 34:21 [b]Neh. 10:31 [c]Neh. 9:29; 13:21

16 [1]Lit., *in it*

17 [1]Or, *contended with* [2]Lit., *and* [a]Neh. 13:11, 25

18 [a]Ezra 9:13; Jer. 17:21

19 [1]Lit., *and commanded* [a]Lev. 23:32

21 [1]Lit., *witnessed against* [2]Lit., *send a hand against* [a]Neh. 13:15

22 [a]1 Chr. 15:12; Neh. 12:30 [b]Neh. 13:14, 31

23 [1]Lit., *given dwelling to* [a]Ezra 9:2; Neh. 10:30 [b]Neh. 4:7 [c]Ezra 9:1; Neh. 13:1

24 [1]Lit., *according to the tongue of people and people*

25 [a]Neh. 13:11, 17 [b]Deut. 25:2 [c]Neh. 10:29, 30

26 [a]1 Kin. 11:1 [b]1 Kin. 3:13; 2 Chr. 1:12

27 [1]Or, *Is it reported* [2]Lit., *giving dwelling to* [a]Ezra 10:2; Neh. 13:23

28 [a]Neh. 2:10, 19

29 [1]Lit., *for the defilings of* [a]Neh. 6:14 [b]Num. 25:13

30 [a]Neh. 10:30

31 [a]Neh. 10:34 [b]Neh. 13:14, 22

THE BOOK OF ESTHER

The Banquets of the King

NOW it took place in the days of
[a]Ahasuerus, the Ahasuerus who
reigned [b]from India to [1]Ethiopia
over [c]127 provinces,
2 in those days as King Ahasuerus sat on his royal throne which
was in [a]Susa the capital,
3 in the third year of his reign, [a]he
gave a banquet for all his princes
and attendants, the army *officers* of
Persia and Media, the nobles, and
the princes of his provinces being in
his presence,
4 when he displayed the riches of
his royal glory and the splendor of
his great majesty for many days,
180 days.
5 And when these days were
completed, the king gave a banquet
lasting seven days for all the people
who were present in Susa the capital, from the greatest to the least, in
the court of [a]the garden of the king's
palace.
6 *There were hangings of* fine
white and violet linen held by cords
of fine purple linen on silver rings
and marble columns, [a]*and* couches
of gold and silver on a mosaic pavement of porphyry, marble, mother-
of-pearl, and precious stones.
7 Drinks were served in golden
vessels of various kinds, and the
royal wine was plentiful [a]according
to the king's [1]bounty.
8 And the drinking was *done* according to the law, there was no
compulsion, for so the king had giv-
en orders to each official of his
household that he should do according to the desires of each person.
9 Queen Vashti also gave a banquet for the women in the [1]palace
which belonged to King Ahasuerus.

Queen Vashti's Refusal

10 On the seventh day, when the
heart of the king was [a]merry with
wine, he commanded Mehuman,
Biztha, Harbona, Bigtha, Abagtha,
Zethar, and Carkas, the seven eunuchs who served in the presence of
King Ahasuerus,
11 to bring Queen Vashti before
the king with *her* royal [a]crown in
order to display her beauty to the
people and the princes, for she was
beautiful.
12 But Queen Vashti refused to
come at the king's command delivered by the eunuchs. Then the king
became very angry and his wrath
burned within him.
13 Then the king said to [a]the wise
men [b]who understood the times—
for it was the custom of the king so
to speak before all who knew law
and justice,
14 and were close to him: Carshe-
na, Shethar, Admatha, Tarshish,
Meres, Marsena, and Memucan, the
seven princes of Persia and Media
[a]who [1]had access to the king's presence and sat in the first place in the
kingdom—
15 "According to law, what is to be
done with Queen Vashti, because
she did not [1]obey the command of
King Ahasuerus *delivered* by the eunuchs?"
16 And in the presence of the king
and the princes, Memucan said,
"Queen Vashti has wronged not
only the king but *also* all the
princes, and all the peoples who are
in all the provinces of King Ahasuerus.
17 "For the queen's conduct will
[1]become known to all the women
causing them [2]to look with contempt on their husbands by saying, 'King Ahasuerus commanded
Queen Vashti to be brought in to his
presence, but she did not come.'
18 "And this day the ladies of Persia and Media who have heard of the
queen's conduct will speak in *the
same way* to all the king's princes,
and there will be plenty of contempt
and anger.
19 "If it pleases the king, let a royal
[1]edict be issued by him and let it be
written in the laws of Persia and
Media so [a]that it cannot [2]be re-
pealed, that Vashti should come no
more into the presence of King
Ahasuerus, and let the king give her
royal position to [3]another who is
more worthy than she.
20 "And when the king's edict
which he shall make is heard
throughout all his kingdom, [1]great
as it is, then [a]all women will give
honor to their husbands, great and
small."
21 And *this* word pleased the king
and the princes, and the king did [1]as
Memucan proposed.
22 So he sent letters to all the
king's provinces, [a]to each province
according to its script and to every
people according to their language,

1 [1]Lit., *Cush* [a]Ezra 4:6; Dan. 9:1 [b]Esth. 8:9 [c]Esth. 9:30

2 [a]Neh. 1:1

3 [a]Esth. 2:8

5 [a]Esth. 7:7-8

6 [a]Ezek. 23:41; Amos 6:4

7 [1]Lit., *hand* [a]Esth. 2:18

9 [1]Lit., *royal house*

10 [a]Judg. 16:25

11 [a]Esth. 2:17; 6:8

13 [a]Jer. 10:7; Dan. 2:2 [b]1 Chr. 12:32

14 [1]Lit., *saw the face of the king* [a]2 Kin. 25:19; Matt. 18:10

15 [1]Lit., *do*

17 [1]Lit., *go forth* [2]Lit., *to despise . . . in their eyes*

19 [1]Lit., *word go forth from* [2]Lit., *pass away* [3]Lit., *her neighbor* [a]Esth. 8:8; Dan. 6:8

20 [1]Lit., *for great is it* [a]Eph. 5:22; Col. 3:18

21 [1]Lit., *according to the word of*

22 [a]Esth. 3:12; 8:9

that every man should be the master
in his own house and the one who
speaks in the language of his own
people.

Chapter 2

Vashti's Successor Sought

AFTER these things [a]when the anger of King Ahasuerus had subsided, he remembered Vashti and
what she had done and [b]what had
been decreed against her.
2 Then the king's attendants,
who served him, said, "Let beautiful
young virgins be sought for the
king.
3 "And let the king appoint overseers in [a]all the provinces of his
kingdom that they may gather every
beautiful young virgin to Susa the
capital, to the harem, into the custody of [b]Hegai, the king's eunuch,
who was in charge of the women;
and [c]let their cosmetics be given
them.
4 "Then let the young lady who
pleases the king be queen in place of
Vashti." And the matter pleased the
king, and he did accordingly.
5 *Now* there was a Jew in Susa
the capital whose name was [a]Mor-
decai, the son of Jair, the son of
Shimei, the son of Kish, a Benjamite,
6 [a]who had been taken into exile
from Jerusalem with the captives
who had been exiled with Jeconiah
king of Judah, whom Nebuchadnezzar the king of Babylon had exiled.
7 And he was bringing up Hadas-
sah, that is [a]Esther, his uncle's
daughter, for she had neither father
nor mother. Now the young lady
was beautiful of form and [1]face, and
when her father and her mother
died, Mordecai took her as his own
daughter.

Esther Finds Favor

8 So it came about when the command and decree of the king were
heard and [a]many young ladies were
gathered to Susa the capital into the
custody of [b]Hegai, that Esther was
taken to the king's [1]palace into the
custody of Hegai, who was in
charge of the women.
9 Now the young lady pleased
him and found favor with him. So he
quickly provided her with her [a]cos-
metics and [1]food, gave her seven
choice maids from the king's palace,
and transferred her and her maids
to the best place in the harem.
10 [a]Esther did not make known
her people or her kindred, for Mordecai had instructed her that she
should not make *them* known.
11 And every day Mordecai
walked back and forth in front of
the court of the harem to learn how
Esther was and how she fared.
12 Now when the turn of each
young lady came to go in to King
Ahasuerus, after the end of her
twelve months under the regulations for the women—for the days
of their beautification were completed as follows: six months with
oil of myrrh and six months with
spices and the cosmetics for
women—
13 the young lady would go in to
the king in this way: anything that
she [1]desired was given her to take
with her from the harem to the
king's palace.
14 In the evening she would go in
and in the morning she would return
to the second harem, to the [1]custody
of Shaashgaz, the king's eunuch
who was in charge of the concubines. She would not again go in to
the king unless the king delighted in
her and she was summoned by
name.
15 Now when the turn of Esther,
[a]the daughter of Abihail the uncle of
Mordecai who had taken her as his
daughter, came to go in to the king,
she did not request anything except
what [b]Hegai, the king's eunuch who
was in charge of the women, [1]ad-
vised. And Esther found favor in the
eyes of all who saw her.
16 So Esther was taken to King
Ahasuerus to his royal palace in the
tenth month which is the month Te-
beth, in the seventh year of his
reign.

Esther Becomes Queen

17 And the king loved Esther more
than all the women, and she found
favor and kindness with him more
than all the virgins, so that [a]he set
the royal crown on her head and
made her queen instead of Vashti.
18 Then [a]the king gave a great
banquet, Esther's banquet, for all
his princes and his servants; he also
made a holiday for the provinces
and gave gifts [b]according to the
king's bounty.
19 And [a]when the virgins were
gathered together the second time,
then Mordecai [b]was sitting at the
king's gate.
20 [a]Esther had not yet made
known her kindred or her people,
even as Mordecai had commanded
her, for Esther did [1]what Mordecai

1 [a]Esth. 7:10 [b]Esth. 1:19, 20
3 [a]Esth. 1:1, 2 [b]Esth. 2:8, 15 [c]Esth. 2:9, 12
5 [a]Esth. 3:2
6 [a]2 Kin. 24:14, 15
7 [1]Lit., *good of appearance* [a]Esth. 2:15
8 [1]Lit., *house* [a]Esth. 2:3 [b]Esth. 2:3, 15
9 [1]Lit., *portions* [a]Esth. 2:3, 12
10 [a]Esth. 2:20
13 [1]Lit., *said*
14 [1]Lit., *hand*
15 [1]Lit., *said* [a]Esth. 2:7; 9:29 [b]Esth. 2:3, 8
17 [a]Esth. 1:11
18 [a]Esth. 1:3 [b]Esth. 1:7
19 [a]Esth. 2:3, 4 [b]Esth. 2:21; 3:2
20 [1]Lit., *the word of Mordecai* [a]Esth. 2:10

told her as she had done [b]when under his care.

Mordecai Saves the King

21 In those days, while Mordecai
was sitting at the king's gate, [a]Big-
than and Teresh, two of the king's
officials from those who guarded
the door, became angry and sought
to [1]lay hands on King Ahasuerus.
22 But the [1]plot became known to
Mordecai, and [a]he told Queen Esther, and Esther [2]informed the king
in Mordecai's name.
23 Now when the plot was investigated and found *to be so,* they were
both hanged on a [1]gallows; and it
was written in [a]the Book of the
Chronicles in the king's presence.

CHAPTER 3

Haman's Plot against the Jews

AFTER these events King Ahasuerus [a]promoted Haman, the son of
Hammedatha [b]the Agagite, and [c]ad-
vanced him and [1]established his authority over all the princes who
were with him.
2 And all the king's servants who
were at the king's gate bowed down
[1]and paid homage to Haman; for so
the king had commanded concerning him. But [a]Mordecai neither
bowed down nor paid homage.
3 Then the king's servants who
were at [a]the king's gate said to Mordecai, "[b]Why are you transgressing
the king's command?"
4 Now it was when they had spoken daily to him and he would not
listen to them, that they told Haman
to see whether Mordecai's reason
would stand; for he had told them
that he was a Jew.
5 When Haman saw that Mordecai neither bowed down nor paid
homage to him, Haman was filled
with rage.
6 But he [1]disdained to [2]lay hands
on Mordecai alone, for they had told
him *who* the people of Mordecai
were; therefore Haman sought to
destroy all the Jews, the people of
Mordecai, who *were* throughout the
whole kingdom of Ahasuerus.
7 In the first month, which is the
month Nisan, in the twelfth year of
King Ahasuerus, [1]Pur, that is the lot,
was [a]cast before Haman from day to
day and from month *to month,* [2]un-
til the twelfth month, that is [b]the
month Adar.
8 Then Haman said to King Ahasuerus, "There is a certain people
scattered and dispersed among the
peoples in all the provinces of your
kingdom; [a]their laws are different
from *those* of all *other* people, and
they do not observe the king's laws,
so it is not in the king's interest to let
them remain.
9 "If it is pleasing to the king, let it
be [1]decreed that they be destroyed,
and I will pay ten thousand talents
of silver into the hands of those who
carry on the king's business, to put
into the king's treasuries."
10 Then [a]the king took his signet
ring from his hand and gave it to
Haman, the son of Hammedatha
[b]the Agagite, the enemy of [c]the
Jews.
11 And the king said to Haman,
"The silver is [1]yours, and the people
also, to do with them as you please."
12 [a]Then the king's scribes were
summoned on the thirteenth day of
the first month, and it was written
just as Haman commanded to [b]the
king's satraps, to the governors who
were over each province, and to the
princes of each people, each province according to its script, each
people according to its language,
being written [c]in the name of King
Ahasuerus and sealed with the
king's signet ring.
13 And letters were sent by [a]couri
ers to all the king's provinces [b]to destroy, to kill, and to annihilate all the
Jews, both young and old, women
and children, [c]in one day, the thirteenth *day* of the twelfth month,
which is the month Adar, and to
[d]seize their possessions as plunder.
14 [a]A copy of the edict to be [1]is-
sued as law in every province was
published to all the peoples so that
they should be ready for this day.
15 The couriers went out impelled
by the king's command while the
decree was [1]issued in Susa the capital; and while the king and Haman
sat down to drink, [a]the city of Susa
was in confusion.

CHAPTER 4

Esther Learns of Haman's Plot

WHEN Mordecai learned [a]all that
had been done, [1]he tore his clothes,
put on sackcloth and ashes, and
went out into the midst of the city
and wailed loudly and bitterly.
2 And he went as far as the king's
gate, for no one was to enter the
king's gate clothed in sackcloth.
3 And in each and every province
where the command and decree of
the king came, there was great
mourning among the Jews, with

20 [b]Esth. 2:7

21 [1]Lit., *send a hand against* [a]Esth. 6:2

22 [1]Lit., *matter,* so also v. 23 [2]Lit., *told* [a]Esth. 6:1, 2

23 [1]Lit., *tree* [a]Esth. 10:2

1 [1]Lit., *set his seat* [a]Esth. 5:11 [b]Esth. 3:10; 8:3 [c]Esth. 5:11

2 [1]Lit., *and prostrated themselves before* [a]Esth. 5:9

3 [a]Esth. 2:19 [b]Esth. 3:2

6 [1]Lit., *despised in his eyes* [2]Lit., *send a hand against*

7 [1]Lit., *he cast Pur . . . before* [2]Gk., *and the lot fell on the thirteenth day of* [a]Esth. 9:24-26 [b]Ezra 6:15

8 [a]Ezra 4:12-15; Acts 16:20, 21

9 [1]Lit., *written*

10 [a]Gen. 41:42; Esth. 8:2 [b]Esth. 3:1 [c]Esth. 7:6

11 [1]Lit., *given to you*

12 [a]Esth. 8:9 [b]Ezra 8:36 [c]1 Kin. 21:8; Esth. 8:8, 10

13 [a]2 Chr. 30:6; Esth. 8:10, 14 [b]Esth. 7:4 [c]Esth. 8:12 [d]Esth. 8:11; 9:10

14 [1]Lit., *given* [a]Esth. 8:13, 14

15 [1]Lit., *given* [a]Esth. 8:15

1 [1]Lit., *Mordecai* [a]2 Sam. 1:11; Esth. 3:8-10; Jon. 3:5,6

[a]fasting, weeping, and wailing; and
many lay on sackcloth and ashes.
4 Then Esther's maidens and her
eunuchs came and told her, and the
queen writhed in great anguish. And
she sent garments to clothe Mordecai that he might remove his sackcloth from him, but he did not accept *them.*
5 Then Esther summoned Hathach from the king's eunuchs,
whom [1]the king had appointed to attend her, and ordered him *to go* to
Mordecai to learn what this *was* and
why it *was.*
6 So Hathach went out to Mordecai to the city square in front of the
king's gate.
7 And Mordecai told him all that
had happened to him, and [a]the exact
amount of money that Haman had
promised to pay to the king's treasuries for the destruction of the
Jews.
8 He also gave him [a]a copy of the
text of the edict which had been issued in Susa for their destruction,
that he might show Esther and inform her, and to order her to go in to
the king to implore his favor and to
plead with him for her people.
9 And Hathach came back and
related Mordecai's words to Esther.
10 Then Esther spoke to Hathach
and ordered him *to reply* to Mordecai:
11 "All the king's servants and the
people of the king's provinces know
that for any man or woman who
[a]comes to the king to the inner court
who is not summoned, [b]he has but
one law, that he be put to death, unless the king holds out [c]to him the
golden scepter so that he may live.
And I have not been summoned to
come to the king for these thirty
days."
12 And they related Esther's
words to Mordecai.
13 Then Mordecai told *them* to reply to Esther, "Do not imagine that
you in the king's palace can escape
any more than all the Jews.
14 "For if you remain silent at this
time, relief and deliverance will
arise for the Jews from another
place and you and your father's
house will perish. And who knows
whether you have not attained royalty for such a time as this?"

Esther Plans to Intercede

15 Then Esther told *them* to reply
to Mordecai,
16 "Go, assemble all the Jews who
are found in Susa, and fast for me;
do not eat or drink for [a]three days,
night or day. I and my maidens also
will fast in the same way. And thus
I will go in to the king, which is not
according to the law; and if I perish,
I perish."
17 So Mordecai went away and
did just as Esther had commanded
him.

CHAPTER 5

Esther Plans a Banquet

NOW it came about [a]on the third
day that Esther put on her royal
robes and stood [b]in the inner court
of the king's palace in front of the
king's [1]rooms, and the king was sitting on his royal throne in the
[2]throne room, opposite the entrance
to the palace.
2 And it happened when the king
saw Esther the queen standing in
the court, [a]she obtained favor in his
sight; and [b]the king extended to Esther the golden scepter which was
in his hand. So Esther came near
and touched the top of the scepter.
3 Then the king said to her,
"What is *troubling* you, Queen Esther? And what is your request?
[a]Even to half of the kingdom it will
be given to you."
4 And Esther said, "If it please
the king, may the king and Haman
come this day to the banquet that I
have prepared for him."
5 Then the king said, "[a]Bring Haman quickly that we may do [1]as Esther desires." So the king and Haman came to the banquet which
Esther had prepared.
6 And, [1]as they drank their wine
at the banquet, [a]the king said to Esther, "[b]What is your petition, for it
shall be granted to you. And what is
your request? Even to half of the
kingdom it shall be done."
7 So Esther answered and said,
"My petition and my request is:
8 [a]if I have found favor in the
sight of the king, and if it please the
king to grant my petition and do
[1]what I request, may the king and
Haman come to [b]the banquet which
I shall prepare for them, and tomorrow I will do [2]as the king says."

Haman's Pride

9 Then Haman went out that day
glad and pleased of heart; but when
Haman saw Mordecai [a]in the king's
gate, and [b]that he did not stand up
or [1]tremble before him, Haman was
filled with anger against Mordecai.
10 Haman controlled himself,
however, went to his house, and

3 [a]Esth. 4:16
5 [1]Lit., *he*
7 [a]Esth. 3:9
8 [a]Esth. 3:14
11 [a]Esth. 5:1; 6:4 [b]Dan. 2:9 [c]Esth. 5:2; 8:4
16 [a]Esth. 5:1
1 [1]Lit., *house* [2]Lit., *royal house* [a]Esth. 4:16 [b]Esth. 4:11; 6:4
2 [a]Esth. 2:9 [b]Esth. 4:11; 8:4
3 [a]Esth. 7:2; Mark 6:23
5 [1]Lit., *the word of Esther* [a]Esth. 6:14
6 [1]Lit., *at the banquet of wine* [a]Esth. 7:2 [b]Esth. 5:3
8 [1]Lit., *my request* [2]Lit., *according to the word of the king* [a]Esth. 7:3; 8:5 [b]Esth. 6:14
9 [1]Or, *move for* [a]Esth. 2:19 [b]Esth. 3:5

[1]sent for his friends and his wife [a]Zeresh.

11 Then Haman recounted to them the glory of his riches, and the [1a]number of his sons, and every *instance* where the king had magnified him, and how he had [2b]promoted him above the princes and servants of the king.

12 Haman also said, "Even Esther the queen let no one but me come with the king to the banquet which she had prepared; and [a]tomorrow also I am [1]invited by her with the king.

13 "Yet all of this [1]does not satisfy me every time I see Mordecai the Jew sitting at [a]the king's gate."

14 Then Zeresh his wife and all his friends said to him, "[a]Have a [1]gallows fifty cubits high made and in the morning ask the king to have Mordecai hanged on it, then go joyfully with the king to the banquet." And the [2]advice pleased Haman, so he had the gallows made.

Chapter 6

The King Plans to Honor Mordecai

[a]DURING that night [1]the king [b]could not sleep so he gave an order to bring [c]the book of records, the chronicles, and they were read before the king.

2 And it was found written what [a]Mordecai had reported concerning Bigthana and Teresh, two of the king's eunuchs who were doorkeepers, that they had sought to lay hands on King Ahasuerus.

3 And the king said, "What honor or dignity has been bestowed on Mordecai for this?" Then the king's servants who attended him said, "Nothing has been done for him."

4 So the king said, "Who is in the court?" Now Haman had just [a]entered the outer court of the king's palace in order to speak to the king about [b]hanging Mordecai on the gallows which he had prepared for him.

5 And the king's servants said to him, "Behold, Haman is standing in the court." And the king said, "Let him come in."

6 So Haman came in and the king said to him, "What is to be done for the man [a]whom the king desires to honor?" And Haman said [1]to himself, "Whom would the king desire to honor more than me?"

7 Then Haman said to the king, "For the man whom the king desires to honor,

8 let them bring a royal robe which the king has worn, and [a]the horse on which the king has ridden, and on whose head [b]a royal crown has been placed;

9 and let the robe and the horse be handed over to one of the king's most noble princes and let them array the man whom the king desires to honor and lead him on horseback through the city square, [a]and proclaim before him, 'Thus it shall be done to the man whom the king desires to honor.' "

Haman Must Honor Mordecai

10 Then the king said to Haman, "[a]Take quickly the robes and the horse as you have said, and do so for Mordecai the Jew, who is sitting at the king's gate; do not fall short in anything of all that you have said."

11 So Haman took the robe and the horse, and arrayed Mordecai, and led him *on horseback* through the city square, and proclaimed before him, "Thus it shall be done to the man whom the king desires to honor."

12 Then Mordecai returned to the king's gate. But Haman hurried home, mourning, [a]with *his* head covered.

13 And Haman recounted [a]to Zeresh his wife and all his friends everything that had happened to him. Then his wise men and Zeresh his wife said to him, "If Mordecai, before whom you have begun to fall, is [1]of Jewish origin, you will not overcome him, but will surely fall before him."

14 While they were still talking with him, the king's eunuchs arrived and hastily [a]brought Haman to the banquet which Esther had prepared.

Chapter 7

Esther's Plea

NOW the king and Haman came to drink *wine* with Esther the queen.

2 And the king said to Esther on the second day also [1]as they drank their wine at the banquet, "[a]What is your petition, Queen Esther? It shall be granted you. And what is your request? [b]Even to half of the kingdom it shall be done."

3 Then Queen Esther answered and said, "[a]If I have found favor in your sight, O king, and if it please the king, let my life be given me as my petition, and my people as my request;

4 for [a]we have been sold, I and my people, to be destroyed, [b]to be

10 [1]Lit., *sent and brought* [a]Esth. 6:13

11 [1]Lit., *multitude* [2]Lit., *lifted* [a]Esth. 9:7-10 [b]Esth. 3:1

12 [1]Lit., *summoned to her* [a]Esth. 5:8

13 [1]Lit., *is not suitable to me* [a]Esth. 5:9

14 [1]Lit., *tree* [2]Lit., *thing* [a]Esth. 6:4; 7:9, 10

1 [1]Lit., *the king's sleep fled* [a]Esth. 5:8 [b]Dan. 6:18 [c]Esth. 2:23; 10:2

2 [a]Esth. 2:21, 22

4 [a]Esth. 4:11; 5:1 [b]Esth. 5:14

6 [1]Lit., *in his heart* [a]Esth. 6:7, 9, 11

8 [a]1 Kin. 1:33 [b]Esth. 1:11; 2:17

9 [a]Gen. 41:43

10 [a]Esth. 5:5

12 [a]2 Sam. 15:30

13 [1]Lit., *from the seed of the Jews* [a]Esth. 5:10

14 [a]Esth. 5:8

2 [1]Lit., *at the banquet of wine* [a]Esth. 5:6; 9:12 [b]Esth. 5:3

3 [a]Esth. 5:8; 8:5

4 [a]Esth. 3:19 [b]Esth. 3:13

killed and to be annihilated. Now if
we had only been sold as slaves,
men and women, I would have remained silent, for the [1]trouble
would not be commensurate with
the [2]annoyance to the king."
5 Then King Ahasuerus [1]asked
Queen Esther, "Who is he, and
where is he, [2]who would presume to
do thus?"
6 And Esther said, "[a]A foe and an
enemy, is this wicked Haman!"
Then Haman became terrified before the king and queen.

Haman Is Hanged

7 And the king arose [a]in his anger
from [1]drinking wine *and went* into
[b]the palace garden; but Haman
stayed to beg for his life from Queen
Esther, for he saw that harm had
been determined against him by the
king.
8 Now when the king returned
from the palace garden into the
[1]place where they were drinking
wine, Haman was falling on [a]the
couch where Esther was. Then the
king said, "Will he even assault the
queen with me in the house?" As the
word went out of the king's mouth,
they covered Haman's face.
9 Then Harbonah, one of the eunuchs who *were* before the king
said, "Behold indeed, [a]the gallows
standing at Haman's house fifty cubits high, which Haman made for
Mordecai [b]who spoke good on behalf of the king!" And the king said,
"Hang him on it."
10 [a]So they hanged Haman on the
[1]gallows which he had prepared for
Mordecai, [b]and the king's anger
subsided.

Chapter 8

Mordecai Promoted

ON that day King Ahasuerus gave
the house of Haman, the enemy of
[a]the Jews, to Queen Esther; and
Mordecai came before the king, for
Esther had disclosed [b]what he was
to her.
2 [a]And the king took off his signet ring which he had taken away
from Haman, and gave it to Mordecai. And Esther set Mordecai over
the house of Haman.
3 Then Esther spoke again to the
king, fell at his feet, wept, and implored him to avert the evil *scheme*
of Haman the Agagite and his plot
which he had devised against the
Jews.
4 [a]And the king extended the
golden scepter to Esther. So Esther
arose and stood before the king.
5 Then she said, "[a]If it pleases the
king and if I have found favor before
him and the matter *seems* proper to
the king and I am pleasing in his
sight, let it be written to revoke the
[b]letters devised by Haman, the son
of Hammedatha the Agagite, which
he wrote to destroy the Jews who
are in all the king's provinces.
6"For [a]how can I endure to see
the calamity which shall befall my
people, and how can I endure to see
the destruction of my kindred?"
7 So King Ahasuerus said to
Queen Esther and to Mordecai the
Jew, "Behold, [a]I have given the
house of Haman to Esther, and him
they have hanged on the gallows because he had stretched out his
hands against the Jews.

The King's Decree Avenges the Jews

8"Now you write to the Jews [1]as
you see fit, in the king's name, and
[a]seal *it* with the king's signet ring;
for a decree which is written in the
name of the king and sealed with the
king's signet ring [b]may not be revoked."
9 [a]So the king's scribes were
called at that time in the third
month (that is, the month Sivan), on
the twenty-third [1]day; and it was
written according to all that Mordecai commanded to the Jews, the satraps, the governors, and the
princes of the provinces which *extended* [b]from India to [2]Ethiopia, 127
provinces, to [c]every province according to its script, and to every
people according to their language,
as well as to the Jews according to
their script and their language.
10 And he wrote in the name of
King Ahasuerus, and sealed it with
the king's signet ring, and sent letters by couriers on [a]horses, riding
on steeds sired by the royal stud.
11 [1]In them the king granted the
Jews who were in each and every
city *the right* [a]to assemble and to
defend their lives, [b]to destroy, to
kill, and to annihilate the entire
army of any people or province
which might attack them, including
children and women, and [c]to plunder their spoil,
12 on one day in all the provinces
of King Ahasuerus, the thirteenth
day of the twelfth month (that is,
the month Adar).
13 [a]A copy of the edict to be [1]is-
sued as law in each and every province, was published to all the peoples, so that the Jews should be

4 [1]Or, *enemy could not compensate for the loss* [2]Or, *damage*

5 [1]Lit., *said and said to* [2]Lit., *whose heart has been filled*

6 [a]Esth. 3:10

7 [1]Lit., *the banquet of wine* [a]Esth. 1:12 [b]Esth. 1:5

8 [1]Lit., *house of the banquet of wine* [a]Esth. 1:6

9 [a]Esth. 5:14 [b]Esth. 2:22

10 [1]Lit., *tree* [a]Ps. 7:16; 94:23 [b]Esth. 7:7, 8

1 [a]Esth. 7:6 [b]Esth. 2:7, 15

2 [a]Esth. 3:10

4 [a]Esth. 4:11; 5:2

5 [a]Esth. 5:8; 7:3 [b]Esth. 3:13

6 [a]Esth. 7:4; 9:1

7 [a]Esth. 8:1

8 [1]Lit., *according to the good in your eyes* [a]Esth. 3:12; 8:10 [b]Esth. 1:19

9 [1]Lit., *in it* [2]Lit., *Cush* [a]Esth. 3:12 [b]Esth. 1:1 [c]Esth. 1:22; 3:12

10 [a]1 Kin. 4:28

11 [1]Lit., *Which* [a]Esth. 9:2 [b]Esth. 3:13 [c]Esth. 9:10

13 [1]Lit., *given* [a]Esth. 3:14

ready for this day to avenge themselves on their enemies.
14 The couriers, hastened and impelled by the king's command, went
out, riding on the royal steeds; and
the decree was given out in Susa the
capital.
15 Then Mordecai went out from
the presence of the king [a]in royal
robes of [1]blue and white, with a
large crown of gold and [b]a garment
of fine linen and purple; and the city
of Susa shouted and rejoiced.
16 For the Jews there was light
and gladness and joy and honor.
17 And in each and every province, and in each and every city,
wherever the king's commandment
and his decree arrived, there was
gladness and joy for the Jews, a
feast and a [1a]holiday. And [b]many
among the peoples of the land became Jews, for the dread of the
Jews had fallen on them.

Chapter 9

The Jews Destroy Their Enemies

NOW [a]in the twelfth month (that
is, the month Adar), on [b]the thirteenth [1]day [c]when the king's command and edict [2]were about to be
executed, on the day when the enemies of the Jews hoped to gain the
mastery over them, it was turned to
the contrary so that the Jews themselves gained the mastery over
those who hated them.
2 [a]The Jews assembled in their
cities throughout all the provinces
of King Ahasuerus to lay hands on
those who sought their harm; and
no one could stand before them, [b]for
the dread of them had fallen on all
the peoples.
3 Even all the princes of the provinces, [a]the satraps, the governors,
and those who were doing the king's
business [1]assisted the Jews, because the dread of Mordecai had
fallen on them.
4 Indeed, Mordecai was great in
the king's house, and his fame
spread throughout all the provinces;
for the man Mordecai [a]became
greater and greater.
5 Thus [a]the Jews struck all their
enemies with [1]the sword, killing and
destroying; and they did what they
pleased to those who hated them.
6 And in Susa the capital the
Jews killed and destroyed five hundred men,
7 and Parshandatha, Dalphon,
Aspatha,
8 Poratha, Adalia, Aridatha,
9 Parmashta, Arisai, Aridai, and
Vaizatha,
10 [a]the ten sons of Haman the son
of Hammedatha, the Jews' enemy;
but they did not lay their hands [b]on
the plunder.
11 On that day the number of
those who were killed in Susa the
capital [1]was reported to the king.
12 And the king said to Queen Esther, "The Jews have killed and destroyed five hundred men and the
ten sons of Haman in Susa the capital. What then have they done in the
rest of the king's provinces! [a]Now
what is your petition? It shall even
be granted you. And what is your
further request? It shall also be
done."
13 Then said Esther, "If it pleases
the king, [a]let tomorrow also be
granted to the Jews who are in Susa
to do according to the edict of today;
and let Haman's ten sons be hanged
on the gallows."
14 So the king commanded that it
should be done so; and an edict was
issued in Susa, and Haman's ten
sons were hanged.
15 And the Jews who were in Susa
assembled also on the fourteenth
day of the month Adar and killed
[a]three hundred men in Susa, but
they did not lay their hands [b]on the
plunder.
16 Now [a]the rest of the Jews who
were in the king's provinces assembled, to defend their lives and [1]rid
themselves of their enemies, and kill
75,000 of those who hated them; but
they did not lay their hands on the
plunder.
17 *This was done* on [a]the thirteenth day of the month Adar, and
[b]on the fourteenth [1]day they rested
and made it a day of feasting and
rejoicing.
18 But the Jews who were in Susa
[a]assembled on the thirteenth and
[b]the fourteenth [1]of the same month,
and they rested on the fifteenth [1]day
and made it a day of feasting and
rejoicing.
19 Therefore the Jews of the rural
areas, who live in [a]the rural towns,
make the fourteenth day of the
month Adar *a* [1b]*holiday* for rejoicing and feasting and [c]sending portions *of food* to one another.

The Feast of Purim Instituted

20 Then Mordecai recorded these
events, and he sent letters to all the
Jews who were in all the provinces
of King Ahasuerus, both near and
far,
21 obliging them to celebrate the

15 [1]Or, *violet* [a]Gen. 41:42; Esth. 5:11 [b]Esth. 3:15
17 [1]Lit., *good day* [a]Esth. 9:19 [b]Esth. 9:27
1 [1]Lit., *day in it* [2]Lit., *drew near* [a]Esth. 8:12 [b]Esth. 9:17 [c]Esth. 3:13
2 [a]Esth. 8:11; 9:15-18 [b]Esth. 8:17
3 [1]Lit., *lifted up* [a]Ezra 8:36
4 [a]2 Sam. 3:1
5 [1]Lit., *the stroke of* [a]Esth. 3:13
10 [a]Esth. 5:11 [b]Esth. 8:11
11 [1]Lit., *came*
12 [a]Esth. 7:2
13 [a]Esth. 8:11; 9:15
15 [a]Esth. 9:12 [b]Esth. 9:10
16 [1]Lit., *have rest from* [a]Esth. 9:2
17 [1]Lit., *in it* [a]Esth. 9:1 [b]Esth. 9:21
18 [1]Lit., *in it* [a]Esth. 8:11; 9:2 [b]Esth. 9:21
19 [1]Lit., *good day* [a]Deut. 3:5; Zech. 2:4 [b]Esth. 9:22 [c]Neh. 8:10

fourteenth day of the month Adar,
and the fifteenth day [1]of the same
month, annually,
22 because on those days the Jews
[1]rid themselves of their enemies,
and *it was a* month which was
turned for them from sorrow into
gladness and from mourning into a
[2]holiday; that they should make
them days of feasting and rejoicing
and sending portions *of food* to one
another and gifts to the poor.
23 Thus the Jews undertook what
they had started to do, and what
Mordecai had written to them.
24 For Haman the son of Hammedatha, the Agagite, the adversary of
all the Jews, had schemed against
the Jews to destroy them, and [a]had
cast Pur, that is the lot, to disturb
them and destroy them.
25 But [a]when it came [1]to the king's
attention, he commanded by letter
[b]that his wicked scheme which he
had [2]devised against the Jews,
[c]should return on his own head, and
that he and his sons should be
hanged on the [3]gallows.
26 Therefore they called these
days Purim after the name of Pur.
[1]And [a]because of the instructions in
this letter, both what they had seen
in this regard and what had happened to them,
27 the Jews established and [1]made
a custom for themselves, and for
their [2]descendants, and for [a]all
those who allied themselves with
them, so that [3]they should not fail
[b]to celebrate these two days according to their [4]regulation, and according to their appointed time annually.
28 So these days were to be remembered and celebrated throughout every generation, every family,
every province, and every city; and
these days of Purim were not to [1]fail
from among the Jews, or their memory [2]fade from their [3]descendants.
29 Then Queen Esther, [a]daughter
of Abihail, with Mordecai the Jew,
wrote with full authority to confirm
[b]this second letter about Purim.
30 And he sent letters to all the
Jews, [a]to the 127 provinces of the
kingdom of Ahasuerus, namely,
words of peace and truth,
31 to establish these days of Purim
at their appointed times, just as
Mordecai the Jew and Queen Esther
had established for them, and just
as they had established for themselves and for their [1]descendants
with [2]instructions [a]for their times of
fasting and their lamentations.
32 And the command of Esther established these [1]customs for [a]Pu-
rim, and it was written in the book.

Chapter 10

Mordecai's Greatness

NOW King Ahasuerus laid a tribute on the land and on the [a]coast-
lands of the sea.
2 And all the [1]accomplishments
of his authority and strength, and
the full account of the greatness of
Mordecai, [a]to which the king [2]ad-
vanced him, are they not written in
[b]the Book of the Chronicles of the
Kings of Media and Persia?
3 For Mordecai the Jew was [a]sec-
ond *only* to King Ahasuerus and
great among the Jews, and in favor
with the multitude of his kinsmen,
[b]one who sought the good of his
people and one who spoke for the
welfare of his whole nation.

21 [1]Lit., *in it*
22 [1]Lit., *had rest from* [2]Lit., *good day*
24 [a]Esth. 3:7
25 [1]Lit., *before the king, he* [2]Lit., *schemed* [3]Lit., *tree* [a]Esth. 7:4-10 [b]Esth. 3:6-15 [c]Ps. 7:16
26 [1]Lit., *Therefore because of all the words* [a]Esth. 9:20
27 [1]Lit., *received* [2]Lit., *seed* [3]Lit., *it should not pass away* [4]Lit., *writing* [a]Esth. 8:17 [b]Esth. 9:20, 21
28 [1]Lit., *pass away* [2]Lit., *end* [3]Lit., *seed*
29 [a]Esth. 2:15 [b]Esth. 9:20, 21
30 [a]Esth. 1:1
31 [1]Lit., *seed* [2]Lit., *words* [a]Esth. 4:3
32 [1]Lit., *words* [a]Esth. 9:26
1 [a]Is. 11:11; 24:15
2 [1]Lit., *doings* [2]Lit., *made him great* [a]Esth. 8:15; 9:4 [b]Esth. 2:23
3 [a]Gen. 41:43, 44 [b]Neh. 2:10

THE BOOK OF JOB

Job's Character and Wealth

THERE was a man in the land of
[a]Uz, whose name was [b]Job, and that
man was [c]blameless, upright, [d]fear-
ing God, and [e]turning away from
evil.
2 [a]And seven sons and three
daughters were born to him.
3 [a]His possessions also were
7,000 sheep, 3,000 camels, 500 yoke
of oxen, 500 female donkeys, and
very many servants; and that man
was [b]the greatest of all the [1]men of
the east.
4 And his sons used to go and
hold a feast in the house of each one
on his day, and they would send and
invite their three sisters to eat and
drink with them.
5 And it came about, when the
days of feasting had completed their
cycle, that Job would send and consecrate them, rising up early in the
morning and offering [a]burnt offerings *according to* the number of
them all; for Job said, "[b]Perhaps my
sons have sinned and cursed God in
their hearts." Thus Job did continually.
6 Now there was a day when the
sons of God came to present them-

1 [a]Jer. 25:20; Lam. 4:21 [b]Ezek. 14:14, 20; James 5:11 [c]Gen. 6:9; 17:1; Deut. 18:13 [d]Gen. 22:12; 42:18; Ex. 18:21 [e]Job 28:28
2 [a]Job 42:13
3 [1]Lit., *sons* [a]Job 42:12 [b]Job 29:25; 31:37
5 [a]Job 42:8 [b]Job 8:4

selves before the LORD, and [1]Satan also came among them.

7 And the LORD said to Satan, "From where do you come?" Then Satan answered the LORD and said, "[a]From roaming about on the earth and walking around on it."

8 And the LORD said to Satan, "Have you [1]considered [a]My servant Job? For there is no one like him on the earth, [b]a blameless and upright man, [2]fearing God and turning away from evil."

9 Then Satan answered the [1]LORD, "Does Job fear God for nothing?

10 "[a]Hast Thou not made a hedge about him and his house and all that he has, on every side? [b]Thou hast blessed the work of his hands, and his [c]possessions have increased in the land.

11 "[a]But put forth Thy hand now and [b]touch all that he has; he will surely curse Thee to Thy face."

12 Then the LORD said to Satan, "Behold, all that he has is in your [1]power, only do not put forth your hand on him." So Satan departed from the presence of the LORD.

Satan Allowed to Test Job

13 Now it happened on the day when his sons and his daughters were eating and drinking wine in their oldest brother's house,

14 that a messenger came to Job and said, "The oxen were plowing and the [1]donkeys feeding beside them,

15 and [1]the [a]Sabeans [2]attacked and took them. They also [3]slew the servants with the edge of the sword, and [4]I alone have escaped to tell you."

16 While he was still speaking, another also came and said, "[a]The fire of God fell from heaven and burned up the sheep and the servants and consumed them; and I alone have escaped to tell you."

17 While he was still speaking, another also came and said, "The [a]Chaldeans formed three bands and made a raid on the camels and took them and [1]slew the servants with the edge of the sword; and I alone have escaped to tell you."

18 While he was still speaking, another also came and said, "Your sons and your daughters were eating and drinking wine in their oldest brother's house,

19 and behold, a great wind came from across the wilderness and struck the four corners of the house, and it fell on the young people and they died; and I alone have escaped to tell you."

20 Then Job arose and [a]tore his robe and shaved his head, and he fell to the ground and worshiped.

21 And he said,

"[a]Naked I came from my mother's womb,
And naked I shall return there.
The [b]LORD gave and the LORD has taken away.
Blessed be the name of the LORD."

22 [a]Through all this Job did not sin nor did he [1]blame God.

CHAPTER 2

Job Loses His Health

[a] AGAIN there was a day when the sons of God came to present themselves before the LORD, and Satan also came among them to present himself before the LORD.

2 And the LORD said to Satan, "Where have you come from?" Then Satan answered the LORD and said, "From roaming about on the earth, and walking around on it."

3 And the LORD said to Satan, "Have you [1]considered My servant Job? For there is no one like him on the earth, a blameless and upright man [2]fearing God and turning away from evil. And he still holds fast his integrity, although you incited Me against him, to [3]ruin him without cause."

4 And Satan answered the LORD and said, "Skin for skin! Yes, all that a man has he will give for his life.

5 "[a]However, put forth Thy hand, now, and touch his bone and his flesh; he will curse Thee to Thy face."

6 So the LORD said to Satan, "Behold, he is in your [1]power, only spare his life."

7 Then Satan went out from the presence of the LORD, and smote Job with [a]sore boils from the sole of his foot to the crown of his head.

8 And he took a potsherd to scrape himself while [a]he was sitting among the ashes.

9 Then his wife said to him, "Do you still hold fast your integrity? Curse God and die!"

10 But he said to her, "You speak as one of the foolish women speaks. [a]Shall we indeed accept good from God and not accept adversity?" [b]In all this Job did not sin with his lips.

11 Now when Job's three friends heard of all this adversity that had come upon him, they came each one

6 [1]I.e., the adversary; so through chaps. 1 & 2

7 [a]1 Pet. 5:8

8 [1]Lit., *set your heart to* [2]Or, *revering* [a]Num. 12:7; Josh. 1:2, 7; Job 7:8 [b]Job 1:1

9 [1]Lit., *LORD and said*

10 [a]Job 29:2-6 [b]Job 31:25 [c]Job 1:3; 31:25

11 [a]Job 2:5 [b]Job 19:21

12 [1]Lit., *hand*

14 [1]Lit., *female donkeys*

15 [1]Lit., *Sheba* [2]Lit., *fell upon* [3]Lit., *smote* [4]Lit., *only I alone* so also vs. 16, 17, 19 [a]Job 6:19

16 [a]Gen. 19:24; Lev. 10:2; Num. 11:1-3

17 [1]Lit., *smote* [a]Gen. 11:28, 31

20 [a]Gen. 37:29, 34; Josh. 7:6

21 [a]Eccles. 5:15 [b]1 Sam. 2:7, 8; Job 2:10

22 [1]Lit., *ascribe unseemliness to* [a]Job 2:10

1 [a]Job 1:6-8

3 [1]Lit., *set your heart to* [2]Or, *revering* [3]Lit., *swallow him up*

5 [a]Job 1:11

6 [1]Lit., *hand*

7 [a]Job 7:5; 13:28; 30:17, 18, 30; Deut. 28:35

8 [a]Job 42:6; Jer. 6:26; Jon. 3:6

10 [a]Job 1:21 [b]Job 1:22

from his own place, Eliphaz the [a]Te-
manite, Bildad the Shuhite, and Zophar the Naamathite; and they
made an appointment together to
come to sympathize with him and
comfort him.
12 And when they lifted up their
eyes at a distance, and did not recognize him, they raised their voices
and wept. And each of them [a]tore
his robe, and they [b]threw dust over
their heads toward the sky.
13 [a]Then they sat down on the
ground with him for seven days and
seven nights with no one speaking a
word to him, for they saw that *his*
pain was very great.

Chapter 3

Job's Lament

AFTERWARD Job opened his mouth and cursed [1]the day of his *birth*.

2 And Job [1]said,

3 "[a]Let the day perish on which I was to be born,
And the night *which* said, 'A [1]boy is conceived.'
4 "May that day be darkness;
Let not God above care for it,
Nor light shine on it.
5 "Let darkness and black gloom claim it;
Let a cloud settle on it;
Let the blackness of the day terrify it.
6 "*As for* that night, let darkness seize it;
Let it not rejoice among the days of the year;
Let it not come into the number of the months.
7 "Behold, let that night be barren;
Let no joyful shout enter it.
8 "Let those curse it who curse the day,
Who are [1]prepared to [a]rouse Leviathan.
9 "Let the stars of its twilight be darkened;
Let it wait for light but have none,
Neither let it see the [1a]breaking dawn;
10 Because it did not shut the opening of my *mother's* womb,
Or hide trouble from my eyes.

11 "[a]Why did I not die [1]at birth,
Come forth from the womb and expire?
12 "Why did the knees receive me,
And why the breasts, that I should suck?
13 "For now I [a]would have lain down and been quiet;
I would have slept then, I would have been at rest,
14 With [a]kings and *with* [b]counselors of the earth,
Who rebuilt [c]ruins for themselves;
15 Or with [a]princes [b]who had gold,
Who were filling their houses *with* silver.
16 "Or like a miscarriage which is [1]discarded, I would not be,
As infants that never saw light.
17 "There the wicked cease from raging,
And there the [1]weary are at [a]rest.
18 "The prisoners are at ease together;
They do not hear the voice of the taskmaster.
19 "The small and the great are there,
And the slave is free from his master.

20 "Why is light given to him who suffers,
And life to the bitter of soul;
21 Who [1]long for death, but there is none,
And dig for it more than for hidden treasures;
22 Who rejoice greatly,
They exult when they find the grave?
23 "*Why is light given* to a man [a]whose way is hidden,
And whom [b]God has hedged in?
24 "For [a]my groaning comes at the sight of my food,
And [b]my cries pour out like water.
25 "For [1a]what I fear comes upon me,
And what I dread befalls me.
26 "I [a]am not at ease, nor am I quiet,
And I am not at rest, but turmoil comes."

Chapter 4

Eliphaz: Innocent Do Not Suffer

THEN Eliphaz the Temanite [1]answered,

2 "If one ventures a word with you, will you become impatient?
But [a]who can refrain [1]from speaking?
3 "Behold [a]you have admonished many,
And you have strengthened weak hands.

11 [a]Job 6:19
12 [a]Job 1:20 [b]Josh. 7:6; Lam. 2:10
13 [a]Ezek. 3:15
1 [1]Lit., *his day*
2 [1]Lit., *answered and said*
3 [1]Lit., *man-child* [a]Jer. 20:14-18
8 [1]Or, *skillful* [a]Job 41:25
9 [1]Lit., *eyelids* [a]Job 41:18
11 [1]Lit., *from the womb* [a]Job 10:18, 19
13 [a]Job 3:13-19; 7:8-10, 21; 10:21, 22; 14:10-15, 20-22; 16:22; 17:13-16; 19:25-27; 21:13, 23-26; 24:19, 20; 26:5, 6; 34:22
14 [a]Job 12:18 [b]Job 12:17 [c]Job 15:28; Is. 58:12
15 [a]Job 12:21 [b]Job 27:16, 17
16 [1]Lit., *hidden*
17 [1]Lit., *weary of strength* [a]Job 17:16
21 [1]Lit., *wait*
23 [a]Job 19:6, 8, 12 [b]Job 19:8; Ps. 88:8
24 [a]Job 6:7; 33:20 [b]Job 30:16; Ps. 42:4
25 [1]Lit., *the fear I fear and* [a]Job 9:28; 30:15
26 [a]Job 7:13, 14
1 [1]Lit., *answered and said*
2 [1]Lit., *in words* [a]Job 32:18-20
3 [a]Job 4:3, 4; 29:15, 16, 21, 25

4 “Your words have [1]helped the tottering to stand,
And you have strengthened [2]feeble knees.
5 “But now it has come to you, and you [a]are impatient;
It [b]touches you, and you are dismayed.
6 “Is not your [1a]fear *of God* your confidence,
And the integrity of your ways your hope?

7 “Remember now, [a]who *ever* perished being innocent?
Or where were the upright destroyed?
8 “According to what I have seen, [a]those who plow iniquity
And those who sow trouble harvest it.
9 “By [a]the breath of God they perish,
And [b]by the [1]blast of His anger they come to an end.
10 “The [a]roaring of the lion and the voice of the *fierce* lion,
And the teeth of the young lions are broken.
11 “The [a]lion perishes for lack of prey,
And the [b]whelps of the lioness are scattered.

12 “Now a word [a]was brought to me stealthily,
And my ear received a [b]whisper of it.
13 “Amid disquieting thoughts from the visions of the night,
When deep sleep falls on men,
14 Dread came upon me, and trembling,
And made [1]all my bones shake.
15 “Then a [1]spirit passed by my face;
The hair of my flesh bristled up.
16 “It stood still, but I could not discern its appearance;
A form *was* before my eyes;
There was silence, then I heard a voice:
17 ‘Can [a]mankind be just [1]before God?
Can a man be pure [1]before his [b]Maker?
18 ‘[a]He puts no trust even in His servants;
And against His angels He charges error.
19 ‘How much more those who dwell in [a]houses of clay,
Whose [b]foundation is in the dust,
Who are crushed before the moth!
20 ‘[a]Between morning and evening they are broken in pieces;
Unobserved, they [b]perish forever.
21 ‘Is not their [a]tent-cord plucked up within them?
They die, yet [b]without wisdom.’

CHAPTER 5

God Is Just

“CALL now, is there anyone who will answer you?
And to which of the [a]holy ones will you turn?
2 “For [a]vexation slays the foolish man,
And anger kills the simple.
3 “I have seen the [a]foolish taking root,
And I [b]cursed his abode immediately.
4 “His [a]sons are far from safety,
They are even [1]oppressed in the gate,
Neither is there a deliverer.
5 “[1]His harvest the hungry devour,
And take it to a *place of* thorns;
And the [2a]schemer is eager for their wealth.
6 “For [a]affliction does not come from the dust,
Neither does trouble sprout from the ground,
7 For [a]man is born for trouble,
As sparks fly upward.

8 “But as for me, I would [a]seek God,
And I would place my cause before God;
9 Who [a]does great and unsearchable things,
[1]Wonders without number.
10 “He [a]gives rain on the earth,
And sends water on the fields,
11 So that [a]He sets on high those who are lowly,
And those who mourn are lifted to safety.
12 “He [a]frustrates the plotting of the shrewd,
So that their hands cannot attain success.
13 “He [a]captures the wise by their own shrewdness
And the advice of the cunning is quickly thwarted.
14 “By day they [a]meet with darkness,
And grope at noon as in the night.
15 “But He saves from [a]the sword of their mouth,
And [b]the poor from the hand of the mighty.

4 [1]Lit., *caused* [2]Lit., *bowing*
5 [a]Job 6:14 [b]Job 19:21
6 [1]Or, *reverence* [a]Job 1:1
7 [a]Job 8:20; 36:6, 7; Ps. 37:25
8 [a]Job 15:31, 35; Prov. 22:8; Hos. 10:13; Gal. 6:7
9 [1]Lit., *wind* [a]Job 15:30; Is. 11:4; 30:33; 2 Thess. 2:8 [b]Job 40:11-13
10 [a]Job 5:15; Ps. 58:6
11 [a]Job 29:17 [b]Job 5:4; 20:10; 27:14
12 [a]Job 4:12-17; 33:15-18 [b]Job 26:14
14 [1]Lit., *the multitude of*
15 [1]Or, *breath passed over*
17 [1]Lit., *from* [a]Job 9:2; 25:4 [b]Job 31:15; 32:22; 35:10; 36:3
18 [a]Job 15:15
19 [a]Job 10:9; 33:6 [b]Gen. 2:7; 3:19; Job 22:16
20 [a]Job 14:2 [b]Job 14:20; 20:7
21 [a]Job 8:22 [b]Job 18:21; 36:12
1 [a]Job 15:15
2 [a]Prov. 12:16; 27:3
3 [a]Jer. 12:2 [b]Job 24:18; 31:30
4 [1]Lit., *crushed* [a]Job 4:11
5 [1]Lit., *Whose* [2]Ancient versions read, *thirsty* [a]Job 18:8-10; 22:10
6 [a]Job 15:35
7 [a]Job 14:1
8 [a]Job 13:2, 3
9 [1]Or, *Miracles* [a]Job 9:10; 37:14, 16; 42:3
10 [a]Job 36:27-29; 37:6-11; 38:26
11 [a]Job 22:29; 36:7
12 [a]Ps. 33:10
13 [a]Job 37:24; 1 Cor. 3:19
14 [a]Job 12:25; 15:30; 18:18; 20:26; 24:13
15 [a]Job 4:10, 11; Ps. 35:10 [b]Job 29:17; 34:28; 36:6, 15; 38:15

16"So the helpless has hope,
And [a]unrighteousness must shut its mouth.

17"Behold, how [a]happy is the man whom God reproves,
So do not despise the [b]discipline of [1]the Almighty.
18"For [a]He inflicts pain, and [1]gives relief;
He wounds, and His hands *also* heal.
19"[1]From six troubles He will deliver you,
Even in seven evil will not touch you.
20"In [a]famine He will redeem you from death,
And [b]in war from the power of the sword.
21"You will be [a]hidden from the scourge of the tongue,
[b]Neither will you be afraid of violence when it comes.
22"You will [a]laugh at violence and famine,
[b]Neither will you be afraid of [1]wild beasts.
23"For you will be in league with the stones of the field;
And [a]the beasts of the field will be at peace with you.
24"And you will know that your [a]tent is secure,
For you will visit your abode and fear no loss.
25"You will know also that your [1a]descendants will be many,
And [b]your offspring as the grass of the earth.
26"You will [a]come to the grave in full vigor,
Like the stacking of grain in its season.
27"Behold this, we have investigated it, thus it is;
Hear it, and know for yourself."

Chapter 6

Job's Friends Are No Help

THEN Job [1]answered,
2"[a]Oh that my vexation were actually weighed,
And laid in the balances together with my iniquity!
3"For then it would be [a]heavier than the sand of the seas,
Therefore my words have been rash.
4"For the [a]arrows of the Almighty are within me;
[1]Their [b]poison my spirit drinks;
The [c]terrors of God are arrayed against me.

5"Does the [a]wild donkey bray over *his* grass,
Or does the ox low over his fodder?
6"Can something tasteless be eaten without salt,
Or is there any taste in the [1]white of an egg?
7"My soul [a]refuses to touch *them;*
They are like loathsome food to me.

8"Oh that my request might come to pass,
And that God would grant my longing!
9"Would that God were [a]willing to crush me;
That He would loose His hand and cut me off!
10"But it is still my consolation,
And I rejoice in unsparing pain,
That I [a]have not [1]denied the words of the Holy One.
11"What is my strength, that I should wait?
And what is my end, that I should [1a]endure?
12"Is my strength the strength of stones,
Or is my flesh bronze?
13"Is it that my [a]help is not within me,
And that [1b]deliverance is driven from me?

14"For the [a]despairing man *there should be* kindness from his friend;
Lest he [b]forsake the [1]fear of the Almighty.
15"My brothers have acted [a]deceitfully like a [1]wadi,
Like the torrents of [1]wadis which vanish,
16 Which are turbid because of ice,
And into which the snow [1]melts.
17"When [a]they become waterless, they [1]are silent,
When it is hot, they vanish from their place.
18"The [1]paths of their course wind along,
They go up into nothing and perish.
19"The caravans of [a]Tema looked,
The travelers of [b]Sheba hoped for them.
20"They [a]were [1]disappointed for they had trusted,
They came there and were confounded.
21"Indeed, you have now become such,
You see a terror and are afraid.

16 [a]Ps. 107:42
17 [1]Heb., *Shaddai,* and so throughout chap. 6
[a]Ps. 94:12 [b]Job 36:15, 16; Prov. 3:11; Heb. 12:5-11
18 [1]Lit., *binds*
[a]Deut. 32:39; 1 Sam. 2:6; Is. 30:26; Hos. 6:1
19 [1]Lit., *In*
20 [a]Ps. 33:19; 37:19 [b]Ps. 144:10
21 [a]Job 5:15; Ps. 31:20 [b]Ps. 91:5, 6
22 [1]Lit., *beasts of the earth*
[a]Job 8:21 [b]Ps. 91:13; Ezek. 34:25; Hos. 2:18
23 [a]Is. 11:6-9; 65:25
24 [a]Job 8:6
25 [1]Lit., *seed*
[a]Ps. 112:2 [b]Is. 44:3, 4; 48:19
26 [a]Job 42:17
1 [1]Lit., *answered and said*
2 [a]Job 31:6
3 [a]Job 23:2
4 [1]Lit., *Whose*
[a]Job 16:13; Ps. 38:2 [b]Job 20:16; 21:20 [c]Job 30:15
5 [a]Job 39:5-8
6 [1]Heb., *hallamuth,* meaning uncertain. Perhaps the juice of a plant.
7 [a]Job 3:24; 33:20
9 [a]Num. 11:15; 1 Kin. 19:4; Job 7:16; 9:21; 10:1
10 [1]Lit., *hidden*
[a]Job 22:22; 23:11, 12
11 [1]Lit., *prolong my soul*
[a]Job 21:4
13 [1]So ancient versions
[a]Job 26:2 [b]Job 26:3
14 [1]Or, *reverence*
[a]Job 4:5 [b]Job 1:5; 15:4
15 [1]Or, *brooks*
[a]Jer. 15:18
16 [1]Lit., *hides itself*
17 [1]Or, *cease*
[a]Job 24:19
18 [1]Or, *caravans turn from their course, they go up into the waste and perish.*
19 [a]Gen. 25:15; Is. 21:14; Jer. 25:23 [b]Job 1:15
20 [1]Lit., *ashamed*
[a]Jer. 14:3

22"Have I said, 'Give me *something,*'
Or, 'Offer a bribe for me from your wealth,'
23 Or, 'Deliver me from the hand of the adversary,'
Or, 'Redeem me from the hand of the tyrants'?

24"Teach me, and I will be silent;
And show me how I have erred.
25"Honest words are [1]not painful,
But what does your argument prove?
26"Do you intend to reprove *my* words,
When the [a]words of one in despair belong to the wind?
27"You would even [a]cast *lots* for [b]the orphans,
And [c]barter over your friend.
28"And now please look at me,
And *see* if I [a]lie to your face.
29"Desist now, let there be no injustice;
Even desist, [a]my righteousness is yet in it.
30"Is there injustice on my tongue?
Cannot [a]my palate discern [1]calamities?

Chapter 7

Job's Life Seems Futile

"[1]Is not man [a]forced to labor on earth,
And *are not* his days like the days of [b]a hired man?
2"As a slave who pants for the shade,
And as a hired man who eagerly waits for his wages,
3 So am I allotted months of vanity,
And [a]nights of trouble are appointed me.
4"When I [a]lie down I say,
'When shall I arise?'
But the night continues,
And I am [1]continually tossing until dawn.
5"My [a]flesh is clothed with worms and a crust of dirt;
My skin hardens and runs.
6"My days are [a]swifter than a weaver's shuttle,
And come to an end [b]without hope.

7"Remember that my life [a]is *but* breath,
My eye will [b]not again see good.
8"The [a]eye of him who sees me will behold me no more;
Thine eyes *will be* on me, but [b]I will not be.
9"When a [a]cloud vanishes, it is gone,
So [b]he who goes down to [c]Sheol does not come up.
10"He will not return again to his house,
Nor will [a]his place know him any more.

11"Therefore, [a]I will not restrain my mouth;
I will speak in the anguish of my spirit,
I will complain in the bitterness of my soul.
12"Am I the sea, or [a]the sea monster,
That Thou dost set a guard over me?
13"If I say, '[a]My bed will comfort me,
My couch will [1]ease my complaint,'
14 Then Thou dost frighten me with dreams
And terrify me by visions;
15 So that my soul would choose suffocation,
Death rather than my [1]pains.
16"I [1a]waste away; I will not live forever.
Leave me alone, [b]for my days are *but* a breath.
17"[a]What is man that Thou dost magnify him,
And that Thou [1]art concerned about him,
18 That [a]Thou dost examine him every morning,
And try him every moment?
19"[1a]Wilt Thou never turn Thy gaze away from me,
Nor let me alone until I swallow my spittle?
20"[a]Have I sinned? What have I done to Thee,
O watcher of men?
Why hast Thou set me as Thy target,
So that I am a burden to myself?
21"Why then [a]dost Thou not pardon my transgression
And take away my iniquity?
For now I will [b]lie down in the dust;
And Thou wilt seek me, [c]but I will not be."

Chapter 8

Bildad Says God Rewards the Good

Then Bildad the Shuhite [1]answered,

25 [1]Or, *in what way...?*
26 [a]Job 8:2; 15:2; 16:3
27 [a]Joel 3:3; Nah. 3:10 [b]Job 22:9; 24:3, 9 [c]2 Pet. 2:3
28 [a]Job 27:4; 33:3; 36:4
29 [a]Job 13:18; 19:6; 23:10; 27:5, 6; 34:5; 42:1-6
30 [1]Or, *words* [a]Job 12:11
1 [1]Lit., *Has not man compulsory labor* [a]Job 5:7; 10:17; 14:1, 14 [b]Job 14:6
3 [a]Job 16:7
4 [1]Lit., *sated with* [a]Job 7:13, 14; Deut. 28:67
5 [a]Job 2:7
6 [a]Job 9:25 [b]Job 13:15; 14:19; 17:15, 16; 19:10
7 [a]Job 7:16 [b]Job 9:25
8 [a]Job 8:18; 20:9 [b]Job 7:21
9 [a]Job 30:15 [b]Job 3:13-19 [c]Job 11:8; 14:13; 17:13, 16
10 [a]Job 8:18; 20:9; 27:21, 23
11 [a]Job 10:1; 21:4; 23:2
12 [a]Ezek. 32:2, 3
13 [1]Lit., *bear* [a]Job 7:4; Ps. 6:6
15 [1]Lit., *bones*
16 [1]Or, *loathe* my life [a]Job 6:9; 9:21; 10:1 [b]Job 7:7
17 [1]Lit., *shouldst set Thy heart on* [a]Job 22:2; Ps. 8:4; 144:3; Heb. 2:6
18 [a]Job 14:3
19 [1]Lit., *How long wilt Thou not* [a]Job 9:18; 10:20; 14:6
20 [a]Job 35:3, 6
21 [a]Job 9:28; 10:14 [b]Job 10:9 [c]Job 7:8
1 [1]Lit., *answered and said*

2"How long will you say these
things,
And the [a]words of your mouth
be a mighty wind?
3"Does [a]God pervert justice
Or does [1]the Almighty pervert
what is right?
4"[a]If your sons sinned against
Him,
Then He delivered them into
the [1]power of their transgression.
5"If you would [a]seek God
And implore the compassion of
the Almighty,
6 If you are pure and upright,
Surely now [a]He would rouse
Himself for you
And restore your righteous
[1b]estate.
7"Though your beginning was insignificant,
Yet your [a]end will increase
greatly.

8"Please [a]inquire of past generations,
And consider the things
searched out by their fathers.
9"For we are *only* of yesterday
and know nothing,
Because [a]our days on earth are
as a shadow.
10"Will they not teach you *and* tell
you,
And bring forth words from
their minds?

11"Can the papyrus grow up without marsh?
Can the rushes grow without
water?
12"While it is still green *and* not
cut down,
Yet it withers before any *other*
[1]plant.
13"So are the paths of [a]all who forget God,
And the [b]hope of the godless
will perish,
14 Whose confidence is fragile,
And whose trust a [a]spider's
[1]web.
15"He [1]trusts in his [a]house, but it
does not stand;
He holds fast to it, but it does
not endure.
16"He [1a]thrives before the sun,
And his [b]shoots spread out over
his garden.
17"His roots wrap around a rock
pile,
He [1]grasps a house of stones.
18"If he is [1]removed from [a]his
place,
Then it will deny him, *saying,* 'I
never saw you.'
19"Behold, this is the joy of His
way;
And out of the dust others will
spring.
20"Lo, [a]God will not reject *a man
of* integrity,
Nor will He [1]support the evildoers.
21"He will yet fill [a]your mouth
with laughter,
And your lips with [b]shouting.
22"Those who hate you will be
[a]clothed with shame;
And the [b]tent of the wicked will
be no more."

Chapter 9

Job Says There Is No Umpire between God and Man

THEN Job [1]answered,
2"In truth I know that this is so,
But how can a [a]man be in the
right [1]before God?
3"If one wished to [a]dispute with
Him,
He could not [b]answer Him once
in a thousand *times.*
4"[a]Wise in heart and [b]mighty in
strength,
Who has [1c]defied Him [2]without
harm?
5"[a]*It is God* who removes the
mountains, they know not
how,
When He overturns them in His
anger;
6 Who [a]shakes the earth out of its
place,
And its [b]pillars tremble;
7 Who commands the [a]sun [1]not
to shine,
And sets a seal upon the stars;
8 Who alone [a]stretches out the
heavens,
And [b]tramples down the waves
of the sea;
9 Who makes the [a]Bear, Orion,
and the Pleiades,
And the [b]chambers of the
south;
10 Who [a]does great things, [1]un-
fathomable,
And wondrous works without
number.
11"Were He to pass by me, [a]I
would not see Him;
Were He to move past *me,* I
would not perceive Him.
12"Were He to snatch away, who
could [a]restrain Him?
Who could say to Him, '[b]What
art Thou doing?'

13"God will not turn back His anger;

2 [a]Job 6:26
3 [1]Heb., *Shaddai,* also v. 5 [a]Gen. 18:25; Deut. 32:4; 2 Chr. 19:7; Job 34:10, 12
4 [1]Lit., *hand* [a]Job 1:5, 18, 19
5 [a]Job 5:17-27
6 [1]Lit., *place* [a]Job 22:27; 34:28; Ps. 7:6 [b]Job 5:24
7 [a]Job 42:12
8 [a]Deut. 4:32; 32:7; Job 15:18
9 [a]Job 14:2
12 [1]Lit., *reed*
13 [a]Ps. 9:17 [b]Job 11:20; 13:16; 15:34; 20:5; 27:8
14 [1]Lit., *house* [a]Is. 59:5, 6
15 [1]Lit., *leans on* [a]Job 8:22; 27:18; Ps. 49:11
16 [1]Lit., *is lush* [a]Ps. 37:35; Jer. 11:16 [b]Ps. 80:11
17 [1]Heb., *sees*
18 [1]Lit., *swallowed up* [a]Job 7:10
20 [1]Lit., *strengthen the hand of* [a]Job 4:7
21 [a]Job 5:22; Ps. 126:1, 2 [b]Ps. 132:16
22 [a]Ps. 132:18 [b]Job 8:15; 15:34; 18:14; 21:28
1 [1]Lit., *answered and said*
2 [1]Lit., *with* [a]Job 4:17; 25:4
3 [a]Job 10:2; 13:19; 23:6; 40:2 [b]Job 15:32
4 [1]Lit., *stiffened his neck against* [2]Lit., *and remained safe* [a]Job 11:6; 12:13; 28:23; 38:36, 37 [b]Job 9:19; 23:6 [c]2 Chr. 13:12; Prov. 29:1
5 [a]Job 9:5-10; 26:6-14; 41:11
6 [a]Is. 2:19, 21; 13:13; Hag. 2:6 [b]Ps. 75:3
7 [1]Lit., *and it does not shine* [a]Is. 13:10; Ezek. 32:7, 8
8 [a]Gen. 1:1; Job 37:18; Ps. 104:2; Is. 40:22 [b]Job 38:16; Ps. 77:19
9 [a]Job 38:31, 32; Amos 5:8 [b]Job 37:9
10 [1]Lit., *until there is no searching out* [a]Job 5:9
11 [a]Job 23:8, 9
12 [a]Job 10:7; 11:10 [b]Is. 45:9

Beneath Him crouch the helpers of [a]Rahab.
14 "How then can [a]I [1]answer Him,
And choose my words [2]before Him?
15 "For [a]though I were right, I could not [1]answer;
I would have to [b]implore the mercy of my judge.
16 "If I called and He answered me,
I could not believe that He was listening to my voice.
17 "For He [a]bruises me with a tempest,
And multiplies my wounds without cause.
18 "He will [a]not allow me to get my breath,
But saturates me with [b]bitterness.
19 "If *it is a matter* of power, [a]behold, *He is* the strong one!
And if *it is a matter* of justice, who can summon [1]Him?
20 "[a]Though I am righteous, my mouth will [b]condemn me;
Though I am guiltless, He will declare me guilty.
21 "I am [a]guiltless;
I do not take notice of myself;
I [b]despise my life.
22 "It is *all* one; therefore I say,
'He [a]destroys the guiltless and the wicked.'
23 "If the scourge kills suddenly,
He [a]mocks the despair of the innocent.
24 "The earth [a]is given into the hand of the wicked;
He [b]covers the faces of its judges.
If *it is* not *He*, then who is it?

25 "Now [a]my days are swifter than a runner;
They flee away, [b]they see no good.
26 "They slip by like [a]reed boats,
Like an [b]eagle that swoops on [1]its prey.
27 "Though I say, 'I will forget [a]my complaint,
I will leave off my *sad* countenance and be cheerful,'
28 I am [a]afraid of all my pains,
I know that [b]Thou wilt not acquit me.
29 "I am accounted [a]wicked,
Why then should I toil in vain?
30 "If I should [a]wash myself with snow
And cleanse [b]my hands with lye,
31 Yet Thou wouldst plunge me into the pit,
And [a]my own clothes would abhor me.
32 "For *He is* not a man as I am that [a]I may answer Him,
That we may go to [1]court together.
33 "There is no [a]umpire between us,
Who may lay his hand upon us both.
34 "Let Him [a]remove his rod from me,
And let not dread of Him terrify me.
35 "*Then* I [a]would speak and not fear Him;
But I am not like that in myself.

Chapter 10

Job Despairs of God's Dealings

"[1a]I LOATHE my own life;
I will give full vent to [b]my complaint;
I will speak in the bitterness of my soul.
2 "I will say to God, '[a]Do not condemn me;
Let me know why Thou dost contend with me.
3 'Is it [1]right for Thee indeed to [a]oppress,
To reject [b]the labor of Thy hands,
And [2]to look favorably on [c]the schemes of the wicked?
4 'Hast Thou eyes of flesh?
Or dost Thou [a]see as a man sees?
5 'Are Thy days as the days of a mortal,
Or [a]Thy years as man's years,
6 That [a]Thou shouldst seek for my guilt,
And search after my sin?
7 'According to Thy knowledge [a]I am indeed not guilty;
Yet there is [b]no deliverance from Thy hand.

8 '[a]Thy hands fashioned and made me [1]altogether,
[b]And wouldst Thou destroy me?
9 'Remember now, that Thou hast made me as [a]clay;
And wouldst Thou [b]turn me into dust again?
10 'Didst Thou not pour me out like milk,
And curdle me like cheese;
11 Clothe me with skin and flesh,
And knit me together with bones and sinews?
12 'Thou hast [a]granted me life and lovingkindness;

13 [a]Job 26:12; Ps. 89:10; Is. 30:7; 51:9
14 [1]Or, *plead my case* [2]Lit., *with* [a]Job 9:3, 32
15 [1]Or, *plead my case* [a]Job 9:20, 21; 10:15 [b]Job 8:5
17 [a]Job 16:12, 14; 30:22
18 [a]Job 7:19; 10:20 [b]Job 13:26; 27:2
19 [1]So with Gk., Heb., *me* [a]Job 9:4
20 [a]Job 9:15 [b]Job 9:29; 15:6
21 [a]Job 1:1; 12:4; 13:18 [b]Job 7:16
22 [a]Job 10:7, 8
23 [a]Job 24:12
24 [a]Job 10:3; 12:6; 16:11 [b]Job 12:17
25 [a]Job 7:6 [b]Job 7:7
26 [1]Lit., *food* [a]Is. 18:2 [b]Job 39:29; Hab. 1:8
27 [a]Job 7:11
28 [a]Job 3:25 [b]Job 7:21; 10:14
29 [a]Job 10:2; Ps. 37:33
30 [a]Jer. 2:22 [b]Job 31:7
31 [a]Job 7:17
32 [1]Lit., *judgment* [a]Job 9:3
33 [a]1 Sam. 2:25; Job 9:19; Is. 1:18
34 [a]Job 13:21
35 [a]Job 13:22
1 [1]Lit., *My soul* [a]Job 7:16 [b]Job 7:11
2 [a]Job 9:29
3 [1]Lit., *good* [2]Lit., *you shine forth* [a]Job 9:22-24; 16:11; 19:6; 27:2 [b]Job 10:8; 14:15; Ps. 138:8; Is. 64:8 [c]Job 21:16; 22:18
4 [a]1 Sam. 16:7; Job 28:24; 34:21
5 [a]Job 36:26
6 [a]Job 14:16
7 [a]Job 9:21; 13:18 [b]Job 9:12; 23:13; 27:22
8 [1]Lit., *together round about* [a]Job 10:3; Ps. 119:73 [b]Job 9:22
9 [a]Job 4:19; 33:6 [b]Job 7:21
12 [a]Job 33:4

And Thy care has preserved my spirit.
13 'Yet [a]these things Thou hast concealed in Thy heart;
I know that this is within Thee:
14 If I sin, then Thou wouldst [a]take note of me,
And [b]wouldst not acquit me of my guilt.
15 'If [a]I am wicked, woe to me!
And [b]if I am righteous, I dare not lift up my head.
I am sated with disgrace and [1]conscious of my misery.
16 'And should *my head* be lifted up, [a]Thou wouldst hunt me like a lion;
And again Thou wouldst show Thy [b]power against me.
17 'Thou dost renew [a]Thy witnesses against me,
And increase Thine anger toward me,
[b]Hardship after hardship is with me.

18 '[a]Why then hast Thou brought me out of the womb?
Would that I had died and no eye had seen me!
19 'I should have been as though I had not been,
Carried from womb to tomb.'
20 "Would He not let [a]my few days alone?
[1b]Withdraw from me that I may have a little cheer
21 Before I go—[a]and I shall not return—
To the land of darkness and [b]deep shadow;
22 The land of utter gloom as darkness *itself*,
Of deep shadow without order,
And which shines as the darkness."

Chapter 11

Zophar Rebukes Job

THEN Zophar the Naamathite [1]answered,
2 "Shall a multitude of words go unanswered,
And a [a]talkative man be acquitted?
3 "Shall your boasts silence men?
And shall you [a]scoff and none rebuke?
4 "For [a]you have said, 'My teaching is pure,
And [b]I am innocent in your eyes.'
5 "But would that God might speak,
And open His lips against you,
6 And show you the secrets of wisdom!
For sound wisdom [1a]has two sides.
Know then that God [2]forgets a part of [b]your iniquity.

7 "[a]Can you discover the depths of God?
Can you discover the limits of the Almighty?
8 "*They are* [a]high as [1]the heavens, what can you do?
Deeper than [2b]Sheol, what can you know?
9 "Its measure is longer than the earth,
And broader than the sea.
10 "If He passes by or shuts up,
Or calls an assembly, [a]who can restrain Him?
11 "For [a]He knows false men,
And He [b]sees iniquity [1]without investigating.
12 "And [1a]an idiot will become intelligent
When the [2]foal of a [b]wild donkey is born a man.

13 "[a]If you would [b]direct your heart right,
And [c]spread out your hand to Him;
14 If iniquity is in your hand, [a]put it far away,
And do not let wickedness dwell in your tents.
15 "Then, indeed, you could [a]lift up your face without *moral* defect,
And you would be steadfast and [b]not fear.
16 "For you would [a]forget *your* trouble,
As [b]waters that have passed by, you would remember *it*.
17 "And your [1]life would be [2a]brighter than noonday;
Darkness would be like the morning.
18 "Then you would trust, because there is hope;
And you would look around and rest securely.
19 "You would [a]lie down and none would disturb *you*,
And many would [b]entreat your [1]favor.
20 "But the [a]eyes of the wicked will fail,
And [1]there will [b]be no escape for them;
And their [c]hope is [2d]to breathe their last."

13 [a]Job 23:13
14 [a]Job 7:20 [b]Job 7:21; 9:28
15 [1]Lit., *see* [a]Job 10:7 [b]Job 6:29
16 [a]Is. 38:13; Lam. 3:10; Hos. 13:7 [b]Job 5:9
17 [a]Ruth 1:21; Job 16:8 [b]Job 7:1
18 [a]Job 3:11-13
20 [1]Lit., *Put* [a]Job 14:1 [b]Job 7:19
21 [a]2 Sam. 12:23; Job 3:13-19; 16:22 [b]Job 10:22; 34:22; 38:17
1 [1]Lit., *answered and said*
2 [a]Job 8:2; 15:2; 18:2
3 [a]Job 17:2; 21:3
4 [a]Job 6:10 [b]Job 10:7
6 [1]Lit., *is double* [2]Lit., *causes to be forgotten for you* [a]Job 9:4 [b]Job 15:5; 22:5
7 [a]Job 33:12, 13; 36:26; 37:5, 23
8 [1]Lit., *the heights of heaven* [2]I.e., the nether world [a]Job 22:12; 35:5 [b]Job 26:6; 38:17
10 [a]Job 9:12
11 [1]Or, *even He does not consider* [a]Job 34:21-23 [b]Job 24:23; 28:24; 31:4
12 [1]Lit., *a hollow man* [2]Lit., *donkey* [a]Ps. 39:5, 11; 62:9; 144:4; Eccles. 1:2; 10:11 [b]Job 39:5
13 [a]Job 5:17-27; 11:13-20 [b]Ps. 78:8 [c]Job 22:27; Ps. 88:9; 143:6
14 [a]Job 22:23
15 [a]Job 22:26 [b]Ps. 27:3; 46:2
16 [a]Is. 65:16 [b]Job 22:11
17 [1]Lit., *duration of life* [2]Lit., *above noonday* [a]Job 22:26
19 [1]Lit., *face* [a]Lev. 26:6; Is. 17:2; Mic. 4:4; Zeph. 3:13 [b]Is. 45:14
20 [1]Lit., *escape has perished from them* [2]Lit., *the expiring of the soul* [a]Deut. 28:65; Job 17:5 [b]Job 27:22; 34:22 [c]Job 8:13 [d]Job 6:9

Chapter 12

Job Chides His Accusers

THEN Job [1]responded,
2"Truly then [a]you are the people,
And with you wisdom will die!
3"But [a]I have intelligence as well as you;
I am not inferior to you.
And [1]who does not know such things as these?
4"I am a [a]joke to [1]my friends.
The one who called on God, and He answered him;
The just *and* [b]blameless *man* is a joke.
5"[1]He who is at ease holds calamity in contempt,
As prepared for those whose feet slip.
6"The [a]tents of the destroyers prosper,
And those who provoke God [b]are secure,
[1]Whom God brings [c]into his power.

7"But now ask the beasts, and let them teach you;
And the birds of the heavens, and let them tell you.
8"Or speak to the earth, and let it teach you;
And let the fish of the sea declare to you.
9"Who among all these does not know
That [a]the hand of the LORD has done this,
10 [a]In whose hand is the life of every living thing,
And [b]the breath of all mankind?
11"Does not [a]the ear test words,
As the palate [1]tastes its food?
12"Wisdom is with [a]aged men,
With [1]long life is understanding.

Job Speaks of the Power of God

13"With Him are [a]wisdom and [b]might;
To Him belong counsel and [c]understanding.
14"Behold, He [a]tears down, and it cannot be rebuilt;
He [1b]imprisons a man, and [2]there can be no release.
15"Behold, He [a]restrains the waters, and they dry up;
And He [b]sends them out, and they [1]inundate the earth.
16"With Him are strength and sound wisdom,
The [a]misled and the misleader belong to Him.
17"He makes [a]counselors walk [1b]barefoot,
And makes fools of [c]judges.
18"He [a]loosens the [1]bond of kings,
And binds their loins with a girdle.
19"He makes priests walk [1]barefoot,
And overthrows [a]the secure ones.
20"He deprives the trusted ones of speech,
And [a]takes away the discernment of the elders.
21"He [a]pours contempt on nobles,
And [b]loosens the belt of the strong.
22"He [a]reveals mysteries from the darkness,
And brings the deep darkness into light.
23"He [a]makes the nations great, then destroys them;
He [1]enlarges the nations, then leads them away.
24"He [a]deprives of intelligence the chiefs of the earth's people,
And makes them wander in a pathless waste.
25"They [a]grope in darkness with no light,
And He makes them [b]stagger like a drunken man.

Chapter 13

Job Says His Friends' Proverbs Are Ashes

"[a]BEHOLD, my eye has seen all *this,*
My ear has heard and understood it.
2"[a]What you know I also know.
I am not inferior to you.

3"But [a]I would speak to the [1]Almighty,
And I desire to [b]argue with God.
4"But you [a]smear with lies;
You are all [b]worthless physicians.
5"O that you would [a]be completely silent,
And that it would become your wisdom!
6"Please hear my argument,
And listen to the contentions of my lips.
7"Will you [a]speak what is unjust for God,
And speak what is deceitful for Him?
8"Will you [a]show partiality for Him?
Will you contend for God?

1 [1]Lit., *answered and said*
2 [a]Job 2:3; 16:1, 2; 17:10
3 [1]Lit., *with whom is there not like these?* [a]Job 13:2
4 [1]Lit., *his* [a]Job 17:6; 30:1, 9, 10; 34:7 [b]Job 6:29
5 [1]Lit., *Contempt for calamity is the thought of him who is at ease*
6 [1]Or, *He who brings God into his hand* [a]Job 9:24; 21:9 [b]Job 24:23 [c]Job 22:18
9 [a]Is. 41:20
10 [a]Acts 17:28 [b]Job 27:3; 33:4
11 [1]Lit., *tastes food for itself* [a]Job 34:3
12 [1]Lit., *length of days* [a]Job 15:10; 32:7
13 [a]Job 9:4 [b]Job 9:4 [c]Job 11:6; 26:12; 32:8; 36:5; 38:36
14 [1]Lit., *shuts against* [2]Lit., *it is not opened* [a]Job 19:10; Is. 25:2 [b]Job 37:7
15 [1]Lit., *overturn* [a]Deut. 11:17; 1 Kin. 8:35; 17:1 [b]Gen. 7:11-24
16 [a]Job 13:7, 9
17 [1]Or, *stripped* [a]Job 3:14 [b]Job 19:9 [c]Job 9:24
18 [1]Or, *discipline* [a]Ps. 116:16
19 [1]Or, *stripped* [a]Job 21:7; 22:8; 24:22; 34:24-28; 35:9
20 [a]Job 17:4; 32:9
21 [a]Job 34:19; Ps. 107:40 [b]Job 12:18
22 [a]Dan. 2:22; 1 Cor. 4:5
23 [1]Or, *spreads out* [a]Is. 9:3; 26:15
24 [a]Job 12:20
25 [a]Job 5:14 [b]Is. 24:20
1 [a]Job 12:9
2 [a]Job 12:3
3 [1]Heb., *Shaddai* [a]Job 13:22; 23:4 [b]Job 13:15
4 [a]Ps. 119:69 [b]Jer. 23:32
5 [a]Job 13:13; 21:5
7 [a]Job 27:4
8 [a]Lev. 19:15

9"Will it be well when He examines you?
Or [a]will you deceive Him as one deceives a man?
10"He will surely reprove you,
If you secretly [a]show partiality.
11"Will not [a]His [1]majesty terrify you,
And the dread of Him fall on you?
12"Your memorable sayings are [a]proverbs of ashes,
Your defenses are defenses of clay.

Job Is Sure He Will Be Vindicated

13"[a]Be silent before me so that I may speak;
Then let come on me what may.
14"Why should I take my flesh in my teeth,
And put my life in my [1]hands?
15"[a]Though He slay me,
I [b]will hope in Him.
Nevertheless I will argue my ways [1]before Him.
16"This also will be my [a]salvation,
For [b]a godless man may not come before His presence.
17"Listen carefully to my speech,
And let my declaration *fill* your ears.
18"Behold now, I have [a]prepared my case;
I know that [b]I will be vindicated.
19"Who will contend with me?
For then I would be silent and [a]die.

20"Only two things do not do to me,
Then I will not hide from Thy face:
21 [a]Remove Thy [1]hand from me,
And let not the dread of Thee terrify me.
22"Then call, and [a]I will answer;
Or let me speak, then reply to me.
23"[a]How many are my iniquities and sins?
Make known to me my [1]rebellion and my sin.
24"Why dost Thou [a]hide Thy face,
And consider me [b]Thine enemy?
25"Wilt Thou cause a [a]driven leaf to tremble?
Or wilt Thou pursue the dry [b]chaff?
26"For Thou dost write [a]bitter things against me,
And dost make me to inherit the iniquities of my youth.
27"Thou [a]dost put my feet in the stocks,
And dost watch all my paths;
Thou dost [1]set a limit for the soles of my feet,
28 While [1]I am decaying like a [a]rotten thing,
Like a garment that is moth-eaten.

Chapter 14

Job Speaks of the Finality of Death

"[a]MAN, who is born of woman,
Is [1]short-lived and full of turmoil.
2"[a]Like a flower he comes forth and withers.
He also flees like [b]a shadow and does not remain.
3"Thou also dost [a]open Thine eyes on him,
And bring [1]him into judgment with Thyself.
4"[a]Who can make the clean out of the unclean?
No one!
5"Since his days are determined,
The [a]number of his months is with Thee,
And his limits Thou hast [1]set so that he cannot pass.
6"[a]Turn your gaze from him that he may [1]rest,
Until he [2]fulfills his day like a hired man.

7"For there is hope for a tree,
When it is cut down, that it will sprout again,
And its shoots will not [1]fail.
8"Though its roots grow old in the ground,
And its stump dies in the dry soil,
9 At the scent of water it will flourish
And put forth sprigs like a plant.
10"But [a]man [b]dies and lies prostrate.
Man expires, and where is he?
11"*As* [a]water [1]evaporates from the sea,
And a river becomes parched and dried up,
12 So [a]man lies down and does not rise.
Until the heavens be no more,
[1]He will not awake nor be aroused out of [2]his sleep.

13"Oh that Thou wouldst [a]hide me in [1]Sheol,
That Thou wouldst conceal me [b]until Thy wrath returns *to Thee*,

9 [a]Job 12:16
10 [a]Job 13:8; 32:21; 34:19
11 [1]Lit., *exaltation* [a]Job 31:23
12 [a]Job 27:1; 29:1
13 [a]Job 13:5
14 [1]Lit., *palm*
15 [1]Lit., *to His face* [a]Job 7:6 [b]Job 27:5
16 [a]Job 23:7 [b]Job 34:21-23
18 [a]Job 6:29; 23:4 [b]Job 9:21; 10:7; 12:4
19 [a]Job 7:21; 10:8
21 [1]Lit., *palm* [a]Job 9:34; Ps. 39:10
22 [a]Job 9:16; 14:15
23 [1]Or, *transgression* [a]Job 7:21
24 [a]Ps. 13:1; 44:24; 88:14 [b]Job 19:11; 33:10
25 [a]Lev. 26:36 [b]Job 21:18
26 [a]Job 9:18
27 [1]Lit., *carve for* [a]Job 33:11
28 [1]Lit., *he* [a]Job 2:7
1 [1]Lit., *short of days* [a]Job 5:7
2 [a]Ps. 90:5, 6; 103:15; Is. 40:6, 7 [b]Job 8:9
3 [1]So with some ancient versions; M.T., *me* [a]Ps. 8:4; 144:3
4 [a]Job 15:14; 25:4
5 [1]Lit., *made* [a]Job 21:21
6 [1]Lit., *cease* [2]Lit., *makes acceptable* [a]Job 7:19
7 [1]Or, *cease*
10 [a]Job 3:13; 14:10-15 [b]Job 13:9
11 [1]Lit., *disappears* [a]Is. 19:5
12 [1]Lit., *They* [2]Lit., *their* [a]Job 3:13
13 [1]I.e., the nether world [a]Job 3:13 [b]Is. 26:20

That Thou wouldst set a limit
for me and remember me!
14“If a man dies, will he live *again?*
All the days of my struggle I
will wait,
Until my change comes.
15“Thou wilt call, and I will answer
Thee;
Thou wilt long for [a]the work of
Thy hands.
16“For now Thou dost [a]number my
steps,
Thou dost not [b]observe my sin.
17“My transgression is [a]sealed up
in a bag,
And Thou dost [1]wrap up my iniquity.

18“But the falling mountain
[1]crumbles away,
And the rock moves from its
place;
19 Water wears away stones,
Its torrents wash away the dust
of the earth;
So Thou dost [a]destroy man’s
hope.
20“Thou dost forever overpower
him and he [a]departs;
Thou dost change his appearance and send him away.
21“His sons achieve honor, but he
does not know *it;*
Or they become insignificant,
but he does not perceive it.
22“But his [1]body pains him,
And he mourns only for himself.”

Chapter 15

Eliphaz Says Job Presumes Much

THEN Eliphaz the Temanite [1]re-
sponded,
2“Should a wise man answer with
windy knowledge,
[a]And fill [1]himself with the east
wind?
3“Should he argue with useless
talk,
Or with words which are not
profitable?
4“Indeed, you do away with [1]rev-
erence,
And hinder meditation before
God.
5“For [a]your guilt teaches your
mouth,
And you choose the language of
[b]the crafty.
6“Your [a]own mouth condemns
you, and not I;
And your own lips testify
against you.
7“Were you the first man to be
born,
Or [a]were you brought forth before the hills?
8“Do you hear the [a]secret counsel
of God,
And limit wisdom to yourself?
9“[a]What do you know that we do
not know?
What do you understand that
[1]we do not?
10“Both the [a]gray-haired and the
aged are among us,
Older than your father.
11“Are [a]the consolations of God
too small for you,
Even the [b]word *spoken* gently
with you?
12“Why does your [a]heart carry
you away?
And why do your eyes flash,
13 That you should turn your spirit
against God,
And allow *such* words to go out
of your mouth?
14“What is man, that [a]he should be
pure,
Or [b]he who is born of a woman,
that he should be righteous?
15“Behold, He puts no trust in His
[a]holy ones,
And the [b]heavens are not pure
in His sight;
16 How much less one who is [a]de-
testable and corrupt,
Man, who [b]drinks iniquity like
water!

What Eliphaz Has Seen of Life

17“I will tell you, listen to me;
And what I have seen I will also
declare;
18 What wise men have told,
And have not concealed from
[a]their fathers,
19 To whom alone the land was
given,
And no alien passed among
them.
20“The wicked man writhes [a]in
pain all *his* days,
And [1]numbered are the years
[b]stored up for the ruthless.
21“[1]Sounds of [a]terror are in his
ears,
[b]While at peace the destroyer
comes upon him.
22“He does not believe that he will
[a]return from darkness,
And he is destined for [b]the
sword.
23“He wanders about for food,
saying, ‘Where is it?’
He knows that a day of [a]dark-
ness is [1]at hand.
24“Distress and anguish terrify
him,

15 [a]Job 10:3
16 [a]Job 31:4; 34:21 [b]Job 10:6
17 [1]Lit., *plaster or glue together* [a]Deut. 32:32-34
18 [1]Lit., *withers*
19 [a]Job 7:6
20 [a]Job 4:20; 20:7
22 [1]Lit., *flesh*
1 [1]Lit., *answered and said*
2 [1]Lit., *his belly* [a]Job 6:26
4 [1]Lit., *fear*
5 [a]Job 22:5 [b]Job 5:12, 13
6 [a]Job 18:7
7 [a]Job 38:4, 21
8 [a]Job 29:4; Rom. 11:34
9 [1]Lit., *is not within us?* [a]Job 12:3; 13:2
10 [a]Job 12:12; 32:6, 7
11 [a]Job 5:17-19; 36:15, 16 [b]Job 6:10; 23:12
12 [a]Job 11:13; 36:13
14 [a]Job 14:4 [b]Job 25:4
15 [a]Job 5:1 [b]Job 25:5
16 [a]Ps. 14:1 [b]Job 34:7
18 [a]Job 8:8; 20:4
20 [1]Lit., *the number of years are* [a]Job 15:24 [b]Job 24:1; 27:13
21 [1]Lit., *A sound of terrors* [a]Job 15:24; 18:11; 20:25; 24:17; 27:20 [b]Job 20:21; 1 Thess. 5:3
22 [a]Job 15:30 [b]Job 19:29; 27:14; 33:18; 36:12
23 [1]Lit., *ready at his hand* [a]Job 15:22, 30

They overpower him like a king ready for the attack,
25 Because he has stretched out his hand against God,
And conducts himself [a]arrogantly against [1]the Almighty.
26"He rushes [1]headlong at Him
With [2]his massive shield.
27"For he has [a]covered his face with his fat,
And made his thighs heavy with flesh.
28"And he has [a]lived in desolate cities,
In houses no one would inhabit,
Which are destined to become [1]ruins.
29"He [a]will not become rich, nor will his wealth endure;
And his grain will not bend down to the ground.
30"He will [a]not [1]escape from darkness;
The [b]flame will wither his shoots,
And by [c]the breath of His mouth he will go away.
31"Let him not [a]trust in emptiness, deceiving himself;
For emptiness will be his [1]reward.
32"It will be accomplished [a]before his time,
And his palm [b]branch will not be green.
33"He will drop off his unripe grape like the vine,
And will [a]cast off his flower like the olive tree.
34"For the company of [a]the godless is barren,
And fire consumes [b]the tents of the corrupt.
35"They [a]conceive [1]mischief and bring forth iniquity,
And their [2]mind prepares deception."

Chapter 16

Job Says Friends Are Sorry Comforters

THEN Job [1]answered,
2"I have heard many such things;
[1a]Sorry comforters are you all.
3"Is there *no* limit to [a]windy words?
Or what plagues you that you answer?
4"I too could speak like you,
If I were in your place.
I could compose words against you,
And [a]shake my head at you.
5"I could strengthen you with my mouth,
And the solace of my lips could lessen *your pain.*

Job Says God Shattered Him

6"If I speak, [a]my pain is not lessened,
And if I hold back, what has left me?
7"But now He has [a]exhausted me;
Thou hast laid [b]waste all my company.
8"And Thou hast shriveled me up,
[a]It has become a witness;
And my [b]leanness rises up against me,
It testifies to my face.
9"His anger has [a]torn me and [1]hunted me down,
He has [b]gnashed at me with His teeth;
My [c]adversary [2]glares at me.
10"They have [a]gaped at me with their mouth,
They have [1b]slapped me on the cheek with contempt;
They have [c]massed themselves against me.
11"God hands me over to ruffians,
And tosses me into the hands of the wicked.
12"I was at ease, but [a]He shattered me,
And He has grasped me by the neck and shaken me to pieces;
He has also set me up as His [b]target.
13"His [a]arrows surround me.
Without mercy He splits my kidneys open;
He pours out [b]my gall on the ground.
14"He [a]breaks through me with breach after breach;
He [b]runs at me like a warrior.
15"I have sewed [a]sackcloth over my skin,
And thrust my [b]horn in the dust.
16"My face is flushed from [a]weeping,
[b]And deep darkness is on my eyelids,
17 Although there is no [a]violence in my hands,
And [b]my prayer is pure.

18"O earth, do not cover my blood,
And let there be no *resting* place for my cry.
19"Even now, behold, [a]my witness is in heaven,
And my [1]advocate is [b]on high.

25 [1]Heb., *Shaddai* [a]Job 36:9
26 [1]Lit., *with a stiff neck* [2]Lit., *the thick-bossed shields*
27 [a]Ps. 17:10; 73:7; 119:70
28 [1]Or, *heaps* [a]Job 3:14; Is. 5:8, 9
29 [a]Job 27:16, 17
30 [1]Lit., *turn aside* [a]Job 5:14; 15:22 [b]Job 15:34; 20:26; 22:20; 31:12 [c]Job 4:9
31 [1]Lit., *exchange* [a]Job 35:13; Is. 59:4
32 [a]Job 22:16; Eccles. 7:17 [b]Job 18:16
33 [a]Job 14:2
34 [a]Job 8:13 [b]Job 8:22
35 [1]Or, *pain* [2]Lit., *belly* [a]Ps. 7:14; Is. 59:4
1 [1]Lit., *answered and said*
2 [1]Lit., *Comforters of trouble* [a]Job 13:4; 21:34
3 [a]Job 6:26
4 [a]Ps. 22:7; 109:25; Zeph. 2:15; Matt. 27:39
6 [a]Job 9:27, 28
7 [a]Job 7:3 [b]Job 16:20; 19:13-15
8 [a]Job 10:17 [b]Job 19:20; Ps. 109:24
9 [1]Lit., *borne a grudge against me* [2]Lit., *sharpens his eyes* [a]Job 19:11; Hos. 6:1 [b]Ps. 35:16; Lam. 2:16; Acts 7:54 [c]Job 13:24; 33:10
10 [1]Lit., *struck* [a]Ps. 22:13 [b]Is. 50:6; Lam. 3:30; Acts 23:2 [c]Job 30:12; Ps. 35:15
12 [a]Job 9:17 [b]Job 7:20; Lam. 3:12
13 [a]Job 6:4; 19:12; 25:3 [b]Job 20:25
14 [a]Job 9:17 [b]Joel 2:7
15 [a]Gen. 37:34; Job 2:8; Ps. 69:11 [b]Job 19:9
16 [a]Job 16:20 [b]Job 24:17
17 [a]Is. 59:6; Jon. 3:8 [b]Job 27:4
19 [1]Or, *witness* [a]Gen. 31:50; Job 19:25-27; Phil. 1:8 [b]Job 31:2

20 "My [a]friends are my scoffers;
[b]My eye [1]weeps to God.
21 "O that a man might plead with God
As a man with his neighbor!
22 "For when a few years are past,
I shall go the way [a]of no return.

Chapter 17

Job Says He Has Become a Byword

"MY spirit is broken, my days are extinguished,
The [1a]grave is *ready* for me.
2 "[a]Surely mockers are with me,
And my eye [1]gazes on their provocation.

3 "Lay down, now, a pledge [a]for me with Thyself;
Who is there that will [1]be my guarantor?
4 "For Thou hast [1a]kept their heart from understanding;
Therefore Thou wilt not exalt *them.*
5 "He who [a]informs against friends for a share *of the spoil,*
The [b]eyes of his children also shall languish.

6 "But He has made me a [a]byword of the people,
And I am one at whom men [b]spit.
7 "My eye has also grown [a]dim because of grief,
And all my [b]members are as a shadow.
8 "The upright shall be appalled at this,
And the [a]innocent shall stir up himself against the godless.
9 "Nevertheless [a]the righteous shall hold to his way,
And [b]he who has clean hands shall grow stronger and stronger.
10 "But come again all of [1]you now,
For I [a]do not find a wise man among you.
11 "My [a]days are past, my plans are torn apart,
Even the wishes of my heart.
12 "They make night into day, *saying,*
'The light is near,' in the presence of darkness.
13 "If I look for [a]Sheol as my home,
I [1]make my bed in the darkness;
14 If I call to the [a]pit, 'You are my father';
To the [b]worm, 'my mother and my sister';
15 Where now is [a]my hope?
And who regards my hope?
16 "[1]Will it go down with me to Sheol?
Shall we together [a]go down into the dust?"

Chapter 18

Bildad Speaks of the Wicked

THEN Bildad the Shuhite [1]responded,
2 "How long will you hunt for words?
Show understanding and then we can talk.
3 "Why are we [a]regarded as beasts,
As stupid in your eyes?
4 "O [1]you who tear yourself in your anger—
For your sake is the earth to be abandoned,
Or the rock to be moved from its place?

5 "Indeed, the [a]light of the wicked goes out,
And the [1]flame of his fire gives no light.
6 "The light in his tent is [a]darkened,
And his lamp goes out above him.
7 "His [1]vigorous stride is shortened,
And his [a]own scheme brings him down.
8 "For he is [a]thrown into the net by his own feet,
And he steps on the webbing.
9 "A snare seizes *him* by the heel,
And a trap snaps shut on him.
10 "A noose for him is hidden in the ground,
And a trap for him on the path.
11 "All around [a]terrors frighten him,
And [b]harry him at every step.
12 "His strength is [a]famished,
And calamity is ready at his side.
13 "[1]His skin is devoured by disease,
The first-born of death [a]devours his [2]limbs.
14 "He is [a]torn from [1]the security of his tent,
And [2]they march him before the king of [b]terrors.
15 "[1]There dwells in his tent nothing of his;
[a]Brimstone is scattered on his habitation.
16 "His [a]roots are dried below,
And his [b]branch is cut off above.

20 [1]Or, *drips* [a]Job 16:7 [b]Job 17:7
22 [a]Job 3:13
1 [1]Lit., *graves* [a]Ps. 88:3, 4
2 [1]Lit., *lodges* [a]Job 12:4; 17:6
3 [1]Lit., *strike hands with me* [a]Ps. 119:122; Is. 38:14
4 [1]Lit., *hidden* [a]Job 12:20
5 [a]Lev. 19:13, 16 [b]Job 11:20
6 [a]Job 17:2 [b]Job 30:10
7 [a]Job 16:16 [b]Job 16:8
8 [a]Job 22:19
9 [a]Prov. 4:18 [b]Job 22:30; 31:7
10 [1]With some ancient mss. and versions; M.T., *them* [a]Job 12:2
11 [a]Job 7:6
13 [1]Lit., *spread out* [a]Job 3:13
14 [a]Job 7:5; 13:28; 30:18, 30 [b]Job 21:26; 25:6
15 [a]Job 7:6
16 [1]So the Gk.; Heb. possibly, *Let my limbs sink down to Sheol, since there is rest in the dust for all.* [a]Job 3:17; 21:33
1 [1]Lit., *answered and said*
3 [a]Ps. 73:22
4 [1]Lit., *he . . . tears himself . . . his*
5 [1]Lit., *spark* [a]Job 21:17; Prov. 13:9; 20:20; 24:20
6 [a]Job 12:25
7 [1]Lit., *steps of his strength* [a]Job 15:6
8 [a]Job 22:10; Ps. 9:15; 35:8; Is. 24:17, 18
11 [a]Job 15:21 [b]Job 18:18; 20:8
12 [a]Is. 8:21
13 [1]Heb., *It eats parts of his skin* [2]Or, *parts* [a]Zech. 14:12
14 [1]Lit., *his tent his trust* [2]Or, *you or she shall march* [a]Job 8:22; 18:6; 27:18 [b]Job 15:21
15 [1]A suggested reading is, *Fire dwells in his tent* [a]Ps. 11:6
16 [a]Is. 5:24; Hos. 9:16; Amos 2:9; Mal. 4:1 [b]Job 15:30, 32

17“[a]Memory of him perishes from the earth,
And he has no name abroad.
18“[1]He is driven from light [a]into darkness,
And [b]chased from the inhabited world.
19“He has no [a]offspring or posterity among his people,
Nor any survivor where he sojourned.
20“Those [1]in the west are appalled at [a]his [2]fate,
And those [3]in the east are seized with horror.
21“Surely such are the [a]dwellings of the wicked,
And this is the place of him who does not know God.”

Chapter 19

Job Feels Insulted

Then Job [1]responded,
2“How long will you torment [1]me,
And crush me with words?
3“These ten times you have insulted me,
You are not ashamed to wrong me.
4“Even if I have truly erred,
My error lodges with me.
5“If indeed you [a]vaunt yourselves against me,
And prove my disgrace to me,
6 Know then that [a]God has wronged me,
And has closed [b]His net around me.

Everything Is against Him

7“Behold, [a]I cry, ‘Violence!’ but I get no answer;
I shout for help, but there is no justice.
8“He has [a]walled up my way so that I cannot pass;
And He has put [b]darkness on my paths.
9“He has [a]stripped my honor from me,
And removed the [b]crown from my head.
10“He [a]breaks me down on every side, and I am gone;
And He has uprooted my [b]hope [c]like a tree.
11“He has also [a]kindled His anger against me,
And [b]considered me as His enemy.
12“His [a]troops come together,
And build up their [1]way against me,
And camp around my tent.
13“He has [a]removed my brothers far from me,
And my [b]acquaintances are completely estranged from me.
14“My relatives have failed,
And my [a]intimate friends have forgotten me.
15“Those who live in my house and my maids consider me a stranger.
I am a foreigner in their sight.
16“I call to my servant, but he does not answer,
I have to implore him with my mouth.
17“My breath is [1]offensive to my wife,
And I am loathsome to my own brothers.
18“Even young children [a]despise me;
I rise up and they speak against me.
19“All [1]my [a]associates abhor me,
And those I love have turned against me.
20“My [a]bone clings to my skin and my flesh,
And I have escaped *only* by the skin of my teeth.
21“Pity me, pity me, O you my friends,
For the [a]hand of God has struck me.
22“Why do you [a]persecute me as God *does*,
And are not satisfied with my flesh?

Job Says, “My Redeemer Lives”

23“Oh that my words were written!
Oh that they were [a]inscribed in a book!
24“That with an iron stylus and lead
They were engraved in the rock forever!
25“And as for me, I know that [a]my [1]Redeemer lives,
And [2]at the last He will take His stand on the [3]earth.
26“Even after my skin [1]is destroyed,
Yet from my flesh I shall [a]see God;
27 Whom I [1]myself shall behold,
And whom my eyes shall see and not another.
My [2]heart [a]faints [3]within me.
28“If you say, ‘How shall we persecute him?’
And ‘What pretext for a case against him can we find?’
29 *Then* be afraid of [a]the sword for yourselves,

---

17 [a]Job 24:20; Ps. 34:16; Prov. 10:7
18 [1]Lit., *They drive him . . . And chase him* [a]Job 5:14, Is. 8:21; 15:30; 20:8 [b]Job 27:21-23
19 [a]Job 27:14, 15; Is. 14:22
20 [1]Lit., *who come after* [2]Lit., *day* [3]Lit., *who have gone before* [a]Ps. 37:13; Jer. 50:27; Obad. 12
21 [a]Job 21:28
1 [1]Lit., *answered and said*
2 [1]Lit., *my soul*
5 [a]Ps. 35:26; 38:16; 55:12
6 [a]Job 16:11; 27:2 [b]Job 18:8-10; Ps. 66:11; Lam. 1:13
7 [a]Job 9:24; 30:20, 24; Hab. 1:2
8 [a]Job 3:23; Lam. 3:7, 9 [b]Job 30:26
9 [a]Job 12:17, 19; Ps. 89:44 [b]Job 16:15; Ps. 89:39; Lam. 5:16
10 [a]Job 12:14 [b]Job 7:6 [c]Job 24:20
11 [a]Job 16:9 [b]Job 13:24; 33:10
12 [1]I.e., siegework [a]Job 16:13
13 [a]Job 16:7; Ps. 69:8 [b]Job 16:20; Ps. 88:8, 18
14 [a]Job 19:19
17 [1]Lit., *strange*
18 [a]Job 12:4
19 [1]Lit., *the men of my council* [a]Ps. 38:11; 55:13
20 [a]Job 16:8; 33:21; Ps. 102:5
21 [a]Job 1:11
22 [a]Job 13:24, 25; 19:6; Ps. 16:11; 69:26
23 [a]Is. 30:8; Jer. 36:2
25 [1]Or, *Vindicator, defender;* lit., *kinsman* [2]Or, *as the Last* [3]Lit., *dust* [a]Job 16:19; Ps. 78:35; Prov. 23:11; Is. 43:14
26 [1]Lit., *which they have cut off* [a]Ps. 17:15; Matt. 5:8; 1 Cor. 13:12; 1 John 3:2
27 [1]Or, *on my side* [2]Lit., *kidneys* [3]Lit., *in my loins* [a]Ps. 73:26
29 [a]Job 15:22

For wrath *brings* the punishment of the sword,
So that you may know [b]there is judgment."

CHAPTER 20

Zophar Says, "The Triumph of the Wicked Is Short"

THEN Zophar the Naamathite [1]answered,
2"Therefore my disquieting thoughts make me [1]respond,
Even because of my [2]inward agitation.
3"I listened to [a]the reproof which insults me,
And the spirit of my understanding makes me answer.
4"Do you know this from [a]of old,
From the establishment of man on earth,
5 That the [a]triumphing of the wicked is short,
And [b]the joy of the godless momentary?
6"Though his loftiness [1a]reaches the heavens,
And his head touches the clouds,
7 He [a]perishes forever like his refuse;
Those who have seen him [b]will say, 'Where is he?'
8"He flies away like a [a]dream, and they cannot find him;
Even like a vision of the night he is [b]chased away.
9"The [a]eye which saw him sees him no more,
And [b]his place no longer beholds him.
10"His [a]sons [1]favor the poor,
And his hands [b]give back his wealth.
11"His [a]bones are full of his youthful vigor,
But it lies down with him [1]in the dust.

12"Though [a]evil is sweet in his mouth,
And he hides it under his tongue,
13 *Though* he [1]desires it and will not let it go,
But holds it [a]in his [2]mouth,
14 *Yet* his food in his stomach is changed
To the [1]venom of cobras within him.
15"He swallows riches,
But will [a]vomit them up;
God will expel them from his belly.
16"He sucks [a]the poison of cobras;
The viper's tongue slays him.
17"He does not look at [a]the streams,
The rivers flowing with honey and curds.
18"He [a]returns what he has attained
And cannot swallow *it;*
As to the riches of his trading,
He cannot even enjoy *them.*
19"For he has [a]oppressed *and* forsaken the poor;
He has seized a house which he has not built.

20"Because he knew no quiet [1]within him
He does [a]not retain anything he desires.
21"Nothing remains [1]for him to devour,
Therefore [a]his prosperity does not endure.
22"In [a]the fulness of his plenty he will be cramped;
The [b]hand of everyone who suffers will come *against* him.
23"When he [a]fills his belly,
God will send His fierce anger on him
And will [b]rain *it* on him [1]while he is eating.
24"He may flee from the iron weapon,
But the bronze bow will pierce him.
25"It is drawn forth and comes out of his back,
Even the glittering point from [a]his gall.
[b]Terrors come upon him,
26 Complete [a]darkness is held in reserve for his treasures,
And unfanned [b]fire will devour him;
It will consume the survivor in his tent.
27"The [a]heavens will reveal his iniquity,
And the earth will rise up against him.
28"The [a]increase of his house will depart;
His possessions will flow away [b]in the day of His anger.
29"This is the wicked man's [a]portion from God,
Even the heritage decreed to him by God."

CHAPTER 21

Job Says God Will Deal with the Wicked

THEN Job [1]answered,
2"Listen carefully to my speech,
And let this be your *way of* consolation.

29 [b]Job 22:4; Ps. 1:5; 9:7; Eccles. 12:14
1 [1]Lit., *answered and said*
2 [1]Lit., *return* [2]Lit., *haste within me*
3 [a]Job 19:3
4 [a]Job 8:8
5 [a]Job 8:12, 13; Ps. 37:35, 36 [b]Job 8:13
6 [1]Lit., *goes up to* [a]Is. 14:13, 14; Obad. 3, 4
7 [a]Job 4:20; 14:20 [b]Job 7:10; 8:18
8 [a]Ps. 73:20; 90:5 [b]Job 18:18; 27:21-23
9 [a]Job 7:8; 8:18 [b]Job 7:10
10 [1]Or, *seek the favor of* [a]Job 5:4; 27:14 [b]Job 20:18; 27:16, 17
11 [1]Lit., *on* [a]Job 21:23, 24
12 [a]Job 15:16
13 [1]Lit., *has compassion on* [2]Lit., *palate* [a]Job 20:23; Num. 11:20, 33
14 [1]Lit., *gall*
15 [a]Job 20:10, 20, 21
16 [a]Deut. 32:24, 33
17 [a]Deut. 32:13, 14; Job 29:6
18 [a]Job 20:10, 15
19 [a]Job 24:2-4; 35:9
20 [1]Lit., *in his belly* [a]Eccles. 5:13-15
21 [1]Or, *of what he devours* [a]Job 15:29
22 [a]Job 15:21 [b]Job 5:5
23 [1]Or, *as his food* [a]Job 20:13, 14 [b]Num. 11:20, 33; Ps. 78:30, 31
25 [a]Job 16:13 [b]Job 18:11, 14
26 [a]Job 18:18 [b]Job 15:30
27 [a]Deut. 31:28
28 [a]Deut. 28:31 [b]Job 20:15; 21:30
29 [a]Job 27:13; 31:2, 3
1 [1]Lit., *answered and said*

3 "Bear with me that I may speak;
Then after I have spoken, you may [a]mock.
4 "As for me, is [a]my complaint [1]to man?
And why should [2]I not be impatient?
5 "Look at me, and be astonished,
And [a]put *your* hand over *your* mouth.
6 "Even when I remember, I am disturbed,
And horror takes hold of my flesh.
7 "Why [a]do the wicked *still* live,
Continue on, also become very [b]powerful?
8 "Their [1a]descendants are established with them in their sight,
And their offspring before their eyes,
9 Their houses [a]are safe from fear,
Neither is the rod of God on them.
10 "His ox mates [1]without fail;
His cow calves and does not abort.
11 "They send forth their little ones like the flock,
And their children skip about.
12 "They [1]sing to the timbrel and harp
And rejoice at the sound of the flute.
13 "They [a]spend their days in prosperity,
And [1]suddenly they go down to [2]Sheol.
14 "And they say to God, 'Depart from us!
We do not even desire the knowledge of Thy ways.
15 '[1]Who is [2]the Almighty, that we should serve Him,
And [a]what would we gain if we entreat Him?'
16 "Behold, their prosperity is not in their hand;
The counsel of the wicked is far from me.

17 "How often is [a]the lamp of the wicked put out,
Or *does* their [b]calamity fall on them?
Does [1]God apportion destruction in His anger?
18 "Are they as [a]straw before the wind,
And like [b]chaff which the storm carries away?
19 "*You say,* '[a]God stores away [1]a man's iniquity for his sons.'
Let [2]God repay him so that he may know *it.*
20 "Let his [a]own eyes see his decay,
And let him [b]drink of the wrath of [1]the Almighty.
21 "For what does he care for his household [1]after him,
When the number of his months is cut off?
22 "Can anyone [a]teach God knowledge,
In that He [b]judges those on high?
23 "One [a]dies in his full strength,
Being wholly at ease and [1]satisfied;
24 His [1]sides are filled out with fat,
And the [a]marrow of his bones is moist,
25 While another dies with a bitter soul,
Never even [1]tasting *anything* good.
26 "Together they [a]lie down in the dust,
And [b]worms cover them.

27 "Behold, I know your thoughts,
And the plans by which you would wrong me.
28 "For you say, 'Where is the house of [a]the nobleman,
And where is the [b]tent, the dwelling places of the wicked?'
29 "Have you not asked wayfaring men,
And do you not recognize their [1]witness?
30 "For the [a]wicked is reserved for the day of calamity;
They will be led forth at [b]the day of fury.
31 "Who will confront him with his actions,
And who will repay him for what he has done?
32 "While he is carried to the grave,
Men will keep watch over *his* tomb.
33 "The [a]clods of the valley will [1]gently cover him;
Moreover, [b]all men will [2]follow after him,
While countless ones *go* before him.
34 "How then will you vainly [a]comfort me,
For your answers remain *full of* [1]falsehood?"

Chapter 22

Eliphaz Accuses and Exhorts Job

THEN Eliphaz the Temanite [1]responded,
2 "Can a vigorous [a]man be of use to God,

3 [a]Job 11:3
4 [1]Or, *against* [2]Lit., *my spirit* [a]Job 7:11
5 [a]Judg. 18:19; Job 13:5; 29:9
7 [a]Job 9:24; Ps. 73:3; Jer. 12:1; Hab. 1:13 [b]Job 12:19
8 [1]Lit., *seed* [a]Ps. 17:14
9 [a]Job 12:6
10 [1]Lit., *and does not fail*
12 [1]Lit., *lifted up the voice*
13 [1]So with most versions. M.T., *are shattered by Sheol.* [2]I.e., the nether world [a]Job 21:23; 36:11
15 [1]Lit., *What* [2]Heb., *Shaddai* [a]Job 22:17; 34:9
17 [1]Lit., *He* [a]Job 18:5, 6 [b]Job 31:2, 3
18 [a]Job 13:25; Ps. 83:13 [b]Ps. 1:4; 35:5; Is. 17:13
19 [1]Lit., *his* [2]Lit., *Him* [a]Ex. 20:5; Jer. 31:29; Ezek. 18:2
20 [1]Heb., *Shaddai* [a]Num. 14:28-32; Jer. 31:30; Ezek. 18:4 [b]Ps. 60:3; Is. 51:17; Jer. 25:15; Rev. 14:10
21 [1]I.e., after he dies
22 [a]Job 35:11; 36:22; Is. 40:14; Rom. 11:34 [b]Job 4:18; 15:15
23 [1]Or, *quiet* [a]Job 20:11; 21:13
24 [1]So with Syr.; Heb. uncertain. Some render as, *his pails are full of milk* [a]Prov. 3:8
25 [1]Lit., *eating*
26 [a]Job 3:13; 20:11; Eccles. 9:2 [b]Job 24:20; Is. 14:11
28 [a]Job 1:3; 31:37 [b]Job 8:22
29 [1]Lit., *signs*
30 [a]Job 20:29; Prov. 16:4; 2 Pet. 2:9 [b]Job 17:20
33 [1]Lit., *be sweet to him* [2]Lit., *draw* [a]Job 3:22; 17:16 [b]Job 3:19; 24:24
34 [1]Or, *faithlessness* [a]Job 16:2
1 [1]Lit., *answered and said*
2 [a]Job 35:7; Luke 17:10

Or a wise man be useful to himself?
3 "Is there any pleasure to [1]the Almighty if you are righteous,
Or profit if you make your ways perfect?
4 "Is it because of your [1]reverence that He reproves you,
That He [a]enters into judgment against you?
5 "Is not [a]your wickedness great,
And your iniquities without end?
6 "For you have [a]taken pledges of your brothers without cause,
And [b]stripped [1]men naked.
7 "To the weary you have [a]given no water to drink,
And from the hungry you have [b]withheld bread.
8 "But the earth [a]belongs to the [b]mighty man,
And [c]the honorable man dwells in it.
9 "You have sent [a]widows away empty,
And the [1]strength of the [b]orphans has been crushed.
10 "Therefore [a]snares surround you,
And sudden [b]dread terrifies you,
11 Or [a]darkness, so that you cannot see,
And an [b]abundance of water covers you.

12 "Is not God [a]*in* the height of heaven?
Look also at the [1]distant stars, how high they are!
13 "And you say, '[a]What does God know?
Can He judge through the thick darkness?
14 '[a]Clouds are a hiding place for Him, so that He cannot see;
And He walks on the [1]vault of heaven.'
15 "Will you keep to the ancient path
Which [a]wicked men have trod,
16 Who were snatched away [a]before their time,
Whose [b]foundations were washed away by a river?
17 "They [a]said to God, 'Depart from us!'
And 'What can the Almighty do to them?'
18 "Yet He [a]filled their houses with good *things;*
But [b]the counsel of the wicked is far from me.
19 "The [a]righteous see and are glad,
And the innocent mock them,
20 *Saying,* 'Truly our adversaries are cut off,
And their abundance [a]the fire has consumed.'

21 "[a]Yield now and be at peace with Him;
Thereby good will come to you.
22 "Please receive [1a]instruction from His mouth,
And establish His words in your heart.
23 "If you [a]return to the Almighty, you will be [1]restored;
If you [b]remove unrighteousness far from your tent,
24 And [a]place *your* [1]gold in the dust,
And *the gold of* Ophir among the stones of the brooks,
25 Then the Almighty will be your [1]gold
And choice silver to you.
26 "For then you will [a]delight in the Almighty,
And lift up your face to God.
27 "You will [a]pray to Him, and [b]He will hear you;
And you will pay your vows.
28 "You will also decree a thing, and it will be established for you;
And [a]light will shine on your ways.
29 "When [1]you are cast down, you will speak with [2]confidence
And the [3a]humble person He will save.
30 "He will deliver one who is not innocent,
And he will be [a]delivered through the cleanness of your hands."

CHAPTER 23

Job Says He Longs for God

THEN Job replied,
2 "Even today my [a]complaint is rebellion;
[1]His hand is [b]heavy despite my groaning.
3 "Oh that I knew where I might find Him,
That I might come to His seat!
4 "I would [a]present *my* case before Him
And fill my mouth with arguments.
5 "I would learn the words *which* He would answer,
And perceive what He would say to me.
6 "Would He contend with me by [a]the greatness of *His* power?

3 [1]Heb., *Shaddai,* also vs. 17, 23, 25, 26
4 [1]Or, *fear* [a]Job 14:3; 19:29
5 [a]Job 11:6
6 [1]Lit., *clothing of the naked* [a]Ex. 22:26; Deut. 24:6, 17; Job 24:3, 9; Ezek. 18:16 [b]Job 31:19, 20
7 [a]Job 31:16, 17 [b]Job 31:31
8 [a]Job 9:24 [b]Job 12:19 [c]Is. 3:3; 9:15
9 [1]Lit., *arms* [a]Job 24:3, 21; 29:13; 31:16, 18 [b]Job 6:27
10 [a]Job 18:8 [b]Job 15:21
11 [a]Job 5:14 [b]Job 38:34; Ps. 69:2; 124:5
12 [1]Lit., *head, top-most* [a]Job 11:7-9
13 [a]Ps. 10:11; 59:7; 64:5; 94:7; Is. 29:15; Ezek. 8:12
14 [1]Lit., *circle* [a]Job 26:9
15 [a]Job 34:36
16 [a]Job 15:32; 21:13, 18 [b]Job 14:19; Ps. 90:5; Is. 28:2; Matt. 7:26, 27
17 [a]Job 21:14, 15
18 [a]Job 12:6 [b]Job 21:16
19 [a]Ps. 52:6; 58:10; 107:42
20 [a]Job 15:30
21 [a]Ps. 34:10
22 [1]Or, *law* [a]Job 6:10; 23:12; Prov. 2:6
23 [1]Lit., *built up* [a]Job 8:5; 11:13; Is. 19:22; 31:6; Zech. 1:3 [b]Job 11:14
24 [1]Lit., *ore* [a]Job 31:24, 25
25 [1]Lit., *ore*
26 [a]Job 27:10; Ps. 37:4; Is. 58:14
27 [a]Job 11:13; 33:26; Is. 58:9 [b]Job 34:28
28 [a]Job 11:17; Ps. 112:4
29 [1]Lit., *they cast you down* [2]Lit., *pride* [3]Lit., *lowly of eyes* [a]Job 5:11; 36:7; Matt. 23:12; James 4:6; 1 Pet. 5:5
30 [a]Job 42:7, 8; Ps. 18:20; 24:3, 4
2 [1]So with Gr. and Syr.; M.T., *My* [a]Job 7:11 [b]Job 6:2, 3; Ps. 32:4
4 [a]Job 13:18
6 [a]Job 9:4

No, surely He would pay attention to me.
7 "There the upright would [a]reason with Him;
And I [1]would be [b]delivered forever from my Judge.

8 "Behold, I go forward but He is not *there*,
And backward, but I [a]cannot perceive Him;
9 When He acts on the left, I cannot behold *Him;*
He turns on the right, I cannot see Him.
10 "But He knows the [1]way I take;
When He has [a]tried me, I shall come forth as gold.
11 "My foot has [a]held fast to His path;
I have kept His way and not turned aside.
12 "I have not departed from the command of His lips;
I have treasured the [a]words of His mouth [1]more than my [2]necessary food.
13 "But He is unique and who can turn Him?
And *what* His soul desires, that He does.
14 "For He performs what is appointed for me,
And many such *decrees* are with Him.
15 "Therefore, I would be dismayed at His presence;
When I consider, I am terrified of Him.
16 "*It is* God *who* has made my [a]heart faint,
And the Almighty *who* has dismayed me,
17 But I [a]am not silenced by the darkness,
Nor [b]deep gloom *which* covers *me.*

Chapter 24

Job Says God Seems to Ignore Wrongs

"WHY are [1]times not stored up by the Almighty,
And why do those who know Him not see [a]His days?
2 "[1]Some [a]remove the landmarks;
They seize and [2]devour flocks.
3 "They drive away the donkeys of the [a]orphans;
They take the [b]widow's ox for a pledge.
4 "They push [a]the needy aside from the road;
The [b]poor of the land are made to hide themselves altogether.
5 "Behold, as [a]wild donkeys in the wilderness
They [b]go forth seeking food in their activity,
As [1]bread for *their* children in the desert.
6 "They harvest their fodder in the field,
And they glean the vineyard of the wicked.
7 "They spend the night naked, without clothing,
And have no covering against the cold.
8 "They are wet with the mountain rains,
And they [a]hug the rock for want of a shelter.
9 "[1]Others snatch the [a]orphan from the breast,
And against the poor they take a pledge.
10 "They cause *the poor* to go about naked without clothing,
And they take away the sheaves from the hungry.
11 "Within the walls they produce oil;
They tread wine presses but thirst.
12 "From the city men groan,
And the souls of the wounded cry out;
Yet God [a]does not pay attention to folly.

13 "[1]Others have been with those who rebel against the light;
They do not want to know its ways,
Nor abide in its paths.
14 "The murderer [a]arises at dawn;
He [b]kills the poor and the needy,
And at night he is as a thief.
15 "And the eye of the [a]adulterer waits for the twilight,
Saying, 'No eye will see me.'
And he [1]disguises his face.
16 "In the dark they [a]dig into houses,
They shut themselves up by day;
They do not know the light.
17 "For the morning is the same to him as thick darkness,
For he is familiar with the [a]terrors of thick darkness.

18 "They are [1a]insignificant on the surface of the water;
Their portion is [b]cursed on the earth.
They do not turn [2]toward the [c]vineyards.
19 "Drought and heat [1a]consume the snow waters,

7 [1]Or, *bring forth my justice forever* [a]Job 13:3 [b]Job 13:16; 23:10
8 [a]Job 9:11; 35:14
10 [1]Lit., *way with me* [a]Job 7:18; Ps. 7:9; 11:5; 66:10; Zech. 13:9; 1 Pet. 1:7
11 [a]Job 31:7; Ps. 17:5; 44:18
12 [1]Or, with some versions, *in my breast* [2]Lit., *prescribed portion* [a]Job 6:10; 22:22
16 [a]Deut. 20:3; Job 27:2; Jer. 51:46
17 [a]Job 10:18, 19 [b]Job 19:8
1 [1]I.e., times of judgment [a]Is. 2:12; Jer. 46:10; Obad. 15; Zeph. 1:7
2 [1]Lit., *They* [2]Or, *pasture* [a]Deut. 19:14; 27:17
3 [a]Job 6:27 [b]Job 22:9
4 [a]Job 24:14; 29:16; 30:25; 31:19 [b]Job 29:12; Ps. 41:1; Prov. 14:31; Amos 8:4
5 [1]Lit., *his bread* [a]Job 39:5-8 [b]Ps. 104:23
8 [a]Lam. 4:5
9 [1]Lit., *They* [a]Job 6:27
12 [a]Job 9:23, 24
13 [1]Lit., *They*
14 [a]Mic. 2:1 [b]Ps. 10:8
15 [1]Or, *puts a covering on his face* [a]Prov. 7:9
16 [a]Ex. 22:2; Matt. 6:19
17 [a]Job 15:21
18 [1]Or, *light* or *swift* [2]Lit., *to the path of* [a]Job 22:11, 16; 27:20 [b]Job 5:3 [c]Job 24:6, 11
19 [1]Lit., *seize* [a]Job 6:16, 17

So does [2b]Sheol *those who* have sinned.
20"A [1a]mother will forget him;
The [b]worm feeds sweetly till he is remembered [c]no more.
And wickedness will be broken [d]like a tree.
21"He wrongs the barren woman,
And does no good for [a]the widow.
22"But He drags off the valiant by [a]His power;
He rises, but [b]no one has assurance of life.
23"He provides them [a]with security, and they are supported;
And His [b]eyes are on their ways.
24"They are exalted a [a]little while, then they are gone;
Moreover, they are [b]brought low and like everything gathered up;
Even like the heads of grain they are cut off.
25"Now if it is not so, [a]who can prove me a liar,
And make my speech worthless?"

CHAPTER 25

Bildad Says Man Is Inferior

THEN Bildad the Shuhite answered,
2"[a]Dominion and awe [1]belong to Him
Who establishes peace in [b]His heights.
3"Is there any number to [a]His troops?
And upon whom does His light not rise?
4"How then can a man be [a]just with God?
Or how can he be [b]clean who is born of woman?
5"If even [a]the moon has no brightness
And the [b]stars are not pure in His sight,
6 How much less [a]man, *that* [b]maggot,
And the son of man, *that* worm!"

CHAPTER 26

Job Rebukes Bildad

THEN Job responded,
2"What a help you are to [1a]the weak!
How you have saved the arm [b]without strength!

19 [2]I.e., nether world [a]Job 6:16, 17 [b]Job 21:13
20 [1]Lit., *womb* [a]Is. 49:15 [b]Job 21:26 [c]Job 18:17; Ps. 34:16; Prov. 10:7 [d]Job 19:10
21 [a]Job 22:9
22 [a]Job 9:4 [b]Job 18:20
23 [a]Job 12:6 [b]Job 10:4; 11:11
24 [a]Ps. 37:10 [b]Job 14:21
25 [a]Job 6:28; 27:4
2 [1]Lit., *are with Him* [a]Job 9:4; 36:5, 22; 37:23; 42:2 [b]Job 16:19; 31:2
3 [a]Job 16:13
4 [a]Job 4:17; 9:2 [b]Job 14:4
5 [a]Job 31:26 [b]Job 15:15
6 [a]Job 7:17 [b]Job 17:14
2 [1]Lit., *no power* [a]Job 6:11, 12 [b]Ps. 71:9
3 [1]Lit., *made known*
4 [1]Lit., *breath has gone forth*
5 [1]Or, *shades;* Heb., *Rephaim* [a]Job 3:13; Ps. 88:10
6 [1]I.e., the nether world [2]I.e., place of destruction [a]Job 9:5-10; 26:6-14; 38:17; 41:11 [b]Job 28:22; 31:12
7 [a]Job 9:8
8 [a]Job 37:11; Prov. 30:4
9 [1]Lit., *covers* [2]Or, *throne* [a]Job 22:14; Ps. 97:2; 105:39
10 [a]Job 38:1-11; Prov. 8:29 [b]Job 38:19, 20, 24
12 [a]Is. 51:15; Jer. 31:35 [b]Job 12:13 [c]Job 9:13
13 [1]Lit., *made beautiful* [a]Job 9:8 [b]Is. 27:1
14 [a]Job 4:12 [b]Job 36:29; 37:4, 5
1 [1]Or, *again took up* [a]Job 13:12; 29:1
2 [a]Job 16:11; 34:5 [b]Job 9:18
3 [1]Lit., *breath* [2]Or, *spirit* [a]Job 32:8; 33:4
4 [a]Job 6:28; 33:3

3"What counsel you have given to *one* without wisdom!
What helpful insight you have abundantly [1]provided!
4"To whom have you uttered words?
And whose [1]spirit was expressed through you?

The Greatness of God

5"The [1a]departed spirits tremble
Under the waters and their inhabitants.
6"Naked is [1a]Sheol before Him
And [2b]Abaddon has no covering.
7"He [a]stretches out the north over empty space,
And hangs the earth on nothing.
8"He [a]wraps up the waters in His clouds;
And the cloud does not burst under them.
9"He [1a]obscures the face of the [2]full moon,
And spreads His cloud over it.
10"He has inscribed a [a]circle on the surface of the waters,
At the [b]boundary of light and darkness.
11"The pillars of heaven tremble,
And are amazed at His rebuke.
12"He [a]quieted the sea with His power,
And by His [b]understanding He shattered [c]Rahab.
13"By His breath the [a]heavens are [1]cleared;
His hand has pierced [b]the fleeing serpent.
14"Behold, these are the fringes of His ways;
And how faint [a]a word we hear of Him!
But His mighty [b]thunder, who can understand?"

CHAPTER 27

Job Affirms His Righteousness

THEN Job [1]continued his [a]discourse and said,
2"As God lives, [a]who has taken away my right,
And the Almighty, [b]who has embittered my soul,
3 For as long as [1]life is in me,
And the [2a]breath of God is in my nostrils,
4 My lips certainly will not speak unjustly,
Nor will [a]my tongue mutter deceit.

5"Far be it from me that I should declare you right;
Till I die [a]I will not put away my integrity from me.
6"I [a]hold fast my righteousness and will not let it go.
My heart does not reproach any of my days.

The State of the Godless

7"May my enemy be as the wicked,
And [1]my opponent as the unjust.
8"For what is [a]the hope of the godless [1]when he is cut off,
When God requires [b]his [2]life?
9"Will God [a]hear his cry,
When [b]distress comes upon him?
10"Will he take [a]delight in the Almighty,
Will he call on God at all times?
11"I will instruct you in the [1a]power of God;
What is with the Almighty I will not conceal.
12"Behold, all of you have seen *it;*
Why then do you [1]act foolishly?

13"This is [a]the portion of a wicked man from God,
And the inheritance *which* [b]tyrants receive from the Almighty.
14"Though his sons are many, [1]they are destined [a]for the sword;
And his [b]descendants will not be satisfied with bread.
15"His survivors will be buried because of the plague,
And [1]their [a]widows will not be able to weep.
16"Though he piles up silver like dust,
And prepares garments as *plentiful as* the clay;
17 He may prepare *it,* [a]but the just will wear *it,*
And the innocent will divide the silver.
18"He has built his [a]house like the [1]spider's web,
Or as a hut *which* the watchman has made.
19"He lies down rich, but never [1]again;
He opens his eyes, and [a]it is no more.
20"[a]Terrors overtake him like a flood;
A tempest steals him away [b]in the night.
21"The east [a]wind carries him away, and he is gone,
For it whirls him [b]away from his place.
22"For it will hurl at him [a]without sparing;
He will surely try to [b]flee from its [1]power.
23"*Men* will clap their hands at him,
And will [a]hiss him from his place.

Chapter 28

Job Tells of Earth's Treasures

"SURELY there is a [1]mine for silver,
And a place [2]where they refine gold.
2"Iron is taken from the dust,
And from rock copper is smelted.
3"*Man* puts an end to darkness,
And to the farthest limit he searches out
The rock in gloom and deep shadow.
4"He [1]sinks a shaft far from [2]habitation,
Forgotten by the foot;
They hang and swing to and fro far from men.
5"The earth, from it comes food,
And underneath it is turned up as fire.
6"Its rocks are the [1]source of sapphires,
And its dust *contains* gold.
7"The path no bird of prey knows,
Nor has the falcon's eye caught sight of it.
8"The [1]proud beasts have not trodden it,
Nor has the *fierce* lion passed over it.
9"He puts his hand on the flint;
He overturns the mountains at the [1]base.
10"He hews out channels through the rocks;
And his eye sees anything precious.
11"He dams up the streams from [1]flowing;
And what is hidden he brings out to the light.

The Search for Wisdom Is Harder

12"But [a]where can wisdom be found?
And where is the place of understanding?
13"Man does not know its value,
Nor is it found in the land of the living.

5 [a]Job 6:29
6 [a]Job 2:3; 13:18
7 [1]Lit., *he who rises up against me*
8 [1]Or, *though he gains* [2]Lit., *soul* [a]Job 8:13; 11:20 [b]Job 12:10
9 [a]Job 35:12, 13; Ps. 18:41; Prov. 1:28; Is. 1:15; Jer. 14:12; Mic. 3:4 [b]Prov. 1:27
10 [a]Job 22:26, 27; Ps. 37:4; Is. 58:14
11 [1]Lit., *hand* [a]Job 27:13
12 [1]Or, *speak vanity*
13 [a]Job 20:29 [b]Job 15:20
14 [1]Lit., *the sword is for them* [a]Job 15:22; 18:19 [b]Job 20:10
15 [1]So ancient versions; Heb., *his* [a]Ps. 78:64
17 [a]Job 20:18-21
18 [1]So ancient versions; Heb., *moth* [a]Job 8:15; 18:14
19 [1]So ancient versions; Heb., *will be gathered* [a]Job 7:8, 21; 20:7
20 [a]Job 15:21 [b]Job 20:8; 34:20
21 [a]Job 21:18 [b]Job 7:10
22 [1]Lit., *hand* [a]Jer. 13:14; Ezek. 5:11; 24:14 [b]Job 11:20
23 [a]Job 18:18; 20:8
1 [1]Or, *source* [2]Lit., *for gold they refine*
4 [1]Lit., *breaks open* [2]Lit., *sojourning*
6 [1]Or, *place*
8 [1]Lit., *sons of pride*
9 [1]Lit., *roots*
11 [1]Lit., *weeping*
12 [a]Job 28:23, 28

14 "The deep says, 'It is not in me';
And the sea says, 'It is not with me.'
15 "Pure gold cannot be given in exchange for it,
Nor can silver be weighed as its price.
16 "It cannot be valued in the gold of Ophir,
In precious onyx, or sapphire.
17 "[a]Gold or glass cannot equal it,
Nor can it be exchanged for articles of fine gold.
18 "Coral and crystal are not to be mentioned;
And the acquisition of [a]wisdom is above *that of* pearls.
19 "The topaz of Ethiopia cannot equal it,
Nor can it be valued in [a]pure gold.
20 "[a]Where then does wisdom come from?
And where is the place of understanding?
21 "Thus it is hidden from the eyes of all living,
And concealed from the birds of the sky.
22 "[1a]Abaddon and Death say,
'With our ears we have heard a report of it.'

23 "[a]God understands its way;
And He knows its place.
24 "For He [a]looks to the ends of the earth,
And sees everything under the heavens.
25 "When He imparted [a]weight to the wind,
And [b]meted out the waters by measure,
26 When He set a [a]limit for the rain,
And a course for the [b]thunderbolt,
27 Then He saw it and declared it;
He established it and also searched it out.
28 "And to man He said, 'Behold, the [a]fear of the Lord, that is wisdom;
And to depart from evil is understanding.' "

Chapter 29

Job's Past Was Glorious

1 And Job again took up his [a]discourse and said,
2 "Oh that I were as in months gone by,
As in the days when God [a]watched over me;
3 When His lamp shone over my head,
And [a]by His light I walked through darkness;
4 As I was in [1]the prime of my days,
When the [2a]friendship of God *was* over my tent;
5 When [1]the Almighty was yet with me,
And my children were around me;
6 When my steps were bathed in [a]butter,
And the [b]rock poured out for me streams of oil!
7 "When I went out to [a]the gate of the city,
When I [1]took my seat in the square;
8 The young men saw me and hid themselves,
And the old men arose *and* stood.
9 "The princes [a]stopped talking,
And [b]put *their* hands on their mouths;
10 The voice of the nobles was [1a]hushed,
And their tongue stuck to their palate.
11 "For when [a]the ear heard, it called me blessed;
And when the eye saw, it gave witness of me,
12 Because I delivered [a]the poor who cried for help,
And the [b]orphan who had no helper.
13 "The blessing of the one [a]ready to perish came upon me,
And I made the [b]widow's heart sing for joy.
14 "I [a]put on righteousness, and it clothed me;
My justice was like a robe and a turban.
15 "I was eyes to the blind,
And feet to the lame.
16 "I was a father to [a]the needy,
And I investigated the case which I did not know.
17 "And I [a]broke the jaws of the wicked,
And snatched the prey from his teeth.
18 "Then I [1]thought, 'I shall die [2]in my nest,
And I shall multiply *my* days as the sand.
19 'My [a]root is spread out to the waters,
And [b]dew lies all night on my branch.
20 'My glory is *ever* new with me,
And my [a]bow is renewed in my hand.'

17 [a]Prov. 8:10; 16:16
18 [a]Prov. 8:11
19 [a]Prov. 8:19
20 [a]Job 28:23, 28
22 [1]I.e., Destruction [a]Job 26:6; Prov. 8:22-36
23 [a]Job 9:4; Prov. 8:22-36
24 [a]Ps. 11:4; 33:13, 14; 66:7; Prov. 15:3
25 [a]Ps. 135:7 [b]Job 12:15; 38:8-11
26 [a]Job 37:6, 11, 12; 38:26-28 [b]Job 37:3; 38:25
28 [a]Ps. 111:10; Prov. 1:7; 9:10

1 [a]Num. 23:7; 24:3; Job 13:12; 27:1
2 [a]Jer. 31:28
3 [a]Job 11:17
4 [1]Lit., *the days of my autumn* [2]Lit., *counsel* [a]Job 15:8; Ps. 25:14; Prov. 3:32
5 [1]Heb., *Shaddai*
6 [a]Deut. 32:14; Job 20:17 [b]Deut. 32:13
7 [1]Lit., *sat up* [a]Job 31:21
9 [a]Job 29:21 [b]Job 21:5
10 [1]Lit., *hidden* [a]Job 29:22
11 [a]Job 4:3, 4
12 [a]Job 24:4, 9; 34:28 [b]Job 31:17, 21
13 [a]Job 31:19 [b]Job 22:9
14 [a]Job 27:5, 6; Ps. 132:9; Is. 59:17; 61:10; Eph. 6:14
16 [a]Job 24:4
17 [a]Ps. 3:7
18 [1]Lit., *said* [2]Lit., *with*
19 [a]Jer. 17:8 [b]Hos. 14:5
20 [a]Gen. 49:24; Ps. 18:34

21"To me [a]they listened and
waited,
And kept silent for my counsel.
22"After my words they did not
[a]speak again,
And [b]my speech dropped on
them.
23"And they waited for me as for
the rain,
And opened their mouth as for
the spring rain.
24"I smiled on them when they did
not believe,
And the light of my face they
did not cast down.
25"I chose a way for them and sat
as [a]chief,
And dwelt as a king among the
troops,
As one who [b]comforted the
mourners.

Chapter 30

Job's Present State Is Humiliating

"But now those younger than I
[a]mock me,
Whose fathers I disdained to
put with the dogs of my
flock.
2"Indeed, what *good was* the
strength of their hands to
me?
Vigor had perished from them.
3"From want and famine they are
gaunt
Who gnaw the dry ground by
night in waste and desolation,
4 Who pluck [1]mallow by the
bushes,
And whose food is the root of
the broom shrub.
5"They are driven from the com-
munity;
They shout against them as
against a thief,
6 So that they dwell in dreadful
[1]valleys,
In holes of the earth and of the
rocks.
7"Among the bushes they [1]cry
out;
Under the nettles they are gathered together.
8"[1]Fools, even [2]those without a
name,
They were scourged from the
land.

9"And now I have become their
[1a]taunt,
I have even become a byword
to them.
10"They abhor me *and* stand aloof
from me,
And they do not [1]refrain from
[a]spitting at my face.
11"Because [1]He has loosed [2]His
[3]bowstring and [a]afflicted me,
They have cast off [b]the bridle
before me.
12"On the right hand their [1]brood
arises;
They [a]thrust aside my feet [b]and
build up against me their
ways of destruction.
13"They [a]break up my path,
They profit [1]from my destruction,
No one restrains them.
14"As *through* a wide breach they
come,
[1]Amid the tempest they roll on.
15"[a]Terrors are turned against me,
They pursue my [1]honor as the
wind,
And my [2]prosperity has passed
away [b]like a cloud.

16"And now [a]my soul is poured
out [1]within me;
Days of affliction have seized
me.
17"At night it pierces [a]my bones
[1]within me,
And my gnawing *pains* take no
rest.
18"By a great force my garment is
[a]distorted;
It binds me about as the collar
of my coat.
19"He has cast me into the [a]mire,
And I have become like dust
and ashes.
20"I [a]cry out to Thee for help, but
Thou dost not answer me;
I stand up, and Thou dost turn
Thy attention against me.
21"Thou hast [1]become cruel to me;
With the might of Thy hand
Thou dost [a]persecute me.
22"Thou dost [a]lift me up to the
wind *and* cause me to ride;
And Thou dost dissolve me in a
storm.
23"For I know that Thou [a]wilt
bring me to death
And to the [b]house of meeting
for all living.

24"Yet does not one in a heap of
ruins stretch out *his* hand,
Or in his disaster therefore [a]cry
out for help?
25"Have I not [a]wept for the [1]one
whose life is hard?
Was not my soul grieved for
[b]the needy?
26"When I [a]expected good, then
evil came,
When I waited for light, [b]then
darkness came.

21 [a]Job 4:3; 29:9
22 [a]Job 29:10 [b]Deut. 32:2
25 [a]Job 1:3; 31:37 [b]Job 4:4; 16:5
1 [a]Job 12:4
4 [1]I.e., plant of the salt marshes (Job 24:24) cf. Job 30:4
6 [1]Or, *wadis*
7 [1]Or, *bray*
8 [1]Lit., *Sons of fools* [2]Lit., *sons*
9 [1]Lit., *song* [a]Job 12:4
10 [1]Lit., *withhold spit from my face* [a]Num. 12:14; Deut. 25:9; Job 17:6; Is. 50:6; Matt. 26:67
11 [1]Or, *they* [2]Some mss. read, *my* [3]Or, *cord* [a]Ruth 1:21; Ps. 88:7 [b]Ps. 32:9
12 [1]Possibly *sprout* or *offspring* [a]Ps. 140:4, 5 [b]Job 19:12
13 [1]Lit., *for* [a]Is. 3:12
14 [1]Lit., *Under*
15 [1]Or, *nobility* [2]Or, *welfare* [a]Job 3:25; 31:23; Ps. 55:3-5 [b]Job 7:9; Hos. 13:3
16 [1]Lit., *upon* [a]Job 3:24; Ps. 22:14; 42:4; Is. 53:12
17 [1]Lit., *from upon* [a]Job 30:30
18 [a]Job 2:7
19 [a]Ps. 69:2, 14
20 [a]Job 19:7
21 [1]Lit., *turned to be* [a]Job 10:3; 16:9, 14; 19:6, 22
22 [a]Job 9:17; 27:21
23 [a]Job 9:22; 10:8 [b]Job 3:19; Eccles. 12:5
24 [a]Job 19:7
25 [1]Lit., *hard of day* [a]Ps. 35:13, 14; Rom. 12:15 [b]Job 24:4
26 [a]Job 3:25, 26; Jer. 8:15 [b]Job 19:8

27 "[1]I am seething [a]within, and cannot relax;
Days of affliction confront me.
28 "I go about [a]mourning without comfort;
I stand up in the assembly *and* [b]cry out for help.
29 "I have become a brother to [a]jackals,
And a companion of ostriches.
30 "My [a]skin turns black on me,
And my [b]bones burn with [1]fever.
31 "Therefore my [a]harp [1]is turned to mourning,
And my flute to the sound of those who weep.

Chapter 31

Job Asserts His Integrity

"I HAVE made a covenant with my [a]eyes;
How then could I gaze at a virgin?
2 "And what is [a]the portion of God from above
Or the heritage of the Almighty from on high?
3 "Is it not [a]calamity to the unjust,
And disaster to [b]those who work iniquity?
4 "Does He not [a]see my ways,
And [b]number all my steps?

5 "If I have [a]walked with falsehood,
And my foot has hastened after deceit,
6 Let Him [a]weigh me with [1]accurate scales,
And let God know [b]my integrity.
7 "If my step has [a]turned from the way,
Or my heart [1]followed my eyes,
Or if any spot has stuck to my hands,
8 Let me [a]sow and another eat,
And let my [b]crops be uprooted.

9 "If my heart has been [a]enticed by a woman,
Or I have lurked at my neighbor's doorway,
10 May my wife [a]grind for another,
And let [b]others [1]kneel down over her.
11 "For that would be a [a]lustful crime;
Moreover, it would be an iniquity *punishable by* judges.
12 "For it would be [a]fire that consumes to [1b]Abaddon,
And would [c]uproot all my [2]increase.

13 "If I have [a]despised the claim of my male or female slaves
When they filed a complaint against me,
14 What then could I do when God arises,
And when He calls me to account, what will I answer Him?
15 "Did not [a]He who made me in the womb make him,
And the same one fashion us in the womb?

16 "If I have kept [a]the poor from *their* desire,
Or have caused the eyes of [b]the widow to fail,
17 Or have [a]eaten my morsel alone,
And [b]the orphan has not [1]shared it
18 (But from my youth he grew up with me as with a father,
And from [1]infancy I guided [2]her),
19 If I have seen anyone perish [a]for lack of clothing,
Or that [b]the needy had no covering,
20 If his loins have not [1]thanked me,
And if he has not been warmed with the fleece of my sheep,
21 If I have lifted up my hand against [a]the orphan,
Because I saw [1]I had support [b]in the gate,
22 Let my shoulder fall from the socket,
And my [a]arm be broken off at the elbow.
23 "For [a]calamity from God is a terror to me,
And because of [b]His [1]majesty I can do nothing.

24 "If I have put my confidence *in* [a]gold,
And called fine gold my trust,
25 If I have [a]gloated because my wealth was great,
And because my hand had secured *so* much;
26 If I have [a]looked at the [1]sun when it shone,
Or the moon going in splendor,
27 And my heart became secretly enticed,
And my hand [1]threw a kiss from my mouth,
28 That too would have been [a]an iniquity *calling for* [1]judgment,

---

27 [1]Lit., *My inward parts are boiling* [a]Lam. 2:11
28 [a]Job 30:30; Ps. 38:6; 42:9; 43:2 [b]Job 19:7
29 [a]Ps. 44:19; Mic. 1:8
30 [1]Lit., *heat* [a]Job 2:7 [b]Ps. 102:3
31 [1]Lit., *become* [a]Is. 24:8
1 [a]Matt. 5:28
2 [a]Job 20:29
3 [a]Job 18:12; 21:30 [b]Job 34:22
4 [a]2 Chr. 16:9; Job 24:23; 28:24; 34:21; 36:7; Prov. 5:21; 15:3 [b]Job 14:16; 31:37
5 [a]Job 15:31; Mic. 2:11
6 [1]Lit., *just* [a]Job 6:2, 3 [b]Job 23:10; 27:5, 6
7 [1]Lit., *walked after* [a]Job 23:11
8 [a]Lev. 26:16; Job 20:18; Mic. 6:15 [b]Job 31:12
9 [a]Job 31:1
10 [1]I.e., sexual relations [a]Judg. 16:21; Is. 47:2 [b]Deut. 28:30
11 [a]Lev. 20:10; Deut. 22:24
12 [1]I.e., place of destruction [2]Or, *yield* [a]Job 15:30 [b]Job 26:6 [c]Job 31:8
13 [a]Deut. 24:14
15 [a]Job 10:3
16 [a]Job 5:16; 20:19 [b]Ex. 22:22-24; Job 22:9
17 [1]Lit., *eaten from it* [a]Job 22:7 [b]Job 29:12
18 [1]Lit., *my mother's womb* [2]Cf. v. 16
19 [a]Job 22:6; 29:13 [b]Job 24:4
20 [1]Lit., *blessed*
21 [1]Lit., *my help* [a]Job 29:12; 31:17 [b]Job 29:7
22 [a]Job 38:15
23 [1]Lit., *exaltation* [a]Job 31:3 [b]Job 13:11
24 [a]Job 22:24; Mark 10:24
25 [a]Job 1:3, 10; Ps. 62:10
26 [1]Lit., *light* [a]Deut. 4:19; 17:3; Ezek. 8:16
27 [1]Lit., *kissed my mouth*
28 [1]Lit., *judges* [a]Deut. 17:2-7; Job 31:11

For I would have [b]denied God above.

29 "Have I [a]rejoiced at the extinction of my enemy,
Or [1]exulted when evil befell him?
30 "[1]No, [a]I have not [2]allowed my mouth to sin
By asking for his life in [b]a curse.
31 "Have the men of my tent not said,
'Who can [1]find one who has not been [a]satisfied with his meat'?
32 "The alien has not lodged outside,
For I have opened my doors to the [1]traveler.
33 "Have I [a]covered my transgressions like [1]Adam,
By hiding my iniquity in my bosom,
34 Because I [a]feared the great multitude,
And the contempt of families terrified me,
And kept silent and did not go out of doors?
35 "Oh that I had one to hear me!
Behold, here is my [1]signature;
[a]Let the Almighty answer me!
And the indictment which my [b]adversary has written,
36 Surely I would carry it on my shoulder;
I would bind it to myself like a crown.
37 "I would declare to Him [a]the number of my steps;
Like [b]a prince I would approach Him.

38 "If my [a]land cries out against me,
And its furrows weep together;
39 If I have [a]eaten its [1]fruit without money,
Or have [b]caused [2]its owners to lose their lives,
40 Let [a]briars [1]grow instead of wheat,
And stinkweed instead of barley."
The words of Job are ended.

Chapter 32

Elihu in Anger Rebukes Job

THEN these three men ceased answering Job, because he was [a]right-
eous in his own eyes.
2 But the anger of Elihu the son of
Barachel the Buzite, of the family of
Ram burned; against Job his anger
burned, [a]because he justified himself [1b]before God.
3 And his anger burned against
his three friends because they had
found no answer, and yet had condemned Job.
4 Now Elihu had waited [1]to
speak to Job because they were
years older than he.
5 And when Elihu saw that there
was no answer in the mouth of the
three men his anger burned.
6 So Elihu the son of Barachel the
Buzite [1]spoke out and said,
"I am young in years and you are [a]old;
Therefore I was shy and afraid to tell you [2]what I think.
7 "I [1]thought [2]age should speak,
And [3]increased years should teach wisdom.
8 "But it is a spirit in man,
And the [a]breath of the Almighty gives them [b]understanding.
9 "The [1]abundant *in years* may not be wise,
Nor may [a]elders understand justice.
10 "So I [1]say, 'Listen to me,
I too will tell [2]what I think.'

11 "Behold, I waited for your words,
I listened to your reasonings,
While you [1]pondered what to say.
12 "I even paid close attention to you,
[1]Indeed, there was no one who refuted Job,
Not one of you who answered his words.
13 "[1]Do not say,
'We have found wisdom;
God will [2]rout him, not man.'
14 "For he has not arranged *his* words against me;
Nor will I reply to him with your [1]arguments.

15 "They are dismayed, they answer no more;
Words have [1]failed them.
16 "And shall I wait, because they do not speak,
Because they [1]stop *and* answer no more?
17 "I too will answer my share,
I also will tell my opinion.
18 "For I am full of words;
The spirit within me constrains me.
19 "Behold, my belly is like unvented wine,
Like new wineskins it is about to burst.
20 "Let me speak that I may get relief;

28 [b]Josh. 24:27; Is. 59:13
29 [1]Lit., *lifted myself up* [a]Prov. 17:5; 24:17; Obad. 12
30 [1]Lit., *And* [2]Lit., *given my palate* [a]Ps. 7:4 [b]Job 5:3
31 [1]Lit., *give* [a]Job 22:7
32 [1]M.T., *way*
33 [1]Or, *mankind* [a]Gen. 3:10; Prov. 28:13
34 [a]Ex. 23:2
35 [1]Lit., *mark* [a]Job. 19:7; 30:20, 24, 28; 35:14 [b]Job 27:7
37 [a]Job 31:4 [b]Job 1:3; 29:25
38 [a]Job 24:2
39 [1]Lit., *strength* [2]Lit., *the soul of its owners to expire* [a]Job 24:6, 10-12; James 5:4 [b]1 Kin. 21:19
40 [1]Lit., *come forth* [a]Job 32:13; Is. 5:6
1 [a]Job 10:7; 13:18; 27:2; 31:6
2 [1]Or, *more than* [a]Job 27:5, 6 [b]Job 30:21
4 [1]Lit., *for Job with words,* or possibly, *while they were speaking with Job*
6 [1]Lit., *answered* [2]Lit., *my knowledge* [a]Job 15:10
7 [1]Lit., *said* [2]Lit., *days* [3]Lit., *many*
8 [a]Job 33:4 [b]Job 38:36
9 [1]Or, *nobles* [a]Job 32:7
10 [1]Or, *said* [2]Lit., *my knowledge*
11 [1]Lit., *searched out words*
12 [1]Lit., *Behold*
13 [1]Lit., *Lest you say* [2]Lit., *drive away*
14 [1]Lit., *words*
15 [1]Lit., *moved away from*
16 [1]Lit., *stand*

Let me open my lips and answer.
21 "Let me now [a]be partial to no one;
Nor flatter *any* man.
22 "For I do not know how to flatter,
Else my Maker would soon take me away.

CHAPTER 33

Elihu Claims to Speak for God

"HOWEVER now, Job, please hear my speech,
And listen to all my words.
2 "Behold now, I open my mouth,
My tongue in my [1]mouth speaks.
3 "My words are *from* the uprightness of my heart;
And my lips speak [a]knowledge sincerely.
4 "The [a]Spirit of God has made me,
And the [b]breath of [1]the Almighty gives me life.
5 "[a]Refute me if you can;
Array yourselves before me, take your stand.
6 "Behold, I belong to God like you;
I too have been [1]formed out of the [a]clay.
7 "Behold, no fear of me should terrify you,
Nor should my pressure weigh heavily on you.

8 "Surely you have spoken in my hearing,
And I have heard the sound of *your* words:
9 'I am [a]pure, [b]without transgression;
I am innocent and there [c]is no guilt in me.
10 'Behold, He [1]invents pretexts against me;
He [a]counts me as His enemy.
11 'He [a]puts my feet in the stocks;
He watches all my paths.'
12 "Behold, let me [1]tell you, you are not right in this,
For God is greater than man.

13 "Why do you [a]complain against Him,
That He does not give an account of all His doings?
14 "Indeed [a]God speaks once,
Or twice, *yet* no one notices it.
15 "In a [a]dream, a vision of the night,
When sound sleep falls on men,
While they slumber in their beds,
16 Then [a]He opens the ears of men,
And seals their instruction,
17 That He may turn man aside *from his* conduct,
And [1]keep man from pride;
18 He [a]keeps back his soul from the pit,
And his life from [1]passing over [b]into Sheol.

19 "[1]Man is also chastened with [a]pain on his bed,
And with unceasing complaint in his bones;
20 So that his life [a]loathes bread,
And his soul favorite food.
21 "His [a]flesh wastes away from sight,
And his [b]bones which were not seen stick out.
22 "Then [a]his soul draws near to the pit,
And his life to those who bring death.

23 "If there is an angel *as* [a]mediator for him,
One out of a thousand,
To remind a man what is [1]right for him,
24 Then let him be gracious to him, and say,
'Deliver him from [a]going down to the pit,
I have found a [b]ransom;'
25 Let his flesh become fresher than in youth,
Let him return to the days of his youthful vigor;
26 Then he will [a]pray to God, and He will accept him,
That [b]he may see His face with joy,
And He may restore His righteousness to man.
27 "He will [a]sing to men and say,
'I [b]have sinned and perverted what is right,
And it is not [c]proper for me.
28 'He has redeemed my soul from going to the pit,
And my life shall [a]see the light.'

29 "Behold, God does [a]all these [1]oftentimes with men,
30 To [a]bring back his soul from the pit,
That he may be enlightened with the light of life.
31 "Pay attention, O Job, listen to me;
Keep silent and let me speak.
32 "*Then* if [1]you have anything to say, answer me;
Speak, for I desire to justify you.

21 [a]Lev. 19:15; Job 13:8, 10; 34:19
2 [1]Lit., *palate*
3 [a]Job 6:28; 27:4; 36:4
4 [1]Heb., *Shaddai* [a]Job 10:3; 32:8 [b]Job 27:3
5 [a]Job 33:32
6 [1]Lit., *cut out of* [a]Job 4:19
9 [a]Job 6:10; 9:21; 10:7; 13:18; 16:17 [b]Job 7:21; 13:23; 14:17 [c]Job 10:14
10 [1]Lit., *finds* [a]Job 13:24
11 [a]Job 13:27
12 [1]Lit., *answer*
13 [a]Job 40:2; Is. 45:9
14 [a]Job 33:29; 40:5; Ps. 62:11
15 [a]Job 4:12-17; 33:15-18
16 [a]Job 36:10, 15
17 [1]Lit., *hide*
18 [1]M.T., *perishing by the sword* [a]Job 33:22, 24, 28, 30 [b]Job 15:22
19 [1]Lit., *He* [a]Job 30:17
20 [a]Job 3:24; 6:7; Ps. 107:18
21 [a]Job 16:8 [b]Job 19:20; Ps. 22:17
22 [a]Job 33:18, 28
23 [1]Lit., *his uprightness* [a]Gen. 40:8
24 [a]Job 33:18, 28; Is. 38:17 [b]Job 36:18; Ps. 49:7
26 [a]Job 22:27; 34:28 [b]Job 22:26
27 [a]Job 8:21 [b]2 Sam. 12:13; Luke 15:21 [c]Rom. 6:21
28 [a]Job 22:28
29 [1]Lit., *twice, three times* [a]Eph. 1:11; Phil. 2:13
30 [a]Job 33:18
32 [1]Lit., *there are words*

33 "If not, listen to me;
Keep silent, and I will teach you wisdom."

Chapter 34

Elihu Vindicates God's Justice

THEN Elihu continued and said,
2 "Hear my words, you wise men,
And listen to me, you who know.
3 "For [a]the ear tests words,
As the palate tastes food.
4 "Let us choose for ourselves what is right;
Let us know among ourselves what is good.
5 "For Job has said, '[a]I am righteous,
But [b]God has taken away my right;
6 [1]Should I lie concerning my right?
My [2a]wound is incurable, *though I am* without transgression.'
7 "What man is like Job,
Who [a]drinks up derision like water,
8 Who goes [a]in company with the workers of iniquity,
And walks with wicked men?
9 "For he has said, '[a]It profits a man nothing
When he [1]is pleased with God.'

10 "Therefore, listen to me, you men of understanding.
Far be it from God to [a]do wickedness,
And from the Almighty to do wrong.
11 "For He pays a man according to [a]his work,
And makes [1]him find it according to his way.
12 "Surely, [a]God will not act wickedly,
And the Almighty will not pervert justice.
13 "Who [a]gave Him authority over the earth?
And who [b]has laid *on Him* the whole world?
14 "If He should [1]determine to do so,
If He should [a]gather to Himself His spirit and His breath,
15 All [a]flesh would perish together,
And man would [b]return to dust.

16 "But if *you have* understanding, hear this;
Listen to the sound of my words.
17 "Shall [a]one who hates justice rule?
And [b]will you condemn a righteous mighty one,
18 Who says to a king, 'Worthless one,'
To nobles, 'Wicked ones';
19 Who shows no [a]partiality to princes,
Nor regards the rich above the poor,
For they all are the [b]work of His hands?
20 "In a moment they die, and [a]at midnight
People are shaken and pass away,
And [b]the mighty are taken away without a hand.

21 "For [a]His eyes are upon the ways of a man,
And He sees all his steps.
22 "There is [a]no darkness or deep shadow
Where the workers of iniquity may hide themselves.
23 "For He does not [a]*need to* consider a man further,
That he should go before God in judgment.
24 "He breaks in pieces [a]mighty men without inquiry,
And sets others in their place.
25 "Therefore He [a]knows their works,
And [b]He overthrows *them* in the night,
And they are crushed.
26 "He [a]strikes them like the wicked
[1]In a public place,
27 Because they [a]turned aside from following Him,
And [b]had no regard for any of His ways;
28 So that they caused [a]the cry of the poor to come to Him,
And that He might [b]hear the cry of the afflicted—
29 When He keeps quiet, who then can condemn?
And when He hides His face, who then can behold Him,
That is, in regard to both nation and man?—
30 So that [a]godless men should not rule,
Nor be snares of the people.

31 "For has any one said to God,
'I have [a]borne *chastisement;*
I will not offend *any more;*
32 Teach Thou me what I do not see;
If I have [a]done iniquity,
I will do it no more'?

3 [a]Job 12:11
5 [a]Job 13:18 [b]Job 27:2
6 [1]Or, *Although I am right I am accounted a liar* [2]Lit., *arrow* [a]Job 6:4
7 [a]Job 15:16
8 [a]Job 22:15
9 [1]Or, *takes delight in God* [a]Job 21:15; 35:3; Ps. 50:18
10 [a]Job 8:3; 34:12
11 [1]Lit., *a man* [a]Job 34:25; Ps. 62:12; Prov. 24:12; Jer. 32:19; Ezek. 33:20; Matt. 16:27; Rom. 2:6; 2 Cor. 5:10; Rev. 22:12
12 [a]Job 34:10
13 [a]Job 38:4 [b]Job 38:5
14 [1]Lit., *set His mind on Himself* [a]Job 12:10; Ps. 104:29
15 [a]Gen. 7:21; Job 9:22 [b]Gen. 3:19; Job 10:9
17 [a]2 Sam. 23:3; Job 34:30 [b]Job 40:8
19 [a]Lev. 19:15; Deut. 10:17; 2 Chr. 19:7; Acts 10:34; Rom. 2:11; Gal. 2:6; Eph. 6:9; Col. 3:25; 1 Pet. 1:17 [b]Job 10:3
20 [a]Ex. 12:29; Job 34:25; 36:20 [b]Job 12:19
21 [a]Job 29:23; 31:4; Prov. 5:21; 15:3; Jer. 16:17
22 [a]Ps. 139:11, 12; Amos 9:2, 3
23 [a]Job 11:11
24 [a]Job 12:19
25 [a]Job 34:11 [b]Job 34:20
26 [1]Lit., *In the place of the ones seeing* [a]Ps. 9:5; 11:5
27 [a]1 Sam. 15:11 [b]Job 21:14
28 [a]Job 35:9 [b]Ex. 22:23; Job 22:27
30 [a]Job 5:15; 20:5; 34:17
31 [a]Job 33:27
32 [a]Job 33:27

33"Shall He [a]recompense on your terms, because you have rejected *it?*
For you must choose, and not I;
Therefore declare what you know.
34"Men of understanding will say to me,
And a wise man who hears me,
35 'Job [a]speaks without knowledge,
And his words are without wisdom.
36 'Job ought to be tried [1]to the limit,
Because he answers [a]like wicked men.
37 'For he adds [a]rebellion to his sin;
He [b]claps his hands among us,
And multiplies his words against God.' "

CHAPTER 35

Elihu Sharply Reproves Job

THEN Elihu continued and said,
2"Do you think this is according to [a]justice?
Do you say, 'My righteousness is more than God's'?
3"For you say, '[a]What advantage will it be to [1]You?
[b]What profit shall I have, more than if I had sinned?'
4"I will answer you,
And your friends with you.
5"[a]Look at the heavens and see;
And behold [b]the clouds—they are higher than you.
6"If you have sinned, [a]what do you accomplish against Him?
And if your transgressions are many, what do you do to Him?
7"If you are righteous, [a]what do you give to Him?
Or what does He receive from your hand?
8"Your wickedness is for a man like yourself,
And your righteousness is for a son of man.

9"Because of the multitude of oppressions they cry out;
They cry for help because of the arm [a]of the mighty.
10"But [a]no one says, 'Where is God my Maker,
Who [b]gives songs in the night,
11 Who [a]teaches us more than the beasts of the earth,
And makes us wiser than the birds of the heavens?'

33 [a]Job 41:11
35 [a]Job 35:16
36 [1]Or, *to the end* [a]Job 22:15
37 [a]Job 23:2 [b]Job 27:23
2 [a]Job 27:2
3 [1]Or, *you* [a]Job 34:9 [b]Job 9:30, 31
5 [a]Gen. 15:5; Ps. 8:3 [b]Job 22:12
6 [a]Job 7:20; Prov. 8:36; Jer. 7:19
7 [a]Job 22:2, 3; Prov. 9:12; Luke 17:10
9 [a]Job 12:19
10 [a]Job 24:14; 27:10; 36:13 [b]Job 8:21; Ps. 42:8; 77:6; 149:5; Acts 16:25
11 [a]Job 36:22; Ps. 94:12; Jer. 32:33
13 [1]Or, *falsehood* [a]Job 27:9; Prov. 15:29; Is. 1:15; Jer. 11:11; Mic. 3:4
14 [a]Job 9:11; 23:8, 9 [b]Job 31:35
15 [1]Or, *arrogance*
16 [1]Lit., *vainly* [a]Job 34:35
2 [1]Lit., *are yet words for God*
3 [a]Job 8:3; 37:23
4 [a]Job 33:3 [b]Job 37:16
5 [a]Ps. 22:24; 69:33; 102:17 [b]Job 12:13
6 [a]Job 8:22; 34:26 [b]Job 5:15
7 [a]Ps. 33:18; 34:15 [b]Job 5:11; Ps. 113:8
8 [a]Job 36:15, 21
9 [a]Job 15:25
10 [a]Job 33:16; 36:15 [b]2 Kin. 17:13; Job 36:21; Jon. 3:8

12"There they cry out, but He does not answer
Because of the pride of evil men.
13"Surely [a]God will not listen to [1]an empty *cry,*
Nor will the Almighty regard it.
14"How much less when [a]you say you do not behold Him,
The [b]case is before Him, and you must wait for Him!
15"And now, because He has not visited *in* His anger,
Nor has He acknowledged [1]transgression well,
16 So Job opens his mouth [1]emptily;
He multiplies words [a]without knowledge."

CHAPTER 36

Elihu Speaks of God's Dealings with Men

THEN Elihu continued and said,
2"Wait for me a little, and I will show you
That there [1]is yet more to be said in God's behalf.
3"I will fetch my knowledge from afar,
And I will ascribe [a]righteousness to my Maker.
4"For truly [a]my words are not false;
One who is [b]perfect in knowledge is with you.
5"Behold, God is mighty but does not [a]despise *any;*
He is [b]mighty in strength of understanding.
6"He does not [a]keep the wicked alive,
But gives justice to [b]the afflicted.
7"He does not [a]withdraw His eyes from the righteous;
But [b]with kings on the throne
He has seated them forever, and they are exalted.
8"And if they are bound in fetters,
And are caught in the cords of [a]affliction,
9 Then he declares to them their work
And their transgressions, that they have [a]magnified themselves.
10"And [a]He opens their ear to instruction,
And [b]commands that they return from evil.
11"If they hear and serve *Him,*
They shall end their days in prosperity,
And their years in pleasures.

12"But if they do not hear, they shall [1]perish [a]by the sword,
And they shall [b]die without knowledge.
13"But the godless in heart lay up anger;
They do not cry for help when He binds them.
14"[1]They die in youth,
And their life *perishes* among the [a]cult prostitutes.
15"He delivers the afflicted in [1]their [a]affliction,
And [b]opens their ear [2]in *time of* oppression.
16"Then indeed, He [a]enticed you from the mouth of distress,
Instead of it, a broad place with no constraint;
And that which was set on your table was full of [1]fatness.

17"But you were full of [a]judgment on the wicked;
Judgment and justice take hold *of you.*
18"*Beware* lest [a]wrath entice you to scoffing;
And do not let the greatness of the [b]ransom turn you aside.
19"Will your [1]riches keep *you* from distress,
Or all the forces of *your* strength?
20"Do not long for [a]the night,
When people [1]vanish in their place.
21"Be careful, do [a]not turn to evil;
For you have preferred this to [b]affliction.
22"Behold, God is exalted in His power;
Who is a [a]teacher like Him?
23"Who has appointed Him His way,
And who has said, '[a]Thou hast done wrong'?

24"Remember that you should exalt His work,
Of which men have [a]sung.
25"All men have seen it;
Man beholds from afar.
26"Behold, God is [a]exalted, and we do not know *Him;*
The [b]number of His years is unsearchable.
27"For [a]He draws up the drops of water,
They distill rain from [1]the [2]mist,
28 Which the clouds pour down,
They drip upon man abundantly.
29"Can anyone understand the [a]spreading of the clouds,
The [b]thundering of His [1]pavilion?
30"Behold, He spreads His [1]lightning about Him,
And He covers the depths of the sea.
31"For by these He [a]judges peoples;
He [b]gives food in abundance.
32"He covers *His* hands with the [1]lightning,
And [a]commands it to strike the mark.
33"Its [a]noise declares [1]His presence;
The cattle also, concerning what is coming up.

Chapter 37

Elihu Says God Is Back of the Storm

"At this also my heart trembles,
And leaps from its place.
2"Listen closely to the [a]thunder of His voice,
And the rumbling that goes out from His mouth.
3"Under the whole heaven He lets it loose,
And His [1]lightning to the [a]ends of the earth.
4"After it, a voice roars;
He thunders with His majestic voice;
And He does not restrain [1]*the lightnings* when His voice is heard.
5"God [a]thunders with His voice wondrously,
Doing [b]great things which we cannot comprehend.
6"For to [a]the snow He says, 'Fall on the earth,'
And to the [1b]downpour and the rain, 'Be strong.'
7"He [a]seals the hand of every man,
That all men may know His work.
8"Then the beast goes into its [a]lair,
And remains in its [1]den.
9"Out of the [1a]south comes the storm,
And out of the [2]north the cold.
10"From the breath of God [a]ice is made,
And the expanse of the waters is frozen.
11"Also with moisture He [a]loads the thick cloud;
He [b]disperses [c]the cloud of His [1]lightning.
12"And it changes direction, turning around by His guidance,

12 [1]Lit., *pass away* [a]Job 15:22 [b]Job 4:21
14 [1]Or, *Their soul dies* [a]Deut. 23:17
15 [1]Lit., *his* [2]Or, *in adversity* [a]Job 36:8, 21 [b]Job 36:10
16 [1]Or, *rich food* [a]Hos. 2:14
17 [a]Job 22:5, 10, 11
18 [a]Job 34:33; Jon. 4:4, 9 [b]Job 33:24
19 [1]Or, *cry*
20 [1]Lit., *go up* [a]Job 34:20, 25
21 [a]Job 36:10; Ps. 31:6; 66:18 [b]Job 36:8, 15
22 [a]Job 35:11
23 [a]Job 8:3
24 [a]Ex. 15:1; Judg. 5:1; 1 Chr. 16:9; Ps. 59:16; 138:5
26 [a]Job 11:7-9; 37:23 [b]Job 10:5; Ps. 90:2; 102:24, 27
27 [1]Lit., *its* [2]Or, *flood* [a]Job 5:10; 36:26-29; 37:6, 11; 38:28; Ps. 147:8
29 [1]Lit., *booth* [a]Job 37:11, 16 [b]Job 26:14
30 [1]Lit., *light*
31 [a]Job 37:13 [b]Ps. 104:27; 136:25; Acts 14:17
32 [1]Lit., *light* [a]Job 37:11, 12, 15
33 [1]Lit., *concerning Him* [a]Job 37:2
2 [a]Job 36:33; 37:4, 5; Ps. 29:3-9
3 [1]Lit., *light* [a]Job 28:24; 37:12; 38:13
4 [1]Lit., *them*
5 [a]Job 26:14 [b]Job 5:9; 37:14, 16, 23
6 [1]Lit., *shower of rain and shower of rains* [a]Job 38:22 [b]Job 36:27
7 [a]Job 12:14
8 [1]Lit., *dens* [a]Job 38:40; Ps. 104:22
9 [1]Lit., *chamber* [2]Lit., *scattering winds* [a]Job 9:9
10 [a]Job 38:29; Ps. 147:17
11 [1]Lit., *light* [a]Job 36:27 [b]Job 36:29 [c]Job 37:15

That [1]it may do whatever He [a]commands [2]it
On the [b]face of the inhabited earth.
13 "Whether for [1a]correction, or for [b]His world,
Or for [c]lovingkindness, He causes it to [2]happen.

14 "Listen to this, O Job,
Stand and consider the wonders of God.
15 "Do you know how God establishes them,
And makes the [1]lightning of His cloud to shine?
16 "Do you know about the layers of the thick clouds,
The [a]wonders of one [b]perfect in knowledge,
17 You whose garments are hot,
When the land is still because of the south wind?
18 "Can you, with Him, [a]spread out the skies,
Strong as a molten mirror?
19 "Teach us what we shall say to Him;
We [a]cannot arrange *our case* because of darkness.
20 "Shall it be told Him that I would speak?
[1]Or should a man say that he would be swallowed up?

21 "And now [1]men do not see the light which is bright in the skies;
But the wind has passed and cleared them.
22 "Out of the north comes golden *splendor;*
Around God is awesome majesty.
23 "The Almighty—[a]we cannot find Him;
He is [b]exalted in power;
And [c]He will not do violence [d]to justice and abundant righteousness.
24 "Therefore men fear Him;
He does not [a]regard any who are wise of heart."

Chapter 38

God Speaks Now to Job

THEN the LORD [a]answered Job out of the whirlwind and said,
2 "Who is this that [a]darkens counsel
By words without knowledge?
3 "Now [a]gird up your loins like a man,
And [b]I will ask you, and you instruct Me!

4 "Where were you [a]when I laid the foundation of the earth!
Tell *Me,* if you [1]have understanding,
5 Who set its [a]measurements, since you know?
Or who stretched the line on it?
6 "On what [a]were its bases sunk?
Or who laid its cornerstone,
7 When the morning stars sang together,
And all the [a]sons of God shouted for joy?

8 "Or *who* enclosed the sea with doors,
When, bursting forth, it went out from the womb;
9 When I made a cloud its garment,
And thick darkness its swaddling band,
10 And I [1a]placed boundaries on it,
And I set a bolt and doors,
11 And I said, 'Thus far you shall come, but no farther;
And here shall your proud waves stop'?

God's Mighty Power

12 "Have you [1]ever in your life commanded the morning,
And caused the dawn to know its place;
13 That it might take hold of [a]the ends of the earth,
And [b]the wicked be shaken out of it?
14 "It is changed like clay *under* the seal;
And they stand forth like a garment.
15 "And [a]from the wicked their light is withheld,
And the [b]uplifted arm is broken.

16 "Have you entered into [a]the springs of the sea?
Or have you walked [1]in the recesses of the deep?
17 "Have the gates of death been revealed to you?
Or have you seen the gates of [a]deep darkness?
18 "Have you understood the [1]expanse of [a]the earth?
Tell *Me,* if you know all this.

19 "Where is the way to the dwelling of light?
And darkness, where is its place,
20 That you may take it to [a]its territory,
And that you may discern the paths to its [1]home?

12 [1]Lit., *they* [2]Lit., *them* [a]Job 36:32; Ps. 148:8 [b]Is. 14:21; 27:6
13 [1]Lit., *the rod* [2]Lit., *be found* [a]Ex. 9:18, 23; 1 Sam. 12:18, 19 [b]Job 38:26, 27 [c]1 Kin. 18:45
15 [1]Lit., *light*
16 [a]Job 37:5, 14, 23 [b]Job 36:4
18 [a]Job 9:8; Ps. 104:2; Is. 45:12; Jer. 10:12; Zech. 12:1
19 [a]Job 9:14; Rom. 8:26
20 [1]Or, *If a man speak, surely he shall be swallowed up*
21 [1]Lit., *they*
23 [a]Job 11:7, 8; Rom. 11:13; 1 Tim. 8:16 [b]Job 9:4; 36:5 [c]Is. 63:9; Lam. 3:33; Nah. 1:12 [d]Job 8:3
24 [a]Job 5:13; 1 Cor. 1:26
1 [a]Job 40:6
2 [a]Job 35:16; 42:3
3 [a]Job 40:7 [b]Job 42:4
4 [1]Lit., *know understanding* [a]Job 15:7; Ps. 104:5; Prov. 30:4
5 [a]Prov. 8:29; Is. 40:12
6 [a]Job. 26:7
7 [a]Job 1:6
10 [1]Lit., *broke My decree on it* [a]Gen. 1:9; Ps. 33:7; 104:9; Prov. 8:29; Jer. 5:22
12 [1]Lit., *from your days*
13 [a]Job 28:24; 37:3 [b]Job 34:25, 26; 36:6
15 [a]Job 5:14 [b]Num. 15:30; Ps. 10:15; 37:17
16 [1]Or, *in search of* [a]Gen. 7:11; 8:2; Prov. 8:24, 28
17 [a]Job 10:21; 26:6; 34:22
18 [1]Or, *width* [a]Job 28:24
20 [1]Lit., *house* [a]Job 26:10

21"You know, for [a]you were born then,
And the number of your days is great!
22"Have you entered the storehouses [a]of the snow,
Or have you seen the storehouses of the [b]hail,
23 Which I have reserved for the time of distress,
For the day of war and battle?
24"Where is the way that [a]the light is divided,
Or the east wind scattered on the earth?

25"Who has cleft a channel for the flood,
Or a way for the thunderbolt;
26 To bring [a]rain on a land without [1]people,
On a desert without a man in it,
27 To [a]satisfy the waste and desolate land,
And to make the [1]seeds of grass to sprout?
28"Has [a]the rain a father?
Or who has begotten the drops of dew?
29"From whose womb has come the [a]ice?
And the frost of heaven, who has given it birth?
30"Water [1]becomes hard like stone,
And the surface of the deep is imprisoned.

31"Can you bind the chains of the [a]Pleiades,
Or loose the cords of Orion?
32"Can you lead forth a [1]constellation in its season,
And guide the Bear with her [2]satellites?
33"Do you know the [a]ordinances of the heavens,
Or fix their rule over the earth?

34"Can you lift up your voice to the clouds,
So that an [a]abundance of water may cover you?
35"Can you [a]send forth lightnings that they may go
And say to you, 'Here we are'?
36"Who has [a]put wisdom in the innermost being,
Or has given [b]understanding to the [1]mind?
37"Who can count the clouds by wisdom,
Or [a]tip the water jars of the heavens,
38 When the dust hardens into a mass,
And the clods stick together?

39"Can you hunt the [a]prey for the lion,
Or satisfy the appetite of the young lions,
40 When they [a]crouch in *their* dens,
And lie in wait in *their* lair?
41"Who prepares for [a]the raven its nourishment,
When its young cry to God,
And wander about without food?

Chapter 39

God Speaks of Nature and Its Beings

"Do you know the time the [1a]mountain goats give birth?
Do you observe the calving of the [b]deer?
2"Can you count the months they fulfill,
Or do you know the time they give birth?
3"They kneel down, they bring forth their young,
They get rid of their labor pains.
4"Their offspring become strong, they grow up in the open field;
They leave and do not return to them.

5"Who sent out the [a]wild donkey free?
And who loosed the bonds of the swift donkey,
6 To whom I gave [a]the wilderness for a home,
And the salt land for his dwelling place?
7"He scorns the tumult of the city,
The shoutings of the driver he does not hear.
8"He explores the mountains for his pasture,
And he searches after every green thing.
9"Will the [a]wild ox consent to serve you?
Or will he spend the night at your manger?
10"Can you bind the wild ox in a furrow with [1]ropes?
Or will he harrow the valleys after you?
11"Will you trust him because his strength is great
And leave your labor to him?
12"Will you have faith in him that he will return your [1]grain,
And gather *it from* your threshing floor?

21 [a]Job 15:7
22 [a]Job 37:6 [b]Ex. 9:18; Josh. 10:11; Is. 30:30; Ezek. 13:11, 13; Rev. 16:21
24 [a]Job 26:10
26 [1]Lit., *man* [a]Job 36:27
27 [1]Or, *growth* [a]Ps. 104:13, 14
28 [a]Job 36:27, 28; Ps. 147:8; Jer. 14:22
29 [a]Job 37:10; Ps. 147:17
30 [1]Lit., *hides itself*
31 [a]Job 9:9; Amos 5:8
32 [1]Lit., *Mazzaroth* [2]Lit., *sons*
33 [a]Ps. 148:6; Jer. 31:35, 36
34 [a]Job 22:11; 36:27, 28; 38:37
35 [a]Job 36:32; 37:3
36 [1]Or, *cock* [a]Job 9:4; Ps. 51:6; Eccles. 2:26 [b]Job 32:8
37 [a]Job 38:34
39 [a]Ps. 104:21
40 [a]Job 37:8
41 [a]Ps. 147:9; Matt 6:26; Luke 12:24
1 [1]Lit., *goats of the rock* [a]Deut. 14:5; 1 Sam. 24:2; Ps. 104:18 [b]Ps. 29:9
5 [a]Job 6:5; 11:12; 24:5; Ps. 104:11
6 [a]Job 24:5; Jer. 2:24; Hos. 8:9
9 [a]Num. 23:22; Deut. 33:17; Ps. 22:21; 29:6; 92:10; Is. 34:7
10 [1]Lit., *his rope*
12 [1]Lit., *seed*

13"The ostriches' wings flap joyously
With the pinion and plumage of [1]love,
14 For she abandons her eggs to the earth,
And warms them in the dust,
15 And she forgets that a foot may crush [1]them,
Or that a wild beast may trample [1]them.
16"She treats her young [a]cruelly, as if *they* were not hers;
Though her labor be in vain, *she* is [1]unconcerned;
17 Because God has made her forget wisdom,
And has not given her a share of understanding.
18"When she lifts herself [1]on high,
She laughs at the horse and his rider.

19"Do you give the horse *his* might?
Do you clothe his neck with a mane?
20"Do you make him [a]leap like the locust?
His majestic [b]snorting is terrible.
21"[1]He paws in the valley, and rejoices in *his* strength;
He [a]goes out to meet the weapons.
22"He laughs at fear and is not dismayed;
And he does not turn back from the sword.
23"The quiver rattles against him,
The flashing spear and javelin.
24"With shaking and rage he [1]races over the ground;
And he does not stand still at the voice of the trumpet.
25"As often as the trumpet *sounds* he says, 'Aha!'
And he scents the battle from afar,
And thunder of the captains, and the war cry.

26"Is it by your understanding that the hawk soars,
Stretching his wings toward the south?
27"Is it at your [1]command that the eagle mounts up,
And makes [a]his nest on high?
28"On the cliff he dwells and lodges,
Upon the rocky crag, an inaccessible place.
29"From there he [a]spies out food;
His eyes see *it* from afar.
30"His young ones also suck up blood;
And [a]where the slain are, there is he."

Chapter 40

Job: What Can I Say?

THEN the LORD said to Job,
2"Will the faultfinder [a]contend with the Almighty?
Let him who [b]reproves God answer it."

3 Then Job answered the LORD and said,
4"Behold, I am insignificant; what can I reply to Thee?
I [a]lay my hand on my mouth.
5"Once I have spoken, and [a]I will not answer;
Even twice, and I will add no more."

God Questions Job

6 Then the [a]LORD answered Job out of the storm, and said,
7"Now [a]gird up your loins like a man;
I will [b]ask you, and you instruct Me.
8"Will you really annul My judgment?
Will you [a]condemn Me [b]that you may be justified?
9"Or do you have an arm like God,
And can you [a]thunder with a voice like His?

10"Adorn yourself with eminence and dignity;
And clothe yourself with honor and majesty.
11"Pour out [a]the overflowings of your anger;
And look on everyone who is [b]proud, and make him low.
12"Look on everyone who is proud, *and* [a]humble him;
And [b]tread down the wicked [1]where they stand.
13"[a]Hide them in the dust together;
Bind [1]them in the hidden *place.*
14"Then I will also [1]confess to you,
That your own right hand can save you.

God's Power Shown in Creatures

15"Behold now, [1]Behemoth, which [a]I made [2]as well as you;
He eats grass like an ox.
16"Behold now, his strength in his loins,
And his power in the muscles of his belly.

13 [1]Or, *a stork*
15 [1]Lit., *it*
16 [1]Lit., *without fear* [a]Lam. 4:3
18 [1]Or, *to flee*
20 [a]Joel 2:5 [b]Jer. 8:16
21 [1]Lit., *They paw* [a]Jer. 8:6
24 [1]Or, *swallows up*
27 [1]Lit., *mouth* [a]Jer. 49:16; Obad. 4
29 [a]Job 9:26
30 [a]Matt. 24:28; Luke 17:37
2 [a]Job 9:3; 10:2; 33:13 [b]Job 13:3; 23:4; 31:35
4 [a]Job 21:5; 29:9
5 [a]Job 9:3, 15
6 [a]Job 38:1
7 [a]Job 38:3 [b]Job 38:3; 42:4
8 [a]Job 10:3, 7; 16:11; 19:6; 27:2 [b]Job 13:18; 27:6
9 [a]Job 37:5
11 [a]Is. 42:25; Nah. 1:6, 8 [b]Is. 2:12; Dan. 4:37
12 [1]Lit., *under them* [a]1 Sam. 2:7; Is. 13:11 [b]Is. 63:3
13 [1]Or, *their faces* [a]Is. 2:10-12
14 [1]Or, *praise you*
15 [1]Or, *the hippopotamus* [2]Lit., *with* [a]Job 40:19

17"He bends his tail like a cedar;
The sinews of his thighs are knit together.
18"His bones are tubes of bronze;
His [1]limbs are like bars of iron.

19"He is the [a]first of the ways of God;
Let his [b]maker bring near his sword.
20"Surely the mountains bring him food,
And all the beasts of the field [a]play there.
21"Under the lotus plants he lies down,
In the covert of the reeds and the marsh.
22"The lotus plants cover him with [1]shade;
The willows of the brook surround him.
23"If a river [1]rages, he is not alarmed;
He is confident, though the Jordan rushes to his mouth.
24"Can anyone capture him [1]when he is on watch,
With [2]barbs can anyone pierce *his* nose?

Chapter 41

God's Power Shown in Creatures

"[1]CAN you draw out [2a]Leviathan with a fishhook?
Or press down his tongue with a cord?
2"Can you [a]put a [1]rope in his nose?
Or pierce his jaw with a [2]hook?
3"Will he make many supplications to you?
Or will he speak to you soft words?
4"Will he make a covenant with you?
Will you take him for a servant forever?
5"Will you play with him as with a bird?
Or will you bind him for your maidens?
6"Will the [1]traders bargain over him?
Will they divide him among the merchants?
7"Can you fill his skin with harpoons,
Or his head with fishing spears?
8"Lay your hand on him;
Remember the battle; [1]you will not do it again!
9"[1]Behold, [2]your expectation is false;
Will [3]you be laid low even at the sight of him?
10"No one is so fierce that he dares to [a]arouse him;
Who then is he that can stand before Me?
11"Who has [1]given to Me that I should repay *him?*
Whatever is [a]under the whole heaven is Mine.

12"I will not keep silence concerning his limbs,
Or his mighty strength, or his [1]orderly frame.
13"Who can [1]strip off his outer armor?
Who can come within his double [2]mail?
14"Who can open the doors of his face?
Around his teeth there is terror.
15"*His* [1]strong scales are *his* pride,
Shut up *as with* a tight seal.
16"One is so near to another,
That no air can come between them.
17"They are joined one to another;
They clasp each other and cannot be separated.
18"His sneezes flash forth light,
And his eyes are like the [a]eyelids of the morning.
19"Out of his mouth go burning torches;
Sparks of fire leap forth.
20"Out of his nostrils smoke goes forth,
As *from* a boiling pot and *burning* rushes.
21"His breath kindles coals,
And a flame goes forth from his mouth.
22"In his neck lodges strength,
And dismay leaps before him.
23"The folds of his flesh are joined together,
Firm on him and immovable.
24"His heart is as hard as a stone;
Even as hard as a lower millstone.
25"When he raises himself up, the [1]mighty fear;
Because of the crashing they are bewildered.
26"The sword that reaches him cannot avail;
Nor the spear, the dart, or the javelin.
27"He regards iron as straw,
Bronze as rotten wood.
28"The [1]arrow cannot make him flee;
Slingstones are turned into stubble for him.

18 [1]Lit., *bones*
19 [a]Job 41:33 [b]Job 40:15
20 [a]Ps. 104:26
22 [1]Lit., *his shade*
23 [1]Or, *oppresses*
24 [1]Lit., *in his eyes* [2]Lit., *snares*
1 [1]Ch. 40:25 in Heb. [2]Or, *the crocodile* [a]Job 3:8; Ps. 74:14; 104:26; Is. 27:1
2 [1]Lit., *rope of rushes* [2]Or, *thorn,* or, *ring* [a]2 Kin. 19:28; Is. 37:29
6 [1]Lit., *partners*
8 [1]Lit., *do not add*
9 [1]Chap. 41:1 in Heb. [2]Lit., *his* [3]Lit., *he*
10 [a]Job 3:8
11 [1]Lit., *anticipated* [a]Ex. 19:5; Deut. 10:14; Job 9:5-10; 26:6-14; 28:24; Ps. 24:1; 50:12; 1 Cor. 10:26
12 [1]Or, *graceful*
13 [1]Lit., *uncover the face of his garment* [2]So Gk.; Heb., *bridle*
15 [1]Lit., *rows of shields*
18 [a]Job 3:9
25 [1]Or, *gods*
28 [1]Lit., *son of the bow*

29 "Clubs are regarded as stubble;
He laughs at the rattling of the javelin.
30 "His underparts are *like* sharp potsherds;
He [1]spreads out *like* a threshing sledge on the mire.
31 "He makes the depths boil like a pot;
He makes the sea like a jar of ointment.
32 "Behind him he makes a wake to shine;
One would think the deep to be gray-haired.
33 "[a]Nothing on [1]earth is like him,
One made without fear.
34 "[1]He looks on everything that is high;
He is king over all the [a]sons of pride."

Chapter 42

Job's Confession

THEN Job answered the LORD, and said,
2 "I know that Thou canst do all things,
And that no purpose of Thine can be thwarted.
3 'Who is this that [a]hides counsel without knowledge?'
"Therefore I have declared that which I did not understand,
Things [b]too wonderful for me, which I did not know."
4 'Hear, now, and I will speak;
I will [a]ask Thee, and do Thou instruct me.'
5 "I have [a]heard of Thee by the hearing of the ear;
But now my [b]eye sees Thee;
6 Therefore I retract,
And I repent in dust and ashes."

God Displeased with Job's Friends

7 And it came about after the LORD had spoken these words to Job, that the LORD said to Eliphaz the Temanite, "My wrath is kindled against you and against your two friends, because you have not spoken of Me what is right [a]as My servant Job has.
8 "Now therefore, take for yourselves seven bulls and seven rams, and go to My servant Job, and offer up a [a]burnt offering for yourselves, and My servant Job will pray for you. [b]For I will [1]accept him so that I may not do with you *according to your* folly, because you have not spoken of Me what is right, as My servant Job has."
9 So Eliphaz the Temanite and Bildad the Shuhite *and* Zophar the Naamathite went and did as the LORD told them; and the LORD [1]accepted Job.

God Restores Job's Fortunes

10 And the LORD [a]restored the fortunes of Job when he prayed for his friends, and the LORD increased all that Job had twofold.
11 Then all his [a]brothers, and all his sisters, and all who had known him before, came to him, and they ate bread with him in his house; and they [b]consoled him and comforted him for all the evil that the LORD had brought on him. And each one gave him one [1]piece of money, and each a ring of gold.
12 [a]And the LORD blessed the latter *days* of Job more than his beginning, [b]and he had 14,000 sheep, and 6,000 camels, and 1,000 yoke of oxen, and 1,000 female donkeys.
13 And [a]he had seven sons and three daughters.
14 And he named the first Jemimah, and the second Keziah, and the third Keren-happuch.
15 And in all the land no women were found so fair as Job's daughters; and their father gave them inheritance among their brothers.
16 And after this Job lived 140 years, and saw his sons, and his grandsons, four generations.
17 [a]And Job died, an old man and full of days.

---

30 [1]Or, *moves across*
33 [1]Lit., *dust* [a]Job 40:19
34 [1]Job 41:26 in Heb. [a]Job 28:8
3 [a]Job 38:2 [b]Ps. 40:5; 131:1; 139:6
4 [a]Job 38:3; 40:7
5 [a]Job 26:14 [b]Is. 6:5
7 [a]Job 40:3-5; 42:1-6
8 [1]Lit., *lift up his face* [a]Job 1:5 [b]Job 22:30
9 [1]Lit., *lifted up the face of*
10 [a]Deut. 30:3; Ps. 14:7; 85:1-3; 126:1-6
11 [1]Lit., *Qesitah* [a]Job 19:13 [b]Job 2:11
12 [a]Job 1:10 [b]Job 1:3
13 [a]Job 1:2
17 [a]Gen. 15:15; 25:8; 38:29; Job 5:26

THE PSALMS

The following expressions occur often in the Psalms:

Selah May mean *Pause, Crescendo* or *Musical Interlude*
Maskil Possibly, *Contemplative,* or *Didactic,* or *Skillful Psalm*
Mikhtam Possibly, *Epigrammatic Poem,* or *Atonement Psalm*
Sheol The nether world

BOOK 1

Psalm 1

The Righteous and the Wicked Contrasted.

HOW blessed is the man who [a]does not walk in the [b]counsel of the wicked,
Nor stand in the [1][c]path of sinners,
Nor [d]sit in the seat of scoffers!
2 But his [a]delight is in the law of the LORD,
And in His law he meditates [b]day and night.
3 And he will be like [a]a tree *firmly* planted by streams of water,
Which yields its fruit in its season,
And its leaf does not wither;
And in whatever he does, [b]he prospers.
4 The wicked are not so,
But they are like [a]chaff which the wind drives away.
5 Therefore [a]the wicked will not stand in the [b]judgment,
Nor sinners in the assembly of the righteous.
6 For the LORD [1][a]knows the way of the righteous,
But the way of [b]the wicked will perish.

Psalm 2

The Reign of the LORD's Anointed.

WHY are [a]the [1]nations in an uproar,
And the peoples devising a vain thing?
2 The [a]kings of the earth take their stand,
And the rulers take counsel together
[b]Against the LORD and against His [1]Anointed:
3 "Let us tear their fetters apart,
And cast away their cords from us!"

4 He who [1]sits in the heavens [a]laughs,
The Lord scoffs at them.
5 Then He will speak to them in His [a]anger
And [b]terrify them in His fury:
6 "But as for Me, I have installed [a]My King
Upon Zion, [b]My holy mountain."

7 "I will surely tell of the decree of the LORD:
He said to Me, 'Thou art [a]My Son,
Today I have begotten Thee.
8 'Ask of Me, and [a]I will surely give [b]the [1]nations as Thine inheritance,
And the *very* [c]ends of the earth as Thy possession.
9 'Thou shalt [1][a]break them with a [2]rod of iron,
Thou shalt [b]shatter them like earthenware.' "

10 Now therefore, O kings, [a]show discernment;
Take warning, O [1]judges of the earth.
11 [1]Worship the LORD with [2][a]reverence,
And rejoice with [b]trembling.
12 [1]Do homage to [a]the Son, lest He become angry, and you perish *in* the way,
For His wrath may [2]soon be kindled.
How blessed are all who [b]take refuge in Him!

Psalm 3

Morning Prayer of Trust in God.

A Psalm of David, when [£]he fled from Absalom his son.

O LORD, how [a]my adversaries have increased!
Many are rising up against me.
2 Many are saying [1]of my soul,
"There is no [2][a]deliverance for him in God." [Selah.

3 But Thou, O LORD, art [a]a shield about me,
My [b]glory, and the One who [c]lifts my head.
4 I was crying to the LORD with my voice,
And He [a]answered me from [b]His holy [1]mountain. [Selah.
5 I [a]lay down and slept;

---

1 [1]Or, *way* [a]Prov. 4:14 [b]Ps. 5:9, 10; 10:2-11; 36:1-4 [c]Ps. 17:4; 119:104 [d]Ps. 26:5
2 [a]Ps. 119:14, 16 [b]Ps. 25:5
3 [a]Ps. 92:12-14; Jer. 17:8; Ezek. 19:10 [b]Gen. 39:2, 3, 23
4 [a]Job 21:18; Ps. 35:5; Is. 17:13
5 [a]Ps. 5:5 [b]Ps. 9:7, 8, 16
6 [1]Or, *approves* [a]Nah. 1:7; John 10:14; 2 Tim. 2:19 [b]Ps. 9:5, 6; 11:6

---

1 [1]Or, *Gentiles* [a]Ps. 46:6; 83:2-5; Acts 4:25, 26
2 [1]Or, *Messiah* [a]Ps. 48:4-6 [b]Ps. 74:18, 23
4 [1]Or, *is enthroned* [a]Ps. 37:13
5 [a]Ps. 21:8, 9; 76:7 [b]Ps. 78:49
6 [a]Ps. 45:6 [b]Ps. 48:1, 2
7 [a]Acts 13:33; Heb. 1:5; 5:5
8 [1]Or, *Gentiles* [a]Ps. 21:1, 2 [b]Ps. 22:27 [c]Ps. 65:2
9 [1]Another reading is, *rule* [2]Or, *scepter* [a]Ps. 110:5, 6; Rev. 2:27; 12:5; 19:15 [b]Ps. 28:5; 52:5
10 [1]Or, *leaders* [a]Prov. 8:15; 27:11
11 [1]Or, *Serve* [2]Or, *fear* [a]Ps. 5:7 [b]Ps. 119:119, 120
12 [1]Lit., *Kiss;* some versions: *Do homage purely,* or, *Lay hold of instruction* [2]Or, *quickly, suddenly* [a]Ps. 2:7 [b]Ps. 5:11; 34:22

[£]2 Sam. 15:13-17, 29
1 [a]2 Sam. 15:12; Ps. 69:4
2 [1]Or, *to* [2]Or, *salvation* [a]Ps. 22:7, 8; 71:11
3 [a]Ps. 5:12 [b]Ps. 62:7 [c]Ps. 9:13
4 [1]Or, *hill* [a]Ps. 4:3 [b]Ps. 2:6; 15:1; 43:3
5 [a]Ps. 4:8

I awoke, for the LORD sustains me.
6 I will [a]not be afraid of ten thousands of people
Who have [b]set themselves against me round about.

7 [a]Arise, O LORD; [b]save me, O my God!
For Thou hast [c]smitten all my enemies on the cheek;
Thou hast [d]shattered the teeth of the wicked.
8 [1a]Salvation belongs to the LORD;
Thy [b]blessing *be* upon Thy people! [Selah.

PSALM 4

Evening Prayer of Trust in God.

For the choir director; on stringed instruments. A Psalm of David.

[a]

ANSWER me when [b]I call, O God [1]of my righteousness!
Thou hast [2c]relieved me in my distress;
Be [d]gracious to me and [e]hear my prayer.

2 O sons of men, how long will [a]my honor become [b]a reproach?
How long will you love [c]what is worthless and aim at [d]deception? [Selah.
3 But know that the LORD has [1a]set apart the [b]godly man for Himself;
The LORD [c]hears when I call to Him.

4 [1a]Tremble, [2b]and do not sin;
[3c]Meditate in your heart upon your bed, and be still. [Selah.
5 Offer [1]the [a]sacrifices of righteousness,
And [b]trust in the LORD.

6 Many are saying, "[a]Who will show us *any* good?"
[b]Lift up the light of Thy countenance upon us, O LORD!
7 Thou hast put [a]gladness in my heart,
More than [b]when their grain and new wine abound.
8 In peace I will both [a]lie down and sleep,
For Thou alone, O LORD, dost make me to [b]dwell in safety.

6 [a]Ps. 23:4; 27:3 [b]Ps. 118:10-13
7 [a]Ps. 7:6 [b]Ps. 6:4; 22:21 [c]Job 16:10 [d]Ps. 57:4; 58:6
8 [1]Or, *Deliverance* [a]Ps. 28:8; 35:3 [b]Ps. 29:11

1 [1]I.e., who maintainest my right [2]Lit., *made room for* [a]Ps. 3:4; 17:6 [b]Ps. 18:6 [c]Ps. 18:18, 19 [d]Ps. 25:16 [e]Ps. 17:6; 39:12
2 [a]Ps. 3:3 [b]Ps. 69:7-10, 19, 20 [c]Ps. 12:2; 31:6 [d]Ps. 31:18
3 [1]Another reading is, *dealt wonderfully with* [a]Ps. 135:4 [b]Ps. 31:23; 50:5; 79:2 [c]Ps. 6:8, 9; 17:6
4 [1]I.e., with anger or fear [2]Or, *but* [3]Lit., *Speak* [a]Ps. 99:1 [b]Ps. 119:11; Eph. 4:26 [c]Ps. 77:6
5 [1]Or, *righteous sacrifices* [a]Deut. 33:19; Ps. 51:19 [b]Ps. 37:3, 5
6 [a]Job 7:7; 9:25 [b]Num. 6:26; Ps. 80:3, 7, 19
7 [a]Ps. 97:11, 12 [b]Ps. 119:14, 72
8 [a]Job 11:19; Ps. 3:5 [b]Deut. 12:10

[£] Heb., *Nehiloth*
1 [1]Or, *meditation* [a]Ps. 54:2 [b]Ps. 104:34
2 [a]Ps. 140:6 [b]Ps. 84:3
3 [a]Ps. 88:13 [b]Ps. 130:5
4 [1]Lit., *sojourns* [a]Ps. 11:5; 34:16 [b]Ps. 92:15
5 [a]Ps. 73:3; 75:4 [b]Ps. 1:5 [c]Ps. 11:5; 45:7
6 [a]Ps. 52:4, 5 [b]Ps. 55:23
7 [1]Or, *Toward* [a]Ps. 69:13 [b]Ps. 138:2 [c]Ps. 115:11, 13
8 [a]Ps. 31:3 [b]Ps. 31:1 [c]Ps. 27:11
9 [1]Or, *true* [2]Lit., *his mouth* [a]Ps. 52:3 [b]Ps. 7:14 [c]Rom. 3:13
10 [a]Ps. 9:16 [b]Ps. 36:12 [c]Ps. 107:10, 11
11 [1]Or, *Thou dost shelter* [a]Ps. 2:12 [b]Ps. 33:1; 64:10 [c]Ps. 12:7 [d]Ps. 69:36
12 [a]Ps. 29:11 [b]Ps. 32:7, 10

PSALM 5

Prayer for Protection from the Wicked.

For the choir director; for [£]flute accompaniment.
A Psalm of David.

[a]

GIVE ear to my words, O LORD,
Consider my [1b]groaning.
2 Heed [a]the sound of my cry for help, [b]my King and my God,
For to Thee do I pray.
3 In the morning, O LORD, Thou wilt hear my voice;
In the [a]morning I will order *my prayer* to Thee and *eagerly* [b]watch.

4 For Thou art not a God [a]who takes pleasure in wickedness;
[b]No evil [1]dwells with Thee.
5 The [a]boastful shall not [b]stand before Thine eyes;
Thou [c]dost hate all who do iniquity.
6 Thou [a]dost destroy those who speak falsehood;
The LORD abhors [b]the man of bloodshed and deceit.
7 But as for me, [a]by Thine abundant lovingkindness I will enter Thy house,
[1]At Thy holy temple I will [b]bow in [c]reverence for Thee.

8 O LORD, [a]lead me [b]in Thy righteousness [c]because of my foes;
Make Thy way straight before me.
9 There is [a]nothing [1]reliable in [2]what they say;
Their [b]inward part is destruction *itself*;
Their [c]throat is an open grave;
They flatter with their tongue.
10 Hold them guilty, O God;
[a]By their own devices let them fall!
In the multitude of their transgressions [b]thrust them out,
For they are [c]rebellious against Thee.

11 But let all who [a]take refuge in Thee [b]be glad,
Let them ever sing for joy;
And [1]mayest Thou [c]shelter them,
That those who [d]love Thy name may exult in Thee.
12 For it is Thou who dost [a]bless the righteous man, O LORD,
Thou dost [b]surround him with favor as with a shield.

Psalm 6

Prayer for Mercy in Time of Trouble.

For the choir director; with stringed instruments, [ℓ]upon an eight-stringed lyre. A Psalm of David.

O LORD, [a]do not rebuke me in
Thine anger,
Nor chasten me in Thy wrath.
2 Be gracious to me, O LORD, for
I *am* [a]pining away;
[b]Heal me, O LORD, for [c]my
bones are dismayed.
3 And my [a]soul is greatly dismayed;
But Thou, O LORD —[b]how long?

4 Return, O LORD, [a]rescue my
[1]soul;
Save me because of Thy lovingkindness.
5 For [a]there is no [1]mention of
Thee in death;
In [2]Sheol who will give Thee
thanks?

6 I am [a]weary with my sighing;
Every night I make my bed
swim,
I dissolve my couch with [b]my
tears.
7 My [a]eye has wasted away with
grief;
It has become old because of all
my adversaries.

8 [a]Depart from me, all you who
do iniquity,
For the LORD [b]has heard the
voice of my weeping.
9 The LORD [a]has heard my supplication,
The LORD [b]receives my prayer.
10 All my enemies shall [a]be
ashamed and greatly dis-
mayed;
They shall turn back, they shall
[b]suddenly be ashamed.

Psalm 7

The LORD Implored to Defend the Psalmist against the Wicked.

A [ℓ]Shiggaion of David, which he sang to the Lord concerning Cush, a Benjamite.

O LORD my God, [a]in Thee I have
taken refuge;
Save me from all those who
pursue me, and [b]deliver me,
2 Lest he tear [1]my soul [a]like a
lion,
[2]Dragging me away, while
there is none to deliver.

3 O LORD my God, if I have done
this,
If there is [a]injustice in my
hands,
4 If I have [a]rewarded evil to [1]my
friend,
Or have [b]plundered him who
without cause was my adversary,
5 Let the enemy pursue my soul
and overtake *it;*
And let him trample my life
down to the ground,
And lay my glory in the
dust. [Selah.

6 [a]Arise, O LORD, in Thine anger;
[b]Lift up Thyself against [c]the
rage of my adversaries,
And [d]arouse Thyself [1]for me;
Thou hast appointed judg-
ment.
7 And let the assembly of the
[a]peoples encompass Thee;
And over [1]them return Thou on
high.
8 The LORD [a]judges the peoples;
[1b]Vindicate me, O LORD, according to my righteousness
and my integrity that is in
me.
9 O let [a]the evil of the wicked
come to an end, but [b]estab-
lish the righteous;
For the righteous God [c]tries the
hearts and [1]minds.
10 My [a]shield is with God,
Who [b]saves the upright in
heart.
11 God is a [a]righteous judge,
And a God who has [b]indigna-
tion every day.

12 If [1]a man [a]does not repent, He
will [b]sharpen His sword;
He has [c]bent His bow and
[2]made it ready.
13 He has also prepared for Himself deadly weapons;
He makes His [a]arrows fiery
shafts.
14 Behold, he travails with wickedness,
And he [a]conceives mischief,
and brings forth falsehood.
15 He has dug a pit and hollowed it
out,
And has [a]fallen into the hole
which he made.
16 His [a]mischief will return upon
his own head,
And his [b]violence will descend
upon [1]his own pate.

17 I will give thanks to the LORD
[a]according to His righteousness,

[ℓ] Or, *according to a lower octave* (Heb., *Sheminith*)
1 [a]Ps. 38:1; 118:18
2 [a]Ps. 102:4, 11 [b]Ps. 41:4; 147:3 [c]Ps. 22:14; 31:10
3 [a]Ps. 88:3; John 12:27 [b]Ps. 90:13
4 [1]Or, *life* [a]Ps. 17:13
5 [1]Or, *remembrance* [2]I.e., the nether world [a]Ps. 30:9; 88:10-12; 115:17; Eccles. 9:10; Is. 38:18
6 [a]Ps. 69:3 [b]Ps. 42:3
7 [a]Ps. 31:9; 38:10
8 [a]Ps. 119:115 [b]Ps. 28:6
9 [a]Ps. 116:1 [b]Ps. 66:19, 20
10 [a]Ps. 71:24 [b]Ps. 73:19
[ℓ] I.e., Dithyrambic rhythm, or, wild passionate song
1 [a]Ps. 31:1; 71:1 [b]Ps. 31:15
2 [1]Or, *me* [2]Or, *Rending it in pieces, while* [a]Ps. 57:4
3 [a]1 Sam. 24:11
4 [1]Lit., *him who was at peace with me* [a]Ps. 109:4, 5 [b]1 Sam. 24:7; 26:9
6 [1]One ancient version reads, *O my God* [a]Ps. 3:7 [b]Ps. 94:2 [c]Ps. 138:7 [d]Ps. 35:23
7 [1]Lit., *it* [a]Ps. 22:27
8 [1]Lit., *Judge* [a]Ps. 96:13; 98:9 [b]Ps. 26:1; 35:24; 43:1
9 [1]Lit., *kidneys,* figurative for inner man [a]Ps. 34:21; 94:23 [b]Ps. 37:23; 40:2 [c]Ps. 11:4, 5; Jer. 11:20
10 [a]Ps. 18:2, 30 [b]Ps. 97:10, 11
11 [a]Ps. 50:6 [b]Ps. 90:9
12 [1]Lit., *he* [2]Lit., *fixed it* [a]Ps. 58:4, 5 [b]Deut. 32:41 [c]Ps. 64:7
13 [a]Ps. 18:14; 45:5
14 [a]Job 15:35; Is. 59:4; James 1:15
15 [a]Ps. 57:6
16 [1]I.e., the crown of his own head [a]Ps. 140:9 [b]Ps. 140:11
17 [a]Ps. 71:15, 16

And will [b]sing praise to the name of the LORD Most High.

PSALM 8

The LORD's Glory and Man's Dignity.

For the choir director; on the Gittith.
A Psalm of David.

O LORD, our Lord,
How majestic is Thy name in all the earth,
Who hast [1a]displayed Thy splendor above the heavens!
2 [a]From the mouth of infants and nursing babes Thou hast established [1b]strength,
Because of Thine adversaries,
To make [c]the enemy and the revengeful cease.

3 When I [1]consider [a]Thy heavens, the work of Thy fingers,
The [b]moon and the stars, which Thou hast [2]ordained;
4 [a]What is man, that Thou [1]dost take thought of him?
And the son of man, that Thou dost care for him?
5 Yet Thou hast made him a [a]little lower than [1]God,
And [b]dost crown him with [c]glory and majesty!
6 Thou dost make him to [a]rule over the works of Thy hands;
Thou hast [b]put all things under his feet,
7 All sheep and oxen,
And also the [1]beasts of the field,
8 The birds of the heavens, and the fish of the sea,
Whatever passes through the paths of the seas.

9 O LORD, our Lord,
How majestic is Thy name in all the earth!

PSALM 9

A Psalm of Thanksgiving for God's Justice.

For the choir director; on [£]Muth-labben.
A Psalm of David.

I WILL give thanks to the LORD with all [a]my heart;
I will [b]tell of all Thy [1]wonders.
2 I will be glad and [a]exult in Thee;
I will [b]sing praise to Thy name, O [c]Most High.

3 When my enemies turn back,
They stumble and [a]perish before Thee.
4 For Thou hast [a]maintained [1]my just cause;
Thou dost sit on the throne [2b]judging righteously.
5 Thou hast [a]rebuked the nations,
Thou hast destroyed the wicked;
Thou hast [b]blotted out their name forever and ever.
6 The enemy has come to an end in [a]perpetual ruins,
And Thou hast uprooted the cities;
The very [b]memory of them has perished.

7 But the [a]LORD [1]abides forever;
He has established His [b]throne for judgment,
8 And He will [a]judge the world in righteousness;
He will execute judgment for the peoples with equity.
9 The LORD also will be a [a]stronghold for the oppressed,
A stronghold in times of trouble,
10 And [1]those who [a]know Thy name will put their trust in Thee;
For Thou, O LORD, hast not [b]forsaken those who seek Thee.

11 Sing praises to the LORD, who [a]dwells in Zion;
[b]Declare among the peoples His deeds.
12 For [a]He who [1]requires blood remembers them;
He does not forget [b]the cry of the afflicted.
13 Be gracious to me, O LORD;
Behold my affliction from those [a]who hate me,
Thou who [b]dost lift me up from the gates of death;
14 That I may tell of [a]all Thy praises,
That in the gates of the daughter of Zion
I may [b]rejoice in Thy [1]salvation.
15 The nations have sunk down [a]in the pit which they have made;
In the [b]net which they hid, their own foot has been caught.
16 The LORD has made Himself known;
He has [a]executed judgment.
In the work of his own hands the wicked is snared.
[[1]Higgaion Selah.

17 The wicked will [1a]return to [2]Sheol,
Even all the nations who [b]forget God.

---

17 [b]Ps. 9:2; 66:1, 2, 4

1 [1]Or, *set* [a]Ps. 57:5, 11; 148:13
2 [1]Or, *a bulwark* [a]Matt. 21:16 [b]Ps. 29:1; 118:14 [c]Ps. 44:16
3 [1]Or, *see* [2]Or, *appointed, fixed* [a]Ps. 89:11; 144:5 [b]Ps. 136:9
4 [1]Or, *dost remember him* [a]Job 7:17; Ps. 144:3; Heb. 2:6-8
5 [1]Or, *the angels;* Heb., *Elohim* [a]Gen. 1:26; Ps. 82:6 [b]Ps. 103:4 [c]Ps. 21:5
6 [a]Gen. 1:26, 28 [b]1 Cor. 15:27
7 [1]Or, *animals*

[£] I.e., "Death to the Son"
1 [1]Or, *miracles* [a]Ps. 86:12 [b]Ps. 26:7
2 [a]Ps. 104:34 [b]Ps. 66:2, 4 [c]Ps. 92:1
3 [a]Ps. 27:2
4 [1]Lit., *my right and my cause* [2]Or, *a righteous Judge* [a]Ps. 140:12 [b]Ps. 50:6
5 [a]Ps. 119:21 [b]Ps. 69:28
6 [a]Ps. 40:15 [b]Ps. 34:16
7 [1]Or, *sits as king* [a]Ps. 10:16 [b]Ps. 89:14
8 [a]Ps. 96:13
9 [a]Ps. 59:9, 16, 17
10 [1]Or, *let those . . . name put* [a]Ps. 91:14 [b]Ps. 37:28; 94:14
11 [a]Ps. 76:2 [b]Ps. 105:1
12 [1]I.e., avenges bloodshed [a]Gen. 9:5; Ps. 72:14 [b]Ps. 9:18
13 [a]Ps. 38:19 [b]Ps. 30:3; 86:13
14 [1]Or, *deliverance* [a]Ps. 106:2 [b]Ps. 13:5; 20:5; 35:9
15 [a]Ps. 7:15 [b]Ps. 57:6
16 [1]Perhaps, resounding music, or meditation [a]Ps. 9:4
17 [1]Or, *turn* [2]I.e., the nether world [a]Ps. 49:14 [b]Ps. 50:22

18 For the [a]needy will not always
be forgotten,
Nor the [b]hope of the afflicted
perish forever.
19 [a]Arise, O LORD, do not let man
prevail;
Let the nations be [b]judged before Thee.
20 Put them [a]in fear, O LORD;
Let the nations know that they
are [b]but men. [Selah.

PSALM 10

A Prayer for the Overthrow of the Wicked.

WHY [a]dost Thou stand afar off, O
LORD?
Why [b]dost Thou hide [1]*Thyself*
in times of trouble?
2 In [a]pride the wicked [1]hotly pursue the afflicted;
[2]Let them be [b]caught in the
plots which they have devised.

3 For the wicked [a]boasts of his
[b]heart's desire,
And [1]the greedy man curses
and [c]spurns the LORD.
4 The wicked, in the haughtiness
of his countenance, [a]does not
seek *Him*.
All his thoughts are, "[b]There is
no God."

5 His ways [1a]prosper at all times;
Thy judgments are on high,
[b]out of his sight;
As for all his adversaries, he
snorts at them.
6 He says to himself, "[a]I shall not
be moved;
[1]Throughout all generations I
shall not be in adversity."
7 His [a]mouth is full of curses and
deceit and [b]oppression;
[c]Under his tongue is mischief
and wickedness.
8 He sits in the [a]lurking places of
the villages;
In the hiding places he [b]kills the
innocent;
His eyes [1]stealthily watch for
the [2c]unfortunate.
9 He lurks in a hiding place as [a]a
lion in his lair;
He [b]lurks to catch [c]the afflicted;
He catches the afflicted when
he draws him into his [d]net.
10 He [1]crouches, he [2]bows down,
And the [3]unfortunate fall [4]by
his mighty ones.
11 He [a]says to himself, "God has
forgotten;
He has hidden His face; He will
never see it."

12 Arise, O LORD; O God, [a]lift up
Thy hand.
[b]Do not forget the afflicted.
13 Why has the wicked [a]spurned
God?
He has said to himself, "Thou
wilt not require *it*."
14 Thou hast seen *it*, for Thou hast
beheld [a]mischief and vexation to [1]take it into Thy
hand.
The [2b]unfortunate commits
himself to Thee;
Thou hast been the [c]helper of
the orphan.
15 [a]Break the arm of the wicked
and the evildoer,
[b]Seek out his wickedness until
Thou dost find none.

16 The LORD is [a]King forever and
ever;
[b]Nations have perished from
His land.
17 O LORD, Thou hast heard the
[a]desire of the humble;
Thou wilt [b]strengthen their
heart, [c]Thou wilt incline
Thine ear
18 To [1]vindicate the [a]orphan and
the [b]oppressed,
That man who is of the earth
may cause terror no more.

PSALM 11

The LORD a Refuge and Defense.

For the choir director. A *Psalm*
of David.

IN the LORD I [a]take refuge;
How can you say to my soul,
"Flee *as* a bird to your mountain;
2 For, behold, the wicked [a]bend
the bow,
They [1b]make ready their arrow
upon the string,
To [c]shoot in darkness at the upright in heart.
3 If the [a]foundations are destroyed,
What can the righteous do?"

4 The LORD is in His [a]holy temple,
the LORD's [b]throne is in
heaven;
His [c]eyes behold, His eyelids
test the sons of men.
5 The LORD [a]tests the righteous
and [b]the wicked,
And the one who loves violence
His soul hates.
6 Upon the wicked He will [a]rain
[1]snares;
[b]Fire and brimstone and [c]burning wind will be the portion
of [d]their cup.

18 [a]Ps. 9:12 [b]Ps. 62:5; 71:5
19 [a]Num. 10:35 [b]Ps. 9:5
20 [a]Ps. 14:5 [b]Ps. 62:9

1 [1]Or, Thine eyes [a]Ps. 22:1 [b]Ps. 13:1; 55:1
2 [1]Lit., *burn* [2]Or, *They will be caught* [a]Ps. 73:6, 8 [b]Ps. 9:16
3 [1]Or, *blesses the greedy man* [a]Ps. 49:6; 94:3, 4 [b]Ps. 112:10 [c]Ps. 10:13
4 [a]Ps. 10:13; 36:2 [b]Ps. 14:1; 36:1
5 [1]Lit., *are strong* [a]Ps. 52:7 [b]Ps. 28:5
6 [1]Lit., *To* [a]Ps. 49:11
7 [a]Rom. 3:14 [b]Ps. 73:8 [c]Job 20:12; Ps. 140:3
8 [1]Lit., *lie in wait* [2]Or, *poor* [a]Ps. 11:2 [b]Ps. 94:6 [c]Ps. 72:12
9 [a]Ps. 17:12 [b]Ps. 59:3; Mic. 7:2 [c]Ps. 10:2 [d]Ps. 140:5
10 [1]Or, *is crushed* [2]Or, *is bowed down* [3]Or, *poor* [4]Or, *into his claws*
11 [a]Ps. 10:4
12 [a]Ps. 17:7; Mic. 5:9 [b]Ps. 9:12
13 [a]Ps. 10:3
14 [1]Lit., *put, give* [2]Or, *poor* [a]Ps. 10:7 [b]Ps. 22:11 [c]Ps. 68:5
15 [a]Ps. 37:17 [b]Ps. 140:11
16 [a]Ps. 29:10 [b]Deut. 8:20
17 [a]Ps. 9:18 [b]1 Chr. 29:18 [c]Ps. 34:15
18 [1]Lit., *judge* [a]Ps. 146:9 [b]Ps. 9:9; 74:21

1 [a]Ps. 2:12
2 [1]Or, *fixed* [a]Ps. 7:12; 37:14 [b]Ps. 64:3 [c]Ps. 64:4
3 [a]Ps. 87:1
4 [a]Ps. 18:6; Mic. 1:2; Hab. 2:20 [b]Ps. 103:19; Is. 66:1; Matt. 5:34; Rev. 4:2 [c]Ps. 34:15, 16
5 [a]Gen. 22:1; Ps. 34:19; James 1:12 [b]Ps. 5:5
6 [1]Or, *coals of fire* [a]Ps. 18:13, 14 [b]Gen. 19:24; Ezek. 38:22 [c]Jer. 4:11, 12 [d]Ps. 75:8

7 For the LORD is [a]righteous; [b]He loves [1]righteousness;
The upright will [c]behold His face.

PSALM 12

God a Helper against the Treacherous.

For the choir director; [£]upon an eight-stringed lyre. A Psalm of David.

HELP, LORD, for [a]the godly man ceases to be,
For the faithful disappear from among the sons of men.
2 They [a]speak [1]falsehood to one another;
With [b]flattering [2]lips and with a double heart they speak.
3 May the LORD cut off all flattering lips,
The tongue that [a]speaks great things;
4 Who [a]have said, "With our tongue we will prevail;
Our lips are [1]our own; who is lord over us?"
5 "Because of the [a]devastation of the afflicted, because of the groaning of the needy,
Now [b]I will arise," says the LORD; "I will [c]set him in the safety for which he longs."

6 The [a]words of the LORD are pure words;
As silver [b]tried in a furnace on the earth, refined seven times.
7 Thou, O LORD, wilt keep them;
Thou wilt [a]preserve him from this generation forever.
8 The [a]wicked strut about on every side,
When [1b]vileness is exalted among the sons of men.

PSALM 13

Prayer for Help in Trouble.

For the choir director. A Psalm of David.

HOW long, O LORD? Wilt Thou [a]forget me forever?
How long [b]wilt Thou hide Thy face from me?
2 How long shall I [a]take counsel in my soul,
Having [b]sorrow in my heart all the day?
How long will my enemy be exalted over me?

3 [a]Consider *and* answer me, O LORD, my God;
[b]Enlighten my eyes, lest I sleep the *sleep of* death,

7 [1]Or, *righteous deeds*
[a]Ps. 7:9, 11 [b]Ps. 33:5
[c]Ps. 16:11; 17:15

[£] Or, *according to a lower octave* (Heb., *Sheminith*)
1 [a]Is. 57:1; Mic. 7:2
2 [1]Or, *emptiness* [2]Lit., *lip*
[a]Ps. 41:6 [b]Ps. 28:3; 55:21; Jer. 9:8; Rom. 16:18
3 [a]Dan. 7:8; Rev. 13:5
4 [1]Lit., *with us*
[a]Ps. 73:8, 9
5 [a]Ps. 9:9; 10:18 [b]Is. 33:10 [c]Ps. 34:6; 35:10
6 [a]Ps. 19:8, 10; 119:140 [b]Prov. 30:5
7 [a]Ps. 37:28; 97:10
8 [1]Or, *worthlessness*
[a]Ps. 55:10, 11 [b]Is. 32:5

1 [a]Ps. 44:24
[b]Ps. 89:46
2 [a]Ps. 42:4 [b]Ps. 42:9
3 [a]Ps. 5:1
[b]1 Sam. 14:29; Ezra 9:8; Job 33:30; Ps. 18:28
4 [a]Ps. 12:4 [b]Ps. 25:2; 38:16
5 [a]Ps. 52:8 [b]Ps. 9:14
6 [a]Ps. 96:1, 2
[b]Ps. 116:7; 119:17; 142:7

1 [1]Lit., *doings*
[a]Ps. 10:4; 53:1
[b]Ps. 14:1-3; 130:3; Rom. 3:10-12
2 [1]Or, *act wisely*
[a]Ps. 33:13, 14; 102:19 [b]Ps. 92:6
[c]1 Chr. 22:19
3 [a]Ps. 58:3 [b]Ps. 143:2
4 [a]Ps. 82:5 [b]Ps. 27:2; Jer. 10:25; Amos 8:4; Mic. 3:3 [c]Ps. 79:6; Is. 64:7
5 [a]Ps. 73:15; 112:2
6 [a]Ps. 42:3, 10
[b]Ps. 40:17; 46:1; 142:5
7 [1]Or, *restores the fortunes of His people*
[a]Ps. 53:6 [b]Ps. 85:1, 2

1 [1]Lit., *sojourn*
[a]Ps. 27:5, 6; 61:4
[b]Ps. 24:3
2 [a]Ps. 24:4; Is. 33:15 [b]Zech. 8:16; Eph. 4:25

4 Lest my enemy [a]say, "I have overcome him,"
Lest [b]my adversaries rejoice when I am shaken.

5 But I have [a]trusted in Thy lovingkindness;
My heart shall [b]rejoice in Thy salvation.
6 I will [a]sing to the LORD,
Because He has [b]dealt bountifully with me.

PSALM 14

Folly and Wickedness of Men.

For the choir director. *A Psalm* of David.

THE fool has [a]said in his heart, "There is no God."
They are corrupt, they have committed abominable [1]deeds;
There is [b]no one who does good.
2 The LORD has [a]looked down from heaven upon the sons of men,
To see if there are any who [1b]understand,
Who [c]seek after God.
3 They have all [a]turned aside; together they have become corrupt;
There is [b]no one who does good, not even one.

4 Do all the workers of wickedness [a]not know,
Who [b]eat up my people *as* they eat bread,
And [c]do not call upon the Lord?
5 There they are in great dread,
For God is with the [a]righteous generation.
6 You would [a]put to shame the counsel of the afflicted,
But the LORD is his [b]refuge.

7 O that [a]the salvation of Israel would come out of Zion!
When the LORD [1b]restores His captive people,
Jacob will rejoice, Israel will be glad.

PSALM 15

Description of a Citizen of Zion.

A Psalm of David.

O LORD, who may [1]abide [a]in Thy tent?
Who may dwell on Thy [b]holy hill?
2 He who [a]walks with integrity, and works righteousness,
And [b]speaks truth in his heart.

3 He [a]does not slander [1]with his tongue,
Nor [b]does evil to his neighbor,
Nor [c]takes up a reproach against his friend;
4 In whose eyes a [a]reprobate is despised,
But who [b]honors those who fear the LORD;
He swears to his own hurt, and does not change;
5 He [a]does not put out his money at interest,
Nor [b]does he take a bribe against the innocent.
He who does these things will never be shaken.

PSALM 16

The LORD the Psalmist's Portion in Life and Deliverer in Death.

Mikhtam of David.

[a]PRESERVE me, O God, for [b]I take refuge in Thee.
2 I said to the LORD, "Thou art my Lord;
I [a]have no good besides Thee."
3 As for the [a]saints who are in the earth,
They are the majestic ones [b]in whom is all my delight.
4 The [a]sorrows of those who have bartered for another *god* will be multiplied;
I shall not pour out their libations of [b]blood,
Nor shall I [c]take their names upon my lips.

5 The LORD is the [a]portion of my inheritance and my [b]cup;
Thou dost support my [c]lot.
6 The [a]lines have fallen to me in pleasant places;
Indeed, my heritage is beautiful to me.

7 I will bless the LORD who has [a]counseled me;
Indeed, my [1b]mind instructs me in the night.
8 [a]I have [b]set the LORD continually before me;
Because He is [c]at my right hand, [d]I will not be shaken.
9 Therefore [a]my heart is glad, and [b]my glory rejoices;
My flesh also will [c]dwell securely.
10 For Thou [a]wilt not abandon my soul to Sheol;
Neither wilt Thou [1b]allow Thy [2]Holy One to [3]undergo decay.
11 Thou wilt make known to me [a]the path of life;
In [b]Thy presence is fulness of joy;
In Thy right hand there are [c]pleasures forever.

PSALM 17

Prayer for Protection against Oppressors.

A Prayer of David.

HEAR a [a]just cause, O LORD, [b]give heed to my cry;
[c]Give ear to my prayer, which is not from [d]deceitful lips.
2 Let [a]my [1]judgment come forth from Thy presence;
Let Thine eyes look with [b]equity.
3 Thou hast [a]tried my heart;
Thou hast visited *me* by night;
Thou hast [b]tested me and [c]dost find [1]nothing;
I have [d]purposed that my mouth will not transgress.
4 As for the deeds of men, [a]by the word of Thy lips
I have kept from the [b]paths of the violent.
5 My [a]steps have held fast to Thy paths.
My [b]feet have not slipped.

6 I have [a]called upon Thee, for Thou wilt answer me, O God;
[b]Incline Thine ear to me, hear my speech.
7 [a]Wondrously show Thy lovingkindness,
O [b]Savior of those who take refuge at Thy right hand
From those who rise up *against them*.
8 Keep me as the [a]apple of the eye;
Hide me [b]in the shadow of Thy wings,
9 From the [a]wicked who despoil me,
My deadly enemies, who surround me.
10 They have [a]closed their unfeeling *heart*;
With their mouth they [b]speak proudly.
11 They have now surrounded us in our steps;
They set their eyes to cast *us* down to the ground.
12 He is [a]like a lion that is eager to tear,
And as a young lion lurking in hiding places.

13 [a]Arise, O LORD, confront him, [b]bring him low;
[c]Deliver my soul from the wicked with Thy sword,
14 From men with [a]Thy hand, O LORD,

Ps. 15: 3 [1]Lit., *according to* [a]Ps. 50:20 [b]Ps. 28:3 [c]Ex. 23:1
4 [a]Ps. 53:5; 73:20 [b]Acts 28:10
5 [a]Ex. 22:25; Lev. 25:36; Deut. 23:20; Ezek. 18:8 [b]Ex. 23:8

Ps. 16: 1 [a]Ps. 17:8 [b]Ps. 7:1
2 [a]Ps. 73:25
3 [a]Ps. 101:6 [b]Ps. 119:63
4 [a]Ps. 32:10 [b]Ps. 106:37, 38 [c]Ex. 23:13; Josh. 23:7
5 [a]Ps. 73:26; 119:57; 142:5; Lam. 3:24 [b]Ps. 23:5 [c]Ps. 125:3
6 [a]Ps. 78:55
7 [1]Lit., *kidneys*, figurative for inner man [a]Ps. 73:24 [b]Ps. 77:6
8 [a]Ps. 16:8-11; Acts 2:25-28 [b]Ps. 27:8; 123:1, 2 [c]Ps. 73:23; 110:5; 121:5 [d]Ps. 112:6
9 [a]Ps. 4:7; 13:5 [b]Ps. 30:12; 57:8; 108:1 [c]Ps. 4:8
10 [1]Lit., *give* [2]Or, *godly one* [3]Or, *see corruption* or *the pit* [a]Ps. 49:15; 86:13 [b]Acts 13:35
11 [a]Ps. 139:24; Matt. 7:14 [b]Ps. 21:6; 43:4 [c]Ps. 36:7, 8; 46:4

Ps. 17: 1 [a]Ps. 9:4 [b]Ps. 61:1; 142:6 [c]Ps. 88:2 [d]Is. 29:13
2 [1]I.e., vindication [a]Ps. 103:6 [b]Ps. 98:9; 99:4
3 [1]Or, *no evil device in me* [a]Ps. 26:1, 2 [b]Ps. 66:10; Zech. 13:9; 1 Pet. 1:7 [c]Jer. 50:20 [d]Ps. 39:1
4 [a]Ps. 119:9, 101 [b]Ps. 10:5-11
5 [a]Job 23:11; Ps. 44:18 [b]Ps. 18:36
6 [a]Ps. 86:7 [b]Ps. 88:2
7 [a]Ps. 31:21 [b]Ps. 20:6
8 [a]Deut. 32:10; Zech. 2:8 [b]Ruth 2:12; Ps. 36:7; 57:1; 61:4; 63:7
9 [a]Ps. 31:20
10 [a]Job 15:27; Ps. 73:7 [b]1 Sam. 2:3; Ps. 31:18; 73:8
12 [a]Ps. 7:2
13 [a]Ps. 3:7 [b]Ps. 55:23 [c]Ps. 22:20
14 [a]Ps. 17:7

From men [1]of the world, [b]whose portion is in *this* life;
And whose belly Thou [c]dost fill with Thy treasure;
They are satisfied with children,
And leave their abundance to their babes.
15 As for me, I shall [a]behold Thy face in righteousness;
I will be satisfied [1]with Thy [b]likeness when I awake.

Psalm 18

The Lord Praised for Giving Deliverance.

For the choir director. *A Psalm* of David the servant of the LORD, [ℓ]who spoke to the LORD the words of this song in the day that the LORD delivered him from the hand of all his enemies and from the hand of Saul. And he said,

"I LOVE Thee, O LORD, [a]my strength."
2 The LORD is [a]my [1]rock and [b]my fortress and my [c]deliverer,
My God, my rock, in whom I take refuge;
My [d]shield and the [e]horn of my salvation, my [f]stronghold.
3 I call upon the LORD, who is [a]worthy to be praised,
And I am [b]saved from my enemies.

4 The [a]cords of death encompassed me,
And the [b]torrents of [1]ungodliness [2]terrified me.
5 The [a]cords of Sheol surrounded me;
The snares of death confronted me.
6 In my [a]distress I called upon the LORD,
And cried to my God for help;
He heard my voice [b]out of His temple,
And my [c]cry for help before Him came into His ears.

7 Then the [a]earth shook and quaked;
And the [b]foundations of the mountains were trembling
And were shaken, because He was angry.
8 Smoke went up [1]out of His nostrils,
And [a]fire from His mouth devoured;
Coals were kindled by it.
9 He [a]bowed the heavens also, and came down
With thick [b]darkness under His feet.
10 And He rode upon a [a]cherub and flew;
And He sped upon the [b]wings of the wind.
11 He made [a]darkness His hiding place, His [1]canopy around Him,
Darkness of waters, thick clouds of the skies.
12 From the [a]brightness before Him passed His thick clouds,
Hailstones and [b]coals of fire.
13 The LORD also [a]thundered in the heavens,
And the Most High uttered His voice,
Hailstones and coals of fire.
14 And He [a]sent out His arrows, and scattered them,
And lightning flashes in abundance, and [1]routed them.
15 Then the [a]channels of water appeared,
And the foundations of the world were laid bare
At Thy [b]rebuke, O LORD,
At the blast of the [c]breath of Thy nostrils.

16 He [a]sent from on high, He took me;
He drew me out of [b]many waters.
17 He [a]delivered me from my strong enemy,
And from those who hated me, for they were [b]too mighty for me.
18 They confronted me in [a]the day of my calamity,
But [b]the LORD was my stay.
19 He brought me forth also into a [a]broad place;
He rescued me, because [b]He delighted in me.

20 The LORD has [a]rewarded me according to my righteousness;
According to the [b]cleanness of my hands He has recompensed me.
21 For I have [a]kept the ways of the LORD,
And have [b]not wickedly departed from my God.
22 For all [a]His ordinances were before me,
And I did not put away His [b]statutes from me.
23 I was also [1][a]blameless with Him,
And I [b]kept myself from my iniquity.

14 [1]Or, *whose portion in life is of the world* [b]Ps. 73:3-7; Luke 16:25 [c]Ps. 49:6
15 [1]Or, *with* beholding [a]Ps. 11:7; 16:11; 140:13 [b]Num. 12:8
[ℓ]2 Sam. 22:1-51
1 [a]Ps. 59:17
2 [1]Or, *crag* [a]Deut. 32:18; 1 Sam. 2:2; Ps. 18:31, 46; 28:1; 31:3; 42:9; 71:3; 78:15 [b]Ps. 144:2 [c]Ps. 19:14 [d]Ps. 28:7; 33:20; 59:11; 84:9, 11; Prov. 30:5 [e]Ps. 75:10 [f]Ps. 59:9
3 [a]Ps. 48:1; 96:4; 145:3 [b]Ps. 34:6
4 [1]Or, *destruction;* Heb., *Belial* [2]Or, *were assailing* [a]Ps. 116:3 [b]Ps. 69:2; 124:3, 4
5 [a]Ps. 116:3
6 [a]Ps. 50:15; 120:1 [b]Ps. 3:4 [c]Ps. 34:15
7 [a]Judg. 5:4; Ps. 68:7, 8; Is. 13:13; Hag. 2:6 [b]Ps. 114:4, 6
8 [1]Or, *in His wrath* [a]Ps. 50:3
9 [a]Ps. 144:5 [b]Ps. 97:2
10 [a]Ps. 80:1; 99:1 [b]Ps. 104:3
11 [1]Or, *pavilion* [a]Deut. 4:11
12 [a]Ps. 104:2 [b]Ps. 140:10; Hab. 3:5
13 [a]Ps. 29:3; 104:7
14 [1]Lit., *confused* [a]Ps. 144:6; Hab. 3:11
15 [a]Ps. 106:9 [b]Ps. 76:6 [c]Ps. 18:8
16 [a]Ps. 144:7 [b]Ps. 32:6
17 [a]Ps. 59:1 [b]Ps. 35:10; 142:6
18 [a]Ps. 59:16 [b]Ps. 16:8
19 [a]Ps. 4:1; 31:8; 118:5 [b]Ps. 37:23; 41:11
20 [a]Job 33:26; Ps. 7:8 [b]Job 22:30; Ps. 24:4
21 [a]Ps. 37:34; 119:33; Prov. 8:32 [b]2 Chr. 34:33
22 [a]Ps. 119:30 [b]Ps. 119:83
23 [1]Lit., *complete;* or, *perfect* [a]Ps. 18:32 [b]Ps. 19:12, 13; 25:11

24 Therefore the LORD has [a]recompensed me according to my righteousness;
According to the cleanness of my hands in His eyes.

25 With [a]the kind Thou dost show Thyself kind;
With the [1]blameless [b]Thou dost show Thyself blameless;
26 With the pure Thou dost show Thyself [a]pure;
And with the crooked [b]Thou dost show Thyself [1]astute.
27 For Thou dost [a]save an afflicted people;
But [b]haughty eyes Thou dost abase.
28 For Thou dost [a]light my lamp;
The LORD my God [b]illumines my darkness.
29 For by Thee I can [1a]run upon a troop;
And by my God I can [b]leap over a wall.

30 As for God, His way is [1a]blameless;
The [b]word of the LORD is tried;
He is a [c]shield to all who take refuge in Him.
31 For [a]who is God, but the LORD?
And who is a [b]rock, except our God,
32 The God who [a]girds me with strength,
And makes my way [b]blameless?
33 He [a]makes my feet like hinds' *feet*,
And sets me upon my high places.
34 He [a]trains my hands for battle,
So that my arms can [b]bend a bow of bronze.
35 Thou hast also given me [a]the shield of Thy salvation,
And Thy [b]right hand upholds me;
And [c]Thy [1]gentleness makes me great.
36 Thou dost [a]enlarge my steps under me,
And my [b]feet have not slipped.

37 I [a]pursued my enemies and overtook them,
And I did not turn back [b]until they were consumed.
38 I shattered them, so that they were [a]not able to rise;
They fell [b]under my feet.
39 For Thou hast [a]girded me with strength for battle;
Thou hast [1b]subdued under me those who rose up against me.

24 [a]Ps. 18:20
25 [1]Note v. 23 [a]Ps. 62:12; Matt. 5:7 [b]Ps. 18:30
26 [1]Lit., *twisted* [a]Job 25:5; Hab. 1:13 [b]Lev. 26:23, 24; Prov. 3:34
27 [a]Ps. 72:12 [b]Ps. 101:5; Prov. 6:17
28 [a]1 Kin. 15:4; Job 18:6; Ps. 132:17 [b]Ps. 27:1
29 [1]Or, *crush a troop* [a]Ps. 118:10-12 [b]Ps. 18:33; 40:2
30 [1]Note v. 23 [a]Ps. 19:7; 145:17 [b]Ps. 12:6 [c]Ps. 91:4
31 [a]Ps. 86:8-10; Is. 45:5 [b]Deut. 32:31; Ps. 18:2; 62:2
32 [a]Ps. 18:39; Is. 45:5 [b]Ps. 18:23
33 [a]Hab. 3:19
34 [a]Ps. 144:1 [b]Job 29:20
35 [1]Or, *condescension* [a]Ps. 33:20 [b]Ps. 63:8; 119:117 [c]Ps. 138:6
36 [a]Ps. 18:33 [b]Ps. 66:9
37 [a]Ps. 44:5 [b]Ps. 37:20
38 [a]Ps. 36:12 [b]Ps. 47:3
39 [1]Lit., *caused to bow down* [a]Ps. 18:32 [b]Ps. 18:47
40 [1]Or, *silenced* [a]Ps. 21:12 [b]Ps. 94:23
41 [a]Ps. 50:22 [b]Job 27:9; Prov. 1:28
42 [a]Ps. 83:13
43 [a]2 Sam. 3:1; 19:9; Ps. 35:1 [b]Ps. 89:27 [c]Is. 55:5
44 [1]Lit., *deceive me;* i.e., give feigned obedience [a]Ps. 66:3
45 [a]Ps. 37:2 [b]Mic. 7:17
46 [a]Job 19:25 [b]Ps. 18:2 [c]Ps. 51:14
47 [a]Ps. 94:1 [b]Ps. 18:43; 47:3; 144:2
48 [a]Ps. 3:7 [b]Ps. 27:6 [c]Ps. 11:5
49 [a]Rom. 15:9 [b]Ps. 108:1
50 [1]I.e., victories; lit., *salvations* [2]Lit., *seed* [a]Ps. 21:1 [b]Ps. 28:8 [c]Ps. 89:4
1 [a]Ps. 8:1; 50:6; Rom. 1:19, 20 [b]Gen. 1:6, 7
2 [a]Ps. 74:16 [b]Ps. 139:12

40 Thou hast also made my enemies [a]turn their backs to me,
And I [1b]destroyed those who hated me.
41 They cried for help, but there was [a]none to save,
Even to the LORD, but [b]He did not answer them.
42 Then I beat them fine as the [a]dust before the wind;
I emptied them out as the mire of the streets.

43 Thou hast delivered me from the [a]contentions of the people;
Thou hast placed me as [b]head of the nations;
A [c]people whom I have not known serve me.
44 As soon as they hear, they obey me;
Foreigners [1a]submit to me.
45 Foreigners [a]fade away,
And [b]come trembling out of their fortresses.

46 The LORD [a]lives, and blessed be [b]my rock;
And exalted be [c]the God of my salvation,
47 The God who [a]executes vengeance for me,
And [b]subdues peoples under me.
48 He [a]delivers me from my enemies;
Surely Thou [b]dost lift me above those who rise up against me;
Thou dost rescue me from the [c]violent man.
49 Therefore I will [a]give thanks to Thee among the nations, O LORD,
And I will [b]sing praises to Thy name.
50 He gives great [1a]deliverance to His king,
And shows lovingkindness to [b]His anointed,
To David and [c]his [2]descendants forever.

PSALM 19

The Works and the Word of God.

For the choir director. A Psalm of David.

THE [a]heavens are telling of the glory of God;
And their [b]expanse is declaring the work of His hands.
2 Day to [a]day pours forth speech,
And [b]night to night reveals knowledge.

3 There is no speech, nor are there words;
Their voice is not heard.
4 Their [1a]line has gone out through all the earth,
And their utterances to the end of the world.
In them He has [b]placed a tent for the sun,
5 Which is as a bridegroom coming out of his chamber;
It rejoices as a strong man to run his course.
6 Its [a]rising is from [1]one end of the heavens,
And its circuit to the [2]other end of them;
And there is nothing hidden from its heat.

7 The law of the LORD is [1a]perfect, [b]restoring the soul;
The testimony of the LORD is [c]sure, making [d]wise the simple.
8 The precepts of the LORD are [a]right, [b]rejoicing the heart;
The commandment of the LORD is [c]pure, [d]enlightening the eyes.
9 The fear of the LORD is clean, enduring forever;
The judgments of the LORD are [a]true; they are [b]righteous altogether.
10 They are more desirable than [a]gold, yes, than much fine gold;
[b]Sweeter also than honey and the drippings of the honeycomb.
11 Moreover, by them [a]Thy servant is warned;
In keeping them there is great [b]reward.
12 Who can [a]discern *his* errors?
[b]Acquit me of [c]hidden *faults*.
13 Also keep back Thy servant [a]from presumptuous *sins*;
Let them not [b]rule over me;
Then I shall be [1c]blameless,
And I shall be acquitted of [d]great transgression.
14 Let the words of my mouth and [a]the meditation of my heart
Be acceptable in Thy sight,
O LORD, [b]my rock and my [c]redeemer.

PSALM 20

Prayer for Victory over Enemies.

For the choir director. A Psalm of David.

MAY the LORD answer you [a]in the day of trouble!

4 [1]Another reading is, *sound*
[a]Rom. 10:18 [b]Ps. 104:2
6 [1]Lit., *the* [2]Lit., *the ends*
[a]Ps. 113:3
7 [1]I.e., blameless
[a]Ps. 119:160 [b]Ps. 23:3 [c]Ps. 93:5 [d]Ps. 119:98-100
8 [a]Ps. 119:128 [b]Ps. 119:14 [c]Ps. 12:6 [d]Ps. 36:9
9 [a]Ps. 119:142 [b]Ps. 119:138
10 [a]Ps. 119:72, 127 [b]Ps. 119:103
11 [a]Ps. 17:4 [b]Ps. 24:5, 6; Prov. 29:18
12 [a]Ps. 40:12; 139:6 [b]Ps. 51:1, 2 [c]Ps. 90:8; 139:23, 24
13 [1]Lit., *complete*
[a]Num. 15:30 [b]Ps. 119:133 [c]Ps. 18:32 [d]Ps. 25:11
14 [a]Ps. 104:34 [b]Ps. 18:2 [c]Ps. 31:5

1 [a]Ps. 50:15 [b]Ps. 91:14 [c]Ps. 46:7, 11
2 [a]Ps. 3:4 [b]Ps. 110:2
3 [1]Lit., *fat*
[a]Acts 10:4 [b]Ps. 51:19
4 [1]Or, *purpose*
[a]Ps. 21:2 [b]Ps. 145:19
5 [1]Or, *Let us sing* [2]Or, *salvation*
[a]Ps. 9:14 [b]Ps. 60:4 [c]1 Sam. 1:17
6 [1]Or, *mighty deeds of the victory of His right hand*
[a]Ps. 41:11 [b]Is. 58:9 [c]Ps. 28:8
7 [a]Ps. 33:17 [b]2 Chr. 32:8
8 [a]Is. 2:11, 17 [b]Ps. 37:24; Mic. 7:8
9 [1]Or, *O LORD, save the king; answer us . . .*
[a]Ps. 3:7 [b]Ps. 17:6

1 [1]Or, *victory*
[a]Ps. 59:16, 17
2 [a]Ps. 20:4; 37:4
3 [a]Ps. 59:10 [b]2 Sam. 12:30
4 [a]Ps. 61:6; 133:3 [b]Ps. 91:16
5 [1]Or, *victory*
[a]Ps. 9:14; 20:5 [b]Ps. 8:5; 96:6
6 [1]Lit., *blessings*
[a]1 Chr. 17:27

May the [b]name of the [c]God of Jacob set you *securely* on high!
2 May He send you help [a]from the sanctuary,
And [b]support you from Zion!
3 May He [a]remember all your meal offerings,
And [b]find your burnt offering [1]acceptable! [Selah.

4 May He grant you your [a]heart's desire,
And [b]fulfill all your [1]counsel!
5 [1]We will [a]sing for joy over your [2]victory,
And in the name of our God we will [b]set up our banners.
May the LORD [c]fulfill all your petitions.

6 Now [a]I know that the LORD saves His anointed;
He will [b]answer him from His holy heaven,
With the [1c]saving strength of His right hand.
7 Some *boast* in chariots, and some in [a]horses;
But [b]we will boast in the name of the LORD, our God.
8 They have [a]bowed down and fallen;
But we have [b]risen and stood upright.
9 [1a]Save, O LORD;
May the [b]King answer us in the day we call.

PSALM 21

Praise for Deliverance.

For the choir director. A Psalm of David.

O LORD, in Thy strength the king will [a]be glad,
And in Thy [1]salvation how greatly he will rejoice!
2 Thou hast [a]given him his heart's desire,
And Thou hast not withheld the request of his lips. [Selah.
3 For Thou [a]dost meet him with the blessings of good things;
Thou dost set a [b]crown of fine gold on his head.
4 He asked life of Thee,
Thou [a]didst give it to him,
[b]Length of days forever and ever.
5 His [a]glory is great through Thy [1]salvation,
[b]Splendor and majesty Thou dost place upon him.
6 For Thou dost make him [1]most [a]blessed forever;

Thou dost make him joyful [b]with gladness in Thy presence.

7 For the king [a]trusts in the LORD,
And through the lovingkindness of the Most High [b]he will not be shaken.
8 Your hand will [a]find out all your enemies;
Your right hand will find out those who hate you.
9 You will make them [a]as a fiery oven in the time [1]of your anger;
The LORD will [b]swallow them up in His wrath,
And [c]fire will devour them.
10 Their [1]offspring Thou wilt destroy from the earth,
And their [2a]descendants from among the sons of men.
11 Though they [1a]intended evil against Thee,
And [b]devised a plot,
They will not succeed.
12 For Thou wilt [a]make them turn their back;
Thou wilt [1]aim [b]with Thy bowstrings at their faces.
13 Be Thou exalted, O LORD, in Thy strength;
We will [a]sing and praise Thy power.

PSALM 22

A Cry of Anguish and a Song of Praise.

For the choir director; upon [ε]aijeleth hashshahar.
A Psalm of David.

[a]MY God, my God, why hast Thou forsaken me?
[1b]Far from my deliverance are the words of my [2c]groaning.
2 O my God, I [a]cry by day, but Thou dost not answer;
And by night, but I have no rest.
3 Yet [a]Thou art holy,
O Thou who art enthroned upon [b]the praises of Israel.
4 In Thee our fathers [a]trusted;
They trusted, and Thou didst [b]deliver them.
5 To Thee they cried out, and were delivered;
In Thee they trusted, and were not [1]disappointed.

6 But I am a [a]worm, and not a man,
A [b]reproach of men, and [c]despised by the people.
7 All who see me [a]sneer at me;
They separate with the lip, they [b]wag the head, *saying,*
8 "Commit *yourself* to the LORD; [a]let Him deliver him;
Let Him rescue him, because He delights in him."

9 Yet Thou art He who [a]didst bring me forth from the womb;
Thou didst make me trust *when* upon my mother's breasts.
10 Upon Thee I was cast [a]from [1]birth;
Thou hast been my God from my mother's womb.

11 [a]Be not far from me, for [1]trouble is near;
For there is [b]none to help.
12 Many [a]bulls have surrounded me;
Strong *bulls* of [b]Bashan have encircled me.
13 They [a]open wide their mouth at me,
As a ravening and a roaring [b]lion.
14 I am [a]poured out like water,
And all my [b]bones are out of joint;
My [c]heart is like wax;
It is melted within me.
15 My [a]strength is dried up like a potsherd,
And my tongue cleaves to my jaws;
And Thou dost [b]lay me in the dust of death.
16 For [a]dogs have surrounded me;
A band of evildoers has encompassed me;
They [b]pierced my hands and my feet.
17 I can count all my bones.
They look, they stare at me;
18 They [a]divide my garments among them,
And for my clothing they cast lots.

19 But Thou, O LORD, [a]be not far off;
O Thou my help, [b]hasten to my assistance.
20 Deliver my [1]soul from [a]the sword,
My [b]only *life* from the [2]power of the dog.
21 Save me from the [a]lion's mouth;
And from the horns of the [b]wild oxen Thou dost [c]answer me.

22 I will [a]tell of Thy name to my brethren;

6 [b]Ps. 43:4
7 [a]Ps. 125:1 [b]Ps. 112:6
8 [a]Is. 10:10
9 [1]Or, *of your presence* [a]Mal. 4:1 [b]Lam. 2:2 [c]Ps. 50:3
10 [1]Lit., *fruit* [2]Lit., *seed* [a]Ps. 37:28
11 [1]Lit., *stretched out* [a]Ps. 2:1-3 [b]Ps. 10:2
12 [1]Lit., *make ready* [a]Ps. 18:40 [b]Ps. 7:12, 13
13 [a]Ps. 59:16
[ε]Lit., *the hind of the morning*
1 [1]Or, Why art Thou so *far from helping me,* and from *the words of my groaning?* [2]Lit., *roaring* [a]Matt. 27:46; Mark 15:34 [b]Ps. 10:1 [c]Job 3:24; Ps. 6:6; 32:3; 38:8
2 [a]Ps. 42:3; 88:1
3 [a]Ps. 99:9 [b]Ps. 148:14
4 [a]Ps. 78:53 [b]Ps. 107:6
5 [1]Or, *ashamed*
6 [a]Job 25:6; Is. 41:14 [b]Ps. 31:11 [c]Is. 49:7
7 [a]Ps. 79:4; Is. 53:3 [b]Matt. 27:39; Mark 15:29
8 [a]Matt. 27:43
9 [a]Ps. 71:5, 6
10 [1]Lit., *a womb* [a]Is. 46:3; 49:1
11 [1]Or, *distress* [a]Ps. 71:12 [b]2 Kin. 14:26; Ps. 72:12
12 [a]Ps. 22:21; 68:30 [b]Deut. 32:14; Amos 4:1
13 [a]Ps. 35:21; Job 16:10; Lam. 2:16; 3:46 [b]Ps. 10:9; 17:12
14 [a]Job 30:16 [b]Ps. 31:10; Dan. 5:6 [c]Josh. 7:5; Job 23:16; Ps. 73:26
15 [a]Ps. 38:10 [b]Ps. 104:29
16 [a]Ps. 59:6, 7 [b]Matt. 27:35; John 20:25
18 [a]Matt. 27:35; Luke 23:34; John 19:24
19 [a]Ps. 22:11 [b]Ps. 70:5
20 [1]Or, *life* [2]Lit., *paw* [a]Ps. 37:14 [b]Ps. 35:17
21 [a]Ps. 22:13 [b]Ps. 22:12 [c]Ps. 34:4; 118:5; 120:1
22 [a]Ps. 40:10; Heb. 2:12

In the midst of the assembly I
will praise Thee.
23 [a]You who fear the LORD, praise
Him;
All you [1]descendants of Jacob,
[b]glorify Him,
And [c]stand in awe of Him, all
you [1]descendants of Israel.
24 For He has [a]not despised nor
abhorred the affliction of the
afflicted;
Neither has He [b]hidden His
face from him;
But [c]when he cried to Him for
help, He heard.

25 From Thee *comes* [a]my praise in
the great assembly;
I shall [b]pay my vows before
those who fear Him.
26 The [1]afflicted shall eat and [a]be
satisfied;
Those who seek Him will
[b]praise the LORD.
Let your [c]heart live forever!
27 All the [a]ends of the earth will
remember and turn to the
LORD,
And all the [b]families of the nations will worship before
Thee.
28 For the [a]kingdom is the LORD's,
And He [b]rules over the nations.
29 All the [1a]prosperous of the
earth will eat and worship,
All those who [b]go down to the
dust will bow before Him,
Even he who [c]cannot keep his
soul alive.
30 [a]Posterity will serve Him;
It will be told of the Lord to the
coming generation.
31 They will come and [a]will declare His righteousness
To a people [b]who will be born,
that He has performed *it.*

PSALM 23

The LORD, the Psalmist's Shepherd.

A Psalm of David.

THE LORD is my [a]shepherd,
I [1]shall [b]not want.
2 He makes me lie down in
[a]green pastures;
He leads me beside [1b]quiet waters.
3 He [a]restores my soul;
He [b]guides me in the [1c]paths of
righteousness
For His name's sake.

4 Even though I [a]walk through
the [1]valley of the shadow of
death,
I [b]fear no [2]evil; for [c]Thou art
with me;
Thy [d]rod and Thy staff, they
comfort me.
5 Thou dost [a]prepare a table before me in the presence of my
enemies;
Thou [1]hast [b]anointed my head
with oil;
My [c]cup overflows.
6 [1]Surely [a]goodness and lovingkindness will follow me all
the days of my life,
And I will [2b]dwell in the house
of the LORD forever.

PSALM 24

The King of Glory Entering Zion.

A Psalm of David.

THE [a]earth is the LORD's, and [1]all
it contains,
The [b]world, and those who
dwell in it.
2 For He has founded it upon the
seas,
And established it upon the rivers.
3 Who may [a]ascend into the [b]hill
of the LORD?
And who may stand in His holy
[c]place?
4 He who has [a]clean hands and a
[b]pure heart,
Who has not [c]lifted up his soul
to falsehood,
And has not [d]sworn deceitfully.
5 He shall receive a [a]blessing
from the LORD
And [b]righteousness from the
God of his salvation.
6 This is the generation of those
who [a]seek Him,
Who seek Thy face—*even* Jacob. [Selah.

7 [a]Lift up your heads, O gates,
And be lifted up, O [1]ancient
doors,
That the King of [b]glory may
come in!
8 Who is the King of glory?
The LORD [a]strong and mighty,
The LORD [b]mighty in battle.
9 Lift up your heads, O gates,
And lift them up, O ancient
doors,
That the King of [a]glory may
come in!
10 Who is this King of glory?
The LORD of [a]hosts,
He is the King of glory. [Selah.

---

23 [1]Lit., *seed* [a]Ps. 135:20 [b]Ps. 86:12 [c]Ps. 33:8
24 [a]Ps. 69:33 [b]Ps. 27:9; 69:17; 102:2 [c]Ps. 31:22; Heb. 5:7
25 [a]Ps. 35:18; 40:9, 10 [b]Ps. 61:8
26 [1]Or, *poor* [a]Ps. 107:9 [b]Ps. 40:16 [c]Ps. 69:32
27 [a]Ps. 2:8; 82:8 [b]Ps. 86:9
28 [a]Ps. 47:7; Obad. 21; Zech. 14:9 [b]Ps. 47:8
29 [1]Lit., *fat ones* [a]Ps. 17:10; Is. 10:16; Hab. 1:16 [b]Ps. 28:1 [c]Ps 89:48
30 [a]Ps. 102:28
31 [a]Ps. 40:9; 71:18 [b]Ps. 78:6

1 [1]Or, *do* [a]Ps. 78:52; 80:1; Is. 40:11; Jer. 31:10; Ezek. 34:11-13; John 10:11; 1 Pet. 2:25 [b]Ps. 34:9, 10
2 [1]Lit., *waters of rest* [a]Ps. 65:11-13; Ezek. 34:14 [b]Ps. 36:8; 46:4
3 [1]Lit., *tracks* [a]Ps. 19:7 [b]Ps. 5:8; 31:3 [c]Ps. 85:13; Prov. 4:11; 8:20
4 [1]Or, *valley of deep darkness* [2]Or, *harm* [a]Ps. 107:14 [b]Ps. 27:1 [c]Ps. 16:8; Is. 43:2 [d]Mic. 7:14
5 [1]Or, *dost anoint* [a]Ps. 78:19 [b]Ps. 92:10; Luke 7:46 [c]Ps. 16:5
6 [1]Or, *Only* [2]Another reading is, *return to* [a]Ps. 25:7, 10 [b]Ps. 27:4-6

1 [1]Lit., *its fulness* [a]1 Cor. 10:26 [b]Ps. 89:11
3 [a]Ps. 15:1 [b]Ps. 2:6 [c]Deut. 12:5
4 [a]Job 17:9; Ps. 22:30; 26:6 [b]Ps. 51:10; 73:1; Matt. 5:8 [c]Ezek. 18:15 [d]Ps. 15:4
5 [a]Ps. 115:13 [b]Ps. 36:10
6 [a]Ps. 27:4, 8
7 [1]Lit., *everlasting* [a]Ps. 118:20; Is. 26:2 [b]Ps. 29:2, 9; 1 Cor. 2:8
8 [a]Deut. 4:34; Ps. 96:7 [b]Ex. 15:3
9 [a]Ps. 26:8; 57:11
10 [a]Gen. 32:2; Josh. 5:14

Psalm 25

Prayer for Protection, Guidance and Pardon.

A Psalm of David.

TO Thee, O LORD, I [a]lift up my soul.
2 O my God, in Thee [a]I trust,
Do not let me [b]be ashamed;
Do not let my [c]enemies exult over me.
3 Indeed, [a]none of those who wait for Thee will be ashamed;
[1]Those who [b]deal treacherously without cause will be ashamed.

4 [a]Make me know Thy ways, O LORD;
Teach me Thy paths.
5 Lead me in [a]Thy truth and teach me,
For Thou art the [b]God of my salvation;
For Thee I [c]wait all the day.
6 [a]Remember, O LORD, Thy compassion and Thy lovingkindnesses,
For they have been [1b]from of old.
7 Do not remember the [a]sins of my youth or my transgressions;
[b]According to Thy lovingkindness remember Thou me,
For Thy [c]goodness' sake, O LORD.

8 [a]Good and [b]upright is the LORD;
Therefore He [c]instructs sinners in the way.
9 He [a]leads the [1]humble in justice,
And He [b]teaches the [1]humble His way.
10 All the paths of the LORD are [a]lovingkindness and truth
To [b]those who keep His covenant and His testimonies.
11 For [a]Thy name's sake, O LORD,
[b]Pardon my iniquity, for it is great.

12 Who is the man who [a]fears the LORD?
He will [b]instruct him in the way he should choose.
13 His soul will [a]abide in [1]prosperity,
And his [2]descendants will [b]inherit the [3]land.
14 The [1a]secret of the LORD is for those who fear Him,
And He will [b]make them know His covenant.
15 My [a]eyes are continually toward the LORD,
For He will [b]pluck my feet out of the net.

16 [a]Turn to me and be gracious to me,
For I am [b]lonely and afflicted.
17 The [a]troubles of my heart are enlarged;
Bring me [b]out of my distresses.
18 Look upon my [a]affliction and my [1]trouble,
And [b]forgive all my sins.
19 Look upon my enemies, for they [a]are many;
And they [b]hate me with violent hatred.
20 [a]Guard my soul and deliver me;
Do not let me [b]be ashamed, for I take refuge in Thee.
21 Let [a]integrity and uprightness preserve me,
For [b]I wait for Thee.
22 [a]Redeem Israel, O God,
Out of all his troubles.

Psalm 26

Protestation of Integrity and Prayer for Protection.

A Psalm of David.

[1a]VINDICATE me, O LORD, for I have [b]walked in my integrity;
And I have [c]trusted in the LORD [2d]without wavering.
2 [a]Examine me, O LORD, and try me;
[b]Test my [1]mind and my heart.
3 For Thy [a]lovingkindness is before my eyes,
And I have [b]walked in Thy truth.
4 I do not [a]sit with deceitful men,
Nor will I go with [b]pretenders.
5 I [a]hate the assembly of evildoers,
And I will not sit with the wicked.
6 I shall [a]wash my hands in innocence,
And I will go about [b]Thine altar, O LORD,
7 That I may proclaim with the voice of [a]thanksgiving,
And declare all Thy wonders.

8 O LORD, I [a]love the habitation of Thy house,
And the place where Thy [b]glory dwells.
9 Do not [1]take my soul away *along* with sinners,
Nor my life with [a]men of bloodshed,

---

1 [a]Ps. 86:4; 143:8
2 [a]Ps. 31:1 [b]Ps. 25:20; 31:1 [c]Ps. 41:11
3 [1]Or, *Let those . . . be ashamed* [a]Ps. 37:9; 40:1; Is. 49:23 [b]Ps. 119:158; Is. 21:2; Hab. 1:13
4 [a]Ps. 27:11
5 [a]Ps. 25:10; 43:3 [b]Ps. 79:9 [c]Ps. 40:1
6 [1]Or, *everlasting* [a]Ps. 98:3 [b]Ps. 103:17
7 [a]Job 13:26; 20:11 [b]Ps. 51:1 [c]Ps. 31:19
8 [a]Ps. 86:5 [b]Ps. 92:15 [c]Ps. 32:8
9 [1]Or, *afflicted* [a]Ps. 23:3 [b]Ps. 27:11
10 [a]Ps. 40:11 [b]Ps. 103:18
11 [a]Ps. 79:9 [b]Ex. 34:9
12 [a]Ps. 31:19 [b]Ps. 25:8
13 [1]Lit., *good* [2]Lit., *seed* [3]Or, *earth* [a]Prov. 1:33; Jer. 23:6 [b]Ps. 37:11
14 [1]Or, *counsel* [a]Job 29:4; Prov. 3:32 [b]Gen. 17:1, 2
15 [a]Ps. 123:2 [b]Ps. 31:4; 124:7
16 [a]Ps. 69:16 [b]Ps. 143:4
17 [a]Ps. 40:12 [b]Ps. 107:6
18 [1]Lit., *toil* [a]Ps. 31:7 [b]Ps. 103:3
19 [a]Ps. 3:1 [b]Ps. 9:13
20 [a]Ps. 86:2 [b]Ps. 25:2
21 [a]Ps. 41:12 [b]Ps. 25:3
22 [a]Ps. 130:8
1 [1]Lit., *Judge* [2]Lit., *I do not slide* [a]Ps. 7:8 [b]Prov. 20:7 [c]Ps. 13:5 [d]Heb. 10:23
2 [1]Lit., *kidneys*, figurative for inner man [a]Ps. 139:23 [b]Ps. 7:9
3 [a]Ps. 48:9 [b]Ps. 86:11
4 [a]Ps. 1:1 [b]Ps. 28:3
5 [a]Ps. 31:6; 139:21
6 [a]Ps. 73:13 [b]Ps. 43:3, 4
7 [a]Ps. 9:1
8 [a]Ps. 27:4 [b]Ps. 24:7
9 [1]Lit., *gather* [a]Ps. 139:19

10 In whose hands is a [a]wicked
scheme,
And whose right hand is full of
[b]bribes.
11 But as for me, I shall [a]walk in
my integrity;
[b]Redeem me, and be gracious
to me.
12 My foot stands on a [a]level
place;
In the [b]congregations I shall
bless the LORD.

PSALM 27

A Psalm of Fearless Trust in God.

A Psalm of David.

THE LORD is my [a]light and my
[b]salvation;
Whom shall I fear?
The LORD is the [1c]defense of my
life;
[d]Whom shall I dread?
2 When evildoers came upon me
to [a]devour my flesh,
My adversaries and my en-
emies, they [b]stumbled and
fell.
3 Though a [a]host encamp against
me,
My heart will not fear;
Though war arise against me,
In *spite of* this I [1]shall be [b]con-
fident.

4 One thing I have asked from the
LORD, that I shall seek:
That I may [a]dwell in the house
of the LORD all the days of my
life,
To behold [b]the [1]beauty of the
LORD,
And to [2c]meditate in His temple.
5 For in the [a]day of trouble He
will [b]conceal me in His [1]tab-
ernacle;
In the secret place of His tent
He will [c]hide me;
He will [d]lift me up on a rock.
6 And now [a]my head will be lifted
up above my enemies around
me;
And I will offer in His tent [b]sac-
rifices [1]with shouts of joy;
I will [c]sing, yes, I will sing
praises to the LORD.

7 [a]Hear, O LORD, when I cry with
my voice,
And be gracious to me and [b]an-
swer me.
8 *When Thou didst say,* "[a]Seek
My face," my heart said to
Thee,
"Thy face, O LORD, [b]I shall
seek."
9 [a]Do not hide Thy face from me,
Do not turn Thy servant away
in [b]anger;
Thou hast been [c]my help;
[d]Do not abandon me nor [e]for-
sake me,
O God of my salvation!
10 [1]For my father and [a]my mother
have forsaken me,
But [b]the LORD will take me up.

11 [a]Teach me Thy way, O LORD,
And lead me in a [b]level path,
Because of my foes.
12 Do not deliver me over to the
[1a]desire of my adversaries;
For [b]false witnesses have risen
against me,
And such as [c]breathe out vio-
lence.
13 [1]*I would have despaired* unless
I had believed that I would
see the [a]goodness of the
LORD
In the [b]land of the living.
14 [a]Wait for the LORD;
Be [b]strong, and let your heart
take courage;
Yes, wait for the LORD.

PSALM 28

A Prayer for Help, and Praise for Its Answer.

A Psalm of David.

TO Thee, O LORD, I call;
My [a]rock, do not be deaf to me,
Lest, if Thou [b]be silent to me,
I become like those who [c]go
down to the pit.
2 Hear the [a]voice of my supplications when I cry to Thee for
help,
When I [b]lift up my hands
[c]toward [1]Thy holy [d]sanctu-
ary.
3 [a]Do not drag me away with the
wicked
And with those who work iniquity;
Who [b]speak peace with their
neighbors,
While evil is in their hearts.
4 Requite them [a]according to
their work and according to
the evil of their practices;
Requite them according to the
deeds of their hands;
Repay them their [1]recompense.
5 Because they [a]do not regard the
works of the LORD
Nor the deeds of His hands,
He will tear them down and not
build them up.

10 [a]Ps. 37:7 [b]Ps. 15:5
11 [a]Ps. 26:1 [b]Ps. 44:26; 69:18
12 [a]Ps. 27:11 [b]Ps. 22:22

1 [1]Or, *refuge* [a]Ps. 18:28; Is. 60:20; Mic. 7:8 [b]Ex. 15:2; Ps. 62:7; 118:14; Is. 33:2; Jon. 2:9 [c]Ps. 28:8 [d]Ps. 118:6
2 [a]Ps. 14:4 [b]Ps. 9:3
3 [1]Lit., *am confident* [a]Ps. 3:6 [b]Job 4:6
4 [1]Lit., *delightfulness* [2]Lit., *inquire* [a]Ps. 23:6 [b]Ps. 90:17 [c]Ps. 18:6
5 [1]Or, *shelter* [a]Ps. 50:15 [b]Ps. 31:20 [c]Ps. 17:8 [d]Ps. 40:2
6 [1]Lit., *of shouts* [a]Ps. 3:3 [b]Ps. 107:22 [c]Ps. 13:6
7 [a]Ps. 4:3; 61:1 [b]Ps. 13:3
8 [a]Ps. 105:4; Amos 5:6 [b]Ps. 34:4
9 [a]Ps. 69:17 [b]Ps. 6:1 [c]Ps. 40:17 [d]Ps. 94:14 [e]Ps. 37:28
10 [1]Or, *If my father . . . forsake me, Then the LORD* [a]Is. 49:15 [b]Is. 40:11
11 [a]Ps. 25:4; 86:11 [b]Ps. 5:8; 26:12
12 [1]Lit., *soul* [a]Ps. 41:2 [b]Deut. 19:18; Ps. 35:11; Matt. 26:60 [c]Acts 9:1
13 [1]Or, *Surely I believed* [a]Ps. 31:19 [b]Job 28:13; Ps. 52:5; 116:9; 142:5; Is. 38:11; Jer. 11:19
14 [a]Ps. 25:3; 37:34; 40:1; 62:5; 130:5; Prov. 20:22; Is. 25:9 [b]Ps. 31:24

1 [a]Ps. 18:2 [b]Ps. 35:22; 39:12; 83:1 [c]Ps. 88:4; 143:7
2 [1]Lit., *the innermost place of Thy sanctuary* [a]Ps. 140:6 [b]Ps. 134:2; 141:2; Lam. 2:19; 1 Tim. 2:8 [c]Ps. 5:7; 138:2 [d]1 Kin. 6:5
3 [a]Ps. 26:9 [b]Ps. 12:2; 55:21; 62:4; Jer. 9:8
4 [1]Or, *dealings* [a]Ps. 62:12; 2 Tim. 4:14
5 [a]Is. 5:12

6 Blessed be the LORD,
Because He [a]has heard the voice of my supplication.
7 The LORD is my [a]strength and my [b]shield;
My heart [c]trusts in Him, and I am helped;
Therefore [d]my heart exults,
And with [e]my song I shall thank Him.
8 The LORD is [1]their [a]strength,
And He is a [b]saving defense to His anointed.
9 [a]Save Thy people, and bless [b]Thine inheritance;
Be their [c]shepherd also, and [d]carry them forever.

Psalm 29

The Voice of the LORD in the Storm.

A Psalm of David.

[a]ASCRIBE to the LORD, O sons of the mighty,
Ascribe to the LORD glory and strength.
2 Ascribe to the LORD the glory [1]due to His name;
Worship the LORD [a]in [2]holy array.

3 The [a]voice of the LORD is upon the waters;
The God of glory [b]thunders,
The LORD is over [c]many waters.
4 The voice of the LORD is powerful,
The voice of the LORD is majestic.
5 The voice of the LORD breaks the cedars;
Yes, the LORD breaks in pieces [a]the cedars of Lebanon.
6 And He makes Lebanon [a]skip like a calf,
And [b]Sirion like a young wild ox.
7 The voice of the LORD hews out [1]flames of fire.
8 The voice of the LORD shakes the wilderness;
The LORD shakes the wilderness of [a]Kadesh.
9 The voice of the LORD makes [a]the deer to calve,
And strips the forests bare,
And [b]in His temple everything says, "Glory!"

10 The LORD sat *as King* at the [a]flood;
Yes, the LORD sits as [b]King forever.
11 [1]The LORD will give [a]strength to His people;
[2]The LORD will bless His people with [b]peace.

Psalm 30

Thanksgiving for Deliverance from Death.

A Psalm; a Song at the Dedication of the House.
A Psalm of David.

I WILL [a]extol Thee, O LORD, for Thou hast [b]lifted me up,
And hast not let my [c]enemies rejoice over me.
2 O LORD my God,
I [a]cried to Thee for help, and Thou didst [b]heal me.
3 O LORD, Thou hast [a]brought up my soul from Sheol;
Thou hast kept me alive, [1]that I should not [b]go down to the pit.
4 [a]Sing praise to the LORD, you [b]His godly ones,
And [c]give thanks to His holy [1d]name.
5 For [a]His anger is but for a moment,
His [b]favor is for a lifetime;
Weeping may [c]last for the night,
But a shout of joy *comes* in the morning.

6 Now as for me, [a]I said in my prosperity,
"I will [b]never be moved."
7 O LORD, by Thy favor Thou hast made my mountain to stand strong;
Thou didst [a]hide Thy face, I was dismayed.
8 To Thee, O LORD, I called,
And to the LORD I made supplication:
9 "What profit is there in my blood, if I [a]go down to the pit?
Will the dust praise Thee? Will it declare Thy faithfulness?

10 "[a]Hear, O LORD, and be gracious to me;
O LORD, be Thou my [b]helper."
11 Thou hast turned for me [a]my mourning into dancing;
Thou hast [b]loosed my sackcloth and girded me with [c]gladness;
12 That *my* [1a]soul may sing praise to Thee, and not be silent.
O LORD my God, I will [b]give thanks to Thee forever.

---

6 [a]Ps. 28:2
7 [a]Ps. 59:17 [b]Ps. 3:3 [c]Ps. 13:5; 112:7 [d]Ps. 16:9 [e]Ps. 40:3; 69:30
8 [1]A few mss. read, *the strength of His people* [a]Ps. 89:17 [b]Ps. 27:1; 140:7
9 [a]Ps. 106:47 [b]Deut. 9:29; 32:9; 1 Kin. 8:51; Ps. 33:12; 106:40 [c]Ps. 80:1 [d]Deut. 1:31; Is. 40:11; 46:3

1 [a]1 Chr. 16:28, 29; Ps. 96:7-9
2 [1]Lit., *of His name* [2]Or, *the majesty of holiness* [a]2 Chr. 20:21; Ps. 110:3
3 [a]Ps. 104:7 [b]Job 37:4, 5; Ps. 18:13 [c]Ps. 18:16; 107:23
5 [a]Judg. 9:15; 1 Kin. 5:6; Ps. 104:16; Is. 2:13
6 [a]Ps. 114:4, 6 [b]Deut. 3:9
7 [1]I.e., lightning
8 [a]Num. 13:26
9 [a]Job 39:1 [b]Ps. 26:8
10 [a]Gen. 6:17 [b]Ps. 10:16
11 [1]Or, *May the LORD give . . .* [2]Or, *May the LORD bless . . .* [a]Ps. 28:8; 68:35; Is. 40:29 [b]Ps. 37:11

1 [a]Ps. 118:28; 145:1 [b]Ps. 3:3 [c]Ps. 25:2; 35:19, 24
2 [a]Ps. 88:13 [b]Ps. 6:2; 103:3
3 [1]Some mss. read, *from among those who go down* [a]Ps. 86:13 [b]Ps. 28:1
4 [1]Lit., *memorial* [a]Ps. 149:1 [b]Ps. 50:5 [c]Ps. 97:12 [d]Ex. 3:15; Ps. 135:13; Hos. 12:5
5 [a]Ps. 103:9; Is. 26:20; 54:7, 8 [b]Ps. 118:1 [c]Ps. 126:5; 2 Cor. 4:17
6 [a]Job 29:18 [b]Ps. 10:6; 62:2, 6
7 [a]Deut. 31:17; Ps. 104:29; 143:7
9 [a]Ps. 28:1
10 [a]Ps. 4:1; 27:7 [b]Ps. 27:9; 54:4
11 [a]Ps. 6:8; Eccles. 3:4; Jer. 31:4, 13 [b]Is. 20:2 [c]Ps. 4:7
12 [1]Lit., *glory* [a]Ps. 16:9; 57:8; 108:1 [b]Ps. 44:8

Psalm 31

A Psalm of Complaint and of Praise.

For the choir director. A Psalm
of David.

[a]
IN Thee, O LORD, I have taken refuge;
Let me never [b]be ashamed;
[c]In Thy righteousness deliver
me.
2 [a]Incline Thine ear to me, rescue
me quickly;
Be Thou to me a [b]rock of
[1]strength,
A stronghold to save me.
3 For Thou art my [1]rock and [a]my
fortress;
For [b]Thy name's sake Thou wilt
lead me and guide me.
4 Thou wilt [a]pull me out of the
net which they have secretly
laid for me;
For Thou art my [b]strength.
5 [a]Into Thy hand I commit my
spirit;
Thou hast [b]ransomed me, O
LORD, [c]God of [1]truth.

6 I hate those who [a]regard [1]vain
idols;
But I [b]trust in the LORD.
7 I will [a]rejoice and be glad in
Thy lovingkindness,
Because Thou hast [b]seen my affliction;
Thou hast known the troubles
of my soul,
8 And Thou hast not [a]given me
over into the hand of the enemy;
Thou hast set my feet [b]in a large
place.

9 Be gracious to me, O LORD, for
[a]I am in distress;
My [b]eye is wasted away from
grief, [c]my soul and my body
also.
10 For my life is spent with [a]sor-
row,
And my years with sighing;
My [b]strength has failed because of my iniquity,
And [c]my [1]body has wasted
away.
11 Because of all my adversaries, I
have become a [a]reproach,
Especially to my [b]neighbors,
And an object of dread to my
acquaintances;
Those who see me in the street
flee from me.
12 I am [a]forgotten as a dead man,
out of mind,
I am like a broken vessel.
13 For I have heard the [1a]slander
of many,
Terror is on every side;
While they [b]took counsel together against me,
They [c]schemed to take away
my life.

14 But as for me, I trust in Thee, O
LORD,
I say, "[a]Thou art my God."
15 My [a]times are in Thy hand;
[b]Deliver me from the hand of
my enemies, and from those
who persecute me.
16 Make Thy [a]face to shine upon
Thy servant;
[b]Save me in Thy lovingkindness.
17 Let me not be [a]put to shame, O
LORD, for I call upon Thee;
Let the [b]wicked be put to
shame, let them [c]be silent in
[1]Sheol.
18 Let the [a]lying lips be dumb,
Which [b]speak arrogantly
against the righteous
With [c]pride and contempt.

19 How great is Thy [a]goodness,
Which Thou hast stored up for
those who fear Thee,
Which Thou hast wrought for
those who [b]take refuge in
Thee,
[c]Before the sons of men!
20 Thou dost hide them in the
[a]secret place of Thy presence
from the [b]conspiracies of
man;
Thou dost keep them secretly in
a [1]shelter from the [c]strife of
tongues.
21 [a]Blessed be the LORD,
For He has made [b]marvelous
His lovingkindness to me in a
[c]besieged city.
22 As for me, [a]I said in my alarm,
"I am [b]cut off from before
Thine eyes";
Nevertheless Thou didst [c]hear
the voice of my supplications
When I cried to Thee.

23 O love the LORD, all you [a]His
godly ones!
The LORD [b]preserves the faithful,
And fully [c]recompenses the
proud doer.
24 [a]Be strong, and let your heart
take courage,
All you who [1]hope in the LORD.

1 [a]Ps. 31:1-3; 71:1-3 [b]Ps. 25:2 [c]Ps. 143:1
2 [1]Or, *refuge, protection* [a]Ps. 17:6; 86:1; 102:2 [b]Ps. 18:2; 71:3
3 [1]Or, *crag* [a]Ps. 18:2 [b]Ps. 25:11
4 [a]Ps. 25:15 [b]Ps. 46:1
5 [1]Or, *faithfulness* [a]Luke 23:46; Acts 7:59 [b]Ps. 55:18; 71:23 [c]Deut. 32:4; Ps. 71:22
6 [1]Lit., *empty vanities* [a]Ps. 144:11; Jon. 2:8 [b]Ps. 52:8
7 [a]Ps. 90:14 [b]Ps. 10:14
8 [a]Deut. 32:30; Ps. 37:33 [b]Ps. 4:1
9 [a]Ps. 66:14; 69:17 [b]Ps. 6:7 [c]Ps. 63:1
10 [1]Or, *bones, substance* [a]Ps. 13:2 [b]Ps. 39:11 [c]Ps. 32:3; 38:3; 102:3
11 [a]Ps. 69:19 [b]Job 19:13; Ps. 38:11; 88:8, 18
12 [a]Ps. 88:5
13 [1]Lit., *whispering* [a]Ps. 50:20; Jer. 20:10 [b]Ps. 62:4; Matt. 27:1 [c]Ps. 41:7
14 [a]Ps. 140:6
15 [a]Job 14:5; 24:1 [b]Ps. 143:9
16 [a]Num. 6:25; Ps. 4:6; 80:3 [b]Ps. 6:4
17 [1]I.e., the nether world [a]Ps. 25:20 [b]Ps. 25:3 [c]1 Sam. 2:9; Ps. 94:17; 115:17
18 [a]Ps. 109:2; 120:2 [b]1 Sam. 2:3; Jude 15 [c]Ps. 94:4
19 [a]Ps. 65:4; 145:7; Rom. 2:4; 11:22 [b]Ps. 5:11 [c]Ps. 23:5
20 [1]Or, *pavilion* [a]Ps. 27:5 [b]Ps. 37:12 [c]Job 5:21; Ps. 31:13
21 [a]Ps. 28:6 [b]Ps. 17:7 [c]1 Sam. 23:7; Ps. 87:5
22 [a]Ps. 116:11 [b]Ps. 88:5; Is. 38:11, 12; Lam. 3:54 [c]Ps. 18:6; 66:19; 145:19
23 [a]Ps. 30:4; 37:28; 50:5 [b]Ps. 145:20; Rev. 2:10 [c]Deut. 32:41; Ps. 94:2
24 [1]Or, *wait for* [a]Ps. 27:14

Psalm 32

Blessedness of Forgiveness and of Trust in God.

A Psalm of David. A Maskil.

[a]HOW blessed is he whose transgression is forgiven,
Whose sin is covered!
2 How blessed is the man to whom the LORD [a]does not impute iniquity,
And in whose spirit there is [b]no deceit!

3 When [a]I kept silent *about my sin,* [b]my body wasted away
Through my [c]groaning all day long.
4 For day and night [a]Thy hand was heavy upon me;
My [b]vitality was drained away *as* with the fever-heat of summer. [Selah.
5 I [a]acknowledged my sin to Thee,
And my iniquity I [b]did not hide;
I said, "[c]I will confess my transgressions to the LORD";
And Thou [d]didst forgive the [1]guilt of my sin. [Selah.
6 Therefore, let everyone who is godly pray to Thee [a]in a time when Thou mayest be found;
Surely [b]in a flood of great waters they shall not reach him.
7 Thou art [a]my hiding place;
Thou [b]dost preserve me from trouble;
Thou dost surround me with [1c]songs of deliverance. [Selah.

8 I will [a]instruct you and teach you in the way which you should go;
I will counsel you [b]with My eye upon you.
9 Do not be [a]as the horse or as the mule which have no understanding,
Whose trappings include bit and bridle to hold them in check,
Otherwise they will not come near to you.
10 Many are the [a]sorrows of the wicked;
But [b]he who trusts in the LORD, lovingkindness shall surround him.
11 Be [a]glad in the LORD and rejoice you righteous ones,
And shout for joy all you who are [b]upright in heart.

1 [a]Ps. 85:2; 103:3; Rom. 4:7, 8
2 [a]2 Cor. 5:19 [b]John 1:47
3 [a]Ps. 39:2, 3 [b]Ps. 31:10 [c]Ps. 38:8
4 [a]1 Sam. 5:6; Job 23:2; 33:7; Ps. 38:2; 39:10 [b]Ps. 22:15
5 [1]Or, *iniquity* [a]Lev. 26:40 [b]Job 31:33 [c]Ps. 38:18; 1 John 1:9 [d]Ps. 103:12
6 [a]Ps. 69:13 [b]Ps. 46:1-3; 69:1; 124:5; 144:7; Is. 43:2
7 [1]Or, *shouts* [a]Ps. 31:20; 91:1; 119:114 [b]Ps. 121:7 [c]Ex. 15:1; Judg. 5:1; Ps. 40:3
8 [a]Ps. 25:8 [b]Ps. 33:18
9 [a]Prov. 26:3
10 [a]Ps. 16:4; Prov. 13:21; Rom. 2:9 [b]Ps. 5:11, 12
11 [a]Ps. 64:10; 68:3; 97:12 [b]Ps. 7:10; 64:10
1 [a]Ps. 32:11; Phil. 3:1; 4:4 [b]Ps. 92:1; 147:1
2 [a]Ps. 71:22; 147:7 [b]Ps. 144:9
3 [a]Ps. 40:3; 96:1; 98:1; 144:9; Is. 42:10; Rev. 5:9 [b]Ps. 98:4
4 [a]Ps. 19:8 [b]Ps. 119:90
5 [a]Ps. 11:7; 37:28 [b]Ps. 119:64
6 [a]Gen. 1:6; Ps. 148:5; Heb. 11:3 [b]Ps. 104:30 [c]Gen. 2:1
7 [1]Some versions read, *in a water skin;* i.e., container [a]Ex. 15:8; Josh. 3:16; Ps. 78:13
8 [a]Ps. 67:7 [b]Ps. 96:9
9 [a]Gen. 1:3
10 [a]Ps. 2:1-3; Is. 8:10; 19:3
11 [a]Job 23:13; Prov. 19:21 [b]Ps. 40:5; 92:5; 139:17; Is. 55:8
12 [a]Ps. 144:15 [b]Deut. 7:6; Ps. 28:9
13 [a]Job 28:24; Ps. 14:2 [b]Ps. 11:4
14 [a]1 Kin. 8:39, 43; Ps. 102:19
15 [1]Or, *their heart together* [a]Job 10:8; Ps. 119:73 [b]2 Chr. 16:9; Job 34:21
16 [a]Ps. 44:6
17 [a]Ps. 20:7; 147:10; Prov. 21:31

Psalm 33

Praise to the Creator and Preserver.

[a]SING for joy in the LORD, O you righteous ones;
Praise is [b]becoming to the upright.
2 Give thanks to the LORD with the [a]lyre;
Sing praises to Him with a [b]harp of ten strings.
3 Sing to Him a [a]new song;
Play skillfully with [b]a shout of joy.
4 For the word of the LORD [a]is upright;
And all His work is *done* [b]in faithfulness.
5 He [a]loves righteousness and justice;
The [b]earth is full of the lovingkindness of the LORD.

6 By the [a]word of the LORD the heavens were made,
And [b]by the breath of His mouth [c]all their host.
7 He gathers the [a]waters of the sea together [1]as a heap;
He lays up the deeps in storehouses.
8 Let [a]all the earth fear the LORD;
Let all the inhabitants of the world [b]stand in awe of Him.
9 For [a]He spoke, and it was done;
He commanded, and it stood fast.
10 The LORD [a]nullifies the counsel of the nations;
He frustrates the plans of the peoples.
11 The [a]counsel of the LORD stands forever,
The [b]plans of His heart from generation to generation.
12 Blessed is the [a]nation whose God is the LORD,
The people whom He has [b]chosen for His own inheritance.

13 The LORD [a]looks from heaven;
He [b]sees all the sons of men;
14 From [a]His dwelling place He looks out
On all the inhabitants of the earth,
15 He who [a]fashions [1]the hearts of them all,
He who [b]understands all their works.
16 [a]The king is not saved by a mighty army;
A warrior is not delivered by great strength.
17 A [a]horse is a false hope for victory;

Nor does it deliver anyone by
its great strength.
18 Behold, [a]the eye of the LORD is
on those who fear Him,
On those who [1b]hope for His
lovingkindness,
19 To [a]deliver their soul from
death,
And to keep them alive [b]in famine.
20 Our soul [a]waits for the LORD;
He is our [b]help and our shield.
21 For our [a]heart rejoices in Him,
Because we trust in His holy
name.
22 Let Thy lovingkindness, O
LORD, be upon us,
According as we have [1]hoped
in Thee.

PSALM 34

The LORD a Provider and Deliverer.

A Psalm of David when he
[£]feigned madness before
[•]Abimelech, who drove him away
and he departed.

I WILL [a]bless the LORD at all times;
His [b]praise shall continually be
in my mouth.
2 My soul shall [a]make its boast in
the LORD;
The [b]humble shall hear it and
rejoice.
3 O [a]magnify the LORD with me,
And let us [b]exalt His name together.

4 I [a]sought the LORD, and He answered me,
And [b]delivered me from all my
fears.
5 They [a]looked to Him and were
radiant,
And their faces shall [b]never be
ashamed.
6 This [1]poor man cried and [a]the
LORD heard him;
And saved him out of all his
troubles.
7 The [a]angel of the LORD encamps around those who
fear Him,
And rescues them.

8 O [a]taste and see that the LORD
is good;
How [b]blessed is the man who
takes refuge in Him!
9 O fear the LORD, you [a]His
saints;
For to those who fear Him,
there is [b]no want.
10 The young lions do lack and
suffer hunger;
But they who seek the LORD
shall [a]not be in want of any
good thing.
11 [a]Come, you children, listen to
me;
I will teach you [b]the fear of the
LORD.
12 [a]Who is the man who desires
life,
And loves *length of* days that
he may [b]see good?
13 Keep [a]your tongue from evil,
And your lips from speaking
[b]deceit.
14 [a]Depart from evil, and do good;
Seek peace, and [b]pursue it.

15 The [a]eyes of the LORD are
toward the righteous,
And His ears are *open* to their
cry.
16 The [a]face of the LORD is against
evildoers,
To [b]cut off the memory of them
from the earth.
17 *The righteous* [a]cry and the
LORD hears,
And delivers them out of all
their troubles.
18 The LORD [a]is near to the [b]brokenhearted,
And saves those who are
[1c]crushed in spirit.

19 Many are the [a]afflictions of the
righteous;
But the LORD [b]delivers him out
of them all.
20 He keeps all his bones;
Not one of them is broken.
21 [a]Evil shall slay the wicked;
And those who hate the righteous will be [1]condemned.
22 The LORD [a]redeems the soul of
His servants;
And none of those who [b]take
refuge in Him will be [1]condemned.

PSALM 35

Prayer for Rescue from Enemies.

A Psalm of David.

CONTEND, O LORD, with those
who [a]contend with me;
Fight against those who [b]fight
against me.
2 Take hold of [1a]buckler and
shield,
And rise up for [b]my help.
3 Draw also the spear and the
battle-axe to meet those who
pursue me;
Say to my soul, "I am [a]your salvation."

---

18 [1]Or, *wait* [a]Job 36:7; Ps. 32:8; 34:15; 1 Pet. 3:12 [b]Ps. 32:10
19 [a]Ps. 56:13; Acts 12:11 [b]Job 5:20; Ps. 37:19
20 [a]Ps. 62:1; 130:6; Is. 8:17 [b]Ps. 115:9
21 [a]Ps. 13:5; 28:7; Zech. 10:7; John 16:22
22 [1]Or, *waited for*

£ Or, *changed his behavior*
• Possibly a title of King Achish of Gath. See 1 Sam. 21:10-15
1 [a]Eph. 5:20; 1 Thess. 5:18 [b]Ps. 71:6
2 [a]Ps. 44:8; Jer. 9:24; 1 Cor. 1:31 [b]Ps. 69:32
3 [a]Ps. 35:27; 69:30; Luke 1:46 [b]Ps. 18:46
4 [a]2 Chr. 15:2; Ps. 9:10; Matt. 7:7 [b]Ps. 34:6, 17, 19
5 [a]Ps. 36:9; Is. 60:5 [b]Ps. 25:3
6 [1]Or, *afflicted* [a]Ps. 34:4
7 [a]Ps. 91:11; Dan. 6:22
8 [a]Ps. 119:103; Heb. 6:5; 1 Pet. 2:3 [b]Ps. 2:12
9 [a]Ps. 31:23 [b]Ps. 23:1
10 [a]Ps. 84:11
11 [a]Ps. 66:16 [b]Ps. 111:10
12 [a]Ps. 34:12, 16; 1 Pet. 3:10-12 [b]Eccles. 3:13
13 [a]Ps. 141:3; Prov. 13:3; James 1:26 [b]1 Pet. 2:22
14 [a]Ps. 37:27; Is. 1:16, 17 [b]Rom. 14:19; Heb. 12:14
15 [a]Ps. 33:18
16 [a]Jer. 44:11; Amos 9:4 [b]Job 18:17; Ps. 9:6
17 [a]Ps. 34:6
18 [1]Or, *contrite* [a]Ps. 145:18 [b]Ps. 147:3; Is. 61:1 [c]Ps. 51:17; Is. 57:15
19 [a]Ps. 71:20; 2 Tim. 3:11, 12 [b]Ps. 34:4, 6, 17
21 [1]Or, *held guilty* [a]Ps. 94:23; 140:11
22 [1]Note, v. 21 [a]Ps. 71:23 [b]Ps. 37:40

1 [a]Ps. 18:43; Is. 49:25 [b]Ps. 56:2
2 [1]I.e., small shield [a]Ps. 91:4 [b]Ps. 44:26
3 [a]Ps. 62:2

4 Let those be [a]ashamed and dishonored who seek my [1]life;
Let those be [b]turned back and humiliated who devise evil against me.
5 Let them be [a]like chaff before the wind,
With the angel of the LORD driving *them* on.
6 Let their way be dark and [a]slippery,
With the angel of the LORD pursuing them.
7 For [a]without cause they hid their net for me;
Without cause they dug a [1]pit for my soul.
8 Let [a]destruction come upon him unawares;
And [b]let the net which he hid catch himself;
Into that very [c]destruction let him fall.

9 And my soul shall [a]rejoice in the LORD;
It shall [b]exult in His salvation.
10 All my [a]bones will say, "LORD, [b]who is like Thee,
Who delivers the afflicted from him [c]who is too strong for him,
And [d]the afflicted and the needy from him who robs him?"
11 [a]Malicious witnesses rise up;
They ask me of things that I do not know.
12 They [a]repay me evil for good,
To the bereavement of my soul.
13 But as for me, [a]when they were sick, my [b]clothing was sackcloth;
I [c]humbled my soul with fasting;
And my [d]prayer kept returning to my bosom.
14 I went about as though it were my friend or brother;
I [a]bowed down mourning, as one who sorrows for a mother.
15 But [a]at my [1]stumbling they rejoiced, and gathered themselves together;
The [b]smiters whom I did not know gathered together against me,
They [2c]slandered me without ceasing.
16 Like godless jesters at a feast,
They [a]gnashed at me with their teeth.

17 Lord, [a]how long wilt Thou look on?
Rescue my soul [b]from their ravages,
My [c]only *life* from the lions.
18 I will [a]give Thee thanks in the great congregation;
I will [b]praise Thee among a mighty throng.
19 [a]Do not let those who are wrongfully [b]my enemies rejoice over me;
Neither let those [c]who hate me without cause [1d]wink maliciously.
20 For they do not speak peace,
But they devise [a]deceitful words against those who are quiet in the land.
21 And they [a]opened their mouth wide against me;
They said, "[b]Aha, aha, our eyes have seen it!"

22 [a]Thou hast seen it, O LORD, [b]do not keep silent;
O Lord, [c]do not be far from me.
23 [a]Stir up Thyself, and awake to my right,
And to my cause, my God and my Lord.
24 [a]Judge me, O LORD my God, according to Thy righteousness;
And [b]do not let them rejoice over me.
25 Do not let them say in their heart, "[a]Aha, our desire!"
Do not let them say, "We have [b]swallowed him up!"
26 Let [a]those be ashamed and humiliated altogether who rejoice at my distress;
Let those be clothed with shame and dishonor who [b]magnify themselves over me.

27 Let them [a]shout for joy and rejoice, who favor [b]my vindication;
And [c]let them say continually,
"The LORD be magnified,
Who [d]delights in the prosperity of His servant."
28 And [a]my tongue shall declare Thy righteousness
And Thy praise all day long.

PSALM 36

Wickedness of Men and Lovingkindness of God.

For the choir director. *A Psalm* of David the servant of the LORD.

1 TRANSGRESSION speaks to the ungodly within [1]his heart;
There is [a]no fear of God before his eyes.

4 [1]Or, *soul* [a]Ps. 70:2 [b]Ps. 40:14; 129:5
5 [a]Job 21:18; Ps. 83:13; Is. 29:5
6 [a]Ps. 73:18; Jer. 23:12
7 [1]*Pit* has been transposed from line above [a]Ps. 69:4; 109:3; 140:5
8 [a]Ps. 55:23; Is. 47:11; 1 Thess. 5:3 [b]Ps. 9:15 [c]Ps. 73:18
9 [a]Is. 61:10 [b]Ps. 9:14; 13:5; Luke 1:47
10 [a]Ps. 51:8 [b]Ex. 15:11; Ps. 86:8; Mic. 7:18 [c]Ps. 18:17 [d]Ps. 37:14; 109:16
11 [a]Ps. 27:12
12 [a]Ps. 38:20; 109:5; Jer. 18:20; John 10:32
13 [a]Job 30:25 [b]Ps. 69:11 [c]Ps. 69:10 [d]Matt. 10:13; Luke 10:6
14 [a]Ps. 38:6
15 [1]Or, *limping* [2]Lit., *tore* [a]Obad. 12 [b]Job 30:1, 8, 12 [c]Ps. 7:2
16 [a]Job 16:9; Ps. 37:12; Lam. 2:16
17 [a]Ps. 13:1; Hab. 1:13 [b]Ps. 35:7 [c]Ps. 22:20, 21
18 [a]Ps. 22:22 [b]Ps. 22:25
19 [1]Or, *wink the eye* [a]Ps. 13:4; 30:1; 38:16 [b]Ps. 38:19; 69:4; 119:78 [c]John 15:25 [d]Prov. 6:13; 10:10
20 [a]Ps. 55:21; Jer. 9:8; Mic. 6:12
21 [a]Job 16:10; Ps. 22:13 [b]Ps. 40:15; 70:3
22 [a]Ex. 3:7; Ps. 10:14 [b]Ps. 28:1 [c]Ps. 10:1; 22:11; 38:21; 71:12
23 [a]Ps. 7:6; 44:23; 59:4; 80:2
24 [a]Ps. 9:4; 26:1; 43:1 [b]Ps. 35:19
25 [a]Ps. 35:21 [b]Ps. 56:1; 124:3; Prov. 1:12; Lam. 2:16
26 [a]Ps. 40:14 [b]Job 19:5; Ps. 38:16
27 [a]Ps. 32:11 [b]Ps. 9:4 [c]Ps. 40:16; 70:4 [d]Ps. 147:11; 149:4
28 [a]Ps. 51:14; 71:15, 24
1 [1]Another reading is, *my heart* [a]Rom. 3:18

2 For [1]it [a]flatters him in his *own* eyes,
Concerning the discovery of his iniquity *and* the hatred *of it.*
3 The [a]words of his mouth are wickedness and deceit;
He has [b]ceased to be wise *and* to do good.
4 He [a]plans wickedness upon his bed;
He sets himself on a [b]path that is not good;
He [c]does not despise evil.

5 Thy [a]lovingkindness, O LORD, [1]extends to the heavens,
Thy faithfulness *reaches* to the skies.
6 Thy [a]righteousness is like the mountains of God;
Thy [b]judgments are *like* a great deep.
O LORD, Thou [c]preservest man and beast.
7 How [a]precious is Thy lovingkindness, O God!
And the children of men [b]take refuge in the shadow of Thy wings.
8 They [a]drink their fill of the abundance of Thy house;
And Thou dost give them to drink of the [b]river of Thy delights.
9 For with Thee is the [a]fountain of life;
In Thy light we see light.

10 O continue Thy lovingkindness to [a]those who know Thee,
And Thy [b]righteousness to the upright in heart.
11 Let not the foot of pride come upon me,
And let not the hand of the wicked drive me away.
12 There the doers of iniquity have fallen;
They have been thrust down and [a]cannot rise.

PSALM 37

Security of Those Who Trust in the LORD, and Insecurity of the Wicked.

A Psalm of David.

[a]FRET not yourself because of evildoers,
Be not [b]envious toward wrongdoers.
2 For they will [a]wither quickly like the grass,
And [b]fade like the green herb.
3 [a]Trust in the LORD, and do good;
[b]Dwell in the land and [c]cultivate faithfulness.
4 [a]Delight yourself in the LORD;
And He will [b]give you the desires of your heart.
5 [a]Commit your way to the LORD,
Trust also in Him, and He will do it.
6 And He will bring forth [a]your righteousness as the light,
And your judgment as the noonday.

7 [a]Rest in the LORD and [b]wait patiently for Him;
[c]Fret not yourself because of him who [d]prospers in his way,
Because of the man who carries out wicked schemes.
8 Cease from anger, and [a]forsake wrath;
Fret not yourself, *it leads* only to evildoing.
9 For [a]evildoers will be cut off,
But those who wait for the LORD, they will [b]inherit the land.
10 Yet [a]a little while and the wicked man will be no more;
And you will look carefully for [b]his place, and he will not be *there.*
11 But [a]the humble will inherit the land,
And will delight themselves in abundant prosperity.

12 The wicked [a]plots against the righteous,
And [b]gnashes at him with his teeth.
13 The LORD [a]laughs at him;
For He sees [b]his day is coming.
14 The wicked have drawn the sword and [a]bent their bow,
To cast down the [b]afflicted and the needy,
To [c]slay those who are upright in conduct.
15 Their sword will enter their own heart,
And their [a]bows will be broken.

16 [a]Better is the little of the righteous
Than the abundance of many wicked.
17 For the [a]arms of the wicked will be broken;
But the LORD [b]sustains the righteous.
18 The LORD [a]knows the days of the [1]blameless;
And their [b]inheritance will be forever.

---

2 [1]Or, *he flatters himself* [a]Deut. 29:19; Ps. 10:11; 49:18
3 [a]Ps. 10:7; 12:2 [b]Ps. 94:8; Jer. 4:22
4 [a]Prov. 4:16; Mic. 2:1 [b]Is. 65:2 [c]Ps. 52:3; Rom. 12:9
5 [1]Lit., *is in* [a]Ps. 57:10; 103:11
6 [a]Ps. 71:19 [b]Job 11:8; Ps. 77:19; Rom. 11:33 [c]Neh. 9:6; Ps. 104:14, 15; 145:16
7 [a]Ps. 40:5; 139:17 [b]Ruth 2:12; Ps. 57:1
8 [a]Ps. 63:5; Is. 25:6; Jer. 31:12-14 [b]Job 20:17; Ps. 46:4; Rev. 22:1
9 [a]Jer. 2:13
10 [a]Jer. 22:16 [b]Ps. 24:5
12 [a]Ps. 140:10; Is. 26:14
1 [a]Prov. 23:17; 24:19 [b]Ps. 73:3; Prov. 3:31
2 [a]Job 14:2; Ps. 90:6; 92:7 [b]Ps. 129:6
3 [a]Ps. 62:8 [b]Deut. 30:20 [c]Is. 40:11; Ezek. 34:13, 14
4 [a]Job 22:26; Ps. 94:19; Is. 58:14 [b]Ps. 21:2; 145:19; Matt. 7:7, 8
5 [a]Ps. 55:22; Prov. 16:3; 1 Pet. 5:7
6 [a]Ps. 97:11; Is. 58:8, 10; Mic. 7:9
7 [a]Ps. 62:5 [b]Ps. 40:1 [c]Ps. 37:1, 8 [d]Jer. 12:1
8 [a]Eph. 4:31; Col. 3:8
9 [a]Ps. 37:2, 22 [b]Ps. 25:13; Prov. 2:21; Is. 60:21
10 [a]Job 24:24 [b]Job 7:10; Ps. 37:35, 36
11 [a]Matt. 5:5
12 [a]Ps. 31:13, 20 [b]Ps. 35:16
13 [a]Ps. 2:4 [b]1 Sam. 26:10; Job 18:20
14 [a]Ps. 11:2; Lam. 2:4 [b]Ps. 35:10; 86:1 [c]Ps. 11:2
15 [a]1 Sam. 2:4; Ps. 46:9
16 [a]Ps. 4:7; Prov. 15:16; 16:8
17 [a]Job 38:15; Ps. 10:15; Ezek. 30:21 [b]Ps. 71:6
18 [1]Lit., *complete;* or, *perfect* [a]Ps. 1:6; 31:7 [b]Ps. 37:27, 29

19 They will not be ashamed in the
time of evil;
And [a]in the days of famine they
will have abundance.
20 But the [a]wicked will perish;
And the enemies of the LORD
will be [b]like the [1]glory of the
pastures,
They vanish—[c]like smoke they
vanish away.
21 The wicked borrows and does
not pay back,
But the righteous [a]is gracious
and gives.
22 For those blessed by Him will
[a]inherit the land;
But those [b]cursed by Him will
be cut off.

23 [a]The steps of a man are established by the LORD;
And He [b]delights in his way.
24 When [a]he falls, he shall not be
hurled headlong;
Because [b]the LORD is the One
who holds his hand.
25 I have been young, and now I
am old;
Yet [a]I have not seen the righteous forsaken,
Or [b]his [1]descendants begging
bread.
26 All day long [a]he is gracious and
lends;
And [b]his descendants are a
blessing.

27 [a]Depart from evil, and do good,
[1]So you will abide [b]forever.
28 For the LORD [a]loves justice,
And [b]does not forsake His godly ones;
They are [c]preserved forever;
But the [d]descendants of the
wicked will be cut off.
29 The righteous will [a]inherit the
land,
And [b]dwell in it forever.
30 The mouth of the righteous [a]ut-
ters wisdom,
And his tongue [b]speaks justice.
31 The [a]law of his God is in his
heart;
His [b]steps do not slip.
32 The [a]wicked spies upon the
righteous,
And [b]seeks to kill him.
33 The LORD will [a]not leave him in
his hand,
Or [b]let him be condemned
when he is judged.
34 [a]Wait for the LORD, and keep
His way,
And He will exalt you to inherit
the land;
When the [b]wicked are cut off,
you will see it.

35 I have [a]seen a violent, wicked
man
Spreading himself like a [b]luxu-
riant tree in its native soil.
36 Then he passed away, and lo, he
[a]was no more;
I sought for him, but he could
not be found.
37 Mark the [1a]blameless man, and
behold the [b]upright;
For the man of peace will have
a [c]posterity.
38 But transgressors will be altogether [a]destroyed;
The posterity of the wicked will
be [b]cut off.
39 But the [a]salvation of the righteous is from the LORD;
He is their strength [b]in time of
trouble.
40 And [a]the LORD helps them, and
delivers them;
He [b]delivers them from the
wicked, and saves them,
Because they [c]take refuge in
Him.

PSALM 38

Prayer of a Suffering Penitent.

A Psalm of David, for a memorial.

O LORD, [a]rebuke me not in Thy
wrath;
And chasten me not in Thy
burning anger.
2 For Thine [a]arrows have sunk
deep into me,
And [b]Thy hand has pressed
down on me.
3 There is [a]no soundness in my
flesh [b]because of Thine indignation;
There is no health [c]in my bones
because of my sin.
4 For my [a]iniquities are gone
over my head;
As a heavy burden they weigh
too much for me.
5 My [1]wounds grow foul *and* fes-
ter.
Because of [a]my folly,
6 I am bent over and [a]greatly
bowed down;
I [b]go mourning all day long.
7 For my loins are filled with
[a]burning;
And there is [b]no soundness in
my flesh.
8 I am [a]benumbed and [1]badly
crushed;
I [2b]groan because of the [3]agita-
tion of my heart.
9 Lord, all [a]my desire is [1]before
Thee;

19 [a]Job 5:20
20 [1]I.e., flowers [a]Ps. 73:27 [b]Lev. 3:11 [c]Ps. 68:2
21 [a]Ps. 112:5
22 [a]Ps. 37:9 [b]Job 5:3
23 [a]1 Sam. 2:9; Ps. 40:2; 66:9; 119:5 [b]Ps. 147:11
24 [a]Ps. 145:14; Prov. 24:16; Mic. 7:8 [b]Ps. 147:6
25 [1]Lit., *seed* [a]Ps. 37:28; Is. 41:17; Heb. 13:5 [b]Ps. 109:10
26 [a]Ps. 37:21 [b]Ps. 147:13
27 [1]Or, *And dwell forever* [a]Ps. 34:14 [b]Ps. 37:18; 102:28
28 [a]Ps. 11:7; 33:5 [b]Ps. 37:25 [c]Ps. 31:23 [d]Ps. 21:10; 37:9; Prov. 2:22; Is. 14:20
29 [a]Ps. 37:9 [b]Ps. 37:18
30 [a]Ps. 49:3; Prov. 10:13 [b]Ps. 101:1; 119:13
31 [a]Deut. 6:6; Ps. 40:8; 119:11; Is. 51:7; Jer 31:33 [b]Ps. 26:1; 37:23
32 [a]Ps. 10:8; 17:11 [b]Ps. 37:14
33 [a]Ps. 31:8; 2 Pet. 2:9 [b]Ps. 34:22; 109:31
34 [a]Ps. 27:14; 37:9 [b]Ps. 52:5, 6
35 [a]Job 5:3; Jer. 12:2 [b]Job 8:16
36 [a]Job 20:5; Ps. 37:10
37 [1]Lit., *complete* [a]Ps. 37:18 [b]Ps. 7:10 [c]Is. 57:1, 2
38 [a]Ps. 37:20, 28 [b]Ps. 37:9; 73:17
39 [a]Ps. 3:8; 62:1 [b]Ps. 9:9; 37:19
40 [a]Ps. 54:4 [b]Ps. 22:4; Dan. 3:17; 6:23 [c]Ps. 34:22
1 [a]Ps. 6:1
2 [a]Job 6:4 [b]Ps. 32:4
3 [a]Is. 1:6 [b]Ps. 102:10 [c]Job 33:19; Ps. 6:2; 31:10
4 [a]Ezra 9:6
5 [1]Or, *stripes* [a]Ps. 69:5
6 [a]Ps. 35:14 [b]Job 30:28; Ps. 42:9; 43:2
7 [a]Ps. 102:3 [b]Ps. 38:3
8 [1]Or, *greatly* [2]Lit., *roar* [3]Lit., *growling* [a]Lam. 1:13; 5:17 [b]Job 3:24; Ps. 22:1; 32:3
9 [1]Or, known *to Thee* [a]Ps. 10:17

And my [b]sighing is not hidden from Thee.
10 My heart throbs, [a]my strength fails me;
And the [b]light of my eyes, even that has gone from me.
11 My [a]loved ones and my friends stand aloof from my plague;
And my kinsmen [b]stand afar off.
12 Those who [a]seek my life [b]lay snares *for me;*
And those who [c]seek to injure me have [d]threatened destruction,
And they devise treachery all day long.

13 But I, like a deaf man, do not hear;
And I am like a [a]dumb man who does not open his mouth.
14 Yes, I am like a man who does not hear,
And in whose mouth are no arguments.
15 For [a]I [1]hope in Thee, O LORD;
Thou wilt answer, O Lord my God.
16 For I said, "May they not rejoice over me,
Who, when my foot slips, [a]would magnify themselves against me."
17 For I am [a]ready to fall,
And [b]my [1]sorrow is continually before me.
18 For I [a]confess my iniquity;
I am full of [b]anxiety because of my sin.
19 But my [a]enemies are vigorous *and* [1]strong;
And many are those who hate me wrongfully.
20 And those who [a]repay evil for good,
They [b]oppose me, because I follow what is good.
21 Do not forsake me, O LORD;
O my God, [a]do not be far from me!
22 Make [a]haste to help me,
O Lord, [b]my salvation!

PSALM 39

The Vanity of Life.

For the choir director, for [£]Jeduthun.
A Psalm of David.

I SAID, "I will [a]guard my ways,
That I [b]may not sin with my tongue;
I will guard [c]my mouth as with a muzzle,
While the wicked are in my presence."

9 [b]Ps. 6:6; 102:5
10 [a]Ps. 31:10 [b]Ps. 6:7; 69:3; 88:9
11 [a]Ps. 31:11; 88:18 [b]Luke 23:49
12 [a]Ps. 54:3 [b]Ps. 140:5 [c]Ps. 35:4 [d]Eccles. 10:13; Mic. 7:3
13 [a]Ps. 39:2, 9
15 [1]Or, *wait for* [a]Ps. 39:7
16 [a]Ps. 35:26
17 [1]Lit., *pain* [a]Ps. 35:15 [b]Ps. 13:2
18 [a]Ps. 32:5 [b]2 Cor. 7:9, 10
19 [1]Or, *numerous* [a]Ps. 18:17
20 [a]Ps. 35:12 [b]Ps. 109:4; 1 John 3:12
21 [a]Ps. 22:19; 35:22
22 [a]Ps. 40:13, 17 [b]Ps. 27:1

[£]1 Chr. 16:41
1 [a]1 Kin. 2:4; 2 Kin. 10:31; Ps. 119:9 [b]Job 2:10; Ps. 34:13; James 3:5-12 [c]Ps. 141:3; James 3:2
2 [1]Lit., *with silence* [2]Lit., *kept silence* [3]Lit., *pain* [a]Ps. 38:13
3 [a]Ps. 32:4; Jer. 20:9; Luke 24:32
4 [a]Job 6:11; Ps. 90:12; 119:84 [b]Ps. 78:39; 103:14
5 [1]Lit., *standing firm* [a]Ps. 89:47 [b]Ps. 144:4 [c]Job 14:2; Ps. 62:9
6 [1]Lit., *an image* [a]1 Cor. 7:31; James 1:10, 11; 1 Pet. 1:24 [b]Ps. 127:2; Eccles. 5:17 [c]Ps. 49:10; Eccles. 2:26; 5:14; Luke 12:20
7 [a]Ps. 38:15
8 [a]Ps. 51:9, 14; 79:9 [b]Ps. 44:13
9 [a]Ps. 39:2 [b]2 Sam. 16:10
10 [a]Job 9:34; 13:21
11 [a]Ezek. 5:15; 2 Pet. 2:16 [b]Job 13:28; Ps. 90:7; Is. 50:9 [c]Ps. 39:5
12 [a]Ps. 102:1; 143:1 [b]2 Kin. 20:5; Ps. 56:8 [c]Lev. 25:23; 1 Chr. 29:15; Ps. 119:19; Heb. 11:13; 1 Pet. 2:11
13 [a]Job 7:19; 14:6; Ps. 102:24

1 [1]Or, *intently* [a]Ps. 25:5; 27:14; 37:7 [b]Ps. 34:15

2 I was [a]dumb [1]*and* silent,
I [2]refrained *even* from good;
And my [3]sorrow grew worse.
3 My [a]heart was hot within me;
While I was musing the fire burned;
Then I spoke with my tongue:
4 "LORD, make me to know [a]my end,
And what is the extent of my days,
Let me know how [b]transient I am.
5 "Behold, Thou hast made [a]my days *as* handbreadths,
And my [b]lifetime as nothing in Thy sight,
Surely every man [1]at his best is a mere [c]breath. [Selah.
6 "Surely every man [a]walks about as [1]a phantom;
Surely they make an [b]uproar for nothing;
He [c]amasses *riches,* and does not know who will gather them.

7 "And now, Lord, for what do I wait?
My [a]hope is in Thee.
8 "[a]Deliver me from all my transgressions;
Make me not the [b]reproach of the foolish.
9 "I have become [a]dumb, I do not open my mouth,
Because it is [b]Thou who hast done *it.*
10 "[a]Remove Thy plague from me;
Because of the opposition of Thy hand, I am perishing.
11 "With [a]reproofs Thou dost chasten a man for iniquity;
Thou dost [b]consume as a moth what is precious to him;
Surely [c]every man is a mere breath. [Selah.

12 "[a]Hear my prayer, O LORD, and give ear to my cry;
Do not be silent [b]at my tears;
For I am [c]a stranger with Thee,
A sojourner like all my fathers.
13 "[a]Turn Thy gaze away from me, that I may smile *again,*
Before I depart and am no more."

PSALM 40

God Sustains His Servant.

For the choir director. A Psalm of David.

I [a]WAITED [1]patiently for the LORD;
And He inclined to me, and [b]heard my cry.

2 He brought me up out of the [a]pit of destruction, out of the [1]miry clay;
And [b]He set my feet upon a rock [c]making my footsteps firm.
3 And He put a [a]new song in my mouth, a song of praise to our God;
Many will [b]see and fear,
And will trust in the LORD.

4 How [a]blessed is the man who has made the LORD his trust,
And [b]has not [1]turned to the proud, nor to those who [c]lapse into falsehood.
5 Many, O LORD my God, are [a]the wonders which Thou hast done,
And Thy [b]thoughts toward us;
There is none to compare with Thee;
If I would declare and speak of them,
They [c]would be too numerous to count.

6 [1a]Sacrifice and meal offering Thou hast not desired;
My ears Thou hast [2]opened;
Burnt offering and sin offering Thou hast not required.
7 Then I said, "Behold, I come;
In the scroll of the book it is [1]written of me;
8 I delight to do Thy will, O my God;
[a]Thy Law is within my heart."

9 I have [a]proclaimed glad tidings of righteousness in the great congregation;
Behold, I will [b]not restrain my lips,
O LORD, [c]Thou knowest.
10 I have [a]not hidden Thy righteousness within my heart;
I have [b]spoken of Thy faithfulness and Thy salvation;
I have not concealed Thy lovingkindness and Thy truth from the great congregation.

11 Thou, O LORD, wilt not withhold Thy compassion from me;
[1]Thy [a]lovingkindness and Thy truth will continually preserve me.
12 For evils beyond number have [a]surrounded me;
My [b]iniquities have overtaken me, so that I am not able to see;

2 [1]Lit., *mud of the mire* [a]Ps. 69:2; Jer. 38:6 [b]Ps. 27:5 [c]Ps. 37:23
3 [a]Ps. 32:7; 33:3 [b]Ps. 52:6; 64:9
4 [1]Lit., *regard* [a]Ps. 84:12 [b]Job 37:24 [c]Ps. 125:5
5 [a]Job 5:9; Ps. 136:4 [b]Ps. 139:17; Is. 55:8 [c]Ps. 71:15; 139:18
6 [1]I.e., Blood sacrifice [2]Lit., *dug*, or possibly, *pierced* [a]1 Sam. 15:22; Ps. 51:16; Is. 1:11; Jer. 6:20; 7:22, 23; Amos 5:22; Mic. 6:6-8; Heb. 10:5-7
7 [1]Or, *prescribed for*
8 [a]Ps. 37:31; 2 Cor. 3:3
9 [a]Ps. 22:25 [b]Ps. 119:13 [c]Josh. 22:22; Ps. 139:4
10 [a]Acts 20:20, 27 [b]Ps. 89:1
11 [1]Or, *May . . . preserve* [a]Ps. 43:3; 57:3; 61:7; Prov. 20:28
12 [1]Lit., *forsaken* [a]Ps. 18:5; 116:3 [b]Ps. 38:4; 65:3 [c]Ps. 69:4 [d]Ps. 73:26
13 [a]Ps. 22:19; 71:12
14 [1]Or, *soul* [2]Or, *to injure me* [a]Ps. 35:4, 26; 70:2; 71:13 [b]Ps. 63:9
15 [1]Or, *desolated* [a]Ps. 70:3 [b]Ps. 35:21; 70:3
16 [a]Ps. 35:27
17 [1]Or, *The Lord is mindful* [a]Ps. 70:5; 86:1; 109:22 [b]Ps. 40:5; 1 Pet. 5:7
1 [1]Or, *poor* [2]Or, *evil* [a]Ps. 82:3, 4; Prov. 14:21 [b]Ps. 27:5; 37:19
2 [1]Or, *be blessed* [a]Ps. 37:28 [b]Ps. 37:22 [c]Ps. 27:12
3 [1]Lit., *turn all his bed* [a]Ps. 6:6
4 [a]Ps. 6:2; 103:3; 147:3 [b]Ps. 51:4
5 [a]Ps. 38:12
6 [1]Or, *if he* [2]Or, *emptiness* [a]Ps. 12:2; 62:4; Prov. 26:24-26

They are [c]more numerous than the hairs of my head;
And my [d]heart has [1]failed me.

13 Be pleased, O LORD, to deliver me;
Make [a]haste, O LORD, to help me.
14 Let those be [a]ashamed and humiliated together
Who [b]seek my [1]life to destroy it;
Let those be turned back and dishonored
Who delight [2]in my hurt.
15 Let those [a]be [1]appalled because of their shame
Who [b]say to me, "Aha, aha!"
16 Let all who seek Thee rejoice and be glad in Thee;
Let those who love Thy salvation [a]say continually,
"The LORD be magnified!"
17 Since [a]I am afflicted and needy,
[1b]Let the Lord be mindful of me;
Thou art my help and my deliverer;
Do not delay, O my God.

PSALM 41

The Psalmist in Sickness Complains of Enemies and False Friends.

For the choir director. A Psalm of David.

HOW blessed is he who [a]considers the [1]helpless;
The LORD will deliver him [b]in a day of [2]trouble.
2 The LORD will [a]protect him, and keep him alive,
And he shall [1]be called [b]blessed upon the earth;
And [c]do not give him over to the desire of his enemies.
3 The LORD will sustain him upon his [a]sickbed;
In his illness, Thou dost [1]restore him to health.

4 As for me, I said, "O LORD, be gracious to me;
[a]Heal my soul, for [b]I have sinned against Thee."
5 My enemies [a]speak evil against me,
"When will he die, and his name perish?"
6 And [1]when he comes to see *me*, he [a]speaks [2]falsehood;
His heart gathers wickedness to itself;
When he goes outside, he tells it.

7 All who hate me whisper together against me;
Against me they devise my hurt, *saying,*
8 "A wicked thing is poured out upon him,
That when he lies down, he will [a]not rise up again."
9 Even my [a]close friend, in whom I trusted,
Who ate my bread,
Has lifted up his heel against me.

10 But Thou, O LORD, be gracious to me, and [a]raise me up,
That I may repay them.
11 By this I know that [a]Thou art pleased with me,
Because [b]my enemy does not shout in triumph over me.
12 As for me, [a]Thou dost uphold me in my integrity,
And Thou dost set me [b]in Thy presence forever.

13 [a]Blessed be the LORD, the God of Israel,
From everlasting to everlasting.
Amen, and Amen.

BOOK 2

PSALM 42

Thirsting for God in Trouble and Exile.

For the choir director.
A Maskil of the sons of Korah.

AS the deer [1]pants for the water brooks,
So my soul [1a]pants for Thee, O God.
2 My soul [a]thirsts for God, for the [b]living God;
When shall I come and [1c]appear before God?
3 My [a]tears have been my food day and night,
While *they* [b]say to me all day long, "Where is your God?"
4 These things I remember, and I [a]pour out my soul within me.
For I [b]used to go along with the throng *and* lead them in procession to the house of God,
With the voice of [c]joy and thanksgiving, a multitude keeping festival.

5 Why are you [1a]in despair, O my soul?
And *why* have you become [b]disturbed within me?
[2c]Hope in God, for I shall [3]again praise Him
For the [d]help of His presence.
6 O my God, my soul is [1]in despair within me;
Therefore I [a]remember Thee from [b]the land of the Jordan,
And the [2]peaks of [c]Hermon, from Mount Mizar.
7 Deep calls to deep at the sound of Thy waterfalls;
All Thy [a]breakers and Thy waves have rolled over me.
8 The LORD will [a]command His lovingkindness in the daytime;
And His song will be with me [b]in the night,
A prayer to [c]the God of my life.

9 I will say to God [a]my rock, "Why hast Thou forgotten me?
Why do I go [b]mourning because of the [c]oppression of the enemy?"
10 As a shattering of my bones, my adversaries revile me,
While they [a]say to me all day long, "Where is your God?"
11 Why are you [1a]in despair, O my soul?
And why have you become disturbed within me?
[2]Hope in God, for I shall yet praise Him,
The help of my countenance, and my God.

PSALM 43

Prayer for Deliverance.

[a]VINDICATE me, O God, and [b]plead my case against an ungodly nation;
O deliver me from [c]the deceitful and unjust man!
2 For Thou art the [a]God of my strength; why hast Thou [b]rejected me?
Why do I go [c]mourning [1]because of the oppression of the enemy?

3 O send out Thy [a]light and Thy truth, let them lead me;
Let them bring me to Thy [b]holy hill,
And to Thy dwelling places.
4 Then I will go to [a]the altar of God,
To God [1]my exceeding [b]joy;
And upon the [c]lyre I shall praise Thee, O God, my God.

5 Why are you [1a]in despair, O my soul?

---

8 [a]Ps. 71:10, 11
9 [a]Job 19:13, 19; Ps. 55:12, 13, 20; Jer. 20:10; Mic. 7:5; John 13:18
10 [a]Ps. 3:3
11 [a]Ps. 37:23; 147:11 [b]Ps. 25:2
12 [a]Ps. 18:32; 37:17; 63:8 [b]Job 36:7; Ps. 21:6
13 [a]Ps. 72:18, 19; 89:52; 106:48

---

1 [1]Lit., *longs for* [a]Ps. 119:131
2 [1]Some mss. read, *see the face of God* [a]Ps. 63:1; 84:2; 143:6 [b]Josh. 3:10; Ps. 84:2; Jer. 10:10; Dan. 6:26; Matt. 26:63; Rom. 9:26; 1 Thess. 1:9 [c]Ex. 23:17
3 [a]Ps. 80:5; 102:9 [b]Ps. 79:10; 115:2; Joel 2:17
4 [a]1 Sam. 1:15; Job 30:16; Ps. 62:8; Lam. 2:19 [b]Ps. 55:14; 122:1; Is. 30:29 [c]Ps. 100:4
5 [1]Or, *sunk down* [2]Or, *Wait for* [3]Or, *still* [a]Ps. 38:6; Matt 26:38 [b]Ps. 77:3 [c]Ps. 71:14; Lam. 3:24 [d]Ps. 44:3
6 [1]Or, *sunk down* [2]Lit., *Hermons* [a]Ps. 61:2 [b]2 Sam. 17:22 [c]Deut. 3:8
7 [a]Ps. 69:1, 2; 88:7; Jon. 2:3
8 [a]Ps. 57:3; 133:3 [b]Job 35:10; Ps. 77:6; 149:5 [c]Eccles. 5:18; 8:15
9 [a]Ps. 18:2 [b]Ps. 38:6 [c]Ps. 17:9
10 [a]Ps. 42:3
11 [1]Or, *sunk down* [2]Or, *Wait for* [a]Ps. 42:5

---

1 [a]Ps. 26:1; 35:24 [b]1 Sam. 24:15 [c]Ps. 5:6; 38:12
2 [1]Or, *while the enemy oppresses* [a]Ps. 18:1; 28:7; 31:4 [b]Ps. 44:9; 88:14 [c]Ps. 42:9
3 [a]Ps. 36:9 [b]Ps. 2:6; 42:4; 46:4
4 [1]Lit., *the gladness of my joy* [a]Ps. 26:6 [b]Ps. 21:6 [c]Ps. 33:2; 49:4; 57:8; 71:22
5 [1]Or, *sunk down* [a]Ps. 42:11

And why are you disturbed
within me?
[2]Hope in God, for I shall [3]again
praise Him,
The [4]help of my countenance,
and my God.

PSALM 44

Former Deliverances and Present Troubles.

For the choir director.
A Maskil of the sons of Korah.

O GOD, we have heard with our
ears,
Our [a]fathers have told us,
The [b]work that Thou didst in
their days,
In the [c]days of old.
2 Thou with Thine own hand
didst [a]drive out the nations;
Then Thou didst [b]plant them;
Thou didst [c]afflict the peoples,
Then Thou didst [d]spread them
abroad.
3 For by their own sword they
[a]did not possess the land;
And their own arm did not save
them;
But Thy right hand, and Thine
[b]arm, and the [c]light of Thy
presence,
For Thou didst [d]favor them.

4 Thou art [a]my King, O God;
Command [1]victories for Jacob.
5 Through Thee we will [a]push
back our adversaries;
Through Thy name we will
[b]trample down those who
rise up against us.
6 For I will [a]not trust in my bow,
Nor will my sword save me.
7 But Thou [a]hast saved us from
our adversaries,
And Thou hast put to shame
those who hate us.
8 In God we have [a]boasted all day
long,
And we will [b]give thanks to Thy
name forever. [Selah.

9 Yet Thou [a]hast rejected *us* and
brought us to [b]dishonor,
And [c]dost not go out with our
armies.
10 Thou dost cause us to [a]turn
back from the adversary;
And those who hate us [b]have
taken spoil for themselves.
11 Thou dost give us as [a]sheep [1]to
be eaten,
And hast [b]scattered us among
the nations.
12 Thou dost [a]sell Thy people
cheaply,
And hast not profited by their
sale.
13 Thou dost make us a [a]reproach
to our neighbors,
A scoffing and a [b]derision to
those around us.
14 Thou dost make us [a]a byword
among the nations,
A [b]laughingstock among the
peoples.
15 All day long my dishonor is before me,
And my [a]humiliation has overwhelmed me,
16 Because of the voice of him
who [a]reproaches and reviles,
Because of the presence of the
enemy and the avenger.

17 All this has come upon us, but
we have [a]not forgotten Thee,
And we have not dealt falsely
with Thy covenant.
18 Our heart has not [a]turned back,
And our steps [b]have not devi-
ated from Thy way,
19 Yet Thou hast [a]crushed us in a
place of [b]jackals,
And covered us with the
shadow of death.

20 If we had [a]forgotten the name
of our God,
Or extended our hands to [b]a
strange god;
21 Would not God [a]find this out?
For He knows the secrets of the
heart.
22 But [a]for Thy sake we are killed
all day long;
We are considered as [b]sheep to
be slaughtered.
23 [a]Arouse Thyself, why [b]dost
Thou sleep, O Lord?
Awake, [c]do not reject us forever.
24 Why dost Thou [a]hide Thy face,
And [b]forget our affliction and
our oppression?
25 For our soul has sunk down into
the dust;
Our body cleaves to the earth.
26 [a]Rise up, be our help,
And [b]redeem us for the sake of
Thy lovingkindness.

PSALM 45

A Song Celebrating the King's Marriage.

For the choir director; according
to the Shoshannim. A Maskil of
the sons of Korah.
A Song of Love.

MY heart [1]overflows with a good
theme;
I address my [2]verses to the
[3]King;

---

5 [2]Or, *Wait for* [3]Or, *still* [4]Or, *saving acts of*

1 [a]Ex. 12:26, 27; Deut. 6:20; Judg. 6:13; Ps. 78:3 [b]Ps. 78:12 [c]Deut. 32:7; Ps. 77:5; Is. 51:9; 63:9
2 [a]Josh. 3:10; Neh. 9:24 [b]Ex. 15:17; 2 Sam. 7:10; Jer. 24:6; Amos 9:15 [c]Ps. 135:10-12 [d]Ps. 80:9-11; Zech. 2:6
3 [a]Josh. 24:12 [b]Ps. 77:15 [c]Ps. 4:6; 89:15 [d]Deut. 4:37; 7:7, 8; 10:15
4 [1]Lit., *salvation* [a]Ps. 74:12
5 [a]Deut. 33:17; Ps. 60:12; Dan. 8:4 [b]Ps. 108:13; Zech. 10:5
6 [a]1 Sam. 17:47; Ps. 33:16; Hos. 1:7
7 [a]Ps. 136:24
8 [a]Ps. 34:2 [b]Ps. 30:12
9 [a]Ps. 43:2; 89:38; 108:11 [b]Ps. 69:19 [c]Ps. 60:10
10 [a]Lev. 26:17; Josh. 7:8, 12; Ps. 89:43 [b]Ps. 89:41
11 [1]Lit., *for food* [a]Ps. 44:22 [b]Lev. 26:33; Deut. 4:27; Ezek. 20:23
12 [a]Deut. 32:30; Judg. 2:14; 3:8
13 [a]Ps. 79:4; 89:41 [b]Ps. 80:6; Ezek. 23:32
14 [a]Job 17:6; Ps. 69:11; Jer. 24:9 [b]2 Kin. 19:21
15 [a]2 Chr. 32:21
16 [a]Ps. 74:10
17 [a]Ps. 78:7
18 [a]Ps. 78:57 [b]Job 23:11; Ps. 119:51, 157
19 [a]Ps. 51:8; 94:5 [b]Job 30:29; Is. 13:22; Jer. 9:11
20 [a]Ps. 78:11 [b]Ps. 81:9
21 [a]Ps. 139:1, 2; Jer. 17:10
22 [a]Rom. 8:36 [b]Is. 53:7; Jer. 12:3
23 [a]Ps. 7:6 [b]Ps. 78:65 [c]Ps. 77:7
24 [a]Job 13:24; Ps. 88:14 [b]Ps. 42:9; Lam. 5:20
26 [a]Ps. 35:2 [b]Ps. 6:4; 25:22

1 [1]Lit., *is astir* [2]Lit., *works* [3]Probably refers to Solomon as a type of Christ.

My tongue is the pen of [a]a ready writer.
2 Thou art fairer than the sons of men;
Grace is poured [1]upon Thy lips;
Therefore God has [a]blessed Thee forever.

3 Gird Thy sword on *Thy* thigh, O [1a]Mighty One,
In Thy splendor and Thy majesty!
4 And in Thy majesty ride on victoriously,
For the cause of truth and [a]meekness *and* righteousness;
Let Thy [b]right hand teach Thee [1]awesome things.
5 Thine [a]arrows are sharp;
The [b]peoples fall under Thee;
Thine arrows are [c]in the heart of the King's enemies.

6 [a]Thy throne, O God, is forever and ever;
A scepter of [b]uprightness is the scepter of Thy kingdom.
7 Thou hast [a]loved righteousness, and hated wickedness;
Therefore God, Thy God, has [b]anointed Thee
With the oil of joy above Thy fellows.
8 All Thy garments are fragrant with [a]myrrh and aloes *and* cassia;
Out of ivory palaces [b]stringed instruments have made Thee glad.
9 Kings' daughters are among [a]Thy noble ladies;
At Thy [b]right hand stands the queen in [c]gold from Ophir.

10 Listen, O daughter, give attention and incline your ear;
[a]Forget your people and your father's house;
11 Then the King will desire your beauty;
Because He is your [a]Lord, [b]bow down to Him.
12 And the daughter of [a]Tyre *will come* with a gift;
The [b]rich among the people will entreat your favor.

13 The King's daughter is all glorious within;
Her clothing is [a]interwoven with gold.
14 She will be [a]led to the King [b]in embroidered work;
The [c]virgins, her companions who follow her,
Will be brought to Thee.

1 [a]Ezra 7:6
2 [1]Or, *through* [a]Ps. 21:6
3 [1]Or, *warrior* [a]Is. 9:6
4 [1]Or, *fearful* [a]Zeph. 2:3 [b]Ps. 21:8
5 [a]Ps. 18:14; 120:4; Is. 5:28; 7:13 [b]Ps. 92:9 [c]2 Sam. 18:14
6 [a]Ps. 93:2; Heb. 1:8, 9 [b]Ps. 98:9
7 [a]Ps. 11:7; 33:5 [b]Ps. 2:2
8 [a]Song of Sol. 4:14; John 19:39 [b]Ps. 150:4
9 [a]Song of Sol. 6:8 [b]1 Kin. 2:19 [c]1 Kin. 9:28; Is. 13:12
10 [a]Deut. 21:13; Ruth 1:16, 17
11 [a]Gen. 18:12; 1 Pet. 3:6 [b]Eph. 5:33
12 [a]Ps. 87:4 [b]Ps. 22:29; 68:29; 72:10, 11
13 [a]Ex. 39:2, 3
14 [a]Song of Sol. 1:4 [b]Judg. 5:30; Ezek. 16:10 [c]Ps. 45:9
17 [a]Mal. 1:11 [b]Ps. 138:4
[£] Possibly, *for soprano voices*
1 [a]Ps. 14:6; 62:7, 8 [b]Deut. 4:7; Ps. 145:18 [c]Ps. 9:9
2 [1]Lit., *seas* [a]Ps. 23:4; 27:1 [b]Ps. 82:5 [c]Ps. 18:7
3 [a]Ps. 93:3, 4; Jer. 5:22
4 [a]Ps. 36:8; 65:9; Is. 8:6; Rev. 22:1 [b]Ps. 48:1; 87:3; 101:8; Is. 60:14; Rev. 3:12 [c]Ps. 43:3
5 [a]Deut. 23:14; Is. 12:6; Ezek. 43:7, 9; Hos. 11:9; Joel 2:27; Zech. 2:5 [b]Ps. 37:40; Is. 41:14; Luke 1:54
6 [1]Or, *Gentiles* [2]Lit., *gave forth* [a]Ps. 2:1, 2 [b]Ps. 18:13; 68:33; Jer. 25:30; Joel 2:11; Amos 1:2 [c]Amos 9:5; Mic. 1:4; Nah. 1:5
7 [a]Num. 14:9; 2 Chr. 13:12 [b]Ps. 9:9; 48:3
8 [a]Ps. 66:5 [b]Is. 61:4; Jer. 51:43
9 [a]Is. 2:4; Mic. 4:3 [b]1 Sam. 2:4; Ps. 76:3 [c]Is. 9:5; Ezek. 39:9
10 [1]Or, *Let go, relax* [2]Or, *Gentiles* [a]Ps. 100:3 [b]Is. 2:11, 17

15 They will be led forth with gladness and rejoicing;
They will enter into the King's palace.

16 In place of your fathers will be your sons;
You shall make them princes in all the earth.
17 I will cause [a]Thy name to be remembered in all generations;
Therefore the peoples [b]will give Thee thanks forever and ever.

PSALM 46

God the Refuge of His People.

For the choir director. *A Psalm* of the sons of Korah, [£]set to Alamoth. A Song.

GOD is our [a]refuge and strength,
A very [b]present help [c]in trouble.
2 Therefore we will [a]not fear, though [b]the earth should change,
And though [c]the mountains slip into the heart of the [1]sea;
3 Though its [a]waters roar *and* foam,
Though the mountains quake at its swelling pride. [Selah.

4 There is a [a]river whose streams make glad the [b]city of God,
The holy [c]dwelling places of the Most High.
5 God is [a]in the midst of her, she will not be moved;
God will [b]help her when morning dawns.
6 The [1]nations [a]made an uproar, the kingdoms tottered;
He [2b]raised His voice, the earth [c]melted.
7 The LORD of hosts [a]is with us;
The God of Jacob is [b]our stronghold. [Selah.

8 Come, [a]behold the works of the LORD,
Who has wrought [b]desolations in the earth.
9 He [a]makes wars to cease to the end of the earth;
He [b]breaks the bow and cuts the spear in two;
He [c]burns the chariots with fire.
10 "[1]Cease *striving* and [a]know that I am God;
I will be [b]exalted among the [2]nations, I will be exalted in the earth."

11 The LORD of hosts is with us;
The God of Jacob is our stronghold. [Selah.

PSALM 47

God the King of the Earth.

For the choir director.
A Psalm of the sons of Korah.

O [a]CLAP your hands, all peoples;
Shout to God with the voice of joy.
2 For the LORD Most High is to be [a]feared,
A [b]great King over all the earth.
3 He [a]subdues peoples under us,
And nations under our feet.
4 He chooses our [a]inheritance for us,
The [b]glory of Jacob whom He loves. [Selah.

5 God has [a]ascended with a shout,
The LORD, with the [b]sound of a trumpet.
6 [a]Sing praises to God, sing praises;
Sing praises to [b]our King, sing praises.
7 For God is the [a]King of all the earth;
Sing praises [b]with a [1]skillful psalm.
8 God [a] reigns over the nations,
God [1]sits on [b]His holy throne.
9 The [1][a]princes of the people have assembled themselves *as* the [b]people of the God of Abraham;
For the [c]shields of the earth belong to God;
He [2]is [d]highly exalted.

PSALM 48

The Beauty and Glory of Zion.

A Song; a Psalm of the sons of Korah.

[a]GREAT is the LORD, and greatly to be praised,
In the [b]city of our God, His [c]holy mountain.
2 [a]Beautiful in elevation, [b]the joy of the whole earth,
Is Mount Zion *in* the far north,
The [c]city of the great King.
3 God, in her palaces,
Has made Himself known as a [a]stronghold.

4 For, lo, the [a]kings assembled themselves,
They passed by together.
5 They saw *it,* then they were amazed;
They were [a]terrified, they [1]fled in alarm.
6 [1]Panic seized them there,
Anguish, as of [a]a woman in childbirth.
7 With the [a]east wind
Thou [b]dost break the [c]ships of Tarshish.
8 As we have heard, so have we seen
In the city of the LORD of hosts, in the city of our God;
God will [a]establish her forever. [Selah.

9 We have thought on [a]Thy lovingkindness, O God,
In the midst of Thy temple.
10 As is Thy [a]name, O God,
So is Thy [b]praise to the ends of the earth;
Thy [c]right hand is full of righteousness.
11 Let Mount [a]Zion be glad,
Let the [a]daughters of Judah rejoice,
Because of Thy judgments.
12 Walk about Zion, and go around her;
Count her [a]towers;
13 Consider her [a]ramparts;
Go through her palaces;
That you may [b]tell *it* to the next generation.
14 For [1]such is God,
Our God forever and ever;
He will [a]guide us [2]until death.

PSALM 49

The Folly of Trusting in Riches.

For the choir director.
A Psalm of the sons of Korah.

[a]HEAR this, all peoples;
Give ear, all [b]inhabitants of the world,
2 Both [a]low and high,
Rich and poor together.
3 My mouth will [a]speak wisdom;
And the meditation of my heart *will be* [b]understanding.
4 I will incline my ear to [a]a proverb;
[b]I will express my [c]riddle on the harp.

5 Why should I [a]fear in days of adversity,
When the iniquity of my [1]foes surrounds me,
6 Even those who [a]trust in their wealth,
And boast in the abundance of their riches?

---

1 [a]Ps. 98:8
2 [a]Deut. 7:21; Neh. 1:5; Ps. 66:3, 5; 68:35 [b]Mal. 1:14
3 [a]Ps. 18:47
4 [a]1 Pet. 1:4 [b]Amos 6:8; 8:7; Nah. 2:2
5 [a]Ps. 68:18, 25 [b]Ps. 98:6
6 [a]Ps. 68:4 [b]Ps. 89:18
7 [1]Heb., *Maskil* [a]Zech. 14:9 [b]1 Cor. 14:15
8 [1]Or, *has taken His seat* [a]1 Chr. 16:31; Ps. 22:28 [b]Ps. 97:2
9 [1]Or, *nobles* [2]Lit., *has greatly exalted Himself* [a]Ps. 72:11; 102:22; Is. 49:7, 23 [b]Rom. 4:11, 12 [c]Ps. 89:18 [d]Ps. 97:9

1 [a]1 Chr. 16:25; Ps. 96:4; 145:3 [b]Ps. 46:4 [c]Ps. 2:6; 87:1; Is. 2:3; Mic. 4:1; Zech. 8:3
2 [a]Ps. 50:2 [b]Lam. 2:15 [c]Matt. 5:35
3 [a]Ps. 46:7
4 [a]2 Sam. 10:6-19
5 [1]Lit., *were hurried away* [a]Ex. 15:15
6 [1]Lit., *Trembling* [a]Is. 13:8
7 [a]Jer. 18:17 [b]1 Kin. 22:48 [c]1 Kin. 10:22; Ezek. 27:25
8 [a]Ps. 87:5
9 [a]Ps. 26:3; 40:10
10 [a]Deut. 28:58; Josh. 7:9; Mal. 1:11 [b]Ps. 65:1, 2; 100:1 [c]Is. 41:10
11 [a]Ps. 97:8
12 [a]Neh. 3:1, 11, 25-27
13 [a]Ps. 122:7 [b]Ps. 78:5-7
14 [1]Lit., *this* [2]Lit., *upon.* Some mss. and the Greek version read, *forever.* [a]Ps. 23:4; Is. 58:11

1 [a]Ps. 78:1; Is. 1:2; Mic. 1:2 [b]Ps. 33:8
2 [a]Ps. 62:9
3 [a]Ps. 37:30 [b]Ps. 119:130
4 [a]Ps. 78:2 [b]2 Kin. 3:15 [c]Num. 12:8
5 [1]Lit., *supplanters* [a]Ps. 23:4; 27:1
6 [a]Job 31:24; Ps. 52:7; Prov. 11:28; Mark 10:24

7 No man can by any means [a]redeem *his* brother,
Or give to God a [b]ransom for him—
8 For the redemption of his soul is costly,
And he should cease *trying* forever—
9 That he should [a]live on eternally;
That he should not [1b]undergo decay.

10 For he sees *that even* [a]wise men die;
The [b]stupid and the senseless alike perish,
And [c]leave their wealth to others.
11 Their [1a]inner thought is, *that* their houses [b]are forever,
And their dwelling places to all generations;
They have [c]called their lands after their own names.
12 But [a]man in *his* pomp will not endure;
He is like the beasts that perish.

13 This is the [a]way of those who are foolish,
And of those after them who approve their words. [Selah.
14 As sheep they are appointed [a]for Sheol;
Death shall be their shepherd;
And the [b]upright shall rule over them in the morning;
And their form shall be for Sheol [c]to consume,
So that they have no habitation.
15 But God will [a]redeem my soul from the power of Sheol;
For [b]He will receive me. [Selah.

16 Do not be afraid [a]when a man becomes rich,
When the [1]glory of his house is increased;
17 For when he dies he will [a]carry nothing away;
His [1]glory will not descend after him.
18 Though while he lives he [a]congratulates himself—
And though *men* praise you when you do well for yourself—
19 He shall [a]go to the generation of his fathers;
They shall never see [b]the light.
20 [a]Man in *his* pomp, yet without understanding,
Is like the beasts that perish.

7 [a]Matt. 25:8, 9 [b]Job 36:18, 19
9 [1]Or, *see corruption* [a]Ps. 22:29 [b]Ps. 16:10; 89:48
10 [a]Eccles. 2:16 [b]Ps. 92:6; 94:8 [c]Ps. 39:6; Eccles. 2:18, 21; Luke 12:20
11 [1]Some versions read, *graves are their houses* [a]Ps. 64:6 [b]Ps. 10:6 [c]Deut. 3:14
12 [a]Ps. 49:20
13 [a]Jer. 17:11
14 [a]Ps. 9:17 [b]Dan. 7:18; Mal. 4:3; 1 Cor. 6:2; Rev. 2:26 [c]Job 24:19
15 [a]Ps. 16:10; 56:13; Hos. 13:14 [b]Gen. 5:24; Ps. 16:11
16 [1]Or, *wealth* [a]Ps. 37:7
17 [1]Or, *wealth* [a]Ps. 17:14; 1 Tim. 6:7
18 [a]Deut. 29:19; Ps. 10:3, 6; Luke 12:19
19 [a]Gen. 15:15 [b]Job 33:30; Ps. 56:13
20 [a]Ps. 49:12
1 [a]Josh. 22:22
2 [a]Ps. 48:2; Lam. 2:15 [b]Deut. 33:2; Ps. 80:1
3 [a]Ps. 96:13 [b]Lev. 10:2; Num. 16:35; Ps. 97:3; Dan. 7:10 [c]Ps. 18:12, 13
4 [a]Deut. 4:26; 31:28; 32:1; Is. 1:2
5 [a]Ps. 30:4; 37:28; 52:9 [b]Ex. 24:7; 2 Chr. 6:11; Ps. 25:10 [c]Ps. 50:8
6 [a]Ps. 89:5; 97:6 [b]Ps. 96:13
7 [1]Or, *to* [a]Ps. 49:1; 81:8 [b]Ex. 20:2; Ps. 48:14
8 [a]Ps. 40:6; 51:16; Is. 1:11; Hos. 6:6
11 [1]Or, *in My mind*, lit., *with Me* [a]Matt. 6:26
12 [1]Lit., its fulness [a]Ex. 19:5; Deut. 10:14; Ps. 24:1
13 [a]Ps. 50:9
14 [a]Ps. 27:6; 116:17; Hos. 14:2; Rom. 12:1; Heb. 13:15 [b]Num. 30:2; Deut. 23:21; Ps. 22:25; 56:12; 61:8; 65:1; 76:11
15 [a]Ps. 91:15; 107:6, 13; Zech. 13:9 [b]Ps. 81:7 [c]Ps. 22:23

PSALM 50

God the Judge of the Righteous and the Wicked.

A Psalm of Asaph.

[a]THE Mighty One, God, the LORD, has spoken,
And summoned the earth from the rising of the sun to its setting.
2 Out of Zion, [a]the perfection of beauty,
God [b]has shone forth.
3 May our God [a]come and not keep silence;
[b]Fire devours before Him,
And it is very [c]tempestuous around Him.
4 He [a]summons the heavens above,
And the earth, to judge His people:
5 "Gather My [a]godly ones to Me,
Those who have made a [b]covenant with Me by [c]sacrifice."
6 And the [a]heavens declare His righteousness,
For [b]God Himself is judge. [Selah.

7 "[a]Hear, O My people, and I will speak;
O Israel, I will testify [1]against you;
I am God, [b]your God.
8 "I do [a]not reprove you for your sacrifices,
And your burnt offerings are continually before Me.
9 "I shall take no young bull out of your house,
Nor male goats out of your folds.
10 "For every beast of the forest is Mine,
The cattle on a thousand hills.
11 "I know every [a]bird of the mountains,
And everything that moves in the field is [1]Mine.
12 "If I were hungry, I would not tell you;
For the [a]world is Mine, and [1]all it contains.
13 "Shall I eat the flesh of [a]bulls,
Or drink the blood of male goats?
14 "Offer to God [a]a sacrifice of thanksgiving,
And [b]pay your vows to the Most High;
15 And [a]call upon Me in the day of trouble;
I shall [b]rescue you, and you will [c]honor Me."

16 But to the wicked God says,
"What right have you to tell of My statutes,
And to take [a]My covenant in your mouth?
17 "For you [a]hate discipline,
And you [b]cast My words behind you.
18 "When you see a thief, you [1a]are pleased with him,
And you [b]associate with adulterers.
19 "You [a]let your mouth loose in evil,
And your [b]tongue frames deceit.
20 "You sit and [a]speak against your brother;
You slander your own mother's son.
21 "These things you have done, and [a]I kept silence;
You thought that I was just like you;
I will reprove you, and state *the case* in order before your eyes.

22 "Now consider this, you who [a]forget God,
Lest I [b]tear *you* in pieces, and there be none to deliver.
23 "He who [a]offers a sacrifice of thanksgiving honors Me;
And to him who [1b]orders *his* way *aright*
I shall [c]show the salvation of God."

PSALM 51

A Contrite Sinner's Prayer for Pardon.

For the choir director. A Psalm of David, when [£]Nathan the prophet came to him, after he had gone in to Bathsheba.

[a]BE gracious to me, O God, according to Thy lovingkindness;
According to the greatness of [b]Thy compassion [c]blot out my transgressions.
2 [a]Wash me thoroughly from my iniquity,
And [b]cleanse me from my sin.
3 For I [a]know my transgressions,
And my sin is ever before me.
4 [a]Against Thee, Thee only, I have sinned,
And done what is [b]evil in Thy sight,
So that [c]Thou art justified [1]when Thou dost speak,
And [2]blameless when Thou dost judge.

5 Behold, I was [a]brought forth in iniquity,
And in sin my mother conceived me.
6 Behold, Thou dost desire [a]truth in the innermost being,
And in the hidden part Thou wilt [b]make me know wisdom.
7 Purify me [a]with hyssop, and I shall be clean;
Wash me, and I shall be [b]whiter than snow.
8 Make me to hear [a]joy and gladness,
Let the [b]bones which Thou hast broken rejoice.
9 [a]Hide Thy face from my sins,
And blot out all my iniquities.

10 [a]Create [1]in me a [b]clean heart, O God,
And renew [2]a [c]steadfast spirit within me.
11 [a]Do not cast me away from Thy presence,
And do not take Thy [b]Holy Spirit from me.
12 Restore to me the [a]joy of Thy salvation,
And sustain me with a [b]willing spirit.
13 *Then* I will [a]teach transgressors Thy ways,
And sinners will [1]be [b]converted to Thee.

14 Deliver me from [a]bloodguiltiness, O God, Thou [b]God of my salvation;
Then my [c]tongue will joyfully sing of Thy righteousness.
15 O LORD, [a]open my lips,
That my mouth may [b]declare Thy praise.
16 For Thou dost not delight in sacrifice, otherwise I would give it;
Thou art not pleased with burnt offering.
17 The sacrifices of God are a [a]broken spirit;
A broken and a contrite heart, O God, Thou wilt not despise.

18 [a]By Thy favor do good to Zion;
[b]Build the walls of Jerusalem.
19 Then Thou wilt delight in [a]righteous sacrifices,
In burnt offering and whole burnt offering;
Then young bulls will be offered on Thine altar.

16 [a]Is. 29:13
17 [a]Prov. 5:12; 12:1; Rom. 2:21, 22 [b]1 Kin. 14:9; Neh. 9:26
18 [1]Some ancient versions read, *run together* [a]Rom. 1:32 [b]1 Tim. 5:22
19 [a]Ps. 10:7 [b]Ps. 36:3; 52:2
20 [a]Job 19:18; Matt. 10:21
21 [a]Eccles. 8:11; Is. 42:14; 57:11
22 [a]Job 8:13; Ps. 9:17 [b]Ps. 7:2
23 [1]Lit., *sets* [a]Ps. 50:14 [b]Ps. 85:13 [c]Ps. 91:16
£ 2 Sam. 12:1
1 [a]Ps. 4:1; 109:26 [b]Ps. 69:16; 106:45 [c]Ps. 51:9; Is. 43:25; 44:22; Acts 3:19; Col. 2:14
2 [a]Ps. 51:7; Is. 1:16; 4:4; Jer. 4:14; Acts 22:16; Rev. 1:5 [b]Jer. 33:8; Ezek. 36:33; Heb. 9:14; 1 John 1:7, 9
3 [a]Is. 59:12
4 [1]Many mss. read, *in Thy words* [2]Lit., *pure* [a]Gen. 20:6; 39:9; 2 Sam. 12:13; Ps. 41:4 [b]Luke 15:21 [c]Rom. 3:4
5 [a]Job 14:4; 15:14; Ps. 58:3; Eph. 2:3
6 [a]Job 38:36 [b]Prov. 2:6; Eccles. 2:26; James 1:5
7 [a]Ex. 12:22; Lev. 14:4; Num. 19:18; Heb. 9:19 [b]Is. 1:18
8 [a]Is. 35:10; Joel 1:16 [b]Ps. 35:10
9 [a]Jer. 16:17
10 [1]Lit., *for* [2]Or, *an upright* [a]Eph. 2:10 [b]Ps. 24:4; Matt. 5:8; Acts 15:9 [c]Ps. 78:37
11 [a]2 Kin. 13:23; 24:20; Jer. 7:15 [b]Is. 63:10, 11
12 [a]Ps. 13:5 [b]Ps. 110:3
13 [1]Or, *turn back* [a]Acts 9:21, 22 [b]Ps. 22:27
14 [a]2 Sam. 12:9; Ps. 26:9 [b]Ps. 25:5 [c]Ps. 35:28
15 [a]Ex. 4:15 [b]Ps. 9:14
17 [a]Ps. 34:18
18 [a]Ps. 69:35; Is. 51:3 [b]Ps. 102:16
19 [a]Ps. 4:5

Psalm 52

Futility of Boastful Wickedness.

For the choir director. A Maskil of David, •when Doeg the Edomite came and told Saul, and said to him, "David has come to the house of Ahimelech."

WHY do you [a]boast in evil, O mighty man?
The [b]lovingkindness of God *endures* all day long.
2 Your tongue devises [a]destruction,
Like a [b]sharp razor, [c]O worker of deceit.
3 You [a]love evil more than good,
[b]Falsehood more than speaking what is right. [Selah.
4 You love all words that devour,
O [a]deceitful tongue.

5 [1]But God will break you down forever;
He will snatch you up, and [a]tear you away from *your* tent,
And [b]uproot you from the [c]land of the living. [Selah.
6 And the righteous will [a]see and fear,
And will [b]laugh at him, *saying,*
7 "Behold, the man who would not make God his refuge,
But [a]trusted in the abundance of his riches,
And [b]was strong in [1]his *evil* desire."

8 But as for me, I am like a [a]green olive tree in the house of God;
I [b]trust in the lovingkindness of God forever and ever.
9 I will [a]give Thee thanks forever, because Thou hast done *it,*
And I will wait on Thy name, [b]for *it is* good, in the presence of Thy godly ones.

Psalm 53

Folly and Wickedness of Men.

For the choir director; according to [£]mahalath. A Maskil of David.

[a]THE fool has said in his heart, "There is no God,"
They are corrupt, and have committed abominable injustice;
There is no one who does good.
2 God has looked down from heaven upon the sons of men,
To see if there is anyone who [1]understands,
Who seeks after God.

• 1 Sam. 22:9
1 [a]Ps. 94:4 [b]Ps. 52:8
2 [a]Ps. 5:9 [b]Ps. 57:4; 59:7 [c]Ps. 101:7
3 [a]Ps. 36:4 [b]Ps. 58:3; Jer. 9:5
4 [a]Ps. 120:3
5 [1]Or, *Also* [a]Is. 22:18, 19 [b]Prov. 2:22 [c]Ps. 27:13
6 [a]Ps. 37:34; 40:3 [b]Job 22:19
7 [1]Or, *his destruction* [a]Ps. 49:6 [b]Ps. 10:6
8 [a]Ps. 92:12; 128:3; Jer. 11:16 [b]Ps. 13:5
9 [a]Ps. 30:12 [b]Ps. 54:6

£ I.e., sickness, a sad tone
1 [a]Ps. 14:1-7; 53:1-6
2 [1]Or, *acts wisely*
5 [1]Or, *dread* [2]Or possibly, *those* [a]Lev. 26:17, 36; Prov. 28:1 [b]Ps. 141:7; Jer. 8:1, 2; Ezek. 6:5 [c]Ps. 44:7 [d]2 Kin. 17:20; Jer. 6:30; Lam. 5:22
6 [1]Or, *Jacob will rejoice, Israel will be glad*

• 1 Sam. 23:19
1 [1]Lit., *judge* [a]Ps. 20:1 [b]2 Chr. 20:6
2 [a]Ps. 17:6; 55:1 [b]Ps. 5:1
3 [1]Or, *soul* [a]Ps. 86:14 [b]Ps. 18:48; 86:14; 140:1, 4, 11 [c]1 Sam. 20:1; 25:29; Ps. 40:14; 63:9; 70:2 [d]Ps. 36:1
4 [a]Ps. 30:10; 37:40; 118:7 [b]Ps. 37:17, 24; 41:12; 51:12; 145:14; Is. 41:10
5 [1]Lit., *The evil will return* [2]Or, *those who lie in wait for me* [3]Or, *Put to silence* [4]Or, *truth* [a]Ps. 94:23 [b]Ps. 143:12 [c]Ps. 89:49; 96:13; Is. 42:3
6 [1]Or, *With a freewill offering* [a]Num. 15:3; Ps. 116:17 [b]Ps. 50:14
7 [1]Or, *it,* i.e., His name [2]Or, *distress* [a]Ps. 34:6 [b]Ps. 59:10; 92:11; 112:8; 118:7

3 Every one of them has turned aside; together they have become corrupt;
There is no one who does good, not even one.
4 Have the workers of wickedness no knowledge,
Who eat up My people *as though* they ate bread,
And have not called upon God?
5 There they were in great [1]fear [a]*where* no [1]fear had been;
For God [b]scattered the bones of [2]him who encamped against you;
You [c]put *them* to shame, because [d]God had rejected them.
6 O that the salvation of Israel would come out of Zion!
When God restores His captive people,
[1]Let Jacob rejoice, let Israel be glad.

Psalm 54

Prayer for Defense against Enemies.

For the choir director; on stringed instruments. A Maskil of David, •when the Ziphites came and said to Saul, "Is not David hiding himself among us?"

SAVE me, O God, by [a]Thy name,
And [1]vindicate me by [b]Thy power.
2 [a]Hear my prayer, O God;
[b]Give ear to the words of my mouth.
3 For strangers have [a]risen against me,
And [b]violent men have [c]sought my [1]life;
They have [d]not set God before them. [Selah.

4 Behold, [a]God is my helper;
The Lord is the [b]sustainer of my soul.
5 [1]He will [a]recompense the evil to [2]my foes;
[3b]Destroy them [c]in Thy [4]faithfulness.

6 [1a]Willingly I will sacrifice to Thee;
I will give [b]thanks to Thy name, O LORD, for it is good.
7 For [1]He has [a]delivered me from all [2]trouble;
And my eye has [b]looked *with satisfaction* upon my enemies.

Psalm 55

Prayer for the Destruction of the Treacherous.

For the choir director; on stringed instruments. A Maskil of David.

[a]GIVE ear to my prayer, O God;
And [b]do not hide Thyself from my supplication.
2 Give [a]heed to me, and answer me;
I am restless in my [b]complaint and [c]am surely distracted,
3 Because of the voice of the enemy,
Because of the [a]pressure of the wicked;
For they [b]bring down trouble upon me,
And in anger they [c]bear a grudge against me.

4 My [a]heart is in anguish within me,
And the terrors of [b]death have fallen upon me.
5 Fear and [a]trembling come upon me;
And [b]horror has overwhelmed me.
6 And I said, "O that I had wings like a dove!
I would fly away and [a]be at rest.
7 "Behold, I would wander far away,
I would [a]lodge in the wilderness. [Selah.
8 "I would hasten to my place of refuge
From the [a]stormy wind *and* tempest."

9 Confuse, O Lord, [a]divide their tongues,
For I have seen [b]violence and strife in the city.
10 Day and night they go around her upon her walls;
And iniquity and mischief are in her midst.
11 [a]Destruction is in her midst;
[b]Oppression and deceit do not depart from her streets.

12 For it is not an enemy who reproaches me,
Then I could bear *it;*
Nor is it one who hates me who [a]has exalted himself against me,
Then I could hide myself from him.
13 But it is you, a man my equal,
My companion and my [a]familiar friend.

1 [a]Ps. 54:2; 61:1; 86:6 [b]Ps. 27:9
2 [a]Ps. 66:19; 86:6, 7 [b]1 Sam. 1:16; Job 9:27; Ps. 64:1; 77:3; 142:2 [c]Is. 38:14; 59:11; Ezek. 7:16
3 [a]Ps. 17:9 [b]2 Sam. 16:7, 8 [c]Ps. 71:11
4 [a]Ps. 38:8 [b]Ps. 18:4, 5; 116:3
5 [a]Ps. 119:120 [b]Job 21:6; Is. 21:4; Ezek. 7:18
6 [a]Job 3:13
7 [a]1 Sam. 23:14
8 [a]Is. 4:6; 25:4
9 [a]Gen. 11:9 [b]Ps. 11:5; Jer. 6:7
11 [a]Ps. 5:9 [b]Ps. 10:7
12 [a]Ps. 35:26
13 [a]Job 19:14; Ps. 41:9
14 [1]Lit., *counsel* [a]Ps. 42:4
15 [1]Another reading is, *desolations be upon them* [a]Ps. 64:7; Prov. 6:15; Is. 47:11; 1 Thess. 5:3 [b]Num. 16:30, 33
16 [a]Ps. 57:2, 3
17 [a]Ps. 141:2; Dan. 6:10; Acts 3:1; 10:3, 30 [b]Ps. 5:3; 88:13; 92:2 [c]Acts 10:9
18 [1]Or, *so that none may approach me* [a]Ps. 103:4 [b]Ps. 56:2
19 [1]Or, *afflict* [2]Or, *abides from* [3]Lit., *are no changes* [a]Ps. 78:59 [b]Deut 33:27; Ps. 90:2; 93:2 [c]Job 10:17 [d]Ps. 36:1
20 [a]Ps. 7:4; 120:7 [b]Num. 30:2
21 [1]Lit., *mouth* [a]Ps. 12:2; 28:3; Prov. 5:3, 4 [b]Ps. 57:4; 59:7
22 [1]Or, *what He has given you* [2]Or, *totter* [a]Ps. 37:5; 1 Pet. 5:7 [b]Ps. 15:5
23 [1]Or, *lowest pit* [a]Ps. 73:18; Is. 38:17; Ezek. 28:8 [b]Ps. 5:6 [c]Job 15:32; Prov. 10:27 [d]Ps. 25:2; 56:3
[£] Or, *The silent dove of those who are far off,* or, *The dove of the distant terebinths.*
[Δ] 1 Sam. 21:10, 11
1 [a]Ps. 57:3 [b]Ps. 17:9

14 We who had sweet [1]fellowship together,
[a]Walked in the house of God in the throng.
15 Let [1]death come [a]deceitfully upon them;
Let them [b]go down alive to Sheol,
For evil is in their dwelling, in their midst.

16 As for me, I shall [a]call upon God,
And the LORD will save me.
17 [a]Evening and [b]morning and at [c]noon, I will complain and murmur,
And He will hear my voice.
18 He will [a]redeem my soul in peace [1]from the battle *which is* against me,
For they are [b]many *who strive* with me.
19 God will [a]hear and [1]answer them—
Even the one [b]who [2]sits enthroned from of old— [Selah.
With whom there [3]is no [c]change,
And who [d]do not fear God.
20 He has put forth his hands against [a]those who were at peace with him;
He has [b]violated his covenant.
21 His [1]speech was [a]smoother than butter,
But his heart was war;
His words were [a]softer than oil,
Yet they were drawn [b]swords.

22 [a]Cast [1]your burden upon the LORD, and He will sustain you;
He will never allow the righteous to [2b]be shaken.
23 But Thou, O God, wilt bring them down to the [1a]pit of destruction;
[b]Men of bloodshed and deceit will [c]not live out half their days.
But I will [d]trust in Thee.

Psalm 56

Supplication for Deliverance, and Grateful Trust in God.

For the choir director; according to [£]Jonath elem rehokim. A Mikhtam of David, [Δ]when the Philistines seized him in Gath.

BE gracious, O God, for man has [a]trampled upon me;
Fighting all day long he [b]oppresses me.

2 My foes have [a]trampled upon me all day long,
For they are many who [b]fight proudly against me.
3 [1]When I am [a]afraid,
I will [b]put my trust in Thee.
4 [a]In God, whose word I praise,
In God I have put my trust;
I shall not be afraid.
[b]What can *mere* [1]man do to me?
5 All day long they [a]distort my words;
All their thoughts are against me for evil.
6 They [1a]attack, they lurk,
They [b]watch my [2]steps,
As they have [c]waited *to take* my life.
7 Because of wickedness, [a]cast them forth,
In anger put down the peoples, O God!

8 Thou [a]hast taken account of my wanderings;
Put my [b]tears in Thy bottle;
Are *they* not in [c]Thy book?
9 Then my enemies will [a]turn back [b]in the day when I call;
This I know, [1]that [c]God is for me.
10 In God, *whose* word I praise,
In the LORD, *whose* word I praise,
11 In God I have put my [1]trust, I shall not be afraid.
What can man do to me?
12 Thy [a]vows are *binding* upon me, O God;
I will render thank offerings to Thee.
13 For Thou hast [a]delivered my soul from death,
Indeed [b]my feet from stumbling,
So that I may [c]walk before God
In the [d]light of the living.

PSALM 57

Prayer for Rescue from Persecutors.

For the choir director; *set to* [£]Al-tashheth.
A Mikhtam of David, [Δ]when he fled from Saul, in the cave.

BE gracious to me, O God, be gracious to me,
For my soul [a]takes refuge in Thee;
And in the [b]shadow of Thy wings I will take refuge,
Until destruction [c]passes by.
2 I will cry to God Most High,
To God who [a]accomplishes *all things* for me.
3 He will [a]send from heaven and save me;
He reproaches him who [b]tramples upon me. [Selah.
God will send forth His [c]lovingkindness and His [1]truth.

4 My soul is among [a]lions;
I must lie among those who breathe forth fire,
Even the sons of men, whose [b]teeth are spears and arrows,
And their [c]tongue a sharp sword.
5 [a]Be exalted above the heavens, O God;
Let Thy glory *be* above all the earth.
6 They have [1]prepared a [a]net for my steps;
My soul is [b]bowed down;
They [c]dug a pit before me;
They *themselves* have [d]fallen into the midst of it. [Selah.

7 [a]My [b]heart is steadfast, O God, my heart is steadfast;
I will sing, yes, I will sing praises!
8 Awake, [a]my glory;
Awake, [b]harp and lyre,
I will awaken the dawn!
9 I will give thanks to Thee, O Lord, among the peoples;
I will sing praises to Thee among the nations.
10 For Thy [a]lovingkindness is great to the heavens,
And Thy [1]truth to the clouds.
11 Be exalted above the heavens, O God;
Let Thy glory *be* above all the earth.

PSALM 58

Prayer for the Punishment of the Wicked.

For the choir director; *set to* [£]Al-tashheth.
A Mikhtam of David.

DO you indeed [1]speak righteousness, O [2]gods?
Do you [a]judge [3]uprightly, O sons of men?
2 No, in heart you [a]work unrighteousness;
On earth you [b]weigh out the violence of your hands.
3 The wicked are estranged [a]from the womb;
These who speak lies go astray from birth.
4 They have venom like the [a]venom of a serpent;

---

2 [a]Ps. 35:25; 57:3; 124:3 [b]Ps. 35:1
3 [1]Lit., *In the day* [a]Ps. 55:4, 5 [b]Ps. 11:1
4 [1]Lit., *flesh* [a]Ps. 56:10, 11 [b]Ps. 118:6; Heb. 13:6
5 [a]2 Pet. 3:16
6 [1]Or, *stir up strife* [2]Lit., *heels* [a]Ps. 59:3; 140:2; Is. 54:15 [b]Ps. 17:11 [c]Ps. 71:10
7 [a]Ps. 36:12; Prov. 19:5; Ezek. 17:15; Rom. 2:3
8 [a]Ps. 139:3 [b]2 Kin. 20:5; Ps. 39:12 [c]Mal. 3:16
9 [1]Or, *because* [a]Ps. 9:3 [b]Ps. 102:2 [c]Ps. 41:11; 118:6; Rom. 8:31
11 [1]Or, *trust without fear*
12 [a]Ps. 50:14
13 [a]Ps. 33:19; 49:15; 86:13 [b]Ps. 116:8 [c]Ps. 116:9 [d]Job 33:30

[£] Lit., *Do Not Destroy*
[Δ] 1 Sam. 22:1; 24:3
1 [a]Ps. 2:12; 34:22 [b]Ruth 2:12; Ps. 17:8; 36:7; 63:7; 91:4 [c]Is. 26:20
2 [a]Ps. 138:8
3 [1]Or, *faithfulness* [a]Ps. 18:16; 144:5, 7 [b]Ps. 56:2 [c]Ps. 25:10; 40:11
4 [a]Ps. 35:17; 58:6 [b]Prov. 30:14 [c]Ps. 55:21; 59:7; 64:3; Prov. 12:18
5 [a]Ps. 57:11
6 [1]Or, *spread* [a]Ps. 10:9; 31:4; 35:7; 140:5 [b]Ps. 145:14 [c]Ps. 7:15 [d]Prov. 26:27; 28:10; Eccles. 10:8
7 [a]Ps. 57:7-11; 108:1-5 [b]Ps. 112:7
8 [a]Ps. 16:9; 30:12 [b]Ps. 150:3
10 [1]Or, *faithfulness* [a]Ps. 36:5

[£] Lit., *Do Not Destroy*
1 [1]Another reading is, *speak righteousness in silence* [2]Or, *mighty ones,* or, *judges* [3]Or, *uprightly the sons of men* [a]Ps. 82:2
2 [a]Mal. 3:15 [b]Ps. 94:20; Is. 10:1
3 [a]Ps. 51:5; Is. 48:8
4 [a]Deut. 32:33

Like a deaf cobra that stops up its ear,
5 So that it [a]does not hear the voice of [1b]charmers,
Or a skillful caster of spells.

6 O God, [a]shatter their teeth in their mouth;
Break out the fangs of the young lions, O LORD.
7 Let them [a]flow away like water that runs off;
When he [1b]aims his arrows, let them be as [2]headless shafts.
8 *Let them be* as a snail which [1]melts away as it goes along,
Like the [a]miscarriages of a woman which never see the sun.
9 Before your [a]pots can feel *the fire of* thorns,
He will [b]sweep them away with a whirlwind, the [1]green and the burning alike.

10 The [a]righteous will rejoice when he [b]sees the vengeance;
He will wash his feet in the blood of the wicked.
11 And men will say, "Surely there is a [1a]reward for the righteous;
Surely there is a God who [b]judges on earth!"

PSALM 59

Prayer for Deliverance from Enemies.

For the choir director; *set to* [£]Al-tashheth. A Mikhtam of David, [Δ]when Saul sent *men,* and they watched the house in order to kill him.

[a]DELIVER me from my enemies, O my God;
[b]Set me *securely* on high away from those who rise up against me.
2 Deliver me from [a]those who do iniquity,
And save me from [b]men of bloodshed.
3 For behold, they [a]have set an ambush for my life;
Fierce men [a]launch an attack against me,
[b]Not for my transgression nor for my sin, O LORD,
4 [1a]For no guilt of *mine,* they run and set themselves against me.
[b]Arouse Thyself to [2]help me, and see!

5 And Thou, [a]O LORD God of hosts, the God of Israel,
Awake to [1b]punish all the nations;
[c]Do not be gracious to any *who are* treacherous in iniquity. [Selah.
6 They return at evening, they howl like a [a]dog,
And go around the city.
7 Behold, they [a]belch forth with their mouth;
[b]Swords are in their lips,
For, *they say,* "[c]Who hears?"
8 But Thou, O LORD, dost [a]laugh at them;
Thou dost [b]scoff at all the nations.

9 *Because of* [1]his [a]strength I will watch for Thee,
For God is my stronghold.
10 My God [a]in His lovingkindness will meet me;
God will let me look *triumphantly* upon my foes.
11 Do not slay them, [a]lest my people forget;
[b]Scatter them by Thy power, and bring them down,
O Lord, [c]our shield.
12 *On account of* the [a]sin of their mouth *and* the words of their lips,
Let them even be [b]caught in their pride,
And on account of [c]curses and lies which they utter.
13 [1a]Destroy *them* in wrath, [1]destroy *them,* that they may be no more;
That *men* may [b]know that God [2]rules in Jacob,
To the ends of the earth. [Selah.
14 And they [a]return at evening, they howl like a dog,
And go around the city.
15 They wander about [1]for food,
And [2]growl if they are not satisfied.

16 But as for me, I shall [a]sing of Thy strength;
Yes, I shall [b]joyfully sing of Thy lovingkindness in the [c]morning,
For Thou hast been my [d]stronghold,
And a [e]refuge in the day of my distress.
17 [a]O my strength, I will sing praises to Thee;
For God is my [b]stronghold, the God who shows me lovingkindness.

5 [1]Or, *whisperers* [a]Ps. 81:11; Jer. 8:17 [b]Eccles. 10:11
6 [a]Job 4:10
7 [1]Lit., *bends* [2]Lit., *though they were cut off* [a]Is. 13:7; Ezek. 21:7 [b]Ps. 64:3
8 [1]I.e., secretes slime [a]Job 3:16; Eccles. 6:3
9 [1]Lit., *living* [a]Eccles. 7:6 [b]Job 27:21; Ps. 83:15
10 [a]Job 22:19; Ps. 32:11; 64:10; 107:42 [b]Deut. 32:43; Ps. 91:8; Jer. 11:20; 20:12
11 [1]Lit., *fruit* [a]Ps. 18:20; 19:11; Is. 3:10; Luke 6:23, 35 [b]Ps. 9:8; 67:4; 75:7; 94:2
£ Lit., *Do Not Destroy*
Δ 1 Sam. 19:11
1 [a]Ps. 143:9 [b]Ps. 20:1; 69:29
2 [a]Ps. 14:4; 28:3; 36:12; 53:4; 92:7; 94:16 [b]Ps. 26:9; 139:19
3 [a]Ps. 56:6 [b]1 Sam. 24:11; Ps. 7:3, 4
4 [1]Lit., *Without guilt* [2]Lit., *meet* [a]Ps. 35:19 [b]Ps. 7:6; 35:23
5 [1]Lit., *visit* [a]Ps. 69:6; 80:4; 84:8 [b]Ps. 9:5; Is. 26:14 [c]Is. 2:9
6 [a]Ps. 22:16
7 [a]Ps. 94:4; Prov. 15:2, 28 [b]Ps. 57:4 [c]Job 22:13; Ps. 10:11; 73:11; 94:7
8 [a]Ps. 37:13 [b]Ps. 2:4
9 [1]Many mss. read, *My strength* [a]Ps. 18:17
10 [a]Ps. 21:3
11 [a]Deut. 4:9; 6:12 [b]Ps. 106:27; 144:6; Is. 33:3 [c]Ps. 84:9
12 [a]Prov. 12:13 [b]Zeph. 3:11 [c]Ps. 10:7
13 [1]Lit., *Bring to an end* [2]Or, *is Ruler* [a]Ps. 104:35 [b]Ps. 83:18
14 [a]Ps. 59:6
15 [1]Or, *to devour* [2]Another reading is, *tarry all night*
16 [a]Ps. 21:13 [b]Ps. 101:1 [c]Ps. 5:3; 88:13 [d]Ps. 59:9 [e]2 Sam. 22:3
17 [a]Ps. 59:9 [b]Ps. 59:10

Psalm 60

Lament over Defeat in Battle, and Prayer for Help.

For the choir director; according to [£]Shushan Eduth. Mikhtam of David, to teach; [Δ]when he struggled with Aram-naharaim and with Aram-zobah, and Joab returned, and smote twelve thousand of Edom in the Valley of Salt.

O GOD, [a]Thou hast rejected us.
Thou hast [b]broken us;
Thou hast been [c]angry; O, [d]restore us.
2 Thou hast made the [1a]land quake, Thou hast split it open;
[b]Heal its breaches, for it totters.
3 Thou hast [a]made Thy people experience hardship;
Thou hast given us wine to [b]drink that makes us stagger.
4 Thou hast given a [a]banner to those who fear Thee,
That it may be displayed because of the truth. [Selah.
5 [a]That Thy [b]beloved may be delivered,
[c]Save with Thy right hand, and answer [1]us!

6 God has spoken in His [1a]holiness:
"I will exult, I will portion out [b]Shechem and measure out the valley of [c]Succoth.
7 "[a]Gilead is Mine, and Manasseh is Mine;
[b]Ephraim also is the [1]helmet of My head;
Judah is My [2c]scepter.
8 "[a]Moab is My washbowl;
Over [b]Edom I shall throw My shoe;
Shout loud, O [c]Philistia, because of Me!"

9 Who will bring me into the besieged city?
Who will lead me to Edom?
10 Hast not Thou Thyself, O God, [a]rejected us?
And [b]wilt Thou not go forth with our armies, O God?
11 O give us help against the adversary,
For [a]deliverance by man is in vain.
12 [1]Through God we shall [a]do valiantly,
And it is He who will [b]tread down our adversaries.

[£] Lit., *The lily of testimony*.
[Δ] 2 Sam. 8:3, 13; 1 Chr. 18:12
1 [a]Ps. 44:9 [b]2 Sam. 5:20 [c]Ps. 79:5 [d]Ps. 80:3
2 [1]Or, *earth* [a]Ps. 18:7 [b]2 Chr. 7:14; Is. 30:26
3 [a]Ps. 66:12; 71:20 [b]Ps. 75:8; Is. 51:17, 22; Jer. 25:15
4 [a]Ps. 20:5; Is. 5:26; 11:12; 13:2
5 [1]Or, *me* [a]Ps. 60:5-12; 108:6-13 [b]Deut. 33:12; Ps. 127:2; Is. 5:1; Jer. 11:15 [c]Ps. 17:7
6 [1]Or, *sanctuary* [a]Ps. 89:35 [b]Gen. 12:6; 33:18; Josh. 17:7 [c]Gen. 33:17; Josh. 13:27
7 [1]Lit., *protection* [2]Or, *lawgiver* [a]Josh. 13:31 [b]Deut. 33:17 [c]Gen. 49:10
8 [a]2 Sam. 8:2 [b]2 Sam. 8:14 [c]2 Sam. 8:1
10 [a]Ps. 60:1 [b]Ps. 44:9
11 [a]Ps. 146:3
12 [1]Or, *In*, or, *With* [a]Num. 24:18; Ps. 118:16 [b]Ps. 44:5; Is. 63:3

1 [a]Ps. 64:1 [b]Ps. 86:6
2 [a]Ps. 42:6 [b]Ps. 77:3 [c]Ps. 18:2; 94:22
3 [1]Lit., *from* [a]Ps. 62:7 [b]Ps. 59:9; Prov. 18:10
4 [1]Or, *sojourn* [a]Ps. 23:6; 27:4 [b]Ps. 17:8; 91:4
5 [a]Job 22:27; Ps. 56:12 [b]Deut. 28:58; Neh. 1:11; Ps. 86:11; 102:15; Is. 59:19; Mal. 2:5; 4:2
6 [1]Lit., *add days to* [2]Lit., *days* [a]Ps. 21:4
7 [1]Or, *sit enthroned* [a]Ps. 41:12 [b]Ps. 40:11
8 [a]Judg. 5:3; Ps. 30:4; 33:2; 71:22 [b]Ps. 65:1; Is. 19:21

[£] Cf. 1 Chr. 16:41; Ps. 39 and 77 titles
1 [a]Ps. 37:39
2 [a]Ps. 89:26 [b]Ps. 59:17; 62:6
3 [a]Is. 30:13

Psalm 61

Confidence in God's Protection.

For the choir director; on a stringed instrument.
A Psalm of David.

[a]HEAR my cry, O God;
[b]Give heed to my prayer.
2 From the [a]end of the earth I call to Thee, when my heart is [b]faint;
Lead me to [c]the rock that is higher than I.
3 For Thou hast been a [a]refuge for me,
A [b]tower of strength [1]against the enemy.
4 Let me [1a]dwell in Thy tent forever;
Let me [b]take refuge in the shelter of Thy wings. [Selah.

5 For Thou hast heard my [a]vows, O God;
Thou hast given *me* the inheritance of those who [b]fear Thy name.
6 Thou wilt [1a]prolong the king's [2]life;
His years will be as many generations.
7 He will [1]abide [a]before God forever;
Appoint [b]lovingkindness and truth, that they may preserve him.
8 So I will [a]sing praise to Thy name forever,
That I may [b]pay my vows day by day.

Psalm 62

God Alone a Refuge from Treachery and Oppression.

For the choir director; [£]according to Jeduthun. A Psalm of David.

MY soul *waits* in silence for God only;
From Him [a]is my salvation.
2 He only is my [a]rock and my salvation,
My [b]stronghold; I shall not be greatly shaken.

3 How long will you assail a man,
That you may murder *him*, all of you,
Like a [a]leaning wall, like a tottering fence?
4 They have counseled only to thrust him down from his high position;

They [a]delight in falsehood;
They [b]bless with [1]their mouth,
But inwardly they curse. [Selah.
5 My soul, [a]wait in silence for God only,
For my hope is from Him.
6 He only is [a]my rock and my salvation,
My stronghold; I shall not be shaken.
7 On God my [a]salvation and my glory *rest;*
The rock of my strength, my [b]refuge is in God.
8 [a]Trust in Him at all times, O people;
[b]Pour out your heart before Him;
God is a refuge for us. [Selah.

9 Men of [a]low degree are only [b]vanity, and men of rank are a [c]lie;
In the [d]balances they go up;
They are together lighter than breath.
10 [a]Do not trust in oppression,
And do not [1]vainly hope in [b]robbery;
If riches increase, [c]do not set *your* heart *upon them.*

11 [1]Once God has [a]spoken;
[2]Twice I have heard this:
That [b]power belongs to God;
12 And lovingkindness [a]is Thine, O Lord,
For Thou [b]dost recompense a man according to his work.

Psalm 63

The Thirsting Soul Satisfied in God.

A Psalm of David, [t]when he was in the wilderness of Judah.

O GOD, [a]Thou art my God; I shall seek Thee [1]earnestly;
My soul [b]thirsts for Thee, my flesh [2]yearns for Thee,
In a [c]dry and weary land where there is no water.
2 Thus I have [a]beheld Thee in the sanctuary,
To see Thy power and Thy glory.
3 Because Thy [a]lovingkindness is better than life,
My lips will praise Thee.
4 So I will bless Thee [a]as long as I live;
I will [b]lift up my hands in Thy name.
5 My soul is [a]satisfied as with marrow and fatness,
And my mouth offers [b]praises with joyful lips.
6 When I remember Thee [a]on my bed,
I meditate on Thee in the [b]night watches,
7 For [a]Thou hast been my help,
And in the [b]shadow of Thy wings I sing for joy.
8 My soul [a]clings to Thee;
Thy [b]right hand upholds me.

9 But those who [a]seek my [1]life, to destroy it,
Will go into the [2b]depths of the earth.
10 They will be [a]delivered over to the power of the sword;
They will be a [b]prey for foxes.
11 But the [a]king will rejoice in God;
Everyone who [b]swears by Him will glory,
For the [c]mouths of those who speak lies will be stopped.

Psalm 64

Prayer for Deliverance from Secret Enemies.

For the choir director. A Psalm of David.

HEAR my voice, O God, in [a]my [1]complaint;
[b]Preserve my life from dread of the enemy.
2 Hide me from the [a]secret counsel of evildoers,
From the tumult of those who do iniquity,
3 Who [a]have sharpened their tongue like a sword.
They aimed bitter speech *as* their arrow,
4 To [a]shoot from concealment at the blameless;
Suddenly they shoot at him, and [b]do not fear.
5 They hold fast to themselves an evil purpose;
They talk of [a]laying snares secretly;
They say, "[b]Who can see them?"
6 They devise injustices, *saying,*
"We are ready with a well-conceived plot";
For the [a]inward thought and the heart of a man are deep.

7 But [a]God will shoot at them with an arrow;
Suddenly they will be wounded.
8 So they will [a]make him stumble;
[b]Their own tongue is against them;
All who see them will [c]shake the head.

---

4 [1]Lit., *his* [a]Ps. 4:2 [b]Ps. 28:3
5 [a]Ps. 62:1
6 [a]Ps. 62:2
7 [a]Ps. 85:9 [b]Ps. 46:1
8 [a]Ps. 37:3, 5; 52:8; Is. 26:4 [b]1 Sam. 1:15; Ps. 42:4; Lam. 2:19
9 [a]Ps. 49:2 [b]Job 7:16; Ps. 39:5; Is. 40:17 [c]Ps. 116:11 [d]Is. 40:15
10 [1]Lit., *become vain in robbery* [a]Is. 30:12 [b]Is. 61:8; Ezek. 22:29; Nah. 3:1 [c]Job 31:25; Ps. 49:6; 52:7; Mark 10:24; Luke 12:15; 1 Tim. 6:10
11 [1]Or, *One thing* [2]Or, *These two things I have heard* [a]Job 33:14; 40:5 [b]Ps. 59:17; Rev. 19:1
12 [a]Ps. 86:5; 103:8; 130:7 [b]Job 34:11; Ps. 28:4; 1 Cor. 3:8

---

[t]1 Sam. 23:14
1 [1]Lit., *early* [2]Lit., *faints* [a]Ps. 118:28 [b]Ps. 42:2; 84:2; Matt. 5:6 [c]Ps. 143:6
2 [a]Ps. 27:4
3 [a]Ps. 69:16
4 [a]Ps. 104:33; 146:2 [b]Ps. 28:2
5 [a]Ps. 36:8 [b]Ps. 71:23
6 [a]Ps. 4:4 [b]Ps. 16:7; 42:8; 119:55
7 [a]Ps. 27:9 [b]Ps. 17:8
8 [a]Num. 32:12; Deut. 1:36; Hos. 6:3 [b]Ps. 18:35
9 [1]Lit., *soul* [2]Lit., *lowest places* [a]Ps. 40:14 [b]Ps. 55:15
10 [a]Jer. 18:21; Ezek. 35:5 [b]Lam. 5:18
11 [a]Ps. 21:1 [b]Deut. 6:13; Is. 45:23; 65:16 [c]Job 5:16; Ps. 107:42; Rom. 3:19

---

1 [1]Or, *concern* [a]Ps. 55:2 [b]Ps. 140:1
2 [a]Ps. 56:6
3 [a]Ps. 140:3
4 [a]Ps. 10:8; 11:2 [b]Ps. 55:19
5 [a]Ps. 140:5 [b]Job 22:13
6 [a]Ps. 49:11
7 [a]Ps. 7:12, 13
8 [a]Ps. 9:3 [b]Prov. 12:13; 18:7 [c]Ps. 22:7; 44:14; Jer. 18:16; 48:27; Lam. 2:15

9 Then all men [1]will [a]fear,
And [2]will declare the work of God,
And [3]will consider [4]what He has done.
10 The righteous man will be [a]glad in the LORD, and will [b]take refuge in Him;
And all the upright in heart will glory.

PSALM 65

God's Abundant Favor to Earth and Man.

For the choir director. A Psalm of David. A Song.

THERE will be silence [1]before Thee, *and* praise in Zion, O God;
And to Thee the [a]vow will be performed.
2 O Thou who dost hear prayer,
To Thee [a]all [1]men come.
3 [a]Iniquities prevail against me;
As for our transgressions, Thou dost [b]forgive them.
4 How [a]blessed is the one whom Thou dost choose, and bring near *to Thee,*
To dwell in Thy courts.
We will be [b]satisfied with the goodness of Thy house,
Thy holy temple.

5 By [a]awesome *deeds* Thou dost answer us in righteousness, O [b]God of our salvation,
Thou who art the trust of all the [c]ends of the earth and of the farthest [1d]sea;
6 Who dost [a]establish the mountains by His strength,
Being [b]girded with might;
7 Who dost [a]still the roaring of the seas,
The roaring of their waves,
And the [b]tumult of the peoples.
8 And they who dwell in the [a]ends *of the earth* stand in awe of Thy signs;
Thou dost make the dawn and the sunset shout for joy.

9 Thou dost visit the earth, and [a]cause it to overflow;
Thou dost greatly [b]enrich it;
The [1c]stream of God is full of water;
Thou dost prepare their [d]grain, for thus Thou dost prepare the earth.
10 Thou dost water its furrows abundantly;
Thou dost [1]settle its ridges;
Thou dost soften it [a]with showers;
Thou dost bless its growth.
11 Thou hast crowned the year with Thy [a]bounty,
And Thy paths [b]drip *with* fatness.
12 [a]The pastures of the wilderness drip,
And the [b]hills gird themselves with rejoicing.
13 The meadows are [a]clothed with flocks,
And the valleys are [b]covered with grain;
They [c]shout for joy, yes, they sing.

PSALM 66

Praise for God's Mighty Deeds and for His Answer to Prayer.

For the choir director. A Song. A Psalm.

[a]SHOUT joyfully to God, all the earth;
2 Sing the [a]glory of His name;
Make His [b]praise glorious.
3 Say to God, "How [a]awesome are Thy works!
Because of the greatness of Thy power Thine enemies will [1b]give feigned obedience to Thee.
4 "[a]All the earth will worship Thee,
And will [b]sing praises to Thee;
They will sing praises to Thy name." [Selah.

5 [a]Come and see the works of God,
Who is [b]awesome in *His* deeds toward the sons of men.
6 He [a]turned the sea into dry land;
They passed through [b]the river on foot;
There let us [c]rejoice in Him!
7 He [a]rules by His might forever;
His [b]eyes keep watch on the nations;
Let not the rebellious [c]exalt themselves. [Selah.

8 Bless our God, O peoples,
And [a]sound His praise abroad,
9 Who [a]keeps us in life,
And [b]does not allow our feet to slip.
10 For Thou hast [a]tried us, O God;
Thou hast [b]refined us as silver is refined.
11 Thou [a]didst bring us into the net;
Thou didst lay an oppressive burden upon our loins.

Ps. 64: 9 [1]Or, *feared* [2]Or, *declared* [3]Or, *considered* [4]Lit., *His work* [a]Ps. 40:3
10 [a]Job 22:19; Ps. 32:11 [b]Ps. 11:1; 25:20

Ps. 65: 1 [1]Lit., *to* [a]Ps. 116:18
2 [1]Lit., *flesh* [a]Ps. 86:9; 145:21; Is. 66:23
3 [a]Ps. 38:4; 40:12 [b]Ps. 79:9
4 [a]Ps. 33:12; 84:4 [b]Ps. 36:8
5 [1]Or, *seas* [a]Ps. 45:4; 66:3 [b]Ps. 85:4 [c]Ps. 22:27; 48:10 [d]Ps. 107:23
6 [a]Ps. 95:4 [b]Ps. 93:1
7 [a]Ps. 89:9; 93:3, 4; 107:29; Matt. 8:26 [b]Ps. 2:1; 74:23; Is. 17:12, 13
8 [a]Ps. 2:8; 139:9; Is. 24:16
9 [1]Or, *channel* [a]Lev. 26:4; Job 5:10; Ps. 68:9; 104:13; 147:8 [b]Ps. 104:24 [c]Ps. 46:4 [d]Ps. 104:14; 147:14
10 [1]Or, *smooth* [a]Deut. 32:2; Ps. 72:6; 147:8
11 [a]Ps. 104:28 [b]Job 36:28; Ps. 147:14
12 [a]Job 38:26, 27; Joel 2:22 [b]Ps. 98:8; Is. 55:12
13 [a]Ps. 144:13; Is. 30:23 [b]Ps. 72:16 [c]Ps. 98:8; Is. 44:23

Ps. 66: 1 [a]Ps. 81:1; 95:1; 98:4; 100:1
2 [a]Ps. 79:9; Is. 42:8 [b]Is. 42:12
3 [1]Lit., *deceive* [a]Ps. 47:2; 65:5; 145:6 [b]Ps. 18:44; 81:15
4 [a]Ps. 22:27; 67:7; 86:9; Zech. 14:16 [b]Ps. 67:4
5 [a]Ps. 46:8 [b]Ps. 106:22
6 [a]Ex. 14:21; Ps. 106:9 [b]Josh. 3:16; Ps. 114:3 [c]Ps. 105:43
7 [a]Ps. 145:13 [b]Ps. 11:4 [c]Ps. 140:8
8 [a]Ps. 98:4
9 [a]Ps. 30:3 [b]Ps. 121:3
10 [a]Job 23:10; Ps. 7:9; 17:3; 26:2 [b]Is. 48:10; Zech. 13:9; Mal. 3:3; 1 Pet. 1:7
11 [a]Lam. 1:13; Ezek. 12:13

12 Thou didst make men [a]ride over our heads;
We went through [b]fire and through water;
Yet Thou [c]didst bring us out into *a place of* abundance.
13 I shall [a]come into Thy house with burnt offerings;
I shall [b]pay Thee my vows,
14 Which my lips uttered
And my mouth spoke when I was [a]in distress.
15 I shall [a]offer to Thee burnt offerings of fat beasts,
With the smoke of [b]rams;
I shall make *an offering of* bulls with male goats. [Selah.

16 [a]Come *and* hear, all who [1]fear God,
And I will [b]tell of what He has done for my soul.
17 I cried to Him with my mouth,
And He was [a]extolled with my tongue.
18 If I [a]regard wickedness in my heart,
The [b]Lord will not hear;
19 But certainly [a]God has heard;
He has given heed to the voice of my prayer.
20 [a]Blessed be God,
Who [b]has not turned away my prayer,
Nor His lovingkindness from me.

Psalm 67

The Nations Exhorted to Praise God.

For the choir director; with stringed instruments. A Psalm. A Song.

GOD be gracious to us and [a]bless us,
And [b]cause His face to shine upon us— [Selah.
2 That [a]Thy way may be known on the earth,
Thy salvation among all nations.
3 Let the [a]peoples praise Thee, O God;
Let all the peoples praise Thee.
4 Let the [a]nations be glad and sing for joy;
For Thou wilt [b]judge the peoples with uprightness,
And [c]guide the nations on the earth. [Selah.
5 Let the [a]peoples praise Thee, O God;
Let all the peoples praise Thee.

12 [a]Is. 51:23 [b]Ps. 78:21; Is. 43:2 [c]Ps. 18:19
13 [a]Ps. 96:8; Jer. 17:26 [b]Ps. 22:25; 116:14
14 [a]Ps. 18:6
15 [a]Ps. 51:19 [b]Num. 6:14
16 [1]Or, *revere* [a]Ps. 34:11 [b]Ps. 71:15, 24
17 [a]Ps. 30:1
18 [a]Job 36:21 [b]Job 27:9; Ps. 18:41; Prov. 1:28; 28:9; Is. 1:15; James 4:3
19 [a]Ps. 18:6; 116:1, 2
20 [a]Ps. 68:35 [b]Ps. 22:24

1 [a]Num. 6:25 [b]Ps. 4:6; 31:16; 80:3, 7, 19; 119:135
2 [a]Ps. 98:2; Acts 18:25; Titus 2:11
3 [a]Ps. 66:4
4 [a]Ps. 100:1, 2 [b]Ps. 9:8; 96:10, 13; 98:9 [c]Ps. 47:8
5 [a]Ps. 67:3
6 [a]Lev. 26:4; Ps. 85:12; Ezek. 34:27; Zech. 8:12 [b]Ps. 29:11; 115:12
7 [1]Or, *And let . . . earth fear Him* [a]Ps. 22:27; 33:8

1 [a]Num. 10:35; Ps. 12:5; 132:8
2 [a]Ps. 37:20; Is. 9:18; Hos. 13:3 [b]Ps. 22:14; 97:5; Mic. 1:4 [c]Ps. 9:3; 37:20; 80:16
3 [a]Ps. 32:11; 64:10; 97:12
4 [1]Heb., *YAH* [a]Ps. 66:2 [b]Is. 57:14; 62:10 [c]Ps. 18:10; 68:33; Is. 40:3 [d]Ps. 83:18
5 [1]Lit., *of* [a]Ps. 10:14; 146:9 [b]Deut. 10:18 [c]Deut. 26:15
6 [a]Ps. 113:9 [b]Ps. 69:33; 102:20; 107:10, 14; 146:7; Acts 12:7; 16:26 [c]Ps. 78:17; 107:34, 40
7 [a]Ex. 13:21; Ps. 78:14; Hab. 3:13 [b]Judg. 5:4
8 [1]Lit., *This is Sinai* which [a]Ex. 19:18; Judg. 5:4; 2 Sam. 22:8; Ps. 77:18; Jer. 10:10 [b]Judg. 5:4; Ps. 18:9; Is. 45:8 [c]Ex. 19:18; Judg. 5:5
9 [a]Lev. 26:4; Job 5:10; Ps. 78:24; Ezek. 34:26
10 [a]Ps. 65:9; 74:19; 78:20; 107:9

6 The [a]earth has yielded its produce;
God, our God, [b]blesses us.
7 God blesses us,
[1]That [a]all the ends of the earth may fear Him.

Psalm 68

The God of Sinai and of the Sanctuary.

For the choir director. A Psalm of David. A Song.

LET [a]God arise, let His enemies be scattered;
And let those who hate Him flee before Him.
2 As [a]smoke is driven away, *so* drive *them* away;
As [b]wax melts before the fire,
So let the [c]wicked perish before God.
3 But let the [a]righteous be glad; let them exult before God;
Yes, let them rejoice with gladness.
4 Sing to God, [a]sing praises to His name;
[b]Cast up a highway for Him who [c]rides through the deserts,
Whose [d]name is [1]the LORD, and exult before Him.

5 A [a]father of the fatherless and a [b]judge [1]for the widows,
Is God in His [c]holy habitation.
6 God [a]makes a home for the lonely;
He [b]leads out the prisoners into prosperity,
Only [c]the rebellious dwell in a parched land.

7 O God, when Thou [a]didst go forth before Thy people,
When Thou didst [b]march through the wilderness, [Selah.
8 The [a]earth quaked;
The [b]heavens also dropped *rain* at the presence of God;
[1c]Sinai itself *quaked* at the presence of God, the God of Israel.
9 Thou didst [a]shed abroad a plentiful rain, O God;
Thou didst confirm Thine inheritance, when it was parched.
10 Thy creatures settled in it;
Thou didst [a]provide in Thy goodness for the poor, O God.

11 The Lord gives the [1]command;
The [a]women who proclaim the
good tidings are a great host:
12 "[a]Kings of armies flee, they flee,
And she who remains at home
will [b]divide the spoil!"
13 [1]When you lie down [a]among
the [2]sheepfolds,
You are like the wings of a dove
covered with silver,
And its pinions with glistening
gold.
14 When the Almighty scattered
the kings [1]there,
It was snowing in [a]Zalmon.

15 A [1a]mountain of God is the
mountain of Bashan;
A mountain *of many* peaks is
the mountain of Bashan.
16 Why do you look with envy, O
mountains with *many* peaks,
At the mountain which God has
[a]desired for His abode?
Surely, [b]the LORD will dwell
there forever.
17 The [a]chariots of God are [1]myr-
iads, [b]thousands upon thousands;
[2]The Lord is among them *as at*
Sinai, in holiness.
18 Thou hast [a]ascended on high,
Thou hast led captive *Thy*
captives;
Thou hast received gifts among
men,
Even *among* the rebellious also,
that [1]the LORD God may
dwell *there.*

19 Blessed be the Lord, who daily
[a]bears our burden,
[b]The God *who* is our salvation. [Selah.
20 God is to us a [a]God of deliverances;
And [b]to [1]GOD the Lord belong
escapes from death.
21 Surely God will shatter the
head of His enemies,
The hairy crown of him who
goes on in his guilty deeds.
22 The Lord said, "[a]I will bring
them back from Bashan.
I will bring *them* back from the
depths of the sea;
23 That [a]your foot may shatter
them in blood,
The tongue of your [b]dogs *may
have* its portion from *your*
enemies."

24 They have seen [a]Thy procession, O God,
The procession of my God, my
King, [b]into the sanctuary.
25 The [a]singers went on, the musicians after *them,*
In the midst of the [b]maidens
beating tambourines.
26 [a]Bless God in the congrega-
tions,
Even the LORD, *you who are* of
the [b]fountain of Israel.
27 There is [a]Benjamin, the [1]youn-
gest, ruling them,
The princes of Judah *in* their
throng,
The princes of [b]Zebulun, the
princes of Naphtali.

28 Your God has [a]commanded
your strength;
Show Thyself strong, O God,
[b]who hast acted on our behalf.
29 Because of Thy temple at Jerusalem
[a]Kings will bring gifts to Thee.
30 Rebuke the [a]beasts in the reeds,
The herd of [b]bulls with the
calves of the peoples,
Trampling under foot the
pieces of silver;
He has [c]scattered the peoples
who delight in war.
31 Envoys will come out of [a]Egypt;
[1b]Ethiopia will quickly stretch
out her hands to God.

32 Sing to God, O [a]kingdoms of
the earth;
[b]Sing praises to the Lord,
[Selah.
33 To Him who [a]rides upon the
[b]highest heavens, which are
from ancient times;
Behold, [c]He speaks forth with
His voice, a [d]mighty voice.
34 [a]Ascribe strength to God;
His majesty is over Israel,
And His strength is in the
[1]skies.
35 O God, *Thou art* [a]awesome
from Thy sanctuary.
The God of Israel Himself
[b]gives strength and power to
the people.
[c]Blessed be God!

PSALM 69

A Cry of Distress and Imprecation on Adversaries.

For the choir director; according
to [ɛ]Shoshannim. *A Psalm* of
David.

SAVE me, O God,
For the [a]waters have threatened my life.

11 [1]Lit., *word* [a]Ex. 15:20; 1 Sam. 18:6
12 [a]Judg. 5:19; Ps. 135:11 [b]Judg. 5:30; 1 Sam. 30:24
13 [1]Lit., *If* [2]Or, *cookingstones,* or, *saddle bags* [a]Gen. 49:14
14 [1]Lit., *in it* [a]Judg. 9:48
15 [1]Or, *mighty mountain is* [a]Ps. 36:6
16 [a]Deut. 12:5; Ps. 87:1, 2; 132:13 [b]Ps. 132:14
17 [1]Lit., *twice ten thousand* [2]Another reading, *The Lord came from Sinai into the sanctuary* [a]2 Kin. 6:17; Hab. 3:8 [b]Deut. 33:2; Dan. 7:10
18 [1]Heb., YAH [a]Ps. 7:7; 47:5; Eph. 4:8
19 [a]Ps. 55:22; Is. 46:4 [b]Ps. 65:5
20 [1]YHWH, usually rendered LORD [a]Ps. 106:43 [b]Ps. 49:15; 56:13
22 [a]Amos 9:1-3
23 [a]Ps. 58:10 [b]1 Kin. 21:19; Jer. 15:3
24 [a]Ps. 77:13 [b]Ps. 63:2
25 [a]1 Chr. 13:8; 15:16; Ps. 47:5 [b]Ex. 15:20; Judg. 11:34
26 [a]Ps. 22:22, 23; 26:12 [b]Deut. 33:28; Is. 48:1
27 [1]Or, *smallest* [a]Judg. 5:14; 1 Sam. 9:21 [b]Judg. 5:18
28 [a]Ps. 29:11; 44:4 [b]Is. 26:12
29 [a]1 Kin. 10:10, 25; 2 Chr. 32:23; Ps. 45:12; 72:10; Is. 18:7
30 [a]Job 40:21; Ezek. 29:3 [b]Ps. 22:12 [c]Ps. 18:14; 89:10
31 [1]Lit., *Cush* [a]Is. 19:19, 21 [b]Is. 45:14; Zeph. 3:10
32 [a]Ps. 102:22 [b]Ps. 67:4
33 [a]Deut. 33:26 [b]Deut. 10:14; 1 Kin. 8:27 [c]Ps. 46:6 [d]Ps. 29:4
34 [1]Lit., *clouds* [a]Ps. 29:1
35 [a]Deut. 7:21; 10:17; Ps. 47:2; 66:5 [b]Ps. 29:11; Is. 40:29 [c]Ps. 66:20; 2 Cor. 1:3
[ɛ] Or possibly, *Lilies*
1 [a]Job 22:11; Ps. 32:6; 42:7; 69:14, 15; Jon. 2:5

2 I have sunk in deep [a]mire, and there is no foothold;
I have come into deep waters, and a [1b]flood overflows me.
3 I am [a]weary with my crying; my throat is parched;
My [b]eyes fail while I wait for my God.
4 Those [a]who hate me without a cause are more than the hairs of my head;
Those who would destroy me [b]are powerful,
[c]What I did not steal, I then have to restore.

5 O God, it is Thou who dost know [a]my folly,
And my wrongs are not hidden from Thee.
6 May those who wait for Thee not [a]be ashamed through me, O Lord [1]GOD of hosts;
May those who seek Thee not be dishonored through me, O God of Israel,
7 Because [a]for Thy sake I have borne reproach;
[b]Dishonor has covered my face.
8 I have become [a]estranged from my brothers,
And an alien to my mother's sons.
9 For [a]zeal for Thy house has consumed me,
And [b]the reproaches of those who reproach Thee have fallen on me.
10 When I wept in my soul with fasting,
It became my reproach.
11 When I made [a]sackcloth my clothing,
I became [b]a byword to them.
12 Those who [a]sit in the gate talk about me,
And I *am* the [b]song of the drunkards.

13 But as for me, my prayer is to Thee, O LORD, [a]at an acceptable time;
O God, in the [b]greatness of Thy lovingkindness,
Answer me with Thy saving truth.
14 Deliver me from the [a]mire, and do not let me sink;
May I be [b]delivered from my foes, and from the [c]deep waters.
15 May the [1a]flood of water not overflow me,
And may the deep not swallow me up,
And may the [b]pit not shut its mouth on me.

16 Answer me, O LORD, for [a]Thy lovingkindness is good;
[b]According to the greatness of Thy compassion, [c]turn to me,
17 And [a]do not hide Thy face from Thy servant,
For I am [b]in distress; answer me quickly.
18 Oh draw near to my soul *and* [a]redeem it;
[b]Ransom me because of my enemies!
19 Thou dost know my [a]reproach and my shame and my dishonor;
All my adversaries are [1]before Thee.

20 Reproach has [a]broken my heart, and I am so sick.
And [b]I looked for sympathy, but there was none,
And for comforters, but I found none.
21 They also gave me [a]gall for my food,
And for my thirst they [b]gave me vinegar to drink.

22 May [a]their table before them become a snare;
And [b]when they are in peace, *may it become* a trap.
23 May their [a]eyes grow dim so that they cannot see,
And make their [b]loins shake continually.
24 [a]Pour out Thine indignation on them,
And may Thy burning anger overtake them.
25 May their [a]camp be desolate;
May none dwell in their tents.
26 For they have [a]persecuted him whom [b]Thou Thyself hast smitten,
And they tell of the pain of those whom [c]Thou hast wounded.
27 Do Thou add [a]iniquity to their iniquity,
And may they not come into Thy righteousness.
28 May they be [a]blotted out of the [b]book of life,
And may they not be [c]recorded with the righteous.

29 But I am [a]afflicted and in pain;
May Thy salvation, O God, [b]set me *securely* on high.
30 I will [a]praise the name of God with song,
And shall [b]magnify Him with [c]thanksgiving.
31 And it will [a]please the LORD better than an ox

2 [1]Lit., *flowing stream* [a]Ps. 40:2 [b]Jon. 2:3
3 [a]Ps. 6:6 [b]Deut. 28:32; Ps. 38:10; 119:82, 123; Is. 38:14
4 [a]Ps. 35:19; John 15:25 [b]Ps. 35:19; 38:19; 59:3 [c]Ps. 35:11; Jer. 15:10
5 [a]Ps. 38:5
6 [1]YHWH, usually rendered LORD [a]2 Sam. 12:14
7 [a]Jer. 15:15 [b]Ps. 44:15; Is. 50:6; Jer. 51:51
8 [a]Job 19:13-15
9 [a]Ps. 119:139; John 2:17 [b]Ps. 89:41, 50; Rom. 15:3
11 [a]1 Kin. 20:31; Ps. 35:13 [b]1 Kin. 9:7; Job 17:6; Ps. 44:14; Jer. 24:9
12 [a]Gen. 19:1; Ruth 4:1 [b]Job 30:9
13 [a]Ps. 32:6; Is. 49:8; 2 Cor. 6:2 [b]Ps. 51:1
14 [a]Ps. 69:2 [b]Ps. 144:7 [c]Ps. 69:2
15 [1]Lit., *stream* [a]Ps. 124:4, 5 [b]Num. 16:33
16 [a]Ps. 63:3; 109:21 [b]Ps. 51:1; 106:45 [c]Ps. 25:16
17 [a]Ps. 27:9; 102:2; 143:7 [b]Ps. 31:9; 66:14
18 [a]2 Sam. 4:9; Ps. 26:11; 49:15 [b]Ps. 119:134
19 [1]Or, *known to Thee* [a]Ps. 22:6; 31:11
20 [a]Jer. 23:9 [b]Ps. 142:4
21 [a]Deut. 29:18 [b]Matt. 27:34, 48; Mark 15:23; Luke 23:36; John 19:28
22 [a]Rom. 11:9, 10 [b]1 Thess. 5:3
23 [a]Is. 6:10 [b]Dan. 5:6
24 [a]Ps. 79:6; Jer. 10:25; Ezek. 20:8; Hos. 5:10
25 [a]Matt. 23:38; Luke 13:35; Acts 1:20
26 [a]2 Chr. 28:9; Zech. 1:15 [b]Is. 53:4 [c]Ps. 109:22
27 [a]Neh. 4:5; Ps. 109:14; Rom. 1:28
28 [a]Ex. 32:33; Rev. 3:5 [b]Phil. 4:3; Rev. 13:8; 20:15 [c]Ps. 87:6; Ezek. 13:9; Luke 10:20; Heb. 12:23
29 [a]Ps. 70:5 [b]Ps. 20:1; 59:1
30 [a]Ps. 28:7 [b]Ps. 34:3 [c]Ps. 50:14
31 [a]Ps. 50:13, 14

Or a young bull with horns and hoofs.
32 The [a]humble [1]have seen *it and* are glad;
You who seek God, [b]let your heart [2]revive.
33 For [a]the LORD hears the needy,
And [b]does not despise His *who are* prisoners.

34 Let [a]heaven and earth praise Him,
The seas and everything that moves in them.
35 For God will [a]save Zion and [b]build the cities of Judah,
That they may dwell there and [c]possess it.
36 And the [1a]descendants of His servants will inherit it,
And those who love His name [b]will dwell in it.

PSALM 70

Prayer for Help against Persecutors.

For the choir director. *A Psalm* of David; for a memorial.

[a]O GOD, *hasten* to deliver me;
O LORD, hasten to my help!
2 Let those be ashamed and humiliated
Who seek my [1]life;
Let those be turned back and dishonored
Who delight [2]in my hurt.
3 Let those be [1]turned back because of their shame
Who say, "Aha, aha!"

4 Let all who seek Thee rejoice and be glad in Thee;
And let those who love Thy salvation say continually,
"Let God be magnified."
5 But I am afflicted and needy;
[a]Hasten to me, O God!
Thou art my help and my deliverer;
O LORD, do not delay.

PSALM 71

Prayer of an Old Man for Deliverance.

[a]IN Thee, O LORD, I have taken refuge;
Let me never be ashamed.
2 In Thy righteousness deliver me, and rescue me;
Incline Thine ear to me, and save me.
3 Be Thou to me a rock of [a]habitation, to which I may continually come;
Thou hast given [b]commandment to save me,
For Thou art [c]my rock and my fortress.
4 [a]Rescue me, O my God, out of the hand of the wicked,
Out of the grasp of the wrongdoer and ruthless man,
5 For Thou art my [a]hope;
O Lord [1]GOD, *Thou art* my [b]confidence from my youth.
6 By Thee I have been [a]sustained from *my* birth;
Thou art He who [b]took me from my mother's womb;
My [c]praise is continually of Thee.

7 I have become a [a]marvel to many;
For Thou art [b]my strong refuge.
8 My [a]mouth is filled with Thy praise,
And with [b]Thy glory all day long.
9 Do not cast me off in the [a]time of old age;
Do not forsake me when my strength fails.
10 For my enemies have spoken [1]against me;
And those who [a]watch for my [2]life [b]have consulted together,
11 Saying, "[a]God has forsaken him;
Pursue and seize him, for there is [b]no one to deliver."

12 O God, [a]do not be far from me;
O my God, [b]hasten to my help!
13 Let those who are adversaries of my soul be [a]ashamed *and* consumed;
Let them be [b]covered with reproach and dishonor, who [c]seek to injure me.
14 But as for me, I will [a]hope continually,
And will [1b]praise Thee yet more and more.
15 My [a]mouth shall tell of Thy righteousness,
And of [b]Thy salvation all day long;
For I [c]do not know the [1]sum *of them.*
16 I will come [a]with the mighty deeds of the Lord [1]GOD;
I will [b]make mention of Thy righteousness, Thine alone.

17 O God, Thou [a]hast taught me from my youth;
And I still [b]declare Thy wondrous deeds.

---

32 [1]Some mss. read, *will see* [2]Or, *live*
[a]Ps. 34:2 [b]Ps. 22:26
33 [a]Ps. 12:5 [b]Ps. 68:6
34 [a]Ps. 96:11; 98:7; 148:1-13; Is. 44:23; 49:13
35 [a]Ps. 46:5; 51:18 [b]Ps. 147:2; Is. 44:26 [c]Obad. 17
36 [1]Lit., *seed* [a]Ps. 25:13; 102:28 [b]Ps. 37:29

1 [a]Ps. 40:13-17; 70:1-5
2 [1]Or, *soul* [2]Or, *to injure me*
3 [1]Some mss. read, *appalled;* cf. Ps. 40:15
5 [a]Ps. 141:1

1 [a]Ps. 31:1-3; 71:1-3
3 [a]Deut. 33:27; Ps. 90:1; 91:9 [b]Ps. 7:6; 42:8 [c]Ps. 18:2
4 [a]Ps. 140:1, 4
5 [1]YHWH, usually rendered LORD [a]Ps. 39:7; Jer. 14:8; 17:7, 13, 17; 50:7 [b]Ps. 22:9
6 [a]Ps. 22:10; Is. 46:3 [b]Job 10:18; Ps. 22:9 [c]Ps. 34:1
7 [a]Is. 8:18; 1 Cor. 4:9 [b]Ps. 61:3
8 [a]Ps. 63:5 [b]Ps. 96:6; 104:1
9 [a]Ps. 71:18; 92:14; Is. 46:4
10 [1]Lit., *with reference to* [2]Lit., *soul* [a]Ps. 56:6 [b]Ps. 31:13; 83:3; Matt. 27:1
11 [a]Ps. 3:2 [b]Ps. 7:2
12 [a]Ps. 10:1; 22:11; 35:22; 38:21 [b]Ps. 38:22; 40:13; 70:5
13 [a]Ps. 35:4, 26; 40:14 [b]Ps. 109:29 [c]Esth. 9:2; Ps. 71:24
14 [1]Lit., *add upon all Thy praise* [a]Ps. 130:7 [b]Ps. 71:8
15 [1]Lit., *numbers* [a]Ps. 35:28 [b]Ps. 96:2 [c]Ps. 40:5
16 [1]YHWH, usually rendered LORD [a]Ps. 106:2 [b]Ps. 51:14
17 [a]Deut. 4:5; 6:7 [b]Ps. 26:7; 40:5; 119:27

18 And even when *I am* [a]old and gray, O God, do not forsake me,
Until I [b]declare Thy [1]strength to *this* generation,
Thy power to all who are to come.
19 For Thy [a]righteousness, O God, *reaches* to the heavens,
Thou who hast [b]done great things;
O God, [c]who is like Thee?
20 Thou, who hast [a]shown [1]me many troubles and distresses,
Wilt [b]revive [1]me again,
And wilt bring [1]me up again from the depths of the earth.
21 Mayest Thou increase my [a]greatness,
And turn *to* [b]comfort me.

22 I will also praise Thee with [a]a harp,
Even Thy truth, O my God;
To Thee I will sing praises with the [b]lyre,
O Thou [c]Holy One of Israel.
23 My lips will [a]shout for joy when I sing praises to Thee;
And my [b]soul, which Thou hast redeemed.
24 My [a]tongue also will utter Thy righteousness all day long;
For they are [b]ashamed, for they are humiliated who seek [1]my hurt.

Psalm 72

The Reign of the Righteous King.

A Psalm of Solomon.

GIVE the king [a]Thy judgments, O God,
And [b]Thy righteousness to the king's son.
2 May [1]he [a]judge Thy people with righteousness,
And [b]Thine afflicted with justice.
3 Let the mountains bring [1a]peace to the people,
And the hills in righteousness.
4 May he [a]vindicate the [1]afflicted of the people,
Save the children of the needy,
And crush the oppressor.

5 Let them fear Thee [a]while the sun endures,
And as long as the moon, throughout all generations.
6 May he come down [a]like rain upon the mown grass,
Like [b]showers that water the earth.
7 In his days may the [a]righteous flourish,
And abundance of peace till the moon is no more.

8 May he also rule [a]from sea to sea,
And from the River to the ends of the earth.
9 Let [a]the nomads of the desert [b]bow before him;
And his enemies [c]lick the dust.
10 Let the kings of [a]Tarshish and of the [1b]islands bring presents;
The kings of [c]Sheba and [d]Seba [e]offer gifts.
11 And let all [a]kings bow down before him,
All [b]nations serve him.

12 For he will [a]deliver the needy when he cries for help,
The afflicted also, and him who has no helper.
13 He will have [a]compassion on the poor and needy,
And the lives of the needy he will save.
14 He will [1a]rescue their life from oppression and violence;
And their blood will be [b]precious in his sight;
15 So may he live; and may the [a]gold of Sheba be given to him;
And let [1]them pray for him continually;
Let [1]them bless him all day long.

16 May there be abundance of grain in the earth on top of the mountains;
Its fruit will wave like *the cedars of* [a]Lebanon;
And may those from the city flourish like [b]vegetation of the earth.
17 May his [a]name endure forever;
May his name increase [b]as long as the sun *shines;*
And let *men* [c]bless themselves by him;
[d]Let all nations call him blessed.

18 [a]Blessed be the LORD God, the God of Israel,
Who alone [b]works wonders.
19 And blessed be His [a]glorious name forever;
And may the whole [b]earth be filled with His glory.
Amen, and Amen.

18 [1]Lit., *arm* [a]Ps. 71:9 [b]Ps. 22:31; 78:4, 6
19 [a]Ps. 36:6; 57:10 [b]Ps. 126:2; Luke 1:49 [c]Deut. 3:24
20 [1]Another reading is, *us* [a]Ps. 60:3 [b]Ps. 80:18; 85:6; Hos. 6:2
21 [a]Ps. 18:35 [b]Ps. 23:4; 86:17; Is. 12:1; 49:13
22 [a]Ps. 33:2; 81:2; 144:9 [b]Ps. 33:2; 147:7 [c]Ps. 78:41; 89:18; Is. 1:4
23 [a]Ps. 5:11; 32:11; 132:9, 16 [b]Ps. 34:22; 55:18
24 [1]Or, *to injure me* [a]Ps. 35:28 [b]Ps. 71:13
1 [a]1 Kin. 3:9; 1 Chr. 22:13 [b]Ps. 24:5
2 [1]Or, *He; Many pronouns could be rendered thus, as Psalm 72 typically refers to the Messiah* [a]Is. 9:7; 11:2-5; 32:1 [b]Ps. 82:3
3 [1]Or, *prosperity* [a]Is. 2:4; 9:5, 6
4 [1]Or, *humble* [a]Is. 11:4
5 [a]Ps. 89:36, 37
6 [a]Deut. 32:2; 2 Sam. 23:4; Hos. 6:3 [b]Ps. 65:10
7 [a]Ps. 92:12
8 [a]Ex. 23:31; Zech. 9:10
9 [a]Ps. 74:14; Is. 23:13 [b]Ps. 22:29 [c]Is. 49:23
10 [1]Or, *coastlands* [a]2 Chr. 9:21; Ps. 48:7 [b]Ps. 97:1; Is. 42:4, 10; Zeph. 2:11 [c]1 Kin. 10:1; Job 6:19; Is. 60:6 [d]Gen. 10:7; Is. 43:3 [e]Ps. 45:12
11 [a]Ps. 138:4; Is. 49:23 [b]Ps. 86:9
12 [a]Job 29:12
13 [a]Prov. 19:17; 28:8
14 [1]Lit., *redeem* [a]Ps. 69:18 [b]1 Sam. 26:21; Ps. 116:15
15 [1]Lit., *him* [a]Is. 60:6
16 [a]Ps. 104:16 [b]Job 5:25
17 [a]Ex. 3:15; Ps. 135:13 [b]Ps. 89:36 [c]Gen. 12:3; 22:18 [d]Luke 1:48
18 [a]Ps. 41:13; 89:52; 106:48 [b]Ex. 15:11; Job 5:9; Ps. 77:14; 86:10; 136:4
19 [a]Neh. 9:5; Ps. 96:8 [b]Num. 14:21

20 The prayers of David the son of
Jesse are ended.

BOOK 3

PSALM 73

The End of the Wicked Contrasted with That of the Righteous.

A Psalm of Asaph.

SURELY God is [a]good to Israel,
To those who are [b]pure in heart!
2 But as for me, [a]my feet came
close to stumbling;
My steps had almost slipped.
3 For I was [a]envious of the [1]arro-
gant,
As I saw the [b]prosperity of the
wicked.
4 For there are no pains in their
death;
And their body is [a]fat.
5 They are [a]not in trouble *as other* [1]men;
Nor are they [b]plagued like mankind.
6 Therefore pride is [a]their necklace;
The [b]garment of violence covers them.
7 Their eye bulges from [a]fatness;
The imaginations of *their* heart
[1]run riot.
8 They [a]mock, and wickedly
speak of oppression;
They [b]speak from on high.
9 They have set their mouth
[1]against the heavens,
And their tongue [2]parades
through the earth.

10 Therefore [1]his people return to
this place;
And waters of [a]abundance are
[2]drunk by them.
11 And they say, "[a]How does God
know?
And is there knowledge with
the Most High?"
12 Behold, [a]these are the wicked;
And always [b]at ease, they have
increased *in* wealth.
13 Surely [a]in vain I have [1]kept my
heart pure,
And [b]washed my hands in innocence;
14 For I have been stricken [a]all
day long,
And [b]chastened every morning.

15 If I had said, "I will speak thus";
Behold, I should have betrayed
the generation of Thy children.
16 When I [a]pondered to understand this,
It was [1]troublesome in my sight
17 Until I came into the [a]sanctuary
of God;
Then I perceived their [b]end.
18 Surely Thou dost set them in
[a]slippery places;
Thou dost cast them down to
[1b]destruction.
19 How they are [a]destroyed in a
moment!
They are utterly swept away by
[b]sudden terrors!
20 Like a [a]dream when one
awakes,
O Lord, when [b]aroused, Thou
wilt [c]despise their [1]form.

21 When my [a]heart was embittered,
And I was [b]pierced [1]within,
22 Then I was [a]senseless and ignorant;
I was *like* a [b]beast before Thee.
23 Nevertheless I am continually
with Thee;
Thou hast taken hold of my
right hand.
24 With Thy counsel Thou wilt
[a]guide me,
And afterward [b]receive me [1]to
glory.

25 [a]Whom have I in heaven *but
Thee?*
And besides Thee, I desire
nothing on earth.
26 My [a]flesh and my heart may
fail;
But God is the [1]strength of my
heart and my [b]portion forever.
27 For, behold, those who are far
from Thee will [a]perish;
Thou hast [1]destroyed all those
who [b]are unfaithful to Thee.
28 But as for me, [a]the nearness of
God is my good;
I have made the Lord [1]GOD my
[b]refuge,
That I may [c]tell of all Thy
works.

PSALM 74

An Appeal against the Devastation of the Land by the Enemy.

A Maskil of Asaph.

O GOD, why hast Thou [a]rejected
us forever?
Why does Thine anger [b]smoke
against the [c]sheep of Thy
pasture?

1 [a]Ps. 86:5 [b]Ps. 24:4; 51:10; Matt. 5:8
2 [a]Ps. 94:18
3 [1]Or, *boasters* [a]Ps. 37:1; Prov. 23:17 [b]Ps. 37:7; Jer. 12:1
4 [a]Ps. 10:5
5 [1]Or, *mortals* [a]Job 21:9; Ps. 73:12 [b]Ps. 73:14
6 [a]Gen. 41:42; Prov. 1:9 [b]Ps. 109:18
7 [1]Lit., *overflow* [a]Job 15:27
8 [a]Ps. 1:1 [b]Ps. 17:10; 2 Pet. 2:18; Jude 16
9 [1]Or, *in* [2]Lit., *walks*
10 [1]Or, *His* [2]Lit., *drained out* [a]Ps. 23:5
11 [a]Job 22:13
12 [a]Ps. 49:6; 52:7 [b]Jer. 49:31; Ezek. 23:42
13 [1]Or, *cleansed my heart* [a]Job 21:15; 34:9; 35:3 [b]Ps. 26:6
14 [a]Ps. 38:6 [b]Job 33:19; Ps. 118:18
16 [1]Lit., *labor* [a]Eccles. 8:17
17 [a]Ps. 27:4; 77:13 [b]Ps. 37:38
18 [1]Lit., *ruins* [a]Ps. 35:6 [b]Ps. 35:8; 36:12
19 [a]Num. 16:21; Is. 47:11 [b]Job 18:11
20 [1]Or, *image* [a]Job 20:8 [b]Ps. 78:65 [c]1 Sam. 2:30
21 [1]Lit., *in my kidneys* [a]Judg. 10:16 [b]Acts 2:37
22 [a]Ps. 49:10; 92:6 [b]Job 18:3; Ps. 49:20; Eccles. 3:18
24 [1]Or, *with honor* [a]Ps. 32:8; 48:14; Is. 58:11 [b]Gen. 5:24; Ps. 49:15
25 [a]Ps. 16:2
26 [1]Lit., *rock* [a]Ps. 38:10; 40:12; 84:2; 119:81 [b]Ps. 16:5
27 [1]Or, *silenced* [a]Ps. 37:20 [b]Ex. 34:15; Num. 15:39; Ps. 106:39; Hos. 4:12; 9:1
28 [1]YHWH, usually rendered LORD [a]Ps. 65:4; Heb. 10:22; James 4:8 [b]Ps. 14:6; 71:7 [c]Ps. 40:5; 107:22
1 [a]Ps. 44:9; 77:7 [b]Deut. 29:20; Ps. 18:8; 89:46 [c]Ps. 79:13; 95:7; 100:3

2 Remember Thy congregation, which Thou hast [a]purchased of old,
Which Thou hast [b]redeemed to be the [c]tribe of Thine inheritance;
And Mount Zion, where Thou hast dwelt.
3 Turn Thy footsteps toward the [a]perpetual ruins,
The enemy [b]has damaged everything within the sanctuary.
4 Thine adversaries have [a]roared in the midst of Thy meeting place;
They have set up their [b]own standards [c]for signs.
5 It seems as if one had lifted up *His* [a]axe in a forest of trees.
6 And now [1]all its [a]carved work
They smash with hatchet and [2]hammers.
7 They have [a]burned Thy sanctuary to the ground;
They have [b]defiled the dwelling place of Thy name.
8 They [a]said in their heart, "Let us [1]completely subdue them."
They have burned all the meeting places of God in the land.
9 We do not see our [a]signs,
There is [b]no longer any prophet,
Nor is there any among us who knows [c]how long.
10 How long, O God, will the adversary [a]revile,
And the enemy [b]spurn Thy name forever?
11 Why [a]dost Thou withdraw Thy hand, even Thy right hand?
From within Thy bosom, [b]destroy *them!*

12 Yet God is [a]my king from of old,
Who works deeds of deliverance in the midst of the earth.
13 [1]Thou didst [a]divide the sea by Thy strength;
[1]Thou [b]didst break the heads of the [c]sea monsters in the waters.
14 Thou didst crush the heads of [1a]Leviathan;
Thou didst give him as food for the creatures [b]of the wilderness.
15 Thou didst [a]break open springs and torrents;
Thou didst [b]dry up ever-flowing streams.
16 Thine is the day, Thine is the night;
Thou hast [a]prepared the light and the sun.
17 Thou hast [a]established all the boundaries of the earth;
Thou hast made [b]summer and winter.

18 Remember this, O LORD, that the enemy has [a]reviled;
And a [b]foolish people has spurned Thy name.
19 Do not deliver the soul of Thy [a]turtledove to the wild beast;
[b]Do not forget the life of Thine afflicted forever.
20 Consider the [a]covenant;
For the [b]dark places of the land are full of the habitations of violence.
21 Let not the [a]oppressed return dishonored;
Let the [b]afflicted and needy praise Thy name.

22 Do arise, O God, *and* [a]plead Thine own cause;
Remember how the [b]foolish man reproaches Thee all day long.
23 Do not forget the voice of Thine [a]adversaries,
The [b]uproar of those who rise against Thee which ascends continually.

PSALM 75

God Abases the Proud, but Exalts the Righteous.

For the choir director; *set to* [£]Al-tashheth.
A Psalm of Asaph, a Song.

WE [a]give thanks to Thee, O God, we give thanks,
For Thy name is [b]near;
Men declare [c]Thy wondrous works.
2 "When I select an [a]appointed time;
It is I who [b]judge with equity.
3 "The [a]earth and all who dwell in it [1]melt;
It is I who have firmly set its [b]pillars. [Selah.
4 "I said to the boastful, 'Do not boast,'
And to the wicked, '[a]Do not lift up the horn;
5 Do not lift up your horn on high,
[a]Do not speak with insolent pride.' "

6 For not from the east, nor from the west,

2 [a]Ex. 15:16; Deut. 32:6 [b]Ex. 15:13; Ps. 77:15; 106:10; Is. 63:9 [c]Deut. 32:9
3 [a]Is. 61:4 [b]Ps. 79:1
4 [a]Lam. 2:7 [b]Num. 2:2 [c]Ps. 74:9
5 [a]Jer. 46:22
6 [1]Lit., *altogether* [2]Or, *axes* [a]1 Kin. 6:18, 29
7 [a]2 Kin. 25:9 [b]Ps. 89:39; Lam. 2:2
8 [1]Lit., *altogether* [a]Ps. 83:4
9 [a]Ps. 78:43 [b]1 Sam. 3:1; Lam. 2:9; Ezek. 7:26; Amos 8:11 [c]Ps. 6:3; 79:5; 80:4
10 [a]Ps. 44:16; 79:12; 89:51 [b]Lev. 24:16
11 [a]Lam. 2:3 [b]Ps. 59:13
12 [a]Ps. 44:4
13 [1]Or, *Thou Thyself,* also vs. 14, 15, 16, 17 [a]Ex. 14:21; Ps. 78:13 [b]Is. 51:9 [c]Ps. 148:7; Jer. 51:34
14 [1]Or, *sea monster* [a]Job 41:1; Ps. 104:26 [b]Ps. 72:9
15 [a]Ex. 17:5, 6; Num. 20:11; Ps. 78:15; 105:41; 114:8; Is. 48:21 [b]Ex. 14:21, 22; Josh. 2:10; 3:13; Ps. 114:3
16 [a]Gen. 1:14-18; Ps. 104:19; 136:7, 8
17 [a]Deut. 32:8; Acts 17:26 [b]Ps. 147:16
18 [a]Ps. 74:10 [b]Deut. 32:6; Ps. 14:1
19 [a]Song of Sol. 2:14 [b]Ps. 9:18
20 [a]Gen. 17:7; Ps. 106:45 [b]Ps. 88:6; 143:3
21 [a]Ps. 103:6 [b]Ps. 35:10; Is. 41:17
22 [a]Ps. 43:1; Is. 3:13; 43:26; Ezek. 20:35 [b]Ps. 14:1; 53:1
23 [a]Ps. 74:10 [b]Ps. 65:7
[£] Lit., *Do Not Destroy*
1 [a]Ps. 79:13 [b]Ps. 145:18 [c]Ps. 26:7; 44:1; 71:17
2 [a]Ps. 102:13 [b]Ps. 9:8; 67:4; Is. 11:4
3 [1]Or, *totter* [a]Ps. 46:6; Is. 24:19 [b]1 Sam. 2:8
4 [a]Zech. 1:21
5 [a]1 Sam. 2:3

Nor from the [a]desert *comes* exaltation;
7 But [a]God is the Judge;
He [b]puts down one, and exalts
another.
8 For a [a]cup is in the hand of the
LORD, and the wine foams;
It is [1][b]well mixed, and He pours
out of this;
Surely all the wicked of the
earth must drain *and* [c]drink
down its dregs.

9 But as for me, I will [a]declare *it*
forever,
I will sing praises to the God of
Jacob.
10 And all the [a]horns of the
wicked [1]He will cut off,
But [b]the horns of the righteous
will be lifted up.

PSALM 76

The Victorious Power of the God of Jacob.

For the choir director; on stringed
instruments.
A Psalm of Asaph, a Song.

GOD is [a]known in Judah;
His name is [b]great in Israel.
2 And His [1][a]tabernacle is in [b]Sa-
lem,
His [c]dwelling place also is in
Zion.
3 There He [a]broke the flaming arrows,
The shield, and the sword, and
the weapons of war. [Selah.

4 Thou art resplendent,
More majestic than the mountains of prey.
5 The [a]stouthearted were plundered;
[1]They sank into sleep;
And none of the [2]warriors
could use his hands.
6 At Thy [a]rebuke, O God of Jacob,
Both [1][b]rider and horse were
cast into a dead sleep.
7 Thou, even Thou, art [a]to be
feared;
And [b]who may stand in Thy
presence when once Thou art
angry?

8 Thou didst cause judgment to
be heard from heaven;
The earth [a]feared, and was still,
9 When God [a]arose to judgment,
To save all the humble of the
earth. [Selah.
10 For the [a]wrath of man shall
praise Thee;
With a remnant of wrath Thou
shalt gird Thyself.

11 Make vows to the LORD your
God and [a]fulfill *them;*
Let all who are around Him
[b]bring gifts to Him who is to
be feared.
12 He will cut off the spirit of
princes;
He is [a]feared by the kings of the
earth.

PSALM 77

Comfort in Trouble from Recalling
God's Mighty Deeds.

For the choir director; [f]according
to Jeduthun. A Psalm of Asaph.

MY voice *rises* to God, and I will
[a]cry aloud;
My voice *rises* to God, and He
will hear me.
2 In the [a]day of my trouble I
sought the Lord;
[b]In the night my [c]hand was
stretched out [1]without
weariness;
My soul [d]refused to be comforted.
3 *When* I remember God, then I
am [a]disturbed;
When I [b]sigh, then [c]my spirit
grows faint. [Selah.
4 Thou hast held my eyelids
open;
I am so troubled that I [a]cannot
speak.
5 I have considered the [a]days of
old,
The years of long ago.
6 I will remember my [a]song in the
night;
I [b]will meditate with my heart;
And my spirit [1]ponders.

7 Will the Lord [a]reject forever?
And will He [b]never be favorable again?
8 Has His [a]lovingkindness ceased
forever?
Has *His* [1][b]promise come to an
end [2]forever?
9 Has God [a]forgotten to be gracious?
Or has He in anger [1]withdrawn
His [b]compassion? [Selah.
10 Then I said, "[a]It is my grief,
That the [b]right hand of the
Most High has changed."

11 I shall remember the [a]deeds of
[1]the LORD;
Surely I will [a]remember Thy
wonders of old.
12 I will [a]meditate on all Thy
work,
And muse on Thy deeds.

---

6 [a]Ps. 3:3; 113:7
7 [a]Ps. 50:6 [b]1 Sam. 2:7; Ps. 147:6; Dan. 2:21
8 [1]Lit., *full of mixture* [a]Job 21:20; Ps. 11:6; 60:3; Jer. 25:15 [b]Prov. 23:30 [c]Obad. 16
9 [a]Ps. 22:22; 40:10
10 [1]Heb., *I* [a]Jer. 48:25 [b]1 Sam. 2:1; Ps. 89:17; 92:10; 148:14

1 [a]Ps. 48:3 [b]Ps. 99:3
2 [1]Lit., *shelter* [a]Ps. 27:5; Lam. 2:6 [b]Gen. 14:18 [c]Ps. 9:11; 132:13; 135:21
3 [a]Ps. 46:9
5 [1]Lit., *They slumbered their sleep* [2]Lit., *men of might have found their hands* [a]Is. 10:12; 46:12
6 [1]Lit., *chariot* [a]Ps. 80:16 [b]Ex. 15:1, 21; Ps. 78:53
7 [a]1 Chr. 16:25; Ps. 89:7; 96:4 [b]Ezra 9:15; Ps. 130:3; Nah. 1:6; Mal. 3:2; Rev. 6:17
8 [a]1 Chr. 16:30; Ps. 33:8
9 [a]Ps. 74:22; 82:8
10 [a]Ex. 9:16; Rom. 9:17
11 [a]Ps. 50:14 [b]Ps. 68:29
12 [a]Ps. 47:2

[f]1 Chr. 16:41
1 [a]Ps. 3:4; 142:1
2 [1]Lit., *and did not grow numb* [a]Ps. 50:15; 86:7 [b]Ps. 63:6; Is. 26:9 [c]Job 11:13; Ps. 88:9 [d]Gen. 37:35
3 [a]Ps. 42:5, 11; 43:5 [b]Ps. 55:2; 142:2 [c]Ps. 61:2; 143:4
4 [a]Ps. 39:9
5 [a]Deut. 32:7; Ps. 44:1; 143:5; Is. 51:9
6 [1]Lit., *searched* [a]Ps. 42:8 [b]Ps. 4:4
7 [a]Ps. 44:9 [b]Ps. 85:1, 5
8 [1]Lit., *word* [2]Lit., *from generation to generation* [a]Ps. 89:49 [b]2 Pet. 3:9
9 [1]Lit., *shut up* [a]Is. 49:15 [b]Ps. 25:6; 40:11; 51:1
10 [a]Ps. 31:22; 73:15 [b]Ps. 44:2, 3
11 [1]Heb., YAH [a]Ps. 105:5; 143:5
12 [a]Ps. 145:5

13 Thy way, O God, is [a]holy;
[b]What god is great like our God?
14 Thou art the [a]God who workest wonders;
Thou hast [b]made known Thy strength among the peoples.
15 Thou hast by Thy [1]power [a]redeemed Thy people,
The sons of Jacob and Joseph. [Selah.

16 The [a]waters saw Thee, O God;
The waters saw Thee, they were in anguish;
The deeps also trembled.
17 The [a]clouds poured out water;
The skies [b]gave forth a sound;
Thy [c]arrows flashed here and there.
18 The [a]sound of Thy thunder was in the whirlwind;
The [b]lightnings lit up the world;
The [c]earth trembled and shook,
19 Thy [a]way was in the sea,
And Thy paths in the mighty waters,
And Thy footprints may not be known.
20 Thou [a]didst lead Thy people like a flock,
By the hand of Moses and Aaron.

Psalm 78

God's Guidance of His People in Spite of Their Unfaithfulness.

Maskil of Asaph.

[a]LISTEN, O my people, to my [1]instruction;
[b]Incline your ears to the words of my mouth.
2 I will [a]open my mouth in a parable;
I will utter [b]dark sayings of old,
3 Which we have heard and known,
And our fathers have told us.
4 We will [a]not conceal them from their children,
But tell to the [b]generation to come the praises of the LORD,
And His strength and His [c]wondrous works that He has done.

5 For He established a [a]testimony in Jacob,
And appointed a [b]law in Israel,
Which He [c]commanded our fathers,
That they should [d]teach them to their children;
6 That the generation to come might know, *even* the children *yet* to be born,
That they may arise and tell *them* to their children,
7 That they should put their confidence in God,
And [a]not forget the works of God,
But [b]keep His commandments,
8 And [a]not be like their fathers,
A [b]stubborn and rebellious generation,
A generation that [c]did not [1]prepare its heart,
And whose spirit was not [d]faithful to God.

9 The sons of Ephraim were [a]archers equipped with bows,
Yet [b]they turned back in the day of battle.
10 They [a]did not keep the covenant of God,
And refused to [b]walk in His law;
11 And they [a]forgot His deeds,
And His [1]miracles that He had shown them.
12 [a]He wrought wonders before their fathers,
In the land of Egypt, in the [b]field of Zoan.
13 He [a]divided the sea, and caused them to pass through;
And He made the waters stand [b]up like a heap.
14 Then He led them with the cloud by [a]day,
And all the night with a [b]light of fire.
15 He [a]split the rocks in the wilderness,
And gave *them* abundant drink like the ocean depths.
16 He [a]brought forth streams also from the rock,
And caused waters to run down like rivers.

17 Yet they still continued to sin against Him,
To [a]rebel against the Most High in the desert.
18 And in their heart they [a]put God to the test
By asking [b]food according to their desire.
19 Then they spoke against God;
They said, "[a]Can God prepare a table in the wilderness?
20 "Behold, He [a]struck the rock, so that waters gushed out,
And streams were overflowing;
Can He give bread also?

13 [a]Ps. 63:2; 73:17 [b]Ex. 15:11; Ps. 71:19; 86:8
14 [a]Ps. 72:18 [b]Ps. 106:8
15 [1]Lit., *arm* [a]Ex. 6:6; Deut. 9:29; Ps. 74:2
16 [a]Ex. 14:21; Ps. 114:3; Hab. 3:8, 10
17 [a]Judg. 5:4 [b]Ps. 68:33 [c]Ps. 18:14
18 [a]Ps. 18:13; 104:7 [b]Ps. 97:4 [c]Judg. 5:4
19 [a]Is. 51:10; Hab. 3:15
20 [a]Ex. 13:21; 14:19; Ps. 78:52; 80:1; Is. 63:11-13
1 [1]Or, *law, teaching* [a]Is. 51:4 [b]Is. 55:3
2 [a]Ps. 49:4; Matt. 13:35 [b]Prov. 1:6
4 [a]Ex. 12:26; Deut. 11:19; Job 15:18; Ps. 145:4; Is. 38:19; Joel 1:3 [b]Ps. 22:30 [c]Job 37:16; Ps. 26:7
5 [a]Ps. 19:7; 81:5; Is. 8:20 [b]Ps. 147:19 [c]Deut. 6:4-9 [d]Deut. 4:9
7 [a]Deut. 4:9; 6:12; 8:14 [b]Deut. 4:2; 5:1, 29; 27:1
8 [1]Or, *put right* [a]2 Chr. 30:7 [b]Deut. 9:7, 24; 31:27; Judg. 2:19; Is. 30:9 [c]Job 11:13; Ps. 78:37 [d]Ps. 51:10
9 [a]1 Chr. 12:2 [b]Judg. 20:39
10 [a]Judg. 2:20; 2 Kin. 18:12 [b]Ps. 119:1; Jer. 32:23; 44:10, 23
11 [1]Or, *wonderful works* [a]Ps. 106:13
12 [a]Ex. 7:12; Ps. 106:22 [b]Num. 13:22; Ps. 78:43; Is. 19:11; 30:4; Ezek. 30:14
13 [a]Ex. 14:21; Ps. 74:13; 136:13 [b]Ex. 15:8; Ps. 33:7
14 [a]Ex. 13:21; Ps. 105:39 [b]Ex. 14:24
15 [a]Ex. 17:6; Ps. 105:41; 114:8; Is. 48:21; 1 Cor. 10:4
16 [a]Num. 20:8, 10, 11
17 [a]Deut. 9:22; Is. 63:10
18 [a]Ex. 17:6; Deut. 6:16; Ps. 78:41, 56; 95:9; 106:14; 1 Cor. 10:9 [b]Num. 11:4
19 [a]Ex. 16:3; Num. 11:4; 20:3
20 [a]Ps. 78:15, 16

Will He provide [b]meat for His people?"

21 Therefore the LORD heard and was [a]full of wrath,
And a fire was kindled against Jacob,
And anger also mounted against Israel;
22 Because they [a]did not believe in God,
And did not trust in His salvation.
23 Yet He commanded the clouds above,
And [a]opened the doors of heaven;
24 And He [a]rained down manna upon them to eat,
And gave them [1b]food from heaven.
25 Man did eat the bread of [1]angels;
He sent them [2]food [a]in abundance.
26 He [a]caused the east wind to blow in the heavens;
And by His [1]power He directed the south wind.
27 When He rained [1]meat upon them like the dust,
Even [a]winged fowl like the sand of the seas;
28 Then He let *them* fall in the midst of [1]their camp,
Round about their dwellings.
29 So they [a]ate and were well filled;
And their desire He gave to them.
30 Before they had satisfied their desire,
While their food was in their mouths,
31 The [a]anger of God rose against them,
And killed [1]some of their [b]stoutest ones,
And subdued the choice men of Israel.
32 In spite of all this they [a]still sinned,
And [b]did not believe in His wonderful works.
33 So He brought [a]their days to an end in [1]futility,
And their years in sudden terror.

34 When He killed them, then they [a]sought Him,
And returned and searched [b]diligently for God;
35 And they remembered that God was their [a]rock,
And the Most High God their [b]redeemer.

20 [b]Num. 11:18
21 [a]Num. 11:1
22 [a]Deut. 1:32; 9:23; Heb. 3:18
23 [a]Gen. 7:11; Mal. 3:10
24 [1]Lit., *grain* [a]Ex. 16:4 [b]Ps. 105:40; John 6:31
25 [1]Lit., *mighty ones* [2]Or, *provision* [a]Ex. 16:3
26 [1]Or, *strength* [a]Num. 11:31
27 [1]Lit., *flesh* [a]Ex. 16:13; Ps. 105:40
28 [1]Lit., *His*
29 [a]Num. 11:19, 20
31 [1]Lit., *among their fat ones* [a]Num. 11:33, 34; Job 20:23 [b]Is. 10:16
32 [a]Num. 14:16, 17 [b]Num. 14:11; Ps. 78:11
33 [1]Lit., *vanity, a mere breath* [a]Num. 14:29, 35
34 [a]Num. 21:7; Hos. 5:15 [b]Ps. 63:1
35 [a]Deut. 32:4 [b]Ex. 15:13; Deut. 9:26; Ps. 74:2
36 [a]Ex. 24:7, 8; Ezek. 33:31 [b]Ex. 32:7, 8; Is. 57:11
37 [a]Ps. 51:10; 78:8
38 [1]Lit., *turned away* [a]Ex. 34:6 [b]Num. 14:20
39 [1]Or, *breath* [a]Job 10:9; Ps. 103:14 [b]Gen. 6:3 [c]Job 7:7; Ps. 103:14; James 4:14
40 [a]Ps. 106:43; 107:11 [b]Ps. 95:10; Is. 63:10; Eph. 4:30 [c]Ps. 106:14
41 [a]Num. 14:22 [b]2 Kin. 19:22; Ps. 89:18
42 [1]Lit., *hand* [a]Judg. 8:34 [b]Ps. 44:3 [c]Ps. 106:10
43 [a]Ps. 105:27 [b]Ex. 4:21; 7:3
44 [a]Ps. 105:29
45 [a]Ex. 8:24; Ps. 105:31 [b]Ex. 8:6; Ps. 105:30
46 [a]1 Kin. 8:37; Ps. 105:34 [b]Ex. 10:14
47 [1]Lit., *was killing* [a]Ex. 9:23; Ps. 105:32
48 [a]Ex. 9:19
49 [a]Ex. 15:7
50 [a]Job 27:22 [b]Ex. 12:29, 30

36 But they [a]deceived Him with their mouth,
And [b]lied to Him with their tongue.
37 For their heart was not [a]steadfast toward Him,
Nor were they faithful in His covenant.
38 But He, being [a]compassionate, [b]forgave *their* iniquity, and did not destroy *them;*
And often He [1]restrained His anger,
And did not arouse all His wrath.
39 Thus [a]He remembered that they were but [b]flesh,
A [1c]wind that passes and does not return.

40 How often they [a]rebelled against Him in the wilderness,
And [b]grieved Him in the [c]desert!
41 And again and again they [a]tempted God,
And pained the [b]Holy One of Israel.
42 They [a]did not remember [b]His [1]power,
The day when He [c]redeemed them from the adversary,
43 When He performed His [a]signs in Egypt,
And His [b]marvels in the field of Zoan,
44 And [a]turned their rivers to blood,
And their streams, they could not drink.
45 He sent among them swarms of [a]flies, which devoured them,
And [b]frogs which destroyed them.
46 He gave also their crops to the [a]grasshopper,
And the product of their labor to the [b]locust.
47 He [1]destroyed their vines with [a]hailstones,
And their sycamore trees with frost.
48 He gave over their [a]cattle also to the hailstones,
And their herds to bolts of lightning.
49 He [a]sent upon them His burning anger,
Fury, and indignation, and trouble,
A band of destroying angels.
50 He leveled a path for His anger;
He [a]did not spare their soul from death,
But [b]gave over their life to the plague,

51 And [a]smote all the first-born in Egypt,
The [b]first *issue* of their virility in the tents of [c]Ham.
52 But He [a]led forth His own people like sheep,
And guided them in the wilderness [b]like a flock;
53 And He led them [a]safely, so that they did not fear;
But [b]the sea engulfed their enemies.

54 So [a]He brought them to His holy land,
To this [b]hill country which His right hand had gained.
55 He also [a]drove out the nations before them,
And He [b]apportioned them for an inheritance by measurement,
And made the tribes of Israel dwell in their tents.
56 Yet they [a]tempted and [b]rebelled against the Most High God,
And did not keep His testimonies,
57 But turned back and [a]acted treacherously like their fathers;
They turned aside like a treacherous bow.
58 For they [a]provoked Him with their [b]high places,
And [c]aroused His jealousy with their [d]graven images.
59 When God heard, He was filled with [a]wrath,
And greatly [b]abhorred Israel;
60 So that He [a]abandoned the dwelling place at Shiloh,
The tent [1]which He had pitched among men;
61 And gave up His [a]strength to captivity,
And His glory [b]into the hand of the adversary.
62 He also [a]delivered His people to the sword,
And was filled with wrath at His inheritance.
63 [a]Fire devoured [1]His young men;
And [1]His [b]virgins had no wedding songs.
64 [1]His [a]priests fell by the sword;
And [1]His [b]widows could not weep.

65 Then the Lord [a]awoke as *if from* sleep,
Like a [b]warrior overcome by wine.
66 And He [1a]drove His adversaries backward;
He put on them an everlasting reproach.
67 He also [a]rejected the tent of Joseph,
And did not choose the tribe of Ephraim,
68 But chose the tribe of Judah,
Mount [a]Zion which He loved.
69 And He [a]built His sanctuary like the heights,
Like the earth which He has founded forever.
70 He also [a]chose David His servant,
And took him from the sheepfolds;
71 From [a]the care of the ewes [b]with suckling lambs He brought him,
To [c]shepherd Jacob His people,
And Israel [d]His inheritance.
72 So he shepherded them according to the [a]integrity of his heart,
And guided them with his skillful hands.

Psalm 79

A Lament over the Destruction of Jerusalem, and Prayer for Help.

A Psalm of Asaph.

O GOD, the [a]nations have invaded [b]Thine inheritance;
They have defiled Thy [c]holy temple;
They have [d]laid Jerusalem in ruins.
2 They have given the [a]dead bodies of Thy servants for food to the birds of the heavens,
The flesh of Thy godly ones to the beasts of the earth.
3 They have poured out their blood like water round about Jerusalem;
And there was [a]no one to bury them.
4 We have become a [a]reproach to our neighbors,
A scoffing and derision to those around us.
5 [a]How long, O LORD? Wilt Thou be angry forever?
Will Thy [b]jealousy [c]burn like fire?
6 [a]Pour out Thy wrath upon the nations which [b]do not know Thee,
And upon the kingdoms which [c]do not call upon Thy name.
7 For they have [a]devoured Jacob,
And [b]laid waste his [1]habitation.

51 [a]Ps. 105:36; 135:8; 136:10 [b]Gen. 49:3 [c]Ps. 105:23, 27; 106:22
52 [a]Ex. 15:22 [b]Ps. 77:20
53 [a]Ex. 14:19, 20 [b]Ex. 14:27, 28
54 [a]Ex. 15:17 [b]Ps. 68:16; Is. 11:9
55 [a]Ps. 44:2 [b]Josh. 23:4; Ps. 105:11; 135:12
56 [a]Ps. 78:18 [b]Ps. 78:40
57 [a]Ezek. 20:28
58 [a]Deut. 4:25; 1 Kin. 14:9; Is. 65:3 [b]Lev. 26:30; 1 Kin. 3:2; 2 Kin. 16:4; Jer. 17:3 [c]Deut. 32:16, 21; 1 Kin. 14:22 [d]Ex. 20:4; Lev. 26:1
59 [a]Deut. 1:34; 9:19; Ps. 106:40 [b]Lev. 26:30; Deut. 32:19; Amos 6:8
60 [1]Or, *where He dwelt* [a]1 Sam. 4:11; Ps. 78:67; Jer. 7:12
61 [a]Ps. 63:2; 132:8 [b]1 Sam. 4:17
62 [a]Judg. 20:21; 1 Sam. 4:10
63 [1]Or, *their* [a]Num. 11:1; 21:28; Is. 26:11; Jer. 48:45 [b]Jer. 7:34; 16:9
64 [1]Or, *their* [a]1 Sam. 4:17; 22:18 [b]Job 27:15; Ezek. 24:23
65 [a]Ps. 44:23; 73:20 [b]Is. 42:13
66 [1]Lit., *smote* [a]1 Sam. 5:6
67 [a]Ps. 78:60
68 [a]Ps. 87:2
69 [a]1 Kin. 6:1-38
70 [a]1 Sam. 16:12
71 [a]2 Sam. 7:8 [b]Gen. 33:13 [c]2 Sam. 5:2; 1 Chr. 11:2; Ps. 28:9 [d]1 Sam. 10:1
72 [a]1 Kin. 9:4
1 [a]Lam. 1:10 [b]Ps. 74:2 [c]Ps. 74:3, 7 [d]2 Kin. 25:9, 10; Jer. 26:18
2 [a]Deut. 28:26; Jer. 7:33; 16:4
3 [a]Jer. 14:16
4 [a]Ps. 44:13; 80:6; Dan. 9:16
5 [a]Ps. 13:1; 89:46 [b]Deut. 29:20; Ezek. 36:5; 38:19 [c]Ps. 89:46
6 [a]Ps. 69:24; Ezek. 21:31; Zeph. 3:8 [b]1 Thess. 4:5; 2 Thess. 1:8 [c]Ps. 14:4; 53:4
7 [1]Lit., *pasture* [a]Ps. 53:4 [b]2 Chr. 36:19; Jer. 39:8

8 [a]Do not remember the iniquities of *our* forefathers against us;
Let Thy compassion come quickly to [b]meet us;
For we are [c]brought very low.
9 [a]Help us, O God of our salvation, for the glory of [b]Thy name;
And deliver us, and [c]forgive our sins, for Thy name's sake.
10 [a]Why should the nations say, "Where is their God?"
Let there be known among the nations in our sight,
[b]Vengeance for the blood of Thy servants, which has been shed.
11 Let [a]the groaning of the prisoner come before Thee;
According to the greatness of Thy [1]power preserve those who are [a]doomed to die.
12 And return to our neighbors [a]sevenfold [b]into their bosom
The [c]reproach with which they have reproached Thee, O Lord.
13 So we Thy people and the [a]sheep of Thy pasture
Will [b]give thanks to Thee forever;
To all generations we will [c]tell of Thy praise.

Psalm 80

God Implored to Rescue His People from Their Calamities.

For the choir director; *set to*
[£]El Shoshannim; [•]Eduth.
A Psalm of Asaph.

Oh give ear, [a]Shepherd of Israel,
Thou who dost lead [b]Joseph like a flock;
Thou who [c]art enthroned *above* the cherubim, shine forth!
2 Before [a]Ephraim and Benjamin and Manasseh, [b]stir up Thy power,
And come to save us!
3 O God, [a]restore us,
And [b]cause Thy face to shine *upon us,* [1]and we will be saved.

4 O [a]Lord God *of* hosts,
[b]How long wilt Thou be angry with the prayer of Thy people?
5 Thou hast fed them with the [a]bread of tears,
And Thou hast made them to drink tears in large measure.
6 Thou dost make us [1]an object of contention [a]to our neighbors;
And our enemies laugh among themselves.
7 O God *of* hosts, restore us,
And cause Thy face to shine *upon us,* and we will be saved.

8 Thou didst remove a [a]vine from Egypt;
Thou didst [b]drive out the [1]nations, and didst [c]plant it.
9 Thou didst [a]clear *the ground* before it,
And it [b]took deep root and filled the land.
10 The mountains were covered with its shadow;
And the cedars of God with its [a]boughs.
11 It was sending out its branches [a]to the sea,
And its shoots to the River.
12 Why hast Thou [a]broken down its [1]hedges,
So that all who pass *that* way [b]pick its *fruit?*
13 A boar from the forest [a]eats it away,
And whatever moves in the field feeds on it.

14 O God *of* hosts, [a]turn again now, we beseech Thee;
[b]Look down from heaven and see, and take care of this vine,
15 Even the [1a]shoot which Thy right hand has planted,
And on the [2]son whom Thou hast strengthened for Thyself.
16 It is [a]burned with fire, it is cut down;
They perish at the [b]rebuke of Thy countenance.
17 Let [a]Thy hand be upon the man of Thy right hand,
Upon the son of man whom Thou [b]didst make strong for Thyself.
18 Then we shall not [a]turn back from Thee;
[b]Revive us, and we will call upon Thy name.
19 O Lord God *of* hosts, [a]restore us;
Cause Thy face to shine *upon us,* and we will be saved.

8 [a]Ps. 106:6; Is. 64:9 [b]Ps. 21:3 [c]Deut. 28:43; Ps. 116:6; 142:6; Is. 26:5
9 [a]2 Chr. 14:11 [b]Ps. 31:3 [c]Ps. 25:11; 65:3
10 [a]Ps. 115:2 [b]Ps. 94:1, 2
11 [1]Lit., *arm* [a]Ps. 102:20
12 [a]Gen. 4:15; Lev. 26:21, 28; Ps. 12:6; 119:164; Prov. 6:31; 24:16; Is. 30:26 [b]Ps. 35:13; Is. 65:6, 7; Jer. 32:18; Luke 6:38 [c]Ps. 74:10, 22
13 [a]Ps. 74:1; 95:7; 100:3 [b]Ps. 44:8 [c]Ps. 89:1; Is. 43:21
£ Possibly, *to the Lilies*
• Lit., *A testimony*
1 [a]Ps. 23:1 [b]Ps. 77:15; 78:67; Amos 5:15 [c]Ex. 25:22; 1 Sam. 4:4; 2 Sam. 6:2; Ps. 99:1
2 [a]Num. 2:18-24 [b]Ps. 35:23
3 [1]Or, *that we may,* also vs. 7, 19 [a]Ps. 60:1; 80:7, 19; 85:4; 126:1; Lam. 5:21 [b]Num. 6:25; Ps. 31:16
4 [a]Ps. 59:5; 84:8 [b]Ps. 79:5; 85:5
5 [a]Ps. 42:3; 102:9
6 [1]Lit., *a strife to* [a]Ps. 44:13; 79:4
8 [1]Or, *Gentiles* [a]Ps. 80:15; Is. 5:2, 7; Jer. 2:21; 12:10; Ezek. 17:6; 19:10 [b]Josh. 13:6; 2 Chr. 20:7; Ps. 44:2; Acts 7:45 [c]Jer. 11:17; 32:41; Ezek. 17:23; Amos 9:15
9 [a]Ex. 23:28; Josh. 24:12; Is. 5:2 [b]Hos. 14:5
10 [a]Gen. 49:22
11 [a]Ps. 72:8
12 [1]Or, *walls, fences* [a]Ps. 89:40; Is. 5:5 [b]Deut. 28:63
13 [a]Jer. 5:6
14 [a]Ps. 90:13 [b]Ps. 102:19; Is. 63:15
15 [1]Or, *root* [2]Or, *branch* [a]Ps. 80:8
16 [a]2 Chr. 36:19; Ps. 74:8; Jer. 52:13 [b]Ps. 39:11; 76:6
17 [a]Ps. 89:21 [b]Ps. 80:15
18 [a]Is. 50:5 [b]Ps. 71:20
19 [a]Ps. 80:3

PSALM 81

God's Goodness and Israel's Waywardness.

For the choir director; [£]on the Gittith.
A Psalm of Asaph.

[a]SING for joy to God our [b]strength;
Shout [c]joyfully to the [d]God of Jacob.
2 Raise a song, strike [a]the timbrel,
The sweet sounding [b]lyre with the [c]harp.
3 Blow the trumpet at the [a]new moon,
At the full moon, on our [b]feast day.
4 For it is a statute for Israel,
An ordinance of the God of Jacob.
5 He established it for a testimony in Joseph,
When he [a]went throughout the land of Egypt.
I heard a [b]language that I did not know:

6"I [a]relieved his shoulder of the burden,
His hands were freed from the [1]basket.
7"You [a]called in trouble, and I rescued you;
I [b]answered you in the hiding place of thunder;
I proved you at the [c]waters of Meribah. [Selah.
8"[a]Hear, O My people, and I will admonish you;
O Israel, if you [b]would listen to Me!
9"Let there be no [a]strange god among you;
Nor shall you worship any foreign god.
10"[a]I, the LORD, am your God,
Who brought you up from the land of Egypt;
[b]Open your mouth wide and I will [c]fill it.

11"But My people [a]did not listen to My voice;
And Israel did not obey Me.
12"So I [a]gave them over to the stubbornness of their heart,
To walk in their own devices.
13"Oh that My people [a]would listen to Me,
That Israel would [b]walk in My ways!
14"I would quickly [a]subdue their enemies,
And [b]turn My hand against their adversaries.

[£] Or, *according to*
1 [a]Ps. 51:14; 59:16; 95:1 [b]Ps. 46:1 [c]Ps. 66:1; 95:2; 98:4 [d]Ps. 84:8
2 [a]Ex. 15:20; Ps. 149:3 [b]Ps. 92:3; 98:5; 147:7 [c]Ps. 108:2; 144:9
3 [a]Num. 10:10 [b]Lev. 23:24
5 [a]Ex. 11:4 [b]Deut. 28:49; Ps. 114:1; Jer. 5:15
6 [1]Or, *brick load* [a]Is. 9:4; 10:27
7 [a]Ex. 2:23; 14:10; Ps. 50:15 [b]Ex. 19:19; 20:18 [c]Ex. 17:6, 7; Ps. 95:8
8 [a]Ps. 50:7 [b]Ps. 95:7
9 [a]Ex. 20:3; Deut. 32:12; Ps. 44:20; Is. 43:12
10 [a]Ex. 20:2 [b]Job 29:23 [c]Ps. 37:4; 78:25; 107:9
11 [a]Ps. 106:25
12 [a]Job 8:4; Acts 7:42; Rom. 1:24, 26
13 [a]Deut. 5:29; Ps. 81:8; Is. 48:18 [b]Ps. 128:1; Is. 42:24; Jer. 7:23
14 [a]Ps. 18:47; 47:3 [b]Amos 1:8
15 [a]Ps. 18:44; 66:3
16 [a]Deut. 32:14; Ps. 147:14 [b]Deut. 32:13

1 [a]Is. 3:13 [b]Ps. 58:11 [c]Ex. 21:6; 22:8, 28
2 [a]Ps. 58:1 [b]Deut. 1:17; Prov. 18:5
3 [a]Deut. 24:17; Ps. 10:18; Is. 11:4; Jer. 22:16
4 [a]Job 29:12
5 [a]Ps. 14:4; Jer. 4:22; Mic. 3:1 [b]Prov. 2:13; Is. 59:9; Jer. 23:12 [c]Ps. 11:3
6 [a]Ps. 82:1; John 10:34 [b]Ps. 89:26
7 [a]Job 21:32; Ps. 49:12; Ezek. 31:14 [b]Ps. 83:11
8 [a]Ps. 12:5 [b]Ps. 58:11; 96:13 [c]Ps. 2:8; Rev. 11:15

1 [a]Ps. 28:1; 35:22 [b]Ps. 109:1
2 [a]Ps. 2:1; Is. 17:12 [b]Judg. 8:28; Zech. 1:21
3 [a]Ps. 64:2; Is. 29:15 [b]Ps. 27:5; 31:20
4 [a]Esth. 3:6; Ps. 74:8; Jer. 48:2 [b]Ps. 41:5

15"Those who hate the LORD would [a]pretend obedience to Him;
And their time *of punishment* would be forever.
16"But I would feed you with the [a]finest of the wheat;
And with [b]honey from the rock I would satisfy you."

PSALM 82

Unjust Judgments Rebuked.

A Psalm of Asaph.

GOD takes His [a]stand in His own congregation;
He [b]judges in the midst of the [c]rulers.
2 How long will you [a]judge unjustly,
And [b]show partiality to the wicked? [Selah.
3 [a]Vindicate the weak and fatherless;
Do justice to the afflicted and destitute.
4 [a]Rescue the weak and needy;
Deliver *them* out of the hand of the wicked.

5 They [a]do not know nor do they understand;
They [b]walk about in darkness;
All the [c]foundations of the earth are shaken.
6 I [a]said, "You are gods,
And all of you are [b]sons of the Most High.
7"Nevertheless [a]you will die like men,
And fall like *any* [b]one of the princes."
8 [a]Arise, O God, [b]judge the earth!
For it is Thou who dost [c]possess all the nations.

PSALM 83

God Implored to Confound His Enemies.

A Song, a Psalm of Asaph.

O GOD, [a]do not remain quiet;
[b]Do not be silent, and, O God, do not be still.
2 For, behold, Thine enemies [a]make an uproar;
And those who hate Thee have [b]exalted themselves.
3 They [a]make shrewd plans against Thy people,
And conspire together against [b]Thy treasured ones.
4 They have said, "Come, and [a]let us wipe them out as a nation;
That the [b]name of Israel be remembered no more."

5 For they have [a]conspired together with one mind;
Against Thee do they make a covenant:
6 The tents of [a]Edom and the [b]Ishmaelites;
[c]Moab, and the [d]Hagrites;
7 [a]Gebal, and [b]Ammon, and [c]Amalek;
[d]Philistia with the inhabitants of [e]Tyre;
8 [a]Assyria also has joined with them;
They have become [1]a help to the [b]children of Lot. [Selah.

9 Deal with them [a]as with Midian,
As [b]with Sisera *and* Jabin, at the torrent of Kishon,
10 Who were destroyed at En-dor,
Who became as dung for the ground.
11 Make their nobles like [a]Oreb and Zeeb,
And all their princes like [b]Zebah and Zalmunna,
12 Who said, "[a]Let us possess for ourselves
The [b]pastures of God."

13 O my God, make them like the [1][a]whirling dust;
Like [b]chaff before the wind.
14 Like [a]fire that burns the forest,
And like a flame that [b]sets the mountains on fire,
15 So pursue them [a]with Thy tempest,
And terrify them with Thy storm.
16 [a]Fill their faces with dishonor,
That they may seek Thy name, O LORD.
17 Let them be [a]ashamed and dismayed forever;
And let them be humiliated and perish,
18 That they may know that [a]Thou alone, whose name is the LORD,
Art the [b]Most High over all the earth.

PSALM 84

Longing for the Temple Worship.

For the choir director; [£]on the Gittith.
A Psalm of the sons of Korah.

HOW lovely are Thy [a]dwelling places,
O LORD of hosts!
2 My [a]soul longed and even yearned for the courts of the LORD;
My heart and my flesh sing for joy to the [b]living God.
3 The bird also has found a house,
And the swallow a nest for herself, where she may lay her young,
Even Thine [a]altars, O LORD of hosts,
[b]My King and my God.
4 How [a]blessed are those who dwell in Thy house!
They are [b]ever praising Thee. [Selah.

5 How blessed is the man whose [a]strength is in Thee;
In [1]whose heart are the [b]highways *to Zion!*
6 Passing through the valley of [1]Baca, they make it a spring,
The [a]early rain also covers it with blessings.
7 They [a]go from strength to strength,
Every one of them [b]appears before God in Zion.

8 O [a]LORD God of hosts, hear my prayer;
Give ear, O [b]God of Jacob! [Selah.
9 Behold our [a]shield, O God,
And look upon the face of [b]Thine anointed.
10 For [a]a day in Thy courts is better than a thousand *outside.*
I would rather stand at the [b]threshold of the house of my God,
Than dwell in the tents of wickedness.
11 For the LORD God is [a]a sun and shield;
The LORD gives grace and [b]glory;
No [c]good thing does He withhold from those who walk uprightly.
12 O LORD of hosts,
How [a]blessed is the man who trusts in Thee!

PSALM 85

Prayer for God's Mercy upon the Nation.

For the choir director.
A Psalm of the sons of Korah.

O LORD, Thou didst show [a]favor to Thy land;
Thou didst [b]restore the captivity of Jacob.
2 Thou didst [a]forgive the iniquity of Thy people;
Thou didst [b]cover all their sin. [Selah.

83:5 [a]Ps. 2:2; Dan. 6:7
6 [a]2 Chr. 20:10; Ps. 137:7 [b]Gen. 25:12-16 [c]2 Chr. 20:10 [d]1 Chr. 5:10
7 [a]Josh. 13:5; Ezek. 27:9 [b]2 Chr. 20:10 [c]1 Sam. 15:2 [d]1 Sam. 4:1; 29:1 [e]Ezek. 27:3
8 [1]Lit., *an arm* [a]2 Kin. 15:19 [b]Deut. 2:9
9 [a]Judg. 7:22 [b]Judg. 4:22, 23
11 [a]Judg. 7:25 [b]Judg. 8:21
12 [a]2 Chr. 20:11 [b]Ps. 132:13
13 [1]Or, *tumbleweed* [a]Is. 17:13 [b]Job 21:18; Is. 40:24; Jer. 13:24
14 [a]Is. 9:18 [b]Ex. 19:18; Deut. 32:22
15 [a]Job 9:17
16 [a]Job 10:15; Ps. 109:29; 132:18
17 [a]Ps. 35:4; 70:2
18 [a]Ps. 86:10; Is. 45:21 [b]Ps. 9:2; 18:13; 97:9

[£] Or, *according to*
84:1 [a]Ps. 43:3
2 [a]Ps. 42:2; 63:1 [b]Ps. 42:2
3 [a]Ps. 43:4 [b]Ps. 5:2
4 [a]Ps. 65:4 [b]Ps. 42:5, 11
5 [1]Lit., *their* [a]Ps. 81:1 [b]Ps. 86:11; 122:1; Jer. 31:6
6 [1]Probably, *Weeping,* or *Balsam trees* [a]Ps. 107:35; Joel 2:23
7 [a]Prov. 4:18; Is. 40:31; John 1:16; 2 Cor. 3:18 [b]Ex. 34:23; Deut. 16:16; Ps. 42:2
8 [a]Ps. 59:5; 80:4; 84:1 [b]Ps. 81:1
9 [a]Gen. 15:1; Ps. 3:3; 28:7; 59:11; 115:9-11 [b]1 Sam. 16:6; 2 Sam. 19:21; Ps. 2:2; 132:17
10 [a]Ps. 27:4 [b]1 Chr. 23:5
11 [a]Is. 60:19, 20; Mal. 4:2; Rev. 21:23 [b]Ps. 85:9 [c]Ps. 34:10
12 [a]Ps. 2:12; 40:4

85:1 [a]Ps. 77:7; 106:4 [b]Ezra 1:11; Ps. 14:7; 126:1; Jer. 30:18; Ezek. 39:25; Hos. 6:11; Joel 3:1
2 [a]Num. 14:19; 1 Kin. 8:34; Ps. 78:38; 103:3; Jer. 31:34 [b]Ps. 32:1

3 Thou didst [a]withdraw all Thy fury;
Thou didst [b]turn away from Thy burning anger.

4 [a]Restore us, O God of our salvation,
And [b]cause Thine indignation toward us to cease.
5 Wilt [a]Thou be angry with us forever?
Wilt Thou prolong Thine anger to all generations?
6 Wilt Thou not Thyself [a]revive us again,
That Thy people may [b]rejoice in Thee?
7 Show us Thy lovingkindness, O LORD,
And [a]grant us Thy salvation.

8 I will hear what God the LORD will say;
For He will [a]speak peace to His people, to His godly ones;
But let them not [b]turn back to folly.
9 Surely [a]His salvation is near to those who [1]fear Him,
That [b]glory may dwell in our land.
10 [a]Lovingkindness and truth have met together;
[b]Righteousness and peace have kissed each other.
11 Truth [a]springs from the earth;
And righteousness looks down from heaven.
12 Indeed, [a]the LORD will give what is good;
And our [b]land will yield its produce.
13 [a]Righteousness will go before Him,
And will make His footsteps into a way.

PSALM 86

A Psalm of Supplication and Trust.

A Prayer of David.

[a]INCLINE Thine ear, O LORD, *and* answer me;
For I am [b]afflicted and needy.
2 [a]Do preserve my [1]soul, for I am a [b]godly man;
O Thou my God, save Thy servant who [c]trusts in Thee.
3 Be [a]gracious to me, O LORD,
For [b]to Thee I cry all day long.
4 Make glad the soul of Thy servant,
For to Thee, O Lord, [a]I lift up my soul.
5 For Thou, Lord, art [a]good, and [b]ready to forgive,
And [c]abundant in lovingkindness to all who call upon Thee.
6 [a]Give ear, O LORD, to my prayer;
And give heed to the voice of my supplications!
7 In [a]the day of my trouble I shall call upon Thee,
For [b]Thou wilt answer me.
8 There is [a]no one like Thee among the gods, O Lord;
Nor are there any works [b]like Thine.
9 [a]All nations whom Thou hast made shall come and worship before Thee, O Lord;
And they shall glorify Thy name.
10 For Thou art [a]great and [b]doest wondrous deeds;
Thou alone [c]art God.

11 [a]Teach me Thy way, O LORD;
I will walk in Thy truth;
[b]Unite my heart to fear Thy name.
12 I will [a]give thanks to Thee, O Lord my God, with all my heart,
And will glorify Thy name forever.
13 For Thy lovingkindness toward me is great,
And Thou hast [a]delivered my soul from the depths of Sheol.

14 O God, arrogant men have [a]risen up against me,
And a band of violent men have sought my life,
And they have not set Thee before them.
15 But Thou, O Lord, art a God [a]merciful and gracious,
Slow to anger and abundant in lovingkindness and truth.
16 [a]Turn to me, and be gracious to me;
Oh [b]grant Thy strength to Thy servant,
And save the [c]son of Thy handmaid.
17 [a]Show me a sign for good,
That those who hate me may [b]see *it*, and be ashamed,
Because Thou, O LORD, [c]hast helped me and comforted me.

PSALM 87

The Privileges of Citizenship in Zion.

A Psalm of the sons of Korah. A Song.

HIS [a]foundation is in the holy mountains.

---

3 [a]Ps. 78:38; 106:23 [b]Ex. 32:12; Deut. 13:17; Ps. 106:23; Jon. 3:9
4 [a]Ps. 80:3 [b]Dan. 9:16
5 [a]Ps. 74:1; 79:5; 80:4
6 [a]Ps. 71:20; 80:18 [b]Ps. 33:1; 90:14; 149:2
7 [a]Ps. 106:4
8 [a]Ps. 29:11; Hag. 2:9; Zech. 9:10 [b]Ps. 78:57; 2 Pet. 2:21
9 [1]Or, *reverence* [a]Ps. 34:18; Is. 46:13 [b]Ps. 84:11; Hag. 2:7; Zech. 2:5; John 1:14
10 [a]Ps. 25:10; 89:14; Prov. 3:3 [b]Ps. 72:3; Is. 32:17
11 [a]Is. 45:8
12 [a]Ps. 84:11; James 1:17 [b]Lev. 26:4; Ps. 67:6; Ezek. 34:27; Zech. 8:12
13 [a]Ps. 89:14

1 [a]Ps. 17:6; 31:2; 71:2 [b]Ps. 40:17; 70:5
2 [1]Or, *life* [a]Ps. 25:20 [b]Ps. 4:3; 50:5 [c]Ps. 25:2; 31:14; 56:4
3 [a]Ps. 4:1; 57:1 [b]Ps. 25:5; 88:9
4 [a]Ps. 25:1; 143:8
5 [a]Ps. 25:8 [b]Ps. 130:4 [c]Ex. 34:6; Neh. 9:17; Ps. 103:8; 145:8; Joel 2:13; Jon. 4:2
6 [a]Ps. 55:1
7 [a]Ps. 50:15; 77:2 [b]Ps. 17:6
8 [a]Ex. 15:11; 2 Sam. 7:22; 1 Kin. 8:23; Ps. 89:6; Jer. 10:6 [b]Deut. 3:24
9 [a]Ps. 22:27; 66:4; Is. 66:23; Rev. 15:4
10 [a]Ps. 77:13 [b]Ex. 15:11; Ps. 72:18; 77:14; 136:4 [c]Deut. 6:4; 32:39; Ps. 83:18; Is. 37:16; 44:6, 8; Mark 12:29; 1 Cor. 8:4
11 [a]Ps. 25:5 [b]Jer. 32:39
12 [a]Ps. 111:1
13 [a]Ps. 30:3
14 [a]Ps. 54:3
15 [a]Ps. 86:5
16 [a]Ps. 25:16 [b]Ps. 68:35 [c]Ps. 116:16
17 [a]Judg. 6:17; Ps. 119:122 [b]Ps. 112:10 [c]Ps. 118:13

1 [a]Ps. 78:69; Is. 28:16

2 The LORD [a]loves the gates of Zion
More than all the *other* dwelling places of Jacob.
3 [a]Glorious things are spoken of you,
O [b]city of God. [Selah.
4 "I shall mention [1a]Rahab and Babylon [2]among those who know Me;
Behold, Philistia and [b]Tyre with [3c]Ethiopia:
'This one was born there.' "
5 But of Zion it shall be said, "This one and that one were born in her";
And the Most High Himself will [a]establish her.
6 The LORD shall count when He [a]registers the peoples,
"This one was born there." [Selah.
7 Then those who [a]sing as well as those who [b]play the flutes *shall say,*
"All my [c]springs *of joy* are in you."

PSALM 88

A Petition to be Saved from Death.

A Song. A Psalm of the sons of Korah. For the choir director; according to Mahalath Leannoth. Maskil of Heman [£]the Ezrahite.

O LORD, the [a]God of my salvation,
I have [b]cried out by day and in the night before Thee.
2 Let my prayer [a]come before Thee;
[b]Incline Thine ear to my cry!
3 For my [a]soul has had enough troubles,
And [b]my life has drawn near to Sheol.
4 I am reckoned among those who [a]go down to the pit;
I have become like a man [b]without strength,
5 Forsaken [a]among the dead,
Like the slain who lie in the grave,
Whom Thou dost remember no more,
And they are [b]cut off from Thy hand.
6 Thou hast put me in [a]the lowest pit,
In [b]dark places, in the [c]depths.
7 Thy wrath [a]has rested upon me,
And Thou hast afflicted me with [b]all Thy waves. [Selah.
8 Thou hast removed [a]my acquaintances far from me;
Thou hast made me an [b]object of loathing to them;
I am [c]shut up and cannot go out.
9 My [a]eye has wasted away because of affliction;
I have [b]called upon Thee every day, O LORD;
I have [c]spread out my [1]hands to Thee.

10 Wilt Thou perform wonders for the dead?
Will [a]the departed spirits rise *and* praise Thee? [Selah.
11 Will Thy lovingkindness be declared in the grave,
Thy faithfulness in [1]the place of destruction?
12 Will Thy wonders be made known in the [a]darkness?
And Thy righteousness in the land of forgetfulness?

13 But I, O LORD, have cried out [a]to Thee for help,
And [b]in the morning my prayer comes before Thee.
14 O LORD, why [a]dost Thou reject my soul?
Why dost Thou [b]hide Thy face from me?
15 I was afflicted and [a]about to die from my youth on;
I suffer [b]Thy terrors; I am [1]overcome.
16 Thy [a]burning anger has passed over me;
Thy terrors have [1b]destroyed me.
17 They have [a]surrounded me [b]like water all day long;
They have [c]encompassed me altogether.
18 Thou hast removed [a]lover and friend far from me;
My acquaintances are *in* darkness.

PSALM 89

The LORD's Covenant with David, and Israel's Afflictions.

A Maskil of Ethan [£]the Ezrahite.

I WILL [a]sing of the lovingkindness of the LORD forever;
To all generations I will [b]make known Thy [c]faithfulness with my mouth.
2 For I have said, "[a]Lovingkindness will be built up forever;
In the heavens Thou wilt establish Thy [b]faithfulness."
3 "I have made a covenant with [a]My chosen;
I have [b]sworn to David My servant,

2 [a]Ps. 78:67, 68
3 [a]Is. 60:1 [b]Ps. 46:4; 48:8
4 [1]I.e., Egypt [2]Or, *as* [3]Lit., *Cush* [a]Job 9:13; Ps. 89:10; Is. 19:23-25 [b]Ps. 45:12 [c]Ps. 68:31
5 [a]Ps. 48:8
6 [a]Ps. 69:28; Is. 4:3
7 [a]Ps. 68:25; 149:3 [b]2 Sam. 6:14; Ps. 30:11 [c]Ps. 36:9

[£] 1 Kin. 4:31; 1 Chr. 2:6; Ps. 89:title
1 [a]Ps. 24:5; 27:9 [b]Ps. 22:2; 86:3; Luke 18:7
2 [a]Ps. 18:6 [b]Ps. 31:2; 86:1
3 [a]Ps. 107:26 [b]Ps. 107:18; 116:3
4 [a]Ps. 28:1; 143:7 [b]Job 29:12; Ps. 22:11
5 [a]Ps. 31:12 [b]Ps. 31:22; Is.53:8
6 [a]Ps. 86:13; Lam. 3:55 [b]Ps. 143:3 [c]Ps. 69:15
7 [a]Ps. 32:4; 39:10 [b]Ps. 42:7
8 [a]Job 19:13, 19; Ps. 31:11; 142:4 [b]Job 30:10 [c]Ps. 142:7; Jer. 32:2; 36:5
9 [1]Lit., *palms* [a]Ps. 6:7; 31:9 [b]Ps. 22:2; 86:3 [c]Job 11:13; Ps. 143:6
10 [a]Ps. 6:5; 30:9
11 [1]Lit., *Abaddon*
12 [a]Job 10:21; Ps. 88:6
13 [a]Ps. 30:2 [b]Ps. 5:3; 119:147
14 [a]Ps. 43:2; 44:9 [b]Job 13:24; Ps. 13:1; 44:24
15 [1]Or, *embarrassed* [a]Prov. 24:11 [b]Job 6:4; 31:23
16 [1]Or, *silenced* [a]2 Chr. 28:11; Is. 13:13; Lam. 1:12 [b]Lam. 3:54; Ezek. 37:11
17 [a]Ps. 118:10-12 [b]Ps. 124:4 [c]Ps. 17:11; 22:12, 16
18 [a]Job 19:13; Ps. 88:8; 31:11; 38:11

[£] Ps. 88:title
1 [a]Ps. 59:16; 101:1 [b]Ps. 40:10 [c]Ps. 36:5; 88:11; 89:5, 8, 24, 33, 49; 92:2; 119:90; Is. 25:1; Lam. 3:23
2 [a]Ps. 103:17 [b]Ps. 36:5
3 [a]1 Kin. 8:16 [b]Ps. 132:11

4 I will establish your [a]seed forever,
And build up your [b]throne to all generations." [Selah.

5 And the [a]heavens will praise Thy wonders, O LORD;
Thy faithfulness also [b]in the assembly of the [c]holy ones.
6 For [a]who in the skies is comparable to the LORD?
Who among the [b]sons of the mighty is like the LORD,
7 A God [a]greatly feared in the council of the [b]holy ones,
And [c]awesome above all those who are around Him?
8 O Lord [1]GOD of hosts, [a]who is like Thee, O mighty [2]LORD?
Thy faithfulness also surrounds Thee.
9 Thou dost rule the swelling of the sea;
When its waves rise, Thou [a]dost still them.
10 Thou Thyself didst crush [1a]Rahab like one who is slain;
Thou didst [b]scatter Thine enemies with Thy mighty arm.

11 The [a]heavens are Thine, the earth also is Thine;
The [b]world and all it contains, Thou hast founded them.
12 The [a]north and the south, Thou hast created them;
[b]Tabor and [c]Hermon shout for joy at Thy name.
13 Thou hast a strong arm;
Thy hand is mighty, Thy [a]right hand is exalted.
14 [a]Righteousness and justice are the foundation of Thy throne;
[b]Lovingkindness and truth go before Thee.
15 How blessed are the people who know the [1a]joyful sound!
O LORD, they walk in the [b]light of Thy countenance.
16 In [a]Thy name they rejoice all the day,
And by Thy righteousness they are exalted.
17 For Thou art the glory of [a]their strength,
And by Thy favor our [b]horn is exalted.
18 For our [a]shield belongs to the LORD,
And our king to the [b]Holy One of Israel.

19 Once Thou didst speak in vision to Thy godly ones,
And didst say, "I have given help to one who is [a]mighty;
I have exalted one [b]chosen from the people.
20 "I have [a]found David My servant;
With My holy [b]oil I have anointed him,
21 With whom [a]My hand will be established;
My arm also will [b]strengthen him.
22 "The enemy will not [1]deceive him,
Nor the [a]son of wickedness afflict him.
23 "But I shall [a]crush his adversaries before him,
And strike those who hate him.
24 "And My [a]faithfulness and My lovingkindness will be with him,
And in My name his horn will be exalted.
25 "I shall also set his hand [a]on the sea,
And his right hand on the rivers.
26 "He will cry to Me, 'Thou art [a]my Father,
My God, and the [b]rock of my salvation.'
27 "I also shall make him *My* [a]firstborn,
The [b]highest of the kings of the earth.
28 "My [a]lovingkindness I will keep for him forever,
And My [b]covenant shall be confirmed to him.
29 "So I will establish his [1a]descendants forever,
And his [b]throne as the days of heaven.

30 "If his sons [a]forsake My law,
And do not walk in My judgments,
31 If they violate My statutes,
And do not keep My commandments,
32 Then I will visit their transgression with the [a]rod,
And their iniquity with stripes.
33 "But I will not break off [a]My lovingkindness from him,
Nor deal falsely in My faithfulness.
34 "My [a]covenant I will not violate,
Nor will I [b]alter the utterance of My lips.
35 "[1]Once I have [a]sworn by My holiness;
I will not lie to David.
36 "His [1a]descendants shall endure forever,
And his [b]throne as the sun before Me.

4 [a]2 Sam. 7:16 [b]Is. 9:7; Luke 1:33
5 [a]Ps. 19:1; 97:6 [b]Ps. 149:1 [c]Job 5:1
6 [a]Ps. 86:8; 113:5 [b]Ps. 29:1; 82:1
7 [a]Ps. 47:2; 68:35 [b]Ps. 89:5 [c]Ps. 96:4
8 [1]YHWH, usually rendered LORD [2]Heb., *YAH* [a]Ps. 35:10; 71:19
9 [a]Ps. 65:7
10 [1]I.e., Egypt [a]Ps. 87:4; Is. 30:7; 51:9 [b]Ps. 18:14
11 [a]Gen. 1:1; 1 Chr. 29:11; Ps. 96:5 [b]Ps. 24:1
12 [a]Job 26:7 [b]Josh. 19:22; Judg. 4:6; Jer. 46:18 [c]Deut. 3:8; Josh. 11:17
13 [a]Ps. 98:1; 118:16
14 [a]Ps. 97:2 [b]Ps.85:13
15 [1]Or, *blast of the trumpet, shout of joy* [a]Lev. 23:24; Num. 10:10; Ps. 98:6 [b]Ps. 4:6; 44:3; 67:1; 80:3; 90:8
16 [a]Ps. 105:3
17 [a]Ps. 28:8 [b]Ps. 75:10; 92:10
18 [a]Ps. 47:9 [b]Ps. 71:22; 78:41
19 [a]2 Sam. 17:10 [b]1 Kin. 11:34
20 [a]Acts 13:22 [b]1 Sam. 16:13
21 [a]Ps. 18:35; 80:17 [b]Ps. 18:32
22 [1]Or, *exact usury from him* [a]2 Sam. 7:10
23 [a]2 Sam. 7:9
24 [a]Ps. 89:1
25 [a]Ps. 72:8
26 [a]2 Sam. 7:14; 1 Chr. 22:10; Jer. 3:19 [b]2 Sam. 22:47; Ps. 95:1
27 [a]Ex. 4:22; Ps. 2:7; Jer. 31:9; Col. 1:15, 18 [b]Num. 24:7; Ps. 72:11; Rev. 19:16
28 [a]Ps. 89:33 [b]Ps. 89:3, 34
29 [1]Lit., *seed* [a]Ps. 18:50; 89:4, 36 [b]1 Kin. 2:4; Ps. 89:4; 132:12; Is. 9:7; Jer. 33:17
30 [a]2 Sam. 7:14
32 [a]Job 9:34
33 [a]2 Sam. 7:15
34 [a]Deut. 7:9; Jer. 33:20, 21 [b]Num. 23:19
35 [1]Or, *One thing* [a]Ps. 60:6; Amos 4:2
36 [1]Lit., *seed* [a]Ps. 89:29 [b]Ps. 72:5

37 "It shall be established forever
[a]like the moon,
And the [b]witness in the sky is
faithful." [Selah.

38 But Thou hast [a]cast off and rejected,
Thou hast been full of wrath
against Thine [b]anointed.
39 Thou hast [a]spurned the covenant of Thy servant;
Thou hast [b]profaned [c]his crown
in the dust.
40 Thou hast [a]broken down all his
walls;
Thou hast [b]brought his strongholds to ruin.
41 [a]All who pass along the way
plunder him;
He has become a [b]reproach to
his neighbors.
42 Thou hast [a]exalted the right
hand of his adversaries;
Thou hast [b]made all his enemies rejoice.
43 Thou dost also turn back the
edge of his sword,
And hast [a]not made him stand
in battle.
44 Thou hast made his [a]splendor
to cease,
And cast his throne to the
ground.
45 Thou hast [a]shortened the days
of his youth;
Thou hast [b]covered him with
shame. [Selah.

46 [a]How long, O LORD?
Wilt Thou hide Thyself forever?
Will Thy [b]wrath burn like fire?
47 [a]Remember [1]what my span of
life is;
For what [b]vanity [2]Thou hast
created all the sons of men!
48 What man can live and not [a]see
death?
Can he [b]deliver his soul from
the power of Sheol? [Selah.

49 Where are Thy former lovingkindnesses, O Lord,
Which Thou didst [a]swear to
David in Thy faithfulness?
50 Remember, O Lord, the [a]reproach of Thy servants;
How I do bear in my bosom *the
reproach of* all the many peoples,
51 With which [a]Thine enemies
have reproached, O LORD,
With which they have reproached the footsteps of
[b]Thine anointed.

52 [a]Blessed be the LORD forever!
Amen and Amen.

BOOK 4

PSALM 90

God's Eternity and Man's Transitoriness.

A Prayer of [£]Moses the man of God.

LORD, Thou hast been our
[1a]dwelling place in all generations.
2 Before [a]the mountains were
born,
Or Thou [b]didst give birth to the
earth and the world,
Even [c]from everlasting to everlasting, Thou art God.

3 Thou dost [a]turn man back into
dust,
And dost say, "Return, O children of men."
4 For [a]a thousand years in Thy
sight
Are like [b]yesterday when it
passes by,
[1]Or *as* a [c]watch in the night.
5 Thou [a]hast swept them away
like a flood, they [b]fall asleep;
In the morning they are like
[c]grass which [1]sprouts anew.
6 In the morning it [a]flourishes,
and sprouts anew;
Towards evening it [b]fades, and
[c]withers away.

7 For we have been [a]consumed
by Thine anger,
And by Thy wrath we have
been dismayed.
8 Thou hast [a]placed our iniquities
before Thee,
Our [b]secret *sins* in the light of
Thy presence.
9 For [a]all our days have declined
in Thy fury;
We have finished our years like
a sigh.
10 As for the days of our life, they
contain seventy years,
Or if due to strength, [a]eighty
years,
Yet their pride is *but* [b]labor and
sorrow;
For soon it is gone and we [c]fly
away.
11 Who understands the [a]power of
Thine anger,
And Thy fury, according to the
[b]fear that is due Thee?
12 So [a]teach us to number our
days,
That we may [b]present to Thee a
heart of wisdom.

37 [a]Ps. 72:5 [b]Job 16:19
38 [a]Ps. 44:9 [b]Ps. 20:6; 89:20, 51
39 [a]Ps. 78:59; Lam. 2:7 [b]Ps. 74:7 [c]Lam. 5:16
40 [a]Ps. 80:12 [b]Lam. 2:2, 5
41 [a]Ps. 80:12 [b]Ps. 44:13; 69:9, 19; 79:4
42 [a]Ps. 13:2 [b]Ps. 80:6
43 [a]Ps. 44:10
44 [a]Ezek. 28:7
45 [a]Ps. 102:23 [b]Ps. 44:15; 71:13; 109:29
46 [a]Ps. 13:1; 44:24 [b]Ps. 79:5; 80:4
47 [1]Lit., *of what duration I am* [2]Or, *hast Thou . . . men?* [a]Job 7:7; 10:9; 14:1 [b]Ps. 39:5; 62:9; Eccles. 1:2; 2:11
48 [a]Ps. 22:29; 49:9 [b]Ps. 49:15
49 [a]Jer. 30:9; Ezek. 34:23
50 [a]Ps. 69:9; 74:18, 22
51 [a]Ps. 74:10 [b]Ps. 89:38
52 [a]Ps. 41:13; 72:19; 106:48
[£] Deut. 33:1
1 [1]Or, *place of refuge* [a]Deut. 33:27; Ps. 71:3; 91:1; Ezek. 11:16
2 [a]Job 15:7; Prov. 8:25 [b]Gen. 1:1; Ps. 102:25; 104:5 [c]Ps. 93:2; 102:24, 27; Jer. 10:10
3 [a]Gen. 3:19; Job 34:14, 15; Ps. 104:29
4 [1]Or, *And* [a]2 Pet. 3:8 [b]Ps. 39:5 [c]Ex. 14:24; Judg. 7:19
5 [1]Or, *passes away* [a]Job 22:16; 27:20 [b]Job 14:12; 20:8; Ps. 76:5 [c]Ps. 103:15; Is. 40:6
6 [a]Job 14:2 [b]Ps. 92:7; Matt. 6:30 [c]James 1:11
7 [a]Ps. 39:11
8 [a]Ps. 50:21; Jer. 16:17 [b]Ps. 19:12; Eccles. 12:14
9 [a]Ps. 78:33
10 [a]2 Kin. 19:35 [b]Eccles. 12:2-7; Jer. 20:18 [c]Job 20:8; Ps. 78:39
11 [a]Ps. 76:7 [b]Neh. 5:9
12 [a]Deut. 32:29; Ps. 39:4 [b]Prov. 2:1-6

13 Do [a]return, O LORD; [b]how long *will it be?*
And be [c]sorry for Thy servants.
14 O [a]satisfy us in the morning with Thy lovingkindness,
That we may [b]sing for joy and be glad all our days.
15 [a]Make us glad according to the days Thou hast afflicted us,
And the [b]years we have seen evil.
16 Let Thy [a]work appear to Thy servants,
And Thy [b]majesty to their children.
17 And let the [a]favor of the Lord our God be upon us;
And do [b]confirm for us the work of our hands;
Yes, confirm the work of our hands.

PSALM 91

Security of the One Who Trusts in the LORD.

HE who dwells in the [a]shelter of the Most High
Will abide in the [b]shadow of the Almighty.
2 I will say to the LORD, "My [a]refuge and my [b]fortress,
My God, in whom I [c]trust!"
3 For it is He who delivers you from the [a]snare of the trapper,
And from the deadly [b]pestilence.
4 He will [a]cover you with His pinions,
And [b]under His wings you may seek refuge;
His [c]faithfulness is a [d]shield and bulwark.

5 You [a]will not be afraid of the [b]terror by night,
Or of the [c]arrow that flies by day;
6 Of the [a]pestilence that stalks in darkness,
Or of the [b]destruction that lays waste at noon.
7 A thousand may fall at your side,
And ten thousand at your right hand;
But [a]it shall not approach you.
8 You will only look on with your eyes,
And [a]see the recompense of the wicked.
9 For you have made the LORD, my refuge,
Even the Most High, your dwelling place.
10 [a]No evil will befall you,
Nor will any plague come near your [1]tent.

11 For He will give [a]His angels charge concerning you,
To guard you in all your ways.
12 They will bear you up in their hands,
Lest you strike your foot against a stone.
13 You will [a]tread upon the lion and cobra,
The young lion and the serpent you will trample down.

14 "[a]Because he has loved Me, therefore I will deliver him;
I will [b]set him *securely* on high, because he has [c]known My name.
15 "He will [a]call upon Me, and I will answer him;
I will be with him in trouble;
I will rescue him, and [b]honor him.
16 "With a [a]long life I will satisfy him,
And [b]let him behold My salvation."

PSALM 92

Praise for the LORD's Goodness.

A Psalm, a Song for the Sabbath day.

IT is [a]good to give thanks to the LORD,
And to [b]sing praises to Thy name, O Most High;
2 To [a]declare Thy lovingkindness in the morning,
And Thy [b]faithfulness by night,
3 [1]With the [a]ten-stringed lute, and [1]with the [a]harp;
[1]With resounding music upon the [a]lyre.
4 For Thou, O LORD, hast made me glad by [1]what Thou [a]hast done,
I will [b]sing for joy at the [c]works of Thy hands.

5 How [a]great are Thy works, O LORD!
Thy [b]thoughts are very [c]deep.
6 A [a]senseless man has no knowledge;
Nor does a [a]stupid man understand this:
7 That when the wicked [a]sprouted up like grass,
And all [b]who did iniquity flourished,
It *was only* that they might be [c]destroyed forevermore.

---

13 [a]Ps. 6:4; 80:14 [b]Ps. 6:3; 74:10 [c]Ex. 32:12; Deut. 32:36; Ps. 106:45; 135:14; Amos 7:3, 6; Jon. 3:9
14 [a]Ps. 36:8; 65:4; 103:5; Jer. 31:14 [b]Ps. 31:7
15 [a]Ps. 86:4; [b]Deut. 2:14-16; Ps. 31:10
16 [a]Deut. 32:4; Ps. 44:1; 77:12; 92:4; Hab. 3:2 [b]1 Kin. 8:11; Is. 6:3
17 [a]Ps. 27:4 [b]Ps. 37:23; Is. 26:12; 1 Cor. 3:7

1 [a]Ps. 27:5; 31:20; 32:7 [b]Ps. 17:8; 121:5; Is. 25:4; 32:2
2 [a]Ps. 14:6; 91:9; 94:22 [b]Ps. 18:2; 31:3; Jer. 16:19 [c]Ps. 25:2
3 [a]Ps. 124:7; Prov. 6:5 [b]1 Kin. 8:37; 2 Chr. 20:9; Ps. 91:6
4 [a]Is. 51:16 [b]Ps. 36:7; 57:1; 63:7 [c]Ps. 40:11 [d]Ps. 35:2
5 [a]Job 5:19-23; Ps. 23:4; 27:1 [b]Song of Sol. 3:8 [c]Ps. 64:4
6 [a]2 Kin. 19:35; Ps. 91:10 [b]Job 5:22
7 [a]Gen. 7:23; Josh. 14:10
8 [a]Ps. 37:34; 58:10
10 [1]Or, *dwelling* [a]Prov. 12:21
11 [a]Ps. 34:7; Matt. 4:6; Luke 4:10, 11
13 [a]Judg. 14:6; Dan. 6:22; Luke 10:19
14 [a]Ps. 145:20 [b]Ps. 59:1 [c]Ps. 9:10
15 [a]Job 12:4; Ps. 50:15 [b]1 Sam. 2:30; John 12:26
16 [a]Deut. 6:2; Ps. 21:4 [b]Ps. 50:23

1 [a]Ps. 147:1 [b]Ps. 135:3
2 [a]Ps. 59:16 [b]Ps. 89:1
3 [1]Lit., *Upon* [a]1 Sam. 10:5; 1 Chr. 13:8; Neh. 12:27; Ps. 33:2
4 [1]Lit., *Thy working* [a]Ps. 40:5; 90:16 [b]Ps. 106:47 [c]Ps. 8:6; 111:7; 143:5
5 [a]Ps. 40:5; 111:2; Rev. 15:3 [b]Ps. 33:11; 40:5; 139:17 [c]Ps. 36:6; Rom. 11:33
6 [a]Ps. 49:10
7 [a]Ps. 90:5 [b]Ps. 94:4 [c]Ps. 37:38

8 But Thou, O LORD, art [a]on high
forever.
9 For, behold, Thine enemies, O
LORD,
For, behold, [a]Thine enemies
will perish;
All who do iniquity will be
[b]scattered.

10 But Thou hast exalted my [a]horn
like *that of* the wild ox;
I have been [b]anointed with
fresh oil.
11 And my eye has [a]looked *exul-
tantly* upon my foes,
My ears hear of the evildoers
who rise up against me.
12 The [a]righteous man will flourish like the palm tree,
He will grow like a [b]cedar in
Lebanon.
13 [a]Planted in the house of the
LORD,
They will flourish [b]in the courts
of our God.
14 They will still [1a]yield fruit in old
age;
They shall be [2]full of sap and
very green,
15 To declare that [a]the LORD is upright;
He is my [b]rock, and there is [c]no
unrighteousness in Him.

PSALM 93

The Majesty of the LORD.

[a]THE LORD reigns, He is [b]clothed
with majesty;
The LORD has [c]clothed and
girded Himself with
strength;
Indeed, the [d]world is firmly established, it will not be
moved.
2 Thy [a]throne is established from
of old;
Thou [b]art from everlasting.

3 The [a]floods have lifted up, O
LORD,
The floods have lifted up their
voice;
The floods lift up their pounding waves.
4 More than the sounds of many
waters,
Than the mighty breakers of
the sea,
The LORD [a]on high is mighty.
5 Thy [a]testimonies are fully confirmed;
[b]Holiness befits Thy house,
O LORD, forevermore.

PSALM 94

The LORD Implored to Avenge His People.

O LORD, God of [a]vengeance;
God of vengeance, [b]shine forth!
2 [a]Rise up, O [b]Judge of the earth;
Render recompense [c]to the
proud.
3 How long shall the wicked, O
LORD,
How long shall the [a]wicked
exult?
4 They pour forth *words,* they
[a]speak arrogantly;
All who do wickedness [b]vaunt
themselves.
5 They [a]crush Thy people, O
LORD,
And [b]afflict Thy heritage.
6 They [a]slay the widow and the
stranger,
And murder the orphans.
7 And [a]they have said, "[1]The
LORD does not see,
Nor does the God of Jacob pay
heed."

8 Pay heed, you [a]senseless
among the people;
And when will you understand,
[a]stupid ones?
9 He who [a]planted the ear, [1]does
He not hear?
He who formed the eye, [1]does
He not see?
10 He who [1a]chastens the nations,
will He not rebuke,
Even He who [b]teaches man
knowledge?
11 The LORD [a]knows the thoughts
of man,
That they are a *mere* breath.

12 Blessed is the man whom [a]Thou
dost chasten, O [1]LORD,
And [b]dost teach out of Thy law;
13 That Thou mayest grant him
[a]relief from the [b]days of adversity,
Until [c]a pit is dug for the
wicked.
14 For [a]the LORD will not abandon
His people,
Nor will He [b]forsake His inheritance.
15 For [a]judgment will again be
righteous;
And all the upright in heart will
follow it.
16 Who will [a]stand up for me
against evildoers?
Who will take his stand for me
[b]against those who do wickedness?

8 [a]Ps. 93:4; 113:5
9 [a]Ps. 37:20 [b]Ps. 68:1; 89:10
10 [a]Ps. 75:10; 89:17; 112:9 [b]Ps. 23:5; 45:7
11 [a]Ps. 54:7; 91:8
12 [a]Num. 24:6; Ps. 1:3; 52:8; 72:7; Jer. 17:8; Hos. 14:5, 6 [b]Ps. 104:16; Ezek. 31:3
13 [a]Ps. 80:15; Is. 60:21 [b]Ps. 100:4; 116:19
14 [1]Or, *thrive in* [2]Lit., *fat and* [a]Prov. 11:30; Is. 37:31; John 15:2; James 3:18
15 [a]Ps. 25:8; Job 34:10 [b]Ps. 18:2; 94:22 [c]Rom. 9:14

1 [a]Ps. 96:10; 97:1; 99:1 [b]Ps. 104:1 [c]Ps. 65:6; Is. 51:9 [d]Ps. 96:10
2 [a]Ps. 45:6; Lam. 5:19 [b]Ps. 90:2
3 [a]Ps. 96:11; 98:7, 8
4 [a]Ps. 65:7; 89:6, 9; 92:8
5 [a]Ps. 19:7 [b]Ps. 29:2; 96:9; 1 Cor. 3:17

1 [a]Deut. 32:35; Is. 35:4; Nah. 1:2; Rom. 12:19 [b]Ps. 50:2; 80:1
2 [a]Ps. 7:6 [b]Gen. 18:25 [c]Ps. 31:23
3 [a]Job 20:5
4 [a]Ps. 31:18; 75:5 [b]Ps. 10:3; 52:1
5 [a]Is. 3:15 [b]Ps. 79:1
6 [a]Is. 10:2
7 [1]Heb., *YAH* [a]Job 22:13
8 [a]Ps. 92:6
9 [1]Or, *can* [a]Ex. 4:11; Prov. 20:12
10 [1]Or, *instructs* [a]Ps. 44:2 [b]Job 35:11; Is. 28:26
11 [a]Job 11:11; 1 Cor. 3:20
12 [1]Heb. *YAH* [a]Deut. 8:5; Job 5:17; Ps. 119:71; Prov. 3:11, 12; Heb.12:5, 6 [b]Ps.119:171
13 [a]Job 34:29; Hab. 3:16 [b]Ps. 49:5 [c]Ps. 9:15; 55:23
14 [a]1 Sam. 12:22; Lam. 3:31; Rom. 11:2 [b]Ps. 37:28
15 [a]Ps. 97:2; Is. 42:3; Mic. 7:9
16 [a]Num. 10:35; Is. 28:21; 33:10 [b]Ps. 17:13; 59:2

17 If [a]the LORD had not been my help,
My soul would soon have dwelt in *the abode of* silence.
18 If I should say, "[a]My foot has slipped,"
Thy lovingkindness, O LORD, will hold me up.
19 When my anxious thoughts multiply within me,
Thy [a]consolations delight my soul.
20 Can a [1a]throne of destruction be allied with Thee,
One [b]which devises [2]mischief by decree?
21 They [a]band themselves together against the life of the righteous,
And [b]condemn the innocent to death.
22 But the LORD has been my [a]stronghold,
And my God the [b]rock of my refuge.
23 And He has [a]brought back their wickedness upon them,
And will [1b]destroy them in their evil;
The LORD our God will [1]destroy them.

PSALM 95

Praise to the LORD, and Warning against Unbelief.

O COME, let us [a]sing for joy to the LORD;
Let us shout joyfully to [b]the rock of our salvation.
2 Let us [a]come before His presence [b]with thanksgiving;
Let us shout joyfully to Him [c]with psalms.
3 For the LORD is a [a]great God,
And a great King [b]above all gods,
4 In whose hand are the [a]depths of the earth;
The peaks of the mountains are His also.
5 The sea is His, for it was He [a]who made it;
And His hands formed the dry land.

6 Come, let us [a]worship and bow down;
Let us [b]kneel before the LORD our [c]Maker.
7 For He is our God,
And we are the people of His [a]pasture, and the sheep of His hand.
[b]Today, if you would hear His voice,
8 Do not harden your hearts, as at [1a]Meribah,
As in the day of [2b]Massah in the wilderness;
9 "When your fathers [a]tested Me,
They tried Me, though they had seen My work.
10 "For [a]forty years I loathed *that* generation,
And said they are a people who err in their heart,
And they do not know My ways.
11 "Therefore I [a]swore in My anger,
Truly they shall not enter into My [b]rest."

PSALM 96

A Call to Worship the LORD the Righteous Judge.

SING to the LORD a [a]new song;
Sing to the LORD, all the earth.
2 Sing to the LORD, bless His name;
[a]Proclaim good tidings of His salvation from day to day.
3 Tell of [a]His glory among the nations,
His wonderful deeds among all the peoples.
4 For [a]great is the LORD, and greatly to be praised;
He is to be [b]feared above all gods.
5 For [a]all the gods of the peoples are idols,
But [b]the LORD made the heavens.
6 [a]Splendor and majesty are before Him,
Strength and beauty are in His sanctuary.

7 [1]Ascribe to the LORD, O [a]families of the peoples,
[1b]Ascribe to the LORD glory and strength.
8 [1]Ascribe to the LORD the [a]glory of His name;
Bring an [2b]offering, and come into His courts.
9 [a]Worship the LORD in [1]holy attire;
[b]Tremble before Him, all the earth.
10 Say among the nations, "[a]The LORD reigns;
Indeed, the [a]world is firmly established, it will not be moved;
He will [b]judge the peoples with [1]equity."

11 Let the [a]heavens be glad, and let the [b]earth rejoice;
Let [c]the sea [1]roar, and [2]all it contains;

17 [a]Ps. 124:1, 2
18 [a]Ps. 38:16; 73:2
19 [a]Is. 57:18; 66:13
20 [1]Or, *tribunal* [2]Or, *trouble* [a]Amos 6:3 [b]Ps. 50:16; 58:2
21 [a]Ps. 56:6; 59:3 [b]Ex. 23:7; Ps. 106:38; Prov. 17:15; Matt. 27:4
22 [a]Ps. 9:9; 59:9 [b]Ps. 18:2; 71:7
23 [1]Or, *silence* [a]Ps. 7:16; 140:9, 11 [b]Gen. 19:15

1 [a]Ps. 66:1; 81:1 [b]Ps. 89:26
2 [a]Mic. 6:6 [b]Ps. 100:4; 147:7; Jon. 2:9 [c]Ps. 81:2; Eph. 5:19; James 5:13
3 [a]Ps. 48:1; 135:5; 145:3 [b]Ps. 96:4; 97:9
4 [a]Ps. 135:6
5 [a]Gen. 1:9, 10; Ps. 146:6; Jon. 1:9
6 [a]Ps. 96:9; 99:5, 9 [b]2 Chr. 6:13; Dan. 6:10 [c]Ps. 100:3; 149:2; Is. 17:7; Hos. 8:14
7 [a]Ps. 74:1 [b]Heb. 3:7-11, 15; 4:7
8 [1]Or, *place of strife* [2]Or, *temptation* [a]Ex. 17:7; Num. 20:13 [b]Ex. 17:7; Deut. 6:16
9 [a]Num. 14:22; 1 Cor. 10:9
10 [a]Acts. 7:36; 13:18; Heb. 3:17
11 [a]Num. 14:23, 28-30; Deut. 1:35; Heb. 4:3, 5 [b]Deut. 12:9

1 [a]Ps. 40:3
2 [a]Ps. 71:15
3 [a]Ps. 145:12
4 [a]Ps. 48:1 [b]Ps. 89:7
5 [a]1 Chr. 16:26 [b]Ps. 115:15; Is. 42:5
6 [a]Ps. 104:1
7 [1]Lit., *Give* [a]Ps. 22:27 [b]1 Chr. 16:28, 29; Ps. 29:1, 2
8 [1]Lit., *Give* [2]Or, *meal offering* [a]Ps. 79:9; 115:1 [b]Ps. 45:12; 72:10
9 [1]Or, *the splendor of holiness* [a]1 Chr. 16:29; 2 Chr. 20:21; Ps. 29:2; 110:3 [b]Ps. 33:8; 114:7
10 [1]Or, *uprightness* [a]Ps. 93:1 [b]Ps. 9:8; 58:11; 67:4; 98:9
11 [1]Or, *thunder* [2]Lit., *its fulness* [a]Is. 49:13 [b]Ps. 97:1 [c]Ps. 98:7

12 Let the [a]field exult, and all that
is in it.
Then all the [b]trees of the forest
will sing for joy
13 Before the LORD, [a]for He is
coming;
For He is coming to judge the
earth.
He will judge the world in righteousness,
And the peoples in His faithfulness.

PSALM 97

The LORD's Power and Dominion.

[a]THE LORD reigns; let the [b]earth rejoice;
Let the many [1][c]islands be glad.
2 [a]Clouds and thick darkness surround Him;
[b]Righteousness and justice are
the foundation of His throne.
3 [a]Fire goes before Him,
And [b]burns up His adversaries
round about.
4 His [a]lightnings lit up the world;
The earth saw and [b]trembled.
5 The mountains [a]melted like
wax at the presence of the
LORD,
At the presence of the [b]Lord of
the whole earth.
6 The [a]heavens declare His righteousness,
And [b]all the peoples have seen
His glory.

7 Let all those be ashamed who
serve [a]graven images,
Who boast themselves of
[b]idols;
[c]Worship Him, all you gods.
8 Zion heard *this* and [a]was glad,
And the daughters of Judah
have rejoiced
Because of Thy judgments, O
LORD.
9 For Thou art the LORD [a]Most
High over all the earth;
Thou art exalted far [b]above all
gods.

10 [a]Hate evil, you who love the
LORD,
Who [b]preserves the souls of His
godly ones;
He [c]delivers them from the
hand of the wicked.
11 [a]Light is sown *like seed* for the
righteous,
And [b]gladness for the upright
in heart.
12 Be [a]glad in the LORD, you righteous ones;
And [b]give thanks to His holy
name.

12 [a]Ps. 65:13; Is. 35:1; 55:12, 13 [b]Is. 44:23
13 [a]Ps. 98:9

1 [1]Or, *coastlands* [a]Ps. 90.10 [b]Ps. 96:11 [c]Is. 42:10, 12
2 [a]Ex. 19:9; Deut. 4:11; 1 Kin. 8:12; Ps. 18:11 [b]Ps. 89:14
3 [a]Ps. 18:8; 50:3; Dan. 7:10; Hab. 3:5 [b]Mal. 4:1; Heb. 12:29
4 [a]Ps. 77:18 [b]Ps. 96:9; 104:32
5 [a]Ps. 46:6; Amos 9:5; Mic. 1:4; Nah. 1:5 [b]Josh. 3:11
6 [a]Ps. 50:6 [b]Ps. 98:2; Is. 6:3; 40:5; 66:18
7 [a]Ps. 78:58; Is. 42:17; 44:9, 11; Jer. 10:14 [b]Ps. 106:36; Jer. 50:2; Hab. 2:18 [c]Heb. 1:6
8 [a]Ps. 48:11; Zeph. 3:14
9 [a]Ps. 83:18 [b]Ex. 18:11; Ps. 95:3; 96:4; 135:5
10 [a]Prov. 8:13; Amos 5:15; Rom. 12:9 [b]Ps. 31:23; 145:20; Prov. 2:8 [c]Ps. 37:40; Jer. 15:21; Dan. 3:28
11 [a]Job 22:28; Ps. 112:4; Prov. 4:18 [b]Ps. 64:10
12 [a]Ps. 32:11 [b]Ps. 30:4

1 [a]Ps. 33:3 [b]Ps. 40:5; 96:3 [c]Ex. 15:6 [d]Is. 52:10
2 [a]Rom. 3:25
3 [a]Luke 1:54, 72 [b]Ps. 22:27
4 [a]Ps. 100:1 [b]Is. 44:23
5 [1]Or, *voice of song* [a]Ps. 92:3 [b]Is. 51:3
6 [a]Num. 10:10; 2 Chr. 15:14 [b]Ps. 66:1 [c]Ps. 47:7
7 [a]Ps. 96:11 [b]Ps.24:1
8 [a]Ps. 93:3; Is. 55:12 [b]Ps. 65:12
9 [a]Ps. 96:13

1 [1]Lit., *sits* [a]Ps. 97:1 [b]Ex. 25:22; 1 Sam. 4:4; Ps. 80:1
2 [a]Ps. 48:1; Is. 12:6 [b]Ps. 97:9; 113:4
3 [a]Deut. 28:58; Ps. 76:1 [b]Lev. 19:2; Josh. 24:19; 1 Sam. 2:2; Ps. 22:3; Is. 6:3
4 [a]Ps. 11:7; 33:5

PSALM 98

A Call to Praise the LORD for His Righteousness.

A Psalm.

O SING to the LORD a [a]new song,
For He has done [b]wonderful
things,
His [c]right hand and His [d]holy
arm have gained the victory
for Him.
2 The LORD has made known His
salvation;
He has revealed His [a]righteous-
ness in the sight of the nations.
3 He has [a]remembered His
lovingkindness and His faithfulness to the house of Israel;
[b]All the ends of the earth have
seen the salvation of our
God.

4 [a]Shout joyfully to the LORD, all
the earth;
[b]Break forth and sing for joy
and sing praises.
5 Sing praises to the LORD with
the [a]lyre;
With the lyre and the [1][b]sound
of melody.
6 With [a]trumpets and the sound
of the horn
[b]Shout joyfully before [c]the
King, the LORD.

7 Let the [a]sea roar and all it contains,
The [b]world and those who
dwell in it.
8 Let the [a]rivers clap their hands;
Let the [b]mountains sing together for joy
9 Before the LORD; for He is coming to [a]judge the earth;
He will judge the world with
righteousness,
And the peoples with equity.

PSALM 99

Praise to the LORD for His Fidelity to Israel.

[a]THE LORD reigns, let the peoples
tremble;
He [1][b]is enthroned *above* the
cherubim, let the earth
shake!
2 The LORD is [a]great in Zion,
And He is [b]exalted above all the
peoples.
3 Let them praise Thy [a]great and
awesome name;
[b]Holy is He.
4 And the strength of the King
[a]loves justice;

Thou hast established [b]equity;
Thou hast [c]executed justice
and righteousness in Jacob.
5 [a]Exalt the LORD our God,
And [b]worship at His footstool;
[c]Holy is He.

6 [a]Moses and Aaron were among
His [b]priests,
And [c]Samuel was among those
who [d]called on His name;
They [e]called upon the LORD,
and He answered them.
7 He [a]spoke to them in the pillar
of cloud;
They [b]kept His testimonies,
And the statute that He gave
them.
8 O LORD our God, Thou didst
[a]answer them;
Thou wast a [b]forgiving God to
them,
And *yet* an [c]avenger of their
evil deeds.
9 Exalt the LORD our God,
And worship at His holy hill;
For holy is the LORD our God.

PSALM 100

All Men Exhorted to Praise God.

A Psalm for [£]thanksgiving.

[a]SHOUT joyfully to the LORD, all the
earth.
2 [a]Serve the LORD with gladness;
[b]Come before Him with joyful
singing.
3 Know that [a]the LORD [1]Himself
is God;
It is He who has [b]made us, and
[2]not we ourselves;
We are [c]His people and the
sheep of His pasture.

4 Enter His gates [a]with [1]thanks-
giving,
And His courts with praise.
Give thanks to Him; [b]bless His
name.
5 For [a]the LORD is good;
His lovingkindness is everlasting,
And His [b]faithfulness to all generations.

PSALM 101

The Psalmist's Profession of Uprightness.

A Psalm of David.

I WILL [a]sing of lovingkindness
and justice,
To Thee, O LORD, I will sing
praises.
2 I will [a]give heed to the blameless way.
When wilt Thou come to me?
I will walk within my house in
the integrity of my heart.
3 I will set no [a]worthless thing
before my eyes;
I hate the [1]work of those who
[b]fall away;
It shall not fasten its grip on me.
4 A [a]perverse heart shall depart
from me;
I will know no evil.
5 Whoever secretly [a]slanders his
neighbor, him I will destroy;
No one who has a [b]haughty
look and an arrogant heart
will I endure.

6 My eyes shall be upon the faithful of the land, that they may
dwell with me;
He who walks in a blameless
way is the one who will minister to me.
7 He who [a]practices deceit shall
not dwell within my house;
He who speaks falsehood [b]shall
not maintain his position before me.
8 Every morning I will [a]destroy
all the wicked of the land,
So as to [b]cut off from the [c]city
of the LORD all those who do
iniquity.

PSALM 102

Prayer of an Afflicted Man for Mercy on
Himself and on Zion.

A Prayer of the Afflicted, when he
is faint, and [£]pours out his
complaint before the LORD.

[a]HEAR my prayer, O LORD!
And let my cry for help [b]come
to Thee.
2 [a]Do not hide Thy face from me
in the day of my distress;
[b]Incline Thine ear to me;
In the day when I call [c]answer
me quickly.
3 For my days [a]have been [1]con-
sumed in smoke,
And my [b]bones have been
scorched like a hearth.
4 My heart [a]has been smitten like
grass and has [b]withered
away,
Indeed, I [c]forget to eat my
bread.
5 Because of the loudness of my
groaning
My [a]bones cling to my flesh.
6 I resemble a [a]pelican of the wilderness;

4 [b]Ps. 17:2; 98:9 [c]Ps. 103:6; 146:7; Jer. 23:5
5 [a]Ps. 34:3; 107:32; 118:28 [b]Ps. 132:7 [c]Ps. 99:3
6 [a]Jer. 15:1 [b]Ex. 24:6-8; 29:26; 40:23-27; Lev. 8:1-30 [c]Jer. 15:1 [d]1 Sam. 7:9; 12:18; Ps. 22:4, 5 [e]Ex. 15:25; 32:30
7 [a]Ex. 33:9; Num. 12:5 [b]Ps. 105:28
8 [a]Ps. 106:44 [b]Num. 14:20; Ps. 78:38 [c]Ex. 32:28; Num. 20:12; Ps. 95:11; 107:12

£ Or, *thank offering*
1 [a]Ps. 98:4, 6
2 [a]Deut. 12:11, 12; 28:47 [b]Ps. 95:2
3 [1]Or, *He* [2]Or, *His we are* [a]Deut. 4:35; 1 Kin. 18:39; Ps. 46:10 [b]Job 10:3, 8; Ps. 95:6; 119:73 [c]Ps. 74:1, 2; 95:7; Is. 40:11; Ezek. 34:30, 31
4 [1]Or, *a thank offering* [a]Ps. 95:2 [b]Ps. 96:2
5 [a]Ps. 25:8; 86:5; 106:1; Jer. 33:11; Nah. 1:7 [b]Ps. 119:90

1 [a]Ps. 51:14; 89:1
2 [a]1 Sam. 18:5, 14
3 [1]Or, *practice of apostasy* [a]Deut. 15:9 [b]Ps. 40:4
4 [a]Prov. 11:20
5 [a]Ps. 50:20; Jer. 9:4 [b]Ps. 10:4; 18:27; Prov. 6:17
7 [a]Ps. 43:1; 52:2 [b]Ps. 52:4, 5
8 [a]Ps. 75:10 [b]Ps. 118:10-12 [c]Ps. 46:4

£ Ps. 142:2
1 [a]Ps. 39:12; 61:1 [b]Ex. 2:23; 1 Sam. 9:16
2 [a]Ps. 69:17 [b]Ps. 31:2 [c]Ps. 69:17
3 [1]Or, *finished* [a]Ps. 37:20; James 4:14 [b]Job 30:30
4 [a]Ps. 90:5, 6 [b]Ps. 37:2; Is. 40:7 [c]1 Sam. 1:7; 2 Sam. 12:17
5 [a]Job 19:20; Lam. 4:8
6 [a]Is. 34:11; Zeph. 2:14

I have become like an owl of the waste places.
7 I [a]lie awake,
I have become like a lonely bird on a housetop.

8 My enemies [a]have reproached me all day long;
Those who [b]deride me have used my *name* as a [c]curse.
9 For I have eaten ashes like bread,
And [a]mingled my drink with weeping,
10 [a]Because of Thine indignation and Thy wrath;
For Thou hast [b]lifted me up and cast me away.
11 My days are like a [a]lengthened shadow;
And I [b]wither away like grass.

12 But Thou, O LORD, dost [a]abide forever;
And Thy [b]name to all generations.
13 Thou wilt [a]arise *and* have [b]compassion on Zion;
For [c]it is time to be gracious to her,
For the [d]appointed time has come.
14 Surely Thy servants find pleasure in her stones,
And feel pity for her dust.
15 So the [a]nations will fear the name of the LORD,
And [b]all the kings of the earth Thy glory.
16 For the LORD has [a]built up Zion;
He has [b]appeared in His glory.
17 He has [a]regarded the prayer of the destitute,
And has not despised their prayer.

18 This will be [a]written for the [b]generation to come;
That a people yet to be created may praise [1]the LORD.
19 For He [a]looked down from His holy height;
[b]From heaven the LORD gazed upon the earth,
20 To hear the [a]groaning of the prisoner;
To [b]set free those who were doomed to death;
21 That *men* may tell of the name of the LORD in Zion,
And His praise in Jerusalem;
22 When [a]the peoples are gathered together,
And the kingdoms, to serve the LORD.

7 [a]Ps. 77:4
8 [a]Ps. 31:11 [b]Acts 26:11 [c]2 Sam. 16:5; Is. 65:15
9 [a]Ps. 42:3; 80:5
10 [a]Ps. 38:3 [b]Job 27:21; 30:22
11 [a]Job 14:2; Ps. 109:23 [b]Ps. 102:4
12 [a]Ps. 9:7; 10:16; Lam. 5:19 [b]Ex. 3:15; Ps. 135:13
13 [a]Ps. 12:5; 44:26 [b]Is. 60:10; Zech. 1:12; [c]Ps. 119:126 [d]Ps. 75:2; Dan. 8:19
15 [a]1 Kin. 8:43; Ps. 67:7 [b]Ps. 138:4
16 [a]Ps. 147:2 [b]Is. 60:1, 2
17 [a]Neh. 1:6; Ps. 22:24
18 [1]Heb., YAH [a]Deut. 31:19; 1 Cor. 10:11 [b]Ps. 22:30; 48:13
19 [a]Deut. 26:15; Ps. 14:2; 53:2 [b]Ps. 33:13
20 [a]Ps. 79:11 [b]Ps. 146:7
22 [a]Ps. 22:27; 86:9; Is. 49:22, 23; 60:3; Zech. 8:20
23 [a]Ps. 39:5
24 [a]Ps. 39:13; Is. 38:10 [b]Job 36:26; Ps. 90:2; 102:12; Hab. 1:12
25 [a]Gen. 1:1; Neh. 9:6; Heb. 1:10-12 [b]Ps. 96:5
26 [a]Is. 34:4; 51:6; Matt. 24:35; 2 Pet. 3:10; Rev. 20:11
27 [1]Lit., *He* [a]Is. 41:4; 43:10; Mal. 3:6; James 1:17
28 [1]Lit., *seed* [a]Ps. 69:36 [b]Ps. 89:4
1 [a]Ps. 104:1, 35 [b]Ps. 33:21; 105:3; 145:21; Ezek. 36:21; 39:7
2 [a]Deut. 6:12; 8:11
3 [a]Ex. 34:7; Ps. 86:5; 130:8; Is. 43:25 [b]Ex. 15:26; Ps. 30:2; Jer. 30:17
4 [a]Ps. 49:15 [b]Ps. 5:12
5 [a]Ps. 107:9; 145:16 [b]Is. 40:31
6 [a]Ps. 99:4; 146:7 [b]Ps. 12:5
7 [a]Ex. 33:13; Ps. 99:7; 147:19 [b]Ps. 78:11; 106:22
8 [a]Ex. 34:6; Num. 14:18; Neh. 9:17; Ps. 86:15; Jon. 4:2 [b]Ps. 145:8; Joel 2:13; Nah. 1:3
9 [a]Ps. 30:5; Is. 57:16 [b]Jer. 3:5, 12; Mic. 7:18

23 He has weakened my strength in the way;
He has [a]shortened my days.
24 I say, "O my God, [a]do not take me away in the midst of my days,
Thy [b]years are throughout all generations.
25 "Of old Thou didst [a]found the earth;
And the [b]heavens are the work of Thy hands.
26 "Even they will [a]perish, but Thou dost endure;
And all of them will wear out like a garment;
Like clothing Thou wilt change them, and they will be changed.
27 "But Thou art [1a]the same,
And Thy years will not come to an end.
28 "The [a]children of Thy servants will continue,
And their [1b]descendants will be established before Thee."

PSALM 103

Praise for the LORD's Mercies.

A Psalm of David.

[a]BLESS the LORD, O my soul;
And all that is within me, *bless* His [b]holy name.
2 Bless the LORD, O my soul,
And [a]forget none of His benefits;
3 Who [a]pardons all your iniquities;
Who [b]heals all your diseases;
4 Who [a]redeems your life from the pit;
Who [b]crowns you with lovingkindness and compassion;
5 Who [a]satisfies your years with good things,
So that your youth is [b]renewed like the eagle.

6 The LORD [a]performs righteous deeds,
And judgments for all who are [b]oppressed.
7 He [a]made known His ways to Moses,
His [b]acts to the sons of Israel.
8 The LORD is [a]compassionate and gracious,
[b]Slow to anger and abounding in lovingkindness.
9 He [a]will not always strive *with us;*
Nor will He [b]keep *His anger* forever.

10 He has [a]not dealt with us according to our sins,
Nor rewarded us according to our iniquities.
11 For as high [a]as the heavens are above the earth,
So great is His lovingkindness toward those who [1]fear Him.
12 As far as the east is from the west,
So far has He [a]removed our transgressions from us.
13 Just [a]as a father has compassion on *his* children,
So the LORD has compassion on those who [1]fear Him.
14 For [a]He Himself knows [1]our frame;
He [b]is mindful that we are *but* [c]dust.

15 As for man, his days are [a]like grass;
As a [b]flower of the field, so he flourishes.
16 When the [a]wind has passed over it, it is no more;
And its [b]place acknowledges it no longer.
17 But the [a]lovingkindness of the LORD is from everlasting to everlasting on those who [1]fear Him,
And His righteousness [b]to children's children,
18 To [a]those who keep His covenant,
And who remember His precepts to do them.

19 The LORD has established His [a]throne in the heavens;
And His [1b]sovereignty rules over [2]all.
20 Bless the LORD, you [a]His angels,
[b]Mighty in strength, who [c]perform His word,
[d]Obeying the voice of His word!
21 Bless the LORD, all you [a]His hosts,
You [b]who serve Him, doing His will.
22 Bless the LORD, [a]all you works of His,
In all places of His dominion;
Bless the LORD, O my soul!

PSALM 104

The LORD's Care over All His Works.

[a]BLESS the LORD, O my soul!
O LORD my God, Thou art very great;
Thou art [b]clothed with splendor and majesty,
2 Covering Thyself with [a]light as with a cloak,
[b]Stretching out heaven like a *tent* curtain.
3 He [a]lays the beams of His upper chambers in the waters;
He makes the [b]clouds His chariot;
He walks upon the [c]wings of the wind;
4 He makes [1a]the winds His messengers,
[2]Flaming [b]fire His ministers.

5 He [a]established the earth upon its foundations,
So that it will not totter forever and ever.
6 Thou [a]didst cover it with the deep as with a garment;
The waters were standing above the mountains.
7 At Thy [a]rebuke they fled;
At the [b]sound of Thy thunder they hurried away.
8 The mountains rose; the valleys sank down
To the [a]place which Thou didst establish for them.
9 Thou didst set a [a]boundary that they may not pass over;
That they may not return to cover the earth.

10 He sends forth [a]springs in the valleys;
They flow between the mountains;
11 They [a]give drink to every beast of the field;
The [b]wild donkeys quench their thirst.
12 [1]Beside them the birds of the heavens [a]dwell;
They lift up *their* voices among the branches.
13 He [a]waters the mountains from His upper chambers;
The earth is satisfied with the fruit of His works.

14 He causes the [a]grass to grow for the cattle,
And [b]vegetation for the labor of man,
So that he may bring forth food [c]from the earth,
15 And [a]wine which makes man's heart glad,
[b]So that he may make *his* face glisten with oil,
And food which [c]sustains man's heart.
16 The trees of the LORD [1]drink their fill,
The cedars of Lebanon which He planted,

10 [a]Ezra 9:13; Lam. 3:22
11 [1]Or, *revere* [a]Ps. 36:5; 57:10
12 [a]2 Sam. 12:13; Is. 38:17; Zech. 3:9; Heb. 9:26
13 [1]Or, *revere* [a]Mal. 3:17
14 [1]I.e., what we are made of [a]Is. 29:16 [b]Ps. 78:39 [c]Gen. 3:19; Eccles. 12:7
15 [a]Ps. 90:5; Is. 40:6; 1 Pet. 1:24 [b]Job 14:2; James 1:10, 11
16 [a]Is. 40:7 [b]Job 7:10; 8:18; 20:9
17 [1]Or, *revere* [a]Ps. 25:6 [b]Ex. 20:6; Deut. 5:10; Ps. 105:8
18 [a]Deut. 7:9; Ps. 25:10
19 [1]Or, *kingdom* [2]I.e., the universe [a]Ps. 11:4 [b]Ps. 47:2, 8; Dan. 4:17
20 [a]Ps. 148:2 [b]Ps. 29:1; 78:25 [c]Matt. 6:10 [d]Ps. 91:11; Heb. 1:14
21 [a]1 Kin. 22:19; Neh. 9:6; Ps. 148:2; Luke 2:13 [b]Ps. 104:4
22 [a]Ps. 145:10
1 [a]Ps. 103:22 [b]Ps. 93:1
2 [a]Dan. 7:9 [b]Is. 40:22
3 [a]Amos 9:6 [b]Is. 19:1 [c]Ps. 18:10
4 [1]Or, *His angels, spirits* [2]Or, *His ministers flames of fire* [a]Ps. 148:8; Heb. 1:7 [b]2 Kin. 2:11; 6:17
5 [a]Job 38:4; Ps. 24:2
6 [a]Gen. 1:2
7 [a]Ps. 18:15; 106:9; Is. 50:2 [b]Ps. 29:3; 77:18
8 [a]Ps. 33:7
9 [a]Job 38:10, 11; Jer. 5:22
10 [a]Ps. 107:35; Is. 41:18
11 [a]Ps. 104:13 [b]Job 39:5
12 [1]Or, *Over* [a]Matt. 8:20
13 [a]Ps. 65:9; 147:8
14 [a]Job 38:27; Ps. 147:8 [b]Gen. 1:29 [c]Job 28:5
15 [a]Judg. 9:13; Prov. 31:6; Eccles. 10:19 [b]Ps. 23:5; 92:10; 141:5; Luke 7:46 [c]Gen. 18:5; Judg. 19:5, 8
16 [1]Lit., *are satisfied*

17 Where the [a]birds build their
nests,
And the [b]stork, *whose home* is
the [1]fir trees.
18 The high mountains are for the
[a]wild goats;
The [b]cliffs are a refuge for the
[c]rock badgers.
19 He made the moon [a]for the seasons;
The [b]sun knows the place of its
setting.
20 Thou [a]dost appoint darkness
and it becomes night,
In which all the [b]beasts of the
forest prowl about.
21 The [a]young lions roar after
their prey,
And [b]seek their food from God.
22 *When* the sun rises they withdraw,
And lie down in their [a]dens.
23 Man goes forth to [a]his work
And to his labor until evening.

24 O LORD, how [a]many are Thy
works!
In [b]wisdom Thou hast made
them all;
The [c]earth is full of Thy [1]pos-
sessions.
25 There is the [a]sea, great and
broad,
In which are swarms without
number,
Animals both small and great.
26 There the [a]ships move along,
And [1b]Leviathan, which Thou
hast formed to sport in it.

27 They all [a]wait for Thee,
To [b]give them their food in due
season.
28 Thou dost give to them, they
gather *it* up;
Thou [a]dost open Thy hand, they
are satisfied with good.
29 Thou [a]dost hide Thy face, they
are dismayed;
Thou [b]dost take away their
[1]spirit, they expire,
And [c]return to their dust.
30 Thou dost send forth Thy
[1a]Spirit, they are created;
And Thou dost renew the face
of the ground.

31 Let the [a]glory of the LORD endure forever;
Let the LORD [b]be glad in His
works;
32 He [a]looks at the earth, and it
trembles;
He [b]touches the mountains,
and they smoke.

17 [1]Or, *cypress* [a]Ps. 104:12 [b]Lev. 11:19
18 [a]Job 39:1 [b]Prov. 30:26 [c]Lev. 11:5
19 [a]Gen. 1:14 [b]Ps. 19:6
20 [a]Ps. 74:16; Is. 45:7 [b]Ps. 50:10; Is. 56:9; Mic. 5:8
21 [a]Job 38:39 [b]Ps. 145:15; Joel 1:20
22 [a]Job 37:8
23 [a]Gen. 3:19
24 [1]Or possibly, *creatures* [a]Ps. 40:5 [b]Ps. 136:5; Prov. 3:19; Jer. 10:12; 51:15 [c]Ps. 65:9
25 [a]Ps. 8:8; 69:34
26 [1]Or, *a sea monster* [a]Ps. 107:23; Ezek. 27:9 [b]Job 41:1
27 [a]Ps. 145:15 [b]Job 36:31; 38:41; Ps. 136:25; 147:9
28 [a]Ps. 145:16
29 [1]Or, *breath* [a]Deut. 31:17; Ps. 30:7 [b]Job 34:14; Ps. 146:4; Eccles. 12:7 [c]Gen. 3:19; Job 10:9; Ps. 90:3
30 [1]Or, *breath* [a]Job 33:4; Ezek. 37:9
31 [a]Ps. 86:12; 111:10 [b]Gen. 1:31
32 [a]Judg. 5:5; Ps. 97:4, 5; 114:7 [b]Ex. 19:18; Ps. 144:5
33 [a]Ps. 63:4
34 [a]Ps. 19:14 [b]Ps. 9:2
35 [1]Or, *Hallelujah!* [2]Heb., YAH [a]Ps. 59:13 [b]Ps. 37:10 [c]Ps. 104:1 [d]Ps. 105:45
1 [a]1 Chr. 16:8-22, 34; Ps. 106:1; Is. 12:4 [b]Ps. 99:6 [c]Ps. 145:12
2 [a]Ps. 96:1; 98:5 [b]Ps. 77:12; 119:27
3 [a]Ps. 33:21
4 [a]Ps. 63:2 [b]Ps. 27:8
5 [a]Ps. 40:5; 77:11 [b]Ps.119:13
6 [a]Ps. 105:42 [b]Ps. 135:4 [c]1 Chr. 16:13; Ps. 106:5
7 [a]Is. 26:9
8 [a]Ps. 105:42; 106:45; Luke 1:72 [b]Deut. 7:9
9 [a]Gen. 17:2; 22:16-18; Gal. 3:17 [b]Gen. 26:3
10 [a]Gen. 28:13-15
11 [a]Gen. 13:15; 15:18 [b]Josh. 23:4
12 [a]Gen. 34:30; Deut. 7:7 [b]Gen. 23:4; Heb. 11:9

33 I will sing to the LORD [a]as long
as I live;
I will sing praise to my God
while I have my being.
34 Let my [a]meditation be pleasing
to Him;
As for me, I shall [b]be glad in the
LORD.
35 Let sinners be [a]consumed from
the earth,
And let the [b]wicked be no more.
[c]Bless the LORD, O my soul.
[1d]Praise [2]the LORD!

PSALM 105

The LORD's Wonderful Works in Behalf of Israel.

OH [a]give thanks to the LORD, [b]call
upon His name;
[c]Make known His deeds among
the peoples.
2 Sing to Him, [a]sing praises to
Him;
[b]Speak of all His wonders.
3 Glory in His holy name;
Let the [a]heart of those who
seek the LORD be glad.
4 Seek the LORD and [a]His
strength;
[b]Seek His face continually.
5 Remember His [a]wonders which
He has done,
His marvels, and the [b]judg-
ments uttered by His mouth,
6 O seed of [a]Abraham, His servant,
O sons of [b]Jacob, His [c]chosen
ones!
7 He is the LORD our God;
His [a]judgments are in all the
earth.

8 He has [a]remembered His covenant forever,
The word which He com-
manded to a [b]thousand generations,
9 *The* [a]*covenant* which He made
with Abraham,
And His [b]oath to Isaac.
10 Then He [a]confirmed it to Jacob
for a statute,
To Israel as an everlasting covenant,
11 Saying, "[a]To you I will give the
land of Canaan
As the [b]portion of your inheritance,"
12 When they were only a [a]few
men in number,
Very few, and [b]strangers in it.
13 And they wandered about from
nation to nation,
From *one* kingdom to another
people.

14 He [a]permitted no man to oppress them,
And He [b]reproved kings for their sakes:
15 "[a]Do not touch My anointed ones,
And do My prophets no harm."

16 And He [a]called for a famine upon the land;
He [b]broke the whole staff of bread.
17 He [a]sent a man before them,
Joseph, *who* was [b]sold as a slave.
18 They afflicted his [a]feet with fetters,
He himself was laid in irons;
19 Until the time that his [a]word came to pass,
The word of the LORD [b]tested him.
20 The [a]king sent and released him,
The ruler of peoples, and set him free.
21 He [a]made him lord of his house,
And ruler over all his possessions,
22 To imprison his princes [a]at will,
That he might teach his elders wisdom.
23 [a]Israel also came into Egypt;
Thus Jacob [b]sojourned in the land of Ham.
24 And He [a]caused His people to be very fruitful,
And made them stronger than their adversaries.

25 He [a]turned their heart to hate His people,
To [b]deal craftily with His servants.
26 He [a]sent Moses His servant,
And [b]Aaron whom He had chosen.
27 They [a]performed His wondrous acts among them,
And miracles in the land of Ham.
28 He [a]sent darkness and made *it* dark;
And they did not [b]rebel against His words.
29 He [a]turned their waters into blood,
And caused their fish to die.
30 Their land swarmed with [a]frogs
Even in the [b]chambers of their kings.
31 He spoke, and there came a [a]swarm of flies
And [b]gnats in all their territory.
32 He gave them [a]hail for rain,
And flaming fire in their land.
33 He struck down their vines also and their fig trees,
And shattered the trees of their territory.
34 He spoke, and [a]locusts came,
And young locusts, even without number,
35 And ate up all vegetation in their land,
And ate up the fruit of their ground.
36 He also [a]struck down all the first-born in their land,
The first fruits of all their vigor.

37 Then He brought them out with [a]silver and gold;
And among His tribes there was not one who stumbled.
38 Egypt was [a]glad when they departed;
For the [b]dread of them had fallen upon them.
39 He spread a [a]cloud for a covering,
And [b]fire to illumine by night.
40 They [a]asked, and He brought [b]quail,
And satisfied them with the [c]bread of heaven.
41 He opened the rock, and [a]water flowed out;
It ran in the dry places *like* a river.
42 For He [a]remembered His holy word
With Abraham His servant;
43 And He brought forth His people with joy,
His chosen ones with a joyful [a]shout.
44 He [a]gave them also the lands of the [1]nations,
That they [b]might take possession of *the fruit of* the peoples' labor,
45 So that they might [a]keep His statutes,
And observe His laws,
[1]Praise [2]the LORD!

PSALM 106

Israel's Rebelliousness and the LORD's Deliverances.

1 PRAISE [2]the LORD!
Oh [a]give thanks to the LORD, for He [b]is good;
For [c]His lovingkindness is everlasting.
2 Who can speak of the [a]mighty deeds of the LORD,
Or can show forth all His praise?
3 How blessed are those who keep [1]justice,
[2]Who [a]practice righteousness at all times!

14 [a]Gen. 20:7; 35:5 [b]Gen. 12:17; 20:3, 7
15 [a]Gen. 26:11
16 [a]Gen. 41:54 [b]Lev. 26:26; Is. 3:1; Ezek. 4:16
17 [a]Gen. 45:5 [b]Gen. 37:28, 36; Acts 7:9
18 [a]Gen. 39:20
19 [a]Gen. 40:20, 21 [b]Ps. 66:10
20 [a]Gen. 41:14
21 [a]Gen. 41:40-44
22 [a]Gen. 41:44
23 [a]Gen. 46:6; Acts 7:15 [b]Acts 13:17
24 [a]Ex. 1:7, 9
25 [a]Ex. 1:8; 4:21 [b]Ex. 1:10; Acts 7:19
26 [a]Ex. 3:10; 4:12 [b]Ex. 4:14; Num. 16:5; 17:5-8
27 [a]Ps. 78:43-51; 105:27-36
28 [a]Ex. 10:21, 22 [b]Ps. 99:7
29 [a]Ex. 7:20, 21
30 [a]Ex. 8:6 [b]Ex. 8:3
31 [a]Ex. 8:21 [b]Ex. 8:16
32 [a]Ex. 9:23-25
34 [a]Ex. 10:12-15
36 [a]Ex. 12:29; 13:15; Ps. 135:8; 136:10
37 [a]Ex. 12:35, 36
38 [a]Ex. 12:33 [b]Ex.15:16
39 [a]Ex. 13:21; Neh. 9:12; Ps. 78:14; Is. 4:5 [b]Ex. 40:38
40 [a]Ps. 78:18 [b]Ex. 16:13; Num. 11:31; Ps. 78:27 [c]Ex. 16:15; Neh. 9:15; Ps. 78:24; John 6:31
41 [a]Ex. 17:6; Num. 20:11; Ps. 78:15; 114:8; Is. 48:21; 1 Cor. 10:4
42 [a]Ps. 105:8
43 [a]Ex. 15:1; Ps. 106:12
44 [1]Or, *Gentiles* [a]Josh. 13:7; Ps. 78:55 [b]Deut. 6:10, 11
45 [1]Or, *Hallelujah!* [2]Heb., *YAH* [a]Deut. 4:40
1 [1]Or, *Hallelujah!* [2]Heb., *YAH* [a]Ps. 105:1; 107:1 [b]Ps. 100:5 [c]1 Chr. 16:34, 41
2 [a]Ps. 145:4, 12; 150:2
3 [1]Or, *judgment* [2]Many Heb. mss. read, *The one who performs* [a]Ps. 15:2

4 Remember me, O LORD, in *Thy* [a]favor toward Thy people;
Visit me with Thy salvation,
5 That I may see the [a]prosperity of Thy chosen ones,
That I may [b]rejoice in the gladness of Thy nation,
That I may [c]glory with Thine [1]inheritance.

6 [a]We have sinned [b]like our fathers,
We have committed iniquity, we have behaved wickedly.
7 Our fathers in Egypt did not understand Thy wonders;
They [a]did not remember Thine abundant kindnesses,
But [b]rebelled by the sea, at the [1]Red Sea.
8 Nevertheless He saved them [a]for the sake of His name,
That He might [b]make His power known.
9 Thus He [a]rebuked the Red Sea and it [b]dried up;
And He [c]led them through the deeps, as through the wilderness.
10 So He [a]saved them from the hand of the one who hated *them*,
And [b]redeemed them from the hand of the enemy.
11 And [a]the waters covered their adversaries;
Not one of them was left.
12 Then they [a]believed His words;
They [b]sang His praise.

13 They quickly [a]forgot His works;
They did not wait for His counsel,
14 But [a]craved intensely in the wilderness,
And [b]tempted God in the desert.
15 So He [a]gave them their request,
But [b]sent a wasting disease among them.

16 When they became [a]envious of Moses in the camp,
And of Aaron, the holy one of the LORD,
17 The [a]earth opened and swallowed up Dathan,
And engulfed the company of Abiram.
18 And a [a]fire blazed up in their company;
The flame consumed the wicked.

19 They [a]made a calf in Horeb,
And worshiped a molten image.
20 Thus they [a]exchanged their glory
For the image of an ox that eats grass.
21 They [a]forgot God their Savior,
Who had done great things in Egypt,
22 Wonders in the land of Ham,
And awesome things by the Red Sea.
23 Therefore [a]He said that He would destroy them,
Had not [b]Moses His chosen one stood in the breach before Him,
To turn away His wrath from destroying *them*.
24 Then they [a]despised the [b]pleasant land;
They [c]did not believe in His word,
25 But [a]grumbled in their tents;
They did not listen to the voice of the LORD.
26 Therefore He [a]swore to them,
That He would cast them down in the wilderness,
27 And that He would [a]cast their seed among the nations,
And [b]scatter them in the lands.

28 They [a]joined themselves also to Baal-peor,
And ate [b]sacrifices offered to the dead.
29 Thus they [a]provoked *Him* to anger with their deeds;
And the plague broke out among them.
30 Then Phinehas [a]stood up and interposed;
And so the [b]plague was stayed.
31 And it was [a]reckoned to him for righteousness,
To all generations forever.

32 They also [a]provoked *Him* to wrath at the waters of [1]Meribah,
So that it [b]went hard with Moses on their account;
33 Because they [a]were rebellious against [1]His Spirit,
He spoke rashly with his lips.

34 They [a]did not destroy the peoples,
As [b]the LORD commanded them,
35 But [a]they mingled with the nations,
And learned their practices,
36 And [a]served their idols,
Which became a snare to them.
37 They even [a]sacrificed their sons and their daughters to the demons,

4 [a]Ps. 44:3
5 [1]I.e., people [a]Ps. 1:3 [b]Ps. 118:15 [c]Ps. 105:3
6 [a]1 Kin. 8:47; Ezra 9:7; Neh. 1:7; Jer. 3:25; Dan. 9:5 [b]2 Chr. 30:7; Neh. 9:2; Ps. 78:8, 57
7 [1]Or, *Sea of Reeds*, also vs. 9, 22 [a]Judg. 3:7; Ps. 78:11, 42 [b]Ex. 14:11, 12
8 [a]Ezek. 20:9 [b]Ex. 9:16
9 [a]Ps. 18:15; Nah. 1:4 [b]Ex. 14:21; Is. 51:10 [c]Is. 63:11-13
10 [a]Ex. 14:30 [b]Ps. 78:42; 107:2
11 [a]Ex. 14:28; 15:5; Ps. 78:53
12 [a]Ex. 14:31 [b]Ex. 15:1-21
13 [a]Ex. 15:24
14 [a]Num 11:4; Ps. 78:18; 1 Cor. 10:6 [b]Ex. 17:2; 1 Cor. 10:9
15 [a]Num. 11:31; Ps. 78:29 [b]Is. 10:16
16 [a]Num. 16:3
17 [a]Num. 16:32
18 [a]Num. 16:35
19 [a]Ex. 32:4; Deut. 9:8; Acts 7:41
20 [a]Jer. 2:11; Rom. 1:23
21 [a]Ps. 78:11
23 [a]Ex. 32:10; Deut. 9:14; Ezek. 20:8, 13 [b]Ex. 32:11-14; Deut. 9:25-29
24 [a]Num. 14:31 [b]Deut. 8:7; Jer. 3:19; Ezek. 20:6 [c]Deut. 1:32; 9:23
25 [a]Num. 14:2
26 [a]Num. 14:28-35; Ps. 95:11; Ezek. 20:15; Heb. 3:11
27 [a]Deut. 4:27 [b]Ps. 44:11
28 [a]Num. 25:3; Deut. 4:3; Hos. 9:10 [b]Num. 25:2
29 [a]Num. 25:4
30 [a]Num. 25:7 [b]Num. 25:8
31 [a]Gen. 15:6; Num. 25:11-13
32 [1]Lit., *strife* [a]Num. 20:2-13; Ps. 81:7; 95:9 [b]Num. 20:12
33 [1]Or, *his spirit* [a]Num. 20:3, 10; Ps. 78:40; 107:11
34 [a]Judg. 1:21, 27-36 [b]Deut. 7:2
35 [a]Judg. 3:5, 6
36 [a]Judg. 2:12
37 [a]Deut. 12:31; 32:17; 2 Kin. 17:17; Ezek. 16:20, 21; 1 Cor. 10:20

38 And shed [a]innocent blood,
The blood of their [b]sons and their daughters,
Whom they sacrificed to the idols of Canaan;
And the land was [c]polluted with the blood.
39 Thus they became [a]unclean in their practices,
And [b]played the harlot in their deeds.

40 Therefore the [a]anger of the LORD was kindled against His people,
And He [b]abhorred His [1]inheritance.
41 Then [a]He gave them into the hand of the [1]nations;
And those who hated them ruled over them.
42 Their enemies also [a]oppressed them,
And they were subdued under their power.
43 Many times He would [a]deliver them;
They, however, were rebellious in their [b]counsel,
And *so* [c]sank down in their iniquity.

44 Nevertheless He looked upon their distress,
When He [a]heard their cry;
45 And He [a]remembered His covenant for their sake,
And [b]relented according to the greatness of His lovingkindness.
46 He also made them [a]*objects* of compassion
In the presence of all their captors.

47 [a]Save us, O LORD our God,
And [b]gather us from among the nations,
To give thanks to Thy holy name,
And [c]glory in Thy praise.
48 [a]Blessed be the LORD, the God of Israel,
From everlasting even to everlasting.
And let all the people say, "Amen."
[1]Praise [2]the LORD!

BOOK 5

PSALM 107

The LORD Delivers Men from Manifold Troubles.

OH [a]give thanks to the LORD, for He is good;
For His lovingkindness is everlasting.
2 Let [a]the redeemed of the LORD say *so*,
Whom He has [b]redeemed from the hand of the adversary,
3 And [a]gathered from the lands,
From the east and from the west,
From the north and from the south.

4 They [a]wandered in the wilderness in a desert region;
They did not find a way to an inhabited [b]city.
5 *They were* hungry and thirsty;
Their [a]soul fainted within them.
6 Then they [a]cried out to the LORD in their trouble;
He delivered them out of their distresses.
7 He led them also by a [a]straight way,
To go to [b]an inhabited city.
8 [a]Let them give thanks to the LORD for His lovingkindness,
And for His wonders to the sons of men!
9 For He has [a]satisfied the thirsty soul,
And the [b]hungry soul He has filled with what is good.

10 There were those who [a]dwelt in darkness and in the shadow of death,
[b]Prisoners in misery and chains,
11 Because they had [a]rebelled against the words of God,
And [b]spurned the counsel of the Most High.
12 Therefore He humbled their heart with labor;
They stumbled and there was [a]none to help.
13 Then they [a]cried out to the LORD in their trouble;
He saved them out of their distresses.
14 He [a]brought them out of darkness and the shadow of death,
And [b]broke their bands apart.
15 Let them give thanks to the LORD for His lovingkindness,
And for His wonders to the sons of men!
16 For He has [a]shattered gates of bronze,
And cut bars of iron asunder.

17 Fools, because of their rebellious way,
And [a]because of their iniquities, were afflicted.

38 [a]Ps. 94:21 [b]Deut. 18:10 [c]Num. 35:33; Is. 24:5; Jer. 3:1, 2
39 [a]Lev. 18:24; Ezek. 20:18 [b]Lev. 17:7; Num. 15:39; Judg. 2:17; Hos. 4:12
40 [1]I.e., people [a]Judg. 2:14; Ps. 78:59 [b]Lev. 26:30; Deut. 32:19
41 [1]Or, *Gentiles* [a]Judg. 2:14; Neh. 9:27
42 [a]Judg. 4:3; 10:12
43 [a]Judg. 2:16-18 [b]Ps. 81:12 [c]Judg. 6:6
44 [a]Judg. 3:9; 6:7; 10:10
45 [a]Lev. 26:42; Ps. 105:8 [b]Judg. 2:18
46 [a]1 Kin. 8:50; 2 Chr. 30:9; Ezra 9:9; Neh. 1:11; Jer. 42:12
47 [a]1 Chr. 16:35, 36 [b]Ps. 147:2 [c]Ps. 47:1
48 [1]Or, *Hallelujah!* [2]Heb., *YAH* [a]Ps. 41:13; 72:18; 89:52
1 [a]Ps. 106:1
2 [a]Is. 35:9, 10; 62:12; 63:4 [b]Ps. 78:42; 106:10
3 [a]Deut. 30:3; Neh. 1:9; Ps. 106:47; Is. 11:12; 43:5; 56:8; Ezek. 11:17; 20:34
4 [a]Num. 14:33; 32:13; Deut. 2:7; Josh. 5:6; 14:10 [b]Ps. 107:7, 36
5 [a]Ps. 77:3
6 [a]Ps. 50:15; 107:13, 19, 28
7 [a]Ezra 8:21; Ps. 5:8; Jer. 31:9 [b]Ps. 107:4, 36
8 [a]Ps. 107:15, 21, 31
9 [a]Ps. 22:26; 63:5; 103:5 [b]Ps. 146:7; Matt. 5:6; Luke 1:53
10 [a]Ps. 143:3; Is. 42:7; Mic. 7:8; Luke 1:79 [b]Job 36:8; Ps. 102:20
11 [a]Ps. 78:40; 106:7 [b]Num. 15:31; 2 Chr. 36:16; Prov. 1:25; Is. 5:24
12 [a]Ps. 22:11; 72:12
13 [a]Ps. 107:6
14 [a]Ps. 86:13; 107:10 [b]Ps. 116:16; Jer. 2:20; 30:8; Nah. 1:13; Luke 13:16; Acts 12:7
16 [a]Is. 45:1, 2
17 [a]Is. 65:6, 7; Jer. 30:14, 15; Ezek. 24:23

18 Their [a]soul abhorred all kinds
of food;
And they [b]drew near to the
[c]gates of death.
19 Then they cried out to the LORD
in their trouble;
He saved them out of their distresses.
20 He [a]sent His word and [b]healed
them,
And [c]delivered *them* from their
[1]destructions.
21 Let them give thanks to the
LORD for His lovingkindness,
And for His wonders to the
sons of men!
22 Let them also offer [a]sacrifices
of thanksgiving,
And [b]tell of His works with joyful singing.

23 Those who [a]go down to the sea
in ships,
Who do business on great waters;
24 They have seen the works of
the LORD,
And His wonders in the deep.
25 For He [a]spoke and raised up a
[b]stormy wind,
Which [c]lifted up the waves of
the sea.
26 They rose up to the heavens,
they went down to the
depths;
Their soul [a]melted away in *their*
misery.
27 They reeled and [a]staggered like
a drunken man,
And were at their wits' end.
28 Then they cried to the LORD in
their trouble,
And He brought them out of
their distresses.
29 He [a]caused the storm to be still,
So that the waves of the sea
were hushed.
30 Then they were glad because
they were quiet;
So He guided them to their desired haven.
31 Let them give thanks to the
LORD for His lovingkindness,
And for His [a]wonders to the
sons of men!
32 Let them [a]extol Him also [b]in the
congregation of the people,
And [c]praise Him at the seat of
the elders.

33 He [a]changes rivers into a wilderness,
And springs of water into a
thirsty ground;
34 A [a]fruitful land into a [b]salt
waste,

18 [a]Job 33:20; Ps. 102:4 [b]Job 33:22; Ps. 88:3 [c]Job 38:17; Ps. 9:13
20 [1]Or, *pits* [a]Ps. 147:15, 18; Matt. 8:8 [b]2 Kin. 20:5; Ps. 30:2; 103:3; 147:3 [c]Job 33:28, 30; Ps. 30:3; 49:15; 56:13; 103:4
22 [a]Lev. 7:12; Ps. 50:14; 116:17 [b]Ps. 9:11; 73:28; 118:17
23 [a]Is. 42:10; Jon. 1:3
25 [a]Ps. 105:31, 34 [b]Ps. 148:8; Jon. 1:4 [c]Ps. 93:3, 4
26 [a]Ps. 22:14; 119:28
27 [a]Job 12:25; Is. 24:20
29 [a]Ps. 65:7; 89:9; Matt. 8:26; Luke 8:24
31 [a]Ps. 78:4; 111:4
32 [a]Ps. 34:3; 99:5; Is. 25:1 [b]Ps. 22:22, 25 [c]Ps. 35:18
33 [a]Ps. 74:15; Is. 42:15; 50:2
34 [a]Gen. 13:10; 14:3; 19:24, 25; Deut. 29:23 [b]Job 39:6; Jer. 17:6
35 [a]Ps. 105:41; 114:8; Is. 35:6, 7; 41:18
36 [1]Or, *a habitable city;* lit., *a city of habitation* [a]Ps. 107:4, 7
37 [1]Lit., *acquire fruits of yield* [a]2 Kin. 19:29; Is. 65:21; Amos 9:14
38 [a]Gen. 12:2; 17:20; Ex. 1:7; Deut. 1:10 [b]Deut. 7:14
39 [a]Ezek. 5:11; 29:15 [b]Ps. 38:6; 44:25; 57:6
40 [1]Or, *nobles* [a]Job 12:21 [b]Job 12:24 [c]Deut. 32:10
41 [1]Lit., *in an inaccessibly high place* [a]1 Sam. 2:8; Ps. 59:1; 113:7, 8 [b]Job 21:11; Ps. 113:9
42 [a]Job 22:19; Ps. 52:6 [b]Job 5:16; Ps. 63:11; Rom. 3:19
43 [a]Ps. 64:9; Jer. 9:12; Hos. 14:9 [b]Ps. 107:1
1 [1]Lit., *glory* [a]Ps. 57:7-11; 108:1-5
4 [a]Ps. 113:4
6 [a]Ps. 60:5-12; 108:6-13

Because of the wickedness of
those who dwell in it.
35 He [a]changes a wilderness into a
pool of water,
And a dry land into springs of
water;
36 And there He makes the hungry
to dwell,
So that they may establish [1a]an
inhabited city,
37 And sow fields, and [a]plant vineyards,
And [1]gather a fruitful harvest.
38 Also He blesses them and they
[a]multiply greatly;
And He [b]does not let their cattle decrease.

39 When they are [a]diminished and
[b]bowed down
Through oppression, misery,
and sorrow,
40 He [a]pours contempt upon
[1]princes,
And [b]makes them wander [c]in a
pathless waste.
41 But He [a]sets the needy [1]se-
curely on high away from affliction,
And [b]makes *his* families like a
flock.
42 The [a]upright see it, and are
glad;
But all [b]unrighteousness shuts
its mouth.
43 Who is [a]wise? Let him give
heed to these things;
And consider the [b]lovingkind-
nesses of the LORD.

PSALM 108

God Praised and Supplicated to Give Victory.

A Song, a Psalm of David.

[a]MY heart is steadfast, O God;
I will sing, I will sing praises,
even with my [1]soul.
2 Awake, harp and lyre;
I will awaken the dawn!
3 I will give thanks to Thee, O
LORD, among the peoples;
And I will sing praises to Thee
among the nations.
4 For Thy lovingkindness is great
[a]above the heavens;
And Thy truth *reaches* to the
skies.
5 Be exalted, O God, above the
heavens,
And Thy glory above all the
earth.
6 [a]That Thy beloved may be delivered,
Save with Thy right hand, and
answer me!

7 God has spoken in His [1]holiness:
"I will exult, I will portion out Shechem,
And measure out the valley of Succoth.
8 "Gilead is Mine, Manasseh is Mine;
Ephraim also is the [1]helmet of My head;
Judah is My [2]scepter.
9 "Moab is My washbowl;
Over Edom I shall throw My shoe;
Over Philistia I will shout aloud."

10 Who will bring me into the besieged city?
Who will lead me to Edom?
11 Hast not Thou Thyself, O God, [a]rejected us?
And wilt Thou not go forth with our armies, O God?
12 Oh give us help against the adversary,
For deliverance by man is in vain.
13 [1]Through God we shall do valiantly;
And it is He who will tread down our adversaries.

PSALM 109

Vengeance Invoked upon Adversaries.

For the choir director. A Psalm of David.

O [a]GOD of my praise,
[b]Do not be silent!
2 For they have opened the wicked and [a]deceitful mouth against me;
They have spoken against me with a [b]lying tongue.
3 They have also surrounded me with words of hatred,
And fought against me [a]without cause.
4 In return [a]for my love they act as my accusers;
But [b]I am *in* prayer.
5 Thus they have [a]repaid me evil for good,
And [b]hatred for my love.

6 Appoint a wicked man over him;
And let an [a]accuser stand at his right hand.
7 When he is judged, let him [a]come forth guilty;
And let his [b]prayer become sin.
8 Let [a]his days be few;
Let [b]another take his office.
9 Let his [a]children be fatherless,
And his [b]wife a widow.
10 Let his [a]children wander about and beg;
And let them [b]seek *sustenance* far from their ruined homes.
11 Let [a]the creditor seize all that he has;
And let [b]strangers plunder the product of his labor.
12 Let there be none to [a]extend lovingkindness to him,
Nor [b]any to be gracious to his fatherless children.
13 Let his [a]posterity be cut off;
In a following generation let their [b]name be blotted out.

14 Let [a]the iniquity of his fathers be remembered [1]before the LORD,
And do not let the sin of his mother be [b]blotted out.
15 Let [a]them be before the LORD continually,
That He may [b]cut off their memory from the earth;
16 Because he did not remember to show lovingkindness,
But persecuted the [a]afflicted and needy man,
And the despondent in heart, to [b]put *them* to death.
17 He also loved cursing, so [a]it came to him;
And he did not delight in blessing, so it was far from him.
18 But he [a]clothed himself with cursing as with his garment,
And it [b]entered into [1]his body like water,
And like oil into his bones.
19 Let it be to him as [a]a garment with which he covers himself,
And for a belt with which he constantly [b]girds himself.
20 [1]Let this be the [a]reward of my accusers from the LORD,
And of those who [b]speak evil against my soul.

21 But Thou, O [1]GOD, the Lord, deal *kindly* with me [a]for Thy name's sake;
Because [b]Thy lovingkindness is good, deliver me;
22 For [a]I am afflicted and needy,
And [1]my heart is [b]wounded within me.
23 I am passing [a]like a shadow when it lengthens;
I am shaken off [b]like the locust.
24 My [a]knees [1]are weak from [b]fasting;
And my flesh has grown lean, without fatness.

7 [1]Or, *sanctuary*
8 [1]Lit., *protection* [2]Or, *lawgiver*
11 [a]Ps. 44:9
13 [1]Or, *In*, or, *With*
1 [a]Deut. 10:21 [b]Ps. 28:1; 83:1
2 [a]Ps. 10:7; 52:4 [b]Ps. 120:2
3 [a]Ps. 69:4
4 [a]Ps. 38:20 [b]Ps. 69:13; 141:5
5 [a]Ps. 35:12; 38:20 [b]John 7:7; 10:32
6 [a]Zech. 3:1
7 [a]Ps. 1:5 [b]Prov. 28:9
8 [a]Ps. 55:23 [b]Acts 1:20
9 [a]Ex. 22:24 [b]Jer. 18:21
10 [a]Gen. 4:12; Job 30:5-8; Ps. 59:15 [b]Ps. 37:25
11 [a]Neh. 5:7; Job 20:15 [b]Is. 1:7; Lam. 5:2; Ezek. 7:21
12 [a]Ezra 7:28; 9:9 [b]Job 5:4; Is. 9:17
13 [a]Ps. 21:10; 37:28 [b]Ps. 9:5; Prov. 10:7
14 [1]Lit., *to* [a]Ex. 20:5; Num. 14:18; Is. 65:6, 7; Jer. 32:18 [b]Neh. 4:5; Jer. 18:23
15 [a]Ps. 90:8; Jer. 16:17 [b]Ps. 34:16
16 [a]Ps. 37:14 [b]Ps. 37:32; 94:6
17 [a]Prov. 14:14; Ezek. 35:9; Matt. 7:2
18 [1]Lit., *his inward parts* [a]Ps. 73:6; 109:29; Ezek. 7:27 [b]Num. 5:22
19 [a]Ps. 73:6; 109:29; Ezek. 7:27 [b]2 Sam. 22:40; Ps. 30:11; Is. 11:5
20 [1]Lit., *This is* [a]Ps. 54:5; 94:23; Is. 3:11; 2 Tim. 4:14 [b]Ps. 41:5; 71:10
21 [1]YHWH, usually rendered LORD [a]Ps. 23:3; 25:11; 79:9; 106:8; Ezek. 36:22 [b]Ps. 69:16
22 [1]Lit., *one has pierced my heart within me* [a]Ps. 40:17; 86:1 [b]Job. 24:12; Ps. 143:4; Prov. 18:14
23 [a]Ps. 102:11 [b]Ex. 10:19; Job 39:20
24 [1]Or, *totter* [a]Heb. 12:12 [b]Ps. 35:13

25 I also have become a [a]reproach
to them;
When they see me, they [b]wag
their head.

26 [a]Help me, O LORD my God;
Save me according to Thy
lovingkindness.
27 And let them [a]know that this is
Thy hand;
Thou, LORD, hast done it.
28 [a]Let them curse, but do Thou
bless;
When they arise, they shall be
ashamed,
But Thy [b]servant shall be glad.
29 Let [a]my accusers be clothed
with dishonor,
And let them [b]cover themselves with their own shame
as with a robe.

30 With my mouth I will give
thanks abundantly to the
LORD;
And in the midst of many [a]I will
praise Him.
31 For He stands [a]at the right hand
of the needy,
To save him from those who
judge his soul.

PSALM 110

The LORD Gives Dominion to the King.

A Psalm of David.

[a]THE LORD says to my Lord:
"[b]Sit at My right hand,
Until I make [c]Thine enemies a
footstool for Thy feet."
2 The LORD will stretch forth Thy
strong [a]scepter from Zion,
saying,
"[b]Rule in the midst of Thine enemies."
3 Thy [a]people will volunteer
freely in the day of Thy
power;
[b]In holy array, from the womb
of the dawn,
Thy youth are to Thee *as* the
[c]dew.

4 [a]The LORD has sworn and will
[b]not [1]change His mind,
"Thou art a [c]priest forever
According to the order of Melchizedek."
5 The Lord is [a]at Thy right hand;
He will [b]shatter kings in the
[c]day of His wrath.
6 He will [a]judge among the nations,
He will fill *them* with [b]corpses,
He will shatter the chief men
over a broad country.

25 [a]Ps. 22:6 [b]Ps. 22:7; Jer. 18:16; Lam. 2:15
26 [a]Ps. 119:86
27 [a]Job 37:7
28 [a]2 Sam. 16:11, 12 [b]Is. 65:14
29 [a]Job 8:22; Ps. 132:18 [b]Job 8:22
30 [a]Ps. 22:22
31 [a]Ps. 16:8; 73:23; 110:5; 121:5

1 [a]Matt. 22:44; Mark 12:36; Luke 20:42, 43; Acts 2:34, 35; Heb. 1:13 [b]Matt. 26:64; Eph. 1:20; Col. 3:1; Heb. 1:3; 8:1; 10:12; 12:2 [c]1 Cor. 15:25; Eph 1:22
2 [a]Ps. 45:6; Jer. 48:17; Ezek. 19:14 [b]Ps. 2:9; 72:8; Dan. 7:13, 14
3 [a]Judg. 5:2; Neh. 11:2 [b]1 Chr. 16:29; Ps. 96:9 [c]2 Sam. 17:12; Mic. 5:7
4 [1]Lit., *be sorry* [a]Heb. 7:21 [b]Num. 23:19 [c]Heb. 5:6; Zech 6:13
5 [a]Ps. 109:31 [b]Ps. 68:14; 76:12 [c]Ps. 2:5, 12; Rom. 2:5; Rev. 6:17
6 [a]Is. 2:4; Joel 3:12; Mic. 4:3 [b]Is. 66:24
7 [a]Judg. 7:5, 6 [b]Ps. 27:6

1 [1]Or, *Hallelujah! I will* [2]Heb., YAH [a]Ps. 138:1 [b]Ps. 89:7; 149:1
2 [1]Lit., *sought out* [a]Ps. 92:5
3 [1]Lit., *Splendor and majesty* [a]Ps. 96:6; 145:5 [b]Ps. 112:3, 9
4 [a]Ps. 86:15
5 [1]Lit., *prey* [2]Or, *revere* [a]Matt. 6:31-33 [b]Ps. 105:8
7 [a]Rev. 15:3 [b]Ps. 19:7; 93:5
8 [a]Ps. 119:160; Is. 40:8; Matt. 5:18
9 [a]Luke 1:68 [b]Ps. 99:3
10 [1]Or, *reverence for* [a]Prov. 1:7; 9:10 [b]Ps. 119:98; Prov. 3:4 [c]Ps. 145:2

1 [1]Or, *Hallelujah! Blessed* [2]Heb., YAH [3]Or, *reveres* [a]Ps. 128:1 [b]Ps. 1:2; 119:14
2 [1]Lit., *seed* [2]Or, *in the land* [a]Ps. 127:4

7 He will [a]drink from the brook
by the wayside;
Therefore He will [b]lift up *His*
head.

PSALM 111

The LORD Praised for His Goodness.

[1]PRAISE [2]the LORD!
I [a]will give thanks to the LORD
with all *my* heart,
In the [b]company of the upright
and in the assembly.
2 Great are the [a]works of the
LORD;
They are [1]studied by all who delight in them.
3 [1a]Splendid and majestic is His
work;
And [b]His righteousness endures forever.
4 He has made His wonders to be
remembered;
The LORD is [a]gracious and compassionate.
5 He has [a]given [1]food to those
who [2]fear Him;
He will [b]remember His covenant forever.
6 He has made known to His people the power of His works,
In giving them the heritage of
the nations.

7 The works of His hands are
[a]truth and justice;
All His precepts [b]are sure.
8 They are [a]upheld forever and
ever;
They are performed in truth
and uprightness.
9 He has sent [a]redemption to His
people;
He has ordained His covenant
forever;
[b]Holy and awesome is His
name.
10 The [1a]fear of the LORD is the beginning of wisdom;
A [b]good understanding have all
those who do *His commandments;*
His [c]praise endures forever.

PSALM 112

Prosperity of the One Who Fears the LORD.

[1]PRAISE [2]the LORD!
How [a]blessed is the man who
[3]fears the LORD,
Who greatly [b]delights in His
commandments.
2 His [1a]descendants will be
mighty [2]on earth;

The generation of the [b]upright will be blessed.
3 [a]Wealth and riches are in his house,
And his righteousness endures forever.
4 Light arises in the darkness [a]for the upright;
He is [b]gracious and compassionate and righteous.
5 It is well with the man who [a]is gracious and lends;
He will [1]maintain his cause in judgment.
6 For he will [a]never be shaken;
The [b]righteous will be remembered forever.

7 He will not fear [a]evil tidings;
His [b]heart is steadfast, [c]trusting in the LORD.
8 His [a]heart is upheld, he [b]will not fear,
Until he [c]looks *with satisfaction* on his adversaries.
9 He [a]has given freely to the poor;
His righteousness endures forever;
His [b]horn will be exalted in honor.

10 The [a]wicked will see it and be [1]vexed;
He will [b]gnash his teeth and [c]melt away;
The [d]desire of the wicked will perish.

PSALM 113

The LORD Exalts the Humble.

1 PRAISE [2]the LORD!
[a]Praise, O [b]servants of the LORD.
Praise the name of the LORD.
2 [a]Blessed be the name of the LORD
From this time forth and forever.
3 [a]From the rising of the sun to its setting
The [b]name of the LORD is to be praised.
4 The LORD is [a]high above all nations;
His [b]glory is above the heavens.

5 [a]Who is like the LORD our God,
Who [b]is enthroned on high,
6 Who [a]humbles Himself to behold
The things that are in heaven and in the earth?

7 He [a]raises the poor from the dust,
And lifts the needy from the ash heap,
8 To make *them* [a]sit with princes,
With the princes of His people.
9 He [a]makes the barren woman abide in the house
As a joyful mother of children.
[1]Praise [2]the LORD!

PSALM 114

God's Deliverance of Israel from Egypt.

WHEN Israel went forth [a]from Egypt,
The house of Jacob from a people of strange language,
2 Judah became [a]His sanctuary,
Israel, [b]His dominion.

3 The [a]sea looked and fled;
The [b]Jordan turned back.
4 The mountains [a]skipped like rams,
The hills, like lambs.
5 What [a]ails you, O sea, that you flee?
O Jordan, that you turn back?
6 O mountains, that you skip like rams?
O hills, like lambs?

7 [a]Tremble, O earth, before the Lord,
Before the God of Jacob,
8 Who [a]turned the rock into a [b]pool of water,
The [c]flint into a fountain of water.

PSALM 115

Heathen Idols Contrasted with the LORD.

[a]NOT to us, O LORD, not to us,
But [b]to Thy name give glory
Because of Thy lovingkindness, because of Thy truth.
2 [a]Why should the nations say,
"[b]Where, now, is their God?"
3 But our [a]God is in the heavens;
He [b]does whatever He pleases.
4 Their [a]idols are silver and gold,
The [b]work of man's hands.
5 They have mouths, but they [a]cannot speak;
They have eyes, but they cannot see;
6 They have ears, but they cannot hear;
They have noses, but they cannot smell;

---

2 [b]Ps. 128:4
3 [a]Prov. 3:16; 8:18
4 [a]Job 11:17; Ps. 97:11 [b]Ps. 37:26
5 [1]Or, *conduct his affairs with justice* [a]Ps. 37:21
6 [a]Ps. 15:5; 55:22 [b]Prov. 10:7
7 [a]Prov. 1:33 [b]Ps. 57:7; 108:1 [c]Ps. 56:4
8 [a]Heb. 13:9 [b]Ps. 27:1; 56:11; Prov. 3:24; Is. 12:2 [c]Ps. 54:7
9 [a]2 Cor. 9:9 [b]Ps. 75:10; 89:17
10 [1]Or, *angry* [a]Ps. 86:17 [b]Ps. 35:16; 37:12; Matt. 8:12; 25:30; Luke 13:28 [c]Ps. 58:7 [d]Job 8:13

1 [1]Or, *Hallelujah! Praise* [2]Heb., *YAH* [a]Ps. 135:1 [b]Ps. 34:22; 69:36
2 [a]Ps. 145:21; Dan. 2:20
3 [a]Ps. 50:1 [b]Ps. 18:3; 48:1, 10
4 [a]Ps. 97:9; 99:2 [b]Ps. 8:1; 57:11
5 [a]Ex. 15:11; Ps. 35:10; 89:6 [b]Ps. 103:19
6 [a]Ps. 11:4; 138:6; Is. 57:15
7 [a]1 Sam. 2:8
8 [a]Job 36:7
9 [1]Or, *Hallelujah!* [2]Heb., *YAH* [a]1 Sam. 2:5

1 [a]Ex. 13:3
2 [a]Ex. 15:17; 29:45, 46; Ps. 78:68, 69 [b]Ex. 19:6
3 [a]Ps. 77:16 [b]Josh. 3:13, 16
4 [a]Ex. 19:18; Judg. 5:5; Ps. 18:7; 29:6; Hab. 3:6
5 [a]Hab. 3:8
7 [a]Ps. 96:9
8 [a]Ex. 17:6; Num. 20:11; Ps. 78:15; 105:41 [b]Ps. 107:35 [c]Deut. 8:15

1 [a]Is. 48:11; Ezek. 36:22 [b]Ps. 29:2
2 [a]Ps. 79:10 [b]Ps. 42:3
3 [a]Ps. 103:19 [b]Ps. 135:6; Dan. 4:35
4 [a]Ps. 115:4-8; 135:15-18 [b]Deut. 4:28; 2 Kin. 19:18; Is. 37:19; 44:10
5 [a]Jer. 10:5

7 They have hands, but they cannot feel;
They have feet, but they cannot walk;
They cannot make a sound with their throat.
8 Those who make them will become like them,
Everyone who trusts in them.

9 O [a]Israel, [b]trust in the LORD;
He is their [c]help and their shield.
10 O house of [a]Aaron, trust in the LORD;
He is their help and their shield.
11 You who [1a]fear the LORD, trust in the LORD;
He is their help and their shield.
12 The LORD [a]has been mindful of us; He will bless *us;*
He will bless the house of Israel;
He will bless the house of Aaron.
13 He will [a]bless those who [1]fear the LORD,
The small together with the great.
14 May the LORD [a]give you increase,
You and your children.
15 May you be blessed of the LORD,
[a]Maker of heaven and earth.

16 The heavens are [a]the heavens of the LORD;
But [b]the earth He has given to the sons of men.
17 The [a]dead do not praise [1]the LORD,
Nor *do* any who go down into [b]silence;
18 But as for us, we will [a]bless [1]the LORD
From this time forth and forever.
[2]Praise [1]the LORD!

PSALM 116

Thanksgiving for Deliverance from Death.

[a]I LOVE the LORD, because He [b]hears
My voice *and* my supplications.
2 Because He has [a]inclined His ear to me,
Therefore I shall call *upon Him* as long as I live.
3 The [a]cords of death encompassed me,
And the terrors of Sheol came upon me;
I found distress and sorrow.
4 Then [a]I called upon the name of the LORD:
"O LORD, I beseech Thee, [1b]save my life!"

5 [a]Gracious is the LORD, and [b]righteous;
Yes, our God is [c]compassionate.
6 The LORD preserves [a]the simple;
I was [b]brought low, and He saved me.
7 Return to your [a]rest, O my soul,
For the LORD has [b]dealt bountifully with you.
8 For Thou hast [a]rescued my soul from death,
My eyes from tears,
My feet from stumbling.
9 I shall walk before the LORD
In the [1a]land of the living.
10 I [a]believed when I said,
"I am [b]greatly afflicted."
11 I [a]said in my alarm,
"[b]All men are liars."

12 What shall I [a]render to the LORD
For all His [b]benefits [1]toward me?
13 I shall lift up the [a]cup of salvation,
And [b]call upon the name of the LORD.
14 I shall [a]pay my vows to the LORD,
Oh *may it be* [b]in the presence of all His people.
15 [a]Precious in the sight of the LORD
Is the death of His godly ones.
16 O LORD, [1]surely I am [a]Thy servant,
I am Thy servant, the [b]son of Thy handmaid,
Thou hast [c]loosed my bonds.
17 To Thee I shall offer [a]a sacrifice of thanksgiving,
And [b]call upon the name of the LORD.
18 I shall [a]pay my vows to the LORD,
Oh *may it be* in the presence of all His people,
19 In the [a]courts of the LORD's house,
In the midst of you, O [b]Jerusalem.
[1]Praise [2]the LORD!

PSALM 117

A Psalm of Praise.

[a]PRAISE the LORD, all nations;
Laud Him, all peoples!

---

9 [a]Ps. 118:2; 135:19 [b]Ps. 37:3; 62:8 [c]Ps. 33:20
10 [a]Ps. 118:2; 135:19
11 [1]Or, *revere* [a]Ps. 22:23; 103:11; 135:20
12 [a]Ps. 98:3
13 [1]Or, *revere* [a]Ps. 103:11; 112:1; 128:1
14 [a]Deut. 1:11
15 [a]Gen. 1:1; Neh. 9:6; Ps. 102:25; 121:2; 124:8; 134:3; 146:6; Acts 14:15; Rev. 14:7
16 [a]Ps. 89:11 [b]Ps. 8:6
17 [1]Heb., *YAH* [a]Ps. 6:5 [b]Ps. 31:17
18 [1]Heb., *YAH* [2]Or, *Hallelujah!* [a]Ps. 113:2

1 [a]Ps. 18:1 [b]Ps. 6:8; 66:19; Is. 37:17; Dan. 9:18
2 [a]Ps. 17:6; 31:2; 40:1
3 [a]Ps. 18:4, 5
4 [1]Or, *deliver my soul* [a]Ps. 18:6; 118:5 [b]Ps. 17:13; 22:20
5 [a]Ps. 86:15; 103:8 [b]Ezra 9:15; Neh. 9:8; Ps. 119:137; 145:17; Jer. 12:1; Dan. 9:14 [c]Ex. 34:6
6 [a]Ps. 19:7; Prov. 1:4 [b]Ps. 79:18; 142:6
7 [a]Jer. 6:16; Matt. 11:29 [b]Ps. 13:6; 142:7
8 [a]Ps. 49:15; 56:13; 86:13
9 [1]Lit., *lands* [a]Ps. 27:13
10 [a]2 Cor. 4:13 [b]Ps. 88:7
11 [a]Ps. 31:22 [b]Ps. 62:9; Rom. 3:4
12 [1]Lit., *upon* [a]2 Chr. 32:25; 1 Thess. 3:9 [b]Ps. 103:2
13 [a]Ps. 16:5 [b]Ps. 80:18; 105:1
14 [a]Ps. 50:14 [b]Ps. 22:25
15 [a]Ps. 72:14
16 [1]Or, *because* [a]Ps. 86:16; 119:125; 143:12 [b]Ps. 86:16 [c]Ps. 107:14
17 [a]Ps. 50:14 [b]Ps. 116:13
18 [a]Ps. 116:14
19 [1]Or, *Hallelujah!* [2]Heb., *YAH* [a]Ps. 92:13; 96:8; 135:2 [b]Ps. 102:21

1 [a]Rom. 15:11

2 For His [a]lovingkindness [1]is great toward us,
And the [2][b]truth of the LORD is everlasting.
[3]Praise [4]the LORD!

PSALM 118

Thanksgiving for the LORD's Saving Goodness.

[a]GIVE thanks to the LORD, for He is good;
[b]For His lovingkindness is everlasting.
2 Oh let [a]Israel say,
"His lovingkindness is everlasting."
3 Oh let the [a]house of Aaron say,
"His lovingkindness is everlasting."
4 Oh let those [a]who [1]fear the LORD say,
"His lovingkindness is everlasting."

5 From *my* [a]distress I called upon [1]the LORD;
[1]The LORD answered me *and* [b]*set me* in a large place.
6 The LORD is [a]for me; I will [b]not fear;
[c]What can man do to me?
7 The LORD is for me [a]among those who help me;
Therefore I shall [b]look *with satisfaction* on those who hate me.
8 It is [a]better to take refuge in the LORD
Than to trust in man.
9 It is [a]better to take refuge in the LORD
Than to trust in princes.

10 All nations [a]surrounded me;
In the name of the LORD I will surely [b]cut them off.
11 They surrounded me, yes, they surrounded me;
In the name of the LORD I will surely cut them off.
12 They surrounded me [a]like bees;
They were extinguished as a [b]fire of thorns;
In the name of the LORD I will surely cut them off.
13 You [a]pushed me violently so that I [1]was falling,
But the LORD [b]helped me.
14 [a]The LORD is my strength and song,
And He has become [b]my salvation.

15 The sound of [a]joyful shouting and salvation is in the tents of the righteous;
The [b]right hand of the LORD does valiantly.
16 The [a]right hand of the LORD is exalted;
The right hand of the LORD does valiantly.
17 I [a]shall not die, but live,
And [b]tell of the works of the LORD.
18 The LORD has [a]disciplined me severely,
But He has [b]not given me over to death.

19 [a]Open to me the gates of righteousness;
I shall enter through them, I shall give thanks to the LORD.
20 This is the gate of the LORD;
The [a]righteous will enter through it.
21 I shall give thanks to Thee, for Thou hast [a]answered me;
And Thou hast [b]become my salvation.

22 The [a]stone which the builders rejected
Has become the chief corner *stone*.
23 This is the LORD's doing;
It is marvelous in our eyes.
24 This is the day which the LORD has made;
Let us [a]rejoice and be glad in it.
25 O LORD, [a]do save, we beseech Thee;
O LORD, we beseech Thee, do send [b]prosperity!
26 [a]Blessed is the one who comes in the name of the LORD;
We have [b]blessed you from the house of the LORD.
27 [a]The LORD is God, and He has given us [b]light;
Bind the festival sacrifice with cords to the [c]horns of the altar.
28 [a]Thou art my God, and I give thanks to Thee;
Thou art my God, [b]I extol Thee.
29 [a]Give thanks to the LORD, for He is good;
For His lovingkindness is everlasting.

PSALM 119

Meditations and Prayers Relating to the Law of God.

Aleph.

HOW blessed are those whose way is [1][a]blameless,
Who [b]walk in the law of the LORD.

---

2 [1]Lit., *prevails over us* [2]Or, *faithfulness* [3]Or, *Hallelujah!* [4]Heb., YAH
[a]Ps. 103:11 [b]Ps. 100:5; 146:6

1 [a]Ps. 106:1 [b]Ps. 136:1-26
2 [a]Ps. 115:9
3 [a]Ps. 115:10
4 [1]Or, *revere* [a]Ps. 115:11
5 [1]Heb., YAH, also vs. 14, 17, 18, 19 [a]Ps. 18:6; 86:7; 120:1 [b]Ps. 18:19
6 [a]Job 19:27; Ps. 56:9; Heb. 13:6 [b]Ps. 23:4; 27:1 [c]Ps. 56:4, 11
7 [a]Ps. 54:4 [b]Ps. 54:7
8 [a]2 Chr. 32:7, 8; Ps. 108:12; Is. 31:1, 3; 57:13
9 [a]Ps. 146:3
10 [a]Ps. 3:6; 88:17 [b]Ps. 18:40
12 [a]Deut. 1:44 [b]Ps. 58:9
13 [1]Or, *fell* [a]Ps. 140:4 [b]Ps. 86:17
14 [a]Ex. 15:2; Is. 12:2 [b]Ps. 27:1
15 [a]Ps. 68:3 [b]Ex. 15:6; Ps. 89:13; Luke 1:51
16 [a]Ps. 89:13
17 [a]Ps. 116:8, 9; Hab. 1:12 [b]Ps. 73:28; 107:22
18 [a]Ps. 73:14; Jer. 31:18; 1 Cor. 11:32; 2 Cor. 6:9 [b]Ps. 86:13
19 [a]Is. 26:2
20 [a]Ps. 15:1, 2; 24:3-6; 140:13
21 [a]Ps. 116:1; 118:5 [b]Ps. 118:14
22 [a]Matt. 21:42; Mark 12:10, 11; Luke 20:17; Acts 4:11; Eph. 2:20; 1 Pet. 2:7
24 [a]Ps. 31:7
25 [a]Ps. 106:47 [b]Ps. 122:6, 7
26 [a]Matt. 21:9; 23:39; Mark 11:9; Luke 13:35; 19:38; John 12:13 [b]Ps. 129:8
27 [a]1 Kin. 18:39 [b]Esth. 8:16; Ps. 18:28; 27:1; 1 Pet. 2:9 [c]Ex. 27:2
28 [a]Ps. 63:1; 140:6 [b]Ex. 15:2; Is. 25:1
29 [a]Ps.118:1

1 [1]Lit., *complete*, or, *having integrity* [a]Ps. 101:2, 6; Prov. 11:20; 13:6 [b]Ps. 128:1; Ezek. 11:20; 18:17; Mic. 4:2

2 How blessed are those who [a]observe His testimonies,
Who [b]seek Him [c]with all *their* heart.
3 They also [a]do no unrighteousness;
They walk in His ways.
4 Thou hast [a]ordained Thy precepts,
That we should keep *them* diligently.
5 Oh that my [a]ways may be established
To [b]keep Thy statutes!
6 Then I [a]shall not be ashamed
When I look [1]upon all Thy commandments.
7 I shall [a]give thanks to Thee with uprightness of heart,
When I learn Thy righteous judgments.
8 I shall keep Thy statutes;
Do not [a]forsake me utterly!

Beth.

9 How can a young man keep his way pure?
By [a]keeping *it* according to Thy word.
10 With all my [a]heart I have sought Thee;
Do not let me [b]wander from Thy commandments.
11 Thy word I have [a]treasured in my heart,
That I may not sin against Thee.
12 Blessed art Thou, O LORD;
[a]Teach me Thy statutes.
13 With my lips I have [a]told of
All the [b]ordinances of Thy mouth.
14 I have [a]rejoiced in the way of Thy testimonies,
As much as in all riches.
15 I will [a]meditate on Thy precepts,
And regard [b]Thy ways.
16 I shall [a]delight in Thy statutes;
I shall [b]not forget Thy word.

Gimel.

17 [a]Deal bountifully with Thy servant,
That I may live and keep Thy word.
18 Open my eyes, that I may behold
Wonderful things from Thy law.
19 I am a [a]stranger in the earth;
Do not hide Thy commandments from me.
20 My soul is crushed [a]with longing
After Thine ordinances at all times.
21 Thou dost [a]rebuke the arrogant, the [b]cursed,
Who [c]wander from Thy commandments.
22 [a]Take away reproach and contempt from me,
For I [b]observe Thy testimonies.
23 Even though [a]princes sit and talk against me,
Thy servant [b]meditates on Thy statutes.
24 Thy testimonies also are my [a]delight;
They are my counselors.

Daleth.

25 My [a]soul cleaves to the dust;
[b]Revive me [c]according to Thy word.
26 I have told of my ways, and Thou hast answered me;
[a]Teach me Thy statutes.
27 Make me understand the way of Thy precepts,
So I will [a]meditate on Thy wonders.
28 My [a]soul [1]weeps because of grief;
[b]Strengthen me according to Thy word.
29 Remove the false way from me,
And graciously grant me Thy law.
30 I have chosen the faithful way;
I have placed Thine ordinances *before me.*
31 I [a]cleave to Thy testimonies;
O LORD, do not put me to shame!
32 I shall run the way of Thy commandments,
For Thou wilt [a]enlarge my heart.

He.

33 [a]Teach me, O LORD, the way of Thy statutes,
And I shall observe it to the end.
34 [a]Give me understanding, that I may [b]observe Thy law,
And keep it [c]with all *my* heart.
35 Make me walk in the [a]path of Thy commandments,
For I [b]delight in it.
36 [a]Incline my heart to Thy testimonies,
And not to [b]*dishonest* gain.
37 Turn away my [a]eyes from looking at vanity,
And [b]revive me in Thy ways.
38 [a]Establish Thy word to Thy servant,
As that which produces reverence for Thee.

2 [a]Ps. 25:10; 99:7; 119:22, 168 [b]Deut. 4:29; Ps. 119:10 [c]Deut. 6:5; 10:12; 11:13; 13:3
3 [a]1 John 3:9; 5:18
4 [a]Deut. 4:13; Neh. 9:13
5 [a]Ps. 40:2; Prov. 4:26 [b]Deut. 12:1; 2 Chr. 7:17
6 [1]Lit., *to* [a]Ps. 119:80
7 [a]Ps. 119:62
8 [a]Ps. 38:21; 71:9, 18
9 [a]1 Kin. 2:4; 8:25; 2 Chr. 6:16
10 [a]Ps. 119:2, 145 [b]Ps. 119:21, 118
11 [a]Ps. 37:31; 40:8; Luke 2:19
12 [a]Ps. 119:26, 64, 108, 124, 135, 171
13 [a]Ps. 40:9 [b]Ps. 119:72
14 [a]Ps. 119:111, 162
15 [a]Ps. 1:2; 119:23, 48, 78, 97, 148 [b]Ps. 25:4; 27:11; Is. 58:2
16 [a]Ps. 119:24, 35, 47, 70, 77, 92, 143, 174 [b]Ps. 119:93
17 [a]Ps. 13:6
19 [a]Gen. 47:9; Lev. 25:23; 1 Chr. 29:15; Ps. 39:12; 119:54; Heb. 11:13
20 [a]Ps. 119:40, 131
21 [a]Ps. 68:30 [b]Deut. 27:26; Ps. 37:22 [c]Ps. 119:10, 118
22 [a]Ps. 119:39 [b]Ps. 119:2
23 [a]Ps. 119:161 [b]Ps. 119:15
24 [a]Ps. 119:16
25 [a]Ps. 44:25 [b]Ps. 119:37, 40, 88, 93, 107, 149, 154, 156, 159 [c]Ps. 119:65
26 [a]Ps. 119:12
27 [a]Ps. 105:2
28 [1]Lit., *drops* [a]Ps. 22:14; 107:26 [b]Ps. 20:2; 1 Pet. 5:10
31 [a]Deut. 11:22
32 [a]1 Kin. 4:29; Is. 60:5; 2 Cor. 6:11, 13
33 [a]Ps. 119:5, 12
34 [a]Ps. 119:27, 73, 125, 144, 169 [b]1 Chr. 22:12; Ezek. 44:24 [c]Ps. 119:2, 69
35 [a]Ps. 25:4; Is. 40:14 [b]Ps. 112:1; 119:16
36 [a]1 Kin. 8:58 [b]Luke 12:15; Heb. 13:5
37 [a]Is. 33:15 [b]Ps. 71:20; 119:25
38 [a]2 Sam. 7:25

39 [a]Turn away my reproach which
I dread,
For Thine ordinances are good.
40 Behold, I [a]long for Thy precepts;
Revive me through Thy righteousness.

Vav.

41 May Thy [a]lovingkindnesses
also come to me, O LORD,
Thy salvation [b]according to
Thy word;
42 So I shall have an [a]answer for
him who [b]reproaches me,
For I trust in Thy word.
43 And do not take the word of
truth utterly out of my
mouth,
For I [1a]wait for Thine ordinances.
44 So I will [a]keep Thy law continually,
Forever and ever.
45 And I will [a]walk at liberty,
For I [b]seek Thy precepts.
46 I will also speak of Thy testimonies [a]before kings,
And shall not be ashamed.
47 And I shall [a]delight in Thy commandments,
Which I [b]love.
48 And I shall lift up my hands to
Thy commandments,
Which I [a]love;
And I will [b]meditate on Thy
statutes.

Zayin.

49 Remember the word to Thy servant,
In which Thou hast made me
hope.
50 This is my [a]comfort in my affliction,
That Thy word has revived me.
51 The arrogant [a]utterly deride
me,
Yet I do not [b]turn aside from
Thy law.
52 I have [a]remembered Thine ordinances from of old, O LORD,
And comfort myself.
53 Burning [a]indignation has seized
me because of the wicked,
Who [b]forsake Thy law.
54 Thy statutes are my songs
In the house of my [a]pilgrimage.
55 O LORD, I [a]remember Thy name
[b]in the night,
And keep Thy law.
56 This has become mine,
[1]That I [a]observe Thy precepts.

Heth.

57 The LORD is my [a]portion;
I have promised to [b]keep Thy
words.
58 I [a]entreated Thy favor [b]with all
my heart;
[c]Be gracious to me [d]according
to Thy word.
59 I [a]considered my ways,
And turned my feet to Thy testimonies.
60 I hastened and did not delay
To keep Thy commandments.
61 The [a]cords of the wicked have
encircled me,
But I have [b]not forgotten Thy
law.
62 At [a]midnight I shall rise to give
thanks to Thee
Because of Thy [b]righteous ordinances.
63 I am a [a]companion of all those
who [1]fear Thee,
And of those who keep Thy precepts.
64 [a]The earth is full of Thy lovingkindness, O LORD;
[b]Teach me Thy statutes.

Teth.

65 Thou hast dealt well with Thy
servant,
O LORD, according to Thy word.
66 Teach me good [a]discernment
and knowledge,
For I believe in Thy commandments.
67 [a]Before I was afflicted I went
astray,
But now I keep Thy word.
68 Thou art [a]good and [b]doest
good;
[c]Teach me Thy statutes.
69 The arrogant have [a]forged a lie
against me;
With all *my* heart I will [b]observe Thy precepts.
70 Their heart is [a]covered with fat,
But I [b]delight in Thy law.
71 It is [a]good for me that I was afflicted,
That I may learn Thy statutes.
72 The [a]law of Thy mouth is better
to me
Than thousands of gold and silver *pieces*.

Yodh.

73 [a]Thy hands made me and fashioned me;
[b]Give me understanding, that I
may learn Thy commandments.
74 May those who [1]fear Thee [a]see
me and be glad,
Because I [2b]wait for Thy word.
75 I know, O LORD, that Thy judgments are [a]righteous,

39 [a]Ps. 119:22
40 [a]Ps. 119:20
41 [a]Ps. 119:77 [b]Ps. 119:58, 76
42 [a]Prov. 27:11 [b]Ps. 102:8; 119:39
43 [1]Or, *hope in* [a]Ps. 119:49, 74, 81, 114, 147
44 [a]Ps. 119:33
45 [a]Prov. 4:12 [b]Ps. 119:94, 155
46 [a]Matt. 10:18; Acts 26:1, 2
47 [a]Ps. 119:16 [b]Ps. 119:97, 127, 159
48 [a]Ps. 119:97, 127, 159 [b]Ps. 119:15
50 [a]Job 6:10; Rom. 15:4
51 [a]Job 30:1; Jer. 20:7 [b]Job 23:11; Ps. 44:18; 119:157
52 [a]Ps. 103:18
53 [a]Ex. 32:19; Ezra 9:3; Neh. 13:25; Ps. 119:158 [b]Ps. 89:30
54 [a]Gen. 47:9; Ps. 119:19
55 [a]Ps. 63:6 [b]Ps. 42:8; 92:2; 119:62; Is. 26:9; Acts 16:25
56 [1]Or, *Because* [a]Ps. 119:22, 69
57 [a]Ps. 16:5 [b]Deut. 33:9
58 [a]1 Kin. 13:6 [b]Ps. 119:2 [c]Ps. 41:4; 56:1; 57:1 [d]Ps. 119:41
59 [a]Mark 14:72; Luke 15:17
61 [a]Job 36:8; Ps. 140:5 [b]Ps. 119:83, 141, 153, 176
62 [a]Ps. 119:55 [b]Ps. 119:7
63 [1]Or, *revere* [a]Ps. 101:6
64 [a]Ps. 33:5 [b]Ps. 119:12
66 [a]Phil. 1:9
67 [a]Ps. 119:71, 75; Jer. 31:18, 19; Heb. 12:5-11
68 [a]Ps. 86:5; 100:5; 106:1 [b]Deut. 8:16; 28:63; 30:5; Ps. 125:4 [c]Ps. 119:12
69 [a]Job 13:4 [b]Ps. 119:56
70 [a]Deut. 32:15; Job 15:27; Ps. 17:10; Is. 6:10; Jer. 5:28 [b]Ps. 119:16
71 [a]Ps. 119:67
72 [a]Ps. 19:10; 119:127; Prov. 8:10, 11, 19
73 [a]Job 10:8; 31:15; Ps. 138:8; 139:15, 16 [b]Ps. 119:34
74 [1]Or, *revere* [2]Or, *hope in* [a]Ps. 34:2; 35:27; 107:42 [b]Ps. 119:43
75 [a]Ps. 119:138

And that [b]in faithfulness Thou hast afflicted me.
76 O may Thy lovingkindness comfort me,
According to Thy word to Thy servant.
77 May [a]Thy compassion come to me that I may live,
For Thy law is my [b]delight.
78 May [a]the arrogant be ashamed, for they subvert me [b]with a lie;
But I shall [c]meditate on Thy precepts.
79 May those who [1]fear Thee turn to me,
Even those who know Thy testimonies.
80 May my heart be [1a]blameless in Thy statutes,
That I may not [b]be ashamed.

Kaph.

81 My [a]soul languishes for Thy salvation;
I [1b]wait for Thy word.
82 My [a]eyes fail *with longing* for Thy word,
While I say, "When wilt Thou comfort me?"
83 Though I have [a]become like a wineskin in the smoke,
I do [b]not forget Thy statutes.
84 How many are the [a]days of Thy servant?
When wilt Thou [b]execute judgment on those who persecute me?
85 The arrogant have [a]dug pits for me,
Men who are not in accord with Thy law.
86 All Thy commandments are [a]faithful;
They have [b]persecuted me with a lie; [c]help me!
87 They almost destroyed me on earth,
But as for me, I [a]did not forsake Thy precepts.
88 Revive me according to Thy lovingkindness,
So that I may keep the testimony of Thy mouth.

Lamedh.

89 [a]Forever, O LORD,
Thy word [1]is settled in heaven.
90 Thy [a]faithfulness *continues* [1]throughout all generations;
Thou didst [b]establish the earth, and it [c]stands.
91 They stand this day according to Thine [a]ordinances,
For [b]all things are Thy servants.
92 If Thy law had not been my [a]delight,
Then I would have perished [b]in my affliction.
93 I will [a]never forget Thy precepts,
For by them Thou hast [1b]revived me.
94 I am Thine, [a]save me;
For I have [b]sought Thy precepts.
95 The wicked [a]wait for me to destroy me;
I shall diligently consider Thy testimonies.
96 I have seen a limit to all perfection;
Thy commandment is exceedingly broad.

Mem.

97 O how I [a]love Thy law!
It is my [b]meditation all the day.
98 Thy [a]commandments make me wiser than my enemies,
For they are ever [1]mine.
99 I have more insight than all my teachers,
For Thy testimonies are my [a]meditation.
100 I understand [a]more than the aged,
Because I have [b]observed Thy precepts.
101 I have [a]restrained my feet from every evil way,
That I may keep Thy word.
102 I have not [a]turned aside from Thine ordinances,
For Thou Thyself hast taught me.
103 How [a]sweet are Thy [1]words to my [2]taste!
Yes, sweeter than honey to my mouth!
104 From Thy precepts I [a]get understanding;
Therefore I [b]hate every false way.

Nun.

105 Thy word is a [a]lamp to my feet,
And a light to my path.
106 I have [a]sworn, and I will confirm it,
That I will keep Thy righteous ordinances.
107 I am exceedingly [a]afflicted;
[b]Revive me, O LORD, according to Thy word.
108 O accept the [a]freewill offerings of my mouth, O LORD,
And [b]teach me Thine ordinances.
109 My [1a]life is continually [2]in my hand,
Yet I do not [b]forget Thy law.
110 The wicked have [a]laid a snare for me,

75 [b]Heb. 12:10
77 [a]Ps. 119:41 [b]Ps. 119:16
78 [a]Jer. 50:32 [b]Ps. 119:86 [c]Ps. 119:15
79 [1]Or, *revere*
80 [1]Lit., *complete;* or, *having integrity* [a]Ps. 119:1 [b]Ps. 119:46
81 [1]Or, *hope in* [a]Ps. 84:2 [b]Ps. 119:43
82 [a]Ps. 69:3; 119:123; Is. 38:14; Lam. 2:11
83 [a]Job 30:30 [b]Ps. 119:61
84 [a]Ps. 39:4 [b]Rev. 6:10
85 [a]Ps. 7:15; 57:6; Jer. 18:22
86 [a]Ps. 119:138 [b]Ps. 35:19; 119:78, 161 [c]Ps. 109:26
87 [a]Is. 58:2
89 [1]Lit., *stands firm* [a]Ps. 119:160; Is. 40:8; Matt. 24:35; 1 Pet. 1:25
90 [1]Lit., *to* [a]Ps. 36:5; 89:1, 2 [b]Ps. 148:6 [c]Eccles. 1:4
91 [a]Jer. 31:35 [b]Ps. 104:2-4
92 [a]Ps. 119:16 [b]Ps. 119:50
93 [1]Or, *kept me alive* [a]Ps. 119:16, 83 [b]Ps. 119:25
94 [a]Ps. 119:146 [b]Ps. 119:45
95 [a]Ps. 40:14; Is. 32:7
97 [a]Ps. 119:47, 48, 127, 163, 165 [b]Ps. 119:15
98 [1]Or, *with me* [a]Deut. 4:6; Ps. 119:130
99 [a]Ps. 119:15
100 [a]Job 32:7-9 [b]Ps. 119:22, 56
101 [a]Prov. 1:15
102 [a]Deut. 17:20; Josh. 23:6; 1 Kin. 15:5
103 [1]Or, *promises* [2]Lit., *palate* [a]Ps. 19:10; Prov. 24:13, 14
104 [a]Ps. 119:130 [b]Ps. 119:128
105 [a]Prov. 6:23
106 [a]Neh. 10:29
107 [a]Ps. 119:25, 50 [b]Ps. 119:25
108 [a]Hos. 14:2; Heb. 13:15 [b]Ps. 119:12
109 [1]Lit., *soul* [2]I.e., in danger [a]Judg. 12:3; Job 13:14 [b]Ps. 119:16
110 [a]Ps. 91:3; 140:5; 141:9

Yet I have not [b]gone astray
from Thy precepts.
111 I have [a]inherited Thy testimonies forever,
For they are the [b]joy of my heart.
112 I have [a]inclined my heart to perform Thy statutes
Forever, *even* [b]to the end.

Samekh.

113 I hate those who are [a]double-minded,
But I love Thy [b]law.
114 Thou art my [a]hiding place and my [b]shield;
I [1c]wait for Thy word.
115 [a]Depart from me, evildoers,
That I may [b]observe the commandments of my God.
116 [a]Sustain me according to Thy word, that I may live;
And [b]do not let me be ashamed of my hope.
117 Uphold me that I may be [a]safe,
That I may [b]have regard for Thy statutes continually.
118 Thou hast [1]rejected all those [a]who wander from Thy statutes,
For their deceitfulness is [2]useless.
119 Thou hast removed all the wicked of the earth *like* [a]dross;
Therefore I [b]love Thy testimonies.
120 My flesh [a]trembles for fear of Thee,
And I am [b]afraid of Thy judgments.

Ayin.

121 I have [a]done justice and righteousness;
Do not leave me to my oppressors.
122 Be [a]surety for Thy servant for good;
Do not let the arrogant [b]oppress me.
123 My eyes fail *with longing* for Thy salvation,
And for Thy righteous word.
124 Deal with Thy servant [a]according to Thy lovingkindness,
And [b]teach me Thy statutes.
125 I [a]am Thy servant; [b]give me understanding,
That I may know Thy testimonies.
126 It is time for the LORD to [a]act,
For they have broken Thy law.
127 Therefore I [a]love Thy commandments
Above gold, yes, above fine gold.
128 Therefore I esteem right all *Thy* [a]precepts concerning everything,
I [b]hate every false way.

Pe.

129 Thy testimonies are [a]wonderful;
Therefore my soul [b]observes them.
130 The [a]unfolding of Thy words gives light;
It gives [b]understanding to the simple.
131 I [a]opened my mouth wide and [b]panted,
For I [c]longed for Thy commandments.
132 [a]Turn to me and be gracious to me,
After Thy manner [1]with those who love Thy name.
133 Establish my [a]footsteps in Thy word,
And do not let any iniquity [b]have dominion over me.
134 [a]Redeem me from the oppression of man,
That I may keep Thy precepts.
135 [a]Make Thy face shine upon Thy servant,
And [b]teach me Thy statutes.
136 My eyes shed [a]streams of water,
Because they [b]do not keep Thy law.

Tsadhe.

137 [a]Righteous art Thou, O LORD,
And upright are Thy judgments.
138 Thou hast commanded Thy testimonies in [a]righteousness
And exceeding [b]faithfulness.
139 My [a]zeal has consumed me,
Because my adversaries have forgotten Thy words.
140 Thy [a]word is very pure,
Therefore Thy servant [b]loves it.
141 I am small and [a]despised,
Yet I do not [b]forget Thy precepts.
142 Thy righteousness is an everlasting righteousness,
And [a]Thy law is truth.
143 Trouble and anguish have come upon me;
Yet Thy commandments are my [a]delight.
144 Thy [a]testimonies are righteous forever;
[b]Give me understanding that I may live.

Qoph.

145 I cried [a]with all my heart; answer me, O LORD!

110 [b]Ps. 119:10
111 [a]Deut. 33:4 [b]Ps. 119:14, 162
112 [a]Ps. 119:36 [b]Ps. 119:33
113 [a]1 Kin. 18:21; James 1:8; 4:8 [b]Ps. 119:47
114 [1]Or, *hope in* [a]Ps. 31:20; 32:7; 61:4; 91:1 [b]Ps. 84:9 [c]Ps. 119:74
115 [a]Ps. 6:8; 139:19; Matt. 7:23 [b]Ps. 119:22
116 [a]Ps. 37:17, 24; 54:4 [b]Ps. 25:2, 20; 31:1, 17; Rom. 5:5; 9:33; Phil. 1:20
117 [a]Ps. 12:5; Prov. 29:25 [b]Ps. 119:6, 15
118 [1]Lit., *made light of* [2]Lit., *falsehood* [a]Ps. 119:10, 21
119 [a]Is. 1:22, 25; Ezek. 22:18, 19 [b]Ps. 119:47
120 [a]Job 4:14; Hab. 3:16 [b]Ps. 119:161
121 [a]2 Sam. 8:15; Job 29:14
122 [a]Job 17:3 [b]Ps. 119:134
124 [a]Ps. 51:1; 106:45; 109:26; 119:88, 149, 159 [b]Ps. 119:12
125 [a]Ps. 116:16 [b]Ps. 119:27
126 [a]Jer. 18:23; Ezek. 31:11
127 [a]Ps. 119:47
128 [a]Ps. 19:8 [b]Ps. 119:104
129 [a]Ps. 119:18 [b]Ps. 119:22
130 [a]Prov. 6:23 [b]Ps. 19:7
131 [a]Job 29:23; Ps. 81:10 [b]Ps. 42:1 [c]Ps. 119:20
132 [1]Lit., *to* [a]Ps. 25:16
133 [a]Ps. 17:5 [b]Ps. 19:13
134 [a]Ps. 119:84
135 [a]Num. 6:25; Ps. 4:6; 31:16; 67:1; 80:3, 7, 19 [b]Ps. 119:12
136 [a]Jer. 9:1, 18; 14:17; Lam. 3:48 [b]Ps. 119:158
137 [a]Ezra 9:15; Ps. 116:5; 129:4; 145:17; Jer. 12:1; Lam. 1:18; Dan. 9:7, 14
138 [a]Ps. 119:144, 172 [b]Ps. 119:86
139 [a]Ps. 69:9
140 [a]Ps. 12:6; 19:8 [b]Ps. 119:47
141 [a]Ps. 22:6 [b]Ps. 119:61
142 [a]Ps. 119:151
143 [a]Ps. 119:24
144 [a]Ps. 19:9 [b]Ps. 119:27
145 [a]Ps. 119:10

I will [b]observe Thy statutes.
146 I cried to Thee; [a]save me,
And I shall keep Thy testimonies.
147 I [a]rise before dawn and cry for help;
I wait for Thy words.
148 My eyes anticipate the night watches,
That I may [a]meditate on Thy word.
149 Hear my voice [a]according to Thy lovingkindness;
[b]Revive me, O LORD, according to Thine ordinances.
150 Those who follow after wickedness draw near;
They are far from Thy law.
151 Thou art [a]near, O LORD,
And all Thy commandments are truth.
152 Of old I have [a]known from Thy testimonies,
That Thou hast founded them [b]forever.

Resh.

153 Look upon my [a]affliction and rescue me,
For I do not [b]forget Thy law.
154 [a]Plead my cause and redeem me;
Revive me according to Thy word.
155 Salvation is [a]far from the wicked,
For they [b]do not seek Thy statutes.
156 [a]Great are Thy mercies, O LORD;
Revive me according to Thine ordinances.
157 Many are my [a]persecutors and my adversaries,
Yet I do not turn aside from Thy testimonies.
158 I behold the [a]treacherous and loathe *them*,
Because they do not keep Thy word.
159 Consider how I [a]love Thy precepts;
[b]Revive me, O LORD, according to Thy lovingkindness.
160 The [a]sum of Thy word is [b]truth,
And every one of Thy righteous ordinances [c]is everlasting.

Shin.

161 [a]Princes persecute me without cause,
But my heart [b]stands in awe of Thy words.
162 I [a]rejoice at Thy word,
As one who [b]finds great spoil.
163 I [a]hate and despise falsehood,
But I [b]love Thy law.

145 [b]Ps. 119:22, 55
146 [a]Ps. 3:7
147 [a]Ps. 57:8
148 [a]Ps. 119:15
149 [a]Ps. 119:124 [b]Ps. 119:25
151 [a]Ps. 34:18; 145:18; Is. 50:8
152 [a]Ps. 119:125 [b]Ps. 119:89; Luke 21:33
153 [a]Ps. 119:50 [b]Ps. 119:16; Prov. 3:1; Hos. 4:6
154 [a]1 Sam. 24:15; Ps. 35:1; Mic. 7:9
155 [a]Job 5:4 [b]Ps. 119:45, 94
156 [a]2 Sam. 24:14
157 [a]Ps. 7:1; 119:86, 161
158 [a]Is. 21:2
159 [a]Ps. 119:47 [b]Ps. 119:25
160 [a]Ps. 139:17 [b]Ps. 119:142 [c]Ps. 119:89, 152
161 [a]1 Sam. 24:11; 26:18; Ps. 119:23 [b]Ps. 119:120
162 [a]Ps. 119:14, 111 [b]1 Sam. 30:16; Is. 9:3
163 [a]Ps. 31:6; 119:104, 128; Prov. 13:5 [b]Ps. 119:47
164 [a]Ps. 119:7
165 [a]Ps. 37:11; Prov. 3:2; Is. 26:3 [b]Prov. 3:23; Is. 63:13; 1 John 2:10
166 [a]Gen. 49:18; Ps. 119:81, 174
167 [a]Ps. 119:129 [b]Ps. 119:47
168 [a]Ps. 119:22 [b]Job 24:23; Ps. 139:3; Prov. 5:21
169 [a]Job 16:18; Ps. 18:6; 102:1 [b]Ps. 119:27 [c]Ps. 119:65, 154
170 [a]Ps. 28:2; 130:2; 140:6; 143:1 [b]Ps. 22:20; 31:2
171 [a]Ps. 51:15; 63:3 [b]Ps. 94:12; 119:12; Is. 2:3; Mic. 4:2
172 [a]Ps. 51:14 [b]Ps. 119:138
173 [a]Ps. 37:24; 73:23 [b]Josh. 24:22; Luke 10:42
174 [a]Ps. 119:166 [b]Ps. 119:24
175 [a]Is. 55:3
176 [a]Is. 53:6; Jer. 50:6; Matt. 18:12; Luke 15:4 [b]Ps. 119:16
[£] Ex. 34:24; 1 Kin. 12:27
1 [a]Ps. 18:6; 66:14; 102:2
2 [a]Ps. 109:2; Prov. 12:22 [b]Ps. 52:4; Zeph. 3:13
3 [a]Ps. 52:4; Zeph. 3:13

164 Seven times a day I praise Thee,
Because of Thy [a]righteous ordinances.
165 Those who love Thy law have [a]great peace,
And [b]nothing causes them to stumble.
166 I [a]hope for Thy salvation, O LORD,
And do Thy commandments.
167 My [a]soul keeps Thy testimonies,
And I [b]love them exceedingly.
168 I [a]keep Thy precepts and Thy testimonies,
For all my [b]ways are before Thee.

Tav.

169 Let my [a]cry come before Thee, O LORD;
[b]Give me understanding [c]according to Thy word.
170 Let my [a]supplication come before Thee;
[b]Deliver me according to Thy word.
171 Let my [a]lips utter praise,
For Thou [b]dost teach me Thy statutes.
172 Let my [a]tongue sing of Thy word,
For all Thy [b]commandments are righteousness.
173 Let Thy [a]hand be ready to help me,
For I have [b]chosen Thy precepts.
174 I [a]long for Thy salvation, O LORD,
And Thy law is my [b]delight.
175 Let my [a]soul live that it may praise Thee,
And let Thine ordinances help me.
176 I have [a]gone astray like a lost sheep; seek Thy servant,
For I do [b]not forget Thy commandments.

PSALM 120

Prayer for Deliverance from the Treacherous.

A Song of [£]Ascents.

[a]IN my trouble I cried to the LORD,
And He answered me.
2 Deliver my soul, O LORD, from [a]lying lips,
From a [b]deceitful tongue.
3 What shall be given to you, and what more shall be done to you,
You [a]deceitful tongue?

4 [a]Sharp arrows of the warrior,
With the *burning* [b]coals of the broom tree.

5 Woe is me, for I sojourn in [a]Meshech,
For I dwell among the [b]tents of [c]Kedar!
6 Too long has my soul had its dwelling
With those who [a]hate peace.
7 I [a]am *for* peace, but when I speak,
They are [b]for war.

Psalm 121

The Lord the Keeper of Israel.

A Song of Ascents.

I WILL [a]lift up my eyes to [b]the mountains;
From whence shall my help come?
2 My [a]help *comes* from the Lord,
Who [b]made heaven and earth.
3 He will not [a]allow your foot to slip;
He who [b]keeps you will not slumber.
4 Behold, He who keeps Israel
Will neither slumber nor sleep.

5 The Lord is your [a]keeper;
The Lord is your [b]shade on your right hand.
6 The [a]sun will not smite you by day,
Nor the moon by night.
7 The Lord will [1][a]protect you from all evil;
He will keep your soul.
8 The Lord will [1]guard your going out and your coming in
[a]From this time forth and forever.

Psalm 122

Prayer for the Peace of Jerusalem.

A Song of Ascents, of David.

I WAS glad when they said to me,
"Let us [a]go to the house of the Lord."
2 Our feet are standing
Within your [a]gates, O Jerusalem,
3 Jerusalem, that is [a]built
As a city that is [b]compact together;
4 To which the tribes [a]go up, even the tribes of [1]the Lord—
An [2]ordinance for Israel—
To give thanks to the name of the Lord.

5 For there [a]thrones were set for judgment,
The thrones of the house of David.
6 Pray for the [a]peace of Jerusalem:
"May they prosper who [b]love you.
7 "May peace be within your [a]walls,
And prosperity within your [b]palaces."
8 For the sake of my [a]brothers and my friends,
I will now say, "[b]May peace be within you."
9 For the sake of the house of the Lord our God
I will [a]seek your good.

Psalm 123

Prayer for the Lord's Help.

A Song of Ascents.

TO Thee I [a]lift up my eyes,
O Thou who [b]art enthroned in the heavens!
2 Behold, as the eyes of [a]servants *look* to the hand of their master,
As the eyes of a maid to the hand of her mistress;
So our [b]eyes *look* to the Lord our God,
Until He shall be gracious to us.

3 [a]Be gracious to us, O Lord, be gracious to us;
For we are greatly filled [b]with contempt.
4 Our soul is greatly filled
With the [a]scoffing of [b]those who are at ease,
And with the [c]contempt of the proud.

Psalm 124

Praise for Rescue from Enemies.

A Song of Ascents, of David.

"[a]HAD it not been the Lord who was on our side,"
[b]Let Israel now say,
2 "Had it not been the Lord who was on our side,
When men rose up against us;
3 Then they would have [a]swallowed us alive,
When their [b]anger was kindled against us;
4 Then the [a]waters would have engulfed us,
The stream would have [1]swept over our soul;

---

4 [a]Ps. 45:5; Prov. 25:18; Is. 5:28 [b]Ps. 140:10
5 [a]Gen. 10:2; 1 Chr. 1:5; Ezek. 27:13; 38:2, 3; 39:1 [b]Song of Sol. 1:5 [c]Gen. 25:13; Is. 21:16; 60:7; Jer. 2:10; 49:28; Ezek. 27:21
6 [a]Ps. 35:20
7 [a]Ps. 109:4 [b]Ps. 55:21

1 [a]Ps. 123:1; Is. 40:26 [b]Ps. 87:1
2 [a]Ps. 124:8 [b]Ps. 115:15
3 [a]Ps. 66:9 [b]Ps. 41:2; 127:1
5 [a]Ps. 91:4 [b]Ps. 91:1
6 [a]Is. 49:10; Jon. 4:8; Rev. 7:16
7 [1]Or, *keep* [a]Ps. 91:10-12
8 [1]Or, *keep* [a]Ps. 113:2; 115:18

1 [a]Ps. 42:4; Is. 2:3; Mic. 4:2; Zech. 8:21
2 [a]Ps. 9:14; 87:2; 116:19; Jer. 7:2
3 [a]Ps. 48:13; 147:2 [b]Neh. 4:6
4 [1]Heb., *Yah* [2]Or, *testimony* [a]Deut. 16:16; Ps. 84:5
5 [a]Deut. 17:8; 2 Chr. 19:8; Ps. 89:29
6 [a]Ps. 29:11; Jer. 29:7 [b]Ps. 102:14
7 [a]Ps. 51:18; Is. 62:6 [b]Ps. 48:3, 13; Jer. 17:27
8 [a]Ps. 133:1 [b]1 Sam. 25:6; John 20:19
9 [a]Neh. 2:10; Esth. 10:3

1 [a]Ps. 121:1; 141:8 [b]Ps. 2:4; 11:4
2 [a]Prov. 27:18; Mal. 1:6 [b]Ps. 25:15
3 [a]Ps. 4:1; 51:1 [b]Neh. 4:4; Ps. 119:22
4 [a]Neh. 2:19; Ps. 79:4 [b]Job 12:5; Is. 32:9, 11; Amos 6:1 [c]Neh. 4:4; Ps. 119:22

1 [a]Ps. 94:17 [b]Ps. 129:1
3 [a]Num. 16:30; Ps. 35:25; 56:1; 57:3; Prov. 1:12 [b]Gen. 39:19; Ps. 138:7
4 [1]Or, *passed over* [a]Job 22:11; Ps. 18:16; 32:6; 69:2; 144:7

5 Then the [a]raging waters would have [1]swept over our soul."

6 Blessed be the LORD,
Who has not given us [1]to be [a]torn by their teeth.
7 Our soul has [a]escaped [b]as a bird out of the [c]snare of the trapper;
The snare is broken and we have escaped.
8 Our [a]help is in the name of the LORD,
Who made heaven and earth.

PSALM 125

The LORD Surrounds His People.

A Song of Ascents.

THOSE who trust in the LORD
Are as Mount Zion, which [a]cannot be moved, but [b]abides forever.
2 As the mountains surround Jerusalem,
So [a]the LORD surrounds His people
[b]From this time forth and forever.
3 For the [a]scepter of wickedness shall not rest upon the [1]land of the righteous;
That the righteous [b]may not put forth their hands to do wrong.

4 [a]Do good, O LORD, to those who are good,
And to those who are [b]upright in their hearts.
5 But as for those who [a]turn aside to their [b]crooked ways,
The LORD will lead them away with the [c]doers of iniquity.
[d]Peace be upon Israel.

PSALM 126

Thanksgiving for Return from Captivity.

A Song of Ascents.

WHEN the LORD [a]brought back [1]the captive ones of Zion,
We were [b]like those who dream.
2 Then our [a]mouth was filled with laughter,
And our [b]tongue with joyful shouting;
Then they said among the nations,
"The LORD has [c]done great things for them."
3 The LORD has done great things for us;
We are [a]glad.

5 [1]Or, *passed over* [a]Job 38:11
6 [1]Lit., *as a prey to* [a]Ps. 27:2; Prov. 30:14
7 [a]Ps. 141:10; 2 Cor. 11:33; Heb. 11:34 [b]Prov. 6:5 [c]Ps. 91:3; Hos. 9:8
8 [a]Ps. 121:2

1 [a]Ps. 46:5 [b]Ps. 61:7; Eccles. 1:4
2 [a]Zech. 2:5 [b]Ps. 121:8
3 [1]Lit., *lot* [a]Ps. 89:22; Prov. 22:8; Is. 14:5 [b]1 Sam. 24:10; Ps. 55:20; Acts 12:1
4 [a]Ps. 119:68 [b]Ps. 7:10; 11:2; 32:11; 36:10; 94:15
5 [a]Job 23:11; Ps. 40:4; 101:3 [b]Prov. 2:15; Is. 59:8 [c]Ps. 92:7; 94:4 [d]Ps. 128:6; Gal. 6:16

1 [1]Or, *those who returned to* [a]Ps. 85:1; Jer. 29:14; Hos. 6:11 [b]Acts 12:9
2 [a]Job 8:21 [b]Ps. 51:14; Is. 35:6 [c]1 Sam. 12:24; Ps. 71:19; Luke 1:49
3 [a]Is. 25:9; Zeph. 3:14
4 [1]Lit., *streambeds* [2]Heb., *Negev* [a]Is. 35:6; 43:19
5 [a]Ps. 80:5; Jer. 31:16; Lam. 1:2 [b]Is. 35:10; 51:11; 61:7; Gal. 6:9

1 [a]Ps. 78:69 [b]Ps. 121:4
2 [1]Lit., *delay sitting* [2]Lit., *toils* [a]Gen. 3:17 [b]Ps. 60:5 [c]Job 11:18, 19; Prov. 3:24; Eccles. 5:12
3 [1]Or, *heritage* [a]Gen. 33:5; Ps. 113:9 [b]Deut. 7:13; 28:4; Is. 13:18
4 [a]Ps. 112:2; 120:4
5 [a]Ps. 128:2, 3 [b]Is. 29:21; Amos 5:12 [c]Gen. 34:20

1 [a]Ps. 112:1 [b]Ps. 119:3
2 [1]Lit., *labor* [a]Is. 3:10 [b]Ps. 109:11; Ezek. 23:29; Hag. 2:17 [c]Eccles. 8:12; Eph. 6:3
3 [1]Lit., *In the innermost parts of* [a]Ezek. 19:10 [b]Ps. 52:8; 144:12

4 Restore our captivity, O LORD,
As the [1a]streams in the [2]South.
5 Those who sow in [a]tears shall reap with [b]joyful shouting.
6 He who goes to and fro weeping, carrying *his* bag of seed,
Shall indeed come again with a shout of joy, bringing his sheaves *with him.*

PSALM 127

Prosperity Comes from the LORD.

A Song of Ascents, of Solomon.

UNLESS the LORD [a]builds the house,
They labor in vain who build it;
Unless the LORD [b]guards the city,
The watchman keeps awake in vain.
2 It is vain for you to rise up early,
To [1]retire late,
To [a]eat the bread of [2]painful labors;
For He gives to His [b]beloved [c]*even in his* sleep.

3 Behold, [a]children are a [1]gift of the LORD;
The [b]fruit of the womb is a reward.
4 Like arrows in the hand of a [a]warrior,
So are the children of one's youth.
5 How [a]blessed is the man whose quiver is full of them;
They shall not be ashamed,
When they [b]speak with their enemies [c]in the gate.

PSALM 128

Blessedness of the Fear of the LORD.

A Song of Ascents.

[a]HOW blessed is everyone who fears the LORD,
Who [b]walks in His ways.
2 When you shall [a]eat of the [1b]fruit of your hands,
You will be happy and [c]it will be well with you.
3 Your wife shall be like a [a]fruitful vine,
[1]Within your house,
Your children like [b]olive plants
Around your table.
4 Behold, for thus shall the man be blessed
Who fears the LORD.

5 [a]The LORD bless you [b]from Zion,
And may you see the [c]prosperity of Jerusalem all the days of your life.
6 Indeed, may you see your [a]children's children.
[b]Peace be upon Israel!

PSALM 129

Prayer for the Overthrow of Zion's Enemies.

A Song of Ascents.

"MANY times they have [a]persecuted me from my [b]youth up,"
Let Israel now say,
2 "Many times they have persecuted me from my youth up;
Yet they have [a]not prevailed against me.
3 "The plowers plowed upon my back;
They lengthened their furrows."
4 The LORD [a]is righteous;
He has cut in two the [b]cords of the wicked.

5 May all who [a]hate Zion,
Be [b]put to shame and turned backward,
6 Let them be like [a]grass upon the housetops,
Which withers before it grows up;
7 With which the reaper does not fill his hand,
Or the binder of sheaves his [a]bosom;
8 Nor do those who pass by say,
"The [a]blessing of the LORD be upon you;
We bless you in the name of the LORD."

PSALM 130

Hope in the LORD's Forgiving Love.

A Song of Ascents.

OUT of the [a]depths I have cried to Thee, O LORD.
2 Lord, [a]hear my voice!
Let [b]Thine ears be attentive
To the [c]voice of my supplications.
3 If Thou, [1]LORD, shouldst mark iniquities,
O Lord, who could [a]stand?
4 But there is [a]forgiveness with Thee,
That Thou mayest be [b]feared.

5 [a]Ps. 134:3 [b]Ps. 20:2; 135:21 [c]Ps. 122:9
6 [a]Gen. 48:11; Ps. 103:17; Prov. 17:6 [b]Ps. 125:5

1 [a]Ex. 1:11; Judg. 3:8; Ps. 88:15 [b]Is. 47:12; Jer. 2:2; 22:21; Ezek. 16:22; Hos. 2:15; 11:1
2 [a]Jer. 1:19; 15:20; 20:11; Matt. 16:18; 2 Cor. 4:8
4 [a]Ps. 119:137 [b]Ps. 140:5
5 [a]Mic. 4:11 [b]Ps. 70:3; 71:13
6 [a]2 Kin. 19:26; Ps. 37:2; Is. 37:27
7 [a]Ps. 79:12
8 [a]Ruth 2:4

1 [a]Ps. 42:7; 69:2
2 [a]Ps. 64:1; 119:149 [b]2 Chr. 6:40; Neh. 1:6, 11 [c]Ps. 28:2; 140:6
3 [1]Heb., *YAH* [a]Ps. 76:7; 143:2; Nah. 1:6; Mal. 3:2; Rev. 6:17
4 [a]Ex. 34:7; Neh. 9:17; Ps. 86:5; Is. 55:7; Dan. 9:9 [b]1 Kin. 8:39, 40; Jer. 33:8
5 [1]Lit., *for* [a]Ps. 33:20; 40:1; 62:1, 5; Is. 8:17; 26:8 [b]Ps. 119:74
6 [a]Ps. 63:6
7 [a]Ps. 131:3 [b]Ps. 103:4 [c]Ps. 111:9; Rom. 3:24; Eph. 1:7
8 [a]Luke 1:68; Titus 2:14

1 [1]Or, *lofty* [2]Lit., *go after* [a]2 Sam. 22:28; Ps. 101:5; Is. 2:12; Zeph. 3:11 [b]Prov. 30:13; Is. 5:15 [c]Jer. 45:5; Rom. 12:16 [d]Job 42:3
2 [1]Or, *upon* [a]Ps. 62:1 [b]Matt. 18:3; 1 Cor. 14:20
3 [a]Ps. 130:7 [b]Ps. 113:2

1 [a]2 Sam. 16:12; 1 Chr. 22:14
2 [a]Gen. 49:24; Is. 49:26; 60:16
3 [a]Job 21:28
5 [1]Lit., *Dwelling places* [a]1 Kin. 8:17; 1 Chr. 22:7; Ps. 26:8; Acts 7:46 [b]Ps. 132:2
6 [1]Or, *the wood* [a]Gen. 35:19; 1 Sam. 17:12 [b]1 Sam. 7:1
7 [a]Ps. 43:3 [b]Ps. 5:7; 99:5 [c]1 Chr. 28:2

5 I wait for the LORD, my [a]soul does wait,
And [1b]in His word do I hope.
6 My soul *waits* for the Lord
More than the watchmen [a]for the morning;
Indeed, more than the watchmen for the morning.
7 O Israel, [a]hope in the LORD;
For with the LORD there is [b]lovingkindness,
And with Him is [c]abundant redemption.
8 And He will [a]redeem Israel
From all his iniquities.

PSALM 131

Childlike Trust in the LORD.

A Song of Ascents, of David.

O LORD, my heart is not [a]proud, nor my eyes [1b]haughty;
Nor do I [2]involve myself in [c]great matters,
Or in things [d]too difficult for me.
2 Surely I have [a]composed and quieted my soul;
Like a weaned [b]child *rests* [1]against his mother,
My soul is like a weaned child [1]within me.
3 O Israel, [a]hope in the LORD
[b]From this time forth and forever.

PSALM 132

Prayer for the LORD's Blessing upon the Sanctuary.

A Song of Ascents.

REMEMBER, O LORD, on David's behalf,
All [a]his affliction;
2 How he swore to the LORD,
And vowed to [a]the Mighty One of Jacob,
3 "Surely I will not enter [a]my house,
Nor lie on my bed;
4 I will not give sleep to my eyes,
Or slumber to my eyelids;
5 Until I find a [a]place for the LORD,
[1]A dwelling place for [b]the Mighty One of Jacob."

6 Behold, we heard of it in [a]Ephrathah;
We found it in the [b]field of [1]Jaar.
7 Let us go into His [a]dwelling place;
Let us [b]worship at His [c]footstool.

8 [a]Arise, O LORD, to Thy [b]resting place;
Thou and the ark of Thy [c]strength.
9 Let Thy priests be [a]clothed with righteousness;
And let Thy [b]godly ones sing for joy.

10 For the sake of David Thy servant,
Do not turn away the face of Thine [a]anointed.
11 The LORD has [a]sworn to David,
A truth from which He will not turn back;
"[b]Of the fruit of your body I will set upon your throne.
12 "If your sons will keep My covenant,
And My testimony which I will teach them,
Their sons also shall [a]sit upon your throne forever."

13 For the LORD has [a]chosen Zion;
He has [b]desired it for His habitation.
14 "This is My [a]resting place forever;
Here I will [b]dwell, for I have desired it.
15 "I will abundantly [a]bless her provision;
I will [b]satisfy her needy with bread.
16 "Her [a]priests also I will clothe with salvation;
And her [a]godly ones will sing aloud for joy.
17 "There I will cause the [a]horn of David to spring forth;
I have prepared a [b]lamp for Mine anointed.
18 "His enemies I will [a]clothe with shame;
But upon himself his [b]crown shall shine."

PSALM 133

The Excellency of Brotherly Unity.

A Song of Ascents, of David.

BEHOLD, how good and how pleasant it is
For [a]brothers to dwell together in unity!
2 It is like the precious [a]oil upon the head,
Coming down upon the beard,
Even Aaron's beard,
Coming down upon the [b]edge of his robes.
3 It is like the [a]dew of [b]Hermon,
Coming down upon the [c]mountains of Zion;

8 [a]Num. 10:35; 2 Chr. 6:41; Ps. 68:1 [b]Ps. 132:14 [c]Ps. 78:61
9 [a]Job 29:14 [b]Ps. 30:4; 132:16
10 [a]Ps. 132:17
11 [a]Ps. 89:3, 35 [b]2 Sam. 7:12-16; 2 Chr. 6:16
12 [a]Luke 1:32; Acts 2:30
13 [a]Ps. 78:68 [b]Ps. 68:16
14 [a]Ps. 132:8 [b]Matt. 23:21
15 [a]Ps. 147:14 [b]Ps. 107:9
16 [a]Ps. 132:9
17 [a]Ezek. 29:21; Luke 1:69 [b]1 Kin. 11:36; 15:4; 2 Kin. 8:19; 2 Chr. 21:7
18 [a]Job 8:22; Ps. 35:26; 109:29 [b]Ps. 21:3

1 [a]Gen. 13:8; Heb. 13:1
2 [a]Ex. 29:7; 30:25, 30; Lev. 8:12 [b]Ex. 28:33; 39:24
3 [a]Prov. 19:12; Hos. 14:5; Mic. 5:7 [b]Deut. 3:9; 4:48 [c]Ps. 48:2; 74:2; 78:68 [d]Lev. 25:21; Deut. 28:8; Ps. 42:8 [e]Ps. 21:4

1 [1]Lit., *stand* [a]Ps. 103:21 [b]Ps. 135:1, 2 [c]Deut. 10:8; 1 Chr. 23:30 [d]1 Chr. 9:33
2 [a]Ps. 28:2 [b]Ps. 63:2
3 [a]Ps. 128:5 [b]Ps. 124:8

1 [1]Or, *Hallelujah!* [2]Heb., *YAH,* also vs. 3, 4 [a]Ps. 113:1 [b]Ps. 134:1
2 [a]Ps. 92:13
3 [a]Ps. 100:5; 119:68 [b]Ps. 68:4 [c]Ps. 147:1
4 [a]Deut. 7:6; 10:15; Ps. 105:6 [b]Ex. 19:5; Mal. 3:17; Titus 2:14; 1 Pet. 2:9
5 [a]Ps. 48:1; 145:3 [b]Ps. 97:9
6 [a]Ps. 115:3
7 [a]Jer. 10:13; 51:16 [b]Job 28:25, 26; 38:25, 26; Zech. 10:1 [c]Jer. 10:13; 51:16
8 [1]Lit., *The one who* [a]Ps. 78:51; 105:36
9 [a]Deut. 6:22; Ps. 78:43 [b]Ps. 136:15
10 [1]Lit., *The one who* [a]Ps. 135:10-12; 136:17-21 [b]Ps. 44:2

For there the LORD [d]commanded the blessing—[e]life forever.

PSALM 134

Greetings of Night Watchers.

A Song of Ascents.

BEHOLD, [a]bless the LORD, all [b]servants of the LORD,
Who [1c]serve [d]by night in the house of the LORD!
2 [a]Lift up your hands to the [b]sanctuary,
And bless the LORD.
3 May the LORD [a]bless you from Zion,
He who [b]made heaven and earth.

PSALM 135

Praise the LORD's Wonderful Works.
Vanity of Idols.

[1a]PRAISE [2]the LORD!
Praise the name of the LORD;
Praise *Him,* O [b]servants of the LORD,
2 You who stand in the house of the LORD,
In the [a]courts of the house of our God!
3 Praise the LORD, for [a]the LORD is good;
[b]Sing praises to His name, [c]for it is lovely.
4 For the LORD has [a]chosen Jacob for Himself,
Israel for His [b]own possession.

5 For I know that [a]the LORD is great,
And that our Lord is [b]above all gods.
6 [a]Whatever the LORD pleases, He does,
In heaven and in earth, in the seas and in all deeps.
7 He [a]causes the vapors to ascend from the ends of the earth;
Who [b]makes lightnings for the rain;
Who [c]brings forth the wind from His treasuries.

8 [1]He [a]smote the first-born of Egypt,
Both of man and beast.
9 He sent [a]signs and wonders into your midst, O Egypt,
Upon [b]Pharaoh and all his servants.
10 [1a]He [b]smote many nations,
And slew mighty kings,

11 [a]Sihon, king of the Amorites,
And [b]Og, king of Bashan,
And [c]all the kingdoms of Canaan;
12 And He [a]gave their land as a heritage,
A heritage to Israel His people.
13 Thy [a]name, O LORD, is everlasting,
Thy [1]remembrance, O LORD, [2]throughout all generations.
14 For the LORD will [a]judge His people,
And [b]will have compassion on His servants.
15 The [a]idols of the nations are *but* silver and gold,
The work of man's hands.
16 They have mouths, but they do not speak;
They have eyes, but they do not see;
17 They have ears, but they do not hear;
Nor is there any breath at all in their mouths.
18 Those who make them will be like them,
Yes, everyone who trusts in them.

19 O house of [a]Israel, bless the LORD;
O house of Aaron, bless the LORD;
20 O house of Levi, bless the LORD;
You [a]who [1]revere the LORD, bless the LORD.
21 Blessed be the LORD [a]from Zion,
Who [b]dwells in Jerusalem.
[1]Praise [2]the LORD!

PSALM 136

Thanks for the LORD's Goodness to Israel.

[a]GIVE thanks to the LORD, for He is good;
For [b]His lovingkindness is everlasting.
2 Give thanks to the [a]God of gods,
For His lovingkindness is everlasting.
3 Give thanks to the [a]Lord of lords,
For His lovingkindness is everlasting.
4 To Him who [a]alone does great [1]wonders,
For His lovingkindness is everlasting;
5 To Him who made the heavens [1a]with skill,
For His lovingkindness is everlasting;
6 To Him who [a]spread out the earth above the waters,
For His lovingkindness is everlasting;
7 To Him who [a]made *the* great lights,
For His lovingkindness is everlasting:
8 The [a]sun to rule [1]by day,
For His lovingkindness is everlasting,
9 The [a]moon and stars to rule [1]by night,
For His lovingkindness is everlasting.

10 To Him who [a]smote [1]the Egyptians in their first-born,
For His lovingkindness is everlasting,
11 And [a]brought Israel out from their midst,
For His lovingkindness is everlasting,
12 With a [a]strong hand and an [b]outstretched arm,
For His lovingkindness is everlasting;
13 To Him who [a]divided the [1]Red Sea [2]asunder,
For His lovingkindness is everlasting,
14 And [a]made Israel pass through the midst of it,
For His lovingkindness is everlasting;
15 But [1a]He overthrew Pharaoh and his army in the [2]Red Sea,
For His lovingkindness is everlasting.
16 To Him who [a]led His people through the wilderness,
For His lovingkindness is everlasting;
17 To Him who [a]smote great kings,
For His lovingkindness is everlasting,
18 And slew [1]mighty kings,
For His lovingkindness is everlasting:
19 Sihon, king of the Amorites,
For His lovingkindness is everlasting,
20 And Og, king of Bashan,
For His lovingkindness is everlasting,
21 And gave their land as a heritage,
For His lovingkindness is everlasting,
22 Even a heritage to Israel His [a]servant,
For His lovingkindness is everlasting.

11 [a]Num. 21:21-26; Deut. 29:7 [b]Num. 21:33-35 [c]Josh. 12:7-24
12 [a]Deut. 29:8; Ps. 78:55
13 [1]Or, *memorial* [2]Lit., *to* [a]Ex. 3:15; Ps. 102:12
14 [a]Deut. 32:36; Ps. 50:4 [b]Ps. 90:13; 106:45
15 [a]Ps. 115:4-8; 135:15-18
19 [a]Ps. 115:9
20 [1]Lit., *fear* [a]Ps. 118:4
21 [1]Or, *Hallelujah!* [2]Heb., *YAH* [a]Ps. 128:5; 134:3 [b]Ps. 132:14
1 [a]Ps. 106:1; 118:1 [b]1 Chr. 16:41; 2 Chr. 20:21; Ps. 107:1; 118:1-4
2 [a]Deut. 10:17
3 [a]Deut. 10:17
4 [1]I.e., wonderful acts [a]Deut. 6:22; Job 9:10; Ps. 72:18
5 [1]Lit., *with understanding* [a]Ps. 104:24; Prov. 3:19; Jer. 10:12; 51:15
6 [a]Ps. 24:2; Is. 42:5; 44:24
7 [a]Gen. 1:16; Ps. 74:16
8 [1]Or, *over the* [a]Gen. 1:16
9 [1]Or, *over the* [a]Gen. 1:16
10 [1]Lit., *Egypt* [a]Ex. 12:29; Ps. 78:51; 135:8
11 [a]Ps. 105:43; Ex. 12:51; 13:3
12 [a]Ex. 6:1; 13:9; 1 Kin. 8:42; Neh. 1:10; Ps. 44:3; Jer. 32:21 [b]Ex. 6:6; Deut. 4:34; 5:15; 7:19; 9:29; 11:2; 2 Kin. 17:36; 2 Chr. 6:32; Jer. 32:17
13 [1]Or, *Sea of Reeds* [2]Lit., *in parts* [a]Ex. 14:21; Ps. 66:6; 78:13
14 [a]Ex. 14:22; Ps. 106:9
15 [1]Lit., *shook off* [2]Or, *Sea of Reeds* [a]Ex. 14:27; Ps. 78:53; 106:11
16 [a]Ex. 13:18; 15:22; Deut. 8:15; Ps. 78:52
17 [a]Ps. 135:10-12; 136:17-22
18 [1]Lit., *majestic*
22 [a]Ps. 105:6; Is. 41:8; 44:1; 45:4

23 Who [a]remembered us in our low estate,
For His lovingkindness is everlasting,
24 And has [a]rescued us from our adversaries,
For His lovingkindness is everlasting;
25 Who [a]gives food to all flesh,
For His lovingkindness is everlasting.
26 Give thanks to the [a]God of heaven,
For His lovingkindness is everlasting.

Psalm 137

An Experience of the Captivity.

By the [a]rivers of Babylon,
There we sat down and [b]wept,
When we remembered Zion.
2 Upon the [1a]willows in the midst of it
We [b]hung our [2]harps.
3 For there our captors [a]demanded of us songs,
And [b]our tormentors mirth, *saying,*
"Sing us one of the songs of Zion."

4 How can we sing [a]the LORD's song
In a foreign land?
5 If I [a]forget you, O Jerusalem,
May my right hand [1]forget *her skill.*
6 May my [a]tongue cleave to the roof of my mouth,
If I do not remember you,
If I do not [b]exalt Jerusalem
Above my chief joy.

7 Remember, O LORD, against the sons of [a]Edom
The day of Jerusalem,
Who said, "Raze it, raze it,
[b]To its very foundation."
8 O daughter of Babylon, you [a]devastated one,
How blessed will be the one who [b]repays you
With the recompense with which you have repaid us.
9 How blessed will be the one who seizes and [a]dashes your little ones
Against the rock.

Psalm 138

Thanksgiving for the LORD's Favor.

A Psalm of David.

[a]I WILL give Thee thanks with all my heart;

23 [a]Ps. 9:12; 103:14; 106:45
24 [a]Judg. 6:9; Neh. 9:28
25 [a]Ps. 104:27
26 [a]Gen. 24:3, 7; 2 Chr. 36:23; Ezra 1:2; 5:11; Neh. 1:4

1 [a]Ezek. 1:1, 3 [b]Neh. 1:4
2 [1]Or, *poplars* [2]Lit., *lyres* [a]Lev. 23:40; Is. 44:4 [b]Job 30:31; Is. 24:8; Ezek. 26:13
3 [a]Ps. 80:6 [b]Ps. 79:7; Is. 49:17; 64:11
4 [a]2 Chr. 29:27; Neh. 12:46
5 [1]I.e., become lame [a]Is. 65:11
6 [a]Job 29:10; Ps. 22:15; Ezek. 3:26 [b]Neh. 2:3
7 [a]Ps. 83:4-8; Is. 34:5, 6; Jer. 49:7-22; Lam. 4:21; Ezek. 25:12-14; 35:2; Amos 1:11; Obad, 10-14 [b]Ps. 74:7; Hab. 3:13
8 [a]Is. 13:1-22; 47:1-15; Jer. 25:12; 50:1-46; 51:1-64 [b]Jer. 50:15; 51:24, 35, 36, 49
9 [a]2 Kin. 8:12; Is. 13:16; Hos. 13:16; Nah. 3:10

1 [a]Ps. 111:1 [b]Ps. 95:3; 96:4
2 [a]1 Kin. 8:29; Ps. 5:7; 28:2 [b]Ps. 140:13 [c]Is. 42:21
3 [a]Ps. 118:5 [b]Ps. 28:7; 46:1
4 [a]Ps. 72:11; 102:15
5 [a]Ps. 145:7 [b]Ps. 21:5
6 [a]Ps. 113:4-7 [b]Prov. 3:34; Is. 57:15; Luke 1:48; James 4:6 [c]Ps. 40:4; 101:5
7 [a]Ps. 23:4; 143:11 [b]Ezra 9:8, 9; Ps. 71:20; Is. 57:15 [c]Ex. 7:5; 15:12; Is. 5:25; Jer. 51:25; Ezek. 6:14; 25:13 [d]Ps. 20:6; 60:5
8 [a]Ps. 57:2; Phil. 1:6 [b]Ps. 136:1 [c]Ps. 27:9; 71:9; 119:8 [d]Job 10:3; 14:15; Ps. 100:3

1 [a]Ps. 17:3; 44:21; Jer. 12:3
2 [a]2 Kin. 19:27 [b]Ps. 94:11; Is. 66:18
3 [a]Job 14:16
4 [a]Heb. 4:13
5 [a]Ps. 34:7; 125:2 [b]Job 9:33

I will sing praises to Thee before the [b]gods.
2 I will bow down [a]toward Thy holy temple,
And [b]give thanks to Thy name for Thy lovingkindness and Thy truth;
For Thou hast [c]magnified Thy word according to all Thy name.
3 On the day I [a]called Thou didst answer me;
Thou didst make me bold with [b]strength in my soul.

4 [a]All the kings of the earth will give thanks to Thee, O LORD,
When they have heard the words of Thy mouth.
5 And they will [a]sing of the ways of the LORD.
For [b]great is the glory of the LORD.
6 For [a]though the LORD is exalted,
Yet He [b]regards the lowly;
But the [c]haughty He knows from afar.

7 Though I [a]walk in the midst of trouble, Thou wilt [b]revive me;
Thou wilt [c]stretch forth Thy hand against the wrath of my enemies,
And Thy right hand will [d]save me.
8 The LORD will [a]accomplish what concerns me;
Thy [b]lovingkindness, O LORD, is everlasting;
[c]Do not forsake the [d]works of Thy hands.

Psalm 139

God's Omnipresence and Omniscience.

For the choir director. A Psalm of David.

O LORD, Thou hast [a]searched me and known *me.*
2 Thou [a]dost know when I sit down and when I rise up;
Thou [b]dost understand my thought from afar.
3 Thou [a]dost scrutinize my path and my lying down,
And art intimately acquainted with all my ways.
4 Even before there is a word on my tongue,
Behold, O LORD, Thou [a]dost know it all.
5 Thou hast [a]enclosed me behind and before,
And [b]laid Thy hand upon me.

6 *Such* [a]knowledge is [b]too wonderful for me;
It is *too* high, I cannot attain to it.

7 [a]Where can I go from Thy Spirit?
Or where can I flee from Thy presence?
8 [a]If I ascend to heaven, Thou art there;
If I make my bed in Sheol, behold, [b]Thou art there.
9 If I take the wings of the dawn,
If I dwell in the remotest part of the sea,
10 Even there Thy hand will [a]lead me,
And Thy right hand will lay hold of me.
11 If I say, "Surely the [a]darkness will [1]overwhelm me,
And the light around me will be night,"
12 Even the [a]darkness is not dark to Thee,
And the night is as bright as the day.
[b]Darkness and light are alike *to Thee.*

13 For Thou didst [a]form my [1]inward parts;
Thou didst [b]weave me in my mother's womb.
14 I will give thanks to Thee, for I am fearfully and wonderfully made;
[a]Wonderful are Thy works,
And my soul knows it very well.
15 My [1a]frame was not hidden from Thee,
When I was made in secret,
And skillfully wrought in the [b]depths of the earth.
16 Thine [a]eyes have seen my unformed substance;
And in [b]Thy book they were all written,
The [c]days that were ordained *for me,*
When as yet there was not one of them.

17 How precious also are Thy [a]thoughts to me, O God!
How vast is the sum of them!
18 If I should count them, they would [a]outnumber the sand.
When [b]I awake, I am still with Thee.

19 O that Thou wouldst [a]slay the wicked, O God;
[b]Depart from me, therefore, [c]men of bloodshed.
20 For they [a]speak [1]against Thee wickedly,
And Thine enemies [2b]take *Thy name* in vain.
21 Do I not [a]hate those who hate Thee, O LORD?
And do I not [b]loathe those who rise up against Thee?
22 I hate them with the utmost hatred;
They have become my enemies.

23 [a]Search me, O God, and know my heart;
[b]Try me and know my anxious thoughts;
24 And see if there be any [a]hurtful way in me,
And [b]lead me in the [c]everlasting way.

PSALM 140

Prayer for Protection against the Wicked.

For the choir director. A Psalm of David.

[a]RESCUE me, O LORD, from evil men;
Preserve me from [b]violent men,
2 Who [a]devise evil things in *their* hearts;
They [b]continually stir up wars.
3 They [a]sharpen their tongues as a serpent;
[b]Poison of a viper is under their lips. [Selah.

4 Keep me, O LORD, from the hands of the wicked;
[a]Preserve me from violent men,
Who have [1]purposed to [2b]trip up my feet.
5 The proud have [a]hidden a trap for me, and cords;
They have spread a [b]net by the [1]wayside;
They have set [c]snares for me. [Selah.

6 I [a]said to the LORD, "Thou art my God;
[b]Give ear, O LORD, to the [c]voice of my supplications.
7 "O [1]GOD the Lord, [a]the strength of my salvation,
Thou hast [b]covered my head in the day of [2]battle.
8 "Do not grant, O LORD, the [a]desires of the wicked;
Do not promote [b]his *evil* device, *lest* they be exalted. [Selah.

9 "As for the head of those who surround me,
May the [a]mischief of their lips cover them.

6 [a]Rom. 11:33 [b]Job 42:3
7 [a]Jer. 23:24
8 [a]Amos 9:2-4 [b]Job 26:6; Prov. 15:11
10 [a]Ps. 23:2, 3
11 [1]Or, *cover* [a]Job 22:13
12 [a]Job 34:22; Dan. 2:22 [b]1 John 1:5
13 [1]Lit., *kidneys* [a]Ps. 119:73; Is. 44:24 [b]Job 10:11
14 [a]Ps. 40:5
15 [1]Lit., *bones* [a]Job 10:8-10; Eccles. 11:5 [b]Ps. 63:9
16 [a]Job 10:8-10; Eccles. 11:5 [b]Ps. 56:8 [c]Job 14:5
17 [a]Ps. 92:5
18 [a]Ps. 40:5 [b]Ps. 3:5
19 [a]Is. 11:4 [b]Ps. 6:8; 119:115 [c]Ps. 5:6
20 [1]Or, *of* [2]Some mss. read, *lift themselves up* against Thee [a]Jude 15 [b]Ex. 20:7; Deut. 5:11
21 [a]Ps. 26:5; 31:6 [b]Ps. 119:158
23 [a]Ps. 26:2 [b]Ps. 7:9; Prov. 17:3; Jer. 11:20; 1 Thess. 2:4
24 [a]Ps. 146:9; Prov. 15:9; 28:10; Jer. 25:5; 36:3 [b]Ps. 5:8; 143:10 [c]Ps. 16:11
1 [a]Ps. 17:13; 59:2; 71:4 [b]Ps. 18:48; 86:14; 140:11
2 [a]Ps. 7:14; 36:4; 52:2; Prov. 6:14; Is. 59:4; Hos. 7:15 [b]Ps. 56:6
3 [a]Ps. 57:4; 64:3 [b]Ps. 58:4; Rom. 3:13; James 3:8
4 [1]Or, *devised* [2]Lit., *push violently* [a]Ps. 140:1 [b]Ps. 36:11
5 [1]Lit., *track* [a]Job 18:9; Ps. 35:7; 141:9; 142:3 [b]Ps. 31:4; 57:6; Lam. 1:13 [c]Ps. 141:9; Is. 8:14; Amos 3:5
6 [a]Ps. 16:2; 31:14 [b]Ps. 143:1 [c]Ps. 116:1; 130:2
7 [1]YHWH, usually rendered LORD [2]Lit., *weapons* [a]Ps. 28:8; 118:14 [b]Ps. 144:10
8 [a]Ps. 112:10 [b]Esth. 9:25; Ps. 10:2, 3
9 [a]Ps. 7:16; Prov. 18:7

10 "May [a]burning coals fall upon them;
May they be [b]cast into the fire,
Into [1]deep pits from which they [c]cannot rise.
11 "May a slanderer not be established in the earth;
[a]May evil hunt the violent man speedily."

12 I know that the LORD will [a]maintain the cause of the afflicted,
And [b]justice for the poor.
13 Surely the [a]righteous will give thanks to Thy name;
The [b]upright will dwell in Thy presence.

PSALM 141

An Evening Prayer for Sanctification and Protection.

A Psalm of David.

O LORD, I call upon Thee; [a]hasten to me!
[b]Give ear to my voice when I call to Thee!
2 May my prayer be [1]counted as [a]incense before Thee;
The lifting up of my hands as the [b]evening offering.
3 Set a [a]guard, O LORD, [1]over my mouth;
Keep watch over the [b]door of my lips.
4 [a]Do not incline my heart to any evil thing,
To practice deeds of wickedness
With men who [b]do iniquity;
And [c]do not let me eat of their delicacies.

5 Let the [a]righteous smite me in kindness and reprove me;
It is [b]oil upon the head;
Do not let my head refuse it,
For still my prayer [c]is against their wicked deeds.
6 Their judges are [a]thrown down by the sides of the rock,
And they hear my words, for they are pleasant.
7 As when one [a]plows and breaks open the earth,
Our [b]bones have been scattered at the [c]mouth of Sheol.

8 For my [a]eyes are toward Thee, O [1]GOD, the Lord;
In Thee I [b]take refuge; [c]do not [2]leave me defenseless.
9 Keep me from the [a]jaws of the trap which they have set for me,
And from the [b]snares of those who do iniquity.
10 Let the wicked [a]fall into their own nets,
While I pass by [b]safely.

PSALM 142

Prayer for Help in Trouble.

Maskil of David, when he was [•]in the cave.
A Prayer.

I [a]CRY aloud with my voice to the LORD;
I [b]make supplication with my voice to the LORD.
2 I [a]pour out my complaint before Him;
I declare my [b]trouble before Him.
3 When [a]my spirit [1]was overwhelmed within me,
Thou didst know my path.
In the way where I walk
They have [b]hidden a trap for me.
4 Look to the right and see;
For there is [a]no one who regards me;
There is no [b]escape for me;
[c]No one cares for my soul.

5 I cried out to Thee, O LORD;
I said, "Thou art [a]my refuge,
My [b]portion in the [c]land of the living.
6 "[a]Give heed to my cry,
For I am [b]brought very low;
Deliver me from my persecutors,
For they are too [c]strong for me.
7 "[a]Bring my soul out of prison,
So that I may give thanks to Thy name;
The righteous will surround me,
For Thou wilt [b]deal bountifully with me."

PSALM 143

Prayer for Deliverance and Guidance.

A Psalm of David.

HEAR my prayer, O LORD,
[a]Give ear to my supplications!
Answer me in Thy [b]faithfulness, in Thy [c]righteousness!
2 And [a]do not enter into judgment with Thy servant,
For in Thy sight [b]no man living is righteous.
3 For the enemy has persecuted my soul;

---

10 [1]Lit., *watery* [a]Ps. 11:6 [b]Ps. 21:9; Matt. 3:10 [c]Ps. 36:12
11 [a]Ps. 34:21
12 [a]1 Kin. 8:45, 49; Ps. 9:4; 18:27; 82:3 [b]Ps. 12:5; 35:10
13 [a]Ps. 97:12 [b]Ps. 11:7; 16:11; 17:15

1 [a]Ps. 22:19; 38:22; 70:5 [b]Ps. 5:1; 143:1
2 [1]Lit., *fixed* [a]Ex. 30:8; Luke 1:10; Rev. 5:8; 8:3, 4 [b]Ex. 29:41; 1 Kin. 18:29, 36; Dan. 9:21
3 [1]Lit., *to* [a]Ps. 34:13; 39:1; Prov. 13:3; 21:23 [b]Mic. 7:5
4 [a]Ps. 119:36 [b]Is. 32:6; Hos. 6:8; Mal. 3:15 [c]Prov. 23:6
5 [a]Prov. 9:8; 19:25; 25:12; 27:6; Eccles. 7:5; Gal. 6:1 [b]Ps. 23:5; 133:2 [c]Ps. 35:14
6 [a]2 Chr. 25:12
7 [a]Ps. 129:3 [b]Ps. 53:5 [c]Num. 16:32, 33; Ps. 88:3-5
8 [1]YHWH, usually rendered LORD [2]Lit., *pour out my soul* [a]Ps. 25:15; 123:2 [b]Ps. 2:12; 11:1 [c]Ps. 27:9
9 [a]Ps. 38:12; 64:5; 91:3 [b]Ps. 140:5
10 [a]Ps. 7:15; 57:6 [b]Ps. 124:7

• 1 Sam. 22:1; 24:3
1 [a]Ps. 77:1 [b]Ps. 30:8
2 [a]Ps. 102:title [b]Ps. 77:2
3 [1]Lit., *fainted* [a]Ps. 77:3; 143:4 [b]Ps. 140:5
4 [a]Ps. 31:11; 88:8, 18 [b]Job 11:20; Jer. 25:35 [c]Jer. 30:17
5 [a]Ps. 91:2, 9 [b]Ps. 16:5; 73:26 [c]Ps. 27:13
6 [a]Ps. 17:1 [b]Ps. 79:8; 116:6 [c]Ps. 18:17
7 [a]Ps. 143:11; 146:7 [b]Ps. 13:6

1 [a]Ps. 140:6 [b]Ps. 89:1, 2 [c]Ps. 71:2
2 [a]Job 14:3; 22:4 [b]1 Kin. 8:46; Job 4:17; 9:2; 25:4; Ps. 130:3; Eccles. 7:20

He has crushed my life [a]to the ground;
He [b]has made me dwell in dark places, like those who have long been dead.
4 Therefore [a]my spirit [1]is overwhelmed within me;
My heart is [2b]appalled within me.

5 I [a]remember the days of old;
I [b]meditate on all Thy doings;
I [c]muse on the work of Thy hands.
6 I [a]stretch out my hands to Thee;
My [b]soul *longs* for Thee, as a [1]parched land. [Selah.

7 [a]Answer me quickly, O LORD, my [b]spirit fails;
[c]Do not hide Thy face from me,
Lest I become like [d]those who go down to the pit.
8 Let me hear Thy [a]lovingkindness in the morning;
For I trust [b]in Thee;
Teach me the [c]way in which I should walk;
For to Thee I [d]lift up my soul.
9 [a]Deliver me, O LORD, from my enemies;
I take refuge in Thee.

10 [a]Teach me to do Thy will,
For Thou art my God;
Let [b]Thy good Spirit [c]lead me on level ground.
11 [a]For the sake of Thy name, O LORD, revive me.
[b]In Thy righteousness bring my soul out of trouble.
12 And in Thy lovingkindness [a]cut off my enemies,
And [b]destroy all those who afflict my soul;
For [c]I am Thy servant.

PSALM 144

Prayer for Rescue and Prosperity.

A Psalm of David.

BLESSED be the LORD, [a]my rock,
Who [b]trains my hands for war,
And my fingers for battle;
2 My lovingkindness and [a]my fortress,
My [b]stronghold and my deliverer;
My [c]shield and He in whom I take refuge;
Who [d]subdues [1]my people under me.
3 O LORD, [a]what is man, that Thou dost take knowledge of him?

3 [a]Ps. 44:25 [b]Ps. 88:6; Lam. 3:6
4 [1]Lit., *faints* [2]Or, *desolate* [a]Ps. 142:3 [b]Lam. 3:11
5 [a]Ps. 77:5, 10, 11 [b]Ps. 77:12 [c]Ps. 105:2
6 [1]Lit., *weary* [a]Job 11:13; Ps. 88:9 [b]Ps. 42:2; 63:1
7 [a]Ps. 69:17 [b]Ps. 73:26; 84:2; Jer. 8:18; Lam. 1:22 [c]Ps. 27:9; 69:17; 102:2 [d]Ps. 28:1; 88:4
8 [a]Ps. 90:14 [b]Ps. 25:2 [c]Ps. 27:11; 32:8; 86:11 [d]Ps. 25:1; 86:4
9 [a]Ps. 31:15; 59:1
10 [a]Ps. 25:4, 5; 119:12 [b]Neh. 9:20 [c]Ps. 23:3
11 [a]Ps. 25:11 [b]Ps. 31:1; 71:2
12 [a]Ps. 54:5 [b]Ps. 52:5 [c]Ps. 116:16

1 [a]Ps. 18:2 [b]Ps. 18:34
2 [1]Or, *peoples* [a]Ps. 18:2; 91:2 [b]Ps. 59:9 [c]Ps. 3:3; 28:7; 84:9 [d]Ps. 18:39
3 [a]Ps. 8:4
4 [a]Ps. 39:11 [b]Job 8:9; 14:2; Ps. 102:11; 109:23
5 [a]Ps. 18:9 [b]Is. 64:1 [c]Ps. 104:32
6 [a]Ps. 18:14 [b]Ps. 7:13; 58:7; Hab. 3:11; Zech. 9:14
7 [a]Ps. 18:16 [b]Ps. 69:1, 14 [c]Ps. 18:44; 54:3
8 [a]Ps. 12:2; 41:6 [b]Gen. 14:22; Deut. 32:40; Ps. 106:26; Is. 44:20
9 [a]Ps. 40:3 [b]Ps. 33:2
10 [a]Ps. 18:50 [b]2 Sam. 18:7
11 [a]Ps. 18:44; 54:3 [b]Ps. 12:2; 41:6 [c]Gen. 14:22; Deut. 32:40; Ps. 106:26; Is. 44:20
12 [1]Lit., *cut after the pattern of* [a]Ps. 92:12-14; 128:3 [b]Song of Sol. 4:4; 7:4
13 [a]Prov. 3:9, 10
14 [a]Prov. 14:4 [b]2 Kin. 25:10, 11; Ps. 60:2 [c]Amos 5:3 [d]Is. 24:11; Jer. 14:2
15 [a]Ps. 33:12

1 [a]Ps. 30:1; 66:17 [b]Ps. 5:2 [c]Ps. 34:1

Or the son of man, that Thou dost think of him?
4 [a]Man is like a mere breath;
His [b]days are like a passing shadow.

5 [a]Bow Thy heavens, O LORD, and [b]come down;
[c]Touch the mountains, that they may smoke.
6 Flash forth [a]lightning and scatter them;
Send out Thine [b]arrows and confuse them.
7 Stretch forth Thy hand [a]from on high;
Rescue me and [b]deliver me out of great waters,
Out of the hand of [c]aliens
8 Whose mouths [a]speak deceit,
And whose [b]right hand is a right hand of falsehood.

9 I will sing a [a]new song to Thee, O God;
Upon a [b]harp of ten strings I will sing praises to Thee,
10 Who dost [a]give salvation to kings;
Who [b]dost rescue David His servant from the evil sword.
11 Rescue me, and deliver me out of the hand of [a]aliens,
Whose mouth [b]speaks deceit,
And whose [c]right hand is a right hand of falsehood.

12 Let our sons in their youth be as [a]grown-up plants,
And our daughters as [b]corner pillars [1]fashioned as for a palace;
13 *Let* our [a]garners be full, furnishing every kind of produce,
And our flocks bring forth thousands and ten thousands in our fields;
14 *Let* our [a]cattle bear,
Without [b]mishap and without [c]loss,
Let there be no [d]outcry in our streets!
15 How blessed are the people who are so situated;
How [a]blessed are the people whose God is the LORD!

PSALM 145

The LORD Extolled for His Goodness.

A Psalm of Praise, of David.

I WILL [a]extol Thee, [b]my God, O King;
And I will [c]bless Thy name forever and ever.
2 Every day I will bless Thee,

And I will [a]praise Thy name forever and ever.
3 [a]Great is the LORD, and highly to be praised;
And His [b]greatness is unsearchable.
4 One [a]generation shall praise Thy works to another,
And shall declare Thy mighty acts.
5 On the [a]glorious splendor of Thy majesty,
And [b]on Thy wonderful works, I will meditate.
6 And men shall speak of the power of Thine [a]awesome acts;
And I will [b]tell of Thy greatness.
7 They shall [1]eagerly utter the memory of Thine [a]abundant goodness,
And shall [b]shout joyfully of Thy righteousness.

8 The LORD is [a]gracious and merciful;
Slow to anger and great in lovingkindness.
9 The LORD is [a]good to all,
And His mercies are over all His works.
10 [a]All Thy works shall give thanks to Thee, O LORD,
And Thy [b]godly ones shall bless Thee.
11 They shall speak of the [a]glory of Thy kingdom,
And talk of Thy power;
12 To [a]make known to the sons of men Thy mighty acts,
And the [b]glory of the majesty of Thy kingdom.
13 Thy kingdom is an [a]everlasting kingdom,
And Thy dominion *endures* throughout all generations.

14 The LORD [a]sustains all who fall,
And [b]raises up all who are bowed down.
15 The eyes of all [1a]look to Thee,
And Thou [a]dost give them their food in due time.
16 Thou [a]dost open Thy hand,
And dost satisfy the desire of every living thing.

17 The LORD is righteous in all His ways,
And kind in all His deeds.
18 The LORD is [a]near to all who call upon Him,
To all who call upon Him [b]in truth.
19 He will [a]fulfill the desire of those who fear Him;

2 [a]Ps. 71:6
3 [a]Ps. 48:1; 86:10; 147:5 [b]Job 5:9; 9:10; 11:7; Is. 40:28; Rom. 11:33
4 [a]Ps. 22:30, 31; Is. 38:19
5 [a]Ps. 145:12 [b]Ps. 119:27
6 [a]Deut. 10:21; Ps. 66:3; 106:22 [b]Deut. 32:3
7 [1]Or, *bubble over with* [a]Ps. 31:19; Is. 63:7 [b]Ps. 51:14
8 [a]Ex. 34:6; Ps. 86:5, 15; 103:8
9 [a]Ps. 100:5; 136:1; Jer. 33:11; Nah. 1:7; Matt. 19:17; Mark 10:18
10 [a]Ps. 19:1; 103:22 [b]Ps. 68:26
11 [a]Jer. 14:21
12 [a]Ps. 105:1 [b]Ps. 145:5; Is. 2:10, 19
13 [a]Ps. 10:16; 29:10; 2 Pet. 1:11
14 [a]Ps. 37:24 [b]Ps. 146:8
15 [1]Lit., *wait;* or, *hope for* [a]Ps. 104:27
16 [a]Ps. 104:28
18 [a]Deut. 4:7; Ps. 34:18; 119:151 [b]John 4:24
19 [a]Ps. 21:2; 37:4 [b]Ps. 10:17; Prov. 15:30; 1 John 5:14
20 [a]Ps. 31:23; 91:14; 97:10
21 [a]Ps. 71:8 [b]Ps. 65:2; 150:6 [c]Ps. 145:1, 2

He will also [b]hear their cry and will save them.
20 The LORD [a]keeps all who love Him;
But all the wicked, He will destroy.
21 My [a]mouth will speak the praise of the LORD;
And [b]all flesh will [c]bless His holy name forever and ever.

PSALM 146

The LORD an Abundant Helper.

1 PRAISE [2]the LORD!
[a]Praise the LORD, O my soul!
2 I will praise the LORD [a]while I live;
I will sing praises to my God while I have my being.
3 [a]Do not trust in princes,
In mortal [b]man, in whom there is [c]no salvation.
4 His [a]spirit departs, he [b]returns to the earth;
In that very day his thoughts perish.
5 How [a]blessed is he whose help is the God of Jacob,
Whose [b]hope is in the LORD his God;
6 Who [a]made heaven and earth,
The [b]sea and all that is in them;
Who [c]keeps [1]faith forever;
7 Who [a]executes justice for the oppressed;
Who [b]gives food to the hungry.
The LORD [c]sets the prisoners free.

8 The LORD [a]opens *the eyes of* the blind;
The LORD [b]raises up those who are bowed down;
The LORD [c]loves the righteous;
9 The LORD [a]protects the strangers;
He [b]supports the fatherless and the widow;
But He thwarts the way of the wicked.
10 The LORD will [a]reign forever,
Thy God, O Zion, to all generations.
[1]Praise the LORD!

1 [1]Or, *Hallelujah!* [2]Heb., YAH, also v.10 [a]Ps. 103:1
2 [a]Ps. 63:4
3 [a]Ps. 118:9 [b]Ps. 118:8; Is. 2:22 [c]Ps. 60:11; 108:12
4 [a]Ps. 104:29 [b]Eccles. 12:7
5 [a]Ps. 144:15 [b]Ps. 71:5
6 [1]Or, *truth* [a]Ps. 115:15 [b]Acts 14:15 [c]Ps. 117:2
7 [a]Ps. 103:6 [b]Ps. 107:9; 145:15 [c]Ps. 68:6; Is. 61:1
8 [a]Matt. 9:30; John 9:7 [b]Ps. 145:14 [c]Ps. 11:7
9 [a]Ex. 22:21; Lev. 19:34 [b]Deut. 10:18; Ps. 68:5
10 [1]Or, *Hallelujah!* [a]Ex. 15:18; Ps. 10:16

PSALM 147

Praise for Jerusalem's Restoration and Prosperity.

1 PRAISE [2]the LORD!
For [a]it is good to sing praises to our God;
For [3]it is pleasant *and* praise is [b]becoming.

1 [1]Or, *Hallelujah!* [2]Heb., YAH, also v.20 [3]Or, *He is gracious* [a]Ps. 135:3 [b]Ps. 33:1

2 The LORD [a]builds up Jerusalem;
He [b]gathers the outcasts of Israel.
3 He heals the [a]brokenhearted,
And [b]binds up their wounds.
4 He [a]counts the number of the stars;
He [b]gives names to all of them.
5 [a]Great is our Lord, and abundant in strength;
His [b]understanding is infinite.
6 The LORD [1a]supports the afflicted;
He brings down the wicked to the ground.

7 Sing to the LORD with thanksgiving;
Sing praises to our God on the lyre,
8 Who [a]covers the heavens with clouds,
Who [b]provides rain for the earth,
Who [c]makes grass to grow on the mountains.
9 He [a]gives to the beast its food,
And to the [b]young ravens which cry.
10 He does not delight in the strength of the [a]horse;
He [b]does not take pleasure in the legs of a man.
11 The LORD [a]favors those who fear Him,
[b]Those who wait for His lovingkindness.

12 Praise the LORD, O Jerusalem!
Praise your God, O Zion!
13 For He has strengthened the [a]bars of your gates;
He has [b]blessed your sons within you.
14 He [a]makes peace in your borders;
He satisfies you with [b]the finest of the wheat.
15 He sends forth His [a]command to the earth;
His [b]word runs very swiftly.
16 He gives [a]snow like wool;
He scatters the [b]hoarfrost like ashes.
17 He casts forth His [a]ice as fragments;
Who can stand before His [b]cold?
18 He [a]sends forth His word and melts them;
He [b]causes His wind to blow and the waters to flow.
19 He [a]declares His words to Jacob,
His [b]statutes and His ordinances to Israel.
20 He [a]has not dealt thus with any nation;
And as for His ordinances, they have [b]not known them.
Praise the LORD!

PSALM 148

The Whole Creation Invoked to Praise the LORD.

1 PRAISE [2]the LORD!
Praise the LORD [a]from the heavens;
Praise Him [b]in the heights!
2 Praise Him, [a]all His angels;
Praise Him, [b]all His hosts!
3 Praise Him, sun and moon;
Praise Him, all stars of light!
4 Praise Him, [a]highest heavens,
And the [b]waters that are above the heavens!
5 Let them praise the name of the LORD,
For [a]He commanded and they were created.
6 He has also [a]established them forever and ever;
He has made a decree which will not pass away.

7 Praise the LORD from the earth,
[a]Sea monsters and all [b]deeps;
8 [a]Fire and hail, [b]snow and [c]clouds;
[d]Stormy wind, [e]fulfilling His word;
9 [a]Mountains and all hills;
Fruit [b]trees and all cedars;
10 Beasts and all cattle;
Creeping things and winged fowl;
11 [a]Kings of the earth and all peoples;
Princes and all judges of the earth;
12 Both young men and virgins;
Old men and children.

13 Let them praise the name of the LORD,
For His [a]name alone is exalted;
His [b]glory is above earth and heaven.
14 And He has [a]lifted up a horn for His people,
[b]Praise for all His godly ones;
Even for the sons of Israel, a people [c]near to Him.
Praise the LORD!

PSALM 149

Israel Invoked to Praise the LORD.

1 PRAISE [2]the LORD!
Sing to the LORD a [a]new song,
And His praise [b]in the congregation of the godly ones.

---

2 [a]Ps. 51:18; 102:16 [b]Deut. 30:3; Ps. 106:47; Is. 11:12; 56:8; Ezek. 39:28
3 [a]Ps. 34:18; Is. 61:1 [b]Job 5:18; Is. 30:26; Ezek. 34:16
4 [a]Gen. 15:5 [b]Is. 40:26
5 [a]Ps. 48:1; 145:3 [b]Is. 40:28
6 [1]Or, *relieves* [a]Ps. 37:24; 146:9
8 [a]Job 26:8 [b]Job 5:10; 38:26; Ps. 104:13 [c]Job 38:27
9 [a]Ps. 104:27, 28; 145:15 [b]Job 38:41
10 [a]Ps. 33:17 [b]1 Sam. 16:7
11 [a]Ps. 149:4 [b]Ps. 33:18
13 [a]Neh. 3:3; 7:3 [b]Ps. 37:26
14 [a]Ps. 29:11; Is. 54:13; 60:17, 18 [b]Deut. 32:14
15 [a]Job 37:12; Ps. 148:5 [b]Ps. 104:4
16 [a]Job 37:6; Ps. 148:8 [b]Job 38:29
17 [a]Job 37:10 [b]Job 37:9
18 [a]Ps. 33:9; 107:20; 147:15 [b]Ps. 107:25
19 [a]Deut. 33:3, 4 [b]Mal. 4:4
20 [a]Deut. 4:7, 8, 32-34 [b]Ps. 79:6; Jer. 10:25

1 [1]Or, *Hallelujah!* [2]Heb., YAH, also v.14 [a]Ps. 69:34 [b]Job 16:19; Ps. 102:19; Matt. 21:9
2 [a]Ps. 103:20 [b]Ps. 103:21
4 [a]Deut. 10:14; 1 Kin. 8:27; Neh. 9:6; Ps. 68:33 [b]Gen. 1:7
5 [a]Gen. 1:1
6 [a]Jer. 31:35, 36; 33:20, 25
7 [a]Gen. 1:21; Ps. 74:13 [b]Gen. 1:2; Deut. 33:13
8 [a]Ps. 18:12 [b]Ps. 147:16 [c]Ps. 135:7 [d]Ps. 107:25 [e]Job 37:12
9 [a]Is. 44:23; 49:13 [b]Is. 55:12
11 [a]Ps. 102:15
13 [a]Is. 12:4 [b]Ps. 8:1; 113:4
14 [a]1 Sam. 2:1; Ps. 75:10 [b]Deut. 10:21; Ps. 109:1; Jer. 17:14 [c]Lev. 10:3; Eph. 2:17

1 [1]Or, *Hallelujah!* [2]Heb., YAH, also v.9 [a]Ps. 33:3 [b]Ps. 35:18; 89:5

2 Let Israel be glad in [a]his Maker;
Let the sons of Zion rejoice in their [b]King.
3 Let them praise His name with [a]dancing;
Let them sing praises to Him with [b]timbrel and lyre.
4 For the LORD [a]takes pleasure in His people;
He will [b]beautify the afflicted ones with salvation.

5 Let the [a]godly ones exult in glory;
Let them [b]sing for joy on their beds.
6 *Let* the [a]high praises of God *be* in their mouth,
And a two-edged [b]sword in their hand,
7 To [a]execute vengeance on the nations,
And punishment on the peoples;
8 To bind their kings [a]with chains,
And their [b]nobles with fetters of iron;
9 To [a]execute on them the judgment written;
This is an honor for all His godly ones.
Praise the LORD!

2 [a]Ps. 95:6 [b]Judg. 8:23; Ps. 47:6
3 [a]2 Sam. 6:14; Ps. 150:4 [b]Ex. 15:20; Ps. 81:2
4 [a]Ps. 35:27; 147:11 [b]Ps. 132:16; Is. 61:3
5 [a]Ps. 132:16 [b]Job 35:10
6 [a]Ps. 66:17 [b]Neh. 4:17
7 [a]Ezek. 25:17; Mic. 5:15
8 [a]Job 36:8 [b]Nah. 3:10
9 [a]Ezek. 28:26
1 [1]Or, *Hallelujah!* [2]Heb., YAH, also v.6 [3]Or, *firmament* [a]Ps. 73:17; 102:19 [b]Ps. 19:1
2 [a]Ps. 145:12 [b]Deut. 3:24
3 [a]Ps. 98:6
4 [a]Ps. 149:3 [b]Ps. 45:8; Is. 38:20 [c]Gen. 4:21; Job 21:12
5 [a]2 Sam. 6:5; 1 Chr. 13:8; 15:16; Ezra 3:10; Neh. 12:27
6 [a]Ps. 103:22

PSALM 150

A Psalm of Praise.

1 [1]PRAISE [2]the LORD!
Praise God in His [a]sanctuary;
Praise Him in His mighty [3b]expanse.
2 Praise Him for His [a]mighty deeds;
Praise Him according to His excellent [b]greatness.

3 Praise Him with [a]trumpet sound;
Praise Him with harp and lyre.
4 Praise Him with [a]timbrel and dancing;
Praise Him with [b]stringed instruments and [c]pipe.
5 Praise Him with loud [a]cymbals;
Praise Him with resounding cymbals.
6 Let [a]everything that has breath praise the LORD.
Praise the LORD!

THE PROVERBS

The Usefulness of Proverbs

1 THE [a]proverbs of Solomon [b]the son of David, king of Israel:
2 To know [a]wisdom and instruction,
To discern the sayings of [b]understanding,
3 To [a]receive instruction in wise behavior,
[b]Righteousness, justice and equity;
4 To give [a]prudence to the naive,
To the youth [b]knowledge and discretion,
5 A wise man will hear and [a]increase in learning,
And a [b]man of understanding will acquire wise counsel,
6 To understand a proverb and a figure,
The words of the wise and their [a]riddles.

7 [a]The fear of the LORD is the beginning of knowledge;
Fools despise wisdom and instruction.

1 [a]1 Kin. 4:32; Prov. 10:1; 25:1; [b]Eccles. 1:1
2 [a]Prov. 15:33 [b]Prov. 4:1
3 [a]Prov. 19:20 [b]Prov. 2:9
4 [a]Prov. 8:5, 12 [b]Prov. 2:10, 11
5 [a]Prov. 9:9 [b]Prov. 14:6
6 [a]Num. 12:8; Ps. 49:4; 78:2; Dan. 8:23
7 [a]Job 28:28; Ps. 111:10; Prov. 9:10; 15:33; Eccles. 12:13
8 [a]Prov. 4:1 [b]Prov. 6:20
9 [a]Prov. 4:9 [b]Gen. 41:42; Dan. 5:29
10 [a]Prov. 16:29 [b]Deut. 13:8; Ps. 50:18
11 [a]Prov. 12:6 [b]Ps. 10:8
12 [a]Ps. 124:3 [b]Ps. 28:1
15 [a]Ps. 1:1; Prov. 4:14

The Enticement of Sinners

8 [a]Hear, my son, your father's instruction,
And [b]do not forsake your mother's teaching;
9 Indeed, they are a [a]graceful wreath to your head,
And [b]ornaments about your neck.
10 My son, if sinners [a]entice you,
[b]Do not consent.
11 If they say, "Come with us,
Let us [a]lie in wait for blood,
Let us [b]ambush the innocent without cause;
12 Let us [a]swallow them alive like Sheol,
Even whole, as those who [b]go down to the pit;
13 We shall find all *kinds* of precious wealth,
We shall fill our houses with spoil;
14 Throw in your lot with us,
We shall all have one purse,"
15 My son, [a]do not walk in the way with them.

[b]Keep your feet from their path,
16 For [a]their feet run to evil,
And they hasten to shed blood.
17 Indeed, it is [1]useless to spread the net
In the eyes of any [2]bird;
18 But they [a]lie in wait for their own blood;
They ambush their own lives.
19 So are the ways of everyone who [a]gains by violence;
It takes away the life of its possessors.

Wisdom Warns

20 [a]Wisdom shouts in the street,
She [1]lifts her voice in the square;
21 At the head of the noisy *streets* she cries out;
At the entrance of the gates in the city, she utters her sayings:
22 "How long, O [1a]naive ones, will you love [2]simplicity?
And [b]scoffers delight themselves in scoffing,
And fools [c]hate knowledge?
23 "Turn to my reproof,
Behold, I will [a]pour out my spirit on you;
I will make my words known to you.
24 Because [a]I called, and you [b]refused;
I [c]stretched out my hand, and no one paid attention;
25 And you [a]neglected all my counsel,
And did not [b]want my reproof;
26 I will even [a]laugh at your [b]calamity;
I will mock when your [c]dread comes,
27 When your dread comes like a storm,
And your calamity comes on like a [a]whirlwind,
When distress *and* anguish come on you.
28 "Then they will [a]call on me, but I will not answer;
They will [b]seek me diligently, but they shall not find me,
29 Because they [a]hated knowledge,
And did not choose the fear of the LORD.
30 "They [a]would not accept my counsel,
They spurned all my reproof.
31 "So they shall [a]eat of the fruit of their own way,
And be [b]satiated with their own devices.

15 [b]Ps. 119:101
16 [a]Prov. 6:17, 18; Is. 59:7
17 [1]Lit., *in vain* [2]Lit., *possessor of wing*
18 [a]Prov. 11:19
19 [a]Prov. 15:27
20 [1]Lit., *gives* [a]Prov. 8:1-3; 9:3
22 [1]Lit., *simple ones* [2]Or, *naivete* [a]Prov. 1:4, 32; 8:5; 9:4; 22:3 [b]Ps. 1:1 [c]Prov. 1:29; 5:12
23 [a]Is. 32:15; Joel 2:28
24 [a]Is. 65:12; 66:4; Jer. 7:13 [b]Prov. 15:32; Zech. 7:11 [c]Is. 65:2; Rom. 10:21
25 [a]Ps. 107:11; Luke 7:30 [b]Prov. 15:10
26 [a]Ps. 2:4 [b]Prov. 6:15 [c]Prov. 10:24
27 [a]Prov. 10:25
28 [a]1 Sam. 8:18; Job 27:9; 35:12; Ps. 18:41; Is. 1:15; Jer. 11:11; 14:12; Ezek. 8:18; Mic. 3:4; Zech. 7:13 [b]Prov. 8:17
29 [a]Job 21:14; Prov. 1:22
30 [a]Ps. 81:11; Prov. 1:25
31 [a]Job 4:8; Prov. 5:22, 23; 22:8; Jer. 6:19 [b]Prov. 14:14
32 [1]Lit., *simple ones* [a]Jer. 2:19
33 [1]Lit., *dwell* [a]Ps. 25:12, 13; Prov. 3:24-26
1 [a]Prov. 4:10 [b]Prov. 3:1
2 [a]Prov. 22:17
3 [1]Lit., *give*
4 [a]Prov. 3:14 [b]Job 3:21; Matt. 13:44
5 [a]Prov. 1:7
6 [a]1 Kin. 3:12; Job 32:8; James 1:5
7 [a]Ps. 84:11; Prov. 30:5
8 [a]1 Sam. 2:9; Ps. 66:9
9 [a]Prov. 8:20 [b]Prov. 4:18
10 [a]Prov. 14:33 [b]Prov. 22:18
11 [a]Prov. 4:6; 6:22
12 [a]Prov. 28:26 [b]Prov. 6:12
13 [a]Prov. 21:16 [b]Ps. 82:5; Prov. 4:19; John 3:19, 20
14 [a]Prov. 10:23; Jer. 11:15
15 [a]Ps. 125:5; Prov. 21:8

32 "For the [a]waywardness of the [1]naive shall kill them,
And the complacency of fools shall destroy them.
33 "But [a]he who listens to me shall [1]live securely,
And shall be at ease from the dread of evil."

CHAPTER 2

The Pursuit of Wisdom Brings Security

MY son, if you will [a]receive my sayings,
And [b]treasure my commandments within you,
2 [a]Make your ear attentive to wisdom,
Incline your heart to understanding;
3 For if you cry for discernment,
[1]Lift your voice for understanding;
4 If you seek her as [a]silver,
And search for her as for [b]hidden treasures;
5 Then you will discern the [a]fear of the LORD,
And discover the knowledge of God.
6 For [a]the LORD gives wisdom;
From His mouth *come* knowledge and understanding.
7 He stores up sound wisdom for the upright;
He is a [a]shield to those who walk in integrity,
8 Guarding the paths of justice,
And He [a]preserves the way of His godly ones.
9 Then you will discern [a]righteousness and justice
And equity *and* every [b]good course.
10 For [a]wisdom will enter your heart,
And [b]knowledge will be pleasant to your soul;
11 Discretion will [a]guard you,
Understanding will watch over you,
12 To [a]deliver you from the way of evil,
From the man who speaks [b]perverse things;
13 From those who [a]leave the paths of uprightness,
To walk in the [b]ways of darkness;
14 Who [a]delight in doing evil,
And rejoice in the perversity of evil;
15 Whose paths are [a]crooked,
And who are devious in their ways;

16 To [a]deliver you from the strange woman,
From the [b]adulteress who flatters with her words;
17 That leaves the [a]companion of her youth,
And forgets the covenant of her God;
18 For [a]her house sinks down to death,
And her tracks *lead* to the dead;
19 None who go to her return again,
Nor do they reach the [a]paths of life.
20 So you will walk in the way of good men,
And keep to the [a]paths of the righteous.
21 For [a]the upright will live in the land,
And [b]the blameless will remain in it;
22 But [a]the wicked will be cut off from the land,
And [b]the treacherous will be [c]uprooted from it.

CHAPTER 3

The Rewards of Wisdom

MY son, [a]do not forget my teaching,
But let your heart [b]keep my commandments;
2 For [a]length of days and years of life,
And peace they will add to you.
3 Do not let [a]kindness and truth leave you;
[b]Bind them around your neck,
[c]Write them on the tablet of your heart.
4 So you will [a]find favor and [b]good repute
In the sight of God and man.
5 [a]Trust in the LORD with all your heart,
And [b]do not lean on your own understanding.
6 In all your ways [a]acknowledge Him,
And He will [b]make your paths straight.
7 [a]Do not be wise in your own eyes;
[b]Fear the LORD and turn away from evil.
8 It will be [a]healing to your body,
And [b]refreshment to your bones.
9 [a]Honor the LORD from your wealth,
And from the [b]first of all your produce;

16 [a]Prov. 6:24; 7:5 [b]Prov. 23:27
17 [a]Mal. 2:14, 15
18 [a]Prov. 7:27
19 [a]Ps. 16:11
20 [a]Prov. 4:18
21 [a]Ps. 37:9, 29; Prov. 10:30 [b]Prov. 28:10
22 [a]Ps. 37:38; Prov. 10:30 [b]Prov. 11:3 [c]Deut. 28:63; Ps. 52:5
1 [a]Ps. 119:61; Prov. 4:5 [b]Ex. 20:6; Deut. 30:16
2 [a]Ps. 91:16; Prov. 3:16; 4:10
3 [a]2 Sam. 15:20; Prov. 14:22 [b]Deut. 6:8; 11:18 [c]Prov. 7:3; Jer. 17:1; 2 Cor. 3:3
4 [a]1 Sam. 2:26; Prov. 8:35; Luke 2:52 [b]Ps. 111:10
5 [a]Ps. 37:3, 5; Prov. 22:19 [b]Prov. 23:4; Jer. 9:23
6 [a]1 Chr. 28:9; Prov. 16:3 [b]Is. 45:13
7 [a]Rom. 12:16 [b]Job 1:1; 28:28; Prov. 8:13; 16:6
8 [a]Prov. 4:22 [b]Job 21:24
9 [a]Is. 43:23 [b]Ex. 23:19; Deut. 26:2; Mal. 3:10
10 [a]Deut. 28:8 [b]Joel 2:24
11 [a]Job 5:17; Heb. 12:5, 6
12 [a]Deut. 8:5; Prov. 13:24
13 [a]Prov. 8:32
14 [a]Job 28:15-19; Prov. 8:10, 19
15 [a]Job 28:18; Prov. 8:11 [b]Prov. 3:8
16 [a]Prov. 3:2 [b]Prov. 8:18; 22:4
17 [a]Ps. 119:165
18 [a]Gen. 2:9; Prov. 11:30; 13:12; 15:4; Rev. 2:7
19 [a]Ps. 104:24; Prov. 8:27 [b]Prov. 8:27, 28
20 [a]Gen. 7:11 [b]Deut. 33:28; Job 36:28
21 [a]Prov. 4:21
22 [a]Deut. 32:47; Prov. 4:22; 8:35; 16:22; 21:21 [b]Prov. 1:9
23 [a]Prov. 4:12; 10:9 [b]Ps. 91:12; Is. 5:27; 63:13
24 [a]Job 11:19; Ps. 3:5; Prov. 1:33; 6:22
25 [1]Lit., *storm* [a]Ps. 91:5; 1 Pet. 3:14 [b]Job 5:21
26 [1]Or, *at your side* [a]1 Sam. 2:9
27 [a]Rom. 13:7; Gal. 6:10

10 So your [a]barns will be filled with plenty,
And your [b]vats will overflow with new wine.
11 [a]My son, do not reject the discipline of the LORD,
Or loathe His reproof,
12 For whom the LORD loves He reproves,
Even [a]as a father, the son in whom he delights.

13 [a]How blessed is the man who finds wisdom,
And the man who gains understanding.
14 For its [a]profit is better than the profit of silver,
And its gain than fine gold.
15 She is [a]more precious than jewels;
And [b]nothing you desire compares with her.
16 [a]Long life is in her right hand;
In her left hand are [b]riches and honor.
17 Her ways are pleasant ways,
And all her paths are [a]peace.
18 She is a [a]tree of life to those who take hold of her,
And happy are all who hold her fast.
19 The LORD [a]by wisdom founded the earth;
By understanding He [b]established the heavens.
20 By His knowledge the [a]deeps were broken up,
And the [b]skies drip with dew.
21 My son, [a]let them not depart from your sight;
Keep sound wisdom and discretion,
22 So they will be [a]life to your soul,
And [b]adornment to your neck.
23 Then you will [a]walk in your way securely,
And your foot will not [b]stumble.
24 When you [a]lie down, you will not be afraid;
When you lie down, your sleep will be sweet.
25 [a]Do not be afraid of sudden fear,
Nor of the [1b]onslaught of the wicked when it comes;
26 For the LORD will be [1]your confidence,
And will [a]keep your foot from being caught.

27 [a]Do not withhold good from those to whom it is due,

When it is in your power to do
it.
28 [a]Do not say to your neighbor,
"Go, and come back,
And tomorrow I will give *it,*"
When you have it with you.
29 [a]Do not devise harm against
your neighbor,
While he lives in security beside you.
30 [a]Do not contend with a man
without cause,
If he has done you no harm.
31 [a]Do not envy a man of violence,
And do not choose any of his
ways.
32 For the [a]crooked *man* is an
abomination to the LORD;
But [1]He is [b]intimate with the
upright.
33 The [a]curse of the LORD is on the
house of the wicked,
But He [b]blesses the dwelling of
the righteous.
34 Though [a]He scoffs at the scoffers,
Yet [b]He gives grace to the afflicted.
35 The wise will inherit honor,
But fools [1]display dishonor.

CHAPTER 4

A Father's Instruction

HEAR, O sons, the [a]instruction of
a father,
And [b]give attention that you
may [1]gain understanding,
2 For I give you [1]sound [a]teaching;
[b]Do not abandon my [2]instruction.
3 When I was a son to my father,
[a]Tender and [b]the only son in the
sight of my mother,
4 Then he taught me and said to
me,
"Let your heart [a]hold fast my
words;
[b]Keep my commandments and
live;
5 [a]Acquire wisdom! [b]Acquire understanding!
Do not forget, nor turn away
from the words of my mouth.
6 "Do not forsake her, and she will
guard you;
[a]Love her, and she will watch
over you.
7 "[a]The [1]beginning of wisdom *is:*
[b]Acquire wisdom;
And with all your acquiring, get
understanding.
8 "Prize her, and she will exalt
you;
She will honor you if you embrace her.
9 "She will place [a]on your head a
garland of grace;
She will present you with a
crown of beauty."
10 Hear, my son, and [a]accept my
sayings,
And the [b]years of your life will
be many.
11 I have [a]directed you in the way
of wisdom;
I have led you in upright paths.
12 When you walk, your [a]steps
will not be impeded;
And if you run, you [b]will not
stumble.
13 [a]Take hold of instruction; do
not let go.
Guard her, for she is your [b]life.
14 [a]Do not enter the path of the
wicked,
And do not proceed in the way
of evil men.
15 Avoid it, do not pass by it;
Turn away from it and pass on.
16 For they [a]cannot sleep unless
they do evil;
And [1]they are robbed of sleep
unless they make *someone*
stumble.
17 For they [a]eat the bread of wickedness,
And drink the wine of violence.
18 But the [a]path of the righteous is
like the [b]light of dawn,
That [c]shines brighter and
brighter until the [d]full day.
19 The [a]way of the wicked is like
darkness;
They do not know over what
they [1b]stumble.
20 My son, [a]give attention to my
words;
[b]Incline your ear to my sayings.
21 [a]Do not let them depart from
your sight;
[b]Keep them in the midst of your
heart.
22 For they are [a]life to those who
find them,
And [b]health to all [1]their whole
body.
23 Watch over your heart with all
diligence,
For [a]from it *flow* the springs of
life.
24 Put away from you a [a]deceitful
mouth,
And [b]put devious lips far from
you.
25 Let your eyes look directly
ahead,
And let your [1]gaze be fixed
straight in front of you.
26 [a]Watch the path of your feet,
And all your [b]ways will be established.

28 [a]Lev. 19:13; Deut. 24:15
29 [a]Prov. 6:14; 14:22
30 [a]Prov. 26:17; Rom. 12:18
31 [a]Ps. 37:1; Prov. 24:1
32 [1]Lit., *His private counsel is* [a]Prov. 11:20 [b]Job 29:4; Ps. 25:14
33 [a]Deut. 11:28; Mal. 2:2 [b]Job 8:6
34 [a]James 4:6 [b]1 Pet. 5:5
35 [1]Lit., *raise high*
1 [1]Lit., *know* [a]Prov. 1:8 [b]Prov. 1:2; 2:2
2 [1]Lit., *good* [2]Or, *law* [a]Deut. 32:2; Job 11:4 [b]Ps. 89:30; 119:87; Prov. 3:1
3 [a]1 Chr. 22:5 [b]Zech. 12:10
4 [a]Ps. 119:168 [b]Prov. 7:2
5 [a]Prov. 4:7 [b]Prov. 16:16
6 [a]2 Thess. 2:10
7 [1]Or, *the primary thing is wisdom* [a]Prov. 8:23 [b]Prov. 23:23
9 [a]Prov. 1:9
10 [a]Prov. 2:1 [b]Prov. 3:2
11 [a]1 Sam. 12:23
12 [a]Job 18:7; Ps. 18:36 [b]Prov. 3:23
13 [a]Prov. 3:18 [b]Prov. 3:22; John 6:63
14 [a]Ps. 1:1; Prov. 1:15
16 [1]Lit., *their sleep is robbed* [a]Ps. 36:4; Mic. 2:1
17 [a]Prov. 13:2
18 [a]Is. 26:7 [b]2 Sam. 23:4 [c]Dan. 12:3 [d]Job 11:17
19 [1]Or, *may stumble* [a]Job 18:5, 6; Prov. 2:13; Is. 59:9, 10; Jer. 23:12; John 12:35 [b]John 11:10
20 [a]Prov. 5:1 [b]Prov. 2:2
21 [a]Prov. 3:21 [b]Prov. 7:1, 2
22 [1]Lit., *his* [a]Prov. 3:22 [b]Prov. 3:8; 12:18
23 [a]Matt. 12:34; 15:18, 19; Mark 7:21; Luke 6:45
24 [a]Prov. 6:12; 10:32 [b]Prov. 19:1
25 [1]Or, *eyelids*
26 [a]Prov. 5:21; Heb. 12:13 [b]Ps. 119:5

27 [a]Do not turn to the right nor to the left;
[b]Turn your foot from evil.

CHAPTER 5

Pitfalls of Immorality

My son, [a]give attention to my wisdom,
[b]Incline your ear to my understanding;
2 That you may [a]observe discretion,
And your [b]lips may reserve knowledge.
3 For the lips of an [1a]adulteress [b]drip honey,
And [c]smoother than oil is her [2]speech;
4 But in the end she is [a]bitter as wormwood,
[b]Sharp as a two-edged sword.
5 Her feet [a]go down to death,
Her steps lay hold of Sheol.
6 [1]She does not ponder the [a]path of life;
Her ways are [b]unstable, she [c]does not know *it*.

7 [a]Now then, *my* sons, listen to me,
And [b]do not depart from the words of my mouth.
8 [a]Keep your way far from her,
And do not go near the [b]door of her house,
9 Lest you give your vigor to others,
And your years to the cruel one;
10 Lest strangers be filled with your strength,
And your hard-earned goods go to the house of an alien;
11 And you groan at your latter end,
When your flesh and your body are consumed;
12 And you say, "How I have [a]hated instruction!
And my heart [b]spurned reproof!
13 "And I have not listened to the voice of my [a]teachers,
Nor inclined my ear to my instructors!
14 "I was almost in utter ruin
In the midst of the assembly and congregation."

15 Drink water from your own cistern,
And [1]fresh water from your own well.
16 Should your [a]springs be dispersed abroad,
Streams of water in the streets?

27 [a]Deut. 5:32; 28:14 [b]Prov. 1:15
1 [a]Prov. 4:20 [b]Prov. 22:17
2 [a]Prov. 3:21 [b]Mal. 2:7
3 [1]Lit., *strange woman* [2]Lit., *palate* [a]Prov. 2:16; 5:20; 7:5; 22:14 [b]Song of Sol. 4:11 [c]Ps. 55:21
4 [a]Eccles. 7:26 [b]Ps. 57:4
5 [a]Prov. 7:27
6 [1]Lit., *Lest she watch* [a]Prov. 4:26; 5:21 [b]2 Pet. 2:14 [c]Prov. 30:20
7 [a]Prov. 7:24 [b]Ps. 119:102
8 [a]Prov. 7:25 [b]Prov. 9:14
12 [a]Prov. 1:7, 22, 29 [b]Prov. 1:25; 12:1
13 [a]Prov. 1:8
15 [1]Lit., *flowing*
16 [a]Prov. 5:18; 9:17; Song of Sol. 4:12, 15
18 [a]Prov. 5:18; 9:17; Song of Sol. 4:12, 15 [b]Eccles. 9:9 [c]Mal. 2:14
19 [1]Lit., *intoxicated* [a]Song of Sol. 2:9, 17; 4:5; 7:3
20 [1]Lit., *strange woman* [a]Prov. 5:3 [b]Prov. 2:16; 6:24; 7:5; 23:27
21 [a]Job 14:16; 31:4; 34:21; Ps. 119:168; Prov. 15:3; Jer. 16:17; 32:19; Hos. 7:2; Heb. 4:13 [b]Prov. 4:26
22 [a]Num. 32:23; Ps. 7:15; 9:15; 40:12; Prov. 1:31, 32
23 [a]Job 4:21; 36:12
1 [1]Lit., *clapped your palms* [a]Prov. 11:15; 17:18; 20:16; 22:26; 27:13
3 [1]Lit., *palm*
4 [a]Ps. 132:4
5 [a]Ps. 91:3; 124:7
6 [a]Prov. 30:24, 25 [b]Prov. 6:9; 10:26; 13:4; 20:4; 26:16
7 [a]Prov. 30:27
8 [a]Prov. 10:5

17 Let them be yours alone,
And not for strangers with you.
18 Let your [a]fountain be blessed,
And [b]rejoice in the [c]wife of your youth.
19 *As* a loving [a]hind and a graceful doe,
Let her breasts satisfy you at all times;
Be [1]exhilarated always with her love.
20 For why should you, my son, be exhilarated with an [1a]adulteress,
And embrace the bosom of a [b]foreigner?
21 For the [a]ways of a man are before the eyes of the LORD,
And He [b]watches all his paths.
22 His [a]own iniquities will capture the wicked,
And he will be held with the cords of his sin.
23 He will [a]die for lack of instruction,
And in the greatness of his folly he will go astray.

CHAPTER 6

Parental Counsel

My son, if you have become [a]surety for your neighbor,
Have [1]given a pledge for a stranger,
2 *If* you have been snared with the words of your mouth,
Have been caught with the words of your mouth,
3 Do this then, my son, and deliver yourself;
Since you have come into the [1]hand of your neighbor,
Go, humble yourself, and importune your neighbor.
4 Do not give [a]sleep to your eyes,
Nor slumber to your eyelids;
5 Deliver yourself like a gazelle from *the hunter's* hand,
And like a [a]bird from the hand of the fowler.

6 Go to the [a]ant, O [b]sluggard,
Observe her ways and be wise,
7 Which, having [a]no chief,
Officer or ruler,
8 Prepares her food [a]in the summer,
And gathers her provision in the harvest.
9 How long will you lie down, O sluggard?
When will you arise from your sleep?

10 "[a]A little sleep, a little slumber,
A little folding of the hands to rest"—
11 And your poverty will come in like a vagabond,
And your need like an armed man.

12 A [a]worthless person, a wicked man,
Is the one who walks with a [b]false mouth,
13 Who [a]winks with his eyes, who [1]signals with his feet,
Who points with his fingers;
14 Who *with* [a]perversity in his heart [b]devises evil continually,
Who [c]spreads strife.
15 Therefore [a]his calamity will come suddenly;
[b]Instantly he will be broken, and there will be [c]no healing.

16 There are six things which the LORD hates,
Yes, seven which are an abomination to Him:
17 [a]Haughty eyes, a [b]lying tongue,
And hands that [c]shed innocent blood,
18 A heart that devises [a]wicked plans,
[b]Feet that run rapidly to evil,
19 A [a]false witness *who* utters lies,
And one who [1b]spreads strife among brothers.

20 My son, observe the commandment of your father,
And do not forsake the teaching of your mother;
21 [a]Bind them continually on your heart;
Tie them around your neck.
22 When you [a]walk about, [1]they will guide you;
When you sleep, [1]they will watch over you;
And when you awake, [1]they will talk to you.
23 For [a]the commandment is a lamp, and the teaching is light;
And reproofs for discipline are the way of life,
24 To [a]keep you from the evil woman,
From the smooth tongue of the adulteress.
25 [a]Do not desire her beauty in your heart,
Nor let her catch you with her [b]eyelids.
26 For [a]on account of a harlot *one is reduced* to a loaf of bread,
And an adulteress [b]hunts for the precious life.
27 Can a man take fire in his bosom,
And his clothes not be burned?
28 Or can a man walk on hot coals,
And his feet not be scorched?
29 So is the one who [a]goes in to his neighbor's wife;
Whoever touches her [b]will not [1]go unpunished.
30 Men do not despise a thief if he steals
To [a]satisfy himself when he is hungry;
31 But when he is found, he must [a]repay sevenfold;
He must give all the substance of his house.
32 The one who commits adultery with a woman is [a]lacking [1]sense;
He who would [b]destroy [2]himself does it.
33 Wounds and disgrace he will find,
And his reproach will not be blotted out.
34 For [a]jealousy [1]enrages a man,
And he will not spare in the [b]day of vengeance.
35 He will not [1]accept any ransom,
Nor will he be [2]content though you give many [3]gifts.

CHAPTER 7

The Wiles of the Harlot

MY son, [a]keep my words,
And treasure my commandments within you.
2 [a]Keep my commandments and live,
And my teaching [b]as the [1]apple of your eye.
3 Bind them on your fingers;
[a]Write them on the tablet of your heart.
4 Say to wisdom, "You are my sister,"
And call understanding *your* intimate friend;
5 That they may keep you from an [1]adulteress,
From the foreigner who [2]flatters with her words.

6 For [a]at the window of my house
I looked out [b]through my lattice,
7 And I saw among the [a]naive,
I discerned among the youths,
A young man [b]lacking [1]sense,
8 Passing through the street near [a]her corner;
And he [1]takes the way to [b]her house,

10 [a]Prov. 24:33, 34
12 [a]Prov. 16:27 [b]Prov. 4:24; 10:32
13 [1]Lit., *scrapes* [a]Ps. 35:19; Prov. 10:10
14 [a]Prov. 17:20 [b]Prov. 3:29; Mic. 2:1 [c]Prov. 6:19; 16:28
15 [a]Prov. 24:22 [b]Is. 30:13, 14; Jer. 19:11 [c]2 Cor. 36:16
17 [a]Ps. 18:27; 101:5; Prov. 21:4; 30:13 [b]Ps. 31:18; 120:2; Prov. 12:22; 17:7 [c]Deut. 19:10; Prov. 28:17; Is. 1:15; 59:7
18 [a]Gen. 6:5; Prov. 24:2 [b]Prov. 1:16
19 [1]Lit., *sends out* [a]Ps. 27:12; Prov. 12:17; 19:5, 9; 21:28 [b]Prov. 6:14
21 [a]Prov. 3:3
22 [1]Lit., *she* [a]Prov. 3:23
23 [a]Ps. 119:105
24 [a]Prov. 5:3; 7:5, 21
25 [a]Matt. 5:28 [b]2 Kin. 9:30; Jer. 4:30; Ezek. 23:40
26 [a]Prov. 5:9, 10; 29:3 [b]Prov. 7:23; Ezek. 13:18
29 [1]Lit., *be innocent* [a]Ezek. 18:6; 33:26 [b]Prov. 16:5
30 [a]Job 38:39
31 [a]Ex. 22:1-4
32 [1]Lit., *heart* [2]Lit., *his soul* [a]Prov. 7:7; 9:4, 16; 10:13, 21; 11:12; 12:11 [b]Prov. 7:22, 23
34 [1]Lit., *is the rage of* [a]Prov. 27:4; Song of Sol. 8:6 [b]Lev. 20:10; Prov. 11:4
35 [1]Lit., *lift up the face of any* [2]Lit., *willing* [3]Or, *bribes*
1 [a]Prov. 2:1; 6:20
2 [1]Lit., *pupil* [a]Prov. 4:4 [b]Deut. 32:10; Ps. 17:8; Zech. 2:8
3 [a]Prov. 3:3
5 [1]Lit., *strange woman* [2]Lit., *is smooth*
6 [a]Judg. 5:28 [b]Song of Sol. 2:9
7 [1]Lit., *heart* [a]Prov. 1:22 [b]Prov. 6:32
8 [1]Lit., *steps* [a]Prov. 7:12 [b]Prov. 7:27

9 In the [a]twilight, in the [1]evening,
In the [2]middle of the night and
in the darkness.
10 And behold, a woman *comes* to
meet him,
[a]Dressed as a harlot and cunning of heart.
11 She is [a]boisterous and rebellious;
Her feet do not remain at home;
12 *She is* now in the streets, now
[a]in the squares,
And [b]lurks by every corner.
13 So she seizes him and kisses
him,
[1]And with a [a]brazen face she
says to him:
14 "[1]I was due to offer [a]peace offerings;
Today I have [b]paid my vows.
15 "Therefore I have come out to
meet you,
To seek your presence earnestly, and I have found you.
16 "I have spread my couch with
[a]coverings,
With colored [b]linens of Egypt.
17 "I have sprinkled my bed
With [a]myrrh, aloes and [b]cinna-
mon.
18 "Come, let us drink our fill of
love until morning;
Let us delight ourselves with
caresses.
19 "For [1]the man is not at home,
He has gone on a long journey;
20 He has taken a [a]bag of money
[1]with him,
At full moon he will come
home."
21 With her many persuasions she
entices him;
With her [1a]flattering lips she seduces him.
22 Suddenly he follows her,
As an ox goes to the slaughter,
Or as [1]*one in* fetters to the discipline of a fool,
23 Until an arrow pierces through
his liver;
As a [a]bird hastens to the snare,
So he does not know that it *will*
cost him his life.

24 Now therefore, *my* sons, [a]listen
to me,
And pay attention to the words
of my mouth.
25 Do not let your heart [a]turn
aside to her ways,
Do not stray into her paths.
26 For many are the [1]victims she
has cast down,
And [a]numerous are all her
slain.
27 Her [a]house is the way to Sheol,
Descending to the chambers of
death.

Chapter 8

The Commendation of Wisdom

DOES not [a]wisdom call,
And understanding [1]lift up her
voice?
2 On top of [a]the heights beside
the way,
Where the paths meet, she
takes her stand;
3 Beside the [a]gates, at the opening to the city,
At the entrance of the doors,
she cries out:
4 "To you, O men, I call,
And my voice is to the sons of
men.
5 "O [1a]naive ones, discern pru-
dence;
And, O [b]fools, discern [2]wisdom.
6 "Listen, for I shall speak [a]noble
things;
And the opening of my lips *will*
produce [b]right things.
7 "For my [a]mouth will utter truth;
And wickedness is an abomination to my lips.
8 "All the utterances of my mouth
are in righteousness;
There is nothing [a]crooked or
perverted in them.
9 "They are all [a]straightforward to
him who understands,
And right to those who [b]find
knowledge.
10 "Take my [a]instruction, and not
silver,
And knowledge rather than
choicest gold.
11 "For wisdom is [a]better than
[1]jewels;
And [b]all desirable things can
not compare with her.

12 "I, wisdom, [a]dwell with pru-
dence,
And I find [b]knowledge *and* discretion.
13 "The [a]fear of the LORD is to hate
evil;
[b]Pride and arrogance and [c]the
evil way,
And the [d]perverted mouth, I
hate.
14 "[a]Counsel is mine and [b]sound
wisdom;
I am understanding, [c]power is
mine.
15 "By me [a]kings reign,
And rulers decree justice.
16 "By me princes rule, and nobles,
All who judge rightly.

9 [1]Lit., *evening of the day* [2]Lit., *pupil* (of the eye) [a]Job 24:15
10 [a]Gen. 38:14, 15
11 [a]Prov. 9:13
12 [a]Prov. 9:14 [b]Prov. 23:28
13 [1]Lit., *She makes bold her face and says* [a]Prov. 21:29
14 [1]Lit., *"Sacrifices of peace offerings are with me* [a]Lev. 7:11 [b]Lev. 7:16
16 [a]Prov. 31:22 [b]Is. 19:9; Ezek. 27:7
17 [a]Ps. 45:8 [b]Ex. 30:23
19 [1]I.e., my husband
20 [1]Lit., *in his hand* [a]Gen. 42:35
21 [1]Lit., *smooth* [a]Prov. 5:3; 6:24
22 [1]Or, *as a stag goes into a trap;* so some ancient versions.
23 [a]Eccles. 9:12
24 [a]Prov. 5:7
25 [a]Prov. 5:8
26 [1]Lit., *mortally wounded* [a]Prov. 9:18
27 [a]Prov. 2:18; 5:5; 9:18
1 [1]Lit., *give* [a]Prov. 1:20, 21; 8:1-3
2 [a]Prov. 9:3, 14
3 [a]Job 29:7
5 [1]Lit., *simple* [2]Lit., *heart* [a]Prov. 1:4 [b]Prov. 1:22, 32; 3:35
6 [a]Prov. 22:20 [b]Prov. 23:16
7 [a]Ps. 37:30
8 [a]Deut. 32:5; Prov. 2:15; Phil. 2:15
9 [a]Prov. 14:6 [b]Prov. 3:13
10 [a]Prov. 3:14, 15; 8:19
11 [1]Lit., *corals* [a]Job 28:18 [b]Prov. 3:15
12 [a]Prov. 8:5 [b]Prov. 1:4
13 [a]Prov. 3:7; 16:6 [b]1 Sam. 2:3; Prov. 16:18; Is. 13:11 [c]Prov. 15:9 [d]Prov. 6:12
14 [a]Prov. 1:25; 19:20; Is. 28:29; Jer. 32:19 [b]Prov. 2:7; 3:21; 18:1 [c]Eccles. 7:19; 9:16
15 [a]2 Chr. 1:10; Prov. 29:4

17 "I [a]love those who love me;
And [b]those who diligently seek me will find me.
18 "[a]Riches and honor are with me,
Enduring [b]wealth and righteousness.
19 "My fruit is [a]better than gold, even pure gold,
And my yield than [b]choicest silver.
20 "I walk in the way of righteousness,
In the midst of the paths of justice,
21 To endow those who love me with wealth,
That I may [a]fill their treasuries.

22 "The LORD possessed me [a]at the beginning of His way,
Before His works of old.
23 "From everlasting I was [1]established,
From the beginning, [a]from the earliest times of the earth.
24 "When there were no [a]depths I was [1]brought forth,
When there were no springs abounding with water.
25 "[a]Before the mountains were settled,
Before the hills I was [1]brought forth;
26 While He had not yet made the earth and the fields,
Nor the first dust of the world.
27 "When He [a]established the heavens, I was there,
When [b]He inscribed a circle on the face of the deep,
28 When He made firm the skies above,
When the springs of the deep became [1]fixed,
29 When [a]He set for the sea its boundary,
So that the water should not transgress His command,
When He marked out [b]the foundations of the earth;
30 Then [a]I was beside Him, *as* a master workman;
And I was daily *His* delight,
Rejoicing always before Him,
31 Rejoicing in the world, His earth,
And *having* my delight in the sons of men.

32 "Now therefore, O sons, [a]listen to me,
For [b]blessed are they who keep my ways.
33 "[a]Heed instruction and be wise,
And do not neglect *it*.
34 "[a]Blessed is the man who listens to me,
Watching daily at my gates,
Waiting at my doorposts.
35 "For [a]he who finds me finds life,
And [b]obtains favor from the LORD.
36 "But he who sins against me [a]injures himself;
All those who [b]hate me [c]love death."

CHAPTER 9

Wisdom's Invitation

WISDOM has [a]built her house,
She has hewn out her seven pillars;
2 She has [a]prepared her food, she has [b]mixed her wine;
She has also [c]set her table;
3 She has [a]sent out her maidens, she [b]calls
From the [c]tops of the heights of the city:
4 "[a]Whoever is [1]naive, let him turn in here!"
To him who [b]lacks [2]understanding she says,
5 "Come, [a]eat of my food,
And drink of the wine I have mixed.
6 "Forsake [1]*your* folly and [a]live,
And [b]proceed in the way of understanding."

7 He who [a]corrects a scoffer gets dishonor for himself,
And he who reproves a wicked man *gets* [1]insults for himself.
8 [a]Do not reprove a scoffer, lest he hate you,
[b]Reprove a wise man, and he will love you.
9 Give *instruction* to a wise man, and he will be still wiser,
Teach a righteous man, and he will [a]increase *his* learning.
10 The fear of the LORD is the beginning of wisdom,
And the knowledge of the Holy One is understanding.
11 For [a]by me your days will be multiplied,
And years of life will be added to you.
12 If you are wise, you are wise [a]for yourself,
And if you [b]scoff, you alone will bear it.

13 The [1]woman of folly is [a]boisterous,
She is [2]naive, and [b]knows nothing.
14 And she sits at the doorway of her house,
On a seat by [a]the high places of the city,

17 [a]1 Sam. 2:30; Prov. 4:6; John 14:21 [b]Prov. 2:4, 5; James 1:5
18 [a]Prov. 3:16 [b]Ps. 112:3; Matt. 6:33
19 [a]Prov. 3:14 [b]Prov. 10:20
21 [a]Prov. 24:4
22 [a]Job 28:26-28; Ps. 104:24; Prov. 3:19
23 [1]Or, *consecrated* [a]John 17:5
24 [1]Or, *born* [a]Gen. 1:2; Ex. 15:5; Job 38:16; Prov. 3:20
25 [1]Or, *born* [a]Ps. 90:2
27 [a]Prov. 3:19 [b]Job 26:10
28 [1]Lit., *strong*
29 [a]Job 38:10; Ps. 104:9 [b]Job 38:6; Ps. 104:5
30 [a]John 1:2, 3
32 [a]Prov. 5:7; 7:24 [b]Ps. 119:1, 2; 128:1; Prov. 29:18; Luke 11:28
33 [a]Prov. 4:1
34 [a]Prov. 3:13, 18
35 [a]Prov. 4:22; John 17:3 [b]Prov. 3:4; 12:2
36 [a]Prov. 1:31, 32; 15:32 [b]Prov. 5:12; 12:1 [c]Prov. 21:6
1 [a]1 Cor. 3:9, 10; Eph. 2:20-22; 1 Pet. 2:5
2 [a]Matt. 22:4 [b]Song of Sol. 8:2 [c]Luke 14:16, 17
3 [a]Ps. 68:11; Matt. 22:3 [b]Prov. 8:1, 2 [c]Prov. 9:14
4 [1]Lit., *simple* [2]Lit., *heart* [a]Prov. 8:5; 9:16 [b]Prov. 6:32
5 [a]Song of Sol. 5:1; Is. 55:1; John 6:27
6 [1]Or, *the simple ones* [a]Prov. 8:35; 9:11 [b]Ezek. 11:20; 37:24
7 [1]Lit., *a blemish* [a]Prov. 23:9
8 [a]Prov. 15:12; Matt. 7:6 [b]Ps. 141:5; Prov. 10:8
9 [a]Prov. 1:5
11 [a]Prov. 3:16; 10:27
12 [a]Job 22:2; Prov. 14:14 [b]Prov. 19:29
13 [1]Or, *foolish woman* [2]Lit., *simple* [a]Prov. 7:11 [b]Prov. 5:6
14 [a]Prov. 9:3

15 Calling to those who pass by,
Who are making their paths straight:
16 "[a]Whoever is [1]naive, let him turn in here,"
And to him who lacks [2]understanding she says,
17 "Stolen [a]water is sweet;
And [b]bread *eaten* in secret is pleasant."
18 But he does not know that the dead are there,
That her guests are in the [a]depths of Sheol.

Chapter 10

Contrast of the Righteous and the Wicked

THE [a]proverbs of Solomon.
[b]A wise son makes a father glad,
But [c]a foolish son is a grief to his mother.
2 [a]Ill-gotten gains do not profit,
But righteousness delivers from death.
3 The LORD [a]will not allow the righteous to hunger,
But He [b]will thrust *aside* the craving of the wicked.
4 Poor is he who works with a negligent hand,
But the hand of the diligent makes rich.
5 He who gathers in summer is a son who acts wisely,
But he who sleeps in harvest is a son who acts shamefully.
6 [a]Blessings are on the head of the righteous,
But [b]the mouth of the wicked conceals violence.
7 The [a]memory of the righteous is blessed,
But [b]the name of the wicked will rot.
8 The [a]wise of heart will receive commands,
But a babbling fool will be thrown down.
9 He [a]who walks in integrity walks securely,
But [b]he who perverts his ways will be found out.
10 He [a]who winks the eye causes trouble,
And [b]a babbling fool will be thrown down.
11 The [a]mouth of the righteous is a fountain of life,
But [b]the mouth of the wicked conceals violence.
12 Hatred stirs up strife,
But [a]love covers all transgressions.
13 On [a]the lips of the discerning, wisdom is found,
But [b]a rod is for the back of him who lacks understanding.
14 Wise men [a]store up knowledge,
But with [b]the mouth of the foolish, ruin is at hand.
15 The [a]rich man's wealth is his fortress,
The [b]ruin of the poor is their poverty.
16 The [1a]wages of the righteous is life,
The income of the wicked, punishment.
17 He [a]is *on* the path of life who heeds instruction,
But he who forsakes reproof goes astray.
18 He [a]who conceals hatred *has* lying lips,
And he who spreads slander is a fool.
19 When there are [a]many words, transgression is unavoidable,
But [b]he who restrains his lips is wise.
20 The tongue of the righteous is *as* [a]choice silver,
The heart of the wicked is *worth* little.
21 The [a]lips of the righteous feed many,
But fools [b]die for lack of understanding.
22 It is the [a]blessing of the LORD that makes rich,
And He adds no sorrow to it.
23 Doing wickedness is like [a]sport to a fool;
And *so is* wisdom to a man of understanding.
24 What [a]the wicked fears will come upon him,
And the [b]desire of the righteous will be granted.
25 When the [a]whirlwind passes, the wicked is no more,
But the [b]righteous *has* an everlasting foundation.
26 Like vinegar to the teeth and smoke to the eyes,
So is the [a]lazy one to those who send him.
27 The [a]fear of the LORD prolongs [1]life,
But the [b]years of the wicked will be shortened.
28 The [a]hope of the righteous is gladness,
But the [b]expectation of the wicked perishes.
29 The [a]way of the LORD is a stronghold to the upright,
But [b]ruin to the workers of iniquity.

16 [1]Lit., *simple* [2]Lit., *heart* [a]Prov. 9:4
17 [a]Prov. 5:15 [b]Prov. 20:17
18 [a]Prov. 7:27
1 [a]Prov. 1:1 [b]Prov. 15:20; 29:3 [c]Prov. 17:25
2 [a]Ps. 49:6, 7; Prov. 11:4; 21:6; Ezek. 7:19; Luke 12:19
3 [a]Ps. 34:9, 10; 37:25; Prov. 28:25; Matt. 6:33 [b]Ps. 112:10; Prov. 28:9
6 [a]Prov. 28:20 [b]Prov. 10:11; Obad. 10
7 [a]Ps. 112:6 [b]Ps. 9:5, 6; 109:13; Eccles. 8:10
8 [a]Prov. 9:8; Matt. 7:24
9 [a]Ps. 23:4; Prov. 3:23; 28:18; Is. 33:15, 16 [b]Prov. 26:26; Matt. 10:26; 1 Tim. 5:25
10 [a]Ps. 35:19; Prov. 6:13 [b]Prov. 10:8
11 [a]Ps. 37:30; Prov. 13:14; 18:4 [b]Prov. 10:6
12 [a]Prov. 17:9; 1 Cor. 13:4-7; James 5:20; 1 Pet. 4:8
13 [a]Prov. 10:31 [b]Prov. 19:29; 26:3
14 [a]Prov. 9:9 [b]Prov. 10:8, 10; 13:3; 18:7; 21:15
15 [a]Job 31:24; Ps. 52:7; Prov. 18:11 [b]Prov. 19:7
16 [1]Or, *work* [a]Prov. 11:18, 19
17 [a]Prov. 6:23
18 [a]Prov. 26:24
19 [a]Job 11:2; Prov. 18:21; Eccles. 5:3 [b]Prov. 17:27; James 1:19
20 [a]Prov. 8:19
21 [a]Prov. 10:11 [b]Prov. 5:23; Hos. 4:6
22 [a]Gen. 24:35; 26:12; Deut. 8:18
23 [a]Prov. 2:14
24 [a]Job 15:21; Prov. 1:27; Is. 66:4 [b]Ps. 145:19; Prov. 15:8; Matt. 5:6; 1 John 5:14
25 [a]Job 21:18; Ps. 58:9; Prov. 12:7 [b]Ps. 15:5; Prov. 12:3; Matt. 7:24, 25
26 [a]Prov. 26:6
27 [1]Lit., *days* [a]Prov. 3:2; 9:11; 14:27 [b]Job 15:32, 33; 22:16
28 [a]Prov. 11:23 [b]Job 8:13; 11:20
29 [a]Prov. 13:6 [b]Prov. 21:15

30 The [a]righteous will never be shaken,
But [b]the wicked will not dwell in the land.
31 The [a]mouth of the righteous flows with wisdom,
But the [b]perverted tongue will be cut out.
32 The lips of the righteous bring forth [a]what is acceptable,
But the [b]mouth of the wicked, what is perverted.

CHAPTER 11

Contrast the Upright and the Wicked

A [a]FALSE balance is an abomination to the LORD,
But a [b]just weight is His delight.
2 When [a]pride comes, then comes dishonor,
But with the humble is wisdom.
3 The [a]integrity of the upright will guide them,
But the [b]falseness of the treacherous will destroy them.
4 [a]Riches do not profit in the day of wrath,
But [b]righteousness delivers from death.
5 The [a]righteousness of the blameless will smooth his way,
But [b]the wicked will fall by his own wickedness.
6 The righteousness of the upright will deliver them,
But the treacherous will [a]be caught by *their own* greed.
7 When a wicked man dies, *his* [a]expectation will perish,
And the [b]hope of strong men perishes.
8 The righteous is delivered from trouble,
But the wicked [1]takes his place.
9 With *his* [a]mouth the godless man destroys his neighbor,
But through knowledge the [b]righteous will be delivered.
10 When it [a]goes well with the righteous, the city rejoices,
And when the wicked perish, there is glad shouting.
11 By the blessing of the upright a city is exalted,
But by the mouth of the wicked it is torn down.
12 He who despises his neighbor lacks sense,
But a man of understanding keeps silent.
13 He [a]who goes about as a talebearer reveals secrets,
But he who is trustworthy [b]conceals a matter.
14 Where there is no [a]guidance, the people fall,
But in abundance of counselors there is [1]victory.
15 He who is [a]surety for a stranger will surely suffer for it,
But he who hates going surety is safe.
16 A [a]gracious woman attains honor,
And violent men attain riches.
17 The [a]merciful man does himself good,
But the cruel man [1]does himself harm.
18 The wicked earns deceptive wages,
But he who [a]sows righteousness *gets* a true reward.
19 He who is steadfast in [a]righteousness *will attain* to life,
And [b]he who pursues evil *will bring about* his own death.
20 The perverse in heart are an abomination to the LORD,
But the [a]blameless in *their* [1]walk are His [b]delight.
21 [1]Assuredly, the evil man will not go unpunished,
But the [2]descendants of the righteous will be delivered.
22 *As* a [a]ring of gold in a swine's snout,
So is a beautiful woman who lacks [1]discretion.
23 The desire of the righteous is only good,
But the [a]expectation of the wicked is wrath.
24 There is one who scatters, yet increases all the more,
And there is one who withholds what is justly due, but *it results* only in want.
25 The [1a]generous man will be [2]prosperous,
And he who [b]waters will himself be watered.
26 He who withholds grain, the [a]people will curse him,
But [b]blessing will be on the head of him who [c]sells *it*.
27 He who diligently seeks good seeks favor,
But [a]he who searches after evil, it will come to him.
28 He who [a]trusts in his riches will fall,
But [b]the righteous will flourish like the *green* leaf.
29 He who [a]troubles his own house will [b]inherit wind,
And [c]the foolish will be servant to the wisehearted.

30 [a]Ps. 37:29; 125:1; Prov. 2:21 [b]Prov. 2:22
31 [a]Ps. 37:30; Prov. 10:13 [b]Prov. 17:20
32 [a]Eccles. 12:10 [b]Prov. 2:12; 6:12
1 [a]Lev. 19:35, 36; Deut. 25:13-16; Prov. 20:10, 23; Mic. 6:11 [b]Prov. 16:11
2 [a]Prov. 16:18; 18:12; 29:23
3 [a]Prov. 13:6 [b]Prov. 19:3; 22:12
4 [a]Prov. 10:2; Ezek. 7:19; Zeph. 1:18 [b]Gen. 7:1
5 [a]Prov. 3:6 [b]Prov. 5:22
6 [a]Ps. 7:15, 16; 9:15; Eccles. 10:8
7 [a]Prov. 10:28 [b]Job 8:13, 14
8 [1]Lit., *enters*
9 [a]Prov. 16:29 [b]Prov. 11:6
10 [a]Prov. 28:12
13 [a]Lev. 19:16; Prov. 20:19; 1 Tim. 5:13 [b]Prov. 19:11
14 [1]Lit., *deliverance* [a]Prov. 15:22; 20:18; 24:6
15 [a]Prov. 6:1; 27:13
16 [a]Prov. 31:28, 30
17 [1]Lit., *troubles his flesh* [a]Matt. 5:7; 25:34-36
18 [a]Hos. 10:12; Gal. 6:8, 9; James 3:18
19 [a]Prov. 10:16; 12:28; 19:23 [b]Prov. 21:16; Rom. 6:23; James 1:15
20 [1]Lit., *way* [a]Ps. 119:1; Prov. 13:6 [b]1 Chr. 29:17
21 [1]Lit., *Hand to hand* [2]Lit., *seed*
22 [1]Lit., *taste* [a]Gen. 24:47
23 [a]Prov. 10:28; Rom. 2:8, 9
25 [1]Lit., *soul of blessing* [2]Lit., *made fat* [a]Prov. 3:9, 10; 2 Cor. 9:6, 7 [b]Matt. 5:7
26 [a]Prov. 24:24 [b]Job 29:13 [c]Gen. 42:6
27 [a]Esth. 7:10; Ps. 7:15, 16; 57:6
28 [a]Ps. 49:6; Mark 10:24; 1 Tim. 6:17 [b]Ps. 1:3; 92:12; Jer. 17:8
29 [a]Prov. 15:27 [b]Eccles. 5:16 [c]Prov. 14:19

30 The fruit of the righteous is [a]a tree of life,
And [b]he who is wise [1]wins souls.
31 If [a]the righteous will be rewarded in the earth,
How much more the wicked and the sinner!

Chapter 12

Contrast the Upright and the Wicked

WHOEVER loves [1]discipline loves knowledge,
But he who hates reproof is stupid.
2 A [a]good man will obtain favor from the LORD,
But He will condemn a man [1]who devises evil.
3 A man will [a]not be established by wickedness,
But the root of the [b]righteous will not be moved.
4 An [1a]excellent wife is the crown of her husband,
But she who shames *him* is as [b]rottenness in his bones.
5 The thoughts of the righteous are just,
But the counsels of the wicked are deceitful.
6 The [a]words of the wicked lie in wait for blood,
But the [b]mouth of the upright will deliver them.
7 The [a]wicked are overthrown and are no more,
But the [b]house of the righteous will stand.
8 A man will be praised according to his insight,
But one of perverse [1]mind will be despised.
9 Better is he who is lightly esteemed and has a servant,
Than he who honors himself and lacks bread.
10 A [a]righteous man has regard for the life of his beast,
But the compassion of the wicked is cruel.
11 He who tills his land will have plenty of bread,
But he who pursues vain *things* lacks [1]sense.
12 The [a]wicked desires the [1]booty of evil men,
But the root of the righteous [b]yields *fruit.*
13 [1]An evil man is ensnared by the transgression of his lips,
But the [a]righteous will escape from trouble.
14 A man will be [a]satisfied with good by the fruit of his [1]words,
And the [b]deeds of a man's hands will return to him.
15 The [a]way of a fool is right in his own eyes,
But a wise man is he who listens to counsel.
16 A [a]fool's vexation is known at once,
But a prudent man conceals dishonor.
17 He who [1]speaks truth tells what is right,
But a false witness, deceit.
18 There is one who [a]speaks rashly like the thrusts of a sword,
But the [b]tongue of the wise brings healing.
19 Truthful lips will be established forever,
But a [a]lying tongue is only for a moment.
20 Deceit is in the heart of those who devise evil,
But counselors of peace have joy.
21 [a]No harm befalls the righteous,
But the wicked are filled with trouble.
22 Lying lips are an abomination to the LORD,
But those who deal faithfully are His delight.
23 A [a]prudent man conceals knowledge,
But the heart of fools proclaims folly.
24 The hand of the diligent will rule,
But the [1]slack *hand* will be [a]put to forced labor.
25 [a]Anxiety in the heart of a man weighs it down,
But a [b]good word makes it glad.
26 The righteous is a guide to his neighbor,
But the way of the wicked leads them astray.
27 A [1]slothful man does not [2]roast his prey,
But the [a]precious possession of a man *is* diligence.
28 In the way of righteousness is life,
And in *its* pathway there is no death.

Chapter 13

Contrast the Upright and the Wicked

A [a]WISE son *accepts his* father's discipline,
But a [b]scoffer does not listen to rebuke.

30 [1]Lit., *takes* [a]Prov. 3:18 [b]Prov. 14:25; Dan. 12:3; 1 Cor. 9:19-22; James 5:20
31 [a]2 Sam. 22:21, 25; Prov. 13:21
1 [1]Or, *instruction*
2 [1]Lit., of *evil devices* [a]Prov. 3:4; 8:35
3 [a]Prov. 11:5 [b]Prov. 10:25
4 [1]Or, *virtuous* [a]Prov. 31:11; 1 Cor. 11:7 [b]Prov. 14:30; Hab. 3:16
6 [a]Prov. 1:11, 16 [b]Prov. 14:3
7 [a]Job 34:25; Prov. 10:25 [b]Matt. 7:24-27
8 [1]Lit., *heart*
10 [a]Deut. 25:4
11 [1]Lit., *heart*
12 [1]Lit., *net* [a]Prov. 21:10 [b]Prov. 11:30
13 [1]Lit., *In the transgression of the lips is an evil snare* [a]Prov. 11:8; 21:23; 2 Pet. 2:9
14 [1]Lit., *mouth* [a]Prov. 13:2; 15:23; 18:20 [b]Job 34:11; Prov. 1:31; 24:12; Is. 3:10, 11; Hos. 4:9
15 [a]Prov. 14:12; 16:2; 21:2
16 [a]Prov. 14:33; 27:3; 29:11
17 [1]Lit., *breathes*
18 [a]Ps. 57:4 [b]Prov. 4:22; 15:4
19 [a]Ps. 52:4, 5; Prov. 19:9
21 [a]Ps. 91:10; 121:7; Prov. 1:33; 1 Pet. 3:13
23 [a]Prov. 10:14; 11:13; 13:16; 15:2; 29:11
24 [1]Lit., *slackness* [a]Gen. 49:15; Judg. 1:28; 1 Kin. 9:21
25 [a]Prov. 15:13 [b]Is. 50:4
27 [1]Lit., *slackness* [2]Or, *catch* [a]Prov. 10:4; 13:4
1 [a]Prov. 10:1; 15:20 [b]Prov. 9:7, 8; 15:12

2 From the fruit of a man's mouth
he [1a]enjoys good,
But the [2]desire of the treacherous is [b]violence.
3 The one who [a]guards his mouth
preserves his life;
The one who [b]opens wide his
lips comes to ruin.
4 The soul of the sluggard craves
and *gets* nothing,
But the soul of the diligent is
made fat.
5 A righteous man hates falsehood,
But a wicked man [a]acts disgustingly and shamefully.
6 Righteousness guards the one
whose way is blameless,
But wickedness subverts the
sinner.
7 There is one who [a]pretends to
be rich, but has nothing;
Another pretends to be [b]poor,
but has great wealth.
8 The ransom of a man's life is his
riches,
But the poor hears no rebuke.
9 The [a]light of the righteous [1]rejoices,
But the [b]lamp of the wicked
goes out.
10 Through presumption comes
nothing but strife,
But with those who receive
counsel is wisdom.
11 Wealth *obtained* by fraud
dwindles,
But the one who gathers by labor increases *it.*
12 Hope deferred *makes* the heart
sick,
But desire fulfilled is a tree of
life.
13 The one who [a]despises the
word will be in debt to it,
But the one who fears the commandment will be [b]rewarded.
14 The [1]teaching of the wise is a
[a]fountain of life,
To turn aside from the [b]snares
of death.
15 [a]Good understanding produces
favor,
But the way of the treacherous
is hard.
16 Every prudent man acts with
knowledge,
But a fool [1]displays folly.
17 A wicked messenger falls into
adversity,
But [a]a faithful envoy *brings*
healing.
18 Poverty and shame *will come*
to him who [a]neglects [1]discipline,
But he who regards reproof will
be honored.
19 Desire realized is sweet to the
soul,
But it is an abomination to fools
to depart from evil.
20 [a]He who walks with wise men
will be wise,
But the [b]companion of fools
will suffer harm.
21 [a]Adversity pursues sinners,
But the [b]righteous will be rewarded with prosperity.
22 A good man [a]leaves an inheritance to his [1]children's children,
And the [b]wealth of the sinner is
stored up for the righteous.
23 Abundant food *is in* the fallow
ground of the poor,
But [1]it is swept away by injustice.
24 He who [a]spares his rod hates
his son,
But he who loves him [1b]disciplines him diligently.
25 The [a]righteous [1]has enough to
satisfy his appetite,
But the stomach of the [b]wicked
is in want.

CHAPTER 14

Contrast the Upright and the Wicked

THE wise woman builds her
house,
But the foolish tears it down
with her own hands.
2 He who [a]walks in his uprightness fears the LORD,
But he who is [b]crooked in his
ways despises Him.
3 In the mouth of the foolish is a
rod [1]for *his* back,
But the lips of the wise will preserve them.
4 Where no oxen are, the manger
is clean,
But much increase comes by
the strength of the ox.
5 A [a]faithful witness will not lie,
But a [b]false witness [1c]speaks
lies.
6 A scoffer seeks wisdom, and
finds none,
But knowledge is easy to him
who has understanding.
7 Leave the [a]presence of a fool,
Or you will not [1]discern [2]words
of knowledge.
8 The wisdom of the prudent is to
understand his way,
But the folly of fools is deceit.
9 [a]Fools mock at [1]sin,
But [b]among the upright there is
[2]good will.

2 [1]Lit., *eats* [2]Lit., *soul* [a]Prov. 12:14 [b]Prov. 1:31; Hos. 10:13
3 [a]Prov. 18:21; 21:23; James 3:2 [b]Prov. 18:7; 20:19
5 [a]Prov. 3:35
7 [a]Prov. 11:24; Luke 12:20, 21 [b]Luke 12:33; 2 Cor. 6:10; James 2:5
9 [1]I.e., shines brightly [a]Job 29:3; Prov. 4:18 [b]Job 18:5; Prov. 24:20
13 [a]Num. 15:31; 2 Chr. 36:16 [b]Prov. 13:21
14 [1]Or, *law* [a]Prov. 10:11; 14:27 [b]Ps. 18:5
15 [a]Ps. 111:10; Prov. 3:4
16 [1]Lit., *spreads out*
17 [a]Prov. 25:13
18 [1]Or, *instruction* [a]Prov. 15:5, 32
20 [a]Prov. 2:20; 15:31 [b]Prov. 28:19
21 [a]Ps. 32:10; 54:5; Is. 47:11 [b]Prov. 11:31; 13:13; Is. 3:10
22 [1]Lit., *sons' sons* [a]Ezra 9:12; Ps. 37:25 [b]Job 27:16, 17; Prov. 28:8; Eccles. 2:26
23 [1]Lit., *there is what is swept*
24 [1]Lit., *seeks him diligently with discipline* [a]Prov. 19:18; 22:15; 23:13, 14; 29:15, 17 [b]Deut. 8:5; Prov. 3:12; Heb. 12:7
25 [1]Lit., *eats to the satisfaction of his soul* [a]Ps. 34:10; 103:5; 132:15; Prov. 10:3 [b]Prov. 13:18; Luke 15:14

2 [a]Prov. 19:1; 28:6 [b]Prov. 2:15
3 [1]Lit., *of pride*
5 [1]Lit., *breathes out* [a]Rev. 1:5; 3:14 [b]Ex. 23:1; Deut. 19:16; Prov. 6:19; 12:17 [c]Prov. 19:5
7 [1]Lit., *know* [2]Lit., *lips* [a]Prov. 23:9
9 [1]Lit., *guilt* [2]Or, the *favor* of God [a]Is. 1:11; Hos. 4:19 [b]Prov. 3:34; 11:20

10 The heart knows its own [a]bitterness,
And a stranger does not share its joy.
11 The house of the wicked will be destroyed,
But the tent of the upright will flourish.
12 There [a]is a way *which seems* right to a man,
But its [b]end is the way of death.
13 Even in laughter the heart may be in pain,
And the [a]end of joy may be grief.
14 The backslider in heart will have his [a]fill of his own ways,
But a good man will [b]*be satisfied* [1]with his.
15 The [1]naive believes everything,
But the prudent man considers his steps.
16 A wise man [1]is cautious and [a]turns away from evil,
But a fool is arrogant and careless.
17 A quick-tempered man acts foolishly,
And a man of evil devices is hated.
18 The [1]naive inherit folly,
But the prudent are crowned with knowledge.
19 The [a]evil will bow down before the good,
And the wicked at the gates of the righteous.
20 The poor is hated even by his neighbor,
But those who love the rich are many.
21 He who [a]despises his neighbor sins,
But [b]happy is he who is gracious to the [1]poor.
22 Will they not go astray who [a]devise evil?
But kindness and truth *will be to* those who devise good.
23 In all labor there is profit,
But [1]mere talk *leads* only to poverty.
24 The [a]crown of the wise is their riches,
But the folly of fools is foolishness.
25 A truthful witness saves lives,
But he who [1a]speaks lies is [2]treacherous.
26 In the [1a]fear of the LORD there is strong confidence,
And his children will have refuge.
27 The [1]fear of the LORD is a fountain of life,
That one may avoid the snares of death.

10 [a]1 Sam. 1:10; Job 21:25
12 [a]Prov. 12:15; 16:25 [b]Rom. 6:21
13 [a]Eccles. 2:1, 2
14 [1]Lit., *from himself* [a]Prov. 1:31; 12:21 [b]Prov. 12:14; 18:20
15 [1]Lit., *simple*
16 [1]Lit., *fears* [a]Job 28:28; Ps. 34:14; Prov. 3:7; 22:3
18 [1]Lit., *simple*
19 [a]1 Sam. 2:36; Prov. 11:29
21 [1]Or, *afflicted* [a]Prov. 11:12 [b]Ps. 41:1; Prov. 19:17; 28:8
22 [a]Ps. 36:4; Prov. 3:29; 12:2; Mic. 2:1
23 [1]Lit., *word of lips*
24 [a]Prov. 10:22; 13:8; 21:20
25 [1]Lit., *breathes out* [2]Lit., *treachery* [a]Prov. 14:5
26 [1]Or, *reverence* [a]Prov. 18:10; 19:23; Is. 33:6
27 [1]Or, *reverence*
28 [a]1 Kin. 4:20
29 [1]Lit., *short of spirit* [a]Prov. 16:32; 19:11; Eccles. 7:9; James 1:19
30 [a]Prov. 15:13 [b]Prov. 12:4; Hab. 3:16
32 [1]Or, *calamity* [a]Prov. 6:15; 24:16 [b]Gen. 49:18; Ps. 16:11; 17:15; 37:37; 73:24; 2 Cor. 1:9; 5:8; 2 Tim. 4:18
33 [1]Lit., *midst*
1 [1]Lit., *painful* [a]Judg. 8:1-3; Prov. 15:18; 25:15 [b]1 Sam. 25:10-13
2 [1]Lit., *good* [a]Prov. 15:7 [b]Prov. 12:23; 13:16; 15:28
3 [a]Job 31:4; Heb. 4:13
4 [1]Lit., *healing* [2]Lit., *is the crushing of the spirit.*
5 [1]Or, *despises*
6 [a]Prov. 8:21
8 [a]Prov. 21:27; Eccles. 5:1; Is. 1:11; Jer. 6:20; Mic. 6:7 [b]Prov. 15:29

28 In a [a]multitude of people is a king's glory,
But in the dearth of people is a prince's ruin.
29 He who is [a]slow to anger has great understanding,
But he who is [1]quick-tempered exalts folly.
30 A [a]tranquil heart is life to the body,
But passion is [b]rottenness to the bones.
31 He who oppresses the poor reproaches his Maker,
But he who is gracious to the needy honors Him.
32 The wicked is [a]thrust down by his [1]wrongdoing,
But the [b]righteous has a refuge when he dies.
33 Wisdom rests in the heart of one who has understanding,
But in the [1]bosom of fools it is made known.
34 Righteousness exalts a nation,
But sin is a disgrace to *any* people.
35 The king's favor is toward a servant who acts wisely,
But his anger is toward him who acts shamefully.

CHAPTER 15

Contrast the Upright and the Wicked

A [a]GENTLE answer turns away wrath,
But a [1b]harsh word stirs up anger.
2 The [a]tongue of the wise makes knowledge [1]acceptable,
But the [b]mouth of fools spouts folly.
3 The [a]eyes of the LORD are in every place,
Watching the evil and the good.
4 A [1]soothing tongue is a tree of life,
But perversion in it [2]crushes the spirit.
5 A fool [1]rejects his father's discipline,
But he who regards reproof is prudent.
6 Much wealth is *in* the house of the [a]righteous,
But trouble is in the income of the wicked.
7 The lips of the wise spread knowledge,
But the hearts of fools are not so.
8 The [a]sacrifice of the wicked is an abomination to the LORD,
But [b]the prayer of the upright is His delight.

9 The way of the wicked is an abomination to the LORD,
But He loves him who pursues righteousness.
10 Stern discipline is for him who forsakes the way;
He who hates reproof will die.
11 [a]Sheol and [1]Abaddon *lie open* before the LORD,
How much more the [b]hearts of men!
12 A [a]scoffer does not love one who reproves him,
He will not go to the wise.
13 A [a]joyful heart makes a [1]cheerful face,
But [2]when the heart is [b]sad, the [c]spirit is broken.
14 The [a]mind of the intelligent seeks knowledge,
But the mouth of fools feeds on folly.
15 All the days of the afflicted are bad,
But a [1]cheerful heart *has* a continual feast.
16 [a]Better is a little with the [1]fear of the LORD,
Than great treasure and turmoil with it.
17 [a]Better is a dish of vegetables where love is,
Than a [b]fattened ox and hatred with it.
18 A [a]hot-tempered man stirs up strife,
But the [b]slow to anger [c]pacifies contention.
19 The way of the sluggard is as a hedge of thorns,
But the path of the upright is a highway.
20 A [a]wise son makes a father glad,
But a foolish man [b]despises his mother.
21 Folly is joy to him who lacks [1]sense,
But a man of understanding [a]walks straight.
22 Without consultation, plans are frustrated,
But with many counselors they [1]succeed.
23 A [a]man has joy in an apt answer,
And how delightful is a timely [b]word!
24 The [a]path of life *leads* upward for the wise,
That he may keep away from Sheol below.
25 The LORD will [a]tear down the house of the proud,
But He will [b]establish the boundary of the [c]widow.
26 Evil plans are an abomination to the LORD,
But pleasant words are pure.
27 He who [a]profits illicitly troubles his own house,
But he who [b]hates bribes will live.
28 The heart of the righteous [a]ponders how to answer,
But the [b]mouth of the wicked pours out evil things.
29 The LORD is [a]far from the wicked,
But He [b]hears the prayer of the righteous.
30 [1]Bright eyes gladden the heart;
Good news puts fat on the bones.
31 He whose ear listens to the life-giving reproof
Will dwell among the wise.
32 He who [a]neglects discipline [b]despises himself,
But he who [c]listens to reproof acquires [1]understanding.
33 The [1]fear of the LORD is the instruction for wisdom,
And before honor *comes* humility.

CHAPTER 16

Contrast the Upright and the Wicked

THE [a]plans of the heart belong to man,
But the answer of the tongue is from the LORD.
2 All the ways of a man are clean in his own sight,
But the LORD weighs the [1]motives.
3 [1a]Commit your works to the LORD,
And your plans will be established.
4 The LORD [a]has made everything for [1]its own purpose,
Even the [b]wicked for the day of evil.
5 Everyone who is proud in heart is an abomination to the LORD;
Assuredly, he will not be unpunished.
6 By [a]lovingkindness and truth iniquity is atoned for,
And by the [1b]fear of the LORD one keeps away from evil.
7 When a man's ways are pleasing to the LORD,
He [a]makes even his enemies to be at peace with him.
8 Better is a little with righteousness
Than great income with injustice.

11 [1]I.e., destruction [a]Job 26:6; Ps. 139:8 [b]1 Sam. 16:7; 2 Chr. 6:30; Ps. 44:21; Acts 1:24
12 [a]Prov. 13:1; Amos 5:10
13 [1]Lit., *good* [2]Lit., *in sadness of heart* [a]Prov. 17:22 [b]Prov. 12:25 [c]Prov. 17:22; 18:14
14 [a]Prov. 18:15
15 [1]Lit., *good*
16 [1]Or, *reverence* [a]Ps. 37:16; Prov. 16:8; Eccles. 4:6; 1 Tim. 6:6
17 [a]Prov. 17:1 [b]Matt. 22:4; Luke 15:23
18 [a]Prov. 16:28; 26:21; 29:22 [b]Prov. 14:29 [c]Gen. 13:8; Prov. 16:14; Eccles. 10:4
20 [a]Prov. 10:1; 29:3 [b]Prov. 30:17
21 [1]Lit., *heart* [a]Prov. 14:8; Eph. 5:15
22 [1]Or, *are established*
23 [a]Prov. 12:14 [b]Prov. 25:11; Is. 50:4
24 [a]Is. 4:18
25 [a]Prov. 12:7; 14:11 [b]Deut. 19:14; Prov. 23:10 [c]Ps. 68:5; 146:9
27 [a]Prov. 1:19; 28:25; 1 Tim. 6:10 [b]Ex. 23:8; Deut. 16:19; 1 Sam. 12:3; Is. 33:15
28 [a]1 Pet. 3:15 [b]Prov. 10:32; 15:2
29 [a]Ps. 18:41; Prov. 1:28 [b]Ps. 145:18, 19
30 [1]Lit., *the light of the eyes*
32 [1]Lit., *heart* [a]Prov. 1:7; 8:33 [b]Prov. 8:36 [c]Prov. 15:5
33 [1]Or, *reverence*
1 [a]Prov. 16:9; 19:21
2 [1]Lit., *spirits*
3 [1]Lit., *Roll* [a]Ps. 37:5; 55:22; Prov. 3:6; 1 Pet. 5:7
4 [1]Or, *His* [a]Gen. 1:31; Eccles. 3:11 [b]Job 31:30; Rom. 9:22
6 [1]Or, *reverence* [a]Dan. 4:27; Luke 11:41 [b]Prov. 8:13; 14:16
7 [a]Gen. 33:4; 2 Chr. 17:10

9 The mind of [a]man plans his
way,
But [b]the LORD directs his steps.
10 A divine [a]decision is in the lips
of the king;
His mouth should not [1]err in
judgment.
11 A [a]just balance and scales belong to the LORD;
All the [1]weights of the bag are
His [2]concern.
12 It is an abomination for kings to
commit wickedness,
For a [a]throne is established on
righteousness.
13 Righteous lips are the delight of
kings,
And he who speaks right is
loved.
14 The wrath of a king is *as* messengers of death,
But a wise man will appease it.
15 In the light of a king's face is
life,
And his favor is like a cloud
with the [1a]spring rain.
16 How much [a]better it is to get
wisdom than gold!
And to get understanding is to
be chosen above silver.
17 The highway of the upright is to
depart from evil;
He who watches his way preserves his [1]life.
18 [a]Pride *goes* before destruction,
And a haughty spirit before
stumbling.
19 It is better to be of a [a]humble
spirit with the lowly,
Than to [b]divide the spoil with
the proud.
20 He who gives attention to the
word shall [a]find good,
And [b]blessed is he who trusts in
the LORD.
21 The [a]wise in heart will be called
discerning,
And sweetness of [1]speech [b]in-
creases [2]persuasiveness.
22 Understanding is a fountain of
life to him who has it,
But the discipline of fools is folly.
23 The [a]heart of the wise teaches
his mouth,
And adds [1]persuasiveness to
his lips.
24 [a]Pleasant words are a honeycomb,
Sweet to the soul and [b]healing
to the bones.
25 There is a way *which seems*
right to a man,
But its end is the way of death.
26 A worker's appetite works for
him,
For his [1]hunger urges him *on*.
27 A [a]worthless man digs up evil,
While [1]his words are as a
[b]scorching fire.
28 A perverse man spreads strife,
And a slanderer separates intimate friends.
29 A man of violence [a]entices his
neighbor,
And leads him in a way that is
not good.
30 He who winks his eyes *does so*
to devise perverse things;
He who compresses his lips
brings evil to pass.
31 A [a]gray head is a crown of glory;
It [b]is found in the way of righteousness.
32 He who is slow to anger is better than the mighty,
And he who rules his spirit,
than he who captures a city.
33 The [a]lot is cast into the lap,
But its every [b]decision is from
the LORD.

CHAPTER 17

Contrast the Upright and the Wicked

[a]BETTER is a dry morsel and quietness with it
Than a house full of [1]feasting
with strife.
2 A servant who acts wisely will
rule over a son who acts
shamefully,
And will share in the inheritance among brothers.
3 The [a]refining pot is for silver
and the furnace for gold,
But [b]the LORD tests hearts.
4 An [a]evildoer listens to wicked
lips,
A [1]liar pays attention to a destructive tongue.
5 He who mocks the [a]poor reproaches his Maker;
He who [b]rejoices at calamity
will not go unpunished.
6 [a]Grandchildren are the crown
of old men,
And the [b]glory of sons is their
fathers.
7 [1a]Excellent speech is not fitting
for a fool;
Much less are [b]lying lips to a
prince.
8 A [a]bribe is a [1]charm in the sight
of its owner;
Wherever he turns, he prospers.
9 He who [a]covers a transgression
seeks love,
But he who repeats a matter
[b]separates intimate friends.

9 [a]Prov. 16:1; 19:21 [b]Ps. 37:23; Jer. 10:23; Prov. 20:24
10 [1]Lit., *be unfaithful* [a]1 Kin. 3:28
11 [1]Lit., *stones* [2]Lit., *work* [a]Prov. 11:1
12 [a]Prov. 25:5
15 [1]Lit., *latter* [a]Job 29:23
16 [a]Prov. 8:10, 19
17 [1]Lit., *soul*
18 [a]Prov. 11:2; 18:12; Jer. 49:16; Obad. 3, 4
19 [a]Prov. 3:34; 29:23; Is. 57:15 [b]Ex. 15:9; Judg. 5:30; Prov. 1:13, 14
20 [a]Prov. 19:8 [b]Ps. 2:12; 34:8; Jer. 17:7
21 [1]Lit., *lips* [2]Or, *learning* [a]Hos. 14:9 [b]Prov. 16:23
23 [1]Or, *learning* [a]Ps. 37:30; Prov. 15:28; Matt. 12:34
24 [a]Ps. 19:10; Prov. 15:26; 24:13, 14 [b]Prov. 4:22; 17:22
26 [1]Lit., *mouth*
27 [1]Lit., *on his lips* [a]Prov. 6:12, 14, 18 [b]James 3:6
29 [a]Prov. 1:10; 12:26
31 [a]Prov. 20:29 [b]Prov. 3:1, 2
33 [a]Prov. 18:18 [b]Prov. 29:26
1 [1]Lit., *sacrifices of strife* [a]Prov. 15:17
3 [a]Prov. 27:21 [b]1 Chr. 29:17; Ps. 26:2; Prov. 15:11; Jer. 17:10; Mal. 3:3
4 [1]Lit., *falsehood* [a]Prov. 14:15
5 [a]Prov. 14:31 [b]Job 31:29; Prov. 24:17; Obad. 12
6 [a]Gen. 48:11; Prov. 13:22 [b]Ex. 20:12; Mal. 1:6
7 [1]Lit., *A lip of abundance* [a]Prov. 24:7 [b]Ps. 31:18; Prov. 12:22
8 [1]Lit., *stone of favor* [a]Prov. 21:14; Is. 1:23; Amos 5:12
9 [a]Prov. 10:12; James 5:20; 1 Pet. 4:8 [b]Prov. 16:28

10 A rebuke goes deeper into one
who has understanding
Than a hundred blows into a
fool.
11 A rebellious man seeks only
evil,
So a cruel messenger will be
sent against him.
12 Let a [a]man meet a [b]bear robbed
of her cubs,
Rather than a fool in his folly.
13 He who [a]returns evil for good,
[b]Evil will not depart from his
house.
14 The beginning of strife is *like*
letting out water,
So [a]abandon the quarrel before
it breaks out.
15 He who [a]justifies the wicked,
and he who condemns the
righteous,
Both of them alike are an
abomination to the LORD.
16 Why is there a price in the hand
of a fool to [a]buy wisdom,
When [1]he has no sense?
17 A [a]friend loves at all times,
And a brother is born for adversity.
18 A man lacking in [1]sense
[2a]pledges,
And becomes surety in the
presence of his neighbor.
19 He who [a]loves transgression
loves strife;
He who [b]raises his door seeks
destruction.
20 He who has a crooked [1]mind
[a]finds no good,
And he who is [b]perverted in his
language falls into evil.
21 He who [a]begets a fool *does so* to
his sorrow,
And the father of a fool has no
joy.
22 A [a]joyful heart [1]is good medicine,
But a broken spirit [b]dries up the
bones.
23 A wicked man receives a [a]bribe
from the bosom
To [b]pervert the ways of justice.
24 Wisdom is in the presence of
the one who has understanding,
But the [a]eyes of a fool are on
the ends of the earth.
25 A foolish son is a grief to his
father,
And bitterness to her who bore
him.
26 It is also not good to fine the
righteous,
Nor to strike the noble for *their*
uprightness.
27 He who [a]restrains his words
[1]has knowledge,
And he who has a [b]cool spirit is
a man of understanding.
28 Even a fool, when he [a]keeps silent, is considered wise;
When he closes his lips, he is
counted prudent.

CHAPTER 18

Contrast the Upright and the Wicked

HE who separates himself seeks
his own desire,
He [1]quarrels against all sound
wisdom.
2 A fool does not delight in understanding,
But only [a]in revealing his own
[1]mind.
3 When a wicked man comes,
contempt also comes,
And with dishonor *comes* reproach.
4 The words of a man's mouth
are [a]deep waters;
[1]The fountain of wisdom is a
bubbling brook.
5 To [a]show partiality to the
wicked is not good,
Nor to [b]thrust aside the righteous in judgment.
6 A fool's lips [1]bring strife,
And his mouth calls for blows.
7 A [a]fool's mouth is his ruin,
And his lips are the snare of his
soul.
8 The words of a whisperer are
like dainty morsels,
And they go down into the [1]in-
nermost parts of the body.
9 He also who is [a]slack in his
work
Is brother to him who destroys.
10 The [a]name of the LORD is a
[b]strong tower;
The righteous runs into it and
[c]is [1]safe.
11 A rich man's wealth is his
strong city,
And like a high wall in his own
imagination.
12 Before destruction the heart of
man is haughty,
But humility *goes* before honor.
13 He who [a]gives an answer before he hears,
It is folly and shame to him.
14 The spirit of a man can endure
his sickness,
But a [a]broken spirit who can
bear?
15 The [1]mind of the prudent acquires knowledge,
And the ear of the wise seeks
knowledge.

---

12 [a]2 Sam. 17:8; Hos. 13:8 [b]Prov. 29:9
13 [a]Ps. 35:12; 109:5; Jer. 18:20 [b]2 Sam. 12:10; 1 Kin. 21:22; Prov. 13:21
14 [a]Prov. 20:3; 25:8
15 [a]Ex. 23:7; Prov. 18:5; 24:24; Is. 5:23
16 [1]Lit., *there is no heart* [a]Prov. 23:23
17 [a]Ruth 1:16; Prov. 18:24
18 [1]Lit., *heart* [2]Lit., *shakes hands* [a]Prov. 6:1; 11:15; 22:26
19 [a]Prov. 29:22 [b]Prov. 11:2; 16:18; 29:23
20 [1]Lit., *heart* [a]Prov. 24:20 [b]James 3:8
21 [a]Prov. 10:1; 17:25; 19:13
22 [1]Lit., *causes good healing* [a]Prov. 15:13 [b]Ps. 22:15
23 [a]Prov. 17:8 [b]Ex. 23:8; Mic. 3:11; 7:3
24 [a]Eccles. 2:14
27 [1]Lit., *knows* [a]Prov. 10:19; James 1:19 [b]Prov. 14:29
28 [a]Job 13:5
1 [1]Lit., *breaks out*
2 [1]Lit., *heart* [a]Prov. 12:23; 13:16; Eccles. 10:3
4 [1]Or, *A bubbling brook, a fountain of wisdom* [a]Prov. 20:5
5 [a]Lev. 19:15; Deut. 1:17; 16:19; Ps. 82:2; Prov. 17:15; 24:23; 28:21 [b]Ex. 23:2, 6; Prov. 17:26; 31:5; Mic. 3:9
6 [1]Lit., *come with*
7 [a]Ps. 64:8; 140:9; Prov. 10:14; 12:13; 13:3; Eccles. 10:12
8 [1]Lit., *chambers of the belly*
9 [a]Prov. 10:4
10 [1]Lit., *set on high* [a]Ex. 3:15 [b]2 Sam. 22:2, 3, 33; Ps. 18:2; 61:3; 91:2; 144:2 [c]Prov. 29:25
13 [a]Prov. 20:25; John 7:51
14 [a]Prov. 15:13
15 [1]Lit., *heart*

16 A man's [a]gift makes room for him,
And brings him before great men.
17 The first to plead his case *seems* just,
Until another comes and examines him.
18 The [a]lot puts an end to contentions,
And decides between the mighty.
19 A brother offended *is harder to be won* than a strong city,
And contentions are like the bars of a castle.
20 With the [1]fruit of a man's mouth his stomach will be satisfied;
He will be satisfied *with* the product of his lips.
21 [a]Death and life are in the power of the tongue,
And those who love it will eat its [b]fruit.
22 He who finds a [a]wife finds a good thing,
And obtains favor from the LORD.
23 The [a]poor man utters supplications,
But the [b]rich man [c]answers roughly.
24 A man of *many* friends *comes* to ruin,
But there is a friend who sticks closer than a brother.

CHAPTER 19

On Life and Conduct

BETTER is a poor man who [a]walks in his integrity
Than he who is perverse in [1]speech and is a fool.
2 Also it is not good for a person to be without knowledge,
And he who makes haste with his feet [1]errs.
3 The [a]foolishness of man subverts his way,
And his heart [b]rages against the LORD.
4 [a]Wealth adds many friends,
But a poor man is separated from his friend.
5 A [a]false witness will not go unpunished,
And he who [1]tells lies will not escape.
6 [a]Many will entreat the favor of a [1]generous man,
And every man is a friend to him who [b]gives gifts.
7 All the brothers of a poor man hate him;
How much more do his [a]friends go far from him!
He [b]pursues *them with* words, *but* they are [1]gone.
8 He who gets [1]wisdom loves his own soul;
He who keeps understanding will [a]find good.
9 A [a]false witness will not go unpunished,
And he who [1]tells lies will perish.
10 Luxury is [a]not fitting for a fool;
Much less for a [b]slave to rule over princes.
11 A man's [a]discretion makes him slow to anger,
And it is his glory [b]to overlook a transgression.
12 The king's wrath is like the roaring of a lion,
But his favor is like [a]dew on the grass.
13 A foolish son is destruction to his father,
And the [a]contentions of a wife are a constant dripping.
14 House and wealth are an [a]inheritance from fathers,
But a prudent wife is from the LORD.
15 [a]Laziness casts into a deep sleep,
And an idle [1]man will suffer hunger.
16 He who [a]keeps the commandment keeps his soul,
But he who [1]is careless of his ways will die.
17 He who [a]is gracious to a poor man lends to the LORD,
And He will repay him for his [b]good deed.
18 Discipline your son while there is hope,
And do not desire [1]his death.
19 *A man of* great anger shall bear the penalty,
For if you rescue *him*, you will only have to do it again.
20 [a]Listen to counsel and accept discipline,
That you may be wise [1]the rest of your days.
21 Many are the plans in a man's heart,
But the [a]counsel of the LORD, it will stand.
22 What is desirable in a man is his [1]kindness,
And *it is* better to be a poor man than a liar.
23 The [1a]fear of the LORD *leads* to life,
So that one may sleep [b]satisfied, [2c]untouched by evil.

16 [a]Gen. 32:20; 1 Sam. 25:27
18 [a]Prov. 16:33
20 [1]I.e., speech
21 [a]Prov. 12:13; 13:3; Matt. 12:37 [b]Prov. 13:2; Is. 3:10; Hos. 10:13
22 [a]Gen. 2:18; Prov. 12:4; 19:14; 31:10-31
23 [a]Prov. 19:7 [b]James 2:3, 6 [c]1 Kin. 12:13; 2 Chr. 10:13
1 [1]Lit., *his lips* [a]Ps. 26:11; Prov. 14:2; 20:7
2 [1]Lit., *sins*
3 [a]Prov. 11:3 [b]Ps. 37:7; Is. 8:21
4 [a]Prov. 14:20
5 [1]Lit., *breathes* [a]Ex. 23:1; Deut. 19:16-19; Prov. 19:9; 21:28
6 [1]Or, *noble* [a]Prov. 29:26 [b]Prov. 18:16; 21:14
7 [1]Lit., *not* [a]Ps. 38:11 [b]Prov. 18:23
8 [1]Lit., *heart* [a]Prov. 16:20
9 [1]Lit., *breathes* [a]Prov. 19:5
10 [a]Prov. 17:7; 26:1; Eccles. 10:6, 7 [b]Prov. 30:22
11 [a]Prov. 14:29; 16:32 [b]Matt. 5:44; Eph. 4:32; Col. 3:13
12 [a]Gen. 27:28; Deut. 33:28; Ps. 133:3; Hos. 14:5; Mic. 5:7
13 [a]Prov. 21:9, 19; 27:15
14 [a]2 Cor. 12:14
15 [1]Lit., *soul* [a]Prov. 6:9, 10; 24:33
16 [1]Lit., *despises* [a]Prov. 16:17; Luke 10:28; 11:28
17 [a]Deut. 15:7, 8; Prov. 14:31; 28:27; Eccles. 11:1, 2; Matt. 10:42; 25:40; 2 Cor. 9:6-8; Heb. 6:10 [b]Prov. 12:14; Luke 6:38
18 [1]Lit., *causing him to die*
20 [1]Lit., *in your latter end* [a]Prov. 4:1; 8:33; 12:15
21 [a]Ps. 33:10, 11; Is. 14:26, 27
22 [1]Or, *loyalty*
23 [1]Or, *reverence* [2]Lit., *not visited* [a]Prov. 14:27; 1 Tim. 4:8 [b]Ps. 25:13 [c]Ps. 91:10; Prov. 12:21

24 The sluggard buries his hand [a]in the dish,
And will not even bring it back to his mouth.
25 Strike a scoffer and the [1]naive may become shrewd,
But reprove one who has understanding and he will [2]gain knowledge.
26 He who assaults *his* father *and* drives *his* mother away
Is a shameful and disgraceful son.
27 Cease listening, my son, to discipline,
And you will stray from the words of knowledge.
28 A rascally witness makes a mockery of justice,
And the mouth of the wicked [1a]spreads iniquity.
29 [1]Judgments are prepared for [a]scoffers,
And [b]blows for the back of fools.

CHAPTER 20

On Life and Conduct

[a]WINE is a mocker, [b]strong drink a brawler,
And whoever [1]is intoxicated by it is not wise.
2 The terror of a king is like the growling of a lion;
He who provokes him to anger [1a]forfeits his own life.
3 [1]Keeping away from strife is an honor for a man,
But any fool will [2]quarrel.
4 The sluggard does not plow after the autumn,
So he [1]begs during the harvest and has nothing.
5 A plan in the heart of a man is *like* deep water,
But a man of understanding draws it out.
6 Many a man [a]proclaims his own loyalty,
But who can find a [b]trustworthy man?
7 A righteous man who [a]walks in his integrity—
[b]How blessed are his sons after him.
8 A king who sits on the throne of justice
[1]Disperses all evil with his eyes.
9 [a]Who can say, "I have cleansed my heart,
I am pure from my sin"?
10 [1]Differing weights and differing measures,
Both of them are abominable to the LORD.

11 It is by his deeds that a lad [1a]distinguishes himself
If his conduct is pure and right.
12 The hearing [a]ear and the seeing eye,
The LORD has made both of them.
13 [a]Do not love sleep, lest you become poor;
Open your eyes, *and* you will be satisfied with [1]food.
14 "Bad, bad," says the buyer;
But when he goes his way, then he boasts.
15 There is gold, and an abundance of [1]jewels;
But the lips of knowledge are a more precious thing.
16 Take his garment when he becomes surety for a stranger;
And for foreigners, hold him in pledge.
17 [a]Bread obtained by falsehood is sweet to a man,
But afterward his mouth will be filled with gravel.
18 Prepare [a]plans by consultation,
And [b]make war by wise guidance.
19 He who goes about as a slanderer reveals secrets,
Therefore do not associate with [1]a gossip.
20 He who [a]curses his father or his mother,
His [b]lamp will go out in time of darkness.
21 An inheritance gained hurriedly at the beginning,
Will not be blessed in the end.
22 [a]Do not say, "I will repay evil";
[b]Wait for the LORD, and He will save you.
23 [1]Differing weights are an abomination to the LORD,
And a [2]false scale is not good.
24 Man's steps are *ordained* by the LORD,
How then can man understand his way?
25 It is a snare for a man to say rashly, "It is holy!"
And [a]after the vows to make inquiry.
26 A [a]wise king winnows the wicked,
And [1]drives the [b]*threshing* wheel over them.
27 The [1a]spirit of man is the lamp of the LORD,
Searching all the [2]innermost parts of his being.
28 [1]Loyalty and [a]truth preserve the king,
And he upholds his throne by [1]righteousness.

24 [a]Matt. 26:23; Mark 14:20
25 [1]Lit., *simple* [2]Lit., *discern*
28 [1]Or, *swallows* [a]Job 15:16; 20:12, 13; 34:7
29 [1]Gk., *Rods* [a]Ps. 1:1; Prov. 9:12 [b]Prov. 10:13; 18:6; 26:3
1 [1]Lit., *errs* [a]Gen. 9:21; Prov. 23:29, 30; Is. 28:7; Hos. 4:11 [b]Prov. 31:4; Is. 5:22; 56:12
2 [1]Lit., *sins against* [a]Num. 16:38; 1 Kin. 2:23; Prov. 8:36; Hab. 2:10
3 [1]Lit., *Ceasing* [2]Lit., *burst out*
4 [1]Lit., *asks*
6 [a]Prov. 25:14; Matt. 6:2; Luke 18:11 [b]Ps. 12:1; Luke 18:8
7 [a]Prov. 19:1 [b]Ps. 37:26; 112:2
8 [1]Or, *Sifts*
9 [a]1 Kin. 8:46; 2 Chr. 6:36; Job 14:4; Eccles. 7:20; Rom. 3:9; 1 John 1:8
10 [1]Lit., *A stone and a stone, an ephah and an ephah*
11 [1]Or, *makes himself known* [a]Matt. 7:16
12 [a]Ex. 4:11; Ps. 94:9
13 [1]Lit., *bread* [a]Prov. 6:9, 10; 19:15; 24:33
15 [1]Or, *corals*
17 [a]Prov. 9:17
18 [a]Prov. 11:14; 15:22 [b]Luke 14:31
19 [1]Lit., *one who opens his lips*
20 [a]Ex. 21:17; Lev. 20:9; Prov. 30:11; Matt. 15:4 [b]Job 18:5; Prov. 13:9; 24:20
22 [a]Prov. 24:29; Matt. 5:39; Rom. 12:17, 19; 1 Thess. 5:15; 1 Pet. 3:9 [b]Ps. 27:14
23 [1]Lit., *A stone and a stone* [2]Lit., *balance of deceit*
25 [a]Eccles. 5:4, 5
26 [1]Lit., *turns* [a]Prov. 20:8 [b]Is. 28:27
27 [1]Lit., *breath* [2]Lit., *chambers of the body* [a]1 Cor. 2:11
28 [1]Lit., *Covenant loyalty* [a]Prov. 29:14

29 The glory of young men is their strength,
And the [1]honor of old men is their gray hair.
30 Stripes that wound scour away evil,
And strokes *reach* the [1]innermost parts.

Chapter 21

On Life and Conduct

THE king's heart is *like* channels of water in the hand of the LORD;
He [a]turns it wherever He wishes.
2 Every man's way is right in his own eyes,
But the LORD [a]weighs the hearts.
3 To do [a]righteousness and justice
Is desired by the LORD rather than sacrifice.
4 Haughty eyes and a proud heart,
The [a]lamp of the wicked, is sin.
5 The plans of the diligent *lead* surely to advantage,
But everyone who is hasty *comes* surely to poverty.
6 The [a]getting of treasures by a lying tongue
Is a fleeting vapor, the [1]pursuit of [b]death.
7 The violence of the wicked will drag them away,
Because they [a]refuse to act with justice.
8 The way of a guilty man is [a]crooked,
But as for the pure, his conduct is upright.
9 It is better to live in a corner of a roof,
Than [1]in a house shared with a contentious woman.
10 The soul of the wicked desires evil;
His [a]neighbor finds no favor in his eyes.
11 When the [a]scoffer is punished, the [1]naive becomes wise;
But when the wise is instructed, he receives knowledge.
12 The righteous one considers the house of the wicked,
Turning the [a]wicked to ruin.
13 He who [a]shuts his ear to the cry of the poor
Will also cry himself and not be [b]answered.
14 A [a]gift in secret subdues anger,
And a bribe in the bosom, strong wrath.

29 [1]Or, *splendor*
30 [1]Lit., *chambers of the body*
1 [a]Ezra 6:22
2 [a]Prov. 16:2; 24:12; Luke 16:15
3 [a]Prov. 11:14; 15:22
4 [a]Luke 11:34
6 [1]Lit., *seekers* [a]Ex. 21:17; Lev. 20:9; Prov. 30:11; Matt. 15:4 [b]Job 18:5; Prov. 13:9; 24:20
7 [a]Prov. 24:29; Matt. 5:39; Rom. 12:17, 19; 1 Thess. 5:15; 1 Pet. 3:9
8 [a]Ps. 27:14
9 [1]Lit., *a woman of contentions and a house of association*
10 [a]Jer. 10:23
11 [1]Lit., *simple* [a]Eccles. 5:4, 5
12 [a]Prov. 21:8
13 [a]Matt. 18:30-34; 1 John 3:17 [b]James 2:13
14 [a]Prov. 18:16; 19:6
15 [a]Prov. 10:29
16 [1]Lit., *departed spirits* [a]Ps. 49:14
17 [a]Prov. 23:21
18 [a]Is. 43:3
20 [a]Ps. 112:3; Prov. 8:21; 22:4 [b]Job 20:15, 18
21 [a]Prov. 15:9; Matt. 5:6
22 [1]Lit., *strength of trust* [a]2 Sam. 5:6-9; Prov. 24:5; Eccles. 7:19; 9:15, 16
23 [a]Prov. 12:13; 13:3; 18:21; James 3:2
24 [a]Ps. 1:1; Prov. 1:22; 3:34; 24:9; Is. 29:20 [b]Is. 16:6; Jer. 48:29
26 [1]Lit., *desires desire* [a]Ps. 37:26; 112:5, 9; Matt. 5:42; Eph. 4:28
27 [a]Ps. 50:9; Prov. 15:8; Is. 66:3; Jer. 6:20; Amos 5:22
29 [1]Lit., *makes firm with his face* [a]Eccles. 8:1 [b]Ps. 119:5; Prov. 11:5
30 [a]Is. 8:9, 10; Jer. 9:23; Acts 5:38, 39; 1 Cor. 3:19, 20
31 [a]Ps. 20:7; 33:17; Is. 31:1 [b]Ps. 3:8; Jer. 3:23; 1 Cor. 15:57

15 The execution of justice is joy for the righteous,
But is [a]terror to the workers of iniquity.
16 A man who wanders from the way of understanding
Will [a]rest in the assembly of the [1]dead.
17 He who [a]loves pleasure *will become* a poor man;
He who loves wine and oil will not become rich.
18 The wicked is a [a]ransom for the righteous,
And the treacherous is in the place of the upright.
19 It is better to live in a desert land,
Than with a contentious and vexing woman.
20 There is precious [a]treasure and oil in the dwelling of the wise,
But a foolish man [b]swallows it up.
21 He who [a]pursues righteousness and loyalty
Finds life, righteousness and honor.
22 A [a]wise man scales the city of the mighty,
And brings down the [1]stronghold in which they trust.
23 He who [a]guards his mouth and his tongue,
Guards his soul from troubles.
24 "Proud," "Haughty," "[a]Scoffer," are his names,
Who acts with [b]insolent pride.
25 The desire of the sluggard puts him to death,
For his hands refuse to work;
26 All day long he [1]is craving,
While the righteous [a]gives and does not hold back.
27 The [a]sacrifice of the wicked is an abomination,
How much more when he brings it with evil intent!
28 A false witness will perish,
But the man who listens *to the truth* will speak forever.
29 A wicked man [1a]shows a bold face,
But as for the [b]upright, he makes his way sure.
30 There is [a]no wisdom and no understanding
And no counsel against the LORD.
31 The [a]horse is prepared for the day of battle,
But [b]victory belongs to the LORD.

Chapter 22

On Life and Conduct

A *GOOD* name is to be more desired than great riches,
Favor is better than silver and gold.
2 The rich and the poor [1]have a common bond,
The LORD is the [a]maker of them all.
3 The prudent sees the evil and hides himself,
But the [1]naive go on, and are punished for it.
4 The reward of humility *and* the [1]fear of the LORD
Are riches, honor and life.
5 Thorns *and* snares are in the way of the perverse;
He who guards himself will be far from them.
6 [a]Train up a child [1]in the way he should go,
Even when he is old he will not depart from it.
7 The [a]rich rules over the poor,
And the borrower *becomes* the lender's slave.
8 He who [a]sows iniquity will reap vanity,
And the [b]rod of his fury will perish.
9 He who [1]is [a]generous will be blessed,
For he [b]gives some of his food to the poor.
10 [a]Drive out the scoffer, and contention will go out,
Even strife and dishonor will cease.
11 He who loves [a]purity of heart
And [1]whose speech is gracious, the king is his friend.
12 The eyes of the LORD preserve knowledge,
But He overthrows the words of the treacherous man.
13 The [a]sluggard says, "There is a lion outside;
I shall be slain in the streets!"
14 The mouth of [1a]an adulteress is a deep pit;
He who is [b]cursed of the LORD will fall [2]into it.
15 Foolishness is bound up in the heart of a child;
The [a]rod of discipline will remove it far from him.
16 He who oppresses the poor to make much for himself
Or who gives to the rich, *will* only *come to* poverty.

17 Incline your ear and hear the words of the wise,
And apply your mind to my knowledge;
18 For it will be pleasant if you keep them within you,
[1]That they may be ready on your lips.
19 So that your trust may be in the LORD,
I have [1]taught you today, even you.
20 Have I not written to you [1]excellent things
Of counsels and knowledge,
21 To make you [a]know the [1]certainty of the words of truth
That you may [2b]correctly answer to him who sent you?

22 [a]Do not rob the poor because he is poor,
Or [b]crush the afflicted at the gate;
23 For the LORD will [a]plead their case,
And [1]take the life of those who rob them.

24 Do not associate with a man *given* to anger;
Or go with a [a]hot-tempered man,
25 Lest you [a]learn his ways,
And [1]find a snare for yourself.

26 Do not be among those who give [1]pledges,
Among those who become sureties for debts.
27 If you have nothing with which to pay,
Why should he [a]take your bed from under you?

28 [a]Do not move the ancient boundary
Which your fathers have set.

29 Do you see a man [a]skilled in his work?
He will [b]stand before kings;
He will not stand before obscure men.

Chapter 23

On Life and Conduct

WHEN you sit down to dine with a ruler,
Consider carefully [1]what is before you;
2 And put a knife to your throat,
If you are a man of *great* appetite.
3 Do not desire his [a]delicacies,
For it is deceptive food.

---

2 [1]Lit., *meet together* [a]Job 31:15; Prov. 14:31
3 [1]Lit., *simple*
4 [1]Or, *reverence*
6 [1]Lit., *according to his way* [a]Eph. 6:4
7 [a]Prov. 18:23; James 2:6
8 [a]Job 4:8; Prov. 24:16 [b]Ps. 125:3
9 [1]Lit., *has a good eye* [a]Prov. 19:17; 2 Cor. 9:6 [b]Luke 14:13
10 [a]Gen. 21:9, 10; Prov. 18:6
11 [1]Lit., *has grace on his lips* [a]Ps. 24:4; Matt. 5:8
13 [a]Prov. 26:13
14 [1]Lit., *strange woman* [2]Lit., *there* [a]Prov. 5:3 [b]Eccles. 7:26
15 [a]Prov. 13:24; 23:14
18 [1]Lit., *They together*
19 [1]Lit., *made you know*
20 [1]Or, *previous*
21 [1]Lit., *truth* [2]Lit., *return words of truth* [a]Luke 1:3, 4 [b]Prov. 25:13
22 [a]Ex. 23:6; Job 31:16; Prov. 23:10 [b]Zech. 7:10; Mal. 3:5
23 [1]Lit., *rob the soul* [a]1 Sam. 25:39; Ps. 12:5; 35:10; 140:12; Prov. 23:11; Jer. 51:36
24 [a]Prov. 29:22
25 [1]Lit., *take* [a]1 Cor. 15:33
26 [1]Lit., *strike hands*
27 [a]Ex. 22:26; Prov. 20:16
28 [a]Deut. 19:14; 27:17; Job 24:2; Prov. 23:10
29 [a]Rom. 12:11 [b]Gen. 41:46; 1 Kin. 10:8
1 [1]Or, *who*
3 [a]Ps. 141:4; Dan. 1:5, 8, 13, 15, 16

4 [a]Do not weary yourself to gain wealth,
[b]Cease from your [1]consideration *of it.*
5 [1]When you set your eyes on it, it is gone.
For [a]*wealth* certainly makes itself wings,
Like an eagle that flies *toward* the heavens.

6 [a]Do not eat the bread of a [1b]selfish man,
Or desire his delicacies;
7 For as he [1]thinks within himself, so he is.
He says to you, "Eat and drink!"
But his heart is not with you.
8 You will vomit up [1]the morsel you have eaten,
And waste your [2]compliments.

9 Do not speak in the [1]hearing of a fool,
For he will despise the wisdom of your words.

10 Do not move the ancient boundary,
Or [a]go into the fields of the fatherless;
11 For their [a]Redeemer is strong;
He will plead their case against you.
12 Apply your heart to discipline,
And your ears to words of knowledge.

13 Do not hold back discipline from the child,
Although you [1]beat him with the rod, he will not die.
14 You shall [1]beat him with the rod,
And [a]deliver his soul from Sheol.

15 My son, if your heart is wise,
My own heart also will be glad;
16 And my [1]inmost being will rejoice,
When your lips speak what is right.

17 [a]Do not let your heart envy sinners,
But *live* in the [1]fear of the LORD [2]always.
18 Surely there is a [1a]future,
And your [b]hope will not be cut off.
19 Listen, my son, and [a]be wise,
And [b]direct your heart in the way.
20 Do not be with [a]heavy drinkers of wine,
Or with [b]gluttonous eaters of meat;
21 For the heavy drinker and the glutton will come to poverty,
And drowsiness will clothe *a man* with rags.

22 Listen to your father who begot you,
And do not despise your mother when she is old.
23 [a]Buy truth, and do not sell *it,*
Get wisdom and instruction and understanding.

24 The father of the righteous will greatly rejoice,
And [a]he who begets a wise son will be glad in him.
25 Let your father and your mother be glad,
And let her rejoice who gave birth to you.

26 Give me your heart, my son,
And let your eyes [1a]delight in my ways.
27 For a harlot is a deep pit,
And an [1]adulterous woman is a narrow well.
28 Surely she [a]lurks as a robber,
And increases the [1]faithless among men.

29 Who has [a]woe? Who has sorrow?
Who has contentions? Who has complaining?
Who has wounds without cause?
Who has redness of eyes?
30 Those who [a]linger long over wine,
Those who go to [1]taste [b]mixed wine.
31 Do not look on the wine when it is red,
When it [1]sparkles in the cup,
When it [a]goes down smoothly;
32 At the last it [a]bites like a serpent,
And stings like a [b]viper.
33 Your eyes will see strange things,
And your [1]mind will utter perverse things.
34 And you will be like one who lies down in the [1]middle of the sea,
Or like one who lies down on the top of a [2]mast.
35 "They [a]struck me, *but* I did not become ill;
They beat me, *but* I did not know *it.*

4 [1]Or, *understanding* [a]Prov. 15:27; 28:20; Matt. 6:19; 1 Tim. 6:9; Heb. 13:5 [b]Prov. 3:5, 7; Rom. 12:16
5 [1]Lit., *Will your eyes fly upon it and it is not?* [a]Prov. 27:24; 1 Tim. 6:17
6 [1]Lit., *evil eye* [a]Ps. 141:4 [b]Prov. 28:22
7 [1]Lit., *reckons in his soul*
8 [1]Lit., *your* [2]Lit., *pleasant words*
9 [1]Lit., *ears*
10 [a]Jer. 22:3; Zech. 7:10
11 [a]Job 19:25
13 [1]Lit., *smite*
14 [1]Lit., *smite* [a]1 Cor. 5:5
16 [1]Lit., *kidneys*
17 [1]Or, *reverence* [2]Lit., *all the day* [a]Ps. 37:1; Prov. 24:1, 19
18 [1]Lit., *latter end* [a]Ps. 19:11; 58:11; Prov. 24:14 [b]Ps. 9:18
19 [a]Prov. 6:6 [b]Prov. 4:23; 9:6
20 [a]Prov. 20:1; 23:29, 30; Is. 5:22; Matt. 24:49; Luke 21:34; Rom. 13:13; Eph. 5:18 [b]Deut. 21:20; Prov. 28:7
23 [a]Prov. 4:7; 18:15; Matt. 13:44
24 [a]Prov. 10:1; 15:20; 29:3
26 [1]Another reading is, *observe* [a]Ps. 1:2; 119:24
27 [1]Lit., *strange*
28 [1]Lit., *treacherous* [a]Prov. 6:26; 7:12; Eccles. 7:26
29 [a]Is. 5:11, 22
30 [1]Or, *search out* [a]1 Sam. 25:36; Prov. 20:1; Is. 5:11; 28:7; Eph. 5:18 [b]Ps. 75:8
31 [1]Lit., *gives its eye* [a]Song of Sol. 7:9
32 [a]Job 20:16 [b]Ps. 91:13; Is. 11:8
33 [1]Lit., *heart*
34 [1]Lit., *heart* [2]Or, *lookout*
35 [a]Jer. 5:3

When shall I awake?
I will [b]seek [1]another drink."

Chapter 24

Precepts and Warnings

Do not be [a]envious of evil men,
Nor desire to [b]be with them;
2 For their [1]minds devise [a]violence,
And their lips [b]talk of trouble.

3 By wisdom a house is built,
And by understanding it is established;
4 And by knowledge the rooms are filled
With all precious and pleasant riches.

5 A wise man is [1]strong,
And a man of knowledge [2]increases power.
6 For by wise guidance you will [1]wage war,
And in abundance of counselors there is victory.

7 Wisdom is [a]too high for a fool,
He does not open his mouth [b]in the gate.

8 He who [a]plans to do evil,
Men will call him a [1]schemer.
9 The [a]devising of folly is sin,
And the scoffer is an abomination to men.

10 If you [a]are slack in the day of distress,
Your strength is limited.

11 [a]Deliver those who are being taken away to death,
And those who are staggering to slaughter, O hold *them* back.
12 If you say, "See, we did not know this,"
Does He not [a]consider *it* [b]who weighs the hearts?
And [c]does He not know *it* who [d]keeps your soul?
And will He not [1e]render to man according to his work?

13 My son, eat [a]honey, for it is good,
Yes, the [b]honey from the comb is sweet to your taste;
14 Know *that* wisdom is thus for your soul;
If you find *it*, then there will be a [1]future,
And your hope will not be cut off.

15 [a]Do not lie in wait, O wicked man, against the dwelling of the righteous;
Do not destroy his resting place;
16 For a [a]righteous man falls seven times, and rises again,
But the [b]wicked stumble in *time of* calamity.

17 [a]Do not rejoice when your enemy falls,
And do not let your heart be glad when he stumbles;
18 Lest the LORD see *it* and [1]be displeased,
And He turn away His anger from him.

19 [a]Do not fret yourself because of evildoers,
Or be [b]envious of the wicked;
20 For [a]there will be no [1b]future for the evil man;
The [c]lamp of the wicked will be put out.

21 My son, [1a]fear the LORD and the king;
Do not associate with those who are given to change;
22 For their [a]calamity will rise suddenly,
And who knows the ruin *that comes* from both of them?

23 These also are [a]sayings of the wise.
To [1b]show partiality in judgment is not good.
24 He who says to the wicked, "You are righteous,"
Peoples will curse him, nations will abhor him;
25 But to those who rebuke the *wicked* will be delight,
And a good blessing will come upon them.
26 He kisses the lips
Who gives a [1]right answer.

27 Prepare your work outside,
And make it ready for yourself in the field;
Afterwards, then, build your house.

28 Do not be a [a]witness against your neighbor without cause,
And [b]do not deceive with your lips.
29 [a]Do not say, "Thus I shall do to him as he has done to me;
I will [1]render to the man according to his work."

30 I passed by the field of the sluggard,

35 [1]Lit., *it yet again* [b]Prov. 26:11; Is. 56:12
1 [a]Ps. 37:1; Prov. 3:31; 23:17; 24:19 [b]Ps. 1:1; Prov. 1:15
2 [1]Lit., *hearts* [a]Is. 30:12; Jer. 22:17 [b]Job 15:35; Ps. 10:7; 38:12
5 [1]Lit., *in strength* [2]Lit., *strengthens power*
6 [1]Lit., *make battle for yourself*
7 [a]Ps. 10:5; Prov. 14:6; 17:16 [b]Job 5:4; Ps. 127:5
8 [1]Or, *deviser of evil* [a]Prov. 6:14; 14:22; Rom. 1:30
9 [a]Is. 59:7
10 [a]Deut. 20:8; Job 4:5; Jer. 51:46; Heb. 12:3
11 [a]Ps. 82:4; Is. 58:6, 7
12 [1]Lit., *bring back* [a]1 Sam. 16:7; Prov. 21:2 [b]Eccles. 5:8 [c]Ps. 121:3-8 [d]Ps. 94:9-11 [e]Job 34:11; Prov. 12:14
13 [a]Ps. 19:10; 119:103; Prov. 25:16; Song of Sol. 5:1 [b]Prov. 16:24; 27:7; Song of Sol. 4:11
14 [1]Lit., *latter end*
15 [a]Ps. 10:9, 10
16 [a]Job 5:19; Ps. 37:24; Mic. 7:8 [b]Prov. 6:15; 14:32; 24:22; Jer. 18:17
17 [a]Job 31:29; Ps. 35:15, 19; Prov. 17:5; Obad. 12
18 [1]Lit., *it is evil in His eyes*
19 [a]Ps. 37:1 [b]Prov. 23:17; 24:1
20 [1]Lit., *latter end* [a]Job 15:31 [b]Prov. 23:18 [c]Job 18:5, 6; 21:17; Prov. 13:9; 20:20
21 [1]Or, *reverence* [a]Rom. 13:1-7; 1 Pet. 2:17
22 [a]Prov. 24:16
23 [1]Lit., *regard the face* [a]Prov. 1:6; 22:17 [b]Prov. 18:5; 28:21
26 [1]Or, *honest*
28 [a]Prov. 25:18 [b]Lev. 6:2, 3; 19:11; Eph. 4:25
29 [1]Lit., *bring back* [a]Prov. 20:22; Matt. 5:39; Rom. 12:17

And by the vineyard of the man [a]lacking [1]sense;
31 And behold, it was completely overgrown with thistles,
Its surface was covered with [1a]nettles,
And its stone [b]wall was broken down.
32 When I saw, I [1]reflected upon it;
I looked, *and* received instruction.
33 "A little sleep, a little slumber,
A little folding of the hands to rest,"
34 Then your poverty will come *as* [1]a robber,
And your want like an armed man.

CHAPTER 25

Similitudes, Instructions

THESE also are [a]proverbs of Solomon which the men of Hezekiah, king of Judah, transcribed.
2 It is the glory of God to [a]conceal a matter,
But the glory of [b]kings is to search out a matter.
3 *As* the heavens for height and the earth for depth,
So the heart of kings is unsearchable.
4 Take away the [a]dross from the silver,
And there comes out a vessel for the [b]smith;
5 Take away the [a]wicked *from* before the king,
And his throne will be established in righteousness.
6 Do not claim honor in the presence of the king,
And do not stand in the place of great men;
7 For [a]it is better that it be said to you, "Come up here,"
Than that you should be put lower in the presence of the prince,
Whom your eyes have seen.

8 Do not go out [a]hastily to [1]argue *your case;*
[2]Otherwise, what will you do in [3]the end,
When your neighbor puts you to shame?
9 [1a]Argue your case with your neighbor,
And [b]do not reveal the secret of another,
10 Lest he who hears *it* reproach you,
And the evil report about you not [1]pass away.

11 *Like* apples of gold in settings of silver
Is a [a]word spoken in [1]right circumstances.
12 *Like* [1]an [a]earring of gold and an [b]ornament of [c]fine gold
Is a wise reprover to a [d]listening ear.
13 Like the cold of snow in the [1]time of harvest
Is a faithful messenger to those who send him,
For he refreshes the soul of his masters.
14 *Like* [a]clouds and [b]wind without rain
Is a man who boasts of his gifts falsely.
15 By [1a]forbearance a ruler may be persuaded,
And a soft tongue breaks the bone.
16 Have you [a]found honey? Eat *only* [1]what you need,
Lest you have it in excess and vomit it.
17 Let your foot rarely be in your neighbor's house,
Lest he become [1]weary of you and hate you.
18 *Like* a club and a [a]sword and a sharp [b]arrow
Is a man who bears [c]false witness against his neighbor.
19 *Like* a bad tooth and [1]an unsteady foot
Is confidence in a [a]faithless man in time of trouble.
20 *Like* one who takes off a garment on a cold day, *or like* vinegar on [1]soda,
Is he who sings songs to a [2]troubled heart.
21 [a]If [1]your enemy is hungry, give him food to eat;
And if he is thirsty, give him water to drink;
22 For you will [1]heap burning coals on his head,
And [a]the LORD will reward you.
23 The north wind brings forth rain,
And a [1a]backbiting tongue, an angry countenance.
24 It is better to live in a corner of the roof
Than [1]in a house shared with a contentious woman.
25 *Like* cold water to a weary soul,
So is good news from a distant land.
26 *Like* a [a]trampled spring and a [1]polluted well
Is a righteous man who gives way before the wicked.

30 [1]Lit., *heart* [a]Prov. 6:32
31 [1]I.e., a kind of weed [a]Job 30:7 [b]Is. 5:5
32 [1]Lit., *set my heart*
34 [1]Or, *a vagabond;* lit., *one who walks*
1 [a]Prov. 1:1
2 [a]Deut. 29:29; Rom. 11:33 [b]Ezra 6:1
4 [a]Prov. 26:23; Ezek. 22:18 [b]Mal. 3:2, 3
5 [a]Prov. 20:8
7 [a]Luke 14:7-11
8 [1]Lit., *contend* [2]Lit., *Lest* [3]Lit., *its* [a]Prov. 17:14; Matt. 5:25
9 [1]Lit., *Contend* [a]Matt. 18:15 [b]Prov. 11:13
10 [1]Lit., *return*
11 [1]Lit., *its* [a]Prov. 15:23
12 [1]Or, *a nose ring* [a]Ex. 32:2; 35:22; Ezek. 16:12 [b]2 Sam. 1:24 [c]Job 28:17 [d]Prov. 15:31; 20:12
13 [1]Lit., *day*
14 [a]Jude 12 [b]Jer. 5:13; Mic. 2:11
15 [1]Lit., *length of anger* [a]Gen. 32:4; 1 Sam. 25:24; Eccles. 10:4
16 [1]Lit., *your sufficiency* [a]Judg. 14:8; 1 Sam. 14:25
17 [1]Lit., *surfeited with*
18 [a]Ps. 57:4; Prov. 12:18 [b]Jer. 9:8 [c]Ex. 20:16; Prov. 24:28
19 [1]Lit., *a slipping foot* [a]Job 6:15
20 [1]I.e., natron [2]Lit., *evil*
21 [1]Lit., *one who hates you* [a]Ex. 23:4, 5; 2 Kin. 6:22; 2 Chr. 28:15; Matt. 5:44; Rom. 12:20
22 [1]Lit., *snatch up* [a]Matt. 6:4, 6
23 [1]Lit., *tongue of secrecy* [a]Ps. 101:5
24 [1]Lit., *a woman of contentions and a house of association*
26 [1]Lit., *ruined* [a]Ezek. 32:2; 34:18, 19

27 It is not good to eat much honey,
Nor is it glory to search out [1]one's own glory.
28 *Like* a [a]city that is broken into *and* without walls
Is a man [b]who has no control over his spirit.

Chapter 26

Similitudes, Instructions

LIKE snow in summer and like [a]rain in harvest,
So honor is not [b]fitting for a fool.
2 Like a [a]sparrow in *its* [1]flitting, like a swallow in *its* flying,
So a [b]curse without cause does not [2]alight.
3 A [a]whip is for the horse, a bridle for the donkey,
And a [b]rod for the back of fools.
4 [a]Do not answer a fool according to his folly,
Lest you also be like him.
5 [a]Answer a fool as his folly *deserves*,
Lest he be [b]wise in his own eyes.
6 He cuts off *his own* feet, *and* drinks violence
Who sends a message by the hand of a fool.
7 *Like* the legs *which* hang down from the lame,
So is a proverb in the mouth of fools.
8 Like [1]one who binds a stone in a sling,
So is he who gives honor to a fool.
9 *Like* a thorn *which* [1]falls into the hand of a drunkard,
So is a proverb in the mouth of fools.
10 [1]*Like* an archer who wounds everyone,
So is he who hires a fool or who hires those who pass by.
11 Like [a]a dog that returns to its vomit
Is a fool who [b]repeats [1]his folly.
12 Do you see a man [a]wise in his own eyes?
There is more hope for a fool than for him.
13 The sluggard says, "There is a lion in the road!
A lion is [1]in the open square!"
14 *As* the door turns on its hinges,
So *does* the sluggard on his bed.
15 The sluggard buries his hand in the dish;
He is weary of bringing it to his mouth again.
16 The sluggard is [a]wiser in his own eyes
Than seven men who can [1]give a discreet answer.
17 *Like* one who takes a dog by the ears
Is he who passes by *and* [1]meddles with [a]strife not belonging to him.
18 Like a madman who throws
[a]Firebrands, arrows and death,
19 So is the man who [a]deceives his neighbor,
And says, "Was I not joking?"
20 For lack of wood the fire goes out,
And where there is no [a]whisperer, contention quiets down.
21 *Like* charcoal to hot embers and wood to fire,
So is a contentious man to kindle strife.
22 The words of a whisperer are like dainty morsels,
And they go down into the [1]innermost parts of the body.
23 *Like* an earthen [a]vessel overlaid with silver dross
Are burning lips and a wicked heart.
24 He who [a]hates disguises *it* with his lips,
But he lays up [b]deceit in his [1]heart.
25 When [1]he [a]speaks graciously, do not believe him,
For there are seven abominations in his heart.
26 *Though his* hatred [a]covers itself with guile,
His wickedness will be [b]revealed before the assembly.
27 He who digs a pit will fall into it,
And he who rolls a stone, it will come back on him.
28 A lying tongue hates [1]those it crushes,
And a flattering mouth works ruin.

Chapter 27

Warnings and Instructions

DO not boast about tomorrow,
For you [a]do not know what a day may bring forth.
2 Let [a]another praise you, and not your own mouth;
A stranger, and not your own lips.
3 A stone is heavy and the sand weighty,
But the provocation of a fool is heavier than both of them.

27 [1]Lit., *their*
28 [a]Prov. 16:32 [b]2 Chr. 32:5; Neh. 1:3
1 [a]1 Sam. 12:17 [b]Prov. 17:7
2 [1]Lit., *wandering* [2]Lit., *come* [a]Prov. 27:8; Is. 16:2 [b]Num. 23:8; Deut. 23:5; 2 Sam. 16:12
3 [a]Ps. 32:9 [b]Prov. 10:13; 19:29
4 [a]Prov. 23:9; 29:9
5 [a]Matt. 16:1-4; 21:24-27 [b]Prov. 3:7; 28:11; Rom. 12:16
8 [1]Lit., *the binding of*
9 [1]Lit., *goes up*
10 [1]Or, *A master workman produces all things, But he who hires a fool is like one who hires those who pass by.*
11 [1]Lit., *with his* [a]2 Pet. 2:22 [b]Ex. 8:15
12 [a]Prov. 3:7; 26:5
13 [1]Lit., *within*
16 [1]Lit., *return discreetly* [a]Prov. 27:11; 1 Pet. 3:15
17 [1]Lit., *infuriates himself* [a]Prov. 3:30
18 [a]Is. 50:11
19 [a]Prov. 24:28
20 [a]Prov. 16:28
22 [1]Lit., *chambers of the belly*
23 [a]Matt. 23:27; Luke 11:39
24 [1]Lit., *inward part* [a]Ps. 41:6; Prov. 10:18 [b]Prov. 12:20
25 [1]Lit., *his voice is gracious* [a]Ps. 28:3; Prov. 26:23; Jer. 9:8
26 [a]Matt. 23:28 [b]Luke 8:17
28 [1]Lit., *its crushed ones*
1 [a]Luke 12:19, 20; James 4:14
2 [a]Prov. 25:27; 2 Cor. 10:12, 18; 12:11

4 Wrath is fierce and anger is a flood,
But who can stand before jealousy?
5 Better is [a]open rebuke
Than love that is concealed.
6 Faithful are the [a]wounds of a friend,
But [1]deceitful are the [b]kisses of an enemy.
7 A sated [1]man [2]loathes honey,
But to a famished [1]man any bitter thing is sweet.
8 Like a [a]bird that wanders from her nest,
So is a man who [b]wanders from his [1]home.
9 [a]Oil and perfume make the heart glad,
So a [1]man's counsel is sweet to his friend.
10 Do not forsake your own friend or [a]your father's friend,
And do not go to your brother's house in the day of your calamity;
Better is a neighbor who is near than a brother far away.
11 [a]Be wise, my son, and make my heart glad,
That I may [b]reply to him who reproaches me.
12 A prudent man sees evil *and* hides himself,
The [1]naive proceed *and* pay the penalty.
13 Take his garment when he becomes surety for a stranger;
And for an [1]adulterous woman hold him in pledge.
14 He who blesses his friend with a loud voice early in the morning,
It will be reckoned a curse to him.
15 A constant dripping on a day of steady rain
And a contentious woman are alike;
16 He who would [1]restrain her [1]restrains the wind,
And [2]grasps oil with his right hand.
17 Iron sharpens iron,
So one man sharpens another.
18 He who tends the [a]fig tree will eat its fruit;
And he who [b]cares for his master will be honored.
19 As in water face *reflects* face,
So the heart of man *reflects* man.
20 [1a]Sheol and [2]Abaddon are [b]never satisfied,
Nor are the [c]eyes of man ever satisfied.
21 The crucible is for silver and the furnace for gold,
And a man [a]*is tested* by the praise accorded him.
22 Though you [a]pound a fool in a mortar with a pestle along with crushed grain,
Yet his folly will not depart from him.

23 [a]Know well the [1]condition of your flocks,
And pay attention to your herds;
24 For riches are not forever,
Nor does a [a]crown *endure* to all generations.
25 *When* the grass disappears, the new growth is seen,
And the herbs of the mountains are [a]gathered in,
26 The lambs *will be* for your clothing,
And the goats *will bring* the price of a field,
27 And *there will be* goats' milk enough for your food,
For the food of your household,
And sustenance for your maidens.

CHAPTER 28

Warnings and Instructions

THE wicked [a]flee when no one is pursuing,
But the righteous are [1]bold as a lion.
2 By the transgression of a land [a]many are its princes,
But by a man of understanding *and* knowledge, so it endures.
3 A [a]poor man who oppresses the lowly
Is *like* a driving rain [1]which leaves no food.
4 Those who forsake the law [a]praise the wicked,
But those who keep the law [b]strive with them.
5 Evil men [a]do not understand justice,
But those who seek the LORD [b]understand all things.
6 Better is the poor who walks in his integrity,
Than he who is [1]crooked though he be rich.
7 He who keeps the law is a discerning son,
But he who is a companion of gluttons humiliates his father.

---

5 [a]Prov. 28:23; Gal. 2:14
6 [1]Or, *excessive* [a]Ps. 141:5; Prov. 20:30 [b]Matt. 26:49
7 [1]Lit., *soul* [2]Lit., *tramples on*
8 [1]Lit., *place* [a]Prov. 26:2; Is. 16:2 [b]Gen. 21:14
9 [1]Lit., *soul's* [a]Ps. 23:5; 141:5
10 [a]1 Kin. 12:6-8; 2 Chr. 10:6-8
11 [a]Prov. 10:1; 23:15; 29:3 [b]Ps. 119:42
12 [1]Lit., *simple*
13 [1]Lit., *strange*
16 [1]Lit., *hide(s)* [2]Lit., *encounters*
18 [a]2 Kin. 18:31; Song of Sol. 8:12; Is. 36:16; 1 Cor. 3:8; 9:7; 2 Tim. 2:6 [b]Luke 12:42-44; 19:17
20 [1]I.e., The nether world [2]I.e., the place of perishing [a]Job 26:6; Prov. 15:11 [b]Prov. 30:15, 16; Hab. 2:5 [c]Eccl. 1:8; 4:8
21 [a]Luke 6:26
22 [a]Prov. 23:35; 26:11; Jer. 5:3
23 [1]Lit., *face* [a]Jer. 31:10; Ezek. 34:12; John 10:3
24 [a]Job 19:9; Ps. 89:39; Jer. 13:18; Lam. 5:16; Ezek. 21:26
25 [a]Is. 17:5; Jer. 40:10, 12
1 [1]Lit., *confident* [a]Lev. 26:17, 36; Ps. 53:5
2 [a]1 Kin. 16:8-28; 2 Kin. 15:8-15
3 [1]Lit., *and there is no bread* [a]Matt. 18:28
4 [a]Ps. 49:18; Rom. 1:32 [b]1 Kin. 18:18; Neh. 13:11, 15; Matt. 3:7; 14:4; Eph. 5:11
5 [a]Ps. 92:6; Is. 6:9; 44:18 [b]Ps. 119:100; Prov. 2:9; John 7:17; 1 Cor. 2:15; 1 John 2:20, 27
6 [1]Lit., *perverse of two ways*

8 He who increases his wealth by
[a]interest and usury,
Gathers it [b]for him who is gracious to the poor.
9 He who turns away his ear from
listening to the law,
Even his [a]prayer is an abomination.
10 He who leads the upright astray
in an evil way
Will [a]himself fall into his own
pit,
But the [b]blameless will inherit
good.
11 The rich man is wise in his own
eyes,
But the poor who has understanding [1]sees through him.
12 When the righteous triumph,
there is great glory,
But [a]when the wicked rise, men
[1]hide themselves.
13 He who [a]conceals his transgressions will not prosper,
But he who [b]confesses and forsakes *them* will find compassion.
14 How blessed is the man who
[a]fears always,
But he who [b]hardens his heart
will fall into calamity.
15 *Like* a [a]roaring lion and a rushing bear
Is a [b]wicked ruler over a poor
people.
16 A [a]leader who is a great oppressor lacks understanding,
But he who hates unjust gain
will prolong *his* days.
17 A man who is [a]laden with the
guilt of human blood
Will [1]be a fugitive until death;
let no one support him.
18 He who walks blamelessly will
be delivered,
But he who is [1]crooked will fall
all at once.
19 He who tills his land will have
plenty of food,
But he who follows empty *pursuits* will have poverty in
plenty.
20 A [a]faithful man will abound
with blessings,
But he who [b]makes haste to be
rich will not go unpunished.
21 To [1a]show partiality is not
good,
[b]Because for a piece of bread a
man will transgress.
22 A man with an [a]evil eye hastens
after wealth,
And does not know that want
will come upon him.
23 He who rebukes a man will afterward find *more* favor
Than he who flatters with the
tongue.
24 He who robs his father or his
mother,
And says, "It is not a transgression,"
Is the companion of a man who
destroys.
25 An [1]arrogant man stirs up
strife,
But he who trusts in the LORD
will [2]prosper.
26 He who [a]trusts in his own heart
is a fool,
But he who walks wisely will be
delivered.
27 He who [a]gives to the poor will
never want,
But he who [1]shuts his eyes will
have many curses.
28 When the wicked rise, men
hide themselves;
But when they perish, the righteous increase.

CHAPTER 29

Warnings and Instructions

A MAN who hardens *his* neck after [a]much reproof
Will suddenly be broken [1]beyond remedy.
2 When the [a]righteous [1]increase,
the people rejoice,
But when a wicked man rules,
people groan.
3 A man who [a]loves wisdom
makes his father glad,
But he who [b]keeps company
with harlots wastes *his*
wealth.
4 The [a]king gives stability to the
land by justice,
But a man who takes bribes overthrows it.
5 A man who [a]flatters his neighbor
Is spreading a net for his steps.
6 By transgression an evil man is
[a]ensnared,
But the righteous [b]sings and rejoices.
7 The [a]righteous [1]is concerned
for the rights of the poor,
The wicked does not understand *such* [2]concern.
8 Scorners set a city aflame,
But wise men turn away anger.
9 When a wise man has a controversy with a foolish man,
[1]The foolish man either rages or
laughs, and there is no rest.
10 Men of [a]bloodshed hate the
blameless,
But the upright [1]are concerned
for his life.

8 [a]Ex. 22:25; Lev. 25:36 [b]Job 27:17; Prov. 13:22
9 [a]Ps. 66:18; 109:7; Prov. 15:8; 21:27
10 [a]Ps. 7:15; Prov. 26:27 [b]Matt. 6:33; Heb. 6:12; 1 Pet. 3:9
11 [1]Lit., *examines him*
12 [1]Lit., *will be searched for* [a]Prov. 28:28; Eccles. 10:5, 6
13 [a]Job 31:33; Ps. 32:3 [b]Ps. 32:5; 1 John 1:9
14 [a]Prov. 23:17 [b]Ps. 95:8; Rom. 2:5
15 [a]Prov. 19:12; 1 Pet. 5:8 [b]Ex. 1:14; Prov. 29:2; Matt. 2:16
16 [a]Eccles. 10:16; Is. 3:12
17 [1]Lit., *flee to the pit* [a]Gen. 9:6; Ex. 21:14
18 [1]Lit., *perverse of two ways*
20 [a]Prov. 10:6; Matt. 24:45; 25:21 [b]Prov. 20:21; 28:22; 1 Tim. 6:9
21 [1]Lit., *regard the face* [a]Prov. 24:23 [b]Ezek. 13:19
22 [a]Prov. 23:6
25 [1]Lit., *broad soul* [2]Lit., *be made fat*
26 [a]Prov. 3:5
27 [1]Lit., *hides* [a]Prov. 11:24; 19:17
1 [1]Lit., *and there is no remedy* [a]1 Sam. 2:25; 2 Chr. 36:16; Prov. 1:24-31
2 [1]Or, *become great* [a]Esth. 8:15; Prov. 11:10; 28:12
3 [a]Prov. 10:1; 15:20; 27:11; 28:7 [b]Prov. 5:10; 6:26; Luke 15:30
4 [a]2 Chr. 9:8; Prov. 8:15; 28:14
5 [a]Ps. 5:9
6 [a]Prov. 22:5; Eccles. 9:12 [b]Ex. 15:1
7 [1]Lit., *knows the cause* [2]Lit., *knowledge* [a]Job 29:16; Ps. 41:1; Prov. 31:8, 9
9 [1]Lit., *He*
10 [1]Lit., *seek his soul* [a]Gen. 4:5-8; 1 John 3:12

11 A fool always loses his temper,
But a [a]wise man holds it back.
12 If a [a]ruler pays attention to falsehood,
All his ministers *become* wicked.
13 The poor man and the oppressor have this in common:
The LORD gives [a]light to the eyes of both.
14 If a [a]king judges the poor with truth,
His throne will be established forever.
15 The [a]rod and reproof give wisdom,
But a child who gets his own way brings shame to his mother.
16 When the wicked [1]increase, transgression increases;
But the [a]righteous will see their fall.
17 [a]Correct your son, and he will give you comfort;
He will also delight your soul.
18 Where there is [a]no [1]vision, the people [b]are unrestrained,
But [c]happy is he who keeps the law.
19 A slave will not be instructed by words *alone;*
For though he understands, there will be no response.
20 Do you see a man who is [a]hasty in his words?
There is more hope for a fool than for him.
21 He who pampers his slave from childhood
Will in the end find him to be a son.
22 An angry man stirs up strife,
And a hot-tempered man abounds in transgression.
23 A man's [a]pride will bring him low,
But a [b]humble spirit will obtain honor.
24 He who is a partner with a thief hates his own life;
He [a]hears the oath but tells nothing.
25 The [a]fear of man brings a snare,
But he who [b]trusts in the LORD will be exalted.
26 Many seek the ruler's favor,
But [a]justice for man *comes* from the LORD.
27 An [a]unjust man is abominable to the righteous,
And he who is [b]upright in the way is abominable to the wicked.

CHAPTER 30

The Words of Agur

THE words of Agur the son of Jakeh, the [1]oracle.
The man declares to Ithiel, to Ithiel and Ucal:
2 Surely I am more [a]stupid than any man,
And I do not have the understanding of a man.
3 Neither have I learned wisdom,
Nor do I have the knowledge of the Holy One.
4 Who has [a]ascended into heaven and descended?
Who has gathered the [b]wind in His fists?
Who has [c]wrapped the waters in His garment?
Who has [d]established all the ends of the earth?
What is His [e]name or His son's name?
Surely you know!

5 Every [a]word of God is tested;
He is a [b]shield to those who take refuge in Him.
6 [a]Do not add to His words
Lest He reprove you, and you be proved a liar.

7 Two things I asked of Thee,
Do not refuse me before I die:
8 Keep deception and lies far from me,
Give me neither poverty nor riches;
Feed me with the [a]food that is my portion,
9 Lest I be [a]full and deny [b]*Thee* and say, "Who is the LORD?"
Or lest I be in want and steal,
And [c]profane the name of my God.

10 Do not slander a slave to his master,
Lest he [a]curse you and you be found guilty.

11 There is a [1]kind of *man* who [a]curses his father,
And does not bless his mother.
12 There is a kind who is [a]pure in his own eyes,
Yet is not washed from his filthiness.
13 There is a kind—oh how [a]lofty are his eyes!
And his eyelids are raised *in arrogance.*
14 There is a kind of *man* whose [a]teeth are *like* swords,
And his [b]jaw teeth *like* knives,

11 [a]Prov. 19:11
12 [a]1 Kin. 12:14
13 [a]Ezra 9:8; Ps. 13:3
14 [a]Ps. 72:4; Is. 11:4
15 [a]Prov. 13:24; 22:15
16 [1]Or, *become great* [a]Ps. 37:34, 36; 58:10; 91:8; 92:11; Prov. 21:12
17 [a]Prov. 29:15
18 [1]Or, *revelation* [a]1 Sam. 3:1; Ps. 74:9; Amos 8:11, 12 [b]Ex. 32:25 [c]Ps. 1:1, 2; 106:3; 119:2; Prov. 8:32; John 13:17
20 [a]James 1:19
23 [a]2 Sam. 22:28; Prov. 11:2; 16:18; Dan. 4:30, 31; Matt. 23:12; James 4:6 [b]Prov. 15:33; 18:12; 22:4; Is. 66:2; Luke 14:11; 18:14; James 4:10
24 [a]Lev. 5:1
25 [a]Gen. 12:12; 20:2; Luke 12:4; John 12:42, 43 [b]Ps. 91:1-16; Prov. 18:10; 28:25
26 [a]Is. 49:4; 1 Cor. 4:4
27 [a]Ps. 6:8; 139:21, 22; Prov. 12:8 [b]Ps. 69:4; Prov. 29:10; Matt. 10:22; 24:9; John 15:18; 17:14; 1 John 3:13
1 [1]Or, *burden*
2 [a]Ps. 49:10; Prov. 12:1
4 [a]Ps. 68:18; John 3:13; Eph. 4:8 [b]Ex. 15:10; Ps. 135:7 [c]Job 26:8; 38:8, 9 [d]Ps. 24:2; Is. 45:18 [e]Rev. 19:12
5 [a]Ps. 12:6; 18:30 [b]Ps. 3:3; 84:11; Prov. 2:7
6 [a]Deut. 4:2; 12:32; Rev. 22:18
8 [a]Job 23:12; Matt. 6:11
9 [a]Deut. 8:12; 31:20; Neh. 9:25; Hos. 13:6 [b]Josh. 24:27; Job 31:28 [c]Ex. 20:7
10 [a]Eccles. 7:21
11 [1]Or, *generation,* also vs. 12, 13, 14 [a]Ex. 21:17; Prov. 20:20
12 [a]Prov. 16:2; Luke 18:11
13 [a]Prov. 6:17; Is. 2:11; 5:15
14 [a]Ps. 57:4 [b]Job 29:17

To [c]devour the afflicted from the earth,
And the needy from among men.

15 The leech has two daughters, "Give," "Give."
There are three things that will not be satisfied,
Four that will not say, "Enough":
16 [1a]Sheol, and the [b]barren womb,
Earth that is never satisfied with water,
And fire that never says, "Enough."
17 The eye that [a]mocks a father,
And [1]scorns a mother,
The [b]ravens of the valley will pick it out,
And the young [b]eagles will eat it.

18 There are three things which are too wonderful for me,
Four which I do not understand:
19 The way of an [a]eagle in the sky,
The way of a serpent on a rock,
The way of a ship in the middle of the sea,
And the way of a man with a maid.
20 This is the way of an adulterous woman:
She eats and wipes her mouth,
And says, "I have done no wrong."

21 Under three things the earth quakes,
And under four, it cannot bear up:
22 Under a slave when he becomes king,
And a fool when he is satisfied with food,
23 Under an unloved woman when she gets a husband,
And a maidservant when she supplants her mistress.

24 Four things are small on the earth,
But they are exceedingly wise:
25 The ants are not a strong folk,
But they prepare their food in the summer;
26 The [a]badgers are not mighty folk,
Yet they make their houses in the rocks;
27 The locusts have no king,
Yet all of them go out in [a]ranks;
28 The lizard you may grasp with the hands,
Yet it is in kings' palaces.

29 There are three things which are stately in *their* march,
Even four which are stately when they walk:
30 The lion *which* is [a]mighty among beasts
And does not [1b]retreat before any,
31 The [1]strutting cock, the male goat also,
And a king *when his* army is with him.

32 If you have been foolish in exalting yourself
Or if you have plotted *evil,* [a]*put your* hand on your mouth.
33 For the [1]churning of milk produces butter,
And pressing the nose brings forth blood;
So the [1]churning of anger produces strife.

Chapter 31

The Words of Lemuel

THE words of King Lemuel, the
[1]oracle which his mother taught
him.
2 What, O my son?
And what, O [a]son of my womb?
And what, O son of my [b]vows?
3 Do not give your strength to women,
Or your ways to that which [a]destroys kings.
4 It is not for [a]kings, O Lemuel,
It is not for kings to [b]drink wine,
Or for rulers to desire strong drink.
5 Lest they drink and forget what is decreed,
And [a]pervert the [1]rights of all the [2]afflicted.
6 Give strong drink to him who is [a]perishing,
And wine to him [1b]whose life is bitter.
7 Let him drink and forget his poverty,
And remember his trouble no more.
8 [a]Open your mouth for the dumb,
For the [1]rights of all the [2]unfortunate.
9 Open your mouth, [a]judge righteously,
And [1]defend the [b]rights of the afflicted and needy.

Description of a Worthy Woman

10 An [a]excellent wife, who can find?

14 [c]Ps. 14:4; Amos 8:4
16 [1]I.e., The nether world [a]Prov. 27:20 [b]Gen. 30:1
17 [1]Lit., *despises to obey* [a]Gen. 9:22 [b]Deut. 28:26
19 [a]Deut. 28:49; Jer. 48:40; 49:22
26 [a]Lev. 11:5; Ps. 104:18
27 [a]Joel 2:7
30 [1]Lit., *turn back* [a]Judg. 14:18; 2 Sam. 1:23 [b]Mic. 5:8
31 [1]Heb., *girt in the loins*
32 [a]Job 21:5; 40:4; Mic. 7:16
33 [1]Lit., *pressing*
1 [1]Or, *burden*
2 [a]Is. 49:15 [b]1 Sam. 1:11
3 [a]Deut. 17:17; 1 Kin. 11:1; Neh. 13:26
4 [a]Eccles. 10:17 [b]Prov. 20:1; Is. 5:22; Hos. 4:11
5 [1]Lit., *judgment* [2]Lit., *sons of affliction* [a]Ex. 23:6; Deut. 16:19; Prov. 17:15
6 [1]Lit., *bitter of soul* [a]Job 29:13 [b]Job 3:20; Is. 38:15
8 [1]Lit., *judgment* [2]Lit., *sons of passing away* [a]Job 29:12-17; Ps. 82; Prov. 24:11
9 [1]Lit., *judge the afflicted* [a]Lev. 19:15; Deut. 1:16 [b]Is. 1:17; Jer. 22:16
10 [a]Ruth 3:11; Prov. 12:4; 19:14

For her worth is far [b]above jewels.
11 The heart of her husband trusts in her,
And he will have no lack of gain.
12 She does him good and not evil
All the days of her life.
13 She looks for wool and flax,
And works with her [1]hands [2]in delight.
14 She is like [a]merchant ships;
She brings her food from afar.
15 She [a]rises also while it is still night,
And [b]gives food to her household,
And [1]portions to her maidens.
16 She considers a field and buys it;
From [1]her earnings she plants a vineyard.
17 She [a]girds [1]herself with strength,
And makes her arms strong.
18 She senses that her gain is good;
Her lamp does not go out at night.
19 She stretches out her hands to the distaff,
And her [1]hands grasp the spindle.
20 She [1a]extends her hand to the poor;
And she stretches out her hands to the needy.
21 She is not afraid of the snow for her household,
For all her household are [a]clothed with scarlet.
22 She makes [a]coverings for herself;
Her clothing is [b]fine linen and [c]purple.
23 Her husband is known [a]in the gates,
When he sits among the elders of the land.
24 She makes [a]linen garments and sells *them*,
And [1]supplies belts to the [2]tradesmen.
25 Strength and dignity are her clothing,
And she smiles at the [1]future.
26 She opens her mouth in wisdom,
And the [1]teaching of kindness is on her tongue.
27 She looks well to the ways of her household,
And does not eat the bread of idleness.
28 Her children rise up and bless her;
Her husband *also*, and he praises her, *saying:*
29 "Many daughters have done nobly,
But you excel them all."
30 Charm is deceitful and beauty is vain,
But a woman who [1]fears the LORD, she shall be praised.
31 Give her the [1]product of her hands,
And let her works praise her in the gates.

10 [b]Job 28:18; Prov. 8:11
13 [1]Lit., *palms* [2]Or, *willingly*
14 [a]Ezek. 27:25
15 [1]Or, *prescribed tasks* [a]Prov. 20:13; Rom. 12:11 [b]Luke 12:42
16 [1]Lit., *the fruit of her palms*
17 [1]Lit., *her loins* [a]1 Kin. 18:46; 2 Kin. 4:29; Job 38:3
19 [1]Lit., *palms*
20 [1]Lit., *spreads out her palm* [a]Deut. 15:11; Job 31:16-20; Prov. 22:9; Rom. 12:13; Eph. 4:28
21 [a]2 Sam. 1:24
22 [a]Prov. 7:16 [b]Gen. 41:42; Rev. 19:8, 14 [c]Judg. 8:26; Luke 16:19
23 [a]Ruth 4:1, 11
24 [1]Lit., *gives* [2]Lit., *Canaanite* [a]Judg. 14:12
25 [1]Lit., *latter days*
26 [1]Or, *law*
30 [1]Or, *reverences*
31 [1]Lit., *fruit*

THE BOOK OF ECCLESIASTES

The Futility of All Endeavor

THE words of the [a]Preacher, the son of David, king in Jerusalem.
2 "[1a]Vanity of vanities," says the Preacher,
"[1]Vanity of vanities! All is [2]vanity."

3 [a]What advantage does man have in all his work
Which he does under the sun?
4 A generation goes and a generation comes,
But the [a]earth [1]remains forever.
5 Also, [a]the sun rises and the sun sets;
And [1]hastening to its place it rises there *again*.
6 [1a]Blowing toward the south,
Then turning toward the north,
The wind continues [2]swirling along;
And on its circular courses the wind returns.
7 All the rivers [1]flow into the sea,
Yet the sea is not full.
To the place where the rivers [1]flow,
There they [1]flow again.
8 All things are wearisome;
Man is not able to tell *it*.
[a]The eye is not satisfied with seeing,
Nor is the ear filled with hearing.
9 [a]That which has been is that which will be,

1 [a]Eccles. 1:12; 7:27; 12:8-10
2 [1]Or, *Futility of futilities* [2]Or, *futile* [a]Ps. 39:5, 6; 62:9; 144:4; Eccles. 12:8; Rom. 8:20
3 [a]Eccles. 2:11; 3:9; 5:16
4 [1]Lit., *stands* [a]Ps. 104:5; 119:90
5 [1]Lit., *panting* [a]Ps. 19:4-6
6 [1]Lit., *Going* [2]Lit., *turning* [a]Eccles. 11:5
7 [1]Lit., *go*
8 [a]Prov. 27:20; Eccles. 4:8
9 [a]Eccles. 2:12; 3:15; 6:10

And that which has been done
is that which will be done.
So, there is nothing new under
the sun.
10 Is there anything of which one
might say,
"See this, it is new"?
Already it has existed for ages
Which were before us.
11 There is [a]no remembrance of
[1]earlier things;
And also of the [2]later things
which will occur,
There will be for them no remembrance
Among those who will come
[2]later *still*.

The Futility of Wisdom

12 I, the [a]Preacher, have been king
over Israel in Jerusalem.
13 And I [a]set my [1]mind to seek and
[b]explore by wisdom concerning all
that has been done under heaven. *It*
is a [2]grievous [c]task *which* God has
given to the sons of men to be afflicted with.
14 I have seen all the works which
have been done under the sun, and
behold, all is [1a]vanity and striving
after wind.
15 What is [a]crooked cannot be
straightened, and what is lacking
cannot be counted.
16 I said to myself, "Behold, I have
magnified and increased [a]wisdom
more than all who were over Jerusalem before me; and my [1]mind has
observed a [2]wealth of wisdom and
knowledge."
17 And I [a]set my [1]mind to know
wisdom and to [b]know madness and
folly; I realized that this also is striving after wind.
18 Because [a]in much wisdom
there is much grief, and increasing
knowledge *results in* increasing
pain.

Chapter 2

The Futility of Pleasure and Possessions

I SAID [1]to myself, "Come now, I
will test you with [a]pleasure. So enjoy yourself." And behold, it too
was futility.
2 [a]I said of laughter, "It is madness," and of pleasure, "What does
it accomplish?"
3 I explored with my [1]mind *how*
to [a]stimulate my body with wine
while my [1]mind was guiding *me*
wisely, and how to take hold of [b]fol-
ly, until I could see [c]what good there
is for the sons of men to do under
heaven the few years of their lives.
4 I enlarged my works: I [a]built
houses for myself, I planted [b]vine-
yards for myself;
5 I made [a]gardens and [b]parks for
myself, and I planted in them all
kinds of fruit trees;
6 I made [a]ponds of water for myself from which to irrigate a forest
of growing trees.
7 I bought male and female
slaves, and I had [a]homeborn slaves.
Also I possessed flocks and [b]herds
larger than all who preceded me in
Jerusalem.
8 Also, I collected for myself silver and [a]gold, and the treasure of
[b]kings and provinces. I provided for
myself [c]male and female singers
and the pleasures of men—many
concubines.
9 Then I became [a]great and increased more than all who preceded
me in Jerusalem. My wisdom also
stood by me.
10 And [a]all that my eyes desired I
did not refuse them. I did not withhold my heart from any pleasure,
for my heart was pleased because of
all my labor and this was my [b]re-
ward for all my labor.
11 Thus I considered all my activities which my hands had done and
the labor which I had [1]exerted, and
behold all was [2a]vanity and striving
after wind and there was [b]no profit
under the sun.

Wisdom Excels Folly

12 So I turned to [a]consider wisdom, madness and folly, for what
will the man *do* who will come after
the king *except* [b]what has already
been done?
13 And I saw that [a]wisdom excels
folly as light excels darkness.
14 The wise man's eyes are in his
head, but the [a]fool walks in darkness. And yet I know that [b]one fate
befalls them both.
15 Then I said [1]to myself, "[a]As is
the fate of the fool, it will also befall
me. [b]Why then have I been extremely wise?" So [2]I said to myself,
"This too is vanity."
16 For there is [a]no lasting remembrance of the wise man *as* with the
fool, inasmuch as *in* the coming
days all will be forgotten. And [b]how
the wise man and the fool alike die!
17 So I [a]hated life, for the work
which had been done under the sun
was grievous to me; because everything is futility and striving after
wind.

---

11 [1]Lit., *first* or *former* [2]Lit., *latter* or *after* [a]Eccles. 2:16; 9:5
12 [a]Eccles. 1:12; 7:27; 12:8-10
13 [1]Lit., *heart* [2]Lit., *evil* [a]Eccles. 1:17 [b]Eccles. 3:10, 11; 7:25; 8:17 [c]Eccles. 2:23, 26; 3:10
14 [1]Or, *futility* [a]Eccles. 2:11, 17; 4:4; 6:9
15 [a]Eccles. 7:13
16 [1]Lit., *heart* [2]Lit., *abundance* [a]1 Kin. 3:12; 4:30; 10:23; Eccles. 2:9
17 [1]Lit., *heart* [a]Eccles. 1:13 [b]Eccles. 2:12; 7:25
18 [a]Eccles. 2:23; 12:12
1 [1]Lit., *in my heart* [a]Eccles. 7:4; 8:15
2 [a]Prov. 14:13; Eccles. 7:3, 6
3 [1]Lit., *heart* [a]Judg. 9:13; Ps. 104:15; Eccles. 10:19 [b]Eccles. 7:25 [c]Eccles. 1:24; 3:12, 13; 5:18; 6:12; 8:15; 12:13
4 [a]1 Kin. 7:1-12 [b]Song of Sol. 8:10, 11
5 [a]Song of Sol. 4:16; 5:1 [b]Neh. 2:8
6 [a]Neh. 2:14; 3:15, 16
7 [a]Gen. 14:14; 15:3 [b]1 Kin. 4:23
8 [a]1 Kin. 9:28; 10:10, 14, 21 [b]1 Kin. 20:14; Lam. 1:1 [c]2 Sam. 19:35
9 [a]1 Chr. 29:25; Eccles. 1:16
10 [a]Eccles. 6:2 [b]Eccles. 3:22; 5:18; 9:9
11 [1]Lit., *labored to do* [2]Or, *futility*, and so throughout the chap. [a]Eccles. 1:14; 2:22, 23 [b]Eccles. 1:3; 3:9; 5:16
12 [a]Eccles. 1:17 [b]Eccles. 1:9, 10
13 [a]Eccles. 7:11, 12, 19; 9:18; 10:10
14 [a]Prov. 17:24; 1 John 2:11 [b]Ps. 49:10; Eccles. 3:19; 6:6; 7:2; 9:2
15 [1]Lit., *in my heart* [2]Lit., *I spoke in heart* [a]Eccles. 2:16 [b]Eccles. 6:8, 11
16 [a]Eccles. 1:11; 4:16; 9:5 [b]Eccles. 2:14
17 [a]Eccles. 4:2

The Futility of Labor

18 Thus I hated [a]all the fruit of my
labor for which I had labored under
the sun, for I must [b]leave it to the
man who will come after me.
19 And who knows whether he
will be a wise man or a fool? Yet he
will have control over all the fruit of
my labor for which I have labored
by acting wisely under the sun. This
too is vanity.
20 Therefore I completely despaired of all the fruit of my labor
for which I had labored under the
sun.
21 When there is a man who has
labored with wisdom, knowledge
and [a]skill, then he [b]gives his [1]legacy
to one who has not labored with
them. This too is vanity and a great
evil.
22 For what does a man get in [a]all
his labor and in his striving with
which he labors under the sun?
23 Because all his days his task is
painful and [a]grievous; even at night
his [1]mind [b]does not rest. This too is
vanity.
24 There is [a]nothing better for a
man *than* to eat and drink and tell
himself that his labor is good. This
also I have seen, that it is [b]from the
hand of God.
25 For who can eat and who can
have enjoyment without [1]Him?
26 For to a person who is good in
His sight [a]He has given wisdom and
knowledge and joy, while [b]to the
sinner He has given the task of gathering and collecting so that he may
[c]give to one who is good in God's
sight. This too is [d]vanity and striving after wind.

Chapter 3

A Time for Everything

THERE is an appointed time for
everything. And there is a [a]time for
every [1]event under heaven—

2 A time to give birth, and a [a]time to die;
A time to plant, and a time to uproot what is planted.
3 A time to kill, and a time to heal;
A time to tear down, and a time to build up.
4 A time to [a]weep, and a time to [b]laugh;
A time to mourn, and a time to [c]dance.
5 A time to throw stones, and a time to gather stones;
A time to embrace, and a time to shun embracing.
6 A time to search, and a time to give up as lost;
A time to keep, and a time to throw away.
7 A time to tear apart, and a time to sew together;
A time to [a]be silent, and a time to speak.
8 A time to love, and a time to [a]hate;
A time for war, and a time for peace.

9 [a]What profit is there to the
worker from that in which he toils?
10 I have seen the [a]task which God
has given the sons of men with
which to occupy themselves.

God Set Eternity in the Heart of Man

11 He has [a]made everything [1]ap-
propriate in its time. He has also set
eternity in their heart, [2]yet so that
man [b]will not find out the work
which God has done from the beginning even to the end.
12 I know that there is [a]nothing
better for them than to rejoice and
to do good in one's lifetime;
13 moreover, that every man who
eats and drinks sees good in all his
labor—it is the [a]gift of God.
14 I know that everything God
does will remain forever; there is
nothing to add to it and there is
nothing to take from it, for God has
so worked that men should [1a]fear
Him.
15 That [a]which is has been already, and that which will be has
already been, for God seeks what
has passed by.
16 Furthermore, I have seen under
the sun *that* in the place of justice
there is [a]wickedness, and in the
place of righteousness there is wickedness.
17 I said [1]to myself, "[a]God will
judge both the righteous man and
the wicked man," for a [b]time for every [2]matter and for every deed is
there.
18 I said [1]to myself concerning the
sons of men, "God has surely tested
them in order for them to see that
they are but [a]beasts."
19 [a]For the fate of the sons of men
and the fate of beasts [1]is the same.
As one dies so dies the other; indeed, they all have the same breath
and there is no advantage for man
over beast, for all is [2]vanity.
20 All go to the same place. All
came from the [a]dust and all return
to the dust.

18 [a]Eccles. 1:3; 2:11 [b]Ps. 39:6; 49:10
21 [1]Lit., *share* [a]Eccles. 4:4 [b]Eccles. 2:18
22 [a]Eccles. 1:3; 2:11
23 [1]Lit., *heart* [a]Job 5:7; 14:1; Eccles. 1:18; 5:17 [b]Ps. 127:2
24 [a]Eccles. 2:3; 3:12, 13, 22; 5:18; 6:12; 8:15; 9:7; 1 Tim. 6:17 [b]Eccles. 3:13
25 [1]So Gk.; Heb., *me*
26 [a]Job 32:8; Prov. 2:6 [b]Job 15:20 [c]Job 27:16, 17; Prov. 13:22 [d]Eccles. 1:14
1 [1]Lit., *delight* [a]Eccles. 3:17; 8:6
2 [a]Job 14:5; Heb. 9:27
4 [a]Rom. 12:15 [b]Ps. 126:2 [c]Ex. 15:20
7 [a]Amos 5:13
8 [a]Ps. 101:3; Prov. 13:5
9 [a]Eccles. 1:3; 2:11; 5:16
10 [a]Eccles. 1:13; 2:26
11 [1]Lit., *beautiful* [2]Or, *without which man* [a]Gen. 1:31 [b]Job 5:9; Eccles. 7:23; 8:17; Rom. 11:33
12 [a]Eccles. 2:24
13 [a]Eccles. 2:24; 5:19
14 [1]Or, *be in awe before Him* [a]Eccles. 5:7; 7:18; 8:12, 13; 12:13
15 [a]Eccles. 1:9; 6:10
16 [a]Eccles. 4:1; 5:8; 8:9
17 [1]Lit., *in my heart* [2]Or, *delight* [a]Gen. 18:25; Ps. 96:13; 98:9; Eccles. 11:9; Matt. 16:27; Rom. 2:6-10; 2 Thess. 1:6-9 [b]Eccles. 3:1; 8:6
18 [1]Lit., *in my heart* [a]Ps. 49:12, 20; 73:22
19 [1]Lit., *and they have one fate* [2]Or, *futility* [a]Eccles. 9:12
20 [a]Gen. 3:19; Ps. 103:14; Eccles. 12:7

21 Who knows that the [a]breath of man ascends upward and the breath of the beast descends downward to the earth?

22 And I have seen that [a]nothing is better than that man should be happy in his activities, for that is his lot. For who will bring him to see [b]what will occur after him?

CHAPTER 4

The Evils of Oppression

THEN I looked again at all the acts of [a]oppression which were being done under the sun. And behold *I saw* the tears of the oppressed and *that* they had [b]no one to comfort *them;* and on the side of their oppressors was power, but they had no one to comfort *them.*

2 So [a]I congratulated the dead who are already dead more than the living who are still living.

3 But [a]better *off* than both of them is the one who has never existed, who has never seen the evil activity that is done under the sun.

4 And I have seen that every labor and every [a]skill which is done is *the result of* rivalry between a man and his neighbor. This too is [1b]vanity and striving after wind.

5 The fool [a]folds his hands and [b]consumes his own flesh.

6 One hand full of rest is [a]better than two fists full of labor and striving after wind.

7 Then I looked again at vanity under the sun.

8 There was a certain man without a [1]dependent, having neither a son nor a brother, yet there was no end to all his labor. Indeed, [a]his eyes were not satisfied with riches *and he never asked,* "And [b]for whom am I laboring and depriving myself of pleasure?" This too is vanity and it is a [c]grievous task.

9 Two are better than one because they have a good return for their labor.

10 For if [1]either of them falls, the one will lift up his companion. But woe to the one who falls when there is not [2]another to lift him up.

11 Furthermore, if two lie down together they [1]keep warm, but [a]how can one be warm *alone?*

12 And if [1]one can overpower him who is alone, two can resist him. A cord of three *strands* is not quickly torn apart.

13 A [a]poor, yet wise lad is better than an old and foolish king who no longer knows *how* to receive [1]instruction.

14 For he has come [a]out of prison to become king, even though he was born poor in his kingdom.

15 I have seen all the living under the sun throng to the side of the second lad who [1]replaces him.

16 There is no end to all the people, to all who were before them, and even the ones who will come later will not be happy with him, for this too is [a]vanity and striving after wind.

CHAPTER 5

Your Attitude Toward God

[1][a]GUARD your steps as you go to the house of God, and draw near to listen rather than to offer the [b]sacrifice of fools; for they do not know they are doing evil.

2 [1]Do not be [a]hasty [2]in word or [3]impulsive in thought to bring up a matter in the presence of God. For God is in heaven and you are on the earth; therefore let your [b]words be few.

3 For the dream comes through much [1]effort, and the voice of a [a]fool through many words.

4 When you [a]make a vow to God, do not be late in paying it, for He takes no delight in fools. [b]Pay what you vow!

5 It is [a]better that you should not vow than that you should vow and not pay.

6 Do not let your [1]speech cause [2]you to sin and do not say in the presence of the messenger *of God* that it was a [a]mistake. Why should God be angry on account of your voice and destroy the work of your hands?

7 For in many dreams and in many words there is [1]emptiness. Rather, [2]fear [a]God.

8 If you see [a]oppression of the poor and [b]denial of justice and righteousness in the province, do not be [c]shocked at the [1]sight, for one [2]official watches over another [2]official, and there are [d]higher [3]officials over them.

9 After all, a king who cultivates the field is an advantage to the land.

The Folly of Riches

10 [a]He who loves money will not be satisfied with money, nor he who loves abundance *with its* income. This too is [1]vanity.

11 [a]When good things increase, those who consume them increase.

---

21 [a]Eccles. 12:7
22 [a]Eccles. 2:24 [b]Eccles. 2:18; 6:12; 8:7; 10:14
1 [a]Job 35:9; Ps. 12:5; Eccles. 3:16; 5:8; Is. 5:7 [b]Lam. 1:9
2 [a]Job 3:11-26; Eccles. 2:17
3 [a]Eccles. 6:3
4 [1]Or, *futility,* and so throughout the chap. [a]Eccles. 2:21 [b]Eccles. 1:14
5 [a]Prov. 6:10; 24:33 [b]Is. 9:20
6 [a]Prov. 15:16, 17; 16:8
8 [1]Lit., *second* [a]Prov. 27:20; Eccles. 1:8; 5:10 [b]Eccles. 2:21 [c]Eccles. 1:13
10 [1]Lit., *they fall* [2]Lit., *a second*
11 [1]Lit., *have warmth* [a]1 Kin. 1:1
12 [1]Lit., *he*
13 [1]Or, *warning* [a]Eccles. 7:19; 9:15
14 [a]Gen. 41:14, 41-43
15 [1]Lit., *stands in his stead*
16 [a]Eccles. 1:14
1 [1]Ch. 4:17 in Heb. [a]Ex. 3:5; 30:18-20; Is. 1:12 [b]1 Sam. 15:22; Prov. 15:8; 21:27
2 [1]Ch. 5:1 in Heb. [2]Lit., *with your mouth* [3]Lit., *hurry your heart* [a]Prov. 20:25 [b]Prov. 10:19; Matt. 6:7
3 [1]Lit., *task* [a]Job 11:2; Eccles. 10:14
4 [a]Num. 30:2; Ps. 50:14; 76:11 [b]Ps. 66:13, 14
5 [a]Prov. 20:25; Acts 5:4
6 [1]Lit., *mouth* [2]Lit., *your body* [a]Lev. 4:2, 22; Num. 15:25
7 [1]Lit., *vanity* [2]Or, *revere* [a]Eccles. 3:14; 7:18; 8:12, 13; 12:13
8 [1]Lit., *delight* [2]Lit., *high one* [3]Lit., *ones* [a]Eccles. 4:1 [b]Ezek. 18:18 [c]1 Pet. 4:12 [d]Ex. 2:25; Ps. 12:5
10 [1]Or, *futility* [a]Eccles. 2:10, 11
11 [a]Eccles. 2:9

So what is the advantage to their owners except to [1]look on?

12 The sleep of the working man is [a]pleasant, whether he eats little or much. But the [1]full stomach of the rich man does not allow him to sleep.

13 There is a grievous evil *which* I have seen under the sun: [a]riches being [1]hoarded by their owner to his hurt.

14 When those riches were lost through a [1]bad investment and he had fathered a son, then there was nothing [2]to support him.

15 [a]As he had come naked from his mother's womb, so will he return as he came. He will take [b]nothing from the fruit of his labor that he can carry in his hand.

16 And this also is a grievous evil—exactly as a man [1]is born, thus will he [2]die. So, [a]what is the advantage to him who [b]toils for the wind?

17 Throughout his life *he* also eats in darkness with [a]great vexation, sickness and anger.

18 Here is what I have seen to be [a]good and [1]fitting: to eat, to drink and [2]enjoy oneself in all one's labor in which he toils under the sun *during* the few [3]years of his life which God has given him, for this is his [4b]reward.

19 Furthermore, as for every man to whom [a]God has given riches and wealth, He has also [b]empowered him to eat from them and to receive his [1]reward and rejoice in his labor; this is the [c]gift of God.

20 For he will not often [1]consider the [2]years of his life, because God keeps [3]him occupied with the gladness of his heart.

Chapter 6

The Futility of Life

THERE is an [a]evil which I have seen under the sun and it is prevalent [1]among men—

2 a man to whom God has [a]given riches and wealth and honor so that his soul [b]lacks nothing of all that he desires, but God has not empowered him to eat from them, for a foreigner [1]enjoys them. This is [2]vanity and a sore affliction.

3 If a man fathers a hundred *children* and lives many years, however many [1]they be, but his soul is not satisfied with good things, and he does not even have a *proper* [a]burial, *then* I say, "Better [b]the miscarriage than he,

4 for it comes in futility and goes into obscurity; and its name is covered in obscurity.

5 "It never sees the sun and it never knows *anything;* [1]it is better off than he.

6 "Even if the *other* man lives a thousand years twice and does not [1]enjoy good things—[a]do not all go to one place?"

7 [a]All a man's labor is for his mouth and yet the [1]appetite is not [2]satisfied.

8 For [a]what advantage does the wise man have over the fool? What *advantage* does the poor man have, knowing *how* to walk before the living?

9 What the eyes [a]see is better than what the soul [1]desires. This too is [b]futility and a striving after wind.

10 Whatever [a]exists has already been named, and it is known what man is; for he [b]cannot dispute with him who is stronger than he is.

11 For there are many words which increase futility. What *then* is the advantage to a man?

12 For who knows what is good for a man during *his* lifetime, *during* the few [1]years of his futile life? He will [2]spend them like a shadow. For who can tell a man [a]what will be after him under the sun?

Chapter 7

Wisdom and Folly Contrasted

A [a]GOOD name is better than a
good ointment,
And the [b]day of *one's* death is
better than the day of one's
birth.

2 It is better to go to a house of
mourning
Than to go to a house of feasting,
Because [1]that is the [a]end of every man,
And the living [2b]takes *it* to
[3]heart.

3 [a]Sorrow is better than laughter,
For [b]when a face is sad a heart
may be happy.

4 The [1]mind of the wise is in the
house of mourning,
While the [1]mind of fools is in
the house of pleasure.

5 It is better to [a]listen to the rebuke of a wise man
Than for one to listen to the
song of fools.

6 For as the [1]crackling of [a]thorn
bushes under a pot,
So is the [b]laughter of the fool,
And this too is futility.

11 [1]Lit., *see with their eyes*
12 [1]Lit., *satiety* [a]Prov. 3:24
13 [1]Lit., *guarded* [a]Eccles. 6:2
14 [1]Lit., *evil task* [2]Lit., *in his hand*
15 [a]Job 1:21 [b]Ps. 49:17; 1 Tim. 6:7
16 [1]Lit., *comes* [2]Lit., *go* [a]Eccles. 1:3; 2:11; 3:9 [b]Prov. 11:29
17 [a]Eccles. 2:23
18 [1]Lit., *beautiful* [2]Lit., *see good* [3]Or, *days* [4]Or, *share* [a]Eccles. 2:24 [b]Eccles. 2:10
19 [1]Or, *share* [a]2 Chr. 1:12; Eccles. 6:2 [b]Eccles. 6:2 [c]Eccles. 3:13
20 [1]Lit., *remember* [2]Or, *days* [3]So with Gk.
1 [1]Lit., *upon* [a]Eccles. 5:13
2 [1]Lit., *eats from them* [2]Or, *futility* [a]1 Kin. 3:13 [b]Ps. 17:14; 73:7
3 [1]Lit., *the days of his years* [a]Is. 14:20; Jer. 8:2; 22:19 [b]Job 3:16; Eccles. 4:3
5 [1]Lit., *more rest has this one than that*
6 [1]Lit., *see* [a]Eccles. 2:14
7 [1]Lit., *soul* [2]Lit., *filled* [a]Prov. 16:26
8 [a]Eccles. 2:15
9 [1]Lit., *goes after* [a]Eccles. 11:9 [b]Eccles. 1:14
10 [a]Eccles. 1:9; 3:15 [b]Job 9:32; 40:2; Prov. 21:30; Is. 45:9
12 [1]Lit., *days* [2]Lit., *do* [a]Eccles. 3:22
1 [a]Prov. 22:1 [b]Eccles. 4:2; 7:8
2 [1]I.e., death [2]Lit., *gives* [3]Lit., *his heart* [a]Eccles. 2:16; 3:19, 20; 6:6; 9:2, 3 [b]Ps. 90:12
3 [a]Eccles. 2:2 [b]2 Cor. 7:10
4 [1]Lit., *heart*
5 [a]Ps. 141:5; Prov. 6:23; 13:18; 15:31, 32; 25:12; Eccles. 9:17
6 [1]Lit., *voice* [a]Ps. 58:9; 118:12 [b]Eccles. 2:2

7 For [a]oppression makes a wise man mad,
And a [b]bribe [1]corrupts the heart.
8 The [a]end of a matter is better than its beginning;
[b]Patience of spirit is better than haughtiness of spirit.
9 Do not be [a]eager in your heart to be angry,
For anger resides in the bosom of fools.
10 Do not say, "Why is it that the former days were better than these?"
For it is not from wisdom that you ask about this.
11 Wisdom along with an inheritance is good
And an [a]advantage to those who see the sun.
12 For [a]wisdom is protection *just as* money is protection.
But the advantage of knowledge is that [b]wisdom preserves the lives of its possessors.
13 Consider the [a]work of God,
For who is [b]able to straighten what He has bent?
14 [a]In the day of prosperity be happy,
But [b]in the day of adversity consider—
God has made the one as well as the other
So that man may [c]not discover anything *that will be* after him.

15 I have seen everything during
my [a]lifetime of futility; there is [b]a
righteous man who perishes in his
righteousness, and there is [c]a
wicked man who prolongs *his life* in
his wickedness.
16 Do not be excessively righteous, and do not [a]be overly wise.
Why should you ruin yourself?
17 Do not be excessively wicked,
and do not be a fool. Why should
you [a]die before your time?
18 It is good that you grasp [a]one
thing, and also not [b]let go of the other; for the one who [c]fears God
comes forth with both of them.
19 [a]Wisdom strengthens a wise
man more than ten rulers who are in
a city.
20 Indeed, [a]there is not a righteous
man on earth who *continually* does
good and who never sins.
21 Also, do not take seriously all
words which are spoken, lest you
hear your servant [a]cursing you.
22 For [1]you also have realized that
you likewise have many times
cursed others.

7 [1]Lit., *destroys* [a]Eccles. 4:1; 5:8 [b]Ex. 23:8; Deut. 16:19; Prov. 17:8, 23
8 [a]Eccles. 7:1 [b]Prov. 14:29; 16:32; Gal. 5:22; Eph. 4:2
9 [a]Prov. 14:17; James 1:19
11 [a]Prov. 8:10, 11
12 [a]Eccles. 7:19; 9:18 [b]Prov. 3:18; 8:35
13 [a]Eccles. 3:11; 8:17 [b]Eccles. 1:15
14 [a]Deut. 26:11; Eccles 3:22; 9:7; 11:9 [b]Deut. 8:5 [c]Eccles. 3:22
15 [a]Eccles. 6:12; 9:9 [b]Eccles. 8:14 [c]Eccles. 8:12, 13
16 [a]Rom. 12:3
17 [a]Job 22:16; Ps. 55:23; Prov. 10:27
18 [a]Eccles. 7:16 [b]Eccles. 7:17 [c]Eccles. 3:14; 5:7; 8:12, 13; 12:13
19 [a]Eccles. 7:12; 9:13-18
20 [a]1 Kin. 8:46; 2 Chr. 6:36; Ps. 143:2; Prov. 20:9; Rom. 3:23
21 [a]Prov. 30:1
22 [1]Lit., *your heart knows also*
23 [a]Eccles. 3:11; 8:17
24 [1]Lit., *deep* [a]Rom. 11:33 [b]Job 11:7; 37:23
25 [1]Lit., *turned about* [2]Lit., *heart* [a]Eccles. 1:17; 10:13
26 [a]Prov. 5:4 [b]Prov. 7:23 [c]Prov. 6:23, 24 [d]Prov. 22:14
28 [a]1 Kin. 11:3
29 [a]Gen. 1:27
1 [1]Lit., *his face* [a]Ex. 34:29, 30 [b]Deut. 28:50
2 [a]Ex. 22:11; 2 Sam. 21:7; Ezek. 17:18
3 [1]Lit., *to go out from his presence* [a]Eccles. 10:4
4 [a]Job 9:12; Dan. 4:35
5 [1]Lit., *evil thing* [a]Eccles. 12:13 [b]Prov. 12:21
6 [a]Eccles. 3:1, 17
7 [a]Eccles. 3:22; 6:12; 7:14; 9:12
8 [1]Lit., *its possessors* [a]Ps. 49:7-9 [b]Deut. 20:5-8 [c]Eccles. 8:13
9 [1]Lit., *heart*

23 I tested all this with wisdom,
and I said, "I will be wise," [a]but it
was far from me.
24 What has been is remote and
[a]exceedingly [1]mysterious. [b]Who
can discover it?
25 I [1]directed my [2]mind to know,
to investigate, and to seek wisdom
and an explanation, and to know the
evil of folly and the [a]foolishness of
madness.
26 And I discovered more [a]bitter
than death the woman whose heart
is [b]snares and nets, whose hands are
chains. [c]One who is pleasing to God
will escape from her, but [d]the sinner
will be captured by her.
27 "Behold, I have discovered this,"
says the Preacher, "*adding* one
thing to another to find an explanation,
28 which I am still seeking but
have not found. I have found one
man among a thousand, but I have
not found a [a]woman among all
these.
29 "Behold, I have found only this,
that [a]God made men upright, but
they have sought out many devices."

Chapter 8

Obey Rulers

WHO is like the wise man and
who knows the interpretation of a
matter? A man's wisdom illumines
[1a]him and causes his [b]stern face to
beam.
2 I say, "Keep the command of
the king because of the [a]oath before
God.
3 "Do not be in a hurry [1a]to leave
him. Do not join in an evil matter,
for he will do whatever he pleases."
4 Since the word of the king is
authoritative, [a]who will say to him,
"What are you doing?"
5 He who [a]keeps a *royal* command [b]experiences no [1]trouble, for
a wise heart knows the proper time
and procedure.
6 For there is a proper time and
procedure [a]for every delight, when
a man's trouble is heavy upon him.
7 If no one [a]knows what will happen, who can tell him when it will
happen?
8 [a]No man has authority to restrain the wind with the wind, or authority over the day of death; and
there is no [b]discharge in the time of
war, and evil [c]will not deliver [1]those
who practice it.
9 All this I have seen and applied
my [1]mind to every deed that has

been done under the sun wherein a
man has exercised [a]authority over
another man to his hurt.
10 So then, I have seen the wicked
buried, those who used to go in and
out from the holy place, and they
are [a]*soon* forgotten in the city where
they did thus. This too is futility.
11 Because the [a]sentence against
an evil deed is not executed quickly,
therefore [b]the hearts of the sons of
men among them are given fully to
do evil.
12 Although a sinner does evil a
hundred *times* and may [a]lengthen
his *life,* still I know that it will be
[b]well for those who fear God, who
fear [1]Him openly.
13 But it will [a]not be well for the
evil man and he will not lengthen his
days like a [b]shadow, because he
does not fear God.
14 There is futility which is done
on the earth, that is, there are [a]right-
eous men to whom it [1]happens according to the deeds of the wicked.
On the other hand, there are [b]evil
men to whom it [1]happens according
to the deeds of the righteous. I say
that this too is futility.
15 So I commended pleasure, for
there is nothing good for [a]a man under the sun except to eat and to
drink and to be merry, and this will
stand by him in his [1]toils *throughout*
the days of his life which God has
given him under the sun.
16 When I [a]gave my heart to know
wisdom and to see the task which
has been done on the earth (even
though one should [1b]never sleep day
or night),
17 and I saw every work of God, *I
concluded* that [a]man cannot discover the work which has been done
under the sun. Even though man
should seek laboriously, he will not
discover; and [b]though the wise man
should say, "I know," he cannot discover.

Chapter 9

Men Are in the Hand of God

FOR I have taken all this to my
heart and explain [1]it that righteous
men, wise men, and their deeds are
[a]in the hand of God. [b]Man does not
know whether *it will be* [c]love or hatred; anything [2]awaits him.
2 [a]It is the same for all. There is
[b]one fate for the righteous and for
the wicked; for the good, for the
clean, and for the unclean; for the
man who offers a sacrifice and for
the one who does not sacrifice. As

9 [a]Eccles. 4:1; 5:8; 7:7
10 [a]Eccles. 1:11; 2:16; 4:16; 9:5, 15
11 [a]Ex. 34:6; Ps. 86:15; Rom. 2:4; 2 Pet. 3:9 [b]Eccles. 9:3
12 [1]Lit., *before Him* [a]Eccles. 7:15; Is. 65:20 [b]Deut. 4:40; 12:25; Ps. 37:11; Prov. 1:33; Is. 3:10
13 [a]Eccles. 8:8; Is. 3:11 [b]Job 14:2; Eccles. 6:12
14 [1]Lit., *strikes* [a]Ps. 73:14; Eccles. 7:15 [b]Job 21:7; Ps. 73:3, 12; Jer. 12:1; Mal. 3:15
15 [1]Lit., *labor* [a]Eccles. 2:24; 3:12, 13; 5:18; 9:7
16 [1]Lit., *see no sleep in his eyes* [a]Eccles. 1:13, 14 [b]Eccles. 2:23
17 [a]Eccles. 3:11 [b]Ps. 73:16; Eccles. 7:23; Rom. 11:33
1 [1]Lit., *all this* [2]Lit., *is before them* [a]Deut. 33:3; Job 12:10, Ps. 119:109 [b]Eccles. 10:14 [c]Eccles. 9:6
2 [1]Lit., *fears an oath* [a]Job 9.22, Eccles. 9:11 [b]Eccles. 2:14; 3:19; 6:6; 7:2
3 [a]Eccles. 9:2 [b]Eccles. 8:11 [c]Eccles. 1:17
5 [a]Job 14:21 [b]Ps. 88:12; Eccles. 1:11; 2:16; 8:10; Is. 26:14
6 [a]Eccles. 2:10; 3:22
7 [a]Eccles. 2:24
8 [a]Rev. 3:4 [b]Ps. 23:5
9 [1]Lit., *life of vanity* [a]Eccles. 6:12; 7:15
10 [a]Eccles. 11:6; Rom. 12:11; Col. 3:23 [b]Eccles. 9:5 [c]Gen. 37:35; Job 21:13; Is. 38:10
11 [a]Amos 2:14, 15 [b]2 Chr. 20:15; Ps. 76:5; Is. 40:29; Zech. 4:6 [c]Deut. 8:17, 18 [d]1 Sam. 6:9
12 [a]Eccles. 8:7 [b]Prov. 7:23 [c]Prov. 29:6; Is. 24:18; Hos. 9:8 [d]Luke 21:34, 35
13 [1]Lit., *great it was to me*
15 [1]Or, *might have delivered* [a]Eccles. 4:13

the good man is, so is the sinner; as
the swearer is, so is the one who [1]is
afraid to swear.
3 This is an evil in all that is done
under the sun, that there is [a]one fate
for all men. Furthermore, [b]the
hearts of the sons of men are full of
evil, and [c]insanity is in their hearts
throughout their lives. Afterwards
they go to the dead.
4 For whoever is joined with the
living, there is hope; surely a live
dog is better than a dead lion.
5 For the living know they will
die; but the dead do not [a]know anything, nor have they any longer a
reward, for their [b]memory is forgotten.
6 Indeed their love, their hate,
and their zeal have already perished, and they will no longer have a
[a]share in all that is done under the
sun.
7 Go *then,* [a]eat your bread in happiness, and drink your wine with a
cheerful heart; for God has already
approved your works.
8 Let your [a]clothes be white all
the time, and let not oil be lacking
on your [b]head.
9 Enjoy life with the woman
whom you love all the days of your
[1]fleeting [a]life which He has given to
you under the sun; for this is your
reward in life, and in your toil in
which you have labored under the
sun.

Whatever Your Hand Finds to Do

10 Whatever your hand finds to
do, verily, [a]do *it* with all your might;
for there is no [b]activity or planning
or wisdom in [c]Sheol where you are
going.
11 I again saw under the sun that
the [a]race is not to the swift, and the
[b]battle is not to the warriors, and
neither is bread to the wise, nor
[c]wealth to the discerning, nor favor
to men of ability; for time and
[d]chance overtake them all.
12 Moreover, man does not [a]know
his time: like fish caught in a treacherous net, and [b]birds trapped in a
snare, so the sons of men are [c]en-
snared at an evil time when it [d]sud-
denly falls on them.
13 Also this I came to see as wisdom under the sun, and it [1]im-
pressed me.
14 There was a small city with few
men in it and a great king came to it,
surrounded it, and constructed
large siegeworks against it.
15 But there was found in it a
[a]poor wise man and he [1]delivered

the city [b]by his wisdom. Yet [c]no one
remembered that poor man.
16 So I said, "[a]Wisdom is better
than strength." But the wisdom of
the poor man is despised and his
words are not heeded.
17 The [a]words of the wise heard in
quietness are *better* than the shouting of a ruler among fools.
18 [a]Wisdom is better than weapons of war, but [b]one sinner destroys
much good.

CHAPTER 10

A Little Foolishness

DEAD flies make a [a]perfumer's oil
stink, so a little foolishness is
weightier than wisdom *and* honor.
2 A wise man's heart *directs him*
toward the right, but the foolish
man's heart *directs him* toward the
left.
3 Even when the fool walks along
the road his sense is lacking, and he
[a]demonstrates to everyone *that* he
is a fool.
4 If the ruler's temper rises
against you, [a]do not abandon your
position, because [b]composure allays great offenses.
5 There is an evil I have seen under the sun, like an [a]error which
goes forth from the ruler—
6 [a]folly is set in many exalted
places while rich men sit in humble
places.
7 I have seen [a]slaves *riding* [b]on
horses and princes walking like
slaves on the land.
8 [a]He who digs a pit may fall into
it, and a [b]serpent may bite him who
breaks through a wall.
9 He who quarries stones may be
hurt by them, and he who splits logs
may be endangered by them.
10 If the [1]axe is dull and he does
not sharpen *its* edge, then he must
exert more strength. Wisdom has
the advantage of giving success.
11 If the serpent bites [a]before
[1]being charmed, there is no profit
for the charmer.
12 [a]Words from the mouth of a
wise man are gracious, while the
lips of a [b]fool consume him;
13 the beginning of his talking is
folly, and the end of it is wicked
[a]madness.
14 Yet the [a]fool multiplies words.
No man knows what will happen,
and who can tell him [b]what will
come after him?
15 The toil of a [1]fool *so* wearies
him that he does not *even* know how
to go to a city.
16 Woe to you, O land, whose
[a]king is a lad and whose princes
[1]feast in the morning.
17 Blessed are you, O land, whose
king is of nobility and whose princes
eat at the appropriate time—for
strength, and not for [a]drunkenness.
18 Through [a]indolence the rafters
sag, and through slackness the
house leaks.
19 *Men* prepare a meal for enjoyment, and [a]wine makes life merry,
and [b]money [1]is the answer to everything.
20 Furthermore, [a]in your bed-
chamber do not [b]curse a king, and in
your sleeping rooms do not curse a
rich man, for a bird of the heavens
will carry the sound, and the winged
creature will make the matter
known.

CHAPTER 11

Cast Your Bread on the Waters

[a]CAST your bread on the surface of
the waters, for you [b]will find it after
many days.
2 [a]Divide your portion to seven,
or even to eight, for you do not
know what [b]misfortune may occur
on the earth.
3 If the clouds are full, they pour
out rain upon the earth; and
whether a tree falls toward the
south or toward the north, wherever
the tree falls, there it [1]lies.
4 He who watches the wind will
not sow and he who looks at the
clouds will not reap.
5 Just as you do not [a]know [1]the
path of the wind and [b]how bones *are*
formed in the womb of the [2]preg-
nant woman, so you do not [c]know
the activity of God who makes all
things.
6 Sow your seed [a]in the morning,
and do not be idle in the evening, for
you do not know whether [1]morning
or evening sowing will succeed, or
whether both of them alike will be
good.
7 The light is pleasant, and *it is*
good for the eyes to [a]see the sun.
8 Indeed, if a man should live
many years, let him [a]rejoice in them
all, and let him remember the [b]days
of darkness, for they shall be many.
Everything that is to come *will be*
futility.
9 [a]Rejoice, young man, during
your childhood, and let your heart
be pleasant during the days of
young manhood. And [b]follow the
impulses of your heart and the de-

15 [b]2 Sam. 20:22 [c]Eccles. 2:16; 8:10
16 [a]Eccles. 7:12, 19
17 [a]Eccles. 7:5; 10:12
18 [a]Eccles. 9:16 [b]Josh. 7:1-26; 2 Kin. 21:2-17
1 [a]Ex. 30:25
3 [a]Prov. 13:16; 18:2
4 [a]Eccles. 8:3 [b]1 Sam. 25:24-33; Prov. 25:15
5 [a]Eccles. 5:6
6 [a]Esth. 3:1; Prov. 28:12; 29:2
7 [a]Prov. 19:10 [b]Esth. 6:8
8 [a]Ps. 7:15; Prov. 26:27 [b]Amos 5:19
10 [1]Lit., *iron*
11 [1]Lit., *without enchantment* [a]Ps. 58:4, 5; Jer. 8:17
12 [a]Prov. 10:32; 22:11; Luke 4:22 [b]Prov. 10:14; 18:7; Eccles. 4:5
13 [a]Eccles. 7:25
14 [a]Prov. 15:2; Eccles. 5:3 [b]Eccles. 3:22; 6:12; 7:14; 8:7
15 [1]Lit., *fools*
16 [1]Lit., *eat* [a]Is. 3:4, 12
17 [a]Prov. 31:4; Is. 5:11
18 [a]Prov. 24:30-34
19 [1]Lit., *answers all* [a]Judg. 9:13; Ps. 104:15; Eccles. 2:3 [b]Eccles. 7:12
20 [a]2 Kin. 6:12; Luke 12:3 [b]Ex. 22:28; Acts 23:5
1 [a]Is. 32:20 [b]Deut. 15:10; Prov. 19:17; Matt. 10:42; 2 Cor. 9:8; Gal. 6:9; Heb. 6:10
2 [a]Ps. 112:9; Matt. 5:42; Luke 6:30; 1 Tim. 6:18, 19 [b]Eccles. 11:8; 12:1
3 [1]Lit., *is*
5 [1]Or, with many mss., *how the spirit* enters *the bones in the womb* [2]Lit., *full* [a]John 3:8 [b]Ps. 139:13-16 [c]Eccles. 1:13; 3:10, 11; 8:17
6 [1]Lit., *this or that* [a]Eccles. 9:10
7 [a]Eccles. 6:5; 7:11
8 [a]Eccles. 9:7 [b]Eccles. 12:1
9 [a]Eccles. 2:10 [b]Num. 15:39; Job 31:7

sires of your eyes. Yet know that [c]God will bring you to judgment for all these things.

10 So, remove vexation from your heart and put away [a]pain from your body, because childhood and the prime of life are fleeting.

Chapter 12

Remember God in Your Youth

[a]REMEMBER also your Creator in the days of your youth, before the [b]evil days come and the years draw near when you will say, "[c]I have no delight in them";

2 before the [a]sun, the light, the moon, and the stars are darkened, and clouds return after the rain;

3 in the day that the watchmen of the house tremble, and mighty men [a]stoop, the grinding ones stand idle because they are few, and [b]those who look through windows grow dim;

4 and the [a]doors on the street are shut as the [b]sound of the grinding mill is low, and one will arise at the sound of the bird, and all the [c]daughters of song will sing softly.

5 Furthermore, [1]men are afraid of a high place and of terrors on the road; the almond tree blossoms, the grasshopper drags himself along, and the caperberry is ineffective. For man goes to his eternal [a]home while [b]mourners go about in the street.

6 *Remember Him* before the silver cord is [1]broken and the [a]golden bowl is crushed, the pitcher by the well is shattered and the wheel at the cistern is crushed;

7 then the [a]dust will return to the earth as it was, and the [b]spirit will return to [c]God who gave it.

8 "Vanity of vanities," says the Preacher, "all is vanity!"

Purpose of the Preacher

9 In addition to being a wise man, the Preacher also taught the people knowledge; and he pondered, searched out and arranged [a]many proverbs.

10 The Preacher sought to find [a]delightful words and to write words of truth correctly.

11 The [a]words of wise men are like [b]goads, and masters of *these* collections are like well-driven [c]nails; they are given by one Shepherd.

12 But beyond this, my son, be warned: the writing of [a]many books is endless, and excessive devotion *to books* is wearying to the body.

13 The conclusion, when all has been heard, *is:* [a]fear God and [b]keep His commandments, because this *applies to* [c]every person.

14 Because [a]God will bring every act to judgment, everything which is hidden, whether it is good or evil.

9 [c]Eccles. 3:17; 12:4; Rom. 14:10
10 [a]2 Cor. 7:1; 2 Tim. 2:22
1 [a]Deut. 8:18; Neh. 4:14 [b]Eccles. 11:8 [c]2 Sam. 19:35
2 [a]Is. 5:30; 13:10; Ezek. 32:7, 8; Joel 3:5; Matt. 24:29
3 [a]Ps. 35:14; 38:6 [b]Gen. 27:1; 48:10; 1 Sam. 3:2
4 [a]Ps. 141:3 [b]Jer. 25:10; Rev. 18:22 [c]2 Sam. 19:35
5 [1]Lit., *they* [a]Job 17:13; 30:23 [b]Gen. 50:10; Jer. 9:7
6 [1]So with Gk.; Heb., *removed* [a]Zech. 4:2, 3
7 [a]Gen. 3:19; Eccles. 3:20 [b]Job 34:14; Eccles. 3:21; Luke 23:46; Acts 7:59 [c]Num. 16:22; 27:16
9 [a]1 Kin. 4:32
10 [a]Prov. 10:32
11 [a]Prov. 1:6; 22:17 [b]Acts 2:37 [c]Ezra 9:8; Is. 22:23
12 [a]1 Kin. 4:32, 33
13 [a]Eccles. 3:14 [b]Deut. 4:2; Eccles. 8:5 [c]Deut. 10:12; Mic. 6:8
14 [a]Eccles. 3:17; 11:9; Matt. 10:26; Rom. 2:16; 1 Cor. 4:5

THE SONG OF SOLOMON

The Young Shulammite Bride and Jerusalem's Daughters

THE [1]Song of [a]Songs, which is Solomon's.

2 "[1]May he kiss me with the kisses
of his mouth!
For your love is better than
wine.
3 "Your [a]oils have a pleasing fragrance,
Your [b]name is *like* purified oil;
Therefore the [c]maidens love
you.
4 "Draw me after you *and* let us
run *together!*
The [a]king has brought me into
his chambers."

"[1]**W**e will rejoice in you and be
glad;
We will extol your love more
than wine.
Rightly do they love you."

5 "[1]I am black but lovely,
O [a]daughters of Jerusalem,
Like the [b]tents of [c]Kedar,
Like the curtains of Solomon.
6 "Do not stare at me because I am
[1]swarthy,
For the sun has burned me.
My [a]mother's sons were angry
with me;
They made me [b]caretaker of
the vineyards,
But I have not taken care of my
own vineyard.
7 "Tell me, O you [a]whom my soul
loves,
Where do you [b]pasture *your
flock,*
Where do you make *it* [c]lie down
at noon?

1 [1]Or, *Best of the Songs* [a]1 Kin. 4:32
2 [1]BRIDE
3 [a]John 12:3 [b]Eccles. 7:1 [c]Ps. 45:14
4 [1]CHORUS [a]Ps. 45:14, 15
5 [1]BRIDE [a]Song of Sol. 2:7; 3:5, 10; 5:8, 16; 8:4 [b]Ps. 120:5 [c]Is. 60:7
6 [1]Or, *black* [a]Ps. 69:8 [b]Job 27:18; Song of Sol. 8:11
7 [a]Song of Sol. 3:1-4 [b]Song of Sol. 2:16; 6:3 [c]Is. 13:20; Jer. 33:12

For why should I be like one who [1]veils herself
Beside the flocks of [d]your companions?"

Solomon, the Lover, Speaks

8 "[1]If you yourself do not know,
Most beautiful among women,
Go forth on the trail of the flock,
And pasture your young goats
By the tents of the shepherds.

9 "To me, my darling, you are like
My [a]mare among the chariots of Pharaoh.
10 "Your [a]cheeks are lovely with ornaments,
Your neck with strings of [b]beads."

11 "[1]We will make for you ornaments of gold
With beads of silver."

12 "[1]While the king was at his [2]table,
My [3a]perfume gave forth its fragrance.
13 "My beloved is to me a pouch of [a]myrrh
Which lies all night between my breasts.
14 "My beloved is to me a cluster of [a]henna blossoms
In the vineyards of [b]Engedi."

15 "[1,2]How beautiful [a]you are, my darling,
[2]How beautiful you are!
Your eyes are *like* doves."

16 "[1,2]How handsome you are, my beloved,
And so pleasant!
Indeed, our couch is luxuriant!
17 "The beams of our houses are [a]cedars,
Our rafters, [1b]cypresses.

Chapter 2

The Bride's Admiration

"[1]I AM the [2a]rose of [b]Sharon,
The [c]lily of the valleys."

2 "[1]Like a lily among the thorns,
So is my darling among the maidens."

3 "[1]Like an apple tree among the trees of the forest,
So is my beloved among the young men.
In his shade I took great delight and sat down,
And his [a]fruit was sweet to my taste.
4 "He has brought me to *his* banquet hall,
And his [a]banner over me is love.
5 "Sustain me with [a]raisin cakes,
Refresh me with [b]apples,
Because I am lovesick.
6 "*Let* [a]his left hand be under my head
And [a]his right hand [b]embrace me."

7 "[1]I adjure you, O [a]daughters of Jerusalem,
By the [b]gazelles or by the [c]hinds of the field,
That you will not arouse or awaken *my* love,
Until [2]she pleases."

8 "[1]Listen! My beloved!
Behold, he is coming,
Climbing [a]on the mountains,
Leaping on the hills!
9 "My beloved is like a [a]gazelle or a young stag.
Behold, he is standing behind our wall,
He is looking through the windows,
He is peering [b]through the lattice.

10 "My beloved responded and said to me,
'Arise, my darling, my beautiful one,
And come along.
11 'For behold, the winter is past,
The rain is over *and* gone.
12 'The flowers have *already* appeared in the land;
The time has arrived for pruning *the vines,*
And the voice of the [a]turtledove has been heard in our land.
13 'The [a]fig tree has ripened its figs,
And the [b]vines in blossom have given forth *their* fragrance.
Arise, my darling, my beautiful one,
And come along!'"
14 "[1]O [a]my dove, [b]in the clefts of the [2]rock,
In the secret place of the steep [3]pathway,
Let me see your [4]form,
[c]Let me hear your voice;
For your voice is sweet,
And your [4]form is [d]lovely."

7 [1]Or, *wanders* [d]Song of Sol. 8:13
8 [1]BRIDEGROOM
9 [a]2 Chr. 1:16, 17
10 [a]Song of Sol. 5:13 [b]Gen. 24:53; Is. 61:10
11 [1]CHORUS
12 [1]BRIDE [2]Or, *couch* [3]Lit., *nard* [a]Song of Sol. 4:13, 14; Mark 14:3; John 12:3
13 [a]Ps. 45:8; John 19:39
14 [a]Song of Sol. 4:13 [b]1 Sam. 23:29
15 [1]BRIDEGROOM [2]Lit., *Behold* [a]Song of Sol. 6:4, 10
16 [1]BRIDE [2]Lit., *Behold*
17 [1]Or, *junipers* [a]1 Kin. 6:9, 10; Jer. 22:14 [b]2 Chr. 3:5
1 [1]BRIDE [2]Lit., *crocus* [a]Is. 35:1 [b]Is. 33:9; 35:2 [c]Song of Sol. 5:13; 7:2; Hos. 14:5
2 [1]BRIDEGROOM
3 [1]BRIDE [a]Song of Sol. 4:13, 16; 8:11, 12
4 [a]Ps. 20:5
5 [a]2 Sam. 6:19; 1 Chr. 16:3; Hos. 3:1 [b]Song of Sol. 7:8
6 [a]Song of Sol. 8:3 [b]Prov. 4:8
7 [1]BRIDEGROOM [2]Or, *it* [a]Song of Sol. 1:5 [b]Prov. 6:5; Song of Sol. 2:9, 17; 3:5; 8:14 [c]Gen. 49:21; Ps. 18:33; Hab. 3:19
8 [1]BRIDE [a]Song of Sol. 2:17; Is. 52:7
9 [a]Prov. 6:5; Song of Sol. 2:9, 17 [b]Judg. 5:28
12 [a]Gen. 15:9; Ps. 74:19; Jer. 8:7
13 [a]Matt. 24:32 [b]Song of Sol. 7:12
14 [1]BRIDEGROOM [2]Or, *crag* [3]Or, *cliff* [4]Lit., *appearance* [a]Song of Sol. 5:2; 6:9 [b]Jer. 48:28 [c]Song of Sol. 8:13 [d]Song of Sol. 1:5

15 "[1]Catch the foxes for us,
The [2]little foxes that are ruining the vineyards,
While our [a]vineyards are in blossom."
16 "[1][a]My beloved is mine, and I am his;
He [b]pastures *his flock* among the lilies.
17 "[a]Until [1]the cool of the day when the shadows flee away,
Turn, my beloved, and be like a [b]gazelle
Or a young stag [c]on the mountains of [2]Bether."

Chapter 3

The Bride's Troubled Dream

"[1]On my bed night after night I sought him
[a]Whom my soul loves;
I [b]sought him but did not find him.
2 '[1]I must arise now and [1]go about the city;
In the [a]streets and in the squares
[1]I must seek him whom my soul loves.'
I sought him but did not find him.
3 "[a]The watchmen who make the rounds in the city found me,
And I said, 'Have you seen him whom my soul loves?'
4 "Scarcely had I [1]left them
When I found him whom my soul loves;
I held on to him and would not let him go,
Until I had [a]brought him to my mother's house,
And into the room of her who conceived me."
5 "[1]I [a]adjure you, O daughters of Jerusalem,
By the [b]gazelles or by the hinds of the field,
That you will not arouse or awaken *my* love,
Until [2]she pleases."

Solomon's Wedding Day

6 "[1,2][a]What is this coming up from the wilderness
Like [b]columns of smoke,
Perfumed with [c]myrrh and [d]frankincense,
With all scented powders of the merchant?
7 "Behold, it is the *traveling* couch of Solomon;
Sixty mighty men around it,
Of the mighty men of Israel.
8 "All of them are wielders of the sword,
[a]Expert in war;
Each man has his [b]sword at his side,
Guarding against the [1][c]terrors of the night.
9 "King Solomon has made for himself a sedan chair
From the timber of Lebanon.
10 "He made its posts of silver,
Its [1]back of gold
And its seat of purple fabric,
With its interior lovingly fitted out
By the [a]daughters of Jerusalem.
11 "Go forth, O [a]daughters of Zion,
And gaze on King Solomon with the [1]crown
With which his mother has crowned him
On the [b]day of his wedding,
And on the day of his gladness of heart."

Chapter 4

Solomon's Love Expressed

"[1,2]How beautiful [a]you are, my darling,
[2]How beautiful you are!
Your [b]eyes are *like* doves [c]behind your veil;
Your [d]hair is like a flock of goats
That have descended from Mount [e]Gilead.
2 "Your [a]teeth are like a flock of *newly* shorn ewes
Which have come up from *their* washing,
All of which bear twins,
And not one among them has [1]lost her young.
3 "Your lips are like a scarlet [a]thread,
And your [b]mouth is lovely.
Your [c]temples are like a slice of a pomegranate
Behind your veil.
4 "Your [a]neck is like the tower of David
Built [1]with [b]rows of stones,
On which are [c]hung a thousand shields,
All the round [d]shields of the mighty men.
5 "Your [a]two breasts are like two fawns,
Twins of a gazelle,
Which [b]feed among the lilies.
6 "[a]Until [1]the cool of the day
When the shadows flee away,
I will go my way to the mountain of [b]myrrh
And to the hill of [b]frankincense.

15 [1]CHORUS [2]Or, *young* [a]Song of Sol. 2:13
16 [1]BRIDE [a]Song of Sol. 6:3; 7:10 [b]Song of Sol. 4:5; 6:2, 3
17 [1]Lit., *the day blows* [2]Or, *cleavage; or a kind of spice* [a]Song of Sol. 4:6 [b]Song of Sol. 2:9 [c]Song of Sol. 2:8
1 [1]BRIDE [a]Song of Sol. 1:7 [b]Song of Sol. 5:6
2 [1]Or, *Let me arise ... go ... search* [a]Jer. 5:1
3 [a]Song of Sol. 5:7
4 [1]Lit., *passed* [a]Song of Sol. 8:2
5 [1]BRIDEGROOM [2]Or, *it* [a]Song of Sol. 2:7; 8:4 [b]Song of Sol. 2:7
6 [1]CHORUS [2]Lit., *Who* [a]Song of Sol. 8:5 [b]Ex. 13:21; Joel 2:30 [c]Song of Sol. 1:13; 4:6, 14; Matt. 2:11 [d]Ex. 30:34; Rev. 18:13
8 [1]Lit., *terror in the nights* [a]Jer. 50:9 [b]Ps. 45:3 [c]Ps. 91:5
10 [1]Or, *support* [a]Song of Sol. 1:5
11 [1]Or, *wreath* [a]Is. 3:16, 17; 4:4 [b]Is. 62:5
1 [1]BRIDEGROOM [2]Lit., *Behold* [a]Song of Sol. 1:15 [b]Song of Sol. 1:15; 5:12 [c]Song of Sol. 6:7 [d]Song of Sol. 6:5 [e]Mic. 7:14
2 [1]Or, *miscarried* [a]Song of Sol. 6:6
3 [a]Josh. 2:18 [b]Song of Sol. 5:16 [c]Song of Sol. 6:7
4 [1]Or, *for an arsenal* [a]Song of Sol. 7:4 [b]Neh. 3:19 [c]Ezek. 27:10, 11 [d]2 Sam. 1:21
5 [a]Song of Sol. 7:3 [b]Song of Sol. 2:16; 6:2, 3
6 [1]Lit., *the day blows* [a]Song of Sol. 2:17 [b]Song of Sol. 4:14

7"[a]You are altogether beautiful, my darling,
And there is no blemish in you.
8"*Come* with me from [a]Lebanon, *my* [b]bride,
May you come with me from Lebanon.
[1]Journey down from the summit of [c]Amana,
From the summit of [d]Senir and Hermon,
From the dens of lions,
From the mountains of leopards.
9"You have made my heart beat faster, [a]my sister, *my* bride;
You have made my heart beat faster with a single *glance* of your eyes,
With a single [b]strand of your necklace.
10"[a]How beautiful is your love, my sister, *my* bride!
How much [b]better is your love than wine,
And the [c]fragrance of your oils
Than all *kinds* of [1]spices!
11"Your lips, *my* bride, [a]drip [b]honey;
Honey and milk are under your tongue,
And the fragrance of your garments is like the [c]fragrance of Lebanon.
12"A garden locked is my sister, *my* bride,
A rock garden locked, a [a]spring [b]sealed up.
13"Your shoots are an [a]orchard of [b]pomegranates
With [c]choice fruits, [d]henna with nard plants,
14 [a]Nard and saffron, [b]calamus and cinnamon,
With all the trees of [c]frankincense,
[d]Myrrh and aloes, along with all the finest [1]spices.
15"*You are* a garden spring,
A well of [a]fresh water,
And streams *flowing* from Lebanon."

16"[1]Awake, O north *wind*,
And come, *wind of* the south;
Make my [a]garden breathe out *fragrance*,
Let its [2]spices be wafted abroad.
May [b]my beloved come into his garden
And eat its [c]choice fruits!"

Chapter 5

The Torment of Separation

"[1]I HAVE [a]come into my garden, [b]my sister, *my* bride;
I have gathered my [c]myrrh along with my balsam.
I have eaten my [d]honeycomb and my honey;
I have [e]drunk my wine and my milk.
Eat, [f]friends;
Drink and imbibe deeply, O lovers."

2"[1]I was asleep, but my heart was awake.
A voice! My beloved was knocking:
'Open to me, [a]my sister, my darling,
[b]My dove, my perfect one!
For my head is drenched with dew,
My [c]locks with the damp of the night.'
3"I have [a]taken off my dress,
How can I put it on *again?*
I have [b]washed my feet,
How can I dirty them *again?*
4"My beloved extended his hand through the opening,
And my [a]feelings were aroused for him.
5"I arose to open to my beloved;
And my hands [a]dripped with myrrh,
And my fingers with [1]liquid myrrh,
On the handles of the bolt.
6"I opened to my beloved,
But my beloved had [a]turned away *and* had gone!
My [1]heart went out *to him* as he [b]spoke.
I [c]searched for him, but I did not find him;
I [d]called him, but he did not answer me.
7"The [a]watchmen who make the rounds in the city found me,
They struck me *and* wounded me;
The guardsmen of the walls took away my shawl from me.
8"I [a]adjure you, O daughters of Jerusalem,
If you find my beloved,
As to what you will tell him:
For [b]I am lovesick."

9"[1]What kind of beloved is your beloved,
O [a]most beautiful among women?
What kind of beloved is your beloved,
That thus you adjure us?"

7 [a]Song of Sol. 1:15
8 [1]Or, *Look* [a]1 Kin. 4:33; Ps. 72:16 [b]Song of Sol. 5:1; Is. 62:5 [c]2 Kin. 5:12 [d]Deut. 3:9; 1 Chr. 5:23; Ezek. 27:5
9 [a]Song of Sol. 4:10, 12; 5:1, 2 [b]Gen. 41:42; Prov. 1:9; Ezek. 16:11; Dan. 5:7
10 [1]Or, *balsam odors* [a]Song of Sol. 7:6 [b]Song of Sol. 1:2, 4 [c]Song of Sol. 1:3
11 [a]Prov. 5:3 [b]Ps. 19:10; Prov. 24:13 [c]Gen. 27:27; Hos. 14:6
12 [a]Prov. 5:15-18 [b]Gen. 29:3
13 [a]Neh. 2:8; Eccles. 2:5 [b]Song of Sol. 6:11; 7:12 [c]Song of Sol. 2:3; 4:16; 7:13 [d]Song of Sol. 1:14
14 [1]Or, *balsam odors* [a]Song of Sol. 1:12 [b]Ex. 30:23 [c]Song of Sol. 4:6 [d]Ps. 45:8; Song of Sol. 3:6; John 19:39
15 [a]Zech. 14:8
16 [1]BRIDE [2]Or, *balsam odors* [a]Song of Sol. 5:1; 6:2 [b]Song of Sol. 1:13; 2:3, 8; 6:2 [c]Song of Sol. 4:13
1 [1]BRIDEGROOM [a]Song of Sol. 6:2 [b]Song of Sol. 4:9 [c]Song of Sol. 1:13; 4:14 [d]Song of Sol. 4:11 [e]Prov. 9:5; Is. 55:1 [f]Judg. 14:11, 20; John 3:29
2 [1]BRIDE [a]Song of Sol. 4:9 [b]Song of Sol. 2:14; 6:9 [c]Song of Sol. 5:11
3 [a]Luke 11:7 [b]Gen. 19:2
4 [a]Jer. 31:20
5 [1]Lit., *passing* [a]Song of Sol. 5:13
6 [1]Lit., *soul* [a]Song of Sol. 6:1 [b]Song of Sol. 5:2 [c]Song of Sol. 3:1 [d]Prov. 1:28
7 [a]Song of Sol. 3:3
8 [a]Song of Sol. 2:7; 3:5 [b]Song of Sol. 2:5
9 [1]CHORUS [a]Song of Sol. 1:8; 6:1

Admiration by the Bride

10 "[1]My beloved is dazzling and
[a]ruddy,
[b]Outstanding among ten thousand.
11 "His head is *like* gold, pure gold;
His [a]locks are *like* clusters of
dates,
And black as a raven.
12 "His [a]eyes are like doves,
Beside streams of water,
Bathed in milk,
And reposed in *their* [b]setting.
13 "His cheeks are like a [a]bed of
balsam,
Banks of sweet-scented herbs;
His lips are [b]lilies,
[c]Dripping with liquid myrrh.
14 "His hands are rods of gold
Set with [a]beryl;
His abdomen is carved ivory
Inlaid with [1b]sapphires.
15 "His legs are pillars of alabaster
Set on pedestals of pure gold;
His appearance is like [a]Lebanon,
Choice as the [b]cedars.
16 "His [a]mouth is *full of* sweetness.
And he is wholly [b]desirable.
This is my beloved and this is
my friend,
O daughters of Jerusalem."

CHAPTER 6

Mutual Delight in Each Other

"[1a]WHERE has your beloved
gone,
O [b]most beautiful among
women?
Where has your beloved
turned,
That we may seek him with
you?"

2 "[1]My beloved has gone down to
his [a]garden,
To the [b]beds of balsam,
To [c]pasture *his flock* in the gardens
And gather [d]lilies.
3 "[a]I am my beloved's and my beloved is mine,
He who [b]pastures *his flock*
among the lilies."

4 "[1a]You are as beautiful as [b]Tirzah, my darling,
As [c]lovely as [d]Jerusalem,
As [e]awesome as an army with
banners.
5 "Turn your eyes away from me,
For they have confused me;
[a]Your hair is like a flock of
goats
That have descended from Gilead.
6 "[a]Your teeth are like a flock of
ewes
Which have come up from *their*
washing,
All of which bear twins,
And not one among them has
lost her young.
7 "[a]Your temples are like a slice of
a pomegranate
Behind your veil.
8 "There are sixty [a]queens and
eighty concubines,
And [1b]maidens without number;
9 *But* [a]my dove, my perfect one,
is [1]unique:
She is her mother's [1]only
daughter;
She is the pure *child* of the one
who bore her.
The [2b]maidens saw her and
called her blessed,
The [c]queens and the concubines *also*, and they praised
her, *saying,*

10 'Who is this that grows like the
dawn,
As beautiful as the full [a]moon,
As pure [b]as the sun,
As [c]awesome as [1]an army with
banners?'
11 "I went down to the orchard of
nut trees
To see the blossoms of the valley,
To see whether [a]the vine had
budded
Or the [b]pomegranates had
bloomed.
12 "Before I was aware, my soul set
me
Over the chariots of [1]my noble
people."

13 "[1,2]Come back, come back, O
Shulammite;
Come back, come back, that we
may gaze at you!"

"[3]Why should you gaze at the
Shulammite,
As at the [a]dance of [4b]the two
companies?

CHAPTER 7

Admiration by the Bridegroom

"[1]HOW beautiful are your [2]feet in
sandals,
O [3a]prince's daughter!
The curves of your hips are like
[4]jewels,
The work of the hands of an artist.

10 [1]BRIDE [a]1 Sam. 16:12 [b]Ps. 45:2
11 [a]Song of Sol. 5:2
12 [a]Song of Sol. 1:15; 4:1 [b]Ex. 25:7
13 [a]Song of Sol. 6:2 [b]Song of Sol. 2:1 [c]Song of Sol. 5:5
14 [1]Lit., *lapis lazuli* [a]Ex. 28:20; 39:13; Ezek. 1:16; Dan. 10:6 [b]Ex. 24:10; 28:18; Job 28:16; Is. 54:11
15 [a]Song of Sol. 7:4 [b]1 Kin. 4:33; Ps. 80:10; Ezek. 17:23; 31:8
16 [a]Song of Sol. 7:9 [b]2 Sam. 1:23
1 [1]CHORUS [a]Song of Sol. 5:6 [b]Song of Sol. 1:8
2 [1]BRIDE [a]Song of Sol. 4:16; 5:1 [b]Song of Sol. 5:13 [c]Song of Sol. 1:7 [d]Song of Sol. 2:1; 5:13
3 [a]Song of Sol. 2:16; 7:10 [b]Song of Sol. 2:16; 4:5
4 [1]BRIDEGROOM [a]Song of Sol. 1:15 [b]1 Kin. 14:17 [c]Song of Sol. 1:5 [d]Ps. 48:2; 50:2 [e]Song of Sol. 6:10
5 [a]Song of Sol. 4:1
6 [a]Song of Sol. 4:2
7 [a]Song of Sol. 4:3
8 [1]Or, *virgins* [a]1 Kin. 11:3 [b]Song of Sol. 1:3
9 [1]Lit., *one* [2]Lit., *daughters* [a]Song of Sol. 2:14; 5:2 [b]Gen. 30:13 [c]1 Kin. 11:3
10 [1]Lit., *bannered ones* [a]Job 31:26 [b]Matt. 17:2; Rev. 1:16 [c]Song of Sol. 6:4
11 [a]Song of Sol. 7:12 [b]Song of Sol. 4:13
12 [1]Another reading is *Amminadib*
13 [1]CHORUS [2]Chap. 7:1 in Heb. [3]BRIDEGROOM [4]Or, *Mahanaim* [a]Judg. 21:21 [b]Gen. 32:2; 2 Sam. 17:24
1 [1]Chap. 7:2 in Heb. [2]Lit., *footsteps* [3]Or, *nobleman's* [4]Or, *ornaments* [a]Ps. 45:13

2"Your navel is *like* a round gob-
let
Which never lacks mixed wine;
Your belly is like a heap of
wheat
Fenced about with lilies.
3"Your [a]two breasts are like two
fawns,
Twins of a gazelle.
4"Your [a]neck is *like* a tower of
ivory,
Your eyes *like* the pools in
[b]Heshbon
By the gate of Bath-rabbim;
Your nose is like the tower of
Lebanon,
Which faces toward Damascus.
5"Your head [1]crowns you like
[a]Carmel,
And the flowing locks of your
head are like purple threads;
The king is captivated by *your*
tresses.
6"How [a]beautiful and how delightful you are,
[1]*My* love, with *all* your charms!
7"[1]Your stature is like a palm
tree,
And your breasts are *like its*
clusters.
8"I said, 'I will climb the palm
tree,
I will take hold of its fruit
stalks.'
Oh, may your breasts be like
clusters of the vine,
And the fragrance of your
[1]breath like [2a]apples,
9 And your [1a]mouth like the best
wine!"

"[2]**I**t [b]goes *down* smoothly for my
beloved,
Flowing gently *through* the lips
of those who fall asleep.

The Union of Love

10"[a]I am my beloved's,
And his [b]desire is for me.
11"Come, my beloved, let us go out
into the [1]country,
Let us spend the night in the villages.
12"Let us rise early *and go* to the
vineyards;
Let us [a]see whether the vine
has budded
And its blossoms have opened,
And whether the pomegranates
have bloomed.
There I will give you my love.
13"The [a]mandrakes have given
forth fragrance;
And over our doors are all
[b]choice *fruits,*
Both new and old,
Which I have saved up for you,
my beloved.

CHAPTER 8

The Lovers Speak

"OH that you were like a brother
to me
Who nursed at my mother's
breasts.
If I found you outdoors, I would
kiss you;
No one would despise me, either.
2"I would lead you *and* [a]bring you
Into the house of my mother,
who used to instruct me;
I would give you spiced wine to
drink from the juice of my
pomegranates.
3"Let [a]his left hand be under my
head,
And his right hand embrace
me."

4"[1a]I want you to swear, O daughters of Jerusalem,
[2]Do not arouse or awaken *my*
love,
Until [3]she pleases."

5"[1a]Who is this coming up from
the wilderness,
Leaning on her beloved?"

"[2]**B**eneath the [3b]apple tree I
awakened you;
There your mother was in labor
with you,
There she was in labor *and*
gave you birth.
6"Put me like a [1]seal over your
heart,
Like a [a]seal on your arm.
For love is as strong as death,
[2b]Jealousy is as severe as Sheol;
Its flashes are flashes of fire,
[3]The *very* flame of the LORD.
7"Many waters cannot quench
love,
Nor will rivers overflow it;
If a man were to give all the
riches of his house for love,
It would be utterly despised."

8"[1]We have a little sister,
And she [a]has no breasts;
What shall we do for our sister
On the day when she is spoken
for?
9"If she is a wall,
We shall build on her a battle-
ment of silver;
But if she is a door,
We shall barricade her with
[a]planks of cedar."

3 [a]Song of Sol. 4:5
4 [a]Song of Sol. 4:4 [b]Num. 21:26
5 [1]Lit., *is upon* [a]Is. 35:2
6 [1]Or, With *love among your delights* [a]Song of Sol. 1:15, 16; 4:10
7 [1]Lit., *This stature of yours*
8 [1]Lit., *nose* [2]Or, *apricots* [a]Song of Sol. 2:5
9 [1]Lit., *palate* [2]BRIDE [a]Song of Sol. 5:16 [b]Prov. 23:31
10 [a]Song of Sol. 2:16; 6:3 [b]Ps. 45:11
11 [1]Lit., *field*
12 [a]Song of Sol. 6:11
13 [a]Gen. 30:14 [b]Song of Sol. 2:3; 4:13, 16
2 [a]Song of Sol. 3:4
3 [a]Song of Sol. 2:6
4 [1]BRIDEGROOM [2]Or, *Why should you arouse* [3]Or, *it* [a]Song of Sol. 2:7; 3:5
5 [1]CHORUS [2]BRIDEGROOM [3]Or, *apricot* [a]Song of Sol. 3:6 [b]Song of Sol. 2:3
6 [1]Or, *signet* [2]Or, Its *ardor is as inflexible* [3]Another reading is: *A vehement flame.* [a]Is. 49:16; Jer. 22:24; Hag. 2:23 [b]Prov. 6:34
8 [1]CHORUS [a]Ezek. 16:7
9 [a]1 Kin. 6:15

10"[1]I was a wall, and my breasts were like towers;
Then I became in his eyes as one who finds peace.
11"Solomon had a [a]vineyard at Baal-hamon;
He [b]entrusted the vineyard to [c]caretakers;
Each one was to bring a [d]thousand *shekels* of silver for its [e]fruit.
12"My very own vineyard is at my disposal;
The thousand *shekels* are for you, Solomon,
And two hundred are for those who take care of its fruit."
13"[1]O you who sit in the gardens,
My [a]companions are listening for your voice—
Let me hear it!"
14"[1]Hurry, my beloved,
And be [a]like a gazelle or a young stag
On the [b]mountains of spices."

10 [1]BRIDE
11 [a]Eccles. 2:4 [b]Matt. 21:33 [c]Song of Sol. 1:6 [d]Is. 7:23 [e]Song of Sol. 2:3; 8:12
13 [1]BRIDEGROOM [a]Song of Sol. 1:7
14 [1]BRIDE [a]Song of Sol. 2:7, 9, 17 [b]Song of Sol. 4:6

THE BOOK OF ISAIAH

Rebellion of God's People

THE vision of Isaiah the son of Amoz, concerning [a]Judah and Jerusalem which he saw during the [1]reigns of [b]Uzziah, Jotham, Ahaz, *and* [c]Hezekiah, kings of Judah.

2 [a]Listen, O heavens, and hear, O [b]earth;
For the LORD speaks,
"[c]Sons I have reared and brought up,
But they have [d]revolted against Me.
3"An ox knows its owner,
And a donkey its master's manger,
But Israel does not know,
My people do not understand."

4 Alas, sinful nation,
People weighed down with iniquity,
[1]Offspring of evildoers,
Sons who act corruptly!
They have [a]abandoned the LORD,
They have [b]despised the Holy One of Israel,
They have turned away [2]from Him.

5 Where will you be stricken again,
As you [a]continue in *your* rebellion?
The whole head is [b]sick,
And the whole heart is faint.
6 From the sole of the foot even to the head
There is [a]nothing sound in it,
Only bruises, welts, and raw wounds,
Not pressed out or bandaged,
Nor softened with oil.

7 Your [a]land is desolate,
Your cities are burned with fire,
Your fields—strangers are devouring them in your presence;
[1]It is desolation, as overthrown by strangers.
8 And the daughter of Zion is left like a shelter in a vineyard,
Like a watchman's hut in a cucumber field, like a besieged city.
9 [a]Unless the LORD of hosts
Had left us a few [b]survivors,
We would be like Sodom,
We would be like Gomorrah.

God Has Had Enough

10 Hear the word of the LORD,
You rulers of Sodom;
Give ear to the instruction of our God,
You people of Gomorrah.
11"[a]What are your multiplied sacrifices to Me?"
Says the LORD.
"I [1]have had enough of burnt offerings of rams,
And the fat of fed cattle.
And I take no pleasure in the blood of bulls, lambs, or goats.
12"When you come [a]to appear before Me,
Who requires [1]of you this trampling of My courts?
13"Bring your worthless offerings no longer,
Their incense is an abomination to Me.
[a]New moon and sabbath, the [b]calling of assemblies—
I cannot [c]endure iniquity and the solemn assembly.
14"I hate your new moon *festivals* and your appointed feasts,
They have become a burden to Me.
I am weary of bearing *them.*

1 [1]Lit., *days* [a]Is. 2:1; 40:9 [b]2 Kin. 15:1, 13 [c]2 Kin. 18:1
2 [a]Deut. 32:1 [b]Mic. 1:2 [c]Jer. 3:22 [d]Is. 30:1, 9; 65:2
4 [1]Lit., *Seed* [2]Lit., *backward* [a]Is. 1:28 [b]Is. 5:24
5 [a]Is. 31:6 [b]Is. 33:24; Ezek. 34:4, 16
6 [a]Ps. 38:3
7 [1]Lit., *And* [a]Lev. 26:33; Jer. 44:6
9 [a]Rom. 9:29 [b]Is. 10:20-22; 11:11, 16; 37:4, 31, 32; 46:3
11 [1]Or, *am sated with* [a]Jer. 6:20; Mal. 1:10
12 [1]Lit., *of your hand* [a]Ex. 23:17
13 [a]1 Chr. 23:31 [b]Ex. 12:16 [c]Jer. 7:9, 10

15"So when you [a]spread out your
hands *in prayer,*
I will hide My eyes from you,
Yes, even though you [b]multiply
prayers,
I will not listen.
Your hands are full of
bloodshed.

16"[a]Wash yourselves, [b]make yourselves clean;
Remove the evil of your deeds
from My sight.
[c]Cease to do evil,
17 Learn to do good;
[a]Seek justice,
[b]Reprove the ruthless;
[1]Defend the orphan,
Plead for the widow.

"Let Us Reason"

18"Come now, and [a]let us reason
together,"
Says the LORD,
"[b]Though your sins are as scarlet,
They will be as white as snow;
Though they are red like crimson,
They will be like wool.
19"[a]If you consent and obey,
You will eat the best of the
land;
20"But if you refuse and rebel,
You will be devoured by the
sword."
Truly, the mouth of the LORD
has spoken.

Zion Corrupted, to be Redeemed

21 How the faithful city has become a harlot,
She *who* was full of justice!
Righteousness once lodged in
her,
But now murderers.
22 Your silver has become dross,
Your drink diluted with water.
23 Your [a]rulers are rebels,
And companions of thieves;
Every one [b]loves a bribe,
And chases after rewards.
They [c]do not [1]defend the [2]orphan,
Nor does the widow's plea
come before them.

24 Therefore the Lord [1]GOD of
hosts,
The Mighty One of Israel declares,
"Ah, I will be relieved of My adversaries,
And [a]avenge Myself on My
foes.
25"I will also turn My hand against
you,
And will [a]smelt away your
dross as with lye,
And will remove all your alloy.
26"Then I will restore your [a]judges
as at the first,
And your counselors as at the
beginning;
After that you will be called the
[b]city of righteousness,
A faithful city."

27 Zion will be [a]redeemed with
justice,
And her [1]repentant ones with
righteousness.
28 But [1]transgressors and sinners
will be [a]crushed together,
And those who forsake the
LORD shall come to an end.
29 Surely, [1]you will be ashamed of
the [2a]oaks which you have
desired,
And you will be embarrassed at
the [b]gardens which you have
chosen.
30 For you will be like an [1]oak
whose [a]leaf fades away,
Or as a garden that has no water.
31 And the strong man will become tinder,
His work also a spark.
Thus they shall both [a]burn together,
And there will be none to
quench *them.*

CHAPTER 2

God's Universal Reign

THE word which [a]Isaiah the son of
Amoz saw concerning Judah and
Jerusalem. Now it will come about
that
2 [a]In the last days,
The [b]mountain of the house of
the LORD
Will be established [1]as the chief
of the mountains,
And will be raised above the
hills;
And [c]all the nations will stream
to it.
3 And many peoples will come
and say,
"Come, let us go up to the mountain of the LORD,
To the house of the God of Jacob;
That He may teach us [1]concerning His ways,
And that we may walk in His
paths."

15 [a]1 Kin. 8:22; Lam. 1:17 [b]Mic. 3:4
16 [a]Ps. 26:6 [b]Is. 52:11 [c]Jer. 25:5
17 [1]Or, *Vindicate the fatherless* [a]Jer. 22:3; Zeph. 2:3 [b]Ps. 82:3
18 [a]Is. 41:1, 21; 43:26; Mic. 6:2 [b]Ps. 51:7; Is. 43:25; 44:22; Rev. 7:14
19 [a]Deut. 30:15, 16
23 [1]Or, *vindicate* [2]Or, *fatherless* [a]Hos. 5:10; Mic. 7:3 [b]Ex. 23:8; Mic. 7:3 [c]Jer. 5:28; Ezek. 22:7; Zech. 7:10
24 [1]YHWH, usually rendered LORD [a]Is. 35:4; 59:18
25 [a]Ezek. 22:19-22; Mal. 3:3
26 [a]Is. 60:17; Jer. 33:7, 11 [b]Is. 33:5; 60:14; 62:1, 2; Zech. 8:3
27 [1]Or, *returnees* [a]Is. 35:9; 62:12; 63:4
28 [1]Lit., the *crushing of transgressors and sinners shall be together* [a]Ps. 9:5; Is. 66:24; 2 Thess. 1:8, 9
29 [1]So with some mss.; M.T. *they* [2]Or, *terebinths* [a]Is. 57:5 [b]Is. 65:3; 66:17
30 [1]Or, *terebinth* [a]Is. 64:6
31 [a]Is. 5:24; 9:19; 26:11; 33:11-14
1 [a]Is. 1:1
2 [1]Lit., *on* [a]Mic. 4:1-3 [b]Is. 27:13; 66:20 [c]Is. 56:7
3 [1]Or, *some of*

For the [2]law will go forth [a]from
Zion,
And the word of the LORD from
Jerusalem.
4 And He will judge between the
nations,
And will [1]render decisions for
many peoples;
And [a]they will hammer their
swords into plowshares, and
their spears into pruning
hooks.
[b]Nation will not lift up sword
against nation,
And never again will they learn
war.

5 Come, [a]house of Jacob, and let
us walk in the [b]light of the
LORD.
6 For Thou hast [a]abandoned Thy
people, the house of Jacob,
Because they are filled with in-
fluences from the east,
And *they are* soothsayers [b]like
the Philistines,
And they [c]strike *bargains* with
the children of foreigners.
7 Their land has also been filled
with silver and gold,
And there is no end to their
treasures;
Their land has also been filled
with horses,
And there is no end to their
chariots.
8 Their land has also been [a]filled
with idols;
They worship the [b]work of their
hands,
That which their fingers have
made.
9 So the [a]*common* man has been
humbled,
And the man *of* [a]*importance*
has been abased,
But do not forgive them.
10 [a]Enter the rock and hide in the
dust
[b]From the terror of the LORD
and from the splendor of His
majesty.
11 The [1a]proud look of man will be
abased,
And the [b]loftiness of man will
be humbled,
And the LORD alone will be exalted in that day.

A Day of Reckoning Coming

12 For the LORD of hosts will have
a day of reckoning
Against [a]everyone who is
proud and lofty,
And against everyone who is
lifted up,
That he may be abased.

3 [2]Or, *instruction*
[a]Is. 51:4, 5; Luke 24:47

4 [1]Or, *reprove many*
[a]Is. 32:17, 18; Joel 3:10 [b]Is. 9:5, 7; 11:6-9; Hos. 2:18; Zech. 9:10

5 [a]Is. 58:1 [b]Is. 60:1, 2, 19, 20; 1 John 1:5

6 [a]Deut. 31:17 [b]2 Kin. 1:2 [c]2 Kin. 16:7, 8; Prov. 6:1

8 [a]Is. 10:11 [b]Ps. 115:4-8; Is. 17:8; 37:19; 40:19; 44:17

9 [a]Ps. 49:2; 62:9; Is. 5:15

10 [a]Is. 2:19, 21; Rev. 6:15, 16 [b]2 Thess. 1:9

11 [1]Lit., *eyes of the loftiness of men*
[a]Is. 5:15; 37:23 [b]Ps. 18:27; Is. 13:11; 23:9; 2 Cor. 10:5

12 [a]Job 40:11, 12; Is. 24:4, 21; Mal. 4:1

14 [a]Is. 40:4

15 [a]Is. 25:12

16 [a]1 Kin. 10:22; Is. 23:1, 14; 60:9

18 [a]Is. 21:9; Mic. 1:7

19 [1]Lit., *dust*
[a]Ps. 18:7; Is. 13:13; 24:1, 19, 20; Hag. 2:6, 7; Heb. 12:26

20 [a]Is. 30:22; 31:7

21 [a]Is. 3:19

22 [1]Lit., *Cease from man* [2]Lit., *in what*
[a]Ps. 146:3; Jer. 17:5 [b]Ps. 8:4; 144:3, 4; Is. 40:15, 17; James 4:14

1 [1]YHWH, usually rendered LORD [2]Lit., *staff*
[a]Lev. 26:26; Is. 5:13; 9:20; Ezek. 4:16

2 [a]2 Kin. 24:14; Is. 9:14, 15; Ezek. 17:12, 13

13 And *it will be* against all the
cedars of Lebanon that are
lofty and lifted up,
Against all the oaks of Bashan,
14 Against all the [a]lofty mountains,
Against all the hills that are
lifted up,
15 Against every [a]high tower,
Against every fortified wall,
16 Against all the [a]ships of Tarshish,
And against all the beautiful
craft.
17 And the pride of man will be
humbled,
And the loftiness of men will be
abased,
And the LORD alone will be exalted in that day.
18 But the [a]idols will completely
vanish.
19 And *men* will go into caves of
the rocks,
And into holes of the [1]ground
Before the terror of the LORD,
And before the splendor of His
majesty,
When He arises [a]to make the
earth tremble.
20 In that day men will [a]cast away
to the moles and the bats
Their idols of silver and their
idols of gold,
Which they made for them-
selves to worship,
21 In order to [a]go into the caverns
of the rocks and the clefts of
the cliffs,
Before the terror of the LORD
and the splendor of His majesty,
When He arises to make the
earth tremble.
22 [1a]Stop regarding man, whose
breath *of life* is in his nostrils;
For [2b]why should he be esteemed?

CHAPTER 3

God Will Remove the Leaders

FOR behold, the Lord [1]GOD of
hosts [a]is going to remove from Jerusalem and Judah
Both [2]supply and support, the
whole [2]supply of bread,
And the whole [2]supply of water;
2 [a]The mighty man and the warrior,
The judge and the prophet,
The diviner and the elder,
3 The captain of fifty and the honorable man,

The counselor and the expert artisan,
And the skillful enchanter.
4 And I will make mere [a]lads their princes
And [1]capricious children will rule over them,
5 And the people will be [a]oppressed,
Each one by another, and each one by his [b]neighbor;
The youth will storm against the elder,
And the inferior against the honorable.
6 When a man [a]lays hold of his brother in his father's house, *saying,*
"You have a cloak, you shall be our ruler,
And these ruins will be under your [1]charge,"
7 On that day will he [1]protest, saying,
"I will not be *your* [2a]healer,
For in my house there is neither bread nor cloak;
You should not appoint me ruler of the people."
8 For [a]Jerusalem has stumbled, and Judah has fallen,
Because their [1b]speech and their actions are against the LORD,
To rebel against [2]His glorious presence.
9 [1]The expression of their faces bears witness against them.
And they display their sin like [a]Sodom;
They do not *even* conceal *it.*
Woe to [2]them!
For they have [b]brought evil on themselves.
10 Say to the [a]righteous that *it will* go well *with them,*
For they will eat the fruit of their actions.
11 Woe to the wicked! *It will* go badly *with him,*
For [1a]what he deserves will be done to him.
12 O My people! Their oppressors [1]are [a]children,
And women rule over them.
O My people! [b]Those who guide you lead *you* astray,
And confuse the direction of your paths.

God Will Judge

13 [a]The LORD arises to contend,
And stands to judge the people.
14 The LORD [a]enters into judgment with the elders and princes of His people,
"It is you who have [b]devoured the vineyard;
The [c]plunder of the poor is in your houses.
15 "What do you mean by [a]crushing My people,
And grinding the face of the poor?"
Declares the Lord [1]GOD of hosts.

Judah's Women Denounced

16 Moreover, the LORD said, "Because the daughters of Zion are proud,
And walk with [1]heads held high and seductive eyes,
And go along with mincing steps,
And tinkle the bangles on their feet,
17 Therefore the Lord will afflict the scalp of the daughters of Zion with scabs,
And the LORD will make their foreheads bare."
18 In that day the Lord will take
away the beauty of *their* anklets,
headbands, [a]crescent ornaments,
19 dangling earrings, bracelets,
veils,
20 [a]headdresses, ankle chains,
sashes, perfume boxes, amulets,
21 [1]finger rings, [a]nose rings,
22 festal robes, outer tunics,
cloaks, money purses,
23 hand mirrors, undergarments,
turbans, and veils.
24 Now it will come about that instead of [1]sweet [a]perfume there will be putrefaction;
Instead of a belt, a rope;
Instead of [b]well-set hair, a [c]plucked-out scalp;
Instead of fine clothes, a [d]donning of sackcloth;
And branding instead of beauty.
25 Your men will [a]fall by the sword,
And your [1]mighty ones in battle.
26 And her [1a]gates will lament and mourn;
And deserted she will [b]sit on the ground.

CHAPTER 4

A Remnant Prepared

FOR seven women will take hold
of [a]one man in that day, saying, "We
will eat our own bread and wear our
own clothes, only let us be called by
your name; [b]take away our reproach!"

4 [1]Lit., *arbitrary power will rule* [a]Eccles. 10:16
5 [a]Mic. 7:3-6 [b]Is. 9:19; Jer. 9:3-8
6 [1]Lit., *hand* [a]Is. 4:1
7 [1]Lit., *lift up his voice* [2]Lit., *binder of wounds* [a]Ezek. 34:4; Hos. 5:13
8 [1]Lit., *tongue* [2]Lit., *the eyes of His glory* [a]Is. 1:7; 6:11 [b]Ps. 73:9-11; Is. 9:17; 59:3
9 [1]Or, *Their partiality bears* [2]Lit., *their soul* [a]Gen. 13:13; Is. 1:10 [b]Prov. 8:36; 15:32; Rom. 6:23
10 [a]Deut. 28:1-14; Eccles. 8:12; Is. 54:17
11 [1]Lit., *the dealing of his hands* [a]Deut. 28:15-68; Is. 65:6, 7
12 [1]Or, *deal severely* [a]Is. 3:4 [b]Is. 9:16; 28:14, 15
13 [a]Is. 66:16; Hos. 4:1; Mic. 6:2
14 [a]Job 22:4; Ps. 143:2; Ezek. 20:35, 36 [b]Ps. 14:4; Mic. 3:3 [c]Job 24:9, 14; Ps. 10:9; Prov. 30:14; Is. 10:1, 2; Ezek. 18:12; James 2:6
15 [1]YHWH, usually rendered LORD [a]Ps. 94:5
16 [1]Lit., *outstretched necks*
18 [a]Judg. 8:21, 26
20 [a]Ex. 39:28
21 [1]Or, *signet rings* [a]Gen. 24:47; Ezek. 16:12
24 [1]Or, *balsam oil* [a]Esth. 2:12 [b]1 Pet. 3:3 [c]Is. 22:12; Ezek. 27:31; Amos 8:10 [d]Is. 15:3; Lam. 2:10
25 [1]Lit., *strength* [a]Is. 1:20; 65:12
26 [1]Lit., *entrances* [a]Jer. 14:2; Lam. 1:4 [b]Lam. 2:10
1 [a]Is. 13:12 [b]Gen. 30:23; Is. 54:4

2 In that day the [a]Branch of the
LORD will be beautiful and glorious,
and the [b]fruit of the earth *will* be the
pride and the adornment of the [c]sur-
vivors of Israel.
3 And it will come about that he
who is [a]left in Zion and remains in
Jerusalem will be called [b]holy—everyone who is [c]recorded for life in
Jerusalem.
4 When the LORD has washed
away the filth of the daughters of
Zion, and [1]purged the [a]bloodshed of
Jerusalem from her midst, by the
[b]spirit of judgment and the [c]spirit of
burning,
5 then the LORD will create over
the whole area of Mount Zion and
over her assemblies [a]a cloud by day,
even smoke, and the brightness of a
flaming fire by night; for over all the
glory will be a canopy.
6 And there will be a [a]shelter to
give shade from the heat by day, and
refuge and [1]protection from the
storm and the rain.

CHAPTER 5

Parable of the Vineyard

LET me sing now for my well-
beloved a song of my beloved concerning His vineyard.
My well-beloved had a [a]vine-
yard on a [1]fertile hill.
2 And He dug it all around, removed its stones,
And planted it with [1]the [a]choic-
est vine.
And He built a tower in the
middle of it,
And hewed out a [2]wine vat in it;
Then He [b]expected *it* to produce *good* grapes,
But it produced *only* [3]worthless
ones.

3 "And now, O inhabitants of Jerusalem and men of Judah,
[a]Judge between Me and My
vineyard.
4 "[a]What more was there to do for
My vineyard [1]that I have not
done in it?
Why, when I expected *it* to produce *good* grapes did it produce [2]worthless ones?
5 "So now let Me tell you what I
am going to do to My vineyard:
I will [a]remove its hedge and it
will be consumed;
I will [b]break down its wall and
it will become [c]trampled
ground.
6 "And I will [a]lay it waste;
It will not be pruned or hoed,
But briars and thorns will come
up.
I will also charge the clouds to
[b]rain no rain on it."

7 For the vineyard of the LORD of
hosts is the house of Israel,
And the men of Judah His delightful plant.
Thus He looked for justice, but
behold, [a]bloodshed;
For righteousness, but behold,
a cry of distress.

Woes for the Wicked

8 Woe to those who [a]add house
to house *and* join field to
field,
Until there is no more room,
So that you have to live alone in
the midst of the land!
9 In my ears the LORD of hosts
has sworn, "Surely, [a]many
houses shall become [b]deso-
late,
Even great and fine ones, without occupants.
10 "For [a]ten acres of vineyard will
yield *only* one [1]bath *of wine,*
And a homer of seed will yield
but an [2]ephah of grain."
11 Woe to those who rise early in
the morning that they may
pursue [a]strong drink;
Who stay up late in the evening
that wine may inflame them!
12 And their banquets are *accompanied* by lyre and [a]harp, by
tambourine and flute, and by
wine;
But they [b]do not pay attention
to the deeds of the LORD,
Nor do they consider the work
of His hands.

13 Therefore My people go into
exile for their [a]lack of knowledge;
And [1]their honorable men are
famished,
And their multitude is parched
with thirst.
14 Therefore Sheol has enlarged
its [1]throat and opened its
mouth without measure;
And [2]Jerusalem's splendor, her
multitude, her din *of revelry,*
and the jubilant within her,
descend *into it.*
15 So the *common* man will be
humbled, and the man of *importance* abased,
[a]The eyes of the proud also will
be abased.

2 [a]Is. 11:1; 53:2; Jer. 23:5; 33:15; Zech. 3:8; 6:12 [b]Ps. 72:16 [c]Is. 10:20; 37:31, 32; Joel 2:32; Obad. 17
3 [a]Is. 28:5; 46:3; Rom. 11:4, 5 [b]Is. 52:1; 62:12 [c]Ex. 32:32; Ps. 69:28; Luke 10:20
4 [1]Lit., *rinsed away* [a]Is. 1:15 [b]Is. 28:6 [c]Is. 1:31; 9:19
5 [a]Ex. 13:21, 22; Num. 9:15-23
6 [1]Lit., *a hiding place* [a]Ps. 27:5; Is. 25:4; 32:1, 2
1 [1]Lit., *a horn, the son of fatness* [a]Ps. 80:8; Jer. 12:10; Matt. 21:33; Mark 12:1; Luke 20:9
2 [1]Lit., *a bright red grape* [2]Or, *wine press* [3]Or, *wild grapes* [a]Jer. 2:21 [b]Matt. 21:19; Mark 11:13; Luke 13:6
3 [a]Matt. 21:40
4 [1]Lit., *and I have not done* [2]Or, *wild grapes* [a]2 Chr. 36:15; Jer. 2:5; 7:25, 26; Mic. 6:3; Matt. 23:37
5 [a]Ps. 89:40 [b]Ps. 80:12 [c]Is. 10:6; 28:18; Lam. 1:15; Luke 21:24; Rev. 11:2
6 [a]2 Chr. 36:19-21; Jer. 25:11 [b]1 Kin. 8:35; 17:1; Jer. 14:1-22
7 [a]Is. 3:14, 15; 30:12; 59:13
8 [a]Jer. 22:13-17; Mic. 2:2; Hab. 2:9-12
9 [a]Is. 6:11, 12 [b]Matt. 23:38
10 [1]I.e., about 10½ gal. [2]I.e., approx. one bushel [a]Lev. 26:26; Is. 7:23; Hag. 1:6; 2:16
11 [a]Prov. 23:29, 30; Eccles. 10:16, 17; Is. 22:13; 28:1, 3, 7, 8
12 [a]Amos 6:5, 6 [b]Job 34:27; Ps. 28:5
13 [1]Lit., *their glory are men of famine* [a]Is. 1:3; 27:11; Hos. 4:6
14 [1]Or, *appetite* [2]Lit., *her*
15 [a]Is. 2:11; 10:33

16 But the [a]LORD of hosts will be [b]exalted in judgment,
And the holy God will show Himself [c]holy in righteousness.
17 [a]Then the lambs will graze as in their pasture,
And strangers will eat in the waste places of the wealthy.

18 Woe to those who drag [a]iniquity with the cords of falsehood,
And sin as if with cart ropes;
19 [a]Who say, "Let Him make speed, let Him hasten His work, that we may see *it;*
And let the purpose of the Holy One of Israel draw near
And come to pass, that we may know *it!*"
20 Woe to those who [a]call evil good, and good evil;
Who [b]substitute darkness for light and light for darkness;
Who substitute bitter for sweet, and sweet for bitter!
21 Woe to those who are [a]wise in their own eyes,
And clever in their own sight!
22 [a]Woe to those who are heroes in drinking wine,
And valiant men in mixing strong drink;
23 [a]Who justify the wicked for a bribe,
And [b]take away the rights of the ones who are in the right!

24 Therefore, [a]as a tongue of fire consumes stubble,
And dry grass collapses into the flame,
So their [b]root will become [c]like rot and their blossom blow away as dust;
For they have [d]rejected the law of the LORD of hosts,
And despised the word of the Holy One of Israel.
25 On this account the [a]anger of the LORD has burned against His people,
And He has stretched out His hand against them and struck them down,
And the mountains quaked; and their [b]corpses lay like refuse in the middle of the streets.
[c]For all this His anger is not spent,
But His [d]hand is still stretched out.

26 He will also lift up a [a]standard to the nations afar off,
And will [b]whistle for [1]it [c]from the ends of the earth;
And behold, it will [d]come with speed swiftly.
27 [a]No one in it is weary or stumbles,
None slumbers or sleeps;
Nor is the [b]belt at its waist undone,
Nor its sandal strap broken.
28 [a]Its arrows are sharp, and all its bows are bent;
The hoofs of its horses seem like flint, and its *chariot* [b]wheels like a whirlwind.
29 Its [a]roaring is like a lioness, and it roars like young lions;
It growls as it [b]seizes the prey,
And carries *it* off with [c]no one to deliver *it.*
30 And it shall [a]growl over it in that day like the roaring of the sea.
If one [b]looks to the land, behold, there is darkness *and* distress;
Even the light is darkened by its clouds.

CHAPTER 6

Isaiah's Vision

IN the year of King Uzziah's death, [a]I saw the Lord sitting on a throne, lofty and exalted, with the train of His robe filling the temple.
2 Seraphim stood above Him, [a]each having six wings; with two he covered his face, and with two he covered his feet, and with two he flew.
3 And one called out to another and said, "Holy, Holy, Holy, is the LORD of hosts, the [a]whole earth is full of His glory."
4 And the [1]foundations of the thresholds trembled at the voice of him who called out, while the [2]temple was filling with smoke.
5 Then I said,
"[a]Woe is me, for I am ruined!
Because I am a man of [b]unclean lips,
And I live among a [c]people of unclean lips;
For my eyes have seen the [d]King, the LORD of hosts."
6 Then one of the seraphim flew to me, with a burning coal in his hand which he had taken from the altar with tongs.
7 And he [a]touched my mouth *with it* and said, "Behold, this has touched your lips; and [b]your iniquity is taken away, and your sin is [1]forgiven."

16 [a]Is. 8:13; 29:23; 1 Pet. 3:15 [b]Is. 2:11, 17; 33:5, 10 [c]Is. 8:13; 29:23; 1 Pet. 3:15
17 [a]Is. 7:25; Mic. 2:12; Zeph. 2:6
18 [a]Is. 59:4-8; Jer. 23:10-14
19 [a]Ezek. 12:22; 2 Pet. 3:4
20 [a]Prov. 17:15; Amos 5:7 [b]Job 17:12; Matt. 6:22, 23; Luke 11:34, 35
21 [a]Prov. 3:7; Rom. 12:16; 1 Cor. 3:18-20
22 [a]Prov. 23:20; Is. 6:11; 56:12; Hab. 2:15
23 [a]Ex. 23:8; Is. 1:23; 10:1, 2; Mic. 3:11; 7:3 [b]Ps. 94:21; James 5:6
24 [a]Is. 9:18, 19; Joel 2:5 [b]Job 18:16 [c]Hos. 5:12 [d]Is. 8:6; 30:9, 12; Acts 13:41
25 [a]2 Kin. 22:13, 17; Is. 66:15 [b]2 Kin. 9:37; Jer. 16:4 [c]Is. 9:12, 17, 21; 10:4; Jer. 4:8; Dan. 9:16 [d]Ex. 7:19; Is. 23:11
26 [1]Probably Assyria [a]Is. 13:2, 3 [b]Is. 7:18; Zech. 10:8 [c]Deut. 28:49 [d]Is. 13:4, 5
27 [a]Joel 2:7, 8 [b]Job 12:18; Dan. 5:6
28 [a]Ps. 7:12, 13; 45:5; Is. 13:18 [b]Is. 21:1; Jer. 4:13
29 [a]Jer. 51:38; Zeph. 3:3; Zech. 11:3 [b]Is. 10:6; 49:24, 25; Mic. 5:8 [c]Is. 42:22
30 [a]Is. 17:12; Jer. 6:23; Luke 21:25 [b]Is. 8:22; Jer. 4:23-28; Joel 2:10; Luke 21:25, 26
1 [a]John 12:41; Rev. 4:2, 3; 20:11
2 [a]Rev. 4:8
3 [a]Num. 14:21; Ps. 72:19
4 [1]Lit., *door sockets* [2]Lit., *house*
5 [a]Ex. 33:20; Luke 5:8 [b]Ex. 6:12, 30 [c]Is. 59:3; Jer. 9:3-8 [d]Jer. 51:57
7 [1]Lit., *atoned for* [a]Jer. 1:9; Dan. 10:16 [b]Is. 40:2; 53:5, 6, 11; John 1:7

Isaiah's Commission

8 Then I heard the [a]voice of the
Lord, saying, "Whom shall I send,
and who will go for Us?" Then [b]I
said, "Here am I. Send me!"
9 And He said, "Go, and tell this
people:
'Keep on listening, but do not
perceive;
Keep on looking, but do not understand.'
10 "Render the hearts of this people
insensitive,
Their ears dull,
And their eyes dim,
[a]Lest they see with their eyes,
Hear with their ears,
Understand with their hearts,
And repent and be healed."
11 Then I said, "Lord, [a]how long?"
And He answered,
"Until [b]cities are devastated *and*
without inhabitant,
Houses are without people,
And the land is utterly desolate,
12 "The LORD has removed men far
away,
And the [a]forsaken places are
many in the midst of the
land.
13 "Yet there will be a tenth portion
in it,
And it will again be *subject* to
burning,
Like a terebinth or an [a]oak
Whose stump remains when it
is felled.
The [b]holy seed is its stump."

CHAPTER 7

War against Jerusalem

NOW it came about in the days of
Ahaz, the son of Jotham, the son of
Uzziah, king of Judah, that Rezin
the king of Syria and Pekah the son
of Remaliah, king of Israel, went up
to Jerusalem to *wage* war against it,
but [a]could not conquer it.
2 When it was reported to the
[a]house of David, saying, "Syria [b]has
camped in [c]Ephraim," his heart and
the hearts of his people shook as the
trees of the forest shake with the
wind.
3 Then the LORD said to Isaiah,
"Go out now to meet Ahaz, you and
your son [1]Shear-jashub, at the end
of the [a]conduit of the upper pool, on
the highway to the [2]fuller's field,
4 and say to him, 'Take care, and
be [a]calm, have no [b]fear and [c]do not
be fainthearted because of these
two stubs of smoldering [d]firebrands, on account of the fierce anger of Rezin and Syria, and the [e]son
of Remaliah.
5 'Because [a]Syria, *with* Ephraim
and the son of Remaliah, has
planned evil against you, saying,
6 "Let us go up against Judah and
[1]terrorize it, and make for ourselves
a breach in [2]its walls, and set up the
son of Tabeel as king in the midst of
it,"
7 thus says the Lord [1]GOD, "[a]It
shall not stand nor shall it come to
pass.
8 "For the head of Syria is Damascus and the head of [a]Damascus is
Rezin (now within another 65 years
Ephraim will be shattered, *so that it
is* no longer a people),
9 and the head of Ephraim is Samaria and the head of Samaria is the
son of Remaliah. [a]If you will not believe, you surely shall not [1]last." ' "

The Child Immanuel

10 Then the LORD spoke again to
Ahaz, saying,
11 "Ask a [a]sign for yourself from
the LORD your God; [1]make *it* deep as
Sheol or high as [2]heaven."
12 But Ahaz said, "I will not ask,
nor will I test the LORD!"
13 Then he said, "Listen now, O
[a]house of David! Is it too slight a
thing for you to try the patience of
men, that you will [b]try the patience
of [c]my God as well?
14 "Therefore the Lord Himself will
give you a sign: Behold, [a]a [1]virgin
will be with child and bear a son,
and she will call His name [2b]Immanuel.
15 "He will eat [a]curds and honey
[1]at the time He knows *enough* to refuse evil and choose good.
16 "[a]For before the boy will know
enough to refuse evil and choose
good, [b]the land whose two kings
you dread will be forsaken.

Trials to Come for Judah

17 "The LORD will bring on you, on
your people, and on your father's
house such days as have never come
since the day that [a]Ephraim separated from Judah, the [b]king of Assyria."
18 And it will come about in that
day, that the LORD will [a]whistle for
the fly that is in the [1b]remotest part
of the rivers of Egypt, and for the
bee that is in the land of Assyria.
19 And they will all come and settle on the steep [1]ravines, on the
[a]ledges of the cliffs, [b]on all the thorn
bushes, and on all the [2]watering
places.

8 [a]Ezek. 10:5; Acts 9:4 [b]Acts 26:19
10 [a]Jer. 5:21
11 [a]Ps. 79:5 [b]Lev. 26:31; Is. 1:7; 3:8, 26
12 [a]Jer. 4:29
13 [a]Job 14:7 [b]Deut. 7:6; Ezra 9:2
1 [a]Is. 7:6, 7
2 [a]Is. 7:13; 22:22 [b]Is. 8:12 [c]Is. 9:9
3 [1]I.e., a remnant shall return [2]I.e., laundryman's [a]2 Kin. 18:17; Is. 36:2
4 [a]Ex. 14:13; Is. 30:15; Lam. 3:26 [b]Is. 10:24; Matt. 24:6 [c]Deut. 20:3; 1 Sam. 17:32; Is. 35:4 [d]Amos 4:11; Zech. 3:2 [e]Is. 7:1, 9
5 [a]Is. 7:2
6 [1]Lit., *cause it a sickening dread* [2]Lit., *it*
7 [1]YHWH, usually rendered LORD [a]Ps. 2:4-6; Is. 8:10; 28:18; Acts 4:25, 26
8 [a]Gen. 14:15; Is. 17:1-3
9 [1]Or, *be established* [a]2 Chr. 20:20; Is. 5:24; 8:6-8; 30:12-14
11 [1]So with the versions; M.T. *make the request deep or high* [2]Lit., *heights* [a]2 Kin. 19:29; Is. 37:30; 38:7, 8; 55:13
13 [a]Is. 7:2 [b]Is. 1:14; 43:24 [c]Is. 25:1
14 [1]Or, *maiden* [2]I.e., God is with us [a]Matt. 1:23 [b]Is. 8:8, 10
15 [1]Lit., *with respect to his knowing* [a]Is. 7:22
16 [a]Is. 8:4 [b]Is. 8:14; 17:3; Jer. 7:15; Hos. 5:3, 9, 14; Amos 1:3-5
17 [a]1 Kin. 12:16 [b]2 Chr. 28:20; Is. 8:7, 8; 10:5, 6
18 [1]Or, *mouth of the rivers*, i.e., the Nile Delta [a]Is. 5:26 [b]Is. 13:5
19 [1]Or, *wadis* [2]Or, *pastures* [a]Is. 2:19; Jer. 16:16 [b]Is. 7:24, 25

20 In that day the Lord will [a]shave
with a [b]razor, [c]hired from regions
beyond [d]the [1]Euphrates (*that is,*
with the king of Assyria), the head
and the hair of the legs; and it will
also remove the beard.
21 Now it will come about in that
day that a man may keep alive a
[a]heifer and a pair of sheep;
22 and it will happen that because
of the abundance of the milk produced he will eat curds, for every
one that is left within the land will
eat [a]curds and honey.
23 And it will come about in that
day, [a]that every place where there
used to be a thousand vines, *valued*
at a thousand *shekels* of silver, will
become [b]briars and thorns.
24 *People* will come there with
bows and arrows because all the
land will be briars and thorns.
25 And as for all the hills which
used to be cultivated with the hoe,
you will not go there for fear of
briars and thorns; but they will become a place for [1a]pasturing oxen
and for sheep to trample.

CHAPTER 8

Damascus and Samaria Fall

THEN the LORD said to me, "Take
for yourself a large tablet and [a]write
on it [1]in ordinary letters: [2]Swift is
the booty, speedy is the prey.
2"And [1]I will take to Myself faithful witnesses for testimony, [a]Uriah
the priest and Zechariah the son of
Jeberechiah."
3 So I approached the prophetess, and she conceived and gave
birth to a son. Then the LORD said to
me, "Name him [1]Maher-shalal-
hash-baz;
4 for [a]before the boy knows how
to cry out 'My father' or 'My
mother,' the wealth of Damascus
and the spoil of Samaria will be carried away before the king of Assyria."
5 And again the LORD spoke to
me further, saying,
6 "Inasmuch as these people
have [a]rejected the gently
flowing waters of Shiloah,
And rejoice in Rezin and the
son of Remaliah;
7 "Now therefore, behold, the
Lord is about to bring on
them the strong and abun-
dant [a]waters of the [1]Euphra-
tes,
Even the king of Assyria and
all his glory;
And it will [b]rise up over all its
channels and go over all its
banks.
8 "Then [a]it will sweep on into Judah, it will overflow and pass
through,
It will [b]reach even to the neck;
And the spread of its wings
will [1]fill the breadth of [2]your
land, O [c]Immanuel.

A Believing Remnant

9 "[a]Be broken, O peoples, and be
[1b]shattered;
And give ear all remote places
of the earth.
Gird yourselves, yet be [1]shat-
tered;
Gird yourselves, yet be [1]shat-
tered.
10 "[a]Devise a plan but it will be
thwarted;
State a [1]proposal, but [b]it will
not stand,
For [2c]God is with us."
11 For thus the LORD spoke to me
[1]with [a]mighty power and instructed
me [b]not to walk in the way of this
people, saying,
12 "You are not to say, '*It is* a [a]con-
spiracy!'
In regard to all that this people
call a conspiracy,
And [b]you are not to fear [1]what
they fear or be in dread of *it.*
13 "It is the [a]LORD of hosts [b]whom
you should regard as holy.
And He shall be your fear,
And He shall be your dread.
14 "Then He shall become a [a]sanc-
tuary;
But to both the houses of Israel, a [b]stone to strike and a
rock to stumble over,
And a snare and a [c]trap for the
inhabitants of Jerusalem.
15 "And many will stumble over
them,
Then they will fall and be broken;
They will even be snared and
caught."
16 [a]Bind up the testimony, [b]seal
the [1]law among [c]my disciples.
17 And I will [a]wait for the LORD
[b]who is hiding His face from the
house of Jacob; I will even look eagerly for Him.
18 [a]Behold, I and the children
whom the LORD has given me are for
[b]signs and wonders in Israel from
the LORD of hosts, who [c]dwells on
Mount Zion.
19 And when they say to you,
"[a]Consult the mediums and the
spiritists who whisper and mutter,"

20 [1]Lit., *River* [a]2 Kin. 18:13-16; Is. 24:1 [b]Ezek. 5:1-4 [c]Is. 10:5, 15 [d]Is. 8:7; 11:15; Jer. 2:18
21 [a]Is. 14:30; 27:10; Jer. 39:10
22 [a]Is. 8:15
23 [a]Is. 5:10; 32:13, 14 [b]Is. 5:6
25 [1]Lit., *sending* [a]Is. 5:17
1 [1]Lit., *with the stylus of man* [2]Heb., *Maher-shalal-hash-baz;* cf. v. 3 [a]Is. 30:8; Hab. 2:2
2 [1]Another reading, *take for me* [a]2 Kin. 16:10, 11, 15, 16
3 [1]I.e., Swift is the booty, speedy is the prey; cf. v. 1
4 [a]Is. 1:20; 5:24; 7:9; 30:12
6 [a]Is. 1:20; 5:24; 7:9; 30:12
7 [1]Lit., *River* [a]Is. 17:12, 13 [b]Amos 8:8; 9:5
8 [1]Lit., *be the fulness of* [2]Or, *Your* [a]Is. 10:6 [b]Is. 30:28 [c]Is. 7:14
9 [1]Or, *dismayed* [a]Is. 17:12-14 [b]Dan. 2:34, 35
10 [1]Lit., *word* [2]Heb., *Immanu-el* [a]Job 5:12; Is. 28:18 [b]Is. 7:7 [c]Is. 8:8; Rom. 8:31
11 [1]Lit., *with strength of the hand* [a]Ezek. 3:14 [b]Ezek. 2:8
12 [1]Lit., *their fear* [a]Is. 7:2; 30:1 [b]1 Pet. 3:14, 15
13 [a]Is. 5:16; 29:23 [b]Num. 20:12
14 [a]Is. 4:6; 25:4; Ezek. 11:16 [b]Luke 2:34; Rom. 9:33; 1 Pet. 2:8 [c]Is. 24:17, 18
16 [1]Or, *teaching* [a]Is. 8:1, 2; 29:11, 12 [b]Dan. 12:4 [c]Is. 50:4
17 [a]Is. 25:9; 30:18; Hab. 2:3 [b]Deut. 31:17; Is. 1:15; 45:15; 54:8
18 [a]Heb. 2:13 [b]Luke 2:34 [c]Ps. 9:11; Zech. 8:3
19 [a]Lev. 20:6; 2 Kin. 21:6; 23:24; Is. 19:3; 29:4; 47:12, 13

should not a people [b]consult their
God? *Should they consult* the dead
on behalf of the living?
20 To the [1][a]law and to the testimony! If they do not speak according to this word, it is because they
have no dawn.
21 And they will pass through [1]the
land [a]hard-pressed and famished,
and it will turn out that when they
are hungry, they will be enraged and
curse [2]their king and their God as
they face upward.
22 Then they will [a]look to the
earth, and behold, distress and
darkness, the gloom of anguish; and
they will be driven away into darkness.

CHAPTER 9

Birth and Reign of the Prince of Peace

1
BUT there will be no *more* [a]gloom
for her who was in anguish; in earlier times He [b]treated the land of
[c]Zebulun and the land of Naphtali
with contempt, but later on He shall
make *it* glorious, by the way of the
sea, on the other side of Jordan,
Galilee of the [2]Gentiles.

2 [1]The people who walk in darkness
Will see a great light;
Those who live in a dark land,
The light will shine on them.
3 [a]Thou shalt multiply the nation,
Thou [b]shalt [1]increase [2]their
gladness;
They will be glad in Thy presence
As with the gladness [3]of harvest,
As [4]men rejoice when they divide the spoil.
4 For Thou shalt break the yoke
of their burden and the staff
on their shoulders,
The rod of their [a]oppressor, as
[1]at the battle of Midian.
5 For every boot of the booted
warrior in the *battle* tumult,
And cloak rolled in blood, will
be for burning, fuel for the
fire.
6 For a [a]child will be born to us, a
[b]son will be given to us;
And the [c]government will [1]rest
[d]on His shoulders;
And His name will be called
[e]Wonderful Counselor,
[f]Mighty God,
Eternal [g]Father, Prince of
[h]Peace.
7 There will be [a]no end to the increase of *His* government or
of peace,
On the [b]throne of David and
over his kingdom,
To establish it and to uphold it
with [c]justice and righteousness
From then on and forevermore.
[d]The zeal of the LORD of hosts
will accomplish this.

God's Anger with Israel's Arrogance

8 The Lord sends a [1]message
against Jacob,
And it falls on Israel.
9 And all the people know *it,*
That is, Ephraim and the inhabitants of Samaria,
Asserting in pride and in [a]arro-
gance of heart:
10 "The bricks have fallen down,
But we will [a]rebuild with
smooth stones;
The sycamores have been cut
down,
But we will replace *them* with
cedars."
11 Therefore the LORD raises
against them adversaries
from Rezin,
And spurs their enemies on,
12 The Syrians on the east and the
[a]Philistines on the west;
And they [b]devour Israel with
[1]gaping jaws.
[c]In *spite of* all this His anger
does not turn away,
And His hand is still stretched
out.

13 Yet the people [a]do not turn
back to Him who struck
them,
Nor do they [b]seek the LORD of
hosts.
14 So the LORD cuts off [a]head and
tail from Israel,
Both palm branch and bulrush
[b]in a single day.
15 The head is [a]the elder and honorable man,
And the prophet who teaches
falsehood is the tail.
16 [a]For those who guide this people are leading *them* astray;
And those who are guided by
them are [1]brought to confusion.
17 Therefore the Lord does [a]not
take pleasure in their young
men,
[b]Nor does He have pity on their
[1]orphans or their widows;
For every one of them is [c]god-
less and an evildoer,

19 [b]Is. 30:2; 45:11

20 [1]Or, *teaching* [a]Is. 1:10; 8:16; Luke 16:29

21 [1]Lit., *it* [2]Or, *by their king* [a]Is. 9:20, 21

22 [a]Jer. 13:16; Amos 5:18, 20; Zeph. 1:14, 15

1 [1]Ch. 8:23 in Heb. [2]Or, *nations* [a]Is. 8:22 [b]2 Kin. 15:29; 2 Chr. 16:4 [c]Matt. 4:15, 16

2 [1]Ch. 9:1 in Heb. text

3 [1]Another reading: *not increase* [2]Lit., *the* [3]Lit., *in* [4]Lit., *they* [a]Is. 26:15 [b]Is. 35:10; 65:14, 18, 19; 66:10

4 [1]Lit., *in the day of Midian* [a]Is. 14:4; 49:26; 51:13; 54:14

6 [1]Lit., *be* [a]Is. 7:14; 11:1, 2; 53:2; Luke 2:11 [b]John 3:16 [c]Matt. 28:18; 1 Cor. 15:25 [d]Is. 22:22 [e]Is. 28:29 [f]Deut. 10:17; Neh. 9:32; Is. 10:21 [g]Is. 63:16; 64:8 [h]Is. 26:3, 12; 53:5; 54:10; 66:12

7 [a]Dan. 2:44; Luke 1:32, 33 [b]Is. 16:5 [c]Is. 11:4, 5; 32:1; 42:3, 4; 63:1 [d]Is. 37:32; 59:17

8 [1]Lit., *word*

9 [a]Is. 46:12

10 [a]Mal. 1:4

12 [1]Lit., *the whole mouth* [a]2 Chr. 28:18 [b]Ps. 79:7; Jer. 10:25 [c]Is. 5:25

13 [a]Jer. 5:3; Hos. 7:10 [b]Is. 31:1; Hos. 3:5

14 [a]Is. 19:15 [b]Rev. 18:8

15 [a]Is. 3:2, 3

16 [1]Or, *swallowed up* [a]Is. 3:12; Matt. 15:14; 23:16, 24

17 [1]Or, *fatherless* [a]Jer. 18:21; Amos 4:10; 8:13 [b]Is. 27:11 [c]Is. 10:6; 32:6

And every [d]mouth is speaking foolishness.
In *spite of* all this His anger does not turn away,
And His hand is still stretched out.

18 [a]For wickedness burns like a fire;
It consumes briars and thorns;
It even sets the thickets of the forest aflame,
And they roll upward in a column of smoke.
19 By the [a]fury of the LORD of hosts the [b]land is burned up,
And the [c]people are like fuel for the fire;
No [d]man spares his brother.
20 And [1]they slice off *what is* on the right hand but *still* are [a]hungry,
And [1]they eat *what is* on the left hand but they are not satisfied;
Each of them eats the [b]flesh of his own arm.
21 Manasseh *devours* Ephraim, and Ephraim Manasseh,
[a]*And* together they are against Judah.
In *spite of* all this His anger does not turn away,
And His hand is still stretched out.

CHAPTER 10

Assyria Is God's Instrument

WOE to those who [a]enact evil statutes,
And to those who constantly record [1]unjust decisions,
2 So as [a]to [1]deprive the needy of justice,
And rob the poor of My people of *their* rights,
In order [b]that widows may be their spoil,
And that they may plunder the [2]orphans.
3 Now [a]what will you do in the [b]day of punishment,
And in the devastation which will come [c]from afar?
[d]To whom will you flee for help?
And where will you leave your [1]wealth?
4 Nothing *remains* but to crouch [1]among the [a]captives
Or fall [1]among the [b]slain.
In *spite of* all this His anger does not turn away,
And His hand is still stretched out.

5 Woe to [a]Assyria, the [b]rod of My anger
And the staff in whose hands is [c]My indignation,
6 I send it against a [a]godless nation
And commission it against the [b]people of My fury
[c]To capture booty and [d]to seize plunder,
And to [1]trample them down like [e]mud in the streets.
7 Yet it [a]does not so intend
Nor does [1]it plan so in its heart,
But rather it is [2]its purpose to destroy,
And to cut off [3]many nations.
8 For it says, "Are not my princes [1]all kings?
9 "Is not Calno like Carchemish,
Or Hamath like Arpad,
Or Samaria like Damascus?
10 "As my hand has reached to the [a]kingdoms of the idols,
Whose graven images *were* greater than those of Jerusalem and Samaria,
11 Shall I not [1]do to Jerusalem and her images
Just as I have done to Samaria and [a]her idols?"

12 So it will be that when the Lord has completed all His [a]work on Mount Zion and on Jerusalem, *He will say,* "I will [1]punish the fruit of the arrogant heart of the king of Assyria and [b]the pomp of [2]his haughtiness."

13 For [a]he has said,
"By the power of my hand and by my wisdom I did *this,*
For I have understanding;
And I [b]removed the boundaries of the peoples,
And plundered their treasures,
And like a mighty man I brought down [1]*their* inhabitants,
14 And my hand reached to the riches of the peoples like a [a]nest,
And as one gathers abandoned eggs, I gathered all the earth;
And there was not one that flapped its wing or opened *its* beak or chirped."

15 Is the [a]axe to [b]boast itself over the one who chops with it?
Is the saw to exalt itself over the one who wields it?
That would be like [c]a [1]club wielding those who lift it,
Or like [d]a rod lifting *him who* is not wood.

17 [d]Matt. 12:34
18 [a]Ps. 83:14; Is. 1:7; Nah. 1:10; Mal. 4:1
19 [a]Is. 10:6; 13:9, 13; 42:25 [b]Joel 2:3 [c]Is. 1:31; 24:6 [d]Mic. 7:2, 6
20 [1]Lit., *he* [a]Is. 8:21, 22 [b]Is. 49:26
21 [a]2 Chr. 28:6, 8; Is. 11:13
1 [1]Lit., *mischief* or *misfortune* [a]Ps. 94:20; Is. 29:21; 59:4, 13
2 [1]Lit., *turn aside from* [2]Or, *fatherless* [a]Is. 5:23 [b]Is. 1:23; 3:14, 15
3 [1]Lit., *glory* [a]Job 31:14 [b]Is. 13:6; 26:14, 21; 29:6; Jer. 9:9; Hos. 9:7; Luke 19:44 [c]Is. 5:26 [d]Is. 20:6; 30:57; 31:3
4 [1]Lit., *under* [a]Is. 24:22 [b]Is. 22:2; 34:3; 66:16
5 [a]Is. 7:17; 8:7 [b]Jer. 51:20 [c]Is. 13:5; 30:30; 34:2; 66:14
6 [1]Lit., *make them a trampled place* [a]Is. 9:17 [b]Is. 9:19 [c]Is. 37:26, 27 [d]Is. 59:29 [e]Is. 5:25
7 [1]Lit., *its heart so plan* [2]Lit., *in its heart* [3]Lit., *not a few* [a]Gen. 50:20; Mic. 4:11, 12; Acts 2:23, 24
8 [1]Lit., *altogether*
10 [a]2 Kin. 19:17, 18
11 [1]Lit., *do thus* [a]Is. 2:8
12 [1]Lit., *visit* [2]Lit., *haughtiness of his eyes* [a]2 Kin. 19:31; Is. 28:21, 22; 29:14; 65:7 [b]Is. 37:23
13 [1]Or, *those who sit* on thrones [a]2 Kin. 19:22-24; Is. 37:24-27; Ezek. 28:4; Dan. 4:30 [b]Hab. 2:6-11
14 [a]Jer. 49:16; Obad. 4
15 [1]Lit., *staff* [a]Jer. 51:20 [b]Is. 29:16; 45:9; Rom. 9:20, 21 [c]Is. 10:5 [d]Is. 10:5

16 Therefore the Lord, the [1]GOD of hosts, will send a [a]wasting disease among his [b]stout warriors;
And under his [c]glory a fire will be kindled like a burning flame.
17 And the [a]light of Israel will become a fire and his [b]Holy One a flame,
And it will [c]burn and devour his thorns and his briars in a single day.
18 And He will [a]destroy the glory of his forest and of his fruitful garden, both soul and body;
And it will be as when a sick man wastes away.
19 And the [a]rest of the trees of his forest will be so small in number
That a child could write them down.

A Remnant Will Return

20 Now it will come about in that day that the remnant of Israel, and those of the house of Jacob who have escaped, will never again rely on the one who struck them, but will truly [a]rely on the LORD, the Holy One of Israel.
21 A [a]remnant will return, the remnant of Jacob, to the mighty God.
22 For [a]though your people, O Israel, may be like the sand of the sea,
Only a remnant within them will return;
A [b]destruction is determined, overflowing with righteousness.
23 For a complete destruction, one that is decreed, the Lord [1]GOD of hosts will execute in the midst of the whole land.
24 Therefore thus says the Lord [1]GOD of hosts, "O My people who dwell in [a]Zion, do not fear the Assyrian [2]who [b]strikes you with the rod and lifts up his staff against you, the way Egypt *did*.
25 "For in a very [a]little while My indignation *against you* will be spent, and My anger *will be directed* to their destruction."
26 And the LORD of hosts will [a]arouse a scourge against him like the slaughter of Midian at the rock of Oreb; and His [b]staff will be over the sea, and He will lift it up [c]the way *He did* in Egypt.
27 So it will be in that day, that [1]his [a]burden will be removed from your shoulders and his yoke from your neck, and the yoke will be broken because [b]of fatness.
28 He has come against Aiath,
He has passed through Migron;
At Michmash he deposited his [a]baggage.
29 They have gone through the pass, saying,
"They have made a lodging place in Geba."
Ramah is terrified, and Gibeah of Saul has fled away.
30 Cry aloud with your voice, O daughter of Gallim!
Pay attention, Laishah and [1]wretched Anathoth!
31 Madmenah has fled.
The inhabitants of Gebim have sought refuge.
32 Yet today he will halt at Nob;
He [a]shakes his fist at the mountain of the [1b]daughter of Zion, the hill of Jerusalem.

33 Behold, the Lord, the [1]GOD of hosts, will lop off the boughs with a terrible crash;
Those also who are [a]tall in stature will be cut down,
And those who are lofty will be abased.
34 And He will cut down the thickets of the forest with an iron *axe*,
And Lebanon will fall [1]by the Mighty One.

CHAPTER 11

Righteous Reign of the Branch

THEN a [a]shoot will spring from the [b]stem of Jesse,
And a [c]branch from his roots will bear fruit.
2 And the [a]Spirit of the LORD will rest on Him,
The spirit of [b]wisdom and understanding,
The spirit of counsel and [c]strength,
The spirit of knowledge and the fear of the LORD.
3 And He will delight in the fear of the LORD,
And He will not judge by what His eyes [a]see,
Nor make a decision by what His ears hear;
4 But with [a]righteousness He will judge the [b]poor,
And decide with fairness for the afflicted of the earth;
And He will strike the earth with the [c]rod of His mouth,
And with the [d]breath of His lips He will slay the wicked.

16 [1]YHWH, usually rendered LORD [a]Ps. 106:15 [b]Is. 17:4 [c]Is. 8:7; 10:18
17 [a]Is. 30:33; 31:9 [b]Is. 37:23 [c]Num. 11:1-3; Is. 27:4; 33:12; Jer. 4:4; 7:20
18 [a]Is. 10:33, 34
19 [a]Is. 21:17
20 [a]2 Chr. 14:11; Is. 17:7, 8; 50:10
21 [a]Is. 7:3
22 [a]Rom. 9:27, 28 [b]Is. 28:22; Dan. 9:27; Rom. 9:28
23 [1]YHWH, usually rendered LORD
24 [1]YHWH, usually rendered LORD [2]Lit., *he* [a]Ps. 8:5, 6 [b]Ex. 5:14-16
25 [a]Is. 17:14; Hag. 2:6
26 [a]Is. 37:36-38 [b]Ex. 14:16 [c]Ex. 14:27
27 [1]I.e., the Assyrian [a]Is. 9:4; 14:25 [b]Is. 30:23; 55:2
28 [a]Judg. 18:21; 1 Sam. 17:22
30 [1]An ancient version reads, *Answer her, O Anathoth*
32 [1]Another reading is, *house of* [a]Is. 19:16; Zech. 2:9 [b]Is. 1:8; Jer. 6:23
33 [1]YHWH, usually rendered LORD [a]Is. 37:24, 36-38; Ezek. 31:3; Amos 2:9
34 [1]Or, *as a mighty one*
1 [a]Is. 4:2; 53:2 [b]Is. 9:7; 11:10; Acts 13:23 [c]Is. 6:13; Jer. 23:5; Zech. 3:8
2 [a]Is. 42:1; 48:16; 61:1; Matt. 3:16; John 1:32 [b]John 16:13; 1 Cor. 1:30; Eph. 1:17, 18 [c]2 Tim. 1:7
3 [a]John 2:25; 7:24
4 [a]Is. 9:7; 16:5; 32:1 [b]Ps. 72:2, 14; Is. 3:14 [c]Ps. 2:9; Is. 49:2; Mal. 4:6 [d]Job 4:9; Is. 30:28, 33; 2 Thess. 2:8

5 Also [a]righteousness will be the belt about His loins,
And [b]faithfulness the belt about His waist.

6 And the [a]wolf will dwell with the lamb,
And the leopard will lie down with the kid,
And the calf and the young lion [1]and the fatling together;
And a little boy will lead them.
7 Also the cow and the bear will graze;
Their young will lie down together;
And the [a]lion will eat straw like the ox.
8 And the nursing child will play by the hole of the cobra,
And the weaned child will put his hand on the viper's den.
9 They will [a]not hurt or destroy in all My holy mountain,
For the [b]earth will be full of the knowledge of the LORD
As the waters cover the sea.

10 Then it will come about in that day
That the [a]nations will resort to the [b]root of Jesse,
Who will stand as a [1c]signal for the peoples;
And His resting place will be [2]glorious.

The Restored Remnant

11 Then it will happen on that day that the Lord
Will again recover the second time with His hand
The remnant of His people, who will remain,
From Assyria, Egypt, Pathros, Cush, Elam, Shinar, Hamath,
And from the [1a]islands of the sea.
12 And He will lift up a standard for the nations,
And will [a]assemble the banished ones of Israel,
And will gather the dispersed of Judah
From the four corners of the earth.
13 Then the [a]jealousy of Ephraim will depart,
And those who harass Judah will be cut off;
Ephraim will not be jealous of Judah,
And Judah will not harass Ephraim.
14 And they will [a]swoop down on the slopes of the Philistines on the west;
Together they will [b]plunder the sons of the east;
[1]They will possess Edom and Moab;
And the sons of Ammon will be [2]subject to them.
15 And the LORD will [1a]utterly destroy
The tongue of the [2]Sea of Egypt;
And He will wave His hand over the [3b]River
With His scorching wind;
And He will strike it into seven streams,
And make *men* walk over [4]dry-shod.
16 And there will be a [a]highway from Assyria
For the remnant of His people who will be left,
Just as there was for Israel
In [b]the day that they came up out of the land of Egypt.

CHAPTER 12

Thanksgiving Expressed

THEN you will say on that day,
"[a]I will give thanks to Thee, O LORD;
For [b]although Thou wast angry with me,
Thine anger is turned away,
And Thou dost comfort me.
2 "Behold, [a]God is my salvation,
I will [b]trust and not be afraid;
For [c]the LORD GOD is my strength and song,
And He has become my salvation."
3 Therefore you will joyously [a]draw water
From the [b]springs of salvation.
4 And in that day you will [a]say,
"[b]Give thanks to the LORD, call on His name.
[c]Make known His deeds among the peoples;
[1]Make *them* remember that His name is exalted."
5 [a]Praise the LORD in song, for He has done [1]excellent things;
Let this be known throughout the earth.
6 [a]Cry aloud and shout for joy, O inhabitant of Zion,
For [b]great in your midst is the Holy One of Israel.

CHAPTER 13

Prophecies About Babylon

THE [1]oracle concerning Babylon which Isaiah the son of Amoz saw.

5 [a]Eph. 6:14 [b]Is. 25:1
6 [1]Some versions read, *will feed together* [a]Is. 65:25
7 [a]Is. 65:25
9 [a]Job 5:23; Is. 65:25; Ezek. 34:25; Hos. 2:18 [b]Ps. 98:2, 3; Is. 45:6; 52:10; 66:18-23; Hab. 2:14
10 [1]Or, *standard* [2]Lit., *glory* [a]Luke 2:32; Acts 11:18 [b]Is. 11:1; Rom. 15:12 [c]Is. 11:12; 49:22; 62:10; John 3:14, 15; 12:32
11 [1]Or, *coastlands* [a]Is. 24:15; 42:4, 10, 12; 49:1; 51:5; 60:9; 66:19
12 [a]Is. 56:8; Zeph. 3:10; Zech. 10:6
13 [a]Is. 9:21; Jer. 3:18; Ezek. 37:16, 17, 22; Hos. 1:11
14 [1]Lit., *Edom and Moab will be the outstretching of their hand* [2]Lit., *their obedience* [a]Jer. 48:40; 49:22; Hab. 1:8 [b]Jer. 49:28
15 [1]Another reading is, *dry up the tongue* [2]Perhaps the Red Sea [3]I.e., the Euphrates [4]Lit., *in sandals* [a]Is. 43:16; 44:27; 50:2; 51:10, 11 [b]Is. 7:20; 8:7
16 [a]Is. 19:23; 35:8; 40:3; 62:10 [b]Ex. 14:26-29
1 [a]Ps. 9:1; Is. 25:1 [b]Ps. 30:5; Is. 40:1, 2; 54:7-10
2 [a]Is. 32:2; 45:17; 62:11 [b]Is. 26:3 [c]Ex. 15:2; Ps. 118:14
3 [a]John 4:10; 7:37, 38 [b]Is. 41:18; Jer. 2:13
4 [1]Or, *Proclaim to them that* [a]Is. 24:15; 42:12; 48:20 [b]Ps. 105:1 [c]Ps. 145:4
5 [1]Or, *gloriously* [a]Ex. 15:1; Ps. 98:1; Is. 24:14; 42:10, 11; 44:23
6 [a]Is. 52:9; 54:1; Zeph. 3:14 [b]Is. 1:24; 49:26; 60:16; Zeph. 3:15-17; Zech. 2:5, 10, 11
1 [1]Lit., *burden of*

2 [a]Lift up a standard on the [1b]bare hill,
Raise your voice to them,
[c]Wave the hand that they may [d]enter the doors of the nobles.
3 I have commanded My consecrated ones,
I have even called My [a]mighty warriors,
My proudly exulting ones,
To *execute* My anger.
4 A [a]sound of tumult on the mountains,
Like that of many people!
A sound of the uproar of kingdoms,
Of nations gathered together!
The LORD of hosts is mustering the army for battle.
5 They are coming from a far country
From the [1a]farthest horizons,
The LORD and His instruments of indignation,
To destroy the whole land.

Judgment on the Day of the LORD

6 Wail, for the [a]day of the LORD is near!
It will come as destruction from [1]the Almighty.
7 Therefore all hands will fall limp,
And every man's [a]heart will melt.
8 And they will be [a]terrified,
Pains and anguish will take hold of *them*;
They will [b]writhe like a woman in labor,
They will look at one another in astonishment,
Their faces aflame.
9 Behold, the day of the LORD is coming,
Cruel, with fury and burning anger,
To make the land a desolation;
And He will exterminate its sinners from it.
10 For the [a]stars of heaven and their constellations
Will not flash forth their light;
The [b]sun will be dark when it rises,
And the moon will not shed its light.
11 Thus I will punish the world for its evil,
And the wicked for their iniquity;
I will also put an end to the [a]arrogance of the proud,
And abase the [b]haughtiness of the [1]ruthless.
12 I will make mortal man [1a]scarcer than pure gold,
And mankind than the gold of Ophir.
13 Therefore I shall make the [a]heavens tremble,
And the earth will be shaken from its place
At the fury of the LORD of hosts
In the day of His burning anger.
14 And it will be that like a hunted gazelle,
Or like [a]sheep with none to gather *them*,
They will each turn to his own people,
And each one flee to his own land.
15 Anyone who is found will be [a]thrust through,
And anyone who is captured will fall by the sword.
16 Their [a]little ones also will be dashed to pieces
Before their eyes;
Their houses will be plundered
And their wives ravished.

Babylon Will Fall to the Medes

17 Behold, I am going to stir up the Medes against them,
Who will not value silver or [a]take pleasure in gold,
18 And *their* bows will [1]mow down the [a]young men,
They will not even have compassion on the fruit of the womb,
Nor will their [b]eye pity [2]children.
19 And Babylon, the [a]beauty of kingdoms, the glory of the Chaldeans' pride,
Will be as when God [b]overthrew Sodom and Gomorrah.
20 It will [a]never be inhabited or lived in from generation to generation;
Nor will the [b]Arab pitch *his* tent there,
Nor will shepherds make *their flocks* lie down there.
21 But [a]desert creatures will lie down there,
And their houses will be full of [1]owls,
Ostriches also will live there, and [2]shaggy goats will frolic there.
22 And [1]hyenas will howl in their fortified towers
And jackals in their luxurious [a]palaces.
Her *fateful* time also [2]will soon come
And her days will not be prolonged.

2 [1]Or, *wind-swept mountain* [a]Is. 5:26; Jer. 50:2 [b]Jer. 51:25 [c]Is. 10:32; 19:16 [d]Is. 45:1-3; Jer. 51:58
3 [a]Joel 3:11
4 [a]Is. 5:30; 17:12; Joel 3:14
5 [1]Lit., *end of heaven* [a]Is. 5:26; 7:18
6 [1]Heb., *Shaddai* [a]Is. 2:12; 10:3; 13:9; 34:2, 8; 61:2; Ezek. 30:3; Amos 5:18; Zeph. 1:7
7 [a]Is. 19:1; Ezek. 21:7; Nah. 2:10
8 [a]2 Kin. 19:26; Is. 21:3; Jer. 46:5 [b]Is. 26:17; Jer. 4:31; John 16:21
10 [a]Is. 5:30; Joel 2:10; Matt. 24:29; Mark 13:24; Luke 21:25 [b]Is. 24:23; 50:3; Acts 2:20
11 [1]Or, *tyrants, despots* [a]Is. 2:11; 23:9; Dan. 5:22, 23 [b]Jer. 48:29
12 [1]Lit., *more precious* [a]Is. 4:1; 6:11, 12
13 [a]Is. 34:4; 51:6
14 [a]1 Kin. 22:17; Matt. 9:36; Mark 6:34; 1 Pet. 2:25
15 [a]Is. 14:19; Jer. 50:25; 51:3, 4
16 [a]Ps. 137:8, 9; Is. 13:18; 14:21; Hos. 10:14; Nah. 3:10
17 [a]Prov. 6:34, 35
18 [1]Lit., *dash in pieces* [2]Lit., *sons* [a]2 Kin. 8:12; 2 Chr. 36:17 [b]Ezek. 9:5, 10
19 [a]Dan. 4:30; Rev. 18:11-16, 19 [b]Gen. 19:24; Deut. 29:23; Jer. 49:18; Amos 4:11
20 [a]Is. 14:23; 34:10-15; Jer. 51:37-43 [b]2 Chr. 17:11
21 [1]Or, *howling creatures* [2]Or, *goat demons* [a]Is. 34:11-15; Zeph. 2:14
22 [1]Or, *howling creatures* [2]Lit., *is near to come* [a]Is. 25:2; 32:14; 34:13

CHAPTER 14

Israel's Taunt

WHEN the LORD will [a]have compassion on Jacob, and again [b]choose Israel, and settle them in their own land, then strangers will join them and attach themselves to the house of Jacob.
2 And the peoples will take them along and bring them to their place, and the [a]house of Israel will possess them as an inheritance in the land of the LORD [b]as male and female servants; and they will take them as their captors, and will rule over their oppressors.
3 And it will be in the day when the LORD gives you [a]rest from your pain and turmoil and harsh service in which you have been enslaved,
4 that you will take up this [1]taunt against the king of Babylon, and say,

"How the oppressor has ceased,
And how [2]fury has ceased!
5"The LORD has broken the staff of the wicked,
The scepter of rulers
6 [a]Which used to strike the peoples in fury with unceasing strokes,
Which [1]subdued the nations in anger with unrestrained persecution.
7"The whole earth is at rest *and* is quiet;
They [a]break forth into shouts of joy.
8"Even the cypress trees rejoice over you, *and* the cedars of Lebanon, *saying,*
'Since you were laid low, no *tree* cutter comes up against us.'
9"Sheol from beneath is excited over you to meet you when you come;
It arouses for you the [1]spirits of the dead, all the [2]leaders of the earth;
It raises all the kings of the nations from their thrones.
10"[a]They will all respond and say to you,
'Even you have been made weak as we,
You have become like *us.*
11 'Your [a]pomp *and* the music of your harps
Have been brought down to Sheol;
Maggots are spread out *as your bed* beneath you,
And worms are your covering.'
12"How you have [a]fallen from heaven,
O [1]star of the morning, son of the dawn!
You have been cut down to the earth,
You who have weakened the nations!
13"But you said in your heart,
'I will [a]ascend to heaven;
I will [b]raise my throne above the stars of God,
And I will sit on the mount of assembly
In the recesses of the north.
14 'I will ascend above the heights of the clouds;
I will make myself like the Most High.'
15"Nevertheless you will be thrust down to Sheol,
To the recesses of the pit.
16"Those who see you will gaze at you,
They will [1]ponder over you, *saying,*
'Is this the man who made the earth tremble,
Who shook kingdoms,
17 Who made the world like a wilderness
And overthrew its cities,
Who did not [1]allow his prisoners to go home?'
18"All the kings of the nations lie in glory,
Each in his own [1]tomb.
19"But you have been cast out of your tomb
Like [1]a rejected branch,
[2]Clothed with the slain who are pierced with a sword,
Who go down to the stones of the pit,
Like a [a]trampled corpse.
20"You will not be united with them in burial,
Because you have ruined your country,
You have slain your people.
May the [a]offspring of evildoers not be mentioned forever.
21"Prepare for his sons a place of slaughter
Because of the [a]iniquity of their fathers.
They must not arise and take possession of the earth
And fill the face of the world with cities."

22"And I will rise up against
them," declares the LORD of hosts,
"and will cut off from Babylon
[a]name and survivors, [b]offspring and
posterity," declares the LORD.
23"I will also make it a possession
for the hedgehog, and swamps of

---

1 [a]Ps. 102:13; Is. 49:13, 15; 54:7, 8 [b]Is. 41:8, 9; 44:1; 49:7; Zech. 1:17; 2:12
2 [a]Is. 45:14; 49:23; 54:3 [b]Is. 60:10; 61:5; Dan. 7:18, 27
3 [a]Ezra 9:8, 9; Is. 11:10; 40:2; Jer. 30:10; 46:27
4 [1]Or, *proverb* [2]Amended from the meaningless *medhebah* to *marshebah*
6 [1]Or, *ruled* [a]Is. 10:14; 47:6
7 [a]Ps. 47:1-3; 98:1-9; 126:1-3
9 [1]Or, *shades* (Heb., *Repha'im*) [2]Lit., *male goats*
10 [a]Ezek. 32:21
11 [a]Is. 5:14; Ezek. 28:13
12 [1]Lit., *Helel;* i.e., shining one [a]Is. 34:4; Luke 10:18; Rev. 9:1
13 [a]Ezek. 28:2 [b]Dan. 5:22; 8:10; 2 Thess. 2:4
16 [1]Lit., *show themselves attentive to*
17 [1]Lit., *open*
18 [1]Lit., *house*
19 [1]Lit., *an abhorred branch* [2]Or, *As the clothing of those who are slain* [a]Is. 5:25
20 [a]Job 18:16, 19; Ps. 21:10; 37:28; Is. 1:4; 31:2
21 [a]Ex. 20:5; Lev. 26:39; Is. 13:16; Matt. 23:35
22 [a]Prov. 10:7 [b]Job 18:19; Is. 47:9

water, and I will sweep it with the broom of [a]destruction," declares the LORD of hosts.

Judgment on Assyria

24 The LORD of hosts has sworn saying, "Surely, [a]just as I have intended so it has happened, and just as I have planned so it will stand,
25 to break Assyria in My land, and I will trample him on My mountains. Then his [a]yoke will be removed from them, and his burden removed from their shoulder.
26"This is the [a]plan [1]devised against the whole earth; and this is the [b]hand that is stretched out against all the nations.
27"For [a]the LORD of hosts has planned, and who can frustrate *it*? And as for His stretched-out hand, who can turn it back?"
28 In the [a]year that King Ahaz died this [1]oracle came:

Judgment on Philistia

29"Do not rejoice, O Philistia, all of you,
Because the rod that [a]struck you is broken;
For from the serpent's root a viper will come out,
And its fruit will be a flying serpent.
30"And [1]those who are most [a]helpless will eat,
And the needy will lie down in security;
I will [2]destroy your root with [b]famine,
And it will kill off your survivors.
31"Wail, O [a]gate; cry, O city;
[1]Melt away, O Philistia, all of you;
For smoke comes from the [b]north,
And [c]there is no straggler in his ranks.
32"How then will one answer the [a]messengers of the nation?
That the LORD has founded Zion,
And [b]the afflicted of His people will seek refuge in it."

CHAPTER 15

Judgment on Moab

THE [1]oracle concerning Moab.
Surely in a night Ar of Moab is devastated *and* ruined,
Surely in a night Kir of Moab is devastated *and* ruined.
2 They have gone up to the [1]temple and *to* Dibon, *even* to the high places to weep.
Moab wails over Nebo and Medeba;
Everyone's head is [a]bald and every beard is cut off.
3 In their streets they have girded themselves with [a]sackcloth;
[b]On their housetops and in their squares
Everyone is wailing, [1c]dissolved in tears.
4 Heshbon and Elealeh also cry out,
Their voice is heard all the way to Jahaz;
Therefore the [1]armed men of Moab cry aloud;
His soul trembles within him.
5 My heart cries out for Moab;
His fugitives are as far as Zoar *and* Eglath-shelishiyah,
For they go up the ascent of Luhith weeping;
Surely on the road to Horonaim they raise a cry of distress [a]over *their* ruin.
6 For the [a]waters of Nimrim are [1]desolate.
Surely the grass is withered, the tender grass [2]died out,
There is [b]no green thing.
7 Therefore the [a]abundance *which* they have acquired and stored up
They carry off over the brook of [1]Arabim.
8 For the cry of distress has gone around the territory of Moab,
Its wail *goes* as far as Eglaim and its wailing even to Beer-elim.
9 For the waters of Dimon are full of [1]blood;
Surely I will bring added *woes* upon Dimon,
A [a]lion upon the fugitives of Moab and upon the remnant of the land.

CHAPTER 16

Prophecy of Moab's Devastation

[a]SEND the *tribute* lamb to the ruler of the land,
From [1b]Sela by way of the wilderness to the [c]mountain of the daughter of Zion.
2 Then, like [1a]fleeing birds *or* scattered [2]nestlings,
The daughters of Moab will be at the fords of the Arnon.
3"[1]Give *us* advice, make a decision;
[2]Cast your [a]shadow like night [3]at high noon;
Hide the outcasts, do not betray the fugitive.

14:23 [a]1 Kin. 14:10; Is. 13:6
24 [a]Job 23:13; Is. 46:11; 55:8, 9; Acts 4:28
25 [a]Is. 9:4; 10:27; Nah. 1:13
26 [1]Lit., *planned* [a]Is. 23:9; Zeph. 3:6, 8 [b]Ex. 15:12
27 [a]2 Chr. 20:6; Is. 43:13; Dan. 4:31, 35
28 [1]Or, *burden* [a]2 Kin. 16:20; 2 Chr. 28:27
29 [a]2 Chr. 26:6
30 [1]Lit., *the first-born of the helpless* [2]Lit., *put to death* [a]Is. 3:14, 15; 7:21, 22; 11:4 [b]Is. 8:21; 9:20; 51:19
31 [1]Or, *Become demoralized* [a]Is. 3:26; 24:12; 45:2 [b]Jer. 1:14 [c]Is. 34:16
32 [a]Is. 37:9 [b]Is. 4:6; 25:4; 57:13; Zeph. 3:12; Heb. 11:10; James 2:5
15:1 [1]Or, *burden of*
2 [1]Lit., *house* [a]Lev. 21:5; Jer. 48:37
3 [1]Lit., *going down in weeping* [a]Jon. 3:6-8 [b]Jer. 48:38 [c]Is. 22:4
4 [1]Another reading is, *the loins of*
5 [a]Is. 59:7; Jer. 4:20
6 [1]Lit., *desolations* [2]Lit., *come to an end* [a]Is. 19:5-7; Jer. 48:34 [b]Joel 1:10-12; 2:3
7 [1]Or, *the poplars* [a]Is. 30:6; Jer. 48:36
9 [1]Heb., *dam* (a word-play) [a]2 Kin. 17:25; Jer. 50:17
16:1 [1]I.e., Petra in Edom [a]2 Kin. 3:4; Ezra 7:17 [b]2 Kin. 14:7; Is. 42:11 [c]Is. 10:32
2 [1]Or, *fluttering* [2]Lit., *nest* [a]Prov. 27:8
3 [1]Lit., *Bring* [2]Lit., *Set* [3]Lit., *in the midst of the noon* [a]1 Kin. 18:4; Is. 25:4; 32:2

4 "Let the [1]outcasts of Moab stay with you;
Be a hiding place to them from the destroyer."
For the extortioner has come to an end, destruction has ceased,
[a]Oppressors have completely *disappeared* from the land.
5 A [a]throne will even be established in lovingkindness,
And a judge will sit on it in faithfulness in the tent of [b]David;
Moreover, he will seek justice
And be prompt in righteousness.

6 [a]We have heard of the pride of Moab, an excessive pride;
Even of his arrogance, pride, and fury;
[b]His idle boasts are [1]false.
7 Therefore Moab shall wail; everyone of Moab shall wail.
You shall moan for the [a]raisin cakes of [b]Kir-hareseth
As those who are utterly stricken.
8 For the fields of Heshbon have [1]withered, the vines of Sibmah *as well*;
The lords of the nations have trampled down its choice clusters
Which reached as far as Jazer *and* wandered to the deserts;
[a]Its tendrils spread themselves out *and* passed over the sea.
9 Therefore I will [a]weep bitterly for Jazer, for the vine of Sibmah;
I will drench you with my tears, O Heshbon and Elealeh;
For the shouting over your [b]summer fruits and your harvest has fallen away.
10 And [a]gladness and joy are taken away from the fruitful field;
In the [b]vineyards also there will be no cries of joy or jubilant shouting,
No [c]treader treads out wine in the presses,
For I have made the shouting to cease.
11 Therefore my [1a]heart intones like a harp for Moab,
And my [2]inward feelings for Kir-hareseth.
12 So it will come about when Moab [a]presents himself,
When he [b]wearies himself upon *his* [c]high place,
And comes to his sanctuary to pray,
That he will not prevail.

13 This is the word which the
LORD spoke earlier concerning
Moab.
14 But now the LORD speaks, saying, "Within three years, as [1a]a
hired man would count them, the
glory of [b]Moab will be degraded
along with all *his* great population,
and *his* remnant will be very small
and [2]impotent."

CHAPTER 17

Prophecy About Damascus

THE [1]oracle concerning Damascus.
"Behold, Damascus is about to be [a]removed from being a city,
And it will become a [b]fallen ruin.
2 "The cities [1]of Aroer are forsaken;
They will be for [a]flocks [2]to lie down in,
And there will be [b]no one to frighten *them*.
3 "The [1a]fortified city will disappear from Ephraim,
And [2]sovereignty from Damascus
And the remnant of Syria;
They will be like the [b]glory of the sons of Israel,"
Declares the LORD of hosts.

4 Now it will come about in that day that the [a]glory of Jacob will [1]fade,
And the fatness of his flesh will become lean.
5 It will be [a]even like the [1]reaper gathering the standing grain,
As his arm harvests the ears,
Or it will be like one gleaning ears of grain
In the valley of Rephaim.
6 Yet [a]gleanings will be left in it like the [1]shaking of an olive tree,
Two *or* three olives on the topmost bough,
Four *or* five on the branches of a fruitful tree,
Declares the LORD, the God of Israel.
7 In that day man will [a]have regard for his Maker,
And his eyes will look to the Holy One of Israel.
8 And he will not have regard for the [a]altars, the work of his hands,

4 [1]So the versions; M.T., *My outcasts, as for Moab* [a]Is. 9:4; 14:4; 49:26; 51:13; 54:14
5 [a]Is. 9:6, 7; 32:1; 55:4; Dan. 7:14; Mic. 4:7; Luke 1:33 [b]Is. 9:7
6 [1]Lit., *not so* [a]Jer. 48:29; Amos 2:1; Obad. 3, 4; Zeph. 2:8, 10 [b]Jer. 48:30
7 [a]1 Chr. 16:3 [b]2 Kin. 3:25; Jer. 48:31
8 [1]Or, *languished* [a]Jer. 48:32
9 [a]Jer. 48:32 [b]Jer. 40:10, 12; 48:32
10 [a]Is. 24:8; Jer. 48:33 [b]Judg. 9:27; Is. 24:7; Amos 11:17 [c]Job 24:11; Amos 9:13
11 [1]Lit., *entrails murmur* [2]Lit., *inward part* [a]Is. 15:5; 63:15; Jer. 48:36; Hos. 11:8; Phil. 2:1
12 [a]Num. 22:39-41; Jer. 48:35 [b]1 Kin. 18:29 [c]Is. 15:2
14 [1]Lit., *the years of a hireling* [2]Lit., *not mighty* [a]Job 7:1; 16:6; Is. 21:16 [b]Is. 25:10; Jer. 48:42
1 [1]Or, *burden of* [a]Is. 7:16; 8:4; 10:9 [b]Is. 25:2; Jer. 49:2; Mic. 1:6
2 [1]Gk. reads, *forever and ever* [2]Lit., *and they will lie down* [a]Is. 7:21, 22; Ezek. 25:5; Zeph. 2:6 [b]Mic. 4:4
3 [1]Or, *fortification* [2]Or, *royal power, kingdom* [a]Is. 7:8, 16; 8:4 [b]Is. 17:4; Hos. 9:11
4 [1]Lit., *become thin* [a]Is. 10:3
5 [1]Lit., *gathering of the harvest, the standing grain* [a]Is. 17:11; Jer. 51:33; Joel 3:13; Matt. 13:30
6 [1]Lit., *striking* [a]Deut. 4:27; Is. 24:13; 27:12; Obad. 5
7 [a]Is. 10:20; Hos. 3.5, 6:1; Mic. 7:7
8 [a]2 Chr. 34:7; Is. 27:9

Nor will he look to that which his [b]fingers have made,
Even the [1c]Asherim and [2]incense stands.
9 In that day [1]their strong cities will be like [2]forsaken places in the forest,
Or like [3]branches which they abandoned before the sons of Israel;
And [4]the land will be a desolation.
10 For [a]you have forgotten the [b]God of your salvation
And have not remembered the [c]rock of your refuge.
Therefore you plant delightful plants
And set them with vine slips of a strange *god*.
11 In the day that you plant *it* you carefully [a]fence *it* in,
And in the [b]morning you bring your seed to blossom;
But the harvest will [c]be a heap
In a day of sickliness and incurable pain.

12 Alas, the uproar of many peoples
[a]Who roar like the roaring of the seas,
And the rumbling of nations
Who rush on like the [b]rumbling of mighty waters!
13 The [a]nations rumble on like the rumbling of many waters,
But He will [b]rebuke them and they will flee far away,
And be chased [c]like chaff in the mountains before the wind,
Or like whirling dust before a gale.
14 At evening time, behold, *there is* terror!
Before morning [a]they are no more.
[1]Such *will be* the portion of those who plunder us,
And the lot of those who pillage us.

Chapter 18

Message to Ethiopia

ALAS, oh land of whirring wings
Which lies beyond the rivers of [1]Cush,
2 Which sends envoys by the sea,
Even in [a]papyrus vessels on the surface of the waters.
Go, swift messengers, to a nation [1b]tall and smooth,
To a people feared [2]far and wide,
A powerful and oppressive nation
Whose land the rivers divide.
3 [a]All you inhabitants of the world and dwellers on earth,
As soon as a standard is raised on the mountains, you will see *it*,
And as soon as the trumpet is blown, you will hear *it*.
4 For thus the LORD has told me,
"I will look [1]from My [a]dwelling place quietly
Like dazzling heat in the [2b]sunshine,
Like a cloud of dew in the heat of harvest."
5 For [a]before the harvest, as soon as the bud [1]blossoms
And the flower becomes a ripening grape,
Then He will cut off the sprigs with pruning knives
And remove *and* cut away the spreading branches.
6 They will be left together for mountain birds [a]of prey,
And for the beasts of the earth;
And the birds of prey will spend the summer *feeding* on them,
And all the beasts of the earth will spend harvest time on them.
7 At that time a gift of homage will be brought to the LORD of hosts
[1]From a [a]people [2]tall and smooth,
Even from a people feared [3]far and wide,
A powerful and oppressive nation,
Whose land the rivers divide—
To the [b]place of the name of the LORD of hosts, *even* Mount Zion.

Chapter 19

Message to Egypt

THE [1]oracle concerning Egypt.
Behold, the LORD is [a]riding on a swift cloud, and is about to come to Egypt;
The [b]idols of Egypt will tremble at His presence,
And the [c]heart of the Egyptians will melt within them.
2 "So I will incite Egyptians against Egyptians;
And they will [a]each fight against his brother, and each against his neighbor,
City against city, *and* kingdom against kingdom.

8 [1]I.e., wooden symbols of a female deity [2]Or, *Sun pillars* [b]Is. 2:8, 20; 30:22; 31:7 [c]Ex. 34:13; Deut. 7:5; Mic. 5:14
9 [1]I.e., man's [2]Gk. reads, *the deserted places of the Amorites and the Hivites which they abandoned* [3]Or, *the tree-top* [4]Lit., *it*
10 [a]Is. 51:13 [b]Ps. 68:19; Is. 12:2; 33:2; 61:10; 62:11 [c]Deut. 32:4, 18, 31; Is. 26:4; 30:29; 44:8
11 [a]Matt. 21:23 [b]Ps. 90:6 [c]Job 4:8; Hos. 8:7; 10:13
12 [a]Jer. 6:23; Ezek. 43:2; Luke 21:25 [b]Ps. 18:4
13 [a]Is. 33:3 [b]Ps. 9:5; Is. 41:11 [c]Job 21:18; Ps. 1:4; 83:13; Is. 29:5; 41:15, 16
14 [1]Lit., *This* [a]2 Kin. 19:35; Is. 41:12
1 [1]Or, *Ethiopia*
2 [1]Lit., *drawn out* [2]Lit., *from it and beyond* [a]Is. 18.7 [b]Gen. 10:8, 9; 2 Chr. 12:2-4; 14:9; 16:8
3 [a]Ps. 49:1; Mic. 1:2
4 [1]Lit., *in* [2]Lit., *light* [a]Is. 26:21; Hos. 5:15 [b]2 Sam. 23:4
5 [1]Lit., *is finished* [a]Is. 17:10, 11; Ezek. 17:6-10
6 [a]Is. 46:11; 56:9; Jer. 7:33; Ezek. 32:4-6; 39:17-20
7 [1]So with some ancient versions and DSS; M.T. implies: *Consisting of a people* [2]Lit., *drawn out* [3]Lit., *from it and beyond* [a]Ps. 68:31; Is. 45:14; Zeph. 3:10; Acts 8:27-38 [b]Zech. 14:16, 17
1 [1]Or, *burden of* [a]Ps. 18:9, 10; 104:3; Matt. 26:64; Rev. 1:7 [b]Ex. 12:12; Jer. 43:12; 44:8 [c]Josh. 2:11; Is. 13:7
2 [a]Judg. 7:22; 1 Sam. 14:20; 2 Chr. 20:23; Matt. 10:21, 36

3 "Then the spirit of the Egyptians will be demoralized within them;
And I will confound their strategy,
So that [a]they will resort to idols and ghosts of the dead,
And to [1]mediums and spiritists.
4 "Moreover, I will deliver the Egyptians into the hand of a [a]cruel master,
And a [1]mighty king will rule over them," declares the Lord [2]GOD of hosts.

5 [a]And the waters from the sea will dry up,
And the river will be parched and dry.
6 And the [1a]canals will emit a stench,
The [2b]streams of Egypt will thin out and dry up;
[c]The reeds and rushes will rot away.
7 The bulrushes by the [a]Nile, by the [1]edge of the Nile
And all the sown fields by the Nile
Will become dry, be driven away, and be no more.
8 And the [a]fishermen will lament,
And all those who cast a line into the Nile will mourn,
And those who spread nets on the waters will pine away.
9 Moreover, the manufacturers of linen made from combed flax
And the weavers of white [a]cloth will be [1]utterly dejected.
10 And the [a]pillars *of Egypt* will be crushed;
All the hired laborers will be grieved in soul.

11 The princes of [1]Zoan are mere fools;
The advice of Pharaoh's wisest advisers has become [2]stupid.
How can you *men* say to Pharaoh,
"I am a son of the [a]wise, a son of ancient kings"?
12 Well then, where are your wise men?
Please let them tell you,
And let them [1]understand what the LORD of hosts
Has [a]purposed against Egypt.
13 The princes of [1]Zoan have acted foolishly,
The princes of [a]Memphis are deluded;
Those who are the [b]cornerstone of her tribes
Have [2]led Egypt astray.
14 The LORD has mixed within her a spirit of [a]distortion;
[b]They have led Egypt astray in all [1]that it does,
As a drunken man [2]staggers in his vomit.
15 And there will be no work for Egypt
[a]Which *its* head or tail, *its* palm branch or bulrush, may do.

16 In that day the Egyptians will become like women, and they will tremble and be in [a]dread because of the waving of the hand of the LORD of hosts, which He is going to wave over them.

17 And the land of Judah will become a [1]terror to Egypt; everyone [2]to whom it is mentioned will be in dread of it, because of the [a]purpose of the LORD of hosts which He is purposing against them.

18 In that day five cities in the land of Egypt will be speaking the language of Canaan and [a]swearing *allegiance* to the LORD of hosts; one will be called the City of [1]Destruction.

19 In that day there will be an [a]altar to the LORD in the midst of the land of Egypt, and a [b]pillar to the LORD near its border.

20 And it will become a sign and a witness to the LORD of hosts in the land of Egypt; for they will cry to the LORD because of oppressors, and He will send them a [a]Savior and a [1b]Champion, and He will deliver them.

21 Thus the LORD will make Himself known to Egypt, and the Egyptians will know the LORD in that day. They will even worship with [a]sacrifice and offering, and will make a vow to the LORD and perform it.

22 And the LORD will strike Egypt, striking but [a]healing; so they will [b]return to the LORD, and He will respond to them and will heal them.

23 In that day there will be a [a]highway from Egypt to Assyria, and the Assyrians will come into Egypt and the Egyptians into Assyria, and the Egyptians will [b]worship with the Assyrians.

24 In that day Israel will be the third *party* with Egypt and Assyria, a blessing in the midst of the earth,

25 whom the LORD of hosts has blessed, saying, "Blessed is [a]Egypt My people, and Assyria the work of My hands, and Israel My inheritance."

3 [1]Or, *ghosts and spirits* [a]1 Chr. 10:13; Is. 8:19; Dan. 2:2
4 [1]Or, *fierce* [2]YHWH, usually rendered LORD [a]Is. 20:4; Jer. 46:26; Ezek. 29:19
5 [a]Is. 50:2; Jer. 51:36; Ezek. 30:12
6 [1]Lit., *rivers* [2]Or, *Nile branches;* i.e., the delta [a]Ex. 7:18 [b]Is. 37:25 [c]Ex. 2:3; Job 8:11; Is. 15:6
7 [1]Or, *mouth* [a]Is. 23:3, 10
8 [a]Ezek. 47:10; Hab. 1:15
9 [1]Lit., *ashamed* [a]Prov. 7:16; Ezek. 27:7
10 [a]Ps. 11:13
11 [1]Or, *Tanis* [2]Or, *brutish* [a]Gen. 41:38, 39; 1 Kin. 4:30; Acts 7:22
12 [1]Or, *know* [a]Is. 14:24; Rom. 9:17
13 [1]Or, *Tanis* [2]Or, *have caused Egypt to stagger* [a]Jer. 2:16; 46:14, 19; Ezek. 30:13 [b]Zech. 10:4
14 [1]Lit., *its work* [2]Or, *goes astray* [a]Prov. 12:8; Matt. 17:17 [b]Is. 3:12; 9:16
15 [a]Is. 9:14, 15
16 [a]2 Cor. 5:11; Heb. 10:31
17 [1]Or, *cause of shame* [2]Lit., *who mentions it will be in dread to it* [a]Is. 14:24; Dan. 4:35
18 [1]Some ancient mss. and versions read, *the Sun* [a]Is. 45:23; 65:16
19 [a]Is. 56:7; 60:7 [b]Gen. 28:18; Ex. 24:4; Josh. 22:10, 26, 27
20 [1]Lit., *Mighty One* [a]Is. 43:3, 11; 45:15, 21; 49:26; 60:16; 63:8 [b]Is. 49:25
21 [a]Is. 56:7; 60:7; Zech. 14:16-18
22 [a]Deut. 32:39; Is. 30:26; 57:18; Heb. 12:11 [b]Is. 27:13; 45:14; Hos. 14:1
23 [a]Is. 11:16; 35:8; 49:11; 62:10 [b]Is. 27:13
25 [a]Is. 45:14

Chapter 20

Prophecy About Egypt and Ethiopia

IN the year that the [1]commander
came to Ashdod, when Sargon the
king of Assyria sent him and he
fought against Ashdod and captured it,
2 at that time the LORD spoke
through Isaiah the son of Amoz,
saying, "Go and loosen the [a]sack-
cloth from your hips, and take your
[b]shoes off your feet." And he did so,
going [c]naked and barefoot.
3 And the LORD said, "Even as
My servant Isaiah has gone naked
and barefoot three years as a [1a]sign
and token against Egypt and
[2b]Cush,
4 so the [a]king of Assyria will lead
away the captives of Egypt and the
exiles of Cush, [b]young and old,
naked and barefoot with buttocks
uncovered, to the shame of Egypt.
5 "Then they shall be [a]dismayed
and ashamed because of Cush their
hope and Egypt their [b]boast.
6 "So the inhabitants of this coastland will say in that day, 'Behold,
such is our hope, where we fled [a]for
help to be delivered from the king of
Assyria; and we, [b]how shall we escape?' "

Chapter 21

God Commands That Babylon Be Taken

THE [1]oracle concerning the [2a]wil-
derness of the sea.
As [b]windstorms in the [3]Negev
sweep on,
It comes from the wilderness,
from a terrifying land.
2 A [a]harsh vision has been shown
to me;
The [b]treacherous one still deals
treacherously, *and* the destroyer still destroys.
Go up, Elam, lay siege, Media;
I have made an end of all the
groaning she has caused.
3 For this reason my [a]loins are
full of anguish;
Pains have seized me like the
pains of a [b]woman in labor.
I am so bewildered I cannot
hear, so terrified I cannot see.
4 My mind reels, horror over-
whelms me;
The twilight I longed for has
been [a]turned for me into
trembling.
5 They [a]set the table, they spread
out the cloth, they eat, they
drink;
"Rise up, captains, oil the
shields,"
6 For thus the Lord says to me,
"Go, station the sentry, let him
[a]report what he sees.
7 "When he sees [a]riders, horsemen in pairs,
A train of donkeys, a train of
camels,
Let him pay close attention,
very close attention."
8 Then [1]the sentry called *like* a
lion,
"[a]O Lord, I stand continually by
day on the watchtower,
And I am stationed every night
at my guard post.
9 "Now behold, here comes a
troop of riders, horsemen in
pairs."
And one answered and said,
"[a]Fallen, fallen is Babylon;
And all the [b]images of her gods
[1]are shattered on the
ground."
10 O my [a]threshed *people*, and my
[1]afflicted of the threshing
floor!
What I have heard from the
LORD of hosts,
The God of Israel, I make
known to you.

Oracles About Edom and Arabia

11 The [1]oracle concerning [2a]E-
dom.
One keeps calling to me from
[b]Seir,
"Watchman, [3]how far gone is
the night?
Watchman, [3]how far gone is
the night?"
12 The watchman says,
"Morning comes but also night.
If you would inquire, inquire;
Come back again."

13 The [1]oracle about [a]Arabia.
In the thickets of Arabia you
[2]must spend the night,
O caravans of [b]Dedanites.
14 Bring water [1]for the thirsty,
O inhabitants of the land of [a]Te-
ma,
Meet the fugitive with bread.
15 For they have [a]fled from the
swords,
From the drawn sword, and
from the bent bow,
And from the press of battle.
16 For thus the Lord said to me,
"In a [a]year, as [1]a hired man would
count it, all the splendor of Kedar
will terminate;
17 and the [a]remainder of the number of bowmen, the mighty men of

---

1 [1]Heb., *Tartan*
2 [a]Zech. 13:4; Matt. 3:4 [b]Ezek. 24:17, 23 [c]1 Sam. 19:24; Mic. 1:8
3 [1]Or, *wonder* [2]Or, *Ethiopia*, so in vs. 4, 5 [a]Is. 8:18 [b]Is. 37:9; 43:3
4 [a]Is. 19:4 [b]Is. 47:2, 3
5 [a]2 Kin. 18:21; Is. 30:3-5; 31:1; Ezek. 29:6, 7 [b]Jer. 9:23, 24; 17:5; 1 Cor. 3:21
6 [a]Is. 10:3; 30:7; 31:3; Jer. 30:1, 7, 15-17; 31:1-3 [b]Matt. 23:33; 1 Thess. 5:3; Heb. 2:3

1 [1]Or, *burden of* [2]Or, *sandy wastes, sea country* [3]I.e., South country [a]Is. 13:20-22; 14:23; Jer. 51:42 [b]Dan. 11:40; Zech. 9:14
2 [a]Ps. 60:3 [b]Is. 24:16; 33:1
3 [a]Is. 13:8; 16:11 [b]Ps. 48:6; Is. 13:8; 26:17; 1 Thess. 5:3
4 [a]Deut. 28:67
5 [a]Jer. 51:39, 57; Dan. 5:1-4
6 [a]2 Kin. 9:17-20
7 [a]Is. 21:9
8 [1]Lit., *he;* i.e., the sentry, cf. v. 6 [a]Hab. 2:1
9 [1]Lit., *he has shattered to the earth* [a]Is. 13:19; 47:5, 9; 48:14; Jer. 51:8; Rev. 14:8 [b]Is. 46:1; Jer. 50:2; 51:44
10 [1]Lit., *son* [a]Jer. 51:33; Mic. 4:13
11 [1]Lit., *burden* [2]So the Gk.; Heb., *Dumah, silence* [3]Lit., *what is the time of the night?* [a]Gen. 25:14 [b]Gen. 32:3
13 [1]Or, *burden* [2]Or, *will spend* [a]Jer. 25:23, 24; 49:28 [b]Gen. 10:7; Ezek. 27:15
14 [1]Lit., *to meet* [a]Gen. 25:15; Job 6:19
15 [a]Is. 13:14, 15; 17:13
16 [1]Lit., *the years of a hireling* [a]Is. 16:14
17 [a]Is. 10:19

the sons of Kedar, will be few; for the LORD God of Israel [b]has spoken."

CHAPTER 22

The Valley of Vision

THE [1]oracle concerning the [a]valley of vision.
What is the matter with you now, that you have all gone up to the [b]housetops?
2 You who were full of noise,
You boisterous town, you [a]exultant city;
Your slain were [b]not slain with the sword,
Nor [1]did they die in battle.
3 All your rulers have fled together,
And have been captured [1]without the bow;
All of you who were found were taken captive together,
[2]Though they had fled far away.
4 Therefore I say, "Turn your eyes away from me,
Let me weep bitterly,
Do not [1]try to comfort me concerning the destruction of the daughter of my people."
5 [a]For the Lord [1]GOD of hosts has a [b]day of panic, [c]subjugation, and confusion
[d]In the valley of vision,
A breaking down of walls
And a crying [2]to the mountain.
6 And [a]Elam took up the quiver
With the chariots, [1]infantry, *and* horsemen;
And Kir uncovered the shield.
7 Then your choicest valleys were [a]full of chariots,
And the horsemen took up fixed positions at the gate.
8 And He removed the [1]defense of Judah.
In that day you [2]depended on the weapons of the [a]house of the forest,
9 And you saw that the breaches
In the *wall* of the city of David were many;
And you [a]collected the waters of the lower pool.
10 Then you counted the houses of Jerusalem,
And you tore down houses to fortify the wall.
11 And you made a reservoir [a]between the two walls
For the waters of the [b]old pool.
But you did not [1]depend on Him who made it,
Nor did you [2]take into consideration Him who planned it long ago.
12 Therefore in that day the Lord [1]GOD of hosts, called *you* to [a]weeping, to wailing,
To shaving the head, and to wearing sackcloth.
13 Instead, there is [a]gaiety and gladness,
Killing of cattle and slaughtering of sheep,
Eating of meat and drinking of wine:
"[b]Let us eat and drink, for tomorrow we may die."
14 But the LORD of hosts revealed Himself [1]to me,
"Surely this iniquity shall not be [2]forgiven you
[a]Until you die," says the Lord [3]GOD of hosts.
15 Thus says the Lord [1]GOD of hosts,
"Come, go to this steward,
To Shebna, who is in charge of the *royal* household,
16 'What right do you have here,
And whom do you have here,
That you have [a]hewn a tomb for yourself here,
You who hew a tomb on the height,
You who carve a resting place for [1]yourself in the rock?
17 'Behold, the LORD is about to hurl you headlong, O man.
And He is about to grasp you firmly,
18 *And* roll you tightly like a ball,
To be [a]*cast* into a vast country;
There you will die,
And there your splendid chariots will be,
You shame of your master's house.'
19 "And I will [a]depose you from your office,
And [1]I will pull you down from your station.
20 "Then it will come about in that day,
That I will summon My servant [a]Eliakim the son of Hilkiah
21 And I will clothe him with your tunic,
And tie your sash securely about him,
I will entrust him with your [1]authority,
And he will become a [a]father to the inhabitants of Jerusalem and to the house of Judah.
22 "Then I will set [a]the key of the [b]house of David on his shoulder,

17 [b]Num. 23:19; Zech. 1:6
1 [1]Or, *burden of* [a]Ps. 125:2; Jer. 21:13; Joel 3:12, 14 [b]Is. 15:3
2 [1]Lit., *dead in battle* [a]Is. 23:7; 32:13 [b]Jer. 14:18; Lam. 2:20
3 [1]Lit., *from a bow* [2]So with ancient versions; Heb., *They fled far away*
4 [1]Lit., *insist*
5 [1]YHWH, usually rendered LORD [2]Or, *against* [a]Lam. 1:5; 2:2 [b]Is. 37:3 [c]Is. 10:6; 63:3 [d]Is. 22:1
6 [1]Lit., *man* [a]Is. 21:2; Jer. 49:35
7 [a]2 Chr. 32:1
8 [1]Lit., *screen, covering* [2]Or, *looked to, considered* [a]1 Kin. 7:2; 10:17
9 [a]Neh. 3:16
11 [1]Or, *look to, consider* [2]Lit., *see . . . Him* [a]2 Kin. 25:4; Jer. 39:4 [b]2 Kin. 20:20; 2 Chr. 32:3, 4
12 [1]YHWH, usually rendered LORD [a]Is. 32:11; Joel 1:13; 2:17
13 [a]Is. 5:11, 22; 28:7, 8; Luke 17:26-29 [b]Is. 56:12; 1 Cor. 15:32
14 [1]Lit., *in my ears* [2]Lit., *atoned for* [3]YHWH, usually rendered LORD [a]Is. 65:20
15 [1]YHWH, usually rendered LORD
16 [1]Lit., *himself* [a]2 Sam. 18:18; 2 Chr. 16:14; Matt. 27:60
18 [a]Job 18:18; Is. 17:13
19 [1]So with many ancient versions; Heb., *He* [a]Job 40:11, 12; Ezek. 17:24
20 [a]2 Kin. 18:18; Is. 36:3, 22; 37:2
21 [1]Lit., *rule* [a]Gen. 45:8
22 [a]Rev. 3:7 [b]Is. 7:2, 13

When he opens no one will shut,
When he shuts no one will [c]open.
23 "And I will drive him *like* a [a]peg in a firm place,
And he will become a [b]throne of glory to his father's house.
24 "So they will hang on him all the
glory of his father's house, offspring
and [1]issue, all the least of vessels,
from bowls to all the jars.
25 "In that day," declares the LORD
of hosts, "the [a]peg driven in a firm
place will give way; it will even
[b]break off and fall, and the load
hanging on it will be cut off, for the
[c]LORD has spoken."

CHAPTER 23

The Fall of Tyre

THE [1]oracle concerning [a]Tyre.
Wail, O [b]ships of [c]Tarshish,
For *Tyre* is destroyed, without house *or* [2d]harbor;
It is reported to them from the land of [3e]Cyprus.
2 [a]Be silent, you inhabitants of the coastland,
You merchants of Sidon;
[1]Your messengers crossed the sea
3 And *were* on many waters.
[a]The grain of the [1b]Nile, the harvest of the River was her revenue;
And she was the [c]market of nations.
4 Be ashamed, O [a]Sidon;
For the sea speaks, the stronghold of the sea, saying,
"I have neither travailed nor given birth,
I have neither brought up young men *nor* reared virgins."
5 When the report *reaches* Egypt,
They will be in [a]anguish at the report of Tyre.
6 Pass over to Tarshish;
Wail, O inhabitants of the coastland.
7 Is this your [a]jubilant *city,*
Whose origin is from antiquity,
Whose feet used to carry her to [1]colonize distant places?
8 Who has planned this against Tyre, the bestower of crowns,
Whose merchants were princes, whose traders were the honored of the earth?
9 [a]The LORD of hosts has planned it to [b]defile the pride of all beauty,

22 [c]Job 12:14
23 [a]Ezra 9:8; Zech. 10:4 [b]1 Sam. 2:8; Job 36:7
24 [1]Or perhaps, *leaf*
25 [a]Is. 22:23 [b]Esth. 9:24, 25 [c]Is. 46:11; Mic. 4:4
1 [1]Or, *burden of* [2]Lit., *entering* [3]Heb., *Kittim* [a]Josh. 19:29; 1 Kin. 5:1; Jer. 25:22; 47:4; Ezek. 26:1-28; Amos 1:9; Zech. 9:2-4 [b]Is. 2:16 [c]Gen. 10:4; 1 Kin. 10:22 [d]Is. 24:10 [e]Gen. 10:4; Is. 23:12; Ezek. 27:6
2 [1]So DSS; M.T., *Who passed over the sea, they replenished you.* [a]Is. 47:5
3 [1]Heb., *Shihor* [a]Is. 19:7-9 [b]Josh. 13:3; 1 Chr. 13:5; Jer. 2:18 [c]Ezek 27:3-23
4 [a]Gen. 10:15, 19; Josh. 11:8; Judg. 10:6; Jer. 25:22; 27:3; 47:4; Ezek. 28:21, 22
5 [a]Ex. 15:14-16; Josh. 2:9-11
7 [1]Lit., *sojourn afar off* [a]Is. 22:2; 32:13
9 [a]Is. 2:11; 13:11 [b]Job 40:11, 12; Dan. 4:37 [c]Is. 5:13; 9:15
10 [1]Lit., *Pass over* [2]Perhaps *girdle* or *shipyard*
11 [a]Ex. 14:21; Is. 14:26 [b]Is. 19:5; 50:2 [c]Is. 25:2; Zech. 9:3, 4
12 [1]Heb., *Kittim*
13 [a]Is. 10:5 [b]Is. 13:21; 18:6 [c]Is. 10:7
15 [a]Jer. 25:11, 22
17 [1]Lit., *of the earth on the face of the land* [a]Ezek. 16:25-29; Nah. 3:4
18 [a]Ps. 72:10, 11; Is. 60:5-9; Mic. 4:13 [b]Ex. 28:36; Zech. 14:20
1 [a]Is. 2:19; 13:13; 24:19, 20; 30:32; 32:9
2 [a]Lev. 25:36, 37; Deut. 23:19, 20

To despise all the [c]honored of the earth.
10 [1]Overflow your land like the Nile, O daughter of Tarshish,
There is no more [2]restraint.
11 He has [a]stretched His hand out [b]over the sea,
He has made the kingdoms tremble;
The LORD has given a command concerning Canaan to [c]demolish its strongholds.
12 And He has said, "You shall exult no more, O crushed virgin daughter of Sidon.
Arise, pass over to [1]Cyprus; even there you will find no rest."
13 Behold, the land of the Chalde-
ans—this is the people *which* was
not; [a]Assyria appointed it for [b]des-
ert creatures—they erected their
siege towers, they stripped its palaces, [c]they made it a ruin.
14 Wail, O ships of Tarshish,
For your stronghold is destroyed.
15 Now it will come about in that
day that Tyre will be forgotten for
[a]seventy years like the days of one
king. At the end of seventy years it
will happen to Tyre as *in* the song of
the harlot:
16 Take *your* harp, walk about the city,
O forgotten harlot;
Pluck the strings skillfully, sing many songs,
That you may be remembered.
17 And it will come about at the
end of seventy years that the LORD
will visit Tyre. Then she will go back
to her harlot's wages, and will [a]play
the harlot with all the kingdoms [1]on
the face of the earth.
18 And her [a]gain and her harlot's
wages will be [b]set apart to the LORD;
it will not be stored up or hoarded,
but her gain will become sufficient
food and choice attire for those who
dwell in the presence of the LORD.

CHAPTER 24

Judgment on the Earth

BEHOLD, the LORD [a]lays the earth
waste, devastates it, distorts its surface, and scatters its inhabitants.
2 And the people will be like the
priest, the servant like his master,
the maid like her mistress, the buyer
like the seller, the lender like the
borrower, the [a]creditor like the
debtor.
3 The earth will be completely
laid waste and completely de-

spoiled, for the LORD has spoken
this word.
4 The earth mourns *and* withers,
the world fades *and* withers, the
[a]exalted of the people of the earth
fade away.
5 The earth is also [a]polluted [1]by
its inhabitants, for they transgressed laws, violated statutes,
[b]broke the everlasting covenant.
6 Therefore, a [a]curse devours the
earth, and those who live in it are
held guilty. Therefore, the inhabitants of the earth are burned, and
few men are left.
7 The [a]new wine mourns,
The vine decays,
All the merry-hearted sigh.
8 The gaiety of tambourines
ceases,
The noise of revelers stops,
The gaiety of the harp ceases.
9 They do not drink wine with
song;
[a]Strong drink is [b]bitter to those
who drink it.
10 The [a]city of chaos is broken
down;
[b]Every house is shut up so that
none may enter.
11 There is an [a]outcry in the
streets concerning the wine;
[b]All joy [1]turns to gloom.
The gaiety of the earth is banished.
12 Desolation is left in the city,
And the [a]gate is battered to ruins.
13 For [a]thus it will be in the midst
of the earth among the peo-
ples,
As the [1]shaking of an olive tree,
As the gleanings when the
grape harvest is over.
14 [a]They raise their voices, they
shout for joy.
They cry out from the [1]west
concerning the majesty of
the LORD.
15 Therefore [a]glorify the LORD in
the [1]east,
The [b]name of the LORD, the God
of Israel
In the [2c]coastlands of the sea.
16 From the [a]ends of the earth we
hear songs, "[b]Glory to the
Righteous One,"
But I say, "[1c]Woe to me! [1]Woe
to me! Alas for me!
The [d]treacherous deal treacherously,
And the treacherous deal very
treacherously."
17 Terror and pit and snare
Confront you, O inhabitant of
the earth.
18 Then it will be that he who flees
the [1]report of disaster will
fall into the pit,
And he who [2]climbs out of the
pit will be caught in the
snare;
For the [a]windows [3]above are
opened, and the [b]foundations
of the earth shake.
19 The earth is broken asunder,
The earth is [a]split through,
The earth is shaken violently.
20 The earth [a]reels to and fro like a
drunkard,
And it totters like a [1]shack,
For its [b]transgression is heavy
upon it,
And it will fall, [c]never to rise
again.
21 So it will happen in that day,
That the LORD will [a]punish the
host of heaven, on high,
And the [b]kings of the earth, on
earth.
22 And they will be gathered together
Like [a]prisoners in the [1]dun-
geon,
And will be confined in prison;
And after many days they will
[b]be punished.
23 Then the moon will be abashed
and the sun ashamed,
For the [a]LORD of hosts will
reign on [b]Mount Zion and in
Jerusalem,
And *His* glory will be before His
elders.

CHAPTER 25

Song of Praise for God's Favor

O LORD, Thou art [a]my God;
I will exalt Thee, I will give
thanks to Thy name;
For Thou hast [b]worked wonders,
[c]Plans formed long ago, with
perfect faithfulness.
2 For Thou hast made a city into
a [a]heap,
A fortified city into a ruin;
A [b]palace of strangers is a city
no more,
It will never be rebuilt.
3 Therefore a strong people will
[a]glorify Thee;
[b]Cities of ruthless nations will
revere Thee.
4 For Thou hast been a [a]defense
for the helpless,
A defense for the needy in his
distress,
A [b]refuge from the storm, a
shade from the heat;
For the breath of the [c]ruthless

4 [a]Is. 2:12; 24:21
5 [1]Lit., *under* [a]Gen. 3:17; Num. 35:33; Is. 9:17; 10:6 [b]Is. 33:8
6 [a]Josh. 23:15; Is. 34:5; 43:28; Zech. 5:3, 4
7 [a]Is. 16:10; Joel 1:10, 12
9 [a]Is. 5:11, 22 [b]Is. 5:20
10 [a]Gen. 1:2; Is. 34:11 [b]Is. 23:1
11 [1]Lit., is *darkened* [a]Jer. 14:2; 46:12 [b]Is. 10:10; 32:13
12 [a]Is. 14:31; 45:2
13 [1]Lit., *striking* [a]Is. 17:6; 27:12
14 [1]Lit., *sea* [a]Is. 12:6; 48:20; 52:8; 54:1
15 [1]Lit., *region of light* [2]Or, *islands* [a]Is. 25:3 [b]Mal. 1:1 [c]Is. 11:11; 42:4, 10, 12; 49:1; 51:5; 60:9; 66:19
16 [1]Lit., *Wasting to me!* [a]Is. 11:12; 42:10 [b]Is. 28:5; 60:21 [c]Lev. 26:39 [d]Is. 21:2; 33:1; Jer. 3:20; 5:1
18 [1]Lit., *sound of terror* [2]Lit., *goes up from the midst of* [3]Lit., *from the height;* i.e., heaven [a]Gen. 7:11 [b]Ps. 18:7; 46:2; Is. 2:19, 21; 13:13
19 [a]Num. 16:31, 32; Deut. 11:6
20 [1]Or, *hut* [a]Is. 19:14; 24:1; 28:7 [b]Is. 1:28; 43:27; 66:24 [c]Dan. 11:19; Amos 8:14
21 [a]Is. 10:12; 13:11 [b]Ps. 76:12
22 [1]Lit., *pit* [a]Is. 10:4; 42:22 [b]Ezek. 38:8; Zech. 9:11, 12
23 [a]Is. 60:19, 20; Zech. 14:6, 7; Rev. 21:23; 22:5 [b]Mic. 4:7; Heb. 12:22
1 [a]Ex. 15:2; Ps. 118:28; Is. 7:13; 49:4, 5; 61:10 [b]Ps. 40:5; 98:1 [c]Eph. 1:11
2 [a]Is. 17:1; 26:5; 27:10; 32:19 [b]Is. 13:22; 32:14; 34:13
3 [a]Is. 24:15 [b]Is. 13:11
4 [a]Is. 14:32; 17:10; 27:5; 33:16 [b]Is. 4:6; 32:2 [c]Is. 29:5, 20; 49:25

Is like a *rain* storm *against* a wall.
5 Like heat in drought, Thou dost subdue the [a]uproar of aliens;
Like heat by the shadow of a cloud, the song of the ruthless is silenced.

6 And the LORD of hosts will prepare a lavish banquet for all peoples on this mountain;
A banquet of aged wine, choice pieces with marrow,
And refined, aged wine.
7 And on this mountain He will swallow up the [a]covering which is over all peoples,
Even the veil which is stretched over all nations.
8 He will [a]swallow up death for all time,
And the Lord [1]GOD will [b]wipe tears away from all faces,
And He will remove the [c]reproach of His people from all the earth;
For the LORD has spoken.
9 And it will be said in that day,
"Behold, [a]this is our God for whom we have [b]waited that [c]He might save us.
This is the LORD for whom we have waited;
[d]Let us rejoice and be glad in His salvation."
10 For the hand of the LORD will rest on this mountain,
And Moab will be trodden down in his place
As straw is trodden down in the water of a manure pile.
11 And he will spread out his hands in the middle of it
As a swimmer spreads out *his hands* to swim,
But *the Lord* will [a]lay low his pride together with the trickery of his hands.
12 And the [a]unassailable fortifications of your walls He will bring down,
Lay low, *and* cast to the ground, even to the dust.

CHAPTER 26

Song of Trust in God's Protection

[a]IN that day this song will be sung in the land of Judah:
"We have a [b]strong city;
He sets up walls and ramparts for [1c]security.
2"Open the [a]gates, that the [b]righteous nation may enter,
The one that remains faithful.
3"The steadfast of mind Thou wilt keep in perfect [a]peace,
Because he trusts in Thee.
4"[a]Trust in the LORD forever,
For in [1]GOD the LORD, *we have* an everlasting [b]Rock.
5"For He has brought low those who dwell on high, the unassailable city;
[a]He lays it low, He lays it low to the ground, He casts it to the dust.
6"The foot will trample it,
The feet of the [a]afflicted, the steps of the helpless."

7 The [a]way of the righteous is smooth;
O Upright One, [b]make the path of the righteous level.
8 Indeed, *while following* the way of Thy judgments, O LORD,
We have waited for Thee eagerly;
[a]Thy name, even Thy [b]memory, is the desire of *our* souls.
9 [a]At night my soul longs for Thee,
Indeed, my spirit within me [b]seeks Thee diligently;
For when the earth experiences Thy judgments
The inhabitants of the world [c]learn righteousness.
10 *Though* the wicked is shown favor,
He does not [a]learn righteousness;
He [b]deals unjustly in the land of uprightness,
And does not perceive the majesty of the LORD.

11 O LORD, Thy hand is lifted up *yet* they do not see it.
[1]They see [a]*Thy* zeal for the people and are put to shame;
Indeed, [2]fire will devour Thine enemies.
12 LORD, Thou wilt establish peace for us,
Since Thou hast also performed for us all our works.
13 O LORD our God, [a]other masters besides Thee have ruled us;
But through Thee alone we [1b]confess Thy name.
14 [a]The dead will not live, the [1]departed spirits will not rise;
Therefore Thou hast [b]punished and destroyed them,
And Thou hast wiped out all remembrance of them.
15 [a]Thou hast increased the nation, O LORD,

5 [a]Jer. 51:54-56
7 [a]2 Cor. 3:15, 16; Eph. 4:18
8 [1]YHWH, usually rendered LORD [a]Hos. 13:14; 1 Cor. 15:54 [b]Is. 30:19; 35:10; 51:11; 65:19; Rev. 7:17; 21:4 [c]Ps. 69:9; 89:50, 51; Is. 51:7; 54:4; Matt. 5:11; 1 Pet. 4:14
9 [a]Is. 35:2; 40:9; 52:10 [b]Is. 8:17; 30:18; 33:2 [c]Is. 33:32; 35:4; 49:25, 26; 60:16 [d]Ps. 20:5; Is. 35:1, 2, 10; 65:18; 66:10
11 [a]Is. 16:6, 14
12 [a]Is. 15:1; 25:2; 26:5
1 [1]Or, *salvation* [a]Is. 4:2; 12:1 [b]Is. 14:31; 31:5, 9; 33:5, 6, 20-24 [c]Is. 60:18
2 [a]Is. 60:11, 18; 62:10 [b]Is. 45:25; 54:14, 17; 58:8; 60:21; 61:3; 62:1, 2
3 [a]Is. 26:12; 27:5; 57:19; 66:12
4 [1]YAH, usually rendered LORD [a]Is. 12:2; 50:10; 51:5 [b]Is. 17:10; 30:29; 44:8
5 [a]Job 40:11-13
6 [a]Is. 3:14, 15; 11:4; 29:19
7 [a]Is. 57:2 [b]Ps. 25:4, 5; 27:11; Is. 42:16; 52:12
8 [a]Is. 12:4; 24:15; 25:1; 26:13 [b]Ex. 3:15
9 [a]Ps. 63:5, 6; 77:2; 119:62; Is. 50:10; Luke 6:12 [b]Ps. 63:1; 78:34; Matt. 6:33 [c]Is. 55:6; Hos. 5:15
10 [a]Is. 22:12, 13; 32:6, 7 [b]Hos. 11:7; John 5:37, 38
11 [1]Or, *Let them see . . . and be* [2]Or, *let the fire for Thine adversaries devour them* [a]Is. 9:7; 37:32; 59:17
13 [1]Or, *cause to be remembered* [a]Is. 2:8; 10:11 [b]Is. 63:7
14 [1]Or, *shades* [a]Deut. 4:28; Ps. 135:17; Is. 8:19; Hab. 2:19 [b]Is. 10:3
15 [a]Is. 9:3

Thou hast increased the nation,
Thou art glorified;
Thou hast [b]extended all the borders of the land.
16 O LORD, they sought Thee [a]in distress;
They [1]could only whisper a prayer,
Your chastening was upon them.
17 [a]As the pregnant woman approaches *the time* to give birth,
She writhes *and* cries out in her labor pains,
Thus were we before Thee, O LORD.
18 We were pregnant, we writhed in *labor*,
We [a]gave birth, as it were, *only* to wind.
We could not accomplish deliverance for the earth
Nor were inhabitants of the world born.
19 Your [a]dead will live;
[1]Their corpses will rise.
You who lie in the dust, [b]awake and shout for joy,
For your dew is as the dew of the [2]dawn,
And the earth will give birth to the departed spirits.

20 *Come,* my people, [a]enter into your rooms,
And close your doors behind you;
Hide for a little [1b]while,
Until indignation [2]runs *its* course.
21 For behold, the LORD is about to [a]come out from His place
To punish the inhabitants of the earth for their iniquity;
And the earth will [b]reveal her bloodshed,
And will no longer cover her slain.

CHAPTER 27

The Deliverance of Israel

IN that day the LORD will punish [1a]Leviathan the fleeing serpent,
With His fierce and great and mighty sword,
Even [1]Leviathan the twisted serpent;
And He will kill the dragon who *lives* in the sea.

2 In that day,
"A [1a]vineyard of wine, sing of it!
3 "I, the LORD, am its keeper;
I water it every moment.
Lest anyone damage it,
I [a]guard it night and day.
4 "I have no wrath.
Should someone give Me [a]briars *and* thorns in battle,
Then I would step on them, [b]I would burn them completely.
5 "Or let him rely on My protection,
Let him make peace with Me,
Let him [a]make peace with Me."
6 In the days to come Jacob will take root,
Israel will [a]blossom and sprout;
And they will fill the [1]whole world with fruit.

7 Like the striking of Him who has struck them, has [a]He struck them?
Or like the slaughter of His slain, [1]have they been slain?
8 Thou didst contend with them [1]by banishing them, by [a]driving them away.
With His fierce wind He has expelled *them* on the day of the [b]east wind.
9 Therefore through this Jacob's iniquity will be [a]forgiven;
And this will be [1]the full price of the [2b]pardoning of his sin:
When he makes all the [c]altar stones like pulverized chalk stones;
When [3]Asherim and incense altars will not stand.
10 For the fortified city is isolated,
A homestead forlorn and forsaken like the desert;
There the calf will graze,
And there it will lie down and feed on its branches.
11 When its limbs are dry, they are broken off;
Women come *and* make a fire with them.
For they are not a people of [a]discernment,
Therefore [b]their Maker will not have compassion on them.
And their Creator will not be gracious to them.

12 And it will come about in that
day, that the LORD [a]will start *His*
threshing from the flowing stream
of the Euphrates to the brook of
Egypt; and you will be [b]gathered up
one by one, O sons of Israel.
13 It will come about also in that
day that a great [a]trumpet will be
blown; and those who were perishing in the land of Assyria and who
were scattered in the land of Egypt

15 [b]Is. 33:17; 54:2, 3
16 [1]Lit., *sound forth a whisper* [a]Is. 37:3; Hos. 5:15
17 [a]Is. 13:8; 21:3; John 16:21
18 [a]Is. 33:11; 59:4
19 [1]So with some ancient versions; Heb., *My* [2]Lit., *lights* [a]Is. 25:8; Ezek. 37:1-14; Dan. 12:2; Hos. 13:14 [b]Eph. 5:14
20 [1]Lit., *moment* [2]Lit., *passes over* [a]Ex. 12:22, 23; Ps. 91:1, 4 [b]Ps. 30:5; Is. 54:7, 8; 2 Cor. 4:17
21 [a]Mic. 1:3; Jude 14 [b]Job 16:18; Luke 11:50
1 [1]Or, *sea monster* [a]Job 3:8; 41:1; Ps. 74:14; 104:26
2 [1]Some mss. read, *a vineyard of delight* [a]Ps. 80:8; Is. 5:7; Jer. 2:21
3 [a]1 Sam. 2:9; Is. 31:5; John 10:28
4 [a]2 Sam. 23:6; Is. 10:17 [b]Is. 33:12; Matt. 3:12; Heb. 6:8
5 [a]Job 22:21; Is. 26:3, 12; Rom. 5:1; 2 Cor. 5:20
6 [1]Lit., *face of* [a]Is. 35:1, 2; Hos. 14:5, 6
7 [1]Lit., *he was slain* [a]Is. 10:12, 17; 30:31-33; 31:8, 9; 37:36-38
8 [1]Some ancient versions read, *by exact measure* [a]Is. 50:1; 54:7 [b]Jer. 4:11; Ezek. 19:12; Hos. 13:15
9 [1]Lit., *all the fruit* [2]Lit., *removing* [3]I.e., wooden symbols of a female deity [a]Is. 1:25; 48:10; Dan. 11:35 [b]Rom. 11:27 [c]Ex. 34:13; Deut. 12:3; 2 Kin. 10:26; Is. 17:8
11 [a]Deut. 32:28; Is. 1:3; 5:13; Jer. 8:7 [b]Deut. 32:18; Is. 43:1, 7; 44:2, 21, 24
12 [a]Is. 11:11; 17:6; 24:13; 56:8 [b]Deut. 30:3, 4; Neh. 1:9
13 [a]Lev. 25:9; 1 Chr. 15:24; Matt. 24:31; Rev. 11:15

will come and [b]worship the LORD in the holy mountain at Jerusalem.

CHAPTER 28

Ephraim's Captivity Predicted

WOE to the proud crown of the drunkards of Ephraim,
And to the fading flower of its glorious beauty,
Which is at the head of the fertile valley
Of those who are overcome with wine!
2 Behold, the Lord has a strong and [a]mighty *agent;*
As a storm of hail, a tempest of destruction,
Like a storm of [b]mighty overflowing waters,
He has cast *it* down to the earth with *His* hand.
3 The proud crown of the drunkards of Ephraim is trodden under foot.
4 And the fading flower of its glorious beauty,
Which is at the head of the fertile valley,
Will be like the [a]first-ripe fig prior to summer;
Which one sees,
And as soon as it is in his hand,
He swallows it.
5 In that day the [a]LORD of hosts will become a beautiful [b]crown
And a glorious diadem to the remnant of His people;
6 A [a]spirit of justice for him who sits in judgment,
A [b]strength to those who repel the [1]onslaught at the gate.
7 And these also reel with wine and stagger from strong drink:
[a]The priest and [b]the prophet reel with strong drink,
They are confused by wine, they stagger from [c]strong drink;
They reel while [1]having visions,
They totter *when rendering* judgment.
8 For all the tables are full of filthy [a]vomit, without a *single clean* place.

9 "To [a]whom would He teach knowledge?
And to whom would He interpret the message?
Those *just* weaned from milk?
Those *just* taken from the breast?
10 "For *He says,*
'[1a]Order on order, order on order,
Line on line, line on line,
A little here, a little there.' "
11 Indeed, He will speak to this people
Through [a]stammering lips and a foreign tongue,
12 He who said to them, "Here is [a]rest, give rest to the weary,"
And, "Here is repose," but they would not listen.
13 So the word of the LORD to them will be,
"Order on order, order on order,
Line on line, line on line,
A little here, a little there,"
That they may go and [a]stumble backward, be broken, snared, and taken captive.

Judah Is Warned

14 Therefore, hear the word of the LORD, O [a]scoffers,
Who rule this people who are in Jerusalem,
15 Because you have said, "We have made a [a]covenant with death,
And with [1]Sheol we have made a [2]pact.
[b]The overwhelming [3]scourge will not reach us when it passes by,
For we have made [c]falsehood our refuge and we have concealed ourselves with deception."
16 Therefore thus says the Lord [1]GOD,
"[a]Behold, I am laying in Zion a stone, a tested [b]stone,
A costly cornerstone *for* the foundation, [2]firmly placed.
He who believes *in it* will not be [3]disturbed.
17 "And I will make [a]justice the measuring line,
And righteousness the level;
Then hail shall sweep away the refuge of lies,
And the waters shall overflow the secret place.
18 "And your covenant with death shall be [1]canceled,
And your pact with Sheol shall not stand;
When the overwhelming scourge passes through,
Then you become its [a]trampling *place.*
19 "As [a]often as it passes through, it will [1]seize you.

13 [b]Is. 19:21, 23; 49:7; 66:23; Zech. 14:16; Heb. 12:22
2 [a]Is. 8:7; 40:10 [b]Is. 8:6, 7; 30:28; Nah. 1:8
4 [a]Hos. 9:10; Mic. 7:1; Nah. 3:12
5 [a]Is. 41:16; 45:25; 60:1, 19 [b]Is. 62:3
6 [1]Lit., *battle* [a]1 Kin. 3:28; Is. 11:2; 32:15, 16; John 5:30 [b]2 Chr. 32:6-8; Is. 25:4
7 [1]Lit., *seeing* [a]Is. 24:2 [b]Is. 9:15 [c]Hab. 2:15, 16
8 [a]Jer. 48:26
9 [a]Is. 2:3; 28:26; 30:20; 48:17; 50:4; 54:13
10 [1]Hebrew monosyllables, imitating the babbling of a child, mock the prophet's preaching, also v. 13 [a]2 Chr. 36:15; Neh. 9:30
11 [a]Is. 33:19; 1 Cor. 14:21
12 [a]Is. 11:10; 30:15; 32:17, 18; Jer. 6:16; Matt. 11:28, 29
13 [a]Is. 8:15; Matt. 21:44
14 [a]Is. 29:20
15 [1]I.e., the nether world [2]So some ancient versions; Heb., *seer* [3]Or, *flood* [a]Is. 28:18 [b]Is. 8:8; 28:2; 30:28; Dan. 11:22 [c]Is. 9:15; 30:9; 44:20; 59:3, 4; Ezek. 13:22
16 [1]YHWH, usually rendered LORD [2]Lit., *well-laid* [3]Lit., *in a hurry* [a]Rom. 9:33; 10:11; 1 Pet. 2:6 [b]Ps. 118:22; Is. 8:14, 15; Matt. 21:42; Mark 12:10; Luke 20:17; Acts 4:11; Eph. 2:20
17 [a]2 Kin. 21:13; Is. 5:16; 30:18; 61:8; Amos 7:7-9
18 [1]Lit., *covered over* [a]Is. 28:3; Dan. 8:13
19 [1]Lit., *take* [a]2 Kin. 24:2

For [b]morning after morning it will pass through, *anytime* during the day or night.
And it will be [2]sheer terror to understand [3]what it means."
20 The bed is too short on which to stretch out,
And the [a]blanket is too [1]small to wrap oneself in.
21 For the LORD will rise up as *at* Mount [a]Perazim,
He will be stirred up as in the valley of Gibeon;
To do His [b]task, His [1c]unusual task,
And to work His work, His [2]extraordinary work.
22 And now do not carry on as scoffers,
Lest your fetters be made stronger;
For I have heard from the Lord [1]GOD of hosts,
Of decisive destruction on all the earth.

23 Give ear and hear my voice,
Listen and hear my words.
24 Does the [1]farmer plow [2]continually to plant seed?
Does he *continually* [3]turn and harrow the ground?
25 Does he not level its surface,
And sow dill and scatter [a]cummin,
And [1]plant [b]wheat in rows,
Barley in its place, and [c]rye within its [2]area?
26 For his God instructs and teaches him properly.
27 For dill is not threshed with a [a]threshing sledge,
Nor is the cartwheel [1]driven over cummin;
But dill is beaten out with a rod, and cummin with a club.
28 *Grain for* bread is crushed,
Indeed, he does not continue to thresh it forever.
Because the wheel of *his* cart and his horses *eventually* [1]damage *it,*
He does not thresh it longer.
29 This also comes from the LORD of hosts,
Who has made *His* counsel [a]wonderful and *His* wisdom [b]great.

CHAPTER 29

Jerusalem Is Warned

WOE, O [1]Ariel, [1]Ariel the city *where* David once [a]camped!
Add year to year, [2b]observe *your* feasts on schedule.
2 And I will bring distress to Ariel,
And she shall be *a city of* lamenting and [a]mourning;
And she shall be like an Ariel to me.
3 And I will [a]camp against you [1]encircling *you,*
And I will set siegeworks against you,
And I will raise up battle towers against you.
4 Then you shall [a]be brought low;
From the earth you shall speak,
And from the dust *where* you are prostrate,
Your words *shall come.*
Your voice shall also be like that of a [1]spirit from the ground,
And your speech shall whisper from the dust.

5 But the multitude of your [1]enemies shall become like fine [a]dust,
And the multitude of the ruthless ones like the chaff which [2]blows away;
And it shall happen [b]instantly, suddenly.
6 From the LORD of hosts you will be punished with [a]thunder and earthquake and loud noise,
With whirlwind and tempest and the flame of a consuming fire.
7 And the [a]multitude of all the nations who wage war against [1]Ariel,
Even all who wage war against her and her stronghold, and who distress her,
Shall be like a dream, a [b]vision of the night.
8 And it will be as when a hungry man dreams—
And behold, he is eating;
But when he awakens, his [1]hunger is not satisfied,
Or as when a thirsty man dreams—
And behold, he is drinking,
But when he awakens, behold, he is faint,
And his [1]thirst is not quenched.
[a]Thus the multitude of all the nations shall be,
Who wage war against Mount Zion.

9 Be delayed and wait.
Blind yourselves and be blind.
They become drunk, but not with wine;

19 [2]Lit., *only* [3]Lit., *the report,* or, *the message* [b]Is. 50:4
20 [1]Lit., *narrow* [a]Is. 59:6
21 [1]Lit., *task is strange* [2]Lit., *work is alien* [a]2 Sam. 5:20; 1 Chr. 14:11 [b]Is. 10:12; 29:14; 65:7 [c]Lam. 2:15; 3:33; Luke 19:41-44
22 [1]YHWH, usually rendered LORD
24 [1]Lit., *plowman* [2]Lit., *all day* [3]Lit., *open*
25 [1]Lit., *put* [2]Lit., *region* [a]Matt. 23:23 [b]Ex. 9:32 [c]Amos 1:3
27 [1]Lit., *rolled* [a]Amos 1:3
28 [1]Lit., *discomfit*
29 [a]Is. 9:6 [b]Is. 31:2; Rom. 11:33
1 [1]I.e., Lion of God, or, Jerusalem [2]Lit., *let your feasts run their round* [a]2 Sam. 5:9 [b]Is. 1:14; 5:12; 22:12, 13; 29:9, 13
2 [a]Is. 3:26; Lam. 2:5
3 [1]Lit., *like a circle* [a]Luke 19:43, 44
4 [1]Or, *ghost* [a]Is. 8:19
5 [1]Lit., *strangers* [2]Lit., *passes away* [a]Is. 17:13; 41:15, 16 [b]Is. 17:14; 30:13; 47:11; 1 Thess. 5:3
6 [a]1 Sam. 2:10; Matt. 24:7; Mark 13:8; Luke 21:11; Rev. 11:13, 19; 16:18
7 [1]See note, v. 1 [a]Mic. 4:11, 12; Zech. 12:9 [b]Job 20:8; Ps. 73:20; Is. 17:14
8 [1]Lit., *soul* [a]Is. 54:17

They stagger, but not with strong drink.
10 For the LORD has poured over you a spirit of deep [a]sleep,
He has [b]shut your eyes, the prophets;
And He has covered your heads, the seers.
11 And the entire vision shall be to
you like the words of a sealed
[1a]book, which when they give it to
the one who [2]is literate, saying,
"Please read this," he will say, "I
cannot, for it is sealed."
12 Then the book will be given to
the one who is illiterate, saying,
"Please read this." And he will say,
"I cannot read."
13 Then the Lord said,
"Because [a]this people draw near with their [1]words
And honor Me with their [2]lip service,
But they remove their hearts far from Me,
And their [3]reverence for Me consists of tradition learned *by rote,*
14 Therefore behold, I will once again deal [a]marvelously with this people, wondrously marvelous;
And [b]the wisdom of their wise men shall perish,
And the discernment of their discerning men shall be concealed.

15 Woe to those who deeply [a]hide their [1]plans from the LORD,
And whose deeds are *done* in a dark place,
And they say, "[b]Who sees us?" or "Who knows us?"
16 You turn *things* around!
Shall the potter be considered [1]as equal with the clay,
That [a]what is made should say to its maker, "He did not make me";
Or what is formed say to him who formed it, "He has no understanding"?

Blessing After Discipline

17 Is it not yet just a little while
Before Lebanon will be turned into a [a]fertile field,
And the fertile field will be considered as a forest?
18 And on that day the deaf shall hear words of a book,
And out of *their* gloom and darkness the [a]eyes of the blind shall see.
19 The [a]afflicted also shall increase their gladness in the LORD,
And the [b]needy of mankind shall rejoice in the Holy One of Israel.
20 For the ruthless will come to an end, and the scorner will be finished,
Indeed [a]all who are intent on doing evil will be cut off;
21 Who [1]cause a person to be indicted by a word,
And [a]ensnare him who adjudicates at the gate,
And [2b]defraud the one in the right with [3]meaningless arguments.
22 Therefore thus says the LORD,
who redeemed [a]Abraham, concerning the house of Jacob,
"Jacob shall not now be ashamed, nor shall his face now turn pale;
23 But when [1]he sees his children, the [a]work of My hands, in his midst,
They will sanctify My name;
Indeed, they will [b]sanctify the Holy One of Jacob,
And will stand in awe of the God of Israel.
24 "And those who [a]err in [1]mind will [b]know the truth,
And those who criticize will [c]accept instruction.

CHAPTER 30

Judah Warned against Egyptian Alliance

"WOE to the rebellious children," declares the LORD,
"Who [a]execute a plan, but not Mine,
And [1b]make an alliance, but not of My Spirit,
In order to add sin to sin;
2 Who [a]proceed down to Egypt,
Without [b]consulting [1]Me,
[c]To take refuge in the safety of Pharaoh,
And to seek shelter in the shadow of Egypt!
3 "Therefore the safety of Pharaoh will be [a]your shame,
And the shelter in the shadow of Egypt, your humiliation.
4 "For [a]their princes are at Zoan,
And their ambassadors arrive at Hanes.
5 "Everyone will be [a]ashamed because of a people who cannot profit them,

10 [a]Ps. 69:23; Is. 6:9, 10; Mic. 3:6; Rom. 11:8 [b]Is. 44:18; 2 Thess. 2:9-12
11 [1]Or, *scroll* [2]Lit., *knows books,* also v. 12 [a]Is. 8:16; Dan. 12:4, 9; Matt. 13:11
13 [1]Lit., *mouth* [2]Lit., *lips* [3]Lit., *fear of Me* [a]Ezek. 33:31; Matt. 15:8, 9; Mark 7:6, 7
14 [a]Is. 6:9, 10; 28:21; 65:7; Hab. 1:5 [b]Is. 44:25; Jer. 8:9; 49:7; 1 Cor. 1:19
15 [1]Lit., *counsel* [a]Ps. 10:11, 13; Is. 28:15; 30:1 [b]Ps. 94:7; Is. 47:10; Mal. 2:17
16 [1]Lit., *like* [a]Is. 45:9; 64:8; Jer. 18:1-6; Rom. 9:19-21
17 [a]Ps. 84:6; 107:33, 35; Is. 32:15
18 [a]Ps. 119:18; Prov. 20:12; Is. 32:3
19 [a]Ps. 25:9; 37:11; Is. 11:4; 61:1; Matt. 5:5; 11:29 [b]Is. 3:14, 15; 11:4; 14:30, 32; 25:4; 26:6; Matt. 11:5; James 1:9; 2:5
20 [a]Is. 59:4
21 [1]Lit., *bring a person under condemnation* [2]Lit., *turn aside* [3]Lit., *confusion* [a]Amos 5:10 [b]Is. 32:7; Amos 5:12
22 [a]Is. 41:8; 51:2; 63:16
23 [1]Or, *his children see* [a]Is. 26:12; 45:11; Eph. 2:10 [b]Is. 5:16; 8:13
24 [1]Lit., *spirit* [a]Is. 30:21; Heb. 5:2 [b]Is. 41:20; 60:16 [c]Is. 54:13
1 [1]Lit., *pour out a drink offering* [a]Is. 29:15 [b]Is. 8:11, 12
2 [1]Lit., *My mouth* [a]Is. 31:1; Jer. 43:7 [b]Is. 8:19 [c]Is. 36:9
3 [a]Is. 20:5, 6; 36:6; Jer. 42:18, 22
4 [a]Is. 19:11
5 [a]Jer. 2:36

Who are [b]not for help or profit,
But for shame and also for reproach."

6 The [1]oracle concerning the
[a]beasts of the [b]Negev.
Through a land of [c]distress and anguish,
From [2]where *come* lioness and lion, viper and [d]flying serpent,
They [e]carry their riches on the backs of young donkeys
And their treasures on camels' humps,
To a people who cannot profit *them;*
7 Even Egypt, whose help is vain and empty.
Therefore, I have called [1]her
"[2a]Rahab who has been exterminated."
8 Now go, [a]write it on a tablet before them
And inscribe it on a scroll,
That it may [1]serve in the time to come
[2]As a witness forever.
9 For this is a rebellious people, [a]false sons,
Sons who refuse to [b]listen
To the instruction of the LORD;
10 Who say to the seers, "You must not see *visions";*
And to the prophets, "You must not [a]prophesy to us what is right,
[b]Speak to us pleasant words,
Prophesy illusions.
11 "Get out of the way, turn aside from the path,
Let us hear no more about the Holy One of Israel."
12 Therefore thus says the Holy One of Israel,
"[a]Since you have rejected this word,
And have put your trust in [b]oppression and guile, and have relied on them,
13 Therefore this iniquity will be to you
Like a [a]breach about to fall,
A bulge in a high wall,
Whose collapse comes suddenly in an instant.
14 "And whose collapse is like the smashing of a [a]potter's jar;
So ruthlessly shattered
That a sherd will not be found among its pieces
To take fire from a hearth,
Or to scoop water from a cistern."
15 For thus the Lord [1]GOD, the Holy One of Israel, has said,

5 [b]Is. 10:3; 30:7; 31:3
6 [1]Lit., *burden* [2]Lit., *them* [a]1 Kin. 10:2; Is. 46:1, 2 [b]Gen. 12:9 [c]Ex. 5:10, 21; Deut. 4:20; 8:15; Is. 5:30; 8:22; Jer. 11:4 [d]Deut. 8:15; Is. 14:29 [e]Is. 15:7; 46:1, 2
7 [1]Lit., *this* one [2]M.T. reads; *They are Rahab* (or *arrogance*), *to remain* [a]Job 9:13; Ps. 87:4; 89:10; Is. 51:9
8 [1]Lit., *be* [2]Heb., *Forever and ever* [a]Is. 8:1
9 [a]Is. 28:15; 59:3, 4 [b]Is. 1:10; 5:24; 24:5
10 [a]Is. 5:20; Jer. 11:21; Amos 2:12; 7:13 [b]1 Kin. 22:8, 13; Jer. 6:14; 23:17, 26; Ezek. 13:7; Rom. 16:18; 2 Tim. 4:3, 4
12 [a]Is. 5:24; 7:9; 8:6 [b]Is. 3:14, 15; 5:7; 59:13
13 [a]1 Kin. 20:30; Ps. 62:4; Is. 58:12
14 [a]Ps. 2:9; Jer. 19:10, 11
15 [1]YHWH, usually rendered LORD [2]Lit., *returning* [a]Ps. 116:7; Is. 7:4 [b]Is. 28:12 [c]Is. 32:17
16 [a]Is. 2:7; 31:1
17 [1]Lit., *pole* [a]Lev. 26:36; Deut. 28:25; 32:30; Josh. 23:10; Prov. 28:1 [b]Is. 6:13; 27:11
18 [a]Is. 42:14, 16; 48:9; Jon. 3:4, 10; 2 Pet. 3:9, 15 [b]Is. 2:11, 17; 33:5 [c]Is. 5:16; 28:17; 61:8 [d]Is. 8:17; 25:9
19 [1]M.T. reads: *A people will inhabit Zion, Jerusalem.* [a]Is. 65:9; Ezek. 37:25, 28 [b]Is. 25:8; 60:20; 61:1-3 [c]Ps. 50:15; Is. 58:9; 65:24; Matt. 7:7-11
20 [a]1 Kin. 22:27; Ps. 80:5 [b]Ps. 74:9
21 [a]Ps. 25:8, 9; Prov. 3:6; Is. 35:8, 9; 42:16 [b]Is. 29:24
22 [a]Ex. 32:2, 4; Judg. 17:3, 4; Is. 46:6
23 [a]Ps. 144:13; Is. 32:20; Hos. 4:16
24 [a]Matt. 3.12, Luke 3:17
25 [a]Is. 35:6, 7; 41:18; 43:19, 20

"In [2a]repentance and [b]rest you shall be saved,
In [c]quietness and trust is your strength."
But you were not willing,
16 And you said, "No, for we will flee on [a]horses,"
Therefore you shall flee!
"And we will ride on swift *horses,*"
Therefore those who pursue you shall be swift.
17 [a]One thousand *shall flee* at the threat of one *man,*
You shall flee at the threat of five;
Until you [b]are left as a [1]flag on a mountain top,
And as a signal on a hill.

God Is Gracious and Just

18 Therefore the LORD [a]longs to be gracious to you,
And therefore He waits on [b]high to have compassion on you.
For the LORD is a [c]God of justice;
How blessed are all those who [d]long for Him.
19 [1]O people in Zion, [a]inhabitant
in Jerusalem, you will [b]weep no
longer. He will surely be gracious to
you at the sound of your cry; when
He hears it, He will [c]answer you.
20 Although the Lord has given
you [a]bread of privation and water of
oppression, *He,* your Teacher will
no longer [b]hide Himself, but your
eyes will behold your Teacher.
21 And your ears will hear a word
behind you, "This is the [a]way, walk
in it," whenever you [b]turn to the
right or to the left.
22 And you will defile your graven
[a]images, overlaid with silver, and
your molten [a]images plated with
gold. You will scatter them as an impure
thing; *and* say to them, "Be
gone!"
23 Then He will give *you* rain for
the seed which you will sow in the
ground, and bread *from* the yield of
the ground, and it will be rich and
plenteous; on that day [a]your livestock
will graze in a roomy pasture.
24 Also the oxen and the donkeys
which work the ground will eat
salted fodder, which has been [a]winnowed
with shovel and fork.
25 And on every lofty mountain
and on [a]every high hill there will be
streams running with water on the
day of the great slaughter, when the
towers fall.

26 And [a]the light of the moon will
be as the light of the sun, and the
light of the sun will be seven times
brighter, like the light of seven days,
on the day [b]the LORD binds up the
[c]fracture of His people and [d]heals
the bruise [1]He has inflicted.
27 Behold, [a]the name of the LORD
comes from a [1]remote place;
Burning is His anger, and
[2]dense is *His* [3]smoke;
His lips are filled with [b]indignation,
And His tongue is like a [c]consuming fire;
28 And His [a]breath is like an overflowing torrent,
Which [b]reaches to the neck,
To [c]shake the nations back and forth in a [1]sieve,
And to *put* in the jaws of the peoples [d]the bridle which [2]leads to ruin.
29 You will have [1]songs as in the night when you keep the festival;
And gladness of heart as when one marches to *the sound of* the flute,
To go to the mountain of the LORD, to the Rock of Israel.
30 And the LORD will cause [1]His voice of authority to be heard.
And the [2]descending of His arm to be seen in fierce anger,
And *in* the flame of a consuming fire,
In cloudburst, downpour, and hailstones.
31 For [a]at the voice of the LORD Assyria will be terrified,
When He strikes with the [b]rod.
32 And every [1]blow of the [2a]rod of punishment,
Which the LORD will lay on him,
Will be with *the music of* [b]tambourines and lyres;
And in battles, [c]brandishing weapons, He will fight them.
33 For [1]Topheth has long been ready,
Indeed, it has been prepared for the king.
He has made it deep and large,
[2]A pyre of fire with plenty of wood;
The breath of the LORD, like a torrent of [a]brimstone, sets it afire.

CHAPTER 31

Help Not in Egypt but in God

WOE to those who go down to Egypt for help,
And [a]rely on horses,
And trust in chariots because they are many,
And in horsemen because they are very strong,
But they do not [b]look to the [c]Holy One of Israel, nor seek the LORD!
2 Yet He also is [a]wise and will bring disaster,
And does [b]not retract His words,
But will arise against the house of evildoers,
And against the help of the [c]workers of iniquity.
3 Now the Egyptians are [a]men, and not God,
And their [b]horses are flesh and not spirit;
So the LORD will [c]stretch out His hand,
And he who helps will stumble
And he who is helped will fall,
And all of them will come to an end together.

4 For thus says the LORD to me,
"As the [a]lion or the young lion growls over his prey,
Against which a band of shepherds is called out,
Will not be terrified at their voice, nor disturbed at their noise,
So will the LORD of hosts come down to wage [b]war on Mount Zion and on its hill."
5 Like [1]flying [a]birds so the LORD of hosts will protect Jerusalem.
He will protect and deliver *it;*
He will pass over and rescue *it.*
6 [a]Return to Him from whom
[1]you have deeply defected, O sons
of Israel.
7 For in that day every man will
[a]cast away his silver idols and his
gold idols, which your hands have
made as a sin.
8 And the [a]Assyrian will fall by a sword not of man,
And a sword not of man will devour him.
So he will [1b]not escape the sword,
And his young men will become [c]forced laborers.
9 "And his [a]rock will pass away because of panic,
And his princes will be terrified at the [b]standard,"
Declares the LORD, whose fire is in Zion and whose furnace is in Jerusalem.

26 [1]Lit., *of His blow* [a]Is. 24:23; 60:19, 20; Rev. 21:23; 22:5 [b]Is. 61:1 [c]Is. 1:6; 13:14 [d]Deut. 32:39; Job 5:18; Is. 33:24; Jer. 33:6; Hos. 6:1, 2
27 [1]Lit., *distance* [2]Lit., *heaviness* [3]Lit., *uplifting* [a]Is. 59:19 [b]Is. 10:5; 13:5; 66:14 [c]Is. 66:15
28 [1]Lit., *sifting of the worthless* [2]Lit., *misleads* [a]Is. 11:4; 30:33; 2 Thess. 2:8 [b]Is. 8:8 [c]Amos 9:9 [d]2 Kin. 19:28; Is. 37:29
29 [1]Lit., *the song*
30 [1]Lit., *the majesty of His voice* [2]Lit., *descent*
31 [a]Is. 11:4 [b]Is. 10:26; 11:4
32 [1]Lit., *passing* [2]Lit., *staff of foundation* [a]Is. 10:24 [b]1 Sam. 18:6; Jer. 31:4 [c]Ezek. 32:10
33 [1]I.e., the place of human sacrifice to Molech. [2]Lit., *Its pile* [a]Gen. 19:24; Is. 34:9
1 [a]Deut. 17:16; Ps. 20:7; 33:17; Is. 2:7; 30:16 [b]Is. 9:13; Dan. 9:13; Amos 5:4-8 [c]Is. 10:17; 43:15; Hos. 11:9; Hab. 1:12; 3:3
2 [a]Is. 28:29; Rom. 16:27 [b]Num. 23:19; Jer. 44:29 [c]Is. 22:14; 32:6
3 [a]Ezek. 28:9; 2 Thess. 2:4 [b]Is. 36:9 [c]Is. 9:17; Jer. 15:6; Ezek. 20:33, 34
4 [a]Num. 24:9; Hos. 11:10; Amos 3:8 [b]Is. 42:13; Zech. 12:8
5 [1]Or, *hovering* [a]Deut. 32:11; Ps. 91:4
6 [1]Heb., *they* [a]Is. 44:22; 55:7; Jer. 3:10, 14, 22; Ezek. 18:31, 32
7 [a]Is. 2:20; 30:22
8 [1]Lit., *flee* [a]Is. 10:12; 14:25; 30:31-33; 37:7, 36-38 [b]Is. 21:15 [c]Gen. 49:15; Is. 14:2
9 [a]Deut. 32:31, 37 [b]Is. 5:26; 13:2; 18:3

CHAPTER 32

The Glorious Future

BEHOLD, a [a]king will reign righteously,
And princes will rule justly.
2 And each will be like a [a]refuge from the wind,
And a shelter from the storm,
Like [1b]streams of water in a dry country,
Like the [a]shade of a [2]huge rock in a [3]parched land.
3 Then the eyes of those who see will not be [1]blinded,
And the ears of those who hear will listen.
4 And the [1]mind of the [a]hasty will discern the [2]truth,
And the tongue of the stammerers will hasten to speak clearly.
5 No longer will the [a]fool be called noble,
Or the rogue be spoken of *as* generous.
6 For a fool speaks nonsense,
And his heart [1a]inclines toward wickedness,
To practice [b]ungodliness and to speak error against the LORD,
To [2c]keep the hungry person unsatisfied
And [3]to withhold drink from the thirsty.
7 As for a rogue, his weapons are evil;
He [a]devises wicked schemes
To destroy *the* afflicted with [1]slander,
[b]Even though *the* needy one speaks [2]what is right.
8 But the noble man devises noble plans;
And by noble plans he stands.

9 Rise up you [a]women who are at ease,
And hear my voice;
Give ear to my word,
You complacent daughters.
10 Within a year and *a few* days,
You will be troubled, O complacent daughters;
[a]For the vintage is ended,
And the *fruit* gathering will not come.
11 Tremble, you *women* who are at ease;
[a]Be troubled, you complacent *daughters;*
Strip, undress, and put *sackcloth* on *your* waist,
12 Beat your breasts for the pleasant fields, for the fruitful vine,
13 [a]For the land of my people *in which* thorns *and* briars shall come up;
Yea, for all the joyful houses, *and for* the [b]jubilant city.
14 Because [a]the palace has been abandoned, the [1]populated [b]city forsaken.
[2]Hill and watch-tower have become [c]caves forever,
A delight for wild donkeys, a pasture for flocks;
15 Until the [a]Spirit is poured out upon us from on high,
And the wilderness becomes a [b]fertile field
And the fertile field is considered as a forest.
16 Then [a]justice will dwell in the wilderness,
And righteousness will abide in the fertile field.
17 And the [a]work of righteousness will be peace,
And the service of righteousness, quietness and [1]confidence forever.
18 Then my people will live in a [a]peaceful habitation,
And in secure dwellings and in undisturbed [b]resting places;
19 And it will hail when the forest comes down,
And [a]the city will be utterly laid low.
20 How [a]blessed will you be, you who sow beside all waters,
Who [1]let out freely the ox and the donkey.

CHAPTER 33

The Judgment of God

WOE [a]to you, O destroyer,
While you were not destroyed;
And he [b]who is treacherous, while *others* did not deal treacherously with him.
As soon as you shall finish destroying, [c]you shall be destroyed;
As soon as you shall cease to deal treacherously, *others* shall [d]deal treacherously with you.
2 O LORD, [a]be gracious to us; we have [b]waited for Thee.
Be Thou [1]their [2c]strength every morning,
Our salvation also in the [d]time of distress.
3 At the sound of the tumult peoples flee;
At the [a]lifting up of Thyself nations disperse.

1 [a]Ps. 72:1-4; Is. 9:6, 7; 11:4, 5; Jer. 23:5; 33:15; Ezek. 37:24; Zech. 9:9
2 [1]Lit., *canals* [2]Lit., *heavy* [3]Lit., *exhausted* [a]Is. 4:6; 25:4 [b]Is. 35:6; 41:18; 43:19, 20
3 [1]Or, *turned away*
4 [1]Lit., *heart* [2]Lit., *knowledge* [a]Is. 29:24
5 [a]1 Sam. 25:25
6 [1]Or, *does* [2]Lit., *make empty the hungry soul* [3]Lit., *he causes to lack* [a]Prov. 19:3; 24:7-9; Is. 59:7, 13 [b]Is. 9:17; 10:6 [c]Is. 3:15; 10:2
7 [1]Lit., *words of falsehood* [2]Lit., *justly* [a]Jer. 5:26-28; Mic. 7:3 [b]Is. 5:23
9 [a]Is. 47:8; Zeph. 2:15
10 [a]Is. 5:5, 6; 7:23; 24:7
11 [a]Is. 22:12
13 [a]Is. 5:6, 10, 17; 27:10 [b]Is. 22:2; 23:9
14 [1]Lit., *multitude of* [2]Or, *Ophel* [a]Is. 13:22; 25:2; 34:13 [b]Is. 6:11; 22:2; 24:10, 12 [c]Is. 13:21; 34:13
15 [a]Is. 11:2; 44:3; 59:21; Ezek. 39:29; Joel 2:28 [b]Ps. 107:35; Is. 29:17; 35:1, 2
16 [a]Is. 33:5
17 [1]Or, *security* [a]Ps. 72:2, 3; 85:8; 119:165; Is. 2:4; Rom. 14:17; James 3:18
18 [a]Is. 26:3, 12 [b]Is. 11:10; 14:3; 30:15; Hos. 2:18-23; Zech. 2:5; 3:10
19 [a]Is. 24:10, 12; 26:5; 27:10; 29:4
20 [1]Lit., *send out the foot of the ox* [a]Eccles. 11:1; Is. 30:23, 24
1 [a]Is. 10:6; 21:2 [b]Is. 24:16; 48:8 [c]Is. 10:12; 13:8; 14:25; Hab. 2:8 [d]Jer. 25:12-14; Matt. 7:2
2 [1]Some versions read, *our* [2]Lit., *arm* [a]Is. 30:18, 19 [b]Is. 25:9 [c]Is. 40:10; 51:5; 59:16 [d]Is. 37:3
3 [a]Is. 10:33; 17:13; 59:16-18; Jer. 25:30, 31

4 And your spoil is gathered *as*
the caterpillar gathers;
As locusts rushing about, men
rush about on it.
5 The LORD is [a]exalted, for He
dwells on high;
He has [b]filled Zion with justice
and righteousness.
6 And He shall be the [a]stability of
your times,
A [b]wealth of salvation, wisdom,
and [c]knowledge;
The [d]fear of the LORD is his
treasure.
7 Behold, their brave men cry in
the streets,
The [a]ambassadors of peace
weep bitterly.
8 The highways are desolate, the
[a]traveler has ceased,
He has [b]broken the covenant,
he has despised the cities,
He has no regard for man.
9 [a]The land mourns and pines
away,
[b]Lebanon is shamed and withers;
[c]Sharon is like a desert plain,
And Bashan and Carmel lose
their foliage.
10 "Now [a]I will arise," says the
LORD,
"Now I will be exalted, now I
will be lifted up.
11 "You have [a]conceived [1]chaff,
you will give birth to stubble;
[2]My [b]breath will consume you
like a fire.
12 "And the peoples will be burned
to lime,
[a]Like cut thorns which are
burned in the fire.

13 "You who are far away, [a]hear
what I have done;
And you who are near, [1]ac-
knowledge My might."
14 [a]Sinners in Zion are terrified;
[b]Trembling has seized the godless.
"Who among us can live with
[c]the consuming fire?
Who among us can live with
[1]continual [d]burning?"
15 He who [a]walks righteously, and
speaks with sincerity,
He who rejects [1]unjust gain,
And shakes his hands so that
they hold no bribe;
He who stops his ears from
hearing about bloodshed,
And [b]shuts his eyes from looking upon evil;
16 He will dwell on the heights;
His refuge will be the [1]impreg-
nable rock;
[a]His bread will be given *him;*
His water will be sure.

17 Your eyes will see [a]the King in
His beauty;
They will behold [b]a far-distant
land.
18 Your heart will meditate on terror:
"Where is [a]he who counts?
Where is he who weighs?
Where is he who counts the
towers?"
19 You will no longer see a fierce
people,
A people of [1a]unintelligible
speech [2]which no one com-
prehends,
Of a stammering tongue which
no one understands.
20 [a]Look upon Zion, the city of our
appointed feasts;
Your eyes shall see Jerusalem
an [b]undisturbed habitation,
[c]A tent which shall not be
folded,
Its stakes shall never be pulled
up
Nor any of its cords be torn
apart.
21 But there the majestic *One,* the
LORD, shall be for us
A place of [a]rivers and wide canals,
On which no boat with oars
shall go,
And on which no mighty ship
shall pass—
22 For the LORD is our [a]judge,
The LORD is [b]our lawgiver,
The LORD is [c]our king;
[d]He will save us—
23 Your tackle hangs slack;
It cannot hold the base of its
mast firmly,
Nor spread out the sail.
Then the [a]prey of an abundant
spoil will be divided;
[b]The lame will take the plunder.
24 And no resident will say, "I am
sick";
The people who dwell [1]there
will be [a]forgiven *their* iniquity.

CHAPTER 34

God's Wrath against Nations

DRAW near, [a]O nations, to hear;
and listen, O peoples!
[b]Let the earth and [1]all it contains hear, and the world and
all that springs from it.
2 For the LORD's indignation is
against all the nations,

5 [a]Ps. 97:9 [b]Is. 1:26; 28:6; 32:16
6 [a]Is. 33:20 [b]Is. 45:17; 51:6 [c]Is. 11:9 [d]2 Kin. 18:7; Ps. 112:1-3; Is. 11:3; Matt. 6:33
7 [a]2 Kin. 18:18, 37
8 [a]Is. 35:8 [b]Is. 24:5
9 [a]Is. 3:26; 24:4; 29:2 [b]Is. 2:13; 10:34 [c]Is. 35:2; 65:10
10 [a]Ps. 12:5; Is. 2:19, 21
11 [1]Lit., *dry grass* [2]So one ancient version; M.T. reads: *Your breath will* [a]Ps. 7:14; Is. 26:18; 59:4; James 1:15 [b]Is. 1:31
12 [a]2 Sam. 23:6, 7; Is. 10:17; 27:4
13 [1]Lit., *know* [a]Ps. 48:10; Is. 49:1
14 [1]Lit., *everlasting* [a]Is. 1:28 [b]Is. 32:11 [c]Is. 30:27, 30; Heb. 12:29 [d]Is. 9:18, 19; 10:16; 47:14
15 [1]Lit., *gain of extortioners* [a]Ps. 15:2; 24:4; Is. 58:6-11 [b]Ps. 119:37
16 [1]Lit., *stronghold of rock* [a]Is. 49:10
17 [a]Is. 6:5; 24:23; 33:21, 22 [b]Is. 26:15
18 [a]1 Cor. 1:20
19 [1]Lit., *deepness of lip* [2]Lit., *from hearing* [a]Deut. 28:49, 50; Is. 28:11; Jer. 5:15
20 [a]Ps. 48:12 [b]Ps. 46:5; 125:1, 2; Is. 32:18 [c]Is. 54:2
21 [a]Is. 41:18; 43:19, 20; 48:18; 66:12
22 [a]Is. 2:4; 11:4; 16:5; 51:5 [b]Is. 1:10; 51:4, 7; James 4:12 [c]Ps. 89:18; Is. 33:17; Zech. 9:9 [d]Is. 25:9; 35:4; 49:25, 26; 60:16
23 [a]2 Kin. 7:16 [b]2 Kin. 7:8; Is. 35:6
24 [1]Lit., *in it* [a]Is. 40:2; 44:22; Jer. 50:20; Mic. 7:18, 19; 1 John 1:7-9
1 [1]Lit., *its fulness* [a]Ps. 49:1; Is. 41:1; 43:9 [b]Deut. 32:1; Is. 1:2

And *His* wrath against all their armies;
He has [1]utterly destroyed them,
He has given them over to slaughter.
3 So their slain will be thrown out,
And their corpses [1]will give off their stench,
And the mountains will [2]be drenched with their [a]blood.
4 And [a]all the host of heaven will [1]wear away,
And the [b]sky will be rolled up like a scroll;
All their hosts will also wither away
As a leaf withers from the vine,
Or as *one* withers from the fig tree.
5 For My sword is satiated in heaven,
Behold it shall descend for judgment upon Edom,
And upon the people whom I have [a]devoted to destruction.
6 The sword of the LORD is filled with blood,
It is [1]sated with fat, with the blood of lambs and goats,
With the fat of the kidneys of rams.
For the LORD has a sacrifice in [a]Bozrah,
And a great slaughter in the land of Edom.
7 [a]Wild oxen shall also [1]fall with them,
And [b]young bulls with strong ones;
Thus their land shall be soaked with blood,
And their dust [2]become greasy with fat.
8 For the LORD has a day of [a]vengeance,
A year of recompense for the [1]cause of Zion.
9 And [1]its streams shall be turned into pitch,
And its loose earth into brimstone,
And its land shall become burning pitch.
10 It shall [a]not be quenched night or day;
Its [b]smoke shall go up forever;
From [c]generation to generation it shall be desolate;
[d]None shall pass through it forever and ever.
11 But [1]pelican and hedgehog shall possess it,
And [2]owl and raven shall dwell in it;
And He shall stretch over it the [a]line of [3]desolation
And the [4]plumb line of emptiness.
12 Its nobles—there is [a]no one there
Whom they may proclaim king—
And all its princes shall be nothing.
13 And thorns shall come up in its [a]fortified towers,
Nettles and thistles in its fortified cities;
It shall also be a haunt of [b]jackals
And an abode of ostriches.
14 And the desert [a]creatures shall meet with the [1]wolves,
The [2b]hairy goat also shall cry to its kind;
Yes, the [3]night monster shall settle there
And shall find herself a resting place.
15 The tree snake shall make its nest and lay *eggs* there,
And it will hatch and gather *them* under its [1]protection.
Yes, the [2]hawks shall be gathered there,
Every one with its kind.

16 Seek from the [a]book of the LORD, and read:
Not one of these will be missing;
None will lack its mate.
For [1b]His mouth has commanded,
And His Spirit has gathered them.
17 And He has cast the [a]lot for them,
And His hand has divided it to them by line.
They shall possess it forever;
From generation to generation they shall dwell in it.

CHAPTER 35

Zion's Happy Future

THE [a]wilderness and the desert will be glad,
And the [1b]Arabah will rejoice and blossom;
Like the crocus
2 It will [a]blossom profusely
And [b]rejoice with rejoicing and shout of joy.
The [c]glory of Lebanon will be given to it,
The majesty of Carmel and Sharon.

2 [1]Lit., *put under the ban*
3 [1]Lit., *their stench will go up* [2]Lit., *dissolve* [a]Ezek. 14:19; 35:6; 38:22
4 [1]Lit., *rot* [a]Is. 13:13; 51:6; Ezek. 32:7, 8; Joel 2:31; Matt. 24:29; 2 Pet. 3:10 [b]Rev. 6:12-14
5 [a]Is. 24:6; 43:28
6 [1]Lit., *made fat* [a]Is. 63:1; Jer. 49:13
7 [1]Lit., *go down* [2]Lit., *made fat* [a]Num. 23:22; Ps. 22:21 [b]Ps. 68:30; Jer. 50:27
8 [1]Or, *controversy* [a]Is. 13:6; 35:4; 47:3; 61:2; 63:4
9 [1]I.e., Edom's
10 [a]Is. 1:31; 66:24 [b]Rev. 14:11; 19:3 [c]Is. 13:20-22; 24:1; 34:10-15; Mal. 1:3, 4 [d]Ezek. 29:11
11 [1]Or, *owl;* or, *jackdaw* [2]Or, *great horned owl* [3]Or, *formlessness* [4]Lit., *stones of void* [a]2 Kin. 21:13; Is. 24:10; Lam. 2:8
12 [a]Jer. 27:20; 39:6
13 [a]Is. 13:22; 25:2; 32:13 [b]Ps. 44:19; Jer. 9:11; 10:22
14 [1]Or, *howling creatures* [2]Or, *demon* [3]Heb., *Lilith* [a]Is. 13:21 [b]Is. 30:8
15 [1]Lit., *shade* [2]Or, *kites*
16 [1]So DSS; M.T., *My* [a]Is. 30:8 [b]Is. 1:20; 40:5; 58:14
17 [a]Is. 17:13, 14; Jer. 13:25
1 [1]Or, *desert* [a]Is. 6:11; 7:21-25; 27:10; 41:18; 55:12, 13 [b]Is. 41:19; 51:3
2 [a]Is. 27:6; 32:15 [b]Is. 25:9; 35:10; 55:12, 13; 66:10, 14 [c]Is. 60:13

They will see the [d]glory of the
Lord,
The majesty of our God.
3 [a]Encourage the [1]exhausted,
and strengthen the [2]feeble.
4 Say to those with [a]anxious
heart,
"Take courage, fear not.
Behold, your God will come
with [b]vengeance;
The [c]recompense of God will
come,
But He will [d]save you."
5 Then the [a]eyes of the blind will
be opened,
And the ears of the deaf will be
unstopped.
6 Then the [a]lame will leap like a
deer,
And the [b]tongue of the dumb
will shout for joy.
For waters will break forth in
the [c]wilderness
And streams in the [1]Arabah.
7 And the [1]scorched land will become a pool,
And the thirsty ground [a]springs
of water;
In the [b]haunt of jackals, its resting place,
Grass *becomes* reeds and
rushes.
8 And [a]a highway will be there,
[b]a roadway,
And it will be called "the highway of [c]holiness."
The unclean will not travel on
it,
But it *will* be for him who walks
that way,
And [d]fools will not wander *on*
it.
9 No lion will be there,
Nor will any vicious beast go up
on it;
[1]These will not be found there.
But [a]the redeemed will walk
there,
10 And [a]the ransomed of the Lord
will return,
And come with joyful shouting
to Zion,
With everlasting joy upon their
heads.
They will [1]find gladness and
joy,
And [b]sorrow and sighing will
flee away.

Chapter 36

Sennacherib Invades Judah

Now it came about in the fourteenth year of King Hezekiah, Sennacherib king of Assyria came up against all the fortified cities of Judah and seized them.

2 And the [a]king of Assyria sent
Rabshakeh from Lachish to Jerusalem to King Hezekiah with a large
army. And he stood by the conduit
of the upper pool on the highway of
the [1]fuller's field.
3 Then Eliakim the son of Hilkiah, who was over the household,
and Shebna the scribe, and Joah the
son of Asaph, the recorder, came
out to him.
4 Then [a]Rabshakeh said to them,
"Say now to Hezekiah, 'Thus says
the great king, the king of Assyria,
"What is this confidence that you
[1]have?
5 "I say, 'Your counsel and
strength for the war are only [1]empty
words.' Now on whom do you rely,
that [a]you have rebelled against me?
6 "Behold, you rely on the [a]staff of
this crushed reed, *even* on Egypt; on
which if a man leans, it will go into
his [1]hand and pierce it. [b]So is Pharaoh king of Egypt to all who rely on
him.
7 "But if you say to me, 'We trust
in the Lord our God,' is it not He
[a]whose high places and whose altars Hezekiah has taken away, and
has said to Judah and to Jerusalem,
'You shall worship before this altar'?
8 "Now therefore, [1]come make a
bargain with my master the king of
Assyria, and I will give you two
thousand horses, if you are able on
your part to set riders on them.
9 "How then can you [1]repulse one
[2]official of the least of my master's
servants, and [3a]rely on Egypt for
chariots and for horsemen?
10 "And have I now come up [1]without the Lord's approval against this
land to destroy it? [a]The Lord said to
me, 'Go up against this land, and destroy it.' " ' "
11 Then Eliakim and Shebna and
Joah said to Rabshakeh, "Speak
now to your servants in [a]Aramaic,
for we [1]understand *it*; and do not
speak with us in [2]Judean, in the
hearing of the people who are on the
wall."
12 But Rabshakeh said, "Has my
master sent me only to your master
and to you to speak these words,
and not to the men who sit on the
wall, *doomed* to eat their own dung
and drink their own urine with
you?"
13 Then Rabshakeh stood and
[a]cried with a loud voice in Judean,
and said, "Hear the words of the
great king, the king of Assyria.
14 "Thus says the king, 'Do not let

2 [d]Is. 25:9
3 [1]Lit., *slack hands* [2]Lit., *tottering knees* [a]Job 4:3, 4; Heb. 12:12
4 [a]Is. 32:4 [b]Is. 1:24; 47:3; 61:2; 63:4 [c]Is. 34:8; 59:18 [d]Ps. 145:19; Is. 33:22; 35:4
5 [a]Is. 29:18; 32:3, 4; 42:7, 16; 50:4; Matt. 11:5; John 9:6, 7
6 [1]Or, *desert* [a]Matt. 15:30; John 5:8, 9; Acts 3:8 [b]Matt. 9:32; Luke 11:14 [c]Is. 35:1; 41:18; 43:19; 49:10; 51:3; John 7:38
7 [1]Or, *mirage* [a]Is. 49:10 [b]Is. 13:22; 34:13
8 [a]Is. 11:16; 19:23; 40:3; 49:11; 62:10 [b]Is. 30:21; 51:10 [c]Is. 4:3; 52:1; Matt. 7:13, 14; 1 Pet. 1:15, 16 [d]Is. 33:8; Jer. 14:8
9 [1]Lit., *It* [a]Is. 51:10; 62:12; 63:4
10 [1]Lit., *overtake* [a]Is. 1:27; 51:11 [b]Is. 25:8; 30:19; 65:19; Rev. 7:17; 21:4
2 [1]I.e., launderer's [a]2 Kin. 18:17-20:11; 2 Chr. 32:9-24; Is. 36:2-38:8
4 [1]Lit., *trust* [a]2 Kin. 18:19
5 [1]Lit., *words of lips* [a]2 Kin. 18:7
6 [1]Lit., *palm* [a]Ezek. 29:6, 7 [b]Ps. 146:3; Is. 30:3, 5, 7
7 [a]Deut. 12:2-5; 2 Kin. 18:4, 5
8 [1]Lit., *please exchange pledges*
9 [1]Lit., *turn away the face of* [2]Or, *governor* [3]Lit., *rely on for yourself* [a]Is. 20:5; 30:2-5, 7; 31:3
10 [1]Lit., *without the Lord* [a]1 Kin. 13:18; 22:6, 12
11 [1]Lit., *hear* [2]I.e., Hebrew [a]Ezra 4:7; Dan. 2:4
13 [a]2 Chr. 32:18

Hezekiah [a]deceive you, for he will not be able to deliver you;

15 nor let Hezekiah make you [a]trust in the LORD, saying, "The LORD will surely deliver us, this city shall not be given into the hand of the king of Assyria."

16 'Do not listen to Hezekiah,' for thus says the king of Assyria, '[1]Make your peace with me and come out to me, and eat each of his [a]vine and each of his fig tree and drink each of the [b]waters of his own cistern,

17 until I come and take you away to a land like your own land, a land of grain and new wine, a land of bread and vineyards.

18 '*Beware* lest Hezekiah misleads you, saying, "[a]The LORD will deliver us." Has anyone of the gods of the nations delivered his land from the hand of the king of Assyria?

19 'Where are the gods of [a]Hamath and Arpad? Where are the gods of [a]Sepharvaim? And when have they [b]delivered Samaria from my hand?

20 'Who among all the [a]gods of these lands have delivered their land from my hand, that the [b]LORD should deliver Jerusalem from my hand?' "

21 But they were silent and answered him not a word; for the king's commandment was, "Do not answer him."

22 Then [a]Eliakim the son of Hilkiah, who was over the household, and [b]Shebna the scribe and Joah the son of Asaph, the recorder, came to Hezekiah with their clothes torn and told him the words of Rabshakeh.

CHAPTER 37

Hezekiah Seeks Isaiah's Help

AND [a]when King Hezekiah heard *it*, he tore his clothes, covered himself with sackcloth and entered the house of the LORD.

2 Then he sent [a]Eliakim who was over the household with [b]Shebna the scribe and the elders of the priests, covered with sackcloth, to [c]Isaiah the prophet, the son of Amoz.

3 And they said to him, "Thus says Hezekiah, 'This day is a [a]day of distress, rebuke, and rejection; for [b]children have come to birth, and there is no strength to [1]deliver.

4 'Perhaps the LORD your God will hear the words of Rabshakeh, whom his master the king of Assyria has sent to [a]reproach the living God, and will rebuke the words which the LORD your God has heard. Therefore, offer a prayer for [b]the remnant that is left.' "

5 So the servants of King Hezekiah came to Isaiah.

6 And Isaiah said to them, "Thus you shall say to your master, 'Thus says the LORD, "[a]Do not be afraid because of the words that you have heard, with which the servants of the king of Assyria have blasphemed Me.

7 "Behold, I will put a spirit in him so that he shall [a]hear a rumor and [b]return to his own land. And I will make him fall by the sword in his own land." ' "

8 Then Rabshakeh returned and found the king of Assyria fighting against [a]Libnah, for he had heard that [1]the king had left [b]Lachish.

9 When he [a]heard *them* say concerning Tirhakah king of [1b]Cush, "He has come out to fight against you," and when he heard *it* he sent messengers to Hezekiah, saying,

10 "Thus you shall say to Hezekiah king of [1]Judah, '[a]Do not let your God in whom you trust deceive you, saying, "Jerusalem shall not be given into the hand of the king of Assyria."

11 '[a]Behold, you have heard what the kings of Assyria have done to all the lands, destroying them completely. So will you be [1]spared?

12 'Did the gods of [1]those nations which my fathers have destroyed deliver them, *even* [a]Gozan and [b]Haran and Rezeph and the sons of Eden who *were* in Telassar?

13 'Where is the king of Hamath, the king of Arpad, the king of the city of Sepharvaim, *and of* Hena and Ivvah?' "

Hezekiah's Prayer in the Temple

14 Then Hezekiah took the [1]letter from the hand of the messengers and read it, and he went up to the house of the LORD and [2]spread it out before the LORD.

15 And Hezekiah prayed to the LORD saying,

16 "O LORD of hosts, the God of Israel, [a]who art enthroned *above* the cherubim, Thou art the [b]God, Thou alone, of all the kingdoms of the earth. [c]Thou hast made heaven and earth.

17 "[a]Incline Thine ear, O LORD, and hear; open Thine eyes, O LORD, and see; and [b]listen to all the words of Sennacherib, who sent *them* to [c]reproach the living God.

14 [a]Is. 37:10

15 [a]Is. 36:18, 20; 37:10, 11

16 [1]Lit., *Make with me a blessing* [a]1 Kin. 4:25; Mic. 4:4; Zech. 3:10 [b]Prov. 5:15

18 [a]Is. 36:15

19 [a]Is. 10:9-11; 37:11-13; Jer. 49:23 [b]2 Kin. 17:6

20 [a]1 Kin. 20:23, 28 [b]Is. 36:15

22 [a]Is. 22:20; 36:3 [b]Is. 22:15

1 [a]2 Kin. 19:1-37; Is. 37:1-38

2 [a]Is. 22:20 [b]Is. 22:15 [c]Is. 1:1; 20:2

3 [1]Lit., *give birth* [a]Is. 22:5; 26:16; 33:2 [b]Is. 26:17, 18; 66:9; Hos. 13:13

4 [a]Is. 36:15, 18, 20 [b]Is. 1:9; 10:20-22; 37:31, 32; 46:3

6 [a]Is. 7:4; 35:4

7 [a]Is. 37:9 [b]Is. 37:37, 38

8 [1]Lit., *he* [a]Num. 33:20; Josh. 10:29 [b]Josh. 10:31, 32

9 [1]Or, *Ethiopia* [a]Is. 37:7 [b]Is. 18:1; 20:5

10 [1]Lit., *Judah, saying* [a]Is. 36:15

11 [1]Lit., *delivered* [a]Is. 10:9-11; 36:18-20

12 [1]Lit., *the* [a]2 Kin. 17:6; 18:11 [b]Gen. 11:31; 12:1-4; Acts 7:2

14 [1]Lit., *letters* [2]Lit., *Hezekiah spread*

16 [a]Ex. 25:22; 1 Sam. 4:4; Ps. 80:1; 99:1 [b]Deut. 10:17; Ps. 86:10; 136:2, 3 [c]Is. 42:5; 45:12; Jer. 10:12

17 [a]2 Chr. 6:40; Ps. 17:6; Dan. 9:18 [b]Ps. 74:22 [c]Is. 37:4

18"Truly, O LORD, the kings of Assyria have devastated all the countries and their lands,
19 and have cast their gods into
the fire, for they were not gods but
the [a]work of men's hands, wood and
stone. So they have [b]destroyed
them.
20"And now, O LORD our God, [a]de-
liver us from his hand that [b]all the
kingdoms of the earth may know
that Thou alone, LORD, [1]art God."

God Answers Through Isaiah

21 Then Isaiah the son of Amoz
sent word to Hezekiah, saying,
"Thus says the LORD, the God of Israel, 'Because you have prayed to
Me about Sennacherib king of Assyria,
22 this is the word that the LORD
has spoken against him:
"She has despised you and
mocked you,
The [a]virgin [b]daughter of Zion;
She has [c]shaken *her* head behind you,
The daughter of Jerusalem!
23"Whom have you reproached
and blasphemed?
And against whom have you
raised *your* voice,
And [1]haughtily [a]lifted up your
eyes?
Against the [b]Holy One of Israel!
24"Through your servants you
have reproached the Lord,
And you have said, 'With my
many chariots I came up to
the heights of the mountains,
To the remotest parts of [a]Leba-
non;
And I cut down its tall [b]cedars
and its choice cypresses.
And I will go to its [1]highest
peak, its thickest forest.
25 'I dug *wells* and drank waters,
And [a]with the sole of my feet I
dried up
All the rivers of [1]Egypt.'
26"[a]Have you not heard?
Long ago I did it,
From ancient times I [b]planned
it.
Now I have brought it to pass,
That [c]you should turn fortified
cities into [d]ruinous heaps.
27"Therefore their inhabitants
were short of strength,
They were dismayed and put to
shame;
They were *as* the [a]vegetation of
the field and *as* the green
herb,
As [b]grass on the housetops [1]is
scorched before it is grown
up.

28"But I [a]know your sitting down,
And your going out and your
coming in,
And your raging against Me.
29"Because of your raging against
Me,
And because your [1a]arrogance
has come up to My ears,
Therefore I will put My [b]hook in
your nose,
And My [c]bridle in your lips,
And I will turn you back [d]by the
way which you came.
30"Then this shall be the sign for
you: [1]you shall eat this year what
[a]grows of itself, in the second year
what springs from the same, and in
the third year sow, reap, plant vineyards, and eat their fruit.
31"And the [a]surviving [b]remnant of
the house of Judah shall again [c]take
root downward and bear fruit upward.
32"For out of Jerusalem shall go
forth a [a]remnant, and out of Mount
Zion [1]survivors. The [b]zeal of the
LORD of hosts shall perform this." '
33"Therefore, thus says the LORD
concerning the king of Assyria, 'He
shall not come to this city, or shoot
an arrow there; neither shall he
come before it with a shield, nor
throw up a [a]mound against it.
34 '[a]By the way that he came, by
the same he shall return, and he
shall not come to this city,' declares
the LORD.
35 'For I will [a]defend this city to
save it [b]for My own sake and for My
servant David's sake.' "

Assyrians Destroyed

36 Then the [a]angel of the LORD
went out, and struck 185,000 in the
camp of the Assyrians; and when
[1]men arose early in the morning, behold, all of these were [2]dead.
37 So Sennacherib, king of Assyria, departed and [1]returned *home*,
and lived at [a]Nineveh.
38 And it came about as he was
worshiping in the house of Nisroch
his god, that Adrammelech and
Sharezer his sons killed him with
the sword; and they escaped into the
land of [a]Ararat. And [b]Esarhaddon
his son became king in his place.

CHAPTER 38

Hezekiah Healed

[a]IN those days Hezekiah became
[1]mortally ill. And [b]Isaiah the
prophet the son of Amoz came to
him and said to him, "Thus says the

19 [a]Is. 2:8; 17:8; 41:24, 29 [b]Is. 26:14
20 [1]So DSS and 2 Kin. 19:19; M.T. omits *God* [a]Is. 25:9; 33:22; 35:4 [b]1 Kin. 18:36, 37; Ps. 46:10; Is. 37:16; Ezek. 36:23
22 [a]Jer. 14:17; Lam. 2:13 [b]Ps. 9:14; Zeph. 3:14; Zech. 2:10 [c]Job 16:4
23 [1]Lit., *on high* [a]Is. 2:11; 5:15, 21 [b]Ezek. 39:7; Hab. 1:12
24 [1]Lit., *farthest height* [a]Is. 10:33, 34 [b]Is. 14:8
25 [1]Or, *the besieged place* [a]Deut. 11:10; 1 Kin. 20:10
26 [a]Is. 40:21, 28 [b]Acts 2:23; 4:27, 28; 1 Pet. 2:8 [c]Is. 10:6 [d]Is. 17:1; 25:2
27 [1]So DSS and 2 Kin. 19:26; M.T. *as a plowed field* [a]Is. 40:7 [b]Ps. 129:6
28 [a]Ps. 139:1
29 [1]Lit., *complacency* [a]Is. 10:12 [b]Ezek. 29:4; 38:4 [c]Is. 30:28 [d]Is. 37:34
30 [1]Lit., *eating* [a]Lev. 25:5, 11
31 [a]Is. 4:2; 10:20 [b]Is. 37:4 [c]Is. 27:6
32 [1]Lit., *those who escape* [a]Is. 37:4 [b]2 Kin. 19:31; Is. 9:7; 59:17; Joel 2:18; Zech. 1:14
33 [a]Jer. 6:6; 32:24
34 [a]Is. 37:29
35 [a]2 Kin. 20:6; Is. 31:5; 38:6 [b]Is. 43:25; 48:9, 11
36 [1]Lit., *they* [2]Lit., *dead bodies* [a]2 Kin. 19:35; Is. 10:12, 33, 34
37 [1]Lit., *went and returned* [a]Gen. 10:11; Jon. 1:2; 3:3; 4:11; Zeph. 2:13
38 [a]Gen. 8:4; Jer. 51:27 [b]Ezra 4:2
1 [1]Lit., *sick to the point of death* [a]2 Kin. 20:1-6, 9-11; 2 Chr. 32:24; Is. 38:1-8 [b]Is. 1:1; 37:2

LORD, '[c]Set your house in order, for
you shall die and not live.' "
2 Then Hezekiah turned his face
to the wall, and prayed to the LORD,
3 and said, "[a]Remember now, O
LORD, I beseech Thee, how I have
[b]walked before Thee in truth and
with a [c]whole heart, and [d]have done
what is good in Thy sight." And
Hezekiah [e]wept [1]bitterly.
4 Then the word of the LORD
came to Isaiah, saying,
5"Go and say to Hezekiah, 'Thus
says the LORD, the God of your father David, "I have heard your
prayer, I have seen your tears; behold, I will add [a]fifteen years to your
[1]life.
6"And I will [a]deliver you and this
city from the hand of the king of
Assyria; and I will defend this
city." '
7"And this shall be the [a]sign to
you from the LORD, that the LORD
will do this thing that He has spoken:
8"Behold, I will [a]cause the
shadow on the stairway, which has
gone down with the sun on the stairway of Ahaz, to go back ten steps."
So the [b]sun's *shadow* went back ten
steps on the stairway on which it
had gone down.
9 A writing of Hezekiah king of
Judah, after his illness and [1]recov-
ery:

10 I said, "[a]In the middle of my
[1]life
I am to enter the [b]gates of
Sheol;
I am to be [c]deprived of the rest
of my years."
11 I said, "I shall not see the LORD,
The LORD [a]in the land of the living;
I shall look on man no more
among the inhabitants of the
world.
12"Like a shepherd's [a]tent my
dwelling is pulled up and removed from me;
As a [b]weaver I [c]rolled up my
life.
He [d]cuts me off from the loom;
From [e]day until night Thou dost
make an end of me.
13"I composed *my soul* until morning.
[a]Like a lion—so He [b]breaks all
my bones,
From [c]day until night Thou dost
make an end of me.
14"[a]Like a swallow, *like* a crane, so
I twitter;
I [b]moan like a dove;
My [c]eyes look wistfully to the
heights;

1 [c]2 Sam. 17:23
3 [1]Lit., *great weeping* [a]Neh. 13:14 [b]2 Kin. 18:5, 6; Ps. 26:3 [c]1 Chr. 28:9; 29:19 [d]Deut. 6:18 [e]Ps. 6:6-8
5 [1]Lit., *days* [a]2 Kin. 18:2, 13
6 [a]Is. 31:5; 37:35
7 [a]Judg. 6:17, 21, 36-40; Is. 7:11, 14; 37:30
8 [a]2 Kin. 20:9-11 [b]Josh. 10:12-14
9 [1]Lit., *he lived after his illness*
10 [1]Lit., *days* [a]Ps. 102:24 [b]Ps. 107:18 [c]Job 17:11, 15; 2 Cor. 1:9
11 [a]Ps. 27:13; 116:9
12 [a]2 Cor. 5:1, 4; 2 Pet. 1:13, 14 [b]Job 7:6 [c]Heb. 1:12 [d]Job 6:9 [e]Job 4:20; Ps. 73:14
13 [a]Job 10:16; 16:12 [b]Ps. 51:8; Dan. 6:24 [c]Ps. 32:4
14 [a]Job 30:29; Ps. 102:6 [b]Is. 59:11; Ezek. 7:16; Nah. 2:7 [c]Ps. 119:123 [d]Job 17:3; Ps. 119:122
15 [1]Targum and DSS read, *And what shall I say for He* [a]Ps. 39:9 [b]1 Kin. 21:27 [c]Job 7:11; 10:1; Is. 38:17
16 [1]Lit., *Thou wilt* [a]Ps. 119:71, 75 [b]Ps. 39:13 [c]Ps. 119:25
17 [1]So some versions; Heb., *loved* [2]Or, *destruction* [a]Ps. 30:3; 86:13; Jon. 2:6 [b]Is. 43:25; Jer. 31:34; Mic. 7:19
18 [a]Num. 16:33; Ps. 28:1
19 [a]Ps. 118:17; 119:175 [b]Deut. 6:7; 11:19; Ps. 78:5-7
20 [a]Ps. 33:1-3; 68:24-26 [b]Ps. 104:33; 116:2; 146:2 [c]Ps. 116:17-19
1 [a]2 Kin. 20:12-19; 2 Chr. 32:31; Is. 39:1-8
2 [1]Lit., *rejoiced over them* [a]2 Chr. 32:25, 31; Job 31:25 [b]2 Kin. 18:15, 16
3 [a]2 Sam. 12:1; 2 Chr. 16:7

O Lord, I am oppressed, be my
[d]security.
15"[a]What shall I say?
[1]For He has spoken to me, and
He Himself has done it;
I shall [b]wander about all my
years because of the [c]bitter-
ness of my soul.
16"O Lord, [a]by *these* things *men*
live;
And in all these is the life of my
spirit;
[1b]O restore me to health, and
[c]let me live!
17"Lo, for *my own* welfare I had
great bitterness;
It is Thou who hast [1a]kept my
soul from the pit of [2]nothing-
ness,
For Thou hast [b]cast all my sins
behind Thy back.
18"For Sheol cannot thank Thee,
Death cannot praise Thee;
Those who go down [a]to the pit
cannot hope for Thy faithfulness.
19"It is the [a]living who give thanks
to Thee, as I do today;
A [b]father tells his sons about
Thy faithfulness.
20"The LORD will surely save me;
So we will [a]play my songs on
stringed instruments
[b]All *the* days of our life [c]at the
house of the LORD."

21 Now Isaiah had said, "Let them
take a cake of figs, and apply it to
the boil, that he may recover."
22 Then Hezekiah had said, "What
is the sign that I shall go up to the
house of the LORD?"

CHAPTER 39

Hezekiah Shows His Treasures

[a]AT that time Merodach-baladan
son of Baladan, king of Babylon,
sent letters and a present to Hezekiah, for he heard that he had been
sick and had recovered.
2 And Hezekiah [1]was [a]pleased,
and showed them all his treasure
house, the [b]silver and the gold and
the spices and the precious oil and
his whole armory and all that was
found in his treasuries. There was
nothing in his house, nor in all his
dominion, that Hezekiah did not
show them.
3 Then Isaiah the [a]prophet came
to King Hezekiah and said to him,
"What did these men say, and from
where have they come to you?" And
Hezekiah said, "They have come to

me from a far [b]country, from Babylon."
4 And he said, "What have they
seen in your house?" So Hezekiah
[1]answered, "They have seen all that
is in my house; there is nothing
among my treasuries that I have not
shown them."
5 Then Isaiah said to Hezekiah,
"Hear the [a]word of the LORD of
hosts,
6 'Behold, the days are coming
when [a]all that is in your house, and
all that your fathers have laid up in
store to this day shall be carried to
Babylon; nothing shall be left,' says
the LORD.
7 'And *some* of your sons who
shall issue from you, whom you
shall beget, shall be taken away; and
they shall become officials in the
palace of the king of Babylon.'"
8 [a]Then Hezekiah said to Isaiah,
"The word of the LORD which you
have spoken is good." For he
[1]thought, "For there will be peace
and truth [b]in my days."

CHAPTER 40

The Greatness of God

"[a]COMFORT, O comfort My people," says your God.
2 "[a]Speak [1]kindly to Jerusalem;
And call out to her, that her
[2b]warfare has ended,
That her [3c]iniquity has been removed,
That she has received of the
LORD's hand
[d]Double for all her sins."

3 [a]A voice [1]is calling,
"[b]Clear the way for the LORD in
the wilderness;
Make smooth in the desert a
highway for our God.
4 "Let every valley be [a]lifted up,
And every mountain and hill be
made low;
And let the rough ground become a plain,
And the rugged terrain a broad
valley;
5 [1]Then the [a]glory of the LORD
will be revealed,
And [b]all flesh will see *it* together;
For the mouth of the LORD has
spoken."
6 A voice says, "Call out."
Then [1]he answered, "What
shall I call out?"
[a]All flesh is grass, and all its
[2]loveliness is like the flower
of the field.
7 The [a]grass withers, the flower
fades,
When the breath of the LORD
blows upon it;
Surely the people are grass.
8 The grass withers, the flower
fades,
But [a]the word of our God
stands forever.

9 Get yourself up on a [a]high
mountain,
O Zion, bearer of [b]good news,
Lift up your voice mightily,
O Jerusalem, bearer of good
news;
Lift *it* up, do not fear.
Say to the cities of Judah,
"[c]Here is your God!"
10 Behold, the Lord [1]GOD will
come [a]with might,
With His [b]arm ruling for Him.
Behold, His [c]reward is with
Him,
And His recompense before
Him.
11 Like a shepherd He will [a]tend
His flock,
In His arm He will gather the
lambs,
And carry *them* in His bosom;
He will gently lead the nursing
ewes.

12 Who has [a]measured the [1]wa-
ters in the hollow of His
hand,
And marked off the heavens by
the [2]span,
And [3]calculated the dust of the
earth by the measure,
And weighed the mountains in
a balance,
And the hills in a pair of scales?
13 [a]Who has directed the Spirit of
the LORD,
Or as His [b]counselor has informed Him?
14 [a]With whom did He consult
and *who* [b]gave Him understanding?
And *who* taught Him in the
path of justice and taught
Him knowledge,
And informed Him of the way
of understanding?
15 Behold, the [a]nations are like a
drop from a bucket,
And are regarded as a speck of
[b]dust on the scales;
Behold, He lifts up the [1]islands
like fine dust.
16 Even Lebanon is not enough to
burn,
Nor its beasts enough for a
burnt offering.

3 [b]Deut. 28:49; Jer. 5:15
4 [1]Lit., *said*
5 [a]1 Sam. 13:13, 14; 15:16
6 [a]2 Kin. 24:13; 25:13-15; Jer. 20:5
8 [1]Lit., *said* [a]2 Chr. 32:26 [b]2 Chr. 34:28
1 [a]Is. 12:1; 49:13; 51:3, 12; 52:9; 61:2; 66:13; Jer. 31:10-14; Zeph. 3:14-17; 2 Cor. 1:4
2 [1]Lit., *to the heart of* [2]Or, *hard service* [3]Or, *penalty of iniquity accepted as paid off* [a]Is. 35:4; Zech. 1:13 [b]Is. 41:11-13; 49:25; 54:15, 17 [c]Is. 33:24; 53:5, 6, 11 [d]Jer. 16:18; Zech. 9:12; Rev. 18:6
3 [1]Or, *of one calling out* [a]Matt. 3:3; Mark 1:3; Luke 3:4-6; John 1:23 [b]Mal. 3:1; 4:5, 6
4 [a]Ezek. 17:24
5 [1]Or, *In order that the* [a]Is. 6:3; Hab. 2:14 [b]Is. 52:10; Joel 2:28
6 [1]Another reading is, *I said* [2]Or, *constancy* [a]Job 14:2; Ps. 102:11; 103:15; 1 Pet. 1:24, 25
7 [a]Ps. 90:5, 6; James 1:10, 11
8 [a]Is. 55:11; 59:21; Matt. 5:18
9 [a]Is. 52:7 [b]Is. 61:1 [c]Is. 25:9; 35:2
10 [1]YHWH, usually rendered LORD [a]Is. 9:6, 7 [b]Is. 59:16, 18 [c]Is. 62:11; Rev. 22:12
11 [a]Jer. 31:10; Ezek. 34:12-14, 23, 31; Mic. 5:4; John 10:11, 14-16
12 [1]DSS reads, *waters of the sea* [2]Or, *half cubit;* i.e., 9 inches [3]Lit., *contained, or comprehended* [a]Job 38:8-11; Ps. 102:25, 26; Is. 48:13; Heb. 1:10-12
13 [a]Rom. 11:34; 1 Cor. 2:16 [b]Is. 41:28
14 [a]Job 38:4 [b]Job 21:22; Col. 2:3
15 [1]Or, *coastlands* [a]Jer. 10:10 [b]Is. 17:13; 29:5

17 [a]All the nations are as nothing before Him,
They are regarded by Him as less than nothing and meaningless.

18 [a]To whom then will you liken God?
Or what likeness will you compare with Him?
19 *As for* the [a]idol, a craftsman casts it,
A goldsmith plates it with gold,
And a silversmith *fashions* chains of silver.
20 He who is too impoverished for *such* an offering
Selects a tree that does not rot;
He seeks out for himself a skillful craftsman
To [1]prepare an idol that [a]will not totter.

21 [a]Do you not know? Have you not heard?
Has it not been declared to you from the beginning?
Have you not understood [b]from the foundations of the earth?
22 It is He who [1]sits above the [2a]vault of the earth,
And its inhabitants are like [b]grasshoppers,
Who [c]stretches out the heavens like a [d]curtain
And spreads them out like a [e]tent to dwell in.
23 He *it is* who reduces [a]rulers to nothing,
Who [b]makes the judges of the earth meaningless.
24 [1]Scarcely have they been planted,
[1]Scarcely have they been sown,
[1]Scarcely has their stock taken root in the earth,
But He merely blows on them, and they wither,
And the [a]storm carries them away like stubble.
25 "[a]To whom then will you liken Me
That I should be *his* equal?" says the Holy One.
26 [a]Lift up your eyes on high
And see [b]who has created these *stars,*
The [c]One who leads forth their host by number,
He calls them all by name;
Because of the [d]greatness of His might and the [1]strength of *His* power
[e]Not one *of them* is missing.

27 [a]Why do you say, O Jacob, and assert, O Israel,
"My way is [b]hidden from the LORD,
And the [c]justice due me [1]escapes the notice of [d]my God"?
28 [a]Do you not know? Have you not heard?
The [b]Everlasting God, the LORD, the creator of the ends of the earth
Does not become weary or tired.
His understanding is [c]inscrutable.
29 He gives strength to the [a]weary,
And to *him who* lacks might He [b]increases power.
30 Though [a]youths grow weary and tired,
And vigorous [b]young men stumble badly,
31 Yet those who [1]wait for the LORD
Will [a]gain new strength;
They will [2b]mount up *with* wings like eagles,
They will run and not get tired,
They will walk and not become weary.

CHAPTER 41

Israel Encouraged

"COASTLANDS, listen to Me [a]in silence,
And let the peoples [b]gain new strength;
[c]Let them come forward, then let them speak;
[d]Let us come together for judgment.
2 "[a]Who has aroused one from the east
Whom He [b]calls in righteousness to His [1]feet?
He [c]delivers up nations before him,
And subdues kings.
He makes them like dust with his sword,
As the wind-driven [d]chaff with his bow.
3 "He pursues them, passing on in safety,
By a way he had not been [1]traversing with his feet.
4 "[a]Who has performed and accomplished *it,*
Calling forth the generations from the beginning?
'[b]I, the LORD, am the first, and with the last. [c]I am He.' "

5 The [a]coastlands have seen and are afraid;

17 [a]Is. 29:7
18 [a]Ex. 8:10; 15:11; 1 Sam. 2:2; Is. 40:25; 46:5; Mic. 7:18
19 [a]Ps. 115:4-8; Is. 41:7; 44:10; Hab. 2:18, 19
20 [1]Or, *set up* [a]1 Sam. 5:3, 4; Is. 41:7; 46:7
21 [a]Ps. 19:1; 50:6; Is. 37:26; Acts 14:17; Rom. 1:19 [b]Is. 48:13; 51:13
22 [1]Or, *is enthroned* [2]Or, *circle* [a]Job 22:14; Prov. 8:27 [b]Num. 13:33 [c]Job 9:8; Is. 37:16; 42:5; 44:24 [d]Ps. 104:2 [e]Job 36:29; Ps. 18:11; 19:4
23 [a]Job 12:21; Ps. 107:40; Is. 34:12 [b]Is. 5:21; Jer. 25:18-27
24 [1]Or, *Not even* [a]Is. 17:13; 41:16
25 [a]Is. 40:18
26 [1]So DSS and ancient versions; M.T., *strong* [a]Is. 51:6 [b]Is. 42:5; 48:12, 13 [c]Ps. 147:4 [d]Ps. 89:11-13 [e]Is. 34:16; 48:13
27 [1]Lit., *passes by my God* [a]Is. 49:4, 14 [b]Is. 54:8 [c]Job 27:2; 34:5; Luke 18:7, 8 [d]Is. 25:1
28 [a]Is. 40:21 [b]Gen. 21:33; Ps. 90:2 [c]Ps. 147:5; Rom. 11:33
29 [a]Is. 50:4; Jer. 31:25 [b]Is. 41:10
30 [a]Jer. 6:11; 9:21 [b]Is. 9:17
31 [1]Or, *hope in* [2]Or, *sprout wings* [a]Job 17:9; Ps. 103:5; 2 Cor. 4:8-10, 16 [b]Ex. 19:4; Deut. 32:11; Luke 18:1; 2 Cor. 4:1, 16; Gal. 6:9; Heb. 12:3
1 [a]Hab. 2:20; Zech. 2:13 [b]Is. 40:31 [c]Is. 34:1; 48:16 [d]Is. 1:18; 43:26; 50:8
2 [1]Lit., *foot* [a]Is. 41:25; 45:1-3; 46:11 [b]Is. 42:6 [c]2 Chr. 36:23; Ezra 1:2 [d]Is. 40:24
3 [1]Lit., *going*
4 [a]Is. 41:26; 44:7; 46:10 [b]Is. 43:10; 44:6; Rev. 1:8, 17; 22:13 [c]Is. 43:13; 46:4; 48:12
5 [a]Is. 41:1; Ezek. 26:15, 16

The [b]ends of the earth tremble;
They have drawn near and have come.
6 Each one [a]helps his neighbor,
And says to his brother, "Be strong!"
7 So the craftsman encourages the smelter,
And he who smooths *metal* with the hammer *encourages* him who beats the anvil,
Saying of the soldering, "It is good";
And he fastens it with nails,
[a]*That* it should not totter.
8 "But you, Israel, My servant,
Jacob whom I have chosen,
Descendant of [a]Abraham My [b]friend,
9 "You whom I have [1a]taken from the ends of the earth,
And called from its remotest parts,
And said to you, 'You are My servant,
I have [b]chosen you and not rejected you.
10 'Do not [a]fear, for I am with you;
Do not anxiously look about you, for I am your God.
I will strengthen you, surely [b]I will help you,
Surely I will uphold you with My righteous [c]right hand.'
11 "Behold, all those who are angered at you will be shamed and dishonored;
[a]Those who contend with you will be as nothing, and will perish.
12 "[a]You will seek those who quarrel with you, but will not find them,
Those who war with you will be as nothing, and non-existent.
13 "For I am the LORD your God, [a]who upholds your right hand,
Who says to you, 'Do not fear, I will help you.'
14 "Do not fear, you worm Jacob, you men of Israel;
I will help you," declares the LORD, "[1]and [a]your Redeemer is the Holy One of Israel.
15 "Behold, I have made you a new, sharp threshing sledge with double edges;
[a]You will thresh the mountains, and pulverize *them*,
And will make the hills like chaff.
16 "You will winnow them, and the wind will carry them away,
And the storm will scatter them;
But you will [a]rejoice in the LORD,
You will glory in the Holy One of Israel.

17 "The [1]afflicted and needy are seeking [a]water, but there is none,
And their tongue is parched with thirst;
I, the LORD, [b]will answer them Myself,
As the God of Israel I [c]will not forsake them.
18 "I will open [a]rivers on the bare heights,
And springs in the midst of the valleys;
I will make [b]the wilderness a pool of water,
And the dry land fountains of water.
19 "I will put the cedar in the wilderness,
The acacia, and the [a]myrtle, and the [1]olive tree;
I will place the [a]juniper in the desert,
Together with the box tree and the cypress,
20 That they may see and recognize,
And consider and gain insight as well,
That the [a]hand of the LORD has done this,
And the Holy One of Israel has created it.

21 "[1]Present your case," the LORD says.
"Bring forward your strong *arguments*,"
The King of Jacob says.
22 [a]Let them bring forth and declare to us what is going to take place;
As for the [b]former *events*, declare what they *were*,
That we may consider them, and know their outcome;
Or announce to us what is coming.
23 [a]Declare the things that are going to come afterward,
That we may know that you are gods;
Indeed, [b]do good or evil, that we may anxiously look about us and fear together.
24 Behold, [a]you are of [1]no account,
And your work amounts to nothing;
He who chooses you is an abomination.

5 [b]Josh. 5:1; Ps. 67:7
6 [a]Joel 3:9-11
7 [a]Is. 40:20; 46:7
8 [a]Is. 29:22; 51:2; 63:16 [b]2 Chr. 20:7; James 2:23
9 [1]Or, *taken hold of* [a]Is. 11:11 [b]Deut. 7:6; 14:2; Ps. 135:4
10 [a]Deut. 20:1; 31:6; Josh. 1:9; Ps. 27:1; Is. 41:13, 14; 43:2, 5; Rom. 8:31 [b]Is. 41:14; 44:2; 49:8 [c]Ps. 89:13, 14
11 [a]Is. 17:13; 29:5, 7, 8
12 [a]Job 20:7-9; Ps. 37:35, 36; Is. 17:14
13 [a]Is. 42:6; 45:1
14 [1]Or, *even your Redeemer, the Holy One* [a]Is. 35:10; 43:14; 46:6, 22-24
15 [a]Mic. 4:13; Hab. 3:12
16 [a]Is. 25:9; 35:10; 51:3; 61:10
17 [1]Or, *poor* [a]Is. 43:20; 44:3; 49:10; 55:1 [b]Is. 30:19; 65:24 [c]Is. 42:16; 62:12
18 [a]Is. 30:25; 43:19 [b]Ps. 107:35; Is. 35:6, 7
19 [1]Or, *oleaster* [a]Is. 35:1; 55:13; 60:13
20 [a]Job 12:9; Is. 66:14
21 [1]Lit., *Bring near*
22 [a]Is. 44:7; 45:21; 46:10 [b]Is. 43:9
23 [a]Is. 42:9; 44:7, 8; 45:3; John 13:19 [b]Jer. 10:5
24 [1]Lit., *nothing* [a]Ps. 115:8; Is. 44:9; 1 Cor. 8:4

25"I have aroused [a]one from the north, and he has come;
From the rising of the sun he will call on My name;
And he will come upon rulers as *upon* [b]mortar,
Even as the potter treads clay."
26 Who has [a]declared *this* from the beginning, that we might know?
Or from former times, that we may say, "*He is* right!"?
Surely there was [b]no one who declared,
Surely there was no one who proclaimed,
Surely there was no one who heard your words.
27"[a]Formerly *I said* to Zion, 'Behold, here they are.'
And to Jerusalem, 'I will give a [b]messenger of good news.'
28"But [a]when I look, there is no one,
And there is no [b]counselor [1]among them
Who, if I ask, can give an answer.
29"Behold, all of them are [1]false;
Their [a]works are worthless,
Their molten images are [b]wind and emptiness.

Chapter 42

God's Promise Concerning His Servant

"[a]Behold, My [b]Servant, whom I [1]uphold;
My [c]chosen one *in whom* My [d]soul delights.
I have put My [e]Spirit upon Him;
He will bring forth justice to the [2]nations.
2"He will not cry out or raise *His voice,*
Nor make His voice heard in the street.
3"A [a]bruised reed He will not break,
And a dimly burning wick He will not extinguish;
He will faithfully bring forth [b]justice.
4"He will not be [a]disheartened or crushed,
Until He has established justice in the earth;
And the [b]coastlands will wait expectantly for His [1]law."

5 Thus says God the LORD,
Who [a]created the heavens and [b]stretched them out,
Who spread out the [c]earth and its [1]offspring,

25 [a]Is. 41:2; Jer. 50:3 [b]2 Sam. 22:43; Is. 10:6; Mic. 7:10; Zech. 10:5

26 [a]Is. 41:22; 44:7; 45:21 [b]Hab. 2:18, 19

27 [a]Is. 48:3-8 [b]Is. 40:9; 44:28; 52:7; Nah. 1:15

28 [1]Lit., *out of those* [a]Is. 50:2; 59:16; 63:5 [b]Is. 40:13, 14

29 [1]Another reading is, *nothing* [a]Is. 2:8; 17:8; 41:24 [b]Jer. 5:13

1 [1]Or, *hold fast* [2]Or, *Gentiles* [a]Matt. 12:18-21 [b]Is. 41:8; 43:10; 49:3-6; 52:13; 53:11; Matt. 12:18-21; Phil. 2:7 [c]1 Pet. 2:4, 6 [d]Matt. 3:17; 17:5 [e]Is. 11:2; 59:21; 61:1; Matt. 3:16; Luke 4:18, 19, 21

3 [a]Is. 57:15 [b]Ps. 72:2, 4; 96:13

4 [1]Or, *instruction* [a]Is. 40:28 [b]Is. 11:11; 24:15; 42:10, 12; 49:1; 51:5; 60:9; 66:19

5 [1]Or, *vegetation* [a]Ps. 102:25, 26; Is. 45:18 [b]Ps. 104:2; Is. 40:22 [c]Ps. 24:1, 2; 136:6 [d]Job 12:10; 33:4; Is. 57:16; Dan. 5:23; Acts 17:25

6 [a]Is. 41:2; Jer. 23:5, 6 [b]Is. 26:3; 27:3 [c]Is. 49:6, 8 [d]Is. 51:4; 60:1, 3; Luke 2:32

7 [a]Is. 29:18; 35:5 [b]Is. 49:9; 61:1

8 [1]Or, *idols* [a]Ex. 3:15; Ps. 83:18 [b]Ex. 20:3-5; Is. 48:11

9 [a]Is. 43:19; 48:6

10 [a]Ps. 33:3; 40:3; 98:1 [b]Is. 49:6; 62:11 [c]Ps. 65:5; 107:23 [d]Ex. 20:11; 1 Chr. 16:32; Ps. 96:11

11 [a]Is. 32:16; 35:1, 6 [b]Is. 21:16; 60:7 [c]Is. 16:1 [d]Is. 52:7; Nah. 1:15

13 [a]Is. 9:7; 26:11; 37:32; 59:17 [b]Is. 66:14-16

Who [d]gives breath to the people on it,
And spirit to those who walk in it,
6"I am the LORD, I have [a]called you in righteousness,
I will also hold you by the hand and [b]watch over you,
And I will appoint you as a [c]covenant to the people,
As a [d]light to the nations,
7 To [a]open blind eyes,
To [b]bring out prisoners from the dungeon,
And those who dwell in darkness from the prison.
8"I am the LORD, that is [a]My name;
I will not give My [b]glory to another,
Nor My praise to [1]graven images.
9"Behold, the former things have come to pass,
Now I declare [a]new things;
Before they spring forth I proclaim *them* to you."

10 Sing to the LORD a [a]new song,
Sing His praise from the [b]end of the earth!
[c]You who go down to the sea, and [d]all that is in it.
You islands and those who dwell on them.
11 Let the [a]wilderness and its cities lift up *their voices,*
The settlements where [b]Kedar inhabits.
Let the inhabitants of [c]Sela sing aloud,
Let them shout for joy from the tops of the [d]mountains.
12 Let them give glory to the LORD,
And declare His praise in the coastlands.
13 The LORD will go forth like a warrior,
He will arouse *His* [a]zeal like a man of war.
He will utter a shout, yes, He will raise a war cry.
He will [b]prevail against His enemies.

The Blindness of the People

14"I have kept silent for a long time,
I have kept still and restrained Myself.
Now like a woman in labor I will groan,
I will both gasp and pant.

15 "I will [a]lay waste the mountains
and hills,
And wither all their vegetation;
I will [b]make the rivers into
coastlands,
And dry up the ponds.
16 "And I will [a]lead the blind by a
way they do not know,
In paths they do not know I will
guide them.
I will [b]make darkness into light
before them
And [c]rugged places into plains.
These are the things I will do,
And I will [d]not leave them un-
done."
17 They shall be turned back and
be [a]utterly put to shame,
Who trust in [1]idols,
Who say to molten images,
"You are our gods."

18 [a]Hear, you deaf!
And look, you blind, that you
may see.
19 Who is blind but My servant,
Or so deaf as My [a]messenger
whom I send?
Who is so blind as he that is [1b]at
peace *with Me,*
Or so blind as the servant of the
LORD?
20 You have seen many things, but
you do not observe *them;*
Your ears are open, but none
hears.
21 The LORD was pleased [a]for His
righteousness' sake
To make the law [b]great and glorious.
22 But this is a people plundered
and despoiled;
All of them are [a]trapped in
[1]caves,
Or are hidden away in prisons;
They have become a prey with
none to deliver *them,*
And a spoil, with none to say,
"Give *them* back!"

23 Who among you will give ear to
this?
Who will give heed and listen
hereafter?
24 [a]Who gave Jacob up for spoil,
and Israel to plunderers?
Was it not the LORD, against
whom we have sinned,
And in whose ways they [b]were
not willing to walk,
And whose law they did not
[c]obey?
25 So He poured out on him the
heat of His anger
And the [a]fierceness of battle;
And it set him aflame all
around,

15 [a]Is. 2:12-16; Ezek. 38:19, 20 [b]Is. 44:27; 50:2; Nah. 1:4-6
16 [a]Is. 29:18; 30:21; 32:3; Jer. 31:8, 9; Luke 1:78, 79 [b]Is. 29:18; Eph. 5:8 [c]Is. 40:4; Luke 3:5 [d]Josh. 1:5; Ps. 94:14; Is. 41:17; Heb. 13:5
17 [1]Or, *graven images* [a]Ps. 97:7; Is. 1:29; 44:9, 11; 45:16
18 [a]Is. 29:18; 35:5
19 [1]Or, *the devoted one* [a]Is. 44:26 [b]Is. 26:3; 27:5
21 [a]Is. 43:25 [b]Is. 42:4; 51:4
22 [1]Or, *holes* [a]Is. 24:18
24 [a]Is. 10:5 [b]Is. 30:15 [c]Is. 48:18; 57:17
25 [1]Lit., *did not lay it to heart* [a]Is. 5:25; 9:19 [b]Is. 29:13; 47:7; 57:1; Hos. 7:9
1 [a]Is. 43:15 [b]Is. 43:7, 21; 44:2, 21, 24 [c]Is. 43:5 [d]Is. 44:22, 23; 48:20 [e]Gen. 32:28; Is. 43:7; 45:3, 4 [f]Is. 43:21
2 [a]Ps. 66;12; Is. 8:7, 8 [b]Deut. 31:6, 8 [c]Is. 29:6; 30:27-29; Dan. 3:25, 27
3 [1]Or, *Ethiopia* [a]Is. 19:20; 43:11; 45:15, 21; 49:26; 60:16; 63:8
4 [a]Is. 63:9
5 [a]Is. 8:10; 43:2 [b]Is. 41:8; 49:12; 61:9 [c]Is. 49:12
6 [a]Ps. 107:3 [b]2 Cor. 6:18 [c]Is. 45:22
7 [a]Is. 56:5; 62:2; James 2:7 [b]Ps. 100:3; Is. 29:23; Eph. 2:10 [c]Is. 44:23; 46:13
9 [a]Is. 34:1; 41:1

Yet he did not recognize *it;*
And it burned him, but he
[1b]paid no attention.

CHAPTER 43

Israel Redeemed

BUT now, thus says the LORD, your
[a]creator, O Jacob,
And He who [b]formed you, O Israel,
"Do not [c]fear, for I have [d]re-
deemed you;
I have [e]called you by name; you
are [f]Mine!
2 "When you [a]pass through the
waters, [b]I will be with you;
And through the rivers, they
will not overflow you.
When you [c]walk through the
fire, you will not be scorched,
Nor will the flame burn you.
3 "For I am the LORD your God,
The Holy One of Israel, your
[a]Savior;
I have given Egypt as your ransom,
[1]Cush and Seba in your place.
4 "Since you are precious in My
sight,
Since you are honored and I
[a]love you,
I will give *other* men in your
place and *other* peoples in
exchange for your life.
5 "Do not fear, for [a]I am with you;
I will bring [b]your offspring
from the east,
And [c]gather you from the west.
6 "I will say to the [a]north, 'Give
them up!'
And to the south, 'Do not hold
them back.'
Bring My [b]sons from afar,
And My daughters from the
[c]ends of the earth,
7 Every one who is [a]called by My
name,
And whom I have [b]created for
My [c]glory,
Whom I have formed, even
whom I have made."

Israel Is God's Witness

8 Bring out the people who are
blind, even though they have
eyes,
And the deaf, even though they
have ears.
9 All the nations have [a]gathered
together
In order that the peoples may
be assembled.
Who among them can declare
this

And proclaim to us the former
things?
Let them present [b]their witnesses that they may be justified,
Or let them hear and say, "It is
true."
10"You are My witnesses," declares the LORD,
"And My servant whom I have
chosen,
In order that you may know
and believe Me,
And understand that I am He.
Before Me there was no God
formed,
And there will be none after
Me.
11"I, even I, am the LORD;
And there is no [a]savior [b]besides
Me.
12"It is I who have declared and
saved and proclaimed,
And there was no [a]strange *god*
among you;
So you are My witnesses," declares the LORD,
"And I am God.
13"Even [1a]from eternity I am He;
And there is [b]none who can deliver out of My hand;
[c]I act and who can reverse it?"

Babylon to Be Destroyed

14 Thus says the LORD your [a]Redeemer, the Holy One of Israel,
"For your sake I have sent to
Babylon,
And will bring them all down as
fugitives,
[1]Even the [b]Chaldeans, into the
[c]ships [2]in which they rejoice.
15"I am the LORD, your Holy One,
The Creator of Israel, your
[a]King."
16 Thus says the LORD,
Who [a]makes a way through the
sea
And a [b]path through the mighty
waters,
17 Who brings forth the [a]chariot
and the horse,
The army and the mighty man
(They will lie down together
and not rise again;
They have been [b]quenched *and*
[c]extinguished like a wick):
18"[a]Do not call to mind the former
things,
Or ponder things of the past.
19"Behold, I will do something
[a]new,
Now it will spring forth;
Will you not be aware of it?
I will even [b]make a roadway in
the wilderness,
Rivers in the desert.
20"The beasts of the field will glorify Me;
The jackals and the ostriches;
Because I have [a]given waters in
the wilderness
And rivers in the desert,
To give drink to My chosen people.
21"The people whom I formed for
Myself,
[a]Will declare My praise.

The Shortcomings of Israel

22"Yet you have not called on Me,
O Jacob;
But you have become [a]weary of
Me, O Israel.
23"You have [a]not brought to Me
the sheep of your burnt offerings;
Nor have you [b]honored Me
with your sacrifices.
I have not [c]burdened you with
offerings,
Nor wearied you with [d]incense.
24"You have bought Me no
[1a]sweet cane with money,
Neither have you filled Me with
the fat of your sacrifices;
Rather you have burdened Me
with your sins,
You have [b]wearied Me with
your iniquities.

25"I, even I, am the one who
[a]wipes out your transgressions [b]for My own sake;
And I will [c]not remember your
sins.
26"Put Me in remembrance; let us
argue our case together,
State your *cause*, that you may
be proved right.
27"Your [a]first [1]forefather sinned,
And your [b]spokesmen have
transgressed against Me.
28"So I will [1]pollute the [2]princes of
the sanctuary;
And I will consign Jacob to the
[a]ban, and Israel to [b]revilement.

CHAPTER 44

The Blessings of Israel

"BUT now listen, O Jacob, My
[a]servant;
And Israel, whom I have chosen:
2 Thus says the LORD who made
you

9 [b]Is. 44:9
11 [a]Is. 43:3; 45:21; Hos. 13:4 [b]Is. 44:6, 8
12 [a]Deut. 32:16; Ps. 81:9
13 [1]So with Gk.; Heb., *from the day* [a]Ps. 90:2; Is. 48:16 [b]Ps. 50:22 [c]Job 9:12; Is. 14:27
14 [1]Another reading is: *As for the Chaldeans, their rejoicing* is *turned into lamentations* [2]Lit., *of their rejoicing* [a]Is. 41:14 [b]Is. 23:13 [c]Jer. 51:13
15 [a]Is. 41:21; 44:6
16 [a]Ex. 14:21, 22; Ps. 77:19; Is. 11:15; 44:27; 50:2; 51:10; 63:11, 12 [b]Josh. 3:15, 16
17 [a]Ex. 15:19 [b]Ps. 118:12; Is. 1:31 [c]Ps. 76:5, 6
18 [a]Is. 65:17; Jer. 16:14; 23:7
19 [a]Is. 42:9; 48:6; 2 Cor. 5:17 [b]Ex. 17:6; Num. 20:11; Deut. 8:15; Ps. 78:16; Is. 35:1, 6; 41:18, 19; 49:10; 51:3
20 [a]Is. 41:17, 18; 48:21
21 [a]Ps. 102:18; Is. 42:12; Luke 1:74, 75; 1 Pet. 2:9
22 [a]Mic. 6:3; Mal. 1:13; 3:14
23 [a]Amos 5:25 [b]Zech. 7:5, 6; Mal. 1:6-8 [c]Jer. 7:21-26 [d]Ex. 30:34; Lev. 2:1; 24:7
24 [1]Or, *calamus* [a]Ex. 30:23; Jer. 6:20 [b]Ps. 95:10; Is. 1:14; 7:13; Ezek. 6:9; Mal. 2:17
25 [a]Is. 44:22; 55:7; Jer. 50:20 [b]Is. 37:35; 48:9, 11; Ezek. 36:22 [c]Is. 38:17; Jer. 31:34
27 [1]Lit., *father* [a]Is. 51:2; Ezek. 16:3 [b]Is. 9:15; 28:7; 29:10; Jer. 5:31
28 [1]Or, *pierce through* [2]Or, *holy princes* [a]Is. 24:6; 34:5; Jer. 24:9; Dan. 9:11; Zech. 8:13 [b]Ps. 79:4; Ezek. 5:15
1 [a]Is. 41:8; Jer. 30:10; 46:27, 28

And formed you from the womb, who will help you,
'Do not fear, O Jacob My servant;
And you [a]Jeshurun whom I have chosen.
3 'For I will pour out water on [1]the thirsty *land*
And streams on the dry ground;
I will [a]pour out My Spirit on your [b]offspring,
And My blessing on your descendants;
4 And they will spring up [1]among the grass
Like [a]poplars by streams of water.'
5 "This one will say, 'I am the LORD's';
And that one [1]will call on the name of Jacob;
And another will write [2]*on* his hand, 'Belonging to the LORD,'
And will name Israel's name with honor.

6 "Thus says the LORD, the [a]King of Israel
And his Redeemer, the LORD of hosts:
'I am the [b]first and I am the last,
And there is no God [c]besides Me.
7 'And who is like Me? Let him proclaim and declare it;
Yes, let him recount it to Me in order,
From the time that I established the ancient [1]nation.
And let them declare to them the things that are coming
And the events that are going to take place.
8 'Do not tremble and do not be afraid;
Have I not long since announced it to you and declared it?
And you are My witnesses.
Is there any God [a]besides Me,
Or is there any *other* [b]Rock?
I know of none.' "

The Folly of Idolatry

9 Those who fashion a [1]graven
image are all of them futile, and
their precious things are of no profit;
even their own witnesses fail to see
or know, so that they will be [a]put to
shame.
10 Who has fashioned a god or
cast an [1]idol to [a]no profit?
11 Behold, all his companions will
be put to shame, for the craftsmen
themselves are mere men. Let them
all assemble themselves, let them
stand up, let them tremble, let them
together be put to shame.
12 The [a]man shapes iron into a
cutting tool, and does his work over
the coals, [1]fashioning it with hammers,
and working it with his strong
arm. He also gets hungry and [2]his
strength fails; he drinks no water
and becomes weary.
13 [a]*Another* shapes wood, he extends
a measuring line; he outlines it
with red chalk. He works it with
planes, and outlines it with a compass,
and makes it like the form of a
man, like the beauty of [b]man, so
that it may sit in a [c]house.
14 Surely he cuts cedars for himself,
and takes a [1]cypress or an oak,
and [2]raises *it* for himself among the
trees of the forest. He plants a fir,
and the rain makes it grow.
15 Then it becomes *something* for
a man to burn, so he takes one of
them and warms himself; he also
makes a fire to bake bread. He also
makes a god and worships it; he
makes it a graven image, and [a]falls
down before it.
16 Half of it he burns in the fire;
over *this* half he eats meat as he
roasts a roast, and is satisfied. He
also warms himself and says, "Aha!
I am warm, I have seen the fire."
17 But the rest of it he makes into
a god, his graven image. He falls
down before it and worships; he also
[a]prays to it and says, "Deliver me,
for thou art my god."
18 They do not [a]know, nor do they
understand, for He has [b]smeared
over their eyes so that they cannot
see and their hearts so that they
cannot comprehend.
19 And no one [1]recalls, nor is there
knowledge or understanding to say,
"I have burned half of it in the fire,
and also have baked bread over its
coals. I roast meat and eat *it*. Then [2]I
make the rest of it into an [a]abomination,
[3]I fall down before a block of
wood!"
20 He [1a]feeds on ashes; a [b]deceived
heart has turned him aside.
And he cannot deliver [2]himself, nor
say, "Is there not a lie in my right
hand?"

God Forgives and Redeems

21 "Remember these things, O Jacob,
And Israel, for you are My servant;
I have formed you, you are My servant,
O Israel, you will not be forgotten by Me.

2 [a]Deut. 32:15; 33:5, 26
3 [1]Or, *him who is thirsty* [a]Is. 32:15; Joel 2:28 [b]Is. 61:9; 65:23
4 [1]Another reading is, *like grass among the waters* [a]Lev. 23:40; Job 40:22
5 [1]Another reading is, *will be called by the name of Jacob* [2]Or, *with*
6 [a]Is. 41:21; 43:15 [b]Is. 41:4; 43:10; 48:12; Rev. 1:8, 17; 22:13 [c]Is. 43:11; 44:8; 45:5, 6, 21
7 [1]Or, *people*
8 [a]Deut. 4:35, 39; 1 Sam. 2:2; Is. 45:5; Joel 2:27 [b]Is. 17:10; 26:4; 30:29
9 [1]Or, *idol* [a]Ps. 97:7; Is. 42:17; 44:11; 45:16
10 [1]Or, *graven image* [a]Is. 41:29; Jer. 10:5; Hab. 2:18; Acts 19:26
12 [1]Lit., *and fashions* [2]Lit., *there is no strength* [a]Is. 40:19, 20; 41:6, 7; 46:6, 7; Jer. 10:3-5; Hab. 2:18
13 [a]Is. 41:7 [b]Ps. 115:5-7 [c]Judg. 17:4, 5; Ezek. 8:10, 11
14 [1]Or, *holm-oak* [2]Lit., *makes strong*
15 [a]2 Chr. 25:14
17 [a]1 Kin. 18:26, 28; Is. 45:20
18 [a]Is. 1:3; Jer. 10:8, 14 [b]Ps. 81:12; Is. 6:9, 10; 29:10
19 [1]Lit., *returns to his heart* [2]Or, *shall I make . . .?* [3]Or, *shall I fall . . .?* [a]Deut. 27:15; 1 Kin. 11:5, 7; 2 Kin. 23:14
20 [1]Or, *is a companion of ashes* [2]Lit., *his soul* [a]Ps. 102:9 [b]Job 15:31; Hos. 4:12; Rom. 1:21, 22; 2 Thess. 2:11; 2 Tim. 3:13

22"I have [a]wiped out your transgressions like a thick cloud,
And your sins like a heavy mist.
[b]Return to Me, for I have [c]redeemed you."
23 [a]Shout for joy, O heavens, for the LORD has done *it!*
Shout joyfully, you lower parts of the earth;
[b]Break forth into a shout of joy, you mountains,
O forest, and every tree in it;
For the LORD has redeemed Jacob
And in Israel He shows forth His glory.

24 Thus says the LORD, your Redeemer, and the one who formed you from the womb,
"I, the LORD, am the maker of all things,
[a]Stretching out the heavens by Myself,
And spreading out the earth [1]all alone,
25 Causing the [1]omens of boasters to fail,
[2]Making fools out of diviners,
[a]Causing wise men to draw back,
And [3]turning their knowledge into foolishness,
26 Confirming the word of His servant,
And [1]performing the purpose of His messengers.
It is I who says of Jerusalem, 'She shall be inhabited!'
And of the cities of Judah, '[a]They shall be built.'
And I will raise up her ruins *again.*
27"*It is I* who says to the depth of the sea, 'Be dried up!'
And I will make your rivers [a]dry.
28"*It is I* who says of Cyrus, '*He is* My shepherd!
And he will perform all My desire.'
And [1]he declares of Jerusalem, '[a]She will be built,'
And of the temple, 'Your foundation will be laid.' "

CHAPTER 45

God Uses Cyrus

THUS says the LORD to Cyrus His anointed,
Whom I have taken by the right [a]hand,
To [b]subdue nations before him,
And [1]to [c]loose the loins of kings;
To open doors before him so that gates will not be shut:
2"I will go before you and [a]make the [1]rough places smooth;
I will [b]shatter the doors of bronze, and cut through their iron [c]bars.
3"And I will give you the [1a]treasures of darkness,
And hidden wealth of secret places,
In order that you may know that it is I,
The LORD, the God of Israel, who [b]calls you by your name.
4"For the sake of [a]Jacob My servant,
And Israel My chosen *one,*
I have also [b]called you by your name;
I have given you a title of honor
Though you have [c]not known Me.
5"I am the LORD, and [a]there is no other;
[b]Besides Me there is no God.
I will [c]gird you, though you have not known Me;
6 That [1a]men may know from the rising to the setting of the sun
That there is no one besides Me.
I am the LORD, and there is no other,
7 The One [a]forming light and [b]creating darkness,
Causing [1]well-being and [c]creating calamity;
I am the LORD who does all these.

God's Supreme Power

8"[a]Drip down, O heavens, from above,
And let the clouds pour down righteousness;
Let the [b]earth open up and salvation bear fruit,
[c]And righteousness spring up with it.
I, the LORD, have created it.

9"Woe to *the one* who [a]quarrels with his [1]Maker—
An earthenware vessel [2]among the vessels of earth!
Will the [b]clay say to the [1]potter, 'What are you doing?'
Or the thing you are making *say,* 'He has no hands'?
10"Woe to him who says to a father, 'What are you begetting?'
Or to a woman, 'To what are you [1]giving birth?' "

22 [a]Ps. 51:1, 9; Is. 43:25; Acts 3:19 [b]Is. 31:6; 55:7 [c]Is. 43:1; 48:20; 1 Cor. 6:20; 1 Pet. 1:18, 19
23 [a]Ps. 69:34; 96:11, 12; Is. 42:10; 49:13 [b]Ps. 98:7, 8; 148:7, 9; Is. 55:12
24 [1]Or, *who was with Me?* [a]Is. 40:22; 42:5; 45:12, 18; 51:13
25 [1]Lit., *signs* [2]Lit., *He makes* [3]Lit., *He turns* [a]2 Sam. 15:31; Job 5:12-14; Ps. 33:10; Is. 29:14; Jer. 51:57; 1 Cor. 1:20, 27
26 [1]Lit., *He performs* [a]Jer. 32:15, 44
27 [a]Is. 42:15; 50:2; Jer. 50:38; 51:36
28 [1]Lit., *to say* [a]2 Chr. 36:22, 23; Ezra 1:1; Is. 14:32; 45:13; 54:11
1 [1]Lit., *I will loose* [a]Ps. 73:23; Is. 41:13; 42:6 [b]Is. 41:2, 25; Jer. 50:3, 35; 51:11, 20, 24 [c]Job 12:21; Is. 45:5
2 [1]Another reading is, *mountains* [a]Is. 40:4 [b]Ps. 107:16 [c]Jer. 51:30
3 [1]Or, *hoarded treasures* [a]Jer. 41:8; 50:37 [b]Ex. 33:12, 17; Is. 43:1; 49:1
4 [a]Is. 41:8, 9; 44:1 [b]Is. 43:1 [c]Acts 17:23
5 [a]Is. 45:6, 14, 18, 21; 46:9 [b]Is. 44:6, 8 [c]Ps. 18:39
6 [1]Lit., *they* [a]Ps. 102:15; Mal. 1:11
7 [1]Or, *peace* [a]Is. 42:16 [b]Ps. 104:20; 105:28 [c]Is. 31:2; 47:11; Amos 3:6
8 [a]Ps. 72:6; Hos. 10:12; 14:5; Joel 3:18 [b]Ps. 85:11 [c]Is. 60:21; 61:11
9 [1]Lit., *Fashioner* [2]Lit., *with* [a]Job 15:25; 40:8, 9; Ps. 2:2, 3; Prov. 21:30; Jer. 50:24 [b]Is. 29:16; 64:8; Jer. 18:6; Rom 9:20, 21
10 [1]Lit., *in labor pains with*

11 Thus says the [a]LORD, the Holy
One of Israel, and his [1b]Maker:
"[2c]Ask Me about the things to
come [3]concerning My [d]sons,
And you shall commit to Me the
work of My hands.
12 "It is I who [a]made the earth, and
created man upon it.
I [b]stretched out the heavens
with My hands,
And I [1]ordained [c]all their host.
13 "I have aroused him in righteousness,
And I will make all his ways
smooth;
He will [a]build My city, and will
let My exiles go [b]free,
Without any payment or reward,"
says the LORD of
hosts.

14 Thus says the LORD,
"The [1]products of [a]Egypt and
the merchandise of [2b]Cush
And the Sabeans, men of stature,
Will [c]come over to you and will
be yours;
They will walk behind you, they
will come over in [d]chains
And will [e]bow down to you;
They will make supplication to
you:
'[3]Surely, [f]God is [4]with you, and
there is none else,
No other God.'"
15 Truly, Thou art a God who
[a]hides Himself,
O God of Israel, Savior!
16 They will be put to shame and
even humiliated, all of them;
The [a]manufacturers of idols
will go away together in humiliation.
17 Israel has been saved by the
LORD
With an [a]everlasting salvation;
You will not be put to shame or
humiliated
To all eternity.

18 For thus says the LORD, who
[a]created the heavens
(He is the God who [b]formed the
earth and made it,
He established it and did not
create it [1]a [c]waste place,
But formed it to be [d]inhabited),
"I am the LORD, and [e]there is
none else.
19 "I have not spoken in secret,
In [1]some dark land;
I did not say to the [2]offspring of
Jacob,
'[a]Seek Me in [3]a waste place';

11 [1]Lit., *Fashioner* [2]Or, *Will you ask* [3]Or, *upon*
[a]Is. 43:15; 48:17; Ezek. 39:7 [b]Is. 44:2; 54:5 [c]Is. 8:19 [d]Jer. 31:9

12 [1]Or, *commanded*
[a]Is. 42:5; 45:18; Jer. 27:5 [b]Ps. 104:2; Is. 42:5; 44:24 [c]Gen. 2:1; Neh. 9:6

13 [a]2 Chr. 36:22, 23; Is. 44:28 [b]Is. 52:3

14 [1]Lit., *labor* [2]Or, *Ethiopia* [3]Or, *God is with you alone* [4]Or, *in*
[a]Ps. 68:31; Is. 19:21 [b]Is. 18:1; 43:3 [c]Is. 14:1, 2; 49:23; 54:3 [d]Ps. 149:8 [e]Is. 49:23; 60:14 [f]Jer. 16:19; Zech. 8:20-23; 1 Cor. 14:25

15 [a]Ps. 44:24; Is. 1:15; 8:17; 57:17

16 [a]Is. 44:11

17 [a]Is. 26:4; 51:6; Rom. 11:26

18 [1]Or, *in vain*
[a]Is. 42:5 [b]Is. 45:12 [c]Gen. 1:2 [d]Gen. 1:26; Ps. 115:16 [e]Is. 45:5

19 [1]Lit., *a place of a land of darkness* [2]Lit., *seed* [3]Or, *vain*
[a]2 Chr. 15:2; Ps. 78:34; Jer. 29:13, 14; Hos. 3:5 [b]Ps. 19:8; Is. 45:23; 63:1 [c]Is. 43:12; 44:8

20 [1]Lit., *the wood of their graven image*
[a]Is. 43:9 [b]Is. 44:18, 19; 48:5-7 [c]Is. 46:1, 7; Jer. 10:5 [d]Is. 44:17; 46:6, 7

21 [a]Is. 41:23; 43:9 [b]Is. 41:26; 44:7; 48:14 [c]Is. 43:3, 11

22 [a]Num. 21:8, 9; 2 Chr. 20:12; Mic. 7:7; Zech. 12:10 [b]Is. 30:15; 49:6, 12; 52:10

23 [a]Rom. 14:11; Phil. 2:10

25 [a]1 Kin. 8:32; Is. 53:11

1 [1]Lit., *carried by you*
[a]Is. 2:18; 21:9; Jer. 50:2-4; 51:44

2 [1]Or, *their soul has*
[a]Judg. 18:17, 18, 24; 2 Sam. 5:21; Jer. 43:12, 13; 48:7; Hos. 10:5, 6

I, the LORD, [b]speak righteousness
[c]Declaring things that are upright.

20 "[a]Gather yourselves and come;
Draw near together, you fugitives of the nations;
[b]They have no knowledge,
Who [c]carry about [1]their
wooden idol,
And [d]pray to a god who cannot
save.
21 "[a]Declare and set forth *your
case;*
Indeed, let them consult together.
[b]Who has announced this from
of old?
Who has long since declared it?
Is it not I, the LORD?
And there is no other God besides Me,
A righteous God and a [c]Savior;
There is none except Me.
22 "[a]Turn to Me, and [b]be saved, all
the ends of the earth;
For I am God, and there is no
other.
23 "I have sworn by Myself,
The word has gone forth from
My mouth in righteousness
And will not turn back,
That to Me [a]every knee will
bow, every tongue will swear
allegiance.
24 "They will say of Me, 'Only in
the LORD are righteousness
and strength.'
Men will come to Him,
And all who were angry at Him
shall be put to shame.
25 "In the LORD all the offspring of
Israel
Will be [a]justified, and will glory."

CHAPTER 46

Babylon's Idols and the True God

[a]BEL has bowed down, Nebo
stoops over;
Their images are *consigned* to
the beasts and the cattle.
The things [1]that you carry are
burdensome,
A load for the weary *beast.*
2 They stooped over, they have
bowed down together;
They could not rescue the burden,
But [1]have themselves [a]gone
into captivity.

3"Listen to Me, O house of Jacob,
And all [a]the remnant of the house of Israel,
You who have been borne by Me from [1]birth,
And have been carried from the womb;
4 Even to your old age, [a]I [1]shall be the same,
And even to your [2]graying years I shall bear *you!*
I have [3]done *it,* and I shall carry *you;*
And I shall bear *you,* and I shall deliver *you.*

5"[a]To whom would you liken Me,
And make Me equal and compare Me,
That we should be alike?
6"Those who [a]lavish gold from the purse
And weigh silver on the scale
Hire a goldsmith, and he makes it *into* a god;
They [b]bow down, indeed they worship it.
7"They [a]lift it upon the shoulder and carry it;
They set it in its place and it stands *there.*
[b]It does not move from its place.
Though one may cry to it, it cannot answer;
It cannot [c]deliver him from his distress.

8"[a]Remember this, and be [1]assured;
Recall it to [2]mind, you transgressors.
9"Remember the [a]former things long past,
For I am God, and there is [b]no other;
I am God, and there is [c]no one like Me,
10 Declaring the end from the beginning
And from ancient times things which have not been done,
Saying, '[a]My purpose will be established,
And I will accomplish all My good pleasure';
11 Calling a bird of prey from the east,
The man of [1]My purpose from a far country.
Truly I have [a]spoken; truly I will bring it to pass.
I have planned *it, surely* I will do it.

12"Listen to Me, you [a]stubborn-minded,
Who are far from righteousness.
13"I [a]bring near My righteousness, it is not far off;
And My salvation will not delay.
And I will grant [b]salvation in Zion,
And My glory for Israel.

3 [1]Lit., *the belly* [a]Is. 10:21, 22

4 [1]Lit., *I am He* [2]Lit., *gray hairs* [3]Or, *made* you [a]Is. 41:4; 43:13; 48:12

5 [a]Is. 40:18, 25

6 [a]Is. 40:19; 41:7; 44:12-17; Jer. 10:4 [b]Is. 44:15, 17

7 [a]Is. 45:20; 46:1; Jer. 10:5 [b]Is. 40:20; 41:7 [c]Is. 45:20

8 [1]Lit., *firm* [2]Lit., *heart* [a]Is. 44:21

9 [a]Deut. 32:7; Is. 42:9; 65:17 [b]Is. 45:5, 21 [c]Is. 41:26, 27

10 [a]Ps. 33:11; Prov. 19:21; Is. 14:24; 25:1; 40:8; Acts 5:39

11 [1]Lit., *His* [a]Num. 23:19; Is. 14:24; 37:26

12 [a]Ps. 76:5; Is. 48:4; Zech. 7:11, 12; Mal. 3:13

13 [a]Is. 51:5; 61:11; Rom. 3:21 [b]Is. 61:3; 62:11; Joel 3:17; 1 Pet. 2:6

Chapter 47

Lament for Babylon

"[a]COME down and sit in the dust,
O virgin daughter of Babylon;
Sit on the ground without a throne,
O daughter of the Chaldeans.
For you shall no longer be called [b]tender and delicate.
2"Take the [a]millstones and grind meal.
Remove your [b]veil, strip off the skirt,
Uncover the leg, cross the rivers.
3"Your nakedness will be uncovered,
Your shame also will be exposed;
I will [a]take vengeance and will not [1]spare a man."
4 Our Redeemer, the LORD of hosts is His name,
The Holy One of Israel.
5"[a]Sit silently, and go into darkness,
O daughter of the Chaldeans;
For you will no more be called
The [b]queen of kingdoms.
6"I was angry with My people,
I profaned My heritage,
And gave them into your hand.
You did not show mercy to them,
On the [a]aged you made your yoke very heavy.
7"Yet you said, 'I shall be a queen forever.'
These things you did not [a]consider,
Nor remember the [b]outcome of [1]them.

8"Now, then, hear this, you [a]sensual one,
Who [b]dwells securely,
Who says in [1]your heart,
'[c]I am, and there is no one besides me.
I shall [d]not sit as a widow,
Nor shall I know loss of children.'
9"But these [a]two things shall come on you [b]suddenly in one day:

1 [a]Is. 3:26; Jer. 48:18 [b]Deut. 28:56

2 [a]Ex. 11:5; Jer. 25:10 [b]Gen. 24:65; Is. 3:23; 1 Cor. 11:5

3 [1]Lit., *meet* [a]Is. 34:8; 63:4

5 [a]Is. 23:2; Jer. 8:14; Lam. 2:10 [b]Gen. 16:4, 8, 9; Prov. 30:23; Is. 47:7

6 [a]Deut. 28:50

7 [1]Lit., *it* [a]Is. 42:25; 57:11 [b]Deut. 32:29; Jer. 5:31; Ezek. 7:2, 3

8 [1]Lit., *her* [a]Is. 22:13; 32:9; Jer. 50:11 [b]Is. 32:9, 11; Zeph. 2:15 [c]Is. 45:5, 6, 18; 47:10; Zeph. 2:15 [d]Rev. 18:7

9 [a]Is. 13:16, 18; 14:22 [b]Ps. 73:19; 1 Thess. 5:3; Rev. 18:8, 10

Loss of children and widowhood.
They shall come on you in full measure
In spite of your many [c]sorceries,
In spite of the great power of your spells.
10 "And you felt [a]secure in your wickedness and said,
'[b]No one sees me,'
Your [c]wisdom and your knowledge, [1]they have deluded you;
For you have said in your heart,
'I am, and there is no one besides me.'
11 "But evil will come on you
Which you will not know how to charm away;
And disaster will fall on you
For which you cannot atone,
And [a]destruction about which you do not know
Will come on you suddenly.

12 "Stand *fast* now in your spells
And in your many sorceries
With which you have labored from your youth;
Perhaps you will be able to profit,
Perhaps you may cause trembling.
13 "You are [a]wearied with your many counsels,
Let now the [b]astrologers,
Those who prophesy by the stars,
Those who predict by the new moons,
Stand up and [c]save you from what will come upon you.
14 "Behold, they have become [a]like stubble,
[b]Fire burns them;
They cannot deliver themselves from the power of the flame;
There will be no coal to warm by,
Nor a fire to sit before!
15 "So have those become to you with whom you have labored,
Who have [a]trafficked with you from your youth;
Each has wandered in his own [1]way.
There is none to save you.

CHAPTER 48

Israel's Obstinacy

"[a]HEAR this, O house of Jacob, who are named Israel
And who came forth from the [1b]loins of Judah,
Who [c]swear by the name of the LORD
And invoke the God of Israel,
But not in truth nor in righteousness.
2 "For they call themselves after the [a]holy city,
And [b]lean on the God of Israel;
The LORD of hosts is His name.
3 "I [a]declared the former things long ago
And they went forth from My mouth, and I proclaimed them.
Suddenly I acted, and they came to pass.
4 "Because I know that you are [1a]obstinate,
And your neck is an iron sinew,
And your forehead bronze,
5 Therefore I declared *them* to you long ago,
Before [1]they took place I proclaimed *them* to you,
Lest you should say, 'My [a]idol has done them,
And my graven image and my molten image have commanded them.'
6 "You have heard; look at all this.
And you, will you not declare it?
I proclaim to you [a]new things from this time,
Even hidden things which you have not known.
7 "They are created now and not long ago;
And before today you have not heard them,
Lest you should say, 'Behold, I knew them.'
8 "You have not [a]heard, you have not known.
Even from long ago your ear has not been open,
Because I knew that you would deal very treacherously;
And you have been called a [1b]rebel from [2]birth.
9 "For the sake of My name I [a]delay My wrath,
And *for* My praise I restrain *it* for you,
In order not to cut you off.
10 "Behold, I have refined you, but [a]not as silver;
I have tested you in the [b]furnace of affliction.
11 "[a]For My own sake, for My own sake, I will act;
For how can *My name* be profaned?
And My [b]glory I will not give to another.

9 [c]Is. 47:13; Nah. 3:4; Rev. 18:23
10 [1]Lit., *it has* [a]Ps. 52:7; 62:10; Is. 59:4 [b]Is. 29:15; Ezek. 8:12; 9:9 [c]Is. 5:21; 44:20
11 [a]Jer. 51:8, 43
13 [a]Jer. 51:58, 64 [b]Is. 8:19; 44:25; 47:9; Dan. 2:2, 10 [c]Is. 47:15
14 [a]Is. 5:24; Nah. 1:10; Mal. 4:1 [b]Is. 10:17; Jer. 51:30, 32, 58
15 [1]Lit., *side, region* [a]Rev. 18:11
1 [1]Lit., *waters* [a]Is. 46:12 [b]Num. 24:7; Deut. 33:28; Ps. 68:26 [c]Deut. 6:13; Is. 45:23; 65:16
2 [a]Is. 52:1; 64:10 [b]Is. 10:20; Jer. 7:4; 21:2; Mic. 3:11; Rom. 2:17
3 [a]Is. 41:22; 42:9; 43:9; 44:7, 8; 45:21; 46:10
4 [1]Or, *harsh* [a]Ezek. 2:4; 3:7
5 [1]Lit., *it* [a]Jer. 44:15-18
6 [a]Is. 42:9; 43:19
8 [1]Or, *transgressor* [2]Lit., *the belly* [a]Is. 42:25; 47:11; Hos. 7:9 [b]Deut. 9:7, 24; Ps. 58:3; Is. 46:8
9 [a]Neh. 9:30, 31; Ps. 78:38; 103:8-10; Is. 30:18; 65:8
10 [a]Jer. 9:7; Ezek. 22:18-22 [b]Deut. 4:20; 1 Kin. 8:51; Jer. 11:4
11 [a]1 Sam. 12:22; Ps. 25:11; 106:8; Jer. 14:7; Ezek. 20:9, 14, 22, 44; Dan. 9:17-19 [b]Deut. 32:26, 27; Is. 42:8

Deliverance Promised

12 "Listen to Me, O Jacob, even Israel [1]whom I called;
[a]I am He, I am the first, I am also the last.
13 "Surely My hand [a]founded the earth,
And My right hand spread out the heavens;
When I call to them, they stand together.
14 "Assemble, all of you, and listen!
Who among them has declared these things?
The LORD loves him; he shall carry out His good pleasure on Babylon,
And His arm *shall be against* the Chaldeans.
15 "I, even I, have spoken; indeed I have [a]called him,
I have brought him, and He will make his ways successful.
16 "[a]Come near to Me, listen to this:
From the first I have [b]not spoken in secret,
[c]From the time it took place, I was there.
And now the Lord [1]GOD has sent Me, and His Spirit."

17 Thus says the LORD, your [a]Redeemer, the Holy One of Israel;
"I am the LORD your God, who teaches you to profit,
Who [b]leads you in the way you should go.
18 "If only you had [a]paid attention to My commandments!
Then your [1b]well-being would have been like a river,
And your [c]righteousness like the waves of the sea.
19 "Your [1a]descendants would have been like the sand,
And [2]your offspring like its grains;
Their name would never be cut off or destroyed from My presence."

20 Go forth from Babylon! Flee from the Chaldeans!
Declare with the sound of [a]joyful shouting, proclaim this,
[b]Send it out to the end of the earth;
Say, "The LORD has redeemed His servant Jacob."
21 And they did not [a]thirst when He led them through the deserts.
He [b]made the water flow out of the rock for them;
He split the rock, and [c]the water gushed forth.
22 "[a]There is no peace for the wicked," says the LORD.

CHAPTER 49

Salvation Reaches to the End of the Earth

1 LISTEN to Me, O islands,
And pay attention, you peoples from afar.
The LORD called Me from the womb;
From the [1]body of My mother He named Me.
2 And He has made My [a]mouth like a sharp sword;
In the [b]shadow of His hand He has concealed Me,
And He has also made Me a [1]select [c]arrow;
He has hidden Me in His quiver.
3 And He said to Me, "You are My Servant, Israel,
In Whom I will [1]show My glory."
4 But I said, "I have toiled in vain,
I have spent My strength for nothing and vanity;
Yet surely the justice *due* to Me is with the LORD,
And My [a]reward with My God."
5 And now says the LORD, who formed Me from the womb to be His Servant,
To bring Jacob back to Him, in order that Israel might be gathered to Him
(For I am [a]honored in the sight of the LORD,
And My God is My [b]strength),
6 He says, "It is too [1]small a thing that You should be My Servant
To raise up the tribes of Jacob, and to restore the [a]preserved ones of Israel;
I will also make You a [b]light [2]of the nations
So that My salvation may [3]reach to the end of the earth."
7 Thus says the LORD, the [a]Redeemer of Israel, *and* its Holy One,
To the [b]despised One,
To the One abhorred by the nation,
To the Servant of rulers,
"[c]Kings shall see and arise,
Princes shall also [d]bow down;
Because of the LORD who is faithful, the Holy One of Israel who has chosen You."

---

12 [1]Lit., *My called one* [a]Is. 41:4; 43:10, 13; 46:4

13 [a]Ex. 20:11; Ps. 102:25; Is. 42:5; 45:12, 18; Heb. 1:10-12

15 [a]Is. 41:2; 45:1, 2

16 [1]YHWH, usually rendered LORD [a]Is. 34:1; 41:1; 57:3 [b]Is. 45:19 [c]Is. 43:13

17 [a]Is. 41:14; 43:14; 49:7, 26; 54:5, 8 [b]Ps. 32:8; Is. 30:21; 49:9, 10

18 [1]Or, *peace* [a]Deut. 5:29; 32:29; Ps. 81:13-16 [b]Ps. 119:165; Is. 32:16-18; 66:12 [c]Is. 45:8; 61:10, 11; 62:1; Hos. 10:12; Amos 5:24

19 [1]Lit., *seed* [2]Lit., *the offspring of your inward parts* [a]Gen. 22:17; Is. 10:22; 44:4; 54:3; Jer. 33:22

20 [a]Is. 42:10; 49:13; 52:9 [b]Is. 62:11; Jer. 31:10; 50:2

21 [a]Is. 30:25; 35:6, 7; 41:17, 18; 43:19, 20; 49:10 [b]Ex. 17:6; Ps. 78:15, 16 [c]Ps. 78:20; 105:41

22 [a]Is. 57:21

1 [1]Lit., *inward parts*

2 [1]Or, *sharpened* [a]Is. 11:4; Heb. 4:12; Rev. 1:16; 2:12, 16 [b]Is. 51:16 [c]Hab. 3:11

3 [1]Or, *glorify Myself*

4 [a]Is. 35:4; 59:18

5 [a]Is. 43:4 [b]Is. 12:2

6 [1]Lit., *light* [2]Or, *to* [3]Lit., *be* [a]Ps. 37:28; 97:10 [b]Is. 42:6; 51:4; Acts 13:47

7 [a]Is. 48:17 [b]Ps. 22:6 8; 60:7-9; Is. 53:3 [c]Is. 52:15 [d]Is. 19:21, 23; 27:13; 66:23

8 Thus says the LORD, "In a [a]favorable time I have answered You,
And in a day of salvation I have helped You;
And I will [b]keep You and give You for a covenant of the people,
To [1c]restore the land, to make *them* inherit the desolate heritages;
9 Saying to those who are [a]bound, 'Go forth,'
To those who are in darkness, 'Show yourselves.'
Along the roads they will feed,
And their pasture will be on all bare heights.
10 "They will [a]not hunger or thirst,
Neither will the scorching [b]heat or sun strike them down;
For He who has compassion on them will [c]lead them,
And will guide them to [d]springs of water.
11 "And I will make all My mountains a road,
And My [a]highways will be raised up.
12 "Behold, these shall come from afar;
And lo, these *will come* from the [a]north and from the west,
And these from the land of Sinim."
13 [a]Shout for joy, O heavens! And rejoice, O earth!
Break forth into joyful shouting, O mountains!
For the [b]LORD has comforted His people,
And will [c]have compassion on His afflicted.

Promise to Zion

14 But Zion said, "The LORD has forsaken me,
And the Lord has forgotten me."
15 "Can a woman forget her nursing child,
And have no compassion on the son of her womb?
Even these may forget, but I will not forget you.
16 "Behold, I have [a]inscribed you on the palms *of My hands;*
Your [b]walls are continually before Me.
17 "Your [1]builders hurry;
Your [a]destroyers and devastators
Will depart from you.
18 "[a]Lift up your eyes and look around;
All of them gather together, they come to you.
[b]As I live," declares the LORD,
"You shall surely put on all of them as [1]jewels, and bind them on as a bride.
19 "For [a]your waste and desolate places, and your destroyed land—
Surely now you will be [b]too cramped for the inhabitants,
And those who [c]swallowed you will be far away.
20 "The [a]children of [1]whom you were bereaved will yet say in your ears,
'The place is too cramped for me;
Make room for me that I may live *here*.'
21 "Then you will [a]say in your heart,
'Who has begotten these for me,
Since I have been bereaved of my children,
And am [b]barren, an [c]exile and a wanderer?
And who has reared these?
Behold, I was [d]left alone;
From where did these come?' "

22 Thus says the Lord [1]GOD,
"Behold, I will lift up My hand to the nations,
And set up My [a]standard to the peoples;
And they will [b]bring your sons in *their* bosom,
And your daughters will be carried on *their* shoulders.
23 "And [a]kings will be your guardians,
And their princesses your nurses.
They will [b]bow down to you with their faces to the earth,
And [c]lick the dust of your feet;
And *you* will [d]know that I am the LORD;
Those who hopefully [e]wait for Me will [f]not be put to shame.

24 "Can the prey be taken from the mighty man,
Or the captives of [1]a tyrant be rescued?"
25 Surely, thus says the LORD,
"Even the [a]captives of the mighty man will be taken away,
And the prey of the tyrant will be rescued;
For I will contend with the one who contends with you,
And I will save your sons.
26 "And I will feed your [a]oppressors with their own flesh,

8 [1]Lit., *establish* [a]Ps. 69:13; 2 Cor. 6:2 [b]Is. 26:3; 27:3; 42:6 [c]Is. 44:26
9 [a]Is. 42:7; 61:1; Luke 4:18
10 [a]Is. 33:16; 48:21; Rev. 7:16 [b]Ps. 121:6 [c]Ps. 23:2; Is. 40:11 [d]Is. 35:7; 41:17
11 [a]Is. 11:16; 19:23; 35:8; 62:10
12 [a]Is. 43:5, 6
13 [a]Is. 44:23 [b]Is. 40:1; 51:3, 12 [c]Is. 54:7, 8, 10
16 [a]Song of Sol. 8:6; Hag. 2:23 [b]Ps. 48:12, 13; Is. 62:6, 7
17 [1]So ancient versions and DSS; M.T. reads, *sons* [a]Is. 10:6; 37:18
18 [1]Lit., *an ornament* [a]Is. 60:4; John 4:35 [b]Is. 45:23; 54:9
19 [a]Is. 1:7; 3:8; 5:6; 51:3 [b]Is. 54:1, 2; Zech. 10:10 [c]Ps. 56:1, 2
20 [1]Lit., *your bereavement* [a]Is. 54:1-3
21 [a]Is. 29:23; 54:6, 7 [b]Is. 27:10; Lam. 1:1 [c]Is. 5:13 [d]Is. 1:8
22 [1]YHWH, usually rendered LORD [a]Is. 11:10, 12; 18:3; 62:10 [b]Is. 14:2; 43:6; 60:4
23 [a]Is. 14:1, 2; 60:3, 10, 11 [b]Is. 45:14; 60:14 [c]Ps. 72:9; Mic. 7:17 [d]Is. 41:20; 43:10; 60:16 [e]Ps. 37:9; Is. 25:9; 26:8 [f]Ps. 25:3; Is. 45:17; Joel 2:27
24 [1]So ancient versions and DSS; M.T. reads, *the righteous,* cf. v. 25
25 [a]Is. 10:6; 14:1, 2; Jer. 50:33, 34
26 [a]Is. 9:4; 14:4; 16:4; 51:13; 54:14

And they will become drunk with their own blood as with sweet wine;
And [b]all flesh will know that I, the LORD, am your Savior,
And your Redeemer, the Mighty One of Jacob."

CHAPTER 50

God Helps His Servant

THUS says the LORD,
"Where is the [a]certificate of divorce,
By which I have [b]sent your mother away?
Or to whom of My creditors did I [c]sell you?
Behold, you were sold for your [d]iniquities,
And for your transgressions your mother [e]was sent away.
2 "Why was there no man when I came?
When I called, *why* was there none to answer?
Is My [a]hand so short that it cannot ransom?
Or have I no power to deliver?
Behold, I [b]dry up the sea with My rebuke,
I [c]make the rivers a wilderness;
Their fish stink for lack of water,
And die of thirst.
3 "I [a]clothe the heavens with blackness,
And I make sackcloth their covering."

4 The Lord [1]GOD has given Me the tongue of disciples,
That I may know how to [a]sustain the weary one with a word.
He awakens *Me* [b]morning by morning,
He awakens My ear to listen as a disciple.
5 The Lord GOD has opened My ear;
And I was [a]not disobedient,
Nor did I turn back.
6 I [a]gave My back to those who strike *Me,*
And My cheeks to those who pluck out the beard;
I did not cover My face from humiliation and spitting.
7 For the Lord GOD [a]helps Me,
Therefore, I am [b]not disgraced;
Therefore, I have set My face like [c]flint,
And I know that I shall not be ashamed.
8 He who [a]vindicates Me is near;
Who will contend with Me?
Let us [b]stand up to each other;
Who has a case against Me?
Let him draw near to Me.
9 Behold, the Lord GOD helps Me;
[a]Who is he who condemns Me?
Behold, they will all wear out like a garment;
The moth will eat them.
10 Who is among you that fears the LORD,
That obeys the voice of His [a]servant,
That [b]walks in darkness and has no light?
Let him trust in the name of the LORD and rely on his God.
11 Behold, all you who [a]kindle a fire,
Who [1]encircle yourselves with firebrands,
Walk in the light of your fire
And among the brands you have set ablaze.
This you will have from My hand;
And you will [b]lie down in torment.

CHAPTER 51

Israel Exhorted

"[a]LISTEN to me, you who [b]pursue righteousness,
Who seek the LORD:
Look to the [c]rock from which you were hewn,
And to the [1]quarry from which you were dug.
2 "Look to Abraham your father,
And to Sarah who gave birth to you in pain;
When *he* [a]*was* one I called him,
Then I blessed him and multiplied him."
3 Indeed, the LORD will comfort Zion;
He will comfort all her waste places.
And her [a]wilderness He will make like [b]Eden,
And her desert like the garden of the LORD;
[c]Joy and gladness will be found in her,
Thanksgiving and sound of a melody.

4 "[a]Pay attention to Me, O My people;
And give ear to Me, O My [1]nation;
For a [b]law will go forth from Me,
And I will [2]set My [c]justice for a [d]light of the peoples.

---

26 [b]Is. 45:6; Ezek. 39:7

1 [a]Deut. 24:1, 3; Jer. 3:8 [b]Is. 54:6, 7 [c]Deut. 32:30; 2 Kin. 4:1; Neh. 5:5 [d]Is. 52:3; 59:2 [e]Jer. 3:8

2 [a]Gen. 18:14; Num. 11:23; Is. 59:1 [b]Ex. 14:21; Is. 19:5; 43:16; 44:27 [c]Josh. 3:16; Is. 42:15

3 [a]Is. 13:10; Rev. 6:12

4 [1]YHWH, usually rendered LORD, and so throughout the chap. [a]Is. 57:19; Jer. 31:25 [b]Ps. 5:3; 88:13; 119:147; 143:8

5 [a]Matt. 26:39; John 8:29; 14:31; 15:10; Acts 26:19; Phil. 2:8; Heb. 5:8; 10:7

6 [a]Matt. 26:67; 27:30; Mark 15:19; Luke 22:63

7 [a]Is. 42:1; 49:8 [b]Is. 45:17; 54:4 [c]Ezek. 3:8, 9

8 [a]Is. 45:25; Rom. 8:33, 34 [b]Is. 1:18; 41:1; 43:26

9 [a]Is. 54:17

10 [a]Is. 49:2, 3; 50:4 [b]Is. 9:2; 26:9; Eph. 5:8

11 [1]Lit., *gird* [a]Prov. 26:18; Is. 9:18; James 3:6 [b]Is. 8:22; 65:13-15; Amos 4:9, 10

1 [1]Lit., *the excavation of a pit* [a]Is. 46:3; 48:12; 51:7 [b]Ps. 94:15; Prov. 15:9 [c]Gen. 17:15-17

2 [a]Gen. 12:1; 15:5; Deut. 1:10; Ezek. 33:24

3 [a]Is. 35:1; 41:19 [b]Gen. 2:8; Joel 2:3 [c]Is. 25:9; 41:16; 65:18; 66:10

4 [1]Or, *people* [2]Lit., *cause to rest* [a]Ps. 50:7; 78:1 [b]Deut. 18:18; Is. 2:3; Mic. 4:2 [c]Is. 1:27; 42:4 [d]Is. 42:6; 49:6

5"My [a]righteousness is near, My salvation has gone forth,
And My arms will judge the peoples;
The [b]coastland will wait for Me,
And for My [c]arm they will wait expectantly.
6"[a]Lift up your eyes to the sky,
Then look to the earth beneath;
For the [b]sky will vanish like smoke,
And the [b]earth will wear out like a garment,
And its inhabitants will die [1]in like manner,
But My salvation shall be forever,
And My righteousness shall not [2]wane.
7"Listen to Me, you who know righteousness,
A people in whose [a]heart is My law;
Do not fear the [b]reproach of man,
Neither be dismayed at their revilings.
8"For the moth will eat them like a garment,
And the [a]grub will eat them like wool.
But My righteousness shall be forever,
And My salvation to all generations."

9 Awake, awake, put on strength, O arm of the LORD;
Awake as in the [a]days of old, the generations of long ago.
Was it not Thou who cut Rahab in pieces,
Who pierced the dragon?
10 Was it not Thou who [a]dried up the sea,
The waters of the great deep;
Who made the depths of the sea a pathway
For the [b]redeemed to cross over?
11 So the ransomed of the LORD will return,
And come with joyful shouting to Zion;
And [a]everlasting joy *will be* on their heads.
They will obtain gladness and joy,
And sorrow and sighing will [b]flee away.

12"I, even I, am He who comforts you.
Who are you that you are afraid of [a]man who dies,
And of the son of man who is made [b]like grass;
13 That you have [a]forgotten the LORD your Maker,
Who [b]stretched out the heavens,
And laid the foundations of the earth;
That you fear continually all day long because of the fury of the oppressor,
As he makes ready to destroy?
But where is the fury of the oppressor?
14"The [1a]exile will soon be set free,
and will not die in the dungeon, [b]nor
will his bread be lacking.
15"For I am the LORD your God,
who [a]stirs up the sea and its waves
roar (the LORD of hosts is His name).
16"And I have [a]put My words in
your mouth, and have [b]covered you
with the shadow of My hand, to
[1c]establish the heavens, to found the
earth, and to say to Zion, 'You are
My people.' "
17 Rouse yourself! Rouse yourself! Arise, O Jerusalem,
You who have [a]drunk from the LORD's hand the cup of His anger;
The [1]chalice of reeling you have [2]drained to the dregs.
18 There is [a]none to guide her among all the sons she has borne;
Nor is there one to take her by the hand among all the sons she has reared.
19 These two things have befallen you;
Who will mourn for you?
The [a]devastation and destruction, famine and sword;
How shall I comfort you?
20 Your sons have fainted,
They [a]lie *helpless* at the head of every street,
Like an antelope in a net,
Full of the wrath of the LORD,
The [b]rebuke of your God.

21 Therefore, please hear this, you afflicted,
Who are drunk, but not with wine:
22 Thus says your Lord, the LORD, even your God
Who [a]contends for His people,
"Behold, I have taken out of your hand the cup of reeling;
The [1]chalice of My anger,
You will never drink it again.
23"And I will [a]put it into the hand of your tormentors,
Who have said to [1]you, '[b]Lie down that we may walk over you.'

5 [a]Is. 46:13; 54:17 [b]Is. 42:4; 60:9 [c]Is. 59:16; 63:5
6 [1]Or, *like gnats* [2]Lit., *be broken* [a]Is. 40:26 [b]Ps. 102:25, 26; Is. 13:13; 34:4; Matt. 24:35; Heb. 1:10-12; 2 Pet. 3:10
7 [a]Ps. 37:31 [b]Is. 25:8; 54:4; Matt. 5:11; Acts 5:41
8 [a]Is. 14:11; 66:24
9 [a]Ex. 6:6; Deut. 4:34
10 [a]Is. 11:15, 16; 50:2; 63:11, 12 [b]Ex. 15:13; Ps. 106:10; Is. 63:9, 16
11 [a]Is. 60:19; 61:7 [b]Is. 25:8; 60:20; 65:19; Rev. 7:17; 21:1, 4; 22:3
12 [a]Ps. 118:6; Is. 2:22 [b]Is. 40:6, 7; 1 Pet. 1:24
13 [a]Deut. 6:12; 8:11; Is. 17:10 [b]Job 9:8; Ps. 104:2; Is. 40.22, 45:12, 18; 48:13
14 [1]Lit., *one in chains* [a]Is. 48:20; 52:2 [b]Is. 33:6; 49:10
15 [a]Ps. 107:25; Jer. 31:35
16 [1]Lit., *plant* [a]Deut. 18:18; Is. 59:21 [b]Ex. 33:22; Is. 49:2 [c]Is. 66:17, 22
17 [1]Lit., *bowl of the cup of reeling* [2]Lit., *drunk* [a]Job 21:20; Is. 29:9; 63:6; Jer. 25:15
18 [a]Ps. 88:18; 142:4; Is. 49:21
19 [a]Is. 8:21; 9:20; 14:30
20 [a]Is. 5:25; Jer. 14:16 [b]Is. 66:15
22 [1]Lit., *bowl of the cup of* [a]Is. 3:12, 13; 49:25; Jer. 50:34
23 [1]Lit., *your soul* [a]Is. 49:26; Jer. 25:15-17, 26, 28; Zech. 12:2 [b]Josh. 10:24

You have even made your back
like the ground,
And like the street for those
who walk over *it*."

CHAPTER 52

Cheer for Prostrate Zion

AWAKE, awake,
Clothe yourself in your
strength, O Zion;
Clothe yourself in your [a]beautiful garments,
O Jerusalem, the [b]holy city.
For the uncircumcised and the
unclean
Will no more come into you.
2 Shake yourself from the dust,
[a]rise up,
O captive Jerusalem;
Loose yourself from the chains
around your neck,
O captive daughter of Zion.
3 For thus says the LORD, "You
were [a]sold for nothing and you will
be [b]redeemed without money."
4 For thus says the Lord [1]GOD,
"My people [a]went down at the first
into Egypt to reside there, then the
Assyrian oppressed them without
cause.
5 "Now therefore, what do I have
here," declares the LORD, "seeing
that My people have been taken
away without cause?" *Again* the
LORD declares, "Those who rule
over them howl, and My [a]name is
continually blasphemed all day
long.
6 "Therefore My people shall
know My name; therefore in that
day I am the one who is speaking,
'Here I am.'"
7 How lovely on the mountains
Are the feet of him who brings
[a]good news,
Who announces [1]peace
And brings good news of [2]happiness,
Who announces salvation,
And says to Zion, "Your [b]God
[3]reigns!"
8 Listen! Your watchmen lift up
their [a]voices,
They shout joyfully together;
For they will see [1]with their
own eyes
When the LORD restores Zion.
9 [a]Break forth, shout joyfully together,
You [b]waste places of Jerusalem;
For the LORD has comforted His
people,
He has [c]redeemed Jerusalem.
10 The LORD has bared His holy
[a]arm
In the sight of all the nations;
[1]That [b]all the ends of the earth
may see
The salvation of our God.
11 Depart, depart, go out from
there,
[a]Touch nothing unclean;
Go out of the midst of her, [b]purify yourselves,
You who carry the vessels of
the LORD.
12 But you will not go out in
[a]haste,
Nor will you go [1]as fugitives;
For the [b]LORD will go before
you,
And [c]the God of Israel *will be*
your rear guard.

The Exalted Servant

13 Behold, My servant will prosper,
He will be high and lifted up,
and [1]greatly [a]exalted.
14 Just as many were astonished
at you, *My people,*
So His [a]appearance was
marred more than any man,
And His form more than the
sons of men.
15 Thus He will sprinkle many nations,
Kings will [a]shut their mouths
on account of Him;
For [b]what had not been told
them they will see,
And what they had not heard
they will understand.

CHAPTER 53

The Suffering Servant

[a]WHO has believed our message?
And to whom has the arm of the
LORD been revealed?
2 For He grew up before Him like
a [a]tender [1]shoot,
And like a root out of parched
ground;
He has [b]no *stately* form or majesty
That we should look upon Him,
Nor appearance that we should
[2]be attracted to Him.
3 He was [a]despised and forsaken
of men,
A man of [1]sorrows, and [b]acquainted with [2]grief;
And like one from whom men
hide their face,
He was [c]despised, and we did
not [d]esteem Him.

---

1 [a]Ex. 28:2, 40; 1 Chr. 16:29; Ps. 110:3; Is. 49:18; 61:3, 10; Zech. 3:4 [b]Neh. 11:1; Is. 48:2; 64:10; Zech. 14:20, 21; Matt. 4:5
2 [a]Is. 60:1
3 [a]Ps. 44:12; Jer. 15:13 [b]Is. 1:27; 62:12; 63:4
4 [1]YHWH, usually rendered LORD [a]Gen. 46:6
5 [a]Ezek. 36:20, 23; Rom. 2:24
7 [1]Or, *well-being* [2]Lit., *good* [3]Or, *is King* [a]Is. 40:9; 61:1; Nah. 1:15; Rom. 10:15 [b]Ps. 93:1; Is. 24:23
8 [1]Lit., *eye to eye* [a]Is. 62:6
9 [a]Ps. 98:4; Is. 44:23 [b]Is. 44:26; 51:3; 61:4 [c]Is. 43:1; 48:20
10 [1]Lit., *And . . . earth will see* [a]Ps. 98:1-3; Is. 51:9; 66:18, 19 [b]Is. 45:22; 48:20
11 [a]Num. 19:11, 16 [b]Lev. 22:2; Is. 1:16
12 [1]Lit., *in flight* [a]Ex. 12:11, 33; Deut. 16:3 [b]Is. 26:7; 42:16; 49:10, 11 [c]Ex. 14:19, 20; Is. 58:8
13 [1]Or, *very high* [a]Is. 57:15
14 [a]Is. 53:2, 3
15 [a]Job 21:5 [b]Rom. 15:21
1 [a]John 12:38; Rom. 10:16
2 [1]Lit., *suckling* [2]Lit., *desire* [a]Is. 11:1 [b]Is. 52:14
3 [1]Or, *pains* [2]Or, *sickness* [a]Ps. 22:6; Is. 49:7; Luke 18:31-33 [b]Is. 53:10 [c]Mark 10:33, 34 [d]John 1:10, 11

4 Surely our [1]griefs He Himself
[a]bore,
And our [2]sorrows He carried;
Yet we ourselves esteemed
Him stricken,
[3]Smitten of [b]God, and afflicted.
5 But He was [1]pierced through
for [a]our transgressions,
He was crushed for [b]our iniquities;
The [c]chastening for our [2]well-
being *fell* upon Him,
And by [d]His scourging we are
healed.
6 All of us like sheep have gone
astray,
Each of us has turned to his
own way;
But the LORD has caused the iniquity of us all
To [1]fall on Him.

7 He was oppressed and He was
afflicted,
Yet He did not [a]open His
mouth;
[b]Like a lamb that is led to
slaughter,
And like a sheep that is silent
before its shearers,
So He did not open His mouth.
8 By oppression and judgment
He was taken away;
And as for His generation, who
considered
That He was cut off out of the
land of the [1]living,
[a]For the transgression of my
people to whom the stroke
was due?
9 His grave was assigned to be
with wicked men,
Yet with a [a]rich man in His
death;
[b]Although He had [c]done no violence,
Nor was there any deceit in His
mouth.

10 But the LORD was pleased
To crush Him, [1]putting *Him* to
grief;
If [2]He would render Himself *as*
a guilt [a]offering,
He will see [b]*His* [3]offspring,
He will prolong *His* days,
And the [4]good [c]pleasure of the
LORD will prosper in His
hand.
11 As a result of the [1]anguish of
His soul,
He will [a]see [2]*it* and be satisfied;
By His [b]knowledge the Right-
eous One,
My Servant, will justify the
many,
As He will bear their iniquities.
12 Therefore, I will allot Him a
[a]portion with the great,
And He will divide the booty
with the strong;
Because He poured out [1b]Him-
self to death,
And was [c]numbered with the
transgressors;
Yet He Himself [d]bore the sin of
many,
And interceded for the transgressors.

CHAPTER 54

The Fertility of Zion

"[a]SHOUT for joy, O barren one,
you who have borne no *child;*
Break forth into joyful shouting
and cry aloud, you who have
not travailed;
For the sons of the [b]desolate
one *will be* [c]more numerous
Than the sons of the married
woman," says the LORD.
2"[a]Enlarge the place of your tent;
[1]Stretch out the curtains of
your dwellings, spare not;
Lengthen your [b]cords,
And strengthen your [b]pegs.
3"For you will [a]spread abroad to
the right and to the left.
And your [1]descendants will
[b]possess nations,
And they will [c]resettle the desolate cities.

4"Fear not, for you will not be put
to shame;
Neither feel humiliated, for you
will not be disgraced;
But you will forget the shame of
your youth,
And the [a]reproach of your widowhood you will remember
no more.
5"For your [a]husband is your Maker,
Whose name is the LORD of
hosts;
And your [b]Redeemer is the
Holy One of Israel,
Who is called the [c]God of all the
earth.
6"For the LORD has called you,
Like a wife [a]forsaken and
grieved in spirit,
Even like a wife of *one's* youth
when she is rejected,"
Says your God.
7"[1]For a [a]brief moment I forsook
you,
But with great compassion I
will [b]gather you.

4 [1]Or, *sickness* [2]Or, *pains* [3]Or, *Struck down by* [a]Matt. 8:17 [b]John 19:7

5 [1]Or, *wounded* [2]Or, *peace* [a]Is. 53:8; Heb. 9:28 [b]Is. 53:10; Rom. 4:25; 1 Cor. 15:3 [c]Deut. 11:2; Heb. 5:8 [d]1 Pet. 2:24, 25

6 [1]Lit., *encounter Him*

7 [a]Matt. 26:63; 27:12-14; Mark 14:61; 15:5; Luke 23:9; John 19:9 [b]Acts 8:32, 33

8 [1]Or, *life* [a]Is. 53:5, 12

9 [a]Matt. 27:57-60 [b]Is. 42:1-3 [c]1 Pet. 2:22

10 [1]Lit., *He made Him sick* [2]Lit., *His soul* [3]Lit., *seed* [4]Or, *will of* [a]Is. 53:6-12; John 1:29 [b]Ps. 22:30; Is. 54:3; 61:9; 66:22 [c]Is. 46:10

11 [1]Or, *toilsome labor* [2]Another reading is, *light* [a]John 10:14-18 [b]Is. 45:25; Rom. 5:18, 19

12 [1]Lit., *His soul* [a]Is. 52:13; Phil. 2:9-11 [b]Matt. 26:38, 39, 42 [c]Luke 22:37 [d]Is. 53:6, 11; 2 Cor. 5:21

1 [a]Gal. 4:27 [b]Is. 62:4 [c]1 Sam. 2:5; Is. 49:20

2 [1]Lit., *Let them stretch out* [a]Is. 33:20; 49:19, 20 [b]Ex. 35:18; 39:40

3 [1]Lit., *seed* [a]Gen. 28:14; Is. 43:5, 6; 60:3-11 [b]Is. 14:1, 2; 43:14; 49:23 [c]Is. 49:19

4 [a]Is. 4:1; 25:8; 51:7

5 [a]Jer. 3:14; Hos. 2:19 [b]Is. 43:14; 48:17 [c]Is. 6:3; 11:9; 65:16

6 [a]Is. 49:14-21; 50:1, 2; 62:4

7 [1]Lit., *in* [a]Is. 26:20 [b]Is. 11:12; 43:5; 49:18

8"In an [1a]outburst of anger
I hid My face from you for a moment;
But with everlasting lovingkindness I will [b]have compassion on you,"
Says the LORD your Redeemer.

9"For [1]this is like the days of Noah to Me;
When I swore that the waters of Noah
Should [a]not [2]flood the earth again,
So I have sworn that I will [b]not be angry with you,
Nor will I rebuke you.
10"For the [a]mountains may be removed and the hills may shake,
But My lovingkindness will not be removed from you,
And My [b]covenant of peace will not be shaken,"
Says the LORD who has compassion on you.

11"O afflicted one, storm-tossed, and not comforted,
Behold, I will set your stones in antimony,
And your foundations I will [a]lay in [1]sapphires.
12"Moreover, I will make your battlements of [1]rubies,
And your gates of [2]crystal,
And your entire [3]wall of precious stones.
13"And [a]all your sons will be [1]taught of the LORD;
And the well-being of your sons will be [b]great.
14"In [a]righteousness you will be established;
You will be far from [b]oppression, for you will not fear;
And from terror, for it will not come near you.
15"If anyone fiercely assails *you* it will not be from Me.
[a]Whoever assails you will fall because of you.
16"Behold, I Myself have created the smith who blows the fire of coals,
And brings out a weapon for its work;
And I have created the destroyer to ruin.
17"[a]No weapon that is formed against you shall prosper;
And [b]every tongue that [1]accuses you in judgment you will condemn.
This is the heritage of the servants of the LORD,
And their [c]vindication is from Me," declares the LORD.

CHAPTER 55

The Free Offer of Mercy

"HO! Every one who [a]thirsts, come to the waters;
And you who have [b]no [1]money come, buy and eat.
Come, buy wine and milk
[c]Without money and without cost.
2"Why do you [1]spend money for what is [a]not bread,
And your wages for what does not satisfy?
Listen carefully to Me, and [b]eat what is good,
And delight yourself in abundance.
3"[a]Incline your ear and come to Me.
Listen, that [1]you may [b]live;
And I will make [c]an everlasting covenant with you,
According to the [d]faithful mercies [2]shown to David.
4"Behold, I have made [a]him a witness to the peoples,
A [b]leader and commander for the peoples.
5"Behold, you will call a [a]nation you do not know,
And a nation which knows you not will [b]run to you,
Because of the LORD your God, even the Holy One of Israel;
For He has [c]glorified you."

6 [a]Seek the LORD while He may be found;
[b]Call upon Him while He is near.
7 [a]Let the wicked forsake his way,
And the unrighteous man his [b]thoughts;
And let him [c]return to the LORD,
And He will have [d]compassion on him;
And to our God,
For He will [e]abundantly pardon.
8"For My thoughts are not [a]your thoughts,
Neither are [b]your ways My ways," declares the LORD.
9"For [a]*as* the heavens are higher than the earth,
So are My ways higher than your ways,
And My thoughts than your thoughts.
10"For as the [a]rain and the snow come down from heaven,

8 [1]Lit., *overflowing* [a]Is. 60:10 [b]Is. 49:10, 13
9 [1]Some mss. read, *the waters of Noah this is to me* [2]Lit., *cross over* [a]Gen. 9:11 [b]Is. 12:1; Ezek. 39:29
10 [a]Ps. 102:26; Is. 51:6 [b]2 Sam. 23:5; Ps. 89:34; Is. 55:3; 59:21; 61:8
11 [1]Or, *lapis lazuli* [a]Is. 14:32; 28:16; 44:28
12 [1]I.e., bright red [2]Or, *carbuncles* [3]Lit., *border, boundary*
13 [1]Or, *disciples* [a]John 6:45 [b]Is. 48:18; 66:12
14 [a]Is. 1:26, 27; 9:7; 62:1 [b]Is. 9:4; 14:4
15 [a]Is. 41:11-16
17 [1]Lit., *rises against* [a]Is. 17:12-14; 29:8 [b]Is. 50:8, 9 [c]Is. 45:24; 46:13
1 [1]Lit., *silver* [a]Ps. 42:1, 2; 63:1; 143:6; Is. 41:17; 44:3; John 4:14; 7:37 [b]Lam. 5:4 [c]Hos. 14:4; Matt. 10:8
2 [1]Lit., *weigh out silver* [a]Eccles. 6:2; Hos. 8:7 [b]Ps. 22:26; Is. 1:19; 62:8, 9
3 [1]Lit., *your soul* [2]Lit., *of David* [a]Is. 51:4 [b]Lev. 18:5; Rom. 10:5 [c]Is. 61:8 [d]Acts 13:34
4 [a]Ps. 18:43; Jer. 30:9; Hos. 3:5 [b]Ezek. 34:24; 37:24, 25; Dan. 9:25; Mic. 5:2
5 [a]Is. 45:14, 22-24; 49:6, 12, 23 [b]Zech. 8:22 [c]Is. 60:9
6 [a]Ps. 32:6; Is. 45:19, 22; 49:8; Amos 5:6 [b]Is. 58:9; 65:24
7 [a]Is. 1:16, 19; 58:6 [b]Is. 32:7; 59:7 [c]Is. 31:6; 44:22 [d]Is. 14:1; 54:8, 10 [e]Is. 1:18; 40:2; 43:25; 44:22
8 [a]Is. 65:2; 66:18 [b]Is. 53:6
9 [a]Ps. 103:11
10 [a]Is. 30:23

And do not return there without watering the earth,
And making it bear and sprout,
And furnishing [b]seed to the sower and bread to the eater;
11 So shall My [a]word be which goes forth from My mouth;
It shall [b]not return to Me empty,
Without [c]accomplishing what I desire,
And without succeeding *in the matter* for which I sent it.
12 "For you will go out with [a]joy,
And be led forth with [b]peace;
The [c]mountains and the hills will break forth into shouts of joy before you,
And all the [d]trees of the field will clap *their* hands.
13 "Instead of the thorn bush the cypress will come up;
And instead of the nettle the myrtle will come up;
And [1]it will be a [2a]memorial to the LORD,
For an everlasting sign which [b]will not be cut off."

CHAPTER 56

Rewards for Obedience to God

THUS says the LORD,
"[a]Preserve justice, and do righteousness,
For My [b]salvation is about to come
And My righteousness to be revealed.
2 "How [a]blessed is the man who does this,
And the son of man who takes hold of it;
Who [b]keeps from profaning the sabbath,
And keeps his hand from doing any evil."
3 Let not the foreigner who has joined himself to the LORD say,
"The LORD will surely separate me from His people."
Neither let the eunuch say, "Behold, I am a dry tree."
4 For thus says the LORD,
"To the eunuchs who keep My sabbaths,
And choose what pleases Me,
And hold fast My covenant,
5 To them I will give in My [a]house and within My [b]walls a memorial,
And a name better than that of sons and daughters;
I will give [1]them an everlasting [c]name which will not be cut off.

6 "Also the foreigners who join themselves to the LORD,
To minister to Him, and to love the name of the LORD,
To be His servants, every one who [a]keeps from profaning the sabbath,
And holds fast My covenant;
7 Even [a]those I will bring to My [b]holy mountain,
And [c]make them joyful in My house of prayer.
Their burnt offerings and their sacrifices will be acceptable on My altar;
For [d]My house will be called a house of prayer for all the peoples."
8 The Lord [1]GOD, who gathers the dispersed of Israel, declares,
"Yet [a]*others* I will gather to [2]them, to those *already* gathered."

9 All you [a]beasts of the field,
All you beasts in the forest,
Come to eat.
10 His [a]watchmen are [b]blind,
All of them know nothing.
All of them are dumb dogs unable to bark,
[1]Dreamers lying down, who love to slumber;
11 And the dogs are [1a]greedy, they [2]are not satisfied.
And they are shepherds who have no understanding;
They have all [b]turned to their own way,
Each one to his unjust gain, to the last one.
12 "Come," *they say,* "let [1]us get wine, and let us drink heavily of strong drink;
And [a]tomorrow will be like today, only more so."

CHAPTER 57

Evil Leaders Rebuked

THE righteous man perishes, and no man [a]takes it to heart;
And devout men are taken away, while no one understands.
For the righteous man is taken away from [b]evil,
2 He enters into peace;
They rest in their [1]beds,
Each one who [a]walked in his upright way.
3 "But come here, you sons of a sorceress,
Offspring of an adulterer and [1]a prostitute.

10 [b]2 Cor. 9:10

11 [a]Is. 45:23; Matt. 24:35 [b]Is. 44:26; 59:21 [c]Is. 46:10; 53:10

12 [a]Ps. 105:43; Is. 51:11; 52:9 [b]Is. 54:10, 13; Jer. 29:11 [c]Is. 44:23; 49:13 [d]1 Chr. 16:33

13 [1]I.e., the transformation of the desert [2]Lit., *name* [a]Is. 63:12, 14; Jer. 33:9 [b]Is. 56:5

1 [a]Is. 1:17; 33:5; 61:8 [b]Ps. 85:9; Is. 46:13; 51:5

2 [a]Ps. 112:1; 119:1, 2 [b]Ex. 20:8-11; 31:13-17; Jer. 17:21, 22; Ezek. 20:12, 20

5 [1]So DSS; M.T. reads, *him* [a]Is. 2:2, 3; 56:7; 66:20 [b]Is. 26:1; 60:18 [c]Is. 62:2

6 [a]Is. 56:2, 4

7 [a]Is. 2:2, 3; 60:11; Mic. 4:1, 2 [b]Is. 11:9; 65:25 [c]Is. 61:10 [d]Matt. 21:13; Mark 11:17; Luke 19:46

8 [1]YHWH, usually rendered LORD [2]Lit., *him* [a]Is. 60:3-11; 66:18-21; John 10:16

9 [a]Is. 18:6; 46:11

10 [1]So DSS, M. T., *Ravers* [a]Ezek. 3:17 [b]Is. 29:9-14; Jer. 14:13, 14

11 [1]Lit., *strong of soul/appetite* [2]Lit., *do not know satisfaction* [a]Is. 28:7; Ezek. 13:19; Mic. 3:5, 11 [b]Is. 57:17; Jer. 22:17

12 [1]So DSS and many versions; M. T., *me* [a]Ps. 10:6; Luke 12:19, 20

1 [a]Is. 42:25; 47:7 [b]2 Kin. 22:20; Is. 47:11; Jer. 18:11

2 [1]I.e., graves [a]Is. 26:7

3 [1]Reading with the versions; Heb., *she prostitutes herself*

4"Against whom do you jest?
Against whom do you open wide your mouth
And stick out your tongue?
Are you not children of [a]rebellion,
Offspring of deceit,
5 *Who* inflame yourselves among the [1]oaks,
[a]Under every luxuriant tree,
Who [b]slaughter the children in the [2]ravines,
Under the clefts of the crags?
6"Among the [1a]smooth *stones* of the [2]ravine
Is your portion, [3]they are your lot;
Even to them you have [b]poured out a libation,
You have made a grain offering.
Shall I [4c]relent concerning these things?
7"Upon a [a]high and lofty mountain
You have made your bed.
You also went up there to offer sacrifice.
8"And behind the door and the doorpost
You have set up your sign;
Indeed, far removed from Me, you have uncovered yourself;
And have gone up and made your bed wide.
And you have made an agreement for yourselves with them,
You have loved their [1]bed,
You have looked on *their* [2]manhood.
9"And you have journeyed to the king with oil
And increased your perfumes;
You have [a]sent your envoys a great distance,
And made *them* go down to [1]Sheol.
10"You were tired out by the length of your road,
Yet you did not say, '[a]It is hopeless.'
You found [1]renewed strength,
Therefore you did not [2]faint.

11"Of [a]whom were you worried and fearful,
When you lied, and did [b]not remember Me,
[1]Nor [c]give *Me* a thought?
Was I not silent even for a long time
So you do not fear Me?
12"I will declare your righteousness and your [a]deeds,
But they will not profit you.
13"When you cry out, [a]let your collection *of idols* deliver you.
But the wind will carry all of them up,
And a breath will take *them* away.
But he who [b]takes refuge in Me shall [c]inherit the land,
And shall [d]possess My holy mountain."

14 And it shall be said,
"[a]Build up, build up, prepare the way,
Remove *every* obstacle out of the way of My people."
15 For thus says the [a]high and exalted One
Who [1b]lives forever, whose name is Holy,
"I [c]dwell *on* a high and holy place,
And *also* with the [d]contrite and lowly of spirit
In order to [e]revive the spirit of the lowly
And to revive the heart of the contrite.
16"For I will [a]not contend forever,
[b]Neither will I always be angry;
For the spirit would grow faint before Me,
And the breath *of those whom* I have made.
17"Because of the iniquity of his [a]unjust gain I was angry and struck him;
I hid *My face* and was angry,
And he went on [b]turning away, in the way of his heart.
18"I have seen his ways, but I will [a]heal him;
I will lead him and [b]restore comfort to him and to his mourners,
19 Creating the [1a]praise of the lips.
[b]Peace, peace to him who is [c]far and to him who is near,"
Says the LORD, "and I will heal him."
20 But the [a]wicked are like the tossing sea,
For it cannot be quiet,
And its waters toss up refuse and mud.
21"[a]There is no peace," says my God, "for the wicked."

CHAPTER 58

Observances of Fasts

"[a]CRY loudly, do not hold back;
Raise your voice like a trumpet,
And declare to My people their transgression,
And to the house of Jacob their sins.

4 [a]Is. 48:8

5 [1]Or, *terebinths* [2]Or, *wadis* [a]2 Kin. 16:4; Jer. 2:20; 3:13 [b]2 Kin. 23:10; Ps. 106:37, 38; Jer. 7:31

6 [1]I.e., symbols of fertility gods [2]Or, *wadi* [3]Lit., *they, they* [4]Or, *repent* [a]Jer. 3:9; Hab. 2:19 [b]Jer. 7:18 [c]Jer. 5:9, 29; 9:9

7 [a]Jer. 3:16; Ezek. 16:16

8 [1]Or, *lying down* [2]Lit., *hand*

9 [1]I.e., the nether world [a]Ezek. 23:16, 40

10 [1]Lit., *the life of your hand* [2]Or, *become sick* [a]Jer. 2:25; 18:12

11 [1]Lit., *You did not set it upon your heart* [a]Prov. 29:25; Is. 51:12, 13 [b]Jer. 2:32; 3:21 [c]Ps. 50:21; Is. 42:14

12 [a]Is. 29:15; 59:6; 65:7; 66:18; Mic. 3:2-4

13 [a]Jer. 22:20; 30:14 [b]Ps. 37:3, 9; Is. 25:4 [c]Is. 49:8; 60:21 [d]Is. 65:9

14 [a]Is. 62:10; Jer. 18:15

15 [1]Or, *dwells in eternity* [a]Is. 52:13 [b]Deut. 33:27; Is. 40:28 [c]Is. 33:5; 66:1 [d]Ps. 34:18; 51:17; Is. 66:2 [e]Ps. 147:3; Is. 61:1-3

16 [a]Gen. 6:3 [b]Ps. 85:5; 103:9; Mic. 7:18

17 [a]Is. 2:7; 56:11; Jer. 6:13 [b]Is. 1:4; Jer. 3:14, 22

18 [a]Is. 19:22; 30:26; 53:5 [b]Is. 61:1-3

19 [1]Lit., *fruit of the lips* [a]Is. 6:7; 51:16; 59:21; Heb. 13:15 [b]Is. 26:12; 32:17 [c]Acts 2:39; Eph. 2:17

20 [a]Job 18:5-14; Is. 3:9, 11

21 [a]Is. 48:22; 59:8

1 [a]Is. 40:6, 8

2 "Yet they [a]seek Me day by day, and delight to know My ways,
As a nation that has done [b]righteousness,
And has not forsaken the ordinance of their God.
They ask Me *for* just decisions,
They delight [c]in the nearness of God.
3 'Why have we [a]fasted and Thou dost not see?
Why have we humbled ourselves and Thou dost not [1]notice?'
Behold, on the [b]day of your fast you find *your* desire,
And drive hard all your workers.
4 "Behold, you fast for contention and [a]strife and to strike with a wicked fist.
You do not fast like *you do* today to [b]make your voice heard on high.
5 "Is it a fast like this which I choose, a day for a man to humble himself?
Is it for bowing [1]one's head like a reed,
And for spreading out [a]sackcloth and ashes as a bed?
Will you call this a fast, even an [b]acceptable day to the LORD?
6 "Is this not the fast which I chose,
To [a]loosen the bonds of wickedness,
To undo the bands of the yoke,
And to [b]let the oppressed go free,
And break every yoke?
7 "Is it not to [a]divide your bread [1]with the hungry,
And [b]bring the homeless poor into the house;
When you see the [c]naked, to cover him;
And not to [d]hide yourself from your own flesh?
8 "Then your light will break out like the dawn,
And your [a]recovery will speedily spring forth;
And your [b]righteousness will go before you;
The glory of the [c]LORD will be your rear guard.
9 "Then you will [a]call, and the LORD will answer;
You will cry, and He will say, 'Here I am.'
If you remove the yoke from your midst,
The [1]pointing of the finger, and speaking wickedness,

2 [a]Is. 1:11; Titus 1:16 [b]Is. 48:1; Jer. 7:9, 10 [c]Ps. 119:150; Is. 29:13; 57:3; James 4:8

3 [1]Lit., *know* [a]Mal. 3:14; Luke 18:12 [b]Is. 22:12, 13; Zech. 7:5, 6

4 [a]Is. 3:14, 15; 59:6 [b]Is. 1:15; 59:2; Joel 2:12-14

5 [1]Lit., *his* [a]1 Kin. 21:27 [b]Is. 49:8; 61:2

6 [a]Neh. 5:10-12; Jer. 34:8 [b]Is. 1:17

7 [1]Lit., *for* [a]Job 31:19, 20; Is. 58:10; Ezek. 18:7, 16 [b]Is. 16:3, 4; Heb. 13:2 [c]Matt. 25:35; Luke 3:11 [d]Deut. 22:1-4; Luke 10:31, 32

8 [a]Is. 30:26; 33:24; Jer. 30:17; 33:6 [b]Ps. 85:13; Is. 62:1 [c]Ex. 14:19; Is. 52:12

9 [1]Lit., *sending out* [a]Ps. 50:15; Is. 55:6; 65:24

10 [1]Lit., *furnish* [2]Or, *soul* [a]Deut. 15:7; Is. 58:7 [b]Job 11:17; Ps. 37:6; Is. 42:16; 58:8

11 [1]Or, *soul* [2]Or, *deceive* [a]Is. 49:10; 57:18 [b]Ps. 107.9, Is. 41:17 [c]Is. 66:14 [d]Song of Sol. 4:15; Is. 27:3; Jer. 31:12 [e]John 4:14; 7:38

12 [1]Lit., *paths* [a]Is. 49:8; 61:4; Ezek. 36:10 [b]Is. 44:28 [c]Is. 30:13; Amos 9:11

13 [a]Ex. 31:16, 17; 35:2, 3; Is. 56:2, 4, 6; Jer. 17:21-27 [b]Ps. 27:4; 42:4; 84:2, 10 [c]Is. 55:8

14 [a]Is. 61:10

1 [a]Num. 11:23; Is. 50:2; Jer. 32:17 [b]Is. 58:9; 65:24; Ezek. 8:18

2 [1]So versions; M. T., *faces* [a]Is. 1:15; 50:1 [b]Is. 58:4

10 And if you [1a]give yourself to the hungry,
And satisfy the [2]desire of the afflicted,
Then your [b]light will rise in darkness,
And your gloom *will become* like midday.
11 "And the [a]LORD will continually guide you,
And [b]satisfy your [1]desire in scorched places,
And [c]give strength to your bones;
And you will be like a [d]watered garden,
And like a [e]spring of water whose waters do not [2]fail.
12 "And those from among you will [a]rebuild the ancient ruins;
You will [b]raise up the age-old foundations;
And you will be called the repairer of the [c]breach,
The restorer of the [1]streets in which to dwell.

Keeping the Sabbath

13 "If because of the sabbath, you [a]turn your foot
From doing your *own* pleasure on My holy day,
And call the sabbath a [b]delight, the holy *day* of the LORD honorable,
And shall honor it, desisting from your [c]*own* ways,
From seeking your *own* pleasure,
And speaking *your own* word,
14 Then you will take [a]delight in the LORD,
And I will make you ride on the heights of the earth;
And I will feed you *with* the heritage of Jacob your father,
For the mouth of the LORD has spoken."

CHAPTER 59

Separation from God

BEHOLD, [a]the LORD's hand is not so short
That it cannot save;
[b]Neither is His ear so dull
That it cannot hear.
2 But your [a]iniquities have made a separation between you and your God,
And your sins have hidden [1]His face from you, so that *He* does [b]not hear.

3 For your [a]hands are defiled with blood,
And your fingers with iniquity;
Your lips have spoken [b]falsehood,
Your tongue mutters wickedness.
4 [a]No one sues righteously and [b]no one pleads [1]honestly.
They trust in confusion, and speak lies;
They [c]conceive mischief, and bring forth iniquity.
5 They hatch adders' eggs and [a]weave the spider's web;
He who eats of their eggs dies,
And *from* that which is crushed a snake breaks forth.
6 Their webs will not become clothing,
Nor will they [a]cover themselves with their works;
Their [b]works are works of iniquity,
And an [c]act of violence is in their [1]hands.
7 [a]Their feet run to evil,
And they hasten to shed innocent blood;
[b]Their thoughts are thoughts of iniquity;
Devastation and destruction are in their highways.
8 They do not know the [a]way of peace,
And there is [b]no justice in their tracks;
They have made their paths crooked;
[c]Whoever treads on [1]them does not know peace.

A Confession of Wickedness

9 Therefore, [a]justice is far from us,
And righteousness does not overtake us;
We [b]hope for light, but behold, darkness;
For brightness, but we walk in gloom.
10 We grope along the wall like blind men,
We grope like those who have no eyes;
We [a]stumble at midday as in the twilight,
Among those who are vigorous we are [b]like dead men.
11 All of us growl like bears,
And [a]moan sadly like doves;
We hope for justice, but there is none,
For salvation, *but* it is far from us.
12 For our [a]transgressions are multiplied before Thee,
And our [b]sins [1]testify against us;
For our transgressions are with us,
And [2]we know our iniquities:
13 Transgressing and [a]denying the LORD,
And turning away from our God,
Speaking [b]oppression and revolt,
Conceiving *in* and [c]uttering from the heart lying words.
14 And [a]justice is turned back,
And [b]righteousness stands far away;
For truth has stumbled in the street,
And uprightness cannot enter.
15 Yes, truth is lacking;
And he who turns aside from evil [a]makes himself a prey.

Now the LORD saw,
And it was [1]displeasing in His sight [b]that there was no justice.
16 And He saw that there was no man,
And was astonished that there was no one to intercede;
Then His [a]own arm brought salvation to Him;
And His righteousness upheld Him.
17 And He put on [a]righteousness like a breastplate,
And a helmet of salvation on His head;
And He put on garments of vengeance for clothing,
And wrapped Himself with [b]zeal as a mantle.
18 [a]According to *their* [1]deeds, [2]so He will repay,
Wrath to His adversaries, recompense to His enemies;
To the coastlands He will [3]make recompense.
19 So they will fear the name of the LORD from the west
And His glory from the rising of the sun,
For He will [a]come like a [1]rushing stream,
Which the wind of the LORD drives.
20 "And a [a]Redeemer will come to Zion,
And to those who [b]turn from transgression in Jacob," declares the LORD.
21 "And as for Me, this is My [a]covenant with them," says the LORD:
"My [b]Spirit which is upon you, and

3 [a]Is. 1:15, 21; Jer. 2:30, 34; Ezek. 7:23; Hos. 4:2 [b]Is. 28:15; 30:9; 59:13
4 [1]Lit., *in truth* [a]Is. 5:7; 59:14 [b]Is. 59:14, 15 [c]Job 15:35; Ps. 7:14; Is. 33:11
5 [a]Job 8:14
6 [1]Lit., *palms* [a]Is. 28:20 [b]Is. 57:12; Jer. 6:7 [c]Is. 58:4; Ezek. 7:11
7 [a]Prov. 1:16; 6:17; Rom. 3:15-17 [b]Is. 65:2; 66:18; Mark 7:21, 22
8 [1]Lit., *it* [a]Luke 1:79 [b]Is. 59:9, 11; Hos. 4:1 [c]Is. 57:20, 21
9 [a]Is. 59:14 [b]Is. 5:30; 8:21, 22
10 [a]Is. 8:14, 15; 28:13 [b]Lam. 3:6
11 [a]Is. 38:14; Ezek. 7:16
12 [1]Lit., *answer* [2]Lit., *our iniquities we know them* [a]Ezra 9:6; Is. 58:1 [b]Is. 3:9; Jer. 14:7; Hos. 5:5
13 [a]Josh. 24:27; Prov. 30:9; Matt. 10:33; Titus 1:16 [b]Is. 5:7; 30:12; Jer. 9:3, 4 [c]Is. 59:3, 4; Mark 7:21, 22
14 [a]Is. 1:21; 5:7 [b]Is. 46:12; Hab. 1:4
15 [1]Or, *evil* [a]Is. 5:23; 10:2; 29:21; 32:7 [b]Is. 1:21-23
16 [a]Ps. 98:1; Is. 52:10; 63:5
17 [a]Eph. 6:14 [b]Is. 9:7; 37:32; Zech. 1:4
18 [1]Lit., *recompense* [2]Lit., *accordingly* [3]Lit., *repay* [a]Job 34:11; Is. 65:6, 7; 66:6; Jer. 17:10
19 [1]Lit., *narrow* [a]Is. 30:28; 66:12
20 [a]Rom. 11:26, 27 [b]Ezek. 18:30, 31; Acts 2:38, 39
21 [a]Jer. 31:31-44 [b]Is. 11:2; 32:15; 44:3

My words which I have put in your mouth, shall not depart from your mouth, nor from the mouth of your [1]offspring, nor from the mouth of your [1]offspring's offspring," says the LORD, "from now and forever."

CHAPTER 60

A Glorified Zion

"ARISE, shine; for your [a]light has
come,
And the [b]glory of the LORD has
risen upon you.
2"For behold, [a]darkness will cover the earth,
And deep darkness the peoples;
But the LORD will rise upon you,
And His [b]glory will appear
upon you.
3"And [a]nations will come to your
light,
And kings to the brightness of
your rising.

4"[a]Lift up your eyes round about,
and see;
They all gather together, they
come to you.
Your sons will come from afar,
And your daughters will be
[1]carried in the arms.
5"Then you will see and be [a]radi-
ant,
And your heart will [1]thrill and
rejoice;
Because the [b]abundance of the
sea will be turned to you,
The [c]wealth of the nations will
come to you.
6"A multitude of camels will cover you,
The young camels of Midian
and Ephah;
All those from Sheba will come;
They will bring gold and frankincense,
And will [a]bear good news of the
praises of the LORD.
7"All the flocks of [a]Kedar will be
gathered together to you,
The rams of Nebaioth will minister to you;
They will go up with acceptance on My [b]altar,
And I shall [1]glorify My [2]glori-
ous house.
8"[a]Who are these who fly like a
cloud,
And like the doves to their [1]lat-
tices?
9"Surely the coastlands will wait
for Me;
And the [a]ships of Tarshish *will
come* first,
To [b]bring your sons from afar,
Their silver and their gold with
them,
For the name of the LORD your
God,
And for the Holy One of Israel
because He has [1]glorified
you.

10"And foreigners will build up
your walls,
And their [a]kings will minister
to you;
For in My wrath I struck you,
And in My favor I have had
compassion on you.
11"And your [a]gates will be open
continually;
They will not be closed day or
night,
So that *men* may bring to you
the wealth of the nations,
With [b]their kings led in procession.
12"For the [a]nation and the kingdom which will not serve you
will perish,
And the nations will be utterly
ruined.
13"The glory of Lebanon will come
to you,
The juniper, the box tree, and
the cypress together,
To beautify the place of My
sanctuary;
And I shall make the [a]place of
My feet glorious.
14"And the [a]sons of those who afflicted you will come bowing
to you,
And all those who despised you
will bow themselves at the
soles of your feet;
And they will call you the [b]city
of the LORD,
The [c]Zion of the Holy One of
Israel.

15"Whereas you have been [a]for-
saken and hated
With no one passing through,
I will make you an everlasting
[b]pride,
A joy from generation to generation.
16"You will also suck the milk of
nations,
And will suck the breast of
kings;
Then you will know that I, the
LORD, am your [a]Savior,
And your [b]Redeemer, the
Mighty One of Jacob.
17"Instead of bronze I will bring
gold,
And instead of iron I will bring
silver,

21 [1]Lit., *seed*

1 [a]Is. 60:19, 20 [b]Is. 24:23; 35:2; 58:8

2 [a]Is. 58:10; Jer. 13:16; Col. 1:13 [b]Is. 4:5

3 [a]Is. 2:3; 45:14, 22-25; 49:23

4 [1]Lit., *nursed upon the side* [a]Is. 11:12; 49:18

5 [1]Lit., *tremble and be enlarged* [a]Ps. 34:5 [b]Is. 23:18; 24:14 [c]Is. 61:6

6 [a]Is. 42:10

7 [1]Or, *beautify* [2]Or, *beautiful* [a]Gen. 25:13 [b]Is. 19:19; 56:7

8 [1]Or, *dovecotes, windows* [a]Is. 49:21

9 [1]Lit., *beautified* [a]Ps. 48:7; Is. 2:16 [b]Is. 14:2; 43:6; 49:22; Gal. 3:26

10 [a]Is. 49:23

11 [a]Is. 26:2; 60:18; 62:10 [b]Ps. 149:8; Is. 24:21

12 [a]Is. 14:2; Zech. 14:17

13 [a]1 Chr. 28:2; Ps. 99:5; 132:7

14 [a]Is. 14:1, 2; 45:14, 23; 49:23 [b]Is. 1:26 [c]Heb. 12:22

15 [a]Is. 1:7-9; 6:11-13; Jer. 30:17 [b]Is. 4:2; 65:18

16 [a]Is. 19:2; 43:3, 11; 45:15, 21; 63:8 [b]Is. 59:20; 63:16

And instead of wood, bronze,
And instead of stones, iron.
And I will make peace your administrators,
And righteousness your overseers.
18 "[a]Violence will not be heard again in your land,
Nor [b]devastation or destruction within your borders;
But you will call your [c]walls salvation, and your [d]gates praise.
19 "No longer will you have the [a]sun for light by day,
Nor for brightness will the moon give you light;
But you will have the [b]LORD for an everlasting light,
And your [c]God for your [1]glory.
20 "Your [a]sun will set no more,
Neither will your moon wane;
For you will have the LORD for an everlasting light,
And the days of your [b]mourning will be finished.
21 "Then all your [a]people *will be* righteous;
They will [b]possess the land forever,
The branch of [1]My planting,
The work of My hands,
That I may be glorified.
22 "The [a]smallest one will become a [1]clan,
And the least one a mighty nation.
I, the LORD, will hasten it in its time."

CHAPTER 61

Exaltation of the Afflicted

THE [a]Spirit of the Lord [1]GOD is upon me,
Because the LORD has anointed me
To bring good news to the [2b]afflicted;
He has sent me to [c]bind up the brokenhearted,
To [d]proclaim liberty to captives,
And [3]freedom to prisoners;
2 To [a]proclaim the favorable year of the LORD,
And the [b]day of vengeance of our God;
To [c]comfort all who mourn,
3 To [a]grant those who mourn *in* Zion,
Giving them a garland instead of ashes,
The [b]oil of gladness instead of mourning,

18 [a]Is. 54:14 [b]Is. 51:19 [c]Is. 26:1 [d]Is. 60:11

19 [1]Or, *beauty* [a]Rev. 21:23; 22:5 [b]Is. 2:5; 9:2 [c]Is. 41:16; 45:25; Zech. 2:5

20 [a]Is. 30:26 [b]Is. 35:10; 65:19; Rev. 21:4

21 [1]Lit., *His* [a]Is. 45:24, 25; 52:1 [b]Ps. 37:11, 22; Is. 57:13; 61:7

22 [1]Or, *thousand* [a]Is. 6:13; 10:22; 51:2

1 [1]YHWH, usually rendered LORD [2]Or, *humble* [3]Lit., *opening to those who are bound* [a]Is. 11:2; 48:16; Luke 4:18, 19 [b]Is. 11:4; 28:19; 32:7 [c]Is. 57:15 [d]Is. 42:7; 49:9

2 [a]Is. 49:8; 60:10 [b]Is. 2:12; 13:6; 34:2, 8 [c]Is. 57:18; Jer. 31:13; Matt. 5:4

3 [1]Or, *terebinths* [a]Is. 60:20 [b]Ps. 23:5; 45:7; 104:15 [c]Is. 60:21; Jer. 17:7, 8

4 [a]Is. 49:8; 58:12; Ezek. 36:33; Amos 9:14

5 [1]Lit., *sons of the foreigner* [a]Is. 14:2; 60:10

6 [1]Or, *glory* [a]Is. 66:21 [b]Is. 56:6 [c]Is. 60:5, 11

7 [a]Ps. 16:11

8 [1]Or, *with iniquity* [a]Is. 5:16; 28:17; 30:18 [b]Gen. 17:7; Ps. 105:10; Is. 55:3; Jer. 32:40

10 [a]Is. 4:16; 12:1, 2; 25:9; 51:3 [b]Is. 49:4 [c]Is. 49:18; 52:1

The mantle of praise instead of a spirit of fainting.
So they will be called [1c]oaks of righteousness,
The planting of the LORD, that He may be glorified.

4 Then they will [a]rebuild the ancient ruins,
They will raise up the former devastations,
And they will repair the ruined cities,
The desolations of many generations.
5 And [a]strangers will stand and pasture your flocks,
And [1]foreigners will be your farmers and your vinedressers.
6 But you will be called the [a]priests of the LORD;
You will be spoken of *as* [b]ministers of our God.
You will eat the [c]wealth of nations,
And in their [1]riches you will boast.
7 Instead of your shame *you will have a* double *portion*,
And *instead of* humiliation they will shout for joy over their portion.
Therefore they will possess a double *portion* in their land,
[a]Everlasting joy will be theirs.
8 For I, the LORD, [a]love justice,
I hate robbery [1]in the burnt offering;
And I will faithfully give them their recompense,
And I will make an [b]everlasting covenant with them.
9 Then their offspring will be known among the nations,
And their descendants in the midst of the peoples.
All who see them will recognize them
Because they are the offspring *whom* the LORD has blessed.

10 I will [a]rejoice greatly in the LORD,
My soul will exult in [b]my God;
For He has [c]clothed me with garments of salvation,
He has wrapped me with a robe of righteousness,
As a bridegroom decks himself with a garland,
And as a bride adorns herself with her jewels.
11 For as the earth brings forth its sprouts,
And as a garden causes the things sown in it to spring up,

So the Lord [1]GOD will [a]cause [b]righteousness and praise
To spring up before all the nations.

CHAPTER 62

Zion's Glory and New Name

FOR Zion's sake I will not keep silent,
And for Jerusalem's sake I will not keep quiet,
Until her righteousness goes forth like brightness,
And her [a]salvation like a torch that is burning.
2 And the [a]nations will see your righteousness,
And all kings your glory;
And you will be called by a new [b]name,
Which the mouth of the LORD will designate.
3 You will also be a [a]crown of beauty in the hand of the LORD,
And a royal [1]diadem in the hand of your God.
4 It will no longer be said to you, "[1a]Forsaken,"
Nor to your land will it any longer be said, "[2]Desolate";
But you will be called, "[3]My delight is in her,"
And your land, "[4]Married";
For the [b]LORD delights in you,
And *to Him* your land will be married.
5 For *as* a young man marries a virgin,
So your sons will marry you;
And *as* the [1]bridegroom rejoices over the bride,
So your [a]God will rejoice over you.

6 On your walls, O Jerusalem, I have appointed [a]watchmen;
All day and all night they will never keep silent.
You who [b]remind the LORD, take no rest for yourselves;
7 And [a]give Him no rest until He establishes
And makes [b]Jerusalem a praise in the earth.
8 The LORD has sworn by His right hand and by His strong arm,
"I will [a]never again give your grain *as* food for your enemies;
Nor will [1]foreigners drink your new wine, for which you have labored."
9 But those who [a]garner it will eat it, and praise the LORD;
And those who gather it will drink it in the courts of My sanctuary.

10 Go through, [a]go through the gates;
Clear the way [1]for the people;
[b]Build up, build up the [c]highway;
Remove the stones, lift up a standard over the peoples.
11 Behold, the LORD has proclaimed to the [a]end of the earth,
[b]Say to the daughter of Zion, "Lo, your salvation comes;
[c]Behold His reward is with Him, and His recompense before Him."
12 And they will call them, "[a]The holy people,
The redeemed of the LORD";
And you will be called, "Sought out, a city [b]not forsaken."

CHAPTER 63

God's Vengeance on the Nations

WHO is this who comes from Edom,
With garments of [1]glowing colors from [a]Bozrah,
This One who is majestic in His apparel,
[2]Marching in the greatness of His strength?
"It is I who speak in righteousness, [b]mighty to save."
2 Why is Your apparel red,
And Your garments like the one who [a]treads in the wine press?
3 "I have trodden the wine trough alone,
And from the peoples there was no man with Me.
I also [a]trod them in My anger,
And [b]trampled them in My wrath;
And their [1]lifeblood is sprinkled on My garments,
And I [2]stained all My raiment.
4 "For the [a]day of vengeance was in My heart,
And My year of redemption has come.
5 "And I looked, and there was [a]no one to help,
And I was astonished and there was no one to uphold;
So My own arm brought salvation to Me;
And My wrath upheld Me.

11 [1]YHWH, usually rendered LORD [a]Is. 45:23, 24; 60:18, 21 [b]Ps. 72:3; 85:11

1 [a]Is. 46:13; 52:10

2 [a]Is. 60:3 [b]Is. 56:5; 62:4, 12; 65:15

3 [1]Lit., *turban* [a]Is. 28:5; Zech. 9:16; 1 Thess. 2:19

4 [1]I.e., Azubah [2]I.e., Shemamah [3]I.e., Hephzibah [4]I.e., Beulah [a]Is. 16:15, 18; 54:6, 7 [b]Jer. 32:41; Zeph. 3:17

5 [1]Lit., *exultation of the bridegroom* [a]Is. 65:19

6 [a]Is. 52:8; Jer. 6:17; Ezek. 3:17; 33:7 [b]Ps. 74:2; Jer. 14:21; Lam. 5:1, 20

7 [a]Matt. 15:21-28; Luke 18:1-8 [b]Is. 60:18; Jer. 33:9; Zeph. 3:19, 20

8 [1]Lit., *sons of foreigners* [a]Lev. 26:16; Deut. 28:31, 33; Judg. 6:3-6; Is. 1:7; Jer. 5:17

9 [a]Is. 65:13, 21-23

10 [1]Lit., *of* [a]Is. 26:1; 60:11, 18 [b]Is. 57:14 [c]Is. 11:16; 19:23; 35:8; 49:11

11 [a]Is. 42:10; 49:6 [b]Matt. 21:5; Zech. 9:9 [c]Is. 40:10

12 [a]Deut. 7:6; Is. 4:3; 1 Pet. 2:9 [b]Is. 41:17; 42:16; 62:4

1 [1]Or, *crimson* [2]Lit., *Inclining* [a]Is. 34:6; Jer. 49:13; Amos 1:12 [b]Zeph. 3:7

2 [a]Rev. 19:13, 15

3 [1]Lit., *juice* [2]Lit., *defiled* [a]Is. 22:5; 28:3 [b]Mic. 7:10

4 [a]Is. 34:8; 35:4; 61:2; Jer. 51:6

5 [a]Is. 59:16

6 "And I [a]trod down the peoples in My anger,
And made them drunk in My wrath,
And I [1]poured out their lifeblood on the earth."

God's Ancient Mercies Recalled

7 I shall make mention of the [a]lovingkindnesses of the LORD, the praises of the LORD,
According to all that the LORD has granted us,
And the great [b]goodness toward the house of Israel,
Which He has granted them according to His [c]compassion,
And according to the multitude of His lovingkindnesses.
8 For He said, "Surely, they are [a]My people,
Sons who will not deal falsely."
So He became their Savior.
9 In all their affliction [1a]He was afflicted,
And the [b]angel of His presence saved them;
In His [c]love and in His mercy He [d]redeemed them;
And He [e]lifted them and carried them all the days of old.
10 But they [a]rebelled
And grieved His [b]Holy Spirit;
Therefore, He turned Himself to become their enemy,
He fought against them.
11 Then [a]His people remembered the days of old, of Moses.
Where is [b]He who brought them up out of the sea with the [1]shepherds of His flock?
Where is He who [c]put His Holy Spirit in the midst of [2]them,
12 Who caused His [a]glorious arm to go at the right hand of Moses,
Who [b]divided the waters before them to make for Himself an everlasting name,
13 Who led them through the depths?
Like the horse in the wilderness, they did not [a]stumble;
14 As the cattle which go down into the valley,
The Spirit of the [a]LORD gave [1]them rest.
So didst Thou [b]lead Thy people,
To make for Thyself a glorious name.

"Thou Art Our Father"

15 [a]Look down from heaven, and see from Thy holy and glorious [b]habitation;
Where are Thy [c]zeal and Thy mighty deeds?
The [d]stirrings of Thy heart and Thy compassion are restrained toward me.
16 For Thou art our [a]Father, though [b]Abraham does not know us,
And Israel does not recognize us.
Thou, O LORD, art our Father,
Our [c]Redeemer from of old is Thy name.
17 Why, O LORD, dost Thou [a]cause us to stray from Thy ways,
And [b]harden our heart from fearing Thee?
Return for the sake of Thy servants, the tribes of Thy heritage.
18 Thy holy people possessed Thy sanctuary for a little while,
Our adversaries have [a]trodden *it* down.
19 We have become *like* those over whom Thou hast never ruled,
Like those who were not called by Thy name.

CHAPTER 64

Prayer for Mercy and Help

1 O THAT Thou wouldst rend the heavens *and* [a]come down,
That the mountains might [b]quake at Thy presence—
2 [1]As fire kindles the brushwood, *as* fire causes water to boil—
To make Thy name known to Thine adversaries,
That the [a]nations may tremble at Thy presence!
3 When Thou didst [a]awesome things which we did not expect,
Thou didst come down, the mountains quaked at Thy presence.
4 For from of old [a]they have not heard nor perceived by ear,
Neither has the eye seen a God besides Thee,
Who acts in behalf of the one who [b]waits for Him.
5 Thou dost [a]meet him who rejoices in [b]doing righteousness,
Who [c]remembers Thee in Thy ways.
Behold, Thou wast angry, for we sinned,
We continued in them a long time;
And shall we be saved?

63:6 [1]Lit., *brought down their juice to the earth* [a]Is. 22:5; 34:2; 65:12
7 [a]Ps. 25:6; 92:2; Is. 54:8, 10 [b]1 Kin. 8:66; Neh. 9:25, 35 [c]Ps. 51:1; 86:5, 15; Is. 54:7, 8; Eph. 2:4
8 [a]Ex. 6:7; Is. 3:15; 51:4
9 [1]Another reading is, *He was not an adversary.* [a]Judg. 10:16 [b]Ex. 23:20-23; 33:14, 15 [c]Deut. 7:7, 8 [d]Is. 43:1; 52:9 [e]Deut. 1:31; 32:10-12; Is. 46:3
10 [a]Ps. 78:40; 106:33; Acts 7:51; Eph. 4:30 [b]Ps. 51:11; Is. 63:11
11 [1]Some mss. read, *shepherd* [2]Lit., *him* [a]Ps. 106:44, 45 [b]Is. 51:9, 10 [c]Num. 11:17, 25, 29; Hag. 2:5
12 [a]Ex. 6:6; 15:16 [b]Ex. 14:21, 22; Is. 11:15; 51:10, 11
13 [a]Jer. 31:9
14 [1]Lit., *him* [a]Josh. 21:44; 23:1 [b]Deut. 32:12
15 [a]Deut. 26:15; Ps. 80:14 [b]Ps. 68:5; 123:1 [c]Is. 9:17; 26:11; 37:32; 42:13; 59:17 [d]Jer. 31:20; Hos. 11:8
16 [a]Is. 1:2; 64:8 [b]Is. 29:22; 41:8; 51:2 [c]Is. 41:14; 44:6; 60:16
17 [a]Is. 30:28; Ezek. 14:7-9 [b]Is. 29:13, 14
18 [a]Ps. 74:3-7; Is. 64:11
64:1 [1]Ch. 63:19b in Heb. [a]Ex. 19:18; Ps. 18:9; 144:5; Mic. 1:3, 4; Hab. 3:13 [b]Judg. 5:5; Ps. 68:8; Nah. 1:5
2 [1]Ch. 64:1 in Heb. [a]Ps. 99:1; Jer. 5:22; 33:9
3 [a]Ps. 65:5; 66:3, 5; 106:22
4 [a]1 Cor. 2:9 [b]Is. 25:9; 30:18; 40:31
5 [a]Ex. 20:24 [b]Is. 56:1 [c]Is. 26:13; 63:7

6 For all of us have become like one who is unclean,
And all our [a]righteous deeds are like a filthy garment;
And all of us [b]wither like a leaf,
And our iniquities, like the wind, take us away.
7 And there is [a]no one who calls on Thy name,
Who arouses himself to take hold of Thee;
For Thou hast [b]hidden Thy face from us,
And hast [1]delivered us into the power of our iniquities.

8 But now, O LORD, [a]Thou art our Father,
We are the [b]clay, and Thou our potter;
And all of us are the [c]work of Thy hand.
9 Do not be [a]angry beyond measure, O LORD,
[b]Neither remember iniquity forever;
Behold, look now, all of us are [c]Thy people.
10 Thy [a]holy cities have become a wilderness,
Zion has become a wilderness,
Jerusalem a desolation.
11 Our holy and beautiful [a]house,
Where our fathers praised Thee,
Has been burned *by* fire;
And all our precious things have become a ruin.
12 Wilt Thou restrain Thyself at these things, O LORD?
Wilt Thou keep silent and afflict us beyond measure?

CHAPTER 65

A Rebellious People

"I PERMITTED Myself to be sought by those who did not ask *for Me;*
I permitted Myself to be found by those who did not seek Me.
I said, 'Here am I, here am I,'
To a nation which did [a]not call on My name.
2 "[a]I have spread out My hands all day long to a [b]rebellious people,
Who walk *in* the way which is not good, [1]following their own [c]thoughts,
3 A people who continually [a]provoke Me to My face,
Offering sacrifices in gardens and burning incense on bricks;
4 Who sit among graves, and spend the night in secret places;
Who [a]eat swine's flesh,
And the broth of unclean meat is *in* their pots.
5 "Who say, '[a]Keep to yourself, do not come near me,
For I am holier than you!'
These are smoke in My [1]nostrils,
A fire that burns all the day.
6 "Behold, it is written before Me,
I will [a]not keep silent, but I will repay;
I will even repay into their bosom,
7 Both [1]their own [a]iniquities and the iniquities of their fathers together," says the LORD.
"Because they have [b]burned incense on the mountains,
And [c]scorned Me on the hills,
Therefore I will [d]measure their former work into their bosom."

8 Thus says the LORD,
"As the new wine is found in the cluster,
And one says, 'Do not destroy it, for there is [1]benefit in it',
So I will act on behalf of My servants
In order not to destroy [2]all of them.
9 "And I will bring forth offspring from Jacob,
And an [a]heir of My mountains from Judah;
Even My chosen ones shall inherit it,
And [b]My servants shall dwell there.
10 "And [a]Sharon shall be a pasture land for flocks,
And the valley of Achor a resting place for herds,
For My people who seek Me.
11 "But you who [a]forsake the LORD,
Who forget My [b]holy mountain,
Who set a table for [1]Fortune,
And who fill *cups* with mixed wine for [2]Destiny,
12 I will destine you for the sword,
And all of you shall bow down to the slaughter.
Because I called, but you did [a]not answer;
I spoke, but you did not hear.
And you did evil in My sight,
And chose that in which I did not delight."

13 Therefore, thus says the Lord [1]GOD,

6 [a]Is. 46:12; 48:1 [b]Ps. 90:5, 6; Is. 1:30
7 [1]Reading with the DSS and versions; M.T., *melted* [a]Is. 59:4; Ezek. 22:40 [b]Deut. 31:18; Is. 1:15; 54:8
8 [a]Is. 63:16 [b]Is. 20:16; 45:9 [c]Ps. 100:3; Is. 60:21
9 [a]Is. 57:17; 60:10 [b]Is. 43:25; Mic. 7:18 [c]Ps. 79:13; Is. 63:8
10 [a]Is. 48:2; 52:1
11 [a]2 Kin. 25:9; Ps. 74:5-7; Is. 63:18
1 [a]Hos. 1:10
2 [1]Lit., *after* [a]Rom. 10:21 [b]Is. 1:2, 23; 30:1, 9 [c]Ps. 81:11, 12; Is. 59:7; 66:18
3 [a]Job 1:11; 2:5; Is. 3:8
4 [a]Lev. 11:7; Is. 66:3, 17
5 [1]Lit., *nose* [a]Matt. 9:11; Luke 7:39; 18:9-12
6 [a]Ps. 50:3, 21; Is. 42:14; 64:12
7 [1]Lit., *your* [a]Is. 13:11; 22:14; 26:21; 30:13, 14 [b]Is. 57:7; Hos. 2:13 [c]Ezek. 20:27, 28 [d]Jer. 5:29; 13:25
8 [1]Lit., *blessing* [2]Lit., *the whole*
9 [a]Is. 49:8; 60:21; Amos 9:11-15 [b]Is. 32:18
10 [a]Is. 33:9; 35:2
11 [1]Heb., *Gad* [2]Heb., *Meni* [a]Deut. 29:24, 25; Is. 1:4, 28 [b]Is. 2:2, 3; 66:20
12 [a]2 Chr. 36:15, 16; Prov. 1:24; Is. 41:28; 50:2; 66:4; Jer. 7:13
13 [1]YHWH, usually rendered LORD

"Behold, My servants shall eat,
but you shall be hungry.
Behold, My servants shall drink, but you shall be [a]thirsty.
Behold, My servants shall rejoice, but you shall be put to shame.
14"Behold, My servants shall [a]shout joyfully with a glad heart,
But you shall [b]cry out with a [1]heavy heart,
And you shall wail with a broken spirit.
15"And you will leave your name for a [a]curse to My chosen ones,
And the Lord [1]GOD will slay you.
But [2]My servants will be called by another name.
16"Because he who [1]is blessed in the earth
Shall [1]be blessed by the [a]God of truth;
And he who swears in the earth
Shall [b]swear by the God of truth;
Because the former troubles are forgotten,
And because they are hidden from My sight!

New Heavens and a New Earth

17"For behold, I create [a]new heavens and a new earth;
And the [b]former things shall not be remembered or come to [1]mind.
18"But be [a]glad and rejoice forever in what I create;
For behold, I create Jerusalem *for* rejoicing,
And her people *for* gladness.
19"I will also [a]rejoice in Jerusalem, and be glad in My people;
And there will no longer be heard in her
The voice of weeping and the sound of crying.
20"No longer will there be *in it* an infant *who lives but a few* days,
Or an old man who does [a]not [1]live out his days;
For the youth will die at the age of one hundred
And the [2b]one who does not reach the age of one hundred
Shall be *thought* accursed.
21"And they shall [a]build houses and inhabit *them;*
They shall also [b]plant vineyards and eat their fruit.
22"They shall not build, and [a]another inhabit,
They shall not plant, and another eat;
For [b]as the [1]lifetime of a tree, *so shall be* the days of My people,
And My chosen ones shall [c]wear out the work of their hands.
23"They shall [a]not labor in vain,
Or bear *children* for calamity;
For they are the [1b]offspring of those blessed by the LORD,
And their descendants with them.
24"It will also come to pass that
before they call, I will [a]answer; and
while they are still speaking, I will
hear.
25"The [a]wolf and the lamb shall
graze together, and the lion shall eat
straw like the ox; and [b]dust shall be
the serpent's food. They shall [c]do no
evil or harm in all My holy mountain," says the LORD.

CHAPTER 66

Heaven Is God's Throne

THUS says the LORD,
"[a]Heaven is My throne, and the earth is My footstool.
Where then is a [b]house you could build for Me?
And where is a place that [1]I may rest?
2"For [a]My hand made all these things,
Thus all these things came into being," declares the LORD.
"But to this one I will look,
To him who is humble and [b]contrite of spirit, and who trembles at My word.

Hypocrisy Rebuked

3"*But* he who kills an ox is *like* one who slays a man;
He who sacrifices a lamb is *like* the one who breaks a dog's neck;
He who offers a grain offering *is like one who offers* swine's blood;
He who [1a]burns incense is *like* the one who blesses an idol.
As they have chosen their [b]own ways,
And their soul delights in their abominations,
4 So I will [a]choose their [1]punishments,
And I will [b]bring on them what they dread.

13 [a]Is. 5:13
14 [1]Lit., *pain of* [a]Ps. 66:4; Is. 51:11; James 5:13 [b]Is. 13:6; Matt. 8:12
15 [1]YHWH, usually rendered LORD [2]So with Gk.; Heb., *He will call His servants* [a]Jer. 24:9; 25:18; Zech. 8:13
16 [1]Or, *bless(es) himself* [a]Ex. 34:6; Ps. 31:5 [b]Is. 19:18; 45:23
17 [1]Lit., *heart* [a]Is. 66:22; 2 Pet. 3:13 [b]Is. 43:18; Jer. 3:16
18 [a]Ps. 98; Is. 12:1, 2; 25:9; 35:10; 41:16; 51:3; 61:10
19 [a]Is. 62:4, 5; Jer. 32:41
20 [1]Lit., *fill out* [2]Lit., *one who misses the mark* [a]Deut. 4:40; Job 5:26; Ps. 34:12 [b]Eccles. 8:12, 13; Is. 3:11; 22:14
21 [a]Is. 32:18; Amos 9:14 [b]Is. 30:23; 37:30; Jer. 31:5
22 [1]Lit., *days* [a]Is. 62:8, 9 [b]Ps. 92:12-14 [c]Deut. 32:46, 47; Ps. 21:4; 91:16
23 [1]Lit., *seed* [a]Deut. 28:3-12; Is. 55:2 [b]Is. 61:9; Jer. 32:38, 39; Acts 2:39
24 [a]Ps. 91:15; Is. 55:6; 58:9; Dan. 9:20-23; 10:12
25 [a]Is. 11:6 [b]Gen. 3:14; Mic. 7:17 [c]Is. 11:9; Mic. 4:3
1 [1]Lit., *is My resting place?* [a]1 Kin. 8:27; Ps. 11:4; Matt. 5:34, 35 [b]2 Sam. 7:5-7; Jer. 7:4; John 4:20, 21; Acts 7:48-50
2 [a]Is. 40:26 [b]Ps. 34:18; Is. 57:15; Matt. 5:3, 4; Luke 18:13, 14
3 [1]Lit., *offers a memorial of incense* [a]Lev. 2:2; Is. 1:13 [b]Is. 57:17; 65:2
4 [1]Lit., *ill treatments* [a]Prov. 1:31, 32; Is. 65:7 [b]Prov. 10:24

Because I called, but [c]no one answered;
I spoke, but they did not listen.
And they did [d]evil in My sight,
And chose that in which I did not delight."
5 Hear the word of the LORD, you who tremble at His word:
"Your brothers who [a]hate you, who [b]exclude you for My name's sake,
Have said, 'Let the LORD be glorified, that we may see your joy.'
But [c]they will be put to shame.
6"A voice of uproar from the city, a voice from the temple,
The voice of the LORD who is [a]rendering recompense to His enemies.

7"Before she travailed, she brought forth;
Before her pain came, she gave birth to a boy.
8"Who has heard such a thing? Who has seen such things?
Can a land be [1]born in one day?
Can a nation be brought forth all at once?
As soon as Zion travailed, she also brought forth her sons.
9"Shall I bring to the point of birth, and [a]not give delivery?" says the LORD.
"Or shall I who gives delivery shut *the womb?*" says your God.

Joy in Jerusalem's Future

10"Be [a]joyful with Jerusalem and rejoice for her, all you who [b]love her;
Be exceedingly [c]glad with her, all you who mourn over her,
11 That you may nurse and [a]be satisfied with her comforting breasts,
That you may suck and be delighted with her [b]bountiful bosom."
12 For thus says the LORD, "Behold, I extend [a]peace to her like a river,
And the [b]glory of the nations like an overflowing stream;
And you shall [1]be nursed, you shall be [c]carried on the [2]hip and fondled on the knees.
13"As one whom his mother comforts, so I will comfort you;
And you shall be comforted in Jerusalem."
14 Then you shall [a]see *this,* and your [b]heart shall be glad,

4 [c]Prov. 1:24; Is. 65:12; Jer. 7:13 [d]2 Kin. 21:2, 6; Is. 59:7; 65:12; Jer. 7:30

5 [a]Ps. 38:20; Is. 60:15 [b]Matt. 5:10-12; 10:22; John 9:34; 15:18-20 [c]Luke 13:17

6 [a]Is. 59:18; 65:6; Joel 3:7

8 [1]Lit., *travailed with*

9 [a]Is. 37:3

10 [a]Deut. 32:43; Is. 65:18; Rom. 15:10 [b]Ps. 26:8; 122:6 [c]Ps. 137:6

11 [a]Is. 49:23; 60:16; Joel 3:18 [b]Is. 60:1, 2; 62:2

12 [1]Lit., *nurse* [2]Lit., *side* [a]Ps. 72:3, 7; Is. 48:18 [b]Is. 60:5; 61:6 [c]Is. 60:4

14 [a]Is. 33:20 [b]Zech. 10:7 [c]Prov. 3:8; Is. 58:11 [d]Ezra 7:9; 8:31

16 [a]Is. 30:30; Ezek. 38:22 [b]Is. 65:12; Ezek. 38:21

17 [1]Lit., *After* [a]Is. 1:29; 65:3 [b]Lev. 11:7; Is. 65:4

18 [1]So with Gk.; Heb. omits *know* [2]Lit., *it is coming* [a]Is. 45:22-25; Jer. 3:17

19 [1]So with Gk.; Heb., *Pul* [2]So with Gk.; Heb., *those who draw the bow* [3]I.e., Greece [a]Is. 11:10, 12; 49:22; 62:10 [b]1 Chr. 16:24; Is. 42:12

20 [a]Is. 43:6; 49:22; 60:4 [b]Is. 2:2, 3; 11:9; 56:7; 65:11, 25 [c]Is. 52:11

21 [a]Is. 61:6; 1 Pet. 2:5, 9

22 [a]Is. 65:17; Heb. 12:26, 27; 2 Pet. 3:13; Rev. 21:1 [b]Is. 61:8, 9; 65:22, 23; John 10:27-29; 1 Pet. 1:4, 5

23 [1]Lit., *flesh* [a]Is. 19:21, 23; 27:13; 49:7

And your [c]bones shall flourish like the new grass;
And the [d]hand of the LORD shall be made known to His servants,
But He shall be indignant toward His enemies.
15 For behold, the LORD will come in fire
And His chariots like the whirlwind,
To render His anger with fury,
And His rebuke with flames of fire.
16 For the LORD will execute judgment by [a]fire
And by His [b]sword on all flesh,
And those slain by the LORD will be many.
17"Those who sanctify and purify themselves *to go* to the [a]gardens,
[1]Following one in the center,
Who eat [b]swine's flesh, detestable things, and mice,
Shall come to an end altogether," declares the LORD.
18"For I [1]know their works and
their thoughts; [2]the time is coming
to [a]gather all nations and tongues.
And they shall come and see My glory.
19"And I will set a [a]sign among
them and will send survivors from
them to the nations: Tarshish, [1]Put,
Lud, [2]Meshech, Rosh, Tubal, and
[3]Javan, to the distant coastlands
that have neither heard My fame
nor seen My glory. And they will
[b]declare My glory among the nations.
20"Then they shall [a]bring all your
brethren from all the nations as a
grain offering to the LORD, on
horses, in chariots, in litters, on
mules, and on camels, to My [b]holy
mountain Jerusalem," says the
LORD, "just as the sons of Israel
bring their grain offering in a [c]clean
vessel to the house of the LORD.
21"I will also take some of them for
[a]priests *and* for Levites," says the
LORD.
22"For just as the [a]new heavens and the new earth
Which I make will endure before Me," declares the LORD,
"So your [b]offspring and your name will endure.
23"And it shall be from new moon to new moon
And from sabbath to sabbath,
All [1]mankind will come to [a]bow down before Me," says the LORD.

24"Then they shall go forth and
look
On the corpses of the men
Who have [1]transgressed
against Me.
For their worm shall not die,
[a]And their fire shall not be
quenched;
And they shall be an [b]abhor-
rence to all [2]mankind."

24 [1]Or, *rebelled* [2]Lit., *flesh* [a]Is. 1:31; Matt. 3:12 [b]Dan. 12:2

THE BOOK OF JEREMIAH

Jeremiah's Call and Commission

THE words of [a]Jeremiah, the son
of Hilkiah, of the priests who were
in Anathoth in the land of Benjamin,
2 to whom the word of the LORD
came in the days of [a]Josiah, the son
of Amon, king of Judah, in the thirteenth year of his reign.
3 It came also in the days of [a]Je-
hoiakim, the son of Josiah, king of
Judah, until the end of the eleventh
year of [b]Zedekiah, the son of Josiah,
king of Judah, until the exile of Jerusalem in the fifth month.
4 Now the word of the LORD
came to me saying,
5"Before I [a]formed you in the
womb I knew you,
And [b]before you were born I
consecrated you;
I have [c]appointed you a prophet
to the nations."
6 Then [a]I said, "Alas, Lord [1]GOD!
Behold, I do not know how to
speak,
Because [b]I am a youth."
7 But the LORD said to me,
"Do not say, 'I am a youth,'
[a]Because everywhere I send
you, you shall go,
And all that I command you,
you shall speak.
8"[a]Do not be afraid of them,
For I am with you to deliver
you," declares the LORD.
9 Then the LORD stretched out
His hand and [a]touched my mouth,
and the LORD said to me,
"Behold, I have [b]put My words
in your mouth.
10"See, I have appointed you this
day over the nations and
over the kingdoms,
[a]To pluck up and to break
down,
To destroy and to overthrow,
[b]To build and to plant."

The Almond Rod and Boiling Pot

11 And the word of the LORD came
to me saying, "What do you see,
[a]Jeremiah?" And I said, "I see a rod
of an [1]almond tree."
12 Then the LORD said to me, "You
have seen well, for [a]I am [1]watching
over My word to perform it."
13 And the word of the LORD came
to me a second time saying, "[a]What
do you see?" And I said, "I see a
boiling [b]pot, facing away from the
north."
14 Then the LORD said to me,
"[a]Out of the north the evil [1]will
break forth on all the inhabitants of
the land.
15"For, behold, I am calling [a]all the
families of the kingdoms of the
north," declares the LORD; "and
they will come, and they will [b]set
each one his throne at the entrance
of the gates of Jerusalem, and
against all its walls round about,
and against all the cities of Judah.
16"And I will [1]pronounce My judgments on them concerning all their
wickedness, whereby they have forsaken Me and have [2a]offered sacrifices to other gods, and worshiped
the [b]works of their own hands.
17"Now, [a]gird up your loins, and
arise, and speak to them all which I
command you. [b]Do not be dismayed
before them, lest I dismay you before them.
18"Now behold, I have made you
today as a fortified city, and as a
pillar of iron and as walls of bronze
against the whole land, to the kings
of Judah, to its princes, to its priests
and to the people of the land.
19"And they will fight against you,
but they will not overcome you, for
[a]I am with you to deliver you," declares the LORD.

CHAPTER 2

Judah's Apostasy

NOW the word of the LORD came
to me saying,
2"Go and [a]proclaim in the ears of
Jerusalem, saying, 'Thus says the
LORD,
"I remember concerning you the
[1b]devotion of your youth,
The love of your betrothals,
Your following after Me in the
wilderness,
Through a land not sown.

1 [a]2 Chr. 35:25; 36:12, 21, 22; Ezra 1:1; Dan. 9:2; Matt. 2:17; 16:14; 27:9
2 [a]1 Kin. 13:2; 2 Kin. 21:24; Jer. 3:6; 36:2
3 [a]2 Kin. 23:34; 1 Chr. 3:15; Jer. 25:1 [b]2 Kin. 24:17; 1 Chr. 3:15; Jer. 39:2
5 [a]Ps. 139:15, 16 [b]Is. 49:1, 5 [c]Jer. 1:10; 25:15-26
6 [1]YHWH, usually rendered LORD [a]Ex. 4:10 [b]1 Kin. 3:7
7 [a]Ezek. 2:3, 4
8 [a]Ezek. 2:6
9 [a]Mark 7:33-35 [b]Ex. 4:11-16; Deut. 18:18
10 [a]Jer. 18:7-10; Ezek. 32:18 [b]Is. 44:26-28; Jer. 24:6; 31:28, 40
11 [1]Heb., *shaqed* [a]Jer. 24:3; Amos 7:8
12 [1]Heb., *shoqed* [a]Deut. 32:35; Jer. 31:28
13 [a]Zech. 4:2 [b]Ezek. 11:3, 7
14 [1]Lit., *will be opened* [a]Is. 41:25; Jer. 4:6; 10:22
15 [a]Jer. 25:9 [b]Is. 22:7; Jer. 39:3
16 [1]Lit., *speak* [2]Or, *burned incense* [a]Jer. 7:9; 19:4; 44:17 [b]Is. 2:8; 37:19; Jer. 10:3-5
17 [a]1 Kin. 18:46; Job 38:3 [b]Ezek. 2:6; 3:16-18
19 [a]Jer. 1:8; 20:11
2 [1]Or, *lovingkindness* [a]Is. 58:1; Jer. 7:2; 11:6 [b]Ezek. 16:8

3"Israel was [a]holy to the LORD,
The first of His harvest;
[b]All who ate of it became guilty;
Evil came upon them," declares the LORD.' "
4 Hear the word of the LORD, O
house of Jacob, and all the families
of the house of Israel.
5 Thus says the LORD,
"[a]What injustice did your fathers find in Me,
That they went far from Me
And walked after [b]emptiness and became empty?
6"And they did not say, 'Where is the LORD
Who brought us up out of the land of Egypt,
Who [a]led us through the wilderness,
Through a land of deserts and of pits,
Through a land of drought and of [1]deep darkness,
Through a land that no one crossed
And where no man dwelt?'
7"And I brought you into the [a]fruitful land,
To eat its fruit and its good things,
But you came and [b]defiled My land,
And My inheritance you made an abomination.
8"The [a]priests did not say, 'Where is the LORD?'
And those who handle the law [b]did not know Me;
The [1]rulers also transgressed against Me,
And the [c]prophets prophesied by Baal
And walked after things that [d]did not profit.

9"Therefore I will yet [a]contend with you," declares the LORD,
"And with your sons' sons I will contend.
10"For [a]cross to the coastlands of [1]Kittim and see,
And send to [b]Kedar and observe closely,
And see if there has been such *a thing* as this!
11"Has a nation changed gods,
[a]When they were not gods?
But My people have [b]changed their glory
For that which does not profit.
12"Be appalled, O [a]heavens, at this,
And shudder, be very desolate," declares the LORD.
13"For My people have committed two evils:
They have forsaken Me,
The [a]fountain of living waters,
To hew for themselves cisterns,
Broken cisterns,
That can hold no water.

14"Is Israel a slave? Or is he a homeborn servant?
Why has he become a prey?
15"The young [a]lions have roared at him,
They have [1]roared loudly.
And they have [b]made his land a waste;
His cities have been destroyed, without inhabitant.
16"Also the [1]men of [a]Memphis and Tahpanhes
Have [2]shaved the [b]crown of your head.
17"Have you not [a]done this to yourself,
By your forsaking the LORD your God,
When He [a]led you in the way?
18"But now what are you doing on the road to Egypt,
To drink the waters of the [1]Nile?
Or what are you doing on the road to Assyria,
To drink the waters of the [2]Euphrates?
19"[a]Your own wickedness will correct you,
And your [b]apostasies will reprove you;
Know therefore and see that it is evil and [c]bitter
For you to forsake the LORD your God,
And [d]the dread of Me is not in you," declares the Lord [1]GOD of hosts.

20"For long ago [1a]I broke your yoke
And tore off your bonds;
But you said, 'I will not serve!'
For on every [b]high hill
And under every green tree
You have lain down as a harlot.
21"Yet I [a]planted you a choice vine,
A completely faithful seed.
How then have you turned yourself before Me
Into the [b]degenerate shoots of a foreign vine?
22"Although you [a]wash yourself with lye
And [1]use much soap,
The stain of your iniquity is before Me," declares the Lord [2]GOD.

3 [a]Ex. 19:5, 6; Deut. 7:6; 14:2 [b]Is. 41:11; Jer. 30:16; 50:7
5 [a]Is. 5:4; Mic. 6:3 [b]2 Kin. 17:15; Jer. 8:19
6 [1]Or, *shadow of death* [a]Deut. 8:15; 32:10
7 [a]Deut. 8:7-9; 11:10-12 [b]Ps. 106:38; Jer. 3:2; 16:18
8 [1]Lit., *shepherds* [a]Jer. 10:21 [b]Jer. 4:22; Mal. 2:6, 7 [c]Jer. 23:13 [d]Jer. 16:19; Hab. 2:18
9 [a]Jer. 2:35; Ezek. 20:35, 36
10 [1]I.e., Cyprus and other islands [a]Is. 23:12 [b]Ps. 120:5; Is. 21:16; Jer. 49:28
11 [a]Is. 37:19; Jer. 5:7; 16:20 [b]Ps. 106:20; Rom. 1:23
12 [a]Is. 1:2; Jer. 4:23
13 [a]Ps. 36:9; Jer. 17:13
15 [1]Lit., *given their voice* [a]Jer. 50:17 [b]Jer. 4:7
16 [1]Or, *sons* [2]Lit., *grazed* [a]Is. 19:13; Jer. 44:1; Hos. 9:6 [b]Deut. 33:20; Jer. 48:45
17 [a]Deut. 32:10
18 [1]Heb., *Shihor* [2]Lit., *the River*
19 [1]YHWH, usually rendered LORD [a]Is. 3:9; Jer. 4:18; Hos. 5:5 [b]Jer. 3:6, 8, 11, 14; Hos. 11:7 [c]Job 20:11-16; Amos 8:10 [d]Ps. 36:1; Jer. 5:24
20 [1]Or, *you* [a]Lev. 26:13 [b]Deut. 12:2; Is. 57:5, 7; Jer. 3:2, 6; 17:2
21 [a]Ex. 15:17; Ps. 44:2; 80:8; Is. 5:2 [b]Is. 5:4
22 [1]Lit., *cause to be great to you* [2]YHWH, usually rendered LORD [a]Jer. 4:14

23“[a]How can you say, ‘I am not defiled,
I have not gone after the [b]Baals’?
Look at your way in the [c]valley!
Know what you have done!
You are a swift young camel [d]entangling her ways,
24 A [a]wild donkey accustomed to the wilderness,
That sniffs the wind in her passion.
In *the time of* her [1]heat who can turn her away?
All who seek her will not become weary;
In her month they will find her.
25“Keep your feet from being unshod
And your throat from thirst;
But you said, ‘[a]It is [1]hopeless!
No! For I have [b]loved strangers,
And after them I will walk.’

26“As the [a]thief is shamed when he is discovered,
So the house of Israel is shamed;
They, their kings, their princes,
And their priests, and their prophets,
27 Who say to a tree, ‘You are my father,’
And to a stone, ‘You gave me birth.’
For they have turned *their* [a]back to Me,
And not *their* face;
But in the [b]time of their [1]trouble they will say,
‘Arise and save us.’
28“But where are your [a]gods
Which you made for yourself?
Let them arise, if they can [b]save you
In the time of your [1]trouble;
For [c]*according to* the number of your cities
Are your gods, O Judah.

29“Why do you contend with Me?
You have [a]all transgressed against Me,” declares the LORD.
30“[a]In vain I have struck your sons;
They accepted no chastening.
Your [b]sword has devoured your prophets
Like a destroying lion.
31“O generation, heed the word of the LORD.
Have I been a wilderness to Israel,
Or a land of thick [a]darkness?
Why do My people say, ‘[b]We *are free to* roam;
We will come no more to Thee’?
32“Can a virgin forget her ornaments,
Or a bride her attire?
Yet My people have [a]forgotten Me
Days without number.
33“How well you prepare your way
To seek love!
Therefore even [1]the wicked women
You have taught your ways.
34“Also on your skirts is found
The [a]lifeblood of the innocent poor;
You did not find them [b]breaking in.
But in spite of all these things,
35 Yet you said, ‘I am innocent;
Surely His anger is turned away from me.’
Behold, I will [a]enter into judgment with you
Because you [b]say, ‘I have not sinned.’
36“Why do you [a]go around so much
Changing your way?
Also, you shall be put to shame by Egypt
As you were put to shame by [b]Assyria.
37“From this *place* also you shall go out
With [a]your hands on your head;
For the LORD has rejected those in whom you trust,
And you shall not prosper with them.”

CHAPTER 3

The Polluted Land

GOD [1]says, “[a]If a husband divorces his wife,
And she goes from him,
And belongs to another man,
Will he still return to her?
Will not that land be completely [2]polluted?
But you [b]are a harlot *with* many [3]lovers;
Yet you [c]turn to Me,” declares the LORD.
2“Lift up your eyes to the [a]bare heights and see;
Where have you not been violated?
By the roads you have [b]sat for them
Like an Arab in the desert,
And you have [c]polluted a land
With your harlotry and with your wickedness.

23 [a]Prov. 30:12 [b]Jer. 9:14 [c]Jer. 7:31 [d]Jer. 2:33, 36; 31:22
24 [1]Lit., *occasion* [a]Jer. 14:6
25 [1]Or, *desperate* [a]Jer. 18:12 [b]Deut. 32:16; Jer. 14:10
26 [a]Jer. 48:27
27 [1]Or, *evil* [a]Jer. 18:17; 32:33 [b]Is. 26:16; Jer. 22:23
28 [1]Or, *evil* [a]Deut. 32:37; Is. 45:20; Jer. 1:16 [b]Jer. 11:12, 13 [c]2 Kin. 17:30, 31; Jer. 11:13
29 [a]Jer. 5:1; 6:13; Dan. 9:11
30 [a]Is. 1:5; Jer. 5:3; 7:28 [b]Neh. 9:26; Jer. 26:20-24
31 [a]Is. 45:19 [b]Deut. 32:15; Jer. 2:20, 25
32 [a]Is. 17:10; Jer. 3:21; 13:25; Hos. 8:14
33 [1]Or, *in wickedness*
34 [a]2 Kin. 21:16; 24:4; Jer. 7:6; 19:4 [b]Ex. 22:2
35 [a]Jer. 25:31 [b]Prov. 28:13; 1 John 1:8, 10
36 [a]Jer. 2:23; Hos. 12:1 [b]2 Chr. 28:16, 20, 21
37 [a]2 Sam. 13:19; Jer. 14:3, 4
1 [1]Heb., *saying* [2]Or, *alienated* [3]Lit., *companions* [a]Deut. 24:1-4 [b]Jer. 2:20; Ezek. 16:26, 28, 29 [c]Jer. 4:1; Zech. 1:3
2 [a]Deut. 12:2; Jer. 2:20 [b]Ezek. 16:25 [c]Jer. 2:7

3"Therefore the [a]showers have
been withheld,
And there has been no spring
rain.
Yet you had a harlot's forehead;
You refused to be ashamed.
4"Have you not just now called to
Me,
'[a]My Father, Thou art the
[1b]friend of my youth?
5 '[a]Will He be angry forever?
Will He [1]be indignant to the
end?'
Behold, you have spoken
And have done evil things,
And you have [2]had your way."

Faithless Israel

6 Then the LORD said to me in the days of Josiah the king, "Have you seen what faithless Israel did? She [a]went up on every high hill and under every green tree, and she was a harlot there.
7"And I [1]thought, 'After she has done all these things, she will return to Me'; but she did not return, and her [a]treacherous sister Judah saw it.
8"And I saw that for all the adulteries of faithless Israel, I had sent her away and [a]given her a writ of divorce, yet her [b]treacherous sister Judah did not fear; but she went and was a harlot also.
9"And it came about because of the lightness of her harlotry, that she polluted the [a]land and committed adultery with [b]stones and trees.
10"And yet in spite of all this her treacherous sister Judah did not return to Me with all her heart, but rather in [a]deception," declares the LORD.

God Invites Repentance

11 And the LORD said to me, "[a]Faithless Israel has proved herself more righteous than treacherous Judah.
12"Go, and proclaim these words toward the north and say,
'[a]Return, faithless Israel,' de-
clares the LORD;
'[b]I will not [1]look upon you in anger.
For I am [c]gracious,' declares
the LORD;
'I will not be angry forever.
13 'Only [1a]acknowledge your iniquity,
That you have transgressed
against the LORD your God
And have [b]scattered your [2]fa-
vors to the strangers [c]under
every green tree,
And you have not obeyed My
voice,' declares the LORD.
14 'Return, O faithless sons,' declares the LORD;
'For I am a [a]master to you,
And I will take you one from a
city and two from a family,
And I will bring you to Zion.'
15"Then I will give you [a]shepherds after My own heart, who will [b]feed you on knowledge and understanding.
16"And it shall be in those days when you are multiplied and increased in the land," declares the LORD, "they shall [a]say no more, 'The ark of the covenant of the LORD.' And it shall not come to mind, nor shall they remember it, nor shall they miss *it*, nor shall it be made again.
17"At that time they shall call Jerusalem 'The [a]Throne of the LORD,' and [b]all the nations will be gathered to it, for the [c]name of the LORD in Jerusalem; [d]nor shall they walk any more after the stubbornness of their evil heart.
18"[a]In those days the house of Judah will walk with the house of Israel, and they will come together [b]from the land of the north to the land that I [c]gave your fathers as an inheritance.
19"Then I said,
'How I would set you among
[1]My sons,
And give you a pleasant land,
The most [a]beautiful inheritance
of the nations!'
And I said, 'You shall call Me,
[b]My Father,
And not turn away from following Me.'
20"Surely, as a woman treacherously departs from her [1]lov-
er,
So you have [a]dealt treacherously with Me,
O house of Israel," declares the
LORD.

21 A voice is heard on the [a]bare
heights,
The weeping *and* the supplications of the sons of Israel;
Because they have perverted
their way,
They have [b]forgotten the LORD
their God.
22"Return, O faithless sons,
[a]I will heal your faithlessness."
"Behold, we come to Thee;
For Thou art the LORD our God.
23"Surely, [a]the hills are a deception,
A tumult *on* the mountains.
Surely, in the [b]LORD our God
Is the salvation of Israel.

3 [a]Lev. 26:19; Jer. 14:3-6
4 [1]Lit., *leader* [a]Jer. 3:19; 31:9 [b]Ps. 71:17
5 [1]Lit., *keep it* [2]Lit., *been able* [a]Ps. 103:9; Is. 57:16; Jer. 3:12
6 [a]Jer. 17:2; Ezek. 23:4-10
7 [1]Lit., *said* [a]Jer. 3:11; Ezek. 16:47
8 [a]Deut. 24:1, 3; Is. 50:1 [b]Ezek. 16:46, 47
9 [a]Jer. 2:7; 3:2 [b]Is. 57:6; Jer. 2:27; 10:8
10 [a]Jer. 12:2; Hos. 7:14
11 [a]Ezek. 16:51, 52; 23:11
12 [1]Heb., *cause My countenance to fall* [a]Jer. 3:14, 22 [b]Jer. 3:5 [c]Ps. 86:15; Jer. 12:15; 31:20; 33:26
13 [1]Lit., *know* [2]Lit., *ways* [a]Deut. 30:1-3; Jer. 3:25; 14:20 [b]Jer. 2:20, 25; 3:2, 6 [c]Deut. 12:2
14 [a]Jer. 31:32; Hos. 2:19
15 [a]Jer. 23:4; 31:10; 50:19; Ezek. 34:23 [b]Acts 20:28
16 [a]Is. 65:17
17 [a]Jer. 17:12; Ezek. 43:7 [b]Jer. 3:19; 4:2; 12:15, 16; 16:19 [c]Is. 60:9 [d]Jer. 11:8
18 [a]Jer. 50:4, 5; Hos. 1:11 [b]Jer. 16:15; 31:8 [c]Amos 9:15
19 [1]Lit., *the* [a]Ps. 16:6 [b]Is. 63:16; Jer. 3:4
20 [1]Or, *companion* [a]Is. 48:8
21 [a]Is. 15:2; Jer. 3:2; 7:29 [b]Is. 17:10; Jer. 2:32; 13:25
22 [a]Jer. 30:17; 33:6; Hos. 6:1; 14:4
23 [a]Jer. 17:2 [b]Ps. 3:8; Jer. 17:14; 31:7

24 "But the shameful thing has consumed the labor of our fathers since
our youth, their flocks and their
herds, their sons and their daughters.
25 "Let us lie down in our shame,
and let our humiliation cover us; for
we have [a]sinned against the LORD
our God, we and our fathers, [b]since
our youth even to this day. And we
have not obeyed the voice of the
LORD our God."

CHAPTER 4

Judah Threatened with Invasion

"[a]IF you will return, O Israel," declares the LORD,
"*Then* you should return to Me.
And [b]if you will put away your detested things from My presence,
And will not waver,
2 And you will [a]swear, 'As the LORD lives,'
In truth, in justice, and in righteousness;
Then the [b]nations will bless themselves in Him,
And [c]in Him they will glory."

3 For thus says the LORD to the
men of Judah and to Jerusalem,
"[1][a]Break up your fallow ground,
And do not sow among thorns.
4 "[a]Circumcise yourselves to the LORD
And remove the foreskins of your heart,
Men of Judah and inhabitants of Jerusalem,
Lest My [b]wrath go forth like fire
And burn with [c]none to quench it,
Because of the evil of your deeds."

5 Declare in Judah and proclaim in Jerusalem, and say,
"[a]Blow the trumpet in the land;
Cry aloud and say,
'[b]Assemble yourselves, and let us go
Into the fortified cities.'
6 "Lift up a [a]standard toward Zion!
Seek refuge, do not stand *still,*
For I am bringing [b]evil from the north,
And great destruction.
7 "A [a]lion has gone up from his thicket,
And a [b]destroyer of nations has set out;
He has gone out from his place
To [c]make your land a waste.
Your cities will be ruins
Without inhabitant.
8 "For this, [a]put on sackcloth,
Lament and wail;
For the [b]fierce anger of the LORD
Has not turned back from us."
9 "And it shall come about in that
day," declares the LORD, "that the
[a]heart of the king and the heart of
the princes will fail; and the priests
will be appalled, and the [b]prophets
will be astounded."
10 Then I said, "Ah, Lord [1]GOD!
Surely Thou hast utterly [a]deceived
this people and Jerusalem, saying,
'[b]You will have peace'; whereas a
sword touches the [2]throat."
11 In that time it will be said to this
people and to Jerusalem, "A scorching wind from the bare heights in
the wilderness in the direction of the
daughter of My people—not to winnow, and not to cleanse,
12 a wind too strong for [1]this—
will come [2]at My command; now I
will also pronounce judgments
against them.
13 "Behold, he [a]goes up like clouds,
And his [b]chariots like the whirlwind;
His horses are [c]swifter than eagles.
Woe to us, for [d]we are ruined!"

14 Wash your heart from evil, O Jerusalem,
That you may be saved.
How long will your [a]wicked thoughts
Lodge within you?
15 For a voice declares from Dan,
And proclaims wickedness from Mount Ephraim.
16 "Report *it* to the nations, now!
Proclaim over Jerusalem,
'Besiegers come from a [a]far country,
And [b]lift their voices against the cities of Judah.
17 'Like watchmen of a field they are [a]against her round about,
Because she has [b]rebelled against Me,' declares the LORD.
18 "Your [a]ways and your deeds
Have [1]brought these things to you.
This is your evil. How bitter!
How it has touched your heart!"

Lament Over Judah's Devastation

19 [a]My [1]soul, my [1]soul! I am in anguish! [2]Oh my heart!

25 [a]Ezra 9:7 [b]Jer. 22:21

1 [a]Jer. 3:22; Joel 2:12 [b]Jer. 7:3, 7; 15:19; 35:15

2 [a]Deut. 10:20; Is. 65:16; Jer. 12:16 [b]Gen. 22:18; Jer. 3:17; 12:15, 16 [c]Is. 45:25; Jer. 9:24

3 [1]Lit., *Plow for yourselves plowed ground* [a]Hos. 10:12

4 [a]Deut. 10:16; 30:6; Jer. 9:25, 26; Rom. 2:28, 29 [b]Is. 30:27, 33; Jer. 21:12 [c]Amos 5:6; Mark 9:43, 48

5 [a]Jer. 6:1; Hos. 8:1 [b]Josh. 10:20; Jer. 8:14

6 [a]Is. 62:10; Jer. 4:21; 50:2 [b]Jer. 1:14, 15; 6:1, 22

7 [a]Jer. 5:6; 25:38; 50:17 [b]Jer. 25:9; Ezek. 26:7-10 [c]Is. 1:7; 6:11; Jer. 2:15

8 [a]Is. 22:12; Jer. 6:26 [b]Is. 5:25; 10:4; Jer. 30:24

9 [a]Is. 22:3-5; Jer. 48:41 [b]Is. 29:9, 10; Ezek. 13:9-16

10 [1]YHWH, usually rendered LORD [2]Or, *life* [a]Ezek. 14:9; 2 Thess. 2:11 [b]Jer. 5:12; 14:13

12 [1]Lit., *these* [2]Lit., *for Me*

13 [a]Is. 19:1; Nah. 1:3 [b]Is. 5:28; 66:15 [c]Lam. 4:19 [d]Is. 3:8

14 [a]Prov. 1:22; Jer. 6:19; 13:27

16 [a]Is. 39:3; Jer. 5:15 [b]Ezek. 21:22

17 [a]2 Kin. 25:1, 4 [b]Is. 1:20, 23; Jer. 5:23

18 [1]Lit., *done* [a]Ps. 107:17; Is. 50:1; Jer. 2:17, 19

19 [1]Lit., *inward parts* [2]Lit., *The walls of my heart* [a]Is. 15:5; 16:11; 21:3; 22:4; Jer. 9:1, 10; 20:9

My [b]heart is pounding in me;
I cannot be silent,
Because [3]you have heard, O my soul,
The [c]sound of the trumpet,
The alarm of war.
20 [a]Disaster on disaster is proclaimed,
For the whole land is devastated;
Suddenly my tents are devastated,
My curtains in an instant.
21 How long must I see the standard,
And hear the sound of the trumpet?
22 "[a]For My people are foolish,
They know Me not;
They are stupid children,
And they have no understanding.
They are shrewd to [b]do evil,
But to do good they do not know."

23 I looked on the earth, and behold, *it was* [1a]formless and void;
And to the heavens, and they had no light.
24 I looked on the mountains, and behold, they were [a]quaking,
And all the hills [1]moved to and fro.
25 I looked, and behold, there was no man,
And all the [a]birds of the heavens had fled.
26 I looked, and behold, [1]the [a]fruitful land was a wilderness,
And all its cities were pulled down
Before the LORD, before His fierce anger.

27 For thus says the LORD,
"The [a]whole land shall be a desolation,
Yet I will [b]not execute a complete destruction.
28 "For this the [a]earth shall mourn,
And the [b]heavens above be dark,
Because I have [c]spoken, I have purposed,
And I will not [1]change My mind, nor will I turn from it."
29 At the sound of the horseman and bowman every city flees;
They [a]go into the thickets and climb among the rocks;
Every city is forsaken,
And no man dwells in them.
30 And you, O desolate one, [a]what will you do?

19 [3]Or, *I, my soul, heard* [b]Hab. 3:16 [c]Num. 10:9

20 [a]Ps. 42:7; Ezek. 7:26

22 [a]Jer. 5:4, 21; 10:8 [b]Jer. 9:3; 13:23; Rom. 16:19

23 [1]Or, *a waste and emptiness* [a]Gen. 1:2; Is. 24:19

24 [1]Lit., *moved lightly* [a]Is. 5:25; Jer. 10:10; Ezek. 38:20

25 [a]Jer. 9:10; 12:4; Zeph. 1:3

26 [1]Or, *Carmel* [a]Jer. 9:10

27 [a]Jer. 12:11, 12; 25:11 [b]Jer. 5:10, 18; 30:11; 46:28

28 [1]Lit., *be sorry* [a]Jer. 12:4, 11; 14:2; Hos. 4:3 [b]Is. 5:30; 50:3; Joel 2:30, 31 [c]Num. 23:19; Jer. 23:20; 30:24

29 [a]Is. 2:19-21; Jer. 16:16

30 [1]Lit., *paramours* [a]Is. 10:3; 20:6; Jer. 13:21 [b]2 Kin. 9:30; Ezek. 23:40 [c]Jer. 22:20, 22; Ezek. 23:9, 10, 22

31 [1]Lit., *sound* [2]Lit., *palms* [3]Lit., *my soul faints* [a]Is. 42:14 [b]Is. 1:15; Lam. 1:17

1 [1]Lit., *faithfulness* [a]2 Chr. 16:9; Dan. 12:4 [b]Ezek. 22:30 [c]Gen. 18:26, 32

3 [1]Lit., *faithfulness* [2]Or, *become sick* [a]2 Chr. 16:9 [b]Jer. 7:28; 8:5; Zeph. 3:2 [c]Jer. 7:26; 19:15; Ezek. 3:8

4 [a]Is. 27:11; Jer. 8:7; Hos. 4:6

5 [a]Ex. 32:25; Ps. 2:3; Jer. 2:20

6 [a]Ezek. 22:27; Hab. 1:8; Zeph. 3:3 [b]Hos. 13:7

Although you dress in scarlet,
Although you decorate *yourself with* ornaments of gold,
Although you [b]enlarge your eyes with paint,
In vain you make yourself beautiful;
Your [1c]lovers despise you;
They seek your life.
31 For I heard a [1]cry as of a woman in labor,
The anguish as of one giving birth to her first child,
The [1]cry of the daughter of Zion [a]gasping for breath,
[b]Stretching out her [2]hands, *saying*,
"Ah, woe is me, for [3]I faint before murderers."

CHAPTER 5

Jerusalem's Godlessness

"[a]ROAM to and fro through the streets of Jerusalem,
And look now, and take note.
And seek in her open squares,
If you can find a [b]man,
If there is one who does justice, who seeks [1]truth,
Then I will [c]pardon her.
2 "And although they say, 'As the LORD lives,'
Surely they swear falsely."
3 O LORD, do not [a]Thine eyes look for [1]truth?
Thou hast smitten them,
But they did not [2]weaken;
Thou hast consumed them,
But they [b]refused to take correction.
They have made their faces [c]harder than rock;
They have refused to repent.

4 Then I said, "They are only the poor,
They are foolish;
For they do not [a]know the way of the LORD
Or the ordinance of their God.
5 "I will go to the great
And will speak to them,
For they know the way of the LORD,
And the ordinance of their God."
But they too, with one accord, have [a]broken the yoke
And burst the bonds.
6 Therefore a lion from the forest shall slay them,
A [a]wolf of the deserts shall destroy them,
A [b]leopard is watching their cities.

Every one who goes out of them shall be torn in pieces,
Because their transgressions are many,
Their apostasies are numerous.

7 "Why should I pardon you?
Your sons have forsaken Me
And [a]sworn by those who are [b]not gods.
When I had fed them to the full,
They committed adultery
And trooped to the harlot's house.
8 "They were well-fed lusty horses,
Each one neighing after his [a]neighbor's wife.
9 "Shall I not punish [1]these *people*," declares the LORD,
"And on a nation such as this
Shall I not avenge Myself?

10 "Go up through her [a]vine rows and destroy,
But do not execute a complete destruction;
Strip away her branches,
For they are not the LORD's.
11 "For the [a]house of Israel and the house of Judah
Have dealt very treacherously with Me," declares the LORD.
12 They have lied about the LORD
And said, "[1a]Not He;
Misfortune will [b]not come on us;
And we will [c]not see sword or famine.
13 "And the [a]prophets are *as* wind,
And the word is not in them.
Thus it will be done to them!"

Judgment Proclaimed

14 Therefore, thus says the LORD, the God of hosts,
"Because you have spoken this word,
Behold, I am making My words in your mouth [a]fire
And this people wood, and it will consume them.
15 "Behold, I am [a]bringing a nation against you from afar, O house of Israel," declares the LORD.
"It is an enduring nation,
It is an ancient nation,
A nation whose [b]language you do not know,
Nor can you understand what they say.
16 "Their quiver is like an [a]open grave,
All of them are mighty men.
17 "And they will [a]devour your harvest and your food;
They will devour your sons and your daughters;
They will devour your flocks and your herds;
They will devour your [b]vines and your fig trees;
They will demolish with the sword your [c]fortified cities in which you trust.
18 "Yet even in those days," de-
clares the LORD, "I will not make
you a complete destruction.
19 "And it shall come about [a]when
[1]they say, 'Why has the LORD our
God done all these things to us?'
then you shall say to them, 'As you
have forsaken Me and served foreign gods in your land, so you shall
[b]serve strangers in a land that is not
yours.'
20 "Declare this in the house of Jacob
And proclaim it in Judah, saying,
21 'Hear this, O foolish and [1]senseless people,
Who have [a]eyes, but see not;
Who have ears, but hear not.
22 'Do you not [a]fear Me?' declares the LORD.
'Do you not tremble in My presence?
For I have [b]placed the sand as a boundary for the sea,
An eternal decree, so it cannot cross over it.
Though the waves toss, yet they cannot prevail;
Though they roar, yet they cannot cross over it.
23 'But this people has a [a]stubborn and rebellious heart;
They have turned aside and departed.
24 'They do not say in their heart,
"Let us now fear the LORD our God,
Who [a]gives rain in its season,
Both the autumn rain and the [b]spring rain,
Who keeps for us
The [c]appointed weeks of the harvest."
25 'Your [a]iniquities have turned these away,
And your sins have withheld good from you.
26 'For wicked men are found among My people,
They [a]watch like fowlers [1]lying in wait;
They set a trap,
They catch men.

7 [a]Josh. 23:7; Jer. 12:16; Zeph. 1:5 [b]Deut. 32:21; Jer. 2:11; Gal. 4:8
8 [a]Jer. 29:23; Ezek. 22:11
9 [1]Or, *for these things*
10 [a]Jer. 39:8
11 [a]Jer. 3:6, 7, 20
12 [1]Lit., *He is not* [a]Prov. 30:9; Jer. 14:22; 43:1-4 [b]Jer. 23:17 [c]Jer. 14:13
13 [a]Job 8:2; Jer. 14:13, 15; 22:22
14 [a]Is. 24:6; Jer. 23:29; Zech. 1:6
15 [a]Deut. 28:49; Is. 5:26; Jer. 4:16 [b]Is. 28:11
16 [a]Ps. 5:9; Is. 5:28; 13:18
17 [a]Lev. 26:16; Deut. 28:31, 33; Jer. 8:16; 50:7, 17 [b]Jer. 8:13 [c]Hos. 8:14
19 [1]Or, *you* [a]Deut. 29:24-26; 1 Kin. 9:8, 9; Jer. 16:10-13 [b]Deut. 28:48; Jer. 16:13
21 [1]Lit., *without heart* [a]Is. 6:9; 43:8; Ezek. 12:2; Matt. 13:14
22 [a]Deut. 28:58; Ps. 119:120; Jer. 2:19; 10:7 [b]Job 38:8-11; Ps. 104:9
23 [a]Deut. 21:18; Ps. 78:8; Jer. 4:17; 6:28
24 [a]Ps. 147:8; Jer. 3:3; Matt. 5:45 [b]Joel 2:23 [c]Gen. 8:22
25 [a]Jer. 2:17; 4:18
26 [1]Perhaps, *crouching down* [a]Ps. 10:9; Prov. 1:11; Jer. 18:22; Hab. 1:15

27 'Like a cage full of birds,
So their houses are full of deceit;
Therefore they have become great and rich.
28 'They are [a]fat, they are sleek,
They also [1]excel in deeds of wickedness;
They do not plead the cause,
The cause of the [2][b]orphan, that they may prosper;
And they do not [3]defend the rights of the poor.
29 'Shall I not punish [1]these *people?*' declares the LORD,
'On a nation such as this
Shall I not avenge Myself?'

30 "An appalling and [a]horrible thing
Has happened in the land:
31 The prophets prophesy falsely,
And the priests rule [1]on their *own* authority;
And My people [a]love it so!
But what will you do at the end of it?

CHAPTER 6

Destruction of Jerusalem Impending

"FLEE for safety, O sons of Benjamin,
From the midst of Jerusalem!
Now blow a trumpet in Tekoa,
And raise a signal over [1]Beth-haccerem;
For evil looks down from the [a]north,
And a great destruction.
2 "The comely and [a]dainty one, the daughter of Zion, I will cut off.
3 "[a]Shepherds and their flocks will come to her,
They will [b]pitch *their* tents [1]around her,
They will pasture each in his [2]place.
4 "[1][a]Prepare war against her;
Arise, and let us [2]attack at [b]noon.
Woe to us, for the day declines,
For the shadows of the evening lengthen!
5 "Arise, and let us [1]attack by night
And [a]destroy her [2]palaces!"
6 For thus says the LORD of hosts,
"[a]Cut down her trees,
And cast up a siege against Jerusalem.
This is the city to be punished,
In whose midst there is only [b]oppression.
7 "[a]As a well [1]keeps its waters fresh,
So she [1]keeps fresh her wickedness.
[b]Violence and destruction are heard in her;
[c]Sickness and wounds are ever before Me.
8 "[a]Be warned, O Jerusalem,
Lest [1][b]I be alienated from you;
Lest I make you a desolation,
A land not inhabited."

9 Thus says the LORD of hosts,
"They will [a]thoroughly glean as the vine the [b]remnant of Israel;
Pass your hand again like a grape gatherer
Over the branches."
10 To whom shall I speak and give warning,
That they may hear?
Behold, their ears are [1]closed,
And they cannot listen.
Behold, the word of the LORD has become a reproach to them;
They have no delight in it.
11 But I am [a]full of the wrath of the LORD:
I am [b]weary with holding *it* in.
"[c]Pour *it* out on the children in the street,
And on the [1]gathering of young men together;
For both husband and wife shall be taken,
The aged [2]and the very old.
12 "And their [a]houses shall be turned over to others,
Their fields and their wives together;
For I will [b]stretch out My hand
Against the inhabitants of the land," declares the LORD.
13 "For [a]from the least of them even to the greatest of them,
Every one is [b]greedy for gain,
And from the prophet even to the priest
Every one [1]deals falsely.
14 "And they have [a]healed the wound of My people slightly,
Saying, 'Peace, peace,'
But there is no peace.
15 "Were they [a]ashamed because of the abomination they have done?
They were not even ashamed at all;
They did not even know how to blush.
Therefore they shall fall among those who fall;
At the time that I punish them,

28 [1]Lit., *pass over, or, overlook deeds* [2]Or, *fatherless* [3]Lit., *judge*
[a]Deut. 32:15 [b]Is. 1:23; Jer. 7:6; 22:3; Zech. 7:10

29 [1]Or, *for these things*

30 [a]Jer. 23:14; Hos. 6:10

31 [1]Lit., *over their own hands*
[a]Mic. 2:11

1 [1]I.e., House of the vineyard
[a]Jer. 1:14; 4:6; 6:22

2 [a]Deut. 28:56

3 [1]Lit., *against her round about* [2]Lit., *hand*
[a]Jer. 12:10 [b]2 Kin. 25:1; Jer. 4:17; Luke 19:43

4 [1]Lit., *Sanctify* [2]Lit., *go up*
[a]Jer. 6:23; Joel 3:9 [b]Jer. 15:8; Zeph. 2:4

5 [1]Lit., *go up* [2]Or, *fortified towers*
[a]Is. 32:14; Jer. 52:13

6 [a]Deut. 20:19, 20 [b]Jer. 22:17

7 [1]Lit., *keeps cold*
[a]James 3:10-12 [b]Ps. 59:9-11; Jer. 20:8; Ezek. 7:11, 23 [c]Jer. 30:12, 13

8 [1]Lit., *my soul*
[a]Jer. 7:28; 17:23 [b]Ezek. 23:18; Hos. 9:12

9 [a]Jer. 16:16; 49:9; Obad. 5, 6 [b]Jer. 8:3; 11:23

10 [1]Lit., *uncircumcised*

11 [1]Lit., *council* [2]Lit., *with fulness of days*
[a]Job 32:18, 19; Mic. 3:8 [b]Jer. 15:6; 20:9 [c]Jer. 7:20; 9:21

12 [a]Deut. 28:30; Jer. 8:10; 38:22 [b]Jer. 15:6

13 [1]Or, *makes lies*
[a]Jer. 8:10; 22:17 [b]Is. 56:11; 57:17; Jer. 8:10; 22:17

14 [a]Jer. 8:11, 12; Ezek. 13:10

15 [a]Jer. 3:3; 8:12

They shall be cast down," says the LORD.

16 Thus says the LORD,
"Stand by the ways and see and ask for the [a]ancient paths,
Where the good way is, and walk in it;
And [b]you shall find rest for your souls.
But they said, 'We will not walk *in it.*'
17"And I set [a]watchmen over you, *saying,*
'Listen to the sound of the trumpet!'
But they said, 'We will not listen.'
18"Therefore hear, O nations,
And know, O congregation, what is among them.
19"[a]Hear, O earth: behold, I am bringing disaster on this people,
The [b]fruit of their [1]plans,
Because they have not listened to My words,
And as for My law, they have [c]rejected it also.
20"[a]For what purpose does [b]frankincense come to Me from Sheba,
And the [1c]sweet cane from a distant land?
Your burnt offerings are not acceptable,
And your sacrifices are not pleasing to Me."
21 Therefore, thus says the LORD,
"Behold, [a]I am [1]laying stumbling blocks before this people.
And they will stumble against them,
[b]Fathers and sons together;
Neighbor and [2]friend will perish."

The Enemy from the North

22 Thus says the LORD,
"Behold, a people is coming from the north land,
And a great nation will be aroused from the [a]remote parts of the earth.
23"They seize [a]bow and spear;
They are [b]cruel and have no mercy;
Their voice [c]roars like the sea,
And they ride on horses,
Arrayed as a man for the battle
Against you, O daughter of Zion!"
24 We have [a]heard the report of it;
Our hands are limp.
Anguish has seized us,
Pain as of a woman in childbirth.
25 [a]Do not go out into the field,
And do not walk on the road,
For the enemy has a sword,
Terror is on every side.
26 O daughter of my people, [a]put on sackcloth
And [b]roll in ashes;
[1c]Mourn as for an only son,
A lamentation most bitter.
For suddenly the destroyer
Will come upon us.

27"I have [a]made you an assayer *and* a tester among My people,
That you may know and assay their way."
28 All of them are stubbornly rebellious,
[a]Going about as a talebearer.
They are [b]bronze and iron;
They, all of them, are corrupt.
29 The bellows blow fiercely,
The lead is consumed by the fire;
In vain the refining goes on,
But the [a]wicked are not [1]separated.
30 [a]They call them rejected silver,
Because the LORD has rejected them.

CHAPTER 7

Message at the Temple Gate

THE word that came to Jeremiah
from the LORD, saying,
2"[a]Stand in the gate of the LORD's
house and proclaim there this word,
and say, 'Hear the word of the LORD,
all you of Judah, who enter by these
gates to worship the LORD!' "
3 Thus says the LORD of hosts,
the God of Israel, "[a]Amend your
ways and your deeds, and I will let
you dwell in this place.
4"[a]Do not trust in deceptive
words, saying, '[1]This is the temple
of the LORD, the temple of the LORD,
the temple of the LORD.'
5"For [a]if you truly amend your
ways and your deeds, if you truly
[b]practice justice between a man and
his neighbor,
6 *if* you do not oppress the alien,
the [1a]orphan, or the widow, and do
not shed innocent blood in this
place, nor [b]walk after other gods to
your own ruin,
7 then I will let you [a]dwell in this
place, in the land that I gave to your
fathers forever and ever.
8"Behold, you are trusting in deceptive words to no avail.
9"Will you steal, murder, and
commit adultery, and swear falsely,

16 [a]Is. 8:20; Jer. 12:16; 18:15; 31:21; Mal. 4:4; Luke 16:29 [b]Matt. 11:29

17 [a]Is. 21:11; 58:1; Jer. 25:4; Ezek. 3:17; Hab. 2:1

19 [1]Or, *devices* [a]Is. 1:2; Jer. 22:29 [b]Prov. 1:31 [c]Jer. 8:9

20 [1]Lit., *good* [a]Ps. 40:6; 50:7-9; Is. 1:11; 66:3; Amos 5:21; Mic. 6:6 [b]Is. 60:6 [c]Ex. 30:23

21 [1]Lit., *giving* [2]Lit., *his friend* [a]Is. 8:14; Jer. 13:16 [b]Is. 9:14-17; Jer. 9:21, 22

22 [a]Neh. 1:9

23 [a]Jer. 4:29; Is. 13:18 [b]Jer. 50:42 [c]Is. 5:30

24 [a]Is. 28:19; Jer. 4:19-21

25 [a]Jer. 14:18

26 [1]Lit., *Make for yourself mourning* [a]Jer. 4:8 [b]Jer. 25:34; Mic. 1:10 [c]Amos 8:10; Zech. 12:10

27 [a]Jer. 1:18; 15:20

28 [a]Jer. 9:4 [b]Ezek. 22:18

29 [1]Or, *drawn off* [a]Jer. 15:19

30 [a]Ps. 119:119; Is. 1:22

2 [a]Jer. 17:19

3 [a]Jer. 4:1; 7:5; 18:11; 26:13

4 [1]Lit., *They are* [a]Jer. 7:8; Mic. 3:11

5 [a]Is. 1:19; Jer. 4:1, 2 [b]1 Kin. 6:12, 13; Jer. 21:12; 22:3

6 [1]Or, *fatherless* [a]Ex. 22:21-24; Jer. 5:28 [b]Deut. 6:14, 15; 8:19; 11:28; Jer. 13:10

7 [a]Deut. 4:40; Jer. 4:1

and [a]offer sacrifices to Baal, and
walk after [b]other gods that you have
not known,
10 then [a]come and stand before
Me in [b]this house, which is called by
My name, and say, 'We are delivered!'—that you may do all these
abominations?
11"Has [a]this house, which is called
by My name, become a [b]den of robbers in your sight? Behold, [c]I, even I,
have seen *it*," declares the LORD.
12"But go now to My place which
was in [a]Shiloh, where I [b]made My
name dwell at the first, and [c]see
what I did to it because of the wickedness of My people Israel.
13"And now, because you have
done all these things," declares the
LORD, "and I spoke to you, rising up
early and [a]speaking, but you did not
hear, and I [b]called you but you did
not answer,
14 therefore, I will do to the house
which is called by My name, [a]in
which you trust, and to the place
which I gave you and your fathers,
as I [b]did to Shiloh.
15"And I will [a]cast you out of My
sight, as I have cast out all your
brothers, all the offspring of [b]Ephra-
im.
16"As for you, do not [a]pray for this
people, and do not lift up cry or
prayer for them, and do not intercede with Me; for I do not hear you.
17"Do you not see what they are
doing in the cities of Judah and in
the streets of Jerusalem?
18"The children gather wood, and
the fathers kindle the fire, and the
women knead dough to make cakes
for the queen of heaven; and *they*
[a]pour out libations to other gods in
order to [b]spite Me.
19"[a]Do they spite Me?" declares
the LORD. "Is it not themselves *they*
spite, to their own [b]shame?"
20 Therefore thus says the Lord
[1]GOD, "Behold, My anger and My
wrath will be poured out on this
place, on man and on beast and on
the [a]trees of the field and on the fruit
of the ground; and it will burn and
not be quenched."
21 Thus says the LORD of hosts,
the God of Israel, "[a]Add your burnt
offerings to your sacrifices and [b]eat
flesh.
22"For I did not [a]speak to your fathers, or command them in the day
that I brought them out of the land
of Egypt, concerning burnt offerings
and sacrifices.
23"But this is [1]what I commanded
them, saying, '[a]Obey My voice, and
[b]I will be your God, and you will be
My people; and you will walk in all
the way which I command you, that
it may [c]be well with you.'
24"Yet they did not [a]obey or incline their ear, but walked in *their*
own counsels *and* in the stubbornness of their evil heart, and went
backward and not forward.
25"Since the day that your fathers
came out of the land of Egypt until
this day, I have sent you all My servants the prophets, daily rising early and sending *them*.
26"Yet they did not listen to Me or
incline their ear, but [a]stiffened their
neck; they [b]did evil more than their
fathers.
27"And you shall [a]speak all these
words to them, but they will not listen to you; and you shall call to
them, but they will [b]not answer you.
28"And you shall say to them, 'This
is the nation that did [a]not obey the
voice of the LORD their God [b]or accept correction; truth has perished
and has been cut off from their
mouth.
29 '[a]Cut off your hair and cast *it*
away,
And take up a lamentation on
the bare heights;
For the LORD has [b]rejected and
forsaken
The generation of His wrath.'
30"For the sons of Judah have
done that which is evil in My sight,"
declares the LORD, "they have [a]set
their detestable things in the house
which is called by My name, to defile it.
31"And they have [a]built the high
places of Topheth, which is in the
valley of the son of Hinnom, to
[b]burn their sons and their daughters
in the fire, which I [c]did not command, and it did not come into My
mind.
32"[a]Therefore, behold, days are
coming," declares the LORD, "when
it will no more be called Topheth, or
the valley of the son of Hinnom, but
the valley of the Slaughter; for they
will bury in Topheth because there
is no *other* place.
33"And the [a]dead bodies of this
people will be food for the birds of
the sky, and for the beasts of the
earth; and no one will frighten *them*
away.
34"Then I will make to [a]cease from
the cities of Judah and from the
streets of Jerusalem the voice of joy
and the voice of gladness, the voice
of the bridegroom and the voice of
the bride; for the [b]land will become
a ruin.

9 [a]Jer. 11:13, 17 [b]Jer. 7:6; 19:4
10 [a]Ezek. 23:39 [b]Jer. 7:11, 14, 30
11 [a]Is. 56:7 [b]Matt. 21:13; Mark 11:17; Luke 19:46 [c]Jer. 29:23
12 [a]Judg. 18:31; Jer. 26:6 [b]Josh. 18:1, 10 [c]Jer. 17:19
13 [a]Jer. 4:1; 7:5; 18:11; 26:13 [b]Jer. 7:8; Mic. 3:11
14 [a]Is. 1:19; Jer. 4:1, 2 [b]1 Kin. 6:12, 13; Jer. 21:12; 22:3
15 [a]Ex. 22:21-24; Jer. 5:28 [b]Deut. 6:14, 15; 8:19
16 [a]Deut. 4:40; Jer. 14:11
18 [a]Jer. 19:13 [b]Deut. 32:16, 21; 1 Kin. 14:9; 16:2; Jer. 11:17; Ezek. 8:7
19 [a]Job 35:6 [b]Jer. 9:19; 15:9; 22:22
20 [1]YHWH, usually rendered LORD [a]Jer. 8:13; 11:16
21 [a]Is. 1:11; Jer. 6:20; 14:12; Amos 5:21 [b]Ezek. 33:25; Hos. 8:13
22 [a]1 Sam. 15:22; Ps. 51:16; Hos. 6:6
23 [1]Lit., *the word which*, cf. Ex. 16:32 [a]Ex. 15:26; Deut. 6:3 [b]Ex. 19:5, 6; Lev. 26:12; Jer. 11:4; 13:11 [c]Is. 3:10; Jer. 38:20
24 [a]Ps. 81:11; Jer. 11:8; Ezek. 20:8, 13, 16, 21
26 [a]Neh. 9:17; Jer. 17:23; 19:15 [b]Jer. 16:12; Matt. 23:32
27 [a]Jer. 1:8; 26:2; Ezek. 2:7 [b]Is. 50:2; 65:12; Zech. 7:13
28 [a]Jer. 6:17; 11:10 [b]Is. 59:14, 15; Jer. 9:5
29 [a]Job 1:20; Is. 15:2; 22:12; Jer. 16:6; Mic. 1:16 [b]Jer. 6:30; 14:19
30 [a]2 Kin. 21:4; 2 Chr. 33:4, 5, 7; Jer. 32:34, 35; Ezek. 7:20; Dan. 9:27; 11:31
31 [a]2 Kin. 23:10; Jer. 19:5 [b]2 Kin. 17:17; Ps. 106:38 [c]Deut. 17:3
32 [a]Jer. 19:6, 7
33 [a]Deut. 28:26; Ps. 79:2; Jer. 12:9
34 [a]Is. 24:7, 8; Jer. 16:9; Ezek. 26:13; Hos. 2:11 [b]Is. 1:7; Jer. 4:27

CHAPTER 8

The Sin and Treachery of Judah

"AT that time," declares the
LORD, "they will [a]bring out the
bones of the kings of Judah, and the
bones of its princes, and the bones
of the priests, and the bones of the
prophets, and the bones of the inhabitants of Jerusalem from their
graves.
2"And they will spread them out
to the sun, the moon, and to all the
[a]host of heaven, which they have
loved, and which they have served,
and which they have gone after, and
which they have sought, and which
they have worshiped. They will not
be gathered [b]or buried; they will be
as dung on the face of the ground.
3"And [a]death will be chosen
rather than life by all the remnant
that remains of this evil family, that
remains in all the [b]places to which I
have driven them," declares the
LORD of hosts.
4"And you shall say to them,
'Thus says the LORD,
"Do *men* fall and [a]not get up
again?
Does one turn away and not
[1]repent?
5"Why then has this people, Jerusalem,
[a]Turned away in continual
apostasy?
They [b]hold fast to deceit,
They refuse to return.
6"I [a]have listened and heard,
They have spoken what is not
right;
No man repented of his wickedness,
Saying, 'What have I done?'
Every one turned to his course,
Like a [b]horse charging into the
battle.
7"Even the [a]stork in the sky
Knows her seasons;
And the [b]turtledove and the
swift and the thrush
Observe the time of their [1]mi-
gration;
But My people do not know
The ordinance of the LORD.

8"How can you say, '[a]We are
wise,
And the law of the LORD is with
us'?
But behold, the lying pen of the
scribes
Has made *it* into a lie.
9"The wise men are [a]put to
shame,
They are dismayed and caught;
Behold, they have rejected the
word of the LORD,
And what kind of wisdom do
they have?
10"Therefore I will [a]give their
wives to others,
Their fields to [1]new owners;
Because from the least even to
the greatest
Every one is [b]greedy for gain;
From the prophet even to the
priest
Every one practices deceit.
11"And they [a]heal the brokenness
of the daughter of My people
superficially
By saying, '[1]All is well, all is
well';
But there is no peace.
12"Were they [a]ashamed because
of the abomination they had
done?
They certainly were not
ashamed,
And they did not know how to
blush;
Therefore they shall [b]fall
among those who fall;
At the [c]time of their punishment they shall be brought
down,"
Declares the LORD.

13"I will [a]surely snatch them
away," declares the LORD;
"There will be no grapes on the
vine,
And [b]no figs on the fig tree,
And the leaf shall wither;
And what I have given them
shall pass away." ' "
14 Why are we sitting still?
[a]Assemble yourselves, and let
us [b]go into the fortified cities,
And let us perish there,
Because the LORD our God has
doomed us
And given us [c]poisoned water
to drink,
For [d]we have sinned against the
LORD.
15 *We* [a]waited for peace, but no
good *came;*
For a time of healing, but behold, terror!
16 From [a]Dan is heard the snort-
ing of his horses;
At the sound of the neighing of
his [b]stallions
The whole land quakes;
For they come and devour the
land and its fulness,
The city and its inhabitants.
17"For behold, I am [a]sending serpents against you,
Adders, for which there is [b]no
charm,

1 [a]Ezek. 6:5
2 [a]2 Kin. 23:5; Jer. 19:13; Zeph. 1:5; Acts 7:42 [b]Jer. 22:19; 36:30
3 [a]Job 3:21, 22; 7:15, 16; Jon. 4:3; Rev. 9:6 [b]Deut. 30:1, 4; Jer. 23:3, 8; 29:14
4 [1]Lit., *turn back* [a]Prov. 24:16; Amos 5:2; Mic. 7:8
5 [a]Jer. 5:6; 7:24 [b]Jer. 5:27; 9:6
6 [a]Ps. 74:2; Mal. 3:16 [b]Job 39:21-25
7 [1]Lit., *coming* [a]Prov. 6:6-8; Is. 1:3 [b]Song of Sol. 2:12
8 [a]Job 5:12, 13; Jer. 4:22; Rom. 1:22; 2:17
9 [a]Is. 19:11; Jer. 6:15; 1 Cor. 1:27
10 [1]Lit., *possessing ones* [a]Deut. 28:30; Jer. 6:12, 13; 38:22 [b]Is. 56:11; 57:17; Jer. 6:13
11 [1]Lit., *Peace, peace* [a]Jer. 6:14; 14:13, 14; Lam. 2:14; Ezek. 13:10
12 [a]Ps. 52:1, 7; Is. 3:9; Jer. 3:3; 6:15; Zeph. 3:5 [b]Is. 9:14; Jer. 6:21; Hos. 4:5 [c]Deut. 32:35; Jer. 10:15
13 [a]Jer. 14:12; Ezek. 22:20, 21 [b]Matt. 21:19
14 [a]Jer. 4:5 [b]2 Sam. 20:6; Jer. 35:11 [c]Deut. 29:18; Ps. 69:21; Jer. 9:15; Lam. 3:19; Matt. 27:34 [d]Jer. 3:25; 14:20
15 [a]Jer. 8:11; 14:19
16 [a]Judg. 18:29; Jer. 4:15 [b]Judg. 5:22
17 [a]Num. 21:6; Deut. 32:24 [b]Ps. 58:4, 5

And they will bite you," declares the LORD.

18 [1]My sorrow is [a]beyond healing,
My heart is faint *within me!*
19 Behold, listen! The cry of the daughter of my people from a [a]distant land:
"Is the LORD not in Zion? Is her King not within her?"
"Why have they [b]provoked Me with their graven images, with foreign [1][c]idols?"
20"Harvest is past, summer is ended,
And we are not saved."
21 For the [a]brokenness of the daughter of my people I am broken;
I [b]mourn, dismay has taken hold of me.
22 Is there no [a]balm in Gilead?
Is there no physician there?
[b]Why then has not the [1]health of the daughter of my people [2]been restored?

CHAPTER 9

A Lament Over Zion

1a O THAT my head were waters,
And my eyes a fountain of tears,
That I might weep day and night
For the slain of the [b]daughter of my people!
2 [1][a]O that I had in the desert
A wayfarers' lodging place;
That I might leave my people,
And go from them!
For all of them are adulterers,
An assembly of treacherous men.
3"And they [a]bend their tongue *like* their bow;
Lies and not truth prevail in the land;
For they proceed from evil to evil,
And they do not [b]know Me," declares the LORD.
4"Let every one be on guard against his neighbor,
And do not [a]trust any brother;
Because every [b]brother deals [1]craftily,
And every neighbor [c]goes about as a slanderer.
5"And everyone [a]deceives his neighbor,
And does not speak the truth,
They have taught their tongue to speak lies;
They [b]weary themselves committing iniquity.
6"Your [a]dwelling is in the midst of deceit;
Through deceit they [b]refuse to know Me," declares the LORD.

7 Therefore thus says the LORD of hosts,
"Behold, I will refine them and [a]assay them;
For [b]what *else* can I do, because of the daughter of My people?
8"Their [a]tongue is a deadly arrow;
It speaks deceit;
With his mouth one [b]speaks peace to his neighbor,
But inwardly he [c]sets an ambush for him.
9"[a]Shall I not punish them for these things?" declares the LORD.
"On a nation such as this
Shall I not avenge Myself?

10"For the [a]mountains I will take up a weeping and wailing,
And for the pastures of the [b]wilderness a dirge,
Because they are [c]laid waste, so that no one passes through,
And the lowing of the cattle is not heard;
Both the [d]birds of the sky and the beasts have fled; they are gone.
11"And I will make Jerusalem a [a]heap of ruins,
A haunt of [b]jackals;
And I will make the cities of Judah a [c]desolation, without inhabitant."
12 Who is the [a]wise man that may
understand this? And *who is* he to
whom [b]the mouth of the LORD has
spoken, that he may declare it?
[c]Why is the land ruined, laid waste
like a desert, so that no one passes
through?
13 And the LORD said, "Because
they have [a]forsaken My law which I
set before them, and have not
obeyed My voice nor walked according to it,
14 but have [a]walked after the
stubbornness of their heart and after the [b]Baals, as their [c]fathers
taught them,"
15 therefore thus says the LORD of
hosts, the God of Israel, "behold, I
will feed them, this people, with
wormwood and give them [a]poisoned water to drink.

18 [1]So Gk. and versions [a]Is. 22:4; Lam. 1:16, 17
19 [1]Lit., *vanities* [a]Is. 13:5; 39:3; Jer. 4:16; 9:16 [b]Deut. 32:21; Jer. 7:19 [c]Ps. 31:6
21 [a]Jer. 4:19; 9:1; 14:17 [b]Jer. 14:2; Nah. 2:10
22 [1]Or, *healing* [2]Lit., *gone up* [a]Gen. 37:25; Jer. 46:11 [b]Jer. 14:19; 30:13
1 [1]8:23 in Heb. [a]Is. 22:4; Jer. 8:18; 13:17; Lam. 2:18 [b]Jer. 6:26; 9:21, 22
2 [1]9:1 in Heb. [a]Ps. 55:6, 7; 120:5, 6
3 [a]Ps. 64:3; Is. 59:4; Jer. 9:8 [b]1 Sam. 2:12; Jer. 5:4, 5; Hos. 4:1
4 [1]I.e., like Jacob (a play on words) [a]Jer. 12:6 [b]Gen. 27:35 [c]Ps. 15:3; Prov. 10:18; Jer. 6:28
5 [a]Mic. 6:12 [b]Jer. 12:13; 51:58, 64
6 [a]Ps. 120:5, 6; Jer. 5:27; 8:5 [b]Job 21:14, 15; Jer. 11:10; 13:10; John 3:14, 20
7 [a]Is. 1:25; Jer. 6:27; Mal. 3:3 [b]Hos. 11:8
8 [a]Jer. 9:3 [b]Ps. 28:3 [c]Jer. 5:26
9 [a]Is. 1:24; Jer. 5:9, 29
10 [a]Jer. 4:24; 7:29 [b]Jer. 4:26; Hos. 4:3 [c]Jer. 12:4, 10; Ezek. 14:15; 29:11; 33:28 [d]Jer. 4:25; 12:4; Hos. 4:3
11 [a]Is. 25:2; Jer. 51:37 [b]Is. 13:22; 34:13 [c]Jer. 4:27; 26:9
12 [a]Ps. 107:43; Hos. 14:9 [b]Jer. 9:20; 23:16 [c]Ps. 107:34; Jer 23:10
13 [a]2 Chr. 7:19; Ps. 89:30; Jer. 5:19; 22:9
14 [a]Jer. 7:24; 11:8; Rom. 1:21-24 [b]Jer. 2:8, 23; 23:27 [c]Gal. 1:14; 1 Pet. 1:18
15 [a]Deut. 29:18; Jer. 8:14; 23:15

16"And I will [a]scatter them among
the nations, whom neither they nor
their fathers have known; and I will
send the [b]sword after them until I
have annihilated them."

17 Thus says the LORD of hosts,
"Consider and call for the [a]mourning women, that they may come;
And send for the [1b]wailing women, that they may come!
18"And let them make haste, and take up a wailing for us,
That our [a]eyes may shed tears,
And our eyelids flow with water.
19"For a voice of [a]wailing is heard from Zion,
'[b]How are we ruined!
We are put to great shame,
For we have [c]left the land,
Because they have cast down our dwellings.' "
20 Now hear the word of the LORD, O you [a]women,
And let your ear receive the word of His mouth;
Teach your daughters wailing,
And every one her neighbor a dirge.
21 For [a]death has come up through our windows;
It has entered our palaces
To cut off the [b]children from the streets,
The young men from the town squares.
22 Speak, "Thus declares the LORD,
'The corpses of men will fall like [a]dung on the open field,
And like the sheaf after the reaper,
But no one will gather *them*.' "

23 Thus says the LORD, "[a]Let not a
wise man boast of his wisdom, and
let not the [b]mighty man boast of his
might, let not a [c]rich man boast of
his riches;
24 but let him who boasts [a]boast
of this, that he understands and
knows Me, that I am the LORD who
[b]exercises lovingkindness, justice,
and righteousness on earth; for I
[c]delight in these things," declares
the LORD.
25"Behold, the days are coming,"
declares the LORD, "that I will punish all who are circumcised and yet
[a]uncircumcised—
26 Egypt, and Judah, and Edom,
and the sons of Ammon, and Moab,
and [a]all those inhabiting the desert
who clip the hair on their temples;
for all the nations are uncircumcised, and all the house of Israel are
[b]uncircumcised of heart."

16 [a]Lev. 26:33; Deut. 28:64; Jer. 13:24 [b]Jer. 44:27; Ezek. 5:2, 12
17 [1]Lit., *skilled in mourning for the dead* [a]2 Chr. 35:25; Eccles. 12:5 [b]Amos 5:16
18 [a]Is. 22:4; Jer. 9:1; 14:17
19 [a]Jer. 7:29; Ezek. 7:16-18 [b]Deut. 28:29; Jer. 4:13 [c]Jer. 7:15; 15:1
20 [a]Is. 32:9
21 [a]2 Chr. 36:17; Jer. 15:7; 18:21; Ezek. 9:5, 6; Amos 6:9, 10 [b]Jer. 6:11
22 [a]Ps. 83:10; Is. 5:25; Jer. 8:2; 16:4; 26:33
23 [a]Eccles. 9:11; Is. 47:10; Ezek. 28:3-7 [b]1 Kin. 20:10, 11; Is. 10:8-12 [c]Job 31:24, 25; Ps. 49:6-9
24 [a]Ps. 44:8; Is. 41:16; Jer. 4:2; 1 Cor. 1:31; 2 Cor. 10:17; Gal. 6:14 [b]Ex. 34:6, 7; Ps. 36:5, 7; 51:1 [c]Is. 61:8; Mic. 7:18
25 [a]Jer. 4:4; Rom. 2:8, 9
26 [a]Jer. 25:23 [b]Lev. 26:41; Jer. 4:4; 6:10; Ezek. 44:7; Rom. 2:28
2 [a]Lev. 18:3; Deut. 12:30 [b]Is. 47:12-14
3 [1]Lit., *vanity* [a]Jer. 14:22 [b]Is. 44:9-20
4 [a]Is. 40:19; Jer. 10:14 [b]Is. 40:20; 41:7
5 [a]Is. 46:1, 7 [b]Is. 41:23, 24
6 [a]Deut. 33:26; Jer. 10:16 [b]Ps. 48:1; 96:4; Is. 12:6; Jer. 32:18
7 [a]Ps. 22:28 [b]Dan. 2:27, 28; 1 Cor. 1:19, 20
8 [1]Lit., *vanities, or idols* [2]Lit., *it is*
9 [a]Is. 40:19 [b]Ps. 72:10; Is. 23:6 [c]Dan. 10:5 [d]Ps. 115:4
10 [a]Is. 65:16 [b]Jer. 4:2 [c]Ps. 10:16; 29:10 [d]Ps. 76:7
11 [1]This verse is in Aramaic [a]Ps. 96:5 [b]Is. 2:18; Zeph. 2:11

CHAPTER 10

A Satire on Idolatry

HEAR the word which the LORD
speaks to you, O house of Israel.
2 Thus says the LORD,
"Do not [a]learn the way of the nations;
And do not be terrified by the signs of the heavens
Although the [b]nations are terrified by them;
3 For the customs of the peoples are [1a]delusion;
Because [b]it is wood cut from the forest,
The work of the hands of a craftsman with a cutting tool.
4"They [a]decorate *it* with silver and with gold;
They [b]fasten it with nails and with hammers
So that it will not totter.
5"Like a scarecrow in a cucumber field are they,
And they cannot speak;
They [a]must be carried,
Because they cannot walk!
Do not fear them,
For they [b]can do no harm,
Nor can they do any good."

6 [a]There is none like Thee, O LORD;
Thou art [b]great, and great is Thy name in might.
7 Who would not fear Thee, O [a]King of the nations?
Indeed it is Thy due!
For among all the [b]wise men of the nations,
And in all their kingdoms,
There is none like Thee.
8 But they are altogether stupid and foolish
In their discipline of [1]delusion—[2]their idol is wood!
9 Beaten [a]silver is brought from [b]Tarshish,
And [c]gold from Uphaz,
The work of a craftsman and of the hands of a goldsmith;
Violet and purple are their clothing;
They are all the work of skilled [d]men.
10 But the LORD is the [a]true God;
He is the [b]living God and the [c]everlasting King.
At His wrath the earth quakes,
And the nations cannot [d]endure His indignation.
11 [1]Thus you shall say to them,
"The [a]gods that did not make the
heavens and the earth shall [b]perish

from the earth and from under the [2]heavens."

12 *It is* [a]He who made the earth by His power,
Who [b]established the world by His wisdom;
And by His understanding He has [c]stretched out the heavens.
13 When He utters His [a]voice, *there is* a tumult of waters in the heavens,
And He causes the [b]clouds to ascend from the end of the earth;
He makes lightning for the rain,
And brings out the [c]wind from His storehouses.
14 Every man is stupid, devoid of knowledge;
Every goldsmith is put to shame by his [1]idols;
For his molten images are deceitful,
And there is no breath in them.
15 They are [a]worthless, a work of mockery;
In the [b]time of their punishment they will perish.
16 The [a]portion of Jacob is not like these;
For the [1b]Maker of all is He,
And [c]Israel is the tribe of His inheritance;
The [d]LORD of hosts is His name.

17 [a]Pick up your bundle from the ground,
You who dwell under siege!
18 For thus says the LORD,
"Behold, I am [a]slinging out the inhabitants of the land
At this time,
And will cause them distress,
That they may [1]be found."

19 [a]Woe is me, because of my [1]injury!
My [b]wound is incurable.
But I said, "Truly this is a sickness,
And I [c]must bear it."
20 My [a]tent is destroyed,
And all my ropes are broken;
My [b]sons have gone from me and are no more.
There is [c]no one to stretch out my tent again
Or to set up my curtains.
21 For the shepherds have become stupid
And have not sought the LORD;
Therefore they have not prospered,
And [a]all their flock is scattered.
22 The sound of a [a]report! Behold, it comes—
A great commotion out of the land of the north—
To [b]make the cities of Judah
A desolation, a haunt of jackals.

23 I know, O LORD, that a man's [a]way is not in himself;
[b]Nor is it in a man who walks to direct his steps.
24 [a]Correct me, O LORD, but with justice;
Not with Thine anger, lest Thou [1]bring me to nothing.
25 [a]Pour out Thy wrath on the nations that do not know Thee,
And on the families that do not [b]call Thy name;
For they have devoured Jacob;
They have [c]devoured him and consumed him,
And have laid waste his [1]habitation.

11 [2]Or, *these heavens*
12 [a]Job 38:4-7; Ps. 148:4, 5; Jer. 51:15-19 [b]Ps. 78:69; Is. 45:18 [c]Job 9:8; Is. 40:22
13 [a]Ps. 29:3-9 [b]Job 36:27-29 [c]Ps. 135:7
14 [1]Or, *graven image*
15 [a]Is. 41:24; Jer. 8:19; 14:22 [b]Jer. 8:12; 51:8
16 [1]Lit., *Fashioner* [a]Ps. 73:26; Jer. 51:19 [b]Is. 45:7; Jer. 10:12 [c]Deut. 32:9 [d]Jer. 31:35; 32:18
17 [a]Ezek. 12:3-12
18 [1]Lit., *find* [a]1 Sam. 25:29
19 [1]Lit., *breaking* [a]Jer. 4:31 [b]Jer. 14:17 [c]Ps. 39:9; Mic. 7:9
20 [a]Jer. 4:20; Lam. 2:4 [b]Jer. 31:15; Lam. 1:5 [c]Is. 51:18
21 [a]Jer. 23:2
22 [a]Jer. 4:15 [b]Jer. 9:11; 49:33
23 [a]Prov. 20:24 [b]Is. 26:7
24 [1]Lit., *diminish me* [a]Ps. 6:1
25 [1]Or, *pasture* [a]Ps. 79:6, 7; Zeph. 3:8 [b]Zeph. 1:6 [c]Jer. 8:16; 50:7, 17
2 [a]Jer. 10:6 [b]Ex. 19:5
3 [a]Deut. 27:26; Jer. 17:5; Gal. 3:10
4 [1]Lit., *do them* [a]Ex. 24:3-8; Jer. 31:32 [b]Deut. 4:20; 1 Kin. 8:51 [c]Jer. 24:7; Zech. 8:8
5 [a]Ex. 13:5; Deut. 7:12; Jer. 32:22 [b]Jer. 28:6
6 [a]Jer. 3:12; 7:2
7 [1]Lit., *rising early and warning* [a]1 Sam. 8:9 [b]Ex. 15:26; Jer. 11:4 [c]2 Chr. 36:15; Jer. 7:25
8 [a]Jer. 7:24; 9:14; 35:15; Ezek. 20:8 [b]Lev. 26:14-43

CHAPTER 11

The Broken Covenant

THE word which came to Jeremiah from the LORD, saying,

2 "[a]Hear the words of this [b]covenant, and speak to the men of Judah and to the inhabitants of Jerusalem;

3 and say to them, 'Thus says the LORD, the God of Israel, "[a]Cursed is the man who does not heed the words of this covenant

4 which I commanded your forefathers in the [a]day that I brought them out of the land of Egypt, from the [b]iron furnace, saying, 'Listen to My voice, and [1]do according to all which I command you; so you shall be [c]My people, and I will be your God,'

5 in order to confirm the [a]oath which I swore to your forefathers, to give them a land flowing with milk and honey, as *it is* this day." ' " Then I answered and said, "[b]Amen, O LORD."

6 And the LORD said to me, "[a]Proclaim all these words in the cities of Judah and in the streets of Jerusalem, saying, 'Hear the words of this covenant and do them.

7 'For I solemnly [a]warned your fathers in the [b]day that I brought them up from the land of Egypt, even to this day, [1c]warning persistently, saying, "Listen to My voice."

8 'Yet they did not [a]obey or incline their ear, but walked, each one, in the stubbornness of his evil heart; therefore I brought on them all the [b]words of this covenant,

which I commanded *them* to do, but
they did not.' "
9 Then the LORD said to me, "A
[a]conspiracy has been found among
the men of Judah and among the inhabitants of Jerusalem.
10 "They have [a]turned back to the
iniquities of their [1]ancestors who
[b]refused to hear My words, and they
[c]have gone after other gods to serve
them; the house of Israel and the
house of Judah have [d]broken My
covenant which I made with their
fathers."
11 Therefore thus says the LORD,
"Behold I am [a]bringing disaster on
them which they will [b]not be able to
escape; though they will cry to Me,
yet I will not listen to them.
12 "Then the cities of Judah and the
inhabitants of Jerusalem will [a]go
and cry to the gods to whom they
burn incense, but they surely will
not save them in the time of their
disaster.
13 "For your gods are [1a]as many as
your cities, O Judah; and [1]as many
as the streets of Jerusalem are the
altars you have set up to the shameful thing, altars to [b]burn incense to
Baal.
14 "Therefore do not [a]pray for this
people, nor lift up a cry or prayer for
them; for I will [b]not listen when they
call to Me because of their disaster.

15 "What right has My beloved in
My house
When she has done many vile
deeds?
Can the sacrificial flesh take
away from you your disaster,
[1]So *that* you can rejoice?"
16 The LORD called your name,
"A [a]green olive tree, beautiful in
fruit and form";
With the noise of a great [b]tu-
mult
He has [c]kindled fire on it,
And its branches are worthless.

17 And the LORD of hosts, who
[a]planted you, has pronounced evil
against you because of the evil of
the house of Israel and of the house
of Judah, which they have [1]done to
provoke Me by [2b]offering up sacrifices to Baal.

Plots against Jeremiah

18 Moreover, the LORD [a]made it
known to me and I knew it;
Then Thou didst show me their
deeds.
19 But I was like a gentle [a]lamb led
to the slaughter;
And I did not know that they
had devised plots against me,
saying,
"Let us destroy the tree with its
[1]fruit,
And [b]let us cut him off from the
[c]land of the living,
That his [d]name be remembered
no more."
20 But, O LORD of hosts, who
[a]judges righteously,
Who [b]tries the [1]feelings and the
heart,
Let me see Thy vengeance on
them,
For to Thee have I [2]committed
my cause.

21 Therefore thus says the LORD
concerning the men of [a]Anathoth,
who [b]seek your life, saying, "Do not
prophesy in the name of the LORD,
that you might not [c]die at our
hand";
22 therefore, thus says the LORD of
hosts, "Behold, I am about to punish
them! The [a]young men will die by
the sword, their sons and daughters
will die by famine;
23 and a remnant will [a]not be left
to them, for I will [b]bring disaster on
the men of Anathoth—the year of
their punishment."

CHAPTER 12

Jeremiah's Prayer

[a]RIGHTEOUS art Thou, O LORD,
that I would plead *my* case
with Thee;
Indeed I would [b]discuss matters of justice with Thee:
Why has the [c]way of the
wicked prospered?
Why are all those who deal in
treachery at ease?
2 Thou hast [a]planted them, they
have also taken root;
They grow, they have even produced fruit.
Thou art [b]near [1]to their lips
But far from their [2]mind.
3 But Thou [a]knowest me, O
LORD;
Thou seest me;
And Thou dost [b]examine my
heart's *attitude* toward Thee.
Drag them off like sheep for the
slaughter
And [1]set them apart for a day of
carnage!
4 How long is the land to mourn
And the [a]vegetation of the
countryside to wither?
For the wickedness of those
who dwell in it,
[b]Animals and birds have been
snatched away,

9 [a]Ezek. 22:25; Hos. 6:9
10 [1]Lit., *the former fathers* [a]1 Sam. 15:11; Jer. 3:10, 11 [b]Deut. 9:7; Ps. 78:8-10; Jer. 13:10 [c]Judg. 2:11-13 [d]Jer. 3:6-11; Ezek.16:59
11 [a]2 Kin. 22:16; Jer. 6:19; 11:17 [b]Is. 24:17; Jer. 25:35
12 [a]Deut. 32:37; Jer. 44:17
13 [1]Lit., *the number of* [a]2 Kin. 23:13; Jer. 2:28 [b]Jer. 7:9
14 [a]Ex. 32:10; Jer. 7:16; 14:11 [b]Ps. 66:18; Jer. 11:11; Hos. 5:6
15 [1]Lit., *Then*
16 [a]Ps. 52:8 [b]Ps. 83:2 [c]Ps. 80:16; Is. 27:11; Jer. 21:14
17 [1]Or, *done for themselves* [2]Or, *burning incense* [a]Jer. 2:21; 12:2 [b]Jer. 7:9; 11:13; 32:29
18 [a]1 Sam. 23:11, 12; 2 Kin. 6:9, 10; Ezek. 8:6
19 [1]Lit., *bread* [a]Is. 53:7 [b]Ps. 83:4; Is. 53:8 [c]Job 28:13; Ps. 52:5 [d]Ps. 109:13
20 [1]Lit., *kidneys* [2]Lit., *revealed* [a]Gen. 18:25; Jer. 20:12 [b]Ps. 7:9; Jer. 17:10
21 [a]Jer. 1:1 [b]Jer. 12:5, 6; 20:10 [c]Jer. 26:8; 38:4
22 [a]2 Chr. 36:17; Jer. 18:21
23 [a]Jer. 6:9 [b]Jer. 23:12; Hos. 9:7; Mic. 7:4
1 [a]Ezra 9:15; Ps. 129:4; Jer. 11:20 [b]Job 13:3 [c]Jer. 5:27, 28; Hab. 1:4; Mal. 3:15
2 [1]Lit., *near in their mouth* [2]Lit., *kidneys* [a]Jer. 11:17; 45:4; Ezek. 17:5-10 [b]Is. 29:13; Jer. 3:10; Ezek. 33:31; Titus 1:16
3 [1]Lit., *sanctify them* [a]Ps. 139:1-4 [b]Ps. 7:9; 11:5; Jer. 11:20
4 [a]Joel 1:10-17 [b]Hos. 4:3; Hab. 3:17

Because *men* have said, "He
will not see our latter [c]end-
ing."

5"If you have run with footmen
and they have tired you out,
Then how can you compete
with horses?
If you fall down in a land of
peace,
How will you do in the [1]thicket
of the Jordan?
6"For even your [a]brothers and the
household of your father,
Even they have dealt treacherously with you,
Even they have cried aloud after you.
Do not believe them, although
they may say [b]nice things to
you."

God's Answer

7"I have [a]forsaken My house,
I have abandoned My inheri-
tance;
I have given the [b]beloved of My
soul
Into the hand of her enemies.
8"My inheritance has become to
Me
Like a lion in the forest;
She has [1a]roared against Me;
Therefore I have come to [b]hate
her.
9"Is My inheritance like a
speckled bird of prey to Me?
Are the [a]birds of prey against
her on every side?
Go, gather all the [b]beasts of the
field,
Bring them to devour!
10"Many shepherds have [a]ruined
My [b]vineyard,
They have [c]trampled down My
field;
They have made My [d]pleasant
field
A desolate wilderness.
11"[1]It has been made a desolation,
Desolate, it mourns [2]before Me;
The [a]whole land has been made
desolate,
Because no man [b]lays it to
heart.
12"On all the [1]bare heights in the
wilderness
Destroyers have come,
For a [a]sword of the LORD is devouring
From one end of the land even
to the [2]other;
There is no [b]peace for [3]anyone.
13"They have sown wheat and
have reaped thorns,

4 [c]Jer. 5:31; Ezek. 7:2

5 [1]Lit., *pride*

6 [a]Gen. 37:4-11; Job 6:15; Ps. 69:8; Jer. 9:4, 5 [b]Ps. 12:9; Prov. 26:25

7 [a]Is. 2:6; Jer. 7:29; 23:39 [b]Jer. 11:15; Lam. 2:1; Hos. 11:1-8

8 [1]Lit., *raised her voice* [a]Is. 59:13 [b]Hos. 9:15; Amos 6:8

9 [a]2 Kin. 24:2; Ezek. 23:22-25 [b]Is. 56:9; Jer. 7:33; 15:3; 34:20

10 [a]Jer. 23:1 [b]Ps. 80:8-16; Is. 5:1-7 [c]Is. 63:18 [d]Jer. 3:19; Lam. 1:10

11 [1]Lit., *One has made it* [2]Or, *upon* [a]Jer. 4:20, 27; 25:11 [b]Is. 42:25

12 [1]Or, *caravan trails* [2]Lit., *other end of the land* [3]Lit., *all flesh* [a]Is. 34:6; Jer. 47:6; Amos 9:4 [b]Jer. 16:5; 30:5

13 [1]Lit., *they do not profit* [2]Lit., *products* [a]Is. 55:2; Jer. 9:5 [b]Jer. 17:10 [c]Jer. 4:26; 25:37, 38

14 [a]Jer. 49:1, 7; Zeph. 2:8-10 [b]Jer. 2:3; 50:11, 12; Zech. 2:8 [c]Deut. 30:3; Ps. 106:47; Is. 11:11-16

15 [a]Jer. 48:7; 49:6, 39

16 [a]Is. 42:6; 49:6 [b]Jer. 4:2 [c]Josh. 23:7; Jer. 5:7 [d]Jer. 3:17; 4:2; 16:19

17 [a]Ps. 2:8-12; Is. 60:12

1 [a]Jer. 13:11; 19:1; 27:2; Ezek. 4:1

2 [a]Is. 20:2; Ezek. 2:8

4 [1]Or, *Parah*, cf. Josh. 18:23; so through v. 7 [a]Jer. 51:63

5 [a]Ex. 39:42, 43; 40:16

9 [a]Lev. 26:19; Is. 2:10-17; 23:9; Jer. 15:17; Zeph. 3:11

They have [a]strained themselves
[1]to no profit.
But be ashamed of your [2b]har-
vest
Because of the [c]fierce anger of
the LORD."
14 Thus says the LORD concerning
all My [a]wicked neighbors who
[b]strike at the inheritance with
which I have endowed My people
Israel, "Behold I am about to uproot
them from their land and will [c]up-
root the house of Judah from among
them.
15"And it will come about that after I have uprooted them, I will
[a]again have compassion on them;
and I will bring them back, each one
to his inheritance and each one to
his land.
16"Then it will come about that if
they will really [a]learn the ways of
My people, to [b]swear by My name,
'As the Lord lives,' even as they
taught My people to [c]swear by Baal,
then they will be [d]built up in the
midst of My people.
17"But if they will not listen, then I
will [a]uproot that nation, uproot and
destroy it," declares the LORD.

CHAPTER 13

The Ruined Waistband

THUS the LORD said to me, "Go
and [a]buy yourself a linen waistband,
and put it around your waist, but do
not put it in water."
2 So I bought the waistband in
accordance with the [a]word of the
LORD and put it around my waist.
3 Then the word of the LORD
came to me a second time, saying,
4"Take the waistband that you
have bought, which is around your
waist, and arise, go to [1]the [a]Euphra-
tes and hide it there in a crevice of
the rock."
5 So I went and hid it by the Euphrates, [a]as the LORD had commanded me.
6 And it came about after many
days that the LORD said to me,
"Arise, go to the Euphrates and take
from there the waistband which I
commanded you to hide there."
7 Then I went to the Euphrates
and dug, and I took the waistband
from the place where I had hidden
it; and lo, the waistband was ruined,
it was totally worthless.
8 Then the word of the LORD
came to me, saying,
9"Thus says the LORD, 'Just so
will I destroy the [a]pride of Judah
and the great pride of Jerusalem.

10 'This wicked people, who refuse to listen to My words, who walk in the stubbornness of their hearts and have gone after other gods to serve them and to bow down to them, let them be just like this waistband, which is totally worthless.
11 'For as the waistband clings to the waist of a man, so I made the whole household of Israel and the whole household of Judah [a]cling to Me', declares the LORD, 'that they might be for Me a people, for [1b]renown, for [c]praise, and for glory; but they [d]did not listen.'

Captivity Threatened

12"Therefore you are to speak this word to them, 'Thus says the LORD, the God of Israel, "Every jug is to be filled with wine."' And when they say to you, 'Do we not very well know that every jug is to be filled with wine?'
13 then say to them, 'Thus says the LORD, "Behold I am about to fill all the inhabitants of this land—the kings that sit for David on his throne, the priests, the prophets and all the inhabitants of Jerusalem—with [a]drunkenness!
14"And I will [a]dash them against each other, both the [b]fathers and the sons together," declares the LORD. "I will [c]not show pity nor be sorry nor have compassion that I should not destroy them."'"

15 Listen and give heed, do not be
[a]haughty,
For the LORD has spoken.
16 [a]Give glory to the LORD your
God,
Before He [b]brings darkness
And before your feet stumble
On the dusky mountains,
And while you are hoping for
light
He makes it into deep darkness,
And turns *it* into [c]gloom.
17 But [a]if you will not listen to it,
My soul will [b]sob in secret for
such pride;
And my eyes will bitterly weep
And flow down with tears,
Because the flock of the [c]LORD
has been taken captive.
18 Say to the [a]king and the queen
mother,
"[b]Take a lowly seat,
For your beautiful [c]crown
Has come down from your
head."
19 The cities of the Negev have
been locked up,
And there is no one to open
them;
All Judah has been carried into
exile,
Wholly carried into exile.

20"Lift up your eyes and see
Those coming [a]from the north.
Where is the [b]flock that was
given you,
Your beautiful sheep?
21"What will you say when He ap-
points over you—
And you yourself had taught
them—
Former [1a]companions to be
head over you?
Will not [b]pangs take hold of
you,
Like a woman in childbirth?
22"And if you [a]say in your heart,
'Why have these things hap-
pened to me?'
Because of the [b]magnitude of
your iniquity
Your skirts have been removed,
And your heels have [1]been exposed.
23"[a]Can the Ethiopian change his
skin
Or the leopard his spots?
Then you also can [b]do good
Who are accustomed to do evil.
24"Therefore I will [a]scatter them
like drifting straw
To the desert [b]wind.
25"This is your [a]lot, the portion
measured to you
From Me," declares the LORD,
"Because you have [b]forgotten
Me
And trusted in falsehood.
26"So I Myself have also [a]stripped
your skirts off over your face,
That your shame may be seen.
27"As for your [a]adulteries and
your *lustful* neighings,
The [b]lewdness of your prostitu-
tion
On the [c]hills in the field,
I have seen your abominations.
Woe to you, O Jerusalem!
How [d]long will you remain un-
clean?"

CHAPTER 14

Drought and a Prayer for Mercy

THAT which came as the word of the LORD to Jeremiah in regard to the drought:
2"Judah mourns,
And her gates languish
They sit on the ground [a]in
mourning,
And the [b]cry of Jerusalem has
ascended.

11 [1]Lit., *a name* [a]Ex. 19:5, 6; Deut. 32:10, 11 [b]Jer. 32:20 [c]Is. 43:21; Jer. 33:9 [d]Ps. 81:11; Jer. 7:13, 24, 26

13 [a]Ps. 60:3; 75:8; Jer. 25:27; 51:57

14 [a]Is. 9:20, 21; Jer. 19:9-11 [b]Jer. 6:21; Ezek. 5:10 [c]Deut. 29:20; Is. 27:11; Jer. 16:5; 21:7

15 [a]Prov. 16:5; Is. 28:14-22

16 [a]Ps. 96:8 [b]Is. 5:30; 59:9; Amos 5:18 [c]Ps. 107:10, 14; Jer. 2:6

17 [a]Mal. 2:2 [b]Ps. 119:136; Jer. 9:1; 14:17; Luke 19:41, 42 [c]Ps. 80:1; Jer. 23:1, 2

18 [a]2 Kin. 24:12, 15; Jer. 22:26 [b]2 Chr. 33:12, 19 [c]Ex. 39:28; Is. 3:20; Ezek. 24:17, 23; 44:18

20 [a]Jer. 1:15; 6:22; Hab. 1:6 [b]Jer. 13:17; 23:2

21 [1]Or, *chieftains* [a]Jer. 2:25; 38:22 [b]Is. 13:8; Jer. 4:31

22 [1]Or, *suffered violence* [a]Deut. 7:17 [b]Jer. 2:17-19; 9:2-9

23 [a]Prov. 27:22; Is. 1:5; Matt. 19:24 [b]Jer. 4:22; 9:5

24 [a]Lev. 26:33; Jer. 9:16; Ezek. 5:2, 12 [b]Jer. 4:11; 18:17

25 [a]Ps. 11:6; Matt. 24:51 [b]Ps. 9:17; 106:21, 22; Jer. 2:32; 3:21

26 [a]Lam. 1:8

27 [a]Jer. 5:7, 8 [b]Jer. 11:15 [c]Jer. 2:20 [d]Prov. 1:22; Hos. 8:5

2 [a]Jer. 8:21 [b]Jer. 11:11; 46:12; Zech. 7:13

3"And their nobles have [a]sent
their [1]servants for water;
They have come to the cisterns
and found no water.
They have returned with their
vessels empty;
They have been [b]put to shame
and humiliated,
And they [c]cover their heads.
4"Because the [a]ground is
[1]cracked,
For there has been no rain on
the land;
The [b]farmers have been put to
shame,
They have covered their heads.
5"For even the doe in the field has
given birth only to abandon
her young,
Because there is [a]no grass.
6"And the [a]wild donkeys stand on
the bare heights;
They pant for air like jackals,
Their eyes fail
For there is [b]no vegetation.
7"Although our [a]iniquities testify
against us,
O LORD, act for Thy name's
sake!
Truly our [b]apostasies have
been many,
We have sinned against Thee.
8"Thou [a]Hope of Israel,
Its [b]Savior in [c]time of distress,
Why art Thou like a stranger in
the land
Or like a traveler who has
pitched his *tent* for the night?
9"Why art Thou like a man dismayed,
Like a mighty man who [a]cannot
save?
Yet [b]Thou art in our midst, O
LORD,
And we are [c]called by Thy
name;
Do not forsake us!"
10 Thus says the LORD to this people, "Even so they have [a]loved to
wander; they have not [b]kept their
feet in check. Therefore the LORD
does [c]not accept them; now He will
[d]remember their iniquity and call
their sins to account."
11 So the LORD said to me, "Do not
[a]pray for the welfare of this people.
12"When they fast, I am [a]not going
to listen to their cry; and when they
offer burnt offering and grain offering, I am not going to accept them.
Rather I am going to [b]make an end
of them by the [c]sword, famine and
pestilence."

False Prophets

13 But, "Ah, Lord [1]GOD!" I said,
"Look, the prophets are telling
them, 'You [a]will not see the sword
nor will you have famine, but I will
give you [2]lasting [b]peace in this
place.'"
14 Then the LORD said to me, "The
[a]prophets are prophesying falsehood in My name. I have neither
sent them nor commanded them nor
spoken to them; they are prophesying to you a [b]false vision, divination,
futility and the deception of their
own [1]minds.
15"Therefore thus says the LORD
concerning the prophets who are
prophesying in My name, although
it was not I who sent them—yet
they keep saying, 'There shall be no
sword or famine in this land'—by
[a]sword and famine those prophets
shall [1]meet their end!
16"The people also to whom they
are prophesying will be [a]thrown out
into the streets of Jerusalem because of the famine and the sword;
and there will be no one to bury
them—*neither* them, *nor* their
wives, nor their sons, nor their
daughters—for I shall [b]pour out
their *own* wickedness on them.
17"And you will say this word to
them,
'[a]Let my eyes flow down with
tears night and day,
And let them not cease;
For the virgin [b]daughter of my
people has been crushed
with a mighty blow,
With a sorely infected wound.
18 'If I [a]go out to the country,
Behold, those [1]slain with the
sword!
Or if I enter the city,
Behold, diseases of famine!
For both prophet and priest
Have [2]gone roving about in the
land that they do not
know.'"

19 Hast Thou completely rejected
Judah?
Or hast [1]Thou loathed Zion?
Why hast Thou stricken us so
that we [a]are beyond healing?
[b]*We* waited for peace, but noth-
ing good *came;*
And for a time of healing, but
behold, terror!
20 We [a]know our wickedness, O
LORD,
The iniquity of our fathers, for
we have sinned against Thee.
21 Do not despise *us,* [a]for Thine
own name's sake;
Do not disgrace the [b]throne of
Thy glory;
Remember *and* do not annul
Thy covenant with us.

3 [1]Lit., *little ones* [a]1 Kin. 18:5 [b]Job 6:20; Ps. 40:14 [c]2 Sam. 15:30

4 [1]Lit., *shattered* [a]Joel 1:19, 20 [b]Joel 1:11

5 [a]Is. 15:6

6 [a]Job 39:5, 6; Jer. 2:24 [b]Joel 1:18

7 [a]Is. 59:12; Hos. 5:5 [b]Jer. 5:6; 8:5

8 [a]Jer. 17:13 [b]Is. 43:3; 63:8 [c]Ps. 9:9; 50:15

9 [a]Num. 11:23; Is. 50:2 [b]Ps. 46:5; Jer. 8:19 [c]Is. 63:19; Jer. 15:16

10 [a]Jer. 2:25; 3:13 [b]Ps. 119:101 [c]Jer. 6:20; Amos 5:22 [d]Jer. 44:21-23; Hos. 8:13

11 [a]Ex. 32:10; Jer. 7:16; 11:14

12 [a]Is. 1:15; Jer. 11:11 [b]Jer. 8:13 [c]Jer. 21:9

13 [1]YHWH, usually rendered LORD [2]Lit., *peace of truth* [a]Jer. 5:12; 23:17 [b]Jer. 6:14; 8:11

14 [1]Lit., *hearts* [a]Jer. 5:31; 23:25 [b]Jer. 23:16, 26; 27:9, 10; Ezek. 12:24

15 [1]Lit., *be finished* [a]Ezek. 14:10

16 [a]Ps. 79:2, 3; Jer. 7:33; 15:2, 3 [b]Prov. 1:31; Jer. 13:22-25

17 [a]Jer. 9:1; 13:17 [b]Is. 37:22; Jer. 8:21; Lam. 1:15; 2:13

18 [1]Lit., *pierced* [2]Or, *gone around trading* [a]Jer. 6:25; Lam. 1:20; Ezek. 7:15

19 [1]Lit., *Thy soul* [a]Jer. 30:13 [b]Job 30:26; Jer. 8:15; 1 Thess. 5:3

20 [a]Neh. 9:2; Ps. 32:5; Jer. 3:25

21 [a]Ps. 25:11; Jer. 14:7 [b]Jer. 3:17; 17:12

22 Are there any among the [1a]idols
of the nations who [b]give
rain?
Or can the heavens grant showers?
Is it not Thou, O LORD our God?
Therefore we [2c]hope in Thee,
For Thou art the one who hast
done all these things.

CHAPTER 15

Judgment Must Come

THEN the LORD said to me, "Even
[a]though [b]Moses and [c]Samuel were
to stand before Me, My [1]heart
would not be [2]with this people;
[d]send them away from My presence
and let them go!
2"And it shall be that when they
say to you, 'Where should we go?'
then you are to tell them, 'Thus says
the LORD:
"Those destined [a]for death, to
death;
And those destined for the
sword, to the sword;
And those *destined* for famine,
to famine;
And those *destined* for captivity,
to captivity." '
3"And I shall [a]appoint over them
four kinds *of doom*," declares the
LORD: "the sword to slay, the [b]dogs
to drag off, and the [c]birds of the sky
and the beasts of the earth to devour
and destroy.
4"And I shall [a]make them an object
of horror among all the kingdoms
of the earth because of [b]Manasseh,
the son of Hezekiah, the
king of Judah, for what he did in
Jerusalem.
5"Indeed, who will have [a]pity on
you, O Jerusalem,
Or who will mourn for you,
Or who will turn aside to ask
about your welfare?
6"You who have forsaken Me,"
declares the LORD,
"You keep [a]going backward.
So I will [b]stretch out My hand
against you and destroy you;
I am [c]tired of relenting!
7"And I will [a]winnow them with a
winnowing fork
At the gates of the land;
I will [b]bereave *them* of children,
I will destroy My people;
They did not [1]repent of their
ways.
8"Their [a]widows will be more numerous
before Me
Than the sand of the seas;
I will bring against them,
against the mother of a
young man,
A destroyer at noonday;
I will suddenly bring down on
her
Anguish and dismay.
9"She who [a]bore seven *sons* pines
away;
[1]Her breathing is labored.
Her [b]sun has set while it was
yet day;
She has been shamed and humiliated.
So I shall give over their [c]survivors
to the sword
Before their enemies," declares
the LORD.

10 [a]Woe to me, my mother, that
you have borne me
As a [b]man of strife and a man of
contention to all the land!
I have neither [c]lent, nor have
men lent money to me,
Yet every one curses me.
11 The LORD said, "Surely I will
[a]set you free for *purposes of*
good;
Surely I will cause the enemy to
make supplication to you
In a time of disaster and a time
of distress.

12"Can anyone smash iron,
Iron from the north, or bronze?
13"Your [a]wealth and your treasures
I will give for booty [b]without
cost,
Even for all your sins
And within all your borders.
14"Then I will cause your enemies
to bring [1]*it*
Into a [a]land you do not know;
For a [b]fire has been kindled in
My anger,
It will burn upon you."

Jeremiah's Prayer and God's Answer

15 Thou who knowest, O LORD,
Remember me, take notice of
me,
And take vengeance for me on
my persecutors.
Do *not*, in view of Thy patience,
take me away;
Know that [a]for Thy sake I endure
reproach.
16 Thy words were found and I
[a]ate them,
And Thy [b]words became for me
a joy and the delight of my
heart;
For I have been [c]called by Thy
name,
O LORD God of hosts.

22 [1]Lit., *vanities* [2]Or, *wait for* [a]Is. 41:29; Jer. 10:3 [b]1 Kin. 17:1; Jer. 5:24 [c]Lam. 3:26

1 [1]Lit., *soul* [2]Lit., *toward* [a]Ps. 99:6; Ezek. 14:14, 20 [b]Ex. 32:11-14; Num. 14:13-20; Ps. 106:23 [c]1 Sam. 7:9; 12:23 [d]2 Kin. 17:20; Jer. 7:15; 10:18; 52:3

2 [a]Jer. 14:12; 24:10; 43:11; Ezek. 5:2, 12

3 [a]Lev. 26:16, 22, 25; Ezek. 14:21 [b]1 Kin. 21:23, 24 [c]Deut. 28:26; Is. 18:6; Jer. 7:33

4 [a]Lev. 26:33; Jer. 24:9; 29:18 [b]2 Kin. 21:1-18; 23:26, 27; 24:3, 4

5 [a]Ps. 69:20; Jer. 13:14; 21:7

6 [a]Is. 1:4; Jer. 7:24 [b]Jer. 6:12; Zeph. 1:4 [c]Jer. 6:11; 7:16

7 [1]Lit., *turn back from* [a]Ps. 1:4; Jer. 51:2 [b]Jer. 18:21; Hos. 9:12-16

8 [a]Is. 3:25, 26; 4:1

9 [1]Or, *She has breathed out her soul* [a]1 Sam. 2:5; Is. 47:9 [b]Jer. 6:4; Amos 8:9 [c]Jer. 21:7

10 [a]Job 3:3; Jer. 20:14 [b]Jer. 1:18, 19; 15:20; 20:7, 8 [c]Ex. 22:25; Lev. 25:36, 37; Deut. 23:19

11 [a]Ps. 138:3; Is. 41:10

13 [a]Jer. 17:3; 20:5 [b]Is. 52:3, 5

14 [1]I. e., your possessions [a]Deut. 28:36, 64; Jer. 16:13 [b]Ps. 21:9; Jer. 17:4

15 [a]Ps. 44:22; 69:7-9; Jer. 20:8

16 [a]Ezek. 3:3 [b]Job 23:12; Ps. 119:103 [c]Jer. 14:9

17 I did not [a]sit in the circle of
merrymakers,
Nor did I exult.
Because of Thy hand *upon me* I
sat [b]alone,
For Thou didst fill me with indignation.
18 Why has my pain been perpetual
And my [a]wound incurable, refusing to be healed?
Wilt Thou indeed be to me [b]like
a deceptive *stream*
With water that is unreliable?

19 Therefore, thus says the LORD,
"If you return, then I will restore
you—
Before Me [a]you will stand;
And [b]if you extract the precious
from the worthless,
You will become [1]My spokesman.
They for their part may turn to
you,
But as for you, you must not
turn to them.
20"Then I will [a]make you to this
people
A fortified wall of bronze;
And though they fight against
you,
They will not prevail over you;
For [b]I am with you to save you
And deliver you," declares the
LORD.
21"So I will [a]deliver you from the
hand of the wicked,
And I will [b]redeem you from
the [1]grasp of the violent."

CHAPTER 16

Distresses Foretold

THE word of the LORD also came
to me saying,
2"You shall not take a wife for
yourself nor have sons or daughters
in this place."
3 For thus says the LORD concerning the sons and daughters born
in this place, and concerning their
mothers who bear them, and their
[a]fathers who beget them in this
land:
4"They will [a]die of deadly diseases, they will not be lamented or
buried; they will be as dung on the
surface of the ground and come to
an end by sword and famine, and
their carcasses will become food for
the [b]birds of the sky and for the
beasts of the earth."
5 For thus says the LORD, "Do not
enter a house of [1a]mourning, or go
to lament or to console them; for I
have withdrawn My [b]peace from
this people," declares the LORD,
"*My* [c]lovingkindness and compassion.
6"Both [a]great men and small will
die in this land; they will not be buried, they will not be lamented, nor
will anyone [b]gash himself or shave
his head for them.
7"Neither will men [a]break *bread*
in mourning for them, to comfort
anyone for the dead, nor give them a
cup of consolation to drink for anyone's father or mother.
8"Moreover you shall [a]not go into
a house of feasting to sit with them
to eat and drink."
9 For thus says the LORD of hosts,
the God of Israel: "Behold, I am
going to [1a]eliminate from this place,
before your eyes and in your time,
the voice of rejoicing and the voice
of gladness, the voice of the groom
and the voice of the bride.
10"Now it will come about when
you tell this people all these words
that they will say to you, '[a]For what
reason has the LORD declared all
this great calamity against us? And
what is our iniquity, or what is our
sin which we have committed
against the LORD our God?'
11"Then you are to say to them, '*It
is* [a]because your forefathers have
forsaken Me,' declares the LORD,
'and have followed [b]other gods and
served them and bowed down to
them; but Me they have forsaken
and have not kept My law.
12 'You too have done evil, *even*
more than your forefathers; for behold, you are each one walking according to the [a]stubbornness of his
own [b]evil heart, without listening to
Me.
13 'So I will [a]hurl you out of this
land into the [b]land which you have
not known, neither you nor your fathers; and there you will [c]serve other gods day and night, for I shall
grant you no favor.'

God Will Restore Them

14"[a]Therefore behold, days are
coming," declares the LORD, "when
it will no longer be said, 'As the
LORD lives, who [b]brought up the
sons of Israel out of the land of
Egypt,'
15 but, 'As the LORD lives, who
brought up the sons of Israel from
the [a]land of the north and from all
the countries where He had banished them.' For I will restore them
to their own land which I gave to
their fathers.

17 [a]Jer. 16:8; 2 Cor. 6:17 [b]Ps. 102:7; Jer. 13:17; Lam. 3:28; Ezek. 3:24, 25
18 [a]Job 34:6; Jer. 30:12, 15; Mic. 1:9 [b]Job 6:15, 20; Jer. 14:3
19 [1]Lit., *as My mouth* [a]1 Kin. 17:1; Jer. 15:1; 35:19 [b]Jer. 6:29; Ezek. 22:26; 44:23
20 [a]Jer. 1:18, 19; 6:27; Ezek. 3:9 [b]Ps. 46:7; Is. 41:10; Jer. 1:8, 19; 15:15
21 [1]Lit., *palm* [a]Gen. 48:16; Ps. 37:40; Jer. 20:13; 39:11, 12 [b]Is. 49:26; 60:16; Jer. 31:11; 50:34
3 [a]Jer. 6:21
4 [a]Jer. 15:2 [b]Ps. 79:2; Is. 18:6; Jer. 15:3; 34:20
5 [1]Or, *banqueting* [a]Ezek. 24:16-23 [b]Jer. 12:12; 15:1-4 [c]Ps. 25:6; Is. 27:11; Jer. 13:14
6 [a]2 Chr. 36:17; Ezek. 9:6 [b]Deut. 14:1; Jer. 41:5; 17:5
7 [a]Deut. 26:14; Ezek. 24:17; Hos. 9:4
8 [a]Eccles. 7:2-4; Is. 22:12-14; Jer. 15:17; Amos 6:4-6
9 [1]Lit., *cause to cease* [a]Jer. 7:34; 25:10; Hos. 2:11
10 [a]Deut. 29:24, 25; 1 Kin. 9:8, 9; Jer. 5:19; 13:22
11 [a]Neh. 9:26-29; Ps. 106:35-41; Jer. 5:7-9 [b]Jer. 8:2; Ezek. 11:21; 1 Pet. 4:3
12 [a]1 Sam. 15:23; Jer. 7:24; 9:14; 13:10 [b]Eccles. 9:3; Mark 7:21
13 [a]Deut. 4:26, 27; 2 Chr. 7:20; Jer. 15:1 [b]Jer. 15:14; 17:4 [c]Deut. 4:28; 28:36; Jer. 5:19
14 [a]Is. 43:18, 19; Jer. 23:7, 8; Hos. 3:4, 5 [b]Ex. 20:2; Deut. 15:15
15 [a]Ps. 106:47; Is. 11:11-16; 14:1; Jer. 3:18; 24:6

16"Behold, I am going to send for
many [a]fishermen," declares the
LORD, "and they will fish for them;
and afterwards I shall send for
many hunters, and they will [b]hunt
them [c]from every mountain and every hill, and from the clefts of the
rocks.
17"[a]For My eyes are on all their
ways; they are not hidden from My
face, nor is their iniquity concealed
from My eyes.
18"And I will first doubly [a]repay
their iniquity and their sin, because
they have [b]polluted My land; they
have filled My inheritance with the
carcasses of their detestable idols
and with their abominations."

19 O LORD, my [a]strength and my stronghold,
And my [b]refuge in the day of distress,
To Thee the [c]nations will come
From the ends of the earth and say,
"Our fathers have inherited nothing but falsehood,
Futility and [1]things of no profit."
20 Can man make gods for himself?
Yet they are [a]not gods!

21"Therefore behold, I am going to make them know—
This time I will [a]make them know
My [1]power and My might;
And they shall [b]know that My name is the LORD."

CHAPTER 17

The Deceitful Heart

THE sin of Judah is written down with an iron [a]stylus;
With a diamond point it is [b]engraved upon the tablet of their heart,
And on the horns of [1]their altars,
2 As they remember their [a]children,
So they *remember* their altars and their [1b]Asherim
By [c]green trees on the high hills.
3 O [a]mountain of Mine in the countryside,
I will [b]give over your wealth and all your treasures for booty,
Your high places for sin throughout your borders.
4 And you will, even of yourself, [a]let go of your inheritance
That I gave you;
And I will make you serve your [b]enemies
In the land which you do not know;
For you have [c]kindled a fire in My anger
Which will burn forever.

5 Thus says the LORD,
"[a]Cursed is the man who trusts in mankind
And makes [b]flesh his [1]strength,
And whose heart turns away from the LORD.
6"For he will be like a [a]bush in the desert
And will not see when prosperity comes,
But will live in stony wastes in the wilderness,
A land of [b]salt [1]without inhabitant.
7"[a]Blessed is the man who trusts in the LORD
And whose [b]trust is the LORD.
8"For he will be like a [a]tree planted by the water,
That extends its roots by a stream
And will not fear when the heat comes;
But its leaves will be green,
And it will not be anxious in a year of drought
Nor cease to yield fruit.

9"The heart is more [a]deceitful than all else
And is desperately [b]sick;
Who can understand it?
10"I, the LORD, [a]search the heart,
I test the [1]mind,
Even to give to each man according to his ways,
According to the [2]results of his deeds.
11"As a partridge that hatches eggs which it has not laid,
So is he who makes a fortune, but unjustly;
In the midst of his days it will forsake him,
And in [1]the end he will be a fool."

12 [a]A glorious throne on high from the beginning
Is the place of our sanctuary.
13 O LORD, the [a]hope of Israel,
All who forsake Thee will be put to shame.
Those who turn [1]away on earth will be written down,
Because they have forsaken the fountain of living water, even the LORD.

16 [a]Amos 4:2; Hab. 1:14, 15 [b]1 Sam. 26:20; Mic. 7:2 [c]Is. 2:21; Amos 9:1-3
17 [a]Ps. 90:8; Jer. 23:24; 32:19; Luke 12:2; 1 Cor. 4:5; Heb. 4:13
18 [a]Jer. 17:18; Rev. 18:6 [b]Num. 35:33, 34; Jer. 2:7; 3:9
19 [1]Lit., *there is nothing profitable in them* [a]Ps. 18:1, 2; Is. 25:4; Jer. 15:11 [b]Nah. 1:7 [c]Jer. 3:17; 4:2
20 [a]Ps. 115:4-8; Is. 37:19; Jer. 2:11; 5:7; Hos. 8:4-6
21 [1]Lit., *hand* [a]Ps. 9:16 [b]Ps. 83:18; Is. 43:3; Jer. 33:2; Amos 5:8
1 [1]So ancient versions; M.T., *your* [a]Job 19:24 [b]Prov. 3:3; 7:3; Is. 49:16; 2 Cor. 3:3
2 [1]I.e., wooden symbols of a female deity [a]Jer. 7:18 [b]Ex. 34:13 [c]Jer. 3:6
3 [a]Jer. 26:18; Mic. 3:12 [b]2 Kin. 24:13; Is. 39:4-6; Jer. 15:13; 20:5
4 [a]Jer. 12:7; Lam. 5:2 [b]Deut. 28:48; Is. 14:3; Jer. 15:14; 27:12, 13 [c]Is. 5:25; Jer. 7:20; 15:14
5 [1]Lit., *arm* [a]Ps. 146:3; Is. 2:22; 30:1; Ezek. 29:6, 7 [b]2 Chr. 32:8; Is. 31:3
6 [1]Lit., *and is not inhabited* [a]Jer. 48:6 [b]Deut. 29:23; Job 39:6
7 [a]Ps. 34:8; 84:12 [b]Ps. 40:4
8 [a]Ps. 1:3; 92:12-14; Ezek. 31:3-9
9 [a]Mark 7:21, 22; Rom. 7:11; Eph. 4:22 [b]Eccles. 9:3; Is. 1:6; 6:10; Matt. 13:15; Mark 2:17; Rom. 1:21
10 [1]Lit., *kidneys* [2]Lit., *fruit* [a]1 Sam. 16:7; Jer. 11:20; 20:12; Rom. 8:27
11 [1]Lit., *his*
12 [a]Jer. 3:17; 14:21
13 [1]Heb., *away from Me* [a]Jer. 14:8; 50:7

14 [a]Heal me, O LORD, and I will be
healed;
[b]Save me and I will be saved,
For Thou art my [c]praise.
15 Look, they keep [a]saying to me,
"Where is the word of the LORD?
Let it come now!"
16 But as for me, I have not hurried away from *being* a shepherd after Thee,
Nor have I longed for the woeful day;
Thou Thyself knowest the utterance of my lips
Was in Thy presence.
17 Do not be a [a]terror to me;
Thou art my [b]refuge in the day of disaster.
18 Let those who persecute me be [a]put to shame, but as for me, let me not be put to shame;
Let them be dismayed, but let me not be dismayed.
[b]Bring on them a day of disaster,
And crush them with twofold destruction!

The Sabbath Must Be Kept

19 Thus the LORD said to me, "Go
and stand in the [1]public gate,
through which the kings of Judah
come in and go out, as well as in all
the gates of Jerusalem;
20 and say to them, 'Listen to the
word of the LORD, [a]kings of Judah,
and all Judah, and all inhabitants of
Jerusalem, who come in through
these gates:
21 'Thus says the LORD, "[a]Take
heed for yourselves, and do not
[b]carry any load on the sabbath day
or bring anything in through the
gates of Jerusalem.
22"And you shall not bring a load
out of your houses on the sabbath
day nor do any [a]work, but keep the
sabbath day holy, as I [b]commanded
your [1]forefathers.
23"Yet they did not listen or incline
their ears, but [a]stiffened their necks
in order not to listen or take correction.
24"But it will come about, if you
listen [a]attentively to Me," declares
the LORD, "to bring no load in
through the gates of this city on the
sabbath day, [b]but to keep the sabbath day holy by doing no work on
it,
25 [a]then there will come in
through the gates of this city kings
and princes [b]sitting on the throne of
David, riding in chariots and on
horses, they and their princes, the
men of Judah, and the inhabitants of
Jerusalem; and this city will [c]be inhabited forever.
26"They will come in from the
cities of Judah and from the environs of Jerusalem, from the land of
Benjamin, from the [a]lowland, from
the hill country, and from the [a]Negev, bringing burnt offerings, sacrifices, grain offerings and incense,
and [b]bringing sacrifices of thanksgiving to the house of the LORD.
27"But if you do not listen to Me to
keep the sabbath day holy by not
carrying a load and coming in
through the gates of Jerusalem on
the sabbath day, then I shall kindle a
fire in its gates, and it will [a]devour
the palaces of Jerusalem and [b]not be
quenched." ' "

CHAPTER 18

The Potter and the Clay

THE word which came to Jeremiah from the LORD saying,
2"Arise and [a]go down to the potter's house, and there I shall announce My words to you."
3 Then I went down to the potter's house, and there he was, making something on the [1]wheel.
4 But the vessel that he was making of clay was spoiled in the hand
of the potter; so he remade it into
another vessel, as it pleased the potter to make.
5 Then the word of the LORD
came to me saying,
6"Can I not, O house of Israel,
deal with you as this potter *does?"*
declares the LORD. "Behold, like the
[a]clay in the potter's hand, so are you
in My hand, O house of Israel.
7"At one moment I might speak
concerning a nation or concerning a
kingdom to [a]uproot, to pull down, or
to destroy *it,*
8 [a]if that nation against which I
have spoken turns from its evil, I
will [1]relent concerning the calamity
I planned to bring on it.
9"Or at another moment I might
speak concerning a nation or concerning a kingdom to [a]build up or to
plant *it,*
10 if it does [a]evil in My sight by not
obeying My voice, then I will [1b]think
better of the good with which I had
promised to [2]bless it.
11"So now then, speak to the men
of Judah and against the inhabitants
of Jerusalem saying, 'Thus says the
LORD, "Behold, I am [a]fashioning calamity against you and devising a
plan against you. Oh [b]turn back,

14 [a]Jer. 30:17; 33:6 [b]Ps. 54:1; 60:5 [c]Deut. 10:21; Ps. 109:1
15 [a]Is. 5:19; Amos 5:18
17 [a]Ps. 88:15 [b]Jer. 16:19; Nah. 1:7
18 [a]Ps. 35:4, 26; Jer. 17:13; 20:11 [b]Ps. 35:8
19 [1]Lit., *gate of the sons of the people*
20 [a]Ps. 49:1, 2; Jer. 19:3, 4; Hos. 5:3; Amos 4:1
21 [a]Deut. 4:9; 16:23; Mark 4:24 [b]Num. 15:32-36; Neh. 13:15-21; John 5:9-12
22 [1]Lit., *fathers* [a]Ex. 16:23-29; 20:8-10; Deut. 5:12-14; Is. 56:2-6; 58:13 [b]Ex. 31:13-17; Ezek. 20:12; Zech. 1:4
23 [a]Prov. 29:1; Jer. 7:26; 19:15
24 [a]Ex. 15:26; Deut. 11:13; Is. 21:7; 55:2 [b]Ex. 20:8-11; Ezek. 20:20
25 [a]Jer. 22:4 [b]2 Sam. 7:16; 9:7; Jer. 13:15, 17, 21; Luke 1:32 [c]Ps. 132:13, 14; Heb. 12:22
26 [a]Zech. 7:7 [b]Ps. 107:22; Jer. 33:11
27 [a]Jer. 39:8; Amos 2:5 [b]Jer. 7:20; Ezek. 20:47
2 [a]Jer. 19:1, 2
3 [1]Lit., *pair of stone discs*
6 [a]Is. 45:9; 64:8; Matt. 20:15; Rom. 9:21
7 [a]Jer. 1:10
8 [1]Lit., *repent of* [a]Jer. 7:3-7; 12:16; Ezek. 18:21
9 [a]Jer. 1:10; 31:28; Amos 9:11-15
10 [1]Lit., *repent* [2]Lit., *do it good* [a]Ps. 125:5; Jer. 7:24-28; Ezek. 33:18 [b]1 Sam. 2:30; 13:13
11 [a]Is. 5:5; Jer. 4:6; 11:11 [b]2 Kin. 17:13; Is. 1:16-19; Jer. 4:1; Acts 26:20

each of you from his evil way, and
[1]reform your ways and your
deeds." '
12"But [a]they will say, 'It's hopeless! For we are going to follow our
own plans, and each of us will act
[b]according to the stubbornness of
his evil heart.'
13"Therefore thus says the LORD,
'[a]Ask now among the nations,
Who ever heard the like of this?
The virgin of Israel
Has done a most [b]appalling
thing.
14 'Does the snow of Lebanon forsake the rock of the open
country?
Or is the cold flowing water
from a foreign *land* ever
snatched away?
15 'For [a]My people have forgotten
Me,
[b]They burn incense [1]to worthless gods
And they [2]have stumbled [3]from
their ways,
[3]From the [c]ancient paths,
To walk in bypaths,
Not on a [d]highway,
16 To make their land a [a]desola-
tion,
An object of perpetual hissing;
Everyone who passes by it will
be astonished
And [b]shake his head.
17 'Like an east wind I will [a]scatter
them
Before the enemy;
I will [1]show them My back and
not *My* face
In the day of their calamity.' "
18 Then they said, "Come and let
us [a]devise plans against Jeremiah.
Surely the [b]law is not going to be
lost to the priest, nor [c]counsel to the
sage, nor the *divine* [d]word to the
prophet! [e]Come on and let us strike
at him with *our* tongue, and let us
give [f]no heed to any of his words."
19 Do give heed to me, O LORD,
And listen to [1]what my opponents are saying!
20 Should good be repaid with
evil?
For they have [a]dug a pit for me.
Remember how I [b]stood before
Thee
To speak good on their behalf,
So as to turn away Thy wrath
from them.
21 Therefore, [a]give their children
over to famine,
And deliver them up to the
power of the sword;
And let their wives become
[b]childless and [c]widowed.
Let their men also be smitten to
death,
Their [d]young men struck down
by the sword in battle.
22 May an [a]outcry be heard from
their houses,
When Thou suddenly bringest
raiders upon them;
[b]For they have dug a pit to capture me
And [c]hidden snares for my feet.
23 Yet Thou, O LORD, knowest
All their [1]deadly designs
against me;
Do not [2a]forgive their iniquity
Or blot out their sin from Thy
sight.
But may they be [b]overthrown
before Thee;
Deal with them in the [c]time of
Thine anger!

CHAPTER 19

The Broken Jar

THUS says the LORD, "Go and buy
a [a]potter's earthenware [b]jar, and
take some of the [c]elders of the people and some of the [d]senior priests.
2"Then go out to the [a]valley of
Ben-hinnom, which is by the entrance of the potsherd gate; and proclaim there the words that I shall tell
you,
3 and say, 'Hear the word of the
LORD, O kings of Judah and inhabitants of Jerusalem: thus says the
LORD of hosts, the God of Israel,
"Behold I am about to bring a calamity upon this place, at which the
[a]ears of everyone that hears of it
will tingle.
4"Because they have [a]forsaken
Me and have made this an [b]alien
place and have burned sacrifices in
it to [c]other gods that neither they
nor their forefathers nor the kings of
Judah had *ever* known, and *because*
they have filled this place with the
[d]blood of the innocent
5 and have built the [a]high places
of Baal to burn their [b]sons in the fire
as burnt offerings to Baal, a thing
which I never commanded or spoke
of, nor did it *ever* enter My mind;
6 therefore, behold, days are
coming," declares the LORD, "when
this place will no longer be called
[a]Topheth or the valley of Ben-hinnom, but rather the valley of
Slaughter.
7"And I shall [a]make void the
counsel of Judah and Jerusalem in

11 [1]Lit., *make good*
12 [a]Is. 57:10; Jer. 2:25 [b]Deut. 29:19; Jer. 7:24; 16:12
13 [a]Is. 66:8; Jer. 2:10, 11 [b]Jer. 5:30; 23:14; Hos. 6:10
15 [1]Lit., *to worthlessness* [2]So ancient versions; Heb., *caused them to* [3]Or, *in* [a]Jer. 2:32; 3:21 [b]Is. 65:7; Jer. 7:9; 44:17 [c]Jer. 6:16 [d]Is. 57:14; 62:10
16 [a]Jer. 25:9; 50:13; Ezek. 33:28, 29 [b]Ps. 22:7; Is. 37:22; Jer. 48:27
17 [1]So ancient versions; M.T. reads: *look them in the back and not in the face* [a]Job 27:21; Jer. 13:24
18 [a]Jer. 11:19; 18:11 [b]Jer. 2:8; Mal. 2:7 [c]Job 5:13; Jer. 8:8 [d]Jer. 5:13 [e]Ps. 52:2; Jer. 20:10 [f]Jer. 43:2
19 [1]Lit., *the voice of my opponents*
20 [a]Ps. 35:7; 57:6; Jer. 5:26; 18:22 [b]Ps. 106:23
21 [a]Ps. 109:9-20; Jer. 11:22; 14:16 [b]1 Sam. 15:33; Is. 13:18 [c]Jer. 15:8; Ezek. 22:25 [d]Jer. 9:21; 11:22
22 [a]Jer. 6:26; 25:34, 36 [b]Jer. 18:20 [c]Ps. 140:5
23 [1]Lit., *unto death* [2]Lit., *cover over, atone for* [a]Ps. 109:14; Is. 2:9 [b]Jer. 6:15, 21 [c]Jer. 7:20; 17:4
1 [a]Jer. 18:2 [b]Jer. 19:10 [c]Num. 11:16 [d]2 Kin. 19:2
2 [a]Josh. 15:8; Jer. 7:31, 32
3 [a]1 Sam. 3:11; 4:18
4 [a]Is. 65:11; Jer. 17:13 [b]Ezek. 7:22; Dan. 11:31 [c]Jer. 7:9; 11:13 [d]2 Kin. 21:6, 16; Jer. 2:34; 7:6
5 [a]Num. 22:41; Jer. 32:35 [b]2 Kin. 17:17; Ps. 106:37, 38
6 [a]Is. 30:33
7 [a]Ps. 33:10, 11; Is. 28:17, 18; Jer. 8:8, 9

this place, and I shall cause them to fall by the sword before their enemies and by the hand of those who seek their life; and I shall give over their [b]carcasses as food for the birds of the sky and the beasts of the earth.

8"I shall also make this city a [a]desolation and an *object of* hissing; [b]everyone who passes by it will be astonished and hiss because of all its [1]disasters.

9"And I shall make them [a]eat the flesh of their sons and the flesh of their daughters, and they will eat one another's flesh in the siege and in the distress with which their enemies and those who seek their life will distress them." '

10"Then you are to break the jar in the sight of the men who accompany you

11 and say to them, 'Thus says the LORD of hosts, "Just so shall I [a]break this people and this city, even as one breaks a potter's vessel, which cannot again be repaired; and they will [b]bury in Topheth [1]because there is no *other* place for burial.

12"This is how I shall treat this place and its inhabitants," declares the LORD, "so as to make this city like Topheth.

13"And the [a]houses of Jerusalem and the houses of the kings of Judah will be defiled [b]like the place Topheth, because of all the [c]houses on whose rooftops they burned [1]sacrifices to [d]all the heavenly host and [e]poured out libations to other gods." ' "

14 Then Jeremiah came from Topheth, where the LORD had sent him to prophesy; and he stood in the [a]court of the LORD's house and said to all the people:

15"Thus says the LORD of hosts, the God of Israel, 'Behold, I am about to bring on this city and all its towns the entire calamity that I have declared against it, because they have [a]stiffened their necks so [b]as not to heed My words.' "

CHAPTER 20

Pashhur Persecutes Jeremiah

WHEN Pashhur the priest, the son of [a]Immer, who was [b]chief officer in the house of the LORD, heard Jeremiah prophesying these things,

2 Pashhur had Jeremiah the prophet [a]beaten, and put him in the [b]stocks that were at the upper Benjamin [c]Gate, which was by the house of the LORD.

3 Then it came about on the next day, when Pashhur released Jeremiah from the stocks, that Jeremiah said to him, "Pashhur is not the name the LORD has [a]called you, but rather [1]Magor-missabib.

4"For thus says the LORD, 'Behold, I am going to make you a [a]terror to yourself and to all your friends; and while [b]your eyes look on, they will fall by the sword of their enemies. So I shall give over all Judah to the hand of the king of Babylon, and he will carry them away as exiles to Babylon and will slay them with the sword.

5 'I shall also give over all the [a]wealth of this city, all its produce, and all its costly things; even all the treasures of the kings of Judah I shall give over to the [b]hand of their enemies, and they will plunder them, take them away, and bring them to Babylon.

6 'And you, Pashhur, and all who live in your house will go into captivity; and you will enter Babylon, and there you will die, and there you will be buried, you and all your [a]friends to whom you have falsely prophesied.' "

Jeremiah's Complaint

7 O LORD, Thou hast deceived me
and I was deceived;
Thou hast [a]overcome me and
prevailed.
I have become a [b]laughingstock
all day long;
Everyone [c]mocks me.
8 For each time I speak, I cry
aloud;
I proclaim violence and destruction,
Because for me the [a]word of the
LORD has [1]resulted
In reproach and derision all day
long.
9 But if I say, "I will not [a]remember Him
Or speak any more in His
name,"
Then in my heart it becomes
like a burning fire
Shut up [b]in my bones;
And I am weary of holding *it* in,
And I cannot endure *it*.
10 For I have heard the whispering
of many,
"Terror on every side!
[a]Denounce *him;* yes, let us denounce him!"
[1]All my [b]trusted friends,
Watching for my fall, say:
"Perhaps he will be [2]deceived,
so that we may [c]prevail
against him
And take our revenge on him."

---

7 [b]Ps. 79:2, 3; Jer. 16:4

8 [1]Lit., *blows* [a]Jer. 18:16 [b]1 Kin. 9:8; 2 Chr. 7:21

9 [a]Deut. 28:53, 55; Lam. 4:10; Ezek. 5:10

11 [1]Or, *until there is no place left to bury* [a]Ps. 2:9; Is. 30:14; Rev. 2:27 [b]Jer. 7:32

13 [1]Or, *incense* [a]Jer. 52:13 [b]Ps. 74:7; 79:1; Ezek. 7:21, 22 [c]Jer. 32:29; Zeph. 1:5 [d]Deut. 4:19; 2 Kin. 17:16; Jer. 8:2 [e]Jer. 7:18; 44:18; Ezek. 20:28

14 [a]Jer. 26:2

15 [a]Neh. 9:17, 29; Jer. 7:26; 17:23 [b]Ps. 58:4

1 [a]1 Chr. 24:14; Ezra 2:37, 38 [b]2 Kin. 25:18

2 [a]1 Kin. 22:27; 2 Chr. 16:10; 24:21; Jer. 1:19; Amos 7:10-13 [b]Job 13:27; 33:11 [c]Jer. 37:13; 38:7; Zech. 14:10

3 [1]I. e., Terror on every side [a]Is. 8:3; Hos. 1:4, 9

4 [a]Job 18:11-21; Ezek. 26:21 [b]Jer. 29:21; 39:6, 7

5 [a]Jer. 15:13; 17:3 [b]2 Kin. 20:17, 18; 2 Chr. 36:10; Jer. 27:21, 22

6 [a]Jer. 14:14, 15; 19:4; Lam. 2:14

7 [a]Ezek. 3:14; Mic. 3:8 [b]Lam. 3:14 [c]Ps. 22:7; Jer. 38:19

8 [1]Lit., *become* [a]2 Chr. 36:16; Jer. 6:10

9 [a]1 Kin. 19:3, 4; Jon. 1:2, 3 [b]Job 38:18-20; Ps. 39:3; Jer. 4:19; 23:19; Ezek. 3:14; Acts 4:20

10 [1]Lit., *Every man of my peace* [2]Or, *persuaded* [a]Neh. 6:6-13; Is. 29:21; Jer. 18:18 [b]Ps. 41:9 [c]1 Kin. 19:2; 22:27

11 But the [a]LORD is with me like a dread champion;
Therefore my [b]persecutors will stumble and not prevail.
They will be utterly ashamed, because they have [1]failed,
With an everlasting disgrace that will not be forgotten.
12 Yet, O LORD of hosts, Thou who dost [a]test the righteous,
Who seest the [1]mind and the heart;
Let me [b]see Thy vengeance on them;
For [c]to Thee I have set forth my cause.
13 Sing to the LORD, praise the LORD!
For He has [a]delivered the soul of the needy one
From the hand of evildoers.

14 Cursed be the [a]day when I was born;
Let the day not be blessed when my mother bore me!
15 Cursed be the man who brought the news
To my father, saying,
"A [1a]baby boy has been born to you!"
And made him very happy.
16 But let that man be like the cities
Which the LORD overthrew without [1]relenting,
And let him hear an [a]outcry in the morning
And a [2]shout of alarm at noon;
17 Because he did not [a]kill me [1]before birth,
So that my mother would have been my grave,
And her womb ever pregnant.
18 Why did I ever come forth from the womb
To [a]look on trouble and sorrow,
So that my [b]days have been spent in [c]shame?

CHAPTER 21

Jeremiah's Message for Zedekiah

THE word which came to Jeremiah from the LORD when King Zedekiah sent to him [a]Pashhur the son of Malchijah, and [b]Zephaniah the priest, the son of Maaseiah, saying,
2 "Please inquire of the LORD on our behalf, for [a]Nebuchadnezzar king of Babylon is warring against us; perhaps the LORD will deal with us [b]according to all His [1]wonderful acts, that *the enemy* may withdraw from us."

3 Then Jeremiah said to them, "You shall say to Zedekiah as follows:
4 'Thus says the LORD God of Israel, "Behold, I am about to [a]turn back the weapons of war which are in your hands, with which you are warring against the king of Babylon and the Chaldeans who are besieging you outside the wall; and I shall [b]gather them into the center of this city.
5 "And I [a]Myself shall war against you with an [b]outstretched hand and a mighty arm, even in [c]anger and wrath and great indignation.
6 "I shall also strike down the inhabitants of this city, both man and beast; they will die of a great [a]pestilence.
7 "Then afterwards," declares the LORD, "I shall give over Zedekiah king of Judah and his servants and the people, even those who survive in this city from the pestilence, the sword, and the famine, into the hand of Nebuchadnezzar king of Babylon, and into the hand of their foes, and into the hand of those who seek their lives; and he will strike them down with the edge of the sword. He will not [a]spare them nor have pity nor compassion."'
8 "You shall also say to this people, 'Thus says the LORD, "Behold, I set before you the [a]way of life and the way of death.
9 "He who [a]dwells in this city will die by the sword and by famine and by pestilence; but he who goes out and falls away to the Chaldeans who are besieging you will live, and he will have his own life as booty.
10 "For I have [a]set My face against this city for [1]harm and not for good," declares the LORD. "It will be [b]given into the hand of the king of Babylon, and he will [c]burn it with fire."'
11 "Then *say* to the household of the king of Judah, 'Hear the word of the LORD,
12 O [a]house of David, thus says the LORD:
"[b]Administer justice [1]every [c]morning;
And deliver the *person* who has been robbed from the [2]power of his oppressor,
[d]That My wrath may not go forth like fire
And burn with [e]none to extinguish *it*,
Because of the evil of their deeds.

11 [1]Lit., *not succeeded*, or, *not acted wisely* [a]Jer. 1:8; 15:20 [b]Deut. 32:35, 36; Jer. 15:15

12 [1]Lit., *kidneys* [a]Ps. 7:9; 11:5; 17:3; 139:23; Jer. 11:20; 17:10 [b]Ps. 59:10; Jer. 11:20 [c]Ps. 62:8

13 [a]Ps. 34:6; 69:33; Jer. 15:21

14 [a]Job 3:3-6

15 [1]Lit., *male child* [a]Gen. 21:6, 7

16 [1]Lit., *being sorry* [2]Or, *trumpet blast* [a]Jer. 48:3, 4

17 [1]Lit., *from the womb* [a]Job 3:10, 11, 16; 10:18, 19

18 [a]Job 3:20; 5:7; 14:1; Jer. 15:10 [b]Ps. 90:9; 102:3 [c]Ps. 69:19; Jer. 3:25; 1 Cor. 4:9-13

1 [a]1 Chr. 9:12; Jer. 38:1 [b]2 Kin. 25:18-21; Jer. 29:25, 29; 37:3; 52:24

2 [1]Or, *miracles* [a]2 Kin. 25:1, 2 [b]Ps. 44:1-4; Jer. 32:17

4 [a]Jer. 32:5; 33:5; 37:8-10; 38:2, 3, 17, 18 [b]Is. 5:5; Jer. 39:3; Lam. 2:5, 7; Zech. 14:2

5 [a]Is. 63:10 [b]Deut. 4:34; Jer. 6:12 [c]Is. 5:25; Jer 32:37

6 [a]Jer. 14:12; 32:24

7 [a]2 Chr. 36:17; Jer. 13:14; Ezek. 7:9; Hab. 1:6-10

8 [a]Deut. 30:15, 19; Is. 1:19, 20

9 [a]Jer. 38:2; 39:18; 45:5

10 [1]Lit., *evil* [a]Jer. 44:11, 27; Amos 9:4 [b]Jer. 32:28, 29 [c]2 Chr. 36:19; Jer. 39:8; 52:13

12 [1]Or, *in the* [2]Lit., *hand* [a]Is. 7:2, 13 [b]Ps. 72:1; Is. 1:17; Jer. 7:5; 22:3; Zech. 7:9, 10 [c]Zeph. 3:5 [d]Jer. 4:4; 17:4; Ezek. 20:47, 48; Nah. 1:6 [e]Is. 1:31; Jer. 7:20

13"Behold, I am against you, O
[a]valley dweller,
O [1]rocky plain," declares the
LORD,
"You men who say, '[b]Who will
come down against us?
Or who will enter into our habitations?'
14"But I shall punish you according to the [1]results of your
deeds," declares the LORD,
"And I shall kindle a fire in its
forest
That it may [a]devour all its environs." ' "

CHAPTER 22

Warning of Jerusalem's Fall

THUS says the LORD, "Go down to
the house of the king of Judah, and
there [a]speak this word,
2 and say, 'Hear the word of the
LORD, O king of Judah, who [a]sits on
David's throne, you and your servants and your people who enter
these gates.
3 'Thus says the LORD, "[a]Do justice and righteousness, and deliver
the one who has been robbed from
the power of *his* [b]oppressor. Also
[c]do not mistreat *or* do violence to
the stranger, the orphan, or the
widow; and do not [d]shed innocent
blood in this place.
4"For if you men will indeed perform this thing, then kings will enter
the gates of this house, sitting [1]in
David's place on his throne, riding
in chariots and on horses, *even the
king* himself and his servants and
his people.
5"But if you will not obey these
words, I [a]swear by Myself," declares the LORD, "that this house
will become a desolation." ' "
6 For thus says the LORD concerning the house of the king of Judah:
"You are *like* [a]Gilead to Me,
Like the summit of Lebanon;
Yet most assuredly I shall make
you like a [b]wilderness,
Like cities which are not inhabited.
7"For I shall set apart [a]destroyers
against you,
Each with his weapons;
And they will cut down your
choicest [b]cedars
And throw *them* on the fire.
8"And many nations will pass by
this city; and they will [a]say to one
another, 'Why has the LORD done
thus to this great city?'
9"Then they will [1]answer, 'Because they [a]forsook the covenant of
the LORD their God and bowed
down to other gods and served
them.' "
10 Do not weep for the dead or
mourn for him,
But weep continually for the
one who goes away;
For he will never return
Or see his native land.
11 For thus says the LORD in regard to [1]Shallum the son of Josiah,
king of Judah, who became king in
the place of Josiah his father, who
went forth from this place, "He will
never return there;
12 but in the place where they led
him captive, there he will [a]die and
not see this land again.

Messages About the Kings

13"Woe to him who builds his
house without [a]righteous-
ness
And his [1]upper rooms without
justice,
Who uses his neighbor's services without pay
And does not give him his
wages,
14 Who says, 'I will [a]build myself a
roomy house
With spacious [1]upper rooms,
And cut out its windows,
[2]Paneling *it* with [b]cedar and
painting *it* [3]bright red.'
15"Do you become a king because
you are competing in cedar?
Did not your father eat and
drink,
And [a]do justice and righteousness?
Then it was [b]well with him.
16"He pled the cause of the [a]afflict-
ed and needy;
Then it was well.
[b]Is not that what it means to
know Me?"
Declares the LORD.
17"But your eyes and your heart
Are *intent* only upon your own
[a]dishonest gain,
And on shedding innocent
blood
And on practicing oppression
and extortion."
18 Therefore thus says the LORD in
regard to Jehoiakim the son of Josiah, king of Judah,
"They will not lament for him:
'Alas, my brother!' or, 'Alas, sister!'
They will not lament for him:
'Alas for the master!' or, 'Alas
for his splendor!'

---

13 [1]Lit., *rock of the level place* [a]Ps. 125:2; Is. 22:1 [b]2 Sam. 5:6, 7; Lam. 4:12; Obad. 3, 4

14 [1]Lit., *fruit* [a]2 Chr. 36:19; Jer. 52:13

1 [a]2 Chr. 25:15, 16

2 [a]Is. 9:7; Jer. 22:4, 30; 17:25; Luke 1:32

3 [a]Jer. 7:5; 21:12 [b]Ps. 72:4 [c]Ex. 22:21-24 [d]Jer. 7:6; 19:4; 22:17

4 [1]Lit., *for David*

5 [a]Gen. 22:16; Amos 6:8; Heb. 6:13

6 [a]Gen. 37:25; Num. 32:1; Song of Sol. 4:1 [b]Ps. 107:34; Is. 6:11; Jer. 7:34

7 [a]Is. 10:3-6; Jer. 4:6, 7 [b]Is. 10:33, 34

8 [a]Deut. 29:24-26; 1 Kin. 9:8, 9; 2 Chr. 7:20-22; Jer. 16:10

9 [1]Lit., *say* [a]2 Chr. 34:25; Jer. 11:3

11 [1]I. e., Jehoahaz

12 [a]2 Kin. 23:34; Jer. 22:18

13 [1]Or, *roof chambers* [a]Jer. 17:11; Mic. 3:10; Hab. 2:9

14 [1]Or, *roof chambers* [2]Or, *Paneled* [3]Or, *vermilion* [a]Is. 5:8, 9 [b]2 Sam. 7:2; Hag. 1:4

15 [c]2 Kin. 23:25; Jer. 7:5; 21:12 [b]Jer. 42:6

16 [a]Ps. 72:1-4, 12, 13 [b]1 Chr. 28:9; Jer. 9:24

17 [a]Jer. 6:13; 8:10; Luke 12:15-20

19"He will be [a]buried with a donkey's burial,
Dragged off and thrown out beyond the gates of Jerusalem.
20"Go up to Lebanon and cry out,
And lift up your voice in Bashan;
Cry out also from [a]Abarim,
For all your [b]lovers have been crushed.
21"I spoke to you in your prosperity;
But you said, 'I will not listen!'
This has been your practice from your youth,
That you have not obeyed My voice.
22"The wind will sweep away all your shepherds,
And your [a]lovers will go into captivity;
Then you will surely be ashamed and humiliated
Because of all your wickedness.
23"You who dwell in Lebanon,
Nested in the cedars,
How you will groan when pangs come upon you,
Pain like a woman in childbirth!

24"As I live," declares the LORD,
"even though [1]Coniah the son of Jehoiakim king of Judah were a [a]sig-
net *ring* on My right hand, yet I
would pull [1]you [2]off;
25 and I shall [a]give you over into
the hand of those who are seeking
your life, yes, into the hand of those
whom you dread, even into the hand
of Nebuchadnezzar king of Babylon, and into the hand of the Chaldeans.
26"I shall hurl you and your [a]moth-
er who bore you into another country where you were not born, and
there you will die.
27"But as for the land to which
they desire to return, they will not
return to it.

28"Is this man Coniah a despised, shattered jar?
Or is he an undesirable [a]vessel?
Why have he and his descendants been [b]hurled out
And cast into a land that they had not known?
29"[a]O land, land, land,
Hear the word of the LORD!
30"Thus says the LORD,
'Write this man down [a]childless,
A man who will not [b]prosper in his days;
For no man of his [c]descendants will prosper
Sitting on the throne of David
Or ruling again in Judah.' "

19 [a]1 Kin. 21:23, 24; Jer. 36:30
20 [a]Num. 27:12; Deut. 32:49 [b]Jer. 2:25; 3:1
22 [a]Jer. 30:14
24 [1]I.e., Jehoiachin [2]Lit., *off from there* [a]Song of Sol. 8:6; Is. 49:16; Hag. 2:23
25 [a]2 Kin. 24:15, 16; Jer. 21:7; 34:20, 21
26 [a]2 Kin. 24:8
28 [a]Hos. 8:8 [b]Jer. 15:1
29 [a]Deut. 4:26; Jer. 6:19; Mic. 1:2
30 [a]1 Chr. 3:17; Matt. 1:12 [b]Jer. 2:37; 10:21 [c]Ps. 94:20; Jer. 36:30
1 [a]Ezek. 13:3; 34:2; Zech. 11:17 [b]Is. 56:9-12; Jer. 10:21; 50:6 [c]Ezek. 34:31
2 [1]Lit., *shepherding* [a]Ex. 32:34 [b]Jer. 21:12; 44:22
3 [a]Is. 11:11-16; Jer. 31:7, 8; 32:37
4 [1]Or, *shepherd* [a]Jer. 3:15; 31:10; Ezek. 34:23 [b]John 6:39; 10:28; 1 Pet. 1:5
5 [1]Lit., *Sprout* [2]Or, *succeed* [a]Is. 4:2; 11:1-5; 53:2; Jer. 30:9; 33:15, 16; Zech. 3:8; 6:12, 13 [b]Is. 9:7; 52:13; Luke 1:32, 33 [c]Ps. 72:2
6 [a]Deut. 33:28; Jer. 30:10; Zech. 14:11 [b]Is. 7:14; 9:6; Matt. 1:21-23 [c]Jer. 33:16; Is. 45:24, 25; 54:17; Dan. 9:24; Rom. 3:22
7 [a]Is. 43:18, 19; Jer. 16:14, 15
9 [a]Jer. 8:18; Hab. 3:16
10 [a]Jer. 9:2; Hos. 4:2, 3; Mal. 3:5

CHAPTER 23

The Coming Messiah: the Righteous Branch

"[a]WOE to the shepherds who are
[b]destroying and scattering the
[c]sheep of My pasture!" declares the
LORD.
2 Therefore thus says the LORD
God of Israel concerning the shepherds who are [1]tending My people:
"You have scattered My flock and
driven them away, and have not attended to them; behold, I am about
to [a]attend to you for the [b]evil of your
deeds," declares the LORD.
3"Then I Myself shall gather the
[a]remnant of My flock out of all the
countries where I have driven them
and shall bring them back to their
pasture; and they will be fruitful and
multiply.
4"I shall also raise up [a]shepherds
over them and they will [1]tend them;
and they will not be afraid any
longer, nor be terrified, nor will [b]any
be missing," declares the LORD.

5"Behold, *the* days are coming," declares the LORD,
"When I shall raise up for David a righteous [1a]Branch;
And He will [b]reign as king and [2]act wisely
And [c]do justice and righteousness in the land.
6"In His days Judah will be saved,
And [a]Israel will dwell securely;
And this is His [b]name by which He will be called,
'The [c]LORD our righteousness.'

7"[a]Therefore behold, *the* days are
coming," declares the LORD, "when
they will no longer say, 'As the LORD
lives, who brought up the sons of
Israel from the land of Egypt,'
8 but, 'As the LORD lives, who
brought up and led back the descendants of the household of Israel
from *the* north land and from all the
countries where I had driven them.'
Then they will live on their own
soil."

False Prophets Denounced

9 As for the prophets:
My [a]heart is broken within me,
All my bones tremble;
I have become like a drunken man,
Even like a man overcome with wine,
Because of the LORD
And because of His holy words.
10 For the land is full of [a]adulterers;

For the land mourns because of the curse.
The [b]pastures of the wilderness have dried up.
Their course also is evil,
And their might is not right.
11 "For both prophet and priest are polluted;
Even in My house I have found their wickedness," declares the LORD.
12 "Therefore their way will be like [a]slippery paths to them,
They will be driven away into the [b]gloom and fall down in it;
For I shall bring [c]calamity upon them,
The year of their punishment," declares the LORD.

13 "Moreover, among the prophets of Samaria I saw an [a]offensive thing:
They [b]prophesied by Baal and led My people Israel astray.
14 "Also among the prophets of Jerusalem I have seen a horrible thing:
The committing of adultery and walking in falsehood;
And they strengthen the hands of [a]evildoers,
So that no one has turned back from his wickedness.
All of them have become to Me like [b]Sodom,
And her inhabitants like Gomorrah.
15 "Therefore thus says the LORD of hosts concerning the prophets,
'Behold, I am going to [a]feed them wormwood
And make them drink poisonous water,
For from the prophets of Jerusalem
Pollution has gone forth into all the land.' "

16 Thus says the LORD of hosts,
"[a]Do not listen to the words of the prophets who are prophesying to you.
They are [b]leading you into futility;
They speak a [c]vision of their own [1]imagination,
Not from the mouth of the LORD.
17 "They keep saying to those who [a]despise Me,
'The LORD has said, "[b]You will have peace" ';

10 [b]Ps. 107:34; Jer. 9:10
12 [a]Ps. 35:6; Jer. 13:16 [b]Is. 8:22; John 12:35 [c]Jer. 11:23
13 [a]Hos. 9:7, 8 [b]1 Kin. 18:18-21; Jer. 2:8
14 [a]Jer. 23:22; Ezek. 13:22, 23 [b]Is. 1:9, 10; Jer. 20:16; 49:18; Matt. 11:24
15 [a]Deut. 29:18; Jer. 8:14; 9:15
16 [1]Lit., *heart* [a]Jer. 27:9, 10, 14-17; 1 John 4:1 [b]Matt. 7:15; 2 Cor. 11:13-15; Gal. 1:8, 9 [c]Jer. 14:14; Ezek. 13:3, 6
17 [a]Mic. 2:11 [b]Jer. 8:11 [c]Jer. 5:12; Amos 9:10; Mic. 3:11
18 [1]Another reading is, *My* [a]Job 15:8, 9; Jer. 23:22 [b]Job 33:31
19 [a]Jer. 30:23; Amos 1:14
20 [a]Is. 55:11; Jer. 30:24; Zech. 1:6
22 [a]Jer. 35:15; Zech. 1:4; 1 Thess. 1:9, 10
23 [a]Ps. 139:1-10 [b]Ps. 113:5; Jer. 51:50; Jon. 1:3, 4
24 [a]Job 22:13, 14; Ps. 139:7-12; Is. 29:15; Jer. 49:10 [b]1 Kin. 8:27; Is. 66:1
25 [a]Jer. 8:6; 1 Cor. 4:5 [b]Num. 12:6; Jer. 23:28, 32; 29:8; Joel 2:28
26 [a]1 Tim. 4:1, 2
27 [a]Deut. 13:1-3; Jer. 29:8 [b]Judg. 3:7; 8:33, 34
28 [a]1 Cor. 3:12, 13

And as for every one who walks in the stubbornness of his own heart,
They say, '[c]Calamity will not come upon you.'
18 "But [a]who has stood in the council of the LORD,
That he should see and hear His word?
Who has given [b]heed to [1]His word and listened?
19 "Behold, the [a]storm of the LORD has gone forth in wrath,
Even a whirling tempest;
It will swirl down on the head of the wicked.
20 "The [a]anger of the LORD will not turn back
Until He has performed and carried out the purposes of His heart;
In the last days you will clearly understand it.
21 "I did not send *these* prophets,
But they ran.
I did not speak to them,
But they prophesied.
22 "But if they had stood in My council,
Then they would have [a]announced My words to My people,
And would have turned them back from their evil way
And from the evil of their deeds.

23 "Am I a God who is [a]near," declares the LORD,
"And not a God [b]far off?
24 "Can a man [a]hide himself in hiding places,
So I do not see him?" declares the LORD.
"[b]Do I not fill the heavens and the earth?" declares the LORD.
25 "I have [a]heard what the prophets have said who prophesy falsely
in My name, saying, 'I had a [b]dream,
I had a dream!'
26 "How long? Is there *anything* in
the hearts of the prophets who
prophesy falsehood, even *these*
prophets of the [a]deception of their
own heart,
27 who intend to [a]make My people
forget My name by their dreams
which they relate to one another,
just as their fathers [b]forgot My
name because of Baal?
28 "The prophet who has a dream
may relate *his* dream, but let him
who has My word speak My word in
truth. [a]What does straw have *in
common* with grain?" declares the
LORD.

29“Is not My word like [a]fire?” declares the LORD, “and like a [b]ham-
mer which shatters a rock?
30“Therefore behold, I am against
the prophets,” declares the LORD,
“who steal My words from each other.
31“Behold, I am against the prophets,” declares the LORD, “who use
their tongues and declare, ‘*The Lord*
declares.’
32“Behold, I am against those who
have prophesied [a]false dreams,” declares the LORD, “and related them,
and led My people astray by their
falsehoods and reckless boasting;
yet [b]I did not send them or command them, nor do they [c]furnish
this people the slightest benefit,”
declares the LORD.
33“Now when this people or the
prophet or a priest asks you saying,
‘What is the [1a]oracle of the LORD?’
then you shall say to them, ‘What
[1]oracle?’ The LORD declares, ‘I shall
[b]abandon you.’
34“Then as for the prophet or the
priest or the people who say, ‘The
[a]oracle of the LORD,’ I shall bring
punishment upon that man and his
household.
35“Thus shall each of you say to
his neighbor and to his brother,
‘What has the LORD answered?’ or,
‘[a]What has the LORD spoken?’
36“For you will no longer remember the oracle of the LORD, because
every man’s own word will become
the oracle, and you have [a]perverted
the words of the [b]living God, the
LORD of hosts, our God.
37“Thus you will say to *that*
prophet, ‘What has the LORD answered you?’ and, ‘What has the
LORD spoken?’
38“For if you say, ‘The oracle of
the LORD!’ surely thus says the
LORD, ‘Because you said this word,
“The oracle of the LORD!” I have
also sent to you, saying, “You shall
not say, ‘The oracle of the LORD!’ ” ’
39“Therefore behold, [a]I shall
surely forget you and cast you away
from My presence, along with the
city which I gave you and your fathers.
40“And I will put an everlasting
[a]reproach on you and an everlasting
humiliation which will not be forgotten.”

CHAPTER 24

Baskets of Figs and the Returnees

AFTER [a]Nebuchadnezzar king of
Babylon had carried away captive
Jeconiah the son of Jehoiakim, king
of Judah, and the officials of Judah
with the craftsmen and smiths from
Jerusalem and had brought them to
Babylon, the LORD showed me: behold, two baskets of [b]figs set before
the temple of the LORD!
2 One basket had very good figs,
like [a]first-ripe figs; and the other
basket had [b]very bad figs, which
could not be eaten due to rottenness.
3 Then the LORD said to me,
“[a]What do you see, Jeremiah?” And
I said, “Figs, the good figs, very
good; and the bad *figs,* very bad,
which cannot be eaten due to rottenness.”
4 Then the word of the LORD
came to me, saying,
5“Thus says the LORD God of Israel, ‘Like these good figs, so I will
regard [a]as good the captives of Judah, whom I have sent out of this
place *into* the land of the Chaldeans.
6 ‘For I will set My eyes on them
for good, and I will [a]bring them
again to this land; and I will [b]build
them up and not overthrow them,
and I will [c]plant them and not pluck
them up.
7 ‘And I will give them a [a]heart to
know Me, for I am the LORD; and
they will be [b]My people, and I will
be their God, for they will [c]return to
Me with their whole heart.
8 ‘But like the [a]bad figs which
cannot be eaten due to rottenness—
for thus says the LORD,—so I will
[1]abandon [b]Zedekiah king of Judah
and his officials, and the [c]remnant of
Jerusalem who remain in this land,
and the ones who dwell in the land
of [d]Egypt.
9 ‘And I will [a]make them a terror
and an evil for all the kingdoms of
the earth, as a [b]reproach and a proverb, a taunt and a [c]curse in all places
where I shall scatter them.
10 ‘And I will send the [a]sword, the
famine, and the pestilence upon
them until they are destroyed from
the land which I gave to them and
their forefathers.’ ”

CHAPTER 25

Prophecy of the Captivity

THE word that came to Jeremiah
concerning all the people of Judah,
in the [a]fourth year of [b]Jehoiakim the
son of Josiah, king of Judah (that
was the [c]first year of Nebuchadnezzar king of Babylon),
2 which Jeremiah the prophet
spoke to all the [a]people of Judah and

29 [a]Jer. 5:14; 20:9 [b]2 Cor. 10:4, 5
32 [a]Deut. 13:1, 2; Jer. 23:25 [b]Jer. 23:21; Lam. 3:37 [c]Jer. 7:8; Lam. 2:14
33 [1]Or, *burden,* and so throughout the chap. [a]Is. 13:1; Nah. 1:1; Hab. 1:1; Zech. 9:1 [b]Jer. 12:7; 23:39
34 [a]Lam. 2:14; Zech. 13:3
35 [a]Jer. 33:3; 42:4
36 [a]2 Pet. 3:16 [b]2 Kin. 19:4; Jer. 10:10
39 [a]Jer. 7:14, 15; 23:33; Ezek. 8:18
40 [a]Jer. 20:11; 42:18; Ezek. 5:14, 15
1 [a]2 Kin. 24:10-16; 2 Chr. 36:10; Jer. 27:20; 29:1, 2 [b]Amos 8:1
2 [a]Mic. 7:1; Nah. 3:12 [b]Is. 5:4, 7; Jer. 29:17
3 [a]Jer. 1:11, 13; Amos 8:2; Zech. 4:2
5 [a]Nah. 1:7; Zech. 13:9
6 [a]Jer. 29:10; 32:37; Ezek. 11:17 [b]Jer. 31:4; 33:7 [c]Jer. 32:41; 42:10
7 [a]Jer. 31:33; 32:40 [b]Zech. 8:8; Heb. 8:10 [c]1 Sam. 7:3; Jer. 29:13
8 [1]Lit., *give up* [a]Jer. 29:17 [b]Jer. 39:5; Ezek. 12:13 [c]Jer. 39:9 [d]Jer. 44:26-30
9 [a]Jer. 15:4; 29:18; 34:17 [b]1 Kin. 9:7; Ps. 44:13, 14 [c]Is. 65:15
10 [a]Is. 51:19; Jer. 21:9; 27:8; Ezek. 5:12-17
1 [a]Jer. 36:1; 46:2 [b]2 Kin. 24:1, 2; 2 Chr. 36:4-6 [c]Jer. 32:1
2 [a]Jer. 18:11

to all the inhabitants of Jerusalem,
saying,
3"From the [a]thirteenth year of
[b]Josiah the son of Amon, king of Judah, even to this day, [1]these [c]twen-
ty-three years the word of the LORD
has come to me, and I have spoken
to you [2d]again and again, but you
have not listened.
4"And the LORD has sent to you
all His [a]servants the prophets [1]again
and again, but you have not listened
nor inclined your ear to hear,
5 saying, '[a]Turn now every one
from his evil way and from the evil
of your deeds, and dwell on the land
which the LORD has given to you
and your forefathers [b]forever and
ever;
6 and do not [a]go after other gods
to [1]serve them and to [2]worship
them, and do not provoke Me to anger with the work of your hands,
and I will do you no harm.'
7"Yet you have not listened to
Me," declares the LORD, "in order
that you might [a]provoke Me to anger with the work of your hands to
your own harm.
8"Therefore thus says the LORD of
hosts, 'Because you have not
obeyed My words,
9 behold, I will send and take all
the families of the north,' declares
the LORD, 'and *I will send* to Nebuchadnezzar king of Babylon, [a]My
servant, and will bring them against
this land, and against its inhabitants, and against all these nations
round about; and I will [1]utterly destroy them, and make them a horror, and a hissing, and an everlasting desolation.
10 'Moreover, I will take from
them the voice of joy and the [a]voice
of gladness, the voice of the bridegroom and the voice of the bride,
the [b]sound of the millstones and the
light of the lamp.
11 'And this whole land shall be a
desolation and a horror, and these
nations shall serve the king of Babylon [a]seventy years.

Babylon Will be Judged

12 'Then it will be [a]when seventy
years are completed I will [b]punish
the king of Babylon and that nation,'
declares the LORD, 'for their iniquity, and the land of the Chaldeans;
and I will make it an everlasting
desolation.
13 'And I will bring upon that land
all My words which I have pronounced against it, all that is written
in [a]this book, which Jeremiah has
prophesied against all the nations.

3 [1]Lit., *this*
[2]Lit., *rising early and speaking*
[a]Jer. 1:2 [b]2 Chr. 34:1-3, 8 [c]Jer. 36:2 [d]Jer. 7:25; 11:7; 26:5
4 [1]Lit., *rising early and sending*
[a]Jer. 26:5
5 [a]Is. 55:6, 7; Jer. 4:1; 35:15; Ezek. 18:30; Jon. 3:8-10 [b]Gen. 17:8; Jer. 7:7; 17:25
6 [1]Or, *worship*
[2]Or, *bow down to*
[a]Deut. 6:14; 8:19; 2 Kin. 17:35; Jer. 35:15
7 [a]2 Kin. 17:17; 21:15; Jer. 7:19; 32:30-33
9 [1]Or, *put them under the ban*
[a]Is. 13:3; Jer. 27:6; 43:10
10 [a]Is. 24:8-11; Jer. 16:9; Ezek. 26:13 [b]Eccles. 12:4; Is. 47:2
11 [a]Dan. 9:2; Zech. 7:5
12 [a]Ezra 1:1; Jer. 29:10 [b]Jer. chaps. 50, 51; Is. 13:14
13 [a]Jer. 36:4, 29, 32
14 [a]Jer. 27:7; 50:9; 51:27, 28 [b]Jer. 51:6, 24, 56
15 [a]Ps. 75:8; Is. 51:17, 22; Jer. 51:7
17 [a]Jer. 1:10; 25:28; 27:3; Ezek. 43:3
19 [a]Jer. 46:2-28; Nah. 3:8-10
20 [a]Jer. 25:24; 50:37; Ezek. 30:5 [b]Job 1:1; Lam. 4:21 [c]Is. 20:1
21 [a]Ps. 137:7; Jer. 49:7-22 [b]Jer. 48:1-47; Amos 2:1-3 [c]Jer. 49:1-6; Amos 1:13-15
22 [a]Jer. 47:4; Zech. 9:2-4 [b]Jer. 31:10
23 [a]Is. 21:13; Jer. 49:7, 8 [b]Gen. 22:21 [c]Jer. 9:26; 49:32
24 [a]2 Chr. 9:14
25 [a]Gen. 10:22; Is. 11:11; Jer. 49:34
26 [1]*Possibly a cipher for Babylon*
[a]Jer. 25:9; 50:9 [b]Jer. 51:41
27 [a]Ezek. 21:4, 5
28 [a]Job 34:33
29 [a]Prov. 11:31; Is. 10:12; Jer. 13:13; Ezek. 9:6; 1 Pet. 4:17 [b]1 Kin. 8:43

14 '(For [a]many nations and great
kings shall make slaves of them,
even them; and I will [b]recompense
them according to their deeds, and
according to the work of their
hands.)' "
15 For thus the LORD, the God of
Israel, says to me, "Take this [a]cup of
the wine of wrath from My hand,
and cause all the nations, to whom I
send you, to drink it.
16"And they shall drink and stagger and go mad because of the
sword that I will send among them."
17 Then I took the cup from the
LORD's hand, and [a]made all the nations drink, to whom the LORD sent
me:
18 Jerusalem and the cities of Judah, and its kings *and* its princes, to
make them a ruin, a horror, a hissing, and a curse, as it is this day;
19 [a]Pharaoh king of Egypt, his servants, his princes, and all his people;
20 and all the [a]foreign people, all
the kings of the [b]land of Uz, all the
kings of the land of the Philistines
(even Ashkelon, Gaza, Ekron, and
the remnant of [c]Ashdod);
21 [a]Edom, [b]Moab, and the sons of
[c]Ammon;
22 and all the kings of [a]Tyre, all
the kings of Sidon, and the kings of
[b]the coastlands which are beyond
the sea;
23 and [a]Dedan, Tema, [b]Buz, and
all who cut the [c]corners *of their
hair;*
24 and all the kings of [a]Arabia and
all the kings of the foreign people
who dwell in the desert;
25 and all the kings of Zimri, all
the kings of [a]Elam, and all the kings
of Media;
26 and all the kings of the north,
near and far, one with another; and
[a]all the kingdoms of the earth which
are upon the face of the ground, and
the king of [1b]Sheshach shall drink
after them.
27"And you shall say to them,
'Thus says the LORD of hosts, the
God of Israel, "Drink, be drunk,
vomit, fall, and rise no more because of the [a]sword which I will
send among you." '
28"And it will be, if they [a]refuse to
take the cup from your hand to
drink, then you will say to them,
'Thus says the LORD of hosts: "You
shall surely drink!
29"For behold, I am [a]beginning to
work calamity in *this* city which is
[b]called by My name, and shall you
be completely free from punishment? You will not be free from
punishment; for I am summoning a

sword against all the inhabitants of
the earth," declares the LORD of
hosts.'
30"Therefore you shall prophesy
against them all these words, and
you shall say to them,
'The [a]LORD will [b]roar from on
high,
And utter His voice from His
holy habitation;
He will roar mightily against
His [1]fold.
He will shout like those who
tread *the grapes,*
Against all the inhabitants of
the earth.
31 'A clamor has come to the end
of the earth,
Because the LORD has a controversy with the nations.
He is entering into [a]judgment
with all flesh;
As for the wicked, He has given
them to the sword,' declares
the LORD."

32 Thus says the LORD of hosts,
"Behold, evil is going forth
From [a]nation to nation,
And a great [b]storm is being
stirred up
From the remotest parts of the
earth.
33"And those [a]slain by the LORD on
that day shall be from one end of the
earth to the [1]other. They shall [b]not
be lamented, gathered, or buried;
they shall be like [c]dung on the face
of the ground.
34"Wail, you shepherds, and cry;
And [a]wallow *in ashes,* you masters of the flock;
For the days of your [b]slaughter
and your dispersions [1]have
come,
And you shall fall like a choice
vessel.
35"Flight shall [a]perish from the
shepherds,
And escape from the masters of
the flock.
36"*Hear* the sound of the cry of the
shepherds,
And the wailing of the masters
of the flock!
For the LORD is destroying their
pasture,
37"And the peaceful [1a]folds are
made silent
Because of the fierce anger of
the LORD.
38"He has [a]left His hiding place
like the lion;
For their land has become a
horror
Because of the fierceness of the
[1]oppressing *sword,*
And because of His fierce anger."

30 [1]Or, *pasture* [a]Is. 42:13; Jer. 25:38 [b]Joel 2:11; Amos 1:2
31 [a]Is. 66:16; Ezek. 20:35, 36
32 [a]2 Chr. 15:6; Is. 34:2 [b]Is. 30:30; Jer. 23:19
33 [1]Lit., *other end of the earth* [a]Is. 34:2, 3; 66:16 [b]Ps. 79:3; Jer. 16:4; Ezek. 39:4, 17 [c]Is. 5:25
34 [1]Lit., *are full* [a]Jer. 6:26; Ezek. 27:30 [b]Is. 34:7; Jer. 50:27
35 [a]Job 11:20; Jer. 11:11; Amos 2:14
37 [1]Or, *pastures* [a]Is. 27:10, 11; Jer. 5:17; 13:20
38 [1]Or, *oppressor* [a]Jer. 4:7; 5:6; Hos. 5:14; 13:7, 8
1 [a]2 Kin. 23:36; 2 Chr. 36:4, 5
2 [a]2 Chr. 24:20, 21; Jer. 7:2; 19:14; Luke 19:47, 48 [b]Jer. 1:17; 42:4; Acts 20:20, 27 [c]Deut. 4:2
3 [a]Is. 1:16-19; Jer. 36:3-7
4 [a]Lev. 26:14; 1 Kin. 9:6; Is. 1:20; Jer. 17:27; 22:5 [b]Jer. 32:23; 44:10, 23
5 [1]Lit., *rising early and sending* [a]2 Kin. 9:7; Ezra 9:11; Jer. 25:4
6 [a]1 Sam. 4:10-12, 22; Ps. 78:60, 61; Jer. 7:12, 14 [b]2 Kin. 22:19; Jer. 24:9; 25:18
7 [a]Jer. 5:31; Mic. 3:11
8 [a]Jer. 11:19; 18:23; Lam. 4:13, 14; Matt. 21:35, 36; 23:34, 35
9 [a]Acts 3:11; 5:12
10 [a]Acts 21:31, 32 [b]Jer. 36:10
11 [a]Jer. 18:23 [b]Deut. 18:20; Matt. 26:66 [c]Jer. 38:4; Acts 6:11-14

CHAPTER 26

Cities of Judah Warned

IN the beginning of the reign of [a]Je-
hoiakim the son of Josiah, king of
Judah, this word came from the
LORD, saying,
2"Thus says the LORD, 'Stand in
the [a]court of the LORD's house, and
speak to all the cities of Judah, who
have come to worship *in* the LORD's
house, [b]all the words that I have
commanded you to speak to them.
[c]Do not omit a word!
3 '[a]Perhaps they will listen and
everyone will turn from his evil
way, that I may repent of the calamity which I am planning to do to
them because of the evil of their
deeds.'
4"And you will say to them, 'Thus
says the LORD, "[a]If you will not listen to Me, to [b]walk in My law, which
I have set before you,
5 to listen to the words of [a]My
servants the prophets, whom I have
been sending to you [1]again and
again, but you have not listened;
6 then I will make this house like
[a]Shiloh, and this city I will make a
[b]curse to all the nations of the
earth." ' "

A Plot to Murder Jeremiah

7 And the [a]priests and the prophets and all the people heard Jeremiah speaking these words in the
house of the LORD.
8 And when Jeremiah finished
speaking all that the LORD had commanded *him* to speak to all the people, the priests and the prophets and
all the people seized him, saying,
"[a]You must die!
9"Why have you prophesied in
the name of the LORD saying, 'This
house will be like Shiloh, and this
city will be desolate, without inhabitant'?" And [a]all the people gathered
about Jeremiah in the house of the
LORD.
10 And when the princes of Judah
heard these things, they [a]came up
from the king's house *to* the house
of the LORD and sat in the [b]entrance
of the New Gate of the LORD's
house.
11 Then the priests and the prophets [a]spoke to the officials and to all
the people, saying, "A [b]death sentence for this man! For he has
prophesied [c]against this city as you
have heard in your hearing."

12 Then Jeremiah spoke to all the
officials and to all the people, saying, "The LORD sent me to prophesy
against this house and against this
city all the words that you have
heard.
13"Now therefore [a]amend your
ways and your deeds, and obey the
voice of the LORD your God; and the
LORD will [1]change His mind about
the misfortune which He has pronounced against you.
14"But as for me, behold, I am in
your hands; do with me as is good
and right in your sight.
15"Only know for certain that if
you put me to death, you will bring
[a]innocent blood on yourselves, and
on this city, and on its inhabitants;
for truly the LORD has sent me to
you to speak all these words in your
hearing."

Jeremiah Is Spared

16 Then the officials and all the
people [a]said to the priests and to the
prophets, "No [b]death sentence for
this man! For he has spoken to us in
the name of the LORD our God."
17 Then some of the elders of the
land rose up and spoke to all the assembly of the people, saying,
18"[1][a]Micah of Moresheth prophesied in the days of Hezekiah king of
Judah; and he spoke to all the people of Judah, saying, 'Thus the LORD
of hosts has said,

"[b]Zion will be plowed *as* a field,
And Jerusalem will become ruins,
And the [c]mountain of the house
as the [2]high places of a forest." '

19"Did Hezekiah king of Judah
and all Judah put him to death? Did
he not [a]fear the LORD and entreat
the favor of the LORD, and the LORD
[1]changed His mind about the misfortune which He had pronounced
against them? But we are [b]commit-
ting a great evil against ourselves."
20 Indeed, there was also a man
who prophesied in the name of the
LORD, Uriah the son of Shemaiah
from Kiriath-jearim; and he prophesied against this city and against
this land words similar to all those
of Jeremiah.
21 When King Jehoiakim and all
his mighty men and all the officials
heard his words, then the [a]king
sought to put him to death; but
Uriah heard *it*, and he was afraid
and [b]fled, and went to Egypt.
22 Then King Jehoiakim sent men
to Egypt: [a]Elnathan the son of Ach-

13 [1]Lit., *be sorry for*
[a]Jer. 7:3, 5; 18:11; 35:15

15 [a]Num. 35:33; Prov. 6:16, 17; Jer. 7:6

16 [a]Jer. 26:11; 36:19, 25; 38:7, 13 [b]Acts 5:34-39; 23:9, 29; 25:25; 26:31

18 [1]Lit., *Micaiah the Morasthite* [2]Or, *a wooded height*
[a]Mic. 1:1 [b]Neh. 4:2; Ps. 79:1; Jer. 9:11; Mic. 3:12 [c]Is. 2:2, 3; Jer. 17:3; Mic. 4:1; Zech. 8:3

19 [1]Lit., *was sorry for*
[a]2 Chr. 29:6-11; 32:26; Is. 37:1, 4, 15-20 [b]Jer. 44:7; Hab. 2:10

21 [a]2 Chr. 16:10; Jer. 36:26; Matt. 14:5 [b]1 Kin. 19:2-4; Matt. 10:23, 28

22 [a]Jer. 36:12

23 [1]Lit., *graves* [2]Lit., *sons of the people*
[a]Jer. 2:30

24 [a]2 Kin. 22:12-14; Jer. 39:14; 40:5-7 [b]1 Kin. 18:4; Jer. 1:18, 19

1 [1]Many mss. read, *Jehoiakim*

2 [a]Jer. 30:8 [b]Jer. 28:10, 13

3 [1]Lit., *them* [2]Lit., *by the hand of*
[a]Jer. 25:21, 22

5 [1]Or, *upright*
[a]Ps. 146:5, 6; Jer. 10:12; 51:15 [b]Deut. 9:29; Jer. 32:17 [c]Ps. 115:15, 16; Acts 17:26

6 [a]Jer. 21:7; 22:25; Ezek. 29:18-20 [b]Is. 44:28; Jer. 25:9; 43:10 [c]Jer. 28:14

7 [1]Or, *enslave him*
[a]Jer. 44:30; 46:13 [b]Zech. 2:8, 9 [c]Is. 14:4-6; Jer. 25:12

8 [1]Lit., *them*
[a]Jer. 38:17-19; 42:15, 16; Ezek. 17:19-21 [b]Jer. 24:10; 27:13; 29:17, 18; Ezek. 14:21

9 [a]Ex. 22:18; Deut. 18:10; Is. 8:19; Mal. 3:5

bor and *certain* men with him *went*
into Egypt.
23 And they brought Uriah from
Egypt and led him to King Jehoiakim, who [a]slew him with a sword,
and cast his dead body into the
[1]burial place of the [2]common people.
24 But the hand of [a]Ahikam the
son of Shaphan was with Jeremiah,
so that he was [b]not given into the
hands of the people to put him to
death.

CHAPTER 27

The Nations to Submit to Nebuchadnezzar

IN the beginning of the reign of
[1]Zedekiah the son of Josiah, king of
Judah, this word came to Jeremiah
from the LORD, saying—
2 thus says the LORD to me—
"Make for yourself [a]bonds and
[b]yokes and put them on your neck,
3 and send [1]word to the king of
[a]Edom, to the king of [a]Moab, to the
king of the sons of [a]Ammon, to the
king of [a]Tyre, and to the king of [a]Si-
don [2]by the messengers who come
to Jerusalem to Zedekiah king of Judah.
4"And command them *to go* to
their masters, saying, 'Thus says the
LORD of hosts, the God of Israel,
thus you shall say to your masters,
5"[a]I have made the earth, the men
and the beasts which are on the face
of the earth [b]by My great power and
by My outstretched arm, and I will
[c]give it to the one who is [1]pleasing in
My sight.
6"And now I [a]have given all these
lands into the hand of Nebuchadnezzar king of Babylon, [b]My servant, and I have given him also the
[c]wild animals of the field to serve
him.
7"And [a]all the nations shall serve
him, and his son, and his grandson,
[b]until the time of his own land
comes; then [c]many nations and
great kings will [1]make him their servant.
8"And it will be, *that* the nation or
the kingdom which [a]will not serve
him, Nebuchadnezzar king of Babylon, and which will not put its neck
under the yoke of the king of Babylon, I will punish that nation with
the [b]sword, with famine, and with
pestilence," declares the LORD, "until I have destroyed [1]it by his hand.
9"But as for you, do not [a]listen to
your prophets, your diviners, your

[1]dreamers, your soothsayers, or your sorcerers, who speak to you, saying, 'You shall not serve the king of Babylon.'

10"For they prophesy a [a]lie to you, in order to [b]remove you far from your land; and I will drive you out, and you will perish.

11"But the nation which will bring its neck under the yoke of the king of Babylon and serve him, I will [a]let remain on its land," declares the LORD, "and they will till it and dwell in it." ' "

12 And I spoke words like all these to [a]Zedekiah king of Judah, saying, "Bring your necks under the yoke of the king of Babylon, and serve him and his people, and live!

13"Why will you [a]die, you and your people, by the sword, famine, and pestilence, as the LORD has spoken to that nation which will not serve the king of Babylon?

14"So do not [a]listen to the words of the prophets who speak to you, saying, 'You shall not serve the king of Babylon,' for they prophesy a [b]lie to you;

15 for [a]I have not sent them," declares the LORD, "but they prophesy [b]falsely in My name, in order that I may [c]drive you out, and that you may perish, you and the prophets who prophesy to you."

16 *Then* I spoke to the priests and to all this people, saying, "Thus says the LORD: Do not listen to the words of your prophets who prophesy to you, saying, 'Behold, the [a]vessels of the LORD's house will now shortly be brought again from Babylon'; for they are prophesying a lie to you.

17"Do not listen to them; serve the king of Babylon, and live! Why should this city become a ruin?

18"But [a]if they are prophets, and if the word of the LORD is with them, let them now [b]entreat the LORD of hosts, that the vessels which are left in the house of the LORD, in the house of the king of Judah, and in Jerusalem, may not go to Babylon.

19"For thus says the LORD of hosts concerning the [a]pillars, concerning the sea, concerning the stands, and concerning the rest of the vessels that are left in this city,

20 which Nebuchadnezzar king of Babylon did not take when he [a]carried into exile Jeconiah the son of Jehoiakim, king of Judah, from Jerusalem to Babylon, and all the nobles of Judah and Jerusalem.

21"Yes, thus says the LORD of hosts, the God of Israel, concerning the vessels that are left in the house of the LORD, and in the house of the king of Judah, and in Jerusalem,

22 'They shall be [a]carried to Babylon, and they shall be there until the [b]day I visit them,' declares the LORD. 'Then I will [c]bring them [1]back and restore them to this place.' "

Chapter 28

Hananiah's False Prophecy

NOW it came about in the same year, [a]in the beginning of the reign of [b]Zedekiah king of Judah, in the fourth year, in the fifth month, that [c]Hananiah the son of Azzur, the prophet, who was from [d]Gibeon, spoke to me in the house of the LORD in the presence of the priests and all the people, saying,

2"[a]Thus says the LORD of hosts, the God of Israel, 'I have broken the yoke of the king of Babylon.

3 'Within two years I am going to bring back to this place [a]all the vessels of the LORD's house, which Nebuchadnezzar king of Babylon took away from this place and carried to Babylon.

4 'I am [a]also going to bring back to this place [b]Jeconiah the son of Jehoiakim, king of Judah, and all the [c]exiles of Judah who went to Babylon,' declares the LORD, 'for I will break the [d]yoke of the king of Babylon.' "

5 Then the prophet Jeremiah spoke to the prophet Hananiah in the presence of the priests and in the presence of all the people who were standing in the [a]house of the LORD,

6 and the prophet Jeremiah said, "[a]Amen! May the LORD do so; may the LORD [1b]confirm your words which you have prophesied to bring back the vessels of the LORD's house and all the exiles, from Babylon to this place.

7"Yet [a]hear now this word which I am about to speak in your hearing and in the hearing of all the people!

8"The prophets who were before me and before you from ancient times [a]prophesied against many lands and against great kingdoms, of war and of calamity and of pestilence.

9"The prophet who prophesies of peace, [a]when the word of the prophet shall come to pass, then that prophet will be known *as* one whom the LORD has truly sent."

10 Then Hananiah the prophet took the [a]yoke from the neck of Jeremiah the prophet and [b]broke it.

---

9 [1]Lit., *dreams*

10 [a]Jer. 23:25 [b]Jer. 8:19; 32:31

11 [a]Jer. 21:9; 38:2; 40:9-12; 42:10, 11

12 [a]Jer. 27:3; 28:1

13 [a]Prov. 8:36; Jer. 27:8; 38:23; Ezek. 18:31

14 [a]2 Chr. 11:13-15; Jer. 27:9 [b]Jer. 27:10; Ezek. 13:22

15 [a]Jer. 23:21; 29:9 [b]Jer. 23:25 [c]2 Chr. 25:16; Jer. 27:10

16 [a]2 Kin. 24:13; 2 Chr. 36:7, 10; Jer. 28:3

18 [a]1 Kin. 18:24 [b]1 Sam. 7:8; 12:19, 23; Jer. 18:20

19 [a]1 Kin. 7:15; 2 Kin. 25:13, 17; Jer. 52:17-23

20 [a]2 Kin. 24:12, 14-16; 2 Chr. 36:10, 18; Jer. 22:28; 24:1

22 [1]Lit., *up* [a]Jer. 29:10; 34:2, 3 [b]Jer. 25:11, 12; 27:7; 29:10; 32:5 [c]Ezra 1:7-11; 5:13-15; 7:9, 19

1 [a]Jer. 49:34 [b]Jer. 27:3, 12 [c]Jer. 28:17 [d]Josh. 9:3; 10:12; 1 Kin. 3:4

2 [a]Jer. 28:11

3 [a]2 Kin. 24:13; 2 Chr. 36:10; Jer. 27:16; Dan. 1:2

4 [a]Jer. 22:26, 27 [b]2 Kin. 25:27; Jer. 22:24; 24:1; [c]Jer. 22:10 [d]Jer. 27:8

5 [a]Jer. 28:1

6 [1]Or, *fulfill* [a]1 Kin. 1:36; Ps. 41:13; Jer. 11:5 [b]Jer. 17:16

7 [a]1 Kin. 22:28

8 [a]Lev. 26:14; 1 Kin. 14:15; 17:1; 22:17; Is. 5:5-7; Joel 1:20; Amos 1:2; Nah. 1:2

9 [a]Deut. 18:22

10 [a]Jer. 27:2 [b]1 Kin. 22:11, 24; Jer. 36:23

11 And Hananiah spoke in the
presence of all the people, saying,
"[a]Thus says the LORD, 'Even so will
I break within two full years, the
yoke of Nebuchadnezzar king of
Babylon from the neck of all the nations.' " Then the prophet Jeremiah
went his way.
12 And the [a]word of the LORD
came to Jeremiah, after Hananiah
the prophet had broken the yoke
from off the neck of the prophet Jeremiah, saying,
13"Go and speak to Hananiah, saying, 'Thus says the LORD, "You have
broken the yokes of wood, but you
have made instead of them [a]yokes
of iron."
14 'For thus says the LORD of hosts,
the God of Israel, "I have put a
[a]yoke of iron on the neck of all these
nations, that they may serve Nebuchadnezzar king of Babylon; and
they shall [b]serve him. And [c]I have
also given him the beasts of the
field." ' "
15 Then Jeremiah the prophet said
to Hananiah the prophet, "Listen
now, Hananiah, the LORD has not
sent you, and [a]you have made this
people trust in a lie.
16"Therefore thus says the LORD,
'[a]Behold, I am about to [1]remove you
from the face of the earth. This year
you are going to [b]die, because you
have [2c]counseled rebellion against
the LORD.' "
17 So Hananiah the prophet died
in the same year in the seventh
month.

CHAPTER 29

Message to the Exiles

NOW these are the words of the
[a]letter which Jeremiah the prophet
sent from Jerusalem to the rest of
the elders of the exile, the priests,
the prophets, and all the people
whom Nebuchadnezzar had taken
into exile from Jerusalem to Babylon.
2 (This was after King [a]Jeconiah
and the [b]queen mother, the court officials, the princes of Judah and Jerusalem, the craftsmen and the
smiths had departed from Jerusalem.)
3 *The letter was sent* by the hand
of Elasah the son of Shaphan, and
Gemariah the son of [a]Hilkiah,
whom Zedekiah king of Judah sent
to Babylon to Nebuchadnezzar king
of Babylon, saying,
4"Thus says the LORD of hosts,
the God of Israel, to all the exiles
whom I have [a]sent into exile from
Jerusalem to Babylon,
5 '[a]Build houses and live *in them;*
and plant gardens, and eat their
[1]produce.
6 'Take [a]wives and [1]become the
fathers of sons and daughters, and
take wives for your sons and give
your daughters to husbands, that
they may bear sons and daughters;
and multiply there and do not decrease.
7 'And [a]seek the [1]welfare of the
city where I have sent you into exile,
and [b]pray to the LORD on its behalf;
for in its [1]welfare you will have
[1]welfare.'
8"For thus says the LORD of hosts,
the God of Israel, 'Do not let your
[a]prophets who are in your midst and
your diviners [b]deceive you, and do
not listen to [1c]the dreams which
[2]they dream.
9 'For they [a]prophesy falsely to
you in My name; [b]I have not sent
them,' declares the LORD.
10"For thus says the LORD, 'When
[a]seventy years have been completed
for Babylon, I will visit you and fulfill My [b]good word to you, to bring
you back to this place.
11 'For I know the [a]plans that I
[1]have for you,' declares the LORD,
'plans for [b]welfare and not for calamity to give you a future and a
[c]hope.
12 'Then you will [a]call upon Me
and come and pray to Me, and I will
[b]listen to you.
13 'And you will [a]seek Me and find
Me, when you [b]search for Me with
all your heart.
14 'And I will be [a]found by you,'
declares the LORD, 'and I will [b]re-
store your [1]fortunes and will [c]gather
you from all the nations and from all
the places where I have driven you,'
declares the LORD, 'and I will [d]bring
you back to the place from where I
sent you into exile.'
15"Because you have said, 'The
LORD has raised up prophets for us
in [a]Babylon'—
16 for thus says the LORD concerning the king who sits on the throne
of David, and concerning all the
people who dwell in this city, your
brothers who did [a]not go with you
into exile—
17 thus says the LORD of hosts,
'Behold, I am sending upon them the
[a]sword, famine, and pestilence, and
I will make them like [b]split-open
figs that cannot be eaten due to rottenness.
18 'And I will pursue them with the
sword, with famine and with pesti-

11 [a]Jer. 14:14; 27:10; 28:15
12 [a]Jer. 1:2
13 [a]Ps. 107:16; Is. 45:2
14 [a]Deut. 28:48; Jer. 27:8 [b]Jer. 25:11 [c]Jer. 27:6
15 [a]Jer. 29:31; Lam. 2:14; Ezek. 13:2, 3, 22; 22:28; Zech. 13:3
16 [1]Lit., *send you away* [2]Lit., *spoken* [a]Gen. 7:4; Ex. 32:12; Deut. 6:15; 1 Kin. 13:34 [b]Jer. 20:6 [c]Deut. 13:5; Jer. 29:32
1 [a]2 Chr. 30:1, 6; Esth. 9:20; Jer. 29:25, 29
2 [a]2 Kin. 24:12-16; 2 Chr. 36:9, 10; Jer. 22:24-28; 24:1; 27:20 [b]Jer. 13:18
3 [a]1 Chr. 6:13
4 [a]Is. 10:5, 6; Jer. 24:5
5 [1]Lit., *fruit* [a]Jer. 29:10, 28
6 [1]Lit., *beget* [a]Jer. 16:2-4
7 [1]Or, *peace* [a]Dan. 4:27; 6:4, 5 [b]Ezra 6:10; 7:23; Dan. 4:19; 1 Tim. 2:1, 2
8 [1]Lit., *your* [2]Lit., *you* [a]Jer. 27:9; 29:1 [b]Jer. 14:14; 23:21; 28:15 [c]Jer. 23:25, 27
9 [a]Jer. 27:15; 29:21 [b]Jer. 29:31
10 [a]2 Chr. 36:21-23; Jer. 25:12; Dan. 9:2; Zech. 7:5 [b]Jer. 24:6, 7; Zeph. 2:7
11 [1]Lit., *am planning* [a]Ps. 40:5; Jer. 23:5, 6; 30:9, 10 [b]Is. 40:9-11; Jer. 30:18-22 [c]Jer. 31:17; Hos. 2:15
12 [a]Ps. 50:15; Jer. 33:3 [b]Ps. 145:19
13 [a]Deut. 4:29 [b]1 Chr. 22:19; 2 Chr. 22:9; Jer. 24:7
14 [1]Or, *captivity* [a]Deut. 30:1-10 [b]Jer. 30:3; 32:37-41 [c]Is. 43:5, 6; Jer. 28:8 [d]Jer. 3:14; 12:15; 16:15
15 [a]Jer. 29:21, 24
16 [a]Jer. 38:2, 3, 17-23
17 [a]Jer. 27:8; 29:18; 32:24 [b]Jer. 24:3, 8-10

lence; and I will [a]make them a terror
to all the kingdoms of the earth, to
be a [b]curse, and a horror, and a
[c]hissing, and a reproach among all
the nations where I have driven
them,
19 because they have [a]not listened
to My words,' declares the LORD,
'which I sent to them again and
again by [b]My servants the prophets;
but you did not listen,' declares the
LORD.
20 "You, therefore, hear the word
of the LORD, all you exiles, whom I
have [a]sent away from Jerusalem to
Babylon.
21 "Thus says the LORD of hosts,
the God of Israel, concerning Ahab
the son of Kolaiah and concerning
Zedekiah the son of Maaseiah, who
are [a]prophesying to you falsely in
My name, 'Behold, I will deliver
them into the hand of Nebuchadnezzar king of Babylon, and he shall
slay them before your eyes.
22 'And because of them a [a]curse
shall be used by all the exiles from
Judah who are in Babylon, saying,
"May the LORD make you like Zedekiah and like Ahab, whom the king
of Babylon [b]roasted in the fire,
23 because they have [a]acted foolishly in Israel, and [b]have committed
adultery with their neighbors'
wives, and have spoken words in
My name [c]falsely, which I did not
command them; and I am He who
[d]knows, and am a witness," declares the LORD.' "
24 And to [a]Shemaiah the Nehelamite you shall speak, saying,
25 "Thus says the LORD of hosts,
the God of Israel, 'Because you have
sent [a]letters in your own name to all
the people who are in Jerusalem,
and to [b]Zephaniah the son of Maaseiah, the priest, and to all the
priests, saying,
26 "The LORD has made you priest
instead of Jehoiada the priest, to be
the [a]overseer in the house of the
LORD over every [b]madman who
[c]prophesies, to [d]put him in the
stocks and in the iron collar,
27 now then, why have you not rebuked Jeremiah of [a]Anathoth who
prophesies to you?
28 "For he has [a]sent to us in Babylon, saying, '*The exile* will be [b]long;
[c]build houses and live *in them* and
plant gardens and eat their produce.' " ' "
29 And [a]Zephaniah the priest read
this letter to Jeremiah the prophet.
30 Then came the word of the
LORD to Jeremiah, saying,
31 "Send to [a]all the exiles, saying,
'Thus says the LORD concerning
[b]Shemaiah the Nehelamite, "Because Shemaiah has [c]prophesied to
you, although I did not send him,
and he has [d]made you trust in a lie,"
32 therefore thus says the LORD,
"Behold, I am about to [a]punish
Shemaiah the Nehelamite and his
descendants; he shall [b]not have anyone living among this people, [c]and
he shall not see the good that I am
about to do to My people," declares
the LORD, "because he has
[d]preached rebellion against the
LORD." ' "

CHAPTER 30

Deliverance from Captivity Promised

THE word which came to Jeremiah from the LORD, saying,
2 "Thus says the LORD, the God of
Israel, '[a]Write all the words which I
have spoken to you in a book.
3 'For, behold, [a]days are coming,'
declares the LORD, 'when I will [b]re-
store the fortunes of My people [c]Is-
rael and Judah.' The LORD says, 'I
will also [d]bring them back to the
land that I gave to their forefathers,
and they shall possess it.' "
4 Now these are the words which
the LORD spoke concerning Israel
and concerning Judah,
5 "For thus says the LORD,
'[1]I have heard a sound of [a]terror,
Of dread, and there is no peace.
6 'Ask now, and see,
If a male can give birth.
Why do I see every man
With his [a]hands on his loins, as
a [b]woman in childbirth?
And *why* have all faces turned
pale?
7 'Alas! for that [a]day is great,
There is [b]none like it;
And it is the time of Jacob's
[c]distress,
But he will be [d]saved from it.
8 'And it shall come about on that
day,' declares the LORD of hosts,
'that I will [a]break his yoke from off
[1]their neck, and will tear off [1]their
bonds; and strangers shall no longer
[b]make them their slaves.
9 'But they shall serve the LORD
their God, and [a]David their king,
whom I will raise up for them.
10 '[a]And fear not, O Jacob My servant,' declares the LORD,
'And do not be dismayed, O Israel;
For behold, I will save you from
[b]afar,

18 [a]Jer. 24:9; 34:17; Ezek. 12:15 [b]Is. 65:15; Jer. 42:18 [c]Jer. 25:9; Lam. 2:15, 16
19 [a]Jer. 6:19 [b]Jer. 26:5; 35:15
20 [a]Jer. 24:5; Ezek. 11:9
21 [a]Jer. 14:14; Lam. 2:14
22 [a]Is. 65:15 [b]Dan. 3:6, 21
23 [a]Gen. 34:7; 2 Sam. 13:12 [b]Jer. 5:8; 23:14 [c]Jer. 29:8, 9, 21 [d]Prov. 5:21; Jer. 7:11; 16:17; Mal. 3:5
24 [a]Jer. 29:31
25 [a]Jer. 29:1 [b]2 Kin. 25:18; Jer. 21:1; 29:29; 37:3
26 [a]Jer. 20:1 [b]2 Kin. 9:11; Hos. 9:7; Mark 3:21; John 10:20; Acts 26:24, 25; 2 Cor. 5:13 [c]Deut. 13:1-5; Zech. 13:1-5 [d]Jer. 20:1, 2; Acts 16:24
27 [a]Jer. 1:1
28 [a]Jer. 29:1 [b]Jer. 29:10 [c]Jer. 29:5
29 [a]Jer. 29:25
31 [a]Jer. 29:20 [b]Jer. 29:24 [c]Jer. 14:14; 29:9; Ezek. 13:8 [d]Jer. 28:15
32 [a]Jer. 36:31 [b]1 Sam. 2:30-34; Jer. 22:30 [c]2 Kin. 7:2, 19, 20; Jer. 17:6; 29:10 [d]Deut. 13:5
2 [a]Jer. 25:13; 36:4, 28, 32; Hab. 2:2
3 [a]Jer. 29:10 [b]Ps. 53:6; Jer. 29:14 [c]Jer. 3:18 [d]Jer. 16:15; 23:7, 8; Ezek. 20:42; 36:24
5 [1]Lit., We [a]Is. 5:30; Jer. 6:25; 8:16; Amos 5:16-18
6 [a]Jer. 6:24; 22:23 [b]Jer. 4:31
7 [a]Is. 2:12; Hos. 1:11; Joel 2:11 [b]Lam. 1:12; Dan. 9:12 [c]Jer. 2:27, 28; 14:8 [d]Jer. 30:10; 50:19
8 [1]So Gk.; Heb., *your* [a]Is. 9:4; Jer. 2:20; Ezek. 34:27 [b]Ezek. 34:27
9 [a]Is. 55:3-5; Ezek. 34:23, 24; 37:24, 25; Hos. 3:5; Luke 1:69; Acts 2:30; 13:23, 34, 38
10 [a]Is. 43:5; 44:2; Jer. 46:27, 28 [b]Is. 60:4; Jer. 23:3, 8; 29:14

And your [1]offspring from the land of their captivity.
And Jacob shall return, and shall be [c]quiet and at ease,
And [d]no one shall make him afraid.
11 'For [a]I am with you,' declares the LORD, 'to save you;
For I will [b]destroy completely all the nations where I have scattered you,
Only I will [c]not destroy you completely.
But I will [d]chasten you justly,
And will by no means leave you unpunished.'

12"For thus says the LORD,
'Your wound is incurable,
And your [a]injury is serious.
13 'There is no one to plead your cause;
No healing for *your* sore,
[a]No recovery for you.
14 'All your [a]lovers have forgotten you,
They do not seek you;
For I have [b]wounded you with the wound of an enemy,
With the punishment of a cruel one,
Because your iniquity is great
And your sins are numerous.
15 'Why do you cry out over your injury?
Your pain is incurable.
Because your iniquity is great
And your sins are numerous,
I have done these things to you.
16 'Therefore all who [a]devour you shall be devoured;
And all your adversaries, every one of them, [b]shall go into captivity;
And those who plunder you shall be for plunder,
And all who prey upon you I will give for prey.
17 'For I will [1]restore you to [2a]health
And I will heal you of your wounds,' declares the LORD,
'Because they have called you an [b]outcast, saying:
"It is Zion; no one [3]cares for her." '

Restoration of Jacob

18"Thus says the LORD,
'Behold, I will restore the [1]fortunes of the tents of Jacob
And have compassion on his dwelling places;
And the [a]city shall be rebuilt on its ruin,
And the [b]palace shall stand on its rightful place.
19 'And from them shall proceed [a]thanksgiving
And the voice of those who [1b]make merry;
And I will multiply them, and they shall not be diminished;
I will also [c]honor them, and they shall not be insignificant.
20 '[1]Their children also shall be as formerly,
And [1]their congregation shall be [a]established before Me;
And I will punish all [1]their oppressors.
21 'And [1]their leader shall be one of them,
And [1]their ruler shall come forth from [1]their midst;
And I will [a]bring him near, and he shall approach Me;
For [2]who would dare to risk his life to [b]approach Me?' declares the LORD.
22 'And you shall be [a]My people,
And I will be your God.' "

23 Behold, the [a]tempest of the LORD!
Wrath has gone forth,
A [1]sweeping tempest;
It will burst on the head of the wicked.
24 The fierce anger of the LORD will not turn back,
Until He has performed, and until He has accomplished
The intent of His heart;
In the [a]latter days you will understand this.

CHAPTER 31

Israel's Mourning Turned to Joy

"AT that time," declares the LORD, "I will be the [a]God of all the [b]families of Israel, and they shall be My people."
2 Thus says the LORD,
"The people who survived the sword
[a]Found grace in the wilderness—
Israel, when it went to [b]find its rest."
3 The LORD appeared to [1]him from afar, *saying,*
"I have [a]loved you with an everlasting love;
Therefore I have drawn you with [b]lovingkindness.
4"[a]Again I will build you, and you shall be rebuilt,
O virgin of Israel!

10 [1]Lit., *seed* [c]Is. 35:9; Jer. 33:16; Hos. 2:18 [d]Mic. 4:4
11 [a]Jer. 1:8, 19 [b]Jer. 46:28 [c]Jer. 4:27; 5:10, 18 [d]Jer. 10:24
12 [a]Jer. 15:18; 30:15
13 [a]Jer. 14:19; 46:11
14 [a]Jer. 22:20, 22 [b]Lam. 2:4, 5
16 [a]Jer. 2:3; 8:16; 10:25 [b]Is. 14:2; Joel 3:8
17 [1]Lit., *cause to go up* [2]Or, *healing* [3]Lit., *is seeking* [a]Ps. 107:20; Jer. 8:22; 33:6 [b]Is. 11:12; 56:8; Jer. 33:24
18 [1]Or, *captivity* [a]Jer. 31:4, 38-40 [b]1 Chr. 29:1, 19; Ps. 48:3, 13; 122:7
19 [1]Or, *dance* [a]Is. 12:1; 51:3; Jer. 17:26; 33:11 [b]Ps. 126:1, 2; Is. 51:11; Jer. 31:4; Zeph. 3:14 [c]Is. 55:5; 60:9
20 [1]Lit., *His* [a]Is. 54:14
21 [1]Lit., *his* [2]Lit., *who is he that gives his heart in pledge* [a]Num. 16:5; Ps. 65:4 [b]Ex. 3:5; Jer. 50:44
22 [a]Ex. 6:7; Jer. 32:38; Hos. 2:23; Zech. 13:9
23 [1]Or, *raging* [a]Jer. 23:19, 20
24 [a]Jer. 23:20
1 [a]Jer. 30:22 [b]Gen. 17:7, 8; Is. 41:10; Rom. 11:26-28
2 [a]Num. 14:20 [b]Ex. 33:14; Josh. 1:13
3 [1]Lit., *me* [a]Deut. 4:37; 7:8 [b]Ps. 25:6
4 [a]Jer. 24:6; 33:7

Again you shall [1]take up your [b]tambourines,
And go forth to the dances of the [c]merrymakers.
5"Again you shall [a]plant vineyards
On the [1]hills of Samaria;
The planters shall plant
And shall [2]enjoy *them*.
6"For there shall be a day when watchmen
On the hills of Ephraim shall call out,
'Arise, and let us go up *to* Zion,
To the LORD our God.' "

7 For thus says the LORD,
"[a]Sing aloud with gladness for Jacob,
And shout among the [1b]chiefs of the nations;
Proclaim, give praise, and say,
'O LORD, [c]save Thy people,
The [d]remnant of Israel.'
8"Behold, I am bringing them from the north country,
And I will [a]gather them from the remote parts of the earth,
Among them the [b]blind and the [c]lame,
The woman with child and she who is in labor with child, together;
A great [1]company, they shall return here.
9"With weeping they shall come,
And by supplication I will lead them;
I will make them walk by [a]streams of waters,
On a straight path in which they shall [b]not stumble;
For I am a father to Israel,
And Ephraim is My first-born."

10 Hear the word of the LORD, O nations,
And declare in the [a]coastlands afar off,
And say, "He who scattered Israel will gather him,
And keep him as a [b]shepherd keeps his flock."
11 For the LORD has ransomed Jacob,
And redeemed him from the hand of him who was [a]stronger than he.
12"And they shall come and shout for joy on the [a]height of Zion,
And they shall be [b]radiant over the [1]bounty of the LORD—
Over the [c]grain, and the new wine, and the oil,
And over the young of the flock and the herd;
And their life shall be like a [d]watered garden,
And they shall never [e]languish again.
13"Then the virgin shall rejoice in the [a]dance,
And the young men and the old, together;
For I will [b]turn their mourning into joy,
And will comfort them, and give them [c]joy for their sorrow.
14"And I will [1]fill the soul of the priests with [2]abundance,
And My people shall be [a]satisfied with My goodness," declares the LORD.

15 Thus says the LORD,
"A voice is heard in Ramah,
Lamentation *and* bitter weeping.
Rachel is weeping for her children;
She [a]refuses to be comforted for her children,
Because [b]they are no more."
16 Thus says the LORD,
"[a]Restrain your voice from weeping,
And your eyes from tears;
For your work shall be [b]rewarded," declares the LORD,
"And they shall [c]return from the land of the enemy.
17"And there is [a]hope for your future," declares the LORD,
"And *your* children shall return to their own territory.
18"I have surely heard Ephraim grieving,
'Thou hast [a]chastised me, and I was chastised,
Like an untrained [b]calf;
[c]Bring me back that I may be restored,
For Thou art the LORD my God.
19 'For after I turned back, I [a]repented;
And after I was instructed, I [b]smote on *my* thigh;
I was ashamed, and also humiliated,
Because I bore the reproach of my youth.'
20"Is [a]Ephraim My dear son?
Is he a delightful child?
Indeed, as often as I have spoken against him,
I *certainly still* remember him;
Therefore My [1b]heart yearns for him;
I will surely [c]have mercy on him," declares the LORD.

4 [1]Or, *be adorned with* [b]Is. 30:32 [c]Jer. 30:19
5 [1]Or, *mountains* [2]Lit., *defile* [a]Ps. 107:37; Is. 65:21; Ezek. 28:26
7 [1]Lit., *heads* [a]Ps. 14:7; Jer. 20:13 [b]Deut. 28:13; Is. 61:9 [c]Ps. 28:9 [d]Is. 37:31; Jer. 23:3
8 [1]Or, *assembly* [a]Deut. 30:4; Is. 43:6 [b]Is. 42:16 [c]Is. 40:11; Ezek. 34:16; Mic. 4:6
9 [a]Is. 43:20; 49:10 [b]Is. 63:13
10 [a]Is. 66:19; Jer. 25:22 [b]Is. 40:11
11 [a]Ps. 142:9
12 [1]Lit., *goodness* [a]Ezek. 17:23 [b]Is. 2:2; Mic. 4:1 [c]Hos. 2:22; Joel 3:18 [d]Is. 58:11 [e]Is. 35:10; 60:20; 65:19; John 16:22
13 [a]Judg. 21:21; Ps. 30:11; Zech. 8:4, 5 [b]Is. 61:3 [c]Is. 51:11
14 [1]Lit., *saturate* [2]Lit., *fatness* [a]Jer. 50:19
15 [a]Gen. 37:35; Ps. 77:2 [b]Gen. 5:24; 42:13, 36; Jer. 10:20
16 [a]Is. 25:8; 30:19 [b]Ruth 2:12; Heb. 6:10 [c]Jer. 30:3; Ezek. 11:17
17 [a]Jer. 29:11
18 [a]Job 5:17; Ps. 94:12 [b]Hos. 4:16 [c]Ps. 80:3, 7, 19; Jer. 17:14; Acts 3:26
19 [a]Ezek. 36:31; Zech. 12:10 [b]Ezek. 21:12; Luke 18:13
20 [1]Lit., *inward parts* [a]Hos. 11:8 [b]Gen. 43:30; Judg. 10:16 [c]Is. 55:7; Hos. 14:4

21“Set up for yourself roadmarks,
Place for yourself guideposts;
Direct your [1]mind to the highway,
The way by which you went.
[a]Return, O virgin of Israel,
Return to these your cities.
22“How long will you go here and there,
O [a]faithless daughter?
For the LORD has created a new thing in the earth—
A woman will encompass a man.”
23 Thus says the LORD of hosts,
the God of Israel, “Once again they
will speak this word in the land of
Judah and in its cities, when I restore their [1]fortunes,
‘The LORD bless you, O [a]abode of righteousness,
[b]O holy hill!’
24“And Judah and all its cities will
[a]dwell together in it, the farmer and
they who go about with flocks.
25“[a]For I satisfy the weary ones
and [1]refresh every one who languishes.”
26 At this I [a]awoke and looked,
and my [b]sleep was pleasant to me.

A New Covenant

27“Behold, days are coming,” declares the LORD, “when I will [a]sow
the house of Israel and the house of
Judah with the seed of man and
with the seed of beast.
28“And it will come about that as I
have [a]watched over them to pluck
up, to break down, to overthrow, to
destroy, and to bring disaster, so I
will watch over them to build and to
plant,” declares the LORD.
29“In those days they will not say again,
‘[a]The fathers have eaten sour grapes,
And the children’s teeth are [1]set on edge.’
30“But [a]every one will die for his
own iniquity; each man who eats the
sour grapes, his teeth will be [1]set on
edge.
31“[a]Behold, days are coming,” declares the LORD, “when I will make
a [b]new covenant with the house of
Israel and with the house of Judah,
32 not like the [a]covenant which I
made with their fathers in the day I
[b]took them by the hand to bring
them out of the land of Egypt, My
covenant which they broke, although I was a husband to them,”
declares the LORD.
33“But [a]this is the covenant which
I will make with the house of Israel
after those days,” declares the
LORD, “I will put My law within
them, and on their heart I will write
it; and I will be their God, and they
shall be My people.
34“And they shall not [a]teach again,
each man his neighbor and each
man his brother, saying, ‘Know the
LORD,’ for they shall all [b]know Me,
from the least of them to the greatest of them,” declares the LORD, “for
I will [c]forgive their iniquity, and
their [d]sin I will remember no more.”
35 Thus says the LORD,
Who [a]gives the sun for light by day,
And the [1]fixed order of the moon and the stars for light by night,
Who stirs up the sea so that its waves roar;
The LORD of hosts is His name:
36“[a]If [1]this fixed order departs
From before Me,” declares the LORD,
“Then the offspring of Israel also shall [b]cease
From being a nation before Me [2]forever.”
37 Thus says the LORD,
“[a]If the heavens above can be measured,
And the foundations of the earth searched out below,
Then I will also [b]cast off all the offspring of Israel
For all that they have done,” declares the LORD.
38“Behold, days are coming,” declares the LORD, “when the city shall
be rebuilt for the LORD from the
[a]Tower of Hananel *to* the [b]Corner
Gate.
39“And the measuring line shall go
out farther straight ahead to the hill
Gareb; then it will turn to Goah.
40“And the whole valley of the
dead bodies and of the ashes, and all
the fields as far as the brook [a]Kid-
ron, to the corner of the [b]Horse Gate
toward the east, shall be [c]holy to the
LORD; it shall not be plucked up, or
overthrown any more forever.”

CHAPTER 32

Jeremiah Imprisoned

THE word that came to Jeremiah
from the LORD in the [a]tenth year of
Zedekiah king of Judah, which was
the eighteenth year of Nebuchadnezzar.
2 Now at that time the army of
the king of Babylon was besieging
Jerusalem, and Jeremiah the

21 [1]Lit., *heart* [a]Is. 48:20; 52:11
22 [a]Jer. 49:4
23 [1]Or, *captivity* [a]Is. 1:26; Jer. 50:7 [b]Ps. 48:1; 87:1
24 [a]Jer. 31:12; Ezek. 36:10; Zech. 8:4-8
25 [1]Lit., *fill* [a]Ps. 107:9; Jer. 31:12, 14; Matt. 5:6; John 4:14
26 [a]Zech. 4:1 [b]Prov. 3:24
27 [a]Ezek. 36:9, 11; Hos. 2:23
28 [a]Jer. 44:27; Dan. 9:14
29 [1]Or, *dull* [a]Lam. 5:7; Ezek. 18:2
30 [1]Or, *dull* [a]Deut. 24:16; Is. 3:11; Ezek. 18:4, 20
31 [a]Jer. 31:31-34; Heb. 8:8-12 [b]Jer. 32:40; Ezek. 37:26; Luke 22:20; 1 Cor. 11:25; 2 Cor. 3:6; Heb. 8:8-12
32 [a]Ex. 19:5; 24:6-8; Deut. 5:2, 3 [b]Deut. 1:31; Is. 63:12
33 [a]Heb. 10:16, 17
34 [a]1 Thess. 4:9; 1 John 2:27 [b]Is. 11:9; 54:13; Jer. 24:7; Heb. 2:14 [c]Jer. 50:20; Mic. 7:18 [d]Is. 43:25
35 [1]Lit., *statutes* [a]Gen. 1:14-18; Deut. 4:19; Ps. 19:1-6; 136:7-9
36 [1]Lit., *these statutes* [2]Lit., *all the days* [a]Ps. 89:36, 37; Is. 54:9, 10; Jer. 33:20-26 [b]Amos 9:8, 9
37 [a]Is. 40:12; Jer. 33:22 [b]Jer. 33:24-26; Rom. 11:2-5, 26, 27
38 [a]Neh. 3:1; 12:39; Zech. 14:10 [b]2 Kin. 14:13; 2 Chr. 26:9
40 [a]2 Sam. 15:23; 2 Kin. 23:6, 12; John 18:1 [b]2 Kin. 11:16; 2 Chr. 23:15; Neh. 3:28 [c]Joel 3:17; Zech. 14:20
1 [a]2 Kin. 25:1, 2; Jer. 39:1, 2

prophet was shut up in the court of
the guard, which was *in* the house of
the [a]king of Judah,
3 because Zedekiah king of Judah had [a]shut him up, saying, "Why
do you [b]prophesy, saying, 'Thus
says the LORD, "Behold, I am about
to [c]give this city into the hand of the
king of Babylon, and he will take it;
4 and Zedekiah king of Judah
shall [a]not escape out of the hand of
the Chaldeans, but he shall surely be
given into the hand of the king of
Babylon, and he shall [b]speak with
him face to face, and see him eye to
eye;
5 and he shall [a]take Zedekiah to
Babylon, and he shall be there until
I visit him," declares the LORD. "If
you fight against the Chaldeans, you
shall [b]not succeed" ' ? "
6 And Jeremiah said, "The word
of the LORD came to me, saying,
7 'Behold, Hanamel the son of
Shallum your uncle is coming to
you, saying, "Buy for yourself my
field which is at Anathoth, for you
have the [a]right of redemption to buy
it." '
8 "Then Hanamel my uncle's son
came to me in the court of the guard
according to the word of the LORD,
and said to me, 'Buy my field,
please, that is at Anathoth, which is
in the land of Benjamin; for you
have the right of possession and the
redemption is yours; buy *it* for yourself.' Then I knew that this was the
[a]word of the LORD.
9 "And I bought the field which
was at Anathoth from Hanamel my
uncle's son, and I [a]weighed out the
silver for him, seventeen [b]shekels of
silver.
10 "And I [a]signed and [b]sealed the
deed, and [c]called in witnesses, and
weighed out the silver on the scales.
11 "Then I took the deeds of purchase, both the sealed *copy contain-*
ing the [a]terms and conditions, and
the open *copy;*
12 and I gave the deed of purchase
to Baruch the son of Neriah, the son
of Mahseiah, in the sight of Hanamel my uncle's *son,* and in the sight
of the witnesses who signed the
deed of purchase, before all the
Jews who were sitting in the court
of the guard.
13 "And I commanded Baruch in
their presence, saying,
14 'Thus says the LORD of hosts,
the God of Israel, "Take these
deeds, this sealed deed of purchase,
and this open deed, and put them in
an earthenware jar, that they may
last a long time."
15 'For thus says the LORD of hosts,
the God of Israel, "[a]Houses and
fields and vineyards shall again be
bought in this land." '

Jeremiah Prays and God Explains

16 "After I had given the deed of
purchase to Baruch the son of Neriah, then I [a]prayed to the LORD, saying,
17 'Ah Lord [1]GOD! Behold, Thou
hast [a]made the heavens and the
earth by Thy great power and by
Thine outstretched arm! [b]Nothing is
too difficult for Thee,
18 who [a]showest lovingkindness
to thousands, but repayest the iniquity of [b]fathers into the bosom of
their children after them, O [c]great
and [d]mighty God. The [e]LORD of
hosts is His name;
19 [a]great in counsel and mighty in
deed, whose [b]eyes are open to all
the ways of the sons of men, [c]giving
to every one according to his ways
and according to the fruit of his
deeds;
20 who hast [a]set signs and wonders in the land of Egypt, *and* even
to this day both in Israel and among
mankind; and Thou hast [b]made a
name for Thyself, as at this day.
21 'And Thou didst [a]bring Thy people Israel out of the land of Egypt
with signs and with wonders, and
with a strong hand and with an outstretched arm, and with great terror;
22 and gavest them this land,
which Thou didst [a]swear to their
forefathers to give them, a land
flowing with milk and honey.
23 'And they [a]came in and took
possession of it, but they did not
obey Thy voice or [b]walk in Thy law;
they have done nothing of all that
Thou commandedst them to do;
therefore Thou hast made [c]all this
calamity come upon them.
24 'Behold, the siege mounds have
reached the city to take it; and the
city is given into the hand of the
Chaldeans who fight against it, because of the [a]sword, the famine, and
the pestilence; and what Thou hast
spoken has [b]come to pass; and, behold, Thou seest *it.*
25 'And Thou hast said to me, O
Lord [1]GOD, "Buy for yourself the
field with money, and call in witnesses"—although the city is given
into the hand of the Chaldeans.' "
26 Then the word of the LORD
came to Jeremiah, saying,
27 "Behold, I am the LORD, the
[a]God of all flesh; is anything [b]too
difficult for Me?"

2 [a]Neh. 3:25
3 [a]2 Kin. 6:31, 32 [b]Jer. 26:8, 9; Amos 7:13 [c]Jer. 21:4-7; 32:28, 29; 34:2, 3
4 [a]2 Kin. 25:4-7; Jer. 37:17; 38:18, 23; 39:4-7 [b]Jer. 39:5
5 [a]Jer. 39:7; Ezek. 12:12, 13 [b]Ezek. 17:9, 10
7 [a]Lev. 25:25; Ruth 4:3, 4
8 [a]1 Sam. 9:16, 17; 10:3-7; 1 Kin. 22:25; Jer. 32:25
9 [a]Gen. 23:16 [b]Gen. 24:22; Ex. 21:32; Neh. 5:15; Ezek. 4:10
10 [a]Is. 44:5; Jer. 32:44 [b]Deut. 32:34; Job 14:17 [c]Ruth 4:1, 9; Is. 8:1, 2
11 [a]Luke 2:27
15 [a]Jer. 30:18; 31:5, 12, 24; 32:37, 43, 44; 33:12, 13; Amos 9:14, 15; Zech. 3:10
16 [a]Gen. 32:9-12; Jer. 12:1; Phil. 4:6, 7
17 [1]YHWH, usually rendered LORD [a]2 Kin. 19:15; Ps. 102:25; Is. 40:26-29; Jer. 27:5 [b]Gen. 18:14
18 [a]Ex. 34:6, 7; Deut. 7:9, 10 [b]1 Kin. 14:9, 10; 16:1-3; Matt. 23:32-36 [c]Ps. 145:3 [d]Ps. 50:1; Jer. 20:11 [e]Jer. 10:16; 31:35
19 [a]Is. 9:6; 28:29 [b]Job 34:21; Jer. 23:24 [c]Ps. 62:12; Jer. 17:10; 21:14; Matt. 16:27; John 5:29
20 [a]Ps. 78:43; 105:27 [b]Is. 63:12, 14; Dan. 9:15
21 [a]Deut. 4:34; 7:19; 26:8; 1 Chr. 17:21
22 [a]Ex. 13:5; Deut. 1:8; Ps. 105:9-11; Jer. 11:5
23 [a]Ps. 44:2, 3; 78:54, 55; Jer. 2:7 [b]Ezra 9:7; Jer. 26:4; 44:10 [c]Lam. 1:18; Dan. 9:11
24 [a]Jer. 29:17, 18; 32:36; 34:17; Ezek. 14:21 [b]Deut. 4:26; Josh. 23:15, 16; Zech. 1:6
25 [1]YHWH, usually rendered LORD
27 [a]Num. 16:22; 27:16 [b]Jer. 32:17; Matt. 19:26

28 Therefore thus says the LORD, "Behold, I am about to [a]give this city into the hand of the Chaldeans and into the hand of Nebuchadnezzar king of Babylon, and he shall take it.

29 "And the Chaldeans who are fighting against this city shall enter and [a]set this city on fire and burn it, with the [b]houses where *people* have offered incense to Baal on their roofs and poured out libations to other gods to provoke Me to anger.

30 "Indeed the sons of Israel and the sons of Judah have been doing only evil in My sight from their youth; for the sons of Israel have been only provoking Me to anger by the work of their hands," declares the LORD.

31 "Indeed this city has been to Me *a* [a]*provocation of* My anger and My wrath from the day that they built it, even to this day, that it should be [b]removed from before My face,

32 because of all the evil of the sons of Israel and the sons of Judah, which they have done to provoke Me to anger—they, their [a]kings, their leaders, their priests, their prophets, the men of Judah, and the inhabitants of Jerusalem.

33 "And they have turned *their* back to Me, and not *their* face; though *I* taught them, [1a]teaching again and again, they would not listen [2]and receive instruction.

34 "But they put their detestable things in the house which is called by My name, to defile it.

35 "And they built the [a]high places of Baal that are in the valley of Ben-hinnom to cause their sons and their daughters to pass through *the fire* to [b]Molech, which I had not commanded them nor had it [1]entered My mind that they should do this abomination, to cause Judah to sin.

36 "Now therefore thus says the LORD God of Israel concerning this city of which you say, 'It is given into the hand of the king of Babylon by sword, by famine, and by pestilence.'

37 "Behold, I will [a]gather them out of all the lands to which I have driven them in My anger, in My wrath, and in great indignation; and I will bring them back to this place and [b]make them dwell in safety.

38 "And they shall be My people, and I will be their God;

39 and I will [a]give them one heart and one way, that they may fear Me always, for their own [b]good, and for *the good of* their children after them.

40 "And I will make an [a]everlasting covenant with them that I will not turn away from them, to do them good; and I will put the fear of Me in their hearts so that they will not turn away from Me.

41 "And I will [a]rejoice over them to do them good, and I will [1]faithfully [b]plant them in this land with [c]all My heart and with all My soul.

42 "For thus says the LORD, '[a]Just as I brought all this calamity on this people, so I am going to bring on them all the good that I am promising them.

43 'And [a]fields shall be bought in this land of which you say, "It is a desolation, without man or beast; it is given into the hand of the Chaldeans."

44 'Men shall buy fields for money, [1]sign and seal deeds, and call in witnesses in the land of Benjamin, in the environs of Jerusalem, in the cities of Judah, in the cities of the hill country, in the cities of the lowland, and in the cities of the [2]Negev; for I will restore their [3]fortunes,' declares the LORD."

CHAPTER 33

Restoration Promised

THEN the word of the LORD came to Jeremiah the second time, while he was still [1]confined in the court of the guard, saying,

2 "Thus says the LORD who made [1]*the earth,* the LORD who formed it to establish it, the [a]LORD is His name,

3 '[a]Call to Me, and I will answer you, and I will tell you [b]great and mighty things, which you do not [c]know.'

4 "For thus says the LORD God of Israel concerning the [a]houses of this city, and concerning the houses of the kings of Judah, which are broken down to *make a defense* against the siege mounds and against the sword,

5 'While *they* are coming to [a]fight with the Chaldeans, and to fill them with the corpses of men whom I have slain in My anger and in My wrath, and I have [b]hidden My face from this city because of all their wickedness:

6 'Behold, I will bring to it [a]health and healing, and I will heal them; and I will reveal to them an [b]abundance of peace and truth.

7 'And I will [a]restore the [1]fortunes of Judah and the fortunes of Israel,

---

28 [a]Jer. 19:7-12; 32:3, 24, 36; 34:2, 3
29 [a]2 Chr. 36:19; Jer. 21:10; 39:8 [b]Jer. 19:13; 44:17-19, 25; 52:13
31 [a]1 Kin. 11:7, 8; 2 Kin. 21:4-7, 16; Jer. 5:9-11; 6:6, 7; Matt. 23:37 [b]2 Kin. 23:27; 24:3, 4; Jer. 27:10
32 [a]Ezra 9:7; Is. 1:4-6, 23; Jer. 2:26; 44:17, 21
33 [1]Lit., *rising up early and teaching* [2]Lit., *to* [a]2 Chr. 36:15, 16; Jer. 25:3; 26:5; 35:15; John 8:2
35 [1]Lit., *come up into My heart* [a]2 Chr. 28:2, 3; 33:6; Jer. 7:31; 19:5 [b]Lev. 18:21; 20:2-5; 1 Kin. 11:7; 2 Kin. 23:10; Acts 7:43
37 [a]Deut. 30:3; Ps. 106:47; Is. 11:11-16; Ezek. 11:17; Hos. 1:11; Amos 9:14, 15 [b]Jer. 23:6; Ezek. 34:25, 28; Zech. 14:11
39 [a]2 Chr. 30:12; Jer. 31:33; John 17:21; Acts 4:32 [b]Deut. 11:18-21; Ezek. 37:25
40 [a]Is. 55:3; Jer. 31:33; 50:5
41 [1]Or, *truly* [a]Deut. 30:9; Is. 62:5; 65:19 [b]Jer. 31:28; Amos 9:15 [c]Hos. 2:19, 20
42 [a]Jer. 31:28; Zech. 8:14, 15
43 [a]Jer. 32:15, 25; Ezek. 37:11-14
44 [1]Or, *write . . . on the document* [2]I.e., South country [3]Or, *captivity*
1 [1]Lit., *shut up*
2 [1]Lit., *it* [a]Ex. 3:15; 6:3; 15:3
3 [a]Ps. 50:15; Is. 55:6, 7; Jer. 29:12 [b]Jer. 32:17, 27 [c]Is. 48:6
4 [a]Is. 32:13, 14
5 [a]Jer. 21:4-7; 32:5 [b]Is. 8:17; Jer. 21:10; Mic. 3:4
6 [a]Jer. 17:14; 30:17; Hos. 6:1 [b]Is. 66:12; Gal. 5:22, 23
7 [1]Or, *captivity* [a]Ps. 85:1; Jer. 32:44; 33:26

and I will [b]rebuild them as they
were at first.
8 'And I will [a]cleanse them from
all their iniquity by which they have
sinned against Me, and I will pardon
all their iniquities by which they
have sinned against Me, and by
which they have transgressed
against Me.
9 'And [1]it shall be to Me a [a]name
of joy, praise, and glory before [b]all
the nations of the earth, which shall
hear of all the [c]good that I do for
them, and they shall [d]fear and tremble because of all the good and all
the peace that I make for it.'
10 "Thus says the LORD, 'Yet again
there shall be heard in this place, of
which you say, "It is a waste, without man and without beast," *that is,*
in the cities of Judah and in the
streets of Jerusalem that are desolate, without man and without inhabitant and without beast,
11 the voice of [a]joy and the voice
of gladness, the voice of the bridegroom and the voice of the bride,
the voice of those who say,

"Give thanks to the LORD of
hosts,
For the LORD is good,
For His lovingkindness is everlasting";

and of those who bring a thank offering into the house of the LORD.
For I will restore the fortunes of the
land as they were at first,' says the
LORD.
12 "Thus says the LORD of hosts,
'There shall again be in this place
which is waste, without man or
beast, and in all its cities, a habitation of shepherds who rest their
[a]flocks.
13 'In the cities of the hill country,
in the cities of the lowland, in the
cities of the Negev, in the land of
Benjamin, in the environs of Jerusalem, and in the cities of Judah, the
flocks shall again [a]pass under the
hands of the one who numbers
them,' says the LORD.

The Davidic Kingdom

14 'Behold, days are coming,' declares the LORD, 'when I will [a]fulfill
the good word which I have spoken
concerning the house of Israel and
the house of Judah.
15 'In those days and at that time I
will cause a [a]righteous Branch of
David to spring forth; and He shall
execute [b]justice and righteousness
on the earth.
16 'In those days [a]Judah shall be
saved, and Jerusalem shall dwell in
safety; and this is *the name* by
which she shall be called: the [b]LORD
is our righteousness.'
17 "For thus says the LORD, 'David
shall [a]never lack a man to sit on the
throne of the house of Israel;
18 and the Levitical [a]priests shall
never lack a man before Me to offer
burnt offerings, to burn grain offerings, and to [b]prepare sacrifices continually.' "
19 And the word of the LORD came
to Jeremiah, saying,
20 "Thus says the LORD, 'If you can
[a]break My covenant for the day, and
My covenant for the night, so that
day and night will not be at their
appointed time,
21 then [a]My covenant may also be
broken with David My servant that
he shall not have a son to reign on
his throne, and with the Levitical
priests, My ministers.
22 'As the [a]host of heaven cannot
be counted, and the [b]sand of the sea
cannot be measured, so I will multiply the [1]descendants of David My
servant and the Levites who minister to Me.' "
23 And the word of the LORD came
to Jeremiah, saying,
24 "Have you not observed what
this people have spoken, saying,
'The [a]two families which the LORD
chose, He has rejected them'? Thus
they [b]despise My people, no longer
are they as a nation in their sight.
25 "Thus says the LORD, 'If My
[a]covenant *for* day and night *stand*
not, *and* the [1]fixed patterns of
heaven and earth I have [b]not established,
26 then I would reject the [1]descen-
dants of Jacob and David My servant, [2]not taking from his [1]descen-
dants [a]rulers over the [1]descendants
of Abraham, Isaac, and Jacob. But I
will restore their [3]fortunes and will
have [b]mercy on them.' "

CHAPTER 34

A Prophecy against Zedekiah

THE word which came to Jeremiah from the LORD, when Nebuchadnezzar king of Babylon and all his
army, with [a]all the kingdoms of the
earth that were under his dominion
and all the peoples, were fighting
against Jerusalem and against all its
cities, saying,
2 "Thus says the LORD God of Israel, '[a]Go and speak to Zedekiah
king of Judah and say to him: "Thus
says the LORD, 'Behold, I am giving
this city into the hand of the king of

7 [b]Jer. 30:18; 31:4, 38; Amos 9:14, 15
8 [a]Ps. 51:2; Is. 44:22; Jer. 50:20; Ezek. 36:25, 33; Mic. 7:18, 19; Zech. 13:1; Heb. 9:11-14
9 [1]I.e., this city [a]Is. 62:2, 4; Jer. 13:11 [b]Jer. 3:17, 19; 4:2; 16:19 [c]Jer. 24:6; 32:42 [d]Neh. 6:16; Ps. 40:3; Hos. 3:5
11 [a]Is. 35:10; 51:3, 11
12 [a]Is. 65:10; Jer. 31:12; Ezek. 34:12-14; Zeph. 2:6, 7
13 [a]Lev. 27:32; Luke 15:4
14 [a]Is. 32:1, 2; Jer. 32:42; 33:9; Ezek. 34:23-25; Hag. 2:6-9
15 [a]Is. 4:2; 11:1-5; Jer. 23:5, 6; 30:9; Zech. 3:8; 6:12, 13 [b]Ps. 72:1-5
16 [a]Is. 45:17, 22; Jer. 23:6 [b]Is. 45:24, 25; Jer. 23:6; 1 Cor. 1:30; 2 Cor. 5:21; Phil. 3:9
17 [a]2 Sam. 7:16; 1 Kin. 2:4; 8:25; Ps. 89:29-37
18 [a]Deut. 18:1; 24:8; Josh. 3:3; Ezek. 44:15 [b]Ex. 29:4; Ezra 3:5; Heb. 13:15
20 [a]Ps. 89:37; 104:19-23; Is. 54:9, 10; Jer. 31:35-37; 33:25
21 [a]2 Sam. 23:5; 2 Chr. 7:18; 21:7
22 [1]Lit., *seed* [a]Gen. 15:5 [b]Gen. 22:17
24 [a]Is. 7:17; 11:13; Jer. 3:7, 8, 10, 18; 33:26; Ezek. 37:22 [b]Neh. 4:2-4; Esth. 3:6-8; Ps. 44:13, 14; 83:4; Ezek. 36:2
25 [1]Lit., *statutes* (cf. 31:35) [a]Jer. 31:35, 36; 33:20 [b]Ps. 74:16, 17
26 [1]Lit., *seed* [2]Lit., *from taking* [3]Or, *captivity* [a]Gen. 49:10 [b]Is. 14:1; 54:8; Jer. 31:20; Ezek. 39:25; Hos. 1:7; 2:23
1 [a]Jer. 1:15; 27:7; Dan. 2:37, 38
2 [a]2 Chr. 36:11, 12; Jer. 22:1, 2; 37:1-4

Babylon, and he will burn it with
fire.
3 'And [a]you will not escape from
his hand, for you will surely be captured and delivered into his hand;
and you will [b]see the king of Babylon eye to eye, and he will speak
with you [1]face to face, and you will
go to Babylon.' " '
4"Yet hear the word of the LORD,
O Zedekiah king of Judah! Thus
says the LORD concerning you, 'You
will not die by the sword.
5 'You will die in peace; and as
spices were burned for your fathers,
the former kings who were before
you, so they will [a]burn spices for
you; and they will lament for you,
"Alas, lord!" ' For I have spoken the
word," declares the LORD.
6 Then Jeremiah the prophet
spoke [a]all these words to Zedekiah
king of Judah in Jerusalem
7 when the army of the king of
Babylon was fighting against Jerusalem and against all the remaining
cities of Judah, *that is,* [a]Lachish and
[b]Azekah, for they *alone* remained as
[c]fortified cities among the cities of
Judah.
8 The word which came to Jeremiah from the LORD, after King
Zedekiah had [a]made a covenant
with all the people who were in Jerusalem to [b]proclaim [1]release to
them:
9 that each man should set free
his male servant and each man his
female servant, a [a]Hebrew man or a
Hebrew woman; so that no one
should keep them, a Jew his
brother, in bondage.
10 And all the officials and all the
people obeyed, who had entered
into the covenant that each man
should set free his male servant and
each man his female servant, so that
no one should keep them any longer
in bondage; they obeyed, and set
them free.
11 But [a]afterward they turned
around and took back the male servants and the female servants,
whom they had set free, and
brought them into subjection for
male servants and for female servants.
12 Then the word of the LORD
came to Jeremiah from the LORD,
saying,
13"Thus says the LORD God of Israel, 'I [a]made a covenant with your
forefathers in the day that I
[b]brought them out of the land of
Egypt, from the house of bondage,
saying,
14"[a]At the end of seven years each

3 [1]Lit., *mouth to mouth* [a]2 Kin. 25:4, 5; Jer. 21:7; 34:21 [b]2 Kin. 25:6, 7; Jer. 39:6, 7
5 [a]2 Chr. 16:14; 21:19
6 [a]1 Sam. 3:18; 15:16-24; 1 Kin. 21:18
7 [a]Josh. 10:3, 5; 2 Kin. 14:19; 18:14; Is. 36:2 [b]Josh. 10:10; 2 Chr. 11:9 [c]2 Chr. 11:5-10
8 [1]Or, *liberty* [a]2 Kin. 11:17; 23:2, 3 [b]Lev. 25:10, 39-46; Neh. 5:1-13; Jer. 34:14, 17
9 [a]Gen. 14:13; Ex. 2:6
11 [a]Ps. 78:34-36; Jer. 34:21; 37:5; Hos. 6:4
13 [a]Ex. 24:3, 7, 8; Deut. 5:2, 3, 27; Jer. 31:32 [b]Ex. 20:2
14 [1]Or, *has sold himself* [a]Ex. 21:2; Deut. 15:12; 1 Kin. 9:22 [b]1 Sam. 8:7, 8; 2 Kin. 17:13, 14
15 [1]Or, *liberty* [a]2 Kin. 23:3; Neh. 10:29
16 [1]Lit., *caused them to return* [a]1 Sam. 15:11; Jer. 34:11; Ezek. 3:20; 18:24 [b]Ex. 20:7
17 [1]Or, *liberty* [a]Lev. 26:34, 35; Esth. 7:10; Dan. 6:24; Matt. 7:2 [b]Jer. 32:24; 38:2 [c]Deut. 28:25, 64; Jer. 29:18
18 [a]Deut. 17:2; Hos. 6:7; 8:1 [b]Gen. 15:10
19 [a]Jer. 34:10; Ezek. 22:27; Mic. 7:1-5; Zeph. 3:3, 4
20 [a]1 Sam. 17:44, 46; 1 Kin. 14:11; 16:4; Jer. 19:7
21 [a]2 Kin. 25:18-21; Jer. 32:3, 4; 39:6; 52:10, 24-27; Ezek. 17:16
22 [a]Jer. 4:7 [b]Jer. 33:10; 44:22
1 [a]2 Kin. 23:34-36; 24:1; Jer. 1:3; 27:20; Dan. 1:1

of you shall set free his Hebrew
brother, who [1]has been sold to you
and has served you six years, you
shall send him out free from you;
but your forefathers did not [b]obey
Me, or incline their ear to Me.
15"Although recently you *had*
turned and done what is right in My
sight, each man proclaiming [1]re-
lease to his neighbor, and you had
[a]made a covenant before Me in the
house which is called by My name.
16"Yet you [a]turned and [b]profaned
My name, and each man [1]took back
his male servant and each man his
female servant, whom you had set
free according to their desire, and
you brought them into subjection to
be your male servants and female
servants." '
17"Therefore thus says the LORD,
'You have not obeyed Me in proclaiming [1]release each man to his
brother, and each man to his neighbor. Behold, I am [a]proclaiming a [1]re-
lease to you,' declares the LORD, 'to
the [b]sword, to the pestilence, and to
the famine; and I will make you a
[c]terror to all the kingdoms of the
earth.
18 'And I will give the men who
have [a]transgressed My covenant,
who have not fulfilled the words of
the covenant which they made before Me, *when* they [b]cut the calf in
two and passed between its parts—
19 the [a]officials of Judah, and the
officials of Jerusalem, the court officers, and the priests, and all the people of the land, who passed between
the parts of the calf—
20 and I will give them into the
hand of their enemies and into the
hand of those who seek their life.
And their [a]dead bodies shall be food
for the birds of the sky and the
beasts of the earth.
21 'And [a]Zedekiah king of Judah
and his officials I will give into the
hand of their enemies, and into the
hand of those who seek their life,
and into the hand of the army of the
king of Babylon which has gone
away from you.
22 'Behold, I am going to command,' declares the LORD, 'and I will
bring them back to this city; and
they shall fight against it and take it
and burn it with fire; and I will make
the cities of Judah a [a]desolation
[b]without inhabitant.' "

CHAPTER 35

The Rechabites' Obedience

THE word which came to Jeremiah from the LORD in the days of [a]Je-

hoiakim the son of Josiah, king of Judah, saying,

2"Go to the house of the [a]Rechabites, and speak to them, and bring them into the house of the LORD, into one of the [b]chambers, and give them wine to drink."

3 Then I took Jaazaniah the son of Jeremiah, son of Habazziniah, and his brothers, and all his sons, and the whole house of the Rechabites,

4 and I brought them into the house of the LORD, into the chamber of the sons of Hanan the son of Igdaliah, the [a]man of God, which was near the chamber of the officials, which was above the chamber of Maaseiah the son of Shallum, the doorkeeper.

5 Then I set before the men of the house of the Rechabites pitchers full of wine, and cups; and I said to them, "[a]Drink wine!"

6 But they said, "We will not drink wine, for [a]Jonadab the son of [b]Rechab, our father, commanded us, saying, 'You shall [c]not drink wine, you or your sons, forever.

7 'And you shall not build a house, and you shall not sow seed, and you shall not plant a vineyard or own one; but in [a]tents you shall dwell all your days, that you may live [b]many days in the land where you [c]sojourn.'

8"And we have [a]obeyed the voice of Jonadab the son of Rechab, our father, in all that he commanded us, not to drink wine all our days, we, our wives, our sons, or our daughters,

9 nor to build ourselves houses to dwell in; and we do not [a]have vineyard or field or seed.

10"We have only dwelt in tents, and have obeyed, and have done according to all that Jonadab our father commanded us.

11"But it came about, when [a]Nebuchadnezzar king of Babylon came up against the land, that we said, 'Come and let us go to Jerusalem before the army of the Chaldeans and before the army of the Syrians.' So we have dwelt in Jerusalem."

Judah Rebuked

12 Then the word of the LORD came to Jeremiah, saying,

13"Thus says the LORD of hosts, the God of Israel, 'Go and say to the men of Judah and the inhabitants of Jerusalem, "[a]Will you not receive instruction by listening to My words?" declares the LORD.

14"The words of Jonadab the son of Rechab, which he commanded his sons not to drink wine, are observed. So they do not drink *wine* to this day, for they have obeyed their father's command. But I have spoken to you [1a]again and again; yet you have [b]not listened to Me.

15"Also I have sent to you all My [a]servants the prophets, sending *them* [1]again and again, saying: '[b]Turn now every man from his evil way, and amend your deeds, and do not [c]go after other gods to worship them, then you shall dwell in the land which I have given to you and to your forefathers; but you have not inclined your ear or listened to Me.

16 'Indeed, the sons of Jonadab the son of Rechab have [a]observed the command of their father which he commanded them, but this people has not listened to Me.' " '

17"Therefore thus says the LORD, the God of hosts, the God of Israel, 'Behold, [a]I am bringing on Judah and on all the inhabitants of Jerusalem all the disaster that I have pronounced against them; because I [b]spoke to them but they did not listen, and I have called them but they did not answer.' "

18 Then Jeremiah said to the house of the Rechabites, "Thus says the LORD of hosts, the God of Israel, 'Because you have [a]obeyed the command of Jonadab your father, kept all his commands, and done according to all that he commanded you;

19 therefore thus says the LORD of hosts, the God of Israel, "Jonadab the son of Rechab [a]shall not lack a man to [b]stand before Me always." ' "

CHAPTER 36

Jeremiah's Scroll Read in the Temple

AND it came about in the [a]fourth year of Jehoiakim the son of Josiah, king of Judah, that this word came to Jeremiah from the LORD, saying,

2"Take a [1a]scroll and write on it all the [b]words which I have spoken to you concerning [c]Israel, and concerning [c]Judah, and concerning all the [d]nations, from the [e]day I *first* spoke to you, from the days of Josiah, even to this day.

3"[a]Perhaps the house of Judah will hear all the calamity which I plan to bring on them, in order that every man will [b]turn from his evil way; then I will [c]forgive their iniquity and their sin."

---

2 [a]1 Chr. 2:55 [b]1 Kin. 6:5, 6, 8; 1 Chr. 9:26, 33
4 [a]Deut. 33:1; Josh. 14:6; 1 Kin. 12:22; 2 Kin. 1:9-13
5 [a]Amos 2:12; 2 Cor. 2:9
6 [a]2 Kin. 10:15, 23 [b]1 Chr. 2:55 [c]Lev. 10:9; Num. 6:2-4; Judg. 13:7, 14; Luke 1:15
7 [a]Gen. 25:27; Heb. 11:9 [b]Ex. 20:12; Eph. 6:2, 3 [c]Gen. 36:7; 1 Chr. 16:19
8 [a]Prov. 1:8, 9; 4:1, 2, 10; 6:20; Eph. 6:1; Col. 3:20
9 [a]Ps. 37:16; Jer. 35:7; 1 Tim. 6:6
11 [a]2 Kin. 24:1, 2; Dan. 1:1, 2
13 [a]Is. 28:9-12; Jer. 5:3; 6:8-10; 32:33
14 [1]Lit., *rising early and speaking* [a]2 Chr. 36:15; Jer. 7:13, 25; 11:7; 25:3, 4 [b]Is. 30:9; 50:2
15 [1]Cf. v. 14 [a]Jer. 26:5; 29:19; 32:33 [b]Is. 1:16, 17; Jer. 4:1; 18:11; Ezek. 18:30-32; Acts 26:20 [c]Deut. 6:14; Jer. 7:6; 13:10; 25:6
16 [a]Jer. 35:14; Mal. 1:6
17 [a]Jer. 19:3, 15; 21:4-10; Mic. 3:12 [b]Prov. 1:24, 25; Is. 65:12; 66:4; Jer. 7:13, 26, 27; 26:5; Luke 13:34, 35; Rom. 10:21
18 [a]Ex. 20:12; Eph. 6:1-3
19 [a]1 Chr. 2:55; Jer. 33:17 [b]Jer. 15:19; Luke 21:36
1 [a]2 Kin. 24:1; Jer. 25:1, 3; 45:1; 46:2
2 [1]Lit., *scroll of a book* [a]Ex. 17:14; Jer. 36:6, 23, 28; Zech. 5:1, 2 [b]Jer. 1:9, 10 [c]Jer. 3:3-10; 23:13, 14; 32:30-32 [d]Jer. 1:5, 10; 25:9-29; chaps. 47-51 [e]Jer. 1:2, 3; 25:3
3 [a]Jer. 26:3; 36:7; Ezek. 12:3 [b]Deut. 30:2, 8; 1 Sam. 7:3; Is. 55:7; Jer. 18:8, 11; 35:15 [c]John 3:10; Mark 4:12; Acts 3:19

4 Then Jeremiah called [a]Baruch the son of Neriah, and Baruch wrote [1]at the dictation of Jeremiah all the words of the LORD, which He had spoken to him, on a [b]scroll.

5 And Jeremiah commanded Baruch, saying, "I am [1a]restricted; I cannot go into the house of the LORD.

6 "So you go and [a]read from the scroll which you have [b]written [1]at my dictation the words of the LORD [2]to the people in the LORD's house on a [c]fast day. And also you shall read them [2]to all *the people of* Judah who come from their cities.

7 "[a]Perhaps their supplication will [1]come before the LORD, and everyone will turn from his evil way, for [b]great is the anger and the wrath that the LORD has pronounced against this people."

8 And Baruch the son of Neriah did according to all that Jeremiah the prophet commanded him, [a]reading from the book the words of the LORD in the LORD's house.

9 Now it came about in the [a]fifth year of Jehoiakim the son of Josiah, king of Judah, in the [b]ninth month, that all the people in Jerusalem and all the people who [c]came from the cities of Judah to Jerusalem proclaimed a [d]fast before the LORD.

10 Then Baruch read from the book the words of Jeremiah in the house of the LORD in the [a]chamber of [b]Gemariah the son of Shaphan the [c]scribe, in the upper court, at the [d]entry of the New Gate of the LORD's house, to all the people.

11 Now when [a]Micaiah the son of Gemariah, the son of Shaphan, had heard all the words of the LORD from the book,

12 he went down to the king's house, into the scribe's chamber. And, behold, all the officials were sitting there—[a]Elishama the scribe, and [b]Delaiah the son of Shemaiah, and [c]Elnathan the son of Achbor, and Gemariah the son of Shaphan, and Zedekiah the son of Hananiah, and all the *other* officials.

13 And Micaiah [a]declared to them all the words that he had heard, when Baruch read from the book to the people.

14 Then all the officials sent [a]Jehudi the son of Nethaniah, the son of Shelemiah, the son of Cushi, to Baruch, saying, "Take in your hand the scroll from which you have read to the people and come." So Baruch the son of Neriah [b]took the scroll in his hand and went to them.

15 And they said to him, "Sit down please, and read it to us." So Baruch [a]read it to them.

16 Now it came about when they had heard all the words, they turned in [a]fear one to another and said to Baruch, "We will surely [b]report all these words to the king."

17 And they asked Baruch, saying, "Tell us please, [a]how did you write all these words? *Was it* [1]at his dictation?"

18 Then Baruch said to them, "He [a]dictated all these words to me, and I wrote them with ink on the book."

19 Then the officials said to Baruch, "Go, [a]hide yourself, you and Jeremiah, and do not let anyone know where you are."

The Scroll Is Burned

20 So they went to the [a]king in the court, but they had deposited the scroll in the chamber of [a]Elishama the scribe, and they reported all the words to the king.

21 Then the king sent Jehudi to get the scroll, and he took it out of the chamber of Elishama the scribe. And [a]Jehudi read it to the king as well as to all the officials who stood beside the king.

22 Now the king was sitting in the [a]winter house in the ninth month, with *a fire* burning in the brazier before him.

23 And it came about, when Jehudi had read three or four columns, *the king* cut it with a scribe's knife and [a]threw *it* into the fire that was in the brazier, until all the scroll was consumed in the fire that was in the brazier.

24 Yet the king and all his servants who heard all these words were [a]not afraid, nor did they [b]rend their garments.

25 Even though Elnathan and Delaiah and Gemariah [a]entreated the king not to burn the scroll, he would not listen to them.

26 And the king commanded Jerahmeel the king's son, Seraiah the son of Azriel, and Shelemiah the son of Abdeel to [a]seize Baruch the scribe and Jeremiah the prophet, but the LORD hid them.

The Scroll Is Replaced

27 Then the word of the LORD came to Jeremiah after the king had burned the scroll and the words which Baruch had written at the dictation of Jeremiah, saying,

28 "[a]Take again another scroll and write on it all the former words that

4 [1]Lit., *from the mouth of* [a]Jer. 32:12; 36:18; 43:3 [b]Jer. 36:14; Ezek. 2:9
5 [1]Lit., *shut up* [a]Jer. 32:2; 33:1; 2 Cor. 11:23
6 [1]Lit., *from my mouth* [2]Lit., *in the ears of,* and so throughout this context [a]Jer 36:8 [b]Jer. 36:4 [c]Jer. 36:9; Zech. 8:19
7 [1]Lit., *fall* [a]1 Kin. 8:33; 2 Chr. 33:12, 13; Jer. 26:3; 36:3 [b]2 Kin. 22:13, 17; Jer. 4:4; 21:5; Lam. 4:11
8 [a]Jer. 1:17; 36:6
9 [a]Jer. 36:1 [b]Jer. 36:22 [c]Jer. 36:6 [d]2 Chr. 20:3; Esth. 4:16; Joel 1:14; 2:15; Jon. 3:5
10 [a]Jer. 35:4 [b]Jer. 36:11, 25 [c]2 Sam. 8:17; Jer. 52:25 [d]Jer. 26:10
11 [a]Jer. 36:13
12 [a]Jer. 36:20 [b]Jer. 36:25 [c]Jer. 26:22
13 [a]2 Kin. 22:10
14 [a]Jer. 36:21 [b]Jer. 36:2; Ezek. 2:6, 7
15 [a]Jer. 36:21
16 [a]Jer. 36:24; Acts 24:25 [b]Jer. 13:18; Amos 7:10, 11
17 [1]Lit., *from his mouth,* and so throughout this context [a]John 9:10, 15, 26
18 [a]Jer. 36:4; 43:2, 3
19 [a]1 Kin. 17:3; 18:4, 10; Jer. 26:20-24; 36:26
20 [a]Jer. 36:12
21 [a]2 Kin. 22:10; 2 Chr. 34:18; Ezek. 2:4, 5
22 [a]Amos 3:15
23 [a]1 Kin. 22:8, 27; Prov. 1:30; Is. 5:18, 19; 28:14, 22; Jer. 36:29
24 [a]Ps. 36:1; 64:5; Is. 26:11; Jer. 36:16 [b]1 Kin. 21:27; 2 Kin. 19:1, 2; 22:11, 19; Is. 36:22; 37:1; Jon. 3:6
25 [a]Gen. 37:22, 26, 27; Acts 5:34-39
26 [a]1 Kin. 19:1-3, 10, 14
28 [a]Jer. 28:13, 14; 44:28; Zech. 1:5, 6

were on the first scroll which Jehoiakim the king of Judah burned.
29"And concerning Jehoiakim
king of Judah you shall say, 'Thus
says the LORD, "You have [a]burned
this scroll, saying, '[b]Why have you
written on it that the [c]king of Babylon shall certainly come and destroy
this land, and shall make man and
beast to cease from it?' "
30 'Therefore thus says the LORD
concerning Jehoiakim king of Judah, "He shall have [a]no one to sit on
the throne of David, and his dead
body shall be cast out to the heat of
the day and the frost of the night.
31"I shall also punish him and his
descendants and his servants for
their iniquity, and I shall [a]bring on
them and the inhabitants of Jerusalem and the men of Judah all the
calamity that I have declared to
them—but they did not listen." ' "
32 Then Jeremiah took another
scroll and gave it to Baruch the son
of Neraiah, the scribe, and he [a]wrote
on it at the dictation of Jeremiah all
the words of the book which Jehoiakim king of Judah had burned in the
fire; and many similar words were
added to them.

CHAPTER 37

Jeremiah Warns against Trust in Pharaoh

NOW [a]Zedekiah the son of Josiah
whom Nebuchadnezzar king of
Babylon had [b]made king in the land
of Judah, reigned as king in place of
[c]Coniah the son of Jehoiakim.
2 But [a]neither he nor his servants
nor the people of the land listened to
the words of the LORD which He
spoke through Jeremiah the
prophet.
3 Yet King Zedekiah sent Jehucal
the son of Shelemiah, and [a]Zephani-
ah the son of Maaseiah, the priest, to
Jeremiah the prophet, saying,
"[b]Please pray to the LORD our God
on our behalf."
4 Now Jeremiah was *still* coming
in and going out among the people,
for they had not *yet* put him in the
prison.
5 Meanwhile, [a]Pharaoh's army
had set out from Egypt; and when
the Chaldeans who had been besieging Jerusalem heard the report
about them, they lifted the *siege*
from Jerusalem.
6 Then the word of the LORD
came to Jeremiah the prophet, saying,
7"Thus says the LORD God of Israel, '[a]Thus you are to say to the
king of Judah, who sent you to Me
to inquire of Me: "Behold, [b]Pha-
raoh's army which has come out for
your assistance is going to return to
its own land of Egypt.
8"The Chaldeans will also [a]return
and fight against this city, and they
will capture it and burn it with
fire." '
9"Thus says the LORD, 'Do not
[a]deceive yourselves, saying, "The
Chaldeans will surely go away from
us," for they will not go.
10 'For [a]even if you had defeated
the entire army of Chaldeans who
were fighting against you, and there
were *only* wounded men left among
them, each man in his tent, they
would [b]rise up and burn this city
with fire.' "

Jeremiah Imprisoned

11 Now it happened, when the
army of the Chaldeans had lifted *the*
siege from Jerusalem because of
Pharaoh's army,
12 that Jeremiah went out from
Jerusalem to go to the land of Benjamin in order to take possession of
some [a]property there among the
people.
13 While he was at the [a]Gate of
Benjamin, a captain of the guard
whose name was Irijah, the son of
Shelemiah the son of Hananiah was
there; and he arrested Jeremiah the
prophet, saying, "You are [1b]going
over to the Chaldeans!"
14 But Jeremiah said, "[a]A lie! I am
not [1]going over to the Chaldeans";
yet he would not listen to him. So
Irijah arrested Jeremiah and
brought him to the officials.
15 Then the officials were [a]angry
at Jeremiah and beat him, and they
[b]put him in jail in the house of Jonathan the scribe, which they had
made into the prison.
16 For Jeremiah had come into the
[1]dungeon, that is, the vaulted cell;
and Jeremiah stayed there many
days.
17 Now King Zedekiah sent and
took him *out;* and in his palace the
king secretly [a]asked him and said,
"Is there a [b]word from the LORD?"
And Jeremiah said, "There is!" Then
he said, "You will be [c]given into the
hand of the king of Babylon!"
18 Moreover Jeremiah said to
King Zedekiah, "[a]*In* what *way* have
I sinned against you, or against your
servants, or against this people, that
you have put me in prison?

29 [a]Deut. 29:19; Job 15:24, 25; Is. 45:9 [b]Is. 29:21; 30:10; Jer. 26:9; 32:3 [c]Jer. 25:9-11
30 [a]2 Kin. 24:12-15; Jer. 22:30
31 [a]Deut. 28:15; Prov. 29:1; Jer. 19:15; 35:17
32 [a]Ex. 4:15, 16; 34:1; Jer. 36:4, 23
1 [a]2 Kin. 24:17; 1 Chr. 3:15; 2 Chr. 36:10 [b]Ezek. 17:12-21 [c]2 Kin. 24:12; 1 Chr. 3:16; 2 Chr. 36:9, 10; Jer. 22:24, 28; 24:1; 52:31
2 [a]2 Kin. 24:19, 20; 2 Chr. 36:12-16; Prov. 29:12
3 [a]Jer. 29:25; 52:24 [b]1 Kin. 13:6; Jer. 2:27; 15:11; 21:1, 2; 42:1-4, 20; Acts 8:24
5 [a]2 Kin. 24:7; Jer. 37:7; Ezek. 17:15
7 [a]2 Kin. 22:18; Jer. 21:1, 2; 37:3 [b]Is. 30:1-3; 31:1-3; Jer. 2:18, 36; Lam. 4:17; Ezek. 17:17
8 [a]Jer. 34:22; 38:23; 39:2-8
9 [a]Jer. 29:8; Obad. 3; Matt. 24:4, 5; Eph. 5:6
10 [a]Lev. 26:36-38; Is. 30:17 [b]Joel 2:11
12 [a]1 Kin. 19:3, 9; Jer. 32:8; Matt. 10:23; Acts 17:10, 14
13 [1]Lit., *falling* [a]Jer. 38:7; Zech. 14:10 [b]Jer. 18:18; 20:10; Amos 7:10; Luke 23:2; Acts 6:11; 24:5-9, 13
14 [1]Lit., *falling* [a]Ps. 27:12; 52:1, 2; Jer. 40:4-6; Matt. 5:11, 12
15 [a]Jer. 18:23; 20:1-3; 26:16; Matt. 21:35 [b]Gen. 39:20; 2 Chr. 16:10; 18:26; Acts 5:18
16 [1]Lit., *house of the cistern-pit*
17 [a]1 Kin. 14:1-4; Jer. 38:5, 14-16, 24-27 [b]1 Kin. 22:15, 16; 2 Kin. 3:11-13; Jer. 15:11; 21:1, 2; 37:3 [c]Jer. 21:7; 24:8; Ezek. 12:12, 13; 17:19-21
18 [a]1 Sam. 24:9; 26:18; Dan. 6:22; John 10:32; Acts 25:8, 11, 25

19"[a]Where then are your prophets who prophesied to you, saying, 'The king of Babylon will not come against you or against this land?'

20"But now, please listen, O my lord the king; please let my [a]petition [1]come before you, and do not make me return to the house of Jonathan the scribe, that I may not die there."

21 Then King Zedekiah gave commandment, and they committed Jeremiah to the court of the guardhouse and gave him a loaf of [a]bread daily from the bakers' street, until all the bread in the city was [b]gone. So Jeremiah remained in the court of the guardhouse.

Chapter 38

Jeremiah Thrown into the Cistern

NOW Shephatiah the son of Mattan, and Gedaliah the son of Pashhur, and Jucal the son of Shelemiah, and Pashhur the son of Malchijah heard the words that Jeremiah was speaking to all the people, saying,

2"Thus says the LORD, 'He who stays in this city will die by the sword and by famine and by pestilence, but he who goes out to the Chaldeans will live and have his *own* [a]life as booty and stay alive.'

3"Thus says the LORD, 'This city will certainly be [a]given into the hand of the army of the king of Babylon, and he will capture it.'"

4 Then the [a]officials said to the king, "Now let this man be put to death, inasmuch as he is [1b]discouraging the men of war who are left in this city and [2]all the people, by speaking such words to them; for this man is not seeking the well-being of this people, but rather their harm."

5 So King Zedekiah said, "Behold, he is in your [1]hands; for the king [a]can *do* nothing against you."

6 Then they took Jeremiah and cast him into the [a]cistern *of* Malchijah the king's son, which was in the court of the guardhouse; and they let Jeremiah down with ropes. Now in the cistern there was no water but only [b]mud, and Jeremiah sank into the mud.

7 But Ebed-melech the Ethiopian, a [1a]eunuch, while he was in the king's palace, heard that they had put Jeremiah into the cistern. Now the king was sitting in the [b]Gate of Benjamin;

8 and Ebed-melech went out from the king's palace and spoke to the king, saying,

9"My lord the king, these men have acted wickedly in all that they have done to Jeremiah the prophet whom they have cast into the cistern; and he [1]will die right where he is because of the famine, for there is [a]no more bread in the city."

10 Then the king commanded Ebed-melech the Ethiopian, saying, "Take thirty men from here [1]under your authority, and bring up Jeremiah the prophet from the cistern before he dies."

11 So Ebed-melech took the men under his [1]authority and went into the king's palace to *a place* beneath the storeroom and took from there worn-out clothes and worn-out rags and let them down by ropes into the cistern to Jeremiah.

12 Then Ebed-melech the Ethiopian said to Jeremiah, "Now put these worn-out clothes and rags under your armpits under the ropes"; and Jeremiah did so.

13 So they pulled Jeremiah up with the ropes and lifted him out of the cistern, and Jeremiah stayed in the [a]court of the guardhouse.

14 Then King Zedekiah [a]sent and [1]had Jeremiah the prophet brought to him at the third entrance that is in the house of the LORD; and the king said to Jeremiah, "I am going to [b]ask you something; do not hide anything from me."

15 Then Jeremiah said to Zedekiah, "[a]If I tell you, will you not certainly put me to death? Besides, if I give you advice, you will not listen to me."

16 But King Zedekiah swore to Jeremiah in [a]secret saying, "As the LORD lives, who made this [1b]life for us, surely I will not put you to death nor will I give you over to the hand of [c]these men who are seeking your [1]life."

Interview with Zedekiah

17 Then Jeremiah said to Zedekiah, "Thus says the LORD [a]God of hosts, the [b]God of Israel, 'If you will indeed [c]go out to the officers of the king of Babylon, then [1]you will live, this city will not be burned with fire, and you and your household will [2]survive.

18 'But if you will [a]not go out to the officers of the king of Babylon, then this city [b]will be given over to the hand of the Chaldeans; and they will burn it with fire, and [c]you yourself will not escape from their hand.'"

19 Then King Zedekiah said to Jeremiah, "I [a]dread the Jews who have [1b]gone over to the Chaldeans, lest

---

19 [a]Deut. 32:37, 38; 2 Kin. 3:13; Jer. 2:28
20 [1]Lit., *fall* [a]Jer. 36:7; 38:26
21 [a]Job 5:20; Ps. 33:18, 19; Is. 33:16 [b]2 Kin. 25:3; Jer. 38:9; 52:6
2 [a]Jer. 21:9; 39:18; 45:5
3 [a]Jer. 21:10; 32:3-5
4 [1]Lit., *weakening the hands of* [2]Lit., *the hands of all* [a]Jer. 18:23; 26:11, 21; 36:12 [b]Ex. 5:4; 1 Kin. 18:17, 18; 21:20; Ezra 4:12; Neh. 6:9; Amos 7:10; Acts 16:20
5 [1]Lit., *hand* [a]1 Sam. 15:24; 29:9; 2 Sam. 3:39
6 [a]Jer. 37:16, 21; Acts 16:24 [b]Ps. 40:2; 69:2, 14, 15; Jer. 38:22; Zech. 9:11
7 [1]Or, *official* [a]Jer. 29:2; Acts 8:27 [b]Deut. 21:19; Job 29:7; Jer. 37:13; Amos 5:10
9 [1]M.T. reads: *has died* [a]Jer. 37:21; 52:6
10 [1]Lit., *in your hand*
11 [1]Lit., *hand*
13 [a]Jer. 37:21; 38:6; 39:14, 15; Acts 23:35; 24:27; 28:16, 30
14 [1]Lit., *took Jeremiah to him* [a]Jer. 21:1, 2; 37:17 [b]1 Sam. 3:17, 18; 1 Kin. 22:16; Jer. 15:11; 42:2-5, 20
15 [a]Luke 22:67, 68
16 [1]Lit., *soul* [a]Jer. 37:17; John 3:2 [b]Num. 16:22; 27:16; Is. 57:16; Zech. 12:1 [c]Jer. 34:20; 38:4-6
17 [1]Lit., *your soul* [2]Lit., *live* [a]Ps. 80:7, 14; Amos 5:27 [b]1 Chr. 17:24; Ezek. 8:4 [c]2 Kin. 24:12; 25:27-30; Jer. 21:8-10; 27:12, 17; 38:2
18 [a]Jer. 27:8 [b]2 Kin. 25:4-10; Jer. 24:8-10; 32:3-5; 37:8; 38:3 [c]Jer. 32:4; 34:3
19 [1]Lit., *fallen* [a]Is. 51:12, 13; 57:11; John 12:42; 19:12, 13 [b]Jer. 39:9

they give me over into their hand and they [c]abuse me."

20 But Jeremiah said, "They will not give you over. Please [a]obey the LORD in what I am saying to you, that it may go [b]well with you and [1c]you may live.

21"But if you keep refusing to go out, this is the word which the LORD has shown me:

22 'Then behold, all of the [a]women who have been left in the palace of the king of Judah are going to be brought out to the [1]officers of the king of Babylon; and those women will say,

"[2]Your close friends
Have misled and overpowered
you;
While your feet were sunk in
the mire,
They turned back."

23 'They will also bring out all your wives and your [a]sons to the Chaldeans, and [b]you yourself will not escape from their hand, but will be seized by the hand of the king of Babylon, and [b]this city will be burned with fire.' "

24 Then Zedekiah said to Jeremiah, "Let no man know about these words and you will not die.

25"But if the [a]officials hear that I have talked with you and come to you and say to you, 'Tell us now what you said to the king, and what the king said to you; do not hide *it* from us, and we will not put you to death;'

26 then you are to say to them, 'I was [a]presenting my petition before the king, not to make me return to the house of Jonathan to die there.' "

27 Then all the officials came to Jeremiah and questioned him. So he [a]reported to them in accordance with all these words which the king had commanded; and they ceased speaking with him, since the conversation had not been overheard.

28 So Jeremiah [a]stayed in the court of the guardhouse until the day that Jerusalem was captured.

CHAPTER 39

Jerusalem Captured

1 NOW it came about when Jerusalem was captured [2a]in the ninth year of Zedekiah king of Judah, in the tenth month, Nebuchadnezzar king of Babylon and all his army came to Jerusalem and laid siege to it;

2 in the eleventh year of Zedekiah, in the fourth month, in the ninth *day* of the month, the city *wall* was [a]breached.

3 Then all the officials of the king of Babylon came in and sat down at the [a]Middle Gate: Nergal-sar-ezer, Samgar-nebu, Sar-sekim the [1]Rab-saris, Nergal-sar-ezer *the* [2]Rab-mag, and all the rest of the officials of the king of Babylon.

4 And it came about, when Zedekiah the king of Judah and all the men of war saw them, that they [a]fled and went out of the city at night by way of the king's garden through the gate [b]between the two walls; and he went out toward the [1]Arabah.

5 But the army of the [a]Chaldeans pursued them and overtook Zedekiah in the [b]plains of Jericho; and they seized him and brought him up to Nebuchadnezzar king of Babylon at [c]Riblah in the land of Hamath, and he passed sentence on him.

6 Then the [a]king of Babylon slew the sons of Zedekiah [b]before his eyes at Riblah; the king of Babylon also slew all the [c]nobles of Judah.

7 He then [a]blinded Zedekiah's eyes and bound him in [b]fetters of bronze to bring him to Babylon.

8 The Chaldeans also [a]burned with fire the king's palace and the houses of the people, and they [b]broke down the walls of Jerusalem.

9 And as for the rest of the people who were left in the city, the [a]deserters who had gone over to him and the rest of the people who remained, [b]Nebuzaradan the [c]captain of the bodyguard carried *them* into exile in Babylon.

10 But some of the [a]poorest people who had nothing, [a]Nebuzaradan the captain of the bodyguard left behind in the land of Judah, and gave them vineyards and fields at that time.

Jeremiah Spared

11 Now Nebuchadnezzar king of Babylon gave orders about [a]Jeremiah through Nebuzaradan the captain of the bodyguard, saying,

12"Take him and look after him, and [a]do nothing harmful to him; but rather deal with him just as he tells you."

13 So Nebuzaradan the captain of the bodyguard sent *word*, along with Nebushazban the [1]Rab-saris, and Nergal-sar-ezer the [2]Rab-mag, and all the leading officers of the king of Babylon;

14 they even sent and [a]took Jeremiah out of the court of the guardhouse and entrusted him to Geda-

---

19 [c]2 Chr. 30:10; Neh. 4:1; Jer. 38:22
20 [1]Lit., *your soul* [a]2 Chr. 20:20; Jer. 11:4, 8; 26:13; Dan. 4:27; Acts 26:29 [b]Jer. 7:23 [c]Gen. 19:20; Is. 55:3
22 [1]Or, *princes* [2]Lit., *The men of your peace* [a]Jer. 6:12; 8:10; 43:6
23 [a]2 Kin. 25:7; Jer. 39:6; 41:10 [b]Jer. 38:18
25 [a]Jer. 38:4-6, 27
26 [a]Jer. 37:15, 20
27 [a]1 Sam. 10:15, 16; 16:2-5
28 [a]Ps. 23:4; Jer. 15:20, 21; 37:20, 21; 38:13; 39:13, 14
1 [1]38:28-b in Heb. [2]39:1 in Heb. [a]2 Kin. 25:1-12; Jer. 52:4; Ezek. 24:1, 2
2 [a]2 Kin. 25:4; Jer. 52:7
3 [1]I.e., chief official [2]I.e., title of a high official [a]Jer. 21:4
4 [1]I.e., Jordan valley [a]2 Kin. 25:4; Is. 30:15, 16; Jer. 52:7; Amos 2:14 [b]2 Chr. 32:5
5 [a]Jer. 32:4, 5; 38:18, 23; 52:8; Lam. 4:20 [b]Josh. 4:13; 5:10 [c]Jer. 52:9, 26, 27
6 [a]2 Kin. 25:7; Jer. 52:10 [b]Deut. 28:34 [c]Jer. 21:7; 24:8-10; 34:19-21
7 [a]2 Kin. 25:7; Jer. 52:11; Ezek. 12:13 [b]Judg. 16:21
8 [a]Jer. 21:10; 52:13 [b]2 Kin. 25:10; Neh. 1:3; Jer. 52:14
9 [a]Jer. 38:19; 52:15 [b]2 Kin. 25:11, 20; Jer. 39:13; 40:1; 52:12-16, 26 [c]Gen. 37:36
10 [a]2 Kin. 25:12; Jer. 52:16
11 [a]Job 5:15, 16; Jer. 1:8; 15:20, 21; Acts 24:23
12 [a]Ps. 105:14, 15; Prov. 16:7; 21:1; 1 Pet. 3:13
13 [1]I.e., chief official (Akkad) [2]I.e., title of a high officer
14 [a]Jer. 38:28; 40:1-6

liah, the son of [b]Ahikam, the son of Shaphan, to take him home. So he stayed among the people.

15 Now the word of the LORD had come to Jeremiah while he was confined in the court of the guardhouse, saying,

16 "Go and speak to Ebed-melech the Ethiopian, saying, 'Thus says the LORD of hosts, the God of Israel, "Behold, I am about to bring My words on this city [a]for disaster and not for [1]prosperity; and they will take place [b]before you on that day.

17 "But I will [a]deliver you on that day," declares the LORD, "and you shall not be given into the hand of the men whom you dread.

18 "For I will certainly rescue you, and you will not fall by the sword; but you will have your *own* [a]life as booty, because you have [b]trusted in Me," declares the LORD.' "

CHAPTER 40

Jeremiah Remains in Judah

THE word which came to Jeremiah from the LORD after Nebuzaradan captain of the bodyguard had released him from [a]Ramah, when he had taken him bound in [b]chains, among all the exiles of Jerusalem and Judah, who were being exiled to Babylon.

2 Now the captain of the bodyguard had taken Jeremiah and said to him, "The [a]LORD your God promised this calamity against this place;

3 and the LORD has brought *it* on and done just as He promised. Because you *people* [a]sinned against the LORD and did not listen to His voice, therefore this thing has happened to you.

4 "But now, behold, I am [a]freeing you today from the chains which are on your hands. If [1]you would prefer to come with me to Babylon, come *along,* and I will [2]look after you; but if [3]you would prefer not to come with me to Babylon, [4]never mind. Look, the [b]whole land is before you; go wherever it seems good and right for you to go."

5 As [1]Jeremiah was still not going back, [2]*he said,* "Go on back then to Gedaliah the son of Ahikam, the son of Shaphan, whom the king of Babylon has [a]appointed over the cities of Judah, and stay with him among the people; or else go anywhere it seems right for you to go." So the captain of the bodyguard gave him a [b]ration and a [c]gift and let him go.

14 [b]2 Kin. 22:12, 14; 2 Chr. 34:20; Jer. 26:24

16 [1]Lit., *good* [a]Jer. 21:10; Dan. 9:12; Zech. 1:6 [b]Ps. 91:8, 9

17 [a]Ps. 41:1, 2; 50:15

18 [a]Jer. 21:9; 38:2; 45:5 [b]Ps. 34:22; Jer. 17:7, 8

1 [a]Jer. 31:15 [b]Acts. 12:6, 7; 21:13; 28:20; Eph. 6:20

2 [a]Deut. 29:24-28; Jer. 22:8, 9

3 [a]Jer. 50:7; Rom. 2:5

4 [1]Lit., *it is good in your eyes* [2]Lit., *set my eyes on* [3]Lit., *it is evil in your eyes* [4]Lit., *refrain!* [a]Jer. 39:11, 12 [b]Gen. 13:9; 20:15; 47:6

5 [1]Lit., *he* [2]I.e., Nebuzaradan [a]2 Kin. 25:23 [b]Jer. 52:34 [c]2 Kin. 8:7-9

6 [a]Judg. 20:1; 21:1; 1 Sam. 7:5; 2 Chr. 16:6

7 [1]Or, *princes* [2]Lit., *infants* [a]2 Kin. 25:23, 24 [b]Jer. 39:10; 52:16

8 [a]Jer. 40:14; 41:2 [b]Jer. 40:13, 15; 42:1; 43:2 [c]2 Sam. 23:28, 29; Ezra 2:22; Neh. 7:26 [d]Deut. 3:14; Josh. 12:5; 2 Sam. 10:6, 8

9 [a]1 Sam. 20:16, 17; 2 Kin. 25:24 [b]Jer. 27:11; 38:17-20

10 [a]Deut. 1:38; 1 Kin. 10:8; Jer. 35:19 [b]Jer. 39:10 [c]Is. 16:9; Jer. 40:12; 48:32

11 [a]Num. 22:1; 25:1, 2; Is. 16:4; Jer. 9:26 [b]1 Sam. 11:1; 12:12 [c]Gen. 36:8; Is. 11:14

14 [a]1 Sam. 11:1-3; 2 Sam. 10:1-6; Jer. 25:21; 41:10

15 [a]1 Sam. 26:8

6 Then Jeremiah went to [a]Mizpah to Gedaliah the son of Ahikam and stayed with him among the people who were left in the land.

7 [a]Now all the [1]commanders of the forces that were in the field, they and their men, heard that the king of Babylon had appointed Gedaliah the son of Ahikam over the land and that he had put him in charge of the men, women and [2]children, those of the [b]poorest of the land who had not been exiled to Babylon.

8 So they came to Gedaliah at Mizpah, along with [a]Ishmael the son of Nethaniah, and [b]Johanan and Jonathan the sons of Kareah, and Seraiah the son of Tanhumeth, and the sons of Ephai the [c]Netophathite, and Jezaniah the son of the [d]Maacathite, *both* they and their men.

9 Then Gedaliah the son of Ahikam, the son of Shaphan, [a]swore to them and to their men, saying, "Do not be [b]afraid of serving the Chaldeans; stay in the land and serve the king of Babylon, that it may go well with you.

10 "Now as for me, behold, I am going to stay at Mizpah to [a]stand *for you* before the Chaldeans who come to us; but as for you, [b]gather in wine and [c]summer fruit and oil, and put *them* in your *storage* vessels, and live in your cities that you have taken over."

11 Likewise also all the Jews who were in [a]Moab and among the sons of [b]Ammon and in [c]Edom, and who were in all the *other* countries, heard that the king of Babylon had left a remnant for Judah and that he had appointed over them Gedaliah the son of Ahikam, the son of Shaphan.

12 Then all the Jews returned from all the places to which they had been driven away and came to the land of Judah, to Gedaliah at Mizpah, and gathered in wine and summer fruit in great abundance.

13 Now Johanan the son of Kareah and all the commanders of the forces that were in the field came to Gedaliah at Mizpah,

14 and said to him, "Are you well aware that Baalis the king of the sons of [a]Ammon has sent Ishmael the son of Nethaniah to take your life?" But Gedaliah the son of Ahikam did not believe them.

15 Then Johanan the son of Kareah spoke secretly to Gedaliah in Mizpah, saying, "[a]Let me go and kill Ishmael the son of Nethaniah, and not a man will know! Why should he

[b]take your life, so that all the Jews
who are gathered to you should be
scattered and the [c]remnant of Judah
perish?"
16 But Gedaliah the son of Ahikam
said to Johanan the son of Kareah,
"[a]Do not do this thing, for you are
telling a lie about Ishmael."

Chapter 41

Gedaliah Is Murdered

NOW it [a]came about in the seventh month that [b]Ishmael the son of
Nethaniah, the son of Elishama, of
the royal [1]family and *one* of the
chief officers of the king, along with
ten men, came to Mizpah to [c]Geda-
liah the son of Ahikam. While they
[d]were eating bread together there in
Mizpah,
2 Ishmael the son of Nethaniah
and the ten men who were with him
arose and [a]struck down Gedaliah
the son of Ahikam, the son of Shaphan, with the sword and put to
[b]death the one [c]whom the king of
Babylon had appointed over the
land.
3 Ishmael also struck down all
the Jews who were with him, *that is*
with Gedaliah at Mizpah, and the
Chaldeans who were found there,
the men of war.
4 Now it happened on the [1]next
day after the killing of Gedaliah,
when no one knew about *it*,
5 that eighty men [a]came from
[b]Shechem, from [c]Shiloh, and from
[d]Samaria with their beards shaved
off and their clothes torn and [1]their
bodies [e]gashed, having grain offerings and incense in their hands to
bring to the [f]house of the LORD.
6 Then Ishmael the son of Nethaniah went out from Mizpah to meet
them, [a]weeping as he went; and it
came about as he met them that he
said to them, "Come to Gedaliah the
son of Ahikam!"
7 Yet it turned out that as soon as
they came inside the city, Ishmael
the son of Nethaniah and the men
that were with him [a]slaughtered
them, *and cast them* into the cistern.
8 But ten men who were found
among them said to Ishmael, "Do
not put us to death; for we have
[a]stores of wheat, barley, oil and
honey hidden in the field." So he re-
frained and did not put them to
death along with their companions.
9 Now as for the cistern where
Ishmael had cast all the corpses of
the men whom he had struck down
[1]because of Gedaliah, it was the
[a]one that King Asa had made on
[b]account of Baasha, king of Israel;
Ishmael the son of Nethaniah filled
it with the slain.
10 Then Ishmael took captive all
the remnant of the people who were
in Mizpah, the [a]king's daughters
and all the people who were left in
Mizpah, whom Nebuzaradan the
captain of the bodyguard had put
under the charge of Gedaliah the
son of Ahikam; thus Ishmael the son
of Nethaniah took them captive and
proceeded to cross over to the sons
of [b]Ammon.

Johanan Rescues the People

11 But Johanan the son of Kareah
and all the [a]commanders of the
forces that were with him heard of
all the evil that Ishmael the son of
Nethaniah had done.
12 So they took all the men and
went to [a]fight with Ishmael the son
of Nethaniah and they found him by
the [b]great [1]pool that is in Gibeon.
13 Now it came about, as soon as
all the people who were with Ishmael saw Johanan the son of Kareah and the commanders of the
forces that were with him, they
were glad.
14 So all the people whom Ishmael
had taken captive from Mizpah
turned around and came back, and
went to Johanan the son of Kareah.
15 But Ishmael the son of Nethaniah [a]escaped from Johanan with
eight men and went to the sons of
Ammon.
16 Then Johanan the son of Kareah and all the commanders of the
forces that were with him took from
Mizpah [a]all the remnant of the people whom he had [1]recovered from
Ishmael the son of Nethaniah, after
he had struck down Gedaliah the
son of Ahikam, *that is*, the men who
were [2]soldiers, *the* women, *the* [3]chil-
dren, and *the* eunuchs, whom he had
brought back from Gibeon.
17 And they went and stayed in
[1a]Geruth Chimham, which is beside
Bethlehem, in order to proceed into
Egypt
18 because of the Chaldeans; for
they were [a]afraid of them, since Ishmael the son of Nethaniah had
struck down Gedaliah the son of
Ahikam, whom the king of Babylon
had appointed over the land.

Chapter 42

Warning against Going to Egypt

THEN all the [1]commanders of the
forces, Johanan the son of Kareah,

40:15 [b]2 Sam. 21:17 [c]Jer. 42:2
40:16 [a]Matt. 10:16
41:1 [1]Lit., *seed* [a]2 Kin. 25:25 [b]Jer. 40:8, 14 [c]Jer. 39:14; 40:5, 6 [d]Jer. 40:13, 14
2 [a]2 Sam. 3:27; 20:9, 10; Ps. 41:9; 109:5; John 13:18 [b]2 Kin. 25:25 [c]Jer. 40:5
4 [1]Or, *second*
5 [1]Lit., *having cut themselves* [a]2 Kin. 10:13, 14 [b]Gen. 33:18; 37:12; 1 Kin. 12:1 [c]Josh. 18:1; Judg. 18:31; 1 Sam. 3:21; Ps. 78:60 [d]1 Kin. 16:24, 29 [e]Deut. 14:1; Jer. 16:6 [f]2 Kin. 25:9; Ps. 102:14
6 [a]2 Sam. 3:16; Jer. 50:4
7 [a]Ps. 55:23; Is. 59:7; Ezek. 22:27; 33:24, 26
8 [a]Is. 45:3
9 [1]Or, *by the side of* [a]1 Kin. 15:17-22; 2 Chr. 16:1-6 [b]Judg. 6:2; 1 Sam. 13:6; 2 Sam. 17:9; Heb. 11:38
10 [a]Jer. 43:6 [b]Neh. 2:10, 19; 4:7, 8; 6:17, 18; Jer. 40:14
11 [a]Jer. 40:7, 8, 14-16
12 [1]Lit., *waters* [a]Gen. 14:14-16; 1 Sam. 30:1-8, 18, 20 [b]2 Sam. 2:13
15 [a]1 Sam. 30:17; 1 Kin. 20:20; Job 21:30; Prov. 28:17
16 [1]Lit., *brought back* [2]Lit., *men of war* [3]Lit., *infants* [a]Jer. 42:8; 43:4-7
17 [1]Or., *the lodging place of Chimham* [a]2 Sam. 19:37, 38, 40
18 [a]Is. 51:12, 13; 57:11; Jer. 42:11, 16; 43:2, 3; Luke 12:4, 5
42:1 [1]Or, *princes*

Jezaniah the son of Hoshaiah, and
all the people [a]both small and great
approached
2 and said to Jeremiah the
prophet, "Please let our [a]petition
[1]come before you, and [b]pray for us
to the LORD your God, *that is* for all
this remnant; because we are left
but a [c]few out of many, as your own
eyes *now* see us,
3 that the LORD your God may tell
us the [a]way in which we should
walk and the thing that we should
do."
4 Then Jeremiah the prophet said
to them, "I have heard *you*. Behold,
I am going to [a]pray to the LORD your
God in accordance with your words;
and it will come about that the
whole message which the [b]LORD
will answer you I will tell you. I will
[c]not keep back a word from you."
5 Then they said to Jeremiah,
"May the [a]LORD be a true and faithful witness against us, if we do not
act in accordance with the whole
message with which the LORD your
God will send you to us.
6"Whether *it* is pleasant or unpleasant, we will [a]listen to the voice
of the LORD our God to whom we are
sending you, in order that it may go
[b]well with us when we listen to the
voice of the LORD our God."
7 Now it came about at the [a]end
of ten days that the word of the
LORD came to Jeremiah.
8 Then he called for Johanan the
son of Kareah, and all the [1]com-
manders of the forces that were
with him, and for all the people both
small and great,
9 and said to them, "Thus [a]says
the LORD the God of Israel, to whom
you sent me to present your petition
before Him:
10 'If you will indeed stay in this
land, then I will [a]build you up and
not tear you down, and I will plant
you and not uproot you; for I shall
[b]relent concerning the calamity that
I have inflicted on you.
11 '[a]Do not be afraid of the king of
Babylon, whom you are *now* fearing; do not be afraid of him,' declares the LORD, 'for [b]I am with you
to save you and deliver you from his
hand.
12 'I will also show you compassion, so that [a]he will have compassion on you and restore you to your
own soil.
13 'But if you are going to say, "We
will [a]not stay in this land," so as not
to listen to the voice of the LORD
your God,
14 saying, "No, but we will [a]go to
the land of Egypt, where we shall
not see war or [b]hear the sound of a
trumpet or hunger for bread, and we
will stay there";
15 then [1]in that case listen to the
word of the LORD, O remnant of Judah. Thus says the LORD of hosts,
the God of Israel, "If you really set
your mind to enter [a]Egypt, and go in
to reside there,
16 then it will come about that the
[a]sword, which you are afraid of will
overtake you there in the land of
Egypt; and the famine, about which
you are anxious, will follow closely
after you there *in* Egypt; and you
will die there.
17"So all the men who set their
mind to go to Egypt to reside there
will die by the [a]sword, by famine,
and by pestilence; and they will
have no survivors or refugees from
the calamity that I am going to bring
on them."'"
18 For thus says the LORD of hosts,
the God of Israel, "As My [a]anger
and wrath have been poured out on
the inhabitants of Jerusalem, so My
wrath will be poured out on you
when you enter Egypt. And you will
become a [b]curse, an object of horror, an imprecation, and a reproach;
and you will see this place no more."
19 The LORD has spoken to you, O
remnant of Judah, "Do not [a]go into
Egypt!" You should clearly [b]under-
stand that today I have [c]testified
against you.
20 For you have *only* [1a]deceived
yourselves; for it is you who sent me
to the LORD your God, saying, "Pray
for us to the LORD our God; and
whatever the LORD our God says,
tell us so, and we will do it."
21 So, I have [a]told you today, but
you have not obeyed the LORD your
God, even in whatever He has sent
me to *tell* you.
22 Therefore you should now
clearly understand that you will die
by the sword, by famine, and by pestilence, in the [a]place where you wish
to go to reside.

CHAPTER 43

In Egypt Jeremiah Warns of Judgment

BUT it came about, as soon as Jeremiah whom the LORD their God
had sent, had [a]finished telling all the
people all the words of the LORD
their God—that is, all these
words—
2 that Azariah the son of Hoshaiah, and Johanan the son of Kareah,

1 [a]Jer. 6:13; 8:10; 42:8; 44:12; Acts 8:10
2 [1]Lit., *fall* [a]Jer. 36:7; 37:20 [b]Ex. 8:28; 1 Kin. 13:6; Jer. 37:3; 42:20; Acts 8:24 [c]Deut. 28:62; Is. 1:9; Lam. 1:1
3 [a]Ps. 86:11; Prov. 3:6; Jer. 6:16; Mic. 4:2
4 [a]Ex. 8:29; 1 Sam. 12:23 [b]1 Kin. 22:14; Jer. 23:28 [c]1 Sam. 3:17, 18; Ps. 40:10
5 [a]Gen. 31:50; Judg. 11:10; Jer. 43:2; Mic. 1:2; Mal. 2:14; 3:5
6 [a]Ex. 24:7; Deut. 5:27; Josh. 24:24 [b]Deut. 5:29, 33; Jer. 7:23
7 [a]Ps. 27:14; Is. 30:18
8 [1]Or, *princes*
9 [a]2 Kin. 19:4, 6, 20; 22:15
10 [a]Jer. 24:6; 31:28; Ezek. 36:36 [b]Jer. 18:7, 8; Hos. 11:8; Joel 2:13; Amos 7:3, 6; Jon. 3:10; 4:2
11 [a]Jer. 1:8; 27:12, 17; 41:18 [b]2 Chr. 32:7, 8; Ps. 46:7, 11; Is. 8:9, 10; 43:2, 5; Jer. 1:19; 15:20; Rom. 8:31
12 [a]Neh. 1:11; Ps. 106:46; Prov. 16:7
13 [a]Ex. 5:2; Jer. 44:16
14 [a]Is. 31:1; Jer. 41:17 [b]Ex. 16:3; Num. 11:4; Jer. 4:19, 21
15 [1]Lit., *now therefore* [a]Deut. 17:16; Jer. 42:17; 44:12-14
16 [a]Jer. 44:13, 27; Ezek. 11:8; Amos 9:1-4
17 [a]Jer. 38:2; 42:22; 44:13
18 [a]2 Chr. 36:16-19; Jer. 7:20; 33:5; 39:1-9 [b]Deut. 29:21; Is. 65:15; Jer. 29:18
19 [a]Is. 30:1-7 [b]Ezek. 2:5 [c]Neh. 9:26, 29, 30
20 [1]Or, *acted errantly in your souls* [a]Jer. 41:17; 43:2; Ezek. 14:3
21 [a]Deut. 11:26; Jer. 43:1; Ezek. 2:7; Acts 20:26, 27
22 [a]Hos. 9:6
1 [a]Jer. 26:8; 51:63

and all the arrogant men said to Jeremiah, "You are [a]telling a lie! The
LORD our God has not sent you to
say, 'You are not to enter Egypt to
reside there';
3 but [a]Baruch the son of Neriah is
inciting you against us to give us
over into the hand of the Chaldeans,
so they may put us to death or exile
us to Babylon."
4 So [a]Johanan the son of Kareah
and all the [1]commanders of the
forces, and all the people, did not
[b]obey the voice of the LORD, so as to
[c]stay in the land of Judah.
5 But Johanan the son of Kareah
and all the [1]commanders of the
forces took the [a]entire remnant of
Judah who had returned from all the
nations to which they had been
driven away, in order to reside in the
land of Judah—
6 the men, the women, the children, the king's daughters and [a]ev-
ery person that Nebuzaradan the
captain of the bodyguard had left
with Gedaliah the son of Ahikam
[1]and grandson of Shaphan, together
with [b]Jeremiah the prophet and
Baruch the son of Neriah—
7 and they entered the land of
Egypt (for they did not obey the
voice of the LORD) and went in as far
as Tahpanhes.
8 Then the word of the LORD
came to [a]Jeremiah in [b]Tahpanhes,
saying,
9"Take *some* large stones in your
[1]hands and hide them in the mortar
in the [2]brick *terrace* which is at the
entrance of Pharaoh's [3]palace in
Tahpanhes, in the sight of some *of
the* Jews;
10 and say to them, 'Thus says the
LORD of hosts, the God of Israel,
"Behold, I am going to send and get
Nebuchadnezzar the king of Babylon, [a]My servant, and I am going to
set his throne *right* over these
stones that I have hidden; and he
will spread his [b]canopy over them.
11"He will also come and strike the
land of Egypt; those who are *meant*
for death *will be given over* to death,
and those for captivity to captivity,
and those for the sword to the
sword.
12"And [1]I shall set fire to the temples of the [a]gods of Egypt, and he
will burn them and take them captive. So he will [b]wrap himself with
the land of Egypt as a shepherd
wraps himself with his garment,
and he will depart from there safely.
13"He will also shatter the [1]ob-
elisks of [2]Heliopolis, which is in the
land of Egypt; and the temples of
the gods of Egypt he will burn with
fire."'"

CHAPTER 44

Conquest of Egypt Predicted

THE word that came to Jeremiah
for all the Jews living in the land of
Egypt, those who were living in
Migdol, Tahpanhes, Memphis, and
the land of Pathros, saying,
2"Thus says the LORD of hosts,
the God of Israel, 'You yourselves
have seen all the calamity that I
have brought on Jerusalem and all
the cities of Judah; and behold, this
day they are in [a]ruins and no one
lives in them,
3 [a]because of their wickedness
which they committed so as to [b]pro-
voke Me to anger by continuing to
burn [1]sacrifices *and* to [c]serve other
gods whom they had not known,
neither they, you, nor your fathers.
4 'Yet I [a]sent you all My servants
the prophets, [1]again and again, saying, "Oh, do not do this [b]abominable
thing which I hate."
5 'But they did not listen or incline
their ears to turn from their wickedness, so as not to burn [1]sacrifices to
other gods.
6 'Therefore My [a]wrath and My
anger were poured out and burned
in the [b]cities of Judah and in the
streets of Jerusalem, so they have
become a ruin and a desolation as it
is this day.
7 'Now then thus says the LORD
God of hosts, the God of Israel,
"Why are you [a]doing great harm to
yourselves, so as to [b]cut off from
you man and woman, child and infant, from among Judah, leaving
yourselves without remnant,
8 [a]provoking Me to anger with
the works of your hands, [b]burning
[1]sacrifices to other gods in the land
of Egypt, where you are entering to
reside, so that you might be cut off
and become a [c]curse and a reproach
among all the nations of the earth?
9"Have you forgotten the [a]wick-
edness of your fathers, the wickedness of the kings of Judah, and the
wickedness of their wives, your own
wickedness, and the wickedness of
your wives, which they committed
in the land of Judah and in the
streets of Jerusalem?
10"But they have not become
[1a]contrite even to this day, nor have
they feared nor [b]walked in My law
or My statutes, which I have set before you and before your fathers."'

2 [a]2 Chr. 36:13; Is. 7:9; Jer. 5:12, 13; 42:5
3 [a]Jer. 36:4, 10, 26, 32; 43:6; 45:1
4 [1]Or, *princes* [a]Jer. 42:6 [b]2 Chr. 25:16; Jer. 42:5, 6; 44:5 [c]Ps. 37:3; Jer. 42:10-12
5 [1]Or, *princes* [a]Jer. 40:11
6 [1]Lit., *the son* [a]Jer. 39:10; 40:7 [b]Eccles. 9:1, 2; Lam. 3:1
8 [a]Ps. 139:7; 2 Tim. 2:9 [b]Jer. 2:16; 44:1; 46:14; Ezek. 30:18
9 [1]Lit., *hand* [2]Or, *brickwork* [3]Lit., *house*
10 [a]Is. 44:28; 45:1; Jer. 25:9; 27:6 [b]Ps. 18:11; 27:5; 31:20
12 [1]Some ancient versions read, *he will set* [a]Ex. 12:12; Is. 19:1; Jer. 46:25; Ezek. 30:13 [b]Ps. 104:2; 109:18, 19; Is. 49:18
13 [1]Or, *stone pillars* [2]Heb., *Beth-shemesh;* i.e., the House of the Sun-god
2 [a]Is. 6:11; Jer. 4:7; 9:11; 34:22; Mic. 3:12
3 [1]Or, *incense* [a]Neh. 9:33; Jer. 2:17-19; 44:23; Ezek. 8:17, 18; Dan. 9:5 [b]Is. 3:8; Jer. 7:19; 32:30-32; 44:8 [c]Deut. 13:6; 29:26; 32:17
4 [1]Lit., *rising early and sending* [a]Jer. 7:13, 25; 25:4; 26:5; 35:15; Zech. 7:7 [b]Jer. 16:18; 32:34, 35; Ezek. 8:10
5 [1]Or, *incense*
6 [a]Is. 51:17-20; Jer. 42:18; Ezek. 8:18 [b]Jer. 7:17, 34
7 [a]Jer. 26:19; Ezek. 33:11; Hab. 2:10 [b]Jer. 3:24; 9:21; 51:22
8 [1]Or, *incense* [a]2 Kin. 17:15-17; Jer. 44:3; 1 Cor. 10:21, 22 [b]Jer. 7:9; 11:12, 17; 44:3; Hos. 4:13; Hab. 1:16 [c]1 Kin. 9:7, 8; 2 Chr. 7:20; Jer. 42:18
9 [a]Jer. 7:9, 10, 17, 18; 44:17, 21
10 [1]Lit., *crushed* [a]Jer. 6:15; 8:12 [b]Jer. 26:4; 32:23; 44:23

11"Therefore thus says the LORD of
hosts, the God of Israel, 'Behold, I
am going to [a]set My face against
you for [1]woe, even to cut off all Judah.
12 'And I will [a]take away the remnant of Judah who have set their
mind on entering the land of Egypt
to reside there, and they will all
[b]meet their end in the land of Egypt;
they will fall by the sword *and* meet
their end by famine. Both small and
great will die by the sword and famine; and they will become a [c]curse,
an object of horror, an imprecation
and a reproach.
13 'And I will [a]punish those who
live in the land of Egypt, as I have
punished Jerusalem, with the
sword, with famine, and with pestilence.
14 'So there will be [a]no refugees or
survivors for the remnant of Judah
who have entered the land of Egypt
to reside there and then to return to
the land of Judah, to which they are
[1b]longing to return and live; for
none will [c]return except *a few* refugees.' "
15 Then [a]all the men who were
aware that their wives were burning
sacrifices to other gods, along with
all the women who were standing
by, *as* a large assembly, including
all the people who were living in
Pathros in the land of Egypt, responded to Jeremiah, saying,
16"As for the message that you
have spoken to us in the name of the
LORD, we are not going to listen to
you!
17"But rather we will certainly carry out every word that has proceeded from our mouths, [1]by burning sacrifices to the [a]queen of
heaven and pouring out libations to
her, just as [b]we ourselves, our forefathers, our kings and our princes
did in the cities of Judah and in the
streets of Jerusalem; for *then* we
had [c]plenty of [2]food, and were well
off, and saw no [3]misfortune.
18"But since we stopped burning
sacrifices to the queen of heaven
and pouring out libations to her, we
have [a]lacked everything and have
met our end by the sword and by
famine."
19"And," *said the women,* "when
we were burning sacrifices to the
queen of heaven, and [1]were pouring
out libations to her, was it [a]without
our husbands that we made for her
sacrificial cakes [2]in her image and
poured out libations to her?"

Calamity for the Jews

20 Then Jeremiah said to all the
people, to the men and women—
even to all the people who were giving him *such* an answer—saying,
21"As for the [a]smoking sacrifices
that you burned in the cities of Judah and in the [b]streets of Jerusalem,
you and your forefathers, your
kings and your princes, and the people of the land, did not the LORD [c]re-
member them, and did not *all this*
come into His [1]mind?
22"So the LORD was [a]no longer
able to endure *it,* because of the evil
of your deeds, [b]because of the
abominations which you have committed; thus your land has become a
[c]ruin, an object of horror and a
curse, without an inhabitant, as *it is*
this day.
23"Because you have burned sacrifices and have sinned against the
LORD and [a]not obeyed the voice of
the LORD or [b]walked in His law, His
statutes or His testimonies, therefore this [c]calamity has befallen you,
as *it has* this day."
24 Then Jeremiah said to all the
people, including all the women,
"[a]Hear the word of the LORD, all Judah who are [b]in the land of Egypt,
25 thus says the LORD of hosts, the
God of Israel, as follows: 'As for you
and your wives, you have spoken
with your mouths and fulfilled *it*
with your hands, saying, "We will
[a]certainly perform our vows that we
have vowed, to burn sacrifices to
the queen of heaven and pour out
libations to her." [1]Go ahead and
[b]confirm your vows, and certainly
perform your vows!'
26"Nevertheless hear the word of
the LORD, all Judah who are living in
the land of Egypt, 'Behold, I have
[a]sworn by My great name,' says the
LORD, '[b]never shall My name be invoked again by the mouth of any
man of Judah in all the land of
Egypt, saying, "[c]As the Lord [1]GOD
lives . . ."
27 'Behold, I am watching over
them [a]for harm and not for good,
and [b]all the men of Judah who are in
the land of Egypt will meet their end
by the sword and by famine until
they are completely gone.
28 '[a]And those who escape the
sword will return out of the land of
Egypt to the land of Judah [1b]few in
number. Then all the remnant of Judah who have gone to the land of
Egypt to reside there will know
whose word will stand, [c]Mine or
theirs.

11 [1]Lit., *evil* [a]Lev. 26:17; Jer. 21:10; Amos 9:4
12 [a]Jer. 42:15-18, 22 [b]Is. 1:28; Jer. 16:4; 44:7 [c]Is. 65:15; Jer. 29:18; 42:18
13 [a]Jer. 11:22; 44:27, 28
14 [1]Lit., *lifting up their soul* [a]Jer. 22:10; 44:27 [b]Jer. 22:26, 27 [c]Is. 4:2; 10:20; Jer. 44:28; Rom. 9:27
15 [a]Prov. 11:21; Is. 1:5; Jer. 5:1-5
17 [1]Or, *so as to burn* [2]Lit., *bread* [3]Lit., *evil* [a]2 Kin. 17:16; Jer. 7:18 [b]Neh. 9:34; Jer. 32:32; 44:21 [c]Ex. 16:3; Is. 48:5; Hos. 2:5-9; Phil. 3:19
18 [a]Num. 11:5, 6; Jer. 40:12; Mal. 3:13-15
19 [1]Lit., *to pour* [2]Lit., *to make an image of her* [a]Num. 30:6, 7; Jer. 44:15
21 [1]Lit., *heart* [a]Ezek. 8:10, 11 [b]Jer. 11:13; 44:9, 17; Ezek. 16:24 [c]Ps. 79:8; Is. 64:9; Jer. 14:10; Hos. 7:2; Amos 8:7
22 [a]Is. 7:13; Mal. 2:17 [b]Jer. 4:4; 21:12; 30:14 [c]Jer. 25:11, 18, 38; 29:18; 42:18; 44:13
23 [a]Jer. 7:13-15; 40:3 [b]Jer. 44:10; Ps. 119:136, 150 [c]1 Kin. 9:9; Neh. 13:18; Jer. 44:2
24 [a]Jer. 42:15; 44:16 [b]Jer. 43:7; 44:15, 26
25 [1]Lit., *Surely cause to stand* [a]Jer. 44:17; Matt. 14:9; Acts 23:12 [b]Ezek. 20:39; James 1:14, 15
26 [1]YHWH, usually rendered LORD [a]Gen. 22:16; Deut. 32:40, 41; Jer. 22:5; Amos 6:8; Heb. 6:13, 18 [b]Ps. 50:16; Ezek. 20:39 [c]Is. 48:1, 2; Jer. 5:2
27 [a]Jer. 39:16 [b]2 Kin. 21:14; Jer. 44:14
28 [1]Lit., *men of number* [a]Jer. 44:14 [b]Is. 10:19; 27:12, 13 [c]Ps. 33:11; Is. 14:27; 46:10, 11; Zech. 1:6

29 'And this will be the [a]sign to
you,' declares the LORD, 'that I am
going to punish you in this place, so
that you may know that [b]My words
will surely stand against you for
harm.'
30 "Thus says the LORD, 'Behold, I
am going to give over [a]Pharaoh
Hophra king of Egypt to the hand of
his enemies, to the hand of those
who seek his life, just as I gave over
[b]Zedekiah king of Judah to the hand
of Nebuchadnezzar king of Babylon, *who was* his enemy and was
seeking his life.' "

CHAPTER 45

Message to Baruch

THIS *is* the message which Jeremiah the prophet spoke to [a]Baruch the
son of Neriah, when he had [b]written
down these words in a book [1]at
Jeremiah's dictation, in the [c]fourth
year of Jehoiakim the son of Josiah,
king of Judah, saying:
2 "Thus says the LORD the God of
Israel to you, O Baruch:
3 'You said, "Ah, woe is me! For
the LORD has added sorrow to my
pain; I am [a]weary with my groaning
and have found no rest." '
4 "Thus you are to say to him,
'Thus says the LORD, "Behold, what
I have built I am about to tear down,
and what I have planted I am about
to uproot, that is, the whole land."
5 'But you, are you [a]seeking great
things for yourself? Do not seek
them; for behold, I am going to
[b]bring disaster on all flesh,' declares
the LORD, 'but I will give your life to
you as booty in all the places where
you may go.' "

CHAPTER 46

Defeat of Pharaoh Foretold

THAT which came as the word of
the LORD to Jeremiah the prophet
[a]concerning the nations.
2 To [a]Egypt, concerning the army
of [b]Pharaoh Necho king of Egypt,
which was by the Euphrates River
at [c]Carchemish, which Nebuchadnezzar king of Babylon defeated in
the fourth year of Jehoiakim the son
of Josiah, king of Judah:

3 "[a]Line up the shield and [1]buck-
ler,
And draw near for the battle!
4 "Harness the horses,
And [1]mount the steeds,
And take your stand with hel-
mets *on!*
[a]Polish the spears,
Put on the [b]scale-armor!
5 "Why have I seen *it?*
They are terrified,
They are [a]drawing back,
And their [b]mighty men are de-
feated
And have taken refuge in flight,
Without facing back;
[1]Terror is on every side!"
Declares the LORD.
6 Let not the [a]swift man flee,
Nor the mighty man escape;
In the north beside the river Euphrates
They have [b]stumbled and
fallen.
7 Who is this that rises like the
Nile,
Like the rivers whose waters
surge about?
8 Egypt rises like the Nile,
Even like the rivers whose wa-
ters surge about;
And He has said, "I will [a]rise
and cover *that* land;
I will surely [b]destroy the city
and its inhabitants."
9 Go up, you horses, and [1a]drive
madly, you chariots,
That the mighty men may
[2]march forward:
Ethiopia and [3b]Put, that handle
the shield,
And the [4c]Lydians, that handle
and bend the bow.
10 For that day belongs to the
Lord [1]GOD of hosts,
A day of vengeance, so as to
avenge Himself on His foes;
And the [a]sword will devour and
be satiated
And [2]drink its fill of their blood;
For there will be a [b]slaughter
for the Lord [1]GOD of hosts,
In the land of the north by the
river Euphrates.
11 Go up to Gilead and obtain
balm,
O virgin daughter of Egypt!
In vain have you multiplied
[1]remedies;
There is [a]no healing for you.
12 The nations have heard of your
[a]shame,
And the earth is full of your cry
of distress;
For one warrior has stumbled
over [1]another,
And both of them have fallen
down together.

13 *This is* the [1]message which the
LORD spoke to Jeremiah the prophet
about the coming of Nebuchadnezzar king of Babylon to smite the
land of Egypt:

29 [a]Is. 7:11, 14; 8:18; Jer. 44:30; Matt. 24:15, 16, 32 [b]Prov. 19:21; Is. 40:8
30 [a]Jer. 43:9-13; 46:25; Ezek. 29:3 [b]2 Kin. 25:4-7; Jer. 34:21; 39:5-7
1 [1]Lit., *from the mouth of Jeremiah* [a]Jer. 32:12, 16; 43:3, 6 [b]Jer. 36:4, 18, 32 [c]Jer. 25:1; 36:1; 46:1
3 [a]Ps. 6:6; 69:3; 2 Cor. 4:1, 16; Gal. 6:9
5 [a]1 Kin. 3:9, 11; 2 Kin. 5:26; Matt. 6:25, 32; Rom. 12:16 [b]Is. 66:16; Jer. 25:31
1 [a]Jer. 1:10; 25:15-38
2 [a]Jer. 25:19; 46:14; Ezek. chaps. 29-32 [b]2 Kin. 18:21; 23:29, 33-35 [c]2 Chr. 35:20; Is. 10:9
3 [1]I.e., small shield [a]Is. 21:5; Jer. 51:11; Joel 3:9; Nah. 2:1; 3:14
4 [1]Or, *go up, you horsemen* [a]Ezek. 21:9-11 [b]1 Sam. 17:5, 38; 2 Chr. 26:14; Neh. 4:16; Jer. 51:3
5 [1]Heb., *Magor-missabib,* cf. 20:3 [a]Is. 42:17; Jer. 46:21 [b]Is. 5:25; Ezek. 39:18
6 [a]Is. 30:16 [b]Jer. 46:12, 16; Dan. 11:19
8 [a]Is. 37:24 [b]Is. 10:13
9 [1]Lit., *act like madmen* [2]Lit., *go forth* [3]I.e., Libya (or Somaliland) [4]Heb., *Ludim* [a]Jer. 47:3; Nah. 2:4 [b]Nah. 3:9 [c]Is. 66:19
10 [1]YHWH, usually rendered LORD [2]Lit., *be saturated with* [a]Is. 31:8; Jer. 12:12 [b]Is. 34:6; Zeph. 1:7
11 [1]Lit., *healings* [a]Jer. 30:13; Mic. 1:9; Nah. 3:19
12 [1]Lit., *warrior* [a]Jer. 2:36; Nah. 3:8-10
13 [1]Lit., *word*

14“Declare in Egypt and proclaim
in Migdol,
Proclaim also in Memphis and
Tahpanhes;
Say, ‘Take your stand and get
yourself ready,
For the sword has [a]devoured
those around you.’
15“Why have your [a]mighty ones
become prostrate?
They do not stand because the
LORD has [b]thrust them down.
16“They have repeatedly [a]stumbled;
Indeed, they have fallen one
against another.
Then they said, ‘Get up! And let
us go back
To our own people and our native land
Away from the [1]sword of the
oppressor.’
17“[1]They cried there, ‘Pharaoh
king of Egypt *is* [a]*but* a big
noise;
He has let the appointed time
pass by!’
18“As I live,” declares the [a]King
Whose name is the LORD of
hosts,
“Surely one shall come *who*
looms up like [b]Tabor among
the mountains,
Or like [c]Carmel by the sea.
19“Make your baggage [a]ready for
exile,
O daughter dwelling in Egypt,
For [b]Memphis will become a
desolation;
It will even be burned down
and [1]bereft of inhabitants.
20“Egypt is a pretty heifer,
But a [1]horsefly is coming from
the north—it is coming!
21“Also her [a]mercenaries in her
midst
Are like [1]fattened [b]calves,
For even they too have turned
back *and* have fled away together;
They did not stand *their*
ground.
For the day of their calamity
has come upon them,
The time of their [c]punishment.
22“Its sound moves along like a
serpent;
For they move on [1]like an army
And come to her as woodcutters with axes.
23“They have cut down her forest,” declares the LORD;
“Surely it will no *more* be found,
Even though [1]they are *now*
more numerous than [a]locusts
And are without number.
24“The daughter of Egypt has been
put to shame,
Given over to the [1]power of the
people of the north.”
25 The LORD of hosts, the God of
Israel, says, “Behold, I am going to
punish Amon of [a]Thebes, and Pharaoh, and Egypt along with her
[b]gods and her kings, even Pharaoh
and those who [c]trust in him.
26“And I shall give them over to
the [1]power of those who are [a]seeking their lives, even into the hand of
Nebuchadnezzar king of Babylon
and into the hand of his [2]officers.
[b]Afterwards, however, it will be inhabited as in the days of old,” declares the LORD.
27“But as for you, O Jacob My servant, do not [a]fear,
Nor be dismayed, O Israel!
For, see, I am going to [b]save
you from afar,
And your descendants from the
land of their captivity;
And Jacob shall return and be
undisturbed
And secure, with no one making *him* tremble.
28“O Jacob My servant, do not
fear,” declares the LORD,
“For [a]I am with you.
For I shall make a full end of all
the nations
Where I have driven you,
Yet I shall [b]not make a full end
of you;
But I shall [c]correct you properly
And by no means leave you unpunished.”

CHAPTER 47

Prophecy against Philistia

THAT which came as the word of
the LORD to Jeremiah the prophet
concerning the Philistines, before
Pharaoh [1]conquered [a]Gaza.
2 Thus says the LORD:
“Behold, waters are going to rise
from [a]the north
And become an overflowing
torrent,
And [b]overflow the land and all
its fulness,
The city and those who live in
it;
And the men will [c]cry out,
And every inhabitant of the
land will wail.
3“Because of the noise of the
[1a]galloping hoofs of his [2]stallions,
The tumult of his chariots, *and*
the rumbling of his wheels,

14 [a]Is. 1:20; Jer. 2:30; 46:10; Nah. 2:13
15 [a]Is. 66:15, 16; Jer. 46:5 [b]Ps. 18:14, 39; 68:1, 2
16 [1]Lit., *oppressing sword* [a]Lev. 26:36, 37; Jer. 46:6
17 [1]Some ancient versions read: *Call the name of Pharaoh a big noise* [a]Ex. 15:9, 10; 1 Kin. 20:10, 11; Is. 19:11-16
18 [a]Jer. 48:15; Mal. 1:14 [b]Josh. 19:22; Judg. 4:6; Ps. 89:12 [c]Josh. 12:22; 1 Kin. 18:42
19 [1]Lit., *without* [a]Is. 20:4 [b]Jer. 46:14; Ezek. 30:13
20 [1]Or, possibly, *mosquito*
21 [1]Lit., *of the stall* [a]2 Sam. 10:6; 2 Kin. 7:6; Jer. 46:5 [b]Is. 34:7 [c]Jer. 48:44; Hos. 9:7; Obad. 13; Mic. 7:4
22 [1]Or, *in force*
23 [1]I.e., trees of the forest, the Egyptians [a]Judg. 2:25; 6:5; 7:12
24 [1]Lit., *hand*
25 [a]Ezek. 30:14, 15, 16; Nah. 3:8 [b]Ex. 12:12; Jer. 43:12, 13; Ezek. 30:13; Zeph. 2:11 [c]Is. 20:5
26 [1]Lit., *hand* [2]Lit., *servants* [a]Jer. 44:30; Ezek. 32:11 [b]Ezek. 29:8-14
27 [a]Is. 41:13, 14; Jer. 30:10, 11 [b]Is. 11:11; Jer. 23:3, 4; 29:14; Mic. 7:12
28 [a]Ps. 46:7, 11; Is. 8:9, 10; 43:2; Jer. 1:19 [b]Jer. 4:27; Amos 9:8, 9 [c]Jer. 10:24; Hab. 3:2
1 [1]Lit., *smote* [a]Gen. 10:19; 1 Kin. 4:24; Jer. 25:20
2 [a]Is. 14:31; Jer. 1:14; 6:22; 46:20, 24 [b]Is. 8:7, 8 [c]Is. 15:2-5; Jer. 46:12
3 [1]Lit., *stamping of the* [2]Lit., *mighty ones* [a]Judg. 5:22; Jer. 8:16

The fathers have not turned back for *their* children,
Because of the limpness of *their* hands,
4 On account of the day that is coming
To [a]destroy all the Philistines,
To cut off from Tyre and Sidon
Every ally that is left;
For the LORD is going to destroy the Philistines,
The remnant of the coastland of [b]Caphtor.
5 "[a]Baldness has come upon Gaza;
[b]Ashkelon has been ruined.
O remnant of their valley,
How long will you gash yourself?
6 "Ah, [a]sword of the LORD,
How long will you not be quiet?
Withdraw into your sheath;
Be at rest and stay still.
7 "How can [1]it be quiet,
When the LORD has [a]given it an order?
Against Ashkelon and against the seacoast—
There He has [b]assigned it."

CHAPTER 48

Prophecy against Moab

CONCERNING Moab.
Thus says the LORD of hosts, the God of Israel,
"Woe to [a]Nebo, for it has been destroyed;
[b]Kiriathaim has been put to shame, it has been captured;
The lofty stronghold has been put to shame and [1]shattered.
2 "There is praise for Moab no longer;
In [a]Heshbon they have devised calamity against her:
'Come and let us cut her off from *being* a nation!'
You too, [1]Madmen, will be silenced;
The sword will follow after you.
3 "The sound of an outcry from [a]Horonaim,
'Devastation and great destruction!'
4 "Moab is broken,
Her little ones have sounded out a cry *of distress*.
5 "For by the ascent of [a]Luhith
They will ascend with continual weeping;
For at the descent of Horonaim
They have heard the [1]anguished cry of destruction.
6 "[a]Flee, save your lives,
That you may be like a juniper in the wilderness.
7 "For because of your trust in your own achievements and treasures,
Even you yourself will be captured;
And [a]Chemosh will go off into exile
Together with his priests and his princes.
8 "And a destroyer will come to every city,
So that no city will escape;
The valley also will be ruined,
And the [a]plateau will be destroyed,
As the LORD has said.
9 "Give [1a]wings to Moab,
For she will [2]flee away;
And her cities will become a desolation,
Without inhabitants in them.
10 "Cursed be the one who does the LORD's work [a]negligently,
And cursed be the one who restrains his [b]sword from blood.

11 "Moab has been [a]at ease since his youth;
He has also been [b]undisturbed on his lees,
Neither has he been [c]emptied from vessel to vessel,
Nor has he gone into exile.
Therefore [1]he retains his [d]flavor,
And his aroma has not changed.
12 "Therefore behold, the days are
coming," declares the LORD, "when
I shall send to him those who [a]tip
vessels, and they will tip him over,
and they will empty his vessels and
shatter [1]his jars.
13 "And Moab will be ashamed of
Chemosh, as the house of Israel was
[a]ashamed of [b]Bethel, their confidence.
14 "How can you say, 'We are [a]mighty warriors,
And men valiant for battle'?
15 "Moab has been destroyed, and [1]men have gone up to [2]his cities;
His choicest [3a]young men have also gone down to the slaughter,"
Declares the [b]King, whose name is the LORD of hosts.
16 "The disaster of Moab will soon [a]come,
And his calamity has swiftly hastened.
17 "Mourn for him, all you who *live* around him,
Even all of you who know his name;

4 [a]Is. 14:31 [b]Gen. 10:14; Deut. 2:23; Amos 9:7
5 [a]Jer. 48:37; Mic. 1:16 [b]Judg. 1:18; Jer. 25:20; Amos 1:7, 8; Zeph. 2:4, 7; Zech. 9:5
6 [a]Judg. 7:20; Jer. 12:12; Ezek. 21:3-5
7 [1]Lit., *you* [a]Is. 10:6; Ezek. 14:17 [b]Mic. 6:9
1 [1]Or, *dismayed* [a]Num. 32:3, 37; Jer. 48:22 [b]Num. 32:37; Jer. 48:23; Ezek. 25:9
2 [1]I.e., a city of Moab [a]Num. 21:25; Jer. 48:34, 45; 49:3
3 [a]Is. 15:5; Jer. 48:5, 34
5 [1]Lit., *distresses of outcry* [a]Is. 15:5
6 [a]Jer. 51:6
7 [a]Num. 21:29; 1 Kin. 11:33; Jer. 48:13, 46
8 [a]Josh. 13:9, 17, 21
9 [1]Or, *salt* [2]Or, *fall in ruins* [a]Ps. 11:1; Is. 16:2; Jer. 48:28
10 [a]1 Kin. 20:42; 2 Kin. 13:19 [b]Jer. 47:6, 7
11 [1]Lit., *his flavor has stayed in him* [a]Jer. 22:21; Zech. 1:15 [b]Zeph. 1:12 [c]Nah. 2:2 [d]Ezek. 16:49, 50
12 [1]Lit., *their* [a]Nah. 2:2
13 [a]Is. 45:16; Jer. 48:39 [b]1 Kin. 12:29; Hos. 8:5, 6
14 [a]Ps. 33:16; Is. 10:13-16
15 [1]Lit., *one has* [2]Lit., *her* [3]I.e., warriors [a]Is. 40:30, 31 [b]Jer. 46:18
16 [a]Is. 13:22

Say, 'How has the mighty
[1a]scepter been broken,
A staff of splendor!'
18 "[a]Come down from your glory
And sit [1]on the parched ground,
O [b]inhabitant of [c]Dibon,
For the destroyer of Moab has
come up against you,
He has ruined your strongholds.
19 "Stand by the road and keep
watch,
O inhabitant of [a]Aroer;
[b]Ask him who flees and her
who escapes
And say, 'What has happened?'
20 "Moab has been put to shame,
for it has been shattered.
Wail and cry out;
Declare by the Arnon
That Moab has been destroyed.
21 "Judgment has also come upon
the plain, upon Holon, [a]Jahzah, and
against [b]Mephaath,
22 against Dibon, Nebo, and Beth-
diblathaim,
23 against Kiriathaim, Beth-ga-
mul, and [a]Beth-meon,
24 against [a]Kerioth, Bozrah, and
all the cities of the land of Moab, far
and near.
25 "The [a]horn of Moab has been cut
off, and his [b]arm broken," declares
the LORD.
26 "Make him drunk, for he has
[1]become [a]arrogant toward the
LORD; so Moab will [2]wallow in his
vomit, and he also will become a
laughingstock.
27 "Now was not Israel a [a]laugh-
ingstock to you? Or was he [1]caught
among thieves? For each time you
speak about him you [b]shake *your
head in scorn*.
28 "Leave the cities and dwell
among the [a]crags,
O inhabitants of Moab,
And be like a [b]dove that nests
Beyond the mouth of the
chasm.
29 "[a]We have heard of the pride of
Moab—he *is* very proud—
Of his haughtiness, his [b]pride,
his arrogance and [1]his self-
exaltation.
30 "I know his [a]fury," declares the
LORD,
"But it is [1]futile;
His idle boasts have accomplished [1]nothing.
31 "Therefore I shall [a]wail for
Moab,
Even for all Moab shall I cry
out;
[1]I will moan for the men of
[b]Kir-heres.

17 [1]Or, *rod* [a]Is. 14:5
18 [1]Lit., *in thirst* [a]Jer. 46:19 [b]Josh. 13:9, 17; Jer. 48:22 [c]Is. 47:1
19 [a]Deut. 2:36; Josh. 12:2 [b]1 Sam. 4:13, 14, 16
21 [a]Num. 21:23; Is. 15:4; Jer. 48:34 [b]Josh. 13:18
23 [a]Josh. 13:17
24 [a]Jer. 48:41; Amos 2:2
25 [a]Ps. 75:10; Zech. 1:19-21 [b]Job 22:9; Ps. 10:15
26 [1]Or, *magnified himself against* [2]Or, *splash into* [a]Ex. 5:2; Jer. 48:42; Dan. 5:23
27 [1]Or, *found* [a]Lam. 2:15-17; Mic. 7:8-10 [b]Job 16:4; Jer. 18:16
28 [a]Judg. 6:2; Is. 2:19; Jer. 49:16; Obad. 3 [b]Ps. 55:6; Song of Sol. 2:14
29 [1]Lit., *elevation of his heart* [a]Is. 16:6; Zeph. 2:8 [b]Job 40:11, 12, Ps. 138:6
30 [1]Lit., *not so* [a]Is. 37:28
31 [1]Another reading is, *He* [a]Is. 15:5; 16:7, 11 [b]2 Kin. 3:25; Is. 16:7, 11; Jer. 48:36
32 [a]Is. 16:8, 9 [b]Num. 21:32
33 [a]Is. 16:10; Jer. 25:10; Joel 1:12 [b]Is. 5:10; Hag. 2:16
34 [1]Lit., *given forth* [a]Is. 15:4-6 [b]Num. 32:3, 37 [c]Gen. 13:10; 14:2
35 [1]Or, *offers up in smoke* [a]Is. 16:12 [b]Jer. 7:9; 11:13
36 [1]Lit., *sounds* [a]Is. 16:11 [b]Is. 15:7
37 [a]Is. 15:2; Jer. 16:6 [b]Is. 15:3; 20:2
38 [1]Lit., *all of it is lamentation* [a]Is. 22:1
39 [a]Ezek. 26:16
40 [a]Jer. 49:22; Hos. 8:1 [b]Is. 8:8
41 [a]Jer. 49:22 [b]Jer. 30:6; Mic. 4:9, 10
42 [a]Ps. 83:4; Jer. 48:2

32 "More than the [a]weeping for
[b]Jazer
I shall weep for you, O vine of
Sibmah!
Your tendrils stretched across
the sea,
They reached to the sea of Jazer;
Upon your summer fruits and
your grape harvest
The destroyer has fallen.
33 "So [a]gladness and joy are taken
away
From the fruitful field, even
from the land of Moab.
And I have made the wine to
[b]cease from the wine
presses;
No one will tread *them* with
shouting,
The shouting will not be shouts
of joy.
34 "[a]From the outcry at Heshbon
even to [b]Elealeh, even to Jahaz they
have [1]raised their voice, from [c]Zoar
even to Horonaim *and to* Eglath-
shelishiyah; for even the waters of
Nimrim will become desolate.
35 "And I shall make an end of
Moab," declares the LORD, "the one
who offers *sacrifice* on the [a]high
place and the one who [1b]burns incense to his gods.
36 "Therefore My [a]heart [1]wails for
Moab like flutes; My heart also
[1]wails like flutes for the men of Kir-
heres. Therefore they have lost the
[b]abundance it produced.
37 "For [a]every head is bald and every beard cut short; there are gashes
on all the hands and sackcloth on
the [b]loins.
38 "On all the [a]housetops of Moab
and in its streets [1]there is lamentation everywhere; for I have broken
Moab like an undesirable vessel,"
declares the LORD.
39 "How shattered it is! *How* they
have wailed! How Moab has turned
his back—he is ashamed! So Moab
will become a laughingstock and an
object of [a]terror to all around him."
40 For thus says the LORD,
"Behold, one will [a]fly swiftly like
an eagle,
And [b]spread out his wings
against Moab.
41 "Kerioth has been captured
And the strongholds have been
seized,
So the [a]hearts of the mighty
men of Moab in that day
Will be like the heart of a
[b]woman in labor.
42 "And Moab will be [a]destroyed
from *being* a people

Because he has [1]become [b]arrogant toward the LORD.
43"[a]Terror, pit, and snare are *coming* upon you,
O inhabitant of Moab," declares the LORD.
44"The one who [a]flees from the terror
Will fall into the pit,
And the one who climbs up out of the pit
Will be caught in the snare;
For I shall bring upon her, *even* upon Moab,
The year of their [b]punishment," declares the LORD.

45"In the shadow of Heshbon
The fugitives stand without strength;
For a fire has gone forth from Heshbon,
And a [a]flame from the midst of [b]Sihon,
And it has devoured the [c]forehead of Moab
And the scalps of the [1]riotous revelers.
46"Woe to you, Moab!
The people of [a]Chemosh have perished;
For your sons have been taken away captive,
And your daughters into captivity.
47"Yet I will [a]restore the [1]fortunes of Moab
In the [2]latter days," declares the LORD.
Thus far the judgment on Moab.

CHAPTER 49

Prophecy against Ammon

CONCERNING the sons of Ammon.
Thus says the LORD:
"Does Israel have no sons?
Or has he no heirs?
Why then has [1][a]Malcam taken possession of Gad
And his people settled in its cities?
2"Therefore behold, the days are coming," declares the LORD,
"That I shall cause a [1]trumpet [a]blast of war to be heard
Against [b]Rabbah of the sons of Ammon;
And it will become a desolate heap,
And her [c]towns will be set on fire.
Then Israel will take [d]possession of his possessors,"
Says the LORD.
3"Wail, O [a]Heshbon, for [b]Ai has been destroyed!
Cry out, O daughters of Rabbah,
[c]Gird yourselves with sackcloth and lament,
And rush back and forth inside the walls;
For [1]Malcam will [d]go into exile
Together with his priests and his princes.
4"How boastful you are about the valleys!
Your valley is flowing *away,*
O backsliding daughter
Who trusts in her [a]treasures, *saying,*
'Who will come against me?'
5"Behold, I am going to bring terror upon you,"
Declares the Lord [1]GOD of hosts,
"From all *directions* around you;
And each of you will be [a]driven out [2]headlong,
With no one to gather the [b]fugitives together.
6"But afterward I will [a]restore
The [1]fortunes of the sons of Ammon,"
Declares the LORD.

Prophecy against Edom

7 Concerning Edom.
Thus says the LORD of hosts,
"Is there no longer any [a]wisdom in [b]Teman?
Has good counsel been lost to the prudent?
Has their wisdom decayed?
8"Flee away, turn back, dwell in the depths,
O inhabitants of [a]Dedan,
For I [1]will bring the [b]disaster of Esau upon him
At the time I [2]punish him.
9"[a]If grape gatherers came to you,
Would they not leave gleanings?
If thieves *came* by night,
They would destroy *only* [1]until they had enough.
10"But I have [a]stripped Esau bare,
I have uncovered his hiding places
So that he will not be able to conceal himself;
His [1]offspring has been destroyed along with his [2]relatives
And his neighbors, and he is no more.
11"Leave your [1][a]orphans behind, I will keep *them* alive;
And let your [b]widows trust in Me."

42 [1]Or, *magnified himself against* [b]Is. 37:23; Jer. 48:26
43 [a]Is. 24:17, 18; Lam. 3:47
44 [a]1 Kin. 19:17; Amos 5:19 [b]Jer. 46:21
45 [1]Lit., *sons of tumult* [a]Num. 21:28, 29 [b]Num. 21:21, 26; Ps. 135:11 [c]Num. 24:17
46 [a]Judg. 11:24; 1 Kin. 11:7; Jer. 48:7
47 [1]Or, *captivity* [2]Lit., *end of the days* [a]Jer. 12:14-17; 49:6, 39
1 [1]Or, *Milcom;* cf. 1 Kin. 11:5 [a]1 Kin. 11:5, 33; Zeph. 1:5
2 [1]Or, *shout of* [a]Num. 10:9; Jer. 4:19 [b]Deut. 3:11; 2 Sam. 11:1; Ezek. 21:20 [c]Josh. 17:11, 16 [d]Is. 14:2
3 [1]Cf. v. 1 [a]Jer. 48:2 [b]Josh. 7:2-5; 8:1-29; Ezra 2:28 [c]Jer. 48:37 [d]Jer. 46:25; 48:7
4 [a]Ps. 62:10; Ezek. 28:4, 5; 1 Tim. 6:17
5 [1]YHWH, usually rendered LORD [2]Lit., *before him* [a]Jer. 16:16; 46:5 [b]Lam. 4:15
6 [1]Or, *captivity* [a]Jer. 48:47; 49:39
7 [a]Job 2:11; Jer. 8:9 [b]Gen. 36:11, 15, 34; Jer. 49:20
8 [1]Or, *brought* [2]Or, *punished* [a]Is. 21:13; Jer. 25:23 [b]Jer. 46:21
9 [1]Lit., *their sufficiency* [a]Obad. 5
10 [1]Lit., *seed* [2]Lit., *brothers* [a]Jer. 13:26
11 [1]Or, *fatherless* [a]Ps. 68:5 [b]Ps. 68:5; Zech. 7:10

12 For thus says the LORD, "Behold, those [1]who were not sen-
tenced to drink the [a]cup will certainly drink *it*, and are you the one
who will be [b]completely acquitted?
You will not be acquitted, but you
will certainly drink *it*.
13"For I have [a]sworn by Myself,"
declares the LORD, "that Bozrah will
become an [b]object of horror, a reproach, a ruin and a curse; and all its
cities will become perpetual ruins."
14 I have [a]heard a message from
the LORD,
And an [b]envoy is sent among
the nations, *saying*,
"Gather yourselves together
and come against her,
And rise up for battle!"
15"For behold, I have made you
[a]small among the nations,
Despised among men.
16"As for the [a]terror of you,
The arrogance of your heart has
deceived you,
O you who live in the clefts of
[1]the [b]rock,
Who occupy the height of the
hill.
Though you make your nest as
[c]high as an eagle's,
I will [d]bring you down from
there," declares the LORD.
17"And Edom will become an [a]ob-
ject of horror; everyone who passes
by it will be horrified and will [b]hiss
at all its wounds.
18"Like the overthrow of Sodom
and Gomorrah with its neighbors,"
says the LORD, "[a]no one will live
there, nor will a son of man reside in
it.
19"Behold, one will come up like a
lion from the [1]thickets of the Jordan
against a [2a]perennially watered pasture; for in an instant I shall make
him run away from it, and whoever
is [b]chosen I shall appoint over it. For
who is [c]like Me, and who will summon Me *into court?* And who then is
the shepherd who can stand against
Me?"
20 Therefore hear the [a]plan of the
LORD which He has planned against
Edom, and His purposes which He
has purposed against the inhabitants of Teman: surely they will
drag them off, *even* the little ones of
the flock; surely He will make their
[1]pasture [b]desolate because of them.
21 The [a]earth has quaked at the
noise of their downfall. There is an
outcry! The noise of it has been
heard at the [1]Red Sea.
22 Behold, [1]He will mount up and
[a]swoop like an eagle, and spread out

12 [1]Lit., *whose judgment was not to* [a]Jer. 25:15 [b]Jer. 25:28, 29; 1 Pet. 4:17

13 [a]Gen. 22:16; Is. 45:23; Jer. 44:26 [b]Is. 34:9-15; Jer. 18:16

14 [a]Obad. 1-4 [b]Is. 18:2; 30:4

15 [a]Luke 1:51

16 [1]Or, *Sela* [a]Is. 25:5 [b]2 Kin. 14:7; Jer. 48:28 [c]Job 39:27; Is. 14:13-15 [d]Amos 9:2

17 [a]Jer. 49:13; Ezek. 35:7 [b]1 Kin. 9:8; Jer. 51:37

18 [a]Job 18:15-18; Jer. 49:33

19 [1]Lit., *pride* [2]Or, *enduring habitation* [a]Josh. 3:15; Jer. 12:5 [b]Num. 16:5 [c]Is. 46:9

20 [1]Or, *habitation* [a]Is. 14:24, 27; Jer. 50:45 [b]Mal. 1:3, 4

21 [1]Lit., *Sea of Reeds* [a]Jer. 50:46; Ezek. 26:15, 18

22 [1]Or, *one* [2]Or, *over* [a]Jer. 4:13; 48:40, 41; Hos. 8:1 [b]Is. 13:8; Jer. 30:6; 48:41

23 [a]Num. 13:21; Is. 10:9; Jer. 39:5; Amos 6:2 [b]2 Kin. 18:34; 19:13; Is. 10:9 [c]Ex. 15:15; Nah. 2:10 [d]Is. 57:20

25 [1]Or, *deserted is the city of praise* [a]Jer. 33:9; 51:41

26 [1]Or, *destroyed* [a]Jer. 11:22; 50:30; Amos 4:10

27 [1]Or, *palaces* [a]Jer. 43:12; Amos 1:3-5 [b]1 Kin. 15:18-20

28 [1]Lit., *sons* [a]Gen. 25:13; Is. 21:16, 17; Jer. 2:10; Ezek. 27:21 [b]Is. 11:14

29 [a]Hab. 3:7 [b]1 Chr. 5:21

30 [a]Jer. 25:9, 24; 27:6

31 [a]Judg. 18:7; Is. 47:8 [b]Is. 42:11

His wings [2]against Bozrah; and the
[b]hearts of the mighty men of Edom
in that day will be like the heart of a
woman in labor.

Prophecy against Damascus

23 Concerning Damascus.
"[a]Hamath and [b]Arpad are put to
shame,
For they have heard bad news;
They are [c]disheartened.
There is anxiety by the sea,
It [d]cannot be calmed.
24"Damascus has become helpless;
She has turned away to flee,
And panic has gripped her;
Distress and pangs have taken
hold of her
Like a woman in childbirth.
25"How [1]the [a]city of praise has not
been deserted,
The town of My joy!
26"Therefore, her [a]young men will
fall in her streets,
And all the men of war will be
[1]silenced in that day," declares the LORD of hosts.
27"And I shall [a]set fire to the wall
of Damascus,
And it will devour the [1]fortified
towers of [b]Ben-hadad."

Prophecy against Kedar and Hazor

28 Concerning [a]Kedar and the
kingdoms of Hazor, which Nebuchadnezzar king of Babylon defeated. Thus says the LORD,
"Arise, go up to Kedar
And devastate the [1b]men of the
east.
29"They will take away their tents
and their flocks;
They will carry off for themselves
Their tent [a]curtains, all their
goods, and their [b]camels,
And they will call out to one another, 'Terror on every side!'
30"Run away, flee! Dwell in the
depths,
O inhabitants of Hazor," declares the LORD;
"For [a]Nebuchadnezzar king of
Babylon has formed a plan
against you
And devised a scheme against
you.
31"Arise, go up against a nation
which is [a]at ease,
Which lives securely," declares
the LORD.
"It has [b]no gates or bars;
They dwell alone.
32"And their camels will become
plunder,

And the multitude of their cattle for booty,
And I shall scatter to all the winds those who cut the [a]corners *of their hair;*
And I shall bring their disaster from every side," declares the LORD.
33"And Hazor will become a haunt of [a]jackals,
A desolation forever;
No one will live there,
Nor will a son of man reside in it."

Prophecy against Elam

34 That which came as the word of
the LORD to Jeremiah the prophet
concerning [a]Elam, [b]at the beginning
of the reign of Zedekiah king of Ju-
dah, saying,
35"Thus says the LORD of hosts,
'Behold, I am going to [a]break the bow of Elam,
The [1]finest of their might.
36 'And I shall bring upon Elam the [a]four winds
From the four ends of heaven,
And shall [b]scatter them to all these winds;
And there will be no nation
To which the outcasts of Elam will not go.
37 'So I shall [1]shatter Elam before their enemies
And before those who seek their lives;
And I shall [a]bring calamity upon them,
Even My [b]fierce anger,' declares the LORD,
'And I shall send out the sword after them
Until I have consumed them.
38 'Then I shall set My throne in Elam,
And I shall destroy [1]out of it king and princes,'
Declares the LORD.
39 'But it will come about in the last days
That I shall restore the [1]fortunes of Elam,'"
Declares the LORD.

CHAPTER 50

Prophecy against Babylon

THE word which the LORD spoke
concerning Babylon, the land of the
Chaldeans, through Jeremiah the
prophet:
2"[a]Declare and proclaim among the nations.
Proclaim it and [b]lift up a standard.
Do not conceal *it but* say,
'[c]Babylon has been captured,
[d]Bel has been put to shame,
[1]Marduk has been [2]shattered;
Her [e]images have been put to shame, her idols have been shattered.'
3"For a nation has come up
against her out of the north; it will
make her land [a]an object of horror,
and there will be [b]no inhabitant in it.
Both man and beast have wandered
off, they have gone away!
4"In those days and at that time,"
declares the LORD, "the sons of Israel will come, *both* they and the
sons of Judah [a]as well; they will go
along [b]weeping as they go, and it
will be the LORD their God they will
seek.
5"They will [a]ask for the way to
Zion, *turning* their faces [1]in its direction; [2]they [3]will come that they
may join themselves to the LORD *in*
an [b]everlasting covenant that will
not be forgotten.
6"My people have become [a]lost sheep;
[b]Their shepherds have led them astray.
They have made them turn aside *on* the [c]mountains;
They have gone along from mountain to hill
And have forgotten their [d]resting place.
7"All who came upon them have devoured them;
And their adversaries have said, 'We are not guilty,
Inasmuch as they have sinned against the LORD *who is* the [a]habitation of righteousness,
Even the LORD, the [b]hope of their fathers.'
8"Wander away from the midst of Babylon,
And [1]go forth from the land of the Chaldeans;
Be also like male goats [2]at the head of the flock.
9"For behold, I am going to arouse and bring up against Babylon
A horde of great nations from the land of the north,
And they will draw up *their* battle lines against her;
From there she will be taken captive.
Their arrows will be like [1]an expert warrior
Who does not return emptyhanded.

32 [a]Jer. 9:26; 25:23
33 [a]Is. 13:20-22; Jer. 10:22; 51:37; Zeph. 2:9, 13-15
34 [a]Gen. 10:22; 14:1, 9; Is. 11:11; Jer. 25:25; Ezek. 32:24; Dan. 8:2 [b]2 Kin. 24:17, 18; Jer. 28:1
35 [1]Lit., *first* [a]Ps. 46:9; Is. 22:6; Jer. 51:56
36 [a]Dan. 7:2; 8:8; Rev. 7:1 [b]Jer. 50:32; Ezek. 5:10; Amos 9:9
37 [1]Or, *dismay* [a]Jer. 6:19 [b]Jer. 30:24
38 [1]Or, *from there*
39 [1]Or, *captivity*
2 [1]Heb., *Merodach* [2]Or, *dismayed* [a]Jer. 4:16 [b]Jer. 51:27 [c]Jer. 51:31 [d]Is. 46:1 [e]Jer. 6:19
3 [a]Is. 14:22, 23; Jer. 50:13 [b]Jer. 9:10; Zeph. 1:3
4 [a]Is. 11:12, 13; Jer. 3:18; 31:31; 33:7; Hos. 1:11 [b]Ezra 3:12, 13; Jer. 31:9
5 [1]Lit., *hither* [2]M.T. reads, *come ye!* [3]Or, *will have come* [a]Is. 35:8; Jer. 6:16 [b]Is. 55:3; Jer. 32:40; Heb. 8:6-10
6 [a]Is. 53:6; Ezek. 34:15, 16; Matt. 9:36; 10:6 [b]Jer. 23:11-14 [c]Jer. 13:16; Ezek. 34:6 [d]Jer. 33:12; 50:19
7 [a]Jer. 31:23 [b]Jer. 14:8; 17:13
8 [1]Another reading is: *"Let them go forth"* [2]Or, *in front of*
9 [1]So some mss. and versions; M.T. reads, *a warrior who makes childless*

10 "And [1a]Chaldea will become plunder;
All who plunder her will have enough," declares the LORD.

11 "Because you are glad, because you are jubilant,
O you who [a]pillage My heritage,
Because you skip about [1]like a threshing heifer
And neigh like [2]stallions,
12 Your [a]mother [1]will be greatly ashamed,
She who gave you birth [1]will be humiliated.
Behold, *she will be* the least of the nations,
A [b]wilderness, a parched land, and a desert.
13 "Because of the indignation of the LORD she will not be inhabited,
But she will be completely desolate;
Everyone who passes by Babylon [a]will be horrified
And will hiss because of all her wounds.
14 "Draw up your battle lines against Babylon on every side,
All you who [1]bend the bow;
Shoot at her, do not be sparing with *your* arrows,
For she has [a]sinned against the LORD.
15 "Raise your battle cry against her on every side!
She has [a]given [1]herself up, her pillars have fallen,
Her [b]walls have been torn down.
For this is the vengeance of the LORD:
Take vengeance on her;
As she has done *to others, so* do to her.
16 "Cut off the [a]sower from Babylon,
And the one who wields the sickle at the time of harvest;
From before [1]the sword of the [b]oppressor
They will each turn back to his own people,
And they will each flee to his own land.

17 "Israel is a scattered [1]flock, the
[a]lions have driven *them* away. The
first one *who* devoured him was the
[b]king of Assyria, and this last one
who has broken his bones is [c]Nebu-
chadnezzar king of Babylon.
18 "Therefore thus says the LORD of
hosts, the God of Israel: 'Behold, I
am going to punish the king of
Babylon and his land, just as I [a]pun-
ished the king of Assyria.
19 'And I shall [a]bring Israel back to
his pasture, and he will graze on
Carmel and Bashan, and his [1]desire
will be satisfied in the hill country of
Ephraim and Gilead.
20 'In those days and at that time,'
declares the LORD, 'search will be
made for the iniquity of Israel, but
[a]there will be none; and for the sins
of Judah, but they will not be found;
for I shall pardon those whom I
leave as a remnant.'

21 "Against the land of [1]Merathaim, go up against it,
And against the inhabitants of [2a]Pekod.
Slay and [3]utterly destroy them," declares the LORD,
"And do according to all that I have commanded you.
22 "The [a]noise of battle is in the land,
And great destruction.
23 "How the [a]hammer of the whole earth
Has been cut off and broken!
How Babylon has become
An object of horror among the nations!
24 "I [a]set a snare for you, and you were also [b]caught, O Babylon,
While you yourself were not aware;
You have been found and also seized
Because you have engaged in [c]conflict with the LORD."
25 The LORD has opened His armory
And has brought forth the [a]weapons of His indignation,
For it is a [b]work of the Lord [1]GOD of hosts
In the land of the Chaldeans.
26 Come to her from the [1]farthest border;
[a]Open up her barns,
Pile her up like heaps
And [2]utterly [b]destroy her,
Let nothing be left to her.
27 Put all her young bulls to the [a]sword;
Let them go down to the slaughter!
Woe be upon them, for their [b]day has come,
The time of their punishment.
28 There is a [a]sound of fugitives and refugees from the land of Babylon,
To declare in Zion the [b]vengeance of the LORD our God,
Vengeance for His [c]temple.

10 [1]Or, *the Chaldeans* [a]Jer. 51:24, 35; Ezek. 11:24
11 [1]Another reading is, *in the grass* [2]Lit., *mighty ones* [a]Jer. 12:14
12 [1]Or, *has become* [a]Jer. 15:9 [b]Jer. 22:6; 51:43
13 [a]Jer. 18:16; 49:17
14 [1]Lit., *tread* (in order to string) [a]Hab. 2:8, 17
15 [1]Lit., *her hand* [a]1 Chr. 29:24 [b]Ps. 137:8; Jer. 50:29
16 [1]Or, *the oppressing sword* [a]Joel 1:11 [b]Jer. 25:38; 46:16
17 [1]Lit., *sheep* [a]Jer. 2:15; 4:7 [b]2 Kin. 15:19; 17:6; 18:9-13 [c]2 Kin. 24:1, 10-12; 25:1-7
18 [a]Is. 10:12; Ezek. 31:3, 11, 12; Nah. 1:1; 3:7, 18, 19
19 [1]Lit., *soul* [a]Jer. 31:10; 33:12
20 [a]Is. 43:25; Jer. 31:34; Mic. 7:19
21 [1]Or, *Double Rebellion* [2]Or, *Punishment* [3]Lit., *put under the ban* [a]Ezek. 23:23
22 [a]Jer. 4:19-21; 51:54-56
23 [a]Jer. 51:20-24
24 [a]Jer. 48:43, 44; 51:31 [b]Dan. 5:30, 31 [c]Job 9:4; 40:2, 9
25 [1]YHWH, usually rendered LORD [a]Is. 13:5 [b]Jer. 50:16; 51:12, 25, 55
26 [1]Lit., *end* [2]Lit., *put under the ban* [a]Is. 45:3; Jer. 50:10 [b]Is. 14:23
27 [a]Is. 34:7 [b]Ps. 37:13; Jer. 46:21; Ezek. 7:7
28 [a]Is. 48:20 [b]Ps. 149:6-9; Jer. 50:15; 51:10 [c]Lam. 1:10; 2:6, 7

29"Summon [1]many against Babylon,
All those who [2]bend the bow:
Encamp against her on every side,
Let there be no escape[3].
Repay her according to her work;
[a]According to all that she has done, *so* do to her;
For she has become [b]arrogant against the LORD,
Against the Holy One of Israel.
30"Therefore her young [a]men will fall in her streets,
And all her men of war will be [1]silenced in that day," declares the LORD.
31"Behold, [a]I am against you, O [1]arrogant one,"
Declares the Lord [2]GOD of hosts,
"For your day has come,
The time [3]when I shall punish you.
32"And the [1a]arrogant one will stumble and fall
With no one to raise him up;
And I shall [b]set fire to his cities,
And it will devour all his environs."

33 Thus says the LORD of hosts,
"The sons of Israel are oppressed,
And the sons of Judah as well;
And [a]all who took them captive have held them fast,
They have refused to let them go.
34"Their [a]Redeemer is strong, the LORD of hosts is His name;
He will vigorously [b]plead their case,
So that He may [c]bring rest to [1]the earth,
But turmoil to the inhabitants of Babylon.
35"A [a]sword against the Chaldeans," declares the LORD,
"And against the inhabitants of Babylon,
And against her officials and her [b]wise men!
36"A sword against the [a]oracle priests, and they will become fools!
A sword against her [b]mighty men, and they will be [1c]shattered!
37"A sword against [1]their [a]horses and against [1]their chariots,
And against all the [2b]foreigners who are in the midst of her,
And they will become [c]women!
A sword against her treasures, and they will be plundered!
38"A [1]drought on her waters, and they will be dried up!
For it is a land of idols,
And they are mad over fearsome idols.
39"Therefore the desert creatures will live *there* along with the jackals;
The ostriches also will live in it,
And it will [a]never again be inhabited
Or dwelt in from generation to generation.
40"As when God overthrew [a]Sodom
And Gomorrah with its neighbors," declares the LORD,
"No man will live there,
Nor will *any* son of man reside in it.

41"Behold, a people is coming [a]from the north,
And a great nation and many kings
Will be aroused from the remote parts of the earth.
42"They seize *their* bow and javelin;
They are [a]cruel and have no mercy.
Their voice roars like the sea,
And they ride on [b]horses,
Marshalled like a man [c]for the battle
Against you, O daughter of Babylon.
43"The king of Babylon has heard the report about them,
And his hands hang limp;
[a]Distress has gripped him,
Agony like a woman in childbirth.
44"[a]Behold, one will come up like a
lion from the [1]thicket of the Jordan
to a [2]perennially watered pasture;
for in an instant I shall make them
run away from it, and whoever is
[b]chosen I shall appoint over it. For
who is [c]like Me, and who will summon Me *into court?* And who then is
the shepherd who can [d]stand before
Me?"
45 Therefore hear the [a]plan of the
LORD which He has planned against
Babylon, and His purposes which
He has purposed against the land of
the Chaldeans: surely they will drag
them off, *even* the little ones of the
flock; surely He will make their
[1]pasture desolate because of them.
46 At the [1]shout, "Babylon has
been seized!" the [a]earth is shaken,
and an [b]outcry is heard among the
nations.

29 [1]Another reading is, *archers* [2]Lit., *tread* (in order to string) [3]Some mss. add: *to her* [a]Ps. 137:8; Jer. 50:15; 51:56 [b]Ex. 10:3; Jer. 49:16; Dan. 4:37
30 [1]Or, *made lifeless;* or, *destroyed* [a]Is. 13:17, 18; Jer. 9:21; 18:21; 49:26
31 [1]Lit., *arrogance* [2]YHWH, usually rendered LORD [3]Another reading is, *of your punishment* [a]Jer. 21:13; Nah. 2:13
32 [1]Lit., *arrogance* [a]Is. 10:12-15 [b]Jer. 21:14; 49:27
33 [a]Is. 14:17; 58:6
34 [1]Or, their *land* [a]Is. 43:14; Jer. 15:21; 31:11 [b]Jer. 51:36; Mic. 7:9 [c]Is. 14:3-7
35 [a]Jer. 47:6; Hos. 11:6 [b]Dan. 5:7, 8
36 [1]Or, *dismayed* [a]Is. 44:25 [b]Jer. 49:42 [c]Nah. 3:13
37 [1]Lit., *his* [2]Lit., *mixed multitude* [a]Ps. 20:7, 8; Jer. 51:21, 22 [b]Jer. 25:20; Ezek. 30:5 [c]Jer. 48:41; 51:30
38 [1]Another reading is, *sword*
39 [a]Is. 13:20
40 [a]Jer. 49:18; Luke 17:28-30; 2 Pet. 2:6; Jude 7
41 [a]Is. 13:2-5; Jer. 50:3, 9; 51:27, 28
42 [a]Is. 13:17, 18; 47:6 [b]Jer. 8:16; 47:3; Hab. 1:8 [c]Jer. 50:9, 14; Joel 2:5
43 [a]Jer. 30:6
44 [1]Lit., *pride* [2]Or, *enduring habitation* [a]Jer. 49:19-21 [b]Num. 16:5 [c]Is. 46:9 [d]Job 41:10; Jer. 30:21
45 [1]Or, *habitation* [a]Is. 14:24; Jer. 51:10, 11
46 [1]Lit., *voice* [a]Jer. 10:10; 49:21; Ezek. 26:18; 31:16 [b]Is. 5:7; 15:5; Jer. 46:12; 51:54; Ezek. 27:28

Chapter 51

Babylon Judged for Sins against Israel

THUS says the LORD:
"Behold, I am going to arouse against Babylon
And against the inhabitants of [1]Leb-kamai
[2]The spirit of a [a]destroyer.
2 "And I shall dispatch [1]foreigners to Babylon that they may [a]winnow her
And may devastate her land;
For on every side they will be opposed to her
In the day of *her* calamity.
3 "[1]Let not [2]him who [3]bends his bow [3]bend *it,*
[1]Nor let him rise up in his scale-armor;
So do not spare her young men;
Devote all her army to destruction.
4 "And they will fall down [1]slain in the land of the Chaldeans,
And [a]pierced through in their streets."

5 For [a]neither Israel nor Judah has been [1]forsaken
By his God, the LORD of hosts,
Although their land is [b]full of guilt
[2]Before the Holy One of Israel.
6 Flee from the midst of Babylon,
And each of you save his life!
Do not be [1a]destroyed in her [2]punishment,
For this is the LORD's time of vengeance;
He is going to render recompense to her.
7 Babylon has been a golden [a]cup in the hand of the LORD,
Intoxicating all the earth.
The [b]nations have drunk of her wine;
Therefore the nations are going mad.
8 Suddenly Babylon has fallen and been broken;
[a]Wail over her!
Bring [1]balm for her pain;
Perhaps she may be healed.
9 We applied healing to Babylon, but she was not healed;
Forsake her and [a]let us each go to his own country,
For her judgment has reached to [b]heaven
And [1]towers up to the very skies.
10 The LORD has [a]brought about our vindication;
Come and let us [b]recount in Zion
The work of the LORD our God!

11 [a]Sharpen the arrows, fill the quivers!
The LORD has aroused the spirit of the kings of the Medes,
Because His purpose is against Babylon to destroy it;
For it is the vengeance of the LORD, vengeance for His temple.
12 [a]Lift up a [1]signal against the walls of Babylon;
Post a strong guard,
Station [2]sentries,
Place men in ambush!
For the LORD has both [b]purposed and performed
What He spoke concerning the inhabitants of Babylon.
13 O you who dwell by many waters,
Abundant in [a]treasures,
Your end has come,
The [1]measure of your [b]end.
14 The LORD of hosts has sworn by Himself:
"Surely I will fill you with a [1]population like [a]locusts,
And they will cry out with [2]shouts of victory over you."

15 *It is* [a]He who made the earth by His power,
Who established the world by His wisdom,
And by His understanding He [b]stretched out the heavens.
16 When He utters His [a]voice, *there is* a tumult of waters in the heavens,
And He causes the [b]clouds to ascend from the end of the earth;
He makes lightning for the rain,
And brings forth the [c]wind from His storehouses.
17 [a]All mankind is stupid, devoid of knowledge;
Every goldsmith is put to shame by his [1]idols,
For his molten images are [b]deceitful,
And there is no breath in them.
18 They are worthless, a work of mockery;
In the time of their punishment they will perish.
19 The [a]portion of Jacob is not like these;
For the [1]Maker of all is He,
And of the [2]tribe of His inheritance;
The LORD of hosts is His name.

1 [1]Code name for Chaldea; or else, *the heart of those who rise up against Me* [2]Or, *a destroying wind* [a]Jer. 4:11, 12; 23:19; Hos. 13:15
2 [1]Some versions read, *winnowers* [a]Is. 41:16; Jer. 15:7; Matt. 3:12
3 [1]M.T. reads: *Against him who* [2]I.e., the Chaldean defender [3]Lit., *tread(s)* (in order to string)
4 [1]Or, *wounded* [a]Jer. 13:15; 14:19
5 [1]Lit., *widowed* [2]Lit., *From* [a]Is. 54:7, 8; Jer. 33:24-26 [b]Hos. 4:1, 2
6 [1]Or, *silenced;* or, *made lifeless* [2]Or, *penalty for iniquity* [a]Num. 16:26
7 [a]Jer. 25:15; Hab. 2:16; Rev. 14:8 [b]Rev. 18:3
8 [1]Or, *balsam resin* [a]Is. 13:6
9 [1]Lit., *is lifted* [a]Is. 13:14; Jer. 46:16; 50:16 [b]Ezra 9:6
10 [a]Ps. 37:6; Mic. 7:9 [b]Is. 40:2; Jer. 50:28
11 [a]Jer. 46:4, 9; Joel 3:9, 10
12 [1]Or, *standard* [2]Or, *watchmen* [a]Is. 13:2; Jer. 50:2; 51:27 [b]Jer. 4:28; 23:20; 51:29
13 [1]Lit., *cubit* [a]Is. 45:3 [b]Is. 57:17; Hab. 2:9-11
14 [1]Or, *mankind* [2]I.e., like the song of grape treaders [a]Jer. 51:27; Nah. 3:15
15 [a]Jer. 10:12-16; 51:15, 19 [b]Ps. 146:5, 6; Jer. 32:17; Acts 14:15; Rom. 1:20
16 [a]Job 37:2-6; Ps. 18:13 [b]Ps. 135:7; Jer. 10:13 [c]Jon. 1:4
17 [1]Or, *graven images* [a]Is. 44:18-20; Jer. 10:14 [b]Hab. 2:18, 19
19 [1]Lit., *Fashioner* [2]Or, *Scepter;* cf. Num. 24:17 [a]Ps. 73:26; Jer. 10:16

20 *He says,* "You are My [1a]war-club, *My* weapon of war;
And with you I [b]shatter nations,
And with you I destroy kingdoms.
21 "And with you I [a]shatter the horse and his rider,
22 And with you I shatter the [a]chariot and its rider,
And with you I shatter [b]man and woman,
And with you I shatter old man and [c]youth,
And with you I shatter young man and virgin,
23 And with you I shatter the shepherd and his flock,
And with you I shatter the farmer and his team,
And with you I shatter governors and prefects.

24 "But I will repay Babylon and all the inhabitants of Chaldea for all their evil that they have done in Zion before your eyes," declares the LORD.

25 "Behold, I am against you, O destroying mountain,
Who destroy the whole earth," declares the LORD,
"And I will stretch out My hand against you,
And roll you down from the crags
And I will make you a [a]burnt out mountain.
26 "And they will not take from you *even* a stone for a corner
Nor a stone for foundations,
But you will be [a]desolate forever," declares the LORD.

27 [a]Lift up a [1]signal in the land,
Blow a trumpet among the nations!
Consecrate the nations against her,
Summon against her the kingdoms of [b]Ararat, Minni and [c]Ashkenaz;
Appoint a marshal against her,
Bring up the [d]horses like bristly locusts.
28 Consecrate the nations against her,
The kings of the Medes,
[1]Their governors and all [1]their [2]prefects,
And every land of [3]their dominion.
29 So the [a]land quakes and writhes,
For the purposes of the LORD against Babylon stand,
To make the land of Babylon
A [1b]desolation without inhabitants.
30 The [a]mighty men of Babylon have ceased fighting,
They stay in the strongholds;
[b]Their strength is [1]exhausted,
They are becoming [b]*like* women;
Their dwelling places are set on fire,
The [c]bars of her *gates* are broken.
31 One [1a]courier runs to meet [1]another,
And one [2b]messenger to meet [2]another,
To tell the king of Babylon
That his city has been captured from end *to end;*
32 The fords also have been seized,
And they have burned the marshes with fire,
And the men of war are terrified.

33 For thus says the LORD of hosts, the God of Israel:
"The daughter of Babylon is like a [a]threshing floor
At the time [1]it is stamped firm;
Yet in a little while the time of [b]harvest will come for her."

34 "Nebuchadnezzar king of Babylon has devoured me *and* crushed me,
He has set me down *like* an [a]empty vessel;
He has swallowed me [b]like a monster,
He has filled his stomach with my delicacies;
He has washed me away.
35 "May the [a]violence *done* to me and to my flesh be upon Babylon,"
The [1]inhabitant of Zion will say;
And, "May my blood be upon the inhabitants of Chaldea,"
Jerusalem will say.
36 Therefore thus says the LORD,
"Behold, I am going to [a]plead your case
And [b]exact full vengeance for you;
And I shall dry up her [1]sea
And make her fountain dry.
37 "And Babylon will become a heap *of ruins,* a haunt of jackals,
An object of horror and hissing, without inhabitants.
38 "They will roar together like [a]young lions,
They will growl like lions' cubs.

20 [1]Lit., *shatterer* [a]Is. 41:15, 16; Jer. 50:23 [b]Is. 8:9; 41:15, 16; Mic. 4:12, 13

21 [a]Ex. 15:1

22 [a]Ex. 15:4; Is. 43:17 [b]2 Chr. 36:17 [c]Is. 13:15, 16, 18

25 [a]Rev. 8:8

26 [a]Is. 13:19-22; 50:13; Jer. 51:29

27 [1]Or, *standard* [a]Is. 13:2-5; 18:3; Jer. 50:2; 51:12 [b]Gen. 8:4; 2 Kin. 19:37; Is. 37:38 [c]Gen. 10:3 [d]Jer. 50:42

28 [1]Lit., *Her* [2]I.e., lieutenant governors [3]Lit., *his*

29 [1]Or, *object of horror* [a]Jer. 8:16; 10:10; 50:46; Amos 8:8 [b]Is. 13:19, 20; 47:11; Jer. 51:26, 43

30 [1]Lit., *dried up* [a]Ps. 76:5; Jer. 50:15, 36, 37 [b]Is. 13:7, 8; Nah. 3:13 [c]Is. 45:1, 2; Lam. 2:9; Amos 1:5; Nah. 3:13

31 [1]Lit., *runner* [2]Lit., *announcer* [a]2 Chr. 30:6 [b]2 Sam. 18:19-31

33 [1]Lit., *of treading it* [a]Is. 21:10; 41:15, 16 [b]Hos. 6:11; Joel 3:13

34 [a]Is. 24:1-3 [b]Job 20:15; Jer. 51:44; Amos 8:4

35 [1]Lit., *inhabitress* [a]Ps. 137:8

36 [1]Or, *broad river* [a]Ps. 140:12 [b]Jer. 51:6, 11; Rom. 12:19

38 [a]Jer. 2:15

39"When they become heated up, I shall serve *them* their banquet
And [a]make them drunk, that they may become jubilant
And may [b]sleep a perpetual sleep
And not wake up," declares the LORD.
40"I shall bring them down like [1]lambs [a]to the slaughter,
Like rams together with male goats.

41"How [1a]Sheshak has been captured,
And the praise of the whole earth been seized!
How Babylon has become an object of horror among the nations!
42"The [1a]sea has come up over Babylon;
She has been engulfed with its tumultuous waves.
43"Her cities have become an object of horror,
A parched land and a desert,
A land in which no man [a]lives,
And through which no son of man passes.
44"And I shall punish Bel in Babylon,
And I shall make what he has swallowed [a]come out of his mouth;
And the nations will no longer [b]stream to him.
Even the [c]wall of Babylon has fallen down!

45"[a]Come forth from her midst, My people,
And each of you [b]save yourselves
From the fierce anger of the LORD.
46"Now [a]lest your heart grow faint,
And you be afraid at the [b]report that *will be* heard in the land—
For the report will come [1]one year,
And after that [2]another report in [2]another year,
And violence *will be* in the land
With [c]ruler against ruler—
47 Therefore behold, days are coming
When I shall punish the [a]idols of Babylon;
And her whole land will be [b]put to shame,
And all her slain will fall in her midst.

39 [a]Jer. 25:27; 48:26; 51:57 [b]Ps. 76:5

40 [1]Or, *young rams* [a]Jer. 48:15; 50:27

41 [1]Code name for Babylon [a]Jer. 25:26

42 [1]Or, *broad river* [a]Is. 8:7, 8; Jer. 51:55; Dan. 9:26

43 [a]Is. 13:20; Jer. 2:6

44 [a]Ezra 1:7, 8 [b]Is. 2:2 [c]Jer. 50:15; 51:58

45 [a]Is. 48:20; Jer. 50:8, 28; 51:6 [b]Gen. 19:12-16; Acts 2:40

46 [1]Lit., *in the* [2]Lit., *the* [a]Is. 43:5; Jer. 46:27, 28 [b]2 Kin. 19:7; Is. 13:3-5 [c]Is. 19:2

47 [a]Is. 21:9; 46:1, 2; Jer. 50:2; 51:52 [b]Jer. 50:12, 35-37

48 [a]Is. 44:23; 48:20; 49:13

49 [a]Ps. 137:8; Jer. 50:29

50 [1]Lit., *come upon your heart* [a]Deut. 4:29-31; Ps. 137:6

51 [a]Ps. 74:3-8; Lam. 1:10

53 [1]Lit., *the height of her strength* [a]Job 20:6; Ps. 139:8-10; Is. 14:12, 13; Jer. 49:16 [b]Is. 13:3

55 [1]Or, *voice* [2]Lit., *is given* [a]Ps. 18:4; 69:2; 124:2, 4, 5; Jer. 51:42

56 [a]Jer. 51:48; Hab. 2:8 [b]Ps. 46:9; 76:3 [c]Ps. 94:1, 2; Jer. 51:6, 24

57 [a]Ps. 76:5, 6 [b]Jer. 46:18; 48:15

48"Then [a]heaven and earth and all that is in them
Will shout for joy over Babylon,
For the destroyers will come to her from the north,"
Declares the LORD.
49 [a]Indeed Babylon is to fall *for* the slain of Israel,
As also for Babylon the slain of all the earth have fallen.
50 You who have escaped the sword,
Depart! Do not stay!
[a]Remember the LORD from afar,
And let Jerusalem [1]come to your mind.
51 We are ashamed because we have heard reproach;
Disgrace has covered our faces,
For [a]aliens have entered
The holy places of the LORD's house.

52"Therefore behold, the days are coming," declares the LORD,
"When I shall punish her idols,
And the mortally wounded will groan throughout her land.
53"Though Babylon should [a]ascend to the heavens,
And though she should fortify [1]her lofty stronghold,
From [b]Me destroyers will come to her," declares the LORD.
54 The sound of an outcry from Babylon,
And of great destruction from the land of the Chaldeans!
55 For the LORD is going to destroy Babylon,
And He will make *her* loud [1]noise vanish from her.
And their [a]waves will roar like many waters;
The tumult of their voices [2]sounds forth.
56 For the [a]destroyer is coming against her, against Babylon,
And her mighty men will be captured,
Their [b]bows are shattered;
For the LORD is a God of [c]recompense,
He will fully repay.
57"And I shall make her princes and her wise men drunk,
Her governors, her prefects, and her mighty men,
That they may sleep a [a]perpetual sleep and not wake up,"
Declares the [b]King, whose name is the LORD of hosts.
58 Thus says the LORD of hosts,
"The broad wall of Babylon will be completely razed,

And her high [a]gates will be set
on fire;
So the peoples will [b]toil for
nothing,
And the nations become [c]ex-
hausted *only* for fire."

59 The message which Jeremiah
the prophet commanded Seraiah
the son of [a]Neriah, the grandson of
Mahseiah, when he went with [b]Zed-
ekiah the king of Judah to Babylon
in the fourth year of his reign. (Now
Seraiah was quartermaster.)

60 So Jeremiah [a]wrote in a single
scroll all the calamity which would
come upon Babylon, *that is,* all
these words which have been written concerning Babylon.

61 Then Jeremiah said to Seraiah,
"As soon as you come to Babylon,
then see that you read all these
words aloud,

62 and say, 'Thou, O LORD, hast
[1]promised concerning this place to
[a]cut it off, so that there will be
[b]nothing dwelling in it, whether
man or beast, but it will be a perpetual desolation.'

63 "And it will come about as soon
as you finish reading this scroll, you
will tie a stone to it and [a]throw it
into the middle of the Euphrates,

64 and say, 'Just so shall Babylon
sink down and [a]not rise again, because of the calamity that I am
going to bring upon her; and they
will become [b]exhausted.' " [c]Thus
far are the words of Jeremiah.

CHAPTER 52

Recount the Fall of Jerusalem

[a]ZEDEKIAH was twenty-one years
old when he became king, and he
reigned eleven years in Jerusalem;
and his mother's name was [1]Ham-
utal the daughter of Jeremiah of
[b]Libnah.

2 And he did [a]evil in the sight of
the LORD like all that [b]Jehoiakim
had done.

3 For through the [a]anger of the
LORD *this* came about in Jerusalem
and Judah until He cast them out
from His presence. And Zedekiah
[b]rebelled against the king of Babylon.

4 [a]Now it came about in the ninth
year of his reign, on the tenth day of
the tenth month, that Nebuchadnezzar king of Babylon came, he and
all his army, against Jerusalem,
camped against it, and built a [b]siege
wall all around it.

5 So the city was under siege until the eleventh year of King Zedekiah.

6 On the ninth day of the [a]fourth
month the [b]famine was so severe in
the city that there was no food for
the people of the land.

7 Then the city was [a]broken into,
and all the [b]men of war fled and
went forth from the city at night by
way of the gate between the two
walls which *was* by the king's garden, though the Chaldeans were [1]all
around the city. And they went by
way of the Arabah.

8 But the army of the Chaldeans
pursued the king and [a]overtook
Zedekiah in the [1]plains of Jericho,
and all his army was scattered from
him.

9 Then they captured the king
and [a]brought him up to the king of
Babylon at [b]Riblah in the land of
[c]Hamath; and he [1]passed sentence
on him.

10 And the king of Babylon
[a]slaughtered the sons of Zedekiah
before his eyes, and he also slaughtered all the [1]princes of Judah in
Riblah.

11 Then he [a]blinded the eyes of
Zedekiah; and the king of Babylon
bound him with bronze fetters and
brought him to Babylon, and put
him in prison until the day of his
death.

12 [a]Now on the tenth day of the
fifth month, which was the [b]nine-
teenth year of King Nebuchadnezzar, king of Babylon, Nebuzaradan
the captain of the bodyguard, who
was in the service of the king of
Babylon, came to Jerusalem.

13 And he [a]burned the house of
the LORD, the [b]king's house, and all
the houses of Jerusalem; even every
large house he burned with fire.

14 So all the army of the Chaldeans who *were* with the captain of the
guard [a]broke down all the walls
around Jerusalem.

15 Then Nebuzaradan the captain
of the guard [a]carried away into exile
some of the poorest of the people,
the rest of the people who were left
in the city, the [1b]deserters who had
deserted to the king of Babylon, and
the rest of the artisans.

16 But [a]Nebuzaradan the captain
of the guard left some of the poorest
of the land to be vinedressers and
[1]plowmen.

17 Now the bronze [a]pillars which
belonged to the house of the LORD
and the [b]stands and the bronze [c]sea,
which were in the house of the
LORD, the Chaldeans broke in pieces

58 [a]Is. 45:1, 2 [b]Hab. 2:13 [c]Jer. 9:5; 51:64; Lam. 5:5
59 [a]Jer. 32:12; 36:4; 45:1 [b]Jer. 28:1; 52:1
60 [a]Is. 30:8; Jer. 30:2, 3; 36:2, 4, 32
62 [1]Lit., *spoken* [a]Is. 13:19-22; 14:22, 23; Jer. 50:3, 13, 39, 40 [b]Jer. 51:43; Ezek. 35:9
63 [a]Jer. 19:10, 11; Rev. 18:21
64 [a]Nah. 1:8, 9 [b]Jer. 51:58 [c]Job 31:40; Ps. 72:20
1 [1]Another reading is: *Hamital* [a]2 Kin. 24:18-20; 2 Chr. 36:11-36 [b]Josh. 10:29; 2 Kin. 8:22; Is. 37:8
2 [a]1 Kin. 14:22 [b]Jer. 36:30, 31
3 [a]Is. 3:1, 4, 5 [b]2 Chr. 36:13
4 [a]2 Kin. 25:1-7; Jer. 39:1; Ezek. 24:1, 2 [b]Jer. 32:24
6 [a]Jer. 39:2 [b]2 Kin. 25:3; Jer. 38:9
7 [1]Lit., *against the city on every side* [a]Jer. 39:2 [b]Jer. 39:4-7; 51:32
8 [1]Lit., *Arabah* [a]Jer. 21:7; 32:4; 34:21; 37:17; 38:23
9 [1]Lit., *spoke judgments with* [a]2 Kin. 25:6; Jer. 39:5 [b]Num. 34:11; Jer. 39:5 [c]Num. 13:21; Josh. 13:5
10 [1]Or, *commanders* [a]Jer. 22:30; 39:6
11 [a]Jer. 39:7; Ezek. 12:13
12 [a]2 Kin. 25:8-21 [b]2 Kin. 24:12; 25:8; Jer. 52:29
13 [a]2 Chr. 36:19; Ps. 74:6-8; 79:1; Is. 64:10, 11; Lam. 2:7; Mic. 3:12 [b]Jer. 39:8
14 [a]2 Kin. 25:10; Neh. 1:3
15 [1]Lit., *fallers who had fallen* [a]2 Kin. 25:11 [b]Jer. 39:9
16 [1]Or, *unpaid laborers* [a]2 Kin. 25:12; Jer. 39:10; 40:2-6
17 [a]1 Kin. 7:15-22; Jer. 27:19-22; 52:21-23 [b]1 Kin. 7:27-36 [c]1 Kin. 7:23-26

and carried all their bronze to Babylon.

18 And they also took away the [a]pots, the shovels, the snuffers, the basins, the [1]pans, and all the bronze vessels which were used in *temple* service.

19 The captain of the guard also took away the [a]bowls, the firepans, the basins, the pots, the lampstands, the [1]pans and the libation bowls, what was fine gold and what was fine silver.

20 The two pillars, the one sea, and the twelve bronze bulls that were under [1]the sea, *and* the stands, which King Solomon had made for the house of the LORD—the bronze of all these vessels was [a]beyond weight.

21 As for the pillars, the [a]height of each pillar was eighteen [1]cubits, and it [2]was twelve cubits in [a]circumference and four fingers in thickness, *and* hollow.

22 Now a [a]capital of bronze was on it; and the height of each capital was five cubits, with network and [b]pomegranates upon the capital all around, all of bronze. And the second pillar was like these, including pomegranates.

23 And there were ninety-six exposed pomegranates; all the pomegranates *numbered* a hundred on the network all around.

24 Then the captain of the guard took [a]Seraiah the chief priest and Zephaniah the second priest, with the three [1b]officers of the temple.

25 He also took from the city one official who was overseer of the men of war, and seven [1a]of the king's advisers who were found in the city, and the scribe of the commander of the army who mustered the people of the land, and sixty men of the people of the land who were found in the midst of the city.

26 And Nebuzaradan the captain of the guard took them and [a]brought them to the king of Babylon at Riblah.

27 Then the king of Babylon [a]struck them down and put them to death at Riblah in the land of Hamath. So Judah was [b]led away into exile from its land.

28 These are the people whom [a]Nebuchadnezzar carried away into exile: in the [1]seventh year 3,023 Jews;

29 in the eighteenth year of Nebuchadnezzar 832 persons from Jerusalem;

30 in the twenty-third year of Nebuchadnezzar, Nebuzaradan the captain of the guard carried into exile 745 Jewish people; there were 4,600 persons in all.

31 [a]Now it came about in the thirty-seventh year of the exile of Jehoiachin king of Judah, in the twelfth month, on the twenty-fifth of the month, that [1]Evil-merodach king of Babylon, in the *first* year of his reign, [b]showed favor to Jehoiachin king of Judah and brought him out of prison.

32 Then he spoke kindly to him and set his throne above the thrones of the kings who *were* with him in Babylon.

33 So Jehoiachin [a]changed his prison clothes, and [b]had his meals in the king's presence regularly all the days of his life.

34 And for his allowance, a [a]regular allowance was given him by the king of Babylon, a daily portion all the days of his life until the day of his death.

18 [1]Or, *spoons for incense* [a]1 Kin. 7:40, 45
19 [1]Or, *spoons for incense* [a]1 Kin. 7:49, 50
20 [1]So Gk. and Syriac; Heb. omits *the sea* [a]1 Kin. 7:47
21 [1]A cubit equals approx. 18 inches. [2]Lit., *a line of 12 cubits would encircle it* [a]1 Kin. 7:15
22 [a]1 Kin. 7:16 [b]1 Kin. 7:20, 42
24 [1]Lit., *keepers of the door* [a]2 Kin. 25:18; 1 Chr. 6:14; Ezra 7:1 [b]1 Chr. 9:19; Ps. 84:10; Jer. 35:4
25 [1]Lit., *men of those seeing the king's face* [a]Esth. 1:14; Matt. 18:10
26 [a]2 Kin. 25:20, 21
27 [a]Ezek. 8:11-18 [b]Is. 6:11, 12; 27:10; 32:13, 14; Jer. 13:19; 20:4; 25:9-11; 39:9; Ezek. 33:28; Mic. 4:10
28 [1]Or possibly, *seventeenth* [a]2 Kin. 24:2, 3, 12-16; 2 Chr. 36:20; Ezra 2:1; Neh. 7:6; Dan. 1:1-3
31 [1]Or, *Awil-Marduk* ("Man of Marduk") [a]2 Kin. 25:27-30 [b]Gen. 40:13, 20; Ps. 3:3; 27:6
33 [a]Gen. 41:14, 42 [b]2 Sam. 9:7, 13; 1 Kin. 2:7
34 [a]2 Sam. 9:10

THE LAMENTATIONS OF JEREMIAH

The Sorrows of Zion

HOW lonely sits the city
That was [a]full of people!
She has become like a [b]widow
Who was once [c]great among the nations!
She who was a princess among the [1]provinces
Has become a [d]forced laborer!
2 She [a]weeps bitterly in the night,
And her tears are on her cheeks;
She has none to comfort her
Among all her [b]lovers.
All her friends have [c]dealt treacherously with her;
They have become her enemies.
3 Judah has gone into exile [1]under affliction,
And [1]under [2]harsh servitude;
She dwells [a]among the nations,
But she has found no rest;
All [b]her pursuers have overtaken her
In the midst of [3]distress.
4 The roads [1]of Zion are in mourning
Because [a]no one comes to the appointed feasts.
All her gates are [b]desolate;
Her priests are groaning,
Her virgins are afflicted,
And she herself [2]is bitter.
5 Her adversaries have become [1]her masters,
Her enemies [2]prosper;
For the LORD has [a]caused her grief
Because of the multitude of her transgressions;
Her little ones have gone away
As captives before the adversary.
6 And all her [a]majesty
Has departed from the daughter of Zion;
Her princes have become like bucks
That have found no pasture;
And they have [1b]fled without strength
Before the pursuer.
7 In the days of her affliction and homelessness
Jerusalem remembers all her precious things
That were from the days of old
When her people fell into the hand of the adversary,
And [a]no one helped her.
The adversaries saw her,
They [b]mocked at her [1]ruin.
8 Jerusalem sinned [a]greatly,
Therefore she has become an unclean thing.
All who honored her despise her
Because they have seen her nakedness;
Even she herself groans and turns away.
9 Her [a]uncleanness was in her skirts;
She [1]did not consider her future;
Therefore she has [2b]fallen astonishingly;
[c]She has no comforter.
"See, O LORD, my affliction,
For the enemy has [d]magnified himself!"
10 The adversary has stretched out his hand
Over all her precious things,
For she has seen the [a]nations enter her sanctuary,
The ones whom Thou didst command
That they should not enter into Thy congregation.
11 All her people groan [a]seeking bread;
They have given their precious things for food
To [b]restore their [1]lives themselves.
"See, O LORD, and look,
For I am [c]despised."
12 "Is [a]it nothing to all you who pass this way?
Look and see if there is any [1]pain like my [1]pain
Which was severely dealt out to me,
Which the LORD inflicted on the day of His [b]fierce anger.
13 "From on high He sent fire into my [a]bones,
And it [1]prevailed *over them;*
He has spread a [b]net for my feet;
He has turned me back;
He has made me [c]desolate,
[2]Faint all day long.
14 "The [a]yoke of my transgressions is bound;
By His hand they are knit together;
They have [b]come upon my neck;
He has made my strength [1]fail;
The Lord [c]has given me into the hands

1 [1]Or, *districts* [a]Is. 22:2 [b]Is. 54:4 [c]1 Kin. 4:21; Ezra 4:20; Jer. 31:7 [d]2 Kin. 23:35; Jer. 40:9

2 [a]Ps. 6:6; 77:2-6; Lam. 1:16 [b]Jer. 2:25; 3:1; 22:20-22 [c]Job 19:13, 14; Ps. 31:11; Mic. 7:5

3 [1]Or, *by reason of* [2]Lit., *great* [3]Or, *narrow places* [a]Lev. 26:39; Deut. 28:64-67 [b]2 Kin. 25:4, 5

4 [1]Or, *to* [2]Or, *suffers bitterly* [a]Is. 24:4-6; Lam. 2:6, 7 [b]Jer. 9:11; 10:22

5 [1]Lit., *head* [2]Or, *are at ease* [a]Ps. 90:7, 8; Ezek. 8:17, 18; 9:9, 10

6 [1]Lit., *gone* [a]Ps. 132:13; Jer. 13:18 [b]2 Kin. 25:4, 5

7 [1]Lit., *cessation* [a]Jer. 37:7; Lam. 4:17 [b]Ps. 79:4; Jer. 48:27

8 [a]Is. 59:2-13; Lam. 1:5, 20

9 [1]Lit., *did not remember her latter end* [2]Lit., *come down* [a]Jer. 2:34; Ezek. 24:13 [b]Is. 3:8; Jer. 13:17, 18 [c]Eccles. 4:1; Jer. 16:7 [d]Ps. 74:23; Zeph. 2:10

10 [a]Ps. 74:4-8; Is. 64:10, 11; Jer. 51:51

11 [1]Lit., *soul* [a]Jer. 38:9; 52:6 [b]1 Sam. 30:12 [c]Jer. 15:19

12 [1]Or, *sorrow* [a]Jer. 18:16; 48:27 [b]Is. 13:13; Jer. 4:8

13 [1]Or, *descended, overthrew* [2]Or, *Sick* [a]Job 30:30; Ps. 22:14; Hab. 3:16 [b]Job 19:6; Ps. 66:11 [c]Jer. 44:6

14 [1]Lit., *stumble* [a]Prov. 5:22; Is. 47:6 [b]Jer. 28:13, 14 [c]Jer. 32:3, 5; Ezek. 25:4, 7

Of *those against whom* I am not
able to stand.
15 "The [a]Lord has rejected all my
strong men
In my midst;
He has called an appointed
[1]time against me
To crush my [b]young men;
The Lord has trodden *as in* a
wine press
The virgin daughter of Judah.
16 "For these things I weep;
[1]My eyes run down with water;
Because far from me is a [a]comforter,
One who restores my soul;
My children are desolate
Because the enemy has prevailed."
17 Zion [a]stretches out her hands;
There is no one to comfort her;
The LORD has [b]commanded
concerning Jacob
That the ones round about him
should be his adversaries;
Jerusalem has become an unclean thing among them.
18 "The LORD is [a]righteous;
For I have [b]rebelled against His
[1]command;
Hear now, all peoples,
And behold my [2]pain;
My virgins and my young men
Have gone into captivity.
19 "I [a]called to my lovers, *but* they
deceived me;
My [b]priests and my elders perished in the city,
While they sought food to restore [1]their strength themselves.
20 "See, O LORD, for I am in distress;
My [1a]spirit is greatly troubled;
My heart is overturned within
me,
For I have been very rebellious.
In the street the sword [2]slays;
In the house it is like death.
21 "They have heard that I groan;
There is no one to comfort me;
All my enemies have heard of
my [1]calamity;
They are [a]glad that Thou hast
done *it*.
O that Thou wouldst bring the
day which Thou hast proclaimed,
That they may become [b]like
me.
22 "Let all their wickedness come
before Thee;
And [a]deal with them as Thou
hast dealt with me
For all my transgressions;
For my groans are many, and
my heart is faint."

15 [1]Or, *feast* [a]Is. 41:2; Jer. 13:24; 37:10 [b]Jer. 6:11; 18:21

16 [1]Lit., *My eye, my eye* [a]Ps. 69:20; Eccles. 4:1; Lam. 1:2

17 [a]Is. 1:15; Jer. 4:31 [b]2 Kin. 24:2-4; Jer. 12:9

18 [1]Lit., *mouth* [2]Or, *sorrow* [a]Ps. 119:75; Jer. 12:1 [b]1 Sam. 12:14, 15; Jer. 4:17

19 [1]Lit., *their soul* [a]Job 19:13-19; Lam. 1:2 [b]Jer. 14:15; Lam. 2:20

20 [1]Lit., *inward parts are in ferment* [2]Lit., *bereaves* [a]Is. 16:11; Lam. 2:11

21 [1]Lit., *evil* [a]Ps. 35:15; Jer. 50:11; Lam. 2:15 [b]Is. 14:5, 6; 47:6, 11; Jer. 30:16

22 [a]Neh. 4:4, 5; Ps. 137:7, 8

1 [a]Is. 14:12-15; Ezek. 28:14-16 [b]Is. 64:11 [c]Ps. 99:5; 132:7

2 [a]Ps. 21:9; Lam. 3:43 [b]Is. 25:12; 26:5 [c]Ps. 89:39, 40; Is. 43:28

3 [1]Lit., *Every horn* [a]Ps. 75:5, 10; Jer. 48:25 [b]Ps. 74:11; Jer. 21:4, 5 [c]Is. 42:25; Jer. 21:14

4 [a]Job 6:4; 16:13; Lam. 3:12, 13 [b]Ezek. 24:25 [c]Is. 42:25; Jer. 7:20

5 [a]Jer. 30:14 [b]Jer. 52:13; Lam. 2:2

6 [1]Lit., *booth* [2]Or, *feast* [a]Jer. 52:13 [b]Jer. 17:27; Lam. 1:4; Zeph. 3:18

7 [a]Ps. 78:59-61; Is. 64:11; Ezek. 7:20-22

CHAPTER 2

God's Anger Over Israel

HOW the Lord has covered the
daughter of Zion
With a cloud in His anger!
He has [a]cast from heaven to
earth
The [b]glory of Israel,
And has not remembered His
[c]footstool
In the day of His anger.
2 The Lord has [a]swallowed up;
He has not spared
All the habitations of Jacob.
In His wrath He has thrown
down
The strongholds of the daughter of Judah;
He has [b]brought *them* down to
the ground;
He has [c]profaned the kingdom
and its princes.
3 In fierce anger He has cut off
[1]All the [a]strength of Israel;
He has [b]drawn back His right
hand
From before the enemy.
And He has [c]burned in Jacob
like a flaming fire
Consuming round about.
4 He has bent His [a]bow like an
enemy,
He has set His right hand like
an adversary
And slain all that were [b]pleasant to the eye;
In the tent of the daughter of
Zion
He has [c]poured out His wrath
like fire.
5 The Lord has become like an
[a]enemy.
He has swallowed up Israel;
He has swallowed up all its
[b]palaces;
He has destroyed its strongholds
And multiplied in the daughter
of Judah
Mourning and moaning.
6 And He has violently treated
His [1]tabernacle like a garden
booth;
He has [a]destroyed His appointed [2]meeting place;
The LORD has [b]caused to be forgotten
The appointed feast and sabbath in Zion,
And He has despised king and
priest
In the indignation of His anger.
7 The Lord has [a]rejected His altar,

He has abandoned His sanctuary;
He [b]has delivered into the hand of the enemy
The walls of her palaces.
They have made a [c]noise in the house of the LORD
As in the day of an appointed feast.
8 The LORD [1]determined to destroy
The wall of the daughter of Zion.
He has [a]stretched out a line,
He has not restrained His hand from [2]destroying;
And He has caused rampart and wall to lament;
They have languished together.
9 Her [a]gates have sunk into the ground,
He has destroyed and broken her bars.
Her king and her princes are among the nations;
The law is no more;
Also, her prophets find
[b]No vision from the LORD.
10 The elders of the daughter of Zion
[a]Sit on the ground, they [b]are silent.
They have thrown [c]dust on their heads;
They have girded themselves with [d]sackcloth.
The virgins of Jerusalem
Have bowed their heads to the ground.
11 My eyes fail because of tears,
My [1a]spirit is greatly troubled;
My [2b]heart is poured out on the earth,
Because of the [3]destruction of the daughter of my people,
When [c]little ones and infants faint
In the streets of the city.
12 They say to their mothers,
"[a]Where is grain and wine?"
As they faint like a wounded man
In the streets of the city,
As their [b]life is poured out
On their mothers' bosom.
13 How shall I admonish you?
To what [a]shall I compare you,
O daughter of Jerusalem?
To what shall I liken you as I comfort you,
O virgin daughter of Zion?
For your [1]ruin is as vast as the sea;
Who can [b]heal you?
14 Your [a]prophets have seen for you
False and foolish visions;
And they have not [b]exposed your iniquity
So as to restore you from captivity,
But they have [c]seen for you false and misleading [1]oracles.
15 All who pass along the way
[a]Clap their hands *in derision* at you;
They hiss and [b]shake their heads
At the daughter of Jerusalem,
"Is this the city of which they said,
'[c]The perfection of beauty,
[d]A joy to all the earth'?"
16 All [a]your enemies
Have opened their mouths wide against you;
They hiss and gnash *their* teeth.
They say, "We have [b]swallowed *her* up!
Surely this is the [c]day for which we waited;
We have reached *it,* we have seen *it.*"
17 The LORD has done what He purposed;
He has accomplished His word
Which He commanded from days of old.
He has thrown down without sparing,
And He has caused the enemy to [a]rejoice over you;
He has [b]exalted the [1]might of your adversaries.
18 Their [a]heart cried out to the Lord,
"O [b]wall of the daughter of Zion,
Let *your* tears run down like a river day and night;
Give yourself no relief;
Let your [1]eyes have no rest.
19 "Arise, cry aloud in the [a]night
At the beginning of the night watches;
Pour [b]out your heart like water
Before the presence of the Lord;
Lift up your hands to Him
For the life of your little ones
Who are [c]faint because of hunger
At the head of every street."
20 See, O LORD, and look!
With [a]whom hast Thou dealt thus?
Should women eat their [1]offspring,
The little ones who were [2]born healthy?
Should [b]priest and prophet be slain
In the sanctuary of the Lord?

7 [b]Jer. 33:4, 5; 52:13 [c]Ps. 74:3-8

8 [1]Lit., *thought* [2]Lit., *swallowing up* [a]2 Kin. 21:13; Is. 34:11; Amos 7:7-9

9 [a]Neh. 1:3 [b]Jer. 14:14; 23:16; Ezek. 7:26

10 [a]Job 2:13; Is. 3:26; 47:1 [b]Amos 8:3 [c]Job 2:12; Ezek. 27:30 [d]Is. 15:3; Jon. 3:6-8

11 [1]Lit., *inward parts are in ferment* [2]Lit., *liver* [3]Lit., *breaking* [a]Jer. 4:19 [b]Job 16:13 [c]Jer. 44:7; Lam. 2:19

12 [a]Jer. 1:11; 5:17 [b]Job 30:16; Ps. 42:4; 62:8

13 [1]Lit., *breaking* [a]Lam. 1:12 [b]Jer. 8:22; 30:12-15

14 [1]Lit., *burdens* [a]Jer. 23:25-29; 29:8, 9 [b]Is. 58:1; Mic. 3:8; Ezek. 23:36 [c]Jer. 23:36; Ezek. 22:25, 28

15 [a]Job 27:23; Ezek. 25:6 [b]Ps. 22:7; Is. 37:22; Jer. 18:16 [c]Ps. 50:2 [d]Ps. 48:2

16 [a]Job 16:10; Ps. 22:13; Lam. 3:46 [b]Ps. 56:2; 124:3; Jer. 51:34 [c]Obad. 12-15

17 [1]Lit., *horn* [a]Ps. 35:24, 26; 89:42; Is. 14:29 [b]Deut. 28:43, 44; Lam. 1:5

18 [1]Lit., *the daughter of your eye* [a]Ps. 119:145; Hos. 7:14 [b]Lam. 2:8; Hab. 2:11

19 [a]Ps. 42:3; Is. 26:9 [b]1 Sam. 1:15; Ps. 42:4; 62:8 [c]Is. 51:20

20 [1]Lit., *fruit* [2]Or, *tenderly cared for* [a]Ex. 32:11; Deut. 9:26 [b]Ps. 78:64; Jer. 14:15; 23:11, 12

21 On the ground in the streets
Lie [a]young and old,
My virgins and my young men
Have fallen by the sword.
Thou hast slain *them* in the day of Thine anger,
Thou hast slaughtered, not sparing.
22 Thou didst call as in the day of an appointed feast
My [a]terrors on every side;
And there was [b]no one who escaped or survived
In the day of the LORD's anger.
Those [c]whom I [1]bore and reared,
My enemy annihilated them.

CHAPTER 3

Jeremiah Shares Israel's Affliction

I AM the man who has seen affliction
Because of the rod of His wrath.
2 He has driven me and made me walk
In [a]darkness and not in light.
3 Surely against me He has [a]turned His hand
Repeatedly all the day.
4 He has caused my [a]flesh and my skin to waste away,
He has broken my bones.
5 He has [a]besieged and encompassed me with [b]bitterness and hardship.
6 In [a]dark places He has made me dwell,
Like those who have long been dead.
7 He has [a]walled *me* in so that I cannot go out;
He has made my [1b]chain heavy.
8 Even when I cry out and call for help,
He [a]shuts out my prayer.
9 He has [a]blocked my ways with hewn stone;
He has made my paths crooked.
10 He is to me like a bear lying in wait,
Like a lion in secret places.
11 He has turned aside my ways and [a]torn me to pieces;
He has made me desolate.
12 He bent His bow
And set me as a target for the arrow.
13 He made the [1]arrows of His [a]quiver
To enter into my [2]inward parts.
14 I have become a [a]laughingstock to all my people,
Their *mocking* [b]song all the day.

21 [a]Jer. 6:11
22 [1]Lit., *bore healthy* or, *tenderly cared for* [a]Ps. 31:13; Is. 24:17, 18; Jer. 6:25 [b]Jer. 11:11 [c]Jer. 16:2-4; 44:7
2 [a]Job 30:26; Is. 59:9; Jer. 4:23
3 [a]Ps. 38:2; Is. 5:25
4 [a]Ps. 31:9, 10; 38:2-8; 102:3-5
5 [a]Job 19:8 [b]Ps. 69:21; Jer. 23:15; Lam. 3:19
6 [a]Ps. 88:5, 6; 143:3
7 [1]Lit., *bronze piece* [a]Job 3:23; 19:8 [b]Jer. 40:4
8 [a]Job 30:20; Ps. 22:2
9 [a]Is. 63:17
11 [a]Job 16:12, 13; Jer. 15:3
13 [1]Lit., *sons* [2]Lit., *kidneys* [a]Jer. 5:16
14 [a]Ps. 22:6, 7; 123:3, 4; Jer. 20:7 [b]Job 30:9; Lam. 3:63
16 [a]Ps. 3:7; 58:6 [b]Prov. 20:17 [c]Jer. 6:26
17 [1]Lit., *good* [a]Is. 59:11; Jer. 12:12
18 [a]Job 17:15; Ezek. 37:11
19 [1]Or, *bitterness* [a]Jer. 9:15; Lam. 3:5, 15
20 [a]Ps. 42:5, 6, 11; 43:5; 44:25
21 [a]Ps. 130:7
22 [1]Or, *that we are not consumed* [a]Ps. 78:38; Jer. 3:12; 30:11 [b]Mal. 3:6
23 [a]Zeph. 3:5
24 [a]Ps. 16:5; 73:26 [b]Ps. 23:18
25 [1]Lit., *soul* [a]Ps. 27:14; Is. 25:9 [b]Is. 26:9
29 [1]Lit., *give* [a]Job 16:15; 40:4 [b]Jer. 31:17
30 [1]Lit., *his* [a]Job 16:10; Is. 50:6
31 [a]Ps. 77:7, 10; Is. 54:7-10
32 [a]Ps. 78:38; 106:43-45; Hos. 11:8
33 [1]Lit., *from His heart*
34 [1]Or, *earth*
35 [1]Or, *turn aside a man's case* [a]Ps. 140:12; Prov. 17:15

15 He has filled me with bitterness,
He has made me drunk with wormwood.
16 And He has [a]broken my teeth with [b]gravel;
He has made me cower in the [c]dust.
17 And my soul has been rejected [a]from peace;
I have forgotten [1]happiness.
18 So I say, "My strength has perished,
And *so has* my [a]hope from the LORD."

Hope of Relief in God's Mercy

19 Remember my affliction and my [1]wandering, the [a]wormwood and bitterness.
20 Surely my soul remembers
And is [a]bowed down within me.
21 This I recall to my mind,
Therefore I have [a]hope.
22 The LORD's [a]lovingkindnesses [1]indeed never cease,
[b]For His compassions never fail.
23 *They* are new [a]every morning;
Great is Thy faithfulness.
24 "The LORD is my [a]portion," says my soul,
"Therefore I [b]have hope in Him."
25 The LORD is good to those who [a]wait for Him,
To the [1]person who [b]seeks Him.
26 *It is* good that he waits silently
For the salvation of the LORD.
27 *It is* good for a man that he should bear
The yoke in his youth.
28 Let him sit alone and be silent
Since He has laid *it* on him.
29 Let him [1]put his mouth in the [a]dust,
Perhaps there is [b]hope.
30 Let him give his [a]cheek to [1]the smiter;
Let him be filled with reproach.
31 For the Lord will [a]not reject forever,
32 For if He causes grief,
Then He will have [a]compassion
According to His abundant lovingkindness.
33 For He does not afflict [1]willingly,
Or grieve the sons of men.
34 To crush under His feet
All the prisoners of the [1]land,
35 To [1]deprive a man of [a]justice
In the presence of the Most High,

36 To [1a]defraud a man in his lawsuit—
Of these things the Lord does
not [2]approve.
37 Who is [1]there who speaks and
it comes to pass,
Unless the Lord has com-
manded *it*?
38 *Is it* not from the mouth of the
Most High
That [1]both good and ill [a]go
forth?

39 Why should *any* living [1]mortal,
or *any* man,
Offer [a]complaint [2]in view of his
sins?
40 Let us [a]examine and probe our
ways,
And let us return to the LORD.
41 We [a]lift up our heart [1]and
hands
Toward God in heaven;
42 We have [a]transgressed and rebelled,
Thou hast not pardoned.
43 Thou hast covered *Thyself* with
anger
And pursued us;
Thou hast slain *and* hast not
spared.
44 Thou hast covered Thyself with
a cloud
So that [a]no prayer can pass
through.
45 *Mere* offscouring and refuse
Thou hast made us
In the midst of the peoples.
46 All our enemies have [a]opened
their mouths against us.
47 [a]Panic and pitfall have befallen
us,
Devastation and destruction;
48 My eyes run down with streams
of water
Because of the destruction of
the daughter of my people.
49 My eyes pour down [a]unceas-
ingly,
Without stopping,
50 Until the LORD [a]looks down
And sees from heaven.
51 My [1]eyes bring pain to my soul
Because of all the daughters of
my city.
52 My enemies [a]without cause
Hunted me down [b]like a bird;
53 They have silenced [1]me in the
pit
And have [2]placed a stone on
me.
54 Waters flowed [a]over my head;
I said, "I am cut off!"
55 I called on Thy name, O LORD,
Out of the lowest pit.
56 Thou hast [a]heard my voice,
"Do not [b]hide Thine ear from my
prayer for relief,
From my cry for help."
57 Thou didst [a]draw near when I
called on Thee;
Thou didst say, "Do not [b]fear!"
58 O Lord, Thou didst [a]plead my
soul's cause;
Thou hast [b]redeemed my life.
59 O LORD, Thou hast [a]seen my oppression;
[b]Judge my case.
60 Thou hast seen all their vengeance,
All their schemes against me.
61 Thou hast heard their [a]re-
proach, O LORD,
All their schemes against me.
62 The [a]lips of my assailants and
their whispering
Are against me all day long.
63 Look on their sitting and their
rising;
[a]I am their mocking song.
64 Thou wilt [a]recompense them, O
LORD,
According to the work of their
hands.
65 Thou wilt give them [1a]hardness
of heart,
Thy curse will be on them.
66 Thou wilt pursue them in anger
and destroy them
From under the heavens of the
LORD!

CHAPTER 4

Distress of the Siege Described

HOW [a]dark the gold has become,
How the pure gold has
changed!
The sacred stones are poured
out
At the [1]corner of every street.
2 The precious sons of Zion,
Weighed against fine gold,
How they are regarded as
[a]earthen jars,
The work of a potter's hands!
3 Even [a]jackals offer the breast,
They nurse their young;
But the daughter of my people
has become [b]cruel
Like ostriches in the wilder-
ness.
4 The tongue of the infant cleaves
To the roof of its mouth be-
cause of [a]thirst;
The little ones ask for bread,
But no one breaks *it* for them.
5 Those who ate delicacies
Are desolate in the streets;
Those [1]reared in purple
Embrace ash pits.

36 [1]Lit., *make crooked* [2]Lit., *see* [a]Jer. 22:3; Hab. 1:13
37 [1]Lit., *this*
38 [1]Lit., *the evil things and the good* [a]Job 2:10; Is. 45:7; Jer. 32:42
39 [1]Or, *human being* [2]Or, *on the basis of* [a]Jer. 30:15; Mic. 7:9; Heb. 12:5, 6
40 [a]Ps. 119:59; 139:23, 24; 2 Cor. 13:5
41 [1]Lit., *to* [a]Ps. 25:1; 28:2; 141:2
42 [a]Neh. 9:26; Jer. 14:20; Dan. 9:5
44 [a]Lam. 3:8; Zech. 7:13
46 [a]Job 30:9, 10; Ps. 22:6-8; Lam. 2:16
47 [a]Is. 24:17, 18; Jer. 48:43, 44
49 [a]Ps. 77:2; Jer. 14:17
50 [a]Ps. 80:14; Is. 63:15; Lam. 5:1
51 [1]Lit., *eye*
52 [a]Ps. 35:7, 19 [b]1 Sam. 26:20; Ps. 11:1; 124:7
53 [1]Lit., *my life* [2]Or, *cast stones*
54 [a]Ps. 69:2; Jon. 2:3-5
56 [a]Job 34:28; Ps. 116:12 [b]Ps. 55:1
57 [a]Ps. 145:18 [b]Is. 41:10, 14
58 [a]Jer. 50:34 [b]Ps. 34:22
59 [a]Jer. 18:19, 20 [b]Ps. 26:1; 43:1
61 [a]Ps. 74:18; 89:50; Lam. 5:1; Zeph. 2:8
62 [a]Ps. 59:7, 12; 140:3; Ezek. 36:3
63 [a]Job 30:9; Lam. 3:14
64 [a]Ps. 28:4; Jer. 51:6, 24, 56
65 [1]Or, *insolence* [a]Ex. 14:8; Deut. 2:30; Is. 6:10
1 [1]Lit., *head* [a]2 Kin. 25:9, 10; Ezek. 7:19-22
2 [a]Is. 30:14; Jer. 19:1, 11
3 [a]Is. 13:22; 34:13 [b]Is. 49:15; Ezek. 5:10
4 [a]Jer. 14:3
5 [1]Lit., *established in crimson*

6 For the [1]iniquity of the daughter of my people
Is greater than the [2]sin of Sodom,
Which was [a]overthrown as in a moment,
And no hands were [3]turned toward her.
7 Her [1]consecrated ones were [a]purer than snow,
They were whiter than milk;
They were more ruddy *in* [2]body than corals,
Their polishing *was* like [3]lapis lazuli.
8 Their appearance is [a]blacker than soot,
They are not recognized in the streets;
Their skin is shriveled on their bones,
It is withered, it has become like wood.
9 Better are those [1]slain with the sword
Than those [1]slain with hunger;
For they [2a]pine away, being stricken
For lack of the fruits of [3]the field.
10 The hands of compassionate women
[a]Boiled their own children;
They became [b]food for them
Because of the destruction of the daughter of my people.
11 The LORD has accomplished His wrath,
He has poured out His fierce anger;
And He has kindled a fire in Zion
Which has consumed its foundations.
12 The kings of the earth did not believe,
Nor *did* any of the inhabitants of the world,
That the adversary and the enemy
Could [a]enter the gates of Jerusalem.
13 Because of the sins of her prophets
And the iniquities of her priests,
Who have shed in her midst
The [a]blood of the righteous,
14 They wandered, [a]blind, in the streets;
They were defiled with blood
So that no one could touch their garments.
15 "Depart! [a]Unclean!" [1]they cried of themselves.
"Depart, depart, do not touch!"

6 [1]Or, *punishment for iniquity* [2]Or, *punishment for sin* [3]Or, *wrung over her* [a]Gen. 19:25; Jer. 20:16

7 [1]Or, *Nazirites* [2]Lit., *bones* [3]Heb., *sappir* [a]Ps. 51:7

8 [a]Job 30:30; Lam. 5:10, 14

9 [1]Lit., *pierced* [2]Lit., *flow away* [3]Lit., *my fields* [a]Lev. 26:39; Ezek. 24:23

10 [a]2 Kin. 6:29; Jer. 19:9; Lam. 2:20 [b]Deut. 28:53-55

12 [a]Jer. 21:13

13 [a]Jer. 2:30; 26:8, 9

14 [a]Deut. 28:28, 29; Is. 29:10; 56:10; 59:9, 10

15 [1]Or, *they* (men) *cried to them* [a]Lev. 13:45, 46

16 [1]Lit., *lift up the faces of* [a]Is. 9:14-16; Jer. 52:24-27

17 [1]Lit., *our help* [a]Jer. 37:7; Lam. 1:7 [b]Ezek. 29:6, 7, 16

18 [1]Lit., *full* [a]Jer. 16:16 [b]Jer. 5:31; Ezek. 7:2-12; Amos 8:2

19 [a]Is. 5:26-28; 30:16, 17; Jer. 4:13; Hab. 1:8 [b]1 Sam. 13:6

20 [a]Jer. 39:5 [b]Dan. 4:12

22 [a]Is. 40:2; Jer. 33:7, 8 [b]Jer. 49:10; Mal. 1:3, 4

1 [a]Ps. 44:13-16

2 [a]Is. 1:7; Hos. 8:7, 8

3 [a]Ex. 22:24; Jer. 15:8; 18:21

4 [1]Lit., *We drink our water for silver* [a]Is. 3:1

So they fled and wandered;
Men among the nations said,
"They shall not continue to dwell *with us.*"
16 The presence of the LORD has scattered them;
He will not continue to regard them.
They did not [1a]honor the priests,
They did not favor the elders.
17 Yet our eyes failed;
Looking for [1]help was [a]useless.
In our watching we have watched
For a [b]nation that could not save.
18 They [a]hunted our steps
So that we could not walk in our streets;
Our [b]end drew near,
Our days were [1]finished
For our end had come.
19 Our pursuers were [a]swifter
Than the eagles of the sky.
They chased us on the mountains;
They waited in ambush for us in the [b]wilderness.
20 The breath of our nostrils, the LORD's anointed,
Was [a]captured in their pits,
Of whom we had said, "Under his [b]shadow
We shall live among the nations."
21 Rejoice and be glad, O daughter of Edom,
Who dwells in the land of Uz;
But the cup will come around to you as well,
You will become drunk and make yourself naked.
22 *The punishment* of your iniquity has been [a]completed, O daughter of Zion;
He [b]will exile you no longer.
But He will punish your iniquity, O daughter of Edom;
He will expose your sins!

CHAPTER 5

A Prayer for Mercy

REMEMBER, O LORD, what has befallen us;
Look, and see our [a]reproach!
2 Our inheritance has been turned over to [a]strangers,
Our houses to aliens.
3 We have become orphans [a]without a father,
Our mothers are like widows.
4 [1]We have to pay for our drinking [a]water,
Our wood comes *to us* at a price.

5 [1]Our pursuers are at our necks;
We are worn out, there is [a]no rest for us.
6 We have [1]submitted to Egypt *and* Assyria to get enough bread.
7 Our [a]fathers sinned, *and* are no more;
It is we who have borne their iniquities.
8 [a]Slaves rule over us;
There is [b]no one to deliver us from their hand.
9 We get our bread [1]at the [a]risk of our lives
Because of the sword in the wilderness.
10 Our skin has become as [a]hot as an oven,
Because of [1]the burning heat of famine.
11 They ravished the [a]women in Zion,
The virgins in the cities of Judah.
12 Princes were hung by their hands;
[a]Elders were not respected.
13 Young men [1]worked at the grinding mill;
And youths stumbled under *loads* of wood.
14 Elders are gone from the gate,
Young men from their [a]music.
15 The joy of our hearts has [a]ceased;
Our dancing has been turned into mourning.
16 The [a]crown has fallen from our head;
Woe to us, for we have sinned!
17 Because of this our [a]heart is faint;
Because of these things our [b]eyes are dim;
18 Because of Mount Zion which lies desolate,
Foxes prowl in it.

19 Thou, O LORD, dost [1]rule forever;
Thy [a]throne is from generation to generation.
20 Why dost Thou [a]forget us forever;
Why dost Thou forsake us so long?
21 [a]Restore us to Thee, O LORD, that we may be restored;
Renew [b]our days as of old,
22 Unless [a]Thou hast utterly rejected us,
And art exceedingly [b]angry with us.

5 [1]Lit., *We have been pursued upon* [a]Neh. 9:36, 37
6 [1]Lit., *given the hand to*
7 [a]Jer. 14:20; 16:12
8 [a]Neh. 5:15 [b]Ps. 7:2; Zech. 11:6
9 [1]Lit., *with our soul* [a]Jer. 40:9-12
10 [1]Or, *the ravages of hunger* [a]Job 30:30; Lam. 4:8
11 [a]Is. 13:16; Zech. 14:2
12 [a]Is. 47:6; Lam. 4:16
13 [1]Lit., *carry*
14 [a]Is. 24:8; Jer. 7:34
15 [a]Jer. 25:10; Amos 8:10
16 [a]Job 19:9; Ps. 89:39; Jer. 13:18
17 [a]Is. 1:5 [b]Job 17:7; Lam. 2:11
19 [1]Lit., *sit* [a]Ps. 45:6
20 [a]Ps. 13:1; 44:24
21 [a]Ps. 80:3; Jer. 31:18 [b]Is. 60:20-22
22 [a]Ps. 60:1, 2; Jer. 7:29 [b]Is. 64:9

THE BOOK OF EZEKIEL

The Vision of Four Figures

NOW it came about in the thirtieth year, on the fifth *day* of the fourth month, while I was by the river Chebar among the exiles, the [a]heavens were opened and I saw [1b]visions of God.

2 (On the fifth of the month in the [a]fifth year of King Jehoiachin's exile,

3 the word of the LORD came expressly to Ezekiel the priest, son of Buzi, in the land of the Chaldeans by the river Chebar; and there the hand of the LORD came upon him.)

4 And as I looked, behold, a [a]storm wind was coming from the north, a great cloud with fire flashing forth continually and a bright light around it, and in its midst something like glowing metal in the midst of the fire.

5 And within it there were figures resembling [a]four living beings. And this was their appearance: they had human [b]form.

6 Each of them had [a]four faces and [b]four wings.

7 And their legs were straight and their feet were like a calf's hoof, and they gleamed like [a]burnished bronze.

8 Under their wings on their [a]four sides *were* human [b]hands. As for the faces and wings of the four of them,

9 their wings touched one another; their *faces* did not turn when they moved, each [a]went straight forward.

10 As for the [a]form of their faces, *each* had the [b]face of a man, [1]all four had the face of a lion on the right and the face of a bull on the left, and all four had the face of an eagle.

11 Such were their faces. Their wings were spread out above; each had two touching another *being*, and [a]two covering their bodies.

12 And each went straight forward; [a]wherever the spirit was about to go, they would go, without turning as they went.

13 In the midst of the living beings there was something that looked like burning coals of [a]fire, like torches darting back and forth

1 [1]Or, *a vision* [a]Matt. 3:16; Mark 1:10; Luke 3:21; John 1:15; Acts 7:56; 10:11; Rev. 4:1; 19:11 [b]Ex. 24:10; Num. 12:6; Is. 1:1; 6:1; Ezek. 8:3; 11:24; 40:2; Dan. 8:1, 2
2 [a]2 Kin. 24:12-15; Ezek. 8:1; 20:1
4 [a]Is. 21:1; Jer. 23:19; Ezek. 13:11, 13
5 [a]Ezek. 10:15, 17, 20; Rev. 4:6-8 [b]Ezek. 1:26
6 [a]Ezek 1:10; 10:14, 21 [b]Ezek. 1:23
7 [a]Rev. 1:15; 2:13
8 [a]Ezek. 1:17; 10:11 [b]Ezek. 10:8
9 [a]Ezek. 1:12
10 [a]Rev. 4:7 [b]Ezek. 10:14
11 [a]Is. 6:2; Ezek. 1:23
12 [a]Ezek. 1:20
13 [a]Ps. 104:4

among the living beings. The fire was bright, and lightning was flashing from the fire.

14 And the living beings [a]ran to and fro like bolts of [b]lightning.

15 Now as I looked at the living beings, behold, there was one [a]wheel on the earth beside the living beings, for *each of* the four of them.

16 The [a]appearance of the wheels and their workmanship *was* like sparkling [b]beryl, and all four of them had the same form, their appearance and workmanship *being* as if one wheel were within another.

17 Whenever they [1]moved, they [1]moved in any of their four [2]directions, without [a]turning as they [1]moved.

18 As for their rims they were lofty and awesome, and the rims of all four of them were [a]full of eyes round about.

19 And [a]whenever the living beings [1]moved, the wheels [1]moved with them. And whenever the living beings [b]rose from the earth, the wheels rose *also*.

20 [a]Wherever the spirit was about to go, they would go in that direction[1]. And the wheels rose close beside them; for the spirit of the living [2]beings *was* in the wheels.

21 [a]Whenever those went, these went; and whenever those stood still, these stood still. And whenever those rose from the earth, the wheels rose close beside them; for the spirit of the living [1]beings *was* in the wheels.

Vision of Divine Glory

22 Now [a]over the heads of the living [1]beings *there was* something like an expanse, like the awesome gleam of crystal, extended over their heads.

23 And under the expanse their wings *were stretched out* straight, one toward the other; each one also had [a]two wings covering their bodies on the one side and on the other.

24 I also heard the sound of their wings like the [a]sound of abundant waters as they went, like the [b]voice of [1]the Almighty, a sound of tumult like the [c]sound of an army camp; whenever they stood still, they dropped their wings.

25 And there came a voice from above the [a]expanse that was over their heads; whenever they stood still, they dropped their wings.

26 Now [a]above the expanse that was over their heads there was something [b]resembling a throne, like [1c]lapis lazuli in appearance; and on that which resembled a throne, high up, *was* a figure with the appearance of a [d]man.

27 Then I noticed from the appearance of His loins and upward something [a]like [1]glowing metal that looked like fire all around within it, and from the appearance of His loins and downward I saw something like fire; and *there was* a radiance around Him.

28 As the appearance of the [a]rainbow in the clouds on a rainy day, so *was* the appearance of the surrounding radiance. Such *was* the appearance of the likeness of the glory of the LORD. And when I saw *it,* I [b]fell on my face and heard a voice speaking.

CHAPTER 2

The Prophet's Call

THEN He said to me, "Son of man, [a]stand on your feet that I may speak with you!"

2 And as He spoke to me the [a]Spirit entered me and set me on my feet; and I heard *Him* speaking to me.

3 Then He said to me, "Son of man, I am sending you to the sons of Israel, to a rebellious people who have [a]rebelled against Me; [b]they and their fathers have transgressed against Me to this very day.

4 "And I am sending you to them who are [1a]stubborn and obstinate children; and you shall say to them, 'Thus says the Lord [2]GOD.'

5 "As for them, [a]whether they listen or not—for they are a rebellious house—they will [b]know that a prophet has been among them.

6 "And you, son of man, [a]neither fear them nor fear their words, though [b]thistles and thorns are with you and you sit on scorpions; neither fear their words nor be dismayed at their presence, for they are a rebellious house.

7 "But you shall [a]speak My words to them whether they listen or not, for they are rebellious.

8 "Now you, son of man, listen to what I am speaking to you; do not be rebellious like that rebellious house. Open your mouth and [a]eat what I am giving you."

9 Then I looked, behold, a hand was extended to me; and lo, a [a]scroll *was* in it.

10 When He spread it out before

14 [a]Zech. 4:10 [b]Matt. 24:27; Luke 17:24
15 [a]Ezek. 1:19-21
16 [a]Ezek. 10:9-11 [b]Ezek. 10:9; Dan. 10:6
17 [1]Lit., *went* [2]Lit., *sides* [a]Ezek. 1:9, 12
18 [a]Ezek. 10:12; Rev. 4:6, 8
19 [1]Lit., *went* [a]Ezek. 10:16 [b]Ezek. 10:19
20 [1]M.T. adds: *the spirit to go* [2]M.T. reads: *being* [a]Ezek. 1:12
21 [1]M.T. reads: *being* [a]Ezek. 10:17
22 [1]Or, *being* [a]Ezek. 10:1
23 [a]Ezek. 1:6, 11
24 [1]Heb., *Shaddai* [a]Ezek. 43:2; Rev. 1:15; 19:6 [b]Ezek. 10:5 [c]2 Kin. 7:6; Dan. 10:6
25 [a]Ezek. 1:22
26 [1]Heb., *eben-sappir* [a]Ezek. 1:22; 10:1 [b]Is. 6:1; Ezek. 10:1; Dan. 7-9 [c]Ex. 24:10; Is. 54:11 [d]Ezek. 43:6, 7; Rev. 1:13
27 [1]Or, *electrum* [a]Ezek. 1:4; 8:2
28 [a]Gen. 9:13; Rev. 4:3; 10:1 [b]Gen. 17:3; Ezek. 3:23; Dan. 8:17; Rev. 1:17
1 [a]Dan. 10:11; Acts 9:6
2 [a]Ezek. 3:24; Dan. 8:18
3 [a]1 Sam. 8:7, 8; Jer. 3:25 [b]Ezek. 20:18, 30
4 [1]Lit., *the sons, stiff-faced and hard-hearted* [2]Heb., YHWH, usually rendered LORD [a]Ps. 95:8; Is. 48:4; Jer. 5:3; 6:15; Ezek. 3:7
5 [a]Ezek. 2:7; 3:11, 27; Matt. 10:12-15; Acts 13:46 [b]Ezek. 33:33; Luke 10:10, 11; John 15:22
6 [a]Is. 51:12; Jer. 1:8, 17; Ezek. 3:9 [b]2 Sam. 23:6, 7; Ezek. 28:24; Mic. 7:4
7 [a]Jer. 1:7, 17; Ezek. 3:10, 17
8 [a]Jer. 15:16; Ezek. 3:3
9 [a]Jer. 36:2; Ezek. 3:1; Rev. 5:1-5; 10:8-11

me, it was written on the front and
back; and written on it were lamentations, mourning and [a]woe.

CHAPTER 3

Ezekiel's Commission

THEN He said to me, "Son of man,
eat what you find; eat this scroll,
and go, speak to the house of Israel."
2 So I [a]opened my mouth, and He
fed me this scroll.
3 And He said to me, "Son of
man, feed your stomach, and [a]fill
your [1]body with this scroll which I
am giving you." Then I [b]ate it, and it
was sweet as [c]honey in my mouth.
4 Then He said to me, "Son of
man, [1]go to the house of Israel and
speak with My words to them.
5"For [a]you are not being sent to a
people of [1b]unintelligible speech or
difficult language, *but* to the house
of Israel,
6 nor to many peoples of [1]unin-
telligible speech or difficult language, whose words you cannot understand. [2]But I have sent you to
them [3]who should listen to you;
7 yet the house of Israel will not
be willing to listen to you, since they
are not willing to listen to Me.
Surely the whole house of Israel is
[1]stubborn and obstinate.
8"Behold, I have made your face
as hard as their faces, and your forehead as hard as their foreheads.
9"Like [1]emery harder than flint I
have made your forehead. Do not be
afraid of them or be dismayed before them, though they are a rebellious house."
10 Moreover, He said to me, "Son
of man, take into your heart all My
[a]words which I shall speak to you,
and listen [1]closely.
11"And [1]go to the exiles, to the
sons of your people, and speak to
them and tell them, whether they
listen or [2]not, 'Thus says the Lord
[3]GOD.'"
12 Then the [a]Spirit lifted me up,
and I heard a great [b]rumbling sound
behind me, "Blessed be the glory of
the LORD [1]in His place."
13 And I *heard* the sound of the
wings of the living beings touching
one another, and the sound of the
[a]wheels beside them, even a great
rumbling sound.
14 So the Spirit lifted me up and
took me away; and I went embittered in the rage of my spirit, and
the hand of the LORD was strong on
me.

10 [a]Rev. 8:13
2 [a]Jer. 25:17
3 [1]Lit., *inward parts* [a]Jer. 6:11; 20:9 [b]Jer. 15:16 [c]Ps. 19:10; 119:103; Rev. 10:9, 10
4 [1]Lit., *go, come*
5 [1]Lit., *deepness of lip and heaviness of tongue* [a]Jon. 1:2; Acts 14:11; 26:17 [b]Is. 28:11; 33:19
6 [1]Lit., *deepness of lip and heaviness of tongue* [2]Or, *If I had sent you to them, they would listen to you.* [3]Lit., *they*
7 [1]Lit., *of a hard forehead and a stiff heart*
9 [1]Lit., *corundum*
10 [1]Lit., *with your ears* [a]Job 22:22; Ezek. 2:8; 3:1-3
11 [1]Lit., *go, come* [2]Lit., *forbear* [3]YHWH, usually rendered LORD
12 [1]Or, *from* [a]Ezek. 3:14; 8:3; Acts 8:39 [b]Acts 2:2
13 [a]Ezek. 1:15; 10:16, 17
15 [a]Job 2:13
16 [a]Jer. 42:7
17 [a]Is. 52:8; 56:10; 62:6; Jer. 6:17; Ezek. 33:7-9 [b]2 Chr. 19:10; Is. 58:1; Hab. 2:1
18 [a]Ezek. 3:20; 33:6, 8
19 [a]2 Kin. 17:13, 14; Ezek. 33:3, 9 [b]Ezek. 14:14, 20; Acts 18:6; 1 Tim. 4:16
20 [a]Ps. 125:5; Ezek. 18:24; 33:18; Zeph. 1:6 [b]Is. 8:14; Jer. 6:21; Ezek. 14:3, 7-9
21 [1]Lit., *him, the righteous* [a]Acts 20:31
22 [a]Acts 9:6
23 [a]Ezek. 1:28; Acts 7:55
24 [a]Ezek. 2:2
25 [a]Ezek. 4:8
26 [1]Lit., *your palate* [a]Hos. 4:17; Amos 8:11, 12
27 [1]YHWH, usually rendered LORD

15 Then I came to the exiles who
lived beside the river Chebar at Tel-
abib, and I sat there [a]seven days
where they were living, causing
consternation among them.
16 Now it came about [a]at the end
of seven days that the word of the
LORD came to me, saying,
17"Son of man, I have appointed
you a [a]watchman to the house of Israel; whenever you hear a word
from My mouth, [b]warn them from
Me.
18"When I say to the wicked, 'You
shall surely die'; and you do not
warn him or speak out to warn the
wicked from his wicked way that he
may live, that wicked man shall die
in his iniquity, but his [a]blood I will
require at your hand.
19"Yet if you have [a]warned the
wicked, and he does not turn from
his wickedness or from his wicked
way, he shall die in his iniquity; but
[b]you have delivered yourself.
20"Again, [a]when a righteous man
turns away from his righteousness
and commits iniquity, and I place an
[b]obstacle before him, he shall die;
since you have not warned him, he
shall die in his sin, and his righteous
deeds which he has done shall not
be remembered; but his blood I will
require at your hand.
21"However, if you have [a]warned
[1]the righteous man that the righteous should not sin, and he does not
sin, he shall surely live because he
took warning; and you have delivered yourself."
22 And the hand of the LORD was
on me there, and He said to me,
"Get up, go out to the plain, and
there I will [a]speak to you."
23 So I got up and went out to the
plain; and behold, the [a]glory of the
LORD was standing there, like the
glory which I saw by the river Chebar, and I fell on my face.
24 The [a]Spirit then entered me and
made me stand on my feet, and He
spoke with me and said to me, "Go,
shut yourself up in your house.
25"As for you, son of man, they
will [a]put ropes on you and bind you
with them, so that you cannot go out
among them.
26"Moreover, I will make your
tongue stick to [1]the roof of your
mouth so that you will be dumb, and
cannot be a man who [a]rebukes
them, for they are a rebellious
house.
27"But when I speak to you, I will
open your mouth, and you will say
to them, 'Thus says the Lord [1]GOD.'
He who hears, let him hear; and he

who refuses, let him refuse; for they are a rebellious house.

CHAPTER 4

Siege of Jerusalem Predicted

"NOW you son of man, [a]get yourself a brick, place it before you, and inscribe a city on it, Jerusalem.

2"Then [a]lay siege against it, build a siege wall, [1]raise up a ramp, pitch camps, and place battering rams against it all around.

3"Then get yourself an iron plate and set it up as an iron wall between you and the city, and set your face toward it so that [a]it is under siege, and besiege it. This is a [b]sign to the house of Israel.

4"As for you, lie down on your left side, and lay the iniquity of the house of Israel on it; you shall [a]bear their iniquity for the number of days that you lie on it.

5"For I have assigned you a number of days corresponding to the years of their iniquity, three hundred and ninety days; thus you shall bear the iniquity of the house of Israel.

6"When you have completed these, you shall lie down a second time, *but* on your right side, and bear the iniquity of the house of Judah; I have assigned it to you for forty days, a day for [a]each year.

7"Then you shall set your face toward the siege of Jerusalem with your arm bared, and [a]prophesy against it.

8"Now behold, I will [a]put ropes on you so that you cannot turn from one side to the other, until you have completed the days of your siege.

Defiled Bread

9"But as for you, take wheat, barley, beans, lentils, millet and [a]spelt, put them in one vessel and make them into bread for yourself; you shall eat it according to the number of the days that you lie on your side, three hundred and ninety days.

10"And your food which you eat *shall be* [a]twenty shekels a day by weight; you shall eat it from time to time.

11"And the water you drink will be the sixth part of a hin by measure; you shall drink it from time to time.

12"And you shall eat it as a barley cake, having baked *it* in their sight over human [a]dung."

13 Then the LORD said, "Thus shall the sons of Israel eat their bread [a]unclean among the nations where I shall banish them."

14 But I said, "[a]Ah, Lord [1]GOD! Behold, I have [b]never been defiled; for from my youth until now I have never eaten what [c]died of itself or was torn by beasts, nor has any [d]unclean meat ever entered my mouth."

15 Then He said to me, "See, I shall give you cow's dung in place of human dung over which you will prepare your bread."

16 Moreover, He said to me, "Son of man, behold, I am going to [a]break the staff of bread in Jerusalem, and they will eat bread by [b]weight and with anxiety, and drink water by [c]measure and in horror,

17 because bread and water will be scarce; and they will be appalled with one another and [a]waste away in their iniquity.

CHAPTER 5

Jerusalem's Desolation Foretold

"AS for you, son of man, take a [a]sharp sword; take and [1]use it *as* a barber's razor on your head and beard. Then take [b]scales for weighing and divide [2]the hair.

2"One third you shall burn in the fire at the center of the city, when the [a]days of the siege are completed. Then you shall take one third and strike *it* with the sword all around [1]the city, and one third you shall scatter to the wind; and I will [b]unsheathe a sword behind them.

3"Take also a [a]few in number from [1]them and bind them in the edges of your *robes*.

4"And take again some of them and throw them into the fire, and [a]burn them in the fire; from it a fire will [1]spread to all the house of Israel.

5"Thus says the Lord [1]GOD, 'This is [a]Jerusalem; I have set her at the [b]center of the nations, with lands around her.

6 'But she has rebelled against My ordinances more wickedly than the nations and against My statutes [a]more than the lands which surround her; for they have [b]rejected My ordinances and have not walked [1]in My statutes.'

7"Therefore, thus says the Lord GOD, 'Because you have [a]more turmoil than the nations which surround you, and have not walked in My statutes, nor observed My ordinances, nor observed the ordinances of the nations which surround you,'

---

1 [a]Ex. 5:1; 12:3; Is. 20:2; Jer. 13:1; 18:2; 19:1
2 [1]Lit., *cast* [a]Jer. 6:6; Ezek. 21:22
3 [a]Jer. 39:1, 2; Ezek. 5:2 [b]Is. 8:18; 20:3; Ezek. 12:6, 11; 24:24-27
4 [a]Lev. 10:17; 16:22; Num. 18:1
6 [a]Num. 14:34; Dan. 9:24-26; 12:11, 12; Rev. 11:2, 3
7 [a]Ezek. 21:2
8 [a]Ezek. 3:25
9 [a]Ex. 9:32; Is. 28:25
10 [a]Ezek. 45:12
12 [a]Is. 36:12
13 [a]Dan. 1:8; Hos. 9:3
14 [1]YHWH, usually rendered LORD [a]Jer. 1:6; Ezek. 9:8; 20:49 [b]Acts 10:14 [c]Lev. 17:15; 22:8; Ezek. 44:31 [d]Deut. 14:3; Is. 65:4; 66:17
16 [a]Lev. 26:26; Is. 3:1; Ezek. 5:16; 14:13 [b]Ezek. 4:10, 11; 12:19 [c]Lam. 5:4; Ezek. 12:18, 19
17 [a]Ezek. 24:23; 33:10
1 [1]Lit., *make it pass over your head* [2]Lit., *them* [a]Lev. 21:5; Is. 7:20; Ezek. 44:20 [b]Dan. 5:27
2 [1]Lit., *it* [a]Jer. 39:1, 2; Ezek. 4:2-8 [b]Lev. 26:33
3 [1]Lit., *there* [a]2 Kin. 25:12; Jer. 39:10
4 [1]Lit., *go out* [a]Jer. 42:16, 17, 22
5 [1]YHWH, usually rendered LORD, and so throughout the chap. [a]Jer. 6:6; Ezek. 4:1 [b]Deut. 4:6; Lam. 1:1; Ezek. 16:14
6 [1]Lit., *in them, My statutes* [a]2 Kin. 17:8-20; Ezek. 16:47, 48, 51 [b]Neh. 9:16, 17; Ps. 78:10; Jer. 11:10; Zech. 7:11
7 [a]2 Kin. 21:9-11; 2 Chr. 33:9; Jer. 2:10, 11

8 therefore, thus says the Lord
GOD, 'Behold, I, even I, am [a]against
you, and I will [b]execute judgments
among you in the sight of the nations.
9 'And because of all your abominations, I will do among you what I
have [a]not done, and the like of
which I will never do again.
10 'Therefore, [a]fathers will eat
their sons among you, and sons will
eat their fathers; for I will execute
judgments on you, and [b]scatter all
your remnant to every wind.
11 'So as I live,' declares the Lord
GOD, 'surely, because you have [a]de-
filed My sanctuary with all your [b]de-
testable idols and with all your
abominations, therefore I will also
[c]withdraw, and My eye shall have
no pity and I will not spare.
12 'One third of you will die by
[a]plague or be consumed by famine
among you, one third will fall by the
sword around you, and one third I
will [b]scatter to every wind, and I
will [c]unsheathe a sword behind
them.
13 'Thus My anger will be spent,
and I will [1]satisfy My wrath on
them, and I shall be [2a]appeased;
then they will know that I, the LORD,
have [b]spoken in My zeal when I
have spent My wrath upon them.
14 'Moreover, I will make you a
desolation and a [a]reproach among
the nations which surround you, in
the sight of all who pass by.
15 'So [1]it will be a reproach, a reviling, a [a]warning and an object of horror to the nations who surround
you, when I [b]execute judgments
against you in anger, wrath, and
raging rebukes. I, the LORD, have
spoken.
16 'When I send against them the
[1]deadly arrows of famine which
were for the destruction of those
whom I shall send to destroy you,
then I shall also intensify the famine
upon you, and break the staff of
bread.
17 'Moreover, I will send on you
famine and wild beasts, and they
will bereave you of children; plague
and bloodshed also will pass
through you, and I will bring the
sword on you. I, the LORD, have spoken.' "

CHAPTER 6

Idolatrous Worship Denounced

AND the word of the LORD came to
me saying,
2 "Son of man, set your face
toward the mountains of Israel, and
prophesy against them,
3 and say, 'Mountains of Israel,
listen to the word of the Lord [1]GOD!
Thus says the Lord [1]GOD to the
mountains, the hills, the ravines and
the valleys: "Behold, I Myself am
going to bring a sword on you, and I
will destroy your high places.
4 "So your [a]altars will become
desolate, and your incense altars
will be smashed; and I shall make
your slain fall in front of your idols.
5 "I shall also lay the dead bodies
of the sons of Israel in front of their
idols; and I shall scatter your [a]bones
around your altars.
6 "In all your dwellings, [a]cities
will become waste and the high
places will be desolate, that your altars may become waste and [1]deso-
late, your [b]idols may be broken and
brought to an end, your incense altars may be cut down, and your
works may be blotted out.
7 "And the slain will fall among
you, and you will know that I am the
LORD.
8 "However, I shall leave a [a]rem-
nant, for you will have those who
[b]escaped the sword among the nations when you are scattered among
the countries.
9 "Then those of you who escape
will [a]remember Me among the nations to which they will be carried
captive, how I have [b]been hurt by
their adulterous hearts which
turned away from Me, and by their
eyes, which played the harlot after
their idols; and they will [c]loathe
themselves in their own sight for the
evils which they have committed,
for all their abominations.
10 "Then they will know that I am
the LORD; I have not said in vain
[1]that I would inflict this disaster on
them." '
11 "Thus says the Lord [1]GOD, 'Clap
your hand, [a]stamp your foot, and
say, "[b]Alas, because of all the evil
abominations of the house of Israel,
which will fall by [c]sword, famine,
and plague!
12 "He who is [a]far off will die by the
plague, and he who is near will fall
by the sword, and he who remains
and is besieged will die by the famine. Thus shall I [b]spend My wrath on
them.
13 "Then you will know that I am
the LORD, when their [a]slain are
among their idols around their altars, on [b]every high hill, on all the
tops of the mountains, under every
green tree, and under every leafy

8 [a]Jer. 21:5, 13; Ezek. 15:7; 21:3; Zech. 14:2 [b]Jer. 24:9; Ezek. 5:15; 11:9
9 [a]Dan. 9:12; Matt. 24:21
10 [a]Lev. 26:29; Jer. 19:9 [b]Ps. 44:11; Ezek. 5:2, 12; 6:8; 12:14; Amos 9:9; Zech. 2:6; 7:14
11 [a]Jer. 7:9-11; Ezek. 8:5, 6, 16 [b]Jer. 16:18; Ezek. 7:20 [c]Ps. 107:39
12 [a]Jer. 15:2; 21:9; Ezek. 5:17; 6:11, 12 [b]Ezek. 5:2, 10; Amos 9:9; Zech. 2:6 [c]Jer. 43:10, 11; 44:27; Ezek. 5:2; 12:14
13 [1]Lit., *cause to rest* [2]Lit., *comforted* [a]Is. 1:24 [b]Is. 59:17; Ezek. 36:5, 6; 38:19
14 [a]Ps. 74:3-10; 79:1-4; Ezek. 22:4
15 [1]Ancient versions: *you* [a] Is. 26:9; Jer. 22:8, 9; 1 Cor. 10:11 [b]Is. 66:15, 16; Ezek. 5:8; 25:17
16 [1]Lit., *evil*
3 [1]YHWH, usually rendered LORD
4 [a]Lev. 26:30; 2 Chr. 14:5; Is. 27:9; Ezek. 6:6
5 [a]2 Kin. 23:14, 16, 20; Jer. 8:1, 2
6 [1]So some ancient versions; Heb., *bear their guilt* [a]Lev. 26:31; Is. 6:11; Ezek. 5:14 [b]Ezek. 6:4; Mic. 1:7; Zech. 13:2
8 [a]Is. 6:13; Jer. 30:11 [b]Jer. 44:14, 28; Ezek. 7:16; 14:22
9 [a]Deut. 4:29; 30:2; Jer. 51:50 [b]Ps. 78:40; Is. 7:13; 43:24; Hos. 11:8 [c]Job 42:6; Ezek. 20:43; 36:31
10 [1]Lit., *to do this evil to*
11 [1]YHWH, usually rendered LORD [a]Ezek. 25:6 [b]Ezek. 9:4 [c]Ezek. 5:12; 7:15
12 [a]Dan. 9:7 [b]Lam. 4:11, 22; Ezek. 5:13
13 [a]Ezek. 6:4-7 [b]1 Kin. 14:23; 2 Kin. 16:4; Is. 57:5-7; Ezek. 20:28; Hos. 4:13

oak—the places where they offered
soothing aroma to all their idols.
14"So throughout all their habitations I shall [a]stretch out My hand
against them and make the land
more desolate and waste than the
wilderness toward Diblah; thus they
will know that I am the LORD." ' "

CHAPTER 7

Punishment for Wickedness Foretold

MOREOVER, the word of the
LORD came to me saying,
2"And you, son of man, thus says
the Lord [1]GOD to the land of Israel,
'An [a]end! The end is coming on the
four corners of the land.
3 'Now the end is upon you, and I
shall send My anger against you, I
shall judge you according to your
ways, and I shall bring all your
abominations upon you.
4 'For My eye will have no pity on
you, nor shall I spare *you,* but I shall
[a]bring your ways upon you, and
your abominations will be among
you; then you will [b]know that I am
the LORD!'
5"Thus says the Lord [1]GOD, 'A
[a]disaster, unique disaster, behold it
is coming!
6 'An end is coming; the end has
come! It has [a]awakened against
you; behold, it has come!
7 'Your doom has come to you, O
inhabitant of the land. The [a]time has
come, the [b]day is near—tumult
rather than joyful shouting on the
mountains.
8 'Now I will shortly [a]pour out My
wrath on you, and spend My anger
against you, [b]judge you according
to your ways, and bring on you all
your abominations.
9 'And My eye will show no pity,
nor will I spare. I will [1]repay you
according to your ways, while your
abominations are in your midst;
then you will know that I, the LORD,
do the smiting.
10 'Behold, the day! Behold, it is
coming! *Your* doom has gone forth;
the [a]rod has budded, arrogance has
blossomed.
11 'Violence has grown into a rod
of [a]wickedness. None of them *shall
remain,* none of their multitude,
none of their [b]wealth, nor anything
eminent among them.
12 'The [a]time has come, the day
has arrived. Let not the [b]buyer rejoice nor the seller mourn; for
[c]wrath is against all their multitude.
13 'Indeed, the seller will not [a]re-
gain [1]what he sold as long as they
both live, for the vision regarding all
their multitude will not be averted;
nor will any of them maintain his
life by his iniquity.
14 'They have [a]blown the trumpet
and made everything ready, but no
one is going to the battle; for My
wrath is against all [1]their multitude.
15 'The [a]sword is outside, and the
plague and the famine are within.
He who is in the field will die by the
sword; famine and the plague will
also consume those in the city.
16 'Even when their survivors [a]es-
cape, they will be on the mountains
like [b]doves of the valleys, all of them
[c]mourning, each over his own iniquity.
17 'All [a]hands will hang limp, and
all knees will become like water.
18 'And they will [a]gird themselves
with sackcloth, and [b]shuddering
will overwhelm them; and shame
will be on all faces, and [c]baldness on
all their heads.
19 'They shall [a]fling their silver
into the streets, and their gold shall
become an abhorrent thing; their
[b]silver and their gold shall not be
able to deliver them in the day of the
wrath of the LORD. They cannot satisfy their appetite, nor can they fill
their stomachs, for their iniquity has
become an occasion of stumbling.

The Temple Profaned

20 'And they transformed the
beauty of His ornaments into pride,
and they made the images of their
abominations *and* their detestable
things with it; therefore I will make
it an abhorrent thing to them.
21 'And I shall give it into the
hands of the [a]foreigners as plunder
and to the wicked of the earth as
spoil, and they will profane it.
22 'I shall also turn My [a]face from
them, and they will profane My secret place; then robbers will enter
and profane it.
23 '[a]Make the chain, for the land is
full of [b]bloody crimes, and the city is
[c]full of violence.
24 'Therefore, I shall bring the
worst of the [a]nations, and they will
possess their houses. I shall also
make the [b]pride of the strong ones
cease, and their [c]holy places will be
profaned.
25 'When anguish comes, they will
seek [a]peace, but there will be none.
26 '[a]Disaster will come upon disaster, and [b]rumor will be *added* to rumor; then they will seek a [c]vision
from a prophet, but the [d]law will be
lost from the priest and [e]counsel
from the elders.

14 [a]Is. 5:25; 9:12; Ezek. 14:13; 20:33, 34
2 [1]YHWH, usually rendered LORD [a]Ezek. 7:3, 5, 6; 11:13; Amos 8:2
4 [a]Ezek. 11:21; 22:31; Hos. 9:7 [b]Ezek. 6:7, 14
5 [1]Cf. v. 2 [a]2 Kin. 21:12, 13; Nah. 1:9
6 [a]Zech. 13:7
7 [a]Ezek. 7:12; 12:23-25, 28 [b]Is. 22:5
8 [a]Is. 42:25; Ezek. 9:8; 14:19; Nah. 1:6 [b]Ezek. 7:3; 33:20; 36:19
9 [1]Lit., *give*
10 [a]Ps. 89:32; Is. 10:5
11 [a]Ps. 73:8; 125:3; Is. 59:6-8 [b]Zeph. 1:18
12 [a]Ezek. 7:5-7, 10; 1 Cor. 7:29-31; James 5:8, 9 [b]Prov. 20:14; 1 Cor. 7:30 [c]Is. 5:13, 14; Ezek. 6:11, 12; 7:14
13 [1]Lit., *thing sold,* i.e., his inherited land [a]Lev. 25:24-28, 31
14 [1]Lit., *her* [a]Num. 10:9; Jer. 4:5
15 [a]Jer. 14:18; Ezek. 5:12; 6:11, 12; 12:16
16 [a]Ezra 9:15; Is. 37:31; Ezek. 6:8; 14:22 [b]Is. 38:14 [c]Is. 59:11; Nah. 2:7
17 [a]Is. 13:7; Ezek. 21:7; 22:14; Heb. 12:12
18 [a]Is. 15:3; Ezek. 27:31; Amos 8:10 [b]Job 21:6; Ps. 55:5 [c]Ezek. 27:31
19 [a]Is. 2:20; 30:22 [b]Prov. 11:4; Zeph. 1:18
21 [a]2 Kin. 24:13; Ps. 74:2-8; Jer. 52:13
22 [a]Jer. 18:17; Ezek. 39:23, 24
23 [a]Jer. 27:2 [b]Ezek. 9:9; Hos. 4:2 [c]Ezek. 8:17
24 [a]Ezek. 21:31; 28:7 [b]Ezek. 33:28 [c]2 Chr. 7:20; Ezek. 24:21
25 [a]Ezek. 13:10, 16
26 [a]Is. 47:11; Jer. 4:20 [b]Ezek. 21:7 [c]Jer. 21:2; 37:17 [d]Ps. 74:9; Ezek. 22:26; Mic. 3:6 [e]Jer. 18:18; Ezek. 11:2

27 'The king will mourn, the prince will be [a]clothed with horror, and the hands of the people of the land will [1]tremble. According to their conduct I shall deal with them, and by their judgments I shall judge them. And they will know that I am the LORD.' "

CHAPTER 8

Vision of Abominations in Jerusalem

AND it came about in the sixth year, on the fifth *day* of the sixth month, as I was sitting in my house with the elders of Judah sitting before me, that the hand of the Lord [1]GOD fell on me there.

2 Then I looked, and behold, a likeness as the appearance of [1]a man; from His loins and downward *there was* the [a]appearance of fire, and from His loins and upward the appearance of brightness, like the appearance [b]of [2]glowing metal.

3 And He stretched out the form of a hand and caught me by a lock of my head; and the [a]Spirit lifted me up between earth and heaven and brought me in the visions of God to Jerusalem, to the entrance of the [1]north gate of the inner *court,* where the seat of the idol of jealousy, which provokes to jealousy, was *located.*

4 And behold, the [a]glory of the God of Israel *was* there, like the appearance which I saw in the plain.

5 Then He said to me, "Son of man, [a]raise your eyes, now, toward the north." So I raised my eyes toward the north, and behold, to the north of the altar gate *was* this [b]idol of jealousy at the entrance.

6 And He said to me, "Son of man, do you see what they are doing, the great [a]abominations which the house of Israel are committing here, that I should be far from My sanctuary? But yet you will see still greater abominations."

7 Then He brought me to the entrance of the court, and when I looked, behold, a hole in the wall.

8 And He said to me, "Son of man, now [a]dig through the wall." So I dug through the wall, and behold, an entrance.

9 And He said to me, "Go in and see the wicked abominations that they are committing here."

10 So I entered and looked, and behold, every form of creeping things and beasts *and* detestable things, with all the idols of the house of Israel, were carved on the wall all around.

11 And standing in front of them were [a]seventy [b]elders of the house of Israel, with Jaazaniah the son of Shaphan standing among them, each man with his [c]censer in his hand, and the fragrance of the cloud of incense rising.

12 Then He said to me, "Son of man, do you see what the elders of the house of Israel are committing in the dark, each man in the room of his carved images? For they say, 'The LORD does not see us; the LORD has forsaken the land.' "

13 And He said to me, "Yet you will see still greater abominations which they are committing."

14 Then He brought me to the entrance of the [a]gate of the LORD's house which *was* toward the north; and behold, women were sitting there weeping for Tammuz.

15 And He said to me, "Do you see *this,* son of man? Yet you will see still greater abominations than these."

16 Then He brought me into the inner court of the LORD's house. And behold, at the entrance to the temple of the LORD, between the porch and the altar, *were* about twenty-five men with their [a]backs to the temple of the LORD and their faces toward the east; and [b]they were [1]prostrating themselves eastward toward the sun.

17 And He said to me, "Do you see *this,* son of man? Is it too light a thing for the house of Judah to commit the abominations which they have committed here, that they have [a]filled the land with violence and [b]provoked Me repeatedly? For behold, they are putting the twig to their nose.

18 "Therefore, I indeed shall deal in wrath. My eye will have no pity nor shall I spare; and [a]though they cry in My ears with a loud voice, yet I shall not listen to them."

CHAPTER 9

The Vision of Slaughter

THEN He cried out in my hearing with a loud [a]voice saying, "Draw near, [1]O executioners of the city, each with his destroying weapon in his hand."

2 And behold, six men came from the direction of the upper gate which faces north, each with his shattering weapon in his hand; and among them was a certain man clothed in linen with a [1]writing case

27 [1]Lit., *be terrified* [a]Job 8:22; Ps. 35:26; 109:18, 29; Ezek. 26:16

1 [1]YHWH, usually rendered LORD

2 [1]Heb., *fire* [2]Or, *electrum* [a]Ezek. 1:27 [b]Ezek. 1:4, 27

3 [1]Lit., *facing north* [a]Ezek. 3:12; 11:1

4 [a]Ezek. 1:28

5 [a]Jer. 3:2; Zech. 5:5 [b]Ps. 78:58; Jer. 7:30; 32:34; Ezek. 8:3

6 [a]2 Kin. 23:4, 5; Ezek. 5:11; 8:9, 17

8 [a]Job 34:22; Is. 29:15

11 [a]Num. 11:16, 25; Ezek. 24:1, 9; Luke 10:1 [b]Jer. 19:1 [c]Num. 16:17, 35

14 [a]Ezek. 44:4; 46:9

16 [1]I.e., *worshiping* [a]2 Kin. 8:30; 2 Chr. 29:6; Jer. 2:27; Ezek. 23:39 [b]Deut. 4:19; 17:3; Job 31:26-28; Jer. 44:17

17 [a]Ezek. 7:11, 23; 9:9; Amos 3:10; Mic. 2:2 [b]Jer. 7:18, 19; Ezek. 16:26

18 [a]Is. 1:15; Jer. 11:11; Mic. 3:4; Zech. 7:13

1 [1]Lit., *you who punish* [a]Is. 6:8

2 [1]Or, *scribal inkhorn*

at his loins. And they went in and
stood beside the bronze altar.
3 Then the [a]glory of the God of
Israel went up from the cherub on
which it had been, to the threshold
of the temple. And He called to the
man clothed in linen at whose loins
was the writing case.
4 And the LORD said to him, "Go
through the midst of the city, *even*
through the midst of Jerusalem, and
put a [a]mark on the foreheads of the
men who [b]sigh and groan over all
the abominations which are being
committed in its midst."
5 But to the others He said in my
hearing, "Go through the city after
him and strike; do not let your eye
have pity, and do not spare.
6 "[1]Utterly [a]slay old men, young
men, maidens, little children, and
women, but do not [b]touch any man
on whom is the mark; and you shall
[c]start from My sanctuary." So they
started with the [2]elders who *were*
before the temple.
7 And He said to them, "[a]Defile
the temple and fill the courts with
the slain. Go out!" Thus they went
out and struck down *the people* in
the city.
8 Then it came about as they
were striking and I *alone* was left,
that I [a]fell on my face and cried out
[1]saying, "[b]Alas, Lord [2]GOD! Art
Thou destroying the whole remnant
of Israel [3]by pouring out Thy wrath
on Jerusalem?"
9 Then He said to me, "The iniquity of the house of Israel and Judah
is very, very great, and the land is
[a]filled with blood, and the city is
[b]full of perversion; for [c]they say,
'The LORD has forsaken the land,
and the LORD does not see!'
10 "But as for Me, [a]My eye will
have no pity nor shall I spare, but [b]I
shall bring their conduct upon their
heads."
11 Then behold, the man clothed
in linen at whose loins was the
[1]writing case [2]reported, saying, "I
have done just as Thou hast commanded me."

CHAPTER 10

Vision of God's Glory Departing from the Temple

THEN I looked, and behold, in the
[1a]expanse that was over the heads
of the cherubim something like a
[b]sapphire stone, in appearance resembling a [c]throne, appeared above
them.
2 And He spoke to the man
clothed in linen and said, "Enter between the [a]whirling wheels under
the [1]cherubim, and fill your hands
with [b]coals of fire from between the
cherubim, and scatter *them* over the
city." And he entered in my sight.
3 Now the cherubim were standing on the right side of the [1]temple
when the man entered, and the
cloud filled the [a]inner court.
4 Then the [a]glory of the LORD
went up from the cherub to the
threshold of the temple, and the
[b]temple was filled with the cloud,
and the court was filled with the
[c]brightness of the glory of the LORD.
5 Moreover, the sound of the
wings of the cherubim was heard as
far as the outer court, like the [a]voice
of [1]God Almighty when He speaks.
6 And it came about when He
commanded the man clothed in lin-
en, saying, "Take fire from between
the whirling wheels, from between
the cherubim," he entered and stood
beside a wheel.
7 Then the cherub stretched out
his hand from between the cherubim to the fire which *was* between
the cherubim, took some and put it
into the hands of the one clothed in
linen, who took *it* and went out.
8 And the cherubim appeared to
have the form of a man's hand under
their wings.
9 Then I looked, and behold,
[a]four wheels beside the cherubim,
one wheel beside each cherub; and
the appearance of the wheels *was*
like the gleam of a [1b]Tarshish stone.
10 And as for their appearance, all
four of them had the same likeness,
as if one wheel were within another
wheel.
11 When they moved, they went
[a]in *any of* their four [1]directions
without turning as they went; but
they followed in the direction which
[2]they faced, without turning as they
went.
12 And their [a]whole body, their
backs, their hands, their wings, and
the [b]wheels were full of eyes all
around, the wheels belonging to all
four of them.
13 The wheels were called in my
hearing, the whirling wheels.
14 And [a]each one had four faces.
The first face *was* the face of a
cherub, the second face *was* the face
of a man, the third the face of a lion,
and the fourth the face of an eagle.
15 Then the cherubim rose up.
They are the [a]living beings that I
saw by the river Chebar.

3 [a]Ezek. 10:4; 11:22, 23

4 [a]Ex. 12:7, 13; Ezek. 9:6; 2 Cor. 1:22; 2 Tim. 2:19; Rev. 7:2, 3 [b]Ps. 119:53, 136; Jer. 13:17; Ezek. 6:11; 21:6

6 [1]Lit., To *destruction* [2]Or, *old men*
[a]2 Chr. 36:17 [b]Ex. 12:23; Rev. 9:4 [c]Jer. 25:29; Amos 3:2; Luke 12:47

7 [a]2 Chr. 36:17; Ezek. 7:20-22

8 [1]Lit., *and said* [2]YHWH, usually rendered LORD [3]Lit., *by Thy pouring*
[a]1 Chr. 21:16 [b]Ezek. 11:13; Amos 7:2-6

9 [a]2 Kin. 21:16; Jer. 2:34; Ezek. 7:23; 22:2, 3 [b]Ezek. 22:29; Mic. 3:1-3; 7:3 [c]Job 22:13; Ps. 10:11; 94:7; Is. 29:15; Ezek. 8:12

10 [a]Is. 65:6; Ezek. 8:18; 24:14 [b]Ezek. 7:4; 11:21; Hos. 9:7

11 [1]Or, *scribal inkhorn* [2]Lit., *brought back word*

1 [1]Or, *firmament*
[a]Ezek. 1:22, 26 [b]Ex. 24:10 [c]Rev. 4:2, 3

2 [1]So with Gk.; Heb., *cherub*
[a]Ezek. 1:15-21; 10:13 [b]Ps. 18:10-13; Is. 6:6; Ezek. 1:13; Rev. 8:5

3 [1]Lit., *house*, and so throughout the chap.
[a]Ezek. 8:3, 16

4 [a]Ezek. 9:3; 11:22, 23 [b]Ex. 40:34, 35; Is. 6:1-4 [c]Ezek. 1:28

5 [1]Heb. *El Shaddai*
[a]Job 40:9; Ezek. 1:24; Rev. 10:3

9 [1]Perhaps, *beryl*
[a]Ezek. 1:15-17 [b]Dan. 10:6; Rev. 21:20

11 [1]Lit., *sides* [2]Lit., *the head*
[a]Ezek. 1:17

12 [a]Rev. 4:6, 8 [b]Ezek. 1:18

14 [a]1 Kin. 7:29, 36; Ezek. 1:6, 10; 10:21; Rev. 4:7

15 [a]Ezek. 1:3, 5

16 Now when the cherubim
moved, the wheels would go beside
them; also when the cherubim lifted
up their wings to rise from the
ground, the wheels would not turn
from beside them.
17 When [1]the cherubim [a]stood
still, the [1]wheels would stand still;
and when they rose up, the [1]wheels
would rise with them; for the spirit
of the living beings *was* in them.
18 Then the glory of the LORD departed from the threshold of the
temple and stood [a]over the cherubim.
19 When the cherubim departed,
they lifted their wings and rose up
from the earth in my sight with the
wheels beside them; and they stood
still at the entrance of the east gate
of the LORD's house. And the glory
of the God of Israel [1]hovered over
them.
20 These are the [a]living beings
that I saw beneath the God of Israel
by the river Chebar; so I knew that
they *were* cherubim.
21 [a]Each one had four faces and
each one four wings, and beneath
their wings *was* the form of human
hands.
22 As for the likeness of their
faces, they were the same faces
whose appearance I had seen by the
river Chebar. Each one went
straight ahead.

CHAPTER 11

Evil Rulers to be Judged

MOREOVER, the Spirit [a]lifted me
up and brought me to the east gate
of the LORD's house which faced
eastward. And behold, *there were*
twenty-five men at the entrance of
the gate, and among them I saw Jaazaniah son of Azzur and [b]Pelatiah
son of Benaiah, leaders of the people.
2 And He said to me, "Son of
man, these are the men who devise
iniquity and [a]give evil advice in this
city,
3 who say, '[1]Is not *the time* near
to build houses? [2]This [a]*city* is the
pot and we are the flesh.'
4"Therefore, [a]prophesy against
them, son of man, prophesy!"
5 Then the Spirit of the LORD fell
upon me, and He said to me, "Say,
'Thus says the LORD, "So you think,
house of Israel, for [a]I know [1]your
[b]thoughts.
6"You have [a]multiplied your slain
in this city, filling its streets with
[1]them."
7 'Therefore, thus says the Lord
[1]GOD, "Your [a]slain whom you have
laid in the midst of [2]the city are the
flesh, and this *city* is the pot; but [3]I
shall [b]bring you out of it.
8"You have feared a sword; so I
will [a]bring a sword upon you," the
Lord GOD declares.
9"And I shall bring you out of the
midst of [1]the city, and I shall deliver
you into the hands of [a]strangers and
[b]execute judgments against you.
10"You will [a]fall by the sword. I
shall judge you to the [b]border of Israel; so you shall know that I am the
LORD.
11"This *city* will [a]not be a pot for
you, nor will you be flesh in the
midst of it, *but* I shall judge you to
the border of Israel.
12"Thus you will know that I am
the LORD; for you have not walked
in My statutes nor have you [a]exe-
cuted My ordinances, but have
acted according to the ordinances of
the [b]nations around you." ' "
13 Now it came about as I prophesied, that [a]Pelatiah son of Benaiah
died. Then I fell on my face and
cried out with a loud voice and said,
"[b]Alas, Lord GOD! Wilt Thou bring
the remnant of Israel to a complete
end?"

Promise of Restoration

14 Then the word of the LORD
came to me, saying,
15"Son of man, your brothers,
your [1]relatives, [2]your fellow exiles,
and the whole house of Israel, all of
them, *are those* to whom the inhabitants of Jerusalem have said, 'Go far
from the LORD; this land has been
given [a]us as a possession.'
16"Therefore say, 'Thus says the
Lord GOD, "Though I had removed
them far away among the nations,
and though I had scattered them
among the countries, yet I was a
[a]sanctuary for them a little while in
the countries where they had
gone." '
17"Therefore say, 'Thus says the
Lord GOD, "I shall [a]gather you from
the peoples and assemble you out of
the countries among which you
have been scattered, and I shall give
you the land of Israel." '
18"When they come there, they
will [a]remove all its [b]detestable
things and all its abominations
from it.
19"And I shall [a]give them one
heart, and shall put a new spirit
within [1]them. And I shall take the
heart of [b]stone out of their flesh and
give them a [c]heart of flesh,

17 [1]Lit., *they* [a]Ezek. 1:21
18 [a]Ps. 18:10
19 [1]Lit., *over them from above*
20 [a]Ezek. 1:5, 26; 10:15
21 [a]Ezek. 1:6, 8; 10:14; 41:18, 19
1 [a]Ezek. 3:12, 14; 8:3; 11:24; 43:5 [b]Ezek. 11:13
2 [a]Ps. 2:1, 2; 52:2; Is. 30:1; Jer. 5:5; Mic. 2:1
3 [1]Or, *The time is not near* [2]Or, *This is* [a]Jer. 1:13; Ezek. 11:7, 11; 24:3, 6
4 [a]Ezek. 3:4, 17
5 [1]Lit., *what comes up in your spirit* [a]Jer. 11:20; 17:10 [b]Ezek. 38:10
6 [1]Lit., *the slain* [a]Is. 1:15; Jer. 7:9; Ezek. 7:23; 22:2-6, 9, 12, 27
7 [1]YHWH, usually rendered LORD, and so throughout the chap. [2]Lit., *it* [3]So with Gk.; Heb., *he will bring you out* [a]Ezek. 24:3-13; Mic. 3:2, 3 [b]2 Kin. 25:18-22; Jer. 52:24-27; Ezek. 11:9
8 [a]Job 3:25; Is. 24:17, 18
9 [1]Lit., *it* [a]Deut. 28:36, 49, 50; Ps. 106:41 [b]Ezek. 5:8; 16:41
10 [a]Jer. 52:9, 10 [b]2 Kin. 14:25
11 [a]Ezek. 11:3, 7; 24:3, 6
12 [a]Ezek. 18:8, 9 [b]Ezek. 8:10, 14, 16
13 [a]Ezek. 11:1 [b]Ezek. 9:8
15 [1]Lit., *brothers* [2]So with Gk. and some ancient versions; Heb., *the men of your redemption* [a]Ezek. 33:24
16 [a]Is. 8:14; Jer. 29:7, 11
17 [a]Is. 11:11-16; Jer. 3:12, 18; 24:5; Ezek. 20:41, 42; 28:25
18 [a]Ezek. 37:23 [b]Ezek. 5:11; 7:20
19 [1]So with Gk. and many mss.; Heb., *you* [a]Jer. 24:7; 32:39; Ezek. 18:31; 36:26 [b]Zech. 7:12; Rom. 2:4, 5 [c]2 Cor. 3:3

20 that they may [a]walk in My statutes and keep My ordinances, and
do them. Then they will be [b]My people, and I shall be their God.
21"[1]But as for those whose hearts
go after their [a]detestable things and
abominations, I shall [b]bring their
conduct down on their heads," declares the Lord GOD.
22 Then the cherubim [a]lifted up
their wings with the wheels beside
them, and the glory of the God of
Israel hovered over them.
23 And the [a]glory of the LORD
went up from the midst of the city,
and [b]stood over the mountain which
is east of the city.
24 And the [a]Spirit lifted me up and
brought me in a vision by the Spirit
of God to the exiles [1]in Chaldea. So
the vision that I had seen [b]left me.
25 Then I [a]told the exiles all the
things that the LORD had shown me.

CHAPTER 12

Ezekiel Prepares for Exile

THEN the word of the LORD came
to me saying,
2"Son of man, you live in the
[a]midst of the [b]rebellious house, who
[c]have eyes to see but do not see,
ears to hear but do not hear; for they
are a rebellious house.
3"Therefore, son of man, prepare
for yourself baggage for exile and
go into exile by day in their sight;
even go into exile from your place to
another place in their sight. [a]Per-
haps they will understand though
they are a rebellious house.
4"And bring your baggage out by
day in their sight, as baggage for
exile. Then you will go out [a]at evening in their sight, as those going
into exile.
5"Dig a hole through the wall in
their sight and go out through it.
6"Load *the baggage* on *your*
shoulder in their sight, *and* carry *it*
out in the dark. You shall [a]cover
your face so that you can not see the
land, for I have set you as a [b]sign to
the house of Israel."
7 And I [a]did so, as I had been
commanded. By day I [b]brought out
my baggage like the baggage of an
exile. Then in the evening I dug
through the wall with my hands; I
went out in the dark *and* carried *the*
baggage on *my* shoulder in their
sight.
8 And in the morning the word of
the LORD came to me, saying,
9"Son of man, has not the house
of Israel, the [a]rebellious house, said
to you, '[b]What are you doing?'
10"Say to them, 'Thus says the
Lord [1]GOD, "This [2a]burden *concerns*
the prince in Jerusalem, as well as
all the house of Israel who are in
it." '
11"Say, 'I am a [a]sign to you. As I
have done, so it will be done to
them; they will [b]go into exile, into
captivity'.
12"And the [a]prince who is among
them will load *his baggage* on *his*
shoulder in the dark and go out.
[1]They will dig a hole through the
wall to bring *it* out. He will cover his
face so that he can not see the land
with *his* eyes.
13"I shall also spread My [a]net over
him, and he will be caught in My
snare. And I shall bring him to
Babylon in the land of the Chaldeans; yet he will [b]not see it, though he
will die there.
14"And I shall [a]scatter to every
wind all who are around him, his
helpers and all his troops; and I shall
draw out a sword after them.
15"So they will [a]know that I am
the LORD when I scatter them
among the nations, and spread them
among the countries.
16"But I shall spare a few of them
from the [a]sword, the famine, and
the pestilence that they may tell all
their abominations among the nations where they go, and may [b]know
that I am the LORD."
17 Moreover, the word of the LORD
came to me saying,
18"Son of man, eat your bread
with trembling, and drink your water with quivering and anxiety.
19"Then say to the people of the
land, 'Thus says the Lord GOD concerning the inhabitants of Jerusalem in the land of Israel, "They will
eat their bread with anxiety and
drink their water with horror, because their land will be [a]stripped of
its fulness on account of the violence of all who live in it.
20"And the inhabited [a]cities will
be laid waste, and the [b]land will be a
desolation. So you will know that I
am the LORD." ' "
21 Then the word of the LORD
came to me saying,
22"Son of man, what is this [a]prov-
erb you *people* have concerning the
land of Israel, saying, 'The [b]days are
long and every [c]vision fails'?
23"Therefore say to them, 'Thus
says the Lord GOD, "I will make this
proverb cease so that they will no
longer use it as a proverb in Israel."
But tell them, "The days draw near
as well as the [1]fulfillment of every
vision.

20 [a]Ps. 105:45; Ezek. 36:27 [b]Ezek. 14:11
21 [1]Lit., *And to the heart of their detestable things and their abomination their heart goes.* [a]Jer. 16:18; Ezek. 11:18 [b]Ezek. 9:10; 16:43
22 [a]Ezek. 10:19
23 [a]Ezek. 8:4 [b]Zech. 14:4
24 [1]I.e., Babylonia [a]Ezek. 8:3; 11:1; 37:1; 2 Cor. 12:2-4 [b]Acts 10:16
25 [a]Ezek. 2:7; 3:4, 17, 27
2 [a]Is. 6:5 [b]Ps. 78:40; Is. 1:23; Ezek. 2:7, 8 [c]Jer. 5:21; Matt. 13:13, 14; John 9:39-41
3 [a]Jer. 26:3; 36:3, 7; Luke 20:13; 2 Tim. 2:25
4 [a]2 Kin. 25:4; Jer. 39:4; Ezek. 12:12
6 [a]1 Sam. 28:8; Ezek. 12:12, 13 [b]Is. 8:18; 20:3; Ezek. 4:3; 12:11; 24:24
7 [a]Ezek. 24:18; 37:7, 10 [b]Ezek. 12:3-6
9 [a]Ezek. 2:5-8; 12:1-3 [b]Ezek. 17:12; 20:49; 24:19
10 [1]YHWH, usually rendered LORD, and so throughout the chap. [2]Or, *oracle* [a]2 Kin. 9:25; Is. 13:1; Ezek. 12:3-8
11 [a]Ezek. 12:6 [b]Jer. 15:2; 52:15, 28-30; Ezek. 12:3
12 [1]I.e., the king's attendants [a]2 Kin. 25:4; Jer. 39:4; 52:7; Ezek. 12:6
13 [a]Is. 24:17, 18; Ezek. 17:20; 19:8; Hos. 7:12 [b]Jer. 39:7; 52:11
14 [a]2 Kin. 25:4, 5; Ezek. 5:2; 17:21
15 [a]Ezek. 6:7, 14; 12:16, 20
16 [a]Ezek. 7:15; 14:21 [b]Jer. 22:8, 9
19 [a]Jer. 10:22; Ezek. 6:6, 7, 14; Mic. 7:13; Zech. 7:14
20 [a]Is. 3:26; Jer. 4:7; Ezek. 5:14 [b]Is. 7:23, 24; Jer. 25:9; Ezek. 36:3
22 [a]Ezek. 16:44; 18:2, 3 [b]Jer. 5:12; Ezek. 11:3; 12:27; Amos 6:3; 2 Pet. 3:4 [c]Ezek. 7:26
23 [1]Lit., *word*

24"For there will no longer be any
[1a]false vision or flattering divination
within the house of Israel.
25"For I the LORD shall speak, and
whatever [a]word I speak will be performed. It will no longer be delayed,
for in [b]your days, O [c]rebellious
house, I shall speak the word and
perform it," declares the Lord
GOD.' "
26 Furthermore, the word of the
LORD came to me saying,
27"Son of man, behold, the house
of Israel is saying, 'The vision that
he sees is for [a]many [1]years *from
now,* and he prophesies of times far
off.'
28"Therefore say to them, 'Thus
says the Lord GOD, "None of My
words will be delayed any longer.
Whatever word I speak will be performed," ' " declares the Lord GOD.

CHAPTER 13

False Prophets Condemned

THEN the word of the LORD came
to me saying,
2"Son of man, prophesy against
the [a]prophets of Israel who prophesy, and say to those who prophesy
from their own [1]inspiration, '[b]Listen
to the word of the LORD!
3 'Thus says the Lord [1]GOD, "Woe
to the [a]foolish prophets who are following their own spirit and have
[b]seen nothing.
4"O Israel, your prophets have
been like foxes among ruins.
5"You have not [a]gone up into the
[b]breaches, nor did you build the
wall around the house of Israel to
stand in the battle on the [c]day of the
LORD.
6"They see [1a]falsehood and lying
divination who are saying, 'The
LORD declares,' when the LORD has
not sent them; [b]yet they hope for the
fulfillment of *their* word.
7"[a]Did you not see a false vision
and speak a lying divination when
you said, 'the LORD declares,' but it
is not I who have spoken?" ' "
8 Therefore, thus says the Lord
GOD, "Because you have spoken
[1]falsehood and seen a lie, therefore
behold, I am [a]against you," declares
the Lord GOD.
9"So My hand will be against the
[a]prophets who see false visions and
utter lying divinations. They will
[1]have no place in the council of My
people, [b]nor will they be written
down in the register of the house of
Israel, nor will they enter the land of
Israel, [2]that you may know that I am
the Lord GOD.
10"It is definitely because they
have [a]misled My people by saying,
'[b]Peace!' when there is [c]no peace.
And when anyone builds a wall, behold, they plaster it over with whitewash;
11 *so* tell those who plaster it over
with whitewash, that it will fall. A
[a]flooding rain will come, and you, O
hailstones, will fall; and a violent
wind will break out.
12"Behold, when the wall has
fallen, will you not be asked, 'Where
is the plaster with which you plastered *it?*' "
13 Therefore, thus says the Lord
GOD, "I will make a violent wind
break out in My wrath. There will
also be in My anger a flooding rain
and [a]hailstones to consume *it* in
wrath.
14"So I shall tear down the wall
which you plastered over with
whitewash and bring it down to the
ground, so that its [a]foundation is
laid bare; and when it falls, you will
be [b]consumed in its midst. And you
will [c]know that I am the LORD.
15"Thus I shall spend My wrath on
the wall and on those who have
plastered it over with whitewash;
and I shall say to you, 'The wall [1]is
gone and its plasterers are gone,
16 *along with* the prophets of Israel who prophesy to Jerusalem,
and who [a]see visions of peace for
her when there is [b]no peace,' declares the Lord GOD.
17"Now you, son of man, set your
face against the daughters of your
people who are [a]prophesying [b]from
their own [1]inspiration. Prophesy
against them,
18 and say, 'Thus says the Lord
GOD, "Woe to the women who sew
magic bands on [1]all wrists, and
make veils for the heads of *persons*
of every stature to hunt down [2]lives!
Will you hunt down the [2]lives of My
people, but preserve the [2]lives *of
others* for yourselves?
19"And for handfuls of barley and
fragments of bread, you have profaned Me to My people to put to
death [1]some who should not die and
to [a]keep [1]others alive who should
not live, by your lying to My people
who listen to lies." ' "
20 Therefore, thus says the Lord
GOD, "Behold, I am against your
magic bands by which you hunt
[1]lives there as [2]birds, and I will tear
them off your arms; and I will let
[1]them go, even those [1]lives whom
you hunt as [2]birds.

24 [1]Lit., *vain* [a]Jer. 14:13-16; Ezek. 13:6, 23; Zech. 13:2-4
25 [a]Num. 14:28-34; Is. 14:24; Ezek. 6:10; 12:28 [b]Jer. 16:9; Hab. 1:5 [c]Ezek. 12:2
27 [1]Lit., *days* [a]Ezek. 12:22; Dan. 10:14
2 [1]Lit., *heart* [a]Is. 9:15; Jer. 37:19; Ezek. 22:25, 28 [b]Is. 1:10; Amos 7:16
3 [1]YHWH, usually rendered LORD, and so throughout the chap. [a]Lam. 2:14; Hos. 9:7; Zech. 11:15 [b]Jer. 23:28-32
5 [a]Ps. 106:23; Jer. 23:22; Ezek. 22:30 [b]Is. 58:12 [c]Is. 13:6, 9; Ezek. 7:19
6 [1]Lit., *vanity* [a]Jer. 29:8; Ezek. 22:28 [b]Jer. 28:15; 37:19
7 [a]Ezek. 22:28
8 [1]Lit., *vanity* [a]Ezek. 5:8; 21:3; Nah. 2:13
9 [1]Lit., *not be in* [2]Or, *and you will know* [a]Jer. 20:3-6; 28:15-17 [b]Ps. 69:28; 87:6; Jer. 17:13; Dan. 12:1
10 [a]Jer. 23:32; 50:6 [b]Jer. 8:11; 14:13 [c]Ezek. 7:25; 13:16
11 [a]Ezek. 38:22
13 [a]Ex. 9:24, 25; Ps. 18:12, 13; Is. 30:30; Rev. 11:19; 16:21
14 [a]Mic. 1:6; Hab. 3:13 [b]Jer. 6:15; 14:15 [c]Ezek. 13:9
15 [1]Lit., *is not . . . are not*
16 [a]Jer. 6:14; 8:11; Ezek. 13:10 [b]Is. 57:21
17 [1]Lit., *heart* [a]Judg. 4:4; 2 Kin. 22:14; Luke 2:36; Acts 21:9 [b]Ezek. 13:2; Rev. 2:20
18 [1]Lit., *all joints of the hand;* M.T. reads, *of my hands* [2]Or, *souls*
19 [1]Or, *souls* [a]Jer. 23:14, 17
20 [1]Lit., *souls* [2]Or, *flying ones*

21"I will also tear off your veils and [a]deliver My people from your hands, and they will no longer be in your hands to be hunted; and you will know that I am the LORD.

22"Because you [a]disheartened the righteous with falsehood when I did not cause him grief, but have [1b]encouraged the wicked not to [c]turn from his wicked way *and* preserve his life,

23 therefore, you women will no longer see [1a]false visions or practice divination, and I will [b]deliver My people out of your hand. Thus you will [c]know that I am the LORD."

CHAPTER 14

Idolatrous Elders Condemned

THEN some [a]elders of Israel came to me and [b]sat down before me.

2 And the word of the LORD came to me saying,

3"Son of man, these men have [a]set up their idols in their hearts, and have [b]put right before their faces the stumbling block of their iniquity. Should I be [c]consulted by them at all?

4"Therefore speak to them and tell them, 'Thus says the Lord [1]GOD, "Any man of the house of Israel who sets up his idols in his heart, puts right before his face the stumbling block of his iniquity, and *then* comes to the prophet, I the LORD will be brought to give him an answer in [2]the matter in view of the [a]multitude of his idols,

5 in order to lay hold of [1a]the hearts of the house of Israel who are [2b]estranged from Me through all their idols."'

6"Therefore say to the house of Israel, 'Thus says the Lord GOD, "[a]Repent and turn away from your idols, and turn your faces away from all your [b]abominations.

7"For anyone of the house of Israel or of the [a]immigrants who stay in Israel who separates himself from Me, sets up his idols in his heart, puts right before his face the stumbling block of his iniquity, and *then* comes to the prophet to inquire of Me for himself, [b]I the LORD will be brought to answer him in My own person.

8"And I shall [a]set My face against that man and make him a [b]sign and [1]a proverb, and I shall cut him off from among My people. So you will know that I am the LORD.

9"But if the prophet is [1]prevailed upon to speak a word, it is I, the LORD, who have [1]prevailed upon that prophet, and I will stretch out My hand against him and [a]destroy him from among My people Israel.

10"And they will bear *the punishment of* their iniquity; as the iniquity of the inquirer is, so the iniquity of the prophet will be,

11 in order that the house of Israel may no longer [a]stray from Me and no longer [b]defile themselves with all their transgressions. Thus they will be [c]My people, and I shall be their God,"' declares the Lord GOD."

The City Will Not Be Spared

12 Then the word of the LORD came to me saying,

13"Son of man, if a country sins against Me by [a]committing unfaithfulness, and I stretch out My hand against it, [1]destroy its supply of bread, send famine against it, and cut off from it both man and beast,

14 even [a]*though* these three men, [b]Noah, [c]Daniel, and [d]Job were in its midst, by their *own* righteousness they could *only* deliver [e]themselves," declares the Lord GOD.

15"If I were to cause [a]wild beasts to pass through the land, and they [1]depopulated it, and it became desolate so that no one would pass through it because of the beasts,

16 *though* these three men were in its midst, as I live," declares the Lord GOD, "they could not deliver either *their* sons or *their* daughters. [a]They alone would be delivered, but the country would be desolate.

17"Or *if* I should bring a sword on that country and say, 'Let the sword pass through the country and cut off man and beast from it,'

18 even *though* these three men were in its midst, as I live," declares the Lord GOD, "they could not deliver either *their* sons or *their* daughters, but they alone would be delivered.

19"Or *if* I should send a [a]plague against that country and pour out My wrath in blood on it, to cut off man and beast from it,

20 even *though* Noah, Daniel, and Job were in its midst, as I live," declares the Lord GOD, "they could not deliver either *their* son or *their* daughter. They would deliver only themselves by their righteousness."

21 For thus says the Lord GOD, "How much more when I send My four [1]severe judgments against Jerusalem: sword, famine, wild beasts, and [a]plague to cut off man and beast from it!

22"Yet, behold, [1]survivors will be

13:21 [a]Ps. 91:3; 124:7
22 [1]Lit., *strengthen the hands of* [a]Amos 5:12 [b]Jer. 23:14; 34:16, 22 [c]Ezek. 18:21, 27, 30-32; 33:14-16
23 [1]Lit., *vanity* [a]Ezek. 12:24; 13:6; Mic. 3:6; Zech. 13:3 [b]Ezek. 13:21; 34:10 [c]Ezek. 13:9, 21
14:1 [a]2 Kin. 6:32; Ezek. 8:1; 20:1 [b]Is. 29:13; Ezek. 33:31, 32
3 [a]Ezek. 20:16 [b]Ezek. 7:19; 14:4, 7; Zeph. 1:3 [c]Is. 1:15; Jer. 11:11; Ezek. 20:3, 31
4 [1]YHWH, usually rendered LORD, and so throughout the chap. [2]Lit., *it* [a]1 Kin. 21:20-24; 2 Kin. 1:16; Is. 66:4
5 [1]Lit., *their* [2]Or, *all estranged from Me through their idols* [a]Jer. 17:10; Zech. 7:12 [b]Is. 1:4; Jer. 2:11; Zech. 11:8
6 [a]1 Sam. 7:3; Neh. 1:9; Is. 2:20; 30:22; 55:6, 7; Ezek. 18:30 [b]Ezek. 8:6; 14:4
7 [a]Ex. 12:48; 20:10 [b]Ezek. 14:4
8 [1]Lit., *proverbs* [a]Jer. 44:11; Ezek. 15:7 [b]Is. 65:15; Ezek. 5:15
9 [1]Or, *enticed* [a]Jer. 6:14, 15; 14:15
11 [a]Ezek. 44:10, 15; 48:11 [b]Ezek. 11:18; 37:23 [c]Ezek. 11:20; 34:30; 36:28
13 [1]Lit., *break the staff* [a]Ezek. 15:8; 20:27
14 [a]Jer. 15:1 [b]Gen. 6:8; 7:1; Heb. 11:7 [c]Ezek. 28:3; Dan. 1:6; 9:21; 10:11 [d]Job 1:1, 5; 42:8, 9 [e]Ezek. 16:18, 20; 18:20
15 [1]Lit., *bereave of children* [a]Ezek. 5:17; 14:21
16 [a]Gen. 19:29; Ezek. 18:20
19 [a]Jer. 14:12; Ezek. 5:12; 14:21
21 [1]Lit., *evil* [a]Amos 4:6-10
22 [1]Lit., *escaped ones*

left in it who will be brought out, *both* sons and daughters. Behold, they are going to come forth to you and you will [a]see their conduct and actions; then you will be [b]comforted for the calamity which I have brought against Jerusalem for everything which I have brought upon it.

23"Then they will comfort you when you see their conduct and actions, for you will know that I have not done in vain whatever I did [1]to it," declares the Lord GOD.

CHAPTER 15

Jerusalem Like a Useless Vine

THEN the word of the LORD came to me saying,

2"Son of man, how is the wood of the [a]vine *better* than any wood of a branch which is among the trees of the forest?

3"Can wood be taken from it to make [1]anything, or can *men* take a peg from it on which to hang any vessel?

4"[1]If it has been put into the [a]fire for fuel, *and* the fire has consumed both of its ends, and its middle part has been charred, is it *then* useful for [2]anything?

5"Behold, while it is intact, it is not made into [1]anything. How much less, when the fire has consumed it and it is charred, can it still be made into [1]anything!

6"Therefore, thus says the Lord [1]GOD, 'As the wood of the vine among the trees of the forest, which I have given to the fire for fuel, so have I given up the inhabitants of Jerusalem;

7 and I [a]set My face against them. *Though* they have [b]come out of the fire, yet the fire will consume them. Then you will know that I am the LORD, when I set My face against them.

8 'Thus I will make the land desolate, because they have [a]acted unfaithfully,' " declares the Lord GOD.

CHAPTER 16

God's Grace to Unfaithful Jerusalem

THEN the word of the LORD came to me saying,

2"Son of man, [a]make known to Jerusalem her abominations,

3 and say, 'Thus says the Lord [1]GOD to Jerusalem, "Your origin and your birth are from the land of the Canaanite, your father was an Amorite and your mother a Hittite.

4"As for your birth, on the day you were born your navel cord was not cut, nor were you washed with water for cleansing; you were not rubbed with salt or even wrapped in cloths.

5"No eye looked with pity on you to do any of these things for you, to have compassion on you. Rather you were thrown out into the [1a]open field, [2]for you were abhorred on the day you were born.

6"When I passed by you and saw you squirming in your blood, I said to you *while you were* in your blood, '[a]Live!' I said to you while you were in your blood, 'Live!'

7"I [a]made you [1]numerous like plants of the field. Then you grew up, became tall, and reached the age for fine ornaments; *your* breasts were formed and your hair had grown. Yet you were naked and bare.

8"Then I passed by you and saw you, and behold, [1]you were at the time for love; so I [a]spread My skirt over you and covered your nakedness. I also [b]swore to you and [c]entered into a covenant with you so that you [d]became Mine," declares the Lord GOD.

9"Then I bathed you with water, washed off your blood from you, and [a]anointed you with oil.

10"I also clothed you with [a]embroidered cloth, and put sandals of porpoise skin on your feet; and I wrapped you with fine linen and covered you with silk.

11"And I adorned you with ornaments, put [a]bracelets on your hands, and a [b]necklace around your neck.

12"I also put a [a]ring in your nostril, earrings in your ears, and a [b]beautiful crown on your head.

13"Thus you were adorned with [a]gold and silver, and your dress was of fine linen, silk, and embroidered cloth. You ate fine flour, honey, and oil; so you were exceedingly beautiful and advanced to [b]royalty.

14"Then your [a]fame went forth among the nations on account of your beauty, for it was [b]perfect because of My splendor which I bestowed on you," declares the Lord GOD.

15"But you [a]trusted in your beauty and played the harlot because of your fame, and you poured out your harlotries on every passer-by [1]who might be *willing*.

16"And you took some of your clothes, made for yourself high

---

22 [a]Ezek. 12:16; 36:20 [b]Ezek. 16:54; 31:16; 32:31
23 [1]Or, *in*
2 [a]Ps. 80:8-16; Is. 5:1-7; Hos. 10:1
3 [1]Lit., *a work*
4 [1]Or, *Behold* [2]Lit., *a work* [a]Is. 27:11; Ezek. 15:6; 19:14
5 [1]Lit., *a work*
6 [1]YHWH, usually rendered LORD, and so throughout the chap.
7 [a]Lev. 26:17; Ps. 34:16; Jer. 21:10; Ezek. 14:8 [b]1 Kin. 19:17; Is. 24:18; Amos 9:1-4
8 [a]Ezek. 14:13; 17:20
2 [a]Is. 58:1; Ezek. 20:4; 22:2
3 [1]YHWH, usually rendered LORD, and so throughout the chap.
5 [1]Lit., *surface* [2]Lit., *in the loathing of your soul* [a]Deut. 32:10
6 [a]Ex. 19:4; Ps. 105:10-15
7 [1]Lit., *a myriad* [a]Ex. 1:7; Deut. 1:10
8 [1]Lit., *your time was* [a]Ruth 3:9; Jer. 2:2 [b]Gen. 22:16-18 [c]Ex. 24:7, 8 [d]Ex. 19:5; Ezek. 20:5; Hos. 2:19, 20
9 [a]Ruth 3:3
10 [a]Ex. 26:36; Ezek. 16:13, 18; 26:16; 27:7, 16
11 [a]Gen. 24:22, 47; Is. 3:19; Ezek. 23:42 [b]Gen. 41:42; Prov. 1:9
12 [a]Gen. 24:47; Is. 3:21 [b]Is. 28:5; Jer. 13:18; Ezek. 16:14
13 [a]Ps. 45:13, 14; Ezek. 16:17 [b]1 Sam. 10:1; 1 Kin. 4:21
14 [a]1 Kin. 10:1, 24 [b]Ps. 50:2; Lam. 2:15
15 [1]Lit., *to whom it might be* [a]Ezek. 16:25; 27:3

places of various colors, and played
the harlot on them, [1]which should
never come about nor happen.
17"You also took your beautiful
[1a]jewels *made* of My gold and of My
silver, which I had given you, and
made for yourself male images that
you might play the harlot with
them.
18"Then you took your embroidered cloth and covered them, and
offered My oil and My incense before them.
19"Also My bread which I gave
you, fine flour, oil, and honey with
which I fed you, [1]you would offer
before them for a soothing aroma;
so it happened," declares the Lord
GOD.
20"Moreover, you took your sons
and daughters whom you had borne
to [a]Me, and you [b]sacrificed them to
[1]idols to be devoured. Were your
harlotries so small a matter?
21"You slaughtered My children,
and offered them up to [1]idols by
[a]causing them to pass through *the*
fire.
22"And besides all your abominations and harlotries you did not remember the days of your youth,
when you were naked and bare and
squirming in your blood.
23"Then it came about after all
your wickedness ('Woe, woe to
you!' declares the Lord GOD),
24 that you built yourself a [a]shrine
and made yourself a [b]high place in
every square.
25"You built yourself a high place
at the top of every street, and made
your beauty abominable; and you
spread your legs to every passer-by
to multiply your harlotry.
26"You also played the harlot with
the Egyptians, your [1]lustful neighbors, and multiplied your harlotry to
[a]make Me angry.
27"Behold now, I have stretched
out My hand against you and diminished your rations. And I delivered
you up to the desire of those who
hate you, the [a]daughters of the Philistines, who are ashamed of your
lewd conduct.
28"Moreover, you played the harlot with the [a]Assyrians because you
were not satisfied; you even played
the harlot with them and still were
not satisfied.
29"You also multiplied your harlotry with the land of merchants,
Chaldea, yet even with this you
were not satisfied." ' "
30"How [a]languishing is your
heart," declares the Lord GOD,
"while you do all these things, the
actions of a [1b]bold-faced harlot.
31"When you built your shrine at
the beginning of every street and
made your high place in every
square, in [a]disdaining money, you
were not like a harlot.
32"You adulteress wife, who takes
strangers instead of her husband!
33"[1]Men give gifts to all harlots,
but you [a]give your gifts to all your
lovers to bribe them to come to you
from every direction for your harlotries.
34"Thus you are different from
those women in your harlotries, in
that no one plays the harlot [1]as you
do, because you give money and no
money is given you; thus you are
different."
35 Therefore, O harlot, hear the
word of the LORD.
36 Thus says the Lord GOD, "Because your lewdness was poured
out and your nakedness uncovered
through your harlotries with your
lovers and with all your detestable
[a]idols, and because of the blood of
your sons which you gave to [1]idols,
37 therefore, behold, I shall [a]gath-
er all your lovers with whom you
took pleasure, even all those whom
you loved *and* all those whom you
[b]hated. So I shall gather them
against you from every direction
and [c]expose your nakedness to
them that they may see all your nakedness.
38"Thus I shall [a]judge you, like
women who commit adultery or
shed blood are judged; and I shall
bring on you the blood of [b]wrath
and jealousy.
39"I shall also give you into [1]the
hands of your lovers, and they will
tear down your shrines, demolish
your high places, strip you of your
clothing, take away your [2]jewels,
and will leave you naked and bare.
40"They will [1]incite a [a]crowd
against you, and they will stone you
and cut you to pieces with their
swords.
41"And they will [a]burn your
houses with fire and execute judgments on you in the sight of many
women. Then I shall [b]stop you from
playing the harlot, and you will also
no longer pay [1]your lovers.
42"So I [a]shall calm My fury against
you, and My jealousy will depart
from you, and I shall be pacified and
angry [b]no more.
43"Because you have [a]not remembered the days of your youth but
[1]have [b]enraged Me by all these

16 [1]Lit., *things which had not happened nor will it be*
17 [1]Lit., *articles of beauty* [a]Ezek. 16:11, 12
19 [1]Lit., *and you . . . offer it*
20 [1]Lit., *them* [a]Ex. 13:2, 12; Deut. 29:11, 12 [b]Ps. 106:37, 38; Jer. 7:31; Ezek. 20:31; 23:37
21 [1]Lit., *them* [a]2 Kin. 17:17; Jer. 19:5
24 Jer. 11:30; Ezek. 16:31, 39; 20:28, 29 [b]Ps. 78:58; Is. 57:5, 7
26 [1]Lit., *great of flesh* [a]Jer. 7:18, 19; Ezek. 8:17
27 [a]Is. 9:12; Ezek. 16:57
28 [a]2 Kin. 16:7, 10-18; 2 Chr. 28:16, 20-23; Jer. 2:18, 36; Ezek. 23:12; Hos. 10:6
30 [1]Lit., *domineering* [a]Prov. 9:13; Is. 1:3; Jer. 4:22 [b]Is. 3:9; Jer. 3:3
31 [a]Is. 52:3
33 [1]Lit., *they* [a]Is. 57:9; Ezek. 16:41; Hos. 8:9, 10
34 [1]Lit., *after you*
36 [1]Lit., *them* [a]Jer. 19:5; Ezek. 20:31; 23:37
37 [a]Jer. 13:22, 26; Ezek. 23:9, 22; Hos. 2:3, 10; Nah. 3:5, 6 [b]Ezek. 23:17, 18 [c]Is. 47:3
38 [a]Ezek. 23:45 [b]Ps. 79:3, 5; Jer. 18:21; Ezek. 23:25; Zeph. 1:17
39 [1]Lit., *their hands, and they* [2]Lit., *articles of beauty*
40 [1]Lit., *bring up an assembly* [a]Ezek. 23:47; Hab. 1:6-10
41 [1]Lit., *a harlot's hire* [a]2 Kin. 25:9; Jer. 39:8; 52:13 [b]Ezek. 23:48
42 [a]2 Sam. 24:25; Ezek. 5:13; 21:17; Zech. 6:8 [b]Is. 40:1, 2; 54:9, 10; Ezek. 39:29
43 [1]So with ancient versions; Heb., *are angry against* [a]Ps. 78:42; 106:13; Ezek. 16:22 [b]Is. 63:10; Ezek. 6:9

things, behold, I in turn will [c]bring
your conduct down on your own
head," declares the Lord GOD, "so
that you will not commit this lewdness on top of all your *other* abominations.
44"Behold, every one who quotes
[a]proverbs will quote *this* proverb
concerning you, saying, '[1]Like
mother, [1]like daughter.'
45"You are the daughter of your
mother, who loathed her husband
and children. You are also the [a]sis-
ter of your sisters, who [b]loathed
their husbands and children. Your
mother was a Hittite and your father an Amorite.
46"Now your [a]older sister is Samaria, who lives north of you with
her [1]daughters; and your younger
sister, who lives south of you, is
[b]Sodom with her [1]daughters.
47"Yet you have not merely
walked in their ways or done according to their abominations; but,
as if that were [a]too little, you acted
[b]more corruptly in all your conduct
than they.
48"As I live," declares the Lord
GOD, "Sodom, your sister, and her
daughters, have [a]not done as you
and your daughters have done.
49"Behold, this was the guilt of
your sister Sodom: she and her
daughters had [a]arrogance, [b]abun-
dant food, and careless [c]ease, but
she did not help the [d]poor and
needy.
50"Thus they were haughty and
committed abominations before
Me. Therefore I [a]removed them
[1]when I saw *it*.
51"Furthermore, Samaria did not
commit half of your sins, for you
have multiplied your abominations
more than they. Thus you have
made your sisters appear [a]righteous
by all your abominations which you
have committed.
52"Also bear your disgrace in that
you have made judgment favorable
for your sisters. Because of your
sins in which you acted [a]more
abominably than they, they are
more in the right than you. Yes, be
also ashamed and bear your disgrace, in that you made your sisters
appear righteous.
53"Nevertheless, I will restore
their captivity, the captivity of Sodom and her daughters, the captivity
of Samaria and her daughters, and
along with them [a]your own captivity,
54 in order that you may bear your
humiliation, and feel [a]ashamed for
all that you have done when you become a consolation to them.
55"And your sisters, Sodom with
her daughters and Samaria with her
daughters, [1]will return to their former state, and you with your daughters will *also* return to your former
state.
56"As *the name of* your sister Sodom was [a]not heard from your lips in
your day of pride,
57 before your [a]wickedness was
uncovered, [1]so now you have become the [b]reproach of the daughters of [2]Edom, and of all who are
around her, of the daughters of the
Philistines—those surrounding *you*
who despise you.
58"You have [a]borne *the penalty of*
your lewdness and abominations,"
the LORD declares.
59 For thus says the Lord GOD, "I
will also do with you as you have
done, you who have [a]despised the
oath by breaking the covenant.

The Covenant Remembered

60"Nevertheless, I will remember
My covenant with you in the days of
your youth, and I will establish an
[a]everlasting covenant with you.
61"Then you will [a]remember your
ways and be ashamed when you receive your sisters, *both* your older
and your younger; and I will give
them to you as daughters, but not
because of your covenant.
62"Thus I will [a]establish My covenant with you, and you shall [b]know
that I am the LORD,
63 in order that you may [a]remem-
ber and be ashamed, and [b]never
open your mouth any more because
of your humiliation, when I have
[c]forgiven you for all that you have
done," the Lord GOD declares.

CHAPTER 17

Parable of Two Eagles and a Vine

NOW the word of the LORD came
to me saying,
2"Son of man, [a]propound a riddle,
and speak a parable to the house of
Israel,
3 [1]saying, 'Thus says the Lord
[2]GOD, "A great [a]eagle with [b]great
wings, long pinions and a full plumage of many colors, came to [c]Leba-
non and took away the top of the
cedar.
4"He plucked off the topmost of
its young twigs and brought it to a
land of merchants; he set it in a city
of traders.

43 [c]Ezek. 11:21; 22:31
44 [1]Lit., *Her* [a]1 Sam. 24:13; Ezek. 12:22, 23; 18:2, 3
45 [a]Ezek. 23:2 [b]Gen. 18:20; Is. 1:4; Ezek. 23:37-39; Zech. 11:8
46 [1]I.e., environs; so through v. 55 [a]Jer. 3:8-11; Ezek. 23:4 [b]Gen. 13:11-13; 18:20; Ezek. 16:48, 49, 53-56
47 [a]1 Kin. 16:31 [b]2 Kin. 21:9; Ezek. 5:6; 16:48
48 [a]Matt. 11:23
49 [a]Gen. 19:9; Ps. 138:6; Is. 3:9; Ezek. 28:2, 9, 17 [b]Gen. 13:10; Is. 22:13; Amos 6:4-6 [c]Luke 12:16-20; 16:19 [d]Ezek. 18:7
50 [1]Or, *as you have seen* [a]Gen. 19:24, 25
51 [a]Jer. 3:8-11 Matt. 12:41, 42
52 [a]Ezek. 16:47, 48, 51
53 [a]Is. 19:24, 25
54 [a]Jer. 2:26
55 [1]Heb. includes *will return . . . state* after Sodom also
56 [a]Is. 65:5; Luke 15:28-30
57 [1]Heb., *as at the time of* [2]So with many mss. and one version; M.T., *Syria* [a]Ezek. 16:36, 37 [b]2 Kin. 16:5-7; 2 Chr. 28:5, 6, 18-23; Ezek. 5:14, 15; 22:4
58 [a]Ezek. 23:49
59 [a]Is. 24:5; Ezek. 17:19
60 [a]Is. 55:3; Jer. 32:38-41; Ezek. 37:26
61 [a]Jer. 50:4, 5; Ezek. 6:9
62 [a]Ezek. 20:37; 34:25; 37:26 [b]Jer. 24:7; Ezek. 20:43
63 [a]Ezek. 36:31, 32; Dan. 9:7, 8 [b]Ps. 39:9; Rom. 3:19 [c]Ps. 65:3; 78:38; 79:9
2 [a]Ezek. 20:49; 24:3
3 [1]Lit., *and you shall say* [2]YHWH, usually rendered LORD, and so throughout the chap. [a]Jer. 48:40; Ezek. 17:12; Hos. 8:1 [b]Dan. 4:22 [c]Jer. 22:23

5 "He also took some of the seed of the land and planted it in [a]fertile soil. He placed *it* beside abundant waters; he set it *like* a [b]willow.

6 "Then it sprouted and became a low, spreading vine with its branches turned toward him, but its roots remained under it. So it became a vine, and yielded shoots and sent out branches.

7 "But there was [1]another great eagle with great wings and much plumage; and behold, this vine bent its roots toward him and sent out its branches toward him from the beds where it was [a]planted, that he might water it.

8 "It was planted in good [1]soil beside abundant waters, that it might yield branches and bear fruit, *and* become a splendid vine." '

9 "Say, 'Thus says the Lord GOD, "Will it thrive? Will he not pull up its roots and cut off its fruit, so that it withers—so that all its sprouting leaves wither? And neither by great [1]strength nor by many people can it be raised from its roots *again*.

10 "Behold, though it is planted, will it thrive? Will it not [a]completely wither as soon as the east wind strikes it—wither on the beds where it grew?" ' "

Zedekiah's Rebellion

11 Moreover, the word of the LORD came to me saying,

12 "Say now to the [a]rebellious house, 'Do you not [b]know what these things *mean?*' Say, 'Behold, the [c]king of Babylon came to Jerusalem, took its king and princes, and brought them to him in Babylon.

13 'And he took one of the royal [1a]family and made a covenant with him, [2]putting him under [b]oath. He also took away the [c]mighty of the land,

14 that the kingdom might be [1]in subjection, not exalting itself, *but* keeping his covenant, that it might continue.

15 'But he [a]rebelled against him by sending his envoys to Egypt that they might give him horses and many [1]troops. Will he succeed? Will he who does such things [b]escape? Can he indeed break the covenant and escape?

16 'As I live,' declares the Lord GOD, 'Surely in the [1]country of the king who [2]put him on the throne, whose oath he [a]despised, and whose covenant he broke, [3b]in Babylon he shall die.

17 'And [a]Pharaoh with *his* mighty army and great company will not [1]help him in the war, when they cast up mounds and build siege walls to cut off many lives.

18 'Now he despised the oath by breaking the covenant, and behold, he [1]pledged his allegiance, yet did all these things; he shall not escape.' "

19 Therefore, thus says the Lord GOD, "As I live, surely My oath which he despised and My covenant which he broke, I will [1]inflict on his head.

20 "And I will spread My [a]net over him, and he will be [b]caught in My snare. Then I will bring him to Babylon and [c]enter into judgment with him there *regarding* the unfaithful act which he has committed against Me.

21 "And all the [1a]choice men in all his troops will fall by the sword, and the survivors will be scattered to every wind; and you will know that I, the LORD, have spoken."

22 Thus says the Lord GOD, "I shall also take *a sprig* from the lofty top of the cedar and set *it* out; I shall pluck from the topmost of its young twigs a tender one, and I shall plant *it* on a [a]high and lofty mountain.

23 "On the high mountain of Israel I shall plant it, that it may bring forth boughs and bear fruit, and become a stately [a]cedar. And birds of every [1]kind will [2]nest under it; they will [2]nest in the shade of its branches.

24 "And all the [a]trees of the field will know that I am the LORD; I bring down the high tree, exalt the low tree, dry up the green tree, and make the dry tree [b]flourish. I am the LORD; I have spoken, and I will perform *it*."

CHAPTER 18

God Deals Justly with Individuals

THEN the word of the LORD came to me saying,

2 "[a]What do you mean by using this proverb concerning the land of Israel saying,

'[b]The fathers eat the sour grapes,
But the children's teeth [1]are set on edge'?

3 "As I live," declares the Lord [1]GOD, "you are surely not going to use this proverb in Israel any more.

4 "Behold, [a]all [1]souls are Mine; the [2]soul of the father as well as the [2]soul of the son is Mine. The [3]soul who [b]sins will die.

---

5 [a]Deut. 8:7-9 [b]Is. 44:4
7 [1]So with several ancient versions; M.T., *one* [a]Ezek. 31:4
8 [1]Lit., *field*
9 [1]Lit., *arm*
10 [a]Ezek. 19:14; Hos. 13:15
12 [a]Ezek. 2:3-5 [b]Ezek. 12:9-11; 24:19 [c]2 Kin. 24:11, 12, 15; Ezek. 1:2; 17:3
13 [1]Lit., *seed* [2]Lit., *and caused him to enter into an oath* [a]2 Kin. 24:17; Ezek. 17:5 [b]2 Chr. 36:13 [c]2 Kin. 24:15, 16
14 [1]Lit., *low*
15 [1]Lit., *people* [a]2 Kin. 24:20; 2 Chr. 36:13; Jer. 52:3; Ezek. 17:7 [b]Jer. 34:3; 38:18, 23; Ezek. 17:18
16 [1]Lit., *place* [2]Lit., *made him king* [3]Lit., *with him in Babylon* [a]2 Kin. 24:17, 20; Ezek. 16:59; 17:13, 18, 19 [b]Jer. 52:11; Ezek. 12:13
17 [1]Lit., *act with* [a]Is. 36:6; Jer. 37:5, 7; Ezek. 29:6, 7
18 [1]Lit., *gave his hand*
19 [1]Lit., *give it*
20 [a]Ezek. 12:13; 32:3 [b]Jer. 39:5-7 [c]Jer. 2:35; 20:35
21 [1]So many ancient mss. and versions; M.T., *fugitives* [a]2 Kin. 25:5, 11; Ezek. 5:2, 10, 12
22 [a]Ps. 72:16; Ezek. 20:40; 37:22
23 [1]Lit., *wing* [2]Lit., *dwell* [a]Ps. 92:12; Is. 27:6
24 [a]Ps. 96:12; Is. 55:12 [b]Is. 37:3, 13; Amos 9:11
2 [1]Lit., *become dull* [a]Is. 3:15 [b]Jer. 31:29; Lam. 5:7; Matt. 23:36
3 [1]YHWH, usually rendered LORD, and so throughout the chap.
4 [1]Or, *lives* [2]Or, *life* [3]Or, *person* [a]Num. 16:22; 27:16; Is. 42:5; 57:16 [b]Ezek. 18:20; Rom. 6:23

5"But if a man is righteous, and
practices justice and righteousness,
6 and does not [a]eat at the mountain *shrines* or [b]lift up his eyes to the
idols of the house of Israel, or [c]defile
his neighbor's wife, or approach a
woman during her menstrual period—
7 if a man does not oppress any
one, but [a]restores to the debtor his
pledge, [b]does not commit robbery,
but [c]gives his bread to the hungry,
and covers the naked with clothing,
8 if he does not lend *money* on
[a]interest or take [b]increase, *if* he
keeps his hand from iniquity, *and*
[c]executes true justice between man
and man,
9 *if* he walks in My statutes and
My ordinances so as to deal faithfully—he is righteous *and* will
surely [a]live," declares the Lord GOD.
10"Then he may [1]have a violent
son who sheds blood, and who does
any of these things to a brother
11 (though he himself did not do
any of these things), that is, he even
eats at the mountain *shrines*, and
defiles his neighbor's wife,
12 oppresses the [a]poor and needy,
[b]commits robbery, does not restore
a pledge, but lifts up his eyes to the
idols, *and* [c]commits abomination,
13 he lends *money* on interest and
takes increase; will he live? He will
not live! He has committed all these
abominations, he will surely be put
to death; his [a]blood will be [1]on his
own head.
14"Now behold, he [1]has a son who
has observed all his father's sins
which he committed, and [a]observ-
ing does not do likewise.
15"He does not eat at the mountain
shrines or lift up his eyes to the idols
of the house of Israel, or defile his
neighbor's wife,
16 or oppress anyone, or retain a
pledge, or commit robbery, *but* he
[a]gives his bread to the hungry, and
covers the naked with clothing,
17 he keeps his hand from [1]the
poor, does not take interest or increase, *but* executes My ordinances,
and walks in My statutes; he will not
die for his father's iniquity, he will
surely live.
18"As for his father, because he
practiced extortion, robbed *his*
brother, and did what was not good
among his people, behold, he will
die for his iniquity.
19"Yet you say, '[a]Why should the
son not bear the punishment for the
father's iniquity?' When the son has
practiced [b]justice and righteousness, and has observed all My statutes and done them, he shall surely
live.
20"The person who [a]sins will die.
The [b]son will not bear the punishment for the father's iniquity, nor
will the father bear the punishment
for the son's iniquity; the [c]right-
eousness of the righteous will be
upon himself, and the wickedness of
the wicked will be upon himself.
21"But if the [a]wicked man turns
from all his sins which he has committed and observes all My statutes
and practices justice and righteousness, he shall surely live; he shall not
die.
22"[a]All his transgressions which
he has committed will not be remembered against him; because of
his [b]righteousness which he has
practiced, he will live.
23"[a]Do I have any pleasure in the
death of the wicked," declares the
Lord GOD, "[1]rather than that he
should [b]turn from his ways and live?
24"But when a righteous man
[a]turns away from his righteousness,
commits iniquity, and does according to all the abominations that a
wicked man does, will he live? [b]All
his righteous deeds which he has
done will not be remembered for his
[c]treachery which he has committed
and his sin which he has committed;
for them he will die.
25"Yet you say, '[a]The way of the
Lord is not right.' Hear now, O
house of Israel! Is [b]My way not
right? Is it not your ways that are
not right?
26"When a righteous man turns
away from his righteousness, commits iniquity, and dies because of it,
for his iniquity which he has committed he will die.
27"Again, when a wicked man
turns away from his wickedness
which he has committed and practices justice and righteousness, he
will save his life.
28"Because he considered and
turned away from all his transgressions which he had committed, he
shall surely live; he shall not die.
29"But the house of Israel says,
'The way of the Lord is not right.'
Are My ways not right, O house of
Israel? Is it not your ways that are
not right?
30"Therefore I will judge you, O
house of Israel, each according to
his conduct," declares the Lord
GOD. "[a]Repent and turn away from
all your transgressions, so that iniq-

6 [a]Ezek. 6:13; 18:15; 22:9 [b]Deut. 4:19; Ezek. 18:12, 15; 20:24; 33:25 [c]Ezek. 18:15; 22:11
7 [a]Deut. 24:13; Ezek. 33:15; Amos 2:8 [b]Lev. 19:13; Amos 3:10 [c]Deut. 15:11; Ezek. 18:16; Matt. 25:35-40; Luke 3:11
8 [a]Ex. 22:25; Deut. 23:19, 20 [b]Lev. 25:36 [c]Zech. 7:9; 8:16
9 [a]Hab. 2:4; Rom. 1:17
10 [1]Lit., *beget*
12 [a]Amos 4:1; Zech. 7:10 [b]Is. 59:6, 7; Jer. 22:3, 17; Ezek. 7:23; 18:7, 16, 18 [c]2 Kin. 21:11; Ezek. 8:6, 17
13 [1]Lit., *on him* [a]Ezek. 33:4, 5
14 [1]Lit., *begets* [a]2 Chr. 29:6-10; 34:21
16 [a]Job 31:16, 20; Ps. 41:1; Is. 58:7, 10; Ezek. 18:7
17 [1]So M.T.; Gk. reads: *iniquity* as in v. 8
19 [a]Ex. 20:5; Jer. 15:4; Ezek. 18:2 [b]Ezek. 18:9; 20:18-20; Zech. 1:3-6
20 [a]2 Kin. 14:6; 22:18-20; Ezek. 18:4 [b]Deut. 24:16; Jer. 31:30 [c]1 Kin. 8:32; Is. 3:10, 11; Matt. 16:27; Rom. 2:6-9
21 [a]Ezek. 18:27, 28; 33:12, 19
22 [a]Is. 43:25; Jer. 50:20; Ezek. 18:24; 33:16; Mic. 7:19 [b]Ps. 18:20-24
23 [1]Lit., *is it not* [a]Ezek. 18:32; 33:11; Lam. 3:33; Hos. 11:8 [b]Ps. 147:11; Mic. 7:18
24 [a]1 Sam. 15:11; 2 Chr. 24:2, 17-22; Ezek. 3:20; 18:26; 33:18 [b]Ezek. 18:22; Gal. 3:3, 4 [c]Prov. 21:16; Ezek. 17:20; 20:27
25 [a]Ezek. 18:29; 33:17, 20; Mal. 2:17; 3:13-15 [b]Gen. 18:25; Jer. 12:1; Zeph. 3:5
30 [a]Ezek. 14:6; 33:11; Hos. 12:6

uity may not become a stumbling
block to you.
31 "[a]Cast away from you all your
transgressions which you have
committed, and make yourselves a
[b]new heart and a new spirit! For
why will you die, O house of Israel?
32 "For I have [a]no pleasure in the
death of anyone who dies," declares
the Lord GOD. "Therefore, repent
and live."

CHAPTER 19

Lament for the Princes of Israel

"AS for you, take up a [a]lamentation for the [b]princes of Israel,
2 and say,

'[1]What was your mother?
A lioness among lions!
She lay down among young lions,
She reared her cubs.

3 'When she brought up one of her cubs,
He became a lion,
And he learned to tear *his* prey;
He devoured men.

4 'Then nations heard about him;
He was [a]captured in their pit,
And they brought him with hooks
To the land of Egypt.

5 'When she saw, as she waited,
That her hope was lost,
She took [1]another of her cubs
And made him a young lion.

6 'And he [a]walked about among the lions;
He became a young lion,
He learned to tear *his* prey;
He devoured men.

7 'And he [1]destroyed their [2]fortified towers
And laid waste their cities;
And the land and its fulness were appalled
Because of the sound of his roaring.

8 'Then [a]nations set against him
On every side from *their* provinces,
And they spread their net over him;
He was captured in their pit.

9 'And they put him in a cage with hooks
And [a]brought him to the king of Babylon;
They brought him in hunting nets
So that his voice should be heard no more
On the mountains of Israel.

10 'Your mother was [a]like a vine in your [1]vineyard,
Planted by the waters;
It was fruitful and full of branches
Because of abundant waters.

11 'And it had [1a]strong branches *fit* for scepters of rulers,
And its [b]height was raised above the clouds
So that it was seen in its height with the mass of its branches.

12 'But it was [a]plucked up in fury;
It was [b]cast down to the ground;
And the [c]east wind dried up its fruit.
Its [1d]strong branch [2]was torn off
So that [3]it withered;
The fire consumed it.

13 'And now it is planted in the [a]wilderness,
In a dry and thirsty land.

14 'And [a]fire has gone out from *its* branch;
It has consumed its shoots *and* fruit,
So that there is not in it a [1]strong branch,
A scepter to rule.' "

This is a lamentation, and has become a lamentation.

CHAPTER 20

God's Dealings with Israel Rehearsed

NOW it came about in the seventh
year, in the fifth *month,* on the tenth
of the month, that [1]certain of the [a]elders of Israel came to inquire of the
LORD, and sat before me.
2 And the word of the LORD came
to me saying,
3 "Son of man, speak to the elders
of Israel, and say to them, 'Thus
says the Lord [1]GOD, "Do you come
to inquire of Me? As I live," declares
the Lord GOD, "I will not be inquired
of by you." '
4 "Will you judge them, will you
judge them, son of man? [a]Make
them know the abominations of
their fathers;
5 and say to them, 'Thus says the
Lord GOD, "On the day when I
[a]chose Israel and [1]swore to the [2]descendants of the house of Jacob and
made Myself known to them in the
land of Egypt, when I [1]swore to
them, saying, [b]I am the LORD your
God,
6 on that day I swore to them, to
bring them out from the land of

31 [a]Is. 1:16, 17; 55:7 [b]Ps. 51:10; Ezek. 11:19; 36:26

32 [a]Ezek. 18:23; 33:11

1 [a]Ezek. 2:10; 19:14 [b]2 Kin. 23:29, 30, 34; 24:6, 12; 25:5-7

2 [1]Or, *Why did your mother, a lioness, lie down among lions; among young lions rear her cubs?*

4 [a]2 Kin. 23:34; 2 Chr. 36:4, 6

5 [1]Lit., *one*

6 [a]2 Kin. 24:9; 2 Chr. 36:9

7 [1]So Targum; M.T., *knew* [2]Or, *widows*

8 [a]2 Kin. 24:11

9 [a]2 Kin. 24:15

10 [1]So with some ancient mss.; M.T., *blood* [a]Ps. 80:8-11

11 [1]Lit., *rods of strength* [a]Ps. 80:15 [b]Ezek. 31:3

12 [1]Lit., *rods of her strength* [2]So Gk.; M.T., *they were* [3]So Gk.; M.T., *they* [a]Jer. 31:28 [b]Lam. 2:1; Ezek. 28:17 [c]Ezek. 17:10; Hos. 13:15 [d]Is. 27:11; Ezek. 19:11

13 [a]2 Kin. 24:12-16; Ezek. 19:10; 20:35; Hos. 2:3

14 [1]Lit., *rod of strength* [a]Ezek. 15:4; 20:47, 48

1 [1]Lit., *men* [a]Ezek. 8:1, 11, 12

3 [1]YHWH, usually rendered LORD, and so throughout the chap.

4 [a]Ezek. 16:2; 22:2

5 [1]Lit., *lifted up My hand,* and so throughout the chap. [2]Lit., *seed* [a]Ex. 6:6-8 [b]Ex. 6:2, 3

Egypt into a land that I had [1]selected for them, [a]flowing with milk and honey, which is the glory of all lands.

7"And I said to them, '[a]Cast away, each of you, the detestable things of his eyes, and [b]do not defile yourselves with the idols of Egypt; [c]I am the LORD your God.'

8"But they [a]rebelled against Me and were not willing to listen to Me; [1]they did not cast away the detestable things of their eyes, nor did they forsake the [b]idols of Egypt.

Then I [2]resolved to [c]pour out My wrath on them, to accomplish My anger against them in the midst of the land of Egypt.

9"But I acted [a]for the sake of My name, that it should [b]not be profaned in the sight of the nations among whom they *lived*, in whose sight I made Myself known to them by bringing them out of the land of Egypt.

10"So I took them out of the land of Egypt and brought them into the [a]wilderness.

11"And I gave them My [a]statutes and informed them of My ordinances, by [b]which, if a man [1]observes them, he will live.

12"And also I gave them My sabbaths to be a [a]sign between Me and them, that they might know that I am the LORD who sanctifies them.

13"But the house of Israel [a]rebelled against Me in the wilderness. They did not walk in My statutes, and they rejected My ordinances, by which, if a man [1]observes them, he will live; and My [b]sabbaths they greatly profaned. Then I [2]resolved to [c]pour out My wrath on them in the wilderness, to annihilate them.

14"But I acted for the sake of My name, that it should not be profaned in the sight of the nations, before whose sight I had brought them out.

15"And also I swore to them in the wilderness that I would not bring them into the land which I had given them, flowing with milk and honey, which is the glory of all lands,

16 because they rejected My ordinances, and as for My statutes, they did not walk in them; they even profaned My sabbaths, for their [a]heart continually went after their idols.

17"Yet My eye spared them rather than destroying them, and I did not cause their [a]annihilation in the wilderness.

18"And I said to their [1a]children in the wilderness, '[b]Do not walk in the statutes of your fathers, or keep their ordinances, or defile yourselves with their idols.

19 '[a]I am the LORD your God; walk in My statutes, and keep My ordinances, and [1]observe them.

20 'And sanctify My sabbaths; and they shall be a sign between Me and you, that you may know that I am the LORD your God.'

21"But the [a]children rebelled against Me; they did not walk in My statutes, nor were they careful to observe My ordinances, by which, *if* a man observes them, he will live; they profaned My sabbaths. So I [1]resolved to pour out My wrath on them, to accomplish My anger against them in the wilderness.

22"But I [a]withdrew My hand and acted [b]for the sake of My name, that it should not be profaned in the sight of the nations in whose sight I had brought them out.

23"Also I swore to them in the wilderness that I would [a]scatter them among the nations and disperse them among the lands,

24 because they had not observed My ordinances, but had rejected My statutes, and had profaned My sabbaths, and their eyes were [1]on the idols of their fathers.

25"And I also gave them statutes that were [a]not good and ordinances by which they could not live;

26 and I pronounced them [a]unclean because of their gifts, in that they [b]caused all [1]their first-born to pass through *the fire* so that I might make them desolate, in order that they might [c]know that I am the LORD."'

27"Therefore, son of man, [a]speak to the house of Israel, and say to them, 'Thus says the Lord GOD, "Yet in this your fathers have [b]blasphemed Me by [c]acting treacherously against Me.

28"When I had [a]brought them into the land which I swore to give to them, then they saw every [b]high hill and every leafy tree, and they offered there their sacrifices, and there they presented the provocation of their offering. There also they made their soothing aroma, and there they poured out their libations.

29"Then I said to them, 'What is the high place to which you go?' So its name is called [1]Bamah to this day."'

30"Therefore, say to the house of Israel, 'Thus says the Lord GOD, "Will you defile yourselves [1]after the manner of your [a]fathers and

6 [1]Lit., *spied out* [a]Ex. 13:5; 33:3
7 [a]Ex. 20:4, 5; 22:20 [b]Lev. 18:3; Deut. 29:16, 18 [c]Ex. 20:2
8 [1]Lit., *each one* [2]Lit., *said* [a]Deut. 9:7; Is. 63:10 [b]Ex. 32:1-9 [c]Ezek. 5:13; 7:8; 20:13, 21
9 [a]Ex. 32:11-14; Ezek. 20:14, 22; 36:21, 22 [b]Ezek. 39:7
10 [a]Ex. 19:1
11 [1]Lit., *does* [a]Ex. 20:1-23, 33 [b]Lev. 18:5; Ezek. 20:13
12 [a]Ex. 31:13, 17; Ezek. 20:20
13 [1]Lit., *does* [2]Lit., *said* [a]Num. 14:11, 12, 22; Ezek. 20:8 [b]Is. 56:6; Ezek. 20:21 [c]Ex. 32:10; Deut. 9:8; Ezek. 20:8, 21
16 [a]Ezek. 11:21; 14:3-7; 20:8
17 [a]Jer. 4:27; 5:18; Ezek. 11:13
18 [1]Lit., *sons* [a]Num. 14:31; Deut. 4:3-6 [b]Zech. 1:4
19 [1]Lit., *do* [a]Ex. 6:7; 20:2
21 [1]Lit., *said* [a]Num. 21:5; 25:1-3
22 [a]Job 13:21; Ps. 78:38; Ezek. 20:17 [b]Is. 48:9-11; Jer. 14:7, 21; Ezek. 20:9, 14
23 [a]Lev. 26:33; Deut. 4:27; 28:64
24 [1]Lit., *after*
25 [a]Ps. 81:12; Is. 66:4; Rom. 1:21-25, 28
26 [1]Lit., *that which opens the womb* [a]Lev. 18:21; 20:2-5; Is. 63:17; Ezek. 20:30; Rom. 11:8 [b]Jer. 7:31; 19:4-9 [c]Ezek. 6:7; 20:12, 20
27 [a]Ezek. 3:4, 11, 27; 20:2, 7 [b]Num. 15:30; Rom. 2:24 [c]Ezek. 18:24; 39:23, 26
28 [a]Josh. 23:3, 14; Neh. 9:22-26; Ps. 78:55 [b]1 Kin. 14:23; Ps. 78:58; Is. 57:5-7; Jer. 2:7; 3:6; Ezek. 6:13
29 [1]Or, *High Place*
30 [1]Lit., *in the way of* [a]Judg. 2:19; Jer. 7:26; 16:12

play the harlot after their detestable things?

31 "And [1]when you offer your gifts, when you cause your sons to [a]pass through the fire, you are defiling yourselves with all your idols to this day. And shall I be inquired of by you, O house of Israel? As I live," declares the Lord GOD, "I will not be inquired of by you.

32 "And what comes [1]into your mind will not come about, when you say: 'We will be like the nations, like the tribes of the lands, [a]serving wood and stone.'

God Will Restore Israel to Her Land

33 "As I live," declares the Lord GOD, "surely with a mighty hand and with an outstretched arm and with wrath poured out, I shall be [a]king over you.

34 "And I shall [a]bring you out from the peoples and gather you from the lands where you are scattered, with a mighty hand and with an outstretched arm and with [b]wrath poured out;

35 and I shall bring you into the [a]wilderness of the peoples, and there I shall enter into judgment with you face to face.

36 "As I [a]entered into judgment with your fathers in the [b]wilderness of the land of Egypt, so I will enter into judgment with you," declares the Lord GOD.

37 "And I shall make you [a]pass under the rod, and I shall bring you into the bond of the covenant;

38 and I shall [a]purge from you the rebels and those who transgress against Me; I shall bring them out of the land where they sojourn, but they will [b]not enter the land of Israel. Thus you will know that I am the LORD.

39 "As for you, O house of Israel," thus says the Lord GOD, "[a]Go, serve every one his idols; [1]but later, you will surely listen to Me, and My holy name you will [b]profane no longer with your gifts and with your idols.

40 "For on My holy mountain, on the high mountain of Israel," declares the Lord GOD, "there the whole house of Israel, [a]all of them, will serve Me in the land; there I shall [b]accept them, and there I shall [1]seek your contributions and the choicest of your gifts, with all your holy things.

41 "[1]As a soothing aroma I shall accept you, when I [a]bring you out from the peoples and gather you from the lands where you are scattered; and I shall prove Myself [b]holy among you in the sight of the nations.

42 "And you will know that I am the LORD, when I bring you into the land of Israel, into the [a]land which I swore to give to your forefathers.

43 "And there you will [a]remember your ways and all your deeds, with which you have defiled yourselves; and you will [b]loathe yourselves in your own sight for all the evil things that you have done.

44 "Then you will know that I am the LORD when I have dealt with you for My name's sake, not according to your evil ways or according to your corrupt deeds, O house of Israel," declares the Lord GOD.' "

45 [1]Now the word of the LORD came to me saying,

46 "Son of man, set your face toward [1]Teman, and speak out against the [a]south, and [b]prophesy against the [c]forest [2]land of the Negev,

47 and say to the forest of the Negev, 'Hear the word of the LORD: thus says the Lord GOD, "Behold, I am about to [a]kindle a fire in you, and it shall consume every [1]green tree in you, as well as every dry tree; the blazing flame will not be quenched, and [2b]the whole surface from south to north will be burned by it.

48 "And all flesh will see that I, the LORD, have kindled it; it shall [a]not be quenched." ' "

49 Then I said, "Ah Lord GOD! They are saying of me, 'Is he not *just* speaking [a]parables?' "

CHAPTER 21

Parable of the Sword of the LORD

1 AND the word of the LORD came to me saying,

2 "Son of man, [a]set your face toward Jerusalem, and [1b]speak against the sanctuaries, and prophesy against the land of Israel;

3 and say to the land of Israel, 'Thus says the LORD, "Behold, [a]I am against you; and I shall draw My sword out of its sheath and cut off from you the [b]righteous and the wicked.

4 "Because I shall cut off from you the righteous and the wicked, therefore My sword shall go forth from its sheath against [a]all flesh from south *to* north.

5 "Thus all flesh will know that I, the LORD, have drawn My sword out

31 [1]Lit., *in your lifting up* [a]Ps. 106:37-39; Jer. 7:31; Ezek. 16:20; 20:26
32 [1]Lit., *upon your spirit* [a]Jer. 2:25; 44:17
33 [a]Jer. 51:57
34 [a]Is. 27:12, 13; Ezek. 20:38; 34:16 [b]Jer. 42:18; 44:6; Lam. 2:4
35 [a]Ezek. 19:13; 20:36; Hos. 2:14
36 [a]Num. 11:1-35; Ps. 106:15; Ezek. 20:13, 21; 1 Cor. 10:5-10 [b]Deut. 32:10
37 [a]Lev. 27:32; Jer. 33:13
38 [a]Ezek. 34:17-22; Amos 9:9, 10; Zech. 13:8, 9; Mal. 3:3; 4:1-3 [b]Num. 14:29, 30; Ps. 95:11; Ezek. 13:9; 20:15, 16; Heb. 4:3
39 [1]Or, *and afterwards, if you will not listen to Me, but* [a]Jer. 44:25, 26 [b]Is. 1:13-15; Ezek. 23:38, 39; 43:7
40 [1]Or, *require* [a]Is. 66:23; Ezek. 37:22, 24 [b]Is. 56:7; 60:7; Ezek. 43:12, 27
41 [1]Lit., *With* [a]Is. 27:12, 13; Ezek. 11:17; 28:25 [b]Is. 5:16; Ezek. 28:25; 36:23
42 [a]Ezek. 20:6
43 [a]Ezek. 6:9; 16:61, 63; Hos. 5:15 [b]Jer. 31:18; Ezek. 36:31; Zech. 12:10
45 [1]Chap. 21:1 in Heb.
46 [1]Or, *the South* [2]Lit., *of the field* [a]Jer. 13:19; Ezek. 21:4 [b]Ezek. 21:2; Amos 7:16 [c]Is. 30:6-11
47 [1]Lit., *moist* [2]Or, *all the faces* [a]Is. 9:18, 19; Jer. 21:14 [b]Is. 13:8
48 [a]Jer. 7:20; 17:27
49 [a]Ezek. 17:2; Matt. 13:13, 14; John 16:25
1 [1]Chap. 21:6 in Heb.
2 [1]Lit., *drip* [a]Ezek. 20:46; 25:2; 28:21 [b]Job 29:22; Ezek. 20:46
3 [a]Jer. 21:13; Ezek. 5:8; Nah. 2:13; 3:5 [b]Is. 57:1
4 [a]Jer. 12:12; Ezek. 7:2; 20:47

of its sheath. It will [a]not return *to its sheath* again." '

6"As for you, son of man, groan with breaking heart and bitter grief, groan in their sight.

7"And it will come about when they say to you, 'Why do you groan?' that you will say, 'Because of the [a]news that is coming; and [b]every heart will melt, all hands will be feeble, every spirit will faint, and all knees will be weak as water. Behold, it comes and it will happen,' declares the Lord [1]GOD."

8 Again the word of the LORD came to me saying,

9"Son of man, prophesy and say, 'Thus says the LORD.' Say,

'A sword, a sword sharpened
And also polished!
10 'Sharpened to make a [a]slaughter,
Polished to flash like lightning!'

Or shall we rejoice, the rod of My son [b]despising every tree?

11"And it is given to be polished, that it may be handled; the sword is sharpened and polished, to give it into the hand of the slayer.

12"[a]Cry out and wail, son of man; for it is against My people, it is against all the [b]officials of Israel. They are delivered over to the sword with My people, therefore strike *your* thigh.

13"For *there is* a testing; and what if even the rod which despises will be no more?" declares the Lord GOD.

14"You therefore, son of man, prophesy, and clap *your* hands together; and let the sword be [a]doubled the third time, the sword for the slain. It is the sword for the great one slain, which [b]surrounds them,

15 that *their* [a]hearts may melt, and [b]many fall at all their [c]gates. I have given the glittering sword. Ah! It is made *for striking* like lightning, it is wrapped up *in readiness* for slaughter.

16"Show yourself sharp, go to the right; set yourself; go to the left, wherever your edge is appointed.

17"I shall also clap My hands together, and I shall [a]appease My wrath; I, the LORD, have spoken."

The Instrument of God's Judgment

18 And the word of the LORD came to me saying,

19"As for you, son of man, [1a]make two ways for the sword of the king of Babylon to come; both of them will go out of one land. And [2]make a signpost; make it at the head of the way to the city.

20"You shall [1]mark a way for the sword to come to [a]Rabbah of the sons of Ammon, and to Judah into [b]fortified Jerusalem.

21"For the king of Babylon stands at the [1]parting of the way, at the head of the two ways, to use [a]divination; he [b]shakes the arrows, he consults the [2c]household idols, he looks at the liver.

22"Into his right hand came the divination, 'Jerusalem,' [a]to set battering rams, to open the mouth [1]for slaughter, to lift up the voice with a battle cry, [b]to set battering rams against the gates, to cast up mounds, to build a siege wall.

23"And it will be to them like a false divination in their eyes; [a]they have *sworn* solemn oaths. But he brings iniquity to [b]remembrance, that they may be seized.

24"Therefore, thus says the Lord GOD, 'Because you have made your iniquity to be remembered, in that your transgressions are uncovered, so that in all your deeds your sins appear—because you have come to remembrance, you will be seized with the hand.

25 'And you, O slain, wicked one, the prince of Israel, whose [a]day has come, in the time of the [1]punishment of the end,'

26 thus says the Lord GOD, 'Remove the turban, and take off the [a]crown; this will *be* [1]no more the same. [b]Exalt that which is low, and abase that which is high.

27 'A ruin, a ruin, a ruin, I shall [a]make it. This also will be no more, until He comes whose [b]right it is; and I shall give it *to Him*.'

28"And you, son of man, prophesy and say, 'Thus says the Lord GOD concerning the sons of Ammon and concerning their [a]reproach,' and say: 'A sword, a sword is drawn, polished for the slaughter, to cause it [1]to [b]consume, that it may be like lightning—

29 while they see for you [a]false visions, while they divine lies for you—to place you on the necks of the wicked who are slain, whose day has come in the [b]time of the [1]punishment of the end.

30 '[a]Return *it* to its sheath. In the [b]place where you were created, in the land of your origin, I shall judge you.

31 'And I shall [a]pour out My indignation on you; I shall [b]blow on you

5 [a]1 Sam. 3:12; Jer. 23:20; Ezek. 21:30; Nah. 1:9
7 [1]YHWH, usually rendered LORD, and so throughout the chap. [a]Ezek. 7:26 [b]Is. 13:7; Nah. 2:10
10 [a]Is. 34:5, 6 [b]Ps. 110:5, 6; Ezek. 20:47
12 [a]Ezek. 21:6; Joel 1:13 [b]Ezek. 21:25; 22:6
14 [a]Lev. 26:21, 24; 2 Kin. 24:1, 10-16; 25:1 [b]1 Kin. 22:25
15 [a]Josh. 2:11; 2 Sam. 17:10; Ps. 22:2; Ezek. 21:7 [b]Is. 59:10; Jer. 13:16; 18:15 [c]Jer. 17:27; Ezek. 21:19
17 [a]Ezek. 5:13
19 [1]Or, *set for yourself* [2]Lit., *cut out a hand* [a]Jer. 1:10; Ezek. 4:1-3
20 [1]Lit., *set* [a]Deut. 3:11; Jer. 49:2; Ezek. 25:5; Amos 1:14 [b]Ps. 48:12, 13; 125:1, 2
21 [1]Lit., *mother* [2]Heb., *teraphim;* cf. Gen. 31:19; Judg. 18:17, 20 [a]Num. 22:7; 23:23 [b]Prov. 16:33; 21:1 [c]Gen. 31:19, 30; Judg. 17:5
22 [1]Lit., *in* [a]Ezek. 4:2 [b]Ezek. 26:9
23 [a]Ezek. 17:16, 18 [b]Num. 5:15; Ezek. 21:24; 29:16
25 [1]Or, *iniquity* [a]Ps. 37:13; Ezek. 7:2, 3, 7
26 [1]Lit., *not this* [a]Jer. 13:18; Ezek. 16:12 [b]Ps. 75:7; Ezek. 17:24
27 [a]Hag. 2:21, 22 [b]Ps. 2:6; 72:7, 10; Jer. 23:5, 6; Ezek. 34:24; 37:24
28 [1]Lit., *to finish* [a]Ezek. 36:15; Zeph. 2:8-10 [b]Is. 31:8; Jer. 12:12; 46:10, 14
29 [1]Or, *iniquity* [a]Jer. 27:9; Ezek. 13:6-9; 22:28 [b]Ezek. 21:25; 35:5
30 [a]Jer. 47:6, 7 [b]Ezek. 25:5
31 [a]Ezek. 14:19; 25:7; Nah. 1:6 [b]Ps. 18:15; Is. 30:33; Ezek. 22:20, 21; Hag. 1:9

with the fire of My wrath, and I shall give you into the hand of brutal men, [1c]skilled in destruction.

32 'You will be [1a]fuel for the fire; your blood will be in the midst of the land. You will [b]not be remembered, for I, the LORD, have spoken.' "

CHAPTER 22

The Sins of Israel

THEN the word of the LORD came to me saying,

2"And you, son of man, will you judge, will you judge the bloody city? Then cause her to know all her abominations.

3"And you shall say, 'Thus says the Lord [1]GOD, "A city [a]shedding blood in her midst, so that her time will come, and that makes idols, contrary to her *interest*, for defilement!

4"You have become [a]guilty by [1]the blood which you have shed, and defiled by your idols which you have made. Thus you have brought your [2]day near and have come to your years; therefore I have made you a [b]reproach to the nations, and a mocking to all the lands.

5"Those who are near and those who are far from you will mock you, you of ill repute, full of [a]turmoil.

6"Behold, the [a]rulers of Israel, each according to his [1]power, have been in you for the purpose of shedding blood.

7"They have [a]treated father and mother lightly within you. The alien they have [b]oppressed in your midst; the [c]fatherless and the widow they have wronged in you.

8"You have despised My [a]holy things and profaned My [b]sabbaths.

9"Slanderous men have been in you for the purpose of shedding blood, and in you they have eaten at the mountain *shrines*. In your midst they have [a]committed acts of lewdness.

10"In you [1]they have [a]uncovered *their* fathers' nakedness; in you they have humbled her who was [b]unclean in her menstrual impurity.

11"And one has committed abomination with his [a]neighbor's wife, and another has lewdly defiled his [b]daughter-in-law. And another in you has [c]humbled his sister, his father's daughter.

12"In you they have [a]taken bribes to shed blood; you have taken [b]interest and profits, and you have injured your neighbors for gain by [c]oppression, and you have [d]forgotten Me," declares the Lord GOD.

13"Behold, then, I smite My hand at your [a]dishonest gain which you have acquired and at [1]the bloodshed which is among you.

14"Can your heart endure, or can your hands be strong, in the days that I shall deal with you? I, the LORD, have spoken and shall act.

15"And I shall [a]scatter you among the nations, and I shall disperse you through the lands, and I shall [b]consume your uncleanness from you.

16"And you will profane yourself in the sight of the nations, and you will [a]know that I am the LORD." ' "

17 And the word of the LORD came to me saying,

18"Son of man, the house of Israel has become [a]dross to Me; all of them are [b]bronze and tin and iron and lead in the [c]furnace; they are the dross of silver.

19"Therefore, thus says the Lord GOD, 'Because all of you have become dross, therefore, behold, I am going to gather you into the midst of Jerusalem.

20 'As they gather silver and bronze and iron and lead and tin into the [a]furnace to blow fire on it in order to melt *it*, so I shall gather *you* in My anger and in My wrath, and I shall lay you *there* and melt you.

21 'And I shall gather you and blow on you with the fire of My wrath, and you will be melted in the midst of it.

22 'As silver is melted in the furnace, so you will be melted in the midst of it; and you will know that I, the LORD, have [a]poured out My wrath on you.' "

23 And the word of the LORD came to me saying,

24"Son of man, say to her, 'You are a land that is [a]not cleansed or rained on in the day of indignation.'

25"There is a [a]conspiracy of her prophets in her midst, like a roaring lion tearing the prey. They have [b]devoured lives; they have taken treasure and precious things; they have made many [c]widows in the midst of her.

26"Her [a]priests have done violence to My law and have [b]profaned My holy things; they have made no [c]distinction between the holy and the profane, and they have not taught the difference between the [d]unclean and the clean; and they hide their eyes from My sabbaths, and I am profaned among them.

27"Her princes within her are like wolves tearing the prey, by shed-

31 [1]Or, *artisans of* [c]Jer. 4:7; 6:22, 23; 51:20, 21; Hab. 1:6, 10
32 [1]Lit., *food* [a]Ezek. 20:47, 48; Mal. 4:1 [b]Ezek. 25:10
3 [1]YHWH, usually rendered LORD, and so throughout the chap. [a]Ezek. 22:6, 27; 23:37, 45; Zeph. 3:3
4 [1]Lit., *your* [2]Lit., *days* [a]2 Kin. 21:16; Ezek. 24:7, 8 [b]Ps. 44:13, 14; Ezek. 5:14, 15; 16:57
5 [a]Is. 22:2
6 [1]Lit., *arm* [a]Is. 1:23; Ezek. 22:27
7 [a]Lev. 20:9; Deut. 27:16 [b]Ex. 23:9; Jer. 7:6; Zech. 7:10 [c]Ex. 22:22; Ezek. 22:25; Mal. 3:5
8 [a]Ezek. 22:26 [b]Ezek. 20:13, 21, 24; 23:38, 39
9 [a]Ezek. 23:29; Hos. 4:2, 10, 14
10 [1]Lit., *he has* [a]Lev. 18:8 [b]Lev. 18:19; Ezek. 18:6
11 [a]Ezek. 18:11; 33:26 [b]Lev. 18:15 [c]2 Sam. 13:14
12 [a]Deut. 27:25; Mic. 7: 2, 3 [b]Lev. 25:36 [c]Lev. 19:13 [d]Ps. 106:21; Ezek. 23:35
13 [1]Lit., *your* [a]Is. 33:15; Amos 2:6-8; Mic. 2:2
15 [a]Deut. 4:27; Neh. 1:8; Ezek. 20:23; Zech. 7:14 [b]Ezek. 23:27, 48
16 [a]Ps. 83:18; Ezek. 6:7
18 [a]Ps. 119:119; Is. 1:22; Lam. 4:1 [b]Jer. 6:28-30 [c]Prov. 17:3; Is. 48:10
20 [a]Is. 1:25
22 [a]Ezek. 20:8, 33; Hos. 5:10
24 [a]2 Chr. 28:22; Is. 9:13; Jer. 2:30; Ezek. 24:13; Zeph. 3:2
25 [a]Jer. 11:9; Hos. 6:9 [b]Jer. 2:34; Ezek. 13:19; 22:27 [c]Jer. 15:8; Ezek. 22:7
26 [a]Jer. 2:8, 26; Ezek. 7:26 [b]1 Sam. 2:12-17, 22; Ezek. 22:8 [c]Lev. 10:10; Ezek. 44:23 [d]Hag. 2:11-14

ding blood *and* [a]destroying lives in order to get [b]dishonest gain.

28"And her prophets have smeared whitewash for them, seeing [a]false visions and divining lies for them, saying, 'Thus says the Lord GOD,' when the LORD has not spoken.

29"The people of the land have practiced [a]oppression and committed robbery, and they have wronged the poor and needy and have [b]oppressed the sojourner without justice.

30"And I [a]searched for a man among them who should [b]build up the wall and [c]stand in the gap before Me for the land, that I should not destroy it; but I found no one.

31"Thus I have poured out My [a]indignation on them; I have consumed them with the fire of My wrath; [b]their way I have brought upon their heads," declares the Lord GOD.

CHAPTER 23

Oholah and Oholibah's Sin and Its Consequences

THE word of the LORD came to me again saying,

2"Son of man, there were two women, the daughters of one mother;

3 and they played the harlot in Egypt. They [a]played the harlot in their youth; there their breasts were pressed, and there their virgin bosom was handled.

4"And their names were Oholah the elder and Oholibah her sister. And they became Mine, and they bore sons and daughters. And *as for* their names, Samaria is Oholah, and Jerusalem is Oholibah.

5"And Oholah played the harlot while she was Mine; and she lusted after her lovers, after the [a]Assyrians, *her* neighbors,

6 who were clothed in purple, [a]governors and officials, all of them desirable young men, horsemen riding on horses.

7"And she bestowed her harlotries on them, all of whom *were* the choicest [1]men of Assyria; and with all whom she lusted after, with all their idols she [a]defiled herself.

8"And she did not forsake her harlotries [a]from the time in Egypt; for in her youth [1]men had lain with her, and they handled her virgin bosom and poured out their [2]lust on her.

9"Therefore, I gave her into the hand of her [a]lovers, into the hand of the Assyrians, after whom she lusted.

10"They uncovered her nakedness; they took her sons and her daughters, but they slew her with the sword. Thus she became a [1]byword among women, and they executed judgments on her.

11"Now her sister Oholibah saw *this*, yet she was [a]more corrupt in her lust than she, and her harlotries were more than the harlotries of her sister.

12"She lusted after the Assyrians, governors and officials, the ones near, magnificently dressed, horsemen riding on horses, all of them desirable young men.

13"And I saw that she had defiled herself; they both took the same way.

14"So she increased her harlotries. And she saw men [a]portrayed on the wall, images of the [b]Chaldeans portrayed with vermilion,

15 girded with belts on their loins, with flowing turbans on their heads, all of them looking like officers, like the [1]Babylonians *in* Chaldea, the land of their birth.

16"And [1]when she saw them she [a]lusted after them and sent messengers to them in Chaldea.

17"And the [1a]Babylonians came to her to the bed of love, and they defiled her with their harlotry. And when she had been defiled by them, [2]she became disgusted with them.

18"And she uncovered her harlotries and [a]uncovered her nakedness; then [1]I became [b]disgusted with her, as [1]I had become disgusted with her [c]sister.

19"Yet she multiplied her harlotries, remembering the days of her youth, when she played the harlot in the land of Egypt.

20"And she [a]lusted after their paramours, whose flesh is *like* the flesh of donkeys and whose issue is *like* the issue of horses.

21"Thus you longed for the [a]lewdness of your youth, when [1]the Egyptians handled your bosom because of the breasts of your youth.

22"Therefore, O Oholibah, thus says the Lord [1]GOD, 'Behold I will arouse your lovers against you, from whom [2]you were alienated, and I will bring them against you from every side:

23 the [1a]Babylonians and all the [b]Chaldeans, [c]Pekod and Shoa and Koa, *and* all the [2d]Assyrians with them; desirable young men, governors and officials all of them, offi-

27 [a]Ezek. 22:25 [b]Ezek. 22:13
28 [a]Jer. 23:25-32; Ezek. 13:6
29 [a]Is. 5:7; Ezek. 9:9; 22:7; Amos 3:10 [b]Ex. 23:9
30 [a]Is. 59:16; 63:5; Jer. 5:1 [b]Ezek. 13:5 [c]Ps. 106:23; Jer. 15:1
31 [a]Is. 10:5; 13:5; 30:27; Ezek. 22:20 [b]Ezek. 7:3, 8, 9; 9:10; 16:43; Rom. 2:8, 9
3 [a]Jer. 3:9
5 [a]2 Kin. 15:19; 16:7; 17:3; Ezek. 16:28; Hos. 5:13; 8:9, 10
6 [a]Ezek. 23:12, 13
7 [1]Lit., *sons of Asshur*, also vs. 9, 12 [a]Ezek. 20:7; 22:3, 4; Hos. 5:3; 6:10
8 [1]Lit., *they* [2]Lit., *harlotry* [a]Ex. 32:4; 1 Kin. 12:28; 2 Kin. 10:29; 17:16; Ezek. 23:3, 19
9 [a]Ezek. 16:37; 23:22
10 [1]Lit., *name*
11 [a]Jer. 3:8-11; Ezek. 16:51
14 [a]Ezek. 8:10 [b]Ezek. 16:29
15 [1]Lit., *sons of Babel*
16 [1]Lit., *at the sight of her eyes* [a]Ezek. 23:20; Matt. 5:28
17 [1]Lit., *sons of Babel* [2]Lit., *her soul* [a]2 Kin. 24:17
18 [1]Lit., *My soul* [a]Jer. 8:12; Ezek. 21:24; 23:10 [b]Ps. 78:59; 106:40; Jer. 12:8 [c]Ezek. 23:9; Amos 5:21
20 [a]Ezek. 16:26; 17:15
21 [1]So two mss. M.T., *from Egypt* [a]Jer. 3:9; Ezek. 23:3
22 [1]YHWH, usually rendered LORD, and so throughout the chap. [2]Lit., *your soul was alienated*
23 [1]Lit., *sons of Babylon* [2]Lit., *sons of Assyria* [a]2 Kin. 20:14-17; Ezek. 21:19; 23:14-17 [b]2 Kin. 24:2; Job 1:17; Is. 23:13 [c]Jer. 50:21 [d]Gen. 2:14; 25:18; Ezra 6:22

cers and [3]men of renown, all of them riding on horses.

24 'And they will come against you with weapons, [a]chariots, and [1]wagons, and with a company of peoples. They will set themselves against you on every side with buckler and shield and helmet; and I shall commit the [b]judgment to them, and they will judge you according to their customs.

25 'And I will set My [a]jealousy against you, that they may deal with you in wrath. They will remove your nose and your ears; and your [1]survivors will fall by the sword. They will take your [b]sons and your daughters; and your [1]survivors will be consumed by the fire.

26 'They will also [a]strip you of your clothes and take away your [b]beautiful jewels.

27 'Thus I shall make your lewdness and your harlotry *brought* from the land of Egypt to cease from you, so that you will not lift up your eyes to them or remember Egypt any more.'

28 "For thus says the Lord GOD, 'Behold, I will give you into the hand of those whom you [a]hate, into the hand of those from whom [1]you were alienated.

29 'And they will [a]deal with you in hatred, take all your property, and leave you naked and bare. And the nakedness of your harlotries shall be uncovered, both your lewdness and your harlotries.

30 'These things will be done to you because you have played the harlot with the nations, because you have defiled yourself with their idols.

31 'You have walked in the way of your sister; therefore I will give [a]her cup into your hand.'

32 "Thus says the Lord GOD,
'You will [a]drink your sister's cup,
Which is deep and wide.
[1]You will be [b]laughed at and held in derision;
It contains much.
33 'You will be filled with [a]drunkenness and sorrow,
The cup of horror and desolation,
The cup of your sister Samaria.
34 'And you will [a]drink it and drain it.
Then you will gnaw its fragments
And tear your breasts;
for I have spoken,' declares the Lord GOD.

35 "Therefore, thus says the Lord GOD, 'Because you have [a]forgotten Me and [b]cast Me behind your back, bear now the *punishment* of your lewdness and your harlotries.' "

36 Moreover, the LORD said to me, "Son of man, will you [a]judge Oholah and Oholibah? Then [b]declare to them their abominations.

37 "For they have committed adultery, and blood is on their hands. Thus they have committed adultery with their idols and even caused their sons, whom they bore to Me, to pass through *the fire* to [1]them as food.

38 "Again, they have done this to Me: they have [a]defiled My sanctuary on the same day and have profaned My [b]sabbaths.

39 "For when they had slaughtered their children for their idols, they entered My [a]sanctuary on the same day to profane it; and lo, thus they did within My house.

40 "Furthermore, [1]they have even sent for men who come from afar, to whom a messenger was sent; and lo, they came—for whom you bathed, [a]painted your eyes, and [b]decorated yourselves with ornaments;

41 and you sat on a splendid [a]couch with a [b]table arranged before it, on which you had set My [c]incense and My [c]oil.

42 "And the sound of a [1a]carefree multitude was with her; and [b]drunkards were brought from the wilderness with men of the [2]common sort. And they put [c]bracelets on [3]the hands of the women and beautiful crowns on their heads.

43 "Then I said concerning her who was [a]worn out by adulteries, 'Will they now commit adultery with her when she is *thus?*'

44 "[1]But they went in to her as they would go in to a harlot. Thus they went in to Oholah and to Oholibah, the lewd women.

45 "But they, righteous men, will judge them with the judgment of adulteresses, and with the judgment of women who shed blood, because they are adulteresses and blood is on their hands.

46 "For thus says the Lord GOD, 'Bring up a company against them, and give them over to [a]terror and plunder.

47 'And the company will [a]stone them with stones and cut them down with their swords; they will slay their sons and their daughters and [b]burn their houses with fire.

48 'Thus I shall make lewdness cease from the land, that all women

23 [3]Lit., *the called ones*
24 [1]Lit., *wheels* [a]Jer. 47:3; Ezek. 26:10; Nah. 2:3, 4 [b]Jer. 39:5, 6; Ezek. 16:38; 23:45
25 [1]Lit., *remainder* [a]Ezek. 5:13; 8:17, 18; 34:14; Zeph. 1:8 [b]Ezek. 23:47; Hos. 2:4
26 [a]Jer. 13:22; Ezek. 16:39; 23:29 [b]Is. 3:18-23
28 [1]Lit., *your soul was alienated* [a]Jer. 21:7-10; 34:20; Ezek. 16:37; 23:17, 22
29 [a]Deut. 28:48; Ezek. 23:25, 26, 45-47
31 [a]2 Kin. 21:13; Jer. 7:14, 15; Ezek. 23:33
32 [1]Or, *It will be for jesting and deriding because of its great size* [a]Ps. 60:3; Is. 51:17; Jer. 25:15 [b]Ezek. 5:14, 15; 16:57; 22:4, 5
33 [a]Jer. 25:15, 16, 27; Hab. 2:16
34 [a]Ps. 75:8; Is. 51:17
35 [a]Is. 17:10; Jer. 3:21; Ezek. 22:12; Hos. 8:14; 13:6 [b]1 Kin. 14:9; Jer. 2:27; 32:33
36 [a]Jer. 1:10; Ezek. 20:4; 22:2 [b]Is. 58:1; Ezek. 16:2; Mic. 3:8
37 [1]I.e., idols
38 [a]2 Kin. 21:4, 7; Ezek. 5:11; 7:20 [b]Jer. 17:27; Ezek. 20:13, 24
39 [a]Jer. 7:9-11
40 [1]Or, *you* (women) [a]2 Kin. 9:30; Jer. 4:30 [b]Is. 3:18-23; Ezek. 16:13-16
41 [a]Esth. 1:6; Is. 57:7; Amos 6:4 [b]Is. 65:11; Ezek. 44:16 [c]Jer. 44:17; Hos. 2:8
42 [1]Lit., *at ease* [2]Lit., *multitude of mankind* [3]Lit., *their hands* [a]Ezek. 16:49; Amos 6:3-6 [b]Jer. 51:7 [c]Gen. 24:30; Ezek. 16:11, 12
43 [a]Ezra 9:7; Ps. 106:6; Ezek. 23:3
44 [1]Or, *And*
46 [a]Jer. 15:4; 24:9; 29:18
47 [a]Lev. 20:10; Ezek. 16:40 [b]Jer. 39:8

may be admonished and not commit
[1]lewdness as you have done.
49 'And your lewdness [1]will be [a]re-
quited upon you, and you will bear
the penalty of worshiping your
idols; thus you will know that I am
the Lord GOD.' "

CHAPTER 24

Parable of the Boiling Pot

AND the word of the LORD came to
me in the ninth year, in the tenth
month, on the tenth of the month,
saying,
2"Son of man, write the name of
the day, this very day. The king of
Babylon [1]has [a]laid siege to Jerusalem this very day.
3"And speak a [a]parable to the [b]re-
bellious house, and say to them,
'Thus says the Lord [1]GOD,
"Put on the [c]pot, put *it* on, and
also pour water in it;
4 [1a]Put in it the pieces,
Every good piece, the thigh,
and the shoulder;
Fill *it* with choice bones.
5 "Take the [a]choicest of the flock,
And also pile [1]wood under
[2]the pot.
Make it boil vigorously.
Also seethe its bones in it."

6 'Therefore, thus says the Lord
GOD,
"Woe to the [a]bloody city,
To the pot in which there is
rust
And whose rust has not gone
out of it!
Take out of it piece after piece,
[1]Without making a choice.
7 "For her blood is in her midst;
She placed it on the bare rock;
She did not [a]pour it on the
ground
To cover it with dust.
8 "That it may [a]cause wrath to
come up to take vengeance,
I have put her blood on the
bare rock,
That it may [b]not be covered."
9 'Therefore, thus says the Lord
GOD,
"[a]Woe to the bloody city!
I also shall make the pile great.
10 "Heap on the wood, kindle the
fire,
[1]Boil the flesh well,
And mix in the spices,
And let the bones be burned.
11 "Then [a]set it empty on its coals,
So that it may be hot,
And its bronze may [1]glow,
And its [b]filthiness may be
melted in it,
Its rust consumed.
12 "She has [a]wearied *Me* with toil,
Yet her great rust has not gone
from her;
Let her rust *be* in the fire!
13 "In your filthiness is lewdness.
Because I *would* have
cleansed you,
Yet you are [a]not clean,
You will not be cleansed from
your filthiness again,
Until I have [1b]spent My wrath
on you.
14"I, the LORD, have spoken; it is
[a]coming and I shall act. I shall not
relent, and I shall not [b]pity, and I
shall not be sorry; [c]according to
your ways and according to your
deeds [1]I shall judge you," declares
the Lord GOD.' "
15 And the word of the LORD came
to me saying,

Death of Ezekiel's Wife Is a Sign

16"Son of man, behold, I am about
to take from you the [a]desire of your
eyes with a [b]blow; but you shall not
[c]mourn, and you shall not weep, and
your [d]tears shall not come.
17"Groan silently; make [a]no
mourning for the dead. Bind on your
turban, and put your shoes on your
feet, and do not cover *your* mustache, and do not [b]eat the bread of
men."
18 So I spoke to the people in the
morning, and in the evening my wife
died. And in the morning I did as I
was commanded.
19 And the people said to me,
"Will you not tell us what these
things that you are doing mean for
us?"
20 Then I said to them, "The word
of the LORD came to me saying,
21 'Speak to the house of Israel,
"Thus says the Lord GOD, 'Behold, I
am about to profane My sanctuary,
the pride of your power, the [a]desire
of your eyes, and the delight of your
soul; and your [b]sons and your
daughters whom you have left behind will fall by the sword.
22 'And you will do as I have done;
you will not cover *your* mustache,
and you will not eat the bread of
men.
23 'And your turbans will be on
your heads and your shoes on your
feet. You will not mourn, and you
will not weep; but you will rot away
in your iniquities, and you will
groan [1]to one another.
24 'Thus Ezekiel will be a [a]sign to
you; according to all that he has

48 [1]Lit., *according to your lewdness*
49 [1]Lit., *they will give* [a]Is. 59:18; Ezek. 7:4, 9; 9:10; 23:35
2 [1]Lit., *leaned on* [a]2 Kin. 25:1; Jer. 39:1; 52:4
3 [1]YHWH, usually rendered LORD, and so throughout the chap. [a]Ps. 78:2; Ezek. 17:2; 20:49 [b]Is. 1:2; 30:1, 9; Ezek. 2:3, 6, 8 [c]Jer. 1:13, 14; Ezek. 11:3, 7, 11; 24:6
4 [1]Lit., *Gather her pieces* [a]Ezek. 22:19-22; Mic. 3:2, 3
5 [1]Lit., *bones* [2]Lit., *it* [a]Jer. 39:6; 52:10, 24-27
6 [1]Lit., *No lot has fallen on it* [a]2 Kin. 24:3, 4; Ezek. 22:2, 3, 27; Mic. 7:2; Nah. 3:1
7 [a]Lev. 17:13; Deut. 12:16
8 [a]Is. 26:21 [b]Jer. 22:8, 9
9 [a]Ezek. 24:6; Hab. 2:12
10 [1]Lit., *Complete*
11 [1]Lit., *become hot* [a]Jer. 21:10; Mal. 4:1 [b]Ezek. 22:15; 23:27
12 [a]Jer. 9:5
13 [1]Lit., *caused to rest* [a]Is. 5:4; 9:13; Jer. 6:28-30; Ezek. 22:24 [b]Ezek. 5:13; 8:18
14 [1]So with several ancient mss. and versions; M.T., *they* [a]Ps. 33:9; Is. 55:11 [b]Jer. 13:14; Ezek. 9:10 [c]Is. 3:11; Ezek. 18:30; 36:19
16 [a]Song of Sol. 7:10; Ezek. 24:18 [b]Job 23:2 [c]Jer. 16:5; 22:10 [d]Jer. 13:17
17 [a]Lev. 21:10-12 [b]Jer. 16:7; Hos. 9:4
21 [a]Ps. 27:4; 84:1; Ezek. 24:16 [b]Jer. 6:11; 16:3, 4; Ezek. 23:25, 47
23 [1]Lit., *a man to his brother*
24 [a]Ezek. 4:3; Hos. 1:2; 3:1; Luke 11:29, 30

done you will do; when it comes,
then you will know that I am the
Lord GOD.' "
25 'As for you, son of man, will *it*
not be on the day when I take from
them their [a]stronghold, the joy of
their [1]pride, the desire of their eyes,
and [2]their heart's delight, their sons
and their daughters,
26 that on that day he who [a]es-
capes will come to you with information for *your* ears?
27 'On that day your [a]mouth will
be opened to him who escaped, and
you will speak and be dumb no
longer. Thus you will be a sign to
them, and they will know that I am
the LORD.' "

CHAPTER 25

Judgment on Gentile Nations—Ammon

AND the word of the LORD came to
me saying,
2"Son of man, set your face
toward the sons of Ammon, and
prophesy against them,
3 and say to the sons of Ammon,
'Hear the word of the Lord [1]GOD!
Thus says the Lord GOD, "Because
you said, '[a]Aha!' against My sanctuary when it was profaned, and
against the land of Israel when it
was made desolate, and against the
house of Judah when they went into
exile,
4 therefore, behold, I am going to
give you to the [a]sons of the east for
a possession, and they will set their
encampments among you and make
their dwellings among you; they will
[b]eat your fruit and drink your milk.
5"And I shall make [a]Rabbah a
pasture for camels and the sons of
Ammon a resting place for flocks.
Thus you will know that I am the
LORD."
6 'For thus says the Lord GOD,
"Because you have [a]clapped your
hands and stamped your feet and
[b]rejoiced with all the scorn of your
soul against the land of Israel,
7 therefore, behold, I have
[a]stretched out My hand against you,
and I shall give you for [b]spoil to the
nations. And I shall [c]cut you off
from the peoples and [d]make you
perish from the lands; I shall destroy
you. Thus you will [e]know that I am
the LORD."

Moab

8 'Thus says the Lord GOD, "Because Moab and Seir say, 'Behold,
the house of Judah is like all the nations,'
9 therefore, behold, I am going to
[1]deprive the flank of Moab of *its*
cities, of its cities which are on its
[2]frontiers, the glory of the land,
[a]Beth-jeshimoth, [b]Baal-meon, and
[c]Kiriathaim,
10 and I will give it for a possession, along with the sons of Ammon,
to the [a]sons of the east, that the sons
of Ammon may not be remembered
among the nations.
11"Thus I will execute judgments
on Moab, and they will know that I
am the LORD."

Edom

12 'Thus says the Lord GOD, "Because Edom has acted against the
house of Judah by taking vengeance, and has incurred grievous
guilt, and avenged themselves upon
them,"
13 therefore, thus says the Lord
GOD, "I will also stretch out My
[a]hand against Edom and [b]cut off
man and beast from it. And I will lay
it waste; from [c]Teman even to [d]De-
dan they will fall by the sword.
14"And I will lay My vengeance on
Edom by the hand of My people Israel. Therefore, they will act in
Edom according to My [a]anger and
according to My wrath; thus they
will know My vengeance," declares
the Lord GOD.

Philistia

15 'Thus says the Lord GOD, "Because the Philistines have acted in
[a]revenge and have taken vengeance
with scorn of soul to destroy with
everlasting enmity,"
16 therefore, thus says the Lord
GOD, "Behold, I will [a]stretch out My
hand against the Philistines, even
cut off the [b]Cherethites and destroy
the remnant of the seacoast.
17"And I will execute great vengeance on them with wrathful rebukes; and they will know that I am
the LORD when I lay My vengeance
on them." ' "

CHAPTER 26

Judgment on Tyre

NOW it came about in the eleventh year, on the first of the month,
that the word of the LORD came to
me saying,
2"Son of man, because [a]Tyre has
said concerning Jerusalem, 'Aha,
the [b]gateway of the peoples is broken; it has [1c]opened to me. I shall be
filled, *now that* she is laid waste,'
3 therefore, thus says the Lord
[1]GOD, 'Behold, I am against you, O

---

25 [1]Or, *beauty* [2]Lit., *the lifting up of their soul* [a]Ps. 48:2; 50:2; Ezek. 24:21
26 [a]1 Sam. 4:12; Job 1:15-19
27 [a]Ezek. 3:26; 33:22
3 [1]YHWH, usually rendered LORD, and so throughout the chap. [a]Ps. 70:2, 3; Ezek. 21:28; 25:6; 26:2; 36:2
4 [a]Judg. 6:3, 33; 1 Kin. 4:30 [b]Deut. 28:33, 51; Is. 1:7
5 [a]Deut. 3:11; 2 Sam. 12:26; Jer. 49:2; Ezek. 21:20
6 [a]Job 27:23; Nah. 3:19 [b]Obad. 12; Zeph. 2:8, 10
7 [a]Ezek. 24:13, 16; Zeph. 1:4 [b]Is. 33:4; Ezek. 26:5 [c]Ezek. 21:32 [d]Amos 1:14, 15 [e]Ezek. 6:14
9 [1]Lit., *open* [2]Lit., *end* [a]Num. 33:49; Josh. 12:3; 13:20 [b]Num. 32:3, 38; Josh. 13:17; 1 Chr. 5:8; Jer. 48:23 [c]Num. 32:37; Josh. 13:19; Jer. 48:1, 23
10 [a]Ezek. 24:4
13 [a]Jer. 49:8, 13 [b]Ezek. 29:8; Mal. 1:3, 4 [c]Gen. 36:34; Jer. 49:7; Amos 1:12 [d]Jer. 25:23; 49:8
14 [a]Ezek. 35:11
15 [a]Is. 14:29-31; Ezek. 25:6, 12; Joel 3:4
16 [a]Jer. 25:20; 47:1-7 [b]1 Sam. 30:14; Zeph. 2:5
2 [1]Lit., *turned* [a]2 Sam. 5:11; Is. 23:1; Jer. 25:22 [b]Is. 62:10 [c]Ezek. 25:8; 35:10
3 [1]YHWH, usually rendered LORD, and so throughout the chap.

Tyre, and I will bring up [a]many nations against you, as the [b]sea brings
up its waves.
4 'And they will destroy the
[a]walls of Tyre and break down her
towers; and I will scrape her debris
from her and make her a bare rock.
5 'She will be a place for the
spreading of nets in the midst of the
sea, for I have spoken,' declares the
Lord GOD, 'and she will become
[a]spoil for the nations.
6 'Also her [a]daughters who are
[1]on the mainland will be slain by the
sword, and they will know that I am
the LORD.' "
7 For thus says the Lord GOD,
"Behold, I will bring upon Tyre from
the north Nebuchadnezzar king
of Babylon, [a]king of kings, with
horses, [b]chariots, cavalry, and a
[1]great army.
8 "He will slay your daughters on
the mainland with the sword; and he
will make [a]siege walls against you,
cast up a [b]mound against you, and
raise up a large shield against you.
9 "And the blow of his battering
rams he will direct against your
walls, and with his [1]axes he will
break down your towers.
10 "Because of the multitude of his
[a]horses, the dust *raised by* them will
cover you; your walls will [b]shake at
the noise of cavalry and [1]wagons
and chariots, when he [c]enters your
gates as men enter a city that is
breached.
11 "With the hoofs of his [a]horses he
will trample all your streets. He will
slay your people with the sword;
and your strong pillars will [b]come
down to the ground.
12 "Also they will make a spoil of
your riches and a prey of your [a]mer-
chandise, [b]break down your walls
and destroy your [c]pleasant houses,
and [1]throw your stones and your
timbers and your debris [d]into the
water.
13 "So I will silence the sound of
your [a]songs, and the sound of your
[b]harps will be heard no more.
14 "And I will make you a bare
rock; you will be a place for the
spreading of nets. You will be built
[a]no more, for I the [b]LORD have spoken," declares the Lord GOD.
15 Thus says the Lord GOD to Tyre,
"Shall not the [a]coastlands [b]shake at
the sound of your fall when the
wounded groan, when the slaughter
occurs in your midst?
16 "Then all the princes of the sea
will [a]go down from their thrones, remove their robes, and strip off their
embroidered garments. They will
[b]clothe themselves with trembling;
they will sit on the ground, [c]tremble
every moment, and be appalled at
you.
17 "And they will take up a [a]lamen-
tation over you and say to you,

'[b]How you have perished, O in-
habited one,
From the seas, O renowned
city,
Which was [c]mighty on the sea,
She and her inhabitants,
Who imposed her terror
On all her inhabitants!
18 'Now the [a]coastlands will
tremble
On the day of your fall;
Yes, the coastlands which are
by the sea
Will be terrified at your [b]pass-
ing.' "

19 For thus says the Lord GOD,
"When I shall make you a desolate
city, like the cities which are not inhabited, when I shall [a]bring up the
deep over you, and the great waters
will cover you,
20 then I shall bring you down
with those who [a]go down to the pit,
to the people of old, and I shall make
you dwell in the [b]lower parts of the
earth, like the ancient waste places,
with those who go down to the pit,
so that you will not [1]be inhabited;
but I shall set [c]glory in the land of
the living.
21 "I shall bring [a]terrors on you,
and you will be no more; though you
will be sought, you will never be
found again," declares the Lord
GOD.

CHAPTER 27

Lament Over Tyre

MOREOVER, the word of the
LORD came to me saying,
2 "And you, son of man, [a]take up a
lamentation over Tyre;
3 and say to Tyre, who dwells at
the entrance to the sea, merchant of
the peoples to many coastlands,
'Thus says the Lord [1]GOD,

"O Tyre, you have said, 'I am
perfect in beauty.'
4 "Your borders are in the heart
of the seas;
Your builders have perfected
your beauty.
5 "They have [1]made all *your*
planks of fir trees from [a]Se-
nir;
They have taken a cedar from
Lebanon to make a mast for
you.

---

3 [a]Mic. 4:11 [b]Is. 5:30; Jer. 50:42; 51:42
4 [a]Is. 23:11; Ezek. 26:9; Amos 1:10
5 [a]Ezek. 25:7; 29:19
6 [1]Lit., *in the field* [a]Jer. 47:4; 49:2; Ezek. 16:46, 53; 26:8
7 [1]Lit., *an assembly, even many people* [a]Ezra 7:12; Is. 10:8; Jer. 52:32; Dan. 2:37, 47 [b]Ezek. 23:24; Nah. 2:3, 4
8 [a]Jer. 52:4; Ezek. 21:22 [b]Jer. 6:6; 32:24
9 [1]Lit., *swords*
10 [1]Lit., *wheels* [a]Jer. 4:13; 47:3 [b]Ezek. 26:15; 27:28 [c]Jer. 39:3
11 [a]Is. 5:28; Hab. 1:8 [b]Is. 26:5; Jer. 43:13
12 [1]Lit., *put* [a]Is. 23:8, 18; Ezek. 27:3-27; Zech. 9:3 [b]Jer. 52:14 [c]2 Chr. 32:27; Amos 5:11 [d]Ezek. 27:27, 32
13 [a]Is. 23:16; 24:8, 9; Amos 6:5 [b]Is. 5:12
14 [a]Deut. 13:16; Job 12:14; Mal. 1:4 [b]Is. 14:27
15 [a]Ezek. 26:18; 27:35 [b]Jer. 49:21; Ezek. 31:16
16 [a]Jon. 3:6 [b]Job 8:22; Ps. 35:26; Ezek. 7:27; 1 Pet. 3:4; 5:5 [c]Ezek. 32:10; Hos. 11:10
17 [a]Ezek. 19:1, 14; 27:2, 32; 32:2, 16 [b]Is. 14:12; Jer. 48:39; 50:23 [c]Ezek. 27:3, 10, 11; 28:2
18 [a]Is. 41:5; Ezek. 26:15; 27:35 [b]Is. 23:5-7, 10, 11
19 [a]Ezek. 26:3
20 [1]Or, *return* [a]Is. 14:9, 10; Ezek. 32:30 [b]Ps. 88:6; Amos 9:2; Jon. 2:2, 6 [c]Jer. 33:9; Zech. 2:8
21 [a]Ezek. 26:15, 16; 27:36
2 [a]Jer. 9:10, 17-20; Ezek. 28:12
3 [1]YHWH, usually rendered LORD, and so throughout the chap.
5 [1]Lit., *built* [a]Deut. 3:9; 1 Chr. 5:23; Song of Sol. 4:8

6 "Of [a]oaks from [b]Bashan they
have made your oars;
With ivory they have [1]inlaid
your deck of boxwood from
the coastlands of [c]Cyprus.
7 "Your sail was of fine embroidered linen from Egypt
So that it became your [1]distin-
guishing mark;
Your [2]awning was [3a]blue and
purple from the coastlands of
[b]Elishah.
8 "The inhabitants of Sidon and
[a]Arvad were your rowers;
Your [b]wise men, O Tyre, were
[1]aboard; they were your pilots.
9 "The elders of Gebal and her
wise men were with you repairing your seams;
All the ships of the sea and
their sailors were with you in
order to deal in your merchandise.
10 "[a]Persia and [a]Lud and [a]Put were
in your army, your men of war. They
hung shield and helmet in you; they
set forth your splendor.
11 "The sons of Arvad and your
army were on your walls, *all*
around, and the [1]Gammadim were
in your towers. They hung their
shields on your walls, *all* around;
they perfected your beauty.
12 "Tarshish was your customer
because of the abundance of all
kinds of wealth; with silver, iron,
tin, and lead, they paid for your
wares.
13 "[a]Javan, [a]Tubal, and [b]Meshech,
they were your traders; with the
[c]lives of men and vessels of bronze
they paid for your merchandise.
14 "Those from [a]Beth-togarmah
gave horses and war horses and
mules for your wares.
15 "The sons of [a]Dedan were your
traders. Many coastlands were
[1]your market; [b]ivory tusks and ebo-
ny they brought as your payment.
16 "[1a]Syria was your customer because of the abundance of your
[2]goods; they paid for your wares
with [b]emeralds, purple, [c]embroi-
dered work, fine linen, coral, and ru-
bies.
17 "Judah and the land of Israel,
they were your traders; with the
wheat of [a]Minnith, [1]cakes, honey,
oil, and balm they paid for your merchandise.
18 "[a]Damascus was your customer
because of the abundance of your
[1]goods, because of the abundance of
all *kinds* of wealth, because of the
wine of Helbon and white wool.
19 "Vedan and Javan paid for your
wares [1]from Uzal; wrought iron,
cassia, and [2]sweet cane were among
your merchandise.
20 "Dedan traded with you in sad-
dlecloths for riding.
21 "[a]Arabia and all the princes of
Kedar, they were [1]your customers
for [b]lambs, rams, and goats; for
these they were your customers.
22 "The traders of [a]Sheba and Raamah, they traded with you; they
paid for your wares with the best of
all *kinds* of [b]spices, and with all
kinds of precious stones, and gold.
23 "Haran, Canneh, [a]Eden, the
traders of Sheba, Asshur, *and* Chil-
mad traded with you.
24 "They traded with you in choice
garments, in clothes of [1]blue and
embroidered work, and in carpets of
many colors, *and* tightly wound
cords, *which were* among your merchandise.
25 "The ships of Tarshish were [1]the
carriers for your merchandise.
And you were filled and were
very [2]glorious
In the heart of the seas.

26 "Your rowers have brought you
Into [a]great waters;
The [b]east wind has broken you
In the heart of the seas.
27 "Your wealth, your wares, your
merchandise,
Your sailors, and your pilots,
Your repairers of seams, your
dealers in merchandise,
And all your men of war who
are in you,
With all your company that is
in your midst,
Will fall into the heart of the
seas
On the day of your overthrow.
28 "At the sound of the cry of your
pilots
The pasture lands will [a]shake.
29 "And all who handle the oar,
The [a]sailors, *and* all the pilots
of the sea
Will come down from their
ships;
They will stand on the land,
30 And they will [a]make their voice
heard over you
And will cry bitterly.
They will [b]cast dust on their
heads,
They will [c]wallow in ashes.
31 "Also they will make themselves
[a]bald for you
And [b]gird themselves with
sackcloth;
And they will [c]weep for you in
bitterness of soul
With bitter mourning.

6 [1]Lit., *made* [a]Is. 2:13; Zech. 11:2 [b]Num. 21:33; Is. 2:13; Jer. 22:20 [c]Gen. 10:4; Is. 23:1, 12; Jer. 2:10
7 [1]Or, *standard* [2]Lit., *covering* [3]Or, *violet* [a]Ex. 25:4; Jer. 10:9 [b]Gen. 10:4
8 [1]Lit., *in you* [a]Gen. 10:18; 1 Chr. 1:16; Ezek. 27:11 [b]1 Kin. 9:27
10 [a]Ezek. 30:5; 38:5
11 [1]Or, *valorous ones*
13 [a]Gen. 10:2; Is. 66:19; Ezek. 27:19 [b]Gen. 10:2, 3; Ezek. 38:2; 39:1 [c]Joel 3:3; Rev. 18:13
14 [a]Gen. 10:3; Ezek. 39:6
15 [1]Lit., *the market of your hand* [a]Jer. 25:23; Ezek. 25:13; 27:20 [b]1 Kin. 10:22; Rev. 18:12
16 [1]Lit., *Aram* [2]Lit., *works* [a]Judg. 10:6; Is. 7:1-8; Ezek. 16:57 [b]Ex. 28:18; 39:11; Ezek. 28:13 [c]Ezek. 16:13, 18
17 [1]Lit., *pannag* [a]Judg. 11:33
18 [1]Lit., *works* [a]Gen. 14:15; Is. 7:8; Jer. 49:23; Ezek. 47:16-18
19 [1]Or, *with yarn* [2]Or, *calamus*
21 [1]Lit., *customers of your hand* [a]Is. 21:13 [b]Is. 60:7
22 [a]Gen. 10:7; Is. 60:6; Ezek. 38:13 [b]Gen. 43:11; 1 Kin. 10:2
23 [a]2 Kin. 19:12; Is. 37:12; Amos 1:5
24 [1]Or, *violet*
25 [1]Lit., *your travelers* [2]Lit., *honored*
26 [a]Ezek. 26:19 [b]Ps. 48:7; Jer. 18:17; Acts 27:14
28 [a]Ezek. 26:10, 15, 18
29 [a]Rev. 18:17-19
30 [a]Is. 23:1-6; Ezek. 26:17 [b]1 Sam. 4:12; 2 Sam. 1:2; Lam. 2:10; Rev. 18:19 [c]Jer. 6:26; Jon. 3:6
31 [a]Is. 15:2; Ezek. 29:18 [b]Is. 22:12; Ezek. 7:18 [c]Is. 16:9; 22:4

32"Moreover, in their wailing they will take up a [a]lamentation for you
And lament over you:
'Who is [b]like Tyre,
Like her who is silent in the midst of the sea?
33 'When your wares went out from the seas,
You satisfied many peoples;
With the [a]abundance of your wealth and your merchandise
You enriched the kings of earth.
34 '[1]Now that you are [a]broken by the seas
In the depths of the waters,
Your [b]merchandise and all your company
Have fallen in the midst of you.
35 'All the [a]inhabitants of the coastlands
Are appalled at you,
And their kings are horribly afraid;
They are troubled in countenance.
36 'The merchants among the peoples [a]hiss at you;
You have become [1]terrified,
And you [b]will be no more.' " ' "

CHAPTER 28

Tyre's King Overthrown

THE word of the LORD came again to me saying,
2"Son of man, say to the [1]leader of Tyre, 'Thus says the Lord [2]GOD,
"Because your heart is lifted up
And you have said, '[a]I am a god,
I sit in the seat of [3]gods,
In the heart of the seas';
Yet you are a [b]man and not God,
Although you make your heart like the heart of God—
3 Behold, you are wiser than [a]Daniel;
There is no secret that is a match for you.
4"By your wisdom and understanding
You have acquired [a]riches for yourself,
And have acquired gold and silver for your treasuries.
5"By your great wisdom, by your [a]trade
You have increased your riches,
And your [b]heart is lifted up because of your riches—
6 Therefore, thus says the Lord GOD,
'Because you have [a]made your heart
Like the heart of God,
7 Therefore, behold, I will bring [a]strangers upon you,
The most [b]ruthless of the nations.
And they will draw their swords
Against the beauty of your wisdom
And defile your splendor.
8 'They will bring you down to the pit,
And you will [a]die the death of those who are slain
In the heart of the seas.
9 'Will you still say, "I am a god,"
In the presence of your slayer,
Although you are a man and not God,
In the hands of those who wound you?
10 'You will die the death of the [a]uncircumcised
By the hand of strangers,
For I have spoken!' declares the Lord GOD!" ' "
11 Again the word of the LORD came to me saying,
12"Son of man, [a]take up a lamentation over the king of Tyre, and say to him, 'Thus says the Lord GOD,
"You [1]had the seal of perfection,
Full of wisdom and perfect in beauty.
13"You were in [a]Eden, the garden of God;
[b]Every precious stone was your covering:
The [c]ruby, the topaz, and the diamond;
The beryl, the onyx, and the jasper;
The lapis lazuli, the turquoise, and the emerald;
And the [c]gold, the workmanship of your [1d]settings and [2]sockets,
Was in you.
On the day that you were created
They were prepared.
14"You were the [a]anointed cherub who [1]covers,
And I placed you *there*.
You were on the holy [b]mountain of God;
You walked in the midst of the [c]stones of fire.
15"You were [a]blameless in your ways
From the day you were created,
Until [b]unrighteousness was found in you.

32 [a]Ezek. 26:17; 27:2; 28:12 [b]Lam. 2:13
33 [a]Ezek. 27:12, 18; 28:4, 5
34 [1]Lit., *The time* [a]Ezek. 26:12; 27:26, 27 [b]Zech. 9:3, 4
35 [a]Is. 23:6; Ezek. 26:16
36 [1]Lit., *terrors* [a]Jer. 18:16; 19:8; 49:17; 50:13; Zeph. 2:15 [b]Ps. 37:10, 36
2 [1]Or, *ruler, prince* [2]YHWH, usually rendered LORD, and so throughout the chap. [3]Or, *God* [a]Is. 14:14; 47:8; Ezek. 28:9; 2 Thess. 2:4 [b]Ps. 9:20; 82:6, 7; Is. 31:3; Ezek. 28:9
3 [a]Dan. 1:20; 2:20-23, 28; 5:11, 12
4 [a]Ezek. 27:33; Zech. 9:2, 3
5 [a]Ezek. 27:12; Hos. 12:7, 8 [b]Job 31:24, 25; Ps. 52:7; Ezek. 28:2; Hos. 13:6
6 [a]Ex. 9:17; Ezek. 28:2
7 [a]Ezek. 26:7 [b]Ezek. 30:11; 31:12; 32:12; Hab. 1:6-8
8 [a]Ezek. 27:26, 27, 34
10 [a]1 Sam. 17:26, 36; Ezek. 31:18; 32:30
12 [1]Lit., were *the one sealing a pattern* [a]Ezek. 19:1; 26:17; 27:2
13 [1]Or, *tambourines* [2]Or, *flutes* [a]Gen. 2:8; Is. 51:3; Ezek. 31:8, 9, 16; 36:35 [b]Ezek. 27:16, 22 [c]Ex. 28:17-20 [d]Is. 24:8; 30:32
14 [1]Or, *guards* [a]Ex. 25:17-20; 30:26; 40:9; Ezek. 28:16 [b]Ezek. 20:40; 28:16 [c]Ezek. 28:13, 16; Rev. 18:16
15 [a]Ezek. 27:3, 4; 28:3-6, 12 [b]Is. 14:12; Ezek. 28:17, 18

16"By the [a]abundance of your trade
[1]You were internally [b]filled with violence,
And you sinned;
Therefore I have cast you as profane
From the mountain of God.
And I have destroyed you, O [2]covering cherub,
From the midst of the stones of fire.
17"Your heart was lifted up because of your [a]beauty;
You [b]corrupted your wisdom by reason of your splendor.
I cast you to the ground;
I put you before [c]kings,
That they may see you.
18"By the multitude of your iniquities,
In the unrighteousness of your trade,
You profaned your sanctuaries.
Therefore I have brought [a]fire from the midst of you;
It has consumed you,
And I have turned you to [b]ashes on the earth
In the eyes of all who see you.
19"All who know you among the peoples
Are appalled at you;
You have become [1a]terrified,
And you will be [b]no more."'"

Judgment of Sidon

20 And the word of the LORD came
to me saying,
21"Son of man, [a]set your face
toward [b]Sidon, prophesy against
her,
22 and say, 'Thus says the Lord
GOD,
"Behold, I am against you, O Sidon,
And I shall [1]be glorified in your midst.
Then they will know that I am the LORD, when I [a]execute judgments in her,
And I shall manifest My holiness in her.
23"For I shall send pestilence to her
And blood to her streets,
And the [a]wounded will [1]fall in her midst
By the sword upon her on every side;
Then they will know that I am the LORD.
24"And there will be no more for
the house of Israel a [a]prickling brier
or a painful thorn from any round
about them who scorned them; then
they will know that I am the Lord
GOD."

Israel Regathered

25 'Thus says the Lord GOD,
"When I [a]gather the house of Israel
from the peoples among whom they
are scattered, and shall manifest My
holiness in them in the sight of the
nations, then they will [b]live in their
[1]land which I gave to My servant
Jacob.
26"And they will [a]live in it securely; and they will [b]build houses,
plant vineyards, and live securely,
when I [c]execute judgments upon all
who scorn them round about them.
Then they will know that I am the
LORD their God."'"

CHAPTER 29

Judgment of Egypt

IN the [a]tenth year, in the tenth
month, on the twelfth of the month,
the word of the LORD came to me
saying,
2"Son of man, set your face
against [a]Pharaoh, king of Egypt,
and prophesy against him and
against all [b]Egypt.
3"Speak and say, 'Thus says the
Lord [1]GOD,
"Behold, I am against you, Pharaoh, king of Egypt,
The great [2a]monster that lies in the midst of his [3]rivers,
That [b]has said, 'My Nile is mine, and I myself have made it.'
4"And I shall put [a]hooks in your jaws,
And I shall make the fish of your [1]rivers cling to your scales.
And I shall bring you up out of the midst of your [1]rivers,
And all the fish of your [1]rivers will cling to your scales.
5"And I shall [a]abandon you to the wilderness, you and all the fish of your [1]rivers;
You will fall on the [2]open field; you will not be brought together or [3]gathered.
I have given you for [b]food to the beasts of the earth and to the birds of the sky.
6"Then all the inhabitants of Egypt will know that I am the LORD,
Because they have been *only* a [a]staff *made* of reed to the house of Israel.
7"When they took hold of you with the hand,

16 [1]Lit., *They filled your midst* [2]Or, *guardian* [a]Ezek. 26:17; 27:12 [b]Ezek. 8:17; Hab. 2:8, 17
17 [a]Ezek. 27:3, 4; 28:7 [b]Is. 19:11 [c]Ezek. 26:16
18 [a]Amos 1:9, 10 [b]Mal. 4:3
19 [1]Lit., *terrors* [a]Ezek. 26:21; 27:36 [b]Jer. 51:64
21 [a]Ezek. 6:2; 25:2 [b]Gen. 10:15, 19; Is. 23:2, 4; Ezek. 27:8
22 [1]Or, *glorify Myself* [a]Ezek. 28:26; 30:19
23 [1]Or, *be judged* [a]Jer. 51:52
24 [a]Num. 33:55; Josh. 23:13; Is. 55:13; Ezek. 2:6
25 [1]Lit., *ground* [a]Ps. 106:47; Is. 11:12, 13; Jer. 32:37; Ezek. 20:41; 34:13, 27 [b]Jer. 23:8; 27:11
26 [a]Jer. 23:6; Ezek. 34:25-28; 38:8 [b]Jer. 32:15, 43, 44; Amos 9:13, 14 [c]Ezek. 25:11; 28:22
1 [a]Ezek. 26:1; 29:17; 30:20
2 [a]Jer. 44:30 [b]Is. 19:1-17; Jer. 46:2-26; Ezek. 30:1-32
3 [1]YHWH, usually rendered LORD, and so throughout the chap. [2]Lit., *tannim* [3]Or, *Nile* [a]Is. 27:1; Ezek. 32:2 [b]Is. 10:13; Ezek. 29:9; 30:12
4 [1]Or, *Nile* [a]2 Kin. 19:28; Ezek. 38:4
5 [1]Or, *Nile* [2]Lit., *faces of the field* [3]Or, with several mss. and Targum, *buried;* cf. Jer. 8:2; 25:33 [a]Ezek. 32:4-6 [b]Jer. 7:33; 34:20; Ezek. 39:4
6 [a]Is. 36:6

You [a]broke and tore all their
[1]hands;
And when they leaned on you,
You broke and made all their
loins [2]quake."
8 'Therefore, thus says the Lord
GOD, "Behold, I shall [a]bring upon
you a sword, and I shall cut off from
you man and beast.
9"And the [a]land of Egypt will become a desolation and waste. Then
they will know that I am the LORD.
Because [1]you [b]said, 'The Nile is
mine, and I have made *it*,'
10 therefore, behold, I am [a]against
you and against your [1]rivers, and I
will make the land of Egypt an utter
waste and desolation, from Migdol
to Syene and even to the border of
[2]Ethiopia.
11"A man's foot will [a]not pass
through it, and the foot of a beast
will not pass through it, and it will
not be inhabited for forty years.
12"So I shall make the land of
Egypt a desolation in the [a]midst of
desolated lands. And her cities, in
the midst of cities that are laid
waste, will be desolate forty years;
and I shall [b]scatter the Egyptians
among the nations and disperse
them among the lands."
13 'For thus says the Lord GOD, "At
the end of forty years I shall [a]gather
the Egyptians from the peoples
among whom they were scattered.
14"And I shall turn the fortunes of
Egypt and shall make them return
to the land of [a]Pathros, to the land of
their origin; and there they will be a
lowly kingdom.
15"It will be the [a]lowest of the
kingdoms; and it will never again lift
itself up above the nations. And I
shall make them so small that they
will not [b]rule over the nations.
16"And it will never again be the
[a]confidence of the house of Israel,
[b]bringing to mind the iniquity of
their having turned to Egypt. Then
they will know that I am the Lord
GOD."'"
17 Now in the [a]twenty-seventh
year, in the first *month*, on the first
of the month, the word of the LORD
came to me saying,
18"Son of man, [a]Nebuchadnezzar
king of Babylon made his army labor hard against Tyre; every head
was made [b]bald, and every shoulder
was rubbed bare. But he and his
army had no wages from Tyre for
the labor that he had performed
against it."
19 Therefore, thus says the Lord
GOD, "Behold, I shall give the land
of [a]Egypt to Nebuchadnezzar king
of Babylon. And he will carry off her
[b]wealth, and capture her spoil and
seize her plunder; and it will be
wages for his army.
20"I have given him the land of
Egypt *for* his labor which he [a]per-
formed, because they acted for Me,"
declares the Lord GOD.
21"On that day I shall make a
[a]horn sprout for the house of Israel,
and I shall [b]open your mouth in their
midst. Then they will know that I
am the LORD."

CHAPTER 30

Lament Over Egypt

THE word of the LORD came again
to me saying,
2"Son of man, prophesy and say,
'Thus says the Lord [1]GOD,
"[a]Wail, 'Alas for the day!'
3 "For the day is near,
Even [a]the day of the LORD is
near;
It will be a day of [b]clouds,
A time *of doom* for the nations.
4 "And a sword will come upon
Egypt,
And anguish will be in [1]Ethi-
opia,
When the slain fall in Egypt,
They take away her wealth,
And her foundations are torn
down.
5"Ethiopia, Put, Lud, all [a]Arabia,
Libya, and the people of the land
that is in league will fall with them
by the sword."
6 'Thus says the LORD,
"Indeed, those who support
[a]Egypt will fall,
And the pride of her power
will come down;
From Migdol *to* Syene
They will fall within her by the
sword,"
Declares the Lord GOD.
7 "And they will be desolate
In the [a]midst of the desolated
lands;
And her cities will be
In the midst of the devastated
cities.
8 "And they will [a]know that I am
the LORD,
When I set a [b]fire in Egypt
And all her helpers are broken.
9"On that day [a]messengers will
go forth from Me in ships to frighten
[b]secure Ethiopia; and [c]anguish will
be on them as on the day of Egypt;
for, behold, it comes!"
10 'Thus says the Lord GOD,

7 [1]M.T., *shoulders;* cf. 2 Kin. 18:21; Is. 36:6 [2]Lit., *stand* [a]Jer. 37:5-11; Ezek. 17:15-17
8 [a]Ezek. 14:17
9 [1]Lit., *he* [a]Ezek. 29:10-12; 30:7, 8, 13-18 [b]Prov. 16:18; 18:12; Ezek. 29:3
10 [1]Or, *Nile* [2]Lit., *Cush* [a]Ezek. 13:8; 21:3; 26:3; 29:3
11 [a]Jer. 43:11, 12; 46:19
12 [a]Jer. 25:15-19; 27:6-11; Ezek. 30:7 [b]Jer. 46:19; Ezek. 30:23, 26
13 [a]Is. 19:22
14 [a]Is. 11:11; 30:14; Jer. 44:1
15 [a]Ezek. 17:6, 14; 30:13; Zech. 10:11 [b]Ezek. 31:2; 32:2; Nah. 3:8-10
16 [a]Is. 20:5; 30:1-3; 31:1; 36:6; Ezek. 17:15; 29:6, 7 [b]Is. 64:9; Jer. 14:10; Ezek. 21:23; Hos. 8:13
17 [a]Ezek. 24:1; 26:1; 29:1; 30:20
18 [a]Jer. 25:9; 27:6; Ezek. 26:7-12 [b]Jer. 48:37; Ezek. 27:31
19 [a]Ezek. 30:10, 24, 25; 32:11 [b]Jer. 43:10-13; Ezek. 30:14
20 [a]Is. 10:6, 7; 45:1-3; Jer. 25:9
21 [a]1 Sam. 2:10; Ps. 92:10; 132:17 [b]Ezek. 3:27; 24:27; 33:22; Amos 3:7, 8; Luke 21:15
2 [1]YHWH, usually rendered LORD, and so throughout the chap. [a]Is. 13:6; 15:2; Ezek. 21:12; Joel 1:5, 11, 13
3 [a]Ezek. 7:19; 13:5; Joel 1:15; 2:1; Obad. 15 [b]Ezek. 30:18; 32:7; 34:12
4 [1]Or, *Cush,* also vs. 5, 9
5 [a]Jer. 25:20, 24
6 [a]Is. 20:3-6
7 [a]Jer. 25:18-26; Ezek. 29:12
8 [a]Ps. 58:11; Ezek. 29:6, 9, 16 [b]Ezek. 30:14, 16; 22:31; Amos 1:4, 7, 10, 12, 14
9 [a]Is. 18:1, 2 [b]Is. 47:8; Ezek. 38:11; 39:6 [c]Is. 19:17; 23:5; Ezek. 32:9, 10

"I will also make the [1]multitude
of Egypt cease
By the hand of Nebuchadnezzar king of Babylon.
11 "He and his people with him,
The most ruthless of the nations,
Will be brought in to destroy
the land;
And they will draw their
swords against Egypt
And fill the land with the slain.
12 "Moreover, I will make the
[a]Nile canals dry
And sell the land into the
hands of evil men.
And I will make the land desolate,
And [1]all that is in it,
By the hand of strangers; I, the
LORD, have spoken."

13 'Thus says the Lord GOD,
"I will also [a]destroy the idols
And make the [1]images cease
from [2b]Memphis.
And there will no longer be a
prince in the land of Egypt;
And I will put fear in the land
of Egypt.
14 "And I will make [a]Pathros
desolate,
Set a fire in [b]Zoan,
And execute judgments on
[1c]Thebes.
15 "And I will pour out My wrath
on [1]Sin,
The stronghold of Egypt;
I will also cut off the multitude
of [2]Thebes.
16 "And I will set a fire in Egypt;
[1]Sin will writhe in anguish,
[2]Thebes will be breached,
And [3]Memphis *will have* [4]distresses daily.
17 "The young men of [1a]On and of
Pi-beseth
Will fall by the sword,
And [2]the women will go into
captivity.
18 "And in [a]Tehaphnehes the day
will [1]be [b]dark
When I [c]break there the yoke
bars of Egypt.
Then the pride of her power
will cease in her;
A cloud will cover her,
And her daughters will go into
captivity.
19 "Thus I will [a]execute judgments on Egypt,
And they will know that I am
the LORD."'"

Victory for Babylon

20 And it came about in the [a]eleventh year, in the first *month,* on the
seventh of the month, that the word
of the LORD came to me saying,
21 "Son of man, I have [a]broken the
arm of Pharaoh king of Egypt; and,
behold, it has not been [b]bound up
[1]for healing [2]or wrapped with a bandage, that it may be strong to hold
the sword.
22 "Therefore, thus says the Lord
GOD, 'Behold, I am [a]against Pharaoh
king of Egypt and will break his
arms, both the strong and the [b]broken; and I will make the sword [c]fall
from his hand.
23 'And I will [a]scatter the Egyptians among the nations and disperse them among the lands.
24 'For I will [a]strengthen the arms
of the king of Babylon and put [b]My
sword in his hand; and I will break
the arms of Pharaoh, so that he will
groan before him with the groanings
of a wounded man.
25 'Thus I will strengthen the arms
of the king of Babylon, but the arms
of Pharaoh will fall. Then they will
know that I am the LORD, when I put
My sword into the hand of the king
of Babylon and he [a]stretches it out
against the land of Egypt.
26 'When I scatter the Egyptians
among the nations and disperse
them among the lands, then they
will know that I am the LORD.'"

CHAPTER 31

Pharoah Warned of Assyria's Fate

AND it came about in the [a]eleventh year, in the third *month,* on the
first of the month, that the word of
the LORD came to me saying,
2 "Son of man, say to Pharaoh
king of Egypt, and to his [a]multitude,
'Whom are you like in your
greatness?
3 'Behold, Assyria *was* a [a]cedar
in Lebanon
With beautiful branches and
forest shade,
And [1]very [b]high;
And its top was among the
[2]clouds.
4 'The [a]waters made it grow, the
[1]deep made it high.
With its rivers it continually
[2]extended all around its
planting place,
And it sent out its channels to
all the trees of the field.
5 'Therefore its height was loftier than all the trees of the
field
And its boughs became many
and its branches long

10 [1]Or, *wealth*
12 [1]Lit., *her fulness* [a]Ezek. 29:3, 9
13 [1]Or, *futile ones* [2]Or, *Noph* [a]Is. 2:18 [b]Is. 19:13; Jer. 2:16; 44:1; 46:14; Ezek. 30:16
14 [1]Or, *No* [a]Is. 11:11; Jer. 44:1, 15; Ezek. 29:14 [b]Ps. 78:12, 43; Is. 19:11, 13 [c]Jer. 46:25; Ezek. 30:15, 16; Nah. 3:8
15 [1]Or, *Pelusium* [2]Or, *No*
16 [1]Or, *Pelusium* [2]Or, *No* [3]Or, *Noph* [4]Or, *adversaries*
17 [1]Or, *Aven* [2]Lit., *they* [a]Gen. 41:45; 46:20
18 [1]So with many mss. and ancient versions; M.T., *restrain* [a]Jer. 43:8-13 [b]Ezek. 30:3 [c]Lev. 26:13; Is. 10:27; Jer. 27:2; 28:10, 13; 30:8; Ezek. 34:27
19 [a]Ps. 9:16; Ezek. 5:8, 15; 25:11; 30:14
20 [a]Ezek. 26:1; 29:1, 17; 31:1
21 [1]Lit., *to give healing* [2]Lit., *to put a bandage, to wrap it* [a]Ps. 10:15; 37:17; Ezek. 30:24 [b]Jer. 30:13; 46:11
22 [a]Jer. 46:25; Ezek. 29:3 [b]2 Kin. 24:7; Jer. 37:7 [c]Jer. 46:21
23 [a]Ezek. 29:12; 30:17, 18, 26
24 [a]Neh. 6:9; Is. 45:1, 5; Ezek. 30:10, 25; Zech. 10:12 [b]Is. 10:5, 6, 15; Ezek. 30:11, 25; Zeph. 2:12
25 [a]Josh. 8:18; 1 Chr. 21:16; Is. 5:25
1 [a]Jer. 52:5, 6; Ezek. 30:20; 32:1
2 [a]Ezek. 29:19; 30:10; Nah. 3:8, 9
3 [1]Lit., *high of stature* [2]So Gk.; M.T., *thick boughs* [a]Is. 10:33, 34; Ezek. 17:3, 4, 22; 31:16; Dan. 4:10, 20-23 [b]Is. 10:33; Ezek. 31:5, 10
4 [1]I.e., subterranean waters [2]Lit., *was going* [a]Ezek. 17:5, 8; Rev. 17:1, 15

Because of [a]many waters as it
spread them out.
6 'All the [a]birds of the heavens
nested in its boughs,
And under its branches all the
beasts of the field gave birth,
And all great nations lived under its shade.
7 'So it was beautiful in its greatness, in the length of its
branches;
For its roots extended to many
waters.
8 'The [a]cedars in God's [b]garden
could not match it;
The cypresses could not compare with its boughs,
And the plane trees could not
match its branches.
No tree in God's [b]garden could
compare with it in its beauty.
9 'I made it beautiful with the
multitude of its branches,
And all the trees of [a]Eden,
which were in the [a]garden of
God, were jealous of it.

10 'Therefore, thus says the Lord [1]GOD, "Because it is high in stature, and it has set its top among the clouds, and its [a]heart is haughty in its loftiness,

11 therefore, I will give it into the hand of a [a]despot of the nations; he will thoroughly deal with it. According to its wickedness I have [b]driven it away.

12 "And [a]alien [b]tyrants of the nations have cut it down and left it; on the [c]mountains and in all the valleys its branches have fallen, and its boughs have been broken in all the ravines of the land. And all the peoples of the earth have [d]gone down from its shade and left it.

13 "On its ruin all the [a]birds of the heavens will dwell. And all the beasts of the field will be on its *fallen* branches

14 in order that all the trees by the waters may not be exalted in their stature, nor set their top among the clouds, nor their well-watered mighty ones stand *erect* in their height. For they have all been given over to death, to the earth [a]beneath, among the sons of men, with those who go down to the pit."

15 'Thus says the Lord GOD, "On the day when it went down to Sheol I [a]caused lamentations; I closed the [1]deep over it and held back its rivers. And *its* many waters were stopped up, and I made Lebanon mourn for it, and all the trees of the field wilted away on account of it.

5 [a]Ps. 1:3; Ezek. 17:5
6 [a]Ezek. 17:23; 31:12, 13; Dan. 4:12, 21; Matt. 13:32
8 [a]Ps. 80:10; Ezek. 31:3 [b]Gen. 2:8, 9; 13:10; Is. 51:3; Ezek. 28:13
9 [a]Gen. 2:8, 9; 13:10; Is. 51:3; Ezek. 28:13
10 [1]YHWH, usually rendered LORD, and so throughout the chap. [a]2 Chr. 32:25; Is. 10:12; 14:13, 14; Ezek. 28:17; Dan. 5:20
11 [a]Ezek. 30:10, 11; 32:11, 12; Dan. 5:18, 19 [b]Deut. 18:12; Nah. 3:18
12 [a]Ezek. 7:21; 28:7; 30:12; Hab. 1:6 [b]Ezek. 28:7; 30:11; 32:12 [c]Ezek. 32:5; 35:8 [d]Ezek. 31:17; Dan. 4:14; Nah. 3:17, 18
13 [a]Is. 18:6; Ezek. 29:5; 31:6
14 [a]Num. 16:30, 33; Ps. 63:9; Ezek. 26:20; 31:18; 32:24; Amos 9:2; Jon. 2:2, 6; Eph. 4:9
15 [1]I.e., subterranean waters [a]Ezek. 32:7; Nah. 2:10
16 [a]Ezek. 26:15; 27:28; Hag. 2:7 [b]Is. 14:15; Ezek. 32:18 [c]Is. 14:8; Hab. 2:17 [d]Ezek. 14:22, 23; 32:31
17 [a]Ps. 9:17 [b]Is. 14:9; Ezek. 32:18-20; Nah. 3:17, 18 [c]Ezek. 31:3, 6; Dan. 4:12
18 [a]Jer. 9:25, 26; Ezek. 28:10; 32:19, 21 [b]Ps. 52:7; Matt. 13:19
1 [a]Ezek. 30:20; 31:1; 32:17; 33:21
2 [a]Ezek. 19:1; 27:2; 28:12; 32:16 [b]Jer. 4:7; Ezek. 19:2-6; 38:13; Nah. 2:11-13 [c]Is. 27:1; Ezek. 29:3 [d]Jer. 46:7, 8
3 [1]YHWH, usually rendered LORD, and so throughout the chap.
4 [a]Jer. 8:2; Ezek. 29:5; 31:12, 13; 39:4, 5, 17-20 [b]Is. 18:6
6 [a]Ex. 7:17; Is. 34:3, 7; Ezek. 35:6; Rev. 14:20

16 "I made the nations [a]quake at the sound of its fall when I made it [b]go down to Sheol with those who go down to the pit; and all the well-watered trees of Eden, the choicest and best of [c]Lebanon, were [d]comforted in the earth beneath.

17 "They also [a]went down with it to Sheol to those who were [b]slain by the sword; and those who were its strength lived [c]under its shade among the nations.

18 "To which among the trees of Eden are you thus equal in glory and greatness? Yet you will be brought down with the trees of Eden to the earth beneath; you will lie in the midst of the [a]uncircumcised, with those who were slain by the sword. [b]So is Pharaoh and all his multitude!" ' declares the Lord GOD."

CHAPTER 32

Lament Over Pharoah and Egypt

AND it came about in the [a]twelfth year, in the twelfth *month,* on the first of the month, that the word of the LORD came to me saying,

2 "Son of man, take up a [a]lamentation over Pharaoh king of Egypt, and say to him,
'You compared yourself to a
young [b]lion of the nations,
Yet you are like the [c]monster
in the seas;
And you [d]burst forth in your
rivers,
And muddied the waters with
your feet,
And fouled their rivers.' "
3 Thus says the Lord [1]GOD,
"Now I will spread My net over
you
With a company of many peoples,
And they shall lift you up in
My net.
4 "And I will leave you on the
[a]land;
I will cast you on the open
field.
And I will cause all the [b]birds
of the heavens to dwell on
you,
And I will satisfy the beasts of
the whole earth with you.
5 "And I will lay your flesh on the
mountains,
And fill the valleys with your
refuse.
6 "I will also make the land drink
the discharge of your [a]blood,
As far as the mountains,

And the ravines shall be full of you.
7 "And when *I* [a]extinguish you,
I will [b]cover the heavens, and darken their [c]stars;
I will cover the [d]sun with a cloud,
And the moon shall not give its light.
8 "All the shining [a]lights in the heavens
I will darken over you
And will set darkness on your land,"
Declares the Lord GOD.

9 "I will also [a]trouble the hearts of many peoples, when I [b]bring your destruction among the nations, into lands which you have not known.

10 "And I will make many peoples appalled at you, and their kings shall be horribly afraid of you when I brandish My sword before them; and they shall tremble every moment, every man for his own life, on the day of your fall."

11 For thus says the Lord GOD, "The sword of the king of Babylon shall come upon you.

12 "By the swords of the mighty ones I will cause your multitude to fall; all of them are tyrants of the nations,
And they shall devastate the pride of Egypt,
And all its multitude shall be destroyed.
13 "I will also destroy all its cattle from beside many waters;
And the foot of man shall not muddy them any more,
And the hoofs of beasts shall not muddy them.
14 "Then I will make their waters settle,
And will cause their rivers to run like oil,"
Declares the Lord GOD.
15 "When I make the land of Egypt a [a]desolation,
And the land is destitute of that which filled it,
When I smite all those who live in it,
Then they shall [b]know that I am the LORD.

16 "This is a [a]lamentation and they shall [1]chant it. The daughters of the nations shall [1]chant it. Over Egypt and over all her multitude they shall [1]chant it," declares the Lord GOD.

17 And it came about in the [a]twelfth year, on the [a]fifteenth of the month, that the word of the LORD came to me saying,

18 "Son of man, [a]wail for the multitude of Egypt, and [b]bring it down, her and the daughters of the powerful nations, to the [c]nether world, with those who go down to the pit;
19 'Whom do you surpass in beauty?
Go down and make your bed with the [a]uncircumcised.'

20 "They shall fall in the midst of those who are slain by the sword. [1]She is given over to the sword; they have [a]drawn her and all her multitudes away.

21 "The [a]strong among the mighty ones shall speak of him *and* his helpers from the midst of Sheol, 'They have gone down, they lie still, the uncircumcised, slain by the sword.'

22 "[a]Assyria is there and all her company; [1]her graves are round about [2]her. All of them are slain, fallen by the sword,

23 whose graves are set in the remotest parts of the pit, and her company is round about her grave. All of them are slain, fallen by the sword, who [1]spread terror in the land of the living.

24 "[a]Elam is there and all her multitude around her grave; all of them slain, fallen by the sword, who went down uncircumcised to the [b]lower parts of the earth, who instilled their terror in the [c]land of the living, and [d]bore their disgrace with those who went down to the pit.

25 "They have made a [a]bed for her among the slain with all her multitude. Her graves are around it, they are all uncircumcised, slain by the sword (although their terror was [1]instilled in the land of the living), and they bore their disgrace with those who go down to the pit; [2]they were put in the midst of the slain.

26 "[a]Meshech, [b]Tubal and all their multitude are there; their graves [1]surround them. All of them were slain by the sword [c]uncircumcised, though they instilled their terror in the land of the living.

27 "[a]Nor do they lie beside the fallen [1b]heroes of the uncircumcised, who went down to Sheol with their weapons of war, and whose swords were laid under their heads; but the punishment for their [c]iniquity rested on their bones, though the terror of *these* [1]heroes *was* once in the land of the living.

28 "But in the midst of the uncircumcised you will be broken and lie with those slain by the sword.

29 "There also is [a]Edom, its kings, and all its [1]princes, who [2]for *all* their might are laid with those slain by

7 [a]Job 18:5, 6; Prov. 13:9 [b]Ex. 10:21-23; Is. 34:4; Ezek. 30:3, 18; 34:12 [c]Is. 13:10 [d]Joel 2:2, 31; 3:15; Amos 8:9
8 [a]Gen. 1:14
9 [a]Ezek. 27:29-32; 28:19; Rev. 18:10-15 [b]Ex. 15:14-16
15 [a]Ps. 107:34; Ezek. 29:12, 19, 20 [b]Ex. 7:5; 14:4, 18; Ps. 9:16; 83:17, 18; Ezek. 6:7; 30:19, 26
16 [1]Or, *lament* [a]2 Sam. 1:17; 3:33, 34; 2 Chr. 35:25; Jer. 9:17; Ezek. 26:17; 32:2
17 [a]Ezek. 31:1; 32:1; 33:21
18 [a]Is. 16:9; Ezek. 21:6; 32:2, 16; Mic. 1:8 [b]Jer. 1:10; Ezek. 43:3; Hos. 6:5 [c]Ezek. 31:14, 16, 18; 32:24
19 [a]Jer. 9:25, 26; Ezek. 31:18; 32:21, 24, 29, 30
20 [1]Or, *The sword is given* [a]Ps. 28:3
21 [a]Is. 14:9-12; Ezek. 32:27
22 [1]Lit., *his* [2]Lit., *him* [a]Ezek. 27:23; 31:3, 16
23 [1]Lit., *gave*, and so throughout the chap.
24 [a]Gen. 10:22; 14:1; Is. 11:11; Jer. 25:25; 49:34-39 [b]Ezek. 26:20; 31:14, 18; 32:18 [c]Job 28:13; Ps. 27:13; 52:5; 142:5; Is. 38:11; Jer. 11:19 [d]Ezek. 16:52, 54; 32:25, 30
25 [1]Lit., *given* [2]So with ancient versions; M.T. reads: *he was* [a]Ps. 139:8
26 [1]Lit., *are around him* [a]Gen. 10:2; Ezek. 27:13; 38:2, 3; 39:1 [b]Gen. 10:2; Is. 66:19; Ezek. 27:13; 38:2, 3; 39:1 [c]Ezek. 32:19
27 [1]Or, *mighty ones* [a]Is. 14:18, 19 [b]Job 3:13-15; Ezek. 32:21 [c]Job 20:11; Ps. 109:18
29 [1]Or, *leaders* [2]Or, *in* [a]Is. 34:5-15; Jer. 49:7-22; Ezek. 25:13; 35:9, 15

the sword; they will lie with the uncircumcised, and with those who go
down to the pit.
30"There also are the [1]chiefs of the
[a]north, all of them, and all the [b]Sido-
nians, who in spite of the terror resulting from their might, in shame
went down with the slain. So they
lay down uncircumcised with those
slain by the sword, and bore their
disgrace with those who go down to
the pit.
31"These Pharaoh will see, and he
will be [a]comforted for all his multitude slain by the sword, *even* Pharaoh and all his army," declares the
Lord GOD.
32"Though I instilled a terror of
him in the land of the living, yet he
will be made to lie down among *the*
uncircumcised *along* with those
slain by the sword, *even* Pharaoh
and all his multitude," declares the
Lord GOD.

CHAPTER 33

The Watchman's Duty

AND the word of the LORD came to
me saying,
2"Son of man, speak to the [a]sons
of your people, and say to them, 'If I
bring a sword upon a land, and the
people of the land take one man
from among them and make him
their watchman;
3 and he sees the sword coming
upon the land, and he [a]blows on the
trumpet and warns the people,
4 then he who hears the sound of
the trumpet and does not [a]take
warning, and a sword comes and
takes him away, his blood will be on
his [b]*own* head.
5 'He heard the sound of the trumpet, but did not take warning; his
blood will be on himself. But had he
taken warning, he would have [a]de-
livered his life.
6 'But if the watchman sees the
sword coming and does not blow
the trumpet, and the people are not
warned, and a sword comes and
takes a person from them, he is
[a]taken away [1]in his iniquity; but his
[b]blood I will require from the watchman's hand.'
7"Now as for you, son of man, I
have [1a]appointed you a watchman
for the house of Israel; so you will
hear a [2]message from My mouth,
and give them [b]warning from Me.
8"When I say to the wicked, 'O
wicked man, you shall [a]surely die,'
and you do not speak to warn the
wicked from his way, that wicked
man shall die in his iniquity, but his
blood I will require from your hand.
9"But if you on your part warn a
wicked man to turn from his way,
and he does not [a]turn from his way,
he will die in his iniquity; but you
have [b]delivered your life.
10"Now as for you, son of man, say
to the house of Israel, 'Thus you
have spoken, saying, "Surely our
transgressions and our sins are
upon us, and we are [a]rotting away in
them; [b]how then can we [1]survive?" '
11"Say to them, '[a]As I live!' declares the Lord [1]GOD, 'I take [b]no
pleasure in the death of the wicked,
but rather that the wicked [c]turn
from his way and live. [d]Turn back,
turn back from your evil ways! Why
then will you die, O house of Israel?'
12"And you, son of man, say to
[1]your fellow-citizens, 'The [a]right-
eousness of a righteous man will not
deliver him in the day of his transgression, and as for the wickedness
of the wicked, he will [b]not stumble
because of it in the day when he
turns from his wickedness; whereas
a righteous man will not be able to
live [2]by his righteousness on the day
when he commits sin.'
13"When I say to the righteous he
will surely live, and he *so* trusts in
his righteousness that he [a]commits
iniquity, none of his righteous deeds
will be remembered; but in that
same iniquity of his which he has
committed he will die.
14"But when I say to the wicked,
'You will surely die,' and he [a]turns
from his sin and practices [b]justice
and righteousness,
15 *if a* wicked man restores a
pledge, [a]pays back what he has
taken by robbery, walks by the
[b]statutes [1]which ensure life without
committing iniquity, he will surely
live; he shall not die.
16"[a]None of his sins that he has
committed will be remembered
against him. He has practiced justice and righteousness; he will
surely live.
17"Yet [1]your fellow-citizens say,
'The way of the Lord is not right',
when it is their own way that is not
right.
18"When the righteous turns from
his righteousness and [a]commits iniquity, then he shall die in [1]it.
19"But when the wicked turns
from his wickedness and practices
justice and righteousness, he will
live by them.

30 [1]Or, *princes* [a]Jer. 1:15; 25:26; Ezek. 38:6, 15; 39:2 [b]Jer. 25:22; Ezek. 28:21-23
31 [a]Ezek. 14:22; 31:16
2 [a]Ezek. 3:11; 33:12, 17, 30; 37:18
3 [a]Neh. 4:18-20; Is. 58:1; Ezek. 33:9; Hos. 8:1; Joel 2:1
4 [a]2 Chr. 25:16; Jer. 6:17; Zech. 1:4 [b]Ezek. 18:13; 33:5, 9; Acts 18:6
5 [a]Ex. 9:19-21; Heb. 11:7
6 [1]Or, *for*, and so throughout the chap. [a]Ezek. 18:20, 24; 33:8, 9 [b]Ezek. 3:18, 20
7 [1]Or, *given* [2]Lit., *word* [a]Is. 62:6; Ezek. 3:17-21 [b]Jer. 1:17; 26:2; Ezek. 2:7, 8; Acts 5:20
8 [a]Is. 3:11; Ezek. 18:4, 13, 18, 20; 33:14
9 [a]Acts 13:40, 41, 46 [b]Ezek. 3:19, 21; Acts 20:26
10 [1]Lit., *live* [a]Lev. 26:39; Ezek. 4:17; 24:23 [b]Is. 49:14; Ezek. 37:11
11 [1]YHWH, usually rendered LORD, and so throughout the chap. [a]Is. 49:18; Ezek. 5:11 [b]Ezek. 18:23, 32; Hos. 11:8 [c]1 Tim. 2:4; 2 Pet. 3:9 [d]Is. 55:6, 7; Jer. 3:22; 31:20; Ezek. 18:30, 31; Hos. 14:1; Acts 3:19
12 [1]Lit., *the sons of your people* [2]Lit., *by it* [a]Ezek. 3:18; 18:24; 33:18 [b]2 Chr. 7:14; Ezek. 18:21; 33:19
13 [a]Ezek. 18:26; Heb. 10:38; 2 Pet. 2:20, 21
14 [a]Is. 55:7; Jer. 18:7, 8; Ezek. 18:27; 33:8; Hos. 14:1, 4 [b]Mic. 6:8
15 [1]Lit., *of life* [a]Ex. 22:1-4; Lev. 6:4, 5; Luke 19:8 [b]Ps. 119:59; 143:8; Ezek. 20:11
16 [a]Is. 1:18; 43:25; Ezek. 18:22
17 [1]Lit., *the sons of your people*
18 [1]Lit., *them* [a]Ezek. 3:20; 18:24; 33:12, 13

20"Yet you say, 'The way of the
Lord is not right.' O house of Israel,
I will judge each of you according to
his ways."

Word of Jerusalem's Capture

21 Now it [a]came about in the
[b]twelfth year of our exile, on the
fifth of the tenth month, that the
refugees from Jerusalem came to
me, saying, "The city has been
taken."
22 Now the [a]hand of the LORD had
been upon me in the evening, before the refugees came. And He
[b]opened my mouth at the time *they*
came to me in the morning; so my
mouth was [c]opened, and I was no
longer speechless.
23 Then the word of the LORD
came to me saying,
24"Son of man, they who [a]live in
these waste places in the land of Israel are saying, '[b]Abraham was *only*
one, yet he possessed the land; so to
[c]us who are many the land has been
given as a possession.'
25"Therefore, say to them, 'Thus
says the Lord GOD, "You eat *meat*
with the [a]blood *in it,* lift up your
eyes to your idols as you shed blood.
[b]Should you then possess the land?
26"You [a]rely on your sword, you
commit abominations, and each of
you defiles his neighbor's wife.
Should you then possess the land?" '
27"Thus you shall say to them,
'Thus says the Lord GOD, "As I live,
surely those who are in the waste
places will [a]fall by the sword, and
whoever is in the open field I will
give to the beasts to be devoured,
and those who are in the strongholds and in the [b]caves will die of
pestilence.
28"And I shall make the land a
desolation and a [a]waste, and the
[b]pride of her power will cease; and
the mountains of Israel will be desolate, so that no one will pass
through.
29"Then they will know that I am
the LORD, when I make the land a
desolation and a waste because of
all their abominations which they
have committed." '
30"But as for you, son of man, your
fellow-citizens who talk about you
by the walls and in the doorways of
the houses, speak to one another,
each to his brother, saying, '[a]Come
now, and hear what the message is
which comes forth from the LORD.'
31"And they come to you as people
come, and they sit before you *as* My
people, but they do the lustful desires *expressed* by their [a]mouth, *and*
their heart [b]goes after their gain.
32"And behold, you are to them
like a sensual song by one who has a
[a]beautiful voice and plays well on
an instrument; for they hear your
words, but they do not practice
them.
33"So when it [a]comes to pass—as
surely it will—then they will know
that a prophet has been in their
midst."

CHAPTER 34

Prophecy against the Shepherds of Israel

THEN the word of the LORD came
to me saying,
2"Son of man, prophesy against
the [a]shepherds of Israel. Prophesy
and say to those shepherds, 'Thus
says the Lord [1]GOD, "Woe, shepherds of Israel who have been [2]feed-
ing [b]themselves! Should not the
shepherds [2]feed the [c]flock?
3"You [a]eat the fat and clothe
yourselves with the wool, you
[b]slaughter the fat *sheep* without
[1]feeding the flock.
4"Those who are sickly you have
not strengthened, the [1]diseased you
have not healed, the broken you
have not [a]bound up, the scattered
you have not brought back, nor
have you [b]sought for the lost; but
with force and with severity you
have dominated them.
5"And they were [a]scattered for
lack of a shepherd, and they became
[b]food for every beast of the field and
were scattered.
6"My flock [a]wandered through all
the mountains and on every high
hill, and [b]My flock was scattered
over all the surface of the earth; and
there was [c]no one to search or seek
for them." ' "
7 Therefore, you shepherds, hear
the word of the LORD:
8"As I live," declares the Lord
GOD, "surely because My flock has
become a [a]prey, My flock has even
become food for all the beasts of the
field for lack of a shepherd, and My
shepherds did not search for My
flock, but *rather* the shepherds fed
themselves and did not feed My
flock;
9 therefore, you shepherds, hear
the word of the LORD:
10 'Thus says the Lord GOD, "Behold, I am [a]against the shepherds,
and I shall demand My [1]sheep [2]from

21 [a]Ezek. 31:1; 32:1, 17; 40:1 [b]Jer. 39:1, 2; 52:4-7; Ezek. 24:1, 2
22 [a]Ezek. 1:3; 8:1; 37:1 [b]Ezek. 3:26, 27; 24:27 [c]Luke 1:64
24 [a]Jer. 39:10; 40:7; Ezek. 33:27 [b]Is. 51:2; Acts 7:5 [c]Ezek. 11:15; Luke 3:8; Rom. 4:12
25 [a]Lev. 17:10, 12, 14; Deut. 12:16, 23; 15:23 [b]Jer. 7:9, 10
26 [a]Mic. 2:1, 2; Zeph. 3:3
27 [a]Jer. 15:2-4; 42:22; Ezek. 5:12-14; 33:24 [b]1 Sam. 13:6; Is. 2:19
28 [a]Jer. 42:22; Ezek. 5:15; 6:14; Mic. 7:13 [b]Ezek. 7:24; 24:21; 30:6, 7
30 [a]Is. 29:13; 58:2; Ezek. 14:3; 20:3, 31
31 [a]Ps. 78:36, 37; Is. 29:13; 1 John 3:18 [b]Ezek. 22:13, 27; Luke 12:15
32 [a]Mark 6:20; John 5:35
33 [a]Jer. 28:9; Ezek. 33:29
2 [1]YHWH, usually rendered LORD, and so throughout the chap. [2]Lit., *pasturing, pasture* [a]Jer. 2:8; 3:15; 10:21; 12:10 [b]Jer. 23:1; Ezek. 22:25; 34:8-10; Mic. 3:1-3, 11 [c]Ps. 78:71, 72; Is. 40:11; Ezek. 34:14, 15; John 10:11; 21:15-17
3 [1]Lit., *pasturing* [a]Zech. 11:5, 16 [b]Ezek. 22:25, 27
4 [1]Lit., *sick* [a]Zech. 11:15, 16 [b]Matt. 9:36; 10:6; 18:12, 13; Luke 15:4
5 [a]Jer. 10:21; 50:6, 7 [b]Jer. 23:2; Ezek. 34:8, 28
6 [a]Jer. 40:11, 12; Ezek. 7:16; 1 Pet. 2:25 [b]John 10:16 [c]Ps. 142:4
8 [a]Acts 20:29
10 [1]Or, (a) *flock* [2]Lit., *from their hand* [a]Jer. 21:13; Ezek. 5:8; 13:8; 34:2; Zech. 10:3

them and make them [b]cease from feeding [1]sheep. So the shepherds will not [3]feed themselves any more, but I shall [c]deliver My flock from their mouth, that they may not be food for them." ' "

The Restoration of Israel

11 For thus says the Lord GOD, "Behold, [a]I Myself will search for My sheep and seek them out.

12"[a]As a shepherd cares for his herd in the day when he is among his scattered sheep, so I will [1b]care for My sheep and will deliver them from all the places to which they were scattered on a [c]cloudy and gloomy day.

13"And I will bring them out from the peoples and gather them from the countries and bring them to their own land; and I will [a]feed them on the mountains of Israel, by the [b]streams, and in all the inhabited places of the land.

14"I will feed them in a [a]good pasture, and their grazing ground will be on the mountain heights of Israel. There they will lie down in good grazing ground, and they will feed in [b]rich pasture on the mountains of Israel.

15"[a]I will feed My flock and I will lead them to rest," declares the Lord GOD.

16"I will seek the lost, bring back the scattered, bind up the broken, and strengthen the sick; but the [a]fat and the strong I will destroy. I will feed them with [b]judgment.

17"And as for you, My flock, thus says the Lord GOD, 'Behold, I will [a]judge between one sheep and another, between the rams and the male goats.

18 'Is it too [a]slight a thing for you that you should feed in the good pasture, that you must [b]tread down with your feet the rest of your pastures? Or that you should drink of the clear waters, that you must foul the rest with your feet?

19 'And as for My flock, they must eat what you tread down with your feet, and they must drink what you foul with your feet!' "

20 Therefore, thus says the Lord GOD to them, "Behold, I, even I, will judge between the fat sheep and the lean sheep.

21"Because you [a]push with side and with shoulder, and thrust at all the weak with your horns, until you have scattered them abroad,

22 therefore, I will [a]deliver My flock, and they will no longer be a prey; and I will judge between one sheep and another.

23"Then I will set over them one shepherd, My servant David, and he will feed them; he will feed them himself and be their shepherd.

24"And I, the LORD, will be their God, and My servant [a]David will be prince among them; I, the LORD, have spoken.

25"And I will make a [a]covenant of peace with them and [b]eliminate harmful beasts from the land, so that they may [c]live securely in the wilderness and sleep in the woods.

26"And I will make them and the places around My hill a [a]blessing. And I will cause [b]showers to come down in their season; they will be showers of [c]blessing.

27"Also the tree of the field will yield its fruit, and the earth will yield its increase, and they will be [a]secure on their land. Then they will know that I am the LORD, when I have [b]broken the bars of their yoke and have delivered them from the hand of those who enslaved them.

28"And they will no longer be a prey to the nations, and the beasts of the earth will not devour them; but they will live [a]securely, and no one will make *them* afraid.

29"And I will establish for them a renowned [a]planting place, and they will not again be victims of [b]famine in the land, and they will not [c]endure the insults of the nations any more.

30"Then they will know that [a]I, the LORD their God, am with them, and that they, the house of Israel, are My people," declares the Lord GOD.

31"As for you, [a]My sheep, the sheep of [b]My pasture, you are men, and I am your God," declares the Lord GOD.

CHAPTER 35

Prophecy against Mount Seir

MOREOVER, the word of the LORD came to me saying,

2"Son of man, set your face against [a]Mount Seir, and prophesy against it,

3 and say to it, 'Thus says the Lord [1]GOD,

"Behold, I am against you, Mount Seir,
And I will [a]stretch out My hand against you,
And I will make you a [b]desolation and a waste.

4 "I will [a]lay waste your cities,

10 [1]Or, (a) *flock* [3]Lit., *pasture*, and so throughout the chap. [b]1 Sam. 2:29, 30; Jer. 52:24-27 [c]Ps. 72:12-14
11 [a]Is. 51:12; Ezek. 11:17; 20:41
12 [a]Jer. 31:10 [b]Is. 40:11; 56:8; Jer. 23:3; 31:8; Luke 19:10; John 10:16 [c]Jer. 13:16; Ezek. 30:3; Joel 2:2
13 [a]Ezek. 34:23; 36:29, 30; Mic. 7:14 [b]Is. 30:25
14 [a]Ps. 23:1, 2; Jer. 31:12-14, 25; John 10:9 [b]Ezek. 28:25
15 [a]Ps. 23:1, 2
16 [a]Is. 10:16 [b]Is. 49:26
17 [a]Ezek. 20:38; 34:20-22; Mal. 4:1; Matt. 25:32
18 [a]Num. 16:9, 13; 2 Sam. 7:19; Is. 7:13 [b]Matt. 23:13; Luke 11:52
21 [a]Deut. 33:17; Dan. 8:4; Luke 13:14-16
22 [a]Ps. 72:12-14; Jer. 23:2, 3
24 [a]Is. 55:3-5; Jer. 30:9; Ezek. 37:24, 25; Hos. 3:5
25 [a]Ezek. 16:60; 20:37; 37:26 [b]Job 5:22; Is. 11:6-9 [c]Jer. 33:16; Ezek. 28:26; 34:27, 28
26 [a]Gen. 12:2; Ezek. 34:14 [b]Deut. 11:13-15; 28:12 [c]Lev. 25:21
27 [a]Ezek. 38:8, 11 [b]Lev. 26:13; Is. 52:2, 3; Jer. 30:8
28 [a]Jer. 30:10; Ezek. 39:26
29 [a]Is. 4:2; 60:21; 61:3 [b]Ezek. 34:26 [c]Ezek. 36:6, 15
30 [a]Ps. 46:7, 11; Ezek. 14:11; 36:28
31 [a]Ps. 78:52; 80:1; Ezek. 36:38 [b]Ps. 100:3; Jer. 23:1
2 [a]Gen. 36:8; Ezek. 25:12; 36:5
3 [1]YHWH, usually rendered LORD, and so throughout the chap. [a]Jer. 6:12; 15:6; Ezek. 25:13 [b]Jer. 49:13, 17, 18; Ezek. 35:7
4 [a]Ezek. 6:6; 35:9; Mal. 1:3, 4

And you will become a desolation.
Then you will know that I am
the LORD.
5 "Because you have had everlasting [a]enmity and have [1]delivered
the sons of Israel to the power of the
sword at the time of their calamity,
at the time of the [2b]punishment of
the end,
6 therefore, as I live," declares
the Lord GOD, "I will [1]give you over
to [a]bloodshed, and bloodshed will
pursue you; since you have not
hated bloodshed, therefore bloodshed will pursue you.
7 "And I will make Mount Seir a
waste and a desolation, and I will
cut off from it the one who passes
through and returns.
8 "And I will [a]fill its mountains
with its slain; on your hills and in
your valleys and in all your ravines
those slain by the sword will fall.
9 "I will make you an everlasting
[a]desolation, and your cities will not
be inhabited. Then you will know
that I am the LORD.
10 "Because you have [a]said, 'These
two nations and these two lands will
be mine, and we will possess them,'
although the [b]LORD was there,
11 therefore, as I live," declares
the Lord GOD, "I will deal *with you*
[a]according to your anger and according to your envy which you
showed because of your hatred
against them; so I will [b]make Myself
known among them when I judge
you.
12 "Then you will know that I, the
LORD, have heard all your revilings
which you have spoken against the
mountains of Israel saying, 'They
are laid desolate; they are [a]given to
us for food.'
13 "And you have [a]spoken arrogantly against Me and have multiplied your words against Me; [b]I
have heard."
14 'Thus says the Lord GOD, "As all
the earth [a]rejoices, I will make you a
desolation.
15 "As you [a]rejoiced over the inheritance of the house of Israel because it was desolate, [b]so I will do to
you. You will be a [c]desolation, O
Mount Seir, and all Edom, all of it.
Then they will know that I am the
LORD." '

CHAPTER 36

The Mountains of Israel to Be Blessed

"AND you, son of man, prophesy
to the mountains of Israel and say,
'O mountains of Israel, hear the
word of the LORD.
2 'Thus says the Lord [1]GOD, "Because the enemy has spoken against
you, 'Aha!' and, 'The everlasting
[2a]heights have become our possession,'
3 therefore, prophesy and say,
'Thus says the Lord GOD, "For good
cause they have made you [a]desolate
and [b]crushed you from every side,
that you should become a possession of the rest of the nations, and
you have been taken up in the [c]talk
and the whispering of the people." ' "
4 'Therefore, O [a]mountains of Israel, hear the word of the Lord GOD.
Thus says the Lord GOD to the
mountains and to the hills, to the
ravines and to the valleys, to the
desolate wastes and to the forsaken
cities, which have become a [b]prey
and a derision to the rest of the nations which are round about,
5 therefore, thus says the Lord
GOD, "Surely in the fire of My [a]jeal-
ousy I have spoken against the [b]rest
of the nations, and against all Edom,
who [1]appropriated My land for
themselves as a possession with
wholehearted [c]joy *and* with scorn of
soul, to drive it out for a prey."
6 'Therefore, prophesy concerning the land of Israel, and say to the
mountains and to the hills, to the
ravines and to the valleys, "Thus
says the Lord GOD, 'Behold, I have
spoken in My jealousy and in My
wrath because you have [a]endured
the insults of the nations.'
7 "Therefore, thus says the Lord
GOD, 'I have sworn that surely the
nations which are around you will
themselves endure their insults.
8 'But you, O mountains of Israel,
you will [a]put forth your branches
and bear your fruit for My people
Israel; for they will soon come.
9 'For, behold, I am for you, and I
will [a]turn to you, and you shall be
[b]cultivated and sown.
10 'And I will multiply men on you,
[a]all the house of Israel, all of it; and
the [b]cities will be inhabited, and the
waste places will be rebuilt.
11 'And I will multiply on you man
and beast; and they will increase
and be fruitful; and I will cause you
to be inhabited as you were [a]former-
ly and will treat you [b]better than at
the first. Thus you will know that I
am the LORD.
12 'Yes, I will cause [a]men—My
people Israel—to walk on you and
possess you, so that you will be-

5 [1]Lit., *poured* [2]Or, *iniquity* [a]Ps. 137:7; Ezek. 25:12, 15; 36:5; Amos 1:11; Obad. 10 [b]Ezek. 7:2; 21:25, 29
6 [1]Lit., *prepare you for* [a]Is. 63:2-6; Ezek. 16:38; 32:6
8 [a]Is. 34:5, 6; Ezek. 31:12; 32:4, 5; 39:4, 5
9 [a]Jer. 49:13; Ezek. 25:13
10 [a]Ps. 83:4-12; Ezek. 36:2, 5 [b]Ps. 48:1-3; 132:13, 14; Is. 12:6; Ezek. 48:35; Zeph. 3:15
11 [a]Ps. 137:7; Ezek. 25:14; Amos 1:11 [b]Ps. 9:16; 73:17, 18
12 [a]Jer. 50:7; Ezek. 36:2
13 [a]Is. 10:13, 14; 36:20; Jer. 48:26, 42; Dan. 11:36 [b]Jer. 7:11; 29:23
14 [a]Is. 44:23; 49:13; Jer. 51:48
15 [a]Jer. 50:11; Lam. 4:21 [b]Obad. 12, 15 [c]Is. 34:5, 6; Ezek. 35:3, 4
2 [1]YHWH, usually rendered LORD, and so throughout the chap. [2]Lit., *Bamoth* [a]Deut. 32:13; Ps. 78:69; Is. 58:14; Hab. 3:19
3 [a]Jer. 2:15 [b]Ps. 35:25; Jer. 51:34; Lam. 2:2, 5, 16 [c]Ps. 44:13, 14; Jer. 18:16; Ezek. 35:13
4 [a]Deut. 11:11; Ezek. 36:1, 6, 8 [b]Ezek. 34:8, 28
5 [1]Lit., *gave* [a]Is. 66:15, 16; Ezek. 5:13; 36:6; 38:19 [b]Jer. 25:9, 15-29; Ezek. 36:3 [c]Jer. 50:11; Ezek. 35:15; Mic. 7:8
6 [a]Ps. 74:10; 123:3, 4; Ezek. 34:29
8 [a]Is. 4:2; 27:6; Ezek. 17:23; 34:26-29
9 [a]Lev. 26:9 [b]Ezek. 28:26; 34:14; 36:34
10 [a]Is. 27:6; 49:17-23; Ezek. 37:21, 22 [b]Jer. 31:27; Ezek. 36:33
11 [a]Jer. 30:18; Ezek. 16:55; Mic. 7:14 [b]Job 42:12; Is. 51:3
12 [a]Ezek. 34:13, 14

come their [b]inheritance and never again [c]bereave them of children.'

13"Thus says the Lord GOD, 'Because they say to you, "You are a devourer of men and have bereaved your [1]nation of children,"

14 therefore, you will no longer devour men, and no longer bereave your nation of children,' declares the Lord GOD.

15"And I will not let you hear [a]insults from the nations any more, nor will you bear [b]disgrace from the peoples any longer, nor will you cause your nation to [c]stumble any longer," declares the Lord GOD.' "

16 Then the word of the LORD came to me saying,

17"Son of man, when the house of Israel was living in their own land, they defiled it by their ways and their deeds; their way before Me was like the uncleanness of a woman in her impurity.

18"Therefore, I [a]poured out My wrath on them for the blood which they had shed on the land, because they had defiled it with their idols.

19"Also I [a]scattered them among the nations, and they were dispersed throughout the lands. [b]According to their ways and their deeds I judged them.

20"When they came to the nations where they went, they [a]profaned My holy name, because it was said of them, 'These are the [b]people of the LORD; yet they have come out of His land.'

21"But I had [1]concern for My [a]holy name, which the house of Israel had profaned among the nations where they went.

Israel to Be Renewed for His Name's Sake

22"Therefore, say to the house of Israel, 'Thus says the Lord GOD, "It is not for your sake, O house of Israel, that I am about to [a]act, but for My holy name, which you have profaned among the nations where you went.

23"And I will [a]vindicate the holiness of My great name which has been profaned among the nations, which you have profaned in their midst. Then the [b]nations will know that I am the LORD," declares the Lord GOD, "when I prove Myself holy among you in their sight.

24"For I will [a]take you from the nations, gather you from all the lands, and bring you into your own land.

25"Then I will [a]sprinkle clean water on you, and you will be clean; I will cleanse you from all your [b]filthiness and from all your [c]idols.

26"Moreover, I will give you a [a]new heart and put a new spirit within you; and I will remove the heart of [b]stone from your flesh and give you a heart of flesh.

27"And I will [a]put My Spirit within you and cause you to walk in My statutes, and you will be careful to observe My ordinances.

28"And you will live in the land that I gave to your forefathers; so you will be [a]My people, and I will be your God.

29"Moreover, I will save you from all your uncleanness; and I will call for the grain and multiply it, and I will not [1a]bring a famine on you.

30"And I will [a]multiply the fruit of the tree and the produce of the field, that you may not receive again the disgrace of famine among the nations.

31"Then you will [a]remember your evil ways and your deeds that were not good, and you will loathe yourselves in your own sight for your iniquities and your abominations.

32"I am not doing *this* for your sake," declares the Lord GOD, "let it be known to you. Be ashamed and confounded for your ways, O house of Israel!"

33 'Thus says the Lord GOD, "On the day that I cleanse you from all your iniquities, I will cause the [a]cities to be inhabited, and the [b]waste places will be rebuilt.

34"And the desolate land will be cultivated instead of being a desolation in the sight of everyone who passed by.

35"And they will say, 'This desolate land has become like the [a]garden of Eden; and the waste, desolate, and ruined cities are fortified *and* inhabited.'

36"Then the nations that are left round about you will know that I, the LORD, have rebuilt the ruined places *and* planted that which was desolate; I, the LORD, have spoken and [a]will do it."

37 'Thus says the Lord GOD, "This also I will let the house of Israel ask Me to do for them: I will increase their men like a flock.

38"Like the [a]flock [1]for sacrifices, like the flock at Jerusalem during her appointed feasts, so will the waste cities be filled with [b]flocks of men. Then they will know that I am the LORD." ' "

12 [b]Ezek. 47:14 [c]Num. 13:32
13 [1]Or, *nations,* and so throughout the chap.
15 [a]Is. 54:4; 60:14; Ezek. 34:29; 36:7 [b]Ps. 89:50; Ezek. 22:4 [c]Is. 63:13; Jer. 13:16; 18:15
18 [a]2 Chr. 34:21, 25; Lam. 2:4; 4:11; Ezek. 22:20
19 [a]Deut. 28:64; Ezek. 5:12; 22:15; Amos 9:9 [b]Ezek. 24:14; 39:24; Rom. 2:6
20 [a]Is. 52:5; Ezek. 12:16; 14:22; Rom. 2:24 [b]Jer. 33:24
21 [1]Lit., *compassion* [a]Ps. 74:18; Is. 37:35; 48:9; Ezek. 20:44
22 [a]Deut. 7:7, 8; 9:5-7; Ps. 108:6; Ezek. 36:32
23 [a]Is. 5:16; Ezek. 20:41; 38:23; 39:7, 25; 1 Pet. 3:15 [b]Ps. 102:13, 15; 126:2
24 [a]Is. 43:5, 6; Ezek. 34:13; 37:21
25 [a]Num. 19:17-19; Ps. 51:7; Titus 3:5, 6; Heb. 9:13, 19; 10:22 [b]Is. 4:4; Zech. 13:1 [c]Is. 2:18, 20; Hos. 14:3, 8
26 [a]Ps. 51:10; Ezek. 11:19; 18:31; John 3:3, 5; 2 Cor. 5:17 [b]Ezek. 11:19; Zech. 7:12
27 [a]Is. 44:3; 59:21; Ezek. 37:14; 39:29; Joel 2:28, 29
28 [a]Ezek. 14:11; 37:23, 27
29 [1]Lit., *put* [a]Ezek. 34:27, 29; Hos. 2:21-23
30 [a]Lev. 26:4
31 [a]Ezek. 16:61-63; 20:43
33 [a]Ezek. 36:10; Zech. 8:7, 8 [b]Is. 58:12
35 [a]Is. 51:3; Ezek. 31:9; Joel 2:3
36 [a]Hos. 14:4-9
38 [1]Lit., *of holy things* [a]1 Kin. 8:63; 2 Chr. 35:7-9; John 2:14 [b]Ps. 74:1; 100:3; Jer. 23:1; Zech. 11:17; John 10:7, 9, 16

CHAPTER 37

Vision of the Valley of Dry Bones

THE [a]hand of the LORD was upon
me, and He [b]brought me out [1]by the
Spirit of the LORD and set me down
in the middle of the [c]valley; and it
was full of bones.
2 And He caused me to pass
among them round about, and behold, *there were* very many on the
surface of the valley; and lo, *they*
were very dry.
3 And He said to me, "Son of
man, [a]can these bones live?" And I
answered, "O Lord [1]GOD, [b]Thou
knowest."
4 Again He said to me, "[a]Prophe-
sy over these bones, and say to
them, 'O dry bones, [b]hear the word
of the LORD.'
5"Thus says the Lord GOD to
these bones, 'Behold, I will cause
[1a]breath to enter you that you may
come to life.
6 'And I will put sinews on you,
make flesh grow back on you, cover
you with skin, and put breath in you
that you may come alive; and you
will [a]know that I am the LORD.' "
7 So I prophesied [a]as I was commanded; and as I prophesied, there
was a [1]noise, and behold, a rattling;
and the bones came together, bone
to its bone.
8 And I looked, and behold, sinews were on them, and flesh grew,
and skin covered them; but there
was no breath in them.
9 Then He said to me, "Prophesy
to the breath, prophesy, son of man,
and say to the breath, 'Thus says the
Lord GOD, "Come from the four
winds, O breath, and breathe on
these slain, that they [a]come to
life." ' "
10 So I prophesied as He commanded me, and the breath came
into them, and they came to life, and
stood on their feet, an [a]exceedingly
great army.

The Vision Explained

11 Then He said to me, "Son of
man, these bones are the [a]whole
house of Israel; behold, they say,
'[b]Our bones are dried up, and our
hope has perished. We are [1]com-
pletely [c]cut off.'
12"Therefore prophesy, and say to
them, 'Thus says the Lord GOD, "Behold, I will open your graves and
[a]cause you to come up out of your
graves, My people; and I will bring
you into the land of Israel.
13"Then you will know that I am
the LORD, when I have opened your
graves and caused you to come up
out of your graves, My people.
14"And I will [a]put My [1]Spirit
within you, and you will come to
life, and I will place you on your own
land. Then you will know that I, the
LORD, have spoken and done it," declares the LORD.' "

Reunion of Judah and Israel

15 The word of the LORD came
again to me saying,
16"And you, son of man, take for
yourself [a]one stick and write on it,
'[b]For Judah and for the sons of Israel, his companions'; then take another stick and write on it, 'For [c]Jo-
seph, the stick of Ephraim and all
the house of Israel, his companions.'
17"Then [a]join them for yourself
one to another into one stick, that
they may become one in your hand.
18"And when the sons of your people speak to you saying, 'Will you
not declare to us [a]what you mean by
these?'
19 say to them, 'Thus says the
Lord GOD, "Behold, I will take the
stick of Joseph, which is in the hand
of Ephraim, and the tribes of Israel,
his companions; and I will put them
with it, with the stick of Judah, and
make them one stick, and they will
be one in My hand." '
20"And the sticks on which you
write will be in your hand before
their eyes.
21"And say to them, 'Thus says the
Lord GOD, "Behold, I will [a]take the
sons of Israel from among the nations where they have gone, and I
will gather them from every side
and bring them into their own land;
22 and I will make them [a]one nation in the land, on the mountains of
Israel; and [b]one king will be king for
all of them; and they will no longer
be two nations, and they will no
longer be divided into two kingdoms.
23"And they will no longer defile
themselves with their idols, or with
their detestable things, or with any
of their transgressions; but I will deliver them from all their [1]dwelling
places in which they have sinned,
and will cleanse them. And they will
be My people, and I will be their
God.

The Davidic Kingdom

24"And My servant [a]David will be
king over them, and they will all
have [b]one shepherd; and they will
walk in My ordinances, and keep
My statutes, and observe them.

1 [1]Or, *in* [a]Ezek. 1:3; 33:22; 40:1 [b]Ezek. 8:3; 11:24; 43:5; Acts 8:39 [c]Jer. 7:32-8:2
3 [1]YHWH, usually rendered LORD, and so throughout the chap. [a]Ezek. 26:19 [b]Deut. 32:39; 1 Sam. 2:6
4 [a]Num. 20:8; 1 Kin. 13:2; Ezek. 37:9, 12 [b]Is. 42:18; Jer. 22:29; Ezek. 36:1
5 [1]Or, *spirit*, and so throughout the chap. [a]Gen. 2:7; Ps. 104:29, 30; Ezek. 37:9, 10, 14
6 [a]Is. 49:23; Ezek. 35:9; 38:23; 39:6; Joel 2:27; 3:17
7 [1]Lit., *voice;* or *thunder* [a]Jer. 13:5-7
9 [a]Hos. 13:14
10 [a]Jer. 30:19; 33:22
11 [1]Lit., *cut off to ourselves* [a]Jer. 33:24; Ezek. 36:10; 39:25 [b]Ps. 141:7; Is. 40:27 [c]Ps. 88:5; Lam. 3:54
12 [a]Deut. 32:39; 1 Sam. 2:6; Is. 26:19; 66:14; Hos. 13:14
14 [1]Or, *breath* [a]Is. 32:15; Ezek. 11:19; 36:27; 37:9; 39:29; Joel 2:28, 29; Zech. 12:10
16 [a]Num. 17:2, 3 [b]2 Chr. 10:17; 11:11-17; 15:9 [c]1 Kin. 12:16-20; 2 Chr. 10:19
17 [a]Is. 11:13; Jer. 50:4; Ezek. 37:22-24; Hos. 1:11; Zeph. 3:9
18 [a]Ezek. 12:9; 17:12; 20:49; 24:19
21 [a]Is. 43:5, 6; Jer. 29:14; Ezek. 36:24; 39:27; Amos 9:14, 15
22 [a]Jer. 3:18; 50:4, 5; Ezek. 36:10 [b]Ezek. 34:23, 24; 37:24
23 [1]Another reading is, *backslidings*
24 [a]Jer. 30:9; Ezek. 34:24; 37:25; Hos. 3:5 [b]Ps. 78:71; Is. 40:11; Ezek. 34:23

25"And they shall live on the land
that I gave to Jacob My servant, in
which your fathers lived; and they
will live on it, they, and their sons,
and their sons' sons, forever; and
[a]David My servant shall be their
prince forever.
26"And I will make a [a]covenant of
peace with them; it will be an [b]ever-
lasting covenant with them. And I
will [1]place them and [c]multiply
them, and will set My [d]sanctuary in
their midst forever.
27"My [a]dwelling place also will be
with them; and [b]I will be their God,
and they will be My people.
28"And the nations will know that
I am the LORD [a]who sanctifies Israel,
when My sanctuary is in their midst
forever." ' "

CHAPTER 38

Prophecy About Gog and Future Invasion of Israel

AND the word of the LORD came to
me saying,
2"Son of man, set your face
toward [a]Gog of the land of [b]Magog,
the prince of [c]Rosh, [d]Meshech, and
[d]Tubal, and prophesy against him,
3 and say, 'Thus says the Lord
[1]GOD, "Behold, I am against you, O
Gog, prince of Rosh, Meshech, and
Tubal.
4"And I will turn you about, and
put hooks into your jaws, and I will
[a]bring you out, and all your army,
[b]horses and horsemen, all of them
splendidly attired, a great company
with buckler and shield, all of them
wielding swords;
5 [a]Persia, [1b]Ethiopia, and [c]Put
with them, all of them *with* shield
and helmet;
6 [a]Gomer with all its troops;
Beth-[b]togarmah *from* the remote
parts of the north with all its
troops—many peoples with you.
7"Be prepared, and prepare yourself, you and all your companies
that are assembled about you, and
be a guard for them.
8"[a]After many days you will be
summoned; in the latter years you
will come into the land that is restored from the sword, *whose inhabitants* have been [b]gathered from
many nations to the [c]mountains of
Israel which had been a continual
waste; but its people were brought
out from the nations, and they are
[d]living securely, all of them.
9"And you will go up, you will
come [a]like a storm; you will be like
a [b]cloud covering the land, you and
all your troops, and many peoples
with you."
10 'Thus says the Lord GOD, "It will
come about on that day, that
thoughts will come into your mind,
and you will [a]devise an evil plan,
11 and you will say, 'I will go up
against the land of [a]unwalled villages. I will go against those who are
[b]at rest, that live securely, all of
them living without walls, and having no bars or gates;
12 to [a]capture spoil and to seize
plunder, to turn your hand against
the waste places which are *now* inhabited, and against the people who
are gathered from the nations, who
have acquired cattle and goods, who
live at the center of the world.'
13"[a]Sheba, and [b]Dedan, and the
merchants of [c]Tarshish, with all its
[d]villages, will say to you, 'Have you
come to capture spoil? Have you assembled your company to seize
plunder, to carry away silver and
gold, to take away cattle and goods,
to capture great [e]spoil?' " '
14"Therefore, prophesy, son of
man, and say to Gog, 'Thus says the
Lord GOD, "On that day when My
people Israel are [a]living securely,
will you not know *it*?
15"And you will come from your
place out of the remote parts of the
north, you and many peoples with
you, all of them riding on horses, a
great assembly and a mighty army;
16 and you will come up against
My people Israel like a cloud to cover the land. It will come about in the
last days that I shall bring you
against My land, in order that the
nations may [a]know Me when I shall
be [b]sanctified through you before
their eyes, O Gog."
17 'Thus says the Lord GOD, "Are
you the one of whom I spoke in former days through My servants the
prophets of Israel, who [a]prophesied
in those days for *many* years that I
would bring you against them?
18"And it will come about on that
day, when Gog comes against the
land of Israel," declares the Lord
GOD, "that My fury will mount up in
My [a]anger.
19"And in My [a]zeal and in My blazing wrath I declare *that* on that day
there will surely be a great [b]earth-
quake in the land of Israel.
20"[a]And the fish of the sea, the
birds of the heavens, the beasts of
the field, all the creeping things that
creep on the earth, and all the men
who are on the face of the earth will

25 [a]Is. 11:1; Ezek. 37:24; Zech. 6:12
26 [1]Lit., *give* [a]Ezek. 16:62; 20:37; 34:25 [b]Ps. 89:3, 4; Is. 55:3; 59:21; Ezek. 16:60 [c]Jer. 30:19; Ezek. 36:10, 11, 37 [d]Ezek. 20:40; 43:7
27 [a]John 1:14 [b]Ezek. 37:23; 2 Cor. 6:16
28 [a]Ex. 31:13; Ezek. 20:12
2 [a]Ezek. 38:3, 14, 16, 18; 39:1, 11; Rev. 20:8 [b]Gen. 10:2; Ezek. 39:6; Rev. 20:8 [c]Ezek. 38:3; 39:1 [d]Ezek. 27:13; 38:3; 39:1
3 [1]YHWH, usually rendered LORD, and so throughout the chap.
4 [a]Is. 43:17 [b]Ezek. 38:15; Dan. 11:40
5 [1]Lit., *Cush* [a]2 Chr. 36:20; Ezra 1:1; Ezek. 27:10; Dan. 8:20 [b]Gen. 10:6-8; Ezek. 30:4, 5 [c]Ezek. 27:10; 30:5
6 [a]Gen. 10:2, 3 [b]Gen. 10:3; Ezek. 27:14
8 [a]Is. 24:22 [b]Is. 11:11; Ezek. 36:24; 37:21; 38:12; 39:27, 28 [c]Ezek. 34:13; 36:1-8 [d]Ezek. 38:11, 14; 39:26
9 [a]Is. 5:28; 21:1; 25:4; 28:2; Jer. 4:13 [b]Ezek. 30:18; 39:16; Joel 2:2
10 [a]Ps. 36:4; Mic. 2:1
11 [a]Zech. 2:4 [b]Jer. 49:31
12 [a]Is. 10:6; Ezek. 29:19
13 [a]Ezek. 27:22, 23 [b]Ezek. 25:13; 27:15, 20 [c]Ezek. 27:12 [d]Ezek. 32:2; Nah. 2:11-13 [e]Is. 10:6; 33:23
14 [a]Jer. 23:6; Ezek. 38:8, 11; Zech. 2:5, 8
16 [a]Ps. 83:18; Ezek. 36:23; 38:23 [b]Is. 5:16; 8:13
17 [a]Is. 5:26-29; 34:1-6; 63:1-6; 66:15, 16; Joel 3:9-14
18 [a]Ps. 18:8, 15
19 [a]Deut. 32:22; Ps. 18:7, 8; Ezek. 5:13; 36:5, 6; Nah. 1:2; Heb. 12:29 [b]Ezek. 37:7; Joel 3:16; Hag. 2:6, 7
20 [a]Jer. 4:24, 25; Hos. 4:3; Nah. 1:4-6

shake at My presence; the [b]moun-
tains also will be thrown down, the
steep pathways will collapse, and
every wall will fall to the ground.
21"And I shall call for a [a]sword
against [1]him on all My mountains,"
declares the Lord GOD. "[b]Every
man's sword will be against his
brother.
22"And with pestilence and with
blood I shall enter into [a]judgment
with him; and I shall rain on him,
and on his troops, and on the many
peoples who are with him, a [1]torren-
tial rain, with [b]hailstones, fire, and
brimstone.
23"And I shall magnify Myself,
sanctify Myself, and make [a]Myself
known in the sight of many nations;
and they will know that I am the
LORD."'

CHAPTER 39

Prophecy against Gog—Invaders Destroyed

"AND you, son of man, prophesy
against Gog, and say, 'Thus says the
Lord [1]GOD, "Behold, I am against
you, O Gog, [2]prince of Rosh, Meshech, and Tubal;
2 and I shall turn you around,
drive you on, take you up from the
remotest parts of the north, and
bring you against the mountains of
Israel.
3"And I shall [a]strike your bow
from your left hand, and dash down
your arrows from your right hand.
4"You shall [a]fall on the mountains of Israel, you and all your
troops, and the peoples who are
with you; I shall give you as food to
every [1]kind of [b]predatory bird and
beast of the field.
5"You will fall on the [1]open field;
for it is I who have spoken," declares the Lord GOD.
6"And I shall send [a]fire upon Magog and those who inhabit the
[b]coastlands in safety; and they will
know that I am the LORD.
7"And My [a]holy name I shall
make known in the midst of My people Israel; and I shall not let My holy
name be [b]profaned any more. And
the [c]nations will know that I am the
Lord, the [d]Holy One in Israel.
8"Behold, it is coming and it shall
be done," declares the Lord GOD.
"That is the day of which I have spoken.
9"Then those who inhabit the
cities of Israel will [a]go out, and
make [b]fires with the weapons and
burn *them*, both shields and buck-
lers, bows and arrows, war clubs
and spears and for seven years they
will make fires of them.
10"And they will not take wood
from the field or gather firewood
from the forests, for they will make
fires with the weapons; and they
will take the spoil of those who despoiled them, and seize the [a]plunder
of those who plundered them," declares the Lord GOD.
11"And it will come about on that
day that I shall give Gog a burial
ground there in Israel, the valley of
those who pass by east of the sea,
and it will block off the passers-by.
So they will bury Gog there with all
his multitude, and they will call *it*
the valley of [1]Hamon-gog.
12"For seven months the house of
Israel will be burying them in order
to [a]cleanse the land.
13"Even all the people of the land
will bury *them;* and it will be [1]to
their [a]renown *on* the day that I [b]glo-
rify Myself," declares the Lord GOD.
14"And they will set apart men
who will constantly pass through
the land, [a]burying those who were
passing through, even those left on
the surface of the ground, in order to
cleanse it. At the end of seven
months they will make a search.
15"And as those who pass through
the land pass through and anyone
sees a man's bone, then he will [1]set
up a marker by it until the buriers
have buried it in the valley of [2]Ha-
mon-gog.
16"And even *the* name of *the* city
will be Hamonah. So they will
cleanse the land."'
17"And as for you, son of man,
thus says the Lord GOD, 'Speak to
every [1]kind of [a]bird and to every
[a]beast of the field, "Assemble and
come, gather from every side to My
sacrifice which I am going to [b]sacri-
fice for you, as a great sacrifice on
the mountains of Israel, that you
may eat flesh and drink blood.
18"You shall eat the [a]flesh of
mighty men, and drink the blood of
the princes of the earth, as *though
they were* [b]rams, lambs, goats, and
[c]bulls, all of them fatlings of [d]Ba-
shan.
19"So you will eat fat until you are
glutted, and drink blood until you
are drunk, from My sacrifice which
I have sacrificed for you.
20"And you will be glutted at My
table with [a]horses and charioteers,
with mighty men and all the men of
war," declares the Lord GOD.

20 [b]Zech. 14:4
21 [1]I.e. Gog [a]Ezek. 14:17 [b]Judg. 7:22; 1 Sam. 14:20; 2 Chr. 20:23; Hag. 2:22
22 [1]Lit., *overflowing* [a]Is. 66:16; Jer. 25:31 [b]Ps. 11:6; 18:12-14; Is. 28:17
23 [a]Ps. 9:16; Ezek. 37:28; 38:16
1 [1]YHWH, usually rendered LORD, and so throughout the chap. [2]Or, *chief prince of Meshech*
3 [a]Ps. 76:3; Jer. 21:4, 5; Ezek. 30:21-24; Hos. 1:5
4 [1]Lit., *wing* [a]Is. 14:24, 25; Ezek. 39:17-20 [b]Ezek. 29:5; 32:4, 5; 33:27
5 [1]Lit., *face of the*
6 [a]Ezek. 30:8, 16; 38:19, 22; Amos 1:4, 7, 10; Nah. 1:6 [b]Ps. 72:10; Is. 66:19; Jer. 25:22
7 [a]Ezek. 36:20-22; 39:25 [b]Ex. 20:7; Ezek. 20:9, 14, 39 [c]Ezek. 38:16, 23 [d]Is. 12:6; 43:3, 14; 55:5; 60:9, 14
9 [a]Is. 66:24; Mal. 1:5 [b]Josh. 11:6; Ps. 46:9
10 [a]Is. 14:2; 33:1; Mic. 5:8; Hab. 2:8
11 [1]Or, *the multitude of Gog*
12 [a]Deut. 21:23; Ezek. 39:14, 16
13 [1]Or, *a memorial for them* [a]Jer. 33:9; Zeph. 3:19, 20 [b]Ezek. 28:22
14 [a]Jer. 14:16
15 [1]Lit., *build* [2]Or, *the multitude of Gog*
17 [1]Lit., *wing* [a]Is. 56:9; Jer. 12:9; Ezek. 39:4; Zeph. 1:7; Rev. 19:17, 18 [b]Is. 34:6, 7; Jer. 46:10; Zeph. 1:7
18 [a]Ezek. 29:5; Rev. 19:18 [b]Jer. 51:40 [c]Jer. 50:27 [d]Ps. 22:12; Amos 4:1
20 [a]Ps. 76:5, 6; Ezek. 38:4; Hag. 2:22; Rev. 19:18

21"And I shall set My [a]glory among the nations; and all the nations will see My judgment which I have executed, and My hand which I have laid on them.

22"And the house of Israel will [a]know that I am the LORD their God from that day onward.

23"And the nations will know that the house of Israel went into exile for their [a]iniquity because they acted treacherously against Me, and I [b]hid My face from them; so I gave them into the hand of their adversaries, and all of them fell by the sword.

24"According to their [a]uncleanness and according to their transgressions I dealt with them, and I hid My face from them." ' "

Israel Restored

25 Therefore thus says the Lord GOD, "Now I shall [a]restore the fortunes of Jacob, and have mercy on the whole [b]house of Israel; and I shall be [c]jealous for My holy name.

26"And they shall [1a]forget their disgrace and all their treachery which they perpetrated against Me, when they [b]live securely on their *own* land with [c]no one to make them afraid.

27"When I [a]bring them back from the peoples and gather them from the lands of their enemies, then I shall be [b]sanctified [1]through them in the sight of the many nations.

28"Then they will know that I am the LORD their God because I made them go into exile among the nations, and then gathered them *again* to their own land; and I will leave none of them there any longer.

29"And I will not hide My face from them any longer, for I shall have [a]poured out My Spirit on the house of Israel," declares the Lord GOD.

CHAPTER 40

Vision of the Man with a Measuring Rod

IN the [a]twenty-fifth year of our exile, at the beginning of the year, on the tenth of the month, in the fourteenth year after the city was [b]taken, on that same day the [c]hand of the LORD was upon me and He brought me there.

2 In the [a]visions of God He brought me into the land of Israel, and set me on a very [b]high mountain; and on it to the [c]south *there was* a [d]structure like a city.

3 So He brought me there; and behold, there was a man whose appearance was like the appearance of [a]bronze, with a [b]line of flax and a measuring [1c]rod in his hand; and he was standing in the gateway.

4 And the man said to me, "[a]Son of man, [b]see with your eyes, hear with your ears, and give attention to all that I am going to show you; for you have been brought here in order to show *it* to you. [c]Declare to the house of Israel all that you see."

Measurements Relating to the Temple

5 And behold, there was a [a]wall on the outside of the [1]temple all around, and in the man's hand was a measuring rod of six cubits, *each of which was* a cubit and a [2]handbreadth. So he measured the thickness of the [3]wall, one rod; and the height, one rod.

6 Then he went to the gate which faced [a]east, went up its steps, and measured the threshold of the gate, one rod [1]in width; and the other threshold *was* one rod [1]in width.

7 And the [a]guardroom *was* one rod long and one rod wide; and *there were* five cubits between the guardrooms. And the threshold of the gate by the porch of the gate [1]facing inward *was* one rod.

8 Then he measured the porch of the gate facing inward, one rod.

9 And he measured the porch of the gate, eight cubits; and its side pillars, two cubits. And the porch of the gate was faced inward.

10 And the guardrooms of the gate toward the east *numbered* three on each side; the three of them had the same measurement. The side pillars also had the same measurement on each side.

11 And he measured the width of the [1]gateway, ten cubits, and the length of the gate, thirteen cubits.

12 And *there was* a [1]barrier *wall* one cubit *wide* in front of the guardrooms on each side; and the guardrooms *were* six cubits *square* on each side.

13 And he measured the gate from the roof of the one guardroom to the roof of the other, a width of twenty-five cubits from *one* door to *the* door opposite.

14 And he made the side pillars sixty cubits *high;* the gate *extended* round about to the side pillar of the [a]courtyard.

15 And *from* the front of the entrance gate to the front of the inner porch of the gate *was* fifty cubits.

21 [a]Ex. 9:16; Is. 37:20; Ezek. 36:23; 38:16, 23
22 [a]Jer. 24:7
23 [a]Jer. 22:8, 9; 44:22; Ezek. 36:18, 19 [b]Is. 1:15; 59:2; Ezek. 39:29
24 [a]2 Kin. 17:7; Jer. 2:17, 19; 4:18; Ezek. 36:19
25 [a]Is. 27:12, 13; Jer. 33:7; Ezek. 34:13 [b]Jer. 31:1; Ezek. 36:10; 37:21, 22; Hos. 1:11 [c]Ex. 20:5; Nah. 1:2
26 [1]Another reading is, *bear* [a]Ezek. 16:63; 20:43; 36:31 [b]1 Kin. 4:25; Ezek. 34:25-28 [c]Is. 17:2; Mic. 4:4
27 [1]Lit., *in* [a]Ezek. 36:24; 37:21 [b]Ezek. 36:23; 38:16, 23
29 [a]Is. 32:15; Ezek. 36:27; 37:14; Joel 2:28
1 [a]Ezek. 32:1, 17; 33:21 [b]2 Kin. 25:1-7; Jer. 39:1-9; 52:4-11; Ezek. 33:21 [c]Ezek. 1:3; 3:14, 22; 37:1
2 [a]Ezek. 1:1; 8:3; Dan. 7:1, 7 [b]Is. 2:2, 3; Ezek. 17:23; 20:40; 37:22; Mic. 4:1; Rev. 21:10 [c]1 Chr. 28:12, 19 [d]Ps. 48:2; Is. 14:13
3 [1]Lit., *reed,* and so throughout the chap. [a]Ezek. 1:7; Dan. 10:5, 6; Rev. 1:15 [b]Ezek. 47:3; Zech. 2:1, 2 [c]Rev. 11:1; 21:15
4 [a]Ezek. 2:1, 3, 6, 8; 44:5 [b]Ezek. 2:7, 8; 43:10; 44:5 [c]Is. 21:10; Jer. 26:2; Acts 20:27
5 [1]Lit., *house* [2]I.e., 20.4 inches [3]Lit., *building* [a]Ezek. 42:20
6 [1]Or, *in depth* [a]Ezek. 8:16; 11:1; 40:20; 43:1
7 [1]Lit., *from the house,* also vs. 8, 9 [a]Ezek. 40:10-16, 21, 29, 33, 36
11 [1]Lit., *entrance of the gate*
12 [1]Lit., *border*
14 [a]Ex. 27:9; 1 Chr. 28:6; Ps. 100:4; Is. 62:9; Ezek. 8:7; 42:1

16 And *there were* [a]shuttered windows *looking* toward the guardrooms, and toward their side pillars within the gate all around, and likewise for the porches. And *there were* windows all around inside; and on *each* side pillar *were* [b]palm tree ornaments.
17 Then he brought me into the [a]outer court, and behold, *there were* [b]chambers and a pavement, made for the court all around; thirty chambers faced the pavement.
18 And the pavement (*that is,* the lower [a]pavement) *was* by the side of the gates, corresponding to the length of the gates.
19 Then he measured the width from the front of the lower gate to the front of the exterior of the inner court, a [a]hundred cubits on the east and on the north.
20 And *as for* the [a]gate of the outer court which faced the north, he measured its length and its width.
21 And it had three [a]guardrooms on each side; and its [b]side pillars and its porches had the same measurement as the first gate. Its length *was* [c]fifty cubits, and the width [d]twenty-five cubits.
22 And its [a]windows, and its porches, and its palm tree ornaments *had* the same measurements as the [b]gate which faced toward the east; and it was reached by seven [c]steps, and its porch *was* in front of them.
23 And the inner court had a gate opposite the gate on the north as well as *the gate* on the east; and he measured a [a]hundred cubits from gate to gate.
24 Then he led me toward the [a]south, and behold, there was a gate toward the south; and he measured its [b]side pillars and its porches according to [1]those same measurements.
25 And the gate and its porches had [a]windows all around like those other windows; the length *was* [b]fifty cubits and the width twenty-five cubits.
26 And *there were* seven [a]steps going up to it, and its porches *were* in front of them; and it had [b]palm tree ornaments on its side pillars, one on each side.
27 And the inner court had a gate toward the [a]south; and he measured from gate to gate toward the south, a [b]hundred cubits.
28 Then he brought me to the inner court by the south gate; and he measured the south gate [a]according to those same measurements.
29 Its [a]guardrooms also, its side pillars, and its [b]porches *were* according to those same measurements. And [1]the gate and its porches had [b]windows all around; it *was* [c]fifty cubits long and twenty-five cubits wide.
30 And *there were* [a]porches all around, twenty-five cubits long and five cubits wide.
31 And its porches *were* toward the outer court; and [a]palm tree ornaments *were* on its side pillars, and its stairway had eight [b]steps.
32 And he brought me into the [a]inner court toward the east. And he measured the gate [b]according to those same measurements.
33 Its [a]guardrooms also, its side pillars, and its porches *were* according to those same measurements. And the gate and its porches had [b]windows all around; it *was* [c]fifty cubits long and twenty-five cubits wide.
34 And its [a]porches *were* toward the outer court; and [a]palm tree ornaments *were* on its side pillars, on each side, and its stairway had eight [b]steps.
35 Then he brought me to the [a]north gate; and he measured *it* according to those same measurements,
36 *with* its [a]guardrooms, its side pillars, and its [b]porches. And the gate had [b]windows all around; the length *was* [c]fifty cubits and the width twenty-five cubits.
37 And its side pillars *were* toward the outer court; and [a]palm tree ornaments *were* on its side pillars on each side, and its stairway had eight [b]steps.
38 And a [a]chamber with its doorway was by the side pillars at the gates; there they [b]rinse the burnt offering.
39 And in the porch of the gate *were* two [a]tables on each side, on which to slaughter the [b]burnt offering, the sin offering, and the guilt offering.
40 And on the outer [1]side, [2]as one went up to the [3]gateway toward the north, were two tables; and on the other [1]side of the porch of the gate *were* two tables.
41 Four [a]tables *were* on each side [1]next to the gate; *or,* eight tables on which they slaughter *sacrifices.*
42 And for the burnt offering *there were* [a]four tables of [b]hewn stone, a cubit and a half long, a cubit and a half wide, and one cubit high, on which they lay the instruments with

16 [a]1 Kin. 6:4; Ezek. 41:16, 26 [b]1 Kin. 6:29, 32, 35; 2 Chr. 3:5; Ezek. 40:22, 26, 31, 34, 37; 41:18-20, 25
17 [a]Ezek. 10:5; 42:1; 46:21; Rev. 11:2 [b]2 Kin. 23:11; 1 Chr. 9:26; 23:28; 2 Chr. 31:11; Ezek. 40:38
18 [a]Ezek. 40:23, 27; 46:1, 2
19 [a]Ezek. 40:23
20 [a]Ezek. 40:6
21 [a]Ezek. 40:7 [b]Ezek. 40:16, 30 [c]Ezek. 40:15 [d]Ezek. 40:13
22 [a]Ezek. 40:16 [b]Ezek. 40:6 [c]Ezek. 40:6, 26, 31, 34, 37, 49
23 [a]Ezek. 40:19, 27
24 [1]Lit., *these measurements,* and so throughout the chap. [a]Ezek. 40:6, 20, 35; 46:9 [b]Ezek. 40:21
25 [a]Ezek. 40:16, 22, 29 [b]Ezek. 40:21
26 [a]Ezek. 40:6, 22 [b]Ezek. 40:16
27 [a]Ezek. 40:23, 32 [b]Ezek. 40:19
28 [a]Ezek. 40:32
29 [1]Lit., *it* [a]Ezek. 40:7, 10, 21 [b]Ezek. 40:16, 22, 25 [c]Ezek. 40:21
30 [a]Ezek. 40:16
31 [a]Ezek. 40:16 [b]Ezek. 40:22, 26
32 [a]Ezek. 40:28-31, 35 [b]Ezek. 40:28
33 [a]Ezek. 40:29 [b]Ezek. 40:16 [c]Ezek. 40:21
34 [a]Ezek. 40:16 [b]Ezek. 40:22, 37
35 [a]Ezek. 40:27, 32; 44:4; 47:2
36 [a]Ezek. 40:7, 29 [b]Ezek. 40:16 [c]Ezek. 40:21
37 [a]Ezek. 40:16 [b]Ezek. 40:35
38 [a]1 Chr. 28:12; Neh. 13:5, 9; Jer. 35:4; 36:10; Ezek. 40:17; 41:10; 42:13 [b]2 Chr. 4:6
39 [a]Ezek. 40:42 [b]Ezek. 46:2; Lev. 1:3-17
40 [1]Lit., *shoulder* [2]Lit., *to the one going up* [3]Lit., *entrance of the gate*
41 [1]Lit., *by the shoulder of* [a]Ezek. 40:39, 40
42 [a]Ezek. 40:39 [b]Ex. 20:25

which they slaughter the [c]burnt offering and the sacrifice.

43 And the double hooks, one handbreadth in length, were installed in the house all around; and on the tables *was* the flesh of the offering.

44 And from the outside to the [a]inner gate were [1b]chambers for the [c]singers in the inner court, *one of* which was at the side of the north gate, with [2]its front toward the south, and one at the side of the [3]east gate facing toward the north.

45 And he said to me, "This is the [a]chamber which faces toward the south, *intended* for the priests who [b]keep charge of the temple;

46 but the [a]chamber which faces toward the north is for the priests who [b]keep charge of the altar. These are the [c]sons of Zadok, who from the sons of Levi [d]come near to the LORD to minister to Him."

47 And he measured the court, a *perfect* square, a [a]hundred cubits long and a hundred cubits wide; and the altar was in front of the [1]temple.

48 Then he brought me to the [a]porch of the [1]temple and measured *each* side pillar of the porch, five cubits on each side; and the width of the gate was three cubits on each side.

49 The length of the porch was twenty cubits, and the width eleven cubits; and at the [a]stairway by which it was ascended *were* [b]columns belonging to the side pillars, one on each side.

Chapter 41

The Inner Temple

THEN he [a]brought me to the [1b]nave and measured the [c]side pillars; six cubits wide on each side *was* the width of the [2]side pillar.

2 And the width of the entrance *was* ten cubits, and the sides of the entrance were five cubits on each side. And he measured the length of the nave, [a]forty cubits, and the width, [a]twenty cubits.

3 Then he went [1a]inside and measured each [b]side pillar of the doorway, two cubits, and the doorway, six cubits *high;* and the width of the doorway, seven cubits.

4 And he measured its length, twenty cubits, and the width, [a]twenty cubits, before the [b]nave; and he said to me, "This is the [c]most holy *place.*"

5 Then he measured the wall of the [1]temple, six cubits; and the width of the [a]side chambers, four cubits, all around about the house on every side.

6 And the side chambers were in three stories, one above another, and thirty in each story; and the side chambers [a]extended to the wall which *stood* on their inward side all around, that they might be fastened, and not be fastened into the wall of the temple *itself.*

7 And the side chambers surrounding the temple were wider at each successive story. Because the structure [a]surrounding the temple went upward by stages on all sides of the temple, therefore the width of the temple increased as it went higher; and thus one went up from the lowest *story* to the highest by way of the second *story.*

8 I saw also that the house had a raised platform all around; the foundations of the side chambers were a full rod of [a]six long cubits *in height.*

9 The thickness of the outer wall of the side chambers was five cubits. But the [a]free space between the side chambers belonging to the temple

10 and the [1]*outer* [a]chambers *was* twenty cubits in width all around the temple on every side.

11 And the doorways of the side chambers toward the [a]free space *consisted of* one doorway toward the north and another doorway toward the south; and the width of the [a]free space was five cubits all around.

12 And the [a]building that *was* in front of the [b]separate area at the side toward the west *was* seventy cubits wide; and the wall of the building was five cubits thick all around, and its length *was* ninety cubits.

13 Then he measured the temple, a [a]hundred cubits long; the [b]separate area with the [c]building and its walls *were* also a [a]hundred cubits long.

14 Also the width of the front of the temple and *that of* the separate areas along the east *side totaled* a hundred cubits.

15 And he measured the length of the [a]building along the front of the [b]separate area behind it, with a [c]gallery on each side, a hundred cubits; *he* also *measured* the inner nave and the porches of the court.

16 The [a]thresholds, the [b]latticed windows, and the [c]galleries round about their [d]three stories, opposite the threshold, were [e]paneled with

---

42 [c]Ezek. 40:39
44 [1]Gk. reads: *in two chambers* [2]Lit., *their* [3]Gk. reads: *south* [a]Ezek. 40:23, 27 [b]Ezek. 40:17, 38 [c]1 Chr. 6:31, 32; 16:41-43; 25:1-7
45 [a]Ezek. 40:17, 38 [b]1 Chr. 9:23; Ps. 134:1
46 [a]Ezek. 40:17, 38 [b]Lev. 6:12, 13; Ezek. 44:15 [c]1 Kin. 2:35; Ezek. 43:19; 44:15; 48:11 [d]Lev. 10:3; Num. 16:5, 40; Ezek. 42:13
47 [1]Lit., *house* [a]Ezek. 40:19, 23
48 [1]Lit., *house* [a]1 Kin. 6:3; 2 Chr. 3:4
49 [a]Ezek. 40:31, 34, 37 [b]1 Kin. 7:15-21; 2 Chr. 3:17; Jer. 52:17-23; Rev. 3:12
1 [1]I.e., the main inner hall [2]Heb., *tent* [a]Ezek. 40:2, 3, 17 [b]Ezek. 41:21, 23; 42:8 [c]Ezek. 40:9; 41:3
2 [a]1 Kin. 6:2, 17; 2 Chr. 3:3
3 [1]I.e., of the inner sanctuary [a]Ezek. 40:16 [b]Ezek. 41:1
4 [a]1 Kin. 6:20 [b]1 Kin. 6:5 [c]Ex. 26:33, 34; 1 Kin. 6:16; 7:50; 8:6; 2 Chr. 5:7; Heb. 9:3-8
5 [1]Lit., *house,* and so throughout the chap. [a]1 Kin. 6:5; Ezek. 41:6-11
6 [a]1 Kin. 6:6, 10
7 [a]1 Kin. 6:8
8 [a]Ezek. 40:5
9 [a]Ezek. 41:11
10 [1]Cf. 42:1 [a]Ezek. 40:17
11 [a]Ezek. 41:9
12 [a]Ezek. 41:13, 15; 42:1 [b]Ezek. 41:13-15; 42:1, 10, 13
13 [a]Ezek. 40:47 [b]Ezek. 41:13-15; 42:1, 10, 13 [c]Ezek. 41:13, 15
15 [a]Ezek. 41:13, 15; 42:1 [b]Ezek. 41:13-15; 42:1, 10, 13 [c]Ezek. 41:16; 42:3, 5
16 [a]Is. 6:4; Ezek. 10:18; 40:6; 41:25 [b]1 Kin. 6:4; Ezek. 40:16, 25; 41:26 [c]Ezek. 41:15 [d]Ezek. 42:3 [e]1 Kin. 6:15

wood all around, and *from* the ground to the windows (but the windows were covered),
17 over the entrance, and to the inner house, and on the outside, and on all the wall all around inside and outside, by measurement.
18 And it was carved with [a]cherubim and [b]palm trees; and a palm tree was between cherub and cherub, and every cherub had two faces,
19 a [a]man's face toward the palm tree on one side, and a young [a]lion's face toward the palm tree on the other side; they were carved on all the house all around.
20 From the ground to above the entrance [a]cherubim and [a]palm trees were carved, as well as *on* the wall of the nave.
21 The [a]doorposts of the [b]nave were square; as for the front of the sanctuary, the appearance of one doorpost was like that of the other.
22 The [a]altar *was* of wood, three cubits high, and its length two cubits; its corners, its [1]base, and its [2]sides *were* of wood. And he said to me, "This is the [b]table that is before the LORD."
23 And the [a]nave and the [b]sanctuary each had a double [c]door.
24 And each of the doors had two leaves, two [1a]swinging leaves; two *leaves* for one door and two leaves for the other.
25 Also there were [1]carved on them, on the doors of the nave, [a]cherubim and [a]palm trees like those [1]carved on the walls; and *there was* a [2b]threshold of wood on the front of the porch outside.
26 And *there were* [1a]latticed windows and [b]palm trees on one side and on the other, on the sides of the [c]porch; thus *were* the [d]side chambers of the house and the [2]thresholds.

CHAPTER 42

Chambers of the Temple

THEN he [a]brought me out into the [b]outer court, the way [c]toward the north; and he brought me to the [d]chamber which *was* opposite the [e]separate area and opposite the [f]building toward the north.
2 Along the length, *which was* a [a]hundred cubits, *was* the north door; the width *was* fifty cubits.
3 Opposite the [a]twenty *cubits* which belonged to the inner court, and opposite the [b]pavement which belonged to the outer court, *was* [1c]gallery corresponding to [1]gallery in three stories.
4 And before the [a]chambers *was* an inner walk ten cubits wide, a way of one *hundred* cubits; and their openings *were* on the north.
5 Now the upper chambers *were* [1]smaller because the [2a]galleries took more *space* away from them than from the lower and middle ones in the building.
6 For they *were* in [a]three stories and had no pillars like the pillars of the courts; therefore *the upper chambers* were [1]set back from the ground upward, more than the lower and middle ones.
7 As for the outer [a]wall by the side of the chambers, toward the outer court facing the chambers, its length *was* fifty cubits.
8 For the length of the chambers which *were* in the outer court *was* fifty cubits; and behold, the length of those facing the temple *was* a [a]hundred cubits.
9 And below these chambers *was* the [a]entrance on the east side, as one enters them from the outer court.
10 In the [1]thickness of the [a]wall of the court toward the east, facing the [b]separate area and facing the building, *there were* [c]chambers.
11 And the [a]way in front of them *was* like the appearance of the chambers which *were* on the north, according to their length so was their width; and all their exits *were* both according to their arrangements and openings.
12 And corresponding to the openings of the chambers which were toward the south was an opening at the head of the way, the way in front of the [a]wall toward the east, as one enters them.
13 Then he said to me, "The north chambers *and* the south chambers, which are opposite the [a]separate area, they are the [b]holy chambers where the priests who are [c]near to the LORD shall eat the [d]most holy things. There they shall lay the most holy things, the grain offering, the sin offering, and the guilt offering; for the place is holy.
14 "When the priests enter, then they shall not go out into the outer court from the sanctuary [1]without [a]laying there their [b]garments in which they minister, for they are holy. They shall put on other garments; then they shall approach that which is for the people."

---

18 [a]1 Kin. 6:29, 32, 35; 7:36; Ezek. 41:20, 25 [b]2 Chr. 3:5; Ezek. 40:16
19 [a]Ezek. 1:10; 10:14
20 [a]Ezek. 41:18
21 [a]1 Kin. 6:33; Ezek. 40:9, 14, 16; 41:1 [b]Ezek. 41:1
22 [1]Lit., *length* [2]Lit., *walls* [a]Ex. 30:1-3; 1 Kin. 6:20; Rev. 8:3 [b]Ex. 25:23, 30; Lev. 24:6; Ezek. 23:41; 44:16; Mal. 1:7, 12
23 [a]Ezek. 41:1 [b]Ezek. 41:4 [c]1 Kin. 6:31-35
24 [1]Or, *turning* [a]1 Kin. 6:34
25 [1]Lit., *made* [2]Or, *canopy of wood over* [a]Ezek. 41:18 [b]Ezek. 41:16
26 [1]Or, *framed* [2]Or, *canopies* [a]Ezek. 41:16 [b]Ezek. 40:16 [c]Ezek. 40:9, 48 [d]Ezek. 41:5
1 [a]Ezek. 40:17, 28, 48; 41:1 [b]Ezek. 40:17, 20 [c]Ezek. 40:20 [d]Ezek. 40:17; 42:4 [e]Ezek. 41:12; 42:10, 13 [f]Ezek. 41:12
2 [a]Ezek. 41:13
3 [1]Or, *passageway* [a]Ezek. 41:10 [b]Ezek. 40:17 [c]Ezek. 41:15, 16; 42:5
4 [a]Ezek. 46:19
5 [1]Lit., *shorter* [2]Or, *passageways* [a]Ezek. 42:3
6 [1]Or, *reduced* [a]Ezek. 41:6
7 [a]Ezek. 42:10, 12
8 [a]Ezek. 41:13, 14
9 [a]Ezek. 44:5; 46:19
10 [1]Lit., *width* [a]Ezek. 42:7 [b]Ezek. 42:1, 13 [c]Ezek. 40:17
11 [a]Ezek. 42:4
12 [a]Ezek. 42:7
13 [a]Ezek. 42:1, 10 [b]Ex. 29:31; Lev. 7:6; 10:13, 14, 17 [c]Lev. 10:3; Deut. 21:5; Ezek. 40:46 [d]Lev. 6:25, 29; 14:13; Num. 18:9, 10
14 [1]Lit., *but there they shall lay* [a]Ezek. 44:19 [b]Ex. 29:4-9; Lev. 8:7, 13; Is. 61:10; Zech. 3:4, 5

15 Now when he had finished measuring the inner house, he brought
me out by the way of the [a]gate
which faced toward the east, and
measured it all around.
16 He measured on the east side
with the measuring reed five hundred reeds, by the measuring [a]reed.
17 He measured on the north side
five hundred reeds by the measuring
reed.
18 On the south side he measured
five hundred reeds with the measuring reed.
19 He turned to the west side, *and*
measured five hundred reeds with
the measuring reed.
20 He measured it on the four
sides; it had a [a]wall all around, the
[b]length five hundred and the [b]width
five hundred, to [c]divide between the
holy and the profane.

Chapter 43

Vision of the Glory of God Filling the Temple

THEN he led me to the [a]gate, the
gate facing toward the east;
2 and behold, the [a]glory of the
God of Israel was coming from the
way of the [b]east. And His [c]voice was
like the sound of many waters; and
the earth [d]shone with His glory.
3 And *it was* like the appearance
of the vision which I saw, like the
[a]vision which I saw when [1]He came
to [b]destroy the city. And the visions
were like the vision which I saw by
the [c]river Chebar; and I [d]fell on my
face.
4 And the glory of the LORD came
into the house by the way of the gate
facing toward the [a]east.
5 And the [a]Spirit lifted me up and
brought me into the inner court; and
behold, the [b]glory of the LORD filled
the house.
6 Then I heard one speaking to
me from the house, while a [a]man
was standing beside me.
7 And He said to me, "Son of
man, *this is* the place of My [a]throne
and the place of the soles of My feet,
where I will [b]dwell among the sons
of Israel forever. And the house of
Israel will not again defile My holy
name, neither they nor their kings,
by their harlotry and by the [c]corpses
of their kings when they [d]die,
8 by setting their threshold by
My threshold, and their door post
beside My door post, with *only* the
wall between Me and them. And
they have [a]defiled My holy name by
their abominations which they have
committed. So I have consumed
them in My anger.
9 "Now let them [a]put away their
harlotry and the corpses of their
kings far from Me; and I will [b]dwell
among them forever.
10 "As for you, son of man, [a]de-
scribe the temple to the house of Israel, that they may be [b]ashamed of
their iniquities; and let them measure the plan.
11 "And if they are ashamed of all
that they have done, make known to
them the [1]design of the house, its
structure, its [a]exits, its entrances,
all its [2]designs, all its [3]statutes, and
all its laws. And write *it* [b]in their
sight, so that they may observe its
whole [1]design and all its statutes,
and [c]do them.
12 "This is the law of the house: its
entire area on the top of the [a]moun-
tain all around *shall be* most holy.
Behold, this is the law of the house.

The Altar of Sacrifice

13 "And these are the measurements of the [a]altar by cubits (the
[b]cubit being a cubit and a handbreadth): the base *shall be* a cubit,
and the width a cubit, and its border
on its edge round about one span;
and this *shall be* the *height of the*
base of the altar.
14 "And from the base on the
ground to the lower [a]ledge *shall be*
two cubits, and the width one cubit;
and from the smaller ledge to the
larger ledge *shall be* four cubits, and
the width [1]one cubit.
15 "And the [1]altar hearth *shall be*
four cubits; and from the [1]altar
hearth shall extend upwards four
[a]horns.
16 "Now the [1]altar hearth *shall be*
twelve *cubits* long by twelve wide,
[a]square in its four sides.
17 "And the ledge *shall be* fourteen
cubits long by fourteen wide in its
four sides, the border around it *shall*
be half a cubit, and its base *shall be*
a cubit round about; and its [a]steps
shall [1b]face the east."

The Offerings

18 And He said to me, "[a]Son of
man, thus says the Lord [1]GOD,
'These are the statutes for the altar
on the day it is built, to offer [b]burnt
offerings on it and to [c]sprinkle blood
on it.
19 'And you shall give to the Levitical priests who are from the offspring of [a]Zadok, who draw [b]near to
Me to minister to Me,' declares the

15 [a]Ezek. 40:6
16 [a]Ezek. 40:3
20 [a]Is. 60:18; Ezek. 40:5; Zech. 2:5 [b]Ezek. 45:2; Rev. 21:16 [c]Ezek. 22:26; 44:23; 48:15
1 [a]Ezek. 10:19; 40:6; 42:15; 43:4; 44:1; 46:1
2 [a]Is. 6:3; Ezek. 1:28; 3:23; 10:18, 19 [b]Ezek. 11:23 [c]Ezek. 1:24; Rev. 1:15; 14:2 [d]Ezek. 1:28; 10:4; Rev. 18:1
3 [1]M.T., *I* [a]Ezek. 1:4-28 [b]Jer. 1:10; Ezek. 9:1, 5; 32:18 [c]Ezek. 1:3; 10:20 [d]Ezek. 1:28; 3:23
4 [a]Ezek. 10:19; 11:23; 43:2
5 [a]Ezek. 3:14; 8:3; 11:1, 24; 2 Cor. 12:2-4 [b]Ezek. 10:4
6 [a]Ezek. 1:26
7 [a]Ps. 47:8; Ezek. 1:26 [b]Ezek. 37:26, 28 [c]Ezek. 6:5, 13 [d]Ezek. 20:29, 30
8 [a]Ezek. 8:3, 16
9 [a]Ezek. 18:30, 31 [b]Ezek. 37:26-28; 43:7
10 [a]Ezek. 40:4 [b]Ezek. 16:61, 63; 43:11
11 [1]Or, *form* [2]Or, *forms* [3]M.T. adds, *and all its designs* after *statutes* [a]Ezek. 44:5 [b]Ezek. 12:3 [c]Ezek. 11:20; 36:27
12 [a]Ezek. 40:2; 42:20
13 [a]Ex. 27:1-8; 2 Chr. 4:1 [b]Ezek. 40:5; 41:8
14 [1]Lit., *the* [a]Ezek. 43:17, 20; 45:19
15 [1]Or, *ariel* shall [a]Ex. 27:2; Lev. 9:9; 1 Kin. 1:50; Ps. 118:27
16 [1]Or, *ariel* shall [a]Ex. 27:1
17 [1]Or, *be on the east side* [a]Ex. 20:26 [b]Ezek. 40:6
18 [1]YHWH, usually rendered LORD, and so throughout the chap. [a]Ezek. 2:1 [b]Ex. 40:29 [c]Lev. 1:5, 11; Heb. 9:21, 22
19 [a]1 Kin. 2:35; Ezek. 40:46; 44:15 [b]Num. 16:5, 40

Lord GOD, 'a [c]young bull for a [d]sin offering.

20 'And you shall take some of its blood, and put it on its four [a]horns, and on the four corners of the [b]ledge, and on the border round about; thus you shall [c]cleanse it and make atonement for it.

21 'You shall also take the bull for the sin offering; and it *shall be* [a]burned in the appointed place of the house, outside the sanctuary.

22 'And on the second day you shall offer a [a]male goat without blemish for a sin offering; and they shall [b]cleanse the altar, as they cleansed *it* with the bull.

23 'When you have finished cleansing *it,* you shall present a young [a]bull without blemish and a [b]ram without blemish from the flock.

24 'And you shall present them before the LORD, and the priests shall throw [a]salt on them, and they shall offer them up as a burnt offering to the LORD.

25 '[a]For seven days you shall prepare daily a goat for a sin offering; also a young bull and a ram from the flock, without blemish, shall be prepared.

26 'For seven days they shall make atonement for the altar and purify it; so shall they consecrate it.

27 'And when they have completed the days, it shall be that on the [a]eighth day and onward, the priests shall offer your burnt offerings on the altar, and your [b]peace offerings; and I will [c]accept you,' declares the Lord GOD."

CHAPTER 44

Gate for the Prince

THEN He brought me back by the way of the [a]outer gate of the sanctuary, which faces the east; and it was shut.

2 And the LORD said to me, "This gate shall be shut; it shall not be opened, and no one shall enter by it, for the [a]LORD God of Israel has entered by it; therefore it shall be shut.

3 "As for the [a]prince, he shall sit in it as prince to [b]eat bread before the LORD; he shall [c]enter by way of the [d]porch of the gate, and shall go out [1]by the same way."

4 Then He brought me by way of the [a]north gate to the front of the house; and I looked, and behold, the [b]glory of the LORD filled the house of the LORD, and I [c]fell on my face.

5 And the LORD said to me, "[a]Son of man, [a]mark well, see with your eyes, and hear with your ears all that I say to you concerning all the [b]statutes of the house of the LORD and concerning all its laws; and mark well the entrance of the house, with all exits of the sanctuary.

6 "And you shall say to the [a]rebellious ones, to the house of Israel, 'Thus says the Lord [1]GOD, "[b]Enough of all your abominations, O house of Israel,

7 when you brought in [a]foreigners, uncircumcised in [b]heart and uncircumcised in flesh, to be in My sanctuary to profane it, *even* My house, when you [c]offered My food, the fat and the blood; for they made My covenant [d]void—*this* in addition to all your abominations.

8 "And you have not [a]kept charge of My holy things yourselves, but you have set *foreigners* to keep charge of My sanctuary."

9 'Thus says the Lord GOD, "[a]No foreigner, uncircumcised in heart and uncircumcised in flesh, of all the foreigners who are among the sons of Israel, shall enter My sanctuary.

10 "But the Levites who [a]went far from Me, when Israel went astray, who went astray from Me after their idols, shall [b]bear the punishment for their iniquity.

11 "Yet they shall be [a]ministers in My sanctuary, having oversight at the [b]gates of the house and [c]ministering in the house; they shall [d]slaughter the burnt offering and the sacrifice for the people, and they shall [e]stand before them to minister to them.

12 "Because they ministered to them [a]before their idols and became a stumbling block of iniquity to the house of Israel, therefore I have sworn against them," declares the Lord GOD, "that they shall bear the punishment for their iniquity.

13 "And they shall [a]not come near to Me to serve as a priest to Me, nor come near to any of My holy things, to the things that are most holy; but they shall [b]bear their shame and their abominations which they have committed.

14 "Yet I will appoint them to [a]keep charge of the house, of all its service, and of all that shall be done in it.

Ordinances for the Levites

15 "But the Levitical [a]priests, the sons of Zadok, who [b]kept charge of My sanctuary when the sons of Israel [c]went astray from Me, shall come near to Me to minister to Me;

19 [c]Lev. 4:3; Ezek. 43:23; 45:18, 19 [d]Heb. 7:27
20 [a]Lev. 8:15; 9:9; Ezek. 43:15 [b]Ezek. 43:14, 16, 17 [c]Lev. 16:19; Ezek. 43:22, 26
21 [a]Ex. 29:14; Lev. 4:12; Heb. 13:11
22 [a]Ezek. 43:25 [b]Ezek. 43:20, 26
23 [a]Ex. 29:1, 10; Ezek. 45:18 [b]Ex. 29:1
24 [a]Lev. 2:13; Num. 18:19; Mark 9:49, 50; Col. 4:6
25 [a]Ex. 29:35-37; Lev. 8:33, 35
27 [a]Lev. 9:1 [b]Lev. 3:1; 17:5 [c]Ezek. 20:40
1 [a]Ezek. 40:6, 17; 42:14
2 [a]Ezek. 43:2-4
3 [1]Lit., *by his way* [a]Ezek. 34:24; 37:25 [b]Gen. 31:54; Ex. 24:9-11 [c]Ezek. 46:2, 8-10 [d]Ezek. 40:9
4 [a]Ezek. 40:20, 40 [b]Is. 6:3, 4; Ezek. 1:28; 3:23; 43:4, 5; Hag. 2:7 [c]Ezek. 1:28; 43:3
5 [a]Deut. 32:46; Ezek. 40:4 [b]Deut. 12:32; Ezek. 43:10, 11
6 [1]YHWH, usually rendered LORD, and so throughout the chap. [a]Ezek. 2:5-7; 3:9 [b]Ezek. 45:9; 1 Pet. 4:3
7 [a]Ex. 12:43-49 [b]Lev. 26:41; Deut. 10:16; Jer. 4:4; 9:26 [c]Lev. 22:25 [d]Gen. 17:14
8 [a]Num. 18:7
9 [a]Ezek. 44:7; Joel 3:17; Zech. 14:21
10 [a]2 Kin. 23:8, 9; Ezek. 22:26; 44:12 [b]Num. 18:23
11 [a]Num. 3:5-37; 4:1-33; 18:2-6 [b]1 Chr. 26:1-19 [c]Ezek. 40:45; 44:14 [d]2 Chr. 29:34; 30:17 [e]Num. 16:9
12 [a]2 Kin. 16:10-16; Hos. 4:6; 5:1
13 [a]Num. 18:3 [b]Ezek. 16:61, 63
14 [a]Num. 18:4; 1 Chr. 23:28-32; Ezek. 44:11
15 [a]Jer. 33:18-22 [b]Num. 18:7; Ezek. 40:45 [c]Ezek. 44:10; 48:11

and they shall [d]stand before Me to offer Me the [e]fat and the blood," declares the Lord GOD.

16"They shall [a]enter My sanctuary; they shall come near to My [b]table to minister to Me and keep My charge.

17"And it shall be that when they enter at the gates of the inner court, they shall be clothed with [a]linen garments; and wool shall not be on them while they are ministering in the gates of the inner court and in the house.

18"Linen [a]turbans shall be on their heads, and linen [b]undergarments shall be on their loins; they shall not gird themselves with *anything which makes them* sweat.

19"And when they go out into the outer court, into the outer court to the people, they shall [a]put off their garments in which they have been ministering and lay them in the holy chambers; then they shall put on other garments that they may not transmit [b]holiness to the people with their garments.

20"Also they shall not [a]shave their heads, yet they shall not [b]let their locks grow long; they shall only trim *the hair of* their heads.

21"Nor shall any of the priests drink wine when they enter the inner court.

22"And they shall not marry a widow or a divorced woman but shall take virgins from the offspring of the house of Israel, or a widow who is the widow of a priest.

23"Moreover, they shall teach My people *the* [a]*difference* between the holy and the profane, and cause them to discern between the unclean and the clean.

24"And in a dispute [a]they shall take their stand to judge; they shall judge it according to My ordinances. They shall also keep My laws and My statutes in all My [b]appointed feasts, and sanctify My sabbaths.

25"And they shall not go to a dead person to defile *themselves;* however, for father, for mother, for son, for daughter, for brother, or for a sister who has not had a husband, they may defile themselves.

26"And after he is [a]cleansed, seven days shall elapse for him.

27"And on the day that he goes into the sanctuary, into the inner court to minister in the sanctuary, he shall offer his [a]sin offering," declares the Lord GOD.

28"And it shall be with regard to an inheritance for them, *that* [a]I am their inheritance; and you shall give them no possession in Israel—I am their possession.

29"They shall [a]eat the grain offering, the sin offering, and the guilt offering; and every [1b]devoted thing in Israel shall be theirs.

30"And the first of all the [a]first fruits of every kind and every [1]contribution of every kind, from all your [1]contributions, shall be for the priests; you shall also give to the priest the [b]first of your [2]dough to cause a [c]blessing to rest on your house.

31"The priests shall not eat any bird or beast that [1]has [a]died a natural death or has been torn to pieces.

CHAPTER 45

The LORD's Portion of the Land

"AND when you shall [a]divide by lot the land for inheritance, you shall offer [1]an [b]allotment to the LORD, a [c]holy portion of the land; the length shall be the length of 25,000 [d]*cubits,* and the width shall be [2]10,000. It shall be holy within all its boundary round about.

2"Out of this there shall be for the holy place a square round about five hundred by five hundred *cubits,* and fifty cubits for its [1]open space round about.

3"And from this [1]area you shall measure a length of 25,000 *cubits,* and a width of 10,000 *cubits;* and in it shall be the sanctuary, the most holy place.

4"It shall be the holy portion of the land; it shall be for the [a]priests, the ministers of the sanctuary, who [b]come near to minister to the LORD, and it shall be a place for their houses and a holy place for the sanctuary.

5"And *an area* 25,000 *cubits* in length and 10,000 in width shall be for the Levites, the ministers of the house, *and* for their possession [1]cities to dwell in.

6"And you shall give the [a]city possession of *an area* 5,000 *cubits* wide and 25,000 *cubits* long, alongside the [1]allotment of the holy portion; it shall be for the whole house of Israel.

Portion for the Prince

7"And the [a]prince shall have *land* on either side of the holy [1]allotment and the [2]property of the city, adjacent to the holy [1]allotment and the [2]property of the city, on the west side toward the west and on the east

15 [d]Zech. 3:1, 7 [e]Lev. 3:16, 17; Ezek. 44:7
16 [a]Num. 18:5, 7, 8 [b]Ezek. 41:22; Mal. 1:7, 12
17 [a]Ex. 28:42, 43; 39:27-29; Rev. 19:8
18 [a]Ex. 28:40; Is. 3:20; Ezek. 24:17, 23 [b]Ex. 28:42
19 [a]Lev. 6:10; 16:4, 23, 24; Ezek. 42:14 [b]Lev. 6:27; Ezek. 46:20
20 [a]Lev. 21:5 [b]Num. 6:5
23 [a]Lev. 10:10, 11; Ezek. 22:26; Hos. 4:6; Mic. 3:9-11; Zeph. 3:4; Hag. 2:11-13; Mal. 2:6-8
24 [a]Deut. 17:8, 9; 19:17; 21:5; 1 Chr. 23:4; 2 Chr. 19:8-10 [b]Lev. 23:2, 4, 44
26 [a]Num. 19:13-19
27 [a]Lev. 5:3, 6; Num. 6:9-11
28 [a]Num. 18:20; Deut. 10:9; 18:1, 2; Josh. 13:33
29 [1]Or, *dedicated;* cf. Num. 18:14 [a]Num. 18:9, 14; Josh. 13:14 [b]Lev. 27:21, 28
30 [1]Or, *heave offering* [2]Or, *coarse meal* [a]Num. 18:12; 2 Chr. 31:4-6, 10; Neh. 10:35-37 [b]Num. 15:20, 21 [c]Mal. 3:10
31 [1]Lit., *a corpse* [a]Lev. 22:8; Deut. 14:21; Ezek. 4:14
1 [1]Or, a *contribution* [2]Or, with Gk., *20,000* [a]Num. 34:13; Josh. 13:7; 14:3; Ezek. 47:21; 48:29 [b]Ezek. 48:8, 9 [c]Zech. 14:20, 21 [d]Ezek. 42:16; 45:2
2 [1]Or, *pasture land;* cf. 27:28
3 [1]Lit., *measure*
4 [a]Ezek. 48:10, 11 [b]Num. 16:5; Ezek. 40:45; 43:19
5 [1]So with Gk.; M.T., *twenty chambers*
6 [1]Or, *contribution* [a]Ezek. 48:15-18, 30-35
7 [1]Or, *contribution* [2]Lit., *possession* [a]Ezek. 34:24; 37:24; 46:16-18; 48:21

side toward the east, and in length
comparable to one of the portions,
from the west border to the east
border.
8 "This shall be his land for a possession in Israel; so My princes shall
no longer [a]oppress My people, but
they shall give *the rest of* the land to
the house of Israel [b]according to
their tribes."
9 'Thus says the Lord [1]GOD,
"Enough, you princes of Israel; put
away [a]violence and destruction, and
[b]practice justice and righteousness.
Stop your [c]expropriations from My
people," declares the Lord GOD.
10 "You shall have [a]just balances, a
just [b]ephah, and a just [b]bath.
11 "The ephah and the bath shall be
the same quantity, so that the bath
may contain a tenth of a [a]homer,
and the ephah a tenth of a homer;
their standard shall be according to
the homer.
12 "And the [a]shekel shall be twenty
[a]gerahs; twenty shekels, twenty-
five shekels, *and* fifteen shekels
shall be your [1]maneh.
13 "This is the offering that you
shall offer: a sixth of an ephah from
a homer of wheat; a sixth of an
ephah from a homer of barley;
14 and the prescribed portion of
oil (*namely,* the bath of oil), a tenth
of a bath from *each* kor (*which is* ten
baths *or* a homer, for ten baths are a
homer);
15 and one sheep from *each* flock
of two hundred from the watering
places of Israel—for a grain offering, for a burnt offering, and for
peace offerings, to [a]make atonement for them," declares the Lord
GOD.
16 "[a]All the people of the land shall
[1]give to this offering for the [b]prince
in Israel.
17 "And it shall be the prince's part
to provide the [a]burnt offerings, the
grain offerings, and the libations, at
the [b]feasts, on the [c]new moons, and
on the sabbaths, at all the appointed
feasts of the house of Israel; he shall
provide the sin offering, the grain
offering, the burnt offering, and the
[d]peace offerings, to make atonement for the house of Israel."
18 'Thus says the Lord GOD, "In the
[a]first *month,* on the first of the
month, you shall take a young bull
[b]without blemish and [c]cleanse the
sanctuary.
19 "And the priest shall take some
of the blood from the sin offering
and put *it* on the door posts of the
house, on the [a]four corners of the
[b]ledge of the altar, and on the posts
of the gate of the inner court.
20 "And thus you shall do on the
seventh *day* of the month for every
one who goes [a]astray or is [1]naive; so
you shall make [b]atonement for the
house.
21 "In the first *month,* on the fourteenth day of the month, you shall
have the [a]Passover, a feast of seven
days; unleavened bread shall be eat-
en.
22 "And on that day the prince shall
provide for himself and all the people of the land a [a]bull for a sin offering.
23 "And *during* the [a]seven days of
the feast he shall provide as a [b]burnt
offering to the LORD [c]seven bulls
and seven rams without blemish on
every day of the seven days, and a
male goat daily for a sin offering.
24 "And he shall provide as a [a]grain
offering an ephah [1]with a bull, an
ephah [1]with a ram, and a hin of oil
[1]with an ephah.
25 "In the [a]seventh *month,* on the
fifteenth day of the month, at the
feast, he shall provide like this,
seven days for the sin offering, the
burnt offering, the grain offering,
and the oil."

CHAPTER 46

The Prince's Offerings

'THUS says the Lord [1]GOD, "The
gate of the [a]inner court facing east
shall be [b]shut the six [c]working days;
but it shall be opened on the [d]sab-
bath day, and opened on the day of
the [e]new moon.
2 "And the [a]prince shall enter by
way of the [a]porch of the gate from
outside and stand by the [b]post of the
gate. Then the priests shall provide
his burnt offering and his peace offerings, and he shall worship at the
threshold of the gate and then go
out; but the gate shall not be shut
until the evening.
3 "The [a]people of the land shall
also worship at the doorway of that
gate before the LORD on the sabbaths and on the new moons.
4 "And the [a]burnt offering which
the prince shall offer to the LORD on
the sabbath day shall be [b]six lambs
without blemish and a ram without
blemish;
5 and the [a]grain offering shall be
an ephah [1]with the ram, and the
grain offering [1]with the lambs [2]as
much as he is [b]able to give, and a hin
of oil [1]with an ephah.

8 [a]Is. 11:3-5; Jer. 23:5; Ezek. 19:7; 22:27; 46:18 [b]Josh. 11:23
9 [1]YHWH, usually rendered LORD, and so throughout the chap. [a]Jer. 6:7; Ezek. 7:11, 23; 8:17 [b]Jer. 22:3; Zech. 8:16 [c]Neh. 5:1-5
10 [a]Lev. 19:36; Deut. 25:15; Prov. 16:11; Amos 8:4-6; Mic. 6:10, 11 [b]Is. 5:10
11 [a]Is. 5:10
12 [1]Or, *mina* [a]Ex. 30:13; Lev. 27:25; Num. 3:47
15 [a]Lev. 1:4; 6:30
16 [1]Lit., *be* [a]Ex. 30:14, 15 [b]Is. 16:1
17 [a]1 Kin. 8:64; 1 Chr. 16:2; 2 Chr. 31:3 [b]Lev. 23:1-44; Num. 28:1-29, 39 [c]Is. 66:23 [d]1 Kin. 8:63; Ezek. 43:27
18 [a]Ex. 12:2 [b]Lev. 22:20; Heb. 9:14 [c]Lev. 16:16, 33; Ezek. 43:22, 26
19 [a]Lev. 16:18-20; Ezek. 43:20 [b]Ezek. 43:14, 17, 20
20 [1]Lit., *simple* [a]Lev. 4:27; Ps. 19:12 [b]Lev. 16:20; Ezek. 45:15, 18
21 [a]Ex. 12:1-24; Lev. 23:5-8
22 [a]Lev. 4:14
23 [a]Lev. 23:8 [b]Num. 28:16-25 [c]Num. 23:1, 2; Job 42:8
24 [1]Lit., *for* [a]Num. 28:12-15; Ezek. 46:5-7
25 [a]Lev. 23:33-43; Num. 29:12-38; 2 Chr. 5:3; 7:8, 10
1 [1]YHWH, usually rendered LORD, and so throughout the chap. [a]Ezek. 8:16; 10:3 [b]Ezek. 44:1, 2 [c]Ex. 20:9 [d]Is. 66:23; Ezek. 45:17 [e]Ezek. 45:18; 46:3, 6
2 [a]Ezek. 44:3; 46:8 [b]Ezek. 45:19
3 [a]Luke 1:10
4 [a]Ezek. 45:17 [b]Num. 28:9, 10
5 [1]Lit., *for* [2]Lit., *a gift of his hand* [a]Num. 28:12; Ezek. 45:24; 46:7, 11 [b]Ezek. 46:7

6"And on the day of the new moon *he shall offer* a young bull without blemish, also six lambs and a ram, *which* shall be without blemish.

7"And he shall provide a grain offering, an ephah [1]with the bull, and an ephah [1]with the ram, and [1]with the lambs as [2]much as he is [a]able, and a hin of oil [1]with an ephah.

8"And when the prince enters, he shall go in by way of the porch of the gate and go out [1]by the same way.

9"But when the people of the land come [a]before the LORD at the appointed feasts, he who enters by way of the north gate to worship shall go out by way of the south gate. And he who enters by way of the south gate shall go out by way of the north gate. [1]No one shall return by way of the gate by which he entered but shall go straight out.

10"And when they go in, the prince shall go in [a]among them; and when they go out, [1]he shall go out.

11"And at the [a]festivals and the appointed feasts the grain offering shall be an ephah [1]with a bull and an ephah [1]with a ram, and [1]with the lambs as [2]much as one is able to give, and a hin of oil [1]with an ephah.

12"And when the prince provides a [a]freewill offering, a burnt offering, or peace offerings *as* a freewill offering to the LORD, the gate facing east shall be [b]opened for him. And he shall provide his burnt offering and his peace offerings as he does on the [c]sabbath day. Then he shall go out, and the gate shall be shut after he goes out.

13"And you shall provide a [a]lamb a year old without blemish for a burnt offering to the LORD daily; [b]morning by morning you shall provide it.

14"Also you shall provide a grain offering with it morning by morning, a [a]sixth of an ephah, and a third of a hin of oil to moisten the fine flour, a grain offering to the LORD continually by a perpetual [1]ordinance.

15"Thus they shall provide the lamb, the grain offering, and the oil, morning by morning, for a [a]continual burnt offering."

16 'Thus says the Lord GOD, "If the prince gives a [a]gift *out of* his inheritance to any of his sons, it shall belong to his sons; it is their possession by inheritance.

17"But if he gives a gift from his inheritance to one of his servants, it shall be his until the [a]year of liberty; then it shall return to the prince. His inheritance *shall be* only his sons'; it shall belong to them.

18"And the prince shall [a]not take from the people's inheritance, [1b]thrusting them out of their possession; he shall give his sons inheritance from his own possession so that My people shall not be scattered, anyone from his possession." ' "

The Boiling Places

19 Then he brought me through the [a]entrance, which *was* at the side of the gate, into the holy chambers for the priests, which faced north; and behold, there *was* a place at the extreme rear toward the west.

20 And he said to me, "This is the place where the priests shall boil the [a]guilt offering and the sin offering, *and* where they shall [b]bake the grain offering, in order that they may not bring *them* out into the outer court to transmit holiness to the people."

21 Then he brought me out into the outer court and led me across to the four corners of the court; and behold, in every corner of the court *there was* a *small* court.

22 In the four corners of the court *there were* enclosed courts, forty *cubits* long and thirty wide; these four in the corners *were* [1]the same size.

23 And *there was* a row *of masonry* round about in them, around the four of them, and boiling places were made under the rows round about.

24 Then he said to me, "These are the boiling [1]places where the ministers of the house shall boil the sacrifices of the people."

CHAPTER 47

Water from the Temple

THEN he brought me back to the [a]door of the house; and behold, [b]water was flowing from under the threshold of the house toward the east, for the house faced east. And the water was flowing down from under, from the right side of the house, from south of the altar.

2 And he brought me out by way of the north gate and led me around [1]on the outside to the outer gate by way of *the gate* that faces east. And behold, water was trickling from the south side.

3 When the man went out toward the east with a line in his hand, he measured a thousand cubits, and he led me through the water, water *reaching* the ankles.

7 [1]Lit., *for* [2]Lit., *his hand can reach* [a]Lev. 14:21; Deut. 16:17; Ezek. 46:5

8 [1]Lit., *by its way*

9 [1]Lit., *He shall not* [a]Ex. 34:23; Ps. 84:7; Mic. 6:6

10 [1]So with many mss. and the ancient versions; M.T., *they* [a]2 Sam. 6:14, 15; 1 Chr. 29:20, 21; 2 Chr. 6:3; 7:4; Ps. 42:4

11 [1]Lit., *for* [2]Lit., *a gift of his hand* [a]Ezek. 45:17

12 [a]Lev. 23:38; 2 Chr. 29:31 [b]Ezek. 44:3; 46:1, 2, 8 [c]Ezek. 45:17

13 [a]Num. 28:3-5 [b]Is. 50:4

14 [1]Lit., *statutes* [a]Num. 28:5

15 [a]Ex. 29:42; Num. 28:6

16 [a]2 Chr. 21:3

17 [a]Lev. 25:10

18 [1]Lit., *oppressing* [a]Is. 11:3, 4; Ezek. 45:8 [b]1 Kin. 21:19; Ezek. 22:27; Mic. 2:1, 2

19 [a]Ezek. 42:9; 44:5

20 [a]2 Chr. 35:13; Ezek. 44:29 [b]Lev. 2:4-7

22 [1]Lit., *one measure*

24 [1]Lit., *houses*

1 [a]Ezek. 41:2, 23-25 [b]Ps. 46:4; Is. 30:25; 55:1; Jer. 2:13; Joel 3:18; Zech. 13:1; 14:8; Rev. 22:1, 17

2 [1]Lit., *by way of*

4 Again he measured a thousand
and led me through the water, water
reaching the knees. Again he measured a thousand and led me
through *the water,* water *reaching*
the loins.
5 Again he measured a thousand;
and it was a river that I could not
ford, for the water had risen, *enough*
water to swim in, a [a]river that could
not be forded.
6 And he said to me, "Son of
man, have you [a]seen *this?*" Then he
brought me back to the bank of the
river.
7 Now when I had returned, behold, on the bank of the river there
were very many [a]trees on the one
side and on the other.
8 Then he said to me, "These waters go out toward the eastern region and go down into the [a]Arabah;
then they go toward the sea, being
made to flow into the [b]sea, and the
waters *of the sea* become fresh.
9 "And it will come about that every living creature which swarms in
every place where the river goes,
will live. And there will be very
many fish, for these waters go there,
and *the others* become fresh; so [a]ev-
erything will live where the river
goes.
10 "And it will come about that
[a]fishermen will stand [b]beside it;
from [c]Engedi to Eneglaim there will
be a place for the [d]spreading of nets.
Their fish will be according to their
kinds, like the fish of the [e]Great Sea,
[f]very many.
11 "But its swamps and marshes
will not become fresh; they will be
left for [a]salt.
12 "And [a]by the river on its bank,
on one side and on the other, will
grow all *kinds of* [b]trees for food.
Their [c]leaves will not wither, and
their fruit will not fail. They will
bear every month because their water flows from the sanctuary, and
their fruit will be for food and their
[d]leaves for healing."

Boundaries and Division of the Land

13 Thus says the Lord [1]GOD, "This
shall be the [a]boundary by which you
shall divide the land for an inheritance among the twelve tribes of Israel; Joseph *shall have two* [b]por-
tions.
14 "And you shall divide it for an
inheritance, each one equally with
the other; for I [a]swore to give it to
your forefathers, and this land shall
fall to you [1]as an inheritance.
15 "And this *shall be* the boundary
of the land: on the [a]north side, from
the Great Sea *by* the way of Hethlon, to the entrance of [1b]Zedad;
16 [1a]Hamath, Berothah, Sibraim,
which is between the border of [b]Da-
mascus and the border of Hamath;
Hazer-hatticon, which is by the border of Hauran.
17 "And the boundary shall [1]extend
from the sea *to* Hazar-enan *at* the
border of Damascus, and on the
north toward the north is the border
of Hamath. This is the north side.
18 "And the [a]east side, from between Hauran, Damascus, [b]Gilead,
and the land of Israel, *shall be* the
[c]Jordan; from the *north* border to
the eastern sea you shall measure.
This is the east side.
19 "And the [a]south side toward the
south *shall extend* from [b]Tamar as
far as the waters of [c]Meribath-ka-
desh, to the [d]brook *of Egypt, and* to
the [e]Great Sea. This is the south side
toward the south.
20 "And the [a]west side *shall be* the
Great Sea, from the *south* border to
a point opposite [1b]Lebo-hamath.
This is the west side.
21 "So you shall divide this land
among yourselves according to the
tribes of Israel.
22 "And it will come about that you
shall divide it by [a]lot for an inheritance among yourselves and among
the [b]aliens who stay in your midst,
who bring forth sons in your midst.
And they shall be to you as the native-born among the sons of Israel;
they shall be allotted an [c]inheri-
tance with you among the tribes of
Israel.
23 "And it will come about that in
the tribe with which the alien stays,
there you shall give *him* his inheritance," declares the Lord GOD.

CHAPTER 48

Division of the Land

"NOW [a]these are the names of
the tribes: from the northern extremity, beside the way of Hethlon
to [1]Lebo-hamath, *as far as* Hazar-
enan *at* the border of Damascus,
toward the north beside Hamath,
running from east to west, [b]Dan,
one *portion.*
2 "And beside the border of Dan,
from the east side to the west side,
[a]Asher, one *portion.*
3 "And beside the border of Asher,
from the east side to the west side,
[a]Naphtali, one *portion.*
4 "And beside the border of Naphtali, from the east side to the west
side, [a]Manasseh, one *portion.*

5 [a]Is. 11:9; Hab. 2:14
6 [a]Ezek. 8:6; 40:4; 44:5
7 [a]Is. 60:13, 21; 61:3; Ezek. 47:12
8 [a]Deut. 3:17; Is. 35:6, 7; 41:17-19; 44:3 [b]Josh. 3:16
9 [a]Is. 12:3; 55:1; John 4:14; 7:37, 38; Rev. 21:7
10 [a]Matt. 4:19; 13:47; Luke 5:10 [b]1 Sam. 23:24; 24:1 [c]Gen. 14:7; Josh. 15:62; 1 Sam. 23:29; 24:1; 2 Chr. 20:2 [d]Ezek. 26:5, 14 [e]Num. 34:6; Ps. 104:25; Ezek. 47:15; 48:28 [f]Luke 5:5-9; John 21:6
11 [a]Deut. 29:23
12 [a]Ezek. 47:7; Rev. 22:2 [b]Gen. 2:9 [c]Ps. 1:3; Jer. 17:8 [d]Rev. 22:2
13 [1]YHWH, usually rendered LORD, and so throughout the chap. [a]Num. 34:2-12 [b]Gen. 48:5; 49:26; Ezek. 48:4, 5
14 [1]Lit., *in* [a]Deut. 1:8; Ezek. 20:6
15 [1]Or, *Hamath* [a]Num. 34:7-9 [b]Num. 34:8
16 [1]Or, *Zedad* [a]Num. 13:21; Is. 10:9; Ezek. 47:17, 20; 48:1; Zech. 9:2 [b]Gen. 14:15; Ezek. 47:17, 18; 48:1
17 [1]Lit., *be*
18 [a]Num. 34:10-12 [b]Gen. 37:25; Jer. 50:19 [c]Gen. 13:10, 11
19 [a]Num. 34:3-5 [b]Ezek. 48:28 [c]Deut. 32:51 [d]Num. 34:5; 1 Kin. 8:65; Is. 27:12 [e]Ezek. 47:10, 15
20 [1]Or, *entrance of Hamath* [a]Num. 34:6 [b]Judg. 3:3; 2 Chr. 7:8; Ezek. 48:1; Amos 6:14
22 [a]Num. 26:55, 56 [b]Is. 14:1; 56:6, 7 [c]Acts 11:18; 15:9; Eph. 2:12-14; 3:6; Col. 3:11
1 [1]Or, *the entrance of Hamath* [a]Ex. 1:1 [b]Josh. 19:40-48
2 [a]Josh. 19:24-31
3 [a]Josh. 19:32
4 [a]Josh. 13:29-31; 17:1-11

5"And beside the border of Manasseh, from the east side to the west side, [a]Ephraim, one *portion.*

6"And beside the border of Ephraim, from the east side to the west side, [a]Reuben, one *portion.*

7"And beside the border of Reuben, from the east side to the west side, [a]Judah, one *portion.*

8"And beside the border of Judah, from the east side to the west side, shall be the [1]allotment which you shall [2]set apart, 25,000 [3]*cubits* in width, and in length like one of the portions, from the east side to the west side; and the [a]sanctuary shall be in the middle of it.

9"The allotment that you shall set apart to the LORD *shall be* 25,000 *cubits* in length, and 10,000 in width.

Portion for the Priests

10"And the holy allotment shall be for these, *namely* for the [a]priests, toward the north 25,000 *cubits in length,* toward the west 10,000 in width, toward the east 10,000 in width, and toward the south 25,000 in length; and the sanctuary of the LORD shall be in its midst.

11"*It shall be* for the priests who are sanctified of the [a]sons of Zadok, who have kept My charge, who did not go astray when the sons of Israel went astray, as the [b]Levites went astray.

12"And it shall be an allotment to them from the allotment of the land, a most holy place, by the border of the Levites.

13"And alongside the border of the priests the Levites *shall have* 25,000 *cubits* in length and 10,000 in width. The whole length *shall be* 25,000 *cubits* and the width 10,000.

14"Moreover, they shall not [a]sell or exchange any of it, or alienate this [1]choice *portion* of land; for it is holy to the LORD.

15"And the remainder, 5,000 *cubits* in width and 25,000 [1]in length, shall be for [a]common use for the city, for dwellings and for [2]open spaces; and the city shall be in its midst.

16"And these *shall be* its measurements: the north side 4,500 *cubits,* the south side [a]4,500 *cubits,* the east side 4,500 *cubits,* and the west side 4,500 *cubits.*

17"And the city shall have [1]open spaces: on the north 250 *cubits,* on the south 250 *cubits,* on the east 250 *cubits,* and on the west 250 *cubits.*

18"And the remainder of the length alongside the holy allotment shall be 10,000 *cubits* toward the east, and 10,000 toward the west; and it shall be [1]alongside the holy allotment. And its produce shall be food for the workers of the city.

19"And the workers of the city, out of all the tribes of Israel, shall cultivate it.

20"The whole allotment *shall be* 25,000 by 25,000 *cubits;* you shall [1]set apart the holy allotment, a [2]square, with the [3]property of the city.

Portion for the Prince

21"And the [a]remainder *shall be* for the prince, on the one side and on the other of the holy allotment and of the [1]property of the city; in front of the 25,000 *cubits* of the allotment toward the east border and westward in front of the 25,000 toward the west border, alongside the portions, *it shall be* for the prince. And the holy allotment and the sanctuary of the house shall be in the middle of it.

22"And exclusive of the [1]property of the Levites and the [1]property of the city, *which* are in the middle of that which belongs to the prince, *everything* between the border of Judah and the border of Benjamin shall be for the prince.

Portion for Other Tribes

23"As for the rest of the tribes: from the east side to the west side, [a]Benjamin, one *portion.*

24"And beside the border of Benjamin, from the east side to the west side, [a]Simeon, one *portion.*

25"And beside the border of Simeon, from the east side to the west side, [a]Issachar, one *portion.*

26"And beside the border of Issachar, from the east side to the west side, [a]Zebulun, one *portion.*

27"And beside the border of Zebulun, from the east side to the west side, [a]Gad, one *portion.*

28"And beside the border of Gad, at the south side toward the south, the border shall be from [a]Tamar to the waters of Meribath-kadesh, to the brook *of Egypt,* to the [b]Great Sea.

29"This is the [a]land which you shall divide by lot to the tribes of Israel for an inheritance, and these are their *several* portions," declares the Lord [1]GOD.

The City Gates

30"And these are the exits of the city: on the [a]north side, 4,500 *cubits* by measurement,

5 [a]Josh. 16:5-9; 17:8-10, 14-18

6 [a]Josh. 13:15-21

7 [a]Josh. 15:1-63; 19:9

8 [1]Or, *contribution,* and so throughout the chap. [2]Lit., *offer* [3]Or, possibly, *reeds,* and so throughout the chap. [a]Is. 12:6; 33:20-22; Ezek. 45:3, 4

10 [a]Ezek. 44:28; 45:4

11 [a]Ezek. 40:46; 44:15 [b]Ezek. 44:10, 12

14 [1]Lit., *first* or *first fruits* [a]Lev. 25:32-34

15 [1]Lit., *in front* [2]Or, *pasture land* [a]Ezek. 42:20; 45:6

16 [a]Rev. 21:16

17 [1]Or, *pasture land*

18 [1]Or, *exactly as*

20 [1]Lit., *offer* [2]Lit., *fourth* [3]Or, *possession*

21 [1]Or, *possession* [a]Ezek. 34:24; 45:7; 48:22

22 [1]Or, *possession*

23 [a]Josh. 18:21-28

24 [a]Josh. 19:1-9

25 [a]Josh. 19:17-23

26 [a]Josh. 19:10-16

27 [a]Josh. 13:24-28

28 [a]Gen. 14:7; 2 Chr. 20:2; Ezek. 47:19 [b]Ezek. 47:10, 15, 19, 20

29 [1]YHWH, usually rendered LORD [a]Ezek. 47:13-20

30 [a]Ezek. 48:32, 33, 34

31 shall be the gates of the city, [a]named for the tribes of Israel, three gates toward the north: the gate of Reuben, one; the gate of Judah, one: the gate of Levi, one.
32 "And on the east side, 4,500 *cubits,* [1]shall be three gates: the gate of Joseph, one; the gate of Benjamin, one; the gate of Dan, one.
33 "And on the south side, 4,500 *cubits* by measurement, shall be three gates: the gate of Simeon, one; the gate of Issachar, one; the gate of Zebulun, one.
34 "On the west side, 4,500 *cubits, shall be* three gates: the gate of Gad, one; the gate of Asher, one; the gate of Naphtali, one.
35 "*The city shall be* 18,000 *cubits* round about; and the [a]name of the city from *that* day *shall be,* '[1]The [b]LORD is there.' "

31 [a]Rev. 21:12, 13
32 [1]Lit., *and*
35 [1]Heb., *YHWH-shammah* [a]Jer. 23:6; 33:16 [b]Is. 12:6; 14:32; 24:23; Jer. 3:17; 8:19; 14:9; Ezek. 35:10; Joel 3:21; Zech. 2:10; Rev. 21:3; 22:3

THE BOOK OF DANIEL

The Choice Young Men

IN the third year of the reign of [a]Jehoiakim king of Judah, [b]Nebuchadnezzar king of Babylon came to Jerusalem and besieged it.
2 And the [a]Lord gave Jehoiakim king of Judah into his hand, along with some of the [b]vessels of the house of God; and he brought them to the land of [c]Shinar, to the house of his god, and he brought the vessels into the treasury of his [d]god.
3 Then the king ordered Ashpenaz, the chief of his [1]officials, to bring in some of the sons of Israel, including some of the [2]royal [a]family and of the nobles,
4 youths in whom was [a]no defect, who were good-looking, showing intelligence in every *branch of* wisdom, endowed with understanding, and discerning knowledge, and who had ability for serving in the king's court; and *he ordered him* to teach them the literature and [b]language of the [c]Chaldeans.
5 And the king appointed for them a daily ration from the king's choice food and from the wine which he drank, and *appointed* that they should be educated three years, at the end of which they were to [a]enter the king's personal service.
6 Now among them from the sons of Judah were [a]Daniel, Hananiah, Mishael and Azariah.
7 Then the commander of the officials assigned *new* names to them; and to Daniel he assigned *the name* [a]Belteshazzar, to Hananiah [b]Shadrach, to Mishael [b]Meshach, and to Azariah [b]Abed-nego.

Daniel's Resolve

8 But Daniel [1]made up his mind that he would not [a]defile himself with the [b]king's choice food or with the [c]wine which he drank; so he sought *permission* from the commander of the officials that he might not defile himself.
9 Now God granted Daniel [a]favor and compassion in the sight of the commander of the officials,
10 and the commander of the officials said to Daniel, "I am afraid of my lord the king, who has appointed your food and your drink; for why should he see your faces looking more haggard than the youths who are your own age? Then you would [1]make me forfeit my head to the king."
11 But Daniel said to the overseer whom the commander of the officials had appointed over Daniel, Hananiah, Mishael and Azariah,
12 "Please test your servants for ten days, and let us be given some vegetables to eat and water to drink.
13 "Then let our appearance be [1]observed in your presence, and the appearance of the youths who are eating the king's choice food; and deal with your servants according to what you see."
14 So he listened to them in this matter and tested them for ten days.
15 And at the end of ten days their appearance seemed [a]better and they were fatter than all the youths who had been eating the king's choice food.
16 So the overseer continued to [1]withhold their choice food and the wine they were to drink, and kept giving them vegetables.
17 And as for these four youths, [a]God gave them knowledge and intelligence in every *branch of* [1]literature and wisdom; Daniel even understood all *kinds of* [b]visions and dreams.
18 Then at the end of the days

1 [a]2 Kin. 24:1; 2 Chr. 36:5, 6 [b]Jer. 25:1; 52:12
2 [a]Is. 42:24; Dan. 2:37, 38 [b]2 Chr. 36:7; Jer. 27:19, 20; Dan. 5:2 [c]Gen. 10:10; 11:2; Is. 11:11; Zech. 5:11 [d]Jer. 50:2; 51:44
3 [1]Or, *eunuchs,* and so throughout the chap. [2]Lit., *seed of the* [a]2 Kin. 24:14; Is. 39:7
4 [a]2 Sam. 14:25 [b]Is. 36:11; Jer. 5:15; Dan. 2:4 [c]Dan. 2:2, 4, 5, 10; 3:8; 4:7; 5:7, 11, 30; 9:1
5 [a]1 Sam. 16:22; Jer. 15:1; Dan. 1:19
6 [a]Ezek. 14:14, 20; 28:3; Matt. 24:15
7 [a]Dan. 2:26; 4:8; 5:12 [b]Dan. 2:49; 3:12
8 [1]Lit., *set upon his heart* [a]Lev. 11:47; Ezek. 4:13, 14; Hos. 9:3, 4 [b]Ps. 141:4; Dan. 1:5 [c]Deut. 32:38; Dan. 5:4
9 [a]Job 5:15, 16; Ps. 106:46; Prov. 16:7
10 [1]Lit., *make my head guilty*
13 [1]Lit., *seen*
15 [a]Ex. 23:25; Prov. 10:22
16 [1]Lit., *take away*
17 [1]Or, *writing* [a]1 Kin. 3:12, 28; Job 32:8; Dan. 1:20; 2:21, 23 [b]Dan. 2:19; 7:1; 8:1

which the king had specified for presenting them, the commander of
the officials presented them before
Nebuchadnezzar.
19 And the king talked with them,
and out of them all not one was
found like Daniel, Hananiah, Mishael and Azariah; so they [a]entered
the king's personal service.
20 And as for every matter of [a]wis-
dom and understanding about
which the king consulted them, he
found them [b]ten times [c]better than
all the [d]magicians *and* conjurers
who *were* in all his realm.
21 And Daniel continued until the
[a]first year of Cyrus the king.

Chapter 2

The King's Forgotten Dream

Now in the second year of the
reign of Nebuchadnezzar, Nebuchadnezzar [a]had dreams; and his
spirit was troubled and his [b]sleep
left him.
2 Then the king gave orders to
call in the [a]magicians, the conjurers,
the sorcerers and the [1]Chaldeans, to
tell the king his dreams. So they
came in and stood before the king.
3 And the king said to them, "I
[a]had a dream, and my spirit is anxious to [1]understand the dream."
4 Then the Chaldeans spoke to
the king in [1a]Aramaic: "O king, live
forever! Tell the dream to your servants, and we will declare the interpretation."
5 The king answered and said to
the Chaldeans, "[1]The command
from me is firm: if you do not make
known to me the dream and its interpretation, you will be [a]torn limb
from limb, and your houses will be
made a rubbish heap.
6 "But if you declare the dream
and its interpretation, you will receive from me [a]gifts and a reward
and great honor; therefore declare
to me the dream and its interpretation."
7 They answered a second time
and said, "Let the king tell the
dream to his servants, and we will
declare the interpretation."
8 The king answered and said, "I
know for certain that you are bar-
gaining for time, inasmuch as you
have seen that [1]the command from
me is firm,
9 that if you do not make the
dream known to me, there is only
[a]one [1]decree for you. For you have
agreed together to speak lying and
corrupt words before me until the
situation is changed; therefore tell
me the dream, that I may [b]know
that you can declare to me its interpretation."
10 The Chaldeans answered the
king and said, "There is not a man
on earth who could declare the matter for the king, inasmuch as no
great king or ruler has *ever* asked
anything like this of any magician,
conjurer or Chaldean.
11 "Moreover, the thing which the
king demands is [1]difficult, and there
is no one else who could declare it
[2]to the king except [a]gods, whose
[b]dwelling place is not with *mortal*
flesh."
12 Because of this the king became [a]indignant and very furious,
and gave orders to destroy all the
wise men of Babylon.
13 So the [1]decree went forth that
the wise men should be slain; and
they looked for Daniel and his
friends to [2]kill *them.*
14 Then Daniel replied with discretion and discernment to Arioch,
the captain of the king's [1]body-
guard, who had gone forth to slay
the wise men of Babylon;
15 he answered and said to Arioch, the king's commander, "For
what reason is the [1]decree from the
king *so* [2]urgent?" Then Arioch informed Daniel about the matter.
16 So Daniel went in and requested of the king that he would
[1]give him time, in order that he
might declare the interpretation to
the king.
17 Then Daniel went to his house
and informed his friends, Hananiah,
Mishael and Azariah, about the
matter,
18 in order that they might [a]re-
quest compassion from the God of
heaven concerning this mystery, so
that Daniel and his friends might
not be [b]destroyed with the rest of
the wise men of Babylon.

The Secret Is Revealed to Daniel

19 Then the mystery was revealed
to Daniel in a night [a]vision. Then
Daniel blessed the God of heaven;
20 Daniel answered and said,
"Let the name of God be
[a]blessed forever and ever,
For [b]wisdom and power belong to Him.
21 "And it is He who [a]changes the
times and the epochs;
He [b]removes kings and [1]estab-
lishes kings;

19 [a]Gen. 41:46; 1 Kin. 17; Prov. 22:29; Jer. 15:1; Dan. 1:5
20 [a]1 Kin. 4:30, 31; Dan. 1:17 [b]Gen. 31:7; Num. 14:22; Neh. 4:12; Job 19:3 [c]Dan. 2:27, 28, 46, 48 [d]Is. 19:3; Dan. 2:2; 4:18; 5:7
21 [a]Dan. 6:28; 10:1
1 [a]Gen. 14:1; 40:5-8; Job 33:15-17; Dan. 2:3; 4:5 [b]Esth. 6:1; Dan. 6:18
2 [1]Or, *master astrologers,* and so throughout the chap. [a]Gen. 41:8; Is. 47:12, 13; Dan. 1:20; 2:10, 27; 4:6; 5:7
3 [1]Lit., *know* [a]Gen. 40:8; 41:15; Dan. 4:5
4 [1]The text is in Aramaic from here through 7:28 [a]Ezra 4:7; Is. 36:11
5 [1]Another reading is, *The word has gone from me* [a]Ezra 6:11; Dan. 2:12; 3:29
6 [a]Dan. 2:48; 5:7, 16, 29
8 [1]See v. 5 nt. 1
9 [1]Or, *law* [a]Esth. 4:11; Dan. 3:15 [b]Is. 41:23
11 [1]Or, *rare* [2]Lit., *before* [a]Gen. 41:39; Dan. 5:11 [b]Ex. 29:45; Is. 57:15
12 [a]Ps. 76:10; Dan. 2:5; 3:13, 19
13 [1]Or, *law* [2]Lit., *be killed*
14 [1]Or, *executioners*
15 [1]Or, *law* [2]Or, *harsh*
16 [1]Or, *appoint a time for him*
18 [a]Esth. 4:15, 16; Is. 37:4; Jer. 33:3; Ezek. 36:37; Dan. 2:23 [b]Gen. 18:28; Mal. 3:18
19 [a]Num. 12:6; Job 33:15, 16; Dan. 1:17; 7:2, 7, 13
20 [a]Ps. 103:1, 2; 113:1, 2 [b]1 Chr. 29:11, 12; Job 12:13, 16-22; Dan. 2:21-23
21 [1]Or, *sets up* [a]Ps. 31:15; Dan. 2:9; 7:25 [b]Job 12:18; Ps. 75:6, 7; Dan. 4:17, 32

He gives [c]wisdom to wise men,
And knowledge to [2]men of understanding.
22 "It is He who [a]reveals the profound and hidden things;
[b]He knows what is in the darkness,
And the [c]light dwells with Him.
23 "To Thee, O [a]God of my fathers, I give thanks and praise,
For Thou hast given me [b]wisdom and power;
Even now Thou hast made known to me what we [c]requested of Thee,
For Thou hast made known to us the king's matter."

24 Therefore, Daniel went in to Arioch, whom the king had appointed to destroy the wise men of Babylon; he went and spoke to him as follows: "[a]Do not destroy the wise men of Babylon! Take me [1]into the king's presence, and I will declare the interpretation to the king."

25 Then Arioch hurriedly [a]brought Daniel [1]into the king's presence and spoke to him as follows: "I have found a man among the [2b]exiles from Judah who can make the interpretation known to the king!"

26 The king answered and said to Daniel, whose name was [a]Belteshazzar, "Are you able to make known to me the dream which I have seen and its interpretation?"

27 Daniel answered before the king and said, "As for the mystery about which the king has inquired, neither [a]wise men, conjurers, [1]magicians, *nor* diviners are able to declare *it* to the king.

28 "However, there is a [a]God in heaven who reveals mysteries, and He has made known to King Nebuchadnezzar what will take place in the [1b]latter days. This was your dream and the visions [2]in your mind *while* on your bed.

29 "As for you, O king, *while* on your bed your thoughts [1]turned to what would take place [2]in the future; and He who reveals mysteries has made known to you what will take place.

30 "But as for me, this mystery has not been revealed to me for any [a]wisdom [1]residing in me more than *in* any *other* living man, but for the purpose of [b]making the interpretation known to the king, and that you may [2]understand the [c]thoughts of your [3]mind.

The King's Dream

31 "You, O king, were looking and behold, there was a single great statue; that statue, which was large and [1]of extraordinary splendor, was standing in front of you, and its appearance was [a]awesome.

32 "The head of that statue *was made* of fine gold, its breast and its arms of silver, its belly and its thighs of bronze,

33 its legs of iron, its feet partly of iron and partly of clay.

34 "You [1]continued looking until a stone was cut out [a]without hands, and it struck the statue on its feet of iron and clay, and [b]crushed them.

35 "Then the iron, the clay, the bronze, the silver and the gold were crushed [1]all at the same time, and became [a]like chaff from the summer threshing floors; and the wind carried them away so that [b]not a trace of them was found. But the stone that struck the statue became a great [c]mountain and filled the whole earth.

The Interpretation—Babylon the First Kingdom

36 "This *was* the dream; now we shall tell its interpretation before the king.

37 "You, O king, are the [a]king of kings, to whom the God of heaven has given the [1]kingdom, the [b]power, the strength, and the glory;

38 and wherever the sons of men dwell, *or* the [a]beasts of the field, or the birds of the sky, He has given *them* into your hand and has caused you to rule over them all. You are the head of gold.

Medo Persia and Greece

39 "And after you there will arise another kingdom inferior to you, then another third kingdom of bronze, which will rule over all the earth.

Rome

40 "Then there will be a fourth kingdom as strong as iron; inasmuch as iron crushes and shatters all things, so, like iron that breaks in pieces, it will crush and break all these in pieces.

41 "And in that you saw the feet and toes, partly of potter's clay and partly of iron, it will be a divided kingdom; but it will have in it the toughness of iron, inasmuch as you saw the iron mixed with [1]common clay.

42 "And *as* the toes of the feet *were* partly of iron and partly of pottery,

21 [2]Lit., *knowers* [c]1 Kin. 3:9, 10; 4:29; James 1:5
22 [a]Job 12:22; Dan. 2:19, 28 [b]Job 26:6; Ps. 139:12; Is. 45:7; Jer. 23:24 [c]Ps. 36:9; Dan. 5:11, 14; 1 John 1:5
23 [a]Gen. 31:42; Ex. 3:15 [b]Dan. 1:17; 2:21 [c]Ps. 21:2, 4; Dan. 2:18, 29, 30
24 [1]Lit., *in before the king* [a]Dan. 2:12, 13; Acts 27:24
25 [1]Lit., *in before the king* [2]Lit., *sons of the exile of* [a]Gen. 41:14 [b]Dan. 1:6; 5:13; 6:13
26 [a]Dan. 1:7; 4:8; 5:12
27 [1]Or, *soothsayer priests* [a]Dan. 2:2, 10, 11; 5:7, 8
28 [1]Lit., *end of the days* [2]Lit., *of your head* [a]Gen. 40:8; 41:16; Dan. 2:22, 45 [b]Gen. 49:1; Is. 2:2; Dan. 10:14; Mic. 4:1
29 [1]Lit., *came up* [2]Lit., *after this*
30 [1]Lit., *which is* [2]Lit., *know* [3]Lit., *heart* [a]Gen. 41:16; Dan. 1:17 [b]Is. 45:3 [c]Ps. 139:2; Amos 4:13
31 [1]Lit., *its splendor was surpassing* [a]Is. 25:3-5; Dan. 7:7; Hab. 1:7
34 [1]Lit., *were* [a]Dan. 8:25; Zech. 4:6 [b]Ps. 2:9; Is. 60:12
35 [1]Lit., *like one* [a]Ps. 1:4; Is. 17:13; 41:15, 16; Hos. 13:3 [b]Ps. 37:10, 36 [c]Is. 2:2; Mic. 4:1
37 [1]Or, *sovereignty* [a]Is. 47:5; Jer. 27:6, 7; Ezek. 26:7 [b]Ps. 62:11
38 [a]Ps. 50:10, 11; Dan. 4:21, 22
41 [1]Lit., *clay of mud*

so some of the kingdom will be strong and part of it will be brittle.

43 "And in that you saw the iron mixed with [1]common clay, they will combine with one another [2]in the seed of men; but they will not adhere to one another, even as iron does not combine with pottery.

The Divine Kingdom

44 "And in the days of those kings the God of heaven will [a]set up a [b]kingdom which will never be destroyed, and *that* kingdom will not be [1]left for another people; it will [c]crush and put an end to all these kingdoms, but it will itself endure forever.

45 "Inasmuch as you saw that a stone was cut out of the mountain without hands and that it crushed the iron, the bronze, the clay, the silver, and the gold, the [a]great God has made known to the king what [b]will take place [1]in the future; so the dream is true, and its interpretation is trustworthy."

Daniel Promoted

46 Then King Nebuchadnezzar fell on his face and did [a]homage to Daniel, and gave orders to present to him an offering and [1b]fragrant incense.

47 The king answered Daniel and said, "Surely [a]your God is a [b]God of gods and a Lord of kings and a [c]revealer of mysteries, since you have been able to reveal this mystery."

48 Then the king [1a]promoted Daniel and gave him many great gifts, and he made him ruler over the whole [b]province of Babylon and chief [2]prefect over all the wise men of Babylon.

49 And Daniel made request of the king, and he appointed Shadrach, Meshach and Abed-nego over the administration of the province of Babylon, while Daniel *was* at the king's [1a]court.

CHAPTER 3

The King's Golden Image

NEBUCHADNEZZAR the king made an [a]image of gold, the height of which *was* sixty [1]cubits *and* its width six [1]cubits; he set it up on the plain of Dura in the [b]province of Babylon.

2 Then Nebuchadnezzar the king sent *word* to assemble the [a]satraps, the prefects and the governors, the counselors, the treasurers, the judges, the magistrates and all the rulers of the provinces to come to the dedication of the image that Nebuchadnezzar the king had set up.

3 Then the satraps, the prefects and the governors, the counselors, the treasurers, the judges, the magistrates and all the rulers of the provinces were assembled for the dedication of the image that Nebuchadnezzar the king had set up; and they stood before the image that Nebuchadnezzar had set up.

4 Then the herald [a]loudly proclaimed: "To you the command is given, [b]O peoples, nations and *men of every* language,

5 that at the moment you [a]hear the sound of the horn, flute, [1]lyre, [2]trigon, [3]psaltery, bagpipe, and all kinds of music, you are to fall down and worship the golden image that Nebuchadnezzar the king has set up.

6 "But whoever does not fall down and worship shall [1]immediately be [a]cast into the midst of a [b]furnace of blazing fire."

7 Therefore at that time, when all the peoples heard the sound of the horn, flute, [1]lyre, trigon, psaltery, bagpipe, and all kinds of music, all the peoples, nations and *men of every* [2]language fell down *and* worshiped the golden image that Nebuchadnezzar the king had set up.

Worship of the Image Refused

8 For this reason at that time certain [a]Chaldeans came forward and [1b]brought charges against the Jews.

9 They responded and said to Nebuchadnezzar the king: "[a]O king, live forever!

10 "You yourself, O king, have [a]made a decree that every man who hears the sound of the horn, flute, [1]lyre, trigon, psaltery, and bagpipe, and all kinds of music, is to fall down and worship the golden image.

11 "But whoever does not fall down and worship shall be cast into the midst of a furnace of blazing fire.

12 "There are certain Jews whom you have appointed over the administration of the province of Babylon, *namely* Shadrach, Meshach, and Abed-nego. These men, O king, have disregarded you; they do not serve your gods or worship the golden image which you have set up."

13 Then Nebuchadnezzar in [a]rage and anger gave orders to bring Shadrach, Meshach, and Abed-nego;

43 [1]Lit., *clay of mud* [2]Or, *with*

44 [1]Or, *passed on to* [a]Is. 9:6, 7 [b]Ps. 145:13; Ezek. 37:25; Dan. 4:3, 34; 6:26; 7:14, 27; Mic. 4:7 [c]Ps. 2:9; Is. 60:12; Dan 2:34, 35

45 [1]Lit., *after this* [a]Deut. 10:17; 2 Sam. 7:22; Ps. 48:1; Jer. 32:18, 19; Dan. 2:29; Mal. 1:11 [b]Gen. 41:28, 32

46 [1]Lit., *sweet odors* [a]Dan. 3:5, 7; Acts 10:25; 14:13; Rev. 19:10; 22:8 [b]Lev. 26:31

47 [a]Dan. 3:15; 4:25 [b]Deut. 10:17; Ps. 136:2, 3; Dan. 11:36 [c]Dan. 2:22, 30; Amos 3:7

48 [1]Lit., *made great* [2]Lit., *of the prefects* [a]Gen. 41:39-43; Dan. 2:6; 5:16, 29 [b]Dan. 3:1, 12, 30

49 [1]Lit., *gate* [a]Esth. 2:19, 21; Amos 5:15

1 [1]A cubit equals approx. 18 inches [a]Is. 46:6; Jer. 16:20; Dan. 2:31; Hab. 2:19 [b]Dan. 2:48; 3:30

2 [a]Dan. 3:3, 27; 6:1-7

4 [a]Is. 40:9; 58:1; Dan. 4:14; Rev. 18:2 [b]Dan. 3:7; 4:1; 6:25

5 [1]Or, *zither* [2]I.e., triangular lyre [3]Or, *a type of harp* [a]Dan. 3:7, 10, 15

6 [1]Or, *in the same hour* [a]Dan. 3:11, 15, 21; 6:7 [b]Jer. 29:22; Ezek. 22:18-22; Matt. 13:42, 50; Rev. 9:2; 14:11

7 [1]See notes at v. 5 [2]Lit., *tongue*

8 [1]Lit., *ate the pieces of* [a]Dan. 2:2, 10; 4:7 [b]Ezra 4:12-16; Esth. 3:8, 9; Dan. 6:12, 13

9 [a]Dan. 2:4; 5:10

10 [1]See notes at v. 5 [a]Esth. 3:12-14; Dan. 3:4-6; 6:12

13 [a]Dan. 2:12; 3:19

then these men were brought before
the king.
14 Nebuchadnezzar responded
and said to them, "Is it true, Shadrach, Meshach and Abed-nego,
that you do not serve [a]my gods or
worship the golden image that I
have set up?
15 "Now if you are ready, at the
moment you hear the sound of the
horn, flute, [1]lyre, trigon, psaltery,
and bagpipe, and all kinds of music,
to fall down and worship the image
that I have made, *very well.* But if
you will not worship, you will [2]im-
mediately be cast into the midst of a
furnace of blazing fire; and [a]what
god is there who can deliver you out
of my hands?"
16 [a]Shadrach, Meshach and Abed-
nego answered and said to the king,
"O Nebuchadnezzar, we do not
need to give you an answer concerning this.
17 "[1]If it be *so,* our [a]God whom we
serve is able to deliver us from the
furnace of blazing fire; [2]and He will
deliver us out of your hand, O king.
18 "[a]But *even* if *He does* not, let it
be known to you, O king, that we are
not going to serve your gods or worship the golden image that you have
set up."

Daniel's Friends Protected

19 Then Nebuchadnezzar was
filled with [a]wrath, and his facial expression was altered toward Shadrach, Meshach and Abed-nego. He
answered [1]by giving orders to heat
the furnace [b]seven times more than
it was usually heated.
20 And he commanded certain
valiant warriors who *were* in his
army to tie up Shadrach, Meshach
and Abed-nego, in order to cast
them into the furnace of blazing fire.
21 Then these men were tied up in
their [1]trousers, their [2]coats, their
caps and their *other* clothes, and
were cast into the midst of the furnace of blazing fire.
22 For this reason, because the
king's [1]command *was* [2a]urgent and
the furnace had been made extremely hot, the flame of the fire
slew those men who carried up Shadrach, Meshach and Abed-nego.
23 But these three men, Shadrach,
Meshach and Abed-nego, fell into
the midst of the furnace of blazing
fire *still* tied up.
24 Then Nebuchadnezzar the king
was astounded and stood up in
haste; he responded and said to his
high officials, "Was it not three men
we cast bound into the midst of the
fire?" They answered and said to the
king, "Certainly, O king."
25 He answered and said, "Look! I
see four men loosed *and* [a]walking
about in the midst of the fire [1]with-
out harm, and the appearance of the
fourth is like a son of *the* [b]gods!"
26 Then Nebuchadnezzar came
near to the door of the furnace of
blazing fire; he responded and said,
"Shadrach, Meshach and Abed-
nego, come out, you servants of the
[a]Most High God, and come here!"
Then Shadrach, Meshach and Abed-
nego [b]came out of the midst of the
fire.
27 And the satraps, the prefects,
the governors and the king's high
officials gathered around *and* saw in
regard to these men that the [a]fire
had no [1]effect on [2]the bodies of
these men nor was the hair of their
head singed, nor were their [3b]trou-
sers [4]damaged, nor had the smell of
fire *even* come upon them.
28 Nebuchadnezzar responded
and said, "Blessed be the [a]God of
Shadrach, Meshach, and Abed-
nego, who has [b]sent His angel and
delivered His servants who put their
[c]trust in Him, [1]violating the king's
command, and yielded up their bodies so as not to serve or worship any
god except their own God.
29 "Therefore, I make a decree that
any people, nation or tongue that
speaks anything offensive against
the God of [a]Shadrach, Meshach and
Abed-nego shall be torn limb from
limb and their [b]houses reduced to a
rubbish heap, inasmuch as there is
[c]no other god who is able to deliver
in this way."
30 Then the king [a]caused Shadrach, Meshach and Abed-nego to
prosper in the province of Babylon.

Chapter 4

The King Acknowledges God

1
NEBUCHADNEZZAR the king to
all the peoples, nations, and *men of*
every [2]language that live in all the
earth: "May your [3a]peace abound!
2 "It has seemed good to me to declare the signs and wonders which
the [a]Most High God has done for
me.
3 "How great are His [a]signs,
And how mighty are His wonders!
His [b]kingdom is an everlasting
kingdom,

14 [a]Is. 46:1; Jer. 50:2; Dan. 3:1; 4:8

15 [1]See notes at v. 5 [2]Or, *in the same hour* [a]Ex. 5:2; Is. 36:18-20; Dan. 2:47

16 [a]Dan. 1:7; 3:12

17 [1]Or, *If our God ... is able* [2]Or, *then* [a]Job 5:19; Ps. 27:1, 2; Is. 26:3, 4; Jer. 1:8; 15:20, 21

18 [a]Josh. 24:15; 1 Kin. 19:14, 18; Is. 51:12, 13; Dan. 3:28

19 [1]Lit., *and ordered to* [a]Esth. 7:7; Dan. 3:13 [b]Lev. 26:18, 21, 24, 28

21 [1]Or, *leggings* [2]Or, *cloaks*

22 [1]Lit., *word* [2]Or, *harsh* [a]Ex. 12:33; Dan. 2:15

25 [1]Lit., *there is no injury in them* [a]Ps. 91:3-9; Is. 43:2 [b]Jer. 1:8, 19; 15:21; Ezek. 34:10

26 [a]Dan. 3:17; 4:2 [b]Deut. 4:20; 1 Kin. 8:51; Jer. 11:4

27 [1]Lit., *power over* [2]Lit., *their* [3]Or, *cloaks* [4]Lit., *changed* [a]Is. 43:2; Heb.11:34 [b]Dan. 3:21

28 [1]Lit., *and changed the king's word* [a]Dan. 2:47; 3:15 [b]Ps. 34:7, 8; Is. 37:36; Dan. 3.25; 6:22; Acts 5:19; 12:7 [c]Ps. 22:4, 5; Is. 26:3, 4

29 [a]Dan. 1:7, 19; 2:17, 49; 3:12 [b]Ezra 6:11; Dan. 2:5 [c]Dan. 2:47; 3:15

30 [a]Dan. 2:49; 3:12

1 [1]Chap. 3:31 in Aram. [2]Lit., *tongue* [3]Or, *welfare* or *prosperity* [a]Ezra 4:17; Dan. 6:25

2 [a]Dan. 3:26; 4:17, 24, 25, 32, 34

3 [a]Ps. 77:19; 105:27; Is. 25:1; Dan. 6:27 [b]Dan. 2:44; 4:34; 6:26

And His dominion is from generation to generation.

The Vision of a Great Tree

4 "[1]I, Nebuchadnezzar, was at
ease in my house and [a]flourishing in
my palace.
5 "I saw a dream and it made me
fearful; and *these* fantasies *as I lay*
on my bed and the [a]visions in my
mind kept alarming me.
6 "So I gave orders to [a]bring into
my presence all the wise men of
Babylon, that they might make
known to me the interpretation of
the dream.
7 "Then the [1a]magicians, the conjurers, the [2]Chaldeans, and the diviners came in, and I related the
dream [3]to them; but they could not
make its [b]interpretation known to
me.
8 "But finally Daniel came in before me, whose name is [a]Belteshaz-
zar according to the name of my
god, and in whom is [1b]a spirit of the
holy gods; and I related the dream
[2]to him, *saying,*
9 'O Belteshazzar, [a]chief of the
magicians, since I know that [b]a
spirit of the holy gods is in you and
[c]no mystery baffles you, [d]tell *me* the
visions of my dream which I have
seen, along with its interpretation.
10 'Now *these were* the visions [1]in
my mind *as I lay* on my bed: I was
looking, and behold, *there was* a
tree in the midst of the [2]earth, and
its height *was* great.

11 'The tree grew large and became strong,
And its height [a]reached to the sky,
And it *was* visible to the end of the whole earth.
12 'Its foliage *was* [a]beautiful and its fruit abundant,
And in it *was* food for all.
The [b]beasts of the field found [c]shade under it,
And the [d]birds of the sky dwelt in its branches,
And all [1]living creatures fed themselves from it.

13 'I was looking in the visions in
my mind *as I lay* on my bed, and
behold, an *angelic* watcher, a [a]holy
one, descended from heaven.
14 'He shouted out and spoke as
follows:
"[a]Chop down the tree and cut off its branches,
Strip off its foliage and scatter its fruit;
Let the [b]beasts flee from under it,
And the birds from its branches.
15 "Yet [a]leave the stump [1]with its roots in the ground,
But with a band of iron and bronze *around it*
In the new grass of the field;
And let him be drenched with the dew of heaven,
And let [2]him share with the beasts in the grass of the earth.
16 "Let his [1]mind be changed from *that of* a man,
And let a beast's [1]mind be given to him,
And let [a]seven [2]periods of time [b]pass over him.
17 "This sentence is by the decree of the *angelic* watchers,
And the decision is a command of the holy ones,
In order that the living may [a]know
That the Most High is ruler over the realm of mankind,
And [b]bestows it on whom He wishes,
And sets over it the [c]lowliest of men."

18 'This is the dream *which* I, King
Nebuchadnezzar, have seen. Now
you, Belteshazzar, tell *me* its interpretation, inasmuch as none of the
[a]wise men of my kingdom is able to
make known to me the interpretation; but you are able, for a spirit of
the holy gods is in you.'

Daniel Interprets the Vision

19 "Then Daniel, whose name is
Belteshazzar, was appalled for a
while as his [a]thoughts alarmed him.
The king responded and said, 'Belteshazzar, do not [b]let the dream or its
interpretation alarm you.' Belteshazzar answered and said, '[c]My
lord, *if only* the dream applied to
those who hate you, and its interpretation to [d]your adversaries!
20 'The tree that you saw, which
became large and grew strong,
whose height reached to the sky and
was visible to all the earth,
21 and whose foliage *was* beautiful and its fruit abundant, and in
which *was* food for all, under which
the beasts of the field dwelt and in
whose branches the birds of the sky
lodged—
22 it is [a]you, O king; for you have
become great and grown strong,
and your [1]majesty has become great
and reached to the sky and your
[b]dominion to the end of the earth.
23 'And in that the king saw an *angelic* watcher, a holy one, descend-

4 [1]Chap. 4:1 in Aram. [a]Ps. 30:6; Is. 47:7
5 [a]Dan. 2:28; 4:10
6 [a]Gen. 41:8; Dan. 2:2
7 [1]Or, *soothsayer priests,* and so throughout the chap. [2]Or, *master astrologers* [3]Lit., *before* [a]Dan. 2:10, 27; 5:7 [b]Is. 44:25; Jer. 27:9, 10; Dan. 2:7
8 [1]Or, possibly, *the Spirit of the holy God,* and so throughout the chap. [2]Lit., *before* [a]Dan. 1:7; 2:26; 5:12 [b]Dan. 4:9, 18; 5:11, 14
9 [a]Dan. 1:20; 2:48; 5:11 [b]Gen. 41:38; Dan. 4:8 [c]Ezek. 28:3; Dan. 2:47 [d]Gen. 41:15; Dan. 2:4, 5
10 [1]Lit., *of my head* [2]Or, *land,* and so throughout the chap.
11 [a]Deut. 9:1; Dan. 4:21, 22
12 [1]Lit., *flesh* [a]Ezek. 31:7 [b]Jer. 27:6; Ezek. 31:6 [c]Lam. 4:20 [d]Matt. 13:32; Luke 13:19
13 [a]Deut. 33:2; Ps. 89:7; Dan. 8:13
14 [a]Ezek. 31:10-14; Dan. 4:23; Matt. 3:10; 7:19; Luke 13:7-9 [b]Ezek. 31:12, 13; Dan. 4:12
15 [1]Lit., *of* [2]Lit., *his portion be with* [a]Job 14:7-9
16 [1]Lit., *heart* [2]I.e., years [a]Dan. 4:23, 25, 32; 7:25; 11:13 [b]1 Chr. 29:30
17 [a]Ps. 9:16; 83:18 [b]Jer. 27:5-7; Dan. 4:25; 5:18, 19 [c]1 Sam. 2:8; Dan. 11:21
18 [a]Gen. 41:8; Dan. 4:7; 5:8, 15
19 [a]Jer. 4:19; Dan. 7:15, 28; 8:27; 10:16, 17 [b]1 Sam. 3:17; Dan. 4:4, 5 [c]2 Sam. 18:31; 1 Kin. 18:7; Dan. 4:24; 10:16 [d]2 Sam. 18:32; Jer. 29:7
22 [1]Lit., *greatness* [a]2 Sam. 12:7; Dan. 2:37, 38 [b]Jer. 27:6, 7

ing from heaven and saying, "Chop
down the tree and destroy it; yet
leave the stump [1]with its roots in the
ground, but with a band of iron and
bronze *around it* in the new grass of
the field, and let him be drenched
with the dew of heaven, and let [2]him
share with the beasts of the field until seven [3]periods of time pass over
him";
24 this is the interpretation, O
king, and this is the decree of the
Most High, which has [a]come upon
my lord the king:
25 that you be [a]driven away from
mankind, and your dwelling place
be with the beasts of the field, and
you be given grass to eat like cattle
and be drenched with the dew of
heaven; and seven [1]periods of time
will pass over you, until you
recognize that the [b]Most High is
ruler over the realm of mankind,
and [c]bestows it on whomever He
wishes.
26 'And in that it was commanded
to leave the stump [1]with the roots of
the tree, your kingdom will be [2]as-
sured to you after you recognize
that *it is* [a]Heaven *that* rules.
27 'Therefore, O king, may my [a]ad-
vice be pleasing to you: [1b]break
away now from your sins by *doing*
righteousness, and from your iniquities by [c]showing mercy to *the* poor,
in case there may be a [d]prolonging
of your prosperity.'

The Vision Fulfilled

28"All *this* [a]happened to Nebuchadnezzar the king.
29"[a]Twelve months later he was
walking on the *roof of* the royal palace of Babylon.
30"The king [1]reflected and said, 'Is
this not Babylon the [a]great, which I
myself have built as a royal [2]resi-
dence by the might of my power and
for the glory of my majesty?'
31"While the word *was* in the
king's mouth, a voice [1]came from
heaven, *saying,* 'King Nebuchadnezzar, to you it is declared: [2]sover-
eignty has been removed from you,
32 and you will be driven away
from mankind, and your dwelling
place *will be* with the beasts of the
field. You will be given grass to eat
like cattle, and seven [1]periods of
time will pass over you, until you
recognize that the Most High is
ruler over the realm of mankind,
and bestows it on whomever He
wishes.'
33"Immediately the word concerning Nebuchadnezzar was fulfilled;
and he was [a]driven away from mankind and began eating grass like cattle, and his body was drenched with
the dew of heaven, until his hair had
grown like eagles' *feathers* and his
nails like birds' *claws.*
34"But at the end of [1]that period I,
Nebuchadnezzar, raised my eyes
toward heaven, and my [2]reason returned to me, and I blessed the
[a]Most High and praised and honored Him who [b]lives forever;
For His dominion is an [c]ever-
lasting dominion,
And His kingdom *endures*
from generation to generation.
35 "And [a]all the inhabitants of the
earth are accounted as nothing,
But [b]He does according to His
will in the host of heaven
And *among* the inhabitants of
earth;
And [c]no one can [1]ward off His
hand
Or say to Him, '[d]What hast
Thou done?'
36"At that time my [1a]reason returned to me. And my majesty and
[b]splendor were [2]restored to me for
the glory of my kingdom, and my
counselors and my nobles began
seeking me out; so I was reestab-
lished in my [3]sovereignty, and surpassing [c]greatness was added to
me.
37"Now I Nebuchadnezzar praise,
exalt, and honor the King of [a]heav-
en, for [b]all His works are [1]true and
His ways [2]just, and He is able to
humble those who [c]walk in pride."

Chapter 5

Belshazzar's Feast

BELSHAZZAR the king [1]held a
great [a]feast for a thousand of his
nobles, and he was drinking wine in
the presence of the thousand.
2 When Belshazzar tasted the
wine, he gave orders to bring the
gold and silver [a]vessels which
Nebuchadnezzar his [1]father had
taken out of the temple which *was*
in Jerusalem, in order that the king
and his nobles, his wives, and his
concubines might drink from them.
3 Then they brought the gold vessels that had been taken out of the
temple, the house of God which *was*
in Jerusalem; and the king and his
nobles, his wives, and his concubines drank from them.
4 They [a]drank the wine and
praised the gods of [b]gold and silver,
of bronze, iron, wood, and stone.

23 [1]Lit., *of* [2]Lit., *his portion be with* [3]I.e., years
24 [a]Job 40:11, 12; Ps. 107:40
25 [1]I.e., years [a]Dan. 4:33; 5:21 [b]Ps. 83:18; Jer. 27:5; Dan. 4:2, 17 [c]Dan. 2:37; 4:17; 5:21
26 [1]Lit., *of* [2]Lit., *enduring* [a]Dan. 2:18, 19, 28, 37, 44; 4:31
27 [1]Or, *redeem now your sins* [a]Gen. 41:33-37 [b]Prov. 28:13; Is. 55:6, 7; Ezek. 18:21, 22 [c]Ps. 41:1-3; Is. 58:6, 7, 10 [d]1 Kin. 21:29; Jon. 3:9
28 [a]Num. 23:19; Zech. 1:6
29 [a]2 Pet. 3:9
30 [1]Lit., *answered* [2]Lit., *house* [a]Hab. 2:4
31 [1]Lit., *fell* [2]Or, *kingdom*
32 [1]I.e., years
33 [a]Dan. 4:25; 5:21
34 [1]Lit., *the days* [2]Lit., *knowledge* [a]Dan. 4:2; 5:18, 21 [b]Ps. 102:24; Dan. 6:26; 12:7 [c]Ps. 145:13; Jer. 10:10; Dan. 4:3
35 [1]Lit., *strike against* [a]Is. 40:17 [b]Ps. 135:6; Dan. 6:27 [c]Job 42:2; Is. 43:13 [d]Is. 45:9
36 [1]Lit., *knowledge* [2]Lit., *returning* [3]Or, *kingdom* [a]2 Chr. 33:12, 13; Dan. 4:34 [b]Dan. 2:31 [c]Prov. 22:4; Dan. 4:22
37 [1]Lit., *truth* [2]Lit., *justice* [a]Dan. 4:26; 5:23 [b]Deut. 32:4; Ps. 33:4, 5; Is. 5:16 [c]Ex. 18:11; Job 40:11, 12; Dan. 5:20
1 [1]Lit., *made* [a]Esth. 1:3; Is. 22:12-14
2 [1]Or, *forefather,* and so throughout the chap. [a]2 Kin. 24:13; 25:15; Ezra 1:7-11; Dan. 1:2
4 [a]Is. 42:8; Dan. 5:23 [b]Ps. 115:4; 135:15; Is. 40:19, 20; Dan. 3:1; Hab. 2:19

5 Suddenly the fingers of a man's hand emerged and began writing opposite the lampstand on the plaster of the wall of the king's palace, and the king saw the back of the hand that did the writing.

6 Then the king's [a]face grew pale, and his thoughts alarmed him; and his [b]hip joints went slack, and his [c]knees began knocking together.

7 The king called aloud to bring in the [a]conjurers, the [1]Chaldeans and the diviners. The king spoke and said to the wise men of Babylon, "Any man who can read this inscription and explain its interpretation to me will be [b]clothed with purple, and *have* a [c]necklace of gold around his neck, and have authority as [2d]third *ruler* in the kingdom."

8 Then all the king's wise men came in, but they could not read the inscription or make known its interpretation to the king.

9 Then King Belshazzar was greatly [a]alarmed, his [b]face grew *even* paler, and his nobles were perplexed.

10 The queen entered the banquet hall because of the words of the king and his nobles; the queen spoke and said, "[a]O king, live forever! Do not let your thoughts alarm you or your face be pale.

11"There is a [a]man in your kingdom in whom is [1]a [b]spirit of the holy gods; and in the days of your father, illumination, insight, and wisdom like the wisdom of the gods were found in him. And King Nebuchadnezzar, your father, your father [2]the king, appointed him chief of the [3]magicians, conjurers, [4]Chaldeans, *and* diviners.

12"*This was* because an [a]extraordinary spirit, knowledge and insight, interpretation of dreams, explanation of enigmas, and solving of difficult problems were found in this Daniel, whom the king named [b]Belteshazzar. Let Daniel now be summoned, and he will declare the interpretation."

Daniel Interprets Handwriting on the Wall

13 Then Daniel was brought in before the king. The king spoke and said to Daniel, "Are you that Daniel who is one of the [a]exiles from Judah, whom my father the king [b]brought from Judah?

14"Now I have heard about you that [1]a spirit of the gods is in you, and that illumination, insight, and extraordinary wisdom have been found in you.

15"Just now the wise men *and* the conjurers were brought in before me that they might read this inscription and make its interpretation known to me, but they [a]could not declare the interpretation of the [1]message.

16"But I personally have heard about you, that you are able to give interpretations and solve difficult problems. Now if you are able to read the inscription and make its [a]interpretation known to me, you will be clothed with purple and *wear* a necklace of gold around your neck, and you will have authority as the [1]third *ruler* in the kingdom."

17 Then Daniel answered and said before the king, "Keep your [a]gifts for yourself, or give your rewards to someone else; however, I will read the inscription to the king and make the interpretation known to him.

18"O king, the [a]Most High God [b]granted sovereignty, [c]grandeur, glory, and majesty to Nebuchadnezzar your father.

19"And because of the grandeur which He bestowed on him, all the peoples, nations, and *men of every* language feared and trembled before him; [a]whomever he wished he killed, and whomever he wished he spared alive; and whomever he wished he elevated, and whomever he wished he humbled.

20"But when his heart was [a]lifted up and his spirit became so [1b]proud that he behaved arrogantly, he was [c]deposed from his royal throne, and *his* glory was taken away from him.

21"He was also [a]driven away from [1]mankind, and his heart was made like *that of* beasts, and his dwelling place *was* with the [b]wild donkeys. He was given grass to eat like cattle, and his body was drenched with the dew of heaven, until he recognized that the [c]Most High God is ruler over the realm of mankind, and *that* He sets over it whomever He wishes.

22"Yet [a]you, his [1]son, Belshazzar, have [b]not humbled your heart, [2]even though you knew all this,

23 but you have [a]exalted yourself against the [b]Lord of heaven; and they have brought the vessels of His house before you, and you and your nobles, your wives and your concubines have been drinking wine from them; and you have praised the gods of silver and gold, of bronze, iron, wood and stone, which do not [c]see, hear or understand. But the God [d]in whose hand are your life-breath and your [e]ways, you have not glorified.

6 [a]Dan. 5:9, 10; 7:28 [b]Ps. 69:23; Nah. 2:10 [c]Ezek. 7:17; 21:7

7 [1]Or, *master astrologers* [2]Or, *a triumvir* [a]Is. 44:25; 47:13; Dan. 4:6, 7; 5:11, 15 [b]Gen. 41:42-44; Dan. 5:16, 29 [c]Ezek. 16:11 [d]Dan. 2:48; 5:16, 29; 6:2, 3

9 [a]Job 18:11; Is. 21:2-4; Jer 6:24; Dan. 2:1; 5:6 [b]Is. 13:6-8

10 [a]Dan. 3:9; 6:6

11 [1]Or possibly, *the Spirit of the holy God* [2]Or, *O king* [3]Or, *soothsayer priests* [4]Or, *master astrologers* [a]Gen. 41:11-15; Dan. 2:47 [b]Dan. 4:8, 9, 18; 5:14

12 [a]Dan 5:14; 6:3 [b]Dan. 1:7; 4:8

13 [a]Ezra 4:1; 6:16, 19, 20; Dan. 2:25; 6:13 [b]Dan. 1:1, 2

14 [1]Or possibly, *the Spirit of God*

15 [1]Lit., *word* [a]Is. 47:12; Dan. 5:8

16 [1]Or, *triumvir* [a]Gen. 40:8

17 [a]2 Kin. 5:16

18 [a]Dan. 4:2; 5:21 [b]Dan. 2:37, 38; 4:17 [c]Jer. 25:9; 27:5-7

19 [a]Dan. 2:12, 13; 3:6; 11:3, 16, 36

20 [1]Lit., *strong* [a]Ex. 9:17; Job 15:25; Is. 14:13-15; Dan. 4:30, 31 [b]2 Kin. 17:14; 2 Chr. 36:13 [c]Job 40:11, 12; Jer. 13:18

21 [1]Lit., *the sons of man* [a]Job 30:3-7; Dan. 4:33 [b]Job 39:5-8 [c]Ex. 9:14-16; Ps. 83:17, 18; Ezek. 17:24; Dan. 4:34, 35

22 [1]Or, *descendant* [2]Lit., *inasmuch as you* [a]Ps. 119:46 [b]Ex. 10:3; 2 Chr. 33:23; 36:12

23 [a]2 Kin. 14:10; Is. 2:12; 37:23; Jer. 50:29; Dan. 5:3, 4 [b]Dan. 4:37 [c]Ps. 115:4-8; Is. 37:19; Hab. 2:18, 19 [d]Job 12:10 [e]Job 31:4; Ps. 139:3; Prov. 20:24; Jer. 10:23

24 "Then the hand was sent from Him, and this inscription was written out.

25 "Now this is the inscription that was written out: '[1]MENĒ, [1]MENĒ, [2]TEKĒL, [3]UPHARSIN.'

26 "This is the interpretation of the message: 'MENĒ'—God has numbered your kingdom and [a]put an end to it.

27 " 'TEKĒL'—you have been [a]weighed on the scales and found deficient.

28 " 'PERĒS'—your kingdom has been divided and given over to the [a]Medes and [1]Persians."

29 Then Belshazzar gave orders, and they clothed Daniel with purple and *put* a necklace of gold around his neck, and issued a proclamation concerning him that he *now* had authority as the [1]third *ruler* in the kingdom.

30 That same night Belshazzar the Chaldean king was [a]slain.

31 [1]So [a]Darius the Mede received the kingdom at about the age of sixty-two.

Chapter 6

Daniel Serves Darius

1 It seemed good to Darius to appoint [a]120 satraps over the kingdom, that they should be in charge of the whole kingdom,

2 and over them three commissioners (of whom [a]Daniel was one), that these satraps might be accountable to them, and that the king might not suffer [b]loss.

3 Then this Daniel began distinguishing himself among the commissioners and satraps because he possessed an [a]extraordinary spirit, and the king planned to appoint him over the [b]entire kingdom.

4 Then the commissioners and satraps began [a]trying to find a ground of accusation against Daniel in regard to government affairs; but they could find [b]no ground of accusation or *evidence of* corruption, inasmuch as he was faithful, and no negligence or corruption was *to be* found in him.

5 Then these men said, "We shall not find any ground of accusation against this Daniel unless we find *it* against him with regard to the [a]law of his God."

6 Then these commissioners and satraps came by agreement to the king and spoke to him as follows: "King Darius, [a]live forever!

7 "All the commissioners of the kingdom, the prefects and the satraps, the high officials and the governors have [a]consulted together that the king should establish a statute and enforce an injunction that anyone who makes a petition to any god or man besides you, O king, for thirty days, shall [b]be cast into the lions' [1]den.

8 "Now, O king, [a]establish the injunction and sign the document so that it may not be changed, according to the [b]law of the Medes and Persians, which may not be revoked."

9 Therefore King Darius [a]signed the document, that is, the injunction.

10 Now when Daniel knew that the document was signed, he entered his house (now in his roof chamber he had windows open [a]toward Jerusalem); and he continued [b]kneeling on his knees three times a day, [c]praying and [d]giving thanks before his God, [1]as he had been doing previously.

11 Then these men came [a]by agreement and found Daniel making petition and supplication before his God.

12 Then they approached and [a]spoke before the king about the king's injunction, "Did you not sign an injunction that any man who makes a petition to any god or man besides you, O king, for thirty days, is to be cast into the lions' den?" The king answered and said, "The statement is true, according to the [b]law of the Medes and Persians, which may not be revoked."

13 Then they answered and spoke before the king, "Daniel, who is one of the exiles from Judah, pays [a]no attention to you, O king, or to the injunction which you signed, but keeps making his petition three times a day."

14 Then, as soon as the king heard this statement, he was deeply [a]distressed and set *his* mind on delivering Daniel; and even until sunset he kept exerting himself to rescue him.

15 Then these men came by agreement to the king and said to the king, "Recognize, O king, that it is a [a]law of the Medes and Persians that no injunction or statute which the king establishes may be changed."

25 [1]Or, *a mina* (50 shekels) from verb "to number" [2]Or, *a shekel*—from verb "to weigh" [3]Or, *and half-shekels* (sing.: *perēs*) from verb "to divide"
26 [a]Is. 13:6, 17; Jer. 27:7; 50:41-43
27 [a]Job 31:6; Ps. 62:9
28 [1]Aram.: *Pāras* [a]Is. 21:2; 45:1, 2; Dan. 5:31; 6:8, 28
29 [1]Or, *triumvir*
30 [a]Is. 21:4-9; 47:9; Jer. 51:11, 31, 39, 57
31 [1]Chap. 6:1 in Aram. [a]Dan. 6:1; 9:1
1 [1]Chap. 6:2 in Aram. [a]Esth. 1:1
2 [a]Dan. 2:48, 49; 5:16, 29 [b]Ezra 4:22; Esth. 7:4
3 [a]Dan. 5:12, 14; 9:23 [b]Gen. 41:40; Esth. 10:3
4 [a]Gen. 43:18; Judg. 14:4; Jer. 20:10; Dan. 3:8; Luke 20:20 [b]Luke 20:26; 23:14, 15
5 [a]Acts 24:13-16, 20, 21
6 [a]Dan. 5:10; 6:21
7 [1]Or, *pit*, and so throughout the chap. [a]Ps. 59:3; 62:4; 64:2-6; 83:1-3 [b]Ps. 10:9; Dan. 3:6; 6:16
8 [a]Esth. 3:12; 8:10; Is. 10:1 [b]Esth. 1:19; 8:8; Dan. 6:12, 15
9 [a]Ps. 118:9; 146:3
10 [1]Or, *because* [a]1 Kin. 8:48, 49; Ps. 5:7; Jon. 2:4 [b]Ps. 95:6 [c]Dan. 9:4-19; Luke 14:26; Acts 4:17, 19 [d]Ps. 34:1; Phil. 4:6; 1 Thess. 5:17, 18
11 [a]Ps. 37:32, 33; Dan. 6:6
12 [a]Dan. 3:8-12; Acts 16:19-21 [b]Esth. 1:19; Dan. 6:8
13 [a]Esth. 3:8; Dan. 3:12; Acts 5:29
14 [a]Mark 6:26
15 [a]Esth. 8:8; Ps. 94:20, 21; Dan. 6:8, 12

Daniel in the Lions' Den

16 Then the king gave orders, and Daniel was brought in and [a]cast into the lions' den. The king spoke and said to Daniel, "[1b]Your God whom you constantly serve will Himself deliver you."

17 And a [a]stone was brought and laid over the mouth of the den; and the king sealed it with his own signet ring and with the signet rings of his nobles, so that nothing might be changed in regard to Daniel.

18 Then the king went off to his palace and spent the night [a]fasting, and no entertainment was brought before him; and his [b]sleep fled from him.

19 Then the king arose with the dawn, at the break of day, and went in haste to the lions' den.

20 And when he had come near the den to Daniel, he cried out with a troubled voice. The king spoke and said to Daniel, "Daniel, servant of the living God, has your God, whom you constantly serve, been [a]able to deliver you from the lions?"

21 Then Daniel spoke [1]to the king, "O king, live forever!

22"My God [a]sent His angel and [b]shut the lions' mouths, and they have not harmed me, inasmuch as [1]I was found innocent before Him; and also [2]toward you, O king, I have committed no crime."

23 Then the king was very pleased and gave orders for Daniel to be taken up out of the den. So Daniel was taken up out of the den, and no injury whatever was found on him, because he had [a]trusted in his God.

24 The king then gave orders, and they brought those men who had [1]maliciously accused Daniel, and they [a]cast them, their [b]children, and their wives into the lions' den; and they had not reached the bottom of the den before the lions overpowered them and crushed all their bones.

25 Then Darius the king wrote to all the [a]peoples, nations, and *men of every* [1]language who were living in all the land: "[b]May your [2]peace abound!

26"[1]I [a]make a decree that in all the dominion of my kingdom men are to fear and tremble before the God of Daniel;

For He is the [b]living God and
[c]enduring forever,
And His kingdom is one which
will not be destroyed,
And His dominion *will be* [2]forever.

27 "He delivers and rescues and
performs signs and wonders
In heaven and on earth,
Who has *also* delivered Daniel
from the [1]power of the
lions."

28 So this Daniel enjoyed success in the reign of Darius and in the reign of Cyrus the Persian.

Chapter 7

Vision of the Four Beasts

IN the first year of Belshazzar king of Babylon Daniel saw a [a]dream and visions [1]in his mind *as he lay* on his bed; then he [b]wrote the dream down *and* related the following [2]summary of [3]it.

2 Daniel [1]said, "I was looking in my vision by night, and behold, the [a]four winds of heaven were stirring up the great sea.

3"And four great [a]beasts were coming up from the sea, different from one another.

4"The first *was* like a lion and had *the* wings of an eagle. I kept looking until its wings were plucked, and it was lifted up from the ground and made to stand on two feet like a man; a human [1]mind also was given to it.

5"And behold, another beast, a second one, resembling a bear. And it was raised up on one side, and three ribs *were* in its mouth between its teeth; and thus they said to it, 'Arise, devour much meat!'

6"After this I kept looking, and behold, another one, like a leopard, which had on its [1]back four wings of a bird; the beast also had four heads, and dominion was given to it.

7"After this I kept looking in the night visions, and behold, a fourth beast, dreadful and terrifying and extremely strong; and it had large iron teeth. It devoured and crushed, and trampled down the remainder with its feet; and it was different from all the beasts that were before it, and it had [a]ten horns.

8"While I was contemplating the horns, behold, another horn, a little one, came up among them, and three of the first horns were pulled out by the roots before it; and behold, [1]this horn possessed eyes like the eyes of a man, and a mouth uttering great *boasts*.

The Ancient of Days Reigns

9 "I kept looking
Until thrones were set up,

---

16 [1]Or, *May your God . . . Himself deliver you* [a]2 Sam. 3:39; Jer. 38:5; Dan. 6:7 [b]Job 5:19; Ps. 37:39, 40; Dan. 3:17, 28; 6:20

17 [a]Lam. 3:53; Matt. 27:66

18 [a]2 Sam. 12:16, 17 [b]Esth. 6:1; Ps. 77:4; Dan. 2:1

20 [a]Gen. 18:14; Num. 11:23; Jer. 32:17; Dan. 3:17

21 [1]Lit., *with*

22 [1]Lit., *innocence was found for me* [2]Lit., *before* [a]Num. 20:16; Is. 63:9; Dan. 3:28; Acts 12:11 [b]Ps. 91:11-13; 2 Tim. 4:17; Heb. 11:33

23 [a]1 Chr. 5:20; 2 Chr. 20:20; Ps. 118:8, 9; Is. 26:3; Dan. 3:17, 28

24 [1]Lit., *eaten the pieces of Daniel* [a]Deut. 19:18, 19; Esth. 7:10 [b]Deut. 24:16; 2 Kin. 14:6; Esth. 9:10

25 [1]Lit., *tongue* [2]Or, *welfare* or *prosperity* [a]Ezra 1:1, 2; Esth. 3:12; 8:9; Dan. 4:1 [b]Ezra 4:17; 1 Pet. 1:2

26 [1]Lit., *From me a decree is made* [2]Lit., *to the end* [a]Ezra 6:8-12; 7:13, 21; Dan. 3:29 [b]Dan. 6:20; Hos. 1:10; Rom. 9:26 [c]Ps. 93:1, 2; Mal. 3:6

27 [1]Lit., *hand*

1 [1]Lit., *of his head* [2]Or, *beginning* [3]Lit., *words* [a]Job 33:14-16; Dan. 1:17; 2:1, 26-28; 4:5-9; Joel 2:28 [b]Jer. 36:4, 32

2 [1]Lit., *spoke and said* [a]Rev. 7:1

3 [a]Rev. 13:1

4 [1]Lit., *heart*

6 [1]Or, *sides*

7 [a]Rev. 12:3; 13:1

8 [1]Lit., *in this horn* were *eyes*

And the Ancient of Days took
His seat;
His [a]vesture *was* like white
snow,
And the [b]hair of His head like
pure wool.
His [c]throne *was* ablaze with
flames,
Its [d]wheels *were* a burning
fire.
10 "A river of [a]fire was flowing
And coming out from before
Him;
[b]Thousands upon thousands
were attending Him,
And [c]myriads upon myriads
were standing before Him;
The [d]court sat,
And [e]the books were opened.
11"Then I kept looking because of
the sound of the [1]boastful words
which the horn was speaking; I kept
looking until the beast was slain,
and its body was destroyed and giv-
en to the [a]burning fire.
12"As for the rest of the beasts,
their dominion was taken away, but
an extension of life was granted to
them for an appointed period of
time.

The Son of Man Presented

13 "I kept looking in the night vi-
sions,
And behold, with the clouds of
heaven
One like a [a]Son of Man was
coming,
And He came up to the An-
cient of Days
And was presented before
Him.
14 "And to Him was given [a]domin-
ion,
Glory and [b]a kingdom,
[c]That all the peoples, nations,
and *men of every* language
Might serve Him.
His dominion is an everlasting
dominion
Which will not pass away;
And His kingdom is one
Which will [d]not be destroyed.

The Vision Interpreted

15"As for me, Daniel, my spirit
was distressed [1]within me, and the
visions [2]in my mind kept [a]alarming
me.
16"I approached one of those who
were [a]standing by and began asking
him the exact meaning of all this. So
he [b]told me and made known to me
the interpretation of these things:
17 'These great beasts, which are
four *in number,* are four kings *who*
will arise from the earth.
18 'But the [1a]saints of the Highest
One will [b]receive the kingdom and
possess the kingdom forever, [2]for
all ages to come.'
19"Then I desired to know the
exact meaning of the fourth beast,
which was different from all the others, exceedingly dreadful, with its
teeth of iron and its claws of bronze,
and which devoured, crushed, and
trampled down the remainder with
its feet,
20 and *the meaning* of the ten
horns that *were* on its head, and the
other *horn* which came up, and before which three *of them* fell,
namely, that horn which had eyes
and a mouth uttering great *boasts,*
and [1]which was larger in appearance than its associates.
21"I kept looking, and that horn
was [a]waging war with the [1]saints
and overpowering them
22 until the Ancient of Days came,
and [a]judgment was [1]passed in favor
of the [2]saints of the Highest One,
and the time arrived when the
[2]saints took possession of the kingdom.
23"Thus he said: 'The fourth beast
will be a fourth kingdom on the
earth, which will be different from
all the *other* kingdoms, and it will
devour the whole earth and tread it
down and crush it.
24 'As for the ten horns, out of this
kingdom ten kings will arise; and
another will arise after them, and he
will be different from the previous
ones and will subdue three kings.
25 'And he will [a]speak [1]out against
the [b]Most High and [c]wear down the
[2]saints of the Highest One, and he
will intend to make alterations in
times and in law; and [3]they will be
given into his hand for a [4d]time,
[4]times, and half a [4]time.
26 'But the court will sit *for judgment,* and his dominion will be
[a]taken away, [1]annihilated and destroyed [2]forever.
27 'Then the [1a]sovereignty, the dominion, and the greatness of *all* the
kingdoms under the whole heaven
will be given to the people of the
[2]saints of the Highest One; His kingdom *will be* an [b]everlasting kingdom, and all the dominions will
[c]serve and obey Him.'
28"[1]At this point the revelation
ended. As for me, Daniel, my
thoughts were greatly alarming me
and my [2]face grew pale, but I [a]kept
the matter [3]to myself."

9 [a]Mark 9:3 [b]Rev. 1:14 [c]Ezek. 1:13, 26 [d]Ezek. 10:2, 6
10 [a]Ps. 18:8; 50:3; 97:3; Is. 30:27, 33 [b]Rev. 5:11 [c]Deut. 33:2 [d]Ps. 96:11-13; Dan. 7:22, 26 [e]Dan. 12:1; Rev. 20:11-15
11 [1]Lit., *great* [a]Rev. 19:20; 20:10
13 [a]Matt. 26:64; Mark 14:62
14 [a]Dan. 7:27; 1 Cor. 15:27; Eph. 1:20-22; Phil. 2:9-11; Rev. 1:6 [b]Dan. 2:37 [c]Ps. 72:11; 102:22 [d]Heb. 12:28
15 [1]Lit., *in the midst of* its *sheath* [2]Lit., *of my head* [a]Dan. 4:19; 7:28
16 [a]Zech. 1:9, 19; Rev. 5:5; 7:13, 14 [b]Dan. 8:16, 17
18 [1]Lit., *holy ones* [2]Lit., *and unto the age of the ages* [a]Dan. 7:22, 25, 27 [b]Ps. 149:5-9; Is. 60:12-14; Dan. 7:14; Rev. 2:26, 27; 20:4
20 [1]Lit., *its appearance was larger*
21 [1]Lit., *holy ones* [a]Rev. 13:7
22 [1]Lit., *given for* [2]Lit., *holy ones* [a]Dan. 7:10; 1 Cor. 6:2, 3
25 [1]Lit., *words* [2]Lit., *holy ones* [3]I.e., the saints [4]I.e., year(s) [a]Dan. 11:36; Rev. 13:6 [b]Dan. 3:26; 4:2, 17, 34 [c]Rev. 13:7 [d]Dan. 12:7; Rev. 12:14
26 [1]Lit., *to annihilate and to destroy* [2]Lit., *to the end* [a]Rev. 17:14; 19:2
27 [1]Or, *kingdom* [2]Lit., *holy ones* [a]Is. 54:3; Dan. 7:14, 18, 22; Rev. 20:4 [b]Ps. 145:13; Is. 9:7; Dan. 2:44; 4:34; 7:14 [c]Ps. 2:6-12; 22:27; 72:11; 86:9; Is. 60:12; Rev. 11:1
28 [1]Lit., *To here the end of the word* [2]Lit., *brightness was changing upon me* [3]Lit., *in my heart* [a]Luke 2:19, 51

Chapter 8

Vision of the Ram and Goat

In the third year of the reign of Belshazzar the king a vision appeared
to me, [1]Daniel, subsequent to the
one which appeared to me [2]previ-
ously.
2 And I [a]looked in the vision, and
it came about while I was looking,
that I was in the citadel of [b]Susa,
which is in the province of [c]Elam;
and I looked in the vision, and I myself was beside the Ulai [1]Canal.
3 Then I lifted my gaze and
looked, and behold, a [a]ram which
had two horns was standing in front
of the [1]canal. Now the two horns
were [2]long, but one *was* [2]longer than
the other, with the [2]longer one coming up last.
4 I saw the ram [a]butting westward, northward, and southward,
and no *other* beasts could stand before him, nor was there anyone to
rescue from his [1]power; but he did
as he pleased and magnified *himself.*
5 While I was observing, behold,
a male goat was coming from the
west over the surface of the whole
earth without touching the ground;
and the [1]goat *had* a [a]conspicuous
horn between his eyes.
6 And he came up to the ram that
had the two horns, which I had seen
standing in front of the [1]canal, and
rushed at him in his mighty wrath.
7 And I saw him come beside the
ram, and he was enraged at him;
and he struck the ram and shattered
his two horns, and the ram had no
strength to withstand him. So he
hurled him to the ground and trampled on him, and there was none to
rescue the ram from his [1]power.
8 Then the male goat magnified
himself exceedingly. But as soon as
[a]he was mighty, the large horn was
broken; and in its place there came
up four conspicuous *horns* toward
the [b]four winds of heaven.

The Little Horn

9 And out of one of them came
forth a rather [a]small horn which
grew exceedingly great toward the
south, toward the east, and toward
the [1b]Beautiful *Land.*
10 And it grew up to the host of
heaven and caused some of the host
and some of the [a]stars to fall to the
earth, and it [b]trampled them down.
11 It even [a]magnified *itself* [1]to be
equal with the [2]Commander of the
host; and it removed the [b]regular
sacrifice from Him, and the place of
His sanctuary was thrown down.
12 And on account of transgression the host will be given over *to
the horn* along with the regular sacrifice; and it will [a]fling truth to the
ground and perform *its will* and
prosper.
13 Then I heard a [a]holy one speaking, and another holy one said to
that particular one who was speaking, "[b]How long will the vision
about the regular sacrifice apply,
[1]while the transgression causes horror, so as to allow both the holy
place and the host [2]to be
[c]trampled?"
14 And he said to me, "For [a]2,300
evenings *and* mornings; then the
holy place will be [1]properly restored."

Interpretation of the Vision

15 And it came about when I, Daniel, had seen the vision, that I sought
[1]to understand it; and behold, standing before me was one [2]who looked
like a [a]man.
16 And I heard the voice of a man
between *the banks of* Ulai, and he
called out and said, "[a]Gabriel, give
this *man* an understanding of the vision."
17 So he came near to where I was
standing, and when he came I was
frightened and [a]fell on my face; but
he said to me, "Son of man, understand that the vision pertains to the
[b]time of the end."
18 Now while he was talking with
me, I [a]sank into a deep sleep with
my face to the ground; but he
[b]touched me and made me stand
[1]upright.
19 And he said, "Behold, I am
going to [a]let you know what will occur at the final period of the indignation, for *it* pertains to the appointed
time of the end.

The Ram's Identity

20 "The ram which you saw with
the two horns represents the kings
of Media and Persia.

The Goat

21 "And the shaggy [1]goat *represents* the [2]kingdom of Greece, and
the large horn that is between his
eyes is the first king.
22 "And the broken *horn* and the
four *horns that* arose in its place
represent four kingdoms *which* will
arise from *his* nation, although not
with his power.

1 [1]Lit., *I, Daniel* [2]Lit., *at the beginning*
2 [1]Or, *river* [a]Num. 12:6; Dan. 7:2, 15; 8:3 [b]Neh. 1:1; Esth. 1:2; 2:8 [c]Gen. 10:22; 14:1; Is. 11:11; Jer. 25:25; Ezek. 32:24
3 [1]Or, *river* [2]Lit., *high(er)* [a]Dan. 8:20
4 [1]Lit., *hand* [a]Deut. 33:17; 1 Kin. 22:11; Ezek. 34:21
5 [1]Lit., *buck* [a]Dan. 8:8, 21; 11:3
6 [1]Or, *river*
7 [1]Lit., *hand*
8 [a]2 Chr. 26:16; Dan. 5:20 [b]Dan. 7:2; Rev. 7:1
9 [1]I.e., Palestine [a]Dan. 8:23 [b]Dan. 11:16, 41
10 [a]Is. 14:13 [b]Dan. 7:7; 8:7
11 [1]Lit., *up to the* [2]Or, *Prince* [a]2 Kin. 19:22, 23; 2 Chr. 32:15-17; Is. 37:23; Dan. 8:25; 11:36, 37 [b]Ezek. 46:14; Dan. 11:31; 12:11
12 [a]Is. 59:14
13 [1]Or possibly, *and the transgression that horrifies* [2]Lit., *as a trampling* [a]Dan. 4:13, 23 [b]Ps. 74:10; 79:5; Is. 6:11; Dan. 12:6, 8; Rev. 6:10 [c]Is. 63:18; Jer. 12:10; Luke 21:24; Heb. 10:29; Rev. 11:2
14 [1]Lit., *vindicated* [a]Dan. 7:25; 12:7, 11; Rev. 11:2, 3; 12:14; 13:5
15 [1]Lit., *understanding* [2]Lit., *like the appearance of a man* [a]Dan. 7:13; 10:16, 18
16 [a]Dan. 9:21; Luke 1:19, 26
17 [a]Ezek. 1:28; 44:4; Dan. 2:46 [b]Dan. 8:19; 11:35, 40
18 [1]Lit., *on my standing* [a]Dan. 10:9; Luke 9:32 [b]Ezek. 2:2; Dan. 10:10, 16, 18
19 [a]Dan. 8:15-17
21 [1]Lit., *buck* [2]Lit., *king*

23 “And in the latter period of their rule,
When the transgressors have run *their course,*
A king will arise
Insolent and skilled in intrigue.
24 “And his power will be mighty, but not by his *own* power,
And he will [a]destroy to an extraordinary degree
And prosper and perform *his will;*
He will destroy mighty men and the holy people.
25 “And through his shrewdness
He will cause deceit to succeed by his [1]influence;
And he will magnify *himself* in his heart,
And he will [2]destroy many while *they are* [3]at ease.
He will even [4]oppose the Prince of princes,
But he will be broken without [1a]human agency.
26 “And the vision of the evenings and mornings
Which has been told is true;
But keep the vision secret,
For *it* pertains to many days *in the future.*”

27 Then I, Daniel, was [1a]exhausted and sick for days. Then I got up *again* and carried on the king's business; but I was astounded at the vision, and there was none to [2]explain *it.*

CHAPTER 9

Daniel's Prayer for His People

IN the first year of [a]Darius the son of Ahasuerus, of Median descent, who was made king over the kingdom of the Chaldeans—

2 in the first year of his reign I, Daniel, observed in the books the number of the years which was *revealed as* the word of the LORD to [a]Jeremiah the prophet for the completion of the desolations of Jerusalem, *namely,* [a]seventy years.

3 So I [1]gave my attention to the Lord God to seek *Him by* prayer and supplications, with fasting, sackcloth, and ashes.

4 And I prayed to the LORD my God and confessed and said, “Alas, O Lord, the [a]great and awesome God, who [b]keeps His covenant and lovingkindness for those who love Him and keep His commandments,

5 we have [a]sinned, committed iniquity, acted wickedly, and [b]rebelled, even [c]turning aside from Thy commandments and ordinances.

6 “Moreover, we have not [a]listened to Thy servants the prophets, who spoke in Thy name to our kings, our princes, our fathers, and all the people of the land.

7 “[a]Righteousness belongs to Thee, O Lord, but to us [1b]open shame, as it is this day—to the men of Judah, the inhabitants of Jerusalem, and all Israel, those who are near by and those who are far away in all the countries to which Thou hast driven them, because of their unfaithful deeds which they have committed against Thee.

8 “[1]Open shame belongs to us, O Lord, to our kings, our princes, and our fathers, because we have sinned against Thee.

9 “To the Lord our God belong [a]compassion and forgiveness, [1]for we have [b]rebelled against Him;

10 nor have we obeyed the voice of the LORD our God, to walk in His [1]teachings which He [a]set before us through His servants the prophets.

11 “Indeed all Israel has transgressed Thy law and turned aside, not obeying Thy voice; so the curse has been poured out on us, along with the oath which is written in the law of Moses the servant of God, for we have sinned against Him.

12 “Thus He has [a]confirmed His words which He had spoken against us and against our [1b]rulers who ruled us, to bring on us great calamity; for under the whole heaven there has [c]not been done *anything* like what was done to Jerusalem.

13 “As it is written in the [a]law of Moses, all this calamity has come on us; yet we have [b]not [1]sought the favor of the LORD our God by [c]turning from our iniquity and [2]giving attention to Thy truth.

14 “Therefore, the LORD has [1a]kept the calamity in store and brought it on us; for the LORD our God is [b]righteous with respect to all His deeds which He has done, but we have not obeyed His voice.

15 “And now, O Lord our God, who hast [a]brought Thy people out of the land of Egypt with a mighty hand and hast [b]made a name for Thyself, as it is this day—we have sinned, we have been wicked.

16 “O Lord, in accordance with all Thy [1]righteous acts, let now Thine [a]anger and Thy wrath turn away from Thy city Jerusalem, Thy [b]holy mountain; for because of our sins and the iniquities of our fathers, Je-

24 [a]Dan. 8:11-13; 12:7; Rev. 16:6
25 [1]Lit., *hand* [2]Or, *corrupt* [3]Or, *secure* [4]Lit., *stand against* [a]Job 34:20; Dan. 2:34, 45
27 [1]Or, *done in* [2]Lit., *make me understand* [a]Dan. 7:28; 8:17; Hab. 3:16
1 [a]Dan. 5:31; 11:1
2 [a]2 Chr. 36:21; Ezra 1:1; Jer. 25:11, 12; 29:10; Zech. 7:5
3 [1]Lit., *set my face*
4 [a]Deut. 7:21; Neh. 9:32 [b]Deut. 7:9
5 [a]Ps. 106:6 [b]Lam. 1:18, 20 [c]Ps. 119:176; Is. 53:6; Dan. 9:11
6 [a]Jer. 44:4, 5, 21
7 [1]Lit., *the shame of face* [a]Jer. 23:6; 33:16; Dan. 9:18 [b]Ps. 44:15; Jer. 2:26, 27; 3:25
8 [1]Lit., *The shame of face*
9 [1]Or, *though* [a]Neh. 9:17; Ps. 130:4 [b]Ps. 106:43; Jer. 14:7; Dan. 9:5, 6
10 [1]Or, *laws* [a]2 Kin. 17:13-15; 18:12
12 [1]Lit., *judges who judged us* [a]Is. 44:26; Jer. 44:2-6; Lam. 2:17; Zech. 1:6 [b]Job 12:17; Ps. 82:2-7; 148:11 [c]Lam. 1:12; 2:13; Ezek. 5:9
13 [1]Lit., *softened the face of* [2]Or, *having insight into* [a]Lev. 26:14-45; Deut. 28:15-68; Dan. 9:11 [b]Job 36:13; Is.9:13; Jer. 2:30; 5:3 [c]Jer. 31:18
14 [1]Lit., *watched over the evil* [a]Jer. 31:28; 44:27 [b]Ps. 51:14; Dan. 9:7
15 [a]Deut. 5:15 [b]Neh. 9:10; Jer. 32:20
16 [1]Lit., *righteousnesses* [a]Jer. 32:31, 32 [b]Ps. 87:1-3; Dan. 9:20; Joel 3:17; Zech. 8:3

rusalem and Thy people *have be-*
come a [c]reproach to all those
around us.
17"So now, our God, listen to the
prayer of Thy servant and to his
supplications, and for Thy sake, O
Lord, [a]let Thy face shine on Thy
[b]desolate sanctuary.
18"O my God, [a]incline Thine ear
and hear! Open Thine eyes and [b]see
our desolations and the city which is
[c]called by Thy name; for we are not
[d]presenting our supplications before Thee on account of any merits
of our own, but on account of Thy
great compassion.
19"O Lord, hear! O Lord, forgive! O
Lord, listen and take action! For
Thine own sake, O my God, do not
[a]delay, because Thy city and Thy
people are called by Thy name."

Gabriel Brings an Answer

20 Now while I was [a]speaking and
praying, and confessing my sin and
the sin of [b]my people Israel, and presenting my supplication before the
LORD my God in behalf of the holy
mountain of my God,
21 while I was still speaking in
prayer, then the man [a]Gabriel,
whom I had seen in the vision previously, came to me in *my* extreme
weariness about the time of the
[b]evening offering.
22 And he gave *me* instruction and
talked with me, and said, "O Daniel,
I have now come forth to give you
insight with [a]understanding.
23"At the beginning of your supplications the command was issued,
and I have come to tell *you,* for you
are highly esteemed; so give heed to
the message and gain [a]understand-
ing of the vision.

Seventy Weeks and the Messiah

24"Seventy [1a]weeks have been decreed for your people and your holy
city, to [2]finish the transgression, to
[3]make an end of sin, to [b]make atonement for iniquity, to bring in [c]ever-
lasting righteousness, to seal up vision and [4]prophecy, and to anoint
the most holy *place.*
25"So you are to know and discern
that from the issuing of a [1a]decree to
restore and rebuild Jerusalem until
[2b]Messiah the [c]Prince *there will be*
seven weeks and sixty-two weeks; it
will be built again, with [3]plaza and
moat, even in times of distress.
26"Then after the sixty-two weeks
the [1]Messiah will be [a]cut off and
have [2]nothing, and the people of the
prince who is to come will [b]destroy
the city and the sanctuary. And [3]its
end *will come* with a [c]flood; even to
the end there will be war; desolations are determined.
27"And he will make a firm covenant with the many for one week,
but in the middle of the week he will
put a stop to sacrifice and grain offering; and on the wing of [1a]abomi-
nations *will come* one who [2]makes
desolate, even until a [b]complete destruction, one that is decreed, is
poured out on the one who [2]makes
desolate."

CHAPTER 10

Daniel Is Terrified By a Vision

IN the third year of [a]Cyrus king of
Persia a message was revealed to
Daniel, who was named Belteshazzar; and the message was true and
one of great conflict, but he understood the message and had an [b]un-
derstanding of the vision.
2 In those days I, Daniel, had
been [a]mourning for three entire
weeks.
3 I did not eat any tasty food, nor
did meat or wine enter my mouth,
nor did I use any ointment at all,
until the entire three weeks were
completed.
4 And on the twenty-fourth day
of the first month, while I was by the
bank of the great [a]river, that is, the
[1]Tigris,
5 I lifted my eyes and looked, and
behold, there was a certain man
[a]dressed in linen, whose waist was
[b]girded with *a belt of* pure [c]gold of
Uphaz.
6 His body also was like [1]beryl,
his face [2]had the appearance of
lightning, his eyes were like flaming
torches, his arms and feet like the
gleam of polished bronze, and the
sound of his words like the sound of
a [3]tumult.
7 Now I, Daniel, [a]alone saw the
vision, while the [b]men who were
with me did not see the vision; nevertheless, a great [c]dread fell on
them, and they ran away to hide
themselves.
8 So I was [a]left alone and saw
this great vision; yet no strength
was [b]left in me, for my natural color
turned to a deathly pallor, and I retained no strength.
9 But I heard the sound of his
words; and as soon as I heard the
sound of his words, I [a]fell into a
deep sleep on my face, with my face
to the ground.

16 [c]Ezek. 5:14
17 [a]Num. 6:24-26; Ps. 80:3, 7, 19 [b]Lam. 5:18
18 [a]Is. 37:17 [b]Ps. 80:14 [c]Jer. 7:10-12 [d]Jer. 36:7
19 [a]Ps. 44:23; 74:10, 11
20 [a]Ps. 145:18; Is. 58:9; Dan. 9:3; 10:12 [b]Is. 6:5
21 [a]Dan. 8:16; Luke 1:19, 26 [b]Ex. 29:39; 1 Kin. 18:36; Ezra 9:4
22 [a]Dan. 8:16; 10:21; Zech. 1:9
23 [a]Matt. 24:15
24 [1]Or, *units of seven,* and so throughout the chap. [2]Or, *restrain* [3]Another reading is: *seal up sins* [4]Lit., *prophet* [a]Lev. 25:8; Num. 14:34; Ezek. 4:6 [b]2 Chr. 29:24; Is. 53:10; Rom. 5:10 [c]Is. 51:6, 8; 56:1; Jer. 23:5, 6; Rom. 3:21, 22
25 [1]Lit., *word* [2]Or, *an anointed one* [3]Or, *streets* [a]Ezra 4:24; 6:1-15; Neh. 2:1-8; 3:1 [b]John 1:41; 4:25 [c]Is. 9:6; Dan. 8:11
26 [1]Or, *anointed one* [2]Or, *no one* [3]Or, *his* [a]Is. 53:8; Mark 9:12; Luke 24:26 [b]Matt. 24:2; Mark 13:2; Luke 19:43, 44 [c]Nah. 1:8
27 [1]Or, *detestable things* [2]Or, *causes horror* [a]Dan. 11:31; Matt. 24:15; Mark 13:14; Luke 21:20 [b]Is. 10:23; 28:22
1 [a]Dan. 1:21; 6:28 [b]Dan. 1:17; 2:21
2 [a]Ezra 9:4, 5; Neh. 1:4
4 [1]Heb., *Hiddeqel* [a]Ezek. 1:3; Dan. 8:2
5 [a]Ezek. 9:2; Dan. 12:6, 7 [b]Rev. 1:13; 15:6 [c]Jer. 10:9
6 [1]Or, *yellow serpentine* [2]Lit., *like* [3]Or, *roaring*
7 [a]2 Kin. 6:17 [b]Acts 9:7 [c]Ezek. 12:18
8 [a]Gen. 32:24 [b]Dan. 7:28; 8:27; Hab. 3:16
9 [a]Gen. 15:12; Job 4:13; Dan. 8:18

Daniel Comforted

10 Then behold, a hand touched
me and set me trembling on my
hands and knees.
11 And he said to me, "O Daniel,
man of high esteem, [a]understand
the words that I am about to tell you
and [b]stand upright, for I have now
been sent to you." And when he had
spoken this word to me, I stood up
[c]trembling.
12 Then he said to me, "[a]Do not be
afraid, Daniel, for from the first day
that you set your heart on understanding *this* and on [b]humbling
yourself before your God, your
words were heard, and I have come
in response [c]to your words.
13"But the prince of the kingdom
of Persia was withstanding me for
twenty-one days; then behold, [a]Mi-
chael, one of the chief princes, came
to help me, for I had been left there
with the kings of Persia.
14"Now I have come to give you an
understanding of what will happen
to your people in the [1a]latter days,
for the vision pertains to [b]the days
yet *future*."
15 And when he had spoken to me
according to these words, I turned
my face toward the ground and became [a]speechless.
16 And behold, one who resembled a human being was [a]touching
my lips; then I opened my mouth
and spoke, and said to him who was
standing before me, "O my lord, as a
result of the vision [b]anguish has
come upon me, and I have retained
no strength.
17"For [a]how can such a servant of
my lord talk with such as my lord?
As for me, there remains just now
no strength in me, nor has any
breath been left in me."
18 Then *this* one with human appearance touched me again and
[a]strengthened me.
19 And he said, "O man of high esteem, [a]do not be afraid. Peace [1]be
with you; take [b]courage and be courageous!" Now as soon as he spoke
to me, I received strength and said,
"May my lord speak, for you have
[c]strengthened me."
20 Then he said, "Do you [1]under-
stand why I came to you? But I shall
now return to fight against the
[2]prince of Persia; so I am going
forth, and behold, the [2a]prince of
[3]Greece is about to come.
21"However, I will tell you what is
inscribed in the writing of [a]truth.
(Yet there is no one who stands
firmly with me against these *forces*
except Michael your prince.

Chapter 11

Conflicts to Come

"AND in the [a]first year of Darius
the Mede, I arose to be an encouragement and a protection for him.)
2"And now I will tell you the
[a]truth. Behold, three more kings are
going to arise in Persia. Then a
fourth will gain far more riches than
all *of them;* as soon as he becomes
strong through his riches, he will
arouse the whole *empire* against the
realm of [b]Greece.
3"And a [a]mighty king will arise,
and he will rule with great authority
and [b]do as he pleases.
4"But as soon as he has arisen, his
kingdom will be broken up and parceled out [a]toward the [b]four [1]points
of the compass, though not to his
own descendants, nor according to
his authority which he wielded; for
his sovereignty will be [c]uprooted
and *given* to others besides [2]them.
5"Then the [a]king of the South will
grow strong, [1]along with *one* of his
princes [2]who will gain ascendancy
over him and obtain dominion; his
domain *will be* a great dominion *indeed.*
6"And after some years they will
form an alliance, and the daughter
of the king of the South will come to
the [a]king of the North to carry out [1]a
peaceful arrangement. But she will
not retain her [2]position of power,
nor will he remain with his [3]power,
but she will be given up, along with
those who brought her in, and the
one who sired her, as well as he who
supported her in *those* times.
7"But one of the [1]descendants of
her line will arise in his place, and he
will come against *their* army and enter the [a]fortress of the king of the
North, and he will deal with them
and display *great* strength.
8"And also their [a]gods with their
[1]metal images *and* their precious
vessels of silver and gold he will
take into captivity to Egypt, and he
on his part will [2]refrain from *attacking* the king of the North for *some*
years.
9"Then [1]the latter will enter the
realm of the king of the South, but
will return to his *own* land.
10"And his sons will [1]mobilize and
assemble a multitude of great
forces; and one of them will keep on
coming and [a]overflow and pass

11 [a]Dan. 8:16, 17 [b]Ezek. 2:1 [c]Job 4:14, 15
12 [a]Is. 41:10, 14; Dan. 10:19 [b]Dan. 9:20-23; 10:2, 3 [c]Acts 10:30, 31
13 [a]Dan. 10:21; 12:1; Jude 9; Rev. 12:7
14 [1]Lit., *end of the days* [a]Deut. 31:29; Dan. 2:28 [b]Dan. 8:26; 12:4, 9
15 [a]Ezek. 24:27; Luke 1:20
16 [a]Is. 6:7; Jer. 1:9 [b]Dan. 7:15, 28; 8:17, 27; 10:8, 9
17 [a]Ex. 24:10, 11; Is. 6:1-5
18 [a]Is. 35:3, 4
19 [1]Lit., *to you* [a]Judg. 6:23; Is. 43:1; Dan. 10:12 [b]Josh. 1:6, 7, 9; Is. 35:4 [c]Ps. 138:3; 2 Cor. 12:9
20 [1]Lit., *know* [2]I.e., Satanic angel [3]Heb., *Javan* [a]Dan. 8:21; 11:2
21 [a]Dan. 12:1, 4
1 [a]Dan. 5:31; 9:1
2 [a]Dan. 8:26; 10:1, 21 [b]Dan. 8:21; 10:20
3 [a]Dan. 8:5, 21 [b]Dan. 5:19; 8:4; 11:16, 36
4 [1]Lit., *winds of the heaven* [2]I.e., his descendants [a]Dan. 8:8, 22 [b]Dan. 7:2; 8:8; Jer. 49:36; Ezek. 37:9; Zech. 2:6; Rev. 7:1 [c]Jer. 12:15, 17; 18:7
5 [1]Lit., *and* [2]Lit., *and he* [a]Dan. 11:9, 11, 14, 25, 40
6 [1]Or, *an equitable agreement* [2]Lit., *strength of arm* [3]Lit., *arm* [a]Dan. 11:7, 13, 15, 40
7 [1]Lit., *branch of her roots* [a]Dan. 11:19, 38, 39
8 [1]Lit., *cast images* [2]Or, *stand against the king* [a]Is. 37:19; 46:1, 2; Jer. 43:12, 13
9 [1]Lit., *he will,* and so throughout the chap.
10 [1]Or, *wage war* [a]Is. 8:8; Jer. 46:7, 8; 51:42; Dan. 11:26, 40

through, that he may [2]again wage war up to his *very* fortress.

11"And the king of the South will be enraged and go forth and fight with the king of the North. Then the latter will raise a great multitude, but *that* multitude will be given into the hand of the *former*.

12"When the multitude is carried away, his heart will be lifted up, and he will cause tens of thousands to fall; yet he will not prevail.

13"For the king of the North will again raise a greater multitude than the former, and [1]after an [a]interval of some years he will [2]press on with a great army and much equipment.

14"Now in those times many will rise up against the king of the South; the violent ones among your people will also lift themselves up in order to fulfill the vision, but they will [1]fall down.

15"Then the king of the North will come, cast up a siege [a]mound, and capture a well-fortified city; and the forces of the South will not stand *their ground,* not even their choicest troops, for there will be no strength to make a stand.

16"But he who comes against him will [a]do as he pleases, and [b]no one will *be able to* withstand him; he will also stay *for a time* in the [1c]Beautiful Land, with destruction in his hand.

17"And he will [a]set his face to come with the power of his whole kingdom, [1]bringing with him [2]a proposal of peace which he will put into effect; he will also give him the daughter of women to ruin it. But she will not take a stand *for him* or be [3]on his side.

18"Then he will turn his face to the [a]coastlands and capture many. But a commander will put a stop to his scorn against him; moreover, he will [b]repay him for his scorn.

19"So he will turn his face toward the fortresses of his own land, but he will [a]stumble and fall and be found [b]no more.

20"Then in his place one will arise who will [a]send an [1]oppressor through the [2]Jewel of *his* kingdom; yet within a few days he will be shattered, though neither in anger nor in battle.

21"And in his place a despicable person will arise, on whom the honor of kingship has not been conferred, but he will come in a time of tranquility and seize the kingdom by intrigue.

22"And the overflowing [a]forces will be flooded away before him and shattered, and also the prince of the covenant.

23"And after an alliance is made with him he will practice deception, and he will go up and gain power with a small *force of* people.

24"In a time of tranquility he will enter the [a]richest *parts* of the realm, and he will accomplish what his fathers never did, nor his ancestors; he will distribute plunder, booty, and possessions among them, and he will devise his schemes against strongholds, but *only* for a time.

25"And he will stir up his strength and [1]courage against the king of the South with a large army; so the king of the South will mobilize an extremely large and mighty army for war; but he will not stand, for schemes will be devised against him.

26"And those who eat his choice food will [1]destroy him, and his army will [2a]overflow, but many will fall down slain.

27"As for both kings, their hearts will be *intent* on [a]evil, and they will [b]speak lies *to each other* at the same table; but it will not succeed, for the [c]end is still *to come* at the appointed time.

28"Then he will return to his land with much [1]plunder; but his heart will be *set* against the holy covenant, and he will take action and *then* return to his *own* land.

29"At the appointed time he will return and come into the South, but [1]this last time it will not turn out the way it did before.

30"For ships of [a]Kittim will come against him; therefore he will be disheartened, and will return and become enraged at the holy covenant and take action; so he will come back and show regard for those who forsake the holy covenant.

31"And forces from him will arise, [a]desecrate the sanctuary fortress, and do away with the regular sacrifice. And they will set up the [b]abomination [1]of desolation.

32"And by [a]smooth *words* he will [1]turn to godlessness those who act wickedly toward the covenant, but the people who know their God will display [b]strength and take action.

33"And [1]those who have insight among the people will give understanding to the many; yet they will [a]fall by sword and by flame, by captivity and by plunder, for *many* days.

34"Now when they fall they will be

10 [2]Or, *return and wage*
13 [1]Lit., *at the end of the times, years* [2]Or, *keep on coming* [a]Dan. 4:16; 12:7
14 [1]Lit., *stumble,* and so throughout the chap.
15 [a]Jer. 6:6; Ezek. 4:2; 17:17
16 [1]I.e., Palestine [a]Dan. 5:19; 11:3, 36 [b]Josh. 1:5 [c]Dan. 8:9; 11:41
17 [1]Lit., *and* [2]Lit., *equitable things* [3]Lit., *for him;* i.e., for her father [a]2 Kin. 12:17; Ezek. 4:3, 7
18 [a]Gen. 10:5; Is. 66:19; Jer. 2:10; 31:10; Zeph. 2:11 [b]Hos. 12:14
19 [a]Ps. 27:2; Jer. 46:6 [b]Job 20:8; Ps. 37:36; Ezek. 26:21
20 [1]Or, *exactor* of tribute [2]Lit., *adornment;* i.e., probably Jerusalem and its temple [a]Is. 60:17
22 [a]Dan. 9:26; 11:10
24 [a]Num. 13:20; Neh. 9:25; Ezek. 34:14
25 [1]Lit., *heart*
26 [1]Lit., *break* [2]Or, *be swept away, and many* [a]Dan. 11:10, 40
27 [a]Ps. 52:1; 64:6 [b]Jer. 9:3-5; 41:1-3 [c]Dan. 8:19; 11:35, 40; Hab. 2:3
28 [1]Lit., *possessions*
29 [1]Lit., *it will not happen as the first and as the last*
30 [a]Gen. 10:4; Num. 24:24; Is. 23:1, 12; Jer. 2:10
31 [1]Lit., *that makes desolate,* or *that causes horror* [a]Dan. 8:11-13; 12:11 [b]Dan. 9:27; 12:11; Matt. 24:15; Mark 13:14
32 [1]Or, *pollute those* [a]Dan. 11:21, 34 [b]Mic. 5:7-9; Zech. 9:13-16; 10:3-6
33 [1]Or, *instructors of* the *people* [a]Matt. 24:9; John 16:2; Heb. 11:36-38

granted a little help, and many will
[a]join with them in [b]hypocrisy.
35"And some of those who have
insight will fall, in order to [a]refine,
[b]purge, and make them [c]pure, until
the end time; because *it is* still *to*
come at the appointed time.
36"Then the king will [a]do as he
pleases, and he will exalt and [b]mag-
nify himself above every god, and
will speak [c]monstrous things
against the [d]God of gods; and he will
prosper until the [e]indignation is finished, for that which is [f]decreed will
be done.
37"And he will show no regard for
the [1]gods of his fathers or for the
desire of women, nor will he show
regard for any *other* god; for he will
magnify himself above *them* all.
38"But instead he will honor a god
of fortresses, a god whom his fathers did not know; he will honor
him with gold, silver, costly stones,
and treasures.
39"And he will take action against
the strongest of fortresses with *the*
help of a foreign god; he will give
great honor to those who acknowledge *him,* and he will cause them to
rule over the many, and will parcel
out land for a price.
40"And at the end [a]time the king of
the South will collide with him, and
the king of the North will [b]storm
against him with chariots, with
horsemen, and with many ships;
and he will enter countries, overflow *them,* and pass through.
41"He will also enter the [1]Beautiful
Land, and many *countries* will fall;
but these will be rescued out of his
hand: Edom, [a]Moab and the foremost of the sons of [b]Ammon.
42"Then he will stretch out his
hand against *other* countries, and
the land of Egypt will not escape.
43"But he will gain control over
the hidden treasures of gold and silver, and over all the precious things
of Egypt; and [a]Libyans and [b]Ethio-
pians *will follow* at his heels.
44"But rumors from the East and
from the North will disturb him, and
he will go forth with great wrath to
destroy and annihilate many.
45"And he will pitch the tents of
his royal pavilion between the seas
and the beautiful [a]Holy Mountain;
yet he will come to his end, and no
one will help him.

CHAPTER 12

The Time of the End

"NOW at that time Michael, the
great prince who stands *guard* over
the sons of your people, will arise.
And there will be a time of distress
[a]such as never occurred since there
was a nation until that time; and at
that time your people, everyone
who is found written in the [b]book,
will be rescued.
2"And [a]many of those who sleep
in the dust of the ground will awake,
[b]these to everlasting life, but the
others to disgrace *and* everlasting
contempt.
3"And those who have [a]insight
will [b]shine brightly like the brightness of the expanse of heaven, and
those who [c]lead the many to righteousness, like the stars forever and
ever.
4"But as for you, Daniel, [a]conceal
these words and [b]seal up the book
until the end of [c]time; [d]many will go
back and forth, and knowledge will
increase."
5 Then I, Daniel, looked and behold, two others were standing, one
on this bank of the river, and the
other on that bank of the river.
6 And [a]one said to the man
[b]dressed in linen, who was above
the waters of the river, "[c]How long
will it be until the end of *these* wonders?"
7 And I heard the man dressed in
linen, who was above the waters of
the river, [1]as he [a]raised his right
hand and his left toward heaven,
and swore by Him who lives forever
that it would be for a [2b]time, [2]times,
and half *a* [2]*time;* and as soon as
[3]they finish [c]shattering the [4]power
of the holy people, all these *events*
will be completed.
8 As for me, I heard but could not
understand; so I said, "My lord,
what *will be* the [1]outcome of these
events?"
9 And he said, "Go *your way,*
Daniel, for *these* words are concealed and sealed up until the end
time.
10"Many will be purged, purified
and refined; but the [a]wicked will act
wickedly, and none of the wicked
will understand, but those who
[b]have insight will understand.
11"And from the time that the
regular sacrifice is abolished, and
the [1a]abomination of desolation is
set up, *there will be* 1,290 days.
12"How [a]blessed is he who keeps
waiting and attains to the [b]1,335
days!
13"But as for you, go *your way* to
the end; then you will enter into
[a]rest and rise *again* for your [b]allot-
ted portion at the end of the age."

34 [a]Matt. 7:15; Acts 20:29, 30 [b]Dan. 11:21, 32; Rom. 16:18
35 [a]Deut. 8:16; Prov. 17:3; Dan. 12:10; Zech. 13:9; Mal. 3:2, 3 [b]John 15:2 [c]Rev. 7:14
36 [a]Dan. 5:19; 11:3, 16 [b]Is. 14:13; Dan. 5:20; 8:11, 25; 2 Thess. 2:4 [c]Dan. 7:8, 11; Rev. 13:5, 6 [d]Deut. 10:17; Ps. 136:2; Dan. 2:47 [e]Is. 10:25; 26:20; Dan. 8:19 [f]Dan. 9:27
37 [1]Or, *God*
40 [a]Dan. 11:27, 35; 12:4, 9 [b]Is. 5:28; Jer. 4:13
41 [1]I.e., Palestine [a]Jer. 48:47 [b]Jer. 49:6
43 [a]2 Chr. 12:3; Nah. 3:9 [b]2 Chr. 12:3; Ezek. 30:4, 5; Nah. 3:9
45 [a]Is. 11:9; 27:13; 65:25; 66:20; Dan. 9:16
1 [a]Jer. 30:7; Ezek. 5:9; Dan. 9:12; Matt. 24:21; Mark 13:19 [b]Dan. 7:10; 10:21; 12:4
2 [a]Is. 26:19; Ezek. 37:12-14 [b]John 5:28, 29
3 [a]Dan. 11:33, 35; 12:10 [b]John 5:35 [c]Is. 53:11
4 [a]Dan. 8:26; 12:9 [b]Is. 8:16; Dan. 12:9 [c]Dan. 8:17; 12:9, 13 [d]Is. 11:9; 29:18, 19; Dan. 11:33
6 [a]Dan. 8:16; Zech. 1:12, 13 [b]Ezek. 9:2; Dan. 10:5 [c]Dan. 8:13; 12:8; Matt. 24:3; Mark 13:4
7 [1]Lit., *and* [2]I.e., year(s) [3]Lit., *to finish* [4]Lit., *hand* [a]Ezek. 20:5; Rev. 10:5, 6 [b]Dan. 7:25; Rev. 12:14 [c]Dan. 8:24; Luke 21:24
8 [1]Or, *final end*
10 [a]Is. 32:6, 7 [b]Dan. 12:3; Hos. 14:9
11 [1]Or, *horrible abomination* [a]Dan. 9:27; 11:31; Matt. 24:15; Mark 13:14
12 [a]Is. 30:18 [b]Dan. 8:14; Rev. 11:2; 12:6; 13:5
13 [a]Rev. 14:13 [b]Ps. 16:5

THE BOOK OF HOSEA

Hosea's Wife and Children

THE word of the LORD which came
to [a]Hosea the son of Beeri, during
the days of [b]Uzziah, [c]Jotham, [d]A-
haz, *and* [e]Hezekiah, kings of Judah,
and during the days of Jeroboam the
son of Joash, king of Israel.
2 When the LORD first spoke
through Hosea, the LORD said to Hosea, "[a]Go, take to yourself a wife of
harlotry, and *have* children of harlotry; for the land commits flagrant
harlotry, [1]forsaking the LORD."
3 So he went and took Gomer the
daughter of Diblaim, and she conceived and bore him a son.
4 And the LORD said to him,
"Name him Jezreel; for yet a little
while, and I will [1]punish the house
of Jehu for the bloodshed of Jezreel,
and I will put an end to the kingdom
of the house of Israel.
5 "And it will come about on that
day, that I will [a]break the bow of
Israel in the [b]valley of Jezreel."
6 Then she conceived again and
gave birth to a daughter. And [1]the
LORD said to him, "Name her [2]Lo-
ruhamah, for I will no longer have
compassion on the house of Israel,
that I should ever forgive them.
7 "But I will have [a]compassion on
the house of Judah and [b]deliver
them by the LORD their God, and
will not deliver them by [c]bow,
sword, battle, horses, or horsemen."
8 When she had weaned Lo-ruhamah, she conceived and gave birth
to a son.
9 And [1]the LORD said, "Name
him [2]Lo-ammi, for you are not My
people and I am not [3]your God."

10 [1]Yet the number of the sons of Israel
Will be like the [a]sand of the sea,
Which cannot be measured or numbered;
And it will come about that, in the place
Where it is said to them,
"You are [b]not My people,"
It will be said to them,
"*You are* the [c]sons of the living God."

11 And the sons of Judah and the sons of Israel will be gathered together,
And they will appoint for themselves [a]one leader,
And they will go up from the land,
For great will be the day of Jezreel.

1 [a]Rom. 9:25 [b]2 Chr. 26:1-23; Is. 1:1; Amos 1:1 [c]2 Kin. 15:5, 7, 32-38; 2 Chr. 27:1-9 [d]2 Kin. 16:1-20; 2 Chr. 28:1-27; Is. 1:1; 7:1-17; Mic. 1:1 [e]2 Kin. 18:1-20:21; 2 Chr. 29:1-32:33; Mic. 1:1

2 [1]Lit., *from not following after* [a]Is. 20:2, 3; Hos. 3:1

4 [1]Lit., *visit the bloodshed of Jezreel on the house of Jehu*

5 [a]Jer. 49:35; Ezek. 39:3 [b]Josh. 17:16; Judg. 6:33

6 [1]Lit., *He* [2]I.e., She has not obtained compassion

7 [a]Is. 30:18 [b]Jer. 25:5, 6; Zech. 9:9, 10 [c]Ps. 44:3-7

9 [1]Lit., *He* [2]I.e., Not my people [3]Lit., *yours*

10 [1]Ch. 2:1 in Heb. [a]Gen. 22:17; Jer. 33:22 [b]Is. 65:1; Hos. 1:9 [c]Is. 63:16; 64:8

11 [a]Jer. 30:21; Hos. 3:5

1 [1]Ch. 2:3 in Heb. [2]I.e., My people [3]I.e., She has obtained compassion

2 [a]Ezek. 23:45; Hos. 2:5; 4:5

3 [a]Ezek. 16:7, 22, 39 [b]Is. 32:13, 14; Hos. 13:15 [c]Jer. 14:3; Amos 8:11-13

5 [a]Jer. 2:25; 3:1, 2 [b]Jer. 44:17, 18; Hos. 2:12

6 [1]So with some ancient versions; Heb., *your* [2]Lit., *her wall so that* [a]Job 19:8 [b]Jer. 18:15

7 [a]2 Chr. 28:20-22; Hos. 5:13 [b]Jer. 2:2; 3:1; Ezek. 16:8; 23:4 [c]Jer. 14:22; Hos. 13:6

8 [1]Or, *made into the* [a]Is. 1:3 [b]Ezek. 16:19

9 [1]Lit., *its time*

CHAPTER 2

Israel's Unfaithfulness Condemned

1 SAY to your brothers, "[2]Ammi,"
and to your sisters, "[3]Ruhamah."

2 "Contend with your mother, [a]contend,
For she is not my wife, and I am not her husband;
And let her put away her harlotry from her face,
And her adultery from between her breasts,
3 Lest I strip her [a]naked
And expose her as on the day when she was born.
I will also [b]make her like a wilderness,
Make her like desert land,
And slay her with [c]thirst.
4 "Also, I will have no compassion on her children,
Because they are children of harlotry.
5 "For their mother has played the harlot;
She who conceived them has acted shamefully.
For she said, '[a]I will go after my lovers,
Who [b]give *me* my bread and my water,
My wool and my flax, my oil and my drink.'
6 "Therefore, behold, I will [a]hedge up [1]her way with thorns,
And I will build [2]a wall against her so that she cannot find her [b]paths.
7 "And she will [a]pursue her lovers, but she will not overtake them;
And she will seek them, but will not find *them*.
Then she will say, 'I will go back to my [b]first husband,
For it was [c]better for me then than now!'

8 "For she does [a]not know that it was [b]I who gave her the grain, the new wine, and the oil,
And lavished on her silver and gold,
Which they [1]used for Baal.
9 "Therefore, I will take back My grain at [1]harvest time
And My new wine in its season.
I will also take away My wool and My flax
Given to cover her nakedness.

10“And then I will [a]uncover her
lewdness
In the sight of her lovers,
And no one will rescue her out
of My hand.
11“I will also [a]put an end to all her
gaiety,
Her [b]feasts, her [c]new moons,
her sabbaths,
And all her festal assemblies.
12“And I will [a]destroy her vines
and fig trees,
Of which she said, ‘These are
my wages
Which my lovers have given
me.’
And I will [b]make them a forest,
And the [c]beasts of the field will
devour them.
13“And I will punish her for the
[a]days of the Baals
When she used to [1b]offer sacrifices to them
And adorn herself with her
[2]earrings and jewelry,
And follow her lovers, so that
she forgot Me,” declares the
LORD.

Restoration of Israel

14“Therefore, behold, I will allure
her,
[a]Bring her into the wilderness,
And speak [1]kindly to her.
15“Then I will give her her [a]vine-
yards from there,
And the [b]valley of Achor as a
door of hope.
And she will [1c]sing there as in
the days of her youth,
As in the day when she came up
from the land of Egypt.
16“And it will come about in that
day,” declares the LORD,
“That you will call Me [1a]Ishi
And will no longer call Me
[2]Baali.
17“For I will remove the names of
the Baals from her mouth,
So that they will be [1]mentioned
by their names no more.
18“In that day I will also make a
covenant for them
With the beasts of the field,
The birds of the sky,
And the creeping things of the
ground.
And I will [1a]abolish the bow,
the sword, and war from the
land,
And will make them [b]lie down
in safety.
19“And I will [a]betroth you to Me
forever;
Yes, I will betroth you to Me in
[b]righteousness and in justice,

10 [a]Ezek. 16:37

11 [a]Jer. 7:34; 16:9 [b]Hos. 3:4; Amos 5:21; 8:10 [c]Is. 1:13, 14

12 [a]Jer. 5:17; 8:13 [b]Ps. 80:12; Is. 5:5; 7:23 [c]Is. 32:13-15; Hos. 13:8

13 [1]Or, *burn incense* [2]Or, *nose rings* [a]Hos. 4:13; 11:2 [b]Jer. 7:9

14 [1]Lit., *upon her heart* [a]Ezek. 20:33-38

15 [1]Or, *give answer* [a]Ezek. 28:25, 26 [b]Josh. 7:26 [c]Jer. 2:1-3

16 [1]I.e., my Husband [2]I.e., my Master, or my Baal [a]Is. 54:5; Hos. 2:7

17 [1]Or, *remembered*

18 [1]Lit., *break* [a]Ezek. 39:1-10 [b]Ezek. 34:25

19 [a]Is. 62:4, 5; Jer. 3:14 [b]Is. 1:27; 54:6-8

20 [a]Hos. 6:6; 13:4

21 [a]Is. 55:10; Zech. 8:12; Mal. 3:10, 11

22 [1]I.e., God sows [a]Jer. 31:12; Joel 2:19

23 [1]Heb., *Lo-ruhamah* [2]Heb., *Lo-ammi* [3]Lit., *he* [a]Jer. 31:27 [b]Rom. 9:25 [c]Hos. 1:9

1 [1]I.e., Gomer [2]Lit., *companion* [a]2 Sam. 6:19; 1 Chr. 16:3; Song of Sol. 2:5

2 [1]Heb., *lethech* [a]Ruth 4:10

3 [1]Or, *husband*

4 [1]Heb., *teraphim* [a]Dan. 9:27; 11:31; 12:11; Hos. 2:11 [b]Hos. 10:1, 2 [c]Ex. 28:4-12; 1 Sam. 23:9-12

5 [a]Jer. 50:4, 5 [b]Ezek. 34:24

1 [a]Hos. 12:2; Mic. 6:2

In lovingkindness and in compassion,
20 And I will betroth you to Me in
faithfulness.
Then you will [a]know the LORD.
21“And it will come about in that
day that [a]I will respond,” declares the LORD.
“I will respond to the heavens,
and they will respond to the
earth,
22 And the [a]earth will respond to
the grain, to the new wine,
and to the oil,
And they will respond to [1]Jez-
reel.
23“And I will [a]sow her for Myself
in the land.
I will also have compassion on
[1]her who had not obtained
compassion,
And [b]I will say to [2]those who
were [c]not My people,
‘You are My people!’
And [3]they will say, *‘Thou art
my God!’* ”

CHAPTER 3

Hosea’s Second Symbolic Marriage

THEN the LORD said to me, “Go
again, love a [1]woman *who* is loved
by *her* [2]husband, yet an adulteress,
even as the LORD loves the sons of
Israel, though they turn to other
gods and love raisin [a]cakes.”
2 So I [a]bought her for myself for
fifteen *shekels* of silver and a homer
and a [1]half of barley.
3 Then I said to her, “You shall
stay with me for many days. You
shall not play the harlot, nor shall
you have a [1]man; so I will also be
toward you.”
4 For the sons of Israel will remain for many days without king or
prince, [a]without sacrifice or *sacred*
[b]pillar, and without [c]ephod or
[1]household idols.
5 Afterward the sons of Israel
will [a]return and seek the LORD their
God and [b]David their king; and they
will come trembling to the LORD and
to His goodness in the last days.

CHAPTER 4

God’s Controversy with Israel

LISTEN to the word of the LORD, O
sons of Israel,
For the LORD has a [a]case
against the inhabitants of the
land,

Because there is [b]no [1]faithful-
ness or [2]kindness
Or knowledge of God in the
land.
2 *There is* swearing, deception,
murder, stealing, and adultery.
They employ violence, so that
bloodshed [1]follows bloodshed.
3 Therefore the land [a]mourns,
And every one who lives in it
languishes
Along with the beasts of the
field and the birds of the sky;
And also the fish of the sea [1]dis-
appear.

4 Yet let no one [1a]find fault, and
let none offer reproof;
For your people are like those
who [b]contend with the
priest.
5 So you will [a]stumble by day,
And the prophet also will stumble with you by night;
And I will destroy your [b]moth-
er.
6 My people are destroyed for
lack of knowledge.
Because you have [a]rejected
knowledge,
I also will reject you from being
My priest.
Since you have forgotten the
law of your God,
I also will forget your children.

7 The more they [a]multiplied, the
more they sinned against Me;
I will [b]change their glory into
shame.
8 They feed on the [1]sin of My
people,
And [a]direct their desire toward
their iniquity.
9 And it will be, like people, [a]like
priest;
So I will punish them for their
ways,
And repay them for their deeds.
10 And they will eat, but not have
enough;
They will play the harlot, but
not increase,
Because they have [1]stopped
giving heed to the LORD.

11 Harlotry, wine, and new wine
[a]take away the [1]understand-
ing.
12 My people [a]consult their
wooden idol, and their *diviner's* wand informs them;
For a spirit of harlotry has led
them astray,
And they have played the
harlot, *departing* [1]from their
God.
13 They offer sacrifices on the
[a]tops of the mountains
And [1b]burn incense on the hills,
[c]Under oak, poplar, and terebinth,
Because their shade is pleasant.
Therefore your daughters play
the harlot,
And your [2]brides commit adultery.
14 I will not punish your daughters
when they play the harlot
Or your [1]brides when they commit adultery,
For *the men* themselves go
apart with harlots
And offer sacrifices with temple [a]prostitutes;
So the people without understanding are [2]ruined.

15 Though you, Israel, play the
harlot,
Do not let Judah become guilty;
Also do not go to Gilgal,
Or go up to Beth-aven,
[a]And take the oath:
"As the LORD lives!"
16 Since Israel is [a]stubborn
Like a stubborn heifer,
[1]Can the LORD now [b]pasture
them
Like a lamb in a large field?
17 Ephraim is joined to [a]idols;
[b]Let him alone.
18 Their liquor gone,
They play the harlot continually;
Their [1]rulers dearly love shame.
19 [a]The wind wraps them in its
wings,
And they will be ashamed because of their sacrifices.

CHAPTER 5

The People's Apostasy Rebuked

HEAR this, O priests!
Give heed, O house of Israel!
Listen, O house of the king!
For the judgment applies to
you,
For you have been a snare at
Mizpah,
And a net spread out on Tabor.
2 And the revolters have [1a]gone
deep in depravity,
But I will chastise all of them.
3 I [a]know Ephraim, and Israel is
not hidden from Me;
For now, O Ephraim, you have
played the harlot,

1 [1]Or, *truth* [2]Or, *loyalty* [b]Is. 50:4; Jer. 7:28
2 [1]Lit., *touches*
3 [1]Lit., *are taken away* [a]Is. 24:4; 33:9
4 [1]Lit., *contend* [a]Ezek. 3:26; Amos 5:10, 13 [b]Deut. 17:12
5 [a]Ezek. 14:3, 7; Hos. 5:5 [b]Hos. 2:2, 5
6 [a]Hos. 4:14; Zech. 11:8, 9, 15-17
7 [a]Hos. 10:1; 13:6 [b]Hab. 2:16
8 [1]Or, *sin offering* [a]Is. 56:11; Mic. 3:11
9 [a]Is. 24:2; Jer. 5:31
10 [1]Lit., *forsaken giving heed; or, forsaken the* LORD *to practice* (v. 11) *harlotry.*
11 [1]Lit., *heart* [a]Is. 5:12; 28:7
12 [1]Lit., *from under* [a]Is. 44:19; Jer. 2:27
13 [1]Or, *offer sacrifices* [2]Or, *daughters-in-law* [a]Jer. 3:6 [b]Hos. 2:13; 11:2 [c]Jer. 2:20
14 [1]Or, *daughters-in-law* [2]Lit., *thrust down* [a]Deut. 23:17
15 [a]Jer. 5:2; 44:26
16 [1]Or, *Now the* LORD *will pasture . . . field.* [a]Ps. 78:8 [b]Is. 5:17; 7:25
17 [a]Hos. 13:2 [b]Ps. 81:12; Hos. 4:4
18 [1]Lit., *shields*
19 [a]Hos. 12:1; 13:15
2 [1]Or, *waded deep in slaughter* [a]Hos. 4:2; 6:9
3 [a]Amos 3:2; 5:12

Israel has defiled itself.
4 Their deeds will not allow them
To return to their God.
For a spirit of harlotry is within
them,
And they do not [a]know the
LORD.
5 Moreover, the pride of Israel
testifies against him,
And Israel and Ephraim stumble in their iniquity;
[a]Judah also has stumbled with
them.
6 They will [a]go with their flocks
and herds
To seek the LORD, but they will
[b]not find *Him;*
He has [c]withdrawn from them.
7 They have [a]dealt treacherously
against the LORD,
For they have borne [1b]illegiti-
mate children.
Now the [c]new moon will devour them with their [2]land.

8 Blow the horn in Gibeah,
The trumpet in Ramah.
Sound an alarm at Beth-aven:
"[a]Behind you, Benjamin!"
9 Ephraim will become a [a]desola-
tion in the [b]day of rebuke;
Among the tribes of Israel
I declare what is [c]sure.
10 The princes of Judah have become like those who [a]move a
boundary;
On them I will [b]pour out My
wrath [c]like water.
11 Ephraim is oppressed, crushed
in judgment,
Because he was determined to
[1]follow *man's* command.
12 Therefore I am like a [a]moth to
Ephraim,
And like rottenness to the
house of Judah.
13 When Ephraim saw his sickness,
And Judah his [1]wound,
Then Ephraim went to Assyria
And sent to [2]King Jareb.
But he is unable to heal you,
Or to cure you of your [1]wound.
14 For I *will be* [a]like a lion to E-
phraim,
And like a young lion to the
house of Judah.
[b]I, even I, will tear to pieces and
go away,
I will carry away, and there will
be [c]none to deliver.
15 I will go away *and* return to My
place
Until they [1a]acknowledge their
guilt and seek My face;
In their affliction they will earnestly [b]seek Me.

CHAPTER 6

The Response to God's Rebuke

"[a]COME, let us return to the
LORD.
For He has torn *us,* but He will
heal us;
He has [1]wounded *us,* but He
will [b]bandage us.
2 "He will [a]revive us after two
days;
He will raise us up on the third
day
That we may live before Him.
3 "So let us [a]know, let us press on
to know the LORD.
His [b]going forth is as certain as
the dawn;
And He will come to us like the
[c]rain,
Like the spring rain watering
the earth."

4 What shall I do with you, O E-
phraim?
What shall I do with you, O Judah?
For your [1]loyalty is like a
[a]morning cloud,
And like the dew which goes
away early.
5 Therefore I have [a]hewn *them* in
pieces by the prophets;
I have slain them by the words
of My mouth;
And the judgments on you are
like the light that goes forth.
6 For [a]I delight in loyalty rather
than sacrifice,
And in the knowledge of God
rather than burnt offerings.
7 But like [1]Adam they have
transgressed the covenant;
There they have dealt treacherously against Me.
8 Gilead is a city of wrongdoers,
Tracked with bloody *footprints.*
9 And as raiders wait for a man,
So a band of priests [a]murder on
the way to Shechem;
Surely they have committed
[1b]crime.
10 In the house of Israel I have
seen a [a]horrible thing;
Ephraim's harlotry is there, Israel has defiled itself.
11 Also, O Judah, there is a [a]har-
vest appointed for you,
When I [b]restore the fortunes of
My people.

4 [a]Hos. 4:6, 14
5 [a]Ezek. 23:31-35
6 [a]Hos. 8:13; Mic. 6:6, 7 [b]Is. 1:15; Jer. 14:12 [c]Ezek. 8:6
7 [1]Lit., *strange* [2]Lit., *portions* [a]Is. 48:8; Hos. 6:7 [b]Hos. 2:4 [c]Is. 1:14; Hos. 2:11, 12
8 [a]Judg. 5:14
9 [a]Is. 28:1-4; Hos. 9:11-17 [b]Is. 37:3 [c]Is. 46:10; Zech. 1:6
10 [a]Deut. 27:17 [b]Ezek. 7:8 [c]Ps. 32:6; 93:3, 4
11 [1]Or, with some ancient versions, *follow nothingness*
12 [a]Ps. 39:11; Is. 51:8
13 [1]Or, *ulcer* [2]Or, *the avenging king;* or, *the great king*
14 [a]Ps. 7:2; Hos. 13:7, 8; Amos 3:4 [b]Ps. 50:22 [c]Mic. 5:8
15 [1]Or, *bear their punishment* [a]Is. 64:7-9; Jer. 3:13, 14 [b]Ps. 50:15; 78:34; Jer. 2:27; Hos. 3:5
1 [1]Lit., *struck* [a]Jer. 50:4, 5 [b]Is. 30:26
2 [a]Ps. 30:5
3 [a]Is. 2:3; Mic. 4:2 [b]Ps. 19:6; Mic. 5:2 [c]Joel 2:23
4 [1]Or, *lovingkindness* [a]Ps. 78:34-37; Hos. 13:3
5 [a]1 Sam. 15:32, 33; Jer. 1:10, 18; 5:14
6 [a]Matt. 9:13; 12:7
7 [1]Or, *men*
9 [1]Or, *lewdness* [a]Jer. 7:9, 10; Hos. 4:2 [b]Ezek. 22:9; 23:27; Hos. 2:10
10 [a]Jer. 5:30, 31; 23:14
11 [a]Jer. 51:33; Joel 3:13 [b]Zeph. 2:7

Chapter 7

Ephraim's Iniquity

WHEN I [a]would heal Israel,
The iniquity of Ephraim is uncovered,
And the evil deeds of Samaria,
For they deal falsely;
The thief enters in,
Bandits raid outside,
2 And they do not [1]consider in their hearts
That I [a]remember all their wickedness.
Now their [b]deeds are all around them;
They are before My face.
3 With their wickedness they make the [a]king glad,
And the princes with their lies.
4 They are [a]all adulterers
Like an oven heated by the baker,
Who ceases to stir up *the fire*
From the kneading of the dough until it is leavened.
5 On the [1]day of our king, the princes [a]became sick with the heat of wine;
He stretched out his hand with [b]scoffers,
6 For their hearts are like an [a]oven
As they approach their [1]plotting;
Their [2]anger [3]smolders all night,
In the morning it burns like a flaming fire.
7 All of them are hot like an oven,
And they consume their rulers;
All their kings have fallen.
None of them calls on Me.

8 Ephraim mixes himself with the [1]nations;
Ephraim has become a cake not turned.
9 [a]Strangers devour his strength,
Yet he does not know *it;*
Gray hairs also are sprinkled on him,
Yet he does not know *it.*
10 Though the pride of Israel testifies against him,
Yet they have neither returned to the LORD their God,
Nor have they sought Him, for all this.
11 So Ephraim has become like a silly dove, without [1]sense;
They call to Egypt, they go to Assyria.
12 When they go, I will [a]spread My net over them;
I will bring them down like the birds of the sky.
I will chastise them in accordance with the [1]proclamation to their assembly.
13 Woe to them, for they have [a]strayed from Me!
Destruction is theirs, for they have rebelled against Me!
I [b]would redeem them, but they speak lies against Me.
14 And they do not cry to Me from their heart
When they wail on their beds;
For the sake of grain and new wine they [1a]assemble themselves,
They turn away from Me.
15 Although I trained *and* strengthened their arms,
Yet they [a]devise evil against Me.
16 They turn, *but* not [1]upward,
They are like a [a]deceitful bow;
Their princes will fall by the sword
Because of the [2b]insolence of their tongue.
This *will be* their [c]derision in the land of Egypt.

Chapter 8

Israel Reaps the Whirlwind

PUT the trumpet to your [1]lips!
[a]Like an eagle *the enemy comes* [b]against the house of the LORD,
Because they have transgressed My covenant,
And rebelled against My law.
2 They cry out to Me,
"My God, we of Israel know Thee!"
3 Israel has rejected the good;
The enemy will pursue him.
4 They have set up kings, but not by Me;
They have appointed princes, but I did not know *it.*
With their [a]silver and gold they have made idols for themselves,
That [1]they might be cut off.
5 [1]He has rejected your calf, O Samaria, saying,
"My anger burns against them!"
How long will they be incapable of [a]innocence?
6 For from Israel is even this!
A craftsman made it, so it is not God;
Surely the calf of Samaria will be broken to [1]pieces.
7 For they sow the wind,

7:1 [a]Ezek. 24:13; Hos. 6:4; 7:13; 11:8
7:2 [1]Lit., *say to their heart* [a]Ps. 25:7; Jer. 14:10; Hos. 8:13; 9:9; Amos 8:7 [b]Jer. 2:19; 4:18; Hos. 4:9
7:3 [a]Jer. 28:1-4; Hos. 7:5; Mic. 7:3
7:4 [a]Jer. 9:2; 23:10
7:5 [1]I.e., a festive occasion [a]Is. 28:1, 7, 8 [b]Is. 28:14
7:6 [1]Lit., *ambush* [2]So with some ancient versions; M.T., *baker* [3]Lit., *sleeps* [a]Ps. 21:9
7:8 [1]Lit., *peoples*
7:9 [a]Is. 1:7
7:11 [1]Lit., *heart*
7:12 [1]Lit., *report* [a]Ezek. 12:13
7:13 [a]Jer. 14:10; Ezek. 34:6; Hos. 9:17 [b]Jer. 51:9; Hos. 7:1; Matt. 23:37
7:14 [1]Or, with Gk. and many ancient mss., *gash themselves* [a]Judg. 9:27; Amos 2:8; Mic. 2:11
7:15 [a]Nah. 1:9
7:16 [1]Or possibly, *to the Most High* [2]Lit., *indignation* or *cursing* [a]Ps. 78:57 [b]Ps. 12:3, 4; 17:10; Dan. 7:25; Mal. 3:13, 14 [c]Ezek. 23:32
8:1 [1]Lit., *palate* [a]Hab. 1:8 [b]Deut. 28:49
8:4 [1]Lit., *he* [a]Hos. 2:8; 13:1, 2
8:5 [1]Or, *Your calf has rejected you* [a]Ps. 19:13; Jer. 13:27
8:6 [1]Or, *splinters*

And they reap the [a]whirlwind.
The standing grain has no
[1]heads;
It yields no [2]grain.
Should it yield, strangers would
swallow it up.

8 Israel is [a]swallowed up;
They are now among the nations
Like a [b]vessel in which no one
delights.
9 For they have gone up to Assyria,
Like a wild donkey all alone;
Ephraim has [a]hired [1]lovers.
10 Even though they hire *allies*
among the nations,
Now I will [a]gather them up;
And they will begin [b]to [1]dimin-
ish
Because of the burden of the
[c]king of princes.

11 Since Ephraim has multiplied
altars for sin,
They have become altars of sinning for him.
12 Though I wrote for him ten
thousand *precepts* of My law,
They are regarded as a strange
thing.
13 As for My sacrificial gifts,
They [a]sacrifice the flesh and eat
it,
But the LORD has taken no delight in them.
Now He will [b]remember their
iniquity,
And punish *them* for their sins;
They will return to Egypt.
14 For Israel has [a]forgotten his
Maker and [b]built palaces;
And Judah has multiplied fortified cities,
But I will send a [c]fire on its
cities that it may consume its
palatial dwellings.

CHAPTER 9

Ephraim Punished

[a]DO not rejoice, O Israel, [1]with exultation like the [2]nations!
For you have played the harlot,
[3]forsaking your God.
You have loved *harlots'* earnings on [4]every threshing
floor.
2 Threshing floor and wine press
will not feed them,
And the new wine will fail
[1]them.
3 They will not remain in the
LORD's land,
But Ephraim will return to
Egypt,
And in Assyria they will eat
[a]unclean *food.*
4 They will not pour out libations
of [a]wine to the LORD,
Their sacrifices will not please
Him.
Their bread will [1]*be* like
[2]mourners' bread;
All who eat of it will be [b]defiled,
For their bread will be for
[3]themselves *alone;*
It will not enter the house of the
LORD.
5 [a]What will you do on the day of
the appointed festival
And on the day of the [b]feast of
the LORD?
6 For behold, they will go be-
cause of destruction;
Egypt will gather them up,
Memphis will bury them.
Weeds will take over their trea-
sures of silver;
[a]Thorns *will be* in their tents.

7 The days of [a]punishment have
come,
The days of [b]retribution have
come;
[1]Let Israel know *this*!
The prophet is a [c]fool,
The [2]inspired man is [d]dement-
ed,
Because of the grossness of
your [e]iniquity,
And *because* your hostility is so
great.
8 Ephraim *was* a watchman with
my God, a prophet;
Yet the snare of a bird catcher
is in all his ways,
And there is *only* hostility in the
house of his God.
9 They have gone [a]deep [1]in depravity
As in the days of Gibeah;
He will [b]remember their iniquity,
He will punish their sins.

10 I found Israel like [a]grapes in the
wilderness;
I saw your forefathers as the
[b]earliest fruit on the fig tree
in its first *season*.
But they came to Baal-peor
and devoted themselves to
[1c]shame,
And they became as [d]detest-
able as that which they
loved.
11 As for Ephraim, their glory will
[a]fly away like a bird—
No birth, no pregnancy, and no
conception!

7 [1]Lit., *growth* [2]Or, *meal* [a]Is. 66:15; Nah. 1:3
8 [a]Jer. 51:34 [b]Jer. 25:34; Hos. 13:15
9 [1]Lit., *loves* [a]Ezek. 16:33
10 [1]Or, *suffer for awhile* [a]Ezek. 22:20 [b]Jer. 42:2 [c]Is. 10:8
13 [a]Jer. 6:20; 7:21 [b]Hos. 7:2; Luke 12:2; 1 Cor. 4:5
14 [a]Hos. 2:13; 4:6; 13:6 [b]Is. 9:9, 10 [c]Jer. 17:27
1 [1]Lit., *to* [2]Lit., *peoples* [3]Lit., *away from your God* [4]Lit., *all threshing floors of grain* [a]Is. 22:12, 13; Hos. 10:5
2 [1]Lit., *her*
3 [a]Ezek. 4:13
4 [1]Lit., *be to them* [2]Or, *bread of misfortune* [3]Lit., *their appetite* [a]Ex. 29:40 [b]Hag. 2:14
5 [a]Is. 10:3; Jer. 5:31 [b]Hos. 2:11; Joel 1:13
6 [a]Is. 5:6; 7:23; Hos. 10:8
7 [1]Or, *Israel will know it* [2]Lit., *man of the spirit* [a]Is. 10:3; Jer. 10:15; Mic. 7:4 [b]Is. 34:8; Jer. 16:18; 25:14 [c]Lam. 2:14; Ezek. 13:3, 10 [d]Is. 44:25 [e]Ezek. 14:9, 10
9 [1]Lit., *they have corrupted* [a]Is. 31:6 [b]Hos. 7:2; 8:13
10 [1]I.e., Baal [a]Mic. 7:1 [b]Jer. 24:2 [c]Jer. 11:13; Hos. 4:18 [d]Ezek. 20:8
11 [a]Hos. 4:7; 10:5

12 Though they bring up their children,
Yet I will bereave them [1]until not a man is left.
Yes, woe to them indeed when I depart from them!
13 Ephraim, as I have seen,
Is planted in a pleasant meadow like Tyre;
But Ephraim will bring out his children for slaughter.
14 Give them, O LORD— what wilt Thou give?
Give them a [a]miscarrying womb and dry breasts.

15 All their evil is at Gilgal;
Indeed, I came to hate them there!
Because of the [a]wickedness of their deeds
I will drive them out of My house!
I will love them no more;
All their princes are [b]rebels.
16 Ephraim is stricken, their root is dried up,
They will bear no fruit.
Even though they bear children,
I will slay the [a]precious ones of their womb.
17 My God will cast them away
Because they have not listened to Him;
And they will be wanderers among the nations.

CHAPTER 10

Retribution for Israel's Sin

ISRAEL is a [1]luxuriant [a]vine;
He produces fruit for himself.
The more his fruit,
The more altars he [b]made;
The [2]richer his land,
The better [3]he made the *sacred* [c]pillars.
2 Their heart is [1a]faithless;
Now they must bear their [b]guilt.
[2]The LORD will [c]break down their altars
And destroy their *sacred* pillars.

3 Surely now they will say, "We have [a]no king,
For we do not revere the LORD.
As for the king, what can he do for us?"
4 They speak *mere* words,
[1]With worthless [a]oaths they make covenants;
And [b]judgment sprouts like poisonous weeds in the furrows of the field.
5 The inhabitants of Samaria will fear
For the [1]calf of Beth-aven.
Indeed, its people will mourn for it,
And its idolatrous priests [2]will cry out over it,
Over its glory, since it has departed from it.
6 The thing itself will be carried to Assyria
As tribute to [1]King Jareb;
Ephraim will [2]be seized with shame,
And Israel will be ashamed of its [a]own counsel.
7 Samaria will be [a]cut off *with* her king,
Like a stick on the surface of the water.
8 Also the [a]high places of Aven, the [b]sin of Israel, will be destroyed;
[c]Thorn and thistle will grow on their altars,
Then they will [d]say to the mountains,
"Cover us!" And to the hills, "Fall on us!"
9 From the days of Gibeah you have sinned, O Israel;
There they stand!
Will not the battle against the sons of iniquity overtake them in Gibeah?
10 When it is My [a]desire, I will [1]chastise them;
And the peoples will be gathered against them
When they are bound for their double guilt.

11 And Ephraim is a trained [a]heifer that loves to thresh,
But I will [b]come over her fair neck *with a yoke;*
I will [c]harness Ephraim,
Judah will plow, Jacob will harrow for himself.
12 [a]Sow with a view to righteousness,
Reap in accordance with [1]kindness;
[b]Break up your fallow ground,
For it is time to seek the LORD
Until He comes to [2c]rain righteousness on you.
13 You have [a]plowed wickedness, you have reaped injustice,
You have eaten the fruit of [b]lies.
Because you have trusted in your way, in your [c]numerous warriors,
14 Therefore, a tumult will arise among your people,

12 [1]Lit., *without a man*
14 [a]Hos. 9:11
15 [a]Hos. 4:9; 7:2; 12:2 [b]Hos. 5:2
16 [a]Ezek. 24:21
1 [1]Or, *degenerate* [2]Or, *better* [3]Lit., *they* [a]Is. 5:1-7; Ezek. 15:1-5 [b]Jer. 2:28; Hos. 8:11; 12:11 [c]1 Kin. 14:23; Hos. 3:4
2 [1]Lit., *smooth* [2]Lit., *He* [a]1 Kin. 18:21; Zeph. 1:5 [b]Hos. 13:16 [c]Hos. 10:8; Mic. 5:13
3 [a]Ps. 12:4; Is. 5:19
4 [1]Or, *Swearing falsely in making a covenant* [a]Ezek. 17:13-19; Hos. 4:2 [b]Deut. 31:16, 17; 2 Kin. 17:3, 4
5 [1]So with some ancient versions; Heb., *calves* [2]Or, *who used to rejoice over*
6 [1]Or, *the avenging king;* or, *the great king* [2]Lit., *receive shame* [a]Is. 30:3; Jer. 7:24
7 [a]Hos. 13:11
8 [a]Hos. 4:13 [b]1 Kin. 12:28-30; 13:34 [c]Is. 32:13; Hos. 9:6; 10:2 [d]Luke 23:30; Rev. 6:16
10 [1]Or, *bind* [a]Ezek. 5:13
11 [a]Jer. 50:11; Hos. 4:16 [b]Jer. 28:14 [c]Ps. 66:12
12 [1]Or, *loyalty* [2]Or, *teach* [a]Prov. 11:18 [b]Jer. 4:3 [c]Is. 44:3; 45:8
13 [a]Job 4:8; Gal. 6:7 [b]Hos. 4:2; 7:3; 11:12 [c]Ps. 33:16

And all your [a]fortresses will be destroyed,
As Shalman destroyed Beth-arbel on the day of battle,
When [b]mothers were dashed in pieces with *their* children.
15 Thus it will be done to you at Bethel because of your great wickedness.
At dawn the king of Israel will be completely cut off.

Chapter 11

God Yearns Over His People

WHEN Israel *was* a youth I loved him,
And [a]out of Egypt I [b]called My son.
2 The more [1a]they called them,
The more they went from [1]them;
They kept sacrificing to the Baals
And [b]burning incense to idols.
3 Yet it is I who taught Ephraim to walk,
[1]I [a]took them in [1]My arms;
But they did not know that I [b]healed them.
4 I [a]led them with cords of a man, with bonds of love,
And I became to them as one who lifts the yoke from their jaws;
And I bent down *and* [b]fed them.

5 [1]They will not return to the land of Egypt;
But Assyria—he will be [2]their king,
Because they refused to return *to Me.*
6 And the sword will whirl against [1]their cities,
And will demolish [1]their gate bars
And [a]consume *them* because of their [b]counsels.
7 So My people are bent on [a]turning from Me.
Though [1]they call [2]them to *the One* on high,
None at all exalts *Him.*

8 [a]How can I give you up, O Ephraim?
How can I surrender you, O Israel?
How can I [1]make you like [b]Admah?
How can I treat you like [b]Zeboiim?
My heart is turned over within Me,

14 [a]Is. 17:3 [b]Hos. 13:16

1 [a]Hos. 2:15; 12:9, 13; 13:4 [b]Matt. 2:15

2 [1]I.e., God's prophets [a]2 Kin. 17:13-15 [b]Is. 65:7; Jer. 18:15

3 [1]So ancient versions; Heb., *He . . . His* [a]Deut. 1:31; 32:10, 11 [b]Ps. 107:20; Jer. 30:17

4 [a]Jer. 31:2, 3 [b]Ex. 16:32

5 [1]Lit., *He* [2]Lit., *his*

6 [1]Lit., *his* [a]Lam. 2:9 [b]Hos. 4:16, 17

7 [1]I.e., God's prophets [2]Lit., *him;* i.e., Israel [a]Jer. 8:5

8 [1]Lit., *give* [2]Lit., *Together* [a]Hos. 6:4; 7:1 [b]Gen. 14:8; Deut. 29:23

9 [1]Lit., *excitement* [a]Deut. 13:17 [b]Jer. 26:3; 30:11 [c]Is. 5:24; 12:6; 41:14, 16

10 [a]Hos. 3:5; 6:1-3 [b]Is. 31:4; Joel 3:16; Amos 1:2 [c]Is. 66:2, 5

11 [a]Is. 11:11 [b]Is. 60:8; Hos. 7:11 [c]Ezek. 34:27, 28

12 [1]Chap. 12:1 in Heb.

1 [1]Chap. 12:2 in Heb. [2]Lit., *they make* [a]Jer. 22:22 [b]Gen. 41:6; Ezek. 17:10

2 [a]Hos. 4:1 [b]Hos. 4:9; 7:2

3 [a]Gen. 25:26 [b]Gen. 32:28

4 [a]Gen. 32:26 [b]Gen. 28:13-15; 35:10-15

5 [1]Lit., *memorial* [a]Ex. 3:15

6 [1]Or, *loyalty* [a]Mic. 7:7

7 [1]Or, *Canaanite* [a]Hos. 7:14 [b]Prov. 11:1; Amos 8:5; Mic. 6:11

[2]All my compassions are kindled.
9 I will [a]not execute My fierce anger;
I will not destroy Ephraim [b]again.
For I am God and not man, the [c]Holy One in your midst,
And I will not come in [1]wrath.
10 They will [a]walk after the LORD,
He will [b]roar like a lion;
Indeed He will roar,
And His sons will come [c]trembling from the west.
11 They will come trembling like birds from [a]Egypt,
And like [b]doves from the land of [a]Assyria;
And I will [c]settle them in their houses, declares the LORD.

12 [1]Ephraim surrounds Me with lies,
And the house of Israel with deceit;
Judah is also unruly against God,
Even against the Holy One who is faithful.

Chapter 12

Ephraim Reminded

1 EPHRAIM feeds on [a]wind,
And pursues the east [b]wind continually;
He multiplies lies and violence.
Moreover, [2]he makes a covenant with Assyria,
And oil is carried to Egypt.
2 The LORD also has a [a]dispute with Judah,
And will punish Jacob [b]according to his ways;
He will repay him according to his deeds.
3 In the womb he [a]took his brother by the heel,
And in his maturity he [b]contended with God.
4 Yes, he wrestled with the angel and prevailed;
He wept and [a]sought His favor.
He found Him at [b]Bethel,
And there He spoke with us,
5 Even the LORD, the God of hosts;
The LORD is His [1a]name.
6 Therefore, return to your God,
Observe [1]kindness and justice,
And [a]wait for your God continually.
7 A [1a]merchant, in whose hands are false [b]balances,
He loves to oppress.

8 And Ephraim said, "Surely I
have become [a]rich,
I have found wealth for myself;
In all my labors they will find in
me
[b]No iniquity, which *would be*
sin."
9 But I *have been* the LORD your
God since the land of Egypt;
I will make you [a]live in tents
again,
As in the days of the appointed
festival.
10 I have also spoken to the
[a]prophets,
And I gave numerous visions;
And through the prophets I
gave [b]parables.
11 Is there iniquity *in* Gilead?
Surely they are worthless.
In Gilgal they sacrifice bulls,
Yes, their altars are like the
stone heaps
Beside the furrows of the field.

12 Now [a]Jacob fled to the land of
Aram,
And [b]Israel worked for a wife,
And for a wife he kept *sheep.*
13 But by a [a]prophet the LORD
brought Israel from Egypt,
And by a prophet he was kept.
14 [a]Ephraim has provoked to bitter anger;
So his Lord will leave his
[b]bloodguilt on him,
And bring back his [c]reproach to
him.

CHAPTER 13

Ephraim's Idolatry

[a]WHEN Ephraim [1]spoke, *there
was* trembling.
He [b]exalted himself in Israel,
But through [c]Baal he [2]did
wrong and died.
2 And now they sin more and
more,
And make for themselves [a]mol-
ten images,
Idols [b]skillfully made from
their silver,
All of them the [c]work of craftsmen.
They say of them, "Let the men
who sacrifice kiss the
calves!"
3 Therefore, they will be like the
morning cloud,
And like dew which [1]soon disappears,
Like [a]chaff which is blown
away from the threshing
floor,
And like [b]smoke from a [2]chim-
ney.

4 Yet I *have been* the LORD your
God
Since the land of Egypt;
And you were not to know [a]any
god except Me,
For there is no savior [b]besides
Me.
5 I [1a]cared for you in the wilderness,
In the land of drought.
6 As *they had* their pasture, they
became [a]satisfied,
And being satisfied, their heart
became proud;
Therefore, they [b]forgot Me.
7 So I will be like a lion to them;
Like a [a]leopard I will [1]lie in wait
by the wayside.
8 I will encounter them like a
bear robbed of her cubs,
And I will tear open [1]their
chests;
There I will also [a]devour them
like a lioness,
As a wild beast would tear
them.

9 *It is* your destruction, O Israel,
[1]That *you are* [a]against Me,
against your [b]help.
10 Where now is your [a]king
That he may save you in all
your cities,
And your judges of whom you
[1]requested,
"Give me a king and princes"?
11 I [a]gave you a king in My anger,
And [b]took him away in My
wrath.

12 The iniquity of Ephraim is
bound up;
His sin is [a]stored up.
13 The pains of [a]childbirth come
upon him;
He is [b]not a wise son,
For [1]it is not the time that he
should [c]delay at the opening
of the womb.
14 I will [a]ransom them from the
[1]power of Sheol;
I will redeem them from death.
[b]O Death, where are your
thorns?
O Sheol, where is your sting?
[c]Compassion will be hidden
from My sight.

15 Though he [a]flourishes among
the [1]reeds,
An [b]east wind will come,
The wind of the LORD coming
up from the wilderness;

8 [a]Ps. 62:10; Hos. 13:6 [b]Hos. 4:8; 14:1
9 [a]Lev. 23:42
10 [a]Jer. 7:25 [b]Ezek. 17:2; 20:49
12 [a]Gen. 28:5 [b]Gen. 29:20
13 [a]Ex. 14:19-22; Is. 63:11-14
14 [a]2 Kin. 17:7-18 [b]Ezek. 18:10-13 [c]Dan. 11:18; Mic. 6:16
1 [1]Or, *spoke with trembling* [2]Or, *became guilty* [a]Job 29:21, 22 [b]Judg. 8:1; 12:1 [c]Hos. 2:8-17; 11:2
2 [a]Is. 46:6; Jer. 10:4; Hos. 2:8 [b]Is. 44:17-20 [c]Hos. 8:6
3 [1]Lit., *goes away early* [2]Lit., *window* [a]Ps. 1:4; Is. 17:13; Dan. 2:35 [b]Ps. 68:2
4 [a]Ex. 20:3; 2 Kin. 18:35 [b]Is. 43:11; 45:21, 22
5 [1]Or, *knew* [a]Deut. 32:10
6 [a]Deut. 8:12, 14; 32:13-15; Jer. 5:7 [b]Hos. 2:13; 4:6; 8:14
7 [1]Or, *watch* [a]Jer. 5:6
8 [1]Lit., *the enclosure of their heart* [a]Ps. 50:22
9 [1]Or, *But in Me is your help* [a]Jer. 2:17, 19; Mal. 1:12, 13 [b]Deut. 33:26, 29
10 [1]Lit., *said* [a]2 Kin. 17:4; Hos. 8:4
11 [a]1 Sam. 8:7 [b]1 Kin. 14:7-10; Hos. 10:7
12 [a]Deut. 32:34, 35; Job 14:17; Rom. 2:5
13 [1]Lit., *it is the time that he should not tarry at the breaking forth of children* [a]Mic. 4:9, 10 [b]Deut. 32:6; Hos. 5:4 [c]Is. 37:3; 66:9
14 [1]Lit., *hand* [a]Ps. 49:15; Ezek. 37:12, 13 [b]1 Cor. 15:55 [c]Jer. 20:16; 31:35-37
15 [1]Or, *brothers* [a]Gen. 49:22; Hos. 10:1 [b]Gen. 41:6; Ezek. 17:10; 19:12

And his fountain will [c]become
dry,
And his spring will be dried up;
It will [d]plunder *his* treasury of
every precious article.
16 [1]Samaria will be held guilty,
For she has rebelled against her
God.
They will fall by the sword,
Their little ones will be dashed
in pieces,
And their pregnant [a]women
will be ripped open.

CHAPTER 14

Israel's Future Blessing

1a RETURN, O Israel, to the LORD
your God,
For you have stumbled [2]be-
cause of your [b]iniquity.
2 Take words with you and return to the LORD.
Say to Him, "[a]Take away all iniquity,
And [1]receive *us* graciously,
That we may [b]present [2]the fruit
of our lips.
3 "Assyria will not save us,
We will [a]not ride on horses;
Nor will we say again, '[b]Our
god,'
To the [c]work of our hands;
For in [d]Thee the orphan finds
mercy."
4 I will [a]heal their apostasy,
I will [b]love them freely,
For My anger has [c]turned away
from them.
5 I will be like the [a]dew to Israel;
He will blossom like the [b]lily,
And he will take root like *the
cedars of* Lebanon.
6 His shoots will [1]sprout,
And his [2]beauty will be like the
[a]olive tree,
And his fragrance like *the ce-
dars of* [b]Lebanon.
7 Those who [a]live in his shadow
Will [1]again raise grain,
And they will blossom like the
vine.
His renown *will be* like the wine
of Lebanon.

8 O Ephraim, what more have I to
do with [a]idols?
It is I who answer and look af-
ter [1]you.
I am like a luxuriant [b]cypress;
From [c]Me comes your fruit.

9 [a]Whoever is wise, let him understand these things;
Whoever is discerning, let him
know them.
For the [b]ways of the LORD are
right,
And the [c]righteous will walk in
them,
But [d]transgressors will stumble
in them.

15 [c]Jer. 51:36 [d]Jer. 20:5
16 [1]Ch. 14:1 in Heb. [a]2 Kin. 15:16
1 [1]Ch. 14:2 in Heb. [2]Or, *in* [a]Hos. 6:1; 10:12; 12:6 [b]Hos. 4:8; 5:5; 9:7
2 [1]Or, *accept that which is good* [2]So with ancient versions; M.T., *our lips as bulls* [a]Mic. 7:18, 19 [b]Ps. 51:16, 17; Hos. 6:6
3 [a]Is. 31:1 [b]Hos. 8:6; 13:2 [c]Hos. 4:12 [d]Ps. 68:5
4 [a]Is. 57:18; Hos. 6:1 [b]Zeph. 3:17 [c]Is. 12:1
5 [a]Is. 26:19 [b]Song of Sol. 2:1; Matt. 6:28
6 [1]Lit., go [2]Or, *splendor* [a]Jer. 11:16 [b]Song of Sol. 4:11
7 [1]Or, *return, they will raise grain* [a]Ezek. 17:23
8 [1]Lit., *him* [a]Job 34:32; Hos. 14:3 [b]Is. 41:19 [c]Ezek. 17:23
9 [a]Ps. 107:43; Jer. 9:12 [b]Ps. 111:7, 8; Zeph. 3:5 [c]Is. 26:7 [d]Is. 1:28

THE BOOK OF JOEL

The Devastation of Locusts

THE [a]word of the LORD that came
to [b]Joel, the son of Pethuel.
2 [a]Hear this, O [b]elders,
And listen, all inhabitants of the
land.
Has *anything like* this happened in [c]your days
Or in your fathers' days?
3 [a]Tell your sons about it,
And *let* your sons *tell* their
sons,
And their sons the next generation.

4 What the [a]gnawing locust has
left, the swarming locust has
eaten;
And what the swarming locust
has left, the [b]creeping locust
has eaten;
And what the creeping locust
has left, the [c]stripping locust
has eaten.
5 Awake, drunkards, and weep;
And wail, all you wine drinkers,
On account of the sweet wine
That is cut off from your mouth.
6 For a [a]nation has [1]invaded my
land,
Mighty and without number;
Its teeth are the teeth of a lion,
And it has the fangs of a lioness.
7 It has [a]made my vine a waste,
And my fig tree [1]splinters.
It has stripped them bare and
cast *them* away;
Their branches have become
white.
8 Wail like a virgin [a]girded with
sackcloth
For the bridegroom of her
youth.

1 [a]Jer. 1:2; Ezek. 1:3; Hos. 1:1 [b]Acts 2:16
2 [a]Hos. 4:1; 5:1 [b]Job 8:8; Joel 1:14 [c]Jer. 30:7; Joel 2:2
3 [a]Ex. 10:2; Ps. 78:4
4 [a]Joel 2:25; Amos 4:9 [b]Nah. 3:15, 16 [c]Is. 33:4
6 [1]Lit., *come up against* [a]Joel 2:2, 11, 25
7 [1]Or, *a stump* [a]Amos 4:9
8 [a]Joel 1:13; Amos 8:10

9 The [a]grain offering and the libation are cut off
From the house of the LORD.
The priests mourn,
The ministers of the LORD.
10 The field is [a]ruined,
The land mourns,
For the grain is ruined,
The new wine dries up,
Fresh oil [1]fails.
11 [1a]Be ashamed, O farmers,
Wail, O vinedressers,
For the wheat and the barley;
Because the [b]harvest of the field is destroyed.
12 The [a]vine dries up,
And the fig tree [1]fails;
The [b]pomegranate, the [c]palm also, and the [2d]apple tree,
All the trees of the field dry up.
Indeed, [e]rejoicing dries up
From the sons of men.

13 Gird yourselves *with sackcloth,*
And lament, O priests;
[a]Wail, O ministers of the altar!
Come, [b]spend the night in sackcloth,
O ministers of my God,
For the grain offering and the libation
Are withheld from the house of your God.

Starvation and Drought

14 Consecrate a fast,
Proclaim a solemn assembly;
Gather the elders
And all the inhabitants of the land
To the house of the LORD your God,
And [a]cry out to the LORD.
15 [a]Alas for the day!
For the day of the LORD is near,
And it will come as [b]destruction from the [1]Almighty.
16 Has not [a]food been cut off before our eyes,
Gladness and [b]joy from the house of our God?
17 The [1a]seeds shrivel under their [2]clods;
The storehouses are desolate,
The barns are torn down,
For the grain is dried up.
18 How the beasts groan!
The herds of cattle wander aimlessly
Because there is no pasture for them;
Even the flocks of sheep [1]suffer.
19 [a]To Thee, O LORD, I cry;
For [b]fire has devoured the pastures of the wilderness,
And the flame has burned up all the trees of the field.

9 [a]Hos. 9:4; Joel 1:13; 2:14

10 [1]Lit., *wastes away* [a]Is. 24:4, 7

11 [1]Or, *The farmers are ashamed, The vinedressers wail* [a]Jer. 14:4; Amos 5:16 [b]Is. 17:11; Jer. 9:12

12 [1]Lit., *wastes away* [2]Or, *apricot* [a]Hab. 3:17, 18 [b]Hag. 2:19 [c]Song of Sol. 7:8 [d]Song of Sol. 2:3 [e]Is. 16:10; 24:11

13 [a]Jer. 9:10 [b]1 Kin. 21:27

14 [a]Jon. 3:8

15 [1]Heb., *Shaddai* [a]Jer. 30:7; Amos 5:16 [b]Is. 13:6; Ezek. 7:2-12

16 [a]Is. 3:7; Amos 4:6, 7 [b]Deut. 12:6, 7; Ps. 43:4

17 [1]Or, *dried figs* [2]Or, *shovels* [a]Is. 17:10, 11

18 [1]Lit., *bear punishment*

19 [a]Ps. 50:15; Mic. 7:7 [b]Jer. 9:10; Amos 7:4

20 [1]Lit., *long for* [a]Ps. 104:21; 147:9; Joel 1:18 [b]1 Kin. 17:7; 18:5

1 [a]Joel 2:15; Zeph. 1:16 [b]Joel 1:15; 2:11, 31; 3:14

2 [a]Joel 2:10, 31; Zeph. 1:15 [b]Joel 1:6; 2:11, 25 [c]Lam. 1:12; Dan. 9:12; 12:1; Joel 1:2

3 [a]Ps. 97:3; Is. 9:18, 19 [b]Is. 51:3; Ezek. 36:35 [c]Ex. 10:5, 15; Ps. 105:34, 35

4 [a]Rev. 9:7

5 [1]Lit., *Like the noise of chariots* [2]Lit., *noise* [a]Rev. 9:9 [b]Is. 5:24; 30:30

6 [1]Or, *become flushed* [a]Is. 13:8; Nah. 2:10 [b]Jer. 30:6

7 [1]Lit., *in his ways* [a]Is. 5:26, 27

8 [1]Lit., *fall* [2]Lit., *weapon,* probably *javelin*

20 Even the beasts of the field [1a]pant for Thee;
For the [b]water brooks are dried up,
And fire has devoured the pastures of the wilderness.

CHAPTER 2

The Terrible Visitation

[a]BLOW a trumpet in Zion,
And sound an alarm on My holy mountain!
Let all the inhabitants of the land tremble,
For the [b]day of the LORD is coming;
Surely it is near,
2 A day of [a]darkness and gloom,
A day of clouds and thick darkness.
As the dawn is spread over the mountains,
So there is a [b]great and mighty people;
There has [c]never been *anything* like it,
Nor will there be again after it
To the years of many generations.
3 A [a]fire consumes before them,
And behind them a flame burns.
The land is [b]like the garden of Eden before them,
But a [c]desolate wilderness behind them,
And nothing at all escapes them.
4 Their [a]appearance is like the appearance of horses;
And like war horses, so they run.
5 [1]With a [a]noise as of chariots
They leap on the tops of the mountains,
Like the [2]crackling of a [b]flame of fire consuming the stubble,
Like a mighty people arranged for battle.
6 Before them the people are in [a]anguish;
All [b]faces [1]turn pale.
7 They run like [a]mighty men;
They climb the wall like soldiers;
And they each march [1]in line,
Nor do they deviate from their paths.
8 They do not crowd each other;
They march every one in his path.
When they [1]burst through the [2]defenses,
They do not break ranks.

9 They rush on the city,
They run on the wall;
They climb into the [a]houses,
They [b]enter through the windows like a thief.
10 Before them the earth [a]quakes,
The heavens tremble,
The [b]sun and the moon grow dark,
And the stars lose their brightness.
11 And the LORD [a]utters His voice before His army;
Surely His camp is very great,
For [b]strong is He who carries out His word.
The [c]day of the LORD is indeed great and very awesome,
And [d]who can endure it?
12 "Yet even now," declares the LORD,
"[a]Return to Me with all your heart,
And with fasting, weeping, and mourning;
13 And rend your heart and not your garments."
Now return to the LORD your God,
For He is [a]gracious and compassionate,
Slow to anger, abounding in lovingkindness,
And [b]relenting of evil.
14 Who knows whether He will *not* turn and relent,
And leave a [a]blessing behind Him,
Even a grain offering and a libation
For the LORD your God?
15 Blow a trumpet in Zion,
Consecrate a fast, proclaim a solemn assembly,
16 Gather the people, sanctify the congregation,
Assemble the elders,
Gather the children and the nursing infants.
Let the [a]bridegroom come out of his room
And the bride out of her *bridal* chamber.
17 Let the priests, the LORD's ministers,
[a]Weep between the porch and the altar,
And let them say, "[b]Spare Thy people, O LORD,
And do not make Thine inheritance a [c]reproach,
A byword among the nations.
Why should they among the peoples say,
'[d]Where is their God?' "

9 [a]Ex. 10:6 [b]Jer. 9:21
10 [a]Ps. 18:7; Joel 3:16; Nah. 1:5 [b]Is. 13:10; 34:4; Jer. 4:23; Ezek. 32:7; Joel 2:31; 3:15
11 [a]Ps. 46:6; Is. 13:4; Joel 3:16 [b]Jer. 50:34; Rev. 18:8 [c]Joel 1:15, 31; 3:14 [d]Ezek. 22:14
12 [a]Deut. 4:29; Ezek. 33:11
13 [a]Ex. 34:6 [b]Jer. 18:8; 42:10; Amos 7:3, 6
14 [a]Hag. 2:19
16 [a]Ps. 19:5
17 [a]2 Chr. 8:12; Ezek. 8:16 [b]Is. 37:20; Amos 7:2, 5 [c]Ps. 44:13; 74:10 [d]Ps. 79:10; 115:2
18 [1]Or, *was zealous* [2]Or, *had pity* [a]Zech. 1:14; 8:2 [b]Is. 60:10; 63:9, 15
19 [1]Or, *answered and said* [2]Lit., *it* [a]Ezek. 34:29; 36:15
20 [a]Jer. 1:14, 15 [b]Zech. 14:8 [c]Deut. 11:24 [d]Is. 34:3; Amos 4:10
21 [a]Is. 54:4; Jer. 30:10; Zeph. 3:16, 17 [b]Ps. 126:3; Joel 2:26
22 [1]Lit., *their wealth*
23 [1]I.e., autumn; or possibly, *the teacher for righteousness* [2]I.e., autumn [3]I.e., spring [4]So with ancient versions; Heb., *in the first* [a]Is. 12:2-6 [b]Deut. 11:14; Jer. 5:24 [c]Hos. 6:3; Zech. 10:1
24 [a]Lev. 26:10; Amos 9:13; Mal. 3:10
25 [a]Joel 1:4-7; 2:2-11
26 [a]Deut. 11:15; Is. 62:9 [b]Deut. 12:7; Ps. 67:5-7 [c]Ps. 126:2, 3; Is. 25:1 [d]Is. 45:17

Deliverance Promised

18 Then the LORD [1]will be [a]zealous for His land,
And [2]will have [b]pity on His people.
19 And the LORD [1]will answer and say to His people,
"Behold, I am going to send you grain, new wine, and oil,
And you will be satisfied *in full* with [2]them;
And I will [a]never again make you a reproach among the nations.
20 "But I will remove the [a]northern *army* far from you,
And I will drive it into a parched and desolate land,
And its vanguard into the [b]eastern sea,
And its rear guard into the [c]western sea.
And its [d]stench will arise and its foul smell will come up,
For it has done great things."

21 Do not [a]fear, O land, rejoice and be glad,
For the LORD has done [b]great things.
22 Do not fear, beasts of the field,
For the pastures of the wilderness have turned green,
For the tree has borne its fruit,
The fig tree and the vine have yielded [1]in full.
23 So rejoice, O sons of Zion,
And [a]be glad in the LORD your God;
For He has [b]given you [1]the early rain for *your* vindication.
And He has poured down for you the rain,
The [2]early and [3][c]latter rain [4]as before.
24 And the threshing [a]floors will be full of grain,
And the vats will overflow with the new wine and oil.
25 "Then I will make up to you for the years
That the swarming [a]locust has eaten,
The creeping locust, the stripping locust, and the gnawing locust,
My great army which I sent among you.
26 "And you shall have plenty to [a]eat and be satisfied,
And [b]praise the name of the LORD your God,
Who has [c]dealt wondrously with you;
Then My people will never be [d]put to shame.

27"Thus you will [a]know that I am in the midst of Israel,
And that I am the LORD your God
And there is [b]no other;
And My people will never be put to shame.

The Promise of the Spirit

28"[1]And it will come about after this
That I will pour out My [a]Spirit on all [2b]mankind;
And your sons and daughters will prophesy,
Your old men will dream dreams,
Your young men will see visions.
29"And even on the [a]male and female servants
I will pour out My Spirit in those days.

The Day of the LORD

30"And I will [a]display wonders in the sky and on the earth,
Blood, fire, and columns of smoke.
31"The [a]sun will be turned into darkness,
And the moon into blood,
Before the [b]great and awesome day of the LORD comes.
32"And it will come about that [a]whoever calls on the name of the LORD
Will be delivered;
For on Mount Zion and in Jerusalem
There will be those who [b]escape,
As the LORD has said,
Even among the survivors whom the LORD calls.

CHAPTER 3

The Nations Will Be Judged

"[1]FOR behold, in those days and at that time,
When I restore the fortunes of Judah and Jerusalem,
2 I will [a]gather all the nations,
And bring them down to the [b]valley of [1]Jehoshaphat.
Then I will [c]enter into judgment with them there
On behalf of My people and My inheritance, Israel,
Whom they have [d]scattered among the nations;
And they have [e]divided up My land.

3"They have also [a]cast lots for My people,
[1b]Traded a boy for a harlot,
And sold a girl for wine that they may drink.
4"Moreover, what are you to Me,
O Tyre, Sidon, and all the regions of
Philistia? Are you rendering Me a
recompense? But if you do recompense Me, swiftly and speedily I will
return your recompense on your
head.
5"Since you have [a]taken My silver and My gold, brought My precious [1]treasures to your temples,
6 and sold the sons of Judah and
Jerusalem to the [1]Greeks in order to
remove them far from their territory,
7 behold, I am going to arouse
them from the place where you have
sold them, and return your recompense on your head.
8"Also I will sell your sons and
your daughters into the hand of the
sons of Judah, and they will sell
them to the Sabeans, to a distant nation," for the LORD has spoken.
9 [a]Proclaim this among the nations:
[b]Prepare a war; [c]rouse the mighty men!
Let all the soldiers draw near, let them come up!
10 [a]Beat your plowshares into swords,
And your pruning hooks into spears;
Let the weak say, "I am a mighty man."
11 [1]Hasten and come, all you surrounding nations,
And gather yourselves there.
Bring down, O LORD, Thy [a]mighty ones.
12 Let the nations be aroused
And come up to the [a]valley of [1]Jehoshaphat,
For there I will sit to [b]judge
All the surrounding nations.
13 Put in the sickle, for the [a]harvest is ripe.
Come, tread, for the wine press is full;
The vats overflow, for their [b]wickedness is great.
14 [a]Multitudes, multitudes in the [b]valley of [1]decision!
For the [c]day of the LORD is near in the valley of [1]decision.
15 The [a]sun and moon grow dark,
And the stars lose their brightness.
16 And the LORD [a]roars from Zion
And utters His voice from Jerusalem,

27 [a]Joel 3:17, 21 [b]Is. 45:5, 6

28 [1]Chap. 3:1 in Heb. [2]Lit., *flesh* [a]Is. 32:15; 44:3; Ezek. 39:29 [b]Is. 40:5; 49:6

29 [a]1 Cor. 12:13

30 [a]Luke 21:11, 25, 26; Acts 2:19

31 [a]Is. 13:9, 10; 34:4; Joel 2:10; 3:15; Matt. 24:29; Mark 13:24; Acts 2:20 [b]Zeph. 1:14-16; Mal. 4:1, 5

32 [a]Jer. 33:3; Acts 2:21; Rom. 10:13 [b]Is. 4:2; Obad. 17

1 [1]Chap. 4:1 in Heb.

2 [1]I.e., YHWH judges [a]Is. 66:18; Mic. 4:12 [b]Joel 3:14 [c]Is. 66:16; Jer. 25:31 [d]Jer. 50:17; Ezek. 34:6 [e]Ezek. 35:10; 36:1-5

3 [1]Lit., *Given* [a]Obad. 11; Nah. 3:10 [b]Amos 2:6

5 [1]Lit., *goodly things* [a]2 Kin. 12:18; 2 Chr. 21:16, 17

6 [1]Lit., *sons of Javan*

9 [a]Jer. 51:27, 28 [b]Jer. 6:4; Mic. 3:5 [c]Is. 8:9, 10; Jer. 46:3, 4; Zech. 14:2, 3

10 [a]Is. 2:4; Mic. 4:3

11 [1]Or, *Lend aid* [a]Is. 13:3

12 [1]I.e., YHWH judges [a]Joel 3:2, 14 [b]Ps. 7:6; 98:9; Is. 3:13

13 [a]Jer. 51:33; Hos. 6:11 [b]Gen. 18:20

14 [1]I.e., God's verdict [a]Is. 34:2-8 [b]Joel 3:2, 12 [c]Joel 1:15; 2:1, 11, 31

15 [a]Joel 2:10, 31

16 [a]Hos. 11:10; Amos 1:2

And the [b]heavens and the earth
tremble.
But the LORD is a [c]refuge for His
people
And a [d]stronghold to the sons
of Israel.
17 Then you will know that I am
the LORD your God,
Dwelling in Zion My [a]holy
mountain.
So Jerusalem will be [b]holy,
And [c]strangers will pass
through it no more.

Judah Will Be Blessed

18 And it will come about in that
day
That the [a]mountains will drip
with [1]sweet wine,

16 [b]Ezek. 38:19; Joel 2:10; Hag. 2:6 [c]Ps. 61:3; Is. 33:16; Jer. 17:17 [d]Jer. 16:19; Nah. 1:7

17 [a]Is. 11:9; 56:7; Ezek. 20:40 [b]Is. 4:3; Obad. 17 [c]Is. 52:1; Nah. 1:15

18 [1]Lit., *freshly pressed out grape juice* [2]Or, *acacias* [a]Amos 9:13 [b]Ex. 3:8 [c]Is. 30:25; 35:6 [d]Ezek. 47:1-12

19 [a]Obad. 10

20 [a]Ezek. 37:25; Amos 9:15

21 [a]Is. 4:4; Ezek. 36:25

And the hills will [b]flow with
milk,
And all the [c]brooks of Judah
will flow with water;
And a [d]spring will go out from
the house of the LORD,
To water the valley of [2]Shittim.
19 Egypt will become a waste,
And Edom will become a desolate wilderness,
Because of the [a]violence done
to the sons of Judah,
In whose land they have shed
innocent blood.
20 But Judah will be [a]inhabited
forever,
And Jerusalem for all generations.
21 And I will [a]avenge their blood
which I have not avenged,
For the LORD dwells in Zion.

THE BOOK OF AMOS

Judgment on Neighbor Nations

THE words of Amos, who was
among the sheepherders from [a]Te-
koa, which he [1]envisioned in visions
concerning Israel in the days of Uzziah king of Judah, and in the days
of Jeroboam son of Joash, king of
Israel, two years before the [b]earth-
quake.
2 And he said,
"The [a]LORD roars from Zion,
And from Jerusalem He utters
His voice;
And the shepherds' [b]pasture
grounds mourn,
And the [1]summit of Carmel
dries up."

3 Thus says the LORD,
"For three transgressions of Damascus and for four
I will [a]not [1]revoke its *punishment,*
Because they threshed Gilead
with *implements* of sharp
iron.
4"So I will send fire upon the
house of Hazael,
And it will consume the citadels of Ben-hadad.
5"I will also [a]break the *gate* bar of
Damascus,
And cut off the inhabitant from
the [1]valley of Aven,
And him who holds the scepter,
from Beth-eden;
So the people of Syria will go
exiled to Kir,"

1 [1]Lit., *concerning saw* [a]2 Sam. 14:2; Jer. 6:1 [b]Zech. 14:5

2 [1]Lit., *head* [a]Is. 42:13; Jer. 25:30; Joel 3:16 [b]Jer. 12:4; Joel 1:18, 19

3 [1]Lit., *cause it to turn back,* and so throughout the chap. [a]Is. 8:4

5 [1]Possibly *Baalbek* [a]Jer. 51:30; Lam. 2:9

6 [a]1 Sam. 6:17; Jer. 47:1, 5; Zeph. 2:4 [b]Ezek. 35:5; Obad. 11

8 [1]Lit., *cause to return* [2]Lit., *hand* [3]YHWH, usually rendered LORD [a]2 Chr. 26:6; Amos 3:9; Zech. 9:6 [b]Jer. 47:5; Zeph. 2:4 [c]Is. 14:29-31; Ezek. 25:16

9 [1]Lit., *brothers* [a]Is. 23:1-18; Jer. 25:22; Ezek. 26:2-4 [b]1 Kin. 5:1; 9:11-14

11 [a]Is. 34:5, 6; 63:1-6; Jer. 49:7-22

Says the LORD.
6 Thus says the LORD,
"For three transgressions of
[a]Gaza and for four
I will not revoke its *punishment,*
Because they deported an entire population
To deliver *it* up to [b]Edom.
7"So I will send fire upon the wall
of Gaza,
And it will consume her citadels.
8"I will also cut off the inhabitant
from [a]Ashdod,
And him who holds the scepter,
from [b]Ashkelon;
I will even [1]unleash My [2]power
upon Ekron,
And the remnant of the [c]Philis-
tines will perish,"
Says the Lord [3]GOD.

9 Thus says the LORD,
"For three transgressions of
[a]Tyre and for four
I will not revoke its *punishment,*
Because they delivered up an
entire population to Edom
And did not remember *the* covenant of [1b]brotherhood.
10"So I will send fire upon the wall
of Tyre,
And it will consume her citadels."

11 Thus says the LORD,
"For three transgressions of
[a]Edom and for four

I will not revoke its *punishment,*
Because he [b]pursued his brother with the sword,
While he [1]stifled his compassion;
His anger also [c]tore continually,
And he maintained his fury forever.
12 "So I will send fire upon [a]Teman,
And it will consume the citadels of Bozrah."

13 Thus says the LORD,
"For three transgressions of the sons of [a]Ammon and for four
I will not revoke its *punishment,*
Because they [b]ripped open the pregnant women of Gilead
In order to [c]enlarge their borders.
14 "So I will kindle a fire on the wall of Rabbah,
And it will consume her citadels
Amid [1a]war cries on the day of battle
And a [b]storm on the day of tempest.
15 "Their [a]king will go into exile,
He and his princes together,"
says the LORD.

CHAPTER 2

Judgment on Judah and Israel

THUS says the LORD,
"For three transgressions of [a]Moab and for four
I will not [1]revoke its *punishment,*
Because he burned the bones of the king of Edom to lime.
2 "So I will send fire upon Moab,
And it will consume the citadels of [a]Kerioth;
And Moab will die amid [b]tumult,
With [1]war cries and the sound of a trumpet.
3 "I will also cut off the [1a]judge from her midst,
And slay all her princes with him," says the LORD.

4 Thus says the LORD,
"For three transgressions of [a]Judah and for four
I will not revoke its *punishment,*
Because they [b]rejected the law of the LORD
And have not kept His statutes;
Their [1c]lies also have led them astray,
Those after which their [d]fathers walked.
5 "So I will [a]send fire upon Judah,
And it will consume the citadels of Jerusalem."

6 Thus says the LORD,
"For three transgressions of Israel and for four
I will not revoke its *punishment,*
Because they [a]sell the righteous for money
And the needy for a pair of sandals.
7 "These who [1]pant after the *very* dust of the earth on the head of the [a]helpless
Also turn aside the way of the humble;
And a [b]man and his father [2]resort to the same [3]girl
In order to profane My holy name.
8 "And on garments [a]taken as pledges they stretch out beside every altar,
And in the house of their God they drink the wine of those who have been fined.

9 "Yet it was I who destroyed the Amorite before them,
[1]Though his height *was* like the height of cedars
And he *was* strong as the oaks;
I even destroyed his [a]fruit above and his root below.
10 "And it was I who brought you up from the land of Egypt,
And I led you in the wilderness [a]forty years
[1]That you might take possession of the land of the Amorite.
11 "Then I [a]raised up some of your sons to be prophets
And some of your young men to be [b]Nazirites.
Is this not so, O sons of Israel?" declares the LORD.
12 "But you made the Nazirites drink wine,
And you commanded the prophets saying, 'You shall not [a]prophesy!'
13 "Behold, I am [1a]weighted down beneath you
As a wagon [2]is weighted down when filled with sheaves.
14 "[1a]Flight will perish from the swift,
And the stalwart will not strengthen his power,
Nor the [b]mighty man save his [2]life.

11 [1]Lit., *corrupted* [b]Num. 20:14-21; 2 Chr. 28:17; Obad. 10-12 [c]Is. 57:16; Mic. 7:18
12 [a]Jer. 49:7, 20
13 [a]Jer. 49:1-6; Ezek. 25:2-7; Zeph. 2:8, 9 [b]2 Kin. 15:16; Hos. 13:16 [c]Is. 5:8; Ezek. 35:10
14 [1]Or, *shouts* [a]Ezek. 21:22; Amos 2:2 [b]Is. 29:6; 30:30
15 [a]Jer. 49:3
1 [1]Lit., *cause it to turn back,* and so throughout the chap. [a]Is. 15:1-16:14; Jer. 48:1-47; Zeph. 2:8, 9
2 [1]Or, *shouts* [a]Jer. 48:24, 41 [b]Jer. 48:45
3 [1]Or, *executive officer* [a]Ps. 2:10; 141:6; Amos 5:7, 12; 6:12
4 [1]Or, *false gods* [a]2 Kin. 17:19; Hos. 12:2; Amos 3:2 [b]Judg. 2:17-20; 2 Kin. 22:11-17; Jer. 6:19; 8:9 [c]Is. 9:15, 16; 28:15; Hab. 2:18 [d]Jer. 9:14; 16:11, 12; Ezek. 20:18, 24, 30
5 [a]Jer. 17:27; 21:10
6 [a]Joel 3:3; Amos 5:11, 12; 8:6
7 [1]Or, *trample the head of the helpless on the dust;* or, *snap at,* etc. [2]Lit., *go* [3]Possibly a harlot, or a temple prostitute [a]Amos 8:4; Mic. 2:2, 9 [b]Hos. 4:14
8 [a]Ex. 22:26
9 [1]Lit., *Whose height* [a]Ezek. 17:9; Mal. 4:1
10 [1]Lit., *To possess* [a]Deut. 2:7
11 [a]Deut. 18:17; Jer. 7:25 [b]Num. 6:2, 3
12 [a]Jer. 11:21; Amos 7:13, 16
13 [1]Or, *tottering* [2]Or, *totters* [a]Joel 3:13
14 [1]Or, *A place of refuge* [2]Lit., *soul* [a]Is. 30:16, 17 [b]Jer. 9:23

15 "He who grasps the bow will not stand *his ground,*
The swift of foot will not escape,
Nor will he who [a]rides the horse save his [1]life.
16 "Even the bravest among the warriors will [a]flee naked in that day," declares the LORD.

CHAPTER 3

All the Tribes Are Guilty

HEAR this word which the LORD has spoken against you, sons of Israel, against the entire [1a]family which [2]He brought up from the land of Egypt,
2 "[a]You only have I [1]chosen among all the families of the earth;
Therefore, I will [2]punish you for all your iniquities."
3 Do two men [a]walk together unless they have made an [1]appointment?
4 Does a lion [a]roar in the forest when he has no prey?
Does a young lion [1]growl from his den unless he has captured *something?*
5 Does a bird fall into a trap on the ground when there is no [1]bait in it?
Does a trap spring up from the earth when it captures nothing at all?
6 If a [a]trumpet is blown in a city will not the people tremble?
If a [b]calamity occurs in a city has not the LORD done it?
7 [1]Surely the LORD God does nothing
Unless He [a]reveals His secret counsel
To His servants the prophets.
8 A lion has roared! Who will not fear?
The [a]Lord [1]GOD has spoken! [b]Who can but prophesy?

9 Proclaim on the citadels in Ashdod and on the citadels in the land of Egypt and say, "Assemble yourselves on the [a]mountains of Samaria and see *the* great tumults within her and *the* [b]oppressions in her midst.
10 "But they do not [a]know how to do what is right," declares the LORD, "these who [b]hoard up [1]violence and devastation in their citadels."
11 Therefore, thus says the Lord GOD,
"An enemy, even one surrounding the land,
Will pull down your [1]strength from you
And your citadels will be looted."
12 Thus says the LORD,
"Just as the shepherd [1a]snatches from the lion's mouth a couple of legs or a piece of an ear,
So will the sons of Israel dwelling in Samaria be [2]snatched away—
With *the* corner of a bed and *the* [3]cover of a couch!
13 "Hear and [a]testify against the house of Jacob,"
Declares the Lord GOD, the God of hosts.
14 "For on the day that I punish Israel's transgressions,
I will also punish the altars of [a]Bethel;
The horns of the altar will be cut off,
And they will fall to the ground.
15 "I will also smite the [1a]winter house together with the [b]summer house;
The houses of [2c]ivory will also perish
And the great houses will come to an end,"
Declares the LORD.

CHAPTER 4

"Yet You Have Not Returned to Me"

HEAR this word, you cows of [a]Bashan who are on the mountain of Samaria,
Who oppress the poor, who crush the needy,
Who say to [1]your husbands, "Bring now, that we may drink!"
2 The Lord [1]GOD has sworn by His [a]holiness,
"Behold, the days are coming upon you
When [2]they will take you away with [b]meat hooks,
And the last of you with [c]fish hooks.
3 "You will [a]go out *through* breaches *in the walls,*
Each one straight before her,
And you [1]will be cast to Harmon," declares the LORD.

4 "Enter Bethel and transgress;
In Gilgal multiply transgression!
Bring your sacrifices every morning,
Your tithes every three days.
5 "[1]Offer a [a]thank offering also from that which is leavened,

15 [1]Lit., *soul* [a]Is. 31:3
16 [a]Judg. 4:17; Jer. 48:41
1 [1]I.e., nation [2]Lit., *I* [a]Jer. 8:3; 13:11
2 [1]Lit., *known* [2]Lit., *visit* [a]Gen. 18:19; Ex. 19:5, 6; Deut. 4:32-37
3 [1]Or, *agreement* [a]Lev. 26:23, 24
4 [1]Lit., *give his voice* [a]Ps. 104:21; Hos. 5:14; 11:10
5 [1]Or, *striker-bar set*
6 [a]Jer. 4:5, 19, 21; 6:1; Hos. 5:8; Zeph. 1:16 [b]Is. 14:24-27; 45:7
7 [1]Or, *For* [a]Gen. 18:17; Jer. 23:22; Dan. 9:22
8 [1]YHWH, usually rendered LORD, and so throughout the chap. [a]Jon. 1:1-3; 3:1-3 [b]Jer. 20:9
9 [a]Is. 28:1; Ezek. 37:22; Amos 4:1; 6:1 [b]Amos 4:1; 5:11; 8:6
10 [1]I.e., the booty from violence, etc. [a]Ps. 14:4; Jer. 4:22; Amos 5:7; 6:12 [b]Hab. 2:8-11; Zeph. 1:9; Zech. 5:3, 4
11 [1]Or, *stronghold*
12 [1]Or, *delivers* [2]Or, *delivered* [3]Lit., *damask* [a]1 Sam. 17:34-37
13 [a]Ezek. 2:7
14 [a]Hos. 10:5-8, 14, 15; Amos 4:4; 5:5, 6; 7:10, 13
15 [1]Or, *autumn* [2]I.e., ivory inlay [a]Jer. 36:22 [b]Judg. 3:20 [c]1 Kin. 22:39; Ps. 45:8
1 [1]Lit., *their lords* [a]Ps. 22:12; Ezek. 39:18
2 [1]YHWH, usually rendered LORD, and so throughout the chap. [2]Lit., *he* [a]Ps. 89:35 [b]Is. 37:29; Ezek. 38:4 [c]Ezek. 29:4
3 [1]So Gk.; M.T. reads, *will cast* [a]Jer. 52:7
5 [1]Lit., *Offer up in smoke* [a]Lev. 7:13

And proclaim [b]freewill offerings, make them known.
For so you [c]love *to do*, you sons of Israel,"
Declares the Lord GOD.

6 "But I gave you also [a]cleanness of teeth in all your cities
And lack of bread in all your places,
Yet you have [b]not returned to Me," declares the LORD.
7 "And furthermore, I [a]withheld the rain from you
While there *were* still three months until harvest.
Then I would send rain on one city
And on [b]another city I would not send rain;
One part would be rained on,
While the part not rained on would dry up.
8 "So two or three cities would stagger to another city to drink [a]water,
But would [b]not be satisfied;
Yet you have [c]not returned to Me," declares the LORD.
9 "I [a]smote you with scorching *wind* and mildew;
And the [b]caterpillar was devouring
Your many gardens and vineyards, fig trees and olive trees;
Yet you have not returned to Me," declares the LORD.
10 "I sent a [a]plague among you after the manner of Egypt;
I slew your [b]young men by the sword along with your [c]captured horses,
And I made the [d]stench of your camp rise up in your nostrils;
Yet you have [e]not returned to Me," declares the LORD.
11 "I overthrew you as [a]God overthrew Sodom and Gomorrah,
And you were like a [b]firebrand snatched from a blaze;
Yet you have [c]not returned to Me," declares the LORD.
12 "Therefore, thus I will do to you, O Israel;
Because I shall do this to you,
Prepare to [a]meet your God, O Israel."
13 For behold, He who [a]forms mountains and [b]creates the wind
And [c]declares to man what are His thoughts,
He who [d]makes dawn into darkness
And [e]treads on the high places of the earth,
The LORD God of hosts is His name.

CHAPTER 5

"Seek Me That You May Live"

HEAR this word which I take up for you as a [a]dirge, O house of Israel.
2 She has fallen, she will not rise again—
The [a]virgin Israel.
She *lies* neglected on her land;
There is [b]none to raise her up.
3 For thus says the Lord [1]GOD,
"The city which goes forth a thousand *strong*
Will have a [a]hundred left,
And the *one* which goes forth a hundred *strong*
Will have ten left to the house of Israel."

4 For thus says the LORD to the house of Israel,
"[a]Seek Me that you may live.
5 "But do not [1]resort to Bethel,
And do not come to Gilgal,
Nor cross over to Beersheba;
For Gilgal will certainly go into captivity,
And Bethel will [2]come to trouble.
6 "[a]Seek the LORD that you may live,
Lest He break forth like a [b]fire,
[1]O house of Joseph,
And it consume with none to quench *it* for Bethel,
7 *For* those who turn [a]justice into wormwood
And [1]cast righteousness down to the earth."

8 He who made the [a]Pleiades and Orion
And [b]changes deep darkness into morning,
Who also [1]darkens day *into* night,
Who [c]calls for the waters of the sea
And pours them out on the surface of the earth,
The LORD is His name.
9 It is He who [a]flashes forth *with* destruction upon the strong,
So that [b]destruction comes upon the fortress.

10 They hate him who [a]reproves in the [1]gate,
And they [b]abhor him who speaks *with* integrity.
11 Therefore, because you [1]impose heavy rent on the poor

---

5 [b]Lev. 22:18-21 [c]Jer. 7:9, 10; Hos. 9:1, 10
6 [a]Is. 3:1; Jer. 14:18 [b]Is. 9:13; Jer. 5:3; Hag. 2:17
7 [a]Deut. 11:17; 2 Chr. 7:13; Is. 5:6 [b]Ex. 9:4, 26; 10:22, 23
8 [a]1 Kin. 18:5; Jer. 14:4 [b]Ezek. 4:16; Hag. 1:6 [c]Jer. 3:7
9 [a]Deut. 28:22; Hag. 2:17 [b]Joel 1:4, 7; Amos 7:1, 2
10 [a]Lev. 26:25; Deut. 28:27, 60 [b]Jer. 11:22; 18:21; 48:15 [c]2 Kin. 13:3, 7 [d]Joel 2:20 [e]Is. 9:13
11 [a]Gen. 19:25; Deut. 29:23 [b]Zech. 3:2 [c]Jer. 23:14
12 [a]Is. 32:11; 64:2; Jer. 5:22
13 [a]Job 38:4-7; Ps. 65:6; Is. 40:12 [b]Ps. 135:7; Jer. 10:13 [c]Ps. 139:2; Dan. 2:30 [d]Jer. 13:16; Joel 2:2; Amos 5:8 [e]Mic. 1:3
1 [a]Jer. 7:29; 9:10, 17; Ezek. 19:1
2 [a]Jer. 14:17 [b]Is. 51:18; Jer. 50:32
3 [1]YHWH, usually rendered LORD, and so throughout the chap. [a]Is. 6:13
4 [a]Deut. 4:29; 32:46, 47
5 [1]Lit., *seek* [2]Or, *become iniquity*
6 [1]Or, *in the house* [a]Is. 55:3, 6, 7; Amos 5:14 [b]Deut. 4:24
7 [1]Lit., *they have put down* [a]Amos 2:3; 5:12; 6:12
8 [1]Lit., *He darkened* [a]Job 9:9; 38:31 [b]Job 12:22; 38:12; Is. 42:16 [c]Ps. 104:6-9; Amos 9:6
9 [a]Job 5:3; Is. 29:5; Amos 2:14 [b]Mic. 5:11
10 [1]I.e., the place where court was held [a]Is. 29:21; Amos 5:15 [b]Is. 59:15; Jer. 17:16-18
11 [1]Another reading is: *trample upon*

And exact a tribute of grain
from them,
Though you have built houses
of well-hewn stone,
Yet you will not live in them;
You have planted pleasant
vineyards, yet you will [a]not
drink their wine.
12 For I know your transgressions
are many and your sins are
great,
You who [a]distress the righteous
and accept bribes,
And [1]turn aside the poor in the
[2]gate.
13 Therefore, at [1]such a time the
prudent person [a]keeps silent,
for it is an evil time.

14 Seek good and not evil, that you
may live;
And thus may the LORD God of
hosts be with you,
Just as you have said!
15 [a]Hate evil, love good,
And establish justice in the
[1]gate!
Perhaps the LORD God of hosts
[b]May be gracious to the [c]rem-
nant of Joseph.

16 Therefore, thus says the LORD
God of hosts, the Lord,
"There is [a]wailing in all the pla-
zas,
And in all the streets they say,
'Alas! Alas!'
They also call the [b]farmer to
mourning
And [1c]professional mourners to
lamentation.
17"And in all the [a]vineyards *there*
is wailing,
Because I shall pass through
the midst of you," says the
LORD.

18 Alas, you who are longing for
the [a]day of the LORD,
For what purpose *will* the day
of the LORD *be* to you?
It *will be* [b]darkness and not
light;
19 As when a man [a]flees from a
lion,
And a bear meets him,
[1]Or goes home, leans his hand
against the wall,
And a snake bites him.
20 *Will* not the day of the LORD *be*
[a]darkness instead of light,
Even gloom with no brightness
in it?

21"I hate, I [a]reject your festivals,
Nor do I [1b]delight in your solemn assemblies.
22"Even though you [a]offer up to
Me burnt offerings and your
grain offerings,
I will not accept *them;*
And I will not *even* look at the
[b]peace offerings of your fatlings.
23"Take away from Me the noise
of your songs;
I will not even listen to the
sound of your harps.
24"But let [a]justice roll down like
waters
And righteousness like an ever-
flowing stream.

25"[1a]Did you present Me with sacrifices and grain offerings in the wilderness for forty years, O house of
Israel?
26"[a]You also carried along [1]Sik-
kuth your king and [2]Kiyyun, your
images, [3]the star of your gods which
you made for yourselves.
27"Therefore, I will make you go
into exile beyond Damascus," says
the LORD, whose name is the God of
hosts.

CHAPTER 6

"Those at Ease in Zion"

[a]WOE to those who are at ease in
Zion,
And to those who *feel* secure in
the mountain of Samaria,
The [b]distinguished men of the
foremost of nations,
To whom the house of Israel
comes.
2 Go over to [a]Calneh and look,
And go from there to [b]Hamath
the great,
Then go down to [c]Gath of the
Philistines.
Are [1]they better than these
kingdoms,
Or is their territory greater than
yours?
3 Do you [a]put off the day of calamity,
And would you [b]bring near the
seat of violence?

4 Those who recline on beds of
ivory
And sprawl on their couches,
And [a]eat lambs from the flock
And calves from the midst of
the stall,
5 Who improvise to the sound of
the harp,
And like David have [1a]com-
posed songs for themselves,
6 Who drink wine from [1]sacrifi-
cial bowls

11 [a]Mic. 6:15
12 [1]Lit., *they turn* [2]I.e., the place where court was held [a]Is. 1:23; 5:23
13 [1]Lit., *that time* [a]Eccles. 3:7; Hos. 4:4
15 [1]I.e., the place where court was held [a]Ps. 97:10 [b]Joel 2:14 [c]Mic. 5:3, 7, 8
16 [1]Lit., *those who know lamentation* [a]Jer. 9:10, 18-20; Amos 8:3 [b]Joel 1:11 [c]2 Chr. 35:25
17 [a]Is. 16:10; Jer. 48:33
18 [a]Is. 5:19; Joel 1:15; 2:1, 11, 31 [b]Is. 5:30; 9:19; Jer. 30:7
19 [1]Or, *Then* [a]Job 20:24; Is. 24:17, 18; Jer. 15:2, 3
20 [a]Is. 13:10; Zeph. 1:15
21 [1]Lit., *like to smell* [a]Is. 1:11-16; 66:3; Amos 4:4, 5; 8:10 [b]Lev. 26:31; Jer. 14:12; Hos. 5:6
22 [a]Mic. 6:6, 7 [b]Lev. 7:11-15; Amos 4:5
24 [a]Jer. 22:3; Ezek. 45:9; Mic. 6:8
25 [1]Or, *You presented Me with the sacrifices and a grain offering* [a]Acts 7:42
26 [1]Or, *Sakkuth (Saturn);* or else, *shrine of your Moloch* [2]Or, *Kaiwan (Saturn);* or else, *stands of* [3]Or, *your star gods* [a]Acts 7:43
1 [a]Is. 32:9-11; Zeph. 1:12 [b]Ex. 19:5; Amos 3:2
2 [1]Or, *you* [a]Gen. 10:10; Is. 10:9 [b]1 Kin. 8:65; 2 Kin. 18:34; Is. 10:9 [c]1 Sam. 5:8; 2 Chr. 26:6
3 [a]Is. 56:12; Amos 9:10 [b]Ps. 94:20
4 [a]Ezek. 34:2, 3
5 [1]Or, *invented musical instruments* [a]1 Chr. 15:16
6 [1]Lit., *sprinkling basins*

While they anoint themselves
with the finest of oils,
Yet they have not [a]grieved over
the ruin of Joseph.
7 Therefore, they will now go into
exile at the head of the exiles,
And the [a]sprawlers' [1]banqueting will [2]pass away.

8 The Lord [1]GOD has sworn by
Himself, the LORD God of
hosts has declared:
"I [a]loathe the arrogance of Jacob,
And I [2]detest his citadels;
Therefore, I will [b]deliver up *the*
city and [3]all it contains."
9 And it will be, if ten men are left
in one house, they will die.
10 Then one's uncle, or his [a]undertaker, will lift him up to carry out
his bones from the house, and he
will say to the one who is in the innermost part of the house, "Is anyone else with you?" And that one
will say, "No one." Then he will answer, "[b]Keep quiet. For the name of
the LORD is [c]not to be mentioned."
11 For behold, the LORD is going to
command that the great house be
smashed to pieces and the small
house to fragments.
12 Do horses run on rocks?
Or does one plow [1]them with
oxen?
Yet you have turned [a]justice
into poison,
And the fruit of righteousness
into [2]wormwood,
13 You who rejoice in [1][a]Lo-debar,
[2]And say, "Have we not by our
own strength [b]taken [3]Karnaim for ourselves?"
14"For behold, I am going to raise
up a nation against you,
O house of Israel," declares the
LORD God of hosts,
"And they will afflict you from
the [a]entrance of Hamath
To the [a]brook of the Arabah.

CHAPTER 7

Warning Through Visions

THUS the Lord [1]GOD showed me,
and behold, He was forming a [a]locust-swarm when the spring crop
began to sprout. And behold, the
spring crop *was* after the king's
mowing.
2 And it came about, when it had
[a]finished eating the vegetation of
the land, that I said,
"[b]Lord GOD, please pardon!
How can Jacob stand,
For he is [c]small?"
3 The LORD [1][a]changed His mind
about this.
"It shall not be," said the LORD.
4 Thus the Lord GOD showed me,
and behold, the Lord GOD was calling to contend *with them* by [a]fire,
and it consumed the great deep and
began to consume the farm land.
5 Then I said,
"[a]Lord GOD, please stop!
How can Jacob stand, for he is
small?"
6 The LORD [1][a]changed His mind
about this.
"This too shall not be," said the
Lord GOD.
7 Thus He showed me, and behold, the Lord was standing by a
vertical wall, with a plumb line in
His hand.
8 And the LORD said to me,
"What do you see, [a]Amos?" And I
said, "A plumb line." Then the LORD
said,
"Behold I am about to put a
[b]plumb line
In the midst of My people Israel.
I will spare them [c]no longer.
9"The [a]high places of Isaac will
be desolated
And the [b]sanctuaries of Israel
laid waste.
Then shall I [c]rise up against the
house of Jeroboam with the
sword."

Amos Accused, Answers

10 Then Amaziah, the [a]priest of
Bethel, sent *word* to Jeroboam, king
of Israel, saying, "Amos has [b]conspired against you in the midst of
the house of Israel; the land is unable to endure all his words.
11"For thus Amos says, 'Jeroboam
will die by the sword and Israel will
certainly go from its land into
exile.' "
12 Then Amaziah said to Amos,
"[a]Go, you seer, flee away to the land
of Judah, and there eat bread and
there do your prophesying!
13"But no longer [a]prophesy at
Bethel, for it is a [b]sanctuary of the
king and a royal [1]residence."
14 Then Amos answered and said
to Amaziah, "I am not a prophet,
nor am I the [a]son of a prophet; for I
am a herdsman and a [1]grower of
sycamore figs.
15"But the LORD took me from
[1]following the flock and the LORD
said to me, 'Go [a]prophesy to My
people Israel.'
16"And now hear the word of the

6 [a]Ezek. 9:4
7 [1]Or, *cultic feasts* [2]Lit., *turn aside*
[a]1 Kin. 20:16-20; Dan. 5:4-6, 30
8 [1]YHWH, usually rendered LORD [2]Lit., *hate* [3]Lit., *its fulness* [a]Lev. 26:30; Deut. 32:19; Ps. 106:40; Amos 5:21 [b]Hos. 11:6
10 [a]1 Sam. 31:12 [b]Amos 5:13; 8:3 [c]Jer. 44:26; Ezek. 20:39
12 [1]Another reading is: *the sea with oxen* [2]I.e., bitterness
[a]1 Kin. 21:7-13; Is. 59:13, 14; Amos 5:7, 11, 12
13 [1]Lit., *a thing of nothing* [2]Lit., *Who* [3]Lit., *a pair of horns*
[a]Job 8:14, 15; Ps. 2:2-4; Luke 12:19, 20 [b]Ps. 75:4, 5; Is. 28:14, 15
14 [a]Num. 34:7, 8; 2 Kin. 14:25
1 [1]YHWH, usually rendered LORD, and so throughout the chap.
[a]Joel 1:4; Amos 4:9; Nah. 3:15
2 [a]Ex. 10:15 [b]Jer. 14:7, 20, 21; Ezek. 9:8; 11:13 [c]Is. 37:4; Jer. 42:2
3 [1]Or, *relented* [a]Jer. 26:19; Hos. 11:8; Amos 5:15
4 [a]Deut. 32:22; Is. 66:15, 16; Amos 2:5
5 [a]Ps. 85:4; Joel 2:17
6 [1]Or, *relented* [a]Ps. 106:45; Amos 7:3; Jon. 3:10
8 [a]Jer. 1:11; Amos 8:2 [b]Is. 28:17; 34:11; Lam. 2:8 [c]Jer. 15:6; Ezek. 7:2-9; Amos 8:2
9 [a]Hos. 10:8; Mic. 1:5 [b]Lev. 26:31; Is. 63:18; Jer. 51:51; Amos 7:13 [c]2 Kin. 15:8-10; Amos 7:11
10 [a]1 Kin. 12:31, 32; 13:33 [b]Jer. 26:8-11; 38:4
12 [a]Matt. 8:34
13 [1]Lit., *house* [a]Amos 2:12; Acts 4:18 [b]1 Kin. 12:29, 32; Amos 7:9
14 [1]Or, *nipper* [a]2 Kin. 2:3; 4:38; 2 Chr. 19:2
15 [1]Lit., *behind* [a]Jer. 1:7; Ezek. 2:3, 4

LORD: you are saying, 'You shall not
[a]prophesy against Israel nor shall
you [1b]preach against the house of
Isaac.'
17"Therefore, thus says the LORD,
'Your [a]wife will become a harlot in
the city, your [b]sons and your daughters will fall by the sword, your land
will be parceled up by a *measuring*
line, and you yourself will die [1]upon
[c]unclean soil. Moreover, Israel will
certainly go from its land into
exile.'"

CHAPTER 8

Basket of Fruit and Israel's Captivity

THUS the Lord [1]GOD showed me,
and behold, *there was* a basket of
summer fruit.
2 And He said, "What do you see,
Amos?" And [a]I said, "A basket of
summer fruit." Then the LORD said
to me, "The [b]end has come for My
people Israel. I will [1]spare them no
longer.
3"[1]The [a]songs of the palace will
turn to wailing in that day," declares the Lord GOD. "Many *will be*
the corpses; in every place [2]they will
cast them forth [3]in silence."
4 Hear this, you who [1]trample the
[a]needy, to do away with the humble
of the land,
5 saying,
"When will the [a]new moon [1]be over,
So that we may buy grain,
And the [b]sabbath, that we may open the wheat *market*,
To make the [2]bushel smaller and the shekel bigger,
And to [c]cheat with [3]dishonest scales,
6 So as to buy the helpless for [1]money
And the needy for a pair of sandals,
And *that* we may sell the refuse of the wheat?"

7 The LORD has sworn by the [a]pride of Jacob,
"Indeed, I will [b]never forget any of their deeds.
8"Because of this will not the land [a]quake
And everyone who dwells in it [b]mourn?
Indeed, all of it will [c]rise up like the Nile,
And it will be tossed about,
And subside like the Nile of Egypt.
9"And it will come about in that day," declares the Lord GOD,
"That I shall make the [a]sun go down at noon
And [b]make the earth dark in [1]broad daylight.
10"Then I shall turn your [a]festivals into mourning
And all your songs into [1]lamentation;
And I will bring [b]sackcloth on everyone's loins
And baldness on every head.
And I will make it [c]like *a time of* mourning for an only son,
And the end of it will be like a bitter day.

11"Behold, days are coming," declares the Lord GOD,
"When I will send a famine on the land,
Not a famine for bread or a thirst for water,
But rather for hearing the words of the LORD.
12"And people will stagger from sea to sea,
And from the north even to the east;
They will go to and fro to [a]seek the word of the LORD,
But they will not find *it*.
13"In that day the beautiful [a]virgins
And the young men will [b]faint from thirst.
14"*As for* those who swear by the [1a]guilt of Samaria,
Who say, 'As your god lives, O [b]Dan,'
And, 'As the way of Beersheba lives,'
They will fall and not rise again."

CHAPTER 9

God's Judgment Unavoidable

I SAW the Lord standing beside the altar, and He said,
"Smite the [a]capitals so that the thresholds will shake,
And break them on the heads of them all!
Then I will slay the rest of them with the sword;
They will not have a [b]fugitive who will flee,
Or a refugee who will escape.
2"Though they dig into [a]Sheol,
From there shall My hand take them;
And though they [b]ascend to heaven,

16 [1]Lit., *drip* [a]Amos 2:12; 7:13 [b]Deut. 32:2; Ezek. 20:46; 21:2

17 [1]Or, *in an unclean land* [a]Hos. 4:13, 14 [b]Jer. 14:16 [c]2 Kin. 17:6; Ezek. 4:13; Hos. 9:3

1 [1]YHWH, usually rendered LORD, and so throughout the chap.

2 [1]Lit., *pass him by* [a]Jer. 24:3 [b]Ezek. 7:2, 3, 6

3 [1]Or, *They will howl the palace songs* [2]Lit., *he has thrown* [3]Or, *hush!* [a]Amos 5:23; 6:4, 5; 8:10

4 [1]Or, *snap at* [a]Amos 2:7; 5:11, 12

5 [1]Lit., *pass by* [2]Lit., *ephah* [3]Lit., *balances of deception* [a]Num. 28:11; 2 Kin. 4:23 [b]Ex. 31:13-17 [c]Hos. 12:7

6 [1]Lit., *silver*

7 [a]Deut. 33:26, 29; Ps. 68:34 [b]Ps. 10:11; Jer. 17:1; Hos. 7:2

8 [a]Ps. 18:7; 60:2; Is. 5:25 [b]Hos. 4:3 [c]Jer. 46:7, 8; Amos 9:5

9 [1]Lit., *a day of light* [a]Is. 13:10; Jer. 15:9; Mic. 3:6 [b]Is. 59:9, 10; Amos 4:13; 5:8

10 [1]Or, *a dirge* [a]Job 20:23; Amos 5:21 [b]Ezek. 7:18 [c]Jer. 6:26; Zech. 12:10

12 [a]Ezek. 20:3, 31

13 [a]Lam. 1:18; 2:21 [b]Is. 41:17; Hos. 2:3

14 [1]Or, *Ashimah* [a]Hos. 8:5 [b]1 Kin. 12:28, 29

1 [a]Zeph. 2:14 [b]Jer. 11:11

2 [a]Ps. 139:8 [b]Jer. 51:53; Obad. 4

From there will I bring them down.
3 "And though they hide on the summit of Carmel,
I will [a]search them out and take them from there;
And though they [b]conceal themselves from My sight on the floor of the sea,
From there I will command the [c]serpent and it will bite them.
4 "And though they go into [a]captivity before their enemies,
From there I will command the sword that it slay them,
And I will [b]set My eyes against them for evil and not for good."

5 And the Lord [1]GOD of hosts,
The One who [a]touches the land so that it melts,
And all those who dwell in it mourn,
And all of it rises up like the Nile
And subsides like the Nile of Egypt;
6 The One who builds His [1]upper [a]chambers in the heavens,
And has founded His vaulted dome over the earth,
He who calls for the waters of the sea
And [b]pours them out on the face of the earth,
The LORD is His name.

7 "Are you not as the sons of [a]Ethiopia to Me,
O sons of Israel?" declares the LORD.
"Have I not brought up Israel from the land of Egypt,
And the Philistines from Caphtor and [1]the Syrians from Kir?
8 "Behold, the eyes of the Lord GOD are on the sinful kingdom,
And I will [a]destroy it from the face of the earth;
Nevertheless, I will [b]not totally destroy the house of Jacob,"
Declares the LORD.
9 "For behold, I am commanding,
And I will [a]shake the house of Jacob among all nations
As *grain* is shaken in a sieve,
But not a [1]kernel will fall to the ground.
10 "All the [a]sinners of My people will die by the sword,
Those who say, 'The calamity will not overtake or confront us.'

The Restoration of Israel

11 "In that day I will [a]raise up the fallen [1][b]booth of David,
And wall up its [c]breaches;
I will also raise up its ruins,
And rebuild it as in the [d]days of old;
12 That they may possess the remnant of Edom
And all the [1]nations who are [a]called by My name,"
Declares the LORD who does this.

13 "Behold, days are coming," declares the LORD,
"When the [a]plowman will overtake the reaper
And the treader of grapes him who sows seed;
When the [b]mountains will drip sweet wine,
And all the hills will be dissolved.
14 "Also I will [a]restore the [1]captivity of My people Israel,
And they will [b]rebuild the ruined cities and live *in them*,
They will also plant vineyards and drink their wine,
And make gardens and eat their fruit.
15 "I will also plant them on their land,
And they will not again be rooted out from their land
Which I have given them,"
Says the LORD your God.

3 [a]Jer. 16:16 [b]Job 34:22; Ps. 139:9-12; Jer. 16:16, 17 [c]Is. 27:1

4 [a]Lev. 26:33 [b]Jer. 21:10; 39:16; 44:11

5 [1]YHWH, usually rendered LORD, and so throughout the chap. [a]Ps. 104:32; 144:5; Is. 64:1

6 [1]Or, *stairs* [a]Ps. 104:3, 13 [b]Ps. 104:6

7 [1]Lit., *Aram* [a]2 Chr. 14:9, 12; Is. 20:4; 43:3

8 [a]Amos 3:12; 7:17; 9:10 [b]Jer. 5:10; 30:11; 31:35, 36; Joel 2:32

9 [1]Or, *pebble* [a]Is. 30:28; Luke 22:31

10 [a]Is. 33:14; Zech. 13:8, 9

11 [1]Or, *shelter;* or, *tabernacle* [a]Acts 15:16-18 [b]Is. 16:5 [c]Ps. 80:12 [d]Is. 63:11; Jer. 46:26

12 [1]Or, *Gentiles* [a]Is. 43:7

13 [a]Lev. 26:5 [b]Joel 3:18

14 [1]Or, *fortunes* [a]Ps. 53:6; Is. 60:4; Jer. 30:18 [b]Is. 61:4; 65:21

THE BOOK OF OBADIAH

Edom Will Be Humbled

1 THE vision of Obadiah.
Thus says the Lord [1]GOD concerning [a]Edom—
[b]We have heard a report from the LORD,
And an [c]envoy has been sent among the nations saying,
"[d]Arise and let us go against her for battle"—
2 "Behold, I will make you [a]small among the nations;
You are greatly despised.
3 "The [a]arrogance of your heart has deceived you,
You who live in the clefts of [1]the [b]rock,
In the loftiness of your dwelling place,
Who say in your heart,
'[c]Who will bring me down to earth?'
4 "Though you [a]build high like the eagle,
Though you set your nest among the [b]stars,
From there I will bring you down," declares the LORD.
5 "If [a]thieves came to you,
If [1]robbers by night—
O how you will be ruined!—
Would they not steal *only* [2]until they had enough?
If grape gatherers came to you,
Would they not leave *some* gleanings?
6 "O how Esau will be [a]ransacked,
And his hidden treasures searched out!
7 "All the [a]men [1]allied with you
Will send you forth to the border,
And the men at [b]peace with you
Will deceive you and overpower you.
They who eat your [c]bread
Will set an ambush for you.
(There is no [d]understanding [2]in him.)
8 "Will I not on that day," declares the LORD,
"[a]Destroy wise men from Edom
And understanding from the mountain of Esau?
9 "Then your [a]mighty men will be dismayed, O Teman,
In order that every one may be [b]cut off from the mountain of Esau by slaughter.

10 "Because of [a]violence to your brother Jacob,
[1]You will be covered *with* shame,
And you will be cut off forever.
11 "On the day that you [a]stood aloof,
On the day that strangers carried off his wealth,
And foreigners entered his gate
And [b]cast lots for Jerusalem—
[c]You too were as one of them.
12 "Do not [1a]gloat over your brother's day,
The day of his misfortune.
And do not [b]rejoice over the sons of Judah
In the day of their destruction;
Yes, do not [2c]boast
In the day of *their* distress.
13 "Do not enter the gate of My people
In the [a]day of their disaster.
Yes, you, do not [1]gloat over their calamity
In the day of their disaster.
And do not [b]loot their wealth
In the day of their disaster.
14 "And do not [a]stand at the fork of the road
To cut down their fugitives;
And do not imprison their survivors
In the day of their distress.

The Day of the LORD and the Future

15 "For the [a]day of the LORD draws near on all the nations.
[b]As you have done, it will be done to you.
Your [c]dealings will return on your own head.
16 "Because just as you drank on My holy mountain,
All the nations will drink continually.
They will drink and [1]swallow,
And become as if they had never existed.
17 "But on Mount [a]Zion there will be those who escape,
And it will be holy.
And the house of Jacob will [b]possess their possessions.
18 "Then the house of Jacob will be a [a]fire
And the house of Joseph a flame;
But the house of Esau *will be* as stubble.
And they will set [1]them on fire and consume [1]them,
So that there will be [b]no survivor of the house of Esau,"
For the LORD has spoken.

1 [1]YHWH, usually rendered LORD [a]Ps. 137:7; Is. 34:1-17; 63:1-6; Jer. 49:7-22; Ezek. 25:12-14 [b]Jer. 49:14-16; Obad. 1-4 [c]Is. 18:2; 30:4 [d]Jer. 6:4, 5

2 [a]Num. 24:18; Is. 23:9

3 [1]Or, *Sela* [a]Is. 16:6; Jer. 49:16 [b]2 Kin. 14:7; 2 Chr. 25:12 [c]Is. 14:13-15

4 [a]Job 20:6, 7; Hab. 2:9 [b]Is. 14:12-15

5 [1]Lit., *devastators of the night* [2]Lit., *their sufficiency* [a]Jer. 49:9

6 [a]Jer. 49:10

7 [1]Lit., *of your covenant* [2]I.e., in Esau; or, *of it* [a]Jer. 30:14 [b]Jer. 38:22 [c]Ps. 41:9 [d]Jer. 49:7

8 [a]Job 5:12-14

9 [a]Jer. 49:22 [b]Is. 34:5-8; 63:1-3; Obad. 5

10 [1]Lit., *Shame will cover you* [a]Ezek. 25:12; Joel 3:19; Amos 1:11

11 [a]Ps. 83:5, 6; 137:7; Amos 1:6, 9 [b]Joel 3:3; Nah. 3:10 [c]Ezek. 35:10

12 [1]Lit., *look on* [2]Lit., *make your mouth large* [a]Mic. 4:11; 7:10 [b]Ezek. 35:15; 36:5 [c]Ps. 31:18; Ezek. 35:12

13 [1]Lit., *look on* [a]Ezek. 35:5 [b]Ezek. 35:10; 36:2, 3

14 [a]Is. 16:3, 4

15 [a]Joel 1:15; 2:1, 11, 31; Amos 5:18, 20 [b]Jer. 50:29; 51:56 [c]Ezek. 35:11

16 [1]Or, *stagger*

17 [a]Is. 4:2, 3 [b]Is. 14:1, 2; Amos 9:11-15

18 [1]I.e., the people of Esau [a]Is. 5:24; 9:18, 19 [b]Jer. 11:23; Amos 1:8

19 Then *those of* the [1]Negev will
[a]possess the mountain of
Esau,
And *those of* the [2]shephelah the
[b]Philistine *plain;*
Also, they will [c]possess the territory of Ephraim and the territory of Samaria,
And Benjamin *will possess* Gilead.
20 And the exiles of this host of
the sons of Israel,
Who are *among* the Canaanites
as far as Zarephath,
And the exiles of Jerusalem
who are in Sepharad
Will possess the [a]cities of the
Negev.
21 The [a]deliverers will ascend
Mount Zion
To judge the mountain of Esau,
And the [b]kingdom will be the
LORD'S.

19 [1]I.e., South country [2]I.e., the foothills [a]Is. 11:14; Amos 9:12 [b]Is. 11:14 [c]Jer. 31:5; 32:44
20 [a]Jer. 32:44; 33:13
21 [a]Neh. 9:27 [b]Ps. 22:28; 47:7-9; 67:4; Zech. 14:9

THE BOOK OF JONAH

Jonah's Disobedience

THE word of the LORD came to
[a]Jonah the son of Amittai saying,
2 "Arise, go to [a]Nineveh the great
city, and [b]cry against it, for their
[c]wickedness has come up before
Me."
3 But Jonah rose up to flee to Tarshish [a]from the presence of the
LORD. So he went down to Joppa,
found a ship which was going to
Tarshish, paid the fare, and went
down into it to go with them to Tarshish from the presence of the LORD.
4 And the LORD hurled a great
wind on the sea and there was a
great storm on the sea so that the
ship was about to break up.
5 Then the sailors became afraid,
and every man cried to [a]his god, and
they [b]threw the cargo which was in
the ship into the sea to lighten *it* for
them. But Jonah had gone below
into the hold of the ship, lain down,
and fallen sound asleep.
6 So the captain approached him
and said, "How is it that you are
sleeping? Get up, [a]call on your god.
Perhaps *your* [b]god will be concerned about us so that we will not
perish."
7 And each man said to his mate,
"Come, let us cast lots so we may
learn on whose account this calamity *has struck* us." So they cast lots
and the [a]lot fell on Jonah.
8 Then they said to him, "[a]Tell us,
now! On whose account *has* this calamity *struck* us? What is your [b]occupation? And where do you come
from? What is your country? From
what people are you?"
9 And he said to them, "I am a
[a]Hebrew, and I [b]fear the LORD [c]God
of heaven who [d]made the sea and
the dry land."
10 Then the men became extremely frightened and they said to
him, "[1]How could you do this?" For
the men knew that he was [a]fleeing
from the presence of the LORD, because he had told them.
11 So they said to him, "What
should we do to you that the sea
may become calm for us?"—for the
sea was becoming increasingly
stormy.
12 And he said to them, "[a]Pick me
up and throw me into the sea. Then
the sea will become calm for you,
for I know that [b]on account of me
this great storm *has come* upon
you."
13 However, the men rowed *desperately* to return to land but they
[a]could not, for the sea was becoming *even* stormier against them.
14 Then they called on the [a]LORD
and said, "We earnestly pray, O
LORD, do not let us perish on account of this man's life and do not
put innocent blood on us; for Thou,
O LORD, hast done as Thou hast
pleased."
15 So they picked up Jonah, threw
him into the sea, and the sea
[a]stopped its raging.
16 Then the men feared the LORD
greatly, and they offered a sacrifice
to the LORD and made [a]vows.
17 [1]And the LORD appointed a
great fish to swallow Jonah, and Jonah was in the stomach of the fish
three days and three nights.

CHAPTER 2

Jonah's Prayer

1
THEN Jonah prayed to the LORD
his God [a]from the stomach of the
fish,
2 and he said,
"I [a]called out of my distress to
the LORD,
And He answered me.

1 [a]2 Kin. 14:25; Matt. 12:39-41; 16:4; Luke 11:29, 30, 32
2 [a]Gen. 10:11; 2 Kin. 19:36; Is. 37:37; Nah. 1:1; Zeph. 2:13 [b]Is. 58:1 [c]Gen. 18:20; Hos. 7:2
3 [a]Ps. 139:7, 9
5 [a]1 Kin. 18:26 [b]Acts 27:18, 19
6 [a]Ps. 107:28 [b]2 Sam. 12:22; Amos 5:15; Jon. 3:9
7 [a]Num. 32:23; Prov. 16:33
8 [a]Josh. 7:19; 1 Sam. 14:43 [b]Gen. 47:3; 1 Sam. 30:13
9 [a]Gen. 14:13; Ex. 1:15; 2:13 [b]2 Kin. 17:25, 28, 32, 33 [c]Ezra 1:2; Neh. 1:4; Ps. 136:26; Dan. 2:18 [d]Neh. 9:6; Ps. 95:5; 146:6
10 [1]Lit., *What is this you have done* [a]Job 27:22; Jon. 1:3
12 [a]2 Sam. 24:17 [b]1 Chr. 21:17
13 [a]Prov. 21:30
14 [a]Ps. 107:28; Jon. 1:16
15 [a]Ps. 65:7; 93:3, 4; 107:29
16 [a]Ps. 50:14; 66:13, 14
17 [1]Chap. 2:1 in Heb.
1 [1]Chap. 2:2 in Heb. [a]Job 13:15; Ps. 130:1, 2; Lam. 3:53-56
2 [a]1 Sam. 30:6; Ps. 18:4-6; 22:24

I cried for help from the [1]depth
of Sheol;
Thou didst hear my voice.
3"For Thou hadst [a]cast me into
the deep,
Into the heart of the seas,
And the current engulfed me.
All Thy [b]breakers and billows
passed over me.
4"So I said, 'I have been [a]expelled
from Thy sight.
Nevertheless I will look again
[b]toward Thy holy temple.'
5"[a]Water encompassed me to the
point of death.
The great [b]deep engulfed me,
Weeds were wrapped around
my head.
6"I [a]descended to the roots of the
mountains.
The earth with its [b]bars *was*
around me forever,
But Thou hast [c]brought up my
life from [1]the pit, O LORD my
God.
7"While [1]I was [a]fainting away,
I [b]remembered the LORD;
And my [c]prayer came to Thee,
Into Thy holy temple.
8"Those who regard [1]vain idols
Forsake their faithfulness,
9 But I will [a]sacrifice to Thee
With the voice of thanksgiving.
That which I have vowed I will
[b]pay.
[c]Salvation is from the LORD."
10 Then the LORD commanded the
fish, and it vomited Jonah up onto
the dry land.

CHAPTER 3

Nineveh Repents

NOW the word of the LORD came
to Jonah the second time, saying,
2"Arise, go to Nineveh the great
city and [a]proclaim to it the proclamation which I am going to tell
you."
3 So Jonah arose and went to
Nineveh according to the word of
the LORD. Now Nineveh was [1]an
[a]exceedingly great city, a three
days' walk.
4 Then Jonah began to go
through the city one day's walk; and
he [a]cried out and said, "Yet forty
days and Nineveh will be overthrown."
5 Then the people of Nineveh believed in God; and they called a [a]fast
and put on sackcloth from the greatest to the least of them.
6 When the word reached the
king of Nineveh, he arose from his
throne, laid aside his robe from him,
covered *himself* with sackcloth, and
sat on the [1]ashes.
7 And he issued a [a]proclamation
and it said, "In Nineveh by the decree of the king and his nobles: Do
not let man, beast, herd, or flock
taste a thing. Do not let them eat or
drink water.
8"But both man and beast must
be covered with sackcloth; and let
[1]men [a]call on God earnestly that
each may [b]turn from his wicked
way and from the violence which is
in [2]his hands.
9"[a]Who knows, God may turn
and relent, and withdraw His burning anger so that we shall not perish?"
10 When God saw their deeds,
that they [a]turned from their wicked
way, then [b]God relented concerning
the calamity which He had declared
He would [1]bring upon them. And He
did not do *it*.

CHAPTER 4

Jonah's Displeasure Rebuked

BUT it greatly displeased Jonah,
and he became angry.
2 And he [a]prayed to the LORD and
said, "Please LORD, was not this
[1]what I said while I was still in my
own country? Therefore, [2]in order to
forestall this I fled to Tarshish, for I
knew that Thou art a [b]gracious and
compassionate God, slow to anger
and abundant in lovingkindness,
and one who relents concerning calamity.
3"Therefore now, O LORD, please
[a]take my [1]life from me, for death is
[b]better to me than life."
4 And the LORD said, "Do you
have good reason to be angry?"
5 Then Jonah went out from the
city and sat east of [1]it. There he
made a shelter for himself and [a]sat
under it in the shade until he could
see what would happen in the city.
6 So the LORD God appointed a
[1]plant and it grew up over Jonah to
be a shade over his head to deliver
him from his discomfort. And Jonah
was [2a]extremely happy about the
[1]plant.
7 But God appointed a worm
when dawn came the next day, and
it attacked the plant and it [a]with-
ered.
8 And it came about when the
sun came up that God appointed a
scorching [a]east wind, and the [b]sun
beat down on Jonah's head so that
he became faint and begged with *all*

2 [1]Lit., *belly*
3 [a]Ps. 69:1, 2, 14, 15; Lam. 3:54 [b]Ps. 42:7
4 [a]Ps. 31:22; Jer. 7:15 [b]1 Kin. 8:38; 2 Chr. 6:38; Ps. 5:7
5 [a]Lam. 3:54 [b]Ps. 69:1, 2
6 [1]Or, *corruption* [a]Ps. 18:5; 116:3 [b]Is. 38:10; Matt. 16:18 [c]Job 33:28; Ps. 16:10; 30:3; Is. 38:17
7 [1]Lit., *my soul . . . within me* [a]Ps. 142:3 [b]Ps. 77:10, 11; 143:5 [c]2 Chr. 30:27; Ps. 18:6
8 [1]Lit., *empty vanities*
9 [a]Ps. 50:14, 23; Jer. 33:11; Hos. 14:2 [b]Job 22:27; Eccles. 5:4, 5 [c]Ps. 3:8; Is. 45:17
2 [a]Jer. 1:17; Ezek. 2:7
3 [1]Lit., *a great city to God* [a]Jon. 1:2; 4:11
4 [a]Matt. 12:41; Luke 11:32
5 [a]Dan. 9:3; Joel 1:14
6 [1]Or, *dust*
7 [a]2 Chr. 20:3; Ezra 8:21; Jon. 3:5
8 [1]Lit., *them* [2]Lit., *their* [a]Ps. 130:1; Jon. 1:6, 14 [b]Is. 1:16-19; 55:6, 7; Jer. 18:11
9 [a]2 Sam. 12:22; Joel 2:14
10 [1]Lit., *do* [a]1 Kin. 21:27-29; Jer. 31:18 [b]Ex. 32:14; Jer. 18:8; Amos 7:3, 6
2 [1]Lit., *my word* [2]Lit., *I was beforehand in fleeing* [a]Jer. 20:7 [b]Ex. 34:6; Num. 14:18; Ps. 86:5, 15; Joel 2:13; Mic. 7:8
3 [1]Lit., *soul* [a]1 Kin. 19:4; Job 6:8, 9; Jon. 3:8 [b]Job 7:15, 16; Eccles. 7:1
5 [1]Lit., *the city* [a]1 Kin. 19:9, 13
6 [1]Probably a castor oil plant, and so in vs. 7, 9 and 10 [2]Lit., *greatly* [a]Amos 6:13
7 [a]Joel 1:12
8 [a]Ezek. 19:12; Hos. 13:15 [b]Ps. 121:6; Is. 49:10

his soul to die, saying, "Death is better to me than life."
9 Then God said to Jonah, "Do
you have good reason to be angry
about the plant?" And he said, "I
have good reason to be angry, even
to death."
10 Then the LORD said, "You had
compassion on the plant for which
you did not work, and *which* you did
not cause to grow, which *came up*
[1]overnight and perished [1]overnight.
11"And should I not [a]have compassion on Nineveh, the great city in
which there are more than 120,000
persons who do not [b]know *the difference* between their right and left
hand, as well as many [c]animals?"

10 [1]Lit., *a son of a night*

11 [a]Jon. 3:10 [b]Deut. 1:39; Is. 7:16 [c]Ps. 36:6

THE BOOK OF MICAH

Destruction in Israel and Judah

THE word of the LORD which came
to [a]Micah of Moresheth in the days
of Jotham, Ahaz, *and* Hezekiah,
kings of Judah, which he saw concerning Samaria and Jerusalem.
2 Hear, O peoples, all of [1]you;
[a]Listen, O earth and [2]all it contains,
And let the Lord [3]GOD be a [b]witness against you,
The Lord from His holy temple.
3 For behold, the LORD is [a]coming forth from His place.
He will come down and [b]tread on the high places of the [1]earth.
4 [a]The mountains will melt under Him,
And the valleys will be split,
Like wax before the fire,
Like water poured down a steep place.
5 All this is for the rebellion of Jacob
And for the sins of the house of Israel.
What is the rebellion of Jacob?
Is it not [a]Samaria?
What is the [b]high [1]place of Judah?
Is it not Jerusalem?
6 For I will make Samaria a heap of ruins [1]in the open country,
[a]Planting places for a vineyard.
I will [b]pour her stones down into the valley,
And will [c]lay bare her foundations.
7 All of her [a]idols will be smashed,
All of her [b]earnings will be burned with fire,
And all of her images I will make desolate,
For she collected *them* from a harlot's earnings,
And to the earnings of a harlot they will return.
8 Because of this I must lament and wail,
I must go [a]barefoot and naked;
I must make a lament like the [b]jackals
And a mourning like the ostriches.
9 For her [1a]wound is incurable,
For it has come to Judah;
It has reached the [b]gate of my people,
Even to Jerusalem.
10 [a]Tell it not in Gath,
Weep not at all.
At [1]Beth-le-aphrah roll yourself in the dust.
11 [1]Go on your way, inhabitant of [2]Shaphir, in [a]shameful nakedness.
The inhabitant of [3b]Zaanan does not [4]escape.
The lamentation of [5]Beth-ezel: "He will take from you its [6]support."
12 For the inhabitant of [1]Maroth
Becomes weak [a]waiting for good,
Because a calamity has come down from the LORD
To the gate of Jerusalem.
13 [a]Harness the chariot to the team of horses,
O inhabitant of [b]Lachish—
She was the beginning of sin
To the daughter of Zion—
Because in you were found
The rebellious acts of Israel.
14 Therefore, you will give parting [a]gifts
On behalf of Moresheth-gath;
The houses of [b]Achzib *will* become a [c]deception
To the kings of Israel.
15 Moreover, I will bring on you
The one who takes possession,
O inhabitant of [1a]Mareshah.
The glory of Israel will enter [b]Adullam.
16 Make yourself [a]bald and cut off your hair,

1 [a]Jer. 26:18

2 [1]Lit., *them* [2]Lit., *its fulness* [3]YHWH, usually rendered LORD [a]Jer. 6:19; 22:29 [b]Is. 50:7

3 [1]Or, *land* [a]Is. 26:21 [b]Amos 4:13

4 [a]Ps. 97:5; Is. 64:1, 2; Nah. 1:5

5 [1]Lit., *places* [a]Is. 7:9; 28:1; Amos 8:14 [b]2 Chr. 34:3, 4

6 [1]Lit., *of the field* [a]Jer. 31:5; Amos 5:11 [b]Lam. 4:1 [c]Ezek. 13:14

7 [a]Deut. 9:21; 2 Chr. 34:7 [b]Deut. 23:18; Is. 23:17

8 [a]Is. 32:11 [b]Is. 13:21, 22

9 [1]Lit., *wounds* [a]Jer. 30:12, 15; Is. 3:26 [b]Mic. 1:12

10 [1]I.e., House of dust [a]2 Sam. 1:20

11 [1]I.e., Go into captivity [2]I.e., Pleasantness [3]I.e., Going out [4]Lit., *go out* [5]I.e., House of removal [6]Lit., *standing place* [a]Ezek. 23:29 [b]Josh. 15:37

12 [1]I.e., Bitterness [a]Is. 59:9-11; Jer. 14:19

13 [a]Amos 2:14 [b]Josh. 10:3; 2 Kin. 14:19; Is. 36:2

14 [a]2 Kin. 16:8 [b]Josh. 15:44 [c]Jer. 15:18

15 [1]I.e., Possession [a]Josh. 15:44 [b]Josh. 12:14; 15:35; 2 Sam. 23:13

16 [a]Is. 22:12

Because of the children of your
delight;
Extend your baldness like the
eagle,
For they will [b]go from you into
exile.

CHAPTER 2

Woe to Oppressors

WOE to those who [a]scheme iniquity,
Who work out evil on their
beds!
[1b]When morning comes, they
do it,
For it is in the [c]power of their
hands.
2 They [a]covet fields and then
[b]seize *them,*
And houses, and take *them*
away.
They [1c]rob a man and his house,
A man and his inheritance.
3 Therefore, thus says the LORD,
"Behold, I am [a]planning against
this [b]family a calamity
From which you [c]cannot remove your necks;
And you will not walk [d]haughti-
ly,
For it will be an [e]evil time.
4"On that day they will [a]take up
against you a [1]taunt
And [2b]utter a bitter lamentation *and* say,
'We are completely [c]destroyed!
He exchanges the portion of my
people;
How He removes it from me!
To the apostate He [d]apportions
our fields.'
5"Therefore, you will have no one
[1a]stretching a measuring line
For you by lot in the assembly
of the LORD.

6 'Do not [1a]speak out,' *so* they
[1]speak out.
But if [2]they do [b]not [1]speak out
concerning these things,
Reproaches will not be turned
back.
7"Is it being said, O house of Jacob:
'Is the Spirit of the LORD [a]impa-
tient?
Are these His doings?'
Do not My words [b]do good
To the one [c]walking uprightly?
8"[1]Recently My people have
arisen as an [a]enemy—
You [b]strip the [2]robe off a fel-
low-Israelite,
From [c]unsuspecting passers-
by,

16 [b]Amos 7:11, 17

1 [1]Lit., *In the light of the morning* [a]Ps. 36:4; Is. 32:7; Nah. 1:11 [b]Hos. 7:6, 7 [c]Gen. 31:29; Deut. 28:32; Prov. 3:27

2 [1]Lit., *oppress* [a]Jer. 22:17; Amos 8:4 [b]Is. 5:8 [c]1 Kin. 21:1-15

3 [a]Deut. 28:48; Jer. 18:11 [b]Jer. 8:3; Amos 3:1, 2 [c]Lam. 1:14; 5:5 [d]Is. 2:11, 12 [e]Amos 5:13

4 [1]Or, *proverb* [2]Lit., *lament* [a]Hab. 2:6 [b]Jer. 9:10, 17-21; Mic. 1:8 [c]Is. 6:11; 24:3; Jer. 4:13 [d]Jer. 6:12; 8:10

5 [1]Lit., *casting* [a]Num. 34:13, 16-29; Josh. 18:4, 10

6 [1]Lit., *drip* [2]I.e., God's prophets [a]Is. 30:10; Amos 2:12; 7:16 [b]Is. 29:10; Mic. 3:6

7 [a]Is. 50:2; 59:1 [b]Ps. 119:65, 68, 116; Jer. 15:16 [c]Ps. 15:2; 84:11

8 [1]Lit., *And yesterday* [2]Or, *ornaments* [a]Jer. 12:8 [b]Mic. 3:2, 3; 7:2, 3 [c]Ps. 120:6, 7

9 [a]Jer. 10:20 [b]Ezek. 39:21; Hab. 2:14

10 [a]Deut. 12:9 [b]Ps. 106:38

11 [1]Lit., *drip* [2]Lit., *one who drips* [a]Is. 30:10, 11

12 [a]Mic. 5:7, 8; 7:18

1 [a]Is. 1:10; Mic. 3:9 [b]Ps. 82:1-5; Jer. 5:5

2 [a]Ps. 53:4; Ezek. 22:27; Mic. 2:8; 7:2, 3

3 [a]Ps. 14:4; 27:2; Zeph. 3:3 [b]Ezek. 34:2, 3 [c]Ezek. 11:3, 6, 7

4 [a]Deut. 31:17; Is. 59:2 [b]Is. 3:11; Mic. 7:13

From those returned from war.
9"The women of My people you
[a]evict,
Each *one* from her pleasant
house.
From her children you take My
[b]splendor forever.
10"Arise and go,
For this is no place [a]of rest
Because of the [b]uncleanness
that brings on destruction,
A painful destruction.
11"If a man walking after wind and
falsehood
Had told lies *and said,*
'I will [1]speak out to you concerning wine and liquor,'
He would be [2]spokesman to
[a]this people.

12"I will surely assemble all of you,
Jacob,
I will surely gather the [a]rem-
nant of Israel.
I will put them together like
sheep in the fold;
Like a flock in the midst of its
pasture
They will be noisy with men.
13"The breaker goes up before
them;
They break out, pass through
the gate, and go out by it.
So their king goes on before
them,
And the LORD at their head."

CHAPTER 3

Rulers Denounced

AND I said,
"[a]Hear now, heads of Jacob
And rulers of the house of Israel.
Is it not for you to [b]know justice?
2"You who hate good and love
evil,
Who [a]tear off their skin from
them
And their flesh from their
bones,
3 And who [a]eat the flesh of my
people,
[b]Strip off their skin from them,
Break their bones,
And [c]chop *them* up as for the
pot
And as meat in a kettle."
4 Then they will cry out to the
LORD,
But He will not answer them.
Instead, He will [a]hide His face
from them at that time,
Because they have [b]practiced
evil deeds.

5 Thus says the LORD concerning the prophets
Who [a]lead my people astray;
When they have *something* to [b]bite with their teeth,
They [c]cry, "Peace,"
But against him who puts nothing in their mouths,
They declare holy war.
6 Therefore *it will be* [a]night for you—without vision,
And darkness for you—without divination.
The [b]sun will go down on the prophets,
And the day will become dark over them.
7 The seers will be [a]ashamed
And the [b]diviners will be embarrassed.
Indeed, they will all cover *their* [1]mouths
Because there is [c]no answer from God.
8 On the other hand [a]I am filled with power—
With the Spirit of the LORD—
And with justice and courage
To make [b]known to Jacob his rebellious act,
Even to Israel his sin.
9 Now hear this, heads of the house of Jacob
And rulers of the house of Israel,
Who [a]abhor justice
And twist everything that is straight,
10 Who [a]build Zion with bloodshed
And Jerusalem with violent injustice.
11 Her leaders pronounce [a]judgment for a bribe,
Her [b]priests instruct for a price,
And her prophets divine for money.
Yet they lean on the LORD saying,
"[c]Is not the LORD in our midst?
Calamity will not come upon us."
12 Therefore, on account of you,
[a]Zion will be plowed as a field,
[b]Jerusalem will become a heap of ruins,
And the mountain of the [1]temple *will become* high places of a forest.

CHAPTER 4

Peaceful Latter Days

AND it will come about in the [a]last days
That the [b]mountain of the house of the LORD
Will be established [1]as the chief of the mountains.
It will be raised above the hills,
And the [c]peoples will stream to it.
2 And [a]many nations will come and say,
"[b]Come and let us go up to the mountain of the LORD
And to the house of the God of Jacob,
That [c]He may teach us about His ways
And that we may walk in His paths."
For [d]from Zion will go forth the law,
Even the word of the LORD from Jerusalem.
3 And He will [a]judge between many peoples
And render decisions for mighty, [1]distant nations.
Then they will hammer their swords into plowshares
And their spears into pruning hooks;
Nation will not lift up sword against nation,
And never again will they [2]train for war.
4 And each of them will sit under his vine
And under his fig tree,
With [a]no one to make *them* afraid,
For the [b]mouth of the LORD of hosts has spoken.
5 Though all the peoples walk
Each in the [a]name of his god,
As for us, we will walk
In the name of the LORD our God forever and ever.

6 "In that day," declares the LORD,
"I will assemble the [a]lame,
And gather the outcasts,
Even those whom I have afflicted.
7 "I will make the lame a [a]remnant,
And the outcasts a strong nation,
And the [b]LORD will reign over them in Mount Zion
From now on and forever.
8 "And as for you, [1][a]tower of the flock,
[2]Hill of the daughter of Zion,
To you it will come—
Even the [b]former dominion will come,
The kingdom of the daughter of Jerusalem.

5 [a]Is. 3:12; 9:15, 16; Jer. 14:14, 15 [b]Is. 56:9-11 [c]Jer. 6:14
6 [a]Is. 8:20-22; 29:10-12 [b]Is. 59:10
7 [1]Lit., *mustache* [a]Zech. 13:4 [b]Is. 44:25; 47:12-14 [c]1 Sam. 28:6; Mic. 3:4
8 [a]Is. 61:1, 2; Jer. 1:18 [b]Is. 58:1
9 [a]Ps. 58:1, 2; Is. 1:23
10 [a]Jer. 22:13, 17; Hab. 2:12
11 [a]Is. 1:23; Mic. 7:3 [b]Jer. 6:13 [c]Is. 48:2
12 [1]Lit., *house* [a]Jer. 26:18 [b]Jer. 9:11
1 [1]Lit., *on* [a]Dan. 2:28; 10:14; Hos. 3:5 [b]Mic. 3:12; Ezek. 43:12; Zech. 8:3 [c]Ps. 22:27; 86:9; Jer. 3:17
2 [a]Zech. 2:11; 14:16 [b]Is. 2:3; Jer. 31:6 [c]Ps. 25:8, 9, 12; Is. 54:13 [d]Is. 42:1-4; Zech. 14:8, 9
3 [1]Lit., *at a distance* [2]Lit., *learn* [a]Is. 2:4; 11:3-5
4 [a]Lev. 26:6; Jer. 30:10 [b]Is. 1:20; 40:5
5 [a]2 Kin. 17:29
6 [a]Zeph. 3:19
7 [a]Mic. 5:7, 8; 7:18 [b]Is. 24:23
8 [1]Heb., *Migdal-eder* [2]Heb., *Ophel of* [a]Ps. 48:3, 12; 61:3 [b]Is. 1:26; Zech. 9:10

9 "Now, why do you [a]cry out
loudly?
Is there no king among you,
Or has your [b]counselor perished,
That agony has gripped you like
a woman in childbirth?
10 "Writhe and labor to give birth,
Daughter of Zion,
Like a woman in childbirth,
For now you will [a]go out of the
city,
Dwell in the field,
And go to Babylon.
[b]There you will be rescued;
[c]There the LORD will redeem
you
From the hand of your enemies.
11 "And now [a]many nations have
been assembled against you
Who say, 'Let her be polluted,
And let our eyes [1]gloat over
Zion.'
12 "But they do not [a]know the
thoughts of the LORD,
And they do not understand His
purpose;
For He has gathered them like
sheaves to the threshing
floor.
13 "Arise and [a]thresh, daughter of
Zion,
For your horn I will make iron
And your hoofs I will make
bronze,
That you may [b]pulverize many
peoples,
That you may [c]devote to the
LORD their unjust gain
And their wealth to the Lord of
all the earth.

CHAPTER 5

Birth of the King in Bethlehem

"[1]NOW [a]muster yourselves in
troops, daughter of troops;
[2]They have laid siege against
us;
With a rod they will [b]smite the
judge of Israel on the cheek.
2 "[1]But as for [a]you, Bethlehem
Ephrathah,
Too little to be among the clans
of Judah,
From [b]you One will go forth for
Me to be [c]ruler in Israel.
[2]His goings forth are [d]from long
ago,
From the days of eternity."
3 Therefore, He will [a]give them
up until the time
When she who is in labor has
borne a child.
Then the [b]remainder of His
brethren
Will return to the sons of Israel.
4 And He will arise and [a]shep-
herd *His flock*
In the strength of the LORD,
In the majesty of the name of
the LORD His God.
And they will [1]remain,
Because [2]at that time He will be
great
To the [b]ends of the earth.
5 And this One will be *our* peace.

When the [a]Assyrian invades
our land,
When he tramples on our [1]cita-
dels,
Then we will raise against him
Seven shepherds and eight
leaders of men.
6 And they will [a]shepherd the
land of Assyria with the
sword,
The land of [b]Nimrod at its entrances;
And He will [c]deliver *us* from
the Assyrian
When he attacks our land
And when he tramples our territory.

7 Then the [a]remnant of Jacob
Will be among many peoples
Like [b]dew from the LORD,
Like [c]showers on vegetation
Which do not wait for man
Or delay for the sons of men.
8 And the remnant of Jacob
Will be among the nations,
Among many peoples
[a]Like a lion among the beasts of
the forest,
Like a young lion among flocks
of sheep,
Which, if he passes through,
[b]Tramples down and [c]tears,
And there is [d]none to rescue.
9 Your hand will be lifted up
against your adversaries,
And all your enemies will be cut
off.

10 "And it will be in that day," declares the LORD,
"That I will cut off your horses
from among you
And destroy your chariots.
11 "I will also cut off the [a]cities of
your land
And tear down all your [b]fortifi-
cations.
12 "I will cut off [a]sorceries from
your hand,
And you will have fortunetell-
ers no more.
13 "[a]I will cut off your carved images

9 [a]Jer. 8:19 [b]Is. 3:1-3; 28:29
10 [a]2 Kin. 20:18; Hos. 2:14 [b]Is. 43:14; 45:13; Mic. 7:8-12 [c]Is. 48:20; 52:9-12
11 [1]Lit., *look on* [a]Is. 5:25-30; 17:12-14
12 [a]Ps. 147:19, 20
13 [a]Is. 41:15 [b]Jer. 51:20-23 [c]Is. 60:9
1 [1]Chap. 4:14 in Heb. [2]Lit., *He has* [a]Jer. 5:7 [b]1 Kin. 22:24; Job 16:10; Lam. 3:30
2 [1]Chap. 5:1 in Heb. [2]Or, *His appearances are from long ago, from days of old* [a]Matt. 2:6 [b]Is. 11:1; Luke 2:4 [c]Jer. 30:21; Zech. 9:9 [d]Ps. 102:25; Prov. 8:22, 23
3 [a]Hos. 11:8; Mic. 4:10; 7:13 [b]Is. 10:20-22; Mic. 5:7, 8
4 [1]Or, *live in safety* [2]Lit., *now* [a]Is. 40:11; 49:9; Ezek. 34:13-15, 23, 24; Mic. 7:14 [b]Is. 45:22; 52:10
5 [1]Or, *palaces* [a]Is. 8:7, 8; 10:24-27
6 [a]Nah. 2:11-13; Zeph. 2:13 [b]Gen. 10:8-11 [c]Is. 14:25; 37:36, 37
7 [a]Mic. 2:12; 4:7; 5:3; 7:18 [b]Deut. 32:2; Ps. 110:3; Hos. 14:5 [c]Ps. 72:6; Is. 44:3
8 [a]Gen. 49:9; Num. 24:9 [b]Ps. 44:5; Is. 41:15, 16; Mic. 4:13; Zech. 10:5 [c]Hos. 5:14 [d]Ps. 50:22
11 [a]Is. 1:7; 6:11 [b]Is. 2:12-17; Hos. 10:14; Amos 5:9
12 [a]Deut. 18:10-12; Is. 2:6; 8:19
13 [a]Is. 2:18; 17:8; Ezek. 6:9

And your *sacred* pillars from among you,
So that you will no longer bow down
To the work of your hands.
14 "I will root out your [1a]Asherim from among you
And destroy your cities.
15 "And I will [a]execute vengeance in anger and wrath
On the nations which have not obeyed."

Chapter 6

God's Indictment of His People

HEAR now what the LORD is saying,
"Arise, plead your case [1]before the mountains,
And let the hills hear your voice.
2 "Listen, you mountains, to the indictment of the LORD,
And you enduring [a]foundations of the earth,
Because the [b]LORD has a case against His people;
Even with Israel He will dispute.
3 "[a]My people, [b]what have I done to you,
And [c]how have I wearied you? Answer Me.
4 "Indeed, I [a]brought you up from the land of Egypt
And [b]ransomed you from the house of slavery,
And I sent before you [c]Moses, Aaron, and [d]Miriam.
5 "My people, remember now
What [a]Balak king of Moab counseled
And what Balaam son of Beor answered him,
And from Shittim to Gilgal,
In order [1]that you might know the [b]righteous acts of the LORD."

What God Requires of Man

6 [a]With what shall I come to the LORD
And bow myself before the God on high?
Shall I come to Him with [b]burnt offerings,
With yearling calves?
7 Does the LORD take delight in [a]thousands of rams,
In ten thousand rivers of oil?
Shall I present my [b]first-born *for* my rebellious acts,
The fruit of my body for the sin of my soul?
8 He has [a]told you, O man, what is good;
And [b]what does the LORD require of you
But to [c]do justice, to [d]love [1]kindness,
And to walk [2e]humbly with your God?

9 The voice of the LORD will call to the city—
And it is sound wisdom to fear Thy name:
"Hear, O [a]tribe. Who has appointed [1]its time?
10 "Is there yet a man in the wicked house,
Along with treasures of [a]wickedness,
And a [1b]short measure *that is* cursed?
11 "Can I justify wicked [a]scales
And a bag of deceptive weights?
12 "For the rich men of *the* [1]city are full of violence,
Her residents speak lies,
And their [a]tongue is deceitful in their mouth.
13 "So also I will make *you* sick, striking you down,
[a]Desolating *you* because of your sins.
14 "You will eat, but you will [a]not be satisfied,
And your [1]vileness will be in your midst.
You will *try to* remove *for safekeeping,*
But you will [b]not preserve *anything,*
And what you do preserve I will give to the sword.
15 "You will sow but you will [a]not reap.
You will tread the olive but will not anoint yourself with oil;
And the grapes, but you will [b]not drink wine.
16 "The statutes of [a]Omri
And all the works of the house of [b]Ahab are observed;
And in their devices you [c]walk.
Therefore, I will give you up for [d]destruction
And [1]your inhabitants for [e]derision,
And you will bear the [f]reproach of My people."

Chapter 7

The Prophet Acknowledges

WOE is me! For I am
Like the fruit pickers and the [a]grape gatherers.

---

14 [1]I.e., wooden symbols of a female deity [a]Ex. 34:13; Is. 17:8; 27:9
15 [a]Is. 1:24; 65:12
1 [1]Lit., *with*
2 [a]2 Sam. 22:16; Ps. 104:5 [b]Is. 1:18; Hos. 4:1; 12:2
3 [a]Ps. 50:7 [b]Jer. 2:5 [c]Is. 43:22, 23
4 [a]Ex. 20:2 [b]Deut. 7:8 [c]Ps. 77:20 [d]Ex. 15:20
5 [1]Lit., *to know* [a]Num. 22:5, 6 [b]1 Sam. 12:7; Is. 1:27
6 [a]Ps. 40:6-8 [b]Ps. 51:16, 17
7 [a]Is. 40:16 [b]Lev. 18:21; 20:1-5; Jer. 7:31
8 [1]Or, *loyalty* [2]Or, *circumspectly* [a]Deut. 30:15 [b]Deut. 10:12 [c]Is. 56:1; Jer. 22:3 [d]Hos. 6:6 [e]Is. 57:15; 66:2
9 [1]Lit., *it* [a]Job 5:6-8, 17; Is. 11:4
10 [1]Lit., *shrunken ephah* [a]Jer. 5:26, 27; Amos 3:10 [b]Ezek. 45:9, 10; Amos 8:5
11 [a]Lev. 19:36; Hos. 12:7
12 [1]Lit., *her* [a]Is. 3:8
13 [a]Is. 1:7; 6:11
14 [1]Or possibly, *garbage* or *excreta* [a]Is. 9:20 [b]Is. 30:6
15 [a]Deut. 28:38-40; Jer. 12:13 [b]Amos 5:11; Zeph. 1:13
16 [1]Lit., *her* [a]1 Kin. 16:25, 26 [b]1 Kin. 16:29-33 [c]Jer. 7:24 [d]Jer. 18:16; Mic. 6:13 [e]Jer. 19:8; 25:9, 18; 29:18 [f]Ps. 44:13; Jer. 51:51; Hos. 12:14
1 [a]Is. 24:13

There is not a cluster of grapes to eat,
Or a [b]first-ripe fig *which* [1]I crave.
2 The [1]godly person has [a]perished from the land,
And there is no upright *person* among men.
All of them lie in wait for [b]bloodshed;
Each of them hunts the other with a [c]net.
3 Concerning evil, both hands do it [a]well.
The prince asks, also the judge, for a [b]bribe,
And a great man speaks the desire of his soul;
So they weave it together.
4 The best of them is like a [a]briar,
The most upright like a [b]thorn hedge.
The day when you post a watchman,
Your [c]punishment will come.
Then their [d]confusion will occur.
5 Do not [a]trust in a neighbor;
Do not have confidence in a friend.
From her who lies in your bosom
Guard [1]your lips.
6 For son treats father contemptuously,
Daughter rises up against her mother,
Daughter-in-law against her mother-in-law;
[a]A man's enemies are the men of his own household.

God Is the Source of Salvation and Light

7 But as for me, I will [a]watch expectantly for the LORD;
I will [b]wait for the God of my salvation.
My [c]God will hear me.
8 Do not rejoice over me, O my enemy.
Though I fall I will [a]rise;
Though I dwell in darkness, the LORD is a [b]light for me.
9 I will bear the indignation of the LORD
Because I have sinned against Him,
Until He [a]pleads my case and executes justice for me.
He will bring me out to the [b]light,
And I will see His [1c]righteousness.
10 Then my enemy will see,
And shame will cover her who [a]said to me,
"Where is the LORD your God?"
My eyes will look on her;
[1]At that time she will [2]be [b]trampled down,
Like mire of the streets.
11 *It will be* a day for [a]building your walls.
On that day will your [b]boundary be extended.
12 It *will be* a day when [1]they will [a]come to you
From Assyria and the cities of Egypt,
From Egypt even to [2]the Euphrates,
Even from sea to sea and mountain to mountain.
13 And the earth will become [a]desolate because of her inhabitants,
On account of the [b]fruit of their deeds.

14 Shepherd Thy people with Thy [a]scepter,
The flock of Thy [1]possession
Which dwells by itself in the woodland,
In the midst of [2]a fruitful field.
Let them feed in Bashan and Gilead
[b]As in the days of old.
15 "As in the days when you came out from the land of Egypt,
I will show [1a]you miracles."
16 Nations will see and be ashamed
Of all their might.
They will [a]put *their* hand on *their* mouth,
Their ears will be deaf.
17 They will [a]lick the dust like a serpent,
Like reptiles of the earth.
They will come trembling out of their [1]fortresses;
To the LORD our God they will come in [b]dread,
And they will be afraid before Thee.
18 Who is a God like Thee, who [a]pardons iniquity
And passes over the rebellious act of the [b]remnant of His [1]possession?
He does not [c]retain His anger forever,
Because He [d]delights in [2]unchanging love.
19 He will again have compassion on us;
[a]He will tread our iniquities underfoot.
Yes, Thou wilt [b]cast all [1]their sins
Into the depths of the sea.

1 [1]Lit., *my soul* [b]Is. 28:4; Hos. 9:10
2 [1]Or, *loyal* [a]Is. 57:1 [b]Mic. 3:10; Is. 59:7 [c]Jer. 5:26; Hos. 5:1
3 [a]Prov. 4:16, 17 [b]Amos 5:12; Mic. 3:11
4 [a]Ezek. 2:6; 28:24 [b]Nah. 1:10 [c]Is. 10:3; Hos. 9:7 [d]Is. 22:5
5 [1]Lit., *openings of your mouth* [a]Jer. 9:4
6 [a]Matt. 10:36
7 [a]Hab. 2:1 [b]Ps. 130:5; Is. 25:9 [c]Ps. 4:3
8 [a]Amos 9:11 [b]Is. 9:2
9 [1]I.e., right dealing [a]Jer. 50:34 [b]Ps. 37:6; Is. 42:7, 16 [c]Is. 46:13; 56:1
10 [1]Lit., *Now* [2]Lit., *become a trampled* place [a]Joel 2:17 [b]Is. 51:23; Zech. 10:5
11 [a]Is. 54:11; Amos 9:11 [b]Zeph. 2:2
12 [1]Lit., *he* [2]Lit., the *River* [a]Is. 19:23-25; 60:4, 9
13 [a]Jer. 25:11; Mic. 6:13 [b]Is. 3:10, 11; Mic. 3:4
14 [1]Or, *inheritance* [2]Or, *Carmel* [a]Lev. 27:32; Ps. 23:4 [b]Amos 9:11
15 [1]Lit., *him* [a]Ex. 3:20; 34:10; Ps. 78:12
16 [a]Mic. 3:7
17 [1]Lit., *fastnesses* [a]Ps. 72:9; Is. 49:23 [b]Is. 25:3; 59:19
18 [1]Or, *inheritance* [2]Or, *lovingkindness* [a]Ex. 34:7, 9; Is. 43:25 [b]Mic. 2:12; 4:7; 5:7, 8 [c]Ps. 103:8, 9, 13 [d]Jer. 32:41
19 [1]Several ancient versions read, *our* [a]Jer. 50:20 [b]Is. 38:17; 43:25; Jer. 31:34

20 Thou wilt give [a]truth to Jacob
And unchanging love to Abraham,
Which Thou didst [b]swear to our forefathers
From the days of old.

20 [a]Gen. 24:27; 32:10 [b]Deut. 7:8, 12

THE BOOK OF NAHUM

God Is Awesome

THE [1a]oracle of Nineveh. The book of the vision of Nahum the Elkoshite.

2 A jealous and avenging God is the LORD;
The LORD is [a]avenging and wrathful.
The LORD takes [b]vengeance on His adversaries,
And He reserves wrath for His enemies.
3 The LORD is [a]slow to anger and great in power,
And the LORD will by no means leave *the guilty* unpunished.
In [b]whirlwind and storm is His way,
And [c]clouds are the dust beneath His feet.
4 He [a]rebukes the sea and makes it dry;
He dries up all the rivers.
[b]Bashan and Carmel wither;
The blossoms of Lebanon wither.
5 Mountains [a]quake because of Him,
And the hills [b]dissolve;
Indeed the earth is [c]upheaved by His presence,
The [d]world and all the inhabitants in it.
6 Who can stand before His [a]indignation?
Who can endure the [b]burning of His anger?
His [c]wrath is poured out like fire,
And the [d]rocks are broken up by Him.
7 The LORD is [a]good,
A stronghold in the day of trouble,
And He knows those who take refuge in Him.
8 But with an [a]overflowing flood
He will make a complete end of [1]its site,
And will pursue His enemies into [b]darkness.

9 Whatever you [a]devise against the LORD,
He will make a [b]complete end of it.
Distress will not rise up twice.
10 Like tangled [a]thorns,
And like those who are [b]drunken with their drink,
They are [c]consumed
As stubble completely withered.
11 From you has gone forth
One who [a]plotted evil against the LORD,
A wicked [b]counselor.
12 Thus says the LORD,
"Though they are at full *strength* and likewise many,
Even so, they will be [a]cut off and pass away.
Though I have afflicted you,
I will afflict you no longer.
13 "So now, I will [a]break his yoke bar from upon you,
And I will tear off your shackles."

14 The LORD has issued a command concerning [1]you:
"Your name will no longer be perpetuated.
I will cut off [2a]idol and [3]image
From the house of your gods.
I will prepare your [b]grave,
For you are contemptible."

15 [1]Behold, [a]on the mountains the feet of him who brings good news,
Who announces peace!
[b]Celebrate your feasts, O Judah;
Pay your vows.
For never again will the [2]wicked one [c]pass through you;
He is [d]cut off completely.

CHAPTER 2

The Overthrow of Nineveh

1 THE one who [a]scatters has come up against [2]you.
Man the fortress, watch the road;
[3]Strengthen your back, [4]summon all *your* strength.
2 For the LORD will restore the [a]splendor of Jacob
[b]Like the splendor of Israel,

1 [1]Or, *burden* [a]Is. 13:1; 19:1; Jer. 23:33, 34; Hab. 1:1; Zech. 9:1; Mal. 1:1
2 [a]Deut. 32:35, 41 [b]Ps. 94:1
3 [a]Ex. 34:6, 7 [b]Is. 29:6; Amos 1:1 [c]Ps. 104:3; Is. 19:1
4 [a]Ps. 106:9; Is. 50:2 [b]Is. 33:9
5 [a]Ex. 19:18 [b]Mic. 1:4 [c]Is. 24:1, 20 [d]Ps. 98:7
6 [a]Jer. 10:10 [b]Is. 13:13 [c]Is. 66:15 [d]1 Kin. 19:11
7 [a]Ps. 25:8; 37:39, 40
8 [1]I.e., Nineveh's [a]Is. 28:2, 18 [b]Is. 13:9, 10
9 [a]Nah. 1:11 [b]Is. 28:22
10 [a]Mic. 7:4 [b]Is. 56:12 [c]Is. 5:24; 10:17
11 [a]Is. 10:7-11; Nah. 1:9 [b]Ezek. 11:2
12 [a]Is. 10:16-19, 33, 34
13 [a]Is. 9:4; 10:27; Jer. 2:20
14 [1]I.e., the king of Nineveh [2]Or, *a graven image* [3]Lit., *cast* metal *image* [a]Is. 46:1, 2; Mic. 5:13, 14 [b]Ezek. 32:22, 23
15 [1]Chap. 2:1 in Heb. [2]Or, *worthless one;* Heb., *Belial* [a]Is. 40:9; 52:7; Rom. 10:15 [b]Lev. 23:2, 4 [c]Is. 52:1; Joel 3:17 [d]Is. 29:7, 8
1 [1]Chap. 2:2 in Heb. [2]Lit., *your face* [3]Lit., *Make strong your loins* [4]Lit., *strengthen power greatly* [a]Jer. 51:20-23
2 [a]Is. 60:15 [b]Ezek. 37:21-23

Even though devastators have [c]devastated them
And [d]destroyed their vine branches.

3 The shields of [1]his mighty men are *colored* red,
The warriors are dressed in scarlet,
The chariots are *enveloped* in [2]flashing steel
[3]When he is prepared *to march,*
And the cypress *spears* are brandished.
4 The [a]chariots race madly in the streets,
They rush wildly in the [1]squares,
Their appearance is like torches,
They [b]dash to and fro like lightning flashes.
5 He remembers his nobles;
They stumble in their march,
They hurry to her wall,
And the [1]mantelet is set up.
6 The gates of the rivers are opened,
And the palace is dissolved.
7 And it is fixed:
She is stripped, she is carried away,
And her handmaids are moaning like the sound of doves,
Beating on their [1]breasts.

8 Though Nineveh *was* like a pool of water throughout her days,
Now they are fleeing;
"Stop, stop,"
But [a]no one turns back.
9 Plunder the silver!
Plunder the gold!
For there is no limit to the treasure—
Wealth from every kind of desirable object.
10 She is [a]emptied! Yes, she is desolate and waste!
[b]Hearts are melting and knees knocking!
Also anguish is in [1]the whole body,
And all their [c]faces are grown pale!
11 Where is the den of the lions
And the feeding place of the young lions,
Where the lion, lioness, and lion's cub prowled,
With nothing to disturb *them?*
12 The lion tore enough for his cubs,
[1]Killed *enough* for his lionesses,
And filled his lairs with prey
And his dens with torn flesh.

2 [c]Jer. 48:11 [d]Ps. 80:12, 13

3 [1]I.e., those attacking Nineveh [2]Lit., *fire of steel* [3]Lit., *On the day of his preparation*

4 [1]Lit., *broad places* [a]Is. 66:15; Ezek. 26:10; Nah. 3:2, 3 [b]Jer. 4:13

5 [1]Lit., *covering* used in a siege

7 [1]Lit., *hearts*

8 [a]Jer. 46:5; 47:3

10 [1]Lit., *all the loin* [a]Is. 24:1; 34:10-15; Nah. 2:2 [b]Ps. 22:14; Is. 13:7, 8; Ezek. 21:7 [c]Joel 2:6

12 [1]Lit., *Strangled*

13 [a]Jer. 21:13; Ezek. 5:8; Nah. 3:5 [b]Josh. 11:6, 9; Ps. 46:9

1 [a]Ezek. 24:6, 9

2 [1]Lit., *skipping* [a]Job 39:22-25; Jer. 47:3; Nah. 2:3, 4

3 [1]Lit., *there is no end to* [2]Lit., *their* [a]Hab. 3:11 [b]Is. 34:3; 66:16 [c]Is. 37:36; Ezek. 39:4

5 [1]Lit., *uncover your* [a]Jer. 50:31; Ezek. 26:3; Nah. 2:13 [b]Jer. 13:26 [c]Ezek. 16:37

6 [1]Lit., *detestable things* [a]Job 9:31 [b]Job 30:8; Mal. 2:9 [c]Is. 14:16; Jer. 51:37

7 [1]Lit., *flee* [a]Is. 51:19; Jer. 15:5

8 [1]I.e., the city of Amon: Thebes [2]I.e., the Nile [a]Jer. 46:25; Ezek. 30:14-16 [b]Is. 19:6-8

9 [1]Lit., *your* [a]Is. 20:5

13"Behold, [a]I am against you," declares the LORD of hosts. "I will [b]burn up her chariots in smoke, a sword will devour your young lions, I will cut off your prey from the land, and no longer will the voice of your messengers be heard."

CHAPTER 3

Nineveh's Complete Ruin

[a]WOE to the bloody city, completely full of lies *and* pillage;
Her prey never departs.
2 The [a]noise of the whip,
The noise of the rattling of the wheel,
Galloping horses,
And [1]bounding chariots!
3 Horsemen charging,
Swords flashing, spears [a]gleaming,
[b]Many slain, a mass of corpses,
And [1c]countless dead bodies—
They stumble over [2]the dead bodies!
4 *All* because of the many harlotries of the harlot,
The charming one, the mistress of sorceries,
Who sells nations by her harlotries
And families by her sorceries.
5"Behold, [a]I am against you," declares the LORD of hosts;
"And I will [1b]lift up your skirts over your face,
And [c]show to the nations your nakedness
And to the kingdoms your disgrace.
6"I will [a]throw [1]filth on you
And [b]make you vile,
And set you up as a [c]spectacle.
7"And it will come about that all who see you
Will [1]shrink from you and say,
'Nineveh is devastated!
[a]Who will grieve for her?'
Where will I seek comforters for you?"

8 Are you better than [1a]No-amon,
Which was situated by the [b]waters of the Nile,
With water surrounding her,
Whose rampart *was* [2]the sea,
Whose wall *consisted* of [2]the sea?
9 [a]Ethiopia was *her* might,
And Egypt too, without limits.
Put and Lubim were among [1]her helpers.

10 Yet she [a]became an exile,
She went into captivity;
Also her [b]small children were dashed to pieces
At the head of every street;
They [c]cast lots for her honorable men,
And all her great men were bound with fetters.
11 You too will become [a]drunk,
You will be hidden.
You too will search for a refuge from the enemy.
12 All your fortifications are fig trees with [1a]ripe fruit—
When shaken, they fall into the eater's mouth.
13 Behold, your people are [a]women in your midst!
The gates of your land are [b]opened wide to your enemies;
Fire consumes your gate bars.
14 [a]Draw for yourself water for the siege!
[b]Strengthen your fortifications!
Go into the clay and tread the mortar!
Take hold of the brick mold!
15 There [a]fire will consume you,
The sword will cut you down;
It will consume you as the locust *does*.
Multiply yourself like the creeping locust,
Multiply yourself like the swarming locust.
16 You have increased your traders more than the stars of heaven—
The creeping locust [1]strips and flies away.
17 Your [1]guardsmen are like the swarming locust.
Your marshals are like hordes of grasshoppers
Settling in the stone walls on a cold day.
The sun rises and they flee,
And the place where they are is not known.
18 Your shepherds are [a]sleeping, O king of Assyria;
Your nobles are lying down.
Your people are [b]scattered on the mountains,
And there is no one to regather *them*.
19 There is no [a]relief for your breakdown,
Your [b]wound is incurable.
All who hear [1]about you
Will [c]clap *their* hands over you,
For on whom has not your evil passed continually?

10 [a]Is. 19:4; 20:4 [b]Hos. 1:16 [c]Joel 3:3; Obad. 11
11 [a]Is. 49:26; Jer. 25:27
12 [1]Lit., *first fruits* [a]Is. 28:4; Hab. 1:10
13 [a]Is. 19:16; Jer. 51:30 [b]Is. 45:1, 2; Nah. 2:6
14 [a]2 Chr. 32:3, 4, 11 [b]Nah. 2:1
15 [a]Is. 66:15, 16; Nah. 2:13; 3:13
16 [1]I.e., strips vegetation; or, *molts*
17 [1]Or, *officials*
18 [a]Ps. 76:5, 6; Is. 56:10; Jer. 51:57 [b]1 Kin. 22:17; Is. 13:14
19 [1]Lit., *your report* [a]Jer. 46:11; Mic. 1:9 [b]Jer. 30:12 [c]Job 27:23; Lam. 2:15

THE BOOK OF HABAKKUK

Chaldeans Used to Punish Judah

THE [1a]oracle which Habakkuk the prophet saw.
2 [a]How long, O LORD, will I call for help,
And Thou wilt not hear?
I cry out to Thee, "Violence!"
Yet Thou dost [b]not save.
3 Why dost Thou make me see iniquity,
And cause *me* to look on wickedness?
Yes, [a]destruction and violence are before me;
[b]Strife exists and contention arises.
4 Therefore, the [a]law is ignored
And justice is never upheld.
For the wicked [b]surround the righteous;
Therefore, justice comes out [c]perverted.

5 "Look among the nations! Observe!
Be astonished! [a]Wonder!
Because *I* am doing [b]something in your days—
You would not believe if you were told.
6 "For behold, I am [a]raising up the Chaldeans,
That fierce and impetuous people
Who march throughout the earth
To [b]seize dwelling places which are not theirs.
7 "They are dreaded and [a]feared.
Their [b]justice and [1]authority [2]originate with themselves.
8 "Their horses are swifter than leopards
And [1]keener than wolves in the evening.
Their [2]horsemen come galloping,
Their horsemen come from afar;
They fly like an [a]eagle swooping *down* to devour.
9 "All of them come for violence.

1 [1]Or, *burden* [a]Is. 13:1; Nah. 1:1
2 [a]Ps. 13:1, 2; 22:1, 2 [b]Jer. 14:9
3 [a]Jer. 20:8 [b]Jer. 15:10
4 [a]Ps. 119:126; Is. 59:12-14 [b]Ps. 22:12; Is. 1:21-23 [c]Is. 5:20; Ezek. 9:9
5 [a]Is. 29:9 [b]Is. 29:14; Ezek. 12:22-28
6 [a]2 Kin. 24:2; Jer. 4:11-13 [b]Jer. 8:10
7 [1]Lit., *eminence* [2]Lit., *proceeds from* [a]Is. 18:2, 7 [b]Jer. 39:5-9
8 [1]Or, *more eager* to attack [2]Or, *steeds paw* the ground [a]Ezek. 17:3; Hos. 8:1

[1]Their [a]horde of faces *moves*
forward.
They collect captives like sand.
10 "They [a]mock at kings,
And rulers are a laughing matter to them.
They [b]laugh at every fortress,
And [c]heap up rubble to capture it.
11 "Then they will sweep through
like the wind and pass on.
But they will be held [a]guilty,
They whose [b]strength is their god."

12 Art Thou not from everlasting,
O LORD, my God, my Holy One?
We will not die.
Thou, O LORD, hast [a]appointed them to judge;
And Thou, O [b]Rock, hast established them to correct.
13 *Thine* eyes are too [a]pure to [1]approve evil,
And Thou canst not look on wickedness *with favor.*
Why dost Thou [b]look with favor
On those who deal [c]treacherously?
Why art Thou [d]silent when the wicked swallowed up
Those more righteous than they?
14 *Why* hast Thou made men like the fish of the sea,
Like creeping things without a ruler over them?
15 *The Chaldeans* [a]bring all of them up with a hook,
[b]Drag them away with their net,
And gather them together in their fishing net.
Therefore, they rejoice and are glad.
16 Therefore, they offer a sacrifice to their net.
And [1]burn incense to their fishing net;
Because through [a]these things their [2]catch is [3]large,
And their food is [4]plentiful.
17 Will they therefore empty their [a]net
And continually [b]slay nations without sparing?

CHAPTER 2

God Answers the Prophet

I WILL [a]stand on my guard post
And station myself on the rampart;
And I will [b]keep watch to see
[c]what He will speak to me,

9 [1]Or, *The eagerness of their faces* [a]2 Kin. 12:17; Dan. 11:17

10 [a]2 Chr. 36:6, 10; Is. 37:13 [b]Is. 10:9; 14:16 [c]Jer. 32:24; Ezek. 26:8

11 [a]Jer. 2:3 [b]Dan. 4:30; Hab. 1:16

12 [a]Is. 10:5, 6; Mal. 3:5 [b]Deut. 32:4

13 [1]Lit., *look at* [a]Ps. 11:4-6; 34:16 [b]Jer. 12:1, 2 [c]Is. 24:16 [d]Ps. 50:21

15 [a]Jer. 16:16; Amos 4:2 [b]Ps. 10:9

16 [1]Or, *sacrifice* [2]Lit., *portion* [3]Lit., *fat* or *plentiful* [4]Lit., *the fat portion* [a]Jer. 44:17

17 [a]Is. 19:8 [b]Is. 14:5, 6

1 [1]Lit., *upon my reproof* [a]Is. 21:8 [b]Ps. 5:3 [c]Ps. 85:8

2 [1]Or, *one may read it fluently* [2]Or, *is to proclaim it* [a]Deut. 27:8; Rev. 1:19

3 [1]Lit., *pants* [2]Or, *lie* [a]Dan. 8:17, 19 [b]Ps. 27:14

4 [1]Or, *faithfulness* [a]Ps. 49:18; Is. 13:11 [b]Rom. 1:17; Gal. 3:11

5 [a]2 Kin. 14:10 [b]Is. 5:11-15

6 [1]Lit., *heavy* [a]Is. 14:4-10; Jer. 50:13 [b]Job 20:15-29; Hab. 2:12

7 [1]Lit., *those who bite you* [2]Lit., *violently shake you* [a]Prov. 29:1

8 [a]Is. 33:1; Jer. 27:7; Zech. 2:8

9 [a]Jer. 22:13; Ezek. 22:27 [b]Is. 47:7; Jer. 49:16

10 [a]2 Kin. 9:26; Nah. 1:14; Hab. 2:16

And how I may reply [1]when I am reproved.
2 Then the LORD answered me and said,
"[a]Record the vision
And inscribe *it* on tablets,
That [1]the one who [2]reads it may run.
3 "For the vision is yet for the [a]appointed time;
It [1]hastens toward the goal, and it will not [2]fail.
Though it tarries, [b]wait for it;
For it will certainly come, it will not delay.

4 "Behold, as for the [a]proud one,
His soul is not right within him;
But the [b]righteous will live by his [1]faith.
5 "Furthermore, wine betrays the haughty man,
So that he does not [a]stay at home.
He [b]enlarges his appetite like Sheol,
And he is like death, never satisfied.
He also gathers to himself all nations
And collects to himself all peoples.

6 "Will not all of these [a]take up a taunt-song against him,
Even mockery *and* insinuations against him,
And say, '[b]Woe to him who increases what is not his—
For how long—
And makes himself [1]rich with loans?'
7 "Will not [1]your creditors [a]rise up suddenly,
And those who [2]collect from you awaken?
Indeed, you will become plunder for them.
8 "Because you have [a]looted many nations,
All the remainder of the peoples will loot you—
Because of human bloodshed and violence done to the land,
To the town and all its inhabitants.

9 "Woe to him who gets [a]evil gain for his house
To [b]put his nest on high
To be delivered from the hand of calamity!
10 "You have devised a [a]shameful thing for your house
By cutting off many peoples;

So you are sinning against
yourself.
11"Surely the [a]stone will cry out
from the wall,
And the rafter will answer it
from the framework.

12"Woe to him who [a]builds a city
with bloodshed
And founds a town with violence!
13"Is it not indeed from the LORD
of hosts
That peoples [a]toil for fire,
And nations grow weary for
nothing?
14"For the earth will be [a]filled
With the knowledge of the glory of the LORD,
As the waters cover the sea.

15"Woe to you who make your
neighbors drink,
Who mix in your venom even to
make *them* drunk
So as to look on their nakedness!
16"You will be filled with disgrace
rather than honor.
Now you yourself drink and expose your *own* nakedness.
The [a]cup in the LORD's right
hand will come around to
you,
And [b]utter disgrace *will come*
upon your glory.
17"For the [a]violence done to Lebanon will overwhelm you,
And the devastation of *its*
beasts by which you terrified
them,
[b]Because of human bloodshed
and [c]violence *done* to the
land,
To the town and all its inhabitants.

18"What [a]profit is the [1]idol when
its maker has carved it,
Or [2]an image, a [b]teacher of
falsehood?
For *its* maker [c]trusts in his *own*
handiwork
When he fashions speechless
idols.
19"Woe to him who says to a *piece*
of wood, '[a]Awake!'
To a dumb stone, 'Arise!'
And that is *your* teacher?
Behold, it is overlaid with [b]gold
and silver,
And there is [c]no breath at all
inside it.
20"But the LORD is in His holy temple.
[1]Let all the earth [a]be silent before Him."

CHAPTER 3

God's Deliverance of His People

A PRAYER of Habakkuk the
prophet, according to [1]Shigionoth.
2 LORD, I have [a]heard [1]the report
about Thee [2]*and* I [b]fear.
O LORD, [c]revive [d]Thy work in
the midst of the years,
In the midst of the years make
it known;
In wrath remember [3]mercy.

3 God comes from Teman,
And the Holy One from Mount
Paran. [Selah.
His [a]splendor covers the heavens,
And the [b]earth is full of His
praise.
4 *His* [a]radiance is like the sun-
light;
He has rays *flashing* from His
hand,
And there is the hiding of His
[b]power.
5 Before Him goes [a]pestilence,
And [b]plague comes [1]after Him.
6 He stood and surveyed the
earth;
He looked and [a]startled the nations.
Yes, the perpetual mountains
were shattered,
The ancient hills [1]collapsed.
His ways are everlasting.
7 I saw the tents of Cushan under
[a]distress,
The tent curtains of the land of
Midian were trembling.

8 Did the LORD rage against the
[a]rivers,
Or *was* Thine anger against the
rivers,
Or *was* Thy wrath against the
[b]sea,
That Thou didst [c]ride on Thy
horses,
On Thy [d]chariots of salvation?
9 Thy [a]bow was made bare,
The rods of [1b]chastisement
were sworn. [Selah.
Thou didst [c]cleave the earth
with rivers.
10 The mountains saw Thee *and*
quaked;
The downpour of waters swept
by.
The deep [a]uttered forth its
voice,
It lifted high its hands.
11 [a]Sun *and* moon stood in their
places;
They went away at the [b]light of
Thine arrows,

11 [a]Josh. 24:27; Luke 19:40
12 [a]Mic. 3:10; Nah. 3:1
13 [a]Is. 50:11; 55:2; Jer. 51:58
14 [a]Ps. 22:27; Is. 11:9; Zech. 14:8, 9
16 [a]Jer. 25:15, 27 [b]Nah. 3:6
17 [a]Joel 3:19; Zech. 11:1 [b]Ps. 55:23; Hab. 2:8 [c]Jer. 51:35; Hab. 2:8
18 [1]Or, *a graven image* [2]Lit., *a cast* metal *image* [a]Is. 42:17; 44:9; Jer. 2:27, 28 [b]Jer. 10:8, 14; Zech. 10:2 [c]Ps. 115:4, 8
19 [a]1 Kin. 18:26-29 [b]Jer. 10:9, 14 [c]Ps. 135:17
20 [1]Lit., *Hush before Him, all the earth.* [a]Zeph. 1:7; Zech. 2:13
1 [1]I.e., a highly emotional poetic form
2 [1]Or, *Thy report* [2]Or, *I stand in awe of Thy work, O LORD; In the midst of the years revive it,* [3]Or, *compassion* [a]Job 42:5, 6 [b]Ps. 119:120; Jer. 10:7 [c]Ps. 71:20; 85:6 [d]Ps. 44:1-8; Hab. 1:5 [e]Num. 14:19; 2 Sam. 24:15-17; Is. 54:8
3 [a]Ps. 113:4; 148:13 [b]Ps. 48:10
4 [a]Ps. 18:12 [b]Job 26:14
5 [1]Lit., *at His feet* [a]Ex. 12:29, 30; Num. 16:46-49 [b]Num. 11:1-3; Ps. 18:12, 13
6 [1]Lit., *bowed* or *sank down* [a]Job 21:18; Ps. 35:5
7 [a]Ex. 15:14-16
8 [a]Ex. 7:19, 20; Josh. 3:16; Is. 50:2 [b]Ex. 14:16, 21; Ps. 114:3, 5 [c]Deut. 33:26; Ps. 18:10 [d]Ps. 68:17
9 [1]Lit., *word* [a]Ps. 7:12, 13; Hab. 3:11 [b]Gen. 26:3; Deut. 7:8 [c]Ps. 78:16; 105:41
10 [a]Ps. 93:3; 98:7, 8
11 [a]Josh 10:12-14; Ps. 18:9, 11 [b]Ps. 18:14

At the radiance of Thy gleaming spear.
12 In indignation Thou didst [a]march through the earth;
In anger Thou didst [b]trample the nations.
13 Thou didst go forth for the [a]salvation of Thy people,
For the salvation of Thine [b]anointed.
Thou didst strike the [c]head of the house of the evil
To lay him open from [d]thigh to neck. [Selah.
14 Thou didst pierce with his [a]own spears
The head of his throngs.
They [b]stormed in to scatter us;
Their exultation *was* like those
Who [c]devour the oppressed in secret.
15 Thou didst tread on the sea with Thy horses,
On the [a]surge of many waters.

16 I heard and my [1]inward parts [a]trembled;
At the sound my lips quivered.
Decay enters my [b]bones,
And in my place I tremble.
Because I must [c]wait quietly for the day of distress,
[2]For the people to [d]arise *who* will invade us.
17 Though the fig tree should not blossom,
And there be no [1]fruit on the vines,
Though the yield of the [a]olive should fail,
And the fields produce no food,
Though the [b]flock should be cut off from the fold,
And there be [c]no cattle in the stalls,
18 Yet I will [a]exult in the LORD,
I will [b]rejoice in the [c]God of my salvation.
19 The Lord [1]GOD is my [a]strength,
And He has made my feet like hinds' *feet*,
And makes me walk on my high places.

For the choir director, on my stringed instruments.

12 [a]Ps. 68:7 [b]Is. 41:15; Jer. 51:33; Mic. 4:13
13 [a]Ex. 15:2; Ps. 68:19, 20 [b]Ps. 20:6; 28:8 [c]Ps. 68:21; 110:6 [d]Ezek. 13:14
14 [a]Judg. 7:22 [b]Dan. 11:40; Zech. 9:14 [c]Ps. 10:8; 64:2-5
15 [a]Ex. 15:8
16 [1]Lit., *belly* [2]Or, *To come upon the people who will* [a]Dan. 10:8; Hab. 3:2 [b]Job 30:17, 30; Jer. 23:9 [c]Luke 21:19 [d]Jer. 5:15
17 [1]Lit., *produce* [a]Mic. 6:15 [b]Joel 1:18 [c]Jer. 5:17
18 [a]Ex. 15:1, 2; Is. 61:10; Rom. 5:2, 3; Phil. 4:4 [b]Ps. 46:1-5 [c]Ps. 25:5; 27:1; Is. 12:2
19 [1]YHWH, usually rendered LORD [a]Ps. 18:32, 33; Is. 45:24

THE BOOK OF ZEPHANIAH

Day of Judgment on Judah

THE word of the LORD which came
to Zephaniah son of Cushi, son of
Gedaliah, son of Amariah, son of
Hezekiah, in the days of Josiah son
of Amon, king of Judah:
2"I will completely [a]remove all *things*
From the face of the earth," declares the LORD.
3"I will remove [a]man and beast;
I will remove the [b]birds of the sky
And the fish of the sea,
And the [c]ruins along with the wicked;
And I will cut off man from the face of the earth," declares the LORD.
4"So I will [a]stretch out My hand against Judah
And against all the inhabitants of Jerusalem.
And I will [b]cut off the remnant of Baal from this place,
And the names of the idolatrous priests along with the priests.
5"And those who bow down on the housetops to the [a]host of heaven,
And those who bow down *and* [b]swear to the LORD and *yet* swear by [1]Milcom,
6 And those who have [a]turned back from following the LORD,
And those who have [b]not sought the LORD or inquired of Him."

7 [1a]Be silent before the Lord [2]GOD!
For the day of the LORD is near,
For the LORD has prepared a [b]sacrifice,
He has [c]consecrated His guests.
8"Then it will come about on the day of the LORD's sacrifice,
That I will [a]punish the princes, the king's sons,
And all who clothe themselves with [b]foreign garments.
9"And I will punish on that day all who leap on the *temple* threshold,
Who fill the house of their [1]lord with [a]violence and deceit.
10"And on that day," declares the LORD,
"There will be the sound of a cry from the [a]Fish Gate,

2 [a]Jer. 7:20; Ezek. 33:27, 28
3 [a]Is. 6:11, 12 [b]Jer. 4:25; 9:10 [c]Ezek. 7:19; 14:3, 4, 8
4 [a]Jer. 6:12; Ezek. 6:14 [b]Mic. 5:13
5 [1]Or, *their king;* M.T., *Malcam* [a]2 Kin. 23:12; Jer. 19:13 [b]Jer. 5:2, 7; 7:9, 10
6 [a]Is. 1:4 [b]Is. 9:13
7 [1]Lit., *Hush* [2]YHWH, usually rendered LORD [a]Hab. 2:20; Zech. 2:13 [b]Is. 34:6; Jer. 46:10 [c]1 Sam. 16:5; Is. 13:3
8 [a]Is. 24:21; Hab. 1:10 [b]Is. 2:6
9 [1]Or, *Lord* [a]Jer. 5:27; Amos 3:10
10 [a]2 Chr. 33:14

A wail from the [1b]Second Quarter,
And a loud crash from the [c]hills.
11 "Wail, O inhabitants of the [1]Mortar,
For all the [2]people of Canaan will be silenced;
All who weigh out [a]silver will be cut off.
12 "And it will come about at that time
That I will [a]search Jerusalem with lamps,
And I will punish the men
Who are [1b]stagnant in spirit,
Who say in their hearts,
'The LORD will [c]not do good or evil!'
13 "Moreover, their wealth will become [a]plunder,
And their houses desolate;
Yes, [b]they will build houses but not inhabit *them*,
And plant vineyards but not drink their wine."

14 Near is the [a]great [b]day of the LORD,
Near and coming very quickly;
Listen, the day of the LORD!
[1]In it the warrior [c]cries out bitterly.
15 A day of wrath is that day,
A day of [a]trouble and distress,
A day of destruction and desolation,
A day of [b]darkness and gloom,
A day of clouds and thick darkness,
16 A day of [a]trumpet and battle cry,
Against the [b]fortified cities
And the high corner towers.
17 And I will bring [a]distress on men,
So that they will walk [b]like the blind,
Because they have sinned against the LORD;
And their [c]blood will be poured out like dust,
And their [d]flesh like dung.
18 Neither their silver nor their gold
Will be able to deliver them
On the day of the LORD's wrath;
And all the earth will be devoured
In the fire of His jealousy,
For He will [a]make a complete end,
Indeed a terrifying one,
Of all the inhabitants of the earth.

10 [1]I.e., a district of Jerusalem [b]2 Chr. 34:22 [c]2 Sam. 5:7; Ezek. 6:13
11 [1]I.e., a district of Jerusalem [2]Or, *merchant people will* [a]Job 27:16, 17; Hos. 9:6
12 [1]Lit., *thickening on their lees* [a]Jer. 16:16, 17; Ezek. 9:4-11; Amos 9:1-3 [b]Jer. 48:11; Amos 6:1 [c]Ezek. 8:12; 9:9
13 [a]Jer. 15:13; 17:3 [b]Amos 5:11; Mic. 6:15
14 [1]Lit., *There* [a]Jer. 30:7; Joel 2:11; Mal. 4:5 [b]Ezek. 7:7, 12; 30:3; Joel 1:15; 3:14; Zeph. 1:7 [c]Ezek. 7:16-18
15 [a]Is. 22:5 [b]Joel 2:2, 31; Amos 5:18-20
16 [a]Jer. 4:19 [b]Is. 2:12-15
17 [a]Jer. 10:18 [b]Deut. 28:29 [c]Ezek. 24:7, 8 [d]Jer. 8:2; 9:22
18 [a]Ezek. 7:5-7
1 [1]Or, *longing* [a]2 Chr. 20:4; Joel 1:14 [b]Jer. 3:3; 6:15
2 [1]Lit., *is born* [a]Is. 17:13; Hos. 13:3 [b]Lam. 4:11; Nah. 1:6
3 [1]Or, *land* [2]Or, *justice* [a]Ps. 105:4; Amos 5:6 [b]Ps. 22:26; Is. 11:4 [c]Amos 5:14, 15 [d]Ps. 57:1; Is. 26:20
4 [a]Amos 1:7, 8; Zech. 9:5-7
5 [1]I.e., a segment of the Philistines with roots in Crete [a]Amos 3:1 [b]Is. 14:29, 30
6 [1]Or, *meadows;* or, *wells* [a]Is. 7:25
7 [a]Is. 11:14; Jer. 32:44 [b]Is. 32:14 [c]Ex. 4:31; Ps. 80:14 [d]Ps. 126:4; Zeph. 3:20
8 [1]Lit., *reproach* [2]Lit., *reproached* [3]Lit., *made* themselves *great* [a]Ezek. 25:8 [b]Ezek. 25:3 [c]Amos 1:13

CHAPTER 2

Judgments on Judah's Enemies

GATHER yourselves together, yes, [a]gather,
O nation [b]without [1]shame,
2 Before the decree [1]takes effect—
The day passes [a]like the chaff—
Before the [b]burning anger of the LORD comes upon you,
Before the day of the LORD's anger comes upon you.
3 [a]Seek the LORD,
All you [b]humble of the [1]earth
Who have carried out His [2]ordinances;
[c]Seek righteousness, seek humility.
Perhaps you will be [d]hidden
In the day of the LORD's anger.

4 For [a]Gaza will be abandoned,
And Ashkelon a desolation;
[a]Ashdod will be driven out at noon,
And [a]Ekron will be uprooted.
5 Woe to the inhabitants of the seacoast,
The nation of the [1]Cherethites!
The word of the LORD is [a]against you,
O Canaan, land of the Philistines;
And I will [b]destroy you,
So that there will be no inhabitant.
6 So the seacoast will be [a]pastures,
With [1]caves for shepherds and folds for flocks.
7 And the coast will be
For the [a]remnant of the house of Judah,
They will [b]pasture on it.
In the houses of Ashkelon they will lie down at evening;
For the LORD their God will [c]care for them
And [d]restore their fortune.

8 "I have heard the [1a]taunting of Moab
And the [b]revilings of the sons of Ammon,
With which they have [2]taunted My people
And [3c]become arrogant against their territory.
9 "Therefore, as I live," declares the LORD of hosts,
The God of Israel,
"Surely Moab will be like Sodom,
And the sons of Ammon like Gomorrah—

A place possessed by nettles and salt pits,
And a perpetual desolation.
The remnant of My people will [a]plunder them,
And the remainder of My nation will inherit them."
10 This they will have in return for
their [a]pride, because they have
[1]taunted and [2]become arrogant
against the people of the LORD of
hosts.
11 The LORD will be [a]terrifying to
them, for He will [1]starve all the gods
of the earth; and all the [b]coastlands
of the nations will [c]bow down to
Him, every one from his *own* place.
12 "You also, O [a]Ethiopians, will be slain by My sword."
13 And He will stretch out His hand against the north
And destroy Assyria,
And He will make [a]Nineveh a desolation,
Parched like the wilderness.
14 And flocks will lie down in her midst,
[1]All beasts which range in herds;
Both the [2][a]pelican and the hedgehog
Will lodge in [3]the tops of her pillars;
[4]Birds will sing in the window,
Desolation *will be* on the threshold;
For He has laid bare the cedar work.
15 This is the [a]exultant city
Which [b]dwells securely,
Who says in her heart,
"[c]I am, and there is no one besides me."
How she has become a [d]desolation,
A resting place for beasts!
[e]Every one who passes by her will hiss
And wave his hand *in contempt*.

CHAPTER 3

Woe to Jerusalem and the Nations

WOE to her who is [a]rebellious and [b]defiled,
The [c]tyrannical city!
2 She [a]heeded no voice;
She [b]accepted no instruction.
She did not [c]trust in the LORD;
She did not [d]draw near to her God.
3 Her [a]princes within her are roaring lions,
Her judges are [b]wolves at evening;
They leave nothing for the morning.
4 Her prophets are [a]reckless, treacherous men;
Her [b]priests have profaned the sanctuary.
They have done violence to the law.
5 The LORD is [a]righteous within her;
He will do no [b]injustice.
[c]Every morning He brings His justice to light;
He does not fail.
But the unjust knows no shame.
6 "I have cut off nations;
Their corner towers are in ruins.
I have made their streets [a]desolate,
With no one passing by;
Their [b]cities are laid waste,
Without a man, without an inhabitant.
7 "I said, 'Surely you will revere Me,
Accept instruction.'
So her dwelling will [a]not be cut off
According to all that I have appointed concerning her.
But they were eager to [b]corrupt all their deeds.

8 "Therefore, [a]wait for Me," declares the LORD,
"For the day when I rise up to the prey.
Indeed, My decision is to [b]gather nations,
To assemble kingdoms,
To pour out on them My indignation,
All My burning anger;
For all the earth will be devoured
By the fire of My zeal.
9 "For then I will [1]give to the peoples [a]purified lips,
That all of them may [b]call on the name of the LORD,
To serve Him [2]shoulder to shoulder.
10 "From beyond the rivers of Ethiopia
My [1]worshipers, [2]My dispersed ones,
Will [a]bring My offerings.
11 "In that day you will [a]feel no shame
Because of all your deeds
By which you have rebelled against Me;
For then I will remove from your midst

9 [a]Is. 11:14

10 [1]Lit., *reproached* [2]Lit., *made* themselves *great* [a]Is. 16:6

11 [1]Lit., *make lean* [a]Joel 2:11 [b]Is. 24:15 [c]Ps. 72:8-11; Zeph. 3:9

12 [a]Is. 20:4, 5; Ezek. 30:4-9

13 [a]Nah. 3:7

14 [1]Or, *All* kinds of *beasts in crowds;* lit., *Every* kind of *beast of a nation* [2]Or, *owl;* or, *jackdaw* [3]Lit., *her capitals* [4]Lit., *A voice* [a]Is. 14:23; 34:11-15

15 [a]Is. 22:2 [b]Is. 32:9, 11; 47:8 [c]Is. 47:8; Ezek. 28:2, 9 [d]Is. 32:14 [e]Jer. 18:16; 19:8

1 [a]Jer. 5:23 [b]Ezek. 23:30 [c]Jer. 6:6

2 [a]Jer. 7:23-28 [b]Jer. 2:30; 5:3 [c]Ps. 78:22; Jer. 13:25 [d]Ps. 73:28

3 [a]Ezek. 22:27 [b]Jer. 5:6; Hab. 1:8

4 [a]Judg. 9:4 [b]Ezek. 22:26; Mal. 2:7, 8

5 [a]Deut. 32:4 [b]Ps. 92:15 [c]Job 7:18

6 [a]Jer. 9:12 [b]Is. 6:11

7 [a]Jer. 7:7 [b]Hos. 9:9

8 [a]Ps. 27:14; Is. 30:18; Hab. 2:3 [b]Ezek. 38:14-23; Joel 3:2

9 [1]Lit., *change* [2]Lit., *with one shoulder* [a]Is. 19:18; 57:19 [b]Ps. 22:27; 86:9; Hab. 2:14; Zeph. 2:11

10 [1]Or, *suppliants* [2]Lit., *the daughter of My dispersed ones* [a]Is. 60:6, 7

11 [a]Is. 45:17; 54:4; Joel 2:26, 27

Your [b]proud, exulting ones,
And you will never again be
haughty
On My [c]holy mountain.

A Remnant of Israel

12 "But I will leave among you
A [a]humble and lowly people,
And they will [b]take refuge in
the name of the LORD.
13 "The [a]remnant of Israel will [b]do
no wrong
And [c]tell no lies,
Nor will a deceitful tongue
Be found in their mouths;
For they shall feed and lie down
With no one to make them
tremble."

14 Shout for joy, O daughter of
Zion!
Shout *in triumph*, O Israel!
Rejoice and exult with all *your*
heart,
O daughter of Jerusalem!
15 The LORD has taken away *His*
judgments against you,
He has cleared away your enemies.
The King of Israel, the LORD, is
[a]in your midst;
You will [b]fear disaster no more.
16 In that day it will be said to Jerusalem:
"[a]Do not be afraid, O Zion;
Do not let your hands fall limp.
17 "The LORD your God is in your
midst,
A [1a]victorious warrior.
He will [b]exult over you with
joy,
He will [2]be quiet in His love,
He will rejoice over you with
shouts of joy.
18 "I will gather those who [a]grieve
about the appointed feasts—
They [1]came from you, *O Zion;*
The reproach *of exile* is a burden on [2]them.
19 "Behold, I am going to deal at
that time
With all your [a]oppressors,
I will save the lame
And gather the outcast,
And I will turn their [b]shame
into [c]praise and renown
In all the earth.
20 "At that time I will [a]bring you in,
Even at the time when I gather
you together;
Indeed, I will give you [b]renown
and praise
Among all the peoples of the
earth,
When I [c]restore your fortunes
before your eyes,"
Says the LORD.

11 [b]Is. 2:12; 5:15 [c]Is. 11:9; 56:7; Ezek. 20:40

12 [a]Is. 14:30, 32; Zech. 13:8, 9 [b]Is. 50:10; Nah. 1:7

13 [a]Is. 10:20-22; Mic. 4:7; Zeph. 2:7 [b]Ps. 119:3; Jer. 31:33; Zeph. 3:5 [c]Zech. 8:3, 16

15 [a]Ezek. 37:26-28; Zeph. 3:5 [b]Is. 54:14

16 [a]Is. 35:3, 4

17 [1]Lit., *A warrior who saves* [2]Or, with some ancient versions, *renew you in* [a]Is. 63:1 [b]Is. 62:5

18 [1]Lit., *were* [2]Lit., *her* [a]Ps. 42:2-4; Ezek. 9:4, 6

19 [a]Is. 60:14; Zech. 8:23 [b]Ezek. 16:27, 57 [c]Is. 60:18; 62:7

20 [a]Ezek. 37:12, 21 [b]Deut. 26:18, 19; Is. 56:5; 66:22 [c]Jer. 29:14; Joel 3:1; Zeph. 2:7

THE BOOK OF HAGGAI

Haggai Begins Temple Building

IN the second year of Darius the
king, on the first day of the sixth
month, the word of the LORD came
by the prophet [a]Haggai to Zerubbabel the son of Shealtiel, [b]governor of
Judah, and to Joshua the son of Jehozadak, the high priest saying,
2 "Thus says the LORD of hosts,
'This people says, "The time has not
come, *even* the time for the house of
the LORD to be rebuilt." ' "
3 Then the word of the LORD
came by Haggai the prophet saying,
4 "Is it time for you yourselves to
dwell in your paneled houses while
this house [a]*lies* desolate?"
5 Now therefore, thus says the
LORD of hosts, "Consider your
ways!
6 "You have [a]sown much, but
[1]harvest little; *you* eat, but *there is*
not *enough* to be satisfied; *you*
drink, but *there is* not *enough* [2]to
become drunk; *you* put on clothing,
but no one is warm *enough;* and he
who earns, earns wages *to put* into a
purse with holes."
7 Thus says the LORD of hosts,
"Consider your ways!
8 "Go up to the [1]mountains, bring
wood and rebuild the [2]temple, that I
may be [a]pleased with it and be glorified," says the LORD.
9 "*You* look for much, but behold,
it comes to little; when you bring *it*
home, I [a]blow it *away*. Why?" declares the LORD of hosts, "Because
of My house which *lies* desolate,
while each of you runs to his own
house.
10 "Therefore, because of you the
[a]sky has withheld [1]its dew, and the
earth has withheld its produce.
11 "And I called for a [a]drought on
the land, on the mountains, on the
grain, on the new wine, on the oil, on
what the ground produces, on [b]men,
on cattle, and on all the labor of
[1]your hands."
12 Then Zerubbabel the son of
Shealtiel, and Joshua the son of Jehozadak, the high priest, with all the

1 [a]Ezra 5:1; 6:14; Hag. 1:3, 12, 13; 2:1, 10, 20 [b]1 Kin. 10:15; Ezra 5:3

4 [a]Jer. 33:10, 12; Hag. 1:9

6 [1]Lit., *bring in* [2]Lit., *not becoming drunk* [a]Deut. 28:38-40; Hos. 8:7; Hag. 1:9, 10; 2:16, 17

8 [1]Lit., *mountain* [2]Lit., *house* [a]Ps. 132:13, 14

9 [a]Is. 40:7

10 [1]Lit., *from dew* [a]Deut. 28:23-24; 1 Kin. 17:1; Joel 1:18-20

11 [1]Lit., *the palms* [a]Jer. 14:2-6; Mal. 3:9, 11 [b]Deut. 28:22

remnant of the people, [a]obeyed the
voice of the LORD their God and the
words of Haggai the prophet, as the
LORD their God had sent him. And
the people [b]showed reverence for
the LORD.
13 Then Haggai, the [a]messenger of
the LORD, spoke by the commission
of the LORD to the people saying,
“ ‘[b]I am with you,’ declares the
LORD.”
14 So the LORD stirred up the spirit
of [a]Zerubbabel the son of Shealtiel,
[a]governor of Judah, and the spirit of
Joshua the son of Jehozadak, the
high priest, and the spirit of all the
[b]remnant of the people; and they
came and [c]worked on the house of
the LORD of hosts, their God,
15 on the twenty-fourth day of the
sixth month in the second year of
Darius the king.

CHAPTER 2

The Builders Encouraged

ON the twenty-first of the seventh
month, the word of the LORD came
by [a]Haggai the prophet saying,
2 “Speak now to [a]Zerubbabel the
son of Shealtiel, [a]governor of Judah,
and to [a]Joshua the son of Jehozadak, the high priest, and to the [b]rem-
nant of the people saying,
3 ‘Who is [a]left among you who
saw this temple in its former glory?
And how do you see it now? Does it
not seem to you like nothing in comparison?
4 ‘But now [a]take courage, Zerubbabel,’ declares the LORD, ‘take
courage also, Joshua son of Jehozadak, the high priest, and all you people of the land take courage,’ declares the LORD, ‘and work; for [b]I am
with you,’ says the LORD of hosts.
5 ‘As for the promise which I
[a]made you when you came out of
Egypt, My [b]Spirit is abiding in your
midst; [c]do not fear!’
6 “For thus says the LORD of hosts,
‘[a]Once more in a [b]little while, I am
going to shake the heavens and the
earth, the sea also and the dry land.
7 ‘And I will shake [a]all the nations; and they will come with the
[b]wealth of all nations; and I will [c]fill
this house with glory,’ says the
LORD of hosts.
8 ‘The [a]silver is Mine, and the gold
is Mine,’ declares the LORD of hosts.
9 ‘The latter [a]glory of this house
will be greater than the former,’
says the LORD of hosts, ‘and in this
place I shall give [b]peace,’ declares
the LORD of hosts.”
10 On the twenty-fourth of the
ninth *month,* in the second year of
Darius, the word of the LORD came
to Haggai the prophet saying,
11 “Thus says the LORD of hosts,
‘[a]Ask now the priests *for* a ruling:
12 ‘If a man carries [a]holy meat in
the fold of his garment, and touches
bread with this fold, or cooked food,
wine, oil, or any *other* food, will it
become holy?’ ” And the priests answered and said, “No.”
13 Then Haggai said, “[a]If one who
is unclean from a [1]corpse touches
any of these, will *the latter* become
unclean?” And the priests answered
and said, “It will become unclean.”
14 Then Haggai answered and
said, “ ‘[a]So is this people. And so is
this nation before Me,’ declares the
LORD, ‘and so is every work of their
hands; and what they offer there is
unclean.
15 ‘But now, do [1]consider from this
day [2]onward: before one [a]stone was
placed on another in the temple of
the LORD,
16 [1]from that time *when* one came
to a *grain* heap of twenty *measures,*
there would be only ten; and *when*
one came to the wine vat to draw
fifty [2]measures, there would be *only*
twenty.
17 ‘I smote you *and* every work of
your hands with [a]blasting wind, mildew, and hail; yet you did not [1]come
back to me,’ declares the LORD.
18 ‘Do [1a]consider from this day
[2]onward, from the twenty-fourth
day of the ninth *month;* from the
day when the temple of the LORD
was [b]founded, [1]consider:
19 ‘Is the seed still in the barn?
Even including the vine, the fig tree,
the pomegranate, and the olive tree,
it has not borne fruit. Yet from this
day on I will [a]bless *you.*’ ”
20 Then the word of the LORD
came a second time to Haggai on
the twenty-fourth *day* of the month
saying,
21 “Speak to Zerubbabel governor
of Judah saying, ‘I am going to
shake the heavens and the earth.
22 ‘And I will overthrow the
[a]thrones of kingdoms and destroy
the [b]power of the kingdoms of the
[1]nations; and I will overthrow the
[c]chariots and their riders, and the
horses and their riders will go down,
[d]every one by the sword of another.’
23 ‘On that day,’ declares the LORD
of hosts, ‘I will take you, Zerubbabel, son of Shealtiel, my servant,’
declares the LORD, ‘and I will make
you like a [1a]signet *ring,* for [b]I have
chosen you,’ ” declares the LORD of
hosts.

12 [a]Is. 1:19; 1 Thess. 2:13 [b]Deut. 31:12, 13; Ps. 112:1; Is. 50:10
13 [a]Is. 44:26; Ezek. 3:17; Mal. 2:7; 3:1 [b]Ps. 46:11; Is. 41:10; 43:2
14 [a]Hag. 1:1; 2:2, 21 [b]Hag. 1:12 [c]Ezra 5:2; Neh. 4:6
1 [a]Hag. 1:1
2 [a]Hag. 1:1 [b]Hag. 1:12
3 [a]Ezra 3:12
4 [a]Deut. 31:23; 1 Chr. 22:13; 28:20; Zech. 8:9; Eph. 6:10 [b]2 Sam. 5:10; Acts 7:9
5 [a]Ex. 19:4-6; 33:12-14; 34:8-10 [b]Neh. 9:20; Is. 63:11, 14 [c]Is. 41:10, 13; Zech. 8:13
6 [a]Heb. 12:26 [b]Is. 10:25; 29:17
7 [a]Dan. 2:44; Joel 3:9, 16 [b]Is. 60:4-9 [c]1 Kin. 8:11; Is. 60:7
8 [a]1 Chr. 29:14, 16; Is. 60:17
9 [a]Zech. 2:5 [b]Is. 9:6, 7; 66:12
11 [a]Deut. 17:8-11; Mal. 2:7
12 [a]Ex. 29:37; Lev. 6:27, 29; 7:6; Ezek. 44:19; Matt. 23:19
13 [1]Lit., *soul* [a]Lev. 22:4-6; Num. 19:22
14 [a]Prov. 15:8; Is. 1:11-15
15 [1]Lit., *set your heart* [2]Or, *backward* [a]Ezra 3:10; 4:24
16 [1]Lit., *since they were* [2]Or, *troughs full*
17 [1]Heb. obscure; perhaps, *but what did we have in common?* [a]Deut. 28:22; 1 Kin. 8:37; Amos 4:9
18 [1]Lit., *set your heart* [2]Or, *backward* [a]Deut. 32:29; Hag. 2:15 [b]Ezra 5:1, 2; Zech. 8:9, 12
19 [a]Ps. 128:1-6; Jer. 31:12, 14; Mal. 3:10
22 [1]Or, *Gentiles* [a]Ezek. 26:16; Zeph. 3:8 [b]Mic. 7:16 [c]Ps. 46:9; Ezek. 39:20; Mic. 5:10 [d]Judg. 7:22; 2 Chr. 20:23
23 [1]Or, *seal* [a]Song of Sol. 8:6; Jer. 22:24 [b]Is. 42:1; 43:10

THE BOOK OF ZECHARIAH

A Call to Repentance

IN the eighth month of the second year of Darius, the word of the LORD came to Zechariah the prophet, the son of Berechiah, the son of Iddo saying,

2 "The LORD was very [a]angry with your fathers.

3 "Therefore say to them, 'Thus says the LORD of hosts, "[a]Return to Me," declares the LORD of hosts, "that I may return to you," says the LORD of hosts.

4 "Do not be [a]like your fathers, to whom the [b]former prophets proclaimed, saying, 'Thus says the LORD of hosts, "[c]Return now from your evil ways and from your evil deeds." ' But they did not [d]listen or give heed to Me," declares the LORD.

5 "Your fathers, where are they? And the [a]prophets, do they live forever?

6 "But did not My words and My statutes, which I commanded My servants the prophets, [a]overtake your fathers? Then they repented and said, '[b]As the LORD of hosts purposed to do to us in accordance with our ways and our deeds, so He has dealt with us.' " ' "

Patrol of the Earth

7 On the twenty-fourth day of the eleventh month, which is the month Shebat, in the second year of Darius, the word of the LORD came to Zechariah the prophet, the son of Berechiah, the son of Iddo, as follows:

8 I saw at night, and behold, a man was riding on a red horse, and he was standing among the [a]myrtle trees which were in the ravine, with red, sorrel, and white horses behind him.

9 Then I said, "My [a]lord, what are these?" And the angel who was speaking with me said to me, "I will show you what these are."

10 And the man who was standing among the myrtle trees answered and said, "These are those whom the LORD has sent to [1a]patrol the earth."

11 So they answered the angel of the LORD who was standing among the myrtle trees, and said, "We have [1]patrolled the earth, and behold, [a]all the earth is [2]peaceful and quiet."

12 Then the angel of the LORD answered and said, "O LORD of hosts, [a]how long wilt Thou [b]have no compassion for Jerusalem and the cities of Judah, with which Thou hast been [c]indignant these [d]seventy years?"

13 And the LORD answered the angel who was speaking with me with [1]gracious words, [a]comforting words.

14 So the angel who was speaking with me said to me, "[a]Proclaim, saying, 'Thus says the LORD of hosts, "I am exceedingly jealous for Jerusalem and Zion.

15 "But I am very angry with the nations who are [a]at ease; for while I was only a little angry, they [1b]furthered the disaster."

16 'Therefore, thus says the LORD, "I will [a]return to Jerusalem with compassion; My [b]house will be built in it," declares the LORD of hosts, "and a measuring [c]line will be stretched over Jerusalem." '

17 "Again, proclaim, saying, 'Thus says the LORD of hosts, "My [a]cities will again overflow with prosperity, and the LORD will again [b]comfort Zion and again choose Jerusalem." ' "

18 [1]Then I lifted up my eyes and looked, and behold, *there were* four horns.

19 So I said to the angel who was speaking with me, "What are these?" And he answered me, "These are the [a]horns which have scattered Judah, Israel, and Jerusalem."

20 Then the LORD showed me four [a]craftsmen.

21 And I said, "What are these coming to do?" And he said, "These are the [a]horns which have scattered Judah, so that no man lifts up his head; but these *craftsmen* have come to terrify them, to [b]throw down the horns of the nations who have lifted up *their* horns against the land of Judah in order to scatter it."

CHAPTER 2

God's Favor to Zion

[1]THEN I lifted up my eyes and looked, and behold, *there was* a man with a [a]measuring line in his hand.

2 So I said, "Where are you going?" And he said to me, "To [a]measure Jerusalem, to see how wide it is and how long it is."

3 And behold, the angel who was speaking with me was going out,

---

2 [a]2 Chr. 36:16; Jer. 44:6; Zech. 1:15

3 [a]Is. 31:6; Mal. 3:7

4 [a]Ps. 78:8; 106:6, 7 [b]2 Chr. 24:19; 36:15 [c]Is. 1:16-19; Jer. 4:1; Ezek. 33:11 [d]Jer. 6:17; 11:7, 8

5 [a]John 8:52

6 [a]Jer. 12:16, 17; 44:28, 29; Amos 9:10 [b]Lam. 2:17

8 [a]Neh. 8:15; Is. 41:19; 55:13; Zech. 1:10, 11

9 [a]Zech. 1:19; 4:4, 5, 13; 6:4

10 [1]Lit., *walk about through* [a]Job 1:7; Zech. 1:11; 4:10; 6:5-8

11 [1]Lit., *walked about through* [2]Lit., *sitting* [a]Is. 14:7; Zech. 1:15

12 [a]Ps. 74:10; Jer. 12:4; Hab. 1:2 [b]Ps. 102:13; Jer. 30:18 [c]Ps. 102:10; Jer. 15:17 [d]Jer. 25:11; 29:10; Dan. 9:2; Zech. 7:5

13 [1]Lit., *good* [a]Is. 40:1, 2; 57:18

14 [a]Is. 40:2, 6; Zech. 1:17

15 [1]Lit., *helped for evil* [a]Ps. 123:4; Jer. 48:11 [b]Amos 1:11

16 [a]Is. 54:8-10; Zech. 2:10, 11 [b]Ezra 6:14, 15; Zech. 4:9 [c] Jer. 31:39; Zech. 2:2, 4

17 [a]Is. 44:26; 61:4 [b]Is. 51:3

18 [1]Ch. 2:1 in Heb.

19 [a]1 Kin. 22:11; Ps. 75:4, 5; Amos 6:13

20 [a]Is. 44:12; 54:16

21 [a]Zech. 1:17 [b]Ps. 73:10

1 [1]Ch. 2:5 in Heb. [a]Jer. 31:39; Ezek. 40:3; 47:3; Zech. 1:16

2 [a]Jer. 31:39; Ezek. 40:3; Rev. 21:15-17

and another angel was coming out to meet him,

4 and said to him, "Run, speak to that [a]young man, saying, 'Jerusalem will be inhabited [b]without walls, because of the [c]multitude of men and cattle within it.

5 'For I,' declares the LORD, 'will be a [a]wall of fire [1]around her, and I will be the [b]glory in her midst.' "

6 "[1]Ho there! [a]Flee from the land of the north," declares the LORD, "for I have [b]dispersed you as the four winds of the heavens," declares the LORD.

7 "Ho, Zion! [a]Escape, you who are living with the daughter of Babylon."

8 For thus says the LORD of hosts, "After [1a]glory He has sent me against the nations which plunder you, for he who touches you, touches the [2b]apple of His eye.

9 "For behold, I will [a]wave My hand over them, so that they will be [b]plunder for their slaves. Then you will know that the LORD of hosts has sent Me.

10 "[a]Sing for joy and be glad, O daughter of Zion; for behold I am coming and I will dwell in your midst," declares the LORD.

11 "And [a]many nations will join themselves to the LORD in that day and will become My people. Then I will dwell in your midst, and you will know that the LORD of hosts has sent Me to you.

12 "And the LORD will [1a]possess Judah as His portion in the holy land, and will again [b]choose Jerusalem.

13 "[1a]Be silent, all flesh, before the LORD; for He is [b]aroused from His holy habitation."

CHAPTER 3

Joshua, the High Priest

THEN he showed me [a]Joshua the high priest standing before the angel of the LORD, and [1b]Satan standing at his right hand to accuse him.

2 And the LORD said to Satan, "The LORD rebuke you, Satan! Indeed, the LORD who has [a]chosen Jerusalem rebuke you! Is this not a brand plucked from the fire?"

3 Now Joshua was clothed with [a]filthy garments and standing before the angel.

4 And he spoke and said to those who were standing before him saying, "[a]Remove the filthy garments from him." Again he said to him, "See, I have [b]taken your iniquity away from you and [1]will [c]clothe you with festal robes."

5 Then I said, "Let them put a clean [a]turban on his head." So they put a clean turban on his head and clothed him with garments, while the angel of the LORD was standing by.

6 And the angel of the LORD admonished Joshua saying,

7 "Thus says the LORD of hosts, 'If you will [a] walk in My ways, and if you will perform My service, then you will also [b]govern My house and also have charge of My [c]courts, and I will grant you [1]free access among these who are standing *here*.

The Branch

8 'Now listen, Joshua the high priest, you and your friends who are sitting in front of you—indeed they are men who are a [a]symbol, for behold, I am going to bring in My servant the [1b]Branch.

9 'For behold, the stone that I have set before Joshua; on one stone are seven eyes. Behold, I will engrave an inscription on it,' declares the LORD of hosts, 'and I will remove the iniquity of that land in one day.

10 'In that day,' declares the LORD of hosts, 'every one of you will invite his neighbor to *sit* under *his* [a]vine and under *his* fig tree.' "

CHAPTER 4

The Golden Lampstand and Olive Trees

THEN the angel who was speaking with me returned, and [a]roused me as a man who is awakened from his sleep.

2 And he said to me, "[a]What do you see?" And I said, "I see, and behold, a [b]lampstand all of gold with its bowl on the top of it, and its [c]seven lamps on it with seven spouts belonging to each of the lamps which are on the top of it;

3 also [a]two olive trees by it, one on the right side of the bowl and the other on its left side."

4 Then I answered and said to the angel who was speaking with me saying, "What are these, my lord?"

5 So the angel who was speaking with me answered and said to me, "Do you not know what these are?" And I said, "No, my lord."

6 Then he answered and [1]said to me, "This is the word of the LORD to [a]Zerubbabel saying, '[b]Not by might nor by power, but by My [c]Spirit,' says the LORD of hosts.

7 'What are you, O great moun-

4 [a]Jer. 1:6; Dan. 1:4; 1 Tim. 4:12 [b]Ezek. 38:11 [c]Is. 49:20; Jer. 30:19; 33:22
5 [1]Lit., *to her* [a]Is. 4:5; 26:1; 60:18 [b]Hag. 2:9; Zech. 2:10, 11
6 [1]Lit., *Ho! ho!* [a]Jer. 3:18 [b]Jer. 31:10; Ezek. 11:16
7 [a]Is. 48:20; Jer. 51:6
8 [1]Or, *the glory* [2]Lit., *pupil* [a]Is. 60:7-9 [b]Deut. 32:10; Ps. 17:8
9 [a]Is. 19:16 [b]Is. 14:2
10 [a]Is. 65:18, 19; Zech. 9:9
11 [a]Mic. 4:2
12 [1]Or, *inherit* [a]Deut. 32:9; Ps. 33:12; Jer. 10:16 [b]2 Chr. 6:6; Ps. 132:13, 14; Zech. 1:17
13 [1]Lit., *Hush* [a]Hab. 2:20; Zeph. 1:7 [b]Ps. 78:65; Is. 51:9
1 [1]Or, the *Adversary* or, *Accuser* [a]Ezra 5:2; Hag. 1:1; Zech. 6:11 [b]1 Chr. 21:1; Job 1:6; Ps. 109:6
2 [a]Zech. 2:12
3 [a]Ezra 9:15; Is. 4:4; 64:6
4 [1]Lit., *to clothe* [a]Is. 43:25; Ezek. 36:25 [b]Mic. 7:18, 19; Zech. 3:9 [c]Is. 52:1; 61:10
5 [a]Job 29.14, Is. 3:23
7 [1]Lit., *goings* [a]1 Kin. 3:14 [b]Deut. 17:9, 12 [c]Is. 62:9
8 [1]Lit., *Sprout* [a]Is. 8:18; 20:3; Ezek. 12:11 [b]Is. 11:1; 53:2; Jer. 33:15; Zech. 6:12
10 [a]1 Kin. 4:25; Is. 36:16; Mic. 4:4
1 [a]1 Kin. 19:5-7; Jer. 31:26
2 [a]Jer. 1:13; Zech. 5:2 [b]Ex. 25:31, 37; Jer. 52:19 [c]Rev. 4:5
3 [a]Zech. 4:11; Rev. 11:4
6 [1]Lit., *said to me, saying* [a]Hag. 2:4, 5 [b]Is. 11:2-4; 30:1; Hos. 1:7 [c]2 Chr. 32:7, 8; Eph. 6:17

tain? Before Zerubbabel *you will be-*
come a plain; and he will bring forth
the top stone with [a]shouts of
"Grace, grace to it!" ' "
8 Also the word of the LORD came
to me saying,
9 "The hands of Zerubbabel have
[a]laid the foundation of this house,
and his hands will [b]finish *it*. Then
you will know that the LORD of hosts
has sent me to you.
10 "For who has despised the day
of [a]small things? But these [b]seven
will be glad when they see the
[c]plumb line in the hand of Zerubbabel—*these are* the eyes of the LORD
which range to and fro throughout
the earth."
11 Then I answered and said to
him, "What are these two olive trees
on the right of the lampstand and on
its left?"
12 And I answered the second
time and said to him, "What are the
two olive [1]branches which are beside the two golden pipes, which
empty the golden *oil* from themselves?"
13 So he answered me saying, "Do
you not know what these are?" And
I said, "No, my lord."
14 Then he said, "These are the
two [1a]anointed ones, who are
[b]standing by the [c]Lord of the whole
earth."

CHAPTER 5

The Flying Scroll

THEN I lifted up my eyes again
and looked, and behold, *there was* a
flying [a]scroll.
2 And he said to me, "What do
you see?" And I answered, "I see a
flying scroll; its length is twenty [1]cu-
bits and its width ten cubits."
3 Then he said to me, "This is the
[a]curse that is going forth over the
face of the whole [1]land; surely everyone who [b]steals will be purged
away according to [2]the writing on
one side, and everyone who swears
will be purged away according to
[2]the writing on the other side.
4 "I will [a]make it go forth," declares the LORD of hosts, "and it will
[b]enter the house of the [c]thief and the
house of the one who swears falsely
by My name; and it will spend the
night within that house and [d]con-
sume it with its timber and stones."
5 Then the angel who was speaking with me went out, and said to
me, "Lift up now your eyes, and see
what this is, going forth."
6 And I said, "What is it?" And he
said, "This is the [1a]ephah going
forth." Again he said, "This is their
[2]appearance in all the [3]land
7 (and behold, a lead cover was
lifted up); and this is a woman sitting inside the ephah."
8 Then he said, "This is [a]Wicked-
ness!" And he threw her down into
the middle of the ephah and cast the
lead weight on its [1]opening.
9 Then I lifted up my eyes and
looked, and there two women were
coming out with the wind in their
wings; and they had wings like the
wings of a [a]stork, and they lifted up
the ephah between the earth and the
heavens.
10 And I said to the angel who was
speaking with me, "Where are they
taking the ephah?"
11 Then he said to me, "To build a
[1]temple for her in the land of [a]Shi-
nar; and when it is prepared, she
will be set there on her own pedestal."

CHAPTER 6

The Four Chariots

NOW I lifted up my eyes again and
looked, and behold, [a]four chariots
were coming forth from between
the two mountains; and the mountains *were* bronze mountains.
2 With the first chariot *were* red
horses, with the second chariot
black horses,
3 with the third chariot white
horses, and with the fourth chariot
strong dappled horses.
4 Then I spoke and said to the angel who was speaking with me,
"What are these, my lord?"
5 And the angel answered and
said to me, "These are the [a]four spirits of heaven, going forth after
standing before the Lord of all the
earth,
6 with one of which the black
horses are going forth to the [a]north
country; and the white ones go forth
after them, while the dappled ones
go forth to the [b]south country.
7 "When the strong ones went out,
they [1]were eager to go to [2]patrol the
earth." And He said, "Go, [2]patrol
the earth." So they [3]patrolled the
earth.
8 Then He cried out to me and
spoke to me saying, "See, those who
are going to the land of the north
have [1a]appeased My wrath in the
land of the north."
9 The word of the LORD also came
to me saying,

7 [a]Ezra 3:10, 11; Ps. 84:11

9 [a]Ezra 3:8-10; 5:16; Hag. 2:18 [b]Ezra 6:14, 15; Zech. 6:12, 13

10 [a]Neh. 4:2-4; Amos 7:2, 5; Hag. 2:3 [b]Zech. 3:9; Rev. 8:2 [c]Amos 7:7, 8

12 [1]Or, *clusters*

14 [1]Lit., *sons of fresh oil* [a]Ex. 29:7; 40:15; 1 Sam. 16:1, 12, 13; Is. 61:1-3; Dan. 9:24-26 [b]Zech. 3:1-7 [c]Mic. 4:13

1 [a]Jer. 36:2; Ezek. 2:9

2 [1]A cubit equals 18 in.

3 [1]Or, *earth* [2]Lit., *it* [a]Is. 24:6; 43:28; Jer. 26:6 [b]Ex. 20:15; Lev. 19:11; Mal. 3:8, 9

4 [a]Mal. 3:5 [b]Hos. 4:2, 3 [c]Jer. 2:26 [d]Lev. 14:34-35; Job 18:15

6 [1]I.e., a bushel measure [2]Lit., *eye;* some ancient versions read, *iniquity* [3]Or, *earth* [a]Lev. 19:36; Amos 8:5

8 [1]Lit., *mouth* [a]Hos. 12:7; Amos 8:5; Mic. 6:11

9 [a]Lev. 11:13, 19; Ps. 104:17; Jer. 8:7

11 [1]Lit., *house* [a]Gen. 10:10; 11:2; 14:1; Is. 11:11; Dan. 1:2

1 [a]Dan. 7:3; 8:22; Zech. 1:18; 6:5

5 [a]Jer. 49:36; Ezek. 37:9; Dan. 7:2; 11:4; Matt. 24:31; Rev. 7:1

6 [a]Jer. 1:14, 15; 4:6; 6:1; 25:9; 46:10; Ezek. 1:4 [b]Is. 43:6; Dan. 11:5

7 [1]Lit., *sought to go* [2]Lit., *walk about through* [3]Lit., *walked about through*

8 [1]Lit., *caused My spirit to rest in* [a]Ezek. 5:13; 24:13; Zech. 1:15

10"[a]Take *an offering* from the exiles, from Heldai, Tobijah, and Jedaiah; and you go the same day and enter the house of Josiah the son of Zephaniah, where they have arrived from Babylon.

The Symbolic Crowns

11"And take silver and gold, make an *ornate* [a]crown, and set *it* on the head of [b]Joshua the son of Jehozadak, the high priest.

12"Then say to him, 'Thus says the LORD of hosts, "Behold, a man whose name is [1a]Branch, for He will [2b]branch out from where He is; and He will [c]build the temple of the LORD.

13"Yes, it is He who will build the temple of the LORD, and He who will [a]bear the honor and sit and [b]rule on His throne. Thus, He will be a [c]priest on His throne, and the counsel of peace will be between the two offices." '

14"Now the crown will become a reminder in the temple of the LORD to Helem, Tobijah, [1]Jedaiah, and Hen the son of Zephaniah.

15"And [a]those who are far off will come and build the temple of the LORD." Then you will know that the LORD of hosts has sent me to you. And it will take place, if you completely [b]obey the LORD your God.

CHAPTER 7

Hearts Like Flint

THEN it came about in the fourth year of King Darius, that the word of the LORD came to Zechariah on the fourth *day* of the ninth month, *which is* Chislev.

2 Now *the town of* Bethel had sent Sharezer and Regemmelech and their men to [a]seek the favor of the LORD,

3 speaking to the [a]priests who belong to the house of the LORD of hosts, and to the prophets saying, "Shall I weep in the fifth month and abstain, as I have done these many years?"

4 Then the word of the LORD of hosts came to me saying,

5"Say to all the people of the land and to the priests, 'When you fasted and mourned in the fifth and seventh months these [a]seventy years, was it actually for [b]Me that you fasted?

6 'And when you eat and drink, do you not eat for yourselves and do you not drink for yourselves?

7 'Are not *these* the words which the LORD [a]proclaimed by the former prophets, when Jerusalem was inhabited and [b]prosperous with its cities around it, and the [1c]Negev and the [2]foothills were inhabited?' "

8 Then the word of the LORD came to Zechariah saying,

9"Thus has the LORD of hosts said, '[a]Dispense true justice, and practice [b]kindness and compassion each to his brother;

10 and do not [a]oppress the widow or the [1]orphan, the [2]stranger or the poor; and do [b]not devise evil in your hearts against one another.'

11"But they [a]refused to pay attention, and [b]turned a stubborn shoulder and [c]stopped their ears from hearing.

12"And they made their [a]hearts like [b]flint so that they could not hear the law and the words which the LORD of hosts had sent by His Spirit through the [c]former prophets; therefore great [d]wrath came from the LORD of hosts.

13"And it came about that just as [a]He called and they would not listen, so [b]they called and I would not listen," says the LORD of hosts;

14"but I [1a]scattered them with a [b]storm wind among all the nations whom they have not known. Thus the land is [c]desolated behind them, [2]so that [d]no one went back and forth, for they [e]made the pleasant land desolate."

CHAPTER 8

The Coming Peace and Prosperity of Zion

THEN the word of the LORD of hosts came saying,

2"Thus says the LORD of hosts, 'I am exceedingly jealous for Zion, yes, with great wrath I am jealous for her.'

3"Thus says the LORD, 'I will return to Zion and will dwell in the midst of Jerusalem. Then Jerusalem will be called the City of Truth, and the mountain of the LORD of hosts *will be called* the Holy Mountain.'

4"Thus says the LORD of hosts, '[a]Old men and old women will again sit in the [1]streets of Jerusalem, each man with his staff in his hand because of [2]age.

5 'And the [1]streets of the city will be filled with [a]boys and girls playing in its [1]streets.'

6"Thus says the LORD of hosts, 'If it is [1a]too difficult in the sight of the remnant of this people in those

---

10 [a]Ezra 7:14-16; 8:26-30; Jer. 28:6

11 [a]2 Sam. 12:30; Ps. 21:3; Song of Sol. 3:11 [b]Ezra 3:2; Hag. 1:1; Zech. 3:1

12 [1]Lit., *Sprout* [2]Lit., *sprout up* [a]Is. 4:2; 11:1; Jer. 23:5; 33:15; Zech. 3:8 [b]Is. 53:2 [c]Ezra 3:8, 10; Amos 9:11; Zech. 4:6-9

13 [a]Is. 9:6; 11:10; 22:24; 49:5, 6 [b]Is. 9:7 [c]Ps. 110:1, 4

14 [1]I.e., Josiah

15 [a]Is. 56:6-8; 60:10 [b]Is. 58:10-14; Jer. 7:23; Zech. 3:7

2 [a]1 Kin. 13:6; Jer. 26:19; Zech. 8:21

3 [a]Ezra 3:10-12

5 [a]Zech. 1:12 [b]Is. 1:11, 12; 58:5

7 [1]I.e., South country [2]Heb., *shephelah* [a]Is. 1:16-20; Jer. 7:5, 23; Zech. 1:4 [b]Jer. 22:21 [c]Jer. 13:19; 32:44

9 [a]Ezek. 18:8; 45:9; Zech. 8:16 [b]2 Sam. 9:7; Job 6:14; Mic. 6:8

10 [1]Or, *fatherless* [2]Or, *resident alien* [a]Ex. 22:22; Ps. 72:4; Jer. 7:6 [b]Ps. 21:11; Mic. 2:1; Zech. 8:17

11 [a]Jer. 5:3; 8:5; 11:10 [b]Jer. 7:26; 17:23 [c]Ps. 58:4; Jer. 5:21

12 [a]2 Chr. 36:13; Ezek. 2:4; 3:7-9 [b]Jer. 17:1; Ezek. 3:9 [c]Neh. 9:30 [d]2 Chr. 36:16; Dan. 9:11, 12

13 [a]Jer. 11:10, 14; 14:12 [b]Prov. 1:24-28; Is. 1:15

14 [1]Lit., *stormed them away upon all* [2]Lit., *from passing and from returning* [a]Deut. 4:27; 28:64 [b]Jer. 23:19 [c]Jer. 44:6 [d]Is. 60:15 [e]Jer. 12:10

4 [1]Or, *squares* [2]Lit., *the multitude of days* [a]Is. 65:20

5 [1]Or, *squares* [a]Jer. 30:19, 20; 31:12, 13

6 [1]Or, *wonderful* [a]Ps. 118:23; 126:1-3

days, will it also be [1]too difficult in
[b]My sight?' declares the LORD of
hosts.
7"Thus says the LORD of hosts,
'Behold, I am going to save My people from the land of the [a]east and
from the land of the west;
8 and I will [a]bring them *back,* and
they will [b]live in the midst of Jerusalem, and they will be [c]My people
and I will be their God in truth and
righteousness.'
9"Thus says the LORD of hosts,
'Let your hands be [a]strong, you who
are listening in these days to these
words from the mouth of the
[b]prophets, *those* who *spoke* in the
day that the foundation of the house
of the LORD of hosts was laid, to the
end that the temple might be built.
10 'For before those days there was
[a]no wage for man or any wage for
animal; and for him who went out or
came in there was no [b]peace because of his enemies, and I [c]set all
men one against another.
11 'But now I will [a]not treat the
remnant of this people as in the former days,' declares the LORD of
hosts.
12 'For *there will be* peace for the
seed: the vine will yield its fruit, the
land will yield its produce, and the
heavens will give their [a]dew; and I
will cause the remnant of this people to inherit [b]all these *things.*
13 'And it will come about that just
as you were a [a]curse among the nations, O house of Judah and house of
Israel, so I will save you that you
may become a [b]blessing. Do not
fear; let your hands be strong.'
14"For thus says the LORD of hosts,
'Just as I [a]purposed to do harm to
you when your fathers provoked Me
to wrath,' says the LORD of hosts,
'and I have not [b]relented,
15 so I have again purposed in
these days to [a]do good to Jerusalem
and to the house of Judah. Do not
fear!
16 'These are the things which you
should do: speak the [a]truth to one
another; judge with truth and judgment for peace in your [1]gates.
17 'Also let none of you [a]devise evil
in your heart against another, and
do not love [b]perjury; for all these are
what I [c]hate,' declares the LORD."
18 Then the word of the LORD of
hosts came to me saying,
19"Thus says the LORD of hosts,
'The fast of the [a]fourth, the fast of
the fifth, the fast of the [b]seventh,
and the fast of the [c]tenth *months*
will become [d]joy, gladness, and

6 [1]Or, *wonderful* [b]Jer. 32:17, 27
7 [a]Ps. 107:3; Is. 11:11; 27:12, 13; 43:5
8 [a]Zeph. 3:20; Zech. 10:10 [b]Jer.3:17; Ezek. 37:25 [c]Ezek. 11:20; 36:28; Zech. 2:11
9 [a]1 Chr. 22:13; Is. 35:4; Hag. 2:4 [b]Ezra 5:1; 6:14
10 [a]Hag. 2:15-19 [b]2 Chr. 15:5 [c]Is. 19:2; Amos 3:6; 9:4
11 [a]Ps. 103:9; Is. 12:1; Hag. 2:19
12 [a]Gen. 27:28; Deut. 33:13, 28; Hos. 13:3 [b]Is. 61:7; Obad. 17
13 [a]Jer. 29:18; Dan. 9:11 [b]Ps. 72:17; Is. 19:24, 25; Ezek. 34:26; Zech. 14:11
14 [a]Jer. 31:28 [b]Jer. 4:28; Ezek. 24:14
15 [a]Jer. 29:11; Mic. 7:18-20
16 [1]I.e., law courts [a]Ps. 15:2; Prov. 12:17-19; Zech. 8:3
17 [a]Prov. 3:29; Jer. 4:14; Zech. 7:10 [b]Zech. 5:4; Mal. 3:5 [c]Prov. 6:16-19; Hab. 1:13
19 [a]2 Kin. 25:3, 4; Jer. 39:2 [b]2 Kin. 25:25; Zech. 7:5 [c]Jer. 52:4 [d]Ps. 30:11; Is. 12:1 [e]Zech. 8:16; Luke 1:74, 75
20 [a]Ps. 117:1; Jer. 16:19; Mic. 4:2, 3; Zech. 2:11; 14:16
22 [a]Is. 2:2, 3; 25:7; 49:6, 22, 23; 60:3-12
23 [a]Is. 45:14, 24; 60:14
1 [1]Or, *oracle* [a]Is. 17:1
2 [1]Or, *because* [2]I.e., they think they are (cf. Ezek. 28:2) [a]Jer. 49:23 [b]Ezek. 28:3-5, 12 [c]Ezek. 28:21
3 [a]Josh. 19:29; 2 Sam. 24:7 [b]Job 27:16; Ezek. 27:33; 28:4, 5 [c]1 Kin. 10:21, 27
4 [a]Ezek. 26:3-5 [b]Ezek. 28:18
6 [1]Lit., *bastard will*

cheerful feasts for the house of Judah; so [e]love truth and peace.'
20"Thus says the LORD of hosts, '*It
will* yet *be* that [a]peoples will come,
even the inhabitants of many cities;
21 and the inhabitants of one will
go to another saying, "Let us go at
once to entreat the favor of the
LORD, and to seek the LORD of hosts;
I will also go."
22 'So [a]many peoples and mighty
nations will come to seek the LORD
of hosts in Jerusalem and to entreat
the favor of the LORD.'
23"Thus says the LORD of hosts, 'In
those days ten men from the nations
of every language will [a]grasp the
garment of a Jew saying, "Let us go
with you, for we have heard that
God is with you." ' "

CHAPTER 9

Prophecies against Neighboring Nations

THE [1]burden of the word of the
LORD is against the land of Hadrach,
with [a]Damascus as its resting place
(for the eyes of men, especially of all
the tribes of Israel, are toward the
LORD),
2 And [a]Hamath also, which borders on it;
[b]Tyre and [c]Sidon, [1]though they are [b]very [2]wise.
3 For Tyre built herself a [a]fortress
And [b]piled up silver like dust,
And [c]gold like the mire of the streets.
4 Behold, the Lord will [a]dispossess her
And cast her wealth into the sea;
And she will be [b]consumed with fire.
5 Ashkelon will see *it* and be afraid.
Gaza too will writhe in great pain;
Also Ekron, for her expectation has been confounded.
Moreover, the king will perish from Gaza,
And Ashkelon will not be inhabited.
6 And a [1]mongrel race will dwell in Ashdod,
And I will cut off the pride of the Philistines.
7 And I will remove their blood from their mouth,
And their detestable things from between their teeth.
Then they also will be a remnant for our God,

And be like a [1]clan in Judah,
And Ekron like a Jebusite.
8 But I will camp around My house [1]because of an army,
Because of [a]him who passes by and returns;
And [b]no oppressor will pass over them any more,
For now I have seen with My eyes.
9 [a]Rejoice greatly, O daughter of Zion!
Shout *in triumph,* O daughter of Jerusalem!
Behold, your [b]king is coming to you;
He is [1c]just and [d]endowed with salvation,
[e]Humble, and mounted on a donkey,
Even on a [f]colt, the [2]foal of a donkey.
10 And I will cut off the chariot from Ephraim,
And the horse from Jerusalem;
And the bow of war will be cut off.
And He will speak [a]peace to the nations;
And His [b]dominion will be from sea to sea,
And from [1]the River to the ends of the earth.

Deliverance of Judah and Ephraim

11 As for you also, because of the [a]blood of *My* covenant with you,
I have set your [b]prisoners free from the [1]waterless pit.
12 Return to the [1a]stronghold, O prisoners [2]who have the hope;
This very day I am declaring that I will restore [b]double to you.
13 For I will [a]bend Judah [1]as My bow,
I will fill the bow with Ephraim.
And I will stir up your sons, O Zion, against your sons, O [b]Greece;
And I will make you like a warrior's sword.
14 Then the LORD will appear [a]over them,
And His [b]arrow will go forth like lightning;
And the Lord [1]GOD will blow the [c]trumpet,
And will march in the [d]storm winds of the south.
15 The LORD of hosts will defend them.
And they will devour, and [a]trample on the sling stones;
And they will drink, *and* be [b]boisterous as with wine;
And they will be filled like a *sacrificial* basin,
Drenched like the [c]corners of the altar.
16 And the LORD their God will [a]save them in that day
As the flock of His people;
For *they are as* the stones of a [b]crown,
[1]Sparkling in His land.
17 For what [1a]comeliness and [b]beauty *will be* [2]theirs!
Grain will make the young men flourish, and new wine the virgins.

CHAPTER 10

God Will Bless Judah and Ephraim

ASK [a]rain from the LORD at the time of the spring rain—
The LORD who [b]makes the [1]storm clouds;
And He will give them [c]showers of rain, vegetation in the field to *each* man.
2 For the [a]teraphim speak [1]iniquity,
And the [b]diviners see [2]lying visions,
And tell [c]false dreams;
They comfort in vain.
Therefore *the people* [3]wander like [d]sheep,
They are afflicted, because there is no shepherd.
3 "My [a]anger is kindled against the shepherds,
And I will punish the [1]male goats;
For the LORD of hosts has [b]visited His flock, the house of Judah,
And will make them like His majestic horse in battle.
4 "From [1]them will come the cornerstone,
From [1]them the tent peg,
From [1]them the bow of [a]battle,
From [1]them every [2]ruler, *all* of them together.
5 "And they will be as mighty men,
[a]Treading down *the enemy* in the mire of the streets in battle;
And they will fight, for the LORD *will be* with them;
And the [b]riders on horses will be put to shame.

7 [1]Or, *chief*
8 [1]Or, *as a guard, so that none will go back and forth* [a]Is. 52:1; Joel 3:1 [b]Is. 54:14; 60:18
9 [1]Or, *vindicated and victorious* [2]Lit., *son of a female donkey* [a]Zeph. 3:14, 15; Zech. 2:10 [b]Ps. 110:1; Is. 9:6, 7; Jer. 23:5, 6; Matt. 21:5; John 12:15 [c]Zeph. 3:5 [d]Is. 43:3, 11 [e]Is. 57:15 [f]Judg. 10:4; Is. 30:6
10 [1]I.e., the Euphrates [a]Is. 57:19; Mic. 4:2-4 [b]Ps. 72:8; Is. 60:12
11 [1]Lit., *cistern in which there is no water* [a]Ex. 24:8; Heb. 10:2 [b]Is. 24:22; 51:14
12 [1]Or, *Stronghold* [2]Lit., *of the hope* [a]Jer. 16:19; Joel 3:16 [b]Is. 61:7
13 [1]Lit., *for Me* [a]Jer. 51:20 [b]Joel 3:6
14 [1]YHWH, usually rendered LORD [a]Is. 31:5; Zech. 2:5 [b]Ps. 18:14; Hab. 3:11 [c]Is. 27:13 [d]Is. 21:1; 66:15
15 [a]Job 41:28 [b]Ps. 78:65 [c]Ex. 27:2
16 [1]Or, *Displayed over* [a]Jer. 31:10, 11 [b]Is. 62:3
17 [1]Lit., *goodness* [2]Lit., *his* [a]Jer. 31:12, 14 [b]Ps. 27:4; Is. 33:17
1 [1]Or, *thunderbolts* [a]Joel 2:23 [b]Jer. 10:13 [c]Is. 30:23
2 [1]Or, *futility* [2]Lit., *a lie* [3]Lit., *journey* [a]Ezek. 21:21; Hos. 3:4 [b]Jer. 27:9 [c]Jer. 23:32 [d]Ezek. 34:5, 8
3 [1]I.e., leaders [a]Jer. 25:34-36 [b]Ezek. 34:12
4 [1]Lit., *him* [2]Or, *oppressor* [a]Jer. 51:20; Zech. 9:10
5 [a]2 Sam. 22:43 [b]Amos 2:15; Hag. 2:22

6 "And I shall strengthen the house of Judah,
And I shall save the house of Joseph,
And I shall bring them back,
Because I have had [a]compassion on them;
And they will be as though I had [b]not rejected them,
For I am the LORD their God, and I will answer them.
7 "And Ephraim will be like a mighty man,
And their heart will be glad as if *from* wine;
Indeed, their [a]children will see *it* and be glad,
Their heart will rejoice in the LORD.
8 "I will [a]whistle for them to gather them together,
For I have redeemed them;
And they will be as [b]numerous as they [c]were before.
9 "When I scatter them among the peoples,
They will [a]remember Me in far countries,
And they with their children will live and come back.
10 "I will [a]bring them back from the land of Egypt,
And gather them from Assyria;
And I will bring them into the land of [b]Gilead and Lebanon,
[1]Until [c]no *room* can be found for them.
11 "And He will pass through the [a]sea *of* distress,
And strike the waves in the sea,
So that all the depths of the [b]Nile will dry up;
And the pride of [c]Assyria will be brought down,
And the scepter of [d]Egypt will depart.
12 "And I shall strengthen them in the LORD,
And in His name [a]they will walk," declares the LORD.

CHAPTER 11

The Doomed Flock

OPEN your doors, O Lebanon,
That a [a]fire may feed on your [b]cedars.
2 Wail, O [1]cypress, for the cedar has fallen,
Because the glorious *trees* have been destroyed;
Wail, O oaks of Bashan,
For the [2]impenetrable forest has come down.
3 There is a sound of the shepherds' [a]wail,
For their glory is ruined;
There is a [b]sound of the young lions' roar,
For the [1]pride of the Jordan is ruined.

4 Thus says the LORD my God:
"Pasture the flock *doomed* to
slaughter.
5 "Those who buy them slay them
and go [a]unpunished, and *each of*
those who sell them says, 'Blessed
be the LORD, for [b]I have become
rich!' And their [c]own shepherds
have no pity on them.
6 "For I shall [a]no longer have pity
on the inhabitants of the land," declares the LORD; "but behold, I shall
[b]cause the men to [1]fall into one another's [2]power and into the [2]power
of his king; and they will strike the
land, and I shall [c]not deliver *them*
from their [2]power."
7 So I pastured the flock *doomed*
to slaughter, [1]hence the [a]afflicted of
the flock. And I took for myself two
[b]staffs: the one I called [2c]Favor, and
the other I called [3d]Union; so I pastured the flock.
8 Then I annihilated the three
shepherds in [a]one month, for my
soul was impatient with them, and
their soul also [1]was weary of me.
9 Then I said, "I will not pasture
you. What is to [a]die, [1]let it die, and
what is to be annihilated, [2]let it be
annihilated; and [3]let those who are
left eat one another's flesh."
10 And I took my staff, [1]Favor,
and cut it in pieces, to [2a]break my
covenant which I had made with all
the peoples.
11 So it was [1]broken on that day;
and [2]thus the [a]afflicted of the flock
who were watching me realized that
it was the word of the LORD.
12 And I said to them, "If it is good
in your sight, give *me* my [a]wages;
but if not, [1]never mind!" So they
weighed out [b]thirty *shekels* of silver
as my wages.
13 Then the LORD said to me,
"Throw it to the [a]potter, *that* magnificent price at which I was valued
by them." So I took the thirty *shekels* of silver and threw them to the
potter in the house of the LORD.
14 Then I cut my second staff,
[1]Union, in pieces, to [a]break the
brotherhood between Judah and Israel.
15 And the LORD said to me, "Take
again for yourself the equipment of
a [1a]foolish shepherd.
16 "For behold, I am going to raise
up a shepherd in the land who will

6 [a]Is. 54:8; Zech. 1:16 [b]Is. 54:4
7 [a]Is. 54:13; Ezek. 37:25
8 [a]Is. 5:26; 7:18, 19 [b]Jer. 33:22 [c]Jer. 30:20; Ezek. 36:11
9 [a]1 Kin. 8:47, 48; Ezek. 6:9
10 [1]Lit., *And* [a]Is. 11:11 [b]Jer. 50:19 [c]Is. 49:19, 20
11 [a]Is. 51:9, 10 [b]Is. 19:5-7 [c]Zeph. 2:13 [d]Ezek. 30:13
12 [a]Mic. 4:5
1 [a]Jer. 22:6, 7 [b]Ezek. 31:3
2 [1]Or, *juniper* [2]Another reading is: *forest of the vintage*
3 [1]Or, *jungle* [a]Jer. 25:34-36 [b]Jer. 2:15; 50:44
5 [a]Jer. 50:7 [b]Hos. 12:8; 1 Tim. 6:9 [c]Ezek. 34:2, 3
6 [1]Lit., *find* [2]Lit., *hand* [a]Jer. 13:14 [b]Is. 9:19-21; Mic. 7:2-6; Zech. 14:13 [c]Ps. 50:22; Mic. 5:8
7 [1]Another reading is: *for the sheep dealers* [2]Or, *Pleasantness* [3]Or, *Cords* [a]Jer. 39:10; Zeph. 3:12 [b]Ezek. 37:16 [c]Ps. 27:4; 90:17; Zech. 11:10 [d]Ps. 133:1; Ezek. 37:16-23; Zech. 11:14
8 [1]Or, *detested* [a]Hos. 5:7
9 [1]Or, *will die* [2]Or, *will be annihilated* [3]Or, *those . . . will eat* [a]Jer. 15:2
10 [1]Or, *Pleasantness* [2]Or, *annul* [a]Ps. 89:39; Jer. 14:21
11 [1]Or, *annulled* [2]Another reading is: *the sheep dealers who* [a]Zeph. 3:12
12 [1]Lit., *cease* [a]1 Kin. 3:5 [b]Gen. 37:28; Ex. 21:32; Matt. 26:15; 27:9, 10
13 [a]Matt. 27:3-10; Acts 1:18, 19
14 [1]Or, *Cords* [a]Is. 9:21; Zech. 11:6
15 [1]Or, *useless* [a]Is. 6:10-12; Zech. 11:17

not [a]care for the perishing, seek the
scattered, heal the broken, or sustain the one standing, but will [b]de-
vour the flesh of the fat *sheep* and
tear off their hoofs.
17 "[a]Woe to the worthless shepherd
Who leaves the flock!
A sword will be on his arm
And on his right eye!
His arm will be totally withered,
And his right eye will be
[1]blind."

CHAPTER 12

Jerusalem to Be Attacked

THE [1]burden of the word of the
LORD concerning Israel.
Thus declares the LORD who
[a]stretches out the heavens, [b]lays the
foundation of the earth, and [c]forms
the spirit of man within him:
2"Behold, I am going to make Jerusalem a [a]cup [1]that causes reeling
to all the peoples around; and when
the siege is against Jerusalem, it will
also be against Judah.
3"And it will come about in that
day that I will make Jerusalem a
heavy [a]stone for all the peoples; all
who lift it will be [b]severely [1]injured.
And all the nations of the earth will
be gathered against it.
4"In that day," declares the LORD,
"I will strike every horse with bewilderment, and his rider with madness. But I will [1]watch over the
house of Judah, while I strike every
horse of the peoples with blindness.
5"Then the clans of Judah will say
in their hearts, '[1]A strong support
for us are the inhabitants of Jerusalem through the LORD of hosts, their
God.'
6"In that day I will make the clans
of Judah like a [a]firepot among
pieces of wood and a flaming torch
among sheaves, so they will consume on the right hand and on the
left all the surrounding peoples,
while the inhabitants of Jerusalem
again dwell on their own sites in Jerusalem.
7"The LORD also will [a]save the
tents of Judah first in order that the
glory of the house of [b]David and the
glory of the inhabitants of Jerusalem may not be magnified above Judah.
8"In that day the LORD will [a]de-
fend the inhabitants of Jerusalem,
and the one who [1b]is feeble among
them in that day will be like David,
and the house of David *will be* like
[c]God, like the [d]angel of the LORD before them.
9"And it will come about in that
day that I will [1]set about to destroy
all the nations that come against Jerusalem.
10"And I will [a]pour out on the
house of David and on the inhabitants of Jerusalem, [1]the Spirit of
grace and of supplication, so that
they will look on Me whom they
have [b]pierced; and they will mourn
for Him, as one [c]mourns for an only
son, and they will weep bitterly over
Him, like the bitter weeping over a
first-born.
11"In that day there will be great
[a]mourning in Jerusalem, like the
mourning of Hadadrimmon in the
[1]plain of [2]Megiddo.
12"And the land will mourn, every
family by itself; the family of the
house of David by itself, and their
wives by themselves; the family of
the house of Nathan by itself, and
their wives by themselves;
13 the family of the house of Levi
by itself, and their wives by themselves; the family of the Shimeites
by itself, and their wives by themselves;
14 all the families that remain, every family by itself, and their wives
by themselves.

CHAPTER 13

False Prophets Ashamed

"IN that day a [a]fountain will be
opened for the house of David and
for the inhabitants of Jerusalem, for
[b]sin and for [c]impurity.
2"And it will come about in that
day," declares the LORD of hosts,
"that I will [a]cut off the names of the
idols from the land, and they will no
longer be remembered; and I will
also remove the [b]prophets and the
[c]unclean spirit from the land.
3"And it will come about that if
anyone still [a]prophesies, then his father and mother who gave birth to
him will say to him, 'You shall [b]not
live, for you have spoken [c]falsely in
the name of the LORD'; and his [d]fa-
ther and mother who gave birth to
him will pierce him through when
he prophesies.
4"Also it will come about in that
day that the prophets will each be
[a]ashamed of his vision when he
prophesies, and they will not put on
a [b]hairy robe in order to deceive;

16 [a]Jer. 23:2 [b]Ezek. 34:2-6

17 [1]Lit., *completely dimmed* [a]Jer. 23:1; Zech. 10:2; 11:15

1 [1]Or, *oracle* [a]Is. 42:5; 44:24; Jer. 51:15 [b]Job 26:7; Ps. 102:25, 26; Heb. 1:10-12 [c]Is. 57:16; Heb. 12:9

2 [1]Lit., *of reeling* [a]Ps. 75:8; Is. 51:22, 23

3 [1]Lit., *scratched* [a]Dan. 2:34, 35, 44, 45 [b]Matt. 21:44

4 [1]Lit., *open My eyes*

5 [1]Lit., *My strength is*

6 [a]Is. 10:17, 18; Obad. 18; Zech. 11:1

7 [a]Jer. 30:18 [b]Amos 9:11

8 [1]Or, *stumbles* [a]Joel 3:16; Zech. 9:14, 15 [b]Lev. 26:8; Josh. 23:10; Mic. 7:8 [c]Ps. 8:5; 82:6 [d]Ex. 14:19; 33:2

9 [1]Lit., *seek to*

10 [1]Or, *a spirit* [a]Is. 44:3; Ezek. 39:29; Joel 2:28, 29 [b]John 19:37; Rev. 1:7 [c]Jer. 6:26; Amos 8:10

11 [1]I.e., broad valley [2]Heb., *Megiddon* [a]Matt. 24:30; Rev. 1:7

1 [a]Jer. 2:13; 17:13 [b]Ps. 51:2, 7; Is. 1:16-18; John 1:29 [c]Num. 19:17; Is. 4:4; Ezek. 36:25

2 [a]Ex. 23:13; Hos. 2:17 [b]Jer. 23:14, 15 [c]1 Kin. 22:22; Ezek. 36:25, 29

3 [a]Jer. 23:34 [b]Deut. 18:20; Ezek. 14:9 [c]Jer. 23:25 [d]Deut. 13:6-11; Matt. 10:37

4 [a]Jer. 6:15; 8:9; Mic. 3:7 [b]2 Kin. 1:8; Is. 20:2; Matt. 3:4

5 but he will say, 'I am [a]not a
prophet; I am a tiller of the ground,
for a man [1]sold me as a slave in my
youth.'
6"And one will say to him, 'What
are these wounds between your
[1]arms?' Then he will say, '*Those*
with which I was wounded in the
house of [2]my friends.'
7 "Awake, O sword, against My
[a]Shepherd,
And against the man, My [b]As-
sociate,"
Declares the LORD of hosts.
"[c]Strike the Shepherd that the
sheep may be scattered;
And I will [d]turn My hand
[1]against the little ones.
8 "And it will come about in all
the land,"
Declares the LORD,
"That [a]two parts in it will be cut
off *and* perish;
But the third will be left in it.
9 "And I will bring the third part
through the [a]fire,
Refine them as silver is refined,
And test them as gold is
tested.
They will [b]call on My name,
And I will [c]answer them;
I will say, 'They are [d]My people,'
And they will say, 'The LORD is
my God.' "

CHAPTER 14

God Will Battle Jerusalem's Foes

BEHOLD, a [a]day is coming for the
LORD when the spoil taken from you
will be divided among you.
2 For I will gather all the nations
against Jerusalem to battle, and the
city will be captured, the [a]houses
plundered, the women ravished,
and half of the city exiled, but the
rest of the people will not be cut off
from the city.
3 Then the LORD will go forth and
fight against those nations, as
[1]when He fights on a day of battle.
4 And in that day His feet will
[a]stand on the Mount of Olives,
which is in front of Jerusalem on the
east; and the Mount of Olives will be
[b]split in its middle from east to west
by a very large valley, so that half of
the mountain will move toward the
north and the other half toward the
south.
5 And you will flee by the valley
of My mountains, for the valley of
the mountains will reach to Azel;
yes, you will flee just as you fled before the [a]earthquake in the days of
Uzziah king of Judah. Then the
LORD, my God, will come, *and* all
the holy ones with [1]Him!
6 And it will come about in that
day that there will be [a]no light; the
[1]luminaries will dwindle.
7 For it will be [a]a unique day
which is [b]known to the LORD, neither day nor night; but it will come
about that at [c]evening time there
will be light.
8 And it will come about in that
day that [a]living waters will flow out
of Jerusalem, half of them toward
the eastern sea and the other half
toward the western sea; it will be in
summer as well as in winter.

God Will Be King Over All

9 And the LORD will be [a]king over
all the earth; in that day the LORD
will be *the only* [b]one, and His name
the only one.
10 All the land will be changed
into a plain from [a]Geba to [b]Rimmon
south of Jerusalem; but [1]Jerusalem
will [c]rise and [d]remain on its site
from [e]Benjamin's Gate as far as the
place of the First Gate to the [f]Corner
Gate, and from the [g]Tower of Hananel to the king's wine presses.
11 And [1]people will live in it, and
there will be [a]no more curse, for Jerusalem will [b]dwell in security.
12 Now this will be the plague
with which the LORD will strike all
the peoples who have gone to war
against Jerusalem; their flesh will
[a]rot while they stand on their feet,
and their eyes will rot in their sockets, and their tongue will rot in their
mouth.
13 And it will come about in that
day that a great panic from the LORD
will [1]fall on them; and they will
seize one another's hand, and the
hand of one will [2]be lifted against
the hand of another.
14 And Judah also will fight at Jerusalem; and the [a]wealth of all the
surrounding nations will be gathered, gold and silver and garments
in great abundance.
15 So also like this plague, will be
the plague on the horse, the mule,
the camel, the donkey, and all the
cattle that will be in those camps.
16 Then it will come about that
any who are left of all the nations
that went against Jerusalem will [a]go
up from year to year to worship the
King, the LORD of hosts, and to celebrate the [b]Feast of Booths.
17 And it will be that whichever of
the families of the earth does not go

5 [1]Lit., *caused another to buy me* [a]Amos 7:14
6 [1]Lit., *hands* [2]Lit., *those who love me*
7 [1]Or, *upon* [a]Is. 40:11; Ezek. 34:23, 24, 37.24, Mic. 5:2, 4 [b]Ps. 2:2; Jer. 23:5, 6 [c]Is. 53:4, 5, 10; Matt. 26:31; Mark 14:27 [d]Is. 1:25
8 [a]Is. 6:13; Ezek. 5:2-4, 12
9 [a]Is. 48:10; Mal. 3:3 [b]Ps. 34:15-17; 50:15; Zech. 12:10 [c]Is. 58:9; 65:24; Jer. 29:11-13; Zech. 10:6 [d]Hos. 2:23
1 [a]Is. 13:6, 9; Joel 2:1; Mal. 4:1
2 [a]Is. 13:16
3 [1]Lit., *His day of fighting*
4 [a]Ezek. 11:23 [b]Is. 64:1, 2; Ezek. 47:1-10; Mic. 1:3, 4; Hab. 3:6; Zech. 4:7; 14:8
5 [1]So the versions; Heb., *Thee* [a]Is. 29:6; Amos 1:1
6 [1]Lit., *glorious ones will congeal* [a]Is. 13:10; Jer. 4:23; Ezek. 32:7, 8; Joel 2:30, 31; Acts 2:16, 19
7 [a]Jer. 30:7; Amos 8:9 [b]Is. 45:21; Acts 15:18 [c]Is. 58:10; Rev. 22:5
8 [a]Ezek. 47:1-12; Joel 3:18; Rev. 22:1, 2
9 [a]Is. 2:2-4; 45:23; Zech. 9:9; 14:16, 17 [b]Deut. 6:4; Is. 45:21-24
10 [1]Lit., *it* [a]1 Kin. 15:22 [b]Josh. 15:32; Judg. 20:45, 47 [c]Is. 2:2; Amos 9:11 [d]Jer. 30:18; Zech. 12:6 [e]Jer. 37:13; 38:7 [f]2 Kin. 14:13 [g]Jer. 31:8
11 [1]Lit., *they* [a]Zech. 8:13; Rev. 22:3 [b]Jer. 23:5, 6; Ezek. 34:25-28
12 [a]Lev. 26:16; Deut. 28:21, 22
13 [1]Lit., *be among* [2]Lit., *rise up against*
14 [a]Is. 23:18; Zech. 14:1
16 [a]Is. 60:6-9; 66:18-21, 23 [b]Lev. 23:34-44

up to Jerusalem to worship the
King, the LORD of hosts, there will
be [a]no rain on them.
18 And if the family of Egypt does
not go up or enter, then no *rain will*
fall on them; it will be the plague
with which the LORD smites the nations who do not go up to celebrate
the Feast of Booths.
19 This will be the [1]punishment of
Egypt, and the [1]punishment of all
the nations who do not go up to celebrate the Feast of Booths.
20 In that day there will *be in-*
scribed on the bells of the horses,
"[a]HOLY TO THE LORD." And the
[b]cooking pots in the LORD's house
will be like the bowls before the altar.
21 And every cooking pot in Jerusalem and in Judah will be [a]holy to
the LORD of hosts; and all who sacrifice will come and take of them and
boil in them. And there will no
longer be a [1]Canaanite in the house
of the LORD of hosts in that day.

17 [a]Jer. 14:3-6; Amos 4:7
19 [1]Lit., *sin*
20 [a]Ex. 28:36-38 [b]Ezek. 46:20
21 [1]Or, *merchant* [a]Neh. 8:10; Rom. 14:6, 7; 1 Cor. 10:31

THE BOOK OF MALACHI

God's Love for Jacob

THE [1a]oracle of the word of the
LORD to Israel through [2]Malachi.
2 "I have [a]loved you," says the
LORD. But you say, "How hast Thou
loved us?" "*Was* not Esau Jacob's
brother?" declares the LORD. "Yet I
[b]have loved Jacob;
3 but I have hated Esau, and I
have made his mountains a desolation, and *appointed* his inheritance
for the jackals of the wilderness."
4 Though Edom says, "We have
been [a]beaten down, but we will [1b]re-
turn and build up the ruins"; thus
says the LORD of hosts, "They may
[c]build, but I will tear down; and *men*
will call them the [2]wicked territory,
and the people [3]toward whom the
LORD is indignant forever."
5 And your eyes will see this and
you will say, "The LORD [1a]be magnified beyond the [2]border of Israel!"

Sin of the Priests

6 "A son [a]honors *his* father, and a
servant his master. Then if I am a
[b]father, where is My honor? And if I
am a master, where is My [1]respect?
says the LORD of hosts to you, O
[c]priests who despise My name. But
you say, 'How have we despised
Thy name?'
7 "*You* are presenting defiled
[1a]food upon My altar. But you say,
'How have we defiled Thee?' In that
you say, 'The table of the LORD is to
be despised.'
8 "But when you present the
[a]blind for sacrifice, is it not evil?
And when you present the lame and
sick, is it not evil? [1]Why not offer it
to your governor? Would he be
pleased with you? Or would he receive you kindly?" says the LORD of
hosts.
9 "But now [1]will you not [a]entreat
God's favor, that He may be gracious to us? [2]With such an offering
on your part, will He [b]receive any of
you kindly?" says the LORD of hosts.
10 "Oh that there were one among
you who would [a]shut the [1]gates,
that you might not uselessly kindle
fire on My altar! I am not pleased
with you," says the LORD of hosts,
"nor will I [b]accept an offering from
[2]you.
11 "For from the [a]rising of the sun,
even to its setting, My name *will be*
great among the nations, and in every place [b]incense is going to be offered to My name, and a grain offering *that is* pure; for My name *will be*
[c]great among the nations," says the
LORD of hosts.
12 "But you are profaning it, in that
you say, 'The table of the LORD is
defiled, and as for its fruit, its food is
to be despised.'
13 "You also say, '[1]My, how [a]tire-
some it is!' And you disdainfully
sniff at it," says the LORD of hosts,
"and you bring what was taken by
[b]robbery, and *what is* lame or sick;
so you bring the offering! Should I
receive that from your hand?" says
the LORD.
14 "But cursed be the swindler who
has a male in his flock, and vows it,
but sacrifices a [a]blemished animal
to the Lord, for I am a great [b]King,"
says the LORD of hosts, "and My
name is [1c]feared among the [2]na-
tions."

CHAPTER 2

Priests to Be Disciplined

"AND now, this commandment is
for you, O priests.
2 "If you do [a]not listen, and if you
do not take it to heart to give honor
to My name," says the LORD of

1 [1]Lit., *burden* [2]Or, *My messenger* [a]Is. 13:1; Nah. 1:1; Hab. 1:1; Zech. 9:1
2 [a]Rom. 9:13 [b]Jer. 49:16-18; Ezek. 35:8, 15
4 [1]Or, *rebuild the ruins* [2]Lit., *border of wickedness* [3]Or, *whom the LORD has cursed* [a]Jer. 5:17 [b]Is. 9:9, 10 [c]Amos 3:15; 5:11; 6:11
5 [1]Or, *will be great* [2]Or, *territory* [a]Ps. 35:27; Mic. 5:4
6 [1]Lit., *fear* [a]Ex. 20:12; Prov. 30:11, 17 [b]Deut. 1:31; Is. 1:2; Jer. 3:4; Mal. 2:10 [c]Zeph. 3:4; Mal. 2:1-9
7 [1]Lit., *bread* [a]Lev. 21:6, 8
8 [1]Lit., *Offer, please* [a]Deut. 15:21
9 [1]Lit., *entreat please* [2]Lit., *This has been from your hand* [a]Jer. 27:18; Joel 2:12-14 [b]Amos 5:22
10 [1]Or, *doors* [2]Lit., *your hand* [a]Is. 1:13 [b]Jer. 14:10, 12; Hos. 5:6
11 [a]Is. 45:6 [b]Is. 60:6 [c]Is. 12:4, 5; 54:5; Jer. 10:6, 7
13 [1]Lit., *Behold it is weariness* [a]Is. 43:22 [b]Lev. 6:4; Is. 61:8
14 [1]Or, *revered* [2]Or, *Gentiles* [a]Lev. 22:18-20; Acts 5:1-4 [b]Zech. 14:9 [c]Zeph. 2:11
2 [a]Lev. 26:14, 15; Deut. 28:15

hosts, "then I will send the [b]curse
upon you, and I will curse your
blessings; and indeed, I have cursed
them *already,* because you are not
taking *it* to heart.
3"Behold, I am going to [a]rebuke
your offspring, and I will [b]spread refuse on your faces, the refuse of
your [c]feasts; and you will be taken
away with it.
4"Then you will know that I have
sent this commandment to you, that
My [a]covenant may continue with
Levi," says the LORD of hosts.
5"My covenant with him was *one
of* life and [a]peace, and I gave them
to him *as an object of* reverence; so
he [b]revered Me, and stood in awe of
My name.
6"[a]True instruction was in his
mouth, and unrighteousness was
not found on his lips; he walked
[b]with Me in peace and uprightness,
and he [c]turned many back from iniquity.
7"For the lips of a priest should
preserve [a]knowledge, and men
should [b]seek instruction from his
mouth; for he is the messenger of
the LORD of hosts.
8"But as for you, you have turned
aside from the way; you have
caused many to [a]stumble by the instruction; you have [b]corrupted the
covenant of Levi," says the LORD of
hosts.
9"So I also have made you despised and abased before all the
people, just as you are not keeping
My ways, but are showing [a]partiali-
ty in the instruction.

Sin in the Family

10"Do we not all have [a]one father?
Has not one God created us? Why
do we deal [b]treacherously each
against his brother so as to profane
the [c]covenant of our fathers?
11"Judah has dealt [a]treacherously,
and an abomination has been committed in Israel and in Jerusalem;
for Judah has [b]profaned the sanctuary of the LORD which He loves, and
has married the daughter of a foreign god.
12"*As* for the man who does this,
may the [a]LORD cut off from the tents
of Jacob *everyone* who awakes and
answers, or who presents an offering to the LORD of hosts.
13"And this is another thing you
do: you cover the altar of the LORD
with tears, with weeping and with
groaning, because He [a]no longer regards the offering or accepts *it with*
favor from your hand.
14"Yet you say, 'For what reason?'
Because the LORD has been a witness between you and the wife of
your youth, against whom you have
dealt [a]treacherously, though she is
your companion and your wife by
covenant.
15"But not one has [a]done *so* who
has a remnant of the Spirit. And
what did *that* one *do* while he was
seeking a [b]godly offspring? Take
heed then, to your spirit, and let no
one deal [c]treacherously against the
wife of your youth.
16"For I hate [a]divorce," says the
LORD, the God of Israel, "and him
who covers his garment with
[b]wrong," says the LORD of hosts.
"So take heed to your spirit, that
you do not deal treacherously."
17 You have [a]wearied the LORD
with your words. Yet you say, "How
have we wearied *Him?*" In that you
say, "[b]Everyone who does evil is
good in the sight of the LORD, and
He [c]delights in them," or, "Where is
the God of [d]justice?"

CHAPTER 3

The Purifier

"[a]BEHOLD, I am going to send
My [1]messenger, and he will [2]clear
the way before Me. And the Lord,
whom you seek, will suddenly come
to His temple; [3]and the [1b]messenger
of the covenant, in whom you delight, behold, He is coming," says
the LORD of hosts.
2"But who can [a]endure the day of
His coming? And who can stand
when He appears? For He is like a
[b]refiner's fire and like [1]fullers' soap.
3"And He will sit as a smelter and
purifier of silver, and He will [a]purify
the sons of Levi and refine them like
gold and silver, so that they may
[b]present to the LORD [1]offerings in
righteousness.
4"Then the [1]offering of Judah and
Jerusalem will be [a]pleasing to the
LORD, as in the [b]days of old and as in
former years.
5"Then I will draw near to you for
judgment; and I will be a swift witness against the [a]sorcerers and
against the [b]adulterers and against
those who [c]swear falsely, and
against those who oppress the
[d]wage earner in his wages, the [e]wid-
ow and the [1]orphan, and those who
turn aside the [2f]alien, and do not
[3]fear Me," says the LORD of hosts.
6"For [1]I, the LORD, do not change;
therefore you, O sons of Jacob, [2]are
not consumed.
7"From the days of your fathers

2 [b]Deut. 28:16-20
3 [a]Lev. 26:16; Deut. 28:38 [b]Nah. 3:6 [c]Ex. 29:14
4 [a]Num. 3:45; 18:21
5 [a]Num. 25:12 [b]Num. 25:7, 8, 13
6 [a]Ps. 119:142, 151, 160 [b]Deut. 33:8, 9; Ps. 37:37 [c]Jer. 23:22
7 [a]Lev. 10:11; Neh. 8:7 [b]Num. 27:21; Deut. 17:8-11
8 [a]Jer. 18:15 [b]Ezek. 44:10
9 [a]Deut. 1:17; Mic. 3:11
10 [a]Is. 63:16; 64:8; Jer. 31:9 [b]Jer. 9:4, 5 [c]Ex. 19:4-6; 24:3, 7, 8
11 [a]Jer. 3:7-9 [b]Ezra 9:1, 2
12 [a]Ezek. 24:21; Hos. 9:12
13 [a]Jer. 11:14; 14:12
14 [a]Jer. 9:2; Mal. 3:5
15 [a]Gen. 2:24; Matt. 19:4, 5 [b]Ruth 4:12; 1 Sam. 2:20 [c]Ex. 20:14; Lev. 20:10
16 [a]Deut. 24:1; Matt. 5:31; 19:6-8 [b]Ps. 73:6; Is. 59:6
17 [a]Is. 43:22, 24 [b]Is. 5:20; Zeph. 1:12 [c]Job 9:24 [d]Is. 5:19; Jer. 17:15
1 [1]Or, *angel* [2]Or, *prepare* [3]Or, *even* [a]Matt. 11:10, 14; Mark 1:2; Luke 7:27 [b]Is. 63:9
2 [1]Lit., *laundrymen's* [a]Is. 33:14; Ezek. 22:14 [b]Zech. 13:9; Matt. 3:10-12; 1 Cor. 3:13-15
3 [1]Or, *grain offerings* [a]Is. 1:25; Dan 12:10 [b]Ps. 4:5; 51:19
4 [1]Or, *grain offering* [a]Ps. 51:17-19 [b]2 Chr. 7:1-3, 12
5 [1]Or, *fatherless* [2]Or, *sojourner* [3]Or, *revere* [a]Deut. 18:10; Jer. 27:9, 10 [b]Ezek. 22:9-11 [c]Jer. 5:2; 7:9; Zech. 5:4 [d]Lev. 19:13 [e]Ex. 22:22-24 [f]Deut. 27:19
6 [1]Or, *I am the LORD; I do not* [2]Or, *have not come to an end*

you have turned aside from My statutes, and have not kept *them.* [a]Re-
turn to Me, and I will return to you,"
says the Lord of hosts. "But you say,
'How shall we return?'

You Have Robbed God

8"Will a man [1]rob God? Yet you
are robbing Me! But you say, 'How
have we robbed Thee?' In [a]tithes
and [2]contributions.
9"You are cursed with a curse, for
you are [1]robbing Me, the whole nation *of you!*
10"Bring the whole tithe into the
storehouse, so that there may be
[1]food in My house, and test Me now
in this," says the LORD of hosts, "if I
will not [a]open for you the windows
of heaven, and [b]pour out for you a
blessing until there is [2c]no more
need.
11"Then I will rebuke the [a]devour-
er for you, so that it may not destroy
the fruits of the ground; nor will
your vine in the field cast *its
grapes,*" says the LORD of hosts.
12"And [a]all the nations will call
you blessed, for you shall be a [b]de-
lightful land," says the LORD of
hosts.
13"Your words have been arrogant
against Me," says the LORD. "Yet
you say, 'What have we spoken
against Thee?'
14"You have said, 'It is [a]vain to
serve God; and what [b]profit is it that
we have kept His charge, and that
we have walked in mourning before
the LORD of hosts?
15 'So now we call the arrogant
blessed; not only are the doers of
wickedness built up, but they also
test God and [a]escape.' "

The Book of Remembrance

16 Then those who [1]feared the
LORD spoke to one another, and the
LORD [a]gave attention and heard *it,*
and a [b]book of remembrance was
written before Him for those who
[2]fear the LORD and who esteem His
name.
17"And they will be [a]Mine," says
the LORD of hosts, "on the [b]day that
I prepare *My* [c]own possession, and I
will spare them as a man [d]spares his
own son who serves him."
18 So you will again [a]distinguish
between the righteous and the
wicked, between one who serves
God and one who does not serve
Him.

CHAPTER 4

Final Admonition

"[1]FOR behold, the day is coming,
[a]burning like a furnace; and all the
arrogant and every evildoer will be
[b]chaff; and the day that is coming
will [c]set them ablaze," says the
LORD of hosts, "so that it will leave
them neither root nor branch."
2"But for you who [1]fear My name
the [a]sun of righteousness will rise
with [b]healing in its wings; and you
will go forth and [c]skip about like
calves from the stall.
3"And you will [a]tread down the
wicked, for they shall be [b]ashes under the soles of your feet on the day
which I am preparing," says the
LORD of hosts.
4"[1a]Remember the law of Moses
My servant, *even the* statutes and
ordinances which I commanded him
in Horeb for all Israel.
5"Behold, I am going to send you
[a]Elijah the prophet before the coming of the great and terrible day of
the LORD.
6"And he will [a]restore the hearts
of the fathers to *their* children, and
the hearts of the children to their
fathers, lest I come and [b]smite the
land with a curse."

7 [a]Zech. 1:3
8 [1]Or, *defraud* [2]Or, *heave offerings* [a]Neh. 13:11
9 [1]Or, *defrauding*
10 [1]Lit., *prey* [2]Or, *not room enough* [a]Ps. 78:23-29 [b]Ezek. 34:26 [c]Lev. 26:3-5
11 [a]Joel 1:4; 2:25
12 [a]Is. 61:9 [b]Is. 62:4
14 [a]Jer. 2:25; 18:12 [b]Is. 58:3
15 [a]Jer. 7:10
16 [1]Or, *revered* [2]Or, *revere* [a]Ps. 34:15; Jer. 31:18-20 [b]Is. 4:3; Dan. 12:1
17 [a]Is. 43:1 [b]Is. 4:2 [c]Ex. 19:5; Deut. 7:6; Is. 43:21; 1 Pet. 2:9 [d]Neh. 13:22; Ps. 103:13; Is. 26:20
18 [a]Gen. 18:25; Amos 5:15
1 [1]In Heb., chap. 3:19 [a]Ps. 21:9; Nah. 1:5, 6; Mal. 3:2, 3 [b]Is. 5:24; Obad. 18 [c]Is. 9:18, 19
2 [1]Or, *revere* [a]2 Sam. 23:4; Is. 30:26; 60:1 [b]Jer. 30:17; 33:6 [c]Is. 35:6
3 [a]Job 40:12; Is. 26:6; Mic. 5:8 [b]Ezek. 28:18
4 [1]In. Heb., chap. 3:22 [a]Deut. 4:23; 8:11, 19
5 [a]Matt. 11:14; Mark 9:11-13; Luke 1:17
6 [a]Luke 1:17 [b]Is. 11:4; Rev. 19:15

New

American Standard

Bible

New Testament

THE GOSPEL
ACCORDING TO
MATTHEW

Genealogy of Jesus Christ

THE book of the genealogy of Jesus Christ, [a]the son of David, [b]the son of Abraham.

2 To Abraham was born Isaac; and to Isaac, Jacob; and to Jacob, [1]Judah and his brothers;

3 and to Judah were born Perez and Zerah by Tamar; and to [a]Perez was born Hezron; and to Hezron, [1]Ram;

4 and to Ram was born Amminadab; and to Amminadab, Nahshon; and to Nahshon, Salmon;

5 and to Salmon was born Boaz by Rahab; and to Boaz was born Obed by Ruth; and to Obed, Jesse;

6 and to Jesse was born David the king.

And to David [a]was born Solomon by her *who had been the wife* of Uriah;

7 and to Solomon [a]was born Rehoboam; and to Rehoboam, Abijah; and to Abijah, [1]Asa;

8 and to Asa was born Jehoshaphat; and to Jehoshaphat, [1]Joram; and to Joram, Uzziah;

9 and to Uzziah was born [1]Jotham; and to Jotham, Ahaz; and to Ahaz, Hezekiah;

10 and to Hezekiah was born Manasseh; and to Manasseh, [1]Amon; and to Amon, Josiah;

11 and to Josiah were born [1]Jeconiah and his brothers, at the time of the [a]deportation to Babylon.

12 And after the [a]deportation to Babylon, to Jeconiah was born [1]Shealtiel; and to Shealtiel, Zerubbabel;

13 and to Zerubbabel was born [1]Abiud; and to Abiud, Eliakim; and to Eliakim, Azor;

14 and to Azor was born Zadok; and to Zadok, Achim; and to Achim, Eliud;

15 and to Eliud was born Eleazar; and to Eleazar, Matthan; and to Matthan, Jacob;

16 and to Jacob was born Joseph the husband of Mary, by whom was born Jesus, [a]who is called [1]Christ.

17 Therefore all the generations from Abraham to David are fourteen generations; and from David to the [a]deportation to Babylon fourteen generations; and from the [a]deportation to Babylon to *the time of* [1]Christ fourteen generations.

Conception and Birth of Jesus

18 Now the birth of Jesus Christ was as follows. When His [a]mother Mary had been betrothed to Joseph, before they came together she was [b]found to be with child by the Holy Spirit.

19 And Joseph her husband, being a righteous man, and not wanting to disgrace her, desired to put her away secretly.

20 But when he had considered this, behold, an angel of the Lord appeared to him in a dream, saying, "Joseph, son of David, do not be afraid to take Mary as your wife; for that which has been [1]conceived in her is of the Holy Spirit.

21 "And she will bear a Son; and [a]you shall call His name Jesus, for it is He who [b]will save His people from their sins."

22 Now all this took place that what was spoken by the Lord through the prophet might be fulfilled, saying,

23 "[a]BEHOLD, THE VIRGIN SHALL BE WITH CHILD, AND SHALL BEAR A SON, AND THEY SHALL CALL HIS NAME [1]IMMANUEL," which translated means, "GOD WITH US."

24 And Joseph arose from his sleep, and did as the angel of the Lord commanded him, and [1]took *her* as his wife,

25 and kept her a virgin until she gave birth to a Son; and [a]he called His name Jesus.

CHAPTER 2

Visit of the Wise Men

NOW after Jesus was [a]born in Bethlehem of Judea in the days of [b]Herod the king, behold, magi from the east arrived in Jerusalem, saying,

2 "Where is He who has been born [a]King of the Jews? For we saw [b]His star in the east, and have come to worship Him."

3 And when Herod the king heard it, he was troubled, and all Jerusalem with him.

4 And gathering together all the chief priests and scribes of the peo-

1 [a]2 Sam. 7:12-16; Ps. 89:3f.; 132:11; Is. 9:6f.; 11:1; Matt. 9:27; Luke 1:32, 69; John 7:42; Acts 13:23; Rom. 1:3; Rev. 22:16 [b]Gen. 22:18; Matt. 1:1-6: *Luke 3:32-34*

2 [1]Gr., *Judas.* Names of Old Testament characters will be given in their Old Testament form throughout this version.

3 [1]Gr., *Aram* [a]Ruth 4:18-22; 1 Chr. 2:1-15; Matt. 1:3-6

6 [a]2 Sam. 11:27; 12:24

7 [1]Gr., *Asaph* [a]1 Chr. 3:10ff.

8 [1]Gr., *Jehoram*

9 [1]Gr., *Joatham*

10 [1]Gr., *Amos*

11 [1]Or, *Jehoiachin* [a]2 Kin. 24:14f.; Jer. 27:20; Matt. 1:17

12 [1]Gr., *Salathiel* [a]2 Kin. 24:14f.

13 [1]Gr., *Abihud*

16 [1]I.e., the Messiah [a]Matt. 27:17, 22; Luke 2:11; John 4:25

17 [1]Cf. v. 16[1] [a]2 Kin. 24:14f.; Jer. 27:20; Matt. 1:11, 12

18 [a]Matt. 12:46; Luke 1:27 [b]Luke 1:35

20 [1]Gr., *begotten*

21 [a]Luke 1:31; 2:21 [b]Luke 2:11; John 1:29; Acts 13:23

23 [1]Or, *Emmanuel* [a]Is. 7:14

24 [1]Or, *took his wife to himself*

25 [a]Matt. 1:21

1 [a]Luke 2:4-7 [b]Luke 1:5

2 [a]Jer. 23:5; 30:9; Zech. 9:9; Matt. 27:11; Luke 19:38; 23:38; John 1:49 [b]Num. 24:17; Rev. 22:16

ple, he *began* to inquire of them
where [1]the Christ was to be born.
5 And they said to him, "[a]In Bethlehem of Judea, for so it has been
written [1]by the prophet,
6 '[a]AND YOU, BETHLEHEM, LAND
OF JUDAH,
ARE BY NO MEANS LEAST
AMONG THE LEADERS OF JU-
DAH;
FOR OUT OF YOU SHALL COME
FORTH A RULER,
WHO WILL [b]SHEPHERD MY PEO-
PLE ISRAEL.' "
7 Then Herod secretly called the
magi, and ascertained from them
[1]the time the star appeared.
8 And he sent them to Bethlehem, and said, "Go and make careful search for the Child; and when
you have found *Him,* report to me,
that I too may come and worship
Him."
9 And having heard the king,
they went their way; and lo, the star,
which they had seen in the east,
went on before them, until it came
and stood over where the Child was.
10 And when they saw the star,
they rejoiced exceedingly with
great joy.
11 And they came into the house
and saw the Child with [a]Mary His
mother; and they fell down and worshiped Him; and opening their treasures they presented to Him gifts of
gold and frankincense and myrrh.
12 And having been [a]warned *by
God* in a dream not to return to Herod, they departed for their own
country by another way.

The Flight to Egypt

13 Now when they had departed,
behold, an angel of the Lord *[a]ap-
peared to Joseph in a dream, saying,
"Arise and take the Child and His
mother, and flee to Egypt, and remain there until I tell you; for Herod
is going to search for the Child to
destroy Him."
14 And he arose and took the
Child and His mother by night, and
departed for Egypt;
15 and was there until the death of
Herod, that what was spoken by the
Lord through the prophet might be
fulfilled, saying, "[a]OUT OF EGYPT
DID I CALL [b]MY SON."
16 Then when Herod saw that he
had been tricked by the magi, he became very enraged, and sent and
slew all the male children who were
in Bethlehem and in all its environs,
from two years old and under, according to the time which he had
ascertained from the magi.

4 [1]I.e., the Messiah
5 [1]Lit., *through* [a]John 7:42
6 [a]Mic. 5:2 [b]John 21:16
7 [1]Lit., *the time of the appearing star*
11 [a]Matt. 1:18; 12:46
12 [a]Matt. 2:13, 19, 22; Luke 2:26; Acts 10:22; Heb. 8:5; 11:7
13 [a]Matt. 2:12, 19
15 [a]Hos. 11:1 [b]Ex. 4:22f.
18 [a]Jer. 31:15
19 [a]Matt. 2:12, 13, 22
22 [a]Matt. 2:12
23 [a]Luke 1:26 [b]Is. 11:1 [c]Mark 1:24
1 [1]Or, *arrived* [2]Or, *proclaiming as a herald* [a]Matt. 3:1-12: *Mark 1:3-8; Luke 3:2-17;* John 1:6-8, 19-28 [b]Josh. 15:61 Judg. 1:16
2 [1]Lit., *of the heavens* [2]Lit., *has come near* [a]Matt. 4:17 [b]Dan. 2:44; Matt. 4:17, 23; 6:10; 10:7; Mark 1:15; Luke 10:9f.; 11:20; 21:31
3 [1]Lit., *through* [a]Is. 40:3 [b]John 1:23
4 [1]Lit., *his garment* [a]2 Kin. 1:8; Zech. 13:4 [b]Lev. 11:22
5 [a]Luke 3:3
7 [a]Matt. 16:1ff.; 23:13, 15 [b]Matt. 16:1ff.; 22:23; Acts 4:1; 5:17; 23:6ff.

17 Then that which was spoken
through Jeremiah the prophet was
fulfilled, saying,
18 "[a]A VOICE WAS HEARD IN RA-
MAH,
WEEPING AND GREAT MOURN-
ING,
RACHEL WEEPING FOR HER
CHILDREN;
AND SHE REFUSED TO BE COM-
FORTED,
BECAUSE THEY WERE NO
MORE."

Herod Slaughters Babies

19 But when Herod was dead, behold, an angel of the Lord *[a]ap-
peared in a dream to Joseph in
Egypt, saying,
20"Arise and take the Child and
His mother, and go into the land of
Israel; for those who sought the
Child's life are dead."
21 And he arose and took the
Child and His mother, and came
into the land of Israel.
22 But when he heard that Archelaus was reigning over Judea in
place of his father Herod, he was
afraid to go there. And being
[a]warned *by God* in a dream, he departed for the regions of Galilee,
23 and came and resided in a city
called [a]Nazareth, that what was
spoken through the prophets might
be fulfilled, "[b]He shall be called a
[c]Nazarene."

CHAPTER 3

John the Baptist Preaches

NOW [a]in those days John the Baptist *[1]came, [2]preaching in the [b]wil-
derness of Judea, saying,
2"[a]Repent, for [b]the kingdom of
[1]heaven [2]is at hand."
3 For this is the one referred to
[1]by Isaiah the prophet, saying,
"[a]THE VOICE OF ONE CRYING IN
THE WILDERNESS,
'[b]MAKE READY THE WAY OF THE
LORD,
MAKE HIS PATHS STRAIGHT!' "
4 Now John himself had [1a]a garment of camel's hair, and a leather
belt about his waist; and his food
was [b]locusts and wild honey.
5 Then Jerusalem was going out
to him, and all Judea, and all [a]the
district around the Jordan;
6 and they were being baptized
by him in the Jordan River, as they
confessed their sins.
7 But when he saw many of the
[a]Pharisees and [b]Sadducees coming
for baptism, he said to them, "You

[c]brood of vipers, who warned you to flee from [d]the wrath to come?

8 "Therefore bring forth fruit [a]in keeping with *your* repentance;

9 and do not suppose that you can say to yourselves, '[a]We have Abraham for our father'; for I say to you, that God is able from these stones to raise up children to Abraham.

10 "And the axe is already laid at the root of the trees; [a]every tree therefore that does not bear good fruit is cut down and thrown into the fire.

11 "As for me, [a]I baptize you [1]in water for repentance, but He who is coming after me is mightier than I, and I am not *even* fit to remove His sandals; [b]He Himself will baptize you [1]with the Holy Spirit and fire.

12 "And His [a]winnowing fork is in His hand, and He will thoroughly clean His threshing floor; and He will [b]gather His wheat into the barn, but He will burn up the chaff with [c]unquenchable fire."

The Baptism of Jesus

13 [a]Then Jesus *arrived [b]from Galilee at the Jordan *coming* to John, to be baptized by him.

14 But John tried to prevent Him, saying, "I have need to be baptized by You, and do You come to me?"

15 But Jesus answering said to him, "Permit *it* at this time; for in this way it is fitting for us to fulfill all righteousness." Then he *permitted Him.

16 And after being baptized, Jesus went up immediately from the water; and behold, the heavens were opened, and [1a]he saw the Spirit of God descending as a dove, *and* coming upon Him,

17 and behold, a voice out of the heavens, saying, "[a]This is [1]My beloved Son, in whom I am well-pleased."

CHAPTER 4

Temptation of Jesus

[a]THEN Jesus was led up by the Spirit into the wilderness to be tempted by the devil.

2 And after He had [a]fasted forty days and forty nights, He [1]then became hungry.

3 And [a]the tempter came and said to Him, "If You are the Son of God, command that these stones become [1]bread."

4 But He answered and said, "It is written, '[a]MAN SHALL NOT LIVE ON BREAD ALONE, BUT ON EVERY WORD THAT PROCEEDS OUT OF THE MOUTH OF GOD.' "

5 Then the devil *took Him into [a]the holy city; and he stood Him on the pinnacle of the temple,

6 and *said to Him, "If You are the Son of God throw Yourself down; for it is written,

'[a]HE WILL GIVE HIS ANGELS CHARGE CONCERNING YOU;
And ON THEIR HANDS THEY WILL BEAR YOU UP,
LEST YOU STRIKE YOUR FOOT AGAINST A STONE.' "

7 Jesus said to him, "[1]On the other hand, it is written, '[a]YOU SHALL NOT [2]TEMPT THE LORD YOUR GOD.' "

8 Again, the devil *took Him to a very high mountain, and *showed Him all the kingdoms of the world, and their glory;

9 and he said to Him, "All these things will I give You, if You fall down and worship me."

10 Then Jesus *said to him, "Begone, Satan! For it is written, '[a]YOU SHALL WORSHIP THE LORD YOUR GOD, AND [1]SERVE HIM ONLY.' "

11 Then the devil *left Him; and behold, [a]angels came and *began* to minister to Him.

Jesus Begins His Ministry

12 Now when He heard that [a]John had [1]been taken into custody, [b]He withdrew into Galilee;

13 and leaving Nazareth, He came and [a]settled in Capernaum, which is by the sea, in the region of Zebulun and Naphtali.

14 *This was* to fulfill what was spoken through Isaiah the prophet, saying,

15 "[a]THE LAND OF ZEBULUN AND THE LAND OF NAPHTALI,
[1]BY THE WAY OF THE SEA, BEYOND THE JORDAN, GALILEE OF THE [2]GENTILES—

16 "[a]THE PEOPLE WHO WERE SITTING IN DARKNESS SAW A GREAT LIGHT,
AND TO THOSE WHO WERE SITTING IN THE LAND AND SHADOW OF DEATH,
UPON THEM A LIGHT DAWNED."

17 [a]From that time Jesus began to [1]preach and say, "[b]Repent, for the kingdom of heaven is at hand."

The First Disciples

18 [a]And walking by [b]the Sea of Galilee, He saw two brothers, [c]Simon who was called Peter, and Andrew his brother, casting a net into the sea; for they were fishermen.

7 [c]Matt. 12:34; 23:33 [d]1 Thess. 1:10
8 [a]Acts 26:20
9 [a]John 8:33, 39
10 [a]Matt. 7:19
11 [1]The Greek here can be translated *in, with* or *by* [a]John 1:26 [b]John 1:33
12 [a]Is. 30:24; Luke 3:17 [b]Matt. 13:30 [c]Mark 9:43, 48
13 [a]Matt. 3:13-17: *Mark 1:9-11; Luke 3:21, 22;* John 1:31-34 [b]Matt. 2:22
16 [1]Or, *He* [a]John 1:32
17 [1]Lit., *My Son, the Beloved* [a]Is. 42:1; Matt. 12:18; 17:5; Mark 9:7; Luke 9:35
1 [a]Matt. 4:1-11: *Mark 1:12, 13; Luke 4:1-13*
2 [1]Lit., *later, afterward* [a]Ex. 34:28; 1 Kin. 19:8
3 [1]Lit., *loaves* [a]1 Thess. 3:5
4 [a]Deut. 8:3
5 [a]Neh. 11:1, 18; Dan. 9:24; Matt. 27:53
6 [a]Ps. 91:11-12
7 [1]Lit., *Again* [2]Or, *put to the test* [a]Deut. 6:16
10 [1]Or, *fulfill religious duty to Him* [a]Deut. 6:13
11 [a]Matt. 26:53; Luke 22:43
12 [1]Lit., *been delivered up* [a]Matt. 14:3; Mark 1:14; Luke 3:20; John 3:24 [b]Mark 1:14; Luke 4:14; John 1:43; 2:11
13 [a]Matt. 11:23; Mark 1:21; 2:1; Luke 4:23, 31; John 2:12; 4:46f.
15 [1]Or, *Toward the sea* [2]Or, *nations* [a]Is. 9:1
16 [a]Is. 9:2
17 [1]Or, *proclaim* [a]Mark 1:14, 15 [b]Matt. 3:2
18 [a]Matt. 4:18-22: *Mark 1:16-20;* Luke 5:2-11; John 1:40-42 [b]Matt. 15:29; Mark 7:31; Luke 5:1; John 6:1 [c]Matt. 10:2; 16:18; John 1:40, 42

19 And He *said to them, "Follow
Me, and I will make you fishers of
men."
20 And they immediately left the
nets, and followed Him.
21 And going on from there He
saw two other brothers, [a]James the
son of Zebedee, and John his
brother, in the boat with Zebedee
their father, mending their nets; and
He called them.
22 And they immediately left the
boat and their father, and followed
Him.

Ministry in Galilee

23 And *Jesus* was going about [a]in
all Galilee, [b]teaching in their synagogues, and [c]proclaiming the gospel
of the kingdom, and [d]healing every
kind of disease and every kind of
sickness among the people.
24 And the news about Him went
out [a]into all Syria; and they brought
to Him all who were ill, taken with
various diseases and pains, [b]demo-
niacs, [c]epileptics, [d]paralytics; and
He healed them.
25 And great multitudes [a]followed
Him from Galilee and [b]Decapolis
and Jerusalem and Judea and *from*
beyond the Jordan.

CHAPTER 5

The Sermon on the Mount
The Beatitudes

[a]AND when He saw the multitudes,
He went up on [b]the mountain; and
after He sat down, His disciples
came to Him.
2 And [a]opening His mouth He *be-*
gan to teach them, saying,
3"[a]Blessed are the poor in spirit,
for [b]theirs is the kingdom of heaven.
4"Blessed are [a]those who mourn,
for they shall be comforted.
5"Blessed are [a]the gentle, for they
shall inherit the earth.
6"Blessed are [a]those who hunger
and thirst for righteousness, for
they shall be satisfied.
7"Blessed are the merciful, for
they shall receive mercy.
8"Blessed are [a]the pure in heart,
for [b]they shall see God.
9"Blessed are the peacemakers,
for [a]they shall be called sons of God.
10"Blessed are those who have
been [a]persecuted for the sake of
righteousness, for [b]theirs is the
kingdom of heaven.
11"Blessed are you when *men* [a]re-
vile you, and persecute you, and say
all kinds of evil against you falsely,
on account of Me.

21 [a]Matt. 10:2; 20:20
23 [a]Mark 1:39; Luke 4:15, 44 [b]Matt. 9:35; 13:54; Mark 1:21; Luke 4:15; 6:6; John 6:59 [c]Matt. 3:2; Mark 1:14; Luke 4:43; 16:16; Acts 20:25 [d]Matt. 8:16; 9:35; 21:14; Mark 1:34; 3:10; Luke 4:40
24 [a]Mark 7:26; Luke 2:2; Acts 15:23; Gal. 1:21 [b]Matt. 8:16, 28, 33; 9:32; Mark 1:32; 5:15; Luke 8:36; John 10:21 [c]Matt. 17:15 [d]Matt. 8:6; Mark 2:3; Luke 5:24
25 [a]Mark 3:7, 8; Luke 6:17 [b]Mark 5:20; 7:31
1 [a]Matt. 5-7; Luke 6:20-49 [b]Mark 3:13; Luke 6:17
2 [a]Matt. 13:35; Acts 8:35; 10:34
3 [a]Matt. 5:3-12; Luke 6:20-23 [b]Matt. 5:10; Mark 10:14; Luke 6:20; 22:29f.
4 [a]Is. 61:2; Rev. 7:17
5 [a]Ps. 37:11
6 [a]Is. 55:1, 2; John 4:14; 6:48ff.
8 [a]Ps. 24:4 [b]Heb. 12:14; 1 John 3:2; Rev. 22:4
9 [a]Matt. 5:45; Luke 6:35
10 [a]1 Pet. 3:14 [b]Matt. 5:3; 19:14; 25:34; Mark 10:14; Luke 6:20
11 [a]1 Pet. 4:14
12 [a]2 Chr. 36:16; Matt. 23:37; Acts 7:52; 1 Thess. 2:15; Heb. 11:33ff.; James 5:10
13 [a]Mark 9:50; Luke 14:34f.
14 [a]John 8:12
15 [a]Mark 4:21; Luke 8:16; 11:33
16 [a]1 Pet. 2:12
18 [a]Matt. 24:35; Luke 16:17
21 [a]Matt. 5:27, 33, 38, 43 [b]Ex. 20:13; Deut. 5:17 [c]Deut. 16:18; 2 Chr. 19:5f.
22 [1]Some mss. insert here: *without cause*
[2] Or, *empty-head*
[a]Deut. 16:18 [b]Matt. 10:17; Mark 13:9; Luke 22:66; John 11:47; Acts 4:15; 5:21; 24:20 [c]Matt. 23:15, 33; Mark 9:43ff.; Luke 12:5

12"Rejoice, and be glad, for your
reward in heaven is great, for [a]so
they persecuted the prophets who
were before you.

Disciples and the World

13"You are the salt of the earth;
but [a]if the salt has become tasteless,
how will it be made salty *again*? It is
good for nothing any more, except
to be thrown out and trampled under foot by men.
14"You are [a]the light of the world.
A city set on a hill cannot be hidden.
15"[a]Nor do *men* light a lamp, and
put it under the peck-measure, but
on the lampstand; and it gives light
to all who are in the house.
16"Let your light shine before men
in such a way that they may [a]see
your good works, and glorify your
Father who is in heaven.
17"Do not think that I came to
abolish the Law or the Prophets; I
did not come to abolish, but to fulfill.
18"For truly I say to you, [a]until
heaven and earth pass away, not the
smallest letter or stroke shall pass
away from the Law, until all is accomplished.
19"Whoever then annuls one of the
least of these commandments, and
so teaches others, shall be called
least in the kingdom of heaven; but
whoever keeps and teaches *them*,
he shall be called great in the kingdom of heaven.
20"For I say to you, that unless
your righteousness surpasses *that*
of the scribes and Pharisees, you
shall not enter the kingdom of
heaven.

Personal Relationships

21"[a]You have heard that the ancients were told, '[b]YOU SHALL NOT
COMMIT MURDER' and 'Whoever
commits murder shall be liable to
[c]the court.'
22"But I say to you that every one
who is angry with his brother[1] shall
be guilty before [a]the court; and
whoever shall say to his brother,
'[2]Raca,' shall be guilty before [b]the
supreme court; and whoever shall
say, 'You fool,' shall be guilty
enough to go into the [c]hell of fire.
23"If therefore you are presenting
your offering at the altar, and there
remember that your brother has
something against you,
24 leave your offering there before
the altar, and go your way; first be

reconciled to your brother, and then
come and present your offering.
25 "[a]Make friends quickly with
your opponent at law while you are
with him on the way, in order that
your opponent may not deliver you
to the judge, and the judge to the
officer, and you be thrown into
prison.
26 "Truly I say to you, you shall not
come out of there, until you have
paid up the last [1]cent.
27 "[a]You have heard that it was
said, '[b]YOU SHALL NOT COMMIT
ADULTERY';
28 but I say to you, that every one
who looks on a woman to lust for
her has committed adultery with
her already in his heart.
29 "And [a]if your right eye makes
you [1]stumble, tear it out, and throw
it from you; for it is better for you
that one of the parts of your body
perish, [2]than for your whole body to
be thrown into [3b]hell.
30 "And [a]if your right hand makes
you stumble, cut it off, and throw it
from you; for it is better for you that
one of the parts of your body perish,
than for your whole body to go into
[b]hell.
31 "And it was said, '[a]WHOEVER DI-
VORCES HIS WIFE, LET HIM GIVE HER A
CERTIFICATE OF DISMISSAL';
32 [a]but I say to you that every one
who divorces his wife, except for
the cause of unchastity, makes her
commit adultery; and whoever marries a divorced woman commits
adultery.
33 "Again, [a]you have heard that the
ancients were told, '[b]YOU SHALL NOT
MAKE FALSE VOWS, BUT SHALL FUL-
FILL YOUR VOWS TO THE LORD.'
34 "But I say to you, [a]make no oath
at all, either by heaven, for it is [b]the
throne of God,
35 or by the earth, for it is the
[a]footstool of His feet, or by Jerusalem, for it is [b]THE CITY OF THE GREAT
KING.
36 "Nor shall you make an oath by
your head, for you cannot make one
hair white or black.
37 "But let your statement be, 'Yes,
yes' *or* 'No, no'; and anything beyond these is of [1a]evil.
38 "[a]You have heard that it was
said, '[b]AN EYE FOR AN EYE, AND A
TOOTH FOR A TOOTH.'
39 "But I say to you, do not resist
him who is evil; but [a]whoever slaps
you on your right cheek, turn to him
the other also.
40 "And if any one wants to sue
you, and take your [1]shirt, let him
have your [2]coat also.
41 "And whoever shall force you to
go one mile, go with him two.
42 "[a]Give to him who asks of you,
and do not turn away from him who
wants to borrow from you.
43 "[a]You have heard that it was
said, '[b]YOU SHALL LOVE YOUR NEIGH-
BOR, and hate your enemy.'
44 "But I say to you, [a]love your enemies, and pray for those who persecute you
45 in order that you may [1]be [a]sons
of your Father who is in heaven; for
He causes His sun to rise on *the* evil
and *the* good, and sends rain on *the*
righteous and *the* unrighteous.
46 "For [a]if you love those who love
you, what reward have you? Do not
even the [1]tax-gatherers do the
same?
47 "And if you greet your brothers
only, what do you do more *than others*? Do not even the Gentiles do the
same?
48 "Therefore [a]you are to be perfect, as your heavenly Father is perfect.

CHAPTER 6

Concerning Alms and Prayer

"BEWARE of practicing your
righteousness before men [a]to be noticed by them; otherwise you have
no reward with your Father who is
in heaven.
2 "When therefore you [1]give alms,
do not sound a trumpet before you,
as the hypocrites do in the synagogues and in the streets, that they
[a]may be honored by men. [b]Truly I
say to you, they have their reward in
full.
3 "But when you give alms, do not
let your left hand know what your
right hand is doing
4 that your alms may be in secret;
and [a]your Father who sees in secret
will repay you.
5 "And when you pray, you are
not to be as the hypocrites; for they
love to [a]stand and pray in the synagogues and on the street corners, [b]in
order to be seen by men. [c]Truly I say
to you, they have their reward in
full.
6 "But you, when you pray, [a]GO
INTO YOUR INNER ROOM, AND WHEN
YOU HAVE SHUT YOUR DOOR, pray to
your Father who is in secret, and
[b]your Father who sees in secret will
repay you.
7 "And when you are praying, do
not use meaningless repetition, as

25 [a]Luke 12:58
26 [1]I.e., 1/64 of a denarius
27 [a]Matt. 5:21, 33, 38, 43 [b]Ex. 20:14; Deut. 5:18
29 [1]I.e., cause to sin [2]Lit., *not your whole body* [3]Gr., *Gehenna* [a]Matt. 17:27; 18:9; Mark 9:47 [b]Matt. 5:22
30 [a]Matt. 17:27; 18:8; Mark 9:43 [b]Matt. 5:22
31 [a]Deut. 24:1, 3
32 [a]Matt. 19:9; Mark 10:11f.; Luke 16:18; 1 Cor. 7:11f.
33 [a]Matt. 5:21, 27, 38, 43; 23:16ff. [b]Lev. 19:12; Num. 30:2; Deut. 23:21
34 [a]James 5:12 [b]Is. 66:1; Matt. 23:22
35 [a]Is. 66:1; Acts 7:49 [b]Ps. 48:2
37 [1]Or, *from the evil one* [a]Matt. 6:13; 13:19, 38; John 17:15; 2 Thess. 3:3; 1 John 2:13f.; 3:12; 5:18f.
38 [a]Matt. 5:21, 27, 33, 43 [b]Ex. 21:24; Lev. 24:20; Deut. 19:21
39 [a]Matt. 5:39-42: *Luke 6:29, 30;* 1 Cor. 6:7
40 [1]*Tunic* or garment worn next to the body [2]*Cloak* or outer garment
42 [a]Luke 6:34f.
43 [a]Matt. 5:21, 27, 33, 38 [b]Lev. 19:18
44 [a]Luke 6:27f.; 23:34; Acts 7:60
45 [1]Or, *show yourselves to be* [a]Matt. 5:9
46 [1]Publicans who collected Roman taxes on commission [a]Luke 6:32
48 [a]Lev. 19:2
1 [a]Matt. 6:5, 16; 23:5
2 [1]Or, *do an act of charity* [a]Matt. 6:5, 16; 23:5 [b]Matt. 6:5, 16; Luke 6:24
4 [a]Matt. 6:6, 18
5 [a]Mark 11:25; Luke 18:11, 13 [b]Matt. 6:1, 16 [c]Matt. 6:2, 16; Luke 6:24
6 [a]Is. 26:20 [b]Matt. 6:4, 18

the Gentiles do, for they suppose
that they will be heard for their
[a]many words.
8 "Therefore do not be like them;
for [a]your Father knows what you
need, before you ask Him.
9 "[a]Pray, then, in this way:
'Our Father who art in heaven,
Hallowed be Thy name.
10 '[a]Thy kingdom come.
Thy will be done,
On earth as it is in heaven.
11 '[a]Give us this day our daily
bread.
12 'And forgive us our debts, as
we also have forgiven our
debtors.
13 'And do not lead us into temptation, but deliver us from
[1a]evil. [2][For Thine is the kingdom, and the power, and the
glory, forever. Amen].'
14 "[a]For if you forgive men for their
transgressions, your heavenly Father will also forgive you.
15 "But if you do not forgive men,
then your Father will not forgive
your transgressions.

Concerning Fasting
True Treasure
Mammon

16 "And [a]whenever you fast, do not
put on a gloomy face as the hypocrites *do*, for they neglect their appearance in order to be seen fasting
by men. [b]Truly I say to you, they
have their reward in full.
17 "But you, when you fast, anoint
your head, and wash your face
18 so that you may not be seen
fasting by men, but by your Father
who is in secret; and your [a]Father
who sees in secret will repay you.
19 "Do not lay up for yourselves
treasures upon earth, where moth
and rust destroy, and where thieves
break in and steal.
20 "But lay up for yourselves [a]trea-
sures in heaven, where neither moth
nor rust destroys, and where thieves
do not break in or steal;
21 for [a]where your treasure is,
there will your heart be also.
22 "[a]The lamp of the body is the
eye; if therefore your eye is clear,
your whole body will be full of light.
23 "But if [a]your eye is bad, your
whole body will be full of darkness.
If therefore the light that is in you is
darkness, how great is the darkness!
24 "[a]No one can serve two masters;
for either he will hate the one and
love the other, or he will hold to one
and despise the other. You cannot
serve God and [b]mammon.

7 [a]1 Kin. 18:26f.
8 [a]Matt. 6:32
9 [a]Matt. 6:9-13: *Luke 11:2-4*
10 [a]Matt. 3:2
11 [a]Prov. 30:8
13 [1]Or, *the evil one* [2]This clause omitted in the earliest manuscripts [a]Matt. 5:37
14 [a]Matt. 18:35; Mark 11:25f.
16 [a]Is. 58:5 [b]Matt. 6:2
18 [a]Matt. 6:4, 6
20 [a]Matt. 19:21; Luke 12:33; 1 Tim. 6:19
21 [a]Luke 12:34
22 [a]Matt. 6:22, 23: *Luke 11:34, 35*
23 [a]Matt. 20:15; Mark 7:22
24 [a]Luke 16:13 [b]Luke 16:9, 11, 13
25 [1]Or, *stop being anxious* [a]Matt. 6:25-33: *Luke 12:22-31* [b]Matt. 6:27, 28, 31, 34; Luke 10:41; 12:11, 22; Phil. 4:6; 1 Pet. 5:7
26 [a]Matt. 10:29ff.
27 [1]I.e., approximately 18 inches [2]Or, *height* [a]Matt. 6:25, 28, 31, 34; Luke 10:41; 12:11, 22; Phil. 4:6; 1 Pet. 5:7 [b]Ps. 39:5
28 [a]Matt. 6:25, 27, 31, 34; Luke 10:41; 12:11, 22; Phil. 4:6; 1 Pet. 5:7
29 [a]1 Kin. 10:4-7
30 [a]Matt. 8:26; 14:31; 16:8
31 [a]Matt. 6:25, 27, 28, 34; Luke 10:41; 12:11, 22; Phil. 4:6; 1 Pet. 5:7
32 [a]Matt. 6:8
33 [a]Matt. 19:28; Mark 10:29f.; Luke 18:29f.; 1 Tim. 4:8
34 [1]Or, *will worry about itself* [a]Matt. 6:25, 27, 28, 31; Luke 10:41; 12:11, 22; Phil. 4:6; 1 Pet. 5:7
1 [1]Or, *Do not pass judgments* [a]Matt. 7:1-5: *Luke 6:37f., 41f.*
2 [1]Lit., *by what measure you measure* [a]Mark 4:24; Luke 6:38
4 [1]Lit., *will*

The Cure for Anxiety

25 "[a]For this reason I say to you,
[1]do not be [b]anxious for your life, *as*
to what you shall eat, or what you
shall drink; nor for your body, *as to*
what you shall put on. Is not life
more than food, and the body than
clothing?
26 "[a]Look at the birds of the air,
that they do not sow, neither do they
reap, nor gather into barns, and *yet*
your heavenly Father feeds them.
Are you not worth much more than
they?
27 "And which of you by being
[a]anxious can [b]add a *single* [1]cubit to
his [2]life's span?
28 "And why are you [a]anxious
about clothing? Observe how the lilies of the field grow; they do not toil
nor do they spin,
29 yet I say to you that even [a]Sol-
omon in all his glory did not clothe
himself like one of these.
30 "But if God so arrays the grass of
the field, which is *alive* today and
tomorrow is thrown into the furnace, *will He* not much more *do so*
for you, [a]O men of little faith?
31 "Do not be [a]anxious then, saying, 'What shall we eat?' or 'What
shall we drink?' or 'With what shall
we clothe ourselves?'
32 "For all these things the Gentiles
eagerly seek; for [a]your heavenly Father knows that you need all these
things.
33 "But seek first His kingdom and
His righteousness; and [a]all these
things shall be added to you.
34 "Therefore do not be [a]anxious
for tomorrow; for tomorrow will
[1]care for itself. *Each* day has
enough trouble of its own.

Chapter 7

Concerning Judging Others

"[1a]Do not judge lest you be
judged *yourselves*.
2 "For in the way you judge, you
will be judged; and [1a]by your standard of measure, it shall be measured to you.
3 "And why do you look at the
speck in your brother's eye, but do
not notice the log that is in your own
eye?
4 "Or how [1]can you say to your
brother, 'Let me take the speck out
of your eye,' and behold, the log is in
your own eye?
5 "You hypocrite, first take the log
out of your own eye, and then you
will see clearly *enough* to take the
speck out of your brother's eye.

6"Do not give what is holy to
dogs, and do not throw your pearls before swine, lest they trample them under their feet, and turn and tear you to pieces.

Encouragement to Pray

7"[a]Ask, and [b]it shall be given to
you; seek, and you shall find; knock, and it shall be opened to you.
8"For every one who asks re-
ceives, and he who seeks finds, and to him who knocks it shall be opened.
9"Or what man is there among
you, [1]when his son shall ask him for a loaf, [2]will give him a stone?
10"Or [1]if he shall ask for a fish, he
will not give him a snake, will he?
11"If you then, being evil, know
how to give good gifts to your children, how much more shall your Father who is in heaven give what is good to those who ask Him!
12"[a]Therefore whatever you want
others to do for you, [1]do so for them, for [b]this is the Law and the Prophets.

Ways Contrasted
Fruits Contrasted

13"[a]Enter by the narrow gate; for
the gate is wide, and the way is broad that leads to destruction, and many are those who enter by it.
14"For the gate is small, and the
way is narrow that leads to life, and few are those who find it.
15"Beware of the [a]false prophets,
who come to you in sheep's clothing, but inwardly are [b]ravenous wolves.
16"You will know them [a]by their
fruits. [1]Grapes are not gathered from thorn *bushes,* nor figs from thistles, are they?
17"Even so, every good tree bears
good fruit; but the rotten tree bears bad fruit.
18"A good tree cannot produce
bad fruit, nor can a rotten tree produce good fruit.
19"[a]Every tree that does not bear
good fruit is cut down and thrown into the fire.
20"So then, you will know them
[a]by their fruits.
21"[a]Not every one who says to Me,
'Lord, Lord,' will enter the kingdom of heaven; but he who does the will of My Father who is in heaven.
22"[a]Many will say to Me on [b]that
day, 'Lord, Lord, did we not prophesy in Your name, and in Your name cast out demons, and in Your name perform many miracles?'
23"And then I will declare to them,
'I never knew you; [a]DEPART FROM ME, YOU WHO PRACTICE LAWLESSNESS.'

The Two Foundations

24"Therefore [a]every one who
hears these words of Mine, and [1]acts upon them, [2]may be compared to a wise man, who built his house upon the rock.
25"And the rain descended, and
the [1]floods came, and the winds blew, and burst against that house; and *yet* it did not fall, for it had been founded upon the rock.
26"And every one who hears these
words of Mine, and does not [1]act upon them, will be like a foolish man, who built his house upon the sand.
27"And the rain descended, and
the [1]floods came, and the winds blew, and burst against that house; and it fell, and great was its fall."
28 [a]The result was that when Je-
sus had finished these words, [b]the multitudes were amazed at His teaching;
29 for He was teaching them as
one having authority, and not as their scribes.

CHAPTER 8

Jesus Cleanses a Leper
The Centurion's Faith

AND when He had come down
from the mountain, great multitudes followed Him.
2 And behold, a leper [a]came to
Him, and [b]bowed down to Him, saying, "Lord, if You are willing, You can make me clean."
3 And stretching out His hand,
He touched him, saying, "I am willing; be cleansed." And immediately his leprosy was cleansed.
4 And Jesus *said to him, "[a]See
that you tell no one; but [b]go, [c]SHOW YOURSELF TO THE PRIEST, and present the offering that Moses prescribed, for a testimony to them."
5 And [a]when He had entered Ca-
pernaum, a centurion came to Him, entreating Him,
6 and saying, "Sir, my [1]servant is
[2]lying [a]paralyzed at home, [3]suffering great pain."
7 And He *said to him, "I will
come and heal him."
8 But the centurion answered
and said, "Lord, I am not qualified for You to come under my roof, but just say the word, and my servant will be healed.

7 [a]Matt. 7:7-11: *Luke 11:9-13* [b]Matt. 18:19; 21:22; Mark 11:24; John 14:13; 15:7, 16; 16:23f.; James 1:5f.; 1 John 3:22; 5:14f.
9 [1]Lit., *whom* [2]Lit., *he will not give him a stone, will he?*
10 [1]Lit., *also*
12 [1]Or, *you, too, do so* [a]Luke 6:31 [b]Matt. 22:40; Rom. 13:8ff.; Gal. 5:14
13 [a]Luke 13:24
15 [a]Matt. 24:11, 24; Mark 13:22; Luke 6:26; Acts 13:6; 2 Pet. 2:1; 1 John 4:1; Rev. 16:13; 19:20; 20:10 [b]Ezek. 22:27; John 10:12; Acts 20:29
16 [1]Lit., *They do not gather* [a]Matt. 7:20; 12:33; Luke 6:44; James 3:12
19 [a]Matt. 3:10; Luke 13:7
20 [a]Matt. 7:16; 12:33; Luke 6:44; James 3:12
21 [a]Luke 6:46
22 [a]Matt. 25:11f.; Luke 13:25ff. [b]Matt. 10:15
23 [a]Ps. 6:8; Matt. 25:41; Luke 13:27
24 [1]Lit., *does* [2]Lit., *will be compared to* [a]Matt. 7:24-27: *Luke 6:47-49;* James 1:22-25
25 [1]Lit., *rivers*
26 [1]Lit., *do*
27 [1]Lit., *rivers*
28 [a]Matt. 11:1; 13:53; 19:1; 26:1 [b]Matt. 13:54; 22:33; Mark 1:22; 6:2; 11:18; Luke 4:32; John 7:46
2 [a]Matt. 8:2-4: *Mark 1:40-44; Luke 5:12-14* [b]Matt. 9:18; 15:25; 18:26; 20:20; John 9:38; Acts 10:25
4 [a]Matt. 9:30; 12:16; 17:9; Mark 1:44; 3:12; 5:43; 7:36; 8:30; 9:9; Luke 4:41; 8:56; 9:21 [b]Mark 1:44; Luke 5:14; 17:14 [c]Lev. 13:49; 14:2ff.
5 [a]Matt. 8:5-13: *Luke 7:1-10*
6 [1]Lit., *boy* [2]Lit., *throwing* [3]Lit., *fearfully tormented* [a]Matt. 4:24

9"For I, too, am a man under authority, with soldiers under me; and I say to this one, 'Go!' and he goes, and to another, 'Come!' and he comes, and to my slave, 'Do this!' and he does *it*."
10 Now when Jesus heard *this*, He marveled, and said to those who were following, "Truly I say to you, I have not found such great faith [1]with anyone in Israel.
11"And I say to you, that many [a]shall come from east and west, and [1]recline *at table* with Abraham, and Isaac, and Jacob, in the kingdom of heaven;
12 but [a]the sons of the kingdom shall be cast out into [b]the outer darkness; in that place [c]there shall be weeping and gnashing of teeth."
13 And Jesus said to the centurion, "Go your way; let it be done to you [a]as you have believed." And the servant was healed that *very* hour.

Peter's Mother-in-law Healed
Many Healed

14 [a]And when Jesus had come to Peter's home, He saw his mother-in-law lying sick in bed with a fever.
15 And He touched her hand, and the fever left her; and she arose, and began to [1]wait on Him.
16 And when evening had come, they brought to Him many [a]who were demon-possessed; and He cast out the spirits with a word, and [b]healed all who were ill
17 in order that what was spoken through Isaiah the prophet might be fulfilled, saying, "[a]HE HIMSELF TOOK OUR INFIRMITIES, AND [1]CARRIED AWAY OUR DISEASES."

Discipleship Tested

18 Now when Jesus saw a crowd around Him, [a]He gave orders to depart to the other side.
19 [a]And a certain scribe came and said to Him, "Teacher, I will follow You wherever You go."
20 And Jesus *said to him, "The foxes have holes, and the birds of the [1]air *have* [2]nests; but [a]the Son of Man has nowhere to lay His head."
21 And another of the disciples said to Him, "Lord, permit me first to go and bury my father."
22 But Jesus *said to him, "[a]Follow Me; and allow the dead to bury their own dead."
23 [a]And when He got into the boat, His disciples followed Him.
24 And behold, there arose [1]a great storm in the sea, so that the boat was covered with the waves; but He Himself was asleep.
25 And they came to *Him*, and awoke Him, saying, "Save *us*, Lord; we are perishing!"
26 And He *said to them, "Why are you timid, [a]you men of little faith?" Then He arose, and rebuked the winds and the sea; and it became perfectly calm.
27 And the men marveled, saying, "What kind of a man is this, that even the winds and the sea obey Him?"

Jesus Casts Out Demons

28 [a]And when He had come to the other side into the country of the Gadarenes, two men who were [b]demon-possessed met Him as they were coming out of the tombs; *they were* so exceedingly violent that no one could pass by that road.
29 And behold, they cried out, saying, "[a]What do we have to do with You, Son of God? Have You come here to torment us before [1]the time?"
30 Now there was at a distance from them a herd of many swine feeding.
31 And the demons *began* to entreat Him, saying, "If You are *going to* cast us out, send us into the herd of swine."
32 And He said to them, "Begone!" And they came out, and went into the swine, and behold, the whole herd rushed down the steep bank into the sea and perished in the waters.
33 And the herdsmen fled, and went away to the city, and reported everything, [1]including the *incident* of the [a]demoniacs.
34 And behold, the whole city came out to meet Jesus; and when they saw Him, they entreated *Him* to depart from their region.

CHAPTER 9

A Paralytic Cured

AND getting into a boat, He crossed over, and came to [a]His own city.
2 [a]And behold, they were bringing to Him a [b]paralytic, [1]lying on a bed; and Jesus seeing their faith said to the paralytic, "[c]Take courage, *My* [2]son, [d]your sins [3]are forgiven."
3 And behold, some of the scribes said to themselves, "This *fellow* blasphemes."
4 And Jesus [a]knowing their

10 [1]Some manuscripts read, *not even in Israel*
11 [1]Or, *dine* [a]Is. 49:12; 59:19; Mal. 1:11; Luke 13:29
12 [a]Matt. 13:38 [b]Matt. 22:13; 25:30 [c]Matt. 13:42, 50; 22:13; 24:51; 25:30; Luke 13:28
13 [a]Matt. 9:22, 29
14 [a]Matt. 8:14-16: *Mark 1:29-34; Luke 4:38-41*
15 [1]Or, *serve*
16 [a]Matt. 4:24 [b]Matt. 4:23; 8:33
17 [1]Or, *removed* [a]Is. 53:4
18 [a]Mark 4:35; Luke 8:22
19 [a]Matt. 8:19-22: *Luke 9:57-60*
20 [1]Or, *sky* [2]Gr., *roosting places* [a]Dan. 7:13; Matt. 9:6; 12:8, 32, 40; 13:41; 16:13, 27f.; 17:9; 19:28; 26:64; Mark 8:38; Luke 12:8; 18:8; 21:36; John 1:51; 3:13f.; 6:27; 12:34; Acts 7:56
22 [a]Matt. 9:9; Mark 2:14; Luke 9:59; John 1:43; 21:19
23 [a]Matt. 8:23-27: *Mark 4:36-41; Luke 8:22-25*
24 [1]Lit., *a shaking*
26 [a]Matt. 6:30; 14:31; 16:8
28 [a]Matt. 8:28-34: *Mark 5:1-17; Luke 8:26-37* [b]Matt. 4:24
29 [1]I.e., the appointed time of judgment [a]Judg. 11:12; 2 Sam. 16:10; 19:22; 1 Kin. 17:18; 2 Kin. 3:13; 2 Chr. 35:21; Mark 1:24; 5:7; Luke 4:34; 8:28; John 2:4
33 [1]Lit., *and* [a]Matt. 4:24
1 [a]Matt. 4:13; Mark 5:21
2 [1]Lit., *thrown* [2]Gr., *child* [3]Lit., *are being forgiven* [a]Matt. 9:2-8: *Mark 2:3-12; Luke 5:18-26* [b]Matt. 4:24; 9:6 [c]Matt. 9:22; 14:27; Mark 6:50; 10:49; John 16:33; Acts 23:11 [d]Mark 2:5, 9; Luke 5:20, 23; 7:48
4 [a]Matt. 12:25; Luke 6:8; 9:47

thoughts said, "Why are you thinking evil in your hearts?
5"For which is easier, to say,
'[a]Your sins are forgiven,' or to say,
'Rise, and walk'?
6"But in order that you may know
that [a]the Son of Man has authority
on earth to forgive sins"—then He
*said to the [b]paralytic, "Rise, take
up your bed, and go home."
7 And he rose, and went to his
home.
8 But when the multitudes saw
this, they were filled with awe, and
[a]glorified God, who had given such
authority to men.

Matthew Called

9 [a]And as Jesus passed on from
there, He saw a man, called [b]Mat-
thew, sitting in the tax office; and He
*said to him, "[c]Follow Me!" And he
rose, and followed Him.
10 And it happened that as He was
reclining *at table* in the house, behold many [1]tax-gatherers and [2]sin-
ners came and joined Jesus and His
disciples *at the table.*
11 And when the Pharisees saw
this, they said to His disciples,
"[a]Why does your Teacher eat with
the tax-gatherers and sinners?"
12 But when He heard this, He
said, "*It is* not [a]those who are
healthy who need a physician, but
those who are ill.
13"But go and learn [a]what *this*
means, '[b]I DESIRE COMPASSION, AND
NOT SACRIFICE,' for [c]I did not come
to call *the* righteous, but sinners."
14 Then the disciples of John
*came to Him, saying, "Why do we
and [a]the Pharisees fast, but Your
disciples do not fast?"
15 And Jesus said to them, "The
attendants of the bridegroom cannot mourn as long as the bridegroom is with them, can they? But
the days will come when the bridegroom is taken away from them,
and then they will fast.
16"But no one puts a patch of unshrunk cloth on an old garment; for
the patch pulls away from the garment, and a worse tear results.
17"Nor do *men* put new wine into
old wineskins; otherwise the wineskins burst, and the wine pours out,
and the wineskins are ruined; but
they put new wine into fresh wineskins, and both are preserved."

Miracles of Healing

18 [a]While He was saying these
things to them, behold, there came a
synagogue official, and [b]bowed

5 [a]Mark 2:5, 9; Luke 5:20, 23; 7:48
6 [a]Matt. 8:20 [b]Matt. 4:24; 9:2
8 [a]Matt. 5:16; 15:31; Mark 2:12; Luke 2:20; 5:25, 26; 7:16; 13:13; 17:15; 23:47; John 15:8; Acts 4:21; 11:18; 21:20; 2 Cor. 9:13; Gal. 1:24
9 [a]Matt. 9:9-17: *Mark 2:14-22; Luke 5:27-38* [b]Matt. 10:3; Mark 2:14; 3:18; Luke 6:15; Acts 1:13 [c]Matt. 8:22
10 [1]Publicans who collected Roman taxes for profit [2]I.e., irreligious or non-practicing Jews
11 [a]Matt. 11:19; Mark 2:16; Luke 5:30; 15:2
12 [a]Mark 2:17; Luke 5:31
13 [a]Matt. 12:7 [b]Hos. 6:6 [c]Mark 2:17; Luke 5:32; 1 Tim. 1:15
14 [a]Luke 18:12
18 [a]Matt. 9:18-26: *Mark 5:22-43; Luke 8:41-56* [b]Matt. 8:2
20 [a]Num. 15:38; Deut. 22:12; Matt. 14:36; 23:5
21 [a]Matt. 14:36; Mark 3:10; Luke 6:19
22 [a]Matt. 9:2 [b]Matt. 9:29; 15:28; Mark 5:34; 10:52; Luke 7:50; 8:48; 17:19; 18:42
23 [a]2 Chr. 35:25; Jer. 9:17; 16:6; Ezek. 24:17
24 [a]John 11:13; Acts 20:10
26 [a]Matt. 4:24; 9:31; 14:1; Mark 1:28, 45; Luke 4:14, 37; 5:15; 7:17
27 [a]Matt. 1:1; 12:23; 15:22; 20:30, 31; 21:9, 15; 22:42; Mark 10:47, 48; 12:35; Luke 18:38, 39; 20:41f.
29 [a]Matt. 8:13; 9:22
30 [a]Matt. 8:4
31 [a]Matt. 4:24; 9:26; 14:1; Mark 1:28, 45; Luke 4:14, 37; 5:15; 7:17
32 [a]Matt. 12:22, 24 [b]Matt. 4:24
33 [a]Mark 2:12
34 [a]Matt. 12:24; Mark 3:22; Luke 11:15; John 7:20f.
35 [a]Matt. 4:23

down before Him, saying, "My
daughter has just died; but come
and lay Your hand on her, and she
will live."
19 And Jesus rose and *began* to
follow him, and *so did* His disciples.
20 And behold, a woman who had
been suffering from a hemorrhage
for twelve years, came up behind
Him and touched [a]the fringe of His
cloak;
21 for she was saying to herself,
"If I only [a]touch His garment, I shall
get well."
22 But Jesus turning and seeing
her said, "Daughter, [a]take courage;
[b]your faith has made you well." And
at once the woman was made well.
23 And when Jesus came into the
official's house, and saw [a]the flute-
players, and the crowd in noisy disorder,
24 He *began* to say, "Depart; for
the girl [a]is not dead, but is asleep."
And they were laughing at Him.
25 But when the crowd had been
put out, He entered and took her by
the hand; and the girl arose.
26 And [a]this news went out into all
that land.
27 And as Jesus passed on from
there, two blind men followed Him,
crying out, and saying, "Have mercy on us, [a]Son of David!"
28 And after He had come into the
house, the blind men came up to
Him, and Jesus *said to them, "Do
you believe that I am able to do
this?" They *said to Him, "Yes,
Lord."
29 Then He touched their eyes,
saying, "Be it done to you [a]accord-
ing to your faith."
30 And their eyes were opened.
And Jesus [a]sternly warned them,
saying, "See *here,* let no one know
about this!"
31 But they went out, and [a]spread
the news about Him in all that land.
32 And as they were going out, behold, [a]a dumb man, [b]demon-pos-
sessed, was brought to Him.
33 And after the demon was cast
out, the dumb man spoke; and
the multitudes marveled, saying,
"[a]Nothing like this was ever seen in
Israel."
34 But the Pharisees were saying,
"He casts out the demons [a]by the
ruler of the demons."
35 And Jesus was going about all
the cities and the villages, [a]teaching
in their synagogues, and proclaiming the gospel of the kingdom, and

[b]healing every kind of disease and every kind of sickness.

36 And [a]seeing the multitudes, He felt compassion for them, [b]because they were distressed and downcast like sheep without a shepherd.

37 Then He *said to His disciples, "[a]The harvest is plentiful, but the workers are few.

38 "[a]Therefore beseech the Lord of the harvest to send out workers into His harvest."

Chapter 10

The Twelve Disciples
Instructions for Service

AND [a]having summoned His twelve disciples, He gave them authority over unclean spirits, to cast them out, and to [b]heal every kind of disease and every kind of sickness.

2 [a]Now the names of the twelve apostles are these: The first, [b]Simon, who is called Peter, and [c]Andrew his brother; and James the *son* of Zebedee, and John his brother;

3 [a]Philip and Bartholomew; [b]Thomas and [c]Matthew the tax-gatherer; [d]James the *son* of Alphaeus, and [e]Thaddaeus;

4 Simon the Cananaean, and [a]Judas Iscariot, the one who betrayed Him.

5 [a]These twelve Jesus sent out after instructing them, saying, "Do not go in *the* way of *the* Gentiles, and do not enter *any* city of the [b]Samaritans;

6 but rather go to [a]the lost sheep of the house of Israel.

7 "And as you go, preach, saying, '[a]The kingdom of heaven is at hand.'

8 "Heal *the* sick, raise *the* dead, cleanse *the* lepers, cast out demons; freely you received, freely give.

9 "[a]Do not acquire gold, or silver, or copper for your money belts;

10 or a bag for *your* journey, or even two tunics, or sandals, or a staff; for [a]the worker is worthy of his support.

11 "And into whatever city or village you enter, inquire who is worthy in it; and abide there until you go away.

12 "And as you enter the house, [a]give it your greeting.

13 "And if the house is worthy, let your *greeting of* peace come upon it; but if it is not worthy, let your *greeting of* peace return to you.

14 "And whoever does not receive you, nor heed your words, as you go out of that house or that city, [a]shake off the dust of your feet.

15 "Truly I say to you, [a]it will be more tolerable for *the* land of [b]Sodom and Gomorrah in [c]the day of judgment, than for that city.

A Hard Road Before Them

16 "[a]Behold, I send you out as sheep in the midst of wolves; therefore be [b]shrewd as serpents, and [c]innocent as doves.

17 "But beware of men; for they will deliver you up to *the* [a]courts, and scourge you [b]in their synagogues;

18 and you shall even be brought before governors and kings for My sake, as a testimony to them and to the Gentiles.

19 "[a]But when they deliver you up, [b]do not become anxious about how or what you will speak; for it shall be given you in that hour what you are to speak.

20 "For [a]it is not you who speak, but *it is* the Spirit of your Father who speaks in you.

21 "[a]And brother will deliver up brother to death, and a father *his* child; and [b]CHILDREN WILL RISE UP AGAINST PARENTS, and cause them to be put to death.

22 "And [a]you will be hated by all on account of My name, but [b]it is the one who has endured to the end who will be saved.

23 "But whenever they [a]persecute you in this city, flee to the next; for truly I say to you, you shall not finish *going through* the cities of Israel, [b]until the Son of Man comes.

The Meaning of Discipleship

24 "[a]A disciple is not above his teacher, nor a slave above his master.

25 "It is enough for the disciple that he become as his teacher, and the slave as his master. [a]If they have called the head of the house [b]Beelzebul, how much more the members of his household!

26 "Therefore do not [a]fear them, [b]for there is nothing covered that will not be revealed, and hidden that will not be known.

27 "[a]What I tell you in the darkness, speak in the light; and what you hear *whispered* in *your* ear, proclaim [b]upon the housetops.

28 "And do not fear those who kill the body, but are unable to kill the soul; but rather [a]fear Him who is able to destroy both soul and body in [b]hell.

35 [b]Mark 1:14
36 [a]Matt. 14:14; 15:32 [b]Num. 27:17; Ezek. 34:5; Zech. 10:2; Mark 6:34
37 [a]Luke 10:2
38 [a]Luke 10:2
1 [a]Mark 3:13-15; 6:7 [b]Matt. 9:35; Luke 9:1
2 [a]Matt. 10:2-4: *Mark 3:16-19; Luke 6:14-16; Acts 1:13* [b]Matt. 4:18 [c]Matt. 4:18
3 [a]John 1:45ff. [b]John 11:16; 14:5 [c]Matt. 9:9 [d]Mark 15:40 [e]Mark 3:18; Luke 6:16
4 [a]Matt. 26:14; Luke 22:3; John 6:71; 13:2, 26
5 [a]Mark 6:7; Luke 9:2 [b]2 Kin. 17:24ff.; Luke 9:52; 10:33; 17:16; John 4:9, 39f.; 8:48; Acts 8:25
6 [a]Matt. 15:24
7 [a]Matt. 3:2
9 [a]Matt. 10:9-15: *Mark 6:8-11; Luke 9:3-5; 10:4-12;* Luke 22:35
10 [a]1 Cor. 9:14; 1 Tim. 5:18
12 [a]1 Sam. 25:6; Ps. 122:7, 8
14 [a]Acts 13:51
15 [a]Matt. 11:22, 24 [b]Matt. 11:24; 2 Pet. 2:6; Jude 7 [c]Matt. 7:22; 11:22, 24; 12:36; Acts 17:31; 1 Thess. 5:4; Heb. 10:25; 2 Pet. 2:9; 3:7
16 [a]Luke 10:3 [b]Gen. 3:1; Matt. 24:25; Rom. 16:19 [c]Hos. 7:11
17 [a]Matt. 5:22 [b]Matt. 23:34; Mark 13:9; Luke 12:11; Acts 5:40; 22:19; 26:11
19 [a]Matt. 10:19-22: *Mark 13:11-13; Luke 21:12-17* [b]Matt. 6:25
20 [a]Luke 12:12; Acts 4:8; 13:9
21 [a]Matt. 10:35, 36 [b]Mic. 7:6
22 [a]Matt. 24:9 [b]Matt. 24:13
23 [a]Matt. 23:34 [b]Matt. 16:27f.
24 [a]Luke 6:40; John 13:16; 15:20
25 [a]Matt. 9:34 [b]2 Kin. 1:2; Matt. 12:24, 27; Mark 3:22; Luke 11:15
26 [a]Matt. 10:26-33: *Luke 12:2-9* [b]Mark 4:22
27 [a]Luke 12:3 [b]Matt. 24:17
28 [a]Heb. 10:31 [b]Matt. 5:22

29 "[a]Are not two sparrows sold for
a [1]cent? And *yet* not one of them will
fall to the ground apart from your
Father.
30 "But [a]the very hairs of your head
are all numbered.
31 "Therefore do not fear; [a]you are
of more value than many sparrows.
32 "Every one therefore who shall
confess Me before men, I will also
confess [a]him before My Father who
is in heaven.
33 "But [a]whoever shall deny Me before men, I will also deny him before
My Father who is in heaven.
34 "[a]Do not think that I came to
bring peace on the earth; I did not
come to bring peace, but a sword.
35 "For I came to [a]SET A MAN
AGAINST HIS FATHER, AND A DAUGH-
TER AGAINST HER MOTHER, AND A
DAUGHTER-IN-LAW AGAINST HER
MOTHER-IN-LAW;
36 and [a]A MAN'S ENEMIES WILL BE
THE MEMBERS OF HIS HOUSEHOLD.
37 "[a]He who loves father or mother
more than Me is not worthy of Me;
and he who loves son or daughter
more than Me is not worthy of Me.
38 "And [a]he who does not take his
cross and follow after Me is not worthy of Me.
39 "[a]He who has found his [1]life
shall lose it, and he who has lost his
life for My sake shall find it.
40 "[a]He who receives you receives
Me, and [b]he who receives Me receives Him who sent Me.
41 "He who receives a prophet in
the name of a prophet shall receive
a prophet's reward; and he who receives a righteous man in the name
of a righteous man shall receive a
righteous man's reward.
42 "And [a]whoever in the name of a
disciple gives to one of these little
ones even a cup of cold water to
drink, truly I say to you he shall not
lose his reward."

CHAPTER 11

John's Questions

[a]AND it came about that when Jesus had finished giving instructions
to His twelve disciples, He departed
from there [b]to teach and preach in
their cities.
2 [a]Now when [b]John in prison
heard of the works of Christ, he sent
word by his disciples,
3 and said to Him, "Are You [a]the
Coming One, or shall we look for
someone else?"

29 [1]Gr., *assarion*, the smallest copper coin [a]Luke 12:6
30 [a]1 Sam. 14:45; 2 Sam. 14:11; 1 Kin. 1:52; Luke 21:18; Acts 27:34
31 [a]Matt. 12:12
32 [a]Luke 12:8; Rev. 3:5
33 [a]Mark 8:38; Luke 9:26; 2 Tim. 2:12
34 [a]Matt. 10:34, 35: *Luke 12:51-53*
35 [a]Mic. 7:6; Matt. 10:21
36 [a]Mic. 7:6; Matt. 10:21
37 [a]Luke 14:26
38 [a]Matt. 16:24; Mark 8:34; Luke 9:23; 14:27
39 [a]Matt. 16:25; Mark 8:35; Luke 9:24; 17:33; John 12:25
40 [a]Matt. 18:5; Luke 10:16; John 13:20; Gal. 4:14 [b]Mark 9:37; Luke 9:48; John 12:44
42 [a]Matt. 25:40; Mark 9:41
1 [a]Matt. 7:28 [b]Matt. 9:35
2 [a]Matt. 11:2-19: *Luke 7:18-35* [b]Matt. 14:3; Mark 6:17; Luke 9:7ff.
3 [a]Ps. 118:26; Matt. 11:10; John 6:14; 11:27; Heb. 10:37
5 [a]Is. 35:5f.; 61:1
6 [a]Matt. 5:29; 13:21, 57; 24:10; 26:31; Mark 6:3; John 6:61; 16:1
7 [a]Matt. 3:1
9 [a]Matt. 14:5; 21:26; Luke 1:76; 20:6
10 [a]Mal. 3:1; Mark 1:2
12 [a]Luke 16:16
13 [a]Luke 16:16
14 [a]Mal. 4:5; Matt. 17:10-13; Mark 9:11-13; Luke 1:17; John 1:21
15 [a]Matt. 13:9, 43; Mark 4:9, 23; Luke 8:8; 14:35; Rev. 2:7, 11, 17, 29; 3:6, 13, 22; 13:9
18 [a]Matt. 3:4 [b]Luke 1:15 [c]Matt. 9:34; John 7:20; 8:48f., 52; 10:20
19 [1]Or, *wine-drinker* [2]Or, *publicans* who collected Roman taxes for profit [3]Lit., *And* [a]Matt. 9:11; Luke 15:2

4 And Jesus answered and said to
them, "Go and report to John the
things which you hear and see:
5 [a]*the* BLIND RECEIVE SIGHT and
the lame walk, *the* lepers are
cleansed and *the* deaf hear, and *the*
dead are raised up, and *the* POOR
HAVE THE GOSPEL PREACHED to
them.
6 "And blessed is he who [a]keeps
from stumbling over Me."

Jesus' Tribute to John

7 And as these were going *away*,
Jesus began to say to the multitudes
concerning John, "What did you go
out into [a]the wilderness to look at?
A reed shaken by the wind?
8 "But what did you go out to see?
A man dressed in soft *clothing*? Behold, those who wear soft *clothing*
are in kings' palaces.
9 "But why did you go out? To see
[a]a prophet? Yes, I tell you, and one
who is more than a prophet.
10 "This is the one about whom it
was written,

'[a]BEHOLD, I SEND MY MESSEN-
GER BEFORE YOUR FACE,
WHO WILL PREPARE YOUR WAY
BEFORE YOU.'

11 "Truly, I say to you, among
those born of women there has not
arisen *anyone* greater than John the
Baptist; yet he who is least in the
kingdom of heaven is greater than
he.
12 "And [a]from the days of John the
Baptist until now the kingdom of
heaven suffers violence, and violent
men take it by force.
13 "For [a]all the prophets and the
Law prophesied until John.
14 "And if you care to accept *it*, he
himself is [a]Elijah, who was to come.
15 "[a]He who has ears to hear, let
him hear.
16 "But to what shall I compare this
generation? It is like children sitting
in the market places, who call out to
the other *children*,
17 and say, 'We played the flute
for you, and you did not dance; we
sang a dirge, and you did not
mourn.'
18 "For John came neither [a]eating
nor [b]drinking, and they say, '[c]He has
a demon!'
19 "The Son of Man came eating
and drinking, and they say, 'Behold,
a gluttonous man and a [1]drunkard,
[a]a friend of [2]tax-gatherers and sinners!' [3]Yet wisdom is vindicated by
her deeds."

The Unrepenting Cities

20 Then He began to reproach the
cities in which most of His miracles
were done, because they did not repent.
21 "[a]Woe to you, Chorazin! Woe to
you, [b]Bethsaida! For if the miracles
had occurred in [c]Tyre and [c]Sidon
which occurred in you, they would
have repented long ago in [d]sack-
cloth and ashes.
22 "Nevertheless I say to you, [a]it
shall be more tolerable for Tyre and
Sidon in [b]*the* day of judgment, than
for you.
23 "And you, [a]Capernaum, will not
be exalted to heaven, will you? You
shall [b]descend to [c]Hades; for if the
miracles had occurred in [d]Sodom
which occurred in you, it would
have remained to this day.
24 "Nevertheless I say to you that
[a]it shall be more tolerable for the
land of [b]Sodom in [b]*the* day of judgment, than for you."

Come to Me

25 **[a]At that time Jesus [b]answered**
and said, "I praise Thee, O [c]Father,
Lord of heaven and earth, that
[d]Thou didst hide these things from
the wise and intelligent and didst reveal them to babes.
26 "Yes, [a]Father, for thus it was
well-pleasing in Thy sight.
27 "[a]All things have been handed
over to Me by My Father; and no
one knows the Son, except the Father; nor does anyone know the Father, [b]except the Son, and anyone to
whom the Son wills to reveal *Him.*
28 "[a]Come to Me, all who are weary
and heavy-laden, and I will give you
rest.
29 "Take My yoke upon you, and
[a]learn from Me, for I am gentle and
humble in heart; and [b]YOU SHALL
FIND REST FOR YOUR SOULS.
30 "For My yoke is easy, and My
load is light."

CHAPTER 12

Sabbath Questions

[a]
AT that time Jesus went on the
Sabbath through the grainfields,
and His disciples became hungry
and began to [b]pick the heads *of*
grain and eat.
2 But when the Pharisees saw it,
they said to Him, "Behold, Your disciples do what [a]is not lawful to do
on a Sabbath."
3 But He said to them, "Have you
not read what David did, when he
became hungry, he and his companions;
4 how he entered the house of
God, and [a]they ate the consecrated
bread, which was not lawful for him
to eat, nor for those with him, but
for the priests alone?
5 "Or have you not read in the
Law, that on the Sabbath the priests
in the temple break the Sabbath,
and are innocent?
6 "But I say to you, that something
[a]greater than the temple is here.
7 "But if you had known what this
means, '[a]I DESIRE COMPASSION, AND
NOT A SACRIFICE,' you would not
have condemned the innocent.

Lord of the Sabbath

8 "For [a]the Son of Man is Lord of
the Sabbath."
9 [a]And departing from there, He
went into their synagogue.
10 And behold, *there was* a man
with a withered hand. And they
questioned Him, saying, "[a]Is it lawful to heal on the Sabbath?"—in order that they might accuse Him.
11 And He said to them, "What
man shall there be among you, who
shall have one sheep, and if it falls
into a pit on the Sabbath, will he not
take hold of it, and lift it out?
12 "Of [a]how much more value then
is a man than a sheep! So then, it is
lawful to do good on the Sabbath."
13 Then He *said to the man,
"Stretch out your hand!" And he
stretched it out, and it was restored
to [1]normal, like the other.
14 But the Pharisees went out, and
[a]counseled together against Him, *as*
to how they might destroy Him.
15 But Jesus, aware of *this,* withdrew from there. And many followed Him, and [a]He healed them all,
16 and [a]warned them not to make
Him known,
17 in order that what was spoken
through Isaiah the prophet, might
be fulfilled, saying,
18 "[a]BEHOLD, MY SERVANT WHOM
I HAVE CHOSEN;
[b]MY BELOVED IN WHOM MY
SOUL IS WELL-PLEASED;
[c]I WILL PUT MY SPIRIT UPON
HIM,
[a]AND HE SHALL PROCLAIM JUS-
TICE TO THE GENTILES.
19 "[a]HE WILL NOT QUARREL, NOR
CRY OUT;
NOR WILL ANY ONE HEAR HIS
VOICE IN THE STREETS.
20 "[a]A BATTERED REED HE WILL
NOT BREAK OFF,

21 [a]Matt. 11:21-23: *Luke 10:13-15* [b]Mark 6:45; 8:22; Luke 9:10; John 1:44; 12:21 [c]Matt. 11:22; 15:21; Mark 3:8; 7:24, 31; Luke 4:26; 6:17; Acts 12:20; 27:3 [d]Rev. 11:3
22 [a]Matt. 10:15; 11:24 [b]Matt. 10:15
23 [a]Matt. 4:13 [b]Is. 14:13, 15; Ezek. 26:20; 31:14; 32:18, 24 [c]Matt. 16:18; Luke 10:15; 16:23; Acts 2:27, 31; Rev. 1:18; 6:8; 20:13f. [d]Matt. 10:15
24 [a]Matt. 10:15; 11:22 [b]Matt. 10:15
25 [a]Matt. 11:25-27: *Luke 10:21, 22* [b]Acts 3:12 [c]Luke 22:42; 23:34; John 11:41; 12:27, 28 [d]1 Cor. 1:26ff.
26 [a]Luke 22:42; 23:34; John 11:41; 12:27, 28
27 [a]Matt. 28:18; John 3:35; 13:3; 17:2 [b]John 7:29; 10:15; 17:25
28 [a]Jer. 31:25; John 7:37
29 [a]John 13:15; Eph. 4:20; Phil. 2:5; 1 Pet. 2:21; 1 John 2:6 [b]Jer. 6:16
1 [a]Matt. 12:1-8: *Mark 2:23-28; Luke 6:1-5* [b]Deut. 23:25
2 [a]Matt. 12:10; Luke 13:14; 14:3; John 5:10; 7:23; 9:16
4 [a]1 Sam. 21:6
6 [a]Matt. 12:41, 42
7 [a]Hos. 6:6
8 [a]Matt. 8:20; 12:32, 40
9 [a]Matt. 12:9-14: *Mark 3:1-6; Luke 6:6-11*
10 [a]Matt. 12:2; Luke 13:14; 14:3; John 5:10; 7:23
12 [a]Matt. 10:31
13 [1]Lit., *health*
14 [a]Matt. 26:4; Mark 14:1; Luke 22:2; John 7:30, 44; 8:59; 10:31, 39; 11:53
15 [a]Matt. 4:23
16 [a]Matt. 8:4
18 [a]Is. 42:1 [b]Matt. 3:17; 17:5 [c]Luke 4:18; John 3:34
19 [a]Is. 42:2
20 [a]Is. 42:3

And a smoldering wick He will not put out,
Until He [1]leads [2]justice to victory.

21 "[a]And in His name the Gentiles will hope."

The Pharisees Rebuked

22 [a]Then there was brought to Him a [b]demon-possessed man *who was* blind and dumb, and He healed him, so that the dumb man spoke and saw.

23 And all the multitudes were amazed, and *began* to say, "This *man* cannot be the [a]Son of David, can he?"

24 But when the Pharisees heard it, they said, "This man casts out demons only [a]by [1]Beelzebul the ruler of the demons."

25 [a]And [b]knowing their thoughts He said to them, "Any kingdom divided against itself is laid waste; and any city or house divided against itself shall not stand.

26 "And if [a]Satan casts out [a]Satan, he is divided against himself; how then shall his kingdom stand?

27 "And if I [a]by [1]Beelzebul cast out demons, [b]by whom do your sons cast them out? Consequently they shall be your judges.

28 "But if I cast out demons by the Spirit of God, then the kingdom of God has come upon you.

29 "Or how can anyone enter the strong man's house and carry off his property, unless he first binds the strong *man*? And then he will plunder his house.

The Unpardonable Sin

30 "[a]He who is not with Me is against Me; and he who does not gather with Me scatters.

31 "[a]Therefore I say to you, any sin and blasphemy shall be forgiven men, but blasphemy against the Spirit shall not be forgiven.

32 "And whoever shall speak a word against the Son of Man, it shall be forgiven him; but whoever shall speak against the Holy Spirit, it shall not be forgiven him, either in [a]this age, or in the *age* to come.

Words Reveal Character

33 "Either make the tree good, and its fruit good; or make the tree rotten, and its fruit rotten; for [a]the tree is known by its fruit.

34 "[a]You brood of vipers, how can you, being evil, speak what is good? [b]For the mouth speaks out of that which fills the heart.

35 "The good man out of *his* good treasure brings forth [1]what is good; and the evil man out of *his* evil treasure brings forth [2]what is evil.

36 "And I say to you, that every [1]careless word that men shall speak, they shall render account for it in [a]the day of judgment.

37 "For by your words you shall be justified, and by your words you shall be condemned."

The Desire for Signs

38 Then some of the scribes and Pharisees answered Him, saying, "Teacher, [a]we want to see a [1]sign from You."

39 But He answered and said to them, "[a]An evil and adulterous generation craves for a sign; and *yet* no sign shall be given to it but the sign of Jonah the prophet;

40 for just as [a]Jonah was three days and three nights in the belly of the sea monster, so shall [b]the Son of Man be [c]three days and three nights in the heart of the earth.

41 "[a]The men of Nineveh shall stand up with this generation at the judgment, and shall condemn it because [b]they repented at the preaching of Jonah; and behold, [c]something greater than Jonah is here.

42 "[a]*The* Queen of *the* South shall rise up with this generation at the judgment and shall condemn it, because she came from the ends of the earth to hear the wisdom of Solomon; and behold, [b]something greater than Solomon is here.

43 "[a]Now when the unclean spirit goes out of a man, it passes through waterless places, seeking rest, and does not find *it*.

44 "Then it says, 'I will return to my house from which I came'; and when it comes, it finds it unoccupied, swept, and put in order.

45 "Then it goes, and takes along with it seven other spirits more wicked than itself, and they go in and live there; and [a]the last state of that man becomes worse than the first. That is the way it will also be with this evil generation."

Changed Relationships

46 [a]While He was still speaking to the multitudes, behold, His [b]mother and His [c]brothers were standing outside, seeking to speak to Him.

47 And someone said to Him, "Behold, Your mother and Your brothers are standing outside seeking to speak to You."

48 But He answered the one who was telling Him and said, "Who is

20 [1]Or, *puts forth* [2]Or, *judgment*
21 [a]Is. 42:4; Rom. 15:12
22 [a]Matt. 12:22, 24: *Luke 11:14, 15;* Matt. 9:32, 34 [b]Matt. 4:24
23 [a]Matt. 9:27
24 [1]Or, *Beezebul;* others read *Beelzebub* [a]Matt. 9:34
25 [a]Matt. 12:25-29: *Mark 3:23-27; Luke 11:17-22* [b]Matt. 9:4
26 [a]Matt. 4:10
27 [1]v. 24 [a]Matt. 9:34 [b]Acts 19:13
30 [a]Mark 9:40; Luke 9:50; 11:23
31 [a]Matt. 12:31, 32; Mark 3:28-30; Luke 12:10
32 [a]Matt. 13:22, 39; Mark 10:30; Luke 16:8; 18:30; 20:34, 35; Eph. 1:21; 1 Tim. 6:17; 2 Tim. 4:10; Titus 2:12; Heb. 6:5
33 [a]Matt. 7:16
34 [a]Matt. 3:7; 23:33 [b]1 Sam. 24:13; Matt. 12:34, 35; 15:18; Luke 6:45; Eph. 4:29; James 3:2-12
35 [1]Lit., *good things* [2]Lit., *evil things*
36 [1]Or, *useless* [a]Matt. 10:15
38 [1]Or, *attesting miracle* [a]Matt. 16:1; Mark 8:11, 12; Luke 11:16; John 2:18; 6:30; 1 Cor. 1:22
39 [a]Matt. 12:39-42: *Luke 11:29-32;* Matt. 16:4
40 [a]Jon. 1:17 [b]Matt. 8:20 [c]Matt. 16:21
41 [a]Jon. 1:2 [b]Jon. 3:5 [c]Matt. 12:6, 42
42 [a]1 Kin. 10:1; 2 Chr. 9:1 [b]Matt. 12:6, 41
43 [a]Matt. 12:43-45: *Luke 11:24-26*
45 [a]2 Pet. 2:20
46 [a]Matt. 12:46-50: *Mark 3:31-35; Luke 8:19-21* [b]Matt. 1:18; 2:11ff.; 13:55; Luke 1:43; 2:33f., 48, 51; John 2:1, 5, 12; 19:25f.; Acts 1:14 [c]Matt. 13:55; Mark 6:3; John 2:12; 7:3, 5, 10; Acts 1:14; 1 Cor. 9:5; Gal. 1:19

My mother and who are My brothers?"
49 And stretching out His hand
toward His disciples, He said, "Behold, My mother and My brothers!
50 "For whoever shall do the will of
My Father who is in heaven, he is
My brother and sister and mother."

CHAPTER 13

Jesus Teaches in Parables

ON that day Jesus went out of [a]the
house, and was sitting [b]by the sea.
2 And great multitudes gathered
about Him, so that [a]He got into a
boat and sat down, and the whole
multitude was standing on the
beach.
3 And He spoke many things to
them in [a]parables, saying, "Behold,
the sower went out to sow;
4 and as he sowed, some *seeds*
fell beside the road, and the birds
came and devoured them.
5 "And others fell upon the rocky
places, where they [1]did not have
much soil; and immediately they
sprang up, because they had no
depth of soil.
6 "But when the sun had risen,
they were scorched; and because
they had no root, they withered
away.
7 "And others fell [1]among the
thorns, and the thorns came up and
choked them out.
8 "And others fell on the good soil,
and *yielded a crop, some a [a]hun-
dredfold, some sixty, and some
thirty.
9 "[a]He who has ears, let him
hear."

An Explanation

10 And the disciples came and
said to Him, "Why do You speak to
them in parables?"
11 And He answered and said to
them, "[a]To you it has been granted
to know the mysteries of the kingdom of heaven, but to them it has
not been granted.
12 "[a]For whoever has, to him shall
more be given, and he shall have an
abundance; but whoever does not
have, even what he has shall be
taken away from him.
13 "Therefore I speak to them in
parables; because while [a]seeing
they do not see, and while hearing
they do not hear, nor do they understand.
14 "And [1]in their case the prophecy
of Isaiah is being fulfilled, which
says,

'[2][a]YOU WILL KEEP ON HEARING,
[3]BUT WILL NOT UNDERSTAND;
AND [4]YOU WILL KEEP ON SEE-
ING, BUT WILL NOT PERCEIVE;
15 [a]FOR THE HEART OF THIS PEO-
PLE HAS BECOME DULL,
AND WITH THEIR EARS THEY
SCARCELY HEAR,
AND THEY HAVE CLOSED THEIR
EYES
LEST THEY SHOULD SEE WITH
THEIR EYES,
AND HEAR WITH THEIR EARS,
AND UNDERSTAND WITH THEIR
HEART AND TURN AGAIN,
AND I SHOULD HEAL THEM.'
16 "[a]But blessed are your eyes, be-
cause they see; and your ears, be-
cause they hear.
17 "For truly I say to you, that
[a]many prophets and righteous men
desired to see what you see, and did
not see *it*; and to hear what you
hear, and did not hear *it*.

The Sower Explained

18 "[a]Hear then the parable of the
sower.
19 "When any one hears [a]the word
of the kingdom, and does not understand it, [b]the evil *one* comes and
snatches away what has been sown
in his heart. This is the one on whom
seed was sown beside the road.
20 "And the one on whom seed was
sown on the rocky places, this is the
man who hears the word, and immediately receives it with joy;
21 yet he has no *firm* root in himself, but is *only* temporary, and
when affliction or persecution arises
because of the word, immediately
he [1][a]falls away.
22 "And the one on whom seed was
sown among the thorns, this is the
man who hears the word, and the
worry of [a]the [1]world, and the [b]de-
ceitfulness of riches choke the
word, and it becomes unfruitful.
23 "And the one on whom seed was
sown on the good ground, this is the
man who hears the word and understands it; who indeed bears fruit,
and brings forth, some [a]a hundredfold, some sixty, and some thirty."

Tares Among Wheat

24 He presented another parable
to them, saying, "[a]The kingdom of
heaven [1]may be compared to [b]a
man who sowed good seed in his
field.
25 "But while men were sleeping,
his enemy came and sowed [1]tares
also among the wheat, and went
away.

1 [a]Matt. 9:28; 13:36; Mark 3:19 [b]Matt. 13:1-15: *Mark 4:1-12; Luke 8:4-10*
2 [a]Luke 5:3
3 [a]Matt. 13:10ff.; Mark 4:2ff.
5 [1]Lit., *were not having*
7 [1]Lit., *upon*
8 [a]Gen. 26:12; Matt. 13:23
9 [a]Matt. 11:15
11 [a]Matt. 19:11; 20:23; John 6:65; 1 Cor. 2:10; Col. 1:27; 1 John 2:20, 27
12 [a]Matt. 25:29; Mark 4:25; Luke 8:18; 19:26
13 [a]Deut. 29:4; Is. 42:19, 20; Jer. 5:21; Ezek. 12:2
14 [1]Lit., *for them* [2]Lit., *With a hearing you will hear* [3]Lit., *and* [4]Lit., *seeing you will see* [a]Is. 6:9; Mark 4:12; Luke 8:10; John 12:40; Acts 28:26, 27; Rom. 10:16; 11:8
15 [a]Is. 6:10
16 [a]Matt. 13:16, 17: *Luke 10:23, 24*
17 [a]John 8:56; Heb. 11:13; 1 Pet. 1:10-12
18 [a]Matt. 13:18-23: *Mark 4:13-20; Luke 8:11-15*
19 [a]Matt. 4:23 [b]Matt. 5:37
21 [1]Lit., *is caused to stumble* [a]Matt. 11:6
22 [1]Or, *age* [a]Matt. 12:32; 13:39; Mark 4:19; Rom. 12:2; 1 Cor. 1:20; 2:6, 8; 3:18; 2 Cor. 4:4; Gal. 1:4; Eph. 2:2 [b]Matt. 19:23; 1 Tim. 6:9, 10, 17
23 [a]Matt. 13:8
24 [1]Lit., *was compared to* [a]Matt. 13:31, 33, 45, 47; 18:23; 20:1; 22:2; 25:1; Mark 4:30; Luke 13:18, 20 [b]Mark 4:26-29
25 [1]Or, *darnel*, a weed resembling wheat

26 "But when the [1]wheat sprang up
and bore grain, then the tares became evident also.
27 "And the slaves of the landowner came and said to him, 'Sir,
did you not sow good seed in your
field? [1]How then does it have tares?'
28 "And he said to them, 'An [1]ene-
my has done this!' And the slaves
*said to him, 'Do you want us, then,
to go and gather them up?'
29 "But he *said, 'No; lest while you
are gathering up the tares, you may
root up the wheat with them.
30 'Allow both to grow together
until the harvest; and in the time of
the harvest I will say to the reapers,
"First gather up the tares and bind
them in bundles to burn them up;
but [a]gather the wheat into my
barn." ' "

The Mustard Seed

31 He presented another parable
to them, saying, "[a]The kingdom of
heaven is like [b]a mustard seed,
which a man took and sowed in his
field;
32 and this is smaller than all *other*
seeds; but when it is full grown, it is
larger than the garden plants, and
becomes a tree, so that [a]THE BIRDS
OF THE [1]AIR come and NEST IN ITS
BRANCHES."

The Leaven

33 He spoke another parable to
them, "[a]The kingdom of heaven is
like leaven, which a woman took,
and hid in [b]three [1]pecks of meal, until it was all leavened."
34 All these things Jesus spoke to
the multitudes in parables, and He
was not talking to them [a]without a
parable,
35 so that what was spoken
through the prophet might be fulfilled, saying,

"[a]I WILL OPEN MY MOUTH IN
PARABLES;
I WILL UTTER THINGS HIDDEN
SINCE THE FOUNDATION OF
THE WORLD."

The Tares Explained

36 Then He left the multitudes,
and went into [a]the house. And His
disciples came to Him, saying, "[b]Ex-
plain to us the parable of the [1]tares
of the field."
37 And He answered and said,
"The one who sows the good seed is
[a]the Son of Man,
38 and the field is the world; and
as for the good seed, these are [a]the
sons of the kingdom; and the tares
are [b]the sons of [c]the evil *one;*

39 and the enemy who sowed
them is the devil, and the harvest is
[a]the [1]end of the age; and the reapers
are angels.
40 "Therefore just as the tares are
gathered up and burned with fire, so
shall it be at [a]the [1]end of the age.
41 "[a]The Son of Man [b]will send
forth His angels, and they will
gather out of His kingdom all
[1c]STUMBLING BLOCKS, AND THOSE
WHO COMMIT LAWLESSNESS,
42 and [a]will cast them into the furnace of fire; in that place [b]there shall
be weeping and gnashing of teeth.
43 "[a]Then THE RIGHTEOUS WILL
SHINE FORTH AS THE SUN in the kingdom of their Father. [b]He who has
ears, let him hear.

Hidden Treasure

44 "[a]The kingdom of heaven is like
a treasure hidden in the field, which
a man found and hid; and from joy
over it he goes and [b]sells all that he
has, and buys that field.

A Costly Pearl

45 "Again, [a]the kingdom of heaven
is like a merchant seeking fine
pearls,
46 and upon finding one pearl of
great value, he went and sold all
that he had, and bought it.

A Dragnet

47 "Again, [a]the kingdom of heaven
is like a dragnet cast into the sea,
and gathering *fish* of every kind;
48 and when it was filled, they
drew it up on the beach; and they sat
down, and gathered the good *fish*
into containers, but the bad they
threw away.
49 "So it will be at [a]the [1]end of the
age; the angels shall come forth, and
[2]take out the wicked from among
the righteous,
50 and [a]will cast them into the furnace of fire; [b]there shall be weeping
and gnashing of teeth.
51 "Have you understood all these
things?" They *said to Him, "Yes."
52 And He said to them, "Therefore every scribe who has become a
disciple of the kingdom of heaven is
like a head of a household, who
brings forth out of his treasure
things new and old."

Jesus Revisits Nazareth

53 [a]And it came about that when
Jesus had finished these parables,
He departed from there.
54 [a]And coming to [1]His hometown
He [2b]*began* teaching them in their
synagogue, so that [c]they became as-

26 [1]Lit., *grass*
27 [1]Lit., *From where*
28 [1]Lit., *enemy man*
30 [a]Matt. 3:12
31 [a]Matt. 13:31, 32: *Mark 4:30-32; Luke 13:18, 19;* Matt. 13:24 [b]Matt. 17:20; Luke 17:6
32 [1]Or, *sky* [a]Ps. 104:12; Ezek. 17:23; 31:6; Dan. 4:12
33 [1]Gr., *sata* [a]Matt. 13:33: *Luke 13:21;* Matt. 13:24 [b]Gen. 18:6; Judg. 6:19; 1 Sam. 1:24
34 [a]Mark 4:34; John 10:6; 16:25
35 [a]Ps. 78:2
36 [1]Or, *darnel* cf. v. 25 [a]Matt. 13:1 [b]Matt. 15:15
37 [a]Matt. 8:20
38 [a]Matt. 8:12 [b]John 8:44; Acts 13:10; 1 John 3:10 [c]Matt. 5:37
39 [1]Or, *consummation* [a]Matt. 12:32; 13:22, 40, 49; 24:3, 28:20, 1 Cor. 10:11; Heb. 9:26
40 [1]Or, *consummation* [a]Matt. 12:32; 13:22, 39, 49; 24:3; 28:20; 1 Cor. 10:11; Heb. 9:26
41 [1]Or, *everything that is offensive* [a]Matt. 8:20 [b]Matt. 24:31 [c]Zeph. 1:3
42 [a]Matt. 13:50 [b]Matt. 8:12
43 [a]Dan. 12:3 [b]Matt. 11:15
44 [a]Matt. 13:24 [b]Matt. 13:46
45 [a]Matt. 13:24
47 [a]Matt. 13:44
49 [1]Or, *consummation* [2]Or, *separate* [a]Matt. 13:39, 40
50 [a]Matt. 13:42 [b]Matt. 8:12
53 [a]Matt. 7:28
54 [1]Or, *His own part of the country* [2]Or, *was teaching* [a]Matt. 13:54-58: *Mark 6:1-6* [b]Matt. 4:23 [c]Matt. 7:28

tonished, and said, "Where *did* this
man *get* this wisdom, and *these* [3]mi-
raculous powers?
55"Is not this the carpenter's son?
Is not [a]His mother called Mary, and
His [a]brothers, James and Joseph
and Simon and Judas?
56"And [a]His sisters, are they not
all with us? Where then *did* this man
get all these things?"
57 And they took [a]offense at Him.
But Jesus said to them, "[b]A prophet
is not without honor except in his
home town, and in his *own* household."
58 And He did not do many miracles there because of their unbelief.

CHAPTER 14

John the Baptist Beheaded

[a]AT that time [b]Herod the tetrarch
heard the news about Jesus,
2 and said to his servants, "[a]This
is John the Baptist; he has risen
from the dead; and that is why mi-
raculous powers are at work in
him."
3 For [a]Herod had seized John,
and bound him, and put him [b]in
prison on account of [c]Herodias, the
wife of his brother Philip.
4 For John had been saying to
him, "[a]It is not lawful for you to
have her."
5 And although he wanted to put
him to death, he feared the multitude, because they regarded him as
[a]a prophet.
6 But when Herod's birthday
came, the daughter of [a]Herodias
danced before *them* and pleased
[b]Herod.
7 Thereupon he promised with an
oath to give her whatever she asked.
8 And having been prompted by
her mother, she *said, "Give me
here on a platter the head of John
the Baptist."
9 And although he was grieved,
the king commanded *it* to be given
because of his oaths, and because of
his dinner guests.
10 And he sent and had John beheaded in the prison.
11 And his head was brought on a
platter and given to the girl; and she
brought *it* to her mother.
12 And his disciples came and
took away the body and buried it;
and they went and reported to Jesus.

Five Thousand Fed

13 [a]Now when Jesus heard *it*, He
withdrew from there in a boat, to a
lonely place by Himself; and when
the multitudes heard *of this*, they
followed Him on foot from the
cities.
14 And when He came out, He
[a]saw a great multitude, and felt
compassion for them, and [b]healed
their sick.
15 And when it was evening, the
disciples came to Him, saying, "The
place is desolate, and the time is already past; so send the multitudes
away, that they may go into the villages and buy food for themselves."
16 But Jesus said to them, "They
do not need to go away; you give
them *something* to eat!"
17 And they *said to Him, "We
have here only [a]five loaves and two
fish."
18 And He said, "Bring them here
to Me."
19 And ordering the multitudes to
recline on the grass, He took the five
loaves and the two fish, and looking
up toward heaven, He [a]blessed *the
food*, and breaking the loaves He
gave them to the disciples, and the
disciples *gave* to the multitudes,
20 and they all ate, and were satisfied. And they picked up what was
left over of the broken pieces,
twelve full [a]baskets.
21 And there were about five thousand men who ate, aside from
women and children.

Jesus Walks on the Water

22 [a]And immediately He made the
disciples get into the boat, and go
ahead of Him to the other side,
while He sent the multitudes away.
23 And after He had sent the multitudes away, [a]He went up to the
mountain by Himself to pray; and
when it was evening, He was there
alone.
24 But the boat was already many
[1]stadia away from the land, battered by the waves; for the wind was
contrary.
25 And in [a]the [1]fourth watch of the
night He came to them, walking
upon the sea.
26 And when the disciples saw
Him walking on the sea, they were
frightened, saying, "It is [a]a ghost!"
And they cried out for fear.
27 But immediately Jesus spoke to
them, saying, "[a]Take courage, it is I;
[b]do not be afraid."
28 And Peter answered Him and
said, "Lord, if it is You, command
me to come to You on the water."
29 And He said, "Come!" And Peter got out of the boat, and walked

54 [3]Or, *miracles*
55 [a]Matt. 12:46
56 [a]Mark 6:3
57 [a]Matt. 11:6 [b]Mark 6:4; Luke 4:24; John 4:44
1 [a]Matt. 14:1-12: *Mark 6:14-29;* Matt. 14:1, 2: *Luke 9:7-9* [b]Mark 8:15; Luke 3:1, 19; 8:3; 13:31; 23:7f., 11f., 15; Acts 4:27; 12:1
2 [a]Matt. 16:14; Mark 6:14; Luke 9:7
3 [a]Matt. 14:1-12: *Mark 6:14-29; Matt. 14:1, 2; Luke 9:7-9;* Mark 8:15; Luke 3:1, 19; 8:3; 13:31; 23:7f., 11f., 15; Acts 4:27; 12:1 [b]Matt. 4:12; 11:2 [c]Matt. 14:6; Mark 6:17, 19, 22; Luke 3:19
4 [a]Lev. 18:16; 20:21
5 [a]Matt. 11:9
6 [a]Matt. 14:3; Mark 6:17, 19, 22; Luke 3:19 [b]Matt. 14:1-12: *Mark 6:14-29;* Matt. 14:1, 2: *Luke 9:7-9;* Mark 8:15; Luke 3:1, 19; 8:3; 13:31; 23:7f., 11f., 15; Acts 4:27; 12:1
13 [a]Matt. 14:13-21: *Mark 6:32-44; Luke 9:10-17; John 6:1-13;* Matt. 15:32-38
14 [a]Matt. 9:36 [b]Matt. 4:23
17 [a]Matt. 16:9
19 [a]1 Sam. 9:13; Matt. 15:36; 26:26; Mark 6:41; 8:7; 14:22; Luke 24:30; Acts 27:35; Rom. 14:6
20 [a]Matt. 16:9; Mark 6:43; 8:19; Luke 9:17; John 6:13
22 [a]Matt. 14:22-33: *Mark 6:45-51; John 6:15-21*
23 [a]Mark 6:46; Luke 6:12; 9:28; John 6:15
24 [1]A stadion was about 600 feet
25 [1]I.e., 3-6 a.m. [a]Matt. 24:43; Mark 13:35
26 [a]Luke 24:37
27 [a]Matt. 9:2 [b]Matt. 17:7; 28:5, 10; Mark 6:50; Luke 1:13; 30; 2:10; 5:10; 12:32; John 6:20; Rev. 1:17

on the water and came toward Jesus.

30 But seeing the wind, he became afraid, and beginning to sink, he cried out, saying, "Lord, save me!"

31 And immediately Jesus stretched out His hand and took hold of him, and *said to him, "[a]O you of little faith, why did you doubt?"

32 And when they got into the boat, the wind stopped.

33 And those who were in the boat worshiped Him, saying, "You are certainly [a]God's Son!"

34 [a]And when they had crossed over, they came to [1]land at [b]Gennesaret.

35 And when the men of that place [1]recognized Him, they sent into all that surrounding district and brought to Him all who were ill;

36 and they *began* to entreat Him that they might just touch [a]the fringe of His cloak; and as many as [b]touched *it* were cured.

CHAPTER 15

Tradition and Commandment

[a]THEN some Pharisees and scribes *came to Jesus [b]from Jerusalem, saying,

2 "Why do Your disciples transgress the tradition of the elders? For they [a]do not wash their hands when they eat bread."

3 And He answered and said to them, "And why do [1]you yourselves transgress the commandment of God for the sake of your tradition?

4 "For God said, '[a]HONOR YOUR FATHER AND MOTHER,' and, '[b]HE WHO SPEAKS EVIL OF FATHER OR MOTHER, LET HIM [1]BE PUT TO DEATH.'

5 "But you say, 'Whoever shall say to *his* father or mother, "Anything of mine you might have been helped by has been [1]given *to God*,"

6 he is not to honor his father [1]or his mother[2].' And *thus* you invalidated the [3]word of God for the sake of your tradition.

7 "You hypocrites, rightly did Isaiah prophesy of you, saying,

8 '[a]THIS PEOPLE HONORS ME WITH THEIR LIPS,
BUT THEIR HEART IS FAR AWAY FROM ME.

9 [a]BUT IN VAIN DO THEY WORSHIP ME,
TEACHING AS THEIR [b]DOCTRINES THE PRECEPTS OF MEN.' "

10 And He called to Himself the multitude, and said to them, "Hear, and understand.

11 "[a]Not what enters into the mouth defiles the man, but what proceeds out of the mouth, this defiles the man."

12 Then the disciples *came and *said to Him, "Do You know that the Pharisees were [1]offended when they heard this statement?"

13 But He answered and said, "[a]Every plant which My heavenly Father did not plant shall be rooted up.

14 "Let them alone; [a]they are blind guides [1]of the blind. And [b]if a blind man guides a blind man, both will fall into a pit."

The Heart of Man

15 And Peter answered and said to Him, "[a]Explain the parable to us."

16 And He said, "Are you also still without understanding?

17 "Do you not understand that everything that goes into the mouth passes into the [1]stomach, and is [2]eliminated?

18 "But [a]the things that proceed out of the mouth come from the heart, and those defile the man.

19 "[a]For out of the heart come evil thoughts, murders, adulteries, [1]fornications, thefts, false witness, slanders.

20 "These are the things which defile the man; but to eat with unwashed hands does not defile the man."

The Syrophoenician Woman

21 [a]And Jesus went away from there, and withdrew into the district of [b]Tyre and [b]Sidon.

22 And behold, a Canaanite woman came out from that region, and *began* to cry out, saying, "Have mercy on me, O Lord, [a]Son of David; my daughter is cruelly [b]demon-possessed."

23 But He did not answer her a word. And His disciples came to *Him* and kept asking Him, saying, "Send her away, for she is shouting out after us."

24 But He answered and said, "I was sent only to [a]the lost sheep of the house of Israel."

25 But she came and [a]*began* [1]to bow down before Him, saying, "Lord, help me!"

26 And He answered and said, "It is not [1]good to take the children's bread and throw *it* to the dogs."

27 But she said, "Yes, Lord; [1]but even the dogs feed on the crumbs

---

31 [a]Matt. 6:30; 8:26; 16:8
33 [a]Matt. 4:3
34 [1]Lit., *the land* [a]Matt. 14:34-36: *Mark 6:53-56;* John 6:24, 25 [b]Mark 6:53; Luke 5:1
35 [1]Or, *knew*
36 [a]Matt. 9:20 [b]Matt. 9:21; Mark 3:10; 6:56; 8:22; Luke 6:19
1 [a]Matt. 15:1-20: *Mark 7:1-23* [b]Mark 3:22; 7:1; John 1:19; Acts 25:7
2 [a]Luke 11:38
3 [1]Or, *you also*
4 [1]Lit., *die the death* [a]Ex. 20:12; Deut. 5:16 [b]Ex. 21:17; Lev. 20:9
5 [1]Or, *a gift, an offering*
6 [1]Many mss. do not contain, *or his mother* [2]I.e., by supporting them with it [3]Some mss. read, *law*
8 [a]Is. 29:13
9 [a]Is. 29:13 [b]Col. 2:22
11 [a]Matt. 15:18; Acts 10:14, 15; 1 Tim. 4:3
12 [1]Lit., *caused to stumble*
13 [a]Is. 60:21; 61:3; John 15:2; 1 Cor. 3:9
14 [1]Some mss. do not contain *of the blind* [a]Matt. 23:16, 24 [b]Luke 6:39
15 [a]Matt. 13:36
17 [1]Lit., *belly* [2]Lit., *cast out into the latrine*
18 [a]Matt. 12:34; Mark 7:20
19 [1]I.e., sexual immorality [a]Gal. 5:19ff.
21 [a]Matt. 15:21-28: *Mark 7:24-30* [b]Matt. 11:21
22 [a]Matt. 9:27 [b]Matt. 4:24
24 [a]Matt. 10:6
25 [1]Or, *to worship* [a]Matt. 8:2
26 [1]Or, *proper*
27 [1]Lit., *for*

which fall from their master's table."

28 Then Jesus answered and said to her, "O woman, [a]your faith is great; be it done for you as you wish." And her daughter was healed [1]at once.

Healing Multitudes

29 [a]And departing from there, Jesus went along by [b]the Sea of Galilee, and having gone up to the mountain, He was sitting there.

30 And great multitudes came to Him, bringing with them *those who were* lame, crippled, blind, dumb, and many others, and they laid them down at His feet; and [a]He healed them,

31 so that the multitude marveled as they saw the dumb speaking, the crippled restored, and the lame walking, and the blind seeing; and they [a]glorified the God of Israel.

Four Thousand Fed

32 [a]And Jesus summoned to Himself His disciples, and said, "[b]I feel compassion for the multitude, because they have remained with Me now for three days and have nothing to eat; and I do not wish to send them away hungry, lest they faint on the way."

33 And the disciples *said to Him, "Where would we get so many loaves in a desert place to satisfy such a great multitude?"

34 And Jesus *said to them, "How many loaves do you have?" And they said, "Seven, and a few small fish."

35 And He directed the multitude to [1]sit down on the ground;

36 and He took the seven loaves and the fish; and [a]giving thanks, He broke *them* and started giving *them* to the disciples, and the disciples *in turn*, to the multitudes.

37 And they all ate, and were satisfied, and they picked up what was left over of the broken pieces, seven large [a]baskets full.

38 And those who ate were four thousand men, besides women and children.

39 And dismissing the multitudes, He got into [a]the boat, and came to the region of [b]Magadan.

Chapter 16

Pharisees Test Jesus

[a]AND the [b]Pharisees and Sadducees came up, and testing Him [c]asked Him to show them a sign from heaven.

2 [1]But He answered and said to them, "[a]When it is evening, you say, '*It will be* fair weather, for the sky is red.'

3 "And in the morning, '*There will be* a storm today, for the sky is red and threatening.' Do you know how to discern the [1]appearance of the sky, but cannot *discern* the signs of the times?

4 "[a]An evil and adulterous generation seeks after a sign; and a sign will not be given it, except the sign of Jonah." And He left them, and went away.

5 And the disciples came to the other side and had forgotten to take bread.

6 And Jesus said to them, "Watch out and [a]beware of the [1]leaven of the [b]Pharisees and Sadducees."

7 And they began to discuss among themselves, saying, "*It is* because we took no bread."

8 But Jesus, aware of this, said, "[a]You men of little faith, why do you discuss among yourselves because you have no bread?

9 "Do you not yet understand or remember [a]the five loaves of the five thousand, and how many [b]baskets you took up?

10 "Or [a]the seven loaves of the four thousand, and how many large [b]baskets you took up?

11 "How is it that you do not understand that I did not speak to you concerning bread? But [a]beware of the [1]leaven of the [b]Pharisees and Sadducees."

12 Then they understood that He did not say to beware of the leaven of bread, but of the teaching of the [a]Pharisees and Sadducees.

Peter's Confession of Christ

13 [a]Now when Jesus came into the district of [b]Caesarea Philippi, He *began* asking His disciples, saying, "Who do people say that [c]the Son of Man is?"

14 And they said, "Some *say* [a]John the Baptist; some, [1b]Elijah; and others, [2]Jeremiah, or one of the prophets."

15 He *said to them, "But who do you say that I am?"

16 And Simon Peter answered and said, "Thou art [1a]the Christ, [b]the Son of [c]the living God."

17 And Jesus answered and said to him, "Blessed are you, [a]Simon [1]Barjona, because [b]flesh and blood

---

28 [1]Lit., *from that hour* [a]Matt. 9:22
29 [a]Matt. 15:29-31; Mark 7:31-37 [b]Matt. 4:18
30 [a]Matt. 4:23
31 [a]Matt. 9:8
32 [a]Matt. 15:32-39: *Mark 8:1-10;* Matt. 14:13-21 [b]Matt. 9:36
35 [1]Lit., *recline*
36 [a]Matt. 14:19
37 [a]Matt. 16:10; Mark 8:8, 20; Acts 9:25
39 [a]Mark 3:9 [b]Mark 8:10
1 [a]Matt. 16:1-12: *Mark 8:11-21* [b]Matt. 3:7; 16:6, 11, 12 [c]Matt. 12:38
2 [1]The earliest mss. do not contain vs. 2 & 3 [a]Luke 12:54f.
3 [1]Lit., *face*
4 [a]Matt. 12:39
6 [1]Or, *yeast* [a]Matt. 16:11; Mark 8:15; Luke 12:1 [b]Matt. 3:7; 16:1, 11, 12
8 [a]Matt. 6:30; 8:26; 14:31
9 [a]Matt. 14:17-21 [b]Matt. 14:20
10 [a]Matt. 15:34-38 [b]Matt. 15:37
11 [1]Or, *yeast* [a]Matt. 16:6; Mark 8:15; Luke 12:1 [b]Matt. 3:7; 16:6, 12
12 [a]Matt. 3:7; 16:6, 11
13 [a]Matt. 16:13-16: *Mark 8:27-29; Luke 9:18-20* [b]Mark 8:27 [c]Matt. 8:20; 16:27, 28
14 [1]Gr., *Elias* [2]Gr., *Jeremias* [a]Matt. 14:2 [b]Matt. 17:10; Mark 6:15; Luke 9:8; John 1:21
16 [1]I.e., the Messiah [a]Matt. 1:16; 16:20; John 11:27 [b]Matt. 4:3 [c]Ps. 42:2; Matt. 26:63; Acts 14:15; Rom. 9:26; 2 Cor. 3:3; 6:16; 1 Thess. 1:9; 1 Tim. 3:15; 4:10; Heb. 3:12; 9:14; 10:31; 12:22; Rev. 7:2
17 [1]I.e., son of Jonah [a]John 1:42; 21:15-17 [b]1 Cor. 15:50; Gal. 1:16; Eph. 6:12; Heb. 2:14

did not reveal *this* to you, but My
Father who is in heaven.
18 "And I also say to you that you
are [1a]Peter, and upon this [2]rock I
will build My church; and the gates
of [b]Hades shall not overpower it.
19 "I will give you [a]the keys of the
kingdom of heaven; and [b]whatever
you shall bind on earth shall have
been bound in heaven, and whatever you shall loose on earth shall
have been loosed in heaven."
20 [a]Then He warned the disciples
that they should tell no one that He
was [b]the Christ.

Jesus Foretells His Death

21 [a]From that time Jesus Christ
began to show His disciples that He
must go to Jerusalem, and [b]suffer
many things from the elders and
chief priests and scribes, and be
killed, and be raised up on the third
day.
22 And Peter took Him aside and
began to rebuke Him, saying, "God
forbid *it,* Lord! This shall never happen to You."
23 But He turned and said to Peter,
"Get behind Me, [a]Satan! You are a
stumbling block to Me; for you are
not setting your mind on God's interests, but man's."

Discipleship is Costly

24 Then Jesus said to His disciples, "If any one wishes to come after Me, let him deny himself, and
[a]take up his cross, and follow Me.
25 "For [a]whoever wishes to save
his life shall lose it; but whoever
loses his life for My sake shall find
it.
26 "For what will a man be profited,
if he gains the whole world, and forfeits his soul? Or what will a man
give in exchange for his soul?
27 "For the [a]Son of Man [b]is going to
come in the glory of His Father with
His angels; and [c]WILL THEN RECOM-
PENSE EVERY MAN ACCORDING TO HIS
DEEDS.
28 "Truly I say to you, there are
some of those who are standing here
who shall not taste death until they
see the [a]Son of Man [b]coming in His
kingdom."

Chapter 17

The Transfiguration

[a]AND six days later Jesus *took
with Him [b]Peter and James and
John his brother, and *brought
them up to a high mountain by
themselves.
2 And He was transfigured before them; and His face shone like
the sun, and His garments became
as white as light.
3 And behold, Moses and Elijah
appeared to them, talking with Him.
4 And Peter [a]answered and said
to Jesus, "Lord, it is good for us to
be here; if You wish, [b]I will make
three tabernacles here, one for You,
and one for Moses, and one for Elijah."
5 While he was still speaking, behold, a bright cloud overshadowed
them; and behold, [a]a voice out of the
cloud, saying, "[b]This is My beloved
Son, with whom I am well-pleased;
hear Him!"
6 And when the disciples heard
this, they fell on their faces and
were much afraid.
7 And Jesus came to *them* and
touched them and said, "Arise, and
[a]do not be afraid."
8 And lifting up their eyes, they
saw no one, except Jesus Himself
alone.
9 [a]And as they were coming
down from the mountain, Jesus
commanded them, saying, "[b]Tell
the vision to no one until [c]the Son of
Man has [d]risen from the dead."
10 And His disciples asked Him,
saying, "Why then do the scribes
say that [a]Elijah must come first?"
11 And He answered and said,
"Elijah is coming and will restore all
things;
12 but I say to you, that Elijah already came, and they did not recognize him, but did to him whatever
they wished. So also [a]the Son of
Man is going to suffer at their
hands."
13 Then the disciples understood
that He had spoken to them about
John the Baptist.

The Demoniac

14 [a]And when they came to the
multitude, a man came up to Him,
falling on his knees before Him, and
saying,
15 "Lord, have mercy on my son,
for he is a [a]lunatic, and is very ill; for
he often falls into the fire, and often
into the water.
16 "And I brought him to Your disciples, and they could not cure
him."
17 And Jesus answered and said,
"O unbelieving and perverted generation, how long shall I be with
you? How long shall I put up with
you? Bring him here to Me."
18 And Jesus rebuked him, and

18 [1]Gr., *Petros,* a stone [2]Gr., *petra,* large rock, bed-rock [a]Matt. 4:18 [b]Matt. 11:23
19 [a]Is. 22:22; Rev. 1:18; 3:7 [b]Matt. 18:18; John 20:23
20 [a]Matt. 8:4; Mark 8:30; Luke 9:21 [b]Matt. 1:16; 16:16; John 11:27
21 [a]Matt. 16:21-28: *Mark 8:31-9:1; Luke 9:22-27* [b]Matt. 12:40; 17:9, 12, 22f.; 20:18f.; 27:63; Mark 9:12, 31; Luke 17:25; 18:32; 24:7; John 2:19
23 [a]Matt. 4:10
24 [a]Matt. 10:38
25 [a]Matt. 10:39
27 [a]Matt. 8:20 [b]Matt. 10:23; 24:3, 27, 37, 39; 26:64; Mark 8:38; 13:26; Luke 21:27; John 21:22; Acts 1:11; 1 Cor. 15:23; 1 Thess. 1:10; 4:16; 2 Thess. 1:7, 10; 2:1, 8; James 5:7f.; 2 Pet. 1:16; 3:4, 12; 1 John 2:28; Rev. 1:7 [c]Ps. 62:12; Prov. 24:12; Rom. 2:6; 14:12; 1 Cor. 3:13; 2 Cor. 5:10; Eph. 6:8; Col. 3:25; Rev. 2:23; 20:12; 22:12
28 [a]Matt. 8:20 [b]Matt. 10:23; 24:3, 27, 37, 39; 26:64; Mark 8:38; 13:26; Luke 21:27; John 21:22; Acts 1:11; 1 Cor. 15:23; 1 Thess. 1:10; 4:16; 2 Thess. 1:7, 10; 2:1, 8; James 5:7f.; 2 Pet. 1:16; 3:4, 12; 1 John 2:28; Rev. 1:7
1 [a]Matt. 17:1-8: *Mark 9:2-8; Luke 9:28-36* [b]Matt. 26:37; Mark 5:37; 13:3
4 [a]Acts 3:12 [b]Mark 9:5; Luke 9:33
5 [a]2 Pet. 1:17f. [b]Matt. 3:17
7 [a]Matt. 14:27
9 [a]Matt. 17:9-13: *Mark 9:9-13* [b]Matt. 8:4 [c]Matt. 8:20; 17:12, 22 [d]Matt. 16:21
10 [a]Matt. 11:14; 16:14
12 [a]Matt. 8:20; 17:9, 22
14 [a]Matt. 17:14-19: *Mark 9:14-28;* Matt. 17:14-18: *Luke 9:37-42*
15 [a]Matt. 4:24

the demon came out of him, and the boy was cured at once.

19 Then the disciples came to Jesus privately and said, "Why could we not cast it out?"

20 And He *said to them, "Because of the littleness of your faith; for truly I say to you, [a]if you have faith as [b]a mustard seed, you shall say to [c]this mountain, 'Move from here to there,' and it shall move; and [d]nothing shall be impossible to you.

21 [[1a]"But this kind does not go out except by prayer and fasting."]

22 [a]And while they were gathering together in Galilee, Jesus said to them, "The Son of Man is going to be delivered into the hands of men;

23 and [a]they will kill Him, and He will be raised again on the third day." And they were deeply grieved.

The Tribute Money

24 And when they had come to Capernaum, those who collected [a]the [1]two-drachma *tax* came to Peter, and said, "Does your teacher not pay [a]the [1]two-drachma *tax*?"

25 He *said, "Yes." And when he came into the house, Jesus spoke to him first, saying, "What do you think, Simon? From whom do the kings of the earth collect [a]customs or [b]poll-tax, from their sons or from strangers?"

26 And upon his saying, "From strangers," Jesus said to him, "Consequently the sons are [1]exempt.

27 "But, lest we [a]give them offense, go to the sea, and throw in a hook, and take the first fish that comes up; and when you open its mouth, you will find a [1]stater. Take that and give it to them for you and Me."

Chapter 18

Rank in the Kingdom

[a]At that time the disciples came to Jesus, saying, "Who then is greatest in the kingdom of heaven?"

2 And He called a child to Himself and stood him in their midst,

3 and said, "Truly I say to you, unless you are converted and [a]become like children, you shall not enter the kingdom of heaven.

4 "Whoever then humbles himself as this child, he is the greatest in the kingdom of heaven.

5 "And whoever receives one such child in My name receives Me;

6 but [a]whoever [b]causes one of these little ones who believe in Me to stumble, it is better for him that a heavy millstone be hung around his neck, and that he be drowned in the depth of the sea.

Stumbling Blocks

7 "Woe to the world because of *its* stumbling blocks! For [a]it is inevitable that stumbling blocks come; but woe to that man through whom the stumbling block comes!

8 "And [a]if your hand or your foot [b]causes you to stumble, cut it off and throw it from you; it is better for you to enter life crippled or lame, than having two hands or two feet, to be cast into the eternal fire.

9 "And [a]if your eye [b]causes you to stumble, pluck it out, and throw it from you. It is better for you to enter life with one eye, than having two eyes, to be cast into the [c]hell of fire.

10 "See that you do not despise one of these little ones, for I say to you, that [a]their angels in heaven continually behold the face of My Father who is in heaven.

11 ["[1a]For the Son of Man has come to save that which was lost.]

Ninety-nine Plus One

12 "What do you think? [a]If any man has a hundred sheep, and one of them has gone astray, does he not leave the ninety-nine on the mountains and go and search for the one that is straying?

13 "And if it turns out that he finds it, truly I say to you, he rejoices over it more than over the ninety-nine which have not gone astray.

14 "Thus it is not *the* will of your Father who is in heaven that one of these little ones perish.

Discipline and Prayer

15 "And [a]if your brother sins[1], go and reprove him in private; if he listens to you, you have won your brother.

16 "But if he does not listen *to you*, take one or two more with you, so that [a]BY THE MOUTH OF TWO OR THREE WITNESSES EVERY FACT MAY BE CONFIRMED.

17 "And if he refuses to listen to them, [a]tell it to the church; and if he refuses to listen even to the church, [b]let him be to you as a Gentile and a [1]tax-gatherer.

18 "Truly I say to you, [a]whatever you shall bind on earth shall have been bound in heaven; and whatever you loose on earth shall have been loosed in heaven.

19 "Again I say to you, that if two of you agree on earth about anything

---

20 [a]Matt. 21:21f.; Mark 11:23f.; Luke 17:6 [b]Matt. 13:31; Luke 17:6 [c]Matt. 17:9; 1 Cor. 13:2 [d]Mark 9:23; John 11:40

21 [1]Many mss. do not contain this verse [a]Mark 9:29

22 [a]Matt. 17:22, 23: *Mark 9:30-32; Luke 9:44, 45*

23 [a]Matt. 16:21; 17:9

24 [1]Equivalent to two denarii or two days' wages paid as a temple tax [a]Ex. 30:13; 38:26

25 [a]Rom. 13:7 [b]Matt. 22:17, 19

26 [1]Or, *free*

27 [1]Or, *shekel*, worth four drachmas [a]Matt. 5:29, 30; 18:6, 8, 9; Mark 9:42, 43, 45, 47; Luke 17:2; John 6:61; 1 Cor. 8:13

1 [a]Matt. 18:1-5: *Mark 9:33-37; Luke 9:46-48*

3 [a]Matt. 19:14; Mark 10:15; Luke 18:17; 1 Cor. 14:20; 1 Pet. 2:2

6 [a]Mark 9:42; Luke 17:2; 1 Cor. 8:12 [b]Matt. 17:27

7 [a]Luke 17:1; 1 Cor. 11:19; 1 Tim. 4:1

8 [a]Matt. 5:30; 17:27; Mark 9:43 [b]Matt. 17:27

9 [a]Matt. 5:29; 17:27; Mark 9:47 [b]Matt. 17:27 [c]Matt. 5:22

10 [a]1 Kin. 10:8; 2 Kin. 25:19; Luke 1:19; Acts 12:15; Rev. 8:2

11 [1]Most ancient mss. do not contain this verse [a]Luke 19:10

12 [a]Matt. 18:12-14; Luke 15:4-7

15 [1]Many mss. add here: *against you* [a]Lev. 19:17; Luke 17:3; Gal. 6:1; 2 Thess. 3:15; James 5:19

16 [a]Deut. 19:15; John 8:17; 2 Cor. 13:1; 1 Tim. 5:19; Heb. 10:28

17 [1]A publican who collected Roman taxes [a]1 Cor. 6:1ff. [b]2 Thess. 3:6, 14f.

18 [a]Matt. 16:19; John 20:23

that they may ask, [a]it shall be done
for them [1]by My Father who is in
heaven.
20 "For where two or three have
gathered together in My name,
there I am in their midst."

Forgiveness

21 Then Peter came and said to
Him, "Lord, [a]how often shall my
brother sin against me and I forgive
him? Up to [b]seven times?"
22 Jesus *said to him, "I do not say
to you, up to seven times, but up to
[a]seventy times seven.
23 "For this reason [a]the kingdom of
heaven may be compared to a certain king who wished to [b]settle accounts with his slaves.
24 "And when he had begun to settle *them,* there was brought to him
one who owed him [1]ten thousand
talents.
25 "But since he [1a]did not have *the
means* to repay, his lord commanded him [b]to be sold, along with
his wife and children and all that he
had, and repayment to be made.
26 "The slave therefore falling
down, [a]prostrated himself before
him, saying, 'Have patience with
me, and I will repay you everything.'
27 "And the lord of that slave felt
compassion and released him and
forgave him the [1]debt.
28 "But that slave went out and
found one of his fellow-slaves who
owed him a hundred [1]denarii; and
he seized him and *began* to choke
him, saying, 'Pay back what you
owe.'
29 "So his fellow-slave fell down
and *began* to entreat him, saying,
'Have patience with me and I will
repay you.'
30 "He was unwilling however, but
went and threw him in prison until
he should pay back what was owed.
31 "So when his fellow-slaves saw
what had happened, they were
deeply grieved and came and reported to their lord all that had happened.
32 "Then summoning him, his lord
*said to him, 'You wicked slave, I
forgave you all that debt because
you entreated me.
33 'Should you not also have had
mercy on your fellow-slave, even as
I had mercy on you?'
34 "And his lord, moved with anger, handed him over to the tortur-
ers until he should repay all that was
owed him.
35 "[a]So shall My heavenly Father
also do to you, if each of you does

19 [1]Lit., *from* [a]Matt. 7:7

21 [a]Matt. 18:15 [b]Luke 17:4

22 [a]Gen. 4:24

23 [a]Matt. 13:24 [b]Matt. 25:19

24 [1]About $10,000,000 in silver content but worth much more in buying power

25 [1]Or, *was unable to* [a]Luke 7:42 [b]Ex. 21:2; Lev. 25:39; 2 Kin. 4:1; Neh. 5:5

26 [a]Matt. 8:2

27 [1]Or, *loan*

28 [1]The denarius was worth 18 cents in silver, equivalent to a day's wage

35 [1]Lit., *your hearts* [a]Matt. 6:14

1 [a]Matt. 7:28 [b]Matt. 19:1-9: *Mark 10:1-12*

2 [a]Matt. 4:23

3 [a]Matt. 5:31

4 [a]Gen. 1:27; 5:2

5 [a]Gen. 2:24; Eph. 5:31 [b]1 Cor. 6:16

7 [a]Deut. 24:1-4

8 [1]Or, *With reference to*

9 [1]I.e., sexual immorality [2]Some early mss. read: *makes her commit adultery* [3]Some early mss. add: *and he who marries a divorced woman commits adultery* [a]Matt. 5:32

11 [a]1 Cor. 7:7ff. [b]Matt. 13:11

13 [a]Matt. 19:13-15: *Mark 10:13-16; Luke 18:15-17*

not forgive his brother from [1]your
heart."

Chapter 19

Concerning Divorce

[a]AND it came about that when Jesus had finished these words, He departed from Galilee, and [b]came into
the region of Judea beyond the Jordan;
2 and great multitudes followed
Him, and [a]He healed them there.
3 And *some* Pharisees came to
Him, testing Him, and saying, "[a]Is it
lawful *for a man* to divorce his wife
for any cause at all?"
4 And He answered and said,
"Have you not read, [a]that He who
created *them* from the beginning
MADE THEM MALE AND FEMALE,
5 and said, '[a]FOR THIS CAUSE A
MAN SHALL LEAVE HIS FATHER AND
MOTHER, AND SHALL CLEAVE TO HIS
WIFE; AND [b]THE TWO SHALL BECOME
ONE FLESH'?
6 "Consequently they are no more
two, but one flesh. What therefore
God has joined together, let no man
separate."
7 They *said to Him, "[a]Why then
did Moses command to GIVE HER A
CERTIFICATE AND DIVORCE HER?"
8 He *said to them, "[1]Because of
your hardness of heart, Moses permitted you to divorce your wives;
but from the beginning it has not
been this way.
9 "And I say to you, [a]whoever divorces his wife, except for [1]immo-
rality, and marries another [2]com-
mits adultery."[3]
10 The disciples *said to Him, "If
the relationship of the man with his
wife is like this, it is better not to
marry."
11 But He said to them, "[a]Not all
men *can* accept this statement, but
[b]*only* those to whom it has been giv-
en.
12 "For there are eunuchs who
were born that way from their
mother's womb; and there are eunuchs who were made eunuchs by
men; and there are *also* eunuchs
who made themselves eunuchs for
the sake of the kingdom of heaven.
He who is able to accept *this,* let him
accept *it.*"

Jesus Blesses Little Children

13 [a]Then *some* children were
brought to Him so that He might lay
His hands on them and pray; and the
disciples rebuked them.

14 But Jesus said, “[1a]Let the children alone, and do not hinder them from coming to Me; for [b]the kingdom of heaven belongs to such as these.”

15 And after laying His hands on them, He departed from there.

The Rich Young Ruler

16 [a]And behold, one came to Him and said, “Teacher, what good thing shall I do that I may obtain [b]eternal life?”

17 And He said to him, “Why are you asking Me about what is good? There is *only* One who is good; but [a]if you wish to enter into life, keep the commandments.”

18 He *said to Him, “Which ones?” And Jesus said, “[a]YOU SHALL NOT COMMIT MURDER; YOU SHALL NOT COMMIT ADULTERY; YOU SHALL NOT STEAL; YOU SHALL NOT BEAR FALSE WITNESS;

19 [a]HONOR YOUR FATHER AND MOTHER; and [b]YOU SHALL LOVE YOUR NEIGHBOR AS YOURSELF.”

20 The young man *said to Him, “All these things I have kept; what am I still lacking?”

21 Jesus said to him, “If you wish to be [1]complete, go *and* [a]sell your possessions and give to *the* poor, and you shall have [b]treasure in heaven; and come, follow Me.”

22 But when the young man heard this statement, he went away grieved; for he was one who owned much property.

23 And Jesus said to His disciples, “Truly I say to you, [a]it is hard for a rich man to enter the kingdom of heaven.

24“And again I say to you, [a]it is easier for a camel to go through the eye of a needle, than for a rich man to enter the kingdom of God.”

25 And when the disciples heard *this*, they were very astonished and said, “Then who can be saved?”

26 And looking upon *them* Jesus said to them, “[a]With men this is impossible, but with God all things are possible.”

The Disciples’ Reward

27 Then Peter answered and said to Him, “Behold, we have left everything and followed You; what then will there be for us?”

28 And Jesus said to them, “Truly I say to you, that you who have followed Me, in the regeneration when [a]the Son of Man will sit on [1]His glorious throne, [b]you also shall sit upon twelve thrones, judging the twelve tribes of Israel.

29“And [a]everyone who has left houses or brothers or sisters or father or mother[1] or children or farms for My name’s sake, shall receive [2]many times as much, and shall inherit eternal life.

30“[a]But many *who are* first will be last; and *the* last, first.

CHAPTER 20

Laborers in the Vineyard

“FOR [a]the kingdom of heaven is like [1]a landowner who went out early in the morning to hire laborers [2]for his [b]vineyard.

2“And when he had agreed with the laborers for a [1]denarius for the day, he sent them into his vineyard.

3“And he went out about the [1]third hour and saw others standing idle in the market place;

4 and to those he said, ‘You too go into the vineyard, and whatever is right I will give you.’ And *so* they went.

5“Again he went out about the [1]sixth and the ninth hour, and did [2]the same thing.

6“And about the [1]eleventh *hour* he went out, and found others standing; and he *said to them, ‘Why have you been standing here idle all day long?’

7“They *said to him, ‘Because no one hired us.’ He *said to them, ‘You too go into the vineyard.’

8“And when [a]evening had come, the [1]owner of the vineyard *said to his [b]foreman, ‘Call the laborers and pay them their wages, beginning with the last *group* to the first.’

9“And when those *hired* about the eleventh hour came, each one received a [1]denarius.

10“And when those *hired* first came, they thought that they would receive more; and they also received each one a denarius.

11“And when they received it, they grumbled at the landowner,

12 saying, ‘These last men have worked *only* one hour, and you have made them equal to us who have borne the burden and the [a]scorching heat of the day.’

13“But he answered and said to one of them, ‘[a]Friend, I am doing you no wrong; did you not agree with me for a denarius?

14 ‘Take what is yours and go your way, but I wish to give to this last man the same as to you.

---

14 [1]Or, *Permit the children* [a]Matt. 18:3; Mark 10:15; Luke 18:17; 1 Cor. 14:20; 1 Pet. 2:2 [b]Matt. 5:3

16 [a]Matt. 19:16-29: *Mark 10:17-30; Luke 18:18-30;* Luke 10:25-28 [b]Matt. 25:46

17 [a]Lev. 18:5; Neh. 9:29; Ezek. 20:21

18 [a]Ex. 20:13-16; Deut. 5:17-20

19 [a]Ex. 20:12; Deut. 5:16 [b]Lev. 19:18

21 [1]Or, *perfect* [a]Luke 12:33; 16:9; Acts 2:45; 4:34f. [b]Matt. 6:20

23 [a]Matt. 13:22; Mark 10:23f.; Luke 18:24

24 [a]Mark 10:25; Luke 18:25

26 [a]Gen. 18:14; Job 42:2; Jer. 32:17; Zech. 8:6; Mark 10:27; Luke 1:37; 18:27

28 [1]Lit., *the throne of His glory* [a]Matt. 25:31 [b]Luke 22:30; Rev. 3:21; 4:4; 11:16; 20:4

29 [1]Many mss. add here, *or wife* [2]Many mss. read, *a hundredfold* [a]Matt. 6:33; Mark 10:29f.; Luke 18:29f.

30 [a]Matt. 20:16; Mark 10:31; Luke 13:30

1 [1]Lit., *a man, a landowner* [2]Lit., *into* [a]Matt. 13:24 [b]Matt. 21:28, 33

2 [1]The denarius was worth 18 cents in silver, equivalent to one day’s wage

3 [1]I.e., 9 a.m.

5 [1]I.e., Noon and 3 p.m. [2]Lit., *similarly*

6 [1]I.e., 5 p.m.

8 [1]Or, *lord* [a]Lev. 19:13 [b]Luke 8:3

9 [1]The denarius was worth 18 cents in silver, equivalent to one day’s wage

12 [a]Jon. 4:8; Luke 12:55; James 1:11

13 [a]Matt. 22:12; 26:50

15 'Is it not lawful for me to do
what I wish with what is my own?
Or is your [a]eye [1]envious because I
am [2]generous?'
16 "Thus [a]the last shall be first, and
the first last."

Death, Resurrection Foretold

17 [a]And as Jesus was about to go
up to Jerusalem, He took the twelve
disciples aside by themselves, and
on the way He said to them,
18 "Behold, we are going up to Jerusalem; and the Son of Man [a]will
be [1]delivered up to the chief priests
and scribes, and they will condemn
Him to death,
19 and [a]will deliver Him up to the
Gentiles to mock and scourge and
crucify *Him*, and on [b]the third day
He will be raised up."

Preferment Asked

20 [a]Then the mother of [b]the sons
of Zebedee came to Him with her
sons, [c]bowing down, and making a
request of Him.
21 And He said to her, "What do
you wish?" She *said to Him, "Command that in Your kingdom these
two sons of mine [a]may sit, one on
Your right and one on Your left."
22 But Jesus answered and said,
"You do not know what you are asking for. Are you able [a]to drink the
cup that I am about to drink?" They
*said to Him, "We are able."
23 He *said to them, "[a]My cup you
shall drink; but to sit on My right
and on *My* left, this is not Mine to
give, [b]but *it is* for those for whom it
has been [c]prepared by My Father."
24 And hearing *this*, the ten became indignant at the two brothers.
25 [a]But Jesus called them to Himself, and said, "You know that the
rulers of the Gentiles lord it over
them, and *their* great men exercise
authority over them.
26 "It is not so among you, [a]but
whoever wishes to become great
among you shall be your servant,
27 and whoever wishes to be first
among you shall be your slave;
28 just as [a]the Son of Man [b]did not
come to be served, but to serve, and
to give His [1]life a ransom for many."

Sight for the Blind

29 [a]And as they were going out
from Jericho, a great multitude followed Him.
30 And behold, two blind men sitting by the road, hearing that Jesus
was passing by, cried out, saying,
"Lord, [a]have mercy on us, [b]Son of
David!"
31 And the multitude sternly told
them to be quiet; but they cried out
all the more, saying, "Lord, have
mercy on us, [a]Son of David!"
32 And Jesus stopped and called
them, and said, "What do you wish
Me to do for you?"
33 They *said to Him, "Lord, we
want our eyes to be opened."
34 And moved with compassion,
Jesus touched their eyes; and immediately they received their sight, and
followed Him.

CHAPTER 21

The Triumphal Entry

[a]AND when they had approached
Jerusalem and had come to Bethphage, to [b]the Mount of Olives, then
Jesus sent two disciples,
2 saying to them, "Go into the village opposite you, and immediately
you will find a donkey tied *there* and
a colt with her; untie *them*, and
bring *them* to Me.
3 "And if anyone says something
to you, you shall say, 'The Lord has
need of them,' and immediately he
will send them."
4 [a]Now this took place that what
was spoken through the prophet
might be fulfilled, saying,
5 "[a]SAY TO THE DAUGHTER OF
ZION,
'BEHOLD YOUR KING IS COMING
TO YOU,
GENTLE, AND MOUNTED UPON A
DONKEY,
EVEN UPON A COLT, THE FOAL
OF A BEAST OF BURDEN.' "
6 And the disciples went and did
just as Jesus had directed them,
7 and brought the donkey and the
colt, and laid on them their garments, [1]on which He sat.
8 And most of the multitude
[a]spread their garments in the road,
and others were cutting branches
from the trees, and spreading them
in the road.
9 And the multitudes going before Him, and those who followed
after were crying out, saying,
"[a]HOSANNA to the [b]Son of David;
[a]BLESSED IS HE WHO COMES IN
THE NAME OF THE LORD;
HOSANNA [c]in the highest!"
10 And when He had entered Jerusalem, all the city was stirred, saying, "Who is this?"
11 And the multitudes were say-

15 [1]Lit., *evil* [2]Lit., *good* [a]Deut. 15:9; Matt. 6:23; Mark 7:22
16 [a]Matt. 19:30
17 [a]Matt. 20:17-19: *Mark 10:32-34; Luke 18:31-33*
18 [1]Or, *betrayed* [a]Matt. 16:21
19 [a]Matt. 27:2; Acts 2:23; 3:13; 4:27; 21:11 [b]Matt. 16:21
20 [a]Matt. 20:20-28: *Mark 10:35-45* [b]Matt. 4:21; 10:2 [c]Matt. 8:2
21 [a]Matt. 19:28
22 [a]Is. 51:17, 22; Jer. 49:12; Matt. 26:39, 42; Luke 22:42; John 18:11
23 [a]Acts 12:2; Rev. 1:9 [b]Matt. 13:11 [c]Matt. 25:34
25 [a]Matt. 20:25-28; Luke 22:25-27
26 [a]Matt. 23:11; Mark 9:35; 10:43
28 [1]Or, *soul* [a]Matt. 8:20 [b]Matt. 26:28; John 13:13ff.; 2 Cor. 8:9; Phil. 2:7; 1 Tim. 2:6; Titus 2:14; Heb. 9:28; Rev. 1:5
29 [a]Matt. 20:29-34: *Mark 10:46-52; Luke 18:35-43;* Matt. 9:27-31
30 [a]Matt. 20:31 [b]Matt. 9:27
31 [a]Matt. 9:27
1 [a]Matt. 21:1-9: *Mark 11:1-10; Luke 19:29-38* [b]Matt. 24:3; 26:30; Mark 11:1; 13:3; 14:26; Luke 19:29, 37; 21:37; 22:39; John 8:1; Acts 1:12
4 [a]Matt. 21:4-9: *John 12:12-15*
5 [a]Is. 62:11; Zech. 9:9
7 [1]Lit., *on them*
8 [a]2 Kin. 9:13
9 [a]Ps. 118:26f. [b]Matt. 9:27 [c]Luke 2:14

ing, "This is [a]the prophet Jesus,
from [b]Nazareth in Galilee."

Cleansing the Temple

12 [a]And Jesus entered the temple
and cast out all those who were buying and selling in the temple, and
overturned the tables of the [b]mon-
eychangers and the seats of those
who were selling [1c]doves.
13 And He *said to them, "It is
written, '[a]MY HOUSE SHALL BE
CALLED A HOUSE OF PRAYER'; but you
are making it a robbers' [1]den."
14 And *the* blind and *the* lame
came to Him in the temple, and [a]He
healed them.
15 But when the chief priests and
the scribes saw the wonderful
things that He had done, and the
children who were crying out in the
temple and saying, "Hosanna to the
[a]Son of David," they became indignant,
16 and said to Him, "Do You hear
what these are saying?" And Jesus
*said to them, "Yes; have you never
read, '[a]OUT OF THE MOUTH OF IN-
FANTS AND NURSING BABES THOU
HAST PREPARED PRAISE FOR THY-
SELF'?"
17 And He left them and went out
of the city to [a]Bethany, and lodged
there.

The Barren Fig Tree

18 [a]Now in the morning, when He
returned to the city, He became
hungry.
19 And seeing a lone fig tree by the
road, He came to it, and found nothing on it except leaves only; and He
*said to it, "No longer shall there
ever be *any* fruit from you." And at
once the fig tree withered.
20 And seeing *this,* the disciples
marveled, saying, "How did the fig
tree wither at once?"
21 And Jesus answered and said to
them, "Truly I say to you, [a]if you
have faith, and do not doubt, you
shall not only do what was done to
the fig tree, but even if you say to
this mountain, 'Be taken up and cast
into the sea,' it shall happen.
22"And [a]everything you ask in
prayer, believing, you shall receive."

Authority Challenged

23 [a]And when He had come into
the temple, the chief priests and the
elders of the people came to Him as
He was teaching, and said, "By
what authority are You doing these
things, and who gave You this authority?"
24 But Jesus answered and said to
them, "I will ask you one [1]thing too,
which if you tell Me, I will also tell
you by what authority I do these
things.
25"The baptism of John was from
what *source,* from heaven or from
men?" And they *began* reasoning
among themselves, saying, "If we
say, 'From heaven,' He will say to
us, 'Then why did you not believe
him?'
26"But if we say, 'From men,' we
fear the multitude; for they all hold
John to be [a]a prophet."
27 And they answered Jesus and
said, "We do not know." He also
said to them, "Neither will I tell you
by what authority I do these things.

Parable of Two Sons

28"But what do you think? A man
had two [1]sons, and he came to the
first and said, '[2]Son, go work today
in the [a]vineyard.'
29"And he answered and said, '[1]I
will, sir'; and he did not go.
30"And he came to the second and
said [1]the same thing. But he answered and said, '[2]I will not'; *yet* he
afterward regretted *it* and went.
31"Which of the two did the will of
his father?" They *said, "The latter." Jesus *said to them, "Truly I
say to you that [a]the [1]tax-gatherers
and harlots [2]will get into the kingdom of God before you.
32"For John came to you in the
way of righteousness and you did
not believe him; but [a]the tax-gatherers and harlots did believe him; and
you, seeing this, did not even feel
remorse afterward so as to believe
him.

Parable of the Landowner

33"Listen to another parable.
[a]There was a [1]landowner who
[b]PLANTED A [c]VINEYARD AND PUT A
WALL AROUND IT AND DUG A [d]WINE
PRESS IN IT, AND [d]BUILT A TOWER,
and rented it out to [2]vine-growers,
and [e]went on a journey.
34"And when the [1]harvest time approached, he [a]sent his slaves to the
vine-growers to receive his produce.
35"And the vine-growers took his
slaves and beat one, and killed another, and stoned a third.
36"Again he [a]sent another group of
slaves larger than the first; and they
did [1]the same thing to them.
37"But afterward he sent his son to
them, saying, 'They will respect my
son.'
38"But when the vine-growers saw
the son, they said among them-

11 [a]Matt. 21:26; Mark 6:15; Luke 7:16, 39; 13:33; 24:19; John 1:21, 25; 4:19; 6:14; 7:40; 9:17; Acts 3:22f.; 7:37 [b]Matt. 2:23

12 [1]Lit. *the doves* [a]Matt. 21:12-16: *Mark 11:15-18; Luke 19:45-47;* Matt. 21:12, 13: *John 2:13-16* [b]Ex. 30:13 [c]Lev. 1:14; 5:7; 12:8

13 [1]Lit., *cave* [a]Is. 56:7; Jer. 7:11

14 [a]Matt. 4:23

15 [a]Matt. 9:27

16 [a]Ps. 8:2

17 [a]Matt. 26:6; Mark 11:1, 11, 12; 14:3; Luke 19:29; 24:50; John 11:1, 18; 12:1

18 [a]Matt. 21:18-22: *Mark 11:12-14, 20-24*

21 [a]Matt. 17:20; Mark 11:23; Luke 17:6; James 1:6

22 [a]Matt. 7:7

23 [a]Matt. 21:23-27: *Mark 11:27-33; Luke 20:1-8*

24 [1]Lit., *word*

26 [a]Matt. 11:9; Mark 6:20

28 [1]Lit., *children* [2]Lit., *Child* [a]Matt. 20:1; 21:33

29 [1]Some mss. read *'I will not'; yet he afterward regretted and went*

30 [1]Lit., *likewise* [2]Some mss. read *'I will'; and he did not go*

31 [1]A publican who collected Roman taxes [2]Or, *are getting into* [a]Luke 7:29, 37-50

32 [a]Luke 3:12

33 [1]Lit., *a man, a householder* [2]Or, *tenant farmers* (Here and in vs. 34, 35, 38, 40) [a]Matt. 21:33-46: *Mark 12:1-12; Luke 20:9-19* [b]Ps. 80:8; Is. 5:1ff. [c]Matt. 20:1; 21:28 [d]Is. 5:2 [e]Matt. 25:14

34 [1]Lit., *the season of the fruits* [a]Matt. 22:3

36 [1]Lit., *likewise* [a]Matt. 22:4

selves, 'This is the heir; come, let us
kill him, and seize his inheritance.'
39"And they took him, and cast
him out of the vineyard, and killed
him.
40"Therefore when the [1]owner of
the vineyard comes, what will he do
to those vine-growers?"
41 They *said to Him, "He will
bring those wretches to a wretched
end, and [a]will rent out the vineyard
to other vine-growers, who will pay
him the proceeds at the *proper* seasons."
42 Jesus *said to them, "Did you
never read in the Scriptures,
'[a]THE STONE WHICH THE BUILD-
ERS REJECTED,
THIS BECAME THE CHIEF COR-
NER *stone;*
THIS CAME ABOUT FROM THE
LORD,
AND IT IS MARVELOUS IN OUR
EYES'?
43"Therefore I say to you, the kingdom of God will be taken away from
you, and be given to a nation producing the fruit of it.
44"And he who falls on this stone
will be broken to pieces; but on
whomever it falls, it will scatter him
like dust."
45 And when the chief priests and
the Pharisees heard His parables,
they understood that He was speaking about them.
46 And when they sought to seize
Him, they [a]became afraid of the
multitudes, because they held Him
to be a [b]prophet.

CHAPTER 22

Parable of the Marriage Feast

AND Jesus [a]answered and spoke
to them again in parables, saying,
2"[a]The kingdom of heaven may
be compared to [1]a king, who [2]gave a
wedding feast for his son.
3"And he [a]sent out his slaves to
call those who had been invited to
the wedding feast, and they were
unwilling to come.
4"Again he [a]sent out other slaves
saying, 'Tell those who have been
invited, "Behold, I have prepared
my dinner; my oxen and my fattened livestock are *all* butchered
and everything is ready; come to the
wedding feast."'
5"But they paid no attention and
went their way, one to his own
[1]farm, another to his business,
6 and the rest seized his slaves
and mistreated them and killed
them.
7"But the king was enraged and
sent his armies, and destroyed those
murderers, and set their city on fire.
8"Then he *said to his slaves, 'The
wedding is ready, but those who
were invited were not worthy.
9 'Go therefore to [a]the main highways, and as many as you find *there,*
invite to the wedding feast.'
10"And those slaves went out into
the streets, and gathered together
all they found, both evil and good;
and the wedding hall was filled with
[1]dinner guests.
11"But when the king came in to
look over the dinner guests, he saw
there [a]a man not dressed in wedding
clothes,
12 and he *said to him, '[a]Friend,
how did you come in here [1]without
wedding clothes?' And he was
speechless.
13"Then the king said to the servants, 'Bind him hand and foot, and
cast him into [a]the outer darkness; in
that place [a]there shall be weeping
and gnashing of teeth.'
14"For many are [1a]called, but few
are [a]chosen."

Tribute to Caesar

15 [a]Then the Pharisees went and
counseled together how they might
trap Him [1]in what He said.
16 And they *sent their disciples
to Him, along with the [a]Herodians,
saying, "Teacher, we know that You
are truthful and teach the way of
God in truth, and [1]defer to no one;
for You are not partial to any.
17"Tell us therefore, what do You
think? Is it [1]lawful to give a [a]poll-tax
to [b]Caesar, or not?"
18 But Jesus perceived their [1]mal-
ice, and said, "Why are you testing
Me, you hypocrites?
19"Show Me the [a]coin *used* for the
poll-tax." And they brought Him a
[1]denarius.
20 And He *said to them, "Whose
likeness and inscription is this?"
21 They *said to Him, "Caesar's."
Then He *said to them, "[a]Then render to Caesar the things that are
Caesar's; and to God the things that
are God's."
22 And hearing *this,* they marveled, and [a]leaving Him, they went
away.

Jesus Answers the Sadducees

23 [a]On that day *some* [b]Sadducees
(who say [c]there is no resurrection)
came to Him and questioned Him,

40 [1]Lit., *lord*
41 [a]Matt. 8:11f.; Acts 13:46; 18:6; 28:28
42 [a]Ps. 118:22; Acts 4:11; Rom. 9:33; 1 Pet. 2:7
46 [a]Matt. 21:26 [b]Matt. 21:11
1 [a]Acts 3:12
2 [1]Lit., *a man, a king* [2]Lit., *made* [a]Matt. 13:24; 22:2-14; Luke 14:16-24
3 [a]Matt. 21:34
4 [a]Matt. 21:36
5 [1]Or, *field*
9 [a]Ezek. 21:21; Obad. 14
10 [1]Lit., *those reclining at table*
11 [a]2 Kin. 10:22
12 [1]Lit., *not having* [a]Matt. 20:13; 26:50
13 [a]Matt. 8:12
14 [1]Or, *invited* [a]Matt. 24:22; 2 Pet. 1:10; Rev. 17:14
15 [1]Lit., *in word* [a]Matt. 22:15-22: *Mark 12:13-17; Luke 20:20-26*
16 [1]I.e., you court no man's favor [a]Mark 3:6; 8:15; 12:13
17 [1]Or, *permissible* [a]Matt. 17:25 [b]Luke 2:1; 3:1
18 [1]Or, *wickedness*
19 [1]The denarius was worth 18 cents in silver, equivalent to one day's wage [a]Matt. 17:25
21 [a]Mark 12:17; Luke 20:25; Rom. 13:7
22 [a]Mark 12:12
23 [a]Matt. 22:23-33: *Mark 12:18-27; Luke 20:27-40* [b]Matt. 3:7 [c]Acts 23:8

24 saying, "Teacher, Moses said, '[a]IF A MAN DIES, HAVING NO CHILDREN, HIS BROTHER AS NEXT OF KIN SHALL MARRY HIS WIFE, AND RAISE UP AN OFFSPRING TO HIS BROTHER.'

25 "Now there were seven brothers with us; and the first married and died, and having no offspring left his wife to his brother;

26 so also the second, and the third, down to the seventh.

27 "And last of all, the woman died.

28 "In the resurrection therefore whose wife of the seven shall she be? For they all had her."

29 But Jesus answered and said to them, "You are mistaken, [a]not understanding the Scriptures, or the power of God.

30 "For in the resurrection they neither [a]marry, nor are given in marriage, but are like angels[1] in heaven.

31 "But regarding the resurrection of the dead, have you not read that which was spoken to you by God, saying,

32 '[a]I AM THE GOD OF ABRAHAM, AND THE GOD OF ISAAC, AND THE GOD OF JACOB'? God is not *the God* of *the* dead but of *the* living."

33 And when the multitudes heard *this,* [a]they were astonished at His teaching.

34 [a]But when the Pharisees heard that He had put [b]the Sadducees to silence, they gathered themselves together.

35 And one of them, [1][a]a lawyer, asked Him a question, testing Him,

36 "Teacher, which is the great commandment in the Law?"

37 And He said to him, " '[a]YOU SHALL LOVE THE LORD YOUR GOD WITH ALL YOUR HEART, AND WITH ALL YOUR SOUL, AND WITH ALL YOUR MIND.'

38 "This is the great and foremost commandment.

39 "And a second is like it, '[a]YOU SHALL LOVE YOUR NEIGHBOR AS YOURSELF.'

40 "[a]On these two commandments depend the whole Law and the Prophets."

41 [a]Now while the Pharisees were gathered together, Jesus asked them a question,

42 saying, "What do you think about the Christ, whose son is He?" They *said to Him, "[a]*The son* of David."

43 He *said to them, "Then how does David [a]in the Spirit call Him 'Lord,' saying,

44 '[a]THE LORD SAID TO MY LORD,
"SIT AT MY RIGHT HAND,

24 [a]Deut. 25:5
29 [a]John 20:9
30 [1]Other mss. add: *of God* [a]Matt. 24:38; Luke 17:27
32 [a]Ex. 3:6
33 [a]Matt. 7:28
34 [a]Matt. 22:34-40: *Mark 12:28-31;* Luke 10:25-37 [b]Matt. 3:7
35 [1]I.e., an expert in the Mosaic law [a]Luke 7:30; 10:25; 11:45, 46, 52; 14:3; Titus 3:13
37 [a]Deut. 6:5
39 [a]Lev. 19:18; Matt. 19:19; Gal. 5:14
40 [a]Matt. 7:12
41 [a]Matt. 22:41-46: *Mark 12:35-37; Luke 20:41-44*
42 [a]Matt. 9:27
43 [a]2 Sam. 23:2; Rev. 1:10; 4:2
44 [a]Ps. 110:1; Matt. 26:64; Mark 16:19; Acts 2:34f.; 1 Cor. 15:25; Heb. 1:13; 10:13
46 [a]Mark 12:34; Luke 14:6; 20:40
1 [a]Matt. 23:1-7: *Mark 12:38, 39; Luke 20:45, 46*
2 [a]Deut. 33:3f.; Ezra 7:6, 25; Neh. 8:4
4 [a]Luke 11:46; Acts 15:10
5 [1]I.e., small boxes containing Scripture texts worn for religious purposes [a]Matt. 6:1, 5, 16 [b]Ex. 13:9; Deut. 6:8; 11:18 [c]Matt. 9:20
6 [a]Luke 11:43; 14:7; 20:46
7 [a]Matt. 23:8; 26:25, 49; Mark 9:5; 10:51; 11:21; John 1:38, 49; 3:2, 26; 4:31; 6:25; 9:2; 11:8; 20:16
8 [a]James 3:1 [b]Matt. 23:7; 26:25, 49; Mark 9:5; 10:51; 11:21; 14:45; John 1:38, 49; 3:2, 26; 4:31; 6:25; 9:2; 11:8; 20:16
9 [a]Matt. 6:9; 7:11
11 [a]Matt. 20:26
12 [a]Luke 14:11; 18:14
13 [a]Matt. 23:15, (16), 23, 25, 27, 29 [b]Luke 11:52
14 [1]This verse not found in the earliest mss. [a]Mark 12:40; Luke 20:47

UNTIL I PUT THINE ENEMIES BENEATH THY FEET?" '

45 "If David then calls Him 'Lord', how is He his son?"

46 And [a]no one was able to answer Him a word, nor did anyone dare from that day on to ask Him another question.

CHAPTER 23

Pharisaism Exposed

[a]THEN Jesus spoke to the multitudes and to His disciples,

2 saying, "[a]The scribes and the Pharisees have seated themselves in the chair of Moses;

3 therefore all that they tell you, do and observe, but do not do according to their deeds; for they say *things,* and do not do *them.*

4 "And [a]they tie up heavy loads, and lay them on men's shoulders; but they themselves are unwilling to move them with *so much as* a finger.

5 "But they do all their deeds [a]to be noticed by men; for they [b]broaden their [1]phylacteries, and lengthen [c]the tassels *of their garments.*

6 "And they [a]love the place of honor at banquets, and the chief seats in the synagogues,

7 and respectful greetings in the market places, and being called by men, [a]Rabbi.

8 "But [a]do not be called [b]Rabbi; for One is your Teacher, and you are all brothers.

9 "And do not call *anyone* on earth your father; for [a]One is your Father, He who is in heaven.

10 "And do not be called leaders; for One is your Leader, *that is,* Christ.

11 "[a]But the greatest among you shall be your servant.

12 "And [a]whoever exalts himself shall be humbled; and whoever humbles himself shall be exalted.

Seven Woes

13 "[a]But woe to you, scribes and Pharisees, hypocrites, [b]because you shut off the kingdom of heaven from men; for you do not enter in yourselves, nor do you allow those who are entering to go in.

14 ["[1]Woe to you, scribes and Pharisees, hypocrites, because [a]you devour widows' houses, even while for a pretense you make long prayers; therefore you shall receive greater condemnation.]

15 "Woe to you, scribes and Pharisees, hypocrites, because you travel

about on sea and land to make one
[1a]proselyte; and when he becomes
one, you make him twice as much a
son of [2b]hell as yourselves.
16 "Woe to you, [a]blind guides, who
say, '[b]Whoever swears by the [1]tem-
ple, that is nothing; but whoever
swears by the gold of the [1]temple,
he is obligated.'
17 "You fools and blind men;
[a]which is [1]more important, the gold,
or the temple that sanctified the
gold?
18 "And, 'Whoever swears by the
altar, *that* is nothing, but whoever
swears by the [1]offering upon it, he is
obligated.'
19 "You blind men, [a]which is [1]more
important, the offering or the altar
that sanctifies the offering?
20 "Therefore he who swears,
swears *both* by the altar and by everything on it.
21 "And he who swears by the temple, swears *both* by the temple and
by Him who [a]dwells within it.
22 "And he who swears by heaven,
[a]swears *both* by the throne of God
and by Him who sits upon it.
23 "[a]Woe to you, scribes and Pharisees, hypocrites! For you tithe mint
and dill and [1]cummin, and have neglected the weightier provisions of
the law: justice and mercy and faithfulness; but these are the things you
should have done without neglecting the others.
24 "You [a]blind guides, who strain
out a gnat and swallow a camel!
25 "[a]Woe to you, scribes and Pharisees, hypocrites! For [a]you clean the
outside of the cup and of the dish,
but inside they are full [1]of robbery
and self-indulgence.
26 "You blind Pharisee, first [a]clean
the inside of the cup and of the dish,
so that the outside of it may become
clean also.
27 "[a]Woe to you, scribes and Pharisees, hypocrites! For you are like
whitewashed tombs which on the
outside appear beautiful, but inside
they are full of dead men's bones
and all uncleanness.
28 "Even so you too outwardly appear righteous to men, but inwardly
you are full of hypocrisy and lawlessness.
29 "[a]Woe to you, scribes and Pharisees, hypocrites! For you build the
tombs of the prophets and adorn the
monuments of the righteous,
30 and say, 'If we had been *living*
in the days of our fathers, we would
not have been partners with them in
shedding the blood of the prophets.'
31 "Consequently you bear witness
against yourselves, that you [a]are
[1]sons of those who murdered the
prophets.
32 "[1]Fill up then the measure *of the
guilt* of your fathers.
33 "You serpents, [a]you brood of vipers, how shall you escape the [1]sen-
tence of [2b]hell?
34 "[a]Therefore, behold, [b]I am sending you prophets and wise men and
scribes; some of them you will kill
and crucify, and some of them you
will [c]scourge in your synagogues,
and [d]persecute from city to city,
35 that upon you may fall *the guilt
of* all the righteous blood shed on
earth, from the blood of righteous
[a]Abel to the blood of Zechariah, the
[b]son of Berechiah, whom [c]you murdered between the [1]temple and the
altar.
36 "Truly I say to you, all these
things shall come upon [a]this generation.

Lament Over Jerusalem

37 "[a]O Jerusalem, Jerusalem, who
[b]kills the prophets and stones those
who are sent to her! How often I
wanted to gather your children together, [c]the way a hen gathers her
chicks under her wings, and you
were unwilling.
38 "Behold, [a]your house is being
left to you [1]desolate!
39 "For I say to you, from now on
you shall not see Me until you say,
'[a]BLESSED IS HE WHO COMES IN THE
NAME OF THE LORD!' "

CHAPTER 24

Signs of Christ's Return

[a]AND Jesus [b]came out from the
temple and was going away [1]when
His disciples came up to point out
the temple buildings to Him.
2 And He answered and said to
them, "Do you not see all these
things? Truly I say to you, [a]not one
stone here shall be left upon another, which will not be torn down."
3 And as He was sitting on [a]the
Mount of Olives, the disciples came
to Him privately, saying, "Tell us,
when will these things be, and what
will be the sign of [b]Your [1]coming,
and of the [2]end of the age?"
4 And Jesus answered and said to
them, "[a]See to it that no one misleads you.
5 "For [a]many will come in My
name, saying, 'I am the [1]Christ,' and
will mislead many.

15 [1]Or, *convert* [2]Lit., *Gehenna* [a]Acts 2:10; 6:5; 13:43 [b]Matt. 5:22
16 [1]Or, *sanctuary* [a]Matt. 15:14; 23:24; [b]Matt. 5:33-35
17 [1]Lit., *greater* [a]Ex. 30:29
18 [1]Or, *gift*
19 [1]Lit., *greater* [a]Ex. 29:37
21 [a]1 Kin. 8:13; Ps. 26:8; 132:14
22 [a]Matt. 5:34
23 [1]Similar to caraway seeds [a]Matt. 23:13; Luke 11:42
24 [a]Matt. 23:16
25 [1]Or, *as a result of* [a]Mark 7:4; Luke 11:39f.
26 [a]Mark 7:4; Luke 11:39f.
27 [a]Luke 11:44; Acts 23:3
29 [a]Luke 11:47f.
31 [1]Or, *descendants* [a]Matt. 23:34, 37; Acts 7:51f.
32 [1]Lit., *And fill up*
33 [1]Or, *judgment* [2]Gr., *Gehenna* [a]Matt. 3:7 [b]Matt. 5:22
34 [a]Matt. 23:34-36; Luke 11:49-51 [b]2 Chr. 36:15, 16 [c]Matt. 10:17 [d]Matt. 10:23
35 [1]Or, *sanctuary* [a]Gen. 4:8ff.; Heb. 11:4 [b]Zech. 1:1 [c]2 Chr. 24:21
36 [a]Matt. 10:23; 24:34
37 [a]Matt. 23:37-39: *Luke 13:34, 35* [b]Matt. 5:12 [c]Ruth 2:12
38 [1]Some mss. do not contain, *desolate*
[a]1 Kin. 9:7f.; Jer. 22:5
39 [a]Ps. 118:26; Matt. 21:9
1 [1]Lit., *and* [a]Matt. 24:1-51: *Mark 13; Luke 21:5-36* [b]Matt. 21:23
2 [a]Luke 19:44
3 [1]Or, *presence* [2]Or, *consummation* [a]Matt. 21:1 [b]Matt. 16:27f.; 24:27, 37, 39
4 [a]Jer. 29:8
5 [1]I.e., Messiah [a]Matt. 24:11, 24; Acts 5:36f.; 1 John 2:18; 4:3

6"And you will be hearing of wars
and rumors of wars; see that you are
not frightened, for *those things* must
take place, but *that* is not yet the
end.
7"For [a]nation will rise against nation, and kingdom against kingdom,
and in various places there will be
[b]famines and earthquakes.
8"But all these things are *merely*
the beginning of birth pangs.
9"[a]Then they will deliver you up
to tribulation, and will kill you, and
[b]you will be hated by all nations on
account of My name.
10"And at that time many will [a]fall
away and will betray one another
and hate one another.
11"And many [a]false prophets will
arise, and will mislead many.
12"And because lawlessness is increased, [1]most people's love will
grow cold.
13"[a]But the one who endures to the
end, it is he who shall be saved.
14"And this [a]gospel of the kingdom [b]shall be preached in the whole
[c]world for a witness to all the nations, and then the end shall come.

Perilous Times

15"Therefore when you see the
[a]ABOMINATION OF DESOLATION which
was spoken of through Daniel the
prophet, standing in [b]the holy place
([c]let the reader understand),
16 then let those who are in Judea
flee to the mountains;
17 let him who is on [a]the housetop
not go down to get the things out
that are in his house;
18 and let him who is in the field
not turn back to get his cloak.
19"But [a]woe to those who are with
child and to those who nurse babes
in those days!
20"But pray that your flight may
not be in the winter, or on a Sabbath;
21 for then there will be a [a]great
tribulation, such as has not occurred
since the beginning of the world until now, nor ever shall.
22"And unless those days had been
cut short, no life would have been
saved; but for [a]the sake of the elect
those days shall be cut short.
23"[a]Then if any one says to you,
'Behold, here is the [1]Christ,' or
'There *He is,*' do not believe *him.*
24"For false Christs and [a]false
prophets will arise and will show
great [b]signs and wonders, so as to
mislead, if possible, even [c]the elect.
25"Behold, I have told you in advance.
26"If therefore they say to you,
'Behold, He is in the wilderness,' do
not go forth, *or,* 'Behold, He is in the
inner rooms,' do not believe *them.*
27"[a]For just as the lightning comes
from the east, and flashes even to
the west, so shall the [b]coming of the
[c]Son of Man be.
28"[a]Wherever the corpse is, there
the vultures will gather.

The Glorious Return

29"But immediately after the [a]trib-
ulation of those days [b]THE SUN WILL
BE DARKENED, AND THE MOON WILL
NOT GIVE ITS LIGHT, AND [c]THE STARS
WILL FALL from the sky, and the
powers of the heavens will be
shaken,
30 and then [a]the sign of the Son of
Man will appear in the sky, and then
all the tribes of the earth will mourn,
and they will see [b]the SON OF MAN
COMING ON THE CLOUDS OF THE SKY
with power and great glory.
31"And [a]He will send forth His angels WITH [b]A GREAT TRUMPET and
THEY WILL GATHER TOGETHER His
[c]elect FROM [d]THE FOUR WINDS,
[e]FROM ONE END OF THE SKY TO THE
OTHER.

Parable of the Fig Tree

32"Now learn the parable from the
fig tree: when its branch has already
become tender, and puts forth its
leaves, you know that summer is
near;
33 even so you too, when you see
all these things, recognize that He is
near, *right* [a]at the door.
34"Truly I say to you, [a]this generation will not pass away until all
these things take place.
35"[a]Heaven and earth will pass
away, but My words shall not pass
away.
36"But [a]of that day and hour no
one knows, not even the angels of
heaven, nor the Son, but the Father
alone.
37"For the [a]coming of the Son of
Man will be [b]just like the days of
Noah.
38"For as in those days which were
before the flood they were eating
and drinking, they were [a]marrying
and giving in marriage, until the day
that [b]NOAH ENTERED THE ARK,
39 and they did not understand until the flood came and took them all
away, so shall the [a]coming of the
Son of Man be.
40"Then there shall be two men in
the field; one will be taken, and one
will be left.

7 [a]2 Chr. 15:6; Is. 19:2 [b]Acts 11:28
9 [a]Matt. 10:17; John 16:2 [b]Matt. 10:22
10 [a]Matt. 11:6
11 [a]Matt. 7:15
12 [1]Lit., *the love of many*
13 [a]Matt. 10:22
14 [a]Matt. 4:23 [b]Rom. 10:18; Col. 1:6, 23 [c]Luke 2:1; 4:5; Acts 11:28; Rom. 10:18; Heb. 1:6; 2:5; Rev. 3:10
15 [a]Dan. 9:27 [b]Mark 13:14; Luke 21:20; John 11:48; Acts 6:13f.; 21:28 [c]Mark 13:14; Rev. 1:3
17 [a]1 Sam. 9:25; 2 Sam. 11:2; Matt. 10:27; Luke 5:19; 12:3; Acts 10:9
19 [a]Luke 23:29
21 [a]Dan. 12:1; Joel 2:2; Matt. 24:29
22 [a]Matt. 22:14; 24:24, 31; Luke 18:7
23 [1]Or, *Messiah* [a]Luke 17:23f.
24 [a]Matt. 7:15; 24:11 [b]John 4:48; 2 Thess. 2:9 [c]Matt. 22:14 [Gr.]; 24:22, 31; Luke 18:7
27 [a]Luke 17:23f. [b]Matt. 24:3, 37, 39 [c]Matt. 8:20
28 [a]Job 39:30; Ezek. 39:17; Hab. 1:8; Luke 17:37
29 [a]Matt. 24:21 [b]Is. 13:10; 24:23; Ezek. 32:7; Amos 5:20; 8:9; Zeph. 1:15; Acts 2:20; Rev. 6:12; 8:12 [c]Is. 34:4; Rev. 6:13
30 [a]Matt. 24:3; Rev. 1:7 [b]Dan. 7:13; Matt. 16:27; 24:3, 37, 39
31 [a]Matt. 13:41 [b]Ex. 19:16; Is. 27:13; Zech. 9:14; 1 Cor. 15:52; 1 Thess. 4:16; Heb. 12:19; Rev. 8:2; 11:15 [c]Matt. 24:22 [d]Dan. 7:2; Zech. 2:6; Rev. 7:1 [e]Deut. 4:32
33 [a]James 5:9; Rev. 3:20
34 [a]Matt. 10:23
35 [a]Matt. 5:18; Mark 13:31; Luke 21:33
36 [a]Mark 13:32; Acts 1:7
37 [a]Matt. 16:27; 24:3, 30, 39 [b]Gen. 6:5; 7:6-23
38 [a]Matt. 22:30 [b]Gen. 7:7
39 [a]Matt. 16:27; 24:3

41 "[a]Two women *will be* grinding at the [b]mill; one will be taken, and one will be left.

Be Ready for His Coming

42 "Therefore [a]be on the alert, for you do not know which day your Lord is coming.

43 "But [1]be sure of this, that [a]if the head of the house had known [b]at what time of the night the thief was coming, he would have been on the alert and would not have allowed his house to be [2]broken into.

44 "For this reason [a]you be ready too; for [b]the Son of Man is coming at an hour when you do not think *He will.*

45 "[a]Who then is the [b]faithful and [c]sensible slave whom his [1]master [d]put in charge of his household to give them their food at the proper time?

46 "Blessed is that slave whom his [1]master finds so doing when he comes.

47 "Truly I say to you, that [a]he will put him in charge of all his possessions.

48 "But if that evil slave says in his heart, 'My [1]master is not coming for a long time,'

49 and shall begin to beat his fellow-slaves and eat and drink with [1]drunkards;

50 the [1]master of that slave will come on a day when he does not expect *him* and at an hour which he does not know,

51 and shall [1]cut him in pieces and [2]assign him a place with the hypocrites; [a]weeping shall be there and the gnashing of teeth.

Chapter 25

Parable of Ten Virgins

"THEN [a]the kingdom of heaven will be comparable to ten virgins, who took their [b]lamps, and went out to meet the bridegroom.

2 "And five of them were foolish, and five were [a]prudent.

3 "For when the foolish took their lamps, they took no oil with them,

4 but the [a]prudent took oil in flasks along with their lamps.

5 "Now while the bridegroom was delaying, they all got drowsy and *began* to sleep.

6 "But at midnight there was a shout, 'Behold, the bridegroom! Come out to meet *him.*'

7 "Then all those virgins arose, and trimmed their lamps.

8 "And the foolish said to the prudent, 'Give us some of your oil, for our lamps are going out.'

9 "But the [a]prudent answered, saying, 'No, there will not be enough for us and you *too;* go instead to the dealers and buy *some* for yourselves.'

10 "And while they were going away to make the purchase, the bridegroom came, and those who were [a]ready went in with him to [b]the wedding feast; and [c]the door was shut.

11 "And later the other virgins also came, saying, '[a]Lord, lord, open up for us.'

12 "But he answered and said, 'Truly I say to you, I do not know you.'

13 "[a]Be on the alert then, for you do not know the day nor the hour.

Parable of the Talents

14 "[a]For *it is* just like a man [b]*about* to go on a journey, who called his own slaves, and entrusted his possessions to them.

15 "And to one he gave five [1a]talents, to another, two, and to another, one, each according to his own ability; and he [b]went on his journey.

16 "Immediately the one who had received the five [a]talents went and traded with them, and gained five more talents.

17 "In the same manner the one who had *received* the two *talents* gained two more.

18 "But he who received the one *talent* went away and dug in the ground, and hid his [1]master's money.

19 "Now after a long time the master of those slaves *came and *[a]settled accounts with them.

20 "And the one who had received the five [a]talents came up and brought five more talents, saying, 'Master, you entrusted five talents to me; see, I have gained five more talents.'

21 "His master said to him, 'Well done, good and [a]faithful slave; you were faithful with a few things, I will put you in charge of many things, enter into the joy of your [1]master.'

22 "The one also who had *received* the two [a]talents came up and said, 'Master, you entrusted to me two talents; see, I have gained two more talents.'

23 "His master said to him, 'Well done, good and [a]faithful slave; you were faithful with a few things, I

---

41 [a]Luke 17:35 [b]Ex. 11:5; Deut. 24:6; Is. 47:2
42 [a]Matt. 24:43, 44; 25:10, 13; Luke 12:39f.; 21:36
43 [1]Lit., *know this* [2]Lit., *dug through* [a]Matt. 24:42, 44; 25:10, 13; Luke 12:39f.; 21:36 [b]Matt. 14:25; Mark 6:48; 13:35; Luke 12:38
44 [a]Matt. 24:42, 43; 25:10, 13; Luke 12:39f.; 21:36 [b]Matt. 24:27
45 [1]Or, *lord* [a]Matt. 24:45-51: *Luke 1:42-46* [b]Matt. 25:21, 23; Luke 16:10 [c]Matt. 7:24; 10:16; 25:2ff. [d]Matt. 25:21, 23
46 [1]Or, *lord*
47 [a]Matt. 25:21, 23
48 [1]Or, *lord*
49 [1]Lit., *those who get drunk*
50 [1]Or, *lord*
51 [1]Or, *severely scourge him* [2]Lit., *appoint his portion* [a]Matt. 8:12
1 [a]Matt. 13:24 [b]John 18:3; Acts 20:8; Rev. 4:5; 8:10 [Gr.]
2 [a]Matt. 7:24; 10:16; 25:2ff.
4 [a]Matt. 7:24; 10:16; 25:2ff.
9 [a]Matt. 7:24; 10:16; 25:2ff.
10 [a]Matt. 24:42ff. [b]Luke 12:35f. [c]Matt. 7:21ff.; Luke 13:25
11 [a]Matt. 7:21ff.; Luke 13:25
13 [a]Matt. 24:42ff.
14 [a]Matt. 25:14-30; Luke 19:12-27 [b]Matt. 21:33
15 [1]A talent was $1,000 in silver content, much more in buying power. [a]Matt. 18:24; Luke 19:13 [b]Matt. 21:33
16 [a]Matt. 18:24; Luke 19:13
18 [1]Or, *lord's*
19 [a]Matt. 18:23
20 [a]Matt. 18:24; Luke 19:13
21 [1]Or, *lord* [a]Matt. 24:45, 47; 25:23
22 [a]Matt. 18:24; Luke 19:13
23 [a]Matt. 24:45, 47; 25:21

will put you in charge of many
things; enter into the joy of your
master.'
24"And the one also who had received the one [a]talent came up and
said, 'Master, I knew you to be a
hard man, reaping where you did
not sow, and gathering where you
scattered no *seed*.
25 'And I was afraid, and went
away and hid your talent in the
ground; see, you have what is
yours.'
26"But his master answered and
said to him, 'You wicked, lazy slave,
you knew that I reap where I did not
sow, and gather where I scattered
no *seed*.
27 'Then you ought to have put my
money [1]in the bank, and on my arrival I would have received my
money back with interest.
28 'Therefore take away the talent
from him, and give it to the one who
has the ten talents.'
29"[a]For to everyone who has shall
more be given, and he shall have an
abundance; but from the one who
does not have, even what he does
have shall be taken away.
30"And cast out the worthless
slave into [a]the outer darkness; in
that place there shall be weeping
and gnashing of teeth.

The Judgment

31"But when [a]the Son of Man
comes in His glory, and all the angels with Him, then [b]He will sit on
His glorious throne.
32"And all the nations will be gathered before Him; and He will separate them from one another, [a]as the
shepherd separates the sheep from
the goats;
33 and He will put the sheep [a]on
His right, and the goats [b]on the left.
34"Then the King will say to those
on His right, 'Come, you who are
blessed of My Father, [a]inherit the
kingdom prepared for you [b]from the
foundation of the world.
35 'For [a]I was hungry, and you
gave Me *something* to eat; I was
thirsty, and you gave Me drink; [b]I
was a stranger, and you invited Me
in;
36 [a]naked, and you clothed Me; I
was sick, and you [b]visited Me; [c]I
was in prison, and you came to Me.'
37"Then the righteous will answer
Him, saying, 'Lord, when did we see
You hungry, and feed You, or
thirsty, and give You drink?
38 'And when did we see You a
stranger, and invite You in, or
naked, and clothe You?
39 'And when did we see You sick,
or in prison, and come to You?'
40"And [a]the King will answer and
say to them, 'Truly I say to you, [b]to
the extent that you did it to one of
these brothers of Mine, *even* the
least *of them*, you did it to Me.'
41"Then He will also say to those
on His left, '[a]Depart from Me, accursed ones, into the [b]eternal fire
which has been prepared for [c]the
devil and his angels;
42 for I was hungry, and you gave
Me *nothing* to eat; I was thirsty, and
you gave Me nothing to drink;
43 I was a stranger, and you did
not invite Me in; naked, and you did
not clothe Me; sick, and in prison,
and you did not visit Me.'
44"Then they themselves also will
answer, saying, 'Lord, when did we
see You hungry, or thirsty, or a
stranger, or naked, or sick, or in
prison, and did not [1]take care of
You?'
45"Then He will answer them, saying, 'Truly I say to you, to the extent
that you did not do it to one of the
least of these, you did not do it to
Me.'
46"And these will go away into
[a]eternal punishment, but the righteous into [b]eternal life."

Chapter 26

The Plot to Kill Jesus

[a]AND it came about that when Jesus had finished all these words, He
said to His disciples,
2"[a]You know that after two days
[b]the Passover is coming, and the
Son of Man is *to be* [c]delivered up for
crucifixion."
3 [a]Then the chief priests and the
elders of the people were gathered
together in [b]the court of the high
priest, named [c]Caiaphas;
4 and they [a]plotted together to
seize Jesus by stealth, and kill *Him*.
5 But they were saying, "Not during the festival, [a]lest a riot occur
among the people."

The Precious Ointment

6 [a]Now when Jesus was in [b]Beth-
any, at the home of Simon the leper,
7 a woman came to Him with an
alabaster vial of very costly perfume, and she poured it upon His
head as He reclined *at table*.
8 But the disciples were indignant when they saw *this*, and said,
"What is the point of this waste?
9"For this *perfume* might have

24 [a]Matt. 18:24; Luke 19:13
27 [1]Lit., *to the bankers*
29 [a]Matt. 13:12
30 [a]Matt. 8:12
31 [a]Matt. 16:27f. [b]Matt. 19:28
32 [a]Ezek. 34:17, 20
33 [a]1 Kin. 2:19; Ps. 45:9 [b]Eccles. 10:2
34 [a]Matt. 5:3; 19:29; Luke 12:32; 1 Cor. 6:9; 15:50; Gal. 5:21; James 2:5 [b]Matt. 13:35; Luke 11:50; John 17:24; Eph. 1:4; Heb. 4:3; 9:26; 1 Pet. 1:20; Rev. 13:8; 17:8
35 [a]Is. 58:7; Ezek. 18:7, 16; James 2:15, 16 [b]Job 31:32; Heb. 13:2
36 [a]Is. 58:7; Ezek. 18:7, 16; James 2:15, 16 [b]James 1:27 [c]2 Tim. 1:16f.
40 [a]Matt. 25:34; Luke 19:38; Rev. 17:14; 19:16 [b]Prov. 19:17; Matt. 10:42; Heb. 6:10
41 [a]Matt. 7:23 [b]Mark 9:48; Luke 16:24; Jude 7 [c]Matt. 4:10; Rev. 12:9
44 [1]Or, *serve*
46 [a]Dan. 12:2; John 5:29; Acts 24:15 [b]Matt. 19:29; John 3:15f., 36; 5:24; 6:27, 40, 47, 54; 17:2f.; Acts 13:46, 48; Rom. 2:7; 5:21; 6:23; Gal. 6:8; 1 John 5:11
1 [a]Matt. 7:28
2 [a]Matt. 26:2-5: *Mark 14:1-2; Luke 22:1-2* [b]John 11:55; 13:1 [c]Matt. 10:4
3 [a]John 11:47 [b]Matt. 26:58, 69; 27:27; Mark 14:54, 66; 15:16; Luke 11:21; 22:55; John 18:15 [c]Matt. 26:57; Luke 3:2; John 11:49; 18:13, 14, 24, 28; Acts 4:6
4 [a]Matt. 12:14
5 [a]Matt. 27:24
6 [a]Matt. 26:6-13: *Mark 14:3-9;* Luke 7:37-39; John 12:1-8 [b]Matt. 21:17

been sold for a high price and *the*
money given to the poor."
10 But Jesus, aware of this, said to
them, "Why do you bother the
woman? For she has done a good
deed to Me.
11 "For [a]the poor you have with
you always; but you do not always
have Me.
12 "For when she poured this perfume upon My body, she did it [a]to
prepare Me for burial.
13 "Truly I say to you, [a]wherever
this gospel is preached in the whole
world, what this woman has done
shall also be spoken of in memory of
her."

Judas' Bargain

14 [a]Then one of the twelve, named
[b]Judas Iscariot, went to the chief
priests,
15 and said, "What are you willing
to give me to [a]deliver Him up to
you?" And [b]they weighed out to him
thirty [1]pieces of silver.
16 And from then on he *began*
looking for a good opportunity to
[1]betray Him.
17 [a]Now on the first *day* of [b]the
Feast of Unleavened Bread the disciples came to Jesus, saying,
"Where do You want us to prepare
for You to eat the Passover?"
18 And He said, "Go into the city
to [a]a certain man, and say to him,
'The Teacher says, "[b]My time is at
hand; I *am to* keep the Passover at
your house with My disciples." ' "
19 And the disciples did as Jesus
had directed them; and they prepared the Passover.

The Last Passover

20 [a]Now when evening had come,
He was reclining *at table* with the
twelve disciples.
21 And as they were eating, He
said, "[a]Truly I say to you that one of
you will betray Me."
22 And being deeply grieved, they
each one began to say to Him,
"Surely not I, Lord?"
23 And He answered and said,
"[a]He who dipped his hand with Me
in the bowl is the one who will betray Me.
24 "The Son of Man *is to* go, [a]just as
it is written of Him; but woe to that
man through whom the Son of Man
is betrayed! [b]It would have been
good [1]for that man if he had not
been born."
25 And [a]Judas, who was betraying
Him, answered and said, "Surely it
is not I, [b]Rabbi?" He *said to him,
"[c]You have said *it* yourself."

The Lord's Supper Instituted

26 [a]And while they were eating,
Jesus took *some* bread, and [b]after a
blessing, He broke it and gave *it* to
the disciples, and said, "Take, eat;
this is My body."
27 And He took a cup and gave
thanks, and gave *it* to them, saying,
"Drink from it, all of you;
28 for [a]this is My blood of the covenant, which is *to be* shed on behalf
of [b]many for forgiveness of sins.
29 "But I say to you, I will not drink
of this fruit of the vine from now on
until that day when I drink it new
with you in My Father's kingdom."
30 [a]And after singing a hymn, they
went out to [b]the Mount of Olives.
31 Then Jesus *said to them, "You
will all [a]fall away because of Me this
night, for it is written, '[b]I WILL
STRIKE DOWN THE SHEPHERD, AND
THE SHEEP OF THE FLOCK SHALL BE
[c]SCATTERED.'
32 "But after I have been raised, [a]I
will go before you to Galilee."
33 But Peter answered and said to
Him, "*Even* though all may fall
away because of You, I will never
fall away."
34 Jesus said to him, "[a]Truly I say
to you that [b]this *very* night, before a
cock crows, you shall deny Me three
times."
35 Peter *said to Him, "[a]Even if I
must die with You, I will not deny
You." All the disciples said the same
thing too.

The Garden of Gethsemane

36 [a]Then Jesus *came with them
to a place called [b]Gethsemane, and
*said to His disciples, "Sit here
while I go over there and pray."
37 And He took with Him [a]Peter
and the two sons of Zebedee, and
began to be grieved and distressed.
38 Then He *said to them, "[a]My
soul is deeply grieved, to the point
of death; remain here and [b]keep
watch with Me."
39 And He went a little beyond
them, and fell on His face and
prayed, saying, "My Father, if it is
possible, let [a]this cup pass from Me;
[b]yet not as I will, but as Thou wilt."
40 And He *came to the disciples
and *found them sleeping, and *said
to Peter, "So, you *men* could not
[a]keep watch with Me for one hour?
41 "[a]Keep watching and praying,
that you may not enter into temptation; [b]the spirit is willing, but the
flesh is weak."
42 He went away again a second
time and prayed, saying, "My Fa-

11 [a]Deut. 15:11; Mark 14:7; John 12:8
12 [a]John 19:40
13 [a]Mark 14:9
14 [a]Matt. 26:14-16: *Mark 14:10, 11; Luke 22:3-6* [b]Matt. 10:4; 26:25, 47; 27:3; John 6:71; 12:4; 13:26; Acts 1:16
15 [1]Or, *silver shekels* [a]Matt. 10:4 [b]Ex. 21:32; Zech. 11:12
16 [1]Or, *deliver Him up*
17 [a]Matt. 26:17-19: *Mark 14:12-16; Luke 22:7-13* [b]Ex. 12:18-20
18 [a]Mark 14:13; Luke 22:10 [b]John 7:6, 8
20 [a]Matt. 26:20-24: *Mark 14:17-21*
21 [a]Luke 22:21-23; John 13:21f.
23 [a]John 13:18, 26
24 [1]Lit., *for him if that man had not been born* [a]Matt. 26:31, 54, 56; Mark 9:12; Luke 24:25-27, 46; Acts 17:2f.; 26:22f.; 1 Cor. 15:3; 1 Pet. 1:10f. [b]Matt. 18:7; Mark 14:21
25 [a]Matt. 26:14 [b]Matt. 23:7; 26:49 [c]Matt. 26:64; 27:11; Luke 22:70
26 [a]Matt. 26:26-29: *Mark 14:22-25; Luke 22:17-20; 1 Cor. 11:23-25;* 1 Cor. 10:16 [b]Matt. 14:19
28 [a]Heb. 9:20 [b]Matt. 20:28
30 [a]Matt. 26:30-35: *Mark 14:26-31; Luke 22:31-34* [b]Matt. 21:1
31 [a]Matt. 11:6 [b]Zech. 13:7 [c]John 16:32
32 [a]Matt. 28:7, 10, 16; Mark 16:7
34 [a]Matt. 26:75; John 13:38 [b]Mark 14:30
35 [a]John 13:37
36 [a]Matt. 26:36-46: *Mark 14:32-42; Luke 22:40-46* [b]Mark 14:32; Luke 22:39; John 18:1
37 [a]Matt. 4:21; 17:1; Mark 5:37
38 [a]John 12:27 [b]Matt. 26:40, 41
39 [a]Matt. 20:22 [b]Matt. 26:42; Mark 14:36; Luke 22:42; John 6:38
40 [a]Matt. 26:38
41 [a]Matt. 26:38 [b]Mark 14:38

ther, if this [a]cannot pass away unless I drink it, [b]Thy will be done."
43 And He came back and found
them sleeping, for their eyes were
heavy.
44 And He left them again, and
went away and prayed a third time,
saying the same thing once more.
45 Then He *came to the disciples,
and *said to them, "Are you still
sleeping and taking your rest? Behold, [a]the hour is at hand and the
Son of Man is being betrayed into
the hands of sinners.
46"Arise, let us be going; behold,
the one who betrays Me is at hand!"

Jesus' Betrayal and Arrest

47 [a]And while He was still speaking, behold, [b]Judas, one of the
twelve, came up, accompanied by a
great multitude with swords and
clubs, from the chief priests and elders of the people.
48 Now he who was betraying
Him gave them a sign, saying,
"Whomever I shall kiss, He is the
one; seize Him."
49 And immediately he came to
Jesus and said, "Hail, [a]Rabbi!" and
kissed Him.
50 And Jesus said to him,
"[a]Friend, *do* what you have come
for." Then they came and laid hands
on Jesus and seized Him.
51 And behold, [a]one of those who
were with Jesus reached and drew
out his [b]sword, and struck the [c]slave
of the high priest, and cut off his ear.
52 Then Jesus *said to him, "Put
your sword back into its place; for
[a]all those who take up the sword
shall perish by the sword.
53"Or do you think that I cannot
appeal to My Father, and He will at
once put at My disposal more than
twelve [1a]legions of [b]angels?
54"How then shall [a]the Scriptures
be fulfilled, that it must happen this
way?"
55 At that time Jesus said to the
multitudes, "Have you come out
with swords and clubs to arrest Me
as though *I were* a robber? [a]Every
day I used to sit in the temple teaching and you did not seize Me.
56"But all this has taken place that
[a]the Scriptures of the prophets may
be fulfilled." Then all the disciples
left Him and fled.

Jesus Before Caiaphas

57 [a]And those who had seized Jesus led Him away to [b]Caiaphas, the
high priest, where the scribes and
the elders were gathered together.
58 But [a]Peter also followed Him at
a distance as far as the [b]courtyard of
the high priest, and entered in, and
sat down with the [1c]officers to see
the outcome.
59 Now the chief priests and the
whole [1a]Council kept trying to obtain false testimony against Jesus,
in order that they might put Him to
death;
60 and they did not find it, even
though many false witnesses came
forward. But later on [a]two came forward,
61 and said, "This man stated, '[a]I
am able to destroy the temple of
God and to rebuild it in three
days.'"
62 And the high priest stood up
and said to Him, "Do You make no
answer? What is it that these men
are testifying against You?"
63 But [a]Jesus kept silent. [b]And the
high priest said to Him, "I [1c]adjure
You by [d]the living God, that You tell
us whether You are [2]the Christ, [e]the
Son of God."
64 Jesus *said to him, "[a]You have
said it *yourself;* nevertheless I tell
you, hereafter you shall see [b]THE
SON OF MAN SITTING AT THE RIGHT
HAND OF POWER, *and* [c]COMING ON
THE CLOUDS OF HEAVEN."
65 Then the high priest [a]tore his
robes, saying, "He has blasphemed!
What further need do we have of
witnesses? Behold, you have now
heard the blasphemy;
66 what do you think?" They answered and said, "[a]He is deserving
of death!"
67 [a]Then they [b]spat in His face and
beat Him with their fists; and others
slapped Him,
68 and said, "[a]Prophesy to us, You
[1]Christ; who is the one who hit
You?"

Peter's Denials

69 [a]Now Peter was sitting outside
in the [b]courtyard, and a certain servant-girl came to him and said,
"You too were with Jesus the Galilean."
70 But he denied *it* before them all,
saying, "I do not know what you are
talking about."
71 And when he had gone out to
the gateway, another *servant-girl*
saw him and *said to those who
were there, "This man was with Jesus of Nazareth."
72 And again he denied *it* with an
oath, "I do not know the man."
73 And a little later the bystanders
came up and said to Peter, "Surely

42 [a]Matt. 20:22 [b]Matt. 26:39; Mark 14:36; Luke 22:42; John 6:38
45 [a]Mark 14:41; John 12:27; 13:1
47 [a]Matt. 26:47-56: *Mark 14:43-50; Luke 22:47-53; John 18:3-11* [b]Matt. 26:14
49 [a]Matt. 23:7; 26:25
50 [a]Matt. 20:13; 22:12
51 [a]Mark 14:47; Luke 22:50; John 18:10 [b]Luke 22:38 [c]Mark 14:47; Luke 22:50; John 18:10
52 [a]Gen. 9:6; Rev. 13:10
53 [1]A legion equaled 6,000 troops [a]Mark 5:9, 15; Luke 8:30 [b]Matt. 4:11
54 [a]Matt. 26:24
55 [a]Mark 12:35; 14:49; Luke 4:20; 19:47; 20:1; 21:37; John 7:14, 28; 8:2, 20; 18:20
56 [a]Matt. 26:24
57 [a]Matt. 26:57-68: *Mark 14:53-65; John 18:12f., 19-24* [b]Matt. 26:3
58 [1]Or, *servants* [a]John 18:15 [b]Matt. 26:3 [c]Matt. 5:25; John 7:32, 45f.; 19:6; Acts 5:22, 26
59 [1]Or, *Sanhedrin* [a]Matt. 5:22
60 [a]Deut. 19:15
61 [a]Matt. 27:40; Mark 14:58; 15:29; John 2:19; Acts 6:14
63 [1]Or, *charge You under oath* [2]I.e., the Messiah [a]Matt. 27:12, 14; John 19:9 [b]Matt. 26:63-66; Luke 22:67-71 [c]Lev. 5:1 [d]Matt. 16:16 [e]Matt. 4:3
64 [a]Matt. 26:25 [b]Ps. 110:1 [c]Dan. 7:13; Matt. 16:27f.
65 [a]Num. 14:6; Mark 14:63; Acts 14:14
66 [a]Lev. 24:16; John 19:7
67 [a]Matt. 26:67, 68; Luke 22:63-65; John 18:22 [b]Matt. 27:30; Mark 10:34
68 [1]I.e., the Messiah [a]Mark 14:65; Luke 22:64
69 [a]Matt. 26:69-75: *Mark 14:66-72; Luke 22:55-62; John 18:16-18, 25-27* [b]Matt. 26:3

you too are *one* of them; [a]for the
way you talk [1]gives you away."
74 Then he began to curse and
swear, "I do not know the man!"
And immediately a cock crowed.
75 And Peter remembered the
word which Jesus had said, "[a]Be-
fore a cock crows, you will deny Me
three times." And he went out and
wept bitterly.

Chapter 27

Judas' Remorse

[a]Now when morning had come, all
the chief priests and the elders of
the people took counsel against Jesus to put Him to death;
2 and they bound Him, and led
Him away, and [a]delivered Him up to
[b]Pilate the governor.
3 Then when [a]Judas, who had betrayed Him, saw that He had been
condemned, he felt remorse and returned [b]the thirty [1]pieces of silver to
the chief priests and elders,
4 saying, "I have sinned by betraying innocent blood." But they
said, "What is that to us? [a]See *to*
that yourself!"
5 And he threw the pieces of silver into [a]the sanctuary and departed; and [b]he went away and
hanged himself.
6 And the chief priests took the
pieces of silver and said, "It is not
lawful to put them into the temple
treasury, since it is the price of
blood."
7 And they counseled together
and with the money bought the Potter's Field as a burial place for
strangers.
8 [a]For this reason that field has
been called the Field of Blood to this
day.
9 Then that which was spoken
through Jeremiah the prophet was
fulfilled, saying, "[a]AND [1]THEY TOOK
THE THIRTY PIECES OF SILVER, THE
PRICE OF THE ONE WHOSE PRICE HAD
BEEN SET BY THE SONS OF ISRAEL;
10 AND [1]THEY GAVE THEM FOR THE
POTTER'S FIELD, AS THE LORD DI-
RECTED ME."

Jesus Before Pilate

11 [a]Now Jesus stood before the
governor, and the governor questioned Him, saying, "Are You the
[b]King of the Jews?" And Jesus said
to him, "[c]*It is as* you say."
12 And while He was being accused by the chief priests and elders, [a]He made no answer.
13 Then Pilate *said to Him, "Do
You not hear how many things they
testify against You?"
14 And [a]He did not answer him
with regard to even a *single* charge,
so that the governor was quite
amazed.
15 [a]Now at *the* feast the governor
was accustomed to release for the
multitude *any* one prisoner whom
they wanted.
16 And they were holding at that
time a notorious prisoner, called
Barabbas.
17 When therefore they were
gathered together, Pilate said to
them, "Whom do you want me to
release for you? Barabbas, or Jesus
[a]who is called Christ?"
18 For he knew that because of
envy they had delivered Him up.
19 And [a]while he was sitting on
the judgment seat, his wife sent to
him, saying, "Have nothing to do
with that [b]righteous Man; for [1]last
night I suffered greatly [c]in a dream
because of Him."
20 But the chief priests and the elders persuaded the multitudes to
[a]ask for Barabbas, and to put Jesus
to death.
21 But the governor answered and
said to them, "Which of the two do
you want me to release for you?"
And they said, "Barabbas."
22 Pilate *said to them, "What
then shall I do with Jesus [a]who is
called Christ?" They all *said, "Let
Him be crucified!"
23 And he said, "Why, what evil
has He done?" But they kept shouting all the more, saying, "Let Him be
crucified!"
24 And when Pilate saw that he
was accomplishing nothing, but
rather that [a]a riot was starting, he
took water and [b]washed his hands
in front of the multitude, saying, "I
am innocent of [1c]this Man's blood;
[d]see *to that* yourselves."
25 And all the people answered
and said, "[a]His blood *be* on us and
on our children!"
26 Then he released Barabbas [1]for
them; but Jesus he [a]scourged and
delivered over to be crucified.

Jesus Is Mocked

27 [a]Then the soldiers of the governor took Jesus into [b]the Praetorium
and gathered the whole *Roman*
[1c]cohort around Him.
28 And they stripped Him, and
[a]put a scarlet robe on Him.
29 [a]And after weaving a crown of
thorns, they put it on His head, and
a [1]reed in His right hand; and they
kneeled down before Him and

73 [1]Lit., *makes you evident* [a]Mark 14:70; Luke 22:59; John 18:26
75 [a]Matt. 26:34
1 [a]Mark 15:1; Luke 22:66; John 18:28
2 [a]Matt. 20:19 [b]Luke 3:1; 13:1; 23:12; Acts 3:13; 4:27; 1 Tim. 6:13
3 [1]Or, *silver shekels* [a]Matt. 26:14 [b]Matt. 26:15
4 [a]Matt. 27:24
5 [a]Matt. 26:61 marg.; Luke 1:9, 21 [b]Acts 1:18
8 [a]Acts 1:19
9 [1]Some mss. read, *I took* [a]Zech. 11:12, 13; cf., Jer. 18:2; 19:2, 11; 32:6-9
10 [1]Some mss. read, *I gave*
11 [a]Matt. 27:11-14: *Mark 15:2-5; Luke 23:2-3; John 18:29-38* [b]Matt. 2:2 [c]Matt. 26:25
12 [a]Matt. 26:63; John 19:9
14 [a]Matt. 27:12; Mark 15:5; Luke 23:9; John 19:9
15 [a]Matt. 27:15-26: *Mark 15:6-15; Luke 23:[17]-25;* John 18:39-19:16
17 [a]Matt. 1:16; 27:22
19 [1]Lit., *today* [a]John 19:13; Acts 12:21 marg.; 18:12, 16f.; 25:6, 10, 17 [b]Matt. 27:24 [c]Gen. 20:6; 31:11; Num. 12:6; Job 33:15; Matt. 1:20; 2:12f., 19, 22
20 [a]Acts 3:14
22 [a]Matt. 1:16
24 [1]Many mss. read, *the blood of this righteous Man* [a]Matt. 26:5 [b]Deut. 21:6-8 [c]Matt. 27:19 [d]Matt. 27:4
25 [a]Josh. 2:19; Acts 5:28
26 [1]Or, *to them* [a]Mark 15:15; Luke 23:16; John 19:1
27 [1]Or, *battalion* [a]Matt. 27:27-31: *Mark 15:16-20* [b]Matt. 26:3; John 18:28, 33; 19:9 [c]Acts 10:1
28 [a]Mark 15:17; John 19:2
29 [1]Or, *staff* (made of a reed) [a]Mark 15:17; John 19:2

mocked Him, saying, "[b]Hail, King of the Jews!"

30 And [a]they spat on Him, and took the reed and *began* to beat Him on the head.

31 [a]And after they had mocked Him, they took His robe off and put His garments on Him, and led Him away to crucify *Him*.

32 [a]And as they were coming out, they found a certain [b]Cyrenian named Simon; this man they pressed into service to bear His cross.

The Crucifixion

33 [a]And when they had come to a place called [b]Golgotha, which means Place of a Skull,

34 [a]THEY GAVE HIM [b]WINE TO DRINK MINGLED WITH GALL; and after tasting *it*, He was unwilling to drink.

35 And when they had crucified Him, [a]THEY DIVIDED UP HIS GARMENTS AMONG THEMSELVES, CASTING LOTS;

36 and sitting down, they *began* to [a]keep watch over Him there.

37 And they put up above His head the charge against Him which read, "[a]THIS IS JESUS THE KING OF THE JEWS."

38 At that time two robbers *were crucified with Him, one on the right and one on the left.

39 And those who were passing by were hurling abuse at Him, [a]WAGGING THEIR HEADS,

40 and saying, "[a]You who destroy the temple and rebuild it in three days, save Yourself! [b]If You are the Son of God, come down from the cross."

41 In the same way the chief priests, along with the scribes and elders, were mocking *Him*, and saying,

42 "[a]He saved others; He cannot save Himself. [b]He is the King of Israel; let Him now come down from the cross, and we shall believe in Him.

43 "[a]HE TRUSTS IN GOD; LET HIM DELIVER *Him* now, IF HE TAKES PLEASURE IN HIM; for He said, 'I am the Son of God.' "

44 [a]And the robbers also who had been crucified with Him were casting the same insult at Him.

45 [a]Now from the [1]sixth hour darkness fell upon all the land until the [2]ninth hour.

46 And about the ninth hour Jesus cried out with a loud voice, saying, "ELI, ELI, LAMA SABACHTHANI?" that is, "[a]MY GOD, MY GOD, WHY HAST THOU FORSAKEN ME?"

47 And some of those who were standing there, when they heard it, *began* saying, "This man is calling for Elijah."

48 And [a]immediately one of them ran, and taking a sponge, he filled it with sour wine, and put it on a reed, and gave Him a drink.

49 But the rest *of them* said, "Let us see whether Elijah will come to save Him."[1]

50 And Jesus [a]cried out again with a loud voice, and yielded up *His* spirit.

51 [a]And behold, [b]the veil of the temple was torn in two from top to bottom, and [c]the earth shook; and the rocks were split,

52 and the tombs were opened; and many bodies of the saints who had [a]fallen asleep were raised;

53 and coming out of the tombs after His resurrection they entered [a]the holy city and appeared to many.

54 [a]Now the centurion, and those who were with him [b]keeping guard over Jesus, when they saw [c]the earthquake and the things that were happening, became very frightened and said, "Truly this was [d]the Son of God!"

55 [a]And many women were there looking on from a distance, who had followed Jesus from Galilee, [b]ministering to Him,

56 among whom was [a]Mary Magdalene, *along with* Mary the mother of James and Joseph, and [b]the mother of the sons of Zebedee.

Jesus Is Buried

57 [a]And when it was evening, there came a rich man from Arimathea, named Joseph, who himself had also become a disciple of Jesus.

58 This man came to Pilate and asked for the body of Jesus. Then Pilate ordered *it* to be given over *to him*.

59 And Joseph took the body and wrapped it in a clean linen cloth,

60 and laid it in his own new tomb, which he had hewn out in the rock; and he rolled [a]a large stone against the entrance of the tomb and went away.

61 And [a]Mary Magdalene was there, and the other Mary, sitting opposite the grave.

62 Now on the next day, which is *the one* after [a]the preparation, the chief priests and the Pharisees gathered together with Pilate,

29 [b]Mark 15:18; John 19:1
30 [a]Matt. 26:67; Mark 10:34
31 [a]Mark 15:20
32 [a]Matt. 27:32: *Mark 15:21; Luke 23:26;* John 19:17 [b]Acts 2:10; 6:9
33 [a]Matt. 27:34-44: *Mark 15:22-32; Luke 23:33-43; John 19:17-24* [b]Luke 23:33 and marg.; John 19:17
34 [a]Ps. 69:21 [b]Mark 15:23
35 [a]Ps. 22:18
36 [a]Matt. 27:54
37 [a]Mark 15:26; Luke 23:38
39 [a]Job 16:4; Ps. 22:7; 109:25; Lam. 2:15; Mark 15:29
40 [a]Matt. 26:61 [b]Matt. 27:42
42 [a]Mark 15:31; Luke 23:35 [b]Matt. 27:37; Luke 23:37; John 1:49; 12:13
43 [a]Ps. 22:8
44 [a]Luke 23:39-43
45 [1]I.e., noon [2]I.e., 3 p.m. [a]Matt. 27:45-56: *Mark 15:33-41; Luke 23:44-49*
46 [a]Ps. 22:1
48 [a]Mark 15:36; Luke 23:36; John 19:29
49 [1]Some early mss. add: *And another took a spear and pierced His side, and there came out water and blood.* (cf. John 19:34)
50 [a]Mark 15:37; Luke 23:46; John 19:30
51 [a]Matt. 27:51-56: *Mark 15:38-41;* Luke 23:47-49 [b]Ex. 26:31ff.; Mark 15:38 [c]Matt. 27:54
52 [a]Acts 7:60
53 [a]Matt. 4:5
54 [a]Mark 15:39; Luke 23:47 [b]Matt. 27:36 [c]Matt. 27:51 [d]Matt. 4:3; 27:43
55 [a]Mark 15:40f.; Luke 23:49; John 19:25 [b]Mark 15:41; Luke 8:2, 3
56 [a]Matt. 28:1; Mark 15:40, 47; John 19:25; 20:1, 18 [b]Matt. 20:20
57 [a]Matt. 27:57-61: *Mark 15:42-47; Luke 23:50-56; John 19:38-42*
60 [a]Matt. 27:66; 28:2; Mark 16:4
61 [a]Matt. 27:56
62 [a]Mark 15:42; Luke 23:54; John 19:14, 31, 42

63 and said, "Sir, we remember that when He was still alive that deceiver said, '[a]After three days I *am to* rise again.'

64 "Therefore, give orders for the grave to be made secure until the third day, lest the disciples come and steal Him away and say to the people, 'He has risen from the dead,' and the last deception will be worse than the first."

65 Pilate said to them, "You have a [a]guard; go, make it *as* secure as you know how."

66 And they went and made the grave secure, and along with [a]the guard they set a [b]seal on [c]the stone.

Chapter 28

[a] *Jesus Is Risen!*

NOW after the Sabbath, as it began to dawn toward the first *day* of the week, [b]Mary Magdalene and the other Mary came to look at the grave.

2 And behold, a severe earthquake had occurred, for [a]an angel of the Lord descended from heaven and came and rolled away [b]the stone and sat upon it.

3 And [a]his appearance was like lightning, and his garment as white as snow;

4 and the guards shook for fear of him, and became like dead men.

5 And the angel answered and said to the women, "[a]Do not be afraid; for I know that you are looking for Jesus who has been crucified.

6 "He is not here, for He has risen, [a]just as He said. Come, see the place where He was lying.

7 "And go quickly and tell His disciples that He has risen from the dead; and behold, He is going before you [a]into Galilee, there you will see Him; behold, I have told you."

8 And they departed quickly from the tomb with fear and great joy and ran to report it to His disciples.

9 And behold, Jesus met them and greeted them. And they came up and took hold of His feet and worshiped Him.

10 Then Jesus *said to them, "[a]Do not be afraid; go and take word to [b]My brethren to leave [c]for Galilee, and there they shall see Me."

11 Now while they were on their way, behold, some of [a]the guard came into the city and reported to the chief priests all that had happened.

12 And when they had assembled with the elders and counseled together, they gave a large sum of money to the soldiers,

13 and said, "You are to say, 'His disciples came by night and stole Him away while we were asleep.'

14 "And if this should come to [a]the governor's ears, we will win him over and [1]keep you out of trouble."

15 And they took the money and did as they had been instructed; and this story was widely [a]spread among the Jews, *and is* [b]to this day.

The Great Commission

16 But the eleven disciples proceeded [a]to Galilee, to the mountain which Jesus had designated.

17 And when they saw Him, they worshiped *Him*; but [a]some were doubtful.

18 And Jesus came up and spoke to them, saying, "[a]All authority has been given to Me in heaven and on earth.

19 "[a]Go therefore and [b]make disciples of [c]all the nations, [d]baptizing them in the name of the Father and the Son and the Holy Spirit,

20 teaching them to observe all that I commanded you; and lo, [a]I am with you [1]always, even to [b]the end of the age."

---

63 [a]Matt. 16:21
65 [a]Matt. 27:66; 28:11
66 [a]Matt. 27:65; 28:11 [b]Dan. 6:17 [c]Matt. 27:60; 28:2; Mark 16:4
1 [a]Matt. 28:1-8: *Mark 16:1-8; Luke 24:1-10;* John 20:1-8 [b]Matt. 27:56, 61
2 [a]Luke 24:4; John 20:12 [b]Matt. 27:66; 28:2; Mark 16:4
3 [a]Dan. 7:9; 10:6; Mark 9:3; John 20:12; Acts 1:10
5 [a]Matt. 14:27; 28:10
6 [a]Matt. 12:40; 16:21; 27:63
7 [a]Matt. 26:32; 28:10, 16
10 [a]Matt. 14:27; 28:5 [b]John 20:17; Rom. 8:29; Heb. 2:11f., 17 [c]Matt. 26:32; 28:7, 16
11 [a]Matt. 27:65, 66
14 [1]Lit., *make you free from care* [a]Matt. 27:2
15 [a]Matt. 9:31; Mark 1:45 [b]Matt. 27:8
16 [a]Matt. 26:32; 28:7, 10
17 [a]Mark 16:11
18 [a]Dan. 7:13f.; Matt. 11:27; 26:64; Rom. 14:9; Eph. 1:20-22; Phil. 2:9f.; Col. 2:10; 1 Pet. 3:22
19 [a]Mark 16:15f. [b]Matt. 13:52; Acts 14:21 [c]Matt. 25:32; Luke 24:47 [d]Acts 2:38; 8:16; Rom. 6:3; 1 Cor. 1:13, 15ff.; Gal. 3:27
20 [1]Lit., *all the days* [a]Matt. 18:20; Acts 18:10 [b]Matt. 13:39

THE GOSPEL
ACCORDING TO
MARK

Preaching of John the Baptist

THE beginning of the gospel of Jesus Christ, [1][a]the Son of God.

2 [a]As it is written in Isaiah the prophet,

"[b]BEHOLD, I SEND MY MESSENGER BEFORE YOUR FACE,
WHO WILL PREPARE YOUR WAY;

3 "[a]THE VOICE OF ONE CRYING IN THE WILDERNESS,
'MAKE READY THE WAY OF THE LORD,
MAKE HIS PATHS STRAIGHT.' "

4 John the Baptist appeared in the wilderness [1][a]preaching a baptism of repentance for the [b]forgiveness of sins.

5 And all the country of Judea was going out to him, and all the people of Jerusalem; and they were being baptized by him in the Jordan River, confessing their sins.

6 And John was clothed with camel's hair and *wore* a leather belt around his waist, and [1]his diet was locusts and wild honey.

7 And he was [1]preaching, and saying, "After me comes One who is mightier than I, and I am not *even* fit to stoop down and untie the thong of His sandals.

8 "I baptized you [1]with water; but He will baptize you [1]with the Holy Spirit."

The Baptism of Jesus

9 [a]And it came about in those days that Jesus [b]came from Nazareth in Galilee, and was baptized by John in the Jordan.

10 And immediately coming up out of the water, He saw the heavens [1]opening, and the Spirit like a dove descending upon Him;

11 and a voice came out of the heavens: "[a]Thou art My beloved Son, in Thee I am well-pleased."

12 [a]And immediately the Spirit *impelled Him *to go* out into the wilderness.

13 And He was in the wilderness forty days being tempted by [a]Satan; and He was with the wild beasts, and the angels were ministering to Him.

Jesus Preaches in Galilee

14 [a]And after John had been [1]taken into custody, Jesus came into Galilee, [2][b]preaching the gospel of God,

15 and saying, "[a]The time is fulfilled, and the kingdom of God is at hand; [b]repent and [1]believe in the gospel."

16 [a]And as He was going along by the Sea of Galilee, He saw Simon and Andrew, the brother of Simon, casting a net in the sea; for they were fishermen.

17 And Jesus said to them, "Follow Me, and I will make you become fishers of men."

18 And they immediately left the nets and followed Him.

19 And going on a little farther, He saw [1]James the *son* of Zebedee, and John his brother, who were also in the boat mending the nets.

20 And immediately He called them; and they left their father Zebedee in the boat with the hired servants, and went away [1]to follow Him.

21 [a]And they *went into Capernaum; and immediately on the Sabbath [b]He entered the synagogue and *began* to teach.

22 And [a]they were amazed at His teaching; for He was teaching them as *one* having authority, and not as the scribes.

23 And just then there was in their synagogue a man with an unclean spirit; and he cried out,

24 saying, "[a]What do we have to do with You, Jesus of [1][b]Nazareth? Have You come to destroy us? I know who You are—[c]the Holy One of God!"

25 And Jesus rebuked him, saying, "Be quiet, and come out of him!"

26 And throwing him into convulsions, the unclean spirit cried out with a loud voice, and came out of him.

27 And they were all [a]amazed, so that they debated among themselves, saying, "What is this? A new teaching with authority! He commands even the unclean spirits, and they obey Him."

28 And immediately the news about Him went out everywhere

---

1 [1]Many mss. do not contain *the Son of God* [a]Matt. 4:3
2 [a]Mark 1:2-8: *Matt. 3:1-11; Luke 3:2-16* [b]Mal. 3:1; Matt. 11:10; Luke 7:27
3 [a]Is. 40:3; Matt. 3:3; Luke 3:4; John 1:23
4 [1]Or, *proclaiming* [a]Acts 13:24 [b]Luke 1:77
6 [1]Lit., *he was eating*
7 [1]Or, *proclaiming*
8 [1]The Greek here can be translated *in, with* or *by*
9 [a]Mark 1:9-11: *Matt. 3:13-17; Luke 3:21, 22* [b]Matt. 2:23; Luke 2:51
10 [1]Or, *being parted*
11 [a]Matt. 3:17; Luke 3:22
12 [a]Mark 1:12, 13: *Matt. 4:1-11; Luke 4:1-13*
13 [a]Matt. 4:10
14 [1]Lit., *delivered up* [2]Or, *proclaiming* [a]Matt. 4:12 [b]Matt. 4:23
15 [1]Or, *put your trust in* [a]Gal. 4:4; Eph. 1:10; 1 Tim. 2:6; Titus 1:3 [b]Acts 20:21
16 [a]Mark 1:16-20: *Matt. 4:18-22;* Luke 5:2-11; John 1:40-42
19 [1]Or, *Jacob*
20 [1]Lit., *after Him*
21 [a]Mark 1:21-28; Luke 4:31-37 [b]Matt. 4:23; Mark 1:39; 10:1
22 [a]Matt. 7:28
24 [1]Lit., *Nazarene* [a]Matt. 8:29 [b]Matt. 2:23; Mark 10:47; 14:67; 16:6; Luke 4:34; 24:19; Acts 24:5 [c]Luke 1:35; 4:34; John 6:69; Acts 3:14
27 [a]Mark 10:24, 32; 14:33; 16:5, 6

into all the surrounding district of
Galilee.

Multitudes Healed

29 [a]And immediately [1]after they
had come [b]out of the synagogue,
they came into the house of Simon
and Andrew, with [2]James and John.
30 Now Simon's mother-in-law
was lying sick with a fever; and immediately they *spoke to Him about
her.
31 And He came to her and raised
her up, taking her by the hand, and
the fever left her, and she began to
[1]wait on them.
32 [a]And [b]when evening had come,
[b]after the sun had set, they *began*
bringing to Him all who were ill and
those who were [c]demon-possessed.
33 And the whole [a]city had gathered at the door.
34 And He [a]healed many who
were ill with various diseases, and
cast out many demons; and He was
not permitting the demons to speak,
because they [1]knew who He was.
35 [a]And in the early morning,
while it was still dark, He arose and
went out and departed to a lonely
place, and [b]was praying there.
36 And Simon and his companions
hunted for Him;
37 and they found Him, and *said
to Him, "Everyone is looking for
You."
38 And He *said to them, **"Let us
go somewhere else to the towns
nearby, in order that I may [1]preach
there also; for that is what I came
out for."**
39 [a]And He went into their synagogues throughout all Galilee,
[1]preaching and casting out the demons.
40 [a]And a leper *came to Him, be-
seeching Him and [b]falling on his
knees before Him, and saying to
Him, "If You are willing, You can
make me clean."
41 And moved with compassion,
He stretched out His hand and
touched him, and *said to him, **"I
am willing; be cleansed."**
42 And immediately the leprosy
left him and he was cleansed.
43 And He sternly warned him and
immediately sent him away,
44 and He *said to him, **"[a]See that
you say nothing to anyone; but [b]go,
show yourself to the priest and offer
for your cleansing what Moses commanded, for a testimony to them."**
45 But he went out and began to
[a]proclaim it freely and to [a]spread
the news about, to such an extent
that Jesus could no longer publicly
enter a city, but [1]stayed out in un-
populated areas; and [b]they were
coming to Him from everywhere.

Chapter 2

The Paralytic Healed

AND when He had come back to
Capernaum several days afterward,
it was heard that He was at home.
2 And [a]many were gathered together, so that there was no longer
room, even near the door; and He
was speaking the word to them.
3 [a]And they *came, bringing to
Him a [b]paralytic, carried by four
men.
4 And being unable to [1]get to
Him on account of the crowd, they
[a]removed the roof [2]above Him; and
when they had dug an opening, they
let down the pallet on which the
[b]paralytic was lying.
5 And Jesus seeing their faith
*said to the paralytic, **"My [1]son,
[a]your sins are forgiven."**
6 But there were some of the
scribes sitting there and reasoning
in their hearts,
7 "Why does this man speak that
way? He is blaspheming; [a]who can
forgive sins [1]but God alone?"
8 And immediately Jesus, perceiving [1]in His spirit that they were
reasoning that way within themselves, *said to them, **"Why are you
reasoning about these things in your
hearts?**
9 **"Which is easier, to say to the
[a]paralytic, 'Your sins are forgiven';
or to say, 'Arise, and take up your
pallet and walk'?**
10 **"But in order that you may know
that the Son of Man has authority on
earth to forgive sins,"** He *said to
the paralytic,
11 **"I say to you, rise, take up your
pallet and go home."**
12 And he rose and immediately
took up the pallet and went out in
the sight of all; so that they were all
amazed and [a]were glorifying God,
saying, "[b]We have never seen anything like this."
13 And He went out again by the
seashore; and [a]all the multitude
were coming to Him, and He was
teaching them.

Levi (Matthew) Called

14 [a]And as He passed by, He saw
[b]Levi the *son* of Alpheus sitting in
the tax office, and He *said to him,
"[c]Follow Me!" And he rose and followed Him.

29 [1]Some mss. read: *after He had come out, He came* [2]Or, *Jacob* [a]Mark 1:29-31: *Matt. 8:14, 15; Luke 4:38, 39* [b]Mark 1:21, 23

31 [1]Or, *serve*

32 [a]Mark 1:32-34: *Matt. 8:16, 17; Luke 4:40, 41* [b]Matt. 8:16; Luke 4:40 [c]Matt. 4:24

33 [a]Mark 1:21

34 [1]Some mss. read: *knew Him to be Christ* [a]Matt. 4:23

35 [a]Mark 1:35-38: *Luke 4:42, 43* [b]Matt. 14:23; Luke 5:16

38 [1]Or, *proclaim*

39 [1]Or, *proclaiming* [a]Matt. 4:23; Mark 1:23; 3:1

40 [a]Mark 1:40-44: *Matt. 8:2-4; Luke 5:12-14* [b]Matt. 8:2; Mark 10:17; Luke 5:12

44 [a]Matt. 8:4 [b]Matt. 8:4

45 [1]Lit., *was* [a]Matt. 28:15; Luke 5:15 [b]Mark 2:2, 13; 3:7; Luke 5:17; John 6:2

2 [a]Mark 1:45; 2:13

3 [a]Mark 2:3-12: *Matt. 9:2-8; Luke 5:18-26* [b]Matt. 4:24

4 [1]Lit., *bring to* [2]Lit., *where He was* [a]Luke 5:19 [b]Matt. 4:24

5 [1]Lit., *child* [a]Matt. 9:2

7 [1]Lit., *if not one, God* [a]Is. 43:25

8 [1]Lit., *by*

9 [a]Matt. 4:24

12 [a]Matt. 9:8 [b]Matt. 9:33

13 [a]Mark 1:45

14 [a]Mark 2:14-17: *Matt. 9:9-13; Luke 5:27-32* [b]Matt. 9:9 [c]Matt. 8:22

15 And it [1]came about that He was reclining *at table* in his house, and many [2]tax-gatherers and sinners [3]were dining with Jesus and His disciples; for there were many of them, and they were following Him.

16 And when [a]the scribes of the Pharisees saw that He was eating with the sinners and tax-gatherers, they *began* saying to His disciples, "[b]Why is He eating and drinking with tax-gatherers and sinners?"

17 And hearing this, Jesus *said to them, "[a]*It is* not those who are healthy who need a physician, but those who are sick; I did not come to call *the* righteous, but sinners."

18 [a]And John's disciples and the Pharisees were fasting; and they *came and *said to Him, "Why do John's disciples and the disciples of the Pharisees fast, but Your disciples do not fast?"

19 And Jesus said to them, "While the bridegroom is with them, [1]the attendants of the bridegroom do not fast, do they? So long as they have the bridegroom with them, they cannot fast.

20"But the [a]days will come when the bridegroom is taken away from them, and then they will fast in that day.

21"No one sews [1]a patch of unshrunk cloth on an old garment; otherwise [2]the patch pulls away from it, the new from the old, and a worse tear results.

22"And no one puts new wine into old [1]wineskins; otherwise the wine will burst the skins, and the wine is lost, and the skins *as well;* but *one puts* new wine into fresh wineskins."

Question of the Sabbath

23 [a]And it came about that He was passing through the grainfields on the Sabbath, and His disciples began to make their way along while [b]picking the heads *of grain.*

24 And the Pharisees were saying to Him, "See here, [a]why are they doing what is not lawful on the Sabbath?"

25 And He *said to them, "Have you never read what David did when he was in need and became hungry, he and his companions:

26 how he entered into the house of God in the time of [a]Abiathar *the* high priest, and ate the [1]consecrated bread, which is not lawful for *anyone* to eat except the priests, and he gave *it* also to those who were with him?"

27 And He was saying to them, "[a]The Sabbath [1]was made [2]for man, and [b]not man [2]for the Sabbath.

28"Consequently, the Son of Man is Lord even of the Sabbath."

CHAPTER 3

Jesus Heals on the Sabbath

[a] AND He [b]entered again into a synagogue; and a man was there with a withered hand.

2 And [a]they were watching Him *to see* if He would heal him on the Sabbath, [b]in order that they might accuse Him.

3 And He *said to the man with the withered hand, "[1]Rise and *come* forward!"

4 And He *said to them, "Is it lawful on the Sabbath to do good or to do harm, to save a life or to kill?" But they kept silent.

5 And after [a]looking around at them with anger, grieved at their hardness of heart, He *said to the man, "Stretch out your hand." And he stretched it out, and his hand was restored.

6 And the Pharisees went out and immediately *began* [1]taking counsel with the [a]Herodians against Him, *as to* how they might destroy Him.

7 [a]And Jesus withdrew to the sea with His disciples; and [b]a great multitude from Galilee followed; and *also* from Judea,

8 and from Jerusalem, and from [a]Idumea, and beyond the Jordan, and the vicinity of [b]Tyre and Sidon, a great multitude heard of all that He was doing and came to Him.

9 And He told His disciples that a boat should stand ready for Him because of the multitude, in order that they might not crowd Him;

10 for He had [a]healed many, with the result that all those who had [b]afflictions pressed about Him in order to [c]touch Him.

11 And whenever the unclean spirits beheld Him, they would fall down before Him and cry out, saying, "You are [a]the Son of God!"

12 And He [a]earnestly warned them not to [1]reveal His identity.

The Twelve Are Chosen

13 And He *went up to [a]the mountain and *[b]summoned those whom He Himself wanted, and they came to Him.

14 And He appointed twelve[1], that they might be with Him, and that He might send them out to preach,

15 [1]Lit., *comes* [2]Publicans who collected Roman taxes for profit [3]Lit., *were reclining with*
16 [a]Luke 5:30; Acts 23:9 [b]Matt. 9:11
17 [a]Matt. 9:12, 13; Luke 5:31, 32
18 [a]Mark 2:18-22: *Matt. 9:14-17; Luke 5:33-38*
19 [1]Lit., *sons of the bridal-chamber*
20 [a]Matt. 9:15; Luke 17:22
21 [1]Lit., *that which is put on* [2]Lit., *that which fills up*
22 [1]I.e., skins used as bottles
23 [a]Mark 2:23-28: *Matt. 12:1-8; Luke 6:1-5* [b]Deut. 23:25
24 [a]Matt. 12:2
26 [1]Or, *showbread;* lit., *loaves of presentation* [a]1 Sam. 21:1; 2 Sam. 8:17; 1 Chr. 24:6
27 [1]Or, *came into being* [2]Lit., *for the sake of* [a]Ex. 23:12; Deut. 5:14 [b]Col. 2:16
1 [a]Mark 3:1-6: *Matt. 12:9-14; Luke 6:6-11* [b]Mark 1:21, 39
2 [a]Luke 6:7; 14:1; 20:20 [b]Matt. 12:10; Luke 6:7; 11:54
3 [1]Lit., *Arise into the midst*
5 [a]Luke 6:10
6 [1]Lit., *giving* [a]Matt. 22:16; Mark 12:13
7 [a]Mark 3:7-12: *Matt. 12:15, 16; Luke 6:17-19* [b]Matt. 4:25; Luke 6:17
8 [a]Josh. 15:1, 21; Ezek. 35:15; 36:5 [b]Matt. 11:21
10 [a]Matt. 4:23 [b]Mark 5:29, 34; Luke 7:21 [c]Matt. 9:21; 14:36; Mark 6:56; 8:22
11 [a]Matt. 4:3
12 [1]Lit., *make Him manifest* [a]Matt. 8:4
13 [a]Matt. 5:1; Luke 6:12 [b]Matt. 10:1; Mark 6:7; Luke 9:1-6
14 [1]Some early mss. add: *whom He named apostles*

15 and to have authority to cast out the demons.

16 And He appointed the twelve: [a]Simon (to whom He gave the name Peter),

17 and [1]James, the *son* of Zebedee, and John the brother of [1]James (to them He gave the name Boanerges, which means, "Sons of Thunder");

18 and Andrew, and Philip, and Bartholomew, and Matthew, and Thomas, and [1]James the *son* of Alphaeus, and Thaddaeus, and Simon [2]the Cananaean;

19 and Judas Iscariot, who also betrayed Him.

20 And He *came [1a]home, and the [b]multitude *gathered again, [c]to such an extent that they could not even eat [2]a meal.

21 And when [a]His own [1]people heard *of this,* they went out to take custody of Him; for they were saying, "[b]He has lost His senses."

22 And the scribes who came down [a]from Jerusalem were saying, "He is possessed by [1b]Beelzebul," and "[c]He casts out the demons by the ruler of the demons."

23 [a]And He called them to Himself and began speaking to them in [b]parables, "How can [c]Satan cast out Satan?

24 "And if a kingdom is divided against itself, that kingdom cannot stand.

25 "And if a house is divided against itself, that house will not be able to stand.

26 "And if [a]Satan has risen up against himself and is divided, he cannot stand, but [1]he is finished!

27 "[a]But no one can enter the strong man's house and plunder his property unless he first binds the strong man, and then he will plunder his house.

28 "[a]Truly I say to you, all sins shall be forgiven the sons of men, and whatever blasphemies they utter;

29 but whoever blasphemes against the Holy Spirit never has forgiveness, but is guilty of an eternal sin" —

30 because they were saying, "He has an unclean spirit."

31 [a]And His mother and His brothers *arrived, and standing outside they sent *word* to Him, and called Him.

32 And a multitude was sitting around Him, and they *said to Him, "Behold, Your mother and Your brothers[1] are outside looking for You."

16 [a]Mark 3:16-19: *Matt. 10:2-4; Luke 6:14-16;* Acts 1:13

17 [1]Or, *Jacob*

18 [1]Or, *Jacob* [2]Or, *the Zealot*

20 [1]Lit., *into a house* [2]Lit., *bread* [a]Mark 2:1; 7:17; 9:28 [b]Mark 1:45; 3:7 [c]Mark 6:31

21 [1]Or, *kinsmen* [a]Mark 3:31f. [b]John 10:20; Acts 26:24

22 [1]Or, *Beezebul;* others read: *Beelzebub* [a]Matt. 15:1 [b]Matt. 10:25; 11:18 [c]Matt. 9:34

23 [a]Mark 3:23-27: *Matt. 12:25-29; Luke 11:17-22* [b]Matt. 13:3ff.; Mark 4:2ff. [c]Matt. 4:10

26 [1]Lit., *he has an end* [a]Matt. 4:10

27 [a]Is. 49:24, 25

28 [a]Matt. 12:31, 32; Mark 3:28-30; Luke 12:10

31 [a]Mark 3:31-35: *Matt. 12:46-50; Luke 8:19-21*

32 [1]Later mss. add: *and Your sisters*

1 [1]Lit., *is gathered* [a]Mark 4:1-12: *Matt. 13:1-15; Luke 8:4-10* [b]Mark 2:13; 3:7

2 [a]Matt. 13:3ff.; Mark 3:23; 4:2ff.

9 [a]Matt. 11:15; Mark 4:23

10 [1]Lit., *those about Him*

11 [a]1 Cor. 5:12f.; Col. 4:5; 1 Thess. 4:12; 1 Tim. 3:7 [b]Mark 3:23; 4:2

12 [a]Is. 6:9; Matt. 13:14

13 [a]Mark 4:13-20: *Matt. 13:18-23; Luke 8:11-15*

33 And answering them, He *said, "Who are My mother and My brothers?"

34 And looking about on those who were sitting around Him, He *said, "Behold, My mother and My brothers!

35 "For whoever does the will of God, he is My brother and sister and mother."

Chapter 4

Parable of the Sower and Soils

[a]AND He began to teach again [b]by the seashore. And such a very great multitude [1]gathered before Him that He got into a boat in the sea and sat down; and all the multitude were by the seashore on the land.

2 And He was teaching them many things in [a]parables, and was saying to them in His teaching,

3 "Listen *to this*! Behold, the sower went out to sow;

4 and it came about that as he was sowing, some *seed* fell beside the road, and the birds came and ate it up.

5 "And other *seed* fell on the rocky *ground* where it did not have much soil; and immediately it sprang up because it had no depth of soil.

6 "And after the sun had risen, it was scorched; and because it had no root, it withered away.

7 "And other *seed* fell among the thorns, and the thorns grew up and choked it, and it yielded no crop.

8 "And other *seeds* fell into the good soil and as they grew up and increased, they were yielding a crop and were producing thirty, sixty, and a hundredfold."

9 And He was saying, "[a]He who has ears to hear, let him hear."

10 And as soon as He was alone, [1]His followers, along with the twelve, *began* asking Him *about* the parables.

11 And He was saying to them, "To you has been given the mystery of the kingdom of God; but [a]those who are outside get everything [b]in parables,

12 [a]in order that WHILE SEEING, THEY MAY SEE AND NOT PERCEIVE; AND WHILE HEARING, THEY MAY HEAR AND NOT UNDERSTAND LEST THEY RETURN AGAIN AND BE FORGIVEN."

Explanation

13 [a]And He *said to them, "Do you not understand this parable? And

how will you understand all the parables?
14"The sower sows the word.
15"And these are the ones who are
beside the road where the word is
sown; and when they hear, immediately [a]Satan comes and takes away
the word which has been sown in
them.
16"And in a similar way these are
the ones on whom seed was sown on
the rocky *places,* who, when they
hear the word, immediately receive
it with joy;
17 and they have no *firm* root in
themselves, but are *only* temporary;
then, when affliction or persecution
arises because of the word, immediately they [1]fall away.
18"And others are the ones on
whom seed was sown among the
thorns; these are the ones who have
heard the word,
19 and the worries of [a]the [1]world,
and the deceitfulness of riches, and
the desires for other things enter in
and choke the word, and it becomes
unfruitful.
20"And those are the ones on
whom seed was sown on the good
ground; and they hear the word and
accept it, and bear fruit, thirty,
sixty, and a hundredfold."
21 And He was saying to them,
"[a]A lamp is not brought to be put
under a peck-measure, is it, or under
a bed? Is it not *brought* to be put on
the lampstand?
22"[a]For nothing is hidden, except
to be revealed; nor has *anything*
been secret, but that it should come
to light.
23"[a]If any man has ears to hear, let
him hear."
24 And He was saying to them,
"Take care what you listen to. [1a]By
your standard of measure it shall be
measured to you; and more shall be
given you besides.
25"[a]For whoever has, to him shall
more be given; and whoever does
not have, even what he has shall be
taken away from him."

Parable of the Seed

26 And He was saying, "[a]The kingdom of God is like a man who casts
seed upon the ground;
27 and goes to bed at night and
gets up by day, and the seed sprouts
up and grows — how, he himself
does not know.
28"The earth produces crops by itself; first the blade, then the head,
then the mature grain in the head.
29"But when the crop permits, he
immediately [1]puts in the sickle, because the harvest has come."

Parable of the Mustard Seed

30 [a]And He said, "How shall we
[1b]picture the kingdom of God, or by
what parable shall we present it?
31"*It is* like a mustard seed,
which, when sown upon the ground,
though it is smaller than all the
seeds that are upon the ground,
32 yet when it is sown, grows up
and becomes larger than all the
garden plants and forms large
branches; so that the birds of the
[1]air can nest under its shade."
33 And with many such parables
He was speaking the word to them
as they were able to hear it;
34 and He was not speaking to
them [a]without [1]parables; but He
was explaining everything privately
to His own disciples.

Jesus Stills the Sea

35 [a]And on that day, when evening
had come, He *said to them, "Let us
go over to the other side."
36 And [1]leaving the multitude,
they *took Him along with them,
just as He was, [a]in the boat; and other boats were with Him.
37 And there *arose a fierce gale
of wind, and the waves were breaking over the boat so much that the
boat was already filling up.
38 And He Himself was in the
stern, asleep on the cushion; and
they *awoke Him and *said to Him,
"Teacher, do You not care that we
are perishing?"
39 And being aroused, He rebuked
the wind and said to the sea, "Hush,
be still." And the wind died down
and [1]it became perfectly calm.
40 And He said to them, "Why are
you so timid? How is it that you
have no faith?"
41 And they became very much
afraid and said to one another,
"Who then is this, that even the
wind and the sea obey Him?"

CHAPTER 5

The Gerasene Demoniac

[a]

AND they came to the other side of
the sea, into the country of the Gera-
senes.
2 And when He had come out of
[a]the boat, immediately a man from
the tombs [b]with an unclean spirit
met Him,
3 and he had his dwelling among
the tombs. And no one was able to

15 [a]Matt. 4:10
17 [1]Lit., *are caused to stumble*
19 [1]Or, *age* [a]Matt. 13:22
21 [a]Matt. 5:15; Luke 8:16; 11:33
22 [a]Matt. 10:26; Luke 8:17; 12:2
23 [a]Matt. 11:15; Mark 4:9
24 [1]Lit., *by what measure you measure* [a]Matt. 7:2; Luke 6:38
25 [a]Matt. 13:12
26 [a]Matt. 13:24-30; Mark 4:26-29
29 [1]Lit., *sends forth*
30 [1]Lit., *compare* [a]Mark 4:30-32: *Matt. 13:31, 32; Luke 13:18, 19* [b]Matt. 13:24
32 [1]Or, *sky*
34 [1]Lit., *a parable* [a]Matt. 13:34; John 10:6; 16:25
35 [a]Mark 4:35-41: *Matt. 8:18, 23-27; Luke 8:22, 25*
36 [1]Or, *sending away* [a]Mark 3:9; 4:1; 5:2, 21
39 [1]Lit., *a great calm occurred*
1 [a]Mark 5:1-17: *Matt. 8:28-34; Luke 8:26-37*
2 [a]Mark 3:9; 4:1, 36; 5:21 [b]Mark 1:23

bind him any more, even with a chain;

4 because he had often been bound with shackles and chains, and the chains had been torn apart by him, and the shackles broken in pieces, and no one was strong enough to subdue him.

5 And constantly night and day, among the tombs and in the mountains, he was crying out and gashing himself with stones.

6 And seeing Jesus from a distance, he ran up and bowed down before Him;

7 and crying out with a loud voice, he *said, "[a]What do I have to do with You, Jesus, [b]Son of [c]the Most High God? I implore You by God, do not torment me!"

8 For He had been saying to him, "Come out of the man, you unclean spirit!"

9 And He was asking him, "What is your name?" And he *said to Him, "My name is [a]Legion; for we are many."

10 And he *began* to entreat Him earnestly not to send them out of the country.

11 Now there was a big herd of swine feeding there on the mountain side.

12 And they entreated Him, saying, "Send us into the swine so that we may enter them."

13 And He gave them permission. And coming out, the unclean spirits entered the swine; and the herd rushed down the steep bank into the sea, about two thousand *of them;* and they [1]were drowned in the sea.

14 And those who tended them ran away and reported it in the city and *out* in the country. And *the people* came to see what it was that had happened.

15 And they *came to Jesus and *observed the man who had been [a]demon-possessed sitting down, [b]clothed and [c]in his right mind, the very man who had had the "[d]legion"; and they became frightened.

16 And those who had seen it described to them how it had happened to the [a]demon-possessed man, and *all* about the swine.

17 And they began to entreat Him to depart from their region.

18 [a]And as He was getting into the boat, the man who had been [b]demon-possessed was entreating Him that he might [1]accompany Him.

19 And He did not let him, but He *said to him, "Go home to your people and report to them [1]what great things the Lord has done for you, and *how* He had mercy on you."

20 And he went off and began to proclaim in [a]Decapolis [1]what great things Jesus had done for him; and everyone marveled.

Miracles and Healing

21 [a]And when Jesus had crossed over again in [b]the boat to the other side, a great multitude gathered about Him; and He [1]stayed [c]by the seashore.

22 [a]And one of [b]the synagogue [1]officials named Jairus *came up, and upon seeing Him, *fell at His feet,

23 and *entreated Him earnestly, saying, "My little daughter is at the point of death; *please* come and [a]lay Your hands on her, that she may [1]get well and live."

24 And He went off with him; and a great multitude was following Him and pressing in on Him.

25 And a woman who had had a hemorrhage for twelve years,

26 and had endured much at the hands of many physicians, and had spent all that she had and was not helped at all, but rather had grown worse,

27 after hearing about Jesus, came up in the crowd behind *Him,* and touched His [1]cloak.

28 For she [1]thought, "If I just touch His garments, I shall [2]get well."

29 And immediately the flow of her blood was dried up; and she felt in her body that she was healed of her [a]affliction.

30 And immediately Jesus, perceiving in Himself that [a]the power *proceeding* from Him had gone forth, turned around in the crowd and said, "Who touched My garments?"

31 And His disciples said to Him, "You see the multitude pressing in on You, and You say, 'Who touched Me?' "

32 And He looked around to see the woman who had done this.

33 But the woman fearing and trembling, aware of what had happened to her, came and fell down before Him, and told Him the whole truth.

34 And He said to her, "Daughter, [a]your faith has [1]made you well; [b]go in peace, and be healed of your [c]affliction."

35 While He was still speaking, they *came from the *house of* the [a]synagogue official, saying, "Your

7 [a]Matt. 8:29 [b]Matt. 4:3 [c]Luke 8:28; Acts 16:17; Heb. 7:1

9 [a]Matt. 26:53; Mark 5:15; Luke 8:30

13 [1]Lit., *were drowning*

15 [a]Matt. 4:24; Mark 5:16, 18 [b]Luke 8:27 [c]Luke 8:35 [d]Mark 5:9

16 [a]Matt. 4:24; Mark 5:15

18 [1]Lit., *be with Him* [a]Mark 5:18-20: *Luke 8:38, 39* [b]Matt. 4:24; Mark 5:15, 16

19 [1]Or, *everything that*

20 [1]Or, *everything that* [a]Matt. 4:25; Mark 7:31

21 [1]Lit., *was* [a]Matt. 9:1; Luke 8:40 [b]Mark 4:36 [c]Mark 4:1

22 [1]Or, *rulers* [a]Mark 5:22-43: *Matt. 9:18-26; Luke 8:41-56* [b]Matt. 9:18; Mark 5:35, 36, 38; Luke 8:49; 13:14; Acts 13:15; 18:8, 17

23 [1]Lit., *be saved* [a]Mark 6:5; 7:32; 8:23; 16:18; Luke 4:40; 13:13; Acts 6:6; 9:17; 28:8

27 [1]Or, *outer garment*

28 [1]Lit., *was saying* [2]Lit., *be saved*

29 [a]Mark 3:10; 5:34

30 [a]Luke 5:17

34 [1]Lit., *saved you* [a]Matt. 9:22 [b]Luke 7:50; 8:48; Acts 16:36; James 2:16 [c]Mark 3:10; 5:29

35 [a]Mark 5:22

daughter has died; why trouble the
Teacher any more?"
36 But Jesus, overhearing what
was being spoken, *said to the [a]syn-
agogue official, "[b]Do not be afraid
any longer, only [1]believe."
37 And He allowed no one to follow with Him, except [a]Peter and
[1]James and John the brother of
[1]James.
38 And they *came to the house of
the [a]synagogue official; and He *beheld a commotion, and *people*
loudly weeping and wailing.
39 And entering in, He *said to
them, "Why make a commotion and
weep? The child has not died, but is
asleep."
40 And they were laughing at Him.
But putting them all out, He *took
along the child's father and mother
and His own companions, and *entered the *room* where the child was.
41 And taking the child by the
hand, He *said to her, "Talitha
kum!" (which translated means,
"Little girl, [a]I say to you, arise!")
42 And immediately the girl got up
and *began* to walk; for she was
twelve years old. And immediately
they were completely astounded.
43 And He [a]gave them strict orders that no one should know about
this; and He said that *something*
should be given her to eat.

Chapter 6

Teaching at Nazareth

[a]AND He went out from there, and
He *came into [b]His home town; and
His disciples *followed Him.
2 And when the Sabbath had
come, He began [a]to teach in the
synagogue; and the [b]many listeners
were astonished, saying, "Where
did this man *get* these things, and
what is *this* wisdom given to Him,
and such miracles as these performed by His hands?
3 "Is not this [a]the carpenter, [b]the
son of Mary, and brother of [1]James,
and Joses, and Judas, and Simon?
Are not [c]His sisters here with us?"
And they [2]took [d]offense at Him.
4 And Jesus said to them, "[a]A
prophet is not without honor except
in [1b]his home town and among his
own relatives and in his *own* household."
5 And He could do no [1]miracle
there except that He [a]laid His hands
upon a few sick people and healed
them.
6 And He wondered at their unbelief.

[a]And He was going around the villages teaching.

The Twelve Sent Out

7 [a]And [b]He *[1]summoned the
twelve and began to send them out
[c]in pairs; and He was giving them
authority over the unclean spirits;
8 [a]and He instructed them that
they should take nothing for *their*
journey, except a mere staff; no
bread, no [1]bag, no money in their
belt;
9 but [1]*to* wear sandals; and *He
added,* "Do not put on two [2]tunics."
10 And He said to them, "Wherever you enter a house, stay there
until you [1]leave town.
11 "And any place that does not receive you or listen to you, as you go
out from there, [a]shake off the dust
[1]from the soles of your feet for a
testimony against them."
12 [a]And they went out and
[1]preached that *men* should repent.
13 And they were casting out
many demons and [a]were anointing
with oil many sick people and healing them.

John's Fate Recalled

14 [a]And King Herod heard *of it,*
for His name had become well
known; and *people* were saying,
"[b]John the Baptist has risen from
the dead, and therefore these mi-
raculous powers are at work in
Him."
15 But others were saying, "*He is*
[a]Elijah." And others were saying,
"*He is* [b]a prophet, like one of the
prophets *of old.*"
16 But when Herod heard *of it,* he
kept saying, "John, whom I beheaded, He has risen!"
17 For Herod himself had sent and
had John arrested and bound in
prison on account of [a]Herodias, the
wife of his brother Philip, because
he had married her.
18 For John had been saying to
Herod, "[a]It is not lawful for you to
have your brother's wife."
19 And [a]Herodias had a grudge
against him and wanted to kill him;
and could not *do so;*
20 for [a]Herod was afraid of John,
knowing that he was a righteous
and holy man, and kept him safe.
And when he heard him, he was
very perplexed; [1]but he [2]used to enjoy listening to him.
21 And a strategic day came when
Herod on his birthday [a]gave a banquet for his lords and [1]military com-

36 [1]Or, *keep on believing* [a]Mark 5:22 [b]Luke 8:50
37 [1]Or, *Jacob* [a]Matt. 17:1; 26:37
38 [a]Mark 5:22
41 [a]Luke 7:14; Acts 9:40
43 [a]Matt. 8:4
1 [a]Mark 6:1-6: *Matt. 13:54-58* [b]Matt. 13:54, 57; Luke 4:16, 23
2 [a]Matt. 4:23; Mark 10:1 [b]Matt. 7:28
3 [1]Or, *Jacob* [2]Lit., *were being made to stumble* [a]Matt. 13:55 [b]Matt. 12:46 [c]Matt. 13:56 [d]Matt. 11:6
4 [1]Or, *his own part of the country* [a]Matt. 13:57 [b]Mark 6:1
5 [1]Or, *work of power* [a]Mark 5:23
6 [a]Matt. 9:35; Mark 1:39; 10:1; Luke 13:22
7 [1]Lit., *summons* [a]Mark 6:7-11: *Matt. 10:1, 9-14; Luke 9:1, 3-5;* Luke 10:4-11 [b]Matt. 10:1, 5; Mark 3:13; Luke 9:1 [c]Luke 10:1
8 [1]Or, *knapsack* or, *beggar's bag* [a]Matt. 10:10
9 [1]Lit., *being shod with* [2]Or, *inner garments*
10 [1]Lit., *go out from there*
11 [1]Lit., *under your feet* [a]Matt. 10:14
12 [1]Or, *proclaimed as a herald* [a]Matt. 11:1; Luke 9:6
13 [a]James 5:14
14 [a]Mark 6:14-29: *Matt. 14:1-12;* Mark 6:14-16: *Luke 9:7-9* [b]Matt. 14:2
15 [a]Matt. 16:14; Mark 8:28 [b]Matt. 21:11
17 [a]Matt. 14:3
18 [a]Matt. 14:4
19 [a]Matt. 14:3
20 [1]Lit., *and* [2]Lit., *was hearing him gladly* [a]Matt. 21:26
21 [1]I.e., chiliarchs in command of a thousand troops [a]Esther 1:3; 2:18

manders and the leading men [b]of
Galilee;
22 and when the daughter of [a]He-
rodias herself came in and danced,
she pleased Herod and [1]his dinner
guests; and the king said to the girl,
"Ask me for whatever you want and
I will give it to you."
23 And he swore to her, "Whatever you ask of me, I will give it to
you; up to [a]half of my kingdom."
24 And she went out and said to
her mother, "What shall I ask for?"
And she said, "The head of John the
Baptist."
25 And immediately she came in
haste before the king and asked,
saying, "I want you to give me right
away the head of John the Baptist
on a platter."
26 And although the king was very
sorry, *yet* because of his oaths and
because of [1]his dinner guests, he
was unwilling to refuse her.
27 And immediately the king sent
an executioner and commanded
him to bring *back* his head. And he
went and beheaded him in the
prison,
28 and brought his head on a platter, and gave it to the girl; and the
girl gave it to her mother.
29 And when his disciples heard
about this, they came and took
away his body and laid it in a tomb.
30 [a]And the [b]apostles *gathered
together with Jesus; and they reported to Him all that they had done
and taught.
31 And He *said to them, "Come
away by yourselves to a lonely place
and rest a while." (For there were
many *people* coming and going, and
[a]they did not even have time to eat.)
32 [a]And they went away in [b]the
boat to a lonely place by themselves.

Five Thousand Fed

33 And *the people* saw them going,
and many recognized *them,* and
they ran there together on foot from
all the cities, and got there ahead of
them.
34 And [1]disembarking, He [a]saw a
great multitude, and He felt compassion for them because [a]they
were like sheep without a shepherd;
and He began to teach them many
things.
35 And when it was already quite
late, His disciples came up to Him
and *began* saying, "The place is
desolate and it is already quite late;
36 send them away so that they
may go into the surrounding countryside and villages and buy themselves [1]something to eat."
37 But He answered and said to
them, "You give them something to
eat!" [a]And they *said to Him, "Shall
we go and spend two hundred [1b]de-
narii on bread and give them something to eat?"
38 And He *said to them, "How
many loaves do you have? Go look!"
And when they found out, they
*said, "Five and two fish."
39 And He commanded them all to
recline by groups on the green
grass.
40 And they reclined in companies
of hundreds and of fifties.
41 And He took the five loaves and
the two fish, and looking up toward
heaven, He [a]blessed *the food* and
broke the loaves and He kept giving
them to the disciples to set before
them; and He divided up the two
fish among them all.
42 And they all ate and were satisfied.
43 And they picked up twelve full
[a]baskets of the broken pieces, and
also of the fish.
44 And there were [a]five thousand
men who ate the loaves.

Jesus Walks on the Water

45 [a]And immediately He made His
disciples get into [b]the boat and go
ahead of *Him* to the other side to
[c]Bethsaida, while He Himself was
sending the multitude away.
46 And after [a]bidding them farewell, He departed [b]to the mountain
to pray.
47 And when it was evening, the
boat was in the midst of the sea, and
He *was* alone on the land.
48 And seeing them [1]straining at
the oars, for the wind was against
them, at about the [2a]fourth watch of
the night, He *came to them, walking on the sea; and He intended to
pass by them.
49 But when they saw Him walking on the sea, they supposed that it
was a ghost, and cried out;
50 for they all saw Him and were
[1]frightened. But immediately He
spoke with them and *said to them,
"[a]Take courage; it is I, [b]do not be
afraid."
51 And He got into [a]the boat with
them, and the wind stopped; and
they were greatly astonished,
52 for [a]they [1]had not gained any
insight from the *incident of* the
loaves, but [2]their heart [b]was hardened.

21 [b]Luke 3:1

22 [1]Lit., *those who reclined at table with him* [a]Matt. 14:3

23 [a]Esther 5:3, 6; 7:2

26 [1]Lit., *those reclining at table*

30 [a]Luke 9:10 [b]Matt. 10:2 [Mark 3:14 in Gr.]; Luke 6:13; 9:10; 17:5; 22:14; 24:10; Acts 1:2, 26

31 [a]Mark 3:20

32 [a]Mark 6:32-44: *Matt. 14:13-21; Luke 9:10-17; John 6:5-13;* Mark 8:2-9 [b]Mark 3:9; 4:36; 6:45

34 [1]Lit., *having come forth* [a]Matt. 9:36

36 [1]Lit., *what they may eat*

37 [1]A denarius represented a day's wages for a common laborer [a]John 6:7 [b]Matt. 18:28; Luke 7:41

41 [a]Matt. 14:19

43 [a]Matt. 14:20

44 [a]Matt. 14:21

45 [a]Mark 6:45-51: *Matt. 14:22-32; John 6:15-21* [b]Mark 6:32 [c]Matt. 11:21; Mark 8:22

46 [a]Acts 18:18, 21; 2 Cor. 2:13 [b]Matt. 14:23

48 [1]Lit., *harassed in rowing* [2]I.e., 3-6 a.m. [a]Matt. 24:43; Mark 13:35

50 [1]Or, *troubled* [a]Matt. 9:2 [b]Matt. 14:27

51 [a]Mark 6:32

52 [1]Lit., *had not understood on the basis of* [2]Or, *their mind was closed, made dull, or insensible* [a]Mark 8:17ff. [b]Rom. 11:7

Healing at Gennesaret

53 [a]And when they had crossed over they came to land at Gennesaret, and moored to the shore.

54 And when they had come out of the boat, immediately *the people* recognized Him,

55 and ran about that whole country and began to carry about on their pallets those who were sick, to [1]the place they heard He was.

56 And wherever He entered villages, or cities, or countryside, they were laying the sick in the market places, and entreating Him that they might just [a]touch [b]the fringe of His cloak; and as many as touched it were being cured.

CHAPTER 7

Followers of Tradition

[a]AND the Pharisees and some of the scribes gathered together around Him when they had come [b]from Jerusalem,

2 and had seen that some of His disciples were eating their bread with [a]impure hands, that is, unwashed.

3 (For the Pharisees and all the Jews do not eat unless they [1]carefully wash their hands, *thus* observing the [a]traditions of the elders;

4 and *when they come* from the market place, they do not eat unless they [1]cleanse themselves; and there are many other things which they have received in order to observe, such as the [2]washing of [a]cups and pitchers and copper pots.)

5 And the Pharisees and the scribes *asked Him, "Why do Your disciples not walk according to the [a]tradition of the elders, but eat their bread with [b]impure hands?"

6 And He said to them, "Rightly did Isaiah prophesy of you hypocrites, as it is written,

'[a]THIS PEOPLE HONORS ME WITH THEIR LIPS,
BUT THEIR HEART IS FAR AWAY FROM ME.

7 '[a]BUT IN VAIN DO THEY WORSHIP ME,
TEACHING AS DOCTRINES THE PRECEPTS OF MEN.'

8 "Neglecting the commandment of God, you hold to the [a]tradition of men."

9 He was also saying to them, "You nicely set aside the commandment of God in order to keep your [a]tradition.

10 "For Moses said, '[a]HONOR YOUR FATHER AND YOUR MOTHER'; and, '[b]HE WHO SPEAKS EVIL OF FATHER OR MOTHER, LET HIM [1]BE PUT TO DEATH';

11 but you say, 'If a man says to *his* father or *his* mother, anything of mine you might have been helped by is [a]Corban (that is to say, [1]*given to God*),'

12 you no longer permit him to do anything for *his* father or *his* mother;

13 *thus* invalidating the word of God by your [a]tradition which you have handed down; and you do many things such as that."

The Heart of Man

14 And summoning the multitude again, He *began* saying to them, "Listen to Me, all of you, and understand:

15 there is nothing outside the man which going into him can defile him; but the things which proceed out of the man are what defile the man.

16 ["[1]If any man has ears to hear, let him hear."]

17 And when leaving the multitude, He had entered [a]the house, [b]His disciples questioned Him about the parable.

18 And He *said to them, "Are you too so uncomprehending? Do you not see that whatever goes into the man from outside cannot defile him;

19 because it does not go into his heart, but into his stomach, and [1]is eliminated?" (*Thus He* declared [a]all foods [b]clean.)

20 And He was saying, "[a]That which proceeds out of the man, that is what defiles the man.

21 "For from within, out of the heart of men, proceed the evil thoughts and [1]fornications, thefts, murders, adulteries,

22 deeds of coveting *and* wickedness, *as well as* deceit, sensuality, [1a]envy, slander, [2]pride *and* foolishness.

23 "All these evil things proceed from within and defile the man."

The Syrophoenecian Woman

24 [a]And from there He arose and went away to the region of [b]Tyre[1]. And when He had entered a house, He wanted no one to know *of it;* [2]yet He could not escape notice.

25 But after hearing of Him, a woman whose little daughter had an unclean spirit, immediately came and fell at His feet.

26 Now the woman was a [1]Gentile, of the Syrophoenician race.

---

53 [a]Mark 6:53-56: *Matt. 14:34-36; John 6:24, 25*
55 [1]Or, *where they were hearing that He was*
56 [a]Mark 3:10 [b]Matt. 9:20
1 [a]Mark 7:1-23: *Matt. 15:1-20* [b]Matt. 15:1
2 [a]Matt. 15:2; Mark 7:5; Luke 11:38; Acts 10:14, 28; 11:8; Rom. 14:14; Heb. 10:29; Rev. 21:27
3 [1]Lit., *with the fist* [a]Mark 7:5, 8, 9, 13; Gal. 1:14
4 [1]Or, *sprinkle* [2]Lit., *baptizing* [a]Matt. 23:25
5 [a]Mark 7:3, 8, 9, 13; Gal. 1:14 [b]Mark 7:2
6 [a]Is. 29:13
7 [a]Is. 29:13
8 [a]Mark 7:3, 5, 9, 13; Gal. 1:14
9 [a]Mark 7:3, 5, 8, 13; Gal. 1:14
10 [1]Lit., *die the death* [a]Ex. 20:12; Deut. 5:16 [b]Ex. 21:17; Lev. 20:9
11 [1]Or, *a gift, an offering* [a]Lev. 1:2; Matt. 27:6
13 [a]Mark 7:3, 5, 8, 9; Gal. 1:14
16 [1]Many mss. do not contain this verse
17 [a]Mark 2:1; 3:19; 9:28 [b]Matt. 15:15
19 [1]Lit., *goes out into the latrine* [a]Rom. 14:1-12; Col. 2:16 [b]Luke 11:41; Acts 10:15; 11:9
20 [a]Matt. 15:18; Mark 7:23
21 [1]I.e., acts of sexual immorality
22 [1]Lit., *an evil eye* [2]Or, *arrogance* [a]Matt. 6:23; 20:15
24 [1]Some early mss. add: *and Sidon* [2]Lit., *and* [a]Mark 7:24-30: *Matt. 15:21-28* [b]Matt. 11:21; Mark 7:31
26 [1]Lit., *Greek*

And she kept asking Him to cast the
demon out of her daughter.
27 And He was saying to her, "Let
the children be satisfied first, for it is
not [1]good to take the children's
bread and throw it to the dogs."
28 But she answered and *said to
Him, "Yes, Lord, *but* even the dogs
under the table feed on the children's crumbs."
29 And He said to her, "Because of
this [1]answer go your way; the demon has gone out of your daughter."
30 And going back to her home,
she found the child [1]lying on the
bed, [2]the demon having departed.
31 [a]And again He went out from
the region of [b]Tyre, and came
through Sidon to [c]the Sea of Galilee,
within the region of [d]Decapolis.
32 And they *brought to Him one
who was deaf and spoke with difficulty, and they *entreated Him to
[a]lay His hand upon him.
33 And [a]He took him aside from
the multitude by himself, and put
His fingers into his ears, and after
[a]spitting, He touched his tongue
with the saliva;
34 and looking up to heaven with a
deep [a]sigh, He *said to him, "Eph-
phatha!" that is, "Be opened!"
35 And his ears were opened, and
the [1]impediment of his tongue [2]was
removed, and he *began* speaking
plainly.
36 And [a]He gave them orders not
to tell anyone; but the more He ordered them, the more widely they
[b]continued to proclaim it.
37 And they were utterly astonished, saying, "He has done all
things well; He makes even the deaf
to hear, and the dumb to speak."

CHAPTER 8

Four Thousand Fed

IN those days again, when there
was a great multitude and they had
nothing to eat, [a]He summoned His
disciples and *said to them,
2 "[a]I feel compassion for the multitude because they have remained
with Me now three days, and have
nothing to eat;
3 and if I send them away fasting
to their home, they will faint on the
way; and some of them have come
from a distance."
4 And His disciples answered
Him, "Where will anyone be able to
find enough to satisfy these men
with [1]bread here in the wilderness?"
5 And He was asking them,
"How many loaves do you have?"
And they said, "Seven."
6 And He *directed the multitude
to [1]sit down on the ground; and taking the seven loaves, He gave
thanks and broke them, and *began*
giving them to His disciples to
[2]serve to them, and they [2]served
them to the multitude.
7 They also had a few small fish;
and [a]after He had blessed them, He
ordered these to be [1]served as well.
8 And they ate and were satisfied; and they picked up seven large
[a]baskets full of what was left over of
the broken pieces.
9 And about four thousand were
there; and He sent them away.
10 And immediately He entered
the boat with His disciples, and
came to the district of [a]Dalmanutha.
11 [a]And the Pharisees came out
and began to argue with Him, [b]seek-
ing from Him a [1]sign from heaven,
[2]to test Him.
12 And [a]sighing deeply [1]in His
spirit, He *said, "Why does this generation seek for a [2]sign? Truly I say
to you, [3]no [2]sign shall be given to
this generation."
13 And leaving them, He again
embarked and went away to the
other side.
14 And they had forgotten to take
bread; and [1]did not have more than
one loaf in the boat with them.
15 And He was giving orders to
them, saying, "[a]Watch out! Beware
of the leaven of the Pharisees and
the leaven of [b]Herod."
16 And they *began* to discuss with
one another *the fact* that they had
no bread.
17 And Jesus, aware of this, *said
to them, "Why do you discuss *the
fact* that you have no bread? [a]Do
you not yet see or understand? Do
you have a [1]hardened heart?
18 "[a]HAVING EYES, DO YOU NOT SEE?
AND HAVING EARS, DO YOU NOT
HEAR? And do you not remember,
19 when I broke [a]the five loaves
for the five thousand, how many
[b]baskets full of broken pieces you
picked up?" They *said to Him,
"Twelve."
20 "And when *I broke* [a]the seven
for the four thousand, how many
large [b]baskets full of broken pieces
did you pick up?" And they *said to
Him, "Seven."
21 And He was saying to them,
"[a]Do you not yet understand?"
22 And they *came to [a]Bethsaida.
And they *brought a blind man to
Him, and *entreated Him to [b]touch
him.

27 [1]Or, *proper*
29 [1]Lit., *word*
30 [1]Lit., *thrown* [2]Lit., *and the*
31 [a]Mark 7:31-37: *Matt. 15:29-31* [b]Matt. 11:21; Mark 7:24 [c]Matt. 4:18 [d]Matt. 4:25; Mark 5:20
32 [a]Mark 5:23
33 [a]Mark 8:23
34 [a]Mark 8:12
35 [1]Or, *bond* [2]Lit., *was loosed*
36 [a]Matt. 8:4 [b]Mark 1:45
1 [a]Mark 8:1-9: *Matt. 15:32-39;* [Mark 6:34-44]
2 [a]Matt. 9:36; Mark 6:34
4 [1]Lit., *loaves*
6 [1]Lit., *recline* [2]Lit., *set before*
7 [1]Lit., *set before* [a]Matt. 14:19
8 [a]Matt. 15:37; Mark 8:20
10 [a]Matt. 15:39
11 [1]Or, *attesting miracle* [2]Lit., *testing Him* [a]Mark 8:11-21: *Matt. 16:1-12* [b]Matt. 12:38
12 [1]Or, *to Himself* [2]Or, *attesting miracle* [3]Lit., *if a sign shall be given* [a]Mark 7:34
14 [1]Lit., *were not having*
15 [a]Matt. 16:6; Luke 12:1 [b]Matt. 14:1; 22:16
17 [1]Or, *dull, insensible* [a]Mark 6:52
18 [a]Ezek. 12:2
19 [a]Mark 6:41-44 [b]Matt. 14:20
20 [a]Mark 8:6-9 [b]Mark 8:8
21 [a]Mark 6:52
22 [a]Matt. 11:21; Mark 6:45 [b]Mark 3:10

23 And taking the blind man by
the hand, He [a]brought him out of the
village; and after [a]spitting on his
eyes, and [b]laying His hands upon
him, He asked him, "Do you see
anything?"
24 And he [1]looked up and said, "I
see men, for [2]I am seeing *them* like
trees, walking about."
25 Then again He laid His hands
upon his eyes; and he looked intently and was restored, and *began* to
see everything clearly.
26 And He sent him to his home,
saying, "[a]Do not even enter [b]the village."

Peter's Confession of Christ

27 [a]And Jesus went out, along
with His disciples, to the villages of
[b]Caesarea Philippi; and on the way
He questioned His disciples, saying
to them, "Who do people say that I
am?"
28 [a]And they told Him, saying,
"John the Baptist; and others *say*
Elijah; but still others, one of the
prophets."
29 And He *continued* by questioning them, "But who do you say that
I am?" Peter *answered and *said to
Him, "Thou art [1]the Christ."
30 And [a]He [1]warned them to tell
no one about Him.
31 [a]And He began to teach them
that [b]the Son of Man must suffer
many things and be rejected by the
elders and the chief priests and the
scribes, and be killed, and after
three days rise again.
32 And He was stating the matter
[a]plainly. And Peter took Him aside
and began to rebuke Him.
33 But turning around and seeing
His disciples, He rebuked Peter, and
*said, "Get behind Me, [a]Satan; for
you are not setting your mind on
[1]God's interests, but man's."
34 And He summoned the multitude with His disciples, and said to
them, "If anyone wishes to come after Me, let him deny himself, and
[a]take up his cross, and follow Me.
35 "For [a]whoever wishes to save
his [1]life shall lose it; and whoever
loses his [1]life for My sake and the
gospel's shall save it.
36 "For what does it profit a man to
gain the whole world, and forfeit his
[1]soul?
37 "For what shall a man give in
exchange for his [1]soul?
38 "For [a]whoever is ashamed of Me
and My words in this adulterous and
sinful generation, [b]the Son of Man
will also be ashamed of him when
He [c]comes in the glory of His Father
with the holy angels."

Chapter 9

The Transfiguration

AND He was saying to them,
"[a]Truly I say to you, there are some
of those who are standing here who
shall not taste of death until they see
the kingdom of God after it has
come with power."
2 [a]And six days later, Jesus *took
with Him [b]Peter and [1]James and
John, and *brought them up to a
high mountain by themselves. And
He was transfigured before them;
3 and [a]His garments became radiant and exceedingly white, as no
launderer on earth can whiten them.
4 And Elijah appeared to them
along with Moses; and they were
conversing with Jesus.
5 And Peter *answered and *said
to Jesus, "[a]Rabbi, it is good for us to
be here; and [b]let us make three [1]tab-
ernacles, one for You, and one for
Moses, and one for Elijah."
6 For he did not know what to answer; for they became terrified.
7 Then a cloud [1]formed, over-
shadowing them, and [a]a voice
[1]came out of the cloud, "[b]This is My
beloved Son, [2]listen to Him!"
8 And all at once they looked
around and saw no one with them
any more, except Jesus only.
9 [a]And as they were coming
down from the mountain, He [b]gave
them orders not to relate to anyone
what they had seen, [1]until the Son of
Man should rise from the dead.
10 And they [1]seized upon [2]that
statement, discussing with one another [3]what rising from the dead
might mean.
11 And they *began* questioning
Him, saying, "*Why is it* that the
scribes say that first [a]Elijah must
come?"
12 And He said to them, "Elijah
does first come and restore everything. And *yet* how is it written of
[a]the Son of Man that [b]He should suffer many things and be treated with
contempt?
13 "But I say to you, that Elijah
has [1]indeed come, and they did to
him whatever they wished, just as it
is written of him."

All Things Possible

14 [a]And when they came *back* to
the disciples, they saw a large
crowd around them, and *some*
scribes arguing with them.

---

23 [a]Mark 7:33 [b]Mark 5:23
24 [1]Or, *gained sight* [2]Or, *they look to me*
26 [a]Matt. 8:4 [b]Mark 8:23
27 [a]Mark 8:27-29: *Matt. 16:13-16; Luke 9:18-20* [b]Matt. 16:13
28 [a]Mark 6:14
29 [1]I.e., the Messiah
30 [1]Or, *strictly admonished* [a]Matt. 8:4; 16:20; Luke 9:21
31 [a]Mark 8:31-9:1: *Matt. 16:21-28; Luke 9:22-27* [b]Matt. 16:21
32 [a]John 10:24; 11:14; 16:25, 29; 18:20
33 [1]Lit., *the things of God* [a]Matt. 4:10
34 [a]Matt. 10:38
35 [1]Gr., *soul-life* [a]Matt. 10:39
36 [1]Gr., *soul-life*
37 [1]Gr., *soul-life*
38 [a]Matt. 10:33; Luke 9:26; Heb. 11:16 [b]Matt. 8:20 [c]Matt. 16:27; Mark 13:26: Luke 9:27
1 [a]Matt. 16:27; Mark 13:26; Luke 9:27
2 [1]Or, *Jacob* [a]Mark 9:2-8: *Matt. 17:1-8; Luke 9:28-36* [b]Mark 5:37
3 [a]Matt. 28:3
5 [1]Or, *sacred tents* [a]Matt. 23:7 [b]Matt. 17:4; Luke 9:33
7 [1]Or, *occurred* [2]Or, *give constant heed* [a]2 Pet. 1:17f. [b]Matt. 3:17; Mark 1:11
9 [1]Lit., *except when* [a]Mark 9:9-13: *Matt. 17:9-13* [b]Matt. 8:4; Mark 5:43; 7:36; 8:30
10 [1]Or, *kept to themselves* [2]Lit., *the statement* [3]Lit., *what was the rising from the dead*
11 [a]Matt. 11:14
12 [a]Mark 9:31 [b]Matt. 16:21; 26:24
13 [1]Lit., *also*
14 [a]Mark 9:14-28: *Matt. 17:14-19; Luke 9:37-42*

15 And immediately, when the entire crowd saw Him, they were
[a]amazed, and *began* running up to
greet Him.
16 And He asked them, "What are
you discussing with them?"
17 And one of the crowd answered
Him, "Teacher, I brought You my
son, possessed with a spirit which
makes him mute;
18 and [1]whenever it seizes him, it
[2]dashes him *to the ground* and he
foams *at the mouth,* and grinds his
teeth, and [3]stiffens out. And I told
Your disciples to cast it out, and
they could not *do it.*"
19 And He *answered them and
*said, "O unbelieving generation,
how long shall I be with you? How
long shall I put up with you? Bring
him to Me!"
20 And they brought [1]the boy to
Him. And when he saw Him, immediately the spirit threw him into a
convulsion, and falling to the
ground, he *began* rolling about and
foaming *at the mouth.*
21 And He asked his father, "How
long has this been happening to
him?" And he said, "From childhood.
22 "And it has often thrown him
both into the fire and into the water
to destroy him. But if You can do
anything, take pity on us and help
us!"
23 And Jesus said to him, " 'If You
can!' [a]All things are possible to him
who believes."
24 Immediately the boy's father
cried out and *began* saying, "I do
believe; help my unbelief."
25 And when Jesus saw that [a]a
crowd was [1]rapidly gathering, He
rebuked the unclean spirit, saying to
it, "You deaf and dumb spirit, I
[2]command you, come out of him
and do not enter him [3]again."
26 And after crying out and throwing him into terrible convulsions, it
came out; and *the boy* became so
much like a corpse that most *of
them* said, "He is dead!"
27 But Jesus took him by the hand
and raised him; and he got up.
28 And when He had come [a]into
the house, His disciples *began* questioning Him privately, "Why is it
that we could not cast it out?"
29 And He said to them, "This
kind cannot come out by anything
but prayer.[1]"

Death and Resurrection Foretold

30 [a]And from there they went out
and *began* to go through Galilee,
and He was unwilling for anyone to
know *about it.*
31 For He was teaching His disciples and telling them, "[a]The Son of
Man is to be [1]delivered up into the
hands of men, and they will kill
Him; and when He has been killed,
He will rise again three days later."
32 But [a]they [1]did not understand
this statement, and they were afraid
to ask Him.
33 [a]And they came to Capernaum;
and when He [1]was in [b]the house, He
began to question them, "What
were you discussing on the way?"
34 But they kept silent, for on the
way [a]they had discussed with one
another which *of them was* the
greatest.
35 And sitting down, He called the
twelve and *said to them, "[a]If any
one wants to be first, [1]he shall be
last of all, and servant of all."
36 And taking a child, He stood
him in the midst of them; and taking
him in His arms, He said to them,
37 "[a]Whoever receives [1]one child
like this in My name is receiving Me;
and whoever receives Me is not receiving Me, but Him who sent Me."

Dire Warnings

38 [a]John said to Him, "Teacher,
we saw someone casting out demons in Your name, and [b]we tried to
hinder him because he was not following us."
39 But Jesus said, "Do not hinder
him, for there is no one who shall
perform a miracle in My name, and
be able soon afterward to speak evil
of Me.
40 "[a]For he who is not against us is
[1]for us.
41 "For [a]whoever gives you a cup
of water to drink [1]because of your
name as *followers* of Christ, truly I
say to you, he shall not lose his reward.
42 "And [a]whoever causes one of
these little ones who believe to
stumble, it [1]would be better for him
if, with a heavy millstone hung
around his neck, he [2]had been cast
into the sea.
43 "And [a]if your hand causes you to
stumble, cut it off; it is better for you
to enter life crippled, than having
your two hands, to go into [1b]hell,
into the [c]unquenchable fire,
44 [[1]where THEIR WORM DOES NOT
DIE, AND THE FIRE IS NOT QUENCHED.]
45 "And if your foot causes you to
stumble, cut it off; it is better for you
to enter life lame, than having your
two feet, to be cast into [1a]hell,

15 [a]Mark 14:33; 16:5, 6

18 [1]Or, *wherever* [2]Or, *tears him* [3]Or, *withers away*

20 [1]Lit., *him*

23 [a]Matt. 17:20; John 11:40

25 [1]Or, *running together* [2]Or, *I Myself command* [3]Or, *from now on* [a]Mark 9:15

28 [a]Mark 2:1; 7:17

29 [1]Many mss. add: *and fasting*

30 [a]Mark 9:30-32: *Matt. 17:22-23; Luke 9:43-45*

31 [1]Or, *betrayed* [a]Matt. 16:21; Mark 8:31; 9:12

32 [1]Lit., *were not knowing* [a]Luke 2:50; 9:45; 18:34; John 12:16

33 [1]Lit., *had become* [a]Mark 9:33-37: *Matt. [17:24] 18:1-5; Luke 9:46-48* [b]Mark 3:19

34 [a]Mark 9:50; Luke 22:24

35 [1]Or, *let him be* [a]Matt. 20:26

37 [1]Lit., *one of such children* [a]Matt. 10:40

38 [a]Mark 9:38-40: *Luke 9:49-50* [b]Num. 11:27-29

40 [1]Or, *on our side* [a]Matt. 12:30

41 [1]Lit., *in a name that you are Christ's* [a]Matt. 10:42

42 [1]Lit., *is better for him if a millstone turned by a donkey is hung* [2]Lit., *has been cast* [a]Matt. 18:6; Luke 17:2; 1 Cor. 8:12

43 [1]Lit., *Gehenna* [a]Matt. 5:30; 17:27; 18:8 [b]Matt. 5:22 [c]Math. 3:12; 25:41

44 [1]Verses 44 and 46, which are identical with verse 48, are not found in the best ancient mss.

45 [1]Lit., *Gehenna* [a]Matt. 5:22

46 [[1]where THEIR WORM DOES NOT DIE, AND THE FIRE IS NOT QUENCHED.]
47 "And [a]if your eye causes you to stumble, cast it out; it is better for you to enter the kingdom of God with one eye, than having two eyes, to be cast into [1][b]hell,
48 [a]where THEIR WORM DOES NOT DIE, AND [b]THE FIRE IS NOT QUENCHED.
49 "For everyone will be salted with fire.
50 "Salt is good; but [a]if the salt becomes unsalty, with what will you [1]make it salty *again?* [b]Have salt in yourselves, and [c]be at peace with one another."

CHAPTER 10

Jesus' Teaching About Divorce

[a]AND rising up, He *went from there to the region of Judea, and beyond the Jordan; and crowds *gathered around Him again, and, [b]according to His custom, He once more *began* to teach them.
2 And *some* Pharisees came up to Him, testing Him, and *began* to question Him whether it was lawful for a man to divorce a wife.
3 And He answered and said to them, "What did Moses command you?"
4 And they said, "[a]Moses permitted *a man* to write a certificate of divorce and [1]send *her* away."
5 But Jesus said to them, "[1][a]Because of your hardness of heart he wrote you this commandment.
6 "But [a]from the beginning of creation, *God* [b]MADE THEM MALE AND FEMALE.
7 "[a]FOR THIS CAUSE A MAN SHALL LEAVE HIS FATHER AND MOTHER,[1]
8 [a]AND THE TWO SHALL BECOME ONE FLESH; consequently they are no longer two, but one flesh.
9 "What therefore God has joined together, let no man separate."
10 And in the house the disciples *began* questioning Him about this again.
11 And He *said to them, "[a]Whoever divorces his wife and marries another woman commits adultery against her;
12 and [a]if she herself divorces her husband and marries another man, she is committing adultery."

Jesus Blesses Little Children

13 [a]And they *began* bringing children to Him, so that He might touch them; and the disciples rebuked them.
14 But when Jesus saw this, He was indignant and said to them, "Permit the children to come to Me; do not hinder them; [a]for the kingdom of God belongs to such as these.
15 "Truly I say to you, [a]whoever does not receive the kingdom of God like a child shall not enter it *at all.*"
16 And He [a]took them in His arms and *began* blessing them, laying His hands upon them.

The Rich Young Ruler

17 [a]And as He was setting out on a journey, a man ran up to Him and [b]knelt before Him, and *began* asking Him, "Good Teacher, what shall I do to [c]inherit eternal life?"
18 And Jesus said to him, "Why do you call Me good? No one is good except God alone.
19 "You know the commandments, '[a]DO NOT MURDER, DO NOT COMMIT ADULTERY, DO NOT STEAL, DO NOT BEAR FALSE WITNESS, Do not defraud, HONOR YOUR FATHER AND MOTHER.' "
20 And he said to Him, "Teacher, I have kept [a]all these things from my youth up."
21 And looking at him, Jesus felt a love for him, and said to him, "One thing you lack: go and sell all you possess, and give *it* to the poor, and you shall have [a]treasure in heaven; and come, follow Me."
22 But at these words [1]his face fell, and he went away grieved, for he was one who owned much property.
23 And Jesus, looking around, *said to His disciples, "[a]How hard it will be for those who are wealthy to enter the kingdom of God!"
24 And the disciples [a]were amazed at His words. But Jesus *answered again and *said to them, "Children, how hard it is [1]to enter the kingdom of God!
25 "[a]It is easier for a camel to go through the eye of [1]a needle than for a rich man to enter the kingdom of God."
26 And they were even more astonished and said [1]to Him, "[2]Then who can be saved?"
27 Looking upon them, Jesus *said, "[a]With men it is impossible, but not with God; for all things are possible with God."
28 [a]Peter began to say to Him, "Behold, we have left everything and followed You."
29 Jesus said, "Truly I say to you, [a]there is no one who has left house or brothers or sisters or mother or

46 [1]See v. 44, mg. nt. 1
47 [1]Lit., *Gehenna* [a]Matt. 5:29; 17:27; 18:9 [b]Matt. 5:22
48 [a]Is. 66:24 [b]Matt. 3:12; 25:41
50 [1]Lit., *season it* [a]Matt. 5:13; Luke 14:34f. [b]Col. 4:6 [c]Mark 9:34; Rom. 12:18; 2 Cor. 13:11; 1 Thess. 5:13
1 [a]Mark 10:1-12: *Matt. 19:1-9* [b]Matt. 4:23; 26:55; Mark 1:21; 2:13; 4:2; 6:2, 6, 34; 12:35; 14:49
4 [1]Or, *divorce her* [a]Deut. 24:1, 3
5 [1]Or, *With reference to* [a]Matt. 19:8
6 [a]Mark 13:19; 2 Pet. 3:4 [b]Gen. 1:27; 5:2
7 [1]Some mss. add: *and shall cleave to his wife* [a]Gen. 2:24
8 [a]Gen. 2:24
11 [a]Matt. 5:32
12 [a]1 Cor. 7:11, 13
13 [a]Mark 10:13-16: *Matt. 19:13-15; Luke 18:15-17*
14 [a]Matt. 5:3
15 [a]Matt. 18:3; 19:14; Luke 18:17; 1 Cor. 14:20; 1 Pet. 2:2
16 [a]Mark 9:36
17 [a]Mark 10:17-31: *Matt. 19:16-30; Luke 18:18-30* [b]Mark 1:40 [c]Matt. 25:34; Luke 10:25; 18:18; Acts 20:32; Eph. 1:18; 1 Pet. 1:4
19 [a]Ex. 20:12-16; Deut. 5:16-20
20 [a]Matt. 19:20
21 [a]Matt. 6:20
22 [1]Or, *he became gloomy*
23 [a]Matt. 19:23
24 [1]Later mss. insert: *for those who trust in wealth* [a]Mark 1:27
25 [1]Lit., *the* [a]Matt. 19:24
26 [1]Later mss. read, *to one another* [2]Lit., *And*
27 [a]Matt. 19:26
28 [a]Matt. 4:20-22
29 [a]Matt. 6:33; 19:29; Luke 18:29f.

father or children or farms, for My
sake and for the gospel's sake,
30 but that he shall receive a hundred times as much now in the
[1]present age, houses and brothers
and sisters and mothers and children and farms, along with persecu-
tions; and in [a]the [2]world to come,
eternal life.
31"But [a]many *who are* first, will be
last; and the last, first."

Jesus' Sufferings Foretold

32 [a]And they were on the road,
going up to Jerusalem, and Jesus
was walking on ahead of them; and
they [b]were amazed, and those who
followed were fearful. And again He
took the twelve aside and began to
tell them what was going to happen
to Him,
33 *saying,* "Behold, we are going
up to Jerusalem, and [a]the Son of
Man will be [1]delivered up to the
chief priests and the scribes; and
they will condemn Him to death,
and will [2]deliver Him up to the Gentiles.
34"And they will mock Him and
[a]spit upon Him, and scourge Him,
and kill *Him,* and three days later
He will rise again."
35 [a]And [1]James and John, the two
sons of Zebedee, *came up to Him,
saying to Him, "Teacher, we want
You to do for us whatever we ask of
You."
36 And He said to them, "What do
you want Me to do for you?"
37 And they said to Him, "[1]Grant
that we [a]may sit in Your glory, one
on Your right, and one on *Your* left."
38 But Jesus said to them, "You do
not know what you are asking for.
Are you able [a]to drink the cup that I
drink, or [b]to be baptized with the
baptism with which I am baptized?"
39 And they said to Him, "We are
able." And Jesus said to them, "The
cup that I drink [a]you shall drink; and
you shall be baptized with the baptism with which I am baptized.
40"But to sit on My right or on *My*
left, this is not Mine to give; [a]but *it is*
for those for whom it has been prepared."
41 [a]And hearing this, the ten began to feel indignant toward [1]James
and John.
42 And calling them to Himself,
Jesus *said to them, "You know
that those who are recognized as
rulers of the Gentiles lord it over
them; and their great men exercise
authority over them.
43"But it is not so among you, [a]but
whoever wishes to become great
among you shall be your servant;
44 and whoever wishes to be first
among you shall be slave of all.
45"For even the Son of Man [a]did
not come to be served, but to serve,
and to give His [1]life a ransom for
many."

Bartimaeus Receives His Sight

46 [a]And they *came to Jericho.
And [b]as He was going out from Jericho with His disciples and a great
multitude, a blind beggar *named*
Bartimaeus, the son of Timaeus,
was sitting by the road.
47 And when he heard that it was
Jesus the [a]Nazarene, he began to
cry out and say, "Jesus, [b]Son of David, have mercy on me!"
48 And many were sternly telling
him to be quiet, but he *began* crying
out all the more, "[a]Son of David,
have mercy on me!"
49 And Jesus stopped and said,
"Call him *here.*" And they *called
the blind man, saying to him, "[a]Take
courage, arise! He is calling for
you."
50 And casting aside his cloak, he
jumped up, and came to Jesus.
51 And answering him, Jesus said,
"What do you want Me to do for
you?" And the blind man said to
Him, "[1a]Rabboni, *I want* to regain
my sight!"
52 And Jesus said to him, "Go
your way; [a]your faith has [1]made you
well." And immediately he received
his sight and *began* following Him
on the road.

CHAPTER 11

The Triumphal Entry

[a]AND as they *approached Jerusalem, at Bethphage and [b]Bethany,
near [c]the Mount of Olives, He *sent
two of His disciples,
2 and *said to them, "Go into the
village opposite you, and immediately as you enter it, you will find a
colt tied *there,* on which no one yet
has ever sat; untie it and bring it
here.
3"And if anyone says to you,
'Why are you doing this?' you say,
'The Lord has need of it;' and immediately he [1]will send it back here."
4 And they went away and found
a colt tied at the door outside in the
street; and they *untied it.
5 And some of the bystanders
were saying to them, "What are you
doing, untying the colt?"
6 And they spoke to them just as

30 [1]Lit., *this time* [2]Or, *age* [a]Matt. 12:32
31 [a]Matt. 19:30
32 [a]Mark 10:32-34: *Matt. 20:17-19; Luke 18:31-33* [b]Mark 1:27
33 [1]Or, *betrayed* [2]Or, *betray* [a]Mark 8:31; 9:12
34 [a]Matt. 16:21; 26:67; 27:30; Mark 9:31; 14:65
35 [1]Or, *Jacob* [a]Mark 10:35-45: *Matt. 20:20-28*
37 [1]Lit., *Give to us* [a]Matt. 19:28
38 [a]Matt. 20:22 [b]Luke 12:50
39 [a]Acts 12:2; Rev. 1:9
40 [a]Matt. 13:11
41 [1]Or, *Jacob* [a]Mark 10:42-45; Luke 22:25-27
43 [a]Matt. 20:26; Mark 9:35
45 [1]Or, *soul* [a]Matt. 20:28
46 [a]Mark 10:46-52: *Matt. 20:29-34; Luke 18:35-43* [b]Luke 18:35; 19:1
47 [a]Mark 1:24 [b]Matt. 9:27
48 [a]Matt. 9:27
49 [a]Matt. 9:2
51 [1]I.e., My Master [a]Matt. 23:7; John 20:16
52 [1]Lit., *saved you* [a]Matt. 9:22
1 [a]Mark 11:1-10: *Matt. 21:1-9; Luke 19:29-38* [b]Matt. 21:17 [c]Matt. 21:1
3 [1]Lit., *sends*

Jesus had told *them,* and they gave them permission.

7 [a]And they *brought the colt to Jesus and put their garments on it; and He sat upon it.

8 And many spread their garments in the road, and others *spread* leafy branches which they had cut from the fields.

9 And those who went before, and those who followed after, were crying out,

"[a]HOSANNA!
BLESSED IS HE WHO COMES IN THE NAME OF THE LORD;
10 Blessed *is* the coming kingdom of our father David;
HOSANNA [a]in the highest!"

11 And [a]He entered Jerusalem *and came* into the temple; and after looking all around, [b]He departed for Bethany with the twelve, since it was already late.

12 [a]And on the next day, when they had departed from Bethany, He became hungry.

13 And seeing at a distance a fig tree in leaf, He went *to see* if perhaps He would find anything on it; and when He came to it, He found nothing but leaves, for it was not the season for figs.

14 And He answered and said to it, "May no one ever eat fruit from you again!" And His disciples were listening.

Jesus Drives Moneychangers from the Temple

15 [a]And they *came to Jerusalem. And He entered the temple and began to cast out those who were buying and selling in the temple, and overturned the tables of the moneychangers and the seats of those who were selling [1]doves;

16 and He would not permit anyone to carry [1]goods through the temple.

17 And He *began* to teach and say to them, "Is it not written, '[a]MY HOUSE SHALL BE CALLED A HOUSE OF PRAYER FOR ALL THE NATIONS'? [b]But you have made it a robbers' [1]den."

18 And the chief priests and the scribes heard *this,* and [a]*began* seeking how to destroy Him; for they were afraid of Him, for [b]all the multitude was astonished at His teaching.

19 And [a]whenever evening came, [1]they would go out of the city.

20 [a]And as they were passing by in the morning, they saw the fig tree withered from the roots *up.*

21 And being reminded, Peter *said to Him, "[a]Rabbi, behold, the fig tree which You cursed has withered."

22 And Jesus *answered saying to them, "[a]Have faith in God.

23 "Truly I say to you, whoever says to this mountain, 'Be taken up and cast into the sea,' and does not doubt in his heart, but believes that what he says is going to happen, it shall be *granted* him.

24 "Therefore I say to you, [a]all things for which you pray and ask, believe that you have received them, and they shall be *granted* you.

25 "And whenever you [a]stand praying, [b]forgive, if you have anything against anyone; so that your Father also who is in heaven may forgive you your transgressions.

26 ["[1a]But if you do not forgive, neither will your Father who is in heaven forgive your transgressions."]

Jesus' Authority Questioned

27 And they *came again to Jerusalem. [a]And as He was walking in the temple, the chief priests, and scribes, and elders *came to Him,

28 and *began* saying to Him, "By what authority are You doing these things, or who gave You this authority to do these things?"

29 And Jesus said to them, "I will ask you one question, and you answer Me, and *then* I will tell you by what authority I do these things.

30 "Was the baptism of John from heaven, or from men? Answer Me."

31 And they *began* reasoning with one another, saying, "If we say, 'From heaven,' He will say, 'Then why did you not believe him?'

32 "But [1]shall we say, 'From men'?"—they were afraid of the multitude, for all considered John to have been a prophet indeed.

33 And answering Jesus, they *said, "We do not know." And Jesus *said to them, "Neither [1]will I tell you by what authority I do these things."

CHAPTER 12

Parable of the Vine-growers

[a]AND He began to speak to them in parables: "[b]A man [c]PLANTED A VINEYARD, AND PUT A [1]WALL AROUND IT, AND DUG A VAT UNDER THE WINE PRESS, AND BUILT A TOWER, and rented it out to [2]vine-growers and went on a journey.

2 "And at the *harvest* time he sent a slave to the vine-growers, in order

7 [a]Mark 11:7-10: *John 12:12-15*
9 [a]Ps. 118:26; Matt. 21:9
10 [a]Matt. 21:9
11 [a]Matt. 21:12 [b]Matt. 21:17
12 [a]Mark 11:12-14 [20-24]: *Matt. 21:18-22*
15 [1]Lit., *the doves* [a]Mark 11:15-18: *Matt. 21:12-16; Luke 19:45-47;* John 2:13-16
16 [1]Lit., *a vessel,* i.e., a receptacle or implement of any kind
17 [1]Lit., *cave* [a]Is. 56:7 [b]Jer. 7:11
18 [a]Matt. 21:46; Mark 12:12; Luke 20:19; John 7:1 [b]Matt. 7:28
19 [1]I.e., Jesus and His disciples [a]Matt. 21:17; Mark 11:11; Luke 21:37
20 [a]Mark 11:20-24 [Mark 11:12-14]: *Matt. 21:19-22*
21 [a]Matt. 23:7
22 [a]Matt. 17:20; 21:21f.
24 [a]Matt. 7:7f.
25 [a]Matt. 6:5 [b]Matt. 6:14
26 [1]Many mss. do not contain this verse [a]Matt. 6:15; 18:35
27 [a]Mark 11:27-33: *Matt. 21:23-27; Luke 20:1-8*
32 [1]Or, *if we say*
33 [1]Lit., *do I tell*
1 [1]Or, *fence* [2]Here and in vs. 2, 7, and 9: or, *tenant farmers* [a]Mark 3:23; 4:2ff. [b]Mark 12:1-12: *Matt. 21:33-46; Luke 20:9-19* [c]Is. 5:2

to receive *some* of the produce of
the vineyard from the vine-growers.
3"And they took him, and beat
him, and sent him away empty-
handed.
4"And again he sent them another slave, and they wounded him
in the head, and treated him shamefully.
5"And he sent another, and that
one they killed; and *so with* many
others, beating some, and killing
others.
6"He had one more *to send*, a beloved son; he sent him last *of all* to
them, saying, 'They will respect my
son.'
7"But those vine-growers said to
one another, 'This is the heir; come,
let us kill him, and the inheritance
will be ours!'
8"And they took him, and killed
him, and threw him out of the vineyard.
9"What will the [1]owner of the
vineyard do? He will come and destroy the vine-growers, and will give
the vineyard to others.
10"Have you not even read this
scripture:

'[a]THE STONE WHICH THE BUILD-
ERS REJECTED,
THIS BECAME THE CHIEF COR-
NER *stone;*
11 [a]THIS CAME ABOUT FROM THE
LORD,
AND IT IS MARVELOUS IN OUR
EYES'?"

12 And [a]they were seeking to seize
Him; and *yet* they feared the multitude; for they understood that He
had spoken the parable against
them. And *so* [b]they left Him, and
went away.

Jesus Answers the Pharisees, Sadducees and Scribes

13 [a]And they *sent some of the
Pharisees and [b]Herodians to Him, in
order to [c]trap Him in a statement.
14 And they *came and *said to
Him, "Teacher, we know that You
are truthful, and [1]defer to no one;
for You are not partial to any, but
teach the way of God in truth. Is it
[2]lawful to pay a poll-tax to Caesar,
or not?
15"Shall we pay, or shall we not
pay?" But He, knowing their hypocrisy, said to them, "Why are you
testing Me? Bring Me a [1]denarius to
look at."
16 And they brought *one*. And He
*said to them, "Whose likeness and
inscription is this?" And they said to
Him, "Caesar's."
17 And Jesus said to them,
"[a]Render to Caesar the things that
are Caesar's, and to God the things
that are God's." And they [1]were
amazed at Him.
18 [a]And *some* Sadducees (who say
that there is no resurrection) *came
to Him, and *began* questioning Him,
saying,
19"Teacher, Moses wrote for us *a*
law that [a]IF A MAN'S BROTHER DIES,
and leaves behind a wife, AND
LEAVES NO CHILD, HIS BROTHER
SHOULD TAKE THE WIFE, AND RAISE
UP OFFSPRING TO HIS BROTHER.
20"There were seven brothers; and
the first one took a wife, and died,
leaving no offspring.
21"And the second one took her,
and died, leaving behind no offspring; and the third likewise;
22 and *so* [1]all seven left no offspring. Last of all the woman died
too.
23"In the resurrection, [1]when they
rise again, which one's wife will she
be? For [2]all seven had her as wife."
24 Jesus said to them, "Is this not
the reason you are mistaken, that
you do not [1]understand the Scriptures, or the power of God?
25"For when they rise from the
dead, they neither marry, nor are
given in marriage, but are like angels in heaven.
26"But [1]regarding the fact that the
dead rise again, have you not read in
the book of Moses, [a]in the *passage*
about the burning bush, how God
spoke to him, saying, '[b]I AM THE GOD
OF ABRAHAM, AND THE GOD OF
ISAAC, AND THE GOD OF JACOB'?
27"[a]He is not *the* God [1]of *the* dead,
but of *the* living; you are greatly
mistaken."
28 [a]And one of the scribes came
and heard them arguing, and [b]rec-
ognizing that He had answered
them well, asked Him, "What commandment is the [1]foremost of all?"
29 Jesus answered, "The foremost
is, '[a]HEAR, O ISRAEL; THE LORD OUR
GOD IS ONE LORD;
30 [a]AND YOU SHALL LOVE THE LORD
YOUR GOD WITH ALL YOUR HEART,
AND WITH ALL YOUR SOUL, AND WITH
ALL YOUR MIND, AND WITH ALL YOUR
STRENGTH.'
31"The second is this, '[a]YOU SHALL
LOVE YOUR NEIGHBOR AS YOURSELF.'
There is no other commandment
greater than these."
32 And the scribe said to Him,
"Right, Teacher, You have truly
stated that [a]HE IS ONE; AND THERE IS
NO ONE ELSE BESIDES HIM;
33 [a]AND TO LOVE HIM WITH ALL THE

9 [1]Lit., *lord*
10 [a]Ps. 118:22
11 [a]Ps. 118:23
12 [a]Mark 11:18 [b]Matt. 22:22
13 [a]Mark 12:13-17: *Matt. 22:15-22; Luke 20:20-26* [b]Matt. 22:16 [c]Luke 11:54
14 [1]Lit., *it is not a concern to You about anyone,* i.e., You court no man's favor [2]Or, *permissible*
15 [1]The denarius was worth 18 cents in silver, equivalent to a day's wage
17 [1]Or, *were greatly marveling* [a]Matt. 22:21
18 [a]Mark 12:18-27: *Matt. 22:23-33; Luke 20:27-38*
19 [a]Deut. 25:5
22 [1]Lit., *the seven*
23 [1]Most ancient mss. do not contain: *when they rise again* [2]Lit., *the seven*
24 [1]Or, *know*
26 [1]Lit., *concerning the dead, that they rise* [a]Luke 20:37; Rom. 11:2 [b]Ex. 3:6
27 [1]Or, *of corpses* [a]Matt. 22:32; Luke 20:38
28 [1]Or, *first* [a]Mark 12:28-34: *Matt. 22:34-40;* Luke 10:25-28; 20:39f. [b]Matt. 22:34; Luke 20:39
29 [a]Deut. 6:4
30 [a]Deut. 6:5
31 [a]Lev. 19:18
32 [a]Deut. 4:35
33 [a]Deut. 6:5

HEART AND WITH ALL THE UNDERSTANDING AND WITH ALL THE STRENGTH, AND TO LOVE ONE'S NEIGHBOR AS HIMSELF, [b]is much more than all burnt offerings and sacrifices."

34 And when Jesus saw that he had answered intelligently, He said to him, "You are not far from the kingdom of God." [a]And after that, no one would venture to ask Him any more questions.

35 [a]And Jesus answering *began* to say, as He [b]taught in the temple, "How *is it that* the scribes say that [1]the Christ is the [c]son of David?

36 "David himself said [1]in the Holy Spirit,

> '[a]THE LORD SAID TO MY LORD,
> "SIT AT MY RIGHT HAND,
> UNTIL I PUT THINE ENEMIES BENEATH THY FEET." '

37 "David himself calls Him 'Lord'; and *so* in what sense is He his son?" And [a]the great crowd [1]enjoyed listening to Him.

38 [a]And in His teaching He was saying: "Beware of the scribes who like to walk around in long robes, and *like* [b]respectful greetings in the market places,

39 and chief seats in the synagogues, and places of honor at banquets.

40 "[a]They *are* the ones who devour widows' houses, and for appearance's sake offer long prayers; these will receive greater condemnation."

The Widow's Mite

41 [a]And He sat down opposite [b]the treasury, and *began* observing how the multitude were [c]putting [1]money into the treasury; and many rich people were putting in large sums.

42 And a poor widow came and put in two [1]small copper coins, which amount to a [2]cent.

43 And calling His disciples to Him, He said to them, "Truly I say to you, this poor widow put in more than all [1]the contributors to the treasury;

44 for they all put in out of their [1]surplus, but she, out of her poverty, put in all she owned, [2]all she had [a]to live on."

CHAPTER 13

Things to Come

[a]AND as He was going out of the temple, one of His disciples *said to Him, "Teacher, behold [1]what wonderful stones and [1]what wonderful buildings!"

2 And Jesus said to him, "Do you see these great buildings? [a]Not one stone shall be left upon another which will not be torn down."

3 And as He was sitting on [a]the Mount of Olives opposite the temple, [b]Peter and [1]James and John and Andrew were questioning Him privately,

4 "Tell us, when will these things be, and what *will be* the [1]sign when all these things are going to be fulfilled?"

5 And Jesus began to say to them, "See to it that no one misleads you.

6 "Many will come in My name, saying, '[a]I am *He!*' and will mislead many.

7 "And when you hear of wars and rumors of wars, do not be frightened; *those things* must take place; but *that is* not yet the end.

8 "For nation will arise against nation, and kingdom against kingdom; there will be earthquakes in various places; there will *also* be famines. These things are *merely* the beginning of birth pangs.

9 "But [1]be on your guard; for they will [a]deliver you up to *the* [2]courts, and you will be flogged [b]in *the* synagogues, and you will stand before governors and kings for My sake, as a testimony to them.

10 "[a]And the gospel must first be preached to all the nations.

11 "[a]And when they [1]arrest you and deliver you up, do not be anxious beforehand about what you are to say, but say whatever is given you in that hour; for it is not you who speak, but *it is* the Holy Spirit.

12 "And brother will deliver up brother to death, and a father *his* child; and children will rise up against parents and [1]cause them to be put to death.

13 "And [a]you will be hated by all on account of My name, but it is the one who has endured to the end who will be saved.

14 "But [a]when you see the [b]ABOMINATION OF DESOLATION standing where it should not be (let the reader understand), then let those who are in Judea flee to the mountains.

15 "And let him who is on the housetop not go down, or enter in, to get anything out of his house;

16 and let him who is in the field not turn back to get his cloak.

17 "But woe to those who are with child and to those who nurse babes in those days!

18 "But pray that it may not happen in the winter.

33 [b]1 Sam. 15:22; Hos. 6:6; Mic. 6:6-8; Matt. 9:13; 12:7

34 [a]Matt. 22:46

35 [1]I.e., the Messiah [a]Mark 12:35-37: *Matt. 22:41-46; Luke 20:41-44* [b]Matt. 26:55; Mark 10:1 [c]Matt. 9:27

36 [1]Or, *by* [a]Ps. 110:1

37 [1]Lit., *was gladly hearing Him* [a]John 12:9

38 [a]Mark 12:38-40: *Matt. 23:1-7; Luke 20:45-47* [b]Matt. 23:6; Luke 11:43

40 [a]Luke 20:47

41 [1]I.e., copper coins [a]Mark 12:41-44: *Luke 21:1-4* [b]John 8:20 [c]2 Kin. 12:9

42 [1]Lit., *lepta* [2]Lit., *quadrans,* i.e., 1/64 of a denarius

43 [1]Lit., *those who were putting in*

44 [1]Or, *abundance* [2]Lit., *her whole livelihood* [a]Luke 8:43; 15:12, 30; 21:4

1 [1]Lit., *how great* [a]Mark 13:1-37: *Matt. 24; Luke 21:5-36*

2 [a]Luke 19:44

3 [1]Or, *Jacob* [a]Matt. 21:1 [b]Matt. 17:1

4 [1]Or, *attesting miracle*

6 [a]John 8:24

9 [1]Lit., *look to yourselves* [2]Or, *Sanhedrin,* or council [a]Matt. 10:17 [b]Matt. 10:17

10 [a]Matt. 24:14

11 [1]Lit., *lead* [a]Mark 13:11-13: *Matt. 10:19-22; Luke 21:12-17*

12 [1]Lit., *put them to death*

13 [a]John 15:21

14 [a]Matt. 24:15 [b]Dan. 9:27; 11:31; 12:11

19"For those days will be a *time of*
tribulation such as has not occurred
[a]since the beginning of the creation
which God created, until now, and
never shall.
20"And unless the Lord had shortened *those* days, no [1]life would have
been saved; but for the sake of the
[2]elect whom He chose, He shortened the days.
21"And then if anyone says to you,
'Behold, here is [1]the Christ'; or, 'Behold, *He is* there'; do not believe
him;
22 for false Christs and [a]false
prophets will arise, and will show
[1b]signs and [b]wonders, in order, if
possible, to lead the elect astray.
23"But take heed; behold, I have
told you everything in advance.

The Return of Christ

24"But in those days, after that
tribulation, [a]THE SUN WILL BE DARK-
ENED, AND THE MOON WILL NOT GIVE
ITS LIGHT,
25 [a]AND THE STARS WILL BE FALL-
ING from heaven, and the powers
that are in [1]the heavens will be
shaken.
26"[a]And then they shall see the
Son of Man [b]coming in clouds with
great power and glory.
27"And then He will send forth the
angels, and [a]WILL GATHER TOGETHER
His [1]elect FROM THE FOUR WINDS,
[b]FROM THE FARTHEST END of the
earth, TO THE FARTHEST END OF
HEAVEN.
28"Now learn the parable from the
fig tree: when its branch has already
become tender, and puts forth its
leaves, you know that the summer is
near.
29"Even so you too, when you see
these things happening, [1]recognize
that [2]He is near, *right* at the [3]door.
30"Truly I say to you, this [1]genera-
tion will not pass away until all
these things take place.
31"Heaven and earth will pass
away, but My words will not pass
away.
32"[a]But of that day or hour no one
knows, not even the angels in
heaven, nor the Son, but the Father
alone.
33"Take heed, [a]keep on the alert;
for you do not know when the *appointed* time is.
34"*It is* like a man, away on a journey, *who* upon leaving his house and
[1]putting his slaves in charge, *assign-
ing* to each one his task, also commanded the doorkeeper to stay on
the alert.
35"Therefore, [a]be on the alert —
for you do not know when the [1]mas-
ter of the house is coming, whether
in the evening, at midnight, at
[b]cockcrowing, or [c]in the morning—
36 lest he come suddenly and find
you [a]asleep.
37"And what I say to you I say to
all, '[a]Be on the alert!' "

CHAPTER 14

Death Plot and Anointing

[a]NOW *the feast of* [b]the Passover
and Unleavened Bread was two
days off; and the chief priests and
the scribes [c]were seeking how to
seize Him by stealth, and kill *Him;*
2 for they were saying, "Not during the festival, lest there be a riot of
the people."
3 [a]And while He was in [b]Bethany
at the home of Simon the leper, and
reclining *at table,* there came a
woman with an alabaster vial of
[c]costly perfume of pure nard; *and*
she broke the vial and poured it over
His head.
4 But some were indignantly *remarking* to one another, "For what
purpose has this perfume been
wasted?
5"For this perfume might have
been sold for over three hundred
[1]denarii, and *the money* given to the
poor." And they were scolding her.
6 But Jesus said, "Let her alone;
why do you bother her? She has
done a good deed to Me.
7"For [a]the poor you always have
with you, and whenever you wish,
you can do them good; but you do
not always have Me.
8"She has done what she could;
[a]she has anointed My body beforehand for the burial.
9"And truly I say to you, [a]wherev-
er the gospel is preached in the
whole world, that also which this
woman has done shall be spoken of
in memory of her."
10 [a]And Judas Iscariot, [b]who was
one of the twelve, went off to the
chief priests, in order to [1]betray
Him to them.
11 And they were glad when they
heard *this,* and promised to give him
money. And he *began* seeking how
to betray Him at an opportune time.

The Last Passover

12 [a]And on the first day of *the
feast of* [b]Unleavened Bread, when
[1]the Passover *lamb* was being [c]sac-
rificed, His disciples *said to Him,
"Where do You want us to go and

19 [a]Mark 10:6
20 [1]Lit., *flesh* [2]Or, *chosen ones*
21 [1]I.e., the Messiah
22 [1]Or, *attesting miracles* [a]Matt. 7:15 [b]Matt. 24:24; John 4:48
24 [a]Is. 13:10
25 [1]Or, *heaven* [a]Is. 34:4
26 [a]Dan. 7:13 [b]Matt. 16:27; Mark 8:38
27 [1]Or, *chosen ones* [a]Deut. 30:4 [b]Zech. 2:6
29 [1]Lit., *know* [2]Or, *it* [3]Lit., *doors*
30 [1]Or, *race*
32 [a]Matt. 24:36; Acts 1:7
33 [a]Eph. 6:18; Col. 4:2
34 [1]Lit., *giving the authority to*
35 [1]Lit., *lord* [a]Matt. 24:42; Mark 13:37 [b]Mark 14:30 [c]Matt. 14:25; Mark 6:48
36 [a]Rom. 13:11
37 [a]Matt. 24:42; Mark 13:35
1 [a]Mark 14:1, 2: *Matt. 26:2-5; Luke 22:1, 2* [b]Mark 14:12; John 11:55; 13:1 [c]Matt. 12:14
3 [a]Mark 14:3-9: *Matt. 26:6-13;* Luke 7:37-39; John 12:1-8 [b]Matt. 21:17 [c]Matt. 26:6f.; John 12:3
5 [1]The denarius was worth 18 cents in silver, equivalent to a day's wage
7 [a]Deut. 15:11; Matt. 26:11; John 12:8
8 [a]John 19:40
9 [a]Matt. 26:13
10 [1]Or, *deliver Him up* [a]Mark 14:10, 11: *Matt. 26:14-16; Luke 22:3-6* [b]John 6:71
12 [1]Lit., *they were sacrificing* [a]Mark 14:12-16: *Matt. 26:17-19; Luke 22:7-13* [b]Matt. 26:17 [c]Deut. 16:5; Mark 14:1; Luke 22:7; 1 Cor. 5:7

prepare for You to eat the Passover?"
13 And He *sent two of His disciples, and *said to them, "Go into the
city, and a man will meet you carrying a pitcher of water; follow him;
14 and wherever he enters, say to
the owner of the house, 'The
Teacher says, "Where is My [a]guest
room in which I may eat the Passover with My disciples?"'
15"And he himself will show you a
large upper room furnished *and*
ready; and prepare for us there."
16 And the disciples went out, and
came to the city, and found *it* just as
He had told them; and they prepared the Passover.
17 [a]And when it was evening He
*came with the twelve.
18 And as they were reclining *at
table* and eating, Jesus said, "Truly I
say to you that one of you will [1]be-
tray Me —[2]one who is eating with
Me."
19 They began to be grieved and to
say to Him one by one, "Surely not
I?"
20 And He said to them, "*It is* one
of the twelve, [1]one who dips with
Me in the bowl.
21"For the Son of Man *is to* go, just
as it is written of Him; but woe to
that man [1]by whom the Son of Man
is betrayed! *It would have been*
good [2]for that man if he had not
been born."

The Lord's Supper

22 [a]And while they were eating,
He took *some* bread, and [1]after a
[b]blessing He broke *it;* and gave *it* to
them, and said, "Take *it;* this is My
body."
23 And He took a cup, and when
He had given thanks, He gave *it* to
them; and they all drank from it.
24 And He said to them, "This is
My blood of the covenant, which is
to be shed on behalf of many.
25"Truly I say to you, I shall never
again drink of the fruit of the vine
until that day when I drink it new in
the kingdom of God."
26 [a]And after singing a hymn, they
went out to [b]the Mount of Olives.
27 [a]And Jesus *said to them, "You
will all [1]fall away, because it is written, '[b]I WILL STRIKE DOWN THE SHEP-
HERD, AND THE SHEEP SHALL BE
SCATTERED.'
28"But after I have been raised, I
will go before you to Galilee."
29 But Peter said to Him, "*Even*
though all may [1]fall away, yet I will
not."
30 And Jesus *said to him, "Truly
I say to you, that you yourself [1a]this
very night, before [b]a cock crows
twice, shall three times deny Me."
31 But *Peter* kept saying insis-
tently, "*Even* if I have to die with
You, I will not deny You!" And they
all were saying the same thing, too.

Jesus in Gethsemane

32 [a]And they *came to a place
named Gethsemane; and He *said
to His disciples, "Sit here until I
have prayed."
33 And He *took with Him Peter
and [1]James and John, and began to
be very [a]distressed and troubled.
34 And He *said to them, "[a]My
soul is deeply grieved to the point of
death; remain here and keep
watch."
35 And He went a little beyond
them, and [1]fell to the ground, and
began praying that if it were possible, [a]the hour might [2]pass Him by.
36 And He was saying, "[a]Abba!
Father! All things are possible for
Thee; remove this cup from Me; [b]yet
not what I will, but what Thou wilt."
37 And He *came and *found
them sleeping, and *said to Peter,
"Simon, are you asleep? Could you
not keep watch for one hour?
38"[a]Keep watching and praying,
that you may not come into temptation; the spirit is willing, but the
flesh is weak."
39 And again He went away and
prayed, saying the same [1]words.
40 And again He came and found
them sleeping, for their eyes were
very heavy; and they did not know
what to answer Him.
41 And He *came the third time,
and *said to them, "[1]Are you still
sleeping and taking your rest? It is
enough; [a]the hour has come; behold,
the Son of Man is being [2]betrayed
into the hands of sinners.
42"Arise, let us be going; behold,
the one who betrays Me is at hand!"

Betrayal and Arrest

43 [a]And immediately while He
was still speaking, Judas, one of the
twelve, *came up, [1]accompanied by
a multitude with swords and clubs,
from the chief priests and the
scribes and the elders.
44 Now he who was betraying
Him had given them a signal, saying, "Whomever I shall kiss, He is
the one; seize Him, and lead Him
away [1]under guard."
45 And after coming, he immediately went up to Him, saying,
"[a]Rabbi!" and kissed Him.

14 [a]Luke 2:7 Gr.; 22:11

17 [a]Mark 14:17-21: *Matt. 26:20-24; Luke 22:14, 21-23;* John 13:18ff.

18 [1]Or, *deliver Me up* [2]Or, *the one*

20 [1]Or, *the one*

21 [1]Or, *through* [2]Lit., *for him if that man had not been born*

22 [1]Lit., *having blessed* [a]Mark 14:22-25: *Matt. 26:26-29; Luke 22:17-20; 1 Cor. 11:23-25;* [b]Mark 10:16 [b]Matt. 14:19

26 [a]Matt. 26:30 [b]Matt. 21:1

27 [1]Or, *stumble* [a]Mark 14:27-31: *Matt. 26:31-35* [b]Zech. 13:7

29 [1]Or, *stumble*

30 [1]Lit., *today, on this night* [a]Matt. 26:34 [b]Mark 14:68, 72; John 13:38

32 [a]Mark 14:32-42: *Matt. 26:36-46; Luke 22:40-46*

33 [1]Or, *Jacob* [a]Mark 9:15; 16:5, 6

34 [a]Matt. 26:38; John 12:27

35 [1]Lit., *was falling* [2]Lit., *pass from Him* [a]Matt. 26:45; Mark 14:41

36 [a]Rom. 8:15; Gal. 4:6 [b]Matt. 26:39

38 [a]Matt. 26:41

39 [1]Lit., *word*

41 [1]Or, *Keep on sleeping therefore* [2]Or, *delivered up* [a]Mark 14:35

43 [1]Lit., *and with him* [a]Mark 14:43-50: *Matt. 26:47-56; Luke 22:47-53; John 18:3-11*

44 [1]Lit., *safely*

45 [a]Matt. 23:7

46 And they laid hands on Him, and seized Him.
47 But a certain one of those who stood by drew his sword, and struck the slave of the high priest, and [1]cut off his ear.
48 And Jesus answered and said to them, "Have you come out with swords and clubs to arrest Me, as though I were a robber?
49 "Every day I was with you [a]in the temple teaching, and you did not seize Me; but [1]*this has happened* that the Scriptures might be fulfilled."
50 And they all left Him and fled.
51 And a certain young man was following Him, wearing *nothing but* a linen sheet over *his* naked *body;* and they *seized him.
52 But he left the linen sheet behind, and escaped naked.

Jesus Before His Accusers

53 [a]And they led Jesus away to the high priest; and all the chief priests and the elders and the scribes *gathered together.
54 And Peter had followed Him at a distance, [a]right into [b]the courtyard of the high priest; and he was sitting with the [1]officers, and [c]warming himself at the [2]fire.
55 Now the chief priests and the whole [1a]Council kept trying to obtain testimony against Jesus to put Him to death; and they were finding none.
56 For many were giving false testimony against Him, and *yet* their testimony was not consistent.
57 And some stood up and *began* to give false testimony against Him, saying,
58 "We heard Him say, '[a]I will destroy this [1]temple made with hands, and in three days I will build another made without hands.'"
59 And not even in this respect was their testimony consistent.
60 And the high priest arose *and came* forward and questioned Jesus, saying, "Do You make no answer [1]to what these men are testifying against You?"
61 [a]But He kept silent, and made no answer. [b]Again the high priest was questioning Him, and [1]saying to Him, "Are You [2]the Christ, the Son of the Blessed *One?*"
62 And Jesus said, "I am; and you shall see the [a]SON OF MAN SITTING AT THE RIGHT HAND OF POWER, and [b]COMING WITH THE CLOUDS OF HEAVEN."
63 And [a]tearing his clothes, the high priest *said, "What further need do we have of witnesses?
64 "You have heard the blasphemy; how does it seem to you?" And they all condemned Him to be deserving of death.
65 And some began to [a]spit at Him, and [1b]to blindfold Him, and to beat Him with their fists, and to say to Him, "[c]Prophesy!" And the officers [2]received Him with [3]slaps *in the face.*

Peter's Denials

66 [a]And as Peter was below in [b]the courtyard, one of the servant-girls of the high priest *came,
67 and seeing Peter [a]warming himself, she looked at him, and *said, "You, too, were with Jesus the [b]Nazarene."
68 But he denied *it,* saying, "I neither know nor understand what you are talking about." And he [a]went out onto the [1]porch.[2]
69 And the maid saw him, and began once more to say to the bystanders, "This is *one* of them!"
70 But again [a]he was denying it. And after a little while the bystanders were again saying to Peter, "Surely you are *one* of them, [b]for you are a Galilean too."
71 But he began to curse and swear, "I do not know this fellow you are talking about!"
72 And immediately a cock crowed a second time. And Peter remembered how Jesus had made the remark to him, "Before [a]a cock crows twice, you will deny Me three times." [1]And he *began* to weep.

CHAPTER 15

Jesus Before Pilate

[a]AND early in the morning the chief priests with the elders and scribes, and the whole [1b]Council, immediately held a consultation; and binding Jesus, they led Him away, and delivered Him up to Pilate.
2 [a]And Pilate questioned Him, "Are You the King of the Jews?" And answering He *said to him, "*It is as* you say."
3 And the chief priests *began* to accuse Him [1]harshly.
4 And Pilate was questioning Him again, saying, "Do You make no answer? See how many charges they bring against You!"
5 But Jesus [a]made no further answer; so that Pilate was astonished.
6 [a]Now at *the* feast he used to re-

47 [1]Lit., *took off*
49 [1]Or possibly: *let the Scriptures be fulfilled* [a]Mark 12:35
53 [a]Mark 14:53-65: *Matt. 26:57-68; John 18:12f.; 19-24*
54 [1]Or, *servants* [2]Lit., *light* [a]Mark 14:68 [b]Matt. 26:3 [c]Mark 14:67; John 18:18
55 [1]Or, *Sanhedrin* [a]Matt. 5:22
58 [1]Or, *sanctuary* [a]Matt. 26:61; Mark 15:29
60 [1]Or, *what do these testify?*
61 [1]Lit., *says* [2]I.e., the Messiah [a]Matt. 26:63 [b]Mark 14:61-63: *Matt. 26:63ff.; Luke 22:67-71*
62 [a]Ps. 110:1; Mark 13:26 [b]Dan. 7:13
63 [a]Num. 14:6; Matt. 26:65; Acts 14:14
65 [1]Or, *cover over His face* [2]Or, *treated* [3]Or possibly: *blows with rods* [a]Matt. 26:67; Mark 10:34 [b]Esther 7:8 [c]Matt. 26:68; Luke 22:64
66 [a]Mark 14:66-72: *Matt. 26:69-75; Luke 22:56-62; John 18:16-18, 25-27* [b]Mark 14:54
67 [a]Mark 14:54 [b]Mark 1:24
68 [1]Or, *forecourt, gateway* [2]Later mss. add: *and a cock crowed* [a]Mark 14:54
70 [a]Mark 14:68 [b]Matt. 26:73; Luke 22:59
72 [1]Or, *Thinking of this, he* began *weeping;* or, *Rushing out, he* began *weeping* [a]Mark 14:30, 68
1 [1]Or, *Sanhedrin* [a]Matt. 27:1 [b]Matt. 5:22
2 [a]Mark 15:2-5: *Matt. 27:11-14; Luke 23:2, 3; John 18:29-38*
3 [1]Or, *of many things*
5 [a]Matt. 27:12
6 [a]Mark 15:6-15: *Matt. 27:15-26; Luke 23:18-25; John 18:39-19:16*

lease for them *any* one prisoner whom they requested.

7 And the man named Barabbas had been imprisoned with the insurrectionists who had committed murder in the insurrection.

8 And the multitude went up and began asking him *to do* as he had been accustomed to do for them.

9 And Pilate answered them, saying, "Do you want me to release for you the King of the Jews?"

10 For he was aware that the chief priests had delivered Him up because of envy.

11 But the chief priests stirred up the multitude [a]*to ask* him to release Barabbas for them instead.

12 And answering again, Pilate was saying to them, "Then what shall I do to Him whom you call the King of the Jews?"

13 And they shouted [1]back, "Crucify Him!"

14 But Pilate was saying to them, "Why, what evil has He done?" But they shouted all the more, "Crucify Him!"

15 And wishing to satisfy the multitude, Pilate released Barabbas for them, and after having Jesus [a]scourged, he delivered Him over to be crucified.

Jesus Is Mocked

16 [a]And the soldiers took Him away into [b]the palace (that is, the Praetorium), and they *called together the whole *Roman* [c]cohort.

17 And they *dressed Him up in [1]purple, and after weaving a crown of thorns, they put it on Him;

18 and they began to acclaim Him, "Hail, King of the Jews!"

19 And they kept beating His head with a [1]reed, and spitting at Him, and kneeling and bowing before Him.

20 And after they had mocked Him, they took the purple off Him, and put His garments on Him. And they *led Him out to crucify Him.

21 [a]And they *pressed into service a passerby coming from the country, Simon of Cyrene (the father of Alexander and Rufus), that he might bear His cross.

The Crucifixion

22 [a]And they *brought Him to the place [b]Golgotha, which is translated, Place of a Skull.

23 And they tried to give Him [a]wine mixed with myrrh; but He did not take it.

24 And they *crucified Him, and *[a]DIVIDED UP HIS GARMENTS AMONG THEMSELVES, CASTING LOTS FOR THEM, *to decide* what each should take.

25 And it was the [1a]third hour when they crucified Him.

26 And the inscription of the charge against Him [1]read, "[a]THE KING OF THE JEWS."

27 And they *crucified two robbers with Him, one on the right and one on the left.

28 [[1]And the Scripture was fulfilled which says, "And He was reckoned with transgessors."]

29 And those passing by were [1]hurling abuse at Him, [a]WAGGING THEIR HEADS, and saying, "Ha! You who *were going to* [b]destroy the temple and rebuild it in three days,

30 save Yourself, and come down from the cross!"

31 In the same way the chief priests along with the scribes were also mocking *Him* among themselves and saying, "[a]He saved others; [1]He cannot save Himself.

32 "Let *this* Christ, [a]the King of Israel, now come down from the cross, so that we may see and believe!" And [b]those who were crucified with Him were casting the same insult at Him.

33 [a]And when the [1b]sixth hour had come, darkness [2]fell over the whole land until the [3b]ninth hour.

34 And at the [a]ninth hour Jesus cried out with a loud voice, "[b]ELOI, ELOI, LAMA SABACHTHANI?" which is translated, "MY GOD, MY GOD, WHY HAST THOU FORSAKEN ME?"

35 And when some of the bystanders heard it, they *began* saying, "Behold, He is calling for Elijah."

36 And someone ran and filled a sponge with sour wine, put it on a reed, and gave Him a drink, saying, "Let us see whether Elijah will come to take Him down."

37 [a]And Jesus uttered a loud cry, and breathed His last.

38 [a]And the veil of the temple was torn in two from top to bottom.

39 [a]And when the centurion, who was standing [1]right in front of Him, saw [2]the way He breathed His last, he said, "Truly this man was [3]the Son of God!"

40 [a]And there were also *some* women looking on from afar, among whom *were* Mary Magdalene, and Mary the mother of [1]James [b]the [2]Less and Joses, and [c]Salome.

41 And when He was in Galilee, they used to follow Him and [1a]minister to Him; and *there were* many other women who had come up with Him to Jerusalem.

11 [a]Acts 3:14
13 [1]Or, *again*
15 [a]Matt. 27:26
16 [a]Mark 15:16-20: *Matt. 27:27-31* [b]Matt. 26:3; 27:27 [c]Acts 10:1
17 [1]A term for shades varying from rose to purple
19 [1]Or, *staff* (made of a reed)
21 [a]Mark 15:21: *Matt. 27:32; Luke 23:26*
22 [a]Mark 15:22-32: *Matt. 27:33-44; Luke 23:33-43; John 19:17-24* [b]Luke 23:33; John 19:17
23 [a]Matt. 27:34
24 [a]Ps. 22:18; John 19:24
25 [1]I.e., 9 a.m. [a]Mark 15:33; John 19:14
26 [1]Lit., *had been inscribed* [a]Matt. 27:37
28 [1]Many mss. do not contain this verse
29 [1]Or, *blaspheming* [a]Ps. 22:8; Matt. 27:39 [b]Mark 14:58
31 [1]Or, *can He not save Himself?* [a]Matt. 27:42; Luke 23:35
32 [a]Matt. 27:42 [b]Matt. 27:44; Mark 15:27; Luke 23:39-43
33 [1]I.e., noon [2]Or, *occurred* [3]I.e., 3 p.m. [a]Mark 15:33-41: *Matt. 27:45-56; Luke 23:44-49* [b]Matt. 27:45f.; Mark 15:25; Luke 23:44
34 [a]Matt. 27:45f.; Mark 15:25; Luke 23:44 [b]Ps. 22:1; Matt. 27:46
37 [a]Matt. 27:50; Luke 23:46; John 19:30
38 [a]Matt. 27:51; Luke 23:45
39 [1]Or, *opposite Him* [2]Lit., *that He thus* [3]Or, possibly: *a son of God*, or, *son of a god* [a]Matt. 27:54; Mark 15:45; Luke 23:47
40 [1]Or, *Jacob* [2]Lit., *little* (either in stature or age) [a]Mark 15:40, 41: *Matt. 27:55f.;* Luke 23:49; John 19:25 [b]Luke 19:3 [c]Mark 16:1
41 [1]Or, *wait on* [a]Matt. 27:55f.

Jesus Is Buried

42 [a]And when evening had already
come, because it was [b]the preparation day, that is, the day before the
Sabbath,
43 Joseph of Arimathea came, a
[a]prominent member of the Council,
a man who was himself [b]waiting for
the kingdom of God; and he [c]gath-
ered up courage and went in before
Pilate, and asked for the body of
Jesus.
44 And Pilate wondered if He was
dead by this time, and summoning
the centurion, he questioned him as
to whether He was already dead.
45 And ascertaining this from [a]the
centurion, he granted the body to
Joseph.
46 And *Joseph* bought a linen
sheet, took Him down, wrapped
Him in the linen sheet, and laid Him
in a tomb which had been hewn out
in the rock; and he rolled a stone
against the entrance of the tomb.
47 And [a]Mary Magdalene and
Mary the *mother* of Joses were looking on *to see* where He was laid.

CHAPTER 16

The Resurrection

[a]AND when the Sabbath was over,
[b]Mary Magdalene, and Mary the
mother of James, and Salome,
[c]bought spices, that they might
come and anoint Him.
2 And very early on the first day
of the week, they *came to the tomb
when the sun had risen.
3 And they were saying to one
another, "Who will roll away [a]the
stone for us from the entrance of the
tomb?"
4 And looking up, they *saw that
the stone had been rolled away, although it was extremely large.
5 And [a]entering the tomb, they
saw a young man sitting at the right,
wearing a white robe; and they
[b]were amazed.
6 And he *said to them, "[a]Do not
be amazed; you are looking for Jesus the [b]Nazarene, who has been
crucified. [c]He has risen; He is not
here; behold, *here is* the place where
they laid Him.
7 "But go, tell His disciples and
Peter, '[a]He is going before you into
Galilee; there you will see Him, just
as He said to you.'"
8 And they went out and fled
from the tomb, for trembling and astonishment had gripped them; and
they said nothing to anyone, for
they were afraid.
9 [[1]Now after He had risen early
on the first day of the week, He first
appeared to [a]Mary Magdalene, from
whom He had cast out seven demons.
10 [a]She went and reported to
those who had been with Him, while
they were mourning and weeping.
11 And when they heard that He
was alive, and had been seen by her,
[a]they refused to believe it.
12 And after that, [a]He appeared in
a different form [b]to two of them,
while they were walking along on
their way to the country.
13 And they went away and reported it to the others, but they [a]did
not believe them either.

The Disciples Commissioned

14 And afterward [a]He appeared
[b]to the eleven themselves as they
were reclining *at table;* and He reproached them for their [c]unbelief
and hardness of heart, because they
had not believed those who had
seen Him after He had risen.
15 And He said to them, "[a]Go into
all the world and preach the gospel
to all creation.
16 "[a]He who has believed and has
been baptized shall be saved; but he
who has disbelieved shall be condemned.
17 "And these signs will accompany those who have believed: [a]in
My name they will cast out demons,
they will [b]speak with new tongues;
18 they will [a]pick up serpents, and
if they drink any deadly *poison,* it
shall not hurt them; they will [b]lay
hands on the sick, and they will recover."
19 So then, when the Lord Jesus
had [a]spoken to them, He [b]was received up into heaven, and [c]SAT
DOWN AT THE RIGHT HAND OF GOD.
20 And they went out and
preached everywhere, while the
Lord worked with them, and confirmed the word by the signs that
followed.]
[[1]*And they promptly reported all
these instructions to Peter and his
companions. And after that, Jesus
Himself sent out through them from
east to west the sacred and imperishable proclamation of eternal salvation.*]

42 [a]Mark 15:42-47: *Matt. 27:57-61; Luke 23:50-56; John 19:38-42* [b]Matt. 27:62
43 [a]Matt. 27:57; Luke 23:51 [b]Matt. 27:57; Luke 2:25, 38 [c]John 19:38
45 [a]Mark 15:39
47 [a]Matt. 27:56
1 [a]Mark 16:1-8: *Matt. 28:1-8; Luke 24:1-10;* John 20:1-8 [b]Mark 15:47 [c]Luke 23:56; John 19:39f.
3 [a]Matt. 27:60; Mark 15:46; 16:3
5 [a]John 20:11, 12 [b]Mark 9:15
6 [a]Mark 9:15 [b]Mark 1:24 [c]Matt. 28:6
7 [a]Matt. 26:32
9 [1]Some of the oldest mss. do not contain vs. 9-20. [a]Matt. 27:56; John 20:14
10 [a]John 20:18
11 [a]Matt. 28:17; Mark 16:13, 14; Luke 24:11, 41
12 [a]John 21:1 [b]Luke 24:13-35
13 [a]Matt. 28:17; Luke 24:11, 41
14 [a]Mark 16:12 [b]Luke 24:36; John 20:19, 26; 1 Cor. 15:5 [c]Matt. 28:17; Luke 24:11, 41; John 20:25
15 [a]Matt. 28:19
16 [a]John 3:18, 36; Acts 16:31
17 [a]Mark 9:38; Luke 10:17; Acts 5:16; 8:7; 16:18; 19:12 [b]Acts 2:4; 10:46; 19:6; 1 Cor. 12:10, 28, 30; 13:1; 14:2
18 [a]Luke 10:19; Acts 28:3-5 [b]Mark 5:23
19 [a]Acts 1:3 [b]Luke 9:51; 24:51; John 6:62; 20:17; Acts 1:2; 1 Tim 3:16 [c]Ps. 110:1; Acts 7:55f.; Rom. 8:34; Eph. 1:20; Col. 3:1; Heb. 1:3; 8:1; 10:12; 12:2
20 [1]A few later mss. and versions contain this paragraph, usually after v. 8

THE GOSPEL
ACCORDING TO
LUKE

Introduction

INASMUCH as many have undertaken to compile an account of the things [a]accomplished among us,

2 just as those who [a]from the beginning [1]were [b]eyewitnesses and [2c]servants of [d]the [3]Word have handed them down to us,

3 it seemed fitting for me as well, [a]having [1]investigated everything carefully from the beginning, to write *it* out for you [b]in consecutive order, [c]most excellent [d]Theophilus;

4 so that you might know the exact truth about the things you have been [a]taught.

Birth of John the Baptist Foretold

5 [a]In the days of Herod, king of Judea, there [1]was a certain priest named [2]Zacharias, of the [b]division of [3]Abijah; and he had a wife [4]from the daughters of Aaron, and her name was Elizabeth.

6 And they were both [a]righteous in the sight of God, walking [b]blamelessly in all the commandments and requirements of the Lord.

7 And they had no child, because Elizabeth was barren, and they were both advanced in years.

8 Now it came about, while [a]he was performing his priestly service before God in the *appointed* order of his division,

9 according to the custom of the priestly office, he was chosen by lot [a]to enter the temple of the Lord and burn incense.

10 And the whole multitude of the people were in prayer [a]outside at the hour of the incense offering.

11 And [a]an angel of the Lord appeared to him, standing to the right of the altar of incense.

12 And Zacharias was troubled when he saw *him*, and fear gripped him.

13 But the angel said to him, "[a]Do not be afraid, Zacharias, for your petition has been heard, and your wife Elizabeth will bear you a son, and [b]you will give him the name John.

14 "And you will have joy and gladness, and many will rejoice at his birth.

15 "For he will be great in the sight of the Lord, and he will [a]drink no wine or liquor; and he will be filled with the Holy Spirit, while yet in his mother's womb.

16 "And he will turn back many of the sons of Israel to the Lord their God.

17 "And it is he who will [a]go *as a forerunner* before Him in the spirit and power of [b]Elijah, [c]TO TURN THE HEARTS OF THE FATHERS BACK TO THE CHILDREN, and the disobedient to the attitude of the righteous; so as to [a]make ready a people prepared for the Lord."

18 And Zacharias said to the angel, "How shall I know this *for certain?* For I am an old man, and my wife is advanced in years."

19 And the angel answered and said to him, "I am [a]Gabriel, who [b]stands in the presence of God; and I have been sent to speak to you, and to bring you this good news.

20 "And behold, you shall be silent and unable to speak until the day when these things take place, because you did not believe my words, which shall be fulfilled in their proper time."

21 And the people were waiting for Zacharias, and were wondering at his delay in the temple.

22 But when he came out, he was unable to speak to them; and they realized that he had seen a vision in the temple; and he [a]kept [1]making signs to them, and remained mute.

23 And it came about, when the days of his priestly service were ended, that he went back home.

24 And after these days Elizabeth his wife became pregnant; and she kept herself in seclusion for five months, saying,

25 "This is the way the Lord has dealt with me in the days when He looked *with favor* upon *me*, to [a]take away my disgrace among men."

Jesus' Birth Foretold

26 Now in the sixth month the angel [a]Gabriel was sent from God to a city in Galilee, called [b]Nazareth,

27 to [a]a virgin engaged to a man whose name was Joseph, [b]of the descendants of David; and the virgin's name was Mary.

28 And coming in, he said to her, "Hail, [1]favored one! The Lord [2]*is* with you."[3]

1 [a][Gr., in] Rom. 4:21; 14:5; Col. 2:2; 4:12; 1 Thess. 1:5; 2 Tim. 4:5, 17; Heb. 6:11; 10:22
2 [1]Lit., *became* [2]Or, *ministers* [3]I.e., Gospel [a]John 15:27; Acts 1:21f. [b]2 Pet. 1:16; 1 John 1:1 [c]Acts 26:16; 1 Cor. 4:1; Heb. 2:3 [d]Mark 4:14; 16:20; Acts 8:4; 14:25; 16:6; 17:11
3 [1]Or, *followed* [a]1 Tim. 4:6; 2 Tim. 3:10 [in Gr.] [b]Acts 11:4; 18:23 [c]Acts 23:26; 24:3; 26:25 [d]Acts 1:1
4 [a]Acts 18:25; Rom. 2:18; 1 Cor. 14:19; Gal. 6:6 [Gr.]
5 [1]Lit., *came into being* [2]I.e., Zechariah [3]Gr., Abia [4]I.e., of priestly descent [a]Matt. 2:1 [b]1 Chr. 24:10
6 [a]Gen. 7:1; Acts 2:25; 8:21 [b]Phil. 2:15; 3:6; 1 Thess. 3:13 [Gr.]
8 [a]1 Chr. 24:19; 2 Chr. 8:14; 31:2
9 [a]Ex. 30:7f.
10 [a]Lev. 16:17
11 [a]Luke 2:9; Acts 5:19
13 [a]Matt. 14:27; Luke 1:30 [b]Luke 1:60, 63
15 [a]Num. 6:3; Judg. 13:4; Matt. 11:18; Luke 7:33
17 [a]Luke 1:76 [b]Matt. 11:14 [c]Mal. 4:6
19 [a]Dan. 8:16; 9:21; Luke 1:26 [b]Matt. 18:10
22 [1]Or, *beckoning to*, or, *nodding to* [a]Luke 1:62
25 [a]Gen. 30:23; Is. 4:1
26 [a]Luke 1:19 [b]Matt. 2:23
27 [a]Matt. 1:18 [b]Matt. 1:16, 20; Luke 2:4
28 [1]Or, *O woman richly blessed* [2]Or, *be* [3]Later mss. add: *you are blessed among women*

29 But she [a]was greatly troubled
at *this* statement, and kept pondering what kind of salutation this
might be.
30 And the angel said to her, "[a]Do
not be afraid, Mary; for you have
found favor with God.
31 "And behold, you will conceive
in your womb, and bear a son, and
you [a]shall name Him Jesus.
32 "He will be great, and will be
called the Son of [a]the Most High;
and the Lord God will give Him the
throne of His father David;
33 [a]and He will reign over the
house of Jacob forever; [b]and His
kingdom will have no end."
34 And Mary said to the angel,
"How [1]can this be, since I [2]am a virgin?"
35 And the angel answered and
said to her, "[a]The Holy Spirit will
come upon you, and the power of
[b]the Most High will overshadow
you; and for that reason [c]the [1]holy
offspring shall be called [d]the Son of
God.
36 "And behold, even your relative
Elizabeth has also conceived a son
in her old age; and [1]she who was
called barren is now in her sixth
month.
37 "For [1a]nothing will be impossible with God."
38 And [1]Mary said, "Behold, the
[2]bondslave of the Lord; be it done to
me according to your word." And
the angel departed from her.

Mary Visits Elizabeth

39 Now [1]at this time Mary arose
and went with haste to [a]the hill
country, to a city of Judah,
40 and entered the house of
Zacharias and greeted Elizabeth.
41 And it came about that when
Elizabeth heard Mary's greeting,
the baby leaped in her womb; and
Elizabeth was [a]filled with the Holy
Spirit.
42 And she cried out with a loud
voice, and said, "Blessed among
women *are* you, and blessed *is* the
fruit of your womb!
43 "And [1]how has it *happened* to
me, that the mother of [a]my Lord
should come to me?
44 "For behold, when the sound of
your greeting reached my ears, the
baby leaped in my womb for joy.
45 "And [a]blessed *is* she who believed [1]that there would be a fulfillment of what had been spoken to
her [2]by the Lord."

29 [a]Luke 1:12
30 [a]Matt. 14:27; Luke 1:13
31 [a]Matt. 1:21, 25; Luke 2:21
32 [a]Mark 5:7; Luke 1:35, 76; 6:35; Acts 7:48
33 [a]Matt. 1:1 [b]Dan. 2:44; 7:14, 18, 27; Matt. 28:18
34 [1]Lit., *shall* [2]Lit., *know no man*
35 [1]Lit., *the holy thing begotten* [a]Matt. 1:18 [b]Luke 1:32 [c]Mark 1:24 [d]Matt. 4:3
36 [1]Lit., *this is the sixth month to her who*
37 [1]Lit., *not any word* [a]Matt. 19:26
38 [1]Gr. *Mariam*, i.e., Miriam; so throughout Luke [2]I.e., female slave
39 [1]Lit., *in these days* [a]Josh. 20:7; 21:11; Luke 1:65
41 [a]Luke 1:67
43 [1]Lit., *whence this to me* [a]Luke 2:11
45 [1]Or, possibly: *because there will be* [2]Lit., *from* [a]Luke 1:20, 48
46 [1]Lit., *makes great* [a]Luke 1:46-53: *1 Sam. 2:1-10* [b]Ps. 34:2f.
47 [a]Ps. 35:9 [b]1 Tim. 1:1; 2:3; Titus 1:3; 2:10; 3:4; Jude 25
48 [1]I.e., female slave [a]Luke 1:45
50 [1]Lit., *unto generations and generations* [a]Ps. 103:17
51 [1]Lit., *might* [2]Lit., *thought, attitude* [a]Ps. 98:1; 118:15
53 [a]Ps. 107:9
54 [1]Lit., *So as to remember*
55 [1]Lit., *seed* [a]Gen. 17:19; Ps. 132:11; Gal. 3:16
57 [1]Lit., *was fulfilled*
58 [1]Lit., *magnified* [a]Gen. 19:19
59 [1]Lit., *after the name of* [a]Gen. 17:12; Lev. 12:3; Luke 2:21; Phil. 3:5
60 [a]Luke 1:13, 63
62 [a]Luke 1:22
63 [a]Luke 1:13, 60

The Magnificat

46 And Mary said:
"[a]My soul [1b]exalts the Lord,
47 "And [a]my spirit has rejoiced in
[b]God my Savior.
48 "For He has had regard for the
humble state of His [1]bond-
slave;
For behold, from this time on
all generations will count me
[a]blessed.
49 "For the Mighty One has done
great things for me;
And holy is His name.
50 "[a]AND HIS MERCY IS [1]UPON GEN-
ERATION AFTER GENERATION
TOWARDS THOSE WHO FEAR
HIM.
51 "[a]He has done [1]mighty deeds
with His arm;
He has scattered *those who
were* proud in the [2]thoughts
of their heart.
52 "He has brought down rulers
from *their* thrones,
And has exalted those who
were humble.
53 "[a]HE HAS FILLED THE HUNGRY
WITH GOOD THINGS;
And sent away the rich empty-
handed.
54 "He has given help to Israel His
servant,
[1]In remembrance of His mercy,
55 [a]As He spoke to our fathers,
To Abraham and his [1]offspring
forever."
56 And Mary stayed with her
about three months, and *then* returned to her home.

John Is Born

57 Now the time [1]had come for
Elizabeth to give birth, and she
brought forth a son.
58 And her neighbors and her relatives heard that the Lord had [1a]dis-
played His great mercy toward her;
and they were rejoicing with her.
59 And it came about that on [a]the
eighth day they came to circumcise
the child, and they were going to
call him Zacharias, [1]after his father.
60 And his mother answered and
said, "No indeed; but [a]he shall be
called John."
61 And they said to her, "There is
no one among your relatives who is
called by that name."
62 And they [a]made signs to his father, as to what he wanted him
called.
63 And he asked for a tablet, and
wrote as follows, "[a]His name is
John." And they were all astonished.

64 [a]And at once his mouth was opened and his tongue *loosed*, and he *began* to speak in praise of God.

65 And fear came on all those living around them; and all these matters were being talked about in all [a]the hill country of Judea.

66 And all who heard them kept them in mind, saying, "What then will this child *turn out to* be?" For [a]the hand of the Lord was certainly with him.

Zacharias' Prophecy

67 And his father Zacharias [a]was filled with the Holy Spirit, and [b]prophesied, saying:

68 "Blessed *be* the Lord God of Israel,
For He has visited us and accomplished [a]redemption for His people,
69 And has raised up a [a]horn of salvation for us
In the house of David [b]His servant—
70 [a]As He spoke by the mouth of His holy prophets [b]from of old—
71 [1a]Salvation [b]FROM OUR ENEMIES,
And FROM THE HAND OF ALL WHO HATE US;
72 [a]To show mercy toward our fathers,
[b]And to remember His holy covenant,
73 [a]The oath which He swore to Abraham our father,
74 To grant us that we, being delivered from the hand of our enemies,
Might serve Him without fear,
75 In holiness and righteousness before Him all our days.
76 "And you, child, will be called the [a]prophet of [b]the Most High;
For you will go on [c]BEFORE THE LORD TO [d]PREPARE HIS WAYS;
77 To give to His people *the* knowledge of salvation
[1]By [a]the forgiveness of their sins,
78 Because of the tender mercy of our God,
With which [a]the Sunrise from on high shall visit us,
79 [a]TO SHINE UPON THOSE WHO SIT IN DARKNESS AND THE SHADOW OF DEATH,
To guide our feet into the way of peace."

80 [a]And the child continued to grow, and to become strong in spirit, and he lived in the deserts until the day of his public appearance to Israel.

CHAPTER 2

Jesus' Birth in Bethlehem

NOW it came about in those days that a decree went out from [a]Caesar Augustus, that a census be taken of [b]all [1]the inhabited earth.

2 [1]This was the first census taken while [2]Quirinius was governor of [a]Syria.

3 And all were proceeding to register for the census, everyone to his own city.

4 And Joseph also went up from Galilee, from the city of Nazareth, to Judea, to the city of David, which is called Bethlehem, because [a]he was of the house and family of David,

5 in order to register, along with Mary, who was engaged to him, and was with child.

6 And it came about that while they were there, the days were completed for her to give birth.

7 And she gave birth to her firstborn son; and she wrapped Him in cloths, and laid Him in a [1]manger, because there was no room for them in the inn.

8 And in the same region there were *some* shepherds staying out in the fields, and keeping watch over their flock by night.

9 And [a]an angel of the Lord suddenly [b]stood before them, and the glory of the Lord shone around them; and they were terribly frightened.

10 And the angel said to them, "[a]Do not be afraid; for behold, I bring you good news of a great joy which shall be for all the people;

11 for today in the city of David there has been born for you a [a]Savior, who is [1b]Christ [c]the Lord.

12 "And [a]this *will be* a sign for you: you will find a baby wrapped in cloths, and lying in a [1]manger."

13 And suddenly there appeared with the angel a multitude of the heavenly host praising God, and saying,

14 "[a]Glory to God in the highest,
And on earth peace among men [1b]with whom He is pleased."

15 And it came about when the angels had gone away from them into heaven, that the shepherds *began* saying to one another, "Let us go straight to Bethlehem then, and see

---

64 [a]Luke 1:20
65 [a]Luke 1:39
66 [a]Acts 11:21
67 [a]Luke 1:41 [b]Joel 2:28
68 [a]Luke 1:71; 2:38; Acts 1:6; Heb. 9:12
69 [a]1 Sam. 2:1, 10; Ps. 18:2; 89:17; 132:17; Ezek. 29:21 [b]Matt. 1:1
70 [a]Rom. 1:2 [b]Acts 3:21
71 [1]Or, *Deliverance* [a]Luke 1:68 [b]Ps. 106:10
72 [a]Mic. 7:20 [b]Ps. 105:8f.; 106:45
73 [a]Gen. 22:16ff.
76 [a]Matt. 11:9 [b]Luke 1:32 [c]Mal. 3:1 [d]Luke 1:17
77 [1]Or, *Consisting in* [a]Jer. 31:34; Mark 1:4
78 [a]Mal. 4:2; Eph. 5:14; 2 Pet. 1:19
79 [a]Is. 9:1, 2; 59:8; Matt. 4:16
80 [a]Luke 2:40
1 [1]I.e., the Roman empire [a]Matt. 22:17; Luke 3:1 [b]Matt. 24:14
2 [1]Or, *This took place as a first census* [2]Gr., *Kyrenios* [a]Matt. 4:24
4 [a]Luke 1:27
7 [1]Or, *feeding trough*
9 [a]Luke 1:11; Acts 5:19 [b]Luke 24:4; Acts 12:7
10 [a]Matt. 14:27
11 [1]I.e., Messiah [a]Matt. 1:21; John 4:42; Acts 5:31 [b]Matt. 1:16; 16:16, 20; John 11:27 [c]Luke 1:43; Acts 2:36; 10:36
12 [1]Or, *feeding trough* [a]1 Sam. 2:34; 2 Kin. 19:29; 20:8f.; Is. 7:11, 14
14 [1]Lit., *of His good pleasure;* or possibly, *of good will* [a]Matt. 21:9; Luke 19:38 [b]Luke 3:22; Eph. 1:9; Phil. 2:13

this thing that has happened which the Lord has made known to us."

16 And they came in haste and found their way to Mary and Joseph, and the baby as He lay in the [1]manger.

17 And when they had seen this, they made known the statement which had been told them about this Child.

18 And all who heard it wondered at the things which were told them by the shepherds.

19 But Mary [a]treasured up all these things, pondering them in her heart.

20 And the shepherds went back, [a]glorifying and praising God for all that they had heard and seen, just as had been told them.

Jesus Presented at the Temple

21 And when [a]eight days were completed [1]before His circumcision, [b]His name was *then* called Jesus, the name given by the angel before He was conceived in the womb.

22 And when the days for their purification according to the law of Moses were completed, they brought Him up to Jerusalem to present Him to the Lord

23 (as it is written in the Law of the Lord, "[a]EVERY *first-born* MALE THAT OPENS THE WOMB SHALL BE CALLED HOLY TO THE LORD"),

24 and to offer a sacrifice according to what was said in the Law of the Lord, "[a]A PAIR OF TURTLEDOVES, OR TWO YOUNG PIGEONS."

25 And behold, there was a man in Jerusalem whose name was Simeon; and this man was [a]righteous and devout, [b]looking for the consolation of Israel; and the Holy Spirit was upon him.

26 And [a]it had been revealed to him by the Holy Spirit that he would not [b]see death before he had seen the Lord's [1]Christ.

27 And he came in the Spirit into the temple; and when the parents brought in the child Jesus, [1a]to carry out for Him the custom of the Law,

28 then he took Him into his arms, and blessed God, and said,

29 "Now Lord, Thou dost let Thy
bond-servant depart
In peace, [a]according to Thy
word;

30 For my eyes have [a]seen Thy
salvation,

31 Which Thou hast prepared in
the presence of all peoples,

32 [a]A LIGHT [1]OF REVELATION TO
THE GENTILES,

16 [1]Or, *feeding trough*

19 [a]Luke 2:51

20 [a]Matt. 9:8

21 [1]Lit., *so as to circumcise Him* [a]Luke 1:59 [b]Luke 1:31

23 [a]Ex. 13:2, 12

24 [a]Lev. 5:11; 12:8

25 [a]Luke 1:6 [b]Mark 15:43; Luke 2:38; 23:51

26 [1]Or, *Messiah* [a]Matt. 2:12 [b]Ps. 89:48; John 8:51; Heb. 11:5

27 [1]Lit., *to do for Him according to* [a]Luke 2:22

29 [a]Luke 2:26

30 [a]Is. 52:10; Luke 3:6

32 [1]Or, *for* [a]Is. 42:6; 49:6; Acts 13:47; 26:23

33 [a]Matt. 12:46

34 [1]Or, *resurrection* [a]Matt. 12:46 [b]Matt. 21:44; 1 Cor. 1:23; 2 Cor. 2:16; 1 Pet. 2:8

36 [1]Or, *Hannah* [2]Lit., *days* [3]Lit., *virginity* [a]Luke 2:38; Acts 21:9 [b]Josh. 19:24 [c]1 Tim. 5:9

37 [a]Luke 5:33; Acts 13:3; 14:23; 1 Tim. 5:5

38 [1]Lit., *hour* [a]Luke 1:68; 2:25

39 [a]Matt. 2:23; Luke 1:26; 2:51; 4:16

40 [1]Lit., *becoming full of* [a]Luke 1:80; 2:52

41 [a]Ex. 23:15; Deut. 16:1-6

43 [a]Ex. 12:15

And the glory of Thy people
Israel."

33 And His father and [a]mother were amazed at the things which were being said about Him.

34 And Simeon blessed them, and said to Mary [a]His mother, "Behold, this *Child* is appointed for [b]the fall and [1]rise of many in Israel, and for a sign to be opposed —

35 and a sword will pierce even your own soul — to the end that thoughts from many hearts may be revealed."

36 And there was a [a]prophetess, [1]Anna the daughter of Phanuel, of [b]the tribe of Asher. She was advanced in [2]years, [c]having lived with a husband seven years after her [3]marriage,

37 and then as a widow to the age of eighty-four. And she *never* left the temple, serving night and day with [a]fastings and prayers.

38 And at that very [1]moment she came up and *began* giving thanks to God, and continued to speak of Him to all those who were [a]looking for the redemption of Jerusalem.

Return to Nazareth

39 And when they had performed everything according to the Law of the Lord, they returned to Galilee, to [a]their own city of Nazareth.

40 [a]And the Child continued to grow and become strong, [1]increasing in wisdom; and the grace of God was upon Him.

Visit to Jerusalem

41 And His parents used to go to Jerusalem every year at [a]the Feast of the Passover.

42 And when He became twelve, they went up *there* according to the custom of the Feast;

43 and as they were returning, after spending the [a]full number of days, the boy Jesus stayed behind in Jerusalem. And His parents were unaware of it,

44 but supposed Him to be in the caravan, and went a day's journey; and they *began* looking for Him among their relatives and acquaintances.

45 And when they did not find Him, they returned to Jerusalem, looking for Him.

46 And it came about that after three days they found Him in the temple, sitting in the midst of the teachers, both listening to them, and asking them questions.

47 And all who heard Him were

amazed at His understanding and His answers.

48 And when they saw Him, they were astonished; and [a]His mother said to Him, "[1]Son, why have You treated us this way? Behold, [b]Your father and I [2]have been anxiously looking for You."

49 And He said to them, "Why is it that you were looking for Me? Did you not know that I had to be in My Father's [1]*house?*"

50 And [a]they did not understand the statement which He [1]had made to them.

51 And He went down with them, and came to [a]Nazareth; and He continued in subjection to them; and [b]His mother [1c]treasured all *these* [2]things in her heart.

52 And Jesus kept increasing in wisdom and [1]stature, and in [a]favor with God and men.

CHAPTER 3

John the Baptist Preaches

NOW in the fifteenth year of the reign of Tiberius Caesar, when [a]Pontius Pilate was governor of Judea, and [b]Herod was tetrarch of Galilee, and his brother Philip was tetrarch of the region of Ituraea and Trachonitis, and Lysanias was tetrarch of Abilene,

2 in the high priesthood of [a]Annas and [b]Caiaphas, [c]the word of God came to John, the son of Zacharias, in the wilderness.

3 And he came into all [a]the district around the Jordan, preaching a baptism of repentance for forgiveness of sins;

4 as it is written in the book of the words of Isaiah the prophet, "[a]THE VOICE OF ONE CRYING IN THE WILDERNESS,
'MAKE READY THE WAY OF THE LORD,
MAKE HIS PATHS STRAIGHT.
5 '[a]EVERY RAVINE SHALL BE FILLED UP,
AND EVERY MOUNTAIN AND HILL SHALL BE [1]BROUGHT LOW;
AND THE CROOKED SHALL BECOME STRAIGHT,
AND THE ROUGH ROADS SMOOTH;
6 [a]AND ALL [1]FLESH SHALL [b]SEE THE SALVATION OF GOD.'"

7 He therefore *began* saying to the multitudes who were going out to be baptized by him, "You brood of vipers, who warned you to flee from the wrath to come?

8 "Therefore bring forth fruits in keeping with your repentance, and [a]do not begin to say [1]to yourselves, 'We have Abraham for our father,' for I say to you that God is able from these stones to raise up children to Abraham.

9 "And also the axe is already laid at the root of the trees; every tree therefore that does not bear good fruit is cut down and thrown into the fire."

10 And the multitudes were questioning him, saying, "Then what shall we do?"

11 And he would answer and say to them, "Let the man who has two tunics share with him who has none; and let him who has food do likewise."

12 And *some* [1]tax-gatherers also came to be baptized, and they said to him, "Teacher, what shall we do?"

13 And he said to them, "[1]Collect no more than what you have been ordered to."

14 And *some* [1]soldiers were questioning him, saying, "And *what about* us, what shall we do?" And he said to them, "Do not take money from anyone by force, or accuse *anyone* falsely, and be content with your wages."

15 Now while the people were in a state of expectation and all were [1]wondering in their hearts about John, [a]as to whether he might be [2]the Christ,

16 [a]John answered and said to them all, "As for me, I baptize you with water; but He who is mightier than I is coming, and I am not fit to untie the thong of His sandals; He Himself will baptize you [1]in the Holy Spirit and fire.

17 "And His [a]winnowing fork is in His hand to clean out His threshing floor, and to gather the wheat into His barn; but He will burn up the chaff with [b]unquenchable fire."

18 So with many other exhortations also he preached the gospel to the people.

19 But when [a]Herod the tetrarch was reproved by him on account of [a]Herodias, his brother's wife, and on account of all the wicked things which [b]Herod had done,

20 he added this also to them all, that [a]he locked John up in prison.

Jesus Is Baptized

21 [a]Now it came about when all the people were baptized, that Jesus also was baptized, and while He was [b]praying, heaven was opened,

48 [1]Lit., *Child* [2]Lit., *are looking* [a]Matt. 12:46 [b]Luke 2:49; 3:23; 4:22

49 [1]Or, *affairs;* lit., *in the things of My Father*

50 [1]Lit., *had spoken* [a]Mark 9:32

51 [1]Lit., *was treasuring* [2]Lit., *words* [a]Luke 2:39 [b]Matt. 12:46 [c]Luke 2:19

52 [1]Or, *age* [a]Luke 2:40

1 [a]Matt. 27:2 [b]Matt. 14:1

2 [a]John 18:13, 24; Acts 4:6 [b]Matt. 26:3 [c]Luke 3:3-10: *Matt. 3:1-10; Mark 1:3-5*

3 [a]Matt. 3:5

4 [a]Is. 40:3

5 [1]Or, *leveled* [a]Is. 40:4

6 [1]Or, *mankind* [a]Is. 40:5 [b]Luke 2:30

8 [1]Or, *in* [a]Luke 5:21; 13:25, 26; 14:9

12 [1]Publicans who collected Roman taxes on commission

13 [1]Or, *Exact*

14 [1]I.e., men in active military service

15 [1]Or, *reasoning,* or *debating* [2]I.e., the Messiah [a]John 1:19f.

16 [1]Or, *with* [a]Luke 3:16, 17: *Matt. 3:11, 12; Mark 1:7, 8*

17 [a]Is. 30:24 [b]Mark 9:43, 48

19 [a]Matt. 14:3; Mark 6:17 [b]Matt. 14:1; Luke 3:1

20 [a]John 3:24

21 [a]Luke 3:21, 22: *Matt. 3:13-17; Mark 1:9-11* [b]Matt. 14:23; Luke 5:16; 9:18, 28f.

22 and the Holy Spirit descended
upon Him in bodily form like a dove,
and a voice came out of heaven,
"[a]Thou art My beloved Son, in Thee
I am well-pleased."

Genealogy of Jesus

23 And [a]when He began His ministry, Jesus Himself was about thirty
years of age, being [1]supposedly *the*
son of [b]Joseph, the *son* of [2]Eli,
24 the *son* of Matthat, the *son* of
Levi, the *son* of Melchi, the *son* of
Jannai, the *son* of Joseph,
25 the *son* of Mattathias, the *son*
of Amos, the *son* of Nahum, the *son*
of [1]Hesli, the *son* of Naggai,
26 the *son* of Maath, the *son* of
Mattathias, the *son* of Semein, the
son of Josech, the *son* of Joda,
27 the *son* of Joanan, the *son* of
Rhesa, [a]the *son* of Zerubbabel, the
son of [1]Shealtiel, the *son* of Neri,
28 the *son* of Melchi, the *son* of
Addi, the *son* of Cosam, the *son* of
Elmadam, the *son* of Er,
29 the *son* of [1]Joshua, the *son* of
Eliezer, the *son* of Jorim, the *son* of
Matthat, the *son* of Levi,
30 the *son* of Simeon, the *son* of
[1]Judah, the *son* of Joseph, the *son* of
Jonam, the *son* of Eliakim,
31 the *son* of Melea, the *son* of
Menna, the *son* of Mattatha, the *son*
of Nathan, the *son* of David,
32 [a]the *son* of Jesse, the *son* of
Obed, the *son* of Boaz, the *son* of
[1]Salmon, the *son* of [2]Nahshon,
33 the *son* of Amminadab, the *son*
of Admin, the *son* of [1]Ram, the *son*
of Hezron, the *son* of Perez, the *son*
of Judah,
34 the *son* of Jacob, the *son* of
Isaac, [a]the *son* of Abraham, the *son*
of Terah, the *son* of Nahor,
35 the *son* of Serug, the *son* of
[1]Reu, the *son* of Peleg, the *son* of
[2]Heber, the *son* of Shelah,
36 the *son* of Cainan, the *son* of
Arphaxad, the *son* of Shem, [a]the *son*
of Noah, the *son* of Lamech,
37 the *son* of Methuselah, the *son*
of Enoch, the *son* of Jared, the *son* of
Mahalaleel, the *son* of Cainan,
38 the *son* of Enosh, the *son* of
Seth, the *son* of Adam, the *son* of
God.

CHAPTER 4

The Temptation of Jesus

[a]AND Jesus, full of the Holy Spirit,
[b]returned from the Jordan and was
led about [1]by the Spirit in the wilderness
2 for forty days, while tempted
by the devil. And He ate nothing
during those days; and when they
had ended, He became hungry.
3 And the devil said to Him, "If
You are the Son of God, tell this
stone to become bread."
4 And Jesus answered him, "It is
written, '[a]MAN SHALL NOT LIVE ON
BREAD ALONE.'"
5 [a]And he led Him up and
showed Him all the kingdoms of
[1b]the world in a moment of time.
6 And the devil said to Him, "I
will give You all this domain and [1]its
glory; [a]for it has been handed over
to me, and I give it to whomever I
wish.
7 "Therefore if You [1]worship before me, it shall all be Yours."
8 And Jesus answered and said to
him, "It is written, '[a]YOU SHALL
WORSHIP THE LORD YOUR GOD AND
SERVE HIM ONLY.'"
9 [a]And he led Him to Jerusalem
and set Him on the pinnacle of the
temple, and said to Him, "If You are
the Son of God, cast Yourself down
from here;
10 for it is written,
'[a]HE WILL GIVE HIS ANGELS
CHARGE CONCERNING YOU TO
GUARD YOU,'
11 and,
'[a]ON THEIR HANDS THEY WILL
BEAR YOU UP,
LEST YOU STRIKE YOUR FOOT
AGAINST A STONE.'"
12 And Jesus answered and said to
him, "It is said, '[a]YOU SHALL NOT
[1]FORCE A TEST ON THE LORD YOUR
GOD.'"
13 And when the devil had finished every temptation, he departed
from Him until an opportune time.

Jesus' Public Ministry

14 And [a]Jesus returned to Galilee
in the power of the Spirit; and [b]news
about Him spread through all the
surrounding district.
15 And He *began* [a]teaching in their
synagogues and was praised by all.
16 And He came to [a]Nazareth,
where He had been brought up; and
as was His custom, [b]He entered the
synagogue on the Sabbath, and
[c]stood up to read.
17 And the [1]book of the prophet
Isaiah was handed to Him. And He
opened the [1]book, and found the
place where it was written,
18 "[a]THE SPIRIT OF THE LORD IS
UPON ME,
BECAUSE HE ANOINTED ME TO
PREACH THE GOSPEL TO THE
POOR.

---

22 [a]Matt. 3:17
23 [1]Lit., *as it was being thought* [2]Also spelled *Heli* [a]Matt. 4:17; Acts 1:1 [b]Matt. 1:16; Luke 3:23-27
25 [1]Also spelled *Esli*
27 [1]Gr., *Salathiel* [a]Matt. 1:12
29 [1]Gr., *Jesus*
30 [1]Gr., *Judas*
32 [1]Gr., *Sala* [2]Gr., *Naasson* [a]Luke 3:32-34: *Matt. 1:1-6*
33 [1]Gr., *Arni*
34 [a]Luke 3:34-36: *Gen. 11:26-30; 1 Chr. 1:24-27*
35 [1]Gr., *Ragau* [2]Gr., *Eber*
36 [a]Luke 3:36-38: *Gen. 5:3-32; 1 Chr. 1:1-4*
1 [1]Or, *under the influence of,* lit., *in* [a]Luke 4:1-13: *Matt. 4:1-11; Mark 1:12, 13* [b]Luke 3:3, 21
4 [a]Deut. 8:3
5 [1]Lit., *the inhabited earth* [a]Matt. 4:8-10 [b]Matt. 24:14
6 [1]Lit., *their* (referring to the kingdoms) [a]1 John 5:19
7 [1]Or, *bow down*
8 [a]Deut. 6:13
9 [a]Matt. 4:5-7
10 [a]Ps. 91:11
11 [a]Ps. 91:12
12 [1]Or, *tempt* [a]Deut. 6:16
14 [a]Matt. 4:12 [b]Matt. 9:26; Luke 4:37
15 [a]Matt. 4:23
16 [a]Luke 2:39, 51 [b]Matt. 13:54; Mark 6:1f. [c]Acts 13:14-16
17 [1]Or, *scroll*
18 [a]Is. 61:1; Matt. 11:5; 12:18; John 3:34

HE HAS SENT ME TO PROCLAIM RELEASE TO THE CAPTIVES,
AND RECOVERY OF SIGHT TO THE BLIND,
TO SET FREE THOSE WHO ARE DOWNTRODDEN,
19 [a]TO PROCLAIM THE FAVORABLE YEAR OF THE LORD."

20 And He [a]closed the book, and gave it back to the attendant, and [b]sat down; and the eyes of all in the synagogue were fixed upon Him.

21 And He began to say to them, "Today this Scripture has been fulfilled in your hearing."

22 And all were speaking well of Him, and wondering at the gracious words which were falling from His lips; and they were saying, "[a]Is this not Joseph's son?"

23 And He said to them, "No doubt you will quote this proverb to Me, 'Physician, heal yourself; whatever we heard was done [a]at Capernaum, do here in [b]your home town as well.' "

24 And He said, "Truly I say to you, [a]no prophet is welcome in his home town.

25 "But I say to you in truth, there were many widows in Israel [a]in the days of Elijah, when the sky was shut up for three years and six months, when a great famine came over all the land;

26 and yet Elijah was sent to none of them, but [a]only to [1]Zarephath, in the land of [b]Sidon, to a woman who was a widow.

27 "And there were many lepers in Israel in the time of Elisha the prophet; and none of them was cleansed, but [a]only Naaman the Syrian."

28 And all in the synagogue were filled with rage as they heard these things;

29 and they rose up and [a]cast Him out of the city, and led Him to the brow of the hill on which their city had been built, in order to throw Him down the cliff.

30 But [a]passing through their midst, He went His way.

31 And [a]He came down to [b]Capernaum, a city of Galilee. And He was teaching them on Sabbath days;

32 and [a]they were *continually* amazed at His teaching, for [b]His message was with authority.

33 And there was a man in the synagogue [1]possessed by the spirit of an unclean demon, and he cried out with a loud voice,

34 "[1]Ha! [a]What do we have to do with You, Jesus of [2b]Nazareth? Have You come to destroy us? I know who You are — [b]the Holy One of God!"

35 And Jesus [a]rebuked him, saying, "Be quiet and come out of him!" And when the demon had thrown him down in *their* midst, he went out of him without doing him any harm.

36 And amazement came upon them all, and they *began* discussing with one another, and saying, "What is [1]this message? For [a]with authority and power He commands the unclean spirits, and they come out."

37 And [a]the report about Him was getting out into every locality in the surrounding district.

Many Are Healed

38 [a]And He arose and *left* the synagogue, and entered Simon's home. Now Simon's mother-in-law was [b]suffering from a high fever; and they made request of Him on her behalf.

39 And standing over her, He [a]rebuked the fever, and it left her; and she immediately arose and *began* to wait on them.

40 [a]And while [b]the sun was setting, all who had any sick with various diseases brought them to Him; and [c]laying His hands on every one of them, He was [d]healing them.

41 And demons also were coming out of many, crying out and saying, "You are [a]the Son of God!" And [b]rebuking them, He would [c]not allow them to speak, because they knew Him to be [1]the Christ.

42 [a]And when day came, He departed and went to a lonely place; and the multitudes were searching for Him, and came to Him, and tried to keep Him from going away from them.

43 But He said to them, "I must preach the kingdom of God to the other cities also, [a]for I was sent for this purpose."

44 And He kept on preaching in the synagogues [a]of [1]Judea.

CHAPTER 5

The First Disciples

[a] NOW it came about that while the multitude were pressing around Him and listening to the word of God, He was standing by [b]the lake of Gennesaret;

2 and He saw two boats lying at the edge of the lake; but the fisher-

19 [a]Lev. 25:10; Is. 61:2
20 [a]Luke 4:17 [b]Matt. 26:55
22 [a]Matt. 13:55; Mark 6:3; John 6:42
23 [a]Matt. 4:13; Mark 1:21ff.; 2:1ff.; Luke 4:35ff.; John 4:46ff. [b]Mark 6:1; Luke 2:39, 51; 4:16
24 [a]Matt. 13:57; Mark 6:4; John 4:44
25 [a]1 Kin. 17:1; 18:1; James 5:17
26 [1]Gr., *Serepta* [a]1 Kin. 17:9 [b]Matt. 11:21
27 [a]2 Kin. 5:1-14
29 [a]Num. 15:35; Acts 7:58; Heb. 13:12
30 [a]John 10:39
31 [a]Luke 4:31-37: *Mark 1:21-28* [b]Matt. 4:13; Luke 4:23
32 [a]Matt. 7:28 [b]Luke 4:36; John 7:46
33 [1]Lit., *having a spirit*
34 [1]Or possibly, *Let us alone* [2]Lit., *Nazarene* [a]Matt. 8:29 [b]Mark 1:24
35 [a]Matt. 8:26; Mark 4:39; Luke 4:39, 41; 8:24
36 [1]Or, *this word, that with authority . . . come out?* [a]Luke 4:32
37 [a]Luke 4:14
38 [a]Luke 4:38, 39: *Matt. 8:14, 15; Mark 1:29-31* [b]Matt. 4:24
39 [a]Luke 4:35, 41
40 [a]Luke 4:40, 41: *Matt. 8:16, 17; Mark 1:32-34* [b]Mark 1:32 [c]Mark 5:23 [d]Matt. 4:23
41 [1]I.e., the Messiah [a]Matt. 4:3 [b]Luke 4:35 [c]Matt. 8:4; Mark 1:34
42 [a]Luke 4:42, 43: *Mark 1:35-38*
43 [a]Mark 1:38
44 [1]I.e., the country of the Jews (including Galilee); some mss. read, *Galilee* [a]Matt. 4:23
1 [a]Matt. 4:18-22; Mark 1:16-20; Luke 5:1-11; John 1:40-42 [b]Num. 34:11; Deut. 3:17; Josh. 12:3; 13:27; Matt. 4:18

men had gotten out of them, and were washing their nets.

3 And [a]He got into one of the boats, which was Simon's, and asked him to put out a little way from the land. And He sat down and *began* teaching the multitudes from the boat.

4 And when He had finished speaking, He said to Simon, "Put out into the deep water and [a]let down your nets for a catch."

5 And Simon answered and said, "[a]Master, we worked hard all night and caught nothing, but at Your [1]bidding I will let down the nets."

6 And when they had done this, they enclosed a great quantity of fish; and their nets *began* to break;

7 and they signaled to their partners in the other boat, for them to come and help them. And they came, and filled both of the boats, so that they began to sink.

8 But when Simon Peter saw *that,* he fell down at Jesus' [1]feet, saying, "Depart from me, for I am a sinful man, O Lord!"

9 For amazement had seized him and all his companions because of the catch of fish which they had taken;

10 and so also [1]James and John, sons of Zebedee, who were partners with Simon. And Jesus said to Simon, "[a]Do not fear, from now on you will be [b]catching men."

11 And when they had brought their boats to land, [a]they left everything and followed Him.

The Leper and the Paralytic

12 [a]And it came about that while He was in one of the cities, behold, *there was* a man full of leprosy; and when he saw Jesus, he fell on his face and implored Him, saying, "Lord, if You are willing, You can make me clean."

13 And He stretched out His hand, and touched him, saying, "I am willing; be cleansed." And immediately the leprosy left him.

14 And He ordered him to tell no one, "But go and [a]SHOW YOURSELF TO THE PRIEST, and make an offering for your cleansing, just as Moses commanded, for a testimony to them."

15 But [a]the news about Him was spreading even farther, and great multitudes were gathering to hear *Him* and to be healed of their sicknesses.

16 But He Himself would *often* slip away [1]to the [2]wilderness and [a]pray.

17 And it came about [1]one day that He was teaching; and [a]there were *some* Pharisees and [b]teachers of the law sitting *there,* who had [c]come from every village of Galilee and Judea and *from* Jerusalem; and [d]the power of the Lord was *present* for Him to perform healing.

18 [a]And behold, *some* men *were* carrying on a [1]bed a man who was paralyzed; and they were trying to bring him in, and to set him down in front of Him.

19 And not finding any *way* to bring him in because of the crowd, they went up on [a]the roof and let him down [b]through the tiles with his stretcher, right in the center, in front of Jesus.

20 And seeing their faith, He said, "[1]Friend, [a]your sins are forgiven you."

21 And the scribes and the Pharisees [a]began to reason, saying, "Who is this *man* who speaks blasphemies? [b]Who can forgive sins, but God alone?"

22 But Jesus, [1]aware of their reasonings, answered and said to them, "Why are you reasoning in your hearts?

23 "Which is easier, to say, 'Your sins have been forgiven you,' or to say, 'Rise and walk'?

24 "But in order that you may know that the Son of Man has authority on earth to forgive sins," He said to the [a]paralytic, "I say to you, rise, and take up your stretcher and go home."

25 And at once he rose up before them, and took up what he had been lying on, and went home, [a]glorifying God.

26 And they were all seized with astonishment and *began* [a]glorifying God; and they were filled [b]with fear, saying, "We have seen remarkable things today."

Call of Levi (Matthew)

27 [a]And after that He went out, and noticed a [1]tax-gatherer named [b]Levi, sitting in the tax office, and He said to him, "Follow Me."

28 And he [a]left everything behind, and rose up and *began* to follow Him.

29 And [a]Levi gave a big [1]reception for Him in his house; and there was a great crowd of [b]tax-gatherers and other *people* who were reclining *at table* with them.

30 And the Pharisees and [a]their scribes *began* grumbling at His disciples, saying, "Why do you eat and

3 [a]Matt. 13:2; Mark 4:1
4 [a]John 21:6
5 [1]Or, *word* [a]Gr. as in Luke 8:24; 9:33, 49; 17:13
8 [1]Lit., *knees*
10 [1]Or, *Jacob* [a]Matt. 14:27 [b]2 Tim. 2:26
11 [a]Matt. 4:20, 22; 19:29; Mark 1:18, 20; Luke 5:28
12 [a]Luke 5:12-14: *Matt. 8:2-4; Mark 1:40-44*
14 [a]Lev. 13:49; 14:2ff.
15 [a]Matt. 9:26
16 [1]Lit., *in* [2]Or, *lonely places* [a]Matt. 14:23; Mark 1:35; Luke 6:12
17 [1]Lit., *on one of the days* [a]Matt. 15:1 [b]Luke 2:46 [c]Mark 1:45 [d]Mark 5:30; Luke 6:19; 8:46
18 [1]Or, *stretcher* [a]Luke 5:18-26: *Matt. 9:2-8; Mark 2:3-12*
19 [a]Matt. 24:17 [b]Mark 2:4
20 [1]Lit., *Man* [a]Matt. 9:2
21 [a]Luke 3:8 [b]Is. 43:25
22 [1]Or, *perceiving*
24 [a]Matt. 4:24
25 [a]Matt. 9:8
26 [a]Matt. 9:8 [b]Luke 1:65; 7:16
27 [1]Publicans who collected Roman taxes on commission [a]Luke 5:27-39: *Matt. 9:9-17; Mark 2:14-22* [b]Matt. 9:9
28 [a]Luke 5:11
29 [1]Or, *banquet* [a]Matt. 9:9 [b]Luke 15:1
30 [a]Mark 2:16; Acts 23:9

drink with the tax-gatherers and
sinners?"
31 And Jesus answered and said to
them, "[a]*It is* not those who are well
who need a physician, but those
who are sick.
32 "I have not come to call righteous men but sinners to repentance."
33 And they said to Him, "[a]The
disciples of John often fast and offer
prayers; the *disciples* of the Pharisees also do [1]the same; but Yours
eat and drink."
34 And Jesus said to them, "You
cannot make the [1]attendants of the
bridegroom fast while the bridegroom is with them, can you?
35 "[a]But *the* days will come; and
when the bridegroom is taken away
from them, then they will fast in
those days."
36 And He was also telling them a
parable: "No one tears a piece from
a new [1]garment and puts it on an old
[1]garment; otherwise he will both
tear the new, and the piece from the
new will not match the old.
37 "And no one puts new wine into
old [1]wineskins; otherwise the new
wine will burst the [1]skins, and it will
be spilled out, and the [1]skins will be
ruined.
38 "But new wine must be put into
fresh wineskins.
39 "And no one, after drinking old
wine wishes for new; for he says,
'The old is good *enough.*'"

Chapter 6

Jesus Is Lord of the Sabbath

[a]NOW it came about that on a *certain* [1]Sabbath He was passing
through *some* grainfields; and His
disciples [b]were picking and eating
the heads *of wheat,* rubbing them in
their hands.
2 But some of the Pharisees said,
"Why do you do what [a]is not lawful
on the Sabbath?"
3 And Jesus answering them
said, "Have you not even read [a]what
David did when he was hungry, he
and those who were with him,
4 how he entered the house of
God, and took and ate the [1]conse-
crated bread which is not lawful for
any to eat except the priests alone,
and gave it to his companions?"
5 And He was saying to them,
"The Son of Man is Lord of the Sabbath."
6 [a]And it came about [b]on another
Sabbath, that He entered [c]the synagogue and was teaching; and there
was a man there [1]whose right hand
was withered.
7 And the scribes and the Pharisees [a]were watching Him closely, *to
see* if He healed on the Sabbath, in
order that they might find *reason* to
accuse Him.
8 But He [a]knew [1]what they were
thinking, and He said to the man
with the withered hand, "Arise and
[2]come forward!" And he arose and
[3]came forward.
9 And Jesus said to them, "I ask
you, is it lawful on the Sabbath to do
good, or [1]to do evil, to save a life, or
to destroy it?"
10 And after [a]looking around at
them all, He said to him, "Stretch
out your hand!" And he did *so;* and
his hand was *completely* restored.
11 But they themselves were filled
with [1]rage, and discussed together
what they might do to Jesus.

Choosing the Twelve

12 And it was [1]at this time that He
went off to [a]the mountain to [b]pray,
and He spent the whole night in
prayer to God.
13 And when day came, [a]He called
His disciples to Him; and chose
twelve of them, whom He also
named as [b]apostles:
14 Simon, whom He also named
Peter, and Andrew his brother;
[1]James and John; Philip and Bartholomew;
15 [a]Matthew and Thomas; James
the son of Alphaeus, and Simon who
was called the Zealot;
16 Judas *the son* of James, and Judas Iscariot, who became a traitor.
17 And He [a]descended with them,
and stood on a level place; and *there
was* [b]a great multitude of His disciples, and a great throng of people
from all Judea and Jerusalem and
the coastal region of [c]Tyre and Sidon,
18 [1]who had come to hear Him,
and to be healed of their diseases;
and those who were troubled with
unclean spirits were being cured.
19 And all the multitude were trying to [a]touch Him, for [b]power was
coming from Him and healing *them*
all.

The Beatitudes

20 And turning His gaze on His
disciples, He *began* to say,
"[a]Blessed *are* you *who are* poor, for
[b]yours is the kingdom of God.
21 "Blessed *are* you who hunger
now, for you shall be satisfied.
Blessed *are* you who weep now, for
you shall laugh.

31 [a]Matt. 9:12, 13; Mark 2:17
33 [1]Or, *likewise* [a]Matt. 9:14; Mark 2:18
34 [1]Lit., *sons of the bridal-chamber*
35 [a]Matt. 9:15; Mark 2:20; Luke 17:22
36 [1]Or, *cloak*
37 [1]I.e., skins used as bottles
1 [1]Many mss. read, *the second-first Sabbath;* i.e., the second Sabbath after the first [a]Luke 5:1-5: *Matt. 12:1-8; Mark 2:23-28* [b]Deut. 23:25
2 [a]Matt. 12:2
3 [a]1 Sam. 21:6
4 [1]Or, *showbread,* lit., *loaves of presentation*
6 [1]Lit., *and his* [a]Luke 5:6-11: *Matt. 12:9-14; Mark 3:1-6* [b]Luke 6:1 [c]Matt. 4:23
7 [a]Mark 3:2
8 [1]Lit., *their thoughts* [2]Lit., *stand* or *stood into the midst* [3]Lit., *stood* [a]Matt. 9:4
9 [1]Or, *to harm*
10 [a]Mark 3:5
11 [1]Lit., *folly*
12 [1]Lit., *in these days* [a]Matt. 5:1 [b]Matt. 14:23; Luke 5:16; 9:18, 28
13 [a]Luke 6:13-16: *Matt. 10:2-4; Mark 3:16-19; Acts 1:13* [b]Mark 6:30
14 [1]Here and in verses 15 and 16, Gr., *Jacob*
15 [a]Matt. 9:9
17 [a]Luke 6:12 [b]Matt. 4:25; Mark 3:7, 8 [c]Matt. 11:21
18 [1]Most English versions begin verse 18 with, *and those who*
19 [a]Matt. 9:21; 14:36; Mark 3:10 [b]Luke 5:17
20 [a]Matt. 5:3-12; Luke 6:20-23 [b]Matt. 5:3

22"Blessed are you when men hate
you, and [a]ostracize you, and heap
insults upon you, and spurn your
name as evil, for the sake of the Son
of Man.
23"Be glad in that day, and [a]leap
for joy, for behold, your reward is
great in heaven; for in the same way
their fathers used to [1]treat the
prophets.
24"But woe to [a]you who are rich,
for [b]you are receiving your comfort
in full.
25"Woe to you who are [1]well-fed
now, for you shall be hungry. Woe
to you who laugh now, for you shall
mourn and weep.
26"Woe *to you* when all men speak
well of you, for in the same way
their fathers used to [1]treat the [a]false
prophets.
27"But I say to you who hear, [a]love
your enemies, do good to those who
hate you,
28 bless those who curse you,
[a]pray for those who [1]mistreat you.
29"[a]Whoever hits you on the
cheek, offer him the other also; and
whoever takes away your [1]coat, do
not withhold your [2]shirt from him
either.
30"Give to everyone who asks of
you, and whoever takes away what
is yours, do not demand it back.
31"[a]And just as you want men to
[1]treat you, [1]treat them in the same
way.
32"And [a]if you love those who love
you, what credit is *that* to you? For
even sinners love those who love
them.
33"And if you do good to those
who do good to you, what credit is
that to you? For even sinners do the
same thing.
34"[a]And if you lend to those from
whom you expect to receive, what
credit is *that* to you? Even sinners
lend to sinners, in order to receive
back the same *amount*.
35"But [a]love your enemies, and do
good, and lend, [1]expecting nothing
in return; and your reward will be
great, and you will be [b]sons of [c]the
Most High; for He Himself is kind to
ungrateful and evil *men*.
36"[1]Be merciful, just as your Father is merciful.
37"[a]And [1]do not pass judgment
and you will not be judged; and do
not condemn, and you shall not be
condemned; [2b]pardon, and you will
be pardoned.
38"Give, and it will be given to you;
[a]good measure, pressed down,
shaken together, running over, they
will pour [b]into your lap. For whatever measure you deal out *to others*,
it will be dealt to you in return."
39 And He also spoke a parable to
them: "[a]A blind man cannot guide a
blind man, can he? Will they not
both fall into a pit?
40"[a]A [1]pupil is not above his
teacher; but everyone, after he has
been fully trained, will [2]be like his
teacher.
41"And why do you look at the
speck that is in your brother's eye,
but do not notice the log that is in
your own eye?
42"Or how can you say to your
brother, 'Brother, let me take out
the speck that is in your eye,' when
you yourself do not see the log that
is in your own eye? You hypocrite,
first take the log out of your own
eye, and then you will see clearly to
take out the speck that is in your
brother's eye.
43"[a]For there is no good tree which
produces bad fruit; nor, [1]on the other hand, a bad tree which produces
good fruit.
44"[a]For each tree is known by its
own fruit. For men do not gather
figs from thorns, nor do they pick
grapes from a briar bush.
45"[a]The good man out of the good
[1]treasure of his heart brings forth
what is good; and the evil *man* out
of the evil [1]*treasure* brings forth
what is evil; [b]for his mouth speaks
from [2]that which fills his heart.

Builders and Foundations

46"And [a]why do you call Me,
'Lord, Lord,' and do not do what I
say?
47"[a]Everyone who comes to Me,
and hears My words, and [1]acts upon
them, I will show you whom he is
like:
48 he is like a man building a
house, who [1]dug deep and laid a
foundation upon the rock; and when
a flood arose, the river burst against
that house and could not shake it,
because it had been well built.
49"But the one who has heard, and
has not acted *accordingly*, is like a
man who built a house upon the
ground without any foundation; and
the river burst against it and immediately it collapsed, and the ruin of
that house was great."

Chapter 7

Jesus Heals a Centurion's Servant

[a]WHEN He had completed all His
discourse in the hearing of the people, [b]He went to Capernaum.

22 [a]John 9:22; 16:2
23 [1]Lit., *do to* [a]Mal. 4
24 [a]Luke 16:25; James 5:1 [b]Matt. 6:2
25 [1]Lit., *having been filled*
26 [1]Lit., *do to* [a]Matt. 7:15
27 [a]Matt. 5:44; Luke 6:35
28 [1]Or, *revile* [a]Matt. 5:44; Luke 6:35
29 [1]Or, *cloak*, i.e., outer garment [2]Or, *tunic*, i.e., garment worn next to body [a]Luke 6:29, 30: *Matt. 5:39-42*
31 [1]Or, *do to* [a]Matt. 7:12
32 [a]Matt. 5:46
34 [a]Matt. 5:42
35 [1]Or, *not despairing at all* [a]Luke 6:27 [b]Matt. 5:9 [c]Luke 1:32
36 [1]Or, *Become*
37 [1]Lit., *do not judge* [2]Lit., *release* [a]Luke 6:37-42: *Matt. 7:1-5* [b]Matt. 6:14; Luke 23:16; Acts 3:13
38 [a]Mark 4:24 [b]Ps. 79:12; Is. 65:6, 7; Jer. 32:18
39 [a]Matt. 15:14
40 [1]Or, *disciple* [2]Or, *reach his teacher's level* [a]Matt. 10:24
43 [1]Lit., *again* [a]Luke 6:43, 44: *Matt. 7:16, 18, 20*
44 [a]Matt. 7:16
45 [1]Or, *treasury, storehouse* [2]Lit., *the abundance of* [a]Matt. 12:35 [b]Matt. 12:34
46 [a]Mal. 1:6; Matt. 7:21
47 [1]Lit., *does* [a]Luke 6:47-49: *Matt. 7:24-27*
48 [1]Lit., *dug and went deep*
1 [a]Matt. 7:28 [b]Luke 7:1-10: *Matt. 8:5-13*

2 And a certain centurion's slave,
[1]who was highly regarded by him,
was sick and about to die.
3 And when he heard about Jesus, [a]he sent some [1]Jewish elders
asking Him to come and [2]save the
life of his slave.
4 And when they had come to Jesus, they earnestly entreated Him,
saying, "He is worthy for You to
grant this to him;
5 for he loves our nation, and it
was he who built us our synagogue."
6 Now Jesus *started* on His way
with them; and when He was already not far from the house, the
centurion sent friends, saying to
Him, "[1]Lord, do not trouble Yourself further, for I am not fit for You
to come under my roof;
7 for this reason I did not even
consider myself worthy to come to
You, but just [1]say the word, and my
[2]servant will be healed.
8 "For indeed, I am a man under
authority, with soldiers under me;
and I say to this one, 'Go!' and he
goes; and to another, 'Come!' and he
comes; and to my slave, 'Do this!'
and he does it."
9 And when Jesus heard this, He
marveled at him, and turned and
said to the multitude that was following Him, "I say to you, [a]not even
in Israel have I found such great
faith."
10 And when those who had been
sent returned to the house, they
found the slave in good health.
11 And it came about [1]soon afterwards, that He went to a city called
Nain; and His disciples were going
along with Him, [2]accompanied by a
large multitude.
12 Now as He approached the gate
of the city, behold, [1]a dead man was
being carried out, the [2]only son of
his mother, and she was a widow;
and a sizeable crowd from the city
was with her.
13 And when [a]the Lord saw her,
He felt compassion for her, and said
to her, "[1]Do not weep."
14 And He came up and touched
the coffin; and the bearers came to a
halt. And He said, "Young man, I
say to you, arise!"
15 And the [1]dead man sat up, and
began to speak. And *Jesus* gave him
back to his mother.
16 And [a]fear gripped them all, and
they *began* [b]glorifying God, saying,
"A great [c]prophet has arisen among
us!" and, "God has [1]visited His people!"
17 [a]And this report concerning
Him went out all over Judea, and in
all the surrounding district.

A Deputation from John

18 [a]And the disciples of John reported to him about all these things.
19 And summoning [1]two of his
disciples, John sent them to [a]the
Lord, saying, "Are You the One who
is coming, or do we look for someone [2]else?"
20 And when the men had come to
Him, they said, "John the Baptist
has sent us to You, saying, 'Are You
the One who is coming, or do we
look for someone else?'"
21 At that [1]very time He [a]cured
many *people* of diseases and [b]afflic-
tions and evil spirits; and He
granted sight to many *who were*
blind.
22 And He answered and said to
them, "Go and report to John what
you have seen and heard: *the* [a]BLIND
RECEIVE SIGHT, *the* lame walk, *the*
lepers are cleansed, and *the* deaf
hear, *the* dead are raised up, *the*
[a]POOR HAVE THE GOSPEL PREACHED
TO THEM.
23 "And blessed is he [1]who keeps
from stumbling over Me."
24 And when the messengers of
John had left, He began to speak to
the multitudes about John, "What
did you go out into the wilderness to
look at? A reed shaken by the wind?
25 "[1]But what did you go out to
see? A man dressed in soft [2]cloth-
ing? Behold, those who are splendidly clothed and live in luxury are
found in royal palaces.
26 "But what did you go out to see?
A prophet? Yes, I say to you, and
one who is more than a prophet.
27 "This is the one about whom it
[1]is written,

'[a]BEHOLD, I SEND MY MESSEN-
GER BEFORE YOUR FACE,
WHO WILL PREPARE YOUR WAY
BEFORE YOU.'

28 "I say to you, among those born
of women, there is no one greater
than John; yet he who is [1]least in the
kingdom of God is greater than he."
29 And when all the people and
the [1]tax-gatherers heard *this,* they
[2]acknowledged [a]God's justice,
[b]having been baptized with [c]the
baptism of John.
30 But the Pharisees and the
[1a]lawyers rejected God's purpose
for themselves, not having been
baptized by [2]John.
31 "To what then shall I compare
the men of this generation, and
what are they like?

2 [1]Lit., *to whom he was honorable*

3 [1]Lit., *elders of the Jews* [2]Lit., *bring safely through, rescue* [a]Matt. 8:5

6 [1]Or, *Sir*

7 [1]Lit., *speak with a word* [2]Or, *boy*

9 [a]Matt. 8:10; Luke 7:50

11 [1]Some mss. read, *on the next day* [2]Lit., *and*

12 [1]Lit., *one who had died* [2]Or, *only begotten*

13 [1]Or, *Stop weeping* [a]Luke 7:19; 10:1; 11:1, 39; 12:42; 13:15; 17:5, 6; 18:6; 19:8; 22:61; 24:34; John 4:1; 6:23; 11:2

15 [1]Or, *corpse*

16 [1]Or, *cared for* [a]Luke 5:26 [b]Matt. 9:8 [c]Matt. 21:11; Luke 7:39

17 [a]Matt. 9:26

18 [a]Luke 7:18-35: *Matt. 11:2-19*

19 [1]Lit., *a certain two* [2]Some early mss. read, *one who is different* [a]Luke 7:13; 10:1; 11:1, 39; 12:42; 13:15; 17:5, 6; 18:6; 19:8; 22:61; 24:34; John 4:1; 6:23; 11:2

21 [1]Lit., *hour* [a]Matt. 4:23 [b]Mark 3:10

22 [a]Is. 61:1

23 [1]Lit., *whoever*

25 [1]Or, *Well then, what* [2]Or, *garments*

27 [1]Lit., *has been written* [a]Mal. 3:1; Matt. 11:10; Mark 1:2

28 [1]Lit., *less*

29 [1]Publicans who collected Roman taxes on commission [2]Or, *justified God* [a]Luke 7:35 [b]Matt. 21:32; Luke 3:12 [c]Acts 18:25; 19:3

30 [1]I.e., experts on the Mosaic law [2]Lit., *him* [a]Matt. 22:35

32 "They are like children who sit in the market place and call to one another; and they say, 'We played the flute for you, and you did not dance; we sang a dirge, and you did not weep.'

33 "For John the Baptist has come [a]eating no bread and drinking no wine; and you say, 'He has a demon!'

34 "The Son of Man has come eating and drinking; and you say, 'Behold, a gluttonous man, and a [1]drunkard, a friend of [2]tax-gatherers and sinners!'

35 "[1]Yet wisdom [a]is vindicated by all her children."

36 Now one of the Pharisees was requesting Him to [1]dine with him. And He entered the Pharisee's house, and reclined *at table.*

37 [a]And behold, there was a woman in the city who was a [1]sinner; and when she learned that He was reclining *at table* in the Pharisee's house, she brought an alabaster vial of perfume,

38 and standing behind *Him* at His feet, weeping, she began to wet His feet with her tears, and kept wiping them with the hair of her head, and kissing His feet, and anointing them with the perfume.

39 Now when the Pharisee who had invited Him saw this, he said [1]to himself, "If this man were [2a]a prophet He would know who and what sort of person this woman is who is touching Him, that she is a [3]sinner."

Parable of Two Debtors

40 And Jesus answered and said to him, "Simon, I have something to say to you." And he [1]replied, "Say it, Teacher."

41 "A certain moneylender had two debtors: one owed five hundred [1a]denarii, and the other fifty.

42 "When they [a]were unable to repay, he graciously forgave them both. Which of them therefore will love him more?"

43 Simon answered and said, "I suppose the one whom he forgave more." And He said to him, "You have judged correctly."

44 And turning toward the woman, He said to Simon, "Do you see this woman? I entered your house; you [a]gave Me no water for My feet, but she has wet My feet with her tears, and wiped them with her hair.

45 "You [a]gave Me no kiss; but she, since the time I came in, [1]has not ceased to kiss My feet.

46 "[a]You did not anoint My head with oil, but she anointed My feet with perfume.

47 "For this reason I say to you, her sins, which are many, have been forgiven, for she loved much; but he who is forgiven little, loves little."

48 And He said to her, "[a]Your sins have been forgiven."

49 And those who were reclining *at table* with Him began to say [1]to themselves, "Who is this *man* who even forgives sins?"

50 And He said to the woman, "[a]Your faith has saved you; [b]go in peace."

CHAPTER 8

Ministering Women

AND it came about soon afterwards, that He *began* going about from one city and village to another, [a]proclaiming and preaching the kingdom of God; and the twelve were with Him,

2 and *also* [a]some women who had been healed of evil spirits and sicknesses: [a]Mary who was called Magdalene, from whom seven demons had gone out,

3 and Joanna the wife of Chuza, [a]Herod's [b]steward, and Susanna, and many others who were contributing to their support out of their private means.

Parable of the Sower

4 [a]And when a great multitude were coming together, and those from the various cities were journeying to Him, He spoke by way of a parable:

5 "The sower went out to sow his seed; and as he sowed, some fell beside the road; and it was trampled under foot, and the birds of the [1]air devoured it.

6 "And other *seed* fell on rocky *soil,* and as soon as it grew up, it withered away, because it had no moisture.

7 "And other *seed* fell among the thorns; and the thorns grew up with it, and choked it out.

8 "And other *seed* fell into the good ground, and grew up, and produced a crop a hundred times as great." As He said these things, He would call out, "[a]He who has ears to hear, let him hear."

9 [a]And His disciples *began* questioning Him as to what this parable might be.

10 And He said, "[a]To you it is granted to know the mysteries of

33 [a]Luke 1:15

34 [1]Or, *wine-drinker* [2]Publicans who collected Roman taxes on commission

35 [1]Lit., *And* [a]Luke 7:29

36 [1]Lit., *eat*

37 [1]I.e., an immoral woman [a]Matt. 26:6-13; Mark 14:3-9; Luke 7:37-39; John 12:1-8

39 [1]Lit., *to himself, saying* [2]Some mss. read, *the prophet* [3]I.e., an immoral woman [a]Luke 7:16; John 4:19

40 [1]Lit., *says*

41 [1]The denarius was worth 18 cents in silver, equivalent to a day's wage [a]Matt. 18:28; Mark 6:37

42 [a]Matt. 18:25

44 [a]Gen. 18:4; 19:2; 43:24; Judg. 19:21; 1 Tim. 5:10

45 [1]Lit., *was not ceasing* [a]2 Sam. 15:5

46 [a]2 Sam. 12:20; Ps. 23:5; Eccles. 9:8; Dan. 10:3

48 [a]Matt. 9:2

49 [1]Or, *among*

50 [a]Matt. 9:22 [b]Mark 5:34; Luke 8:48

1 [a]Matt. 4:23

2 [a]Matt. 27:55f.; Luke 23:49

3 [a]Matt. 14:1 [b]Matt. 20:8

4 [a]Luke 8:4-8: *Matt. 13:2-9; Mark 4:1-9*

5 [1]Lit., *heaven*

8 [a]Matt. 11:15

9 [a]Luke 8:9-15: *Matt. 13:10-23; Mark 4:10-20*

10 [a]Matt. 13:11

the kingdom of God, but to the rest *it is* in parables; in order that [b]SEEING THEY MAY NOT SEE, AND HEARING THEY MAY NOT UNDERSTAND.

11 "Now the parable is this: [a]the seed is the word of God.

12 "And those beside the road are those who have heard; then the devil comes and takes away the word from their heart, so that they may not believe and be saved.

13 "And those on the rocky *soil are* those who, when they hear, receive the word with joy; and these have no *firm* root; [1]they believe for a while, and in time of temptation fall away.

14 "And the *seed* which fell among the thorns, these are the ones who have heard, and as they go on their way they are choked with worries and riches and pleasures of *this* life, and bring no fruit to maturity.

15 "And the *seed* in the good ground, these are the ones who have heard the word in an honest and good heart, and hold it fast, and bear fruit with [1]perseverance.

Parable of the Lamp

16 "Now [a]no one after lighting a lamp covers it over with a container, or puts it under a bed; but he puts it on a lampstand, in order that those who come in may see the light.

17 "[a]For nothing is hidden that shall not become evident, nor *anything* secret that shall not be known and come to light.

18 "Therefore take care how you listen; [a]for whoever has, to him shall *more* be given; and whoever does not have, even what he [1]thinks he has shall be taken away from him."

19 [a]And His mother came to Him and *His* brothers *also,* and they were unable to get to Him because of the crowd.

20 And it was reported to Him, "Your mother and Your brothers are standing outside, wishing to see You."

21 But He answered and said to them, "My mother and My brothers are these [a]who hear the word of God and do it."

Jesus Stills the Sea

22 [a]Now it came about on one of *those* days, that He and His disciples got into a boat, and He said to them, "Let us go over to the other side of [b]the lake." And they launched out.

23 But as they were sailing along He fell asleep; and a fierce gale of wind descended upon [a]the lake, and they *began* to be swamped and to be in danger.

24 And they came to Him and woke Him up, saying, "[a]Master, Master, we are perishing!" And being aroused, He [b]rebuked the wind and the surging waves, and they stopped, and [1]it became calm.

25 And He said to them, "Where is your faith?" And they were fearful and amazed, saying to one another, "Who then is this, that He commands even the winds and the water, and they obey Him?"

The Demoniac Cured

26 [a]And they sailed to the country of the [1]Gerasenes, which is opposite Galilee.

27 And when He had come out onto the land, He was met by a certain man from the city who was possessed with demons; and who had not put on any clothing for a long time, and was not living in a house, but in the tombs.

28 And seeing Jesus, he cried out and fell before Him, and said in a loud voice, "[a]What do I have to do with You, Jesus, Son of [b]the Most High God? I beg You, do not torment me."

29 For He [1]had been commanding the unclean spirit to come out of the man. For it had seized him many times; and he was bound with chains and shackles and kept under guard; and *yet* he would burst his fetters and be driven by the demon into the desert.

30 And Jesus asked him, "What is your name?" And he said, "[a]Legion"; for many demons had entered him.

31 And they were entreating Him not to command them to depart into [a]the abyss.

32 Now there was a herd of many swine feeding there on the mountain; and *the demons* entreated Him to permit them to enter [1]the swine. And He gave them permission.

33 And the demons came out from the man and entered the swine; and the herd rushed down the steep bank into [a]the lake, and were drowned.

34 And when those who tended them saw what had happened, they ran away and reported it in the city and *out* in the country.

35 And *the people* went out to see what had happened; and they came to Jesus, and found the man from whom the demons had gone out, sitting down [a]at the feet of Jesus,

10 [b]Is. 6:9; Matt. 13:14
11 [a]1 Pet. 1:23
13 [1]Lit., *who believe*
15 [1]Or, *steadfastness*
16 [a]Matt. 5:15; Mark 4:21; Luke 11:33
17 [a]Matt. 10:26; Mark 4:22; Luke 12:2
18 [1]Or, *seems to have* [a]Matt. 13:12; Luke 19:26
19 [a]Luke 8:19-21: *Matt. 12:46-50; Mark 3:31-35*
21 [a]Luke 11:28
22 [a]Luke 8:22-25: *Matt. 8:23-27; Mark 4:36-41* [b]Luke 5:1f.; 8:23
23 [a]Luke 5:1f.; 8:22
24 [1]Lit., *a calm occurred* [a]Luke 5:5 [b]Luke 4:39
26 [1]Other mss. read, *Gergesenes,* or *Gadarenes* [a]Luke 8:26-37: *Matt. 8:28-34; Mark 5:1-17*
28 [a]Matt. 8:29 [b]Mark 5:7
29 [1]Or, *was commanding*
30 [a]Matt. 26:53
31 [a]Rom. 10:7; Rev. 9:1f., 11; 11:7; 17:8; 20:1, 3
32 [1]Lit., *them*
33 [a]Luke 5:1f.; 8:22
35 [a]Luke 10:39

clothed and in his right mind; and they became frightened.

36 And those who had seen it reported to them how the man who was [a]demon-possessed had been [1]made well.

37 And all the people of the country of the [1]Gerasenes and the surrounding district asked Him to depart from them; for they were gripped with great fear; and He got into a boat, and returned.

38 [a]But the man from whom the demons had gone out was begging Him that he might [1]accompany Him; but He sent him away, saying,

39 "Return to your house and describe what great things God has done for you." And he departed, proclaiming throughout the whole city what great things Jesus had done for him.

Miracles of Healing

40 [a]And as Jesus returned, the multitude welcomed Him, for they had all been waiting for Him.

41 [a]And behold, there came a man named Jairus, and he was an [1b]official of the synagogue; and he fell at Jesus' feet, and *began* to entreat Him to come to his house;

42 for he had an [1]only daughter, about twelve years old, and she was dying. But as He went, the multitudes were pressing against Him.

43 And a woman who had a hemorrhage for twelve years, [1]and could not be healed by anyone,

44 came up behind Him, and touched the fringe of His [1]cloak; and immediately her hemorrhage stopped.

45 And Jesus said, "Who is the one who touched Me?" And while they were all denying it, Peter said,[1] "[a]Master, the multitudes are crowding and pressing upon You."

46 But Jesus said, "Someone did touch Me, for I was aware that [a]power had gone out of Me."

47 And when the woman saw that she had not escaped notice, she came trembling and fell down before Him, and declared in the presence of all the people the reason why she had touched Him, and how she had been immediately healed.

48 And He said to her, "Daughter, [a]your faith has [1]made you well; [b]go in peace."

49 While He was still speaking, someone *came from *the house of* [a]the synagogue official, saying, "Your daughter has died; do not trouble the Teacher any more."

50 But when Jesus heard *this,* He answered him, "[a]Do not be afraid *any longer;* only believe, and she shall be [1]made well."

51 And when He had come to the house, He did not allow anyone to enter with Him, except Peter, John and James, and the girl's father and mother.

52 Now they were all weeping and [a]lamenting for her; but He said, "Stop weeping, for she has not died, but [b]is asleep."

53 And they *began* laughing at Him, knowing that she had died.

54 He, however, took her by the hand and called, saying, "Child, arise!"

55 And her spirit returned, and she rose up immediately; and He gave orders for *something* to be given her to eat.

56 And her parents were amazed; but He [a]instructed them to tell no one what had happened.

CHAPTER 9

Ministry of the Twelve

[a]AND He called the twelve together, and gave them power and authority over all the demons, and to heal diseases.

2 And He sent them out to [a]proclaim the kingdom of God, and [1]to perform healing.

3 And He said to them, "[a]Take nothing for *your* journey, [b]neither a staff, nor a [1]bag, nor bread, nor money; and do not *even* have [2]two tunics apiece.

4 "And whatever house you enter, stay there, and take your leave from there.

5 "And as for those who do not receive you, when you depart from that city, [a]shake off the dust from your feet as a testimony against them."

6 And departing, they *began* going about [1]among the villages, [a]preaching the gospel, and healing everywhere.

7 [a]Now [b]Herod the tetrarch heard of all that was happening; and he was greatly perplexed, because it was said by some that [c]John had risen from the dead,

8 and by some that [a]Elijah had appeared, and by others, that one of the prophets of old had risen again.

9 And Herod said, "I myself had John beheaded; but who is this man about whom I hear such things?" And [a]he kept trying to see Him.

36 [1]Or, *saved* [a]Matt. 4:24

37 [1]Other mss. read, *Gergesenes,* or *Gadarenes*

38 [1]Lit., *be with* [a]Luke 8:38, 39: *Mark 5:18-20*

40 [a]Matt. 9:1; Mark 5:21

41 [1]Lit., *ruler* [a]Luke 8:41-56: *Matt. 9:18-26; Mark 5:22-43* [b]Mark 5:22; Luke 8:49

42 [1]Or, *only begotten*

43 [1]Some mss. add, *who had spent all her living upon physicians*

44 [1]Or, *outer garment*

45 [1]Some early mss. add, *and those with him* [a]Luke 5:5

46 [a]Luke 5:17

48 [1]Lit., *saved you* [a]Matt. 9:22 [b]Mark 5:34; Luke 7:50

49 [a]Luke 8:41

50 [1]Or, *saved* [a]Mark 5:36

52 [a]Matt. 11:17; Luke 23:27 [b]John 11:13

56 [a]Matt. 8:4

1 [a]Matt. 10:5; Mark 6:7

2 [1]Some mss. read, *to heal the sick* [a]Matt. 10:7

3 [1]Or, *knapsack,* or *beggar's bag* [2]Or, *inner garment* [a]Luke 9:3-5: *Matt. 10:9-15; Mark 6:8-11;* Luke 10:4-12; 22:35 [b]Matt. 10:10; Mark 6:8; Luke 22:35f.

5 [a]Luke 10:11; Acts 13:51

6 [1]Or, *from village to village* [a]Mark 6:12; Luke 8:1

7 [a]Luke 9:7-9: *Matt. 14:1, 2;* Mark 6:14f. [b]Matt. 14:1; Luke 3:1; 13:31; 23:7 [c]Matt. 14:2

8 [a]Matt. 16:14

9 [a]Luke 23:8

10 [a]And when the [b]apostles returned, they gave an account to Him
of all that they had done. [c]And taking them with Him, He withdrew
privately to a city called [d]Bethsaida.
11 But the multitudes were aware
of this and followed Him; and welcoming them, He *began* speaking to
them about the kingdom of God and
curing those who had need of healing.

Five Thousand Fed

12 And the day began to decline,
and the twelve came and said to
Him, "Send the multitude away,
that they may go into the surrounding villages and countryside and
find lodging and get [1]something to
eat; for here we are in a desolate
place."
13 But He said to them, "You give
them something to eat!" And they
said, "We have no more than five
loaves and two fish, unless perhaps
we go and buy food for all these people."
14 (For there were about five thousand men). And He said to His disciples, "Have them recline *to eat* [a]in
groups of about fifty each."
15 And they did so, and had them
all recline.
16 And He took the five loaves and
the two fish, and looking up to
heaven, He blessed them, and broke
them, and kept giving *them* to the
disciples to set before the multitude.
17 And they all ate and were satisfied; and that which was left over
[a]baskets them of the broken pieces
was picked up, twelve [a]baskets *full.*
18 [a]And it came about that while
He was [b]praying alone, the disciples
were with Him, and He questioned
them, saying, "Who do the multitudes say that I am?"
19 And they answered and said,
"John the Baptist; but others *say,*
Elijah; and others, that one of the
prophets of old has risen again."
20 And He said to them, "But who
do you say that I am?" And Peter
answered and said, "[a]The [1]Christ of
God."
21 But He [1a]warned them, and instructed *them* not to tell this to anyone,
22 [a]saying, "[b]The Son of Man
must suffer many things, and be rejected by the elders and chief priests
and scribes, and be killed, and be
raised up on the third day."
23 And He was saying to *them* all,
"If anyone wishes to come after Me,
let him deny himself, and [a]take up
his cross daily, and follow Me.

10 [a]Mark 6:30 [b]Mark 6:30 [c]Luke 9:10-17: *Matt. 14:13-21; Mark 6:32-44; John 6:5-13* [d]Matt. 11:21

12 [1]Lit., *provisions*

14 [a]Mark 6:39

17 [a]Matt. 14:20

18 [a]Luke 9:18-20: *Matt. 16:13-16; Mark 8:27-29* [b]Matt. 14:23; Luke 6:12; 9:28

20 [1]I.e., Messiah [a]John 6:68f.

21 [1]Or, *strictly admonished* [a]Matt. 8:4; 16:20; Mark 8:30

22 [a]Luke 9:22-27: *Matt. 16:21-28; Mark 8:31-9:1* [b]Matt. 16:21; Luke 9:44

23 [a]Matt. 10:38

24 [1]Gr., *soul-life* [a]Matt. 10:39

25 [a]Heb. 10:34

26 [a]Matt. 10:33; Luke 12:9

27 [a]Matt. 16:28

28 [a]Luke 9:28-36: *Matt. 17:1-8; Mark 9:2-8* [b]Matt. 17:1 [c]Matt. 5:1 [d]Luke 3:21; 5:16; 6:12; 9:18

29 [1]Lit., *flashing like lightning* [a]Luke 3:21; 5:16; 6:12; 9:18 [b]Mark 16:12

31 [1]Or, *splendor* [a]2 Pet. 1:15

32 [a]Matt. 26:43; Mark 14:40

33 [1]Lit., *they* [2]Or, *sacred tents* [a]Luke 5:5; 9:49 [b]Matt. 17:4; Mark 9:5 [c]Mark 9:6

34 [1]Or, *occurred*

35 [a]2 Pet. 1:17f. [b]Matt. 3:17; Luke 3:22

36 [1]Lit., *occurred* [a]Matt. 17:9; Mark 9:9f.

37 [a]Luke 9:37-42: *Matt. 17:14-18; Mark 9:14-27*

38 [1]Or, *only begotten*

24 "For [a]whoever wishes to save
his [1]life shall lose it, but whoever
loses his [1]life for My sake, he is the
one who will save it.
25 "For what is a man profited if he
gains the whole world, and [a]loses or
forfeits himself?
26 "[a]For whoever is ashamed of Me
and My words, of him will the Son
of Man be ashamed when He comes
in His glory, and *the glory* of the Father and of the holy angels.
27 "But I tell you truly, [a]there are
some of those standing here who
shall not taste death until they see
the kingdom of God."

The Transfiguration

28 [a]And some eight days after
these sayings, it came about that He
took along [b]Peter and John and
James, and [c]went up to the mountain [d]to pray.
29 And while He was [a]praying, the
appearance of His face [b]became different, and His clothing *became*
white *and* [1]gleaming.
30 And behold, two men were
talking with Him; and they were
Moses and Elijah,
31 who, appearing in [1]glory, were
speaking of His [a]departure which
He was about to accomplish at Jerusalem.
32 Now Peter and his companions
[a]had been overcome with sleep; but
when they were fully awake, they
saw His glory and the two men
standing with Him.
33 And it came about, as [1]these
were parting from Him, Peter said
to Jesus, "[a]Master, it is good for us
to be here; and [b]let us make three
[2]tabernacles: one for You, and one
for Moses, and one for Elijah"—
[c]not realizing what he was saying.
34 And while he was saying this, a
cloud [1]formed and *began* to overshadow them; and they were afraid
as they entered the cloud.
35 And [a]a voice came out of the
cloud, saying, "[b]This is My Son, *My*
Chosen One; listen to Him!"
36 And when the voice [1]had spoken, Jesus was found alone. And
[a]they kept silent, and reported to no
one in those days any of the things
which they had seen.
37 [a]And it came about on the next
day, that when they had come down
from the mountain, a great multitude met Him.
38 And behold, a man from the
multitude shouted out, saying,
"Teacher, I beg You to look at my
son, for he is my [1]only *boy,*

39 and behold, a spirit seizes him,
and he suddenly screams, and it
throws him into a convulsion with
foaming *at the mouth,* and as it
mauls him, it scarcely leaves him.
40 "And I begged Your disciples to
cast it out, and they could not."
41 And Jesus answered and said,
"O unbelieving and perverted generation, how long shall I be with
you, and put up with you? Bring
your son here."
42 And while he was still approaching, the demon [1]dashed him
to the ground, and threw him into a
violent convulsion. But Jesus rebuked the unclean spirit, and healed
the boy, and gave him back to his
father.
43 And they were all amazed at
the [1a]greatness of God.
[b]But while everyone was marveling at all that He was doing, He said
to His disciples,
44 "Let these words sink into your
ears; [a]for the Son of Man is going to
be delivered into the hands of men."
45 But [a]they did not understand
this statement, and it was concealed
from them so that they might not
perceive it; and they were afraid to
ask Him about this statement.

The Test of Greatness

46 [a]And an argument arose among
them as to which of them might be
the greatest.
47 But Jesus, [a]knowing [1]what they
were thinking in their heart, took a
child and stood him by His side,
48 and said to them, "[a]Whoever
receives this child in My name receives Me; and whoever receives
Me receives Him who sent Me; [b]for
he who is least among you, this is
the one who is great."
49 [a]And John answered and said,
"[b]Master, we saw someone casting
out demons in Your name; and we
tried to hinder him because he does
not follow along with us."
50 But Jesus said to him, "Do not
hinder *him;* [a]for he who is not
against you is for you."
51 And it came about, when the
days were approaching for [a]His [1]as-
cension, that He resolutely set His
face [b]to go to Jerusalem;
52 and He sent messengers on
ahead of Him. And they went, and
entered a village of the [a]Samaritans,
to make arrangements for Him.
53 And they did not receive Him,
[a]because He was journeying with
His face toward Jerusalem.
54 And when His disciples [a]James
and John saw *this,* they said, "Lord,
do You want us to command fire to
come down from heaven and consume them[1]?"
55 But He turned and rebuked
them.[1]
56 And they went on to another
village.

Exacting Discipleship

57 And [a]as they were going along
the road, [b]someone said to Him, "I
will follow You wherever You go."
58 And Jesus said to him, "The
foxes have holes, and the birds of
the [1]air *have* [2]nests, but [a]the Son of
Man has nowhere to lay His head."
59 And He said to another, "[a]Fol-
low Me." But he said, "[1]Permit me
first to go and bury my father."
60 But He said to him, "Allow the
dead to bury their own dead; but as
for you, go and [a]proclaim everywhere the kingdom of God."
61 And another also said, "I will
follow You, Lord; but [a]first permit
me to say good-bye to those at
home."
62 But Jesus said to him, "[a]No one,
after putting his hand to the plow
and looking back, is fit for the kingdom of God."

CHAPTER 10

The Seventy Sent Out

NOW after this [a]the Lord appointed [1]seventy [b]others, and sent
them [c]two and two ahead of Him to
every city and place where He Himself was going to come.
2 And He was saying to them,
"[a]The harvest is plentiful, but the laborers are few; therefore beseech
the Lord of the harvest to send out
laborers into His harvest.
3 "Go your ways; [a]behold, I send
you out as lambs in the midst of
wolves.
4 "[a]Carry no purse, no [1]bag, no
shoes; and greet no one on the way.
5 "And whatever house you enter,
first say, 'Peace *be* to this house.'
6 "And if a [1]man of peace is there,
your peace will rest upon him; but if
not, it will return to you.
7 "And stay in [1]that house, eating
and drinking [2]what they give you;
for [a]the laborer is worthy of his
wages. Do not keep moving from
house to house.
8 "And whatever city you enter,
and they receive you, [a]eat what is
set before you;

42 [1]Or, *tore him*
43 [1]Or, *majesty* [a]2 Pet. 1:16 [b]Luke 9:43-45: *Matt. 17:22f.; Mark 9:30-32*
44 [a]Luke 9:22
45 [a]Mark 9:32
46 [a]Luke 9:46-48: *Matt. 18:1-5; Mark 9:33-37*
47 [1]Lit., *the reasoning or argument* [a]Matt. 9:4
48 [a]Matt. 10:40 [b]Luke 22:26
49 [a]Luke 9:49, 50: *Mark 9:38-40* [b]Luke 5:5; 9:33
50 [a]Matt. 12:30; Luke 11:23
51 [1]Lit., *taking up* [a]Mark 16:19 [b]Luke 13:22; 17:11; 18:31; 19:11, 28
52 [a]Matt. 10:5; Luke 10:33; 17:16; John 4:4
53 [a]John 4:9
54 [1]Some mss. add, *as Elijah did* [a]Mark 3:17
55 [1]Later mss. add, *and said, "You do not know what kind of spirit you are of.* 56 *"For the Son of Man did not come to destroy men's lives, but to save them."*
57 [a]Luke 9:51 [b]Luke 9:57-60: *Matt. 8:19-22*
58 [1]Or, *sky* [2]Gr., *roosting-places* [a]Matt. 8:20
59 [1]Some mss. add, *Lord* [a]Matt. 8:22
60 [a]Matt. 4:23
61 [a]1 Kin. 19:20
62 [a]Phil. 3:13
1 [1]Some mss. read, *seventy-two* [a]Luke 7:13 [b]Luke 9:1f., 52 [c]Mark 6:7
2 [a]Matt. 9:37, 38; John 4:35
3 [a]Matt. 10:16
4 [1]Gr., *knapsack,* or *beggar's bag* [a]Matt. 10:9-14; Mark 6:8-11; Luke 9:3-5; 10:4-12
6 [1]Lit., *son*
7 [1]Or, *the house itself* [2]Lit., *the things from them* [a]Matt. 10:10; 1 Cor. 9:14; 1 Tim. 5:18
8 [a]1 Cor. 10:27

9 and heal those in it who are sick, and say to them, '[a]The kingdom of God has come near to you.'

10 "But whatever city you enter and they do not receive you, go out into its streets and say,

11 '[a]Even the dust of your city which clings to our feet, we wipe off *in protest* against you; yet [1]be sure of this, that [b]the kingdom of God has come near.'

12 "I say to you, [a]it will be more tolerable in that day for [b]Sodom, than for that city.

13 "[a]Woe to you, [b]Chorazin! Woe to you, [b]Bethsaida! For if the [1]miracles had been performed in [b]Tyre and Sidon which occurred in you, they would have repented long ago, sitting in [c]sackcloth and ashes.

14 "But it will be more tolerable for [a]Tyre and Sidon in the judgment, than for you.

15 "And you, [a]Capernaum, will not be exalted to heaven, will you? You will be brought down to [b]Hades!

16 "[a]The one who listens to you listens to Me, and [b]the one who rejects you rejects Me; and he who rejects Me rejects the One who sent Me."

The Happy Results

17 And the [1]seventy returned with joy, saying, "Lord, even [a]the demons are subject to us in Your name."

18 And He said to them, "I was watching [a]Satan fall from heaven like lightning.

19 "Behold, I have given you authority to [a]tread upon serpents and scorpions, and over all the power of the enemy, and nothing shall injure you.

20 "Nevertheless do not rejoice in this, that the spirits are subject to you, but rejoice that [a]your names are recorded in heaven."

21 [a]At that very [1]time He rejoiced greatly in the Holy Spirit, and said, "I [2]praise Thee, O Father, Lord of heaven and earth, that Thou didst hide these things from *the* wise and intelligent and didst reveal them to babes. Yes, Father, for thus it was well-pleasing in Thy sight.

22 "All things have been handed over to Me by My Father, and no one knows who the Son is except the Father, and who the Father is except the Son, and anyone to whom the Son wills to reveal *Him.*"

23 [a]And turning to the disciples, He said privately, "Blessed *are* the eyes which see the things you see,

24 for I say to you, that many prophets and kings wished to see the things which you see, and did not see *them,* and to hear the things which you hear, and did not hear *them.*"

25 [a]And behold, a certain [1][b]lawyer stood up and put Him to the test, saying, "Teacher, what shall I do to inherit eternal life?"

26 And He said to him, "What is written in the Law? How [1]does it read to you?"

27 And he answered and said, "[a]YOU SHALL LOVE THE LORD YOUR GOD WITH ALL YOUR HEART, AND WITH ALL YOUR SOUL, AND WITH ALL YOUR STRENGTH, AND WITH ALL YOUR MIND; AND YOUR NEIGHBOR AS YOURSELF."

28 And He said to him, "You have answered correctly; [a]DO THIS, AND YOU WILL LIVE."

29 But wishing [a]to justify himself, he said to Jesus, "And who is my neighbor?"

The Good Samaritan

30 Jesus replied and said, "A certain man was [a]going down from Jerusalem to Jericho; and he fell among robbers, and they stripped him and [1]beat him, and went off leaving him half dead.

31 "And by chance a certain priest was going down on that road, and when he saw him, he passed by on the other side.

32 "And likewise a Levite also, when he came to the place and saw him, passed by on the other side.

33 "But a certain [a]Samaritan, who was on a journey, came upon him; and when he saw him, he felt compassion,

34 and came to him, and bandaged up his wounds, pouring oil and wine on *them;* and he put him on his own beast, and brought him to an inn, and took care of him.

35 "And on the next day he took out two [1]denarii and gave them to the innkeeper and said, 'Take care of him; and whatever more you spend, when I return, I will repay you.'

36 "Which of these three do you think proved to be a neighbor to the man who fell into the robbers' *hands?*"

37 And he said, "The one who showed mercy toward him." And Jesus said to him, "Go and do [1]the same."

Martha and Mary

38 Now as they were traveling along, He entered a certain village; and a [1]woman named [a]Martha welcomed Him into her home.

9 [a]Matt. 3:2; 10:7; Luke 10:11

11 [1]Lit., *know* [a]Matt. 10:14; Mark 6:11; Luke 9:5 [b]Matt. 3:2; 10:7; Luke 10:9

12 [a]Matt. 10:15; 11:24 [b]Matt. 10:15

13 [1]Or, *works of power* [a]Luke 10:13-15: *Matt. 11:21-23* [b]Matt. 11:21 [c]Rev. 11:3

14 [a]Matt. 11:21

15 [a]Matt. 4:13 [b]Matt. 11:23

16 [a]Matt. 10:40; John 13:20; Gal. 4:14 [b]John 12:48; 1 Thess. 4:8

17 [1]Some mss. read, *seventy-two* [a]Mark 16:17

18 [a]Matt. 4:10

19 [a]Mark 16:18

20 [a]Ex. 32:32; Ps. 69:28; Is. 4:3; Ezek. 13:9; Dan. 12:1; Phil. 4:3; Heb. 12:23; Rev. 3:5; 13:8; 17:8; 20:12, 15; 21:27

21 [1]Lit., *hour* [2]Or, *acknowledge to Thy praise* [a]Luke 10:21, 22: *Matt. 11:25-27*

23 [a]Luke 10:23, 24: *Matt. 13:16, 17*

25 [1]I.e., an expert in the Mosaic law [a]Luke 10:25-28: *Matt. 22:34-40; Mark 12:28-31;* Matt. 19:16-19 [b]Matt. 22:35

26 [1]Lit., *do you read*

27 [a]Lev. 19:18; Deut. 6:5

28 [a]Lev. 18:5; Matt. 19:17

29 [a]Luke 16:15

30 [1]Lit., *laid blows upon* [a]Luke 18:31; 19:28

33 [a]Matt. 10:5; Luke 9:52

35 [1]The denarius was worth 18 cents in silver, equivalent to a day's wage

37 [1]Or, *likewise*

38 [1]Lit., *certain woman* [a]Luke 10:40f.; John 11:1, 5, 19ff., 30, 39; 12:2

39 And she had a sister called [a]Mary, who moreover was listening to the Lord's word, [b]seated at His feet.

40 But [a]Martha was distracted with all her preparations; and she came up *to Him*, and said, "Lord, do You not care that my sister has left me to do all the serving alone? Then tell her to help me."

41 But the Lord answered and said to her, "[a]Martha, Martha, you are [b]worried and bothered about so many things;

42 [1a]but *only* a few things are necessary, really *only* one, for [b]Mary has chosen the good part, which shall not be taken away from her."

CHAPTER 11

Instruction About Prayer

AND it came about that while He was praying in a certain place, after He had finished, one of His disciples said to Him, "[a]Lord, teach us to pray just as John also taught his disciples."

2 And He said to them, "[a]When you pray, say:

'[1]Father, hallowed be Thy name.
Thy kingdom come.
3 'Give us [a]each day our daily bread.
4 'And forgive us our sins,
For we ourselves also forgive everyone who [a]is indebted to us.
And lead us not into temptation.' "

5 And He said to them, "[1]Suppose one of you shall have a friend, and shall go to him at midnight, and say to him, 'Friend, lend me three loaves;

6 for a friend of mine has come to me from a journey, and I have nothing to set before him';

7 and from inside he shall answer and say, 'Do not bother me; the door has already been shut and my children and I are in bed; I cannot get up and give you *anything*.'

8 "I tell you, even though he will not get up and give him *anything* because he is his friend, yet [a]because of his [1]persistence he will get up and give him as much as he needs.

9 "And I say to you, [1a]ask, and it shall be given to you; [2]seek, and you shall find; [3]knock, and it shall be opened to you.

10 "For everyone who asks, receives; and he who seeks, finds; and to him who knocks, it shall be opened.

11 "Now [1]suppose one of you fathers is asked by his son for a [2]fish; he will not give him a snake instead of a fish, will he?

12 "Or *if* he is asked for an egg, he will not give him a scorpion, will he?

13 "[a]If you then, being evil, know how to give good gifts to your children, how much more shall *your* [1]heavenly Father give the [b]Holy Spirit to those who ask Him?"

Pharisees' Blasphemy

14 [a]And He was casting out a demon, *and it was* dumb; and it came about that when the demon had gone out, the dumb man spoke; and the multitudes marveled.

15 But some of them said, "He casts out demons [a]by [1b]Beelzebul, the ruler of the demons."

16 And others, [1]to test *Him*, [a]were demanding of Him a sign from heaven.

17 [a]But He knew their thoughts, and said to them, "[1]Any kingdom divided against itself is laid waste; and [2]a house divided against itself falls.

18 "And if [a]Satan also is divided against himself, how shall his kingdom stand? For you say that I cast out demons by [b]Beelzebul.

19 "And if I by [a]Beelzebul cast out demons, by whom do your sons cast them out? Consequently they shall be your judges.

20 "But if I cast out demons by the [a]finger of God, then [b]the kingdom of God has come upon you.

21 "When a strong *man* fully armed guards his own [a]homestead, his possessions are undisturbed;

22 but when someone stronger than he attacks him and overpowers him, he takes away from him all his armor on which he had relied, and distributes his plunder.

23 "[a]He who is not with Me is against Me; and he who does not gather with Me, scatters.

24 "[a]When the unclean spirit goes out of a man, it passes through waterless places seeking rest, and not finding any, it says, 'I will return to my house from which I came.'

25 "And when it comes, it finds it swept and put in order.

26 "Then it goes and takes *along* seven other spirits more evil than itself, and they go in and live there; and the last state of that man becomes worse than the first."

39 [a]Luke 10:42; John 11:1f., 19f., 28, 31f., 45; 12:3 [b]Luke 8:35; Acts 22:3
40 [a]Luke 10:38, 41; John 11:1, 5, 19ff., 30, 39; 12:2
41 [a]Luke 10:38, 40; John 11:1, 5, 19ff., 30, 39; 12:2 [b]Matt. 6:25
42 [1]Some mss. read, *but one thing is necessary* [a]Ps. 27:4; John 6:27 [b]Luke 10:39; John 11:1f., 19f., 28, 31f., 45; 12:3
1 [a]Luke 7:13
2 [1]Some mss. insert phrases from Matt. 6:9-13 to make the two passages closely similar [a]Luke 11:2-4: *Matt. 6:9-13*
3 [a]Acts 17:11
4 [a]Luke 13:4 marg.
5 [1]Lit., *Which one of you*
8 [1]Or, *shamelessness* [a]Luke 18:1-6
9 [1]Or, *keep asking* [2]Or, *keep seeking* [3]Or, *keep knocking* [a]Luke 11:9 13: *Matt. 7:7-11*
11 [1]Lit., *which of you shall a son ask the father* [2]Some early mss. insert: *loaf, he will not give him a stone, will he, or for a*
13 [1]Lit., *Father from heaven* [a]Luke 18:7f. [b]Matt. 7:11
14 [a]Luke 11:14, 15: *Matt. 12:22, 24;* Matt. 9:32-34
15 [1]Here and in verses 18 and 19 some mss. read, *Beezebul* [a]Matt. 9:34 [b]Matt. 10:25
16 [1]Lit., *were testing* [a]Matt. 12:38
17 [1]Lit., *every* [2]Lit., *a house against a house falls* [a]Luke 11:17-22: *Matt. 12:25-29; Mark 3:23-27*
18 [a]Matt. 4:10 [b]Matt. 10:25
19 [a]Matt. 10:25
20 [a]Ex. 8:19 [b]Matt. 3:2
21 [a]Matt. 26:3
23 [a]Matt. 12:30
24 [a]Luke 11:24-26: *Matt. 12:43-45*

27 And it came about while He said these things, one of the women in the crowd raised her voice, and said to Him, "[a]Blessed is the womb that bore You, and the breasts at which You nursed."

28 But He said, "On the contrary, blessed are [a]those who hear the word of God, and observe it."

The Sign of Jonah

29 And as the crowds were increasing, He began to say, "[a]This generation is a wicked generation; it [b]seeks for a [1]sign, and *yet* no [1]sign shall be given to it but the [1]sign of Jonah.

30 "For just as Jonah became a [1]sign to the Ninevites, so shall the Son of Man be to this generation.

31 "The Queen of the South shall rise up with the men of this generation at the judgment and condemn them, because she came from the ends of the earth to hear the wisdom of Solomon; and behold, something greater than Solomon is here.

32 "The men of Nineveh shall stand up with this generation at the judgment and condemn it, because they repented at the preaching of Jonah; and behold, something greater than Jonah is here.

33 "No [a]one, after lighting a lamp, puts it away in a cellar, nor under a peck-measure, but on the lampstand, in order that those who enter may see the light.

34 "[a]The lamp of your body is your eye; when your eye is [1]clear, your whole body also is full of light; but when it is bad, your body also is full of darkness.

35 "Then watch out that the light in you may not be darkness.

36 "If therefore your whole body is full of light, with no dark part in it, it shall be wholly illumined, as when the lamp illumines you with its rays."

Woes upon the Pharisees

37 Now when He had spoken, a Pharisee *asked Him to have lunch with him; and He went in, and reclined *at table.*

38 And when the Pharisee saw it, he was surprised that He had not first [1a]ceremonially washed before the [2]meal.

39 But [a]the Lord said to him, "Now [b]you Pharisees clean the outside of the cup and of the platter; but [1]inside of you, you are full of robbery and wickedness.

40 "[a]You foolish ones, did not He who made the outside make the inside also?

41 "But [a]give that which is within as charity, and [1]then all things are [b]clean for you.

42 "[a]But woe to you Pharisees! For you [b]pay tithe of mint and rue and every *kind of* garden herb, and *yet* disregard justice and the love of God; but these are the things you should have done without neglecting the others.

43 "Woe to you Pharisees! For you [a]love the front seats in the synagogues, and the respectful greetings in the market places.

44 "[a]Woe to you! For you are like [1]concealed tombs, and the people who walk over *them* are unaware *of it.*"

45 And one of the [1a]lawyers *said to Him in reply, "Teacher, when You say this, You insult us too."

46 But He said, "Woe to you [a]lawyers as well! For [b]you weigh men down with burdens hard to bear, [1]while you yourselves will not even touch the burdens with one of your fingers.

47 "[a]Woe to you! For you build the [1]tombs of the prophets, and *it was* your fathers *who* killed them.

48 "Consequently, you are witnesses and approve the deeds of your fathers; because it was they who killed them, and you build *their tombs.*

49 "For this reason also [a]the wisdom of God said, '[b]I will send to them prophets and apostles, and *some* of them they will kill and *some* they will [1]persecute,

50 in order that the blood of all the prophets, shed [a]since the foundation of the world, may be [1]charged against this generation,

51 from the blood of Abel to the blood of Zechariah, who perished between the altar and the house *of God;* yes, I tell you, it shall be [1]charged against this generation.'

52 "Woe to you [1a]lawyers! For you have taken away the key of knowledge; [b]you did not enter in yourselves, and those who were entering in you hindered."

53 And when He left there, the scribes and the Pharisees began to be very hostile and to question Him closely on many subjects,

54 [a]plotting against Him, [b]to catch [1]*Him* in something He might say.

27 [a]Luke 23:29
28 [a]Luke 8:21
29 [1]Or, *attesting miracle* [a]Luke 11:29-32: *Matt. 12:39-42* [b]Matt. 12:38; Luke 11:16
30 [1]Or, *attesting miracle*
33 [a]Matt. 5:15; Mark 4:21; Luke 8:16
34 [1]Or, *healthy* [a]Luke 11:34, 35: *Matt. 6:22, 23*
38 [1]Gr., *baptized* [2]Or, *lunch* [a]Matt. 15:2; Mark 7:3f.
39 [1]Lit., *your inside is full* [a]Luke 7:13 [b]Matt. 23:25f.
40 [a]Luke 12:20; 1 Cor. 15:36
41 [1]Lit., *behold* [a]Luke 12:33; 16:9 [b]Mark 7:19; Titus 1:15
42 [a]Matt. 23:23 [b]Luke 18:12
43 [a]Matt. 23:6f.; Mark 12:38f.; Luke 14:7; 20:46
44 [1]Or, *indistinct, unseen* [a]Matt. 23:27
45 [1]I.e., experts in the Mosaic law [a]Matt. 22:35; Luke 11:46, 52
46 [1]Lit., *and* [a]Matt. 22:35; Luke 11:45, 52 [b]Matt. 23:4
47 [1]Or, *monuments to* [a]Matt. 23:29ff.
49 [1]Or, *drive out* [a]1 Cor. 1:24, 30; Col. 2:3 [b]Matt. 23:34-36; Luke 11:49-51
50 [1]Or, *required of* [a]Matt. 25:34
51 [1]Or, *required of*
52 [1]I.e., experts in the Mosaic law [a]Matt. 22:35; Luke 11:45, 46 [b]Matt. 23:13
54 [1]Lit., *something out of His mouth* [a]Mark 3:2; Luke 20:20; Acts 23:21 [b]Mark 12:13

Chapter 12

God Knows and Cares

UNDER these circumstances, after [1]so many thousands of the multitude had gathered together that they were stepping on one another, He began saying to His disciples first *of all,* "[a]Beware of the leaven of the Pharisees, which is hypocrisy.

2 "[a]But there is nothing covered up that will not be revealed, and hidden that will not be known.

3 "Accordingly whatever you have said in the dark shall be heard in the light, and what you have [1]whispered in the inner rooms shall be proclaimed upon [a]the housetops.

4 "And I say to you, [a]My friends, do not be afraid of those who kill the body, and after that have no more that they can do.

5 "But I will [1]warn you whom to fear: [a]fear the One who after He has killed has authority to cast into [2b]hell; yes, I tell you, fear Him!

6 "Are not [a]five sparrows sold for two [1]cents? And *yet* not one of them is forgotten before God.

7 "[a]Indeed the very hairs of your head are all numbered. Do not fear; you are of more value than many sparrows.

8 "And I say to you, everyone who confesses Me before men, the Son of Man shall confess him also [a]before the angels of God;

9 but [a]he who denies Me before men shall be denied [b]before the angels of God.

10 "[a]And everyone who will speak a word against the Son of Man, it shall be forgiven him; but he who blasphemes against the Holy Spirit, it shall not be forgiven him.

11 "And when they bring you before [a]the synagogues and the rulers and the authorities, do not become [b]anxious about how or what you should speak in your defense, or what you should say;

12 for [a]the Holy Spirit will teach you in that very hour what you ought to say."

Covetousness Denounced

13 And someone [1]in the crowd said to Him, "Teacher, tell my brother to divide the *family* inheritance with me."

14 But He said to him, "[a]Man, who appointed Me a judge or arbiter over you?"

15 And He said to them, "[a]Beware, and be on your guard against every form of greed; for not *even* when one has an abundance does his life consist of his possessions."

16 And He told them a parable, saying, "The land of a certain rich man was very productive.

17 "And he began reasoning to himself, saying, 'What shall I do, since I have no place to store my crops?'

18 "And he said, 'This is what I will do: I will tear down my barns and build larger ones, and there I will store all my grain and my goods.

19 'And I will say to my soul, "Soul, [a]you have many goods laid up for many years *to come;* take your ease, eat, drink *and* be merry." '

20 "But God said to him, '[a]You fool! This *very* night [1b]your soul is required of you; and [c]*now* who will own what you have prepared?'

21 "So is the man who [a]lays up treasure for himself, and is not rich toward God."

22 And He said to His disciples, "[a]For this reason I say to you, do not be anxious for *your* [1]life, *as to* what you shall eat; nor for your body, *as to* what you shall put on.

23 "For life is more than food, and the body than clothing.

24 "Consider the [a]ravens, for they neither sow nor reap; and they have no storeroom nor [b]barn; and *yet* God feeds them; how much more valuable you are than the birds!

25 "And which of you by being anxious can add a *single* [1a]cubit to his [2]life's span?

26 "If then you cannot do even a very little thing, why are you anxious about other matters?

27 "Consider the lilies, how [1]they grow; they neither toil nor spin; but I tell you, even [a]Solomon in all his glory did not clothe himself like one of these.

28 "But if God so *arrays* the grass in the field, which is *alive* today and tomorrow is thrown into the furnace, how much more *will He clothe* you, [a]O men of little faith!

29 "And do not seek what you shall eat, and what you shall drink, and do not [a]keep worrying.

30 "For [1]all these things the nations of the world eagerly seek; but your Father knows that you need these things.

31 "But seek for His kingdom, and [a]these things shall be added to you.

32 "[a]Do not be afraid, [b]little flock, for [c]your Father has chosen gladly to give you the kingdom.

33 "[a]Sell your possessions and give to charity; make yourselves purses which do not wear out, [b]an unfailing

1 [1]Gr., *myriads* [a]Matt. 16:6, 11ff.; Mark 8:15
2 [a]Luke 12:2-9: *Matt. 10:26-33;* Matt. 10:26; Mark 4:22; Luke 8:17
3 [1]Lit., *spoken in the ear* [a]Matt. 10:27; 24:17
4 [a]John 15:13-15
5 [1]Or, *show* [2]Gr., *Gehenna* [a]Heb. 10:31 [b]Matt. 5:22
6 [1]Gr., *assaria,* the smallest of copper coins [a]Matt. 10:29
7 [a]Matt. 10:30
8 [a]Matt. 10:32; Luke 15:10; Rom. 10:9
9 [a]Matt. 10:33; Luke 9:26 [b]Matt. 10:32; Luke 15:10; Rom. 10:9
10 [a]Matt. 12:31, 32; Mark 3:28-30
11 [a]Matt. 10:17 [b]Matt. 6:25; 10:19; Mark 13:11; Luke 12:22; 21:14
12 [a]Matt. 10:20; Luke 21:15
13 [1]Lit., *out of*
14 [a]Mic. 6:8; Rom. 2:1, 3; 9:20
15 [a]1 Tim. 6:6-10
19 [a]Eccles. 11:9
20 [1]Lit., *they are demanding your soul from you* [a]Jer. 17:11; Luke 11:40 [b]Job 27:8 [c]Ps. 39:6
21 [a]Luke 12:33
22 [1]Gr., *soul-life* [a]Luke 12:22-31: *Matt. 6:25-33*
24 [a]Job 38:41 [b]Luke 12:18
25 [1]I.e., 18 inches [2]Or, *height* [a]Ps. 39:5
27 [1]Some mss. omit, *they grow* [a]1 Kin. 10:4-7
28 [a]Matt. 6:30
29 [a]Matt. 6:31
30 [1]Or, *these things all the nations of the world*
31 [a]Matt. 6:33
32 [a]Matt. 14:27 [b]John 21:15-17 [c]Eph. 1:5, 9
33 [a]Matt. 19:21; Luke 11:41; 18:22 [b]Matt. 6:20; Luke 12:21

treasure in heaven, where no thief
comes near, nor moth destroys.
34"For [a]where your treasure is,
there will your heart be also.

Be in Readiness

35"[1a]Be dressed in [b]readiness, and
keep your lamps alight.
36"And be like men who are waiting for their master when he returns
from the wedding feast, so that they
may immediately open *the door* to
him when he comes and knocks.
37"Blessed are those slaves whom
the master shall find [a]on the alert
when he comes; truly I say to you,
that [b]he will gird himself *to serve,*
and have them recline *at table,* and
will come up and wait on them.
38"Whether he comes in the [1a]sec-
ond watch, or even in the [2a]third,
and finds *them* so, blessed are those
slaves.
39"[a]And [1]be sure of this, that if the
head of the house had known at
what hour the thief was coming, he
would not have allowed his house to
be [2b]broken into.
40"[a]You too, be ready; for the Son
of Man is coming at an hour that you
do not [1]expect."
41 And Peter said, "Lord, are You
addressing this parable to us, or [a]to
everyone *else* as well?"
42 And [a]the Lord said, "[b]Who then
is the faithful and sensible [c]steward,
whom his master will put in charge
of his [1]servants, to give them their
rations at the proper time?
43"Blessed is that [a]slave whom his
[1]master finds so doing when he
comes.
44"Truly I say to you, that he will
put him in charge of all his possessions.
45"But if that slave says in his
heart, 'My master [1]will be a long
time in coming,' and begins to beat
the slaves, *both* men and women,
and to eat and drink and get drunk;
46 the master of that slave will
come on a day when he does not
expect *him,* and at an hour he does
not know, and will cut him in pieces,
and assign him a place with the unbelievers.
47"And that slave who knew his
master's will and did not get ready
or act in accord with his will, shall
[a]receive many lashes,
48 but the one who did not [a]know
it, and committed deeds worthy of
[1]a flogging, will receive but few.
[b]And from everyone who has been
given much shall much be required;
and to whom they entrusted much,
of him they will ask all the more.

Christ Divides Men

49"I [1]have come to cast fire upon
the earth; and [2]how I wish it were
already kindled!
50"But I have a [a]baptism to [1]un-
dergo, and how distressed I am until
it is accomplished!
51"[a]Do you suppose that I came to
grant peace on earth? I tell you, no,
but rather division;
52 for from now on five *members*
in one household will be divided,
three against two, and two against
three.
53"They will be divided, [a]father
against son, and son against father;
mother against daughter, and
daughter against mother; mother-
in-law against daughter-in-law, and
daughter-in-law against mother-in-
law."
54 And He was also saying to the
multitudes, "[a]When you see a cloud
rising in the west, immediately you
say, 'A shower is coming,' and so it
turns out.
55"And when *you see* a south wind
blowing, you say, 'It will be a [a]hot
day,' and it turns out *that way.*
56"You hypocrites! [a]You know
how to analyze the appearance of
the earth and the sky, but [1]why do
you not analyze this present time?
57"And [a]why do you not even on
your own initiative judge what is
right?
58"For [a]while you are going with
your opponent to appear before the
magistrate, on *your* way *there* make
an effort to [1]settle with him, in order
that he may not drag you before the
judge, and the judge turn you over
to the constable, and the constable
throw you into prison.
59"I say to you, you shall not get
out of there until you have paid the
very last [1a]cent."

Chapter 13

Call to Repent

Now on the same occasion there
were some present who reported to
Him about the Galileans, whose
blood [a]Pilate had [1]mingled with
their sacrifices.
2 And He answered and said to
them, "[a]Do you suppose that these
Galileans were *greater* sinners than
all *other* Galileans, because they
suffered this *fate?*
3"I tell you, no, but, unless you
[1]repent, you will all likewise perish.
4"Or do you suppose that those
eighteen on whom the tower in [a]Si-
loam fell and killed them, were

34 [a]Matt. 6:21
35 [1]Lit., *Let your loins be girded* [a]Matt. 25:1ff.; Luke 12:35, 36 [b]Eph. 6:14; 1 Pet. 1:13
37 [a]Matt. 24:42 [b]Luke 17:8; John 13:4
38 [1]I.e., 9 p.m. to midnight [2]I.e., midnight to 3 a.m. [a]Matt. 24:43
39 [1]Lit., *know* [2]Lit., *dug through* [a]Luke 12:39, 40: *Matt. 24:43, 44* [b]Matt. 6:19
40 [1]Lit., *think, suppose* [a]Mark 13:33; Luke 21:36
41 [a]Luke 12:47, 48
42 [1]Lit., *service* [a]Luke 7:13 [b]Luke 12:42-46: *Matt. 24:45-51* [c]Matt. 24:45; Luke 16:1ff.
43 [1]Or, *lord* [a]Luke 12:42
45 [1]Lit., *is delaying to come*
47 [a]Deut. 25:2
48 [1]Lit., *blows* [a]Lev. 5:17; Num. 15:29f. [b]Matt. 13:12
49 [1]Or, *came* [2]Lit., *what do I wish if . . . ?*
50 [1]Lit., *be baptized with* [a]Mark 10:38
51 [a]Luke 12:51-53: *Matt. 10:34-36*
53 [a]Mic. 7:6; Matt. 10:21
54 [a]Matt. 16:2f.
55 [a]Matt. 20:12
56 [1]Lit., *how* [a]Matt. 16:3
57 [a]Luke 21:30
58 [1]Lit., *be released from him* [a]Luke 12:58, 59: *Matt. 5:25, 26*
59 [1]Lit., *lepton,* i.e., 1/128 of a denarius [a]Mark 12:42
1 [1]Or, *shed along with* [a]Matt. 27
2 [a]John 9:2f.
3 [1]Or, *are repentant*
4 [a]Is. 8:6 [Neh. 3:15]; John 9:7, 11

worse [1b]culprits than all the men who live in Jerusalem?

5"I tell you, no, but, unless you repent, you will all likewise perish."

6 And He *began* telling this parable: "A certain man had [a]a fig tree which had been planted in his vineyard; and he came looking for fruit on it, and did not find any.

7"And he said to the vineyard-keeper, 'Behold, for three years I have come looking for fruit on this fig tree [1]without finding any. [a]Cut it down! Why does it even use up the ground?'

8"And he answered and said to him, 'Let it alone, sir, for this year too, until I dig around it and put in fertilizer;

9 and if it bears fruit next year, *fine;* but if not, cut it down.' "

Healing on the Sabbath

10 And He was [a]teaching in one of the synagogues on the Sabbath.

11 And behold, there was a woman who for eighteen years had had [a]a sickness caused by a spirit; and she was bent double, and could not straighten up at all.

12 And when Jesus saw her, He called her over and said to her, "Woman, you are freed from your sickness."

13 And He [a]laid His hands upon her; and immediately she was made erect again, and *began* [b]glorifying God.

14 And [a]the synagogue official, indignant because Jesus [b]had healed on the Sabbath, *began* saying to the multitude in response, "[c]There are six days in which work should be done; therefore come during them and get healed, and not on the Sabbath day."

15 But [a]the Lord answered him and said, "You hypocrites, [b]does not each of you on the Sabbath untie his ox or his donkey from the stall, and lead him away to water *him?*

16"And this woman, [a]a daughter of Abraham as she is, whom [b]Satan has bound for eighteen long years, should she not have been released from this bond on the Sabbath day?"

17 And as He said this, all His opponents were being humiliated; and [a]the entire multitude was rejoicing over all the glorious things being done by Him.

Parables of Mustard Seed and Leaven

18 Therefore [a]He was saying, "[b]What is the kingdom of God like, and to what shall I compare it?

19"It is like a mustard seed, which a man took and threw into his own garden; and it grew and became a tree; and the birds of the [1]air nested in its branches."

20 And again He said, "[a]To what shall I compare the kingdom of God?

21"[a]It is like leaven, which a woman took and hid in [b]three [1]pecks of meal, until it was all leavened."

Teaching in the Villages

22 And He was passing through from one city and village to another, teaching, and [a]proceeding on His way to Jerusalem.

23 And someone said to Him, "Lord, are there *just* a few who are being saved?" And He said to them,

24"[a]Strive to enter by the narrow door; for many, I tell you, will seek to enter and will not be able.[1]

25"Once the head of the house gets up and [a]shuts the door, and you [b]begin to stand outside and knock on the door, saying, '[c]Lord, open up to us!' [1]then He will answer and say to you, '[d]I do not know where you are from.'

26"Then you will [a]begin to say, 'We ate and drank in Your presence, and You taught in our streets';

27 and He will say, 'I tell you, [a]I do not know where you are from; [b]DEPART FROM ME, ALL YOU EVILDOERS.'

28"[a]There will be weeping and gnashing of teeth there when you see Abraham and Isaac and Jacob and all the prophets in the kingdom of God, but yourselves being cast out.

29"And they [a]will come from east and west, and from north and south, and will recline *at table* in the kingdom of God.

30"And behold, [a]*some* are last who will be first and *some* are first who will be last."

31 Just at that time some Pharisees came up, saying to Him, "Go away and depart from here, for [a]Herod wants to kill You."

32 And He said to them, "Go and tell that fox, 'Behold, I cast out demons and perform cures today and tomorrow, and the third *day* I [1a]reach My goal.'

33"Nevertheless [a]I must journey on today and tomorrow and the next *day;* for it cannot be that a [b]prophet should perish outside of Jerusalem.

34"[a]O Jerusalem, Jerusalem, *the city* that kills the prophets and stones those sent to her! How often I wanted to gather your children to-

4 [1]Lit., *debtors* [b]Matt. 6:12; Luke 11:4
6 [a]Matt. 21:19
7 [1]Lit., *and I do not find* [a]Matt. 3:10; 7:19; Luke 3:9
10 [a]Matt. 4:23
11 [a]Luke 13:16
13 [a]Mark 5:23 [b]Matt. 9:8
14 [a]Mark 5:22 [b]Matt. 12:2; Luke 14:3 [c]Ex. 20:9; Deut. 5:13
15 [a]Luke 7:13 [b]Luke 14:5
16 [a]Luke 19:9 [b]Matt. 4:10; Luke 13:11
17 [a]Luke 18:43
18 [a]Luke 13:18, 19: *Matt. 13:31, 32; Mark 4:30-32* [b]Matt. 13:24; Luke 13:20
19 [1]Or, *sky*
20 [a]Matt. 13:24; Luke 13:18
21 [1]Gr., *sata* [a]Luke 13:20, 21: *Matt. 13:33* [b]Matt. 13:33
22 [a]Luke 9:51
24 [1]Or, *able, once* [a]Matt. 7:13
25 [1]Lit., *and* [a]Matt. 25:10 [b]Luke 3:8 [c]Matt. 7:22; 25:11 [d]Matt. 7:23; 25:12; Luke 13:27
26 [a]Luke 3:8
27 [a]Luke 13:25 [b]Ps. 6:8; Matt. 25:41
28 [a]Matt. 8:12
29 [a]Matt. 8:11
30 [a]Matt. 19:30
31 [a]Matt. 14:1; Luke 3:1; 9:7; 23:7
32 [1]Or possibly, *am perfected* [a]Heb. 2:10; 5:9; 7:28
33 [a]John 11:9 [b]Matt. 21:11
34 [a]Luke 13:34, 35: *Matt. 23:37-39;* Luke 19:41

gether, [b]just as a hen *gathers* her brood under her wings, and you would not *have it!*

35 "Behold, your house is left to you [1]*desolate;* and I say to you, you shall not see Me until *the time* comes when you say, '[a]BLESSED *is* HE WHO COMES IN THE NAME OF THE LORD!' "

CHAPTER 14

Jesus Heals on the Sabbath

AND it came about when He went into the house of one of the [1]leaders of the Pharisees on *the* Sabbath to eat bread, that [a]they were watching Him closely.

2 And [1]there, in front of Him was a certain man suffering from dropsy.

3 And Jesus [a]answered and spoke to the [1b]lawyers and Pharisees, saying, "[c]Is it lawful to heal on the Sabbath, or not?"

4 But they kept silent. And He took hold of him, and healed him, and sent him away.

5 And He said to them, "[a]Which one of you shall have a [1]son or an ox fall into a well, and will not immediately pull him out on a Sabbath day?"

6 [a]And they could make no reply to this.

Parable of the Guests

7 And He *began* speaking a parable to the invited guests when He noticed how [a]they had been picking out the places of honor *at the table;* saying to them,

8 "When you are invited by someone to a wedding feast, [a]do not [1]take the place of honor, lest someone more distinguished than you may have been invited by him,

9 and he who invited you both shall come and say to you, 'Give place to this man', and then [a]in disgrace you [1]proceed to occupy the last place.

10 "But when you are invited, go and recline at the last place, so that when the one who has invited you comes, he may say to you, 'Friend, [a]move up higher'; then you will have honor in the sight of all who [1]are at the table with you.

11 "[a]For everyone who exalts himself shall be humbled, and he who humbles himself shall be exalted."

12 And He also went on to say to the one who had invited Him, "When you give a luncheon or a dinner, do not invite your friends or your brothers or your relatives or rich neighbors, lest they also invite you in return, and repayment come to you.

13 "But when you give a [1]reception, invite *the* poor, *the* crippled, *the* lame, *the* blind,

14 and you will be [1]blessed, since they [2]do not have *the means* to repay you; for you will be repaid at [a]the resurrection of the righteous."

15 And when one of those who were reclining *at table* with Him heard this, he said to Him, "[a]Blessed is everyone who shall eat bread in the kingdom of God!"

Parable of the Dinner

16 But He said to him, "[a]A certain man was giving a big dinner, and he invited many;

17 and at the dinner hour he sent his slave to say to those who had been invited, 'Come; for everything is ready now.'

18 "But they all alike began to make excuses. The first one said to him, 'I have bought a [1]piece of land and I need to go out and look at it; [2]please consider me excused.'

19 "And another one said, 'I have bought five yoke of oxen, and I am going to try them out; [1]please consider me excused.'

20 "And another one said, '[a]I have married a wife, and for that reason I cannot come.'

21 "And the slave came *back* and reported this to his master. Then the head of the household became angry and said to his slave, 'Go out at once into the streets and lanes of the city and bring in here the poor and crippled and blind and lame.'

22 "And the slave said, 'Master, what you commanded has been done, and still there is room.'

23 "And the master said to the slave, 'Go out into the highways and along the hedges, and compel *them* to come in, that my house may be filled.

24 'For I tell you, none of those men who were invited shall taste of my dinner.' "

Discipleship Tested

25 Now great multitudes were going along with Him; and He turned and said to them,

26 "[a]If anyone comes to Me, and does not [1]hate his own father and mother and wife and children and brothers and sisters, yes, and even his own life, he cannot be My disciple.

---

34 [b]Matt. 23:37

35 [1]Later mss. add, *desolate* [a]Ps. 118:26; Matt. 21:9; Luke 19:38

1 [1]I.e., members of the Sanhedrin [a]Mark 3:2

2 [1]Lit., *behold*

3 [1]I.e., experts in Mosaic Law [a]Acts 3:12 [b]Matt. 22:35 [c]Matt. 12:2; Luke 13:14

5 [1]Some ancient mss. read, *donkey* [a]Luke 13:15

6 [a]Matt. 22:46; Luke 20:40

7 [a]Matt. 23:6

8 [1]Lit., *recline at* [a]Prov. 25:6, 7

9 [1]Lit., *begin* [a]Luke 3:8

10 [1]Lit., *recline at table* [a]Prov. 25:6, 7

11 [a]Matt. 23:12; Luke 18:14

13 [1]Or, *banquet*

14 [1]Or, *happy* [2]Or, *are unable to* [a]John 5:29; Acts 24:15; Rev. 20:4, 5 [?]

15 [a]Rev. 19:9

16 [a]Matt. 22:2-14; Luke 14:16-24

18 [1]Or, *field* [2]Lit., *I request you*

19 [1]Lit., *I request you*

20 [a]Deut. 24:5; 1 Cor. 7:33

26 [1]I.e., by comparison of his love for Me [a]Matt. 10:37f.

27"Whoever does not [a]carry his
own cross and come after Me cannot be My disciple.
28"For which one of you, when he
wants to build a tower, does not first
sit down and calculate the cost, to
see if he has enough to complete it?
29"Otherwise, when he has laid a
foundation, and is not able to finish,
all who observe it begin to ridicule
him,
30 saying, 'This man began to
build and was not able to finish.'
31"Or what king, when he sets out
to meet another king in battle, will
not first sit down and take counsel
whether he is strong enough with
ten thousand *men* to encounter the
one coming against him with twenty
thousand?
32"Or else, while the other is still
far away, he sends [1]a delegation and
asks terms of peace.
33"So therefore, no one of you can
be My disciple who [a]does not give
up all his own possessions.
34"Therefore, salt is good; but [a]if
even salt has become tasteless, with
what will it be seasoned?
35"It is useless either for the soil or
for the manure pile; [1]it is thrown
out. [a]He who has ears to hear, let
him hear."

CHAPTER 15

The Lost Sheep

NOW all the [1a]tax-gatherers and
the [2]sinners were coming near Him
to listen to Him.
2 And both the Pharisees and the
scribes [1]*began* to grumble, saying,
"This man receives sinners and
[a]eats with them."
3 And He told them this parable,
saying,
4"[a]What man among you, if he
has a hundred sheep and has lost
one of them, does not leave the
ninety-nine in the [1]open pasture,
and go after the one which is lost,
until he finds it?
5"And when he has found it, he
lays it on his shoulders, rejoicing.
6"And when he comes home, he
calls together his friends and his
neighbors, saying to them, 'Rejoice
with me, for I have found my sheep
which was lost!'
7"I tell you that in the same way,
there will be *more* joy in heaven
over one sinner who repents, than
over ninety-nine righteous persons
who need no repentance.

The Lost Coin

8"Or what woman, if she has ten
[1]silver coins and loses one coin,
does not light a lamp and sweep the
house and search carefully until she
finds it?
9"And when she has found it, she
calls together her [1]friends and
neighbors, saying, 'Rejoice with me,
for I have found the coin which I had
lost!'
10"In the same way, I tell you,
there is joy [a]in the presence of the
angels of God over one sinner who
repents."

The Prodigal Son

11 And He said, "A certain man
had two sons;
12 and the younger of them said to
his father, 'Father, give me [a]the
share of the estate that falls to me.'
And he divided his [1b]wealth between them.
13"And not many days later, the
younger son gathered everything together and went on a journey into a
distant country, and there he squandered his estate with loose living.
14"Now when he had spent everything, a severe famine occurred in
that country, and he began to be in
need.
15"And he went and [1]attached
himself to one of the citizens of that
country, and he sent him into his
fields to feed swine.
16"And he was longing [1]to fill his
[2]stomach with the [3]pods that the
swine were eating, and no one was
giving *anything* to him.
17"But when he came to [1]his
senses, he said, 'How many of my
father's hired men have more than
enough bread, but I am dying here
with hunger!
18 'I will get up and go to my father, and will say to him, "Father, I
have sinned against heaven, and [1]in
your sight;
19"I am no longer worthy to be
called your son; make me as one of
your hired men."'
20"And he got up and came to [1]his
father. But while he was still a long
way off, his father saw him, and felt
compassion *for him,* and ran and
[2a]embraced him, and [3]kissed him.
21"And the son said to him, 'Father, I have sinned against heaven
and in your sight; I am no longer
worthy to be called your son.[1]'
22"But the father said to his slaves,
'Quickly bring out [a]the best robe
and put it on him, and [b]put a ring on
his hand and sandals on his feet;

27 [a]Matt. 10:38
32 [1]Or, *an embassy*
33 [a]Phil. 3:7; Heb. 11:26
34 [a]Matt. 5:13; Mark 9:50
35 [1]Lit., *they throw it out* [a]Matt. 11:15
1 [1]Publicans who collected Roman taxes for profit [2]I.e., irreligious or non-practicing Jews [a]Luke 5:29
2 [1]Lit., *grumble among themselves* [a]Matt. 9:11
4 [1]Lit., *wilderness* [a]Matt. 18:12-14; Luke 15:4-7
8 [1]Gr., *drachmas,* one drachma was equivalent to a day's wages
9 [1]Lit., *women friends and neighbors*
10 [a]Matt. 10:32; Luke 15:7
12 [1]Lit., *living* [a]Deut. 21:17 [b]Mark 12:44; Luke 15:30
15 [1]Lit., *was joined to*
16 [1]Some mss. read, *to be satisfied with* [2]Lit., *belly* [3]I.e., of the carob tree
17 [1]Lit., *himself*
18 [1]Lit., *before you*
20 [1]Lit., *his own* [2]Lit., *fell on his neck* [3]Lit., *kissed him again and again* [a]Gen. 45:14; 46:29; Acts 20:37
21 [1]Some ancient mss. add: *make me as one of your hired men*
22 [a]Zech. 3:4; Rev. 6:11 [b]Gen. 41:42

23 and bring the fattened calf, kill
it, and let us eat and be merry;
24 for this son of mine was [a]dead,
and has come to life again; he was
lost, and has been found.' And they
began to be merry.
25"Now his older son was in the
field, and when he came and approached the house, he heard music
and dancing.
26"And he summoned one of the
servants and *began* inquiring what
these things might be.
27"And he said to him, 'Your
brother has come, and your father
has killed the fattened calf, because
he has received him back safe and
sound.'
28"But he became angry, and was
not willing to go in; and his father
came out and *began* entreating him.
29"But he answered and said to his
father, 'Look! For so many years I
have been serving you, and I have
never [1]neglected a command of
yours; and *yet* you have never given
me a [2]kid, that I might be merry
with my friends;
30 but when this son of yours
came, who has devoured your
[1a]wealth with harlots, you killed the
fattened calf for him.'
31"And he said to him, '*My* child,
you [1]have always been with me, and
all that is mine is yours.
32 'But [1]we had to be merry and
rejoice, for this brother of yours was
[a]dead and *has begun* to live, and
was lost and has been found.' "

Chapter 16

The Unrighteous Steward

NOW He was also saying to the
disciples, "There was a certain rich
man who had a steward, and this
steward was [1]reported to him as
[a]squandering his possessions.
2"And he called him and said to
him, 'What is this I hear about you?
Give an account of your stewardship, for you can no longer be steward.'
3"And the steward said to himself, 'What shall I do, since my
[1]master is taking the stewardship
away from me? I am not strong
enough to dig; I am ashamed to beg.
4 'I [1]know what I shall do, so that
when I am removed from the stewardship, they will receive me into
their homes.'
5"And he summoned each one of
his [1]master's debtors, and he *began*
saying to the first, 'How much do
you owe my master?'
6"And he said, 'A hundred [1]mea-
sures of oil.' And he said to him,
'Take your bill, and sit down quickly
and write fifty.'
7"Then he said to another, 'And
how much do you owe?' And he
said, 'A hundred [1]measures of
wheat.' He *said to him, 'Take your
bill, and write eighty.'
8"And his [1]master praised the unrighteous steward because he had
acted shrewdly; for the sons of [a]this
age are more shrewd in relation to
their own [2]kind than the [b]sons of
light.
9"And I say to you, [a]make friends
for yourselves by means of the
[1b]mammon of unrighteousness; that
when it fails, [c]they may receive you
into the eternal dwellings.
10"[a]He who is faithful in a very little thing is faithful also in much; and
he who is unrighteous in a very little
thing is unrighteous also in much.
11"If therefore you have not been
faithful in the *use of* unrighteous
[1a]mammon, who will entrust the
true *riches* to you?
12"And if you have not been faithful in *the use of* that which is another's, who will give you that which is
[1]your own?
13"[a]No [1]servant can serve two
masters; for either he will hate the
one, and love the other, or else he
will hold to one, and despise the other. You cannot serve God and
[2b]mammon."
14 Now the Pharisees, who were
[a]lovers of money, were listening to
all these things, and they [b]were
scoffing at Him.
15 And He said to them, "You are
those who [a]justify yourselves [1]in
the sight of men, but [b]God knows
your hearts; for that which is
[2]highly esteemed among men is detestable [3]in the sight of God.
16"[a]The Law and the Prophets
were proclaimed until John; since
then [b]the gospel of the kingdom of
God is preached, and every one is
forcing his way into it.
17"[a]But it is easier for heaven and
earth to pass away than for one
[1]stroke of a letter of the Law to fail.
18"[a]Every one who divorces his
wife and marries another commits
adultery; and he who marries one
who is divorced from a husband
commits adultery.

The Rich Man and Lazarus

19"Now there was a certain rich
man, and he habitually dressed in
purple and fine linen, gaily living in
splendor every day.

24 [a]Matt. 8:22; Luke 9:60; 15:32; Rom. 11:15; Eph. 2:1, 5; 5:14; Col. 2:13; 1 Tim. 5:6
29 [1]Or, *disobeyed* [2]Or, *young goat*
30 [1]Lit., *living* [a]Prov. 29:3; Luke 15:12
31 [1]Lit., *are always with me*
32 [1]Lit., *it was necessary* [a]Luke 15:24
1 [1]Or, *accused* [a]Luke 15:13
3 [1]Or, *lord*
4 [1]Lit., *have come to the knowledge of*
5 [1]Or, *lord's*
6 [1]Gr., *baths,* one bath equals between 8 and 9 gallons
7 [1]Gr., *kors,* one kor equals between 10 and 12 bushels
8 [1]Or, *lord* [2]Lit., *generation* [a]Matt. 12:32; Luke 20:34 [b]John 12:36; Eph. 5:8; 1 Thess. 5:5
9 [1]Or, *riches* [a]Matt. 19:21; Luke 11:41; 12:33 [b]Matt. 6:24; Luke 16:11, 13 [c]Luke 16:4
10 [a]Matt. 25:21, 23
11 [1]Or, *riches* [a]Luke 16:9
12 [1]Some mss. read, *our own*
13 [1]Or, *house-servant* [2]Or, *riches* [a]Matt. 6:24 [b]Luke 16:9
14 [a]2 Tim. 3:2 [b]Luke 23:35
15 [1]Lit., *before men* [2]Lit., *high* [3]Lit., *before God* [a]Luke 10:29; 18:9, 14 [b]1 Sam. 16:7; Prov. 21:2; Acts 1:24; Rom. 8:27
16 [a]Matt. 11:12f. [b]Matt. 4:23
17 [1]I.e., projection of a letter (serif) [a]Matt. 5:18
18 [a]Matt. 5:32

20 "And a certain poor man named Lazarus [a]was laid at his gate, covered with sores,
21 and longing to be fed with the *crumbs* which were falling from the rich man's table; besides, even the dogs were coming and licking his sores.
22 "Now it came about that the poor man died and he was carried away by the angels to [a]Abraham's bosom; and the rich man also died and was buried.
23 "And in [a]Hades [1]he lifted up his eyes, being in torment, and *saw Abraham far away, and Lazarus in his bosom.
24 "And he cried out and said, '[a]Father Abraham, have mercy on me, and send Lazarus, that he may dip the tip of his finger in water and cool off my tongue; for I am in agony in [b]this flame.'
25 "But Abraham said, 'Child, remember that [a]during your life you received your good things, and likewise Lazarus bad things; but now he is being comforted here, and you are in agony.
26 'And [1]besides all this, between us and you there is a great chasm fixed, in order that those who wish to come over from here to you may not be able, and *that* none may cross over from there to us.'
27 "And he said, 'Then I beg you, Father, that you send him to my father's house —
28 for I have five brothers — that he may [a]warn them, lest they also come to this place of torment.'
29 "But Abraham *said, 'They have [a]Moses and the Prophets; let them hear them.'
30 "But he said, 'No, [a]Father Abraham, but if someone goes to them from the dead, they will repent!'
31 "But he said to him, 'If they do not listen to Moses and the Prophets, neither will they be persuaded if someone rises from the dead.' "

Chapter 17

Instructions

AND He said to His disciples, "[a]It is inevitable that [1]stumbling blocks should come, but woe to him through whom they come!
2 "[a]It would be better for him if a millstone were hung around his neck and he were thrown into the sea, than that he should cause one of these little ones to stumble.

20 [a]Acts 3:2
22 [a]John 1:18; 13:23
23 [1]Lit., *having lifted up* [a]Matt. 11:23
24 [a]Luke 3:8; 16:30; 19:9 [b]Matt. 25:41
25 [a]Luke 6:24
26 [1]Lit., *in all these things*
28 [a]Acts 2:40; 8:25; 10:42; 18:5; 20:21ff.; 23:11; 28:23; Gal. 5:3; Eph. 4:17; 1 Thess. 2:11; 4:6
29 [a]Luke 4:17; John 5:45-47; Acts 15:21
30 [a]Luke 3:8; 16:24; 19:9
1 [1]Or, *temptations to sin* [a]Matt. 18:7; 1 Cor. 11:19; 1 Tim. 4:1
2 [a]Matt. 18:6; Mark 9:42; 1 Cor. 8:12
3 [1]Lit., *Take heed to yourselves* [a]Matt. 18:15
4 [1]Lit., *you shall forgive* [a]Matt. 18:21f.
5 [a]Mark 6:30 [b]Luke 7:13
6 [1]Gr., *have obeyed* [a]Luke 7:13 [b]Matt. 13:31; 17:20; Mark 4:31; Luke 13:19 [c]Luke 19:4
7 [1]Lit., *recline*
8 [1]Lit., *gird* [2]Lit., *after these things* [a]Luke 12:37
11 [1]Lit., *through the midst of*, or, *along the borders of* [a]Luke 9:51 [b]Luke 9:52ff.; John 4:3f.
12 [a]Lev. 13:45f.
13 [a]Luke 5:5
14 [a]Matt. 8:4; Luke 5:14
15 [a]Matt. 9:8
16 [a]Matt. 10:5
18 [1]Lit., *Were there not found those who* [a]Matt. 9:8
19 [1]Lit., *has saved you* [a]Matt. 9:22; Luke 18:42

3 "[1]Be on your guard! [a]If your brother sins, rebuke him; and if he repents, forgive him.
4 "And if he sins against you [a]seven times a day, and returns to you seven times, saying, 'I repent,' [1]forgive him."
5 And [a]the apostles said to [b]the Lord, "Increase our faith!"
6 And [a]the Lord said, "If you had faith like [b]a mustard seed, you would say to this [c]mulberry tree, 'Be uprooted and be planted in the sea'; and it would [1]obey you.
7 "But which of you, having a slave plowing or tending sheep, will say to him when he has come in from the field, 'Come immediately and [1]sit down to eat'?
8 "But will he not say to him, '[a]Prepare something for me to eat, and *properly* [1]clothe yourself and serve me until I have eaten and drunk; and [2]afterward you will eat and drink'?
9 "He does not thank the slave because he did the things which were commanded, does he?
10 "So you too, when you do all the things which are commanded you, say, 'We are unworthy slaves; we have done *only* that which we ought to have done.' "

Ten Lepers Cleansed

11 And it came about while He was [a]on the way to Jerusalem, that [b]He was passing [1]between Samaria and Galilee.
12 And as He entered a certain village, there met Him ten leprous men, who [a]stood at a distance;
13 and they raised their voices, saying, "Jesus, [a]Master, have mercy on us!"
14 And when He saw them, He said to them, "[a]Go and show yourselves to the priests." And it came about that as they were going, they were cleansed.
15 Now one of them, when he saw that he had been healed, turned back, [a]glorifying God with a loud voice,
16 and he fell on his face at His feet, giving thanks to Him. And he was a [a]Samaritan.
17 And Jesus answered and said, "Were there not ten cleansed? But the nine — where are they?
18 "[1]Were none found who turned back to [a]give glory to God, except this foreigner?"
19 And He said to him, "Rise, and go your way; [a]your faith [1]has made you well."

20 Now having been questioned
by the Pharisees [a]as to when the
kingdom of God was coming, He answered them and said, "The kingdom of God is not coming with
[b]signs to be observed;
21 nor will [a]they say, 'Look, here *it*
is!' or, 'There *it is!*' For behold, the
kingdom of God is in your midst."

Second Coming Foretold

22 And He said to the disciples,
"[a]The days shall come when you
will long to see one of the days of the
Son of Man, and you will not see it.
23 "[a]And they will say to you, 'Look
there! Look here!' Do not go away,
and do not run after *them*.
24 "[a]For just as the lightning, when
it flashes out of one part of the sky,
shines to the other part of the sky,
so will the Son of Man be in His day.
25 "[a]But first He must suffer many
things and be rejected by this generation.
26 "[a]And just as it happened [b]in the
days of Noah, so it shall be also in
the days of the Son of Man:
27 they were eating, they were
drinking, they were marrying, they
were being given in marriage, until
the day that Noah entered the ark,
and the flood came and destroyed
them all.
28 "It was the same as happened in
[a]the days of Lot: they were eating,
they were drinking, they were buying, they were selling, they were
planting, they were building;
29 but on the day that Lot went out
from Sodom it rained fire and [1]brim-
stone from heaven and destroyed
them all.
30 "It will be just the same on the
day that the Son of Man [a]is revealed.
31 "On that day, let not the one who
is [a]on the housetop and whose
goods are in the house go down to
take them away; and likewise let not
the one who is in the field turn back.
32 "[a]Remember Lot's wife.
33 "[a]Whoever seeks to keep his
[1]life shall lose it, and whoever loses
his life shall preserve it alive.
34 "I tell you, on that night there
will be two men in one bed; one will
be taken, and the other will be left.
35 "[a]There will be two women
grinding at the same place; one will
be taken, and the other will be left.
36 ["[1a]Two men will be in the field;
one will be taken and the other will
be left."]
37 And answering they *said to
Him, "Where, Lord?" And He said
to them, "[a]Where the body *is*, there
also will the vultures be gathered."

Chapter 18

Parables on Prayer

NOW He was telling them a parable to show that at all times they
[a]ought to pray and not to [b]lose
heart,
2 saying, "There was in a certain
city a judge who did not fear God,
and did not [a]respect man.
3 "And there was a widow in that
city, and she kept coming to him,
saying, 'Give me legal protection
from my opponent.'
4 "And for a while he was unwilling; but afterward he said to himself, 'Even though I do not fear God
nor [a]respect man,
5 yet [a]because this widow bothers me, I will give her legal protection, lest by continually coming she
[b]wear me out.' "
6 And [a]the Lord said, "Hear what
the unrighteous judge *said;
7 now shall not God [a]bring about
justice for His [b]elect, who cry to
Him day and night, [1]and will He [c]de-
lay long over them?
8 "I tell you that He will bring
about justice for them speedily.
However, when the Son of Man
comes, [a]will He find [1]faith on the
earth?"

The Pharisee and the Publican

9 And He also told this parable to
certain ones who [a]trusted in themselves that they were righteous, and
[b]viewed others with contempt:
10 "Two men [a]went up into the
temple to pray, one a Pharisee, and
the other a [1]tax-gatherer.
11 "The Pharisee [a]stood and was
praying thus to himself, 'God, I
thank Thee that I am not like other
people: swindlers, unjust, adulterers, or even like this [1]tax-gatherer.
12 'I [a]fast twice a week; I [b]pay
tithes of all that I get.'
13 "But the [1]tax-gatherer, [a]stand-
ing some distance away, [b]was even
unwilling to lift up his eyes to
heaven, but [c]was beating his breast,
saying, 'God, be [2]merciful to me, the
sinner!'
14 "I tell you, this man went down
to his house justified rather than the
other; [a]for every one who exalts
himself shall be humbled, but he
who humbles himself shall be exalted."
15 [a]And they were bringing even
their babies to Him, in order that He

20 [a]Luke 19:11; Acts 1:6 [b]Luke 14:1 [Gr.]
21 [a]Luke 17:23
22 [a]Matt. 9:15; Mark 2:20; Luke 5:35
23 [a]Matt. 24:23; Mark 13:21; Luke 21:8
24 [a]Matt. 24:27
25 [a]Matt. 16:21; Luke 9:22
26 [a]Luke 17:26, 27: *Matt. 24:37-39* [b]Gen. 7
28 [a]Gen. 19
29 [1]Or, *sulphur*
30 [a]Matt. 16:27; 1 Cor. 1:7; Col. 3:4; 2 Thess. 1:7; 1 Pet. 1:7; 4:13; 1 John 2:28
31 [a]Matt. 24:17, 18; Mark 13:15f.; Luke 21:21
32 [a]Gen. 19:26
33 [1]Or, *soul-life* [a]Matt. 10:39
35 [a]Matt. 24:41
36 [1]Many mss. do not contain this verse [a]Matt. 24:40
37 [a]Matt. 24:28
1 [a]Luke 11:5-10 [b]2 Cor. 4:1
2 [a]Luke 18:4; 20:13; Heb. 12:9
4 [a]Luke 18:2; 20:13; Heb. 12:9
5 [a]Luke 11:8 [b]1 Cor. 9:27
6 [a]Luke 7:13
7 [1]Or, *and yet He is long-suffering over them* [a]Rev. 6:10 [b]Matt. 24:22; Rom. 8:33; Col. 3:12; 2 Tim. 2:10; Titus 1:1 [c]2 Pet. 3:9
8 [1]Lit., *the faith* [a]Luke 17:26ff.
9 [a]Luke 16:15 [b]Rom. 14:3, 10
10 [1]A publican who collected Roman taxes for profit [a]1 Kin. 10:5; 2 Kin. 20:5, 8; Acts 3:1
11 [1]Note, verse 10 [a]Matt. 6:5; Mark 11:25; Luke 22:41
12 [a]Matt. 9:14 [b]Luke 11:42
13 [1]Note, verse 10 [2]Or, *propitious* [a]Matt. 6:5; Mark 11:25; Luke 22:41 [b]Ezra 9:6 [c]Luke 23:48
14 [a]Matt. 23:12; Luke 14:11
15 [a]Luke 18:15-17: *Matt. 19:13-15; Mark 10:13-16*

might touch them, but when the disciples saw it, they *began* rebuking
them.
16 But Jesus called for them, saying, "Permit the children to come to
Me, and stop hindering them, for the
kingdom of God belongs to such as
these.
17 "Truly I say to you, [a]whoever
does not receive the kingdom of
God like a child shall not enter it *at
all.*"

The Rich Young Ruler

18 [a]And a certain ruler questioned
Him, saying, "Good Teacher, what
shall I do to obtain eternal life?"
19 And Jesus said to him, "Why do
you call Me good? No one is good
except God alone.
20 "You know the commandments,
'[a]DO NOT COMMIT ADULTERY, DO NOT
MURDER, DO NOT STEAL, DO NOT
BEAR FALSE WITNESS, HONOR YOUR
FATHER AND MOTHER.' "
21 And he said, "All these things I
have kept from *my* youth."
22 And when Jesus heard *this*, He
said to him, "One thing you still
lack; [a]sell all that you possess, and
distribute it to the poor, and you
shall have [b]treasure in heaven; and
come, follow Me."
23 But when he had heard these
things, he became very sad; for he
was extremely rich.
24 And Jesus looked at him and
said, "[a]How hard it is for those who
are wealthy to enter the kingdom of
God!
25 "For [a]it is easier for a camel to
[1]go through the eye of a needle, than
for a rich man to enter the kingdom
of God."
26 And they who heard it said,
"[1]Then who can be saved?"
27 But He said, "[a]The things impossible with men are possible with
God."
28 And Peter said, "Behold, [a]we
have left [1]our own *homes*, and followed You."
29 And He said to them, "Truly I
say to you, [a]there is no one who has
left house or wife or brothers or parents or children, for the sake of the
kingdom of God,
30 who shall not receive many
times as much at this time and in
[a]the age to come, eternal life."
31 [a]And He took the twelve aside
and said to them, "Behold, [b]we are
going up to Jerusalem, and [c]all
things which are written through
the prophets about the Son of Man
will be accomplished.
32 "[a]For He will be [1]delivered up to
the Gentiles, and will be mocked
and mistreated and spit upon,
33 and after they have scourged
Him, they will kill Him; and the
third day He will rise again."
34 And [a]they understood none of
these things, and this saying was
hidden from them, and they did not
comprehend the things that were
said.

Bartimaeus Receives Sight

35 [a]And it came about that [b]as He
was approaching Jericho, a certain
blind man was sitting by the road,
begging.
36 Now hearing a multitude going
by, he *began* to inquire what this
might be.
37 And they told him that Jesus of
Nazareth was passing by.
38 And he called out, saying, "Jesus, [a]Son of David, have mercy on
me!"
39 And those who led the way
were sternly telling him to be quiet;
but he kept crying out all the more,
"[a]Son of David, have mercy on me!"
40 And Jesus [1]stopped and commanded that he be brought to Him;
and when he had come near, He
questioned him,
41 "What do you want Me to do for
you?" And he said, "Lord, *I want* to
receive my sight!"
42 And Jesus said to him, "Receive your sight; [a]your faith has
[1]made you well."
43 And immediately he received
his sight, and *began* following Him,
[a]glorifying God; and when [b]all the
people saw it, they gave praise to
God.

CHAPTER 19

Zaccheus Converted

AND He [a]entered and was passing
through Jericho.
2 And behold, there was a man
called by the name of Zaccheus; and
he was a chief [1]tax-gatherer, and he
was rich.
3 And he was trying to see who
Jesus was, and he was unable because of the crowd, for he was small
in stature.
4 And he ran on ahead and
climbed up into a [1a]sycamore tree in
order to see Him, for He was about
to pass through that way.
5 And when Jesus came to the
place, He looked up and said to him,
"Zaccheus, hurry and come down,
for today I must stay at your house."

17 [a]Matt. 18:3; 19:14; Mark 10:15; 1 Cor. 14:20; 1 Pet. 2:2
18 [a]Luke 18:18-30: *Matt. 19:16-29; Mark 10:17-30;* Luke 10:25-28
20 [a]Ex. 20:12-16; Deut. 5:16-20
22 [a]Matt. 19:21; Luke 12:33 [b]Matt. 6:20
24 [a]Matt. 19:23; Mark 10:23f.
25 [1]Lit., *enter* [a]Matt. 19:24; Mark 10:25
26 [1]Lit., *And*
27 [a]Matt. 19:26
28 [1]Lit., *our own things* [a]Luke 5:11
29 [a]Matt. 6:33; 19:29; Mark 10:29f.
30 [a]Matt. 12:32
31 [a]Luke 18:31-33: *Matt. 20:17-19; Mark 10:32-34* [b]Luke 9:51 [c]Ps. 22, Is. 53
32 [1]Or, *betrayed* [a]Matt. 16:21
34 [a]Mark 9:32; Luke 9:45
35 [a]Luke 18:35-43: *Matt. 20:29-34; Mark 10:46-52* [b]Matt. 20:29; Mark 10:46; Luke 19:1
38 [a]Matt. 9:27; Luke 18:39
39 [a]Luke 18:38
40 [1]Lit., *stood*
42 [1]Or, *saved you* [a]Matt. 9:22
43 [a]Matt. 9:8 [b]Luke 9:43; 13:17; 19:37
1 [a]Luke 18:35
2 [1]A publican who collected Roman taxes for profit
4 [1]I.e., a fig-mulberry [a]1 Kin. 10:27; 1 Chr. 27:28; 2 Chr. 1:15; 9:27; Ps. 78:47; Is. 9:10; Luke 17:6 [?]

6 And he hurried and came down,
and received Him [1]gladly.
7 And when they saw it, they all
began to [1]grumble, saying, "He has
gone [2]to be the guest of a man who
is a sinner."
8 And Zaccheus [1]stopped and
said to [a]the Lord, "Behold, Lord,
half of my possessions I will give to
the poor, and if I have [b]defrauded
anyone of anything, I will give back
[c]four times as much."
9 And Jesus said to him, "Today
salvation has come to this house,
because he, too, is [a]a son of Abraham.
10"For [a]the Son of Man has come
to seek and to save that which was
lost."

Parable of Money Usage

11 And while they were listening
to these things, He went on to tell a
parable, because [a]He was near Jerusalem, and they supposed that [b]the
kingdom of God was going to appear immediately.
12 He said therefore, "[a]A certain
nobleman went to a distant country
to receive a kingdom for himself,
and *then* return.
13"And he called ten of his slaves,
and gave them ten [1]minas, and said
to them, 'Do business *with this* [2]un-
til I come *back.*'
14"But his citizens hated him, and
sent [1]a delegation after him, saying,
'We do not want this man to reign
over us.'
15"And it came about that when he
returned, after receiving the kingdom, he ordered that these slaves,
to whom he had given the money, be
called to him in order that he might
know what business they had done.
16"And the first appeared, saying,
'[1]Master, your [2]mina has made ten
minas more.'
17"And he said to him, 'Well done,
good slave, because you have been
[a]faithful in a very little thing, be in
authority over ten cities.'
18"And the second came, saying,
'Your [1]mina, [2]master, has made five
minas.'
19"And he said to him also, 'And
you are to be over five cities.'
20"And another came, saying,
'Master, behold your mina, which I
kept put away in a handkerchief;
21 for I was afraid of you, because
you are an exacting man; you take
up what you did not lay down, and
reap what you did not sow.'
22"He *said to him, '[1]By your own
words I will judge you, you worthless slave. Did you know that I am
an exacting man, taking up what I
did not lay down, and reaping what
I did not sow?
23 '[1]Then why did you not put the
money in the bank, and having
come, I would have collected it with
interest?'
24"And he said to the bystanders,
'Take the mina away from him, and
give it to the one who has the ten
minas.'
25"And they said to him, 'Master,
he has ten minas *already.*'
26"[a]I tell you, that to everyone who
has shall *more* be given, but from
the one who does not have, even
what he does have shall be taken
away.
27"But [a]these enemies of mine,
who did not want me to reign over
them, bring them here, and [b]slay
them in my presence."

Triumphal Entry

28 And after He had said these
things, He [a]was going on ahead, [b]as-
cending to Jerusalem.
29 And it came about that [a]when
He approached Bethphage and
[b]Bethany, near the [1]mount that is
called [2c]Olivet, He sent two of the
disciples,
30 saying, "Go into the village opposite *you,* in which as you enter
you will find a colt tied, on which no
one yet has ever sat; untie it, and
bring it *here.*
31"And if anyone asks you, 'Why
are you untying it?' thus shall you
speak, 'The Lord has need of it.' "
32 And those who were sent went
away and found it just as He had
told them.
33 And as they were untying the
colt, its [1]owners said to them, "Why
are you untying the colt?"
34 And they said, "The Lord has
need of it."
35 And they brought it to Jesus,
[a]and they threw their garments on
the colt, and put Jesus *on it.*
36 And as He was going, they were
spreading their garments in the
road.
37 And as He was now approaching, near the descent of [a]the Mount
of Olives, the whole multitude of the
disciples began to [b]praise God [1]joy-
fully with a loud voice for all the
[2]miracles which they had seen,
38 saying,

"[a]BLESSED IS THE [b]KING WHO
COMES IN THE NAME OF THE
LORD;
Peace in heaven and [c]glory in
the highest!"

39 [a]And some of the Pharisees

6 [1]Lit., *rejoicing*
7 [1]Lit., *grumble among themselves* [2]Or, *to find lodging*
8 [1]Lit., *stood* [a]Luke 7:13 [b]Luke 3:14 [c]Ex. 22:1; Lev. 6:5; Num. 5:7; 2 Sam. 12:6
9 [a]Luke 3:8; 13:16; Rom. 4:16; Gal. 3:7
10 [a]Matt. 18:11
11 [a]Luke 9:51 [b]Luke 17:20
12 [a]Matt. 25:14-30; Luke 19:12-27
13 [1]A mina is equal to about 100 days' wages or nearly $20 [2]Lit., *while I am coming*
14 [1]Or, *an embassy*
16 [1]Lit., *Lord* [2]Note, verse 13
17 [a]Luke 16:10
18 [1]Note, verse 13 [2]Lit., *lord*
22 [1]Lit., *Out of your own mouth*
23 [1]Lit., *And*
26 [a]Matt. 13:12; Luke 8:18
27 [a]Luke 19:14 [b]Matt. 22:7; Luke 20:16
28 [a]Mark 10:32 [b]Luke 9:51
29 [1]Or, *hill* [2]Or, *Olive Grove* [a]Luke 19:29-38: *Matt. 21:1-9; Mark 11:1-10* [b]Matt. 21:17 [c]Luke 21:37; Acts 1:12
33 [1]Lit., *lords*
35 [a]Luke 19:35-38: *John 12:12-15*
37 [1]Lit., *as they were rejoicing* [2]Or, *works of power* [a]Matt. 21:1; Luke 19:29 [b]Luke 18:43
38 [a]Ps. 118:26 [b]Matt. 2:2; 25:34 [c]Matt. 21:9; Luke 2:14
39 [a]Matt. 21:15f.

[1]in the multitude said to Him,
"Teacher, rebuke Your disciples."
40 And He answered and said, "I
tell you, if these become silent, [a]the
stones will cry out!"
41 And when He approached, He
saw the city and [a]wept over it,
42 saying, "If you had known in
this day, even you, the things which
make for peace! But now they have
been hidden from your eyes.
43 "For the days shall come upon
you [1]when your enemies will [a]throw
up a [2]bank before you, and [b]sur-
round you, and hem you in on every
side,
44 and will level you to the ground
and your children within you, and
[a]they will not leave in you one stone
upon another, because you did not
recognize [b]the time of your visitation."

Traders Driven from the Temple

45 [a]And He entered the temple
and began to cast out those who
were selling,
46 saying to them, "It is written,
'[a]AND MY HOUSE SHALL BE A HOUSE
OF PRAYER,' but you have made it a
robbers' [1]den."
47 And [a]He was teaching daily in
the temple; but the chief priests and
the scribes and the leading men
among the people [b]were trying to
destroy Him,
48 and they could not find [1]any-
thing that they might do, for all the
people were hanging upon [2]His
words.

CHAPTER 20

Jesus' Authority Questioned

[a]AND it came about on one of the
days while [b]He was teaching the
people in the temple and [c]preaching
the gospel, that the chief priests and
the scribes with the elders [d]con-
fronted *Him*,
2 and they spoke, saying to Him,
"Tell us by what authority You are
doing these things, or who is the one
who gave You this authority?"
3 And He answered and said to
them, "I shall also ask you a [1]ques-
tion, and you tell Me:
4 "Was the baptism of John from
heaven or from men?"
5 And they reasoned among
themselves, saying, "If we say,
'From heaven,' He will say, 'Why
did you not believe him?'
6 "But if we say, 'From men,' all
the people will stone us to death, for
they are convinced that John was a
[a]prophet."
7 And they answered that they
did not know where *it came* from.
8 And Jesus said to them, "Neither [1]will I tell you by what authority I am doing these things."

Parable of the Vine-growers

9 [a]And He began to tell the people this parable: "A man planted a
vineyard and rented it out to [1]vine-
growers, and went on a journey for
a long time.
10 "And at the *harvest* time he sent
a slave to the vine-growers, in order
that they might give him *some* of the
produce of the vineyard; but the
vine-growers beat him and sent him
away empty-handed.
11 "And he proceeded to send another slave; and they beat him also
and treated him shamefully, and
sent him away empty-handed.
12 "And he proceeded to send a
third; and this one also they
wounded and cast out.
13 "And the [1]owner of the vineyard
said, 'What shall I do? I will send my
beloved son; perhaps they will [a]re-
spect him.'
14 "But when the vine-growers saw
him, they reasoned with one another, saying, 'This is the heir; let us
kill him that the inheritance may be
ours.'
15 "And they cast him out of the
vineyard and killed him. What,
therefore, will the [1]owner of the
vineyard do to them?
16 "He will come and [a]destroy
these vine-growers and will give the
vineyard to others." And when they
heard it, they said, "[b]May it never
be!"
17 But He looked at them and said,
"What then is this that is written,
'[a]THE STONE WHICH THE BUILD-
ERS REJECTED,
THIS BECAME [b]THE CHIEF COR-
NER *stone*'?
18 "[a]Every one who falls on that
stone will be broken to pieces; but
on whomever it falls, it will scatter
him like dust."

Tribute to Caesar

19 And the scribes and the chief
priests [a]tried to lay hands on Him
that very hour, and they feared the
people; for they understood that He
spoke this parable against them.
20 [a]And they watched Him, and
sent spies who [1]pretended to be
righteous, in order [b]that they might
[2]catch Him in some statement, so as

39 [1]Lit., *from*
40 [a]Hab. 2:11
41 [a]Luke 13:34, 35
43 [1]Lit., *and* [2]I.e., a dirt wall or mound for siege purposes [a]Eccles. 9:14; Is. 29:3; 37:33; Jer. 6:6; Ezek. 4:2; 26:8 [b]Luke 21:20
44 [a]Matt. 24:2; Mark 13:2; Luke 21:6 [b]1 Pet. 2:12
45 [a]Luke 19:45, 46: *Matt. 21:12-16; Mark 11:15-18;* John 2:13-16
46 [1]Lit., *cave* [a]Is. 56:7; Jer. 7:11; Matt. 21:13; Mark 11:17
47 [a]Matt. 26:55 [b]Luke 20:19
48 [1]Lit., *what they might do* [2]Lit., *Him, listening*
1 [a]Luke 20:1-8: *Matt. 21:23-27; Mark 11:27-33* [b]Matt. 26:55 [c]Luke 8:1 [d]Acts 4:1; 6:12
3 [1]Lit., *word*
6 [a]Matt. 11:9; Luke 7:29, 30
8 [1]Lit., *do I tell*
9 [1]Here and in verses 10, 14 and 16, or, *tenant farmers* [a]Luke 20:9-19: *Matt. 21:33-46; Mark 12:1-12*
13 [1]Lit., *lord* [a]Luke 18:2
15 [1]Lit., *lord*
16 [a]Matt. 21:41; Mark 12:9; Luke 19:27 [b]Rom. 3:4, 6, 31; 6:2, 15; 7:7, 13; 9:14; 11:1, 11; 1 Cor. 6:15; Gal. 2:17; 3:21; 6:14
17 [a]Ps. 118:22 [b]Eph. 2:20; 1 Pet. 2:6
18 [a]Matt. 21:44
19 [a]Luke 19:47
20 [1]Lit., *feigned themselves* [2]Lit., *take hold of His word* [a]Luke 20:20-26: *Matt. 22:15-22; Mark 12:13-17;* Mark 3:2 [b]Luke 11:54; 20:26

to deliver Him up to the rule and the
authority of [c]the governor.
21 And they questioned Him, saying, "Teacher, we know that You
speak and teach correctly, and You
[1]are not partial to any, but teach the
way of God in truth.
22 "Is it [1]lawful for us [a]to pay taxes
to Caesar, or not?"
23 But He detected their trickery
and said to them,
24 "Show Me a [1]denarius. Whose
[2]head and inscription does it have?"
And they said, "Caesar's."
25 And He said to them, "Then
[a]render to Caesar the things that are
Caesar's, and to God the things that
are God's."
26 And they were unable to
[1a]catch Him in a saying in the presence of the people; and marveling at
His answer, they became silent.

Is There a Resurrection?

27 [a]Now there came to Him some
of the Sadducees (who say that
there is no resurrection),
28 and they questioned Him, saying, "Teacher, Moses wrote us that
[a]IF A MAN'S BROTHER DIES, having a
wife, AND HE IS CHILDLESS, HIS
BROTHER SHOULD TAKE THE WIFE
AND RAISE UP OFFSPRING TO HIS
BROTHER.
29 "Now there were seven brothers; and the first took a wife, and
died childless;
30 and the second
31 and the third took her; and in
the same way the seven also [1]died,
leaving no children.
32 "Finally the woman died also.
33 "In the resurrection therefore,
which one's wife will the woman
be? For the seven had her as wife."
34 And Jesus said to them, "The
sons of [a]this age marry and are giv-
en in marriage,
35 but those who are considered
worthy to attain to [a]that age and the
resurrection from the dead, neither
marry, nor are given in marriage;
36 for neither can they die any
more, for they are like angels, and
are [a]sons of God, being sons of the
resurrection.
37 "But that the dead are raised,
even Moses showed, in [a]the *passage
about the burning* bush, where he
calls the Lord [b]THE GOD OF ABRA-
HAM, AND THE GOD OF ISAAC, AND
THE GOD OF JACOB.
38 "[a]Now He is not the God of the
dead, but of the living; for [b]all live to
Him."
39 And some of the scribes answered and said, "Teacher, You
have spoken well."
40 For [a]they did not have courage
to question Him any longer about
anything.
41 [a]And He said to them, "How *is
it that* they say [1]the Christ is [b]Da-
vid's son?
42 "For David himself says in the
book of Psalms,
'[a]THE LORD SAID TO MY LORD,
"SIT AT MY RIGHT HAND,
43 [a]UNTIL I MAKE THINE ENE-
MIES A FOOTSTOOL FOR THY
FEET."'
44 "David therefore calls Him
'Lord,' and how is He his son?"
45 [a]And while all the people were
listening, He said to the disciples,
46 "Beware of the scribes, [a]who
like to walk around in long robes,
and love respectful greetings in the
market places, and chief seats in the
synagogues, and places of honor at
banquets,
47 who devour widows' houses,
and for appearance's sake offer long
prayers; these will receive greater
condemnation."

CHAPTER 21

The Widow's Gift

[a]AND He looked up and saw the
rich putting their gifts into the treasury.
2 And He saw a certain poor
widow putting [1]in [a]two [2]small copper coins.
3 And He said, "Truly I say to
you, this poor widow put in more
than all *of them;*
4 for they all out of their [1]surplus
put into the [2]offering; but she out of
her poverty put in all [3]that she had
[a]to live on."
5 [a]And while some were talking
about the temple, that it was
adorned with beautiful stones and
votive gifts, He said,
6 "*As for* these things which you
are looking at, the days will come in
which [a]there will not be left one
stone upon another which will not
be torn down."
7 And they questioned Him, saying, "Teacher, when therefore will
these things be? And what *will be*
the [1]sign when these things are
about to take place?"
8 And He said, "Take heed that
you be not misled; for many will
come in My name, saying, '[a]I am
He,' and, 'The time is at hand'; [b]do
not go after them.

20 [c]Matt. 27:2
21 [1]Lit., *do not receive a face*
22 [1]Or, *permissible* [a]Matt. 17:25; Luke 23:2
24 [1]The denarius was worth 18 cents in silver, equivalent to one day's wages [2]Lit., *image*
25 [a]Matt. 22:21; Mark 12:17
26 [1]Lit., *take hold of His saying* [a]Luke 11:54; 20:26
27 [a]Luke 20:27-40: *Matt. 22:23-33; Mark 12:18-27*
28 [a]Deut. 25:5
31 [1]Lit., *left no children, and died*
34 [a]Matt. 12:32; Luke 16:8
35 [a]Matt. 12:32; Luke 16:8
36 [a]Rom. 8:16f.; 1 John 3:1, 2
37 [a]Mark 12:26 [b]Ex. 3:6
38 [a]Matt. 22:32; Mark 12:27 [b]Rom. 14:8
40 [a]Matt. 22:46; Luke 14:6
41 [1]I.e., the Messiah [a]Luke 20:41-44: *Matt. 22:41-46; Mark 12:35-37* [b]Matt. 9:27
42 [a]Ps. 110:1
43 [a]Ps. 110:1
45 [a]Luke 20:45-47: *Matt. 23:1-7; Mark 12:38-40*
46 [a]Luke 11:43; 14:7
1 [a]Luke 21:1-4: *Mark 12:41-44*
2 [1]Or, *therein* [2]Lit., *lepta* [a]Mark 12:42
4 [1]Or, *abundance* [2]Lit., *gifts* [3]Lit., *the living that she had* [a]Mark 12:44
5 [a]Luke 21:5-36: *Matt. 24; Mark 13*
6 [a]Luke 19:44
7 [1]Or, *attesting miracle*
8 [a]John 8:24 [b]Luke 17:23

9 "And when you hear of wars and
disturbances, do not be terrified; for
these things must take place first,
but the end *does* not *follow* immediately."

Things to Come

10 Then He continued by saying to
them, "Nation will rise against nation, and kingdom against kingdom,
11 and there will be great earthquakes, and in various places
plagues and famines; and there will
be terrors and great [1]signs from
heaven.
12 "But before all these things,
[a]they will lay their hands on you and
will persecute you, delivering you to
the synagogues and prisons, [1]bring-
ing you before kings and governors
for My name's sake.
13 "[a]It will lead to an [1]opportunity
for your testimony.
14 "[a]So make up your minds not to
prepare beforehand to defend yourselves;
15 for [a]I will give you [1]utterance
and wisdom which none of your opponents will be able to resist or refute.
16 "But you will be betrayed even
by parents and brothers and relatives and friends, and they will put
some of you to death,
17 and you will be hated by all on
account of My name.
18 "Yet [a]not a hair of your head will
perish.
19 "[a]By your perseverance you will
win your souls.
20 "But when you see Jerusalem
[a]surrounded by armies, then [1]recog-
nize that her desolation is at hand.
21 "Then let those who are in Judea
flee to the mountains, and let those
who are in the midst of [1]the city depart, and [a]let not those who are in
the country enter [1]the city;
22 because these are [a]days of vengeance, in order that all things
which are written may be fulfilled.
23 "Woe to those who are with
child and to those who nurse babes
in those days; for [a]there will be
great distress upon the [1]land, and
wrath to this people,
24 and they will fall by [a]the edge of
the sword, and will be led captive
into all the nations; and [b]Jerusalem
will be [c]trampled underfoot by the
Gentiles until [d]the times of the Gentiles be fulfilled.

The Return of Christ

25 "And there will be [1]signs in sun
and moon and stars, and upon the
earth dismay among nations, in perplexity at the roaring of the sea and
the waves,
26 men fainting from fear and the
expectation of the things which are
coming upon the [1]world; for the
powers of [2]the heavens will be
shaken.
27 "And [a]then will they see [b]THE
SON OF MAN COMING IN A CLOUD with
power and great glory.
28 "But when these things begin to
take place, straighten up and lift up
your heads, because [a]your redemption is drawing near."
29 And He told them a parable:
"Behold the fig tree, and all the
trees;
30 as soon as they put forth *leaves,*
you see it and [a]know for yourselves
that the summer is now near.
31 "Even so you, too, when you see
these things happening, [1]recognize
that [a]the kingdom of God is near.
32 "Truly I say to you, this [1]genera-
tion will not pass away until all
things take place.
33 "[a]Heaven and earth will pass
away, but My words will not pass
away.
34 "[a]Be on guard, that your hearts
may not be weighted down with dissipation and drunkenness and the
worries of life, and that day come on
you suddenly like a trap;
35 for it will come upon all those
who dwell on the face of all the
earth.
36 "But [a]keep on the alert at all
times, praying in order that you may
have strength to escape all these
things that are about to take place,
and to [b]stand before the Son of
Man."
37 Now [1]during the day He was
[a]teaching in the temple, but [2][b]at
evening He would go out and spend
the night on [3][c]the mount that is
called [4]Olivet.
38 And all the people would get up
[a]early in the morning *to come* to
Him in the temple to listen to Him.

CHAPTER 22

Preparing the Passover

[a]NOW the Feast of Unleavened
Bread, which is called the [b]Pass-
over, was approaching.
2 And the chief priests and the
scribes [a]were seeking how they
might put Him to death; for they
were afraid of the people.
3 [a]And [b]Satan entered into Judas
who was called Iscariot, [1]belonging
to the number of the twelve.

11 [1]Or, *attesting miracles*
12 [1]Lit., *being brought* [a]Luke 21:12-17: *Matt. 10:19-22; Mark 13:11-13*
13 [1]Lit., *a testimony for you* [a]Phil. 1:12
14 [a]Luke 12:11
15 [1]Lit., *a mouth* [a]Luke 12:12
18 [a]Matt. 10:30; Luke 12:7
19 [a]Matt. 10:22; 24:13; Rom. 2:7; 5:3f.; Heb. 10:36; James 1:3; 2 Pet. 1:6
20 [1]Lit., *know* [a]Luke 19:43
21 [1]Lit., *her* [a]Luke 17:31
22 [a]Is. 63:4; Dan. 9:24-27; Hos. 9:7
23 [1]Or, *earth* [a]Dan. 8:19; 1 Cor. 7:26
24 [a]Gen. 34:26; Ex. 17:13; Heb. 11:34 [b]Is. 63:18; Dan. 8:13; Rev. 11:2 [c]Rev. 11:2 [d]Rom. 11:25
25 [1]Or, *attesting miracles*
26 [1]Lit., *inhabited earth* [2]Or, *heaven*
27 [a]Matt. 16:27; 24:30; 26:64; Mark 13:26 [b]Dan. 7:13
28 [a]Luke 18:7
30 [a]Luke 12:57
31 [1]Lit., *know* [a]Matt. 3:2
32 [1]Or, *race*
33 [a]Matt. 5:18; Luke 16:17
34 [a]Matt. 24:42-44; Mark 4:19; Luke 12:40, 45; 1 Thess. 5:2ff.
36 [a]Mark 13:33; Luke 12:40 [b]Luke 1:19; Rev. 7:9; 8:2; 11:4
37 [1]Lit., *days* [2]Lit., *nights* [3]Or, *the hill* [4]Or, *Olive Grove* [a]Matt. 26:55 [b]Mark 11:19 [c]Matt. 21:1
38 [a]John 8:2
1 [a]Luke 22:1, 2: *Matt. 26:2-5; Mark 14:1, 2* [b]John 11:55; 13:1
2 [a]Matt. 12:14
3 [1]Lit., *being of* [a]Luke 22:3-6: *Matt. 26:14-16; Mark 14:10, 11* [b]Matt. 4:10; John 13:2, 27

4 And he went away and discussed with the chief priests and [a]officers how he might betray Him to them.

5 And they were delighted, and agreed to give him money.

6 And he consented, and *began* seeking a good opportunity to betray Him to them [1]apart from the multitude.

7 [a]Then came the day of Unleavened Bread on which [b]the Passover *lamb* had to be sacrificed.

8 And He sent [a]Peter and John, saying, "Go and prepare the Passover for us, that we may eat it."

9 And they said to Him, "Where do You want us to prepare it?"

10 And He said to them, "Behold, when you have entered the city, a man will meet you carrying a pitcher of water; follow him into the house that he enters.

11 "And you shall say to the owner of the house, 'The Teacher says to you, "Where is the guest room in which I may eat the Passover with My disciples?"'

12 "And he will show you a large, furnished, upper room; prepare it there."

13 And they departed and found *everything* just as He had told them; and they prepared the Passover.

The Lord's Supper

14 [a]And when the hour had come He reclined *at table,* and [b]the apostles with Him.

15 And He said to them, "I have earnestly desired to eat this Passover with you before I suffer;

16 for I say to you, I shall never again eat it [a]until it is fulfilled in the kingdom of God."

17 [a]And having taken a cup, [b]when He had given thanks, He said, "Take this and share it among yourselves;

18 for [a]I say to you, I will not drink of the fruit of the vine from now on until the kingdom of God comes."

19 And having taken *some* bread, [a]when He had given thanks, He broke *it,* and gave *it* to them, saying, "This is My body [1]which is given for you; do this in remembrance of Me."

20 And in the same way *He took* the cup after they had eaten, saying, "This cup which is [a]poured out for you is the [b]new covenant in My blood.

21 "[a]But behold, the hand of the one betraying Me is with Me on the table.

22 "For indeed, the Son of Man is going [a]as it has been determined; but woe to that man through whom He is betrayed!"

23 And they began to discuss among themselves which one of them it might be who was going to do this thing.

Who Is Greatest

24 And there arose also [a]a dispute among them *as to* which one of them was regarded to be greatest.

25 [a]And He said to them, "The kings of the Gentiles lord it over them; and those who have authority over them are called 'Benefactors.'

26 "But not so with you, [a]but let him who is the greatest among you become as [b]the youngest, and the leader as the servant.

27 "For [a]who is greater, the one who reclines *at table,* or the one who serves? Is it not the one who reclines *at table?* But [b]I am among you as the one who serves.

28 "And you are those who have stood by Me in My [a]trials;

29 and just as My Father has granted Me a [a]kingdom, I grant you

30 that you may [a]eat and drink at My table in My [b]kingdom, and [c]you will sit on thrones judging the twelve tribes of Israel.

31 "Simon, Simon, behold, [a]Satan has [1]demanded *permission* to [b]sift you like wheat;

32 but I [a]have prayed for you, that your faith may not fail; and you, when once you have turned again, [b]strengthen your brothers."

33 [a]And he said to Him, "Lord, with You I am ready to go both to prison and to death!"

34 And He said, "I tell you, Peter, the cock will not crow today until you have denied three times that you know Me."

35 And He said to them, "[a]When I sent you out without purse and bag and sandals, you did not lack anything, did you?" And they said, "*No,* nothing."

36 And He said to them, "But now, let him who has a purse take it along, likewise also a bag, and let him who has no sword sell his [1]robe and buy one.

37 "For I tell you, that this which is written must be fulfilled in Me, '[a]AND HE WAS CLASSED AMONG CRIMINALS'; for [b]that which refers to Me has *its* fulfillment."

38 And they said, "Lord, look, here are two [a]swords." And He said to them, "It is enough."

---

4 [a]1 Chr. 9:11; Neh. 11:11; Luke 22:52; Acts 4:1; 5:24, 26
6 [1]Or, *without a disturbance*
7 [a]Luke 22:7-13: *Matt. 26:17-19; Mark 14:12-16* [b]Mark 14:12
8 [a]Acts 3:1, 11; 4:13, 19; 8:14; Gal. 2:9
14 [a]Matt. 26:20; Mark 14:17 [b]Mark 6:30
16 [a]Luke 14:15; 22:18, 30; Rev. 19:9
17 [a]Luke 22:17-20: *Matt. 26:26-29; Mark 14:22-25; 1 Cor. 11:23-25;* 10:16 [b]Matt. 14:19
18 [a]Matt. 26:29; Mark 14:25
19 [1]Some ancient mss. do not contain the remainder of verse 19 and all of verse 20 [a]Matt. 14:19
20 [a]Matt. 26:28; Mark 14:24 [b]Ex. 24:8; Jer. 31:31; 1 Cor. 11:25; 2 Cor. 3:6; Heb. 8:8, [13]; 9:15
21 [a]Luke 22:21-23: *Matt. 26:21-24; Mark 14:18-21;* John 13:18, 21, 22, 26
22 [a]Acts 2:23; 4:28; 10:42; 17:31
24 [a]Mark 9:34; Luke 9:46
25 [a]Luke 22:25-27: *Matt. 20:25-28; Mark 10:42-45*
26 [a]Luke 9:48 [b]1 Pet. 5:5
27 [a]Luke 12:37 [b]Matt. 20:28
28 [a]Heb. 2:18; 4:15
29 [a]Matt. 5:3; 2 Tim. 2:12
30 [a]Luke 22:16 [b]Matt. 5:3; 2 Tim. 2:12 [c]Matt. 19:28
31 [1]Or, *obtained by asking* [a]Job 1:6-12; 2:1-6; Matt. 4:10 [b]Amos 9:9
32 [a]John 17:9, 15 [b]John 21:15-17
33 [a]Luke 22:33, 34: *Matt. 26:33-35; Mark 14:29-31; John 13:37, 38*
35 [a]Matt. 10:9f.; Mark 6:8; Luke 9:3ff.; 10:4
36 [1]Or, *outer garment*
37 [a]Is. 53:12 [b]John 17:4; 19:30
38 [a]Luke 22:36, 49

The Garden of Gethsemane

39 [a]And He came out and proceeded [b]as was His custom to [c]the Mount of Olives; and the disciples also followed Him.
40 [a]And when He arrived at the place, He said to them, "[b]Pray that you may not enter into temptation."
41 And He withdrew from them about a stone's throw, and He [a]knelt down and *began* to pray,
42 saying, "Father, if Thou art willing, remove this [a]cup from Me; [b]yet not My will, but Thine be done."
43 [1]Now an [a]angel from heaven appeared to Him, strengthening Him.
44 And [a]being in agony He was praying very fervently; and His sweat became like drops of blood, falling down upon the ground.
45 And when He rose from prayer, He came to His disciples and found them sleeping from sorrow,
46 and said to them, "Why are you sleeping? Rise and [a]pray that you may not enter into temptation."

Jesus Betrayed by Judas

47 [a]While He was still speaking, behold, a multitude *came,* and the one called Judas, one of the twelve, was preceding them; and he approached Jesus to kiss Him.
48 But Jesus said to him, "Judas, are you betraying the Son of Man with a kiss?"
49 And when those who were around Him saw what was going to happen, they said, "Lord, shall we strike with the [a]sword?"
50 And a certain one of them struck the slave of the high priest and cut off his right ear.
51 But Jesus answered and said, "[1]Stop! No more of this." And He touched his ear and healed him.
52 And Jesus said to the chief priests and [a]officers of the temple and elders who had come against Him, "Have you come out with swords and clubs [b]as against a robber?
53 "While I was with you daily in the temple, you did not lay hands on Me; but [1]this hour and the power of darkness are yours."

Jesus' Arrest

54 [a]And having arrested Him, they led Him *away,* and brought Him to the house of the high priest; but [b]Peter was following at a distance.
55 [a]And after they had kindled a fire in the middle of [b]the courtyard and had sat down together, Peter was sitting among them.
56 And a certain servant-girl, seeing him as he sat in the firelight, and looking intently at him, said, "This man was with Him too."
57 But he denied *it,* saying, "Woman, I do not know Him."
58 And a little later, [a]another saw him and said, "You are *one* of them too!" But Peter said, "Man, I am not!"
59 And after about an hour had passed, another man *began* to insist, saying, "Certainly this man also was with Him, [a]for he is a Galilean too."
60 But Peter said, "Man, I do not know what you are talking about." And immediately, while he was still speaking, a cock crowed.
61 And [a]the Lord turned and looked at Peter. And Peter remembered the word of the Lord, how He had told him, "[b]Before a cock crows today, you will deny Me three times."
62 And he went outside and wept bitterly.
63 [a]And the men who were holding [1]Jesus in custody were mocking Him, and beating Him,
64 and they blindfolded Him and were asking Him, saying, "[a]Prophesy, who is the one who hit You?"
65 And they were saying many other things against Him, [a]blaspheming.

Jesus Before the Sanhedrin

66 [a]And when it was day, [b]the [1]Council of elders of the people assembled, both chief priests and scribes, and they led Him away to their [c]council *chamber,* saying,
67 "[a]If You are the [1]Christ, tell us." But He said to them, "If I tell you, you will not believe;
68 and if I ask a question, you will not answer.
69 "[a]But from now on [b]THE SON OF MAN WILL BE SEATED AT THE RIGHT HAND of the power OF GOD."
70 And they all said, "Are You [a]the Son of God, then?" And He said to them, "[1b]Yes, I am."
71 And they said, "What further need do we have of testimony? For we have heard it ourselves from His own mouth."

CHAPTER 23

Jesus Before Pilate

THEN the whole body of them arose and [a]brought Him before Pilate.

39 [a]Matt. 26:30; Mark 14:26; John 18:1 [b]Luke 21:37 [c]Matt. 21:1
40 [a]Luke 22:40-46: *Matt. 26:36-46; Mark 14:32-42* [b]Matt. 6:13; Luke 22:46
41 [a]Matt. 26:39; Mark 14:35; Luke 18:11
42 [a]Matt. 20:22 [b]Matt. 26:39
43 [1]Some ancient mss. do not contain verses 43 and 44 [a]Matt. 4:11
44 [a]Heb. 5:7
46 [a]Luke 22:40
47 [a]Luke 22:47-53: *Matt. 26:47-56; Mark 14:43-50; John 18:3-11*
49 [a]Luke 22:38
51 [1]Or, *"Let Me at least do this," and He touched*
52 [a]Luke 22:4 [b]Luke 22:37
53 [1]Lit., *this is your hour and power of darkness*
54 [a]Matt. 26:57; Mark 14:53 [b]Matt. 26:58; Mark 14:54; John 18:15
55 [a]Luke 22:55-62: *Matt. 26:69-75; Mark 14:66-72; John 18:16-18, 25-27* [b]Matt. 26:3
58 [a]John 18:26
59 [a]Matt. 26:73; Mark 14:70
61 [a]Luke 7:13 [b]Luke 22:34
63 [1]Lit., *Him* [a]Matt. 26:67f.; Mark 14:65; John 18:22f.
64 [a]Matt. 26:68; Mark 14:65
65 [a]Matt. 27:39
66 [1]Or, *Sanhedrin* [a]Matt. 27:1f.; Mark 15:1; John 18:28 [b]Acts 22:5 [c]Matt. 5:22
67 [1]I.e., Messiah [a]Matt. 26:63-66; Mark 14:61-63; Luke 22:67-71; John 18:19-21
69 [a]Matt. 26:64; Mark 14:62; 16:19 [b]Ps. 110:1
70 [1]Lit., *you say that I am* [a]Matt. 4:3 [b]Matt. 26:64; 27:11; Luke 23:3
1 [a]Matt. 27:2; Mark 15:1; John 18:28

2 [a]And they began to accuse Him, saying, "We found this man [b]misleading our nation and [c]forbidding to pay taxes to Caesar, and saying that He Himself is [1]Christ, a King."

3 And Pilate asked Him, saying, "Are You the King of the Jews?" And He answered him and said, "[a]*It is as* you say."

4 And Pilate said to the chief priests and the multitudes, "[a]I find no guilt in this man."

5 But they kept on insisting, saying, "He stirs up the people, teaching all over Judea, [a]starting from Galilee, even as far as this place."

6 But when Pilate heard it, he asked whether the man was a Galilean.

7 And when he learned that He belonged to Herod's jurisdiction, he sent Him to [a]Herod, who himself also was in Jerusalem [1]at that time.

Jesus Before Herod

8 Now Herod was very glad when he saw Jesus; for [a]he had wanted to see Him for a long time, because he had been hearing about Him and was hoping to see some [1]sign performed by Him.

9 And he questioned Him [1]at some length; but [a]He answered him nothing.

10 And the chief priests and the scribes were standing there, accusing Him vehemently.

11 And Herod with his soldiers, after treating Him with contempt and mocking Him, [a]dressed Him in a gorgeous robe and sent Him back to Pilate.

12 Now [a]Herod and Pilate became friends with one another that very day; for before they had been at enmity with each other.

Pilate Seeks Jesus' Release

13 And Pilate summoned the chief priests and the [a]rulers and the people,

14 and said to them, "You brought this man to me as one who [a]incites the people to rebellion, and behold, having examined Him before you, I [b]have found no guilt in this man regarding the charges which you make against Him.

15 "No, nor has [a]Herod, for he sent Him back to us; and behold, nothing deserving death has been done by Him.

16 "I will therefore [a]punish Him and release Him."

17 [[1]Now he was obliged to release to them at the feast one prisoner.]

18 But they cried out all together, saying, "[a]Away with this man, and release for us Barabbas!"

19 (He was one who had been thrown into prison for a certain insurrection made in the city, and for murder.)

20 And Pilate, wanting to release Jesus, addressed them again,

21 but they kept on calling out, saying, "Crucify, crucify Him!"

22 And he said to them the third time, "Why, what evil has this man done? I have found in Him no guilt *demanding* death; I will therefore [a]punish Him and release Him."

23 But they were insistent, with loud voices asking that He be crucified. And their voices *began* to prevail.

24 And Pilate pronounced sentence that their demand should be granted.

25 And he released the man they were asking for who had been thrown into prison for insurrection and murder, but he turned Jesus over to their will.

Simon Bears the Cross

26 [a]And when they led Him away, they laid hold of one Simon, a [b]Cyrenian, coming in from the country, and placed on him the cross to carry behind Jesus.

27 And there were following Him a great multitude of the people, and of women who were [1a]mourning and lamenting Him.

28 But Jesus turning to them said, "Daughters of Jerusalem, stop weeping for Me, but weep for yourselves and for your children.

29 "For behold, the days are coming when they will say, '[a]Blessed are the barren, and the wombs that never bore, and the breasts that never nursed.'

30 "Then they will begin TO [a]SAY TO THE MOUNTAINS, 'FALL ON US,' AND TO THE HILLS, 'COVER US.'

31 "For if they do these things in the green tree, what will happen in the dry?"

32 [a]And two others also, who were criminals, were being led away to be put to death with Him.

The Crucifixion

33 [a]And when they came to the place called [1]The Skull, there they crucified Him and the criminals, one on the right and the other on the left.

2 [1]I.e., Messiah [a]Luke 23:2, 3: *Matt. 27:11-14; Mark 15:2-5; John 18:29-37* [b]Luke 23:14 [c]Luke 20:22; John 18:33ff.; 19:12; Acts 17:7

3 [a]Luke 22:70

4 [a]Matt. 27:23; Mark 15:14; Luke 23:14, 22; John 18:38; 19:4, 6

5 [a]Matt. 4:12

7 [1]Lit., *in these days* [a]Matt. 14:1; Mark 6:14; Luke 3:1; 9:7; 13:31

8 [1]Or, *attesting miracle* [a]Luke 9:9

9 [1]Lit., *in many words* [a]Matt. 27:12, 14; Mark 15:5; John 19:9

11 [a]Matt. 27:28

12 [a]Acts 4:27

13 [a]Luke 23:35; John 7:26, 48; 12:42; Acts 3:17; 4:5, 8; 13:27

14 [a]Luke 23:2 [b]Luke 23:4

15 [a]Luke 9:9

16 [a]Matt. 27:26; Mark 15:15; Luke 23:22; John 19:1; Acts 16:37

17 [1]Many mss. do not contain this verse

18 [a]Luke 23:18-25: *Matt. 27:15-26; Mark 15:6-15;* John 18:39-19:16

22 [a]Luke 23:16

26 [a]Luke 23:26: *Matt. 27:32; Mark 15:21;* John 19:17 [b]Matt. 27:32

27 [1]Lit., *beating the breast* [a]Luke 8:52

29 [a]Matt. 24:19; Luke 11:27; 21:23

30 [a]Is. 2:19, 20; Hos. 10:8; Rev. 6:16

32 [a]Matt. 27:38; Mark 15:27; John 19:18

33 [1]In Latin, *Calvarius,* or *Calvary* [a]Luke 23:33-43: *Matt. 27:33-44; Mark 15:22-32; John 19:17-24*

34 [1]But Jesus was saying, "[a]Father forgive them; for they do not know what they are doing." [b]AND THEY CAST LOTS, DIVIDING UP HIS GARMENTS AMONG THEMSELVES.

35 And the people stood by, looking on. And even the [a]rulers were sneering at Him, saying, "He saved others; [b]let Him save Himself if this is the Christ of God, His Chosen One."

36 And the soldiers also mocked Him, coming up to Him, [a]offering Him sour wine,

37 and saying, "[a]If You are the King of the Jews, save Yourself!"

38 Now there was also an inscription above Him, "[a]THIS IS THE KING OF THE JEWS."

39 [a]And one of the criminals who were hanged *there* was hurling abuse at Him, saying, "Are You not the Christ? [b]Save Yourself and us!"

40 But the other answered, and rebuking him said, "Do you not even fear God, since you are under the same sentence of condemnation?

41 "And we indeed justly, for we are receiving what we deserve for our deeds; but this man has done nothing wrong."

42 And he was saying, "Jesus, remember me when You come in Your kingdom!"

43 And He said to him, "Truly I say to you, today you shall be with Me in [a]Paradise."

44 [a]And it was now about [1b]the sixth hour, and darkness fell over the whole land until [2]the ninth hour,

45 the sun being obscured; and [a]the veil of the temple was torn in two.

46 And Jesus, [a]crying out with a loud voice, said, "Father, [b]INTO THY HANDS I COMMIT MY SPIRIT." And having said this, He breathed His last.

47 [a]Now when the centurion saw what had happened, he *began* [b]praising God, saying, "Certainly this man was innocent."

48 And all the multitudes who came together for this spectacle, when they observed what had happened, *began* to return, [a]beating their breasts.

49 [a]And all His acquaintances and [a]the women who accompanied Him from Galilee, were standing at a distance, seeing these things.

Jesus Is Buried

50 [a]And behold, a man named Joseph, who was a [b]member of the Council, a good and righteous man

51 (he had not consented to their plan and action), *a man* from Arimathea, a city of the Jews, who was [a]waiting for the kingdom of God;

52 this man went to Pilate and asked for the body of Jesus.

53 And he took it down and wrapped it in a linen cloth, and laid Him in a tomb cut into the rock, where no one had ever lain.

54 And it was [a]the preparation day, and the Sabbath was about to begin.

55 Now [a]the women who had come with Him out of Galilee followed after, and saw the tomb and how His body was laid.

56 And they returned and [a]prepared spices and perfumes.

And on the Sabbath they rested according to [b]the commandment.

Chapter 24

The Resurrection

[a]BUT on the first day of the week, at early dawn, they came to the tomb, bringing the spices which they had prepared.

2 And they found the stone rolled away from the tomb,

3 but when they entered, they did not find the body of [a]the Lord Jesus.

4 And it happened that while they were perplexed about this, behold, [a]two men suddenly [b]stood near them in dazzling apparel;

5 and as *the women* were terrified and bowed their faces to the ground, *the men* said to them, "Why do you seek the living One among the dead?

6 "[1]He is not here, but He [a]has [2]risen. Remember how He spoke to you [b]while He was still in Galilee,

7 saying that [a]the Son of Man must be delivered into the hands of sinful men, and be crucified, and the third day rise again."

8 And [a]they remembered His words,

9 and returned from the tomb and reported all these things to the eleven and to all the rest.

10 Now they were [a]Mary Magdalene and Joanna and Mary the *mother* of James; also the other women with them were telling these things to [b]the apostles.

11 And these words appeared to them as nonsense, and they [a]would not believe them.

12 [[1]But Peter arose and [a]ran to the tomb; [a]stooping and looking in, he *saw the linen wrappings only;

34 [1]Some mss. do not contain *"But Jesus was saying... doing."* [a]Matt. 11:25; Luke 22:42 [b]Ps. 22:18; John 19:24
35 [a]Luke 23:13 [b]Matt. 27:43
36 [a]Matt. 27:48
37 [a]Matt. 27:43
38 [a]Matt. 27:37; Mark 15:26; John 19:19
39 [a]Matt. 27:44; Mark 15:32; Luke 23:39-43 [b]Luke 23:35, 37
43 [a]Gen. 2:8; 2 Cor. 12:4; Rev. 2:7
44 [1]I.e., 12 noon [2]I.e., 3 p.m. [a]Luke 23:44-49: *Matt. 27:45-56; Mark 15:33-41* [b]John 19:14
45 [a]Matt. 27:51
46 [a]Matt. 27:50; Mark 15:37; John 19:30 [b]Ps. 31:5
47 [a]Matt. 27:54; Mark 15:39 [b]Matt. 9:8
48 [a]Luke 8:52; 18:13
49 [a]Matt. 27: 55f.; Mark 15:40f.; Luke 8:2; John 19:25
50 [a]Luke 23:50-56: *Matt. 27:57-61; Mark 15:42-47; John 19:38-42* [b]Mark 15:43
51 [a]Mark 15:43; Luke 2:25
54 [a]Matt. 27:62; Mark 15:42
55 [a]Luke 23:49
56 [a]Mark 16:1; Luke 24:1 [b]Ex. 20:10
1 [a]Luke 24:1-10: *Matt. 28:1-8; Mark 16:1-8;* John 20:1-8
3 [a]Luke 7:13; Acts 1:21
4 [a]John 20:12 [b]Luke 2:9; Acts 12:7
6 [1]Some ancient mss. do not contain *He is not here, but He has risen* [2]Or, *been raised* [a]Mark 16:6 [b]Matt. 17:22f.; Mark 9:30f.; Luke 9:44; 24:44
7 [a]Matt. 16:21
8 [a]John 2:22
10 [a]Matt. 27:56 [b]Mark 6:30
11 [a]Mark 16:11
12 [1]Some ancient mss. do not contain v. 12 [a]John 20:3-6

and he went away [b]to his home, marveling at that which had happened.]

The Road to Emmaus

13 And behold, [a]two of them were going that very day to a village named Emmaus, which was [1]about seven miles from Jerusalem.

14 And they were conversing with each other about all these things which had taken place.

15 And it came about that while they were conversing and discussing, Jesus Himself approached, and *began* traveling with them.

16 But [a]their eyes were prevented from recognizing Him.

17 And He said to them, "What are these words that you are exchanging with one another as you are walking?" And they stood still, looking sad.

18 And one of them, named Cleopas, answered and said to Him, "[1]Are You the only one visiting Jerusalem and unaware of the things which have happened here in these days?"

19 And He said to them, "What things?" And they said to Him, "The things about [a]Jesus the Nazarene, who was a [b]prophet mighty in deed and word in the sight of God and all the people,

20 and how the chief priests and our [a]rulers delivered Him up to the sentence of death, and crucified Him.

21 "But we were hoping that it was He who was going to [a]redeem Israel. Indeed, besides all this, it is the third day since these things happened.

22 "But also some women among us amazed us. [a]When they were at the tomb early in the morning,

23 and did not find His body, they came, saying that they had also seen a vision of angels, who said that He was alive.

24 "And some of those who were with us went to the tomb and found it just exactly as the women also had said; but Him they did not see."

25 And He said to them, "O foolish men and slow of heart to believe in all that [a]the prophets have spoken!

26 "[a]Was it not necessary for the [1]Christ to suffer these things and to enter into His glory?"

27 And beginning with [a]Moses and with all the [b]prophets, He explained to them the things concerning Himself in all the Scriptures.

28 And they approached the village where they were going, and [a]He acted as though He would go farther.

29 And they urged Him, saying, "Stay with us, for it is *getting* toward evening, and the day is now nearly over." And He went in to stay with them.

30 And it came about that when He had reclined *at table* with them, He took the bread and [a]blessed *it*, and breaking *it*, He *began* giving *it* to them.

31 And their [a]eyes were opened and they recognized Him; and He vanished from [1]their sight.

32 And they said to one another, "[1]Were not our hearts burning within us while He was speaking to us on the road, while He [a]was explaining the Scriptures to us?"

33 And they arose that very hour and returned to Jerusalem, and [a]found gathered together the eleven and [b]those who were with them,

34 saying, "[a]The Lord has really risen, and [b]has appeared to Simon."

35 And they *began* to relate their experiences on the road and how [a]He was recognized by them in the breaking of the bread.

Other Appearances

36 And while they were telling these things, [a]He Himself stood in their midst.[1]

37 But they were startled and frightened and thought that they were seeing [a]a spirit.

38 And He said to them, "Why are you troubled, and why do doubts arise in your hearts?

39 "[a]See My hands and My feet, that it is I Myself; [b]touch Me and see, for a spirit does not have flesh and bones as you see that I have."

40 [[1]And when He had said this, He showed them His hands and His feet.]

41 And while they still [1a]could not believe *it* for joy and were marveling, He said to them, "[b]Have you anything here to eat?"

42 And they gave Him a piece of a broiled fish;

43 and He took it and [a]ate *it* in their sight.

44 Now He said to them, "[a]These are My words which I spoke to you while I was still with you, that all things which are written about Me in the [b]Law of Moses and [b]the Prophets and [c]the Psalms must be fulfilled."

45 Then He [a]opened their [1]minds to understand the Scriptures,

12 [b]John 20:10
13 [1]I.e., 60 stadia, one stadion equals 600 feet [a]Mark 16:12
16 [a]Luke 24:31; John 20:14; 21:4
18 [1]Or, *Are You visiting Jerusalem alone*
19 [a]Mark 1:24 [b]Matt. 21:11
20 [a]Luke 23:13
21 [a]Luke 1:68
22 [a]Luke 24:1ff.
25 [a]Matt. 26:24
26 [1]I.e., Messiah [a]Luke 24:7, 44ff.; Heb. 2:10; 1 Pet. 1:11
27 [a]Gen. 3:15; 12:3; Num. 21:9 [John 3:14]; Deut. 18:15 [John 1:45]; John 5:46 [b]2 Sam. 7:12-16; Is. 7:14 [Matt. 1:23]; 9:1f. [Matt. 4:15f.]; 42:1 [Matt. 12:18ff.]; 53:4 [Matt. 8:17; Luke 22:37]; Dan. 7:13 [Matt. 24:30]; Mic. 5:2 [Matt. 2:6]; Zech. 9:9 [Matt. 21:5]; Acts 13:27
28 [a]Mark 6:48
30 [a]Matt. 14:19
31 [1]Lit., *them* [a]Luke 24:16
32 [1]Lit., *Was not our heart* [a]Luke 24:45
33 [a]Mark 16:13 [b]Acts 1:14
34 [a]Luke 24:6 [b]1 Cor. 15:5
35 [a]Luke 24:30f.
36 [1]Some ancient mss. insert, *And He says to them, "Peace be to you."* [a]Mark 16:14
37 [a]Matt. 14:26; Mark 6:49
39 [a]John 20:20, 27 [b]John 20:27; 1 John 1:1
40 [1]Many mss. do not contain this verse
41 [1]Lit., *were disbelieving* [a]Luke 24:11 [b]John 21:5
43 [a]Acts 10:41
44 [a]Luke 9:22, 44f.; 18:31-34; 22:37 [b]Luke 24:27 [c]Ps. 2 [Acts 13:33]; Ps. 16 [Acts 2:27]; Ps. 22 [Matt. 27:34-46]; Ps. 69 [John 19:28ff.]; Ps. 72; 110 [Matt. 22:43f.]; Ps. 118 [Matt. 21:42]
45 [1]Lit., *mind* [a]Luke 24:32; Acts 16:14; 1 John 5:20

46 and He said to them, "[a]Thus it
is written, that the Christ should
suffer and [b]rise again from the dead
the third day;
47 and that [a]repentance for forgiveness of sins should be proclaimed in His name to [b]all the nations, beginning from Jerusalem.
48"You are [a]witnesses of these
things.
49"And behold, [a]I am sending
forth the promise of My Father upon
you; but [b]you are to stay in the city
until you are clothed with power
from on high."

The Ascension

50 And He led them out as far as
[a]Bethany, and He lifted up His
hands and blessed them.
51 And it came about that while
He was blessing them, He parted
from them.[1]
52 And they returned to Jerusalem
with great joy,
53 and were continually in the
temple, praising God.

46 [a]Luke 24:26, 44 [b]Luke 24:7
47 [a]Acts 5:31; 10:43; 13:38; 26:18 [b]Matt. 28:19
48 [a]Acts 1:8, 22; 5:32; 10:39, 41; 13:31; 1 Pet. 5:1
49 [a]John 14:26 [b]Acts 1:4
50 [a]Matt. 21:17; Acts 1:12
51 [1]Some mss. add, *and was carried up into heaven*

THE GOSPEL
ACCORDING TO
JOHN

The Deity of Jesus Christ

[a]
IN the beginning was [b]the Word,
and the Word was [c]with God, and
the Word was God.
2 He was in the beginning with
God.
3 [a]All things came into being by
Him; and apart from Him nothing
came into being that has come into
being.
4 [a]In Him was life; and the life
was [b]the light of men.
5 And the light shines in the darkness; and the darkness did not
[1]comprehend it.

The Witness of John

6 There came a man, sent from
God, whose name was John.
7 He came [a]for a witness, that he
might bear witness of the light,
[b]that all might believe through him.
8 [a]He was not the light, but *came*
that he might bear witness of the
light.
9 There was [a]the true light which,
coming into the world, enlightens
every man.
10 He was in the world, and [a]the
world was made through Him, and
the world did not know Him.
11 He came to His own, and those
who were His own did not receive
Him.
12 But as many as received Him,
to them He gave the right to become
[a]children of God, *even* [b]to those who
believe in His name,
13 [a]who were born not of blood,
nor of the will of the flesh, nor of the
will of man, but of God.

The Word Made Flesh

14 And [a]the Word [b]became flesh,
and [c]dwelt among us, and [d]we beheld His glory, glory as of the only
begotten from the Father, full of
[e]grace and [f]truth.
15 John *[a]bore witness of Him,
and cried out, saying, "This was He
of whom I said, '[b]He who comes after me has a higher rank than I, [c]for
He existed before me.' "
16 For of His [a]fulness we have all
received, and grace upon grace.
17 For [a]the law was given through
Moses; [b]grace and [c]truth were realized through Jesus Christ.
18 [a]No man has seen God at any
time; [b]the only begotten [1]God, who
is [c]in the bosom of the Father, He
has explained *Him.*

The Testimony of John

19 And this is [a]the witness of John,
when [b]the Jews sent to him priests
and Levites [c]from Jerusalem to ask
him, "Who are you?"
20 And he confessed, and did not
deny, and he confessed, "[a]I am not
the Christ."
21 And they asked him, "What
then? Are you [a]Elijah?" And he
*said, "I am not." "Are you [b]the
Prophet?" And he answered, "No."
22 They said then to him, "Who
are you, so that we may give an answer to those who sent us? What do
you say about yourself?"
23 He said, "[a]I am a voice of one
crying in the wilderness, '[b]MAKE
STRAIGHT THE WAY OF THE LORD,' as
Isaiah the prophet said."
24 Now they had been sent from
the Pharisees.

1 [a]Gen. 1:1 [b]John 1:14 [c]John 17:5
3 [a]John 1:10
4 [a]John 5:26 [b]John 8:12; 9:5
5 [1]Or, *overpower*
7 [a]John 1:15, 19 [b]John 1:12
8 [a]John 1:20
9 [a]1 John 2:8
10 [a]1 Cor. 8:6
12 [a]John 11:52 [b]John 1:7; 3:18
13 [a]John 3:5f.
14 [a]Rev. 19:13 [b]Rom. 1:3; 1 Tim. 3:16 [c]Rev. 21:3 [d]Luke 9:32; John 2:11 [e]John 1:17; Rom. 5:21 [f]John 8:32
15 [a]John 1:7 [b]Matt. 3:11; John 1:27, 30 [c]John 1:30
16 [a]Eph. 1:23; 3:19
17 [a]John 7:19 [b]John 1:14; Rom. 5:21; 6:14 [c]John 8:32; 14:6; 18:37
18 [1]Some later mss. read, *Son* [a]Ex. 33:20; 1 John 4:12 [b]John 3:16, 18; 1 John 4:9 [c]Luke 16:22
19 [a]John 1:7 [b]John 2:18, 20; 8:22; 9:18; 10:24 [c]Matt. 15:1
20 [a]John 3:28
21 [a]Matt. 11:14; 16:14 [b]Deut. 18:15, 18
23 [a]Matt. 3:3 [b]Is. 40:3

25 And they asked him, and said to
him, "Why then are you baptizing, if
you are not the [1]Christ, nor Elijah,
nor [a]the Prophet?"
26 John answered them saying, "[a]I
baptize in water, *but* among you
stands One whom you do not know.
27"*It is* [a]He who comes after me,
the [b]thong of whose sandal I am not
worthy to untie."
28 These things took place in Bethany [a]beyond the Jordan, where John
was baptizing.
29 The next day he *saw Jesus
coming to him, and *said, "Behold,
[a]the Lamb of God who [b]takes away
the sin of the world!
30"This is He on behalf of whom I
said, '[a]After me comes a Man who
has a higher rank than I, [b]for He existed before me.'
31"And I did not recognize [1]Him,
but in order that He might be manifested to Israel, I came baptizing in
water."
32 And John [a]bore witness saying,
"[b]I have beheld the Spirit descending as a dove out of heaven; and He
remained upon Him.
33"And I did not recognize Him,
but He who sent me to baptize in
water said to me, 'He upon whom
you see the Spirit descending and
remaining upon Him, [a]this is the one
who baptizes in the Holy Spirit.'
34"And I have seen, and have
borne witness that this is [a]the Son of
God."

Jesus' Public Ministry, First Converts

35 Again [a]the next day John was
standing, and two of his disciples;
36 and he looked upon Jesus as He
walked, and *said, "Behold, [a]the
Lamb of God!"
37 And the two disciples heard
him speak, and they followed Jesus.
38 And Jesus turned, and beheld
them following, and *said to them,
"What do you seek?" And they said
to Him, "[a]Rabbi (which translated
means Teacher), where are You
staying?"
39 He *said to them, "Come, and
you will see." They came therefore
and saw where He was staying; and
they stayed with Him that day, for it
was about the [1]tenth hour.
40 [a]One of the two who heard
John *speak,* and followed Him, was
Andrew, Simon Peter's brother.
41 He *found first his own brother
Simon, and *said to him, "We have
found the [a]Messiah" (which translated means Christ).
42 He brought him to Jesus. Jesus
looked at him, and said, "You are
Simon the son of [a]John; you shall be
called [b]Cephas" (which translated
means [1c]Peter).
43 [a]The next day *He* purposed to
go forth into [b]Galilee, and He
*found [c]Philip, and Jesus *said to
him, "[d]Follow Me."
44 Now [a]Philip was from [b]Bethsa-
ida, of the city of Andrew and Peter.
45 [a]Philip *found [b]Nathanael, and
*said to him, "We have found Him
of whom [c]Moses in the Law and also
[c]the Prophets wrote, Jesus of [d]Naz-
areth, [e]the son of Joseph."
46 And Nathanael *said to him,
"[a]Can any good thing come out of
Nazareth?" [b]Philip *said to him,
"Come and see."
47 Jesus saw Nathanael coming to
Him, and *said of him, "Behold, an
[a]Israelite indeed, in whom is no
guile!"
48 Nathanael *said to Him, "How
do You know me?" Jesus answered
and said to him, "Before [a]Philip
called you, when you were under
the fig tree, I saw you."
49 Nathanael answered Him,
"[a]Rabbi, You are [b]the Son of God;
You are the [c]King of Israel."
50 Jesus answered and said to
him, "Because I said to you that I
saw you under the fig tree, do you
believe? You shall see greater things
than these."
51 And He *said to him, "Truly,
truly, I say to you, you shall see [a]the
heavens opened, and [b]the angels of
God ascending and descending
upon [c]the Son of Man."

CHAPTER 2

Miracle at Cana

AND on [a]the third day there was a
wedding in [b]Cana of Galilee; and the
[c]mother of Jesus was there;
2 and Jesus also was invited, and
His [a]disciples, to the wedding.
3 And when the wine gave out,
the mother of Jesus *said to Him,
"They have no wine."
4 And Jesus *said to her, "[a]Wom-
an, [b]what do I have to do with you?
[c]My hour has not yet come."
5 His [a]mother *said to the servants, "Whatever He says to you, do
it."
6 Now there were six stone waterpots set there [a]for the Jewish custom of purification, containing
twenty or thirty gallons each.
7 Jesus *said to them, "Fill the
waterpots with water." And they
filled them up to the brim.

25 [1]I.e., Messiah [a]Deut. 18:15, 18; Matt. 21:11
26 [a]Matt. 3:11; Mark 1:8; Luke 3:16
27 [a]Matt. 3:11; John 1:30 [b]Matt. 3:11; Mark 1:7
28 [a]John 3:26
29 [a]Is. 53:7; John 1:36; Rev. 5:6, 8, 12f.; 6:1 [b]Matt. 1:21
30 [a]Matt. 3:11; John 1:27 [b]John 1:15
31 [1]I.e., as the Messiah
32 [a]John 1:7 [b]Matt. 3:16
33 [a]Matt. 3:11; Mark 1:8; Luke 3:16
34 [a]Matt. 4:3; John 1:49
35 [a]John 1:29
36 [a]John 1:29
38 [a]Matt. 23:7f.; John 1:49
39 [1]I.e., 4 p.m.
40 [a]Matt. 4:18-22; Mark 1:16-20; Luke 5:2-11; John 1:40-42
41 [a]Dan. 9:25
42 [1]I.e., Rock or Stone [a]John 21:15-17 [b]1 Cor. 1:12; 3:22; 9:5; 15:5; Gal. 1:18; 2:9, 11, 14 [c]Matt. 16:18
43 [a]John 1:29, 35 [b]Matt. 4:12 [c]Matt. 10:3; John 1:44-48; 6:5, 7 [d]Matt. 8:22
44 [a]Matt. 10:3; John 1:44-48; 6:5, 7; 12:21f.; 14:8f. [b]Matt. 11:21
45 [a]Matt. 10:3; John 1:44-48; 6:5, 7; 12:21f.; 14:8f. [b]John 1:46-49; 21:2 [c]Luke 24:27 [d]Matt. 2:23 [e]Luke 2:48; 3:23; 4:22; John 6:42
46 [a]John 7:41, 52 [b]Matt. 10:3; John 1:44-48; 6:5
47 [a]Rom. 9:4
48 [a]Matt. 10:3; John 1:44-48; 6:5
49 [a]John 1:38 [b]John 1:34 [c]Matt. 2:2; 27:42
51 [a]Ezek. 1:1; Matt. 3:16; Rev. 19:11 [b]Gen. 28:12 [c]Matt. 8:20
1 [a]John 1:29, 35, 43 [b]John 2:11; 4:46; 21:2 [c]Matt. 12:46
2 [a]John 1:40-49; 2:12, 17, 22
4 [a]John 19:26 [b]Matt. 8:29 [c]John 7:6, 8, 30; 8:20
5 [a]Matt. 12:46
6 [a]Mark 7:3f.; John 3:25

8 And He *said to them, "Draw *some* out now, and take it to the headwaiter." And they took it *to him.*

9 And when the headwaiter tasted the water [a]which had become wine, and did not know where it came from (but the servants who had drawn the water knew), the headwaiter *called the bridegroom,

10 and *said to him, "Every man serves the good wine first, and when *men* [a]have drunk freely, *then* that which is poorer; you have kept the good wine until now."

11 This beginning of *His* [a]signs Jesus did in Cana of [b]Galilee, and manifested His [c]glory, and His disciples believed in Him.

12 After this He went down to [a]Capernaum, He and His [b]mother, and *His* [b]brothers, and His [c]disciples; and there they stayed a few days.

First Passover—Cleansing the Temple

13 And [a]the Passover of the Jews was at hand, and Jesus [b]went up to Jerusalem.

14 [a]And He found in the temple those who were selling oxen and sheep and doves, and the moneychangers seated.

15 And He made a scourge of cords, and drove *them* all out of the temple, with the sheep and the oxen; and He poured out the coins of the moneychangers, and overturned their tables;

16 and to those who were selling [a]the doves He said, "Take these things away; stop making [b]My Father's house a house of merchandise."

17 His [a]disciples remembered that it was written, "[b]ZEAL FOR THY HOUSE WILL CONSUME ME."

18 [a]The Jews therefore answered and said to Him, "[b]What sign do You show to us, seeing that You do these things?"

19 Jesus answered and said to them, "[a]Destroy this temple, and in three days I will raise it up."

20 [a]The Jews therefore said, "It took [b]forty-six years to build this temple, and will You raise it up in three days?"

21 But He was speaking of [a]the temple of His body.

22 When therefore He was raised from the dead, His [a]disciples [b]remembered that He said this; and they believed [c]the Scripture, and the word which Jesus had spoken.

23 Now when He was in Jerusalem at [a]the Passover, during the feast, many believed in His name, [b]beholding His signs which He was doing.

24 But Jesus, on His part, was not entrusting Himself to them, for He knew all men,

25 and because He did not need anyone to bear witness concerning man [a]for He Himself knew what was in man.

CHAPTER 3

The New Birth

NOW there was a man of the Pharisees, named [a]Nicodemus, a [b]ruler of the Jews;

2 this man came to Him by night, and said to Him, "[a]Rabbi, we know that You have come from God *as* a teacher; for no one can do these [b]signs that You do unless [c]God is with him."

3 Jesus answered and said to him, "Truly, truly, I say to you, unless one [a]is born again, he cannot see [b]the kingdom of God."

4 Nicodemus *said to Him, "How can a man be born when he is old? He cannot enter a second time into his mother's womb and be born, can he?"

5 Jesus answered, "Truly, truly, I say to you, unless one is born of [a]water and the Spirit, he cannot enter into [b]the kingdom of God.

6 "[a]That which is born of the flesh is flesh; and that which is born of the Spirit is spirit.

7 "Do not marvel that I said to you, 'You must be born again.'

8 "[a]The wind blows where it wishes and you hear the sound of it, but do not know where it comes from and where it is going; so is every one who is born of the Spirit."

9 Nicodemus answered and said to Him, "How can these things be?"

10 Jesus answered and said to him, "Are you [a]the teacher of Israel, and do not understand these things?

11 "Truly, truly, I say to you, [a]we speak that which we know, and [b]bear witness of that which we have seen; and [b]you do not receive our witness.

12 "If I told you earthly things and you do not believe, how shall you believe if I tell you heavenly things?

13 "And [a]no one has ascended into heaven, but [b]He who descended from heaven, *even* [c]the Son of Man.[1]

14 "And as [a]Moses lifted up the serpent in the wilderness, even so must [b]the Son of Man [c]be lifted up;

9 [a]John 4:46
10 [a]Matt. 24:49; Luke 12:45; Acts 2:15; 1 Cor. 11:21; Eph. 5:18; 1 Thess. 5:7; Rev. 17:2, 6
11 [a]John 2:23; 3:2; 4:54; 6:2, 14, 26 [b]John 1:43 [c]John 1:14
12 [a]Matt. 4:13 [b]Matt. 12:46 [c]John 2:2
13 [a]John 5:1 marg.; 6:4; 11:55 [b]Deut. 16:1-6; Luke 2:41
14 [a]John 2:14-16: *Matt. 21:12ff.; Mark 11:15, 17; Luke 19:45f.;* Mal. 3:1ff.
16 [a]Matt. 21:12 [b]Luke 2:49
17 [a]John 2:2 [b]Ps. 69:9
18 [a]John 1:19 [b]Matt. 12:38
19 [a]Matt. 26:61; Mark 14:58; 15:29; Acts 6:14
20 [a]John 1:19 [b]Ezra 5:16
21 [a]1 Cor. 6:19
22 [a]John 2:2 [b]Luke 24:8 [c]Ps. 16:10; Luke 24:26f.; John 20:9; Acts 13:33
23 [a]John 2:13 [b]John 2:11
25 [a]Matt. 9:4; John 1:42, 47
1 [a]John 7:50; 19:39 [b]Luke 23:13; John 7:26
2 [a]Matt. 23:7; John 3:26 [b]John 2:11 [c]John 9:33; 10:38; 14:10f.; Acts 2:22
3 [a]2 Cor. 5:17, 1 Pet. 1:23 [b]Matt. 19:24; Mark 9:47
5 [a]Ezek. 36:25-27; Eph. 5:26; Titus 3:5 [b]Matt. 19:24; 21:31; Mark 9:47; 10:14f.; John 3:3
6 [a]John 1:13; 1 Cor. 15:50
8 [a]Ps. 135:7; Eccles. 11:5; Ezek. 37:9
10 [a]Luke 2:46; 5:17; Acts 5:34
11 [a]John 1:18; 7:16f.; 8:26, 28 [b]John 3:32
13 [1]Later manuscripts add, *who is in heaven* [a]Deut. 30:12; Prov. 30:4; Acts 2:34; Rom. 10:6; Eph. 4:9 [b]John 3:31; 6:38, 42 [c]Matt. 8:20
14 [a]Num. 21:9 [b]Matt. 8:20 [c]John 8:28; 12:34

15 that whoever [1]believes may [a]in Him have eternal life.

16"For God so [a]loved the world, that He [b]gave His [c]only begotten Son, that whoever [d]believes in Him should not perish, but have eternal life.

17"For God [a]did not send the Son into the world [b]to judge the world; but that the world should be saved through Him.

18"[a]He who believes in Him is not judged; he who does not believe has been judged already, because he has not believed in the name of [b]the only begotten Son of God.

19"And this is the judgment, that [a]the light is come into the world, and men loved the darkness rather than the light; for [b]their deeds were evil.

20"[a]For everyone who does evil hates the light, and does not come to the light, lest his deeds should be exposed.

21"But he who [a]practices the truth comes to the light, that his deeds may be manifested as having been wrought in God."

John's Last Testimony

22 After these things Jesus and His [a]disciples came into the land of Judea; and there He was spending time with them, and [b]baptizing.

23 And John also was baptizing in Aenon near Salim, because there was much water there; and they were coming, and were being baptized.

24 For [a]John had not yet been thrown into prison.

25 There arose therefore a discussion on the part of John's disciples with a Jew about [a]purification.

26 And they came to John, and said to him, "[a]Rabbi, He who was with you [b]beyond the Jordan, to whom you [c]have borne witness, behold, He is baptizing, and all are coming to Him."

27 John answered and said, "[a]A man can receive nothing, unless it has been given him from heaven.

28"You yourselves bear me witness, that I said, '[a]I am not the [1]Christ', but, 'I have been sent before Him.'

29"He who has the bride is [a]the bridegroom; but the friend of the bridegroom, who stands and hears him, rejoices greatly because of the bridegroom's voice. And so this [b]joy of mine has been made full.

30"He must increase, but I must decrease.

31"[a]He who comes from above is above all, he who is of the earth is from the earth and speaks [b]of the earth. [a]He who comes from heaven is above all.

32"What He has seen and heard, of that He [a]bears witness; and [a]no man receives His witness.

33"He who has received His witness [a]has set his seal to *this,* that God is true.

34"For He whom God has [a]sent speaks the words of God; [b]for He gives the Spirit without measure.

35"[a]The Father loves the Son, and has given all things into His hand.

36"He who [a]believes in the Son has eternal life; but he who [b]does not obey the Son shall not see life, but the wrath of God abides on him."

Chapter 4

Jesus Goes to Galilee

WHEN therefore [a]the Lord knew that the Pharisees had heard that Jesus was making and [b]baptizing more disciples than John

2 (although [a]Jesus Himself was not baptizing, but His [b]disciples were),

3 He left [a]Judea, and departed [b]again into Galilee.

4 And He had to pass through [a]Samaria.

5 So He *came to a city of [a]Samaria, called Sychar, near the parcel of ground that [b]Jacob gave to his son Joseph;

6 and Jacob's well was there. Jesus therefore, being wearied from His journey, was sitting thus by the well. It was about [1]the sixth hour.

The Woman of Samaria

7 There *came a woman of Samaria to draw water. Jesus *said to her, "Give Me a drink."

8 For His [a]disciples had gone away into [b]the city to buy food.

9 The [a]Samaritan woman therefore *said to Him, "How is it that You, being a Jew, ask me for a drink since I am a Samaritan woman?" (For [b]Jews have no dealings with Samaritans.)

10 Jesus answered and said to her, "If you knew the gift of God, and who it is who says to you, 'Give Me a drink,' you would have asked Him, and He would have given you [a]living water."

11 She *said to Him, "Sir, You have nothing to draw with and the well is deep; where then do You get that [a]living water?

15 [1]Some mss. read, *believes in Him may have eternal life* [a]John 20:31; 1 John 5:11-13
16 [a]Rom. 5:8; Eph. 2:4; 2 Thess. 2:16; 1 John 4:10; Rev. 1:5 [b]Rom. 8:32; 1 John 4:9 [c]John 1:18; 3:18; 1 John 4:9 [d]John 3:36
17 [a]John 3:34; 5:36, 38; 6:29, 38; 10:36; 11:42; 17:3; 20:21 [b]Luke 19:10; John 8:15; 12:47; 1 John 4:14
18 [a]Mark 16:16; John 5:24 [b]John 1:18; 1 John 4:9
19 [a]John 1:4 [b]John 7:7
20 [a]John 3:20, 21; Eph. 5:11, 13
21 [a]1 John 1:6
22 [a]John 2:2 [b]John 4:1, 2
24 [a]Matt. 4:12
25 [a]John 2:6
26 [a]Matt. 23:7; John 3:2 [b]John 1:28 [c]John 1:7
27 [a]1 Cor. 4:7; Heb. 5:4
28 [1]I.e., Messiah [a]John 1:20, 23
29 [a]Matt. 9:15; 25:1 [b]John 15:11; 16:24; 17:13; Phil. 2:2; 1 John 1:4
31 [a]John 3:13; 8:23 [b]1 John 4:5
32 [a]John 3:11
33 [a]John 6:27; Rom. 4:11; 15:28; 1 Cor. 9:2; 2 Cor. 1:22; Eph. 1:13; 4:30; 2 Tim. 2:19; Rev. 7:3-8
34 [a]John 3:17 [b]Matt. 12:18; Luke 4:18; Acts 1:2; 10:38
35 [a]Matt. 28:18; John 5:20; 17:2
36 [a]John 3:16 [b]Acts 14:2; Heb. 3:18
1 [a]Luke 7:13 [b]John 3:22, 26; 1 Cor. 1:17
2 [a]John 3:22, 26; 1 Cor. 1:17 [b]John 2:2
3 [a]John 3:22 [b]John 2:11f.
4 [a]Luke 9:52
5 [a]Luke 9:52 [b]Gen. 33:19; 48:22; Josh. 24:32; John 4:12
6 [1]I.e., noon
8 [a]John 2:2 [b]John 4:5, 39
9 [a]Luke 9:52 [b]Ezra 4:3-6, 11ff.; Matt. 10:5; John 8:48
10 [a]John 7:37f.; Rev. 21:6; 22:17
11 [a]John 7:37f.; Rev. 21:6; 22:17

12 "You are not greater than our father Jacob, are You, who [a]gave us the well, and drank of it himself, and his sons, and his cattle?"

13 Jesus answered and said to her, "Everyone who drinks of this water shall thirst again;

14 but whoever drinks of the water that I shall give him [a]shall never thirst; but the water that I shall give him shall become in him a well of water springing up to [b]eternal life."

15 The woman *said to Him, "[1]Sir, [a]give me this water, so I will not be thirsty, nor come all the way here to draw."

16 He *said to her, "Go, call your husband, and come here."

17 The woman answered and said, "I have no husband." Jesus *said to her, "You have well said, 'I have no husband';

18 for you have had five husbands; and the one whom you now have is not your husband; this you have said truly."

19 The woman *said to Him, "[1]Sir, I perceive that You are [a]a prophet.

20 "[a]Our fathers worshiped in [b]this mountain; and you *people* say that [c]in Jerusalem is the place where men ought to worship."

21 Jesus *said to her, "Woman, believe Me, [a]an hour is coming when [b]neither in this mountain, nor in Jerusalem, shall you worship the Father.

22 "[a]You worship that which you do not know; we worship that which we know; for [b]salvation is from the Jews.

23 "But [a]an hour is coming, and now is, when the true worshipers shall worship the Father [b]in spirit and truth; for such people the Father seeks to be His worshipers.

24 "God is [1]spirit; and those who worship Him must worship [a]in spirit and truth."

25 The woman *said to Him, "I know that [a]Messiah is coming ([b]He who is called Christ); when that One comes, He will declare all things to us."

26 Jesus *said to her, "[a]I who speak to you am *He.*"

27 And at this point His [a]disciples [b]came, and they marveled that He had been speaking with a woman; yet no one said, "What do You seek?" or, "Why do You speak with her?"

28 So the woman left her waterpot, and went into the city, and *said to the men,

29 "Come, see a man [a]who told me all the things that I *have* done; [b]this is not [1]the Christ, is it?"

30 They went out of the city, and were coming to Him.

31 In the meanwhile the disciples were requesting Him, saying, "[a]Rabbi, eat."

32 But He said to them, "I have food to eat that you do not know about."

33 The [a]disciples therefore were saying to one another, "No one brought Him *anything* to eat, did he?"

34 Jesus *said to them, "My food is to [a]do the will of Him who sent Me, and to [b]accomplish His work.

35 "Do you not say, 'There are yet four months, and *then* comes the harvest'? Behold, I say to you, lift up your eyes, and look on the fields, that they are white [a]for harvest.

36 "Already he who reaps is receiving [a]wages, and is gathering [b]fruit for [c]life eternal; that he who sows and he who reaps may rejoice together.

37 "For in this *case* the saying is true, '[a]One sows, and another reaps.'

38 "I sent you to reap that for which you have not labored; others have labored, and you have entered into their labor."

The Samaritans

39 And from [a]that city many of the Samaritans believed in Him because of the word of the woman who testified, "[b]He told me all the things that I *have* done."

40 So when the Samaritans came to Him, they were asking Him to stay with them; and He stayed there two days.

41 And many more believed because of His word;

42 and they were saying to the woman, "It is no longer because of what you said that we believe, for we have heard for ourselves and know that this One is indeed [a]the Savior of the world."

43 And after [a]the two days He went forth from there into Galilee.

44 For Jesus Himself testified that [a]a prophet has no honor in his own country.

45 So when He came to Galilee, the Galileans received Him, [a]having seen all the things that He did in Jerusalem at the feast; for they themselves also went to the feast.

Healing a Nobleman's Son

46 He came therefore again to [a]Cana of Galilee [b]where He had

12 [a]John 4:6
14 [a]John 6:35; 7:38 [b]Matt. 25:46; John 6:27
15 [1]Or, *Lord* [a]John 6:34
19 [1]Or, *Lord* [a]Matt. 21:11; Luke 7:39
20 [a]Gen. 33:20 [John 4:12] [b]Deut. 11:29; Josh. 8:33 [c]Luke 9:53
21 [a]John 4:23; 5:25, 28; 16:2, 32 [b]Mal. 1:11; 1 Tim. 2:8
22 [a]2 Kin. 17:28-41 [b]Is. 2:3; Rom. 3:1f.; 9:4f.
23 [a]John 4:21; 5:25, 28; 16:2, 32 [b]Phil. 3:3
24 [1]Or, *God is a Spirit* [a]Phil. 3:3
25 [a]John 1:41 [b]Matt. 1:16
26 [a]John 8:24; 9:35-37
27 [a]John 4:8 [b]John 2:2
29 [1]I.e., the Messiah [a]John 4:17f. [b]Matt. 12:23; John 7:26, 31
31 [a]Matt. 23:7
33 [a]John 2:2
34 [a]John 5:30; 6:38 [b]John 5:36; 17:4; 19:28, 30
35 [a]Luke 10:2
36 [a]1 Cor. 9:17f. [b]Rom. 1:13 [c]John 4:14
37 [a]Job 31:8; Mic. 6:15
39 [a]John 4:5, 30 [b]John 4:29
42 [a]Luke 2:11; Acts 5:31; 13:23; 1 Tim. 4:10; 1 John 4:14
43 [a]John 4:40
44 [a]Matt. 13:57
45 [a]John 2:23
46 [a]John 2:1 [b]John 2:9

made the water wine. And there was a certain royal official, whose son was sick at [c]Capernaum.

47 When he heard that Jesus had come [a]out of Judea into Galilee, he went to Him, and was requesting *Him* to come down and heal his son; for he was at the point of death.

48 Jesus therefore said to him, "Unless you *people* see [1a]signs and [a]wonders, you *simply* will not believe."

49 The royal official *said to Him, "[1]Sir, come down before my child dies."

50 Jesus *said to him, "Go your way; your son lives." The man believed the word that Jesus spoke to him, and he started off.

51 And as he was now going down, *his* slaves met him, saying that his [1]son was living.

52 So he inquired of them the hour when he began to get better. They said therefore to him, "Yesterday at the [1]seventh hour the fever left him."

53 So the father knew that *it was* at that hour in which Jesus said to him, "Your son lives"; and he himself believed, and [a]his whole household.

54 This is again a [a]second [1]sign that Jesus performed, when He had [b]come out of Judea into Galilee.

CHAPTER 5

The Healing at Bethesda

AFTER these things there was [1]a feast of the Jews; and Jesus went up to Jerusalem.

2 Now there is in Jerusalem by [a]the sheep *gate* a pool, which is called [b]in [1]Hebrew [2]Bethesda, having five porticoes.

3 In these lay a multitude of those who were sick, blind, lame, and withered, [[1]waiting for the moving of the waters;

4 for an angel of the Lord went down at certain seasons into the pool, and stirred up the water; whoever then first, after the stirring up of the water, stepped in was made well from whatever disease with which he was afflicted.]

5 And a certain man was there, who had been thirty-eight years in his sickness.

6 When Jesus saw him lying there, and knew that he had already been a long time *in that condition,* He *said to him, "Do you wish to get well?"

7 The sick man answered Him, "Sir, I have no man to put me into the pool when [a]the water is stirred up, but while I am coming, another steps down before me."

8 Jesus *said to him, "[a]Arise, take up your pallet, and walk."

9 And immediately the man became well, and took up his pallet and *began* to walk.

[a]Now it was the Sabbath on that day.

10 Therefore [a]the Jews were saying to him who was cured, "It is the Sabbath, and [b]it is not permissible for you to carry your pallet."

11 But he answered them, "He who made me well was the one who said to me, 'Take up your pallet and walk.' "

12 They asked him, "Who is the man who said to you, 'Take up *your* pallet, and walk'?"

13 But he who was healed did not know who it was; for Jesus had slipped away while there was a crowd in *that* place.

14 Afterward Jesus *found him in the temple, and said to him, "Behold, you have become well; do not [a]sin any more, [b]so that nothing worse may befall you."

15 The man went away, and told [a]the Jews that it was Jesus who had made him well.

16 And for this reason [a]the Jews were persecuting Jesus, because He was doing these things on the Sabbath.

17 But He answered them, "My Father is working until now, and I Myself am working."

Jesus' Equality with God

18 For this cause therefore [a]the Jews [b]were seeking all the more to kill Him, because He not only was breaking the Sabbath, but also was calling God His own Father, [c]making Himself equal with God.

19 Jesus therefore answered and was saying to them, "Truly, truly, I say to you, [a]the Son can do nothing of Himself, unless *it is* something He sees the Father doing; for whatever *the Father* does, these things the Son also does in like manner.

20 "[a]For the Father loves the Son, and shows Him all things that He Himself is doing; and [b]greater works than these will He show Him, that you may marvel.

21 "For just as the Father raises the dead and [a]gives them life, even so [b]the Son also gives life to whom He wishes.

46 [c]Luke 4:23; John 2:12

47 [a]John 4:3, 54

48 [1]Or, *attesting miracles* [a]Dan. 4:2f.; 6:27; Matt. 24:24; Mark 13:22; Acts 2:19, 22, 43; 4:30; 5:12; 6:8; 7:36; 14:3; 15:12; Rom. 15:19; 1 Cor. 1:22; 2 Cor. 12:12; 2 Thess. 2:9; Heb. 2:4

49 [1]Or, *Lord*

51 [1]Or, *boy*

52 [1]I.e., 1 p.m.

53 [a]Acts 11:14

54 [1]Or, *attesting miracle* [a]John 2:11 [b]John 4:45f.

1 [1]Many good mss. read, *the feast,* i.e., the Passover

2 [1]I.e., Jewish Aramaic [2]Many good mss. read, *Bethsaida* or *Bethzatha* [a]Neh. 3:1, 32; 12:39 [b]John 19:13, 17, 20; 20:16; Acts 21:40; Rev. 9:11; 16:16

3 [1]Many mss. do not contain the remainder of v. 3, nor v. 4

7 [a]John 5:4

8 [a]Matt. 9:6; Mark 2:11; Luke 5:24

9 [a]John 9:14

10 [a]John 1:19; 5:15, 16, 18 [b]Neh. 13:19; Jer. 17:21f.; Matt. 12:2; John 7:23; 9:16

14 [a]Mark 2:5; John 8:11 [b]Ezra 9:14

15 [a]John 1:19; 5:16, 18

16 [a]John 1:19; 5:10, 15, 18

18 [a]John 1:19; 5:15, 16 [b]John 5:16; 7:1 [c]John 10:33; 19:7

19 [a]John 5:30; 8:28; 12:49; 14:10

20 [a]John 3:35 [b]John 14:12

21 [a]Rom. 4:17; 8:11 [b]John 11:25

22 "For not even the Father judges
any one, but [a]He has given all judgment to the Son,
23 in order that all may honor the
Son, even as they honor the Father.
[a]He who does not honor the Son
does not honor the Father who sent
Him.
24 "Truly, truly, I say to you, he
who hears My word, and [a]believes
Him who sent Me, has eternal life,
and [b]does not come into judgment,
but has [c]passed out of death into
life.

Two Resurrections

25 "Truly, truly, I say to you, [a]an
hour is coming and now is, when
[b]the dead shall hear the voice of the
Son of God; and those who [c]hear
shall live.
26 "For just as the Father has life in
Himself, even so He [a]gave to the
Son also to have life in Himself;
27 and He gave Him authority to
[a]execute judgment, because He is
the Son of Man.
28 "Do not marvel at this; for [a]an
hour is coming, in which [b]all who
are in the tombs shall hear His
voice,
29 and shall come forth; [a]those
who did the good *deeds,* to a resurrection of life, those who committed
the evil *deeds* to a resurrection of
judgment.
30 "[a]I can do nothing on My own
initiative. As I hear, I judge; and
[b]My judgment is just, because I do
not seek My own will, but [c]the will
of Him who sent Me.
31 "[a]If I *alone* bear witness of Myself, My testimony is not [1]true.
32 "There is [a]another who bears
witness of Me; and I know that the
testimony which He bears of Me is
true.

Witness of John

33 "You have sent to John, and he
[a]has borne witness to the truth.
34 "But [a]the witness which I receive is not from man; but I say
these things, that you may be saved.
35 "He was [a]the lamp that was
burning and was shining and you
[b]were willing to rejoice for a while
in his light.

Witness of Works

36 "But the witness which I have is
greater than *that of* John; for [a]the
works which the Father has given
Me [b]to accomplish, the very works
that I do, bear witness of Me, that
the Father [c]has sent Me.

Witness of the Father

37 "And the Father who sent Me,
[a]He has borne witness of Me. You
have neither heard His voice at any
time, nor seen His form.
38 "And you do not have [a]His word
abiding in you, for you do not believe Him whom He [b]sent.

Witness of the Scripture

39 "[1a]You search the Scriptures,
because you think that in them you
have eternal life; and it is [b]these that
bear witness of Me;
40 and you are unwilling to come
to Me, that you may have life.
41 "[a]I do not receive glory from
men;
42 but I know you, that you do not
have the love of God in yourselves.
43 "I have come in My Father's
name, and you do not receive Me; [a]if
another shall come in his own name,
you will receive him.
44 "How can you believe, when you
[a]receive glory from one another,
and you do not seek [b]the glory that
is from [c]the *one and* only God?
45 "Do not think that I will accuse
you before the Father; the one who
accuses you is [a]Moses, in whom you
have set your hope.
46 "For if you believed Moses, you
would believe Me; for [a]he wrote of
Me.
47 "But [a]if you do not believe his
writings, how will you believe My
words?"

Chapter 6

Five Thousand Fed

AFTER these things [a]Jesus went
away to the other side of [b]the Sea of
Galilee (or [c]Tiberias).
2 And a great multitude was following Him, because they were seeing the [a]signs which He was performing on those who were sick.
3 And Jesus went up on [a]the
mountain, and there He sat with His
disciples.
4 Now [a]the Passover, the feast of
the Jews, was at hand.
5 Jesus therefore lifting up His
eyes, and seeing that a great multitude was coming to Him, *said to
[a]Philip, "Where are we to buy
bread, that these may eat?"
6 And this He was saying to test
him; for He Himself knew what He
was intending to do.
7 [a]Philip answered Him, "[b]Two
hundred [1]denarii worth of bread is

22 [a]John 5:27; 9:39; Acts 10:42; 17:31
23 [a]Luke 10:16; 1 John 2:23
24 [a]John 3:18; 12:44; 20:31; 1 John 5:13 [b]John 3:18 [c]1 John 3:14
25 [a]John 4:21, 23; 5:28 [b]Luke 15:24 [c]John 6:60; 8:43, 47; 9:27
26 [a]John 1:4; 6:57
27 [a]John 9:39; Acts 10:42; 17:31
28 [a]John 4:21 [b]John 11:24; 1 Cor. 15:52
29 [a]Dan. 12:2; Matt. 25:46; Acts 24:15
30 [a]John 5:19 [b]John 8:16 [c]John 4:34; 6:38
31 [1]I.e., admissible as legal evidence [a]John 8:14
32 [a]John 5:37
33 [a]John 1:7
34 [a]John 5:32; 1 John 5:9
35 [a]2 Sam. 21:17; 2 Pet. 1:19 [b]Mark 1:5
36 [a]Matt. 11:4; John 2:23; 10:25, 38; 14:11; 15:24 [b]John 4:34 [c]John 3:17
37 [a]Luke 24:27; John 8:18
38 [a]1 John 2:14 [b]John 3:17
39 [1]Or, (a command) *Search the Scriptures!* [a]John 7:52; Rom. 2:17ff. [b]Luke 24:25, 27; Acts 13:27
41 [a]John 5:44; 7:18
43 [a]Matt. 24:5
44 [a]John 5:41 [b]Rom. 2:29 [c]John 17:3; 1 Tim. 1:17
45 [a]John 9:28; Rom. 2:17ff.
46 [a]Luke 24:27
47 [a]Luke 16:29, 31
1 [a]John 6:1-13: *Matt. 14:13-21; Mark 6:32-44; Luke 9:10-17* [b]Matt. 4:18; Luke 5:1 [c]John 6:23; 21:1
2 [a]John 2:11
3 [a]Matt. 5:1; John 6:15
4 [a]John 2:13
5 [a]John 1:43
7 [1]A denarius represented a days wages for a common laborer [a]John 1:43 [b]Mark 6:37

not sufficient for them, for every one
to receive a little."
8 One of His [a]disciples, [b]Andrew,
Simon Peter's brother, *said to Him,
9"There is a lad here, who has five
barley loaves, and two [a]fish; but
what are these for so many people?"
10 Jesus said, "Have the people
[1]sit down." Now there was [a]much
grass in the place. So the men [1]sat
down, in number about [b]five thousand.
11 Jesus therefore took the loaves;
and [a]having given thanks, He distributed to those who were seated;
likewise also of the [b]fish as much as
they wanted.
12 And when they were filled, He
*said to His [a]disciples, "Gather up
the leftover fragments that nothing
may be lost."
13 And so they gathered them up,
and filled twelve [a]baskets with fragments from the five barley loaves,
which were left over by those who
had eaten.
14 When therefore the people saw
the [1]sign which He had performed,
they said, "This is of a truth the
[a]Prophet who is to come into the
world."

Jesus Walks on the Water

15 Jesus therefore perceiving that
they were [1]intending to come and
take Him by force, [a]to make Him
king, [b]withdrew again to [c]the mountain by Himself alone.
16 Now when evening came, His
[a]disciples went down to the sea,
17 and after getting into a boat,
they *started to* cross the sea [a]to Capernaum. And it had already become dark, and Jesus had not yet
come to them.
18 And the sea *began* to be stirred
up because a strong wind was blowing.
19 When therefore they had rowed
about [1]three or four miles, they *beheld Jesus walking on the sea and
drawing near to the boat; and they
were frightened.
20 But He *said to them, "It is I;
[1a]do not be afraid."
21 They were willing therefore to
receive Him into the boat; and immediately the boat was at the land
to which they were going.
22 The next day [a]the multitude
that stood on the other side of the
sea saw that there was no other
small boat there, except one, and
that Jesus [b]had not entered with His
disciples into the boat, but *that* His
disciples had gone away alone.
23 There came other small boats
from [a]Tiberias near to the place
where they ate the bread after the
[b]Lord [c]had given thanks.
24 When the multitude therefore
saw that Jesus was not there, nor
His disciples, they themselves got
into the small boats, and [a]came to
Capernaum, seeking Jesus.
25 And when they found Him on
the other side of the sea, they said to
Him, "[a]Rabbi, when did You get
here?"

Words to the People

26 Jesus answered them and said,
"Truly, truly, I say to you, you [a]seek
Me, not because you saw [b]signs, but
because you ate of the loaves, and
were filled.
27"Do not [a]work for the food
which perishes, but for the food
which endures to [b]eternal life,
which [c]the Son of Man shall give to
you, for on Him the Father, *even*
God, [d]has set His seal."
28 They said therefore to Him,
"What shall we do, that we may
work the works of God?"
29 Jesus answered and said to
them, "This is [a]the work of God,
that you believe in Him whom He
[b]has sent."
30 They said therefore to Him,
"[a]What then do You do for a [b]sign,
that we may see, and believe You?
What work do You perform?
31"[a]Our fathers ate the manna in
the wilderness; as it is written, '[b]HE
GAVE THEM BREAD OUT OF HEAVEN TO
EAT.'"
32 Jesus therefore said to them,
"Truly, truly, I say to you, it is not
Moses who has given you the bread
out of heaven, but it is My Father
who gives you the true bread out of
heaven.
33"For the bread of God is [1]that
which [a]comes down out of heaven,
and gives life to the world."
34 They said therefore to Him,
"Lord, evermore [a]give us this
bread."
35 Jesus said to them, "[a]I am the
bread of life; he who comes to Me
shall not hunger, and he who believes in Me [b]shall never thirst.
36"But [a]I said to you, that you have
seen Me, and yet do not believe.
37"[a]All that the Father gives Me
shall come to Me; and the one who
comes to Me I will certainly not cast
out.
38"For [a]I have come down from
heaven, [b]not to do My own will, but
[c]the will of Him who [d]sent Me.

8 [a]John 2:2 [b]John 1:40
9 [a]John 6:11; 21:9, 10, 13
10 [1]Lit., *recline(d)* [a]Mark 6:39; John 6:4 [b]Matt. 14:21
11 [a]Matt. 15:36; John 6:23 [b]John 6:9; 21:9, 10, 13
12 [a]John 2:2
13 [a]Matt. 14:20
14 [1]Or, *attesting miracle* [a]Matt. 11:3; 21:11; John 1:21
15 [1]Or, *about* [a]John 18:36f. [b]John 6:15-21: *Matt. 14:22-33; Mark 6:45-51* [c]John 6:3
16 [a]John 2:2
17 [a]Mark 6:45; John 6:24, 59
19 [1]I.e., 25 or 30 stadia
20 [1]Or, *stop fearing* [a]Matt. 14:27
22 [a]John 6:2 [b]John 6:15ff.
23 [a]John 6:1 [b]Luke 7:13 [c]John 6:11
24 [a]Matt. 14:34; Mark 6:53; John 6:17, 59
25 [a]Matt. 23:7
26 [a]John 6:24 [b]John 6:2, 14, 30
27 [a]Is. 55:2 [b]John 3:15f.; 4:14; 6:40, 47, 54; 10:28; 17:2f. [c]Matt. 8:20; John 6:53, 62 [d]John 3:33
29 [a]1 Thess. 1:3; James 2:22; 1 John 3:23; Rev. 2:26 [b]John 3:17
30 [a]Matt. 12:38 [b]John 6:2, 14, 26
31 [a]Ex. 16:21; Num. 11:8; John 6:49, 58 [b]Ex. 16:4, 15; Neh. 9:15; Ps. 78:24; 105:40
33 [1]Or, *He who comes* [a]John 6:41, 50
34 [a]John 4:15
35 [a]John 6:48, 51 [b]John 4:14
36 [a]John 6:26
37 [a]John 6:39; 17:2, 24
38 [a]John 3:13 [b]Matt. 26:39 [c]John 4:34; 5:30 [d]John 6:29

39 "And this is the will of Him who sent Me, that of [a]all that He has given Me I [b]lose nothing, but [c]raise it up on the last day.

40 "For this is the will of My Father, that every one who [a]beholds the Son, and [b]believes in Him, may have eternal life; and I Myself will [c]raise him up on the last day."

Words to the Jews

41 [a]The Jews therefore were grumbling about Him, because He said, "I am the bread that [b]came down out of heaven."

42 And they were saying, "[a]Is not this Jesus, the son of Joseph, whose father and mother [b]we know? How does He now say, '[c]I have come down out of heaven'?"

43 Jesus answered and said to them, "Do not grumble among yourselves.

44 "No one can come to Me, unless the Father who sent Me [a]draws him; and I will [b]raise him up on the last day.

45 "It is written [a]in the prophets, '[b]AND THEY SHALL ALL BE [c]TAUGHT OF GOD.' Every one who has heard and learned from the Father, comes to Me.

46 "[a]Not that any man has seen the Father, except the One who is from God; He has seen the Father.

47 "Truly, truly, I say to you, he who believes [a]has eternal life.

48 "[a]I am the bread of life.

49 "[a]Your fathers ate the manna in the wilderness, and they died.

50 "This is the bread which [a]comes down out of heaven, so that one may eat of it and [b]not die.

51 "[a]I am the living bread that [b]came down out of heaven; if any one eats of this bread, [c]he shall live forever; and the bread also which I shall give [d]for the life of the world is [e]My flesh."

52 [a]The Jews therefore [b]*began* to argue with one another, saying, "How can this man give us *His* flesh to eat?"

53 Jesus therefore said to them, "Truly, truly, I say to you, unless you eat the flesh of [a]the Son of Man and drink His blood, you have no life in yourselves.

54 "He who eats My flesh and drinks My blood has eternal life; and I will [a]raise him up on the last day.

55 "For My flesh is true food, and My blood is true drink.

56 "He who eats My flesh and drinks My blood [a]abides in Me, and I in him.

39 [a]John 6:37; 17:2, 24 [b]John 17:12; 18:9 [c]Matt. 10:15; John 6:40
40 [a]John 12:45; 14:17, 19 [b]John 3:16 [c]Matt. 10:15; John 6:39, 44, 54
41 [a]John 1:19; 6:52 [b]John 6:33
42 [a]Luke 4:22 [b]John 7:27f. [c]John 6:38, 62
44 [a]Jer. 31:3; Hos. 11:4; John 6:65 [b]John 6:39
45 [a]Acts 7:42; 13:40; Heb. 8:11 [b]Is. 54:13; Jer. 31:34 [c]Phil. 3:15; 1 Thess. 4:9
46 [a]John 1:18
47 [a]John 3:36; 5:24; 6:51, 58
48 [a]John 6:35
49 [a]John 6:31
50 [a]John 6:33 [b]John 3:36; 5:24
51 [a]John 6:35, 48 [b]John 6:41, 58 [c]John 3:36; 5:24 [d]John 1:29; 3:14f.; 1 John 4:10 [e]John 6:53-56
52 [a]John 1:19; 6:41 [b]John 9:16
53 [a]Matt. 8:20; John 6:27, 62
54 [a]John 6:39
56 [a]John 15:4f.; 1 John 2:24
57 [a]Matt. 16:16; John 5:26 [b]John 3:17; 6:29, 38
58 [a]John 6:33, 41, 51 [b]John 6:31, 49 [c]John 3:36; 5:24; 6:47, 51
59 [a]Matt. 4:23 [b]John 6:24
60 [a]John 2:2; 7:3 [b]John 6:52
61 [a]John 6:64 [b]Matt. 11:6
62 [a]Matt. 8:20; John 6:27, 53 [b]Mark 16:19
63 [a]2 Cor. 3:6 [b]John 6:68
64 [a]John 6:60, 66 [b]John 2:25 [c]Matt. 10:4; John 6:71
65 [a]John 6:37, 44 [b]Matt. 13:11
66 [a]John 2:2; 7:3 [b]John 6:60, 64
67 [a]Matt. 10:2; John 2:2; 6:70f.
68 [a]Matt. 16:16 [b]John 6:63
69 [a]Mark 1:24
70 [a]John 15:16, 19 [b]Matt. 10:2; John 2:2; 6:71; 20:24 [c]John 8:44
71 [a]John 12:4 [b]Mark 14:10 [c]Matt. 10:2; John 2:2
1 [a]John 4:3; 6:1; 11:54 [b]John 1:19 [c]John 5:18; 7:19; 8:37, 40

57 "As the [a]living Father [b]sent Me, and I live because of the Father, so he who eats Me, he also shall live because of Me.

58 "This is the bread which [a]came down out of heaven; not as [b]the fathers ate, and died, he who eats this bread [c]shall live forever."

Words to the Disciples

59 These things He said [a]in the synagogue, as He taught [b]in Capernaum.

60 Many therefore of His [a]disciples, when they heard *this* said, "[b]This is a difficult statement; who can listen to it?"

61 But Jesus, [a]conscious that His disciples grumbled at this, said to them, "Does this [b]cause you to stumble?

62 "*What* then if you should behold [a]the Son of Man [b]ascending where He was before?

63 "[a]It is the Spirit who gives life; the flesh profits nothing; [b]the words that I have spoken to you are spirit and are life.

64 "But there are [a]some of you who do not believe." For Jesus [b]knew from the beginning who they were who did not believe, and [c]who it was that would betray Him.

65 And He was saying, "For this reason I have [a]said to you, that no one can come to Me, unless [b]it has been granted him from the Father."

Peter's Confession of Faith

66 As a result of this many of His [a]disciples [b]withdrew, and were not walking with Him any more.

67 Jesus said therefore to [a]the twelve, "You do not want to go away also, do you?"

68 [a]Simon Peter answered Him, "Lord, to whom shall we go? You have [b]words of eternal life.

69 "And we have believed and have come to know that You are [a]the Holy One of God."

70 Jesus answered them, "[a]Did I Myself not choose you, [b]the twelve, and *yet* one of you is [c]a devil?"

71 Now He meant Judas [a]*the son* of Simon Iscariot, for he, [b]one of [c]the twelve, was going to betray Him.

CHAPTER 7

Jesus Teaches at the Feast

AND after these things Jesus [a]was walking in Galilee; for He was unwilling to walk in Judea, because [b]the Jews [c]were seeking to kill Him.

2 Now the feast of the Jews, [a]the
Feast of Booths, was at hand.
3 His [a]brothers therefore said to
Him, "Depart from here, and go into
Judea, that Your [b]disciples also may
behold Your works which You are
doing.
4"For no one does anything in secret, when he himself seeks to be
known publicly. If You do these
things, show Yourself to the world."
5 For not even His [a]brothers were
believing in Him.
6 Jesus therefore *said to them,
"[a]My time is not yet at hand; but
your time is always opportune.
7"[a]The world cannot hate you;
but it hates Me, because I testify of
it, that [b]its deeds are evil.
8"Go up to the feast yourselves; I
do not go up to this feast because
[a]My time has not yet fully come."
9 And having said these things to
them, He stayed in Galilee.
10 But when His [a]brothers had
gone up to the feast, then He Himself also went up, not publicly, but
as it were, in secret.
11 [a]The Jews therefore [b]were
seeking Him at the feast, and were
saying, "Where is He?"
12 And there was much grumbling
among the multitudes concerning
Him; [a]some were saying, "He is a
good man"; others were saying,
"No, on the contrary, He leads the
multitude astray."
13 Yet no one was speaking
openly of Him for [a]fear of the Jews.
14 But when it was now the midst
of the feast Jesus went up into the
temple, and *began to* [a]teach.
15 [a]The Jews therefore were marveling, saying, "How has this man
[b]become learned, having never been
educated?"
16 Jesus therefore answered them,
and said, "[a]My teaching is not Mine,
but His who sent Me.
17"[a]If any man is willing to do His
will, he shall know of the teaching,
whether it is of God, or *whether* I
speak from Myself.
18"He who speaks from himself
[a]seeks his own glory; but He who is
seeking the glory of the one who
sent Him, He is true, and there is no
unrighteousness in Him.
19"[a]Did not Moses give you the
law, and *yet* none of you carries out
the law? Why do you [b]seek to kill
Me?"
20 The multitude answered, "[a]You
have a demon! Who seeks to kill
You?"
21 Jesus answered and said to
them, "I did [a]one deed, and you all
marvel.
22"On this account [a]Moses has
given you circumcision (not because it is from Moses, but from
[b]the fathers); and on *the* Sabbath
you circumcise a man.
23"[a]If a man receives circumcision
on *the* Sabbath that the Law of
Moses may not be broken, are you
angry with Me because I made an
entire man well on *the* Sabbath?
24"Do not [a]judge according to appearance, but judge with righteous
judgment."
25 Therefore some of the people of
Jerusalem were saying, "Is this not
the man whom they are seeking to
kill?
26"And look, He is speaking publicly, and they are saying nothing to
Him. [a]The rulers do not really know
that this is [1]the Christ, do they?
27"However [a]we know where this
man is from; but whenever the
Christ may come, no one knows
where He is from."
28 Jesus therefore cried out in the
temple, [a]teaching and saying, "[b]You
both know Me, and know where I
am from; and [c]I have not come of
Myself, but He who sent Me is true,
whom you do not know.
29"[a]I know Him; because [b]I am
from Him, and [c]He sent Me."
30 They [a]were seeking therefore
to seize Him; and no man laid his
hand on Him, because His [b]hour had
not yet come.
31 But [a]many of the multitude believed in Him; and they were saying,
"[b]When the Christ shall come, He
will not perform more [c]signs than
those which this man has, will He?"
32 The Pharisees heard the multitude muttering these things about
Him; and the chief priests and the
Pharisees sent [a]officers to [b]seize
Him.
33 Jesus therefore said, "[a]For a little while longer I am with you, then
[b]I go to Him who sent Me.
34"[a]You shall seek Me, and shall
not find Me; and where I am, you
cannot come."
35 [a]The Jews therefore said to one
another, "[b]Where does this man intend to go that we shall not find
Him? He is not intending to go to
[c]the Dispersion among [d]the Greeks,
and teach the Greeks, is He?
36"What is this statement that He
said, '[a]You will seek Me, and will
not find Me; and where I am, you
cannot come'?"
37 Now on [a]the last day, the great

2 [a]Lev. 23:34; Deut. 16:16; Zech. 14:16-19
3 [a]Matt. 12:46; Mark 3:21; John 7:5, 10 [b]John 6:60
5 [a]Matt. 12:46; John 7:3, 10
6 [a]Matt. 26:18; John 2:4; 7:8, 30
7 [a]John 15:18f. [b]John 3:19f.
8 [a]John 7:6
10 [a]Matt. 12:46; Mark 3:21
11 [a]John 7:13, 15, 35 [b]John 11:56
12 [a]John 7:40-43
13 [a]John 9:22
14 [a]Matt. 26:55; John 7:28
15 [a]John 1:19 [b]Acts 26:24 [Gr.]
16 [a]John 3:11
17 [a]Ps. 25:9, 14; Prov. 3:32; Dan. 12:10; John 3:21
18 [a]John 5:41
19 [a]John 1:17 [b]Mark 11:18
20 [a]Matt. 11:18; John 8:48f., 52
21 [a]John 5:2-9, 16
22 [a]Lev. 12:3 [b]Gen. 17:10ff.; 21:4; Acts 7:8
23 [a]Matt. 12:2; John 5:10
24 [a]Lev. 19:15; Is. 11:3; Zech. 7:9; John 8:15
26 [1]I.e., the Messiah [a]Luke 23:13; John 3:1
27 [a]John 6:42
28 [a]John 7:14 [b]John 6:42; 7:14f.; 9:29 [c]John 8:42
29 [a]Matt. 11:27; John 8:55; 17:25 [b]John 6:46 [c]John 3:17
30 [a]Matt. 21:46; John 7:32, 44; 10:39 [b]John 7:6; 8:20
31 [a]John 2:23; 8:30; 12:11, 42 [b]John 7:26 [c]John 2:11
32 [a]Matt. 26:58; John 7:45f. [b]Matt. 12:14
33 [a]John 12:35; 16:16-19 [b]John 14:12, 28; 16:5
34 [a]John 7:36
35 [a]John 7:1 [b]John 8:22 [c]Ps. 147:2; Is. 11:12; 56:8; Zeph. 3:10; James 1:1; 1 Pet. 1:1 [d]John 12:20; Acts 14:1; 17:4; 18:4; Rom. 1:16
36 [a]John 7:34
37 [a]Lev. 23:36; Num. 29:35; Neh. 8:18

day of the feast, Jesus stood and cried out, saying, "[b]If any man is thirsty, let him come to Me and drink.

38"He who believes in Me, [a]as the Scripture said, 'From his innermost being shall flow rivers of [b]living water.'"

39 But this He spoke [a]of the Spirit, whom those who believed in Him were to receive; [1]for [b]the Spirit was not yet *given,* because Jesus was not yet [c]glorified.

Division of People over Jesus

40 *Some* of the multitude therefore, when they heard these words, were saying, "This certainly is [a]the Prophet."

41 Others were saying, "This is [1]the Christ." Still others were saying, "[a]Surely [1]the Christ is not going to come from Galilee, is He?

42"Has not the Scripture said that the Christ comes from [a]the offspring of David, and from Bethlehem, the village where David was?"

43 So [a]there arose a division in the multitude because of Him.

44 And [a]some of them wanted to seize Him, but no one laid hands on Him.

45 The [a]officers therefore came to the chief priests and Pharisees, and they said to them, "Why did you not bring Him?"

46 The [a]officers answered, "[b]Never did a man speak the way this man speaks."

47 The Pharisees therefore answered them, "[a]You have not also been led astray, have you?

48"[a]No one of [b]the rulers or Pharisees has believed in Him, has he?

49"But this multitude which does not know the Law is accursed."

50 [a]Nicodemus *said to them (he who came to Him before, being one of them),

51"[a]Our Law does not judge a man, unless it first hears from him and knows what he is doing, does it?"

52 They answered and said to him, "[a]You are not also from Galilee, are you? Search, and see that no prophet arises out of Galiiee."

53 [[1]And everyone went to his home.

CHAPTER 8

The Adulterous Woman

BUT Jesus went to [a]the Mount of Olives.

2 And early in the morning He came again into the temple, and all the people were coming to Him; and [a]He sat down and *began* to teach them.

3 And the scribes and the Pharisees *brought a woman caught in adultery, and having set her in the midst,

4 they *said to Him, "Teacher, this woman has been caught in adultery, in the very act.

5"Now in the Law [a]Moses commanded us to stone such women; what then do You say?"

6 And they were saying this, [a]testing Him, [b]in order that they might have grounds for accusing Him. But Jesus stooped down, and with His finger wrote on the ground.

7 But when they persisted in asking Him, [a]He straightened up, and said to them, "[b]He who is without sin among you, let him *be the* [c]first to throw a stone at her."

8 And again He stooped down, and wrote on the ground.

9 And when they heard it, they *began* to go out one by one, beginning with the older ones, and He was left alone, and the woman, *where she had been,* in the midst.

10 And [a]straightening up, Jesus said to her, "Woman, where are they? Did no one condemn you?"

11 And she said, "No one, Lord." And Jesus said, "[a]Neither do I condemn you; go your way; from now on [b]sin no more."]

Jesus Is the Light of the World

12 Again therefore Jesus spoke to them, saying, "[a]I am the light of the world; [b]he who follows Me shall not walk in the darkness, but shall have the light of life."

13 The Pharisees therefore said to Him, "[a]You are bearing witness of Yourself; Your witness is not true."

14 Jesus answered and said to them, "[a]Even if I bear witness of Myself, My witness is true; for I know [b]where I came from, and where I am going; but [c]you do not know where I come from, or where I am going.

15"[a]You people judge according to the flesh; [b]I am not judging any one.

16"But even [a]if I do judge, My judgment is true; for I am not alone *in it,* but I and [1]He who sent Me.

17"Even in [a]your law it has been written, that the testimony of [b]two men is true.

18"I am He who bears witness of Myself, and [a]the Father who sent Me bears witness of Me."

37 [b]John 4:10, 14; 6:35
38 [a]Is. 44:3; 55:1; 58:11 [b]John 4:10
39 [1]Other mss. read, *for the Holy Spirit was not yet given* [a]Joel 2:28; John 1:33 [b]John 20:22; Acts 1:4f.; 2:4, 33; 19:2 [c]John 12:16, 23; 13:31f.; 16:14; 17:1
40 [a]Matt. 21:11; John 1:21
41 [1]I.e., the Messiah [a]John 1:46; 7:52
42 [a]Ps. 89:4; Mic. 5:2; Matt. 1:1; 2:5f.; Luke 2:4ff.
43 [a]John 9:16; 10:19
44 [a]John 7:30
45 [a]John 7:32
46 [a]John 7:32 [b]Matt. 7:28
47 [a]John 7:12
48 [a]John 12:42 [b]Luke 23:13; John 7:26
50 [a]John 3:1; 19:39
51 [a]Ex. 23:1; Deut. 17:6; 19:15; Prov. 18:13; Acts 23:3
52 [a]John 1:46; 7:41
53 [1]John 7:53-8:11 is not found in most of the old mss.
1 [a]Matt. 21:1
2 [a]Matt. 26:55; John 8:20
5 [a]Lev. 20:10; Deut. 22:22f.
6 [a]Matt. 16:1; 19:3; 22:18, 35; Mark 8:11; 10:2; 12:15; Luke 10:25; 11:16 [b]Mark 3:2
7 [a]John 8:10 [b]Matt. 7:1; Rom. 2:1 [c]Deut. 17:7
10 [a]John 8:7
11 [a]John 3:17 [b]John 5:14
12 [a]John 1:4; 12:35 [b]Matt. 5:14
13 [a]John 5:31
14 [a]John 18:37; Rev. 1:5; 3:14 [b]John 8:42; 13:3; 16:28 [c]John 7:28; 9:29
15 [a]1 Sam. 16:7; John 7:24 [b]John 3:17
16 [1]Or, *the Father who sent Me* [a]John 5:30
17 [a]Deut. 17:6; 19:15 [b]Matt. 18:16
18 [a]John 5:37; 1 John 5:9

19 And so they were saying to
Him, "Where is Your Father?" Jesus answered, "You know neither
Me, nor My Father; [a]if you knew
Me, you would know My Father
also."
20 These words He spoke in [a]the
treasury, as [b]He taught in the temple; and no one seized Him, because
[c]His hour had not yet come.
21 He said therefore again to
them, "I go away, and [a]you shall
seek Me, and [b]shall die in your sin;
where I am going, you cannot
come."
22 Therefore [a]the Jews were saying, "Surely He will not kill Himself,
will He, since He says, '[b]Where I am
going, you cannot come'?"
23 And He was saying to them,
"[a]You are from below, I am from
above; [b]you are of this world; [c]I am
not of this world.
24"I said therefore to you, that you
[a]shall die in your sins; for unless you
believe that [1b]I am *He,* [a]you shall die
in your sins."
25 And so they were saying to
Him, "Who are You?" Jesus said to
them, "What have I been saying to
you *from* the beginning?
26"I have many things to speak
and to judge concerning you, but
[a]He who sent Me is true; and [b]the
things which I heard from Him,
these I speak to the world."
27 They did not realize that He had
been speaking to them about the Father.
28 Jesus therefore said, "When
you [a]lift up the Son of Man, then you
will know that [1b]I am *He,* and [c]I do
nothing on My own initiative, but I
speak these things as the Father
taught Me.
29"And He who sent Me is with
Me; [a]He has not left Me alone, for [b]I
always do the things that are pleasing to Him."
30 As He spoke these things,
[a]many came to believe in Him.

The Truth Shall Make You Free

31 Jesus therefore was saying to
those Jews who had believed Him,
"[a]If you abide in My word, *then* you
are truly [b]disciples of Mine;
32 and [a]you shall know the truth,
and [b]the truth shall make you free."
33 They answered Him, "[a]We are
Abraham's offspring, and have never yet been enslaved to anyone; how
is it that You say, 'You shall become
free'?"
34 Jesus answered them, "Truly,
truly, I say to you, [a]every one who
commits sin is the slave of sin.
35"And [a]the slave does not remain
in the house forever; [b]the son does
remain forever.
36"If therefore the Son [a]shall make
you free, you shall be free indeed.
37"I know that you are [a]Abra-
ham's offspring; yet [b]you seek to kill
Me, because My word has no place
in you.
38"I speak the things which I have
seen with *My* Father; therefore you
also do the things which you heard
from [a]*your* father."
39 They answered and said to
Him, "Abraham is [a]our father." Jesus *said to them, "[b]If you are Abraham's children, do the deeds of
Abraham.
40"But as it is, [a]you are seeking to
kill Me, a man who has [b]told you the
truth, which I heard from God; this
Abraham did not do.
41"You are doing the deeds of
[a]your father." They said to Him,
"We were not born of fornication;
[b]we have one Father, *even* God."
42 Jesus said to them, "If God
were your Father, [a]you would love
Me; [b]for I proceeded forth and have
come from God, for I have [c]not even
come on My own initiative, but [d]He
sent Me.
43"Why do you not understand
[a]what I am saying? *It is* because you
cannot [b]hear My word.
44"[a]You are of [b]*your* father the
devil, and [c]you want to do the desires of your father. [d]He was a murderer from the beginning, and does
not stand in the truth, because
[e]there is no truth in him. Whenever
he speaks a lie, he [f]speaks from his
own *nature;* for he is a liar, and the
father of lies.
45"But because [a]I speak the truth,
you do not believe Me.
46"Which one of you convicts Me
of sin? If [a]I speak truth, why do you
not believe Me?
47"[a]He who is of God hears the
words of God; for this reason you do
not hear *them,* because you are not
of God."
48 [a]The Jews answered and said to
Him, "Do we not say rightly that
You are a [b]Samaritan and [c]have a
demon?"
49 Jesus answered, "I do not [a]have
a demon; but I honor My Father, and
you dishonor Me.
50"But [a]I do not seek My glory;
there is One who seeks and judges.
51"Truly, truly, I say to you, if anyone [a]keeps My word he shall never
[b]see death."

19 [a]John 7:28; 8:55; 14:7, 9; 16:3
20 [a]Mark 12:41, 43; Luke 21:1 [b]John 7:14; 8:2 [c]John 7:30
21 [a]John 7:34 [b]John 8:24
22 [a]John 1:19; 8:48, [b]John 7:35
23 [a]John 3:31 [b]1 John 4:5 [c]John 17:14, 16
24 [1]Most auth. connect this with Ex. 3:14, *I AM WHO I AM* [a]John 8:21 [b]Mark 13:6; Luke 21:8 [Matt. 24:5]; John 4:26; 8:28; 13:19
26 [a]John 3:33; 7:28 [b]John 8:40
28 [1]Cf. v. 24 [a]John 3:14; 12:32 [b]Mark 13:6; Luke 21:8 [Matt. 24:5]; John 4:26; 8:24; 13:19 [c]John 3:11
29 [a]John 8:16; 16:32 [b]John 4:34
30 [a]John 7:31
31 [a]John 15:7; 2 John 9 [b]John 2:2
32 [a]John 1:14, 17 [b]John 8:36; Rom. 8:2; 2 Cor. 3:17; Gal. 5:1, 13; James 2:12
33 [a]Matt. 3:9; John 8:37, 39
34 [a]Rom. 6:16; 2 Pet. 2:19
35 [a]Gen. 21:10; Gal. 4:30 [b]Luke 15:31
36 [a]John 8:32
37 [a]Matt. 3:9; John 8:39 [b]John 7:1
38 [a]John 8:41
39 [a]Matt. 3:9; John 8:37 [b]Rom. 9:7; Gal. 3:7
40 [a]John 7:1; 8:37 [b]John 8:26
41 [a]John 8:38, 44 [b]Deut. 32:6; Is. 63:16; 64:8
42 [a]1 John 5:1 [b]John 13:3; 16:28, 30; 17:8 [c]John 7:28 [d]John 3:17
43 [a]John 8:33, 39, 41 [b]John 5:25
44 [a]1 John 3:8 [b]John 8:38, 41 [c]John 7:17 [d]Gen. 3:4; 1 John 3:8, 15 [e]1 John 2:4 [f]Matt. 12:34
45 [a]John 18:37
46 [a]John 18:37
47 [a]1 John 4:6
48 [a]John 1:19 [b]Matt. 10:5; John 4:9 [c]John 7:20
49 [a]John 7:20
50 [a]John 5:41
51 [a]John 8:55; 14:23; 15:20; 17:6 [b]Matt. 16:28; Luke 2:26; John 8:52; Heb. 2:9

52 [a]The Jews said to Him, "Now we know that You [b]have a demon. Abraham died, and the prophets *also;* and You say, 'If anyone [c]keeps My word, he shall never [d]taste of death.'

53 "Surely You [a]are not greater than our father Abraham, who died? The prophets died too; whom do You make Yourself out *to be?*"

54 Jesus answered, "[a]If I glorify Myself, My glory is nothing; [b]it is My Father who glorifies Me, of whom you say, 'He is our God';

55 and [a]you have not come to know Him, [b]but I know Him; and if I say that I do not know Him, I shall be [c]a liar like you, [b]but I do know Him, and [d]keep His word.

56 "[a]Your father Abraham [b]rejoiced [1]to see My day; and he saw *it,* and was glad."

57 [a]The Jews therefore said to Him, "You are not yet fifty years old, and have You seen Abraham?"

58 Jesus said to them, "Truly, truly, I say to you, before Abraham [1]was born, [a]I AM."

59 Therefore they [a]picked up stones to throw at Him; but Jesus [1b]hid Himself, [2]and went out of the temple.

Chapter 9

Healing the Man Born Blind

AND as He passed by, He saw a man blind from birth.

2 And His disciples asked Him, saying, "[a]Rabbi, who sinned, [b]this man or his [c]parents, that he should be born blind?"

3 Jesus answered, "*It was* neither *that* this man sinned, nor his parents; but *it was* in order [a]that the works of God might be displayed in him.

4 "We must work the works of Him who sent Me, [a]as long as it is day; night is coming, when no man can work.

5 "While I am in the world, I am [a]the light of the world."

6 When He had said this, He [a]spat on the ground, and made clay of the spittle, and applied the clay to his eyes,

7 and said to him, "Go, wash in [a]the pool of Siloam" (which is translated, Sent). And so he went away and washed, and [b]came *back* seeing.

8 The neighbors therefore, and those who previously saw him as a beggar, were saying, "Is not this the one who used to [a]sit and beg?"

9 Others were saying, "This is he," *still* others were saying, "No, but he is like him." He kept saying, "I am the one."

10 Therefore they were saying to him, "How then were your eyes opened?"

11 He answered, "The man who is called Jesus made clay, and anointed my eyes, and said to me, 'Go to [a]Siloam, and wash'; so I went away and washed, and I received sight."

12 And they said to him, "Where is He?" He *said, "I do not know."

Controversy over the Man

13 They *brought to the Pharisees him who was formerly blind.

14 [a]Now it was a Sabbath on the day when Jesus made the clay, and opened his eyes.

15 [a]Again, therefore, the Pharisees also were asking him how he received his sight. And he said to them, "He applied clay to my eyes, and I washed, and I see."

16 Therefore some of the Pharisees were saying, "[a]This man is not from God, because He does not keep the Sabbath." But others were saying, "How can a man who is a sinner perform such [1b]signs?" And [c]there was a division among them.

17 They *said therefore to the blind man [a]again, "What do you say about Him, since He opened your eyes?" And he said, "He is a [b]prophet."

18 [a]The Jews therefore did not believe *it* of him, that he had been blind, and had received sight, until they called the parents of the very one who had received his sight,

19 and questioned them, saying, "Is this your son, who you say was born blind? Then how does he now see?"

20 His parents answered them and said, "We know that this is our son, and that he was born blind;

21 but how he now sees, we do not know; or who opened his eyes, we do not know. Ask him; he is of age, he shall speak for himself."

22 His parents said this because they [a]were afraid of the Jews; for the Jews [b]had already agreed, that if any one should confess Him to be [1]Christ, [c]he should be put out of the synagogue.

23 For this reason his parents said, "[a]He is of age; ask him."

24 So a second time they called the man who had been blind, and said to

52 [a]John 1:19 [b]John 7:20 [c]John 8:55; 14:23; 15:20; 17:6 [d]John 8:51

53 [a]John 4:12

54 [a]John 8:50 [b]John 7:39

55 [a]John 8:19; 15:21 [b]John 7:29 [c]John 8:44 [d]John 8:51; 15:10

56 [1]Lit., *in order that he might see* [a]John 8:37, 39 [b]Matt. 13:17; Heb. 11:13

57 [a]John 1:19

58 [1]Lit., *came into being* [a]John 1:1; 17:5, 24

59 [1]Lit., *was hidden* [2]Some mss. add, *and going through the midst of them went His way and so passed by* [a]Matt. 12:14; John 10:31; 11:8 [b]John 12:36

2 [a]Matt. 23:7 [b]Luke 13:2; John 9:34; Acts 28:4 [c]Ex. 20:5

3 [a]John 11:4

4 [a]John 7:33; 11:9; 12:35; Gal. 6:10

5 [a]John 1:4; 8:12; 12:46

6 [a]Mark 7:33; 8:23

7 [a]Luke 13:4; John 9:11 [b]John 11:37

8 [a]Acts 3:2, 10

11 [a]John 9:7

14 [a]John 5:9

15 [a]John 9:10

16 [1]Or, *attesting miracles* [a]Matt. 12:2 [b]John 2:11 [c]John 6:52; 7:43; 10:19

17 [a]John 9:15 [b]Matt. 21:11

18 [a]John 1:19; 9:22

22 [1]I.e., the Messiah [a]John 7:13 [b]John 7:45-52 [c]Luke 6:22; John 12:42; 16:2

23 [a]John 9:21

him, "[a]Give glory to God; we know
that [b]this man is a sinner."
25 He therefore answered,
"Whether He is a sinner, I do not
know; one thing I do know, that,
whereas I was blind, now I see."
26 They said therefore to him,
"What did He do to you? How did
He open your eyes?"
27 He answered them, "[a]I told you
already, and you did not [b]listen; why
do you want to hear *it* again? You do
not want to become His disciples
too, do you?"
28 And they reviled him, and said,
"You are His disciple; but [a]we are
disciples of Moses.
29"We know that God has spoken
to Moses; but as for this man, [a]we
do not know where He is from."
30 The man answered and said to
them, "Well, here is an amazing
thing, that you do not know where
He is from, and *yet* He opened my
eyes.
31"We know that [a]God does not
hear sinners; but if any one is God-
fearing, and does His will, He hears
him.
32"[1]Since the beginning of time it
has never been heard that any one
opened the eyes of a person born
blind.
33"[a]If this man were not from God,
He could do nothing."
34 They answered and said to him,
"[a]You were born entirely in sins,
and are you teaching us?" And they
[b]put him out.

Jesus Affirms His Deity

35 Jesus heard that they had [a]put
him out; and finding him, He said,
"Do you believe in the [b]Son of
Man?"
36 He answered and said, "And
[a]who is He, [1]Lord, that I may believe
in Him?"
37 Jesus said to him, "You have
both seen Him, and [a]He is the one
who is talking with you."
38 And he said, "Lord, I believe."
And he [a]worshiped Him.
39 And Jesus said, "[a]For judgment
I came into this world, that [b]those
who do not see may see; and that
[c]those who see may become blind."
40 Those of the Pharisees who
were with Him heard these things,
and said to Him, "[a]We are not blind
too, are we?"
41 Jesus said to them, "[a]If you
were blind, you would have no sin;
but since you say, '[b]We see'; your
sin remains.

Chapter 10

Parable of the Good Shepherd

"TRULY, truly, I say to you, he
who does not enter by the door into
the fold of the sheep, but climbs up
some other way, he is [a]a thief and a
robber.
2"But he who enters by the door
is [a]a shepherd of the sheep.
3"To him the doorkeeper opens,
and the sheep hear [a]his voice, and
he calls his own sheep by name, and
[b]leads them out.
4"When he puts forth all his own,
he goes before them, and the sheep
follow him because they know [a]his
voice.
5"And a stranger they simply will
not follow, but will flee from him,
because they do not know [a]the voice
of strangers."
6 This [a]figure of speech Jesus
spoke to them, but they did not understand what those things were
which He had been saying to them.
7 Jesus therefore said to them
again, "Truly, truly, I say to you, I
am [a]the door of the sheep.
8"All who came before Me are
[a]thieves and robbers; but the sheep
did not hear them.
9"[a]I am the door; if anyone enters
through Me, he shall be saved, and
shall go in and out, and find pasture.
10"The thief comes only to steal,
and kill, and destroy; I came that
they [a]might have life, and might
[1]have *it* abundantly.
11"[a]I am the good shepherd; the
good shepherd [b]lays down His life
for the sheep.
12"He who is a hireling, and not a
[a]shepherd, who is not the owner of
the sheep, beholds the wolf coming,
and leaves the sheep, and flees, and
the wolf snatches them, and scatters *them*.
13 *"He flees* because he is a hireling, and is not concerned about the
sheep.
14"[a]I am the good shepherd; and [b]I
know My own, and My own know
Me,
15 even as [a]the Father knows Me
and I know the Father; and [b]I lay
down My life for the sheep.
16"And I have [a]other sheep, which
are not of this fold; I must bring
them also, and they shall hear My
voice; and they shall become [b]one
flock *with* [c]one shepherd.
17"For this reason the Father loves
Me, because I [a]lay down My life that
I may take it again.

24 [a]Josh. 7:19; Ezra 10:11; Rev. 11:13 [b]John 9:16
27 [a]John 9:15 [b]John 5:25
28 [a]John 5:45; Rom. 2:17
29 [a]John 8:14
31 [a]Job 27:8f.; 35:13; Ps. 34:15f.; 66:18; 145:19; Prov. 15:29; 28:9; Is. 1:15; James 5:16ff.
32 [1]Lit., *From antiquity it was not heard*
33 [a]John 3:2; 9:16
34 [a]John 9:2 [b]John 9:22, 35; 3 John 10
35 [a]John 9:22, 34; 3 John 10 [b]Matt. 4:3
36 [1]Or, *Sir* [a]Rom. 10:14
37 [a]John 4:26
38 [a]Matt. 8:2
39 [a]John 3:19; 5:22, 27 [b]Luke 4:18 [c]Matt. 13:13; 15:14
40 [a]Rom. 2:19
41 [a]John 15:22, 24 [b]Prov. 26:12
1 [a]John 10:8
2 [a]John 10:11f.
3 [a]John 10:4f., 16, 27 [b]John 10:9
4 [a]John 10:5, 16, 27
5 [a]John 10:4f., 16, 27
6 [a]John 16:25, 29; 2 Pet. 2:22
7 [a]John 10:1f., 9
8 [a]Jer. 23:1f.; Ezek. 34:2ff.; John 10:1
9 [a]John 10:1f., 9
10 [1]Or, *have abundance* [a]John 5:40
11 [a]Is. 40:11; Ezek. 34:11-16, 23; John 10:14; Heb. 13:20; 1 Pet. 5:4; Rev. 7:17 [b]John 10:15, 17, 18; 15:13; 1 John 3:16
12 [a]John 10:2
14 [a]John 10:11 [b]John 10:27
15 [a]Matt. 11:27 [b]John 10:11, 17, 18
16 [a]Is. 56:8 [b]John 11:52; 17:20f.; Eph. 2:13-18; 1 Pet. 2:25 [c]Ezek. 34:23; 37:24
17 [a]John 10:11, 15, 18

18"[a]No one [1]has taken it away
from Me, but I [b]lay it down on My
own initiative. I have authority to
lay it down, and I have authority to
take it up again. [c]This commandment I received from My Father."
19 [a]There arose a division again
among the Jews because of these
words.
20 And many of them were saying,
"He [a]has a demon, and [b]is insane;
why do you listen to Him?"
21 Others were saying, "These are
not the sayings of one [a]demon-pos-
sessed. [b]A demon cannot open the
eyes of the blind, can he?"

Jesus Asserts His Deity

22 At that time the Feast of the
Dedication took place at Jerusalem;
23 it was winter, and Jesus was
walking in the temple in the portico
of [a]Solomon.
24 [a]The Jews therefore gathered
around Him, and were saying to
Him, "How long will You keep us in
suspense? If You are [1]the Christ, tell
us [b]plainly."
25 Jesus answered them, "[a]I told
you, and you do not believe; [b]the
works that I do in My Father's
name, these bear witness of Me.
26"But you do not believe, because
[a]you are not of My sheep.
27"My sheep [a]hear My voice, and
[b]I know them, and they follow Me;
28 and I give [a]eternal life to them,
and they shall never perish; and [b]no
one shall snatch them out of My
hand.
29"[1]My Father, who has given
them to Me, is greater than all; and
no one is able to snatch *them* out of
the Father's hand.
30"[a]I and the Father are one."
31 The Jews [a]took up stones again
to stone Him.
32 Jesus answered them, "I
showed you many good works from
the Father; for which of them are
you stoning Me?"
33 The Jews answered Him, "For a
good work we do not stone You, but
for [a]blasphemy; and because You,
being a man, [b]make Yourself out *to
be* God."
34 Jesus answered them, "Has it
not been written in [a]your [b]Law, 'I
said, [c]YOU ARE GODS'?
35"If he called them gods, to whom
the word of God came (and the
Scripture cannot be broken),
36 do you say of Him, whom the
Father [a]sanctified and [b]sent into the
world, 'You are blaspheming,' because I said, '[c]I am the Son of God'?

18 [1]Or, *takes*
[a]Matt. 26:53;
John 2:19; 5:26
[b]John 10:11, 15,
17 [c]John 14:31;
15:10; Phil. 2:8;
Heb. 5:8
19 [a]John 7:43
20 [a]John 7:20
[b]Mark 3:21
21 [a]Matt. 4:24
[b]Ex. 4:11; John
9:32f.
23 [a]Acts 3:11
24 [1]I.e., the
Messiah
[a]John 1:19; 10:31,
33 [b]Luke 22:67;
John 16:25
25 [a]John 8:56,
58 [b]John 5:36;
10:38
26 [a]John 8:47
27 [a]John 10:4,
16 [b]John 10:14
28 [a]John 17:2f.;
1 John 2:25; 5:11
[b]John 6:37, 39
29 [1]Or, *What
My Father has
given Me is
greater than all*
30 [a]John 17:21ff.
31 [a]John 8:59
33 [a]Lev. 24:16
[b]John 5:18
34 [a]John 8:17
[b]John 12:34;
15:25; Rom. 3:19;
1 Cor. 14:21 [c]Ps.
82:6
36 [a]Jer. 1:5;
John 6:69 [b]John
3:17 [c]John 5:17f.;
10:30
37 [a]John 10:25;
15:24
38 [a]John 10:25;
14:11 [b]John
14:10f., 20; 17:21,
23
39 [a]John 7:30
[b]Luke 4:30; John
8:59
40 [a]John 1:28
41 [a]John 2:11
[b]John 1:27, 30,
34; 3:27-30
42 [a]John 7:31
1 [a]Matt. 21:17;
John 11:18 [b]Luke
10:38; John 11:5,
19ff.
2 [a]Luke 7:38;
John 12:3 [b]Luke
7:13; John 11:3,
21, 32; 13:13f.
3 [a]Luke 7:13;
John 11:2, 21, 32;
13:13f. [b]John
11:5, 11, 36
4 [a]John 9:3;
10:38; 11:40
5 [a]John 11:1
7 [a]John 10:40
8 [a]Matt. 23:7
[b]John 8:59; 10:31
9 [a]Luke 13:33;
John 9:4; 12:35
11 [a]John 11:3
[b]Matt. 27:52;
Mark 5:39; John
11:13; Acts 7:60

37"[a]If I do not do the works of My
Father, do not believe Me;
38 but if I do them, though you do
not believe Me, believe [a]the works,
that you may know and understand
that [b]the Father is in Me, and I in the
Father."
39 Therefore [a]they were seeking
again to seize Him; and [b]He eluded
their grasp.
40 And He went away [a]again beyond the Jordan to the place where
John was first baptizing; and He
was staying there.
41 And many came to Him; and
they were saying, "While John performed no [a]sign, yet [b]everything
John said about this man was true."
42 And [a]many believed in Him
there.

CHAPTER 11

The Death and Resurrection of Lazarus

NOW a certain man was sick,
Lazarus of [a]Bethany, the village of
Mary and her sister [b]Martha.
2 And it was the Mary who [a]a-
nointed [b]the Lord with ointment,
and wiped His feet with her hair,
whose brother Lazarus was sick.
3 The sisters therefore sent to
Him, saying, "[a]Lord, behold, [b]he
whom You love is sick."
4 But when Jesus heard it, He
said, "This sickness is not unto
death, but for [a]the glory of God, that
the Son of God may be glorified by
it."
5 Now Jesus loved [a]Martha, and
her sister, and Lazarus.
6 When therefore He heard that
he was sick, He stayed then two
days *longer* in the place where He
was.
7 Then after this He *said to the
disciples, "[a]Let us go to Judea
again."
8 The disciples *said to Him,
"[a]Rabbi, the Jews were just now
seeking [b]to stone You; and are You
going there again?"
9 Jesus answered, "[a]Are there
not twelve hours in the day? If anyone walks in the day, he does not
stumble, because he sees the light of
this world.
10"But if anyone walks in the
night, he stumbles, because the light
is not in him."
11 This He said, and after that He
*said to them, "Our [a]friend Lazarus
[b]has fallen asleep; but I go, that I
may awaken him out of sleep."

12 The disciples therefore said to
Him, "Lord, if he has fallen asleep,
he will recover."
13 Now [a]Jesus had spoken of his
death; but they thought that He was
speaking of literal sleep.
14 Then Jesus therefore said to
them plainly, "Lazarus is dead,
15 and I am glad for your sakes
that I was not there, so that you may
believe; but let us go to him."
16 [a]Thomas therefore, who is
called [1b]Didymus, said to *his* fellow
disciples, "Let us also go, that we
may die with Him."
17 So when Jesus came, He found
that he had already been in the tomb
[a]four days.
18 Now [a]Bethany was near Jerusalem, about [1]two miles off;
19 and many of [a]the Jews had
come to [b]Martha and Mary, [c]to console them concerning *their* brother.
20 [a]Martha therefore, when she
heard that Jesus was coming, went
to meet Him; but [a]Mary still sat in
the house.
21 Martha therefore said to Jesus,
"[a]Lord, [b]if You had been here, my
brother would not have died.
22"Even now I know that [a]what-
ever You ask of God, God will give
You."
23 Jesus *said to her, "Your
brother shall rise again."
24 Martha *said to Him, "[a]I know
that he will rise again in the resurrection on the last day."
25 Jesus said to her, "[a]I am the resurrection and the life; he who believes in Me shall live even if he dies,
26 and everyone who lives and believes in Me [a]shall never die. Do you
believe this?"
27 She *said to Him, "Yes, Lord; I
have believed that You are [1a]the
Christ, the Son of God, *even* [2b]He
who comes into the world."
28 And when she had said this, she
[a]went away, and called Mary her
sister, saying secretly, "[b]The
Teacher is here, and is calling for
you."
29 And when she heard it, she
*arose quickly, and was coming to
Him.
30 Now Jesus had not yet come
into the village, but [a]was still in the
place where Martha met Him.
31 [a]The Jews then who were with
her in the house, and [b]consoling her,
when they saw that Mary rose up
quickly and went out, followed her,
supposing that she was going to the
tomb to weep there.
Therefore, when Mary came
where Jesus was, she saw Him, and
fell at His feet, saying to Him,
"[a]Lord, [b]if You had been here, my
brother would not have died."
33 When Jesus therefore saw her
weeping, and [a]the Jews who came
with her, *also* weeping, He [b]was
deeply moved in spirit, and [c]was
troubled,
34 and said, "Where have you laid
him?" They *said to Him, "Lord,
come and see."
35 Jesus [a]wept.
36 And so [a]the Jews were saying,
"Behold how He [1b]loved him!"
37 But some of them said, "Could
not this man, who [a]opened the eyes
of him who was blind, have kept this
man also from dying?"
38 Jesus therefore again being
deeply moved within, *came to the
tomb. Now it was a [a]cave, and a
stone was lying against it.
39 Jesus *said, "Remove the
stone." Martha, the sister of the deceased, *said to Him, "Lord, by this
time [1]there will be a stench; for he
has been dead [a]four days."
40 Jesus *said to her, "[a]Did I not
say to you, if you believe, you will
see the glory of God?"
41 And so they removed the
[a]stone. And Jesus [b]raised His eyes,
and said, "[c]Father, I thank Thee that
Thou heardest Me.
42"And I knew that Thou hearest
Me always; but [a]because of the people standing around I said it, that
they may believe that [b]Thou didst
send Me."
43 And when He had said these
things, He cried out with a loud
voice, "Lazarus, come forth."
44 He who had died came forth,
[a]bound hand and foot with wrappings; and [b]his face was wrapped
around with a cloth. Jesus *said to
them, "Unbind him, and let him go."
45 [a]Many therefore of the Jews,
[b]who had come to Mary and [c]beheld
what He had done, believed in Him.
46 But some of them went away to
the [a]Pharisees, and told them the
things which Jesus had done.

Conspiracy to Kill Jesus

47 Therefore [a]the chief priests and
the Pharisees [b]convened a [c]council,
and were saying, "What are we
doing? For this man is performing
many [d]signs.
48"If we let Him *go on* like this, all
men will believe in Him, and the Romans will come and take away both
our [a]place and our nation."
49 But a certain one of them,
[a]Caiaphas, [b]who was high priest

13 [a]Matt. 9:24; Luke 8:52
16 [1]I.e., the Twin [a]Matt. 10:3; Mark 3:18; Luke 6:15; John 14:5; 20:26-28; Acts 1:13 [b]John 20:24; 21:2
17 [a]John 11:39
18 [1]I.e., 15 stadia (9,090 ft.) [a]John 11:1
19 [a]John 1:19; 11:8 [b]John 11:1 [c]1 Sam. 31:13; 1 Chr. 10:12; Job 2:11; John 11:31
20 [a]Luke 10:38
21 [a]John 11:2 [b]John 11:32, 37
22 [a]John 9:31
24 [a]Dan. 12:2; John 5:28f.
25 [a]John 1:4; 5:26; 6:39f.; Rev. 1:18
26 [a]John 6:47, 50, 51; 8:51
27 [1]I.e., the Messiah [2]The Coming One was the Messianic title [a]Matt. 16:16; Luke 2:11 [b]John 6:14
28 [a]John 11:30 [b]Matt. 26:18; Mark 14:14; Luke 22:11; John 13:13
30 [a]John 11:20
31 [a]John 11:19, 33 [b]John 11:19
32 [a]John 11:2 [b]John 11:21
33 [a]John 11:19 [b]John 11:38 [c]John 12:27; 13:21
35 [a]Luke 19:41; John 11:33
36 [1]Lit., *was loving* [a]John 11:19 [b]John 11:3
37 [a]John 9:7
38 [a]Matt. 27:60; Mark 15:46; Luke 24:2; John 20:1
39 [1]Lit., *he stinks* [a]John 11:17
40 [a]John 11:4
41 [a]Matt. 27:60; Mark 15:46; Luke 24:2; John 20:1 [b]John 17:1; Acts 7:55 [c]Matt. 11:25
42 [a]John 12:30; 17:21 [b]John 3:17
44 [a]John 19:40 [b]John 20:7
45 [a]John 7:31 [b]John 11:19; 12:17f. [c]John 2:23
46 [a]John 7:32
47 [a]John 7:32, 45; 11:57 [b]Matt. 26:3 [c]Matt. 5:22 [d]John 2:11
48 [a]Matt. 24:15
49 [a]Matt. 26:3 [b]John 11:51

that year, said to them, "You know nothing at all,

50 nor do you take into account that [a]it is expedient for you that one man should die for the people, and that the whole nation should not perish."

51 Now this he did not say [1]on his own initiative; but [a]being high priest that year, he [b]prophesied that Jesus was going to die for the nation;

52 and not for the nation only, but that He might also [a]gather together into one the children of God who are scattered abroad.

53 So from that day on they [a]planned together to kill Him.

54 Jesus therefore [a]no longer continued to walk publicly among the Jews, but went away from there to the country near the wilderness, into a city called [b]Ephraim; and there He stayed with the disciples.

55 Now [a]the Passover of the Jews was at hand, and many went up to Jerusalem out of the country before the Passover, [b]to purify themselves.

56 Therefore they [a]were seeking for Jesus, and were saying to one another, as they stood in the temple, "What do you think; that He will not come to the feast at all?"

57 Now [a]the chief priests and the Pharisees had given orders that if any one knew where He was, he should report it, that they might seize Him.

Chapter 12

Mary Anoints Jesus

[a]JESUS, therefore, six days before [b]the Passover, came to [c]Bethany where Lazarus was, whom Jesus had raised from the dead.

2 So they made Him a supper there; and [a]Martha was serving; but Lazarus was one of those reclining *at the table* with Him.

3 [a]Mary therefore took a pound of very costly, [b]genuine spikenard ointment, and anointed the feet of Jesus, and wiped His feet with her hair; and the house was filled with the fragrance of the ointment.

4 But [a]Judas Iscariot, one of His disciples, who was intending to [1]betray Him, *said,

5 "Why was this ointment not sold for [1]three hundred denarii, and given to poor *people?*"

6 Now he said this, not because he was concerned about the poor, but because he was a thief, and as he [a]had the money box, he used to pilfer [b]what was put into it.

7 Jesus therefore said, "Let her alone, in order that she may keep [1]it for [a]the day of My burial.

8 "[a]For the poor you always have with you; but you do not always have Me."

9 The [a]great multitude therefore of the Jews learned that He was there; and they came, not for Jesus' sake only, but that they might also see Lazarus, [b]whom He raised from the dead.

10 But the chief priests took counsel that they might put Lazarus to death also;

11 because [a]on account of him [b]many of the Jews were going away, and were believing in Jesus.

Jesus Enters Jerusalem

12 On the next day [1a]the great multitude who had come to [b]the feast, when they heard that Jesus was coming to Jerusalem,

13 took the branches of the palm trees, and went out to meet Him, and *began* to cry out, "[a]Hosanna! BLESSED *is* HE WHO COMES IN THE NAME OF THE LORD, even the [b]King of Israel."

14 And Jesus, finding a young donkey, sat on it; as it is written,

15 "[a]FEAR NOT, DAUGHTER OF ZION; BEHOLD, YOUR KING COMES SITTING ON A DONKEY'S COLT."

16 [a]These things His disciples did not understand at the first; but when Jesus [b]was glorified, then they remembered that these things were written of Him, and that they had done these things to Him.

17 And so [a]the multitude who were with Him when He called Lazarus out of the tomb, and raised him from the dead, were bearing Him witness.

18 [a]For this cause also the multitude went and met Him, [b]because they heard that He had performed this [1]sign.

19 The Pharisees therefore said to one another, "You see that you are not doing any good; look, the world has gone after Him."

Greeks Seek Jesus

20 Now there were certain [a]Greeks among those who were going up to worship at [b]the feast;

21 these therefore came to [a]Philip, who was from [b]Bethsaida of Galilee, and *began to* ask him, saying, "Sir, we wish to see Jesus."

22 Philip *came and *told [a]Andrew; Andrew and Philip *came, and they *told Jesus.

---

50 [a]John 18:14
51 [1]Lit., *from himself* [a]John 18:13 [b]Ex. 28:30; Num. 27:21; 1 Sam. 23:9; 30:7; Ezra 2:63
52 [a]John 10:16
53 [a]Matt. 26:4
54 [a]John 7:1 [b]2 Chr. 13:19 marg.
55 [a]Matt. 26:1f.; Mark 14:1; Luke 22:1; John 2:13; 12:1; 13:1 [b]Num. 9:10; 2 Chr. 30:17f.; John 18:28
56 [a]John 7:11
57 [a]John 11:47
1 [a]John 12:1-8: *Matt. 26:6-13; Mark 14:3-9; Luke 7:37-39* [b]John 11:55; 12:20 [c]Matt. 21:17; John 11:43f.
2 [a]Luke 10:38
3 [a]John 11:2 [b]Mark 14:3
4 [1]Or, *deliver Him up* [a]John 6:71
5 [1]Monetary value $50, but equal to 11 months' wages
6 [a]John 13:29 [b]Luke 8:3
7 [1]I.e., The custom of anointing for burial [a]John 19:40
8 [a]Deut. 15:11; Matt. 26:11; Mark 14:7
9 [a]Mark 12:37; John 12:12 marg. [b]John 11:43f.; 12:1, 17f.
11 [a]John 11:45f.; 12:18 [b]John 7:31; 11:42
12 [1]Or, *the common people* [a]John 12:12-15: *Matt. 21:4-9; Mark 11:7-10; Luke 19:35-38* [b]John 12:1
13 [a]Ps. 118:25f. [b]John 1:49
15 [a]Zech. 9:9
16 [a]Mark 9:32; John 2:22; 14:26 [b]John 7:39; 12:23
17 [a]John 11:42
18 [1]Or, *attesting miracle* [a]Luke 19:37; John 12:12 [b]John 12:11
20 [a]John 7:35 [b]John 12:1
21 [a]John 1:44 [b]Matt. 11:21
22 [a]John 1:44

23 And Jesus *answered them,
saying, "[a]The hour has come for the
Son of Man to [b]be glorified.
24"Truly, truly, I say to you, [a]un-
less a grain of wheat falls into the
earth and dies, it remains by itself
alone; but if it dies, it bears much
fruit.
25"[a]He who loves his life loses it;
and he who [b]hates his life in this
world shall keep it to life eternal.
26"If any one serves Me, let him
follow Me; and [a]where I am, there
shall My servant also be; if any one
serves Me, the Father will [b]honor
him.

Jesus Foretells His Death

27"[a]Now My soul has become
troubled; and what shall I say, '[b]Fa-
ther, save Me from [c]this hour'? But
for this purpose I came to this hour.
28"[a]Father, glorify Thy name."
There came therefore a [b]voice out of
heaven: "I have both glorified it, and
will glorify it again."
29 The multitude therefore, who
stood by and heard it, were saying
that it had thundered; others were
saying, "[a]An angel has spoken to
Him."
30 Jesus answered and said,
"[a]This voice has not come for My
sake, but for your sakes.
31"[a]Now judgment is upon this
world; now [b]the ruler of this world
shall be cast out.
32"And I, if I [a]be lifted up from the
earth, will [b]draw all men to Myself."
33 But He was saying this [a]to indicate the kind of death by which He
was to die.
34 The multitude therefore answered Him, "We have heard out of
[a]the Law that [b]the Christ is to remain forever; and how can You say,
'The [c]Son of Man must be [d]lifted
up'? Who is this [c]Son of Man?"
35 Jesus therefore said to them,
"[a]For a little while longer [b]the light
is among you. [c]Walk while you have
the light, that darkness may not
overtake you; he who [d]walks in the
darkness does not know where he
goes.
36"While you have the light, [a]be-
lieve in the light, in order that you
may become [b]sons of light."
These things Jesus spoke, and He
departed and [c]hid Himself from
them.
37 But though He had performed
so many signs before them, *yet* they
were not believing in Him;
38 that the word of Isaiah the
prophet might be fulfilled, which he
spoke, "[a]LORD, WHO HAS BELIEVED
OUR REPORT? AND TO WHOM HAS THE
ARM OF THE LORD BEEN REVEALED?"
39 For this cause they could not
believe, for Isaiah said again,
40"[a]HE HAS BLINDED THEIR EYES,
AND HE [b]HARDENED THEIR HEART;
LEST THEY SEE WITH THEIR EYES, AND
PERCEIVE WITH THEIR HEART, AND BE
CONVERTED, AND I HEAL THEM."
41 These things Isaiah said, because [a]he saw His glory, and [b]he
spoke of Him.
42 Nevertheless [a]many even of
[b]the rulers believed in Him, but [c]be-
cause of the Pharisees they were not
confessing *Him*, lest they should be
[d]put out of the synagogue;
43 [a]for they loved the approval of
men rather than the approval of
God.
44 And Jesus cried out and said,
"[a]He who believes in Me does not
believe in Me, but in Him who sent
Me.
45"And [a]he who beholds Me beholds the One who sent Me.
46"[a]I have come *as* light into the
world, that everyone who believes
in Me may not remain in darkness.
47"And if any one hears My sayings, and does not keep them, I do
not judge him; for [a]I did not come to
judge the world, but to save the
world.
48"[a]He who rejects Me, and does
not receive My sayings, has one who
judges him; [b]the word I spoke is
what will judge him at [c]the last day.
49"[a]For I did not speak [1]on My
own initiative, but the Father Himself who sent Me [b]has given Me
commandment, what to say, and
what to speak.
50"And I know that [a]His commandment is eternal life; therefore
the things I speak, I speak [b]just as
the Father has told Me."

CHAPTER 13

The Last Passover—The Upper Room

NOW before the Feast of [a]the
Passover, Jesus knowing that [b]His
hour had come that He should depart out of this world [c]to the Father,
having loved His own who were in
the world, He loved them to the end.
2 And during supper, [a]the devil
having already put into the heart of
[b]Judas Iscariot, *the son* of Simon, to
betray Him,
3 *Jesus*, [a]knowing that the Father
had given all things into His hands,
and that [b]He had come forth from

23 [a]Matt. 26:45; Mark 14:35, 41; John 13:1, 32; 17:1 [b]John 7:39
24 [a]Rom. 14:9; 1 Cor. 15:36
25 [a]Matt. 10:39 [b]Luke 14:26
26 [a]John 14:3; 17:24; 2 Cor. 5:8 1 Thess. 4:17 [b]1 Sam. 2:30; Ps. 91:15; Luke 12:37
27 [a]Matt. 26:38; Mark 14:34; John 11:33 [b]Matt. 11:25 [c]John 12:23
28 [a]Matt. 11:25 [b]Matt. 3:17; 17:5; Mark 1:11; 9:7; Luke 3:22; 9:35
29 [a]Acts 23:9
30 [a]John 11:42
31 [a]John 3:19; 9:39; 16:11 [b]John 14:30; 16:11; 2 Cor. 4:4; Eph. 2:2; 6:12; 1 John 4:4; 5:19
32 [a]John 3:14; 8:28; 12:34 [b]John 6:44
33 [a]John 18:32
34 [a]John 10:34 [b]Ps. 110:4; Is. 9:7; Ezek. 37:25; Dan. 7:14 [c]Matt. 8:20 [d]John 3:14; 8:28
35 [a]John 7:33; 9:4; 1 John 2:10 [b]John 12:46 [c]Gal. 6:10; Eph. 5:8 [d]1 John 1:6; 2:11
36 [a]John 12:46 [b]Luke 16:8; John 8:12 [c]John 8:59
38 [a]Is. 53:1; Rom. 10:16
40 [a]Is. 6:10; Matt. 13:14f. [b]Mark 6:52
41 [a]Is. 6:1ff. [b]Luke 24:27
42 [a]John 7:48; 12:11 [b]Luke 23:13 [c]John 7:13 [d]John 9:22
43 [a]John 5:41
44 [a]Matt. 10:40; John 5:24
45 [a]John 14:9
46 [a]John 1:4; 3:19; 8:12; 9:5; 12:35f.
47 [a]John 3:17
48 [a]Luke 10:16 [b]Deut. 18:18f.; John 5:45ff.; 8:47 [c]Matt. 10:15
49 [1]Lit., *of Myself* [a]John 3:11 [b]John 14:31; 17:8
50 [a]John 6:68 [b]John 8:28
1 [a]John 2:13; 11:55 [b]John 12:23 [c]John 13:3; 16:28
2 [a]John 6:70; 13:27 [b]John 6:71
3 [a]John 3:35 [b]John 8:42

God, and was going back to God,
4 *rose from supper, and *laid
aside His garments; and taking a
towel, [a]girded Himself about.

Jesus Washes the Disciples' Feet

5 Then He *poured water into the
basin, and began to [a]wash the disciples' feet, and to wipe them with the
towel with which He was girded.
6 And so He *came to Simon Peter. He *said to Him, "Lord, do You
wash my feet?"
7 Jesus answered and said to
him, "What I do you do not realize
now; but you shall understand
[a]hereafter."
8 Peter *said to Him, "Never
shall You wash my feet!" Jesus answered him, "If I do not wash you,
[a]you have no part with Me."
9 Simon Peter *said to Him,
"Lord, not my feet only, but also my
hands and my head."
10 Jesus *said to him, "He who
has bathed needs only to wash his
feet, but is completely clean; and
[a]you are clean, but not all *of you.*"
11 For [a]He knew the one who was
betraying Him; for this reason He
said, "Not all of you are clean."
12 And so when He had washed
their feet, and [a]taken His garments,
and reclined *at table* again, He said
to them, "Do you know what I have
done to you?
13 "You call Me [a]Teacher and
[b]Lord; and you are right; for *so* I am.
14 "If I then, [a]the Lord and the
Teacher, washed your feet, you also
ought to wash one another's feet.
15 "For I gave you [a]an example that
you also should do as I did to you.
16 "Truly, truly, I say to you, [a]a
slave is not greater than his master;
neither [b]one who is sent greater
than the one who sent him.
17 "If you know these things, you
are [a]blessed if you do them.
18 "[a]I do not speak of all of you. I
know the ones I have [b]chosen; but *it*
is [c]that the Scripture may be fulfilled, '[d]HE WHO EATS MY BREAD HAS
LIFTED UP HIS HEEL AGAINST ME.'
19 "From now on [a]I am telling you
before *it* comes to pass, so that
when it does occur, you may believe
that [b]I am *He.*
20 "Truly, truly, I say to you, [a]he
who receives whomever I send receives Me; and he who receives Me
receives Him who sent Me."

Jesus Predicts His Betrayal

21 When Jesus had said this, He
[a]became troubled in spirit, and testified, and said, "Truly, truly, I say to
you, that [b]one of you will betray
Me."
22 The disciples *began* looking at
one another, [a]at a loss *to know* of
which one He was speaking.
23 There was reclining on [a]Jesus'
breast one of His disciples, [b]whom
Jesus loved.
24 Simon Peter therefore *ges-
tured to him, and *said to him, "Tell
us who it is of whom He is speaking."
25 He, [a]leaning back thus on Jesus' breast, *said to Him, "Lord,
who is it?"
26 Jesus therefore *answered,
"That is the one for whom I shall dip
the morsel and give it to him." So
when He had dipped the morsel, He
*took and *gave it to Judas, [a]*the son*
of Simon Iscariot.
27 And after the morsel, [a]Satan
then [b]entered into him. Jesus therefore *said to him, "What you do, do
quickly."
28 Now no one of those reclining
at table knew for what purpose He
had said this to him.
29 For some were supposing, because Judas [a]had the money box,
that Jesus was saying to him, "Buy
the things we have need of [b]for the
feast"; or else, that he should [c]give
something to the poor.
30 And so after receiving the morsel he went out immediately; and [a]it
was night.
31 When therefore he had gone
out, Jesus *said, "Now is [a]the Son of
Man [b]glorified, and [c]God is glorified
in Him;
32 [1]if God is glorified in Him, [a]God
will also glorify Him in Himself, and
will glorify Him immediately.
33 "[a]Little children, I am with you
[b]a little while longer. [c]You shall
seek Me; and as I said to the Jews,
'Where I am going, you cannot
come,' now I say to you also.
34 "A [a]new commandment I give to
you, [b]that you love one another,
[c]even as I have loved you, that you
also love one another.
35 "[a]By this all men will know that
you are My disciples, if you have
love for one another."
36 Simon Peter *said to Him,
"Lord, where are You going?" Jesus
answered, "[a]Where I go, you cannot
follow Me now; but [b]you shall follow later."
37 Peter *said to Him, "Lord, why
can I not follow You right now? [a]I
will lay down my life for You."

4 [a]Luke 12:37
5 [a]Luke 7:44
7 [a]John 13:12ff.
8 [a]Deut. 12:12; 2 Sam. 20:1; 1 Kin. 12:16
10 [a]John 15:3
11 [a]John 6:64
12 [a]John 13:4
13 [a]John 11:28 [b]John 11:2; 1 Cor. 12:3; Phil. 2:11
14 [a]John 11:2; 1 Cor. 12:3
15 [a]1 Pet. 5:3
16 [a]Matt. 10:24 [b]2 Cor. 8:23; Phil. 2:25
17 [a]Matt. 7:24ff.; Luke 11:28
18 [a]John 13:10f. [b]John 6:70; 15:16, 19 [c]John 15:25; 17:12; 18:32; 19:24, 36; [d]Ps. 41:9; Matt. 26:21ff.; Mark 14:18f.; Luke 22:21ff.; John 13:18, 21, 22, 26
19 [a]John 14:29; 16:4 [b]John 8:24
20 [a]Matt. 10:40; Luke 10:16
21 [a]John 11:33 [b]Matt. 26:21f.; Mark 14:18ff.; Luke 22:21ff.; John 13:18, 21
22 [a]Matt. 26:21ff.; Mark 14:18ff.; Luke 22:21ff.; John 13:18, 21, 22, 26
23 [a]John 1:18 [b]John 19:26; 20:2
25 [a]John 21:20
26 [a]John 6:71
27 [a]Matt. 4:10 [b]Luke 22:3; John 13:2
29 [a]John 12:6 [b]John 13:1 [c]John 12:5
30 [a]Luke 22:53
31 [a]Matt. 8:20 [b]John 7:39 [c]John 14:13; 17:4; 1 Pet. 4:11
32 [1]Some ancient mss. do not contain this phrase [a]John 17:1
33 [a]1 John 2:1 [b]John 7:33 [c]John 7:34
34 [a]John 15:12, 17; 1 John 2:7f.; 3:11, 23; 2 John 5 [b]Lev. 19:18; Matt. 5:44; Gal. 5:14; 1 Thess. 4:9; Heb. 13:1; 1 Pet. 1:22; 1 John 4:7 [c]Eph. 5:2
35 [a]1 John 3:14
36 [a]John 13:33; 14:2; 16:5 [b]John 21:18f.; 2 Pet. 1:14
37 [a]John 13:37, 38: *Matt. 26:33-35; Mark 14:29-31; Luke 22:33-34*

38 Jesus *answered, "Will you lay down your life for Me? Truly, truly, I say to you, [a]a cock shall not crow, until you deny Me three times.

Chapter 14

Jesus Comforts His Disciples

"[a]LET not your heart be troubled; [1]believe in God, believe also in Me.

2"In My Father's house are many dwelling places; if it were not so, I would have told you; for [a]I go to prepare a place for you.

3"And if I go and prepare a place for you, [a]I will come again, and receive you to Myself; that [b]where I am, *there* you may be also.

4"[1]And you know the way where I am going."

5 [a]Thomas *said to Him, "Lord, we do not know where You are going; how do we know the way?"

6 Jesus *said to him, "I am [a]the way, and [b]the truth, and [c]the life; no one comes to the Father, but through Me.

Oneness with the Father

7"[a]If you had known Me, you would have known My Father also; from now on you [b]know Him, and have [c]seen Him."

8 [a]Philip *said to Him, "Lord, show us the Father, and it is enough for us."

9 Jesus *said to him, "Have I been so long with you, and *yet* you have not come to know Me, Philip? [a]He who has seen Me has seen the Father; how do you say, 'Show us the Father'?

10"Do you not believe that [a]I am in the Father, and the Father is in Me? [b]The words that I say to you I do not speak on My own initiative, but the Father abiding in Me does His works.

11"Believe Me that [a]I am in the Father, and the Father in Me; otherwise [b]believe on account of the works themselves.

12"Truly, truly, I say to you, he who believes in Me, the works that I do shall he do also; and [a]greater *works* than these shall he do; because [b]I go to the Father.

13"And [a]whatever you ask in My name, that will I do, that [b]the Father may be glorified in the Son.

14"If you ask Me anything [a]in My name, I will do *it*.

15"[a]If you love Me, you will keep My commandments.

38 [a]Mark 14:30
1 [1]Or, *you believe in God* [a]John 14:27
2 [a]John 13:33
3 [a]John 14:18, 28 [b]John 12:26
4 [1]Some mss. read, *And where I go you know, and the way you know*
5 [a]John 11:16
6 [a]Rom. 5:2 [b]John 1:14 [c]John 1:4; 11:25
7 [a]John 8:19 [b]1 John 2:13 [c]John 6:46
8 [a]John 1:43
9 [a]John 1:14; 12:45; Col. 1:15
10 [a]John 10:38; 14:11, 20 [b]John 5:19; 14:24
11 [a]John 10:38; 14:10, 20 [b]John 5:36
12 [a]John 4:37f.; 5:20 [b]John 7:33
13 [a]Matt. 7:7 [b]John 13:31
14 [a]John 15:16
15 [a]John 14:21, 23; 15:10
16 [1]Or, *Intercessor* [a]John 7:39; Rom. 8:26; 1 John 2:1
17 [a]John 15:26 [b]1 Cor. 2:14
18 [a]John 14:3
19 [a]John 7:33 [b]John 16:16, 22 [c]John 6:57
20 [a]John 16:23, 26 [b]John 10:38
21 [a]John 14:15, 23; 15:10 [b]John 14:23; 16:27 [c]Ex. 33:18f.; Prov. 8:17
22 [a]Matt. 10:3; Luke 6:16; Acts 1:13 [b]Acts 10:40
23 [a]John 14:15, 21; 15:10; 1 John 5:3; 2 John 6 [b]John 8:51; 1 John 2:5 [c]John 14:21 [d]2 Cor. 6:16 for O.T.; Eph. 3:17; 1 John 2:24
24 [a]John 14:23 [b]John 7:16; 14:10
26 [a]John 14:16 [b]Luke 24:49; John 1:33; Acts 2:33 [c]John 16:13f.; 1 John 2:20, 27 [d]John 2:22
27 [a]John 16:33; Col. 3:15 [b]John 14:1
28 [a]John 14:2-4 [b]John 14:3, 18 [c]John 14:12 [d]John 10:29
29 [a]John 13:19
30 [a]John 12:31 [b]Heb. 4:15
31 [a]John 10:18

Role of the Spirit

16"And I will ask the Father, and He will give you another [1a]Helper, that He may be with you forever;

17 *that is* [a]the Spirit of truth, [b]whom the world cannot receive, because it does not behold Him or know Him, *but* you know Him because He abides with you, and will be in you.

18"I will not leave you as orphans; [a]I will come to you.

19"[a]After a little while [b]the world will behold Me no more; but you *will* behold Me; [c]because I live, you shall live also.

20"[a]In that day you shall know that [b]I am in My Father, and you in Me, and I in you.

21"[a]He who has My commandments and keeps them, he it is who loves Me; and [b]he who loves Me shall be loved by My Father, and I will love him, and will [c]disclose Myself to him."

22 [a]Judas (not Iscariot) *said to Him, "Lord, what then has happened [b]that You are going to disclose Yourself to us, and not to the world?"

23 Jesus answered and said to him, "[a]If anyone loves Me, he will [b]keep My word; and [c]My Father will love him, and We [d]will come to him, and make Our abode with him.

24"He who does not love Me [a]does not keep My words; and [b]the word which you hear is not Mine, but the Father's who sent Me.

25"These things I have spoken to you, while abiding with you.

26"But the [a]Helper, the Holy Spirit, [b]whom the Father will send in My name, [c]He will teach you all things, and [d]bring to your remembrance all that I said to you.

27"[a]Peace I leave with you; My peace I give to you; not as the world gives, do I give to you. [b]Let not your heart be troubled, nor let it be fearful.

28"[a]You heard that I said to you, 'I go away, and [b]I will come to you.' If you loved Me, you would have rejoiced, because [c]I go to the Father; for [d]the Father is greater than I.

29"And now [a]I have told you before it comes to pass, that when it comes to pass, you may believe.

30"I will not speak much more with you, for [a]the ruler of the world is coming, and [b]he has nothing in Me;

31 but that the world may know that I love the Father, and as [a]the

Father gave Me commandment, even so I do. Arise, [b]let us go from here.

Chapter 15

Jesus Is the Vine—Followers are Branches

"[a]I AM the true vine, and My Father is the [b]vinedresser.

2"Every branch in Me that does not bear fruit, He takes away; and every *branch* that bears fruit, He prunes it, that it may bear more fruit.

3"[a]You are already clean because of the word which I have spoken to you.

4"[a]Abide in Me, and I in you. As the branch cannot bear fruit of itself, unless it abides in the vine, so neither *can* you, unless you abide in Me.

5"I am the vine, you are the branches; he who abides in Me, and I in him, he [a]bears much fruit; for apart from Me you can do nothing.

6"If anyone does not abide in Me, he is [a]thrown away as a branch, and dries up; and they gather them, and cast them into the fire, and they are burned.

7"If you abide in Me, and My words abide in you, [a]ask whatever you wish, and it shall be done for you.

8"[a]By this is My Father glorified, that you bear much fruit, and so [b]prove to be My disciples.

9"Just as [a]the Father has loved Me, I have also loved you; abide in My love.

10"[a]If you keep My commandments, you will abide in My love; just as [b]I have kept My Father's commandments, and abide in His love.

11"[a]These things I have spoken to you, that My joy may be in you, and *that* your [b]joy may be made full.

Disciples' Relation to Each Other

12"This is [a]My commandment, that you love one another, just as I have loved you.

13"[a]Greater love has no one than this, that one [b]lay down his life for his friends.

14"You are My [a]friends, if [b]you do what I command you.

15"No longer do I call you slaves; for the slave does not know what his master is doing; but I have called you friends, for [a]all things that I have heard from My Father I have made known to you.

16"[a]You did not choose Me, but I chose you, and appointed you, that you should go and [b]bear fruit, and *that* your fruit should remain, that [c]whatever you ask of the Father in My name, He may give to you.

17"This [a]I command you, that you love one another.

Disciples' Relation to the World

18"[a]If the world hates you, you know that it has hated Me before *it hated* you.

19"[a]If you were of the world, the world would love its own; but because you are not of the world, but [b]I chose you out of the world, [c]therefore the world hates you.

20"Remember the word that I said to you, '[a]A slave is not greater than his master.' If they persecuted Me, [b]they will also persecute you; if they [c]kept My word, they will keep yours also.

21"But all these things they will do to you [a]for My name's sake, [b]because they do not know the One who sent Me.

22"[a]If I had not come and spoken to them, they would not have sin, but now they have no excuse for their sin.

23"He who hates Me hates My Father also.

24"[a]If I had not done among them [b]the works which no one else did, they would not have sin; but now they have both seen and hated Me and My Father as well.

25"But *they have done this* in order that the word may be fulfilled that is written in their [a]Law, '[b]THEY HATED ME WITHOUT A CAUSE.'

26"When the [1a]Helper comes, [b]whom I will send to you from the Father, *that is* [c]the Spirit of truth, who proceeds from the Father, [d]He will bear witness of Me,

27 [1]and [a]you *will* bear witness also, because you have been with Me [b]from the beginning.

Chapter 16

Jesus' Warning

"[a]THESE things I have spoken to you, that you may be kept from [b]stumbling.

2"They will [a]make you outcasts from the synagogue; but [b]an hour is coming for everyone [c]who kills you to think that he is offering service to God.

3"And these things they will do, [a]because they have not known the Father, or Me.

---

31 [b]John 13:1; 18:1
1 [a]Ps. 80:8ff.; Is. 5:1ff.; Ezek. 19:10ff.; Matt. 21:33ff. [b]Matt. 15:13; Rom. 11:17; 1 Cor. 3:9
3 [a]John 13:10; 17:17; Eph. 5:26
4 [a]John 6:56; 15:4-7; 1 John 2:6
5 [a]John 15:16
6 [a]John 15:2
7 [a]Matt. 7:7; John 15:16
8 [a]Matt. 5:16 [b]John 8:31
9 [a]John 3:35; 17:23, 24, 26
10 [a]John 14:15 [b]John 8:29
11 [a]John 17:13 [b]John 3:29
12 [a]John 13:34
13 [a]Rom. 5:7f. [b]John 10:11
14 [a]Luke 12:4 [b]Matt. 12:50
15 [a]John 8:26; 16:12
16 [a]John 6:70; 13:18; 15:19 [b]John 15:5 [c]John 14:13; 15:7; 16:23
17 [a]John 15:12
18 [a]John 7:7; 1 John 3:13
19 [a]Matt. 10:22; 24:9 [b]John 15:16 [c]John 17:14
20 [a]John 13:16 [b]1 Cor. 4:12; 2 Cor. 4:9; 2 Tim. 3:12 [c]John 8:51
21 [a]Matt. 10:22; 24:9; Mark 13:13; Luke 21:12, 17; Acts 4:17; 5:41; 9:14; 26:9; 1 Pet. 4:14; Rev. 2:3 [b]John 8:19, 55; 16:3; 17:25; Acts 3:17; 1 John 3:1
22 [a]John 9:41; 15:24
24 [a]John 9:41; 15:21 [b]John 5:36; 10:37
25 [a]John 10:34 [b]Ps. 35:19; 69:4
26 [1]Or, *Intercessor* [a]John 14:16 [b]John 14:26 [c]John 14:17 [d]1 John 5:7
27 [1]Or, (imperative) *and bear witness* [a]Luke 24:48; John 19:35; 21:24; 1 John 1:2; 4:14 [b]Luke 1:2
1 [a]John 15:18-27 [b]Matt. 11:6
2 [a]John 9:22 [b]John 4:21; 16:25 [c]Is. 66:5; Acts 26:9-11; Rev. 6:9
3 [a]John 8:19, 55; 15:21; 17:25; Acts 3:17; 1 John 3:1

4 "But these things I have spoken to you, [a]that when their hour comes, you [1]may remember that I told you of them. And these things I did not say to you [b]at the beginning, because I was with you.

The Holy Spirit Promised

5 "But now [a]I am going to Him who sent Me; and none of you asks Me, '[b]Where are You going?'

6 "But because I have said these things to you, [a]sorrow has filled your heart.

7 "But I tell you the truth, it is to your advantage that I go away; for if I do not go away, the [1a]Helper shall not come to you; but if I go, [b]I will send Him to you.

8 "And He, when He comes, will convict the world concerning sin, and righteousness, and judgment;

9 concerning sin, [a]because they do not believe in Me;

10 and concerning [a]righteousness, because [b]I go to the Father, and you no longer behold Me;

11 [a]and concerning judgment, because the ruler of this world has been judged.

12 "I have many more things to say to you, but you cannot bear *them* now.

13 "But when He, [a]the Spirit of truth, comes, He will [b]guide you into all the truth; for He will not speak on His own initiative, but whatever He hears, He will speak; and He will disclose to you what is to come.

14 "He shall [a]glorify Me; for He shall take of Mine, and shall disclose *it* to you.

15 "[a]All things that the Father has are Mine; therefore I said, that He takes of Mine, and will disclose *it* to you.

Jesus' Death and Resurrection Foretold

16 "[a]A little while, and [b]you *will* no longer behold Me; and again a little while, and [c]you will see Me."

17 *Some* of His disciples therefore said to one another, "What is this thing He is telling us, '[a]A little while, and you *will* not behold Me; and again a little while, and you will see Me'; and, 'because [b]I go to the Father'?"

18 And so they were saying, "What is this that He says, 'A little while'? We do not know what He is talking about."

19 [a]Jesus knew that they wished to question Him, and He said to them, "Are you deliberating together about this, that I said, 'A little while, and you *will* not behold Me, and again a little while, and you *will* see Me'?

20 "Truly, truly, I say to you, that [a]you will weep and lament, but the world will rejoice; you will be sorrowful, but [b]your sorrow will be turned to joy.

21 "[a]Whenever a woman is in travail she has sorrow, because her hour has come; but when she gives birth to the child, she remembers the anguish no more, for joy that a [1]child has been born into the world.

22 "Therefore [a]you, too, now have sorrow; but [b]I will see you again, and your heart will rejoice, and no one takes your joy away from you.

Prayer Promises

23 "And [a]in that day [b]you will [1]ask Me no question. Truly, truly, I say to you, [c]if you shall ask the Father for anything, He will give it to you in My name.

24 "[a]Until now you have asked for nothing in My name; ask, and you will receive, that your [b]joy may be made full.

25 "These things I have spoken to you in [1a]figurative language; [b]an hour is coming, when I will speak no more to you in [1]figurative language, but will tell you plainly of the Father.

26 "[a]In that day [b]you will ask in My name; and I do not say to you that I will request the Father on your behalf;

27 for [a]the Father Himself loves you, because you have loved Me, and [b]have believed that [c]I came forth from the Father.

28 "[a]I came forth from the Father, and have come into the world; I am leaving the world again, and [b]going to the Father."

29 His disciples *said, "Lo, now You are speaking plainly, and are not using [a]a [1]figure of speech.

30 "Now we know that You know all things, and have no need for anyone to question You; by this we [a]believe that You [b]came from God."

31 Jesus answered them, "Do you now believe?

32 "Behold, [a]an hour is coming, and has *already* come, for [b]you to be scattered, each to [c]his own *home,* and to leave Me alone; and *yet* [d]I am not alone, because the Father is with Me.

33 "These things I have spoken to you, that [a]in Me you may have

4 [1]Lit., *may remember them, that I told you* [a]John 13:19 [b]Luke 1:2
5 [a]John 7:33; 16:10, 17, 28 [b]John 13:36; 14:5
6 [a]John 14:1; 16:22
7 [1]Gr. *Paracletos,* equals one called alongside to help, or, *Intercessor* [a]John 14:16 [b]John 14:26
9 [a]John 15:22, 24
10 [a]Acts 3:14; 7:52; 17:31; 1 Pet. 3:18 [b]John 16:5
11 [a]John 12:31
13 [a]John 14:17 [b]John 14:26
14 [a]John 7:39
15 [a]John 17:10
16 [a]John 7:33 [b]John 14:18-24; 16:16-24 [c]John 16:22
17 [a]John 16:16 [b]John 16:5
19 [a]Mark 9:32; John 6:61
20 [a]Mark 16:10; Luke 23:27 [b]John 20:20
21 [1]Lit., *human being* [a]Is. 13:8; 21:3; 26:17; 66:7; Hos. 13:13; Mic. 4:9; 1 Thess. 5:3
22 [a]John 16:6 [b]John 16:16
23 [1]Lit., *question Me nothing* [a]John 14:20; 16:26 [b]John 16:19, 30 [c]John 15:16
24 [a]John 14:14 [b]John 3:29; 15:11
25 [1]Lit., *proverbs* or, *figures of speech* [a]Matt. 13:34; John 10:6; 16:29 [b]John 16:2
26 [a]John 14:20; 16:23 [b]John 16:19, 30
27 [a]John 14:21, 23 [b]John 2:11; 16:30 [c]John 8:42; 16:30
28 [a]John 8:42; 16:30 [b]John 13:1, 3; 16:5, 10, 17
29 [1]Lit., *proverb* [a]Matt. 13:34; John 10:6; 16:25
30 [a]John 2:11; 16:27 [b]John 8:42; 16:28
32 [a]John 4:23; 16:2, 25 [b]Zech. 13:7; Matt. 26:31 [c]John 19:27 [d]John 8:29
33 [a]John 14:27

peace. [b]In the world you have tribulation, but [c]take courage; [d]I have
overcome the world."

CHAPTER 17

The High Priestly Prayer

THESE things Jesus spoke; and
[a]lifting up His eyes to heaven, He
said, "Father, the hour has come;
[b]glorify Thy Son, that the Son may
glorify Thee,
2 even as [a]Thou gavest Him authority over all mankind, that [b]to all
whom Thou hast given Him, [c]He
may give eternal life.
3 "And this is eternal life, that
they may know Thee, [a]the only true
God, and Jesus Christ whom [b]Thou
hast sent.
4 "[a]I glorified Thee on the earth,
[b]having accomplished the work
which Thou hast given Me to do.
5 "And now, [a]glorify Thou Me together with Thyself, Father, with
the glory which I had [b]with Thee before the world was.
6 "[a]I manifested Thy name to the
men whom [b]Thou gavest Me out of
the world; [c]Thine they were, and
Thou gavest them to Me, and they
have [d]kept Thy word.
7 "Now they have come to know
that everything Thou hast given Me
is from Thee;
8 for [a]the words which [a]Thou
gavest Me [b]I have given to them;
and they received *them*, and truly
understood that [c]I came forth from
Thee, and they believed that [d]Thou
didst send Me.
9 "[a]I ask on their behalf; [b]I do not
ask on behalf of the world, but of
those whom [c]Thou hast given Me;
for [d]they are Thine;
10 and [a]all things that are Mine are
Thine, and Thine are Mine; and I
have been glorified in them.
11 "And I am no more in the world;
and *yet* [a]they themselves are in the
world, and [b]I come to Thee. [c]Holy
Father, keep them in Thy name, *the
name* [d]which Thou hast given Me,
that [e]they may be one, even as We
are.
12 "While I was with them, I was
keeping them in Thy name [a]which
Thou hast given Me; and I guarded
them, and [b]not one of them perished
but [c]the son of perdition, that the
[d]Scripture might be fulfilled.

The Disciples in the World

13 "But now [a]I come to Thee; and
[b]these things I speak in the world,

33 [b]John 15:18ff. [c]Matt. 9:2 [d]Rom. 8:37; 2 Cor. 2:14; 4:7ff.; 6:4ff.; Rev. 3:21; 12:11
1 [a]John 11:41 [b]John 7:39
2 [a]John 3:35 [b]John 6:37, 39; 17:6, 9, 24 [c]John 10:28
3 [a]John 5:44 [b]John 3:17; 17:8
4 [a]John 13:31 [b]Luke 22:37
5 [a]John 17:1 [b]John 1:1; 8:58
6 [a]John 17:26 [b]John 6:37, 39; 17:2, 9, 24 [c]John 17:9 [d]John 8:51
8 [a]John 6:68; 12:49 [b]John 15:15; 17:14, 26 [c]John 8:42; 16:27, 30 [d]John 3:17
9 [a]Luke 22:32; John 14:16 [b]Luke 23:34 [c]John 6:37, 39; 17:2, 6, 24 [d]John 17:6
10 [a]John 16:15
11 [a]John 13:1 [b]John 7:33; 17:13 [c]John 17:25 [d]John 17:6; Phil. 2:9; Rev. 19:12 [e]John 17:21f.; Rom. 12:5
12 [a]John 17:6; Rev. 19:12 [b]John 6:39; 18:9 [c]John 6:70 [d]Ps. 41:9
13 [a]John 7:33; 17:11 [b]John 15:11 [c]John 3:29
14 [a]John 15:19 [b]John 8:23; 17:16
15 [a]Matt. 5:37
16 [a]John 17:14
17 [a]John 15:3
18 [a]John 3:17 [b]Matt. 10:5; John 4:38; 20:21
19 [a]John 15:13 [b]John 15:3 [c]2 Cor. 7:14
21 [a]John 10:38; 17:11, 23 [b]John 17:8 [c]John 3:17
22 [a]John 1:14
23 [a]John 10:38; 17:11, 21 [b]John 3:17 [c]John 16:27
24 [a]John 17:2 [b]John 12:26 [c]John 1:14 [d]Matt. 25:34
25 [a]John 17:11; 1 John 1:9 [b]John 7:29; 15:21 [c]John 3:17; 17:3, 8, 18
26 [a]John 17:6 [b]John 15:9
1 [a]Matt. 26:30, 36; Mark 14:26, 32 [b]2 Sam. 15:23; 1 Kin. 2:37; 15:13; 2 Chr. 15:16; Jer. 31:40 [c]Matt. 26:36; Mark 14:32; John 18:26
2 [a]Luke 21:37

that they may have My [c]joy made
full in themselves.
14 "I have given them Thy word;
and [a]the world has hated them, because [b]they are not of the world,
even as I am not of the world.
15 "I do not ask Thee to take them
out of the world, but to keep them
from [a]the evil *one*.
16 "[a]They are not of the world, even
as I am not of the world.
17 "[a]Sanctify them in the truth; Thy
word is truth.
18 "As [a]Thou didst send Me into the
world, [b]I also have sent them into
the world.
19 "And for their sakes I [a]sanctify
Myself, that they themselves also
may be [b]sanctified [c]in truth.
20 "I do not ask in behalf of these
alone, but for those also who believe
in Me through their word;
21 that they may all be one; [a]even
as Thou, Father, *art* in Me, and I in
Thee, that they also may be in Us;
[b]that the world may believe that
[c]Thou didst send Me.

Their Future Glory

22 "And the [a]glory which Thou hast
given Me I have given to them; that
they may be one, just as We are one;
23 [a]I in them, and Thou in Me, that
they may be perfected in unity, that
the world may know that [b]Thou
didst send Me, and didst [c]love them,
even as Thou didst love Me.
24 "Father, I desire that [a]they also,
whom Thou hast given Me, [b]be with
Me where I am, in order that they
may behold My [c]glory, which Thou
hast given Me; for Thou didst love
Me before [d]the foundation of the
world.
25 "O [a]righteous Father, although
[b]the world has not known Thee, yet
I have known Thee; and these have
known that [c]Thou didst send Me;
26 and [a]I have made Thy name
known to them, and will make it
known; that [b]the love wherewith
Thou didst love Me may be in them,
and I in them."

CHAPTER 18

Judas Betrays Jesus

WHEN Jesus had spoken these
words, [a]He went forth with His disciples over [b]the ravine of the Kidron, where there was [c]a garden, into
which He Himself entered, and His
disciples.
2 Now Judas also, who was betraying Him, knew the place; for Jesus had [a]often met there with His
disciples.

3 [a]Judas then, having received [b]the *Roman* [1]cohort, and [c]officers from the chief priests and the Pharisees, *came there with lanterns and [d]torches and weapons.

4 Jesus therefore, [a]knowing all the things that were coming upon Him, went forth, and *said to them, "[b]Whom do you seek?"

5 They answered Him, "Jesus the Nazarene." He *said to them, "I am *He.*" And Judas also who was betraying Him, was standing with them.

6 When therefore He said to them, "I am *He*", they drew back, and fell to the ground.

7 Again therefore He asked them, "[a]Whom do you seek?" And they said, "Jesus the Nazarene."

8 Jesus answered, "I told you that I am *He;* if therefore you seek Me, let these go their way,"

9 that the word might be fulfilled which He spoke, "[a]Of those whom Thou hast given Me I lost not one."

10 Simon Peter therefore [a]having a sword, drew it, and struck the high priest's slave, and cut off his right ear; and the slave's name was Malchus.

11 Jesus therefore said to Peter, "Put the sword into the sheath; [a]the cup which the Father has given Me, shall I not drink it?"

Jesus Before the Priests

12 [a]So [b]the *Roman* [1]cohort and the [2]commander, and the [b]officers of the Jews, arrested Jesus and bound Him,

13 and led Him to [a]Annas first; for he was father-in-law of [b]Caiaphas, who was high priest that year.

14 Now Caiaphas was the one who had advised the Jews that [a]it was expedient for one man to die on behalf of the people.

15 And [a]Simon Peter was following Jesus, and *so was* another disciple. Now that disciple was known to the high priest, and entered with Jesus into [b]the court of the high priest,

16 [a]but Peter was standing at the door outside. So the other disciple, who was known to the high priest, went out and spoke to the doorkeeper, and brought in Peter.

17 [a]The slave-girl therefore who kept the door *said to Peter, "[b]You are not also *one* of this man's disciples, are you?" He *said, "I am not."

18 Now the slaves and the [a]officers were standing *there,* [b]having made [c]a charcoal fire, for it was cold and they were warming themselves; and Peter also was with them, standing and warming himself.

19 [a]The high priest therefore questioned Jesus about His disciples, and about His teaching.

20 Jesus answered him, "I [a]have spoken openly to the world; I always [b]taught in [1]synagogues, and [c]in the temple, where all the Jews come together; and I spoke nothing in secret.

21 "Why do you question Me? Question those who have heard what I spoke to them; behold, these know what I said."

22 And when He had said this, one of the [a]officers standing by [b]gave Jesus a blow, saying, "Is that the way You answer the high priest?"

23 [a]Jesus answered him, "If I have spoken wrongly, bear witness of the wrong; but if rightly, why do you strike Me?"

24 [a]Annas therefore sent Him bound to [a]Caiaphas the high priest.

Peter's Denial of Jesus

25 [a]Now [b]Simon Peter was standing and warming himself. They said therefore to him, "[c]You are not also *one* of His disciples, are you?" He denied *it,* and said, "I am not."

26 One of the slaves of the high priest, being a relative of the one [a]whose ear Peter cut off, *said, "Did I not see you in [b]the garden with Him?"

27 Peter therefore denied *it* again; and immediately [a]a cock crowed.

Jesus Before Pilate

28 [a]They *led Jesus therefore from [b]Caiaphas into [c]the Praetorium; and it was early; and they themselves did not enter into [c]the Praetorium in order that [d]they might not be defiled, but might eat the Passover.

29 [a]Pilate therefore went out to them, and *said, "What accusation do you bring against this Man?"

30 They answered and said to him, "If this Man were not an evildoer, we would not have delivered Him up to you."

31 Pilate therefore said to them, "Take Him yourselves, and judge Him according to your law." The Jews said to him, "We are not permitted to put any one to death,"

32 that [a]the word of Jesus might be fulfilled, which He spoke, signifying by what kind of death He was about to die.

33 Pilate therefore [a]entered again into the Praetorium, and summoned

3 [1]Or, *battalion* [a]John 18:3-11: *Matt. 26:47-56; Mark 14:43-50; Luke 22:47-53* [b]John 18:12; Acts 10:1 [c]John 7:32; 18:12, 18 [d]Matt. 25:1 and marg.
4 [a]John 6:64; 13:1, 11 [b]John 18:7
7 [a]John 18:4
9 [a]John 17:12
10 [a]Matt. 26:51; Mark 14:47
11 [a]Matt. 20:22
12 [1]Or, *battalion* [2]Lit., *chiliarch,* in command of a thousand troops [a]John 18:12f.: *Matt. 26:57ff.* [b]John 18:3
13 [a]Luke 3:2; John 18:24 [b]Matt. 26:3; John 11:49, 51
14 [a]John 11:50
15 [a]Matt. 26:58; Mark 14:54; Luke 22:54 [b]Matt. 26:3; John 18:24, 28
16 [a]John 18:16-18: *Matt. 26:69f.; Mark 14:66-68; Luke 22:55-57*
17 [a]Acts 12:13 [b]John 18:25
18 [a]John 18:3 [b]Mark 14:54, 67 [c]John 21:9
19 [a]John 18:19-24: *Matt. 26:59-68; Mark 14:55-65; Luke 22:63-71*
20 [1]Lit., *synagogue* [a]John 7:26; 8:26 [b]Matt. 4:23; John 6:59 [c]Matt. 26:55
22 [a]John 18:3 [b]John 19:3
23 [a]Matt. 5:39; Acts 23:2-5
24 [a]John 18:13
25 [a]John 18:25-27: *Matt. 26:71-75; Mark 14:69-72; Luke 22:58-62* [b]John 18:18 [c]John 18:17
26 [a]John 18:10 [b]John 18:1
27 [a]John 13:38
28 [a]Matt. 27:2; Mark 15:1; Luke 23:1 [b]John 18:13 [c]Matt. 27:27; John 18:33; 19:9 [d]John 11:55; Acts 11:3
29 [a]John 18:29-38: *Matt. 27:11-14; Mark 15:2-5; Luke 23:2, 3*
32 [a]Matt. 20:19; 26:2; Mark 10:33f.; Luke 18:32f.; John 3:14; 8:28; 12:32f.
33 [a]John 18:28, 29; 19:9

Jesus, and said to Him, "[b]You are the King of the Jews?"

34 Jesus answered, "Are you saying this on your own initiative, or did others tell you about Me?"

35 Pilate answered, "I am not a Jew, am I? Your own nation and the chief priests delivered You up to me; what have You done?"

36 Jesus answered, "[a]My kingdom is not of this world. If My kingdom were of this world, then My servants would be fighting, that I might not be delivered up to the Jews; but as it is, My kingdom is not of this realm."

37 Pilate therefore said to Him, "So You are a king?" Jesus answered, "[a]You say *correctly* that I am a king. For this I have been born, and for this I have come into the world, [b]to bear witness to the truth. [c]Every one who is of the truth hears My voice."

38 Pilate *said to Him, "What is truth?"

And when he had said this, he [a]went out again to the Jews, and *said to them, "[b]I find no guilt in Him.

39 "[a]But you have a custom, that I should release someone for you at the Passover; do you wish then that I release for you the King of the Jews?"

40 Therefore they cried out again, saying, "[a]Not this Man, but Barabbas." Now Barabbas was a robber.

CHAPTER 19

The Crown of Thorns

THEN Pilate therefore took Jesus, and [a]scourged Him.

2 [a]And the soldiers wove a crown of thorns and put it on His head, and arrayed Him in a purple robe;

3 and they *began* to come up to Him, and say, "[a]Hail, King of the Jews!" and to [b]give Him blows in the face.

4 And Pilate [a]came out again, and *said to them, "Behold, I am bringing Him out to you, that you may know that [b]I find no guilt in Him."

5 Jesus therefore came out, [a]wearing the crown of thorns and the purple robe. And *Pilate* *said to them, "Behold, the Man!"

6 When therefore the chief priests and the [a]officers saw Him, they cried out, saying, "Crucify, crucify!" Pilate *said to them, "Take Him yourselves, and crucify Him, for [b]I find no guilt in Him."

7 The Jews answered him, "[a]We have a law, and by that law He ought to die because He [b]made Himself out *to be* the Son of God."

8 When Pilate therefore heard this statement, he was the more afraid;

9 and he [a]entered into the Praetorium again, and *said to Jesus, "Where are You from?" But [b]Jesus gave him no answer.

10 Pilate therefore *said to Him, "You do not speak to me? Do You not know that I have authority to release You, and I have authority to crucify You?"

11 Jesus answered, "[a]You would have no authority over Me, unless it had been given you from above; for this reason [b]he who delivered Me up to you has *the* greater sin."

12 As a result of this Pilate made efforts to release Him, but the Jews cried out, saying, "[a]If you release this Man, you are no friend of Caesar; every one who makes himself out *to be* a king [1]opposes Caesar."

13 When Pilate therefore heard these words, he brought Jesus out, and [a]sat down on the judgment seat at a place called [1]The Pavement, but [b]in [2]Hebrew, Gabbatha.

14 Now it was [a]the day of preparation for the Passover; it was about the [1b]sixth hour. And he *said to the Jews, "Behold, [c]your King!"

15 They therefore cried out, "[a]Away with *Him*, away with *Him*, crucify Him!" Pilate *said to them, "Shall I crucify your King?" The chief priests answered, "We have no king but Caesar."

The Crucifixion

16 And so he then [a]delivered Him up to them to be crucified.

17 [a]They took Jesus therefore, and He went out, [b]bearing His own cross, to the place called [c]the Place of a Skull, which is called [d]in [1]Hebrew, Golgotha.

18 There they crucified Him, and with Him [a]two other men, one on either side, and Jesus in between.

19 And Pilate wrote an inscription also, and put it on the cross. And it was written, "[a]JESUS THE NAZARENE, [b]THE KING OF THE JEWS."

20 Therefore this inscription many of the Jews read, for the place where Jesus was crucified was near the city; and it was written [a]in [1]Hebrew, Latin, *and* in Greek.

21 And so the chief priests of the Jews were saying to Pilate, "Do not

33 [b]Luke 23:3; John 19:12
36 [a]Matt. 26:53; Luke 17:21; John 6:15
37 [a]Matt. 27:11; Mark 15:2; Luke 22:70; 23:3 [b]John 1:14; 3:32; 8:14 [c]John 8:47; 1 John 4:6
38 [a]John 18:33; 19:4 [b]Luke 23:4; John 19:4
39 [a]John 18:39-19:16: *Matt. 27:15-18, 20-23; Mark 15:6-15; Luke 23:18-25*
40 [a]Acts 3:14
1 [a]Matt. 27:26
2 [a]Matt. 27:27-30: *Mark 15:16-19*
3 [a]Matt. 27:29; Mark 15:18 [b]John 18:22
4 [a]John 18:33, 38 [b]Luke 23:4; John 18:38; 19:6
5 [a]John 19:2
6 [a]Matt. 26:58; John 18:3 [b]Luke 23:4; John 18:38; 19:4
7 [a]Lev. 24:16; Matt. 26:63-66 [b]John 5:18; 10:33
9 [a]John 18:33 [b]Matt. 26:63; 27:12, 14; John 18:34-37
11 [a]Rom. 13:1 [b]John 18:13f., 28ff.; Acts 3:13
12 [1]Or, *speaks against* [a]Luke 23:2; John 18:33ff.
13 [1]Gr., *The Lithostrotos* [2]I.e., Jewish Aramaic [a]Matt. 27:19 [b]John 5:2; 19:17
14 [1]I.e., noon [a]Matt. 27:62; John 19:31, 42 [b]Matt. 27:45; Mark 15:25 [c]John 19:19, 21
15 [a]Luke 23:18
16 [a]Matt. 27:26; Mark 15:15; Luke 23:25
17 [1]I.e., Jewish Aramaic [a]John 19:17-24: *Matt. 27:33-44; Mark 15:22-32; Luke 23:33-43* [b]Matt. 27:32; Mark 15:21; Luke 14:27; 23:26 [c]Luke 23:33 and marg. [d]John 19:13
18 [a]Luke 23:32
19 [a]Matt. 27:37; Mark 15:26; Luke 23:38 [b]John 19:14, 21
20 [1]I.e., Jewish Aramaic [a]John 19:13

write, '[a]The King of the Jews'; but that He said, 'I am [a]King of the Jews.' "

22 Pilate answered, "[a]What I have written I have written."

23 [a]The soldiers therefore, when they had crucified Jesus, took His outer garments and made [b]four parts, a part to every soldier and *also* the [1]tunic; now the tunic was seamless, woven in one piece.

24 They said therefore to one another, "[a]Let us not tear it, but cast lots for it, *to decide* whose it shall be"; [b]that the Scripture might be fulfilled, "THEY [c]DIVIDED MY OUTER GARMENTS AMONG THEM, AND FOR MY CLOTHING THEY CAST LOTS."

25 Therefore the soldiers did these things. [a]But there were standing by the cross of Jesus [b]His mother, and His mother's sister, Mary the *wife* of [c]Clopas, and [d]Mary Magdalene.

26 When Jesus therefore saw His mother, and [a]the disciple whom He loved standing nearby, He *said to His mother, "[b]Woman, behold, your son!"

27 Then He *said to the disciple, "Behold, your mother!" And from that hour the disciple took her into [a]his own *household.*

28 After this, Jesus, [a]knowing that all things had already been accomplished, [b]in order that the Scripture might be fulfilled, *said, "[c]I am thirsty."

29 A jar full of sour wine was standing there; so [a]they put a sponge full of the sour wine upon *a branch of* hyssop, and brought it up to His mouth.

30 When Jesus therefore had received the sour wine, He said, "[a]It is finished!" And He bowed His head, and [b]gave up His spirit.

Care of the Body of Jesus

31 The Jews therefore, because it was [a]the day of preparation, so that [b]the bodies should not remain on the cross on the Sabbath (for that Sabbath was a [c]high *day),* asked Pilate that their legs might be broken, and *that* they might be taken away.

32 The soldiers therefore came, and broke the legs of the first man, and of the other man who was [a]crucified with Him;

33 but coming to Jesus, when they saw that He was already dead, they did not break His legs;

34 but one of the soldiers pierced His side with a spear, and immediately there came out [a]blood and water.

35 And he who has seen has [a]borne witness, and his witness is true; and he knows that he is telling the truth, so that you also may believe.

36 For these things came to pass, [a]that the Scripture might be fulfilled, "[b]NOT A BONE OF HIM SHALL BE BROKEN."

37 And again another Scripture says, "[a]THEY SHALL LOOK ON HIM WHOM THEY PIERCED."

38 [a]And after these things Joseph of Arimathea, being a disciple of Jesus, but a [b]secret *one,* for [c]fear of the Jews, asked Pilate that he might take away the body of Jesus; and Pilate granted permission. He came therefore, and took away His body.

39 And [a]Nicodemus came also, who had first come to Him by night; [b]bringing a [1]mixture of [c]myrrh and aloes, about a [d]hundred [2]pounds *weight.*

40 And so they took the body of Jesus, and [a]bound it in [b]linen wrappings with the spices, as is the burial custom of the Jews.

41 Now in the place where He was crucified there was a garden; and in the garden a [a]new tomb, [b]in which no one had yet been laid.

42 Therefore on account of the Jewish day of [a]preparation, because the tomb was [b]nearby, they laid Jesus there.

CHAPTER 20

The Empty Tomb

[a]NOW on the first *day* of the week [b]Mary Magdalene *came early to the tomb, while it *was still dark, and *saw [c]the stone *already* taken away from the tomb.

2 And so she *ran and *came to Simon Peter, and to the other [a]disciple whom Jesus loved, and *said to them, "[b]They have taken away the Lord out of the tomb, and we do not know where they have laid Him."

3 [a]Peter therefore went forth, and the other disciple, and they were going to the tomb.

4 And the two were running together; and the other disciple ran ahead faster than Peter, and came to the tomb first;

5 and [a]stooping and looking in, he *saw the [b]linen wrappings lying *there;* but he did not go in.

6 Simon Peter therefore also *came, following him, and entered the tomb; and he *beheld the linen wrappings lying *there,*

---

21 [a]John 19:14
22 [a]Gen. 43:14; Esth. 4:16
23 [1]Gr., *khiton,* the garment worn next to the skin [a]Matt. 27:35; Mark 15:24; Luke 23:34 [b]Acts 12:4
24 [a]Ex. 28:32; Matt. 27:35; Mark 15:24; Luke 23:34 [b]John 19:28, 36f. [c]Ps. 22:18
25 [a]Matt. 27:55f.; Mark 15:40f.; Luke 23:49 [b]Matt. 12:46 [c]Luke 24:18 [d]Luke 8:2
26 [a]John 13:23 [b]John 2:4
27 [a]Luke 18:28; John 1:11; 16:32
28 [a]John 13:1; 17:4 [b]John 19:24, 36f. [c]Ps. 69:21
29 [a]John 19:29, 30: *Matt. 27:48, 50; Mark 15:36f.; Luke 23:36*
30 [a]John 17:4 [b]Matt. 27:50; Mark 15:37; Luke 23:46
31 [a]John 19:14, 42 [b]Deut. 21:23; Josh. 8:29; 10:26f. [c]Ex. 12:16
32 [a]John 19:18
34 [a]1 John 5:6, 8
35 [a]John 15:27
36 [a]John 19:24, 28 [b]Ex. 12:46; Num. 9:12; Ps. 34:20
37 [a]Zech. 12:10
38 [a]John 19:38-42: *Matt. 27:57-61; Mark 15:42-47; Luke 23:50-56* [b]Mark 15:43 [c]John 7:13
39 [1]Another reading, *package of* [2]I.e., 100 litras (12 oz. each) [a]John 3:1 [b]Mark 16:1 [c]Ps. 45:8; Prov. 7:17; Song of Sol. 4:14; Matt. 2:11 [d]John 12:3
40 [a]Matt. 26:12; Mark 14:8; John 11:44 [b]Luke 24:12; John 20:5
41 [a]Matt. 27:60 [b]Luke 23:53
42 [a]John 19:14, 31 [b]John 19:20
1 [a]John 20:1-8: *Matt. 28:1-8; Mark 16:1-8; Luke 24:1-10* [b]John 19:25 [c]Matt. 27:60; Mark 15:46; 16:3f.; Luke 24:2
2 [a]John 13:23 [b]John 20:13
3 [a]Luke 24:12
5 [a]John 20:11 [b]John 19:40

7 and [a]the face-cloth, which had been on His head, not lying with the [b]linen wrappings, but rolled up in a place by itself.

8 Then entered in therefore the other disciple also, who [a]had first come to the tomb, and he saw, and believed.

9 For as yet [a]they did not understand the Scripture, [b]that He must rise again from the dead.

10 So the disciples went away again [a]to their own homes.

11 [a]But Mary was standing outside the tomb weeping; and so, as she wept, she [b]stooped and looked into the tomb;

12 and she *beheld [a]two angels in white sitting, one at the head, and one at the feet, where the body of Jesus had been lying.

13 And they *said to her, "[a]Woman, why are you weeping?" She *said to them, "Because [b]they have taken away my Lord, and I do not know where they have laid Him."

14 When she had said this, she turned around, and *[a]beheld Jesus standing *there,* and [b]did not know that it was Jesus.

15 Jesus *said to her, "[a]Woman, why are you weeping? Whom are you seeking?" Supposing Him to be the gardener, she *said to Him, "Sir, if you have carried Him away, tell me where you have laid Him, and I will take Him away."

16 Jesus *said to her, "Mary!" She *turned and *said to Him [a]in [1]Hebrew, "[b]Rabboni!" (which means, Teacher).

17 Jesus *said to her, "Stop clinging to Me; for I have not yet ascended to the Father; but go to [a]My brethren, and say to them, 'I [b]ascend to My Father and your Father, and My God and your God.'"

18 [a]Mary Magdalene *came, [b]announcing to the disciples, "I have seen the Lord," and *that* He had said these things to her.

Jesus among His Disciples

19 When therefore it was evening, on that day, the first *day* of the week, and when the doors were shut where the disciples were, for [a]fear of the Jews, Jesus came and stood in their midst, and *said to them, "[1b]Peace *be* with you."

20 And when He had said this, [a]He showed them both His hands and His side. The disciples therefore [b]rejoiced when they saw the Lord.

21 Jesus therefore said to them again, "[1a]Peace *be* with you; [b]as the Father has sent Me, I also send you."

22 And when He had said this, He breathed on them, and *said to them, "Receive the Holy Spirit.

23 "[a]If you forgive the sins of any, *their sins* [1]have been forgiven them; if you retain the *sins* of any, they have been retained."

24 But [a]Thomas, one of [b]the twelve, called [1a]Didymus, was not with them when Jesus came.

25 The other disciples therefore were saying to him, "We have seen the Lord!" But he said to them, "Unless I shall see in [a]His hands the imprint of the nails, and put my finger into the place of the nails, and put my hand into His side, [b]I will not believe."

26 And [1]after eight days again His disciples were inside, and Thomas with them. Jesus *came, the doors having been [2]shut, and stood in their midst, and said, "[a]Peace *be* with you."

27 Then He *said to Thomas, "[a]Reach here your finger, and see My hands; and reach here your hand, and put it into My side; and be not unbelieving, but believing."

28 Thomas answered and said to Him, "My Lord and my God!"

29 Jesus *said to him, "Because you have seen Me, have you believed? [a]Blessed *are* they who did not see, and *yet* believed."

Why This Gospel Was Written

30 [a]Many other [1b]signs therefore Jesus also performed in the presence of the disciples, which are not written in this book;

31 but these have been written [a]that you may believe that Jesus is [1]the Christ, [b]the Son of God; and that [c]believing you may have life in His name.

Chapter 21

Jesus Appears at the Sea of Galilee

AFTER these things Jesus [1a]manifested Himself [b]again to the disciples at the [c]Sea of Tiberias; and He manifested *Himself* in this way.

2 There were together Simon Peter, and [a]Thomas called [1]Didymus, and [b]Nathanael of [c]Cana in Galilee, and [d]the *sons* of Zebedee, and two others of His disciples.

3 Simon Peter *said to them, "I am going fishing." They *said to him, "We will also come with you." They went out, and got into the

7 [a]John 11:44 [b]John 19:40
8 [a]John 20:4
9 [a]Matt. 22:29; John 2:22 [b]Luke 24:26ff., 46
10 [a]Luke 24:12
11 [a]Mark 16:5 [b]John 20:5
12 [a]Matt. 28:2f.; Mark 16:5; Luke 24:4
13 [a]John 20:15 [b]John 20:2
14 [a]Matt. 28:9; Mark 16:9 [b]John 21:4
15 [a]John 20:13
16 [1]I.e., Jewish Aramaic [a]John 5:2 [b]Matt. 23:7; Mark 10:51
17 [a]Matt. 28:10 [b]Mark 12:26; 16:19; John 7:33
18 [a]John 20:1 [b]Mark 16:10; Luke 24:10, 23
19 [1]Lit., *Peace to you* [a]John 7:13 [b]Luke 24:36; John 14:27; 20:21, 26
20 [a]Luke 24:39, 40; John 19:34 [b]John 16:20, 22
21 [1]Here as in verses 19 and 26 [a]Luke 24:36; John 14:27; 20:19, 26 [b]John 17:18
23 [1]I.e., have previously been forgiven [a]Matt. 16:19; 18:18
24 [1]I.e., the Twin [a]John 11:16 [b]John 6:67
25 [a]John 20:20 [b]Mark 16:11
26 [1]Or, *a week later* [2]Or, *locked* [a]Luke 24:36; John 14:27; 20:19, 21
27 [a]Luke 24:40; John 20:25
29 [a]1 Pet. 1:8
30 [1]Or, *attesting miracles* [a]John 21:25 [b]John 2:11
31 [1]I.e., the Messiah [a]John 19:35 [b]Matt. 4:3 [c]John 3:15
1 [1]Or, *made Himself visible* [a]Mark 16:12; John 21:14 [b]John 20:19, 26 [c]John 6:1
2 [1]I.e., the Twin [a]John 11:16 [b]John 1:45ff. [c]John 2:1 [d]Matt. 4:21; Mark 1:19; Luke 5:10

boat; and [a]that night they caught
nothing.
4 But when the day was now
breaking, Jesus stood on the beach;
yet the disciples did not [a]know that
it was Jesus.
5 Jesus therefore *said to them,
"Children, [a]you do not have any
[1]fish, do you?" They answered Him,
"No."
6 And He said to them, "[a]Cast the
net on the right-hand side of the
boat, and you will find *a catch.*"
They cast therefore, and then they
were not able to haul it in because of
the great number of fish.
7 [a]That disciple therefore whom
Jesus [1]loved *said to Peter, "It is the
Lord." And so when Simon Peter
heard that it was the Lord, he put his
outer garment on (for he was
stripped *for work),* and threw himself into the sea.
8 But the other disciples came in
the little boat, for they were not far
from the land, but about [1]one hundred yards away, dragging the net
full of fish.
9 And so when they got out upon
the land, they *saw a charcoal [a]fire
already laid, and [b]fish placed on it,
and bread.
10 Jesus *said to them, "Bring
some of the [a]fish which you have
now caught."
11 Simon Peter went up, and drew
the net to land, full of large fish, a
hundred and fifty-three; and although there were so many, the net
was not torn.

Jesus Provides

12 Jesus *said to them, "Come
and have [a]breakfast." None of the
disciples ventured to question Him,
"Who are You?" knowing that it
was the Lord.
13 Jesus *came and *took [a]the
bread, and *gave them, and the [b]fish
likewise.
14 This is now the [a]third time that
Jesus [1]was manifested to the disciples, after He was raised from the
dead.

The Love Motivation

15 So when they had [a]finished
breakfast, Jesus *said to Simon Peter, "Simon, [1]*son* of John, do you
[2b]love Me more than these?" He
*said to Him, "Yes, Lord; You know
that I [3]love You." He *said to him,
"Tend [c]My lambs."
16 He *said to him again a second
time, "Simon, *son* of John, do you
[1]love Me?" He *said to Him, "Yes,
Lord; You know that I [2]love You."
He *said to him, "[a]Shepherd My
sheep."
17 He *said to him the third time,
"Simon, *son* of John, do you [1]love
Me?" Peter was grieved because He
said to him [a]the third time, "Do you
[1]love Me?" And he said to Him,
"Lord, [b]You know all things; You
know that I [1]love You." Jesus *said
to him, "[c]Tend My sheep.

Our Times Are in His Hand

18"Truly, truly, I say to you, when
you were younger, you used to gird
yourself, and walk wherever you
wished; but when you grow old, you
will stretch out your hands, and
someone else will gird you, and
bring you where you do not wish to
go."
19 Now this He said, [a]signifying
by [b]what kind of death he would
glorify God. And when He had spoken this, He *said to him, "[c]Follow
Me!"
20 Peter, turning around, *saw the
[a]disciple whom Jesus loved following *them;* the one who also had
[b]leaned back on His breast at the
supper, and said, "Lord, who is the
one who betrays You?"
21 Peter therefore seeing him
*said to Jesus, "Lord, and what
about this man?"
22 Jesus *said to him, "If I want
him to remain [a]until I come, what *is*
that to you? You [b]follow Me!"
23 This saying therefore went out
among [a]the brethren that that disciple would not die; yet Jesus did not
say to him that he would not die, but
only, "If I want him to remain [b]until
I come, what *is that* to you?"
24 This is the disciple who [a]bears
witness of these things, and wrote
these things; and we know that his
witness is true.
25 And there are also [a]many other
things which Jesus did, which if
they *were written in detail, I suppose that even the world itself
*would not contain the books which
*were written.

3 [a]Luke 5:5
4 [a]Luke 24:16; John 20:14
5 [1]Lit., *something eaten with bread* [a]Luke 24:41
6 [a]Luke 5:4ff.
7 [1]Lit., *was loving* [a]John 13:23; 21:20
8 [1]Lit., *200 cubits*
9 [a]John 18:18 [b]John 6:9, 11; 21:10, 13
10 [a]John 6:9, 11; 21:10, 13
12 [a]John 21:15
13 [a]John 21:9 [b]John 6:9, 11; 21:9, 10
14 [1]Or, *made Himself visible* [a]John 20:19, 26
15 [1]Here and in verses 16 and 17 some mss. read, *son of Jonas* [2]Gr., agapao [3]Gr., phileo [a]John 21:12 [b]Matt. 26:33; Mark 14:29; John 13:37 [c]Luke 12:32
16 [1]Gr., agapao [2]Gr., phileo [a]Matt. 2:6; Acts 20:28; 1 Pet. 5:2; Rev. 7:17
17 [1]Gr., phileo [a]John 13:38 [b]John 16:30 [c]John 21:16
19 [a]John 12:33; 18:32 [b]2 Pet. 1:14 [c]Matt. 8:22; 16:24; John 21:22
20 [a]John 21:7 [b]John 13:25
22 [a]Matt. 16:27f.; 1 Cor. 4:5; 11:26; James 5:7; Rev. 2:25 [b]Matt. 8:22; 16:24; John 21:19
23 [a]Acts 1:15 [b]Matt. 16:27f.; 1 Cor. 4:5; 11:26; James 5:7; Rev. 2:25
24 [a]John 15:27
25 [a]John 20:30

THE ACTS OF THE APOSTLES

Introduction

THE first account I composed, [a]Theophilus, about all that Jesus [b]began to do and teach,

2 until the day when He [a]was taken up, after He [b]had by the Holy Spirit given orders to [c]the apostles whom He had [d]chosen.

3 To these [a]He also presented Himself alive, after His suffering, by many convincing proofs, appearing to them over *a period of* forty days, and speaking of [b]the things concerning the kingdom of God.

4 And gathering them together, He commanded them [a]not to leave Jerusalem, but to wait for [b]what the Father had promised, "Which," *He said,* "you heard of from Me;

5 for [a]John baptized with water, but you shall be baptized with the Holy Spirit [b]not many days from now."

6 And so when they had come together, they were asking Him, saying, "Lord, [a]is it at this time You are restoring the kingdom to Israel?"

7 He said to them, "It is not for you to know times or epochs which [a]the Father has fixed by His own authority;

8 but you shall receive power [a]when the Holy Spirit has come upon you; and you shall be [b]My witnesses both in Jerusalem, and in all Judea and [c]Samaria, and even to [d]the remotest part of the earth."

The Ascension

9 And after He had said these things, [a]He was lifted up while they were looking on, and a cloud received Him out of their sight.

10 And as they were gazing intently into the sky while He was departing, behold, [a]two men in white clothing stood beside them;

11 and they also said, "[a]Men of Galilee, why do you stand looking into the sky? This Jesus, who [b]has been taken up from you into heaven, will [c]come in just the same way as you have watched Him go into heaven."

The Upper Room

12 Then they [a]returned to Jerusalem from the [b]mount called Olivet, which is near Jerusalem, a Sabbath day's journey away.

13 And when they had entered, they went up to [a]the upper room, where they were staying; [b]that is, Peter and John and [1]James and Andrew, Philip and Thomas, Bartholomew and Matthew, [1]James *the son* of Alphaeus, and Simon the Zealot, and [c]Judas *the son* of [1]James.

14 These all with one mind [a]were continually devoting themselves to prayer, along with [b]*the* women, and Mary the [c]mother of Jesus, and with His [c]brothers.

15 And at this time Peter stood up in the midst of [a]the brethren (a gathering of about one hundred and twenty persons was there together), and said,

16 "Brethren, [a]the Scripture had to be fulfilled, which the Holy Spirit foretold by the mouth of David concerning Judas, [b]who became a guide to those who arrested Jesus.

17 "For he was [a]counted among us, and received his portion in [b]this ministry."

18 (Now this man [a]acquired a field with [b]the price of his wickedness; and falling headlong, he burst open in the middle and all his bowels gushed out.

19 And it became known to all who were living in Jerusalem; so that in [a]their own language that field was called [1]Hakeldama, that is, Field of Blood).

20 "For it is written in the book of Psalms,

'[a]LET HIS HOMESTEAD BE MADE DESOLATE,
AND LET NO MAN DWELL IN IT';
and,
'[b]HIS OFFICE LET ANOTHER MAN TAKE.'

21 "It is therefore necessary that of the men who have accompanied us all the time that [a]the Lord Jesus went in and out among us—

22 [a]beginning with the baptism of John, until the day that He [b]was taken up from us—one of these should become a [c]witness with us of His resurrection."

23 And they put forward two men, Joseph called Barsabbas (who was also called Justus), and [a]Matthias.

24 And they [a]prayed, and said, "Thou, Lord, [b]who knowest the hearts of all men, show which one of these two Thou hast chosen

---

1 [a]Luke 1:3 [b]Luke 3:23
2 [a]Mark 16:19; Acts 1:9, 11, 22 [b]Matt. 28:19f.; John 20:21f.; Acts 10:42 [c]Mark 6:30 [d]John 13:18
3 [a]Matt. 28:17; Luke 24:34, 36; John 20:19, 26; 21:1, 14; 1 Cor. 15:5-7 [b]Acts 8:12
4 [a]Luke 24:49 [b]John 14:16, 26
5 [a]Matt. 3:11; Acts 11:16 [b]Acts 2:1-4
6 [a]Matt. 17:11; Mark 9:12
7 [a]Matt. 24:36
8 [a]Acts 2:1-4 [b]Luke 24:48; John 15:27 [c]Acts 8:1, 5, 14 [d]Matt. 28:19; Mark 16:15
9 [a]Acts 1:2
10 [a]Luke 24:4
11 [a]Acts 2:7; 13:31 [b]Mark 16:19; Acts 1:9, 22 [c]Matt. 16:27f.; Acts 3:21
12 [a]Luke 24:50, 52 [b]Matt. 21:1
13 [1]Or, *Jacob* [a]Mark 14:15; Luke 22:12 [b]Acts 1:13: *Matt. 1:2-4; Mark 3:16-19; Luke 6:14-16* [c]John 14:22
14 [a]Acts 2:42; 6:4; Rom. 12:12 [b]Luke 8:2f. [c]Matt. 12:46
15 [a]John 21:23; Acts 6:3; 9:30; 10:23; 16:2, 40; 17:6, 10; 18:18; 21:7, 17; 22:5; Rom. 1:13
16 [a]John 13:18; 17:12; Acts 1:20 [b]Matt. 26:47; Mark 14:43
17 [a]John 6:70f. [b]Acts 1:25; 20:24
18 [a]Matt. 27:3-10 [b]Matt. 26:14f.
19 [1]Or, *Hakeldamach* [a]Matt. 27:8; Acts 21:40
20 [a]Ps. 69:25 [b]Ps. 109:8
21 [a]Luke 24:3
22 [a]Mark 1:1-4 [b]Acts 1:2 [c]Acts 1:8; 2:32
23 [a]Acts 1:26
24 [a]Acts 6:6 [b]1 Sam. 16:7; Rom. 8:27

25 to occupy [a]this ministry and [b]a-
postleship from which Judas turned
aside to go to his own place."
26 And they [a]drew lots for them,
and the lot fell to [b]Matthias; and he
was numbered with [c]the eleven
apostles.

Chapter 2

The Day of Pentecost

AND when [a]the day of Pentecost
had come, they were all together in
one place.
2 And suddenly there came from
heaven a noise like a violent, rushing wind, and it filled [a]the whole
house where they were sitting.
3 And there appeared to them
tongues as of fire distributing themselves, and they rested on each one
of them.
4 And they were all [a]filled with
the Holy Spirit and began to [b]speak
with other tongues, as the Spirit was
giving them utterance.
5 Now there were Jews living in
Jerusalem, [a]devout men, from every
nation under heaven.
6 And when [a]this sound occurred, the multitude came together, and were bewildered, because they were each one hearing
them speak in his own language.
7 And [a]they were amazed and
marveled, saying, "Why, are not all
these who are speaking [b]Galileans?
8"And how is it that we each hear
them in our own language to which
we were born?
9"Parthians and Medes and Elamites, and residents of Mesopotamia,
Judea and [a]Cappadocia, [b]Pontus
and [1c]Asia,
10 [a]Phrygia and [b]Pamphylia,
Egypt and the districts of Libya
around [c]Cyrene, and [1d]visitors from
Rome, both Jews and [2e]proselytes,
11 Cretans and Arabs—we hear
them in our *own* tongues speaking
of the mighty deeds of God."
12 And [a]they continued in amazement and great perplexity, saying to
one another, "What does this
mean?"
13 But others were mocking and
saying, "[a]They are full of sweet
wine."

Peter's Sermon

14 But Peter, taking his stand with
[a]the eleven, raised his voice and declared to them: "Men of Judea, and
all you who live in Jerusalem, let
this be known to you, and give heed
to my words.
15"For these men are not drunk, as
you suppose, [a]for it is *only* the [1]third
hour of the day;
16 but this is what was spoken of
through the prophet Joel:
17 '[a]AND IT SHALL BE IN THE LAST
DAYS,' GOD SAYS,
'THAT I WILL POUR FORTH OF
MY SPIRIT UPON ALL [1]MAN-
KIND;
AND YOUR SONS AND YOUR
DAUGHTERS SHALL PROPHESY,
AND YOUR YOUNG MEN SHALL
SEE VISIONS,
AND YOUR OLD MEN SHALL
DREAM DREAMS;
18 EVEN UPON MY BONDSLAVES,
BOTH MEN AND WOMEN,
I WILL IN THOSE DAYS POUR
FORTH OF MY SPIRIT
And they shall prophesy.
19 'AND I WILL GRANT WONDERS IN
THE SKY ABOVE,
AND SIGNS ON THE EARTH BE-
NEATH,
BLOOD, AND FIRE, AND VAPOR
OF SMOKE.
20 'THE SUN SHALL BE TURNED
INTO DARKNESS,
AND THE MOON INTO BLOOD,
BEFORE THE GREAT AND GLORI-
OUS DAY OF THE LORD SHALL
COME.
21 'AND IT SHALL BE, THAT [a]EVERY
ONE WHO CALLS ON THE NAME
OF THE LORD SHALL BE
SAVED.'
22"Men of Israel, listen to these
words: [a]Jesus the Nazarene, [b]a man
attested to you by God with miracles and [c]wonders and signs which
God performed through Him in your
midst, just as you yourselves
know—
23 this *Man*, delivered up by the
[a]predetermined plan and foreknowledge of God, [b]you nailed to a
cross by the hands of godless men
and put *Him* to death.
24"And [a]God raised Him up again,
putting an end to the agony of
death, since it [b]was impossible for
Him to be held in its power.
25"For David says of Him,
'[a]I WAS ALWAYS BEHOLDING
THE LORD IN MY PRESENCE;
FOR HE IS AT MY RIGHT HAND,
THAT I MAY NOT BE SHAKEN.
26 'THEREFORE MY HEART WAS
GLAD AND MY TONGUE EX-
ULTED;
MOREOVER MY FLESH ALSO
WILL ABIDE IN HOPE;
27 BECAUSE THOU WILT NOT
ABANDON MY SOUL TO
[a]HADES,

25 [a]Acts 1:17 [b]Rom. 1:5; 1 Cor. 9:2; Gal. 2:8
26 [a]Lev. 16:8; Josh. 14:2; 1 Sam. 14:41f.; Neh. 10:34; 11:1; Prov. 16:33 [b]Acts 1:23 [c]Acts 2:14
1 [a]Lev. 23:15f.; Acts 20:16; 1 Cor. 16:8
2 [a]Acts 4:31
4 [a]Matt. 10:20; Acts 1:5, 8; 4:8, 31; 6:3, 5; 7:55; 8:17; 9:17; 11:15; 13:9, 52 [b]Mark 16:17; 1 Cor. 12:10f.; 14:21
5 [a]Luke 2:25; Acts 8:2
6 [a]Acts 2:2
7 [a]Acts 2:12 [b]Matt. 26:73; Acts 1:11
9 [1]I.e., west coast province of Asia Minor [a]1 Pet. 1:1 [b]Acts 18:2; 1 Pet. 1:1 [c]Acts 6:9; 16:6; 19:10; 20:4; 21:27; 24:18; 27:2; Rom. 16:5; 1 Cor. 16:19; 2 Cor. 1:8; 2 Tim. 1:15; Rev. 1:4
10 [1]Lit., *the sojourning Romans* [2]I.e., Gentile converts to Judaism [a]Acts 16:6; 18:23 [b]Acts 13:13; 14:24; 15:38; 27:5 [c]Matt. 27:32 [d]Acts 17:21 [e]Matt. 23:15
12 [a]Acts 2:7
13 [a]1 Cor. 14:23
14 [a]Acts 1:26
15 [1]I.e., 9 a.m. [a]1 Thess. 5:7
17 [1]Lit., *flesh* [a]Joel 2:28-32
21 [a]Rom. 10:13
22 [a]Acts 3:6; 4:10; 10:38 [b]John 3:2 [c]John 4:48; Acts 2:19, 43
23 [a]Luke 22:22; Acts 3:18; 4:28; 1 Pet. 1:20 [b]Luke 24:20; Acts 3:13
24 [a]Acts 2:32; 3:15; 10:40; 13:30, 33, 34, 37; 17:31; Rom. 4:24; 6:4; 8:11; 10:9; 1 Cor. 6:14; 15:15; 2 Cor. 4:14; Gal. 1:1; Eph. 1:20; Col. 2:12; 1 Thess. 1:10; Heb. 13:20; 1 Pet. 1:21 [b]John 20:9
25 [a]Ps. 16:8-11
27 [a]Matt. 11:23; Acts 2:31

[b]NOR ALLOW THY HOLY ONE TO
UNDERGO DECAY.
28 'THOU HAST MADE KNOWN TO
ME THE WAYS OF LIFE;
THOU WILT MAKE ME FULL OF
GLADNESS WITH THY PRESENCE.'

29 "Brethren, I may confidently say to you regarding the [a]patriarch David that he both [b]died and [c]was buried, and [d]his tomb is with us to this day.

30 "And so, because he was [a]a prophet, and knew that [b]God had sworn to him with an oath to seat *one* of his descendants upon his throne,

31 he looked ahead and spoke of the resurrection of the Christ, that He was neither abandoned to [a]Hades, nor did His flesh suffer decay.

32 "This Jesus [a]God raised up again, to which we are all [b]witnesses.

33 "Therefore having been exalted [a]to the right hand of God, and [b]having received from the Father [c]the promise of the Holy Spirit, He has [d]poured forth this which you both see and hear.

34 "For it was not David who ascended into heaven, but he himself says:

'[a]THE LORD SAID TO MY LORD,
"SIT AT MY RIGHT HAND,
35 UNTIL I MAKE THINE ENEMIES A
FOOTSTOOL FOR THY FEET." '

36 "Therefore let all the [a]house of Israel know for certain that God has made Him both [b]Lord and [1]Christ—this Jesus [c]whom you crucified."

The Ingathering

37 Now when they heard *this*, they were pierced to the heart, and said to Peter and the rest of the apostles, "Brethren, [a]what shall we do?"

38 And Peter *said* to them, "[a]Repent, and let each of you be [b]baptized in the name of Jesus Christ for the forgiveness of your sins; and you shall receive the gift of the Holy Spirit.

39 "For [a]the promise is for you and your children, and for all who are [b]far off, as many as the Lord our God shall call to Himself."

40 And with many other words he solemnly [a]testified and kept on exhorting them, saying, "Be saved from this [b]perverse generation!"

41 So then, those who had received his word were baptized; and there were added that day about three thousand [a]souls.

27 [b]Acts 13:35
29 [a]Acts 7:8f.; Heb. 7:4 [b]Acts 13:36 [c]1 Kin. 2:10 [d]Neh. 3:16
30 [a]Matt. 22:43 [b]2 Sam. 7:12f.; Ps. 89:3f.; 132:11
31 [a]Matt. 11:23; Acts 2:27
32 [a]Acts 2:24; 3:15, 26; 4:10; 5:30; 10:40; 13:30; Rom. 4:24; 6:4; 1 Cor. 6:14; 2 Cor. 4:14; Gal. 1:1; Eph. 1:20; Col. 2:12; 1 Thess. 1:10; Heb. 13:20; 1 Pet. 1:21 [b]Acts 1:8
33 [a]Mark 16:19; Acts 5:31 [b]Acts 1:4 [c]John 7:39; Gal. 3:14 [d]Acts 2:17
34 [a]Ps. 110:1; Matt. 22:44f.
36 [1]I.e., Messiah [a]Ezek. 36:22, 32, 37; 45:6 [b]Luke 2:11 [c]Acts 2:23
37 [a]Luke 3:10, 12, 14
38 [a]Mark 1:15; Luke 24:47; Acts 3:19 [b]Mark 16:16; Acts 8:12
39 [a]Is. 44:3; 54:13; 57:19; Joel 2:32 [b]Eph. 2:13, 17
40 [a]Luke 16:28 [b]Deut. 32:5; Matt. 17:17; Phil. 2:15
41 [a]Acts 3:23; 7:14; 1 Pet. 3:20; Rev. 16:3
42 [a]Acts 1:14 [b]Luke 24:30; Acts 2:46; 20:7; 1 Cor. 10:16
43 [1]Some ancient mss. add, *in Jerusalem; and great fear was upon all* [a]Acts 2:22
44 [a]Acts 4:32, 37; 5:2
45 [a]Matt. 19:21; Acts 4:34
46 [a]Acts 5:42 [b]Luke 24:30; Acts 2:42; 20:7; 1 Cor. 10:16
47 [a]Acts 5:13 [b]Acts 2:41; 4:4; 5:14; 17:12 [c]1 Cor. 1:18
1 [1]I.e., 3 p.m. [a]Luke 22:8; Acts 3:3, 4, 11 [b]Ps. 55:17; Matt. 27:45; Acts 10:30
2 [a]Acts 14:8 [b]Luke 16:20 [c]John 9:8; Acts 3:10
3 [a]Luke 22:8; Acts 3:1, 4, 11
4 [a]Acts 10:4
6 [a]Acts 2:22
8 [a]Acts 14:10
9 [a]Acts 4:16, 21

42 And they were [a]continually devoting themselves to the apostles' teaching and to fellowship, to [b]the breaking of bread and [a]to prayer.

43 And everyone kept feeling a sense of awe; and many [a]wonders and signs were taking place through the apostles[1].

44 And all those who had believed were together, and [a]had all things in common;

45 and they [a]*began* selling their property and possessions, and were sharing them with all, as anyone might have need.

46 [a]And day by day continuing with one mind in the temple, and [b]breaking bread from house to house, they were taking their meals together with gladness and sincerity of heart,

47 praising God, and [a]having favor with all the people. And the Lord [b]was adding to their number day by day [c]those who were being saved.

CHAPTER 3

Healing the Lame Beggar

NOW [a]Peter and John were going up to the temple at the [1]ninth *hour*, [b]the hour of prayer.

2 And [a]a certain man who had been lame from his mother's womb was being carried along, whom they [b]used to set down every day at the gate of the temple which is called Beautiful, [c]in order to beg alms of those who were entering the temple.

3 And when he saw [a]Peter and John about to go into the temple, he *began* asking to receive alms.

4 And Peter, along with John, [a]fixed his gaze upon him and said, "Look at us!"

5 And he *began* to give them his attention, expecting to receive something from them.

6 But Peter said, "I do not possess silver and gold, but what I do have I give to you: [a]In the name of Jesus Christ the Nazarene—walk!"

7 And seizing him by the right hand, he raised him up; and immediately his feet and his ankles were strengthened.

8 [a]And with a leap, he stood upright and *began* to walk; and he entered the temple with them, walking and leaping and praising God.

9 And [a]all the people saw him walking and praising God;

10 and they were taking note of him as being the one who used to

[a]sit at the Beautiful Gate of the temple to *beg* alms, and they were filled with wonder and amazement at what had happened to him.

Peter's Second Sermon

11 And while he was clinging to [a]Peter and John, all the people ran together to them at the so-called [1b]portico of Solomon, full of amazement.

12 But when Peter saw *this*, he [a]replied to the people, "Men of Israel, why do you marvel at this, or why do you gaze at us, as if by our own power or piety we had made him walk?

13 "[a]The God of Abraham, Isaac, and Jacob, [b]the God of our fathers, has glorified His [c]servant Jesus, *the one* whom [d]you delivered up, and disowned in the presence of [e]Pilate, when he had [f]decided to release Him.

14 "But you disowned [a]the Holy and Righteous One, and [b]asked for a murderer to be granted to you,

15 but put to death the [1a]Prince of life, *the one* whom [b]God raised from the dead, *a fact* to which we are [c]witnesses.

16 "And on the basis of faith [a]in His name, *it is* the name of [1]Jesus which has strengthened this man whom you see and know; and the faith which *comes* through Him has given him this perfect health in the presence of you all.

17 "And now, brethren, I know that you acted [a]in ignorance, just as your [b]rulers did also.

18 "But the things which [a]God announced beforehand by the mouth of all the prophets, [b]that His [1]Christ should suffer, He has thus fulfilled.

19 "[a]Repent therefore and return, that your sins may be wiped away, in order that [b]times of refreshing may come from the presence of the Lord;

20 and that He may send Jesus, the Christ appointed for you,

21 [a]whom heaven must receive until *the* period of [b]restoration of all things about which [c]God spoke by the mouth of His holy prophets from ancient time.

22 "Moses said, '[a]THE LORD GOD SHALL RAISE UP FOR YOU A PROPHET LIKE ME FROM YOUR BRETHREN; TO HIM YOU SHALL GIVE HEED IN EVERYTHING HE SAYS TO YOU.

23 '[a]AND IT SHALL BE THAT EVERY [b]SOUL THAT DOES NOT HEED THAT PROPHET SHALL BE UTTERLY DESTROYED FROM AMONG THE PEOPLE.'

24 "And likewise, [a]all the prophets who have spoken, from Samuel and *his* successors onward, also announced these days.

25 "It is you who are [a]the sons of the prophets, and of the [b]covenant which God made with your fathers, saying to Abraham, '[c]AND IN YOUR SEED ALL THE FAMILIES OF THE EARTH SHALL BE BLESSED.'

26 "For you [a]first, God [b]raised up His Servant, and sent Him to bless you by turning every one *of you* from your wicked ways."

CHAPTER 4

Peter and John Arrested

AND as they were speaking to the people, the priests and [a]the captain of the temple *guard*, and [b]the Sadducees, [c]came upon them,

2 being greatly disturbed because they were teaching the people and proclaiming [a]in Jesus the resurrection from the dead.

3 And they laid hands on them, and [a]put them in jail until the next day, for it was already evening.

4 But many of those who had heard the message believed; and [a]the number of the men came to be about five thousand.

5 And it came about on the next day, that their [a]rulers and elders and scribes were gathered together in Jerusalem;

6 and [a]Annas the high priest *was there*, and [b]Caiaphas and John and Alexander, and all who were of high-priestly descent.

7 And when they had placed them in the center, they *began to* inquire, "By what power, or in what name, have you done this?"

8 Then Peter, [a]filled with the Holy Spirit, said to them, "[b]Rulers and elders of the people,

9 if we are on trial today for [a]a benefit done to a sick man, as to how this man has been made well,

10 let it be known to all of you, and to all the people of Israel, that [a]by the name of Jesus Christ the Nazarene, whom you crucified, whom [b]God raised from the dead—by this *name* this man stands here before you in good health.

11 "[1a]He is the [b]STONE WHICH WAS [c]REJECTED by you, THE BUILDERS, *but* WHICH BECAME THE VERY CORNER *stone*.

12 "And there is salvation in [a]no one else; for there is no other name under heaven that has been given

---

10 [a]John 9:8; Acts 3:2
11 [1]Or, *colonnade* [a]Luke 22:8; Acts 3:3, 4 [b]John 10:23; Acts 5:12
12 [a]Matt. 11:25; 17:4; 22:1; Luke 14:3; Acts 5:8; 10:46
13 [a]Matt. 22:32 [b]Ex. 3:13, 15; Acts 5:30; 7:32; 22:14 [c]Acts 3:26; 4:27, 30 [d]Matt. 20:19; John 19:11; Acts 2:23 [e]Matt. 27:2 [f]Luke 23:4
14 [a]Mark 1:24; Acts 4:27; 7:52; 2 Cor. 5:21 [b]Matt. 27:20; Mark 15:11; Luke 23:18-25
15 [1]Or, *Author* [a]Acts 5:31; Heb. 2:10; 12:2 [b]Acts 2:24 [c]Luke 24:48
16 [1]Lit., *His* [a]Acts 3:6
17 [a]Luke 23:34; John 15:21; Acts 13:27; 26:9; Eph. 4:18 [b]Luke 23:13
18 [1]Or, *Anointed One, Messiah* [a]Acts 2:23 [b]Luke 24:27; Acts 17:3; 26:23
19 [a]Acts 2:38; 26:20 [b]2 Thess. 1:7; Heb. 4:1ff.
21 [a]Acts 1:11 [b]Matt. 17:11; Rom. 8:21 [c]Luke 1:70
22 [a]Deut. 18:15; Acts 7:37
23 [a]Deut. 18:19 [b]Acts 2:41
24 [a]Luke 24:27; Acts 17:3; 26:23
25 [a]Acts 2:39 [b]Rom. 9:4f. [c]Gen. 22:18
26 [a]Matt. 15:24; John 4:22; Acts 13:46; Rom. 1:16; 2:9f. [b]Acts 2:24
1 [a]Luke 22:4 [b]Matt. 3:7 [c]Luke 20:1; Acts 6:12
2 [a]Acts 3:15; 17:18
3 [a]Acts 5:18
4 [a]Acts 2:41
5 [a]Luke 23:13; Acts 4:8
6 [a]Luke 3:2 [b]Matt. 26:3
8 [a]Acts 2:4; 13:9 [b]Luke 23:13; Acts 4:5
9 [a]Acts 3:7f.
10 [a]Acts 2:22; 3:6 [b]Acts 2:24
11 [1]Lit., *This One* [a]Matt. 21:42 [b]Ps. 118:22 [c]Mark 9:12
12 [a]Matt. 1:21; Acts 10:43; 1 Tim. 2:5

among men, by which we must be saved."

Threat and Release

13 Now as they observed the [a]confidence of [b]Peter and John, and understood that they were uneducated and untrained men, they were marveling, and [c]*began* to recognize them [1]as having been with Jesus.

14 And seeing the man who had been healed standing with them, they had nothing to say in reply.

15 But when they had ordered them to go aside out of the [1a]Council, they *began* to confer with one another,

16 saying, "[a]What shall we do with these men? For the fact that a [b]noteworthy miracle has taken place through them is apparent to all who live in Jerusalem, and we cannot deny it.

17 "But in order that it may not spread any further among the people, let us warn them to speak no more to any man [a]in this name."

18 And when they had summoned them, they [a]commanded them not to speak or teach at all in the name of Jesus.

19 But [a]Peter and John answered and said to them, "[b]Whether it is right in the sight of God to give heed to you rather than to God, you be the judge;

20 for [a]we cannot stop speaking what we have seen and heard."

21 And when they had threatened them further, they let them go (finding no basis on which they might punish them) [a]on account of the people, because they were all [b]glorifying God for what had happened;

22 for the man was more than forty years old on whom this miracle of healing had been performed.

23 And when they had been released, they went to their own *companions,* and reported all that the chief priests and the elders had said to them.

24 And when they heard *this,* they lifted their voices to God with one accord and said, "O [1]Lord, it is Thou who [a]DIDST MAKE THE HEAVEN AND THE EARTH AND THE SEA, AND ALL THAT IS IN THEM,

25 who [a]by the Holy Spirit, *through* the mouth of our father David Thy servant, didst say,

'[b]WHY DID THE GENTILES RAGE,
AND THE PEOPLES DEVISE FUTILE THINGS?

26 '[a]THE KINGS OF THE EARTH
[1]TOOK THEIR STAND,
AND THE RULERS WERE GATHERED TOGETHER
AGAINST THE LORD, AND AGAINST HIS [2b]CHRIST.'

27 "For truly in this city there were gathered together against Thy holy [1a]servant Jesus, whom Thou didst anoint, both [b]Herod and [c]Pontius Pilate, along with [d]the [2]Gentiles and the peoples of Israel,

28 to do whatever Thy hand and [a]Thy purpose predestined to occur.

29 "And now, Lord, take note of their threats, and grant that Thy bond-servants may [a]speak Thy word with all [b]confidence,

30 while Thou dost extend Thy hand to heal, and [a]signs and wonders take place through the name of Thy holy [b]servant Jesus."

31 And when they had prayed, the [a]place where they had gathered together was shaken, and they were all [b]filled with the Holy Spirit, and *began* to [c]speak the word of God with [d]boldness.

Sharing Among Believers

32 And the [1]congregation of those who believed were of one heart and soul; and not one *of them* claimed that anything belonging to him was his own; but [a]all things were common property to them.

33 And [a]with great power the apostles were giving [b]witness to the resurrection of the Lord Jesus[1], and abundant grace was upon them all.

34 For there was not a needy person among them, for all who were owners of land or houses [a]would sell them and bring the [1]proceeds of the sales,

35 and [a]lay them at the apostles' feet; and they would be [b]distributed to each, as any had need.

36 And Joseph, a Levite of [a]Cyprian birth, who was also called [b]Barnabas by the apostles (which translated means, Son of [1c]Encouragement),

37 and who owned a tract of land, sold it and brought the money and [a]laid it at the apostles' feet.

Chapter 5

Fate of Ananias and Sapphira

BUT a certain man named Ananias, with his wife Sapphira, sold a piece of property,

2 and [a]kept back *some* of the price for himself, with his wife's [1]full knowledge, and bringing a por-

13 [1]Lit., *that they had been* [a]Acts 4:31 [b]Luke 22:8; Acts 4:19 [c]John 7:15
15 [1]Or, *Sanhedrin* [a]Matt. 5:22
16 [a]John 11:47 [b]Acts 3:7-10
17 [a]John 15:21
18 [a]Acts 5:28f.
19 [a]Acts 4:13 [b]Acts 5:28f.
20 [a]1 Cor. 9:16
21 [a]Acts 5:26 [b]Matt. 9:8
24 [1]Or, *Master* [a]Ex. 20:11; Ps. 146:6
25 [a]Acts 1:16 [b]Ps. 2:1
26 [1]Or, *approached* [2]I.e., Messiah, Anointed One [a]Ps. 2:2 [b]Dan. 9:24f.; Luke 4:18; Acts 10:38; Heb. 1:9
27 [1]Or, *Child* [2]Or, *nations* [a]Acts 3:13; 4:30 [b]Matt. 14:1 [c]Matt. 27:2; Luke 23:12 [d]Matt. 20:19
28 [a]Acts 2:23
29 [a]Phil. 1:14 [b]Acts 4:13, 31; 14:3
30 [a]John 4:48 [b]Acts 3:13; 4:27
31 [a]Acts 2:1 [b]Acts 2:4 [c]Phil. 1:14 [d]Acts 4:13; 14:3
32 [1]Or, *multitude* [a]Acts 2:44
33 [1]Some mss. add, *Christ* [a]Acts 1:8 [b]Luke 24:48
34 [1]Lit., *the prices of the things being sold* [a]Matt. 19:21; Acts 2:45
35 [a]Acts 4:37; 5:2 [b]Acts 2:45; 6:1
36 [1]Or, *Exhortation,* or, *Consolation* [a]Acts 11:19f.; 13:4; 15:39; 21:3, 16; 27:4 [b]Acts 9:27; 11:22, 30; 12:25; 13:15; 1 Cor. 9:6; Gal. 2:1, 9, 13; Col. 4:10 [c]Acts 2:40; 11:23; 13:15; 1 Cor. 14:3; 1 Thess. 2:3
37 [a]Acts 4:35; 5:2
2 [1]Or, *collusion* [a]Acts 5:3

tion of it, he [b]laid it at the apostles' feet.

3 But Peter said, "Ananias, why has [a]Satan filled your heart to lie [b]to the Holy Spirit, and to [c]keep back *some* of the price of the land?

4 "While it remained *unsold,* did it not remain your own? And after it was sold, was it not [1]under your control? Why is it that you have [2]conceived this deed in your heart? You have not lied to men, but [a]to God."

5 And as he heard these words, Ananias [a]fell down and breathed his last; and [b]great fear came upon all who heard of it.

6 And the [1]young men arose and [a]covered him up, and after carrying him out, they buried him.

7 Now there elapsed an interval of about three hours, and his wife came in, not knowing what had happened.

8 And Peter [a]responded to her, "Tell me whether you sold the land [1b]for such and such a price?" And she said, "Yes, [1]that was the price."

9 Then Peter *said* to her, "Why is it that you have agreed together to [a]put [b]the Spirit of the Lord to the test? Behold, the feet of those who have buried your husband are at the door, and they shall carry you out *as well.*"

10 And she [a]fell immediately at his feet, and breathed her last; and the young men came in and found her dead, and they carried her out and buried her beside her husband.

11 And [a]great fear came upon the whole church, and upon all who heard of these things.

12 And [1]at the hands of the apostles many [a]signs and wonders were taking place among the people; and they were all with one accord in [b]Solomon's portico.

13 But none of the rest dared to associate with them; however, [a]the people [1]held them in high esteem.

14 And all the more [a]believers in the Lord, multitudes of men and women, were constantly [b]added to *their number;*

15 to such an extent that they even carried the sick out into the streets, and laid them on cots and pallets, so that when Peter came by, [a]at least his shadow might fall on any one of them.

16 And also the [1]people from the cities in the vicinity of Jerusalem were coming together, bringing people who were sick [2]or afflicted with unclean spirits; and they were all being healed.

Imprisonment and Release

17 But the high priest rose up, along with all his associates (that is [a]the sect of [b]the Sadducees), and they were filled with jealousy;

18 and they laid hands on the apostles, and [a]put them in a public jail.

19 But [a]an angel of the Lord during the night opened the gates of the prison, and taking them out he said,

20 "Go your way, stand and [1]speak to the people in the temple [2a]the whole message of this Life."

21 And upon hearing *this,* they entered into the temple [a]about daybreak, and *began* to teach. Now when [b]the high priest and his associates had come, they called [c]the [1]Council together, even all the Senate of the sons of Israel, and sent *orders* to the prison house for them to be brought.

22 But [a]the officers who came did not find them in the prison; and they returned, and reported back,

23 saying, "We found the prison house locked quite securely and the guards standing at the doors; but when we had opened up, we found no one inside."

24 Now when [a]the captain of the temple *guard* and the chief priests heard these words, they were greatly perplexed about them as to what [1]would come of this.

25 But someone came and reported to them, "Behold, the men whom you put in prison are standing in the temple and teaching the people!"

26 Then [a]the captain went along with [b]the officers and *proceeded* to bring them *back* without violence; (for [c]they were afraid of the people, lest they should be stoned).

27 And when they had brought them, they stood them [1]before [a]the Council. And the high priest questioned them,

28 saying, "We gave you [a]strict orders not to continue teaching in this name, and behold, you have filled Jerusalem with your teaching, and [b]intend to bring this man's blood upon us."

29 But Peter and the apostles answered and said, "[a]We must obey God rather than men.

30 "[a]The God of our fathers [b]raised up Jesus, [1]whom you had [c]put to death by hanging Him on a [2]cross.

2 [b]Acts 4:35, 37
3 [a]Matt. 4:10; Luke 22:3; John 13:2, 27 [b]Acts 5:4, 9 [c]Acts 5:2
4 [1]Or, *in your authority* [2]Or, *placed* [a]Acts 5:3, 9
5 [a]Ezek. 11:13; Acts 5:10 [b]Acts 2:43; 5:11
6 [1]Lit., *younger* [a]John 19:40
8 [1]Lit., *for so much* [a]Acts 3:12 [b]Acts 5:2
9 [a]Acts 15:10 [b]Acts 5:3, 4
10 [a]Ezek. 11:13; Acts 5:5
11 [a]Acts 2:43; 5:5
12 [1]Lit., *through* [a]John 4:48 [b]John 10:23; Acts 3:11
13 [1]Lit., *were holding* [a]Acts 2:47; 4:21
14 [a]2 Cor. 6:15 [b]Acts 2:47; 11:24
15 [a]Acts 19:12
16 [1]Lit., *multitude* [2]Lit., *and*
17 [a]Acts 15:5 [b]Matt. 3:7; Acts 4:1
18 [a]Acts 4:3
19 [a]Matt. 1:20, 24; 2:13, 19; 28:2; Luke 1:11; 2:9; Acts 8:26; 10:3; 12:7, 23; 27:23
20 [1]Or, *continue to speak* [2]Lit., *all the words* [a]John 6:63, 68
21 [1]Or, *Sanhedrin* [a]John 8:2 [b]Acts 4:6 [c]Matt. 5:22; Acts 5:27, 34, 41
22 [a]Matt. 26:58; Acts 5:26
24 [1]Lit., *this would become* [a]Acts 4:1; 5:26
26 [a]Acts 5:24 [b]Acts 5:22 [c]Acts 4:21; 5:13
27 [1]Lit., *in* [a]Matt. 5:22; Acts 5:21, 34, 41
28 [a]Acts 4:18 [b]Matt. 23:35; 27:25; Acts 2:23, 36; 3:14f.; 7:52
29 [a]Acts 4:19
30 [1]Or, *on whom you had laid violent hands* [2]Lit., *wood* [a]Acts 3:13 [b]Acts 2:24 [c]Acts 10:39; 13:29; Gal. 3:13; 1 Pet. 2:24

31 "[a]He is the one whom God exalted to His right hand as a [b]Prince and a [c]Savior, to grant [d]repentance to Israel, and forgiveness of sins.

32 "And we are [a]witnesses[1] of these things; and [b]so *is* the Holy Spirit, whom God has given to those who obey Him."

Gamaliel's Counsel

33 But when they heard this, they were [a]cut to the quick and were intending to slay them.

34 But a certain Pharisee named [a]Gamaliel, a [b]teacher of the Law, respected by all the people, stood up in [c]the Council and gave orders to put the men outside for a short time.

35 And he said to them, "Men of Israel, take care what you propose to do with these men.

36 "For some time ago Theudas rose up, [a]claiming to be somebody; and a group of about four hundred men joined up with him. And he was slain; and all who followed him were dispersed and came to nothing.

37 "After this man Judas of Galilee rose up in the days of [a]the census, and drew away *some* people after him, he too perished, and all those who followed him were scattered.

38 "And so in the present case, I say to you, stay away from these men and let them alone, for if this plan or action should [a]be of men, it will be overthrown;

39 but if it is of God, you will not be able to overthrow them; or else you may even be found [a]fighting against God."

40 And they took his advice; and after calling the apostles in, they [a]flogged them and ordered them to speak no more in the name of Jesus, and *then* released them.

41 So they went on their way from the presence of the [1a]Council, [b]rejoicing that they had been considered worthy to suffer shame [c]for [2]*His* name.

42 [a]And every day, in the temple and from house to house, they kept right on teaching and [b]preaching Jesus *as* the Christ.

CHAPTER 6

Choosing of the Seven

NOW at this time while the [a]disciples were increasing [b]*in number,* a complaint arose on the part of the [c]Hellenistic *Jews* against the *native* [d]Hebrews, because their [e]widows were being overlooked in [f]the daily serving *of food.*

2 And the twelve summoned the congregation of the disciples and said, "It is not desirable for us to neglect the word of God in order to serve tables.

3 "But select from among you, [a]brethren, seven men of good reputation, [b]full of the Spirit and of wisdom, whom we may put in charge of this task.

4 "But we will [a]devote ourselves to prayer, and to the ministry of the word."

5 And the statement found approval with the whole congregation; and they chose [a]Stephen, a man [b]full of faith and of the Holy Spirit, and [c]Philip, Prochorus, Nicanor, Timon, Parmenas and Nicolas, a [d]proselyte from [e]Antioch.

6 And these they brought before the apostles; and after [a]praying, they [b]laid their hands on them.

7 And [a]the word of God kept on spreading; and [b]the number of the disciples continued to increase greatly in Jerusalem, and a great many of the priests were becoming obedient to [c]the faith.

8 And Stephen, full of grace and power, was performing great [a]wonders and signs among the people.

9 But some men from what was called the Synagogue of the Freedmen, *including* both [a]Cyrenians and [b]Alexandrians, and some from [c]Cilicia and [1d]Asia, rose up and argued with Stephen.

10 And *yet* they were unable to cope with the wisdom and the Spirit with which he was speaking.

11 Then they secretly induced men to say, "We have heard him speak blasphemous words against Moses and *against* God."

12 And they stirred up the people, the elders and the scribes, and they [a]came upon him and dragged him away, and brought him before [b]the [1]Council.

13 And they put forward [a]false witnesses who said, "This man incessantly speaks against this [b]holy place, and the Law;

14 for we have heard him say that [a]this Nazarene, Jesus, will destroy this place and alter [b]the customs which Moses handed down to us."

15 And fixing their gaze on him, all who were sitting in the [a]Council saw his face like the face of an angel.

31 [a]Acts 2:33 [b]Acts 3:15 [c]Luke 2:11 [d]Luke 24:47; Acts 2:38
32 [1]Some mss. add, *in Him* or, *of Him* [a]Luke 24:48 [b]John 15:26; Acts 15:28; Rom. 8:16; Heb. 2:4
33 [a]Acts 2:37; 7:54
34 [a]Acts 22:3 [b]Luke 2:46; 5:17 [c]Acts 5:21
36 [a]Acts 8:9; Gal. 2:6; 6:3
37 [a]Luke 2:2
38 [a]Mark 11:30
39 [a]Prov. 21:30; Acts 11:17
40 [a]Matt. 10:17
41 [1]Or, *Sanhedrin* [2]Lit., the *name* (par excellence) [a]Acts 5:21 [b]1 Pet. 4:14, 16 [c]John 15:21
42 [a]Acts 2:46 [b]Acts 8:35; 11:20; 17:18; Gal. 1:16
1 [a]Acts 11:26 [b]Acts 2:47; 6:7 [c]Acts 9:29; 11:20 marg. [d]2 Cor. 11:22; Phil. 3:5 [e]Acts 9:39, 41; 1 Tim. 5:3 [f]Acts 4:35
3 [a]John 21:23; Acts 1:15 [b]Acts 2:4
4 [a]Acts 1:14
5 [a]Acts 6:8ff.; 11:19; 22:20 [b]Acts 6:3; 11:24 [c]Acts 8:5ff.; 21:8 [d]Matt. 23:15 [e]Acts 11:19
6 [a]Acts 1:24 [b]Num. 8:10; 27:18; Deut. 34:9; Mark 5:23; Acts 8:17ff.; 9:17; 13:3; 19:6; 1 Tim. 4:14; 2 Tim. 1:6
7 [a]Acts 12:24; 19:20 [b]Acts 6:1 [c]Acts 13:8; 14:22; Gal. 1:23; 6:10
8 [a]John 4:48
9 [1]I.e., west coast province of Asia Minor [a]Matt. 27:32; Acts 2:10 [b]Acts 18:24 [c]Acts 15:23, 41; 21:39; 22:3; 23:34; 27:5; Gal. 1:21 [d]Acts 16:6; 19:10; 21:27; 24:18
12 [1]Or, *Sanhedrin* [a]Luke 20:1; Acts 4:1 [b]Matt. 5:22
13 [a]Matt. 26:59-61; Acts 7:58 [b]Matt. 24:15; Acts 21:28; 25:8
14 [a]Matt. 26:61 [b]Acts 15:1; 21:21; 26:3; 28:17
15 [a]Matt. 5:22

Chapter 7

Stephen's Defense

AND the high priest said, "Are these things so?"

2 And he said, "Hear me, [a]brethren and fathers! [b]The God of glory [c]appeared to our father Abraham when he was in Mesopotamia, before he lived in [1]Haran,

3 AND SAID TO HIM, '[a]DEPART FROM YOUR COUNTRY AND YOUR RELATIVES, AND COME INTO THE LAND THAT I WILL SHOW YOU.'

4 "[a]Then he departed from the land of the Chaldeans, and settled in [1]Haran. And [b]from there, after his father died, God removed him into this country in which you are now living.

5 "And He gave him no inheritance in it, not even a foot of ground; and *yet,* even when he had no child, [a]He promised that HE WOULD GIVE IT TO HIM AS A POSSESSION, AND TO HIS OFFSPRING AFTER HIM.

6 "But [a]God spoke to this effect, that HIS OFFSPRING WOULD BE ALIENS IN A FOREIGN LAND, AND THAT THEY WOULD [1]BE ENSLAVED AND MISTREATED FOR FOUR HUNDRED YEARS.

7 " 'AND WHATEVER NATION TO WHICH THEY SHALL BE IN BONDAGE I MYSELF WILL JUDGE,' said God, 'AND [a]AFTER THAT THEY WILL COME OUT AND [1]SERVE ME IN THIS PLACE.'

8 "And He [a]gave him [1]the covenant of circumcision; and so [b]*Abraham* became the father of Isaac, and circumcised him on the eighth day; and [c]Isaac *became the father of* Jacob, and [d]Jacob *of* the twelve [e]patriarchs.

9 "And the patriarchs [a]BECAME JEALOUS OF JOSEPH AND SOLD HIM INTO EGYPT. And *yet* God WAS WITH HIM,

10 and rescued him from all his afflictions, and [a]GRANTED HIM FAVOR and wisdom IN THE SIGHT OF PHARAOH, KING OF EGYPT; AND HE MADE HIM GOVERNOR OVER EGYPT AND ALL HIS HOUSEHOLD.

11 "Now [a]A FAMINE CAME OVER ALL EGYPT AND CANAAN, and great affliction *with it;* and our fathers [1]could find no [2]food.

12 "But [a]WHEN JACOB HEARD THAT THERE WAS GRAIN IN EGYPT, he sent our fathers *there* the first time.

13 "And on the second *visit* [a]Joseph [1]made himself known to his brothers, and Joseph's family was disclosed to Pharaoh.

14 "And [a]Joseph sent *word* and invited Jacob his father and all his relatives to come to him, [b]seventy-five [c]persons *in all.*

15 "And [a]Jacob WENT DOWN TO EGYPT AND *there* PASSED AWAY, he and our fathers.

16 "And *from there* they were removed to [1a]Shechem, and laid in the tomb which Abraham had purchased for a sum of money from the sons of [2]Hamor in [1]Shechem.

17 "But as the time of the promise was approaching which God had assured to Abraham, [a]the people increased and multiplied in Egypt,

18 until [a]THERE AROSE ANOTHER KING OVER EGYPT WHO KNEW NOTHING ABOUT JOSEPH.

19 "It was he who took [a]shrewd advantage of our race, and mistreated our fathers so that they would [1]expose their infants and they would not survive.

20 "And it was at this time that [a]Moses was born; and he was lovely [1]in the sight of God; and he was nurtured three months in his father's home.

21 "And after he had been [1]exposed, [a]Pharaoh's daughter [2]took him away, and nurtured him as her own son.

22 "And Moses was educated in all [a]the learning of the Egyptians, and he was a man of power in words and deeds.

23 "But when he was approaching the age of forty, [a]it entered his [1]mind to visit his brethren, the sons of Israel.

24 "And when he saw one *of them* being treated unjustly, he defended him and took vengeance for the oppressed by striking down the Egyptian.

25 "And he [1]supposed that his brethren understood that God was granting them [2]deliverance [3]through him; but they did not understand.

26 "[a]And on the following day he appeared to them as they were fighting together, and he tried to reconcile them in peace, saying, 'Men, you are brethren, why do you injure one another?'

27 "[a]BUT THE ONE WHO WAS INJURING HIS NEIGHBOR pushed him away, saying, 'WHO MADE YOU A RULER AND JUDGE OVER US?

28 '[a]YOU DO NOT MEAN TO KILL ME AS YOU KILLED THE EGYPTIAN YESTERDAY, DO YOU?'

29 "AND AT THIS REMARK [a]MOSES FLED, AND BECAME AN ALIEN IN THE LAND OF [1]MIDIAN, where he became the father of two sons.

2 [1]Gr., *Kharran* [a]Acts 22:1 [b]Ps. 29:3; 1 Cor. 2:8 [c]Gen. 11:31; 15:7
3 [a]Gen. 12:1
4 [1]Gr., *Kharran* [a]Gen. 11:31; 15:7 [b]Gen. 12:5
5 [a]Gen. 12:7; 17:8
6 [1]Lit., *enslave them and mistreat them* [a]Gen. 15:13f.
7 [1]Or, *worship* [a]Ex. 3:12
8 [1]Or, *a* [a]Gen. 17:10ff. [b]Gen. 21:2-4 [c]Gen. 25:26 [d]Gen. 29:31ff.; 30:5ff.; 35:23ff. [e]Acts 2:29
9 [a]Gen. 37:11, 28; 39:2, 21f.; 45:4
10 [a]Gen. 39:21; 41:40-46; Ps. 105:21
11 [1]Lit., *were not finding* [2]Or, *fodder* [a]Gen. 41:54f.; 42:5
12 [a]Gen. 42:2
13 [1]Or, *was made known* [a]Gen. 45:1-4
14 [a]Gen. 45:9f. [b]Gen. 46:26f.; Ex. 1:5; Deut. 10:22 [c]Acts 2:41
15 [a]Gen. 46:5; 49:33; Ex. 1:6
16 [1]Gr., *Sychem* [2]Gr., *Emmor* [a]Gen. 23:16; 33:19; 50:13; Josh. 24:32
17 [a]Ex. 1:7f.
18 [a]Ex. 1:8
19 [1]Or, *put out to die* [a]Ex. 1:10f., 16ff.
20 [1]Lit., *to God* [a]Ex. 2:2
21 [1]Or, *put out to die* [2]Or, *adopted him* [a]Ex. 2:5f., 10
22 [a]1 Kin. 4:30; Is. 19:11
23 [1]Lit., *heart* [a]Ex. 2:11f.
25 [1]Lit., *was thinking* [2]Or, *salvation* [3]Lit., *through his hand*
26 [a]Ex. 2:13f.
27 [a]Ex. 2:14; Acts 7:35
28 [a]Ex. 2:14
29 [1]Gr., *Madiam* [a]Ex. 2:15, 22

30"And after forty years had passed, [a]AN ANGEL APPEARED TO HIM IN THE WILDERNESS OF MOUNT Sinai, IN THE FLAME OF A BURNING THORN BUSH.

31"And when Moses saw it, he *began* to marvel at the sight; and as he approached to look *more* closely, there came the voice of the Lord:

32 '[a]I AM THE GOD OF YOUR FATHERS, THE GOD OF ABRAHAM AND ISAAC AND JACOB.' And Moses shook *with fear* and would not venture to look.

33"BUT THE LORD SAID TO HIM, '[a]TAKE OFF THE SANDALS FROM YOUR FEET, FOR THE PLACE ON WHICH YOU ARE STANDING IS HOLY GROUND.

34 '[a]I HAVE CERTAINLY SEEN THE OPPRESSION OF MY PEOPLE IN EGYPT, AND HAVE HEARD THEIR GROANS, AND I HAVE COME DOWN TO DELIVER THEM; [b]COME NOW, AND I WILL SEND YOU TO EGYPT.'

35"This Moses whom they [a]disowned, saying, 'WHO MADE YOU A RULER AND A JUDGE?' is the one whom God sent *to be* both a ruler and a deliverer with the help of the angel who appeared to him in the thorn bush.

36"[a]This man led them out, performing [b]wonders and signs in the land of Egypt and in the Red Sea and in the [c]wilderness for forty years.

37"This is the Moses who said to the sons of Israel, 'GOD SHALL RAISE UP FOR YOU [a]A PROPHET LIKE ME FROM YOUR BRETHREN.'

38"This is the one who was in [a]the [1]congregation in the wilderness together with [b]the angel who was speaking to him on Mount Sinai, and *who was* with our fathers; and he received [c]living [d]oracles to pass on to you.

39"And our fathers were unwilling to be obedient to him, but [a]repudiated him and in their hearts turned back to Egypt,

40 SAYING TO AARON, '[a]MAKE FOR US GODS WHO WILL GO BEFORE US; FOR THIS MOSES WHO LED US OUT OF THE LAND OF EGYPT—WE DO NOT KNOW WHAT HAPPENED TO HIM.'

41"And at that time [a]they made a calf and brought a sacrifice to the idol, and were rejoicing in [b]the works of their hands.

42"But God [a]turned away and delivered them up to [1]serve the [2]host of heaven; as it is written in the book of the prophets, '[b]IT WAS NOT TO ME THAT YOU OFFERED VICTIMS AND SACRIFICES [c]FORTY YEARS IN THE WILDERNESS, WAS IT, O HOUSE OF ISRAEL?

43 '[a]YOU ALSO TOOK ALONG THE TABERNACLE OF MOLOCH AND THE STAR OF THE GOD [1]ROMPHA, THE IMAGES WHICH YOU MADE TO WORSHIP THEM. I ALSO WILL REMOVE YOU BEYOND BABYLON.'

44"Our fathers had [a]the tabernacle of testimony in the wilderness, just as He who spoke to Moses directed *him* to make it according to the pattern which he had seen.

45"And having received it in their turn, our fathers [a]brought it in with [1]Joshua upon dispossessing the [2]nations whom God drove out before our fathers, until the time of David.

46"And [a]*David* found favor in God's sight, and asked that he might find a dwelling place for the [1]God of Jacob.

47"But it was [a]Solomon who built a house for Him.

48"However, [a]the Most High does not dwell in *houses* made by *human* hands; as the prophet says:

49 '[a]HEAVEN IS MY THRONE,
AND EARTH IS THE FOOTSTOOL OF MY FEET;
WHAT KIND OF HOUSE WILL YOU BUILD FOR ME?' says the Lord;
'OR WHAT PLACE IS THERE FOR MY REPOSE?

50 '[a]WAS IT NOT MY HAND WHICH MADE ALL THESE THINGS?'

51"You men who are [a]stiff-necked and uncircumcised in heart and ears are always resisting the Holy Spirit; you are doing just as your fathers did.

52"[a]Which one of the prophets did your fathers not persecute? And they killed those who had previously announced the coming of [b]the Righteous One, whose betrayers and murderers [c]you have now become;

53 you who received the law as [a]ordained by angels, and *yet* did not keep it."

Stephen Put to Death

54 Now when they heard this, they were [a]cut to the quick, and they *began* gnashing their teeth at him.

55 But being [a]full of the Holy Spirit, he [b]gazed intently into heaven and saw the glory of God, and Jesus standing [c]at the right hand of God;

56 and he said, "Behold, I see the [a]heavens opened up and [b]the Son of Man standing at the right hand of God."

30 [a]Ex. 3:1f.
32 [a]Ex. 3:6
33 [a]Ex. 3:5
34 [a]Ex. 3:7 [b]Ex. 3:10
35 [a]Acts 7:27
36 [a]Ex. 12:41; 33:1; Heb. 8:9 [b]Ex. 7:3; John 4:48 [c]Ex. 16:35; Num. 14:33; Ps. 95:8-10; Acts 7:42; 13:18; Heb. 3:8f.
37 [a]Deut. 18:15; Acts 3:22
38 [1]Or, *church* (Gr., ekklesia) [a]Ex. 19:17 [b]Acts 7:53 [c]Deut. 32:47; Heb. 4:12 [d]Rom. 3:2; Heb. 5:12; 1 Pet. 4:11
39 [a]Num. 14:3f.
40 [a]Ex. 32:1, 23
41 [a]Ex. 32:4, 6 [b]Rev. 9:20
42 [1]Or, *worship* [2]I.e., heavenly bodies [a]Josh. 24:20; Is. 63:10; Jer. 19:13; Ezek. 20:39 [b]Amos 5:25 [c]Acts 7:36
43 [1]Other mss. spell it: *Romphan*, or *Rempham*, or *Raiphan*, or *Rephan* [a]Amos 5:26, 27
44 [a]Ex. 25:8, 9; 38:21
45 [1]Gr., *Jesus* [2]Or, *Gentiles* [a]Deut. 32:49; Josh. 3:14ff.; 18:1; 23:9; 24:18; Ps. 44:2f.
46 [1]The earliest mss. read *house* instead of *God;* the Septuagint reads, *God* [a]2 Sam. 7:8ff.; Ps. 132:1-5; Acts 13:22
47 [a]1 Kin. 8:20
48 [a]Luke 1:32
49 [a]Is. 66:1; Matt. 5:34f.
50 [a]Is. 66:2
51 [a]Ex. 32:9; 33:3, 5; Lev. 26:41; Num. 27:14; Is. 63:10; Jer. 6:10; 9:26
52 [a]2 Chr. 36:15f.; Matt. 5:12; 23:31, 37 [b]Acts 3:14; 22:14; 1 John 2:1 [c]Acts 3:14; 5:28
53 [a]Deut. 33:2 [Septuagint]; Acts 7:38; Gal. 3:19; Heb. 2:2
54 [a]Acts 5:33
55 [a]Acts 2:4 [b]John 11:41 [c]Mark 16:19
56 [a]John 1:51 [b]Matt. 8:20

57 But they cried out with a loud
voice, and covered their ears, and
they rushed upon him with one im-
pulse.
58 And when they had [a]driven him
out of the city, they *began* stoning
him, and [b]the witnesses [c]laid aside
their robes at the feet of [d]a young
man named Saul.
59 And they went on stoning Stephen as he [a]called upon *the Lord*
and said, "Lord Jesus, receive my
spirit!"
60 And [a]falling on his knees, he
cried out with a loud voice, "Lord,
[b]do not hold this sin against them!"
And having said this, he [1c]fell
asleep.

Chapter 8

Saul Persecutes the Church

AND [a]Saul was in hearty agreement with putting him to death.
And on that day a great persecution arose against [b]the church in Jerusalem; and they were all [c]scat-
tered throughout the regions of
Judea and [d]Samaria, except the
apostles.
2 And *some* devout men buried
Stephen, and made loud lamentation over him.
3 But [a]Saul *began* ravaging the
church, entering house after house;
and [b]dragging off men and women,
he would put them in prison.

Philip in Samaria

4 Therefore, those [a]who had been
scattered went about [1b]preaching
the word.
5 And [a]Philip went down to the
city of Samaria and *began* proclaiming [1]Christ to them.
6 And the multitudes with one
accord were giving attention to
what was said by Philip, as they
heard and saw the [1]signs which he
was performing.
7 For *in the case of* many who
had [a]unclean spirits, they were coming out *of them* shouting with a loud
voice; and many who had been [b]par-
alyzed and lame were healed.
8 And there was [a]much rejoicing
in that city.
9 Now there was a certain man
named Simon, who formerly was
practicing [a]magic in the city, and as-
tonishing the people of Samaria,
[b]claiming to be someone great;
10 and they all, from smallest to
greatest, were giving attention to
him, saying, "[a]This man is what is
called the Great Power of God."
11 And they were giving him attention because he had for a long
time astonished them with his
[a]magic arts.
12 But when they believed Philip
[a]preaching the good news about the
kingdom of God and the name of
Jesus Christ, they were being [b]bap-
tized, men and women alike.
13 And even Simon himself believed; and after being baptized, he
continued on with Philip; and as he
observed [a]signs and [b]great miracles
taking place, he was constantly
amazed.
14 Now when [a]the apostles in Jerusalem heard that Samaria had received the word of God, they sent
them [b]Peter and John,
15 who came down and prayed for
them, [a]that they might receive the
Holy Spirit.
16 For He had not yet fallen upon
any of them; they had simply been
[a]baptized [1]in the name of the Lord
Jesus.
17 Then they [a]*began* laying their
hands on them, and they were [b]re-
ceiving the Holy Spirit.
18 Now when Simon saw that the
Spirit was bestowed through the
laying on of the apostles' hands, he
offered them money,
19 saying, "Give this authority to
me as well, so that everyone on
whom I lay my hands may receive
the Holy Spirit."
20 But Peter said to him, "May
your silver perish with you, because
you thought you could [a]obtain the
gift of God with money!
21 "You have [a]no part or portion in
this [1]matter, for your heart is not
[b]right before God.
22 "Therefore repent of this wickedness of yours, and pray the Lord
that if possible, the intention of your
heart may be forgiven you.
23 "For I see that you are in the gall
of bitterness and in [a]the [1]bondage of
iniquity."
24 But Simon answered and said,
"Pray to the Lord for me yourselves,
so that nothing of what you have
said may come upon me."

An Ethiopian Receives Christ

25 And so, when they had solemnly [a]testified and spoken [b]the
word of the Lord, they started back
to Jerusalem, and were [c]preaching
the gospel to many villages of the
[d]Samaritans.
26 But [a]an angel of the Lord spoke
to [b]Philip saying, "Arise and go
south to the road that descends

58 [a]Lev. 24:14, 16; Luke 4:29 [b]Deut. 13:9f.; 17:7; Acts 6:13 [c]Acts 22:20 [d]Acts 8:1; 22:20; 26:10
59 [a]Acts 9:14, 21; 22:16; Rom. 10:12, 13f.; 1 Cor. 1:2; 2 Tim. 2:22
60 [1]Or, *expired* [a]Luke 22:41 [b]Matt. 5:44; Luke 23:34 [c]Dan. 12:2; Matt. 27:52; John 11:11f.; Acts 13:36; 1 Cor. 15:6, 18, 20; 1 Thess. 4:13ff.; 2 Pet. 3:4
1 [a]Acts 7:58; 22:20; 26:10 [b]Acts 9:31 [c]Acts 8:4; 11:19 [d]Acts 1:8; 8:5, 14; 9:31
3 [a]Acts 9:1, 13, 21; 22:4, 19; 26:10f.; 1 Cor. 15:9; Gal. 1:13; Phil. 3:6; 1 Tim. 1:13 [b]James 2:6
4 [1]Or, *bringing the good tidings of* [a]Acts 8:1 [b]Acts 8:12; 15:35
5 [1]I.e., the Messiah [a]Acts 6:5; 8:26, 30
6 [1]Or, *attesting miracles*
7 [a]Mark 16:17 [b]Matt. 4:24
8 [a]John 4:40-42; Acts 8:39
9 [a]Acts 8:11; 13:6 [b]Acts 5:36
10 [a]Acts 14:11; 28:6
11 [a]Acts 8:9; 13:6
12 [a]Acts 1:3; 8:4 [b]Acts 2:38
13 [a]Acts 8:6 [b]Acts 19:11
14 [a]Acts 8:1 [b]Luke 22:8
15 [a]Acts 2:38; 19:2
16 [1]Lit., *into* [a]Matt. 28:19
17 [a]Mark 5:23; Acts 6:6 [b]Acts 2:4
20 [a]2 Kin. 5:16; Is. 55:1; Dan. 5:17; Matt. 10:8; Acts 2:38
21 [1]Or, *teaching;* lit., *word* [a]Deut. 10:9; 12:12; Eph. 5:5 [b]Ps. 78:37
23 [1]Or, *fetter* [a]Is. 58:6
25 [a]Luke 16:28 [b]Acts 13:12 [c]Acts 8:40 [d]Matt. 10:5
26 [a]Acts 5:19; 8:29 [b]Acts 8:5

from Jerusalem to [c]Gaza." (This is a
desert *road.*)
27 And he arose and went; and behold, [a]there was an Ethiopian eunuch, a court official of Candace,
queen of the Ethiopians, who was in
charge of all her treasure; and he
[b]had come to Jerusalem to worship.
28 And he was returning and sitting in his chariot, and was reading
the prophet Isaiah.
29 And [a]the Spirit said to Philip,
"Go up and join this chariot."
30 And when Philip had run up, he
heard him reading Isaiah the
prophet, and said, "Do you understand what you are reading?"
31 And he said, "Well, how could
I, unless someone guides me?" And
he invited Philip to come up and sit
with him.
32 Now the passage of Scripture
which he was reading was this:
"[a]HE WAS LED AS A SHEEP TO
SLAUGHTER;
AND AS A LAMB BEFORE ITS
SHEARER IS SILENT,
SO HE DOES NOT OPEN HIS
MOUTH.
33 "[a]IN HUMILIATION HIS JUDG-
MENT WAS TAKEN AWAY;
WHO SHALL RELATE HIS GEN-
ERATION?
FOR HIS LIFE IS REMOVED FROM
THE EARTH."
34 And the eunuch answered
Philip and said, "Please *tell me,* of
whom does the prophet say this? Of
himself, or of someone else?"
35 And Philip [a]opened his mouth,
and [b]beginning from this Scripture
he [c]preached Jesus to him.
36 And as they went along the
road they came to some water; and
the eunuch *said, "Look! Water!
[a]What prevents me from being baptized?"
37 [[1]And Philip said, "If you believe with all your heart, you may."
And he answered and said, "I believe that Jesus Christ is the Son of
God."]
38 And he ordered the chariot to
stop; and they both went down into
the water, Philip as well as the eunuch; and he baptized him.
39 And when they came up out of
the water, [a]the Spirit of the Lord
snatched Philip away; and the eunuch saw him no more, but went on
his way rejoicing.
40 But Philip found himself at
[a]Azotus; and as he passed through
he [b]kept preaching the gospel to all
the cities, until he came to [c]Caesa-
rea.

26 [c]Gen. 10:19
27 [a]Ps. 68:31; 87:4; Is. 56:3ff. [b]1 Kin. 8:41f.; John 12:20
29 [a]Acts 8:39; 10:19; 11:12; 13:2; 21:11; 28:25; Heb. 3:7
32 [a]Is. 53:7
33 [a]Is. 53:8f.
35 [a]Matt. 5:2 [b]Luke 24:27; Acts 17:2; 18:28; 28:23 [c]Acts 5:42
36 [a]Acts 10:47
37 [1]Many mss. do not contain this verse
39 [a]1 Kin. 18:12; 2 Kin. 2:16; Ezek. 3:12, 14; 8:3; 11:1, 24; 43:5; 2 Cor. 12:2
40 [a]Josh. 11:22; 1 Sam. 5:1 [b]Acts 8:25 [c]Acts 9:30; 10:1, 24; 11:11; 12:19; 18:22; 21:8, 16; 23:23, 33
1 [a]Acts 9:1-22; 22:3-16; 26:9-18 [b]Acts 8:3; 9:13-21
2 [a]Acts 9:14, 21; 22:5; 26:10 [b]Matt. 10:17 [c]Gen. 14:15; 2 Cor. 11:32; Gal. 1:17 [d]John 14:6; Acts 18:25f.; 19:9, 23; 22:4; 24:14, 22
3 [a]1 Cor. 15:8
4 [a]Acts 22:7
6 [a]Acts 9:16
7 [a]Acts 26:14 [b]Acts 22:9
8 [a]Acts 9:18; 22:11 [b]Gen. 14:15; 2 Cor. 11:32; Gal. 1:17
10 [a]Gen. 14:15; 2 Cor. 11:32; Gal. 1:17 [b]Acts 22:12 [c]Acts 10:3, 17, 19; 11:5; 12:9; 16:9f.
11 [a]Acts 9:30; 11:25; 21:39; 22:3
12 [1]Some mss. do not contain *in a vision* [a]Mark 5:23; Acts 6:6; 9:17
13 [a]Acts 8:3 [b]Acts 9:32, 41; 26:10; Rom 1:7; 15:25f., 31; 16:2, 15; 1 Cor. 1:2
14 [a]Acts 9:2, 21 [b]Acts 7:59
15 [a]Acts 13:2; Rom. 1:1; 9:23; Gal. 1:15; Eph. 3:7 [b]Acts 22:21; 26:17; Rom. 1:5; 11:13; 15:16; Gal. 1:16; 2:7ff.; Eph. 3:2, 8; 1 Tim. 2:7; 2 Tim. 4:17 [c]Acts 25:22f.; 26:1, 32; 2 Tim. 4:16
16 [a]Acts 20:23; 21:11 [4 and 13]; 1 Thess. 3:3; 2 Cor. 6:4f.; 11:23

CHAPTER 9

The Conversion of Saul

[a]NOW Saul, still [b]breathing threats
and murder against the disciples of
the Lord, went to the high priest,
2 and asked for [a]letters from him
to [b]the synagogues at [c]Damascus,
so that if he found any belonging to
[d]the Way, both men and women, he
might bring them bound to Jerusalem.
3 And it came about that as he
journeyed, he was approaching Damascus, and [a]suddenly a light from
heaven flashed around him;
4 and [a]he fell to the ground, and
heard a voice saying to him, "Saul,
Saul, why are you persecuting Me?"
5 And he said, "Who art Thou,
Lord?" And He *said,* "I am Jesus
whom you are persecuting,
6 but rise, and enter the city, and
[a]it shall be told you what you must
do."
7 And the men who traveled with
him [a]stood speechless, [b]hearing the
voice, but seeing no one.
8 And Saul got up from the
ground, and [a]though his eyes were
open, he could see nothing; and
leading him by the hand, they
brought him into [b]Damascus.
9 And he was three days without
sight, and neither ate nor drank.
10 Now there was a certain disciple at [a]Damascus, named [b]Ananias;
and the Lord said to him in [c]a vision,
"Ananias." And he said, "Behold,
here am I, Lord."
11 And the Lord *said* to him,
"Arise and go to the street called
Straight, and inquire at the house of
Judas for a man from [a]Tarsus
named Saul, for behold, he is praying,
12 and he has seen [1]in a vision a
man named Ananias come in and
[a]lay his hands on him, so that he
might regain his sight."
13 But Ananias answered, "Lord, I
have heard from many about this
man, [a]how much harm he did to
[b]Thy saints at Jerusalem;
14 and here he [a]has authority from
the chief priests to bind all who [b]call
upon Thy name."
15 But the Lord said to him, "Go,
for [a]he is a chosen instrument of
Mine, to bear My name before [b]the
Gentiles and [c]kings and the sons of
Israel;
16 for [a]I will show him how much
he must suffer for My name's sake."
17 And Ananias departed and en-

tered the house, and after [a]laying
his hands on him said, "[b]Brother
Saul, the Lord Jesus, who appeared
to you on the road by which you
were coming, has sent me so that
you may regain your sight, and be
[c]filled with the Holy Spirit."
18 And immediately there fell
from his eyes something like scales,
and he regained his sight, and he
arose and was baptized;
19 and he took food and was
strengthened.

Saul Begins to Preach Christ

Now [a]for several days he was with
[b]the disciples who were at Damascus,
20 and immediately he *began* to
proclaim Jesus [a]in the synagogues,
[1]saying, "He is [b]the Son of God."
21 And all those hearing him continued to be amazed, and were saying, "Is this not he who in Jerusalem
[a]destroyed those who [b]called on this
name, and *who* had come here for
the purpose of bringing them bound
before the chief priests?"
22 But Saul kept increasing in
strength and confounding the Jews
who lived at Damascus by proving
that this *Jesus* is the [1]Christ.
23 And when [a]many days had
elapsed, [b]the Jews plotted together
to do away with him,
24 but [a]their plot became known
to Saul. And [b]they were also watching the gates day and night so that
they might put him to death;
25 but his disciples took him by
night, and let him down through *an*
opening in the wall, lowering him in
a large basket.
26 And [a]when he had come to Jerusalem, he was trying to associate
with the disciples; and they were all
afraid of him, not believing that he
was a disciple.
27 But [a]Barnabas took hold of him
and brought him to the apostles and
described to them how he had [b]seen
the Lord on the road, and that He
had talked to him, and how [c]at Damascus he had [d]spoken out boldly in
the name of Jesus.
28 And he was with them moving
about freely in Jerusalem, [a]speaking
out boldly in the name of the Lord.
29 And he was talking and arguing
with the [a]Hellenistic *Jews;* but they
were attempting to put him to
death.
30 But when [a]the brethren learned
of it, they brought him down to
[b]Caesarea and [c]sent him away to
[d]Tarsus.
31 So [a]the church throughout all
Judea and Galilee and Samaria enjoyed peace, being built up; and,
going on in the fear of the Lord and
in the comfort of the Holy Spirit, it
continued to increase.

Peter's Ministry

32 Now it came about that as Peter
was traveling through all *those*
parts, he came down also to [a]the
saints who lived at [b]Lydda.
33 And there he found a certain
man named Aeneas, who had been
bedridden eight years, for he was
paralyzed.
34 And Peter said to him, "Aeneas,
Jesus Christ heals you; arise, and
make your bed." And immediately
he arose.
35 And all who lived at [a]Lydda and
[b]Sharon saw him, and they [c]turned
to the Lord.
36 Now in [a]Joppa there was a certain disciple named Tabitha (which
translated *in Greek* is called [1]Dor-
cas); this woman was abounding
with deeds of kindness and charity,
which she continually did.
37 And it came about at that time
that she fell sick and died; and when
they had washed her body, they laid
it in an [a]upper room.
38 And since Lydda was near
[a]Joppa, [b]the disciples, having heard
that Peter was there, sent two men
to him, entreating him, "Do not delay to come to us."
39 And Peter arose and went with
them. And when he had come, they
brought him into the [a]upper room;
and all the [b]widows stood beside
him weeping, and showing all the
tunics and garments that Dorcas
used to make while she was with
them.
40 But Peter [a]sent them all out and
[b]knelt down and prayed, and turning to the body, he said, "[c]Tabitha,
arise." And she opened her eyes,
and when she saw Peter, she sat up.
41 And he gave her his hand and
raised her up; and calling [a]the
[1]saints and [b]widows, he presented
her alive.
42 And it became known all over
[a]Joppa, and [b]many believed in the
Lord.
43 And it came about that he
stayed many days in [a]Joppa with [b]a
certain tanner, Simon.

Chapter 10

Cornelius' Vision

NOW *there was* a certain man at
[a]Caesarea named Cornelius, a cen-

17 [a]Mark 5:23; Acts 6:6; 9:12 [b]Acts 22:13 [c]Acts 2:4
19 [a]Acts 26:20 [b]Acts 9:26, 38; 11:26
20 [1]Lit., *that* [a]Acts 13:5, 14; 14:1; 16:13; 17:2, 10; 18:4, 19; 19:8; 28:17 [b]Matt. 4:3; Acts 9:22; 13:33
21 [a]Acts 8:3; 9:13; Gal. 1:13, 23 [b]Acts 9:14
22 [1]I.e., Messiah
23 [a]Gal. 1:17, 18 [b]1 Thess. 2:16
24 [a]Acts 20:3, 19; 23:12, 30; 25:3 [b]2 Cor. 11:32f.
26 [a]Acts 22:17-20; 26:20
27 [a]Acts 4:36 [b]Acts 9:3-6 [c]Acts 9:20, 22 [d]Acts 4:13, 29; 9:29
28 [a]Acts 4:13, 29; 9:29
29 [a]Acts 6:1
30 [a]Acts 1:15 [b]Acts 8:40 [c]Gal. 1:21 [d]Acts 9:11
31 [a]Acts 5:11; 8:1; 16:5
32 [a]Acts 9:13 [b]1 Chr. 8:12; Ezra 2:33; Neh. 7:37; 11:35
35 [a]1 Chr. 8:12; Ezra 2:33; Neh. 7:37; 11:35 [b]1 Chr. 5:16; 27:29; Is. 33:9; 35:2; 65:10 [c]Acts 2:47; 9:42; 11:21
36 [1]Or, *Gazelle* [a]Josh. 19:46; 2 Chr. 2:16; Ezra 3:7; Jon. 1:3; Acts 9:38, 42f.; 10:5, 8, 23, 32; 11:5, 13
37 [a]Acts 1:13; 9:39
38 [a]Josh. 19:46; 2 Chr. 2:16; Ezra 3:7; Jon. 1:3; Acts 9:36, 42f.; 10:5, 8, 23, 32; 11:5, 13 [b]Acts 11:26
39 [a]Acts 1:13; 9:37 [b]Acts 6:1
40 [a]Matt. 9:25 [b]Luke 22:41; Acts 7:60 [c]Mark 5:41
41 [1]Note v. 32 [a]Acts 9:13 [b]Acts 6:1
42 [a]Josh. 19:46; 2 Chr. 2:16; Jon. 1:3; Acts 9:38, 42f.; 10:5, 8, 23, 32; 11:5, 13 [b]Acts 9:35
43 [a]Josh. 19:46; 2 Chr. 2:16; Ezra 3:7; Jon. 1:3; Acts 9:38, 42f.; 10:5, 8, 23, 32; 11:13, 15 [b]Acts 10:6
1 [a]Acts 8:40; 10:24

turion of what was [b]called the Italian [1]cohort,

2 a devout man, and [a]one who feared God with all his household, and [b]gave many alms to the *Jewish* people, and prayed to God continually.

3 About [a]the [1]ninth hour of the day he clearly saw [b]in a vision [c]an angel of God who had *just* come in to him, and said to him, "Cornelius!"

4 And [a]fixing his gaze upon him and being much alarmed, he said, "What is it, Lord?" And he said to him, "Your prayers and alms [b]have ascended [c]as a memorial before God.

5 "And now dispatch *some* men to [a]Joppa, and send for a man *named* Simon, who is also called Peter;

6 he is staying with a certain tanner *named* [a]Simon, whose house is by the sea."

7 And when the angel who was speaking to him had departed, he summoned two of his servants and a devout soldier of those who were in constant attendance upon him,

8 and after he had explained everything to them, he sent them to [a]Joppa.

9 And on the next day, as they were on their way, and approaching the city, [a]Peter went up on [b]the housetop about [c]the [1]sixth hour to pray.

10 And he became hungry, and was desiring to eat; but while they were making preparations, he [a]fell into a trance;

11 and he *beheld [a]the sky opened up, and a certain object like a great sheet coming down, lowered by four corners to the ground,

12 and there were in it all *kinds of* four-footed animals and [1]crawling creatures of the earth and birds of the [2]air.

13 And a voice came to him, "Arise, Peter, kill and eat!"

14 But Peter said, "By no means, [a]Lord, for [b]I have never eaten anything unholy and unclean."

15 And again a voice *came* to him a second time, "[a]What God has cleansed, no *longer* consider unholy."

16 And this happened three times; and immediately the [1]object was taken up into the [2]sky.

17 Now while Peter was greatly perplexed in mind as to what [a]the vision which he had seen might be, behold, [b]the men who had been sent by Cornelius, having asked directions for Simon's house, appeared at the gate;

18 and calling out, they were asking whether Simon, who was also called Peter, was staying there.

19 And while Peter was reflecting on [a]the vision, [b]the Spirit said to him, "Behold, [1]three men are looking for you.

20 "But arise, go downstairs, and [a]accompany them without misgivings; for I have sent them Myself."

21 And Peter went down to the men and said, "Behold, I am the one you are looking for; what is the reason for which you have come?"

22 And they said, "Cornelius, a centurion, a righteous and [a]God-fearing man well spoken of by the entire nation of the Jews, [b]was *divinely* directed by a [c]holy angel to send for you *to come* to his house and hear [d]a [1]message from you."

23 And so he invited them in and gave them lodging.

Peter at Caesarea

And on the next day he arose and went away with them, and [a]some of [b]the brethren from [c]Joppa accompanied him.

24 And on the following day he entered [a]Caesarea. Now Cornelius was waiting for them, and had called together his relatives and close friends.

25 And when it came about that Peter entered, Cornelius met him, and fell at his feet and [1a]worshiped *him.*

26 But Peter raised him up, saying, "[a]Stand up; I too am *just* a man."

27 And as he talked with him, he entered, and found [a]many people assembled.

28 And he said to them, "You yourselves know how [a]unlawful it is for a man who is a Jew to associate with a foreigner or to visit him; and *yet* [b]God has shown me that I should not call any man [1]unholy or unclean.

29 "That is why I came without even raising any objection when I was sent for. And so I ask for what reason you have sent for me."

30 And Cornelius said, "[a]Four days ago to this hour, I was praying in my house during [b]the [1]ninth hour; and behold, [c]a man stood before me in shining garments,

31 and he *said, 'Cornelius, your prayer has been heard and your alms have been remembered before God.

32 'Send therefore to [a]Joppa and invite Simon, who is also called Peter, to come to you; he is [1]staying at

1 [1]Or, *battalion* [b]Matt. 27:27; Mark 15:16; John 18:3, 12; Acts 21:31; 27:1
2 [a]Acts 10:22, 35; 13:16, 26 [b]Luke 7:4f.
3 [1]I.e., 3 p.m. [a]Acts 3:1 [b]Acts 9:10; 10:17, 19 [c]Acts 5:19
4 [a]Acts 3:4 [b]Rev. 8:4 [c]Matt. 26:13; Phil. 4:18; Heb. 6:10
5 [a]Acts 9:36
6 [a]Acts 9:43
8 [a]Acts 9:36
9 [1]I.e., noon [a]Acts 10:9-32; 11:5-14 [b]Jer. 19:13; 32:29; Zeph. 1:5; Matt. 24:17 [c]Ps. 55:17; Acts 10:3
10 [a]Acts 11:5; 22:17
11 [a]John 1:51
12 [1]Or possibly, *reptiles* [2]Or, *heaven*
14 [a]Matt. 8:2ff.; John 4:11ff.; Acts 9:5; 22:8 [b]Lev. 11:20-25; Deut. 14:4-20; Ezek. 4:14; Dan. 1:8; Acts 10:28
15 [a]Matt. 15:11; Mark 7:19; Rom. 14:14; 1 Cor. 10:25ff.; 1 Tim. 4:4f.; Titus 1:15
16 [1]Or, *vessel* [2]Or, *heaven*
17 [a]Acts 10:3 [b]Acts 10:8
19 [1]One early ms. reads, *two* [a]Acts 10:3 [b]Acts 8:29
20 [a]Acts 15:7-9
22 [1]Lit., *words* [a]Acts 10:2 [b]Matt. 2:12 [c]Mark 8:38; Luke 9:26; Rev. 14:10 [d]Acts 11:14
23 [a]Acts 10:45; 11:12 [b]Acts 1:15 [c]Acts 9:36
24 [a]Acts 8:40; 10:1
25 [1]Or, *prostrated himself in reverence* [a]Matt. 8:2
26 [a]Acts 14:15; Rev. 19:10; 22:8f.
27 [a]Acts 10:24
28 [1]Or, *profane;* lit., *common* [a]John 4:9; 18:28; Acts 11:3 [b]Acts 10:14f., 35; 15:9
30 [1]I.e., 3 to 4 p.m. [a]Acts 10:9, 22f. [b]Acts 3:1; 10:3 [c]Acts 10:3-6, 30-32
32 [1]Or, *lodging* [a]John 4:9; 18:28; Acts 11:3

the house of Simon *the* tanner by the sea.'

33"And so I sent to you immediately, and you have been kind enough to come. Now then, we are all here present before God to hear all that you have been commanded by the Lord."

34 And [a]opening his mouth, Peter said:

Gentiles Hear Good News

"I most certainly understand *now* that [b]God is not one to show partiality,

35 but [a]in every nation the man who [b]fears Him and does what is right, is welcome to Him.

36"[1]The word which He sent to the sons of Israel, [a]preaching [b]peace through Jesus Christ (He is [c]Lord of all)—

37 you yourselves know the thing which took place throughout all Judea, starting from Galilee, after the baptism which John proclaimed.

38"*You know of* [a]Jesus of Nazareth, how God [b]anointed Him with the Holy Spirit and with power, [c]and *how* He went about doing good, and healing all who were oppressed by the devil; for [d]God was with Him.

39"And we are [a]witnesses of all the things He did both in the land of the Jews and in Jerusalem. And they also [b]put Him to death by hanging Him on a cross.

40"[a]God raised Him up on the third day, and granted that He should become visible,

41 [a]not to all the people, but to [b]witnesses who were chosen beforehand by God, *that is,* to us, [c]who ate and drank with Him after He arose from the dead.

42"And He [a]ordered us to preach to the people, and solemnly to [b]testify that this is the One who has been [c]appointed by God as [d]Judge of the living and the dead.

43"Of Him [a]all the prophets bear witness that through [b]His name every one who believes in Him receives forgiveness of sins."

44 While Peter was still speaking these words, [a]the Holy Spirit fell upon all those who were listening to the message.

45 And [a]all the [1]circumcised believers who had come with Peter were amazed, because the gift of the Holy Spirit had been [b]poured out upon the Gentiles also.

46 For they were hearing them [a]speaking with tongues and exalting God. Then Peter [b]answered,

34 [a]Matt. 5:2 [b]Deut. 10:17; 2 Chr. 19:7; Rom. 2:11; Gal. 2:6; Eph. 6:9; Col. 3:25; 1 Pet. 1:17
35 [a]Acts 10:28 [b]Acts 10:2
36 [1]Or, *He sent the word to* [a]Acts 13:32 [b]Luke 1:79; 2:14; Rom. 5:1; Eph. 2:17 [c]Matt. 28:18; Acts 2:36; Rom. 10:12
38 [a]Acts 2:22 [b]Acts 4:26 [c]Matt. 4:23 [d]John 3:2
39 [a]Luke 24:48; Acts 10:41 [b]Acts 5:30
40 [a]Acts 2:24
41 [a]John 14:19, 22; 15:27 [b]Luke 24:48; Acts 10:39 [c]Luke 24:43; Acts 1:4 marg.
42 [a]Acts 1:2 [b]Luke 16:28 [c]Luke 22:22 [d]John 5:22, 27; Acts 17:31; 2 Tim. 4:1; 1 Pet. 4:5
43 [a]Acts 3:18 [b]Luke 24:47; Acts 2:38; 4:12
44 [a]Acts 11:15
45 [1]Lit., *believers from among the circumcision;* i.e., Jewish Christians [a]Acts 10:23 [b]Acts 2:33, 38
46 [a]Mark 16:17; Acts 2:4; 19:6 [b]Acts 3:12
47 [a]Acts 8:36 [b]Acts 2:4; 10:44f.; 11:17; 15:8
48 [a]1 Cor. 1:14-17 [b]Acts 2:38; 8:16; 19:5
1 [a]Acts 1:15
2 [1]Lit., *those of the circumcision;* i.e., Jewish Christians [a]Acts 10:45
3 [a]Matt. 9:11; Acts 10:28; Gal. 2:12
4 [a]Luke 1:3
5 [a]Acts 10:9-32; 11:5-14 [b]Acts 9:10
6 [1]Lit., *and I saw* [2]Or possibly, *reptiles*
9 [a]Acts 10:15
11 [a]Acts 8:40
12 [1]Or, *without making any distinction* [a]Acts 8:29 [b]Acts 15:9; Rom. 3:22 [c]Acts 10:23
13 [1]Or, *after he had stood in his house and said*
14 [a]Acts 10:22 [b]John 4:53; Acts 10:2; 16:15, 31-34; 18:8; 1 Cor. 1:16

47"[a]Surely no one can refuse the water for these to be baptized who [b]have received the Holy Spirit just as we *did,* can he?"

48 And he [a]ordered them to be baptized [b]in the name of Jesus Christ. Then they asked him to stay on for a few days.

Chapter 11

Peter Reports at Jerusalem

NOW the apostles and [a]the brethren who were throughout Judea heard that the Gentiles also had received the word of God.

2 And when Peter came up to Jerusalem, [1a]those who were circumcised took issue with him,

3 saying, "[a]You went to uncircumcised men and ate with them."

4 But Peter began *speaking* and *proceeded* to explain to them [a]in orderly sequence, saying,

5"[a]I was in the city of Joppa praying; and in a trance I saw [b]a vision, a certain object coming down like a great sheet lowered by four corners from the sky; and it came right down to me,

6 and when I had fixed my gaze upon it and was observing it [1]I saw the four-footed animals of the earth and the wild beasts and the [2]crawling creatures and the birds of the air.

7"And I also heard a voice saying to me, 'Arise, Peter; kill and eat.'

8"But I said, 'By no means, Lord, for nothing unholy or unclean has ever entered my mouth.'

9"But a voice from heaven answered a second time, '[a]What God has cleansed, no longer consider unholy.'

10"And this happened three times, and everything was drawn back up into the sky.

11"And behold, at that moment three men appeared before the house in which we were *staying,* having been sent to me from [a]Caesarea.

12"And [a]the Spirit told me to go with them [1b]without misgivings. And [c]these six brethren also went with me, and we entered the man's house.

13"And he reported to us how he had seen the angel [1]standing in his house, and saying, 'Send to Joppa, and have Simon, who is also called Peter, brought here;

14 and he shall speak [a]words to you by which you will be saved, you and [b]all your household.'

15 "And as I began to speak, [a]the Holy Spirit fell upon them, just [b]as *He did* upon us at the beginning.

16 "And I remembered the word of the Lord, how He used to say, '[a]John baptized with water, but you shall be baptized with the Holy Spirit.'

17 "If [a]God therefore gave to them the same gift as *He gave* to us also after believing in the Lord Jesus Christ, [b]who was I that I could stand in God's way?"

18 And when they heard this, they quieted down, and [a]glorified God, saying, "Well then, God has granted to the Gentiles also the [b]repentance *that leads* to life."

The Church at Antioch

19 [a]So then those who were scattered because of the persecution that arose in connection with Stephen made their way to [b]Phoenicia and [c]Cyprus and [d]Antioch, speaking the word to no one except to Jews alone.

20 But there were some of them, men of [a]Cyprus and [b]Cyrene, who came to [c]Antioch and *began* speaking to the [1d]Greeks also, [e]preaching the Lord Jesus.

21 And [a]the hand of the Lord was with them, and [b]a large number who believed turned to the Lord.

22 And the news about them reached the ears of the church at Jerusalem, and they sent [a]Barnabas off to [b]Antioch.

23 Then when he had come and witnessed [a]the grace of God, he rejoiced and *began* to encourage them all with resolute heart to remain *true* to the Lord;

24 for he was a good man, and [a]full of the Holy Spirit and of faith. And [b]considerable numbers were brought to the Lord.

25 And he left for [a]Tarsus to look for Saul;

26 and when he had found him, he brought him to [a]Antioch. And it came about that for an entire year they met with the church, and taught considerable numbers; and [b]the disciples were first called [c]Christians in [a]Antioch.

27 Now at this time [a]some prophets [b]came down from Jerusalem to [c]Antioch.

28 And one of them named [a]Agabus stood up and *began* to indicate by the Spirit that there would certainly be a great famine [b]all over the world. And this took place in the *reign* of [c]Claudius.

29 And in the proportion that any of [a]the disciples had means, each of them determined to send *a contribution* for the relief of [b]the brethren living in Judea.

30 [a]And this they did, sending it in charge of [b]Barnabas and Saul to the [c]elders.

Chapter 12

Peter's Arrest and Deliverance

NOW about that time [1]Herod the king laid hands on some who belonged to the church, in order to mistreat them.

2 And he [a]had James the brother of John [b]put to death with a sword.

3 And when he saw that it [a]pleased the Jews, he proceeded to arrest Peter also. Now it was during [b]the days of *the Feast of* Unleavened Bread.

4 And when he had seized him, he put him in prison, delivering him to four [a]squads of soldiers to guard him, intending after [b]the Passover to bring him out before the people.

5 So Peter was kept in the prison, but prayer for him was being made fervently by the church to God.

6 And on the very night when Herod was about to bring him forward, Peter was sleeping between two soldiers, [a]bound with two chains; and guards in front of the door were watching over the prison.

7 And behold, [a]an angel of the Lord suddenly [b]appeared, and a light shone in the cell; and he struck Peter's side and roused him, saying, "Get up quickly." And [c]his chains fell off his hands.

8 And the angel said to him, "Gird yourself and put on your sandals." And he did so. And he *said to him, "Wrap your cloak around you and follow me."

9 And he went out and continued to follow, and he did not know that what was being done by the angel was real, but thought he was seeing [a]a vision.

10 And when they had passed the first and second guard, they came to the iron gate that leads into the city, which [a]opened for them by itself; and they went out and went along one street; and immediately the angel departed from him.

11 And when Peter [a]came to himself, he said, "Now I know for sure that [b]the Lord has sent forth His angel and rescued me from the hand of Herod and from all that the Jewish people were expecting."

---

15 [a]Acts 10:44 [b]Acts 2:4
16 [a]Acts 1:5
17 [a]Acts 10:45, 47 [b]Acts 5:39
18 [a]Matt. 9:8 [b]2 Cor. 7:10
19 [a]Acts 8:1, 4 [b]Acts 15:3; 21:2 [c]Acts 4:36 [d]Acts 6:5; 18:22
20 [1]Some mss. read, *Greek-speaking Jews* [a]Acts 4:36 [b]Matt. 27:32; Acts 2:10; 6:9; 13:1 [c]Acts 6:5; 11:19, 22, 27; 13:1; 14:26; 15:22f., 30, 35; 18:22; Gal. 2:11 [d]John 7:35 [e]Acts 5:42
21 [a]Luke 1:66 [b]Acts 2:47
22 [a]Acts 4:36 [b]Acts 6:5; 11:19, 20, 27; 18:22; Gal. 2:11
23 [a]Acts 13:43
24 [a]Acts 2:4 [b]Acts 2:47; 5:14; 11:21
25 [a]Acts 9:11
26 [a]Acts 6:5; 11:20; 14:26; 15:22f., 30; 18:22; Gal. 2:11 [b]John 2:2; Acts 1:15; 6:1f.; 11:29; 13:52 [c]Acts 26:28
27 [a]Luke 11:49; Acts 2:17; 13:1; 1 Cor. 12:10, 28f. [b]Acts 18:22 [c]Acts 6:5; 11:20, 22, 26; 13:1; 14:26; 15:22f., 30, 35; 18:22; Gal. 2:11
28 [a]Acts 21:10 [b]Matt. 24:14 [c]Acts 18:2
29 [a]John 2:2; Acts 1:15; 6:1f.; 9:19, 25; 13:52; 14:20, 22, 28 [b]Acts 11:1
30 [a]Acts 12:25 [b]Acts 4:36 [c]Acts 14:23; 16:4; 20:17; 21:18; 1 Tim. 5:17, 19; Titus 1:5; James 5:14; 1 Pet. 5:1; 2 John 1; 3 John 1
1 [1]I.e., Herod Agrippa I
2 [a]Matt. 4:21; 20:23 [b]Mark 10:39
3 [a]Acts 24:27; 25:9 [b]Ex. 12:15; 23:15; Acts 20:6
4 [a]John 19:23 [b]Mark 14:1; Acts 12:3
6 [a]Acts 21:33
7 [a]Acts 5:19 [b]Luke 2:9; 24:4 [c]Acts 16:26
9 [a]Acts 9:10
10 [a]Acts 5:19
11 [a]Luke 15:17 [b]Dan. 3:28; 6:22

12 And when he realized *this,* he went to the house of Mary, the mother of [a]John who was also called Mark, where many were gathered together and [b]were praying.

13 And when he knocked at the door of the gate, [a]a servant-girl named Rhoda came to answer.

14 And when she recognized Peter's voice, [a]because of her joy she did not open the gate, but ran in and announced that Peter was standing in front of the gate.

15 And they said to her, "You are out of your mind!" But she kept insisting that it was so. And they kept saying, "It is [a]his angel."

16 But Peter continued knocking; and when they had opened *the door,* they saw him and were amazed.

17 But [a]motioning to them with his hand to be silent, he described to them how the Lord had led him out of the prison. And he said, "Report these things to [1b]James and [c]the brethren." And he departed and went to another place.

18 Now when day came, there was no small disturbance among the soldiers *as to* what could have become of Peter.

19 And when Herod had searched for him and had not found him, he examined the guards and ordered that they [a]be led away *to execution.* And he went down from Judea to [b]Caesarea and was spending time there.

Death of Herod

20 Now he was very angry with the people of [a]Tyre and Sidon; and with one accord they came to him, and having won over Blastus the king's chamberlain, they were asking for peace, because [b]their country was fed by the king's country.

21 And on an appointed day Herod, having put on his royal apparel, took his seat on the rostrum and *began* delivering an address to them.

22 And the people kept crying out, "The voice of a god and not of a man!"

23 And immediately [a]an angel of the Lord struck him because he did not give God the glory, and he was eaten by worms and [1]died.

24 But [a]the word of the Lord continued to grow and to be multiplied.

25 And [a]Barnabas and [a]Saul returned [1]from Jerusalem [b]when they had fulfilled their [2]mission, taking along with *them* [c]John, who was also called Mark.

12 [a]Acts 12:25; 13:5, 13; 15:37, 39; Col. 4:10; 2 Tim. 4:11; Philem. 24; 1 Pet. 5:13 [b]Acts 12:5
13 [a]John 18:16f.
14 [a]Luke 24:41
15 [a]Matt. 18:10
17 [1]Or, *Jacob* [a]Acts 13:16; 19:33; 21:40 [b]Mark 6:3; Acts 15:13; 21:18; 1 Cor. 15:7; Gal. 1:19; 2:9, 12 [c]Acts 1:15
19 [a]Acts 16:27; 27:42 [b]Acts 8:40
20 [a]Matt. 11:21 [b]1 Kin. 5:11; Ezra 3:7; Ezek. 27:17
23 [1]Lit., *breathed his last* [a]2 Sam. 24:16; 2 Kin. 19:35; Acts 5:19
24 [a]Acts 6:7; 19:20
25 [1]Some ancient mss. read, *to Jerusalem* [2]Lit., *ministry* [a]Acts 4:36; 13:1ff. [b]Acts 11:30 [c]Acts 12:12
1 [a]Acts 11:19 [b]Acts 11:26 [c]Acts 11:27; 15:32; 19:6; 21:9; 1 Cor. 11:4f.; 13:2, 8f.; 14:29, 32, 37 [d]Rom. 12:6f.; 1 Cor. 12:28f.; Eph. 4:11; James 3:1 [e]Acts 4:36; 13:1ff. [f]Matt. 27:32; Acts 11:20 [g]Matt. 14:1
2 [a]Acts 8:29; 13:4 [b]Acts 4:36; 13:1ff. [c]Acts 9:15
3 [a]Acts 1:24 [b]Acts 6:6 [c]Acts 13:4; 14:26
4 [a]Acts 13:2f. [b]Acts 4:36
5 [a]Acts 9:20; 13:14 [b]Acts 12:12
6 [a]Acts 8:9 [b]Matt. 7:15
7 [a]Acts 13:8, 12; 18:12; 19:38
8 [a]Acts 8:9 [b]Acts 13:7, 12; 18:12; 19:38 [c]Acts 6:7
9 [a]Acts 2:4; 4:8
10 [a]Matt. 13:38; John 8:44 [b]Hos. 14:9; 2 Pet. 2:15
11 [a]Ex. 9:3; 1 Sam. 5:6f.; Job 19:21; Ps. 32:4; Heb. 10:31
12 [a]Acts 13:7, 8; 18:12; 19:38 [b]Acts 8:25; 13:49; 15:35f.; 19:10, 20
13 [a]Acts 13:6 [b]Acts 14:25 [c]Acts 2:10; 14:24; 15:38; 27:5 [d]Acts 12:12

Chapter 13

First Missionary Journey

NOW there were at [a]Antioch, in the [b]church that was *there,* [c]prophets and [d]teachers: [e]Barnabas, and Simeon who was called Niger, and Lucius of [f]Cyrene, and Manaen who had been brought up with [g]Herod the tetrarch, and [e]Saul.

2 And while they were ministering to the Lord and fasting, [a]the Holy Spirit said, "Set apart for Me [b]Barnabas and Saul for [c]the work to which I have called them."

3 Then, when they had fasted and [a]prayed and [b]laid their hands on them, [c]they sent them away.

4 So, being [a]sent out by the Holy Spirit, they went down to Seleucia and from there they sailed to [b]Cyprus.

5 And when they reached Salamis, they *began* to proclaim the word of God in [a]the synagogues of the Jews; and they also had [b]John as their helper.

6 And when they had gone through the whole island as far as Paphos, they found a certain [a]magician, a Jewish [b]false prophet whose name was Bar-Jesus,

7 who was with the [a]proconsul, Sergius Paulus, a man of intelligence. This man summoned Barnabas and Saul and sought to hear the word of God.

8 But Elymas the [a]magician (for thus his name is translated) was opposing them, seeking to turn the [b]proconsul away from [c]the faith.

9 But Saul, who was also *known as* Paul, [a]filled with the Holy Spirit, fixed his gaze upon him,

10 and said, "You who are full of all deceit and fraud, you [a]son of the devil, you enemy of all righteousness, will you not cease to make crooked [b]the straight ways of the Lord?

11 "And now, behold, [a]the hand of the Lord is upon you, and you will be blind and not see the sun for a time." And immediately a mist and a darkness fell upon him, and he went about seeking those who would lead him by the hand.

12 Then the [a]proconsul believed when he saw what had happened, being amazed at [b]the teaching of the Lord.

13 Now Paul and his companions put out to sea from [a]Paphos and came to [b]Perga in [c]Pamphylia; and [d]John left them and returned to Jerusalem.

14 But going on from Perga, they
arrived at [a]Pisidian [b]Antioch, and
on [c]the Sabbath day they went into
[d]the synagogue and sat down.
15 And after [a]the reading of the
Law and [b]the Prophets [c]the synagogue officials sent to them, saying,
"Brethren, if you have any word of
exhortation for the people, say it."
16 And Paul stood up, and [a]mo-
tioning with his hand, he said,
"**M**en of Israel, and [b]you who fear
God, listen:
17 "The God of this people Israel
[a]chose our fathers, and made the
people great during their stay in the
land of Egypt, and with an uplifted
arm He led them out from it.
18 "And for [a]a period of about forty
years [b]He [1]put up with them in the
wilderness.
19 "And [a]when He had destroyed
[b]seven nations in the land of Canaan, He [c]distributed their land as
an inheritance—*all of which took*
[d]about four hundred and fifty years.
20 "And after these things He [a]gave
them judges until [b]Samuel the
prophet.
21 "And then they [a]asked for a
king, and God gave them [b]Saul the
son of Kish, a man of the tribe of
Benjamin, for forty years.
22 "And after He had [a]removed
him, He raised up David to be their
king, concerning whom He also testified and said, 'I have found [b]David
the son of Jesse, a man after My
heart, who will do all My will.'
23 "[a]From the offspring of this
man, [b]according to promise, God
has brought to Israel [c]a Savior, Jesus,
24 after [a]John had proclaimed before His coming a baptism of repentance to all the people of Israel.
25 "And while John [a]was complet-
ing his course, [b]he kept saying,
'What do you suppose that I am? I
am not *He*. But behold, one is coming after me the sandals of whose
feet I am not worthy to untie.'
26 "Brethren, sons of Abraham's
family, and those among you who
fear God, to us the word of [a]this salvation is sent out.
27 "For those who live in Jerusalem, and their [a]rulers, [b]recognizing
neither Him nor the utterances of
[c]the prophets which are [d]read every
Sabbath, fulfilled *these* by con-
demning *Him*.
28 "And though they found no
ground for *putting Him to* death,
they [a]asked Pilate that He be executed.

14 [a]Acts 14:24 [b]2 Tim. 3:11 [c]Acts 17:2; 18:4 [d]Acts 9:20; 13:5
15 [a]Acts 15:21 [b]Acts 13:27 [c]Mark 5:22
16 [a]Acts 12:17 [b]Acts 10:2; 13:26
17 [a]Ex. 6:1, 6; 13:14, 16; Deut. 7:6-8; Acts 7:17ff.
18 [1]Or, *bore them up in His arms as a nurse in the wilderness* [a]Acts 7:36 [b]Deut. 1:31
19 [a]Acts 7:45 [b]Deut. 7:1 [c]Josh. 19:51; Ps. 78:55 [d]Judg. 11:26; 1 Kin. 6:1
20 [a]Judg. 2:16 [b]Acts 3:24
21 [a]1 Sam. 8:5 [b]1 Sam. 9:1f.; 10:1
22 [a]1 Sam. 15:23, 26, 28; 16:1, 13 [b]1 Sam. 13:14; Ps. 89:20; Acts 7:46
23 [a]Matt. 1:1 [b]Acts 13:32f. [c]Luke 2:11
24 [a]Mark 1:1-4; Acts 1:22; 19:4
25 [a]Acts 20:24 [b]Matt. 3:11; Mark 1:7; Luke 3:16
26 [a]John 6:68; Acts 4:12; 5:20
27 [a]Luke 23:13 [b]Acts 3:17 [c]Luke 24:27 [d]Acts 13:15
28 [a]Acts 3:14
29 [a]Acts 26:22 [b]Luke 23:53 [c]Acts 5:30
30 [a]Acts 2:24
31 [a]Acts 1:11 [b]Luke 24:48
32 [a]Acts 5:42; 14:15 [b]Acts 13:23; 26:6; Rom. 1:2
33 [1]Or, *to us their children* [a]Acts 2:24; 13:30, 34, 37 [b]Ps. 2:7
34 [a]Acts 2:24 [b]Is. 55:3
35 [a]Ps. 16:10
36 [a]Acts 2:29 [b]Acts 13:22; 20:27 [c]1 Kin. 2:10
37 [a]Acts 2:24; 13:30
38 [a]Luke 24:47
39 [1]In the Greek text the remainder of this v. is part of v. 38 [a]Acts 10:43; Rom. 3:28; 10:4
40 [a]Luke 24:44; John 6:45
41 [a]Hab. 1:5
42 [a]Acts 13:14
43 [1]I.e., Gentile converts to Judaism [a]Acts 13:50; 18:7 [b]Matt. 23:15 [c]Acts 11:23

29 "And when they had [a]carried out
all that was written concerning
Him, [b]they took Him down from
[c]the cross and laid Him in a tomb.
30 "But God [a]raised Him from the
dead;
31 and for many days He appeared
to those who came up with Him
[a]from Galilee to Jerusalem, the very
ones who are now [b]His witnesses to
the people.
32 "And we [a]preach to you the
good news of [b]the promise made to
the fathers,
33 that God has fulfilled this *promise* [1]to our children in that He
[a]raised up Jesus, as it is also written
in the second Psalm, '[b]THOU ART MY
SON; TODAY I HAVE BEGOTTEN THEE.'
34 "*And as for the fact* that He
[a]raised Him up from the dead, no
more to return to decay, He has spoken in this way: '[b]I WILL GIVE YOU
THE HOLY *and* SURE *blessings* OF DA-
VID.'
35 "Therefore He also says in another *Psalm*, '[a]THOU WILT NOT AL-
LOW THY HOLY ONE TO UNDERGO DE-
CAY.'
36 "For [a]David, after he had served
[b]the purpose of God in his own generation, [c]fell asleep, and was laid
among his fathers, and underwent
decay;
37 but He whom God [a]raised did
not undergo decay.
38 "Therefore let it be known to
you, brethren, that [a]through Him
forgiveness of sins is proclaimed to
you,
39 and through Him [a]everyone
who believes is freed[1] from all
things, from which you could not be
freed through the Law of Moses.
40 "Take heed therefore, so that the
thing spoken of [a]in the Prophets
may not come upon *you*:
41 '[a]BEHOLD, YOU SCOFFERS, AND
MARVEL, AND PERISH;
FOR I AM ACCOMPLISHING A
WORK IN YOUR DAYS,
A WORK WHICH YOU WILL NEV-
ER BELIEVE, THOUGH SOME-
ONE SHOULD DESCRIBE IT TO
YOU.' "
42 And as Paul and Barnabas were
going out, the people kept begging
that these things might be spoken to
them the next [a]Sabbath.
43 Now when *the meeting of* the
synagogue had broken up, many of
the Jews and of the [a]God-fearing
[1b]proselytes followed Paul and Barnabas, who, speaking to them, were
urging them to continue in [c]the
grace of God.

Paul Turns to the Gentiles

44 And the next [a]Sabbath nearly the whole city assembled to hear the word of [1]God.

45 But when [a]the Jews saw the crowds, they were filled with jealousy, and *began* contradicting the things spoken by Paul, and were blaspheming.

46 And Paul and Barnabas spoke out boldly and said, "It was necessary that the word of God should be spoken to you [a]first; since you repudiate it, and judge yourselves unworthy of eternal life, behold, [b]we are turning to the Gentiles.

47"For thus the Lord has commanded us,

'[a]I HAVE PLACED YOU AS A [b]LIGHT FOR THE GENTILES,
THAT YOU SHOULD BRING SALVATION TO THE END OF THE EARTH.' "

48 And when the Gentiles heard this, they *began* rejoicing and glorifying [a]the word of [1]the Lord; and as many as [b]had been appointed to eternal life believed.

49 And [a]the word of the Lord was being spread through the whole region.

50 But [a]the Jews aroused the [b]devout women [c]of prominence and the leading men of the city, and instigated a persecution against Paul and Barnabas, and drove them out of their district.

51 But [a]they shook off the dust of their feet *in protest* against them and went to [b]Iconium.

52 And the disciples were continually [a]filled with joy and with the Holy Spirit.

CHAPTER 14

Acceptance and Opposition

AND it came about that in [a]Iconium [b]they entered the synagogue of the Jews together, and spoke in such a manner [c]that a great multitude believed, both of Jews and of [d]Greeks.

2 But [a]the Jews who [b]disbelieved stirred up the minds of the Gentiles, and embittered them against [c]the brethren.

3 Therefore they spent a long time *there* [a]speaking boldly *with reliance* upon the Lord, who was bearing witness to the word of His grace, granting that [b]signs and wonders be done by their hands.

4 [a]But the multitude of the city was divided; and some sided with [b]the Jews, and some with [c]the apostles.

5 And when an attempt was made by both the Gentiles and [a]the Jews with their rulers, to mistreat and to [b]stone them,

6 they became aware of it and fled to the cities of [a]Lycaonia, [b]Lystra and [c]Derbe, and the surrounding region;

7 and there they continued to [a]preach the gospel.

8 And at [a]Lystra there was sitting [b]a certain man, without strength in his feet, lame from his mother's womb, who had never walked.

9 This man was listening to Paul as he spoke, who, [a]when he had fixed his gaze upon him, and had seen that he had [b]faith to be made well,

10 said with a loud voice, "Stand upright on your feet." [a]And he leaped up and *began* to walk.

11 And when the multitudes saw what Paul had done, they raised their voice, saying in the [a]Lycaonian language, "[b]The gods have become like men and have come down to us."

12 And they *began* calling Barnabas, [1]Zeus, and Paul, [2]Hermes, because he was the chief speaker.

13 And the priest of Zeus, whose *temple* was just outside the city, brought oxen and garlands to the gates, and [a]wanted to offer sacrifice with the crowds.

14 But when [a]the apostles, Barnabas and Paul, heard of it, they [b]tore their robes and rushed out into the crowd, crying out

15 and saying, "Men, why are you doing these things? We are also [a]men of the same nature as you, and [b]preach the gospel to you in order that you should turn from these [c]vain things to a [d]living God, [e]WHO MADE THE HEAVEN AND THE EARTH AND THE SEA, AND ALL THAT IS IN THEM.

16"And in the generations gone by He [a]permitted all the nations to [b]go their own ways;

17 and yet [a]He did not leave Himself without witness, in that He did good and [b]gave you rains from heaven and fruitful seasons, satisfying your hearts with food and gladness."

18 And *even* saying these things, they with difficulty restrained the crowds from offering sacrifice to them.

---

44 [1]Or, *the Lord* [a]Acts 13:14
45 [a]Acts 13:50; 14:2, 4, 5, 19; 1 Thess. 2:16
46 [a]Acts 3:26; 9:20; 13:5, 14 [b]Acts 18:6; 19:9, 15; 22:21; 26:20
47 [a]Is. 49:6 [b]Luke 2:32
48 [1]Or, *God* [a]Acts 13:12 [b]Rom. 8:28ff.; Eph. 1:4f., 11
49 [a]Acts 13:12
50 [a]Acts 13:45; 14:2, 4, 5, 19; 1 Thess. 2:16 [b]Acts 13:43; 18:7 [c]Mark 15:43
51 [a]Matt. 10:14; Acts 18:6 [b]Acts 14:1, 19, 21; 16:2; 2 Tim. 3:11
52 [a]Acts 2:4
1 [a]Acts 13:51; 2 Tim. 3:11 [b]Acts 13:5 [c]Acts 2:47 [d]John 7:35; Acts 18:4
2 [a]Acts 13:45, 50; 1 Thess. 2:16 [b]John 3:36 [c]Acts 1:15
3 [a]Acts 4:29f.; 20:32; Heb. 2:4 [b]John 4:48
4 [a]Acts 17:4f.; 19:9; 28:24 [b]Acts 13:45; 1 Thess. 2:16 [c]Acts 14:14
5 [a]Acts 13:45; 1 Thess. 2:16 [b]Acts 14:19
6 [a]Acts 14:11 [b]Acts 14:8, 21; 16:1f.; 2 Tim. 3:11 [c]Acts 14:20; 16:1; 20:4
7 [a]Acts 14:15
8 [a]Acts 14:6, 21; 16:1f.; 2 Tim. 3:11 [b]Acts 3:2
9 [a]Acts 3:4; 10:4 [b]Matt. 9:28
10 [a]Acts 3:8
11 [a]Acts 14:6 [b]Acts 8:10; 28:6
12 [1]Lat., Jupiter [2]Lat., Mercurius
13 [a]Dan. 2:46
14 [a]Acts 14:4 [b]Num. 14:6; Matt. 26:65; Mark 14:63
15 [a]Acts 10:26; James 5:17 [b]Acts 13:32; 14:7, 21 [c]Deut. 32:21; 1 Sam. 12:21; Jer. 8:19; 14:22; 1 Cor. 8:4 [d]Matt. 16:16 [e]Ex. 20:11; Ps. 146:6; Acts 4:24; 17:24; Rev. 14:7
16 [a]Acts 17:30 [b]Ps. 81:12; Mic. 4:5
17 [a]Acts 17:26f.; Rom. 1:19f. [b]Deut. 11:14; Job 5:10; Ps. 65:10f.; Ezek. 34:26f.; Joel 2:23

19 But [a]Jews came from [b]Antioch
and [c]Iconium, and having won over
the multitudes, they [d]stoned Paul
and dragged him out of the city,
supposing him to be dead.
20 But while [a]the disciples stood
around him, he arose and entered
the city. And the next day he went
away with Barnabas to [b]Derbe.
21 And after they had [a]preached
the gospel to that city and had
[b]made many disciples, they returned to [c]Lystra and to [d]Iconium
and to [e]Antioch,
22 strengthening the souls of [a]the
disciples, encouraging them to continue in [b]the faith, and *saying,*
"[c]Through many tribulations we
must enter the kingdom of God."
23 And when [a]they had appointed
[b]elders for them in every church,
having [c]prayed with fasting, they
[d]commended them to the Lord in
whom they had believed.
24 And they passed through [a]Pi-
sidia and came into [b]Pamphylia.
25 And when they had spoken the
word in [a]Perga, they went down to
Attalia;
26 and from there they sailed to
[a]Antioch, from [b]which they had
been [c]commended to the grace of
God for the work that they had accomplished.
27 And when they had arrived and
gathered the church together, they
began to [a]report all things that God
had done with them and how He had
opened a [b]door of faith to the Gentiles.
28 And they spent a long time with
[a]the disciples.

Chapter 15

The Council at Jerusalem

AND [a]some men came down from
Judea and *began* teaching [b]the
brethren, "Unless you are [c]circum-
cised according to [d]the custom of
Moses, you cannot be saved."
2 And when Paul and Barnabas
had great dissension and [a]debate
with them, [b]*the brethren* determined that Paul and Barnabas and
certain others of them, should go up
to Jerusalem to the [c]apostles and elders concerning this issue.
3 Therefore, being [a]sent on their
way by the church, they were passing through both [b]Phoenicia and Samaria, [c]describing in detail the conversion of the Gentiles, and were
bringing great joy to all [d]the brethren.
4 And when they arrived at Jerusalem, they were received by the
church and [a]the apostles and the elders, and they [b]reported all that God
had done with them.
5 But certain ones of [a]the sect of
the [b]Pharisees who had believed,
stood up, saying, "It is necessary to
[c]circumcise them, and to direct
them to observe the Law of Moses."
6 And [a]the apostles and the elders came together to look into this
matter.
7 And after there had been much
[a]debate, Peter stood up and said to
them, "Brethren, you know that in
the early days [b]God made a choice
among you, that by my mouth the
Gentiles should hear the word of
[c]the gospel and believe.
8 "And God, [a]who knows the
heart, bore witness to them, [b]giving
them the Holy Spirit, just as He also
did to us;
9 and [a]He made no distinction
between us and them, [b]cleansing
their hearts by faith.
10 "Now therefore why do you [a]put
God to the test by placing upon the
neck of the disciples a yoke which
[b]neither our fathers nor we have
been able to bear?
11 "But we believe that we are
saved through [a]the grace of the
Lord Jesus, in the same way as they
also are."
12 And all the multitude kept silent, and they were listening to Barnabas and Paul as they were [a]relat-
ing what [b]signs and wonders God
had done through them among the
Gentiles.

James' Judgment

13 And after they had stopped
speaking, [1a]James answered, say-
ing, "Brethren, listen to me.
14 "[a]Simeon has related how God
first concerned Himself about tak-
ing from among the Gentiles a peo-
ple for His name.
15 "And with this the words of [a]the
Prophets agree, just as it is written,
16 '[a]AFTER THESE THINGS [b]I WILL
RETURN,
AND I WILL REBUILD THE TAB-
ERNACLE OF DAVID WHICH
HAS FALLEN,
AND I WILL REBUILD ITS RUINS,
AND I WILL RESTORE IT,
17 [a]IN ORDER THAT THE REST OF
MANKIND MAY SEEK THE
LORD,
AND ALL THE GENTILES [b]WHO
ARE CALLED BY MY NAME,

19 [a]Acts 13:45, 50; 1 Thess. 2:16 [b]Acts 13:14; 14:21, 26 [c]Acts 13:51 [d]Acts 14:5; 2 Cor. 11:25; 2 Tim. 3:11
20 [a]Acts 11:26; 14:22, 28 [b]Acts 14:6
21 [a]Acts 14:7 [b]Acts 2:47 [c]Acts 14:6 [d]Acts 13:51 [e]Acts 14:19, 26
22 [a]Acts 11:26; 14:28 [b]Acts 6:7 [c]Mark 10:30; John 15:18, 20; 16:33; Acts 9:16; 2 Tim. 3:12; 1 Pet. 2:21; Rev. 1:9
23 [a]2 Cor. 8:19; Titus 1:5 [b]Acts 11:30 [c]Acts 1:24; 13:3 [d]Acts 20:32
24 [a]Acts 13:14 [b]Acts 13:13
25 [a]Acts 13:13
26 [a]Acts 11:19 [b]Acts 13:3 [c]Acts 11:23
27 [a]Acts 15:3, 4, 12; 21:19 [b]1 Cor. 16:9; 2 Cor. 2:12; Col. 4:3; Rev. 3:8
28 [a]Acts 11:26, 14:22
1 [a]Acts 15:24 [b]Acts 1:15; 15:3, 22, 32 [c]Acts 15:5; 1 Cor. 7:18 [d]Acts 6:14
2 [a]Acts 15:7 [b]Gal. 2:2 [c]Acts 11:30
3 [a]Acts 20:38; 21:5; Rom. 15:24; 2 Cor. 1:16 [b]Acts 11:19 [c]Acts 14:27; 15:4, 12 [d]Acts 1:15; 15:22
4 [a]Acts 11:30 [b]Acts 14:27; 15:12
5 [a]Acts 5:17; 28:22 [b]Matt. 3:7; Acts 26:5 [c]1 Cor. 7:18; Gal. 2:11
6 [a]Acts 11:30; 15:4
7 [a]Acts 15:2 [b]Acts 10:19f. [c]Acts 20:24
8 [a]Acts 1:24 [b]Acts 10:47
9 [a]Acts 10:28, 34; 11:12 [b]Acts 10:43
10 [a]Acts 5:9 [b]Matt. 23:4; Gal. 5:1
11 [a]Rom. 3:24; 5:15; 2 Cor. 13:14
12 [a]Acts 14:27; 15:3, 4 [b]John 4:48
13 [1]Or, *Jacob* [a]Acts 12:17
14 [a]Acts 15:7
15 [a]Acts 13:40
16 [a]Amos 9:11 [b]Jer. 12:15
17 [a]Amos 9:12 [b]Deut. 28:10; Is. 63:19; Jer. 14:9; Dan. 9:19; James 2:7

18 [a]SAYS THE LORD, WHO [b]MAKES
THESE THINGS KNOWN FROM
OF OLD.'
19"Therefore it is [a]my judgment
that we do not trouble those who are
turning to God from among the
Gentiles,
20 but that we write to them that
they abstain from [a]things contami-
nated by idols and from fornication
and from [b]what is strangled and
from blood.
21"For [a]Moses from ancient generations has in every city those who
preach him, since he is read in the
synagogues every Sabbath."
22 Then it seemed good to [a]the
apostles and the elders, with the
whole church, to choose men from
among them to send to [b]Antioch
with Paul and Barnabas—Judas
called Barsabbas, and [c]Silas, leading men among [d]the brethren,
23 and they sent this letter by
them,
"[a]The apostles and the
brethren who are elders, to
[b]the brethren in [c]Antioch
and [d]Syria and [e]Cilicia who
are from the Gentiles,
[f]greetings.
24 "Since we have heard that
[a]some of our number to
whom we gave no instruc-
tion have [b]disturbed you
with *their* words, unsettling
your souls,
25 [a]it seemed good to us, having [1]become of one mind, to
select men to send to you
with our beloved Barnabas
and Paul,
26 men who have [a]risked their
lives for the name of our
Lord Jesus Christ.
27 "Therefore we have sent [a]Ju-
das and [b]Silas, who themselves will also report the
same things by word *of
mouth*.
28 "For [a]it seemed good to [b]the
Holy Spirit and to [c]us to lay
upon you no greater burden
than these essentials:
29 that you abstain from
[a]things sacrificed to idols
and from [a]blood and from
[a]things strangled and from
[a]fornication; if you keep
yourselves free from such
things, you will do well.
Farewell."
30 So, when they were sent away,
[a]they went down to Antioch; and
having gathered the congregation
together, they delivered the letter.
31 And when they had read it, they
rejoiced because of its encouragement.
32 And [a]Judas and [b]Silas, also
being [c]prophets themselves, encouraged and strengthened [d]the
brethren with a lengthy message.
33 And after they had spent time
there, they were sent away from the
brethren [a]in peace to those who had
[b]sent them out.
34 [[1]But it seemed good to Silas to
remain there.]
35 But [a]Paul and Barnabas stayed
in Antioch, teaching and [b]preach-
ing, with many others also, [c]the
word of the Lord.

Second Missionary Journey

36 And after some days Paul said
to Barnabas, "Let us return and visit
the brethren in [a]every city in which
we proclaimed [b]the word of the
Lord, *and see* how they are."
37 And Barnabas was desirous of
taking [a]John, called Mark, along
with them also.
38 But Paul kept insisting that
they should not take him along who
had [a]deserted them in Pamphylia
and had not gone with them to the
work.
39 And there arose such a sharp
disagreement that they separated
from one another, and Barnabas
took [a]Mark with him and sailed
away to [b]Cyprus.
40 But Paul chose [a]Silas and departed, being [b]committed by the
brethren to the grace of the Lord.
41 And he was traveling through
[a]Syria and [b]Cilicia, strengthening
the churches.

CHAPTER 16

The Macedonian Vision

AND he came also to [a]Derbe and to
[a]Lystra. And behold, a certain disciple was there, named [b]Timothy, the
son of a [c]Jewish woman who was a
believer, but his father was a Greek,
2 and he was well spoken of by
[a]the brethren who were in [b]Lystra
and [c]Iconium.
3 Paul wanted this man to go
with him; and he [a]took him and circumcised him because of the Jews
who were in those parts, for they all
knew that his father was a Greek.
4 Now while they were passing
through the cities, they were delivering [a]the decrees, which had been
decided upon by [b]the apostles and
[c]elders who were in Jerusalem, for
them to observe.

18 [a]Amos 9:12 [b]Is. 45:21
19 [a]Acts 15:28; 21:25
20 [a]Dan. 1:8; Acts 15:29; 1 Cor. 8:7; Rev. 2:14, 20 [b]Gen. 9:4; Lev. 3:17; 7:26; 17:10; Deut. 12:16, 23; 1 Sam. 14:33
21 [a]Acts 13:15; 2 Cor. 3:14f.
22 [a]Acts 15:2 [b]Acts 11:20 [c]Acts 15:27, 32, 40; 18:5; 2 Cor. 1:19; 1 Thess. 1:1; 2 Thess. 1:1; 1 Pet. 5:12 [d]Acts 15:1
23 [a]Acts 15:2 [b]Acts 15:1 [c]Acts 11:20 [d]Matt. 4:24; Acts 15:41; Gal. 1:21 [e]Acts 6:9 [f]Acts 23:26; James 1:1
24 [a]Acts 15:1 [b]Gal. 1:7; 5:10
25 [a]Acts 15:28
26 [a]Acts 9:23ff.
27 [a]Acts 15:22, 32 [b]Acts 15:22
28 [a]Acts 15:25 [b]Acts 5:32; 15:8 [c]Acts 15:19, 25
29 [a]Acts 15:20
30 [a]Acts 15:22f.
32 [a]Acts 15:22, 27 [b]Acts 15:22 [c]Acts 13:1 [d]Acts 15:1
33 [a]Mark 5:34; Acts 16:36; 1 Cor. 16:11; Heb. 11:31 [b]Acts 15:22
34 [1]Many mss. do not contain this verse
35 [a]Acts 12:25 [b]Acts 8:4 [c]Acts 13:12
36 [a]Acts 13:4 [b]Acts 13:12
37 [a]Acts 12:12
38 [a]Acts 13:13
39 [a]Acts 12:12 [b]Acts 4:36
40 [a]Acts 15:22 [b]Acts 11:23; 14:26
41 [a]Matt. 4:24 [b]Acts 6:9
1 [a]Acts 14:6 [b]Acts 17:14f.; Rom. 16:21; 1 Cor. 4:17; 16:10; 2 Cor. 1:1, 19; Phil. 1:1; 2:19; Col. 1:1; 1 Thess. 1:1; 3:2, 6; 1 Tim. 1:2, 18; 6:20; 2 Tim. 1:2; Philem. 1; Heb. 13:23 [c]2 Tim. 1:5
2 [a]Acts 16:40 [b]Acts 14:6 [c]Acts 13:51
3 [a]Gal. 2:3
4 [a]Acts 15:28f. [b]Acts 15:2 [c]Acts 11:30

5 So [a]the churches were being
strengthened in the faith, and were
[b]increasing in number daily.
6 And they passed through the
[1a]Phrygian and [b]Galatian region,
having been forbidden by the Holy
Spirit to speak the word in [2c]Asia;
7 and when they had come to
[a]Mysia, they were trying to go into
[b]Bithynia, and the [c]Spirit of Jesus
did not permit them;
8 and passing by [a]Mysia, they
came down to [b]Troas.
9 And [a]a vision appeared to Paul
in the night: a certain man of [b]Mac-
edonia was standing and appealing
to him, and saying, "Come over to
Macedonia and help us."
10 And when he had seen [a]the vision, immediately [b]we sought to go
into Macedonia, concluding that
God had called us to [c]preach the
gospel to them.
11 Therefore putting out to sea
from [a]Troas, we ran [b]a straight
course to Samothrace, and on the
day following to Neapolis;
12 and from there to [a]Philippi,
which is a leading city of the district
of [b]Macedonia, [c]a *Roman* colony;
and we were staying in this city for
some days.
13 And on [a]the Sabbath day we
went outside the gate to a riverside,
where we were supposing that there
would be a place of prayer; and we
sat down and began speaking to the
women who had assembled.

First Convert in Europe

14 And a certain woman named
Lydia, from the city of [a]Thyatira, a
seller of purple fabrics, [b]a worshiper
of God, was listening; and the Lord
[c]opened her heart to respond to the
things spoken by Paul.
15 And when she and [a]her household had been baptized, she urged
us, saying, "If you have judged me
to be faithful to the Lord, come into
my house and stay." And she prevailed upon us.
16 And it happened that as we
were going to [a]the place of prayer, a
certain slave-girl having [b]a spirit of
divination met us, who was bringing
her masters much profit by fortune-
telling.
17 Following after Paul and us, she
kept crying out, saying, "These men
are bond-servants of [a]the Most High
God, who are proclaiming to you the
way of salvation."
18 And she continued doing this
for many days. But Paul was greatly
annoyed, and turned and said to the
spirit, "I command you [a]in the name
of Jesus Christ to come out of her!"
And it came out at that very moment.
19 But when her masters saw that
their hope of [a]profit was gone, they
seized [b]Paul and Silas and [c]dragged
them into the market place before
the authorities,
20 and when they had brought
them to the chief magistrates, they
said, "These men are throwing our
city into confusion, being Jews,
21 and [a]are proclaiming customs
which it is not lawful for us to accept or to observe, being [b]Romans."

Paul and Silas Imprisoned

22 And the crowd rose up together
against them, and the chief magistrates tore their robes off them, and
proceeded to order *them* to be
[a]beaten with rods.
23 And when they had inflicted
many blows upon them, they threw
them into prison, commanding [a]the
jailer to guard them securely;
24 and he, having received such a
command, threw them into the inner prison, and fastened their feet in
[a]the stocks.
25 But about midnight [a]Paul and
Silas were praying and [b]singing
hymns of praise to God, and the
prisoners were listening to them;
26 and suddenly [a]there came a
great earthquake, so that the foundations of the prison house were
shaken; and immediately [b]all the
doors were opened, and everyone's
[c]chains were unfastened.
27 And when [a]the jailer had been
roused out of sleep and had seen the
prison doors opened, he drew his
sword and was about [b]to kill himself, supposing that the prisoners
had escaped.
28 But Paul cried out with a loud
voice, saying, "Do yourself no harm,
for we are all here!"
29 And he called for lights and
rushed in and, trembling with fear,
he fell down before [a]Paul and Silas,
30 and after he brought them out,
he said, "Sirs, [a]what must I do to be
saved?"

The Jailer Converted

31 And they said, "[a]Believe in the
Lord Jesus, and you shall be saved,
you and [b]your household."
32 And they spoke the word of
[1]the Lord to him together with all
who were in his house.
33 And he took them [a]that *very*
hour of the night and washed their

5 [a]Acts 9:31 [b]Acts 2:47
6 [1]Or, *Phrygia and the Galatian region* [2]I.e., west coast province of Asia Minor [a]Acts 2:10; 18:23 [b]Acts 18:23; 1 Cor. 16:1; Gal. 1:2; 3:1; 2 Tim. 4:10; 1 Pet. 1:1 [c]Acts 2:9
7 [a]Acts 16:8 [b]1 Pet. 1:1 [c]Luke 24:49; Acts 8:29; Rom. 8:9; Gal. 4:6; Phil. 1:19; 1 Pet. 1:11
8 [a]Acts 16:7 [b]Acts 16:11; 20:5f.; 2 Cor. 2:12; 2 Tim. 4:13
9 [a]Acts 9:10 [b]Acts 16:10, 12; 18:5; 27:2; Rom. 15:26
10 [a]Acts 9:10 [b][we] Acts 16:10-17; 27:1-28:16 [c]Acts 14:7
11 [a]Acts 16:8; 20:5f.; 2 Cor. 2:12; 2 Tim. 4:13 [b]Acts 21:1
12 [a]Acts 20:6; Phil. 1:1; 1 Thess. 2:2 [b]Acts 16:9, 10; 18:5; 19:21f., 29; 20:1, 3; 27:2; Rom. 15:26 [c]Acts 16:21
13 [a]Acts 13:14
14 [a]Rev. 1:11; 2:18, 24 [b]Acts 13:43; 18:7 [c]Luke 24:45
15 [a]Acts 11:14
16 [a]Acts 16:13 [b]Lev. 19:31; 20:6, 27; Deut. 18:11; 1 Sam. 28:3, 7; 2 Kin. 21:6; 1 Chr. 10:13; Is. 8:19
17 [a]Mark 5:7
18 [a]Mark 16:17
19 [a]Acts 16:16; 19:25f. [b]Acts 15:22, 40; 16:25, 29 [c]Acts 8:3; 17:6f.; 21:30; James 2:6
21 [a]Esther 3:8 [b]Acts 16:12
22 [a]2 Cor. 11:25; 1 Thess. 2:2
23 [a]Acts 16:27
24 [a]Job 13:27; 33:11; Jer. 20:2f.; 29:26
25 [a]Acts 16:19 [b]Eph. 5:19
26 [a]Acts 4:31 [b]Acts 12:10 [c]Acts 12:7
27 [a]Acts 16:23, 36 [b]Acts 12:19
29 [a]Acts 16:19
30 [a]Acts 2:37
31 [a]Mark 16:16 [b]Acts 11:14; 16:15
32 [1]Or, God
33 [a]Acts 16:25

wounds, and immediately he was
baptized, he and all his *household*.
34 And he brought them into his
house and set [1]food before them,
and rejoiced [2]greatly, having believed in God with [a]his whole household.
35 Now when day came, the chief
magistrates sent their policemen,
saying, "Release those men."
36 And [a]the jailer reported these
words to Paul, *saying*, "The chief
magistrates have sent to release
you. Now therefore come out and go
[b]in peace."
37 But Paul said to them, "They
have beaten us in public without
trial, [a]men who are Romans, and
have thrown us into prison; and now
are they sending us away secretly?
No indeed! But let them come themselves and bring us out."
38 And the policemen reported
these words to the chief magistrates. And [a]they were afraid when
they heard that they were Romans,
39 and they came and appealed to
them, and when they had brought
them out, they kept begging them
[a]to leave the city.
40 And they went out of the prison
and entered *the house of* [a]Lydia, and
when they saw [b]the brethren, they
encouraged them and departed.

CHAPTER 17

Paul at Thessalonica

NOW when they had traveled
through Amphipolis and Apollonia,
they came to [a]Thessalonica, where
there was a synagogue of the Jews.
2 And [a]according to Paul's custom, he went to them, and for three
[b]Sabbaths reasoned with them from
[c]the Scriptures,
3 explaining and giving evidence
that the Christ [a]had to suffer and
[b]rise again from the dead, and *say-*
ing, "[c]This Jesus whom I am proclaiming to you is the Christ."
4 [a]And some of them were persuaded and joined [b]Paul and Silas,
along with a great multitude of the
[c]God-fearing [d]Greeks and a number
of the [e]leading women.
5 But [a]the Jews, becoming jealous and taking along some wicked
men from the market place, formed
a mob and set the city in an uproar;
and coming upon the house of [b]Ja-
son, they were seeking to bring
them out to the people.
6 And when they did not find
them, they *began* [a]dragging Jason
and some brethren before the city
authorities, shouting, "These men
who have upset [1b]the world have
come here also;
7 [1]and Jason [a]has welcomed
them, and they all act [b]contrary to
the decrees of Caesar, saying that
there is another king, Jesus."
8 And they stirred up the crowd
and the city authorities who heard
these things.
9 And when they had received a
pledge from [a]Jason and the others,
they released them.

Paul at Berea

10 And [a]the brethren immediately
sent [b]Paul and Silas away by night
to [c]Berea; [1]and when they arrived,
they went into [d]the synagogue of
the Jews.
11 Now these were more noble-
minded than those in [a]Thessalonica,
for they received the word with
great eagerness, examining the
Scriptures daily, *to see* whether
these things were so.
12 [a]Many of them therefore believed, along with a number of
[b]prominent Greek [c]women and
men.
13 But when the Jews of [a]Thessa-
lonica found out that the word of
God had been proclaimed by Paul in
[b]Berea also, they came there likewise, agitating and stirring up the
crowds.
14 And then immediately [a]the
brethren sent Paul out to go as far as
the sea; and [b]Silas and [c]Timothy remained there.
15 Now [a]those who conducted
Paul brought him as far as [b]Athens;
and receiving a command for [c]Silas
and Timothy to [d]come to him as
soon as possible, they departed.

Paul at Athens

16 Now while Paul was waiting for
them at [a]Athens, his spirit was
being provoked within him as he
was beholding the city full of idols.
17 So he was reasoning [a]in the
synagogue with the Jews and [b]the
God-fearing *Gentiles*, and in the
market place every day with those
who happened to be present.
18 And also some of the Epicurean
and Stoic philosophers were [1]con-
versing with him. And some were
saying, "What would [a]this [2]idle babbler wish to say?" Others, "He
seems to be a proclaimer of strange
[3]deities,"—because he was preaching [b]Jesus and the resurrection.

34 [1]Lit., *a table* [2]Or, *greatly with his whole household, having believed in God* [a]Acts 11:14; 16:15
36 [a]Acts 16:27 [b]Acts 15:33
37 [a]Acts 22:25-29
38 [a]Acts 22:29
39 [a]Matt. 8:34
40 [a]Acts 16:14 [b]Acts 1:15; 16:2
1 [a]Acts 17:11, 13; 20:4; 27:2; Phil. 4:16; 1 Thess. 1:1; 2 Thess. 1:1; 2 Tim. 4:10
2 [a]Acts 9:20; 17:10, 17 [b]Acts 13:14 [c]Acts 8:35
3 [a]Acts 3:18 [b]John 20:9 [c]Acts 9:22; 18:5, 28
4 [a]Acts 14:4 [b]Acts 15:22, 40; 17:10, 14f. [c]Acts 13:43; 17:17 [d]John 7:35 [e]Acts 13:50
5 [a]Acts 17:13; 1 Thess. 2:16 [b]Acts 17:6, 7, 9; Rom. 16:21
6 [1]Lit., *the inhabited earth* [a]Acts 16:19f. [b]Matt. 24:14; Acts 17:31
7 [1]Lit., *whom Jason has welcomed* [a]Luke 10:38; James 2:25 [b]Luke 23:2
9 [a]Acts 17:5
10 [1]Lit., *who when . . . arrived went* [a]Acts 1:15; 17:6, 14f. [b]Acts 17:4 [c]Acts 17:13; 20:4 [d]Acts 17:2
11 [a]Acts 17:1
12 [a]Acts 2:47 [b]Mark 15:43 [c]Acts 13:50
13 [a]Acts 17:1 [b]Acts 17:10; 20:4
14 [a]Acts 1:15; 17:6, 10 [b]Acts 15:22; 17:4, 10 [c]Acts 16:1
15 [a]Acts 15:3 [b]Acts 17:16, 21f.; 18:1; 1 Thess. 3:1 [c]Acts 17:14 [d]Acts 18:5
16 [a]Acts 17:15, 21f.; 18:1; 1 Thess. 3:1
17 [a]Acts 9:20; 17:2 [b]Acts 17:4
18 [1]Or, *disputing* [2]I.e., one who makes his living by picking up scraps [3]Lit., *demons* [a]1 Cor. 1:20; 4:10 [b]Acts 4:2; 17:31f.

19 And they [a]took him and brought him to the [b]Areopagus, saying, "May we know what [c]this new teaching is which you are proclaiming?

20 "For you are bringing some strange things to our ears; we want to know therefore what these things mean."

21 (Now all the Athenians and the strangers [a]visiting there used to spend their time in nothing other than telling or hearing something new.)

Sermon on Mars Hill

22 And Paul stood in the midst of the Areopagus and said, "Men of [a]Athens, I observe that you are very [b]religious in all respects.

23 "For while I was passing through and examining the [a]objects of your worship, I also found an altar with this inscription, 'TO AN UNKNOWN GOD.' What therefore [b]you worship in ignorance, this I proclaim to you.

24 "[a]The God who made the world and all things in it, since He is [b]Lord of heaven and earth, does not [c]dwell in temples made with hands;

25 neither is He served by human hands, [a]as though He needed anything, since He Himself gives to all life and breath and all things;

26 and [a]He made from [1]one, every nation of mankind to live on all the face of the earth, having [b]determined *their* appointed times, and the boundaries of their habitation,

27 that they should seek God, if perhaps they might grope for Him and find Him, [a]though He is not far from each one of us;

28 for [a]in Him we live and move and [1]exist, as even some of your own poets have said, 'For we also are His offspring.'

29 "Being then the offspring of God, we [a]ought not to think that the Divine Nature is like gold or silver or stone, an image formed by the art and thought of man.

30 "Therefore having [a]overlooked [b]the times of ignorance, God is [c]now declaring to men that all everywhere should repent,

31 because He has fixed [a]a day in which [b]He will judge [c]the world in righteousness through a Man whom He has [d]appointed, having furnished proof to all men by [e]raising Him from the dead."

32 Now when they heard of [a]the resurrection of the dead, some *began* to sneer, but others said, "We shall hear you again concerning this."

33 So Paul went out of their midst.

34 But some men joined him and believed, among whom also was Dionysius the [a]Areopagite and a woman named Damaris and others with them.

CHAPTER 18

Paul at Corinth

AFTER these things he left [a]Athens and went to [b]Corinth.

2 And he found a certain Jew named [a]Aquila, a native of [b]Pontus, having recently come from [c]Italy with his wife [a]Priscilla, because [d]Claudius had commanded all the Jews to leave Rome. He came to them,

3 and because he was of the same trade, he stayed with them and [a]they were working; for by trade they were tent-makers.

4 And he was reasoning [a]in the synagogue every [b]Sabbath and trying to persuade [c]Jews and Greeks.

5 But when [a]Silas and Timothy [b]came down from [c]Macedonia, Paul *began* devoting himself completely to the word, solemnly [d]testifying to the Jews that [e]Jesus was the [1]Christ.

6 And when they resisted and blasphemed, he [a]shook out his garments and said to them, "[b]Your blood *be* upon your own heads! I am clean. From now on I shall go [c]to the Gentiles."

7 And he departed from there and went to the house of a certain man named Titius Justus, [a]a worshiper of God, whose house was next to the synagogue.

8 And [a]Crispus, [b]the leader of the synagogue, believed in the Lord [c]with all his household, and many of the [d]Corinthians when they heard were believing and being baptized.

9 And the Lord said to Paul in the night by [a]a vision, **"Do not be afraid *any longer*, but go on speaking and do not be silent;**

10 **for I am with you, and no man will attack you in order to harm you, for I have many people in this city."**

11 And he settled *there* a year and six months, teaching the word of God among them.

12 But while Gallio was [a]proconsul of [b]Achaia, [c]the Jews with one accord rose up against Paul and brought him before [d]the judgment seat,

---

19 [a]Acts 23:19 [b]Acts 17:22 [c]Mark 1:27
21 [a]Acts 2:10
22 [a]Acts 17:15 [b]Acts 25:19
23 [a]2 Thess. 2:4 [b]John 4:22
24 [a]Is. 42:5; Acts 14:15 [b]Deut. 10:14; Ps. 115:16 [c]Acts 7:48
25 [a]Job 22:2; Ps. 50:10-12
26 [1]Or, *one blood* [a]Mal. 2:10 [b]Deut. 32:8; Job 12:23
27 [a]Deut. 4:7; Jer. 23:23f.
28 [1]Lit., *are* [a]Job 12:10; Dan. 5:23
29 [a]Is. 40:18ff.; Rom. 1:23
30 [a]Acts 14:16; Rom. 3:25 [b]Acts 17:23 [c]Luke 24:47; Acts 26:20
31 [a]Matt. 10:15 [b]Ps. 9:8; 96:13; 98:9; John 5:22, 27; Acts 10:42 [c]Matt. 24:14; Acts 17:6 [d]Luke 22:22 [e]Acts 2:24
32 [a]Acts 17:18, 31
34 [a]Acts 17:19
1 [a]Acts 17:15 [b]Acts 18:8; 19:1; 1 Cor. 1:2; 2 Tim. 4:20
2 [a]Acts 18:18, 26; Rom. 16:3; 1 Cor. 16:19; 2 Tim. 4:19 [b]Acts 2:9 [c]Acts 27:1, 6; Heb. 13:24 [d]Acts 11:28
3 [a]Acts 20:34; 1 Cor. 4:12; 9:15; 2 Cor. 11:7; 12:13; 1 Thess. 2:9; 4:11
4 [a]Acts 9:20; 18:19 [b]Acts 13:14 [c]Acts 14:1
5 [1]I.e., Messiah [a]Acts 15:22; 16:1; 17:14 [b]Acts 17:15 [c]Acts 16:9 [d]Luke 16:28; Acts 20:21 [e]Acts 17:3; 18:28
6 [a]Neh. 5:13 [b]2 Sam. 1:16; 1 Kin. 2:33; Ezek. 18:13; 33:4, 6, 8; Matt. 27:25; Acts 20:26 [c]Acts 13:46
7 [a]Acts 13:43; 16:14
8 [a]1 Cor. 1:14 [b]Mark 5:22 [c]Acts 11:14 [d]Acts 18:1; 19:1; 1 Cor. 1:2; 2 Tim. 4:20
9 [a]Acts 9:10
12 [a]Acts 13:7 [b]Acts 18:27; 19:21; Rom. 15:26; 1 Cor. 16:15; 2 Cor. 1:1 1 Thess. 1:7f. [c]1 Thess. 2:16 [d]Matt. 27:19

13 saying, "This man persuades men to worship God contrary to [a]the law."

14 But when Paul was about to [a]open his mouth, Gallio said to the Jews, "If it were a matter of wrong or of vicious crime, O Jews, it would be reasonable for me to put up with you;

15 but if there are [a]questions about words and names and your own law, look after it yourselves; I am unwilling to be a judge of these matters."

16 And he drove them away from [a]the judgment seat.

17 And they all took hold of [a]Sosthenes, [b]the leader of the synagogue, and *began* beating him in front of [c]the judgment seat. And Gallio was not concerned about any of these things.

18 And Paul, having remained many days longer, [a]took leave of [b]the brethren and put out to sea for [c]Syria, and with him were [d]Priscilla and [d]Aquila. In [e]Cenchrea he [f]had his hair cut, for he was keeping a vow.

19 And they came to [a]Ephesus, and he left them there. Now he himself entered [b]the synagogue and reasoned with the Jews.

20 And when they asked him to stay for a longer time, he did not consent,

21 but [a]taking leave of them and saying, "I will return to you again [b]if God wills," he set sail from [c]Ephesus.

22 And when he had landed at [a]Caesarea, he went up and greeted the church, and went down to [b]Antioch.

Third Missionary Journey

23 And having spent some time *there*, he departed and passed successively through the [a]Galatian region and Phrygia, strengthening all the disciples.

24 Now a certain Jew named [a]Apollos, an [b]Alexandrian by birth, an eloquent man, came to [c]Ephesus; and he was mighty in the Scriptures.

25 This man had been instructed in [a]the way of the Lord; and being fervent in spirit, he was speaking and teaching accurately the things concerning Jesus, being acquainted only with [b]the baptism of John;

26 and he began to speak out boldly in the synagogue. But when [a]Priscilla and Aquila heard him, they took him aside and explained to him [b]the way of God more accurately.

27 And when he wanted to go across to [a]Achaia, [b]the brethren encouraged him and wrote to [c]the disciples to welcome him; and when he had arrived, he helped greatly those who had believed through grace;

28 for he powerfully refuted the Jews in public, demonstrating [a]by the Scriptures that [b]Jesus was the [1]Christ.

Chapter 19

Paul at Ephesus

AND it came about that while [a]Apollos was at [b]Corinth, Paul having passed through the [c]upper country came to [d]Ephesus, and found some disciples,

2 and he said to them, "[a]Did you receive the Holy Spirit when you believed?" And they *said* to him, "No, [b]we have not even heard whether there is a Holy Spirit."

3 And he said, "Into what then were you baptized?" And they said, "[a]Into John's baptism."

4 And Paul said, "[a]John baptized with the baptism of repentance, telling the people [b]to believe in Him who was coming after him, that is, in Jesus."

5 And when they heard this, they were [a]baptized in the name of the Lord Jesus.

6 And when Paul had [a]laid his hands upon them, the Holy Spirit came on them, and they *began* [b]speaking with tongues and [c]prophesying.

7 And there were in all about twelve men.

8 And he entered [a]the synagogue and continued speaking out boldly for three months, reasoning and persuading *them* [b]about the kingdom of God.

9 But when [a]some were becoming hardened and disobedient, speaking evil of [b]the Way before the multitude, he withdrew from them and took away [c]the disciples, reasoning daily in the school of Tyrannus.

10 And this took place for [a]two years, so that all who lived in [1b]Asia heard [c]the word of the Lord, both Jews and Greeks.

Miracles at Ephesus

11 And God was performing [a]extraordinary miracles by the hands of Paul,

13 [a]John 19:7; Acts 18:15
14 [a]Matt. 5:2
15 [a]Acts 23:29
16 [a]Matt. 27:19
17 [a]1 Cor. 1:1 [b]Acts 18:8 [c]Matt. 27:19
18 [a]Mark 6:46 [b]Acts 1:15; 18:27 [c]Matt. 4:24 [d]Acts 18:2, 26 [e]Rom. 16:1 [f]Num. 6:2, 5, 9
19 [a]Acts 18:21; 20:16f.; 1 Cor. 15:32; 16:8; Eph. 1:1; 1 Tim. 1:3; 2 Tim. 1:18; 4:12; Rev. 1:11; 2:1 [b]Acts 18:4
21 [a]Mark 6:46 [b]Rom. 1:10; 15:32; 1 Cor. 4:19; 16:7; Heb. 6:3; James 4:15; 1 Pet. 3:17 [c]Acts 18:19; 1 Cor. 15:32; 16:8; Eph. 1:1; 1 Tim. 1:3; 2 Tim. 1:18; 4:12
22 [a]Acts 8:40 [b]Acts 11:19
23 [a]Acts 16:6
24 [a]Acts 19:1; 1 Cor. 1:12; 3:5; Titus 3:13 [b]Acts 6:9 [c]Acts 18:19
25 [a]Acts 9:2; 18:26 [b]Luke 7:29; Acts 19:3
26 [a]Acts 18:2, 18 [b]Acts 18:25
27 [a]Acts 18:12; 19:1 [b]Acts 18:18 [c]Acts 11:26
28 [1]I.e., Messiah [a]Acts 8:35 [b]Acts 18:5
1 [a]Acts 18:24; 1 Cor. 1:12; 3:5, 6; Titus 3:13 [b]Acts 18:1 [c]Acts 18:23 [d]Acts 18:21, 24; 1 Cor. 15:32; 16:8; Eph. 1:1; 1 Tim. 1:3; 2 Tim. 1:18; 4:12; Rev. 1:11; 2:1
2 [a]Acts 8:15f.; 11:16f. [b]John 7:39
3 [a]Luke 7:29
4 [a]Acts 13:24 [b]John 1:7
5 [a]Acts 8:12, 16; 10:48
6 [a]Acts 6:6; 8:17 [b]Mark 16:17; Acts 2:4; 10:46 [c]Acts 13:1
8 [a]Acts 9:20; 18:26 [b]Acts 1:3
9 [a]Acts 14:4 [b]Acts 9:2; 19:23 [c]Acts 11:26; 19:30
10 [1]I.e., west coast province of Asia Minor [a]Acts 19:8; 20:31 [b]Acts 16:6; 19:22, 26, 27 [c]Acts 13:12; 19:20
11 [a]Acts 8:13

12 [a]so that handkerchiefs or
aprons were even carried from his
body to the sick, and the diseases
left them and [b]the evil spirits went
out.
13 But also some of the Jewish
[a]exorcists, who went from place to
place, attempted to name over those
who had the evil spirits the name of
the Lord Jesus, saying, "I adjure you
by Jesus whom Paul preaches."
14 And seven sons of one Sceva, a
Jewish chief priest, were doing this.
15 And the evil spirit answered
and said to them, "I recognize Jesus,
and I know about Paul, but who are
you?"
16 And the man, in whom was the
evil spirit, leaped on them and subdued both of them and overpowered
them, so that they fled out of that
house naked and wounded.
17 And this became known to all,
both Jews and Greeks, who lived in
[a]Ephesus; and fear fell upon them
all and the name of the Lord Jesus
was being magnified.
18 Many also of those who had believed kept coming, confessing and
disclosing their practices.
19 And many of those who practiced magic brought their books together and *began* burning them in
the sight of all; and they counted up
the price of them and found it [1]fifty
thousand [a]pieces of silver.
20 So [a]the word of the Lord [b]was
growing mightily and prevailing.
21 Now after these things were
finished, Paul purposed in the [1]spirit
to [a]go to Jerusalem [b]after he had
passed through [c]Macedonia and
[d]Achaia, saying, "After I have been
there, [e]I must also see Rome."
22 And having sent into [a]Macedo-
nia two of [b]those who ministered to
him, [c]Timothy and [d]Erastus, he himself stayed in [1e]Asia for a while.
23 And about that time there arose
no small disturbance concerning
[a]the Way.
24 For a certain man named Demetrius, a silversmith, who made
silver shrines of [1]Artemis, [a]was
bringing no little business to the
craftsmen;
25 these he gathered together with
the workmen of similar *trades,* and
said, "Men, you know that our prosperity depends upon this business.
26 "And you see and hear that not
only in [a]Ephesus, but in almost all of
[1b]Asia, this Paul has persuaded and
turned away a considerable number
of people, saying that [c]gods made
with hands are no gods *at all.*
27 "And not only is there danger
that this trade of ours fall into disre-
pute, but also that the temple of the
great goddess [1]Artemis be regarded
as worthless and that she whom all
of [2a]Asia and [b]the world worship
should even be dethroned from her
magnificence."
28 And when they heard *this* and
were filled with rage, they *began*
crying out, saying, "Great is [1]Arte-
mis of the [a]Ephesians!"
29 And the city was filled with the
confusion, and they rushed with one
accord into the theater, dragging
along [a]Gaius and [b]Aristarchus,
Paul's traveling [c]companions from
[d]Macedonia.
30 And when Paul wanted to go
into the assembly, [a]the disciples
would not let him.
31 And also some of the [1]Asiarchs
who were friends of his sent to him
and repeatedly urged him not to
venture into the theater.
32 [a]So then, some were shouting
one thing and some another, for the
[1]assembly was in confusion, and the
majority did not know for what
cause they had come together.
33 And some of the crowd [1]con-
cluded *it was* Alexander, since the
Jews had put him forward; and having [a]motioned with his hand, Alexander was intending to make a defense to the [2]assembly.
34 But when they recognized that
he was a Jew, a *single* outcry arose
from them all as they shouted for
about two hours, "Great is [1]Artemis
of the Ephesians!"
35 And after quieting the multitude, the town clerk *said, "Men of
[a]Ephesus, what man is there after
all who does not know that the city
of the Ephesians is guardian of the
temple of the great [1]Artemis, and of
the *image* which fell down from
[2]heaven?
36 "Since then these are undeniable
facts, you ought to keep calm and to
do nothing rash.
37 "For you have brought these
men *here* who are neither [a]robbers
of temples nor blasphemers of our
goddess.
38 "So then, if Demetrius and the
craftsmen who are with him have a
complaint against any man, the
courts are in session and [1a]procon-
suls are *available;* let them bring
charges against one another.
39 "But if you want anything beyond this, it shall be settled in the
[1]lawful [2]assembly.
40 "For indeed we are in danger of

12 [a]Acts 5:15 [b]Mark 16:17
13 [a]Matt. 12:27; Luke 11:19
17 [a]Acts 18:19
19 [1]Or probably, fifty thousand Greek drachmas. A drachma approximated a day's wage. [a]Luke 15:8
20 [a]Acts 19:10 [b]Acts 6:7; 12:24
21 [1]Or, *Spirit* [a]Acts 20:16, 22; 21:15; Rom. 15:25; 2 Cor. 1:16 [b]Acts 20:1; 1 Cor. 16:5 [c]Acts 16:9; 19:22, 29; Rom. 15:26; 1 Thess. 1:7f. [d]Acts 18:12 [e]Acts 23:11; Rom. 15:24, 28
22 [1]I.e., west coast province of Asia Minor [a]Acts 16:9; 19:21, 29 [b]Acts 13:5; 19:29; 20:34; 2 Cor. 8:19 [c]Acts 16:1 [d]Rom. 16:23; 2 Tim. 4:20 [e]Acts 19:10
23 [a]Acts 19:9
24 [1]Latin, *Diana* [a]Acts 16:16, 19f.
26 [1]Note v. 22 [a]Acts 18:19 [b]Acts 19:10 [c]Deut. 4:28; Ps. 115:4; Is. 44:10-20; Jer. 10:3ff.; Acts 17:29; 1 Cor. 8:4; 10:19; Rev. 9:20
27 [1]Latin, *Diana* [2]Note v. 22 [a]Acts 19:10 [b]Matt. 24:14
28 [1]Latin, *Diana* [a]Acts 18:19
29 [a]Acts 20:4 [b]Acts 20:4; 27:2; Col. 4:10; Philem. 24 [c]Acts 13:5; 19:22; 20:34; 2 Cor. 8:19 [d]Acts 16:9; 19:22
30 [a]Acts 19:9
31 [1]I.e., political or religious officials of the province of Asia
32 [1]Gr., ekklesia [a]Acts 21:34
33 [1]Or, *instructed Alexander* [2]Lit., *people* [a]Acts 12:17
34 [1]Latin, *Diana*
35 [1]Latin, *Diana* [2]Lit., *Zeus* or, *Jupiter* [a]Acts 18:19
37 [a]Rom. 2:22
38 [1]Or, *provincial governors* [a]Acts 13:7
39 [1]Or, *regular* [2]Gr., ekklesia

being accused of a riot in connection with today's affair, since there is no *real* cause *for it;* and in this connection we shall be unable to account for this disorderly gathering."

41 And after saying this he dismissed the [1]assembly.

CHAPTER 20

Paul in Macedonia and Greece

AND after the uproar had ceased, Paul sent for [a]the disciples and when he had exhorted them and taken his leave of them, he departed [b]to go to [c]Macedonia.

2 And when he had gone through those districts and had given them much exhortation, he came to Greece.

3 And *there* he spent three months, and when [a]a plot was formed against him by the Jews as he was about to set sail for [b]Syria, he determined to return through [c]Macedonia.

4 And he was accompanied by Sopater of [a]Berea, *the son* of Pyrrhus; and by [b]Aristarchus and Secundus of the [c]Thessalonians; and [d]Gaius of [e]Derbe, and [f]Timothy; and [g]Tychicus and [h]Trophimus of [1i]Asia.

5 But these had gone on ahead and were waiting for [a]us at [b]Troas.

6 And [a]we sailed from [b]Philippi after [c]the days of Unleavened Bread, and came to them at [d]Troas within five days; and there we stayed seven days.

7 And on [a]the first day of the week, when [b]we were gathered together to [c]break bread, Paul *began* talking to them, intending to depart the next day, and he prolonged his message until midnight.

8 And there were many [a]lamps in the [b]upper room where we were gathered together.

9 And there was a certain young man named Eutychus sitting on the window sill, sinking into a deep sleep; and as Paul kept on talking, he was overcome by sleep and fell down from the third floor, and was picked up dead.

10 But Paul went down and [a]fell upon him and after embracing him, he [b]said, "Do not be troubled, for his life is in him."

11 And when he had gone *back* up, and had [a]broken the bread and eaten, he talked with them a long while, until daybreak, and so departed.

12 And they took away the boy alive, and were greatly comforted.

Troas to Miletus

13 But [a]we, going ahead to the ship, set sail for Assos, intending from there to take Paul on board; for thus he had arranged it, intending himself to go by land.

14 And when he met us at Assos, we took him on board and came to Mitylene.

15 And sailing from there, we arrived the following day opposite Chios; and the next day we crossed over to Samos; and [1]the day following we came to [a]Miletus.

16 For Paul had decided to sail past [a]Ephesus in order that he might not have to spend time in [b]Asia; for he was hurrying [c]to be in Jerusalem, if possible, [d]on the day of Pentecost.

Farewell to Ephesus

17 And from Miletus he sent to [a]Ephesus and called to him [b]the elders of the church.

18 And when they had come to him, he said to them,

"You yourselves know, [a]from the first day that I set foot in [1a]Asia, how I was with you the whole time,

19 serving the Lord with all humility and with tears and with trials which came upon me through [a]the plots of the Jews;

20 how I [a]did not shrink from declaring to you anything that was profitable, and teaching you publicly and from house to house,

21 solemnly [a]testifying to both Jews and Greeks of [b]repentance toward God and [c]faith in our Lord Jesus Christ.

22 "And now, behold, bound in [1]spirit, [a]I am on my way to Jerusalem, not knowing what will happen to me there,

23 except that [a]the Holy Spirit solemnly [b]testifies to me in every city, saying that [c]bonds and afflictions await me.

24 "But [a]I do not consider my life of any account as dear to myself, in order that I may [b]finish my course, and [c]the ministry which I received from the Lord Jesus, to [d]testify solemnly of the gospel of [e]the grace of God.

25 "And now, behold, I know that you all, among whom I went about [a]preaching the kingdom, will see my face no more.

26 "Therefore I testify to you this day, that [a]I am innocent of the blood of all men.

27 "For I [a]did not shrink from declaring to you the whole [b]purpose of God.

41 [1]Gr., ekklesia
1 [a]Acts 11:26 [b]Acts 19:21 [c]Acts 16:9; 20:3
3 [a]Acts 9:24; 20:19 [b]Matt. 4:24 [c]Acts 16:9; 20:1
4 [1]I.e., west coast province of Asia Minor [a]Acts 17:10 [b]Acts 19:29 [c]Acts 17:1 [d]Acts 19:29 [e]Acts 14:6 [f]Acts 16:1 [g]Eph. 6:21; Col. 4:7; 2 Tim. 4:12; Titus 3:12 [h]Acts 21:29; 2 Tim. 4:20 [i]Acts 16:6; 20:16, 18
5 [a]Acts 16:10; 20:5-15 [b]Acts 16:8
6 [a]Acts 16:10; 20:5-15 [b]Acts 16:12 [c]Acts 12:3 [d]Acts 16:8
7 [a]1 Cor. 16:2; Rev. 1:10 [b]Acts 16:10; 20:5-15 [c]Acts 2:42; 20:11
8 [a]Matt. 25:1 [b]Acts 1:13
10 [a]1 Kin. 17:21; 2 Kin. 4:34 [b]Matt. 9:23f.; Mark 5:39
11 [a]Acts 2:42; 20:7
13 [a]Acts 16:10; 20:5-15
15 [1]Later mss. add, *after staying at Trogyllium, the day following* [a]Acts 20:17; 2 Tim. 4:20
16 [a]Acts 18:19 [b]Acts 16:6; 20:4, 18 [c]Acts 19:21; 20:6, 22; 1 Cor. 16:8 [d]Acts 2:1
17 [a]Acts 18:19 [b]Acts 11:30
18 [1]Note v. 16 [a]Acts 18:19; 19:1, 10; 20:4, 16
19 [a]Acts 20:3
20 [a]Acts 20:27
21 [a]Luke 16:28; Acts 18:5; 20:23, 24 [b]Acts 2:38; 11:18; 26:20 [c]Acts 24:24; 26:18; Eph. 1:15; Col. 2:5; Philem. 5
22 [1]Or, *the Spirit* [a]Acts 17:16; 20:16
23 [a]Acts 8:29 [b]Luke 16:28; Acts 18:5; 20:21, 24 [c]Acts 9:16; 21:33
24 [a]Acts 21:13 [b]Acts 13:25 [c]Acts 1:17 [d]Luke 16:28; Acts 18:5; 20:21 [e]Acts 11:23; 20:32
25 [a]Matt. 4:23; Acts 28:31
26 [a]Acts 18:6
27 [a]Acts 20:20 [b]Acts 13:36

28 "Be on guard for yourselves and for all [a]the flock, among which the Holy Spirit has made you [1]overseers, to shepherd [b]the church of [2]God which [c]He [3]purchased with His own blood.

29 "I know that after my departure [a]savage wolves will come in among you, not sparing [b]the flock;

30 and from among your own selves men will arise, speaking perverse things, to draw away [a]the disciples after them.

31 "Therefore be on the alert, remembering that night and day for a period of [a]three years I did not cease to admonish each one [b]with tears.

32 "And now I [a]commend you to God and to [b]the word of His grace, which is able to [c]build *you* up and to give *you* [d]the inheritance among all those who are sanctified.

33 "[a]I have coveted no one's silver or gold or clothes.

34 "You yourselves know that [a]these hands ministered to my *own* needs and to the [b]men who were with me.

35 "In every thing I showed you that by working hard in this manner you must help the weak and remember the words of the Lord Jesus, that He Himself said, '**It is more blessed to give than to receive.**' "

36 And when he had said these things, he [a]knelt down and prayed with them all.

37 And they *began* to weep aloud and [a]embraced Paul, and repeatedly kissed him,

38 grieving especially over [a]the word which he had spoken, that they should see his face no more. And they were [b]accompanying him to the ship.

Chapter 21

Paul Sails from Miletus

AND when it came about that [a]we had parted from them and had set sail, we ran [b]a straight course to Cos and the next day to Rhodes and from there to Patara;

2 and having found a ship crossing over to [a]Phoenicia, we went aboard and set sail.

3 And when we had come in sight of [a]Cyprus, leaving it on the left, we kept sailing to [b]Syria and landed at [c]Tyre; for [d]there the ship was to unload its cargo.

4 And after looking up [a]the disciples, we stayed there seven days; and they kept telling Paul [b]through the Spirit not to set foot in Jerusalem.

5 And when it came about that our days there were ended, we departed and started on our journey, while they all, with wives and children, [a]escorted us until *we were* out of the city. And after [b]kneeling down on the beach and praying, we said farewell to one another.

6 Then we went on board the ship, and they returned [a]home again.

7 And when we had finished the voyage from [a]Tyre, we arrived at Ptolemais; and after greeting [b]the brethren, we stayed with them for a day.

8 And on the next day we departed and came to [a]Caesarea; and entering the house of [b]Philip the [c]evangelist, who was [b]one of the seven, we stayed with him.

9 Now this man had four virgin daughters who were [a]prophetesses.

10 And as we were staying there for some days, a certain prophet named [a]Agabus came down from Judea.

11 And coming to us, he [a]took Paul's belt and bound his own feet and hands, and said, "This [b]is what the Holy Spirit says: 'In this way the Jews at Jerusalem will [c]bind the man who owns this belt and [d]deliver him into the hands of the Gentiles.' "

12 And when we had heard this, we as well as the local residents *began* begging him [a]not to go up to Jerusalem.

13 Then Paul answered, "What are you doing, weeping and breaking my heart? For [a]I am ready not only to be bound, but even to die at Jerusalem for [b]the name of the Lord Jesus."

14 And since he would not be persuaded, we fell silent, remarking, "[a]The will of the Lord be done!"

Paul at Jerusalem

15 And after these days we got ready and [a]started on our way up to Jerusalem.

16 And *some* of [a]the disciples from [b]Caesarea also came with us, taking us to Mnason of [c]Cyprus, a [d]disciple of long standing with whom we were to lodge.

17 And when we had come to Jerusalem, [a]the brethren received us gladly.

18 And now the following day Paul went in with us to [a]James, and all [b]the elders were present.

---

28 [1]Or, *bishops* [2]Some ancient mss. read, *the Lord* [3]Lit., *acquired* [a]Luke 12:32; John 21:15-17; Acts 20:29; 1 Pet. 5:2f. [b]Matt. 16:18; Rom. 16:16; 1 Cor. 10:32 [c]Eph. 1:7, 14; Titus 2:14; 1 Pet. 1:19; 2:9; Rev. 5:9
29 [a]Ezek. 22:27; Matt. 7:15 [b]Luke 12:32; John 21:15-17; Acts 20:28; 1 Pet. 5:2f.
30 [a]Acts 11:26
31 [a]Acts 19:1, 8, 10; 24:17 [b]Acts 20:19
32 [a]Acts 14:23 [b]Acts 14:3; 20:24 [c]Acts 9:31 [d]Acts 26:18; Eph. 1:14; 5:5; Col. 1:12; 3:24; Heb. 9:15; 1 Pet. 1:4
33 [a]1 Cor. 9:4-18; 2 Cor. 11:7-12; 12:14-18; 1 Thess. 2:5f.
34 [a]Acts 18:3 [b]Acts 19:22
36 [a]Acts 9:40; 21:5; Luke 22:41
37 [a]Luke 15:20
38 [a]Acts 20:25 [b]Acts 15:3
1 [a][we] Acts 16:10; 21:1-18 [b]Acts 16:11
2 [a]Acts 11:19
3 [a]Acts 4:36; 21:16 [b]Matt. 4:24 [c]Acts 12:20; 21:7 [d]Acts 21:2
4 [a]Acts 11:26; 21:16 [b]Acts 20:23; 21:11
5 [a]Acts 15:3 [b]Luke 22:41; Acts 9:40
6 [a]John 19:27
7 [a]Acts 12:20; 21:3 [b]Acts 1:15
8 [a]Acts 8:40; 21:16 [b]Acts 6:5 [c]Eph. 4:11; 2 Tim. 4:5
9 [a]Luke 2:36; Acts 13:1; 1 Cor. 11:5
10 [a]Acts 11:28
11 [a]1 Kin. 22:11; Is. 20:2; Jer. 13:1-11; 19:1, 11; John 18 [b]Acts 8:29 [c]Acts 9:16; 21:33 [d]Matt. 20:19
12 [a]Acts 21:15
13 [a]Acts 20:24 [b]Acts 5:41; 9:16
14 [a]Luke 22:42
15 [a]Acts 21:12
16 [a]Acts 21:4 [b]Acts 8:40 [c]Acts 4:36; 21:3 [d]Acts 15:7
17 [a]Acts 1:15
18 [a]Acts 12:17 [b]Acts 11:30

19 And after he had greeted them,
he [a]*began* to relate one by one the
things which God had done among
the Gentiles through his [b]ministry.
20 And when they heard it they *be-*
gan [a]glorifying God; and they said
to him, "You see, brother, how
many thousands there are among
the Jews of those who have believed, and they are all [b]zealous for
the Law;
21 and they have been told about
you, that you are [a]teaching all the
Jews who are among the Gentiles to
forsake Moses, telling them [b]not to
circumcise their children nor to
walk according to [c]the customs.
22"What, then, is *to be done?* They
will certainly hear that you have
come.
23"Therefore do this that we tell
you. We have four men who [a]are under a vow;
24 take them and [a]purify yourself
along with them, and pay their ex-
penses in order that they may
[b]shave their heads; and all will
know that there is nothing to the
things which they have been told
about you, but that you yourself
also walk orderly, keeping the Law.
25"But concerning the Gentiles
who have believed, we wrote, [a]hav-
ing decided that they should abstain
from meat sacrificed to idols and
from blood and from what is strangled and from fornication."
26 Then Paul took the men, and
the next day, [a]purifying himself
along with them, [b]went into the
temple, giving notice of the completion of the days of purification, until
the sacrifice was offered for each
one of them.

Paul Seized in the Temple

27 And when [a]the seven days were
almost over, [b]the Jews from [1c]Asia,
upon seeing him in the temple, *be-*
gan to stir up all the multitude and
laid hands on him,
28 crying out, "Men of Israel,
come to our aid! [a]This is the man
who preaches to all men everywhere against our people, and the
Law, and this place; and besides he
has even brought Greeks into the
temple and has [b]defiled this [a]holy
place."
29 For they had previously seen
[a]Trophimus the [b]Ephesian in the
city with him, and they supposed
that Paul had brought him into the
temple.
30 And all the city was aroused,
and the people rushed together; and
taking hold of Paul, they [a]dragged
him out of the temple; and immediately the doors were shut.
31 And while they were seeking to
kill him, a report came up to the
[1]commander of the [a]*Roman* [2]cohort
that all Jerusalem was in confusion.
32 And at once he [a]took along
some soldiers and centurions, and
ran down to them; and when they
saw the [1]commander and the soldiers, they stopped beating Paul.
33 Then the [1]commander came up
and took hold of him, and ordered
him to be [a]bound with [b]two chains;
and he *began* asking who he was
and what he had done.
34 But among the crowd [a]some
were shouting one thing *and* some
another, and when he could not find
out the facts on account of the uproar, he ordered him to be brought
into [b]the barracks.
35 And when he got to [a]the stairs,
it so happened that he was carried
by the soldiers because of the violence of the mob;
36 for the multitude of the people
kept following behind, crying out,
"[a]Away with him!"
37 And as Paul was about to be
brought into [a]the barracks, he said
to the [1]commander, "May I say
something to you?" And he *said,
"Do you know Greek?
38"Then you are not [a]the Egyptian
who some time ago stirred up a revolt and led the four thousand men
of the Assassins out [b]into the wilderness?"
39 But Paul said, "[a]I am a Jew of
Tarsus in [b]Cilicia, a citizen of no insignificant city; and I beg you, allow
me to speak to the people."
40 And when he had given him
permission, Paul, standing on [a]the
stairs, [b]motioned to the people with
his hand; and when there was a
great hush, he spoke to them in the
[1c]Hebrew dialect, saying,

CHAPTER 22

Paul's Defense Before the Jews

"[a]BRETHREN and fathers, hear
my defense which I now *offer* to
you."
2 And when they heard that he
was addressing them in the [1a]He-
brew dialect, they became even
more quiet; and he *said,
3"[a]I am [b]a Jew, born in [c]Tarsus
of [d]Cilicia, but brought up in this
city, [e]educated [1]under [f]Gamaliel,
[g]strictly according to the law of our
fathers, being zealous for God, just
as [h]you all are today.

19 [a]Acts 14:27 [b]Acts 1:17
20 [a]Matt. 9:8 [b]Acts 15:1; 22:3; Rom. 10:2; Gal. 1:14
21 [a]Acts 21:28 [b]Acts 15:19ff.; 1 Cor. 7:18f. [c]Acts 6:14
23 [a]Acts 18:18
24 [a]John 11:55; Acts 21:26; 24:18 [b]Acts 18:18
25 [a]Acts 15:19f., 29
26 [a]John 11:55; Acts 21:24; 24:18 [b]Num. 6:13; Acts 24:18
27 [1]I.e., west coast province of Asia Minor [a]Num. 6:9, 13-20 [b]Acts 20:19; 24:18 [c]Acts 16:6
28 [a]Acts 6:13 [b]Matt. 24:15; Acts 6:13f.; 24:6
29 [a]Acts 20:4 [b]Acts 18:19
30 [a]2 Kin. 11:15; Acts 16:19; 26:21
31 [1]Lit., *chiliarch,* in command of one thousand troops [2]Or, *battalion* [a]Acts 10:1
32 [1]V. 31 note [a]Acts 23:27
33 [1]V. 31 note [a]Acts 20:23; 21:11; 22:29; 26:29; 28:20; Eph. 6:20; 2 Tim. 1:16; 2:9 [b]Acts 12:6
34 [a]Acts 19:32 [b]Acts 21:37; 22:24; 23:10, 16, 32
35 [a]Acts 21:40
36 [a]Luke 23:18; John 19:15; Acts 22:22
37 [1]V. 31 note [a]Acts 21:34; 22:24; 23:10, 16, 32
38 [a]Acts 5:36 [b]Matt. 24:26
39 [a]Acts 9:11; 22:3 [b]Acts 6:9
40 [1]I.e., Jewish Aramaic [a]Acts 21:35 [b]Acts 12:17 [c]John 5:2; Acts 1:19; 22:2; 26:14
1 [a]Acts 7:2
2 [1]I.e., Jewish Aramaic [a]Acts 21:40
3 [1]Lit., *at the feet of* [a]Acts 9:1-22; 22:3-16; 26:9-18 [b]Acts 21:39 [c]Acts 9:11 [d]Acts 6:9 [e]Deut. 33:3; 2 Kin. 4:38; Luke 10:39 [f]Acts 5:34 [g]Acts 23:6; 26:5; Phil. 3:6 [h]Acts 21:20

4“And [a]I persecuted this [b]Way to
the death, binding and putting both
men and women into prisons,
5 as also [a]the high priest and all
[b]the Council of the elders can testify. From them I also [c]received letters to [d]the brethren, and started off
for [e]Damascus in order to bring
even those who were there to Jerusalem as prisoners to be punished.
6“[a]And it came about that as I
was on my way, approaching Damascus about noontime, a very
bright light suddenly flashed from
heaven all around me,
7 and I fell to the ground and
heard a voice saying to me, ‘Saul,
Saul, why are you persecuting Me?’
8“And I answered, ‘Who art
Thou, Lord?’ And He said to me, ‘I
am [a]Jesus the Nazarene, whom you
are persecuting.’
9“And those who were with me
[a]beheld the light, to be sure, but [b]did
not understand the voice of the One
who was speaking to me.
10“And I said, ‘[a]What shall I do,
Lord?’ And the Lord said to me,
‘Arise and go on into Damascus; and
there you will be told of all that has
been appointed for you to do.’
11“But since I [a]could not see because of the brightness of that light,
I was led by the hand by those who
were with me, and came into Damascus.
12“And a certain [a]Ananias, a man
who was devout by the standard of
the Law, *and* [b]well spoken of by all
the Jews who lived there,
13 came to me, and standing near
said to me, ‘[a]Brother Saul, receive
your sight!’ And [b]at that very time I
looked up at him.
14“And he said, ‘[a]The God of our
fathers has [b]appointed you to know
His will, and to [c]see the [d]Righteous
One, and to hear an utterance from
His mouth.
15 ‘For you will be [a]a witness for
Him to all men of [b]what you have
seen and heard.
16 ‘And now why do you delay?
[a]Arise, and be baptized, and [b]wash
away your sins, [c]calling on His
name.’
17“And it came about when I [a]re-
turned to Jerusalem and was praying in the temple, that I [b]fell into a
trance,
18 and I saw Him saying to me,
‘[a]Make haste, and get out of Jerusalem quickly, because they will not
accept your testimony about Me.’
19“And I said, ‘Lord, they themselves understand that in one synagogue after another [a]I used to imprison and [b]beat those who believed
in Thee.
20 ‘And [a]when the blood of Thy
witness Stephen was being shed, I
also was standing by approving, and
watching out for the cloaks of those
who were slaying him.’
21“And He said to me, ‘Go! For I
will send you far away [a]to the Gentiles.’ ”
22 And they listened to him up to
this statement, and *then* they raised
their voices and said, “[a]Away with
such a fellow from the earth, for [b]he
should not be allowed to live!”
23 And as they were crying out
and [a]throwing off their cloaks and
[b]tossing dust into the air,
24 the [1]commander ordered him
to be brought into [a]the barracks,
stating that he should be [b]examined
by scourging so that he might find
out the reason why they were shouting against him that way.
25 And when they stretched him
out [1]with thongs, Paul said to the
centurion who was standing by, “Is
it lawful for you to scourge [a]a man
who is a Roman and uncon-
demned?”
26 And when the centurion heard
this, he went to the [1]commander
and told him, saying, “What are you
about to do? For this man is a Roman.”
27 And the [1]commander came and
said to him, “Tell me, are you a Roman?” And he said, “Yes.”
28 And the [1]commander answered, “I acquired this citizenship
with a large sum of money.” And
Paul said, “But I was actually born *a
citizen.*”
29 Therefore those who were
about to [a]examine him immediately
[1]let go of him; and the [2]commander
also [b]was afraid when he found out
that he was a Roman, and because
he had [3]put him in chains.
30 But on the next day, [a]wishing to
know for certain why he had been
accused by the Jews, he [b]released
him and ordered the chief priests
and all [c]the [1]Council to assemble,
and brought Paul down and set him
before them.

CHAPTER 23

Paul Before the Council

AND Paul, looking intently at [a]the
[1]Council, said, “[b]Brethren, [c]I have
[2]lived my life with a perfectly good

4 [a]Acts 8:3; 22:19f. [b]Acts 9:2
5 [a]Acts 9:1 [b]Luke 22:66 [Gr.]; Acts 5:21 [Gr.]; 1 Tim. 4:14 [Gr.] [c]Acts 9:2 [d]Acts 2:29; 3:17; 13:26; 23:1; 28:17, 21; Rom. 9:3 [e]Acts 9:2
6 [a]Acts 22:6-11: *Acts 9:3-8; 26:12-18*
8 [a]Acts 26:9
9 [a]Acts 26:13 [b]Acts 9:7
10 [a]Acts 16:30
11 [a]Acts 9:8
12 [a]Acts 9:10 [b]Acts 6:3; 10:22
13 [a]Acts 9:17 [b]Acts 9:18
14 [a]Acts 3:13 [b]Acts 9:15; 26:16 [c]Acts 9:17; 26:16; 1 Cor. 9:1; 15:8 [d]Acts 7:52
15 [a]Acts 23:11; 26:16 [b]Acts 22:14
16 [a]Acts 9:18 [b]Acts 2:38; 1 Cor. 6:11; Eph. 5:26; Heb. 10:22 [c]Acts 7:59
17 [a]Acts 9:26; 26:20 [b]Acts 10:10
18 [a]Acts 9:29
19 [a]Acts 8:3; 22:4 [b]Matt. 10:17; Acts 26:11
20 [a]Acts 7:58f.; 8:1; 26:10
21 [a]Acts 9:15
22 [a]Acts 21:36; 1 Thess. 2:16 [b]Acts 25:24
23 [a]Acts 7:58 [b]2 Sam. 16:13
24 [1]Lit., *chiliarch,* in command of one thousand troops [a]Acts 21:34 [b]Acts 22:29
25 [1]Lit., *for the thongs* [a]Acts 16:37
26 [1]V. 24 note
27 [1]V. 24 note
28 [1]V. 24 note
29 [1]Or, *withdrew from* [2]V. 24 note [3]Lit., *bound him* [a]Acts 22:24 [b]Acts 16:38 [c]Acts 22:24f.
30 [1]Or, *Sanhedrin* [a]Acts 23:28 [b]Acts 21:33 [c]Matt. 5:22
1 [1]Or, *Sanhedrin* [2]Or, *conducted myself as a citizen* [a]Acts 22:30; 23:6, 15, 20, 28 [b]Acts 22:5 [c]Acts 24:16; 2 Cor. 1:12; 2 Tim. 1:3

conscience before God up to this
day."
2 And the high priest [a]Ananias
commanded those standing beside
him [b]to strike him on the mouth.
3 Then Paul said to him, "God is
going to strike you, [a]you white-
washed wall! And do you [b]sit to try
me according to the Law, and in violation of the Law order me to be
struck?"
4 But the bystanders said, "Do
you revile God's high priest?"
5 And Paul said, "I was not
aware, brethren, that he was high
priest; for it is written, '[a]YOU SHALL
NOT SPEAK EVIL OF A RULER OF YOUR
PEOPLE.' "
6 But perceiving that one part
were [a]Sadducees and the other
Pharisees, Paul *began* crying out in
[b]the [1]Council, "[c]Brethren, [d]I am a
Pharisee, a son of Pharisees; I am on
trial for [e]the hope and resurrection
of the dead!"
7 And as he said this, there arose
a dissension between the Pharisees
and Sadducees; and the assembly
was divided.
8 For [a]the Sadducees say that
there is no resurrection, nor an angel, nor a spirit; but the Pharisees
acknowledge them [1]all.
9 And there arose a great uproar;
and some of [a]the scribes of the
Pharisaic party stood up and *began*
to argue heatedly, saying, "[b]We find
nothing wrong with this man; [c]sup-
pose a spirit or an angel has spoken
to him?"
10 And as a great dissension was
developing, the [1]commander was
afraid Paul would be torn to pieces
by them and ordered the troops to
go down and take him away from
them by force, and bring him into
[a]the barracks.
11 But on [a]the night *immediately*
following, the Lord stood at his side
and said, "[b]Take courage; for [c]as
you have [d]solemnly witnessed to
My cause at Jerusalem, so you must
witness at Rome also."

A Conspiracy to Kill Paul

12 And when it was day, [a]the Jews
formed a [1]conspiracy and [b]bound
themselves under an oath, saying
that they would neither eat nor
drink until they had killed Paul.
13 And there were more than forty
who formed this plot.
14 And they came to the chief
priests and the elders, and said, "We
have [a]bound ourselves under a solemn oath to taste nothing until we
have killed Paul.
15 "Now, therefore, you [1]and [a]the
[2]Council notify the [3]commander to
bring him down to you, as though
you were going to determine his
case by a more thorough investigation; and we for our part are ready
to slay him before he comes near *the
place.*"
16 But the son of Paul's sister
heard of their ambush, [1]and he
came and entered [a]the barracks and
told Paul.
17 And Paul called one of the centurions to him and said, "Lead this
young man to the [1]commander, for
he has something to report to him."
18 So he took him and led him to
the [1]commander and *said, "Paul
[a]the prisoner called me to him and
asked me to lead this young man to
you since he has something to tell
you."
19 And the [1]commander took him
by the hand and stepping aside, *began* to inquire of him privately,
"What is it that you have to report
to me?"
20 And he said, "[a]The Jews have
agreed to ask you to bring Paul
down tomorrow to [b]the [1]Council, as
though they were going to inquire
somewhat more thoroughly about
him.
21 "So do not [1]listen to them, for
more than forty of them are [a]lying in
wait for him who have [b]bound
themselves under a curse not to eat
or drink until they slay him; and
now they are ready and waiting for
the promise from you."
22 Therefore the [1]commander let
the young man go, instructing him,
"Tell no one that you have notified
me of these things."

Paul Moved to Caesarea

23 And he called to him two of the
centurions, and said, "Get two hundred soldiers ready by [1]the third
hour of the night to proceed to
[a]Caesarea, [2]with seventy horsemen
and two hundred [3]spearmen."
24 *They were* also to provide
mounts to put Paul on and bring him
safely to [a]Felix the governor.
25 And he wrote a letter having
this form:
26 "Claudius Lysias, to the
[a]most excellent governor
Felix, [b]greetings.
27 "When this man was ar-
rested by the Jews and
[a]was about to be slain by
them, [a]I came upon them
with the troops and rescued
him, [b]having learned that
he was a Roman.

2 [a]Acts 24:1 [b]John 18:22
3 [a]Matt. 23:27 [b]Lev. 19:15; Deut. 25:2; John 7:51
5 [a]Ex. 22:28
6 [1]Or, *Sanhedrin* [a]Matt. 3:7; 22:23 [b]Acts 22:30; 23:1, 15, 20, 28 [c]Acts 22:5 [d]Acts 26:5; Phil. 3:5 [e]Acts 24:15, 21; 26:8
8 [1]Lit., *both* [a]Matt. 22:23; Acts 3:7
9 [a]Mark 2:16; Luke 5:30 [b]Acts 23:29 [c]John 12:29; Acts 22:6ff.
10 [1]Lit., *chiliarch,* in command of one thousand troops [a]Acts 21:34; 23:16, 32
11 [a]Acts 18:9 [b]Matt. 9:2 [c]Acts 19:21 [d]Luke 16:28; Acts 28:23
12 [1]Or, *mob* [a]Acts 9:23; 23:30; 1 Thess. 2:16 [b]Acts 23:14, 21
14 [a]Acts 23:12, 21
15 [1]Lit., *with* [2]Or, *Sanhedrin* [3]V. 10 note [a]Acts 22:30; 23:1, 6, 20, 28
16 [1]Or, *having been present* with them, *and he entered* [a]Acts 21:34; 23:10, 32
17 [1]V. 10 note
18 [1]V. 10 note [a]Eph. 3:1
19 [1]V. 10 note
20 [1]Or, *Sanhedrin* [a]Acts 23:14f. [b]Acts 22:30; 23:1, 6, 15, 28
21 [1]Lit., *be persuaded by them* [a]Luke 11:54 [b]Acts 23:12, 14
22 [1]V. 10 note
23 [1]I.e., 9 p.m. [2]Lit., *and* [3]Or, *slingers* or *bowmen* [a]Acts 8:40; 23:33
24 [a]Acts 23:26, 33; 24:1, 3, 10; 25:14
26 [a]Luke 1:3; Acts 24:3; 26:25 [b]Acts 15:23
27 [a]Acts 21:32f. [b]Acts 22:25-29

28 "And [a]wanting to ascertain
the charge for which they
were accusing him, I
[b]brought him down to their
[1c]Council;
29 and I found him to be accused over [a]questions
about their Law, but under
[b]no accusation deserving
death or imprisonment.
30 "And when I was [a]informed
that there would be [b]a plot
against the man, I sent him
to you at once, also in-
structing [c]his accusers to
[1]bring charges against him
before you.[2]"
31 So the soldiers, in accordance
with their orders, took Paul and
brought him by night to Antipatris.
32 But the next day, leaving [a]the
horsemen to go on with him, they
returned to [b]the barracks.
33 And when these had come to
[a]Caesarea and delivered the letter to
[b]the governor, they also presented
Paul to him.
34 And when he had read it, he
asked from what [a]province he was;
and when he learned that [b]he was
from Cilicia,
35 he said, "I will give you a hearing after your [a]accusers arrive
also," giving orders for him to be
[b]kept in Herod's [1]Praetorium.

Chapter 24

Paul Before Felix

AND after [a]five days the high
priest [b]Ananias came down with
some elders, with a certain attorney
named Tertullus; and they brought
charges to [c]the governor against
Paul.
2 And after *Paul* had been summoned, Tertullus began to accuse
him, saying *to the governor,*
"**S**ince we have through you attained much peace, and since by
your providence reforms are being
carried out for this nation,
3 we acknowledge *this* in every
way and everywhere, [a]most excellent Felix, with all thankfulness.
4"But, that I may not weary you
any further, I beg you to grant us, by
your kindness, a brief hearing.
5"For we have found this man a
real pest and a fellow who stirs up
dissension among all the Jews
throughout the world, and a ring-
leader of the [a]sect of the Nazarenes.
6"And he even tried to [a]desecrate
the temple; and [1]then we arrested
him. [[2]And we wanted to judge him
according to our own Law.
7 "But Lysias the commander
came along, and with much violence
took him out of our hands,
8 ordering his accusers to come
before you.] And by examining him
yourself concerning all these matters, you will be able to ascertain the
things of which we accuse him."
9 And [a]the Jews also joined in the
attack, asserting that these things
were so.
10 And when [a]the governor had
nodded for him to speak, Paul responded:
"**K**nowing that for many years you
have been a judge to this nation, I
cheerfully make my defense,
11 since you can take note of the
fact that no more than [a]twelve days
ago I went up to Jerusalem to worship.
12"And [a]neither in the temple, nor
in the synagogues, nor in the city
itself did they find me carrying on a
discussion with anyone or [b]causing
[1]a riot.
13"[a]Nor can they prove to you the
charges of which they now accuse
me.
14"But this I admit to you, that according to [a]the Way which they call
a [b]sect I do serve [1c]the God of our
fathers, [d]believing everything that
is in accordance with the Law, and
that is written in the Prophets;
15 having a hope in God, which
[a]these men cherish themselves, that
there shall certainly be a resurrection of both the righteous and the
wicked.
16"In view of this, [a]I also [1]do my
best to maintain always a blameless
conscience *both* before God and before men.
17"Now [a]after several years I
[b]came to bring [1]alms to my nation
and to present offerings;
18 in which they found me *occupied* in the temple, having been [a]pu-
rified, without *any* [b]crowd or uproar. But *there were* certain [c]Jews
from [1]Asia—
19 who ought to have been present
before you, and to [a]make accusation, if they should have anything
against me.
20"Or else let these men themselves tell what misdeed they found
when I stood before [a]the [1]Council,
21 other than for this one statement which [a]I shouted out while
standing among them, 'For the resurrection of the dead I am on trial
before you today.' "

28 [1]Or, *Sanhedrin* [a]Acts 22:30 [b]Acts 23:10 [c]Acts 23:1
29 [a]Acts 18:15; 25:19 [b]Acts 23:9; 25:25; 26:31; 28:18
30 [1]Lit., *speak against him* [2]Some mss. add, *Farewell* [a]Acts 23:20f. [b]Acts 9:24; 23:12 [c]Acts 23:35; 24:19; 25:16
32 [a]Acts 23:23 [b]Acts 23:10
33 [a]Acts 8:40; 23:23 [b]Acts 23:24, 26; 24:1, 3, 10; 25:14
34 [a]Acts 25:1 [b]Acts 6:9; 21:39
35 [1]Or, *governor's official residence* [a]Acts 23:30; 24:19; 25:16 [b]Acts 24:27
1 [a]Acts 24:11 [b]Acts 23:2 [c]Acts 23:24
3 [a]Acts 23:26; 26:25
5 [a]Acts 15:5; 24:14
6 [1]Lit., *also* [2]Many mss. do not contain the remainder of v. 6, v. 7, nor the first part of v. 8 [a]Acts 21:28
9 [a]1 Thess. 2:16
10 [a]Acts 23:24
11 [a]Acts 21:18, 27; 24:1
12 [1]Lit., *an attack of a mob* [a]Acts 25:8 [b]Acts 24:18
13 [a]Acts 25:7
14 [1]Lit., *the ancestral god* [a]Acts 9:2; 24:22 [b]Acts 15:5; 24:5 [c]Acts 3:13 [d]Acts 25:8; 26:4ff., 22f.; 28:23
15 [a]Dan. 12:2; John 5:28f.; 11:24; Acts 23:6
16 [1]Lit., *practice myself* [a]Acts 23:1
17 [1]Or, *gifts to charity* [a]Acts 20:31 [b]Acts 11:29f.; Rom. 15:25-28; 1 Cor. 16:1-4; 2 Cor. 8:1-4; 9:1, 2, 12; Gal. 2:10
18 [1]I.e., west coast province of Asia Minor [a]Acts 21:26 [b]Acts 24:12 [c]Acts 21:27
19 [a]Acts 23:30
20 [1]Or, *Sanhedrin* [a]Matt. 5:22
21 [a]Acts 23:6; 24:15

22 But Felix, having a more exact
knowledge about [a]the Way, put
them off, saying, "When Lysias the
[1]commander comes down, I will decide your case."
23 And he gave orders to the centurion for him to be [a]kept in custody
and *yet* [b]have *some* freedom, and
not to prevent any of [c]his friends
from ministering to him.
24 But some days later, Felix arrived with Drusilla, his [1]wife who
was a Jewess, and sent for Paul, and
heard him *speak* about [a]faith in
Christ Jesus.
25 And as he was discussing
[a]righteousness, [b]self-control and
[c]the judgment to come, Felix became frightened and said, "Go away
for the present, and when I find
time, I will summon you."
26 At the same time too, he was
hoping that [a]money would be given
him by Paul; therefore he also used
to send for him quite often and converse with him.
27 But after two years had passed,
Felix [1]was succeeded by Porcius
[a]Festus; and [b]wishing to do the Jews
a favor, Felix left Paul [c]imprisoned.

Chapter 25

Paul Before Festus

FESTUS therefore, having arrived
in [a]the province, three days later
went up to Jerusalem from [b]Caesa-
rea.
2 And the chief priests and the
leading men of the Jews [a]brought
charges against Paul; and they were
urging him,
3 requesting a [1]concession
against [2]Paul, that he might [3]have
him brought to Jerusalem, (*at the
same time,* [a]setting an ambush to
kill him on the way).
4 Festus then [a]answered that
Paul [b]was being kept in custody at
[c]Caesarea and that he himself was
about to leave shortly.
5 "Therefore," he *said, "let the
influential men among you [1]go there
with me, and if there is anything
wrong [2]about the man, let them
[3]prosecute him."
6 And after he had spent not
more than eight or ten days among
them, he went down to [a]Caesarea;
and on the next day he took his seat
on [b]the tribunal and ordered Paul to
be brought.
7 And after he had arrived, the
Jews who had come down from Jerusalem stood around him, bringing
[a]many and serious charges against
him [b]which they could not prove;
8 while Paul said in his own defense, "[a]I have committed no offense either against the Law of the
Jews or against the temple or
against Caesar."
9 But Festus, [a]wishing to do the
Jews a favor, answered Paul and
said, "[b]Are you willing to go up to
Jerusalem and [1]stand trial before
me on these charges?"
10 But Paul said, "I am standing
before Caesar's [a]tribunal, where I
ought to be tried. I have done no
wrong to *the* Jews, as you also very
well know.
11 "If then I am a wrongdoer, and
have committed anything worthy of
death, I do not refuse to die; but if
none of those things is *true* of which
these men accuse me, no one can
hand me over to them. I [a]appeal to
Caesar."
12 Then when Festus had conferred with [1]his council, he answered, "You have appealed to Caesar, to Caesar you shall go."
13 Now when several days had
elapsed, King Agrippa and Bernice
arrived at [a]Caesarea, [1]and paid their
respects to Festus.
14 And while they were spending
many days there, Festus laid Paul's
case before the king, saying, "There
is a certain man [a]left a prisoner by
Felix;
15 and when I was at Jerusalem,
the chief priests and the elders of
the Jews [a]brought charges against
him, asking for a sentence of condemnation upon him.
16 "And I [a]answered them that it is
not the custom of the Romans to
hand over any man before [b]the accused meets his accusers face to
face, and has an opportunity to
make his defense against the
charges.
17 "And so after they had assembled here, I made no delay, but on
the next day took my seat on [a]the
tribunal, and ordered the man to be
brought.
18 "And when the accusers stood
up, they *began* bringing charges
against him not of such crimes as I
was expecting;
19 but they *simply* had some
[a]points of disagreement with him
about their own [1b]religion and about
a certain dead man, Jesus, whom
Paul asserted to be alive.
20 "And [a]being at a loss how to investigate [1]such matters, I asked
whether he was willing to go to Je-

22 [1]Lit., *chiliarch,* in command of one thousand troops [a]Acts 24:14
23 [a]Acts 23:35 [b]Acts 28:16 [c]Acts 23:16; 27:3
24 [1]Lit., *own wife* [a]Acts 20:21
25 [a]Titus 2:12 [b]Gal. 5:23; Titus 1:8; 2 Pet. 1:6 [c]Acts 10:42
26 [a]Acts 24:17
27 [1]Lit., *received a successor, Porcius Festus* [a]Acts 25:1, 4, 9, 12; 26:24f., 32 [b]Acts 12:3; 25:9 [c]Acts 23:35; 25:14
1 [a]Acts 23:34 [b]Acts 8:40; 25:4, 6, 13
2 [a]Acts 24:1; 25:15
3 [1]Or, *favor* [2]Lit., *him* [3]Lit., *send for him to Jerusalem* [a]Acts 9:24
4 [a]Acts 25:16 [b]Acts 24:23 [c]Acts 8:40; 25:1, 6, 13
5 [1]Lit., *go down* [2]Lit., *in* [3]Or, *accuse*
6 [a]Acts 8:40; 25:1, 4, 13 [b]Matt. 27:19; Acts 25:10, 17
7 [a]Acts 24:5f. [b]Acts 24:13
8 [a]Acts 6:13; 24:12; 28:17
9 [1]Lit., *be judged* [a]Acts 12:3; 24:27 [b]Acts 25:20
10 [a]Matt. 27:19; Acts 25:10, 17
11 [a]Acts 25:21, 25; 26:32; 28:19
12 [1]A different body from that mentioned in Acts 4:15 and subsequently [e.g. Acts 24:20]
13 [1]Lit., *greeting Festus* [a]Acts 8:40; 25:1, 4, 6
14 [a]Acts 24:27
15 [a]Acts 24:1; 25:2
16 [a]Acts 25:4f. [b]Acts 23:30
17 [a]Matt. 27:19; Acts 25:6, 10
19 [1]Or, *superstition* [a]Acts 18:15; 23:29 [b]Acts 17:22
20 [1]Lit., *these* [a]Acts 25:9

rusalem and there stand trial on
these matters.
21 "But when Paul [a]appealed to be
held in custody for [1]the Emperor's
decision, I ordered him to be kept in
custody until I send him to Caesar."
22 And [a]Agrippa *said* to Festus, "I
also would like to hear the man myself." "Tomorrow," he *said, "you
shall hear him."

Paul Before Agrippa

23 And so, on the next day when
[a]Agrippa had come [1]together with
[a]Bernice, amid great pomp, and had
entered the auditorium [2]accom-
panied by the [3]commanders and
the prominent men of the city, at
the command of Festus, Paul was
brought in.
24 And Festus *said, "King Agrippa, and all you gentlemen here present with us, you behold this man
about whom [a]all the people of the
Jews appealed to me, both at Jerusalem and here, loudly declaring
that [b]he ought not to live any longer.
25 "But I found that he had committed [a]nothing worthy of death;
and since he himself [b]appealed to
[1]the Emperor, I decided to send him.
26 "Yet I have nothing definite
about him to write to my lord.
Therefore I have brought him before
you *all* and especially before you,
King Agrippa, so that after the investigation has taken place, I may
have something to write.
27 "For it seems absurd to me in
sending a prisoner, not to indicate
also the charges against him."

Chapter 26

Paul's Defense Before Agrippa

AND [a]Agrippa said to Paul, "You
are permitted to speak for yourself." Then Paul stretched out his
hand and *proceeded* to make his defense:
2 "In regard to all the things of
which I am accused by the Jews, I
consider myself fortunate, King A-
grippa, that I am about to make my
defense before you today;
3 [1]especially because you are an
expert in all [a]customs and [2]ques-
tions among *the* Jews; therefore I
beg you to listen to me patiently.
4 "So then, all Jews know [a]my
manner of life from my youth up,
which from the beginning was spent
among my *own* nation and at Jerusalem;
5 since they have known about
me for a long time previously, if
they are willing to testify, that I
lived *as* a [a]Pharisee [b]according to
the strictest [c]sect of our religion.
6 "And now I am [1]standing trial
[a]for the hope of [b]the promise made
by God to our fathers;
7 *the promise* [a]to which our
twelve tribes hope to attain, as they
earnestly serve *God* night and day.
And for this [b]hope, O King, I am
being [c]accused by Jews.
8 "Why is it considered incredible
among you *people* [a]if God does raise
the dead?
9 "So then, [a]I thought to myself
that I had to do many things hostile
to [b]the name of Jesus of Nazareth.
10 "And this is [1]just what I [a]did in
Jerusalem; not only did I lock up
many of the [2]saints in prisons, having [b]received authority from the
chief priests, but also when they
were being put to death I [c]cast my
vote against them.
11 "And [a]as I punished them often
in all the synagogues, I tried to force
them to blaspheme; and being [b]furi-
ously enraged at them, I kept pursuing them [c]even to [1]foreign cities.
12 "[1]While thus engaged [a]as I was
journeying to Damascus with the
authority and commission of the
chief priests,
13 at midday, O King, I saw on the
way a light from heaven, [1]brighter
than the sun, shining all around me
and those who were journeying
with me.
14 "And when we had [a]all fallen to
the ground, I heard a voice saying to
me in the [1b]Hebrew dialect, 'Saul,
Saul, why are you persecuting Me?
It is hard for you to kick against the
goads.'
15 "And I said, 'Who art Thou,
Lord?' And the Lord said, 'I am Jesus whom you are persecuting.
16 'But arise, and [a]stand on your
feet; for this purpose I have appeared to you, to [b]appoint you a
[c]minister and [d]a witness not only to
the things which you have [1]seen,
but also to the things in which I will
appear to you;
17 [a]delivering you [b]from the *Jewish* people and from the Gentiles, to
whom I am sending you,
18 to [a]open their eyes so that they
may turn from [b]darkness to light
and from the dominion of [c]Satan to
God, in order that they may receive
[d]forgiveness of sins and an [e]inheri-
tance among those who have been
sanctified by [f]faith in Me.'
19 "Consequently, King Agrippa, I
did not prove disobedient to the
heavenly vision,

21 [1]Lit., *the Augustus* (in this case Nero) [a]Acts 25:11f.
22 [a]Acts 9:15
23 [1]Lit., *and Bernice* [2]Lit., *and with* [3]Lit., *chiliarchs*, in command of one thousand troops [a]Acts 25:13; 26:30
24 [a]Acts 25:2, 7 [b]Acts 22:22
25 [1]Note v. 21 [a]Acts 23:29 [b]Acts 25:11f.
1 [a]Acts 9:15
3 [1]Or, *because you are especially expert* [2]Or, *controversial issues* [a]Acts 6:14; 25:19; 26:7
4 [a]Gal. 1:13f.; Phil. 3:5
5 [a]Acts 23:6 [b]Acts 22:3 [c]Acts 15:5
6 [1]Lit., *being tried* [a]Acts 24:15; 28:20 [b]Acts 13:32
7 [a]James 1:1 [b]Acts 24:15; 28:20 [c]Acts 26:2
8 [a]Acts 23:6
9 [a]John 16:2; 1 Tim. 1:13 [b]John 15:21
10 [1]Lit., *also* [2]I.e., true believers; lit., *holy ones* [a]Acts 8:3; 9:13 [b]Acts 9:1f. [c]Acts 22:20
11 [1]Or, *outlying* [a]Matt. 10:17; Acts 22:19 [b]Acts 9:1 [c]Acts 22:5
12 [1]Lit., *In which things* [a]Acts 26:12-18: *9:3-8; 22:6-11*
13 [1]Lit., *above the brightness of*
14 [1]I.e., Jewish Aramaic [a]Acts 9:7 [b]Acts 21:40
16 [1]Some early mss. read, *seen Me* [a]Ezek. 2:1; Dan. 10:11 [b]Acts 22:14 [c]Luke 1:2 [d]Acts 22:15
17 [a]Jer. 1:8, 19 [b]1 Chr. 16:35; Acts 9:15
18 [a]Is. 35:5; 42:7, 16; Eph. 5:8; Col. 1:13; 1 Pet. 2:9 [b]John 1:5; Eph. 5:8; Col. 1:12f.; 1 Thess. 5:5; 1 Pet. 2:9 [c]Matt. 4:10 [d]Luke 24:47; Acts 2:38 [e]Acts 20:32 [f]Acts 20:21

20 but *kept* declaring both [a]to those of Damascus first, and *also* [b]at Jerusalem and *then* throughout all the region of Judea, and *even* [c]to the Gentiles, that they should [d]repent and turn to God, performing deeds [e]appropriate to repentance.
21 "For this reason *some* Jews [a]seized me in the temple and tried [b]to put me to death.
22 "And so, having obtained help from God, I stand to this day [a]testifying both to small and great, stating nothing but what [b]the Prophets and Moses said was going to take place;
23 [1][a]that [2]the Christ was to suffer, *and* [1]that [b]by reason of *His* resurrection from the dead He should be the first to proclaim [c]light both to the *Jewish* people and to the Gentiles."
24 And while *Paul* was saying this in his defense, Festus *said in a loud voice, "Paul, you are out of your mind! *Your* great [a]learning is driving you mad."
25 But Paul *said, "I am not out of my mind, [a]most excellent Festus, but I utter words of sober truth.
26 "For the king [a]knows about these matters, and I speak to him also with confidence, since I am persuaded that none of these things escape his notice; for this has not been done in a corner.
27 "King Agrippa, do you believe the Prophets? I know that you do."
28 And Agrippa *replied* to Paul, "[1]In a short time you [2]will persuade me to [3]become a [a]Christian."
29 And Paul *said,* "[1]I would to God, that whether in a short or long time, not only you, but also all who hear me this day, might become such as I am, except for these [a]chains."
30 And [a]the king arose and the governor and Bernice, and those who were sitting with them,
31 and when they had drawn aside, they *began* talking to one another, saying, "[a]This man is not doing anything worthy of death or imprisonment."
32 And Agrippa said to Festus, "This man might have been [a]set free if he had not [b]appealed to Caesar."

CHAPTER 27

Paul Is Sent to Rome

AND when it was decided that [a]we [b]should sail for [c]Italy, they proceeded to deliver Paul and some other prisoners to a centurion of the Augustan [1][d]cohort named Julius.
2 And embarking in an Adramyttian ship, which was about to sail to the regions along the coast of [a]Asia, we put out to sea, accompanied by [b]Aristarchus, a [c]Macedonian of [d]Thessalonica.
3 And the next day we put in at [a]Sidon; and Julius [b]treated Paul with consideration and [c]allowed him to go to his friends and receive care.
4 And from there we put out to sea and sailed under the shelter of [a]Cyprus because [b]the winds were contrary.
5 And when we had sailed through the sea along the coast of [a]Cilicia and [b]Pamphylia, we landed at Myra in Lycia.
6 And there the centurion found an [a]Alexandrian ship sailing for [b]Italy, and he put us aboard it.
7 And when we had sailed slowly for a good many days, and with difficulty had arrived off Cnidus, [a]since the wind did not permit us *to* go farther, we sailed under the shelter of [b]Crete, off Salmone;
8 and with difficulty [a]sailing past it we came to a certain place called Fair Havens, near which was the city of Lasea.
9 And when considerable time had passed and the voyage was now dangerous, since even [a]the [1]fast was already over, Paul *began* to admonish them,
10 and said to them, "Men, I perceive that the voyage will certainly be *attended* with [a]damage and great loss, not only of the cargo and the ship, but also of our lives."
11 But the centurion was more persuaded by the [a]pilot and the [1]captain of the ship, than by what was being said by Paul.
12 And because the harbor was not suitable for wintering, the majority reached a decision to put out to sea from there, if somehow they could reach Phoenix, a harbor of [a]Crete, facing [1]northeast and southeast, and spend the winter *there.*
13 And [1]when a moderate south wind came up, supposing that they had gained their purpose, they weighed anchor and *began* [a]sailing along [b]Crete, close *inshore.*

Shipwreck

14 But before very long there [a]rushed down from [1]the land a violent wind, called [2]Euraquilo;
15 and when the ship was caught

20 [a]Acts 9:19ff. [b]Acts 9:26-29; 22:17-20 [c]Acts 9:15; 13:46 [d]Acts 3:19 [e]Matt. 3:8; Luke 3:8
21 [a]Acts 21:27, 30 [b]Acts 21:31
22 [a]Luke 16:28 [b]Acts 10:43; 24:14
23 [1]Lit., *whether* [2]I.e., the Messiah [a]Matt. 26:24; Acts 3:18 [b]1 Cor. 15:20, 23; Col. 1:18; Rev. 1:5 [c]Luke 2:32; 2 Cor. 4:4
24 [a]John 7:15; 2 Tim. 3:15
25 [a]Acts 23:26; 24:3
26 [a]Acts 26:3
28 [1]Or, *With a little* [2]Or, *try to convince* [3]Lit., *make* [a]Acts 11:26
29 [1]Lit., *I would pray to* [a]Acts 21:33
30 [a]Acts 25:23
31 [a]Acts 23:29
32 [a]Acts 28:18 [b]Acts 25:11
1 [1]Or, *battalion* [a][we] Acts 16:10; 27:1-28 [b]Acts 25:12, 25 [c]Acts 18:2; 27:6 [d]Acts 10:1
2 [a]Acts 2:9 [b]Acts 19:29 [c]Acts 16:9 [d]Acts 17:1
3 [a]Matt. 11:21 [b]Acts 27:43 [c]Acts 24:23
4 [a]Acts 4:36 [b]Acts 27:7
5 [a]Acts 6:9 [b]Acts 13:13
6 [a]Acts 28:11 [b]Acts 18:2; 27:1
7 [a]Acts 27:4 [b]Acts 2:11; 27:12f., 21; Titus 1:5, 12
8 [a]Acts 27:13 [Gr.]
9 [1]I.e., Day of Atonement in October [a]Lev. 16:29-31; 23:27-29; Num. 29:7
10 [a]Acts 27:21
11 [1]Or, *owner* [a]Rev. 18:17
12 [1]Or possibly, *southwest and northwest* [a]Acts 2:11; 27:13, 21; Titus 1:5, 12
13 [1]Lit., *a south wind having gently blown* [a]Acts 27:8 [Gr.] [b]Acts 2:11; 27:12f., 21; Titus 1:5, 12
14 [1]Lit., *it* [2]I.e., *a northeaster* [a]Mark 4:37

in it, and could not face the wind, we gave way *to it,* and let ourselves be driven along.

16 And running under the shelter of a small island called [1]Clauda, we were scarcely able to get the *ship's* boat under control.

17 And after they had hoisted it up, they used [1]supporting cables in undergirding the ship; and fearing that they might [a]run aground on *the shallows* of Syrtis, they let down the [2]sea anchor, and so let themselves be driven along.

18 The next day as we were being violently storm-tossed, [1]they began to [a]jettison the cargo;

19 and on the third day they threw the ship's tackle overboard with their own hands.

20 And since neither sun nor stars appeared for many days, and no small storm was assailing *us,* from then on all hope of our being saved was gradually abandoned.

21 And [1]when they had gone a long time without food, then Paul stood up in their midst and said, "[a]Men, you ought to have [2]followed my advice and not to have set sail from [b]Crete, and [3]incurred this [a]damage and loss.

22 "And *yet* now I urge you to [a]keep up your courage, for there shall be no loss of life among you, but *only* of the ship.

23 "For this very night [a]an angel of the God to whom I belong and [b]whom I serve [c]stood before me,

24 saying, 'Do not be afraid, Paul; [a]you must stand before Caesar; and behold, God has granted you [b]all those who are sailing with you.'

25 "Therefore, [a]keep up your courage, men, for I believe God, that [1]it will turn out exactly as I have been told.

26 "But we must [a]run aground on a certain [b]island."

27 But when the fourteenth night had come, as we were being driven about in the Adriatic Sea, about midnight the sailors *began* to surmise that [1]they were approaching some land.

28 And they took soundings, and found *it to be* twenty fathoms; and a little farther on they took another sounding and found *it to be* fifteen fathoms.

29 And fearing that we might [a]run aground somewhere on the [1]rocks, they cast four anchors from the stern and [2]wished for daybreak.

30 And as the sailors were trying to escape from the ship, and had let down [a]the *ship's* boat into the sea, on the pretense of intending to lay out anchors from the bow,

31 Paul said to the centurion and to the soldiers, "Unless these men remain in the ship, you yourselves cannot be saved."

32 Then the soldiers cut away the [a]ropes of the *ship's* boat, and let it fall away.

33 And until the day was about to dawn, Paul was encouraging them all to take some food, saying, "Today is the fourteenth day that you have been constantly watching and going without eating, having taken nothing.

34 "Therefore I encourage you to take some food, for this is for your preservation; for [a]not a hair from the head of any of you shall perish."

35 And having said this, he took bread and [a]gave thanks to God in the presence of all; and he broke it and began to eat.

36 And all [a]of them [1]were encouraged, and they themselves also took food.

37 And all of us in the ship were two hundred and seventy-six [1a]persons.

38 And when they had eaten enough, they *began* to lighten the ship by [a]throwing out the wheat into the sea.

39 And when day came, [a]they [1]could not recognize the land; but they [2]did observe a certain bay with a beach, and they [3]resolved to [4]drive the ship onto it if they could.

40 And casting off [a]the anchors, they [1]left them in the sea while at the same time they were loosening the ropes of the rudders, and hoisting the foresail to the wind, they were heading for the beach.

41 But striking a [1]reef where two seas met, they ran the vessel aground; and the prow stuck fast and remained immovable, but the stern *began* to be broken up by the force *of the waves.*

42 And the soldiers' plan was to [a]kill the prisoners, that none *of them* should swim away and escape;

43 but the centurion, [a]wanting to bring Paul safely through, kept them from their intention, and commanded that those who could swim should [1]jump overboard first and get to land,

44 and the rest *should follow,* some on planks, and others on various things from the ship. And thus it happened that [a]they all were brought safely to land.

16 [1]Some ancient mss. read, *Cauda*

17 [1]Lit., *helps* [2]Or possibly, *sail* [a]Acts 27:26, 29

18 [1]Lit., *they were doing a throwing out* [a]Jon. 1:5; Acts 27:38

21 [1]Lit., *there being much abstinence from food* [2]Lit., *obeyed me* [3]Lit., *gained* [a]Acts 27:10 [b]Acts 27:7

22 [a]Acts 27:25, 36

23 [a]Acts 5:19 [b]Rom. 1:9 [c]Acts 18:9; 23:11; 2 Tim. 4:17

24 [a]Acts 23:11 [b]Acts 27:31, 42, 44

25 [1]Lit., *it will be* [a]Acts 27:22, 36

26 [a]Acts 27:17, 29 [b]Acts 28:1

27 [1]Lit., *some land was approaching them*

29 [1]Lit., *rough places* [2]Lit., *they were praying for it to become day* [a]Acts 27:17, 26

30 [a]Acts 27:16

32 [a]John 2:15 [Gr.]

34 [a]Matt. 10:30

35 [a]Matt. 14:19

36 [1]Lit., *became cheerful* [a]Acts 27:22, 25

37 [1]Lit., *souls* [a]Acts 2:41

38 [a]Jon. 1:5; Acts 27:18

39 [1]Or, *were not recognizing* [2]Or, *were observing* [3]Or, *were resolving* [4]Some ancient mss. read, *bring the ship safely ashore* [a]Acts 28:1

40 [1]Or, *were leaving* [a]Acts 27:29

41 [1]Lit., *place*

42 [a]Acts 12:19

43 [1]Lit., *cast themselves* [a]Acts 27:3

44 [a]Acts 27:22, 31

CHAPTER 28

Safe at Malta

AND when [a]they had been brought safely through, [b]then we found out that [c]the island was called [1]Malta.

2 And [a]the [1]natives showed us extraordinary kindness; for because of the rain that had set in and because of the cold, they kindled a fire and [b]received us all.

3 But when Paul had gathered a bundle of sticks and laid them on the fire, a viper came out [1]because of the heat, and fastened on his hand.

4 And when [a]the [1]natives saw the creature hanging from his hand, they *began* saying to one another, "[b]Undoubtedly this man is a murderer, and though he has been saved from the sea, [2]justice has not allowed him to live."

5 However [a]he shook the creature off into the fire and suffered no harm.

6 But they were expecting that he was about to swell up or suddenly fall down dead. But after they had waited a long time and had seen nothing unusual happen to him, they changed their minds and [a]*began* to say that he was a god.

7 Now in the neighborhood of that place were lands belonging to the leading man of the island, named Publius, who welcomed us and entertained us courteously three days.

8 And it came about that the father of Publius was lying *in bed* afflicted with *recurrent* fever and dysentery; and Paul went in *to see* him and after he had [a]prayed, he [b]laid his hands on him and healed him.

9 And after this had happened, the rest of the people on the island who had diseases were coming to him and getting cured.

10 And they also honored us with many [1]marks of respect; and when we were setting sail, they [2]supplied *us* with [3]all we needed.

Paul Arrives at Rome

11 And at the end of three months we set sail on [a]an Alexandrian ship which had wintered at the island, and which had [1]the Twin Brothers for its figurehead.

12 And after we put in at Syracuse, we stayed there for three days.

13 And from there we [1]sailed around and arrived at Rhegium, and a day later a south wind sprang up, and on the second day we came to Puteoli.

14 [1]There we found *some* [a]brethren, and were invited to stay with them for seven days; and thus we came to Rome.

15 And the [a]brethren, when they heard about us, came from there as far as the [1]Market of Appius and [2]Three Inns to meet us; and when Paul saw them, he thanked God and took courage.

16 And when we entered Rome, Paul was [a]allowed to stay by himself, with the soldier who was guarding him.

17 And it happened that after three days he called together those who were [a]the leading men of the Jews, and when they had come together, he *began* saying to them, "[b]Brethren, [c]though I had done nothing against our people, or [d]the customs of our [1]fathers, yet I was delivered prisoner from Jerusalem into the hands of the Romans.

18 "And when they had examined me, they [a]were willing to release me because there was [b]no ground [1]for putting me to death.

19 "But when the Jews [1]objected, I was forced to [a]appeal to Caesar; not that I had any accusation against my nation.

20 "For this reason therefore, I [1]requested to see you and to speak with you, for I am wearing [a]this chain for [b]the sake of the hope of Israel."

21 And they said to him, "We have neither received letters from Judea concerning you, nor have any of [a]the brethren come here and reported or spoken anything bad about you.

22 "But we desire to hear from you what [1]your views are; for concerning this [a]sect, it is known to us that [b]it is spoken against everywhere."

23 And when they had set a day for him, they came to him at [a]his lodging in large numbers; and he was explaining to them by solemnly [b]testifying about the kingdom of God, and trying to persuade them concerning Jesus, [c]from both the Law of Moses and from the Prophets, from morning until evening.

24 And [a]some were being persuaded by the things spoken, but others would not believe.

25 And when they did not agree with one another, they *began* leaving after Paul had spoken one parting word, "The Holy Spirit rightly spoke through Isaiah the prophet to your fathers,

1 [1]Or, *Melita.* Some mss. read, *Melitene* [a][we] Acts 16:10; 27:1 [b]Acts 27:39 [c]Acts 27:26
2 [1]Lit., *barbarians* [a]Acts 28:4; Rom. 1:14; 1 Cor. 14:11; Col. 3:11 [b]Rom. 14:1
3 [1]Or, *from the heat*
4 [1]Lit., *barbarians* [2]I.e., personification of a goddess [a]Acts 28:2 [b]Luke 13:2, 4
5 [a]Mark 16:18
6 [a]Acts 14:11
8 [a]Acts 9:40; James 5:14f. [b]Mark 5:23
10 [1]Lit., *honors* [2]Or, *put on board* [3]Lit., *the things pertaining to the needs*
11 [1]Gr., *the Dioscuri,* i.e., Castor and Pollux, twin sons of Zeus [a]Acts 27:6
13 [1]Some early mss. read, *weighed anchor*
14 [1]Lit., *where* [a]Acts 1:15
15 [1]Lat., Appii Forum, a station about 43 miles from Rome [2]Lat., Tres Tabernae, a station about 33 miles from Rome [a]Acts 1:15
16 [a]Acts 24:23
17 [1]Or, *forefathers* [a]Acts 13:50; 25:2 [b]Acts 22:5 [c]Acts 25:8 [d]Acts 6:14
18 [1]Lit., *of death in me* [a]Acts 26:32 [b]Acts 23:29
19 [1]Lit., *spoke against it* [a]Acts 25:11
20 [1]Or, *invited you to see me and speak with me* [a]Acts 21:33 [b]Acts 26:6f.
21 [a]Acts 22:5
22 [1]Lit., *you think* [a]Acts 24:14 [b]1 Pet. 2:12; 3:16; 4:14, 16
23 [a]Philem. 22 [b]Luke 16:28; Acts 1:3; 23:11 [c]Acts 8:35
24 [a]Acts 14:4

26 saying,
'[a]GO TO THIS PEOPLE AND SAY,
"[b]YOU WILL KEEP ON HEARING,
BUT WILL NOT UNDERSTAND;
AND YOU WILL KEEP ON SEEING,
BUT WILL NOT PERCEIVE;
27 [a]FOR THE HEART OF THIS PEOPLE HAS BECOME DULL,
AND WITH THEIR EARS THEY SCARCELY HEAR,
AND THEY HAVE CLOSED THEIR EYES;
LEST THEY SHOULD SEE WITH THEIR EYES,
AND HEAR WITH THEIR EARS,
AND UNDERSTAND WITH THEIR HEART AND TURN AGAIN,
AND I SHOULD HEAL THEM."'

28 "Let it be known to you therefore, that [a]this salvation of God has
been sent [b]to the Gentiles; they will
also listen."
29 [[1]And when he had spoken
these words, the Jews departed,
having a great dispute among themselves.]
30 And he stayed two full years [1]in
his own rented quarters, and was
welcoming all who came to him,
31 [1a]preaching the kingdom of
God, and teaching concerning the
Lord Jesus Christ [b]with all openness, unhindered.

26 [a]Is. 6:9 [b]Matt. 13:14f.; Acts 28:26, 27
27 [a]Is. 6:10
28 [a]Ps. 98:3; Luke 2:30; Acts 13:26 [b]Acts 9:15; 13:46
29 [1]Many mss. do not contain this verse
30 [1]Or, *at his own expense*
31 [1]Or, *proclaiming* [a]Matt. 4:23; Acts 20:25; 28:23 [b]2 Tim. 2:9

THE EPISTLE OF PAUL TO THE

ROMANS

The Gospel Exalted

PAUL, a bond-servant of Christ
Jesus, [a]called *as* an apostle, [b]set
apart for [c]the gospel of God,
2 which He [a]promised beforehand through His [b]prophets in the
holy Scriptures,
3 concerning His Son, who was
born [a]of a descendant of David [b]according to the flesh,
4 who was declared [a]the Son of
God with power by the resurrection
from the dead, according to the
Spirit of holiness, Jesus Christ our
Lord,
5 through whom we have received grace and [a]apostleship to
bring about *the* [b]obedience of faith
among [c]all the Gentiles, for His
name's sake,
6 among whom you also are the
[a]called of Jesus Christ;
7 to all who are [a]beloved of God
in Rome, called *as* [b]saints: Grace to
you and peace from God our Father
and the Lord Jesus Christ.
8 First, [a]I thank my God through
Jesus Christ for you all, because
[b]your faith is being proclaimed
throughout the whole world.
9 For [a]God, whom I [b]serve in my
spirit in the *preaching of the* gospel
of His Son, is my witness *as to* how
unceasingly [c]I make mention of you,
10 always in my prayers making
request, if perhaps now at last by
[a]the will of God I may succeed in
coming to you.
11 For [a]I long to see you in order
that I may impart some spiritual gift
to you, that you may be established;
12 that is, that I may be encouraged together with you *while*
among you, each of us by the other's
faith, both yours and mine.
13 And [a]I do not want you to be
unaware, [b]brethren, that often I
[c]have planned to come to you (and
have been prevented thus far) in order that I might obtain some [d]fruit
among you also, even as among the
rest of the Gentiles.
14 [a]I am under obligation both to
Greeks and to [b]barbarians, both to
the wise and to the foolish.
15 Thus, [a]for my part, I am eager
to [b]preach the gospel to you also
who are in Rome.
16 For I am not [a]ashamed of the
gospel, for [b]it is the power of God
for salvation to every one who believes, to the [c]Jew first and also to
[d]the Greek.
17 For in it [a]*the* righteousness of
God is revealed from faith to faith;
as it is written, "[b]BUT THE RIGHTEOUS *man* SHALL LIVE BY FAITH."

Unbelief and Its Consequences

18 For [a]the wrath of God is revealed from heaven against all ungodliness and unrighteousness of
men, who [b]suppress the truth in unrighteousness,
19 because [a]that which is known
about God is evident within them;
for God made it evident to them.
20 For [a]since the creation of the
world His invisible attributes, His
eternal power and divine nature,
have been clearly seen, [b]being understood through what has been
made, so that they are without excuse.

1 [a]1 Cor. 1:1; 9:1 [b]Acts 9:15 [c]Mark 1:14; 2 Cor. 2:12
2 [a]Titus 1:2 [b]Luke 1:70
3 [a]Matt. 1:1 [b]John 1:14; Rom. 4:1
4 [a]Matt. 4:3
5 [a]Acts 1:25; Gal. 1:16 [b]Acts 6:7 [c]Acts 9:15
6 [a]Jude 1; Rev. 17:14
7 [a]Rom. 5:5ff.; 8:39 [b]Acts 9:13; Rom. 8:28ff.
8 [a]1 Cor. 1:4; Philem. 4 [b]Acts 28:22; Rom. 16:19
9 [a]Rom. 9:1 [b]Acts 24:14 [c]Eph. 1:16; Phil. 1:3f.; 1 Thess. 1:2f.; 2 Tim. 1:3
10 [a]Acts 18:21
11 [a]Acts 19:21
13 [a]Rom. 11:25 [b]Acts 1:15; Rom. 7:1; 1 Cor. 1:10; 14:20, 26; Gal. 3:15 [c]Acts 19:21 [d]John 4:36; 15:16
14 [a]1 Cor. 9:16 [b]Acts 28:2
15 [a]Rom. 12:18 [b]Rom. 15:20
16 [a]2 Tim. 1:8, 12, 16 [b]1 Cor. 1:18, 24 [c]Acts 3:26; Rom. 2:9 [d]John 7:35
17 [a]Rom. 3:21; 9:30; Phil. 3:9 [b]Hab. 2:4; Gal. 3:11
18 [a]Rom. 5:9 [b]2 Thess. 2:6f.
19 [a]Acts 14:17
20 [a]Mark 10:6 [b]Job 12:7-9; Ps. 19:1-6; Jer. 5:21f.

21 For even though they knew God, they did not honor Him as God, or give thanks; but they became [a]futile in their speculations, and their foolish heart was darkened.

22 [a]Professing to be wise, they became fools,

23 and [a]exchanged the glory of the incorruptible God for an image in the form of corruptible man and of birds and four-footed animals and crawling creatures.

24 Therefore [a]God gave them over in the lusts of their hearts to impurity, that their bodies might be [b]dishonored among them.

25 For they exchanged the truth of God for a [a]lie, and worshiped and served the creature rather than the Creator, [b]who is blessed forever. Amen.

26 For this reason [a]God gave them over to [b]degrading passions; for their women exchanged the natural function for that which is unnatural,

27 and in the same way also the men abandoned the natural function of the woman and burned in their desire towards one another, [a]men with men committing indecent acts and receiving in their own persons the due penalty of their error.

28 And just as they did not see fit to acknowledge God any longer, [a]God gave them over to a depraved mind, to do those things which are not proper,

29 being filled with all unrighteousness, wickedness, greed, malice; full of envy, murder, strife, deceit, malice; *they are* [a]gossips,

30 slanderers, [a]haters of God, insolent, arrogant, boastful, inventors of evil, [b]disobedient to parents,

31 without understanding, untrustworthy, [a]unloving, unmerciful;

32 and, although they know the ordinance of God, that those who practice such things are worthy of [a]death, they not only do the same, but also [b]give hearty approval to those who practice them.

Chapter 2

The Impartiality of God

THEREFORE you are [a]without excuse, [b]every man *of you* who passes judgment, for in that [c]you judge another, you condemn yourself; for you who judge practice the same things.

2 And we know that the judgment of God rightly falls upon those who practice such things.

3 And do you suppose this, [a]O man, when you pass judgment upon those who practice such things and do the same *yourself,* that you will escape the judgment of God?

4 Or do you think lightly of [a]the riches of His [b]kindness and [c]forbearance and [d]patience, not knowing that [e]the kindness of God leads you to repentance?

5 But because of your stubbornness and unrepentant heart [a]you are storing up wrath for yourself [b]in the day of wrath and revelation of the righteous judgment of God,

6 [a]who WILL RENDER TO EVERY MAN ACCORDING TO HIS DEEDS:

7 to those who by [a]perseverance in doing good seek for [b]glory and honor and [c]immortality, [d]eternal life;

8 but to those who are [a]selfishly ambitious and [b]do not obey the truth, but obey unrighteousness, wrath and indignation.

9 *There will be* [a]tribulation and distress for every soul of man who does evil, of the Jew [b]first and also of the Greek,

10 but [a]glory and honor and peace to every man who does good, to the Jew [b]first and also to the Greek.

11 For [a]there is no partiality with God.

12 For all who have sinned [a]without the Law will also perish without the Law; and all who have sinned under the Law will be judged by the Law;

13 for [a]not the hearers of the Law are just before God, but the doers of the Law will be justified.

14 For when Gentiles who do not have the Law do [a]instinctively the things of the Law, these, not having the Law, are a law to themselves,

15 in that they show [a]the work of the Law written in their hearts, their conscience bearing witness, and their thoughts alternately accusing or else defending them,

16 on the day when, [a]according to my gospel, [b]God will judge the secrets of men through Christ Jesus.

The Jew is Condemned by the Law

17 But if you bear the name "Jew," and [a]rely upon the Law, and boast in God,

18 and know *His* will, and [a]approve the things that are essential, being instructed out of the Law,

---

21 [a]2 Kin. 17:15; Jer. 2:5; Eph. 4:17f.
22 [a]Jer. 10:14; 1 Cor. 1:20
23 [a]Ps. 106:20; Jer. 2:11; Acts 17:29
24 [a]Rom. 1:26, 28; Eph. 4:19 [b]Eph. 2:3
25 [a]Is. 44:20; Jer. 10:14; [b]Rom. 9:5
26 [a]Rom. 1:24 [b]1 Thess. 4:5
27 [a]Lev. 18:22
28 [a]Rom. 1:24
29 [a]2 Cor. 12:20
30 [a]Ps. 5:5 [b]2 Tim. 3:2
31 [a]2 Tim. 3:3
32 [a]Rom. 6:21 [b]Luke 11:48; Acts 8:1; 22:20
1 [a]Rom. 1:20 [b]Luke 12:14; Rom. 2:3; 9:20 [c]2 Sam. 12:5-7; Matt. 7:1
3 [a]Luke 12:14; Rom. 2:1; 9:20
4 [a]Rom. 9:23; 11:33; 2 Cor. 8:2; Phil. 4:19; Col. 1:27; 2:2; Titus 3:6 [b]Rom. 11:22 [c]Rom. 3:25 [d]Ex. 34:6; Rom. 9:22; 1 Tim. 1:16 [e]2 Pet. 3:9
5 [a]Deut. 32:34f.; Prov. 1:18 [b]Ps. 110:5; 2 Cor. 5:10; 2 Thess. 1:5; Jude 6
6 [a]Ps. 62:12; Matt. 16:27
7 [a]Luke 8:15; Heb. 10:36 [b]Rom. 2:10; Heb. 2:7; 1 Pet. 1:7 [c]1 Cor. 15:42, 50, 53f.; Eph. 6:24; 2 Tim. 1:10 [d]Matt. 25:46
8 [a]2 Cor. 12:20; Gal. 5:20; Phil. 1:17; 2:3; James 3:14, 16 [b]2 Thess. 2:12
9 [a]Rom. 8:35 [b]Acts 3:26; Rom. 1:16; 1 Pet. 4:17
10 [a]Rom. 2:7; Heb. 2:7; 1 Pet. 1:7 [b]Rom. 2:9
11 [a]Acts 10:34
12 [a]Acts 2:23; 1 Cor. 9:21
13 [a]Matt. 7:21, 24ff.; John 13:17; James 1:22f., 25
14 [a]Acts 10:35; Rom. 1:19; 2:15
15 [a]Rom. 2:14
16 [a]Rom. 16:25; 1 Cor. 15:1; Gal. 1:11; 1 Tim. 1:11; 2 Tim. 2:8 [b]Acts 10:42; 17:31; Rom. 3:6; 14:10
17 [a]Mic. 3:11; John 5:45; Rom. 2:23
18 [a]Phil. 1:10

19 and are confident that you
yourself are a guide to the blind, a
light to those who are in darkness,
20 a [1]corrector of the foolish, a
teacher of [2]the immature, having in
the Law [a]the embodiment of knowledge and of the truth,
21 you, therefore, [a]who teach another, do you not teach yourself?
You who preach that one should not
steal, do you steal?
22 You who say that one should
not commit adultery, do you commit adultery? You who abhor idols,
do you [a]rob temples?
23 You who [a]boast in the Law,
through your breaking the Law, do
you dishonor God?
24 For "[a]THE NAME OF GOD IS BLAS-
PHEMED AMONG THE GENTILES [b]BE-
CAUSE OF YOU," just as it is written.
25 For indeed circumcision is of
value, if you [a]practice the Law; but
if you are a transgressor of the Law,
[b]your circumcision has become uncircumcision.
26 [a]If therefore [b]the uncircumcised man [c]keeps the requirements
of the Law, will not his uncircumcision be regarded as circumcision?
27 And will not [a]he who is physi-
cally uncircumcised, if he keeps the
Law, will he not [b]judge you who
though having the letter *of the Law*
and circumcision are a transgressor
of the Law?
28 For [a]he is not a Jew who is one
outwardly; neither is circumcision
that which is outward in the flesh.
29 But [a]he is a Jew who is one inwardly; and circumcision is that
which is of the heart, by the [b]Spirit,
not by the letter; [c]and his praise is
not from men, but from God.

CHAPTER 3

All the World Guilty

THEN what advantage has the
Jew? Or what is the benefit of circumcision?
2 Great in every respect. First of
all, that [a]they were entrusted with
the [b]oracles of God.
3 What then? If [a]some did not believe, their unbelief will not nullify
the faithfulness of God, will it?
4 [a]May it never be! Rather, let
God be found true, though every
man *be found* [b]a liar, as it is written,
"[c]THAT THOU MIGHTEST BE JUS-
TIFIED IN THY WORDS,
AND MIGHTEST PREVAIL WHEN
THOU ART JUDGED."
5 But if our unrighteousness
[a]demonstrates the righteousness of
God, [b]what shall we say? The God
who inflicts wrath is not unrighteous, is He? ([c]I am speaking in human terms.)
6 [a]May it never be! For otherwise
how will [b]God judge the world?
7 But if through my lie [a]the truth
of God abounded to His glory, [b]why
am I also still being judged as a sinner?
8 And why not *say* (as we are
slanderously reported and as some
affirm that we say), "[a]Let us do evil
that good may come"? [1]Their condemnation is just.
9 What then? [a]Are we better than
they? Not at all; for we have already
charged that both [b]Jews and
[c]Greeks are [d]all under sin;
10 as it is written,
"[a]THERE IS NONE RIGHTEOUS,
NOT EVEN ONE;
11 THERE IS NONE WHO UNDER-
STANDS,
THERE IS NONE WHO SEEKS FOR
GOD;
12 ALL HAVE TURNED ASIDE, TO-
GETHER THEY HAVE BECOME
USELESS;
THERE IS NONE WHO DOES
GOOD,
THERE IS NOT EVEN ONE."
13 "[a]THEIR THROAT IS AN OPEN
GRAVE,
WITH THEIR TONGUES THEY
KEEP DECEIVING,"
"THE POISON OF ASPS IS UNDER
THEIR LIPS;"
14 "[a]WHOSE MOUTH IS FULL OF
CURSING AND BITTERNESS;"
15 "[a]THEIR FEET ARE SWIFT TO
SHED BLOOD,
16 DESTRUCTION AND MISERY ARE
IN THEIR PATHS,
17 AND THE PATH OF PEACE HAVE
THEY NOT KNOWN."
18 "[a]THERE IS NO FEAR OF GOD BE-
FORE THEIR EYES."
19 Now we know that whatever
the [a]Law says, it speaks to [b]those
who are [1]under the Law, that every
mouth may be closed, and [c]all the
world may become accountable to
God;
20 because [a]by the works of the
Law no flesh will be justified in His
sight; for [b]through the Law *comes*
the knowledge of sin.

Justification by Faith

21 But now apart [1]from the Law
[a]*the* righteousness of God has been
manifested, being [b]witnessed by the
Law and the Prophets,
22 even *the* [a]righteousness of God
through [b]faith [c]in Jesus Christ for

20 [1]Or, *instructor* [2]Lit., *infants* [a]Rom. 3:31; 2 Tim. 1:13
21 [a]Matt. 23:3ff.
22 [a]Acts 19:37
23 [a]Mic. 3:11; John 5:45; Rom. 2:17; 9:4
24 [a]Is. 52:5 [b]Ezek. 36:20ff.; 2 Pet. 2:2
25 [a]Rom. 2:13f., 27 [b]Jer. 4:4; 9:25f.
26 [a]1 Cor. 7:19 [b]Rom. 3:30; Eph. 2:11 [c]Rom. 2:25, 27; 8:4
27 [a]Rom. 3:30; Eph. 2:11 [b]Matt. 12:41
28 [a]John 8:39; Rom. 2:17; 9:6; Gal. 6:15
29 [a]Phil. 3:3; Col. 2:11 [b]Rom. 2:27; 7:6; 2 Cor. 3:6 [c]John 5:44; 12:43; 1 Cor. 4:5; 2 Cor. 10:18
2 [a]Deut. 4:8; Ps. 147:19; Rom. 9:4 [b]Acts 7:38
3 [a]Rom. 10:16; Heb. 4:2
4 [a]Luke 20:16; Rom. 3:6, 31 [b]Ps. 116:11; Rom. 3:7 [c]Ps. 51:4
5 [a]Rom. 5:8; 2 Cor. 6:4; 7:11 [Gr.]; Gal. 2:18 [Gr.] [b]Rom. 4:1; 7:7; 8:31; 9:14, 30 [c]Rom. 6:19; 1 Cor. 9:8; 15:32; Gal. 3:15
6 [a]Luke 20:16; Rom. 3:4, 31 [b]Rom. 2:16
7 [a]Rom. 3:4 [b]Rom. 9:19
8 [1]Lit., *Whose* [a]Rom. 6:1
9 [a]Rom. 3:1 [b]Rom. 2:1-29 [c]Rom. 1:18-32 [d]Rom. 3:19, 23; 11:32; Gal. 3:22
10 [a]Ps. 14:1-3; 53:1-4
13 [a]Ps. 5:9; 140:3
14 [a]Ps. 10:7
15 [a]Is. 59:7f.
18 [a]Ps. 36:1
19 [1]Lit., *in* [a]John 10:34 [b]Rom. 2:12 [c]Rom. 3:9
20 [a]Ps. 143:2; Acts 13:39; Gal. 2:16 [b]Rom. 4:15; 5:13, 20; 7:7
21 [1]Or, *from law* [a]Rom. 1:17; 9:30 [b]Acts 10:43; Rom. 1:2
22 [a]Rom. 1:17; 9:30 [b]Rom. 4:5 [c]Acts 3:16; Gal. 2:16, 20; 3:22; Eph. 3:12

[d]all those who believe; for [e]there is
no distinction;
23 for all [a]have sinned and fall
short of the glory of God,
24 being justified as a gift [a]by His
grace through [b]the redemption
which is in Christ Jesus;
25 whom God displayed publicly
as [a]a propitiation [b]in His blood
through faith. *This was* to demonstrate His righteousness, because in
the [c]forbearance of God He [d]passed
over the sins previously committed;
26 for the demonstration, *I say,* of
His righteousness at the present
time, that He might be just and the
justifier of the one who has faith in
Jesus.
27 Where then is [a]boasting? It is
excluded. By [b]what kind of law? Of
works? No, but by a law of faith.
28 [1]For [a]we maintain that a man is
justified by faith apart from works
[2]of the Law.
29 Or [a]is God *the God* of Jews
only? Is He not *the God* of Gentiles
also? Yes, of Gentiles also,
30 since indeed [a]God [b]who will
justify the circumcised by faith and
the uncircumcised through faith [c]is
one.
31 Do we then nullify the Law
through faith? [a]May it never be! On
the contrary, we [b]establish the Law.

CHAPTER 4

Justification by Faith Evidenced in Old Testament

WHAT then shall we say that
Abraham, our forefather [a]according
to the flesh, has found?
2 For if Abraham was justified by
works, he has something to boast
about; but [a]not before God.
3 For what does the Scripture
say? "[a]AND ABRAHAM BELIEVED
GOD, AND IT WAS RECKONED TO HIM
AS RIGHTEOUSNESS."
4 Now to the one who [a]works, his
wage is not reckoned as a favor but
as what is due.
5 But to the one who does not
work, but [a]believes in Him who justifies the ungodly, his faith is reckoned as righteousness,
6 just as David also speaks of the
blessing upon the man to whom God
reckons righteousness apart from
works:
7 "[a]BLESSED ARE THOSE WHOSE
LAWLESS DEEDS HAVE BEEN
FORGIVEN,
AND WHOSE SINS HAVE BEEN
COVERED.
8 "[a]BLESSED IS THE MAN WHOSE
SIN THE LORD WILL NOT [b]TAKE
INTO ACCOUNT."
9 Is this blessing then upon [a]the
circumcised, or upon the uncircumcised also? For [b]we say, "[c]FAITH
WAS RECKONED TO ABRAHAM AS
RIGHTEOUSNESS."
10 How then was it reckoned?
While he was circumcised, or uncircumcised? Not while circumcised,
but while uncircumcised;
11 and he [a]received the sign of circumcision, [b]a seal of the righteousness of the faith which he had while
uncircumcised, that he might be
[c]the father of [d]all who believe without being circumcised, that righteousness might be reckoned to
them,
12 and the father of circumcision
to those who not only are of the circumcision, but who also follow in
the steps of the faith of our father
Abraham which he had while uncircumcised.
13 For [a]the promise to Abraham
or to his descendants [b]that he would
be heir of the world was not through
the Law, but through the righteousness of faith.
14 For [a]if those who are of the Law
are heirs, faith is made void and the
promise is nullified;
15 for [a]the Law brings about
wrath, but [b]where there is no law,
neither is there violation.
16 For this reason *it is* [1]by faith,
that *it might be* in accordance with
[a]grace, in order that the promise
may be certain to [b]all the [2]descen-
dants, not only to [3]those who are of
the Law, but also to [3]those who are
of the faith of Abraham, who is [c]the
father of us all,
17 (as it is written, "[a]A FATHER OF
MANY NATIONS HAVE I MADE YOU")
in the sight of Him whom he believed, *even* God, [b]who gives life to
the dead and [1c]calls into being [d]that
which does not exist.
18 In hope against hope he believed, in order that he might become [a]a father of many nations, according to that which had been
spoken, "[b]SO SHALL YOUR DESCEND-
ANTS BE."
19 And without becoming weak in
faith he contemplated his own body,
now [a]as good as dead since [b]he was
about a hundred years old, and [c]the
deadness of Sarah's womb;
20 yet, with respect to the promise
of God, he did not waver in unbelief,
but grew strong in faith, [a]giving glory to God,

22 [d]Rom. 4:11, 16; 10:4 [e]Rom. 10:12; Gal. 3:28; Col. 3:11
23 [a]Rom. 3:9
24 [a]Rom. 4:4f., 16; Eph. 2:8 [b]1 Cor. 1:30; Eph. 1:7; Col. 1:14; Heb. 9:15
25 [a]1 John 2:2; 4:10 [b]1 Cor. 5:7; Heb. 9:14, 28; 1 Pet. 1:19; Rev. 1:5 [c]Rom. 2:4 [d]Acts 14:16; 17:30
27 [a]Rom. 2:17, 23; 4:2; 1 Cor. 1:29ff. [b]Rom. 9:31
28 [1]Some ancient mss. read, *Therefore* [2]Or, *of law* [a]Acts 13:39; Rom. 3:20, 21; Eph. 2:9; James 2:20, 24, 26
29 [a]Acts 10:34f.; Rom. 9:24; 10:12; 15:9; Gal. 3:28
30 [a]Rom. 10:12 [b]Rom. 3:22; 4:11f., 16; Gal. 3:8 [c]Deut. 6:4
31 [a]Luke 20:16; Rom. 3:4 [b]Matt. 5:17; Rom. 4:3; 8:4
1 [a]Rom. 1:3
2 [a]1 Cor. 1:31
3 [a]Gen. 15:6; Rom. 4:9, 22; Gal. 3:6; James 2:23
4 [a]Rom. 11:6
5 [a]John 6:29; Rom. 3:22
7 [a]Ps. 32:1
8 [a]Ps. 32:2 [b]2 Cor. 5:19
9 [a]Rom. 3:30 [b]Rom. 4:3 [c]Gen. 15:6
11 [a]Gen. 17:10f. [b]John 3:33 [c]Luke 19:9; Rom. 4:16f. [d]Rom. 3:22; 4:16
13 [a]Rom. 9:8; Gal. 3:16 [b]Gen. 17:4-6; 22:17f.
14 [a]Gal. 3:18
15 [a]Rom. 7:7, 10-25; 1 Cor. 15:56; Gal. 3:10 [b]Rom. 3:20
16 [1]Or, *of* [2]Lit., *seed* [3]Lit., *that which is* [a]Rom. 3:24 [b]Rom. 4:11; 9:8; 15:8 [c]Luke 19:9; Rom. 4:11
17 [1]Lit., *calls the things which do not exist as existing* [a]Gen. 17:5 [b]John 5:21 [c]Is. 48:13; 51:2 [d]1 Cor. 1:28
18 [a]Rom. 4:17 [b]Gen. 15:5
19 [a]Heb. 11:12 [b]Gen. 17:17 [c]Gen. 18:11
20 [a]Matt. 9:8

21 and [a]being fully assured that [b]what He had promised, He was able also to perform.

22 Therefore also [a]IT WAS RECKONED TO HIM AS RIGHTEOUSNESS.

23 Now [a]not for his sake only was it written, that "IT WAS RECKONED TO HIM,"

24 but for our sake also, to whom it will be reckoned, as those [a]who believe in Him who [b]raised Jesus our Lord from the dead,

25 *He* who was [a]delivered up because of our transgressions, and was [b]raised because of our justification.

Chapter 5

Results of Justification

[a]THEREFORE having been justified by faith, [1b]we have peace with God through our Lord Jesus Christ,

2 through whom also we have [a]obtained our introduction by faith into this grace [b]in which we stand; and we exult in hope of the glory of God.

3 [a]And not only this, but [1]we also [b]exult in our tribulations, knowing that tribulation brings about [c]perseverance;

4 and [a]perseverance, [b]proven character; and proven character, hope;

5 and hope [a]does not disappoint, because the love of God has been [b]poured out within our hearts through the Holy Spirit who was given to us.

6 For while we were still [a]helpless, [b]at the right time [c]Christ died for the ungodly.

7 For one will hardly die for a righteous man; though perhaps for the good man someone would dare even to die.

8 But God [a]demonstrates [b]His own love toward us, in that while we were yet sinners, [c]Christ died for us.

9 Much more then, having now been justified [a]by His blood, we shall be saved [b]from the wrath *of God* through Him.

10 For if while we were [a]enemies, we were reconciled to God through the death of His Son, much more, having been reconciled, we shall be saved [b]by His life.

11 [a]And not only this, but we also exult in God through our Lord Jesus Christ, through whom we have now received [b]the reconciliation.

12 Therefore, just as through [a]one man sin entered into the world, and [b]death through sin, and [c]so death spread to all men, because all sinned—

13 for until the Law sin was in the world; but [a]sin is not imputed when there is no law.

14 Nevertheless death reigned from Adam until Moses, even over those who had not sinned [a]in the likeness of Adam's offense, who is a [b]type of Him who was to come.

15 But the free gift is not like the transgression. For if by the transgression of [a]the one [b]the many died, much more did the grace of God and the gift by [c]the grace of the one Man, Jesus Christ, abound to [b]the many.

16 And the gift is not like *that which came* through the one who sinned; for on the one hand [a]the judgment *arose* from one *transgression* resulting in condemnation, but on the other hand the free gift *arose* from many transgressions resulting in justification.

17 For if by the transgression of the one, death reigned [a]through the one, much more those who receive the abundance of grace and of the gift of righteousness will [b]reign in life through the One, Jesus Christ.

18 So then as through [a]one transgression there resulted condemnation to all men, even so through one [b]act of righteousness there resulted [c]justification of life to all men.

19 For as through the one man's disobedience [a]the many [b]were made sinners, even so through [c]the obedience of the One [a]the many will be made righteous.

20 And [a]the Law came in that the transgression might increase; but where sin increased, [b]grace abounded all the more,

21 that, as [a]sin reigned in death, even so [b]grace might reign through righteousness to eternal life through Jesus Christ our Lord.

Chapter 6

Believers Are Dead to Sin, Alive to God

[a]WHAT shall we say then? Are we to [b]continue in sin that grace might increase?

2 [a]May it never be! How shall we who [b]died to sin still live in it?

3 Or do you not know that all of us who have been [a]baptized into [b]Christ Jesus have been baptized into His death?

4 Therefore we have been [a]buried with Him through baptism into

21 [a]Rom. 14:5 [b]Gen. 18:14
22 [a]Rom. 4:3
23 [a]Rom. 15:4; 1 Cor. 9:9f.; 10:11
24 [a]Rom. 10:9 [b]Acts 2:24
25 [a]Rom. 5:6, 8; Eph. 5:2 [b]Rom. 5:18; 1 Cor. 15:17
1 [1]Or, *let us have* [a]Rom. 3:28 [b]Rom. 5:11
2 [a]Eph. 2:18; 3:12; 1 Pet. 3:18 [b]1 Cor. 15:1
3 [1]Or, *let us also exult* [a]Rom. 5:11; 8:23 [b]Matt. 5:12; James 1:2f. [c]Luke 21:19
4 [a]Luke 21:19 [b]Phil. 2:22; James 1:12
5 [a]Ps. 119:116; Rom. 9:33; Heb. 6:18f. [b]Acts 2:33; 10:45; Gal. 4:6
6 [a]Rom. 5:8, 10 [b]Gal. 4:4 [c]Rom. 4:25; 5:8; 8:32
8 [a]Rom. 3:5 [b]John 3:16; 15:13; Rom. 8:39 [c]Gal. 2:20; Eph. 5:2
9 [a]Rom. 3:25 [b]Rom. 1:18; 1 Thess. 1:10
10 [a]Rom. 11:28; 2 Cor. 5:18f.; Eph. 2:3; Col. 1:21f. [b]Rom. 8:34
11 [a]Rom. 5:3; 8:23; 9:10; 2 Cor. 8:19 [b]Rom. 5:10
12 [a]Gen. 2:17; 1 Cor. 15:21f. [b]Rom. 6:23; James 1:15 [c]Rom. 5:14, 19, 21
13 [a]Rom. 4:15
14 [a]Hos. 6:7 [b]1 Cor. 15:45
15 [a]Rom. 5:12, 18 [b]Rom. 5:18, 19 [c]Acts 15:11
16 [a]1 Cor. 11:32
17 [a]Gen. 2:17; 1 Cor. 15:21f. [b]2 Tim. 2:12
18 [a]Rom. 5:12, 15 [b]Rom. 3:25 [c]Rom. 4:25
19 [a]Rom. 5:15, 18 [b]Rom. 5:12; 11:32 [c]Phil. 2:8
20 [a]Rom. 3:20; 7:7f.; Gal. 3:19 [b]Rom. 6:1; 1 Tim. 1:14
21 [a]Rom. 5:12, 14 [b]John 1:17
1 [a]Rom. 3:5 [b]Rom. 3:8; 6:15
2 [a]Luke 20:16; Rom. 6:15 [b]Rom. 6:11; 7:4, 6; Gal. 2:19; Col. 2:20
3 [a]Matt. 28:19 [b]Acts 2:38; 8:16
4 [a]Col. 2:12

death, in order that as Christ was
[b]raised from the dead through the
[c]glory of the Father, so we too might
walk in [d]newness of life.
5 For [a]if we have become united
with *Him* in the likeness of His
death, certainly we shall be also *in
the likeness* of His resurrection,
6 knowing this, that our [a]old [1]self
was [b]crucified with *Him,* that our
[c]body of sin might be done away
with, that we should no longer be
slaves to sin;
7 for [a]he who has died is freed
from sin.
8 Now [a]if we have died with
Christ, we believe that we shall also
live with Him,
9 knowing that Christ, having
been [a]raised from the dead, is never
to die again; [b]death no longer is
master over Him.
10 For the death that He died, He
died to sin, once for all; but the life
that He lives, He lives to God.
11 Even so consider yourselves to
be [a]dead to sin, but alive to God in
Christ Jesus.
12 Therefore do not let sin [a]reign
in your mortal body that you should
obey its lusts,
13 and do not go on [a]presenting
the members of your body to sin *as*
instruments of unrighteousness; but
[b]present yourselves to God as those
alive from the dead, and your members *as* instruments of righteousness to God.
14 For [a]sin shall not [b]be master
over you, for [c]you are not under law,
but [d]under grace.
15 What then? [a]Shall we sin because we are not under law but under grace? [b]May it never be!
16 Do you not [a]know that when
you present yourselves to someone
as [b]slaves for obedience, you are
slaves of the one whom you obey,
either of sin resulting in death, or of
obedience resulting in righteousness?
17 But [a]thanks be to God that
though you were slaves of sin, you
became obedient from the heart to
that [b]form of teaching to which you
were committed,
18 and having been [a]freed from
sin, you became slaves of righteousness.
19 [a]I am speaking in human terms
because of the weakness of your
flesh. For just [b]as you presented
your members *as* slaves to impurity
and to lawlessness, resulting in *further* lawlessness, so now present
your members *as* slaves to righteousness, resulting in sanctification.
20 For [a]when you were slaves of
sin, you were free in regard to righteousness.
21 Therefore what [a]benefit were
you then deriving from the things of
which you are now ashamed? For
the outcome of those things is
[b]death.
22 But now having been [a]freed
from sin and [b]enslaved to God, you
derive your [c]benefit, resulting in
sanctification, and [d]the outcome,
eternal life.
23 For the wages of [a]sin is death,
but the free gift of God is [b]eternal
life in Christ Jesus our Lord.

Chapter 7

Believers United to Christ

OR do you not know, [a]brethren
(for I am speaking to those who
know the law), that the law has jurisdiction over a person as long as
he lives?
2 For [a]the married woman is
bound by law to her husband while
he is living; but if her husband dies,
she is released from the law concerning the husband.
3 So then if, while her husband is
living, she is joined to another man,
she shall be called an adulteress; but
if her husband dies, she is free from
the law, so that she is not an adulteress, though she is joined to another
man.
4 Therefore, my brethren, you
also were [a]made to die [b]to the Law
[c]through the body of Christ, that
you might be joined to another, to
Him who was raised from the dead,
that we might bear fruit for God.
5 For while we were [a]in the flesh,
the sinful passions, which were
[b]*aroused* by the Law, were at work
[c]in the members of our body to bear
fruit for death.
6 But now we have been [a]re-
leased from the Law, having [b]died
to that by which we were bound, so
that we serve in [c]newness of [d]the
Spirit and not in oldness of the letter.
7 [a]What shall we say then? Is the
Law sin? [b]May it never be! On the
contrary, [c]I would not have come to
know sin except through the Law;
for I would not have known about
coveting if the Law had not said,
"[d]YOU SHALL NOT COVET."
8 But sin, [a]taking opportunity
[b]through the commandment, pro-

4 [b]Acts 2:24; Rom. 6:9 [c]John 11:40; 2 Cor. 13:4 [d]Rom. 7:6; 2 Cor. 5:17; Gal. 6:15; Eph. 4:23f.; Col. 3:10
5 [a]2 Cor. 4:10; Phil. 3:10f.; Col. 2:12
6 [1]Lit., *man* [a]Eph. 4:22; Col. 3:9 [b]Gal. 2:20; 5:24; 6:14 [c]Rom. 7:24
7 [a]1 Pet. 4:1
8 [a]Rom. 6:4; 2 Cor. 4:10; 2 Tim. 2:11
9 [a]Acts 2:24; Rom. 6:4 [b]Rev. 1:18
11 [a]Rom. 6:2; 7:4, 6; Gal. 2:19; Col. 2:20; 3:3; 1 Pet. 2:24
12 [a]Rom. 6:14
13 [a]Rom. 6:16, 19; 7:5; Col. 3:5 [b]Rom. 12:1; 2 Cor. 5:14f.
14 [a]Rom. 8:2, 12 [b]Rom. 6:12 [c]Rom. 5:18; 7:4, 6; Gal. 4:21 [d]Rom. 5:17
15 [a]Rom. 6:1 [b]Luke 20:16
16 [a]Rom. 11:2; 1 Cor. 3:16; 5:6; 6:2, 3, 9, 15, 16, 19; 9:13, 24 [b]John 8:34; 2 Pet. 2:19
17 [a]Rom. 1:8; 2 Cor. 2:14 [b]2 Tim. 1:13
18 [a]John 8:32; Rom. 6:22; 8:2
19 [a]Rom. 3:5 [b]Rom. 6:13
20 [a]Matt. 6:24
21 [a]Jer. 12:13; Ezek. 16:63; Rom. 7:5 [b]Rom. 1:32; 5:12; 6:16, 23; 8:6, 13; Gal. 6:8
22 [a]John 8:32; Rom. 6:18; 8:2 [b]1 Cor. 7:22; 1 Pet. 2:16 [c]Rom. 7:4 [d]1 Pet. 1:9
23 [a]Rom. 1:32; 5:12; 6:16, 21; 8:6, 13; Gal. 6:8 [b]Matt. 25:46; Rom. 5:21; 8:39
1 [a]Rom. 1:13
2 [a]1 Cor. 7:39
4 [a]Rom. 6:2; 7:6 [b]Rom. 8:2; Gal. 2:19; 5:18 [c]Col. 1:22
5 [a]Rom. 8:8f.; 2 Cor. 10:3 [b]Rom. 7:7f. [c]Rom. 6:13
6 [a]Rom. 7:2 [b]Rom. 6:2 [c]Rom. 6:4 [d]Rom. 2:29
7 [a]Rom. 3:5 [b]Luke 20:16 [c]Rom. 3:20; 4:15; 5:20 [d]Ex. 20:17; Deut. 5:21
8 [a]Rom. 7:11 [b]Rom. 3:20; 7:11

duced in me coveting of every kind;
for [c]apart from the Law sin *is* dead.
9 And I was once alive apart from
the Law; but when the commandment came, sin became alive, and I
died;
10 and this commandment, which
was [a]to result in life, proved to result in death for me;
11 for sin, [a]taking opportunity
[b]through the commandment, [c]de-
ceived me, and through it killed me.
12 [a]So then, the Law is holy, and
the commandment is holy and righteous and good.
13 Therefore did that which is
good become *a cause of* death for
me? [a]May it never be! Rather it was
sin, in order that it might be shown
to be sin by effecting my death
through that which is good, that
through the commandment sin
might become utterly sinful.

The Conflict of Two Natures

14 For we know that the Law is
[a]spiritual; but I am [a]of flesh, [b]sold
[c]into bondage to sin.
15 For that which I am doing, [a]I do
not understand; for I am not practicing [b]what I *would* like to *do,* but I
am doing the very thing I hate.
16 But if I do the very thing I do
not wish *to do,* I agree with [a]the
Law, *confessing* that it is good.
17 So now, no longer am I the one
doing it, but sin which indwells me.
18 For I know that nothing good
dwells in me, that is, in my [a]flesh;
for the wishing is present in me, but
the doing of the good *is* not.
19 For [a]the good that I wish, I do
not do; but I practice the very evil
that I do not wish.
20 But if I am doing the very thing
I do not wish, [a]I am no longer the
one doing it, but sin which dwells in
me.
21 I find then [a]the principle that
evil is present in me, the one who
wishes to do good.
22 For I joyfully concur with the
law of God in [a]the inner man,
23 but I see [a]a different law in the
members of my body, waging war
against the [b]law of my mind, and
making me a prisoner of [c]the law of
sin which is in my members.
24 Wretched man that I am! Who
will set me free from [a]the body of
this [b]death?
25 [a]Thanks be to God through Jesus Christ our Lord! So then, on the
one hand I myself with my mind am
serving the law of God, but on the
other, with my flesh [b]the law of sin.

8 [c]1 Cor. 15:56
10 [a]Lev. 18:5; Luke 10:28; Rom. 10:5
11 [a]Rom. 7:8 [b]Rom. 3:20; 7:8 [c]Gen. 3:13
12 [a]Rom. 7:16; 1 Tim. 1:8
13 [a]Luke 20:16
14 [a]1 Cor. 3:1 [b]1 Kin. 21:20, 25; Rom. 6:6; Gal. 4:3 [c]Rom. 3:9
15 [a]John 15:15 [b]Rom. 7:19; Gal. 5:17
16 [a]Rom. 7:12; 1 Tim. 1:8
18 [a]John 3:6
21 [a]Rom. 7:23
22 [a]2 Cor. 4:16; Eph. 3:16
23 [a]Rom. 6:19; 1 Pet. 2:11 [b]Rom. 7:25 [c]Rom. 7:21
24 [a]Rom. 6:6; Col. 2:11 [b]Rom. 8:2
25 [a]1 Cor. 15:57 [b]Rom. 7:21, 23
1 [a]Rom. 5:16; 8:34 [b]Rom. 8:9f. [c]Rom. 8:2, 11, 39
2 [1]Some ancient mss. read, *me* [a]1 Cor. 15:45 [b]Rom. 8:1, 11, 39; 16:3 [c]John 8:32, 36; Rom. 6:14, 18
3 [a]Acts 13:39; Heb. 10:1ff. [b]Rom. 7:18f; Heb. 7:18 [c]Phil. 2:7; Heb. 2:14, 17
4 [a]Luke 1:6; Rom. 2:26 [b]Gal. 5:16, 25
5 [a]Gal. 5:19-21 [b]Gal. 5:22-25
6 [a]Gal. 6:8 [b]Rom. 6:21; 8:13
7 [a]James 4:4
8 [a]Rom. 7:5
9 [a]Rom. 7:5 [b]John 14:23; Rom. 8:11; 2 Cor. 6:16; 2 Tim. 1:14 [c]John 14:17; Gal. 4:6; Phil. 1:19
10 [a]John 17:23; Gal. 2:20
11 [a]Acts 2:24; Rom. 6:4 [b]John 5:21 [c]Rom. 8:1, 2
13 [a]Rom. 8:6 [b]Col. 3:5
14 [a]Gal. 5:18 [b]Hos. 1:10; [Rom. 9:26]; Matt. 5:9; John 1:12; 2 Cor. 6:18; Gal. 3:26; 1 John 3:1
15 [a]2 Tim. 1:7; Heb. 2:15 [b]Rom. 8:23; Gal. 4:5f. [c]Mark 14:36; Gal. 4:6
16 [a]Acts 5:32 [b]Hos. 1:10; [Rom. 9:26]; Matt. 5:9; John 1:12; 2 Cor. 6:18; Gal. 3:26; 1 John 3:1

CHAPTER 8

Deliverance from Bondage

THERE is therefore now no [a]con-
demnation for those who are [b]in
[c]Christ Jesus.
2 For [a]the law of the Spirit of life
in [b]Christ Jesus [c]has set [1]you free
from the law of sin and of death.
3 For [a]what the Law could not
do, [b]weak as it was through the
flesh, God *did:* sending His own Son
in [c]the likeness of sinful flesh and *as*
an offering for sin, He condemned
sin in the flesh,
4 in order that the [a]requirement
of the Law might be fulfilled in us,
who [b]do not walk according to the
flesh, but according to the Spirit.
5 For those who are according to
the flesh set their minds on [a]the
things of the flesh, but those who
are according to the Spirit, [b]the
things of the Spirit.
6 [a]For the mind set on the flesh is
[b]death, but the mind set on the
Spirit is life and peace,
7 because the mind set on the
flesh is [a]hostile toward God; for it
does not subject itself to the law of
God, for it is not even able *to do so;*
8 and those who are [a]in the flesh
cannot please God.
9 However you are not [a]in the
flesh but in the Spirit, if indeed the
Spirit of God [b]dwells in you. But [c]if
anyone does not have the Spirit of
Christ, he does not belong to Him.
10 And [a]if Christ is in you, though
the body is dead because of sin, yet
the spirit is alive because of righteousness.
11 But if the Spirit of Him who
[a]raised Jesus from the dead dwells
in you, [b]He who raised [c]Christ Jesus
from the dead will also give life to
your mortal bodies through His
Spirit who indwells you.
12 So then, brethren, we are under
obligation, not to the flesh, to live
according to the flesh—
13 for [a]if you are living according
to the flesh, you must die; but if by
the Spirit you are [b]putting to death
the deeds of the body, you will live.
14 For all who are [a]being led by
the Spirit of God, these are [b]sons of
God.
15 For you [a]have not received a
spirit of slavery leading to fear
again, but you [b]have received a
spirit of adoption as sons by which
we cry out, "[c]Abba! Father!"
16 The Spirit Himself [a]bears witness with our spirit that we are
[b]children of God,

17 and if children, [a]heirs also,
heirs of God and fellow-heirs with
Christ, [b]if indeed we suffer with
Him in order that we may also be
glorified with *Him*.
18 For I consider that the sufferings of this present time [a]are not
worthy to be compared with the
[b]glory that is to be revealed to us.
19 For the [a]anxious longing of the
creation waits eagerly for [b]the revealing of the [c]sons of God.
20 For the creation [a]was subjected
to [b]futility, not of its own will, but
because of Him who subjected it, in
hope
21 that [a]the creation itself also will
be set free from its slavery to corruption into the freedom of the glory
of the children of God.
22 For we know that the whole
creation [a]groans and suffers the
pains of childbirth together until
now.
23 [a]And not only this, but also we
ourselves, having [b]the first fruits of
the Spirit, even we ourselves [c]groan
within ourselves, [d]waiting eagerly
for *our* adoption as sons, [e]the redemption of our body.
24 For [a]in hope we have been
saved, but [b]hope that is seen is not
hope; for why does one also hope for
what he sees?
25 But [a]if we hope for what we do
not see, with perseverance we wait
eagerly for it.

Our Victory in Christ

26 And in the same way the Spirit
also helps our weakness; for [a]we do
not know how to pray as we should,
but [b]the Spirit Himself intercedes
for *us* with groanings too deep for
words;
27 and [a]He who searches the
hearts knows what [b]the mind of the
Spirit is, because He [c]intercedes for
the saints according to *the will of*
God.
28 And we know that [1]God causes
[a]all things to work together for good
to those who love God, to those who
are [b]called according to *His* purpose.
29 For whom He [a]foreknew, He
also [b]predestined *to become* [c]con-
formed to the image of His Son, that
He might be the [d]first-born among
many brethren;
30 and whom He [a]predestined,
these He also [b]called; and whom He
called, these He also [c]justified; and
whom He justified, these He also
[d]glorified.
31 [a]What then shall we say to
these things? [b]If God *is* for us, who
is against us?
32 He who [a]did not spare His own
Son, but [b]delivered Him up for us
all, how will He not also with Him
freely give us all things?
33 Who will bring a charge against
[a]God's elect? God is the one who
justifies;
34 who is the one who [a]condemns?
Christ Jesus is He who [b]died, yes,
rather who was [1c]raised, who is [d]at
the right hand of God, who also intercedes for us.
35 Who shall separate us from
[a]the love of [1]Christ? Shall [b]tribula-
tion, or distress, or [c]persecution, or
[c]famine, or [c]nakedness, or [c]peril, or
sword?
36 Just as it is written,
"[a]FOR THY SAKE WE ARE BEING
PUT TO DEATH ALL DAY LONG;
WE WERE CONSIDERED AS
SHEEP TO BE SLAUGHTERED."
37 But in all these things we over-
whelmingly [a]conquer through Him
who loved us.
38 For I am convinced that neither
[a]death, nor life, nor [b]angels, nor
principalities, nor things present,
nor things to come, nor powers,
39 nor height, nor depth, nor any
other created thing, shall be able to
separate us from [a]the love of God,
which is in Christ Jesus our Lord.

CHAPTER 9

Solicitude for Israel

[a]I AM telling the truth in Christ, I
am not lying, my conscience bearing me witness in the Holy Spirit,
2 that I have great sorrow and
unceasing grief in my heart.
3 For [a]I could wish that I myself
were [b]accursed, *separated* from
Christ for the sake of my brethren,
my kinsmen [c]according to the flesh,
4 who are [a]Israelites, to whom
belongs [b]the adoption as sons and
[c]the glory and [d]the covenants and
[e]the giving of the Law and [f]the *tem-*
ple service and [g]the promises,
5 whose are [a]the fathers, and
[b]from whom is the Christ according
to the flesh, [c]who is over all, [d]God
blessed forever. Amen.
6 But *it is* not as though [a]the
word of God has failed. [b]For they
are not all Israel who are *descended*
from Israel;
7 neither are they all children
[a]because they are Abraham's descendants, but: "[b]THROUGH ISAAC
YOUR DESCENDANTS WILL BE
NAMED."

17 [a]Acts 20:32; Rev. 21:7 [b]2 Cor. 1:5, 7; Phil. 3:10
18 [a]2 Cor. 4:17 [b]Col. 3:4
19 [a]Phil. 1:20 [b]Rom. 8:18; 1 John 3:2 [c]Hos. 1:10; [Rom. 9:26]
20 [a]Gen. 3:17-19 [b]Ps. 39:5f.; Eccl. 1:2
21 [a]Acts 3:21
22 [a]Jer. 12:4, 11
23 [a]Rom. 5:3 [b]Rom. 8:16 [c]2 Cor. 5:2, 4 [d]Rom. 8:15, 19 [e]Rom. 7:24
24 [a]Rom. 8:20 [b]Rom. 4:18
25 [a]1 Thess. 1:3
26 [a]Matt. 20:22; 2 Cor. 12:8 [b]John 14:16
27 [a]Ps. 139:1f.; Rev. 2:23 [b]Rom. 8:6 [c]Rom. 8:34
28 [1]Or, *all things work together for good* [a]Rom. 8:32 [b]Rom. 8:30; 9:24; 11:29
29 [a]Rom. 11:2 [b]Rom. 9:23 [c]1 Cor. 15:49; Phil. 3:21 [d]Col. 1:18
30 [a]Rom. 9:23 [b]Rom. 8:28; 9:24 [c]1 Cor. 6:11 [d]John 17:22
31 [a]Rom. 3:5; 4:1 [b]Ps. 118:6; Matt. 1:23
32 [a]John 3:16 [b]Rom. 4:25
33 [a]Luke 18:7
34 [1]Or, *raised from the dead* [a]Rom. 8:1 [b]Rom. 5:6f. [c]Acts 2:24 [d]Mark 16:19
35 [1]Or, *God* [a]Rom. 8:37f. [b]Rom. 2:9; 2 Cor. 4:8 [c]1 Cor. 4:11
36 [a]Ps. 44:22
37 [a]John 16:33
38 [a]1 Cor. 3:22 [b]1 Cor. 15:24
39 [a]Rom. 5:8
1 [a]Rom. 1:9
3 [a]Ex. 32:32 [b]1 Cor. 12:3; 16:22; Gal. 1:8f. [c]Rom. 1:3
4 [a]Rom. 9:6 [b]Ex. 4:22; Rom. 8:15 [c]Ex. 40:34; 1 Kin. 8:11 [d]Gen. 17:2 [e]Deut. 4:13f.; Ps. 147:19 [f]Deut. 7:6; 14:1f.; Heb. 9:1, 6 [g]Acts 2:39
5 [a]Acts 3:13; Rom. 11:28 [b]Matt. 1:1-16; Rom. 1:3 [c]Col. 1:16-19 [d]John 1:1
6 [a]Num. 23:19 [b]John 1:47
7 [a]John 8:33, 39 [b]Gen. 21:12

8 That is, it is not the children of the flesh who are [a]children of God, but the [b]children of the promise are regarded as descendants.

9 For this is a word of promise: "[a]AT THIS TIME I WILL COME, AND SARAH SHALL HAVE A SON."

10 [a]And not only this, but there was [b]Rebekah also, when she had conceived *twins* by one man, our father Isaac;

11 for though *the twins* were not yet born, and had not done anything good or bad, in order that [a]God's purpose according to *His* choice might stand, not because of works, but because of Him who calls,

12 it was said to her, "[a]THE OLDER WILL SERVE THE YOUNGER."

13 Just as it is written, "[a]JACOB I LOVED, BUT ESAU I HATED."

14 [a]What shall we say then? [b]There is no injustice with God, is there? [c]May it never be!

15 For He says to Moses, "[a]I WILL HAVE MERCY ON WHOM I HAVE MERCY, AND I WILL HAVE COMPASSION ON WHOM I HAVE COMPASSION."

16 So then it *does* not *depend* on the man who wills or the man who [a]runs, but on [b]God who has mercy.

17 For the Scripture says to Pharaoh, "[a]FOR THIS VERY PURPOSE I RAISED YOU UP, TO DEMONSTRATE MY POWER IN YOU, AND THAT MY NAME MIGHT BE PROCLAIMED THROUGHOUT THE WHOLE EARTH."

18 So then He has mercy on whom He desires, and He [a]hardens whom He desires.

19 [a]You will say to me then, "[b]Why does He still find fault? For [c]who resists His will?"

20 On the contrary, who are you, [a]O man, who [b]answers back to God? [c]The thing molded will not say to the molder, "Why did you make me like this," will it?

21 Or does not the potter have a right over the clay, to make from the same lump one vessel for honorable use, and another for common use?

22 What if God, although willing to demonstrate His wrath and to make His power known, endured with much [a]patience vessels of wrath [b]prepared for destruction?

23 And *He did so* in order that He might make known [a]the riches of His glory upon [b]vessels of mercy, which He [c]prepared beforehand for glory,

24 *even* us, whom He also [a]called, [b]not from among Jews only, but also from among Gentiles.

25 As He says also in Hosea,
"[a]I WILL CALL THOSE WHO WERE NOT MY PEOPLE, 'MY PEOPLE,'
AND HER WHO WAS NOT BELOVED, 'BELOVED.'"

26 "[a]AND IT SHALL BE THAT IN THE PLACE WHERE IT WAS SAID TO THEM, 'YOU ARE NOT MY PEOPLE,'
THERE THEY SHALL BE CALLED SONS OF [b]THE LIVING GOD."

27 And Isaiah cries out concerning Israel, "[a]THOUGH THE NUMBER OF THE SONS OF ISRAEL BE [b]AS THE SAND OF THE SEA, IT IS [c]THE REMNANT THAT WILL BE SAVED;

28 [a]FOR THE LORD WILL EXECUTE HIS WORD UPON THE EARTH, THOROUGHLY AND QUICKLY."

29 And just as Isaiah foretold,
"[a]EXCEPT [b]THE LORD OF [1]SABAOTH HAD LEFT TO US A [2]POSTERITY,
[c]WE WOULD HAVE BECOME AS SODOM, AND WOULD HAVE [3]RESEMBLED GOMORRAH."

30 [a]What shall we say then? That Gentiles, who did not pursue righteousness, attained righteousness, even [b]the righteousness which is by faith;

31 but Israel, [a]pursuing a law of righteousness, did not [b]arrive at *that* law.

32 Why? Because *they did* not *pursue it* by faith, but as though *it were* by works. They stumbled over [a]THE STUMBLING STONE,

33 just as it is written,
"[a]BEHOLD, I LAY IN ZION A STONE OF STUMBLING AND A ROCK OF OFFENSE,
[b]AND HE WHO BELIEVES IN HIM [c]WILL NOT BE [1]DISAPPOINTED."

CHAPTER 10

The Word of Faith Brings Salvation

BRETHREN, my heart's desire and my prayer to God for them is for *their* salvation.

2 For I bear them witness that they have [a]a zeal for God, but not in accordance with knowledge.

3 For not knowing about [a]God's righteousness, and [b]seeking to establish their own, they did not subject themselves to the righteousness of God.

4 For [a]Christ is the end of the law for righteousness to [b]everyone who believes.

5 For Moses writes that the man who practices the righteousness

8 [a]Rom. 8:14 [b]Rom. 4:13, 16; Gal. 3:29; 4:28; Heb. 11:11
9 [a]Gen. 18:10
10 [a]Rom. 5:3 [b]Gen. 25:21
11 [a]Rom. 4:17; 8:28
12 [a]Gen. 25:23
13 [a]Mal. 1:2f.
14 [a]Rom. 3:5 [b]2 Chr. 19:7; Rom. 2:11 [c]Luke 20:16
15 [a]Ex. 33:19
16 [a]Gal. 2:2 [b]Eph. 2:8
17 [a]Ex. 9:16
18 [a]Ex. 4:21; 7:3; 9:12; 10:20, 27; 11:10; 14:4, 17; Deut. 2:30; Josh. 11:20; John 12:40; Rom. 11:7, 25
19 [a]Rom. 11:19; 1 Cor. 15:35; James 2:18 [b]Rom. 3:7 [c]2 Chr. 20:6; Job 9:12; Dan. 4:35
20 [a]Rom. 2:1 [b]Job 33:13 [c]Is. 29:16; 45:9; 64:8; Jer. 18:6; Rom. 9:22f.; 2 Tim. 2:20
22 [a]Rom. 2:4 [b]Prov. 16:4; 1 Pet. 2:8
23 [a]Rom. 2:4; Eph. 3:16 [b]Acts 9:15 [c]Rom. 8:29f.
24 [a]Rom. 8:28 [b]Rom. 3:29
25 [a]Hos. 2:23; 1 Pet. 2:10
26 [a]Hos. 1:10 [b]Matt. 16:16
27 [a]Is. 10:22 [b]Gen. 22:17; Hos. 1:10 [c]Rom. 11:5
28 [a]Is. 10:23
29 [1]I.e., Hosts [2]Lit., *seed* [3]Lit., *been made like* [a]Is. 1:9 [b]James 5:4 [c]Deut. 29:23; Is. 13:19; Jer. 49:18; 50:40; Amos 4:11
30 [a]Rom. 9:14 [b]Rom. 1:17; 3:21f.; 10:6; Gal. 2:16; 3:24; Phil. 3:9; Heb. 11:7
31 [a]Is. 51:1; Rom. 9:30; 10:2f., 20; 11:7 [b]Gal. 5:4
32 [a]Is. 8:14; 1 Pet. 2:6, 8
33 [1]Lit., *put to shame* [a]Is. 28:16 [b]Rom. 10:11 [c]Rom. 5:5
2 [a]Acts 21:20
3 [a]Rom. 1:17 [b]Is. 51:1; Rom. 8:30; 10:2f., 20; 11:7
4 [a]Rom. 7:1-4; Gal. 3:24; 4:5 [b]Rom. 3:22

which is [1]based on law [a]shall live
[2]by that righteousness.
6 But [a]the righteousness based
on faith speaks thus, "[b]DO NOT SAY
IN YOUR HEART, 'WHO WILL ASCEND
INTO HEAVEN?' (that is, to bring
Christ down),
7 or 'WHO WILL DESCEND INTO
THE [a]ABYSS?' (that is, to [b]bring
Christ up from the dead)."
8 But what does it say? "[a]THE
WORD IS NEAR YOU, IN YOUR MOUTH
AND IN YOUR HEART"—that is, the
word of faith which we are preaching,
9 [1]that [a]if you confess with your
mouth Jesus *as* Lord, and [b]believe in
your heart that [c]God raised Him
from the dead, you shall be saved;
10 for with the heart man believes,
resulting in righteousness, and with
the mouth he confesses, resulting in
salvation.
11 For the Scripture says, "[a]WHO-
EVER BELIEVES IN HIM WILL NOT BE
[1]DISAPPOINTED."
12 For [a]there is no distinction between Jew and Greek; for the same
Lord is [b]Lord of [c]all, abounding in
riches for all who call upon Him;
13 for "[a]WHOEVER WILL CALL UPON
THE NAME OF THE LORD WILL BE
SAVED."
14 How then shall they call upon
Him in whom they have not believed? And how shall they believe
in Him [a]whom they have not heard?
And how shall they hear without [b]a
preacher?
15 And how shall they preach unless they are sent? Just as it is written, "[a]HOW BEAUTIFUL ARE THE FEET
OF THOSE WHO [1b]BRING GLAD TIDINGS
OF GOOD THINGS!"
16 However, they [a]did not all heed
the [1]glad tidings; for Isaiah says,
"[b]LORD, WHO HAS BELIEVED OUR RE-
PORT?"
17 So faith *comes* from [a]hearing,
and hearing by [b]the word [1]of Christ.
18 But I say, surely they have never heard, have they? Indeed they
have:

"[a]THEIR VOICE HAS GONE OUT
INTO ALL THE EARTH,
AND THEIR WORDS TO THE ENDS
OF THE WORLD."

19 But I say, surely Israel did not
know, did they? At the first Moses
says,

"[a]I WILL [b]MAKE YOU JEALOUS BY
THAT WHICH IS NOT A NATION,
BY A NATION WITHOUT UNDER-
STANDING WILL I ANGER
YOU."

20 And Isaiah is very bold and
says,

"[a]I WAS FOUND BY THOSE WHO
SOUGHT ME NOT,
I BECAME MANIFEST TO THOSE
WHO DID NOT ASK FOR ME."

21 But as for Israel He says, "[a]ALL
THE DAY LONG I HAVE STRETCHED
OUT MY HANDS TO A DISOBEDIENT
AND OBSTINATE PEOPLE."

CHAPTER 11

Israel Is Not Cast Away

I SAY then, God has not [a]rejected
His people, has He? [b]May it never
be! For [c]I too am an Israelite, [1]a descendant of Abraham, of the tribe of
Benjamin.
2 God [a]has not rejected His people whom He [b]foreknew. [c]Or do you
not know what the Scripture says in
the passage about Elijah, how he
pleads with God against Israel?
3 "Lord, [a]THEY HAVE KILLED THY
PROPHETS, THEY HAVE TORN DOWN
THINE ALTARS, AND I ALONE AM LEFT,
AND THEY ARE SEEKING MY [1]LIFE."
4 But what is the divine response
to him? "[a]I HAVE KEPT for Myself
SEVEN THOUSAND MEN WHO HAVE
NOT BOWED THE KNEE TO BAAL."
5 In the same way then, there has
also come to be at the present time
[a]a remnant according to *God's* [1]gra-
cious choice.
6 But [a]if it is by grace, it is no
longer on the basis of works, otherwise grace is no longer grace.
7 What then? That which [a]Israel
is seeking for, it has not obtained,
but [1]those who were chosen obtained it, and the rest were [b]hard-
ened;
8 just as it is written,

"[a]GOD GAVE THEM A SPIRIT OF
STUPOR,
EYES TO SEE NOT AND EARS TO
HEAR NOT,
DOWN TO THIS VERY DAY."

9 And David says,

"[a]LET THEIR TABLE BECOME A
SNARE AND A TRAP,
AND A STUMBLING BLOCK AND A
RETRIBUTION TO THEM.
10 "[a]LET THEIR EYES BE DARKENED
TO SEE NOT,
AND BEND THEIR BACKS FOR-
EVER."

11 [a]I say then, they did not stumble so as to fall, did they? [b]May it
never be! But by their transgression
[c]salvation *has come* to the Gentiles,
to [d]make them jealous.

5 [1]Lit., *out of, from* [2]Lit., *by it* [a]Lev. 18:5; Neh. 9:29; Ezek. 20:11, 13, 21; Rom. 7:10
6 [a]Rom. 9:30 [b]Deut. 30:12f.
7 [a]Luke 8:31 [b]Heb. 13:20
8 [a]Deut. 30:14
9 [1]Or, *because* [a]Matt. 10:32; Luke 12:8; Rom. 14:9; 1 Cor. 12:3; Phil. 2:11 [b]Acts 16:31; Rom. 4:24 [c]Acts 2:24
11 [1]Lit., *put to shame* [a]Is. 28:16; Rom. 9:33
12 [a]Rom. 3:22, 29 [b]Acts 10:36 [c]Rom. 3:29
13 [a]Joel 2:32; Acts 2:21
14 [a]Eph. 2:17; 4:21 [b]Acts 8:31; Titus 1:3
15 [1]Or, *preach the gospel* [a]Is. 52:7 [b]Rom. 1:15; 15:20
16 [1]Lit., *gospel* [a]Rom. 3:3 [b]Is. 53:1; John 12:38
17 [1]Or, *concerning Christ* [a]Gal. 3:2, 5 [b]Col. 3:16
18 [a]Ps. 19:4; Rom. 1:8; Col. 1:6, 23; 1 Thess. 1:8
19 [a]Deut. 32:21 [b]Rom. 11:11, 14
20 [a]Is. 65:1; Rom. 9:30
21 [a]Is. 65:2
1 [1]Lit., *of the seed of Abraham* [a]1 Sam. 12:22; Jer. 31:37; 33:24-26 [b]Luke 20:16 [c]2 Cor. 11:22; Phil. 3:5
2 [a]Ps. 94:14 [b]Rom. 8:29 [c]Rom. 6:16
3 [1]Gr., *soul-life* [a]1 Kin. 19:10
4 [a]1 Kin. 19:18
5 [1]Lit., *choice of grace* [a]2 Kin. 19:4; Rom. 9:27
6 [a]Rom. 4:4
7 [1]Lit., *the election* [a]Rom. 9:31 [b]Mark 6:52; Rom. 9:18; 11:25; 2 Cor. 3:14
8 [a]Deut. 29:4; Is. 29:10; Matt. 13:13f.
9 [a]Ps. 69:22f.
10 [a]Ps. 69:23
11 [a]Rom. 11:1 [b]Luke 20:16 [c]Acts 28:28 [d]Rom. 11:14

12 Now if their transgression be riches for the world and their failure be riches for the Gentiles, how much more will their [a]fulfillment be!

13 But I am speaking to you who are Gentiles. Inasmuch then as [a]I am an apostle of Gentiles, I magnify my ministry,

14 if somehow I might [a]move to jealousy [b]my fellow-countrymen and [c]save some of them.

15 For if their rejection be the [a]reconciliation of the world, what will *their* acceptance be but [b]life from the dead?

16 And if the [a]first piece *of dough* be holy, the lump is also; and if the root be holy, the branches are too.

17 But if some of the [a]branches were broken off, and [b]you, being a wild olive, were grafted in among them and became partaker with them of the rich root of the olive tree,

18 do not be arrogant toward the branches; but if you are arrogant, *remember that* [a]it is not you who supports the root, but the root *supports* you.

19 [a]You will say then, "Branches were broken off so that I might be grafted in."

20 Quite right, they were broken off for their unbelief, and you [a]stand *only* by your faith. [b]Do not be conceited, but fear;

21 for if God did not spare the natural branches, neither will He spare you.

22 Behold then the kindness and severity of God; to those who fell, severity, but to you, God's [a]kindness, [b]if you continue in His kindness; otherwise you also [c]will be cut off.

23 And they also, [a]if they do not continue in their unbelief, will be grafted in; for God is able to graft them in again.

24 For if you were cut off from what is by nature a wild olive tree, and were grafted contrary to nature into a cultivated olive tree, how much more shall these who are the natural *branches* be grafted into their own olive tree?

25 For [a]I do not want you, brethren, to be uninformed of this [b]mystery, lest you be [c]wise in your own estimation, that a partial [d]hardening has happened to Israel until the [e]fulness of the Gentiles has come in;

26 and thus all Israel will be saved; just as it is written,

"[a]THE DELIVERER WILL COME
FROM ZION,
HE WILL REMOVE UNGODLINESS
FROM JACOB."

27 "[a]AND THIS IS MY COVENANT
WITH THEM,
WHEN I TAKE AWAY THEIR
SINS."

28 From the standpoint of the gospel they are [a]enemies for your sake, but from the standpoint of *God's* choice they are beloved for [b]the sake of the fathers;

29 for the gifts and the [a]calling of God [b]are irrevocable.

30 For just as you once were disobedient to God but now have been shown mercy because of their disobedience,

31 so these also now have been disobedient, in order that because of the mercy shown to you they also may now be shown mercy.

32 For [a]God has shut up all in disobedience that He might show mercy to all.

33 Oh, the depth of [a]the riches both of the [b]wisdom and knowledge of God! [c]How unsearchable are His judgments and unfathomable His ways!

34 For [a]WHO HAS KNOWN THE MIND OF THE LORD, OR WHO BECAME HIS COUNSELOR?

35 Or [a]WHO HAS FIRST GIVEN TO HIM THAT IT MIGHT BE PAID BACK TO HIM AGAIN?

36 For [a]from Him and through Him and to Him are all things. [b]To Him *be* the glory forever. Amen.

Chapter 12

Dedicated Service

[a]I URGE you therefore, brethren, by the mercies of God, to [b]present your bodies a living and holy sacrifice, acceptable to God, *which is* your spiritual service of worship.

2 And do not [a]be conformed to [b]this world, but be transformed by the [c]renewing of your mind, that you may [d]prove what the will of God is, that which is good and acceptable and perfect.

3 For through [a]the grace given to me I say to every man among you [b]not to think more highly of himself than he ought to think; but to think so as to have sound judgment, as God has allotted to [c]each a measure of faith.

4 For [a]just as we have many members in one body and all the members do not have the same function,

12 [a]Rom. 11:25
13 [a]Acts 9:15
14 [a]Rom. 11:11 [b]Gen. 29:14; 2 Sam. 19:12f.; Rom. 9:3 [c]1 Cor. 1:21; 7:16; 9:22; 1 Tim. 1:15; 2:4; 2 Tim. 1:9
15 [a]Rom. 5:11 [b]Luke 15:24, 32
16 [a]Num. 15:18ff.; Neh. 10:37; Ezek. 44:30
17 [a]Jer. 11:16; John 15:2 [b]Eph. 2:11ff.
18 [a]John 4:22
19 [a]Rom. 9:19
20 [a]Rom. 5:2; 2 Cor. 1:24 [b]Rom. 12:16; 1 Tim. 6:17; 1 Pet. 1:17
22 [a]Rom. 2:4 [b]1 Cor. 15:2; Heb. 3:6, 14 [c]John 15:2
23 [a]2 Cor. 3:16
25 [a]Rom. 1:13 [b]Matt. 13:11; 1 Cor. 2:7-10; Eph. 3:3-5, 9 [c]Rom. 12:16 [d]Rom. 11:7 [e]Luke 21:24; John 10:16
26 [a]Is. 59:20, 21
27 [a]Is. 27:9; Heb. 8:10, 12
28 [a]Rom. 5:10 [b]Deut. 7:8; 10:15; Rom. 9:5
29 [a]Rom. 8:28; 1 Cor. 1:26; Eph. 1:18; 4:1, 4; Phil. 3:14; 2 Tim. 1:9; Heb. 3:1; 2 Pet. 1:10 [b]Heb. 7:21
32 [a]Rom. 3:9; Gal. 3:22f.
33 [a]Rom. 2:4; Eph. 3:8 [b]Eph. 3:10; Col. 2:3 [c]Job 5:9
34 [a]Is. 40:13f.; 1 Cor. 2:16
35 [a]Job 35:7; 41:11
36 [a]1 Cor. 8:6; 11:12; Col. 1:16; Heb. 2:10 [b]Rom. 16:27; Eph. 3:21; Phil. 4:20; 1 Tim. 1:17; 2 Tim. 4:18; 1 Pet. 4:11; 5:11; 2 Pet. 3:18; Jude 25; Rev. 1:6; 5:13
1 [a]1 Cor. 1:10; 2 Cor. 10:2 [b]Rom. 6:13, 16, 19; 1 Cor. 6:20; Heb. 13:15
2 [a]1 Pet. 1:14 [b]Matt. 13:22; Gal. 1:4; 1 John 2:15 [c]Eph. 4:23; Titus 3:5 [d]Eph. 5:10, 17
3 [a]Rom. 1:5; 15:15; 1 Cor. 3:10; 15:10; Gal. 2:9; Eph. 3:7f. [b]Rom. 11:20; 12:16 [c]1 Cor. 7:17; 2 Cor. 10:13; Eph. 4:7; 1 Pet. 4:11
4 [a]1 Cor. 12:12-14; Eph. 4:4, 16

5 so we, [a]who are many, are [b]one
body in Christ, and individually
members one of another.
6 And since we have gifts that
[a]differ according to the grace given
to us, *let each exercise them accord-*
ingly: if [b]prophecy, according to the
proportion of his faith;
7 if [a]service, in his serving; or he
who [b]teaches, in his teaching;
8 or he who [a]exhorts, in his exhortation; he who gives, with [b]liber-
ality; [c]he who leads, with diligence;
he who shows mercy, with [d]cheer-
fulness.
9 Let [a]love be without hypocrisy.
[b]Abhor what is evil; cling to what is
good.
10 Be [a]devoted to one another in
brotherly love; give preference to
one another [b]in honor;
11 not lagging behind in diligence,
[a]fervent in spirit, [b]serving the Lord;
12 [a]rejoicing in hope, [b]persevering
in tribulation, [c]devoted to prayer,
13 [a]contributing to the needs of
the saints, [b]practicing hospitality.
14 [a]Bless those who persecute
you; bless and curse not.
15 [a]Rejoice with those who rejoice, and weep with those who
weep.
16 [a]Be of the same mind toward
one another; do not be haughty in
mind, [b]but associate with the lowly.
[c]Do not be wise in your own estimation.
17 [a]Never pay back evil for evil to
anyone. [b]Respect what is right in
the sight of all men.
18 If possible, [a]so far as it depends
on you, [b]be at peace with all men.
19 [a]Never take your own revenge,
beloved, but leave room for the
wrath *of God,* for it is written,
"[b]VENGEANCE IS MINE, I WILL RE-
PAY, SAYS THE LORD."
20 "[a]BUT IF YOUR ENEMY IS HUNGRY,
FEED HIM, AND IF HE IS THIRSTY, GIVE
HIM A DRINK; FOR [b]IN SO DOING YOU
WILL HEAP BURNING COALS UPON HIS
HEAD."
21 Do not be overcome by evil, but
overcome evil with good.

CHAPTER 13

Be Subject to Government

LET every [a]person be in [b]subjec-
tion to the governing authorities.
For [c]there is no authority except
from God, and those which exist are
established by God.
2 Therefore he who resists authority has opposed the ordinance
of God; and they who have opposed
will receive condemnation upon
themselves.
3 For [a]rulers are not a cause of
fear for good behavior, but for evil.
Do you want to have no fear of authority? Do what is good, and you
will have praise from the same;
4 for it is a minister of God to you
for good. But if you do what is evil,
be afraid; for it does not bear the
sword for nothing; for it is a minister of God, an [a]avenger who brings
wrath upon the one who practices
evil.
5 Wherefore it is necessary to be
in subjection, not only because of
wrath, but also [a]for conscience'
sake.
6 For because of this you also pay
taxes, for *rulers* are servants of God,
devoting themselves to this very
thing.
7 [a]Render to all what is due them:
[b]tax to whom tax *is due;* [c]custom to
whom custom; fear to whom fear;
honor to whom honor.
8 Owe nothing to anyone except
to love one another; for [a]he who
loves his neighbor has fulfilled *the*
law.
9 For this, "[a]YOU SHALL NOT COM-
MIT ADULTERY, YOU SHALL NOT MUR-
DER, YOU SHALL NOT STEAL, YOU
SHALL NOT COVET," and if there is
any other commandment, it is
summed up in this saying, "[b]YOU
SHALL LOVE YOUR NEIGHBOR AS
YOURSELF."
10 Love does no wrong to a neighbor; [a]love therefore is the fulfillment
of *the* law.
11 And this *do,* knowing the time,
that it is [a]already the hour for you to
[b]awaken from sleep; for now salvation is nearer to us than when we
believed.
12 [a]The night is almost gone, and
[b]the day is at hand. Let us therefore
lay aside [c]the deeds of darkness and
put on [d]the armor of light.
13 Let us [a]behave properly as in
the day, [b]not in carousing and
drunkenness, not in sexual promiscuity and sensuality, not in strife
and jealousy.
14 But [a]put on the Lord Jesus
Christ, and make no provision for
the flesh [b]in regard to *its* lusts.

CHAPTER 14

Principles of Conscience

NOW [a]accept the one who is
[b]weak in faith, *but* not for *the pur-*
pose of passing judgment on his
opinions.

---

5 [a]1 Cor. 10:17, 33 [b]1 Cor. 12:20
6 [a]Rom. 12:3; 1 Pet. 4:10f. [b]Acts 13:1; 1 Cor. 12:10
7 [a]Acts 6:1; 1 Cor. 12:5, 28 [b]Acts 13:1; 1 Cor. 12:28
8 [a]Acts 4:36; 11:23; 13:15 [b]2 Cor. 8:2 [c]1 Cor. 12:28 [d]2 Cor. 9:7
9 [a]2 Cor. 6:6 [b]1 Thess. 5:21f.
10 [a]John 13:34; Heb. 13:1; 2 Pet. 1:7 [b]Rom. 13:7
11 [a]Acts 18:25 [b]Acts 20:19
12 [a]Rom. 5:2 [b]Heb. 10:32, 36 [c]Acts 1:14
13 [a]Rom. 15:25; Heb. 6:10 [b]Matt. 25:35
14 [a]Matt. 5:44; Luke 6:28; 1 Cor. 4:12
15 [a]Job 30:25
16 [a]Rom. 15:5; Phil. 2:2; 4:2; 1 Pet. 3:8 [b]Rom. 11:20; 12:3 [c]Prov. 3:7
17 [a]Prov. 20:22 [b]2 Cor. 8:21
18 [a]Rom. 1:15 [b]Mark 9:50
19 [a]Prov. 20:22 [b]Deut. 32:35; Ps. 94:1; 1 Thess. 4:6
20 [a]Prov. 25:21f. [b]2 Kin. 6:22
1 [a]Acts 2:41 [b]Titus 3:1; 1 Pet. 2:13f. [c]Dan. 2:21
3 [a]1 Pet. 2:14
4 [a]1 Thess. 4:6
5 [a]Eccl. 8
7 [a]Matt. 22:21 [b]Luke 20:22; 23:2 [c]Matt. 17:25
8 [a]Matt. 7:12; 22:39f.
9 [a]Ex. 20:13ff. [b]Lev. 19:18
10 [a]Matt. 7:12; 22:39f.; John 13:34; Rom. 13:8
11 [a]1 Cor. 7:29f.; 10:11; James 5:8; 1 Pet. 4:7; 2 Pet. 3:9, 11; 1 John 2:18 [b]Mark 13:37; 1 Cor. 15:34
12 [a]1 Cor. 7:29f.; 1 Pet. 4:7; 2 Pet. 3:9, 11 [b]Heb. 10:25; 1 John 2:8; Rev. 1:3; 22:10 [c]Eph. 5:11 [d]2 Cor. 6:7; 10:4; Eph. 6:11
13 [a]1 Thess. 4:12 [b]Luke 21:34; Gal. 5:21; Eph. 5:18
14 [a]Job 29:14; Gal. 3:27 [b]Gal. 5:16
1 [a]Acts. 28:2 [b]Rom. 14:2; 15:1; 1 Cor. 8:9ff.

2 [a]One man has faith that he may
eat all things, but he who is [b]weak
eats vegetables *only*.
3 Let not him who eats [a]regard
with contempt him who does not
eat, and let not him who does not eat
[b]judge him who eats, for God has
[c]accepted him.
4 [a]Who are you to judge the servant of another? To his own master
he stands or falls; and stand he will,
for the Lord is able to make him
stand.
5 [a]One man regards one day
above another, another regards every day *alike*. Let each man be [b]fully
convinced in his own mind.
6 He who observes the day, observes it for the Lord, and he who
eats, does so for the Lord, for he
[a]gives thanks to God; and he who
eats not, for the Lord he does not
eat, and gives thanks to God.
7 For not one of us [a]lives for himself, and not one dies for himself;
8 for if we live, we live for the
Lord, or if we die, we die for the
Lord; therefore [a]whether we live or
die, we are the Lord's.
9 For to this end [a]Christ died and
lived *again*, that He might be [b]Lord
both of the dead and of the living.
10 But you, why do you judge your
brother? Or you again, why do you
[a]regard your brother with contempt? For [b]we shall all stand before the judgment seat of God.
11 For it is written,
"[a]AS I LIVE, SAYS THE LORD,
[b]EVERY KNEE SHALL BOW TO
ME,
AND EVERY TONGUE SHALL
GIVE PRAISE TO GOD."
12 So then [a]each one of us shall
give account of himself to God.
13 Therefore let us not [a]judge one
another any more, but rather determine this — [b]not to put an obstacle
or a stumbling block in a brother's
way.
14 I know and am convinced in the
Lord Jesus that [a]nothing is unclean
in itself; but to him who [b]thinks anything to be unclean, to him it is unclean.
15 For if because of food your
brother is hurt, you are no longer
[a]walking according to love. [b]Do not
destroy with your food him for
whom Christ died.
16 Therefore [a]do not let what is for
you a good thing be spoken of as
evil;
17 for the kingdom of God [a]is not
eating and drinking, but righteousness and [b]peace and [b]joy in the Holy
Spirit.

2 [a]Rom. 14:14 [b]Rom. 14:1; 15:1; 1 Cor. 8:9ff.; 9:22
3 [a]Luke 18:9 [b]Rom. 14:10, 13; Col. 2:16 [c]Acts 28:2; Rom. 11:15
4 [a]Rom. 9:20
5 [a]Gal. 4:10 [b]Luke 1:1; Rom. 4:21
6 [a]Matt. 14:19; 1 Cor. 10:30
7 [a]Rom. 8:38; 2 Cor. 5:15
8 [a]Luke 20:38; 1 Thess. 5:10
9 [a]Rev. 1:18; 2:8 [b]Matt. 28:18; John 12:24; Phil. 2:11; 1 Thess. 5:10
10 [a]Luke 18:9; Rom. 14:3 [b]Rom. 2:16; 2 Cor. 5:10
11 [a]Is. 45:23 [b]Phil. 2:10f.
12 [a]Matt. 12:36; 16:27; 1 Pet. 4:5
13 [a]Matt. 7:1 [b]1 Cor. 8:13
14 [a]Acts 10:15; Rom. 14:2, 20 [b]1 Cor. 8:7
15 [a]Eph. 5:2 [b]Rom. 14:20; 1 Cor. 8:11
16 [a]1 Cor. 10:30
17 [a]1 Cor. 8:8 [b]Rom. 15:13
18 [a]Rom. 16:18 [b]2 Cor. 8:21; Phil. 4:8; 1 Pet. 2:12
19 [1]Or, *we pursue* [a]Ps. 34:14; Rom. 12:18; 1 Cor. 7:15; 2 Tim. 2:22; Heb. 12:14 [b]Rom. 15:2; 1 Cor. 10:23; 14:3f., 26; 2 Cor. 12:19; Eph. 4:12
20 [a]Rom. 14:15 [b]Acts 10:15; Rom. 14:2, 14 [c]1 Cor. 8:9-12
21 [a]1 Cor. 8:13
22 [a]1 John 3:21
23 [a]Rom. 14:5
1 [a]Rom. 14:1; Gal. 6:2; 1 Thess. 5:14
2 [a]1 Cor. 9:22; 10:24, 33; 2 Cor. 13:9 [b]Rom. 14:19; 1 Cor. 10:23; 14:3f., 26; 2 Cor. 12:19; Eph. 4:12
3 [a]2 Cor. 8:9 [b]Ps. 69:9
4 [a]Rom. 4:23f.; 2 Tim. 3:16
5 [a]2 Cor. 1:3 [b]Rom. 12:16
6 [a]Rev. 1:6
7 [1]Some mss. read, *you* [a]Rom. 14:1
8 [a]Matt. 15:24; Acts 3:26 [b]Rom. 4:16; 2 Cor. 1:20
9 [a]Rom. 3:29; 11:30 [b]Matt. 9:8 [c]2 Sam. 22:50

18 For he who in this *way* [a]serves
Christ is [b]acceptable to God and approved by men.
19 So then [1]let us [a]pursue the
things which make for peace and
the [b]building up of one another.
20 [a]Do not tear down the work of
God for the sake of food. [b]All things
indeed are clean, but [c]they are evil
for the man who eats and gives offense.
21 [a]It is good not to eat meat or to
drink wine, or *to do anything* by
which your brother stumbles.
22 The faith which you have, have
as your own conviction before God.
Happy is he who [a]does not condemn
himself in what he approves.
23 But [a]he who doubts is condemned if he eats, because *his eating is* not from faith; and whatever
is not from faith is sin.

CHAPTER 15

Self-denial Denial on Behalf of Others

NOW we who are strong ought to
bear the weaknesses of [a]those without strength and not *just* please ourselves.
2 Let each of us [a]please his neighbor for his good, to his [b]edification.
3 For even [a]Christ did not please
Himself; but as it is written, "[b]THE
REPROACHES OF THOSE WHO RE-
PROACHED THEE FELL UPON ME."
4 For [a]whatever was written in
earlier times was written for our instruction, that through perseverance and the encouragement of the
Scriptures we might have hope.
5 Now may the [a]God who gives
perseverance and encouragement
grant you [b]to be of the same mind
with one another according to
Christ Jesus;
6 that with one accord you may
with one voice glorify [a]the God and
Father of our Lord Jesus Christ.
7 Wherefore, [a]accept one another, just as Christ also accepted
[1]us to the glory of God.
8 For I say that Christ has become a servant to [a]the circumcision
on behalf of the truth of God to confirm [b]the promises *given* to the fathers,
9 and for [a]the Gentiles to [b]glorify
God for His mercy; as it is written,
"[c]THEREFORE I WILL GIVE
PRAISE TO THEE AMONG THE
GENTILES,
AND I WILL SING TO THY
NAME."

10 And again he says,
"[a]REJOICE, O GENTILES, WITH
HIS PEOPLE."
11 And again,
"[a]PRAISE THE LORD ALL YOU
GENTILES,
AND LET ALL THE PEOPLES
PRAISE HIM."
12 And again Isaiah says,
"[a]THERE SHALL COME [b]THE ROOT
OF JESSE,
AND HE WHO ARISES TO RULE
OVER THE GENTILES,
[c]IN HIM SHALL THE GENTILES
HOPE."
13 Now may the God of hope fill
you with all [a]joy and peace in believing, that you may abound in
hope [b]by the power of the Holy
Spirit.
14 And concerning you, my brethren, I myself also am convinced that
you yourselves are full of [a]good-
ness, filled with [b]all knowledge, and
able also to admonish one another.
15 But I have written very boldly
to you on some points, so as to remind you again, because of [a]the
grace that was given me [1]from God,
16 to be [a]a minister of Christ Jesus
to the Gentiles, ministering as a
priest the [b]gospel of God, that *my*
[c]offering of the Gentiles might become acceptable, sanctified by the
Holy Spirit.
17 Therefore in Christ Jesus I have
found [a]reason for boasting in
[b]things pertaining to God.
18 For I will not presume to speak
of anything except what [a]Christ has
accomplished through me, resulting
in the obedience of the Gentiles by
word and deed,
19 in the power of [a]signs and
[a]wonders, [b]in the power of the
Spirit; so that [c]from Jerusalem and
round about as [d]far as Illyricum I
have fully preached the gospel of
Christ.
20 And thus I aspired to [a]preach
the gospel, not where Christ was *already* named, [b]that I might not build
upon another man's foundation;
21 but as it is written,
"[a]THEY WHO HAD NO NEWS OF
HIM SHALL SEE,
AND THEY WHO HAVE NOT
HEARD SHALL UNDERSTAND."
22 For this reason [a]I have often
been hindered from coming to you;
23 but now, with no further place
for me in these regions, and since I
[a]have had for many years a longing
to come to you
24 whenever I [a]go to Spain — for I
hope to see you in passing, and to be
[b]helped on my way there by you,
when I have first [c]enjoyed your
company for a while —
25 but now, [a]I am going to Jerusalem [b]serving the saints.
26 For [a]Macedonia and [b]Achaia
have been pleased to make a contribution for the poor among the saints
in Jerusalem.
27 Yes, they were pleased *to do so,*
and they are indebted to them. For
[a]if the Gentiles have shared in their
spiritual things, they are indebted to
minister to them also in material
things.
28 Therefore, when I have finished
this, and [a]have put my seal on this
fruit of theirs, I will [b]go on by way of
you to Spain.
29 And I know that when [a]I come
to you, I will come in the fulness of
the blessing of Christ.
30 Now I urge you, brethren, by
our Lord Jesus Christ and by [a]the
love of the Spirit, to [b]strive together
with me in your prayers to God for
me,
31 that I may be [a]delivered from
those who are disobedient in Judea,
and *that* my [b]service for Jerusalem
may prove acceptable to the [c]saints;
32 so that [a]I may come to you in
joy by [b]the will of God and find *refreshing* rest in your company.
33 Now [a]the God of peace be with
you all. Amen.

CHAPTER 16

Greetings and Love Expressed

I [a]COMMEND to you our sister
Phoebe, who is a servant of the
church which is at [b]Cenchrea;
2 that you [a]receive her in the
Lord in a manner worthy of the
[b]saints, and that you help her in
whatever matter she may have need
of you; for she herself has also been
a helper of many, and of myself as
well.
3 Greet [a]Prisca and [a]Aquila, my
fellow-workers [b]in [c]Christ Jesus,
4 who for my life risked their own
necks, to whom not only do I give
thanks, but also all the churches of
the Gentiles;
5 also *greet* [a]the church that is in
their house. Greet Epaenetus, my
beloved, who is the [b]first convert to
Christ from [1c]Asia.
6 Greet Mary, who has worked
hard for you.
7 Greet Andronicus and [1]Junias,
my [a]kinsmen, and my [b]fellow prisoners, who are outstanding among
the apostles, who also were [c]in
Christ before me.

10 [a]Deut. 32:43
11 [a]Ps. 117:1
12 [a]Is. 11:10 [b]Rev. 5:5; 22:16 [c]Matt. 12:21
13 [a]Rom. 14:17 [b]Rom. 15:19; 1 Cor. 2:4
14 [a]Eph. 5:9 [b]1 Cor. 1:5; 8:1, 7
15 [1]Or, *by God* [a]Rom. 12:3
16 [a]Acts 9:15 [b]Rom. 1:1; 15:19, 20 [c]Rom. 12:1
17 [a]Phil. 3:3 [b]Heb. 2:17; 5:1
18 [a]Acts 15:12; 21:19; Rom. 1:5
19 [a]John 4:48 [b]Rom. 15:13; 1 Cor. 2:4 [c]Acts 22:17-21 [d]Acts 20:1f.
20 [a]Rom. 1:15 [b]1 Cor. 3:10
21 [a]Is. 52:15
22 [a]Rom. 1:13; 1 Thess. 2:18
23 [a]Acts 19:21; Rom. 1:10f.
24 [a]Rom. 15:28 [b]Acts 15:3 [c]Rom. 1:12
25 [a]Acts 19:21 [b]Acts 24:17
26 [a]Acts 16:9; 1 Cor. 16:5; 2 Cor. 1:16; 11:9; Phil. 4:15; 1 Thess. 1:7f. [b]Acts 18:12; 19:21
27 [a]1 Cor. 9:11
28 [a]John 3:33 [b]Rom. 15:24
29 [a]Acts 19:21; Rom. 1:10f.
30 [a]Gal. 5:22; Col. 1:8 [b]2 Cor. 1:11; Col. 4:12
31 [a]2 Cor. 1:10; 2 Tim. 3:11; 4:17 [b]Rom. 15:25f.; 2 Cor. 8:4; 9:1 [c]Acts 9:13, 15
32 [a]Rom. 15:23 [b]Acts 18:21; Rom. 1:10
33 [a]Rom. 16:20; 2 Cor. 13:11; Phil. 4:9; 1 Thess. 5:23
1 [a]2 Cor. 3:1 [b]Acts 18:18
2 [a]Phil. 2:29 [b]Acts 9:13, 15
3 [a]Acts 18:2 [b]Rom. 8:1ff.; 16:7, 9, 10; 2 Cor. 5:17; 12:2; Gal. 1:22 [c]Rom. 8:1
5 [1]I.e., west coast province of Asia Minor [a]1 Cor. 16:19; Col. 4:15; Philem. 2 [b]1 Cor. 16:15 [c]Acts 16:6
7 [1]Or, *Junia* (fem.) [a]Rom. 9:3; 16:11, 21 [b]Col. 4:10; Philem. 23 [c]Rom. 8:1ff.; 16:3, 9, 10; 2 Cor. 5:17; 12:2

8 Greet Ampliatus, my beloved in
the Lord.
9 Greet Urbanus, our fellow-
worker [a]in Christ, and Stachys my
beloved.
10 Greet Apelles, the approved [a]in
Christ. Greet [b]those who are of the
household of Aristobulus.
11 Greet Herodion, my [a]kinsman.
[b]Greet those of the *household* of
Narcissus, who are in the Lord.
12 Greet Tryphaena and Try-
phosa, workers in the Lord. Greet
Persis the beloved, who has worked
hard in the Lord.
13 Greet [a]Rufus, a choice man in
the Lord, also his mother and mine.
14 Greet Asyncritus, Phlegon,
Hermes, Patrobas, Hermas and the
brethren with them.
15 Greet Philologus and Julia, Ne-
reus and his sister, and Olympas,
and all [a]the saints who are with
them.
16 [a]Greet one another with a holy
kiss. All the churches of Christ greet
you.
17 Now I urge you, brethren, keep
your eye on those who cause dissensions and hindrances [a]contrary to
the teaching which you learned, and
[b]turn away from them.
18 For such men are [a]slaves not of
our Lord Christ but of [b]their own
appetites; and by their [c]smooth and
flattering speech they deceive the
hearts of the unsuspecting.
19 For the report of your obedience [a]has reached to all; therefore I
am rejoicing over you, but [b]I want
you to be wise in what is good, and
innocent in what is evil.
20 And [a]the God of peace will soon
crush [b]Satan under your feet.
[c]The grace of our Lord Jesus be
with you.
21 [a]Timothy my fellow-worker
greets you; and *so do* [b]Lucius and
[c]Jason and [d]Sosipater, my [e]kins-
men.
22 I, Tertius, who [a]write this letter,
greet you in the Lord.
23 [a]Gaius, host to me and to the
whole church, greets you. [b]Erastus,
the city treasurer greets you, and
Quartus, the brother.
24 [[1]The grace of our Lord Jesus
Christ be with you all. Amen.]
25 [a]Now to Him who is able to establish you [b]according to my gospel
and the preaching of Jesus Christ,
according to the revelation of [c]the
mystery which has been kept secret
for [d]long ages past,
26 but now is manifested, and by
[a]the Scriptures of the prophets, according to the commandment of the
eternal God, has been made known
to all the nations, *leading* to [b]obedi-
ence of faith;
27 to the only wise God, through
Jesus Christ, [a]be the glory forever.
Amen.

9 [a]Rom. 8:1ff.; 16:3, 7, 10; 2 Cor. 5:17; 12:2
10 [a]Rom. 8:1ff.; 16:3, 7, 9; 2 Cor. 5:17; 12:2; Gal. 1:22 [b]1 Cor. 1:11
11 [a]Rom. 9:3; 16:7, 21 [b]1 Cor. 1:11
13 [a]Mark 15:21
15 [a]Rom. 16:2, 14
16 [a]1 Cor. 16:20; 2 Cor. 13:12
17 [a]1 Tim. 1:3; 6:3 [b]Matt. 7:15
18 [a]Rom. 14:18 [b]Phil. 3:19 [c]Col. 2:4; 2 Pet. 2:3
19 [a]Rom. 1:8 [b]Jer. 4:22
20 [a]Rom. 15:33 [b]Matt. 4:10 [c]1 Cor. 16:23
21 [a]Acts 16:1 [b]Acts 13:1 [?] [c]Acts 17:5 [?] [d]Acts 20:4 [?] [e]Rom. 9:3; 16:7
22 [a]1 Cor. 16:21
23 [a]Acts 20:4 [?]; 1 Cor. 1:14 [b]Acts 19:22
24 [1]Many mss. do not contain this verse
25 [a]Eph. 3:20; Jude 24 [b]Rom. 2:16 [c]Matt. 13:35; 1 Cor. 2:1, 7; 4:1 [d]2 Tim. 1:9
26 [a]Rom. 1:2 [b]Rom. 1:5
27 [a]Rom. 11:36

THE FIRST EPISTLE OF PAUL TO THE

CORINTHIANS

Appeal to Unity

PAUL, [a]called *as* an apostle of Jesus Christ by [b]the will of God, and
Sosthenes our brother,
2 to [a]the church of God which is
at [b]Corinth, to those who have been
sanctified in Christ Jesus, saints [c]by
calling, with all who in every place
[d]call upon the name of our Lord Jesus Christ, their *Lord* and ours:
3 [a]Grace to you and peace from
God our Father and the Lord Jesus
Christ.
4 [a]I thank my God always concerning you, for the grace of God
which was given you in Christ Jesus,
5 that in everything you were
[a]enriched in Him, in all [b]speech and
[b]all knowledge,
6 even as [a]the testimony concerning Christ was confirmed in
you,
7 so that you are not lacking in
any gift, [a]awaiting eagerly the revelation of our Lord Jesus Christ,
8 [a]who shall also confirm you to
the end, blameless in [b]the day of our
Lord Jesus Christ.
9 [a]God is faithful, through whom
you were [b]called into [c]fellowship
with His Son, Jesus Christ our Lord.
10 Now [a]I exhort you, [b]brethren,
by the name of our Lord Jesus
Christ, that you all agree, and there
be no [c]divisions among you, but you
be made complete in the same mind
and in the same judgment.
11 For I have been informed concerning you, my brethren, by [a]Chlo-
e's *people*, that there are quarrels
among you.

1 [a]Rom. 1:1 [b]Rom. 1:10; 15:32
2 [a]1 Cor. 10:32 [b]Acts 18:1 [c]Rom. 1:7; 8:28 [d]Acts 7:59
3 [a]Rom. 1:7
4 [a]Rom. 1:8
5 [a]2 Cor. 9:11 [b]Rom. 15:14
6 [a]2 Thess. 1:10
7 [a]Luke 17:30; Rom. 8:19, 23
8 [a]Rom. 8:19; Phil. 1:6; Col. 2:7 [b]Luke 17:24, 30
9 [a]Deut. 7:9 [b]Rom. 8:28 [c]1 John 1:3
10 [a]Rom. 12:1 [b]Rom. 1:13 [c]1 Cor. 11:18
11 [a]Rom. 16:10f.

12 Now I mean this, that [a]each one
of you is saying, "I am of Paul," and
"I of [b]Apollos," and "I of [c]Cephas,"
and "I of Christ."
13 Has Christ been divided? Paul
was not crucified for you, was he?
Or were you [a]baptized in the name
of Paul?
14 I thank God that I [a]baptized
none of you except [a]Crispus and
[b]Gaius,
15 that no man should say you
were baptized in my name.
16 Now I did baptize also the
[a]household of Stephanas; beyond
that, I do not know whether I baptized any other.
17 [a]For Christ did not send me to
baptize, but to preach the gospel,
[b]not in cleverness of speech, that
the cross of Christ should not be
made void.

The Wisdom of God

18 For the word of the cross is to
[a]those who are perishing [b]foolish-
ness, but to us who are being saved
it is [c]the power of God.
19 For it is written,
"[a]I WILL DESTROY THE WISDOM
OF THE WISE,
AND THE CLEVERNESS OF THE
CLEVER I WILL SET ASIDE."
20 [a]Where is the wise man? Where
is the scribe? Where is the debater
of [b]this age? Has not God [c]made
foolish the wisdom of [d]the world?
21 For since in the wisdom of God
[a]the world through its wisdom did
not *come to* know God, [b]God was
well-pleased through the [c]foolish-
ness of the message preached to
[d]save those who believe.
22 For indeed [a]Jews ask for signs,
and Greeks search for wisdom;
23 but we preach [a]Christ crucified,
[b]to Jews a stumbling block, and to
Gentiles [c]foolishness,
24 but to those who are [a]the
called, both Jews and Greeks, Christ
[b]the power of God and [c]the wisdom
of God.
25 Because the [a]foolishness of
God is wiser than men, and [b]the
weakness of God is stronger than
men.
26 For consider your [a]calling,
brethren, that there were [b]not many
wise according to the flesh, not
many mighty, not many noble;
27 but [a]God has chosen the foolish
things of [b]the world to shame the
wise, and God has chosen the weak
things of [b]the world to shame the
things which are strong,
28 and the base things of [a]the
world and the despised, God has
chosen, [b]the things that are not, that
He might [c]nullify the things that are,
29 that [a]no man should boast before God.
30 But by His doing you are in
[a]Christ Jesus, who became to us
[b]wisdom from God, and [c]right-
eousness and [d]sanctification, and
[e]redemption,
31 that, just as it is written, "[a]LET
HIM WHO BOASTS, BOAST IN THE
LORD."

CHAPTER 2

Paul's Reliance upon the Spirit

AND when I came to you, brethren, I [a]did not come with superiority
of speech or of wisdom, proclaiming
to you [b]the [1]testimony of God.
2 For I determined to know nothing among you except [a]Jesus Christ,
and Him crucified.
3 And I [a]was with you in [b]weak-
ness and in [c]fear and in much trembling.
4 And my message and my
preaching were [a]not in persuasive
words of wisdom, but in demonstration of [b]the Spirit and of power,
5 that your faith should not [1]rest
on the wisdom of men, but on [a]the
power of God.
6 Yet we do speak wisdom
among those who are [a]mature; a
wisdom, however, not of [b]this age,
nor of the rulers of [b]this age, who
are [c]passing away;
7 but we speak God's wisdom in
a [a]mystery, the hidden *wisdom*,
which God [b]predestined before the
[c]ages to our glory;
8 *the wisdom* [a]which none of the
rulers of [b]this age has understood;
for if they had understood it, they
would not have crucified [c]the Lord
of glory;
9 but just as it is written,
"[a]THINGS WHICH EYE HAS NOT
SEEN AND EAR HAS NOT
HEARD,
AND *which* HAVE NOT ENTERED
THE HEART OF MAN,
ALL THAT GOD HAS PREPARED
FOR THOSE WHO LOVE HIM."
10 [a]For to us God revealed *them*
[b]through the Spirit; for the Spirit
searches all things, even the [c]depths
of God.
11 For who among men knows the
thoughts of a man except the [a]spirit
of the man, which is in him? Even so
the *thoughts* of God no one knows
except the Spirit of God.
12 Now we [a]have received, not the
spirit of [b]the world, but the Spirit

12 [a]Matt. 23:8 [b]Acts 18:24; 1 Cor. 3:22 [c]John 1:42; 1 Cor. 3:22
13 [a]Matt. 28:19
14 [a]Acts 18:8 [b]Rom. 16:23
16 [a]1 Cor. 16:15
17 [a]John 4:2; Acts 10:48 [b]1 Cor. 2:1
18 [a]Acts 2:47; 2 Cor. 2:15 [b]1 Cor. 1:21 [c]Rom. 1:16
19 [a]Is. 29:14
20 [a]Job 12:17 [b]Matt. 13:22 [c]Rom. 1:20ff. [d]John 12:31
21 [a]John 12:31; 1 Cor. 1:27f.; 6:2; 11:32; James 4:4 [b]Luke 12:32 [c]1 Cor. 1:18, 23 [d]Rom. 11:14
22 [a]Matt. 12:38
23 [a]1 Cor. 2:2; Gal. 3:1; 5:11 [b]Luke 2:34; 1 Pet. 2:8 [c]1 Cor. 1:18
24 [a]Rom. 8:28 [b]Rom. 1:16; 1 Cor. 1:18 [c]Luke 11:49; 1 Cor. 1:30
25 [a]1 Cor. 1:18 [b]2 Cor. 13:4
26 [a]Rom. 11:29 [b]Matt. 11:25
27 [a]James 2:5 [b]1 Cor. 1:20
28 [a]1 Cor. 1:20 [b]Rom. 4:17 [c]Job 34:19; 1 Cor. 2:6
29 [a]Eph. 2:9
30 [a]Rom. 8:1 [b]1 Cor. 1:24 [c]Jer. 23:5f.; 33:16 [d]1 Cor. 1:2 [e]Rom. 3:24
31 [a]Jer. 9:23f.
1 [1]Or, *mystery* [a]1 Cor. 1:17; 2:4, 13 [b]1 Cor. 2:7
2 [a]1 Cor. 1:23
3 [a]Acts 18:1, 6, 12 [b]1 Cor. 4:10; 2 Cor. 11:30; 12:5, 9f.; 13:9 [c]Is. 19:16; 2 Cor. 7:15
4 [a]1 Cor. 1:17; 2:1, 13 [b]Rom. 15:19
5 [1]Lit., *be* [a]2 Cor. 4:7; 6:7
6 [a]Eph. 4:13; Heb. 5:14; 6:1 [b]Matt. 13:22 [c]1 Cor. 1:28
7 [a]Rom. 11:25; 16:25f.; 1 Cor. 2:1 [b]Rom. 8:29f. [c]Heb. 1:2; 11:3
8 [a]1 Cor. 1:26; 2:6 [b]Matt. 13:22; 1 Cor. 1:20 [c]Acts 7:2; James 2:1
9 [a]Is. 64:4
10 [a]Matt. 11:25 [b]John 14:26 [c]Rom. 11:33ff.
11 [a]Prov. 20:27
12 [a]Rom. 8:15 [b]1 Cor. 1:27

who is from God, that we might
know the things freely given to us
by God,
13 which things we also speak,
[a]not in words taught by human
wisdom, but in those taught by
the Spirit, combining spiritual
thoughts with spiritual *words.*
14 But a [a]natural man [b]does not
accept the things of the Spirit of
God; for they are [c]foolishness to
him, and he cannot understand
them, because they are spiritually
appraised.
15 But he who is [a]spiritual ap-
praises all things, yet he himself is
appraised by no man.
16 For [a]WHO HAS KNOWN THE MIND
OF THE LORD, THAT HE SHOULD IN-
STRUCT HIM? But [b]we have the mind
of Christ.

CHAPTER 3

Foundations for Living

AND I, brethren, could not speak
to you as to [a]spiritual men, but as to
[b]men of flesh, as to [c]babes in Christ.
2 I gave you [a]milk to drink, not
solid food; for you [b]were not yet
able *to receive it.* Indeed, even now
you are not yet able,
3 for you are still fleshly. For
since there is [a]jealousy and strife
among you, are you not fleshly, and
are you not walking [b]like mere men?
4 For when [a]one says, "I am of
Paul," and another, "I am of Apollos," are you not *mere* [b]men?
5 What then is Apollos? And
what is Paul? [a]Servants through
whom you believed, even [b]as the
Lord gave *opportunity* to each one.
6 [a]I planted, [b]Apollos watered,
but [c]God was causing the growth.
7 So then neither the one who
plants nor the one who waters is
anything, but God who causes the
growth.
8 Now he who plants and he who
waters are one; but each will [a]re-
ceive his own reward according to
his own labor.
9 For we are God's [a]fellow-work-
ers; you are God's [b]field, God's
[c]building.
10 According to [a]the grace of God
which was given to me, as a wise
master builder [b]I laid a foundation,
and [c]another is building upon it. But
let each man be careful how he
builds upon it.
11 For no man can lay a [a]founda-
tion other than the one which is laid,
which is Jesus Christ.
12 Now if any man builds upon the
foundation with gold, silver, precious stones, wood, hay, straw,
13 [a]each man's work will become
evident; for [b]the day will show it,
because it is *to be* revealed with fire;
and the fire itself will test the quality
of each man's work.
14 If any man's work which he has
built upon it remains, he shall [a]re-
ceive a reward.
15 If any man's work is burned up,
he shall suffer loss; but he himself
shall be saved, yet [a]so as through
fire.
16 [a]Do you not know that [b]you are
a temple of God, and *that* the Spirit
of God dwells in you?
17 If any man destroys the temple
of God, God will destroy him, for the
temple of God is holy, and that is
what you are.
18 [a]Let no man deceive himself. [b]If
any man among you thinks that he
is wise in [c]this age, let him become
foolish that he may become wise.
19 For [a]the wisdom of this world is
foolishness before God. For it is
written, "*He is* [b]THE ONE WHO
CATCHES THE WISE IN THEIR CRAFTI-
NESS";
20 and again, "[a]THE LORD KNOWS
THE REASONINGS of the wise, THAT
THEY ARE USELESS."
21 So then [a]let no one boast in
men. For [b]all things belong to you,
22 [a]whether Paul or Apollos or Cephas or the world or [b]life or death or
things present or things to come; all
things belong to you,
23 and [a]you belong to Christ; and
[b]Christ belongs to God.

CHAPTER 4

Servants of Christ

LET a man regard us in this manner, as [a]servants of Christ, and
[b]stewards of [c]the mysteries of God.
2 In this case, moreover, it is required of stewards that one be
found trustworthy.
3 But to me it is a very small thing
that I should be examined by you, or
by *any* human court; in fact, I do not
even examine myself.
4 I [a]am conscious of nothing
against myself, yet I am not by this
[b]acquitted; but the one who examines me is the Lord.
5 Therefore [a]do not go on passing
judgment before the time, *but wait*
[b]until the Lord comes who will both
[c]bring to light the things hidden in
the darkness and disclose the mo-

13 [a]1 Cor. 1:17; 2:1
14 [a]1 Cor. 15:44, 46 [b]John 14:17 [c]1 Cor. 1:18
15 [a]1 Cor. 3:1
16 [a]Is. 40:13; Rom. 11:34 [b]John 15:15
1 [a]1 Cor. 2:15 [b]Rom. 7:14 [c]1 Cor. 2:6; Eph. 4:14; Heb. 5:13
2 [a]Heb. 5:12f. [b]John 16:12
3 [a]Rom. 13:13 [b]1 Cor. 3:4
4 [a]1 Cor. 1:12 [b]1 Cor. 3:3
5 [a]Rom. 15:16; 2 Cor. 3:3, 6; Eph. 3:7; Col. 1:25; 1 Tim. 1:12 [b]Rom. 12:6; 1 Cor. 3:10
6 [a]Acts 18:4-11, 18; 1 Cor. 4:15 [b]Acts 18:27; 1 Cor. 1:12 [c]1 Cor. 15:10
8 [a]1 Cor. 3:14; 4:5
9 [a]Mark 16:20; 2 Cor. 6:1 [b]Is. 61:3; Matt. 15:13 [c]1 Cor. 3:16; Eph. 2:20-22; Col. 2:7
10 [a]Rom. 12:3 [b]Rom. 15:20 [c]1 Thess. 3:2
11 [a]Is. 28:16; Eph. 2:20; 1 Pet. 2:4ff.
13 [a]1 Cor. 4:5 [b]Matt. 10:15; 1 Cor. 1:8; 4:3 marg.; 2 Thess. 1:7-10; 2 Tim. 1:12, 18
14 [a]1 Cor. 3:8; 4:5; 9:17; Gal. 6:4
15 [a]Job 23:10; Ps. 66:10, 12; Jude 23
16 [a]Rom. 6:16 [b]Rom. 8:9; 1 Cor. 6:19; 2 Cor. 6:16; Eph. 2:21f.
18 [a]Is. 5:21 [b]1 Cor. 8:2; Gal. 6:3 [c]1 Cor. 1:20
19 [a]1 Cor. 1:20 [b]Job 5:13
20 [a]Ps. 94:11
21 [a]1 Cor. 4:6 [b]Rom. 8:32
22 [a]1 Cor. 1:12; 3:5, 6 [b]Rom. 8:38
23 [a]1 Cor. 15:23; 2 Cor. 10:7; Gal. 3:29 [b]1 Cor. 11:3
1 [a]Luke 1:2 [b]1 Cor. 9:17; Titus 1:7; 1 Pet. 4:10 [c]Rom. 11:25
4 [a]Acts 23:1; 2 Cor. 1:12 [b]Ps. 143:2; Rom. 2:13
5 [a]Matt. 7:1; Rom. 2:1 [b]John 21:22; Rom. 2:16 [c]1 Cor. 3:13

tives of *men's* hearts; and then each man's [d]praise will come to him from God.

6 Now these things, brethren, I have figuratively applied to myself and Apollos for your sakes, that in us you might learn not to exceed [a]what is written, in order that no one of you might [b]become arrogant [c]in behalf of one against the other.

7 For who regards you as superior? And [a]what do you have that you did not receive? But if you did receive it, why do you boast as if you had not received it?

8 You are [a]already filled, you have already become rich, you have become kings without us; and *I* would indeed that you had become kings so that we also might reign with you.

9 For, I think, God has exhibited us apostles last of all, as men [a]condemned to death; because we [b]have become a spectacle to the world, both to angels and to men.

10 We are [a]fools for Christ's sake, but [b]you are prudent in Christ; [c]we are weak, but you are strong; you are distinguished, but we are without honor.

11 To this present hour we are both [a]hungry and thirsty, and are poorly clothed, and are roughly treated, and are homeless;

12 and we toil, [a]working with our own hands; when we are [b]reviled, we bless; when we are [c]persecuted, we endure;

13 when we are slandered, we try to conciliate; we have [a]become as the scum of the world, the dregs of all things, *even* until now.

14 I do not write these things to [a]shame you, but to admonish you as my beloved [b]children.

15 For if you were to have countless [a]tutors in Christ, yet *you would* not *have* many fathers; for in [b]Christ Jesus I [c]became your father through the [d]gospel.

16 I exhort you therefore, be [a]imitators of me.

17 For this reason I [a]have sent to you [b]Timothy, who is my [c]beloved and faithful child in the Lord, and he will remind you of my ways which are in Christ, [d]just as I teach everywhere in every church.

18 Now some have become [a]arrogant, as though I were not [b]coming to you.

19 But I [a]will come to you soon, [b]if the Lord wills, and I shall find out, not the words of those who are [c]arrogant, but their power.

5 [d]Rom. 2:29; 1 Cor. 3:8; 2 Cor. 10:18
6 [a]1 Cor. 1:19, 31; 3:19f. [b]1 Cor. 4:18f.; 8:1; 13:4 [c]1 Cor. 1:12; 3:4
7 [a]John 3:27; Rom. 12:3, 6
8 [a]Rev. 3:17f.
9 [a]Rom. 8:36 [b]Heb. 10:33
10 [a]Acts 17:18 [b]1 Cor. 1:19f. [c]1 Cor. 2:3; 2 Cor. 13:9
11 [a]Rom. 8:35
12 [a]Acts 18:3 [b]1 Pet. 3:9 [c]John 15:20; Rom. 8:35
13 [a]Lam. 3:45
14 [a]1 Cor. 6:5; 15:34 [b]2 Cor. 6:13; 12:14
15 [a]Gal. 3:24f. [b]1 Cor. 1:30; [c]Num. 11:12; 1 Cor. 3:8; Gal. 4:19; Philem. 10 [d]1 Cor. 9:12, 14
16 [a]1 Cor. 11:1; Phil. 3:17; 4:9
17 [a]1 Cor. 16:10 [b]Acts 16:1 [c]1 Cor. 4:14; 1 Tim. 1:2, 18; 2 Tim. 1:2 [d]1 Cor. 7:17; 11:34; 14:33; 16:1
18 [a]1 Cor. 4:6 [b]1 Cor. 4:21
19 [a]Acts 19:21; 20:2; 1 Cor. 11:34; 16:5f.; 16:8; 2 Cor. 1:15f. [b]Acts 18:21 [c]1 Cor. 4:6
20 [a]1 Cor. 2:4
21 [a]2 Cor. 1:23
1 [a]Lev. 18:8; Deut. 22:30; 27:20
2 [a]1 Cor. 4:6 [b]2 Cor. 7:7-10 [c]1 Cor. 5:13
3 [a]Col. 2:5; 1 Thess. 2:17
4 [a]2 Thess. 3:6 [b]John 20:23; 2 Cor. 2:6, 10
5 [1]Some ancient mss. do not contain *Jesus* [a]Prov. 23:14; 1 Tim. 1:20 [b]Matt. 4:10 [c]1 Cor. 1:8
6 [a]1 Cor. 5:2; James 4:16 [b]Rom. 6:16 [c]Hos. 7:4; Matt. 16:6, 12
7 [a]Mark 14:12
8 [a]Ex. 12:19; 13:7; Deut. 16:3
9 [a]2 Cor. 6:14; 2 Thess. 3:6
10 [a]1 Cor. 10:27
11 [a]Acts 1:15; 2 Thess. 3:6 [b]1 Cor. 10:7, 14
12 [a]Mark 4:11 [b]1 Cor. 5:3-5; 6:1
13 [a]Deut. 13:5; 17:7, 12; 21:21; 22:21

20 For the kingdom of God does [a]not consist in words, but in power.

21 What do you desire? [a]Shall I come to you with a rod or with love and a spirit of gentleness?

Chapter 5

Immorality Rebuked

It is actually reported that there is immorality among you, and immorality of such a kind as does not exist even among the Gentiles, that someone has [a]his father's wife.

2 And you [a]have become arrogant, and have not [b]mourned instead, in order that the one who had done this deed might be [c]removed from your midst.

3 For I, on my part, though [a]absent in body but present in spirit, have already judged him who has so committed this, as though I were present.

4 [a]In the name of our Lord Jesus, when you are assembled, and I with you in spirit, [b]with the power of our Lord Jesus,

5 *I have decided* to [a]deliver such a one to [b]Satan for the destruction of his flesh, that his spirit may be saved in [c]the day of the Lord [1]Jesus.

6 [a]Your boasting is not good. [b]Do you not know that [c]a little leaven leavens the whole lump *of dough?*

7 Clean out the old leaven, that you may be a new lump, just as you are *in fact* unleavened. For Christ our [a]Passover also has been sacrificed.

8 Let us therefore celebrate the feast, [a]not with old leaven, nor with the leaven of malice and wickedness, but with the unleavened bread of sincerity and truth.

9 I wrote you in my letter [a]not to associate with immoral people;

10 I *did* not at all *mean* with the immoral people of this world, or with the covetous and swindlers, or with [a]idolaters; for then you would have to go out of the world.

11 But actually, I wrote to you not to associate with any so-called [a]brother if he should be an immoral person, or covetous, or [b]an idolater, or a reviler, or a drunkard, or a swindler—not even to eat with such a one.

12 For what have I to do with judging [a]outsiders? [b]Do you not judge those who are within *the church?*

13 But those who are outside, God judges. [a]Remove the wicked man from among yourselves.

CHAPTER 6

Lawsuits Discouraged

DOES any one of you, when he has a case against his neighbor, dare to go to law before the unrighteous, and [a]not before the saints?

2 Or [a]do you not know that [b]the saints will judge [c]the world? And if the world is judged by you, are you not competent *to constitute* the smallest law courts?

3 [a]Do you not know that we shall judge angels? How much more, matters of this life?

4 If then you have law courts dealing with matters of this life, do you appoint them as judges who are of no account in the church?

5 [a]I say *this* to your shame. *Is it* so, *that* there is not among you one wise man who will be able to decide between his [b]brethren,

6 but brother goes to law with brother, and that before [a]unbelievers?

7 Actually, then, it is already a defeat for you, that you have lawsuits with one another. [a]Why not rather be wronged? Why not rather be defrauded?

8 On the contrary, you yourselves wrong and defraud, and that *your* [a]brethren.

9 Or [a]do you not know that the unrighteous shall not [b]inherit the kingdom of God? [c]Do not be deceived; [d]neither fornicators, nor idolaters, nor adulterers, nor effeminate, nor homosexuals,

10 nor thieves, nor *the* covetous, nor drunkards, nor revilers, nor swindlers, shall [a]inherit the kingdom of God.

11 And [a]such were some of you; but you were [b]washed, but you were [c]sanctified, but you were [d]justified in the name of the Lord Jesus Christ, and in the Spirit of our God.

The Body Is the Lord's

12 [a]All things are lawful for me, but not all things are profitable. All things are lawful for me, but I will not be mastered by anything.

13 [a]Food is for the stomach, and the stomach is for food; but God will [b]do away with both of them. Yet the body is not for immorality, but [c]for the Lord; and [d]the Lord is for the body.

14 Now God has not only [a]raised the Lord, but [b]will also raise us up through His power.

15 [a]Do you not know that [b]your bodies are members of Christ? Shall I then take away the members of Christ and make them members of a harlot? [c]May it never be!

16 Or [a]do you not know that the one who joins himself to a harlot is one body *with her?* For He says, "[b]THE TWO WILL BECOME ONE FLESH."

17 But the one who joins himself to the Lord is [a]one spirit *with Him.*

18 [a]Flee immorality. Every *other* sin that a man commits is outside the body, but the immoral man sins against his own body.

19 Or [a]do you not know that [b]your body is a temple of the Holy Spirit who is in you, whom you have from God, and that [c]you are not your own?

20 For [a]you have been bought with a price: therefore glorify God in [b]your body.

CHAPTER 7

Advice on Marriage

NOW concerning the things about which you wrote, it is [a]good for a man not to touch a woman.

2 But because of immoralities, let each man have his own wife, and let each woman have her own husband.

3 Let the husband fulfill his duty to his wife, and likewise also the wife to her husband.

4 The wife does not have authority over her own body, but the husband *does;* and likewise also the husband does not have authority over his own body, but the wife *does.*

5 [a]Stop depriving one another, except by agreement for a time that you may devote yourselves to prayer, and come together again lest [b]Satan tempt you because of your lack of self-control.

6 But this I say by way of concession, [a]not of command.

7 Yet I wish that all men were [a]even as I myself am. However, [b]each man has his own gift from God, one in this manner, and another in that.

8 But I say to the unmarried and to widows that it is [a]good for them if they remain [b]even as I.

9 But if they do not have self-control, [a]let them marry; for it is better to marry than to burn.

10 But to the married I give instructions, [a]not I, but the Lord, that the wife should not leave her husband

11 (but if she does leave, let her

1 [a]Matt. 18:17
2 [a]Rom. 6:16 [b]Dan. 7:18, 22, 27; Matt. 19:28 [c]1 Cor. 1:20
3 [a]Rom. 6:16
5 [a]1 Cor. 4:14; 15:34 [b]Acts 1:15; 9:13; 1 Cor. 6:1
6 [a]2 Cor. 6:14f.
7 [a]Matt. 5:39f.
8 [a]1 Thess. 4:6
9 [a]Rom. 6:16 [b]Acts 20:32; 1 Cor. 15:50; Gal. 5:21; Eph. 5:5 [c]Luke 21:8; 1 Cor. 15:33; Gal. 6:7; James 1:16; 1 John 3:7 [d]Rom. 13:13; 1 Cor. 5:11; Gal. 5:19-21; Eph. 5:5; 1 Tim. 1:10; Rev. 21:8; 22:15
10 [a]Acts 20:32; 1 Cor. 15:50; Gal. 5:21; Eph. 5:5
11 [a]1 Cor. 12:2; Eph. 2:2f.; Col. 3:5-7; Titus 3:3-7 [b]Acts 22:16; Eph. 5:26 [c]1 Cor. 1:2, 30 [d]Rom. 8:30
12 [a]1 Cor. 10:23
13 [a]Matt. 15:17 [b]Col. 2:22 [c]1 Cor. 6:15, 19 [d]Gal. 5:24; Eph. 5:23
14 [a]Acts 2:24 [b]John 6:39f.; 1 Cor. 15:23
15 [a]1 Cor. 6:3 [b]Rom. 12:5, 27; 1 Cor. 6:13; Eph. 5:30 [c]Luke 20:16
16 [a]1 Cor. 6:3 [b]Gen. 2:24; Matt. 19:5; Mark 10:8
17 [a]John 17:21-23; Rom. 8:9-11; 1 Cor. 6:15; Gal. 2:20
18 [a]1 Cor. 6:9; 2 Cor. 12:21; Eph. 5:3; Col. 3:5; Heb. 13:4
19 [a]1 Cor. 6:3 [b]John 2:21 [c]Rom. 14:7f.
20 [a]Acts 20:28; 1 Cor. 7:23; 1 Pet. 1:18f.; 2 Pet. 2:1; Rev. 5:9 [b]Rom. 12:1; Phil. 1:20
1 [a]1 Cor. 7:8
5 [a]Ex. 19:15; 1 Sam. 21:5 [b]Matt. 4:10
6 [a]2 Cor. 8:8
7 [a]1 Cor. 7:8; 9:5 [b]Matt. 19:11f.; Rom. 12:6; 1 Cor. 12:4, 11
8 [a]1 Cor. 7:1, 26 [b]1 Cor. 7:7; 9:5
9 [a]1 Tim. 5:14
10 [a]Mal. 2:16; Matt. 5:32; 19:3-9; Mark 10:2-12; Luke 16:18; 1 Cor. 7:6

remain unmarried, or else be reconciled to her husband), and that the
husband should not [1]send his wife
away.
12 But to the rest [a]I say, not the
Lord, that if any brother has a wife
who is an unbeliever, and she consents to live with him, let him not
[1]send her away.
13 And a woman who has an unbelieving husband, and he consents to
live with her, let her not [1]send her
husband away.
14 For the unbelieving husband is
sanctified through his wife, and the
unbelieving wife is sanctified
through [1]her believing husband; for
otherwise your children are unclean, but now they are [a]holy.
15 Yet if the unbelieving one
leaves, let him leave; the brother or
the sister is not under bondage in
such *cases,* but God has called [1]us
[2a]to peace.
16 For how do you know, O wife,
whether you will [a]save your husband? Or how do you know, O husband, whether you will save your
wife?
17 Only, [a]as the Lord has assigned
to each one, as God has called each,
in this manner let him walk. And
[b]thus I direct in [c]all the churches.
18 Was any man called *already*
circumcised? Let him not become
uncircumcised. Has anyone been
called in uncircumcision? [a]Let him
not be circumcised.
19 [a]Circumcision is nothing, and
uncircumcision is nothing, but *what
matters is* [b]the keeping of the commandments of God.
20 [a]Let each man remain in that
[1]condition in which he was called.
21 Were you called while a slave?
[1]Do not worry about it; but if you
are able also to become free, rather
[2]do that.
22 For he who was called in the
Lord while a slave, is [a]the Lord's
freedman; likewise he who was
called while free, is [b]Christ's slave.
23 [a]You were bought with a price;
do not become slaves of men.
24 Brethren, [a]let each man remain
with God in that *condition* in which
he was called.
25 Now concerning virgins I have
[a]no command of the Lord, but I give
an opinion as one who [1b]by the mercy of the Lord is trustworthy.
26 I think then that this is good in
view of the [1]present [a]distress, that
[b]it is good for a man [2]to remain as he
is.
27 Are you bound to a wife? Do
not seek to be released. Are you released from a wife? Do not seek a
wife.
28 But if you should marry, you
have not sinned; and if a virgin
should marry, she has not sinned.
Yet such will have [1]trouble in this
life, and I am trying to spare you.
29 But this I say, brethren, [a]the
time has been shortened, so that
from now on both those who have
wives should be as though they had
none;
30 and those who weep, as though
they did not weep; and those who
rejoice, as though they did not rejoice; and those who buy, as though
they did not possess;
31 and those who use the world, as
though they did not [a]make full use
of it; for [b]the form of this world is
passing away.
32 But I want you to be free from
concern. One who is [a]unmarried is
concerned about the things of the
Lord, how he may please the Lord;
33 but one who is married is concerned about the things of the
world, how he may please his [1]wife,
34 and *his interests* are divided.
And the woman who is unmarried,
and the virgin, is concerned about
the things of the Lord, that she may
be holy both in body and spirit; but
one who is married is concerned
about the things of the world, how
she may please her husband.
35 And this I say for your own
benefit; not to put a restraint upon
you, but to promote what is seemly,
and *to secure* undistracted devotion
to the Lord.
36 But if any man thinks that he is
acting unbecomingly toward his virgin *daughter,* if she should be of full
age, and if it must be so, let him do
what he wishes, he does not sin; let
[1]her marry.
37 But he who stands firm in his
heart, [1]being under no constraint,
but has authority [2]over his own will,
and has decided this in his own
heart, to keep his own [3]virgin
daughter, he will do well.
38 So then both he who gives his
own virgin *daughter* in marriage
does well, and he who does not give
her in marriage will do better.
39 [a]A wife is bound as long as her
husband lives; but if her husband [1]is
dead, she is free to be married to
whom she wishes, only [b]in the Lord.
40 But [a]in my opinion she is hap-
pier if she remains as she is; and I
think that I also have the Spirit of
God.

11 [1]Or, *leave his wife*
12 [1]Or, *leave her* [a]1 Cor. 7:6; 2 Cor. 11:17
13 [1]Or, *leave her husband*
14 [1]Lit., *the brother* [a]Ezra 9:2; Mal. 2:15
15 [1]Some ancient mss. read, *you* [2]Lit., *in* [a]Rom. 14:19
16 [a]Rom. 11:14; 1 Pet. 3:1
17 [a]Rom. 12:3 [b]1 Cor. 4:17 [c]1 Cor. 11:16; 14:33; 2 Cor. 8:18; 11:28; Gal. 1:22; 1 Thess. 2:14; 2 Thess. 1:4
18 [a]Acts 15:1ff.
19 [a]Rom. 2:27, 29; Gal. 3:28; 5:6; 6:15; Col. 3:11 [b]Rom. 2:25
20 [1]Lit., *calling* [a]1 Cor. 7:24
21 [1]Lit., *Let it not be a care to you* [2]Lit., *use*
22 [a]John 8:32, 36; Philem. 16 [b]Eph. 6:6; Col. 3:24; 1 Pet. 2:16
23 [a]1 Cor. 6:20
24 [a]1 Cor. 7:20
25 [1]Lit., *has had mercy shown on him by the Lord to be trustworthy* [a]1 Cor. 7:6 [b]2 Cor. 4:1; 1 Tim. 1:13, 16
26 [1]Or, *impending* [2]Lit., *so to be* [a]Luke 21:23; 2 Thess. 2:2 [b]1 Cor. 7:1, 8
28 [1]Lit., *tribulation in the flesh*
29 [a]Rom. 13:11f.; 1 Cor. 7:31
31 [a]1 Cor. 9:18 [b]1 Cor. 7:29; 1 John 2:17
32 [a]1 Tim. 5:5
33 [1]Some mss. read, *wife. And there is a difference also between the wife and the virgin. One who is unmarried is concerned*
36 [1]Lit., *them*
37 [1]Lit., *having no necessity* [2]Lit., *pertaining to* [3]Or, *virgin*
39 [1]Lit., *has fallen asleep* [a]Rom. 7:2 [b]2 Cor. 6:14
40 [a]1 Cor. 7:6, 25

Chapter 8

Take Care with Your Liberty

NOW concerning [a]things sacrificed to idols, we know that we all have [b]knowledge. Knowledge [c]makes arrogant, but love [d]edifies.

2 [a]If any one supposes that he knows anything, he has not yet [b]known as he ought to know;

3 but if any one loves God, he [a]is known by Him.

4 Therefore concerning the eating of [a]things sacrificed to idols, we know that there is [b]no such thing as an idol in the world, and that [c]there is no God but one.

5 For even if [a]there are so-called gods whether in heaven or on earth, as indeed there are many gods and many lords,

6 yet for us [a]there is *but* one God, [b]the Father, [c]from whom are all things, and we *exist* for Him; and [d]one Lord, Jesus Christ, [e]through whom are all things, and we *exist* through Him.

7 However not all men [a]have this knowledge; but [b]some, being accustomed to the idol until now, eat food as if it were sacrificed to an idol; and their conscience being weak is defiled.

8 But [a]food will not commend us to God; we are neither the worse if we do not eat, nor the better if we do eat.

9 But [a]take care lest this liberty of yours somehow become a stumbling block to the [b]weak.

10 For if someone sees you, who have [a]knowledge, dining in an idol's temple, will not his conscience, if he is weak, be strengthened to eat [b]things sacrificed to idols?

11 For through [a]your knowledge he who is weak [b]is ruined, the brother for whose sake Christ died.

12 [a]And thus, by sinning against the brethren and wounding their conscience when it is weak, you sin [b]against Christ.

13 Therefore, [a]if food causes my brother to stumble, I will never eat meat again, that I might not cause my brother to stumble.

Chapter 9

Paul's Use of Liberty

AM I not [a]free? Am I not an [b]apostle? Have I not [c]seen Jesus our Lord? Are you not [d]my work in the Lord?

2 If to others I am not an apostle, at least I am to you; for you are the [a]seal of my [b]apostleship in the Lord.

3 My defense to those who examine me is this:

4 [a]Do we not have a right to eat and drink?

5 [a]Do we not have a right to take along a believing wife, even as the rest of the apostles, and the [b]brothers of the Lord, and [c]Cephas?

6 Or do only [a]Barnabas and I not have a right to refrain from working?

7 Who at any time serves [a]as a soldier at his own expense? Who [b]plants a vineyard, and does not eat the fruit of it? Or who tends a flock and does not use the milk of the flock?

8 I am not speaking these things [a]according to human judgment, am I? Or does not the Law also say these things?

9 For it is written in the Law of Moses, "[a]YOU SHALL NOT MUZZLE THE OX WHILE HE IS THRESHING." God is not concerned about [b]oxen, is He?

10 Or is He speaking altogether for our sake? Yes, [a]for our sake it was written, because [b]the plowman ought to plow in hope, and the thresher *to thresh* in hope of sharing *the crops.*

11 [a]If we sowed spiritual things in you, is it too much if we should reap material things from you?

12 If others share the right over you, do we not more? Nevertheless, we [a]did not use this right, but we endure all things, [b]that we may cause no hindrance to the [c]gospel of Christ.

13 [a]Do you not know that those who [b]perform sacred services eat the *food* of the temple, *and* those who attend regularly to the altar have their share with the altar?

14 So also [a]the Lord directed those who proclaim the [b]gospel to [c]get their living from the gospel.

15 But I have [a]used none of these things. And I am not writing these things that it may be done so in my case; for it would be better for me to die than have any man make [b]my boast an empty one.

16 For if I preach the gospel, I have nothing to boast of, for [a]I am under compulsion; for woe is me if I do not preach [b]the gospel.

17 For if I do this voluntarily, I have a [a]reward; but if against my will, I have a [b]stewardship entrusted to me.

18 What then is my [a]reward? That, when I preach the gospel, I may offer the gospel [b]without charge, so as

---

Chapter 8
1 [a]Acts 15:20 [b]Rom. 15:14 [c]1 Cor. 4:6 [d]Rom. 14:19
2 [a]1 Cor. 3:18 [b]1 Cor. 13:8, 9
3 [a]Ps. 1:6; Jer. 1:5; Amos 3:2
4 [a]Acts 15:20 [b]Acts 14:15 [c]Deut. 4:35
5 [a]2 Thess. 2:4
6 [a]Deut. 4:35 [b]Mal. 2:10; Eph. 4:6 [c]Rom. 11:36 [d]John 13:13 [e]John 1:3
7 [a]1 Cor. 8:4ff. [b]Rom. 14:14, 22f.
8 [a]Rom. 14:17
9 [a]Rom. 14:13, 21 [b]Rom. 14:1
10 [a]1 Cor. 8:4ff. [b]Acts 15:20
11 [a]1 Cor. 8:4ff. [b]Rom. 14:15, 20
12 [a]Matt. 18:6 [b]Matt. 25:45
13 [a]Rom. 14:21; 2 Cor. 6:3; 11:29

Chapter 9
1 [a]1 Cor. 9:19; 10:29 [b]Acts 14:14; 2 Tim. 1:11 [c]Acts 9:3, 17; 18:9 [d]1 Cor. 3:6; 4:15
2 [a]John 3:33 [b]Acts 1:25
4 [a]1 Cor. 9:14
5 [a]1 Cor. 7:7f. [b]Matt. 12:46 [c]Matt. 8:14
6 [a]Acts 4:36
7 [a]2 Cor. 10:4 [b]Deut. 20:6; Prov. 27:18; 1 Cor. 3:6, 8
8 [a]Rom. 3:5
9 [a]Deut. 25:4; 1 Tim. 5:18 [b]Deut. 22:1-4
10 [a]Rom. 4:23f. [b]2 Tim. 2:6
11 [a]Rom. 15:27; 1 Cor. 9:14
12 [a]Acts 18:3; 20:33; 1 Cor. 9:15, 18 [b]2 Cor. 6:3; 11:12 [c]1 Cor. 4:15
13 [a]Rom. 6:16 [b]Lev. 6:16, 26
14 [a]Matt. 10:10; Luke 10:7; 1 Tim. 5:18 [b]1 Cor. 4:15; 2 Cor. 2:12 [c]Luke 10:8; 1 Cor. 9:4
15 [a]Acts 18:3; 20:33; 1 Cor. 9:12, 18 [b]2 Cor. 11:10
16 [a]Acts 9:15; Rom. 1:14 [b]1 Cor. 4:15; 9:12, 14, 18
17 [a]John 4:36 [Gr.]; 1 Cor. 3:8; 9:18 [b]1 Cor. 4:1
18 [a]John 4:36 [Gr.]; 1 Cor. 3:8; 9:17 [b]Acts 18:3

[c]not to make full use of my right in
the gospel.
19 For though I am [a]free from all
men, I have made myself [b]a slave to
all, that I might [c]win the more.
20 And [a]to the Jews I became as a
Jew, that I might win Jews; to those
who are under the Law, as under the
Law, though [b]not being myself under the Law, that I might win those
who are under the Law;
21 to those who are [a]without law,
[b]as without law, though not being
without the law of God but [c]under
the law of Christ, that I might win
those who are without law.
22 To the [a]weak I became weak,
that I might win the weak; I have
become [b]all things to all men, [c]that
I may by all means save some.
23 And I do all things for the sake
of the gospel, that I may become a
fellow-partaker of it.
24 [a]Do you not know that those
who run in a race all run, but *only*
one receives [b]the prize? [c]Run in
such a way that you may win.
25 And everyone who [a]competes
in the games exercises self-control
in all things. They then *do it* to receive a perishable [b]wreath, but we
an imperishable.
26 Therefore I [a]run in such a way,
as not without aim; I box in such a
way, as not [b]beating the air;
27 but I buffet [a]my body and make
it my slave, lest possibly, after I
have preached to others, I myself
should be disqualified.

Chapter 10

Avoid Israel's Mistakes

For [a]I do not want you to be unaware, brethren, that our fathers
were all [b]under the cloud, and all
[c]passed through the sea;
2 and all [1]were [a]baptized into
Moses in the cloud and in the sea;
3 and all [a]ate the same spiritual
food;
4 and all [a]drank the same spiritual drink, for they were drinking
from a spiritual rock which followed
them; and the rock was [1]Christ.
5 Nevertheless, with most of
them God was not well-pleased; for
[a]they were laid low in the wilderness.
6 Now these things happened as
[a]examples for us, that we should not
crave evil things, as [b]they also
craved.
7 And do not be [a]idolaters, as
some of them were; as it is written,

18 [c]1 Cor. 7:31; 9:12
19 [a]1 Cor. 9:1 [b]2 Cor. 4:5; Gal. 5:13 [c]Matt. 18:15
20 [a]Acts 16:3; 21:23 [b]Gal. 2:19
21 [a]Rom. 2:12, 14 [b]Gal. 2:3; 3:2 [c]1 Cor. 7:22
22 [a]Rom. 14:1 [b]1 Cor. 10:33 [c]Rom. 11:14
24 [a]1 Cor. 9:13 [b]Phil. 3:14; Col. 2:18 [c]Gal. 2:2; 2 Tim. 4:7
25 [a]Eph. 6:12 [b]2 Tim. 4:8; James 1:12; 1 Pet. 5:4; Rev. 2:10
26 [a]Gal. 2:2; 2 Tim. 4:7; Heb. 12:1 [b]1 Cor. 14:9
27 [a]Rom. 8:13
1 [a]Rom. 1:13 [b]Ex. 13:21; Ps. 105:39 [c]Ex. 14:22
2 [1]Some ancient mss. read, *received baptism* [a]Rom. 6:3; 1 Cor. 1:13; Gal. 3:27
3 [a]Ex. 16:4, 35; Deut. 8:3; Neh. 9:15, 20; Ps. 78:24f.; John 6:31
4 [1]I.e., the Messiah [a]Ex. 17:6; Num. 20:11; Ps. 78:15
5 [a]Num. 14:29ff., 37; 26:65; Heb. 3:17
6 [a]1 Cor. 10:11 [b]Num. 11:4, 34
7 [a]Ex. 32:4 [b]Ex. 32:6 [c]Ex. 32:19
8 [a]Num. 25:1ff. [b]Num. 25:9
9 [a]Num. 21:5f.
10 [a]Num. 16:41; 17:5, 10 [b]Num. 16:49 [c]Ex. 12:23; 1 Chr. 21:15
11 [a]1 Cor. 10:6 [b]Rom. 4:23 [c]Rom. 13:11
12 [a]Rom. 11:20
13 [a]1 Cor. 1:9 [b]2 Pet. 2:9
14 [a]Heb. 6:9 [b]1 Cor. 10:7, 19f.
16 [a]Matt. 26:27f. [b]Matt. 26:26
17 [a]Rom. 12:5
18 [a]Rom. 1:3 [b]Lev. 7:6, 14f.
19 [a]1 Cor. 8:4
20 [a]Deut. 32:17
21 [a]2 Cor. 6:16 [b]Is. 65:11
22 [a]Deut. 32:21 [b]Eccl. 6:10
23 [a]1 Cor. 6:12 [b]Rom. 14:19
24 [a]Rom. 15:2
25 [a]Acts 10:15
26 [a]Ps. 24:1; 50:12; 1 Tim. 4:4

"[b]The people sat down to eat and
drink, and stood up to [c]play."
8 Nor let us act immorally, as
[a]some of them did, and [b]twenty-
three thousand fell in one day.
9 Nor let us try the Lord, as
[a]some of them did, and were destroyed by the serpents.
10 Nor grumble, [a]as some of them
did, and [b]were destroyed by the [c]de-
stroyer.
11 Now these things happened to
them as an [a]example, and [b]they
were written for our instruction,
upon whom [c]the ends of the ages
have come.
12 Therefore let him who [a]thinks
he stands take heed lest he fall.
13 No temptation has overtaken
you but such as is common to man;
and [a]God is faithful, who will not
allow you to be [b]tempted beyond
what you are able, but with the
temptation will provide the way of
escape also, that you may be able to
endure it.
14 Therefore, my [a]beloved, flee
from [b]idolatry.
15 I speak as to wise men; you
judge what I say.
16 Is not the [a]cup of blessing
which we bless a sharing in the
blood of Christ? Is not the [b]bread
which we break a sharing in the
body of Christ?
17 Since there is one bread, we
[a]who are many are one body; for we
all partake of the one bread.
18 Look at the nation [a]Israel; are
not those who [b]eat the sacrifices
sharers in the altar?
19 What do I mean then? That a
thing sacrificed to idols is anything,
or [a]that an idol is anything?
20 No, but *I say* that the things
which the Gentiles sacrifice, they
[a]sacrifice to demons, and not to
God; and I do not want you to become sharers in demons.
21 [a]You cannot drink the cup of
the Lord and the cup of demons; you
cannot partake of the table of the
Lord and the table of demons.
22 Or do we [a]provoke the Lord to
jealousy? We are not [b]stronger than
He, are we?
23 [a]All things are lawful, but not
all things are profitable. All things
are lawful, but not all things [b]edify.
24 Let no one [a]seek his own *good,*
but that of his neighbor.
25 [a]Eat anything that is sold in the
meat market, without asking questions for conscience' sake;
26 [a]For the earth is the Lord's,
and all it contains.

27 If [a]one of the unbelievers invites you, and you wish to go, [b]eat anything that is set before you, without asking questions for conscience' sake.

28 But [a]if anyone should say to you, "This is meat sacrificed to idols," do not eat *it,* for the sake of the one who informed *you,* and for conscience' sake;

29 I mean not your own conscience, but the other *man's;* for [a]why is my freedom judged by another's conscience?

30 If I partake with thankfulness, [a]why am I slandered concerning that for which I [b]give thanks?

31 Whether, then, you eat or drink or [a]whatever you do, do all to the glory of God.

32 [a]Give no offense either to Jews or to Greeks or to [b]the church of God;

33 just as I also [a]please all men in all things, [b]not seeking my own profit, but the *profit* of the many, [c]that they may be saved.

Chapter 11

Christian Order

[a]Be imitators of me, just as I also am of Christ.

2 Now [a]I praise you because you [b]remember me in everything, and [c]hold firmly to the traditions, just as I delivered them to you.

3 But I want you to understand that [1]Christ is the [a]head of every man, and [b]the man is the head of a woman, and God is the [c]head of [1]Christ.

4 Every man who has *something* on his head while praying or [a]prophesying, disgraces his head.

5 But every [a]woman who has her head uncovered while praying or prophesying, disgraces her head; for she is one and the same with her whose head is [b]shaved.

6 For if a woman does not cover her head, let her also have her hair cut off; but if it is disgraceful for a woman to have her hair cut off or her head shaved, let her cover her head.

7 For a man ought not to have his head covered, since he is the [a]image and glory of God; but the woman is the glory of man.

8 For [a]man does not originate from woman, but woman from man;

9 for indeed man was not created for the woman's sake, but [a]woman for the man's sake.

27 [a]1 Cor. 5:10 [b]Luke 10:8
28 [a]1 Cor. 8:7, 10-12
29 [a]Rom. 14:16; 1 Cor. 9:19
30 [a]1 Cor. 9:1 [b]Rom. 14:6
31 [a]Col. 3:17; 1 Pet. 4:11
32 [a]Acts 24:16; 1 Cor. 8:13 [b]Acts 20:28; 1 Cor. 1:2; 7:17; 11:22; 15:9; 2 Cor. 1:1; Gal. 1:13; Phil. 3:6; 1 Tim. 3:5, 15
33 [a]Rom. 15:2; 1 Cor. 9:22; Gal. 1:10 [b]Rom. 15:2; 1 Cor.13:5; 2 Cor. 12:14; Phil. 2:21 [c]Rom. 11:14; 1 Thess. 2:16
1 [a]1 Cor. 4:16
2 [a]1 Cor. 11:17, 22 [b]1 Cor. 4:17; 15:2; 1 Thess. 1:6; 3:6 [c]2 Thess. 2:15; 3:6
3 [1]I.e., the Messiah [a]Eph. 1:22; 4:15; 5:23; Col. 1:18; 2:19 [b]Gen. 3:16; Eph. 5:23 [c]1 Cor. 3:23
4 [a]Acts 13:1; 1 Thess. 5:20
5 [a]Luke 2:36; Acts 21:9; 1 Cor. 14:34 [b]Deut. 21:12
7 [a]Gen. 1:26; 5:1; 9:6; James 3:9
8 [a]Gen. 2:21-23; 1 Tim. 2:13
9 [a]Gen. 2:18
12 [a]2 Cor. 5:18 [b]Rom. 11:36
13 [a]Luke 12:57
16 [a]1 Cor. 4:5; 9:1-3, 6 [b]1 Cor. 7:17
17 [a]1 Cor. 11:2, 22
18 [a]1 Cor. 1:10; 3:3
19 [1]Or, *manifest* [a]Matt. 18:7; Luke 17:1; 1 Tim. 4:1; 2 Pet. 2:1 [b]Deut. 13:3; 1 John 2:19
21 [a]Jude 12
22 [a]1 Cor. 10:32 [b]James 2:6 [c]1 Cor. 11:2, 17
23 [a]1 Cor. 15:3; Gal. 1:12; Col. 3:24 [b]1 Cor. 11:23-25: *Matt. 26:26-28; Mark 14:22-24; Luke 22:17-20;* 1 Cor. 10:16
24 [1]Some ancient mss. read, *is broken*
25 [a]1 Cor. 10:16 [b]Luke 22:20; 2 Cor. 3:6
26 [a]John 21:22; 1 Cor. 4:5

10 Therefore the woman ought to have *a symbol of* authority on her head, because of the angels.

11 However, in the Lord, neither is woman independent of man, nor is man independent of woman.

12 For as the woman originates from the man, so also the man has his birth through the woman; and [a]all things originate [b]from God.

13 [a]Judge for yourselves: is it proper for a woman to pray to God *with head* uncovered?

14 Does not even nature itself teach you that if a man has long hair, it is a dishonor to him,

15 but if a woman has long hair, it is a glory to her? For her hair is given to her for a covering.

16 But if one is inclined to be contentious, [a]we have no other practice, nor have [b]the churches of God.

17 But in giving this instruction, [a]I do not praise you, because you come together not for the better but for the worse.

18 For, in the first place, when you come together as a church, I hear that [a]divisions exist among you; and in part, I believe it.

19 For there [a]must also be factions among you, [b]in order that those who are approved may have become [1]evident among you.

20 Therefore when you meet together, it is not to eat the Lord's Supper,

21 for in your eating each one takes his own supper first; and one is hungry and [a]another is drunk.

22 What! Do you not have houses in which to eat and drink? Or do you despise the [a]church of God, and [b]shame those who have nothing? What shall I say to you? Shall [c]I praise you? In this I will not praise you.

The Lord's Supper

23 For [a]I received from the Lord that which I also delivered to you, that [b]the Lord Jesus in the night in which He was betrayed took bread;

24 and when He had given thanks, He broke it, and said, "This is My body, which [1]is for you; do this in remembrance of Me."

25 In the same way *He took* [a]the cup also, after supper, saying, "This cup is the [b]new covenant in My blood; do this, as often as you drink *it,* in remembrance of Me."

26 For as often as you eat this bread and drink the cup, you proclaim the Lord's death [a]until He comes.

27 Therefore whoever eats the bread or drinks the cup of the Lord in an unworthy manner, shall be [a]guilty of the body and the blood of the Lord.

28 But let a man [a]examine himself, and so let him eat of the bread and drink of the cup.

29 For he who eats and drinks, eats and drinks judgment to himself, if he does not judge the body rightly.

30 For this reason many among you are weak and sick, and a number [a]asleep.

31 But if we judged ourselves rightly, we should not be judged.

32 But when we are judged, we are [a]disciplined by the Lord in order that we may not be condemned along with [b]the world.

33 So then, my brethren, when you come together to eat, wait for one another.

34 If anyone is [a]hungry, let him eat [b]at home, so that you may not come together for judgment. And the remaining matters I shall [c]arrange [d]when I come.

Chapter 12

The Use of Spiritual Gifts

NOW concerning [a]spiritual *gifts,* brethren, [b]I do not want you to be unaware.

2 [a]You know that when you were pagans, *you were* [b]led astray to the [c]dumb idols, however you were led.

3 Therefore I make known to you, that no one speaking [a]by the Spirit of God says, "Jesus is [b]accursed"; and no one can say, "Jesus is [c]Lord," except [a]by the Holy Spirit.

4 Now there are [a]varieties of gifts, but the same Spirit.

5 And there are varieties of ministries, and the same Lord.

6 And there are varieties of effects, but the same [a]God who works all things in all *persons.*

7 But to each one is given the manifestation of the Spirit [a]for the common good.

8 For to one is given the word of [a]wisdom through the Spirit, and to another the word of [b]knowledge according to the same Spirit;

9 to another [a]faith by the same Spirit, and to another [b]gifts of healing by the one Spirit,

10 and to another the [1]effecting of [2a]miracles, and to another [b]prophecy, and to another the [3c]distinguishing of spirits, to another *various* [d]kinds of tongues, and to another the [e]interpretation of tongues.

11 But one and the same Spirit works all these things, [a]distributing to each one individually just as He wills.

12 For even [a]as the body is one and *yet* has many members, and all the members of the body, though they are many, are one body, [b]so also is Christ.

13 For [a]by one Spirit we were all baptized into one body, whether [b]Jews or Greeks, whether slaves or free, and we were all made to [c]drink of one Spirit.

14 For [a]the body is not one member, but many.

15 If the foot should say, "Because I am not a hand, I am not *a part* of the body," it is not for this reason any the less *a part* of the body.

16 And if the ear should say, "Because I am not an eye, I am not *a part* of the body," it is not for this reason any the less *a part* of the body.

17 If the whole body were an eye, where would the hearing be? If the whole were hearing, where would the sense of smell be?

18 But now God has [a]placed the members, each one of them, in the body, [b]just as He desired.

19 And if they were all one member, where would the body be?

20 But now [a]there are many members, but one body.

21 And the eye cannot say to the hand, "I have no need of you"; or again the head to the feet, "I have no need of you."

22 On the contrary, [1]it is much truer that the members of the body which seem to be weaker are necessary;

23 and those *members* of the body, which we [1]deem less honorable, [2]on these we bestow more abundant honor, and our unseemly *members come to* have more abundant seemliness,

24 whereas our seemly *members* have no need *of it.* But God has *so* composed the body, giving more abundant honor to that *member* which lacked,

25 that there should be no [1]division in the body, but *that* the members should have the same care for one another.

26 And if one member suffers, all the members suffer with it; if *one* member is [1]honored, all the members rejoice with it.

27 [a]Heb. 10:29
28 [a]Matt. 26:22; 2 Cor. 13:5; Gal. 6:4
30 [a]Acts 7:60
32 [a]2 Sam. 7:14; Ps. 94:12; Heb. 12:7-10; Rev. 3:19 [b]1 Cor. 1:20
34 [a]1 Cor. 11:21 [b]1 Cor. 11:22 [c]1 Cor. 4:17; 7:17; 16:1 [d]1 Cor. 4:19
1 [a]1 Cor. 12:4; 14:1 [b]Rom. 1:13
2 [a]1 Cor. 6:11; Eph. 2:11f.; 1 Pet. 4:3 [b]1 Thess. 1:9 [c]Ps. 115:5; Is. 46:7; Jer. 10:5; Hab. 2:18f.
3 [a]Matt. 22:43; 1 John 4:2f.; Rev. 1:10 [b]Rom. 9:3 [c]John 13:13; Rom. 10:9
4 [a]Rom. 12:6f.; 1 Cor. 12:11; Eph. 4:4ff., 11; Heb. 2:4
6 [a]1 Cor. 15:28; Eph. 1:23; 4:6
7 [a]1 Cor. 12:12-30; 14:26; Eph. 4:12
8 [a]1 Cor. 2:6; 2 Cor. 1:12 [b]Rom. 15:14; 1 Cor. 2:11, 16; 2 Cor. 2:14; 4:6; 8:7; 11:6
9 [a]1 Cor. 13:2; 2 Cor. 4:13 [b]1 Cor. 12:28, 30
10 [1]Lit., *effects* [2]Or, *works of power* [3]Lit., *distinguishings* [a]1 Cor. 12:28f.; Gal. 3:5 [b]1 Cor. 11:4; 13:2, 8 [c]1 Cor. 14:29; 1 John 4:1 [d]Mark 16:17; 1 Cor. 12:28, 30; 13:1; 14:2ff. [e]1 Cor. 12:30; 14:26
11 [a]1 Cor. 12:4 and ref.
12 [a]Rom. 12:4; 1 Cor. 10:17 [b]1 Cor. 12:27
13 [a]Eph. 2:18 [b]Rom. 3:22; Gal. 3:28; Eph. 2:13-18; Col. 3:11 [c]John 7:37-39
14 [a]1 Cor. 12:20
18 [a]1 Cor. 12:28 [b]Rom. 12:6; 1 Cor. 12:11
20 [a]1 Cor. 12:12, 14
22 [1]Lit., *to a much greater degree the members*
23 [1]Or, *think to be* [2]Or, *these we clothe with*
25 [1]Lit., *schism*
26 [1]Lit., *glorified*

27 Now you are [a]Christ's body, and [b]individually members of it.

28 And God has [a]appointed in [b]the church, first [c]apostles, second [d]prophets, third [e]teachers, then [f]miracles, then [g]gifts of healings, helps, [h]administrations, *various* [i]kinds of tongues.

29 All are not apostles, are they? All are not prophets, are they? All are not teachers, are they? All are not *workers of* miracles, are they?

30 All do not have gifts of healings, do they? All do not speak with tongues, do they? All do not [a]interpret, do they?

31 But [a]earnestly desire the greater gifts.

And I show you a still more excellent way.

Chapter 13

The Excellence of Love

If I speak with the [a]tongues of men and of [b]angels, but do not have love, I have become a noisy gong or a [c]clanging cymbal.

2 And if I have *the gift of* [a]prophecy, and know all [b]mysteries and all [c]knowledge; and if I have [d]all faith, so as to [e]remove mountains, but do not have love, I am nothing.

3 And if I [a]give all my possessions to feed *the poor,* and if I [b]deliver my body to be burned, but do not have love, it profits me nothing.

4 Love [a]is patient, love is kind, *and* [b]is not jealous; love does not brag *and* is not [c]arrogant,

5 does not act unbecomingly; it [a]does not seek its own, is not provoked, [b]does not take into account a wrong *suffered,*

6 [a]does not rejoice in unrighteousness, but [b]rejoices with the truth;

7 [a]bears all things, believes all things, hopes all things, endures all things.

8 Love never fails; but if *there are gifts of* [a]prophecy, they will be done away; if *there are* [b]tongues, they will cease; if *there is* knowledge, it will be done away.

9 For we [a]know in part, and we prophesy in part;

10 but when the perfect comes, the partial will be done away.

11 When I was a child, I used to speak as a child, think as a child, reason as a child; when I became a man, I did away with childish things.

12 For now we [a]see in a mirror dimly, but then [b]face to face; now I know in part, but then I shall know fully just as I also [c]have been fully known.

13 But now abide faith, hope, love, these three; but the greatest of these is [a]love.

Chapter 14

Prophecy a Superior Gift

[a]Pursue love, yet [b]desire earnestly [c]spiritual *gifts,* but especially that you may [d]prophesy.

2 For one who [a]speaks in a tongue does not speak to men, but to God; for no one understands, but in *his* spirit he speaks [b]mysteries.

3 But one who prophesies speaks to men for [a]edification and [b]exhortation and consolation.

4 One who [a]speaks in a tongue [b]edifies himself; but one who [c]prophesies [b]edifies the church.

5 Now I wish that you all [a]spoke in tongues, but [b]*even* more that you would prophesy; and greater is one who prophesies than one who [a]speaks in tongues, unless he interprets, so that the church may receive [c]edifying.

6 But now, brethren, if I come to you speaking in tongues, what shall I profit you, unless I speak to you either by way of [a]revelation or of [b]knowledge or of [c]prophecy or of [d]teaching?

7 Yet *even* lifeless things, either flute or harp, in producing a sound, if they do not produce a distinction in the tones, how will it be known what is played on the flute or on the harp?

8 For if [a]the bugle produces an indistinct sound, who will prepare himself for battle?

9 So also you, unless you utter by the tongue speech that is clear, how will it be known what is spoken? For you will be [a]speaking into the air.

10 There are, perhaps, a great many kinds of languages in the world, and no *kind* is without meaning.

11 If then I do not know the meaning of the language, I shall be to the one who speaks a [a]barbarian, and the one who speaks will be a barbarian to me.

12 So also you, since you are zealous of spiritual *gifts,* seek to abound for the [a]edification of the church.

13 Therefore let one who speaks in a tongue pray that he may interpret.

14 For if I pray in a tongue, my

---

27 [a]1 Cor. 1:2; Col. 1:18, 24; 2:19 [b]Rom. 12:5
28 [a]1 Cor. 12:18 [b]1 Cor. 10:32 [c]Eph. 4:11 [d]Acts 13:1; Eph. 2:20; 3:5 [e]Acts 13:1 [f]1 Cor. 12:10, 29 [g]1 Cor. 12:9, 30 [h]Rom. 12:8 [i]1 Cor. 12:10
30 [a]1 Cor. 12:10
31 [a]1 Cor. 14:1
1 [a]1 Cor. 12:10 [b]2 Cor. 12:4; Rev. 14:2 [c]Ps. 150:5
2 [a]Matt. 7:22; Acts 13:1; 1 Cor. 11:4; 13:8; 14:1, 39 [b]1 Cor. 14:2; 15:51 [c]Rom. 15:14 [d]1 Cor. 12:9 [e]Matt. 17:20
3 [a]Matt. 6:2 [b]Dan. 3:28
4 [a]Prov. 10:12; 17:9; 1 Thess. 5:14; 1 Pet. 4:8 [b]Acts 7:9 [c]1 Cor. 4:6
5 [a]1 Cor. 10:24 [b]2 Cor. 5:19
6 [a]2 Thess. 2:12 [b]2 John 4; 3 John 3f.
7 [a]1 Cor. 9:12
8 [a]1 Cor. 13:2 [b]1 Cor. 13:1
9 [a]1 Cor. 8:2
12 [a]2 Cor. 5:7; Phil. 3:12; James 1:23 [b]Gen. 32:30; Num. 12:8; 1 John 3:2 [c]1 Cor. 8:3
13 [a]Gal. 5:6
1 [a]1 Cor. 16:14 [b]1 Cor. 12:31; 14:39 [c]1 Cor. 12:1 [d]1 Cor. 13:2
2 [a]Mark 16:17; 1 Cor. 12:10, 28 [b]1 Cor. 13:2
3 [a]Rom. 14:19 [b]Acts 4:36
4 [a]Mark 16:17; 1 Cor. 12:10, 28, [b]Rom. 14:19; 1 Cor. 14:5, 12, 17, 26 [c]1 Cor. 13:2
5 [a]Mark 16:17; 1 Cor. 12:10, 28 [b]Num. 11:29 [c]Rom. 14:19; 1 Cor. 14:4, 12
6 [a]1 Cor. 14:26; Eph. 1:17 [b]1 Cor. 12:8 [c]1 Cor. 13:2 [d]Acts 2:42; Rom. 6:17; 1 Cor. 14:26
8 [a]Num. 10:9; Jer. 4:19; Ezek. 33:3-6
9 [a]1 Cor. 9:26
11 [a]Acts 28:2
12 [a]Rom. 14:19; 1 Cor. 14:4, 5, 17

spirit prays, but my mind is unfruitful.
15 [a]What is *the outcome* then? I
shall pray with the spirit and I shall
pray with the mind also; I shall [b]sing
with the spirit and I shall sing with
the mind also.
16 Otherwise if you bless in the
spirit *only,* how will the one who
fills the place of the ungifted say
[a]the "Amen" at your [b]giving of
thanks, since he does not know
what you are saying?
17 For you are giving thanks well
enough, but the other man is not
[a]edified.
18 I thank God, I speak in tongues
more than you all;
19 however, in the church I desire
to speak five words with my mind,
that I may instruct others also,
rather than ten thousand words in a
tongue.

Instruction for the Church

20 [a]Brethren, [b]do not be children
in your thinking; yet in evil [c]be
babes, but in your thinking be mature.
21 In [a]the Law it is written, "[b]BY
MEN OF STRANGE TONGUES AND BY
THE LIPS OF STRANGERS I WILL SPEAK
TO THIS PEOPLE, AND EVEN SO THEY
WILL NOT LISTEN TO ME," says the
Lord.
22 So then tongues are for a sign,
not to those who believe, but to unbelievers; but [a]prophecy *is for a
sign,* not to unbelievers, but to those
who believe.
23 If therefore the whole church
should assemble together and all
speak in tongues, and ungifted men
or unbelievers enter, will they not
say that [a]you are mad?
24 But if all [a]prophesy, and an unbeliever or an ungifted man enters,
he is [b]convicted by all, he is called to
account by all;
25 [a]the secrets of his heart are disclosed; and so he will [b]fall on his
face and worship God, [c]declaring
that God is certainly among you.
26 [a]What is *the outcome* then,
[b]brethren? When you assemble,
[c]each one has a [d]psalm, has a
[e]teaching, has a [e]revelation, has a
[f]tongue, has an [g]interpretation. Let
[h]all things be done for edification.
27 If any one speaks in a [a]tongue,
it should be by two or at the most
three, and *each* in turn, and let one
[b]interpret;
28 but if there is no interpreter, let
him keep silent in the church; and
let him speak to himself and to God.

15 [a]Acts 21:22; 1 Cor. 14:26 [b]Eph. 5:19; Col. 3:16
16 [a]Deut. 27:15-26; 1 Chr. 16:36; Neh. 5:13; 8:6; Ps. 106:48; Jer. 11:5 [b]Matt. 15:36
17 [a]Rom. 14:19; 1 Cor. 14:4, 5, 12
20 [a]Rom. 1:13 [b]Eph. 4:14; Heb. 5:12f. [c]Ps. 131:2; Matt. 18:3; Rom. 16:19; 1 Pet. 2:2
21 [a]John 10:34; 1 Cor. 14:34 [b]Is. 28:11f.
22 [a]1 Cor. 14:1
23 [a]Acts 2:13
24 [a]1 Cor. 14:1 [b]John 16:8
25 [a]John 4:19 [b]Luke 17:16 [c]Is. 45:14; Dan. 2:47; Zech. 8:23
26 [a]1 Cor. 14:15 [b]Rom. 1:13 [c]1 Cor. 12:8-10 [d]Eph. 5:19 [e]1 Cor. 14:6 [f]1 Cor. 14:2 [g]1 Cor. 12:10 [h]Rom. 14:19
27 [a]1 Cor. 14:2 [b]1 Cor. 12:10
29 [a]1 Cor. 13:2; 14:32, 37 [b]1 Cor. 12:10
33 [a]1 Cor. 14:40 [b]1 Cor. 4:17; 7:17 [c]Acts 9:13
34 [a]1 Cor. 11:5, 13 [b]1 Tim. 2:11f.; 1 Pet. 3:1 [c]1 Cor. 14:21
37 [a]2 Cor. 10:7 [b]1 Cor. 2:15 [c]1 Cor. 7:40
38 [1]Or, *is ignorant, let him be ignorant*
39 [a]1 Cor. 12:31 [b]1 Cor. 13:2; 14:1
40 [a]1 Cor. 14:33
1 [a]Rom. 2:16; Gal. 1:11 [b]Rom. 2:16; 1 Cor. 3:6; 4:15 [c]Rom. 5:2; 11:20; 2 Cor. 1:24
2 [a]Rom. 11:22 [b]Gal. 3:4
3 [a]1 Cor. 11:23 [b]John 1:29; Gal. 1:4; Heb. 5:1, 3; 1 Pet. 2:24 [c]Is. 53:5-12; Matt. 26:24; Luke 24:25-27; Acts 8:32f.
4 [a]Matt. 16:21; John 2:21f.; Acts 2:24 [b]Ps. 16:8ff.; Acts 2:31; 26:22f.
5 [a]Luke 24:34 [b]1 Cor. 1:12 [c]Mark 16:14
6 [a]Acts 7:60; 1 Cor. 15:18, 20
7 [a]Acts 12:17 [b]Luke 24:33, 36f.; Acts 1:3f.

29 And let two or three [a]prophets
speak, and let the others [b]pass judgment.
30 But if a revelation is made to
another who is seated, let the first
keep silent.
31 For you can all prophesy one by
one, so that all may learn and all
may be exhorted;
32 and the spirits of prophets are
subject to prophets;
33 for God is not *a God* of [a]confu-
sion but of peace, as in [b]all the
churches of the [c]saints.
34 Let the women [a]keep silent in
the churches; for they are not permitted to speak, but [b]let them subject themselves, just as [c]the Law
also says.
35 And if they desire to learn anything, let them ask their own husbands at home; for it is improper for
a woman to speak in church.
36 Was it from you that the word
of God *first* went forth? Or has it
come to you only?
37 [a]If any one thinks he is a
prophet or [b]spiritual, let him recognize that the things which I write to
you [c]are the Lord's commandment.
38 But if any one [1]does not recognize *this,* he is not recognized.
39 Therefore, my brethren, [a]desire
earnestly to [b]prophesy, and do not
forbid to speak in tongues.
40 But [a]let all things be done properly and in an orderly manner.

CHAPTER 15

The Fact of Christ's Resurrection

NOW [a]I make known to you,
brethren, the [b]gospel which I
preached to you, which also you received, [c]in which also you stand,
2 by which also you are saved, [a]if
you hold fast the word which I
preached to you, [b]unless you believed in vain.
3 For [a]I delivered to you as of
first importance what I also received, that Christ died [b]for our sins
[c]according to the Scriptures,
4 and that He was buried, and
that He was [a]raised on the third day
[b]according to the Scriptures,
5 and that [a]He appeared to [b]Ce-
phas, then [c]to the twelve.
6 After that He appeared to more
than five hundred brethren at one
time, most of whom remain until
now, but some [a]have fallen asleep;
7 then He appeared to [a]James,
then to [b]all the apostles;
8 and last of all, as it were to one

untimely born, [a]He appeared to me
also.
9 For I am [a]the least of the apostles, who am not fit to be called an
apostle, because I [b]persecuted the
church of God.
10 But by [a]the grace of God I am
what I am, and His grace toward me
did not prove vain; but I [b]labored
even more than all of them, yet [c]not
I, but the grace of God with me.
11 Whether then *it was* I or they,
so we preach and so you believed.
12 Now if Christ is preached, that
He has been raised from the dead,
how do some among you say that
there [a]is no resurrection of the
dead?
13 But if there is no resurrection of
the dead, not even Christ has been
raised;
14 and [a]if Christ has not been
raised, then our preaching is vain,
your faith also is vain.
15 Moreover we are even found *to
be* false witnesses of God, because
we witnessed [1]against God that He
[a]raised [2]Christ, whom He did not
raise, if in fact the dead are not
raised.
16 For if the dead are not raised,
not even Christ has been raised;
17 and if Christ has not been
raised, your faith is worthless; [a]you
are still in your sins.
18 Then those also who [a]have
fallen asleep in Christ have perished.
19 If we have only hoped in Christ
in this life, we are [a]of all men most
to be pitied.

The Order of Resurrection

20 But now Christ [a]has been
raised from the dead, the [b]first fruits
of those who [c]are asleep.
21 For since [a]by a man *came*
death, by a man also *came* the resurrection of the dead.
22 For [a]as in Adam all die, so also
in [1]Christ all shall be made alive.
23 But each in his own order:
Christ [a]the first fruits, after that
[b]those who are Christ's at [c]His coming,
24 then *comes* the end, when He
delivers up [a]the kingdom to the
[b]God and Father, when He has abolished [c]all rule and all authority and
power.
25 For He must reign [a]until He has
put all His enemies under His feet.
26 The last enemy that will be
[a]abolished is death.
27 For [a]HE HAS PUT ALL THINGS IN
SUBJECTION UNDER HIS FEET. But
when He says, "[b]All things are put

8 [a]Acts 9:3-8; 22:6-11; 26:12-18; 1 Cor. 9:1
9 [a]2 Cor. 12:11; Eph. 3:8; 1 Tim. 1:15 [b]Acts 8:3
10 [a]Rom. 12:3 [b]2 Cor. 11:23; Col. 1:29; 1 Tim. 4:10 [c]1 Cor. 3:6; 2 Cor. 3:5; Phil. 2:13
12 [a]Acts 17:32; 23:8; 2 Tim. 2:18
14 [a]1 Thess. 4:14
15 [1]Or, *concerning* [2]I.e., the Messiah [a]Acts 2:24
17 [a]Rom. 4:25
18 [a]1 Cor. 15:6; 1 Thess. 4:16; Rev. 14:13
19 [a]1 Cor. 4:9; 2 Tim. 3:12
20 [a]Acts 2:24; 1 Pet. 1:3 [b]Acts 26:23; 1 Cor. 15:23; Rev. 1:5 [c]1 Cor. 15:6; 1 Thess. 4:16; Rev. 14:13
21 [a]Rom. 5:12
22 [1]I.e., the Messiah [a]Rom. 5:14-18
23 [a]Acts 26:23; 1 Cor. 15:20; Rev. 1:5 [b]1 Cor. 6:14; 15:52; 1 Thess. 4:16 [c]1 Thess. 2:19
24 [a]Dan. 2:44; 7:14, 27; 2 Pet. 1:11 [b]Eph. 5:20 [c]Rom. 8:38
25 [a]Ps. 110:1; Matt. 22:44
26 [a]2 Tim. 1:10; Rev. 20:14; 21:4
27 [a]Ps. 8:6 [b]Matt. 11:27; 28:18; Eph. 1:22; Heb. 2:8
28 [a]Phil. 3:21 [b]1 Cor. 3:23; 12:6
30 [a]2 Cor. 11:26
31 [a]Rom. 8:36
32 [1]Lit., *according to man* [a]2 Cor. 1:8 [b]Acts 18:19; 1 Cor. 16:8f. [c]Is. 22:13; 56:12; Luke 12:19
33 [a]1 Cor. 6:9
34 [a]Rom. 13:11 [b]Matt. 22:29; Acts 26:8 [c]1 Cor. 6:5
35 [a]Rom. 9:19 [b]Ezek. 37:3
36 [a]Luke 11:40 [b]John 12:24
38 [a]Gen. 1:11
42 [a]Dan. 12:3; Matt. 13:43 [b]Rom. 8:21; 1 Cor. 15:50; Gal. 6:8 [c]Rom. 2:7
43 [a]Phil. 3:21; Col. 3:4
44 [a]1 Cor. 2:14 [b]1 Cor. 15:50
45 [a]Gen. 2:7 [b]Rom. 5:14 [c]John 5:21; 6:57f.; Rom. 8:2

in subjection," it is evident that He
is excepted who put all things in
subjection to Him.
28 And when [a]all things are subjected to Him, then the Son Himself
also will be subjected to the One
who subjected all things to Him,
that [b]God may be all in all.
29 Otherwise, what will those do
who are baptized for the dead? If the
dead are not raised at all, why then
are they baptized for them?
30 Why are we also [a]in danger every hour?
31 I protest, brethren, by the
boasting in you, which I have in
Christ Jesus our Lord, [a]I die daily.
32 If [1]from human motives I
[a]fought with wild beasts at [b]Ephe-
sus, what does it profit me? If the
dead are not raised, [c]LET US EAT AND
DRINK, FOR TOMORROW WE DIE.
33 [a]Do not be deceived: "Bad company corrupts good morals."
34 [a]Become sober-minded as you
ought, and stop sinning; for some
have [b]no knowledge of God. [c]I
speak *this* to your shame.
35 But [a]some one will say, "How
are [b]the dead raised? And with what
kind of body do they come?"
36 [a]You fool! That which you [b]sow
does not come to life unless it dies;
37 and that which you sow, you do
not sow the body which is to be, but
a bare grain, perhaps of wheat or of
something else.
38 But God gives it a body just as
He wished, and [a]to each of the seeds
a body of its own.
39 All flesh is not the same flesh,
but there is *one flesh* of men, and
another flesh of beasts, and another
flesh of birds, and another of fish.
40 There are also heavenly bodies
and earthly bodies, but the glory of
the heavenly is one, and the *glory* of
the earthly is another.
41 There is one glory of the sun,
and another glory of the moon, and
another glory of the stars; for star
differs from star in glory.
42 [a]So also is the resurrection of
the dead. It is sown [b]a perishable
body, it is raised [c]an imperishable
body;
43 it is sown in dishonor, it is
raised in [a]glory; it is sown in weakness, it is raised in power;
44 it is sown a [a]natural body, it is
raised a [b]spiritual body. If there is a
natural body, there is also a spiritual
body.
45 So also it is written, "The first
[a]MAN, Adam, BECAME A LIVING
SOUL." The [b]last Adam *became* a
[c]life-giving spirit.

46 However, the spiritual is not first, but the natural; then the spiritual.
47 The first man is [a]from the earth, [b]earthy; the second man is from heaven.
48 As is the earthy, so also are those who are earthy; and as is the heavenly, [a]so also are those who are heavenly.
49 And just as we have [a]borne the image of the earthy, we [b]shall also bear the image of the heavenly.

The Mystery of Resurrection

50 Now I say this, brethren, that [a]flesh and blood cannot [b]inherit the kingdom of God; nor does the perishable inherit [c]the imperishable.
51 Behold, I tell you a [a]mystery; we shall not all sleep, but we shall all be [b]changed,
52 in a moment, in the twinkling of an eye, at the last trumpet; for [a]the trumpet will sound, and [b]the dead will be raised imperishable, and [c]we shall be changed.
53 For this perishable must put on [a]the imperishable, and this [b]mortal must put on immortality.
54 But when this perishable will have put on the imperishable, and this mortal will have put on immortality, then will come about the saying that is written, "[a]DEATH IS SWALLOWED UP IN VICTORY.
55 "[a]O DEATH, WHERE IS YOUR VICTORY? O DEATH, WHERE IS YOUR STING?"
56 The sting of [a]death is sin, and [b]the power of sin is the law;
57 but [a]thanks be to God, who gives us the [b]victory through our Lord Jesus Christ.
58 [a]Therefore, my beloved brethren, be steadfast, immovable, always abounding in [b]the work of the Lord, knowing that your toil is not *in* vain in the Lord.

CHAPTER 16

Instructions and Greetings

NOW concerning [a]the collection for [b]the saints, as [c]I directed the churches of [d]Galatia, so do you also.
2 On [a]the first day of every week let each one of you put aside and save, as he may prosper, that [b]no collections be made when I come.
3 And when I arrive, [a]whomever you may approve, I shall send them with letters to carry your gift to Jerusalem;
4 and if it is fitting for me to go also, they will go with me.

47 [a]John 3:31 [b]Gen. 2:7; 3:19
48 [a]Phil. 3:20f.
49 [a]Gen. 5:3 [b]Rom. 8:29
50 [a]Matt. 16:17; John 3:5f. [b]1 Cor. 6:9 [c]Rom. 2:7
51 [a]1 Cor. 13:2 [b]2 Cor. 5:2, 4
52 [a]Matt. 24:31 [b]John 5:28 [c]1 Thess. 4:15, 17
53 [a]Rom. 2:7 [b]2 Cor. 5:4
54 [a]Is. 25:8
55 [a]Hos. 13:14
56 [a]Rom. 5:12 [b]Rom. 3:20; 4:15
57 [a]Rom. 7:25; 2 Cor. 2:14 [b]Rom. 8:37; Heb. 2:14f.; 1 John 5:4
58 [a]2 Pet. 3:14 [b]1 Cor. 16:10
1 [a]Acts 24:17 [b]Acts 9:13 [c]1 Cor. 4:17 [d]Acts 16:6
2 [a]Acts 20:7 [b]2 Cor. 9:4f.
3 [a]2 Cor. 3:1
5 [a]1 Cor. 4:19 [b]Rom. 15:26 [c]Acts 19:21
6 [a]Acts 15:3
7 [a]2 Cor. 1:15f. [b]Acts 18:21
8 [a]Acts 18:19 [b]Acts 2:1
9 [a]Acts 14:27 [b]Acts 19:9
10 [a]Acts 16:1; 1 Cor. 4:17; 2 Cor. 1:1 [b]1 Cor. 15:58
11 [a]1 Tim. 4:12; Titus 2:15 [b]Acts 15:3; 1 Cor. 16:6 [c]Acts 15:33
12 [a]Acts 18:24 [1 Cor. 1:12; 3:5f.]
13 [a]Matt. 24:42 [b]1 Cor. 15:1; Gal. 5:1; Phil. 1:27; 4:1 [c]1 Sam. 4:9; 2 Sam. 10:12; Is. 46:8 [d]Ps. 31:24
14 [a]1 Cor. 14:1
15 [a]1 Cor. 1:16 [b]Rom. 16:5 [c]Acts 18:12 [d]Rom. 15:31 [e]1 Cor. 16:1
16 [a]1 Thess. 5:12; Heb. 13:17
17 [a]2 Cor. 7:6f. [b]2 Cor. 11:9
18 [a]2 Cor. 7:13 [b]Phil. 2:29
19 [a]Acts 16:6 [b]Acts 18:2 [c]Rom. 16:5
20 [a]Rom. 16:16
21 [a]Rom. 16:22; Gal. 6:11; Col. 4:18
22 [1]Gr., anathema [2]I.e., O [our] Lord come! [a]Rom. 9:3 [b]Phil. 4:5; Rev. 22:20
23 [a]Rom. 16:20

5 But I [a]shall come to you after I go through [b]Macedonia, for I [c]am going through Macedonia;
6 and perhaps I shall stay with you, or even spend the winter, that you may [a]send me on my way wherever I may go.
7 For I do not wish to see you now [a]*just* in passing; for I hope to remain with you for some time, [b]if the Lord permits.
8 But I shall remain in [a]Ephesus until [b]Pentecost;
9 for a [a]wide door for effective *service* has opened to me, and [b]there are many adversaries.
10 Now if [a]Timothy comes, see that he is with you without cause to be afraid; for he is doing [b]the Lord's work, as I also am.
11 [a]Let no one therefore despise him. But [b]send him on his way [c]in peace, so that he may come to me; for I expect him with the brethren.
12 But concerning [a]Apollos our brother, I encouraged him greatly to come to you with the brethren; and it was not at all *his* desire to come now, but he will come when he has opportunity.
13 [a]Be on the alert, [b]stand firm in the faith, [c]act like men, [d]be strong.
14 Let all that you do be done [a]in love.
15 Now I urge you, brethren (you know the [a]household of Stephanas, that they were the [b]first fruits of [c]Achaia, and that they have devoted themselves for [d]ministry to [e]the saints),
16 that [a]you also be in subjection to such men and to everyone who helps in the work and labors.
17 And I rejoice over the [a]coming of Stephanas and Fortunatus and Achaicus; because they have supplied [b]what was lacking on your part.
18 For they [a]have refreshed my spirit and yours. Therefore [b]acknowledge such men.
19 The churches of [a]Asia greet you. [b]Aquila and Prisca greet you heartily in the Lord, with [c]the church that is in their house.
20 All the brethren greet you. [a]Greet one another with a holy kiss.
21 The greeting is in [a]my own hand—Paul.
22 If any one does not love the Lord, let him be [1a]accursed. [2b]Maranatha.
23 [a]The grace of the Lord Jesus be with you.
24 My love be with you all in Christ Jesus. Amen.

THE SECOND EPISTLE OF PAUL TO THE

CORINTHIANS

Introduction

PAUL, [a]an apostle of [b]Christ Jesus
[c]by the will of God, and [d]Timothy
our brother, to [e]the church of God
which is at [f]Corinth with all the
saints who are throughout [g]Achaia:
2 [a]Grace to you and peace from
God our Father and the Lord Jesus
Christ.
3 [a]Blessed *be* the God and Father
of our Lord Jesus Christ, the Father
of mercies and [b]God of all comfort;
4 who [a]comforts us in all our affliction so that we may be able to
comfort those who are in any affliction with the comfort with which we
ourselves are comforted by God.
5 For just [a]as the sufferings of
Christ are ours in abundance, so
also our comfort is abundant
through Christ.
6 But if we are afflicted, it is [a]for
your comfort and salvation; or if we
are comforted, it is for your comfort, which is effective in the patient
enduring of the same sufferings
which we also suffer;
7 and our hope for you is firmly
grounded, knowing that [a]as you are
sharers of our sufferings, so also you
are *sharers* of our comfort.
8 For [a]we do not want you to be
unaware, brethren, of our [b]affliction
which came *to us* in [1c]Asia, that we
were burdened excessively, beyond
our strength, so that we despaired
even of life;
9 indeed, we had the sentence of
death within ourselves in order that
we should not trust in ourselves, but
in God who raises the dead;
10 who [a]delivered us from so great
a *peril of* death, and will deliver *us*,
He [b]on whom we have set our hope.
And He will yet deliver us,
11 you also joining in [a]helping us
through your prayers, that thanks
may be given by [b]many persons on
our behalf for the favor bestowed
upon us through *the prayers of*
many.

Paul's Integrity

12 For our proud confidence is
this, the testimony of [a]our conscience, that in holiness and [b]godly
sincerity, [c]not in fleshly wisdom but
in the grace of God, we have conducted ourselves in the world, and
especially toward you.
13 For we write nothing else to
you than what you read and understand, and I hope you will understand [a]until the end;
14 just as you also partially did understand us, that we are your reason
to be proud as you also are ours, in
[a]the day of our Lord Jesus.
15 And in this confidence I intended at first to [a]come to you, that
you might twice receive a [b]blessing;
16 that is, to [a]pass your way into
[b]Macedonia, and again from Macedonia to come to you, and by you to
be [c]helped on my journey [d]to Judea.
17 Therefore, I was not vacillating
when I intended to do this, was I? Or
that which I purpose, do I purpose
[a]according to the flesh, that with me
there should be yes, yes and no, no
at the same time?
18 But as [a]God is faithful, [b]our
word to you is not yes and no.
19 For [a]the Son of God, Christ Jesus, who was preached among you
by us—by me and [b]Silvanus and
[c]Timothy—was not yes and no, but
is yes [d]in Him.
20 For [a]as many as may be the
promises of God, [b]in Him they are
yes; wherefore also by Him is [c]our
Amen to the glory of God through
us.
21 Now He who [a]establishes us
with you in Christ and [b]anointed us
is God,
22 who also [a]sealed us and [b]gave
us the Spirit in our hearts as a
pledge.
23 But [a]I call God as witness [1]to
my soul, that [b]to spare you I came
no more to [c]Corinth.
24 Not that we [a]lord it over your
faith, but are workers with you for
your joy; for in your faith you are
[b]standing firm.

CHAPTER 2

Reaffirm Your Love

BUT I determined this for my own
sake, that I [a]would not come to you
in sorrow again.
2 For if I cause you sorrow, who
then makes me glad but the one
whom I made sorrowful?
3 And this is the very thing I
[a]wrote you, lest, [b]when I came, I
should have sorrow from those who
ought to make me rejoice; having

1 [a]Rom. 1:1; Gal. 1:1; Eph. 1:1; Titus 1:1 [b]Gal. 3:26 [c]1 Cor. 1:1 [d]Acts 16:1 [e]1 Cor. 10:32 [f]Acts 18:1 [g]Acts 18:12
2 [a]Rom. 1:7
3 [a]Eph. 1:3; 1 Pet. 1:3 [b]Rom. 15:5
4 [a]Is. 51:12; 66:13; 2 Cor. 7:6
5 [a]2 Cor. 4:10; Phil. 3:10; Col. 1:24
6 [a]2 Cor. 4:15; 12:15; Eph. 3:1, 13; 2 Tim. 2:10
7 [a]Rom. 8:17
8 [1]I.e., west coast province of Asia Minor [a]Rom. 1:13 [b]Acts 19:23; 1 Cor. 15:32 [c]Acts 16:6
10 [a]Rom. 15:31 [b]1 Tim. 4:10
11 [a]Rom. 15:30; Phil. 1:19; Philem. 22 [b]2 Cor. 4:15
12 [a]Acts 23:1 [b]2 Cor. 2:17 [c]1 Cor. 1:17; James 3:15
13 [a]1 Cor. 1:8
14 [a]1 Cor. 1:8
15 [a]1 Cor. 4:19 [b]Rom. 1:11; 15:29
16 [a]Acts 19:21 [b]Rom. 15:26 [c]Acts 15:3; 1 Cor. 16:6, 11 [d]Acts 19:21
17 [a]2 Cor. 10:2f.
18 [a]1 Cor. 1:9 [b]2 Cor. 2:17
19 [a]Matt. 4:3; 16:16; 26:63 [b]Acts 15:22; 1 Pet. 5:12 [c]2 Cor. 1:1 [d]Heb. 13:8
20 [a]Rom. 15:8 [b]Heb. 13:8 [c]1 Cor. 14:16; Rev. 3:14
21 [a]1 Cor. 1:8 [b]1 John 2:20, 27
22 [a]John 3:33 [b]Rom. 8:16; 2 Cor. 5:5
23 [1]Lit., *upon* [a]Rom. 1:9; Gal. 1:20 [b]1 Cor. 4:21 [c]2 Cor. 1:1
24 [a]2 Cor. 4:5 [b]Rom 11:20
1 [a]1 Cor. 4:21
3 [a]2 Cor. 2:9; 7:8, 12 [b]1 Cor. 4:21; 2 Cor. 12:21

[c]confidence in you all, that my joy
would be *the joy* of you all.
4 For out of much affliction and
anguish of heart I [a]wrote to you
with many tears; not that you
should be made sorrowful, but that
you might know the love which I
have especially for you.
5 But [a]if any has caused sorrow,
he has caused sorrow not to me, but
in some degree—in order not to say
too much—to all of you.
6 Sufficient for such a one is [a]this
punishment which was *inflicted by*
the majority,
7 so that on the contrary you
should rather [a]forgive and comfort
him, lest somehow such a one be
overwhelmed by excessive sorrow.
8 Wherefore I urge you to reaffirm *your* love for him.
9 For to this end also [a]I wrote
that I might [b]put you to the test,
whether you are [c]obedient in all
things.
10 But whom you forgive anything, I *forgive* also; for indeed what
I have forgiven, if I have forgiven
anything, *I did it* for your sakes [a]in
the presence of Christ,
11 in order that no advantage be
taken of us by [a]Satan; for [b]we are
not ignorant of his schemes.
12 Now when I came to [a]Troas for
the [b]gospel of Christ and when a
[c]door was opened for me in the
Lord,
13 I [a]had no rest for my spirit, not
finding [b]Titus my brother; but [c]tak-
ing my leave of them, I went on to
[d]Macedonia.
14 [a]But thanks be to God, who always [b]leads us in His triumph in
Christ, and manifests through us the
[c]sweet aroma of the [d]knowledge of
Him in every place.
15 For we are a [a]fragrance of
Christ to God among [b]those who are
being saved and among those who
are perishing;
16 [a]to the one an aroma from
death to death, to the other an aroma from life to life. And who is [b]ad-
equate for these things?
17 For we are not like many, [a]ped-
dling the word of God, but [b]as from
sincerity, but as from God, we speak
in Christ [c]in the sight of God.

CHAPTER 3

Ministers of a New Covenant

ARE we beginning to [a]commend
ourselves again? Or do we need, as
some, [b]letters of commendation to
you or from you?

3 [c]Gal. 5:10; 2 Thess. 3:4
4 [a]2 Cor. 2:9
5 [a]1 Cor. 5:1f.
6 [a]1 Cor. 5:4f.
7 [a]Gal. 6:1
9 [a]2 Cor. 2:3f. [b]2 Cor. 8:2; Phil. 2:22 [c]2 Cor. 7:15
10 [a]1 Cor. 5:4
11 [a]Matt. 4:10 [b]Luke 22:31; 2 Cor. 4:4
12 [a]Acts 16:8 [b]Rom. 1:1; 2 Cor. 4:3, 4; 8:18; 9:13; 10:14; 11:4, 7; 1 Thess. 3:2 [c]Acts 14:27
13 [a]2 Cor. 7:5 [b]2 Cor. 7:6, 13f.; Gal. 2:1, 3; 2 Tim. 4:10; Titus 1:4 [c]Mark 6:46 [d]Rom. 15:26
14 [a]Rom. 1:8; 2 Cor. 8:16; 9:15 [b]Col. 2:15 [Gr.] [c]Song of Sol. 1:3; Ezek. 20:41; Eph. 5:2; Phil. 4:18 [d]1 Cor. 12:8
15 [a]Song of Sol. 1:3; Ezek. 20:41; Eph. 5:2; Phil. 4:18 [b]1 Cor. 1:18
16 [a]Luke 2:34; John 9:39; 1 Pet. 2:7f. [b]2 Cor. 3:5f.
17 [a]2 Cor. 4:2; Gal. 1:6-9 [b]1 Cor. 5:8; 1 Pet. 4:11 [c]2 Cor. 12:19
1 [a]2 Cor. 5:12 [b]Acts 18:27; Rom. 16:1; 1 Cor. 16:3
2 [a]1 Cor. 9:2
3 [a]2 Cor. 3:6 [b]Matt. 16:16 [c]Ex. 24:12; 2 Cor. 3:7 [d]Prov. 3:3; 7:3; Jer. 17:1 [e]Jer. 31:33
4 [a]Eph. 3:12
5 [a]1 Cor. 15:10
6 [a]1 Cor. 3:5 [b]Luke 22:20 [c]Rom. 2:29 [d]John 6:63; Rom. 7:6
7 [a]Rom. 4:15; 5:20; Gal. 3:10, 21f. [b]Ex. 24:12; 31:18 [c]Ex. 34:29-35
9 [a]Deut. 27:26; 2 Cor. 3:7; Heb. 12:18-21 [b]Rom. 1:17; 3:21f.
12 [a]2 Cor. 7:4 [b]Acts 4:13, 29; 2 Cor. 7:4
13 [a]2 Cor. 3:7
14 [a]Rom. 11:7; 2 Cor. 4:4 [b]Acts 13:15 [c]2 Cor. 3:6
16 [a]Ex. 34:34
17 [a]Is. 61:1f.; Gal. 4:6 [b]John 8:32; Gal. 5:1, 13
18 [a]1 Cor. 13:12 [b]2 Cor. 4:4, 6; John 17:22, 24 [c]Rom. 8:29 [d]2 Cor. 3:17

2 [a]You are our letter, written in
our hearts, known and read by all
men;
3 being manifested that you are a
letter of Christ, [a]cared for by us,
written not with ink, but with the
Spirit of [b]the living God, not on [c]tab-
lets of stone, but on [d]tablets of [e]hu-
man hearts.
4 And such [a]confidence we have
through Christ toward God.
5 Not that we are adequate in
ourselves to consider anything as
coming from ourselves, but [a]our
adequacy is from God,
6 who also made us adequate *as*
[a]servants of a [b]new covenant, not of
[c]the letter, but of the Spirit; for the
letter kills, but [d]the Spirit gives life.
7 But if the [a]ministry of death, [b]in
letters engraved on stones, came
with glory, [c]so that the sons of Israel
could not look intently at the face of
Moses because of the glory of his
face, fading *as* it was,
8 how shall the ministry of the
Spirit fail to be even more with glory?
9 For if [a]the ministry of condemnation has glory, much more does
the [b]ministry of righteousness
abound in glory.
10 For indeed what had glory, in
this case has no glory on account of
the glory that surpasses *it.*
11 For if that which fades away
was with glory, much more that
which remains *is* in glory.
12 [a]Having therefore such a hope,
[b]we use great boldness in *our*
speech,
13 and *are* not as Moses, [a]*who*
used to put a veil over his face that
the sons of Israel might not look intently at the end of what was fading
away.
14 But their minds were [a]hard-
ened; for until this very day at the
[b]reading of [c]the old covenant the
same veil remains unlifted, because
it is removed in Christ.
15 But to this day whenever Moses
is read, a veil lies over their heart;
16 [a]BUT WHENEVER A MAN TURNS
TO THE LORD, THE VEIL IS TAKEN
AWAY.
17 Now the Lord is the Spirit; and
where [a]the Spirit of the Lord is,
[b]*there* is liberty.
18 But we all, with unveiled face
[a]beholding as in a mirror the [b]glory
of the Lord, are being [c]transformed
into the same image from glory to
glory, just as from [d]the Lord, the
Spirit.

Chapter 4

Paul's Apostolic Ministry

THEREFORE, since we have this
[a]ministry, as we [b]received mercy,
we [c]do not lose heart,
2 but we have renounced the
[a]things hidden because of shame,
not walking in craftiness or [b]adul-
terating the word of God, but by the
manifestation of truth [c]commend-
ing ourselves to every man's conscience in the sight of God.
3 And even if our [a]gospel is
[b]veiled, it is veiled to [c]those who are
perishing,
4 in whose case [a]the god of [b]this
world has [c]blinded the minds of the
unbelieving, that they might not see
the [d]light of the gospel of the [e]glory
of Christ, who is the [f]image of God.
5 For we [a]do not preach ourselves but Christ Jesus as Lord, and
ourselves as your bond-servants for
Jesus' sake.
6 For God, who said, "[a]Light
shall shine out of darkness," is the
One who has [b]shone in our hearts to
give the [c]light of the knowledge of
the glory of God in the face of
Christ.
7 But we have this treasure in
[a]earthen vessels, that the surpassing greatness of [b]the power may be
of God and not from ourselves;
8 *we are* [a]afflicted in every way,
but not [b]crushed; [c]perplexed, but
not despairing;
9 [a]persecuted, but not [b]forsaken;
[c]struck down, but not destroyed;
10 [a]always carrying about in the
body the dying of Jesus, that [b]the
life of Jesus also may be manifested
in our body.
11 For we who live are constantly
being delivered over to death for Jesus' sake, that the life of Jesus also
may be manifested in our mortal
flesh.
12 So death works in us, but life in
you.
13 But having the same [a]spirit of
faith, according to what is written,
"[b]I BELIEVED, THEREFORE I SPOKE,"
we also believe, therefore also we
speak;
14 knowing that He who [a]raised
the Lord Jesus [b]will raise us also
with Jesus and will [c]present us with
you.
15 For all things *are* [a]for your
sakes, that the grace which is
[b]spreading to more and more people
may cause the giving of thanks to
abound to the glory of God.

1 [a]1 Cor. 3:5 [b]1 Cor. 7:25 [c]Luke 18:1; 2 Cor. 4:16; Gal. 6:9; Eph. 3:13
2 [a]Rom. 6:21; 1 Cor. 4:5 [b]2 Cor. 2:17 [c]2 Cor. 5:11f.
3 [a]2 Cor. 2:12 [b]1 Cor. 2:6ff. [c]1 Cor. 1:18
4 [a]John 12:31 [b]Matt. 13:22 [c]2 Cor. 3:14 [d]Acts 26:18; 2 Cor. 4:6 [e]2 Cor. 3:18; 4:6 [f]John 1:18
5 [a]1 Cor. 4:15f.; 1 Thess. 2:6f.
6 [a]Gen. 1:3 [b]2 Pet. 1:19 [c]Acts 26:18; 2 Cor. 4:4
7 [a]Job 4:19; 10:9; 33:6; Lam. 4:2; 2 Cor. 5:1; 2 Tim. 2:20 [b]Judg. 7:2; 1 Cor. 2:5
8 [a]2 Cor. 1:8; 7:5 [b]2 Cor. 6:12 [c]Gal. 4:20
9 [a]John 15:20; Rom. 8:35f. [b]Ps. 129:2; Heb. 13:5 [c]Ps. 37:24; Prov. 24:16; Mic. 7:8
10 [a]Rom. 6:5 [b]Rom. 6:8
13 [a]1 Cor. 12:9 [b]Ps. 116:10
14 [a]Acts 2:24 [b]1 Thess. 4:14 [c]Luke 21:36; Eph. 5:27; Col. 1:22
15 [a]Rom. 8:28; 2 Cor. 1:6 [b]1 Cor. 9:19; 2 Cor. 1:11
16 [a]2 Cor. 4:1 [b]Rom. 7:22 [c]Is. 40:29, 31
17 [a]Rom. 8:18
18 [a]Rom. 8:24; 2 Cor. 5:7; Heb. 11:1, 13
1 [a]Job 4:19; 1 Cor. 15:47; 2 Cor. 4:7 [b]2 Pet. 1:13f. [c]Mark 14:58; Acts 7:48; Heb. 9:11
2 [a]Rom. 8:23; 2 Cor. 5:4 [b]1 Cor. 15:53f.; 2 Cor. 5:4
4 [a]2 Cor. 5:2 [b]1 Cor. 15:53f.; 2 Cor. 5:2 [c]1 Cor. 15:54
5 [a]Rom. 8:23; 2 Cor. 1:22
6 [a]Heb. 11:13f.
7 [a]1 Cor. 13:12
8 [a]Phil. 1:23 [b]John 12:26
9 [a]Rom. 14:18; Col. 1:10
10 [a]Matt. 16:27; Acts 10:42; Rom. 2:16
11 [a]Heb. 10:31 [b]2 Cor. 4:2
12 [a]2 Cor. 3:1 [b]2 Cor. 1:14; Phil. 1:26

16 Therefore we [a]do not lose heart,
but though our outer man is decaying, yet our [b]inner man is [c]being renewed day by day.
17 For momentary, [a]light affliction
is producing for us an eternal
weight of glory far beyond all comparison,
18 while we [a]look not at the things
which are seen, but at the things
which are not seen; for the things
which are seen are temporal, but the
things which are not seen are eternal.

Chapter 5

The Temporal and Eternal

FOR we know that if the [a]earthly
[b]tent which is our house is torn
down, we have a building from God,
a house [c]not made with hands, eternal in the heavens.
2 For indeed in this *house* we
[a]groan, longing to be [b]clothed with
our dwelling from heaven;
3 inasmuch as we, having put it
on, shall not be found naked.
4 For indeed while we are in this
tent, we [a]groan, being burdened, because we do not want to be un-
clothed, but to be [b]clothed, in order
that what is [c]mortal may be swallowed up by life.
5 Now He who prepared us for
this very purpose is God, who [a]gave
to us the Spirit as a pledge.
6 Therefore, being always of
good courage, and knowing that
[a]while we are at home in the body
we are absent from the Lord—
7 for [a]we walk by faith, not by
sight—
8 we are of good courage, I say,
and [a]prefer rather to be absent from
the body and [b]to be at home with
the Lord.
9 Therefore also we have as our
ambition, whether at home or absent, to be [a]pleasing to Him.
10 For we must all appear before
[a]the judgment seat of Christ, that
each one may be recompensed for
his deeds in the body, according to
what he has done, whether good or
bad.
11 Therefore knowing the [a]fear of
the Lord, we persuade men, but we
are made manifest to God; and I
hope that we are [b]made manifest
also in your consciences.
12 We are not [a]again commending
ourselves to you but *are* giving you
an [b]occasion to be proud of us, that
you may have *an answer* for those

who take pride in appearance, and not in heart.

13 For if we are [a]beside ourselves, it is for God; if we are of sound mind, it is for you.

14 For the love of Christ [a]controls us, having concluded this, that [b]one died for all, therefore all died;

15 and He died for all, that they who live should no longer [a]live for themselves, but for Him who died and rose again on their behalf.

16 Therefore from now on we recognize no man [a]according to the flesh; even though we have known Christ according to the flesh, yet now we know *Him thus* no longer.

17 Therefore if any man is [a]in Christ, *he is* [b]a new creature; [c]the old things passed away; behold, new things have come.

18 Now [a]all *these* things are from God, [b]who reconciled us to Himself through Christ, and gave us the [c]ministry of reconciliation,

19 namely, that [a]God was in Christ reconciling the world to Himself, [b]not counting their trespasses against them, and He has committed to us the word of reconciliation.

20 Therefore, we are [a]ambassadors for Christ, [b]as though God were entreating through us; we beg you on behalf of Christ, be [c]reconciled to God.

21 He made Him who [a]knew no sin *to be* [b]sin on our behalf, that we might become the [c]righteousness of God in Him.

CHAPTER 6

Their Ministry Commended

AND [a]working together *with Him,* [b]we also urge you not to receive [c]the grace of God in vain—

2 for He says,

"[a]AT THE ACCEPTABLE TIME I LISTENED TO YOU,
AND ON THE DAY OF SALVATION I HELPED YOU";

behold, now is "THE ACCEPTABLE TIME," behold, now is "THE DAY OF SALVATION"—

3 [a]giving no cause for offense in anything, in order that the ministry be not discredited,

4 but in everything [a]commending ourselves as [b]servants of God, [c]in much endurance, in afflictions, in hardships, in distresses,

5 in [a]beatings, in [a]imprisonments, in [b]tumults, in labors, in sleeplessness, in [c]hunger,

6 in purity, in [a]knowledge, in [b]patience, in kindness, in the [c]Holy Spirit, in [d]genuine love,

7 in [a]the word of truth, in [b]the power of God; by [c]the weapons of righteousness for the right hand and the left,

8 by glory and [a]dishonor, by [b]evil report and good report; *regarded* as [c]deceivers and yet [d]true;

9 as unknown yet well-known, as [a]dying yet behold, [b]we live; as punished yet not put to death,

10 as [a]sorrowful yet always [a]rejoicing, as [b]poor yet making many rich, as [c]having nothing yet possessing [d]all things.

11 [a]Our mouth has spoken freely to you, O Corinthians, our [b]heart is opened wide.

12 You are not restrained by us, but [a]you are restrained in your own affections.

13 Now in a like [a]exchange—I speak as to [b]children—open wide *to us* also.

14 [a]Do not be bound together with [b]unbelievers; for what [c]partnership have righteousness and lawlessness, or what fellowship has light with darkness?

15 Or what [a]harmony has Christ with Belial, or what has a [b]believer in common with an [c]unbeliever?

16 Or [a]what agreement has the temple of God with idols? For we are [b]the temple of [c]the living God; just as God said,

"[d]I WILL [e]DWELL IN THEM AND [f]WALK AMONG THEM;
AND I WILL BE THEIR GOD, AND THEY SHALL BE MY PEOPLE.

17 "[a]Therefore, [b]COME OUT FROM THEIR MIDST AND BE SEPARATE," says the Lord.
"AND DO NOT TOUCH WHAT IS UNCLEAN;
AND I WILL WELCOME YOU.

18 "[a]AND I WILL BE A FATHER TO YOU,
AND YOU SHALL BE [b]SONS and daughters TO ME,"
SAYS THE LORD ALMIGHTY.

CHAPTER 7

Paul Reveals His Heart

THEREFORE, having these promises, [a]beloved, [b]let us cleanse ourselves from all defilement of flesh and spirit, perfecting holiness in the fear of God.

2 [a]Make room for us *in your hearts;* we wronged no one, we corrupted no one, we took advantage of no one.

13 [a]Mark 3:21
14 [a]Acts 18:5 [b]Rom. 5:15; 6:6f.
15 [a]Rom. 14:7-9
16 [a]John 8:15
17 [a]Rom. 16:7 [b]John 3:3; Rom. 6:4 [c]Is. 43:18f.
18 [a]1 Cor. 11:12 [b]Rom. 5:10; Col. 1:20 [c]1 Cor. 3:5
19 [a]Col. 2:9 [b]Rom. 4:8; 1 Cor. 13:5
20 [a]Mal. 2:7; Eph. 6:20 [b]2 Cor. 6:1 [c]Rom. 5:10
21 [a]Acts 3:14; 1 Pet. 2:22; 1 John 3:5 [b]Rom. 3:25 [c]Rom. 1:17; 3:21f.; 1 Cor. 1:30
1 [a]1 Cor. 3:9 [b]2 Cor. 5:20 [c]Acts 11:23
2 [a]Is. 49:8
3 [a]1 Cor. 8:9
4 [a]Rom. 3:5 [b]1 Cor. 3:5; 2 Tim. 2:24f. [c]Acts 9:16; 2 Cor. 4:8-11; 6:4ff.
5 [a]Acts 16:23 [b]Acts 19:23ff. [c]1 Cor. 4:11
6 [a]1 Cor. 12:8; 2 Cor. 11:6 [b]2 Cor. 1:23; 2:10; 13:10 [c]1 Cor. 2:4 [d]Rom. 12:9
7 [a]2 Cor. 2:17; 4:2 [b]1 Cor. 2:5 [c]Rom. 13:12
8 [a]1 Cor. 4:10 [b]Rom. 3:8; 1 Cor. 4:13; 2 Cor. 12:16 [c]Matt. 27:63 [d]2 Cor. 1:18; 4:2; 1 Thess. 2:3f.
9 [a]Rom. 8:36 [b]2 Cor. 1:8, 10
10 [a]John 16:22; 2 Cor. 7:4; Phil. 2:17; 4:4; Col. 1:24; 1 Thess. 1:6 [b]1 Cor. 1:5; 2 Cor. 8:9 [c]Acts 3:6 [d]Rom. 8:32
11 [a]Ezek. 33:22; Eph. 6:19 [b]Is. 60:5
12 [a]2 Cor. 7:2
13 [a]Gal. 4:12 [b]1 Cor. 4:14
14 [a]Deut. 22:10 [b]1 Cor. 6:6 [c]Eph. 5:7, 11; 1 John 1:6
15 [a]1 Cor. 10:21 [b]Acts 5:14; 1 Pet. 1:21 [c]1 Cor. 6:6
16 [a]1 Cor. 10:21 [b]1 Cor. 3:16 [c]Matt. 16:16 [d]Ex. 29:45; Lev. 26:12; Jer. 31:1; Ezek. 37:27 [e]Ex. 25:8; John 14:23 [f]Rev. 2:1
17 [a]Is. 52:11 [b]Rev. 18:4
18 [a]Is. 43:6; Hos. 1:10 [b]Rom. 8:14
1 [a]Heb. 6:9 [b]1 Pet. 1:15f.
2 [a]2 Cor. 6:12f.

3 I do not speak to condemn you; for I have said [a]before that you are [b]in our hearts to die together and to live together.

4 Great is my [a]confidence in you, great is my [b]boasting on your behalf; I am filled with [c]comfort. I am overflowing with [d]joy in all our affliction.

5 For even when we came into [a]Macedonia our flesh had no rest, but we were [b]afflicted on every side: [c]conflicts without, fears within.

6 But [a]God, who comforts the depressed, [b]comforted us by the coming of [c]Titus;

7 and not only by his coming, but also by the comfort with which he was comforted in you, as he reported to us your longing, your mourning, your zeal for me; so that I rejoiced even more.

8 For though I [a]caused you sorrow by my letter, I do not regret it; though I did regret it—*for* I see that that letter caused you sorrow, though only for a while—

9 I now rejoice, not that you were made sorrowful, but that you were made sorrowful to *the point of* repentance; for you were made sorrowful according to *the will of* God, in order that you might not suffer loss in anything through us.

10 For the sorrow that is according to *the will of* God produces a [a]repentance [1]without regret, *leading* to salvation; but the sorrow of the world produces death.

11 For behold what earnestness this very thing, this [1]godly sorrow, has produced in you: what vindication of yourselves, what indignation, what fear, what [a]longing, what zeal, what [b]avenging of wrong! In everything you [c]demonstrated yourselves to be innocent in the matter.

12 So although [a]I wrote to you *it was* not for the sake of [b]the offender, nor for the sake of the one offended, but that your earnestness on our behalf might be made known to you in the sight of God.

13 For this reason we have been [a]comforted.

And besides our comfort, we rejoiced even much more for the joy of [b]Titus, because his [c]spirit has been refreshed by you all.

14 For if in anything I have [a]boasted to him about you, I was not put to shame; but as we spoke all things to you in truth, so also our boasting before [b]Titus proved to be *the* truth.

15 And his affection abounds all the more toward you, as he remembers the [a]obedience of you all, how you received him with [b]fear and trembling.

16 I rejoice that in everything [a]I have confidence in you.

Chapter 8

Great Generosity

Now, brethren, we *wish to* make known to you the grace of God which has been [a]given in the churches of [b]Macedonia,

2 that in a great ordeal of affliction their abundance of joy and their deep poverty overflowed in the [a]wealth of their liberality.

3 For I testify that [a]according to their ability, and beyond their ability *they gave* of their own accord,

4 begging us with much entreaty for the [a]favor of participation in the [1b]support of the saints,

5 and *this,* not as we had expected, but they first [a]gave themselves to the Lord and to us by [b]the will of God.

6 Consequently we [a]urged [b]Titus that as he had previously [c]made a beginning, so he would also complete in you [d]this gracious work as well.

7 But just as you [a]abound [b]in everything, in faith and utterance and knowledge and in all earnestness and in the [1]love we inspired in you, *see* that you [a]abound in this gracious work also.

8 I [a]am not speaking *this* as a command, but as proving through the earnestness of others the sincerity of your love also.

9 For you know [a]the grace of our Lord Jesus Christ, that [b]though He was rich, yet for your sake He became poor, that you through His poverty might become rich.

10 And I [a]give *my* opinion in this matter, for this is to your advantage, who were the first to begin [b]a year ago not only to do *this,* but also to desire *to do it.*

11 But now finish doing it also; that just as *there was* the [a]readiness to desire it, so *there may be* also the completion of it by your ability.

12 For if the readiness is present, it is acceptable [a]according to what *a man* has, not according to what he does not have.

13 For *this* is not for the ease of others *and* for your affliction, but by way of equality—

---

3 [a]2 Cor. 6:11f. [b]Phil. 1:7
4 [a]2 Cor. 3:12 [b]2 Cor. 7:14; 8:24; 9:2f.; 10:8; Phil. 1:26; 2 Thess. 1:4 [c]2 Cor. 1:4 [d]2 Cor. 6:10
5 [a]Rom. 15:26; 2 Cor. 2:13 [b]2 Cor. 4:8 [c]Deut. 32:25
6 [a]2 Cor. 1:3f. [b]2 Cor. 7:13 [c]2 Cor. 2:13; 7:13f.
8 [a]2 Cor. 2:2
10 [1]Or, *leading to a salvation without regret* [a]Acts 11:18
11 [1]Lit., *sorrow according to God* [a]2 Cor. 7:7 [b]2 Cor. 2:6 [c]Rom. 3:5
12 [a]2 Cor. 2:3, 9; 7:8 [b]1 Cor. 5:1f.
13 [a]2 Cor. 7:6 [b]2 Cor. 2:13; 7:6, 14 [c]1 Cor. 16:18
14 [a]2 Cor. 7:4; 8:24; 9:2f.; 10:8; Phil. 1:26; 2 Thess. 1:4 [b]2 Cor. 2:13; 7:6, 13
15 [a]2 Cor. 2:9 [b]1 Cor. 2:3; Phil. 2:12
16 [a]2 Cor. 2:3
1 [a]2 Cor. 8:5 [b]Acts 16:9
2 [a]Rom. 2:4
3 [a]1 Cor. 16:2; 2 Cor. 8:11
4 [1]Lit., *service to the saints* [a]Acts 24:17; Rom. 15:25f. [b]Rom. 15:31; 2 Cor. 8:19f.; 9:1, 12f.
5 [a]2 Cor. 8:1 [b]1 Cor. 1:1
6 [a]2 Cor. 8:17; 12:18 [b]2 Cor. 2:13; 8:16, 23 [c]2 Cor. 8:10 [d]Acts 24:17; Rom. 15:25f.
7 [1]Lit., *love from us in you;* some ancient mss. read, *your love for us* [a]2 Cor. 9:8 [b]Rom. 15:14; 1 Cor. 1:5; 12:8
8 [a]1 Cor. 7:6
9 [a]2 Cor. 13:14 [b]Matt. 20:28; 2 Cor. 6:10; Phil. 2:6f.
10 [a]1 Cor. 7:25, 40 [b]1 Cor. 16:2f.; 2 Cor. 9:2
11 [a]2 Cor. 8:12, 19; 9:2
12 [a]Mark 12:43f.; Luke 21:3; 2 Cor. 9:7

14 at this present time your abundance *being a supply* for [a]their
want, that their abundance also may
become *a supply* for [a]your want,
that there may be equality;
15 as it is written, "[a]HE WHO *gathered* MUCH DID NOT HAVE TOO MUCH,
AND HE WHO *gathered* LITTLE HAD NO
LACK."
16 But [a]thanks be to God, who
[b]puts the same earnestness on your
behalf in the heart of [c]Titus.
17 For he not only accepted our
[a]appeal, but being himself very earnest, he has gone to you of his own
accord.
18 And we have sent along with
him [a]the brother whose fame in *the
things of* the [b]gospel *has spread*
through [c]all the churches;
19 [a]and not only *this,* but he has
also been [b]appointed by the
churches to travel with us in [c]this
gracious work, which is being ad-
ministered by us for the glory of the
Lord Himself, and *to show* our
[d]readiness,
20 taking precaution that no one
should discredit us in our administration of this generous gift;
21 for we [a]have regard for what is
honorable, not only in [b]the sight of
the Lord, but also in the sight of
men.
22 And we have sent with them
our brother, whom we have often
tested and found diligent in many
things, but now even more diligent,
because of *his* great confidence in
you.
23 As for [a]Titus, *he is* my [b]partner
and fellow-worker among you; as
for our [c]brethren, *they are* [1d]mes-
sengers of the churches, [e]a glory to
Christ.
24 Therefore openly before the
churches show them the proof of
your love and of our [a]reason for
boasting about you.

CHAPTER 9

God Gives Most

FOR [a]it is superfluous for me to
write to you about this [b]ministry to
the saints;
2 for I know your readiness, of
which I [a]boast about you to the
[b]Macedonians, *namely,* that [c]Acha-
ia has been prepared since [d]last
year, and your zeal has stirred up
most of them.
3 But I have sent the brethren,
that our [a]boasting about you may
not be made empty in this case, that,

14 [a]Acts 4:34; 2 Cor. 9:12
15 [a]Ex. 16:18
16 [a]2 Cor. 2:14 [b]Rev. 17:17 [c]2 Cor. 2:13; 8:6, 23
17 [a]2 Cor. 8:6; 12:18
18 [a]1 Cor. 16:3; 2 Cor. 12:18 [b]2 Cor. 2:12 [c]1 Cor. 4:17; 7:17
19 [a]Rom. 5:3 [b]Acts 14:23; 1 Cor. 16:3f. [c]2 Cor. 8:4, 6 [d]2 Cor. 8:11, 12; 9:2
21 [a]Rom. 12:17 [b]Rom. 14:18
23 [1]Lit., *apostles* [a]2 Cor. 8:6 [b]Philem. 17 [c]2 Cor. 8:18, 22 [d]John 13:16; Phil. 2:25 [e]1 Cor. 11:7
24 [a]2 Cor. 7:4
1 [a]1 Thess. 4:9 [b]2 Cor. 8:4
2 [a]2 Cor. 7:4 [b]Rom. 15:26 [c]Acts 18:12 [d]2 Cor. 8:10
3 [a]2 Cor. 7:4 [b]1 Cor. 16:2
4 [a]Rom. 15:26
5 [a]2 Cor. 9:3 [b]Gen. 33:11; Judg. 1:15; 2 Cor. 9:6 [c]Phil. 4:17 [d]2 Cor. 12:17f.
6 [a]Prov. 11:24f.; 22:9; Gal. 6:7, 9
7 [a]Deut. 15:10; 1 Chr. 29:17; Rom. 12:8; 2 Cor. 8:12 [b]Ex. 25:2; Prov. 22:8; 2 Cor. 8:12
8 [a]Eph. 3:20
9 [a]Ps. 112:9
10 [a]Is. 55:10 [b]Hos. 10:12
11 [a]1 Cor. 1:5 [b]2 Cor. 1:11
12 [a]2 Cor. 8:14 [b]2 Cor. 1:11
13 [1]Or, *sharing with them* [a]Rom. 15:31; 2 Cor. 8:4 [b]Matt. 9:8 [c]1 Tim. 6:12f.; Heb. 3:1; 4:14; 10:23 [d]2 Cor. 2:12
15 [a]2 Cor. 2:14 [b]Rom. 5:15f.
1 [1]Lit., *lowly* [a]Gal. 5:2; Eph. 3:1; Col. 1:23 [b]Rom. 12:1 [c]Matt. 11:29; 1 Cor. 4:21; Phil. 4:5 [d]1 Cor. 2:3f.; 2 Cor. 10:10

[b]as I was saying, you may be prepared;
4 lest if any [a]Macedonians come
with me and find you unprepared,
we (not to speak of you) should be
put to shame by this confidence.
5 So I thought it necessary to
urge the [a]brethren that they would
go on ahead to you and arrange beforehand your previously promised
[b]bountiful gift, that the same might
be ready as a [c]bountiful gift, and not
[d]affected by covetousness.
6 Now this *I say,* [a]he who sows
sparingly shall also reap sparingly;
and he who sows bountifully shall
also reap bountifully.
7 Let each one *do* just as he has
purposed in his heart; not [a]grudg-
ingly or under compulsion; for [b]God
loves a cheerful giver.
8 And [a]God is able to make all
grace abound to you, that always
having all sufficiency in everything,
you may have an abundance for every good deed;
9 as it is written,
"[a]HE SCATTERED ABROAD, HE
GAVE TO THE POOR,
HIS RIGHTEOUSNESS ABIDES
FOREVER."
10 Now He who supplies [a]seed to
the sower and bread for food, will
supply and multiply your seed for
sowing and [b]increase the harvest of
your righteousness;
11 you will be [a]enriched in everything for all liberality, which
through us is producing [b]thanksgiv-
ing to God.
12 For the ministry of this service
is not only fully supplying [a]the
needs of the saints, but is also overflowing [b]through many thanksgivings to God.
13 Because of the proof given by
this [a]ministry they will [b]glorify God
for *your* obedience to your [c]confes-
sion of the [d]gospel of Christ, and for
the liberality of your [1]contribution
to them and to all,
14 while they also, by prayer on
your behalf, yearn for you because
of the surpassing grace of God in
you.
15 [a]Thanks be to God for His in-
describable [b]gift!

CHAPTER 10

Paul Describes Himself

NOW [a]I, Paul, myself [b]urge you by
the [c]meekness and gentleness of
Christ—I who [d]am [1]meek when
face to face with you, but bold
toward you when absent!

2 I ask that [a]when I am present I may not be bold with the confidence with which I propose to be courageous against [b]some, who regard us as if we walked [c]according to the flesh.

3 For though we walk in the flesh, we do not war [a]according to the flesh,

4 for the [a]weapons of our warfare are not of the flesh, but [b]divinely powerful [c]for the destruction of fortresses.

5 *We are* destroying speculations and every [a]lofty thing raised up against the knowledge of God, and *we are* taking every thought captive to the [b]obedience of Christ,

6 and we are ready to punish all disobedience, whenever [a]your obedience is complete.

7 [a]You are looking at things as they are outwardly. [b]If any one is confident in himself that he is Christ's, let him consider this again within himself, that just as he is Christ's, [c]so also are we.

8 For even if [a]I should boast somewhat further about our [b]authority, which the Lord gave for building you up and not for destroying you, I shall not be put to shame,

9 for I do not wish to seem as if I would terrify you by my letters.

10 For they say, "His letters are weighty and strong, but his personal presence is [a]unimpressive, and [b]his speech contemptible."

11 Let such a person consider this, that what we are in word by letters when absent, such persons *we are* also in deed when present.

12 For we are not bold to class or compare ourselves with some of those who [a]commend themselves; but when they measure themselves by themselves, and compare themselves with themselves, they are without understanding.

13 But we will not boast [a]beyond *our* measure, but [b]within the measure of the sphere which God apportioned to us as a measure, to reach even as far as you.

14 For we are not overextending ourselves, as if we did not reach to you, for [a]we were the first to come even as far as you in the [b]gospel of Christ;

15 not boasting [a]beyond *our* measure, *that is,* in [b]other men's labors, but with the hope that as [c]your faith grows, we shall be, within our sphere, [d]enlarged even more by you,

16 so as to [a]preach the gospel even to [b]the regions beyond you, *and* not to boast [c]in what has been accomplished in the sphere of another.

17 But [a]HE WHO BOASTS, LET HIM BOAST IN THE LORD.

18 For not he who [a]commends himself is approved, but [b]whom the Lord commends.

CHAPTER 11

Paul Defends His Apostleship

I WISH that you would [a]bear with me in a little [b]foolishness; but indeed you are bearing with me.

2 For I am jealous for you with a godly jealousy; for I [a]betrothed you to one husband, that to Christ I might [b]present you *as* a pure virgin.

3 But I am afraid, lest as the [a]serpent deceived Eve by his craftiness, your minds should be led astray from the simplicity and purity *of devotion* to Christ.

4 For if one comes and preaches [a]another Jesus whom we have not preached, or you receive a [b]different spirit which you have not received, or a [c]different gospel which you have not accepted, you [d]bear *this* [e]beautifully.

5 For I consider myself [a]not in the least inferior to the most eminent apostles.

6 But even if I am [a]unskilled in speech, yet I am not *so* in [b]knowledge; in fact, in every way we have [c]made *this* evident to you in all things.

7 Or [a]did I commit a sin in humbling myself that you might be exalted, because I preached the [b]gospel of God to you [c]without charge?

8 I robbed other churches, [a]taking wages *from them* to serve you;

9 and when I was present with you and was in need, I was [a]not a burden to anyone; for when [b]the brethren came from [c]Macedonia, they fully supplied my need, and in everything I kept myself from [a]being a burden to you, and will continue to do so.

10 [a]As the truth of Christ is in me, [b]this boasting of mine will not be stopped in the regions of [c]Achaia.

11 Why? [a]Because I do not love you? [b]God knows *I do!*

12 But what I am doing, I will continue to do, [a]that I may cut off opportunity from those who desire an opportunity to be regarded just as we are in the matter about which they are boasting.

13 For such men are [a]false apostles, [b]deceitful workers, disguising themselves as apostles of Christ.

2 [a]1 Cor. 4:21; 2 Cor. 13:2, 10 [b]1 Cor. 4:18f. [c]Rom. 8:4; 2 Cor. 1:17
3 [a]Rom. 8:4
4 [a]1 Cor. 9:7; 2 Cor. 6:7; 1 Tim. 1:18 [b]Acts 7:20 [c]Jer. 1:10; 2 Cor. 10:8
5 [a]Is. 2:11f. [b]2 Cor. 9:13
6 [a]2 Cor. 2:9
7 [a]John 7:24; 2 Cor. 5:12 [b]1 Cor. 1:12; 14:37 [c]1 Cor. 9:1; 2 Cor. 11:23; Gal. 1:12
8 [a]2 Cor. 7:4 [b]2 Cor. 13:10
10 [a]1 Cor. 2:3; 2 Cor. 12:7; Gal. 4:13f. [b]1 Cor. 1:17; 2 Cor. 11:6
12 [a]2 Cor. 3:1; 10:18
13 [a]2 Cor. 10:15 [b]Rom. 12:3; 2 Cor. 10:15f.
14 [a]1 Cor. 3:6 [b]2 Cor. 2:12
15 [a]2 Cor. 10:13 [b]Rom. 15:20 [c]2 Thess. 1:3 [d]Acts 5:13
16 [a]2 Cor. 11:7 [b]Acts 19:21 [c]Rom. 15:20
17 [a]Jer. 9:24
18 [a]2 Cor. 10:12 [b]Rom. 2:29; 1 Cor. 4:5
1 [a]Matt. 17:17; 2 Cor. 11:4, 16, 19f. [b]2 Cor. 5:13
2 [a]Hos. 2:19f. [b]2 Cor. 4:14
3 [a]Gen. 3:4, 13; John 8:44; 1 Tim. 2:14; Rev. 12:9, 15
4 [a]1 Cor. 3:11 [b]Rom. 8:15 [c]Gal. 1:6 [d]2 Cor. 11:1 [e]Mark 7:9
5 [a]2 Cor. 12:11; Gal. 2:6
6 [a]1 Cor. 1:17 [b]1 Cor. 12:8; Eph. 3:4 [c]2 Cor. 4:2
7 [a]2 Cor. 12:13 [b]Rom. 1:1; 2 Cor. 2:12 [c]Acts 18:3; 1 Cor. 9:18
8 [a]1 Cor. 4:12; 9:6; Phil. 4:15, 18
9 [a]2 Cor. 12:13f., 16 [b]Acts 18:5 [c]Rom. 15:26
10 [a]Rom. 1:9; 9:1; 2 Cor. 1:23; Gal. 2:20 [b]1 Cor. 9:15 [c]Acts 18:12
11 [a]2 Cor. 12:15 [b]Rom. 1:9; 2 Cor. 2:17; 11:31; 12:2f.
12 [a]1 Cor. 9:12
13 [a]Acts 20:30; Gal. 1:7; 2:4; Phil. 1:15; Titus 1:10f.; 2 Pet. 2:1; Rev. 2:2 [b]Phil. 3:2

14 And no wonder, for even [a]Satan disguises himself as an [b]angel of light.
15 Therefore it is not surprising if his servants also disguise themselves as servants of righteousness; [a]whose end shall be according to their deeds.
16 [a]Again I say, let no one think me foolish; but if *you do*, receive me even as foolish, that I also may boast a little.
17 That which I am speaking, I am not speaking [a]as the Lord would, but as [b]in foolishness, in this confidence of boasting.
18 Since [a]many boast [b]according to the flesh, I will boast also.
19 For you, [a]being *so* wise, bear with the foolish gladly.
20 For you bear with anyone if he [a]enslaves you, if he [b]devours you, if he [c]takes advantage of you, if he [d]exalts himself, if he [e]hits you in the face.
21 To *my* [a]shame I *must* say that we have been [b]weak *by comparison*. But in whatever respect anyone *else* [c]is bold (I [d]speak in foolishness), I am just as bold myself.
22 Are they [a]Hebrews? [b]So am I. Are they [c]Israelites? [c]So am I. Are they [d]descendants of Abraham? [e]So am I.
23 Are they [a]servants of Christ? (I speak as if insane) I more so; in [b]far more labors, in [c]far more imprisonments, [d]beaten times without number, often in [e]danger of death.
24 Five times I received from the Jews [a]thirty-nine *lashes*.
25 Three times I was [a]beaten with rods, once I was [b]stoned, three times I was shipwrecked, a night and a day I have spent in the deep.
26 *I have been* on frequent journeys, in dangers from rivers, dangers from robbers, dangers from *my* [a]countrymen, dangers from the [b]Gentiles, dangers in the [c]city, dangers in the wilderness, dangers on the sea, dangers among [d]false brethren;
27 *I have been* in [a]labor and hardship, through many sleepless nights, in [b]hunger and thirst, often [c]without food, in cold and [d]exposure.
28 Apart from *such* external things, there is the daily pressure upon me *of* concern for [a]all the churches.
29 Who is [a]weak without my being weak? Who is led into sin without my intense concern?
30 If I have to boast, I will boast of what pertains to my [a]weakness.
31 The God and Father of the Lord Jesus, [a]He who is blessed forever, [b]knows that I am not lying.
32 In [a]Damascus the ethnarch under Aretas the king was [b]guarding the city of the Damascenes in order to seize me,
33 and I was let down in a basket [a]through a window in the wall, and *so* escaped his hands.

Chapter 12

Paul's Vision

[a]BOASTING is necessary, though it is not profitable; but I will go on to visions and [b]revelations of the Lord.
2 I know a man [a]in Christ who fourteen years ago—whether in the body I do not know, or out of the body I do not know, [b]God knows—such a man was [c]caught up to the [d]third heaven.
3 And I know how such a man—whether in the body or apart from the body I do not know, [a]God knows—
4 was [a]caught up into [b]Paradise, and heard inexpressible words, which a man is not permitted to speak.
5 [a]On behalf of such a man will I boast; but on my own behalf I will not boast, except in regard to *my* [b]weaknesses.
6 For if I do wish to boast I shall not be [a]foolish, [b]for I shall be speaking the truth; but I refrain *from this*, so that no one may credit me with more than he sees *in* me or hears from me.

A Thorn in the Flesh

7 And because of the surpassing greatness of the [a]revelations, for this reason, to keep me from exalting myself, there was given me a [b]thorn in the flesh, a [c]messenger of Satan to buffet me—to keep me from exalting myself!
8 Concerning this I entreated the Lord [a]three times that it might depart from me.
9 And He has said to me, "My grace is sufficient for you, for [a]power is perfected in weakness." Most gladly, therefore, I will rather [b]boast about my weaknesses, that the power of Christ may dwell in me.
10 Therefore [a]I am well content with weaknesses, with insults, with [b]distresses, with [c]persecutions, with [b]difficulties, [d]for Christ's sake;

14 [a]Matt. 4:10; Eph. 6:12; Col. 1:13 [b]Col. 1:12
15 [a]Rom. 2:6
16 [a]2 Cor. 11:1
17 [a]1 Cor. 7:12, 25 [b]2 Cor. 11:21
18 [a]Phil. 3:3f. [b]2 Cor. 5:16
19 [a]1 Cor. 4:10
20 [a]2 Cor. 1:24 [b]Mark 12:40 [c]Luke 5:5 [d]2 Cor. 10:5 [e]1 Cor. 4:11
21 [a]2 Cor. 6:8 [b]2 Cor. 10:10 [c]2 Cor. 10:2 [d]2 Cor. 11:17
22 [a]Acts 6:1 [b]Phil. 3:5 [c]Rom. 9:4 [d]Gal. 3:16 [e]Rom. 11:1
23 [a]1 Cor. 3:5 [b]1 Cor. 15:10 [c]2 Cor 6:5 [d]Acts 16:23; 2 Cor. 6:5 [e]Rom. 8:36
24 [a]Deut. 25:3
25 [a]Acts 16:22 [b]Acts 14:19
26 [a]Acts 9:23 [b]Acts 14:5, 19 [c]Acts 21:31 [d]Gal. 2:4
27 [a]1 Thess. 2:9 [b]1 Cor. 4:11; Phil. 4:12 [c]2 Cor. 6:5 [d]1 Cor. 4:11
28 [a]1 Cor. 7:17
29 [a]1 Cor. 8:9, 13
30 [a]1 Cor. 2:3
31 [a]Rom. 1:25 [b]2 Cor. 11:11
32 [a]Acts 9:2 [b]Acts 9:24
33 [a]Acts 9:25
1 [a]2 Cor. 11:16, 18, 30; 12:5, 9 [b]1 Cor. 14:6; 2 Cor. 12:7
2 [a]Rom. 16:7 [b]2 Cor. 11:11 [c]Ezek. 8:3; Acts 8:39; 2 Cor. 12:4; 1 Thess. 4:17; Rev. 12:5 [d]Deut. 10:14; Ps. 148:4
3 [a]2 Cor. 11:11
4 [a]Ezek. 8:3; Acts 8:39 [b]Luke 23:43
5 [a]2 Cor. 12:1 [b]1 Cor. 2:3; 2 Cor. 12:9f.
6 [a]2 Cor. 5:13 [b]2 Cor. 7:14
7 [a]2 Cor. 12:1 [b]Num. 33:55; Ezek. 28:24; Hos. 2:6 [c]Job 2:6; Matt. 4:10
8 [a]Matt. 26:44
9 [a]1 Cor. 2:5; Eph. 3:16; Phil. 4:13 [b]1 Cor. 2:3; 2 Cor. 12:5
10 [a]Rom. 5:3; 8:35 [b]2 Cor. 6:4 [c]2 Thess. 1:4 [d]2 Cor. 5:15, 20

for [e]when I am weak, then I am strong.

11 I have become [a]foolish; you yourselves compelled me. Actually I should have been commended by you, for [b]in no respect was I inferior to the most eminent apostles, even though [c]I am a nobody.

12 The [a]signs of a true apostle were performed among you with all perseverance, by signs and wonders and miracles.

13 For in what respect were you treated as inferior to the rest of the churches, except that [a]I myself did not become a burden to you? Forgive me [b]this wrong!

14 Here [a]for this third time I am ready to come to you, and I [b]will not be a burden to you; for I [c]do not seek what is yours, but [d]you; for [e]children are not responsible to save up for *their* parents, but [f]parents for *their* children.

15 And I will [a]most gladly spend and be expended for your souls. If [b]I love you the more, am I to be loved the less?

16 But be that as it may, I [a]did not burden you myself; nevertheless, crafty fellow that I am, I [b]took you in by deceit.

17 [a]Certainly I have not taken advantage of you through any of those whom I have sent to you, have I?

18 I [a]urged [b]Titus *to go,* and sent [c]the brother with him. Titus did not take any advantage of you, did he? Did we not conduct ourselves in the same [d]spirit *and walk* [e]in the same steps?

19 All this time you have been thinking that we are defending ourselves to you. *Actually,* [a]it is in the sight of God that we have been speaking in Christ; and [b]all for your upbuilding, [c]beloved.

20 For I am afraid that perhaps [a]when I come I may find you to be not what I wish and may be found by you to be not what you wish; that perhaps *there may be* [b]strife, jealousy, [c]angry tempers, [d]disputes, [e]slanders, [f]gossip, [g]arrogance, [h]disturbances;

21 I am afraid that when I come again my God may humiliate me before you, and I may mourn over many of those who have [a]sinned in the past and not repented of the [b]impurity, immorality and sensuality which they have practiced.

CHAPTER 13

Examine Yourselves

[a]THIS is the third time I am coming to you. [b]EVERY FACT IS TO BE CONFIRMED BY THE TESTIMONY OF TWO OR THREE WITNESSES.

2 I have previously said when present the second time, and though now absent I say in advance to those who have [a]sinned in the past and to all the rest as well, that [b]if I come again, I will not [c]spare *anyone,*

3 since you are [a]seeking for proof of the [b]Christ who speaks in me, and who is not weak toward you, but [c]mighty in you.

4 For indeed He was [a]crucified because of weakness, yet He lives [b]because of the power of God. For we also are [c]weak [1]in Him, yet [d]we shall live with Him because of the power of God *directed* toward you.

5 [a]Test yourselves *to see* if you are in the faith; [b]examine yourselves! Or do you not recognize this about yourselves, that Jesus Christ is in you—unless indeed you [c]fail the test?

6 But I trust that you will realize that we ourselves do not fail the test.

7 Now we pray to God that you do no wrong; not that we ourselves may appear approved, but that you may do what is right, even though we should appear unapproved.

8 For we can do nothing against the truth, but *only* for the truth.

9 For we rejoice when we ourselves are [a]weak but you are strong; this we also pray for, that you be [b]made complete.

10 For this reason I am writing these things while absent, in order that when present [a]I may not use [b]severity, in accordance with the [c]authority which the Lord gave me, for building up and not for tearing down.

11 [a]Finally, brethren, rejoice, [b]be made complete, be comforted, [c]be like-minded, [d]live in peace; and [e]the God of love and peace shall be with you.

12 [a]Greet one another with a holy kiss.

13 [a]All the saints greet you.

14 [a]The grace of the Lord Jesus Christ, and the [b]love of God, and the [c]fellowship of the Holy Spirit, be with you all.

10 [e]2 Cor. 13:4
11 [a]2 Cor. 5:13 [b]1 Cor. 15:10 [c]1 Cor. 3:7; 13:2
12 [a]John 4:48; Rom. 15:19; 1 Cor. 9:1
13 [a]1 Cor. 9:12 [b]2 Cor. 11:7
14 [a]2 Cor. 1:15; 13:1, 2 [b]1 Cor. 9:12, 18 [c]1 Cor. 10:24, 33 [d]1 Cor. 9:19 [e]1 Cor. 4:14f.; Gal. 4:19 [f]Prov. 19:14
15 [a]Rom. 9:3; 2 Cor. 1:6; Phil. 2:17; Col. 1:24 [b]2 Cor. 11:11
16 [a]2 Cor. 11:9 [b]2 Cor. 11:20
17 [a]2 Cor. 9:5
18 [a]2 Cor. 8:6 [b]2 Cor. 2:13 [c]2 Cor. 8:18 [d]1 Cor. 4:21 [e]Rom. 4:12
19 [a]Rom. 9:1; 2 Cor. 2:17 [b]Rom. 14:19 [c]Heb. 6:9
20 [a]1 Cor. 4:21 [b]1 Cor. 1:11; 3:3 [c]Gal. 5:20 [d]Rom. 2:8; 1 Cor. 11:19 [e]Rom. 1:30; James 4:11; 1 Pet. 2:1 [f]Rom. 1:29 [g]1 Cor. 4:6, 18; 5:2 [h]1 Cor. 14:33
21 [a]2 Cor. 13:2 [b]1 Cor. 6:9, 18
1 [a]2 Cor. 12:14 [b]Deut. 19:15
2 [a]2 Cor. 12:21 [b]1 Cor. 4:21 [c]2 Cor. 1:23; 10:11
3 [a]2 Cor. 10:1, 10 [b]Matt. 10:20 [c]2 Cor. 9:8; 10:4
4 [1]Some early mss. read, *with Him* [a]Phil. 2:7f.; 1 Pet. 3:18 [b]Rom. 1:4 [c]1 Cor. 2:3; 2 Cor. 13:9 [d]Rom. 6:8
5 [a]John 6:6 [b]1 Cor. 11:28 [c]1 Cor. 9:27
9 [a]2 Cor. 12:10; 13:4 [b]1 Cor. 1:10; 2 Cor. 13:11
10 [a]2 Cor. 2:3 [b]Titus 1:13 [c]1 Cor. 5:4
11 [a]1 Thess. 4:1; 2 Thess. 3:1 [b]1 Cor. 1:10 [c]Rom. 12:16 [d]Mark 9:50 [e]Rom. 15:33; Eph. 6:23
12 [a]Rom. 16:16
13 [a]Phil. 4:22
14 [a]Rom. 16:20; 2 Cor. 8:9 [b]Rom. 5:5; Jude 21 [c]Phil. 2:1

THE EPISTLE OF PAUL TO THE

GALATIANS

Introduction

PAUL, [a]an apostle ([b]not *sent* from
men, nor through the agency of
man, but [c]through Jesus Christ, and
God the Father, who [d]raised Him
from the dead),
2 and all [a]the brethren who are
with me, to [b]the churches of Galatia:
3 [a]Grace to you and peace from
God our Father, and the Lord Jesus
Christ,
4 who [a]gave Himself for our sins,
that He might deliver us out of [b]this
present evil age, according to the
will of [c]our God and Father,
5 [a]to whom *be* the glory forevermore. Amen.

Perversion of the Gospel

6 I am amazed that you are [a]so
quickly deserting [b]Him who called
you by the grace of Christ, for a
[c]different gospel;
7 which is *really* not another;
only there are some who are [a]dis-
turbing you, and want to distort the
gospel of Christ.
8 But even though we, or [a]an angel from heaven, should preach to
you a gospel contrary to that which
we have preached to you, let him be
[b]accursed.
9 As we [a]have said before, so I
say again now, [b]if any man is
preaching to you a gospel contrary
to that which you received, let him
be [c]accursed.
10 For am I now [a]seeking the favor
of men, or of God? Or am I striving
to please men? If I were still trying
to please men, I would not be a
[b]bond-servant of Christ.

Paul Defends His Ministry

11 For [a]I would have you know,
brethren, that the gospel which was
preached by me is [b]not according to
man.
12 For [a]I neither received it from
man, nor was I taught it, but *I received it* through a [b]revelation of Jesus Christ.
13 For you have heard of [a]my former manner of life in Judaism, how
I [b]used to persecute [c]the church of
God beyond measure, and [d]tried to
destroy it;
14 and I [a]was advancing in Judaism beyond many of my contempo-
raries among my countrymen, being
more extremely zealous for my [b]an-
cestral traditions.
15 But when He who had set me
apart, *even* from my mother's
womb, and [a]called me through His
grace, was [b]pleased
16 to reveal His Son in me, that I
might [a]preach Him among the Gentiles, [b]I did not immediately consult
with [c]flesh and blood,
17 [a]nor did I go up to Jerusalem to
those who were apostles before me;
but I went away to Arabia, and returned once more to [b]Damascus.
18 Then [a]three years later I went
up [b]to Jerusalem to become acquainted with [c]Cephas, and stayed
with him fifteen days.
19 But I did not see any other of
the apostles except [a]James, the
Lord's brother.
20 (Now in what I am writing to
you, I assure you [a]before God *that* I
am not lying.)
21 Then [a]I went into the regions of
[b]Syria and [c]Cilicia.
22 And I was *still* unknown by
sight to [a]the churches of Judea
which were [b]in Christ;
23 but only, they kept hearing,
"He who once persecuted us is now
preaching [a]the faith which he once
[b]*tried to* destroy."
24 And they [a]were glorifying God
because of me.

CHAPTER 2

The Council at Jerusalem

THEN after an interval of fourteen
years I [a]went up again to Jerusalem
with [b]Barnabas, taking [c]Titus along
also.
2 And it was because of a [a]revela-
tion that I went up; and I submitted
to them the [b]gospel which I preach
among the Gentiles, but I did so in
private to those who were of reputation, for fear that I might be [c]run-
ning, or had run, in vain.
3 But not even [a]Titus who was
with me, though he was a Greek,
was [b]compelled to be circumcised.
4 But *it was* because of the [a]false
brethren who [b]had sneaked in to spy
out our [c]liberty which we have in
Christ Jesus, in order to [d]bring us
into bondage.
5 But we did not yield in subjection to them for even an hour, so

---

1 [a]2 Cor. 1:1 [b]Gal. 1:11f. [c]Acts 9:15; 20:24; Gal. 1:15f. [d]Acts 2:24
2 [a]Phil. 4:21 [b]Acts 16:6
3 [a]Rom. 1:7
4 [a]Matt. 20:28; Rom. 4:25; 1 Cor. 15:3; Gal. 2:20 [b]Matt. 13:22; Rom. 12:2; 2 Cor. 4:4 [c]Phil. 4:20
5 [a]Rom. 11:36
6 [a]Acts 16:6; 18:23; Gal. 4:13 [b]Rom. 8:28; Gal. 1:15; 5:8 [c]2 Cor. 11:4; Gal. 1:7, 11; 2:2
7 [a]Acts 15:24
8 [a]2 Cor. 11:14 [b]Rom. 9:3
9 [a]Acts 18:23 [b]Rom. 16:17 [c]Rom. 9:3
10 [a]1 Cor. 10:33 [b]Rom. 1:1; Phil. 1:1
11 [a]Rom. 2:16 [b]1 Cor. 3:4; 9:8
12 [a]1 Cor. 11:23; Gal. 1:1 [b]1 Cor. 2:10; 2 Cor. 12:1
13 [a]Acts 26:4f. [b]Acts 8:3 [c]1 Cor. 10:32 [d]Acts 9:21
14 [a]Acts 22:3 [b]Jer. 9:14; Matt. 15:2; Mark 7:3; Col. 2:8
15 [a]Gal. 1:6 [b]Is. 49:1, 5; Jer. 1:5
16 [a]Acts 9:15; Gal. 2:9 [b]Acts 9:20 [c]Matt. 16:17
17 [a]Acts 9:19-22 [b]Acts 9:2
18 [a]Acts 9:22f. [b]Acts 9:26f. [c]John 1:42
19 [a]Matt. 12:46
20 [a]Rom. 9:1
21 [a]Acts 9:30 [b]Acts 15:23, 41 [c]Acts 6:9
22 [a]1 Cor. 7:17 [b]Rom. 16:7
23 [a]Acts 6:7; Gal. 6:10 [b]Acts 9:21
24 [a]Matt. 9:8
1 [a]Acts 15:2 [b]Acts 4:36; Gal. 2:9, 13 [c]2 Cor. 2:13; Gal. 2:3
2 [a]Acts 15:2; Gal. 1:12 [b]Gal. 1:6 [c]Rom. 9:16
3 [a]2 Cor. 2:13 [b]Acts 16:3
4 [a]Acts 15:1 [b]2 Pet. 2:1; Jude 4 [c]Gal. 5:1, 13; James 1:25 [d]Rom. 8:15; 2 Cor. 11:20

that [a]the truth of the gospel might remain with you.

6 But from those who were of high [a]reputation (what they were makes no difference to me; [b]God shows no partiality)—well, those who were of reputation contributed nothing to me.

7 But on the contrary, seeing that I had been [a]entrusted with the [b]gospel to the uncircumcised, just as [c]Peter with *the gospel* to the circumcised

8 (for He who effectually worked for Peter in *his* [a]apostleship to the circumcised effectually worked for me also to the Gentiles),

9 and recognizing [a]the grace that had been given to me, [b]James and [c]Cephas and John, who were [d]reputed to be [e]pillars, gave to me and [f]Barnabas the [g]right hand of fellowship, that we might [h]go to the Gentiles, and they to the circumcised.

10 *They* only *asked* us to remember the poor—[a]the very thing I also was eager to do.

Peter (Cephas) Opposed by Paul

11 But when [a]Cephas came to [b]Antioch, I opposed him to his face, because he stood condemned.

12 For prior to the coming of certain men from [a]James, he used to [b]eat with the Gentiles; but when they came, he *began* to withdraw and hold himself aloof, [c]fearing the party of the circumcision.

13 And the rest of the Jews joined him in hypocrisy, with the result that even [a]Barnabas was carried away by their hypocrisy.

14 But when I saw that they [a]were not straightforward about [b]the truth of the gospel, I said to [c]Cephas in the presence of all, "If you, being a Jew, [d]live like the Gentiles and not like the Jews, how *is it that* you compel the Gentiles to live like Jews?[1]

15 "We *are* [a]Jews by nature, and not [b]sinners from among the Gentiles;

16 nevertheless knowing that [a]a man is not justified by the works of the Law but through faith in Christ Jesus, even we have believed in Christ Jesus, that we may be justified by [b]faith in Christ, and not by the works of the Law; since [c]by the works of the Law shall no flesh be justified.

17 "But if, while seeking to be justified in Christ, we ourselves have also been found [a]sinners, is Christ then a minister of sin? [b]May it never be!

18 "For if I rebuild what I have *once* destroyed, I [a]prove myself to be a transgressor.

19 "For through the Law I [a]died to the Law, that I might live to God.

20 "I have been [a]crucified with Christ; and it is no longer I who live, but [b]Christ lives in me; and the *life* which I now live in the flesh I live by faith in [c]the Son of God, who [d]loved me, and [e]delivered Himself up for me.

21 "I do not nullify the grace of God; for [a]if righteousness *comes* through the Law, then Christ died needlessly."

Chapter 3

Faith Brings Righteousness

YOU foolish [a]Galatians, who has bewitched you, before whose eyes Jesus Christ [b]was publicly portrayed *as* crucified?

2 This is the only thing I want to find out from you: did you receive the Spirit by the works of the Law, or by [a]hearing with faith?

3 Are you so foolish? Having begun by the Spirit, are you now being perfected by the flesh?

4 Did you suffer so many things in vain—[a]if indeed it was in vain?

5 Does He then, who [a]provides you with the Spirit and [b]works miracles among you, do it by the works of the Law, or by [c]hearing with faith?

6 Even so [a]Abraham [b]BELIEVED GOD, AND IT WAS RECKONED TO HIM AS RIGHTEOUSNESS.

7 Therefore, be sure that [a]it is those who are of faith that are [b]sons of Abraham.

8 And the Scripture, foreseeing that God would justify the [1]Gentiles by faith, preached the gospel beforehand to Abraham, *saying,* "[a]ALL THE NATIONS SHALL BE BLESSED IN YOU."

9 So then [a]those who are of faith are blessed with Abraham, the believer.

10 For as many as are of the works of the Law are under a curse; for it is written, "[a]CURSED IS EVERY ONE WHO DOES NOT ABIDE BY ALL THINGS WRITTEN IN THE BOOK OF THE LAW, TO PERFORM THEM."

11 Now that [a]no one is justified by the Law before God is evident; for, "[b]THE RIGHTEOUS MAN SHALL LIVE BY FAITH."

5 [a]Gal. 1:6; 2:14; Col. 1:5
6 [a]2 Cor. 11:5; 12:11; Gal. 2:9; 6:3 [b]Acts 10:34
7 [a]1 Cor. 9:17; 1 Thess. 2:4; 1 Tim. 1:11 [b]Acts 9:15; Gal. 1:16 [c]Gal. 1:18; 2:9, 11, 14
8 [a]Acts 1:25
9 [a]Rom. 12:3 [b]Acts 12:17; Gal. 2:12 [c]Luke 22:8; Gal. 1:18; 2:7, 11, 14 [d]2 Cor. 11:5; 12:11; Gal. 2:2, 6; 6:3 [e]1 Tim. 3:15; Rev. 3:12 [f]Acts 4:36; Gal. 2:1, 13 [g]2 Kin. 10:15; Ezra 10:19 [h]Gal. 1:16
10 [a]Acts 24:17
11 [a]Gal. 1:18; 2:6, 9, 14 [b]Acts 11:19; 15:1
12 [a]Acts 12:17; Gal. 2:9 [b]Acts 11:3 [c]Acts 11:2
13 [a]Acts 4:36; Gal. 2:1, 9
14 [1]Some close the direct quotation here, others extend it through v. 21. [a]Heb. 12:13 [b]Gal. 1:6; 2:5; Col. 1:5 [c]Gal. 1:18; 2:7, 9, 11 [d]Acts. 10:28; Gal. 2:12
15 [a]Phil. 3:4f. [b]1 Sam. 15:18; Luke 24:7; 1 Cor. 6:1
16 [a]Acts 13:39; Gal. 3:11 [b]Rom. 9:30 [c]Ps. 143:2; Rom. 3:20
17 [a]Gal. 2:15 [b]Luke 20:16; Gal. 3:21
18 [a]Rom. 3:5 [Gr.]
19 [a]Rom. 6:2; 7:4; 1 Cor. 9:20
20 [a]Rom. 6:6; Gal. 5:24; 6:14 [b]Rom. 8:10 [c]Matt. 4:3 [d]Rom. 8:37 [e]Gal. 1:4
21 [a]Gal. 3:21
1 [a]Gal. 1:2 [b]1 Cor. 1:23; Gal. 5:11
2 [a]Rom. 10:17
4 [a]1 Cor. 15:2
5 [a]2 Cor. 9:10; Phil. 1:19 [b]1 Cor. 12:10 [c]Rom. 10:17
6 [a]Rom. 4:3 [b]Gen. 15:6
7 [a]Gal. 3:9 [b]Luke 19:9; Gal. 6:16
8 [1]Lit., *nations* [a]Gen. 12:3
9 [a]Gal. 3:7
10 [a]Deut. 27:26
11 [a]Gal. 2:16 [b]Hab. 2:4; Rom. 1:17; Heb. 10:38

12 However, the Law is not of
faith; on the contrary, "[a]HE WHO
PRACTICES THEM SHALL LIVE BY
THEM."
13 Christ [a]redeemed us from the
curse of the Law, having become a
curse for us—for it is written,
"[b]CURSED IS EVERY ONE WHO HANGS
ON [c]A TREE"—
14 in order that [a]in Christ Jesus
the blessing of Abraham might
come to the Gentiles, so that we
[b]might receive [c]the promise of the
Spirit through faith.

Intent of the Law

15 [a]Brethren, [b]I speak in terms of
human relations: [c]even though it is
only a man's covenant, yet when it
has been ratified, no one sets it aside
or adds conditions to it.
16 Now the promises were spoken
[a]to Abraham and to his seed. He
does not say, "AND TO SEEDS," as
referring to many, but *rather* to one,
"[b]AND TO YOUR SEED," that is,
Christ.
17 What I am saying is this: the
Law, which came [a]four hundred and
thirty years later, does not invalidate a covenant previously ratified
by God, so as to nullify the promise.
18 For [a]if the inheritance is based
on law, it is no longer based on a
promise; but [b]God has granted it to
Abraham by means of a promise.
19 [a]Why the Law then? It was
added because of transgressions,
having been [b]ordained through angels [c]by the agency of a mediator,
until [d]the seed should come to
whom the promise had been made.
20 Now [a]a mediator is not for one
party only; whereas God is *only* one.
21 Is the Law then contrary to the
promises of God? [a]May it never be!
For [b]if a law had been given which
was able to impart life, then righteousness would indeed have been
based on law.
22 But the Scripture has [a]shut up
all [b]men under sin, that the promise
by faith in Jesus Christ might be giv-
en to those who believe.
23 But before faith came, we were
kept in custody under the law,
[a]being shut up to the faith which
was later to be revealed.
24 Therefore the Law has become
our [a]tutor *to lead us* to Christ, that
[b]we may be justified by faith.
25 But now that faith has come,
we are no longer under a [a]tutor.
26 For you are all [a]sons of God
through faith in [b]Christ Jesus.
27 For all of you who were [a]bap-
tized into Christ have [b]clothed yourselves with Christ.
28 [a]There is neither Jew nor
Greek, there is neither slave nor free
man, there is neither male nor female; for [b]you are all one in [c]Christ
Jesus.
29 And if [a]you belong to Christ,
then you are Abraham's offspring,
heirs according to [b]promise.

CHAPTER 4

Sonship in Christ

NOW I say, as long as the heir is a
child, he does not differ at all from a
slave although he is owner of everything,
2 but he is under guardians and
managers until the date set by the
father.
3 So also we, while we were children, were held [a]in bondage under
the [b]elemental things of the world.
4 But when [a]the fulness of the
time came, God sent forth His Son,
[b]born of a woman, born [c]under the
Law,
5 in order that He might redeem
those who were under the Law, that
we might receive the adoption as
[a]sons.
6 And because you are sons,
[a]God has sent forth the Spirit of His
Son into our hearts, crying, "[b]Abba!
Father!"
7 Therefore you are no longer a
slave, but a son; and [a]if a son, then
an heir through God.
8 However at that time, [a]when
you did not know God, you were
[b]slaves to [c]those which by nature
are no gods.
9 But now that you have come to
know God, or rather to be [a]known
by God, [b]how is it that you turn back
again to the weak and worthless [c]el-
emental things, to which you desire
to be enslaved all over again?
10 You [a]observe days and months
and seasons and years.
11 I fear for you, that perhaps I
have labored [1]over you in vain.
12 I beg of you, [a]brethren, [b]be-
come as *I am,* for I also *have become*
as you *are.* You have done me no
wrong;
13 but you know that it was because of a bodily illness that I
preached the gospel to you the first
time;
14 and that which was a trial to
you in my bodily condition you did
not despise or loathe, but [a]you received me as an angel of God, as
[b]Christ Jesus *Himself.*

12 [a]Lev. 18:5; Rom. 10:5
13 [a]Gal. 4:5 [b]Deut. 21:23 [c]Acts 5:30
14 [a]Rom. 4:9, 16; Gal. 3:28 [b]Gal. 3:2 [c]Acts 2:33; Eph. 1:13
15 [a]Acts 1:15; Rom. 1:13; Gal. 6:18 [b]Rom. 3:5 [c]Heb. 6:16
16 [a]Luke 1:55 [b]Acts 3:25
17 [a]Gen. 15:13f.
18 [a]Rom. 4:14 [b]Heb. 6:14
19 [a]Rom. 5:20 [b]Acts 7:53 [c]Ex. 20:19; Deut. 5:5 [d]Gal. 3:16
20 [a]1 Tim. 2:5; Heb. 8:6; 9:15
21 [a]Luke 20:16; Gal. 2:17 [b]Gal. 2:21
22 [a]Rom. 11:32 [b]1 Cor. 1:27
23 [a]Rom. 11:32
24 [a]1 Cor. 4:15 [b]Gal. 2:16
25 [a]1 Cor. 4:15
26 [a]Rom. 8:14; Gal. 4:5 [b]Rom. 8:1; Gal. 3:28; 4:14; 5:6, 24; Eph. 1:1; Phil. 1:1; Col. 1:4; 1 Tim. 1:12
27 [a]Matt. 28:19; Rom. 6:3; 1 Cor. 10:2 [b]Rom. 13:14
28 [a]Rom. 3:22; 1 Cor. 12:13; Col. 3:11 [b]John 17:11; Eph. 2:15 [c]Rom. 8:1; Gal. 3:26; 4:14; 5:6, 24; Eph. 1:1; Phil. 1:1; Col. 1:4; 1 Tim. 1:12
29 [a]1 Cor. 3:23 [b]Rom. 9:8; Gal. 3:18; 4:28
3 [a]Gal. 2:4; 4:8f., 24f. [b]Gal. 4:9; Col. 2:8, 20; Heb. 5:12
4 [a]Mark 1:15 [b]John 1:14; Rom. 1:3; 8:3; Phil. 2:7 [c]Luke 2:21f., 27
5 [a]Rom. 8:14; Gal. 3:26
6 [a]Acts 16:7; Rom. 5:5; 8:9, 16; 2 Cor. 3:17 [b]Mark 14:36; Rom. 8:15
7 [a]Rom. 8:17
8 [a]1 Cor. 1:21; 1 Thess. 4:5; 2 Thess. 1:8 [b]Gal. 4:3 [c]2 Chr. 13:9; Is. 37:19; Jer. 2:11; 1 Cor. 8:4f.
9 [a]1 Cor. 8:3 [b]Col. 2:20 [c]Gal. 4:3
10 [a]Rom. 14:5
11 [1]Or, *for*
12 [a]Gal. 6:18 [b]2 Cor. 6:11, 13
14 [a]Matt. 10:40; 1 Thess. 2:13 [b]Gal. 3:26

15 Where then is that sense of blessing you had? For I bear you witness, that if possible, you would have plucked out your eyes and given them to me.
16 Have I therefore become your enemy [a]by telling you the truth?
17 They eagerly seek you, not commendably, but they wish to shut you out, in order that you may seek them.
18 But it is good always to be eagerly sought in a commendable manner, and [a]not only when I am present with you.
19 [a]My children, with whom [b]I am again in labor until [c]Christ is formed in you —
20 but I could wish to be present with you now and to change my tone, for [a]I am perplexed about you.

Bond and Free

21 Tell me, you who want to be under law, do you not [a]listen to the law?
22 For it is written that Abraham had two sons, one by the bondwoman and one by the free woman.
23 But [a]the son by the bondwoman was born according to the flesh, and [b]the son by the free woman through the promise.
24 [a]This is allegorically speaking: for these *women* are two covenants, one *proceeding* from [b]Mount Sinai bearing children who are to be [c]slaves; she is Hagar.
25 Now this Hagar is Mount Sinai in Arabia, and corresponds to the present Jerusalem, for she is in slavery with her children.
26 But [a]the Jerusalem above is free; she is our mother.
27 For it is written,

"[a]REJOICE, BARREN WOMAN WHO DOES NOT BEAR;
BREAK FORTH AND SHOUT, YOU WHO ARE NOT IN LABOR;
FOR MORE ARE THE CHILDREN OF THE DESOLATE
THAN OF THE ONE WHO HAS A HUSBAND."

28 And you brethren, [a]like Isaac, are [b]children of promise.
29 But as at that time [a]he who was born according to the flesh [b]persecuted him *who was born* according to the Spirit, [c]so it is now also.
30 But what does the Scripture say?

"[a]CAST OUT THE BONDWOMAN AND HER SON,
FOR [b]THE SON OF THE BONDWOMAN SHALL NOT BE AN HEIR WITH THE SON OF THE FREE WOMAN."

16 [a]Amos 5:10
18 [a]Gal. 4:13f.
19 [a]1 John 2:1 [b]1 Cor. 4:15 [c]Eph. 4:13
20 [a]2 Cor. 4:8
21 [a]Luke 16:29
23 [a]Rom. 9:7; Gal. 4:29 [b]Gen. 17:16ff.; 18:10ff.; 21:1; Gal. 4:28; Heb. 11:11
24 [a]1 Cor. 10:11 [b]Deut. 33:2 [c]Gal. 4:3
26 [a]Heb. 12:22; Rev. 3:12; 21:2, 10
27 [a]Is. 54:1
28 [a]Gal. 4:23 [b]Rom. 9:7ff.; Gal. 3:29
29 [a]Gal. 4:23 [b]Gen. 21:9 [c]Gal. 5:11
30 [a]Gen. 21:10, 12 [b]John 8:35
1 [a]John 8:32, 36; Rom. 8:15; 2 Cor. 3:17; Gal. 2:4; 5:13 [b]1 Cor. 16:13 [c]Acts 15:10; Gal. 2:4
2 [a]2 Cor. 10:1 [b]Acts 15:1; Gal. 5:3, 6, 11
3 [a]Luke 16:28 [b]Acts 15:1; Gal. 5:2, 6, 11 [c]Rom. 2:25
4 [1]Or, *would be* [a]Heb. 12:15; 2 Pet. 3:17
5 [a]Rom. 8:23; 1 Cor. 1:7
6 [a]Gal. 3:26 [b]1 Cor. 7:19; Gal. 6:15 [c]Col. 1:4f.; 1 Thess. 1:3; James 2:18, 20, 22
7 [a]Gal. 2:2
8 [a]Rom. 8:28; Gal. 1:6
9 [a]1 Cor. 5:6
10 [a]2 Cor. 2:3 [b]Gal. 5:7; Phil. 3:15 [c]Gal. 1:7; 5:12
11 [a]Gal. 4:29; 6:12 [b]Rom. 9:33; 1 Cor. 1:23
12 [1]Or, *cut themselves off* [a]Gal. 2:4; 5:10 [b]Deut. 23:1
13 [a]Gal. 5:1 [b]1 Cor. 8:9; 1 Pet. 2:16 [c]1 Cor. 9:19; Eph. 5:21
14 [a]Matt. 7:12; 22:40; Rom. 13:8, 10; Gal. 6:2 [b]Lev. 19:18; Matt. 19:19; John 13:34
15 [a]Gal. 5:20; Phil. 3:2
16 [a]Rom. 8:4; 13:14; Gal. 5:24f. [b]Rom. 13:14; Eph. 2:3
17 [a]Rom. 7:18, 23; 8:5ff.

31 So then, brethren, we are not children of a bondwoman, but of the free woman.

CHAPTER 5

Walk By the Spirit

[a]IT was for freedom that Christ set us free; therefore [b]keep standing firm and do not be subject again to a [c]yoke of slavery.
2 Behold I, [a]Paul, say to you that if you receive [b]circumcision, Christ will be of no benefit to you.
3 And I [a]testify again to every man who receives [b]circumcision, that he is under obligation to [c]keep the whole Law.
4 You have been severed from Christ, you who [1]are seeking to be justified by law; you have [a]fallen from grace.
5 For we through the Spirit, by faith, are [a]waiting for the hope of righteousness.
6 For in [a]Christ Jesus [b]neither circumcision nor uncircumcision means anything, but [c]faith working through love.
7 You were [a]running well; who hindered you from obeying the truth?
8 This persuasion *did* not *come* from [a]Him who calls you.
9 [a]A little leaven leavens the whole lump *of dough.*
10 [a]I have confidence in you in the Lord, that you [b]will adopt no other view; but the one who is [c]disturbing you shall bear his judgment, whoever he is.
11 But I, brethren, if I still preach circumcision, why am I still [a]persecuted? Then [b]the stumbling block of the cross has been abolished.
12 Would that [a]those who are troubling you would even [1b]mutilate themselves.
13 For you were called to [a]freedom, brethren; [b]only *do* not *turn* your freedom into an opportunity for the flesh, but through love [c]serve one another.
14 For [a]the whole Law is fulfilled in one word, in the *statement,* "[b]YOU SHALL LOVE YOUR NEIGHBOR AS YOURSELF."
15 But if you [a]bite and devour one another, take care lest you be consumed by one another.
16 But I say, [a]walk by the Spirit, and you will not carry out [b]the desire of the flesh.
17 For [a]the flesh sets its desire against the Spirit, and the Spirit

against the flesh; for these are in opposition to one another, [b]so that you
may not do the things that you
please.
18 But if you are [a]led by the Spirit,
[b]you are not under the Law.
19 Now the deeds of the flesh are
evident, which are: [a]immorality, impurity, sensuality,
20 idolatry, [a]sorcery, enmities,
[b]strife, jealousy, outbursts of anger,
[c]disputes, dissensions, [d]factions,
21 envyings, [a]drunkenness, carousings, and things like these, of
which I forewarn you just as I have
forewarned you that those who
practice such things shall not [b]in-
herit the kingdom of God.
22 But [a]the fruit of the Spirit is
[b]love, joy, peace, patience, kindness, goodness, faithfulness,
23 gentleness, [a]self-control;
against such things [b]there is no law.
24 Now those who belong to
[a]Christ Jesus have [b]crucified the
flesh with its passions and [c]desires.
25 If we live by the Spirit, let us
also walk [a]by the Spirit.
26 Let us not become [a]boastful,
challenging one another, envying
one another.

Chapter 6

Bear One Another's Burdens

[a]BRETHREN, even if a man is
caught in any trespass, you who are
[b]spiritual, [c]restore such a one [d]in a
spirit of gentleness; *each one* looking to yourself, lest you too be
tempted.
2 [a]Bear one another's burdens,
and thus fulfill [b]the law of Christ.
3 For [a]if anyone thinks he is
something when he is nothing, he
deceives himself.
4 But let each one [a]examine his
own work, and then he will have
reason for [b]boasting in regard to
himself alone, and not in regard to
another.
5 For [a]each one shall bear his
own load.
6 And [a]let the one who is taught
[b]the word share all good things with
him who teaches.
7 [a]Do not be deceived, [b]God is
not mocked; for [c]whatever a man
sows, this he will also reap.
8 [a]For the one who sows to his
own flesh shall from the flesh reap
[b]corruption, but [c]the one who sows
to the Spirit shall from the Spirit
reap eternal life.
9 And [a]let us not lose heart in
doing good, for in due time we shall
reap if we [b]do not grow weary.
10 So then, [a]while we have opportunity, let us do good to all men, and
especially to those who are of the
[b]household of [c]the faith.
11 See with what large letters I am
writing to you [a]with my own hand.
12 Those who desire [a]to make a
good showing in the flesh try to
[b]compel you to be circumcised, simply that they [c]may not be persecuted for the cross of Christ.
13 For those who are circumcised
do not even [a]keep the Law themselves, but they desire to have you
circumcised, that they may [b]boast
in your flesh.
14 But [a]may it never be that I
should boast, [b]except in the cross of
our Lord Jesus Christ, [c]through
which the world has been crucified
to me, and [d]I to the world.
15 For [a]neither is circumcision
anything, nor uncircumcision, but a
[b]new creation.
16 And those who will walk by this
rule, peace and mercy *be* upon
them, and upon the [a]Israel of God.
17 From now on let no one cause
trouble for me, for I bear on my
body the [a]brand-marks of Jesus.
18 [a]The grace of our Lord Jesus
Christ be [b]with your spirit, [c]breth-
ren. Amen.

17 [b]Rom. 7:15ff.
18 [a]Rom. 8:14 [b]Rom. 6:14; 7:4
19 [a]1 Cor. 6:9, 18
20 [a]Rev. 21:8 [b]2 Cor. 12:20 [c]Rom. 2:8 [d]1 Cor. 11:19
21 [a]Rom. 13:13 [b]1 Cor. 6:9
22 [a]Matt. 7:16ff. [b]Rom. 5:1-5
23 [a]Acts 24:25 [b]Gal. 5:18
24 [a]Gal. 3:26 [b]Rom. 6:6 [c]Gal. 5:16f.
25 [a]Gal. 5:16
26 [a]Phil. 2:3
1 [a]Gal. 6:18 [b]1 Cor. 2:15 [c]2 Cor. 2:7 [d]1 Cor. 4:21
2 [a]Rom. 15:1 [b]Rom. 8:2
3 [a]Acts 5:36
4 [a]1 Cor. 11:28 [b]Phil. 1:26
5 [a]Prov. 9:12
6 [a]1 Cor. 9:11, 14 [b]2 Tim. 4:2
7 [a]1 Cor. 6:9 [b]Job 13:9 [c]2 Cor. 9:6
8 [a]Job 4:8 [b]1 Cor. 15:42 [c]Rom. 8:11
9 [a]1 Cor. 15:58; 2 Cor. 4:1 [b]Matt. 10:22; Heb. 12:3
10 [a]Prov. 3:27; John 12:35 [b]Eph. 2:19 [c]Acts 6:7; Gal. 1:23
11 [a]1 Cor. 16:21
12 [a]Matt. 23:27f. [b]Acts 15:1 [c]Gal. 5:11
13 [a]Rom. 2:25 [b]Phil. 3:3
14 [a]Luke 20:16 [in the Gr.]; Gal. 2:17; 3:21 [b]1 Cor. 2:2 [c]Gal. 2:20; Col. 2:20 [d]Rom. 6:2, 6; Gal. 2:19f.
15 [a]Rom. 2:26, 28 [b]2 Cor. 5:17
16 [a]Rom. 9:6
17 [a]Is. 44:5
18 [a]Rom. 16:20 [b]2 Tim. 4:22 [c]Acts 1:15; Rom. 1:13; Gal. 3:15

THE EPISTLE OF PAUL TO THE

EPHESIANS

The Blessings of Redemption

PAUL, [a]an apostle of [b]Christ Jesus
[c]by the will of God, to the [d]saints
who are at Ephesus, and *who are*
faithful in [b]Christ Jesus:
2 [a]Grace to you and peace from
God our Father and the Lord Jesus
Christ.
3 [a]Blessed *be* the God and Father
of our Lord Jesus Christ, who has
blessed us with every spiritual
blessing in [b]the heavenly *places* in
Christ,
4 just as [a]He chose us in Him before [b]the foundation of the world,
that we should be [c]holy and blameless before Him. [d]In love
5 He [a]predestined us to [b]adoption
as sons through Jesus Christ to
Himself, [c]according to the kind intention of His will,
6 [a]to the praise of the glory of His
grace, which He freely bestowed on
us in the Beloved.
7 [a]In Him we have [b]redemption
[c]through His blood, the [d]forgiveness
of our trespasses, according to [e]the
riches of His grace,
8 which He lavished upon us. In
all wisdom and insight
9 He [a]made known to us the mystery of His will, [b]according to His
kind intention which He purposed
in Him
10 with a view to an administration suitable to [a]the fulness of the
times, *that is,* [b]the summing up of
all things in Christ, things in the
heavens and things upon the earth.
In Him
11 also we [a]have obtained an inheritance, having been [b]predestined
[c]according to His purpose who
works all things [d]after the counsel
of His will,
12 to the end that we who were the
first to hope in Christ should be to
the praise of His glory.
13 In Him, you also, after listening
to [a]the message of truth, the gospel
of your salvation—having also believed, you were [b]sealed in Him with
[c]the Holy Spirit of promise,
14 who is [a]given as a pledge of
[b]our inheritance, with a view to the
[c]redemption of [d]*God's own* possession, to the praise of His glory.
15 For this reason I too, [a]having
heard of the faith in the Lord Jesus
which *exists* among you, and your
love for all the saints,
16 [a]do not cease giving thanks for
you, while making mention *of you* in
my prayers;
17 that the [a]God of our Lord Jesus
Christ, [b]the Father of glory, may
give to you a spirit of [c]wisdom and
of revelation in the knowledge of
Him.
18 *I pray that* [a]the eyes of your
heart may be enlightened, so that
you may know what is the [b]hope of
His [c]calling, what are [d]the riches of
the glory of [e]His inheritance in [f]the
saints,
19 and what is the surpassing
greatness of His power toward us
who believe. [a]*These are* in accordance with the working of the
strength of His might
20 which He brought about in
Christ, when He [a]raised Him from
the dead, and [b]seated Him at His
right hand in the heavenly *places,*
21 far above [a]all rule and authority
and power and dominion, and every
[b]name that is named, not only in this
age, but also in the one to come.
22 And He [a]put all things in subjection under His feet, and gave
Him as [b]head over all things to the
church,
23 which is His [a]body, the [b]fulness
of Him who [c]fills all in all.

CHAPTER 2

Made Alive in Christ

AND you were [a]dead in your trespasses and sins,
2 in which you [a]formerly walked
according to the course of [b]this
world, according to [c]the prince of
the power of the air, of the spirit
that is now working in the sons of
disobedience.
3 Among them we too all [a]for-
merly lived in [b]the lusts of our flesh,
indulging the desires of the flesh
and of the mind, and were [c]by nature [d]children of wrath, [e]even as the
rest.
4 But God, being [a]rich in mercy,
because of [b]His great love with
which He loved us,
5 even when we were [a]dead in
our transgressions, made us alive
together [1]with Christ (by grace you
have been saved),

1 [a]2 Cor. 1:1 [b]Rom. 8:1; Gal. 3:26 [c]1 Cor. 1:1 [d]Acts 9:13; Phil. 1:1
2 [a]Rom. 1:7
3 [a]2 Cor. 1:3 [b]Eph. 1:20; 2:6
4 [a]Eph. 2:10 [b]Matt. 25:34 [c]Eph. 5:27 [d]Eph. 4:2, 15, 16
5 [a]Acts 13:48 [b]Rom. 8:14ff. [c]Luke 12:32; 1 Cor. 1:21; Gal. 1:15
6 [a]Eph. 1:12, 14
7 [a]Col. 1:14 [b]Rom. 3:24 [c]Acts 20:28; Rom. 3:25 [d]Acts 2:38 [e]Rom. 2:4; Eph. 1:18; 2:7
9 [a]Rom. 11:25 [b]Luke 12:32; Col. 1:19
10 [a]Mark 1:15 [b]Eph. 3:15; Phil. 2:9f.
11 [a]Deut. 4:20; 9:26 [b]Eph. 1:5 [c]Rom. 8:28f.; Eph. 3:11 [d]Rom. 9:11
13 [a]Acts 13:26 [b]John 3:33 [c]Acts 1:4f.
14 [a]2 Cor. 1:22 [b]Acts 20:32 [c]Eph. 1:7 [d]Eph. 1:11
15 [a]Rom. 1:8
16 [a]Rom. 1:8f.
17 [a]John 20:17 [b]Acts 7:2 [c]Col. 1:9
18 [a]Acts 26:18 [b]Eph. 4:4 [c]Rom. 11:29 [d]Eph. 1:7 [e]Eph. 1:11 [f]Acts 9:13
19 [a]Eph. 3:7
20 [a]Acts 2:24 [b]Mark 16:19
21 [a]Matt. 28:18 [b]John 17:11
22 [a]1 Cor. 15:27 [b]1 Cor. 11:3
23 [a]1 Cor. 12:27 [b]John 1:16; Eph. 3:19 [c]Eph. 4:10
1 [a]Luke 15:24, 32
2 [a]Rom. 13:13 [b]Eph. 1:21 [c]John 12:31; Eph. 6:12
3 [a]Eph. 2:2 [b]Gal. 5:16f. [c]Rom. 2:14 [d]Rom. 5:10 [e]Rom. 5:12, 19
4 [a]Eph. 1:7 [b]John 3:16
5 [1]Or, *in Christ* [a]Eph. 2:1

6 and [a]raised us up with Him, and [b]seated us with Him in [c]the heavenly *places,* in [d]Christ Jesus,

7 in order that in the ages to come He might show the surpassing [a]riches of His grace in kindness toward us in Christ Jesus.

8 For [a]by grace you have been saved [b]through faith; and that not of yourselves, *it is* the gift of God;

9 [a]not as a result of works, that no one should boast.

10 For we are His workmanship, [a]created in [b]Christ Jesus for [c]good works, which God [d]prepared beforehand, that we should [e]walk in them.

11 Therefore remember, that [a]formerly [b]you, the Gentiles in the flesh, who are called "[c]Uncircumcision" by the so-called "[c]Circumcision," *which is* performed in the flesh by human hands—

12 *remember* that you were at that time separate from Christ, [a]excluded from the commonwealth of Israel, and strangers to [b]the covenants of promise, having [c]no hope and [d]without God in the world.

13 But now in [a]Christ Jesus you who [b]formerly were far off have been brought near by the blood of Christ.

14 For He Himself is [a]our peace, who made both *groups into* one, and broke down the barrier of the dividing wall,

15 by [a]abolishing in His flesh the enmity, *which is* [b]the Law of commandments *contained* in ordinances, that in Himself He might [c]make the two into [d]one new man, *thus* establishing [e]peace,

16 and might [a]reconcile them both in [b]one body to God through the cross, by it having put to death the enmity.

17 AND [a]HE CAME AND PREACHED [b]PEACE TO YOU WHO WERE [c]FAR AWAY, AND PEACE TO THOSE WHO WERE [c]NEAR;

18 for through Him we both have [a]our access in [b]one Spirit to [c]the Father.

19 So then you are no longer [a]strangers and aliens, but you are [b]fellow-citizens with the saints, and are of [c]God's household,

20 having been [a]built upon [b]the foundation of [c]the apostles and prophets, [d]Christ Jesus Himself being the [e]corner *stone,*

21 [a]in whom the whole building, being fitted together is growing into [b]a holy temple in the Lord;

22 in whom you also are being [a]built together into a [b]dwelling of God in the Spirit.

CHAPTER 3

Paul's Stewardship

FOR this reason I, Paul, [a]the prisoner of [b]Christ Jesus [c]for the sake of you [d]Gentiles—

2 if indeed you have heard of the [a]stewardship of God's grace which was given to me for you;

3 [a]that [b]by revelation there was [c]made known to me [d]the mystery, [e]as I wrote before in brief.

4 And by referring to this, when you read you can understand [a]my insight into the [b]mystery of Christ,

5 which in other generations was not made known to the sons of men, as it has now been revealed to His holy [a]apostles and prophets in the Spirit;

6 *to be specific,* that the Gentiles are [a]fellow-heirs and [b]fellow-members of the body, and [c]fellow-partakers of the promise in [d]Christ Jesus through the gospel,

7 [a]of which I was made a [b]minister, according to the gift of [c]God's grace which was given to me [d]according to the working of His power.

8 To me, [a]the very least of all saints, this grace was given, to preach to the Gentiles the unfathomable riches of Christ,

9 and to bring to light what is the administration of the [a]mystery which for ages has been [b]hidden in God, [c]who created all things;

10 in order that the manifold [a]wisdom of God might now be [b]made known through the church to the rulers and the authorities in the heavenly *places.*

11 *This was* in [a]accordance with the eternal purpose which He carried out in [b]Christ Jesus our Lord,

12 in whom we have [a]boldness and confident access through faith in Him.

13 Therefore I ask you not to lose heart at my tribulations on your behalf, for they are your glory.

14 For this reason, I bow my knees before the Father,

15 from whom every family in heaven and on earth derives its name,

16 that He would grant you, according to [a]the riches of His glory, to be [b]strengthened with power through His Spirit in the inner man;

17 so that [a]Christ may dwell in your hearts through faith; *and* that

6 [a]Col. 2:12 [b]Eph. 1:20 [c]Eph. 1:3 [d]Eph. 1:1
7 [a]Rom. 2:4
8 [a]Acts 15:11; Eph. 2:5 [b]1 Pet. 1:5
9 [a]Rom. 3:28
10 [a]Col. 3:10 [b]Eph. 1:1; 2:6, 13 [c]Titus 2:14 [d]Eph. 1:4 [e]Eph. 4:1
11 [a]Rom. 13:13 [b]1 Cor. 12:2; Eph. 5:8 [c]Rom. 2:28f.
12 [a]Rom. 9:4 [b]Gal. 3:17 [c]1 Thess. 4:13 [d]Gal. 4:8
13 [a]Eph. 1:1; 2:6, 10 [b]Rom. 13:13
14 [a]Is. 9:6
15 [a]Eph. 2:16; Col. 1:21f. [b]Col. 2:14, 20 [c]Eph. 2:10 [d]Gal. 3:28; Col. 3:10f. [e]Is. 9:6
16 [a]2 Cor. 5:18; Col. 1:20, 22 [b]1 Cor. 10:17
17 [a]Is. 57:19 [b]Acts 10:36 [c]Is. 57:19
18 [a]Rom. 5:2 [b]1 Cor. 12:13 [c]Col. 1:12
19 [a]Eph. 2:12 [b]Phil. 3:20; Heb. 12:22f. [c]Gal. 6:10
20 [a]1 Cor. 3:9 [b]Matt. 16:18 [c]1 Cor. 12:28 [d]1 Cor. 3:11 [e]Luke 20:17
21 [a]Eph. 4:15f.; Col. 2:19 [b]1 Cor. 3:16f.
22 [a]1 Cor. 3:9 [b]Eph. 3:17
1 [a]Acts 23:18; Eph. 4:1 [b]Gal. 5:24 [c]2 Cor. 1:6 [d]Eph. 3:8
2 [a]Eph. 1:10; 3:9; Col. 1:25
3 [a]Acts 22:17, 21; 26:16ff. [b]Gal. 1:12 [c]Eph. 1:9; 3:4, 9 [d]Rom. 11:25; 16:25 [e]Eph. 1:9f.; Heb. 13:22
4 [a]2 Cor. 11:6 [b]Rom. 11:25
5 [a]1 Cor. 12:28
6 [a]Gal. 3:29 [b]Eph. 2:16 [c]Eph. 5:7 [d]Gal. 5:24
7 [a]Col. 1:23, 25 [b]1 Cor. 3:5 [c]Acts 9:15 [d]Eph. 1:19
8 [a]1 Cor. 15:9
9 [a]Rom. 11:25 [b]Col. 3:3 [c]Rev. 4:11
10 [a]Rom. 11:33; 1 Cor. 2:7 [b]Eph. 1:23; 1 Pet. 1:12
11 [a]Eph. 1:11 [b]Gal. 5:24
12 [a]Heb. 4:16; 10:19
16 [a]Eph. 1:18; 3:8 [b]1 Cor. 16:13
17 [a]John 14:23;

you, being [b]rooted and [c]grounded in love,

18 may be able to comprehend with [a]all the saints what is [b]the breadth and length and height and depth,

19 and to know [a]the love of Christ which [b]surpasses knowledge, that you may be [c]filled up to all the [d]fulness of God.

20 [a]Now to Him who is [b]able to do exceeding abundantly beyond all that we ask or think, [c]according to the power that works within us,

21 [a]to Him *be* the glory in the church and in Christ Jesus to all generations forever and ever. Amen.

CHAPTER 4

Unity of the Spirit

I, THEREFORE, [a]the prisoner of the Lord, [b]entreat you to [c]walk in a manner worthy of the [d]calling with which you have been [e]called,

2 with all [a]humility and gentleness, with patience, showing forbearance to one another [b]in love,

3 being diligent to preserve the unity of the Spirit in the [a]bond of peace.

4 *There is* [a]one body and one Spirit, just as also you were called in one [b]hope of your calling;

5 [a]one Lord, one faith, one baptism,

6 one God and Father of all [a]who is over all and through all and in all.

7 But [a]to each one of us [b]grace was given according to the measure of Christ's gift.

8 Therefore it says,

"[a]WHEN HE ASCENDED ON HIGH,
HE [b]LED CAPTIVE A HOST OF CAPTIVES,
AND HE GAVE GIFTS TO MEN."

9 (Now this *expression,* "He [a]ascended," what does it mean except that He also had descended into [b]the lower parts of the earth?

10 He who descended is Himself also He who ascended [a]far above all the heavens, that He might [b]fill all things.)

11 And He [a]gave [b]some *as* apostles, and some *as* prophets, and some *as* [c]evangelists, and some *as* pastors and teachers,

12 [a]for the equipping of the saints for the work of service, to the building up of [b]the body of Christ;

13 until we all attain to [a]the unity of the faith, and of the [b]knowledge of the Son of God, to a [c]mature man, to the measure of the stature which belongs to the [d]fulness of Christ.

14 As a result, we are [a]no longer to be children, [b]tossed here and there by waves, and carried about by every wind of doctrine, by the trickery of men, by [c]craftiness in deceitful scheming;

15 but speaking the truth [a]in love, we are to [b]grow up in all *aspects* into Him, who is the [c]head, *even* Christ,

16 from whom [a]the whole body, being fitted and held together by that which every joint supplies, according to the proper working of each individual part, causes the growth of the body for the building up of itself [b]in love.

The Christian's Walk

17 [a]This I say therefore, and [b]affirm together with the Lord, [c]that you walk no longer just as the Gentiles also walk, in the [d]futility of their mind,

18 being [a]darkened in their understanding, excluded from [b]the life of God, because of the [c]ignorance that is in them, because of the [d]hardness of their heart;

19 and they, having [a]become callous, [b]have given themselves over to [c]sensuality, for the practice of every kind of impurity with greediness.

20 But you did not [a]learn Christ in this way,

21 if indeed you [a]have heard Him and have [b]been taught in Him, just as truth is in Jesus,

22 that, in reference to your former manner of life, you [a]lay aside the [b]old self, which is being corrupted in accordance with the [c]lusts of deceit,

23 and that you be [a]renewed in the spirit of your mind,

24 and [a]put on the [b]new self, which [c]in *the likeness of* God has been created in righteousness and holiness of the truth.

25 Therefore, [a]laying aside falsehood, [b]SPEAK TRUTH, EACH ONE *of you,* WITH HIS NEIGHBOR, for we are [c]members of one another.

26 [a]BE ANGRY, AND *yet* DO NOT SIN; do not let [b]the sun go down on your anger,

27 and do not [a]give the devil an opportunity.

28 Let him who steals steal no longer; but rather [a]let him labor, [b]performing with his own hands what is good, in order that he may have *something* to share with him who has need.

17 [b]1 Cor. 3:6; Col. 2:7 [c]Col. 1:23
18 [a]Eph. 1:15 [b]Job 11:8f.
19 [a]Rom. 8:35, 39 [b]Phil. 4:7 [c]Col. 2:10 [d]Eph. 1:23
20 [a]Rom. 16:25 [b]2 Cor. 9:8 [c]Eph. 3:7
21 [a]Rom. 11:36
1 [a]Eph. 3:1 [b]Rom. 12:1 [c]Eph. 2:10; Col. 1:10 [d]Rom. 11:29 [e]Rom. 8:28f.
2 [a]Col. 3:12f. [b]Eph. 1:4
3 [a]Col. 3:14f.
4 [a]1 Cor. 12:4ff.; Eph. 2:16, 18 [b]Eph. 1:18
5 [a]1 Cor. 8:6
6 [a]Rom. 11:36
7 [a]1 Cor. 12:7, 11 [b]Eph. 3:2
8 [a]Ps. 68:18 [b]Judg. 5:12
9 [a]John 3:13 [b]Ps. 63:9; Is. 44:23
10 [a]Eph. 1:20f.; Heb. 4:14; 7:26; 9:24 [b]Eph. 1:23
11 [a]Eph. 4:8 [b]Acts 13:1; 1 Cor. 12:28 [c]Acts 21:8
12 [a]2 Cor. 13:9 [b]1 Cor. 12:27
13 [a]Eph. 4:3, 5 [b]John 6:69 [c]1 Cor. 14:20; Col. 1:28; Heb. 5:14 [d]John 1:16
14 [a]1 Cor. 14:20 [b]James 1:6; Jude 12 [c]1 Cor. 3:19
15 [a]Eph. 1:4 [b]Eph. 2:21 [c]Eph. 1:22
16 [a]Rom. 12:4f.; 1 Cor. 10:17; Col. 2:19 [b]Eph. 1:4
17 [a]Col. 2:4 [b]Luke 16:28 [c]Eph. 2:2; 4:22 [d]Rom. 1:21; Col. 2:18
18 [a]Rom. 1:21 [b]Eph. 2:1, 12 [c]Acts 3:17; 1 Pet. 1:14 [d]Mark 3:5; Rom. 11:7
19 [a]1 Tim. 4:2 [b]Rom. 1:24 [c]Col. 3:5
20 [a]Matt. 11:29
21 [a]Rom. 10:14; Col. 1:5 [b]Col. 2:7
22 [a]Eph. 4:25, 31 [b]Rom. 6:6 [c]2 Cor. 11:3; Heb. 3:13
23 [a]Rom. 12:2
24 [a]Rom. 13:14 [b]Rom. 6:4; 7:6 [c]Eph. 2:10
25 [a]Eph. 4:22 [b]Zech. 8:16 [c]Rom. 12:5
26 [a]Ps. 4:4 [b]Deut. 24:15
27 [a]Rom. 12:19
28 [a]Acts 20:35 [b]1 Thess. 4:11

29 Let no [a]unwholesome word
proceed from your mouth, but only
such *a word* as is good for [b]edifica-
tion according to the need *of the
moment,* that it may give grace to
those who hear.
30 And [a]do not grieve the Holy
Spirit of God, by whom you were
[b]sealed for the day of redemption.
31 [a]Let all bitterness and wrath
and anger and clamor and slander
be [b]put away from you, along with
all [c]malice.
32 And [a]be kind to one another,
tender-hearted, forgiving each other, [b]just as God in Christ also has
forgiven [1]you.

Chapter 5

Be Imitators of God

[a]THEREFORE be imitators of God,
as beloved children;
2 and [a]walk in love, just as Christ
also [b]loved [1]you, and [c]gave Himself
up for us, an [d]offering and a sacrifice
to God as a [e]fragrant aroma.
3 But do not let [a]immorality or
any impurity or greed even be
named among you, as is proper
among saints;
4 and *there must be no* [a]filthiness
and silly talk, or coarse jesting,
which [b]are not fitting, but rather
[c]giving of thanks.
5 For this you know with certainty, that [a]no immoral or impure
person or covetous man, who is an
idolater, has an inheritance in the
kingdom [b]of Christ and God.
6 [a]Let no one deceive you with
empty words, for because of these
things [b]the wrath of God comes
upon [c]the sons of disobedience.
7 Therefore do not be [a]partakers
with them;
8 for [a]you were formerly [b]dark-
ness, but now you are light in the
Lord; walk as [c]children of light
9 (for [a]the fruit of the light *consists* in all [b]goodness and righteousness and truth),
10 [a]trying to learn what is pleasing
to the Lord.
11 And [a]do not participate in the
unfruitful [b]deeds of [c]darkness, but
instead even [d]expose them;
12 for it is disgraceful even to
speak of the things which are done
by them in secret.
13 But all things become visible
[a]when they are exposed by the light,
for everything that becomes visible
is light.
14 For this reason [a]it says,
"[b]AWAKE, SLEEPER,
AND ARISE FROM [c]THE DEAD,
AND CHRIST [d]WILL SHINE ON
YOU."
15 Therefore be careful how you
[a]walk, not [b]as unwise men, but as
wise,
16 [a]making the most of your time,
because [b]the days are evil.
17 So then do not be foolish, but
[a]understand what the will of the
Lord is.
18 And [a]do not get drunk with
wine, for that is [b]dissipation, but be
[c]filled with the Spirit,
19 [a]speaking to one another in
[b]psalms and [c]hymns and spiritual
[d]songs, [e]singing and making melody
with your heart to the Lord;
20 [a]always giving thanks for all
things in the name of our Lord Jesus
Christ to [b]God, even the Father;
21 [a]and be subject to one another
in the [b]fear of Christ.

Marriage Like Christ and the Church

22 [a]Wives, [b]*be subject* to your own
husbands, [c]as to the Lord.
23 For [a]the husband is the head of
the wife, as Christ also is the [b]head
of the church, He Himself [c]*being* the
Savior of the body.
24 But as the church is subject to
Christ, so also the wives *ought to be*
to their husbands in everything.
25 [a]Husbands, love your wives,
just as Christ also loved the church
and [b]gave Himself up for her;
26 [a]that He might sanctify her,
having [b]cleansed her by the [c]wash-
ing of water with [d]the word,
27 that He might [a]present to Himself the church in all her glory, having no spot or wrinkle or any such
thing; but that she should be [b]holy
and blameless.
28 So husbands ought also to [a]love
their own wives as their own bodies.
He who loves his own wife loves
himself;
29 for no one ever hated his own
flesh, but nourishes and cherishes it,
just as Christ also *does* the church,
30 because we are [a]members of
His [b]body.
31 [a]FOR THIS CAUSE A MAN SHALL
LEAVE HIS FATHER AND MOTHER, AND
SHALL CLEAVE TO HIS WIFE; AND THE
TWO SHALL BECOME ONE FLESH.
32 This mystery is great; but I am
speaking with reference to Christ
and the church.
33 Nevertheless let each individual among you also [a]love his own

---

29 [a]Matt. 12:34; Eph. 5:4; Col. 3:8 [b]Eccl. 10:12
30 [a]Is. 63:10 [b]John 3:33
31 [a]Rom. 3:14; Col. 3:8, 19 [b]Eph. 4:22 [c]1 Pet. 2:1
32 [1]Or, *us* [a]1 Cor. 13:4; Col. 3:12f.; 1 Pet. 3:8 [b]Matt. 6:14f.
1 [a]Matt. 5:48
2 [1]Or, *us* [a]Rom. 14:15; Col. 3:14 [b]John 13:34; Rom. 8:37 [c]John 6:51; Rom. 4:25 [d]Heb. 7:27 [e]Ex. 29:18, 25
3 [a]Col. 3:5
4 [a]Matt. 12:34 [b]Rom. 1:28 [c]Eph. 5:20
5 [a]1 Cor. 6:9; Col. 3:5 [b]Col. 1:13
6 [a]Col. 2:8 [b]Rom. 1:18; Col. 3:6 [c]Eph. 2:2; Col. 3:6
7 [a]Eph. 3:6
8 [a]Eph. 2:2 [b]Acts 26:18; Col. 1:12f. [c]Luke 16:8
9 [a]Gal. 5:22 [b]Rom. 15:14
10 [a]Rom. 12:2
11 [a]1 Cor. 5:9; 2 Cor. 6:14 [b]Rom. 13:12 [c]Acts 26:18; Col. 1:12f. [d]1 Tim. 5:20
13 [a]John 3:20f.
14 [a]Is. 26:19 [b]Rom. 13:11 [c]Eph. 2:1 [d]Luke 1:78f.
15 [a]Eph. 5:2 [b]Col. 4:5
16 [a]Col. 4:5 [b]Gal. 1:4; Eph. 6:13
17 [a]Rom. 12:2
18 [a]Prov. 20:1 [b]Titus 1:6; 1 Pet. 4:4 [c]Luke 1:15
19 [a]Col. 3:16; James 5:13 [b]1 Cor. 14:26 [c]Acts 16:25 [d]Rev. 5:9 [e]1 Cor. 14:15
20 [a]Rom. 1:8 [b]1 Cor. 15:24
21 [a]Gal. 5:13 [b]2 Cor. 5:11
22 [a]Eph. 5:22 [b]1 Cor. 14:34f. [c]Eph. 6:5
23 [a]1 Cor. 11:3 [b]Eph. 1:22 [c]1 Cor. 6:13
25 [a]Eph. 5:28 [b]Eph. 5:2
26 [a]Heb. 10:10; Titus 2:14 [b]2 Pet. 1:9 [c]Acts 22:16 [d]John 15:3
27 [a]2 Cor. 4:14; 11:2; Col. 1:22 [b]Eph. 1:4
28 [a]Eph. 5:25
30 [a]1 Cor. 6:15; 12:27 [b]Eph. 1:23
31 [a]Gen. 2:24
33 [a]Eph. 5:25, 28

wife even as himself; and *let* the
wife *see to it* that she [b]respect her
husband.

CHAPTER 6

Family Relationships

[a]CHILDREN, obey your parents in
the Lord, for this is right.
2 [a]HONOR YOUR FATHER AND
MOTHER (which is the first commandment with a promise),
3 [a]THAT IT MAY BE WELL WITH
YOU, AND THAT YOU MAY LIVE LONG
ON THE EARTH.
4 And, [a]fathers, do not provoke
your children to anger; but [b]bring
them up in the discipline and instruction of the Lord.
5 [a]Slaves, be obedient to those
who are your masters according to
the flesh, with [b]fear and trembling,
in the sincerity of your heart, [c]as to
Christ;
6 [a]not by way of eyeservice, as
[b]men-pleasers, but as [c]slaves of
Christ, doing the will of God from
the heart.
7 With good will render service,
[a]as to the Lord, and not to men,
8 [a]knowing that [b]whatever good
thing each one does, this he will receive back from the Lord, [c]whether
slave or free.
9 And, masters, do the same
things to them, and [a]give up threatening, knowing that [b]both their
Master and yours is in heaven, and
there is [c]no partiality with Him.

The Armor of God

10 Finally, [a]be strong in the Lord,
and in [b]the strength of His might.
11 [a]Put on the full armor of God,
that you may be able to stand firm
against the [b]schemes of the devil.
12 For our [a]struggle is not against
[b]flesh and blood, but [c]against the
rulers, against the powers, against
the [d]world forces of this [e]darkness,
against the [f]spiritual *forces* of wickedness in the heavenly *places*.
13 Therefore, take up [a]the full armor of God, that you may be able to
[b]resist in [c]the evil day, and having
done everything, to stand firm.
14 Stand firm therefore, [a]HAVING
GIRDED YOUR LOINS WITH TRUTH,
and HAVING [b]PUT ON THE [c]BREAST-
PLATE OF RIGHTEOUSNESS,
15 and having [a]shod YOUR FEET
WITH THE PREPARATION OF THE GOS-
PEL OF PEACE;
16 in addition to all, taking up the
[a]shield of faith with which you will
be able to extinguish all the [b]flaming
missiles of [c]the evil *one*.
17 And take the [a]HELMET OF SAL-
VATION, and the [b]sword of the Spirit,
which is [c]the word of God.
18 With all [a]prayer and petition
[b]pray at all times [c]in the Spirit, and
with this in view, [d]be on the alert
with all perseverance and petition
for all the saints,
19 and [a]*pray* on my behalf, that utterance may be given to me [b]in the
opening of my mouth, to make
known with [c]boldness the mystery
of the gospel,
20 for which I am an [a]ambassador
[b]in chains; that in *proclaiming* it I
may speak [c]boldly, as I ought to
speak.
21 [a]But that you also may know
about my circumstances, how I am
doing, [b]Tychicus, [c]the beloved
brother and faithful minister in the
Lord, will make everything known
to you.
22 And [a]I have sent him to you for
this very purpose, so that you may
know about us, and that he may
[b]comfort your hearts.
23 [a]Peace be to the brethren, and
[b]love with faith, from God the Father and the Lord Jesus Christ.
24 Grace be with all those who
love our Lord Jesus Christ with *a
love* incorruptible.

33 [b]1 Pet. 3:2, 5f.
1 [a]Prov. 6:20
2 [a]Ex. 20:12
3 [a]Ex. 20:12
4 [a]Col. 3:21 [b]Gen. 18:19
5 [a]Col. 3:22 [b]1 Cor. 2:3 [c]Eph. 5:22
6 [a]Col. 3:22 [b]Gal. 1:10 [c]1 Cor. 7:22
7 [a]Col. 3:23
8 [a]Col. 3:24 [b]Matt. 16:27 [c]1 Cor. 12:13; Col. 3:11
9 [a]Lev. 25:43 [b]Job 31:13ff.; John 13:13 [c]Acts 10:34; Col. 3:25
10 [a]1 Cor. 16:13; 2 Tim. 2:1 [b]Eph. 1:19
11 [a]Rom. 13:12; Eph. 6:13 [b]Eph. 4:14
12 [a]1 Cor. 9:25 [b]Matt. 16:17 [c]Eph. 1:21; 2:2; 3.10 [d]John 12:31 [e]Acts 26:18; Col. 1:13 [f]Eph. 3:10
13 [a]Eph. 6:11 [b]James 4:7 [c]Eph. 5:16
14 [a]Is. 11:5 [b]Rom. 13:12; Eph. 6:13 [c]Is. 59:17; 1 Thess. 5:8
15 [a]Is. 52:7
16 [a]1 Thess. 5:8 [b]Ps. 7:13; 120:4 [c]Matt. 5:37
17 [a]Is. 59:17 [b]Is. 49:2 [c]Eph. 5:26; Heb. 6:5
18 [a]Phil. 4:6 [b]Luke 18:1; Col. 1:3; 4:2 [c]Rom. 8:26f. [d]Mark 13:33
19 [a]Col. 4:3 [b]2 Cor. 6:11 [c]2 Cor. 3:12
20 [a]2 Cor. 5:20 [b]Acts 21:33 [c]2 Cor. 3:12
21 [a]Eph. 6:21 [b]Acts 20:4 [c]Col. 4:7
22 [a]Col. 4:8 [b]Col. 2:2; 4:8
23 [a]Rom. 15:33 [b]Gal. 5:6

THE EPISTLE OF PAUL TO THE
PHILIPPIANS

Thanksgiving

[a]Paul and [b]Timothy, [c]bond-servants of [d]Christ Jesus, to [e]all the [f]saints in Christ Jesus who are in [g]Philippi, including the [h]overseers and [i]deacons:

2 [a]Grace to you and peace from God our Father and the Lord Jesus Christ.

3 [a]I thank my God in all my remembrance of you,

4 always offering prayer with joy in [a]my every prayer for you all,

5 in view of your [a]participation in the [b]gospel [c]from the first day until now.

6 *For I am* confident of this very thing, that He who began a good work in you will perfect it until [a]the day of Christ Jesus.

7 For [a]it is only right for me to feel this way about you all, because I [b]have you in my heart, since both in my [c]imprisonment and in the [d]defense and confirmation of the [e]gospel, you all are partakers of grace with me.

8 For [a]God is my witness, how I long for you all with the affection of [b]Christ Jesus.

9 And this I pray, that [a]your love may abound still more and more in [b]real knowledge and all discernment,

10 so that you may [a]approve the things that are excellent, in order to be sincere and blameless until [b]the day of Christ;

11 having been filled with the [a]fruit of righteousness which *comes* through Jesus Christ, to the glory and praise of God.

The Gospel Is Preached

12 Now I want you to know, brethren, that my circumstances [a]have turned out for the greater progress of the [b]gospel,

13 so that my [a]imprisonment in *the cause of* Christ has become well known throughout the whole praetorian guard and to [b]everyone else,

14 and that most of the brethren, trusting in the Lord because of my [a]imprisonment, have [b]far more courage to speak the word of God without fear.

15 [a]Some, to be sure, are preaching Christ even from envy and strife, but some also from good will;

16 [1]the latter *do it* out of love, knowing that I am [a]appointed for the defense of the [b]gospel;

17 the former proclaim Christ [a]out of selfish ambition, rather than from pure motives, thinking to cause me distress in my [b]imprisonment.

18 What then? Only that in every way, whether in pretense or in truth, Christ is proclaimed; and in this I rejoice, yes, and I will rejoice.

19 For I know that this shall turn out for my deliverance [a]through your prayers and the provision of [b]the Spirit of Jesus Christ,

20 according to my [a]earnest expectation and [b]hope, that I shall not be put to shame in anything, but *that* with [c]all boldness, Christ shall even now, as always, be [d]exalted in my body, [e]whether by life or by death.

To Live Is Christ

21 For to me, [a]to live is Christ, and to die is gain.

22 But if *I am* to live *on* in the flesh, this *will mean* [a]fruitful labor for me; and I do not know which to choose.

23 But I am hard-pressed from both *directions,* having the [a]desire to depart and [b]be with Christ, for *that* is very much better;

24 yet to remain on in the flesh is more necessary for your sake.

25 And [a]convinced of this, I know that I shall remain and continue with you all for your progress and joy in the faith,

26 so that your [a]proud confidence in me may abound in Christ Jesus through my coming to you again.

27 Only conduct yourselves in a manner [a]worthy of the [b]gospel of Christ; so that whether I come and see you or remain absent, I may hear of you that you are [c]standing firm in [d]one spirit, with one mind [e]striving together for the faith of the gospel;

28 in no way alarmed by *your* opponents—which is a [a]sign of destruction for them, but of salvation for you, and that *too,* from God.

29 For to you [a]it has been granted for Christ's sake, not only to believe in Him, but also to [b]suffer for His sake,

30 experiencing the same [a]conflict

---

1 [a]2 Cor. 1:1; Col. 1:1; 1 Thess. 1:1; Philem. 1 [b]Acts 16:1 [c]Rom. 1:1; Gal. 1:10 [d]Gal. 3:26; Phil. 1:8; 2:5 [e]2 Cor. 1:1; Col. 1:2 [f]Acts 9:13 [g]Acts 16:12 [h]Acts 20:28 [i]1 Tim. 3:8ff.
2 [a]Rom. 1:7
3 [a]Rom. 1:8
4 [a]Rom. 1:9
5 [a]Acts 2:42; Phil. 4:15 [b]Phil. 1:7, 12 [c]Acts 16:12-40
6 [a]1 Cor. 1:8
7 [a]2 Pet. 1:13 [b]2 Cor. 7:3 [c]Acts 21:33; Eph. 6:20 [d]Phil. 1:16 [e]Phil. 1:5, 12, 16, 27
8 [a]Rom. 1:9 [b]Gal. 3:26; Phil. 1:1; 2:5
9 [a]1 Thess. 3:12 [b]Col. 1:9
10 [a]Rom. 2:18 [b]1 Cor. 1:8
11 [a]James 3:18
12 [a]Luke 21:13 [b]Phil. 1:5, 7, 16
13 [a]Phil. 1:7; 2 Tim. 2:9 [b]Acts 28:30
14 [a]Phil. 1:7; 2 Tim. 2:9 [b]Acts 4:31; 2 Cor. 3:12; 7:4
15 [a]2 Cor. 11:13
16 [1]Some later mss. reverse the order of vs. 16 and 17 [a]1 Cor. 9:17 [b]Phil. 1:5, 7, 12, 27
17 [a]Rom. 2:8; Phil. 2:3 [b]Phil. 1:7
19 [a]2 Cor. 1:11 [b]Acts 16:7
20 [a]Rom. 8:19 [b]Rom. 5:5; 1 Pet. 4:16 [c]Acts 4:31; 2 Cor. 3:12; 7:4; Phil. 1:14 [d]1 Cor. 6:20 [e]Rom. 14:8
21 [a]Gal. 2:20
22 [a]Rom. 1:13
23 [a]2 Cor. 5:8; 2 Tim. 4:6 [b]John 12:26
25 [a]Phil. 2:24
26 [a]2 Cor. 5:12
27 [a]Eph. 4:1 [b]Phil. 1:5 [c]1 Cor. 16:13; Phil. 4:1 [d]Acts 4:32 [e]Jude 3
28 [a]2 Thess. 1:5
29 [a]Matt. 5:12 [b]Acts 14:22
30 [a]Col. 1:29; 2:1; 1 Thess. 2:2; 2 Tim. 4:7; Heb. 10:32; 12:1 [Gr.]

which [b]you saw in me, and now hear
to be in me.

CHAPTER 2

Be Like Christ

IF therefore there is any encouragement in Christ, if there is any
consolation of love, if there is any
[a]fellowship of the Spirit, if any [b]af-
fection and compassion,
2 [a]make my joy complete by
[b]being of the same mind, maintain-
ing the same love, united in spirit,
intent on one purpose.
3 Do nothing from [a]selfishness or
[b]empty conceit, but with humility of
mind let [c]each of you regard one another as more important than himself;
4 [a]do not *merely* look out for your
own personal interests, but also for
the interests of others.
5 [a]Have this attitude in yourselves which was also in [b]Christ Jesus,
6 who, although He [a]existed in
the [b]form of God, [c]did not regard
equality with God a thing to be
grasped,
7 but [a]emptied Himself, taking
the form of a [b]bond-servant, *and*
[c]being made in the likeness of men.
8 And being found in appearance
as a man, [a]He humbled Himself by
becoming [b]obedient to the point of
death, even [c]death on a cross.
9 [a]Therefore also God [b]highly exalted Him, and bestowed on Him
[c]the name which is above every
name,
10 that at the name of Jesus [a]every
knee should bow, of [b]those who are
in heaven, and on earth, and under
the earth,
11 and that every tongue should
confess that Jesus Christ is [a]Lord, to
the glory of God the Father.
12 So then, my beloved, [a]just as
you have always obeyed, not as in
my presence only, but now much
more in my absence, work out your
[b]salvation with [c]fear and trembling;
13 for it is [a]God who is at work in
you, both to will and to work [b]for
His good pleasure.
14 Do all things without [a]grum-
bling or disputing;
15 that you may prove yourselves
to be [a]blameless and innocent, [b]chil-
dren of God above reproach in the
midst of a [c]crooked and perverse
generation, among whom you [d]ap-
pear as [e]lights in the world,
16 holding fast the word of life, so
that in [a]the day of Christ I may have

30 [b]Acts 16:19-40; Phil. 1:13
1 [a]2 Cor. 13:14 [Gr.] [b]Col. 3:12
2 [a]John 3:29 [b]Rom. 12:16; Phil. 4:2
3 [a]Rom. 2:8; Phil. 1:17 [b]Gal. 5:26 [c]Rom. 12:10; Eph. 5:21
4 [a]Rom. 15:1f.
5 [a]Matt. 11:29; Rom. 15:3 [b]Phil. 1:1
6 [a]John 1:1 [b]2 Cor. 4:4 [c]John 5:18; 10:33; 14:28
7 [a]2 Cor. 8:9 [b]Matt. 20:28 [c]John 1:14; Rom. 8:3; Gal. 4:4; Heb. 2:17
8 [a]2 Cor. 8:9 [b]Matt. 26:39; John 10:18; Rom. 5:19; Heb. 5:8 [c]Heb. 12:2
9 [a]Heb. 1:9 [b]Matt. 28:18; Acts 2:33; Heb. 2:9 [c]Eph. 1:21
10 [a]Rom. 14:11 [b]Eph. 1:10
11 [a]John 13:13
12 [a]Phil. 1:5, 6; 4:15 [b]Heb. 5:9 [c]2 Cor. 7:15
13 [a]Rom. 12:3; 1 Cor. 12:6; 15:10; Heb. 13:21 [b]Eph. 1:5
14 [a]1 Cor. 10:10
15 [a]Luke 1:6; Phil. 3:6 [b]Matt. 5:45; Eph. 5:1 [c]Acts 2:40 [d]Matt. 24:27 [e]Gen. 1:16
16 [a]Phil. 1:6 [b]Gal. 2:2 [c]Is. 49:4; Gal. 4:11; 1 Thess. 3:5
17 [a]2 Cor. 12:15; 2 Tim. 4:6 [b]Num. 28:6, 7; Rom. 15:16
19 [a]Phil. 2:23 [b]Phil. 1:1
20 [a]1 Cor. 16:10; 2 Tim. 3:10
21 [a]1 Cor. 10:24; 13:5; Phil. 2:4
22 [a]Rom. 5:4 [Gr.] [b]1 Cor. 16:10; 2 Tim. 3:10 [c]1 Cor. 4:17
23 [a]Phil. 2:19
24 [a]Phil. 1:25
25 [a]Phil. 4:18 [b]Rom. 16:3, 9, 21; Phil. 4:3; Philem. 1, 24 [c]Philem. 2 [d]John 13:16; 2 Cor. 8:23 [e]Phil. 4:18
29 [a]Rom. 16:2 [b]1 Cor. 16:18
30 [a]Acts 20:24 [b]1 Cor. 16:17; Phil. 4:10
1 [a]Phil. 2:18; 4:4

cause to glory because I did not [b]run
in vain nor [c]toil in vain.
17 But even if I am being [a]poured
out as a drink offering upon [b]the
sacrifice and service of your faith, I
rejoice and share my joy with you
all.
18 And you too, *I urge you,* rejoice
in the same way and share your joy
with me.

Timothy and Epaphroditus

19 But I hope in the Lord Jesus to
[a]send [b]Timothy to you shortly, so
that I also may be encouraged when
I learn of your condition.
20 For I have no one *else* [a]of kindred spirit who will genuinely be
concerned for your welfare.
21 For they all [a]seek after their
own interests, not those of Christ
Jesus.
22 But you know [a]of his proven
worth that [b]he served with me in the
furtherance of the gospel [c]like a
child *serving* his father.
23 [a]Therefore I hope to send him
immediately, as soon as I see how
things go with me;
24 and [a]I trust in the Lord that I
myself also shall be coming shortly.
25 But I thought it necessary to
send to you [a]Epaphroditus, my
brother and [b]fellow-worker and
[c]fellow-soldier, who is also your
[d]messenger and [e]minister to my
need;
26 because he was longing for you
all and was distressed because you
had heard that he was sick.
27 For indeed he was sick to the
point of death, but God had mercy
on him, and not on him only but also
on me, lest I should have sorrow
upon sorrow.
28 Therefore I have sent him all
the more eagerly in order that when
you see him again you may rejoice
and I may be less concerned *about
you.*
29 Therefore [a]receive him in the
Lord with all joy, and [b]hold men like
him in high regard;
30 because he came close to death
[a]for the work of Christ, risking his
life to [b]complete what was deficient
in your service to me.

CHAPTER 3

The Goal of Life

FINALLY, my brethren, [a]rejoice in
the Lord. To write the same things
again is no trouble to me, and it is a
safeguard for you.

2 Beware of the [a]dogs, beware of
the [b]evil workers, beware of the
false circumcision;
3 for [a]we are the *true* circumcision, who [b]worship in the Spirit of
God and [c]glory in [d]Christ Jesus and
put no confidence in the flesh,
4 although [a]I myself might have
confidence even in the flesh. If anyone else has a mind to put confidence in the flesh, I far more:
5 [a]circumcised the eighth day, of
the [b]nation of Israel, of the [c]tribe of
Benjamin, a [b]Hebrew of Hebrews;
as to the Law, [d]a Pharisee;
6 as to zeal, [a]a persecutor of the
church; as to the [b]righteousness
which is in the Law, found [c]blame-
less.
7 But [a]whatever things were gain
to me, those things I have counted
as loss for the sake of Christ.
8 More than that, I count all
things to be loss in view of the surpassing value of [a]knowing [b]Christ
Jesus my Lord, for whom I have suffered the loss of all things, and
count them but rubbish in order that
I may gain Christ,
9 and may be found in Him, not
having [a]a righteousness of my own
derived from *the* Law, but that
which is through faith in Christ, [b]the
righteousness which *comes* from
God on the basis of faith,
10 that I may [a]know Him, and [b]the
power of His resurrection and [c]the
fellowship of His sufferings, being
[d]conformed to His death;
11 in order that I may [a]attain to
the resurrection from the dead.
12 Not that I have already [a]ob-
tained *it,* or have already [b]become
perfect, but I press on in order that
I may [c]lay hold of that for which
also I [d]was laid hold of by Christ
Jesus.
13 Brethren, I do not regard myself as having laid hold of *it* yet; but
one thing *I do:* [a]forgetting what *lies*
behind and reaching forward to
what *lies* ahead,
14 I [a]press on toward the goal for
the prize of the [b]upward call of God
in [c]Christ Jesus.
15 Let us therefore, as many as are
[a]perfect, have this attitude; and if in
anything you have a [b]different attitude, [c]God will reveal that also to
you;
16 however, let us keep [a]living by
that same *standard* to which we
have attained.
17 Brethren, [a]join in following my
example, and observe those who
walk according to the [b]pattern you
have in us.

2 [a]Ps. 22:16, 20 [b]2 Cor. 11:13
3 [a]Rom. 2:29; 9:6; Gal. 6:15 [b]Gal. 5:25 [c]Rom. 15:17; Gal. 6:14 [d]Rom. 8:39; Phil. 1:1
4 [a]2 Cor. 5:16
5 [a]Luke 1:59 [b]Rom. 11:1; 2 Cor. 11:22 [c]Rom. 11:1 [d]Acts 22:3
6 [a]Acts 8:3 [b]Phil. 3:9 [c]Phil. 2:15
7 [a]Luke 14:33
8 [a]Jer. 9:23f.; John 17:3; Eph. 4:13 [b]Rom. 8:39
9 [a]Rom. 10:5; Phil. 3:6 [b]Rom. 9:30; 1 Cor. 1:30
10 [a]Jer. 9:23f.; John 17:3; Eph. 4:13 [b]Rom. 6:5 [c]Rom. 8:17 [d]Rom. 6:5; 8:36
11 [a]Acts 26:7
12 [a]1 Cor. 9:24f. [b]1 Cor. 13:10 [c]1 Tim. 6:12, 19 [d]Acts 9:5f.
13 [a]Luke 9:62
14 [a]1 Cor. 9:24; Heb. 6:1 [b]Rom. 8:28; 11:29; 2 Tim. 1:9 [c]Phil. 3:3
15 [a]Matt. 5:48; 1 Cor. 2:6 [b]Gal. 5:10 [c]John 6:45
16 [a]Gal. 6:16
17 [a]1 Cor. 4:16; Phil. 4:9 [b]1 Pet. 5:3
18 [a]2 Cor. 11:13 [b]Acts 20:31 [c]Gal. 6:14
19 [a]Rom. 16:18; Titus 1:12 [b]Rom. 6:21; Jude 13 [c]Rom. 8:5f.; Col. 3:2
20 [a]Eph. 2:19; Phil. 1:27; Col. 3:1 [b]1 Cor. 1:7
21 [a]1 Cor. 15:43-53 [b]Rom. 8:29; Col. 3:4 [c]1 Cor. 15:43, 49 [d]Eph. 1:19 [e]1 Cor. 15:28
1 [a]Phil. 1:8 [b]1 Cor. 16:13; Phil. 1:27
2 [a]Phil. 2:2
3 [a]Phil. 2:25 [b]Luke 10:20
4 [a]Phil. 3:1
5 [a]1 Cor. 16:22 marg.; Heb. 10:37
6 [a]Matt. 6:25 [b]Eph. 6:18
7 [a]Is. 26:3 [b]Phil. 3:19 [c]1 Pet. 1:5 [d]2 Cor. 10:5 [e]Phil. 1:1; 4:19, 21
8 [a]Rom. 14:18
9 [a]Phil. 3:17 [b]Rom. 15:33
10 [a]2 Cor. 11:9

18 For [a]many walk, of whom I often told you, and now tell you even
[b]weeping, *that they are* enemies of
[c]the cross of Christ,
19 whose end is destruction,
whose god is *their* [a]appetite, and
whose [b]glory is in their shame, who
[c]set their minds on earthly things.
20 For [a]our citizenship is in
heaven, from which also we eagerly
[b]wait for a Savior, the Lord Jesus
Christ;
21 who will [a]transform the body of
our humble state into [b]conformity
with the [c]body of His glory, [d]by the
exertion of the power that He has
even to [e]subject all things to Himself.

Chapter 4

Think of Excellence

THEREFORE, my beloved breth-
ren whom I [a]long *to see,* my joy and
crown, so [b]stand firm in the Lord,
my beloved.
2 I urge Euodia and I urge Syn-
tyche to [a]live in harmony in the
Lord.
3 Indeed, true comrade, I ask you
also to help these women who have
shared my struggle in *the cause of*
the gospel, together with Clement
also, and the rest of my [a]fellow-
workers, whose [b]names are in the
book of life.
4 [a]Rejoice in the Lord always;
again I will say, rejoice!
5 Let your forbearing *spirit* be
known to all men. [a]The Lord is near.
6 [a]Be anxious for nothing, but in
everything by [b]prayer and supplication with thanksgiving let your requests be made known to God.
7 And [a]the peace of God, which
[b]surpasses all comprehension, shall
[c]guard your hearts and your [d]minds
in [e]Christ Jesus.
8 Finally, brethren, [a]whatever is
true, whatever is honorable, whatever is right, whatever is pure,
whatever is lovely, whatever is of
good repute, if there is any excellence and if anything worthy of
praise, let your mind dwell on these
things.
9 The things you have learned
and received and heard and seen [a]in
me, practice these things; and [b]the
God of peace shall be with you.

God's Provisions

10 But I rejoiced in the Lord
greatly, that now at last [a]you have

revived your concern for me; indeed, you were concerned *before*,
but you lacked opportunity.
11 Not that I speak from want; for
I have learned to be [a]content in
whatever circumstances I am.
12 I know how to get along with
humble means, and I also know how
to live in prosperity; in any and every circumstance I have learned the
secret of being filled and going
[a]hungry, both of having abundance
and [b]suffering need.
13 I can do all things through Him
who [a]strengthens me.
14 Nevertheless, you have done
well to [a]share *with me* in my affliction.
15 And you yourselves also know,
Philippians, that at the [a]first preaching of the gospel, after I departed
from [b]Macedonia, no church
[c]shared with me in the matter of giving and receiving but you alone;
16 for even in [a]Thessalonica you
sent *a gift* more than once for my
needs.
17 [a]Not that I seek the gift itself,
but I seek for the profit which increases to your account.
18 But I have received everything
in full, and have an abundance; I am
amply supplied, having received
from [a]Epaphroditus what you have
sent, [b]a fragrant aroma, an acceptable sacrifice, well-pleasing to God.
19 And [a]my God shall supply all
your needs according to His [b]riches
in glory in Christ Jesus.
20 Now to [a]our God and Father
[b]*be* the glory forever and ever.
Amen.
21 Greet every saint in Christ Jesus. [a]The brethren who are with me
greet you.
22 [a]All the [b]saints greet you, especially those of Caesar's household.
23 [a]The grace of the Lord Jesus
Christ [b]be with your spirit.

11 [a]2 Cor. 9:8; 1 Tim. 6:6, 8; Heb. 13:5
12 [a]1 Cor. 4:11 [b]2 Cor. 11:9
13 [a]2 Cor. 12:9; Eph. 3:16; Col. 1:11
14 [a]Heb. 10:33; Rev. 1:9 [Gr.]
15 [a]Phil. 1:5 [b]Rom. 15:26 [c]2 Cor. 11:9
16 [a]Acts 17:1; 1 Thess. 2:9
17 [a]1 Cor. 9:11f.; 2 Cor. 9:5
18 [a]Phil. 2:25 [b]2 Cor. 2:14; Eph. 5:2
19 [a]2 Cor. 9:8 [b]Rom. 2:4
20 [a]Gal. 1:4 [b]Rom. 11:36
21 [a]Gal. 1:2
22 [a]2 Cor. 13:13 [b]Acts 9:13
23 [a]Rom. 16:20 [b]2 Tim. 4:22

THE EPISTLE OF PAUL TO THE

COLOSSIANS

Thankfulness for Spiritual Attainments

[a]PAUL, [b]an apostle of Jesus Christ
[c]by the will of God, and [d]Timothy
our brother,
2 to the [a]saints and faithful brethren in Christ *who are* at Colossae:
[b]Grace to you and peace from God
our Father.
3 [a]We give thanks to God, [b]the
Father of our Lord Jesus Christ,
praying always for you,
4 [a]since we heard of your faith in
Christ Jesus and the [b]love which
you have for [c]all the saints;
5 because of the [a]hope [b]laid up
for you in heaven, of which you previously [c]heard in the word of truth,
the gospel,
6 which has come to you, just as
[a]in all the world also it is constantly
bearing [b]fruit and increasing, even
as *it has been doing* in you also since
the day you [c]heard *of it* and understood the grace of God in truth;
7 just as you learned *it* from [a]Ep-
aphras, our [b]beloved fellow bond-
servant, who is a faithful servant of
Christ on [1]our behalf,
8 and he also informed us of your
[a]love in the Spirit.
9 For this reason also, [a]since the
day we heard *of it*, [b]we have not
ceased to pray for you and to ask
that you may be filled with the
[c]knowledge of His will in all spiritual [d]wisdom and understanding,
10 so that you may [a]walk in a manner worthy of the Lord, [b]to please
Him in all respects, [c]bearing fruit in
every good work and increasing in
the knowledge of God;
11 [a]strengthened with all power,
according to His glorious might, for
the attaining of all steadfastness
and patience; joyously
12 giving thanks to [a]the Father,
who has qualified us to share in [b]the
inheritance of the saints in [c]light.

The Incomparable Christ

13 For He delivered us from the
[a]domain of darkness, and transferred us to the kingdom of [b]His beloved Son,
14 [a]in whom we have redemption,
the forgiveness of sins.
15 And He is the [a]image of the [b]in-
visible God, the [c]first-born of all creation.
16 For [a]by Him all things were created, [a]*both* in the heavens and on
earth, visible and invisible, whether
[b]thrones or dominions or rulers or
authorities—[c]all things have been
created by Him and for Him.

1 [a]Phil. 1:1 [b]2 Cor. 1:1 [c]1 Cor. 1:1 [d]2 Cor. 1:1
2 [a]Acts 9:13 [b]Rom. 1:7
3 [a]Rom. 1:8 [b]Rom. 15:6
4 [a]Eph. 1:15 [b]Gal. 5:6 [c]Eph. 6:18
5 [a]Acts 23:6 [b]2 Tim. 4:8 [c]Eph. 1:13
6 [a]Rom. 10:18 [b]Rom. 1:13 [c]Eph. 4:21; Col. 1:5
7 [1]Some later mss. read, *your* [a]Col. 4:12 [b]Col. 4:7
8 [a]Rom. 15:30
9 [a]Col. 1:4 [b]Eph. 1:16 [c]Eph. 5:17; Phil. 1:9 [d]Eph. 1:17
10 [a]Eph. 4:1; Col. 2:6 [b]2 Cor. 5:9; Eph. 5:10 [c]Rom. 1:13
11 [a]1 Cor. 16:13
12 [a]Eph. 2:18 [b]Acts 20:32 [c]Acts 26:18
13 [a]Acts 26:18 [b]Matt. 3:17
14 [a]Rom. 3:24
15 [a]2 Cor. 4:4 [b]John 1:18 [c]Rom. 8:29
16 [a]Eph. 1:10 [b]Eph. 1:20f.; Col. 2:15 [c]John 1:3

17 And He [a]is before all things, and in Him all things hold together.

18 He is also [a]head of [b]the body, the church; and He is [c]the beginning, [d]the first-born from the dead; so that He Himself might come to have first place in everything.

19 For it was [a]the *Father's* good pleasure for all [b]the fulness to dwell in Him,

20 and through Him to [a]reconcile all things to Himself, having made [b]peace through [c]the blood of His cross; through Him, *I say,* [d]whether things on earth or things in heaven.

21 And although you were [a]formerly alienated and hostile in mind, *engaged* in evil deeds,

22 yet He has now [a]reconciled you in His fleshly [b]body through death, in order to [c]present you before Him [d]holy and blameless and beyond reproach—

23 if indeed you continue in the faith firmly [a]established and steadfast, and not moved away from the [b]hope of the gospel that you have heard, which was proclaimed [c]in all creation under heaven, [d]and of which I, Paul, was made a [e]minister.

24 [a]Now I rejoice in my sufferings for your sake, and in my flesh [b]I do my share on behalf of [c]His body (which is the church) in filling up that which is lacking in Christ's afflictions.

25 [a]Of *this church* I was made a minister according to the [b]stewardship from God bestowed on me for your benefit, that I might fully carry out the *preaching of* the word of God,

26 *that is,* [a]the mystery which has been hidden from the *past* ages and generations; but has now been manifested to His saints,

27 to whom [a]God willed to make known what is [b]the riches of the glory of this mystery among the Gentiles, which is [c]Christ in you, the [d]hope of glory.

28 And we proclaim Him, [a]admonishing every man and teaching every man with all [b]wisdom, that we may [c]present every man [d]complete in Christ.

29 And for this purpose also I [a]labor, [b]striving [c]according to His power, which mightily works within me.

Chapter 2

You Are Built Up in Christ

FOR I want you to know how great a [a]struggle I have on your behalf, and for those who are at [b]Laodicea, and for all those who have not personally seen my face,

2 that their [a]hearts may be encouraged, having been [b]knit together in love, and *attaining* to all [c]the wealth that comes from the [d]full assurance of understanding, *resulting* in a [e]true knowledge of [f]God's mystery, *that is,* Christ *Himself,*

3 in whom are hidden all [a]the treasures of wisdom and knowledge.

4 [a]I say this in order that no one may delude you with [b]persuasive argument.

5 For even though I am [a]absent in body, nevertheless I am with you in spirit, rejoicing to see your [b]good discipline and the [c]stability of your faith in Christ.

6 As you therefore have received [a]Christ Jesus the Lord, *so* [b]walk in Him,

7 having been firmly [a]rooted *and now* being [b]built up in Him and [c]established in your faith, just as you [d]were instructed, *and* overflowing with gratitude.

8 [a]See to it that no one takes you captive through [b]philosophy and empty deception, according to the tradition of men, according to the [c]elementary principles of the world, rather than according to Christ.

9 For in Him all the [a]fulness of Deity dwells in bodily form,

10 and in Him you have been [a]made complete, and [b]He is the head over all [c]rule and authority;

11 and in Him [a]you were also circumcised with a circumcision made without hands, in the removal of [b]the body of the flesh by the circumcision of Christ;

12 having been [a]buried with Him in baptism, in which you were also [b]raised up with Him through faith in the working of God, who raised Him from the dead.

13 And when you were [a]dead in your transgressions and the uncircumcision of your flesh, He [b]made you alive together with Him, having forgiven us all our transgressions,

14 having cancelled out [a]the certificate of debt consisting of decrees against us *and* which was hostile to us; and [b]He has taken it out of the way, having nailed it to the cross.

15 When He had [a]disarmed the [b]rulers and authorities, He [c]made a public display of them, having triumphed over them through Him.

17 [a]John 1:1
18 [a]Eph. 1:22 [b]Eph. 1:23; Col. 1:24; 2:19 [c]Rev. 3:14 [d]Acts 26:23
19 [a]Eph. 1:5 [b]John 1:16
20 [a]2 Cor. 5:18; Eph. 2:16 [b]Rom. 5:1; Eph. 2:14 [c]Eph. 2:13 [d]Col. 1:16
21 [a]Rom. 5:10
22 [a]2 Cor. 5:18; Eph. 2:16 [b]Rom. 7:4 [c]Eph. 5:27 [d]Eph. 1:4
23 [a]Eph. 3:17; Col. 2:7 [b]Col. 1:5 [c]Mark 16:15; Acts 2:5; Col. 1:6 [d]Eph. 3:7; Col. 1:25 [e]1 Cor. 3:5
24 [a]Rom. 8:17; Phil. 2:17 [b]2 Tim. 1:8; 2:10 [c]Col. 1:18
25 [a]Col. 1:23 [b]Eph. 3:2
26 [a]Rom. 16:25f.
27 [a]Matt. 13:11 [b]Eph. 1:7, 18; 3:16 [c]Rom. 8:10 [d]1 Tim. 1:1
28 [a]Acts 20:31; Col. 3:16 [b]1 Cor. 2:6f.; Col. 2:3 [c]Col. 1:22 [d]Matt. 5:48
29 [a]1 Cor. 15:10 [b]Col. 2:1; 4:12 [c]Eph. 1:19
1 [a]Col. 1:29; 4:12 [b]Col. 4:13
2 [a]1 Cor. 14:31 [b]Col. 2:19 [c]Eph. 1:7, 18; 3:16 [d]Luke 1:1 [Gr.] [e]Matt. 13:11 [f]Rom. 16:25f.
3 [a]Is. 11:2
4 [a]Eph. 4:17 [b]Rom. 16:18
5 [a]1 Cor. 5:3 [b]1 Cor. 14:40 [c]1 Pet. 5:9
6 [a]Gal. 3:26 [b]Col. 1:10
7 [a]Eph. 3:17 [b]1 Cor. 3:9; Eph. 2:20 [c]1 Cor. 1:8 [d]Eph. 4:21
8 [a]1 Cor. 8:9; 10:12 [b]Eph. 5:6 [c]Gal. 4:3
9 [a]2 Cor. 5:19
10 [a]Eph. 3:19 [b]Eph. 1:21f. [c]1 Cor. 15:24; Eph. 3:10
11 [a]Rom. 2:29; Eph. 2:11 [b]Rom. 6:6; 7:24
12 [a]Rom. 6:4f. [b]Rom. 6:5
13 [a]Eph. 2:1 [b]Eph. 2:1, 5
14 [a]Eph. 2:15; Col. 2:20 [b]1 Pet. 2:24
15 [a]Eph. 4:8 [b]1 Cor. 15:24; Eph. 3:10; Col. 2:10 [c]Is. 53:12

16 Therefore let no one [a]act as
your judge in regard to [b]food or
[b]drink or in respect to a [c]festival or
a [d]new moon or a [e]Sabbath day—
17 things which are [a]a *mere*
shadow of what is to come; but the
substance belongs to Christ.
18 Let no one keep [a]defrauding
you of your prize by [b]delighting in
self-abasement and the worship of
the angels, taking his stand on *vi-*
sions he has seen, [c]inflated without
cause by his [d]fleshly mind,
19 and not holding fast to [a]the
head, from whom [b]the entire body,
being supplied and held together by
the joints and ligaments, grows with
a growth which is from God.
20 [a]If you have died with Christ to
the [b]elementary principles of the
world, [c]why, as if you were living in
the world, do you submit yourself to
[d]decrees, such as,
21 "Do not handle, do not taste, do
not touch!"
22 (which all *refer* [a]*to* things destined to perish with the using)—in
accordance with the [b]command-
ments and teachings of men?
23 These are matters which have,
to be sure, the appearance of wisdom in [a]self-made religion and self-
abasement and [b]severe treatment of
the body, *but are* of no value against
[c]fleshly indulgence.

Chapter 3

Put On the New Self

If then you have been [a]raised up
with Christ, keep seeking the things
above, where Christ is, [b]seated at
the right hand of God.
2 [a]Set your mind on the things
above, not on the things that are on
earth.
3 For you have [a]died and your life
is hidden with Christ in God.
4 When Christ, [a]who is our life, is
revealed, [b]then you also will be revealed with Him in glory.
5 [a]Therefore consider [b]the members of your earthly body as dead to
[c]immorality, impurity, passion, evil
desire, and greed, which amounts to
idolatry.
6 For it is on account of these
things that [a]the wrath of God will
come[1],
7 and [a]in them you also once
walked, when you were living in
them.
8 But now you also, [a]put them all
aside: [b]anger, wrath, malice, slander, *and* [c]abusive speech from your
mouth.
9 [a]Do not lie to one another, since
you [b]laid aside the old self with its
evil practices,
10 and have [a]put on the new self
who is being [b]renewed to a true
knowledge [c]according to the image
of the One who [d]created him,
11 —*a renewal* in which [a]there is
no *distinction between* Greek and
Jew, [b]circumcised and uncircumcised, [c]barbarian, Scythian, [d]slave
and freeman, but [e]Christ is all, and
in all.
12 And so, as those who have been
[a]chosen of God, holy and beloved,
[b]put on a [c]heart of compassion,
kindness, [d]humility, gentleness and
[e]patience;
13 [a]bearing with one another, and
[b]forgiving each other, whoever has
a complaint against any one; [b]just
as the Lord forgave you, so also
should you.
14 And beyond all these things *put
on* love, which is [a]the perfect bond
of [b]unity.
15 And let [a]the peace of Christ rule
in your hearts, to which indeed you
were called in [b]one body; and be
thankful.
16 Let [a]the word of Christ richly
dwell within you, with all wisdom
[b]teaching and admonishing one another [c]with psalms *and* hymns *and*
spiritual songs, [d]singing with thankfulness in your hearts to God.
17 And [a]whatever you do in word
or deed, *do* all in the name of the
Lord Jesus, [b]giving thanks through
Him to God the Father.

Family Relations

18 [a]Wives, [b]be subject to your
husbands, as is fitting in the Lord.
19 [a]Husbands, love your wives,
and do not be embittered against
them.
20 [a]Children, be obedient to your
parents in all things, for this is well-
pleasing to the Lord.
21 [a]Fathers, do not exasperate
your children, that they may not
lose heart.
22 [a]Slaves, in all things obey those
who are your masters on earth, [b]not
with external service, as those who
merely please men, but with sincerity of heart, fearing the Lord.
23 Whatever you do, do your work
heartily, [a]as for the Lord rather than
for men;
24 [a]knowing that from the Lord
you will receive the reward of [b]the
inheritance. It is the Lord Christ
whom you [c]serve.
25 For [a]he who does wrong will re-

16 [a]Rom. 14:3 [b]Mark 7:19; Rom. 14:17; Heb. 9:10 [c]Lev. 23:2; Rom. 14:5 [d]1 Chr. 23:31; 2 Chr. 31:3; Neh. 10:33 [e]Mark 2:27f.; Gal. 4:10f.
17 [a]Heb. 8:5
18 [a]1 Cor. 9:24 [b]Col. 2:23 [c]1 Cor. 4:6 [d]Rom. 8:7
19 [a]Eph. 1:22 [b]Eph. 1:23; 4:16
20 [a]Rom. 6:2 [b]Col. 2:8 [c]Gal. 4:9 [d]Col. 2:14, 16
22 [a]1 Cor. 6:13 [b]Is. 29:13
23 [a]Col. 2:18 [b]1 Tim. 4:3 [c]Rom. 13:14

Colossians 3
1 [a]Col. 2:12 [b]Mark 16:19
2 [a]Matt. 16:23
3 [a]Rom. 6:2
4 [a]John 11:25; Gal. 2:20 [b]1 Cor. 1:7; Phil. 3:21
5 [a]Rom. 8:13 [b]Col. 2:11 [c]Mark 7:21f.
6 [1]Some early mss. add, *upon the sons of disobedience* [a]Rom. 1:18
7 [a]Eph. 2:2
8 [a]Eph. 4:22 [b]Eph. 4:31 [c]Eph. 4:29
9 [a]Eph. 4:25 [b]Eph. 4:22
10 [a]Eph. 4:24 [b]Rom. 12:2 [c]Rom. 8:29 [d]Eph. 2:10
11 [a]Rom. 10:12 [b]1 Cor. 7:19; Gal. 5:6 [c]Acts 28:2 [d]Eph. 6:8 [e]Eph. 1:23
12 [a]Luke 18:7 [b]Eph. 4:24 [c]Luke 1:78 [d]Eph. 4:2; Phil. 2:3 [e]1 Cor. 13:4
13 [a]Eph. 4:2 [b]Rom. 15:7
14 [a]Eph. 4:3 [b]John 17:23; Heb. 6:1
15 [a]John 14:27 [b]Eph. 2:16
16 [a]Rom. 10:17 1 Thess. 1:8 [b]Eph. 5:19; Col. 1:28 [c]Eph. 5:19 [d]1 Cor. 14:15
17 [a]1 Cor. 10:31 [b]Eph. 5:20
18 [a]Col. 3:18-4:1: *Eph. 5:22-6:9* [b]Eph. 5:22
19 [a]Eph. 5:25
20 [a]Eph. 6:1
21 [a]Eph. 6:4
22 [a]Eph. 6:5 [b]Eph. 6:6
23 [a]Eph. 6:7
24 [a]Eph. 6:8 [b]Acts 20:32; 1 Pet. 1:4 [c]1 Cor. 7:22
25 [a]Eph. 6:8

ceive the consequences of the wrong which he has done, and [b]that without partiality.

Chapter 4

Fellow-workers

MASTERS, grant to your slaves justice and fairness, knowing that you too have a Master in heaven.

2 [a]Devote yourselves to prayer, keeping alert in it with *an attitude of* thanksgiving;

3 praying at the same time [a]for us as well, that God may open up to us a [b]door for [c]the word, so that we may speak forth [d]the mystery of Christ, for which I have also [e]been imprisoned;

4 in order that I may make it clear [a]in the way I ought to speak.

5 [1a]Conduct yourselves with wisdom toward [b]outsiders, [2c]making the most of the opportunity.

6 [a]Let your speech always be [1]with grace, seasoned, *as it were,* with [b]salt, so that you may know how you should [c]respond to each person.

7 [a]As to all my affairs, [b]Tychicus, *our* [c]beloved brother and faithful servant and fellow-bondslave in the Lord, will bring you information.

8 [a]For I have sent him to you for this very purpose, that you may know *about* our circumstances and that he may [b]encourage your hearts;

9 and with him [a]Onesimus, *our* faithful and [b]beloved brother, [c]who is one of your *number.* They will inform you about the whole situation here.

10 [a]Aristarchus, my [b]fellow prisoner, sends you his greetings; and *also* [c]Barnabas' cousin Mark (about whom you received instructions: [d]if he comes to you, welcome him);

11 and *also* Jesus who is called Justus; these are the only [a]fellow-workers for the kingdom of God [b]who are from the circumcision; and they have proved to be an encouragement to me.

12 [a]Epaphras, [b]who is one of your number, a bondslave of Jesus Christ, sends you his greetings, always [c]laboring earnestly for you in his prayers, that you may stand [d]perfect and [e]fully assured in all the will of God.

13 For I bear him witness that he has a deep concern for you and for those who are in [a]Laodicea and Hierapolis.

14 [a]Luke, the beloved physician, sends you his greetings, and *also* [b]Demas.

15 Greet the brethren who are in [a]Laodicea and also [1]Nympha and [b]the church that is in [2]her house.

16 And [a]when this letter is read among you, have it also read in the church of the Laodiceans; and you, for your part [a]read my letter *that is coming* from [b]Laodicea.

17 And say to [a]Archippus, "Take heed to the [b]ministry which you have received in the Lord, that you may fulfill it."

18 I, Paul, [a]write this greeting with my own hand. [b]Remember my [c]imprisonment. [d]Grace be with you.

[b]Acts 10:34; Eph. 6:9
2 [a]Acts 1:14
3 [a]Eph. 6:19 [b]Acts 14:27 [c]2 Tim. 4:2 [d]Eph. 3:3, 4; 6:19 [e]Eph. 6:20
4 [a]Eph. 6:20
5 [1]Lit., *Walk* [2]Lit., *redeeming the time* [a]Eph. 5:15 [b]Mark 4:11 [c]Eph. 5:16
6 [a]Eph. 4:29 [b]Mark 9:50 [c]1 Pet. 3:15
7 [a]Col. 4:7-9: *Eph. 6:21, 22* [b]Acts 20:4 [c]Eph. 6:21; Col. 1:7
8 [a]Eph. 6:22 [b]Col. 2:2
9 [a]Philem. 10 [b]Col. 1:7 [c]Col. 4:12
10 [a]Acts 19:29 [b]Rom. 16:7 [c]Acts 4:36; 12:12; 15:37, 39 [d]2 Tim. 4:11
11 [a]Rom. 16:3 [b]Acts 11:2
12 [a]Col. 1:7 [b]Col. 4:9 [c]Rom. 15:30 [d]Col. 1:28 [e]Luke 1:1
13 [a]Col. 2:1
14 [a]2 Tim. 4:11 [b]2 Tim. 4:10
15 [1]Or, *Nymphas* (masc.) [2]Some ancient mss. read, *their* [a]Col. 2:1; 4:13, 16 [b]Rom. 16:5
16 [a]1 Thess. 5:27 [b]Col. 2:1; 4:13, 15
17 [a]Philem. 2
18 [a]1 Cor. 16:21 [b]Heb. 13:3 [c]Phil. 1:7; Col. 4:3 [d]1 Tim. 6:21

THE FIRST EPISTLE OF PAUL TO THE THESSALONIANS

Thanksgiving for These Believers

[a]PAUL and Silvanus and Timothy to the church of the Thessalonians in God the Father and the Lord Jesus Christ: Grace to you and peace.

2 [a]We give thanks to God always for all of you, making mention *of you* in our prayers;

3 constantly bearing in mind your [a]work of faith and labor of [b]love and steadfastness of hope in our Lord Jesus Christ in the presence of our God and Father,

4 knowing, [a]brethren beloved by God, *His* choice of you;

5 for our [a]gospel did not come to you in word only, but also [b]in power and in the Holy Spirit and with full conviction; just as you know what kind of men we proved to be among you for your sake.

6 You also became [a]imitators of us and of the Lord, [b]having received the word in much tribulation with the joy of the Holy Spirit,

7 so that you became an example to all the believers in [a]Macedonia and in [b]Achaia.

8 For [a]the word of the Lord has sounded forth from you, not only in Macedonia and Achaia, but also in

1 [a]2 Thess. 1:1
2 [a]Rom. 1:8
3 [a]John 6:29 [b]1 Cor. 13:13
4 [a]Rom. 1:7
5 [a]1 Cor. 9:14 [b]Rom. 15:19
6 [a]1 Cor. 4:16; 11:1f. [b]Acts 17:5
7 [a]Rom. 15:26 [b]Acts 18:12
8 [a]Col. 3:16

every place your faith toward God
has gone forth, so that we have no
need to say anything.
9 For they themselves report
about us what kind of a [a]reception
we had with you, and how you
[b]turned to God [c]from idols to serve
[d]a living and true God,
10 and to [a]wait for His Son from
heaven, whom He [b]raised from the
dead, *that is* Jesus, who [c]delivers us
from [d]the wrath to come.

CHAPTER 2

Paul's Ministry

FOR you yourselves know, brethren, that our [a]coming to you [b]was
not in vain,
2 but after we had already suffered and been [a]mistreated in [b]Phi-
lippi, as you know, we had the boldness in our God [c]to speak to you the
[d]gospel of God amid much [e]opposi-
tion.
3 For our [a]exhortation does not
come from [b]error or [c]impurity or by
way of [d]deceit;
4 [a]but just as we have been approved by God to be [b]entrusted with
the gospel, so we speak, [c]not as
pleasing men but God, who [d]exam-
ines our hearts.
5 For we never came with flattering speech, as you know, nor
with [a]a pretext for greed—[b]God is
witness —
6 nor did we [a]seek glory from
men, either from you or from others,
even though as [b]apostles of Christ
we might have asserted our authority.
7 But we proved to be [1a]gentle
among you, [b]as a nursing *mother*
tenderly cares for her own children.
8 Having thus a fond affection for
you, we were well-pleased to [a]im-
part to you not only the [b]gospel of
God but also our own lives, because
you had become very dear to us.
9 For you recall, brethren, our
[a]labor and hardship, *how* [b]working
night and day so as not to be a [c]bur-
den to any of you, we proclaimed to
you the [d]gospel of God.
10 You are witnesses, and *so is*
[a]God, [b]how devoutly and uprightly
and blamelessly we behaved toward
you believers;
11 just as you know how we *were*
[a]exhorting and encouraging and
[b]imploring each one of you as [c]a father *would* his own children,
12 so that you may [a]walk in a manner worthy of the God who [b]calls
you into His own kingdom and [c]glo-
ry.
13 And for this reason we also
constantly [a]thank God that when
you received from us the [b]word of
God's message, you accepted *it* [c]not
as the word of men, but *for* what it
really is, the word of God, [d]which
also performs its work in you who
believe.
14 For you, brethren, became [a]im-
itators of [b]the churches of God in
Christ Jesus that are [c]in Judea, for
[d]you also endured the same sufferings at the hands of your own countrymen, [e]even as they *did* from the
Jews,
15 [a]who both killed the Lord Jesus
and [b]the prophets, and drove us out.
They are not pleasing to God, but
hostile to all men,
16 [a]hindering us from speaking to
the Gentiles [b]that they might be
saved; with the result that they always [c]fill up the measure of their
sins. But [d]wrath has come upon
them to the utmost.
17 But we, brethren, having been
bereft of you for a short while—[a]in
person, not in spirit—were all the
more eager with great desire [b]to see
your face.
18 For [a]we wanted to come to
you—I, Paul, [b]more than once—and
yet [c]Satan [d]thwarted us.
19 For who is our hope or [a]joy or
crown of exultation? Is it not even
you, in the presence of our Lord Jesus at His [b]coming?
20 For you are [a]our glory and joy.

CHAPTER 3

Encouragement of Timothy's Visit

THEREFORE [a]when we could endure *it* no longer, we thought it best
to be left behind at [b]Athens alone;
2 and we sent [a]Timothy, our
brother and God's fellow-worker in
the gospel of Christ, to strengthen
and encourage you as to your faith,
3 so that no man may be disturbed by these afflictions; for you
yourselves know that [a]we have been
destined for this.
4 For indeed when we were with
you, we *kept* telling you in advance
that we were going to suffer affliction; [a]and so it came to pass, as you
know.
5 For this reason, [a]when I could
endure *it* no longer, I also [b]sent to
find out about your faith, for fear

9 [a]1 Thess. 2:1 [b]Acts 14:15 [c]1 Cor. 12:2 [d]Matt. 16:16
10 [a]Matt. 16:27f.; 1 Cor. 1:7 [b]Acts 2:24 [c]Rom. 5:9 [d]Matt. 3:7
1 [a]1 Thess. 1:9 [b]2 Thess. 1:10
2 [a]Acts 14:5; Phil. 1:30 [b]Acts 16:22-24 [c]Acts 17:1-9 [d]Rom. 1:1 [e]Phil. 1:30
3 [a]Acts 13:15 [b]2 Thess. 2:11 [c]1 Thess. 4:7 [d]2 Cor. 4:2
4 [a]2 Cor. 2:17 [b]Gal. 2:7 [c]Gal. 1:10 [d]Rom. 8:27
5 [a]Acts 20:33; 2 Pet. 2:3 [b]Rom. 1:9; 1 Thess. 2:10
6 [a]John 5:41, 44; 2 Cor. 4:5 [b]1 Cor. 9:1f.
7 [1]Or, *babes* [a]2 Tim. 2:24 [b]Gal. 4:19; 1 Thess. 2:11
8 [a]2 Cor. 12:15 [b]Rom. 1:1
9 [a]Phil. 4:16; 2 Thess. 3:8 [b]Acts 18:3 [c]1 Cor. 9:4f.; 2 Cor. 11:9 [d]Rom. 1:1
10 [a]1 Thess. 2:5 [b]2 Cor. 1:12
11 [a]1 Thess. 5:14 [b]Luke 16:28 [c]1 Cor. 4:14
12 [a]Eph. 4:1 [b]Rom. 8:28 [c]2 Cor. 4:6
13 [a]Rom. 1:8 [b]Rom. 10:17; Heb. 4:2 [c]Matt. 10:20; Gal. 4:14 [d]Heb. 4:12
14 [a]1 Thess. 1:6 [b]1 Cor. 7:17; 10:32 [c]Gal. 1:22 [d]Acts 17:5 [e]Heb. 10:33f.
15 [a]Luke 24:20; Acts 2:23 [b]Matt. 5:12
16 [a]Acts 9:23; 13:45 [b]1 Cor. 10:33 [c]Gen. 15:16; Dan. 8:23; Matt. 23:32 [d]1 Thess. 1:10
17 [a]1 Cor. 5:3 [b]1 Thess. 3:10
18 [a]Rom. 15:22 [b]Phil. 4:16 [c]Matt. 4:10 [d]Rom. 1:13
19 [a]Phil. 4:1 [b]Matt. 16:27; Mark 8:38; John 21:22
20 [a]2 Cor. 1:14
1 [a]Phil. 2:19; 1 Thess. 3:5 [b]Acts 17:15f.
2 [a]2 Cor. 1:1
3 [a]Acts 9:16; 14:22
4 [a]1 Thess. 2:14
5 [a]Phil. 2:19; 1 Thess. 3:1 [b]1 Thess. 3:2

that the tempter might have
tempted you, and our labor should
be in vain.
6 But now that [a]Timothy has
come to us from you, and has
brought us good news of [b]your faith
and love, and that you always [c]think
kindly of us, longing to see us just as
we also long to see you,
7 for this reason, brethren, in all
our distress and affliction we were
comforted about you through your
faith;
8 for now we *really* live, if you
[a]stand firm in the Lord.
9 For [a]what thanks can we render to God for you in return for all
the joy with which we rejoice before
our God on your account,
10 as we [a]night and day keep praying most earnestly that we may [b]see
your face, and may [c]complete what
is lacking in your faith?
11 [a]Now may [b]our God and Father
[c]Himself and Jesus our Lord [d]direct
our way to you;
12 and may the Lord cause you to
increase and [a]abound in love for one
another, and for all men, just as we
also *do* for you;
13 so that He may [a]establish your
hearts [b]unblamable in holiness before [c]our God and Father at the
[d]coming of our Lord Jesus [e]with all
His saints.

Chapter 4

Sanctification and Love

[a]FINALLY then, [b]brethren, we request and exhort you in the Lord Jesus, that, as you received from us
instruction as to how you ought to
[c]walk and [d]please God (just as you
actually do walk), that you may [e]ex-
cel still more.
2 For you know what commandments we gave you by *the authority
of* the Lord Jesus.
3 For this is the will of God, your
sanctification; *that is,* that you [a]ab-
stain from sexual immorality;
4 that [a]each of you know how to
possess his own [1b]vessel in sanctification and [c]honor,
5 not in [a]lustful passion, like the
Gentiles who do not know God;
6 *and* that no man transgress and
[a]defraud his brother [b]in the matter
because [c]the Lord is *the* avenger in
all these things, just as we also [d]told
you before and solemnly warned
you.
7 For [a]God has not called us for
[b]the purpose of impurity, but in
sanctification.
8 Consequently, he who rejects
this is not rejecting man but the God
who [a]gives His Holy Spirit to you.
9 Now as to the [a]love of the
brethren, you [b]have no need for
anyone to write to you, for you
yourselves are [c]taught by God to
love one another;
10 for indeed [a]you do practice it
toward all the brethren who are in
all Macedonia. But we urge you,
brethren, to [b]excel still more,
11 and to make it your ambition
[a]to lead a quiet life and [b]attend to
your own business and [c]work with
your hands, just as we commanded
you;
12 so that you may [a]behave properly toward [b]outsiders and [c]not be
in any need.

Those Who Died in Christ

13 But [a]we do not want you to be
uninformed, brethren, about those
who [b]are asleep, that you may not
grieve, as do [c]the rest who have no
hope.
14 For if we believe that Jesus died
and rose again, [a]even so God will
bring with Him [b]those who have
fallen asleep in Jesus.
15 For this we say to you [a]by the
word of the Lord, that [b]we who are
alive, and remain until [c]the coming
of the Lord, shall not precede those
who have fallen asleep.
16 For the Lord [a]Himself [b]will descend from heaven with a [c]shout,
with the voice of [d]*the* archangel, and
with the [e]trumpet of God; and [f]the
dead in Christ shall rise first.
17 Then [a]we who are alive and remain shall be [b]caught up together
with them [c]in the clouds to meet the
Lord in the air, and thus we shall
always [d]be with the Lord.
18 Therefore comfort one another
with these words.

Chapter 5

The Day of the Lord

NOW as to the [a]times and the
epochs, brethren, you [b]have no need
of anything to be written to you.
2 For you yourselves know full
well that [a]the day of the Lord will
come [b]just like a thief in the night.
3 While they are saying, "[a]Peace
and safety!" then [b]destruction will
come upon them suddenly like birth
pangs upon a woman with child;
and they shall not escape.
4 But you, brethren, are not in
[a]darkness, that the day should overtake you [b]like a thief;

6 [a]Acts 18:5 [b]1 Thess. 1:3 [c]1 Cor. 11:2
8 [a]1 Cor. 6:13
9 [a]1 Thess. 1:2
10 [a]2 Tim. 1:3 [b]1 Thess. 2:17 [c]2 Cor. 13:9
11 [a]2 Thess. 2:16 [b]Gal. 1:4; 1 Thess. 3:13 [c]1 Thess. 4:16; 5:23 [d]2 Thess. 3:5
12 [a]Phil. 1:9
13 [a]1 Cor. 1:8 [b]Luke 1:6 [c]Gal. 1:4; 1 Thess. 3:11 [d]1 Thess. 2:19 [e]Matt. 25:31
1 [a]2 Cor. 13:11; 2 Thess. 3:1 [b]Gal. 6:1; 1 Thess. 5:12 [c]Eph. 4:1 [d]2 Cor. 5:9 [e]Phil. 1:9; 1 Thess. 3:12
3 [a]1 Cor. 6:18
4 [1]I.e., body; or possibly, wife [a]1 Cor. 7:2, 9 [b]2 Cor. 4:7; 1 Pet. 3:7 [c]Rom. 1:24
5 [a]Rom. 1:26
6 [a]1 Cor. 6:8 [b]2 Cor. 7:11 [c]Rom. 12:19; 13:4; Heb. 13:4 [d]Luke 16:28
7 [a]1 Pet. 1:15 [b]1 Thess. 2:3
8 [a]Rom. 5:5
9 [a]John 13:34 [b]2 Cor. 9:1 [c]Jer. 31:33f.; John 6:45
10 [a]1 Thess. 1:7 [b]1 Thess. 3:12
11 [a]2 Thess. 3:12 [b]1 Pet. 4:15 [c]Acts 18:3; Eph. 4:28
12 [a]Rom. 13:13; Col. 4:5 [b]Mark 4:11 [c]Eph. 4:28
13 [a]Rom. 1:13 [b]Acts 7:60 [c]Eph. 2:3; 1 Thess. 5:6
14 [a]Rom. 14:9 [b]1 Cor. 15:18
15 [a]1 Kin. 13:17f.; Gal. 1:12 [b]1 Cor. 15:52; 1 Thess. 5:10 [c]1 Thess. 2:19
16 [a]1 Thess. 3:11 [b]1 Thess. 1:10; 2 Thess. 1:7 [c]Joel 2:11 [d]Jude 9 [e]Matt. 24:31 [f]1 Cor. 15:23
17 [a]1 Cor. 15:52 [b]2 Cor. 12:2 [c]Dan. 7:13 [d]John 12:26
1 [a]Acts 1:7 [b]1 Thess. 4:9
2 [a]1 Cor. 1:8 [b]Luke 21:34
3 [a]Jer. 6:14; 8:11 [b]2 Thess. 1:9
4 [a]Acts 26:18; 1 John 2:8 [b]Luke 21:34

5 for you are all [a]sons of light and
sons of day. We are not of night nor
of [b]darkness;
6 so then let us not [a]sleep as [b]oth-
ers do, but let us be alert and [c]sober.
7 For those who sleep do their
sleeping at night, and those who get
drunk get [a]drunk at night.
8 But since [a]we are of *the* day, let
us [b]be sober, having put on the
[c]breastplate of [d]faith and love, and
as a [e]helmet, the hope of salvation.
9 For God has not destined us for
[a]wrath, but for [b]obtaining salvation
through our Lord Jesus Christ,
10 [a]who died for us, that whether
we are awake or asleep, we may live
together with Him.
11 Therefore encourage one another, and [a]build up one another,
just as you also are doing.

Christian Conduct

12 But we request of you, brethren, that you [a]appreciate those
[b]who diligently labor among you,
and have charge over you in the
Lord and give you instruction,
13 and that you esteem them very
highly in love because of their work.
[a]Live in peace with one another.
14 And we urge you, brethren, admonish [a]the unruly, encourage [b]the
fainthearted, help [c]the weak, be [d]pa-
tient with all men.
15 See that [a]no one repays another
with evil for evil, but always [b]seek
after that which is good for one another and for all men.
16 [a]Rejoice always;
17 [a]pray without ceasing;
18 in everything [a]give thanks; for
this is God's will for you in Christ
Jesus.
19 [a]Do not quench the Spirit;
20 do not despise [a]prophetic utterances.
21 But [a]examine everything *carefully;* [b]hold fast to that which is
good;
22 abstain from every form of evil.
23 Now [a]may the God of peace
[b]Himself sanctify you entirely; and
may your [c]spirit and soul and body
be preserved complete, [d]without
blame at the coming of our Lord Jesus Christ.
24 [a]Faithful is He who [b]calls you,
and He also will bring it to pass.
25 Brethren, [a]pray for us.
26 [a]Greet all the brethren with a
holy kiss.
27 I adjure you by the Lord to
[a]have this letter read to all the
[b]brethren.
28 [a]The grace of our Lord Jesus
Christ be with you.

5 [a]Luke 16:8 [b]Acts 26:18
6 [a]Rom. 13:11 [b]Eph. 2:3 [c]1 Pet. 1:13
7 [a]Acts 2:15
8 [a]1 Thess. 5:5 [b]1 Pet. 1:13 [c]Eph. 6:14 [d]Eph. 6:23 [e]Eph. 6:17
9 [a]1 Thess. 1:10 [b]2 Thess. 2:13f.
10 [a]Rom. 14:9
11 [a]Eph. 4:29
12 [a]Ps. 144:3 [b]Rom. 16:6, 12
13 [a]Mark 9:50
14 [a]2 Thess. 3:6, 7, 11 [b]Is. 35:4 [c]Rom. 14:1f. [d]1 Cor. 13:4
15 [a]Matt. 5:44 [b]Rom. 12:9; Gal. 6:10
16 [a]Phil. 4:4
17 [a]Eph. 6:18
18 [a]Eph. 5:20
19 [a]Eph. 4:30
20 [a]Acts 13:1
21 [a]1 Cor. 14:29; 1 John 4:1 [b]Rom. 12:9; Gal. 6:10
23 [a]Rom. 15:33 [b]1 Thess. 3:11 [c]Luke 1:46f.; Heb. 4:12 [d]James 1:4
24 [a]1 Cor. 1:9 [b]1 Thess. 2:12
25 [a]Eph. 6:19
26 [a]Rom. 16:16
27 [a]Col. 4:16 [b]Acts 1:15
28 [a]Rom. 16:20

THE SECOND EPISTLE OF PAUL TO THE

THESSALONIANS

Thanksgiving for Faith and Perseverance

[a]PAUL and [b]Silvanus and [c]Timothy
to the [d]church of the Thessalonians
in God our Father and the Lord Jesus Christ:
2 [a]Grace to you and peace from
God the Father and the Lord Jesus
Christ.
3 We ought always [a]to give
thanks to God for you, [b]brethren, as
is *only* fitting, because your faith is
greatly enlarged, and the [c]love of
each one of you toward one another
grows *ever* greater;
4 therefore, we ourselves [a]speak
proudly of you among [b]the churches
of God for your perseverance and
faith [b]in the midst of all your perse-
cutions and afflictions which you
endure.
5 *This is* a [a]plain indication of
God's righteous judgment so that
you may be [b]considered worthy of
the kingdom of God, for which indeed you are suffering.
6 For after all [a]it is *only* just for
God to repay with affliction those
who afflict you,
7 and *to give* relief to you who are
afflicted and to us as well [a]when the
Lord Jesus shall be revealed [b]from
heaven [c]with His mighty angels [d]in
flaming fire,
8 dealing out retribution to those
who [a]do not know God and to those
who [b]do not obey the gospel of our
Lord Jesus.
9 And these will pay the penalty
of [a]eternal destruction, [b]away from
the presence of the Lord and from
the glory of His power,
10 when He comes to be [a]glorified
in His saints on that [b]day, and to be
marveled at among all who have believed—for our [c]testimony to you
was believed.

1 [a]1 Thess. 1:1 [b]2 Cor. 1:19 [c]Acts 16:1 [1 Thess. 1:1] [d]Acts 17:1
2 [a]Rom. 1:7
3 [a]Rom. 1:8 [b]1 Thess. 4:1 [c]1 Thess. 3:12
4 [a]2 Cor. 7:4 [b]1 Cor. 7:17
5 [a]Phil. 1:28 [b]Luke 20:35
6 [a]Ex. 23:22
7 [a]Luke 17:30 [b]1 Thess. 4:16 [c]Jude 14 [d]Ex. 3:2; Ezek. 1:13f.; Dan. 7:9; Matt. 25:41
8 [a]Gal. 4:8 [b]Rom 2:8
9 [a]Phil. 3:19; 1 Thess. 5:3 [b]Is. 2:10, 19, 21
10 [a]Is. 49:3 [b]Is. 2:11ff. [c]1 Cor. 1:6

11 To this end also we [a]pray for you always that our God may [b]count you worthy of your [c]calling, and fulfill every desire for [d]goodness and the [e]work of faith with power;

12 in order that the [a]name of our Lord Jesus may be glorified in you, and you in Him, according to the grace of our God and the Lord Jesus Christ.

Chapter 2

Man of Lawlessness

NOW we request you, [a]brethren, with regard to the [b]coming of our Lord Jesus Christ, and our [c]gathering together to Him,

2 that you may not be quickly shaken from your composure or be disturbed either by a [a]spirit or a [b]message or a [c]letter as if from us, to the effect that [d]the day of the Lord [e]has come.

3 [a]Let no one in any way deceive you, for *it will not come* unless the [b]apostasy comes first, and the [c]man of [1]lawlessness is revealed, the [d]son of destruction,

4 who opposes and exalts himself above [a]every so-called god or object of worship, so that he takes his seat in the temple of God, [b]displaying himself as being God.

5 Do you not remember that [a]while I was still with you, I was telling you these things?

6 And you know [a]what restrains him now, so that in his time he may be revealed.

7 For [a]the mystery of lawlessness is already at work; only [b]he who now restrains *will do so* until he is taken out of the way.

8 And then that lawless one [a]will be revealed whom the Lord will slay [b]with the breath of His mouth and bring to an end by the [c]appearance of His coming;

9 *that is,* the one whose coming is in accord with the activity of [a]Satan, with all power and [b]signs and false wonders,

10 and with all the deception of wickedness for [a]those who perish, because they did not receive the love of [b]the truth so as to be saved.

11 And for this reason [a]God will send upon them a [b]deluding influence so that they might believe what is false,

12 in order that they all may be judged who [a]did not believe the truth, but [b]took pleasure in wickedness.

13 [a]But we should always give thanks to God for you, [b]brethren beloved by the Lord, because [c]God has chosen you from the beginning [d]for salvation [e]through sanctification by the Spirit and faith in the truth.

14 And it was for this He [a]called you through [b]our gospel, that you may gain the glory of our Lord Jesus Christ.

15 So then, brethren, [a]stand firm and [b]hold to the traditions which you were taught, whether [c]by word *of mouth* or [c]by letter from us.

16 [a]Now may our Lord Jesus Christ [b]Himself and God our Father, who has [c]loved us and given us eternal comfort and [d]good hope by grace,

17 [a]comfort and [b]strengthen your hearts in every good work and word.

Chapter 3

Exhortation

[a]FINALLY, brethren, [b]pray for us that [c]the word of the Lord may spread rapidly and be glorified, just as *it did* also with you;

2 and that we may be [a]delivered from perverse and evil men; for not all have faith.

3 But [a]the Lord is faithful, and He will strengthen and protect you from [b]the evil *one.*

4 And we have [a]confidence in the Lord concerning you, that you [b]are doing and will continue to do what we command.

5 And may the Lord [a]direct your hearts into the love of God and into the steadfastness of Christ.

6 Now we command you, brethren, [a]in the name of our Lord Jesus Christ, that you [b]keep aloof from every brother who leads an [c]unruly life and not according to [d]the tradition which you received from us.

7 For you yourselves know how you ought to [a]follow our example, because we did not act in an undisciplined manner among you,

8 nor did we [a]eat anyone's bread without paying for it, but with [b]labor and hardship we *kept* [c]working night and day so that we might not be a burden to any of you;

9 not because we do not have [a]the right *to this,* but in order to offer ourselves [b]as a model for you, that you might follow our example.

10 For even [a]when we were with you, we used to give you this order:

11 [a]Col. 1:9 [b]2 Thess. 1:5 [c]Rom. 11:29 [d]Rom. 15:14 [e]1 Thess. 1:3
12 [a]Is. 24:15; 66:5
1 [a]2 Thess. 1:3 [b]1 Thess. 2:19 [c]Mark 13:27
2 [a]1 Cor. 14:32 [b]1 Thess. 5:2 [c]2 Thess. 3:17 [d]1 Cor. 1:8 [e]1 Cor. 7:26
3 [1]Or, *sin* [a]Eph. 5:6 [b]1 Tim. 4:1 [c]Dan. 7:25; 2 Thess. 2:8; Rev. 13:5ff. [d]John 17:12
4 [a]1 Cor. 8:5 [b]Is. 14:14; Ezek. 28:2
5 [a]1 Thess. 3:4
6 [a]2 Thess. 2:7
7 [a]Rev. 17:5, 7 [b]2 Thess. 2:6
8 [a]Dan. 7:25; 8:25; 11:36; 2 Thess. 2:3; Rev. 13:5ff. [b]Is. 11:4 [c]1 Tim. 6:14
9 [a]Matt. 4:10 [b]Matt. 24:24
10 [a]1 Cor. 1:18 [b]2 Thess. 2:12, 13
11 [a]1 Kin. 22:22 [b]1 Thess. 2:3
12 [a]Rom. 2:8 [b]Rom. 1:32; 1 Cor. 13:6
13 [a]2 Thess. 1:3 [b]1 Thess. 1:4 [c]Eph. 1:4ff. [d]1 Cor. 1:21; 1 Thess. 2:12; 5:9; 1 Pet. 1:5 [e]1 Thess. 4:7
14 [a]1 Thess. 2:12 [b]1 Thess. 1:5
15 [a]1 Cor. 16:13 [b]1 Cor. 11:2; 2 Thess. 3:6 [c]2 Thess. 2:2
16 [a]1 Thess. 3:11 [b]1 Thess. 3:11 [c]John 3:16 [d]Titus 3:7; 1 Pet. 1:3
17 [a]1 Thess. 3:2, 13 [b]2 Thess. 3:3
1 [a]1 Thess. 4:1 [b]1 Thess. 5:25 [c]1 Thess. 1:8
2 [a]Rom. 15:31
3 [a]1 Cor. 1:9 [b]Matt. 5:37
4 [a]2 Cor. 2:3 [b]1 Thess. 4:10
5 [a]1 Thess. 3:11
6 [a]1 Cor. 5:4 [b]Rom. 16:17; 1 Cor. 5:11 [c]1 Thess. 5:14 [d]1 Cor. 11:2
7 [a]1 Thess. 1:6
8 [a]1 Cor. 9:4 [b]1 Thess. 2:9 [c]Acts 18:3
9 [a]1 Cor. 9:4ff. [b]2 Thess. 3:7
10 [a]1 Thess. 3:4

[b]if anyone will not work, neither let
him eat.
11 For we hear that some among
you are [a]leading an undisciplined
life, doing no work at all, but acting
like [b]busybodies.
12 Now such persons we command and [a]exhort in the Lord Jesus
Christ to [b]work in quiet fashion and
eat their own bread.
13 But as for you, [a]brethren, [b]do
not grow weary of doing good.
14 And if anyone does not obey
our instruction [a]in this letter, take
special note of that man [b]and do not
associate with him, so that he may
be [c]put to shame.
15 And *yet* [a]do not regard him as
an enemy, but [b]admonish him as a
[c]brother.
16 Now [a]may the Lord of peace
[b]Himself continually grant you
peace in every circumstance. [c]The
Lord be with you all!
17 I, Paul, write this greeting [a]with
my own hand, and this is a distinguishing mark in every letter; this is
the way I write.
18 [a]The grace of our Lord Jesus
Christ be with you all.

10 [b]1 Thess. 4:11
11 [a]2 Thess. 3:6 [b]1 Tim. 5:13
12 [a]1 Thess. 4:1 [b]1 Thess. 4:11
13 [a]1 Thess. 4:1 [b]2 Cor. 4:1; Gal. 6:9
14 [a]Col. 4:16 [b]2 Thess. 3:6 [c]1 Cor. 4:14
15 [a]Gal. 6:1 [b]1 Thess. 5:14 [c]2 Thess. 3:6, 13
16 [a]Rom. 15:33 [b]1 Thess. 3:11 [c]Ruth 2:4
17 [a]1 Cor. 16:21
18 [a]Rom. 16:20

THE FIRST EPISTLE OF PAUL TO

TIMOTHY

Misleadings in Doctrine and Living

PAUL, [a]an apostle of [b]Christ Jesus
[c]according to the commandment of
God our Savior, and of [b]Christ Jesus, *who is* our hope;
2 to [a]Timothy, [b]*my* true child in
the faith: Grace, mercy *and* peace
from God the Father and Christ Jesus our Lord.
3 As I urged you upon my departure for [a]Macedonia, remain on at
[b]Ephesus, in order that you may instruct certain men not to [c]teach
strange doctrines,
4 nor to pay attention to [a]myths
and endless [b]genealogies, which
give rise to mere speculation rather
than *furthering* the administration
of God which is by faith.
5 But the goal of our [a]instruction
is love [b]from a pure heart and a
good conscience and a sincere faith.
6 For some men, straying from
these things, have turned aside to
[a]fruitless discussion,
7 [a]wanting to be [b]teachers of the
Law, even though they do not understand either what they are saying or the matters about which they
make confident assertions.
8 But we know that [a]the Law is
good, if one uses it lawfully,
9 realizing the fact that [a]law is
not made for a righteous man, but
for those who are lawless and [b]re-
bellious, for the ungodly and sinners, for the unholy and profane, for
those who kill their fathers or mothers, for murderers
10 and [a]immoral men and [b]homo-
sexuals and [c]kidnappers and [d]liars
and perjurers, and whatever else is
contrary to sound teaching,
11 according to [a]the glorious gospel of [b]the blessed God, with which
I have been [c]entrusted.
12 I thank [a]Christ Jesus our Lord,
who has [b]strengthened me, because
He considered me faithful, [c]putting
me into service;
13 even though I was formerly a
blasphemer and a [a]persecutor and a
violent aggressor. And yet I was
[b]shown mercy, because I acted ig-
norantly in unbelief;
14 and the [a]grace of our Lord was
more than abundant, with the [b]faith
and love which are *found* in Christ
Jesus.
15 [a]It is a trustworthy statement,
deserving full acceptance, that
[b]Christ Jesus came into the world to
save sinners, among whom I am
foremost *of all*.
16 And yet for this reason I [a]found
mercy, in order that in me as the
foremost, Jesus Christ might [b]dem-
onstrate His perfect patience, as an
example for those who would believe in Him for eternal life.
17 Now to the [a]King eternal, [b]im-
mortal, [c]invisible, the [d]only God, [e]*be*
honor and glory forever and ever.
Amen.
18 This [a]command I entrust to
you, Timothy, [b]my son, in accordance with the prophecies previously
made concerning you, that by them
you may fight the good fight,
19 keeping [a]faith and a good conscience, which some have rejected
and suffered shipwreck in regard to
their faith.
20 Among these are [a]Hymenaeus
and [b]Alexander, whom I have [c]de-

1 [a]2 Cor. 1:1; 2 Tim. 1:1 [b]1 Tim. 1:12 [c]Titus 1:3
2 [a]Acts 16:1; 2 Tim. 1:2 [b]2 Tim. 1:2; Titus 1:4
3 [a]Rom. 15:26 [b]Acts 18:19 [c]Rom. 16:17
4 [a]1 Tim. 4:7 [b]Titus 3:9
5 [a]1 Tim. 1:18 [b]2 Tim. 2:22
6 [a]Titus 1:10
7 [a]James 3:1 [b]Luke 2:46
8 [a]Rom. 7:12
9 [a]Gal. 5:23 [b]Titus 1:6, 10
10 [a]1 Cor. 6:9 [b]Lev. 18:22 [c]Ex. 21:16; Rev. 18:13 [d]Rev. 21:8, 27; 22:15
11 [a]2 Cor. 4:4 [b]1 Tim. 6:15 [c]Gal. 2:7
12 [a]Gal. 3:26 [b]Acts 9:22 [c]Acts 9:15
13 [a]Acts 8:3; Phil. 3:6 [b]1 Cor. 7:25; 1 Tim. 1:16
14 [a]Rom. 5:20 [b]1 Thess. 1:3
15 [a]1 Tim. 3:1 [b]Mark 2:17
16 [a]1 Cor. 7:25; 1 Tim. 1:13 [b]Eph. 2:7
17 [a]Rev. 15:3 [Gr.] [b]1 Tim. 6:16 [c]Col. 1:15 [d]John 5:44 [e]Rom. 2:7, 10
18 [a]1 Tim. 1:5 [b]1 Tim. 1:2
19 [a]1 Tim. 1:5
20 [a]2 Tim. 2:17 [b]2 Tim. 4:14 [c]1 Cor. 5:5

livered over to Satan, so that they
may be [d]taught not to blaspheme.

Chapter 2

A Call to Prayer

FIRST of all, then, I urge that [a]en-
treaties *and* prayers, petitions *and*
thanksgivings, be made on behalf of
all men,
2 [a]for kings and all who are in authority, in order that we may lead a
tranquil and quiet life in all godliness and dignity.
3 This is good and acceptable in
the sight of [a]God our Savior,
4 [a]who desires all men to be
[b]saved and to [c]come to the knowledge of the truth.
5 For there is [a]one God, *and* [b]one
mediator also between God and
men, *the* [c]man Christ Jesus,
6 who [a]gave Himself as a ransom
for all, the [b]testimony *borne* at [c]the
proper time.
7 [a]And for this I was appointed a
preacher and [b]an apostle ([c]I am telling the truth, I am not lying) as a
teacher of [d]the Gentiles in faith and
truth.
8 Therefore [a]I want the men [b]in
every place to pray, [c]lifting up [d]holy
hands, without wrath and dissension.

Women Instructed

9 Likewise, *I want* [a]women to
adorn themselves with proper clothing, modestly and discreetly, not
with braided hair and gold or pearls
or costly garments;
10 but rather by means of good
works, as befits women making a
claim to godliness.
11 [a]Let a woman quietly receive
instruction with entire submissive-
ness.
12 [a]But I do not allow a woman to
teach or exercise authority over a
man, but to remain quiet.
13 [a]For it was Adam who was first
created, *and* then Eve.
14 And *it was* not Adam *who* was
deceived, but [a]the woman being
quite deceived, fell into transgression.
15 But women shall be preserved
through the bearing of children if
they continue in [a]faith and love and
sanctity with self-restraint.

Chapter 3

Overseers and Deacons

[a]IT is a trustworthy statement; if
any man aspires to the [b]office of

20 [d]1 Cor. 11:32
1 [a]Eph. 6:18
2 [a]Ezra 6:10
3 [a]Luke 1:47
4 [a]Ezek. 18:23,
32; 2 Pet. 3:9
[b]Rom. 11:14
[c]2 Tim. 2:25; 3:7
5 [a]Rom. 3:30
[b]1 Cor. 8:6; Gal.
3:20 [c]Matt. 1:1
6 [a]Matt. 20:28;
Gal. 1:4 [b]1 Cor.
1:6 [c]Mark 1:15
7 [a]Eph. 3:8;
1 Tim. 1:11;
2 Tim. 1:11
[b]1 Cor. 9:1 [c]Rom.
9:1 [d]Acts 9:15
8 [a]Phil. 1:12;
1 Tim. 5:14; Titus
3:8 [Gr.] [b]John
4:21; 1 Cor. 1:2;
1 Thess. 1:8 [c]Ps.
63:4; Luke 24:50
[d]Ps. 24:4
9 [a]1 Pet. 3:3
11 [a]1 Cor. 14:34
12 [a]1 Cor. 14:34
13 [a]Gen. 2:7, 22
14 [a]Gen. 3:6, 13
15 [a]1 Tim. 1:14
1 [a]1 Tim. 1:15
[b]Acts 20:28
2 [a]1 Tim. 3:2-4;
Titus 1:6-8 [b]Luke
2:36f. [c]1 Tim. 3:8,
11; Titus 2:2
[d]Rom. 12:13
[e]2 Tim. 2:24
3 [a]Titus 1:7
[b]1 Tim. 3:8; 6:10
4 [a]1 Tim. 3:12
5 [a]1 Cor. 10:32
6 [a]1 Tim. 6:4;
2 Tim. 3:4 [b]1 Tim.
3:7
7 [a]2 Cor. 8:21
[b]Mark 4:11
[c]1 Tim. 6:9
8 [a]Phil. 1:1;
1 Tim. 3:12
[b]1 Tim. 5:23;
Titus 2:3 [c]1 Tim.
3:3; Titus 1:7;
1 Pet. 5:2
9 [a]1 Tim. 1:5,
19
10 [a]1 Tim. 5:22
11 [a]2 Tim. 3:3;
Titus 2:3 [b]1 Tim.
3:2
12 [a]Phil. 1:1;
1 Tim. 3:8 [b]1 Tim.
3:2 [c]1 Tim. 3:4
13 [a]Matt. 25:21
15 [a]1 Cor. 3:16;
2 Cor. 6:16; Eph.
2:21f.; 1 Pet. 2:5;
4:17 [b]1 Tim. 3:5
[c]Matt. 16:16;
1 Tim. 4:10 [d]Gal.
2:9; 2 Tim. 2:19
16 [1]Some later
mss. read, *God*
[a]Rom. 16:25
[b]John 1:14; 1 Pet.
1:20; 1 John 3:5, 8
[c]Rom. 3:4 [d]Luke
2:13; 24:4; 1 Pet.
1:12 [e]Rom. 16:26;
2 Cor. 1:19; Col.
1:23 [f]2 Thess. 1:10
[g]Mark 16:19

overseer, it is a fine work he desires
to do.
2 [a]An overseer, then, must be
above reproach, [b]the husband of
one wife, [c]temperate, prudent, re-
spectable, [d]hospitable, [e]able to
teach,
3 [a]not addicted to wine or pugnacious, but gentle, uncontentious,
[b]free from the love of money.
4 *He must be* one who [a]manages
his own household well, keeping his
children under control with all dignity
5 (but if a man does not know
how to manage his own household,
how will he take care of [a]the church
of God?);
6 *and* not a new convert, lest he
become [a]conceited and fall into the
[b]condemnation incurred by the devil.
7 And he must [a]have a good reputation with [b]those outside *the
church,* so that he may not fall into
reproach and [c]the snare of the devil.
8 [a]Deacons likewise *must be* men
of dignity, not double-tongued, [b]or
addicted to much wine [c]or fond of
sordid gain,
9 [a]*but* holding to the mystery of
the faith with a clear conscience.
10 And [a]let these also first be
tested; then let them serve as deacons if they are beyond reproach.
11 Women *must* likewise *be* dignified, [a]not malicious gossips, but
[b]temperate, faithful in all things.
12 Let [a]deacons be [b]husbands of
only one wife, *and* [c]good managers
of *their* children and their own
households.
13 For those who have served well
as deacons [a]obtain for themselves a
high standing and great confidence
in the faith that is in Christ Jesus.
14 I am writing these things to
you, hoping to come to you before
long;
15 but in case I am delayed, *I write*
so that you may know how one
ought to conduct himself in [a]the
household of God, which is the
[b]church of [c]the living God, the [d]pil-
lar and support of the truth.
16 And by common confession
great is [a]the mystery of godliness:

[1]He who was [b]revealed in the
flesh,
Was [c]vindicated in the Spirit,
[d]Beheld by angels,
[e]Proclaimed among the nations,
[f]Believed on in the world,
[g]Taken up in glory.

Chapter 4

Apostasy

BUT [a]the Spirit explicitly says that [b]in later times some will fall away from the faith, paying attention to [c]deceitful spirits and [d]doctrines of demons,

2 by means of the hypocrisy of liars [a]seared in their own conscience as with a branding iron,

3 *men* who [a]forbid marriage *and advocate* [b]abstaining from foods, which [c]God has created to be [d]gratefully shared in by those who believe and know the truth.

4 For [a]everything created by God is good, and nothing is to be rejected, if it is [b]received with gratitude;

5 for it is sanctified by means of [a]the word of God and prayer.

A Good Minister's Discipline

6 In pointing out these things to [a]the brethren, you will be a good [b]servant of Christ Jesus, *constantly* nourished on the words of the faith and of the [c]sound doctrine which you [d]have been following.

7 But have nothing to do with [a]worldly [b]fables fit only for old women. On the other hand, discipline yourself for the purpose of [c]godliness;

8 for [a]bodily discipline is only of little profit, but [b]godliness is profitable for all things, since it [c]holds promise for the [d]present life and *also* for the *life* to come.

9 [a]It is a trustworthy statement deserving full acceptance.

10 For it is for this we labor and strive, because we have fixed [a]our hope on [b]the living God, who is [c]the Savior of all men, especially of believers.

11 [a]Prescribe and teach these things.

12 [a]Let no one look down on your youthfulness, but *rather* in speech, conduct, [b]love, faith *and* purity, show yourself [c]an example of those who believe.

13 [a]Until I come, give attention to the *public* [b]reading *of Scripture,* to exhortation and teaching.

14 Do not neglect the spiritual gift within you, which was bestowed upon you through [a]prophetic utterance with [b]the laying on of hands by the [c]presbytery.

15 Take pains with these things; be *absorbed* in them, so that your progress may be evident to all.

16 [a]Pay close attention to yourself and to your teaching; persevere in these things; for as you do this you will [b]insure salvation both for yourself and for those who hear you.

Chapter 5

Honor Widows

[a]DO not sharply rebuke an [b]older man, *but rather* appeal to him as a father, *to* [c]the younger men as brothers,

2 the older women as mothers, *and* the younger women as sisters, in all purity.

3 Honor widows who are [a]widows indeed;

4 but if any widow has children or grandchildren, [a]let them first learn to practice piety in regard to their own family, and to make some return to their parents; for this is [b]acceptable in the sight of God.

5 Now she who is a [a]widow, indeed, and who has been left alone [b]has fixed her hope on God, and continues in [c]entreaties and prayers night and day.

6 But she who [a]gives herself to wanton pleasure is [b]dead even while she lives.

7 [a]Prescribe these things as well, so that they may be above reproach.

8 But if any one does not provide for his own, and especially for those of his household, he has [a]denied the faith, and is worse than an unbeliever.

9 Let a widow be [a]put on the list only if she is not less than sixty years old, *having been* [b]the wife of one man,

10 having a reputation for [a]good works; *and* if she has brought up children, if she has [b]shown hospitality to strangers, if she [c]has washed the saints' feet, if she has [d]assisted those in distress, *and* if she has devoted herself to every good work.

11 But refuse *to put* younger widows *on the list,* for when they feel [a]sensual desires in disregard of Christ, they want to get married,

12 *thus* incurring condemnation, because they have set aside their previous pledge.

13 And at the same time they also learn *to be* idle, as they go around from house to house; and not merely idle, but also [a]gossips and [b]busybodies, talking about [c]things not proper *to mention.*

14 Therefore, [a]I want younger *widows* to get [b]married, bear chil-

---

1 [a]John 16:13; Acts 20:23; 21:11; 1 Cor. 2:10f. [b]2 Thess. 2:3ff.; 2 Tim. 3:1; 2 Pet. 3:3; Jude 18 [c]1 John 4:6 [d]James 3:15
2 [a]Eph. 4:19
3 [a]Heb. 13:4 [b]Col. 2:16, 23 [c]Gen. 1:29; 9:3 [d]Rom. 14:6
4 [a]1 Cor. 10:26 [b]Rom. 14:6; 1 Tim. 4:3
5 [a]Gen. 1:25
6 [a]Acts 1:15 [b]2 Cor. 11:23 [c]1 Tim. 1:10 [d]Luke 1:3
7 [a]1 Tim. 1:9 [b]1 Tim. 1:4 [c]1 Tim. 4:8; 6:3
8 [a]Col. 2:23 [b]1 Tim. 4:7; 6:3, 5f.; 2 Tim. 3:5 [c]Ps. 37:9, 11; Prov. 19:23; 22:4; Matt. 6:33 [d]Matt. 6:33
9 [a]1 Tim. 1:15
10 [a]2 Cor. 1:10 [b]1 Tim. 3:15 [c]John 4:42
11 [a]1 Tim. 5:7; 6:2
12 [a]1 Cor. 16:11; Titus 2:15 [b]1 Tim. 1:14 [c]Titus 2:7
13 [a]1 Tim. 3:14 [b]2 Tim. 3:15ff.
14 [a]1 Tim. 1:18 [b]Acts 6:6; 1 Tim. 5:22; 2 Tim. 1:6 [c]Acts 11:30 [Gr.]
16 [a]Acts 20:28 [b]1 Cor. 1:21
1 [a]Lev. 19:32 [b]Titus 2:2 [c]Titus 2:6
3 [a]Acts 6:1; 9:39, 41; 1 Tim. 5:5, 16
4 [a]Eph. 6:2 [b]1 Tim. 2:3
5 [a]Acts 6:1; 9:39, 41; 1 Tim. 5:3, 16 [b]1 Cor. 7:34; 1 Pet. 3:5 [c]Luke 2:37; 1 Tim. 2:1; 2 Tim. 1:3
6 [a]James 5:5 [b]Luke 15:24
7 [a]1 Tim. 4:11
8 [a]2 Tim. 2:12; Titus 1:16; 2 Pet. 2:1; Jude 4
9 [a]1 Tim. 5:16 [b]1 Tim. 3:2
10 [a]Acts 9:36; 3:8; 1 Pet. 2:12 [b]1 Tim. 3:2 [c]Luke 7:44; John 13:14 [d]1 Tim. 5:16
11 [a]Rev. 18:7
13 [a]3 John 10 [Gr.] [b]2 Thess. 3:11 [c]Titus 1:11
14 [a]1 Tim. 2:8 [b]1 Cor. 7:9; 1 Tim. 4:3

dren, [c]keep house, *and* [d]give the
enemy no occasion for reproach;
15 for some [a]have already turned
aside to follow [b]Satan.
16 If any woman who is a believer
[a]has *dependent* widows, let her
[b]assist them, and let not the church
be burdened, so that it may assist
those who are [c]widows indeed.

Concerning Elders

17 Let [a]the elders who [b]rule well
be considered worthy of double
honor, especially those who [c]work
hard at preaching and teaching.
18 For the Scripture says, "[a]YOU
SHALL NOT MUZZLE THE OX WHILE HE
IS THRESHING," and "[b]The laborer is
worthy of his wages."
19 Do not receive an accusation
against an [a]elder except on the basis
of [b]two or three witnesses.
20 Those who continue in sin, [a]re-
buke in the presence of all, [b]so that
the rest also may be fearful *of sinning.*
21 [a]I solemnly charge you in the
presence of God and of Christ Jesus
and of *His* chosen angels, to maintain these *principles* without bias,
doing nothing in a *spirit of* partiality.
22 [a]Do not lay hands upon any one
too hastily and thus share [b]*responsibility for* the sins of others; keep
yourself free from sin.
23 No longer drink water *exclusively,* but [a]use a little wine for the
sake of your stomach and your frequent ailments.
24 The sins of some men are quite
evident, going before them to judgment; for others, their *sins* [a]follow
after.
25 Likewise also, deeds that are
good are quite evident, and [a]those
which are otherwise cannot be concealed.

CHAPTER 6

Instructions to Those Who Minister

[a]LET all who are under the yoke as
slaves regard their own masters as
worthy of all honor so [b]that the
name of God and *our* doctrine may
not be spoken against.
2 And let those who have believers as their masters not be disre-
spectful to them because they are
[a]brethren, but let them serve them
all the more, because those who partake of the benefit are believers and
beloved. [b]Teach and preach these
principles.
3 If any one [a]advocates a different doctrine, and does not agree
with [b]sound words, those of our
Lord Jesus Christ, and with the doctrine [c]conforming to godliness,
4 he is [a]conceited *and* understands nothing; but he has a morbid
interest in [b]controversial questions
and [c]disputes about words, out of
which arise envy, strife, abusive language, evil suspicions,
5 and constant friction between
[a]men of depraved mind and de-
prived of the truth, who [b]suppose
that godliness is a means of gain.
6 [a]But godliness *actually* is a
means of [b]great gain, when accompanied by [c]contentment.
7 For [a]we have brought nothing
into the world, [1]so we cannot take
anything out of it either.
8 And if we [a]have food and covering, with these we shall be content.
9 [a]But those who want to get rich
fall into temptation and [b]a snare and
many foolish and harmful desires
which plunge men into ruin and destruction.
10 For [a]the love of money is a
[b]root of all sorts of evil, and some by
longing for it have [c]wandered away
from the faith, and pierced themselves with many a pang.
11 But [a]flee from these things, you
[b]man of God; and pursue righteousness, godliness, [c]faith, [d]love, perseverance *and* gentleness.
12 [a]Fight the good fight of [b]faith;
[c]take hold of the eternal life [d]to
which you were called, and you
made the good [e]confession in the
presence of [f]many witnesses.
13 [a]I charge you in the presence of
God, who gives life to all things, and
of [b]Christ Jesus, who testified the
[c]good confession [d]before Pontius
Pilate,
14 that you keep the commandment without stain or reproach, until the [a]appearing of our Lord Jesus
Christ,
15 which He will bring about at
[a]the proper time—He who is [b]the
blessed and [c]only Sovereign, [d]the
King of kings and [e]Lord of lords;
16 [a]who alone possesses immortality and [b]dwells in unapproachable light; [c]whom no man has seen
or can see. [d]To Him *be* honor and
eternal dominion! Amen.
17 Instruct those who are rich in
[a]this present world [b]not to be conceited or to [c]fix their hope on the
uncertainty of riches, but on God,
[d]who richly supplies us with all
things to enjoy.
18 *Instruct them* to do good, to be

14 [c]Titus 2:5 [d]1 Tim. 6:1
15 [a]1 Tim. 1:20 [b]Matt. 4:10
16 [a]1 Tim. 5:4 [b]1 Tim. 5:10 [c]1 Tim. 5:3
17 [a]Acts 11:30; 1 Tim. 4:14 [Gr.]; 5:19 [b]Rom. 12:8 [c]1 Thess. 5:12
18 [a]Deut. 25:4; 1 Cor. 9:9 [b]Lev. 19:13
19 [a]Acts 11:30 [b]Matt. 18:16
20 [a]Gal. 2:14 [b]2 Cor. 7:11
21 [a]Luke 9:26
22 [a]1 Tim. 3:10; 4:14 [b]Eph. 5:11
23 [a]1 Tim. 3:8
24 [a]Rev. 14:13
25 [a]Prov. 10:9
1 [a]Eph. 6:5 [b]Titus 2:5
2 [a]Acts 1:15 [b]1 Tim. 4:11
3 [a]1 Tim. 1:3 [b]1 Tim. 1:10 [c]Titus 1:1
4 [a]1 Tim. 3:6 [b]1 Tim. 1:4 [c]Acts 18:15; 2 Tim. 2:14
5 [a]2 Tim. 3:8; Titus 1:15 [b]Titus 1:11
6 [a]Luke 12:15 [b]1 Tim. 4:8 [c]Phil. 4:11; Heb. 13:5
7 [1]Later mss. read, *it is clear that* [a]Job 1:21
8 [a]Prov. 30:8
9 [a]Prov. 15:27 [b]1 Tim. 3:7
10 [a]Col. 3:5; 1 Tim. 3:3; 6:9 [b]Rom. 11:16ff. [c]James 5:19
11 [a]2 Tim. 2:22 [b]2 Tim. 3:17 [c]1 Tim. 1:14 [d]2 Tim. 3:10
12 [a]1 Cor. 9:25f.; Phil. 1:30; 1 Tim. 1:18 [b]1 Tim. 1:19 [c]Phil. 3:12; 1 Tim. 6:19 [d]Col. 3:15 [e]2 Cor. 9:13 [f]1 Tim. 4:14
13 [a]1 Tim. 5:21 [b]Gal. 3:26 [c]2 Cor. 9:13; 1 Tim. 6:12 [d]Matt. 27:2; John 18:37
14 [a]2 Thess. 2:8
15 [a]1 Tim. 2:6 [b]1 Tim. 1:11 [c]1 Tim. 1:17 [d]Deut. 10:17; Rev. 17:14; 19:16 [e]Ps. 136:3
16 [a]1 Tim. 1:17 [b]Ps. 104:2 [c]John 1:18 [d]1 Tim. 1:17
17 [a]Matt. 12:32; 2 Tim. 4:10; Titus 2:12 [b]Ps. 62:10 [c]1 Tim. 4:10 [d]Acts 14:17

rich in [a]good works, [b]to be generous
and ready to share,
19 [a]storing up for themselves the
treasure of a good foundation for
the future, so that they may [b]take
hold of that which is life indeed.
20 O [a]Timothy, guard [b]what has

18 [a]1 Tim. 5:10 [b]Rom. 12:8
19 [a]Matt. 6:20 [b]1 Tim. 6:12
20 [a]1 Tim. 1:2 [b]2 Tim. 1:12, 14
21 [a]2 Tim. 2:18 [b]1 Tim. 1:19

been entrusted to you, avoiding
worldly *and* empty chatter *and* the
opposing arguments of what is
falsely called "knowledge"—
21 which some have professed and
thus [a]gone astray from [b]the faith.
Grace be with you.

THE SECOND EPISTLE OF PAUL TO TIMOTHY

Timothy Charged to Guard His Trust

PAUL, [a]an apostle of [b]Christ Jesus
[c]by the will of God, according to the
promise of life in Christ Jesus,
2 to [a]Timothy, my beloved [b]son:
[c]Grace, mercy *and* peace from God
the Father and Christ Jesus our
Lord.
3 [a]I thank God, whom I [b]serve
with a [c]clear conscience the way my
forefathers did, [d]as I constantly remember you in my prayers night
and day,
4 [a]longing to see you, [b]even as I
recall your tears, so that I may be
filled with joy.
5 For I am mindful of the [a]sincere
faith within you, which first dwelt in
your grandmother Lois, and [b]your
mother Eunice, and I am sure that *it*
is in you as well.
6 And for this reason I remind
you to kindle afresh [a]the gift of God
which is in you through [a]the laying
on of my hands.
7 For God has not given us a
[a]spirit of timidity, but of power and
love and discipline.
8 Therefore [a]do not be ashamed
of the [b]testimony of our Lord, or of
me [c]His prisoner; but join with *me*
in [d]suffering for the gospel according to the power of God,
9 who has [a]saved us, and [b]called
us with a holy [c]calling, [d]not according to our works, but according to
His own [b]purpose and grace which
was granted us in [e]Christ Jesus
from [f]all eternity,
10 but [a]now has been revealed by
the [b]appearing of our Savior [c]Christ
Jesus, who [d]abolished death, and
brought life and immortality to light
through the gospel,
11 [a]for which I was appointed a
preacher and an apostle and a
teacher.
12 For this reason I also suffer
these things, but [a]I am not ashamed;
for I know [b]whom I have believed

1 [a]2 Cor. 1:1 [b]Gal. 3:26; 1 Tim. 1:12; 2 Tim. 1:2, 9, 13; 2:1, 3, 10; 3:12, 15 [c]1 Cor. 1:1
2 [a]Acts 16:1; 1 Tim. 1:2 [b]1 Tim. 1:2 [c]1 Tim. 1:2
3 [a]Rom. 1:8 [b]Acts 24:14 [c]Acts 23:1 [d]Rom. 1:9
4 [a]2 Tim. 4:9, 21 [b]Acts 20:37
5 [a]1 Tim. 1:5 [b]Acts 16:1; 2 Tim. 3:15
6 [a]1 Tim. 4:14
7 [a]John 14:27
8 [a]Mark 8:38; Rom. 1:16; 2 Tim. 1:12, 16 [b]1 Cor. 1:6 [c]Eph. 3:1 [d]2 Tim. 2:3, 9; 4:5
9 [a]Rom. 11:14 [b]Rom. 8:28f. [c]Rom. 11:29 [d]Eph. 2:9 [e]2 Tim. 1:1 [f]Rom. 16:25
10 [a]Rom. 16:26 [b]2 Thess. 2:8 Titus 2:11 [c]2 Tim. 1:1 [d]1 Cor. 15:26
11 [a]1 Tim. 2:7
12 [a]2 Tim. 1:8, 16 [b]Titus 3:8 [c]1 Tim. 6:20; 2 Tim. 1:14
13 [a]2 Tim. 3:14; Titus 1:9 [b]Rom. 2:20; 6:17 [c]1 Tim. 1:10 [d]2 Tim. 2:2
14 [a]Rom. 8:9 [b]1 Tim. 6:20; 2 Tim. 1:12
15 [a]Acts 2:9 [b]2 Tim. 4:10, 11, 16
16 [a]2 Tim. 4:19 [b]2 Tim. 1:8 [c]Eph. 6:20
18 [a]1 Cor. 1:8 [b]Acts 18:19
1 [a]2 Tim. 1:2 [b]Eph. 6:10 [c]2 Tim. 1:1
2 [a]2 Tim. 1:13 [b]1 Tim. 6:12 [c]1 Tim. 1:18 [d]1 Tim. 1:12
3 [a]2 Tim. 1:8 [b]1 Cor. 9:7; 1 Tim. 1:18 [c]2 Tim. 1:1
4 [a]2 Pet. 2:20
5 [a]1 Cor. 9:25
6 [a]1 Cor. 9:10

and I am convinced that He is able
to [c]guard what I have entrusted to
Him until that day.
13 [a]Retain the [b]standard of [c]sound
words [d]which you have heard from
me, in the faith and love which are
in Christ Jesus.
14 Guard, through the Holy Spirit
who [a]dwells in us, the [b]treasure
which has been entrusted to *you.*
15 You are aware of the fact that
all who are in [a]Asia [b]turned away
from me, among whom are Phy-
gelus and Hermogenes.
16 The Lord grant mercy to [a]the
house of Onesiphorus for he often
refreshed me, and [b]was not
ashamed of my [c]chains;
17 but when he was in Rome, he
eagerly searched for me, and found
me—
18 the Lord grant to him to find
mercy from the Lord on [a]that day—
and you know very well what services he rendered at [b]Ephesus.

CHAPTER 2

Be Strong

YOU therefore, my [a]son, [b]be strong
in the grace that is in [c]Christ Jesus.
2 And the things [a]which you have
heard from me in the presence of
[b]many witnesses, these [c]entrust to
[d]faithful men, who will be able to
teach others also.
3 [a]Suffer hardship with *me,* as a
good [b]soldier of [c]Christ Jesus.
4 No soldier in active service [a]en-
tangles himself in the affairs of ev-
eryday life, so that he may please
the one who enlisted him as a soldier.
5 And also if any one [a]competes
as an athlete, he does not win the
prize unless he competes according
to the rules.
6 [a]The hard-working farmer
ought to be the first to receive his
share of the crops.

7 Consider what I say, for the
Lord will give you understanding in
everything.
8 Remember Jesus Christ, [a]risen
from the dead, [b]descendant of David, [c]according to my gospel,
9 for which I [a]suffer hardship
even to [b]imprisonment as a [c]crimi-
nal; but [d]the word of God [e]is not imprisoned.
10 For this reason [a]I endure all
things for [b]the sake of those who are
chosen, [c]that they also may obtain
the salvation which is in Christ Jesus *and* with *it* eternal glory.
11 [a]It is a trustworthy statement:
For [b]if we died with Him, we
shall also live with Him;
12 If we endure, [a]we shall also
reign with Him;
If we [b]deny Him, He also will
deny us;
13 If we are faithless, [a]He remains faithful; for [b]He cannot deny Himself.

An Unashamed Workman

14 Remind *them* of these things,
and solemnly [a]charge *them* in the
presence of God not to [b]wrangle
about words, which is useless, *and*
leads to the ruin of the hearers.
15 Be diligent to [a]present yourself
approved to God as a workman who
does not need to be ashamed, handling accurately [b]the word of truth.
16 But [a]avoid [b]worldly *and* empty
chatter, for it will lead to further ungodliness,
17 and their talk will spread like
gangrene. Among them are [a]Hyme-
naeus and Philetus,
18 *men* who have gone astray
from the truth saying that [a]the resurrection has already taken place,
and thus they upset [b]the faith of
some.
19 Nevertheless, the [a]firm foundation of God stands, having this [b]seal,
"[c]The Lord knows those who are
His," and, "Let every one who
names the name of the Lord abstain
from wickedness."
20 Now in a large house there are
not only gold and silver vessels, but
also vessels of wood and of earthenware, and [a]some to honor and some
to dishonor.
21 Therefore, if a man cleanses
himself from [a]these *things,* he will
be a vessel for honor, sanctified,
useful to the Master, prepared for
every good work.
22 Now [a]flee from youthful lusts,
and [a]pursue righteousness, [b]faith,
love *and* peace, with those who call
on the Lord from a pure heart.

8 [a]Acts 2:24
[b]Matt. 1:1 [c]Rom.
2:16
9 [a]2 Tim. 1:8;
2:3 [b]Phil. 1:7
[c]Luke 23:32
[d]1 Thess. 1:8
[e]Acts 28:31;
2 Tim. 4:17
10 [a]Col. 1:24
[b]Luke 18:7; Titus
1:1 [c]2 Cor. 1:6;
1 Thess. 5:9
11 [a]1 Tim. 1:15
[b]Rom. 6:8;
1 Thess. 5:10
12 [a]Matt. 19:28;
Luke 22:29; Rom.
5:17; 8:17 [b]Matt.
10:33; 1 Tim. 5:8
13 [a]Rom. 3:3;
1 Cor. 1:9 [b]Num.
23:19; Titus 1:2
14 [a]1 Tim. 5:21;
2 Tim. 4:1 [b]1 Tim.
6:4; 2 Tim. 2:23;
Titus 3:9
15 [a]Rom. 6:13;
James 1:12 [b]Eph.
1:13; James 1:18
16 [a]Titus 3:9
[b]1 Tim. 1:9; 6:20
17 [a]1 Tim. 1:20
18 [a]1 Cor. 15:12
[b]1 Tim. 1:19;
Titus 1:11
19 [a]Is. 28:16f.;
1 Tim. 3:15 [b]John
3:33 [c]John 10:14;
1 Cor. 8:3
20 [a]Rom. 9:21
21 [a]1 Tim. 6:11
22 [a]1 Tim. 6:11
[b]1 Tim. 1:14
23 [a]1 Tim. 6:4
24 [a]1 Tim. 3:3
25 [a]Gal. 6:1
[b]Acts 8:22
[c]1 Tim. 2:4
26 [a]1 Tim. 3:7
[b]Luke 5:10
1 [a]1 Tim. 4:1
2 [a]Phil. 2:21
[b]Luke 16:14
[c]Rom. 1:30
[d]2 Pet. 2:10-12
3 [a]Rom. 1:31
[b]1 Tim. 3:11
[c]Titus 1:8
4 [a]Acts 7:52
[Gr.] [b]Acts 19:36
[Gr.] [c]1 Tim. 3:6
[d]Phil. 3:19
5 [a]Rom. 2:20
[b]1 Tim. 4:7
[c]1 Tim. 5:8 [d]Matt.
7:15; 2 Thess. 3:6
6 [a]Jude 4
[b]1 Tim. 5:6; Titus
3:3 [c]Titus 3:3
7 [a]2 Tim. 2:25
8 [a]Ex. 7:11
[b]Acts 13:8
[c]1 Tim. 6:5
9 [a]Luke 6:11
[Gr.] [b]Ex. 7:12
10 [a]Luke 1:3
[Gr.]; 1 Tim. 4:6
[b]1 Tim 6:11
11 [a]2 Cor. 12:10
[b]2 Cor. 1:5, 7
[c]Acts 13:14, 45,
50 [d]Acts 14:5
12 [a]John 15:20

23 But refuse foolish and ignorant
[a]speculations, knowing that they
produce quarrels.
24 And [a]the Lord's bond-servant
must not be quarrelsome, but be
kind to all, able to teach, patient
when wronged,
25 [a]with gentleness correcting
those who are in opposition, [b]if perhaps God may grant them repentance leading to [c]the knowledge of
the truth,
26 and they may come to their
senses *and escape* from [a]the snare
of the devil, having been [b]held captive by him to do his will.

CHAPTER 3

"Difficult Times Will Come"

BUT realize this, that [a]in the last
days difficult times will come.
2 For men will be [a]lovers of self,
[b]lovers of money, [c]boastful, [c]arro-
gant, [d]revilers, [c]disobedient to parents, ungrateful, unholy,
3 [a]unloving, irreconcilable, [b]ma-
licious gossips, without self-control,
brutal, [c]haters of good,
4 [a]treacherous, [b]reckless, [c]con-
ceited, [d]lovers of pleasure rather
than lovers of God;
5 holding to a [a]form of [b]godli-
ness, although they have [c]denied its
power; and [d]avoid such men as
these.
6 For among them are those who
[a]enter into households and capti-
vate [b]weak women weighed down
with sins, led on by [c]various impulses,
7 always learning and never able
to [a]come to the knowledge of the
truth.
8 And just as [a]Jannes and
Jambres [b]opposed Moses, so these
men also oppose the truth, [c]men of
depraved mind, rejected as regards
the faith.
9 But they will not make further
progress; for their [a]folly will be obvious to all, [b]as also that of those
two came to be.
10 But you [a]followed my teaching,
conduct, purpose, faith, patience,
[b]love, perseverance,
11 [a]persecutions, [b]sufferings, such
as happened to me at [c]Antioch, at
[d]Iconium *and* at Lystra; what perse-
cutions I endured, and out of them
all the Lord delivered me!
12 And indeed, all who desire to
live godly in Christ Jesus [a]will be
persecuted.
13 But evil men and impostors

[a]will proceed *from bad* to worse,
[b]deceiving and being deceived.
14 You, however, [a]continue in the
things you have learned and become
convinced of, knowing from whom
you have learned *them;*
15 and that [a]from childhood you
have known [b]the sacred writings
which are able to [c]give you the
wisdom that leads to salvation
through faith which is in Christ Jesus.
16 [a]All Scripture is inspired by
God and profitable for teaching, for
reproof, for correction, for training
in righteousness;
17 that [a]the man of God may be
adequate, [b]equipped for every good
work.

CHAPTER 4

"Preach the Word"

[a]I SOLEMNLY charge *you* in the
presence of God and of Christ Jesus,
who is to [b]judge the living and the
dead, and by His [c]appearing and His
kingdom:
2 preach [a]the word; be ready in
season *and* out of season; [b]reprove,
rebuke, exhort, with great patience
and instruction.
3 For [a]the time will come when
they will not endure [b]sound doctrine; but *wanting* to have their ears
tickled, they will accumulate for
themselves teachers in accordance
to their own desires;
4 and [a]will turn away their ears
from the truth, and [b]will turn aside
to myths.
5 But you, [a]be sober in all things,
[b]endure hardship, do the work of an
[c]evangelist, [d]fulfill your ministry.
6 For I am already being [a]poured
out as a drink offering, and the time
of [b]my departure has come.
7 [a]I have fought the good fight, I
have finished [b]the course, I have
kept [c]the faith;
8 in the future there [a]is laid up for
me [b]the crown of righteousness,

13 [a]2 Tim. 2:16 [b]Titus 3:3
14 [a]2 Tim. 1:13
15 [a]2 Tim. 1:5 [b]John 5:47; Rom. 2:27 [c]Ps. 119:98f.
16 [a]Rom. 4:23f.
17 [a]1 Tim. 6:11 [b]2 Tim. 2:21
1 [a]1 Tim. 5:21; 2 Tim. 2:14 [b]Acts 10:42 [c]2 Thess. 2:8; 2 Tim. 1:10
2 [a]Gal. 6:6; Col. 4:3 [b]1 Tim. 5:20
3 [a]2 Tim. 3:1 [b]1 Tim. 1:10
4 [a]2 Thess. 2:11; Titus 1:14 [b]1 Tim. 1:4
5 [a]1 Pet. 1:13 [b]2 Tim. 1:8 [c]Acts 21:8 [d]Luke 1:1
6 [a]Phil. 2:17 [b]Phil. 1:23
7 [a]1 Cor. 9:25f. [b]Acts 20:24; 1 Cor. 9:24 [c]2 Tim. 3:10
8 [a]Col. 1:5 [b]1 Cor. 9:25
9 [a]2 Tim. 1:4
10 [1]Some ancient mss. read, *Gaul* [a]Col. 4:14 [b]1 Tim. 6:17 [c]Acts 17:1
11 [a]2 Tim. 1:15 [b]Col. 4:14 [c]Acts 12:12 [d]Col. 4:10
12 [a]Acts 20:4 [b]Acts 18:19
13 [a]Acts 16:8
14 [a]Acts 19:33
16 [a]Acts 7:60
17 [a]1 Tim. 1:12; 2 Tim. 2:1 [b]Titus 1:3 [c]2 Tim. 4:5 [d]Acts 9:15; Phil. 1:12ff. [e]Rom. 15:31; 2 Tim. 3:11
18 [a]1 Cor. 1:21 [b]1 Cor. 15:50 [c]Rom. 11:36
19 [a]Acts 18:2 [b]2 Tim. 1:16
20 [a]Acts 19:22 [b]Acts 18:1 [c]Acts 20:15
21 [a]2 Tim. 4:9 [b]Titus 3:12
22 [a]Gal. 6:18 [b]Col. 4:18

which the Lord, the righteous
Judge, will award to me on that day;
and not only to me, but also to all
who have loved His appearing.

Personal Concerns

9 [a]Make every effort to come to
me soon;
10 for [a]Demas, having loved [b]this
present world, has deserted me and
gone to [c]Thessalonica; Crescens *has
gone* to [1]Galatia, Titus to Dalmatia.
11 [a]Only [b]Luke is with me. Pick up
[c]Mark and bring him with you, [d]for
he is useful to me for service.
12 But [a]Tychicus I have sent to
[b]Ephesus.
13 When you come bring the cloak
which I left at [a]Troas with Carpus,
and the books, especially the parch-
ments.
14 [a]Alexander the coppersmith
did me much harm; the Lord will repay him according to his deeds.
15 Be on guard against him yourself, for he vigorously opposed our
teaching.
16 At my first defense no one supported me, but all deserted me;
[a]may it not be counted against
them.
17 But the Lord stood with me,
and [a]strengthened me, in order that
through me [b]the proclamation
might be [c]fully accomplished, and
that all [d]the Gentiles might hear;
and I was [e]delivered out of the lion's
mouth.
18 The Lord will deliver me from
every evil deed, and will [a]bring me
safely to His [b]heavenly kingdom; [c]to
Him *be* the glory forever and ever.
Amen.
19 Greet Prisca and [a]Aquila, and
[b]the household of Onesiphorus.
20 [a]Erastus remained at [b]Corinth,
but Trophimus I left sick at [c]Mile-
tus.
21 [a]Make every effort to come before [b]winter. Eubulus greets you,
also Pudens and Linus and Claudia
and all the brethren.
22 [a]The Lord be with your spirit.
[b]Grace be with you.

THE EPISTLE OF PAUL TO
TITUS

Salutation

PAUL, [a]a bond-servant of God, and an [b]apostle of Jesus Christ, for the faith of those [c]chosen of God and [d]the knowledge of the truth which is according to godliness,

2 in [a]the hope of eternal life, which God, [b]who cannot lie, [c]promised [d]long ages ago,

3 but [a]at the proper time manifested, *even* His word, in [b]the proclamation [c]with which I was entrusted according to the commandment of God our Savior;

4 to [a]Titus, [b]my true child in a [c]common faith: [d]Grace and peace from God the Father and Christ Jesus our Savior.

Qualifications of Elders

5 For this reason I left you in [a]Crete, that you might set in order what remains, and [b]appoint [c]elders in every city as I directed you,

6 namely, [a]if any man be above reproach, the [b]husband of one wife, having children who believe, not accused of [c]dissipation or [d]rebellion.

7 For the [a]overseer must be above reproach as [b]God's steward, not [c]self-willed, not quick-tempered, not [d]addicted to wine, not pugnacious, not fond of sordid gain,

8 but [a]hospitable, [b]loving what is good, sensible, just, devout, self-controlled,

9 [a]holding fast the faithful word which is in accordance with the teaching, that he may be able both to exhort in [b]sound doctrine and to refute those who contradict.

10 [a]For there are many [b]rebellious men, [c]empty talkers and deceivers, especially [d]those of the circumcision,

11 who must be silenced because they are upsetting [a]whole families, teaching [b]things they should not *teach,* for the sake of sordid gain.

12 One of themselves, a prophet of their own, said, "[a]Cretans are always liars, evil beasts, lazy gluttons."

13 This testimony is true. For this cause [a]reprove them [b]severely that they may be sound in the faith,

14 not paying attention to Jewish [a]myths and [b]commandments of men who [c]turn away from the truth.

15 [a]To the pure, all things are pure; but [b]to those who are defiled and unbelieving, nothing is pure, but both their mind and their conscience are defiled.

16 [a]They profess to know God, but by *their* deeds they [b]deny *Him,* being [c]detestable and [d]disobedient, and worthless for any good deed.

CHAPTER 2

Duties of the Older and Younger

BUT as for you, speak the things which are fitting for [a]sound doctrine.

2 [a]Older men are to be [b]temperate, dignified, [b]sensible, [c]sound [d]in faith, in love, in perseverance.

3 Older women likewise are to be reverent in their behavior, [a]not malicious gossips, nor [b]enslaved to much wine, teaching what is good,

4 that they may encourage the young women to love their husbands, to love their children,

5 *to be* sensible, pure, [a]workers at home, kind, being [b]subject to their own husbands, [c]that the word of God may not be dishonored.

6 Likewise urge [a]the young men to be [b]sensible;

7 in all things show yourself to be [a]an example of good deeds, *with* purity in doctrine, dignified,

8 sound *in* speech which is beyond reproach, in order [a]that the opponent may be put to shame, having nothing bad to say about us.

9 Urge [a]bondslaves to be subject to their own masters in everything, to be well-pleasing, not argumentative,

10 not pilfering, but showing all good faith that they may adorn the doctrine of [a]God our Savior in every respect.

11 For the grace of God has [a]appeared, [b]bringing salvation to all men,

12 instructing us to deny ungodliness and [a]worldly desires and [b]to live sensibly, righteously and godly in the present age,

13 looking for the blessed hope and the [a]appearing of the glory of [b]our great God and Savior, Christ Jesus;

14 who [a]gave Himself for us, [b]that HE MIGHT REDEEM US FROM EVERY LAWLESS DEED and [c]PURIFY FOR

---

1 [a]Rom. 1:1; James 1:1; Rev. 1:1 [b]2 Cor. 1:1 [c]Luke 18:7 [d]1 Tim. 2:4
2 [a]2 Tim. 1:1; Titus 3:7 [b]2 Tim. 2:13 [c]Rom. 1:2 [d]2 Tim. 1:9
3 [a]1 Tim. 2:6 [b]Rom. 16:25; 2 Tim. 4:17 [c]1 Tim. 1:11
4 [a]2 Cor. 2:13 [b]2 Tim. 1:2 [c]2 Pet. 1:1 [d]Rom. 1:7
5 [a]Acts 27:7; Titus 1:12 [b]Acts 14:23 [c]Acts 11:30
6 [a]1 Tim. 3:2-4 [b]1 Tim. 3:2 [c]Eph. 5:18 [d]Titus 1:10
7 [a]1 Tim. 3:2 [b]1 Cor. 4:1 [c]2 Pet. 2:10 [d]1 Tim. 3:3
8 [a]1 Tim. 3:2 [b]2 Tim. 3:3
9 [a]2 Thess. 2:15; 1 Tim. 1:19 [b]1 Tim. 1:10
10 [a]2 Cor. 11:13 [b]Titus 1:6 [c]1 Tim. 1:6 [d]Acts 11:2
11 [a]1 Tim. 5:4 [b]1 Tim. 5:13
12 [a]Acts 2:11; 27:7
13 [a]1 Tim. 5:20 [b]2 Cor. 13:10
14 [a]1 Tim. 1:4 [b]Col. 2:22 [c]2 Tim. 4:4
15 [a]Luke 11:41 [b]Rom. 14:14, 23
16 [a]1 John 2:4 [b]1 Tim. 5:8 [c]Rev. 21:8 [d]Titus 3:3
1 [a]Titus 1:9
2 [a]Philem. 9 [b]1 Tim. 3:2 [c]Titus 1:13 [d]1 Tim. 1:2
3 [a]1 Tim. 3:11 [b]1 Tim. 3:8
5 [a]1 Tim. 5:14 [b]Eph. 5:22 [c]1 Tim. 6:1
6 [a]1 Tim. 5:1 [b]1 Tim. 3:2
7 [a]1 Tim. 4:12
8 [a]2 Thess. 3:14; 1 Pet. 2:12
9 [a]Eph. 6:5
10 [a]Titus 1:3
11 [a]2 Tim. 1:10; Titus 3:4 [b]1 Tim. 2:4
12 [a]1 Tim. 6:9; Titus 3:3 [b]2 Tim. 3:12
13 [a]2 Thess. 2:8 [b]1 Tim. 1:1
14 [a]1 Tim. 2:6 [b]Ps. 130:8; 1 Pet. 1:18f. [c]Ezek. 37:23; Heb. 1:3

HIMSELF A PEOPLE FOR HIS OWN POS-
SESSION, zealous for good deeds.
15 These things speak and [a]exhort
and [a]reprove with all authority. Let
no one disregard you.

CHAPTER 3

Godly Living

[a]REMIND them [b]to be subject to
rulers, to authorities, to be obedient,
to be ready for every good deed,
2 to malign no one, [a]to be uncontentious, [a]gentle, [b]showing every
consideration for all men.
3 [a]For we also once were foolish
ourselves, [b]disobedient, [c]deceived,
enslaved to various lusts and pleasures, spending our life in malice
and [f]envy, hateful, hating one another.
4 But when the [a]kindness of [b]God
our Savior and *His* love for mankind
appeared,
5 [a]He saved us, [b]not on the basis
of deeds which we have done in
righteousness, but [c]according to His
mercy, by the washing of regeneration and renewing by the Holy
Spirit,
6 [a]whom He poured out upon us
[b]richly through Jesus Christ our
Savior,
7 that being justified by His grace
we might be made [a]heirs according
to *the* hope of eternal life.
8 [a]This is a trustworthy statement; and concerning these things I
[b]want you to speak confidently, so
that those who have [c]believed God
may be careful to engage in good
deeds. These things are good and
profitable for men.
9 But [a]shun [b]foolish controversies and [c]genealogies and strife and
[d]disputes about the Law; for they
are unprofitable and worthless.
10 [a]Reject a [b]factious man [c]after a
first and second warning,
11 knowing that such a man is
[a]perverted and is sinning, being self-
condemned.

Personal Concerns

12 When I send Artemas or [a]Tych-
icus to you, [b]make every effort to
come to me at [c]Nicopolis, for I have
decided to spend the winter there.
13 [a]Diligently help Zenas the [b]law-
yer and [c]Apollos on their way so
that nothing is lacking for them.
14 And let [a]our *people* also learn to
[b]engage in good deeds to meet
[c]pressing needs, that they may not
be [d]unfruitful.
15 [a]All who are with me greet you.
Greet those who love us [b]in *the*
faith.
[c]Grace be with you all.

15 [a]1 Tim. 4:13
1 [a]2 Tim. 2:14 [b]Rom. 13:1
2 [a]1 Tim. 3:3 [b]2 Tim. 2:25
3 [a]Rom. 11:30; 1 Cor. 6:11; Col. 3:7 [b]Titus 1:16 [c]2 Tim. 3:13
4 [a]Rom. 2:4; Eph. 2:7; 1 Pet. 2:3 [b]Titus 2:10
5 [a]Rom. 11:14; 2 Tim. 1:9 [b]Eph. 2:9 [c]Eph. 2:4
6 [a]Rom. 5:5 [b]Rom. 2:4
7 [a]Matt. 25:34; Mark 10:17; Rom. 8:17, 24; Titus 1:2
8 [a]1 Tim. 1:15 [b]1 Tim. 2:8 [c]2 Tim. 1:12
9 [a]2 Tim. 2:16 [b]1 Tim. 1:4 [c]1 Tim. 1:4 [d]James 4:1
10 [a]2 John 10 [b]Rom. 16:17 [c]Matt. 18:15f.
11 [a]Titus 1:14
12 [a]Acts 20:4; 2 Tim. 4:12 [b]2 Tim. 4:9 [c]2 Tim. 4:10
13 [a]Acts 15:3 [b]Matt. 22:35 [c]Acts 18:24
14 [a]Titus 2:8 [b]Titus 3:8 [c]Rom. 12:13; Phil. 4:16 [d]Matt. 7:19
15 [a]Acts 20:34 [b]1 Tim. 1:2 [c]Col. 4:18

THE EPISTLE OF PAUL TO

PHILEMON

Salutation

[a]PAUL, [b]a prisoner of [c]Christ Jesus,
and [d]Timothy our brother, to Philemon our beloved *brother* and fellow-worker,
2 and to Apphia [a]our sister, and
to [b]Archippus our [c]fellow-soldier,
and to [d]the church in your house:
3 [a]Grace to you and peace from
God our Father and the Lord Jesus
Christ.

Philemon's Love and Faith

4 [a]I thank my God always, [b]mak-
ing mention of you in my prayers,
5 because I [a]hear of your love,
and of the faith which you have
toward the Lord Jesus, and toward
all the saints;
6 *and I pray* that the fellowship
of your faith may become effective
through the [a]knowledge of every
good thing which is in you for
Christ's sake.
7 For I have come to have much
[a]joy and comfort in your love, because the hearts of the saints have
been [b]refreshed through you,
brother.
8 Therefore, [a]though I have
enough confidence in Christ to order you *to do* that which is [b]proper,
9 yet for love's sake I rather [a]ap-
peal *to you*—since I am such a person as Paul, the [b]aged, and now also
[c]a prisoner of Christ Jesus—

Plea for Onesimus, a Free Man

10 I [a]appeal to you for my [b]child,
whom I have begotten in my imprisonment, [c]Onesimus,
11 who formerly was useless to
you, but now is useful both to you
and to me.
12 And I have sent him back to

1 [a]Phil. 1:1 [b]Eph. 3:1; Philem. 9, 23 [c]Gal. 3:26 [d]2 Cor. 1:1
2 [a]Rom. 16:1 [b]Col. 4:17 [c]Phil. 2:25; 2 Tim. 2:3 [d]Rom. 16:5
3 [a]Rom. 1:7
4 [a]Rom. 1:8 [b]Rom. 1:9
5 [a]Eph. 1:15; Col. 1:4; 1 Thess. 3:6
6 [a]Phil. 1:9; Col. 1:9; 3:10
7 [a]2 Cor. 7:4, 13 [b]1 Cor. 16:18
8 [a]2 Cor. 3:12; 1 Thess. 2:6 [b]Eph. 5:4
9 [a]Rom. 12:1 [b]Titus 2:2 [c]Philem. 1
10 [a]Rom. 12:1 [b]1 Cor. 4:14f. [c]Col. 4:9

you in person, that is, *sending* my
very heart,
13 whom I wished to keep with
me, that in your behalf he might
minister to me in my [a]imprisonment
for the gospel;
14 but without your consent I did
not want to do anything, that your
goodness should [a]not be as it were
by compulsion, but of your own free
will.
15 For perhaps [a]he was for this
reason parted *from you* for a while,
that you should have him back forever,
16 [a]no longer as a slave, but more
than a slave, [b]a beloved brother, especially to me, but how much more
to you, both [c]in the flesh and in the
Lord.
17 If then you regard me a [a]part-
ner, accept him as *you would* me.
18 But if he has wronged you in
any way, or owes you anything,
charge that to my account;
19 [a]I, Paul, am writing this with
my own hand, I will repay it ([b]lest I
should mention to you that you owe
to me even your own self as well).
20 Yes, brother, let me benefit
from you in the Lord; [a]refresh my
heart in Christ.
21 [a]Having confidence in your
obedience, I write to you, since I
know that you will do even more
than what I say.
22 And at the same time also prepare me a [a]lodging; for [b]I hope that
through [c]your prayers [d]I shall be
given to you.
23 [a]Epaphras, my [b]fellow prisoner
in [c]Christ Jesus, greets you,
24 *as do* [a]Mark, [b]Aristarchus, [c]De-
mas, [c]Luke, my [d]fellow-workers.
25 [a]The grace of the Lord Jesus
Christ be [b]with your spirit.[1]

13 [a]Phil. 1:7
14 [a]2 Cor. 9:7
15 [a]Gen. 45:5, 8
16 [a]1 Cor. 7:22 [b]Matt. 23:8; 1 Tim. 6:2 [c]Eph. 6:5; Col. 3:22
17 [a]2 Cor. 8:23
19 [a]1 Cor. 16:21 [b]2 Cor. 9:4
20 [a]Philem. 7
21 [a]2 Cor. 2:3
22 [a]Acts 28:23 [b]Phil. 1:25; 2:24 [c]2 Cor. 1:11 [d]Acts 27:24; Heb. 13:19
23 [a]Col. 1:7 [b]Rom. 16:7; Philem. 1 [c]Philem. 1
24 [a]Acts 12:12 [b]Acts 19:29; Col. 4:10 [c]Col. 4:14 [d]Philem. 1
25 [1]Some ancient mss. add, *Amen* [a]Gal. 6:18 [b]2 Tim. 4:22

THE EPISTLE TO THE

HEBREWS

God's Final Word in His Son

GOD, after He [a]spoke long ago to
the fathers in [b]the prophets in many
portions and [c]in many ways,
2 [a]in these last days [b]has spoken
to us in [c]*His* Son, whom He appointed [d]heir of all things, [e]through
whom also He made the [f]world.
3 And He is the radiance of His
glory and the exact [a]representation
of His nature, and [b]upholds all
things by the word of His power.
When He had made [c]purification of
sins, He [d]sat down at the right hand
of the [e]Majesty on high;
4 having become as much better
than the angels, as He has inherited
a more excellent [a]name than they.
5 For to which of the angels did
He ever say,
"[a]THOU ART MY SON,
TODAY I HAVE BEGOTTEN
THEE"?
And again,
"[b]I WILL BE A FATHER TO HIM,
AND HE SHALL BE A SON TO
ME"?
6 And when He again [a]brings the
first-born into [b]the world, He says,
"[c]AND LET ALL THE ANGELS OF
GOD WORSHIP HIM."
7 And of the angels He says,
"[a]WHO MAKES HIS ANGELS
WINDS,
AND HIS MINISTERS A FLAME
OF FIRE."
8 But of the Son *He says,*
"[a]THY [b]THRONE, O GOD, IS FOR-
EVER AND EVER,
AND THE RIGHTEOUS SCEPTER
IS THE SCEPTER OF [1]HIS KING-
DOM.
9 "[a]THOU HAST LOVED RIGHT-
EOUSNESS AND HATED LAW-
LESSNESS;
[b]THEREFORE GOD, THY GOD,
HATH [c]ANOINTED THEE
WITH THE OIL OF GLADNESS
ABOVE THY COMPANIONS."
10 And,
"[a]THOU, LORD, IN THE BEGIN-
NING DIDST LAY THE FOUNDA-
TION OF THE EARTH,
AND THE HEAVENS ARE THE
WORKS OF THY HANDS;
11 [a]THEY WILL PERISH, BUT THOU
REMAINEST;
[b]AND THEY ALL WILL BECOME
OLD AS A GARMENT,
12 [a]AND AS A MANTLE THOU WILT
ROLL THEM UP;
AS A GARMENT THEY WILL ALSO
BE CHANGED.
BUT THOU ART [b]THE SAME,
AND THY YEARS WILL NOT
COME TO AN END."

1 [a]John 9:29; 16:13; Heb. 2:2f.; 11:18; 12:25 [b]Acts 2:30; 3:21 [c]Num. 12:6, 8; Joel 2:28
2 [a]Matt. 13:39 [b]John 9:29; 12:25; 16:13 [c]John 5:26; 7:28 [d]Ps. 2:8; Matt. 28:18; Heb. 2:8 [e]John 1:3; 1 Cor. 8:6; Col. 1:16 [f]1 Cor. 2:7; Heb. 11:3
3 [a]2 Cor. 4:4 [b]Col. 1:17 [c]Titus 2:14; Heb. 9:14 [d]Mark 16:19; Heb. 8:1; 10:12; 12:2 [e]2 Pet. 1:17
4 [a]Eph. 1:21
5 [a]Ps. 2:7 [b]2 Sam. 7:14
6 [a]Heb. 10:5 [b]Matt. 24:14 [c]Deut. 32:43 [Septuagint]
7 [a]Ps. 104:4
8 [1]Some mss. read, *Thy* [a]Ps. 45:6 [b]Deut. 33:27; Ps. 71:3
9 [a]Ps. 45:7 [b]John 10:17 [c]Is. 61:1, 3
10 [a]Ps. 102:25
11 [a]Ps. 102:26 [b]Is. 51:6
12 [a]Ps. 102:26, 27 [b]Heb. 13:8

13 But to which of the angels has
He ever said,
"[a]SIT AT MY RIGHT HAND,
[b]UNTIL I MAKE THINE ENEMIES
A FOOTSTOOL FOR THY FEET"?
14 Are they not all [a]ministering
spirits, sent out to render service for
the sake of those who will [b]inherit
[c]salvation?

CHAPTER 2

Give Heed

FOR this reason we must pay
much closer attention to what we
have heard, lest [a]we drift away *from*
it.
2 For if the word [a]spoken
through [b]angels proved unalterable,
and [c]every transgression and disobedience received a just [d]recom-
pense,
3 [a]how shall we escape if we neglect so great a [b]salvation? After it
was at the first [c]spoken through the
Lord, it was [d]confirmed to us by
those who heard,
4 God also bearing witness with
them, both by [a]signs and [a]wonders
and by [b]various miracles and by
[c]gifts of the Holy Spirit [d]according
to His own will.

Earth Subject to Man

5 For He did not subject to angels
[a]the world to come, concerning
which we are speaking.
6 But one has [a]testified [b]some-
where, saying,
"[c]WHAT IS MAN, THAT THOU RE-
MEMBEREST HIM?
OR THE SON OF MAN, THAT
THOU ART CONCERNED ABOUT
HIM?
7 "[a]THOU HAST MADE HIM FOR A
LITTLE WHILE LOWER THAN
THE ANGELS;
THOU HAST CROWNED HIM
WITH GLORY AND HONOR,
[1]AND HAST APPOINTED HIM
OVER THE WORKS OF THY
HANDS;
8 [a]THOU HAST PUT ALL THINGS IN
SUBJECTION UNDER HIS FEET."
For in subjecting all things to him,
He left nothing that is not subject to
him. But now [b]we do not yet see all
things subjected to him.

Jesus Briefly Humbled

9 But we do see Him who has
been [a]made for a little while lower
than the angels, *namely,* Jesus, [b]be-
cause of the suffering of death
[c]crowned with glory and honor, that
[d]by the grace of God He might [e]taste
death [f]for every one.
10 For [a]it was fitting for Him, [b]for
whom are all things, and [b]through
whom are all things, in bringing
many sons to glory, to [c]perfect the
[d]author of their salvation through
sufferings.
11 For both He who sanctifies and
those who [b]are sanctified are all
[c]from one *Father;* for which reason
He is not ashamed to call them
[d]brethren,
12 saying,
"[a]I WILL PROCLAIM THY NAME
TO MY BRETHREN,
IN THE MIDST OF THE CONGRE-
GATION I WILL SING THY
PRAISE."
13 And again,
"[a]I WILL PUT MY TRUST IN HIM."
And again,
"[b]BEHOLD, I AND THE CHILDREN
WHOM GOD HAS GIVEN ME."
14 Since then the children share in
[a]flesh and blood, [b]He Himself likewise also partook of the same, that
[c]through death He might render
powerless [d]him who had the power
of death, that is, the devil;
15 and might deliver those who
through [a]fear of death were subject
to slavery all their lives.
16 For assuredly He does not give
help to angels, but He gives help to
the descendant of Abraham.
17 Therefore, He had [a]to be made
like His brethren in all things, that
He might [b]become a merciful and
faithful [c]high priest in [d]things pertaining to God, to [e]make propitiation for the sins of the people.
18 For since He Himself was
[a]tempted in that which He has suffered, He is able to come to the aid
of those who are tempted.

CHAPTER 3

Jesus Our High Priest

THEREFORE, [a]holy brethren, partakers of a [b]heavenly calling, consider Jesus, [c]the Apostle and [d]High
Priest of our [e]confession.
2 He was faithful to Him who appointed Him, as [a]Moses also was in
all His house.
3 [a]For He has been counted worthy of more glory than Moses, by
just so much as the builder of the
house has more honor than the
house.
4 For every house is built by
someone, but the builder of all
things is God.

---

13 [a]Ps. 110:1; Matt. 22:44; Heb. 1:3 [b]Josh 10:24; Heb. 10:13
14 [a]Ps. 103:20f.; Dan. 7:10 [b]Matt. 25:34; Mark 10:17; Titus 3:7; Heb. 6:12 [c]Rom. 11:14; 1 Cor. 1:21; Heb. 2:3; 5:9; 9:28
1 [a]Prov. 3:21
2 [a]Heb. 1:1 [b]Acts 7:53 [c]Heb. 10:28 [d]Heb. 10:35; 11:26
3 [a]Heb. 10:29; 12:25 [b]Rom. 11:14; 1 Cor. 1:21; Heb. 1:14; 5:9; 9:28 [c]Heb. 1:1 [d]Mark 16:20; Luke 1:2; 1 John 1:1
4 [a]John 4:48 [b]Mark 6:14 [c]1 Cor. 12:4, 11; Eph. 4:7 [d]Eph. 1:5
5 [a]Matt. 24:14; Heb. 1:6; 6:5
6 [a]1 Thess. 4:6 [b]Heb. 4:4 [c]Ps. 8:4
7 [1]Some ancient mss. do not contain *And . . . hands* [a]Ps. 8:5, 6
8 [a]Ps. 8:6; 1 Cor. 15:27 [b]1 Cor. 15:25
9 [a]Heb. 2:7 [b]Phil. 2:9; Heb. 1:9 [c]Acts 2:33; 3:13; 1 Pet. 1:21 [d]John 3:16 [e]Matt. 16:28; John 8:52 [f]Heb. 6:20; 7:25
10 [a]Luke 24:26 [b]Rom. 11:36 [c]Luke 13:32; Heb. 5:9; 7:28 [d]Acts 3:15; 5:31
11 [a]Heb. 13:12 [b]Heb. 10:10 [c]Acts 17:28 [d]Matt. 25:40; Mark 3:34f.; John 20:17
12 [a]Ps. 22:22
13 [a]Is. 8:17 [b]Is. 8:18
14 [a]Matt. 16:17 [b]John 1:14 [c]1 Cor. 15:54-57; 2 Tim. 1:10 [d]John 12:31; 1 John 3:8
15 [a]Rom. 8:15
17 [a]Phil. 2:7; Heb. 2:14 [b]Heb. 4:15f.; 5:2 [c]Heb. 3:1 [d]Rom. 15:17; Heb. 5:1 [e]Dan. 9:24; 1 John 2:2
18 [a]Heb. 4:15
1 [a]Acts 1:15; Heb. 2:11; 3:12; 10:19; 13:22 [b]Phil. 3:14 [c]John 17:3 [d]Heb. 2:17; 4:14f.; 10:21 [e]2 Cor. 9:13
2 [a]Ex. 40:16; Num. 12:7; Heb. 3:5
3 [a]2 Cor. 3:7-11

5 Now [a]Moses was faithful in all His house as [b]a servant, [c]for a testimony of those things [d]which were to be spoken later;

6 but Christ *was faithful* as [a]a Son over His house [b]whose house we are, [c]if we hold fast our [d]confidence and the boast of our [e]hope firm until the end.

7 Therefore, just as [a]the Holy Spirit says,

"[b]TODAY IF YOU HEAR HIS VOICE,
8 [a]DO NOT HARDEN YOUR HEARTS AS WHEN THEY PROVOKED ME,
AS IN THE DAY OF TRIAL IN THE WILDERNESS,
9 [a]WHERE YOUR FATHERS TRIED *Me* BY TESTING *Me*,
AND SAW MY WORKS FOR [b]FORTY YEARS.
10 "[a]THEREFORE I WAS ANGRY WITH THIS GENERATION,
AND SAID, 'THEY ALWAYS GO ASTRAY IN THEIR HEART;
AND THEY DID NOT KNOW MY WAYS';
11 [a]AS I SWORE IN MY WRATH,
'THEY SHALL NOT ENTER MY REST.' "

The Peril of Unbelief

12 [a]Take care, brethren, lest there should be in any one of you an evil, unbelieving heart, in falling away from [b]the living God.

13 But [a]encourage one another day after day, as long as it is *still* called "Today," lest any one of you be hardened by the [b]deceitfulness of sin.

14 For we have become partakers of Christ, [a]if we hold fast the beginning of our [b]assurance firm until the end;

15 while it is said,

"[a]TODAY IF YOU HEAR HIS VOICE,
DO NOT HARDEN YOUR HEARTS, AS WHEN THEY PROVOKED ME."

16 For who [a]provoked *Him* when they had heard? Indeed, [b]did not all those who came out of Egypt *led* by Moses?

17 And with whom was He angry for forty years? Was it not with those who sinned, [a]whose bodies fell in the wilderness?

18 And to whom did He swear [a]that they should not enter His rest, but to those who were [b]disobedient?

19 And *so* we see that they were not able to enter because of [a]unbelief.

CHAPTER 4

The Believer's Rest

THEREFORE, let us fear lest, while a promise remains of entering His rest, any one of you should seem to have [a]come short of it.

2 For indeed we have had good news preached to us, just as they also; but [a]the word they heard did not profit them, because it was not united by faith in those who heard.

3 [1]For we who have believed enter that rest, just as He has said,

"[a]AS I SWORE IN MY WRATH,
THEY SHALL NOT ENTER MY REST,"

although His works were finished [b]from the foundation of the world.

4 For He has thus said [a]somewhere concerning the seventh *day*, "[b]AND GOD [c]RESTED ON THE SEVENTH DAY FROM ALL HIS WORKS";

5 and again in this *passage*, "[a]THEY SHALL NOT ENTER MY REST."

6 Since therefore it remains for some to enter it, and those who formerly had good news preached to them failed to enter because of [a]disobedience,

7 He again fixes a certain day, "Today," saying through David after so long a time just [a]as has been said before,

"[b]TODAY IF YOU HEAR HIS VOICE,
DO NOT HARDEN YOUR HEARTS."

8 For [a]if Joshua had given them rest, He would not have [b]spoken of another day after that.

9 There remains therefore a Sabbath rest for the people of God.

10 For the one who has entered His rest has himself also [a]rested from his works, as [b]God did from His.

11 Let us therefore be diligent to enter that rest, lest anyone fall through *following* the same [a]example of [b]disobedience.

12 For [a]the word of God is [b]living and [c]active and sharper than any two-edged [d]sword, and piercing as far as the division of [e]soul and [e]spirit, of both joints and marrow, and [f]able to judge the thoughts and intentions of the heart.

13 And [a]there is no creature hidden from His sight, but all things are [b]open and laid bare to the eyes of Him with whom we have to do.

14 Since then we have a great [a]high priest who has [b]passed through the heavens, Jesus [c]the Son

---

5 [a]Ex. 40:16; Num. 12:7; Heb. 3:2 [b]Ex. 14:31; Num. 12:7 [c]Deut. 18:18f. [d]Heb. 1:1
6 [a]Heb. 1:2 [b]1 Cor. 3:16; 1 Tim. 3:15 [c]Rom. 11:22; Heb. 3:14; 4:14 [d]Eph. 3:12; Heb. 4:16; 10:19, 35 [e]Heb. 6:11; 7:19; 10:23; 11:1; 1 Pet. 1:3
7 [a]Acts 28:25; Heb. 9:8; 10:15 [b]Ps. 95:7; Heb. 3:15; 4:7
8 [a]Ps. 95:8
9 [a]Ps. 95:9, 10 [b]Acts 7:36
10 [a]Ps. 95:10
11 [a]Ps. 95:11; Heb. 4:3, 5
12 [a]Col. 2:8; Heb. 12:25 [b]Matt. 16:16; Heb. 9:14; 10:31; 12:22
13 [a]Heb. 10:24f. [b]Eph. 4:22
14 [a]Heb. 3:6 [b]Heb. 11:1 [Gr.]
15 [a]Ps. 95:7f.
16 [a]Jer. 32:29; 44:3, 8 [b]Num. 14:2, 11, 30; Deut. 1:35, 36, 38
17 [a]Num. 14:29; 1 Cor. 10:5
18 [a]Num. 14:23; Deut. 1:34f.; Heb. 4:2 [b]Rom. 11:30-32; Heb. 4:6, 11
19 [a]John 3:36
1 [a]Heb. 12:15
2 [a]1 Thess. 2:13
3 [1]Some ancient mss. read, *Therefore* [a]Ps. 95:11; Heb. 3:11 [b]Matt. 25:34
4 [a]Heb. 2:6 [b]Gen. 2:2 [c]Ex. 20:11; 31:17
5 [a]Ps. 95:11; Heb. 3:11
6 [a]Heb. 3:18
7 [a]Heb. 3:7f. [b]Ps. 95:7f.
8 [a]Josh. 22:4 [b]Heb. 1:1
10 [a]Rev. 14:13 [b]Heb. 4:4
11 [a]2 Pet. 2:6 [b]Heb. 3:18; 4:6
12 [a]Jer. 23:29; Eph. 5:26; Heb. 6:5; 1 Pet. 1:23 [b]Acts 7:38 [c]1 Thess. 2:13 [d]Eph. 6:17 [e]1 Thess. 5:23 [f]John 12:48; 1 Cor. 14:24f.
13 [a]2 Chr. 16:9; Ps. 33:13-15 [b]Job 26:6
14 [a]Heb. 2:17 [b]Eph. 4:10; Heb. 6:20; 8:1; 9:24 [c]Matt. 4:3; Heb. 1:2; 6:6; 7:3; 10:29

of God, let us hold fast our [d]confession.

15 For we do not have [a]a high priest who cannot sympathize with our weaknesses, but one who has been [b]tempted in all things as *we are, yet* [c]without sin.

16 Let us therefore [a]draw near with [b]confidence to the throne of grace, that we may receive mercy and may find grace to help in time of need.

CHAPTER 5

The Perfect High Priest

FOR every high priest [a]taken from among men is appointed on behalf of men in [b]things pertaining to God, in order to [c]offer both gifts and sacrifices [d]for sins;

2 [a]he can deal gently with the [b]ignorant and [c]misguided, since he himself also is [d]beset with weakness;

3 and because of it he is obligated to offer *sacrifices* [a]for sins, [b]as for the people, so also for himself.

4 And [a]no one takes the honor to himself, but *receives it* when he is called by God, even [b]as Aaron was.

5 So also Christ [a]did not glorify Himself so as to become a [b]high priest, but He who [c]said to Him,

"[d]THOU ART MY SON,
TODAY I HAVE BEGOTTEN THEE";

6 just as He says also in another *passage,*

"[a]THOU ART A PRIEST FOREVER
ACCORDING TO [b]THE ORDER OF MELCHIZEDEK."

7 In the days of His flesh, [a]He offered up both prayers and supplications with [b]loud crying and tears to the One [c]able to save Him from death, and He was heard because of His [d]piety.

8 Although He was [a]a Son, He learned [b]obedience from the things which He suffered.

9 And having been made [a]perfect, He became to all those who obey Him the source of eternal salvation,

10 being designated by God as [a]a high priest according to [b]the order of Melchizedek.

11 Concerning him we have much to say, and *it is* hard to explain, since you have become dull of hearing.

12 For though by this time you ought to be teachers, you have need again for some one to teach you [a]the [b]elementary principles of the [c]oracles of God, and you have come to need [d]milk and not solid food.

13 For every one who partakes *only* of milk is not accustomed to the word of righteousness, for he is a [a]babe.

14 But solid food is for [a]the mature, who because of practice have their senses [b]trained to [c]discern good and evil.

CHAPTER 6

The Peril of Falling Away

THEREFORE [a]leaving [b]the elementary teaching about the Christ, let us press on to [c]maturity, not laying again a foundation of repentance from [d]dead works and of faith toward God,

2 of [a]instruction about washings, and [b]laying on of hands, and the [c]resurrection of the dead, and [c]eternal judgment.

3 And this we shall do, [a]if God permits.

4 For in the case of those who have once been [a]enlightened and have tasted of [b]the heavenly gift and have been made [c]partakers of the Holy Spirit,

5 and [a]have tasted the good [b]word of God and the powers of [c]the age to come,

6 and *then* have fallen away, it is [a]impossible to renew them again to repentance, [b]since they again crucify to themselves the Son of God, and put Him to open shame.

7 For ground that drinks the rain which often falls upon it and brings forth vegetation useful to those [a]for whose sake it is also tilled, receives a blessing from God;

8 but if it yields thorns and thistles, it is worthless and [a]close to being cursed, and it ends up being burned.

Better Things for You

9 But, [a]beloved, we are convinced of better things concerning you, and things that accompany salvation, though we are speaking in this way.

10 For [a]God is not unjust so as to forget [b]your work and the love which you have shown toward His name, in having [c]ministered and in still ministering to the saints.

11 And we desire that each one of you show the same diligence so as to realize the [a]full assurance of [b]hope until the end,

14 [d]Heb. 3:1
15 [a]Heb. 2:17 [b]Heb. 2:18 [c]2 Cor. 5:21; Heb. 7:26
16 [a]Heb. 7:19 [b]Heb. 3:6
1 [a]Ex. 28:1 [b]Heb. 2:17 [c]Heb. 7:27; 8:3f.; 9:9; 10:11 [d]1 Cor. 15:3; Heb. 7:27
2 [a]Heb. 2:18; 4:15 [b]Eph. 4:18; Heb. 9:7 marg. [c]James 5:19; 1 Pet. 2:25 [d]Heb. 7:28
3 [a]1 Cor. 15:3; Heb. 7:27; 10:12 [b]Lev. 9:7; 16:6; Heb. 7:27; 9:7
4 [a]Num. 16:40; 18:7; 2 Chr. 26:18 [b]Ex. 28:1; 1 Chr. 23:13
5 [a]John 8:54 [b]Heb. 2:17; 5:10 [c]Heb. 1:1, 5 [d]Ps. 2:7
6 [a]Ps. 110:4; Heb. 7:17 [b]Heb. 5:10; 6:20; 7:11
7 [a]Matt. 26:39, 42, 44; Mark 14:36, 39; Luke 22:41, 44 [b]Matt. 27:46, 50; Luke 23:46 [c]Mark 14:36 [d]Heb. 11:7
8 [a]Heb. 1:2 [b]Phil. 2:8
9 [a]Heb. 2:10
10 [a]Heb. 2:17; 5:5 [b]Heb. 5:6
12 [a]Gal. 4:3 [b]Heb. 6:1 [c]Acts 7:38 [d]1 Cor. 3:2
13 [a]1 Cor. 3:1
14 [a]1 Cor. 2:6; Eph. 4:13; Heb. 6:1 [b]1 Tim. 4:7 [c]Rom. 14:1
1 [a]Phil. 3:13f. [b]Heb. 5:12 [c]Heb. 5:14 [d]John 8:21; Heb. 9:14
2 [a]John 3:25; Acts 19:3f. [b]Acts 6:6 [c]Acts 17:31f.
3 [a]Acts 18:21
4 [a]2 Cor. 4:4, 6; Heb. 10:32 [b]John 4:10; Eph. 2:8 [c]Gal. 3:2; Heb. 2:4
5 [a]1 Pet. 2:3 [b]Eph. 6:17 [c]Heb. 2:5
6 [a]Matt. 19:26; Heb. 10:26f.; 2 Pet. 2:21; 1 John 5:16 [b]Heb. 10:29
7 [a]2 Tim. 2:6
8 [a]Deut. 29:22ff.
9 [a]1 Cor. 10:14; 1 Pet. 2:11; 2 Pet. 3:1; 1 John 2:7
10 [a]Prov. 19:17; Matt. 10:42 [b]1 Thess. 1:3 [c]Rom. 15:25; Heb. 10:32-34
11 [a]Luke 1:1; Heb. 10:22 [b]Heb. 3:6

12 that you may not be sluggish, but [a]imitators of those who through [b]faith and patience [c]inherit the promises.

13 For [a]when God made the promise to Abraham, since He could swear by no one greater, He [b]swore by Himself,

14 saying, "[a]I WILL SURELY BLESS YOU, AND I WILL SURELY MULTIPLY YOU."

15 And thus, [a]having patiently waited, he obtained the promise.

16 [a]For men swear by one greater *than themselves*, and with them [b]an oath *given* as confirmation is an end of every dispute.

17 [1]In the same way God, desiring even more to show to [a]the heirs of the promise [b]the unchangeableness of His purpose, [2]interposed with an oath,

18 in order that by two unchangeable things, in which [a]it is impossible for God to lie, we may have strong encouragement, we who have fled for refuge in laying hold of [b]the hope set before us.

19 [1]This hope we have as an anchor of the soul, a *hope* both sure and steadfast and one which [a]enters [2]within the veil,

20 [a]where Jesus has entered as a forerunner for us, having become a [b]high priest forever according to the order of Melchizedek.

CHAPTER 7

Melchizedek's Priesthood Like Christ's

FOR this [a]Melchizedek, king of Salem, priest of the [b]Most High God, who met Abraham as he was returning from the slaughter of the kings and blessed him,

2 to whom also Abraham apportioned a tenth part of all *the spoils*, was first of all, by the translation *of his name*, king of righteousness, and then also king of Salem, which is king of peace.

3 Without father, without mother, [a]without genealogy, having neither beginning of days nor end of life, but made like [b]the Son of God, he abides a priest perpetually.

4 Now observe how great this man was to whom Abraham, the [a]patriarch, gave a tenth of the choicest spoils.

5 And those indeed of [a]the sons of Levi who receive the priest's office have commandment [1]in the Law to collect [2]a tenth from the people, that is, from their brethren, although these [3]are descended from Abraham.

6 But the one [a]whose genealogy is not traced from them [b]collected [1]a tenth from Abraham, and [b]blessed the one who [c]had the promises.

7 But without any dispute the lesser is blessed by the greater.

8 And in this case mortal men receive tithes, but in that case one *receives them*, [a]of whom it is witnessed that he lives on.

9 And, so to speak, through Abraham even Levi, who received tithes, paid tithes,

10 for he was still in the loins of his father when Melchizedek met him.

11 [a]Now if perfection was through the Levitical priesthood (for on the basis of it [b]the people received the Law), what further need *was there* for another priest to arise [c]according to the order of Melchizedek, and not be designated according to the order of Aaron?

12 For when the priesthood is changed, of necessity there takes place a change of law also.

13 For [a]the one concerning whom [b]these things are spoken belongs to another tribe, from which no one has officiated at the altar.

14 For it is evident that our Lord [1]was [a]descended from Judah, a tribe with reference to which Moses spoke nothing concerning priests.

15 And this is clearer still, if another priest arises according to the likeness of Melchizedek,

16 who has become *such* not on the basis of a law of [a]physical requirement, but according to the power of [b]an indestructible life.

17 For it is witnessed *of Him*,

"[a]THOU ART A PRIEST FOREVER
ACCORDING TO THE ORDER OF
MELCHIZEDEK."

18 For, on the one hand, there is a setting aside of a former commandment [a]because of its weakness and uselessness

19 (for [a]the Law made nothing perfect), and on the other hand there is a bringing in of a better [b]hope, through which we [c]draw near to God.

20 And inasmuch as *it was* not without an oath

21 (for they indeed became priests without an oath, but He with an oath through the One who said to Him,

"[a]THE LORD HAS SWORN
AND [b]WILL NOT CHANGE HIS
MIND,

---

12 [a]Heb. 13:7 [b]2 Thess. 1:4; James 1:3; Rev. 13:10 [c]Heb. 1:14
13 [a]Gal. 3:15, 18 [b]Gen. 22:16; Luke 1:73
14 [a]Gen. 22:16f.
15 [a]Gen. 12:4; 21:5
16 [a]Gal. 3:15 [b]Ex. 22:11
17 [1]Or, *Therefore God* [2]Or, *guaranteed* [a]Heb. 11:9 [b]Ps. 110:4; Prov. 19:21; Heb. 6:18
18 [a]Num. 23:19; Titus 1:2 [b]Heb. 3:6; 7:19
19 [1]Lit., *Which we have* [2]Or, *inside* [a]Lev. 16:2; Heb. 9:2f.
20 [a]John 14:2; Heb. 4:14 [b]Heb. 2:17; 5:6
1 [a]Gen. 14:18-20; Heb. 7:6 [b]Mark 5:7
3 [a]Heb. 7:6 [b]Matt. 4:3; Heb. 7:1, 28
4 [a]Acts 2:29
5 [1]Lit., *according to* [2]Or, *tithes* [3]Lit., *have come out of the loins of* [a]Num. 18:21, 26; 2 Chr. 31:4f.
6 [1]Or, *tithes* [a]Heb. 7:3 [b]Heb. 7:1f. [c]Rom. 4:13
8 [a]Heb. 5:6; 6:20
11 [a]Heb. 7:18f.; 8:7 [b]Heb. 9:6; 10:1 [c]Heb. 5:6; 7:17
13 [a]Heb. 7:14 [b]Heb. 7:11
14 [1]Lit., *rose from* [a]Num. 24:17; Is. 11:1; Matt. 2:6 [Mic. 5:2]; Rev. 5:5
16 [a]Heb. 9:10 [b]Heb. 9:14
17 [a]Ps. 110:4; Heb. 5:6; 7:21
18 [a]Rom. 8:3; Gal. 3:21; Heb. 7:11
19 [a]Acts 13:39; Rom. 3:20; 7:7f.; Gal. 2:16; 3:21; Heb. 9:9; 10:1 [b]Heb. 3:6 [c]Lam. 3:57; Heb. 4:16; 7:25; 10:1, 22; James 4:8
21 [a]Ps. 110:4; Heb. 5:6; 7:17 [b]Num. 23:19; 1 Sam. 15:29; Rom. 11:29

'THOU ART A PRIEST [c]FOR-
EVER' ");
22 so much the more also Jesus
has become the [a]guarantee of [b]a
better covenant.
23 And the *former* priests, on the
one hand, existed in greater numbers, because they were prevented
by death from continuing,
24 but He, on the other hand, because He abides [a]forever, holds His
priesthood permanently.
25 Hence, also, He is able to [a]save
[1]forever those who [b]draw near to
God through Him, since He always
lives to [c]make intercession for
them.
26 For it was fitting that we should
have such a [a]high priest, [b]holy, [c]in-
nocent, undefiled, separated from
sinners and [d]exalted above the
heavens;
27 who does not need daily, like
those high priests, to [a]offer up sacrifices, [b]first for His own sins, and
then for the *sins* of the people, because this He did [c]once for all when
He [d]offered up Himself.
28 For the Law appoints men as
high priests [a]who are weak, but the
word of the oath, which came after
the Law, *appoints* [b]a Son, [c]made
perfect forever.

CHAPTER 8

A Better Ministry

NOW the main point in what has
been said *is this:* we have such a
[a]high priest, who has taken His seat
at [b]the right hand of the throne of
the [b]Majesty in the heavens,
2 a [a]minister [1]in the sanctuary,
and [1]in the [b]true [2]tabernacle, which
the Lord [c]pitched, not man.
3 For every [a]high priest is appointed [b]to offer both gifts and sacrifices; hence it is necessary that
this *high priest* also have something
to offer.
4 Now if He were on earth, He
would not be a priest at all, since
there are those who [a]offer the gifts
according to the Law;
5 who serve [a]a copy and [b]shadow
of the heavenly things, just as
Moses [1]was [c]warned *by God* when
he was about to erect the [2]taberna-
cle; for, "[d]SEE," He says, "THAT YOU
MAKE ALL THINGS ACCORDING TO THE
PATTERN WHICH WAS SHOWN YOU ON
THE MOUNTAIN."
6 But now He has obtained a
more excellent ministry, by as much
as He is also the [a]mediator of [b]a better covenant, which has been en-
acted on better promises.

A New Covenant

7 For [a]if that first *covenant* had
been faultless, there would have
been no occasion sought for a sec-
ond.
8 For finding fault with them, He
says,
"[a]BEHOLD, DAYS ARE COMING,
SAYS THE LORD,
[1]WHEN I WILL EFFECT [b]A NEW
COVENANT
WITH THE HOUSE OF ISRAEL
AND WITH THE HOUSE OF JU-
DAH;
9 [a]NOT LIKE THE COVENANT
WHICH I MADE WITH THEIR
FATHERS
ON THE DAY WHEN I [b]TOOK
THEM BY THE HAND
TO LEAD THEM OUT OF THE
LAND OF EGYPT;
FOR THEY DID NOT CONTINUE IN
MY COVENANT,
AND I DID NOT CARE FOR THEM,
SAYS THE LORD.
10 "[a]FOR [b]THIS IS THE COVENANT
THAT I WILL MAKE WITH THE
HOUSE OF ISRAEL
AFTER THOSE DAYS, SAYS THE
LORD:
I WILL PUT MY LAWS INTO
THEIR MINDS,
AND I WILL WRITE THEM [c]UPON
THEIR HEARTS.
AND I WILL BE THEIR GOD,
AND THEY SHALL BE MY PEO-
PLE.
11 "[a]AND THEY SHALL NOT TEACH
EVERY ONE HIS FELLOW-CITI-
ZEN,
AND EVERY ONE HIS BROTHER,
SAYING, 'KNOW THE LORD,'
FOR [b]ALL SHALL KNOW ME,
FROM THE LEAST TO THE
GREATEST OF THEM.
12 "[a]FOR I WILL BE MERCIFUL TO
THEIR INIQUITIES,
[b]AND I WILL REMEMBER THEIR
SINS NO MORE."
13 [1]When He said, "[a]A new *cov-
enant*," He has made the first obso-
lete. [b]But whatever is becoming ob-
solete and growing old is [2]ready to
disappear.

CHAPTER 9

The Old and the New

NOW even the first *covenant* had
[a]regulations of divine worship and
[b]the earthly sanctuary.
2 For there was [a]a [1]tabernacle
prepared, the [2]outer one, in which

21 [c]Heb. 7:23f., 28
22 [a]Ps. 119:122; Is. 38:14 [b]Heb. 8:6
24 [a]Heb. 7:23f.
25 [1]Or, *completely* [a]1 Cor. 1:21 [b]Heb. 7:19 [c]Rom. 8:34; Heb. 9:24
26 [a]Heb. 2:17 [b]2 Cor. 5:21; Heb. 4:15 [c]1 Pet. 2:22 [d]Heb. 4:14
27 [a]Heb. 5:1 [b]Heb. 5:3 [c]Heb. 9:12, 28; 10:10 [d]Eph. 5:2; Heb. 9:14, 28; 10:10, 12
28 [a]Heb. 5:2 [b]Heb. 1:2 [c]Heb. 2:10
1 [a]Heb. 2:17 [b]Heb. 1:3
2 [1]Or, *of* [2]Or, *sacred tent* [a]Heb. 10:11 [b]Heb. 9:11, 24 [c]Ex. 33:7
3 [a]Heb. 2:17 [b]Heb. 5:1; 8:4
4 [a]Heb. 5:1; 8:3
5 [1]Lit., *is* [2]Or, *sacred tent* [a]Heb. 9:23 [b]Col. 2:17; Heb. 10:1 [c]Matt. 2:12; Heb. 11:7; 12:25 [d]Ex. 25:40
6 [a]1 Tim. 2:5 [b]Luke 22:20; Heb. 7:22; 8:8; 9:15; 12:24
7 [a]Heb. 7:11
8 [1]Lit., *And* [a]Jer. 31:31 [b]Luke 22:20; 2 Cor. 3:6; Heb. 7:22; 8:6, 13; 9:15; 12:24
9 [a]Jer. 31:32 [b]Ex. 19:5f.; Heb. 2:16 marg.
10 [a]Jer. 31:33 [b]Rom. 11:27; Heb. 10:16 [c]2 Cor. 3:3
11 [a]Jer. 31:34 [b]Is. 54:13; John 6:45; 1 John 2:27
12 [a]Jer. 31:34 [b]Heb. 10:17
13 [1]Or, *In His saying* [2]Or, *near* [a]Luke 22:20; 2 Cor. 3:6; Heb. 7:22; 8:6, 8; 9:15; 12;24 [b]2 Cor. 5:17; Heb. 1:11
1 [a]Heb. 9:10 [b]Ex. 25:8; Heb. 8:2; 9:11, 24
2 [1]Or, *sacred tent* [2]Lit., *first* [a]Ex. 25:8, 9

were [b]the lampstand and [c]the table
and [d]the sacred bread; this is called
the holy place.
3 And behind [a]the second veil,
there was a tabernacle which is
called the [b]Holy of Holies,
4 having a golden [a]altar of incense and [b]the ark of the covenant
covered on all sides with gold, in
which *was* [c]a golden jar holding the
manna, and [d]Aaron's rod which
budded, and [e]the tables of the covenant.
5 And above it *were* the [a]cheru-
bim of glory [b]overshadowing the
mercy seat; but of these things we
cannot now speak in detail.
6 Now when these things have
been thus prepared, the priests [a]are
continually entering [b]the outer tabernacle, performing the divine worship,
7 but into [a]the second only [b]the
high priest *enters,* [c]once a year, [d]not
without *taking* blood, which he [e]of-
fers for himself and for the [f]sins of
the people committed in ignorance.
8 [a]The Holy Spirit *is* signifying
this, [b]that the way into the holy
place has not yet been disclosed,
while the outer tabernacle is still
standing,
9 which *is* [a]a symbol for the present time. Accordingly both gifts and
sacrifices are [b]offered which cannot
[c]make the worshiper perfect in conscience,
10 since they *relate* only to [a]food
and [b]drink and various [c]washings,
[d]regulations for the body imposed
until [e]a time of reformation.
11 But when Christ appeared *as* a
[a]high priest of the [b]good things [1]to
come, *He entered* through [c]the
greater and more perfect tabernacle, [d]not made with hands, that is to
say, [e]not of this creation;
12 and not through [a]the blood of
goats and calves, but [b]through His
own blood, He [c]entered the holy
place [d]once for all, having obtained
[e]eternal redemption.
13 For if [a]the blood of goats and
bulls and [b]the ashes of a heifer
sprinkling those who have been defiled, sanctify for the cleansing of
the flesh,
14 how much more will [a]the blood
of Christ, who through [b]the eternal
Spirit [c]offered Himself without
blemish to God, [d]cleanse [1]your conscience from dead works to serve
the living God?
15 And for this reason [a]He is the
[b]mediator of a [c]new covenant, in order that since a death has taken
place for the redemption of the
transgressions that were *committed*
under the first covenant, those who
have been [d]called may receive the
promise of the eternal inheritance.
16 For where a covenant is, there
must of necessity be the death of the
one who made it.
17 For a covenant is valid *only*
when men are dead, for it is never in
force while the one who made it
lives.
18 Therefore even the first *covenant* was not inaugurated without
blood.
19 For when every commandment
had been [a]spoken by Moses to all
the people according to the Law, [b]he
took the [c]blood of the calves and the
goats, with [d]water and scarlet wool
and hyssop, and sprinkled both [e]the
book itself and all the people,
20 saying, "[a]THIS IS THE BLOOD OF
THE COVENANT WHICH GOD COM-
MANDED YOU."
21 And in the same way he sprinkled both the [a]tabernacle and all the
vessels of the ministry with the
blood.
22 And according to the Law, *one
may* [a]almost *say,* all things are
cleansed with blood, and [b]without
shedding of blood there is no forgiveness.
23 Therefore it was necessary for
the [a]copies of the things in the heavens to be cleansed with these, but
[a]the heavenly things themselves
with better sacrifices than these.
24 For Christ [a]did not enter a holy
place made with hands, a *mere* copy
of [b]the true one, but into [c]heaven
itself, now [d]to appear in the presence of God for us;
25 nor was it that He should offer
Himself often, as [a]the high priest enters [b]the holy place [a]year by year
with blood not his own.
26 Otherwise, He would have
needed to suffer often since [a]the
foundation of the world; but now
[b]once at [c]the consummation of the
ages He has been [d]manifested to put
away sin [e]by the sacrifice of Himself.
27 And inasmuch as [a]it is appointed for men to die once and after this [b]*comes* judgment,
28 so Christ also, having been [a]of-
fered once to [b]bear the sins of many,
shall appear [c]a second time for [f]sal-
vation [d]without *reference to* sin, to
those who [e]eagerly await Him.

2 [b]Ex. 25:31-39 [c]Ex. 25:23-29 [d]Ex. 25:30; Lev. 24:5ff.
3 [a]Ex. 26:31-33 [b]Ex. 26:33
4 [a]Ex. 30:1-5; 37:25f. [b]Ex. 25:10ff.; 37:1ff. [c]Ex. 16:32f. [d]Num. 17:10 [e]Ex. 31:18; 32:15
5 [a]Ex. 25:18ff. [b]Ex. 25:17, 20
6 [a]Num. 28:3 [b]Ex. 25:8, 9
7 [a]Heb. 9:3 [b]Lev. 16:12ff. [c]Ex. 30:10 [d]Lev. 16:11, 14 [e]Heb. 5:3 [f]Num. 15:25
8 [a]Heb. 3:7 [b]John 14:6
9 [a]Heb. 10:1; 11:19 [b]Heb. 5:1 [c]Heb. 7:19
10 [a]Lev. 11:2ff. [b]Num. 6:3 [c]Lev. 11:25 [d]Heb. 7:16 [e]Heb. 7:12
11 [1]Or, *that have come* [a]Heb. 2:17 [b]Heb. 10:1 [c]Heb. 8:2; 9:24 [d]Mark 14:58; 2 Cor. 5:1 [e]2 Cor. 4:18; Heb. 12:27
12 [a]Lev. 4:3; 16:6 [b]Heb. 9:14; 13:12 [c]Heb. 9:24 [d]Heb. 7:27 [e]Heb. 5:9
13 [a]Heb. 9:19; 10:4 [b]Num. 19:9
14 [1]Or, *our* [a]Heb. 9:12; 13:12 [b]1 Cor. 15:45; 1 Pet. 3:18 [c]Eph. 5:2 [d]Acts 15:9; Titus 2:14
15 [a]Rom. 3:24 [b]1 Tim. 2:5; Heb. 8:6; 12:24 [c]Heb. 8:8 [d]Matt. 22:3ff.
19 [a]Heb. 1:1 [b]Ex. 24:6ff. [c]Heb. 9:12 [d]Lev. 14:4, 7 [e]Ex. 24:7
20 [a]Ex. 24:8
21 [a]Ex. 24:6
22 [a]Lev. 5:11f. [b]Lev. 17:11
23 [a]Heb. 8:5
24 [a]Heb. 4:14; 9:12 [b]Heb. 8:2 [c]Heb. 9:12 [d]Matt. 18:10; Heb. 7:25
25 [a]Heb. 9:7 [b]Heb. 9:2; 10:19
26 [a]Matt. 25:34; Heb. 4:3 [b]Heb. 7:27; 9:12 [c]Matt. 13:39; Heb. 1:2 [d]1 John 3:5, 8 [e]Heb. 9:12
27 [a]Gen. 3:19 [b]2 Cor. 5:10
28 [a]Heb. 7:27 [b]1 Pet. 2:24 [c]Acts 1:11 [d]Heb. 4:15 [e]1 Cor. 1:7; Titus 2:13 [f]Heb. 5:9

CHAPTER 10

One Sacrifice of Christ Is Sufficient

FOR the Law, since it has *only* [a]a
shadow of [b]the good things to come
and not the very form of things, can
[c]never by the same sacrifices year
by year, which they offer continually, [d]make perfect those who draw
near.
2 Otherwise, would they not have
ceased to be offered, because the
worshipers, having once been
cleansed, would no longer have had
[a]consciousness of sins?
3 But [a]in those *sacrifices* there is
a reminder of sins year by year.
4 For it is [a]impossible for the
[b]blood of bulls and goats to take
away sins.
5 Therefore, [a]when He comes
into the world, He says,
"[b]SACRIFICE AND OFFERING
THOU HAST NOT DESIRED,
BUT [c]A BODY THOU HAST PRE-
PARED FOR ME;
6 [a]IN WHOLE BURNT OFFERINGS
AND *sacrifices* FOR SIN THOU
HAST TAKEN NO PLEASURE.
7 "[a]THEN I SAID, 'BEHOLD, I HAVE
COME
(IN [b]THE ROLL OF THE BOOK IT IS
WRITTEN OF ME)
TO DO THY WILL, O GOD.'"
8 After saying above, "[a]SACRI-
FICES AND OFFERINGS AND [b]WHOLE
BURNT OFFERINGS AND *sacrifices*
[c]FOR SIN THOU HAST NOT DESIRED,
NOR HAST THOU TAKEN PLEASURE *in
them*" (which are offered according
to the Law),
9 then He said, "[a]BEHOLD, I HAVE
COME TO DO THY WILL." He takes
away the first in order to establish
the second.
10 By this will we have been [a]sanc-
tified through [b]the offering of [c]the
body of Jesus Christ [d]once for all.
11 And every priest stands daily
ministering and [a]offering time after
time the same sacrifices, which [b]can
never take away sins;
12 but He, having offered one sacrifice [a]for sins [b]for all time, [c]sat
down at the right hand of God,
13 waiting from that time onward
[a]UNTIL HIS ENEMIES BE MADE A FOOT-
STOOL FOR HIS FEET.
14 For by one offering He has [a]per-
fected [b]for all time those who are
sanctified.
15 And [a]the Holy Spirit also bears
witness to us; for after saying,
16 "[a]THIS IS THE COVENANT THAT I
WILL MAKE WITH THEM
AFTER THOSE DAYS, SAYS THE
LORD:
I WILL PUT MY LAWS UPON
THEIR HEART,
AND UPON THEIR MIND I WILL
WRITE THEM,"
He then says,
17 "[a]AND THEIR SINS AND THEIR
LAWLESS DEEDS
I WILL REMEMBER NO MORE."
18 Now where there is forgiveness
of these things, there is no longer
any offering for sin.

A New and Living Way

19 Since therefore, brethren, we
[a]have confidence to [b]enter the holy
place by the blood of Jesus,
20 by [a]a new and living way which
He inaugurated for us through [b]the
veil, that is, His flesh,
21 and since *we have* [a]a great
priest [b]over the house of God,
22 let us [a]draw near with a sincere
heart in [b]full assurance of faith, having our hearts [c]sprinkled *clean* from
an evil conscience and our bodies
[d]washed with pure water.
23 Let us hold fast the [a]confession
of our [b]hope without wavering, for
[c]He who promised is faithful;
24 and let us consider how [a]to
stimulate one another to love and
[b]good deeds,
25 not forsaking our own [a]assem-
bling together, as is the habit of
some, but [b]encouraging *one another;* and all the more, as you see
[c]the day drawing near.

Christ or Judgment

26 For if we go on [a]sinning will-
fully after receiving [b]the knowledge
of the truth, there no longer remains
a sacrifice for sins,
27 but a certain terrifying expectation of [a]judgment, and THE [b]FURY OF
A FIRE WHICH WILL CONSUME THE AD-
VERSARIES.
28 [a]Anyone who has set aside the
Law of Moses dies without mercy
on *the testimony of* two or three witnesses.
29 [a]How much severer punishment do you think he will deserve
[b]who has trampled under foot the
Son of God, and has regarded as unclean [c]the blood of the covenant [d]by
which he was sanctified, and has
[e]insulted the Spirit of grace?
30 For we know Him who said,
"[a]VENGEANCE IS MINE, I WILL RE-
PAY." And again, "[b]THE LORD WILL
JUDGE HIS PEOPLE."

1 [a]Heb. 8:5 [b]Heb. 9:11 [c]Rom. 8:3; Heb. 9:9; 10:4, 11 [d]Heb. 7:19
2 [a]1 Pet. 2:19
3 [a]Heb. 9:7
4 [a]Heb. 10:1, 11 [b]Heb. 9:12f.
5 [a]Heb. 1:6 [b]Ps. 40:6 [c]Heb. 2:14; 5:7; 1 Pet. 2:24
6 [a]Ps. 40:6
7 [a]Ps. 40:7, 8 [b]Ezra 6:2; Ezek. 2:9
8 [a]Ps. 40:6; Heb. 10:5f. [b]Mark 12:33 [c]Rom. 8:3
9 [a]Ps. 40:7, 8; Heb. 10:7
10 [a]John 17:19; Eph. 5:26; Heb. 2:11; 10:14, 29; 13:12 [b]John 6:51; Eph. 5:2; Heb. 7:27; 9:14, 28; 10:12 [c]Heb. 2:14; 5:7; 1 Pet. 2:24 [d]Heb. 7:27
11 [a]Heb. 5:1 [b]Mic. 6:6-8; Heb. 10:1, 4
12 [a]Heb. 5:1 [b]Heb. 10:14 [c]Heb. 1:3
13 [a]Ps. 110:1
14 [a]Heb. 10:1 [b]Heb. 10:12
15 [a]Heb. 3:7
16 [a]Jer. 31:33
17 [a]Jer. 31:34
19 [a]Heb. 3:6; 10:35 [b]Heb. 9:25
20 [a]Heb. 9:8 [b]Heb. 6:19; 9:3
21 [a]Heb. 2:17 [b]1 Tim. 3:15
22 [a]Heb. 7:19; 10:1 [b]Heb. 6:11 [c]Ezek. 36:25; Heb. 9:19; 12:24; 1 Pet. 1:2 [d]Acts 22:16; 1 Cor. 6:11; Eph. 5:26; Titus 3:5; 1 Pet. 3:21
23 [a]Heb. 3:1 [b]Heb. 3:6 [c]1 Cor. 1:9; 10:13; Heb. 11:11
24 [a]Heb. 13:1 [b]Titus 3:8
25 [a]Acts 2:42 [b]Heb. 3:13 [c]1 Cor. 3:13
26 [a]Num. 15:30; Heb. 5:2; 6:4-8; 2 Pet. 2:20f. [b]1 Tim. 2:4
27 [a]John 5:29; Heb. 9:27 [b]Is. 26:11; 2 Thess. 1:7
28 [a]Deut. 17:2-6; Matt. 18:16
29 [a]Heb. 2:3 [b]Heb. 6:6 [c]Matt. 26:28; Heb. 13:20 [d]Eph. 5:26; Heb. 9:13f.; Rev. 1:5 [e]1 Cor. 6:11; Eph. 4:30; Heb. 6:4
30 [a]Deut. 32:35; Rom. 12:19 [b]Deut. 32:36

31 It is a [a]terrifying thing to fall
into the hands of the [b]living God.
32 But remember [a]the former
days, when, after being [b]enlight-
ened, you endured a great [c]conflict
of sufferings,
33 partly, by being [a]made a public
spectacle through reproaches and
tribulations, and partly by becoming [b]sharers with those who were so
treated.
34 For you [a]showed sympathy to
the prisoners, and accepted [b]joyful-
ly the seizure of your property,
knowing that you have for yourselves [c]a better possession and an
abiding one.
35 Therefore, do not throw away
your [a]confidence, which has a great
[b]reward.
36 For you have need of [a]endur-
ance, so that when you have done
the will of God, you may [b]receive
what was promised.
37 [a]FOR YET IN A VERY LITTLE
WHILE,
[b]HE WHO IS COMING WILL
COME, AND WILL NOT DELAY.
38 [a]BUT MY RIGHTEOUS ONE
SHALL LIVE BY FAITH;
AND IF HE SHRINKS BACK, MY
SOUL HAS NO PLEASURE IN
HIM.
39 But we are not of those who
shrink back to destruction, but of
those who have faith to the preserving of the soul.

CHAPTER 11

The Triumphs of Faith

NOW faith is the [a]assurance of
things [b]hoped for, the conviction of
[c]things not seen.
2 For by it the [a]men of old
[b]gained approval.
3 By faith we understand that the
[a]worlds were prepared [b]by the
[c]word of God, so that what is seen
[d]was not made out of things which
are visible.
4 By faith [a]Abel offered to God a
better sacrifice than Cain, through
which he [b]obtained the testimony
that he was righteous, God testifying about his [c]gifts, and through
faith, though [d]he is dead, he still
speaks.
5 By faith [a]Enoch was taken up
so that he should not [b]see death; and
he was not found because God took
him up; for he obtained the witness
that before his being taken up he
was pleasing to God.
6 And without faith it is impossible to please *Him,* for he who
[a]comes to God must believe that He
is, and *that* He is a rewarder of those
who seek Him.
7 By faith [a]Noah, being [b]warned
by God about [c]things not yet seen,
[d]in reverence [e]prepared an ark for
the salvation of his household, by
which he condemned the world, and
became an heir of [f]the righteousness which is according to faith.
8 By faith [a]Abraham, when he
was called, obeyed by going out to a
place which he was to [b]receive for
an inheritance; and he went out, not
knowing where he was going.
9 By faith he lived as an alien in
[a]the land of promise, as in a foreign
land, [b]dwelling in tents with Isaac
and Jacob, [c]fellow-heirs of the same
promise;
10 for he was looking for [a]the city
which has [b]foundations, [c]whose architect and builder is God.
11 By faith even [a]Sarah herself received ability to conceive, even beyond the proper time of life, since
she considered Him [b]faithful who
had promised;
12 therefore, also, there was born
of one man, and [a]him as good as
dead at that, *as many descendants*
[b]AS THE STARS OF HEAVEN IN NUM-
BER, AND INNUMERABLE AS THE SAND
WHICH IS BY THE SEASHORE.
13 [a]All these died in faith, [b]with-
out receiving the promises, but
[c]having seen them and having welcomed them from a distance, and
[d]having confessed that they were
strangers and exiles on the earth.
14 For those who say such things
make it clear that they are seeking a
country of their own.
15 And indeed if they had been
thinking of that *country* from which
they went out, [a]they would have had
opportunity to return.
16 But as it is, they desire a better
country, that is a [a]heavenly one.
Therefore [b]God is not ashamed to be
[c]called their God; for [d]He has prepared a city for them.
17 By faith [a]Abraham, when he
was tested, offered up Isaac; and he
who had [b]received the promises
was offering up his only begotten
son;
18 *it was he* to whom it was said,
"[a]IN ISAAC YOUR DESCENDANTS
SHALL BE CALLED."
19 He considered that [a]God is able
to raise *men* even from the dead;
from which he also received him
back as a [b]type.
20 By faith [a]Isaac blessed Jacob

31 [a]2 Cor. 5:11 [b]Matt. 16:16
32 [a]Heb. 5:12 [b]Heb. 6:4 [c]Phil. 1:30
33 [a]1 Cor. 4:9; Heb. 12:4 [b]Phil. 4:14 [Gr.]; 1 Thess. 2:14
34 [a]Heb. 13:3 [b]Matt. 5:12 [c]Heb. 9:15; 11:16; 13:14
35 [a]Heb. 10:19 [b]Heb. 2:2
36 [a]Luke 21:19 [b]Heb. 9:15
37 [a]Hab. 2:3; Heb. 10:25; Rev. 22:20 [b]Matt. 11:3
38 [a]Hab. 2:4; Rom. 1:17
1 [a]Heb. 3:14 [Gr.] [b]Heb. 3:6 [c]Rom. 8:24; 2 Cor. 4:18; 5:7; Heb. 11:7, 27
2 [a]Heb. 1:1 [b]Heb. 11:4, 39
3 [a]Heb. 1:2 [b]Gen. 1; Heb. 1:2 [c]Heb. 6:5; 2 Pet. 3:5 [d]Rom. 4:17
4 [a]Gen. 4:4; Matt. 23:35; 1 John 3:12 [b]Heb. 11:2 [c]Heb. 5:1 [d]Gen. 4:8-10; Heb. 12:24
5 [a]Gen. 5:21-24 [b]Luke 2:26; John 8:51; Heb. 2:9
6 [a]Heb. 7:19
7 [a]Gen. 6:13-22 [b]Heb. 8:5 [c]Heb. 11:1 [d]Heb. 5:7 [e]1 Pet. 3:20 [f]Gen. 6:9; Ezek. 14:14, 20; Rom. 4:13
8 [a]Gen. 12:1-4; Acts 7:2-4 [b]Gen. 12:7
9 [a]Acts 7:5 [b]Gen. 12:8; 13:3, 18; 18:1, 9 [c]Heb. 6:17
10 [a]Heb. 12:22; 13:14 [b]Rev. 21:14ff. [c]Heb. 11:16
11 [a]Gen. 17:19 [b]Heb. 10:23
12 [a]Rom. 4:19 [b]Gen. 15:5; 22:17
13 [a]Matt. 13:17 [b]Heb. 11:39 [c]John 8:56; Heb. 11:27 [d]Gen. 23:4; 47:9; Ps. 39:12; Eph. 2:19; 1 Pet. 1:1
15 [a]Gen. 24:6-8
16 [a]2 Tim. 4:18 [b]Mark 8:38; Heb. 2:11 [c]Gen. 26:24; 28:13; Ex. 3:6, 15; 4:5 [d]Heb. 11:10; Rev. 21:2
17 [a]Gen. 22:1-10; James 2:21 [b]Heb. 11:13
18 [a]Gen. 21:12; Rom. 9:7
19 [a]Rom. 4:21 [b]Heb. 9:9
20 [a]Gen. 27:27

and Esau, even regarding things to
come.
21 By faith [a]Jacob, as he was
dying, blessed each of the sons of
Joseph, and [b]worshiped, *leaning* on
the top of his staff.
22 By faith [a]Joseph, when he was
dying, made mention of the exodus
of the sons of Israel, and gave orders
concerning his bones.
23 By faith [a]Moses, when he was
born, was hidden for three months
by his parents, because they saw he
was a beautiful child; and they were
not afraid of the [b]king's edict.
24 By faith Moses, [a]when he had
grown up, refused to be called the
son of Pharaoh's daughter;
25 choosing rather to [a]endure ill-
treatment with the people of God,
than to enjoy the passing pleasures
of sin;
26 [a]considering the reproach of
Christ greater riches than the treasures of Egypt; for he was looking to
the [b]reward.
27 By faith he [a]left Egypt, not
[b]fearing the wrath of the king; for he
endured, as [c]seeing Him who is unseen.
28 By faith he [a]kept the Passover
and the sprinkling of the blood, so
that [b]he who destroyed the first-
born might not touch them.
29 By faith they [a]passed through
the Red Sea as though *they were*
passing through dry land; and the
Egyptians, when they attempted it,
were drowned.
30 By faith [a]the walls of Jericho
fell down, [b]after they had been encircled for seven days.
31 By faith [a]Rahab the harlot did
not perish along with those who
were disobedient, after she had welcomed the spies in peace.
32 And what more shall I say? For
time will fail me if I tell of [a]Gideon,
[b]Barak, [c]Samson, [d]Jephthah, of
[e]David and [f]Samuel and the prophets,
33 who by faith [a]conquered kingdoms, [b]performed *acts of* righteousness, [c]obtained promises, [d]shut the
mouths of lions,
34 [a]quenched the power of fire,
[b]escaped the edge of the sword,
from weakness were made strong,
[c]became mighty in war, [c]put foreign
armies to flight.
35 [a]Women received *back* their
dead by resurrection; and others
were tortured, not accepting their
release, in order that they might obtain a better resurrection;
36 and others experienced mock-

21 [a]Gen. 48:1, 5, 16, 20 [b]Gen. 47:31
22 [a]Gen. 50:24f.; Ex. 13:19
23 [a]Ex. 2:2 [b]Ex. 1:16, 22
24 [a]Ex. 2:10
25 [a]Heb. 11:37
26 [a]Luke 14:33; Phil. 3:7f. [b]Heb. 2:2
27 [a]Ex. 2:15; 12:50f.; 13:17f. [b]Ex. 2:14; 10:28f. [c]Col. 1:15
28 [a]Ex. 12:21ff. [b]Ex. 12:23, 29f.
29 [a]Ex. 14:22-29
30 [a]Josh. 6:20 [b]Josh. 6:15f.
31 [a]Josh. 2:9ff.
32 [a]Judg. 6-8 [b]Judg. 4-5 [c]Judg. 13-16 [d]Judg. 11-12 [e]1 Sam. 16:1, 13 [f]1 Sam. 1:20
33 [a]Judg. 4, 7, 11, 14; 2 Sam. 5:17; 8:2; 10:12 [b]1 Sam. 12:4; 2 Sam. 8:15 [c]2 Sam. 7:11f. [d]Judg. 14:6; 1 Sam. 17:34
34 [a]Dan. 3:23ff. [b]Ex. 18:4; 1 Sam. 18:11; 19:10; 1 Kin. 19; 2 Kin. 6; Ps. 144:10 [c]Judg. 7:21; 15:8, 15f.; 1 Sam. 17:51f.; 2 Sam. 8:1-6; 10:15ff.
35 [a]1 Kin. 17:23
36 [a]Gen. 39:20; Jer. 20:2; 37:15
37 [a]1 Kin. 21:13; 2 Chr. 24:21 [b]2 Sam. 12:31; 1 Chr. 20:3 [c]1 Kin. 19:10; Jer. 26:23 [d]1 Kin. 19:13, 19; 2 Kin. 2:8, 13f.; Zech. 13:4 [e]Heb. 11:25; 13:3
38 [a]1 Kin. 18:4
39 [a]Heb. 11:2 [b]Heb. 10:36; 11:13
40 [a]Heb. 11:16 [b]Rev. 6:11
1 [a]Heb. 10:39 [b]Rom. 13:12; Eph. 4:22 [Gr.] [c]1 Cor. 9:24; Gal. 2:2 [d]Heb. 10:36
2 [a]Heb. 2:10 [b]Phil. 2:8f.; Heb. 2:9 [c]1 Cor. 1:18, 23; Heb. 13:13 [d]Heb. 1:3
3 [a]Matt. 10:24; Rev. 2:3 [b]Gal. 6:9
4 [a]Heb. 10:32ff.; 13:13 [b]Phil. 2:8
5 [a]Prov. 3:11 [b]Heb. 12:3
6 [a]Prov. 3:12 [b]Ps. 119:75; Rev. 3:19
7 [a]Deut. 8:5; 2 Sam. 7:14; Prov. 13:24; 19:18
8 [a]1 Pet. 5:9

ings and scourgings, yes, also
[a]chains and imprisonment.
37 They were [a]stoned, they were
[b]sawn in two, they were tempted,
they were [c]put to death with the
sword; they went about [d]in sheep-
skins, in goatskins, being destitute,
afflicted, [e]ill-treated
38 (*men* of whom the world was
not worthy), [a]wandering in deserts
and mountains and caves and holes
in the ground.
39 And all these, having [a]gained
approval through their faith, [b]did
not receive what was promised,
40 because God had provided
[a]something better for us, so that
[b]apart from us they should not be
made perfect.

Chapter 12

Jesus, the Example

THEREFORE, since we have so
great a cloud of witnesses surrounding us, let [a]us also [b]lay aside every
encumbrance, and the sin which so
easily entangles us, and let us [c]run
with [d]endurance the race that is set
before us,
2 fixing our eyes on Jesus, the
[a]author and perfecter of faith, who
for the joy set before Him [b]endured
the cross, [c]despising the shame, and
has [d]sat down at the right hand of
the throne of God.
3 For [a]consider Him who has endured such hostility by sinners
against Himself, so that you may
not grow weary [b]and lose heart.
4 [a]You have not yet resisted [b]to
the point of shedding blood in your
striving against sin;
5 and you have forgotten the exhortation which is addressed to you
as sons,
"[a]MY SON, DO NOT REGARD
LIGHTLY THE DISCIPLINE OF
THE LORD,
NOR [b]FAINT WHEN YOU ARE RE-
PROVED BY HIM;

A Father's Discipline

6 [a]FOR THOSE [b]WHOM THE LORD
LOVES HE DISCIPLINES,
AND HE SCOURGES EVERY SON
WHOM HE RECEIVES."
7 It is for discipline that you endure; [a]God deals with you as with
sons; for what son is there whom *his*
father does not discipline?
8 But if you are without discipline, [a]of which all have become
partakers, then you are illegitimate
children and not sons.

9 Furthermore, we had earthly
fathers to discipline us, and we [a]re-
spected them; shall we not much
rather be subject to [b]the Father of
spirits, and [c]live?
10 For they disciplined us for a
short time as seemed best to them,
but He disciplines us for *our* good,
[a]that we may share His holiness.
11 All discipline [a]for the moment
seems not to be joyful, but sorrowful; yet to those who have been
trained by it, afterwards it yields the
[b]peaceful fruit of righteousness.
12 Therefore, [a]strengthen the
hands that are weak and the knees
that are feeble,
13 and [a]make straight paths for
your feet, so that *the limb* which is
lame may not be put out of joint, but
rather [b]be healed.
14 [a]Pursue peace with all men, and
the [b]sanctification without which no
one will [c]see the Lord.
15 See to it that no one [a]comes
short of the grace of God; that no
[b]root of bitterness springing up
causes trouble, and by it many be
[c]defiled;
16 that *there be* no [a]immoral or
[b]godless person like Esau, [c]who sold
his own birthright for a *single* meal.
17 For you know that even afterwards, [a]when he desired to inherit
the blessing, he was rejected, for he
found no place for repentance,
though he sought for it with tears.

Contrast of Sinai and Zion

18 [a]For you have not come to [b]*a*
mountain that may be touched and
to a blazing fire, and to darkness
and gloom and whirlwind,
19 and to the [a]blast of a trumpet
and the [b]sound of words which
sound was such that those who
heard [c]begged that no further word
should be spoken to them.
20 For they could not bear the
command, "[a]IF EVEN A BEAST
TOUCHES THE MOUNTAIN, IT WILL BE
STONED."
21 And so terrible was the sight,
that Moses said, "[a]I AM FULL OF
FEAR AND TREMBLING."
22 But [a]you have come to Mount
Zion and to [b]the city of [c]the living
God, [d]the heavenly Jerusalem, and
to [e]myriads of angels,
23 to the general assembly and
[a]church of the first-born who [b]are
enrolled in heaven, and to God, [c]the
Judge of all, and to the [d]spirits of
righteous men made perfect,
24 and to Jesus, the [a]mediator of a
new covenant, and to the [b]sprinkled

9 [a]Luke 18:2 [b]Num. 16:22; 27:16; Rev. 22:6 [c]Is. 38:16
10 [a]2 Pet. 1:4
11 [a]1 Pet. 1:6 [b]Is. 32:17; 2 Tim. 4:8; James 3:17f.
12 [a]Is. 35:3
13 [a]Prov. 4:26; Gal. 2:14 [b]Gal. 6:1; James 5:16
14 [a]Rom. 14:19 [b]Rom. 6:22; Heb. 12:10 [c]Matt. 5:8
15 [a]2 Cor. 6:1; Gal. 5:4; Heb. 4:1 [b]Deut. 29:18 [c]Titus 1:15
16 [a]Heb. 13:4 [b]1 Tim. 1:9 [c]Gen. 25:33f.
17 [a]Gen. 27:30
18 [a]2 Cor. 3:7-13; Heb. 12:18ff. [b]Ex. 19:12, 16ff.
19 [a]Ex. 19:16, 19; 20:18; Matt. 24:31 [b]Ex. 19:19; Deut. 4:12 [c]Ex. 20:19; Deut. 5:25
20 [a]Ex. 19:12f.
21 [a]Deut. 9:19
22 [a]Rev. 14:1 [b]Eph. 2:19; Phil. 3:20 [c]Heb. 3:12 [d]Gal. 4:26; Heb. 11:16 [e]Rev. 5:11
23 [a]Ex. 4:22; Heb. 2:12 marg. [b]Luke 10:20 [c]Gen. 18:25; Ps. 50:6; 94:2 [d]Heb. 11:40; Rev. 6:9, 11
24 [a]1 Tim. 2:5 [b]Heb. 9:19; 10:22; 1 Pet. 1:2 [c]Heb. 11:4
25 [a]Heb. 3:12 [b]Heb. 1:1 [c]Heb. 2:2f.; 10:28f. [d]Heb. 12:19 [Gr.] [e]Heb. 8:5; 11:7
26 [a]Ex. 19:18; Judg. 5:4f. [b]Hag. 2:6
27 [a]Is. 34:4; 1 Cor. 7:31
28 [a]Dan. 2:44 [b]Heb. 13:15, 21
29 [a]Deut. 4:24; 2 Thess. 1:7
1 [a]Rom. 12:10
2 [a]Matt. 25:35 [b]Gen. 18:3
3 [a]Col. 4:18 [b]Matt. 25:36
4 [a]1 Cor. 7:38; 1 Tim. 4:3 [b]1 Cor. 6:9; Gal. 5:19, 21
5 [a]Eph. 5:3; Col. 3:5; 1 Tim. 3:3 [b]Phil. 4:11 [c]Deut. 31:6
6 [a]Ps. 118:6
7 [a]Heb. 13:17, 24 [b]Luke 5:1 [c]Heb. 6:12
8 [a]2 Cor. 1:19
9 [a]Eph. 4:14; Jude 12 [b]2 Cor. 1:21; Col. 2:7

blood, which speaks better than [c]*the*
blood of Abel.

The Unshaken Kingdom

25 [a]See to it that you do not refuse
Him who is [b]speaking. For [c]if those
did not escape when they [d]refused
him who [e]warned *them* on earth,
much less *shall* we *escape* who turn
away from Him who [e]*warns* from
heaven.
26 And [a]His voice shook the earth
then, but now He has promised, saying, "[b]YET ONCE MORE I WILL SHAKE
NOT ONLY THE EARTH, BUT ALSO THE
HEAVEN."
27 And this *expression,* "Yet once
more," denotes [a]the removing of
those things which can be shaken,
as of created things, in order that
those things which cannot be
shaken may remain.
28 Therefore, since we receive a
[a]kingdom which cannot be shaken,
let us show gratitude, by which we
may [b]offer to God an acceptable service with reverence and awe;
29 for [a]our God is a consuming
fire.

Chapter 13

The Changeless Christ

LET [a]love of the brethren continue.
2 Do not neglect to [a]show hospitality to strangers, for by this some
have [b]entertained angels without
knowing it.
3 [a]Remember [b]the prisoners, as
though in prison with them, and
those who are ill-treated, since you
yourselves also are in the body.
4 [a]*Let* marriage *be held* in honor
among all, and let the *marriage* bed
be undefiled; [b]for fornicators and
adulterers God will judge.
5 Let your character be [a]free
from the love of money, [b]being content with what you have; for He
Himself has said, "[c]I WILL NEVER
DESERT YOU, NOR WILL I EVER FOR-
SAKE YOU,"
6 so that we confidently say,
"[a]THE LORD IS MY HELPER, I
WILL NOT BE AFRAID.
WHAT SHALL MAN DO TO ME?"
7 Remember [a]those who led you,
who spoke [b]the word of God to you;
and considering the result of their
conduct, [c]imitate their faith.
8 [a]Jesus Christ *is* the same yesterday and today, *yes* and forever.
9 [a]Do not be carried away by
varied and strange teachings; for
it is good for the heart to [b]be
strengthened by grace, not by

[c]foods, [d]through which those who
were thus occupied were not bene-
fited.
10 We have an altar, [a]from which
those [b]who serve the tabernacle
have no right to eat.
11 For [a]the bodies of those animals whose blood is brought into
the holy place by the high priest *as*
an offering for sin, are burned outside the camp.
12 Therefore Jesus also, [a]that He
might sanctify the people [b]through
His own blood, suffered [c]outside the
gate.
13 Hence, let us go out to Him outside the camp, [a]bearing His reproach.
14 For here [a]we do not have a lasting city, but we are seeking [b]*the city*
which is to come.

God-pleasing Sacrifices

15 [a]Through Him then, let us continually offer up a [b]sacrifice of
praise to God, that is, [c]the fruit of
lips that [1]give thanks to His name.
16 And do not neglect doing good
and [a]sharing; for [b]with such sacrifices God is pleased.
17 [a]Obey your leaders, and submit
to them; for [b]they keep watch over
your souls, as those who will give an

9 [c]Col. 2:16 [d]Heb. 9:10
10 [a]1 Cor. 10:18 [b]Heb. 8:5
11 [a]Ex. 29:14; Lev. 4:12, 21; Num. 19:3, 7
12 [a]Eph. 5:26; Heb. 2:11 [b]Heb. 9:12 [c]John 19:17
13 [a]Luke 9:23
14 [a]Heb. 10:34; 12:27 [b]Eph. 2:19
15 [1]Lit., *confess* [a]1 Pet. 2:5 [b]Lev. 7:12 [c]Is. 57:19
16 [a]Rom. 12:13 [b]Phil. 4:18
17 [a]1 Cor. 16:16; Heb. 13:7, 24 [b]Is. 62:6; Ezek. 3:17
18 [a]1 Thess. 5:25 [b]Acts 24:16
19 [a]Philem. 22
20 [a]Rom. 15:33 [b]Acts 2:24; Rom. 10:7 [c]Is. 63:11 [d]Zech. 9:11; Heb. 10:29 [e]Is. 55:3
21 [a]1 Pet. 5:10 [b]Phil. 2:13 [c]Heb. 12:28; 1 John 3:22 [d]Rom. 11:36
22 [a]Acts 13:15 [b]Heb. 3:1 [c]1 Pet. 5:12
23 [a]Acts 16:1
24 [a]1 Cor. 16:16 [b]Acts 9:13 [c]Acts 18:2
25 [a]Col. 4:18

account. Let them do this with joy
and not with grief, for this would be
unprofitable for you.
18 [a]Pray for us, for we are sure
that we have a [b]good conscience,
desiring to conduct ourselves hon-
orably in all things.
19 And I urge *you* all the more to
do this, [a]that I may be restored to
you the sooner.

Benediction

20 Now [a]the God of peace, who
[b]brought up from the dead the
[c]great Shepherd of the sheep
through [d]the blood of the [e]eternal
covenant, *even* Jesus our Lord,
21 [a]equip you in every good thing
to do His will, [b]working in us that
[c]which is pleasing in His sight,
through Jesus Christ, [d]to whom *be*
the glory forever and ever. Amen.
22 But [a]I urge you, [b]brethren, bear
with this [b]word of exhortation, for [c]I
have written to you briefly.
23 Take notice that [a]our brother
Timothy has been released, with
whom, if he comes soon, I shall see
you.
24 Greet [a]all of your leaders and
all the [b]saints. Those from [c]Italy
greet you.
25 [a]Grace be with you all.

THE EPISTLE OF
JAMES

Testing Your Faith

[a]JAMES, a [b]bond-servant of God
and [c]of the Lord Jesus Christ, to
[d]the twelve tribes who are dispersed
abroad, greetings.
2 [a]Consider it all joy, my brethren, when you encounter various
trials,
3 knowing that [a]the testing of
your [b]faith produces [c]endurance.
4 And let [a]endurance have *its*
perfect result, that you may be [b]per-
fect and complete, lacking in nothing.
5 But if any of you [a]lacks wisdom, let him ask of God, who gives
to all men generously and without
reproach, and [b]it will be given to
him.
6 But let him [a]ask in faith [b]with-
out any doubting, for the one who
doubts is like the surf of the sea
[c]driven and tossed by the wind.
7 For let not that man expect that

1 [a]Acts 12:2, 17 [b]Titus 1:1 [c]Rom. 1:1; 2 Pet. 1:1; Jude 1 [d]Luke 22:30; Acts 26:7
2 [a]Matt. 5:12
3 [a]1 Pet. 1:7 [b]Heb. 6:12 [c]Luke 21:19
4 [a]Luke 21:19 [b]Matt. 5:48
5 [a]1 Kin. 3:9ff. [b]Matt. 7:7
6 [a]Matt. 21:21 [b]Mark 11:23; Acts 10:20 [c]Eph. 4:14
8 [a]James 4:8 [b]2 Pet. 2:14
9 [a]Luke 14:11
10 [a]1 Cor. 7:31
11 [a]Matt. 20:12 [b]Ps. 102:4, 11
12 [a]Luke 6:22; [b]1 Cor. 9:25
13 [a]Gen. 22:1

he will receive anything from the
Lord,
8 *being* a [a]double-minded man,
[b]unstable in all his ways.
9 [a]But let the brother of humble
circumstances glory in his high position;
10 and *let* the rich man *glory* in his
humiliation, because [a]like flowering
grass he will pass away.
11 For the sun rises with [a]a
scorching wind, and [b]withers the
grass; and its flower falls off, and the
beauty of its appearance is destroyed; so too the rich man in the
midst of his pursuits will fade away.
12 [a]Blessed is a man who perseveres under trial; for once he has
been approved, he will receive [b]the
crown of life, which *the Lord* has
promised to those who love Him.
13 Let no one say when he is
tempted, "[a]I am being tempted by
God"; for God cannot be tempted by

evil, and He Himself does not tempt any one.

14 But each one is tempted when he is carried away and enticed by his own lust.

15 Then [a]when lust has conceived, it gives birth to sin; and when [b]sin is accomplished, it brings forth death.

16 [a]Do not be deceived, [b]my beloved brethren.

17 Every good thing bestowed and every perfect gift is [a]from above, coming down from [b]the Father of lights, [c]with whom there is no variation, or shifting shadow.

18 In the exercise of [a]His will He [b]brought us forth by [c]the word of truth, so that we might be, as it were, the [d]first fruits among His creatures.

19 *This* [a]you know, [b]my beloved brethren. But let every one be quick to hear, [c]slow to speak *and* [d]slow to anger;

20 for [a]the anger of man does not achieve the righteousness of God.

21 Therefore [a]putting aside all filthiness and *all* that remains of wickedness, in humility receive [b]the word implanted, which is able to save your souls.

22 [a]But prove yourselves doers of the word, and not merely hearers who delude themselves.

23 For if any one is a hearer of the word and not a doer, he is like a man who looks at his natural face [a]in a mirror;

24 for *once* he has looked at himself and gone away, he has immediately forgotten what kind of person he was.

25 But one who looks intently at the perfect law, [a]the *law* of liberty, and abides by it, not having become a forgetful hearer but an effectual doer, this man shall be [b]blessed in what he does.

26 If any one thinks himself to be religious, and yet does not [a]bridle his tongue but deceives his *own* heart, this man's religion is worthless.

27 This is pure and undefiled religion [a]in the sight of *our* God and Father, to [b]visit [c]orphans and widows in their distress, *and* to keep oneself unstained by [d]the world.

CHAPTER 2

The Sin of Partiality

[a]MY brethren, [b]do not hold your faith in our [c]glorious Lord Jesus Christ with *an attitude of* [d]personal favoritism.

2 For if a man comes into your assembly with a gold ring and dressed in [a]fine clothes, and there also comes in a poor man in [b]dirty clothes,

3 and you pay special attention to the one who is wearing the [a]fine clothes, and say, "You sit here in a good place," and you say to the poor man, "You stand over there, or sit down by my footstool,"

4 have you not made distinctions among yourselves, and become judges [a]with evil motives?

5 Listen, [a]my beloved brethren: did not [b]God choose the poor of this world *to be* [c]rich in faith and [d]heirs of the kingdom which He [e]promised to those who love Him?

6 But you have dishonored the poor man. Is it not the rich who oppress you and personally [a]drag you into court?

7 [a]Do they not blaspheme the fair name by which you have been called?

8 If, however, you [a]are fulfilling the royal law, according to the Scripture, "[b]YOU SHALL LOVE YOUR NEIGHBOR AS YOURSELF," you are doing well.

9 But if you [a]show partiality, you are committing sin *and* are [b]convicted by the law as transgressors.

10 For whoever keeps the whole law and yet [a]stumbles in one *point*, he has become [b]guilty of all.

11 For He who said, "[a]DO NOT COMMIT ADULTERY," also said, "[b]DO NOT COMMIT MURDER." Now if you do not commit adultery, but do commit murder, you have become a transgressor of the law.

12 So speak and so act, as those who are to be judged by [a]*the* law of liberty.

13 For [a]judgment *will be* merciless to one who has shown no mercy; mercy triumphs over judgment.

Faith and Works

14 [a]What use is it, [b]my brethren, if a man says he has faith, but he has no works? Can that faith save him?

15 [a]If a brother or sister is without clothing and in need of daily food,

16 and one of you says to them, "[a]Go in peace, be warmed and be filled," and yet you do not give them what is necessary for *their* body, what use is that?

17 Even so [a]faith, if it has no works, is dead, *being* by itself.

18 [a]But someone may *well* say, "You have faith, and I have works;

15 [a]Job 15:35; Ps. 7:14; Is. 59:4 [b]Rom. 5:12; 6:23
16 [a]1 Cor. 6:9 [b]Acts 1:15; James 1:2, 19; 2:1, 5, 14
17 [a]John 3:3; James 3:15, 17 [b]Ps. 136:7; 1 John 1:5 [c]Mal. 3:6
18 [a]John 1:13 [b]James 1:15; 1 Pet. 1:3, 23 [c]2 Cor. 6:7; Eph. 1:13; 2 Tim. 2:15 [d]Jer. 2:3; Rev. 14:4
19 [a]1 John 2:21 [b]Acts 1:15; James 1:2, 16; 2:1, 5, 14; 3:1, 10; 4:11; 5:12, 19 [c]Prov. 10:19; 17:27 [d]Prov. 16:32; Eccles. 7:9
20 [a]Matt. 5:22; Eph. 4:26
21 [a]Eph. 4:22; 1 Pet. 2:1 [b]Eph. 1:13
22 [a]Matt. 7:24-27; Luke 6:46-49; Rom. 2:13
23 [a]1 Cor. 13:12
25 [a]John 8:32; Rom. 8:2; Gal. 2:4; 6:2; James 2:12; 1 Pet. 2:16 [b]John 13:17
26 [a]Ps. 39:1; 141:3; James 3:2
27 [a]Rom. 2:13; Gal. 3:11 [b]Matt. 25:36 [c]Deut. 14:29; Job 31:16, 17, 21; Ps. 146:9; Is. 1:17, 23 [d]Matt. 12:32; Eph. 2:2
1 [a]James 1:16 [b]Heb. 12:2 [c]Acts 7:2; 1 Cor. 2:8 [d]Acts 10:34
2 [a]Luke 23:11; James 2:3 [b]Zech. 3:3f.
3 [a]Luke 23:11; James 2:3
4 [a]Luke 18:6; John 7:24
5 [a]James 1:16 [b]Job 34:19; 1 Cor. 1:27f. [c]Luke 12:21; Rev. 2:9 [d]Matt. 5:3; 25:34 [e]James 1:12
6 [a]Acts 8:3
7 [a]Acts 11:26
8 [a]Matt. 7:12 [b]Lev. 19:18
9 [a]Acts 10:34 [b]Deut. 1:17
10 [a]James 3:2 [b]Matt. 5:19
11 [a]Ex. 20:14; Deut. 5:18 [b]Ex. 20:13
12 [a]James 1:25
13 [a]Prov. 21:13
14 [a]James 1:22ff. [b]James 1:16
15 [a]Matt. 25:35f.; Luke 3:11
16 [a]1 John 3:17f.
17 [a]Gal. 5:6
18 [a]Rom. 9:19

show me your [b]faith without the
works, and I will [c]show you my faith
[d]by my works."
19 You believe that [a]God is one.
[b]You do well; [c]the demons also believe, and shudder.
20 But are you willing to recognize, [a]you foolish fellow, that [b]faith
without works is useless?
21 [a]Was not Abraham our father
justified by works, when he offered
up Isaac his son on the altar?
22 You see that [a]faith was working with his works, and as a result of
the [b]works, faith was perfected;
23 and the Scripture was fulfilled
which says, "[a]AND ABRAHAM BE-
LIEVED GOD, AND IT WAS RECKONED
TO HIM AS RIGHTEOUSNESS," and he
was called [b]the friend of God.
24 You see that a man is justified
by works, and not by faith alone.
25 And in the same way was not
[a]Rahab the harlot also justified by
works, [b]when she received the messengers and sent them out by another way?
26 For just as the body without *the*
spirit is dead, so also [a]faith without
works is dead.

CHAPTER 3

The Tongue Is a Fire

[a]LET not many *of you* become
teachers, [b]my brethren, knowing
that as such we shall incur a stricter
judgment.
2 For we all [a]stumble in many
ways. [b]If any one does not stumble
in what he says, he is a [c]perfect
man, able to [d]bridle the whole body
as well.
3 Now [a]if we put the bits into the
horses' mouths so that they may
obey us, we direct their entire body
as well.
4 Behold, the ships also, though
they are so great and are driven by
strong winds, are still directed by a
very small rudder, wherever the inclination of the pilot desires.
5 So also the tongue is a small
part of the body, and *yet* it [a]boasts
of great things. [b]Behold, how great a
forest is set aflame by such a small
fire!
6 And [a]the tongue is a fire, the
very world of iniquity; the tongue is
set among our members as that
which [b]defiles the entire body, and
sets on fire the course of *our* life,
and is set on fire by [c]hell.
7 For every species of beasts and
birds, of reptiles and creatures of

18 [b]Rom. 3:28; 4:6; Heb. 11:33 [c]James 3:13 [d]Matt. 7:16f.; Gal. 5:6
19 [a]Deut. 6:4; Mark 12:29 [b]James 2:8 [c]Matt. 8:29; Mark 1:24
20 [a]Rom. 9:20; 1 Cor. 15:36 [b]Gal. 5:6; James 2:17
21 [a]Gen. 22:9
22 [a]John 6:29; Heb. 11:17 [b]1 Thess. 1:3
23 [a]Gen. 15:6; Rom. 4:3 [b]2 Chr. 20:7; Is. 41:8
25 [a]Heb. 11:31 [b]Josh. 2:4, 6, 15
26 [a]Gal. 5:6
1 [a]Matt. 23:8; Rom. 2:20f.; 1 Tim. 1:7 [b]James 1:16; 3:10
2 [a]James 2:10 [b]Matt. 12:34-37 [c]James 1:4 [d]James 1:26
3 [a]Ps. 32:9
5 [a]Ps. 12:3f.; 73:8f. [b]Prov. 26:20f.
6 [a]Ps. 120:3, 4 [b]Matt. 12:36f.; 15:11, 18f. [c]Matt. 5:22
8 [a]Ps. 140:3; Eccles. 10:11; Rom. 3:13
9 [a]James 1:27 [b]1 Cor. 11:7
12 [a]Matt. 7:16
13 [a]James 2:18 [b]1 Pet. 2:12
14 [a]Rom. 2:8; 2 Cor. 12:20; James 3:16 [b]1 Tim. 2:4; James 1:18; 5:19
15 [a]James 1:17 [b]1 Cor. 2:6; 3:19 [c]2 Cor. 1:12; Jude 19 [d]2 Thess. 2:9f.; 1 Tim. 4:1; Rev. 2:24
16 [a]Rom. 2:8; 2 Cor. 12:20; James 3:14
17 [a]James 1:17 [b]2 Cor. 7:11; James 4:8 [c]Matt. 5:9; Heb. 12:11 [d]Phil. 4:5; Titus 3:2 [e]Luke 6:36; James 2:13 [f]James 2:4 [Gr.] [g]Rom. 12:9
18 [a]Prov. 11:18; Is. 32:17; Hos. 10:12; Amos 6:12; Gal. 6:8; Phil. 1:11
1 [a]Titus 3:9 [b]Rom. 7:23
2 [a]James 5:6
3 [a]1 John 3:22
4 [a]Is. 54:5; Jer. 2:2; Ezek. 16:32; Matt. 12:39 [b]James 1:27 [c]Rom. 8:7; 1 John 2:15 [d]Matt. 6:24; John 15:19

the sea, is tamed, and has been
tamed by the human race.
8 But no one can tame the
tongue; *it is* a restless evil *and* full of
[a]deadly poison.
9 With it we bless [a]*our* Lord and
Father; and with it we curse men,
[b]who have been made in the likeness of God;
10 from the same mouth come
both blessing and cursing. My
brethren, these things ought not to
be this way.
11 Does a fountain send out from
the same opening *both* fresh and bitter *water?*
12 [a]Can a fig tree, my brethren,
produce olives, or a vine produce
figs? Neither *can* salt water produce
fresh.

Wisdom from Above

13 Who among you is wise and understanding? [a]Let him show by his
[b]good behavior his deeds in the gentleness of wisdom.
14 But if you have bitter [a]jealousy
and selfish ambition in your heart,
do not be arrogant and *so* lie against
[b]the truth.
15 This wisdom is not that which
comes down [a]from above, but is
[b]earthly, [c]natural, [d]demonic.
16 For where [a]jealousy and selfish
ambition exist, there is disorder and
every evil thing.
17 But the wisdom [a]from above is
first [b]pure, then [c]peaceable, [d]gentle,
reasonable, [e]full of mercy and good
fruits, [f]unwavering, without [g]hy-
pocrisy.
18 And the [a]seed whose fruit is
righteousness is sown in peace by
those who make peace.

CHAPTER 4

Things to Avoid

WHAT is the source of quarrels
and [a]conflicts among you? Is not the
source your pleasures that wage
[b]war in your members?
2 You lust and do not have; *so*
you [a]commit murder. And you are
envious and cannot obtain; *so* you
fight and quarrel. You do not have
because you do not ask.
3 You ask and [a]do not receive,
because you ask with wrong motives, so that you may spend *it*
on your pleasures.
4 You [a]adulteresses, do you not
know that friendship with [b]the
world is [c]hostility toward God?
[d]Therefore whoever wishes to be a

friend of the world makes himself
an enemy of God.
5 Or do you think that the Scripture [a]speaks to no purpose: "He
jealously desires [b]the Spirit which
He has made to dwell in us"?
6 But [a]He gives a greater grace.
Therefore *it* says, "[b]GOD IS OPPOSED
TO THE PROUD, BUT GIVES GRACE TO
THE HUMBLE."
7 [a]Submit therefore to God. [b]Re-
sist the devil and he will flee from
you.
8 [a]Draw near to God and He will
draw near to you. [b]Cleanse your
hands, you sinners; and [c]purify your
hearts, you [d]double-minded.
9 [a]Be miserable and mourn and
weep; let your laughter be turned
into mourning, and your joy to
gloom.
10 [a]Humble yourselves in the
presence of the Lord, and He will
exalt you.
11 [a]Do not speak against one another, [b]brethren. He who speaks
against a brother, or [c]judges his
brother, speaks against [d]the law,
and judges the law; but if you judge
the law, you are not [e]a doer of the
law, but a judge *of it.*
12 There is *only* one [a]Lawgiver
and Judge, the One who is [b]able to
save and to destroy; but [c]who are
you who judge your neighbor?
13 [a]Come now, you who say, "[b]To-
day or tomorrow, we shall go to
such and such a city, and spend a
year there and engage in business
and make a profit."
14 Yet you do not know what your
life will be like tomorrow. [a]You are
just a vapor that appears for a little
while and then vanishes away.
15 Instead, *you ought* to say, "[a]If
the Lord wills, we shall live and also
do this or that."
16 But as it is, you boast in your
arrogance; [a]all such boasting is evil.
17 Therefore, [a]to one who knows
the right thing to do, and does not do
it, to him it is sin.

CHAPTER 5

Misuse of Riches

[a]COME now, [b]you rich, [c]weep and
howl for your miseries which are
coming upon you.
2 [a]Your riches have rotted and
your garments have become moth-
eaten.
3 Your gold and your silver have
rusted; and their rust will be a witness against you and will consume
your flesh like fire. It is [a]in the last
days that you have stored up your
treasure!
4 Behold, [a]the pay of the laborers
who mowed your fields, *and* which
has been withheld by you, cries out
against you; and [b]the outcry of
those who did the harvesting has
reached the ears of [c]the Lord of Sab-
aoth.
5 You have [a]lived luxuriously on
the earth and led a life of wanton
pleasure; you have fattened your
hearts in [b]a day of slaughter.
6 You have condemned and [a]put
to death [b]the righteous *man;* he
does not resist you.

Exhortation

7 Be patient, therefore, [a]breth-
ren, [b]until the coming of the Lord.
[c]Behold, the farmer waits for the
precious produce of the soil, being
patient about it, until it gets [d]the
early and late rains.
8 [a]You too be patient; [b]strength-
en your hearts, for [c]the coming of
the Lord is [d]at hand.
9 [a]Do not complain, [b]brethren,
against one another, that you yourselves may not be judged; behold,
[c]the Judge is standing [d]right at the
door.
10 As an example, [a]brethren, of
suffering and patience, take [b]the
prophets who spoke in the name of
the Lord.
11 Behold, we count those
[a]blessed who endured. You have
heard of [b]the endurance of Job and
have seen [c]the outcome of the
Lord's dealings, that [d]the Lord is full
of compassion and *is* merciful.
12 But above all, [a]my brethren,
[b]do not swear, either by heaven or
by earth or with any other oath; but
let your yes be yes, and your no, no;
so that you may not fall under judgment.
13 Is anyone among you [a]suffer-
ing? [b]Let him pray. Is anyone cheerful? Let him [c]sing praises.
14 Is anyone among you sick? Let
him call for [a]the elders of the
church, and let them pray over him,
[b]anointing him with oil in the name
of the Lord;
15 and the [a]prayer offered in faith
will [b]restore the one who is sick, and
the Lord will [c]raise him up, and if he
has committed sins, they will be forgiven him.
16 Therefore, [a]confess your sins to
one another, and pray for one an-

5 [a]Num. 23:19 [b]1 Cor. 6:19
6 [a]Is. 54:7f.; Matt. 13:12 [b]Ps. 138:6; Prov. 3:34
7 [a]1 Pet. 5:6 [b]Eph. 4:27; 6:11f.
8 [a]2 Chr. 15:2 [b]Job 17:9 [c]Jer. 4:14 1 John 3:3 [d]James 1:8
9 [a]Neh. 8:9
10 [a]Job 5:11; Ezek. 21:26
11 [a]2 Cor. 12:20 [b]James 1:16; 5:7, 9, 10 [c]Matt. 7:1; Rom. 14:4 [d]James 2:8 [e]James 1:22
12 [a]Is. 33:22; James 5:9 [b]Matt. 10:28 [c]Rom. 14:4
13 [a]James 5:1 [b]Prov. 27:1
14 [a]Job 7:7; Ps. 39:5
15 [a]Acts 18:21
16 [a]1 Cor. 5:6
17 [a]Luke 12:47
1 [a]James 4:13 [b]Luke 6:24; 1 Tim. 6:9 [c]Is. 13:6; 15:3
2 [a]Job 13:28
3 [a]James 5:7, 8
4 [a]Lev. 19:13; Mal. 3:5 [b]Ex. 2:23 [c]Rom. 9:29
5 [a]Ezek. 16:49; Luke 16:19 [b]Jer. 12:3
6 [a]James 4:2 [b]Heb. 10:38; 1 Pet. 4:18
7 [a]James 4:11; 5:9, 10 [b]John 21:22; 1 Thess. 2:19 [c]Gal. 6:9 [d]Deut. 11:14; Jer. 5:24; Joel 2:23
8 [a]Luke 21:19 [b]1 Thess. 3:13 [c]John 21:22; 1 Thess. 2:19 [d]Rom. 13:11, 12; 1 Pet. 4:7
9 [a]James 4:11 [b]James 4:11; 5:7, 10 [c]1 Cor. 4:5 [d]Matt. 24:33
10 [a]James 4:11; 5:7, 9 [b]Matt. 5:12
11 [a]Matt. 5:10; 1 Pet. 3:14 [b]Job 1:21f.; 2:10 [c]Job 42:10, 12 [d]Ex. 34:6
12 [a]James 1:16 [b]Matt. 5:34-37
13 [a]James 5:10 [b]Ps. 50:15 [c]1 Cor. 14:15; Col. 3:16
14 [a]Acts 11:30 [b]Mark 6:13; 16:18
15 [a]James 1:6 [b]1 Cor. 1:21; James 5:20 [c]John 6:39; 2 Cor. 4:14
16 [a]Matt. 3:6; Mark 1:5; Acts 19:18

other, so that you may be [b]healed.
The effective prayer of a righteous
man can accomplish much.
17 Elijah was [a]a man with a nature
like ours, and [b]he prayed earnestly
that it might not rain; and it did not
rain on the earth for three years and
six months.
18 And he [a]prayed again, and [b]the

16 [b]Heb. 12:13
17 [a]Acts 14:15
[b]1 Kin. 17:1; 18:1
18 [a]1 Kin. 18:42
[b]1 Kin. 18:45
19 [a]Matt. 18:15;
Gal. 6:1 [b]James
3:14
20 [a]Rom. 11:14
[b]1 Pet. 4:8

sky poured rain, and the earth produced its fruit.
19 My brethren, [a]if any among you
strays from [b]the truth, and one
turns him back,
20 let him know that he who turns
a sinner from the error of his way
will [a]save his soul from death, and
will [b]cover a multitude of sins.

THE FIRST EPISTLE OF

PETER

A Living Hope, and a Sure Salvation

[a]PETER, an apostle of Jesus Christ,
to those who reside as [b]aliens, [c]scat-
tered throughout [d]Pontus, [e]Galatia,
[d]Cappadocia, [d]Asia, and [f]Bithynia,
[g]who are chosen
2 according to the [a]foreknowl-
edge of God the Father, [b]by the
sanctifying work of the Spirit, that
you may [c]obey Jesus Christ and be
sprinkled with His blood: May grace
and peace be yours in fullest measure.
3 [a]Blessed be the God and Father
of our Lord Jesus Christ, who [b]ac-
cording to His great mercy [c]has
caused us to be born again to a living hope through the resurrection of
Jesus Christ from the dead,
4 to *obtain* an [a]inheritance *which*
is imperishable and undefiled and
[b]will not fade away, reserved in
heaven for you,
5 who are [a]protected by the
power of God [b]through faith for [c]a
salvation ready to be revealed in the
last time.
6 [a]In this you greatly rejoice,
even though now [b]for a little while,
[c]if necessary, you have been distressed by various trials,
7 that the [a]proof of your faith,
being more precious than gold
which is perishable, [b]even though
tested by fire, [c]may be found to result in praise and glory and honor at
the revelation of Jesus Christ;
8 and [a]though you have not seen
Him, you [b]love Him, and though you
do not see Him now, but believe in
Him, you greatly rejoice with joy inexpressible and full of glory,
9 obtaining as [a]the outcome of
your faith the salvation of your
souls.
10 [a]As to this salvation, the prophets who [b]prophesied of the [c]grace

1 [a]2 Pet. 1:1
[b]1 Pet. 2:11
[c]James 1:1 [d]Acts
2:9 [e]Acts 16:6
[f]Acts 16:7 [g]Matt.
24:22; Luke 18:7
2 [a]Rom. 8:29;
1 Pet. 1:20
[b]2 Thess. 2:13
[c]Rom. 1:5
3 [a]2 Cor. 1:3
[b]Gal. 6:16; Titus
3:5 [c]James 1:18
4 [a]Acts 20:32
[b]1 Pet. 5:4
5 [a]John 10:28;
Phil 4:7 [b]Eph. 2:8
[c]1 Cor. 1:21
6 [a]Rom. 5:2
[b]1 Pet. 5:10
[c]1 Pet. 3:17
7 [a]James 1:3
[b]Job 23:10; Ps.
66:10 [c]Rom. 2:7
8 [a]John 20:29
[b]Eph. 3:19
9 [a]Rom. 6:22
10 [a]Matt. 13:17
[b]Matt. 26:24;
Luke 24:27, 44
[c]Col. 3:4
11 [a]Rom. 8:9;
2 Pet. 1:21 [b]Matt.
26:24
12 [a]1 Pet. 1:25;
4:6 [b]Acts 2:2-4
[c]Luke 2:13; Eph.
3:10
13 [a]Eph. 6:14
[b]Rom. 12:3
[c]1 Pet. 1:3 [d]Col.
3:4; 1 Pet. 1:10
[e]Luke 17:30
14 [a]1 Pet. 1:2
[b]Rom. 12:2
15 [a]1 Thess. 4:7;
1 John 3:3 [b]2 Cor.
7:1 [c]James 3:13
16 [a]Lev. 11:44f.
17 [a]Ps. 89:26
[b]Acts 10:34
[c]Matt. 16:27
[d]2 Cor. 7:1
18 [a]Is. 52:3
[b]Eph. 4:17
19 [a]Acts 20:28;
1 Pet. 1:2 [b]John
1:29; Heb. 9:14
20 [a]Acts 2:23
Rev. 13:8 [b]Matt.
25:34 [c]Heb. 9:26
21 [a]Rom. 4:24;
10:9 [b]John 17:5

that *would come* to you made careful search and inquiry,
11 seeking to know what person or
time [a]the Spirit of Christ within
them was indicating as He [b]predict-
ed the sufferings of Christ and the
glories to follow.
12 It was revealed to them that
they were not serving themselves,
but you, in these things which now
have been announced to you
through those who [a]preached the
gospel to you by [b]the Holy Spirit
sent from heaven—things into
which [c]angels long to look.
13 Therefore, [a]gird your minds for
action, [b]keep sober *in spirit,* fix your
[c]hope completely on the [d]grace to
be brought to you at [e]the revelation
of Jesus Christ.
14 As [a]obedient children, do not
[b]be conformed to the former lusts
which were yours in your ignorance,
15 but [a]like the Holy One who
called you, [b]be holy yourselves also
[c]in all *your* behavior;
16 because it is written, "[a]YOU
SHALL BE HOLY, FOR I AM HOLY."
17 And if you [a]address as Father
the One who [b]impartially [c]judges
according to each man's work, conduct yourselves [d]in fear during the
time of your stay *upon earth;*
18 knowing that you were not [a]re-
deemed with perishable things like
silver or gold from your [b]futile way
of life inherited from your forefathers,
19 but with precious [a]blood, as of
a [b]lamb unblemished and spotless,
the blood of Christ.
20 For He was [a]foreknown before
[b]the foundation of the world, but
has [c]appeared in these last times for
the sake of you
21 who through Him are [a]believ-
ers in God, who raised Him from the
dead and [b]gave Him glory, so that
your faith and hope are in God.

22 Since you have [a]in obedience to
the truth [b]purified your souls for a
[c]sincere love of the brethren, fervently love one another from the
heart,
23 for you have been [a]born again
[b]not of seed which is perishable but
imperishable, *that is,* through the
living and abiding [c]word of God.
24 For,
"[a]ALL FLESH IS LIKE GRASS,
AND ALL ITS GLORY LIKE THE
FLOWER OF GRASS.
THE GRASS WITHERS,
AND THE FLOWER FALLS OFF,
25 [a]BUT THE WORD OF THE LORD
ABIDES FOREVER."
And this is [b]the word which was
preached to you.

CHAPTER 2

As Newborn Babes

THEREFORE, [a]putting aside all
malice and all guile and hypocrisy
and envy and all [b]slander,
2 [a]like newborn babes, long for
the [b]pure milk of the word, that by it
you may [c]grow in respect to salvation,
3 if you have [a]tasted [b]the kindness of the Lord.

As Living Stones

4 And coming to Him as to a living stone, [a]rejected by men, but
choice and precious in the sight of
God,
5 [a]you also, as living stones, are
being built up as a [b]spiritual house
for a holy [c]priesthood, to [d]offer up
spiritual sacrifices acceptable to
God through Jesus Christ.
6 For *this* is contained in Scripture:
"[a]BEHOLD I LAY IN ZION A
CHOICE STONE, A [b]PRECIOUS
CORNER *stone,*
AND HE WHO BELIEVES IN
HIM SHALL NOT BE DISAP-
POINTED."
7 [a]This precious value, then, is
for you who believe, but for those
who disbelieve,
"[b]THE STONE WHICH THE BUILD-
ERS [c]REJECTED,
THIS BECAME THE VERY CORNER
stone,"
8 and,
"[a]A STONE OF STUMBLING AND A
ROCK OF OFFENSE";
[b]for they stumble because they are
disobedient to the word, [c]and to this
doom they were also appointed.
9 But you are [a]A CHOSEN RACE, A
ROYAL [b]PRIESTHOOD, A [c]HOLY NA-

22 [a]1 Pet. 1:2 [b]James 4:8 [c]John 13:34; Rom. 12:10; Heb. 13:1
23 [a]John 3:3; 1 Pet. 1:3 [b]John 1:13 [c]Heb. 4:12
24 [a]Is. 40:6ff.; James 1:10f.
25 [a]Is. 40:8 [b]Heb. 6:5
1 [a]Eph. 4:22, 25, 31 [b]James 4:11
2 [a]Matt. 18:3; 19:14; Mark 10:15; Luke 18:17; 1 Cor. 14:20 [b]1 Cor. 3:2 [c]Eph. 4:15f.
3 [a]Heb. 6:5 [b]Ps. 34:8; Titus 3:4
4 [a]1 Pet. 2:7
5 [a]1 Cor. 3:9 [b]Gal. 6:10; 1 Tim. 3:15 [c]Is. 61:6; 66:21; 1 Pet. 2:9; Rev. 1:6 [d]Rom. 15:16
6 [a]Is. 28:16; 1 Pet. 2:6, 8 [b]Eph. 2:20
7 [a]2 Cor. 2:16; 1 Pet. 2:7, 8 [b]Ps. 118:22; Matt. 21:42; Luke 2:34 [c]1 Pet. 2:4
8 [a]Is. 8:14 [b]1 Cor. 1:23; Gal. 5:11 [c]Rom. 9:22
9 [a]Deut. 10:15; Is. 43:20f. [b]Is. 61:6; 66:21; 1 Pet. 2:5; Rev. 1:6 [c]Ex. 19:6; Deut. 7:6 [d]Titus 2:14 [e]Is. 42:16; Acts 26:18
10 [a]Hos. 1:10
11 [a]Heb. 6:9; 1 Pet. 4:12 [b]Rom. 12:1 [c]Lev. 25:23 [d]Rom. 13:14; Gal. 5:16, 24 [e]James 4:1
12 [a]2 Cor. 8:21; Phil. 2:15; Titus 2:8 [b]Acts 28:22 [c]Matt. 5:16; 9:8 [d]Is. 10:3
13 [a]Rom. 13:1
14 [a]Rom. 13:4 [b]Rom. 13:3
15 [a]1 Pet. 3:17 [b]1 Pet. 2:12
16 [a]John 8:32; James 1:25 [b]Rom. 6:22; 1 Cor. 7:22
17 [a]Rom. 12:10; 13:7 [b]1 Pet. 1:22 [c]Prov. 24:21 [d]Prov. 24:21; Matt. 22:21; 1 Pet. 2:13
18 [a]Eph. 6:5 [b]James 3:17
19 [a]Rom. 13:5
20 [a]1 Pet. 3:17
21 [a]Acts 14:22; 1 Pet. 3:9 [b]1 Pet. 3:18; 4:1, 13 [c]Matt. 11:29
22 [a]Is. 53:9
23 [a]Is. 53:7; Heb. 12:3; 1 Pet. 3:9

TION, [d]A PEOPLE FOR *God's* OWN POS-
SESSION, that you may proclaim the
excellencies of Him who has called
you [e]out of darkness into His marvelous light;
10 [a]for you once were NOT A PEO-
PLE, but now you are THE PEOPLE OF
GOD; you had NOT RECEIVED MERCY,
but now you have RECEIVED MERCY.
11 [a]Beloved, [b]I urge you as [c]aliens
and strangers to abstain from
[d]fleshly lusts, which wage [e]war
against the soul.
12 [a]Keep your behavior excellent
among the Gentiles, so that in the
thing in which they [b]slander you as
evildoers, they may on account of
your good deeds, as they observe
them, [c]glorify God [d]in the day of
visitation.

Honor Authority

13 [a]Submit yourselves for the
Lord's sake to every human institution, whether to a king as the one in
authority,
14 or to governors as sent by him
[a]for the punishment of evildoers
and the [b]praise of those who do
right.
15 For [a]such is the will of God that
by doing right you may [b]silence the
ignorance of foolish men.
16 *Act* as [a]free men, and do not
use your freedom as a covering for
evil, but *use it* as [b]bondslaves of
God.
17 [a]Honor all men; [b]love the brotherhood, [c]fear God, [d]honor the king.
18 [a]Servants, be submissive to
your masters with all respect, not
only to those who are good and
[b]gentle, but also to those who are
unreasonable.
19 For this *finds* favor, if for the
sake of [a]conscience toward God a
man bears up under sorrows when
suffering unjustly.
20 For what credit is there if, when
you sin and are harshly treated, you
endure it with patience? But if
[a]when you do what is right and suffer *for it* you patiently endure it, this
finds favor with God.

Christ Is Our Example

21 For [a]you have been called for
this purpose, [b]since Christ also suffered for you, leaving you [c]an example for you to follow in His steps,
22 WHO [a]COMMITTED NO SIN, NOR
WAS ANY DECEIT FOUND IN HIS
MOUTH;
23 and while being [a]reviled, He did
not revile in return; while suffering,
He uttered no threats, but kept en-

trusting *Himself* to Him who judges righteously;

24 and He Himself [a]bore our sins in His body on the [b]cross, that we [c]might die to sin and live to righteousness; for [d]by His wounds you were [e]healed.

25 For you were [a]continually straying like sheep, but now you have returned to the [b]Shepherd and Guardian of your souls.

Chapter 3

Godly Living

1 [a]In the same way, you wives, [b]be submissive to your own husbands so that even if any *of them* are disobedient to the word, they may be [c]won without a word by the behavior of their wives,

2 as they observe your chaste and respectful behavior.

3 [a]And let not your adornment be *merely* external—braiding the hair, and wearing gold jewelry, and putting on dresses;

4 but *let it be* [a]the hidden person of the heart, with the imperishable quality of a gentle and quiet spirit, which is precious in the sight of God.

5 For in this way in former times the holy women also, [a]who hoped in God, used to adorn themselves, being submissive to their own husbands.

6 Thus Sarah obeyed Abraham, [a]calling him lord, and you have become her children if you do what is right [b]without being frightened by any fear.

7 [a]You husbands likewise, live with your wives in an understanding way, as with a weaker [b]vessel, since she is a woman; and grant her honor as a fellow-heir of the grace of life, so that your prayers may not be hindered.

8 To sum up, [a]let all be harmonious, sympathetic, [b]brotherly, [c]kindhearted, and [d]humble in spirit;

9 [a]not returning evil for evil, or [b]insult for insult, but giving a [c]blessing instead; for [d]you were called for the very purpose that you might [e]inherit a blessing.

10 For

"[a]LET HIM WHO MEANS TO LOVE LIFE AND SEE GOOD DAYS
REFRAIN HIS TONGUE FROM EVIL AND HIS LIPS FROM SPEAKING GUILE.

11 "[a]AND LET HIM TURN AWAY FROM EVIL AND DO GOOD;
LET HIM SEEK PEACE AND PURSUE IT.

12 "[a]FOR THE EYES OF THE LORD ARE UPON THE RIGHTEOUS,
AND HIS EARS ATTEND TO THEIR PRAYER,
BUT THE FACE OF THE LORD IS AGAINST THOSE WHO DO EVIL."

13 And [a]who is there to harm you if you prove zealous for what is good?

14 But even if you should [a]suffer for the sake of righteousness, [b]*you are* blessed. [c]AND DO NOT FEAR THEIR [1]INTIMIDATION, AND DO NOT BE TROUBLED,

15 but sanctify [a]Christ as Lord in your hearts, always *being* ready [b]to make a defense to every one who asks you to give an account for the [c]hope that is in you, yet [d]with gentleness and [e]reverence;

16 and keep a [a]good conscience so that in the thing in which [b]you are slandered, those who revile your good behavior in Christ may be put to shame.

17 For [a]it is better, [b]if God should will it so, that you suffer for doing what is right rather than for doing what is wrong.

18 For [a]Christ also died for sins [b]once for all, *the* just for *the* unjust, in order that He might [c]bring us to God, having been put to death [d]in the flesh, but made alive [e]in the spirit;

19 in which also He went and [a]made proclamation to the spirits *now* in prison,

20 who once were disobedient, when the [a]patience of God [b]kept waiting in the days of Noah, during the construction of [c]the ark, in which a few, that is, [d]eight [e]persons, were brought safely through *the* water.

21 [a]And corresponding to that, baptism now saves you—[b]not the removal of dirt from the flesh, but an appeal to God for a [c]good conscience—through [d]the resurrection of Jesus Christ,

22 [a]who is at the right hand of God, [b]having gone into heaven, [c]after angels and authorities and powers had been subjected to Him.

Chapter 4

Keep Fervent in Your Love

1 THEREFORE, since [a]Christ has suffered in the flesh, [b]arm yourselves also with the same purpose,

---

24 [a]Is. 53:4, 11; 1 Cor. 15:3; Heb. 9:28 [b]Acts 5:30 [c]Rom. 6:2, 13 [d]Is. 53:5 [e]Heb. 12:13; James 5:16
25 [a]Is. 53:6 [b]John 10:11; 1 Pet. 5:4
1 [a]1 Pet. 2:18; 3:7 [b]Eph. 5:22 [c]1 Cor. 9:19
3 [a]Is. 3:18ff.; 1 Tim. 2:9
4 [a]Rom. 7:22
5 [a]1 Tim. 5:5; 1 Pet. 1:3
6 [a]Gen. 18:12 [b]1 Pet. 3:14
7 [a]Eph. 5:25; Col. 3:19 [b]1 Thess. 4:4
8 [a]Rom. 12:16 [b]1 Pet. 1:22 [c]Eph. 4:32 [d]Eph. 4:2; Phil. 2:3; 1 Pet. 5:5
9 [a]Rom. 12:17; 1 Thess. 5:15 [b]1 Cor. 4:12; 1 Pet. 2:23 [c]Luke 6:28; Rom. 12:14; 1 Cor. 4:12 [d]1 Pet. 2:21 [e]Gal. 3:14; Heb. 6:14; 12:17
10 [a]Ps. 34:12, 13
11 [a]Ps. 34:14
12 [a]Ps. 34:15, 16
13 [a]Prov. 16:7
14 [1]Lit., *fear* [a]1 Pet. 2:19ff.; 4:15f. [b]James 5:11 [c]Is. 8:12f.; 1 Pet. 3:6
15 [a]1 Pet. 1:3 [b]Col. 4:6 [c]1 Pet. 1:3 [d]2 Tim. 2:25 [e]1 Pet. 1:17
16 [a]1 Tim. 1:5; Heb. 13:18; 1 Pet. 3:21 [b]1 Pet. 2:12, 15
17 [a]1 Pet. 2:20; 4:15f. [b]Acts 18:21; 1 Pet. 1:6; 2:15; 4:19
18 [a]1 Pet. 2:21 [b]Heb. 9:26, 28; 10:10 [c]Rom. 5:2; Eph. 3:12 [d]Col. 1:22; 1 Pet. 4:1 [e]1 Pet. 4:6
19 [a]1 Pet. 4:6
20 [a]Rom. 2:4 [b]Gen. 6:3, 5, 13f. [c]Heb. 11:7 [d]Gen. 8:18; 2 Pet. 2:5 [e]Acts 2:41; 1 Pet. 1:9, 22; 2:25; 4:19
21 [a]Acts 16:33; Titus 3:5 [b]Heb. 9:14; 10:22 [c]1 Tim. 1:5; Heb. 13:18; 1 Pet. 3:16 [d]1 Pet. 1:3
22 [a]Mark 16:19 [b]Heb. 4:14; 6:20 [c]Rom. 8:38f.; Heb. 1:6
1 [a]1 Pet. 2:21 [b]Eph. 6:13

because [c]he who has suffered in the flesh has ceased from sin,

2 [a]so as to live [b]the rest of the time in the flesh no longer for the lusts of men, but for the will of God.

3 For [a]the time already past is sufficient *for you* to have carried out the desire of the Gentiles, [b]having pursued a course of sensuality, lusts, drunkenness, carousals, drinking parties and abominable idolatries.

4 And in *all* this, they are surprised that you do not run with *them* into the same excess of [a]dissipation, and they [b]malign *you;*

5 but they shall give account to Him who is ready to judge [a]the living and the dead.

6 For [a]the gospel has for this purpose been preached even to those who are dead, that though they are judged in the flesh as men, they may live in the spirit according to *the will of* God.

7 [a]The end of all things is at hand; therefore, [b]be of sound judgment and sober *spirit* for the purpose of prayer.

8 Above all, [a]keep fervent in your love for one another, because [b]love covers a multitude of sins.

9 [a]Be hospitable to one another without [b]complaint.

10 [a]As each one has received a *special* gift, employ it in serving one another, as good [b]stewards of the manifold grace of God.

11 [a]Whoever speaks, *let him speak,* as it were, the [b]utterances of God; whoever serves, *let him do so* as [c]by the strength which God supplies; so that [d]in all things God may be glorified through Jesus Christ, [e]to whom belongs the glory and dominion forever and ever. Amen.

Share the Sufferings of Christ

12 [a]Beloved, do not be surprised at the [b]fiery ordeal among you, which comes upon you for your testing, as though some strange thing were happening to you;

13 but to the degree that you [a]share the sufferings of Christ, keep on rejoicing; so that also at the [b]revelation of His glory, [c]you may rejoice with exultation.

14 If you are reviled [a]for the name of Christ, [b]you are blessed, [c]because the Spirit of glory and of God rests upon you.

15 By no means [a]let any of you suffer as a murderer, or thief, or evildoer, or a [b]troublesome meddler;

16 but if *anyone suffers* as a [a]Christian, let him not feel ashamed, but in that name let him [b]glorify God.

17 For *it is* time for judgment [a]to begin with [b]the household of God; and if *it* [c]*begins* with us first, what *will be* the outcome for those [d]who do not obey the [e]gospel of God?

18 [a]AND IF IT IS WITH DIFFICULTY THAT THE RIGHTEOUS IS SAVED, WHAT WILL BECOME OF THE [b]GODLESS MAN AND THE SINNER?

19 Therefore, let those also who suffer according to [a]the will of God entrust their souls to a faithful Creator in doing what is right.

Chapter 5

Serve God Willingly

[a]THEREFORE, I exhort the elders among you, as *your* [b]fellow-elder and [c]witness of the sufferings of Christ, and a [d]partaker also of the glory that is to be revealed,

2 shepherd [a]the flock of God among you, [b]not under compulsion, but voluntarily, according to *the will of* God; and [c]not for sordid gain, but with eagerness;

3 nor yet as [a]lording it over those allotted to your charge, but proving to be [b]examples to the flock.

4 And when the Chief [a]Shepherd appears, you will receive the [b]unfading [c]crown of glory.

5 [a]You younger men, likewise, [b]be subject to your elders; and all of you, clothe yourselves with [c]humility toward one another, for [d]GOD IS OPPOSED TO THE PROUD, BUT GIVES GRACE TO THE HUMBLE.

6 [a]Humble yourselves, therefore, under the mighty hand of God, that He may exalt you at the proper time,

7 casting all your [a]anxiety upon Him, because He cares for you.

8 [a]Be of sober *spirit,* [b]be on the alert. Your adversary, [c]the devil, prowls about like a roaring [d]lion, seeking someone to devour.

9 [a]But resist him, [b]firm in *your* faith, knowing that [c]the same experiences of suffering are being accomplished by your brethren who are in the world.

10 And after you have suffered [a]for a little while, the [b]God of all grace, who [c]called you to His [d]eternal glory in Christ, will Himself [e]perfect, [f]confirm, strengthen *and* establish you.

1 [c]Rom. 6:7
2 [a]Rom. 6:2; Col. 3:3 [b]1 Pet. 1:14
3 [a]1 Cor. 12:2 [b]Rom. 13:13; Eph. 2:2; 4:17ff.
4 [a]Eph. 5:18 [b]1 Pet. 3:16
5 [a]Acts 10:42
6 [a]1 Pet. 1:12
7 [a]Rom. 13:11; Heb. 9:26; James 5:8 [b]1 Pet. 1:13
8 [a]1 Pet. 1:22 [b]Prov. 10:12
9 [a]1 Tim. 3:2; Heb. 13:2 [b]Phil. 2:14
10 [a]Rom. 12:6f. [b]1 Cor. 4:1
11 [a]1 Thess. 2:4 [b]Acts 7:38 [c]Eph. 1:19; 6:10 [d]1 Cor. 10:31; 1 Pet. 2:12 [e]Rom. 11:36; 1 Pet. 5:11
12 [a]1 Pet. 2:11 [b]1 Pet. 1:6f.
13 [a]Rom. 8:17; 2 Cor. 1:5; 4:10; Phil. 3:10 [b]1 Pet. 1:7; 5:1 [c]2 Tim. 2:12
14 [a]John 15:21 [b]Matt. 5:11; Luke 6:22; Acts 5:41 [c]2 Cor. 4:10f., 16
15 [a]1 Pet. 2:19f.; 3:17 [b]1 Thess. 4:11
16 [a]Acts 5:41 [b]1 Pet. 4:11
17 [a]Jer. 25:29 [b]1 Tim. 3:15 [c]Rom. 2:9 [d]2 Thess. 1:8 [e]Rom. 1:1
18 [a]Prov. 11:31 [b]1 Tim. 1:9
19 [a]1 Pet. 3:17
1 [a]Acts 11:30 [b]2 John 1; 3 John 1 [c]Luke 24:48; Heb. 12:1 [d]1 Pet. 1:5, 7; 4:13
2 [a]John 21:16 [b]Philem. 14 [c]1 Tim. 3:8
3 [a]Ezek. 34:4; Matt. 20:25f. [b]John 13:15; Phil. 3:17
4 [a]1 Pet. 2:25 [b]1 Pet. 1:4 [c]1 Cor. 9:25
5 [a]Luke 22:26; 1 Tim. 5:1 [b]Eph. 5:21 [c]1 Pet. 3:8 [d]Prov. 3:34
6 [a]James 4:10
7 [a]Matt. 6:25
8 [a]1 Pet. 1:13 [b]Matt. 24:42 [c]James 4:7 [d]2 Tim. 4:17
9 [a]James 4:7 [b]Col. 2:5 [c]Acts 14:22
10 [a]1 Pet. 1:6 [b]1 Pet. 4:10 [c]1 Cor. 1:9 [d]2 Cor. 4:17 [e]1 Cor. 1:10; Heb. 13:21 [f]Rom. 16:25

11 [a]To Him *be* dominion forever and ever. Amen.

12 Through [a]Silvanus, our faithful brother (for so I regard *him*), [b]I have written to you briefly, exhorting and testifying that this is [c]the true grace of God. [d]Stand firm in it!

11 [a]Rom. 11:36
12 [a]2 Cor. 1:19 [b]Heb. 13:22 [c]Acts 11:23 [d]1 Cor. 15:1
13 [1]Or, *The church which* [a]Acts 12:12
14 [a]Rom. 16:16

13 [1]She who is in Babylon, chosen together with you, sends you greetings, and *so does* my son, [a]Mark.

14 [a]Greet one another with a kiss of love.

Peace be to you all who are in Christ.

THE SECOND EPISTLE OF

PETER

Growth in Christian Virtue

SIMON PETER, a [a]bond-servant and [b]apostle of Jesus Christ, to those who have received [c]a faith of the same kind as ours, by the righteousness of our God and Savior, Jesus Christ:

2 [a]Grace and peace be multiplied to you in [b]the knowledge of God and of Jesus our Lord;

3 seeing that His [a]divine power has granted to us everything pertaining to life and godliness, through the true [b]knowledge of Him who [c]called us by His own glory and excellence.

4 For by these He has granted to us His precious and magnificent [a]promises, in order that by them you might become [b]partakers of *the* divine nature, having [c]escaped the [d]corruption that is in [e]the world by lust.

5 Now for this very reason also, applying all diligence, in your faith [a]supply [b]moral excellence, and in *your* moral excellence, [c]knowledge;

6 and in *your* knowledge, [a]self-control, and in *your* self-control, [b]perseverance, and in *your* perseverance, [c]godliness;

7 and in *your* godliness, [a]brotherly kindness, and in *your* brotherly kindness, *Christian* love.

8 For if these *qualities* are yours and are increasing, they render you neither useless nor [a]unfruitful in the true [b]knowledge of our Lord Jesus Christ.

9 For he who lacks these *qualities* is [a]blind *or* short-sighted, having forgotten *his* [b]purification from his former sins.

10 Therefore, brethren, be all the more diligent to make certain about His [a]calling and [b]choosing you; for as long as you practice these things, you will never [c]stumble;

1 [a]Rom. 1:1; Jude 1 [b]1 Pet. 1:1 [c]Rom. 1:12; 2 Cor. 4:13; Titus 1:4
2 [a]Rom. 1:7; 1 Pet. 1:2 [b]John 17:3; Phil. 3:8
3 [a]1 Pet. 1:5 [b]John 17:3; Phil. 3:8 [c]1 Thess. 2:12; 2 Thess. 2:14; 1 Pet. 5:10
4 [a]2 Pet. 3:9, 13 [b]Eph. 4:13, 24; 1 John 3:2 [c]2 Pet. 2:18, 20 [d]2 Pet. 2:19 [e]James 1:27
5 [a]2 Pet. 1:11 [b]2 Pet. 1:3 [c]Col. 2:3; 2 Pet. 1:2
6 [a]Acts 24:25 [b]Luke 21:19 [c]2 Pet. 1:3
7 [a]Rom. 12:10
8 [a]Col. 1:10 [b]John 17:3
9 [a]1 John 2:11 [b]Eph. 5:26
10 [a]Matt. 22:14 [b]1 Thess. 1:4 [c]James 2:10; 2 Pet. 3:17; Jude 24
11 [a]2 Tim. 4:18 [b]2 Pet. 2:20; 3:18 [c]Rom. 2:4; 1 Tim. 6:17 [d]2 Pet. 1:5
12 [a]Phil. 3:1
13 [a]Phil. 1:7 [b]2 Cor. 5:1, 4
14 [a]2 Cor. 5:1; 2 Tim. 4:6 [b]John 13:36; 21:19
15 [a]Luke 9:31
16 [a]1 Tim. 1:4; 2 Pet. 2:3 [b]Mark 13:26; 14:62 [c]Matt. 17:1ff.
17 [a]Matt. 17:5 [b]Heb. 1:3
18 [a]Ex. 3:5
19 [a]1 Pet. 1:10f. [b]Heb. 2:2 [c]Ps. 119:105 [d]Luke 1:78 [e]Rev. 22:16
20 [a]2 Pet. 3:3 [b]Rom. 12:6
21 [a]Jer. 23:26 [b]2 Sam. 23:2

11 for in this way the entrance into [a]the eternal kingdom of our [b]Lord and Savior Jesus Christ will be [c]abundantly [d]supplied to you.

12 Therefore, [a]I shall always be ready to remind you of these things, even though you *already* know *them*, and have been established in the truth which is present with *you*.

13 And I consider it [a]right, as long as I am in [b]this *earthly* dwelling, to stir you up by way of reminder,

14 knowing that [a]the laying aside of my *earthly* dwelling is imminent, [b]as also our Lord Jesus Christ has made clear to me.

15 And I will also be diligent that at any time after my [a]departure you may be able to call these things to mind.

Eyewitnesses

16 For we did not follow cleverly devised [a]tales when we made known to you the [b]power and coming of our Lord Jesus Christ, but we were [c]eyewitnesses of His majesty.

17 For when He received honor and glory from God the Father, such an [a]utterance as this was made to Him by the [b]Majestic Glory, "This is My beloved Son with whom I am well-pleased"—

18 and we ourselves heard this utterance made from heaven when we were with Him on the [a]holy mountain.

19 And *so* we have [a]the prophetic word *made* more [b]sure, to which you do well to pay attention as to [c]a lamp shining in a dark place, until the [d]day dawns and the [e]morning star arises in your hearts.

20 But [a]know this first of all, that [b]no prophecy of Scripture is *a matter* of one's own interpretation,

21 for [a]no prophecy was ever made by an act of human will, but men [b]moved by the Holy Spirit spoke from God.

CHAPTER 2

The Rise of False Prophets

BUT [a]false prophets also arose among the people, just as there will also be [b]false teachers [c]among you, who will [d]secretly introduce [e]destructive heresies, even [f]denying the [g]Master who [h]bought them, bringing swift destruction upon themselves.
2 And many will follow their [a]sensuality, and because of them [b]the way of the truth will be [c]maligned;
3 and in *their* [a]greed they will [b]exploit you with [c]false words; [d]their judgment from long ago is not idle, and their destruction is not asleep.
4 For [a]if God did not spare angels when they sinned, but cast them into hell and [b]committed them to pits of darkness, reserved for judgment;
5 and did not spare [a]the ancient world, but preserved [b]Noah, a preacher of righteousness, with seven others, when He brought a [c]flood upon the world of the ungodly;
6 and *if* He [a]condemned the cities of Sodom and Gomorrah to destruction by reducing *them* to ashes, having made them an [b]example to those who would [c]live ungodly thereafter;
7 and if He [a]rescued righteous Lot, oppressed by the [b]sensual conduct of [c]unprincipled men
8 (for by what he saw and heard *that* [a]righteous man, while living among them, felt *his* righteous soul tormented day after day with *their* lawless deeds),
9 [a]*then* the Lord knows how to rescue the godly from temptation, and to keep the unrighteous under punishment for the [b]day of judgment,
10 and especially those who [a]indulge the flesh in *its* corrupt desires and [b]despise authority. Daring, [c]self-willed, they do not tremble when they [b]revile angelic majesties,
11 [a]whereas angels who are greater in might and power do not bring a reviling judgment against them before the Lord.
12 But [a]these, like unreasoning animals, [b]born as creatures of instinct to be captured and killed, reviling where they have no knowledge, will in the destruction of those creatures also be destroyed,
13 suffering wrong as [a]the wages of doing wrong. They count it a pleasure to [b]revel in the [c]daytime. They are stains and blemishes, [b]reveling in their deceptions, as they [d]carouse with you;
14 having eyes full of adultery and that never cease from sin; [a]enticing [b]unstable souls, having a heart trained in [c]greed, [d]accursed children;
15 forsaking [a]the right way they have gone astray, having followed [b]the way of Balaam, the *son* of Beor, who loved [c]the wages of unrighteousness,
16 but he received a rebuke for his own transgression; [a]*for* a dumb donkey, speaking with a voice of a man, restrained the madness of the prophet.
17 These are [a]springs without water, and mists driven by a storm, [b]for whom the black darkness has been reserved.
18 For speaking out [a]arrogant *words* of [b]vanity they [c]entice by fleshly desires, by [d]sensuality, those who barely [e]escape from the ones who live in error,
19 promising them freedom while they themselves are slaves of corruption; for [a]by what a man is overcome, by this he is enslaved.
20 For if after they have [a]escaped the defilements of the world by [b]the knowledge of the [c]Lord and Savior Jesus Christ, they are again [d]entangled in them and are overcome, [e]the last state has become worse for them than the first
21 [a]For it would be better for them not to have known the way of righteousness, than having known it, to turn away from [b]the holy commandment [c]delivered to them.
22 It has happened to them according to the true proverb, "[a]A DOG RETURNS TO ITS OWN VOMIT," and, "A sow, after washing, *returns* to wallowing in the mire."

CHAPTER 3

Purpose of This Letter

THIS is now, [a]beloved, the second letter I am writing to you in which I am [b]stirring up your sincere mind by way of reminder,
2 that you should [a]remember the words spoken beforehand by [b]the holy prophets and [c]the commandment of the Lord and Savior *spoken* by your apostles.

1 [a]Deut. 13:1ff.; Jer. 6:13 [b]2 Cor. 11:13 [c]Matt. 7:15; 1 Tim. 4:1 [d]Gal. 2:4; Jude 4 [e]1 Cor. 11:19; Gal. 5:20 [f]Jude 4 [g]Rev. 6:10 [h]1 Cor. 6:20
2 [a]Gen. 19:5ff.; 2 Pet. 2:7, 18; Jude 4 [b]Acts 16:17; 22:4; 24:14 [c]Rom. 2:24 [Gr.]
3 [a]1 Tim. 6:5 [b]2 Cor. 2:17 marg.; 1 Thess. 2:5 [c]Rom. 16:18; 2 Pet. 1:16 [d]Deut. 32:35
4 [a]Gen. 6; Jude 6 [b]Rev. 20:1f.
5 [a]Ezek. 26:20; 2 Pet. 3:6 [b]1 Pet. 3:20 [c]2 Pet. 3:6
6 [a]Gen. 19:24; Jude 7 [b]Matt. 10:15; 11:23; Rom. 9:29 [Is. 1:9]; Jude 7 [c]Jude 15
7 [a]Gen. 19:16, 29 [b]Gen. 19:5ff.; Jude 4 [c]2 Pet. 3:17
8 [a]Heb. 11:4
9 [a]1 Cor. 10:13; Rev. 3:10 [b]Matt. 10:15; Jude 6
10 [a]2 Pet. 3:3; Jude 16, 18 [b]Ex. 22:28; Jude 8 [c]Titus 1:7
11 [a]Jude 9
12 [a]Jude 10 [b]Jer. 12:3; Col. 2:22
13 [a]2 Pet. 2:15 [b]Rom. 13:13 [c]1 Thess. 5:7 [d]1 Cor. 11:21
14 [a]2 Pet. 2:18 [b]James 1:8; 2 Pet. 3:16 [c]2 Pet. 2:3 [d]Eph. 2:3
15 [a]Acts 13:10 [b]Num. 22:5, 7; Deut. 23:4; Neh. 13:2; Jude 11; Rev. 2:14 [c]2 Pet. 2:13
16 [a]Num. 22:21
17 [a]Jude 12 [b]Jude 13
18 [a]Jude 16 [b]Eph. 4:17 [c]2 Pet. 2:14 [d]2 Pet. 2:2 [e]2 Pet. 1:4; 2:20
19 [a]John 8:34
20 [a]2 Pet. 2:18 [b]2 Pet. 1:2 [c]2 Pet. 1:11; 3:18 [d]2 Tim. 2:4 [e]Matt. 12:45
21 [a]Ezek. 18:24; Heb. 6:4ff.; 10:26f.; James 4:17 [b]Gal. 6:2 [c]Jude 3
22 [a]Prov. 26:11
1 [a]1 Pet. 2:11 [b]2 Pet. 1:13
2 [a]Jude 17 [b]Luke 1:70 [c]Gal. 6:2

The Coming Day of the Lord

3 [a]Know this first of all, that [b]in the last days [c]mockers will come with *their* mocking, following after their own lusts,

4 and saying, "[a]Where is the promise of His [b]coming? For *ever* since the fathers [c]fell asleep, all continues just as it was [d]from the beginning of creation."

5 For when they maintain this, it escapes their notice that [a]by the word of God *the* heavens existed long ago and *the* earth was [b]formed out of water and by water,

6 through which [a]the world at that time was [b]destroyed, being flooded with water.

7 But [a]the present heavens and earth by His word are being reserved for [b]fire, kept for [c]the day of judgment and destruction of ungodly men.

8 But do not let this one *fact* escape your notice, [a]beloved, that with the Lord one day is as a thousand years, and [b]a thousand years as one day.

9 [a]The Lord is not slow about His promise, as some count slowness, but [b]is patient toward you, [c]not wishing for any to perish but for all to come to repentance.

A New Heaven and Earth

10 But [a]the day of the Lord [b]will come like a thief, in which [c]the heavens [d]will pass away with a roar and the [e]elements will be destroyed with intense heat, and [f]the earth and its works will be burned up.

11 Since all these things are to be destroyed in this way, what sort of people ought you to be in holy conduct and godliness,

12 [a]looking for and hastening the coming of the day of God, on account of which [b]the heavens will be destroyed by burning, and the [c]elements will melt with intense heat!

13 But according to His [a]promise we are looking for [b]new heavens and a new earth, [c]in which righteousness dwells.

14 [a]Therefore, [b]beloved, since you look for these things, be diligent to be [c]found by Him in peace, spotless and blameless,

15 and regard the [a]patience of our Lord *to be* salvation; just as also [b]our beloved brother Paul, according to the wisdom given him, wrote to you,

16 as also in all *his* letters, speaking in them of [a]these things, [b]in which are some things hard to understand, which the untaught and [c]unstable distort, as *they do* also [d]the rest of the Scriptures, to their own destruction.

17 You therefore, [a]beloved, knowing this beforehand, [b]be on your guard lest, being carried away by [c]the error of unprincipled men, you fall from your own steadfastness,

18 but grow in the grace and [a]knowledge of our [b]Lord and Savior Jesus Christ. [c]To Him *be* the glory, both now and to the day of eternity. Amen.

3 [a]2 Pet. 1:20 [b]1 Tim. 4:1; Heb. 1:2 [c]Jude 18
4 [a]Is. 5:19 [b]1 Thess. 2:19; 2 Pet. 3:12 [c]Acts 7:60 [d]Mark 10:6
5 [a]Gen. 1:6, 9; Heb. 11:3 [b]Ps. 24:2
6 [a]2 Pet. 2:5 [b]Gen. 7:21f.
7 [a]2 Pet. 3:10, 12 [b]Is. 66:15; Dan. 7:9f. [c]Matt. 10:15
8 [a]2 Pet. 3:1 [b]Ps. 90:4
9 [a]Hab. 2:3; Rom. 13:11; Heb. 10:37 [b]Rom. 2:4; Rev. 2:21 [c]1 Tim. 2:4; Rev. 2:21
10 [a]1 Cor. 1:8 [b]Matt. 24:43; 1 Thess. 5:2; Rev. 3:3; 16:15 [c]2 Pet. 3:7, 12 [d]Matt. 24:35; Rev. 21:1 [e]Is. 24:19; 34:4 [f]2 Pet. 3:7
12 [a]1 Cor. 1:7 [b]2 Pet. 3:7, 10 [c]Is. 24:19; 34:4
13 [a]Is. 65:17; 66:22 [b]Rom. 8:21 [c]Is. 60:21; 65:25
14 [a]1 Cor. 15:58; 2 Pet. 1:10 [b]2 Pet. 3:1 [c]1 Pet. 1:7
15 [a]2 Pet. 3:9 [b]Acts 9:17; 15:25; 2 Pet. 3:2
16 [a]2 Pet. 3:14 [b]Heb. 5:11 [c]2 Pet. 2:14 [d]Is. 28:13
17 [a]2 Pet. 3:1 [b]1 Cor. 10:12 [c]2 Pet. 2:18
18 [a]2 Pet. 1:2 [b]2 Pet. 1:11; 2:20 [c]Rom. 11:36

THE FIRST EPISTLE OF

JOHN

Introduction
The Incarnate Word

WHAT was [a]from the beginning,
what we have [b]heard, what we have
[c]seen with our eyes, what we [d]be-
held and our hands [e]handled, concerning the Word of Life—
2 and [a]the life was manifested,
and we have [b]seen and bear witness
and proclaim to you the eternal life,
which was with the Father and was
[a]manifested to us—
3 what we have [a]seen and [b]heard
we proclaim to you also, that you
also may have fellowship with us;
and indeed our [c]fellowship is with
the Father, and with His Son Jesus
Christ.
4 And [a]these things we write, so
that our [b]joy may be made complete.

God Is Light

5 And [a]this is the message we
have heard from Him and announce
to you, that God is light, and in Him
there is no darkness at all.
6 [a]If we say that we have fellowship with Him and *yet* walk in the
darkness, we [b]lie and do not practice the truth;
7 but if we [a]walk in the light as
[b]He Himself is in the light, we have
fellowship with one another, and
the blood of Jesus His Son cleanses
us from all sin.
8 [a]If we say that we have no sin,
we are deceiving ourselves, and the
[b]truth is not in us.
9 [a]If we confess our sins, He is
faithful and righteous to forgive us
our sins and [b]to cleanse us from all
unrighteousness.
10 [a]If we say that we have not
sinned, we [b]make Him a liar, and
His word is not in us.

CHAPTER 2

Christ Is Our Advocate

[a]
MY little children, I am writing
[b]these things to you that you may
not sin. And if anyone sins, [c]we have
an Advocate with the Father, Jesus
Christ the righteous;
2 and He Himself is [a]the propitiation for our sins; and not for ours
only, but also [b]for *those of* the whole
world.
3 And [a]by this we know that we
have come to [b]know Him, if we
[c]keep His commandments.
4 The one who says, "[a]I have
come to [b]know Him," and does not
keep His commandments, is a [c]liar,
and [d]the truth is not in him;
5 but whoever [a]keeps His word,
in him the [b]love of God has truly
been perfected. [c]By this we know
that we are in Him:
6 the one who says he [a]abides in
Him [b]ought himself to walk in the
same manner as He walked.
7 [a]Beloved, I am [b]not writing a
new commandment to you, but an
old commandment which you have
had from the beginning; the old
commandment is the word which
you have heard.
8 On the other hand, I am writing
[a]a new commandment to you,
which is true in Him and in you, because [b]the darkness is passing
away, and the true light is already
shining.
9 The one who says he is in the
light and *yet* [a]hates his [b]brother is in
the darkness until now.
10 [a]The one who loves his brother
abides in the light and there is no
cause for stumbling in him.
11 But the one who [a]hates his
brother is in the darkness and
[b]walks in the darkness, and does not
know where he is going because the
darkness has blinded his eyes.
12 I am writing to you, [a]little children, because [b]your sins are forgiven you for His name's sake.
13 I am writing to you, fathers, because you know Him [a]who has been
from the beginning. I am writing to
you, young men, because [b]you have
overcome the evil one. I have written to you, children, because you
know the Father.
14 I have written to you, fathers,
because you know Him [a]who has
been from the beginning. I have
written to you, young men, because
you are [b]strong, and the [c]word of
God abides in you, and [d]you have
overcome the evil one.

Do Not Love the World

15 Do not love [a]the world, nor the
things in the world. [b]If any one loves
the world, the love of the Father is
not in him.

1 [a]John 1:1f.; 1 John 2:13, 14 [b]Acts 4:20; 1 John 1:3 [c]John 19:35; 2 Pet. 1:16; 1 John 1:2 [d]John 1:14; 1 John 4:14 [e]Luke 24:39; John 20:27
2 [a]John 1:4 [b]John 19:35; 1 John 1:1
3 [a]John 19:35 [b]Acts 4:20; 1 John 1:1 [c]John 17:3, 21
4 [a]1 John 2:1 [b]John 3:29
5 [a]John 1:19
6 [a]John 8:12 [b]John 8:55
7 [a]Is. 2:5 [b]1 Tim. 6:16
8 [a]Job 15:14; Prov. 20:9 [b]John 8:44
9 [a]Ps. 32:5; Prov. 28:13 [b]Titus 2:14; Heb. 9:14
10 [a]Job 15:14; Prov. 20:9; Rom. 3:10ff.; James 3:2 [b]John 3:33
1 [a]John 13:33 [b]1 John 1:4 [c]Rom. 8:34
2 [a]Rom. 3:25 [b]John 4:42
3 [a]1 John 2:5 [b]1 John 2:4; 3:6; 4:7f. [c]John 14:15
4 [a]Titus 1:10 [b]1 John 3:6; 4:7f. [c]1 John 1:6 [d]1 John 1:8
5 [a]John 14:23 [b]1 John 4:12 [c]1 John 2:3; 3:24
6 [a]John 15:4 [b]John 13:15
7 [a]Heb. 6:9 [b]1 John 3:11, 23
8 [a]John 13:34 [b]Rom. 13:12
9 [a]1 John 2:11; 3:15; 4:20 [b]Acts 1:15; 1 John 3:10
10 [a]John 11:9
11 [a]1 John 2:9; 3:15; 4:20 [b]John 12:35; 1 John 1:6
12 [a]1 John 2:1 [b]Acts 13:38
13 [a]1 John 1:1 [b]John 16:33
14 [a]1 John 1:1 [b]Eph. 6:10 [c]John 5:38; 8:37; 1 John 1:10 [d]1 John 2:13
15 [a]Rom. 12:2 [b]James 4:4

16 For all that is in the world, [a]the lust of the flesh and [b]the lust of the eyes and the boastful pride of life, is not from the Father, but is from the world.

17 And [a]the world is passing away, and *also* its lusts; but the one who does the will of God abides forever.

18 Children, [a]it is the last hour; and just as you heard that [b]antichrist is coming, even now many antichrists have arisen; from this we know that it is the last hour.

19 [a]They went out from us, but they were not *really* of us; for if they had been of us, they would have remained with us; but *they went out*, [b]in order that it might be shown that they all are not of us.

20 But you have an [a]anointing from [b]the Holy One, and [1c]you all know.

21 I have not written to you because you do not know the truth, but [a]because you do know it, and because no lie is [b]of the truth.

22 Who is the liar but [a]the one who denies that Jesus is the Christ? This is [b]the antichrist, the one who denies the Father and the Son.

23 [a]Whoever denies the Son does not have the Father; the one who confesses the Son has the Father also.

24 As for you, let that abide in you which you heard [a]from the beginning. If what you heard from the beginning abides in you, you also [b]will abide in the Son and in the Father.

The Promise Is Eternal Life

25 And [a]this is the promise which He Himself made to us: eternal life.

26 These things I have written to you concerning those who are trying to [a]deceive you.

27 And as for you, the [a]anointing which you received from Him abides in you, and you have no need for anyone to teach you; but as His anointing [b]teaches you about all things, and is true and is not a lie, and just as it has taught you, you abide in Him.

28 And now, [a]little children, abide in Him, so that when He [b]appears, we may have [c]confidence and [d]not shrink away from Him in shame at His [e]coming.

29 If you know that [a]He is righteous, you know that every one also who practices righteousness [b]is born of Him.

Chapter 3

Children of God Love One Another

SEE [a]how great a love the Father has bestowed upon us, that we should be called [b]children of God; and *such* we are. For this reason the world does not know us, because it did not know Him.

2 [a]Beloved, now we are [b]children of God, and [c]it has not appeared as yet what we shall be. We know that, when He [d]appears, we shall be [e]like Him, because we shall see Him just as He is.

3 And every one who has this [a]hope *fixed* on Him [b]purifies himself, just as He is pure.

4 Every one who practices sin also practices lawlessness; and [a]sin is lawlessness.

5 And you know that He [a]appeared in order to [b]take away sins; and [c]in Him there is no sin.

6 No one who abides in Him [a]sins; no one who sins has seen Him or [b]knows Him.

7 [a]Little children, let no one [b]deceive you; [c]the one who practices righteousness is righteous, just as He is righteous;

8 the one who practices sin is [a]of the devil; for the devil has sinned from the beginning. [b]The Son of God [c]appeared for this purpose, [d]that He might destroy the works of the devil.

9 No one who is [a]born of God [b]practices sin, because His seed abides in him; and he cannot sin, because he is born of God.

10 By this the [a]children of God and the [b]children of the devil are obvious: any one who does not practice righteousness is not of God, nor the one who [c]does not love his brother.

11 [a]For this is the message [b]which you have heard from the beginning, [c]that we should love one another;

12 not as [a]Cain, *who* was of [b]the evil one, and slew his brother. And for what reason did he slay him? Because [c]his deeds were evil, and his brother's were righteous.

13 Do not marvel, brethren, if [a]the world hates you.

14 We know that we have [a]passed out of death into life, [b]because we love the brethren. He who does not love abides in death.

15 Every one who [a]hates his brother is a murderer; and you know that [b]no murderer has eternal life abiding in him.

---

16 [a]Rom. 13:14 [b]Prov. 27:20
17 [a]1 Cor. 7:31
18 [a]Rom. 13:11 [b]Matt. 24:5
19 [a]Acts 20:30 [b]1 Cor. 11:19
20 [1]Some ancient mss. read, *you know all things* [a]2 Cor. 1:21 [b]Mark 1:24; Acts 10:38 [c]Prov. 28:5
21 [a]James 1:19 [b]John 8:44; 18:37
22 [a]1 John 4:3; 2 John 7 [b]Matt. 24:5, 24
23 [a]John 8:19
24 [a]1 John 2:7 [b]John 14:23
25 [a]John 3:15; 6:40
26 [a]1 John 3:7
27 [a]John 14:16; 1 John 2:20 [b]John 14:26; 1 Cor. 2:12; 1 Thess. 4:9
28 [a]1 John 2:1 [b]Luke 17:30; Col. 3:4; 1 John 3:2 [c]Eph. 3:12; 1 John 3:21; 4:17; 5:14 [d]Mark 8:38 [e]1 Thess. 2:19
29 [a]John 7:18; 1 John 3:7 [b]John 1:13; 3:3
1 [a]John 3:16; 1 John 4:10 [b]John 1:12; 11:52
2 [a]1 John 2:7 [b]John 1:12; 11:52 [c]Rom. 8:19, 23f. [d]Luke 17:30; Col. 3:4; 1 John 2:28 [e]Rom. 8:29; 2 Pet. 1:4
3 [a]Rom. 15:12; 1 Pet. 1:3 [b]John 17:19; 2 Cor. 7:1
4 [a]Rom. 4:15
5 [a]1 John 1:2; 3:8 [b]John 1:29 [c]2 Cor. 5:21; 1 John 2:29
6 [a]1 John 3:9 [b]1 John 2:3
7 [a]1 John 2:1 [b]1 John 2:26 [c]1 John 2:29
8 [a]Matt. 13:38 [b]Matt. 4:3 [c]1 John 3:5 [d]John 12:31; 16:11
9 [a]John 1:13; 3:3 [b]James 1:18
10 [a]John 1:12 [b]Matt. 13:38 [c]Rom. 13:8ff.
11 [a]1 John 1:5 [b]1 John 2:7 [c]John 13:34f.; 15:12
12 [a]Gen. 4:8 [b]Matt. 5:37; 1 John 2:13f. [c]Ps. 38:20; Prov. 29:10
13 [a]John 15:18
14 [a]John 5:24 [b]John 13:35
15 [a]Matt. 5:21f.; John 8:44 [b]Gal. 5:20f.; Rev. 21:8

16 We know love by this, that [a]He laid down His life for us; and [b]we ought to lay down our lives for the [c]brethren.

17 But [a]whoever has the world's goods, and beholds his brother in need and [b]closes his heart against him, [c]how does the love of God abide in him?

18 [a]Little children, let us not love with word or with tongue, but in deed and [b]truth.

19 We shall know by this that we are [a]of the truth, and shall assure our heart before Him,

20 in whatever our heart condemns us; for God is greater than our heart, and knows all things.

21 [a]Beloved, if our heart does not condemn us, we have [b]confidence before God;

22 and [a]whatever we ask we receive from Him, because we [b]keep His commandments and do [c]the things that are pleasing in His sight.

23 And this is His commandment, that we [a]believe in [b]the name of His Son Jesus Christ, and love one another, just as [c]He commanded us.

24 And the one who [a]keeps His commandments [b]abides in Him, and He in him. And [c]we know by this that [d]He abides in us, by the Spirit which He has given us.

Chapter 4

Testing the Spirits

[a]BELOVED, do not believe every [b]spirit, but test the spirits to see whether they are from God; because [c]many false prophets have gone out into the world.

2 By this you know the Spirit of God: [a]every spirit that [b]confesses that Jesus Christ has come in the flesh is from God;

3 and every spirit that [a]does not confess Jesus is not from God; and this is the *spirit* of the [b]antichrist, of which you have heard that it is coming, and [c]now it is already in the world.

4 You are from God, [a]little children, and [b]have overcome them; because [c]greater is He who is in you than he who is in the world.

5 [a]They are from the world; therefore they speak *as* from the world, and the world listens to them.

6 [a]We are from God; [b]he who knows God listens to us; [c]he who is not from God does not listen to us. By this we know the spirit of truth and the spirit of error.

God Is Love

7 [a]Beloved, let us [b]love one another, for love is from God; and [c]every one who loves is born of God and knows God.

8 The one who does not love does not know God, for [a]God is love.

9 By this the love of God was manifested [a]in us, that [b]God has sent His only begotten Son into the world so that we might live through Him.

10 In this is love, [a]not that we loved God, but that [b]He loved us and sent His Son *to be* [c]the propitiation for our sins.

11 [a]Beloved, if God so loved us, [b]we also ought to love one another.

12 [a]No one has beheld God at any time; if we love one another, God abides in us, and His [b]love is perfected in us.

13 [a]By this we know that we abide in Him and He in us, because He has given us of His Spirit.

14 And we have beheld and [a]bear witness that the Father has [b]sent the Son *to be* the Savior of the world.

15 [a]Whoever confesses that [b]Jesus is the Son of God, God [c]abides in him, and he in God.

16 And [a]we have come to know and have believed the love which God has [b]for us. God is love, and the one who abides in love abides in God, and God abides in him.

17 By this, [a]love is perfected with us, that we may have [b]confidence in [c]the day of judgment; because as He is, so also are we in this world.

18 There is no fear in love; but [a]perfect love casts out fear, because fear involves punishment, and the one who fears is not [b]perfected in love.

19 [a]We love, because He first loved us.

20 [a]If some one says, "I love God," and [b]hates his brother, he is a [c]liar; for [d]the one who does not love his brother whom he has seen, cannot love God whom he has not seen.

21 And [a]this commandment we have from Him, that the one who loves God [b]should love his brother also.

Chapter 5

Overcoming the World

[a]WHOEVER believes that Jesus is the Christ is [b]born of God; and who-

16 [a]John 10:11; 15:13 [b]Phil. 2:17 [c]1 John 2:9
17 [a]James 2:15f. [b]Deut. 15:7 [c]1 John 4:20
18 [a]1 John 2:1; 3:7 [b]2 John 1
19 [a]1 John 2:21
21 [a]1 John 2:7 [b]1 John 2:28; 5:14
22 [a]Job 22:26f.; John 9:31 [b]1 John 2:3 [c]John 8:29
23 [a]John 6:29 [b]John 1:12 [c]John 13:34
24 [a]1 John 2:3 [b]John 6:56; 10:38; 1 John 2:6, 24; 4:15 [c]John 14:17; Rom. 8:9 [d]1 John 2:5
1 [a]1 John 2:7 [b]Jer. 29:8 [c]Jer. 14:14
2 [a]1 Cor. 12:3 [b]1 John 2:23
3 [a]1 John 2:22; 2 John 7 [b]1 John 2:18, 22 [c]2 Thess. 2:3-7; 1 John 2:18
4 [a]1 John 2:1 [b]1 John 2:13 [c]2 Kin. 2:16
5 [a]John 15:19
6 [a]John 8:23; 1 John 4:4 [b]John 8:47; 10:3ff.; 18:37 [c]1 Cor. 14:37
7 [a]1 John 2:7 [b]1 John 3:11 [c]1 John 5:1
8 [a]1 John 4:7
9 [a]John 9:3; 1 John 4:16 [b]John 3:16f.
10 [a]Rom. 5:8, 10; 1 John 4:19 [b]John 3:16f.; 1 John 4:9; 5:11 [c]1 John 2:2
11 [a]1 John 2:7 [b]1 John 4:7
12 [a]John 1:18 [b]1 John 2:5; 4:17f.
13 [a]Rom. 8:9
14 [a]John 15:27 [b]John 3:17
15 [a]1 John 2:23 [b]Rom. 10:9 [c]1 John 2:24
16 [a]John 6:69 [b]John 9:3; 1 John 4:9
17 [a]1 John 2:5; 4:12 [b]1 John 2:28 [c]Matt. 10:15
18 [a]Rom. 8:15; Gal. 4:30f. [b]1 John 4:12
19 [a]1 John 4:10
20 [a]1 John 1:6, 8, 10; 2:4 [b]1 John 2:9, 11 [c]1 John 1:6 [d]1 John 3:17
21 [a]Lev. 19:18 [b]1 John 3:11
1 [a]1 John 2:22f.; 4:2, 15 [b]John 1:3; 3:3 marg.; 1 John 2:29; 5:4, 18

ever loves the Father [c]loves the
child born of Him.
2 [a]By this we know that [b]we love
the children of God, when we love
God and observe His commandments.
3 For [a]this is the love of God, that
we [b]keep His commandments; and
[c]His commandments are not burdensome.
4 For whatever is [a]born of God
[b]overcomes the world; and this is
the victory that has overcome the
world—our faith.
5 And who is the one who overcomes the world, but he who [a]be-
lieves that Jesus is the Son of God?
6 This is the one who came [a]by
water and blood, Jesus Christ; not
with the water only, but with the
water and with the blood.
7 And it is [a]the Spirit who bears
witness, because the Spirit is the
truth.
8 For there are [a]three that bear
witness, [1]the Spirit and the water
and the blood; and the three are in
agreement.
9 [a]If we receive the witness of
men, the witness of God is greater;
for the witness of God is this, that
He has borne witness concerning
His Son.
10 The one who believes in the Son
of God [a]has the witness in himself;
the one who does not believe God
has [b]made Him a liar, because he
has not believed in the witness that
God has borne concerning His Son.
11 And the witness is this, that
God has given us [a]eternal life, and
this life is in His Son.
12 [a]He who has the Son has the
life; he who does not have the Son of
God does not have the life.

This Is Written That You May Know

13 [a]These things I have written to
you who [b]believe in the name of the
Son of God, in order that you may
know that you have eternal life.
14 And this is [a]the confidence
which we have before Him, that, [b]if
we ask anything according to His
will, He hears us.
15 And if we know that He hears
us *in* whatever we ask, [a]we know
that we have the requests which we
have asked from Him.
16 If any one sees his brother committing a sin not *leading* to death,
[a]he shall ask and *God* will for him
give life to those who commit sin
not *leading* to death. [b]There is a sin
leading to death; I do not say that he
should make request for this.
17 [a]All unrighteousness is sin, and
[b]there is a sin not *leading* to death.
18 [a]We know that [b]no one who is
born of God sins; but He who was
born of God keeps him and the evil
one does not touch him.
19 [a]We know that [b]we are of God,
and the whole world lies in *the
power of* the evil one.
20 And [a]we know that [b]the Son of
God has come, and has [c]given us understanding, in order that we might
know [d]Him who is true, and we [e]are
in Him who is true, in His Son Jesus
Christ. This is the true God and eternal life.
21 [a]Little children, guard yourselves from [b]idols.

1 [c]John 8:42
2 [a]1 John 2:5 [b]1 John 3:14
3 [a]John 14:15; 2 John 6 [b]1 John 2:3 [c]Matt. 11:30
4 [a]John 1:13; 3:3 marg. [b]1 John 2:13; 4:4
5 [a]1 John 4:15
6 [a]John 19:34
7 [a]John 15:26
8 [1]A few late mss. read *in heaven, the Father, the Word, and the Holy Spirit, and these three are one. And there are three that bear witness on earth, the Spirit* [a]Matt. 18:16
9 [a]John 5:34
10 [a]Rom. 8:16 [b]John 3:18
11 [a]1 John 1:2
12 [a]John 3:15f.
13 [a]John 20:31 [b]1 John 3:23
14 [a]1 John 2:28; 3:21f. [b]Matt. 7:7
15 [a]1 John 5:18
16 [a]James 5:15 [b]Num. 15:30
17 [a]1 John 3:4 [b]1 John 2:1f.; 5:16
18 [a]1 John 5:15, 19, 20 [b]1 John 3:9
19 [a]1 John 5:15, 18, 20 [b]1 John 4:6
20 [a]1 John 5:15, 18, 19 [b]John 8:42; 1 John 5:5 [c]Luke 24:45 [d]John 17:3; Rev. 3:7 [e]John 1:18; 14:9
21 [a]1 John 2:1 [b]1 Cor. 10:7, 14

THE SECOND EPISTLE OF
JOHN

Walk According to His
Commandments

[a]THE elder to the [b]chosen [c]lady and
her children, whom I [d]love in truth;
and not only I, but also all who know
the truth,
2 for [a]the sake of the truth which
abides [b]in us and will be [c]with us
forever:
3 [a]Grace, mercy *and* peace will
be with us, from God the Father and
from Jesus Christ, the Son of the Father, in truth and love.
4 [a]I was very glad to find *some* of
your children walking in truth, just
as we have received commandment
to do from the Father.
5 And now I ask you, lady, [a]not as
writing to you a new commandment, but the one which we have
had [a]from the beginning, that we
[b]love one another.
6 And [a]this is love, that we walk
according to His commandments.
This is the commandment, [b]just as
you have heard [c]from the beginning,
that you should walk in it.
7 For [a]many deceivers have
[b]gone out into the world, those who
[c]do not acknowledge Jesus Christ
as coming in the flesh. This is [a]the
deceiver and the [d]antichrist.
8 [a]Watch yourselves, [b]that you
might not lose what [1]we have accomplished, but that you may receive a full reward.
9 Any one who goes too far and
[a]does not abide in the teaching of
Christ, does not have God; the one
who abides in the teaching, he has
both the Father and the Son.
10 If any one comes to you and
does not bring this teaching, [a]do not
receive him into *your* house, and do
not give him a greeting;
11 for the one who gives him a
greeting [a]participates in his evil
deeds.
12 [a]Having many things to write
to you, I do not want to *do* so with
paper and ink; but I hope to come to
you and speak face to face, that
[1]your [b]joy may be made full.
13 The children of your [a]chosen
sister greet you.

1 [a]Acts 11:30; 3 John 1; 1 Pet. 5:1 [b]Rom. 16:13 [Gr.]; 1 Pet. 5:13; 2 John 13 [c]2 John 5 [d]1 John 3:18
2 [a]2 Pet. 1:12 [b]1 John 1:8 [c]John 14:16
3 [a]Rom. 1:7
4 [a]3 John 3f.
5 [a]1 John 2:7 [b]1 John 3:11
6 [a]1 John 2:5; 5:3 [b]1 John 2:24 [c]1 John 2:7
7 [a]1 John 2:26 [b]1 John 2:19; 4:1 [c]1 John 4:2f. [d]1 John 2:18
8 [1]Or, *you* [a]Mark 13:9 [b]1 Cor. 3:8
9 [a]John 7:16; 8:31
10 [a]1 Kin. 13:16f.
11 [a]1 Tim. 5:22
12 [1]Or, *our* [a]3 John 13, 14 [b]John 3:29
13 [a]2 John 1

THE THIRD EPISTLE OF
JOHN

You Walk in the Truth

[a]THE elder to the beloved Gaius,
whom I [b]love in truth.
2 Beloved, I pray that in all respects you may prosper and be in
good health, just as your soul prospers.
3 For I [a]was very glad when
[b]brethren came and bore witness to
your truth, *that is,* how you [a]are
walking in truth.
4 I have no greater joy than this,
to hear of [a]my children [b]walking in
the truth.
5 Beloved, you are acting faithfully in whatever you accomplish
for the [a]brethren, and especially
when they are [b]strangers;
6 and they bear witness to your
love before the church; and you will
do well to [a]send them on their way
in a manner [b]worthy of God.
7 For they went out for the sake
of [a]the Name, [b]accepting nothing
from the Gentiles.
8 Therefore we ought to support
such men, that we may be fellow-
workers with the truth.
9 I wrote something to the
church; but Diotrephes, who loves
to be first among them, does not accept what we say.
10 For this reason, [a]if I come, I will
call attention to his deeds which he
does, unjustly accusing us with
wicked words; and not satisfied
with this, neither does he himself
[b]receive the [c]brethren, and he forbids those who desire *to do so,* and
[d]puts *them* out of the church.
11 Beloved, [a]do not imitate what is
evil, but what is good. [b]The one who
does good is of God; [c]the one who
does evil has not seen God.
12 Demetrius [a]has received a *good*
testimony from everyone, and from
the truth itself; and we also bear

1 [a]2 John 1 [b]1 John 3:18
3 [a]2 John 4 [b]Acts 1:15; Gal. 6:10
4 [a]1 Cor. 4:14f.; 2 Cor. 6:13 [b]2 John 3
5 [a]Acts 1:15 [b]Rom. 12:13; Heb. 13:2
6 [a]Acts 15:3; Titus 3:13 [b]Col. 1:10; 1 Thess. 2:12
7 [a]John 15:21; Acts 5:41; Phil. 2:9 [b]Acts 20:33, 35
10 [a]2 John 12 [b]2 John 10; 3 John 5 [c]Acts 1:15; Gal. 6:10; 3 John 3, 5 [d]John 9:34
11 [a]Ps. 34:14; 37:27 [b]1 John 2:29; 3:10 [c]1 John 3:6
12 [a]Acts 6:3; 1 Tim. 3:7

witness, and [b]you know that our witness is true.

13 [a]I had many things to write to you, but I am not willing to write *them* to you with pen and ink;

12 [b]John 19:35; 21:24
13 [a]2 John 12
14 [a]John 20:19 [b]John 10:3

14 but I hope to see you shortly, and we shall speak face to face. [a]Peace *be* to you. The friends greet you. Greet the friends [b]by name.

THE EPISTLE OF
JUDE

The Warnings of History to the Ungodly

[a]JUDE, a [b]bond-servant of Jesus Christ, and brother of James, to [c]those who are the called, beloved in God the Father, and [d]kept for Jesus Christ:

2 [a]May mercy and peace and love [b]be multiplied to you.

3 [a]Beloved, while I was making every effort to write you about our [b]common salvation, I felt the necessity to write to you appealing that you [c]contend earnestly for [d]the faith which was once for all delivered to the saints.

4 For certain persons have [a]crept in unnoticed, those who were long beforehand [b]marked out for this condemnation, ungodly persons who turn [c]the grace of our God into [d]licentiousness and [e]deny our only Master and Lord, Jesus Christ.

5 Now I desire to [a]remind you, though [b]you know all things once for all, that the Lord, [c]after saving a people out of the land of Egypt, subsequently destroyed those who did not believe.

6 And [a]angels who did not keep their own domain, but abandoned their proper abode, He has [b]kept in eternal bonds under darkness for the judgment of the great day.

7 Just as [a]Sodom and Gomorrah and the [b]cities around them, since they in the same way as these indulged in gross immorality and [c]went after strange flesh, are exhibited as an [d]example, in undergoing the [e]punishment of eternal fire.

8 Yet in the same manner these men, also by dreaming, [a]defile the flesh, and [a]reject authority, and [a]revile angelic majesties.

9 But [a]Michael [b]the archangel, when he disputed with the devil and argued about [c]the body of Moses, did not dare pronounce against him a railing judgment, but said, "[d]THE LORD REBUKE YOU."

1 [a]Matt. 13:55 [b]Rom. 1:1 [c]Rom. 1:6f. [d]John 17:11f.
2 [a]Gal. 6:16 [b]1 Pet. 1:2
3 [a]Heb. 6:9; Jude 1, 17, 20 [b]Titus 1:4 [c]1 Tim. 6:12 [d]Acts 6:7; Jude 20
4 [a]Gal. 2:4; 2 Tim. 3:6 [b]1 Pet. 2:8 [c]Acts 11:23 [d]2 Pet. 2:7 [e]2 Tim. 2:12; Titus 1:16
5 [a]2 Pet. 1:12f.; 3:1f. [b]1 John 2:20 [c]1 Cor. 10:5-10
6 [a]2 Pet. 2:4 [b]2 Pet. 2:9
7 [a]2 Pet. 2:6 [b]Deut. 29:23; Hos. 11:8 [c]2 Pet. 2:2 [d]2 Pet. 2:6 [e]Matt. 25:41
8 [a]2 Pet. 2:10
9 [a]Dan. 10:13 [b]1 Thess. 4:16; 2 Pet. 2:11 [c]Deut. 34:6 [d]Zech. 3:2
10 [a]2 Pet. 2:12 [b]Phil. 3:19
11 [a]Gen. 4:3-8 [b]Num. 31:16; 2 Pet. 2:15; Rev. 2:14 [c]Num. 16:1
12 [a]1 Cor. 11:20ff.; 2 Pet. 2:13 and marg. [b]Ezek. 34:2, 8, 10 [c]Prov. 25:14; 2 Pet. 2:17 [d]Eph. 4:14
13 [a]Is. 57:20 [b]Phil. 3:19 [c]2 Pet. 2:17
14 [a]Gen. 5:18, 21ff. [b]Deut. 33:2
15 [a]2 Pet. 2:6ff. [b]1 Tim. 1:9
16 [a]Num. 16:11, 41 [b]2 Pet. 2:10; Jude 18 [c]2 Pet. 2:18 [d]2 Pet. 2:3
17 [a]Jude 3 [b]2 Pet. 3:2 [c]Heb. 2:3
18 [a]Acts 20:29; 1 Tim. 4:1; 2 Tim. 3:1f.; 4:3; 2 Pet. 3:3 [b]Jude 4, 16
19 [a]1 Cor. 2:14f.
20 [a]Jude 3 [b]Col. 2:7; 1 Thess. 5:11 [c]Eph. 6:18

10 But [a]these men revile the things which they do not understand; and [b]the things which they know by instinct, [a]like unreasoning animals, by these things they are destroyed.

11 Woe to them! For they have gone [a]the way of Cain, and for pay they have rushed headlong into [b]the error of Balaam, and [c]perished in the rebellion of Korah.

12 These men are those who are hidden reefs [a]in your love-feasts when they feast with you [b]without fear, caring for themselves; [c]clouds without water, [d]carried along by winds; autumn trees without fruit, doubly dead, uprooted;

13 [a]wild waves of the sea, casting up [b]their own shame like foam; wandering stars, [c]for whom the black darkness has been reserved forever.

14 And about these also [a]Enoch, *in* the seventh *generation* from Adam, prophesied, saying, "[b]Behold, the Lord came with many thousands of His holy ones,

15 [a]to execute judgment upon all, and to convict all the ungodly of all their ungodly deeds which they have done in an ungodly way, and of all the harsh things which [b]ungodly sinners have spoken against Him."

16 These are [a]grumblers, finding fault, [b]following after their *own* lusts; they speak [c]arrogantly, flattering people [d]for the sake of *gaining an* advantage.

Keep Yourselves in the Love of God

17 But you, [a]beloved, [b]ought to remember the words that were spoken beforehand by [c]the apostles of our Lord Jesus Christ,

18 that they were saying to you, "[a]In the last time there shall be mockers, [b]following after their own ungodly lusts."

19 These are the ones who cause divisions, [a]worldly-minded, devoid of the Spirit.

20 But you, [a]beloved, [b]building yourselves up on your most holy [a]faith; [c]praying in the Holy Spirit;

21 keep yourselves in the love of
God, [a]waiting anxiously for the
mercy of our Lord Jesus Christ to
eternal life.
22 And [1]have mercy on some, who
are doubting;
23 save others, [a]snatching them
out of the fire; and on some have
mercy with fear, [b]hating even the
garment polluted by the flesh.

21 [a]Titus 2:13
22 [1]Or, *convince*
23 [a]Amos 4:11 [b]Zech. 3:3f.
24 [a]Rom. 16:25 [b]2 Cor. 4:14 [c]1 Pet. 4:13
25 [a]John 5:44; 1 Tim. 1:17 [b]Luke 1:47 [c]Rom. 11:36 [d]Heb. 13:8

24 [a]Now to Him who is able to
keep you from stumbling, and to
[b]make you stand in the presence of
His glory blameless with [c]great joy,
25 to the [a]only [b]God our Savior,
through Jesus Christ our Lord, [c]*be*
glory, majesty, dominion and authority, [d]before all time and now
and forever. Amen.

THE REVELATION TO JOHN

The Revelation of Jesus Christ

1 THE Revelation of Jesus Christ,
which [a]God gave Him to [b]show to
His bond-servants, [c]the things
which must shortly take place; and
He sent and communicated *it* [d]by
His angel to His bond-servant
[e]John,
2 who bore witness to [a]the word
of God and to [b]the testimony of Jesus Christ, *even* to all that he saw.
3 [a]Blessed is he who reads and
those who hear the words of the
prophecy, and heed the things
which are written in it; [b]for the time
is near.

Message to the Seven Churches

4 [a]John to [b]the seven churches
that are in [c]Asia: Grace to you and
peace, from Him who is and who
was and who is to come; and from
the seven Spirits who are before His
throne;
5 and from Jesus Christ, [a]the
faithful witness, the [b]first-born of
the dead, and the [c]ruler of the kings
of the earth. To Him who loves us,
and released us from our sins by His
blood,
6 and He has made us *to be* a
[a]kingdom, [a]priests to [b]His God and
Father; [c]to Him *be* the glory and the
dominion forever and ever. Amen.
7 [a]BEHOLD, HE IS COMING WITH
THE CLOUDS, and [b]EVERY EYE WILL
SEE HIM, EVEN THOSE WHO PIERCED
HIM; AND ALL THE TRIBES OF THE
EARTH WILL [c]MOURN OVER HIM. Even
so. Amen.
8 "I am [a]the Alpha and the
Omega," says the [b]Lord God, "[c]who
is and who was and who is to come,
the Almighty."

The Patmos Vision

9 [a]I, John, your [b]brother and
[c]fellow-partaker in the tribulation
and kingdom and perseverance
which are in Jesus, was on the island called Patmos, because of the

1 [a]John 17:8; Rev. 5:7 [b]Rev. 22:6 [c]Dan. 2:28f.; Rev. 1:19 [d]Rev. 17:1 [e]Rev. 1:4, 9; 22:8
2 [a]1 Cor. 1:6; Rev. 1:9; 6:9 [b]Rev. 12:17
3 [a]Luke 11:28; Rev. 22:7 [b]Rom. 13:11
4 [a]Rev. 1:1, 9; 22:8 [b]Rev. 1:11, 20 [c]Acts 2:9
5 [a]John 8:14; 18:37 [b]1 Cor. 15:20; Col. 1:18 [c]Dan. 2:47
6 [a]Ex. 19:6; Is. 61:6 [b]Rom. 15:6 [c]Rom. 11:36
7 [a]Dan. 7:13; Matt. 16:27f.; 24:30 [b]Zech. 12:10; John 19:37 [c]Luke 23:28
8 [a]Is. 41:4; Rev. 21:6; 22:13 [b]Rev. 4:8; 11:17; 15:3 [c]Rev. 1:4
9 [a]Rev. 1:1 [b]Acts 1:15 [c]Matt. 20:23
10 [a]Matt. 22:43; Rev. 4:2; 17:3; 21:10 [b]Acts 20:7 [c]Rev. 4:1
11 [a]Rev. 1:2, 19 [b]Rev. 1:4, 20
12 [a]Ex. 25:37
13 [a]Rev. 2:1 [b]Ezek. 1:26; Dan. 7:13
14 [a]Dan. 7:9 [b]Dan. 7:9; 10:6
15 [a]Ezek. 1:7; Dan. 10:6; Rev. 2:18 [b]Ezek. 43:2
16 [a]Rev. 1:20; 2:1; 3:1 [b]Is. 49:2; Heb. 4:12 [c]Matt. 17:2; Rev. 10:1
17 [a]Dan. 8:17; 10:9, 10, 15 [b]Dan. 8:18; 10:10, 12
18 [a]Luke 24:5; Rev. 4:9f. [b]Rom. 6:9 [c]Job 38:17
19 [a]Rev. 1:11 [b]Rev. 1:12-16 [c]Rev. 4:1

word of God and the testimony of
Jesus.
10 I was [a]in the Spirit on [b]the
Lord's day, and I heard behind me a
loud voice [c]like *the sound* of a trumpet,
11 saying, "[a]Write in a book what
you see, and send *it* to the [b]seven
churches: to Ephesus and to
Smyrna and to Pergamum and to
Thyatira and to Sardis and to Philadelphia and to Laodicea."
12 And I turned to see the voice
that was speaking with me. And
having turned I saw [a]seven golden
lampstands;
13 and [a]in the middle of the lampstands one [b]like a son of man,
clothed in a robe reaching to the
feet, and girded across His breast
with a golden girdle.
14 And His head and His [a]hair
were white like white wool, like
snow; and [b]His eyes were like a
flame of fire;
15 and His [a]feet *were* like burnished bronze, when it has been
caused to glow in a furnace, and His
[b]voice *was* like the sound of many
waters.
16 And in His right hand He held
[a]seven stars; and out of His mouth
came a [b]sharp two-edged sword;
and His [c]face was like the sun shining in its strength.
17 And when I saw Him, I [a]fell at
His feet as a dead man. And He [b]laid
His right hand upon me, saying,
"Do not be afraid; I am the first and
the last,
18 and the [a]living One; and I [b]was
dead, and behold, I am alive forevermore, and I have [c]the keys of death
and of Hades.
19 "[a]Write therefore [b]the things
which you have seen, and the things
which are, and the things which
shall take place [c]after these things.

20 "As for the [a]mystery of the [b]sev-
en stars which you saw in My right
hand, and the [c]seven golden lampstands: the [b]seven stars are the angels of [d]the seven churches, and the
seven [e]lampstands are the seven
churches.

Chapter 2

Message to Ephesus

"To the angel of the church in
[a]Ephesus write:
The One who holds [b]the seven
stars in His right hand, the One who
walks [c]among the seven golden
lampstands, says this:
2 '[a]I know your deeds and your
toil and perseverance, and that you
cannot endure evil men, and you
[b]put to the test those who call themselves [c]apostles, and they are not,
and you found them *to be* false;
3 and you have perseverance and
have endured [a]for My name's sake,
and have not grown weary.
4 'But I have *this* against you, that
you have [a]left your first love.
5 'Remember therefore from
where you have fallen, and [a]repent
and [b]do the deeds you did at first; or
else I am coming to you, and will
remove your [c]lampstand out of its
place — unless you repent.
6 'Yet this you do have, that you
hate the deeds of the [a]Nicolaitans,
which I also hate.
7 '[a]He who has an ear, let him
hear what the Spirit says to the
churches. [b]To him who overcomes, I
will grant to eat of [c]the tree of life,
which is in the [d]Paradise of God.'

Message to Smyrna

8 "And to the angel of the church
in [a]Smyrna write:
[b]The first and the last, who [c]was
dead, and has come to life, says this:
9 'I know your [a]tribulation and
your [b]poverty (but you are [b]rich),
and the blasphemy by those who
[c]say they are Jews and are not, but
are a synagogue of [d]Satan.
10 'Do not fear what you are about
to suffer. Behold, the devil is about
to cast some of you into prison, that
you may be [a]tested, and you will
have tribulation [b]ten days. Be [c]faith-
ful until death, and I will give you
[d]the crown of life.
11 '[a]He who has an ear, let him
hear what the Spirit says to the
churches. [b]He who overcomes shall
not be hurt by the [c]second death.'

Message to Pergamum

12 "And to the angel of the church
in [a]Pergamum write:
The One who has [b]the sharp two-
edged sword says this:
13 'I know where you dwell, where
[a]Satan's throne is; and you hold fast
My name, and did not deny [b]My
faith, even in the days of Antipas,
My [c]witness, My [d]faithful one, who
was killed among you, [e]where Satan
dwells.
14 'But [a]I have a few things against
you, because you have there some
who hold the [b]teaching of Balaam,
who kept teaching Balak to put a
stumbling block before the sons of
Israel, [c]to eat things sacrificed to
idols, and to commit *acts of* immorality.
15 'Thus you also have some who
in the same way hold the teaching of
the [a]Nicolaitans.
16 '[a]Repent therefore; or else [b]I am
coming to you quickly, and I will
make war against them with [c]the
sword of My mouth.
17 '[a]He who has an ear, let him
hear what the Spirit says to the
churches. [a]To him who overcomes,
to him I will give *some* of the hidden
[b]manna, and I will give him a white
stone, and a [c]new name written on
the stone [d]which no one knows but
he who receives it.'

Message to Thyatira

18 "And to the angel of the church
in [a]Thyatira write:
[b]The Son of God, [c]who has eyes
like a flame of fire, and His feet are
like burnished bronze, says this:
19 '[a]I know your deeds, and your
love and faith and service and perseverance, and that your deeds of late
are greater than at first.
20 'But [a]I have *this* against you,
that you tolerate the woman [b]Jeze-
bel, who calls herself a prophetess,
and she teaches and leads My bond-
servants astray, so that they [c]com-
mit *acts of* immorality and eat
things sacrificed to idols.
21 'And [a]I gave her time to repent;
and she [b]does not want to repent of
her immorality.
22 'Behold, I will cast her upon a
bed *of sickness,* and those who
[a]commit adultery with her into
great tribulation, unless they repent
of her deeds.
23 'And I will kill her children with
pestilence; and all the churches will
know that I am He who [a]searches
the minds and hearts; and I will give
to each one of you according to your
deeds.
24 'But I say to you, the rest who

20 [a]Rom. 11:25 [b]Rev. 1:16; 2:1; 3:1 [c]Ex. 25:37; 37:23; Zech. 4:2; Rev. 1:12; 2:1 [d]Rev. 1:4, 11 [e]Matt. 5:14f.
1 [a]Rev. 1:11 [b]Rev. 1:16 [c]Rev. 1:12f.
2 [a]Rev. 2:19; 3:1, 8, 15 [b]John 6:6; 1 John 4:1 [c]2 Cor. 11:13
3 [a]John 15:21
4 [a]Jer. 2:2; Matt. 24:12
5 [a]Rev. 2:16, 22; 3:3, 19 [b]Heb. 10:32; Rev. 2:2 [c]Matt. 5:14ff.
6 [a]Rev. 2:15
7 [a]Matt. 11:15 [b]Rev. 2:11, 17, 26; 3:5, 12, 21; 21:7 [c]Gen. 2:9; 3:22; Prov. 3:18; 11:30; 13:12; 15:4; Rev. 22:2, 14 [d]Ezek. 31:8 Luke 23:43
8 [a]Rev. 1:11 [b]Rev. 1:17 [c]Rev. 1:18
9 [a]Rev. 1:9 [b]2 Cor. 6:10; 8:9; James 2:5 [c]Rev. 3:9 [d]Matt. 4:10
10 [a]Rev. 3:10; 13:14ff. [b]Dan. 1:12, 14 [c]Rev. 2:13; 12:11; 17:14 [d]1 Cor. 9:25; Rev. 3:11
11 [a]Matt. 11:15; Rev. 2:7, 17, 29 [b]Rev. 2:7, 17, 26 [c]Rev. 20:6, 14
12 [a]Rev. 1:11 [b]Rev. 1:16; 2:16
13 [a]Matt. 4:10 [b]1 Tim. 5:8; Rev. 14:12 [c]Acts 22:20 [d]Rev. 2:10; 12:11; 17:14 [e]Rev. 2:9
14 [a]Rev. 2:20 [b]2 Pet. 2:15 [c]Acts 15:29
15 [a]Rev. 2:6
16 [a]Rev. 2:5 [b]Rev. 22:7, 20 [c]2 Thess. 2:8
17 [a]Rev. 2:7 [b]John 6:49f. [c]Is. 56:5; 62:2; 65:15 [d]Rev. 14:3; 19:12
18 [a]Rev. 1:11; 2:24 [b]Matt. 4:3 [c]Rev. 1:14f.
19 [a]Rev. 2:2
20 [a]Rev. 2:14 [b]1 Kin. 16:31; 21:25; 2 Kin. 9:7 [c]Acts 15:29
21 [a]Rom. 2:4; 2 Pet. 3:9 [b]Rom. 2:5; Rev. 9:20f.
22 [a]Rev. 17:2; 18:9
23 [a]Ps. 7:9; 26:2; 139:1; Jer. 11:20; 17:10

are in [a]Thyatira, who do not hold
this teaching, who have not known
the [b]deep things of Satan, as they
call them — I [c]place no other burden on you.
25 'Nevertheless [a]what you have,
hold fast [b]until I come.
26 'And [a]he who overcomes, and
he who keeps My deeds [b]until the
end, [c]TO HIM I WILL GIVE AUTHORITY
OVER THE NATIONS;
27 AND HE SHALL [a]RULE THEM WITH
A ROD OF IRON, [b]AS THE VESSELS OF
THE POTTER ARE BROKEN TO PIECES,
as I also have received *authority*
from My Father;
28 and I will give him [a]the morning star.
29 '[a]He who has an ear, let him
hear what the Spirit says to the
churches.'

CHAPTER 3

Message to Sardis

"AND to the angel of the church
in [a]Sardis write:
He who has [b]the seven Spirits of
God, and [c]the seven stars, says this:
[d]I know your deeds, that you have a
name that you are alive, and you are
[e]dead.
2 'Wake up, and strengthen the
things that remain, which were
about to die; for I have not found
your deeds completed in the sight of
My God.
3 '[a]Remember therefore what you
have received and heard; and keep
it, and [a]repent. If therefore you will
not wake up, [b]I will come [c]like a
thief, and you will not know at
[d]what hour I will come upon you.
4 'But you have a few [a]people in
[b]Sardis who have not [c]soiled their
garments; and they will walk with
Me [d]in white; for they are worthy.
5 '[a]He who overcomes shall thus
be clothed in [b]white garments; and I
will not [c]erase his name from the
book of life, and [d]I will confess his
name before My Father, and before
His angels.
6 '[a]He who has an ear, let him
hear what the Spirit says to the
churches.'

Message to Philadelphia

7 "And to the angel of the church
in [a]Philadelphia write:
[b]He who is holy, [c]who is true, who
has [d]the key of David, who opens
and no one will shut, and who shuts
and no one opens, says this:
8 '[a]I know your deeds. Behold, I
have put before you [b]an open door
which no one can shut, because you
have a little power, and have kept
My word, and [c]have not denied My
name.
9 'Behold, I will cause *those* of
[a]the synagogue of Satan, who say
that they are Jews, and are not, but
lie — behold, I will make them to
[b]come and bow down at your feet,
and to know that [c]I have loved you.
10 'Because you have [a]kept the
word of [b]My perseverance, [c]I also
will keep you from the hour of [d]test-
ing, that *hour* which is about to
come upon the whole [e]world, to test
[f]those who dwell upon the earth.
11 '[a]I am coming quickly; [b]hold
fast what you have, in order that no
one take your [c]crown.
12 '[a]He who overcomes, I will
make him a [b]pillar in the temple of
My God, and he will not go out from
it any more; and I will write upon
him the [c]name of My God, and [d]the
name of the city of My God, [e]the
new Jerusalem, which comes down
out of heaven from My God, and My
[f]new name.
13 '[a]He who has an ear, let him
hear what the Spirit says to the
churches.'

Message to Laodicea

14 "And to the angel of the church
in [a]Laodicea write:
[b]The Amen, [c]the faithful and true
Witness, [d]the Beginning of the creation of God, says this:
15 '[a]I know your deeds, that you
are neither cold nor hot; [b]I would
that you were cold or hot.
16 'So because you are lukewarm,
and neither hot nor cold, I will spit
you out of My mouth.
17 'Because you say, "[a]I am rich,
and have become wealthy, and have
need of nothing," and you do not
know that you are wretched and
miserable and poor and blind and
naked,
18 'I advise you to [a]buy from Me
[b]gold refined by fire, that you may
become rich, and [c]white garments,
that you may clothe yourself, and
that [d]the shame of your nakedness
may not be revealed; and eyesalve
to anoint your eyes, that you may
see.
19 '[a]Those whom I love, I reprove
and discipline; be zealous therefore,
and [b]repent.
20 'Behold, I stand [a]at the door and
[b]knock; if any one hears My voice
and opens the door, [c]I will come in
to him, and will dine with him, and
he with Me.

24 [a]Rev. 2:18 [b]1 Cor. 2:10 [c]Acts 15:28
25 [a]Rev. 3:11 [b]John 21:22
26 [a]Rev. 2:7 [b]Matt. 10:22; Heb. 3:6 [c]Ps. 2:8; Rev. 3:21; 20:4
27 [a]Rev. 12:5; 19:15 [b]Is. 30:14; Jer. 19:11
28 [a]1 John 3:2
29 [a]Rev. 2:7
1 [a]Rev. 1:11 [b]Rev. 1:4 [c]Rev. 1:16 [d]Rev. 2:2; 3:8, 15 [e]1 Tim. 5:6
3 [a]Rev. 2:5 [b]Rev. 2:5 [c]1 Thess. 5:2; 2 Pet. 3:10; Rev. 16:15 [d]Matt. 24:43
4 [a]Acts 1:15 marg. [b]Rev. 1:11 [c]Jude 23 [d]Eccles. 9:8
5 [a]Rev. 2:7 [b]Rev. 3:4 [c]Luke 10:20; Rev. 13:8 [d]Matt. 10:32; Luke 12:8
6 [a]Rev. 2:7
7 [a]Rev. 1:11 [b]Rev. 6:10 [c]1 John 5:20; Rev. 3:14; 19:11 [d]Job 12:14; Is. 22:22
8 [a]Rev. 3:1 [b]Acts 14:27 [c]Rev. 2:13
9 [a]Rev. 2:9 [b]Is. 45:14; 49:23; 60:14 [c]Is. 43:4; John 17:23
10 [a]John 17:6; Rev. 3:8 [b]Rev. 1:9 [c]2 Tim. 2:12; 2 Pet. 2:9 [d]Rev. 2:10 [e]Matt. 24:14; Rev. 16:14 [f]Rev. 6:10; 8:13; 11:10
11 [a]Rev. 1:3; 22:7, 12, 20 [b]Rev. 2:25 [c]Rev. 2:10
12 [a]Rev. 3:5 [b]1 Kin. 7:21 [c]Rev. 14:1; 22:4 [d]Ezek. 48:35; Rev. 21:2 [e]Gal. 4:26 [f]Rev. 2:17
13 [a]Rev. 3:6
14 [a]Rev. 1:11 [b]2 Cor. 1:20 [c]Rev. 1:5; 3:7 [d]Gen. 49:3; Deut. 21:17; Prov. 8:22
15 [a]Rev. 3:1 [b]Rom. 12:11
17 [a]Hos. 12:8; Zech. 11:5; Matt. 5:3; 1 Cor. 4:8
18 [a]Is. 55:1 [b]1 Pet. 1:7 [c]Rev. 3:4 [d]Rev. 16:15
19 [a]1 Cor. 11:32; Heb. 12:6 [b]Rev. 2:5
20 [a]Matt. 24:33; James 5:9 [b]Luke 12:36; John 10:3 [c]John 14:23

21 '[a]He who overcomes, I will grant to him [b]to sit down with Me on My throne, as [c]I also overcame and sat down with My Father on His throne.
22 '[a]He who has an ear, let him hear what the Spirit says to the churches.' "

CHAPTER 4

Scene in Heaven

AFTER [a]these things I looked, and behold, [b]a door *standing* open in heaven, and the first voice which I had heard, [c]like *the sound* of a trumpet speaking with me, said, "[d]Come up here, and I will [e]show you what must take place after these things."
2 Immediately I was [a]in the Spirit; and behold, [b]a throne was standing in heaven, and [c]One sitting on the throne.
3 And He who was sitting *was* like a [a]jasper stone and a [b]sardius in appearance; and *there was* a [c]rainbow around the throne, like an [d]emerald in appearance.
4 And [a]around the throne *were* [b]twenty-four thrones; and upon the thrones *I saw* [c]twenty-four elders [d]sitting, clothed in [e]white garments, and [f]golden crowns on their heads.

The Throne and Worship of the Creator

5 And from the throne proceed [a]flashes of lightning and sounds and peals of thunder. And *there were* [b]seven lamps of fire burning before the throne, which are [c]the seven Spirits of God;
6 and before the throne *there was*, as it were, a [a]sea of glass like crystal; and in the center and [b]around the throne, [c]four living creatures [d]full of eyes in front and behind.
7 [a]And the first creature *was* like a lion, and the second creature like a calf, and the third creature had a face like that of a man, and the fourth creature *was* like a flying eagle.
8 And the [a]four living creatures, each one of them having [b]six wings, are [c]full of eyes around and within; and [d]day and night they do not cease to say,

"[e]HOLY, HOLY, HOLY, *is* THE [f]LORD GOD, THE ALMIGHTY, [g]who was and who is and who is to come."

9 And when the living creatures give glory and honor and thanks to Him who [a]sits on the throne, to [b]Him who lives forever and ever,
10 the [a]twenty-four elders will [b]fall down before Him who [c]sits on the throne, and will worship [d]Him who lives forever and ever, and will cast their [e]crowns before the throne, saying,
11 "[a]Worthy art Thou, our Lord and our God, to receive glory and honor and power; for Thou [b]didst create all things, and because of Thy will they existed, and were created."

CHAPTER 5

The Book with Seven Seals

AND I saw in the right hand of Him who [a]sat on the throne a [b]book written inside and on the back, [c]sealed up with seven seals.
2 And I saw a [a]strong angel proclaiming with a loud voice, "Who is worthy to open the book and to break its seals?"
3 And no one [a]in heaven, or on the earth, or under the earth, was able to open the book, or to look into it.
4 And I *began* to weep greatly, because no one was found worthy to open the book, or to look into it;
5 and one of the elders *said to me, "Stop weeping; behold, the [a]Lion that is [b]from the tribe of Judah, the [c]Root of David, has overcome so as to open the book and its seven seals."
6 And I saw between the throne (with the four living creatures) and [a]the elders a [b]Lamb standing, as if [c]slain, having seven [d]horns and [e]seven eyes, which are [f]the seven Spirits of God, sent out into all the earth.
7 And He came, and He took [a]*it* out of the right hand of Him who [a]sat on the throne.
8 And when He had taken the book, the [a]four living creatures and the [b]twenty-four elders [c]fell down before the [d]Lamb, having each one a [e]harp, and [f]golden bowls full of incense, which are the [g]prayers of the saints.
9 And they *sang a [a]new song, saying,

"[b]Worthy art Thou to take the book, and to break its seals; for Thou wast [c]slain, and didst [d]purchase for God with Thy blood *men* from [e]every tribe and tongue and people and nation.

21 [a]Rev. 2:7 [b]Matt. 19:28 [c]John 16:33; Rev. 5:5
22 [a]Rev. 2:7
1 [a]Rev. 1:12ff., 19 [b]Ezek. 1:1; Rev. 19:11 [c]Rev. 1:10 [d]Rev. 11:12 [e]Rev. 1:19; 22:6
2 [a]Rev. 1:10 [b]1 Kin. 22:19; Is. 6:1; Ezek. 1:26 [c]Rev. 4:9
3 [a]Rev. 21:11 [b]Rev. 21:20 [c]Ezek. 1:28; Rev. 10:1 [d]Rev. 21:19
4 [a]Rev. 4:6; 5:11; 7:11 [b]Rev. 11:16 [c]Rev. 4:10; 5:6, 8, 14; 19:4 [d]Matt. 19:28; 2 Tim. 2:12; Rev. 2:26; 20:4 [e]Rev. 3:18 [f]Rev. 4:10
5 [a]Ex. 19:16 [b]Ex. 25:37; Zech. 4:2 [c]Rev. 1:4
6 [a]Ezek. 1:22 [b]Rev. 4:4 [c]Ezek. 1:5; Rev. 4:8f. [d]Ezek. 1:18; 10:12
7 [a]Ezek. 1:10; 10:14
8 [a]Ezek. 1:5 [b]Is. 6:2 [c]Ezek. 1:18; 10:12 [d]Rev. 14:11 [e]Is. 6:3 [f]Rev. 1:8 [g]Rev. 1:4
9 [a]Ps. 47:8 [b]Deut. 32:40
10 [a]Rev. 4:4 [b]Rev. 5:8, 14 [c]Ps. 47:8; Is. 6:1; Rev. 4:2 [d]Deut. 32:40; Dan. 4:34; 12:7 [e]Rev. 4:4
11 [a]Rev. 1:6; 5:12 [b]Acts 14:15
1 [a]Rev. 4:9; 5:7, 13 [b]Ezek. 2:9, 10 [c]Is. 29:11; Dan. 12:4
2 [a]Rev. 10:1; 18:21
3 [a]Phil. 2:10
5 [a]Gen. 49:9 [b]Heb. 7:14 [c]Is. 11:1, 10; Rom. 15:12
6 [a]Rev. 4:4; 5:8, 14 [b]John 1:29 [c]Rev. 5:9, 12; 13:8 [d]Dan. 8:3f. [e]Zech. 3:9; 4:10 [f]Rev. 1:4
7 [a]Rev. 5:1
8 [a]Rev. 4:6; 5:6, 11, 14 [b]Rev. 4:4; 5:6, 14 [c]Rev. 4:10 [d]John 1:29 [e]Rev. 14:2; 15:2 [f]Rev. 15:7 [g]Ps. 141:2; Rev. 8:3f.
9 [a]Ps. 40:3; 98:1 [b]Rev. 4:11 [c]Rev. 5:6, 12; 13:8 [d]1 Cor. 6:20; Rev. 14:3f. [e]Dan. 3:4

10 "And Thou hast made them *to*
be a [a]kingdom and [a]priests to
our God; and they will [b]reign
upon the earth."

Angels Exalt the Lamb

11 And I looked, and I heard the
voice of many angels [a]around the
throne and the [b]living creatures and
the [c]elders; and the number of them
was [d]myriads of myriads, and thousands of thousands,

12 saying with a loud voice,
"[a]Worthy is the [b]Lamb that
was [b]slain to receive power
and riches and wisdom and
might and honor and glory
and blessing."

13 And [a]every created thing which
is in heaven and on the earth and
under the earth and on the sea, and
all things in them, I heard saying,
"To Him who [b]sits on the
throne, and to the [c]Lamb, [d]*be*
blessing and honor and glory
and dominion forever and
ever."

14 And the [a]four living creatures
kept saying, "[b]Amen." And the [c]el-
ders [d]fell down and worshiped.

CHAPTER 6

The Book Opened
First Seal a False Christ

AND I saw when the [a]Lamb broke
one of the [b]seven seals, and I heard
one of the [c]four living creatures saying as with a [d]voice of thunder,
"Come.[1]"

2 And I looked, and behold, a
[a]white horse, and he who sat on it
had a bow; and [b]a crown was given
to him; and he went out [c]conquer-
ing, and to conquer.

The Second Seal—War

3 And when He broke the second
seal, I heard the [a]second living creature saying, "Come.[1]"

4 And another, [a]a red horse, went
out; and to him who sat on it, it was
granted to [b]take peace from the
earth, and that *men* should slay one
another; and a great sword was giv-
en to him.

The Third Seal—Famine

5 And when He broke the third
seal, I heard the [a]third living creature saying, "Come.[1]" And I looked,
and behold, a [b]black horse; and he
who sat on it had a [c]pair of scales in
his hand.

6 And I heard as it were a voice in
the center of the [a]four living creatures saying, "A [1]quart of wheat for
a [2]denarius, and three [1]quarts of
barley for a [2]denarius; and [b]do not
harm the oil and the wine."

The Fourth Seal—Death

7 And when He broke the fourth
seal, I heard the voice of the [a]fourth
living creature saying, "Come.[1]"

8 And I looked, and behold, an
[a]ashen horse; and he who sat on it
had the name "[b]Death"; and [b]Hades
was following with him. And authority was given to them over a
fourth of the earth, [c]TO KILL WITH
SWORD AND WITH FAMINE AND WITH
PESTILENCE AND BY THE WILD BEASTS
OF THE EARTH.

The Fifth Seal—Martyrs

9 And when He broke the fifth
seal, I saw [a]underneath the [b]altar
the [c]souls of those who had been
slain [d]because of the word of God,
and because of the testimony which
they had maintained;

10 and they cried out with a loud
voice, saying, "[a]How long, O [b]Lord,
[c]holy and true, wilt Thou refrain
from [d]judging and avenging our
blood on those who dwell on the
earth?"

11 And [a]there was given to each of
them a white robe; and they were
told that they should [b]rest for a little
while longer, [c]until *the number of*
their fellow servants and their
brethren who were to be killed even
as they had been, should be completed also.

The Sixth Seal—Terror

12 And I looked when He broke
the sixth seal, and there was a great
[a]earthquake; and the [b]sun became
black as [c]sackcloth *made* of hair,
and the whole moon became like
blood;

13 and [a]the stars of the sky fell to
the earth, [b]as a fig tree casts its unripe figs when shaken by a great
wind.

14 And [a]the sky was split apart
like a scroll when it is rolled up; and
[b]every mountain and island were
moved out of their places.

15 And [a]the kings of the earth and
the great men and the [1]commanders
and the rich and the strong and every slave and free man, hid themselves in the caves and among the
rocks of the mountains;

16 and they *[a]said to the mountains and to the rocks, "Fall on us
and hide us from the presence of
Him [b]who sits on the throne, and
from the [c]wrath of the Lamb;

---

10 [a]Rev. 1:6 [b]Rev. 3:21; 20:4
11 [a]Rev. 4:4 [b]Rev. 4:6; 5:6, 8, 14 [c]Rev. 4:4; 5:6, 14 [d]Dan. 7:10
12 [a]Rev. 1:6; 4:11; 5:9 [b]John 1:29; Rev. 5:6, 13
13 [a]Phil. 2:10; Rev. 5:3 [b]Rev. 5:1 [c]John 1:29 [d]Rom. 11:36
14 [a]Rev. 4:6; 5:6, 8, 11 [b]1 Cor. 14:16; Rev. 7:12; 19:4 [c]Rev. 4:4; 5:6, 8 [d]Rev. 4:10
1 [1]Some mss. add, *and see* [a]John 1:29 [b]Rev. 5:1 [c]Rev. 4:6; 5:6, 8, 11, 14 [d]Rev. 14:2; 19:6
2 [a]Zech. 1:8; 6:3f.; Rev. 19:11 [b]Zech. 6:11 [c]Rev. 3:21
3 [1]Some mss. add, *and see* [a]Rev. 4:7
4 [a]Zech. 1:8; 6:2 [b]Matt. 10:34
5 [1]Some mss. add, *and see* [a]Rev. 4:7 [b]Zech. 6:2 [c]Ezek. 4:16
6 [1]Lit., *choenix;* a dry measure almost equal to a quart [2]A denarius was worth about 18 cents in silver, equal to a day's wage [a]Rev. 4:6f. [b]Rev. 7:3; 9:4
7 [1]Some mss. add, *and see* [a]Rev. 4:7
8 [a]Zech. 6:3 [b]Prov. 5:5; Hos. 13:14 [c]Jer. 15:2f.; 24:10
9 [a]Ex. 29:12 [b]Rev. 14:18; 16:7 [c]Rev. 20:4 [d]Rev. 1:2, 9
10 [a]Zech. 1:12 [b]Luke 2:29; 2 Pet. 2:1 [c]Rev. 3:7 [d]Deut. 32:43; Ps. 79:10
11 [a]Rev. 3:4, 5; 7:9 [b]2 Thess. 1:7 [c]Heb. 11:40
12 [a]Matt. 24:7 [b]Matt. 24:29 [c]Is. 50:3
13 [a]Matt. 24:29 [b]Is. 34:4
14 [a]Is. 34:4; 2 Pet. 3:10 [b]Is. 54:10; Jer. 4:24
15 [1]Lit., *chiliarchs,* in command of one thousand troops [a]Is. 2:10f., 19, 21
16 [a]Luke 23:30; Rev. 9:6 [b]Rev. 4:9; 5:1 [c]Mark 3:5

17 for [a]the great day of their wrath
has come; and [b]who is able to
stand?"

CHAPTER 7

An Interlude

AFTER this I saw [a]four angels
standing at the [b]four corners of the
earth, holding back [c]the four winds
of the earth, [d]so that no wind should
blow on the earth or on the sea or on
any tree.
2 And I saw another angel ascending [a]from the rising of the sun,
having the [b]seal of [c]the living God;
and he cried out with a loud voice to
the [d]four angels to whom it was
granted to harm the earth and the
sea,
3 saying, "[a]Do not harm the earth
or the sea or the trees, until we have
[b]sealed the bond-servants of our
God on their [c]foreheads."

A Remnant of Israel—144,000

4 And I heard the [a]number of
those who were sealed, [b]one hundred and forty-four thousand sealed
from every tribe of the sons of Israel:
5 from the tribe of Judah, twelve
thousand *were* sealed, from the
tribe of Reuben twelve thousand,
from the tribe of Gad twelve thousand,
6 from the tribe of Asher twelve
thousand, from the tribe of Naphtali
twelve thousand, from the tribe of
Manasseh twelve thousand,
7 from the tribe of Simeon twelve
thousand, from the tribe of Levi
twelve thousand, from the tribe of
Issachar twelve thousand,
8 from the tribe of Zebulun
twelve thousand, from the tribe of
Joseph twelve thousand, from the
tribe of Benjamin, twelve thousand
were sealed.

A Multitude from the Tribulation

9 After these things I looked, and
behold, a great multitude, which no
one could count, from [a]every nation
and *all* tribes and peoples and
tongues, standing [b]before the
throne and [c]before the Lamb,
clothed in [d]white robes, and [e]palm
branches *were* in their hands;
10 and they cry out with a loud
voice, saying,
"[a]Salvation to our God [b]who sits
on the throne, and to the Lamb."
11 And all the angels were standing [a]around the throne and *around*
[a]the elders and the [b]four living crea-

17 [a]Is. 63:4; Jer. 30:7; Joel 1:15; 2:1f., 11, 31; Zeph. 1:14f.; Rev. 16:14 [b]Ps. 76:7; Nah. 1:6; Mal. 3:2; Luke 21:36
1 [a]Rev. 9:14 [b]Is. 11:12; Ezek. 7:2; Rev. 20:8 [c]Jer. 49:36; Zech. 6:5; Matt. 24:31 [d]Rev. 7:3; 8:7; 9:4
2 [a]Is. 41:2; Rev. 16:12 [b]Rev. 7:3; 9:4 [c]Matt. 16:16 [d]Rev. 9:14
3 [a]Rev. 6:6 [b]John 3:33; Rev. 7:3-8 [c]Ezek. 9:4, 6; Rev. 13:16; 14:1, 9; 20:4; 22:4
4 [a]Rev. 9:16 [b]Rev. 14:1, 3
9 [a]Rev. 5:9 [b]Rev. 7:15 [c]Rev. 22:3 [d]Rev. 6:11; 7:14 [e]Lev. 23:40
10 [a]Ps. 3:8; Rev. 12:10; 19:1 [b]Rev. 22:3
11 [a]Rev. 4:4 [b]Rev. 4:6 [c]Rev. 4:10
12 [a]Rev. 5:14 [b]Rev. 5:12
13 [a]Acts 3:12 [b]Rev. 7:9
14 [a]Matt. 24:21 [b]Zech. 3:3-5; Rev. 22:14 [c]Rev. 6:11; 7:9 [d]Heb. 9:14; 1 John 1:7
15 [a]Rev. 7:9 [b]Rev. 4:8; 22:3 [c]Rev. 11:19; 21:22 [d]Rev. 4:9 [e]Lev. 26:11; Ezek. 37:27; John 1:14; Rev. 21:3
16 [a]Ps. 121:5f.; Is. 49:10
17 [1]Lit., *waters* [a]Ps. 23:1f.; Matt. 2:6; John 10:11 [b]John 4:14; Rev. 21:6; 22:1 [c]Is. 25:8; Matt. 5:4; Rev. 21:4
1 [a]Rev. 5:1; 6:1, 3, 5, 7, 9, 12 [b]Rev. 5:9
2 [a]Matt. 18:10; Rev. 1:4; 8:6-13; 9:1, 13; 11:15 [b]1 Cor. 15:52; 1 Thess. 4:16
3 [a]Rev. 7:2 [b]Amos 9:1; Rev. 6:9 [c]Heb. 9:4 [d]Rev. 5:8 [e]Ex. 30:1, 3; Num. 4:11; Rev. 8:5; 9:13
4 [a]Ps. 141:2
5 [a]Lev. 16:12 [b]Ezek. 10:2 [c]Rev. 4:5 [d]Rev. 6:12
6 [a]Rev. 8:2

tures; and they [c]fell on their faces
before the throne and worshiped
God,
12 saying,
"[a]Amen, [b]blessing and glory and
wisdom and thanksgiving and hon-
or and power and might, *be* to our
God forever and ever. [a]Amen."
13 And one of the elders [a]an-
swered, saying to me, "These who
are clothed in the [b]white robes, who
are they, and from where have they
come?"
14 And I said to him, "My lord, you
know." And he said to me, "These
are the ones who come out of the
[a]great tribulation, and they have
[b]washed their robes and made them
[c]white in the [d]blood of the Lamb.
15 "For this reason, they are [a]be-
fore the throne of God; and they
[b]serve Him day and night in His
[c]temple; and [d]He who sits on the
throne shall spread His [e]tabernacle
over them.
16 "[a]They shall hunger no more,
neither thirst any more; neither
shall the sun beat down on them,
nor any heat;
17 for the Lamb in the center of
the throne shall be their [a]shepherd,
and shall guide them to springs of
the [1b]water of life; and [c]God shall
wipe every tear from their eyes."

CHAPTER 8

The Seventh Seal—the Trumpets

AND when He broke the [a]seventh
seal, there was [b]silence in heaven
for about half an hour.
2 And I saw [a]the seven angels
who stand before God; and seven
[b]trumpets were given to them.
3 And [a]another angel came and
stood at the [b]altar, holding a [c]golden
censer; and much [d]incense was giv-
en to him, that he might add it to the
[d]prayers of all the saints upon the
[e]golden altar which was before the
throne.
4 And [a]the smoke of the incense,
with the prayers of the saints, went
up before God out of the angel's
hand.
5 And the angel took the censer;
and he [a]filled it with the fire of the
altar and [b]threw it to the earth; and
there followed [c]peals of thunder and
sounds and flashes of lightning and
an [d]earthquake.
6 [a]And the seven angels who had
the seven trumpets prepared themselves to sound them.

7 And the first sounded, and there came [a]hail and fire, mixed with blood, and they were thrown to the earth; and [b]a third of the earth was burnt up, and [b]a third of the [c]trees were burnt up, and all the green [c]grass was burnt up.

8 And the second angel sounded, and *something* like a great [a]mountain burning with fire was thrown into the sea; and [b]a third of the [c]sea became blood;

9 and [a]a third of the creatures, which were in the sea and had life, died; and a third of the [b]ships were destroyed.

10 And the third angel sounded, and a great star [a]fell from heaven, burning like a torch, and it fell on a [b]third of the rivers and on the [c]springs of waters;

11 and the name of the star is called Wormwood; and a [a]third of the waters became [b]wormwood; and many men died from the waters, because they were made bitter.

12 And the fourth angel sounded, and a [a]third of the [b]sun and a third of the [b]moon and a [a]third of the [b]stars were smitten, so that a [a]third of them might be darkened and the day might not shine for a [a]third of it, and the night in the same way.

13 And I looked, and I heard an eagle flying in [a]midheaven, saying with a loud voice, "[b]Woe, woe, woe, to [c]those who dwell on the earth, because of the remaining blasts of the trumpet of the [d]three angels who are about to sound!"

Chapter 9

The Fifth Trumpet—The Bottomless Pit

AND the [a]fifth angel sounded, and I saw a [b]star from heaven which had fallen to the earth; and the [c]key of the [d]bottomless pit was given to him.

2 And he opened the bottomless pit; and [a]smoke went up out of the pit, like the smoke of a great furnace; and [b]the sun and the air were darkened by the smoke of the pit.

3 And out of the smoke came forth [a]locusts upon the earth; and power was given them, as the [b]scorpions of the earth have power.

4 And they were told that they should not [a]hurt the [b]grass of the earth, nor any green thing, nor any tree, but only the men who do not have the [c]seal of God on their foreheads.

5 And they were not permitted to kill anyone, but to torment for [a]five months; and their torment was like the torment of a [b]scorpion when it stings a man.

6 And in those days [a]men will seek death and will not find it; and they will long to die and death flees from them.

7 And the [a]appearance of the locusts was like horses prepared for battle; and on their heads, as it were, crowns like gold, and their faces were like the faces of men.

8 And they had hair like the hair of women, and their [a]teeth were like *the teeth* of lions.

9 And they had breastplates like breastplates of iron; and the [a]sound of their wings was like the sound of chariots, of many horses rushing to battle.

10 And they have tails like [a]scorpions, and stings; and in their [b]tails is their power to hurt men for [c]five months.

11 They have as king over them, the angel of the [a]abyss; his name in [b]Hebrew is [1c]Abaddon, and in the Greek he has the name [2]Apollyon.

12 [a]The first woe is past; behold, two woes are still coming after these things.

The Sixth Trumpet—Army from the East

13 And the sixth angel sounded, and I heard a voice from the four [a]horns of the [b]golden altar which is before God,

14 one saying to the sixth angel who had the trumpet, "Release the [a]four angels who are bound at the [b]great river Euphrates."

15 And the four angels, who had been prepared for the hour and day and month and year, were [a]released, so that they might kill a [b]third of mankind.

16 And the number of the armies of the horsemen was [a]two hundred million; [b]I heard the number of them.

17 And this is how I saw [a]in the vision the horses and those who sat on them: *the riders* had breastplates *the color* of fire and of hyacinth and of [b]brimstone; and the heads of the horses are like the heads of lions; and [c]out of their mouths proceed fire and smoke and [b]brimstone.

18 A [a]third of mankind was killed by these three plagues, by the [b]fire and the smoke and the brimstone, which proceeded out of their mouths.

19 For the power of the horses is in their mouths and in their tails; for

7 [a]Is. 28:2; Ezek. 38:22; Joel 2:30 [b]Zech. 13:8, 9; Rev. 8:7-12; 9:15, 18; 12:4 [c]Rev. 9:4
8 [a]Jer. 51:25 [b]Zech. 13:8, 9; Rev. 8:7-12; 9:15, 18; 12:4 [c]Ex. 7:17ff.; Rev. 11:6; 16:3
9 [a]Zech. 13:8, 9 [b]Is. 2:16
10 [a]Is. 14:12; Rev. 6:13; 9:1 [b]Zech. 13:8, 9; Rev. 8:7-12; 9:15, 18; 12:4 [c]Rev. 14:7; 16:4
11 [a]Zech. 13:8, 9; Rev. 8:7-12; 9:15, 18; 12:4 [b]Jer. 9:15; 23:15
12 [a]Zech. 13:8, 9; Rev. 8:7-12; 9:15, 18; 12:4 [b]Ex. 10:21ff.; Rev. 6:12f.
13 [a]Rev. 14:6; 19:17 [b]Rev. 9:12; 11:14; 12:12 [c]Rev. 3:10 [d]Rev. 8:2
1 [a]Rev. 8:2 [b]Rev. 8:10 [c]Rev. 1:18 [d]Luke 8:31; Rev. 9:2, 11
2 [a]Gen. 19:28; Ex. 19:18 [b]Joel 2:2, 10
3 [a]Ex. 10:12-15; Rev. 9:7 [b]2 Chr. 10:11, 14; Ezek. 2:6; Rev. 9:5, 10
4 [a]Rev. 6:6 [b]Rev. 8:7 [c]Rev. 7:2, 3
5 [a]Rev. 9:10 [b]2 Chr. 10:11, 14; Ezek. 2:6; Rev. 9:3, 10
6 [a]Job 3:21; 7:15; Jer. 8:3
7 [a]Joel 2:4
8 [a]Joel 1:6
9 [a]Jer. 47:3
10 [a]2 Chr. 10:11; Rev. 8:3, 5 [b]Rev. 9:19 [c]Rev. 9:5
11 [1]Or, *Destruction* [2]Or, *Destroyer* [a]Luke 8:31; Rev. 9:1, 2 [b]John 5:2; Rev. 16:16 [c]Job 26:6; 28:22; 31:12; Ps. 88:11 marg.
12 [a]Rev. 8:13; 11:14
13 [a]Ex. 30:2f., 10 [b]Rev. 8:3
14 [a]Rev. 7:1 [b]Gen. 15:18
15 [a]Rev. 20:7 [b]Rev. 8:7; 9:18
16 [a]Rev. 5:11 [b]Rev. 7:4
17 [a]Dan. 8:2; 9:21 [b]Rev. 9:18; 14:10 [c]Rev. 11:5
18 [a]Rev. 8:7; 9:15 [b]Rev. 9:17

their tails are like serpents and have heads; and with them they do harm.

20 And the rest of [1]mankind, who were not killed by these plagues, [a]did not repent of [b]THE WORKS OF THEIR HANDS, so as not to [c]worship DEMONS, AND [d]THE IDOLS OF GOLD AND OF SILVER AND OF BRASS AND OF STONE AND OF WOOD, WHICH CAN NEITHER SEE NOR HEAR NOR WALK;

21 and they [a]did not repent of their murders nor of their [b]sorceries nor of their [c]immorality nor of their thefts.

CHAPTER 10

The Angel and the Little Book

AND I saw another [a]strong angel [b]coming down out of heaven, clothed with a cloud; and the [c]rainbow was upon his head, and [d]his face was like the sun, and his [e]feet like pillars of fire;

2 and he had in his hand a [a]little book which was open. And he placed [b]his right foot on the sea and his left on the land;

3 and he cried out with a loud voice, [a]as when a lion roars; and when he had cried out, the [b]seven peals of thunder uttered their voices.

4 And when the seven peals of thunder had spoken, [a]I was about to write; and I [b]heard a voice from heaven saying, "[c]Seal up the things which the seven peals of thunder have spoken, and do not write them."

5 And the angel whom I saw standing on the sea and on the land [a]LIFTED UP HIS RIGHT HAND TO HEAVEN,

6 AND SWORE BY [a]HIM WHO LIVES FOREVER AND EVER, WHO [b]CREATED HEAVEN AND THE THINGS IN IT, AND THE EARTH AND THE THINGS IN IT, AND THE SEA AND THE THINGS IN IT, that [c]there shall be delay no longer,

7 but in the days of the voice of the [a]seventh angel, when he is about to sound, then [b]the mystery of God is finished, as He preached to His servants the prophets.

8 And [a]the voice which I heard from heaven, *I heard* again speaking with me, and saying, "Go, take [b]the book which is open in the hand of the angel who [b]stands on the sea and on the land."

9 And I went to the angel, telling him to give me the little book. And he *said to me, "[a]Take it, and eat it; and it will make your stomach bitter, but in your mouth it will be sweet as honey."

10 And I took the little book out of the angel's hand and ate it, and it was in my mouth sweet as honey; and when I had eaten it, my stomach was made bitter.

11 And [a]they *said to me, "You must [b]prophesy again concerning [c]many peoples and nations and tongues and [d]kings."

CHAPTER 11

The Two Witnesses

AND there was given me a [a]measuring rod like a staff; and [b]someone said, "Rise and measure the temple of God, and the altar, and those who worship in it.

2 "And leave out the [a]court which is outside the temple, and do not measure it, for [b]it has been given to the nations; and they will [b]tread under foot [c]the holy city for [d]forty-two months.

3 "And I will grant *authority* to my two [a]witnesses, and they will prophesy for [b]twelve hundred and sixty days, clothed in [c]sackcloth."

4 These are the [a]two olive trees and the two lampstands that stand before the Lord of the earth.

5 And if any one desires to harm them, [a]fire proceeds out of their mouth and devours their enemies; and if any one would desire to harm them, [b]in this manner he must be killed.

6 These have the power to [a]shut up the sky, in order that rain may not fall during [b]the days of their prophesying; and they have power over the waters to [c]turn them into blood, and to smite the earth with every plague, as often as they desire.

7 And when they have finished their testimony, [a]the beast that comes up out of the [b]abyss will [c]make war with them, and overcome them and kill them.

8 And their dead bodies *will lie* in the street of the [a]great city which mystically is called [b]Sodom and [c]Egypt, where also their Lord was crucified.

9 And those from [a]the peoples and tribes and tongues and nations *will* look at their dead bodies for three and a half days, and [b]will not permit their dead bodies to be laid in a tomb.

10 And [a]those who dwell on the earth *will* rejoice over them and

---

20 [1]Lit., *men* [a]Rev. 2:21 [b]Deut. 4:28; Jer. 1:16 [c]1 Cor. 10:20 [d]Ps. 115:4-7

21 [a]Rev. 9:20 [b]Is. 47:9, 12; Rev. 18:23 [c]Rev. 17:2, 5

1 [a]Rev. 5:2 [b]Rev. 18:1; 20:1 [c]Rev. 4:3 [d]Matt. 17:2; Rev. 1:16 [e]Rev. 1:15

2 [a]Rev. 5:1; 10:8-10 [b]Rev. 10:5, 8

3 [a]Is. 31:4; Hos. 11:10 [b]Ps. 29:3-9

4 [a]Rev. 1:11, 19 [b]Rev. 10:8 [c]Dan. 8:26; 12:4, 9

5 [a]Gen. 14:22; Ex. 6:8; Num. 14:30; Deut. 32:40; Ezek. 20:5; Dan 12:7

6 [a]Rev. 4:9 [b]Rev. 4:11 [c]Rev. 6:11; 12:12; 16:17; 21:6

7 [a]Rev. 11:15 [b]Amos 3:7; Rom. 16:25

8 [a]Rev. 10:4 [b]Rev. 10:2

9 [a]Jer. 15:16; Ezek. 2:8; 3:1-3

11 [a]Rev. 11:1 [b]Ezek. 37:4, 9 [c]Rev. 5:9 [d]Rev. 17:10, 12

1 [a]Ezek. 40:3-42:20; Zech. 2:1; Rev. 21:15f. [b]Rev. 10:11

2 [a]Ezek. 40:17, 20 [b]Luke 21:24 [c]Is. 52:1; Matt. 4:5; 27:53; Rev. 21:2, 10; 22:19 [d]Dan. 7:25; 12:7

3 [a]Rev. 1:5; 2:13 [b]Dan. 7:25; 12:7; Rev. 12:6; 13:5 [c]Gen. 37:34; 2 Sam. 3:31

4 [a]Ps. 52:8; Jer. 11:16

5 [a]2 Kin. 1:10-12; Jer. 5:14; Rev. 9:17f. [b]Num. 16:29, 35

6 [a]Luke 4:25 [b]Rev. 11:3 [c]Rev. 8:8

7 [a]Rev. 13:1ff. [b]Rev. 9:1 [c]Dan. 7:21

8 [a]Rev. 14:8; 16:19 [b]Is. 1:9, 10; 3:9 [c]Ezek. 23:3, 8, 19, 27

9 [a]Rev. 5:9; 10:11 [b]1 Kin. 13:22; Ps. 79:2f.

10 [a]Rev. 3:10

make merry; and they will [b]send gifts to one another, because these two prophets tormented [a]those who dwell on the earth.

11 And after the three and a half days [a]the breath of life from God came into them, and they stood on their feet; and great fear fell upon those who were beholding them.

12 And they heard a loud voice from heaven saying to them, "[a]Come up here." And they [b]went up into heaven in the cloud, and their enemies beheld them.

13 And in that hour there was a great [a]earthquake, and a tenth of the city fell; and seven thousand people were killed in the earthquake, and the rest were terrified and [b]gave glory to the [c]God of heaven.

14 The second [a]woe is past; behold, the third woe is coming quickly.

The Seventh Trumpet—Christ's Reign Foreseen

15 And the [a]seventh angel sounded; and there arose [b]loud voices in heaven, saying,

"[c]The kingdom of the world has become *the kingdom* of our Lord, and of [d]His Christ; and [e]He will reign forever and ever."

16 And the twenty-four elders, who [a]sit on their thrones before God, [b]fell on their faces and worshiped God,

17 saying,

"**W**e give Thee thanks, [a]O Lord God, the Almighty, who art and who wast, because Thou hast taken Thy great power and hast begun to [b]reign.

18 "And [a]the nations were enraged, and Thy wrath came, and [b]the time *came* for the dead to be judged, and *the time* to give their reward to Thy [c]bond-servants the prophets and to the saints and to those who fear Thy name, [d]the small and the great, and to destroy those who destroy the earth."

19 And [a]the temple of God which is in heaven was opened; and [b]the ark of His covenant appeared in His temple, and there were flashes of [c]lightning and sounds and peals of thunder and an earthquake and a [d]great hailstorm.

Chapter 12

The Woman, Israel

AND a great [a]sign appeared [b]in heaven: [c]a woman [d]clothed with the sun, and the moon under her feet, and on her head a crown of twelve stars;

2 and she was with child; and she *[a]cried out, being in labor and in pain to give birth.

The Red Dragon, Satan

3 And [a]another sign appeared in heaven: and behold, a great red [b]dragon having [c]seven heads and [d]ten horns, and on his heads *were* [e]seven diadems.

4 And his tail *swept away a [a]third of the stars of heaven, and [b]threw them to the earth. And the [c]dragon stood before the woman who was about to give birth, so that when she gave birth [d]he might devour her child.

The Male Child, Christ

5 And she gave birth to a son, a male *child,* who is to [a]rule all the nations with a rod of iron; and her child was [b]caught up to God and to His throne.

6 And the woman fled into the wilderness where she *had a place prepared by God, so that there she might be nourished for [a]one thousand two hundred and sixty days.

The Angel, Michael

7 And there was war in heaven, [a]Michael and his angels waging war with the [b]dragon. And the dragon and [c]his angels waged war,

8 and they were not strong enough, and there was no longer a place found for them in heaven.

9 And the great [a]dragon was thrown down, the [b]serpent of old who is called the devil and [c]Satan, who [d]deceives the whole world; he was [e]thrown down to the earth, and his angels were thrown down with him.

10 And I heard [a]a loud voice in heaven, saying,

"**N**ow the [b]salvation, and the power, and the [a]kingdom of our God and the authority of His Christ have come, for the [c]accuser of our brethren has been thrown down, who accuses them before our God day and night.

11 "And they [a]overcame him because of [b]the blood of the Lamb and because of [c]the word of their testimony, and they [d]did not love their life even to death.

12 "For this reason, [a]rejoice, O heavens and [b]you who dwell in them. [c]Woe to the earth and the sea; because [d]the devil has come down

10 [b]Neh. 8:10, 12; Esth. 9:19, 22
11 [a]Ezek. 37:5, 9, 10, 14
12 [a]Rev. 4:1, [b]2 Kin. 2:11; Acts 1:9
13 [a]Rev. 6:12; 8:5; 11:19; 16:18 [b]John 9:24; Rev. 14:7; 16:9; 19:7 [c]Rev. 16:11
14 [a]Rev. 8:13; 9:12
15 [a]Rev. 8:2; 10:7 [b]Rev. 16:17; 19:1 [c]Rev. 12:10 [d]Acts 4:26 [Ps. 2:2] [e]Dan. 2:44; 7:14, 27; Luke 1:33
16 [a]Matt. 19:28; Rev. 4:4 [b]Rev. 4:10
17 [a]Rev. 1:8 [b]Rev. 19:6
18 [a]Ps. 2:1 [b]Dan. 7:10; Rev. 20:12 [c]Rev. 10:7; 16:6 [d]Ps. 115:13; Rev. 13:16; 19:5
19 [a]Rev. 4:1; 15:5 [b]Heb. 9:4 [c]Rev. 4:5 [d]Rev. 16:21
1 [a]Matt. 24:30; Rev. 12:3 [b]Rev. 11:19 [c]Gal. 4:26 [d]Ps. 104:2; Song of Sol. 6:10
2 [a]Is. 26:17; 66:6-9; Mic. 4:9, 10
3 [a]Rev. 12:1; 15:1 [b]Is. 27:1; Rev. 12:4, 7, 9, 13, 16f.; 13:2, 4, 11; 16:13; 20:2 [c]Rev. 13:1; 17:3, 7, 9ff. [d]Dan 7:7, 20, 24; Rev. 13:1; 17:12, 16 [e]Rev. 13:1
4 [a]Rev. 8:7, 12 [b]Dan. 8:10 [c]Is. 27:1; Rev. 12:3, 7, 9, 13, 16f.; 13:2, 4, 11; 16:13; 20:2 [d]Matt. 2:16
5 [a]Rev. 2:27 [b]2 Cor. 12:2
6 [a]Rev. 11:3; 13:5
7 [a]Jude 9 [b]Rev. 12:3 [c]Matt. 25:41
9 [a]Rev. 12:3 [b]Gen. 3:1; 2 Cor. 11:3; Rev. 12:15; 20:2 [c]Matt. 4:10; 25:41 [d]Rev. 13:14; 20:3, 8, 10 [e]Luke 10:18
10 [a]Rev. 11:15 [b]Rev. 7:10 [c]Job 1:11; 2:5; Zech. 3:1; Luke 22:31
11 [a]John 16:33; 1 John 2:13; Rev. 15:2 [b]Rev. 7:14 [c]Rev. 6:9 [d]Luke 14:26; Rev. 2:10
12 [a]Ps. 96:11; Is. 44:23; Rev. 18:20 [b]Rev. 13:6 [c]Rev. 8:13 [d]Rev. 12:9

to you, having great wrath, knowing
that he has *only* [e]a short time."
13 And when the [a]dragon saw that
he was thrown down to the earth, he
persecuted [b]the woman who gave
birth to the male *child.*
14 And the [a]two wings of the great
eagle were given to the woman, in
order that she might fly [b]into the
wilderness to her place, where she
*was nourished for [c]a time and
times and half a time, from the presence of the serpent.
15 And the [a]serpent poured water
[b]like a river out of his mouth after
the woman, so that he might cause
her to be swept away with the flood.
16 And the earth helped the
woman, and the earth opened its
mouth and drank up the river which
the dragon poured out of his mouth.
17 And the dragon was enraged
with the woman, and went off to
[a]make war with the rest of her [b]off-
spring, who [c]keep the commandments of God and [d]hold to the testimony of Jesus.

Chapter 13

The Beast from the Sea

AND [1]he stood on the sand of the
seashore.
And I saw a [a]beast coming up out
of the sea, having [b]ten horns and
[b]seven heads, and on his horns *were*
[c]ten diadems, and on his heads *were*
[d]blasphemous names.
2 And the beast which I saw was
[a]like a leopard, and his feet were
like those of [b]a bear, and his mouth
like the mouth of [c]a lion. And the
[d]dragon gave him his power and his
[e]throne and great authority.
3 And *I saw* one of his heads as if
it had been slain, and his [a]fatal
wound was healed. And the whole
earth [b]was amazed *and followed* after the beast;
4 and they worshiped the [a]drag-
on, because he [a]gave his authority
to the beast; and they worshiped the
beast, saying, "[b]Who is like the
beast, and who is able to wage war
with him?"
5 And there was given to him a
mouth [a]speaking arrogant words
and blasphemies; and authority to
act for [b]forty-two months was given
to him.
6 And he opened his mouth in
blasphemies against God, to blaspheme His name and His tabernacle, *that is,* [a]those who dwell in
heaven.
7 And it was given to him to
[a]make war with the saints and to
overcome them; and authority over
[b]every tribe and people and tongue
and nation was given to him.
8 And all who [a]dwell on the earth
will worship him, *every one* [b]whose
name has not been written [c]from the
foundation of the world in the book
of life of [d]the Lamb who has been
slain.
9 [a]If any one has an ear, let him
hear.
10 [a]If any one *is destined* for captivity, to captivity he goes; [b]if any
one kills with the sword, with the
sword he must be killed. Here is [c]the
perseverance and the faith of the
saints.

The Beast from the Earth

11 And [a]I saw another beast coming up out of the earth; and he had
[b]two horns like a lamb, and he
spoke as a [c]dragon.
12 And he [a]exercises all the authority of the first beast [b]in his presence. And he makes [c]the earth and
those who dwell in it to [d]worship the
first beast, whose [e]fatal wound was
healed.
13 And he [a]performs great signs,
so that he even makes [b]fire come
down out of heaven to the earth in
the presence of men.
14 And he [a]deceives [b]those who
dwell on the earth because of [c]the
signs which it was given him to perform [d]in the presence of the beast,
telling those who dwell on the earth
to make an image to the beast who
*had the [e]wound of the sword and
has come to life.
15 And there was given to him to
give breath to the image of the
beast, that the image of the beast
might even speak and cause [a]as
many as do not [b]worship the image
of the beast to be killed.
16 And he causes all, [a]the small
and the great, and the rich and the
poor, and the free men and the
slaves, to be given a [b]mark on their
right hand, or on their forehead,
17 and *he provides* that no one
should be able to buy or to sell, except the one who has the [a]mark, *ei-*
ther [b]the name of the beast or [c]the
number of his name.
18 [a]Here is wisdom. Let him who
has understanding calculate the
number of the beast, for the number
is that [b]of a man; and his number is
[1]six hundred and sixty-six.

12 [e]Rev. 10:6
13 [a]Rev. 12:3 [b]Rev. 12:5
14 [a]Ex. 19:4; Deut. 32:11; Is. 40:31 [b]Rev. 12:6 [c]Dan. 7:25; 12:7
15 [a]Gen. 3:1; 2 Cor. 11:3; Rev. 12:9; 20:2 [b]Is. 59:19; Hos. 5:10
17 [a]Rev. 11:7; 13:7 [b]Gen. 3:15 [c]1 John 2:3; Rev. 14:12 [d]Rev. 1:2; 6:9; [14:12]; 19:10
1 [1]Some mss. read, *I stood* [a]Dan 7:3; Rev. 11:7; 13:14, 15; 15:2; 16:13; 17:8 [b]Rev. 12:3 [c]Rev. 12:3; 17:12 [d]Dan. 7:8; 11:36; Rev. 17:3
2 [a]Dan. 7:6; Hos. 13:7f. [b]Dan. 7:5 [c]Dan. 7:4 [d]Rev. 12:3; 13:4, 12 [e]Rev. 2:13
3 [a]Rev. 13:12, 14 [b]Rev. 17:8
4 [a]Rev. 12:3; 13:2, 12 [b]Ex. 15:11; Is. 46:5
5 [a]Dan. 7:8, 11, 20, 25; 11:36; 2 Thess. 2:3f. [b]Rev. 11:2
6 [a]Rev. 7:15; 12:12
7 [a]Rev. 11:7 [b]Rev. 5:9
8 [a]Rev. 3:10; 13:12, 14 [b]Rev. 3:5 [c]Matt. 25:34; Rev. 17:8 [d]Rev. 5:6
9 [a]Rev. 2:7
10 [a]Is. 33:1; Jer. 15:2; 43:11 [b]Gen. 9:6; Matt. 26:52; Rev. 11:18 [c]Heb. 6:12; Rev. 14:12
11 [a]Rev. 13:1, 14; 16:13 [b]Dan. 8:3 [c]Rev. 13:4
12 [a]Rev. 13:4 [b]Rev. 13:14; 19:20 [c]Rev. 13:8 [d]Rev. 13:15; 19:20; 20:4 [e]Rev. 13:3
13 [a]Matt. 24:24 [b]1 Kin. 18:38; Luke 9:54; Rev. 11:5; 20:9
14 [a]Rev. 12:9 [b]Rev. 13:8 [c]2 Thess. 2:9f. [d]Rev. 13:12; 19:20 [e]Rev. 13:3
15 [a]Dan. 3:3ff. [b]Rev. 13:12; 14:9, 11
16 [a]Rev. 11:18; 19:5, 18 [b]Gal. 6:17; Rev. 7:3; 14:9
17 [a]Gal. 6:17 [b]Rev. 14:11 [c]Rev. 15:2
18 [1]Some mss. read, 616 [a]Rev. 17:9 [b]Rev. 21:17

CHAPTER 14

The Lamb and the 144,000 on Mount Zion

AND I looked, and behold, [a]the
Lamb *was* standing on [b]Mount Zion,
and with Him [c]one hundred and
forty-four thousand, having [d]His
name and the [d]name of His Father
written [e]on their foreheads.
2 And I heard a voice from
heaven, like [a]the sound of many waters and like the [b]sound of loud
thunder, and the voice which I
heard *was* like *the sound* of [c]harp-
ists playing on their harps.
3 And they [1]*sang [a]a new song
before the throne and before the
[b]four living creatures and the [c]el-
ders; and [d]no one could learn the
song except the [e]one hundred and
forty-four thousand who had been
[a]purchased from the earth.
4 [a]These are the ones who have
not been defiled with women, for
they have kept themselves chaste.
These *are* the ones who [b]follow the
Lamb wherever He goes. These
have been [c]purchased from among
men [d]as first fruits to God and to the
Lamb.
5 And no lie was found [a]in their
mouth; they are [b]blameless.

Vision of the Angel with the Gospel

6 And I saw another angel flying
in [a]midheaven, having [b]an eternal
gospel to preach to [c]those who [1]live
on the earth, and to [d]every nation
and tribe and tongue and people;
7 and he said with a loud voice,
"[a]Fear God, and [b]give Him glory,
because the hour of His judgment
has come; and worship Him who
[c]made the heaven and the earth and
sea and [d]springs of waters."
8 And another angel, a second
one, followed, saying, "[a]Fallen,
fallen is [b]Babylon the great, she who
has [c]made all the nations drink of
the [d]wine of the passion of her immorality."

Doom for Worshipers of the Beast

9 And another angel, a third one,
followed them, saying with a loud
voice, "If any one [a]worships the
beast and his [b]image, and receives a
mark on his forehead or upon his
hand,
10 he also will drink of the [a]wine
of the wrath of God, which is mixed
in full strength [b]in the cup of His
anger; and he will be tormented
with [c]fire and brimstone in the presence of the [d]holy angels and in the
presence of the Lamb.
11 "And the [a]smoke of their torment goes up forever and ever; and
[b]they have no rest day and night,
those who [c]worship the beast and
his [c]image, and whoever receives
the [d]mark of his name."
12 Here is [a]the perseverance of the
[1]saints who [b]keep the commandments of God and [2c]their faith in Jesus.
13 And I heard a voice from
heaven, saying, "Write, '[a]Blessed
are the dead who [b]die in the Lord
[c]from now on!'" "Yes," [d]says the
Spirit, "that they may [e]rest from
their labors, for their [f]deeds follow
with them."

The Reapers

14 And I looked, and behold, a
[a]white cloud, and sitting on the
cloud *was* one [b]like [1]a son of man,
having a golden [c]crown on His head,
and a sharp sickle in His hand.
15 And another angel [a]came out of
the temple, crying out with a loud
voice to Him who sat on the cloud,
"[b]Put in your sickle and reap, because the hour to reap has come, because the [c]harvest of the earth is
ripe."
16 And He who sat on the cloud
swung His sickle over the earth; and
the earth was reaped.
17 And another angel [a]came out of
the temple which is in heaven, and
he also had a sharp sickle.
18 And another angel, [a]the one
who has power over fire, came out
from [b]the altar; and he called with a
loud voice to him who had the sharp
sickle, saying, "[c]Put in your sharp
sickle, and gather the clusters from
the vine of the earth, [d]because her
grapes are ripe."
19 And the angel swung his sickle
to the earth, and gathered *the clusters from* the vine of the earth, and
threw them into [a]the great wine
press of the wrath of God.
20 And the wine press was trodden [a]outside the city, and [b]blood
came out from the wine press, up to
the horses' bridles, for a distance of
two hundred miles.

CHAPTER 15

A Scene of Heaven

AND I saw [a]another sign in
heaven, great and marvelous, [b]sev-
en angels who had [c]seven plagues,
which are [d]the last, because in them
the wrath of God is finished.

1 [a]Rev. 5:6 [b]Ps. 2:6; Heb. 12:22 [c]Rev. 7:4; 14:3 [d]Rev. 3:12 [e]Rev. 7:3
2 [a]Rev. 1:15 [b]Rev. 6:1 [c]Rev. 5:8
3 [1]Some ancient mss. read, *sing, as it were, a new song* [a]Rev. 5:9 [b]Rev. 4:6 [c]Rev. 4:4 [d]Rev. 2:17 [e]Rev. 7:4; 14:1
4 [a]Matt. 19:12 [b]Rev. 3:4; 7:17; 17:14 [c]Rev. 5:9 [d]Heb. 12:23
5 [a]Ps. 32:2; 1 Pet. 2:22 [b]Heb. 9:14; 1 Pet. 1:19
6 [1]Lit., *sit* [a]Rev. 8:13 [b]1 Pet. 1:25; Rev. 10:7 [c]Rev. 3:10 [d]Rev. 5:9
7 [a]Rev. 15:4 [b]Rev. 11:13 [c]Rev. 4:11 [d]Rev. 8:10
8 [a]Is. 21:9; Jer. 51:8; Rev. 18:2 [b]Dan. 4:30 [c]Jer. 51:7 [d]Rev. 17:2, 4; 18:3
9 [a]Rev. 13:12; 14:11 [b]Rev. 13:14f.; 14:11
10 [a]Is. 51:17 [b]Ps. 75:8 [c]Ezek. 38:22 [d]Mark 8:38
11 [a]Is. 34:8-10 [b]Rev. 4:8 [c]Rev. 13:12; 14:9 [d]Rev. 13:17
12 [1]I.e., true believers; lit., *holy ones* [2]Lit., *the faith of* [a]Rev. 13:10 [b]Rev. 12:17 [c]Rev. 2:13
13 [a]Rev. 20:6 [b]1 Cor. 15:18 [c]Rev. 11:18 [d]Rev. 2:7; 22:17 [e]Heb. 4:9f.; Rev. 6:11 [f]1 Tim. 5:25
14 [1]Or, *the Son of Man* [a]Matt. 17:5 [b]Rev. 1:13 [c]Ps. 21:3
15 [a]Rev. 11:19 [b]Joel 3:13 [c]Jer. 51:33
17 [a]Rev. 11:19
18 [a]Rev. 16:8 [b]Rev. 6:9; 8:3 [c]Joel 3:13 [d]Joel 3:13
19 [a]Is. 63:2f.
20 [a]Heb. 13:12; Rev. 11:8 [b]Gen. 49:11
1 [a]Rev. 12:1, 3 [b]Rev. 15:6-8; 16:1; 17:1; 21:9 [c]Lev. 26:21 [d]Rev. 9:20

2 And I saw, as it were, a [a]sea of
glass mixed with fire, and those who
had [b]come off victorious from the
[c]beast and from [d]his image and
from the [e]number of his name,
standing on the [a]sea of glass, holding [f]harps of God.
3 And they *sang the [a]song of
Moses [b]the bond-servant of God
and the [c]song of the Lamb, saying,

"[d]GREAT AND MARVELOUS ARE
THY WORKS,
[e]O LORD GOD, THE ALMIGHTY;
RIGHTEOUS AND TRUE ARE THY
WAYS,
THOU [f]KING OF THE [1]NATIONS.

4 "[a]WHO WILL NOT FEAR, O LORD,
AND GLORIFY THY NAME?
FOR THOU ALONE ART HOLY;
FOR [b]ALL THE NATIONS WILL
COME AND WORSHIP BEFORE
THEE,
For Thy [c]righteous acts have
been revealed."

5 After these things I looked, and
[a]the temple of the [b]tabernacle of
testimony in heaven was opened,
6 and the [a]seven angels who had
the seven plagues [b]came out of the
temple, clothed [c]in linen, clean *and*
bright, and [d]girded around their
breasts with golden girdles.
7 And one of the [a]four living creatures gave to the [b]seven angels
seven [c]golden bowls full of the
[d]wrath of God, who lives forever
and ever.
8 And the temple was filled with
[a]smoke from the glory of God and
from His power; and no one was
able to enter the temple until the
seven plagues of the seven angels
were finished.

CHAPTER 16

Six Bowls of Wrath

AND I heard a loud voice from [a]the
temple, saying to the [b]seven angels,
"Go and [c]pour out the [d]seven bowls
of the wrath of God into the earth."
2 And the first *angel* went and
poured out his bowl [a]into the earth;
and it became a loathsome and malignant [b]sore upon the men [c]who
had the mark of the beast and who
worshiped his image.
3 And the second *angel* poured
out his bowl [a]into the sea, and it became blood like *that* of a dead man;
and every living thing in the sea
died.
4 And the third *angel* poured out
his bowl into the [a]rivers and the
springs of waters; and they [b]became
blood.
5 And I heard the angel of the waters saying, "[a]Righteous art Thou,
[b]who art and who wast, O [c]Holy
One, because Thou didst [d]judge
these things;
6 for they poured out [a]the blood
of saints and prophets, and Thou
hast given them [b]blood to drink.
They deserve it."
7 And I heard [a]the altar saying,
"Yes, O [b]Lord God, the Almighty,
true and righteous are Thy judgments."
8 And the fourth *angel* poured
out his bowl upon [a]the sun; [b]and it
was given to it to scorch men with
fire.
9 And men were scorched with
fierce heat; and they [a]blasphemed
the name of God who has the power
over these plagues; and they [b]did
not repent, so as to [c]give Him glory.
10 And the fifth *angel* poured out
his bowl upon the [a]throne of the
beast; and his kingdom became
[b]darkened; and they gnawed their
tongues because of pain,
11 and they [a]blasphemed the [b]God
of heaven because of their pains and
their [c]sores; and they [d]did not repent of their deeds.
12 And the sixth *angel* poured out
his bowl upon the [a]great river, the
Euphrates; and [b]its water was dried
up, that [c]the way might be prepared
for the kings from the east.

Armageddon

13 And I saw *coming* out of the
mouth of the [a]dragon and out of the
mouth of the [b]beast and out of the
mouth of the [c]false prophet, three
[d]unclean spirits like frogs;
14 for they are [a]spirits of demons,
[b]performing signs, which go out to
the kings of the [c]whole world, to
[d]gather them together for the war of
the great day of God, the Almighty.
15 (Behold, [a]I am coming like a
thief. [b]Blessed is the one who stays
awake and keeps his garments, [c]lest
he walk about naked and men see
his shame.)
16 And they [a]gathered them together to the place which [b]in Hebrew is called [1]Har–[c]Magedon.

Seventh Bowl of Wrath

17 And the seventh *angel* poured
out his bowl upon [a]the air; and a
[b]loud voice came out of the [c]temple
from the throne, saying, "[d]It is
done."
18 And there were flashes of

2 [a]Rev. 4:6 [b]Rev. 12:11 [c]Rev. 13:1 [d]Rev. 13:14f. [e]Rev. 13:17 [f]Rev. 5:8
3 [1]Or, *ages* [a]Ex. 15:1ff. [b]Josh. 22:5; Heb. 3:5 [c]Rev. 5:9f., 12f. [d]Deut. 32:3f.; Hos. 14:9 [e]Rev. 1:8 [f]1 Tim. 1:17 marg.
4 [a]Jer. 10:7; Rev. 14:7 [b]Ps. 86:9; Is. 66:23 [c]Rev. 19:8
5 [a]Rev. 11:19 [b]Ex. 38:21; Num. 1:50
6 [a]Rev. 15:1 [b]Rev. 14:15 [c]Ezek. 28:13 [d]Rev. 1:13
7 [a]Rev. 4:6 [b]Rev. 15:1 [c]Rev. 5:8 [d]Rev. 14:10
8 [a]Ex. 19:18
1 [a]Rev. 11:19 [b]Rev. 15:1 [c]Ps. 79:6; Jer. 10:25; Ezek. 22:31; Zeph. 3:8; Rev. 16:2ff. [d]Rev. 5:8
2 [a]Rev. 8:7 [b]Ex. 9:9-11 [c]Rev. 13:15-17; 14:9
3 [a]Ex. 7:17-21
4 [a]Rev. 8:10 [b]Ex. 7:17-20; Rev. 11:6
5 [a]John 17:25 [b]Rev. 11:17 [c]Rev. 15:4 [d]Rev. 6:10
6 [a]Rev. 17:6; 18:24 [b]Is. 49:26; Luke 11:49-51
7 [a]Rev. 6:9; 14:18 [b]Rev. 1:8
8 [a]Rev. 6:12 [b]Rev. 14:18
9 [a]Rev. 16:11, 21 [b]Rev. 2:21 [c]Rev. 11:13
10 [a]Rev. 13:2 [b]Ex. 10:21f.
11 [a]Rev. 16:9, 21 [b]Rev. 11:13 [c]Rev. 16:2 [d]Rev. 2:21
12 [a]Rev. 9:14 [b]Is. 11:15f.; 44:27; Jer. 51:32, 36 [c]Is. 41:2, 25; 46:11
13 [a]Rev. 12:3 [b]Rev. 13:1 [c]Rev. 13:11, 14; 19:20; 20:10 [d]Rev. 18:2
14 [a]1 Tim. 4:1 [b]Rev. 13:13 [c]Rev. 3:10 [d]1 Kin. 22:21-23
15 [a]Rev. 3:3, 11 [b]Luke 12:37 [c]Rev. 3:18
16 [1]Some authorities read, *Armageddon* [a]Rev. 19:19 [b]Rev. 9:11 [c]Judg. 5:19
17 [a]Eph. 2:2 [b]Rev. 11:15 [c]Rev. 14:15 [d]Rev. 10:6; 21:6

[a]lightning and sounds and peals of thunder; and there was [b]a great earthquake, [c]such as there had not been since man came to be upon the earth, so great an earthquake *was it, and* so mighty.

19 And [a]the great city was split into three parts, and the cities of the nations fell. And [b]Babylon the great was [c]remembered before God, to give her [d]the cup of the wine of His fierce wrath.

20 And [a]every island fled away, and the mountains were not found.

21 And [a]huge hailstones, about one hundred pounds each, *came down from heaven upon men; and men [b]blasphemed God because of the [c]plague of the hail, because its plague *was extremely severe.

Chapter 17

The Doom of Babylon

[a]AND one of the [b]seven angels who had the [c]seven bowls came and spoke with me, saying, "Come here, I shall show you [d]the judgment of the [e]great harlot who [f]sits on many waters,

2 with whom [a]the kings of the earth committed *acts of* immorality, and [b]those who dwell on the earth were [c]made drunk with the wine of her immorality."

3 And [a]he carried me away [b]in the Spirit [c]into a wilderness; and I saw a woman sitting on a [d]scarlet beast, full of [e]blasphemous names, having [f]seven heads and ten horns.

4 And the woman [a]was clothed in purple and scarlet, and adorned with gold and precious stones and pearls, having in her hand [b]a gold cup full of abominations and of the unclean things of her immorality,

5 and upon her forehead a name *was* written, a [a]mystery, "[b]BABYLON THE GREAT, THE MOTHER OF HARLOTS AND OF [c]THE ABOMINATIONS OF THE EARTH."

6 And I saw the woman drunk with the [a]blood of the saints, and with the blood of the witnesses of Jesus. And when I saw her, I wondered greatly.

7 And the angel said to me, "Why do you wonder? I shall tell you the [a]mystery of the woman and of the beast that carries her, which has the [b]seven heads and the ten horns.

8 "The beast that you saw [a]was and is not, and is about to [b]come up out of the [c]abyss and [1]to [d]go to destruction. And [e]those who dwell on the earth will [f]wonder, [g]whose name has not been written in the book of life [h]from the foundation of the world, when they see the beast, that [a]he was and is not and will come.

9 "[a]Here is the mind which has wisdom. The [b]seven heads are seven mountains on which the woman sits,

10 and they are seven [a]kings; five have fallen, one is, the other has not yet come; and when he comes, he must remain a little while.

11 "And the beast which [a]was and is not, is himself also an eighth, and is *one* of the seven, and he [b]goes to destruction.

12 "And the [a]ten horns which you saw are ten kings, who have not yet received a kingdom, but they receive authority as kings with the beast [b]for one hour.

13 "These have [a]one purpose and they give their power and authority to the beast.

Victory for the Lamb

14 "These will wage [a]war against the Lamb, and the Lamb will [b]overcome them, because He is [c]Lord of lords and [c]King of kings, and [d]those who are with Him *are the* [e]called and chosen and faithful."

15 And he *said to me, "The [a]waters which you saw where the harlot sits, are [b]peoples and multitudes and nations and tongues.

16 "And the [a]ten horns which you saw, and the beast, these will hate the harlot and will make her [b]desolate and [c]naked, and will [d]eat her flesh and will [e]burn her up with fire.

17 "For [a]God has put it in their hearts to execute His purpose by [b]having a common purpose, and by giving their kingdom to the beast, until the [c]words of God should be fulfilled.

18 "And the woman whom you saw is [a]the great city, which reigns over the kings of the earth."

Chapter 18

Babylon Is Fallen

AFTER these things I saw [a]another angel [b]coming down from heaven, having great authority, and the earth was [c]illumined with his glory.

2 And he cried out with a mighty voice, saying, "[a]Fallen, fallen is

---

18 [a]Rev. 4:5 [b]Rev. 6:12 [c]Dan. 12:1; Matt. 24:21
19 [a]Rev. 11:8; 17:18; 18:10, 18f., 21 [b]Rev. 14:8 [c]Rev. 18:5 [d]Rev. 14:10
20 [a]Rev. 6:14
21 [a]Rev. 8:7; 11:19 [b]Rev. 16:9, 11 [c]Ex. 9:18-25
1 [a]Rev. 1:1; 21:9 [b]Rev. 15:1 [c]Rev. 15:7 [d]Rev. 16:19 [e]Is. 1:21 [f]Jer. 51:13; Rev. 17:15
2 [a]Rev. 2:22; 18:3, 9 [b]Rev. 3:10; 17:8 [c]Rev. 14:8
3 [a]Rev. 21:10 [b]Rev. 1:10 [c]Rev. 12:6, 14; 21:10 [d]Matt. 27:28; Rev. 18:12, 16 [e]Rev. 13:1 [f]Rev. 12:3; 17:7
4 [a]Ezek. 28:13; Rev. 18:12, 16 [b]Jer. 51:7; Rev. 18:6
5 [a]2 Thess. 2:7; Rev. 1:20; 17:7 [b]Rev. 14:8; 16:19 [c]Rev. 17:2
6 [a]Rev. 16:6
7 [a]2 Thess. 2:7 [b]Rev. 17:3
8 [1]Some ancient mss. read, *he goes* [a]Rev. 13:3, 12, 14; 17:11 [b]Rev. 11:7; 13:1 [c]Rev. 9:1; 13:1 [d]Rev. 13:10; 17:11 [e]Rev. 3:10 [f]Rev. 13:3 [g]Rev. 3:5 [h]Matt. 25:34
9 [a]Rev. 13:18 [b]Rev. 17:3
10 [a]Rev. 10:11
11 [a]Rev. 13:3, 12, 14; 17:8 [b]Rev. 13:10; 17:8
12 [a]Rev. 12:3; 13:1; 17:16 [b]Rev. 18:10, 17, 19
13 [a]Rev. 17:17
14 [a]Rev. 16:14 [b]Rev. 3:21 [c]1 Tim. 6:15; Rev. 19:16 [d]Rev. 2:10f. [e]Matt. 22:14
15 [a]Is. 8:7; Jer. 47:2; Rev. 17:1 [b]Rev. 5:9
16 [a]Rev. 17:12 [b]Rev. 18:17, 19 [c]Ezek. 16:37, 39 [d]Rev. 19:18 [e]Rev. 18:8
17 [a]2 Cor. 8:16 [b]Rev. 17:13 [c]Rev. 10:7
18 [a]Rev. 11:8; 16:19
1 [a]Rev. 17:1, 7 [b]Rev. 10:1 [c]Ezek. 43:2
2 [a]Rev. 14:8

Babylon the great! And she [b]has become a dwelling place of demons and a prison of every [c]unclean spirit, and a prison of every unclean and hateful bird.

3 "For all the nations [1]have drunk of the [a]wine of the passion of her immorality, and [b]the kings of the earth have committed *acts of* immorality with her, and the [c]merchants of the earth have become rich by the wealth of her [d]sensuality."

4 And I heard another voice from heaven, saying, "[a]Come out of her, my people, that you may not participate in her sins and that you may not receive of her plagues;

5 for her sins have [a]piled up as high as heaven, and God has [b]remembered her iniquities.

6 "[a]Pay her back even as she has paid, and give back *to her* double according to her deeds; in the [b]cup which she has mixed, mix twice as much for her.

7 "[a]To the degree that she glorified herself and [b]lived [1]sensuously, to the same degree give her torment and mourning; for she says in her heart, '[c]I sit *as* a queen and I am not a widow, and will never see mourning.'

8 "For this reason [a]in one day her plagues will come, pestilence and mourning and famine, and she will be [b]burned up with fire; for the Lord God who judges her [c]is strong.

Lament for Babylon

9 "And [a]the kings of the earth, who committed *acts of* immorality and [b]lived sensuously with her, will [c]weep and lament over her when they [d]see the smoke of her burning,

10 [a]standing at a distance because of the fear of her torment, saying, '[b]Woe, woe, [c]the great city, Babylon, the strong city! For in [d]one hour your judgment has come.'

11 "And the [a]merchants of the earth [b]weep and mourn over her, because no one buys their cargoes any more;

12 cargoes of [a]gold and silver and precious stones and pearls and fine linen and purple and silk and scarlet, and every *kind of* citron wood and every article of ivory and every article *made* from very costly wood and bronze and iron and marble,

13 and cinnamon and spice and incense and perfume and frankincense and wine and olive oil and fine flour and wheat and cattle and sheep, and *cargoes* of horses and chariots and slaves and [a]human lives.

14 "And the fruit you long for has gone from you, and all things that were luxurious and splendid have passed away from you and *men* will no longer find them.

15 "The [a]merchants of [b]these things, who became rich from her, will [c]stand at a distance because of the fear of her torment, weeping and mourning,

16 saying, '[a]Woe, woe, [b]the great city, she who [c]was clothed in fine linen and purple and scarlet, and adorned with gold and precious stones and pearls;

17 for in [a]one hour such great wealth has been laid [b]waste!' And [c]every shipmaster and every passenger and sailor, and as many as make their living by the sea, [a]stood at a distance,

18 and were [a]crying out as they [b]saw the smoke of her burning, saying, '[c]What *city* is like [d]the great city?'

19 "And they threw [a]dust on their heads and were crying out, weeping and mourning, saying, '[b]Woe, woe, the great city, in which all who had ships at sea [c]became rich by her wealth, for in [b]one hour she has been laid [d]waste!'

20 "[a]Rejoice over her, O heaven, and you saints and [b]apostles and prophets, because [c]God has pronounced judgment for you against her."

21 And a [a]strong angel [b]took up a stone like a great millstone and threw it into the sea, saying, "Thus will Babylon, [c]the great city, be thrown down with violence, and will not be found any longer.

22 "And [a]the sound of harpists and musicians and flute-players and trumpeters will not be heard in you any longer; and no craftsman of any craft will be found in you any longer; and the [b]sound of a mill will not be heard in you any longer;

23 and the light of a lamp will not shine in you any longer; and the [a]voice of the bridegroom and bride will not be heard in you any longer; for your [b]merchants were the great men of the earth, because all the nations were deceived [c]by your sorcery.

24 "And in her was found the [a]blood of prophets and of saints and of [b]all who have been slain on the earth."

2 [b]Is. 13:21f.; 34:11, 13-15; Jer. 50:39; 51:37; Zeph. 2:14f. [c]Rev. 16:13
3 [1]Many ancient mss. read, *have fallen by* [a]Rev. 14:8 [b]Rev. 17:2; 18:9 [c]Ezek. 27:9-25; Rev. 18:11, 15, 19, 23 [d]1 Tim. 5:11; Rev. 18:7, 9
4 [a]Is. 52:11; Jer 50:8; 51:6, 9, 45; 2 Cor. 6:17
5 [a]Jer. 51:9 [b]Rev. 16:19
6 [a]Ps. 137:8; Jer. 50:15, 29 [b]Rev. 17:4
7 [1]Or, *luxuriously* [a]Ezek. 28:2-8 [b]1 Tim. 5:11; Rev. 18:3, 9 [c]Is. 47:7f.; Zeph. 2:15
8 [a]Is. 47:9; Jer. 50:31f.; Rev. 18:10 [b]Rev. 17:16 [c]Jer. 50:34; Rev. 11:17f.
9 [a]Rev. 17:2; 18:3 [b]1 Tim. 5:11; Rev. 18:3, 7 [c]Ezek. 26:16f.; 27:35 [d]Rev. 14:11
10 [a]Rev. 18:15, 17 [b]Rev. 18:16, 19 [c]Rev. 11:8; 16:19 [d]Rev. 17:12; 18:8
11 [a]Ezek. 27:9-25; Rev. 18:3, 15, 19, 23 [b]Ezek. 27:27-34
12 [a]Ezek. 27:12-22; Rev. 17:4
13 [a]Ezek. 27:13; 1 Chr. 5:21 marg.; 1 Tim. 1:10
15 [a]Rev. 18:3 [b]Rev. 18:12, 13 [c]Rev. 18:10
16 [a]Rev. 18:10, 19 [b]Rev. 18:10, 18, 19, 21 [c]Rev. 17:4
17 [a]Rev. 18:10 [b]Rev. 17:16; 18:19 [c]Ezek. 27:28f.
18 [a]Ezek. 27:30 [b]Rev. 18:9 [c]Ezek. 27:32; Rev. 13:4 [d]Rev. 18:10
19 [a]Josh. 7:6; Job 2:12; Lam. 2:10 [b]Rev. 18:10 [c]Rev. 18:3, 15 [d]Rev. 17:16; 18:17
20 [a]Jer. 51:48; Rev. 12:12 [b]Luke 11:49f. [c]Rev. 6:10
21 [a]Rev. 5:2; 10:1 [b]Jer. 51:63f. [c]Rev. 18:10
22 [a]Is. 24:8; Ezek. 26:13; Matt. 9:23 [b]Eccles. 12:4
23 [a]Jer. 7:34; 16:9 [b]Is. 23:8; Rev. 6:15; 18:3 [c]Nah. 3:4
24 [a]Rev. 16:6; 17:6 [b]Matt. 23:35

CHAPTER 19

The Fourfold Hallelujah

AFTER these things I heard, as it
were, a [a]loud voice of a great multitude in heaven, saying,
"[b]Hallelujah! [c]Salvation and [d]glory
and power belong to our God;
2 [a]BECAUSE HIS [b]JUDGMENTS ARE
[c]TRUE AND RIGHTEOUS; for He has
judged the [d]great harlot who was
corrupting the earth with her immorality, and HE HAS [e]AVENGED THE
BLOOD OF HIS BOND-SERVANTS ON
HER."
3 And a second time they said,
"[a]HALLELUJAH! HER [b]SMOKE RISES
UP FOREVER AND EVER."
4 And the [a]twenty-four elders
and the [b]four living creatures [c]fell
down and worshiped God who sits
on the throne saying, "[d]Amen. [e]Hal-
lelujah!"
5 And a voice came from the
throne, saying,
"[a]GIVE PRAISE TO OUR GOD, ALL
YOU HIS BOND-SERVANTS, [b]YOU WHO
FEAR HIM, THE SMALL AND THE
GREAT."
6 And I heard, as it were, [a]the
voice of a great multitude and as
[b]the sound of many waters and as
the [c]sound of mighty peals of thunder, saying,
"[a]Hallelujah! For the [d]Lord our
God, the Almighty, reigns.

Marriage of the Lamb

7 "Let us rejoice and be glad and
[a]give the glory to Him, for [b]the marriage of the Lamb has come and His
[c]bride has made herself ready."
8 And it was given to her to
clothe herself in [a]fine linen, bright
and clean; for the fine linen is the
[b]righteous acts of the saints.
9 And [a]he *said to me, "[b]Write,
'[c]Blessed are those who are invited
to the marriage supper of the
Lamb.'" And he *said to me, "These
are true words of God."
10 And [a]I fell at his feet to worship
him. [b]And he *said to me, "Do not
do that; I am a [c]fellow servant of
yours and your brethren who [d]hold
the testimony of Jesus; worship
God. For the testimony of Jesus is
the spirit of prophecy."

The Coming of Christ

11 And I saw [a]heaven opened; and
behold, a [b]white horse, and He who
sat upon it *is* called Faithful and
True; and in righteousness He
judges and wages war.
12 And His [a]eyes *are* a flame of
fire, and upon His head *are* many
[b]diadems; and He has a [c]name written *upon Him* which no one knows
except Himself.
13 And *He is* clothed with a [a]robe
dipped in blood; and His name is
called [b]The Word of God.
14 And the armies which are in
heaven, clothed in [a]fine linen,
[b]white *and* clean, were following
Him on white horses.
15 And [a]from His mouth comes a
sharp sword, so that [b]with it He may
smite the nations; and He will [c]rule
them with a rod of iron; and He
treads the wine press of the fierce
wrath of God, the Almighty.
16 And on His robe and on His
thigh He has [a]a name written,
"[b]KING OF KINGS, AND LORD OF
LORDS."
17 And I saw an angel standing in
the sun; and he cried out with a loud
voice, saying to [a]all the birds which
fly in [b]midheaven, "[c]Come, assemble for the great supper of God;
18 in order that you may [a]eat the
flesh of kings and the flesh of commanders and the flesh of mighty
men and the flesh of horses and of
those who sit on them and the flesh
of all men, [b]both free men and
slaves, and [c]small and great."
19 And I saw [a]the beast and [b]the
kings of the earth and their armies,
assembled to make war against Him
who [c]sat upon the horse, and
against His army.

Doom of the Beast and False Prophet

20 And the beast was seized, and
with him the [a]false prophet who
[b]performed the signs [c]in his presence, by which he [d]deceived those
who had received the [e]mark of the
beast and those who [f]worshiped his
image; these two were thrown alive
into the [g]lake of [h]fire which burns
with brimstone.
21 And the rest were killed with
the sword which [a]came from the
mouth of Him who [b]sat upon the
horse, and [c]all the birds were filled
with their flesh.

CHAPTER 20

Satan Bound

AND I saw [a]an angel coming down
from heaven, having the [b]key of the
abyss and a great chain in his hand.
2 And he laid hold of the [a]dragon,
the serpent of old, who is the devil
and Satan, and [b]bound him for a
thousand years,

1 [a]Jer. 51:48 [b]Ps. 104:35 marg.; Rev. 19:3, 4, 6 [c]Rev. 7:10 [d]Rev. 4:11
2 [a]Ps. 19:9 [b]Rev. 6:10 [c]Rev. 16:7 [d]Rev. 17:1 [e]Deut. 32:43; 2 Kin. 9:7; Rev. 16:6; 18:20
3 [a]Ps. 104:35 [b]Rev. 14:11
4 [a]Rev. 4:4, 10 [b]Rev. 4:6 [c]Rev. 4:10 [d]Ps. 106:48; Rev. 5:14 [e]Ps. 104:35; Rev. 19:3
5 [a]Ps. 115:13; 134:1; 135:1 [b]Rev. 11:18
6 [a]Jer. 51:48 [b]Rev. 1:15 [c]Rev. 6:1 [d]Rev. 1:8
7 [a]Rev. 11:13 [b]Matt. 22:2 [c]Matt. 1:20
8 [a]Rev. 15:6; 19:14 [b]Rev. 15:4
9 [a]Rev. 17:1; 19:10 [b]Rev. 1:19 [c]Luke 14:15
10 [a]Rev. 22:8 [b]Acts 10:26; Rev. 22:9 [c]Rev. 1:1f. [d]Rev. 12:17
11 [a]John 1:51; Rev. 4:1 [b]Rev. 6:2; 19:19, 21
12 [a]Rev. 1:14 [b]Rev. 6:2; 12:3 [c]Rev. 2:17; 19:16
13 [a]Is. 63:3 [b]John 1:1
14 [a]Rev. 19:8 [b]Rev. 3:4; 19:8
15 [a]Rev. 1:16; 19:21 [b]Is. 11:4; 2 Thess. 2:8 [c]Rev. 2:27
16 [a]Rev. 2:17; 19:12 [b]Rev. 17:14
17 [a]Rev. 19:21 [b]Rev. 8:13 [c]1 Sam. 17:44; Jer. 12:9; Ezek. 39:17
18 [a]Ezek. 39:18-20 [b]Rev. 6:15 [c]Rev. 11:18; 13:16; 19:5
19 [a]Rev. 11:7; 13:1 [b]Rev. 16:14, 16 [c]Rev. 19:11, 21
20 [a]Rev. 16:13 [b]Rev. 13:13 [c]Rev. 13:12 [d]Rev. 13:14 [e]Rev. 13:16f. [f]Rev. 13:15 [12] [g]Rev. 20:10, 14f.; 21:8 [h]Is. 30:33
21 [a]Rev. 19:15 [b]Rev. 19:11, 19 [c]Rev. 19:17
1 [a]Rev. 10:1 [b]Rev. 1:18; 9:1
2 [a]Rev. 12:9 [b]Is. 24:22; 2 Pet. 2:4; Jude 6

3 and threw him into the [a]abyss, and shut *it* and [b]sealed *it* over him, so that he should [c]not deceive the nations any longer, until the thousand years were completed; after these things he must be released for a short time.

4 And I saw [a]thrones, and [b]they sat upon them, and [c]judgment was given to them. And I *saw* [d]the souls of those who had been [d]beheaded because of the [e]testimony of Jesus and because of the word of God, and those who had not worshiped the beast or his image, and had not received the mark upon their forehead and upon their hand; and they came to life and reigned with Christ for a thousand years.

5 The rest of the dead did not come to life until the thousand years were completed. [a]This is the first resurrection.

6 [a]Blessed and holy is the one who has a part in the first resurrection; over these the [b]second death has no power, but they will be [c]priests of God and of Christ and will [d]reign with Him for a thousand years.

Satan Freed, Doomed

7 And when the thousand years are completed, Satan will be [a]released from his prison,

8 and will come out to [a]deceive the nations which are in the [b]four corners of the earth, [c]Gog and Magog, to [d]gather them together for the war; the number of them is like the [e]sand of the seashore.

9 And they [a]came up on the broad plain of the earth and surrounded the [b]camp of the saints and the [c]beloved city, and [d]fire came down from heaven and devoured them.

10 And [a]the devil who [a]deceived them was thrown into the [b]lake of fire and brimstone, where the [c]beast and the [c]false prophet are also; and they will be [d]tormented day and night forever and ever.

Judgment at the Throne of God

11 And I saw a great white [a]throne and Him who sat upon it, from whose presence [b]earth and heaven fled away, and [c]no place was found for them.

12 And I saw the dead, the [a]great and the small, standing before the throne, and [b]books were opened; and another book was opened, which is [c]*the book* of life; and the dead [d]were judged from the things which were written in the books, [e]according to their deeds.

13 And the sea gave up the dead which were in it, and [a]death and Hades [b]gave up the dead which were in them; and they were judged, every one *of them* [c]according to their deeds.

14 And [a]death and Hades were thrown into [b]the lake of fire. This is the [c]second death, the lake of fire.

15 And if anyone's name was not found written in [a]the book of life, he was thrown into the lake of fire.

Chapter 21

The New Heaven and Earth

AND I saw [a]a new heaven and a new earth; for [b]the first heaven and the first earth passed away, and there is no longer *any* sea.

2 And I saw [a]the holy city, [b]new Jerusalem, [c]coming down out of heaven from God, [d]made ready as a bride adorned for her husband.

3 And I heard a loud voice from the throne, saying, "Behold, [a]the tabernacle of God is among men, and He shall [b]dwell among them, and they shall be His people, and God Himself shall be among them,[1]

4 and He shall [a]wipe away every tear from their eyes; and [b]there shall no longer be *any* death; [c]there shall no longer be *any* mourning, or crying, or pain; [d]the first things have passed away."

5 And [a]He who sits on the throne said, "Behold, I am [b]making all things new." And He *said, "Write, for [c]these words are faithful and true."

6 And He said to me, "[a]It is done. I am the [b]Alpha and the Omega, the beginning and the end. [c]I will give to the one who thirsts from the spring of the [d]water of life without cost.

7 "[a]He who overcomes shall inherit these things, and [b]I will be his God and he will be My son.

8 "[a]But for the cowardly and unbelieving and abominable and murderers and immoral persons and sorcerers and idolaters and all liars, their part *will be* in [b]the lake that burns with fire and brimstone, which is the [c]second death."

9 [a]And one of the seven angels who had the [b]seven bowls full of the [c]seven last plagues, came and spoke with me, saying, "[d]Come here, I shall show you the [e]bride, the wife of the Lamb."

3 [a]Rev. 20:1 [b]Dan. 6:17; Matt. 27:66 [c]Rev. 12:9; 20:8, 10
4 [a]Dan. 7:9 [b]Matt. 19:28; Rev. 3:21 [c]Dan. 7:22; 1 Cor. 6:2 [d]Rev. 6:9 [e]Rev. 1:9
5 [a]Luke 14:14
6 [a]Rev. 14:13 [b]Rev. 2:11; 20:14 [c]Rev. 1:6 [d]Rev. 3:21; 5:10; 20:4
7 [a]Rev. 20:2
8 [a]Rev. 12:9; 20:3, 10 [b]Rev. 7:1 [c]Ezek. 38:2; 39:1, 6 [d]Rev. 16:14 [e]Heb. 11:12
9 [a]Ezek. 38:9, 16; Hab. 1:6 [b]Deut. 23:14 [c]Ps. 87:2 [d]Ezek. 38:22
10 [a]Rev. 20:2f. [b]Rev. 19:20; 20:14, 15 [c]Rev. 16:13 [d]Rev. 14:10f.
11 [a]Rev. 4:2 [b]Rev. 6:14; 21:1 [c]Dan. 2:35; Rev. 12:8
12 [a]Rev. 11:18 [b]Jer. 17:1, 10; Dan. 7:10 [c]Rev. 3:5; 20:15 [d]Rev. 11:18 [e]Matt. 16:27
13 [a]1 Cor. 15:26 [b]Is. 26:19 [c]Matt. 16:27
14 [a]1 Cor. 15:26 [b]Rev. 19:20; 20:10, 15 [c]Rev. 20:6
15 [a]Rev. 20:12; 3:5
1 [a]Is. 65:17 [b]2 Pet. 3:10; Rev. 20:11
2 [a]Rev. 11:2; 21:10; 22:19 [b]Rev. 3:12; 21:10 [c]Heb. 11:10, 16; Rev. 21:10 [d]Is. 61:10
3 [1]Some ancient mss. add, and be *their God* [a]Lev. 26:11f.; Rev. 7:15 [b]John 14:23; 2 Cor. 6:16
4 [a]Rev. 7:17 [b]1 Cor. 15:26; Rev. 20:14 [c]Is. 25:8; 35:10; 51:11; 65:19 [d]2 Cor. 5:17; Heb. 12:27
5 [a]Rev. 4:9; 20:11 [b]2 Cor. 5:17; Heb. 12:27 [c]Rev. 19:9; 22:6
6 [a]Rev. 10:6; 16:17 [b]Rev. 1:8; 22:13 [c]Is. 55:1 [d]Rev. 7:17
7 [a]Rev. 2:7 [b]2 Sam. 7:14
8 [a]1 Cor. 6:9 [b]Rev. 19:20 [c]Rev. 2:11
9 [a]Rev. 17:1 [b]Rev. 15:7 [c]Rev. 15:1 [d]Rev. 17:1 [e]Rev. 19:7; 21:2

The New Jerusalem

10 And [a]he carried me away [1b]in
the Spirit to a great and high mountain, and showed me [c]the holy city,
Jerusalem, coming down out of
heaven from God,
11 having [a]the glory of God. Her
brilliance was like a very costly
stone, as a [b]stone of [c]crystal-clear
jasper.
12 It had a great and high wall,
[1a]with twelve [b]gates, and at the
gates twelve angels; and names
were written on them, which are
those of the twelve tribes of the sons
of Israel.
13 *There were* three gates on the
east and three gates on the north
and three gates on the south and
three gates on the west.
14 And the wall of the city had
[a]twelve foundation stones, and on
them *were* the twelve names of the
[b]twelve apostles of the Lamb.
15 And the one who spoke with me
had a gold measuring [a]rod to measure the city, and its [b]gates and its
wall.
16 And the city is laid out as a
square, and its length is as great as
the width; and he measured the city
with the rod, fifteen hundred miles;
its length and width and height are
equal.
17 And he measured its wall, seventy-two yards, *according to* [a]hu-
man measurements, which are *also*
[b]angelic *measurements.*
18 And the material of the wall
was [a]jasper; and the city was [b]pure
gold, like clear [c]glass.
19 [a]The foundation stones of the
city wall were adorned with every
kind of precious stone. The first
foundation stone was [b]jasper; the
second, sapphire; the third, chalcedony; the fourth, [c]emerald;
20 the fifth, sardonyx; the sixth,
[a]sardius; the seventh, chrysolite; the
eighth, beryl; the ninth, topaz; the
tenth, chrysoprase; the eleventh, jacinth; the twelfth, amethyst.
21 And the twelve [a]gates were
twelve [b]pearls; each one of the gates
was a single pearl. And the street of
the city was [c]pure gold, like trans-
parent [d]glass.
22 And I saw [a]no temple in it, for
the [b]Lord God, the Almighty, and
the [c]Lamb, are its temple.
23 And the city [a]has no need of the
sun or of the moon to shine upon it,
for [b]the glory of God has illumined
it, and its lamp *is* the [c]Lamb.
24 And [a]the nations shall walk by
its light, and the [b]kings of the earth
shall bring their glory into it.
25 And in the daytime (for [a]there
shall be no night there) [b]its gates
[c]shall never be closed;
26 and [a]they shall bring the glory
and the honor of the nations into it;
27 and nothing unclean and no one
who practices abomination and
lying, [a]shall ever come into it, but
only those whose names are [b]writ-
ten in the Lamb's book of life.

Chapter 22

The River and the Tree of Life

AND [a]he showed me a [b]river of the
[c]water of life, clear [d]as crystal, coming from the throne of God and of
the Lamb,
2 in the middle of [a]its street. And
[b]on either side of the river was [c]the
tree of life, bearing twelve *kinds of*
fruit, yielding its fruit every month;
and the [b]leaves of the tree were for
the healing of the nations.
3 And [a]there shall no longer be
any curse; and [b]the throne of God
and of the Lamb shall be in it, and
His bond-servants shall [c]serve Him;
4 and they shall [a]see His face,
and His [b]name *shall be* on their
[c]foreheads.
5 And [a]there shall no longer be
any night; and they shall not have
need [b]of the light of a lamp nor the
light of the sun, because the Lord
God shall illumine them; and they
shall [c]reign forever and ever.
6 And [a]he said to me, "[b]These
words are faithful and true"; and the
Lord, the [c]God of the spirits of the
prophets, [d]sent His angel to show to
His bond-servants the things which
must shortly take place.
7 "And behold, [a]I am coming
quickly. [b]Blessed is he who heeds
[c]the words of the prophecy of this
book."
8 And [a]I, John, am the one who
heard and saw these things. And
when I heard and saw, [b]I fell down
to worship at the feet of the angel
who showed me these things.
9 And [a]he *said to me, "Do not do
that; I am a [b]fellow servant of yours
and of your brethren the prophets
and of those who heed the words of
[c]this book; worship God."

The Final Message

10 And he *said to me, "[a]Do not
seal up [b]the words of the prophecy
of this book, [c]for the time is near.
11 "[a]Let the one who does wrong,

---

10 [1]Or, *in spirit* [a]Ezek. 40:2; Rev. 17:3 [b]Rev. 1:10 [c]Rev. 21:2
11 [a]Is. 60:1f. [b]Rev. 4:3; 21:18, 19 [c]Rev. 4:6
12 [a]Ezek. 48:31-34 [b]Rev. 21:15, 21
14 [a]Eph. 2:20; Heb. 11:10 [b]Acts 1:26
15 [a]Rev. 11:1 [b]Rev. 21:12, 21, 25
17 [a]Deut. 3:11; Rev. 13:18 [b]Rev. 21:9
18 [a]Rev. 21:11 [b]Rev. 21:21 [c]Rev. 4:6
19 [a]Ex. 28:17-20; Is. 54:11f.; Ezek. 28:13; Rev. 21:19, 20 [b]Rev. 21:11 [c]Rev. 4:3
20 [a]Rev. 4:3
21 [a]Rev. 21:12, 15, 25 [b]Is. 54:12; Rev. 17:4 [c]Rev. 21:18 [d]Rev. 4:6
22 [a]Matt. 24:2; John 4:21 [b]Rev. 1:8 [c]Rev. 5:6; 7:17
23 [a]Is. 24:23 [b]Rev. 21:11 [c]Rev. 5:6
24 [a]Is. 60:3, 5; Rev. 22:2 [b]Ps. 72:10f.
25 [a]Zech. 14:7 [b]Rev. 21:12, 15 [c]Is. 60:11
26 [a]Ps. 72:10f.
27 [a]Is. 52:1; Rev. 22:14f. [b]Rev. 3:5
1 [a]Rev. 1:1; 21:9; 22:6 [b]Ps. 46:4; Ezek. 47:1 [c]Rev. 7:17; 22:17 [d]Rev. 4:6
2 [a]Rev. 21:21 [b]Ezek. 47:12 [c]Rev. 2:7; 22:14
3 [a]Zech. 14:11 [b]Rev. 21:3, 23 [c]Rev. 7:15
4 [a]Ps. 17:15 [b]Rev. 14:1 [c]Rev. 7:3
5 [a]Zech. 14:7; Rev. 21:25 [b]Rev. 21:23 [c]Dan. 7:18, 27
6 [a]Rev. 1:1; 21:9 [b]Rev. 19:9; 21:5 [c]1 Cor. 14:32; Heb. 12:9 [d]Rev. 1:1; 22:16
7 [a]Rev. 1:3; 3:3, 11; 16:15; 22:12, 20 [b]Rev. 1:3; 16:15 [c]Rev. 1:11; 22:9
8 [a]Rev. 1:1 [b]Rev. 19:10
9 [a]Rev. 19:10 [b]Rev. 1:1 [c]Rev. 1:11; 22:10
10 [a]Dan. 8:26; Rev. 10:4 [b]Rev. 1:11; 22:9, 18f. [c]Rev. 1:3
11 [a]Ezek. 3:27; Dan. 12:10

still do wrong; and let the one who is
filthy, still be filthy; and let the one
who is righteous, still practice righteousness; and let the one who is
holy, still keep himself holy.
12 "Behold, [a]I am coming quickly,
and My [b]reward is with Me, [c]to render to every man according to what
he has done.
13 "I am the [a]Alpha and the Omega,
[b]the first and the last, [c]the beginning
and the end."
14 Blessed are those who [a]wash
their robes, that they may have the
right to [b]the tree of life, and may
[c]enter by the [d]gates into the city.
15 [a]Outside are the [b]dogs and the
sorcerers and the immoral persons
and the murderers and the idolaters,
and everyone who loves and practices lying.
16 "[a]I, Jesus, have sent [b]My angel
to testify to you these things [c]for the
churches. I am [d]the root and the
[e]offspring of David, the bright
morning star."
17 And the [a]Spirit and the [b]bride
say, "Come." And let the one who
hears say, "Come." And let the one
who is thirsty come; let the one who
wishes take the water of life without
cost.
18 I testify to everyone who hears
[a]the words of the prophecy of this
book: if anyone [b]adds to them, God
shall add to him the plagues which
are written in this book;
19 and if anyone [a]takes away from
the [b]words of the book of this
prophecy, God shall take away his
part from [c]the tree of life and from
the holy city, which are written in
this book.
20 He who [a]testifies to these
things says, "Yes, I am coming
quickly." Amen. Come, Lord Jesus.
21 [a]The grace of the Lord Jesus be
with [1]all. Amen.

12 [a]Rev. 22:7 [b]Is. 40:10; 62:11 [c]Jer. 17:10
13 [a]Rev. 1:8 [b]Rev. 1:17 [c]Rev. 21:6
14 [a]Rev. 7:14 [b]Rev. 22:2 [c]Rev. 21:27 [d]Rev. 21:12
15 [a]Matt. 8:12 [b]Deut. 23:18
16 [a]Rev. 1:1 [b]Rev. 1:1; 22:6 [c]Rev. 1:4, 11; 3:22 [d]Rev. 5:5 [e]Matt. 1:1
17 [a]Rev. 2:7; 14:13 [b]Rev. 21:2
18 [a]Rev. 22:7 [b]Deut. 4:2; 12:32
19 [a]Deut. 4:2; 12:32; Prov. 30:6 [b]Rev. 22:7 [c]Rev. 22:2
20 [a]Rev. 1:2
21 [1]Or, *the saints* [a]Rom. 16:20

The New American Standard

CONCORDANCE

to the

Old and New Testaments

A collection of the principal common words with their most widely used examples in text and lesser usages in reference. Related words, or synonyms follow the key word. The key word is abbreviated in the text to its first letter, e.g., "abide" is "**a**". Variants add suffixes or prefixes, e.g., "abiding" appears as "**a-ing**".

A

ABANDON—*leave* Judg. 6:13, LORD has **a-ed** us
1 Sam. 12:22; Ps. 94:14, LORD ... **a** His people
2 Kin. 21:14, I will **a** the remnant
Ps. 27:9, Do not **a** me nor forsake me
Jer. 23:33, I shall **a** you
Acts 2:27, Thou wilt not **a** my soul to
27:20, hope of our being saved ... **a-ed**
Ps. 16:10; Prov. 17:14; Is. 2:6; Jer. 12:7; Ezek. 29:5
ABASE—*humble* Ezek. 21:26; Mal. 2:9
ABATE—*decrease* Gen. 8:8,11, water was **a-d**
Deut. 34:7, his vigor **a-d**
ABBA Mark 14:36, saying, **A**! Father
Rom. 8:15, by which we cry out, **A**! Father
Gal. 4:6, crying, **A**! Father
ABHOR—*despise, detest, loathe*
Rom. 12:9, **A** what is evil
Deut. 7:26; Job 19:19; Ps. 78:59; Prov. 24:24; Is. 49:7
ABIDE—*remain, stay* Ps. 9:7, the LORD **a-s** forever
Ps. 15:1, who may **a** in Thy tent
91:1, Will **a** in the shadow
102:12, LORD, dost **a** forever
John 3:36, wrath of God **a-s** on him
5:38, His word **a-ing** in you
8:31, you **a** in My word
14:25, while **a-ing** with you
15:4, **A** in Me ... it **a-s** in the vine ... you **a** in Me
15:6, If anyone does not **a** in Me
15:7, **a** in Me, and My words **a** in you
15:9, **a** in My love
15:10, you will **a** in My love ... **a** in His love
1 Cor. 13:13, But now **a** faith, hope, love
Heb. 10:34, a better possession and an **a-ing** one
1 Pet. 1:23, living and **a-ing** word of God
1:25, BUT THE WORD OF THE LORD A-S FOREVER
1 John 3:17, how does the love of God **a** in him
4:12, God **a-s** in us
ABILITY—*strength* Ezra 2:69, according to ... **a**
Dan. 1:4, who had **a** for serving
Matt. 25:15, according to his own **a**
ABLE—*adequate* 1 Sam. 6:20, Who is **a** to stand
Matt. 3:9, God is **a** from these stones
9:28, believe that I am **a** to do this
10:28, fear Him who is **a** to destroy
20:22, Are you **a** to drink the cup
John 10:29, no one is **a** to snatch them
Acts 6:10, they were **un-a** to cope with the wisdom
Rom. 8:39, shall be **a** to separate us
1 Cor. 10:13, tempted beyond what you are **a**
Eph. 3:18, may be **a** to comprehend
2 Tim. 2:2, who will be **a** to teach
James 4:12, the One who is **a** to save
Jude 24, Now to Him who is **a** to keep
1 Kin. 3:9; 2 Chr. 2:6; Rev. 5:3; 6:17
ABOARD Acts 21:2, went **a** and set sail
ABODE—*habitation* Jer. 31:23; Jude 6
John 14:23, and make Our **a** with him
ABOLISH—*destroy* Matt. 5:17, I did not come to **a**
Eph. 2:15, by **a-ing** in His flesh
2 Tim. 1:10, Christ Jesus, who **a-ed** death
ABOMINABLE—*detestable, rejected*
Jer. 44:4, do not do this **a** thing
Ezek. 16:25, made your beauty **a**
1 Pet. 4:3, drinking parties and **a** idolatries
Ps. 14:1; 53:1; Rev. 21:8
ABOMINATION—*detestable thing*
Ex. 8:26, an **a** to the Egyptians
Prov. 3:32, an **a** to the LORD
8:7, an **a** to my lips
Ezek. 33:29, because of all their **a-s**
Dan. 12:11, the **a** of desolation
Rev. 17:5, the **a-s** of the earth
Lev. 18:26; Deut. 7:26; 29:17
ABOUND—*excel, multiply*
Ex. 34:6, **a-ing** in lovingkindness and truth
Prov. 28:20, a faithful man will **a** with blessings
Dan. 4:1, May your peace **a**
Rom. 15:13, that you may **a** in hope
1 Cor. 15:58, always **a-ing** in the work of the
1 Cor. 14:12; 2 Cor. 7:15; 9:8
ABOVE—*over* Ex. 20:4, what is in heaven **a** or on
Ps. 8:1, Thy splendor **a** the heavens
Matt. 10:24, A disciple is not **a** his teacher
John 3:31, He who comes from **a** is **a** all
8:23, I am from **a**
Phil. 2:9, the name which is **a** every name
Col. 3:1; 2 Thess. 2:4; James 1:17
ABSENT Gen. 31:49, we are **a** one from the other
1 Cor. 5:3, though **a** in body, but present
2 Cor. 5:6, we are **a** from the Lord
5:8, **a** from the body and to be
10:1, but bold toward you when **a**
ABSTAIN—*depart, separate* Num. 6:3
Acts 15:20, that they **a** from things
1 Thess. 5:22, **a** from every form of evil
1 Tim. 4:3, **a-ing** from foods, which
2 Tim. 2:19, who names ... the Lord **a** from wickedness
1 Pet. 2:11, strangers to **a** from fleshly lusts

© LOCKMAN FOUNDATION 1972, 1975

ABUNDANCE—*surplus, plenty, full, plenteous*
Gen. 41:34, seven years of **a**
Ps. 52:7, the **a** of his riches
72:7, And **a** of peace till
Is. 55:2, delight yourself in **a**
Matt. 13:12, and he shall have an **a**
Luke 12:15, when one has an **a** does his life
Rom. 5:17, receive the **a** of grace
Phil. 4:18, everything in full, and have an **a**
Gen. 41:29; Deut. 28:47; Neh. 9:25; Ps. 36:8; 72:16; 73:10; Prov. 24:6; Eccles. 5:10; Phil. 4:12
ABUNDANT—*plenteous* Job 36:28; Ezek. 16:49
Gen. 41:47, land brought forth **a-ly**
Ps. 86:5, **a** in lovingkindness to all
2 Cor. 1:5, our comfort is **a** through Christ
ABUSE Judg. 19:25, **a-d** her all night
1 Chr. 10:4, lest these ... come and **a** me
Matt. 27:39, passing by were hurling **a** at Him
ABUSIVE—*filthy* Col. 3:8, **a** speech from your mouth
ABYSS—*deep, depth* Rom. 10:7, DESCEND INTO THE A
Rev. 20:3, threw him into the **a**
Luke 8:31; Rev. 11:7; 17:8; 20:1
ACCEPT—*receive* Deut. 33:11, And **a** the work
Job 2:10, **a** good from God and not **a** adversity
Jer. 2:30, They **a-ed** no chastening
Mark 4:20, hear the word and **a** it
Rom. 15:7, **a** one another
1 Tim. 1:15, statement, deserving full **a-ance**
ACCEPTABLE—*favorable, pleasing* Ps. 69:13, at an **a** time
Rom. 15:31, may prove **a** to the saints
2 Cor. 6:2, At the **a** time ... the **a** time
Phil. 4:18, an **a** sacrifice
1 Tim. 2:3, good and **a** in the sight
ACCESS Eph. 2:18, have our **a** in one Spirit
Eph. 3:12, confident **a** through faith in Him
ACCOMPLISH—*perform* 1 Kin. 5:9, you shall **a** my desire
Ps. 57:2, God who **a-es** *all things*
John 4:34, and to **a** His work
James 5:16, prayer of a righteous man can **a**
ACCOMPLISHED—*realized, wrought*
Neh. 6:16, work had been **a** ... God
Luke 1:1, things **a** among us
John 17:4, having **a** the work
Rom. 15:18, what Christ has **a** through me
James 1:15, when sin is **a**
Luke 12:50; John 19:28; 1 Pet. 5:9
ACCORD—*unite* Josh. 9:2; Acts 5:12
Acts 4:24, voices to God with one **a**
8:6, the multitudes with one **a**
12:20, one **a** they came to him
18:12, one **a** rose up against Paul
19:29, rushed with one **a** into the
2 Cor. 8:17, gone to you of his own **a**
ACCORDING Gen. 30:34, be **a** to your word
Matt. 16:27; Rom. 2:6, **a** to his deeds
Rom. 8:28, **a** to *His* purpose
Gal. 3:29, heirs **a** to promise
Rev. 22:12, render to every man **a**
Job 34:11; Jer. 17:10; John 7:24; 18:31; Rom. 12:6; 16:25; 2 Cor. 8:12
ACCOUNT—*declaration, sake, tell*
Gen. 2:4, is the **a** of the heavens and the earth
8:21, curse the ground on **a** of man
Esth. 10:2, full **a** of the greatness of Mordecai
1 Sam. 12:22, on **a** of His great name
Matt. 5:11, evil ... falsely on **a** of Me
Luke 1:1, compile an **a** of the things accomplished
Rom. 3:19, become **a-able** to God
Num. 12:11; Judg. 7:15
ACCUMULATE—*heap* 2 Tim. 4:3, **a** for themselves teachers
ACCURATE Job 31:6; Acts 18:25
ACCURSED Is. 65:20; Matt. 25:41
Josh. 6:18, make the camp of Israel **a**
Rom. 9:3, wish that I myself were **a**
1 Cor. 12:3, no one ... says, Jesus is **a**
Gal. 1:8, let him be **a**
ACCUSATION—*charge* Ezra 4:6, wrote an **a** against
Dan. 6:4, find no ground of **a** or
John 18:29, What **a** do you bring against
Acts 28:19, had any **a** against my nation
1 Tim. 5:19, Do not receive an **a** against
ACCUSE—*testify* Matt. 27:12, while He was being **a-d**
John 5:45, I will **a** you before the Father
Acts 22:30, why he had been **a-d** by the Jews
Deut. 19:18; Titus 1:6
ACKNOWLEDGE—*confess* Ps. 32:5, I **a-d** my sin
Prov. 3:6, In all your ways **a** Him
Acts 23:8, Pharisees **a** them all
Rom. 1:28, see fit to **a** God
ACQUAINT Ps. 139:3, **a-ed** with all my ways
Is. 53:3, **a-ed** with grief
ACQUAINTANCE Ps. 88:8, removed my **a-s** far from me
Luke 23:49, all His **a-s** and the women
Job 19:13; Ps. 31:11; 88:18; Luke 2:44
ACQUIRE—*get, purchase* Ruth 4:10; Prov. 1:5; 18:15
Prov. 4:5, **A** wisdom! **A** understanding
4:7, with all your **a-ing**, get understanding
Matt. 10:9, Do not **a** gold, or silver
ACQUIT—*cleanse* Job 10:14; Ps. 19:12
ACT—*behave* Ps. 103:7, made known His ... **a** to the
1 Cor. 16:13, **a** like men, be strong
John 8:4; 1 Cor. 13:5
A-s of Solomon, 1 Kin. 11:41
Jeroboam, 14:19
Rehoboam, 14:29
Abijam, 15:7
Asa, 15:23
Nadab, 15:31
Baasha, 16:5
Elah, 16:14
Zimri, 16:20
Omri, 16:27
Ahab, 22:39
Jehoshaphat, 22:45
Ahaziah, 2 Kin. 1:18
Joram, 8:23
Jehu, 10:34
Joash, 12:19
Jehoahaz, 13:8
Joash, 13:12
Jehoash, 14:15
Amaziah, 14:18
Jeroboam, 14:28
Azariah, 15:6
Zechariah, 15:11
Shallum, 15:15
Menahem, 15:21
Pekahiah, 15:26
Pekah, 15:31
Jotham, 15:36
Ahaz, 16:19
Hezekiah, 20:20
Manasseh, 21:17
Amon, 21:25
Josiah, 23:28
Jehoiakim, 24:5
David, 1 Chr. 29:29
Uzziah, 2 Chr. 26:22
ACTION—*deed, work* Acts 5:38, plan or **a** should be of men
1 Sam. 2:3; Dan. 11:28,32; Luke 23:51
ACTIVITY Eccles. 11:5, you do not know the **a** of God
2 Thess. 2:9, accord with the **a** of Satan
ADDER—*serpent, viper* Is. 59:5, They hatch **a-s**

ADJURE—*implore* 1 Kin. 22:16, many times must I **a**
Matt. 26:63, I **a** You by the living God
Acts 19:13, I **a** you by Jesus
ADMINISTRATION 1 Cor. 12:28, **a-s** ... kinds of tongues
2 Cor. 8:20, in our **a** of this
Eph. 1:10, an **a** suitable to the fulness of the times
3:9, **a** of the mystery
ADMONISH—*warn* Acts 20:31, cease to **a** each one
Acts 27:9, Paul *began* to **a** them
Rom. 15:14, able also to **a** one another
1 Cor. 4:14, to **a** you as my ... children
Col. 1:28, **a-ing** every man
3:16, **a-ing** one another with psalms
1 Thess. 5:14, **a** the unruly
2 Thess. 3:15, **a** him as a brother
ADOPTION Rom. 8:15, spirit of **a** as sons
Rom. 8:23, waiting eagerly for *our* **a** as sons
9:4, to whom belong the **a**
Gal. 4:5, receive the **a** as sons
Eph. 1:5, predestined us to **a**
ADORN—*clothe, array* 1 Tim. 2:9, women to **a** themselves
1 Pet. 3:3, let not your **a-ment**
Rev. 21:2, as a bride **a-ed** for her husband
Job 40:10; Is. 61:10; Ezek. 16:11; Matt. 23:29; Luke 21:5; Rev. 17:4; 18:16; 21:19
ADULTERATING 2 Cor. 4:2, not ... **a** the word of God
ADULTERER Lev. 20:10; Ps. 50:18; Heb. 13:4
ADULTERESS—*strange woman* Prov. 22:14, mouth of an **a**
ADULTERY Ex. 20:14; Deut. 5:18; Matt. 5:27, 28; Luke 18:20; James 2:11; 2 Pet. 2:14
ADVANCE Gen. 24:1; Luke 1:7
ADVANTAGE—*profit* Prov. 21:5; 2 Cor. 2:11
Eccles. 1:3, What **a** does man have in all his work
7:12, the **a** of knowledge
John 16:7, to your **a** that I go away
2 Cor. 12:17, I have not taken **a** of you
ADVERSARY—*opponent, foe*
1 Cor. 16:9, and there are many **a-es**
Heb. 10:27, which will consume the **a-es**
1 Pet. 5:8, Your **a**, the devil
Ex. 23:22; 1 Kin. 11:14; Ps. 27:2; 89:23
ADVERSITY—*distress, privation* Deut. 30:15; Job 2:10
Ps. 10:6, I shall not be in **a**
94:13, relief from the days of **a**
Prov. 17:17, is born for **a**
ADVISE—*inform, counsel* Num. 24:14; Rev. 3:18
ADVOCATE—*witness* Job 16:19, my **a** is on high
1 John 2:1, we have an **A** with the Father
AFFAIRS 1 Chr. 26:32, all the **a** of God and ... the king
2 Tim. 2:4, entangles himself in the **a**
AFFECTION—*devotion, passion*
2 Cor. 6:12, restrained in your own **a-s**
7:15, his **a** abounds
Deut. 10:15; Phil. 1:8; 2:1; 1 Thess. 2:8
AFFLICT—*oppress, distress, trouble*
Deut. 26:6, Egyptians ... **a-ed** us
Judg. 16:5, we may bind him to **a** him
Ps. 82:3, justice to the **a-ed** and destitute
147:6, LORD supports the **a-ed**
Is. 61:1, bring good news to the **a-ed**
63:9, He was **a-ed**
Lam. 3:33, does not **a** willingly
2 Cor. 4:8, *we are* **a-ed** in every way
Ex. 1:11,12; 22:22,23; Num. 24:24; 2 Sam. 7:10; 1 Kin. 11:39; 2 Kin. 17:20; Ps. 105:18; Prov. 15:15; Nah. 1:12
AFFLICTION—*misery, oppression*
Deut. 16:3, the bread of **a**
Job 36:15, delivers the afflicted in their **a**
Ps. 25:18, Look upon my **a**
Mark 4:17, when **a** or persecution arises
5:29, she was healed of her **a**
2 Cor. 2:4, out of much **a** and anguish
8:2, in a great ordeal of **a**
2 Thess. 1:6, **a** those who afflict you
Gen. 29:32; 31:42; 41:52; Job 5:6; 30:16; Eccles. 6:2; Acts 20:23
AFRAID—*dread, fear* Ex. 3:6, **a** to look at God
Deut. 20:8, Who is the man that is **a**
Ps. 56:4, not be **a**. What can *mere* man
91:5, **a** of the terror by night
Is. 51:12, are **a** of man who dies
Matt. 14:27, do not be **a**
21:46, they became **a** of the multitudes
Luke 9:34, they were **a** as they entered
12:4, **a** of those who kill the body
Gen. 3:10; Ex. 20:20; Josh. 11:6; Judg. 7:3; Job 9:28; 19:29; Prov. 31:21; Eccles. 9:2; Matt. 1:20; Mark 4:41; 5:36; 9:32; 11:18; 11:32; Luke 12:32; 19:21; John 9:22; 2 Cor. 11:3; 12:20; Heb. 13:6
AFTER Acts 13:22, a man **a** My heart
Acts 24:17, **a** several years I came
Gal. 2:1, **a** an interval
Gen. 7:4; Judg. 16:22; Dan. 2:39
AFTERWARD—*later, after* Gen. 38:30, And **a** his brother came
Matt. 21:30, he **a** regretted *it*
Mark 16:14, And **a** He appeared
AGAINST Gen. 16:12, hand *will be* **a** everyone
Lev. 20:3, set My face **a** that man
Matt. 12:30, not with Me is **a** Me
Gal. 5:23, **a** such things there is no law
Rev. 2:4, have *this* **a** you
Gen. 4:8; Job 16:4; Luke 4:11; Acts 19:38; 1 Pet. 3:12
AGE—*world, generations, elder*
1 Chr. 23:1, Now when David reached old **a**
Job 12:12, Wisdom is with **a-d** men
Matt. 12:32, this **a**, or in the **a** to come
Luke 16:8, sons of this **a** are more shrewd
John 9:21, he is of **a**, he shall speak
Eph. 2:7, that in the **a-s** to come
Col. 1:26, hidden from the *past* **a-s**
Heb. 6:5, powers of the **a** to come
Job 15:10; 32:7; Jer. 6:11; John 9:23; Philem. 9
AGITATION Ps. 38:8, the **a** of my heart
AGONY Luke 22:44, being in **a** He was praying
Acts 2:24, putting an end to the **a** of death
AGREE—*consent* Matt. 18:19, if two of you **a** on earth
John 9:22, Jews had already **a-d**
Acts 5:9, Why is it that you have **a-d** together
15:15, words of the Prophets **a**
28:25, when they did not **a** with one another
Matt. 20:13; Acts 23:20; 1 Tim. 6:3
AGREEMENT Acts 8:1, Saul was in hearty **a**
2 Cor. 6:16, what **a** has the temple
1 John 5:8, the three are in **a**
AILMENT—*infirmity* 1 Tim. 5:23, and your frequent **a-s**
AIR 1 Cor. 9:26, not beating the **a**
Eph. 2:2, prince of the power of the **a**
1 Thess. 4:17, meet the Lord in the **a**
Job 41:16; 1 Cor. 14:9
ALARM Jer. 4:19, The **a** of war
Num. 10:5,6,7,9; Ps. 31:22; 116:11; Joel 2:1
ALAS—*woe* 2 Kin. 6:5, **A**, my master! For it was
Judg. 6:22; 11:35; Amos 5:16
ALERT—*watch* Matt. 24:42; Acts 20:31, be on the **a**
1 Cor. 16:13, Be on the **a**, stand firm
1 Thess. 5:6, let us be **a** and sober
ALIEN—*stranger, foreigner*
Deut. 10:19, show your love for the **a**
14:21, **a** who is in your town
Acts 7:6, **A-S IN A FOREIGN LAND**
Eph. 2:19, no longer strangers and **a-s**
2 Sam. 1:13; Ps. 69:8; Lam. 5:2
ALIENATED Col. 1:21, you were formerly **a**
ALIVE Num. 16:33; 2 Kin. 5:7; Ps. 55:15
Gen. 43:7; 45:3, Is your father still **a**

ALIVE *(Continued)*
Acts 1:3, presented Himself **a**
Rom. 6:13, those **a** from the dead
1 Cor. 15:22, Christ . . . made **a**
Eph. 2:5, made us **a** together with Christ
1 Pet. 3:18, made **a** in the spirit
Rev. 1:18, I am **a** forevermore
ALL—*whatever* Jer. 1:7, And **a** that I command you
Matt. 6:32, **a** these things the Gentiles
Mark 16:15, Go into **a** the world and preach
Luke 2:10, great joy which shall be for **a** the people
3:6, A FLESH SHALL SEE THE SALVATION OF GOD
4:6, I will give you **a** this domain
Acts 2:1, **a** together in one place
1 Cor. 10:26, LORD'S, AND A IT CONTAINS
ALLEGORY Gal. 4:24, This contains an **a**
ALLIANCE 1 Kin. 3:1, Solomon . . . marriage **a** with Pharaoh
ALLIED 2 Chr. 18:1; Ps. 94:20
ALLOT Job 7:3, I **a-ed** months of vanity
Rom. 12:3, as God has **a-ed** to each a measure of faith
ALLOW Ex. 12:23, **a** the destroyer to come
Ps. 16:10, **a** Thy Holy One to see the pit
Acts 2:27, A THY HOLY ONE TO UNDERGO
22:22, not be **a-ed** to live
1 Cor. 10:13, not **a** you to be tempted
1 Tim. 2:12, do not **a** a woman to teach
ALLOWANCE 2 Kin. 25:30, for his **a**, a regular **a** was given
Jer. 52:34, a regular **a** was given him
ALLY Gen. 14:13, these were **a-es** with Abram
ALMIGHTY Gen. 17:1, I am God **A**
Ps. 91:1, shadow of the **A**
Rev. 4:8, *is* THE LORD GOD, THE **A**
11:17, the **A**, who art and who wast
Ex. 6:3; Job 11:7; 29:5; 37:23
ALMS—*charity* Matt. 6:2, therefore you give **a**
Matt. 6:4, your **a** may be in secret
Acts 10:2; 24:17
ALONE Gen. 2:18, not good for the man to be **a**
Matt. 4:4, MAN SHALL NOT LIVE ON BREAD A
Luke 9:18, He was praying **a**
John 8:16, I am not **a**
Job 7:16; Mark 14:6
ALREADY—*utterly* Eccles. 1:10, **A** it has existed for ages
Matt. 5:28, committed adultery with her **a**
John 3:18, who does not believe . . . judged **a**
9:27, He answered them, I told you **a**
11:17, had **a** been in the tomb four days
1 Cor. 5:3, I . . . have **a** judged him who
6:7, it is **a** a defeat for you
2 Thess. 2:7, mystery of lawlessness is **a** at work
ALTAR Ps. 43:4, I will go to the **a**
Ezek. 6:4, your **a-s** will become desolate
Matt. 5:23, your offering at the **a**
Rev. 9:13, four horns of the golden **a**
Gen. 8:20; Ex. 17:15; Lev. 6:9; Judg. 6:24; Matt. 23:19
ALWAYS—*forever, ever* Matt. 28:20, lo, I am with you **a**
Mark 14:7, you do not **a** have Me
Phil. 4:4, Rejoice in the Lord **a**
1 Thess. 4:17, thus we shall **a** be with the Lord
Deut. 14:23; 2 Tim. 3:7; Heb. 7:25
AM Ex. 3:14, **I A WHO I A**
Matt. 18:20, there I **a** in their midst
1 Cor. 15:10, grace of God I **a** what I **a**
Gal. 4:12, brethren, become as I **a**
AMASS—*heap* Ps. 39:6, He **a-es** *riches*
AMAZE—*astonish, astound*
Matt. 7:28, were **a-d** at His teaching
Luke 9:43, **a-d** at the greatness of God
Rev. 13:3, the whole earth was **a-d**
Mark 2:12; Luke 24:22; John 9:30
AMAZEMENT—*astonishment* Acts 3:10, with wonder and **a**
AMBITION 1 Thess. 4:11, make it your **a** to lead
James 3:14,16, bitter jealousy and selfish **a**
AMBUSH—*wait* Josh. 8:2, Set an **a** for the city
Josh. 8:4,7,12,14,19,21; Jer. 51:12
AMEN Num. 5:22, the woman shall say, **A. A**
Ps. 41:13; 72:19; 89:52, **A** and **A**
Matt. 6:13, *the glory, forever.* **A**
Rev. 3:14, The **A**, the faithful and true Witness
ANALYZE—*discern* Luke 12:56, **a** this present time
ANCIENT—*aged, everlasting, old*
Deut. 33:15, of the **a** mountains
1 Chr. 4:22, the records are **a**
Ps. 24:7, be lifted up, O **a** doors
Dan. 7:9,13,22, **A** of Days
Matt. 5:21, the **a-s** were told
ANGEL Matt. 4:6, GIVE HIS A-S CHARGE
Luke 20:36, for they are like **a-s**
22:43, an **a** from heaven appeared
John 20:12, beheld two **a-s** in white
2 Cor. 11:14, as an **a** of light
Col. 2:18, worship of the **a-s**
Gen. 24:7; Ps. 78:25; Is. 63:9; Matt. 1:20,24; 2:13; Acts 6:15; 23:8; Heb. 13:2; 2 Pet. 2:4; Rev. 2:1,8,12; 9:11
ANGER—*exasperation, wrath, indignation*
Ex. 32:19, Moses' **a** burned
Deut. 13:17, from His burning **a**
Job 5:2, And **a** kills the simple
Ps. 30:5, His **a** is but for a moment
Prov. 15:18, the slow to **a**
22:24, a man given to **a**
Eph. 4:26, sun go down on your **a**
James 1:19, slow to speak *and* slow to **a**
Gen. 39:19; 49:7; Ex. 22:24; Neh. 9:17; Job 9:13; Ps. 37:8; 38:1; Prov. 14:29; Eccles. 5:17; Is. 5:25; 51:17; 54:8; Gal. 5:20
ANGRY—*indignant, enraged*
Prov. 29:22, An **a** man stirs up strife
Is. 64:9, Do not be **a** beyond measure
Eph. 4:26, BE A . . . DO NOT SIN
Gen. 4:6; 18:30; Esth. 1:12; Jon. 4:4; Matt. 5:22; Heb. 3:10
ANGUISH—*distress, pain* Ps. 55:4; Is. 30:6; Jer. 6:24
ANIMAL—*beast, creature, cattle*
Gen. 6:7, from man to **a-s** to creeping things
7:8, Of clean **a-s** and **a-s** that are not
8:20, took of every clean **a** and
Acts 10:12, four-footed **a-s** and crawling creatures
2 Pet. 2:12, like unreasoning **a-s**
Ex. 22:19; Ps. 104:25; Jer. 27:6
ANNOUNCE—*proclaim* Is. 52:7, **a-s** peace . . . **a-s** salvation
ANNUAL 1 Sam. 7:16, used to go **a-ly** on circuit
ANOINT Matt. 6:17, fast, **a** your head
Mark 14:8, she has **a-ed** My body
16:1, they might come and **a**
Ex. 28:41; Ps. 23:5; 105:15; Luke 7:46; Acts 10:38; 2 Cor. 1:21; Rev. 3:18
ANSWER—*respond* Ps. 65:5, Thou dost **a** us
Prov. 15:1, **a** turns away wrath
Eccles. 10:19, money is the **a** to everything
Mic. 3:7, there is no **a** from God
Luke 2:47, amazed at . . . His **a-s**
Deut. 27:15; Ps. 55:19; Prov. 24:26; 26:4,5; Matt. 26:62; Mark 14:60; John 19:9; Acts 12:13
ANT Prov. 6:6, Go to the **a**, O sluggard
Prov. 30:25, The **a-s** are not a strong folk
ANTICHRIST 1 John 2:18, **a** is coming
2 John 7, the deceiver and the **a**
1 John 2:22; 4:3
ANXIETY—*sorrow* Ps. 38:18, full of **a** because of my sin
Jer. 49:23, There is **a** by the sea
ANXIOUS—*worry, concern, thought* Jer. 17:8
Matt. 6:25, do not be **a** for your life
6:27; Luke 12:25, being **a** can add a single
6:31, Do not be **a** then, saying

6:34, be **a** for tomorrow
10:19, **a** about how or what you will speak
Mark 13:11, do not be **a** beforehand about what
Luke 12:26, why are you **a** about other
Phil. 4:6, Be **a** for nothing
APART—*separate, without* Matt. 10:29, **a** from your Father
John 1:3, **a** from Him nothing came into being
Acts 13:2, Set **a** for Me Barnabas and
Rom. 3:28, justified by faith **a** from works
APOSTASY—*backsliding, faithlessness*
Hos. 14:4, I will heal their **a**
2 Thess. 2:3, *not come* unless the **a** comes first
Jer. 2:19; 5:6; 8:5; 14:7
APOSTLE Matt. 10:2, names of the twelve **a-s**
Rom. 1:1, called *as* an **a**
11:13, **a** of the Gentiles
Eph. 4:11, He gave some as **a-s**
Luke 11:49; 1 Cor. 15:9; 2 Cor. 12:11; Gal. 1:19; 1 Tim. 2:7; 2 Tim. 1:11
APPALL—*astound, amaze, astonish*
Job 17:8, upright shall be **a-ed**
Ps. 40:15, Let those be **a-ed** because of their shame
143:4, My heart is **a-ed** within me
Lev. 26:32; Jer. 2:12; Ezek. 4:17; Dan. 4:19
APPAREL—*garment* 2 Sam. 1:24, gold on your **a**
Is. 63:1, is majestic in His **a**
Luke 24:4, two men ... in dazzling **a**
Acts 12:21, put on his royal **a**
APPEAL—*ask, beg, entreat* Acts 25:11, I **a** to Caesar
Acts 28:19, I was forced to **a** to Caesar
1 Tim. 5:1, **a** to him as a father
Philem. 9, for love's sake I rather **a** to you
Acts 25:12,21,25; 26:32
APPEAR—*be seen* Gen. 12:7, LORD **a-ed** to Abram
Ex. 3:2, **a-ed** to him in a blazing
Mal. 3:2, who can stand when He **a-s**
Acts 2:3, **a-ed** to them tongues as of
16:9, a vision **a-ed** to Paul in the
27:20, sun nor stars **a-ed** for many days
2 Cor. 5:10, we must all **a** before
Heb. 9:24, now to **a** in ... of God for us
9:28, shall **a** a second time
1 Pet. 5:4, Chief Shepherd **a-s**
1 John 3:2, it has not **a-ed** ... if He should **a**
Gen. 19:14; Num. 14:10; 2 Sam. 22:11; Matt. 1:20; 2:13; 27:53; Mark 16:9
APPEARANCE—*brightness, radiance, sight*
1 Sam. 16:7, man looks at the *outward* **a**
Matt. 6:16, for they neglect their **a**
28:3, his **a** was like lightning
Phil. 2:8, found in **a** as a man
2 Thess. 2:8, **a** of His coming
Num. 11:7; 1 Sam. 16:12; 2 Sam. 11:2; 14:27; Dan. 1:15; Nah. 2:4; Luke 9:29; Rev. 4:3
APPETITE—*stomach, desire* Prov. 23:2, man of *great* **a**
Phil. 3:19, whose god is *their* **a**
Num. 11:6; Job 38:39; Eccles. 6:7; Hab. 2:5; Rom. 16:18
APPLE Ps. 17:8, **a** of the eye
Prov. 25:11; Song 2:3,5
APPOINT—*name* Num. 3:10, you shall **a** Aaron
1 Chr. 17:9, I will **a** a place for My people
Jon. 1:17, **a-ed** a great fish to swallow
Mark 3:14, He **a-ed** twelve, that they
Heb. 9:27, **a-ed** for men to die
Gen. 4:15; Job 36:23; Jer. 49:19; John 15:16; 1 Tim. 2:7
APPORTION—*distribute* Josh. 13:7, **a** this land for an
Job 21:17, Does God **a** destruction
2 Cor. 10:13, sphere which God **a-ed** to us
APPRAISE—*discern*
1 Cor. 2:14, they are spiritually **a-d**
APPROACH Matt. 21:34, the harvest time **a-ed**
Luke 24:15, Jesus Himself **a-ed**
Lev. 18:14,19; Judg. 19:25
APPROPRIATE Eccles. 3:11, everything **a** in its time
Ezek. 36:5, **a-d** My land for themselves
APPROVAL Heb. 11:2, men of old gained **a**
Heb. 11:39, having gained **a** through
APPROVE—*attest* Rom. 14:18, and **a-d** by men
Rom. 16:10, **a-d** in Christ
2 Tim. 2:15, present yourself **a-d** to God
APRON Acts 19:12, handkerchiefs or **a-s**
ARCHANGEL 1 Thess. 4:16; Jude 9
ARGUE—*dispute, question* Mark 8:11
Prov. 25:8, out hastily to **a** *your case*
25:9, **A** your case with your neighbor
Mark 9:14, *some* scribes **a-ing** with them
Acts 9:29, talking and **a-ing** with Hellenistic Jews
ARGUMENT Job 23:4, fill my mouth with **a-s**
Ps. 38:14, whose mouth are no **a-s**
ARISE—*rise, stand* Gen. 31:13, **a**, leave this land
Job 31:14, do when God **a-s**
Ps. 27:3, war **a** against me
Dan. 11:2, three more kings are going to **a**
Matt. 11:11, has not **a-n** *anyone* greater
24:11, false prophets will **a**
Acts 10:13, **A**, Peter, kill and eat
Eph. 5:14, AND A FROM THE DEAD
2 Pet. 1:19, morning star **a-s** in your hearts
Deut. 9:12; Ps. 3:7; Song 2:13; Matt. 2:13,20; Acts 22:16
ARK Gen. 6:14, an **a** of gopher wood
Heb. 9:4, **a** of the covenant
Ex. 37:1; Matt. 24:38; Rev. 11:19
ARM (n.)—*hand, side* Deut. 33:27, the everlasting **a-s**
Ps. 37:17, **a-s** of the wicked ... broken
Mark 10:16, took them in His **a-s**
Ex. 6:6; Job 26:2; Ps. 98:1; Song 8:6; Is. 60:4; Zech. 13:6
ARM (v.) Num. 31:3, **A** men from among you
Luke 11:21, a strong *man* fully **a-ed**
1 Pet. 4:1, **a** yourselves also
ARMOR—*weapon, harness* 1 Kin. 20:11; 22:34; Luke 11:22
Rom. 13:12, put on the **a** of light
Eph. 6:11,13, full **a** of God
ARMY—*host, war* Deut. 24:5; 1 Chr. 12:22; 2 Chr. 26:11
AROMA Gen. 8:21, LORD smelled the soothing **a**
2 Cor. 2:16, **a** from death ... **a** from life
AROUSE—*raise, stir* Is. 42:13, He will **a** *His* zeal like
Acts 13:50, Jews **a-d** the devout women
Job 14:12; Is. 41:25; 45:13; Jer. 51:11
ARRAY—*adorn, clothe* Matt. 6:30, God so **a-s** the grass
Judg. 20:20; Luke 12:28
ARROGANCE—*pride* Prov. 8:13, Pride and **a** and the evil way
Is. 13:11, **a** of the proud
16:6, *Even* of his **a**, pride, and
Jer. 48:29, his **a** and his self-exaltation
49:16, **a** of your heart has deceived you
ARROGANT—*proud* Jer. 48:26, become **a** toward the LORD
Rom. 1:30, insolent, **a**, boastful
Jude 16, they speak **a-ly**
Rev. 13:5, **a** words and blasphemies
Jer. 50:32; Dan. 5:20; 2 Pet. 2:18
ARROW—*dart, missile* 1 Sam. 20:36, he shot an **a** past him
Job 6:4, **a-s** of the Almighty
Jer. 9:8, Their tongue is a deadly **a**
Job 41:28; Ps. 45:5; Prov. 7:23; Lam. 3:12
ART 2 Chr. 16:14, blended by the perfumers' **a**
Acts 17:29, image formed by the **a**
ASCEND Ps. 24:3, may **a** into the hill of
Ps. 139:8, If I **a** to heaven
John 3:13, no one has **a-ed**
6:62, behold the Son of Man **a-ing**
20:17, I **a** to My Father
Rom. 10:6, WHO WILL A INTO HEAVEN

ASH Gen. 18:27, am *but* dust and **a-es**
Job 13:12, sayings are proverbs of **a-es**
42:6, repent in dust and **a-es**
Ps. 102:9, eat **a-es** like bread
Is. 61:3, a garland instead of **a-es**
Matt. 11:21, repented ... sackcloth and **a-es**
Luke 10:13, sitting in sackcloth and **a-es**
Lev. 6:11; Num. 19:17; 1 Sam. 2:8; 2 Sam. 13:19; 1 Kin. 13:3,5; Esth. 4:1; Job 2:8; 30:19; Ps. 147:16; Is. 44:20; 58:5; Jer. 6:26; Mal. 4:3; Heb. 9:13
ASHAMED—*confused* Ps. 71:1, me never be **a**
Mark 8:38, the Son of Man ... **a** of him
Rom. 1:16, not **a** of the gospel
Heb. 11:16, not **a** to be called their God
Gen. 2:25; Ps. 25:2; Is. 24:23; 2 Tim. 1:8; 1 Pet. 4:16
ASHERAH, ASHERIM (pl.)
1 Kin. 15:13, made a ... image as an **A**
Ex. 34:13; 2 Kin. 17:10; 2 Chr. 19:3; 33:19; Mic. 5:14
ASIDE 1 Sam. 8:3, turned **a** after dishonest gain
1 Pet. 2:1, putting **a** all malice
ASK—*appeal, beg, inquire* 1 Kin. 3:5, **A** what *you wish*
Ps. 27:4, One thing I have **a-ed** from the LORD
Prov. 30:7, Two things I **a-ed** of Thee
Jer. 6:16, **a** for the ancient paths
Matt. 5:42, Give to him who **a-s** of
7:7, **A**, and it shall be given to you
Mark 10:38, not know ... **a-ing** for
John 4:40, they were **a-ing** Him to stay
14:16, I will **a** the Father
James 1:5, let him **a** of God
Ruth 3:11; Job 42:4; Ps. 2:8; Is. 7:11; Zech. 10:1; Matt. 21:22; Mark 10:35; 11:24; Luke 11:11; 1 Cor. 1:22; 10:25; Eph. 3:13; 1 John 5:15
ASLEEP Matt. 9:24, not dead, but **a**
Mark 4:38, was in the stern, **a**
13:36, come suddenly and find you **a**
John 11:11, Our friend Lazarus has fallen **a**
Acts 7:60, having said this, he fell **a**
1 Cor. 15:6, some have fallen **a**
1 Thess. 4:14, those who have fallen **a** in Jesus
5:10, whether ... awake or **a**
Judg. 4:21; 1 Thess. 4:13,15
ASSEMBLE—*gather* 1 Chr. 13:5; 15:3, David **a-d** all Israel
Lev. 8:3; Num. 8:9; 20:8; Deut. 4:10; 31:12; Is. 43:9; Jer. 4:5; 8:14; Ezek. 11:17; Hos. 7:14; Amos 3:9
ASSEMBLY—*band, congregation, convocation*
Ps. 1:5, in the **a** of the righteous
Joel 1:14; 2:15, Proclaim a solemn **a**
Heb. 12:23, to the general **a** and church
Ex. 12:16; Lev. 23:36; Num. 20:10,12; Job 11:10; Ps. 26:5; 111:1; Acts 19:39
ASSERT Acts 25:19, whom Paul **a-ed** to be alive
1 Tim. 1:7, they make confident **a-ions**
ASSIGN—*distribute* 1 Cor. 7:17, Lord has **a-ed** to each
ASSOCIATE Rom. 12:16, but **a** with the lowly
Job 19:19; Ps. 50:18; Zech. 13:7; 2 Thess. 3:14
ASSURANCE—*confidence* Job 24:22, no one has **a** of life
Col. 2:2, full **a** of understanding
Heb. 6:11, full **a** of hope
10:22, full **a** of faith
11:1, faith ... **a** of things hoped for
ASTONISH—*amaze, astound*
Matt. 13:54, so that they became **a-ed**
22:33, they were **a-ed** at His teaching
Mark 6:2, many listeners were **a-ed**
7:37, they were utterly **a-ed**
10:26, they were even more **a-ed**
11:18, all the multitude were **a-ed**
Job 21:5; Matt. 19:25; Luke 1:63
ASTOUND—*amaze, astonish* Jer. 4:9, prophets will be **a-ed**
Dan. 8:27, **a-ed** at the vision
Mark 5:42; 10:26

ASTRAY—*err* Ps. 119:176, gone **a** like a lost sheep
Is. 53:6, sheep have gone **a**
1 Tim. 6:21, gone **a** from the faith
Ps. 119:110; Prov. 10:17; Is. 3:12; 9:16; Matt. 18:13; Heb. 3:10
ATE—*eat* Jer. 15:16, words were found and I **a** them
1 Cor. 10:3, all **a** the same spiritual food
Luke 13:26; 24:43; Acts 9:9
ATONEMENT—*reconciliation* Lev. 23:27; 25:9, the day of **a**
Ex. 30:15; 2 Sam. 21:3
ATTAIN—*acquire* Rom. 9:30, **a-ed** righteousness
Phil. 3:11, **a** to the resurrection
ATTENTION—*heed, regard* Prov. 4:1, give **a** ... gain understanding
16:20, who gives **a** to the word
Is. 5:12, not pay **a** to the deeds
Heb. 2:1, we must pay closer **a**
Ex. 5:9; Job 33:31; Prov. 29:12; 1 Tim. 1:4; 4:13
ATTEST Acts 2:22, a man **a-ed** to you by God
AUTHOR—*source* Heb. 12:2, the **a** and perfecter of faith
AUTHORITY Eccles. 8:8, **a** over the day of death
Matt. 7:29, teaching them as one having **a**
8:9, For I too am a man under **a**
9:6, **a** on earth to forgive
10:1, **a** over unclean spirits
21:23, By what **a** are You doing these things
28:18, **a** has been given to Me
Luke 5:24, Son of Man has **a** on earth to forgive
9:1, gave them power and **a**
19:17, be in **a** over ten cities
20:8, by what **a** I am doing these things
John 5:27, **a** to execute judgment
10:18, **a** to lay it down ... **a** to take it up
17:2, Thou gavest Him **a** over all mankind
Acts 8:19, Give this **a** to me as well, so
Rom. 13:1, no **a** except from God
1 Cor. 15:24, all rule and all **a**
1 Tim. 2:12, to teach or exercise **a**
Titus 2:15, reprove with all **a**
2 Pet. 2:10, and despise **a**
Jude 25, majesty, dominion and **a**
Rev. 2:26, GIVE A OVER THE NATIONS
Num. 27:20; Is. 22:21; Hab. 1:7; Luke 10:19; 12:5
AVAIL—*profit* Jer. 7:8, deceptive words to no **a**
AVENGE—*vengeance, revenge* 1 Sam. 24:12
Jer. 5:9,29, Shall I not **a** Myself
2 Cor. 7:11, what zeal, what **a-ing** of wrong
AVOID—*refuse* Prov. 4:15, **A** it, do not pass by it
1 Tim. 6:20, **a-ing** worldly *and* empty chatter
2 Tim. 3:5, **a** such men as these
AWAIT—*wait* 1 Cor. 1:7, **a-ing** eagerly the revelation
AWAKE—*watch* Ps. 139:18, when I **a**, I am still with Thee
Eph. 5:14, **A**, SLEEPER
Rev. 16:15, Blessed is the one who stays **a**
Judg. 5:12; Ps. 17:15; Is. 51:9; John 11:11; Rom. 13:11
AWARE Luke 8:46, I was **a** that power had gone
AWE—*fear* Ps. 33:8, inhabitants ... in **a** of Him
Ps. 119:161, stands in **a** of Thy words
Heb. 12:28, with reverence and **a**
AWESOME—*fearful* Gen. 28:17, How **a** is this place
Ex. 15:11, **A** in praises
Judg. 13:6, angel of God, very **a**
Neh. 1:5, the great and **a** God
Job 37:22, Around God is **a** majesty
Ps. 89:7, **a** above all those ... around Him
Song 6:4, **a** as an army with banners
Joel 2:31, great and **a** day of the LORD
AXE—*hatchet* 2 Kin. 6:5, **a** head fell into the water
Matt. 3:10, **a** is already laid at the root
Luke 3:9, the **a** ... root of the trees
1 Sam. 13:20; 1 Kin. 6:7

B

BABBLER Acts 17:18, this idle **b**
BABE—*immature* Matt. 11:25, reveal ... to **b-s**
1 Cor. 3:1, to **b-s** in Christ
Heb. 5:13, for he is a **b**
1 Pet. 2:2, like newborn **b-s**
Ps. 8:2; 17:14; Matt. 21:16; Luke 10:21
BABY—*babe, immature* Luke 2:12; 2:16
BACK—*backward* Is. 38:17, sins behind Thy **b**
Num. 24:11; 1 Sam. 10:9; Neh. 9:26; Ezek. 2:10; Mark 13:16
BACKBITING—*slanders* Prov. 25:23, a **b** tongue
BACKSLIDE—*apostasy, faithless*
Prov. 14:14, **b-r** in heart will have his fill
Jer. 49:4, O **b-ing** daughter Who trusts
BACKWARD 2 Kin. 20:10, shadow turn **b** ten steps
Gen. 9:23; 49:17; Job 23:8; Jer. 7:24
BAD—*evil, wrong* Gen. 24:50; 31:24,29; Lev. 27:12,14,33; Num. 13:19; 24:13; 2 Sam. 13:22; 2 Cor. 5:10, good or **b**
Lev. 27:10, good for a **b**, or a **b** for a good
Matt. 7:18, good tree cannot produce **b** fruit
Gen. 43:6; Is. 3:11; Jer. 24:2,3; Matt. 13:48
BAG—*purse* Deut. 25:13; 1 Sam. 17:40
Job 14:17, My transgression is sealed up in a **b**
Matt. 10:10, or a **b** for *your* journey
2 Kin. 5:23; Prov. 7:20; 16:11; Mic. 6:11
BAGGAGE 1 Sam. 17:22, David left his **b**
BAKE Gen. 19:3; 40:17; Ex. 12:39; 16:23; Lev. 2:4; 24:5; 26:26; Num. 11:8; 1 Sam. 28:24; Is. 44:15
BAKER Gen. 40:1, **b** of the king of Egypt
Gen. 41:10; 1 Sam. 8:13; Jer. 37:21; Hos. 7:4
BALANCE—*scale* Lev. 19:36, shall have just **b-s**
Prov. 11:1, A false **b** is an abomination to the LORD
16:11, A just **b** and scales belong to the LORD
Job 6:2; Ps. 62:9; Is. 40:12; Ezek. 45:10; Hos. 12:7
BALD—*baldhead* Lev. 13:41, head becomes **b**
Jer. 48:37; Ezek. 29:18
BALDHEAD—*bald* 2 Kin. 2:23, Go up, you **b**
BALDNESS Mic. 1:16, **b** like an eagle
Lev. 21:5; Ezek. 7:18; Amos 8:10
BALM Jer. 8:22, no **b** in Gilead
Gen. 37:25; 43:11; Jer. 46:11; 51:8; Ezek. 27:17
BAND—*bond, chain, fetter* Ex. 27:10; 28:8; 38:10; Judg. 8:26; Ps. 107:14; Is. 58:6
BANISH 2 Sam. 14:13,14; Ezra 7:26
BANK—*mound* Gen. 41:17, **b** of the Nile
Matt. 25:27, put my money in the **b**
Gen. 41:3; Ex. 2:3; 7:15; Ezek. 47:7; Luke 19:23
BANNER—*standard* Ps. 20:5; 60:4
Song 2:4, his **b** over me is love
6:4, awesome as an army with **b-s**
BANQUET—*feast, supper*
Song 2:4; Dan. 5:10; Amos 6:7
Esth. 5:4, the **b** that I have prepared for him
Matt. 23:6; Mark 12:39; Luke 20:46, place of honor at **b-s**
Mark 6:21, Herod on his birthday gave a **b**
BAPTISM—*washing*
Matt. 3:7; Mark 10:38; 1 Pet. 3:21
Matt. 21:25; Mark 11:30; Luke 7:29, **b** of John
Luke 20:4; Acts 1:22; 18:25; 19:3, **b** of John
Mark 1:4; Luke 3:3; Acts 13:24; 19:4, **b** of repentance
Luke 12:50, I have a **b** to undergo
Rom. 6:4, buried with Him through **b**
Col. 2:12, buried with Him in **b**
Eph. 4:5, one Lord, one faith, one **b**
BAPTIZE Matt. 3:11, I **b** you in water
Matt. 3:14, I have need to be **b-d** by You
28:19, **b-ing** them in the name of the Father
Mark 1:8; Luke 3:16, **b** you with the Holy Sp.
John 3:22, He was ... with them and **b-ing**
Acts 1:5, John **b-d** with water
2:41, those ... were **b-d**
8:16, **b-d** in the name of the Lord Jesus
9:18, Saul ... arose and was **b-d**
19:4, John **b-d** with the baptism
Rom. 6:3, **b-d** into Christ Jesus ... **b-d** into His death
1 Cor. 1:13, were you **b-d** in the name of Paul
12:13, by one Spirit we were all **b-d**
Mark 16:16; Luke 3:7,12,21; 7:29; John 1:25,33; 4:1; Acts 2:38; 8:12,36; 10:47; 16:15,33; 18:8; 22:16; 1 Cor. 10:2; 15:29
BARBARIAN Rom. 1:14; 1 Cor. 14:11
BARBER Ezek. 5:1, use it as a **b-'s** razor
BARE—*naked* Is. 52:10; 1 Cor. 15:37; Heb. 4:13
BARK Ex. 11:7; Is. 56:10
BARLEY Ex. 9:31; Deut. 8:8; Ruth 1:22; John 6:9
BARN Matt. 6:26, nor gather into **b-s**
Luke 12:18, I will tear down my **b-s**
Joel 1:17; Hag. 2:19; Matt. 3:12; 13:30; Luke 12:24
BARRACKS Acts 21:34; 22:24
BARREN—*unfruitful* Gen. 11:30; 29:31; Ex. 23:26; Job 24:21; Is. 54:1; Luke 1:7,36; 23:29
BARS 1 Sam. 23:7; Ps. 107:16; Is. 45:2; Ezek. 38:11
BASE 1 Cor. 1:28, the **b** things of the world
BASIN Ex. 12:22; 1 Chr. 28:17; Jer. 52:19; John 13:5
BASKET Ex. 2:3; 29:23; Judg. 6:19; Jer. 24:2; Amos 8:1; Matt. 14:20; 15:37; 16:9; Mark 6:43; 8:8; 8:19; Luke 9:17; John 6:13
BAT Lev. 11:19; Deut. 14:18; Is. 2:20
BATH—*measure* 1 Kin. 7:26; 2 Chr. 2:10; Ezra 7:22; Is. 5:10
BATHE—*wash* Song 5:12, eyes ... **b-d** in milk
Lev. 15:5,22; 17:16; Num. 19:7; 2 Sam. 11:2
BATTER—*bruise, crush*
Matt. 12:20, **B-ED REED ... NOT BREAK**
BATTLE—*war* 1 Sam. 17:47, **b** is the LORD's
2 Chr. 20:15, the **b** is not yours
1 Sam. 17:20; 1 Chr. 5:20; Job 39:25; 41:8; Ps. 18:39; 55:18; 140:7; 144:1; Eccles. 9:11; Is. 21:15; Jer. 50:22; Luke 14:31
BEACH Matt. 13:2; John 21:4; Acts 21:5
BEAM—*log* 2 Kin. 6:2; Ps. 104:3
BEAR (n.) 1 Sam. 17:34; 2 Sam. 17:8; Prov. 17:12; Is. 11:7; 59:11; Hos. 13:8; Amos 5:19
BEAR (v.)—*carry, sustain* Gen. 43:9; 44:32
Gen. 4:13, punishment is too great to **b**
Ex. 20:16, You shall not **b** false witness
Ps. 91:12, They will **b** you up
Matt. 1:23, VIRGIN ... SHALL **B** A SON
27:32, to **b** His cross
Mark 15:21, that he might **b** His cross
John 1:7, **b** witness of the light
16:12, you cannot **b** *them* now
Rom. 8:16, Spirit Himself **b-s** witness
1 Cor. 13:7, **b-s** all things
15:49, **b** the image of the heavenly
Gal. 6:2, **B** one another's burdens
6:5, each one shall **b** his own load
6:17, I **b** on my body
1 John 1:2, we have seen and **b** witness
Ex. 28:12; Lev. 24:15; Deut. 1:9; Prov. 18:14; Lam. 3:27; Ezek. 23:49; Matt. 1:21; Luke 11:46; John 5:31; 8:18; 15:27; Rom. 13:4; 15:1; Heb 9:28
BEARD Lev. 13:29; 1 Sam. 21:13; 2 Sam. 10:4; 20:9; 1 Chr. 19:5; Ps. 133:2; Ezek. 5:1
BEARING—*carrying* Rom. 2:15; Gal. 4:24
John 19:17, **b** His own cross
Col. 3:13, **b** with one another
Heb. 13:13, **b** His reproach
BEAST—*animal, creature* Lev. 26:22; Job 12:7; 18:3
Ps. 50:10, every **b** of the forest is Mine
147:9, He gives to the **b** its food
Eccles. 3:19, no advantage for man over **b**
1 Cor. 15:32, I fought with wild **b-s**
Ps. 49:12; 73:22; Prov. 12:10; James 3:7
BEAT—*flog, hammer* Judg. 6:11; Matt. 26:67
Prov. 23:14, **b** him with the rod
Joel 3:10, **B** your plowshares into swords
Luke 18:13, was **b-ing** his breast

BEAT *(Continued)*
1 Cor. 9:26, as not **b-ing** the air
2 Cor. 11:23, **b-en** times without number
BEAUTIFUL—*appropriate, lovely* Lev. 23:40
Gen. 6:2, daughters of men were **b**
12:11, you are a **b** woman
Is. 4:2, the Branch of the LORD will be **b**
64:11, Our holy and **b** house
Matt. 23:27, tombs which on the outside appear **b**
Acts 3:2, gate of the temple which is called **B**
Rom. 10:15, How B ARE THE FEET
Judg. 15:2; Ps. 48:2; Song 1:8; 6:4; Is. 52:1; Jer. 11:16; 13:20
BEAUTY 2 Sam. 1:19; Prov. 31:30; Is. 3:18; Zech. 9:17
Ps. 27:4, To behold the **b** of the LORD
50:2, Out of Zion, the perfection of **b**
BECAME Gen. 26:13, and the man **b** rich
Heb. 11:34, **b** mighty in war
BECOME Ps. 33:1, Praise is **b-ing** to the upright
Luke 2:40, Child ... to grow and **b** strong
BED—*pallet* Ps. 63:6, remember Thee on my **b**
Matt. 9:6, Rise, take up your **b**
2 Kin. 4:10; Job 7:13; 33:15; Is. 28:20; Ezek. 17:10; Mark 4:21; Luke 8:16
BEES Deut. 1:44; Judg. 14:8; Ps. 118:12; Is. 7:18
BEFALL—*happen* Gen. 42:4; 49:1; Deut. 31:29
Gen. 44:29, harm **b-s** him
Ps. 91:10, No evil will **b** you
BEFIT—*proper, worthy* Ps. 93:5, Holiness **b-s**
1 Tim. 2:10, as **b-s** women making a claim to godliness
BEG—*appeal, ask* Ps. 37:25, his descendants **b-ing** bread
Luke 16:3, I am ashamed to **b**
18:35, blind man by the road, **b-ing**
John 9:8, the one who used to sit and **b**
Ps. 109:10; Prov. 20:4; Luke 9:38
BEGINNING 1 Sam. 3:12; Prov. 8:22,23
Gen. 1:1, In the **b** God created the heavens
Job 8:7, your **b** was insignificant
Ps. 111:10, **b** of wisdom
Prov. 1:7, **b** of knowledge
Eccles. 7:8, end ... better than its **b**
Luke 24:47, **b** from Jerusalem
John 1:1, In the **b** was the Word
Rev. 21:6, the **b** and the end
Matt. 19:8; John 2:11; 2 Cor. 3:1; 8:6; Col. 1:18; Heb. 3:14; Rev. 22:13
BEGOTTEN—*born* Ps. 2:7, Today I have **b** Thee
Job 38:28; Acts 13:33; Philem. 10; Heb. 1:5; 5:5
BEHALF—*place, sake* Job 36:2, more ... said in God's **b**
2 Cor. 1:11, thanks may be given ... on our **b**
5:20, we beg you on **b** of Christ
BEHAVE—*act* 1 Sam. 18:30, David **b-d** himself more wisely
1 Thess. 2:10, how devoutly ... we **b-d**
BEHAVIOR—*conduct* James 3:13, his good **b**
1 Pet. 1:15, holy ... in all *your* **b**
2:12, keep your **b** excellent
BEHEAD Luke 9:9; Rev. 20:4
Matt. 14:10, had John **b-ed** in prison
Mark 6:16, John whom I **b-ed**
BEHOLD—*look* Num. 24:17; Ps. 37:37
Matt. 18:10, angels ... **b** the face of My Father
John 17:24, that they may **b** My glory
2 Cor. 3:18, **b-ing** as in a mirror
BEING Gen. 2:7, man became a living **b**
Matt. 7:11, **b** evil, know how to give
12:34, **b** evil, speak ... good
John 4:9, **b** a Jew, ask me
1 Cor. 8:7, conscience **b** weak
9:21, **b** without the law
Eph. 2:20, **b** the chief cornerstone
BELIEVE—*faith, trust* Ex. 4:5; Matt. 8:13; 9:28
Num. 14:11, how long will they not **b** in Me
Ps. 78:22, Because they did not **b** in God
Prov. 14:15, The naive **b-s** everything
Matt. 21:22, everything you ask ... **b-ing** you
Mark 5:36, Do not be afraid ... only **b**
9:23, All things are possible to him who **b-s**
Luke 8:13, they **b** for a while
24:25, slow of heart to **b**
John 2:22, they **b-d** the Scripture
7:5, not even His brothers were **b-ing** in Him
8:24, unless you **b** that I am He
10:38, though you do not **b** Me, **b** the works
11:26, everyone who ... **b-s** in Me shall never die
11:27, Yes, Lord; I have **b-d**
11:48, all men will **b** in Him
17:21, that the world may **b** that Thou didst send Me
20:25, Unless I shall see ... I will not **b**
20:29, Blessed *are* they who ... yet **b-d**
Rom. 4:11, the father of all who **b**
Heb. 11:6, he who comes to God must **b** that
James 2:19, You **b** that God is one ... the
1 Pet. 2:6, HE WHO B-S IN HIM SHALL NOT BE
Matt. 21:25; 27:42; Mark 11:24,31; 16:13; Luke 8:50; 24:41; John 1:7; 3:12; 5:44,47; 6:36; 7:48; 10:37; 11:15; 12:36; Acts 4:32; 9:26; 13:39,48; 16:34; Rom. 4:18; 9:33; 10:14; 2 Cor. 4:13; Gal. 3:22; 2 Thess. 1:10
BELLY—*stomach* Gen. 3:14, On your **b** shall you go
BELONG Luke 23:7, He **b-ed** to Herod's
1 Cor. 3:21, all things **b** to you
3:23, **b** to Christ ... **b-s** to God
BELOVED—*chosen* Ps. 127:2, He gives to His **b**
Matt. 3:17; 17:5, This is My **b** Son
Eph. 1:6, bestowed on us in the **B**
5:1, be imitators of God, as **b** children
Col. 1:13, kingdom of His **b** Son
2 Tim. 1:2, to Timothy, my **b** son
Philem. 16, more than a slave, a **b** brother
Jude 1, **b** in God the Father
Deut. 33:12; Jer. 12:7; Mark 1:11; 9:7; Luke 3:22; Rom. 11:28; 12:19; 16:9; 1 Cor. 10:14; 2 Cor. 7:1; 12:19; Phil. 4:1; Col. 4:9; 1 Pet. 2:11; 2 Pet. 1:17
BELOW—*beneath* Gen. 1:9; Deut. 4:39; Prov. 15:24; Jer. 31:37; John 8:23
BELT—*girdle* Mark 1:6, John ... a leather **b**
Acts 21:11, took Paul's **b** and bound his own feet
1 Sam. 18:4; 2 Sam. 18:11; 20:8; Ps. 109:19; Prov. 31:24; Is. 3:24; 5:27; 11:5; Ezek. 23:15; Matt. 3:4
BEND—*bow* Ps. 11:2, the wicked **b** the bow
BENEFACTOR Luke 22:25, those ... called **B-s**
BENEFIT—*profit, blessing* Ps. 103:2, forget none of His **b-s**
Ps. 116:12, For all His **b-s** toward me
1 Tim. 6:2, those who partake of the **b**
2 Chr. 32:25; Is. 65:8; Rom. 3:1; 1 Tim. 6:2
BEREAVE—*deprive* Gen. 27:45; 42:36; Lev. 26:22; Jer. 15:7; Ezek. 5:17; 36:12
BESIDE Ps. 23:2, He leads me **b** quiet waters
Is. 43:11, there is no saviour **b-s** Me
44:6, there is no God **b-s** Me
Matt. 13:4, *seeds* fell **b** the road
2 Cor. 5:13, if we are **b** ourselves, it is for God
Deut. 11:30; Ruth 2:14; 2 Kin. 21:16; Is. 32:20
BESIEGE Deut. 20:19; 2 Sam. 11:1; 1 Kin. 16:17; Is. 1:8; Ezek. 4:3; 6:12
BEST Ps. 39:5, man at his **b** is a mere breath
Luke 15:22, bring out the **b** robe
Gen. 43:11; 1 Sam. 15:9,15; 2 Sam. 18:4
BESTOW—*grant* Ex. 32:29, He may **b** a blessing upon you
1 Chr. 29:25, **b-ed** on him royal majesty
1 Cor. 12:23, we **b** more abundant honor
1 John 3:1, love the Father has **b-ed** on us
BETRAY Matt. 27:4, I have sinned by **b-ing**
Mark 14:11, he *began* seeking how to **b** Him
Luke 22:21, the hand of the one **b-ing** Me
1 Cor. 11:23, the night ... He was **b-ed**
Is. 16:3; Matt. 24:10; 26:16; Mark 14:18; Luke 22:22; John 6:64; 21:20
BETROTH Hos. 2:19,20, I will **b** you to Me
Jer. 2:2; Matt. 1:18; 2 Cor. 11:2

BETTER 1 Sam. 15:22, to obey is **b** than sacrifice
Ps. 63:3, Thy lovingkindness is **b** than life
Heb. 11:16, they desire a **b** country
2 Pet. 2:21, **b** for them not to have known the way
1 Kin. 19:4; Eccles. 2:24; 4:9; 7:10; Song 1:2; Heb. 1:4
BEWARE Deut. 8:11, **B**, lest you forget the LORD
Deut. 15:9, **B**, lest there is a base thought
Matt. 6:1, **B** of practicing your righteousness
10:17, But **b** of men
16:6, **b** of the leaven of the Pharisees
Mark 12:38, **B** of the scribes
Luke 12:15, **B**, and be on your guard against ... greed
Ex. 19:12; Job 36:18; Mark 8:15; Luke 12:1; 20:46; Phil. 3:2
BEWITCHED Gal. 3:1, You foolish Galatians, who has **b**
BEYOND 2 Cor. 8:3, **b** their ability
Gal. 1:13, persecute the church of God **b** measure
Gen. 35:21; Deut. 3:20; John 3:26; Acts 7:43
BIER 2 Sam. 3:31, David walked behind the **b**
BILLOWS—*waves* Jon. 2:3, **b** passed over me
BIND—*wrap* Num. 30:2, an oath to **b** himself
Prov. 6:21, **B** them continually on your heart
Is. 61:1, **b** up the brokenhearted
Matt. 16:19, **b** on earth shall be bound in heaven
Job 38:31; Matt. 12:29; 18:18; Mark 3:27
BIRD—*fowl, swallow* Lev. 20:25, unclean **b**
Ps. 84:3, **b** also has found a house
124:7, Our soul has escaped as a **b**
Matt. 6:26, Look at the **b-s** of the air
8:20, **b-s** of the air *have* nests
Gen. 1:20; 6:7; 2 Sam. 21:10; Ps. 8:8; 11:1; Prov. 1:17; Eccles. 10:20; Jer. 9:10; 12:9; Hos. 9:8; Luke 9:58; Rev. 19:17
BIRTH Eccles. 7:1, better than the day of **b**
Matt. 1:18, **b** of Jesus Christ was
John 9:1, a man blind from **b**
Gen. 38:27; Is. 66:9; Luke 1:14
BIRTHRIGHT Gen. 25:31, First sell me your **b**
Gen. 27:36, Jacob ... took away my **b**
Heb. 12:16, sold his own **b** for a single meal
BIT (n.) Ps. 32:9; James 3:3
BITE Prov. 23:32; Eccles. 10:8; Amos 5:19; 9:3; Mic. 3:5; Gal. 5:15
BITTER Ex. 1:14, **b** with hard labor
Ex. 12:8, unleavened bread and **b** herbs
15:23, waters of Marah ... were **b**
2 Kin. 14:26, affliction of Israel ... was very **b**
Is. 24:9, Strong drink is **b** to those who drink
Matt. 26:75, went out and wept **b-ly**
Job 21:25; Is. 5:20; Luke 22:62
BITTERNESS—*gall* Job 10:1, **b** of my soul
Prov. 14:10; 17:25, heart knows its own **b**
Eph. 4:31, Let all **b** and wrath ... be put away
Heb. 12:15, no root of **b**
1 Sam. 15:32; Is. 38:15; Lam. 3:19; Rom. 3:14
BLACK Matt. 5:36, make one hair **b** or white
Jude 13, for whom the **b** darkness has been reserved
Rev. 6:5, behold a **b** horse
BLADE Judg. 3:22, fat closed over the **b**
Mark 4:28, first the **b**, then the head
BLAMELESS Ps. 119:80, May my heart be **b**
Prov. 11:20, **b** in their walk are His delight
Acts 24:16, maintain always a **b** conscience
1 Cor. 1:8, **b** in the day of our Lord Jesus Christ
Eph. 1:4, holy and **b** before Him
2 Sam. 22:26; Ps. 119:1; Phil. 1:10; 2:15; 3:6; Jude 24; Rev. 14:5
BLASPHEME—*spoke* Is. 52:5, My name is continually **b-d**
Matt. 9:3, This *fellow* **b-s**
26:65, He has **b-d**
Mark 3:29, **b-s** against the Holy Spirit
2 Sam. 12:14; Acts 26:11; Rom. 2:24; 1 Tim. 1:20; James 2:7
BLASPHEMY Matt. 12:31, **b** against the Spirit
Matt. 26:65, you have now heard the **b**
Mark 3:28, whatever **b-es** they utter
Rev. 2:9, the **b** by those who say they are Jews
13:5, arrogant words and **b-es**
Mark 14:64; Luke 5:21; John 10:33
BLEMISH—*spot* Heb. 9:14, offered Himself without **b**
Num. 19:2; Song 4:7; Ezek. 43:22; 45:18; 46:4
BLEND 2 Chr. 16:14, **b-ed** by the perfumers' art
BLESS—*happy* Josh. 17:14, LORD has ... **b-ed**
Ps. 144:15, **b-ed** are the people whose God is the LORD
Prov. 3:13, **b-ed** is the man who finds wisdom
10:7, memory of the righteous is **b-ed**
Luke 6:28, **b** those who curse you
Acts 20:35, more **b-ed** to give than to receive
Titus 2:13, looking for **b-ed** hope
James 3:9, we **b** *our* Lord and Father
Rev. 14:13, Write, **B-ed** are the dead
Gen. 22:17; Deut. 28:3-6; 33:29; Judg. 5:2; 1 Chr. 4:10; Ps. 127:5; Prov. 28:14; Is. 32:20; 65:16; Hag. 2:19; Mal. 3:15; John 13:17; Rom. 12:14; 2 Cor. 11:31; Titus 2:13; James 5:11; 1 Pet. 3:14; 4:14
BLESSING—*benefit* Gen. 39:5, LORD's **b** was upon all
Prov. 10:22, **b** of the LORD that makes rich
28:20, faithful man will abound with **b-s**
Mal. 3:10, pour out for you a **b**
Rom. 15:29, the fulness of the **b** of Christ
1 Cor. 10:16, Is not the cup of **b**
Gen. 27:35; Deut. 11:26; 23:5; Neh. 13:2; Job 29:13; Mal. 2:2; 2 Cor. 1:15; James 3:10; Rev. 5:12
BLIND Ex. 23:8, bribe **b-s** the clear-sighted
Matt. 11:5, *the* B RECEIVE SIGHT
2 Cor. 4:4, **b-ed** the minds of the unbelieving
1 John 2:11, darkness has **b-ed** his eyes
Deut. 16:19; 1 Sam. 12:3
BLINDNESS Deut. 28:28; 2 Kin. 6:18; Zech. 12:4
BLOOD Gen. 9:6, Whoever sheds man's **b**, By man his **b**
Ps. 72:14, their **b** will be precious in his sight
Ezek. 9:9, the land is filled with **b**
Matt. 16:17, because flesh and **b** did not reveal
27:4, by betraying innocent **b**
Luke 22:20, new covenant in My **b**
22:44, His sweat became like drops of **b**
Acts 20:28, He purchased with His own **b**
21:25, abstain from meat ... and from **b**
Rom. 3:25, a propitiation in His **b**
5:9, justified by His **b**
1 Cor. 10:16, sharing in the **b** of Christ
11:27, guilty of the body ... **b** of the Lord
15:50, flesh and **b** cannot inherit the kingdom
Eph. 1:7, redemption through His **b**
Heb. 9:22, shedding of **b** there is no forgiveness
1 Pet. 1:19, the **b** of Christ
Rev. 12:11, the **b** of the Lamb
Gen. 9:4; Ex. 12:22; Lev. 3:17; Josh. 2:19; 1 Kin. 2:32; Is. 9:5; Ezek. 18:13; Matt. 27:25; Mark 14:24; John 1:13; 6:54,55,56; Acts 15:20; 1 Cor. 11:25; Heb. 10:29; Rev. 7:14
BLOSSOM Gen. 40:10; Eccles. 12:5; Is. 17:11; 27:6; 35:1; Hos. 14:5; Hab. 3:17
BLOT—*erase* Ex. 32:32, please **b** me from Thy book
Deut. 9:14, **b** out their name from heaven
Ps. 51:1, Thy compassion **b** out my transgressions
51:9, **b** out all my iniquities
69:28, May they be **b-ed** out of the book of life
Deut. 25:19; 29:20; 2 Kin. 14:27; Neh. 4:5; Ps. 109:13,14; Prov. 6:33; Jer. 18:23
BLOWS Prov. 19:29, **b** for the back of fools

BOAST—*glory, rejoice, talk* Ps. 34:2, soul . . . make its **b**
Ps. 49:6, **b** in the abundance of their riches
Prov. 27:1, do not **b** about tomorrow
Rom. 2:23, You who **b** in the Law
James 4:16, all such **b-ing** is evil
1 Sam. 2:3; 1 Kin. 20:11; 2 Chr. 25:19; Ps. 5:5; 75:4; Prov. 20:14; Rom. 2:17; 3:27; 1 Cor. 5:6; 2 Cor. 11:16; Gal. 5:26; Eph. 2:9; James 3:5; 4:16
BOAT Is. 33:21; John 6:22; Acts 27:16; 27:30
BODILY Luke 3:22, Holy Spirit descended . . . in **b** form
Col. 2:9, fulness of Deity dwells in **b** form
1 Tim. 4:8, **b** discipline is only little profit
BODY—*corpse, flesh* Matt. 6:22, whole **b** . . . full of light
Mark 5:29, she felt in her **b** that she was healed
6:29, his **b** and laid it in a tomb
Luke 12:22, do not be anxious . . . for your **b**
Acts 19:12, carried from his **b** to the sick
Rom. 6:6, that our **b** of sin might be done away
12:1, present your **b-es** a living . . . sacrifice
12:4, many members in one **b**
12:5, we . . . are one **b** in Christ
1 Cor. 9:27, but I buffet my **b**
13:3, if I deliver my **b** to be burned
2 Cor. 5:8, prefer to be absent from the **b**
Gal. 6:17, I bear on my **b** the brand-marks of Jesus
1 Pet. 2:24, bore our sins in His **b**
Gen. 47:18; Eccles. 12:12; Matt. 5:29; 6:23; Luke 11:34; 17:37; John 2:21; Rom. 7:24; 1 Cor. 12:14; 2 Cor. 12:2; Phil. 3:21
BODYGUARD—*guard* Gen. 40:4; Jer. 39:9
BOISTEROUS—*clamor*
Prov. 9:13, woman of folly is **b**
BOLD Prov. 28:1, righteous are **b** as a lion
Acts 13:46, Paul and Barnabas spoke out **b-ly**
Ex. 14:8; Num. 33:3; Rom. 10:20; 2 Cor. 10:2; 10:12
BOLDNESS—*confidence* Acts 4:31, speak . . . with **b**
Eph. 3:12, we have **b** and confident access
Phil. 1:20, with all **b**, Christ . . . be exalted
BOND—*cord* Hos. 11:4, with **b-s** of love
Eph. 4:3, in the **b** of peace
Col. 3:14, perfect **b** of unity
Ezek. 20:37; Luke 13:16; Jude 6
BOND-SERVANT—*servant* Luke 2:29, let Thy **b** depart
Rom. 1:1, Paul, a **b** of Christ Jesus
Phil. 1:1, Paul and Timothy, **b-s** of Christ
Titus 1:1; James 1:1; 2 Pet. 1:1
BONE Ezek. 37:7, **b-s** came together, **b** to its **b**
Luke 24:39, spirit does not have flesh and **b-s**
John 19:36, NOT A B OF HIM SHALL BE BROKEN
Gen. 2:23; Ex. 12:46; Job 20:11; Ps. 51:8; Prov. 12:4; Matt. 23:27
BOOK Is. 34:16, Seek from the **b** of the LORD
Mal. 3:16, **b** of remembrance
John 21:25, world itself would not contain the **b-s**
Phil. 4:3, names are in the **b** of life
Ex. 17:14; Ezra 4:15; Job 19:23; Luke 4:17; Acts 19:19; 1 Tim. 4:13; Rev. 3:5; 13:8; 17:8; 20:12; 21:27; 22:19
BOOTHS Gen. 33:17; Lev. 23:42,43; Neh. 8:14
BOOTY—*plunder* Num. 31:32; Is. 53:12; Jer. 38:2; 49:32
BORDER Gen. 47:21, one end of Egypt's **b** to the other
Ex. 34:24, drive out nations . . . . . . **b-s**
Jer. 15:13, . . . within all your **b-s**
50:26, Come to her from the farthest **b**
Gen. 23:17; Num. 21:13; 34:3; 35:26; Deut. 3:17; Josh. 12:5; 2 Kin. 3:21; 1 Chr. 4:10; Ps. 147:14; Is. 19:19; 60:18; Ezek. 11:10
BORE—*bear, carry, pierce, yield*
Ex. 19:4, how I **b** you on eagles' wings
Is. 53:4, our griefs He Himself **b**
53:12, He Himself **b** the sin of many
1 Pet. 2:24, He Himself **b** our sins
Num. 17:8; 2 Kin. 12:9; Jer. 31:19
BORN—*begotten, forth* Job 5:7, man is **b** for trouble
Job 14:1, Man, who is **b** of woman
Is. 9:6, For a child will be **b** to us
66:8, Can a land be **b** in one day
John 1:13, who were **b** not of blood
3:3, unless one is **b** again
3:6,8, **b** of the Spirit
1 Cor. 15:8, one untimely **b**
1 Pet. 1:3, **b** again to a living hope
1 John 4:7, every one who loves is **b** of God
5:4, whatever is **b** of God overcomes the world
Job 3:3; 15:14; 25:4; Ps. 87:4; 90:2; Prov. 17:17; Matt. 11:11; 1 Pet. 1:23; 1 John 5:1
BORNE Is. 46:3, been **b** by Me from birth
Job 34:31; Lam. 5:7; Matt. 20:12
BORROW Deut. 28:12, you shall not **b**
Prov. 22:7, **b-er** *becomes* the lender's slave
Ex. 22:14; Deut. 15:6; 2 Kin. 4:3; Ps. 37:21; Matt. 5:42
BOSOM—*breast* Prov. 6:27, fire in his **b**
Is. 40:11, carry *them* in His **b**
Luke 16:22, carried . . . to Abraham's **b**
John 1:18, in the **b** of the Father
Ex. 4:6; Job 31:33; Ps. 35:13
BOTHER—*trouble* Matt. 26:10, do you **b** the woman
BOTTLE—*jug, wineskin* Judg. 4:19; Ps. 56:8
BOUGH—*branch* Ps. 80:10, cedars of God with its **b-s**
Gen. 49:22; Lev. 23:40; Deut. 24:20; Ps. 80:10; Is. 17:6; Ezek. 31:6
BOUGHT Luke 14:18, I have **b** a piece of land
1 Cor. 6:20, been **b** with a price
7:23, You were **b** with a price
2 Pet. 2:1, denying the Master who **b** them
BOUND—*gird, yoke* Prov. 22:15, Foolishness is **b** up in
Matt. 16:19, **b** in heaven
Acts 20:22, **b** in spirit, I am on my way to Jerusalem
1 Cor. 7:27, Are you **b** to a wife
2 Cor. 6:14, Do not be **b** together
Gen. 44:30; Mark 5:4
BOUNDARY Prov. 8:29, He set for the sea its **b**
BOUNTIFUL—*generous*
Ps. 13:6, He has dealt **b-ly** with me
116:7, the LORD has dealt **b-ly** with you
2 Cor. 9:6, he who sows **b-ly** . . . reap **b-ly**
Ps. 119:17; 2 Cor. 9:5
BOUNTY 1 Kin. 10:13, according to his royal **b**
BOW—*bend, worship* Is. 66:23, to **b** down
1 Sam. 2:36; Ps. 10:10; Is. 60:14
BOWL—*dish, pitcher* Eccles. 12:6, golden **b** is crushed
Matt. 26:23, who dipped his hand in the **b**
Num. 7:25; 1 Kin. 17:12; Amos 6:6; Zech. 4:2; Mark 14:20
BOY—*child* Is. 11:6, a little **b** will lead them
Joel 3:3, Traded a **b** for a harlot
Gen. 25:27; Zech. 8:5
BRACELET Gen. 24:22; 24:30; 24:47; Ex. 35:22; Num. 31:50; 2 Sam. 1:10; Is. 3:19; Ezek. 16:11; 23:42
BRAMBLE—*briar* Judg. 9:14, trees said to the **b**
Judg. 9:15, fire come out from the **b**
BRANCH—*bough* Jer. 23:5, raise up for David a righteous **B**
Matt. 13:32, THE BIRDS . . . NEST IN ITS B-ES
21:8, others were cutting **b-es**
John 15:2, every **b** that bears fruit
15:4, **b** cannot bear fruit of itself
15:5, I am the vine, you are the **b-es**
Judg. 9:48; Ezek. 31:3; Mark 11:8; Luke 13:19; John 12:13; 15:6; Rom. 11:16
BRAND—*torch* Zech. 3:2; 1 Tim. 4:2

BRAY Job 6:5, wild donkey **b** over *his* grass
BREACH Judg. 21:15, LORD had made a **b** in ... Israel
Job 16:14, breaks through me with **b** after **b**
Gen. 38:29; Ex. 22:9; 1 Kin. 11:27; Neh. 4:7; 6:1; Ps. 60:2; 106:23; Is. 22:9; 30:13; 58:12; Amos 4:3; 9:11
BREAD—*food* Ex. 16:4, I will rain **b** from heaven
Deut. 8:3, man does not live by **b** alone
Job 22:7, you have withheld **b**
Ps. 132:15, satisfy her needy with **b**
Prov. 31:27, does not eat the **b** of idleness
Eccles. 11:1, Cast your **b** on the surface of the waters
Is. 55:2, spend money for what is not **b**
55:10, seed to the sower and **b** to the eater
Matt. 4:3, command these stones become **b**
6:11, Give us this day our daily **b**
Mark 7:27, take the children's **b**
Acts 2:42, the breaking of **b**
20:7, gathered together to break **b**
Ex. 23:25; Josh. 9:5; Judg. 7:13; 1 Kin. 17:6; Job 33:20; Prov. 9:17; 12:11; Matt. 4:4; Luke 4:3,4; 24:35; Acts 27:35; 2 Thess. 3:8
BREAK—*broke, profane* 2 Chr. 32:1, to **b** into them
Is. 42:3, reed He will not **b**
Luke 5:6, their nets began to **b**
24:30, He took the bread ... and **b-ing** it
1 Cor. 10:16, bread which we **b** a sharing in ... Christ
Job 19:10; Jer. 4:3; Hos. 10:12; Matt. 12:5,20; 14:19; Acts 21:13
BREASTPIECE Ex. 25:7; 28:4,15,22,23; 35:9,27; 39:8; Lev. 8:8
BREASTPLATE Is. 59:17, put on righteousness like a **b**
Eph. 6:14, PUT ON THE B OF RIGHTEOUSNESS
1 Thess. 5:8, put on the **b** of faith and love
Neh. 4:16; Rev. 9:9,17
BREATH—*spirit, wind* Gen. 2:7, **b** of life
Job 7:16, my days are *but* a **b**
12:10, the **b** of all mankind
27:3, **b** of God is in my nostrils
Ps. 150:6, Let everything that has **b** praise the LORD
Acts 17:25, He Himself gives to all life and **b**
Gen. 6:17; 7:15; Eccles. 3:21; Is. 2:22; Ezek. 37:5,10
BREATHE Gen. 2:7, **b-d** into his nostrils the breath
Ezek. 37:9, **b** on these slain
Acts 9:1, **b-ing** threats and murder
Deut. 20:16; Josh. 10:40; 11:11,14; Ps. 27:12; John 20:22
BRETHREN—*brother* Ps. 22:22, tell of Thy name to my **b**
Is. 66:20, all your **b** from all the nations
1 Cor. 14:39, my **b**, desire earnestly to prophesy
2 Cor. 11:26, dangers among false **b**
Gal. 1:2, all the **b** who are with me
2:4, because of false **b**
Eph. 6:23, Peace be to the **b**
Col. 1:2, saints and faithful **b** in Christ
1 Thess. 4:9, love of the **b**
1 Pet. 1:22, sincere love of the **b**
1 John 3:14, because we love the **b**
Mic. 5:3; Rom. 1:13; 7:1; 8:12; Heb. 13:1
BRIAR—*thistle* Luke 6:44, nor ... pick grapes from a **b**
BRIBE Ex. 23:8, not take a **b**, for a **b** blinds
Is. 1:23, Every one loves a **b**
5:23, justify the wicked for a **b**
Deut. 10:17; 27:25; 1 Sam. 8:3; 12:3; Ps. 26:10; Is. 33:15; Mic. 7:3
BRICK Gen. 11:3; Ex. 1:14; 5:7; Is. 9:10; 65:3
BRIDE Rev. 21:2, as a **b** adorned for her husband
21:9, the **b**, the wife of the Lamb
22:17, the Spirit and the **b** say, Come
Is. 49:18; 61:10; 62:5; Jer. 2:32; 7:34; 16:9; 25:10; 33:11; Joel 2:16; John 3:29; Rev. 18:23
BRIDEGROOM Jer. 7:34; 16:9; 25:10; 33:11
Matt. 25:1, virgins ... went out to meet the **b**
John 3:29, He who has the bride is the **b**
Rev. 18:23, voice of the **b**
Ex. 4:25; Ps. 19:5; Is. 61:10; 62:5; Joel 2:16; Matt. 9:15; Mark 2:19; John 2:9
BRIDLE—*guard* James 1:26, not **b** his tongue
2 Kin. 19:28; Prov. 26:3; Is. 37:29
BRIGHT Rev. 22:16, **b** morning star
Lev. 13:2; Job 37:21; Matt. 17:5
BRIGHTNESS—*radiance* Is. 60:3, kings to the **b** of your
Is. 62:1, righteousness goes forth like **b**
BRIMSTONE Gen. 19:24; Is. 30:33; Rev. 9:17; 14:10; 19:20
BRISTLE Job 4:15, hair ... **b-d** up
BROAD—*wide* Ps. 119:96, commandment is exceedingly **b**
Matt. 7:13, way is **b** that leads to destruction
1 Chr. 4:40; Ps. 104:25; Matt. 23:5
BROILED Luke 24:42, gave Him a piece of **b** fish
BROKE—*break* John 19:32, **b** the legs of the first man
Eph. 2:14, **b** down the barrier
1 Sam. 4:18; 2 Kin. 23:14; 2 Chr. 34:4; Matt. 15:36; 26:26; Mark 6:41
BROKEN—*loose, void* Job 17:1, My spirit is **b**
Ps. 51:17, a **b** spirit; A **b** and a contrite heart
69:20, Reproach has **b** my heart
119:126, have **b** Thy law
Eccles. 12:6, the silver cord is **b**
Jer. 2:13, **B** cisterns
John 10:35, Scripture cannot be **b**
19:36, NOT A BONE OF HIM SHALL BE B
BROKENHEARTED
Ps. 34:18, Lord is near to the **b**
BRONZE Deut. 28:23; 2 Sam. 22:35; Ezra 8:27; Jer. 15:12
BROOD Matt. 3:7, You **b** of vipers, who warned you
Luke 13:34, a hen *gathers* her **b**
BROOK 1 Sam. 17:40; Ps. 110:7
Ps. 42:1, deer pants for the water **b-s**
BROTHER—*brethren* Gen. 4:9, Am I my **b-'s** keeper
Prov. 18:24, friend who sticks closer than a **b**
Matt. 10:21, **b** will deliver up **b** to death
23:8, you are all **b-s**
Luke 18:29, no one who has left ... **b-s**
John 7:5, not even His **b-s** were
1 Cor. 6:6, **b** goes to law with **b**
Gen. 42:8; Prov. 17:17; 18:9,19; 19:7; Eccles. 4:8; Matt. 5:23; Mark 3:35; 10:29; 2 Thess. 3:15
BROTHERHOOD Amos 1:9, covenant of **b**
BROTHERLY Rom. 12:10, in **b** love
2 Pet. 1:7, *your* **b** kindness
BROUGHT—*escape* Matt. 10:18, shall ... be **b** before governors
BROW Luke 4:29, led Him to the **b** of the hill
BRUISE—*batter, crush* Gen. 3:15, shall **b** you
Is. 1:6, **b-s**, welts, and raw wounds
42:3, A **b-d** reed He will not break
BRUTAL—*senseless, stupid, fierce* Ezek. 21:31; 2 Tim. 3:3
BUCKET Num. 24:7, flow from his **b-s**
Is. 40:15, nations are like a drop from a **b**
BUD—*sprout* Num. 17:8; Is. 18:5
BUFFET—*beat* 2 Cor. 12:7, to **b** me
BUGLE—*trumpet* 1 Cor. 14:8, **b** produces an ... sound
BUILD 1 Chr. 17:12, He shall **b** for Me a house
Ps. 127:1, Unless the LORD **b-s** the house
Eccles. 3:3, a time to **b** up
1 Cor. 3:12, if any man **b-s** upon the foundation
2 Chr. 6:9; Luke 14:30; Acts 20:32; Rom. 15:20
BUILDER—*maker* Ps. 118:22, the **b-s** rejected
Heb. 11:10, whose architect and **b** is God
1 Pet. 2:7, STONE WHICH THE B-S REJECTED
1 Kin. 5:18; Ezra 3:10; Matt. 21:42; Mark 12:10; Luke 20:17; Acts 4:11

BUILDING 1 Cor. 3:9, you are ... God's **b**
2 Cor. 5:1, we have a **b** from God
Eph. 2:21, **b**, being fitted together
BUILT Eccles. 2:4, I **b** houses for myself
Matt. 7:24, **b** his house upon the rock
Eph. 2:22, **b** together into a dwelling of God
BULL Lev. 4:3, a **b** without defect
BULRUSHES Is. 19:7, **b** by the Nile
BUNDLE Gen. 42:35; Acts 28:3
1 Sam. 25:29, bound in the **b** of living
Matt. 13:30, bind them in **b-s** to burn
BURDEN—*load* Ps. 55:22, Cast your **b** upon the LORD
Matt. 20:12, borne the **b** and ... heat of the day
Luke 11:46, weigh men down with **b-s** hard to bear
Gal. 6:2, Bear one another's **b-s**
Acts 15:28; 2 Cor. 11:9; 12:16; 1 Thess. 2:9
BURIAL John 19:40, **b** custom of the Jews
Gen. 23:4; Eccles. 6:3; Jer. 22:19; Matt. 26:12
BURN—*kindle* Ex. 3:2, bush was **b-ing** with fire
Ps. 39:3, While I was musing the fire **b-ed**
Prov. 26:23, **b-ing** lips and a wicked heart
Is. 9:18, wickedness **b-s** like a fire
42:3, dimly **b-ing** wick He will not
Luke 3:17, He will **b** up the chaff
24:32, our hearts **b-ing** within us
John 5:35, He was the lamp that was **b-ing**
1 Cor. 13:3, deliver my body to be **b-ed**
Rev. 18:8, she will be **b-ed** up with fire
Gen. 30:2; Ex. 32:12,19; Ps. 11:6; Is. 33:14; Mal. 4:1; Matt. 13:30; Rom. 12:20; Heb. 6:8; Rev. 4:5; 19:20
BURNT OFFERING Gen. 22:7; Lev. 1:4; 6:9; Is. 61:8
Ps. 40:6, **B** and sin offering Thou hast not required
Jer. 6:20, **b-s** are not acceptable
Hos. 6:6, knowledge of God rather than **b-s**
Mark 12:33, more than all **b-s** and sacrifices
BURST—*break* Job 32:19; Matt. 9:17; Mark 2:22; Luke 5:37
BURY Rom. 6:4, **b-ed** with Him through baptism
1 Cor. 15:4, and that he was **b-ed**
Gen. 23:4; 47:29; Matt. 8:21,22; 14:12; Luke 9:59,60; Acts 8:2; Col. 2:12
BUSHEL—*ephah* Amos 8:5, To make the **b** smaller
BUSINESS—*matter* Ps. 107:23, Who do **b** on great waters
1 Thess. 4:11, attend to your own **b**
James 4:13, engage in **b** and make a profit
Gen. 24:33; Josh. 2:14; Matt. 22:5; Acts 19:25
BUSYBODIES—*meddler* 2 Thess. 3:11, acting like **b**
1 Tim. 5:13, also gossips and **b**
BUTTER—*curds* Job 29:6; Prov. 30:33
Ps. 55:21, His speech was smoother than **b**
BUY Is. 55:1, **b** and eat ... **b** wine and milk
Matt. 13:44, sells all that he has and **b-s** that field
Rev. 3:18, **b** from Me gold refined by fire
13:17, no one should be able to **b** or to sell
Gen. 42:2; 47:19; Lev. 22:11; Ruth 4:4; Prov. 23:23; Matt. 25:9; John 4:8; Rev. 18:11
BUYER Is. 24:2; Ezek. 7:12
Prov. 20:14, Bad, bad, says the **b**
BYWORD—*taunt* Job 30:9
1 Kin. 9:7, Israel will become ... a **b** among all peoples
2 Chr. 7:20, a **b** among all peoples
Job 17:6, a **b** of the people
Ps. 44:14, **b** among the nations

C

CAGE Jer. 5:27, a **c** full of birds
CAKE Gen. 18:6; 1 Kin. 17:13; 2 Kin. 20:7
CALAMITY—*destruction* Job 31:23, **c** from God is a terror
Prov. 1:27, **c** comes on like a whirlwind
2 Sam. 22:19; 24:16; 1 Chr. 21:15; Job 6:30; 21:17; 31:3; Ps. 18:18; Prov. 24:16; 27:10; Jon. 3:10; 4:2
CALCULATE—*count* Is. 40:12, **c-d** the dust of the earth
Luke 14:28, sit down and **c** the cost
CALF Luke 15:23, bring the fattened **c**
Heb. 9:12, blood of goats and **c-ves**
Gen. 18:7; Is. 11:6; Rev. 4:7
CALL—*address* Gen. 4:26, to **c** upon the name
Ps. 4:1, Answer me when I **c**
Is. 7:14, **c** His name Immanuel
Matt. 9:13, not come to **c** *the* righteous
Luke 6:46, why do you **c** Me, Lord, Lord
John 13:13, **c** Me Teacher, and Lord
1 Cor. 1:26, consider your **c**, brethren
1 Thess. 4:7, God has not **c-ed** us for ... impurity
Deut. 4:26; Ruth 1:20; Ps. 18:3; Prov. 8:1; Is. 5:20; Jer. 3:19
CALLING—*summoning* Is. 1:13, the **c** of assemblies
Rom. 11:29, gifts and the **c** of God
2 Tim. 1:9, called us with a holy **c**
Heb. 3:1, partakers of a heavenly **c**
CALM—*still* Is. 7:4, be **c**, have no fear
Jon. 1:11, the sea may become **c**
Matt. 8:26, it became perfectly **c**
Acts 19:36, you ought to keep **c** ... do nothing rash
CAMEL Gen. 24:64; Mark 1:6
Matt. 3:4, John ... a garment of **c-'s** hair
19:24, easier for a **c** ... eye of a needle
23:24, out a gnat and swallow a **c**
CAMP—*settle* Ex. 14:19, before the **c**
Deut. 23:14, God walks ... your **c**
Gen. 32:2; Num. 31:19; Ps. 69:25; Is. 29:3; Zech. 9:8; Rev. 20:9
CANCEL—*blot, erase* Is. 28:18; Col. 2:14
CAPTIVE Luke 4:18, RELEASE TO THE **C**-S
Eph. 4:8, LED **C** A HOST OF **C**-S
Ps. 68:18; Jer. 13:17; Col. 2:8
CAPTIVITY Is. 46:2, have themselves gone into **c**
CAPTURE Job 5:13, **c-s** the wise
CARCASS—*corpse* Gen. 15:11; Judg. 14:8
CARE—*concern, worry*
Gen. 50:24, God ... take **c** of you
Ps. 142:4, No one **c-s** for my soul
Ezek. 34:12, I will **c** for My sheep
Luke 10:34, to an inn, and took **c** of him
1 Tim. 3:5, take **c** of the church
1 Pet. 5:7, because He **c-s** for you
Ps. 8:4; Mark 4:38; 1 Cor. 12:25
CAREFUL—*guard, diligent* Luke 15:8
Prov. 23:1, Consider **c-ly** what is before you
Eph. 5:15, be **c** how you walk
CARELESS—*idle* Matt. 12:36, every **c** word
CARGO—*merchandise* Rev. 18:12, **c-es** of gold
CAROUSE Rom. 13:13, not in **c-ing** and drunkenness
CARPENTER—*craftsmen* 2 Sam. 5:11; 2 Kin. 22:6; Matt. 13:55; Mark 6:3
CARRIED—*wrought* Is. 53:4, our sorrows He **c**
Matt. 8:17, **c** away our diseases
Luke 16:22, was **c** away by the angels
Heb. 13:9, not be **c** away by ... teachings
1 Pet. 4:3, **c** out the desire of the Gentiles
CARRY—*bear, wear* Luke 10:4, **c** no purse, no bag
23:26, placed on him the cross to **c**
2 Cor. 4:10, **c-ing** about in the body the dying of Jesus
Ex. 23:1; Num. 10:17; 11:14; Deut. 1:31; 1 Sam. 2:28; Ps. 126:6; Is. 40:11; 52:11; 63:9; Mark 14:13
CART 1 Sam. 6:8, ark of the LORD ... on the **c**
1 Sam. 6:7,14; Is. 5:18; 28:28
CASE—*matter* Job 19:28; 37:19
Deut. 17:8, any **c** is too difficult for you
Mic. 6:2, the LORD has a **c** against His people
CASSIA Ex. 30:24; Ps. 45:8; Ezek. 27:19

CAST—*drive, throw, thrust*
Ps. 51:11, Do not **c** me away
Eccles. 11:1, **C** your bread on the ... waters
Luke 4:29, **c** Him out of the city
12:49, **c** fire upon the earth
John 6:37, will certainly not **c** out
1 Pet. 5:7, **c-ing** all your anxiety upon Him
Josh. 18:10; Job 6:27; Mark 15:32
CATCH—*trap* Ps. 10:9; Prov. 6:25; Song 2:15; Luke 5:10
CATTLE—*herd* Ps. 50:10, **c** on a thousand hills
Ex. 12:29; 20:10; Lev. 22:19; Num. 31:28; Ps. 104:14; Hab. 3:17
CAUGHT—*seized* 2 Cor. 12:4, was **c** up into Paradise
Gal. 6:1, if a man is **c** in any trespass
Gen. 22:13; Ex. 22:7; Judg. 15:4; John 21:3
CAUSE—*purpose* Gen. 2:24, For this **c** a man shall leave
Ps. 67:1, **c** His face to shine upon us
Prov. 3:30, Do not contend ... without **c**
Matt. 19:5, THIS C A MAN SHALL LEAVE
John 15:25, HATED ME WITHOUT A C
Ps. 112:5; Is. 45:7; Rom. 16:17; 1 Cor. 3:6
CAVE—*shelter* 1 Kin. 18:4; Zeph. 2:6; John 11:38; Heb. 11:38
CEASE Ex. 23:12, day you shall **c** *from labor*
Ps. 46:9, He makes wars to **c**
Luke 7:45, not **c-d** to kiss My feet
1 Cor. 13:8, *are* tongues, they will **c**
1 Thess. 5:17, pray without **c-ing**
Gen. 8:22; Deut. 15:11; Ps. 37:8; Prov. 23:4
CEDAR—*fir* 1 Kin. 5:6; 6:15; Job 40:17; Ps. 92:12
CENSER Ezek. 8:11; Rev. 8:3,5
CENSUS—*tax* Luke 2:1, a **c** ... of all the inhabited earth
Acts 5:37, rose up in the days of the **c**
CENT Matt. 5:26, paid up the last **c**
Matt. 10:29, sparrows sold for a **c**
Mark 12:42, two small copper coins ... a **c**
CERTAIN—*sure* 2 Pet. 1:10, make **c** about His calling
CERTIFICATE Matt. 5:31, A C OF DISMISSAL
CHAFF Ps. 1:4; Matt. 3:12
CHAIN—*band* Acts 12:7, **c-s** fell off his hands
Heb. 11:36, also **c-s** and imprisonment
Judg. 16:21; 1 Kin. 6:21; Eccles. 7:26; Mark 5:3; Luke 8:29; Rev. 20:1
CHALCEDONY Rev. 21:19, the third, **c**
CHAMBER—*room* Gen. 43:30; Judg. 3:20,24; 2 Kin. 4:10; Ps. 19:5; Joel 2:16
CHAMPION 1 Sam. 17:4,23
CHANCE—*happen* Eccles. 9:11, for time and **c** overtake
Luke 10:31, by **c** a certain priest
CHANGE—*transform* Ps. 46:2, earth should **c**
Jer. 13:23, the Ethiopian **c** his skin
Mal. 3:6, I, the LORD, do not **c**
1 Cor. 15:51, we shall all be **c-d**
Gen. 35:2; Job 14:14; Prov. 24:21; Dan. 2:21
CHANNEL Job 28:10, hews out **c-s**
CHARCOAL—*coal, soot* John 18:18; 21:9
CHARGE—*accusation, crime* Lev. 8:35, **c** of the LORD
2 Chr. 23:6, keep the **c** of the LORD
Ps. 91:11, give His angels **c** concerning
Matt. 24:45, master put in **c** of his household
Ex. 23:7; Matt. 4:6; 27:37; Acts 25:27; 1 Cor. 9:18; 1 Tim. 5:21; 1 Pet. 5:3
CHARIOT Ps. 20:7, Some boast in **c-s**
Ps. 104:3, makes the clouds his **c**
Acts 8:28, sitting in his **c** ... reading
Gen. 46:29; 2 Kin. 2:11; Ps. 46:9
CHARITY—*alms* Luke 12:33, sell ... give to **c**
CHARM—*favor* Prov. 31:30, **C** is deceitful
CHARMER—*babbler* Ps. 58:5; Eccles. 10:11
CHASE—*drive* Lev. 26:7,8; Deut. 32:30; Job 20:8
CHASTE—*pure* 1 Pet. 3:2, **c** and respectful behavior
CHASTEN—*discipline* Is. 53:5, **c-ing** for our well-being
Ps. 38:1; 94:12

CHATTER—*babbling* 1 Tim. 6:20; 2 Tim. 2:16
CHEAT—*deceive, mislead*
Gen. 31:7, father has **c-ed** me
CHEEK Job 16:10; Is. 50:6; Matt. 5:39
CHEER—*merry* Judg. 9:13; 1 Sam. 15:32; Prov. 15:13
Prov. 15:15, **c-ful** heart *has* a continual feast
2 Cor. 9:7, God loves a **c-ful** giver
James 5:13, Is anyone **c-ful**
CHEESE 1 Sam. 17:18; 2 Sam. 17:29; Job 10:10
CHICK Matt. 23:37, way a hen gathers her **c-s**
CHILD Prov. 22:6, Train up a **c** ... should go
Prov. 23:13, hold back discipline from the **c**
Is. 9:6, a **c** will be born to us
Matt. 1:18, Mary ... with **c** by the Holy Spirit
2:8, make careful search for the **C**
2:9, stood over where the **C** was
2:13,20, take the **C** and His mother
1 Cor. 13:11, When I was a **c**
Gen. 21:8; Jer. 31:20; Matt. 18:2; Mark 5:39; Luke 8:54
CHILDBIRTH Ps. 48:6; Rom. 8:22
CHILDHOOD Eccles. 11:9, during your **c**
2 Tim. 3:15, from **c** you have known
CHILDREN—*babes, immature* Gen. 3:16; 1 Sam. 16:11
Ps. 103:13, father has compassion on *his* **c**
Prov. 31:28, **c** rise up and bless her
Jer. 31:15, Rachel is weeping for her **c**
Ezek. 18:2, **c-'s** teeth are set on edge
Matt. 2:16, slew all the male **c**
2:18, RACHEL WEEPING FOR HER C
10:21, C WILL RISE UP AGAINST PARENTS
18:3, and become like **c**
Is. 3:4; 49:21; Matt. 3:9; 11:16; 19:14; 1 John 2:1; Rev. 2:23
CHOICE—*pleasant* 1 Sam. 9:2, **c** and handsome man
Rom. 9:11, God's purpose according to *His* **c**
1 Thess. 1:4, knowing ... *His* **c** of you
Gen. 23:6; 2 Sam. 10:9; Song 4:16; Acts 15:7; Rom. 11:5,28
CHOKE Matt. 13:22, riches **c** the word
Mark 4:19, **c** the word
Luke 8:14, **c-d** with worries
CHOOSE—*take* Heb. 11:25, **c-ing** ... endure ill treatment
2 Pet. 1:10, calling and **c-ing** you
Ex. 17:9; Deut. 1:13; Josh. 24:15; Is. 7:15
CHOSEN—*elect, beloved, esteemed, loved, choose*
Is. 65:9, My **c** ones shall inherit
Luke 9:35, This is My son, *My* **C** One
Col. 3:12, who have been **c** of God
2 Tim. 2:10, endure all things ... who are **c**
1 Pet. 2:9, you are A C RACE
Deut. 7:6; Ps. 119:30; Is. 42:1; 45:4; Matt. 12:18; Rom. 11:7; 1 Tim. 5:21; 1 Pet. 1:1; 2 John 1
CHRIST—*Messiah, Lord* 2 Thess. 3:5; 2 John 9
Matt. 16:16, Thou art the **C**, the Son
Luke 24:46, the **C** should suffer
Acts 2:36, made Him both Lord and **C**
1 Cor. 1:23, we preach **C** crucified
Phil. 1:21, to live is **C**
Col. 3:4, **C**, who is our life
1 Thess. 4:16, the dead in **C** shall rise
CHRISTIAN Acts 11:26, first called **C-s** in Antioch
Acts 26:28, persuade me to become a **C**
1 Pet. 4:16, if *anyone suffers* as a **C**
CHURCH Matt. 16:18, rock I will build My **c**
Matt. 18:17, tell it to the **c**; refuses to listen ... **c**
Acts 15:4, received by the **c**
1 Cor. 11:18, come together as a **c**
14:35, for a woman to speak in **c**
2 Cor. 11:8, robbed other **c-es**
Eph. 5:23, Christ ... head of the **c**
1 Tim. 3:5, how will he take care of the **c**
Heb. 12:23, general assembly and **c**
CIRCULATE 1 Sam. 2:24, LORD's people **c-ing**

CIRCUMCISE Phil. 3:5, **c-d** the eighth day
Col. 2:11, in Him you were also **c-d**
Gen. 17:10; Deut. 30:6; Luke 1:59
CIRCUMSTANCE—*degree*
James 1:9, humble **c-s**
CISTERN—*dungeon* Eccles. 12:6, wheel at the **c** is crushed
Jer. 2:13, hew for themselves **c-s**, Broken **c-s**
Prov. 5:15; Jer. 38:6
CITIZEN—*free* Eph. 2:19, fellow-**c-s** with the saints
Luke 15:15; Acts 21:39; 22:28
CITY Num. 35:6; Josh. 15:59, **c** of refuge
Ps. 46:4, make glad the **c** of God
107:4, an inhabited **c**
127:1, Unless the LORD guards the **c**
Zech. 8:3, the **C** of Truth
Matt. 2:23, resided in a **c** called Nazareth
4:5, took Him into the holy **c**
5:14, a **c** set on a hill
10:11, whatever **c** or village you enter
21:10, all the **c** was stirred
Acts 8:8, much rejoicing in that **c**
Heb. 11:10, a **c** which has foundations
12:22, the **c** of the living God
Rev. 21:2, I saw the holy **c**
Gen. 4:17; 11:4; 2 Sam. 19:37; Eccles. 9:14; Is. 1:26; 19:18; 33:20; Matt. 10:14; 21:10; Luke 9:5; 24:49; Acts 7:58
CLAMOR—*boisterous* Eph. 4:31, anger and **c**
CLAN—*thousand* Is. 60:22, become a **c**
CLAP Ps. 47:1, O **c** your hands, all peoples
Is. 55:12, trees of the field will **c**
2 Kin. 11:12; Job 27:23; 34:37; Ps. 98:8; Lam. 2:15; Ezek. 25:6
CLASS—*reckon* Luke 22:37, HE WAS **C-ED**
CLAW—*hoof* Dan. 4:33, nails like birds' **c-s**
CLAY Job 4:19, who dwell in houses of **c**
Job 33:6, formed out of **c**
Jer. 18:6, **c** in the potter's hand
1 Kin. 7:46; Is. 64:8; Dan. 2:33; John 9:6; Rom. 9:21
CLEAN—*cleanse, acquit, purify*
Ps. 19:9, fear of the LORD is **c**
24:4, who has **c** hands
51:10, Create in me a **c** heart
Matt. 3:12, thoroughly **c** His threshing floor
Matt. 8:2; Mark 1:40; Luke 5:12, Thou canst make me **c**
John 15:3, **c** because of the word
1 Cor. 5:7, **C** out the old leaven
2 Kin. 5:12; Job 14:4; Is. 1:16; 52:11; Matt. 23:26; Luke 11:39,41; John 13:10
CLEANSE—*clean, purify, wash*
Matt. 8:3; 10:8; 11:5, I am willing; be **c-d**
Mark 7:4, not eat unless they **c** themselves
Acts 10:15; 11:9, What God has **c-d**
15:9, **c-ing** their hearts by faith
James 4:8, **C** your hands, you sinners
1 John 1:7, blood ... **c-s** us from all sin
Prov. 20:9; Luke 4:27; 7:22; 17:17; 2 Cor. 7:1
CLEAR—*pure, plain* Is. 40:3, **C** the way for the LORD
Matt. 7:5, you will see **c-ly** *enough*
Rom. 1:20, have been **c-ly** seen
Rev. 22:1, water of life, **c** as crystal
Gen. 20:16; Num. 14:18; Job 26:13; Is. 32:4
CLEAVE—*cling* Gen. 2:24, shall **c** to his wife
Hab. 3:9, **c** the earth with rivers
Matt. 19:5; Eph. 5:31
CLEFT Song 2:14; Is. 2:21; Jer. 49:16
CLEVER—*skillful, wise* 1 Cor. 1:17, not in **c-ness**
1 Cor. 1:19, **c-ness** of the **c** I will set aside
2 Pet. 1:16, not follow **c-ly** devised tales
CLIMB 1 Sam. 14:13; Jer. 48:44; Luke 19:4; John 10:1
CLING Josh. 23:8, **c** to the LORD your God
Ps. 63:8, My soul **c-s** to Thee
102:5, My bones **c** to my flesh
John 20:17, Stop **c-ing** to Me
CLOAK—*mantle, coat* Ruth 3:15, Give me the **c** ... on you
Is. 3:7; Matt. 9:20; Acts 12:8; 2 Tim. 4:13

CLOD—*crust* Job 21:33, **c-s** of the valley
CLOSE (adj.)—*intimate, near*
Prov. 18:24, a friend who sticks **c-r** than
Judg. 20:34; Ps. 41:9
CLOSE (v.)—*shut, stop* Gen. 7:16; 8:2, LORD **c-d** *it* behind
Num. 16:33, the earth **c-d** over them
Acts 28:27, THEY HAVE **C-D** THEIR EYES
Rom. 3:19, every mouth may be **c-d**
1 John 3:17, **c-s** his heart against him
Rev. 21:25, its gates shall never be **c-d**
Judg. 19:9
CLOTH 1 Sam. 21:9; Matt. 9:16; Luke 2:7; John 11:44
CLOTHE—*array, adorn, wrap* Job 10:11, **C** me with skin
Matt. 6:29, Solomon ... not **c-d** like
25:36, naked, and you **c-d** Me
1 Pet. 5:5, **c** yourselves with humility
Rev. 7:13, are **c-d** in the white robes
1 Kin. 11:29; Job 40:10; Ps. 65:13; 93:1; Is. 52:1; Luke 24:49; Rev. 3:5
CLOTHES—*dress, garment* Matt. 22:11, not ... in wedding **c**
James 2:3, one who is wearing the fine **c**
Deut. 29:5; Josh. 9:5; 1 Sam. 19:13; 2 Sam. 12:20; Mark 14:63; James 2:2
CLOTHING—*clothes, dress, raiment*
Matt. 6:25, food, and the body than **c**
7:15, come to you in sheep's **c**
1 Tim. 2:9, with proper **c**
Deut. 8:4; Job 24:10; Jer. 10:9
CLOUD—*darkness* Gen. 9:13, My bow in the **c**
Ex. 13:21, a pillar of **c** by day
20:21, Moses approached the thick **c**
24:15, **c** covered the mountain
Matt. 24:30, SON OF MAN COMING ON THE **C-S**
Mark 9:7, a **c** formed ... voice came out of the **c**
Luke 12:54, see a **c** rising in the west
21:27, IN A **C** with power and great glory
Acts 1:9, a **c** received Him out of their sight
1 Thess. 4:17, caught up ... in the **c-s**
Rev. 1:7, HE IS COMING WITH THE **C-S**
Ex. 14:24; 33:9; 1 Kin. 8:12; 2 Chr. 6:1; Ps. 99:7; 105:39; Ezek. 30:3; Jude 12
CLUSTER Is. 65:8, new wine is found in the **c**
Num. 13:23; Mic. 7:1; Rev. 14:18
COAL—*soot, charcoal* Prov. 6:28; Is. 6:6
Prov. 25:22, heap burning **c-s** on his head
Rom. 12:20, HEAP ... **C-S** UPON HIS HEAD
COAST Acts 27:2, the regions along the **c**
COAT—*cloak* Matt. 5:40, let him have your **c** also
COBRA Job 20:16, He sucks the poison of **c-s**
Ps. 58:4, Like a deaf **c**
91:13, tread upon the lion and **c**
COCK Matt. 26:34,75, before a **c** crows
Mark 13:35, at **c**-crowing, or in the morning
COFFIN—*bier* Gen. 50:26; Luke 7:14
COIN—*money* Matt. 22:19, Show Me the **c** *used* for
Luke 15:8, woman ... loses **c**
COLD Prov. 25:25, Like **c** water to a weary soul
Matt. 10:42, a cup of **c** water
24:12, love will grow **c**
Rev. 3:15, that you were **c** or hot
Gen. 8:22; Job 24:7; 37:9; Prov. 25:13; John 18:18; 2 Cor. 11:27
COLLAPSED—*fell* Luke 6:49, immediately it **c**
COLLECT—*exact* Luke 3:13, **C** no more
Luke 19:23, would have **c-ed** it with interest
COLLECTION 1 Cor. 16:1, the **c** for the saints
COLOR Ezek. 16:16, high places of various **c-s**
COLT—*foal* Zech. 9:9, a **c**, the foal of a donkey
Matt. 21:2, a donkey tied *there* and a **c** with her
John 12:15, KING COMES ... ON A DONKEY'S **C**
COMBINE 1 Cor. 2:13, **c-ing** spiritual *thoughts* ... *words*
COME—*enter, return* Ps. 95:6, **C**, let us worship
Zech. 9:9, your king is **c-ing** to you
Matt. 6:10, Thy kingdom **c**
11:28, **C** to Me, all who are weary

Mark 10:14, children to **c** to Me
Luke 21:27, SON OF MAN **C-ING**
John 17:1, Father, the hour has **c**
Rev. 22:20, I am **c-ing** quickly
Mark 14:38; Luke 19:23; 2 Thess. 2:2
COMFORT—*consolation, rest*
Ps. 23:4, Thy rod . . . they **c** me
Is. 61:2, To **c** all who mourn
Matt. 5:4, who mourn, for they shall be **c-ed**
Acts 9:31, in the **c** of the Holy Spirit
2 Cor. 1:3, God of all **c**
1:6, for your **c** and salvation
1 Thess. 4:18, **c** one another
2 Thess. 2:17, **c** and strengthen your hearts
Job 29:25; Ps. 77:2; Prov. 29:17; Eccles. 4:1; Is. 54:11; Lam. 1:21; Matt. 2:18; Luke 6:24; 16:25; 2 Cor. 7:4,13; 2 Thess. 2:16
COMFORTER—*helper* Job 16:2, Sorry **c-s** are you all
Ps. 69:20, looked for . . . **c-s**, but I found none
Nah. 3:7, Where will I seek **c-s** for you
COMING 2 Sam. 3:25, your going out and **c** in
Mal. 3:2, endure the day of His **c**
Matt. 11:3, Are You the **C** One
24:30, SON OF MAN **C**
26:64, **C** ON THE CLOUDS OF HEAVEN
John 5:25, an hour is **c** and now is
James 5:8, **c** of the Lord is at hand
2 Pet. 3:4, promise of His **c**
COMMAND—*declare, spoke* Gen. 18:19; Lev. 24:12; Deut. 2:37
Ps. 33:9, He **c-ed**, and it stood fast
Jon. 2:10, LORD **c-ed** the fish
Matt. 1:24, angel of the Lord **c-ed** him
4:3, Son of God, **c** that these stones
20:21, **C** that . . . these two sons of mine
Luke 8:25, He **c-s** even the winds
9:54, **c** fire to come down from heaven
John 15:14, do what I **c** you
COMMANDER—*general* Judg. 5:9; 1 Chr. 27:34; Is. 55:4
COMMANDMENT—*instruction, duty*
Ex. 20:6, keep My **c-s**
34:28, tablets . . . the Ten **C-s**
Ps. 19:8, **C** of the LORD is pure
Matt. 5:19, one of the least of these **c-s**
22:36, which is the great **c**
John 14:15, If you love Me . . . keep My **c-s**
Prov. 6:20; Eccles. 12:13; Matt. 22:40; John 15:10
COMMEND—*praise* Eccles. 8:15, So I **c-ed** pleasure
Acts 20:32, I **c** you to God
1 Cor. 8:8; 2 Cor. 3:1
COMMISSION Acts 26:12, authority and **c** of . . . priests
COMMIT—*entrust, practice, wrought*
Ex. 20:14, You shall not **c** adultery
Ps. 31:5, into Thy hand I **c** my spirit
37:5, **C** your way to the LORD
Luke 23:46, into Thy hands I **c** My spirit
John 8:34, every one who **c-s** sin
Ex. 32:30; Lev. 20:12; Prov. 16:3; Luke 18:20; 1 Pet. 2:22
COMMON—*prevalent* Lev. 4:27; Jer. 26:23
Acts 2:44, had all things in **c**
Titus 1:4, in a **c** faith
Jude 3, write you about our **c** salvation
COMMOTION—*disturbance* Jer. 10:22, great **c** out of . . . land
COMPANION—*fellow* Prov. 13:20, **c** of fools will suffer
Heb. 1:9, OIL OF GLADNESS ABOVE THY **C-S**
Ex. 2:13; Job 30:29; Eccles. 4:10
COMPANY—*congregation*
Job 15:34, the **c** of the godless
COMPARE Prov. 3:15, nothing . . . **c-s** with her
Matt. 11:16, to what shall I **c** this generation
Rom. 8:18, not worthy . . . **c-d** with the glory
COMPARISON Judg. 8:2; Hag. 2:3
COMPASSION—*lovingkindness, mercy*
Ex. 33:19, **c** on whom I will show **c**
Ps. 25:6, Remember . . . Thy **c**
72:13, **c** on the poor and needy
103:13, father has **c** on *his* children
111:4, LORD is gracious and **c-ate**
Col. 3:12, put on a heart of **c**
Matt. 9:36; 15:32; Luke 15:20; Rom. 9:15
COMPEL—*force, press* Luke 14:23, **c** *them* to come in
COMPETE—*strive* 1 Cor. 9:25, everyone who **c-s**
2 Tim. 2:5, **c-s** as an athlete
COMPLACENCY Prov. 1:32, **c** of fools shall destroy them
COMPLAIN James 5:9, Do not **c** . . . against one another
Job 7:11; Ps. 55:17
COMPLAINING—*babbling*
Prov. 23:29, Who has **c**
COMPLAINT—*grudge* 1 Pet. 4:9 without **c**
COMPLETE—*fulfill, full, utterly*
Is. 2:18, idols will **c-ly** vanish
Col. 2:10, in Him . . . made **c**
James 1:4, that you may be perfect and **c**
1 John 1:4, our joy may be **c**
Rev. 20:3, thousand years were **c-d**
Gen. 2:1; 29:27; Ex. 5:13; Num. 15:31; Esth. 1:5; 1 Cor. 1:10; Rev. 20:7
COMPOSE Job 16:4, I could **c** words against you
COMPOSURE Eccles. 10:4, **c** allays great offenses
COMPREHEND—*calculate*
Job 37:5, things . . . cannot **c**
John 1:5, darkness did not **c** it
COMPREHENSION—*understanding*
Phil. 4:7, peace . . . surpasses all **c**
COMPULSION—*constrain*
1 Pet. 5:2, not under **c**, but
CONCEAL—*cover, hide* Prov. 12:23; Is. 3:9; Jer. 50:2
Ps. 40:10, have not **c-ed** thy lovingkindness
Prov. 27:5, love that is **c-ed**
CONCEIT—*pride*
Phil. 2:3, nothing . . . selfishness or empty **c**
1 Tim. 6:4, is **c-ed** *and* understands nothing
CONCEIVE Num. 11:12; Job 15:35; Ps. 51:5; Matt. 1:20; Acts 5:4; James 1:15
CONCERN—*care* Col. 4:13, he has a deep **c** for you
1 Sam. 1:16; Matt. 4:6; John 12:6; Rom. 1:3; 1 Cor. 7:32; 9:9; 12:1
CONCILIATE—*entreat*
1 Cor. 4:13, slandered, we try to **c**
CONCLUSION
Eccles. 12:13, The **c** when all has been heard
CONDEMN—*discredit, judge*
Is. 50:9, Who . . . **c-s** Me
Mark 16:16, who has disbelieved shall be **c-ed**
Gal. 2:11, because he stood **c-ed**
1 John 3:20, in whatever our heart **c-s** us
Job 9:20; Prov. 12:2; Mark 10:33; Luke 6:37; Rom. 2:1; 14:23
CONDEMNATION—*judgment* Rom. 3:8, Their **c** is just
Rom. 8:1, no **c** for those who are in
Matt. 23:14; Mark 12:40; Luke 20:47; 23:40; Rom. 13:2
CONDUCT—*bring, behavior* Job 33:17; Ezek. 7:27; Acts 17:15
Col. 4:5, **C** yourselves with wisdom
2 Pet. 2:7, sensual **c** of unprincipled men
CONDUIT 2 Kin. 18:17; 20:20; Is. 7:3; 36:2
CONFER—*consult* Acts 4:15; 25:12
CONFESS—*acknowledge* Matt. 3:6, they **c-ed** their sins
Matt. 10:32, **c** Me before men . . . **c** him before My Father
Mark 1:5, baptized . . . **c-ing** their sins
Rom. 10:9, **c** with your mouth
James 5:16, **c** your sins to one another
1 John 1:9, If we **c** our sins, He is
Ps. 32:5; John 1:20; Rom. 10:10

CONFESSION 2 Cor. 9:13, your **c** of the gospel of Christ
1 Tim. 6:13; Heb. 10:23
CONFIDENCE—*boldness, trust* Prov. 3:26; Heb. 3:6
Job 31:24, have put my **c** in gold
Is. 32:17, quietness and **c** forever
2 Cor. 1:12, For our proud **c** is this
Phil. 1:26, your proud **c** in me
3:3, and put no **c** in the flesh
Heb. 4:16, draw near with **c** to the throne of grace
1 John 4:17, we may have **c** in the day of judgment
CONFIDENT Eph. 3:12, **c** access through faith in Him
CONFIRM—*establish* Ps. 90:17, **c** the work of our hands
Rom. 15:8, to **c** the promises *given* to the fathers
1 Cor. 1:8, also **c** you to the end
Matt. 18:16; Mark 16:20
CONFIRMATION Phil. 1:7, defense and **c** of the gospel
Heb. 6:16, an oath *given* as **c** is an end
CONFORM Rom. 8:29, *to become* **c-ed** to the image
Rom. 12:2, do not be **c-ed** to this world
Phil. 3:10, being **c-ed** to His death
CONFOUND Josh. 10:10; Is. 19:3
CONFUSE Gen. 11:7, **c** their language
CONFUSION—*disorder*
1 Sam. 14:20, *was* very great **c**
1 Cor. 14:33, not *a God* of **c**
CONGREGATION—*company, assembly*
Ex. 12:3, Speak to all the **c**
Ps. 82:1, His stand in His own **c**
149:1, **c** of the godly ones
CONQUER Rom. 8:37, **c** through Him
Rev. 6:2, went out **c-ing**, and to **c**
CONSCIENCE Acts 23:1, lived . . . good **c** before God
Rom. 13:5, also for **c** sake
1 Cor. 8:7, their **c** being weak
1 Tim. 3:9, faith with a clear **c**
4:2, **c** as with a branding iron
1 Pet. 3:16, keep a good **c**
Acts 24:16; Rom. 2:15; Heb. 9:14; 10:22
CONSECRATE—*sanctify*
Lev. 11:44, **C** yourselves
1 Sam. 21:4, there is **c-d** bread
Matt. 12:4, They ate **c-d** bread
Ex. 28:38,41; 29:1,21,29,35; 40:9; Lev. 12:4; 16:19; 25:10; Num. 6:11; 1 Sam. 21:6; 1 Kin. 8:64; 9:3,7; 2 Chr. 7:7
CONSENT—*agree* Prov. 1:10; Is. 1:19; Luke 23:51
CONSIDER—*notice, observe*
Ps. 41:1, blessed is he who **c-s** the helpless
Eccles. 7:14, in the day of adversity **c**
Luke 12:24, **C** the ravens, for they
Heb. 10:24, let us **c** . . . one another
11:26, **c-ing** the reproach of Christ
2 Sam. 19:19; Ps. 44:22; 48:13; 77:5
CONSIDERATION
Acts 27:3, Julius treated Paul with **c**
CONSIST Luke 12:15, his life **c** of his possessions
CONSOLATION—*comfort* Job 15:11, Are the **c-s** of God . . . small
Phil. 2:1, if there is any **c** of love
CONSPIRACY—*plot* 2 Sam. 15:12, the **c** was strong
CONSTRAIN—*persuade, urge* Job 32:18
CONSULT—*confer, counsel* 1 Kin. 12:6,8
Gal. 1:16, I did not . . . **c** with flesh and blood
CONSUME—*eat, devour*
Ex. 3:2, yet the bush was not **c-d**
Ex. 24:17; Is. 29:6; 30:27,30; 33:14, **c-ing** fire
Deut. 4:24, God is a **c-ing** fire
Ezek. 15:7, yet the fire will **c** them
Lev. 10:2; Deut. 5:25; 32:24; Ps. 39:11; 49:14; 69:9; 90:7; Eccles. 4:5; Luke 9:54; John 2:17; Gal. 5:15; James 5:3
CONSUMMATION—*end* Heb. 9:26, at the **c**
CONSUMPTION Lev. 26:16; Deut. 28:22
CONTAIN 1 Kin. 8:27; 1 Pet. 2:6
CONTAINER Luke 8:16, covers it over with a **c**
CONTEMPT Rom. 14:10, regard your brother with **c**
2 Cor. 10:10, his speech **c-ible**
Job 12:21; Prov. 18:3; Dan. 12:2
CONTEND—*strive* Is. 50:8, Who will **c** with Me
Is. 57:16, I will not **c** forever
Jude 3, **c** earnestly for the faith
Judg. 8:1; Job 40:2; Prov. 3:30; Is. 49:25; Jer. 2:9
CONTENT—*satisfy* Luke 3:14, be **c** with your wages
Phil. 4:11, I have learned to be **c**
1 Tim. 6:6, accompanied by **c-ment**
2 Cor. 12:10; Heb. 13:5
CONTENTIOUS Prov. 21:19; 25:24; 1 Cor. 11:16
CONTINUAL—*unceasing, constant* Num. 4:16; 28:24
Prov. 15:15, cheerful heart *has* a **c** feast
CONTINUALLY—*perpetual*
1 Chr. 16:11, Seek His face **c**
Ps. 34:1, praise shall **c** be in my mouth
Prov. 6:21; Luke 18:5
CONTINUE—*persevere*
Acts 13:43, **c** in the grace of God
Heb. 13:1, Let love of the brethren **c**
CONTRARY—*hostile*
Matt. 14:24, for the wind was **c**
Rom. 11:24, grafted **c** to nature
16:17, **c** to the teaching
2 Cor. 2:7, on the **c** . . . rather forgive
Gal. 2:7, on the **c**, seeing that I
1 Tim. 1:10, **c** to sound teaching
CONTRIBUTE Rom. 12:13, **c-ing** to the needs of the saints
CONTRIBUTION Rom. 15:26, make a **c** for the poor
CONTRITE—*crush* Ps. 51:17, broken and a **c** heart
Is. 66:2, humble and **c** of spirit
CONTROL—*rule* Prov. 25:28, no **c** over his spirit
2 Cor. 5:14, love of Christ **c-s** us
CONTROVERSY—*dispute*
Jer. 25:31, **c** with the nations
CONVERSE—*discuss*
Luke 24:15, while they were **c-ing**
Acts 17:18, philosophers were **c-ing** with him
CONVERSION Acts 15:3, **c** of the Gentiles
CONVERT—*restore*
Matt. 18:3, unless you are **c-ed**
CONVICT—*reprove*
John 8:46, Which one of you **c-s** Me
16:8, **c** the world concerning sin
Heb. 11:1, the **c-ion** of things not seen
CONVINCE—*persuade* Rom. 14:14, am **c-d** in the Lord Jesus
Heb. 6:9, **c-d** of better things
COOK 1 Sam. 8:13; 9:23,24
COOL Gen. 3:8; Luke 16:24
COPE Acts 6:10, unable to **c** with the wisdom
COPPER Deut. 8:9, you can dig **c**
Matt. 10:9, Do not acquire gold . . . or **c**
COPPERSMITH 2 Tim. 4:14, Alexander the **c**
COPY—*transcribe* Deut. 17:18; Josh. 8:32; Heb. 9:24
CORBAN Mark 7:11, have been helped by is **C**
CORD—*band, chain*
Ps. 18:4, **c-s** of death encompassed me
Prov. 5:22, held with the **c-s** of his sin
Eccles. 12:6, the silver **c** is broken
John 2:15, made a scourge of **c-s**
2 Sam. 22:6; Job 36:8; 38:31; 41:1; Is. 5:18
CORNER Prov. 7:12, lurks by every **c**
Matt. 6:5, synagogues and on the street **c-s**
Acts 10:11, lowered by four **c-s** to the ground
Rev. 7:1, at the four **c-s** of the earth

CORNERSTONE—*corner* Ps. 118:22, the chief **c**
Matt. 21:42, BECAME THE CHIEF **C**
Eph. 2:20, Christ ... being the **c**
Job 38:6; Is. 28:16
CORPSE—*body* Is. 14:19; Nah. 3:3; Matt. 24:28
CORRECT—*reprove*
Prov. 29:17, **C** your son, and he will
Jer. 10:24, **C** me ... but with justice
2 Tim. 3:16, profitable ... for **c-ion**
CORRUPT—*depraved, rotten*
Gen. 6:11, the earth was **c**
Ps. 14:1, They are **c**, they have committed
1 Cor. 15:33, Bad company **c-s** good morals
Job 15:16; Is. 1:4; Jer. 6:28; 2 Cor. 7:2; Eph. 4:22
CORRUPTIBLE—*perish*
Rom. 1:23, in the form of **c** man
CORRUPTION—*decay* Lev. 22:25; Rom. 8:21; 2 Pet. 2:19
Gal. 6:8, shall from the flesh reap **c**
2 Pet. 1:4, the **c** that is in the world
COST—*wealth, price*
Ps. 49:8, redemption ... soul is **c-ly**
Is. 55:1, Without money and without **c**
Matt. 26:7, vial of very **c-ly** perfume
2 Sam. 24:24; 1 Kin. 5:17; Ezra 6:4,8; John 12:3; 1 Tim. 2:9
COUCH—*pallet* Gen. 49:4,9
Ps. 6:6, dissolve my **c** with my tears
COUNCIL Mark 15:43; Luke 23:50
Jer. 23:18, stood in the **c** of the LORD
Acts 5:27, stood them before the **C**
6:12, brought Stephen before the **C**
COUNSEL—*advice, opinion*
Ps. 1:1, not walk in the **c**
33:11, **C** of the LORD stands
73:24, With Thy **c** ... guide me
Prov. 13:10, those who receive **c**
19:20, Listen to **c** and accept
Is. 28:29, made *His* **c** wonderful
John 12:10, chief priests took **c**
Eph. 1:11, after the **c** of His will
Ex. 18:19; Judg. 19:30; 1 Kin. 12:6; 2 Chr. 10:9; Ezra 4:5; Ps. 32:8; 62:4; Matt. 22:15; Luke 14:31
COUNSELOR
Is. 9:6, will be called Wonderful **C**
Rom. 11:34, WHO BECAME HIS **C**
Job 12:17; Prov. 11:14; Mic. 4:9
COUNT—*consider, number* 2 Cor. 5:19; James 5:11
Gen. 15:5, **c** the stars, if you are able
Prov. 17:28, closes his lips ... **c-ed** prudent
1 Cor. 4:15, have **c-less** tutors in Christ
Phil. 3:8, I **c** all things to be loss
2 Pet. 3:9, as some **c** slowness
COUNTENANCE Gen. 4:6, why has your **c** fallen
Num. 6:26, The LORD lift up His **c**
Ps. 4:6; 89:15, light of Thy **c**
COUNTRY—*region*
John 4:44, no honor in his own **c**
Gen. 12:1; Matt. 2:12; Luke 15:13
COURAGE—*cheer* 2 Chr. 15:7, strong and do not lose **c**
Ps. 27:14, let your heart take **c**
John 16:33, take **c**; I have overcome
Matt. 9:2,22; 14:27; Acts 23:11
COURAGEOUS Deut. 31:6; Josh. 1:7
COURSE Ps. 19:5, strong man to run his **c**
2 Tim. 4:7, have finished the **c**
James 3:6, sets on fire the **c** of our life
Judg. 5:20; Acts 20:24
COURT—*council* Ps. 84:10, a day in Thy **c-s**
Ex. 27:9; Ps. 135:2; Matt. 10:17
COURTEOUS Acts 28:7, entertained us **c-ly** three days
COVENANT Job 31:1; Acts 3:25; Gal. 4:24
Gen. 6:18, I will establish My **c**
Num. 10:33, ark of the **c** of the LORD
2 Kin. 23:2, book of the **c**
Ps. 25:10; 103:18, To those who keep His **c**
Matt. 26:28, My blood of the **c**
Luke 22:20, This cup ... is the new **c**
2 Cor. 3:6, servants of a new **c**
3:14, reading of the old **c**
Heb. 7:22, Jesus ... guarantee of a better **c**
8:6, mediator of a better **c**
13:20, blood of the eternal **c**
Rev. 11:19, the ark of His **c**
COVER—*hide* Ps. 32:1, Whose sin is **c-ed**
Ps. 91:4, **c** you with His pinions
Prov. 10:12, love **c-s** all transgressions
Matt. 10:26, nothing **c-ed** that will not be revealed
James 5:20, will **c** a multitude of sins
1 Pet. 4:8, love **c-s** a multitude of sins
Gen. 37:26; Ex. 2:3; Job 36:32; Is. 6:2; 50:6; Luke 23:30
COVERING—*raiment*
Ps. 105:39, spread a cloud for a **c**
1 Cor. 11:15, her hair is given ... for a **c**
Gen. 3:7; 2 Sam. 17:19; Is. 50:3; 1 Tim. 6:8
COVET—*crave, desire* Mic. 2:2; Rom. 13:9
Ex. 20:17, You shall not **c**
Mark 7:22, deeds of **c-ing** *and* wickedness
Acts 20:33, have **c-ed** no one's silver
Rom. 7:8, produced in me **c-ing** of every kind
COW—*ox* Is. 11:7, the **c** and the bear will graze
Lev. 22:28; Job 21:10
COWARDLY—*fearful* Rev. 21:8, for the **c** and unbelieving
CRAFT—*deceit* Job 15:5, language of the **c-y**
Ex. 21:14; Is. 2:16; 2 Cor. 12:16
CRAFTINESS—*shrewd* 2 Cor. 4:2, walking in **c**
CRAFTSMEN 2 Kin. 24:14; Hos. 13:2; Zech. 1:20; Acts 19:24
CRANE—*thrush* Is. 38:14
CRASH Zeph. 1:10, a loud **c** from the hills
CRAVE—*desire, covet* Mic. 7:1
Prov. 13:4, soul of the sluggard **c-s** and gets nothing
21:26, All day long he is **c-ing**
CRAWL—*creep* Acts 10:12, **c-ing** creatures of the earth
CREATE—*form* Gen. 1:1, **c-d** the heavens and the earth
Ps. 51:10, **C** in me a clean heart
Is. 45:12, made the earth, and **c-d** man
Mal. 2:10, Has not one God **c-d** us
Eph. 2:10, **c-d** in Christ Jesus
4:24, God ... **c-d** in righteousness
Col. 1:16, in Him all things were **c-d**
Is. 57:19; 65:17; Mark 13:19; Eph. 3:9; 1 Tim. 2:13
CREATION Mark 10:6, beginning of **c**, *God* MADE THEM
Mark 13:19, **c** which God created
16:15, preach the gospel to all **c**
Rom. 1:20, since the **c** of the world
8:22, whole **c** groans
2 Pet. 3:4, from the beginning of **c**
CREATOR Eccles. 12:1, Remember also your **C**
Is. 40:28, **c** of the ends of the earth
Rom. 1:25, the creature rather than the **C**
1 Pet. 4:19, to a faithful **C**
CREATURE—*animal, beast* Gen. 1:21, every living **c**
Lev. 11:47, the edible **c** and the **c** ... not to be eaten
2 Cor. 5:17, *he is* a new **c**; the old things
Rom. 1:23; James 1:18
CREDIT—*thanks* Luke 6:32, what **c** is *that* to you
CREDITOR Ps. 109:11; Is. 50:1
Deut. 15:2, every **c** shall release what ... loaned
CREEP Gen. 1:26; Ps. 148:10
CRESCENT Is. 3:18, will take away ... **c** ornaments
CRIME Job 31:11; Ezek. 7:23
CRIMINAL 2 Tim. 2:9, suffer hardship ... as a **c**
CRIMSON 2 Chr. 2:7, in purple, **c** and violet
Is. 1:18, like **c**, They will be like wool
CRIPPLE Matt. 18:8, better ... to enter life **c-d**
Luke 14:21, bring in **c-d** and blind

CRITICIZE Is. 29:24, those who **c** ... accept instruction
CROCUS Is. 35:1, blossom; Like the **c**
CROOKED—*perverse* Deut. 32:5; Prov. 21:8; Phil. 2:15
Ps. 125:5, turn aside to their **c** ways
Eccles. 1:15, **c** cannot be straightened
Luke 3:5, THE C SHALL BECOME STRAIGHT
CROP Lev. 1:16, take away its **c**
CROSS—*tree* Matt. 10:38, take his **c**
Matt. 27:40, come down from the **c**
John 19:17, went out, bearing His own **c**
19:25, standing by the **c** of Jesus
Acts 5:30, hanging Him on a **c**
1 Cor. 1:17, that the **c** of Christ should not
Gal. 6:14, except in the **c** of our Lord
Phil. 2:8, even death on a **c**
3:18, enemies of the **c** of Christ
Heb. 12:2, endured the **c**, despising
1 Kin. 1:6; 1 Cor. 1:18; Eph. 2:16; Col. 1:20
CROUCH—*bow* Job 38:40; Ps. 10:10
CROW Matt. 26:74, immediately a cock **c-ed**
Mark 14:72; Luke 22:34; 22:60
CROWD—*press*
Mark 2:4, unable to get to Him ... **c**
5:27, in the **c** behind *Him,* and touched
CROWN—*wreath* Ps. 8:5, **c** him with glory
Ps. 103:4, **c-s** you with lovingkindness
Prov. 12:4, excellent wife is the **c** of
14:18, are **c-ed** with knowledge
14:24, **c** of the wise is their
16:31, gray head is a **c** of glory
17:6, grandchildren are the **c** of old men
Heb. 2:9, Jesus ... **c-ed** with glory and honor
Gen. 49:26; Ps. 21:3; 65:11
CRUCIFIXION Matt. 26:2, delivered up for **c**
CRUCIFY Matt. 27:22, Let Him be **c-ed**
Matt. 28:5, Jesus who has been **c-ed**
Mark 15:13, shouted back, **C** Him
1 Cor. 1:23, we preach Christ **c-ed**
Gal. 2:20, I have been **c-ed** with Christ
6:14, world has been **c-ed** to me
Heb. 6:6, **c** to themselves the Son of God
Matt. 20:19; 27:35; 1 Cor. 1:13; 2 Cor. 13:4
CRUEL—*fierce* Prov. 11:17; Matt. 15:22
CRUMBS Matt. 15:27; Mark 7:28
CRUSH—*batter* Ps. 34:18, saves those ... **c-ed** in spirit
Is. 53:5, **c-ed** for our iniquities
53:10, LORD was pleased to **c** Him
Amos 4:1, who **c** the needy
Rom. 16:20, **c** Satan under your feet
2 Cor. 4:8, but not **c-ed**
Lev. 22:24; 2 Kin. 18:21; Job 39:15; Jer. 17:18
CRUST Job 7:5, flesh is clothed ... a **c** of dirt
CRY—*outcry*
Gen. 4:10, your brother's blood is **c-ing**
Ps. 9:12, the **c** of the afflicted
130:1, Out of the depths I have **c-ed**
Matt. 3:3, ONE C-ING IN THE WILDERNESS
Rev. 21:4, no ... mourning, or **c-ing**
Ex. 2:6; 32:18; Lev. 13:45; Ps. 17:1; 27:7; Is. 42:2; Mark 15:37
CRYSTAL Ezek. 1:22; Rev. 4:6; 21:11
CUB 2 Sam. 17:8; Jer. 51:38; Nah. 2:11
CUBIT Gen. 6:15, length of the ark 300 **c-s**
Esth. 5:14, a gallows fifty **c-s** high
Matt. 6:27, add a single **c** to his life's span
Deut. 3:11; Ezek. 43:13
CUCUMBER Num. 11:5; Is. 1:8
CUD Lev. 11:3; Deut. 14:6
CULTIVATE—*till* Gen. 2:5, no man to **c** the ground
Ps. 37:3, Dwell in the land and **c** faithfulness
Gen. 2:15; Deut. 28:39; 2 Sam. 9:10; Ezek. 36:9
CUMMIN Matt. 23:23, and dill and **c**
CUP Ps. 23:5, My **c** overflows
Matt. 10:42, a **c** of cold water
20:22, able to drink the **c**
23:25, outside of the **c**
26:27, took a **c** and gave thanks
26:39, let this **c** pass from Me
Luke 22:20, **c** ... is the new covenant
John 18:11, the **c** which the Father has given
1 Cor. 10:16, the **c** of blessing
Ps. 116:13; Prov. 23:31; Mark 7:4; 1 Cor. 10:21
CUPBEARER Gen. 40:1; 41:9; 1 Kin. 10:5; 2 Chr. 9:4; Neh. 1:11
CURDLE Job 10:10, and **c** me like cheese
CURDS—*butter* Judg. 5:25; Is. 7:15,22
CURE Luke 7:21, At that very time He **c-d** many
Luke 13:32, perform **c-s** today and tomorrow
CURSE—*oath* Ex. 22:28, You shall not **c** God
Mal. 4:6, smite the land with a **c**
Luke 6:28, bless those who **c** you
Rom. 3:14, WHOSE MOUTH IS FULL OF C-ING
Gal. 3:13, redeemed us from the **c**
Gen. 3:14; 12:3; 27:12; Lev. 19:14; 1 Sam. 3:13; Jer. 42:18; 44:12; Mic. 6:10; Zech. 14:11; Mark 14:71; Rom. 12:14; James 3:9
CURTAIN Ex. 26:1; Song 1:5; Is. 40:22
CUSHION Mark 4:38, asleep on the **c**
CUSTODY—*prison* Esth. 2:3,8,14; Matt. 4:12
CUSTOM—*manner* Luke 4:16, as was His **c**
Acts 16:21, **c-s** which are not lawful
Judg. 11:39; Ezra 4:13; John 18:39; 19:40; Acts 28:17; Rom. 13:7
CUT Matt. 3:10, not bear good fruit is **c** down
Matt. 21:8, others were **c-ing** branches
26:51, and **c** off his ear
Acts 7:54, they were **c** to the quick
Rom. 11:22, you also will be **c** off
Ex. 9:15; Judg. 1:6; Ps. 12:3; Prov. 10:31; Is. 45:2; Jer. 7:29; Matt. 5:30; 24:51
CYMBAL 2 Sam. 6:5; 1 Chr. 15:16; 16:5; Ps. 150:5; 1 Cor. 13:1

D

DAILY—*continual* Ps. 68:19, who **d** bears our burden
Prov. 8:30, I was **d** His delight
Matt. 6:11; Luke 11:3, Give us ... our **d** bread
Luke 9:23, take up his cross **d**
Acts 16:5, churches ... increasing in number **d**
17:11, examining the Scriptures **d**
1 Cor. 15:31, I die **d**
Dan. 1:5; Acts 6:1; James 2:15
DAINTY Gen. 49:20; Jer. 6:2
DAMAGE—*loss* Ezra 4:13,22; Acts 27:10
DANCE—*skip* 2 Sam. 6:14, David was **d-ing** before the LORD
Ps. 30:11, turned ... mourning into **d-ing**
149:3, praise His name with **d-ing**
150:4, Praise Him with timbrel and **d-ing**
Eccles. 3:4, a time to **d**
Matt. 11:17, We played ... you did not **d**
14:6, daughter of Herodias **d-d**
Ex. 32:19; Judg. 21:23; 1 Sam. 18:6; Jer. 31:13; Lam. 5:15; Mark 6:22; Luke 7:32
DANGER Acts 19:27; 27:9
DARE—*presume*
Acts 5:13, none ... **d-d** to associate
Rom. 5:7, someone would **d** even to die
1 Cor. 6:1, **d** to go to law before the unrighteous
Job 41:10; Jude 9
DARK—*dim, shadow* Num. 12:8, not in **d** sayings
Joel 2:10, sun and the moon grow **d**
Luke 12:3, whatever you have said in the **d**
Gen. 15:17; Job 24:16; Is. 9:2; Lam. 4:1
DARKEN—*obscure*
Job 38:2, Who is this that **d-s** counsel
Eccles. 12:2, stars are **d-ed**
Matt. 24:29, THE SUN WILL BE D-ED
Rom. 1:21, their foolish heart was **d-ed**
11:10, LET THEIR EYES BE D-ED TO SEE NOT
Eph. 4:18, being **d-ed** in their understanding
Ex. 10:15; Mark 13:24; Rev. 16:10
DARKNESS—*cloud, gloom* Gen. 1:2, **d** was over the surface
Ex. 10:21, **d** over the land of Egypt ... **d** which
2 Sam. 22:29, the LORD illumines my **d**

Ps. 91:6, pestilence that stalks in **d**
107:10, those who dwelt in **d**
112:4, Light arises in the **d**
Eccles. 2:13, as light excels **d**
2:14, the fool walks in **d**
Matt. 6:23, full of **d**, how great is the **d**
10:27, What I tell you in **d**, speak
22:13, cast him into the outer **d**
Luke 1:79, SHINE UPON THOSE WHO SIT IN D
John 1:5, light shines in the **d**
3:19, men loved the **d** rather than the light
12:35, **d** may not overtake
Acts 26:18, they may turn from **d** to light
Rom. 2:19, a light to those who are in **d**
2 Cor. 6:14, what fellowship has light with **d**
Eph. 5:11, unfruitful deeds of **d**
6:12, world forces of this **d**
1 Pet. 2:9, out of **d** into His marvelous light
1 John 1:5, in Him there is no **d** at all
2:9, hates his brother is in the **d**
Deut. 28:29; 1 Sam. 2:9; 2 Sam. 22:10; Job 3:5; 10:22; 12:25; 30:26; Ps. 18:9,28; 88:12; 97:2; 139:12; Prov. 20:20; Is. 58:10; Matt. 25:30; Luke 22:53; 23:44; Rom. 13:12; 1 Cor. 4:5; 2 Cor. 4:6; Col. 1:13; Heb. 12:18; 2 Pet. 2:4; 1 John 1:6

DART—*arrow, missile* Job 41:26, the **d** or the

DASH—*shatter* Is. 13:16, **d-ed** to pieces
Nah. 2:4, **d** to and fro like lightning
2 Kin. 8:12; Ps. 137:9; Jer. 13:14; Hos. 13:16

DATE—*time* Gal. 4:2, the **d** set by the father

DAUGHTER—Gen. 6:1, **d-s** were born to them
Num. 27:8, transfer his inheritance to his **d**
Prov. 31:29, Many **d-s** have done nobly
Eccles. 12:4, **d-s** of song will sing softly
Is. 22:4, destruction of the **d** of my people
Mic. 7:6, **D** rises up against her mother
Heb. 11:24, son of Pharaoh's **d**
Gen. 24:23,47; 27:46; Ex. 21:7; Deut. 28:53; Judg. 11:34; 2 Sam. 1:20; 12:3; Ps. 45:9; 144:12; Prov. 30:15; Jer. 8:21; 9:1; Lam. 2:11; 3:48; Matt. 10:35; Luke 8:42; 12:53; 13:16

DAWN—*light, morning* Deut. 33:2; Josh. 6:15; Judg. 19:26
Ps. 119:147, I rise before **d** and cry for help
139:9, take the wings of the **d**
2 Pet. 1:19, until the day **d-s**
Job 7:4; 38:12; Joel 2:2

DAY—*age, time* Gen. 1:5, God called the light **d**
1 Chr. 29:15, our **d-s** on the earth are like a shadow
Ps. 19:2, **D** to **d** pours forth speech
41:1, deliver him in a **d** of trouble
84:10, a **d** in Thy courts is better
118:24, This is the **d** which the LORD has made
Prov. 3:2, For length of **d-s** and years of life
27:1, you do not know what a **d** may bring
Eccles. 7:1, **d** of *one's* death is better than
12:1, **d-s** of your youth, before the evil **d-s**
Is. 2:12, LORD of hosts will have a **d** of reckoning
13:6, **d** of the LORD is near
58:5, an acceptable **d** to the LORD
Joel 2:11, **d** of the LORD is indeed great
Zech. 4:10, who has despised the **d** of small things
Mal. 3:2, who can endure the **d** of His coming
Matt. 6:11, this **d** our daily bread
24:36, But of that **d** and hour no one knows
John 6:39, raise it up on the last **d**
8:56, Your father Abraham rejoiced to see My **d**
9:4, We must work ... as long as it is **d**
Rom. 14:5, One man regards one **d** above another
1 Cor. 3:13, the **d** will show it
2 Cor. 6:2, ON THE D OF SALVATION
Phil. 1:6, will perfect it until the **d** of Christ
1 Thess. 5:5, all sons of light and sons of **d**
2 Pet. 3:8, one **d** is as a thousand years
Gen. 27:2; Deut. 4:32; 1 Sam. 25:8; 2 Kin. 7:9; Neh. 4:2; Job 1:4; 7:1; 8:9; 14:6; 21:30; Ps. 77:5; Prov. 4:18; Is. 2:2; 10:3; 13:9; 27:3; 65:20; Joel 1:15; 2:1; Mic. 4:1; Zeph. 1:7,14; Zech. 14:1; Mal. 4:5; Matt. 7:22; 24:50; 25:13; Mark 13:32; Luke 12:46; 21:34; John 11:24; 12:48; Acts 2:17,20; 17:31; Rom. 2:5; 1 Thess. 5:2; 2 Tim. 3:1; Heb. 1:2; James 5:3; 2 Pet. 3:3,10; Rev. 6:17; 16:14; 20:10

DAZZLE—*shine* Song 5:10, My beloved is **d-ing**
Luke 24:4, men ... in **d-ing** apparel

DEAD 1 Sam. 24:14; 2 Sam. 9:8; 16:9, **d** dog
Ps. 31:12, I am forgotten as a **d** man
Eccles. 9:4, a live dog is better than a **d** lion
Is. 26:19, Your **d** will live
Matt. 11:5, and *the* **d** are raised up
22:32, God is not *the God* of *the* **d**
23:27, full of **d** men's bones
John 5:25, **d** shall hear the voice of the Son of God
Acts 10:42, Judge of the living and the **d**
26:23, *His* resurrection from the **d**
Rom. 6:11, consider yourselves to be **d** to sin
14:9, Lord both of the **d** and of the living
1 Cor. 15:15, if in fact the **d** are not raised
2 Cor. 1:9, God who raises the **d**
Eph. 2:1, you were **d** in your trespasses and sins
1 Tim. 5:6, **d** even while she lives
Heb. 6:1, repentance from **d** works
James 2:17, faith, if it has no works, is **d**
2:26, body without the spirit is **d**
Rev. 1:18, I was **d**, and behold, I am alive
3:1, name that you are alive, and you are **d**
14:13, Blessed are the **d** who die in the Lord
Gen. 23:3; Ex. 12:30; Lev. 19:28; Ruth 1:8; Ps. 115:17; Prov. 9:18; Eccles. 4:2; 9:5; 10:1; Jer. 22:10; Matt. 2:19,20; 8:22; 9:24; 10:8; Mark 9:10,26; Luke 7:22; 15:24,32; 16:31; Rom. 7:4; 1 Cor. 15:35; Eph. 5:14; Col. 1:18; 2:13; 1 Thess. 4:16; 2 Tim. 4:1; Heb. 11:4; 13:20; 1 Pet. 4:6; Jude 12; Rev. 1:5; 20:5,12,13

DEADLY 1 Sam. 5:11; Ps. 17:9; Mark 16:18; James 3:8

DEAF Matt. 11:5, lepers are cleansed and *the* **d** hear
Ex. 4:11; Lev. 19:14; Ps. 58:4; Is. 29:18; 42:18; 43:8; Mark 7:37; 9:25; Luke 7:22

DEAL—*allot, treat* Prov. 12:22, those who **d** faithfully are
Ex. 1:10; Lev. 19:11; Ps. 25:3; Is. 21:2; 24:16; 26:10; Jer. 6:13; Hos. 5:7

DEALINGS Judg. 18:7, had no **d** with anyone
John 4:9, Jews have no **d** with Samaritans

DEAR—*beloved* Jer. 31:20, Is Ephraim My **d** son
Acts 20:24, I do not consider my life ... as **d**
1 Thess. 2:8, you had become very **d** to us

DEATH—*grave* Num. 23:10; Judg. 16:16; 2 Sam. 22:5
Judg. 16:30, whom he killed at his **d** were more
Ruth 1:17, if *anything but* **d** parts you and me
1 Sam. 15:32, Surely the bitterness of **d** is past
2 Sam. 1:23, in their **d** they were not parted
Ps. 23:4, valley of the shadow of **d**
89:48, what man can live and not see **d**
107:10, darkness and in the shadow of **d**
116:15, Precious ... Is the **d** of His godly ones
Song 8:6, love is as strong as **d**
Is. 25:8, He will swallow up **d** for all time
Ezek. 33:11, no pleasure in the **d** of the wicked
Matt. 2:15, there until the **d** of Herod
16:28; Mark 9:1; Luke 9:27, shall not taste **d**
26:38; Mark 14:34, to the point of **d**
John 5:24, has passed out of **d** into life
8:51, never see **d**
Acts 10:39, **d** by hanging Him on a cross
Rom. 6:23, the wages of sin is **d**
8:2, free from the law of sin and **d**
8:36, WE ARE BEING PUT TO D ALL DAY LONG

DEATH *(Continued)*
1 Cor. 11:26, proclaim the Lord's **d** until He comes
15:21, by a man *came* **d**
15:56, the sting of **d** is sin
2 Cor. 4:12, **d** works in us
Phil. 2:8, obedient to the point of **d**, even **d** on
Heb. 2:9, suffering of **d** ... He might taste **d**
2:15, through fear of **d** were subject to slavery
James 1:15, sin ... brings forth **d**
5:20, will save his soul from **d**
Rev. 1:18, I have the keys of **d** and of Hades
2:10, Be faithful until **d**
6:8, he who sat on it had the name **D**
9:6, men will seek **d** ... and **d** flees from them
21:4, there shall no longer be *any* **d**
2 Chr. 25:4; Job 3:21; 7:15; 30:23; Ps. 6:5; 13:3; 18:4; 22:15; 49:14; 68:20; 102:20; 116:3; Prov. 7:27; 8:36; 14:12; 16:25; Is. 38:18; Jer. 8:3; Ezek. 18:32; Hos. 13:14; Jon. 4:3,8; Matt. 10:21; 15:4; Mark 7:10; Luke 2:26; 22:33; John 11:4; 12:33; 18:31,32; 21:19; Acts 2:24; Rom. 1:32; 5:10,14,17; 6:5,21; 1 Cor. 3:22; 15:55; 2 Cor. 1:9; 11:23; James 5:6; 1 John 3:14; 5:16; Rev. 2:11; 20:6

DEBATE—*dispute* Acts 15:2,7; 1 Cor. 1:20

DEBT Matt. 6:12, forgive us our **d-s**
1 Sam. 22:2; 2 Kin. 4:7; Neh. 10:31; Prov. 22:26; Matt. 18:27

DEBTOR—*obligation*
Ezek. 18:7, restores to the **d**
Matt. 6:12, as we also have forgiven our **d-s**
Luke 7:41, a certain money-lender had two **d-s**
16:5, summoned each of his master's **d-s**

DECAY—*corruption* Job 21:20, own eyes see his **d**
Acts 2:27, HOLY ONE TO UNDERGO D

DECEIT—*falsehood, deception* Ps. 32:2; 36:3; 50:19
Ps. 10:7, mouth full of curses and **d** and oppression
34:13, your lips from speaking **d**
55:23, Men of bloodshed and **d** will not live
Prov. 12:5, counsels of the wicked are **d-ful**
31:30, Charm is **d-ful** and beauty is vain
Jer. 17:9, heart is more **d-ful** than all else
2 Cor. 11:13, false apostles, **d-ful** workers
1 Pet. 2:22, NOR WAS ANY D FOUND
Prov. 27:6; Is. 57:4; Jer. 5:27; 48:10; Dan. 8:25; Hos. 11:12; Zeph. 1:9; Mark 7:22; 2 Cor. 12:16; Eph. 4:14,22

DECEITFUL—*false* Ps. 120:3, You **d** tongue
Ps. 17:1; 26:4

DECEITFULNESS—*deception*
Matt. 13:22; Mark 4:19, **d** of riches

DECEIVE—*cheat, mislead, steal* Gen. 31:20,27; Num. 25:18
Gen. 29:25, Why then have you **d-d** me
Jer. 42:20, you have *only* **d-d** yourselves
Matt. 27:63, we remember that ... that **d-r** said
Rom. 3:13, THEY KEEP D-ING
2 Cor. 6:8, *regarded* as **d-rs** and yet true
Eph. 5:6, 1 John 3:7, Let no one **d** you
1 John 1:8, If we say ... no sin, we are **d-ing**
2 John 7, many **d-rs** ... This is the **d-r** and the antichrist
Rev. 12:9, Satan, who **d-s** the whole world
Deut. 11:16; Josh. 7:11; 9:22; 1 Kin. 22:22; 2 Kin. 19:10; Is. 37:10; 44:20; Jer. 20:7; 37:9; Obad. 3; 1 Cor. 6:9; 15:33; Gal. 6:7; 2 Thess. 2:3; 1 Tim. 2:14; 2 Tim. 3:13; James 1:16; Rev. 19:20

DECEPTION—*deceit*
Jer. 3:10, return to Me ... in **d**
Matt. 27:64, last **d** will be worse than the first
Col. 2:8, philosophy and empty **d**

DECEPTIVE Mic. 6:11, a bag of **d** weights

DECIDE—*determine* 1 Sam. 20:7, he has **d-d** on evil
2 Chr. 2:1, Solomon **d-d** to build a house
Ex. 21:22; Acts 3:13; 1 Cor. 7:37

DECISION—*rebuke* Prov. 16:33, every **d** is from the LORD
Joel 3:14, day ... is near in the valley of **d**
Mic. 4:3; Zeph. 3:8

DECK Is. 61:10, As a bridegroom **d-s** himself

DECLARATION—*account*
Job 13:17, let my **d** *fill* your ears

DECLARE—*explain, relate* Ps. 75:9, I will **d** it forever
Ps. 92:2, To **d** Thy lovingkindness
145:4, shall **d** Thy mighty acts
Is. 43:21, Will **d** My praise
45:19, **D-ing** things that are upright
46:10, **D-ing** the end from the beginning
John 4:25, He will **d** all things to us
Acts 20:27, **d-ing** to you the whole purpose of God
Rom. 1:4, **d-d** with power *to be* the Son of God
Deut. 30:18; Job 31:37; Ps. 9:11; 30:9; 51:15; Is. 41:26; 45:21; 66:19; Acts 17:30

DECORATE—*deck* Jer. 4:30; 10:4

DECREASE—*abate, subside* Gen. 8:3, the water **d-d**
Ps. 107:38, He does not let their cattle **d**
John 3:30, He must increase, but I must **d**

DECREE—*decide, determine* Job 22:28; Ps. 94:20; 148:6
Dan. 11:36, that which is **d-d** will be done
Prov. 8:15; Dan. 2:9; 9:24; Acts 16:4; 17:7

DEDICATE—*devote*
Ex. 32:29, **D** yourselves today to the
1 Kin. 7:51, Solomon brought things **d-d**
8:63, sons of Israel **d-d** the house of the LORD
Deut. 20:5; Judg. 17:3; 1 Kin. 15:15; 1 Chr. 18:11; 26:27

DEED—*action, practice, work* Gen. 44:15; 2 Sam. 12:14
Ps. 9:1, committed abominable **d-s**
28:4, according to the **d-s** of their hands
Is. 1:16, Remove the evil of your **d-s**
59:18; Jer. 25:4, according to their **d-s**
Luke 24:19, prophet mighty in **d** and word
John 3:19, their **d-s** were evil
Acts 7:22, man of power in words and **d-s**
Gal. 5:19, **d-s** of the flesh are evident
Col. 3:17, whatever you do in word or **d**
Titus 3:1, ready for every good **d**
1 John 3:18, not love with word ... but in **d** and truth
Rev. 2:2, I know your **d-s** and your toil
14:13, for their **d-s** follow with them
Ezra 9:13; Neh. 13:14; Ps. 66:5; Prov. 20:11; Jer. 32:10,44; Luke 11:48; 23:41; John 8:41; Rom. 2:6

DEEP—*abyss, depth*
Gen. 7:11, fountains of the great **d**
Job 28:14, the **d** says, It is not with me
Ps. 36:6, Thy judgments are *like* a great **d**
42:7, **D** calls to **d**
Prov. 19:15, Laziness casts into a **d** sleep
Matt. 26:38; Mark 14:34, soul is **d-ly** grieved
Luke 5:4, Put out into **d** water
Rom. 8:26, groanings too **d** for words
Gen. 8:2; Deut. 33:13; Job 4:13; 38:30; Ps. 33:7; 77:16; 106:9; 107:24; Prov. 22:14; 23:27; Is. 7:11; Luke 6:48; John 4:11

DEER Ps. 42:1, **d** pants for the water brooks
Is. 35:6, lame will leap like a **d**
Deut. 12:15; 14:5; 1 Kin. 4:23

DEFEAT 1 Chr. 18:1, David **d-ed** the Philistines
Jer. 37:10, had **d-ed** the entire army
Gen. 14:15; 36:35; Num. 22:6; Josh. 10:33; 12:1,7; 1 Chr. 1:46; 14:11; 18:3; Jer. 46:2

DEFECT—*spot* Lev. 21:17; Deut. 15:21; 2 Sam. 14:25; Job 11:15; Dan. 1:4

DEFEND—*protect*
Zech. 9:15, LORD of hosts will **d** them
Acts 7:24; Rom. 2:15; 2 Cor. 12:19

DEFENSE Acts 19:33; 22:1
Phil. 1:7, in the **d** ... of the gospel

DEFICIENT—*want* Dan. 5:27, and found **d**

DEFILE—*pollute, profane* Lev. 21:4; Is. 59:3; Jer. 2:7
2 Kin. 23:13, high places ... the king **d-d**
Neh. 13:29, they have **d-d** the priesthood
Ps. 74:7, **d-d** the dwelling place of Thy name
79:1, **d-d** Thy holy temple
Matt. 15:11,18,20; Mark 7:15,20,23, **d** the man
Titus 1:15, to those who are **d-d** ... nothing is pure
Heb. 12:15, by it many are **d-d**
James 3:6, that which **d-s** the entire body
Jude 8, these men also by dreaming **d** the flesh
Ezek. 23:38; 36:17; Dan. 1:8; John 18:28; 1 Cor. 8:7
DEFILEMENT—*filth* 2 Cor. 7:1, from all **d**
DEFRAUD—*deprive, wrong*
1 Cor. 6:7,8; 1 Thess. 4:6, transgress and **d**
1 Sam. 12:3; Lam. 3:36; Mark 10:19
DEGENERATE Jer. 2:21, **d** shoots of a foreign vine
DEGRADE Rom. 1:26, gave them over to **d-ing** passions
DEGREE—*standing* 1 Chr. 17:17; Ps. 62:9
DEITY Col. 2:9, fulness of **D** ... bodily form
DELAY—*hinder, linger*
Ex. 32:1, the people saw that Moses **d-ed**
Deut. 23:21, shall not **d** to pay it
1 Tim. 3:15, in case I am **d-ed**
Rev. 10:6, there shall be **d** no longer
Gen. 24:56; Ex. 22:29; Acts 9:38; 25:17
DELEGATION—*messenger*
Luke 19:14, sent a **d** after him
DELICACY—*dainty, delicate* Ps. 141:4; Prov. 23:3; Lam. 4:5
DELICATE—*dainty* Deut. 28:54,56; Is. 47:1
DELIGHT (n.)—*affection, luxury, observe, pleasure*
2 Sam. 15:26, I have no **d** in you
Ps. 1:2, his **d** is in the law of the LORD
Prov. 8:31, *having* my **d** in the sons of men
11:1, a just weight is His **d**
12:22, those who deal faithfully are His **d**
Job 27:10; Ps. 16:3; 119:24,77,92,143,174; Prov. 8:30; 15:8; 16:13; Song 2:3; Is. 58:13; 62:4
DELIGHT (v.)—*desire*
Job 22:26, you will **d** in the Almighty
Ps. 37:4, **D** yourself in the LORD
37:11, **d** themselves in abundant prosperity
51:16, Thou dost not **d** in sacrifice
Eccles. 5:4, He takes no **d** in fools
Is. 42:1, My chosen one *in whom* My soul **d-s**
55:2, **d** yourself in abundance
Mic. 7:18, He **d-s** in unchanging love
1 Sam. 15:22; Neh. 1:11; Ps. 94:19; Prov. 1:22; 2:14; 18:2; 23:26; Is. 11:3; Hos. 6:6; Mal. 3:1
DELIGHTFUL Mal. 3:12, you shall be a **d** land
DELIVER—*rescue, save* Ex. 3:8; Num. 35:25; Deut. 32:39
Job 5:19, From six troubles He will **d** you
Ps. 56:13, **d-ed** my soul from death
Is. 43:13, none who can **d** out of My hand
50:2, have I no power to **d**
Matt. 6:13, **d** us from evil
10:17, they will **d** you up to *the* courts
10:21, brother will **d** up brother
Acts 2:23, **d-ed** up by the predetermined plan
Rom. 4:25, who was **d-ed** up because of our trangressions
2 Cor. 1:10, **d-ed** us from so great a *peril of* death
Gal. 1:4, He might **d** us out of this present evil age
Jude 3, faith which was ... **d-ed** to the saints
Judg. 7:2; 1 Sam. 10:27; 2 Chr. 20:9; 32:13; Ps. 33:17; Prov. 24:11; Eccles. 9:15; Jer. 1:8; 39:17; Dan. 3:17; 6:14; Joel 2:32; Matt. 26:15; Acts 7:34; 2 Cor. 4:11; 2 Tim. 4:18
DELIVERANCE—*victory, salvation* Gen. 45:7, by a great **d**
Ps. 32:7, surround me with songs of **d**
68:20, God is ... a God of **d-s**

DELUDE 2 Thess. 2:11, God will send ... a **d-ing** influence
DEMON—*satyr* Matt. 8:31, **d-s** *began* to entreat Him
Mark 3:15, authority to cast out the **d-s**
James 2:19, **d-s** also believe and shudder
3:15, is earthly, natural, **d-ic**
Lev. 17:7; Deut. 32:17; Ps. 106:37; Matt. 10:8; 1 Cor. 10:20; Rev. 9:20
DEMONSTRATE—*show* Rom. 5:8, God **d-s** His own love
Rom. 9:22, willing to **d** His wrath
DEMONSTRATION 1 Cor. 2:4, in **d** of the Spirit and of power
DEN Jer. 7:11, Has this house ... become a **d** of robbers
Dan. 6:7, shall be cast into the lions' **d**
Judg. 6:2; Job 37:8; Is. 11:8; Amos 3:4; Matt. 21:13; Mark 11:17
DENOUNCE—*slander* Jer. 20:10, **D** *him;* yes, let us **d** him
DENY—*conceal* Matt. 10:33, whoever shall **d** Me before men
1 Tim. 5:8, he has **d-ed** the faith
2 Tim. 2:13, for He cannot **d** Himself
3:5, they have **d-ed** its power
Titus 2:12, instructing us to **d** ungodliness
Josh. 24:27; Job 6:10; Prov. 30:9; Titus 1:16
DEPART Job 21:14, they say to God, **D** from us
Job 28:28, to **d** from evil is understanding
Ps. 6:8, **D** from me, all you who do iniquity
Prov. 22:6, when he is old he will not **d** from it
27:22, his folly will not **d** from him
Is. 26:14, **d-ed** spirits will not rise
John 13:1, hour had come that He should **d**
2 Cor. 12:8, entreated ... that it might **d**
Phil. 1:23, desire to **d** and be with Christ
Gen. 49:10; Job 22:17; Ps. 18:21; 34:14; 37:27; 105:38; Matt. 2:13,22; 7:23; 25:41; Luke 2:29; 4:13; 13:27; 21:21; Acts 7:3
DEPARTURE—*death* Luke 9:13, His **d**
2 Tim. 4:6, the time of my **d** has come
2 Pet. 1:15, at any time after my **d**
DEPEND—*hang* Matt. 22:40, two commandments **d** ... Law
DEPOSE Dan. 5:20, he was **d-d** from his royal throne
DEPRAVE Rom. 1:28, gave them over to a **d-d** mind
2 Tim. 3:8, men of **d-d** mind
DEPRIVE Is. 38:10, **d-d** of the rest of my years
1 Cor. 7:5, Stop **d-ing** one another
1 Tim. 6:5, **d-d** of the truth
DEPTH—*abyss, deep*
Ps. 95:4, In whose hand are the **d-s** of the earth
107:26, they went down to the **d-s**
Prov. 25:3, heavens for height ... for **d**
Mic. 7:19, cast all their sins Into the **d-s** of the sea
Matt. 13:5, they had no **d** of soil
18:6, better ... be drowned in the **d** of the sea
Mark 4:5, it sprang up because it had no **d** of soil
Rom. 8:39, nor height, nor **d** ... separate us
11:33, **d** of the riches
1 Cor. 2:10, searches all things, even the **d-s** of God
Job 41:31, Ps. 86:13; Prov. 8:24; Is. 63:13
DEPUTY—*proconsul* 1 Kin. 22:47, a **d** was king
DERIDE—*mock, scoff, sneer* Ps. 119:51, utterly **d** me
DERISION—*laughingstock, shame* Ex. 32:25; Ps. 79:4
Ps. 44:13, a **d** to those around us
Jer. 20:8; Ezek. 23:32; 36:4; Hos. 7:16
DESCEND Gen. 28:12, angels of God ... **d-ing**
Matt. 7:25,27, rain **d-ed**, and the floods came
Mark 1:10, Spirit like a dove **d-ing** upon Him
Rom. 10:7, WHO WILL **D** INTO THE ABYSS

DESCEND *(Continued)*
Ps. 49:17; Prov. 30:4; Matt. 11:23; John 1:32,33; Eph. 4:10
DESCENDANT—*seed* Ps. 37:28, **d-s** of the wicked will be
Rom. 4:18, So SHALL YOUR D-S BE
DESCENT Luke 19:37, near the **d** of the Mount
DESCRIPTION Josh. 18:4, write a **d** of it according to
DESERT—*wild* Ps. 78:40, grieved Him in the **d**
Is. 35:1, the **d** will be glad
40:3, in the **d** a highway for our God
43:19, Rivers in the **d**
51:3, her **d** like the garden of the LORD
Prov. 21:19; Jer. 17:6; 25:24; 50:39; Luke 1:80
DESERT—*leave, forsake* 2 Kin. 25:11, the **d-ers** who had
2 Tim. 4:16, but all **d-ed** me
Heb. 13:5, I WILL NEVER D YOU
DESERVE—*due, worthy*
Matt. 26:66, He is **d-ing** of death
Luke 23:41, receiving what we **d** for our deeds
1 Tim. 1:15, statement, **d-ing** full acceptance
Judg. 9:16; Ezra 9:13
DESIGN—*device, devise* Ex. 31:4; 35:32,35; 2 Chr. 2:14
DESIRABLE Ps. 19:10, more **d** than gold
Prov. 19:22, What is **d** in a man is his kindness
Ezek. 23:6,12,23, **d** young men
Gen. 3:6; Prov. 8:11
DESIRE (n.)—*appetite* Job 31:16; Ps. 10:3; 140:8; Prov. 13:12
Gen. 3:16, your **d** shall be for your husband
Ps. 21:2, given him his heart's **d**
37:4, He will give you the **d-s** of your heart
112:10, **d** of the wicked will perish
145:16, satisfy the **d** of every living thing
Prov. 10:24; 11:23, the **d** of the righteous
Mic. 7:3, great man speaks the **d** of his soul
Rom. 10:1, my heart's **d** ... is for *their* salvation
Eph. 2:3, **d-s** of the flesh and of the mind
Phil. 1:23, having the **d** to depart
Prov. 21:25; Ezek. 24:16,21,25; Mark 4:19; Col. 3:5
DESIRE (v.)—*want, wish, crave* Deut. 14:26; 1 Sam. 2:16
Ps. 34:12, Who is the man who **d-s** life
51:6, Thou dost **d** truth
73:25, besides Thee, I **d** nothing on earth
Luke 22:15, earnestly **d-d** to eat this Passover
1 Cor. 12:31, earnestly **d** the greater gifts
14:1, yet **d** earnestly spiritual *gifts*
Gal. 6:12, who **d** to make a good showing in the flesh
Heb. 11:16, they **d** a better *country*
Job 13:3; Ps. 40:6; 45:11; 107:30; Prov. 3:15, 23:3; Eccles. 2:10; Matt. 13:17; Gal. 4:9; 1 Tim. 3:1
DESOLATE—*lonely, waste* Lev. 26:31; Is. 54:1; 62:4
Matt. 23:38, your house is being left to you **d**
Jer. 2:12; 12:10; Ezek. 6:6; Joel 2:3; Zech. 7:14; Luke 13:35; Acts 1:20; Gal. 4:27
DESOLATION—*ruins, waste*
Jer. 25:9; Ezek. 35:9, an everlasting **d**
32:43, a **d** without man or beast
Dan. 9:26, there will be war; **d-s** are determined
11:31; 12:11, abomination of **d**
Zeph. 1:15, day of destruction and **d**
2 Kin. 22:19; Josh. 8:28; Ps. 46:8; Is. 61:4; Luke 21:20
DESPAIR—*faint, sorrow* 1 Sam. 27:1; Job 6:26; Eccles. 2:20
Deut. 28:65, failing of eyes, and **d** of soul
2 Cor. 4:8, perplexed, but not **d-ing**
DESPERATE Jer. 17:9, The heart ... is **d-ly** sick
DESPISE—*reject, scorn, spurn* Gen. 16:4; Num. 15:31
Gen. 25:34, Esau **d-d** his birthright
Job 5:17, do not **d** the discipline of the Almighty
36:5, God is mighty but does not **d** *any*
Ps. 51:17, a contrite heart ... Thou wilt not **d**
Prov. 1:7, Fools **d** wisdom and instruction
15:32, He who neglects discipline **d-s** himself
Eccles. 9:16, wisdom of the poor man is **d-d**
Zech. 4:10, who has **d-d** the day of small things
Matt. 6:24; Luke 16:13, hold to one and **d** the other
18:10, do not **d** one of these little ones
1 Cor. 1:28, base things ... and the **d-d**
Heb. 12:2, endured the cross, **d-ing** the shame
1 Sam. 2:30; 2 Sam. 6:16; Neh. 4:4; Job 19:18; Ps. 73:20; 102:17; 119:163; Prov. 6:30; 13:13; 15:20; Is. 5:24; 49:7; Jer. 49:15; Ezek. 21:10; 22:8; Mal. 1:6; 1 Cor. 11:22; 16:11; 1 Thess. 5:20
DESPONDENCY—*anguish, distress*
Ex. 6:9, on account of *their* **d**
DESTINE—*appoint, name*
1 Thess. 5:9, God has not **d-d** us for wrath
DESTITUTE—*deprive* Ezek. 32:15
Ps. 102:17, regarded the prayer of the **d**
Heb. 11:37, being **d**, afflicted, ill-treated
DESTROY—*defile, pollute, abolish, ruin, waste*
2 Sam. 1:14, **d** the LORD's anointed
Ps. 40:14, seek my life to **d** it
Prov. 1:32, complacency of fools shall **d** them
Is. 23:14, your stronghold is **d-ed**
Matt. 2:13, search ... to **d** Him
6:19, where moth and rust **d**
10:28, fear Him who is able to **d**
12:14; Mark 3:6, they might **d** Him
Mark 14:58, I will **d** this temple
Luke 6:9, is it lawful ... to save a life or **d** it
17:27, flood came and **d-ed** them all
1 Cor. 3:17, If any man **d-s** the temple
Gal. 1:13, church of God ... tried to **d** it
1:23, the faith which he once tried to **d**
2:18, if I rebuild what I *once* **d-ed**
2 Pet. 3:12, heavens will be **d-ed** by burning
1 John 3:8, **d** the works of the devil
Gen. 6:17; Ex. 22:20; Deut. 9:14; 1 Sam. 15:6; Job 10:8; Ps. 63:9; 145:20; Prov. 28:24; 31:3; Eccles. 9:18; Is. 10:7; 11:9; Jer. 13:14; 23:1; Ezek. 9:1; 22:27; Dan. 8:24; Matt. 22:7; Mark 1:24; 11:18; 12:9; 15:29; Luke 4:34; 20:16; John 2:19; Rom. 14:15; James 4:12; 2 Pet. 2:12; 3:11; Jude 5
DESTROYER—*robber* Judg. 16:24, Even the **d** of our country
Job 12:6; 15:21; Is. 49:17; Jer. 22:7
DESTRUCTION—*calamity, ruin* Ps. 35:8, Let **d** come upon him
Ps. 52:2, Your tongue devises **d**
91:6, **d** that lays waste at noon
Prov. 16:18, Pride goes before **d**
Is. 19:18, called the City of **D**
59:7, Devastation and **d** are in their highways
Lam. 2:11; 3:48; 4:10, **d** of the daughter of my people
Matt. 7:13, way is broad that leads to **d**
Rom. 9:22, vessels of wrath prepared for **d**
Phil. 3:19, whose end is **d**
1 Thess. 5:3, **d** will come upon them suddenly
1 Tim. 6:9, desires plunge to ruin and **d**
2 Chr. 22:4; Esth. 8:6; Job 21:17; Ps. 5:9; 57:1; 73:18; Prov. 17:19; 19:13; Is. 10:22; 14:23; 28:2; Jer. 17:18; 50:22; Hos. 13:9; Rom. 3:16; 2 Thess. 1:9; 2 Pet. 2:1,3; 3:16; Rev. 17:8
DESTRUCTIVE—*false* Prov. 17:4, a **d** tongue
2 Pet. 2:1, secretly introduce **d** heresies
DETAIN Judg. 13:15,16; 1 Sam. 21:7
DETERMINE—*decide* Job 14:5, his days are **d-d**
Luke 22:22, Son ... as it has been **d-d**
Acts 17:26, having **d-d** *their* appointed times
1 Cor. 2:2, I **d-d** to know nothing
DETEST—*despise, loathe* Deut. 7:26; Jer. 4:1; Amos 6:8
DETESTABLE—*abominable*
Deut. 14:3, eat any **d** thing
Is. 66:17, swine's flesh, **d** things
Luke 16:15, is **d** in the sight of God

Job 15:16; Jer. 16:18; Ezek. 5:11; 7:20; 11:18; 37:23
DEVASTATE—*waste* Nah. 2:2; 3:7
DEVASTATION—*oppression*
Ps. 12:5, the **d** of the afflicted
DEVICE—*design, plan, scheme*
Prov. 1:31, satiated ... own **d-s**
DEVIOUS—*perverse* Prov. 4:24, put **d** lips far from you
DEVISE—*design, plan, scheme, fashion*
Prov. 3:29, Do not **d** harm against your neighbor
6:14, **d-s** evil continually
14:22, will they not go astray who **d** evil
2 Pet. 1:16, cleverly **d-d** tales
Esth. 9:25; Ps. 2:1; 10:2; 21:11; 35:4; 41:7; 94:20; Prov. 6:18; 12:2; Is. 32:7,8; Zech. 7:10; Acts 4:25
DEVOTE—*dedicate* Rom. 12:10, Be **d-d** to one another
Col. 4:2, **D** yourselves to prayer
Num. 18:14; Ezek. 44:29
DEVOTION Eccles. 12:12, excessive **d** *to books* is wearying
DEVOUR—*consume, swallow*
2 Sam. 2:26, Shall the sword **d** forever
11:25, the sword **d-s** one as well as another
Zeph. 1:18; 3:8, all the earth will be **d-ed**
Matt. 13:4, birds came and **d-ed** them
23:14, you **d** widows' houses
Luke 15:30, son of yours ... has **d-ed** your wealth
Gal. 5:15, if you bite and **d** one another
Gen. 37:20; 2 Sam. 18:8; 22:9; Job 18:13; Ps. 18:8; 50:3; 52:4; Prov. 30:14; Is. 1:7,20; Jer. 2:30; 30:16; Amos 4:9; Mal. 3:11; Mark 12:40; Luke 8:5; 2 Cor. 11:20
DEVOUT—*God-fearing*
Luke 2:25, Simeon ... righteous and **d**
Acts 2:5; 8:2, **d** men
Acts 10:2; 13:50; 22:12
DEW Gen. 27:28, God give you of the **d** of heaven
Judg. 6:37, If there is **d** on the fleece only
2 Sam. 17:12, we will fall on him as the **d** falls
Prov. 3:20, the skies drip with **d**
Is. 18:4, Like a cloud of **d** in the heat of harvest
Dan. 4:15,23,25,33, drenched with the **d** of heaven
Ex. 16:13; Num. 11:9; Deut. 32:2; 33:13; 2 Sam. 1:21; 1 Kin. 17:1; Job 29:19; 38:28; Ps. 110:3; 133:3; Prov. 19:12; Is. 26:19; Hos. 6:4; 13:3; 14:5; Hag. 1:10
DIADEM—*turban* Is. 28:5; 62:3
DIAMOND Ex. 28:18; 39:11; Jer. 17:1; Ezek. 28:13
DID—*put* Gen. 6:22; Job 1:5
2 Chr. 18:23, How **d** the Spirit ... pass
Matt. 13:58, He **d** not do many miracles
John 9:26, What **d** He do to you
15:24, works which no one else **d**
1 Cor. 13:11, **d** away with childish things
DIE—*depart* Gen. 2:17; 20:7; 1 Sam. 14:44; 22:16; 1 Kin. 2:37,42; Ezek. 3:18; 33:8, you shall surely **d**
Deut. 14:21, not eat anything which **d-s** of itself
Ruth 1:17, Where you **d**, I will **d**
1 Sam. 26:16, *all* of you must surely **d**
Job 2:9, his wife said ... Curse God and **d**
3:11, Why did I not **d** at birth
14:14, If a man **d-s**, will he live *again*
21:23, One **d-s** in his full strength
Ps. 49:10, *even* wise men **d**
49:17, when he **d-s** he will carry nothing away
Prov. 10:21, fools **d** for lack of understanding
Eccles. 2:16, wise man and fool alike **d**
Ezek. 18:4, soul who sins will **d**
18:32, no pleasure in ... who **d-s**
Matt. 26:35, Even if I must **d** with you
Luke 8:52, she has not **d-d**, but is asleep
16:22, poor man **d-d** ... rich man also **d-d**
John 6:49, ate the manna ... and they **d-d**
11:25, who believes ... live even if he **d-s**
11:51, that Jesus was going to **d** for the nation
12:24, a grain of wheat falls ... and **d-s**
Rom. 5:6, Christ **d-d** for the ungodly
5:7, one will hardly **d** for a righteous man
6:2, How shall we who **d-d** to sin
14:9, Christ **d-d** and lived *again*
14:15, him for whom Christ **d-d**
1 Cor. 15:31, I **d** daily
2 Cor. 5:14, one **d-d** for all, therefore all **d-d**
Phil. 1:21, to **d** is gain
Col. 2:20, If you have **d-d** with Christ
1 Thess. 4:14, we believe that Jesus **d-d** and rose
5:10, who **d-d** for us, that ... we may live
Heb. 9:27, appointed for men to **d** once
11:13, All these **d-d** in faith
Gen. 3:3; 25:8; 27:4; 45:28; Lev. 10:6; Num. 18:32; Prov. 14:32; 30:7; Jer. 26:8; 27:13; Ezek. 18:20,31; 33:11,14; Matt. 22:25; Mark 5:39; John 11:44; 19:7; Acts 9:37; 21:13; Rom. 6:10; 7:9; 8:34; 14:7; 1 Cor. 8:11; 15:3,22; Gal. 2:19; 2 Tim. 2:11; 1 Pet. 2:24; Rev. 9:6; 14:13
DIFFER Rom. 12:6, we have gifts that **d**
1 Cor. 15:41, star **d-s** from star in glory
Deut. 25:13; Gal. 4:1
DIFFERENCE—*distinction* Ezek. 44:23
DIFFICULT—*hard* Jer. 32:27; Ezek. 3:5
Gen. 18:14, Is anything too **d** for the LORD
1 Kin. 10:1; 2 Chr. 9:1, test Solomon with **d** questions
Jer. 32:17, Nothing is too **d** for Thee
John 6:60, This is a **d** statement
DIG Ex. 21:33; Deut. 6:11; 8:9; Job 3:21; 24:16; Ezek. 12:5; Luke 13:8; 16:3
DIGNITY—*majesty* Gen. 49:3; Esth. 6:3; 1 Tim. 2:2
DILIGENCE—*effort, speed* Ezra 6:12, carried out with all **d**
Prov. 4:23, Watch over your heart with all **d**
Rom. 12:11, not lagging behind in **d**
DILIGENT—*careful, eager, thorough* Prov. 1:28; Heb. 4:11
Prov. 11:27, **d-ly** seeks good seeks favor
Eph. 4:3, **d** to preserve the unity
2 Tim. 2:15, Be **d** to present yourself approved
2 Pet. 1:15, I will also be **d**
DILL Is. 28:25,27
DILUTE—*mix* Is. 1:22, drink **d-d** with water
DIM—*dark* Job 17:7, My eye has also grown **d**
1 Cor. 13:12, see in a mirror **d-ly**
Gen. 27:1; 48:10; Deut. 34:7; 1 Sam. 3:2; Ps. 69:23; Eccles. 12:3
DIMINISH—*dwindle, reduce* Lev. 25:16; Ezek. 16:27
DINE—*eat* Gen. 43:16; Prov. 23:1
DINNER—*lunch, supper* Matt. 22:4; Luke 14:12
Luke 14:16, certain man was giving a big **d**
DIP 2 Kin. 5:14, **d-ed** *himself* seven times in the Jordan
Matt. 26:23, **d-ed** his hand with Me in the bowl
Luke 16:24, **d** the tip of his finger in water and
Rev. 19:13, clothed with a robe **d-ed** in blood
Gen. 37:31; Lev. 4:6; 9:9; Josh. 3:15; Ruth 2:14; 1 Sam. 14:27; Mark 14:20; John 13:26
DIRECT—*arrange, order* Is. 40:13; Jer. 10:23; 1 Thess. 3:11
Prov. 16:9, the LORD **d-s** his steps
23:19, **d** your heart in the way
2 Thess. 3:5, **d** your hearts into the love of God
DIRGE Matt. 11:17, we sang a **d**
DIRTY James 2:2, a poor man in **d** clothes
DISAPPOINT—*frustrate* Ps. 22:5, they trusted ... not **d-ed**
1 Pet. 2:6, SHALL NOT BE D-ED
DISASTER—*evil* Jer. 17:17; Ezek. 7:5
DISCERN—*appraise, analyze, recognize*
1 Kin. 3:9, **d** between good and evil
Matt. 16:3, **d** the appearance of the sky

DISCERN *(Continued)*
Heb. 5:14, senses trained to **d** good and evil
Gen. 41:33; Deut. 32:29; 2 Sam. 14:17; Job 4:16; 6:30; Prov. 7:7; 8:5
DISCERNING—*understanding*
Deut. 1:13, Choose wise and **d**
1 Kin. 3:12, a wise and **d** heart
Prov. 16:21, wise in heart will be called **d**
DISCERNMENT—*judgment*
Ps. 119:66, Teach me good **d**
Is. 27:11, not a people of **d**
1 Sam. 25:33; 1 Kin. 3:11
DISCIPLE—*pupil* Matt. 10:24, A **d** is not above his teacher
Matt. 12:2, Your **d-s** do what is not lawful
26:56, all the **d-s** left Him and fled
28:7, tell His **d-s** that He has risen
28:19, make **d-s** of all nations
Mark 14:14; Luke 22:11, Passover with My **d-s**
Luke 6:13, He called His **d-s** to Him
11:1, just as John also taught his **d-s**
14:26,27, cannot be My **d**
19:37, **d-s** began to praise God joyfully
19:39, Teacher, rebuke Your **d-s**
John 2:11, His **d-s** believed in Him
6:66, many of His **d-s** withdrew
13:5, began to wash the **d-s**' feet
13:35, all men will know you are My **d-s**
19:26, **d** whom He loved standing nearby
Acts 9:26, associate with the **d-s**
11:26, **d-s** were first called Christians
Is. 8:16; Matt. 10:1,42; 11:1; 15:2; 17:16; 19:13; 20:17; 22:16; 26:18,35; 28:13; Mark 2:18; 4:34; 7:2,5; 10:13; Luke 5:30,33; 6:20; 14:33; John 4:2; 6:22; 7:3; 8:31; 9:27,28; 15:8; 18:1,15,16,17,25; 19:38; 20:2,18,26; 21:7,20,23,24; Acts 9:1; 20:30; 21:16
DISCIPLINE—*chasten, exercise*
Job 5:17; Prov. 3:11, not despise **d** of the Almighty
Prov. 16:22, **d** of fools is folly
19:18, **D** your son while there is hope
1 Cor. 11:32, we are **d-d** by the Lord
1 Tim. 4:7, **d** yourself for the purpose of godliness
Heb. 12:6, THE LORD LOVES HE **D-S**
Deut. 4:36; 8:5; 1 Kin. 12:11; Heb. 12:8
DISCONTENTED 1 Sam. 22:2, everyone ... **d**
DISCOURAGE—*dishearten* Num. 32:7,9
DISCOVER—*reveal, find* Job 11:7, **d** the depths of God
DISCREDIT—*condemn*
2 Cor. 6:3, the ministry be not **d-ed**
8:20, no one should **d** us
DISCRETION—*understanding, wisdom*
1 Chr. 22:12, LORD give you **d**
Prov. 11:22, beautiful woman who lacks **d**
DISCUSS—*converse, reason* Matt. 16:7; Mark 9:33; Luke 6:11; 24:15
DISDAIN 1 Sam. 17:42, he **d-ed** him (David)
Job 30:1, whose fathers I **d-ed**
DISEASE—*affliction* Ps. 103:3, heals all your **d-s**
Matt. 4:23, healing every kind of **d**
Luke 9:1, gave them power ... to heal **d-s**
Ex. 15:26; Deut. 7:15; 28:60; 2 Chr. 16:12; Ezek. 34:4; Matt. 4:24; Acts 28:9
DISGRACE—*shame, reproach* Gen. 34:7; Lev. 20:17; Job 10:15; Prov. 6:33; 14:34; Jer. 14:21; 1 Cor. 11:4,5,6
DISGUISE—*pretend* 1 Sam. 21:13, David **d-d** his sanity
1 Sam. 28:8, Saul **d-d** himself
1 Kin. 22:30; 2 Chr. 18:29, king of Israel **d-d** himself
1 Kin. 14:2; 20:38; 2 Chr. 35:22; Job 24:15
DISGUST—*exclude, alienate* Ezek. 23:17, became **d-ed** with
DISH—*bowl* Gen. 27:4; 2 Kin. 21:13
DISHEARTEN Is. 42:4, will not be **d-ed** or crushed
DISHONEST Amos 8:5, cheat with **d** scales
DISHONOR—*disgrace, shame* Ezra 4:14; Ps. 35:26; 71:13
John 8:49, I honor My Father, and you **d** Me
1 Cor. 15:43, it is sown in **d**
2 Cor. 6:8, by glory and **d**
2 Tim. 2:20, some to honor and some to **d**
Ps. 83:16; Prov. 12:16; Rom. 1:24; 2:23; James 2:6
DISLOCATE—*joint*
Gen. 32:25, Jacob's thigh was **d-d**
DISMAY—*astound, discourage*
Deut. 1:21, Do not fear or be **d-ed**
Deut. 31:8; Josh. 1:9; 8:1; 10:25; 1 Sam. 17:11; 1 Chr. 22:13; 28:20; 2 Chr. 20:15,17; 32:7; Job 41:22; Jer. 1:17; 8:9,21; 17:18; 30:10; 46:27; Ezek. 2:6; 3:9; Obad. 9
DISMISS 2 Chr. 23:8; Acts 19:41
DISOBEDIENCE Rom. 5:19, one man's **d**
Eph. 2:2, spirit ... working in the sons of **d**
5:6 wrath of God comes upon the sons of **d**
Heb. 2:2, **d** received a just recompense
DISOBEDIENT—*rebellious* Neh. 9:26; Luke 1:17; Titus 3:3
Acts 26:19, did not prove **d** to the heavenly vision
Rom. 1:30; 2 Tim. 3:2, **d** to parents
10:21, A **D** AND OBSTINATE PEOPLE
1 Pet. 3:20, spirits who once were **d**
DISOBEY 1 Kin. 13:26, **d-ed** the command of the LORD
DISORDER—*confusion* James 3:16, **d** and every evil thing
DISPERSE—*spread* Esth. 3:8; Is. 11:12; Ezek. 20:23; 36:19; Zeph. 3:10
DISPERSION Jer. 25:34; John 7:35
DISPLAY—*declare* Esth. 1:11; Ps. 60:4; Is. 3:9
Ps. 8:1, Who hast **d-ed** Thy splendor above
John 9:3, works of God might be **d-ed**
DISPLEASE Gen. 48:17; Num. 22:34; 1 Sam. 8:6; 18:8; Prov. 24:18; Is. 59:15; Jon. 4:1
DISPLEASURE—*anger, fury*
Deut. 9:19, anger and hot **d**
DISPOSSESS Num. 14:12; Deut. 7:17
DISPUTE—*contend, controversy, debate* Deut. 25:1; Heb. 7:7
Phil. 2:14, Do all things without ... **d-ing**
Jude 9, when he **d-d** with the devil
DISREGARD—*despise* Titus 2:15, Let no one **d** you
DISSENSION—*division* Acts 23:7
Acts 15:2, Paul and Barnabas had great **d**
Rom. 16:17, keep your eye on those who cause **d-s**
1 Tim. 2:8, without wrath and **d**
DISSIPATION Eph. 5:18, wine, for that is **d**
Titus 1:6, accused of **d** or rebellion
DISSOLVE—*melt* Ps. 6:6, I **d** my couch with my tears
Job 30:22; Nah. 2:6
DISTAFF Prov. 31:19, her hands to the **d**
DISTANCE Gen. 22:4; Matt. 26:58
DISTANT—*far* Luke 15:13, into a **d** country
DISTILL—*drip* Deut. 32:2, My speech **d** as the dew
DISTINCTION—*difference* Ex. 11:7; Lev. 11:47; 20:25
Lev. 10:10, **d** between the holy and the profane
Rom. 3:22; 10:12; for there is no **d**
Ezek. 22:26; Acts 15:9; 1 Cor. 14:7
DISTINCTLY—*plain*
Deut. 27:8, all the words ... **d**
DISTINGUISH—*discern* Ezra 3:13; 1 Cor. 12:10
2 Sam. 19:35, Can I **d** between good and bad
Mal. 3:18, **d** between the righteous and the wicked
DISTORT—*pervert* Gal. 1:7, **d** the gospel of Christ
DISTRACTED Luke 10:40, Martha was **d** with
DISTRESS—*adversity, privation* Gen. 35:3; Deut. 4:30
2 Chr. 20:9, cry to Thee in our **d**

Ps. 25:17, Bring me out of my **d-es**
Prov. 1:27, when **d** *and* anguish come on you
Mark 14:33, began to be very **d-ed**
1 Thess. 3:7, in all our **d** and affliction
James 1:27, orphans and widows in their **d**
Deut. 28:53; 1 Sam. 26:24; 2 Sam. 4:9; 24:14; 2 Kin. 19:3; 2 Chr. 33:12; Prov. 24:10; Is. 25:4; 29:2; 33:2; Jer. 16:19; Lam. 1:20; Zeph. 1:17; Luke 21:23; Rom. 2:9; 1 Cor. 7:26; Phil. 1:17; 1 Tim. 5:10

DISTRIBUTE—*apportion*
Luke 18:22, **d** it to the poor
John 6:11, He **d-d** to those who were seated

DISTURBANCES
Luke 21:9, when you hear of war and **d**

DISTURBED 1 Sam. 28:15, Why have you **d** me by bringing
Ps. 42:5; 43:5, Why have you become **d** within me

DIVIDE—*apportion* 1 Kin. 3:25, **D** the living child in two
Ps. 22:18, **d** my garments among them
Prov. 16:19, **d** the spoil with the proud
Luke 11:17, Any kingdom **d-d** against itself
Eph. 2:14, broke down the barrier of the **d-ing** wall
Is. 53:12; Dan. 2:41; Matt. 27:35; Luke 15:12

DIVINATION Acts 16:16, having a spirit of **d**
Num. 22:7; Jer. 14:14; Ezek. 13:6,9

DIVINE Heb. 9:1, regulations of **d** worship
2 Pet. 1:4, partakers of *the* **d** nature
Gen. 30:27; Mic. 3:11; Zech. 10:2

DIVISION—*dissension* Ex. 8:23, put a **d** between My people
1 Chr. 23:6, divided them into **d-s**
John 7:43, arose a **d** in the multitude
1 Cor. 1:10, and there be no **d-s** among you

DIVORCE Lev. 21:14, widow, or a **d-d** woman
Deut. 24:1,3, a certificate of **d**
Jer. 3:8, given her a writ of **d**
Matt. 5:31, WHOEVER **D-S** HIS WIFE

DO—*practice, work* Gen. 11.6, 30:31; 1 Kin. 2:6
Ex. 20:9, Six days . . . labor and **d** all your work
Ps. 1:3, in whatever he **d-es**, he prospers
34:14, Depart from evil and **d** good
Eccles. 3:14, everything God **d-es** will remain forever
Matt. 12:50, whoever shall **d** the will of My Father
John 7:17, If any man is willing to **d** His will
15:5, apart from Me you can **d** nothing
Acts 16:30, what must I **d** to be saved
Rom. 13:3, **D** what is good
1 Cor. 9:23, I **d** all things for the sake of the gospel
11:24, **d** this in remembrance of Me
Gal. 6:10, let us **d** good to all men
2 Tim. 4:5, **d** the work of an evangelist
Heb. 10:7, BEHOLD, I HAVE COME . . . TO **D** THY WILL
1 Pet. 3:11, TURN AWAY FROM EVIL AND **D** GOOD
Prov. 2:14; 21:29; Matt. 23:3; John 2:5; 5:30

DOCTRINE—*teaching*
Eph. 4:14, every wind of **d**
1 Tim. 4:6, of the faith and of the sound **d**
Titus 1:9, able both to exhort in sound **d**

DOER—*workmen* Rom. 2:13, the **d-s** of the Law will be justified
James 1:22, prove yourselves **d-s** of the word
4:11, you are not a **d** of the law

DOG Eccles. 9:4, a live **d** is better than a dead lion
1 Sam. 17:43; 2 Sam. 3:8; Ps. 22:16; 59:6; Is. 56:10; Luke 16:21; Phil. 3:2; Rev. 22:15

DOING—*deeds*
Acts 10:38, He went about **d** good
Rom. 2:7, perseverance in **d** good
Gal. 6:9, let us not lose heart in **d** good
Eph. 6:6, **d** the will of God from the heart
2 Thess. 3:13, do not grow weary of **d** good
2 Cor. 8:11; 1 Pet. 2:15; 3:17

DOMAIN—*estate* Jude 6, angels who did not keep their own **d**
Luke 4:6; Col. 1:13

DOMINION—*kingdom, rule*
Ps. 103:22, in all places of His **d**
Zech. 9:10, His **d** will be from sea to sea
Col. 1:16, thrones or **d-s** or rulers
1 Pet. 4:11, belongs the glory and **d** forever
1 Chr. 29:11; Job 25:2; Eph. 1:21; Rev. 1:6

DONE—*wrought* Matt. 6:10, Thy will be **d**
Matt. 18:19, shall be **d** for them by My Father
Mark 14:6, has **d** a good deed to Me
Gen. 20:9; Ex. 31:15; Eccles. 2:11

DONKEY Zech. 9:9, mounted on a **d**
Matt. 21:2, you will find a **d** tied *there*
Num. 22:30; Prov. 26:3; Jer. 22:19; Matt. 21:5; 2 Pet. 2:16

DOOMED—*silenced* Ps. 79:11, those who are **d** to die
Jer. 8:14, God has **d** us

DOOR—*entrance*
Gen. 4:7, sin is crouching at the **d**
Ex. 12:7, put it on the two **d-posts**
Ps. 141:3, Keep watch over the **d** of my lips
Matt. 6:6, WHEN YOU HAVE SHUT YOUR **D**, pray
John 10:9, I am the **d**
1 Cor. 16:9, a wide **d** for effective *service*
James 5:9, Judge is standing right at the **d**
Rev. 3:8, put before you an open **d**
Gen. 6:16; 18:1; Judg. 4:20; 2 Sam. 11:9; 2 Chr. 12:10; Job 31:9; Prov. 26:14; Ezek. 40:38; Matt. 25:10; John 18:16; Rev. 4:1

DOUBLE—*twice* Gen. 43:12; Ps. 12:2; 1 Tim. 5:17
2 Kin. 2:9, **d** portion of your spirit be upon me
Is. 40:2, **D** for all her sins
James 1:8, *being* a **d-minded** man
Jude 12, without fruit, **d-ly** dead

DOUBT—*misgiving* Matt. 14:31, you of little faith, why did you **d**
Matt. 21:21, if you have faith and do not **d**
28:17, but some were **d-ful**
Luke 24:38, why do **d-s** arise in your hearts
Rom. 14:23, he who **d-s** is condemned if he eats

DOUGH—*flour* 2 Sam. 13:8, Tamar took **d**, kneaded *it*

DOVE Ps. 55:6, O that I had wings like a **d**
Matt. 3:16, Spirit of God descending as a **d**
10:16, shrewd as serpents . . . innocent as **d-s**
Gen. 8:8; Song 1:15; Is. 38:14; John 1:32

DOWN Ps. 23:2, makes me lie **d** in green pastures
Matt. 4:6, Son of God throw Yourself **d**
8:32, whole herd rushed **d** the steep bank
Gen. 12:10; 2 Sam. 3:35; Eccles. 3:21; John 8:6

DRAG—*draw* James 2:6, the rich who . . . **d** you into court
Jer. 12:3; 15:3; Acts 8:3

DRAGON Is. 51:9; Rev. 20:2

DRANK—*drink* 1 Cor. 10:4, all **d** the same spiritual drink
Gen. 9:21; Dan. 1:5; Mark 14:23; John 4:12

DRAW Ps. 69:18, **d** near to my soul
Is. 12:3, **d** water from the springs of salvation
Jer. 31:3, I have **d-n** you with lovingkindness
Luke 21:28, your redemption is **d-ing** near
John 4:11, You have nothing to **d** with
12:32, if I be lifted up . . . will **d** all men to Myself
Heb. 10:22, let us **d** near with a sincere heart
James 4:8, **D** near to God . . . He will **d** near to you
Gen. 24:13; Judg. 3:22; 19:9; Prov. 20:5; Zeph. 3:2; Acts 11:10

DREAD—*fear* Ps. 27:1, Whom shall I **d**
Prov. 1:27, **d** comes like a storm
Deut. 28:66; Job 3:25; Ps. 14:5; Is. 7:16; 8:13

DREAM Gen. 28:12, he had a **d**, and behold, a ladder
Gen. 37:19, Here comes this **d-er**
Dan. 1:17, Daniel understood all . . . **d-s**
Joel 2:28, Your old men will **d** dreams

DREAM *(Continued)*
Matt. 2:12, warned *by God* in a **d**
2:13, appeared to Joseph in a **d**
Jude 8, these men also by **d-ing** defile the flesh
Gen. 20:3; Judg. 7:13; Job 20:8; Ps. 73:20; 126:1; Is. 29:7; Matt. 1:20; 2:19; 27:19; Acts 2:17
DRENCHED—*wet* Dan. 4:15, **d** with the dew of heaven
DRESS—*array, clothe* Mark 15:17; Luke 7:25; 1 Pet. 3:3
Matt. 11:8, A man **d-ed** in soft *clothing*
DREW Gen. 47:29; Matt. 26:51; Acts 5:37
Ex. 2:10, I **d** him out of the water
Acts 1:26, they **d** lots for them
DRIED—*parched, withered* Job 18:16; Jer. 23:10
Gen. 8:7, water was **d** up from the earth
Ps. 22:15, My strength is **d** up
DRIES Joel 1:12, rejoicing **d** up
DRINK—*libation* Lev. 10:9, Do not **d** wine or strong **d**
Job 21:20, **d** the wrath of the Almighty
Ps. 80:5, made them to **d** tears
Prov. 20:1, strong **d** a brawler
Is. 22:13, Let us eat and **d**, for tomorrow
Matt. 11:18, neither eating nor **d-ing**
25:35, I was thirsty and you gave Me **d**
26:27, **D** from it, all of you
26:29, day when I **d** it new with you
27:34, GAVE HIM WINE TO **D** MINGLED WITH GALL
1 Cor. 10:4, all drank the same spiritual **d**
10:21, You cannot **d** the cup of the Lord
11:25, as often as you **d** *it*
Num. 6:3; 1 Kin. 17:6; Prov. 5:15; 7:18; Eccles. 9:7; Is. 24:9; Joel 1:5; Luke 5:39; 17:27; John 6:55; 18:11; Rom. 12:20; Heb. 6:7
DRIP Prov. 27:15, constant **d-ing** on a day of steady rain
Job 36:28; Ps. 65:11; Song 4:11; Is. 45:8
DRIVE—*chase* Ps. 1:4, chaff which the wind **d-s** away
Gen. 4:14; 21:10; Judg. 11:7; 2 Kin. 9:20; Ps. 35:5; Is. 58:3
DROP—*leak, drip* Deut. 32:2; Job 36:27
Is. 40:15, nations are like a **d** from a bucket
Luke 22:44, His sweat became like **d-s** of blood
DROUGHT—*famine* Jer. 14:1, in regard to the **d**
DROVE John 2:15; Acts 13:50
DROWNED Ex. 15:4, his officers are **d** in the Red Sea
Matt. 18:6, **d** in the depth of the sea
DROWSY Matt. 25:5, got **d** and *began* to sleep
DRUNK—*drink* Eph. 5:18, do not get **d** with wine
Lev. 11:34; Deut. 32:42; Is. 29:9; 63:6; John 2:10; 1 Thess. 5:7
DRUNKARD Deut. 21:20; Ps. 69:12; Joel 1:5; 1 Cor. 5:11
DRUNKENNESS
Luke 21:34, weighted down with . . . **d**
Rom. 13:13, not in carousing and **d**
Gal. 5:21, envyings, **d**, carousings and things
DRY—*parch, scorch, wither*
Ezek. 37:4, O **d** bones, hear the word
Gen. 1:9; Ps. 63:1; Prov. 17:1; Ezek. 17:24; Luke 23:31
DUE—*deserve, owe* Gal. 6:9, in **d** time we shall reap
Lev. 10:13; Ps. 104:27
DUG Ps. 7:15; 57:6; Is. 51:1; Ezek. 8:8; Matt. 21:33; 25:18; Luke 6:48
DULL—*red* Gen. 49:12, eyes are **d** from wine
DUMB—*silent* Mark 7:37, deaf to hear, and **d** to speak
Ps. 31:18, Let the lying lips be **d**
Ex. 4:11; Ps. 39:2; Matt. 9:32; 1 Cor. 12:2; 2 Pet. 2:16
DUNGEON—*pit* Gen. 41:14, out of the **d**
DUST Gen. 2:7, LORD God formed man of **d**
Gen. 3:19, you are **d**, And to **d** you shall return
Ps. 103:14, He is mindful we are *but* **d**
Matt. 10:14, shake off the **d** of your feet
Gen. 3:14; 13:16; 1 Sam. 2:8; 2 Sam. 22:43; Job 30:19; 34:15; 42:6; Ps. 18:42; 30:9; 72:9; Is. 26:19; 40:15; 65:25; Dan. 12:2; Luke 10:11; Acts 22:23; Rev. 18:19
DWELL—*abide, remain, live*
Ps. 5:4, No evil **d-s** with Thee
15:1, Who may **d** on Thy holy hill
23:6, will **d** in the house of the LORD
24:1, world, and those who **d** in it
91:1, **d-s** in the shelter of the Most High
Prov. 3:33, He blesses the **d-ing** of the righteous
Luke 16:9, receive you into the eternal **d-ings**
2 Cor. 5:2, our **d-ing** from heaven
Eph. 2:22, **d-ing** of God in the Spirit
3:17, Christ may **d** in your hearts
Phil. 4:8, mind **d** on these things
Col. 1:19, for all the fulness to **d** in Him
1 Tim. 6:16, **d-s** in unapproachable light
2 Pet. 1:14, laying aside . . . *earthly* **d-ing**
Gen. 4:20; Deut. 12:11; 1 Chr. 17:1; Ezra 7:15; Ps. 33:14; Prov. 15:31; Is. 57:15; Luke 21:35
DWELT—*sat* Ps. 107:10, those who **d** in darkness
DWINDLE—*diminish*
Prov. 13:11, wealth . . . by fraud **d-s**

E

EACH Acts 17:27, not far from **e** one of us
Rom. 14:12, **e** one of us shall give account
Phil. 2:3, let **e** of you regard one another
2 Thess. 1:3, the love of **e** one of you
Ex. 18:7; Ps. 85:10; Is. 57:2; Ezek. 4:6; Acts 2:3
EAGER—*hasty* Ps. 17:12; Eccles. 7:9
EAGERLY—*fervently*
Rom. 8:19, creation waits **e** for
Gal. 4:17, They **e** seek you
2 Tim. 1:17, in Rome, he **e** searched for me
EAGLE Ps. 103:5, youth is renewed like the **e**
Is. 40:31, with wings like **e-s**
Ex. 19:4; Deut. 28:49; 2 Sam. 1:23; Job 9:26; 39:27; Ezek. 1:10; 17:3; Dan. 4:33; Obad. 4; Rev. 4:7; 12:14
EAR Prov. 20:12, The hearing **e** and the seeing eye
Prov. 25:12, a wise reprover to a listening **e**
Is. 55:3, Incline your **e** and come to Me
1 Cor. 2:9, EYE HAS NOT SEEN AND **E** HAS NOT HEARD
Rev. 2:7, He who has an **e**, let him hear
Neh. 1:6; Job 12:11; 29:11; 42:5; Ps. 45:10; 58:4; 78:1; 94:9; Prov. 15:31; 18:15; 22:17; Eccles. 1:8; Is. 48:8; 50:4; 59:1; Jer. 9:20; Amos 3:12; Matt. 11:15; 1 Cor. 12:16
EARLY Gen. 26:31; Song 7:12; Hos. 6:4; Mark 16:2; Luke 24:22; John 20:1; James 5:7
EARNEST—*pledge* 2 Cor. 8:8; Phil. 1:20
EARNESTLY—*diligently, fervently*
Ps. 63:1, seek Thee **e**
1 Cor. 12:31, But **e** desire the greater gifts
Col. 4:12, always laboring **e** for you
James 5:17, he prayed **e** that it might not rain
Jude 3, contend **e** for the faith
EARNS Hag. 1:6, he who **e**, **e** wages to put into a purse
EARS—*hearing* 2 Sam. 7:22, heard with our **e**
Job 15:21, Sounds of terror are in his **e**
28:22, With our **e** we have heard
Ps. 34:15, His **e** are open to their cry
115:6, They have **e**, but they cannot hear
Prov. 21:13, shuts his **e** to the cry of the poor
26:17, *Like* one who takes a dog by the **e**
Mark 8:18, HAVING **E**, DO YOU NOT HEAR
2 Tim. 4:3, wanting to have their **e** tickled
James 5:4, reached the **e** of the Lord
1 Pet. 3:12, HIS **E** ATTEND TO THEIR PRAYER
Ps. 135:17; Is. 6:10; Matt. 10:27; 11:15; 13:15,16; 26:51; 28:14; Mark 4:9; 7:33; 14:47; Acts 7:51; 17:20
EARTH—*ground, land, soil*
Gen. 18:25, Shall not the judge of all the **e** deal
Ex. 9:29, the **e** is the LORD's

Num. 14:21, all the **e** will be filled with the glory
Josh. 3:11; Zech. 6:5, Lord of all the **e**
Job 26:7, hangs the **e** on nothing
Ps. 8:1, Thy name in all **e**
24:1, The **e** is the LORD's
33:5, **e** is full of the lovingkindness of the LORD
46:6, raised His voice, the **e** melted
97:1, LORD reigns; let the **e** rejoice
104:5, He established the **e**
104:24, The **e** is full of Thy possessions
Eccles. 1:4, the **e** remains forever
Is. 11:9, **e** will be full of the knowledge
51:6, the **e** will wear out like a garment
66:1, the **e** is My footstool
Jer. 51:15, made the **e** by His power
Mic. 1:2, Listen, O **e** and all it contains
Hab. 2:14, **e** will be filled with the knowledge
3:3, the **e** is full of His praise
Zech. 4:10, eyes of the LORD ... the **e**
Matt. 5:5, gentle, for they shall inherit the **e**
6:10, on **e** as it is in heaven
6:19, treasures upon **e**
16:19; 18:18, shall bind on **e**
Luke 2:14, on **e** peace
John 12:32, lifted up from the **e**
17:4, I glorified Thee on the **e**
1 Cor. 15:47, first man is from the **e**, **e-y**
15:48, As is the **e-y**, so also ... who are **e-y**
Col. 3:2, not on the things that are on **e**
2 Pet. 3:13, new heavens and a new **e**
Rev. 20:11, from whose presence **e** and heaven fled
21:1, a new **e**
Gen. 1:1,11; 7:10; 8:22; 10:25; Deut. 32:1; Josh. 23:14; 1 Kin. 8:27; 2 Kin. 5:17; 2 Chr. 6:18; Job 9:24; 12:8; 19:25; 38:4; 41:33; Ps. 2:8; 16:3; 34:16; 41:2; 46:2,8,10; 47:9; 50:4; 57:5; 58:11; 63:9; 65:8,9; 67:6; 68:8; 71:20; 72:6,16; 73:25; 75:3; 83:18; 90:2; 97:9; 99:1; 102:25; 104:13; 108:5; 112:2; 115:16; 119:19,64,90; 146:4; 147:8; 148:13, Prov. 3:19; 8:23,26; 11:31; 25:3, 30:14,16,21,24; Eccles. 3:21; 12:7; Is. 4:2; 13:13; 14:16; 24:1,19; 26:9,21; 34:1; 40:22,28; 44:24; 45:22; 48:13; 49:13; 65:16; Jer. 31:22; Ezek. 34:27; 43:2; Hos. 2:22; Amos 8:9; Jon. 2:6; Mic. 6:2; 7:17; Nah. 1:5; Zeph. 3:8; Hag. 1:10; Matt. 5:35; 10:34; 23:9; Mark 4:28; 9:3; John 3:31; Acts 8:33; 22:22; Rom. 10:18; 1 Cor. 15:49; Heb. 8:4; 11:13; 12:25,26; James 3:15; 5:5,18; 2 Pet. 3:7,10; Rev. 5:10; 7:3; 18:1; 20:9

EARTHEN Jer. 19:1; Lam. 4:2
2 Cor. 4:7, have this treasure in **e** vessels

EARTHLY John 3:12, If I told you **e** things
2 Cor. 5:1, **e** tent which is our house
Phil. 3:19, set their minds on **e** things
James 3:15, wisdom ... is **e**, natural, demonic

EARTHQUAKE 1 Kin. 19:11; Is. 29:6; Amos 1:1; Zech. 14:5; Matt. 24:7; 27:54; Acts 16:26; Rev. 6:12; 8:5; 11:13; 16:18

EASE—*rest, prosperity* Job 12:5, He who is at **e**
Amos 6:1, Woe to those who are at **e**
Zech. 1:15, nations who are at **e**
Matt. 19:24; Mark 10:25; Luke 18:25, **e-ier** for a camel
Luke 12:19, take your **e**
Heb. 12:1, sin which so **e-ily** entangles us
Ex. 18:22; Job 21:23; Is. 32:9,11

EAST Judg. 6:3; 7:12, 1 Kin. 4:30, sons of the **e**
Ps. 103:12, As far as the **e**
Matt. 2:1, magi from the **e**
2:2, His star in the **e**
Gen. 28:14; Ex. 10:13; Job 1:3; Ps. 48:7; 75:6; Is. 27:8; 43:5; Ezek. 8:16; 17:10; Hos. 12:1; Joel 2:20; Jon. 4:5; Zech. 8:7; 14:4; Matt. 8:11; 24:27; Luke 13:29; Rev. 16:12; 21:13

EASY Prov. 14:6, knowledge is **e** to him
Matt. 11:30, My yoke is **e**

EAT—*consume, dine, feast* Prov. 31:27, not **e** the bread
Is. 55:1, come, buy and **e**
Ezek. 3:1, **e** this scroll
Dan. 4:33, began **e-ing** grass like cattle
Matt. 6:25; Luke 12:22, what you shall **e**
11:19, Son of Man came **e-ing** and drinking
15:20, **e** with unwashed hands
26:26, Take, **e**; this is My body
Mark 2:16, He was **e-ing** with the sinners
Luke 12:19, **e**, drink *and* be merry
15:2, receives sinners and **e-s** with them
22:30, may **e** and drink at My table
John 4:32, food to **e** that you do not know about
Acts 12:23, **e-en** by worms and died
Rom. 14:17, kingdom of God is not **e-ing**
1 Cor. 11:29, **e-s** and drinks judgment to himself
2 Thess. 3:10, not work, neither let him **e**
Heb. 13:10, have no right to **e**
Rev. 2:7, **e** of the tree of life
Gen. 2:16; 3:17; 9:4; Lev. 19:26; Deut. 6:11; 8:10; 12:16; Josh. 5:12; 1 Kin. 19:5; 2 Kin. 6:28; Neh. 5:2; 8:10; Ps. 22:26; 80:13; Prov. 1:31; 24:13; 25:27; Eccles. 5:12; Is. 1:19; 3:10; 4:1; 7:15; 11:7; 65:13, 25; Jer. 24:2; 29:17; 31:29; Ezek. 18:2; Hos. 4:10; 10:13; Mic. 6:14; Hag. 1:6; Matt. 9:11; 12:1; 14:16; Mark 6:31,37; 11:14; Luke 9:13; 10:8; 15:23; John 6:53; Acts 10:13; Rom. 14:2; 1 Cor. 8:13; 9:4; 10:27,31; Rev. 10:10; 19:18

EDGE—*bank* Josh. 3:8; Eccles. 10:10; Jer. 31:30
Prov. 5:4, sharp as a **two-e-d** sword

EDICT—*word* Ezra 6:11, violates this **e**

EDIFICATION Rom. 15:2, please his neighbor ... to his **e**
1 Cor. 14:3, speaks to men for **e**
14:26, all things be done for **e**

EDIFY—*encourage* 1 Cor. 8:1, but love **e-es**
1 Cor. 10:23, lawful, but not all things **e**
14:5, church may receive **e-ing**

EDUCATE Acts 22:3, **e-d** under Gamaliel

EFFECT—*wise* Acts 7:6, God spoke to this **e**

EFFECTIVE 1 Cor. 16:9, door for **e** *service*
James 5:16, The **e** prayer

EFFEMINATE 1 Cor. 6:9, Do not be deceived ... nor **e**

EFFORT—*diligence* 2 Tim. 4:9; Jude 3

EGG Job 6:6; 39:14; Is. 59:5; Jer. 17:11
Luke 11:12, asked for an **e** ... give him a scorpion

ELDERS—*older, aged* 1 Sam. 15:30; Job 12:20; 32:9
Matt. 15:2; Mark 7:3, tradition of the **e**
Acts 14:23, appointed **e** for them in every church
1 Tim. 5:17, Let the **e** who rule
James 5:14, call for the **e**
Prov. 31:23; Titus 1:5; 1 Pet. 5:1; Rev. 4:4; 7:13

ELECT—*chosen* Matt. 24:22; Mark 13:20, sake of the **e**
Matt. 24:24, mislead, if possible, even the **e**
Mark 13:22, to lead the **e** astray
Luke 18:7, God bring about justice for His **e**
Rom. 8:33, charge against God's **e**

ELEMENT Gal. 4:3, **e-al** things
2 Pet. 3:10, **e-s** will be destroyed

ELOQUENT—*skillful* Ex. 4:10, never been **e**
Acts 18:24, Jew named Apollos ... an **e** man

ELUDE—*escape* John 10:39, He **e-d** their grasp

EMBITTERED Acts 14:2, **e** them against

EMBRACE 2 Kin. 4:16, Prov. 5:20; Song 2:6
Gen. 33:4, Esau ran ... and **e-d** him
48:10, Joseph ... and **e-d**
Eccles. 3:5, a time to **e** ... to shun **e-ing**
Luke 15:20, ran and **e-d** him

EMBROIDER—*weave* Ex. 35:35; Ezek. 16:10,13; 27:7,16,24

EMERALD Ex. 28:17; Ezek. 28:13; Rev. 4:3; 21:19

EMINENT—*foremost* 2 Cor. 11:5, inferior ... **e** apostles

EMPTINESS—*vanity* Is. 34:11, plumb line of **e**
Jer. 2:5, And walked after **e**
EMPTY—*vain, void* 2 Kin. 18:20, *they are* only **e** words
Is. 55:11, not return to Me **e**
Eph. 5:6, deceive you with **e** words
1 Tim. 6:20, worldly and **e** chatter
Gen. 31:42; Ex. 3:21; 23:15; Deut. 15:13; Judg. 7:16; Ruth 1:21; 2 Sam. 1:22; 2 Kin. 4:3; Job 22:9; 26:7; Mark 12:3; Luke 1:53; 20:10
ENCAMP Ps. 27:3; 34:7; 53:5; Jer. 50:29
ENCIRCLE Ps. 22:12, bulls of Bashan have **e-d** me
ENCLOSE Job 38:8; Ps. 139:5
ENCOUNTER James 1:2, when you **e** various trials
ENCOURAGE—*strengthen* 2 Chr. 35:2; Is. 41:7
Deut. 1:38; 3:28; 2 Sam. 11:25, **e** him
1 Sam. 23:16, **e-d** him in God
Ezra 6:22, to **e** them in the work
1 Thess. 5:11, Therefore **e** one another
Heb. 3:13, **e** one another
10:25, but **e-ing** *one another*
ENCOURAGEMENT—*consolation*
Acts 4:36, Son of **E**
Rom. 15:5, God who gives perseverance and **e**
Phil. 2:1, if . . . any **e** in Christ
Heb. 6:18, may have strong **e**
ENCUMBRANCE—*weight*
Heb. 12:1, also lay aside every **e**
END—*goal, outcome* Gen. 6:13, **e** of all flesh
Job 6:11, what is my **e**
Ps. 2:8, *very* **e-s** of the earth
7:9, wicked come to an **e**
39:4, LORD, make me to know my **e**
Prov. 14:12, **e** is the way of death
Eccles. 4:8, no **e** to all his labor
Is. 9:7, no **e** to the increase of *His* government
Jer. 8:20, Harvest is past, summer is **e-ed**
Ezek. 21:25; 35:5, punishment of the **e**
Matt. 10:22; Mark 13:13, endured to the **e**
13:39, harvest is the **e** of the age
28:20, with you always, even to the **e**
Luke 1:33, His kingdom will have no **e**
21:9, the **e** *does* not *follow* immediately
John 13:1, He loved them to the **e**
Rom. 10:4, Christ is the **e** of the law
Heb. 7:3, beginning of days, nor **e** of life
Rev. 21:6; 22:13, the beginning and the **e**
Num. 23:10; Ps. 9:6; 19:6; 73:17; 102:27; 107:27; Eccles. 7:8; Jer. 5:31; Lam 4:18; Ezek. 7:2; Dan. 11:45; 12:13; Matt. 24:6,13; Mark 13:7; Heb. 6:8
ENDLESS Eccles. 12:12, writing . . . books is **e**
1 Tim. 1:4, attention to myths and **e** genealogies
ENDOW—*clothe* Gen. 30:20; 2 Chr. 2:13
ENDURANCE—*patience*
James 1:4, let **e** have *its* perfect
5:11, **e** of Job
ENDURE—*persevere* Ps. 104:31, LORD **e** forever
Ps. 111:3; 112:3, His righteousness **e-s** forever
Mal. 3:2, who can **e** the day of His coming
Matt. 10:22, one who has **e-d** to the end
24:13, **e-s** to the end
1 Cor. 9:12, but we **e** all things
13:7, **e-s** all things
2 Tim. 2:12, if we **e**, we shall also reign
4:3, not **e** sound doctrine
James 5:11, count those blessed who **e-d**
Ex. 18:23; Esth. 8:6; Job 6:11; Ps. 72:5,17; Prov. 27:24; Is. 66:22; Ezek. 22:14; Joel 2:11; Mark 13:13; Heb. 12:7
ENEMY—*foe* Ps. 23:5, in the presence of my **e-es**
Ps. 61:3, tower of strength against the **e**
72:9, his **e-es** lick the dust
Prov. 24:17, Do not rejoice when your **e** falls
25:21, **e** is hungry, give him food to eat
Matt. 5:44; Luke 6:27,35, love your **e-es**
10:36, A MAN'S E-ES . . . HIS HOUSEHOLD
Acts 2:35, I MAKE THINE E-ES A FOOTSTOOL
Rom. 5:10, while we were **e-es**, we were reconciled
James 4:4, friend of the world . . . **e** of God
Ex. 23:22; Deut. 32:31; Judg. 5:31; 1 Kin. 21:20; Job 13:24; Ps. 8:2; 119:98; 127:5; Prov. 16:7; 27:6; Is. 63:10; Mic. 7:6; Rom. 12:20; Gal. 4:16
ENGAGE 1 Chr. 9:33; Luke 1:27
ENGINE 2 Chr. 26:15, he made **e-s** of *war*
ENGRAVE—*graven* Ex. 28:11; 32:16; 35:35; 38:23; 39:14; Zech. 3:9; 2 Cor. 3:7
ENGULF Ps. 78:53, the sea **e-ed** their enemies
ENJOY Lev. 26:34, land will **e** its sabbaths
2 Chr. 36:21, land had **e-ed** its sabbaths
Eccles. 2:1, **e** yourself
5:18, **e** oneself in all one's labor
1 Tim. 6:17, supplies us with all things to **e**
Heb. 11:25, **e** the passing pleasures of sin
ENLARGE—*extend* Gen. 9:27; Is. 5:14
Ps. 25:17, troubles of my heart are **e-d**
119:32, Thou wilt **e** my heart
ENLIGHTEN—*illumine*
Ps. 19:8, pure, **e-ing** the eyes
Eph. 1:18, eyes of your heart may be **e-ed**
Heb. 6:4, those who have once been **e-ed**
ENMITY—*hostile* Gen. 3:15; Luke 23:12; Eph. 2:15,16
ENOUGH—*plenty, much* Num. 16:9, **e** . . . that the God of Israel
Matt. 6:34, *Each* day has **e** trouble
Mark 14:41, It is **e**; the hour has come
Luke 15:17, hired men have more than **e** bread
Gen. 45:28; Ex. 36:5; Num. 16:3; 2 Sam. 24:16; 1 Kin. 19:4; 1 Chr. 21:15; Prov. 30:15; Hos. 4:10; Hag. 1:6; Matt. 10:25; 25:9; Luke 22:38
ENRAGE—*angry* Prov. 6:34, jealousy **e-s** man
Matt. 2:16, Herod . . . became very **e-d**
ENRICH 1 Sam. 17:25; Ps. 65:9; Ezek. 27:33
1 Cor. 1:5, in everything you were **e-ed**
2 Cor. 9:11, be **e-ed** in everything
ENSLAVED Titus 3:3, **e** to various lusts and pleasures
ENTANGLE—*trap* 2 Tim. 2:4, No soldier . . . **e-s** himself
Heb. 12:1, sin which so easily **e-s** us
ENTER—*come* Ps. 100:4, **E** His gates with thanksgiving
Ps. 118:20, righteous will **e** through it
Is. 57:2, He **e-s** into peace
Ezek. 44:16, They shall **e** My sanctuary
Matt. 5:20, you shall not **e** the kingdom
7:13, **E** by the narrow gate
10:5; do not **e** . . . city of the Samaritans
10:11, village you **e**, inquire
10:12, **e** the house, give it your greeting
18:8; Mark 9:43, better . . . **e** life crippled
19:17, if you wish to **e** into life, keep
25:21, **e** into the joy of your master
Luke 9:34, afraid as they **e-ed** the cloud
22:46, that you may not **e** into temptation
John 10:1, does not **e** by the door
10:9, if anyone **e-s** through Me
Rom. 5:12, sin **e-ed** into the world
1 Cor. 2:9, *which* HAVE NOT E-ED THE HEART
Gen. 6:18; Job 22:4; 38:16; Is. 2:10; 26:2,20; Ezek. 2:2; Hab. 3:16; Luke 13:24; John 3:5; 2 Tim. 3:6; Heb. 3:11,18; 4:10; 6:20
ENTICE—*deceive, seduce* Judg. 14:15; 16:5; 2 Chr. 18:19
Prov. 1:10, if sinners **e** you
James 1:14, **e-d** by his own lust
2 Pet. 2:14, **e-ing** unstable souls
2:18, they **e** by fleshly desires
ENTRANCE—*door* Ezek. 8:5, jealousy at the **e**
Matt. 27:60, rolled a large stone against the **e**
2 Pet. 1:11, **e** into the eternal kingdom
ENTREAT—*appeal, ask, beg* Ex. 8:8; 32:11; 2 Sam. 24:25
Matt. 8:34, they **e-ed** Him to depart from their region

Mark 5:10, he *began* to **e** Him earnestly
2 Cor. 5:20, as though God were **e-ing** through us
Eph. 4:1, I therefore ... **e** you to walk
1 Tim. 2:1, I urge that **e-es** *and* prayers
1 Kin. 13:6; 2 Chr. 33:12; Job 21:15; Prov. 19:6; Jer. 26:19; Matt. 8:5,31; Luke 8:31; 15:28; 2 Cor. 12:8

ENTRUST—*commit*
Luke 12:48, whom they **e-ed** much

ENVIOUS Ps. 37:1; 73:3
Prov. 24:1, Do not be **e** of evil men
24:19, Or be **e** of the wicked

ENVY (n.)—*jealousy* Matt. 27:18; Mark 15:10
Rom. 1:29, full of **e**, murder
Phil. 1:15, preaching Christ even from **e**
1 Tim. 6:4, out of which arise **e**
Titus 3:3, spending life in malice and **e**
1 Pet. 2:1, putting aside all malice ... and **e**

ENVY (v.) Gen. 26:14, Philistines **e-ed** him
Prov. 3:31, Do not **e** a man of violence
23:17, Do not let your heart **e** sinners
Gal. 5:26, **e-ing** one another

EPHAH—*bushel* Ex. 16:36; 29:40; Lev. 19:36; Ezek. 45:10; Zech. 5:8

EPHOD Ex. 28:4; 39:2; Judg. 8:27; 17:5; 1 Sam. 2:18; 23:9; Hos. 3:4

EPOCH—*season*
Dan. 2:21, changes times and **e-s**
Acts 1:7, to know times or **e-s**

EQUAL—*equity, right* John 5:18, Himself **e** with God
2 Cor. 8:14, that there may be **e-ity**
Phil. 2:6, not regard **e-ity** with God
Job 28:17,19; Ps. 55:13; Is. 40:25; 46:5; Matt. 20:12

EQUIP—*furnish*
2 Tim. 3:17, **e-ed** for every good work
Heb. 13:21, **e** you in every good thing

EQUITY—*equal, uprightness, straight* Ps. 17:2; 98:9
Prov. 1:3, Righteousness, justice, and **e**
2:9, discern righteousness ... and **e**

ERASE—*blot* Rev. 3:5, I will not **e** his name

ERECT—*upright*
Gen. 33:20, Then he **e-ed** there an altar
37:7, sheaf rose ... stood **e**

ERR—*stray, mistake* Ps. 95:10, people who **e**

ERROR—*mistake, sin* Is. 32:6; 2 Pet. 3:17; Jude 11
Ps. 19:12, Who can discern *his* **e-s**
Eccles. 10:5, evil I have seen ... like an **e**
James 5:20, from the **e** of his way
1 John 4:6, we know ... the spirit of **e**

ESCAPE—*deliverance, refuge, elude*
Prov. 19:5, he who tells lies wll not **e**
Eccles. 7:26, who is pleasing to God will **e**
Is. 20:6; Heb. 2:3, how shall we **e**
1 Cor. 10:13, provide the way of **e**
Heb. 11:34, **e-d** the edge of the sword
2 Pet. 1:4, **e-d** the corruption that is in the world
Gen. 19:17; Deut. 23:15; 1 Kin. 18:40; 2 Kin. 9:15; Esth. 4:13; Job 11:20; 19:20; Ps. 124:7; Obad. 17; Matt. 23:33; Mark 14:52; Luke 21:36; Heb. 11:34

ESSENTIAL—*excellent*
Rom. 2:18, approve ... that are **e**

ESTABLISH—*confirm, direct, plant, strengthen*
Ps. 119:5, that my ways may be **e-ed**
119:38, **E** Thy word to Thy servant
Prov. 16:12, throne is **e-ed** on righteousness
Is. 16:5, A throne ... **e-ed** in lovingkindness
Rom. 16:25, able to **e** you according to
1 Thess. 3:13, He may **e** your hearts
2 Pet. 1:12, been **e-ed** in the truth
Gen. 17:19; Job 37:15; Ps. 65:6; Prov. 3:19; Is. 51:16; Jer. 10:12; 51:15; Rom. 3:31; 10:3

ESTATE—*domain, standard* Ps. 136:23, low **e**
Luke 15:13, squandered his **e** with loose living

ESTEEM—*regard, consider*
Ps. 119:128, I **e** right ... precepts
1 Thess. 5:13, you **e** them very highly in love

ESTEEMED—*beloved, chosen, loved* 1 Sam. 18:23; Dan. 9:23
1 Sam. 2:30, despise Me will be lightly **e**
Is. 53:4, we ourselves **e** Him stricken
Luke 16:15, highly **e** among men

ESTIMATION—*imagination*
Rom. 11:25, wise in your own **e**

ESTRANGE Job 19:13; Ps. 58:3; Ezek. 14:5

ETERNAL—*everlasting* Deut. 33:27; Matt. 18:8
Is. 9:6, name will be called ... **E** Father
Matt. 19:16, I may obtain **e** life
19:29, shall inherit **e** life
25:46, righteous into **e** life
Mark 10:17; Luke 10:25, what ... to inherit **e** life
10:30, in the world to come, **e** life
John 3:15, may in Him have **e** life
3:16, whoever believes ... have **e** life
3:36, who believes in the Son has **e** life
5:39, search the Scriptures ... have **e** life
6:68, You have words of **e** life
10:28, I give **e** life to them
12:25, hates his life ... keep it to life **e**
17:3, **e** life, that they may know Thee
Rom. 2:7, seek for glory and honor ... **e** life
5:21, righteousness to **e**
6:23, free gift of God is **e** life
2 Cor. 4:17, an **e** weight of glory
4:18, things which are not seen are **e**
5:1, house ... **e** in the heavens
Gal. 6:8, from the Spirit reap **e** life
Eph. 3:11, in accordance with the **e** purpose
1 Tim. 1:17, Now to the King **e**, immortal
6:12, take hold of the **e** life
Titus 1:2, in the hope of **e** life
Heb. 5:9, source of **e** salvation
9:14, through the **e** Spirit
1 Pet. 5:10, called you to His **e** glory in Christ
1 John 2:25, promise ... made to us, **e** life
5:11, God has given us **e** life
Rev. 14:6, having an **e** gospel to preach
Matt. 25:41,46; Mark 3:29; Luke 16:9; 18:18; John 4:14,36; 6:54; 12:50; 17:2; Acts 13:46,48; Rom. 6:22; 16:26; 2 Thess. 1:9; 2:16; Heb. 6:2; 9:12,15; 1 John 1:2; 3:15; 5:20; Jude 6,7

ETERNITY—*world*
Eccles. 3:11, set **e** in their heart
Mic. 5:2, goings forth ... from the days of **e**

EUNUCH—*chamberlain, official* Esth. 1:10; Is. 56:3; Matt. 19:12; Acts 8:27

EVANGELIST Acts 21:8, Philip the **e**
Eph. 4:11, He gave some ... *as* **e-s**
2 Tim. 4:5, do the work of an **e**

EVAPORATE—*fail, gone* Ex. 16:14; Job 14:11

EVENING—*close* Ps. 104:23, to his labor until **e**
Jer. 6:4, shadows of the **e** lengthen
Zech. 14:7, at **e** time there will be light
Luke 24:29, for it is *getting* toward **e**
Judg. 20:23; 1 Sam. 14:24; 1 Kin. 17:6; Ps. 55:17; 90:6; 141:2; Eccles. 11:6; Matt. 8:16; 14:23; Mark 1:32

EVER—*forever* Ps. 52:8; Matt. 21:19; Mark 11:14; Rev. 14:11
Ps. 48:14, Our God forever and **e**
51:3, my sin is **e** before me
Rev. 11:15, He will reign forever and **e**
22:5, they shall reign forever and **e**

EVERLASTING—*endure, eternal, ancient, perpetual*
Gen. 21:33; Is. 40:28, the **E** God
Deut. 33:27, underneath are the **e** arms
Ps. 90:2, from **e** to **e**, Thou art God
106:1; 107:1; 136:1, lovingkindness is **e**
139:24, lead me in the **e** way
Is. 26:4, in GOD ... *have* an **e** Rock
35:10; 51:11; 61:7, **e** joy
Jer. 31:3, loved you with an **e** love
Gen. 9:16; Ps. 103:17; 119:142; 138:8; Prov. 8:23; 10:25; Is. 45:17; 54:8; 55:13; 56:5; 60:19,20; 63:12; Dan. 4:34; 7:14

EVERMORE—*ever, forever* Ps. 92:7; John 6:34
EVERY Gen. 6:5, **e** intent ... of his heart was only evil
Ps. 119:101, restrained my feet from **e** evil way
119:104, I hate **e** false way
Prov. 30:5, **E** word of God is tested
Eccles. 3:1, a time for **e** event under heaven
Is. 45:23, **e** knee will bow
55:1, Ho! **E** one who thirsts
Jer. 25:5, Turn now **e** one from his evil way
Matt. 4:4, ON E WORD THAT PROCEEDS
7:8, For **e** one who asks receives
John 3:8, so is **e** one who is born of the Spirit
2 Cor. 10:5, taking **e** thought captive
Eph. 1:21, far above all rule ... **e** name
2 Tim. 2:21, prepared for **e** good work
Heb. 12:1, lay aside **e** encumbrance
James 1:17, **E** good thing ... **e** perfect gift
1 John 4:1, do not believe **e** spirit
Rev. 20:13, **e** one of them according to their deeds
22:12, **e** man according to what he has done
Deut. 4:4; Prov. 2:9; 7:12; John 18:37; Rom. 14:11; 1 Tim. 2:8; 2 Tim. 2:19
EVERYONE Ps. 32:6, **e** who is godly pray
Eccles. 10:3, demonstrates to **e** *that* he is a fool
Luke 11:10, For **e** who asks receives
19:26, to **e** who has shall *more* be given
EVERYTHING Prov. 14:15, The naive believes **e**
1 Tim. 4:4, **e** created by God is good
EVERYWHERE Mark 1:45; 16:20; Acts 17:30
EVIDENCE—*mouth* Deut. 17:6, the **e** of two witnesses
EVIDENT—*see* Gal. 3:11; Heb. 7:14
EVIL—*bad, wicked, reproach*
Gen. 38:7, **e** in the sight of the LORD
Deut. 23:9, keep yourself from every **e**
1 Kin. 21:25, sold himself to do **e**
Ps. 15:3, Nor does **e** to his neighbor
23:4, I fear no **e**
34:14; 37:27, Depart from **e**, and do good
91:10, No **e** will befall you
97:10, Hate **e**, you who love the LORD
Jer. 7:26, did **e** more than their fathers
Matt. 5:11, all kinds of **e** against you falsely
6:13, deliver us from **e**
7:11; Luke 11:13, If you then, being **e**
12:45, this **e** generation
27:23; Mark 15:14, what **e** has He done
Mark 9:39, speak **e** of Me
Luke 6:45, **e** *man* out of the **e** *treasure*
John 3:20, does **e** hates the light
Rom. 12:17, Never pay back **e** for **e** to anyone
12:21, overcome **e** with good
Eph. 5:16, because the days are **e**
1 Thess. 5:22, abstain from every form of **e**
1 Tim. 6:10, love of money is a root of all **e**
James 3:8, tongue; *it is* a restless **e**
1 John 2:13, overcome the **e** one
5:19, world lies ... power of the **e** one
Gen. 6:5; 8:21; 50:20; Deut. 31:29; 2 Sam. 14:17; 1 Kin. 3:9; Ezra 4:12; Job 30:26; Ps. 35:12; 40:12; 109:5; Prov. 3:7; 6:18; 14:19; 15:3; 17:13; Is. 5:20; 7:15,16; 57:1; Jer. 2:13,19; Hab. 1:13; Matt. 9:4; 22:10; Luke 6:22,35; Acts 23:5; Rom. 7:19; 1 Thess. 5:15; 3 John 11
EVILDOERS Ps. 37:1, Fret not ... because of **e**
Ps. 37:9, **e** will be cut off
Ps. 119:115; Is. 1:4; 9:17; Luke 13:27; 1 Pet. 4:15
EWE Num. 6:14; 2 Sam. 12:3; Ps. 78:71
EXACT—*lend, collect* Deut. 15:2, he shall not **e** it
Heb. 1:3, **e** representation of His nature
EXALT—*extol, lift, raise* Ps. 34:3, let us **e** His name
Ps. 46:10, I will be **e-ed** in the earth
108:5, Be **e-ed**, O God, above the heavens
Prov. 4:8, Prize her, and she will **e** you
14:34, Righteousness **e-s** a nation
Matt. 11:23; Luke 10:15, **e-ed** to heaven
23:12; Luke 14:11; 18:14, **e-s** himself
Luke 1:46, My soul **e-s** the Lord
Acts 5:31, He is the one whom God **e-ed**
Phil. 1:20, Christ shall ... be **e-ed** in my body
2:9, God highly **e-ed** Him
Ex. 15:1; 1 Sam. 2:10; 1 Chr. 29:11; Job 37:23; Ps. 89:16; 92:10; 97:9; Prov. 11:11; Is. 52:13; Ezek. 21:26; Dan. 4:37; 2 Cor. 12:7; 2 Thess. 2:4; James 4:10; 1 Pet. 5:6
EXAMINE—*investigate, search* Job 7:18; Acts 22:24
Ps. 26:2, **E** me, O LORD
Acts 17:11, **e-ing** the Scriptures daily
1 Cor. 11:28, let a man **e** himself
2 Cor. 13:5, **e** yourselves
EXAMPLE—*model, pattern* James 5:10; 2 Pet. 2:6; Jude 7
John 13:15; I gave you an **e**
1 Cor. 10:6, these things happened as **e-s**
10:11, to them as an **e**
1 Tim. 4:12, an **e** of those who believe
Heb. 4:11, same **e** of disobedience
1 Pet. 2:21, Christ also ... leaving you an **e**
5:3, proving to be **e-s** to the flock
EXASPERATE—*anger*
Col. 3:21, do not **e** your children
EXCEED—*great, surpass, utterly*
Ps. 43:4, God my **e-ing** joy
119:96, Thy commandment is **e-ingly** broad
Prov. 30:24, Four things ... are **e-ingly** wise
Jon. 3:3, Nineveh was an **e-ingly** great city
Mark 9:3, His garments became ... **e-ingly** white
Eph. 3:20, able to do **e-ing** abundantly
Gen. 27:34; Num. 14:7; 1 Kin. 10:7; Matt. 2:10
EXCEL Prov. 31:29, you **e** them all
Eccles. 2:13, wisdom **e-s** folly
1 Thess. 4:1, that you may **e** still more
EXCELLENCE—*great, preeminent*
Ex. 15:7, of Thine **e**
Ruth 3:11, are a woman of **e**
Phil. 4:8, if there is any **e**
2 Pet. 1:5, supply moral **e** ... knowledge
EXCELLENT—*noble* Prov. 12:4, **e** wife is the crown
1 Cor. 12:31, a still more **e** way
Phil. 1:10, approve the things that are **e**
Heb. 1:4, a more **e** name
Prov. 17:7; 22:20; Is. 12:5
EXCEPT—*save* Gen. 14:24; Ps. 18:31
Matt. 11:27, knows the Son, **e** the Father
Luke 18:19, No one is good **e** God alone
Acts 26:29, **e** for these chains
Rom. 9:29, E THE LORD ... HAD LEFT TO US A POSTERITY
EXCESS Is. 16:6; 1 Pet. 4:4
EXCHANGE Matt. 16:26; Mark 8:37, give in **e** for his soul
Luke 24:17, these words that you are **e-ing**
Rom. 1:25, they **e-d** the truth of God
EXCLUDE—*alienated*
Eph. 4:18, **e-d** from the life of God
EXCUSE Luke 14:18, began to make **e-s**
Rom. 1:20, they are without **e**
EXECUTE—*perform* Deut. 33:21; Ps. 149:7
Ps. 9:16, He has **e-d** judgment
John 5:27, Him authority to **e** judgment
Rom. 9:28, LORD WILL E HIS WORD
Jude 15, to **e** judgment
EXEMPT Matt. 17:26, the sons are **e**
EXERCISE Jer. 9:24, the LORD who **e-s** lovingkindness
Matt. 20:25; Mark 10:42, **e** authority over them
EXHAUST Judg. 4:21; 1 Kin. 17:14
EXHORT Acts 2:40, many other words ... **e-ing** them
2 Tim. 4:2, **e**, with great patience
Titus 1:9, able both to **e** in sound doctrine
2:15, **e** and reprove
1 Pet. 5:12, **e-ing** and testifying
EXHORTATION Luke 3:18; Acts 20:2; Rom. 12:8; Heb. 13:22

EXILE 2 Sam. 15:19; Is. 51:14
EXORCISTS Acts 19:13, some of the Jewish **e**
EXPANSE—*firmament* Gen. 1:6; Ezek. 1:25
EXPECT Gen. 48:11; Job 30:26; Luke 6:35; Acts 3:5
EXPECTATION Prov. 10:28; 11:7,23
Phil. 1:20, my earnest **e** and hope
Heb. 10:27, terrifying **e** of judgment
EXPEDIENT—*advantageous*
John 11:50, **e** for you that one
EXPERT Jer. 50:9; Acts 26:3
EXPLAIN Luke 24:27, **e-ed** to them
Luke 24:32, He was **e-ing** the Scriptures
John 1:18, He has **e-ed** *Him*
Acts 18:26, **e-ed** to him the way of God
28:23, **e-ing** to them ... about the kingdom of God
EXPLICIT 1 Tim. 4:1, Spirit **e-ly** says
EXPLORE Eccles. 2:3, I **e-d** with my mind
EXPOSE—*reprove*
Eph. 5:11, instead even **e** them
EXPRESS
Ezek. 1:3, word of the LORD came **e-ly**
EXTEND Is. 44:13, he **e-s** a measuring line
Deut. 12:20; Ezra 7:28; Ps. 109:12; Is. 66:12
EXTOL—*exalt* Ex. 15:2, will **e** Him
Ps. 30:1; 145:1, I will **e** Thee
EXTORTIONER Is. 16:4, **e** has come to an end
EXTRAORDINARY Dan. 5:12; 6:3
EXULT—*rejoicing*
1 Thess. 2:19, or joy or crown of **e-ation**
EYE—*look* Gen. 3:7; 27:1; 49:12; Num. 10:31; 24:3,15
Ex. 21:24; Lev. 24:20; Deut. 19:21; Matt. 5:38, **e** for **e**
Deut. 12:8; Judg. 17:6; 21:25, right in his **e-s**
16:19, bribe blinds the **e-s** of the wise
32:10, as the pupil of His **e**
2 Chr. 16:9, **e-s** of the LORD move
Job 19:27, whom my **e-s** shall see
Ps. 11:4, **e-s** ... test the sons of men
19:8, enlightening the **e-s**
34:15, **e-s** of the LORD are toward the righteous
36:1, no fear of God before his **e-s**
69:3; 119:82; Lam. 2:11, My **e-s** fail
Prov. 6:17, Haughty **e-s**, a lying tongue
27:20, Nor are the **e-s** of man ever satisfied
Is. 33:17, **e-s** will see the King
40:26; Jer. 13:20, Lift up your **e-s**
Jer. 5:21, Who have **e-s**, but see not
16:17, My **e-s** are on all their ways
Zech. 4:10, **e-s** of the LORD which range
Matt. 6:22, lamp of the body is the **e**
13:16, blessed are your **e-s**
18:9, **e** causes you to stumble, pluck it out
Mark 8:18, HAVING E-S, DO YOU NOT SEE
Luke 4:20, **e-s** ... were fixed upon Him
24:16, their **e-s** were prevented from recognizing
John 9:6, applied clay to his **e-s**
Heb. 4:13, laid bare to the **e-s** of Him
1 John 2:16, the lust of the **e-s**
Deut. 3:27; 4:19; 34:7; 1 Kin. 1:20; 8:29,52; 20:6; 2 Kin. 6:17; 2 Chr. 6:20,40; 34:28; Job 10:18; 29:11,15; Ps. 15:4; 33:18; 94:9; 119:18; 132:4; 145:15; Prov. 10:26; 20:12; 23:29; 30:17; Eccles. 1:8; 2:14; 6:9; 11:7; Is. 1:15; 22:4; 29:10; 32:3; 42:7; 52:8; 64:4; Jer. 9:1; 13:17; 14:17; 24:6; Ezek. 12:2; 24:16,25; Hab. 1:13; Matt. 5:29; Luke 11:34; John 11:37; 1 Cor. 2:9; Gal. 3:1; 4:15; Eph. 1:18; 1 Pet. 3:12; 2 Pet. 2:14
EYESALVE Rev. 3:18, **e** to anoint your eyes
EYESERVICE Eph. 6:6, not by way of **e**
EYEWITNESSES Luke 1:2, **e** and servants of the Word
2 Pet. 1:16, we were **e** of His majesty

F

FABLES—*myths* 1 Tim. 4:7, worldly **f** fit only for old women
FACE—*countenance*
Gen. 3:19, By the sweat of your **f**
Num. 6:25, Lord make His **f** shine on you
Ps. 34:16, the **f** of the Lord is against evildoers
67:1, cause His **f** to shine upon us
84:9, look upon the **f** of Thine anointed
Is. 25:8, wipe tears away from all **f-s**
Matt. 6:17, when you fast ... wash your **f**
Luke 24:5, bowed their **f-s** to the ground
John 11:44, his **f** was wrapped around with a cloth
2 Cor. 3:18, with unveiled **f** beholding
1 Pet. 3:12, THE F OF THE LORD IS AGAINST
Rev. 1:16, His **f** was like the sun shining
Gen. 17:3; Ex. 33:11; 33:23; 2 Kin. 14:8; Ezra 9:6; Job 33:26; Ps. 13:1; 24:6; 83:16; Prov. 15:13; 27:19; Eccles. 8:1; Is. 50:6; Jer. 5:3; Matt. 6:16; 26:67
FADE—*wither*
James 1:11, rich man ... will **f** away
1 Pet. 1:4, an inheritance ... will not **f** away
Ps. 90:6; Is. 28:1
FAIL—*spent, lack* Deut. 31:6, He will not **f** you or
Luke 22:32, that your faith may not **f**
1 Cor. 13:8, Love never **f-s**
Deut. 4:31; 1 Sam. 3:19; 17:32; Neh. 4:10; Job 11:20; 19:14; Ps. 38:10; Is. 44:12,25; Hab. 3:17
FAILURE Rom. 11:12, their **f** be riches for the Gentiles
FAINT—*languish* Job 23:16, has made my heart **f**
Ps. 61:2, when my heart is **f**
Luke 21:26, men **f-ing** from fear
Is. 1:5; Jon. 2:7; Matt. 15:32
FAIR Ps. 45:2; Is. 11:4; Matt. 16:2; Acts 27:8; Col. 4:1
FAITH—*believe, trust* Matt. 9:2; 15:28; Mark 4:40
Hab. 2:4, the righteous will live by his **f**
Matt. 6:30, O men of little **f**
17:20, **f** as a mustard seed
Mark 11:22, Have **f** in God
Luke 7:50, Your **f** has saved you
17:5, Increase our **f**
18:8, will He find **f** on earth
22:32, that your **f** may not fail
Acts 14:27, door of **f** to the Gentiles
15:9, cleansing their hearts by **f**
Rom. 5:1, having been justified by **f**
10:17, **f** *comes* from hearing
1 Cor. 15:14, your **f** also is vain
16:13, stand firm in the **f**
2 Cor. 13:5, if you are in the **f**
Gal. 2:16, through **f** in Christ Jesus
Eph. 2:8, by grace ... through **f**
4:5, one Lord, one **f**, one baptism
6:16, taking up the shield of **f**
Col. 2:5, stability of your **f** in Christ
1 Thess. 5:8, breastplate of **f** and love
2 Thess. 1:3, your **f** is greatly enlarged
1 Tim. 4:1, some will fall away from the **f**
2 Tim. 4:7, I have kept the **f**
Heb. 10:22, in full assurance of **f**
12:2, author and perfecter of **f**
James 1:3, testing of your **f** produces endurance
1 Pet. 1:5, power of God through **f**
Jude 20, building ... on your most holy **f**
Rev. 2:13, did not deny My **f**
Luke 8:25; Acts 6:5; 20:21; Rom. 4:14; 1 Cor. 13:2; Gal. 5:5; Phil. 1:25; 1 Thess. 1:3; 1 Tim. 1:2; 3:9; Titus 1:13; 2:2,10; Heb. 10:39; 11:1; James 2:1; 2 Pet. 1:5
FAITHFUL—*trustworthy*
Ps. 31:23, The Lord preserves the **f**
Prov. 12:22, who deal **f-ly** are His
27:6, **F** are the wounds of a friend
1 Cor. 1:9, God is **f**, through whom you were

FAITHFUL *(Continued)*
Eph. 1:1, who are **f** in Christ Jesus
1 Thess. 5:24, **F** is He who calls you
1 Tim. 1:12, He considered me **f**
2 Tim. 2:2, these entrust to **f** men
Heb. 10:23, He who promised is **f**
Rev. 2:10, Be **f** until death
Num. 12:7; Deut. 7:9; 1 Sam. 2:35; 2 Kin. 12:15; Neh. 9:8; Ps. 101:6; 119:86; Prov. 13:17; 14:5; Is. 1:21; Matt. 24:45; 25:23; 1 Pet. 4:19; Rev. 1:5; 19:11
FAITHFULNESS—*truth* Deut. 32:4, A God of **f** and without
Ps. 143:1, Answer me in Thy **f**
Rom. 3:3, nullify the **f** of God
Gal. 5:22, Kindness, goodness, **f**
Deut. 32:20; Ps. 89:1; Is. 11:5; Matt. 23:23
FAITHLESS Jer. 3:6,8,11,12,22; 31:22
FALL Ps. 16:6, The lines have **f-en** ... in pleasant places
Matt. 7:25, house; and *yet* it did not **f**
7:27, and great was its **f**
10:29, not one ... will **f** to the ground
15:14, both will **f** into a pit
Mark 14:27, You will all **f** away
Luke 8:13, in time of temptation **f** away
1 Cor. 10:12, take heed lest he **f**
15:6,18, have **f-en** asleep
Gal. 5:4, you have **f-en** from grace
1 Tim. 3:6, **f** into the condemnation
6:9, rich **f** into temptation
Heb. 6:6, and then have **f-en** away
10:31, **f** into the hands of the living God
Judg. 18:25; Job 4:13; Ps. 5:10; 37:24; 38:17; Prov. 24:16; Eccles. 4:10; 11:3; Dan. 3:5; 11:26; Mic. 7:8; Matt. 12:11; Luke 2:34; Rom. 14:4; Heb. 4:11; 2 Pet. 3:17
FALSE—*deceitful, vain*
Ex. 5:9, pay no attention to **f** words
20:16, you shall not bear **f** witness
23:1, shall not carry a **f** rumor
Ps. 33:17, horse is a **f** hope for victory
119:104,128, I hate every **f** way
Prov. 6:19; 12:17; 14:5; 19:5, **f** witness
Matt. 24:24, **f** Christs and **f** prophets
Ex. 23:7; Lam. 2:14; Zech. 10:2; Matt. 19:18; Mark 13:22; 2 Thess. 2:9
FALSEHOOD—*deceitfulness* Ps. 144:8; Jer. 13:25; Mic. 2:11
Ps. 24:4, lifted up his soul to **f**
119:163, I hate and despise **f**
Prov. 20:17, Bread obtained by **f** is sweet
Jer. 14:14, prophesying **f** in My name
Eph. 4:25, laying aside **f**
FALSELY Jer. 5:31, The prophets prophesy **f**
Matt. 5:11, say ... evil against you **f**
Luke 3:14, accuse *anyone* **f**
1 Tim. 6:20, what is **f** called knowledge
Gen. 21:23; Lev. 6:3; Deut. 19:18; Hos. 7:1
FAME 1 Kin. 10:1, the **f** of Solomon
Is. 66:19, heard My **f**
2 Cor. 8:18, whose **f** *in the* things of
Num. 14:15; Josh. 6:27
FAMILY Gen. 12:3, all the **f-es** of the earth
Eph. 3:15, every **f** in heaven
Gen. 10:5; Deut. 29:18; Judg. 6:15; Job 31:34; Ps. 107:41; Jer. 3:14; 31:1
FAMINE—*drought* Gen. 12:10; 41:27,54; 42:19
Matt. 24:7, there will be **f-s** and earthquakes
Mark 13:8, will *also* be **f-s**
Luke 15:14, a severe **f** occurred in that country
Rom. 8:35, or **f**, or nakedness, or peril
2 Kin. 4:38; 1 Chr. 21:12; 2 Chr. 6:28; Neh. 5:3; Job 5:20; Ps. 33:19; Is. 14:30; Jer. 14:12; Amos 8:11; Acts 7:11; 11:28
FAMISH—*hunger* Gen. 41:55, Egypt was **f-ed**
FAMOUS 1 Chr. 5:24, men of valor, **f** men
FANG Joel 1:6, the **f-s** of a lioness
FAR—*distant* Ps. 22:11, Be not **f** from me
Ps. 103:12, As **f** as the east is from the west
119:155, Salvation is **f** from the wicked
Prov. 15:29, LORD is **f** from the wicked
Jer. 23:23, a God **f** off
Matt. 15:8, THEIR HEART IS **F** AWAY FROM ME
Mark 12:34, are not **f** from the kingdom
Acts 17:27, though He is not **f** from
2 Cor. 4:17, glory **f** beyond all comparison
Eph. 1:21, **f** above all rule
Gen. 18:25; Ex. 23:7; Deut. 13:7; Josh. 9:6; 2 Sam. 20:20; Ps. 97:9; Prov. 4:24; 27:10; Is. 60:4; Ezek. 11:15; John 21:8; Eph. 2:17
FARE Jon. 1:3, Tarshish, paid the **f**
FAREWELL Acts 15:29, you will do well. **F**
FARTHEST—*utmost* Mark 13:27, **F** END of the earth
FASHION—*appearance* Job 10:8, Thy hands **f-ed**
Ps. 33:15, He who **f-s** the hearts
1 Kin. 7:15; Job 31:15; Is. 44:12; Jer. 18:11
FAST Matt. 4:2, after He had **f-ed** forty days
Matt. 6:16, whenever you **f**, do not ... as the
6:17, when you **f**, anoint your head
Acts 13:3, when they had **f-ed** and prayed
Is. 58:3,4,5,6; Joel 1:14; Zech. 7:5; Mark 2:18,19; Luke 18:12
FASTING—*hungry* Ps. 109:24, weak from **f**
Matt. 6:16,18, seen **f** by men
Luke 2:37, serving ... with **f-s** and prayers
Acts 14:23, having prayed with **f**
Esth. 4:3; Ps. 35:13; Joel 2:12; Mark 2:18
FAT Prov. 13:4, soul of the diligent is made **f**
Prov. 15:30, Good news puts **f** on the bones
Luke 15:23, bring the **f-ned** calf
James 5:5, you have **f-ned** your hearts
Gen. 45:18; Judg. 3:17; Neh. 8:10; 9:25; Ps. 73:4; 119:70
FATE Eccles. 2:14; 9:2,3
FATHER Gen. 2:24, leave his **f** and his mother
Gen. 9:23, covered the nakedness of their **f**
17:4, **f** of a multitude of nations
Ex. 20:12, Honor your **f** and your mother
Job 29:16, I was a **f** to the needy
Ps. 22:4, In Thee our **f-s** trusted
103:13, as a **f** has compassion on his
Prov. 10:1, A wise son makes a **f** glad
17:6, glory of sons is their **f-s**
Is. 9:6, Eternal **F**, Prince of Peace
63:16, Thou art our **F**
Matt. 3:9, We have Abraham for our **f**
5:16, glorify your **F** who is in heaven
6:1, your **F** who is in heaven
6:4,6,18, your **F** who sees in secret
6:9, Our **F** who art in heaven
7:21, he who does the will of My **F**
10:35, SET A MAN AGAINST HIS **F**
11:25, I praise Thee O **F**, Lord of
11:27, knows the Son, except the **F**
28:19, baptizing ... name of the **F**
Mark 8:38, comes in the glory of His **F**
Luke 2:49, be in My **F-'s** *house*
11:2, **F**, hallowed be Thy name
23:34, Jesus was saying, **F** forgive them
23:46, **F** ... HANDS I COMMIT
John 2:16, stop making My **F-'s** house a
5:17, My **F** is working until now and
10:15, **F** knows me and I know the **F**
14:2, In My **F-'s** house are many
17:1, **F**, the hour has come; glorify
2 Cor. 1:3, **F** of mercies and God of all
Eph. 3:14, I bow my knees before the **F**
6:4, **f-s**, do not provoke your children
Phil. 2:11, to the glory of God the **F**
Heb. 1:5, I will be a **F** to Him
1 Pet. 1:3, Blessed be the God and **F**
2 Pet. 1:17, honor ... from God the **F**
Jude 1, are the called, beloved in God the **F**
Rev. 1:6, priests to His God and **F**
Gen. 4:20; 43:7; 48:17; Ex. 21:15; Deut. 5:9; 1 Sam. 17:34; 2 Sam. 7:12; Job 17:14; 38:28; Ps. 68:5; 89:26; Prov. 1:8; 6:20; Jer. 3:19; Mal. 2:10; Matt. 11:26; 26:29; Mark 14:36; Luke 10:21; 15:18; 24:49; 1 Cor. 4:15; Heb. 3:9; 1 John 2:13; 2 John 4
FATHERLESS—*orphan*
Prov. 23:10, the fields of the **f**

FATNESS—*abundance*
Ps. 65:11, Thy paths drip *with* **f**
Gen. 27:28; Judg. 9:9; Ps. 63:5; 73:7
FAULT—*offense* 1 Sam. 29:3; Ps. 19:12; Rom. 9:19
FAULTLESS—*blameless*
Heb. 8:7, *covenant* had been **f**
FAVOR—*beauty, charm, grace, pleasure, supplication*
Ps. 90:17, let the **f** of the Lord our God
Prov. 8:35; 12:2; 18:22, obtains **f** from the LORD
13:15, Good understanding produces **f**
Luke 2:52, increasing ... in **f** with God and men
Acts 2:47, having **f** with all the people
Gen. 6:8; 39:21; Ex. 3:21; 33:12; Deut. 33:23; 1 Sam. 13:12; Esth. 2:17; Ps. 5:12; 30:5; 51:18; 85:1; Prov. 14:35; 19:12; Eccles. 9:11; Dan. 1:9; Zech. 11:7
FAVORABLE—*acceptable*
Ps. 77:7, will He never be **f** again
Is. 61:2, proclaim the **f** year of the LORD
FEAR (n.)—*dread, awe, terror* Gen. 9:2; 20:11; Deut. 2:25
Ps. 19:9, the **f** of the LORD is clean
53:5, in great **f** *where* no **f** had been
111:10; Prov. 9:10, **f** ... is the beginning of wisdom
Prov. 1:7, **f** ... is the beginning of knowledge
10:27, **f** of the LORD prolongs life
14:26, **f** of the LORD there is strong confidence
14:27, **f** of the LORD is a fountain of life
15:16, better is a little with the **f** of the LORD
19:23, the **f** of the LORD *leads* to life
29:25, the **f** of man brings a snare
Luke 21:26, men fainting from **f**
John 7:13; 19:38; 20:19, for **f** of the Jews
Rom. 13:3, not a cause of **f** for good behavior
1 Cor. 2:3, in weakness and in **f**
2 Cor. 5:11, knowing the **f** of the Lord
7:5, conflicts without, **f-s** within
7:11, what **f**, what longing, what zeal
Eph. 6:5; Phil. 2:12, with **f** and trembling
Deut. 11:25; 1 Chr. 14:17; Job 4:6; 39:22; Ps. 34:11; 36:1; Prov. 3:25; Is. 8:12; Jer. 32:40; Matt. 14:26; Rom. 3:18; Heb. 2:15; Jude 12,23
FEAR (v.)—*be afraid, revere* Gen. 22:12; 42:18
1 Kin. 18:12, I ... have **f-ed** the LORD from my youth
Job 1:9, Job **f** God for nothing
Ps. 27:1, Whom shall I **f**
118:6, will not **f**; what can man do
Prov. 31:30, woman who **f-s** the LORD, she shall be praised
Eccles. 12:13, **f** God and keep His commandments
Matt. 10:26, Therefore do not **f** them
10:28, do not **f** those who kill the body
10:31, do not **f**; you are of ... value
Luke 23:40, Do you not even **f** God
Ex. 1:21; 14:13; 18:21; Deut. 4:10; 5:29; 28:58; Neh. 7:2; Job 11:15; Ps. 27:3; 31:19; 34:9; 66:16; 76:7; 86:11; 112:7; 115:11; 119:74; Prov. 3:7; 24:21; 28:14; Eccles. 3:14; 5:7; Is. 8:12; 35:4; 41:10; 43:5; Jer. 5:24; 10:7; 33:9; Dan. 6:26; Mal. 3:16; Matt. 14:5; 21:26; Mark 5:33; Luke 12:5; 18:2; 20:19; Acts 10:35; 13:26; Rom. 8:15; 11:20; Gal. 4:11; Col. 3:22; Heb. 4:1; 1 John 4:18
FEARFUL Ps. 139:14, I am **f-ly** and wonderfully made
1 Tim. 5:20, that the rest also may be **f**
FEAST—*banquet* Judg. 14:10; Esth. 9:17
Prov. 15:15, heart *has* a continual **f**
John 7:37, the great *day* of the **f**
Job 1:4; Ps. 35:16; Eccles. 7:2; 10:16; Is. 1:14; Jer. 16:8; Mal. 2:3; Luke 2:42; John 7:8,14; 13:29; 1 Cor. 5:8; Jude 12
FEATHERS—*plumage, wings*
Dan. 4:33, hair ... like eagles' **f**

FED Deut. 8:3, humbled you and **f** you with manna
Ezek. 34:8, shepherds **f** themselves and did not feed
Luke 16:21, longing to be **f** with the *crumbs*
FEEBLE Job 4:4, you have strengthened **f** knees
Is. 35:3, strengthen the **f**
Heb. 12:12, strengthen ... the knees that are **f**
Gen. 30:42; Neh. 4:2
FEED—*tend* 1 Kin. 22:27; Ps. 81:16; Prov. 30:8
Prov. 15:14, the mouth of fools **f-s** on folly
Matt. 6:26, your heavenly Father **f-s** them
25:37, see You hungry and **f** you
Luke 12:24, *yet* God **f-s** them
Rom. 12:20, ENEMY IS HUNGRY, F HIM
Is. 44:20; Jer. 3:15; Hos. 12:1; Matt. 15:27; Mark 7:28
FEEL Gen. 27:12, Perhaps my father will **f** me
Judge. 16:26, Let me **f** the pillars
Ps. 115:7, have hands, but they cannot **f**
1 Tim. 5:11, **f** sensual desires in disregard of
FEET—*footstool* Ps. 8:6, all things under his **f**
Ps. 22:16, pierced my hands and my **f**
31:8, set my **f** in a large place
40:2, set my **f** upon a rock
56:13; 116:8, my **f** from stumbling
66:9, does not allow our **f** to slip
119:105, word is a lamp to my **f**
122:2, **f** are standing within your gates
Prov. 1:16; 6:18; Is. 59:7, their **f** run to evil
5:5, Her **f** go down to death
Is. 49:23; Matt. 10:14; Mark 6:11; Luke 9:5, dust of your **f**
52:7, lovely on the mountains Are the **f**
Dan. 2:33, **f** partly of iron and partly of clay
10:6, **f** ... of polished bronze
Nah. 1:3, clouds are the dust beneath His **f**
1:15, the **f** of him who brings good news
Zech. 14:4, His **f** will stand on the Mount of Olives
Luke 1:79, guide our **f** into the way of peace
8:35, sitting down at the **f** of Jesus
24:39, See My hands and My **f**
John 12:3, anointed the **f** of Jesus
13:5, began to wash the disciples' **f**
Acts 4:35,37; 5:2, laid ... at the apostles' **f**
Rom. 3:15, THEIR F ARE SWIFT TO SHED BLOOD
10:15, HOW BEAUTIFUL ARE THE F OF THOSE WHO
16:20, crush Satan under your **f**
Eph. 6:15, shod your **f** with the preparation
Rev. 1:15, 2:18, **f** like burnished bronze
1:17, I fell at his **f** as a dead man
19.10, I fell at his **f** to worship
22:8, I fell down to worship at the **f** of
Gen. 49:10; Josh. 3:15; Ruth 3:14; 1 Sam. 2:9; 2 Sam. 4:4; 22:37; 2 Kin. 6:32; 9:35; 13:21; Neh. 9:21; Job 29:15; Ps. 73:2; 115:7; Prov. 4:26; 6:13,28; 7:11; 19:2; Song 5:3; 7:1; Is. 3:16; 6:2; 23:7; 26:6; 60:13; Lam. 3:34; Ezek. 2:1,2; 3:24; 24:17,23; 25:6; 32:2; 34:18,19; Matt. 7:6; 18:8; 28:9; Mark 12:36; Luke 7:38; 10:39; John 11:2; 12:3; 20:12; Acts 3:7; 21:11; 1 Cor. 12:21; 1 Tim. 5:10; Rev. 13:2
FELL—*came, collapsed* Gen. 4:5; Josh. 6:20; 1 Kin. 18:38
Matt. 13:4, some seeds **f** beside the road
Luke 8:23, Jesus **f** asleep
10:30, he **f** among robbers
13:4, on whom the tower in Siloam **f**
Acts 1:26, the lot **f** to Matthias
10:44, the Holy Spirit **f** upon all those
19:35, *image* which **f** down from heaven
20:9, Eutychus ... **f** down from the third floor
2 Kin. 6:5; Jon. 1:7; Luke 10:36; Acts 13:36; 2 Pet. 3:4; Rev. 16:19
FELLOW Ps. 45:7, oil of joy above Thy **f-s**
Acts 24:5, pest and a **f** who stirs up
Rom. 8:17, and **f-heirs** with Christ

FELLOW *(Continued)*
Eph. 2:19, **f-citizens** with the saints
3:6, Gentiles are **f-heirs**
2 Kin. 9:11; Matt. 24:49; Acts 22:22; Heb. 8:11
FELLOWSHIP—*share* Ps. 55:14, had sweet **f** together
2 Cor. 6:14, What **f** has light with darkness
13:14, **f** of the Holy Spirit
Gal. 2:9, right hand of **f**
1 John 1:3, our **f** is with the Father
1:7, **f** with one another
FELLOW-WORKER—*helper*
Rom. 16:3, Prisca and Aquila my **f-s**
Phil. 2:25, my brother and **f**
4:3, **f-s**, whose names are in the book
1 Thess. 3:2, **f** in the gospel of Christ
Philem. 24, *as do* ... my **f-s**
3 John 8, **f-s** with the truth
FELT Gen. 27:22, he **f** him and said, The voice
Matt. 9:36, He **f** compassion for them
Ex. 10:21; Mark 5:29
FEMALE Gen. 1:27, male and **f** He created them
Gen. 6:19; Lev. 3:1; 5:6; Num. 5:3; Deut. 4:16; Matt. 19:4; Mark 10:6; Gal. 3:28
FERTILE—*fruit* Is. 5:1, vineyard on a **f** hill
FERTILIZER Luke 13:8, dig around it and ... **f**
FERVENT Acts 18:25, being **f** in spirit
Rom. 12:11, **f** in spirit, serving
1 Pet. 4:8, keep **f** in your love
FERVENTLY Luke 22:44, in agony He was praying very **f**
FESTIVAL—*feast* Amos 5:21; 8:10; Matt. 26:5; Mark 14:2
FETTER—*band, chain* 2 Sam. 3:34; Job 36:8; Ps. 2:3; 105:18; Prov. 7:22; Luke 8:29
FEVER Matt. 8:14, mother-in-law ... sick in bed with a **f**
Luke 4:38, suffering from a high **f**
John 4:52, seventh hour the **f** left him
Deut. 28:22; Matt. 8:15; Acts 28:8
FEW Gen. 47:9, **f** and unpleasant ... years
Matt. 9:37, but the workers are **f**
22:14, many are called, but **f** *are* chosen
25:21, faithful with a **f** things
Mark 8:7, had a **f** small fish
1 Pet. 3:20, a **f**, that is, eight persons
Rev. 2:14, I have a **f** things against you
Gen. 24:55; 29:20; 34:30; Lev. 25:52; Num. 13:18; Deut. 4:27; 33:6; Josh. 7:3; 1 Sam. 14:6; 1 Chr. 16:19; 2 Chr. 29:34; Neh. 2:12; Job 10:20; Ps. 105:12; 109:8; Eccles. 5:2; 9:14; Ezek. 12:16; Luke 12:48; 13:23
FIELD—*garden* Prov. 31:16, She considers a **f**
Matt. 6:28, how the lilies of the **f** grow
13:38, the **f** is the world
27:10, GAVE THEM FOR THE POTTER'S **F**
Luke 2:8, shepherds staying out in the **f-s**
15:15, sent him into his **f-s**
17:36, Two men will be in the **f**
John 4:35, **f-s** ... white for harvest
Acts 1:18, acquired a **f** with the price
1:19, that is, **F** of Blood
Gen. 2:5,20; 23:20; 25:29; Ex. 9:19,22; 10:15; 23:11; Lev. 19:9,19; Num. 23:14; Deut. 11:15; 20:19; Judg. 9:43; Ruth 2:3,8; 1 Sam. 20:24; 30:11; 2 Sam. 14:6; 1 Kin. 11:29; Job 5:23; Ps. 96:12; Prov. 24:30; Is. 1:8; 5:8; Jer. 4:17; 26:18; 32:44; Lam. 4:9; Dan. 4:15; Hos. 2:12; Joel 1:20; James 5:4
FIERCE Rev. 19:15, **f** wrath of God the Almighty
Gen. 49:7; Num. 25:4; Job 41:10; Prov. 27:4; Is. 33:19
FIERY Num. 21:6; Deut. 28:22; Ps. 21:9; 1 Pet. 4:12
FIFTEEN Gen. 5:10; Judg. 8:10; Hos. 3:2; Gal. 1:18
FIFTH Gen. 1:23; Lev. 5:16; Neh. 6:5; Jer. 1:3; Rev. 6:9
FIFTY Lev. 25:10, consecrate the **f-eth** year
Gen. 6:15; Ex. 18:21; 26:5; Lev. 23:16; Esth. 5:14; Luke 9:14; John 8:57; Acts 13:19
FIG Gen. 3:7, they sewed **f** leaves together
Matt. 21:19, the **f** tree withered
Mark 13:28, the parable from the **f** tree
Luke 6:44, men do not gather **f-s** from thorns
James 3:12, Can a **f** tree ... produce olives
Rev. 6:13, as a **f** tree casts its unripe **f-s**
Deut. 8:8; Judg. 9:11; Jer. 29:17; Matt. 7:16; Mark 11:13; John 1:48
FIGHT Ex. 14:14, The LORD will **f** for you
1 Tim. 1:18, you may **f** the good **f**
6:12, **F** the good **f** of faith
James 4:2, *so* you **f** and quarrel
Josh. 9:2; 1 Sam. 8:20; Neh. 4:20; Ps. 35:1
FIGURATIVE 1 Cor. 4:6, I have **f-ly** applied to myself
FIGURE—*graven* Lev. 26:1; Deut. 4:16
FILL Gen. 42:25, gave orders to **f** their bags
Jer. 23:24, **f** the heavens and the earth
Gen. 1:22; Job 41:7; Ps. 83:16; Prov. 7:18; Is. 8:8; 65:11; Mic. 3:8; Matt. 22:10
FILTH—*uncleanness*
Is. 4:4, LORD has washed away the **f**
64:6, deeds are like a **f-y** garment
James 1:21, putting aside all **f-iness**
Is. 28:8; Nah. 3:6
FIND—*discover* Gen. 18:26, If I **f** in Sodom fifty
Num. 32:23, be sure your sin will **f** you out
Deut. 4:29, you will **f** *Him* if you search
Prov. 8:35, he who **f-s** Me **f-s** life
18:22, he who **f-s** a wife **f-s** a good thing
Is. 35:10, They will **f** gladness and joy
Matt. 7:7, Seek, and you shall **f**
10:39, lost his life ... shall **f** it
11:29, YOU SHALL **F** REST FOR YOUR SOULS
Mark 13:36, **f** you asleep
Luke 2:12, you will **f** a baby wrapped
15:8, search ... until she **f-s** it
23:4, I **f** no guilt in this man
John 10:9, go in and out, and **f** pasture
Acts 7:46, **f** a dwelling place for the God of
Gen. 32:5; Ruth 1:9; 2 Sam. 15:25; 20:6; Prov. 1:13; 3:4; Song 3:1; 5:8; Matt. 21:2; Mark 11:2; Luke 11:9; John 18:38; Acts 23:9; 2 Cor. 9:4; Rev. 18:14
FINE—*good* Ps. 19:10, than much **f** gold; Sweeter
Matt. 13:45, merchant seeking **f** pearls
Luke 16:19, in purple and **f** linen
Rev. 19:14, clothed in **f** linen, white
Gen. 41:42; Ex. 16:14; 25:4; Ps. 81:16
FINGER John 8:6, Jesus ... with His **f** wrote on the ground
John 20:25, put my **f** into the place of the nails
20:27, Reach here your **f**
Ex. 8:19; Lev. 4:6; Deut. 9:10; 2 Sam. 21:20; 1 Kin. 12:10; 1 Chr. 20:6; Prov. 6:13; Jer. 52:21; Mark 7:33; Luke 11:20; 16:24
FINISH—*end, spend* 2 Chr. 7:11, Solomon **f-ed** the house
John 19:30, said, It is **f-ed**
Acts 20:24, that I may **f** my course
Ex. 40:33; Ps. 90:9; Mark 3:26; 2 Cor. 8:11
FIR—*cedar* 2 Sam. 6:5; Ps. 104:17; Ezek. 27:5
FIRE—*flame, burn* Ex. 13:21, pillar of **f** by night
Num. 3:4, offered strange **f** before the LORD
1 Kin. 18:38, Then **f** of the LORD fell
Neh. 9:12, with a pillar of **f** by night
Ps. 105:39, **f** to illumine by night
Is. 66:15, the LORD will come in **f**
Dan. 3:25, walking *about* in the midst of the **f**
Matt. 3:11, baptize you ... Holy Spirit and **f**
Mark 9:43, into the unquenchable **f**
Acts 2:3, tongues as of **f**
1 Cor. 3:13, *to be* revealed with **f**
Rev. 3:18, gold refined by **f**
21:8, lake that burns with **f** and brimstone
Gen. 19:24; 22:6; Ex. 3:2; 9:24; Lev. 6:13; Deut. 9:3; Job 18:5; Ps. 46:9; Jer. 23:29; Matt. 3:10,12; Luke 3:17; 12:49; Jude 7
FIREPAN Lev. 16:12, take a **f** full of coals

FIRM—*hard, steadfast* Josh. 3:17, LORD stood **f** on dry
Is. 22:23, *like* a peg in a **f** place
1 Cor. 7:37, stands **f** in his heart
2 Tim. 2:19, the **f** foundation of God stands
Heb. 3:6, hope **f** until the end
1 Pet. 5:9, resist him, **f** in *your* faith
FIRMAMENT—*expanse* Ps. 19:1, **f** is declaring the work of
FIRST—*leader, eminent, foremost* Gen. 38:28
Matt. 6:33, seek **f** His kingdom
7:5, **f** take the log out of
19:30, many *who are* **f** will be last
20:27, be **f** among you
28:1, the **f** *day* of the week
1 John 4:19, because He **f** loved us
Rev. 1:17, I am the **f** and the last
2:4, you have left your **f** love
21:4, the **f** things have passed away
22:13, Omega, the **f** and the last
Deut. 26:10; Prov. 3:9; 18:17; Hos. 2:7; Mark 3:27; 10:44; Acts 1:1
FIRST-BORN Luke 2:7, she gave birth to her **f** son
Heb. 12:23, church of the **f**
Gen. 10:15; 19:37; 27:19; Ex. 11:5
FIRST FRUITS Ex. 23:16, the **f** of your labors
Rom. 8:23, the **f** of the Spirit
James 1:18, the **f** among His creatures
Rev. 14:4, **f** to God and to the Lamb
FISH Matt. 14:17, five loaves and two **f**
Luke 5:6, a great quantity of **f**
11:11, asked by his son for a **f**
Gen. 1:26; Num. 11:5; 2 Chr. 33:14; Is. 50:2; Jon. 1:17; John 21:10
FISHERMEN Is. 19:8; Jer. 16:16
FISHERS—*fishermen* Matt. 4:19, I will make you **f** of men
Mark 1:17, I will make you become **f** of men
FIT—*ready, prepare, worthy*
Matt. 3:11, not . . . **f** to remove His sandals
Luke 9:62, **f** for the kingdom of God
Eph. 2:21, whole building, being **f-ed** together
4:16, whole body, being **f-ed** and held together
FITTING—*opportune* Matt. 3:15, it is **f** for us to fulfill
Eph. 5:4, jesting, which are not **f**
Col. 3:18, as is **f** in the Lord
FIVE 1 Sam. 17:40, **f** smooth stones from the brook
Matt. 14:17, **f** loaves and two fish
25:2, **f** of them were foolish . . . **f**
25:20, who had received the **f** talents
Gen. 5:6; Ex. 22:1; Lev. 26:8; 2 Chr. 4:2; 2 Cor. 11:24; Rev. 17:10
FIXED Luke 16:26, there is a great chasm **f**
FLAG Is. 30:17, a **f** on a mountain top
FLAME—*fire* Is. 4:5, of a **f-ing** fire by night
Rev. 19:12, eyes *are* a **f** of fire
Gen. 3:24; Judg. 13:20; Ps. 106:18; Song 8:6; Is. 5:24; 10:17; Ezek. 20:47; Dan. 7:9; 10:6; Joel 2:5; Acts 7:30; 2 Thess. 1:7
FLASH Job 15:12, why do your eyes **f**
Acts 22:6, bright light suddenly **f-ed** from heaven
Deut. 32:41; Ezek. 1:13; 21:10; Nah. 3:3
FLASK—*vessel* Matt. 25:4, took oil in **f-s**
FLAT Josh. 6:5,20, wall fell down **f**
FLATTER Job 32:21, Nor **f** *any* man
Ps. 5:9, They **f** with their tongue
Prov. 7:21, **f-ing** lips she seduces him
1 Thess. 2:5, we never came with **f-ing** speech
FLAX Ex. 9:31; Judg. 15:14; Ezek. 40:3
FLEA 1 Sam. 24:14; 26:20
FLED—*escape* Matt. 26:56, left Him and **f**
Mark 16:8, **f** from the tomb
Rev. 20:11, whose presence earth and heaven **f**
Gen. 14:10; 31:21; 39:18; Is. 22:3
FLEE—*wander* Lev. 26:17, **f** when no one is pursuing
Ps. 11:1, **F** *as* a bird to your mountain
139:7, I **f** from Thy presence
Prov. 28:1, wicked **f** when no one
Is. 16:2, like **f-ing** birds
Matt. 3:7, **f** from the wrath to come
1 Tim. 6:11, But **f** from these things, you man
2 Tim. 2:22, **f** from youthful lusts
Gen. 16:8; Is. 30:16; Matt. 2:13; Rev. 9:6
FLEECE—*shear* Judg. 6:37; Job 31:20
FLESH—*body, meat, life*
Gen. 2:24, they shall become one **f**
Ps. 84:2, **f** sing for joy to the living God
136:25, Who gives food to all **f**
Is. 40:6, All **f** is grass
Matt. 16:17, because **f** and blood did not reveal
26:41, but the **f** is weak
Luke 24:39, spirit does not have **f** and bones
John 1:14, the Word became **f**
3:6, which is born of the **f** is **f**
Rom. 8:6, mind set on the **f** is death
2 Cor. 1:17, according to the **f** . . . should be
10:4, weapons . . . not of the **f**
Gal. 6:8, **f** shall from the **f** reap
Eph. 2:3, indulging the desires of the **f**
5:31, TWO SHALL BECOME ONE **F**
6:12, struggle is not against **f**
1 Pet. 2:11, abstain from **f-ly** lusts
Gen. 2:23; 7:21; 37:27; Num. 16:22; Job 19:26; 41:23; Ps. 16:9; Rom. 9:8; Jude 23; Rev. 19:21
FLIES—*fly* Job 20:8; Ps. 78:45; Prov. 23:5; Eccles. 10:1
FLIGHT Amos 2:14, **F** will perish from the swift
Matt. 24:20, your **f** may not be in the winter
Heb. 11:34, put foreign armies to **f**
FLINT—*stone* Zech. 7:12, hearts like **f** so
Ex. 4:25; Deut. 8:15; 32:13; Ps. 114:8; Is. 5:28; Ezek. 3:9
FLOCK—*fold, sheep* Gen. 4:2,4; 29:2; 30:31,38
Is. 40:11, Like a shepherd He will tend His **f**
Jer. 23:2, scattered My **f** and driven
Matt. 26:31, SHEEP OF THE **F** SHALL BE SCATTERED
Luke 2:8, keeping watch over their **f** by night
12:32, Do not be afraid, little **f**
John 10:16, become one **f** *with* one Shepherd
1 Pet. 5:2, the **f** of God among you
Ex. 2:16; 10:9; Judg. 5:16; 1 Sam. 16:19; 17:34; 2 Chr. 32:28; Ps. 77:20; Prov. 27:23; Is. 13:20; Ezek. 45:15; Amos 6:4; Hab. 3:17
FLOG Mark 13:9, you will be **f-ed**
FLOOD Gen. 7:17, **f** came upon the earth
Gen. 9:15, never . . . the water become a **f**
Matt. 7:25, **f-s** came, and the winds blew
Luke 17:27, **f** came and destroyed them all
Gen. 6:17; Dan. 9:26
FLOODGATES Gen. 7:11, **f** of the sky were opened
FLOOR Gen. 50:11; Ruth 3:3; 1 Kin. 6:30; 7:7; Joel 2:24; Matt. 3:12
FLOUR—*dough* Ex. 29:2; Lev. 2:1; Ezek. 16:13; Rev. 18:13
FLOURISH—*blossom, green*
Ps. 72:7, may the righteous **f**
92:7, all who did iniquity **f-ed**
103:15, a flower . . . so he **f-es**
Prov. 11:28, will **f** like the *green* leaf
Ezek. 17:24, make the dry tree **f**
FLOW—*gush* Ex. 3:8, land **f-ing** with milk and honey
John 7:38, shall **f** rivers of living water
Job 20:28; Ps. 147:18; Jer. 9:18; Joel 3:18; Mark 5:29
FLOWER Ps. 103:15, As a **f** of the field, so he
1 Pet. 1:24, AND THE **F** FALLS OFF
Job 14:2; Song 2:12; Is. 28:1
FLUENTLY—*well* Ex. 4:14, he speaks **f**
FLUSH Job 16:16, My face is **f-ed** from weeping
FLUTE 1 Sam. 10:5; 1 Kin. 1:40; 1 Cor. 14:7; Rev. 18:22
FLY Job 5:7, As sparks **f** upward
Gen. 1:20; Is. 14:29; Rev. 8:13; 12:14; 19:17

FOAL—*colt* Job 11:12; Zech. 9:9
FOE—*enemy*
1 Chr. 21:12, swept away before your **f-s**
FOLD—*flock* Eccles. 4:5, The fool **f-s** his hands
John 10:16, sheep, which are not of this **f**
Num. 32:24; Ps. 50:9; Prov. 6:10
FOLLOW—*cling, imitate, pursue* Gen. 24:5; 44:4; Ex. 11:8
Ruth 1:16, turn back from **f-ing** you
Ps. 23:6, goodness and lovingkindness will **f** me
Matt. 4:19, He said to them, **F** Me
4:20, left the nets, and **f-ed** Him
8:19, **f** You wherever You go
12:15, And many **f-ed** Him
16:24, take up his cross, and **f** Me
19:21, and come, **f** Me
Luke 22:39, disciples also **f-ed** Him
John 10:27, I know them, and they **f** Me
Jude 16, **f-ing** after their *own* lusts
Rev. 14:4, the ones who **f** the Lamb
Num. 15:39; 1 Sam. 12:14; Ps. 119:150; Jer. 48:2; Mark 5:37; 14:54; Luke 22:10; John 18:15; Acts 5:36; Rev. 14:13
FOLLY—*foolishness*
Prov. 14:18, The naive inherit **f**
15:2, mouth of fools spouts **f**
24:9, devising of **f** is sin
Judg. 19:23; Prov. 15:21
FOND—*greedy* 1 Tim. 3:8, or **f** of sordid gain
FONDLE Is. 66:12, **f-d** on the knees
FOOD—*bread, meat* Ps. 69:21, gall for my **f**
Ps. 136:25, Who gives **f** to all flesh
Matt. 6:25, Is not life more than **f**
John 4:34, My **f** is to do the will of Him
6:55, My flesh is true **f**
1 Cor. 6:13, **F** is for the stomach
James 2:15, in need of daily **f**
Gen. 1:29; 2:9; 3:6; 43:2; Lev. 3:11; Deut. 10:18; Ruth 1:6; Job 38:41; Ps. 78:25; 145:15; Prov. 6:8; 20:13; 23:3; 28:19; 30:8; Is. 65:25; Matt. 3:4; 1 Tim. 6:8
FOOL—*foolish, unwise* Ps. 14:1, The **f** has said in his
Prov. 1:7, **F-s** despise wisdom and instruction
15:5, A **f** rejects his father's discipline
26:3, a rod for the back of **f-s**
29:11, A **f** always loses his temper
Eccles. 10:14, the **f** multiplies words
Rom. 1:22, wise, they became **f-s**
1 Cor. 4:10, We are **f-s** for Christ's sake
1 Sam. 26:21; 2 Sam. 3:33; Prov. 24:7; Hos. 9:7; Matt. 5:22; 23:17
FOOLISH—*fool, boastful, folly, unwise*
Prov. 14:17, quick-tempered man acts **f-ly**
Luke 24:25, O **f** men and slow of heart
Rom. 1:14, the wise and to the **f**
1 Cor. 3:18, let him become **f**
Eph. 5:17, then do not be **f**
Gen. 31:28; Deut. 32:6; Job 5:3; Lam. 2:14; Matt. 25:8; 1 Pet. 2:15
FOOLISHNESS—*folly* Prov. 14:24; Is. 9:17; 2 Cor. 11:21
FOOT Prov. 25:17, **f** rarely be in your neighbor's house
Matt. 4:6, LEST YOU STRIKE YOUR F
Luke 4:11, STRIKE YOUR F AGAINST A STONE
Rev. 10:2, placed his right **f** on the sea
Gen. 8:9; 41:44; Deut. 2:28; 33:24; Num. 11:21; Josh. 14:9; 2 Sam. 8:4; 21:20; 1 Chr. 20:6; Ps. 26:12; 91:12; 121:3; Prov. 3:23; 25:19; Jer. 12:5; Matt. 22:13
FOOTSTOOL—*feet* 1 Chr. 28:2, for the **f** of our God
Ps. 99:5, And worship at His **f**
110:1, Thine enemies a **f**
132:7, Let us worship at His **f**
Is. 66:1, the earth is My **f**
James 2:3, or sit down by my **f**
FORBEARANCE Eph. 4:2, showing **f** to one another
Prov. 25:15; Rom. 3:25
FORBID—*hinder* 1 Cor. 14:39, do not **f** to speak in tongues
1 Tim. 4:3, *men* who **f** marriage *and*
Num. 30:5,8,11; Luke 23:2
FORCE—*compel* Matt. 5:41, **f** you to go one mile
Luke 3:14, Do not take money . . . by **f**
Gen. 31:31; 1 Sam. 2:16; Job 30:18; 36:19; Dan. 11:10; Matt. 11:12; Heb. 9:17
FOREHEAD 1 Sam. 17:49, stone sank into his **f**
Rev. 9:4, seal of God on their **f-s**
17:5, upon her **f** a name *was* written
Ex. 28:38; Lev. 13:42; Is. 48:4; Jer. 3:3; Ezek. 3:8; 9:4
FOREIGN—*strange* Gen. 35:2, Put away the **f** gods
Ex. 2:22, a sojourner in a **f** land
1 Kin. 11:1, Solomon loved many **f** women
Ezra 10:2, have married **f** women
Ps. 137:4, LORD's song in a **f** land
Heb. 11:34, put **f** armies to flight
FOREIGNER—*alien, sojourner*
Ruth 2:10, since I am a **f**
Prov. 5:20, embrace the bosom of a **f**
Deut. 14:21; 15:3; Job 19:15; Obad. 11
FOREMOST—*first*
Matt. 22:38, great and **f** commandment
Mark 12:28, commandment is the **f** of all
1 Tim. 1:15, among whom I am **f** *of all*
FOREST—*wood* Ps. 50:10, every beast of the **f** is Mine
James 3:5, how great a **f** is set aflame
1 Sam. 22:5; 2 Sam. 18:8; 1 Kin. 7:2; 1 Chr. 16:33; Ps. 83:14; Is. 10:18; 44:14; 56:9; Jer. 5:6; 21:14; Ezek. 15:2; Amos 3:4
FOREVER—*always, evermore, utmost* Gen. 3:22; 6:3
1 Chr. 17:14, throne shall be established **f**
Ps. 9:7, the LORD abides **f**
16:11, there are pleasures **f**
23:6, in the house of the LORD **f**
29:10, the LORD sits as King **f**
33:11, counsel of the LORD stands **f**
86:12, will glorify Thy name **f**
89:52, Blessed be the LORD **f**
92:8, O LORD, art on high **f**
102:12, Thou, O LORD, dost abide **f**
119:89, **F**, O LORD, Thy word is settled
121:8, LORD will guard your going out . . . **f**
133:3, the blessing . . . life **f**
Prov. 27:24, riches are not **f**
Eccles. 3:14, everything God does . . . **f**
Is. 40:8, word of our God stands **f**
57:15, exalted One Who lives **f**
57:16, For I will not contend **f**
John 6:51, eats of this bread, he shall live **f**
12:34, the Christ is to remain **f**
14:16, Helper, that he may be with you **f**
Rom. 9:5, God blessed **f**
2 Cor. 11:31, Lord Jesus, He who is blessed **f**
Eph. 3:21, all generations **f** and ever
Heb. 7:25, He is able to save **f**
7:28, a Son, made perfect **f**
13:8, today, *yes* and **f**
Ex. 14:13; Deut. 5:29; 12:28; 32:40; Ps. 12:7; 23:6; 61:4; 73:26; 77:8; 113:2; 115:18; 132:14; 146:6; Prov. 21:28; Is. 26:4; 34:10; Lam. 3:31
FOREVERMORE Rev. 1:18, I am alive **f**
FORFEIT Dan 1:10, make me **f** my head to the king
FORGAVE Ps. 78:38, **f** their iniquity, and
Matt. 18:27, and **f** him the debt
Luke 7:42, he graciously **f** them both
7:43, the one whom he **f** more
FORGET—*neglect, forsake*
Deut. 6:12, lest you **f** the LORD
Ps. 9:17, all the nations who **f** God
13:1, Wilt Thou **f** me forever
74:23, Do not **f** the voice of Thine
88:12, in the land of **f-fulness**
119:176, I do not **f** Thy commandments

Prov. 3:1, My son, do not **f** my teaching
Heb. 6:10, **f** your work and the love
Gen. 27:45; 41:51; Deut. 4:9; Prov. 4:5; 31:5; Is. 54:4; Jer. 2:32; 23:27

FORGIVE—*forgave, pardon*
Ps. 86:5, good, and ready to **f**
99:8, a **f-ing** God to them
Matt. 6:12, **f** us our debts, as we
6:14, if you **f** men for
6:15, if you do not **f** men
9:5, Your sins are **f-n**
9:6, on earth to **f** sins
Mark 2:7, who can **f** sins but God alone
11:26, if you do not **f**
Luke 7:47, sins ... many, have been **f-n**
23:34, Father **f** them
2 Cor. 2:10, whom you **f** anything, I **f** also
Eph. 4:32, **f-ing** each other
Col. 2:13, **f-n** us all our transgressions
1 John 1:9, righteous to **f** us our sins
Gen. 50:17; Ex. 32:32; Num. 30:5; Ps. 25:18; 79:9; Jer. 18:23

FORGIVENESS—*pardon*
Neh. 9:17, art a God of **f**
Ps. 130:4, there is **f** with Thee
Matt. 26:28, for **f** of sins
Mark 1:4; Luke 24:47, repentance for the **f** of sins
3:29, Holy Spirit never has **f**
Acts 10:43, has received **f** of sins
13:38, through Him **f** of sins is proclaimed
26:18, they may receive **f** of sins
Eph. 1:7, the **f** of our trespasses
Col. 1:14, redemption, the **f** of sins
Heb. 9:22, shedding of blood ... no **f**

FORGOT Deut. 32:18, **f** the God who gave you birth

FORGOTTEN—*neglect* Job 19:14, friends have **f** me
Ps. 9:18, needy will not always be **f**
Ezek. 23:35, Because you have **f** Me
Matt. 16:5, had **f** to take bread
Luke 12:6, is **f** before God
James 1:24, **f** what kind of person
Gen. 41:30; Job 28:4; Ps. 31:12; 77:9; Jer. 2:32; Lam. 2:6

FORK 1 Sam. 2:13; Matt. 3:12

FORM—*fashion* Ps. 95:5, His hands **f-ed** the dry land
Is. 53:2, no *stately* **f** or majesty
Mark 4:32, **f-s** large branches
16:12, He appeared in a different **f**
1 Cor. 7:31, the **f** of this world is passing
Gal. 4:19, until Christ is **f-ed** in you
2 Pet. 3:5, earth was **f-ed** out of water
Gen. 1:2; 2:7; Job 4:16; 33:6; Song 2:14; Is. 43:1; 44:13; 45:7; Amos 4:13; 7:1; Acts 17:29

FORMER—*past* 1 Pet. 1:14, conformed to the **f** lusts
Gen. 40:13; Deut. 4:32; 24:4; Ruth 4:7; Is. 42:9; 46:9; 65:16; Ezek. 16:55

FORNICATION—*immorality* Matt. 15:19; John 8:41

FORSAKE—*fail, leave, reject* Job 6:14; Ps. 27:9; 38:21
Josh. 1:5, not fail you or **f** you
2 Chr. 15:2, **f** Him, He will **f** you
Ezra 9:9, our God has not **f-n** us
Ps. 22:1, God, why hast Thou **f-n** me
27:10, father and my mother have **f-n** me
Prov. 1:8, do not **f** your mother's teaching
9:6, **F** *your* folly and live
Is. 53:3, despised and **f-n** of men
55:7, Let the wicked **f** his way
Matt. 27:46, GOD, WHY HAST THOU **F-N** ME
2 Cor. 4:9, persecuted, but not **f**
Heb. 13:5, NOR WILL I EVER **F** YOU
Jer. 5:7; Ezek. 9:9; 20:8; Mark 15:34; 2 Pet. 2:15

FORSOOK—*left, deserted* Deut. 32:15; 1 Kin. 12:8; 2 Chr. 12:1

FORTIFICATION—*stronghold*
Is. 25:12, unassailable **f-s** of

FORTIFY—*strengthen* Num. 32:17; Deut. 3:5; Josh. 10:20; 1 Sam. 6:18; 2 Kin. 3:19; Is. 34:13; Jer. 5:17; 51:53

FORTRESS—*stronghold, power*
2 Sam. 22:2, my rock and my **f**
Ps. 91:2, My refuge and my **f**
2 Sam. 22:33; Ps. 18:2; Dan. 11:19

FORTY Gen. 7:4, the earth **f** days and **f** nights
Ex. 16:35, Israel ate the manna **f** years
Matt. 4:2, fasted **f** days and **f** nights
Gen. 7:17; Ex. 34:28; Num. 33:38; Ps. 95:10; Mark 1:13

FORWARD—*further*
2 Kin. 20:9, shadow go **f** ten steps
Job 23:8; Is. 41:21; Jer. 7:24; Ezek. 1:9; Acts 19:33

FOUGHT—*waged war* Num. 21:1, then he **f** against Israel
Judg. 5:20, stars **f** from heaven
2 Chr. 20:29, the LORD had **f** against
1 Cor. 15:32, I **f** with wild beasts
2 Tim. 4:7, I have **f** the good fight

FOUL Ezek. 32:2; 34:19

FOUND—*caught, proved*
Judg. 14:18, not have **f** out my riddle
Jer. 15:16, Thy words were **f** and I
Dan. 5:27, weighed on the scales and **f** deficient
Matt. 8:10, not **f** such great faith
10:39, He who has **f** his life shall
Mark 14:37, **f** them sleeping
Luke 2:46, they **f** Him in the temple
15:6, I have **f** my sheep
24:2, **f** the stone rolled away
John 1:41, We have **f** the Messiah
Acts 13:22, I have **f** David the son of
1 Cor. 15:15, we are even **f** *to be* false witnesses
Phil. 2:8, being **f** in appearance
Gen. 2:20; 6:8; Lev. 6:3; Deut. 17:2; Ruth 2:10,13; Job 28:12; Ps. 84:3; Prov. 25:16; Eccles. 7:29; Is. 51:3; Dan. 6:11; Mal. 2:6; Matt. 27:32; Mark 11:4; 14:40; Rev. 18:24

FOUNDATION—*habitation, founded* 2 Sam. 22:8; Job 4:19
Ps. 89:14; 97:2, Right and justice are the **f**
Matt. 13:35, SINCE THE **F** OF THE WORLD
Luke 6:48, laid a **f** upon the rock
Rom. 15:20, upon another man's **f**
2 Tim. 2:19, the firm **f** of God stands
Heb. 1:10, DIDST LAY THE **F** OF THE EARTH
6:1, a **f** of repentance
Ps. 87:1; 104:5; Prov. 10:25; Is. 28:16

FOUNDED Ps. 24:2, He has **f** it upon the seas
Prov. 3:19, by wisdom **f** the earth
Matt. 7:25, **f** upon the rock
Ex. 9:18; Amos 9:6

FOUNTAIN—*spring, well* Gen. 7:11, **f-s** of the great deep
Ps. 36:9, with Thee is the **f** of life
Prov. 14:27, fear of the LORD is a **f** of life

FOUR Mark 13:27, FROM THE **F** WINDS
Luke 19:8, give back **f** times as much
Gen. 2:10; Ex. 25:12; 2 Kin. 7:3; Is. 11:12; Matt. 15:38; John 11:39

FOURTEEN Gen. 31:41; 2 Chr. 13:21; 30:15; Is. 36:1; Matt. 1:17; Acts 27:27; 2 Cor. 12:2

FOURTH Gen. 1:19; Ex. 20:5; Judg. 19:5; Matt. 14:25; Rev. 6:7

FOWL—*bird* 1 Kin. 4:23; Ps. 148:10

FOX Judg. 15:4; Neh. 4:3; Song 2:15; Ezek. 13:4; Matt. 8:20; Luke 13:32

FRAGMENT—*piece*
John 6:12, Gather up the left-over **f-s**

FRAGRANCE 2 Cor. 2:15, we are a **f** of Christ
Song 1:3; 2:13

FRANKINCENSE Ex. 30:34; 1 Chr. 9:29; Song 4:6; Matt. 2:11

FRAUD—*mischief*
Acts 13:10, full of all deceit and **f**

FREE Matt. 10:8, **f-ly** you received, **f-ly** give
John 8:32, the truth shall make you **f**
Rom. 6:7, he who has died is **f-d**
6:22, now having been **f-d** from sin
8:2, **f** from the law
Gal. 5:1, that Christ set us **f**
Gen. 2:16; Deut. 15:8; Josh. 2:20; Ps. 110:3; Is. 58:6; Eph. 6:8; Rev. 19:18
FREEDOM—*liberty* 1 Pet. 2:16, use your **f** as a
Rom. 8:21; Gal. 5:13
FREEWILL Lev. 22:18; Ezra 7:16; Ps. 119:108
FREQUENT 1 Tim. 5:23, your **f** ailments
FRESH Prov. 5:15, **f** water from your own well
James 3:11, *both* **f** and bitter water
Job 33:25; Ps. 92:10; James 3:12
FRET Prov. 24:19, Do not **f** yourself because of
FRICTION—*dispute*
1 Tim. 6:5, constant **f** between men
FRIEND Prov. 17:17, A **f** loves at all times
Prov. 18:24, a **f** who sticks closer
Matt. 11:19, a **f** of tax-gatherers and sinners
John 15:13, lay down his life for his **f-s**
Gen. 38:12; Ex. 33:11; Judg. 14:20; Job 16:20; Ps. 38:11; Mic. 7:5; Matt. 20:13
FRIENDSHIP James 4:4, do you not know that **f**
FROGS Ex. 8:2; Ps. 78:45; 105:30; Rev. 16:13
FRONT Ex. 28:27, ephod, on the **f** of it
FROST—*ice* Gen. 31:40; Ex. 16:14; Ps. 78:47; Jer. 36:30
FRUIT—*labor, produce* Ps. 1:3, yields its **f** in its season
Prov. 11:30, **f** of the righteous
Matt. 3:8, Therefore bring forth **f**
7:16, know them by their **f-s**
John 4:36, **f** for life eternal
Rom. 7:4, bear **f** for God
Col. 1:10, bearing **f** in every good work
James 3:17, full of mercy and good **f-s**
Gen. 1:11; 3:6; Lev. 27:30; Ps. 92:14; 128:2; Song 4:16; Jer. 2:7; 6:19
FRUSTRATE Ezra 4:5; Job 5:12; Prov. 15:22; Is. 14:27
FUEL Is. 9:5,19; Ezek. 15:4; 21:32
FUGITIVE Judg. 12:4; Is. 15:5; 52:12
FULFILL—*complete*
Matt. 2:15, prophet might be **f-ed**
2:17, prophet was **f-ed** saying
3:15, fitting for us to **f** all righteousness
5:17, not come to abolish, but to **f**
Luke 22:16, it is **f-ed** in the kingdom
1 Cor. 7:3, husband **f** his duty to his wife
Gal. 6:2, **f** the law of Christ
2 Tim. 4:5, **f** your ministry
1 Chr. 17:11; 2 Chr. 36:21; Ps. 20:5; 148:8; Matt. 1:22
FULL—*complete, whole* 1 Chr. 21:24; Ps. 92:14; Prov. 4:18
Ps. 33:5, earth is **f** of the lovingkindness
Is. 11:9, will be **f** of knowledge
Matt. 6:2,5,16, have their reward in **f**
14:20, twelve **f** baskets
23:27, **f** of dead men's bones
Luke 4:1, **f** of the Holy Spirit
11:34, body also is **f** of light
John 1:14, **f** of grace and truth
Eph. 6:11, the **f** armor of God
James 5:11, the Lord is **f** of compassion
Acts 2:13; 1 Cor. 7:36; Col. 1:25
FULLER—*launderer* 2 Kin. 18:17; Mal. 3:2
FUNCTION Rom. 12:4, members do not have the same **f**
FURIOUS 2 Kin. 9:20; Dan. 2:12
FURNACE—*oven* Ps. 12:6; Is. 31:9; Dan. 3:6,15; Matt. 13:42; Rev. 1:15
FURNISH Deut. 15:14; Mark 14:15
FURNITURE Ex. 31:7, all the **f** of the tent
FURROWS Job 31:38; Ps. 65:10; 129:3
FURTHER Ex. 21:22; Num. 22:26; 1 Sam. 10:3; Matt. 26:65; Acts 24:4; Heb. 12:9
FURY—*displeasure* Gen. 27:44; Ps. 2:5; Ezek. 19:12; Heb. 10:27
FUTILE—*vain* 1 Sam. 12:21, **f** things ... because they are **f**
Acts 4:25, PEOPLES DEVISE **F** THINGS
Rom. 1:21, **f** in their speculations
FUTILITY—*vanity*
Rom. 8:20, creation was subjected to **f**
Eph. 4:17, walk, in the **f** of their mind
FUTURE—*end, reward*
Prov. 24:20, no **f** for the evil man
Deut. 32:29; Jer. 31:17

G

GAIN—*price, profit* Prov. 10:2, Ill-gotten **g-s** do not
Matt. 16:26; Luke 9:25, if he **g-s** the whole world
Phil. 3:8, that I may **g** Christ
1 Tim. 6:5, godliness ... means of **g**
1 Pet. 5:2, not for sordid **g**
1 Sam. 8:3; Prov. 3:14; Is. 33:15; Ezek. 22:12,27
GALE Mark 4:37, arose a fierce **g** of wind
GALL Ps. 69:21, Matt. 27:34; Acts 8:23
GALLERY Ezek. 41:15; 42:3
GALLOWS Esth. 5:14; 7:10; 9:25
GANGRENE 2 Tim. 2:17, will spread like **g**
GARDEN—*field* Gen. 3:8, God walking in the **g**
John 18:1, where there was a **g**
19:41, in the **g** a new tomb
Gen. 2:8; 3:10; Deut. 11:10; Lam. 2:6; Joel 2:3; John 18:26; 20:15
GARMENT—*clothing, dress* Gen. 41:42, in **g-s** ... linen
Ex. 28:2, make holy **g-s** for Aaron
Ps. 22:18, divide my **g-s** among them
102:26, wear out like a **g**
Matt. 27:35, DIVIDED UP HIS **G-S**- ... CASTING
28:3, his **g** as white as snow
Luke 23:34, DIVIDING UP HIS **G-S**
Heb. 1:11, BECOME OLD AS A **G**
Gen. 3:21; 25:25; 38:14; 39:12; Ex. 19:10; Esth. 8:15; Is. 59:17; 63:1; Ezek. 27:24; Joel 2:13; Matt. 3:4; Mark 5:28; John 21:7; Acts 10:30
GARNER—*barn* Ps. 144:13, *Let* our **g-s** be full
GARRISON—*pillars* 1 Sam. 10:5; 14:12; 1 Chr. 18:13
GASH—*cut* Mark 5:5, **g-ing** himself
GATE Gen. 28:17, this is the **g** of heaven
Ps. 24:7, Lift your heads, O **g-s**
100:4, Enter His **g-s** with
Matt. 7:13, Enter by the narrow **g**
16:18, **g-s** of Hades shall not
Gen. 22:17; Judg. 16:3; Is. 38:10; Acts 12:14
GATHER—*assemble* Is. 40:11, His arm ... **g** the lambs
John 4:36, **g-ing** fruit for life
6:12, **G** up the ... fragments
Gen. 1:10; 31:46; 37:7; 41:35; Ps. 33:7; Is. 66:18; Matt. 26:3; Acts 19:40; Rev. 14:19
GAVE—*provide* Gen. 2:20, Adam **g** names to all
Gen. 3:12, Thou **g-st** to *be* with me
Ps. 69:21, they **g** me vinegar to drink
Eccles. 12:7, return to God who **g** it
Mark 8:6, He **g** thanks and broke them
John 3:16, He **g** His only begotten Son
13:26, morsel ... He ... **g** it to Judas
19:30, bowed ... **g** up His spirit
Rom. 1:28, **g** them over to a depraved mind
1 Tim. 2:6, who **g** Himself as a ransom
Is. 50:6; Matt. 10:1; 26:48; Luke 7:44; Eph. 1:22
GAZE Ex. 19:21; Job 31:1
GENEALOGY—*descent* Heb. 7:3,6
GENERAL Heb. 12:23, to the **g** assembly and church
GENERATION—*ages* Deut. 1:35; Luke 21:32; Eph. 3:5
Ps. 90:1, dwelling place in all **g-s**
100:5, His faithfulness to all **g-s**
Matt. 1:17, to David are fourteen **g-s**
24:34, this **g** will not pass away

Luke 1:48, all **g-s** will count me blessed
Eph. 3:21, all **g-s** forever and ever
Phil. 2:15, a crooked and perverse **g**
GENEROUS—*bountiful* Prov. 22:9; Is. 32:5
GENTILE—*nations* Matt. 6:7, as the **G-s** do
Luke 2:32, LIGHT OF REVELATION TO THE **G-S**
Acts 4:25, WHY DID THE **G-S** RAGE
14:2, stirred the minds of the **G-s**
Rom. 11:11, salvation *has come* to the **G-s**
Gal. 1:16, I might preach Him among the **G-s**
GENTLE—*compassionate*
1 Kin. 19:12, sound of a **g** blowing
Prov. 15:1, **g** answer turns away wrath
Matt. 5:5, Blessed are the **g**
1 Cor. 4:21, with love and a spirit of **g-ness**
2 Cor. 10:1, **g-ness** of Christ
Gal. 5:23, **g-ness**, self-control
Eph. 4:2, with all humility and **g-ness**
1 Thess. 2:7, we proved to be **g** among you
1 Tim. 6:11, love, perseverance *and* **g-ness**
Titus 3:2, to be uncontentious, **g**
1 Pet. 3:4, a **g** and quiet spirit
Ps. 18:35; Matt. 21:5; 1 Tim. 3:3; Heb. 5:2; 1 Pet. 2:18
GESTURE—*motion*
John 13:24, Simon Peter therefore **g-d**
GET—*acquire, take* Gen. 34:4; Judg. 11:5; 14:2
Prov. 4:7, with all your acquiring, **g** understanding
Matt. 16:23, **G** behind Me, Satan
Luke 18:12, tithes of all that I **g**
1 Kin. 17:10; Job 9:18; Is. 30:11; 56:12; Jer. 36:21
GIANT—*Rephaim* 1 Chr. 20:6, he ... was descended from **g-s**
GIFT Gen. 25:6, Abraham gave **g-s** while he was
Ps. 68:18, hast received **g-s** among men
127:3, children are a **g** of the LORD
Prov. 18:16, A man's **g** makes room for him
21:14, A **g** in secret subdues anger
Matt. 2:11, presented to Him **g-s**
John 4:10, you knew the **g** of God
Acts 2:38, the **g** of the Holy Spirit
Rom. 6:23, **g** of God is eternal life
James 1:17, every perfect **g** is from above
GIRD—*bound* Ex. 29:5; Job 38:3; Ps. 45:3; John 13:5
John 21:18, when you were younger ... **g** ... will **g** you
Eph. 6:14, **G-ED** YOUR LOINS WITH TRUTH
Rev. 1:13, **g-ed** across His breast with a golden
GIRDLE—*belt, waistband* 2 Kin. 1:8; Rev. 1:13; 15:6, golden **g**
Job 12:18, binds their loins with a **g**
GIRL—*maiden, woman* Gen. 24:55; 34:4; Joel 3:3; Zech. 8:5; Matt. 14:11; 26:69; Mark 6:28; John 18:17; Acts 12:13; 16:16
GIVE Num. 6:26, on you, And **g** you peace
Ps. 21:4, He asked life ... Thou didst **g** it
Prov. 26:16, seven men ... **g** a ... answer
Is. 9:6, a son will be **g-n** to us
Matt. 6:11, **G** us this day our daily
10:8, freely **g**
15:36, **g-ing** thanks, He broke them
16:19, **g** you the keys
26:9, **g-n** to the poor
28:18, All authority has been **g-n** to Me
Luke 6:38, **G**, and it will be **g-n** to you
11:9, ask, and it shall be **g-n** to you
22:19, My body which is **g-n** for you
John 5:22, has **g-n** all judgment
6:11, and having **g-n** thanks
14:27, My peace I **g** to you
Acts 3:6, what I do have I **g** to you
12:23, he did not **g** God the glory
20:35, more blessed to **g** than to
Rom. 12:20, IF HE IS THIRSTY, **G** HIM A DRINK
14:6, he **g-s** thanks to God
1 Cor. 3:10, grace of God which was **g-n**
2 Cor. 12:7, was **g-n** me a thorn in
Eph. 4:27, do not **g** the devil an opportunity
5:20, always **g-ing** thanks
James 4:6, But He **g-s** a greater grace ... **G-S** GRACE
1 John 5:11, has **g-n** us eternal life
Gen. 1:29; Ex. 20:12; Ps. 29:11; 68:11; 80:1; 145:15; Luke 1:77; 19:8; Rev. 19:8
GLAD Ps. 32:11, Be **g** in the LORD
Ps. 100:2, Serve the LORD with **g-ness**
122:1, I was **g** when they said to me
Prov. 10:1, wise son makes a father **g**
Matt. 5:12, Rejoice and be **g**
Luke 1:14, you will have joy and **g-ness**
6:23, Be **g** in that day, and leap
12:32, Father has chosen **g-ly** to give
Acts 2:46, **g-ness** and sincerity of heart
2 Cor. 11:19, bear with the foolish **g-ly**
Ex. 4:14; Num. 10:10; Deut. 28:47; 1 Chr. 16:31; Ps. 16:9; Is. 16:10
GLASS—*crystal* Job 28:17; Rev. 4:6
GLEAMING—*glitter*
Nah. 3:3, Swords flashing, spears **g**
GLEAN Lev. 19:10; Ruth 2:8,15,17; Is. 17:6; Jer. 49:9
GLISTEN Ps. 104:15, make his face **g** with oil
GLOOM Deut. 5:22; Job 3:5
Matt. 6:16, **g-y** face as the hypocrites *do*
Heb. 12:18, darkness and **g** and whirlwind
GLORIFY—*honor* Ps. 86:12, will **g** Thy name forever
Is. 66:5, Let the LORD be **g-ed**
Matt. 5:16, **g** your Father who is in heaven
John 12:28, Father **g** Thy name
13:31, is the Son of Man **g-ed**
16:14, He shall **g** Me
17:1, **g** Thy Son ... **g** Thee
Acts 13:48, **g-ing** the word of the Lord
1 Cor. 6:20, **g** God in your body
Heb. 5:5, Christ did not **g** Himself
GLORIOUS—*exalt, glory, honor*
Neh. 9:5, Thy **g** name
Ps. 87:3, **G** things are spoken of you
1 Tim. 1:11, the **g** gospel of the blessed God
GLORY—*honor, splendor* Ex. 16:7, see ... **g** of the Lord
Ps. 24:7, the King of **g** may come in
Prov. 16:31, gray head is a crown of **g**
Is. 6:3, earth is full of His **g**
66:19, heard ... nor seen My **g** ... **g** among the nations
Matt. 6:13, power, and the **g**
6:29, Solomon in all his **g** did not clothe
Luke 2:9, **g** of the Lord shone around
2:14, **G** to God in the highest
17:18, turned back to give **g** to God
John 5:44, you receive **g** from one another
9:24, Give **g** to God
Rom. 2:7, in doing good seek for **g** and honor
3:23, fall short of the **g** of God
2 Cor. 4:4, gospel of the **g** of Christ
Phil. 3:21, with the body of His **g**
Heb. 2:7, THOU HAST CROWNED HIM WITH **G** AND HONOR
Jude 25, through Jesus Christ ... *be* **g**
Ex. 33:18; 1 Chr. 16:24; 29:11; Job 29:20; Ps. 105:3; Is. 35:2; Jer. 13:16; Ezek. 10:4; Hos. 4:7; John 8:50; James 1:9
GLUTTON Prov. 23:20; Matt. 11:19
GNASH—*grind* Ps. 35:16; 37:12; 112:10; Lam. 2:16; Matt. 8:12
GNAT Matt. 23:24, who strain out a **g**
GNAWED Rev. 16:10, they **g** their tongues
GO Ex. 14:15, Tell the sons of Israel to **g** forward
Ex. 23:23, My angel will **g** before you
33:14, My presence shall **g** with you
Ruth 1:16, where you **g**, I will **g**
Ps. 139:7, Where can I **g** from
Matt. 5:41, force you to **g** one mile, **g** ... two
6:6, when you pray, **G** INTO YOUR INNER ROOM
Luke 10:37, **G** and do the same
John 14:12, I **g** to the Father

GO *(Continued)*
Gen. 12:1; 32:26; Deut. 17:8; 23:23; Job 23:8; Ps. 42:4; Prov. 22:6; Hos. 2:7; Mic. 2:11; Matt. 21:29
GOAD Judg. 3:31; 1 Sam. 13:20,21
Eccles. 12:11, words of wise men are like **g-s**
GOAL Phil. 3:14, press on toward the **g**
1 Tim. 1:5, **g** of our instruction is love
GOAT Ex. 26:7; Lev. 3:12; Num. 15:27; 1 Sam. 19:13; Dan. 8:5; Matt. 25:32; Heb. 9:13
GODDESS 1 Kin. 11:5; Acts 19:27,37
GOD-FEARING Acts 10:22, Cornelius ... a righteous and **G** man
Acts 17:17, reasoning ... with the Jews and **G** *Gentiles*
GODLESS Job 8:13, hope of the **g** will perish
Job 15:34, company of the **g** is barren
Is. 9:17, every one is **g**
Acts 2:23, hands of **g** men and put Him to death
GODLINESS 1 Tim. 2:2, in all **g** and dignity
1 Tim. 3:16, great is the mystery of **g**
4:8, but **g** is profitable
6:6, **g** *actually* is a means ... contentment
2 Tim. 3:5, holding to a form of **g**
2 Pet. 1:7, **g**, brotherly kindness
GODLY 1 Sam. 2:9, keeps the feet of His **g** ones
Ps. 12:1, for the **g** man ceaseth
37:28, not forsake His **g** ones
2 Cor. 1:12, in holiness and **g** sincerity
2 Pet. 2:9, rescue the **g** from temptation
GODS Ex. 20:3, have no other **g** before Me
Judg. 5:8, New **g** were chosen
Is. 37:12, **g** of those nations ... deliver
Jer. 22:9, bowed down to other **g**
Dan. 2:47, your God is a God of **g**
Gal. 4:8, by nature are no **g**
GOING Ps. 121:8, guard your **g** out
Is. 20:2, **g** naked and barefoot
Matt. 25:8, our lamps are **g** out
Mark 1:16, He was **g** along by the sea of Galilee
10:32, road, **g** up to Jerusalem
John 14:5, not know where You are **g**
Gen. 15:12; Mic. 5:2; Matt. 26:46
GOLD Job 22:25, The Almighty will be your **g**
Ps. 19:10, more desirable than **g** ... much fine **g**
Prov. 8:19, **g**, even pure **g**
Matt. 2:11, to Him gifts of **g**
Acts 3:6, Peter said ... not possess silver and **g**
20:33, coveted no one's silver or **g**
1 Pet. 1:7, more precious than **g**
Rev. 3:18, buy from Me **g** refined
Gen. 2:12; 24:22; Ex. 3:22; Job 31:24; Ps. 72:15; Prov. 16:16; 25:11; Lam. 4:1; Zech. 9:3; Matt. 10:9; James 2:2; Rev. 21:15
GOLDEN Job 37:22, Out of the north comes **g** *splendor*
Lev. 8:9; 1 Sam. 6:18; Dan. 3:5; Rev. 1:12
GOLDSMITH Neh. 3:31,32; Is. 40:19; 46:6
GONE Judg. 19:11, the day was almost **g**
Ps. 19:4, line has **g** out through
Prov. 7:19, **g** on a long journey
Hos. 4:18, Their liquor **g**
Mark 5:30, power ... had **g** forth
Rom. 13:12, The night is almost **g**
2 Pet. 2:15, they have **g** astray
Gen. 31:30; Song 2:11; Lam. 1:3
GOOD Gen. 1:4, that the light was **g**
Gen. 50:20, God meant it for **g**
2 Chr. 6:41, godly ones rejoice in what is **g**
Esth. 10:3, sought the **g** of his people
Ps. 106:1; 136:1, give thanks ... for He is **g**
Prov. 22:1, A **g** name ... more desired
Is. 1:17, Learn to do **g**
Jer. 33:11, For the LORD is **g**, For His lovingkindness
Jon. 4:4, Do you have **g** reason
Matt. 3:10, does not bear **g** fruit
19:16, what **g** thing shall I do
Mark 9:50, Salt is **g**, but if the salt
Luke 1:19, to bring you this **g** news
6:27, do **g** to those who hate you
10:42; Mary has chosen the **g** part
John 10:14, I am the **g** shepherd
Acts 23:1, lived my life ... **g** conscience
Rom. 2:7, perseverance in doing **g**
2:10, every man who does **g**
12:21, overcome evil with **g**
Gal. 6:10, do **g** to all men
Phil. 4:8, whatever is of **g** repute
1 Tim. 6:12, Fight the **g** fight of faith
1 Pet. 3:11, TURN ... FROM EVIL AND DO G
Gen. 15:15; Lev. 27:10; Job 7:7; Prov. 25:25; Is. 39:8; Jer. 24:3; Amos 5:14; Matt. 25:23; Luke 18:19; Acts 6:3; Gal. 6:12; 2 Thess. 2:16; James 1:17
GOODNESS Ex. 33:19; 2 Sam. 2:6; Ps. 25:7
Ps. 23:6, Surely **g** and lovingkindness will follow
31:19, How great is Thy **g**
Gal. 5:22, kindness, **g**, faithfulness
2 Thess. 1:11, fulfill every desire for **g**
GOODS—*possessions* Gen. 14:21; Ezek. 38:12; Luke 12:19
GORGEOUS Luke 23:11, dressed Him in a **g** robe
GOSPEL Matt. 4:23, the **g** of the kingdom
Matt. 11:5, HAVE THE G PREACHED
Mark 16:15, preach the **g** to all
Luke 4:18, PREACH THE G TO THE POOR
Rom. 1:16, I am not ashamed of the **g**
2 Cor. 10:14, in the **g** of Christ
11:4, or a different **g**
Gal. 1:7, distort the **g** of Christ
Eph. 1:13, **g** of your salvation
6:15, G OF PEACE
Phil. 1:5, participation in the **g**
Col. 1:23, from the hope of the **g**
Rev. 14:6, an eternal **g**
GOSSIP Rom. 1:29, malice; *they are* **g-s**
2 Cor. 12:20, **g**, arrogance, disturbances
GOVERN—*rule* Gen. 1:16, to **g** the day ... **g** the night
GOVERNMENT—*authority* Is. 9:6, **g** will rest on His
GOVERNOR—*commander*
Matt. 27:11; Acts 7:10
GRACE—*favor* Ps. 45:2; 2 Thess. 2:16
Luke 2:40, the **g** of God was upon Him
John 1:16, received, and **g** upon **g**
Rom. 1:5, through whom we have received **g**
5:2, this **g** in which we stand
16:20, The **g** of our Lord Jesus be with you
2 Cor. 9:8, make all **g** abound
12:9, My **g** is sufficient
1 Thess. 1:1, **G** to you and peace
Philem. 25, **g** of the Lord Jesus Christ
Heb. 4:16, the throne of **g** ... may find **g**
James 4:6, GIVES G TO THE HUMBLE
2 Pet. 3:18, grow in the **g**
GRACIOUS—*kind* Neh. 9:31, art a **g** and compassionate God
Ps. 6:2, Be **g** to me, O LORD
111:4, LORD is **g** and compassionate
Luke 4:22, wondering at the **g** words
Gen. 43:29; Ex. 33:19; Ps. 77:9; 112:4; 119:29; Prov. 19:17, 26:25; Amos 5:15
GRAFT Rom. 11:23, God is able to **g** them in
Rom. 11:24, **g-ed** contrary to nature ... branches be **g-ed**
GRAIN—*kernel* John 12:24, unless a **g** of wheat falls
1 Cor. 15:37, a bare **g**, perhaps of wheat
Gen. 41:5; Lev. 2:14; 2 Sam. 17:19; 2 Kin. 4:42; Jer. 23:28; Amos 9:9; Matt. 12:1; Mark 4:28
GRANDCHILDREN Prov. 17:6, **G** ... crown of old men
GRANDMOTHER 2 Tim. 1:5, in your **g** Lois
GRANT—*give, provide*
Job 10:12, Thou hast **g-ed** me life
Ps. 85:7, **g** us Thy salvation
Prov. 10:24, of the righteous will be **g-ed**
Mark 10:37, **G** that we may sit
Rev. 3:21, He who overcomes, I will **g** ... to sit
Is. 63:7; Luke 22:29

GRAPE Num. 6:3; Deut. 32:14; Jer. 49:9; Matt. 7:16; Luke 6:44
GRASS—*vegetation*
Ps. 103:15, man, his days are like **g**
Is. 40:6, All flesh is **g**
40:7, the **g** withers, the flower
Matt. 6:30, if God so arrays the **g** of the field
1 Pet. 1:24, ALL FLESH IS LIKE G
Num. 22:4; 2 Sam. 23:4; 2 Kin. 19:26; Ps. 102:11; Prov. 27:25; Is. 5:24; 15:6; 37:27; Dan. 5:21
GRASSHOPPER—*caterpillar*
Num. 13:33, we became like **g-s**
Lev. 11:22; 2 Chr. 6:28; Is. 40:22
GRATITUDE 1 Tim. 4:4, is received with **g**
GRAVE—*tomb* Gen. 35:20; 2 Sam. 3:32; Ps. 5:9; Ezek. 37:12; Nah. 1:14
GRAY Gen. 42:38, bring my **g** hair down ... in sorrow
1 Sam. 12:2, I am old and **g**
Deut. 32:25; Job 15:10; Ps. 71:18; Hos. 7:9
GRAZE—*feed* Is. 5:17; 11:7; 27:10; 65:25
GREAT—*excellent, big* Gen. 12:2; 15:1; Ex. 18:11; 32:30
Gen. 1:16, two **g** lights; the **g-er** light
Ps. 48:1, **G** is the LORD
Mal. 4:5, the **g** and terrible day
Matt. 2:10, rejoiced exceedingly, with **g** joy
4:16, DARKNESS SAW A G LIGHT
5:12, your reward in heaven is **g**
7:27, **g** was its fall
11:11, he who is least ... is **g-er** than he
Luke 2:10, good news of a **g** joy
6:23, your reward is **g** in heaven
John 5:20, **g-er** works than these
15:13, **G-er** love has no one
1 Cor. 13:13, **g-est** of these is love
1 Tim. 6:6, godliness ... a means of **g** gain
Jude 24, stand in the presence ... **g** joy
Rev. 8:10, a **g** star fell from heaven
15:3, G AND MARVELOUS ARE THY WORKS
Deut. 1:17; 2 Sam. 5:10; 19:32; 1 Chr. 16:25; Neh. 9:27; Job 31:25; Ps. 57:10; Prov. 15:16; Jer. 9:19; Dan. 4:22; Zeph. 1:14; Matt. 15:28; Luke 5:6; Acts 11:5; 2 Cor. 3:12
GREATLY—*utterly*
Gen. 20:8, men were **g** frightened
John 3:29, rejoices **g** because of the
Phil. 4:10, I rejoiced in the Lord **g**
Gen. 3:16; Num. 14:39; 1 Sam. 28:5; Ps. 89:7; Zech. 9:9; Mark 12:27
GREATNESS—*magnitude* Ps. 51:1, **g** of Thy compassion
Luke 9:43, the **g** of God
2 Cor. 4:7, the surpassing **g** of the power
Eph. 1:19, surpassing **g** of His power toward us
1 Chr. 29:11; Neh. 13:22; Ps. 150:2; Is. 63:1
GREED Is. 56:11, the dogs are **g-y**
Luke 12:15, Beware ... every form of **g**
1 Thess. 2:5, a pretext for **g**
GREEK Acts 16:1; 21:37; Rom. 2:9; 1 Cor. 12:13; Gal. 3:28; Rev. 9:11
GREEN—*luxuriant*
Ps. 23:2, lie down in **g** pastures
Gen. 1:30; Ps. 92:14; Jer. 17:2; Ezek. 17:24; Luke 23:31
GREET Matt. 10:12, house, give it your **g-ing**
1 Cor. 16:20, All the brethren **g** you. **G** one another
1 Pet. 5:14, **G** one another with a kiss
Matt. 23:7; 2 Tim. 4:21
GREW Gen. 21:8; 1 Sam. 2:21
Ex. 16:21, when the sun **g** hot
Mark 4:7, thorns **g** up and choked it
GRIEF—*sorrow* Ps. 77:10, It is my **g**
Prov. 17:25, A foolish son is a **g** to his
Is. 53:4, our **g-s** He Himself bore
Heb. 13:17, with joy and not with **g**
GRIEVE Is. 63:10, And **g-d** His Holy Spirit
Matt. 26:38, My soul is deeply **g-d**
Mark 3:5, **g-d** at their hardness of heart
John 21:17, Peter was **g-d** because He
Eph. 4:30, do not **g** the Holy Spirit of God
Gen. 6:6; 45:5; Neh. 8:10; Ps. 78:40; Amos 6:6; Nah. 3:7
GRIND Is. 3:15, **g-ing** the face of the poor
Matt. 24:41, women ... **g-ing** at the mill
Judg. 16:21; Eccles. 12:3,4; Is. 47:2; Mark 9:18
GROAN Ex. 2:24, God heard their **g-ing**
Acts 7:34, HAVE HEARD THEIR G-S
Rom. 8:22, whole creation **g-s** and suffers
8:26, **g-ings** too deep for words
2 Cor. 5:2, in this *house* we **g**
Job 24:12; Is. 42:14; Ezek. 30:24; Joel 1:18
GROPE Deut. 28:29; Job 12:25; Is. 59:10; Acts 17:27
GROUND—*earth, land, soil*
Gen. 3:17, Cursed is the **g**
4:2, a tiller of the **g**
Matt. 25:25, hid your talent in the **g**
Luke 19:44, will level you to the **g**
John 8:6, His finger wrote on the **g**
9:6, He spat on the **g**
Acts 7:33, ARE STANDING IS HOLY G
9:8, Saul got up from the **g**
Eph. 3:17, rooted and **g-ed** in love
Gen. 2:5,7,9; 8:21; Num. 16:30; Deut. 28:56; Josh. 3:17; 2 Sam. 14:22; Job 5:6; Ps. 89:44; Is. 3:26; 29:4; Jer. 4:3; 14:4; Lam. 2:21; Hos. 10:12; Amos 3:5; 9:9; Matt. 25:18; Mark 4:31; Acts 9:4; 26:14; Heb. 6:7
GROUP Mark 6:39, recline by **g-s** ... grass
GROVE Judg. 15:5, with the vineyards and **g-s**
GROW 1 Sam. 3:2, eyesight had begun to **g** dim
Matt. 6:28, lilies of the field **g**
24:12, people's love will **g** cold
Luke 2:40, And the Child continued to **g**
Acts 12:24, word of the Lord continued to **g**
19:20, word of the Lord was **g-ing** mightily
1 Cor. 3:6, but God was causing the **g-th**
2 Cor. 10:15, as your faith **g-s**
Eph. 4:15, we are to **g** up ... into Him
1 Pet. 2:2, you may **g** in respect
2 Pet. 3:18, **g** in the grace and knowledge
Gen. 26:13; 48:16; Judg. 16:22; 2 Sam. 10:5; 2 Kin. 19:29; Ps. 147:8
GROWL Is. 59:11, All of us **g** like bears
GROWN Ezek. 7:11, Violence has **g** into a rod
Ex. 2:11; Lev. 13:37; Deut. 32:15; 2 Kin. 4:18; Prov. 24:31
GRUDGE Lev. 19:18; 2 Cor. 9:7
GRUMBLE Phil. 2:14, Do all things without **g-ing**
Ex. 17:3; Luke 15:2; John 6:43
GUARANTOR Job 17:3, Who ... will be my **g**
GUARD—*keep, watch* Ps. 39:1, I will **g** my ways
Mark 14:44, lead Him away under **g**
Phil. 4:7, **g** your hearts and minds
1 Tim. 6:20, **g** what has been entrusted to you
1 John 5:21, children, **g** yourselves from idols
Ex. 23:13; 1 Chr. 11:25; Job 7:12; Prov. 2:11; Ezek. 38:7; Acts 5:23; 28:16
GUARDIAN—*overseer*
1 Pet. 2:25, Shepherd and **G** ... souls
GUEST 1 Kin. 1:41; Prov. 9:18; Matt. 22:10
GUIDANCE—*counsel*
Prov. 11:14, Where there is no **g**
20:18, war by wise **g**
GUIDE—*direct, lead* Ps. 48:14, He will **g** us until death
Prov. 12:26, righteous is a **g** to his neighbor
Is. 58:11, And the LORD will ... **g** you
Matt. 15:14, if a blind man **g-s** a blind man
Luke 1:79, **g** our feet ... way of peace
Rom. 2:19, are a **g** to the blind
Deut. 32:12; Job 38:32; Matt. 23:16; Acts 8:31
GUILE—*deceit* John 1:47, in whom is no **g**
1 Pet. 2:1, all malice and all **g**
3:10, LIPS FROM SPEAKING G
GUILT Luke 23:22, found in Him no **g** *demanding* death
1 Cor. 11:27, **g-y** of the body and the blood
James 2:10, one *point*, he has become **g-y** of all

GUILT *(Continued)*
Gen. 42:21; Lev. 6:4; Num. 5:31; 35:31;
Deut. 25:2; 2 Sam. 3:8; 14:13; Ezra 9:6;
Jer. 51:5; Ezek. 22:4; Hos. 10:2; Hab. 1:11;
Luke 23:4; John 18:38; 19:4,6
GUSH—*flow* Ps. 78:20; Is. 48:21; Acts 1:18

H

HABITATION—*abode, camp* Is. 32:18; 33:20; Acts 17:26
Ps. 26:8, I love the **h** of Thy house
71:3, Be Thou to me a rock of **h**
132:13, He has desired it for His **h**
Is. 63:15, Thy holy and glorious **h**
HADES Matt. 16:18; Luke 16:23; Acts 2:31; Rev. 1:18
HAIL Matt. 26:49, **H**, Rabbi
Matt. 27:29, **H**, King of the Jews
Rev. 16:21, **h-stones** . . . came down from heaven upon men
Ex. 9:23; Job 38:22; Ps. 148:8; Is. 28:17; 32:19;
Mark 15:18; Luke 1:28; John 19:3
HAIR 1 Kin. 1:52, not one of his **h-s** will fall
Matt. 3:4, garment of camel's **h**
5:36, cannot make one **h** white
10:30; Luke 12:7, **h-s** of your head . . . numbered
Luke 7:38, wiping them with the **h** of her head
John 11:2, Mary . . . wiped His feet with her **h**
1 Cor. 11:14, if a man has long **h**
1 Tim. 2:9, not with braided **h**
Rev. 1:14, His **h** were white like white wool
Gen. 42:38; 44:29; Judg. 20:16; Neh. 13:25;
Job 4:15; Mark 1:6; 1 Pet. 3:3
HAIRY—*rough* Zech. 13:4, **h** robe in order to deceive
Gen. 25:25; 27:11; 2 Kin. 1:8; Ps. 68:21
HALLELUJAH Rev. 19:1,3,4,6, saying **h**
HALLOWED—*consecrated, sanctified*
Matt. 6:9; Luke 11:2, **H** be Thy name
HAMMER—*beat* Is. 2:4, **h** their swords into plowshares
Judg. 4:21; 1 Kin. 6:7; Is. 41:7; Jer. 23:29; Mic. 4:3
HAND—*power* Ps. 16:11, In Thy right **h** there are pleasures
Ps. 24:4, has clean **h-s** and a pure heart
31:5; Luke 23:46, Into Thy **h** I commit my spirit
90:17, confirm the work of our **h-s**
137:5, my right **h** forget her *skill*
Eccles. 9:10, Whatever your **h** finds to do
Is. 28:4, it is in his **h**
40:12, in the hollow of His **h**
Jer. 18:6, like the clay in the potter's **h**
Lam. 2:4, His right **h** like an adversary
Matt. 3:2; 4:17; 10:7, kingdom . . . is at **h**
4:6, ON THEIR H-S THEY WILL BEAR
11:27, **h-ed** over to Me by My Father
26:18, My time is at **h**
Mark 14:62, SITTING AT THE RIGHT H OF POWER
16:19, SAT DOWN AT THE RIGHT H OF GOD
John 10:28, snatch them out of My **h**
2 Cor. 5:1, a house not made with **h-s**
Heb. 10:31, fall into the **h-s** of the living God
James 4:8, Cleanse your **h-s**
1 Pet. 4:7, end of all things is at **h**
1 John 1:1, our **h-s** handled
Gen. 3:22; 16:12; 24:2; 47:29; Ex. 21:24; 33:22;
Deut. 8:17; 19:21; 33:3; 1 Sam. 5:11; 12:3;
26:18; 2 Sam. 24:14; 1 Kin. 18:44;
2 Kin. 5:11; 1 Chr. 21:13; 29:14; Ezra 7:9;
Neh. 2:8,18; Job 12:10; 19:21; 40:14;
Ps. 68:31; 80:17; 139:10; Prov. 3:16; 10:4;
12:24; 19:24; 26:15; Eccles. 2:24; Is. 5:25;
9:12; 10:4; 14:27; 53:10; 56:2; Ezek. 7:17;
21:7; Dan. 4:35; Mic. 7:3; Hab. 2:9;
Zeph. 3:16; Matt. 3:12; 6:3; 18:8; Mark 9:43;
14:41; Luke 3:17; 9:44; John 20:27;
1 Cor. 12:15; Col. 2:11; 1 Thess. 4:11;
1 Tim. 2:8
HANDBREADTH Ex. 25:25; 1 Kin. 7:26;
2 Chr. 4:5; Ezek. 40:5
Ps. 39:5, Thou hast made my days *as* **h-s**
HANDFUL—*hand* Lev. 2:2; 5:12; 1 Kin. 20:10
1 Kin. 17:12, only a **h** of flour in the bowl
HANDKERCHIEF Acts 19:12, **h-s** . . . carried from his body
HANDLE—*touch* Song 5:5; Jer. 2:8; Ezek. 27:29
2 Tim. 2:15, **h-ing** accurately the word of truth
1 John 1:1, our hands **h-d**, concerning the Word of Life
HANDMAID—*servant, slave* Ps. 86:16; 116:16
HANDSOME—*becoming* 1 Sam. 16:18, and a **h** man
HANG Deut. 21:23, who is **h-ed** is accursed of God
Job 26:7, He . . . **h-s** the earth on nothing
Matt. 27:5, Judas went away and **h-ed** himself
Gal. 3:13, CURSED IS EVERY ONE WHO H-S
HAPPEN—*befall* Lev. 10:19; Deut. 22:6; Judg. 6:13; Dan. 10:14
HAPPINESS—*joy* Deut. 24:5, shall give **h** to his wife
Eccles. 9:7, eat your bread in **h**
HAPPY—*bless* Job 5:17, **h** is the man whom God reproves
Prov. 14:21, **h** is he who is gracious to the poor
Rom. 14:22, **H** is he who does not condemn himself
HARASS Deut. 2:9, Do not **h** Moab
HARBOR—*haven* Acts 27:12, **h** was not suitable
HARD—*difficult, firm* Ex. 1:14; Num. 11:11; Deut. 1:17
Matt. 19:23, is **h** for a rich man to enter . . . heaven
25:24, I knew you to be a **h** man
Mark 10:24, **h** it is to enter the Kingdom of God
Acts 26:14, **h** for you to kick against the goads
2 Tim. 2:3, Suffer **h-ship** . . . as a good soldier
Deut. 15:18; 2 Kin. 2:10; Job 38:30; 41:24;
Prov. 13:15; 18:19; Is. 8:21; Mark 10:23;
Luke 18:24
HARDEN—*hardness* Job 38:38; Prov. 29:1
John 12:40, HE H-ED THEIR HEART
Rom. 9:18, He **h-s** whom He desires
Heb. 3:13, **h-ed** by deceitfulness of sin
3:15; 4:7, DO NOT H YOUR HEARTS
HARDNESS—*stubborn* Matt. 19:8; Mark 10:5, **h** of heart
Mark 3:5, grieved at their **h** of heart
16:14, He reproached . . . **h** of heart
HARLOT Matt. 21:31, **h-s** will get into the kingdom
Luke 15:30, devoured your wealth with **h-s**
Josh. 6:17; Prov. 7:10; 29:3; Is. 1:21; 23:17;
Jer. 2:20; Ezek. 16:15; Joel 3:3; Rev. 17:5
HARM—*evil, hurt* Lev. 19:27; Judg. 15:3; 2 Kin. 4:41
1 Chr. 16:22; Ps. 105:15, do my prophets no **h**
Prov. 12:21, No **h** befalls the righteous
1 Pet. 3:13, who is there to **h** you
Prov. 3:30; Jer. 25:6; Acts 16:28; 28:5; Rev. 6:6
HARMONY 2 Cor. 6:15, what **h** has Christ with
HARNESS—*armor* Jer. 46:4, **H** the horses
HARP—*lyre, instrument* 1 Sam. 16:16; Ps. 33:2; 49:4; 57:8
Job 30:31, my **h** is turned to mourning
Ps. 137:2, Upon the willows . . . hung our **h-s**
Is. 5:12; 24:8; Amos 6:5; 1 Cor. 14:7; Rev. 5:8; 14:2
HARROW—*instrument* Job 39:10, will he **h** the valleys
HARRY Job 18:11, terrors . . . **h** him at every step
HARSH 1 Sam. 20:10, father answers you **h-ly**
Gen. 16:6; 1 Sam. 25:3; Prov. 15:1
HARVEST—*reap, ripe*
Gen. 8:22, Seedtime and **h** . . . cease
Job 4:8, who sow trouble **h** it
Jer. 8:20, **h** is past, summer is ended
Joel 3:13, the **h** is ripe

Matt. 9:37, **h** is plentiful
9:38; Luke 10:2, the Lord of the **h**
13:30, both to grow together until the **h**
13:39, **h** is the end of the age
Mark 4:29, puts in the sickle . . . **h** has come
John 4:35, fields, that they are white for **h**
Rev. 14:15, the **h** of the earth is ripe
Ex. 22:29; 23:16; 34:22; Lev. 19:9; Deut. 24:19; 1 Sam. 12:17; Job 5:5; Prov. 6:8; 10:5; 25:13; 26:1; Is. 9:3; 16:9; 18:4; Jer. 5:17; 51:33

HASTE—*hurry, urgent*
Prov. 7:23, As a bird **h-ns** . . . snare
Prov. 28:22, evil eye **h-ns** after wealth
2 Pet. 3:12, **h-ning** the coming of the day of God
Ex. 12:11; Ps. 22:19; Eccles. 1:5; Is. 52:12; Mark 6:25

HASTILY—*hurried* Prov. 25:8, Do not go out **h** to argue
1 Tim. 5:22, lay hands upon any one *too* **h**

HASTY—*impetuous* Prov. 29:20, a man who is **h**
Eccles. 5:2, Do not be **h** in word

HATCH Jer. 17:11, As a partridge that **h-es** eggs

HATCHET—*axe, war-club* Ps. 74:6, smash with **h** and hammers

HATE Ps. 81:15, Those who **h** the LORD
Ps. 97:10, **H** evil, you who love the LORD
Prov. 6:16, six things which the LORD **h-s**
8:13, fear of the LORD is to **h** evil
13:24, who spares his rod **h-s** his son
15:10, He who **h-s** reproof will die
Eccles. 3:8, A time to love, and a time to **h**
Matt. 6:24, he will **h** the one and love the other
10:22, Mark 13:13; Luke 21:17, will be **h-d**
Luke 6:22, Blessed are you when men **h** you
6:27, do good to those who **h** you
14:26, not **h** his own father and mother
John 3:20, does evil **h-s** the light
12:25, he who **h-s** his life
15:18; 1 John 3:13, If the world **h-s** you
15:23, He who **h-s** Me **h-s** My Father also
Rom. 1:30, slanderers, **h-rs** of God
7:15, I am doing the very thing I **h**
Eph. 5:29, no one ever **h-d** his own flesh
Titus 3:3, hateful, **h-ing** one another
1 John 2:9; 3:15; 4:20, **h-s** his brother
Gen. 24:60; Lev. 19:17; 26:17; 1 Kin. 22:8; 2 Chr. 18:7; 19:2; Ps. 34:21; 36:2; 139:21; Prov. 1:22; Is. 1:14; 61:8; Ezek. 23:29; Amos 5:15; Mic. 3:2; Zech. 8:17; Mal. 1:3; John 7:7; Rom. 9:13

HAUGHTY—*proud, lofty, high*
Ps. 131:1, nor my eyes **h**
Prov. 16:18, **h** spirit before stumbling
Rom. 12:16, do not be **h** in mind
2 Sam. 22:28; Prov. 6:17; 21:24; Zeph. 3:11

HAUNT—*habitation* Is. 34:13, also be a **h** of jackals

HAVEN—*harbor* Gen. 49:13; Ps. 107:30

HAWK Lev. 11:16; Deut. 14:15; Job 39:26

HEAD—*chief* 2 Kin. 6:5, axe **h** fell into the water
Ps. 24:7, Lift up your **h-s**, O gates
Prov. 25:22, burning coals on his **h**
Eccles. 2:14, wise man's eyes are in his **h**
Matt. 14:8, Give me . . . **h** of John the Baptist
27:39, WAGGING THEIR H-S
Luke 21:18, not a hair of your **h** will perish
21:28, straighten up and lift up your **h-s**
John 13:9, also my hands and my **h**
1 Cor. 11:3, Christ is the **h** of every man
Eph. 1:22, Him as **h** over all things
5:23, Christ also is the **h** of the church
Col. 2:19, not holding fast to the **H**
Rev. 1:14, His **h** and His hair were white
Gen. 3:15; 1 Sam. 1:11; 9:22; 2 Kin. 4:19; Ps. 66:12; Is. 3:16; 59:17; Jer. 18:16; Dan. 2:38; 7:6; Matt. 5:36; 6:17; Acts 21:24

HEAL 2 Chr. 7:14, and will **h** their land
Ps. 147:3, He **h-s** the broken-hearted
Prov. 3:8, will be **h-ing** to your body
Is. 53:5, by His scourging we are **h-ed**
Jer. 3:22, I will **h** your faithlessness
Hos. 14:4, I will **h** their apostasy
Matt. 10:8, **H** *the* sick, raise *the* dead
Mark 3:2, He would **h** him on the Sabbath
Luke 4:23, Physician, **h** yourself
9:2, kingdom of God, and to perform **h-ing**
9:11, those who had need of **h-ing**
Acts 9:34, Jesus Christ **h-s** you
1 Cor. 12:9, gifts of **h-ing** by the one Spirit
James 5:16, pray . . . that you may be **h-ed**
Rev. 22:2, the **h-ing** of the nations
Ex. 15:26; Num. 12:13; Deut. 32:39; Job 5:18; Ps. 6:2; Prov. 13:17; Jer. 17:14; 30:13; Matt. 4:23

HEALTH Jer. 30:17, will restore you to **h**
3 John 2, prosper and be in good **h**

HEAP—*store* Prov. 25:22, **h** burning coals on his head
Is. 25:2, made a city into a **h**
Gen. 31:46; Ex. 15:8; Deut. 32:23; Josh. 3:13; Ps. 33:7; Ezek. 24:10; Hab. 1:10

HEAR Job 27:9, Will God **h** his cry
Ps. 4:1, O God . . . **h** my prayer
135:17, have ears, but they do not **h**
Is. 28:14, **h** the word of the LORD
Ezek. 37:4, dry bones, **h** the word of the LORD
Matt. 11:15, ears to **h**, let him **h**
13:13, while **h-ing** they do not **h**
15:10, **H** and understand
17:5, I am well pleased; **h** Him
Mark 7:37, He makes even the deaf to **h**
John 5:24, he who **h-s** My word
10:3, the sheep **h** his voice
12:47, if any one **h-s** My sayings
Acts 17:32, We shall **h** you again
James 1:19, let every one be quick to **h**
Rev. 3:20, if any one **h-s** My voice
Lev. 5:1; Deut. 6:4; 1 Sam. 15:14; 1 Kin. 8:30; Job 15:8; 26:14; Ps. 38:13; 65:2; Is. 1:2; Matt. 10:27; Rom. 11:8

HEARD Matt. 2:18, A VOICE WAS H IN RAMAH
Acts 4:4, who had **h** the message believed
19:10, lived in Asia **h** the word
1 Cor. 2:9, EYE HAS NOT SEEN AND EAR HAS NOT H
2 Cor. 12:4, **h** inexpressible words
Phil. 4:9, learned and received and **h**
Rev. 10:4, I **h** a voice from heaven
Gen. 3:10; Ps. 10:17; Eccles. 12:13; Song 2:12; Is. 65:19; Jer. 31:15; Ezek. 1:24; Matt. 6:7; Luke 1:13

HEARING—*ears* Prov. 20:12, The **h** ear
Prov. 23:9, Do not speak in the **h** of a fool
Matt. 24:6, you will be **h** of wars
Rom. 10:17, So faith *comes* from **h**
Heb. 5:11, since you have become dull of **h**

HEART—*desire, mind*
Gen. 8:21, intent of man's **h** is evil
1 Sam. 16:7, LORD looks at the **h**
1 Kin. 3:9, an understanding **h**
15:3, his **h** was not wholly devoted
1 Chr. 28:9, serve Him with a whole **h**
Ps. 19:14, the meditation of my **h**
44:21, He knows the secrets of the **h**
51:10, Create in me a clean **h**
51:17, broken and contrite **h**
119:11, Thy word I have treasured in my **h**
Prov. 4:23, Watch . . . **h** with all diligence
17:22, joyful **h** is good medicine
25:20, sings songs to a troubled **h**
Jer. 17:9, **h** is more deceitful than all else
17:10, I, the LORD search the **h**
Matt. 5:8, Blessed are the pure in **h**
5:28, committed adultery . . . in his **h**
6:21, treasure is, there will your **h** be
11:29, I am gentle and humble in **h**
15:8, THEIR H IS FAR AWAY FROM ME
19:8, Because of your hardness of **h**
Mark 12:30, LOVE THE LORD . . . YOUR H
Luke 2:19, pondering them in her **h**
2:51, treasured all *these* things in her **h**
24:25, slow of **h** to believe
John 14:1, Let not your **h** be troubled

HEART *(Continued)*
Acts 2:37, they were pierced to the **h**
Rom. 8:27, He who searches the **h-s** knows
10:10, for with the **h** man believes
Eph. 3:17, Christ may dwell in your **h-s**
5:19, making melody with your **h**
6:5, in the sincerity of your **h**
Phil. 4:7, guard your **h-s** and your minds
Col. 3:22, but with sincerity of **h**
2 Thess. 3:5, Lord direct your **h-s** into
Heb. 4:12, thoughts and intentions of the **h**
10:22, draw near with a sincere **h**
James 1:26, deceives his *own* **h**
2 Pet. 1:19, morning star arises in your **h-s**
Ex. 4:21; 31:6; Num. 15:39; Deut. 28:65; Josh. 5:1; Judg. 5:16; 1 Sam. 10:9; 13:14; 2 Sam. 6:16; 2 Chr. 15:15; Job 23:16; 29:13; 41:24; Ps. 4:7; 9:1; 12:2; 15:2; 17:3; 22:14; 27:3; 38:10; 111:1; Prov. 12:20; 16:5; 23:7,26; Eccles. 8:5; 11:9; Song 8:6; Is. 35:4; 47:10; Jer. 11:20; 24:7; Ezek. 11:19; 18:31; 21:7; 44:7,9; Joel 2:13; Mal. 4:6; Matt. 12:34; 2 Cor. 3:3; 6:11; 9:7

HEAT—*outburst* Gen. 8:22; 18:1; Job 24:19; Is. 25:4
2 Pet. 3:10, be destroyed with intense **h**
Rev. 16:9, men were scorched with fierce **h**
Jer. 2:24; Hos. 7:4; Matt. 20:12

HEAVEN—*sky* Gen. 1:1, God created the **h-s**
Gen. 1:8, God called the expanse **h**
28:17, this is the gate of **h**
Ps. 19:1, **h-s** are telling . . . glory of God
103:11, high as the **h-s** are above the earth
Is. 65:17, new **h-s** and a new earth
Mal. 3:10, open for you the windows of **h**
Matt. 3:2, Repent . . . kingdom of **h** is
3:17, behold, a voice out of the **h-s**
5:3, Blessed . . . theirs is the kingdom of **h**
5:12, your reward in **h** is great
6:9, Our Father who art in **h**
6:10, On earth as it is in **h**
6:14, your **h-ly** Father will also forgive
10:7, kingdom of **h** is at hand
16:19, keys of the kingdom of **h**
Mark 13:31, **H** and earth will pass away
Luke 10:20, your names are recorded in **h**
15:18, have sinned against **h**
John 3:13, from **h**, *even* the Son of Man
1 Cor. 15:40, are also **h-ly** bodies
15:47, second man is from **h**
2 Cor. 5:1, eternal in the **h-s**
12:2, was caught up to the third **h**
Gal. 1:8, or an angel from **h**, should preach
Eph. 6:9, their Master and yours is in **h**
Phil. 3:20, our citizenship is in **h**
Heb. 11:12, AS THE STARS OF H
12:23, who are enrolled in **h**
James 5:12, do not swear, either by **h**
Rev. 4:1, a door *standing* open in **h**
21:1, I saw a new **h**
Ex. 20:22; Deut. 33:13; 1 Sam. 2:10; 1 Kin. 8:27; 2 Kin. 7:2; Job 11:8; 22:12,14; Eccles. 5:2; Is. 14:12; Jer. 7:18; 23:24; Ezek. 32:8; John 3:12; 1 Cor. 15:48

HEAVY Matt. 11:28, who are weary and **h** laden
Matt. 26:43, their eyes were **h**
Ex. 17:12; 2 Chr. 10:10,11; Ps. 38:4; Prov. 27:3; Zech. 12:3; Matt. 23:4

HEDGE Luke 14:23, highways and along the **h-s**
Job 1:10; Prov. 15:19; Mic. 7:4

HEED Ps. 17:1; 55:2; Jer. 2:31

HEEL Gen. 3:15; 25:26; 49:17; Ps. 41:9

HEIGHT Rom. 8:39, nor **h**, nor depth
Job 22:12; Prov. 25:3; Rev. 21:16

HEIR Rom. 8:17, **h-s** also, **h-s** of God
Gal. 4:7, an **h** through God
James 2:5, **h-s** of the kingdom
Gen. 15:3; Jer. 49:1; Matt. 21:38

HELD Ezek. 31:15, and **h** back its rivers

HELL Mark 9:47, to be cast into **h**
James 3:6, tongue . . . is set on fire by **h**
2 Pet. 2:4, angels . . . cast them into **h**
Matt. 5:22; 10:28; 23:15

HELMET 1 Sam. 17:5, had a bronze **h** on his head
Is. 59:17, **h** of salvation on His head
Eph. 6:17, take the **h** of salvation

HELP 1 Sam. 7:12, the LORD has **h-ed** us
Ps. 33:20, He is our **h** and our shield
42:11, The **h** of my countenance
46:1, very present **h** in trouble
121:1, whence shall my **h** come
Matt. 15:25, Lord, **h** me
Mark 9:24, **h** *me in* my unbelief
2 Cor. 1:11, **h-ing** us through your prayers
Heb. 4:16, grace to **h** in time of need
Job 5:16; 6:13; Is. 41:6,13; Mark 7:11

HELPER—*comforter*
Gen. 2:18, I will make him a **h**
Ps. 10:14, **h** of the orphan
30:10, O LORD, be Thou my **h**
54:4, Behold, God is my **h**
John 14:16, will give you another **H**
Heb. 13:6, THE LORD IS MY H

HEMORRHAGE—*blood* Matt. 9:20; Mark 5:25; Luke 8:43

HEMORRHOIDS Deut. 28:27; 1 Sam. 5:6; 6:4

HERB Luke 11:42, tithe . . . every garden **h**
2 Kin. 4:39; 19:26; Ps. 37:2; Prov. 27:25; Is. 37:27

HERD—*cattle* Gen. 13:5; Jon. 3:7; Matt. 8:30

HERITAGE—*gift, possession* Ps. 16:6, my **h** is beautiful
Job 20:29; Ps. 135:12; 136:21,22; Is. 49:8

HESITATE 1 Kin. 18:21, How long *will* you **h**

HID—*cover, secret* Gen. 3:8, man and his wife **h** themselves
Matt. 10:26, and **h-en** that will not be known
13:44, treasure **h-en** in the field
25:25, **h** your talent in the ground
Mark 4:22, For nothing is **h-en**
1 Cor. 2:7, **h-en** wisdom, which God predestined
Col. 3:3, your life is **h-en** with Christ
Deut. 33:19; Josh. 2:4; 1 Sam. 20:24; 2 Sam. 17:9; Job 40:13; Ps. 19:6,12; 69:5; Is. 45:3; Dan. 2:22; Luke 8:17; John 8:59; Heb. 11:23

HIDE—*conceal, cover* Gen. 18:17; Job 14:13; 20:12; Ps. 27:5,9; Is. 2:10; Jer. 38:14

HIGH—*rank* Ps. 103:11, **h** as the heavens are above . . . earth
Matt. 4:8, devil took Him to a very **h** mountain
Mark 5:7, Jesus, Son of the Most **H** God
11:10, HOSANNA in the **h-est**
Luke 2:14, Glory to God in the **h-est**
John 19:31, for that Sabbath was a **h** *day*
Heb. 3:1, Jesus, the Apostle and **H** Priest
Gen. 29:7; Job 11:8; 22:12; Ps. 49:2; 91:14; Prov. 24:7; Is. 32:15; Luke 1:78

HIGHWAY—*way*
Num. 20:17, go along the king's **h**
Is. 35:8, **h** . . . called the **h** of holiness
40:3, a **h** for our God
59:7, Devastation and . . . in their **h-s**
Deut. 2:27; Prov. 15:19; Is. 11:16; 19:23; 49:11; 62:10; Matt. 22:9; Luke 14:23

HILL—*mountains*
Ps. 24:3, Who may ascend into the **h**
50:10, cattle on a thousand **h-s**
Matt. 5:14, city set on a **h** cannot be hidden
Luke 4:29, led Him to the brow of the **h**
Gen. 49:26; Deut. 11:11; Ps. 15:1; Is. 5:1; Luke 23:30

HINDER—*delay, forbid, restrain*
Matt. 19:14, do not **h** them from coming to Me
Mark 9:39, But Jesus said, Do not **h** him
Gal. 5:7, who **h-ed** you from obeying
1 Pet. 3:7, your prayers may not be **h-ed**
Mark 9:38; Luke 11:52; 18:16

HINDRANCE 1 Cor. 9:12, cause no **h** to the gospel

HIRE Is. 7:20, shave with a razor, **h-d**
Matt. 20:1, went out early . . . to **h** laborers
20:7, Because no one **h-d** us
Luke 15:19, as one of your **h-d** men

HIT 2 Cor. 11:20, if he **h-s** you in the face
HOARD—*store* Amos 3:10, **h** up violence and devastation
HOLD—*keep, retain*
Prov. 4:13, Take **h** of instruction
Is. 4:1, seven women ... **h** of one man
Matt. 6:24, he will **h** to one
Mark 7:8, **h** to the tradition of men
Luke 8:15, heard the word, and **h** it fast
Phil. 2:16, **h-ing** fast the word of life
1 Thess. 5:21, **h** fast to that which is good
Titus 1:9, **h-ing** fast the faithful word
Job 2:9; 27:6; Ps. 64:5; Prov. 4:4; Is. 33:15; Jer. 20:9; Acts 7:60; Phil. 2:29
HOLE—*opening* Matt. 8:20, foxes have **h-s**
2 Kin. 12:9; Is. 11:8; Ezek. 8:7; Hag. 1:6
HOLINESS—*holy, sanctity* Ex. 15:11
Ps. 93:5, **H** befits Thy house
Is. 35:8, be called the highway of **h**
2 Cor. 7:1, perfecting **h** in the fear of God
1 Thess. 3:13, hearts unblameable in **h**
Heb. 12:10, we may share His **h**
HOLY—*holiness, sacred, sanctify* Ex. 3:5; 28:36
Ex. 20:8, sabbath day, to keep it **h**
Deut. 5:12, Observe the sabbath ... keep it **h**
7:6, you are a **h** people
1 Chr. 16:10, Glory in His **h** name
Ps. 11:4, Lord is in His **h** temple
16:10, allow Thy **H** One to see the pit
145:21, bless His **h** name forever
Is. 6:3, **H**, **H**, **H**, is the Lord of hosts
Hab. 2:20, Lord is in His **h** temple
Matt. 7:6, not give what is **h** to dogs
Luke 1:49, **h** is His name
4:34, the **H** One of God
John 17:11, **H** Father, keep them in Thy name
Acts 2:27, Thy **H** One
Rom. 12:1, your bodies a living and **h** sacrifice
1 Cor. 3:17, the temple of God is **h**
7:34, **h** both in body and spirit
Eph. 1:4, be **h** and blameless before Him
Col. 1:22, **h** and blameless
1 Tim. 2:8, lifting up **h** hands
2 Tim. 1:9, called us with a **h** calling
Lev. 20:7; Deut. 33:2; 1 Sam. 2:2; 2 Kin. 4:9; 1 Chr. 16:29; Job 15:15; Ps. 47:8; 89:5; 99:9; Jer. 17:22,24,27; 31:23; Mark 6:20; Rom. 16:16
HOLY SPIRIT—*spirit*
Matt. 1:20, in her is of the **H**
Matt. 3:11, baptize you with the **H**
Luke 3:22, **H** descended upon Him in bodily
4:1, Jesus, full of the **H**
11:13, give the **H** to those
12:12, **H** will teach you
John 14:26, Helper, the **H**
20:22, Receive the **H**
Acts 2:4, all filled with the **H**
2:38, receive the gift of the **H**
7:51, always resisting the **H**
10:38, the **H** and with power
19:2, Did you receive the **H**
Rom. 9:1, witness in the **H**
Eph. 1:13, with the **H** of promise
4:30, do not grieve the **H** of God
1 Thess. 4:8, God who gives His **H** to you
HOME Eccles. 12:5, man goes to his eternal **h**
2 Cor. 5:6, are at **h** in the body
Titus 2:5, sensible, pure, workers at **h**
Lev. 18:9; Deut. 24:5; 1 Kin. 13:15; 2 Chr. 25:19; Prov. 7:19; Mark 5:19; 1 Cor. 11:34; 14:35
HOMESTEAD—*habitation* Luke 11:21; Acts 1:20
HONEST—*good, true* Gen. 42:11, we are **h** men
Luke 8:15, an **h** and good heart
HONOR—*splendor* Ex. 20:12, **H** your father and your mother
Lev. 19:32, **h** the aged
Prov. 15:33, before **h** *comes* humility
Matt. 6:2, that they may be **h-ed** by men
13:57, A prophet is not without **h**
15:8, **h-s** Me with their lips
John 5:23, all may **h** the Son
Rom. 2:10, glory and **h** and peace
1 Tim. 6:16, To Him *be* **h** and eternal dominion
Heb. 13:4, *Let* marriage *be held* in **h**
1 Pet. 2:17, **H** all men ... **h** the king
3:7, grant her **h** as a fellow-heir
Rev. 5:13, *be* blessing and **h** and glory
1 Sam. 2:30; 9:6; 1 Kin. 3:13; 1 Chr. 29:28; Job 19:9; Ps. 50:23; Eccles. 6:2; Is. 49:5; Matt. 15:4; Rom. 12:10; 13:7; 1 Tim. 5:17
HONORABLE—*noble* Is. 9:15; Nah. 3:10
Rom. 9:21, one vessel for **h** use ... another for common
Phil. 4:8, brethren ... whatever is **h**
Heb. 13:18, conduct ourselves **h-y** in all things
HOOF—*claw* Lev. 11:3,4,5,6,7,26, whatever divides a **h**
Deut. 14:6,7,8; Ps. 69:31; Is. 5:28; Jer. 47:3; Ezek. 32:13; Zech. 11:16
HOOK 2 Kin. 19:28; Is. 37:29, put My **h** in your nose
Job 41:2, pierce his jaw with a **h**
Ezek. 29:4; 38:4; Amos 4:2
HOPE—*comfort, expectation, confidence, trust*
Job 13:15, I will **h** in Him
Ps. 39:7, My **h** is in Thee
62:5, my **h** is from Him
Prov. 13:12, **H** deferred *makes* the heart sick
19:18, Discipline your son while there is **h**
Acts 2:26, my flesh also will abide in **h**
23:6, **h** and resurrection of the dead
28:20, for the sake of the **h** of Israel
Rom. 4:18, **h** against **h** he believed
5:5, **h** does not disappoint
8:24, **h** that is seen is not **h**
12:12, rejoicing in **h**
15:4, Scriptures we might have **h**
1 Cor. 13:7, **h-s** all things
13:13, now abide faith, **h**, love
2 Cor. 3:12, Having therefore such a **h**
Gal. 5:5, waiting for the **h** of righteousness
Eph. 4:4, you were called in one **h**
Col. 1:23, away from the **h** of the gospel
1:27, Christ in you, the **h** of glory
1 Thess. 5:8, as a helmet, the **h** of salvation
1 Tim. 4:10, our **h** on the living God
Titus 3:7, *the* **h** of eternal life
Heb. 6:19, **h** we have as an anchor
11:1, assurance of *things* **h-d** for
1 Pet. 1:3, born again to a living **h**
Ruth 1:12; Job 7:6; Ps. 9:18; 71:5; Prov. 26:12; Eccles. 9:4; Is. 20:5; 57:10; Jer. 29:11; 1 Cor. 9:10; 2 Cor. 1:7; 2 Thess. 2:16
HORN—*trumpet* Gen. 22:13; Lev. 25:9; Josh. 6:5; 2 Sam. 22:3; 1 Chr. 15:28; Dan. 3:5; 7:7; Rev. 5:6
HORRIBLE Jer. 5:30; 23:14; Hos. 6:10
HORROR Ps. 55:5; Jer. 25:18
HORSE Ps. 33:17, A **h** is a false hope
Gen. 49:17; 1 Kin. 10:29; Job 39:19; Ps. 32:9; Prov. 26:3; Jer. 4:13; 46:4; Hos. 14:3
HOSPITABLE 1 Tim. 3:2, must be above reproach ... **h**
Titus 1:8, but **h**, loving what is good
1 Pet. 4:9, Be **h** to one another
HOSPITALITY Rom. 12:13, practicing **h**
HOST—*army, camp, innkeeper*
Ps. 24:10, Lord of **h-s**, He is the King
Luke 2:13, multitude of the heavenly **h**
Deut. 4:19; Josh. 5:15; Ps. 27:3; Is. 48:2; Rom. 16:23
HOSTILE—*enmity, contrary* Lev. 26:21, you act with **h-ity**
Rom. 8:7, mind set on the flesh is **h**
1 Thess. 2:15, but **h** to all men
Heb. 12:3, endured such **h-ity** by sinners
James 4:4, friendship with the world is **h-ity**
HOT—*branding* Ps. 39:3, My heart was **h** within me
Rev. 3:15, are neither cold nor **h**
Ex. 16:21; Deut. 9:19; Job 6:17; Prov. 6:28
HOT-TEMPERED Prov. 29:22, a **h** man abounds

HOUR—*time* Matt. 20:12, men have worked *only* one **h**
Matt. 24:36, day and **h** no one knows
26:40, watch with Me for one **h**
Mark 15:34, ninth **h** Jesus cried out
Luke 22:59, about an **h** had passed
John 5:25, an **h** is coming and now is
12:27, Father, save Me from this **h**
17:1, Father, the **h** has come
Matt. 8:13; Mark 13:32; Luke 12:39; John 11:9; Acts 3:1; Rom. 13:11; Rev. 3:10
HOUSE—*temple* Ps. 23:6, dwell in the **h** of the LORD
Ps. 127:1, Unless the LORD builds the **h**
Prov. 9:1, Wisdom has built her **h**
Matt. 2:11, they came into the **h** and saw
7:25, winds blew, and burst against that **h**
10:12, enter the **h**, give it your greeting
12:25, city or **h** divided against itself
21:13, MY **H** SHALL BE CALLED A **H**
Luke 11:17, a **h** divided against itself falls
John 14:2, Father's **h** are many dwelling places
Acts 2:46, breaking bread from **h** to **h**
7:48, does not dwell in **h-s** ... human hands
7:49, WHAT KIND OF **H** WILL YOU BUILD
Rom. 16:5, church that is in their **h**
2 Cor. 5:1, **h** not made with hands
1 Tim. 5:13, go around from **h** to **h**
1 Pet. 2:5, built up as a spiritual **h**
Gen. 15:3; Ex. 20:2,17; Deut. 8:12; 22:8; 2 Kin. 20:1; Neh. 13:11; Job 27:18; 30:23; Ps. 55:14; 84:3; 93:5; 102:7; Prov. 24:3; Eccles. 7:2; Is. 5:8; Matt. 23:38; Mark 12:40; Luke 10:7
HOUSEHOLD—*home* Prov. 31:27, ways of her **h**
Gal. 6:10, who are of the **h** of the faith
Eph. 2:19, and are of God's **h**
1 Tim. 3:4, manages his own **h** well
3:15, conduct himself in the **h** of God
Gen. 18:19; 26:14; Ex. 1:1; Matt. 10:36; 13:52; John 19:27; 2 Tim. 3:6
HUMBLE—*abase, gentle* Mic. 6:8, walk **h-ly** with your God
Matt. 11:29, I am gentle and **h** in heart
23:12, exalts ... shall be **h-d**; and ... **h-s** himself
Phil. 3:21, body of our **h** state
4:12, get along with **h** means
James 4:6, BUT GIVES GRACE TO THE **H**
1 Pet. 5:6, **H** yourselves under the mighty hand
Ex. 10:3; Num. 12:3; Deut. 8:2; 2 Chr. 34:27; Job 40:12; Ps. 35:13; 37:11; Prov. 6:3; 11:2; Dan. 4:37; Zech. 9:9
HUMILIATE 2 Cor. 12:21, my God may **h** me before you
HUMILIATION—*confusion* Is. 45:16; Jer. 3:25
Acts 8:33, in **h** His judgment was taken
HUMILITY—*humble, self-abasement*
Prov. 15:33, before honor comes **h**
18:12, **h** *goes* before honor
22:4, The reward of **h**
Phil. 2:3, with **h** of mind
Col. 3:12, put on a heart of ... **h**
1 Pet. 5:5, clothe yourselves with **h**
HUNG Ps. 137:2, Upon the willows ... we **h** our harps
Matt. 18:6; Mark 9:4; Luke 17:2, better ... millstone be **h** around his neck
HUNGER Ps. 34:10, lions do lack and suffer **h**
Prov. 10:3, not allow the righteous to **h**
19:15, an idle man will suffer **h**
Is. 49:10, They will not **h** or thirst
Matt. 5:6; Luke 6:21, Blessed are those who **h**
John 6:35, comes to Me shall not **h**
Deut. 28:48; Luke 6:25; 15:17
HUNGRY Ps. 146:7, Who gives food to the **h**
Prov. 25:21, If your enemy is **h**
Matt. 4:2, He then became **h**
12:1, His disciples became **h**
12:3, David did, when he became **h**
15:32, do not wish to send them away **h**
25:35, For I was **h**
Rom. 12:20, BUT IF YOUR ENEMY IS **H**
1 Cor. 11:34, If anyone is **h**
Deut. 8:3; 2 Sam. 17:29; Job 22:7; Ps. 50:12; Is. 29:8; Ezek. 18:7; 1 Cor. 11:21; Phil. 4:12
HUNT Gen. 10:9, a mighty **h-er** before the LORD
Gen. 27:5; 1 Sam. 26:20; Ps. 140:11; Ezek. 13:18; Mic. 7:2
HURRIED Prov. 20:21, inheritance gained **h-ly**
HURRY—*speed* 1 Sam. 20:38, **H**, be quick, do not stay
HURT—*harm* Ps. 15:4, He swears to his own **h**
Is. 11:9; Mark 16:18
HUSBAND—*bridegroom*
Prov. 12:4, wife is a crown of her **h**
John 4:16, Go, call your **h**
Rom. 7:2,3, if her **h** dies
1 Cor. 7:3, **h** fulfill his duty to his wife
Eph. 5:23, **h** is the head of the wife
5:25, **H-s**, love your wives
Rev. 21:2, bride adorned for her **h**
Gen. 3:16; 29:32; 30:20; Is. 54:5; Hos. 3:1; Mark 10:12; 1 Cor. 7:2; 2 Cor. 11:2
HUSH—*silence* Acts 21:40, there was a great **h**
HYMN Matt. 26:30, singing a **h**, they went out
Eph. 5:19, in psalms and **h-s** and spiritual songs
HYPOCRISY Matt. 23:28, you are full of **h**
Rom. 12:9, Let love be without **h**
1 Tim. 4:2, means of the **h** of liars
James 3:17, wisdom from above ... without **h**
HYPOCRITE—*godless* Matt. 6:2, as the **h-s** do ... synagogues
Matt. 6:5, not to be as the **h-s**
6:16, gloomy face as the **h-s** *do*
7:5, You **h**, first take the log
22:18, Why are you testing Me, you **h-s**
23:13, scribes and Pharisees, **h-s**
Luke 12:56, You **h-s**! You know how to analyze

I

ICE—*frost* Job 37:10, breath of God **i** is made
IDLE Prov. 19:15, an **i** man will suffer hunger
Prov. 31:27, not eat the bread of **i-ness**
Matt. 20:6, Why have you been standing ... **i**
1 Tim. 5:13, not merely **i**, but also gossips
IDOL—*image* Ex. 20:4, make for yourself an **i**
Acts 15:20, abstain from ... **i-s**
1 Cor. 10:7, do not be **i-aters**
1 John 5:21, guard yourselves from **i-s**
Lev. 19:4; 26:1; Is. 66:3; Jer. 50:38
IGNORANCE—*unintentionally*
Acts 17:23, What ... worship in **i**
17:30, overlooked the times of **i**
Eph. 4:18, because of the **i** that is in them
1 Pet. 2:15, silence the **i** of foolish men
IGNORANT 2 Cor. 2:11, not **i** of his schemes
2 Tim. 2:23, refuse foolish and **i** speculations
ILLEGITIMATE Deut. 23:2; Heb. 12:8
ILLNESS—*infirmity* Gal. 4:13, a bodily **i**
ILLUMINE Ps. 18:28, God **i-s** my darkness
IMAGE—*likeness* Gen. 1:26, make man in Our **i**
Gen. 9:6, **i** of God He made man
1 Cor. 11:7, **i** and glory of God
Col. 1:15, **i** of the invisible God
IMAGINATION—*estimation*
Prov. 18:11, wall in his own **i**
IMITATE—*follow* 3 John 11, do not **i** what is evil
IMITATORS—*followers* Eph. 5:1, be **i** of God
1 Thess. 2:14, become **i** of the churches of God
IMMATURE—*babes, children*
Rom. 2:20, teacher of the **i**
IMMEDIATELY Matt. 3:16, went up **i** from the water
Matt. 4:20, **i** left the nets
21:2, **i** you will find a donkey tied
26:74, And **i** a cock crowed
Mark 4:15, **i** Satan comes
Luke 12:54, **i** you say, A shower is coming
14:5, **i** pull him out ... Sabbath
21:9, the end does not *follow* **i**

John 5:9, **i** the man became well
19:34, **i** there came out blood and water
Acts 9:18, **i** there fell from his eyes
9:20, **i** he began to proclaim Jesus
21:30, **i** the doors were shut
Rev. 4:2, **i** I was in the Spirit
Matt. 13:21; 26:49; Mark 6:25; Luke 17:7; Acts 13:11

IMMORALITY—*fornication* Matt. 19:9, except for **i**
1 Cor. 6:18, Flee **i**
1 Thess. 4:3, abstain from sexual **i**
Rev. 2:20, they commit *acts of* **i**
17:2, the wine of her **i**

IMMORTALITY 1 Cor. 15:53, mortal ... put on **i**
1 Tim. 6:16, who alone possesses **i**
2 Tim. 1:10, brought life and **i**

IMPATIENT Num. 21:4, people became **i**

IMPEL—*drive* Mark 1:12, the Spirit **i-ed** Him

IMPERISHABLE 1 Cor. 9:25, perishable ... an **i**
1 Cor. 15:52, the dead will be raised **i**
1 Pet. 1:4, *obtain* an inheritance *which is* **i**

IMPETUOUS Hab. 1:6, Chaldeans, That fierce and **i** people

IMPLORE—*adjure* Job 8:5, **i** the compassion of the Almighty
Mark 5:7, I **i** you by God

IMPOSSIBLE Matt. 19:26, With men this is **i**
Luke 1:37, nothing will be **i** with God
Heb. 6:18, it is **i** for God to lie
11:6, without faith it is **i** to

IMPROPER 1 Cor. 14:35, **i** for a woman to speak

IMPROVISE Amos 6:5, Who **i** to the sound of the harp

IMPUTE—*reckon* Rom. 5:13, sin is not **i-d** when there is

INAUGURATED—*dedicated*
Heb. 9:18, first covenant ... not **i**
10:20, way which He **i** for us

INCITE Luke 23:14, one who **i-s** the people

INCLINE Josh. 24:23, **i** your hearts to the LORD
Ps. 119:36, **I** my heart to Thy
Is. 37:17, **I** Thine ear, O LORD

INCREASE—*multiply, produce* Job 31:12, Prov. 28:8
Ps. 62:10, riches **i**, do not set *your* heart
Eccles. 1:18, **i-ing** knowledge results in **i-ing** pain
Luke 2:52, **i-ing** in wisdom and stature
11:29, the crowds were **i-ing**
Col. 1:10, **i-ing** in the knowledge of God

INDEBTED Rom. 15:27, they are **i**

INDEED—*surely, truly* Gen. 3:1, **I**, has God said, You shall
Ex. 4:25, **i** a bridegroom of blood
Num. 14:21, but **i**, as I live
1 Kin. 8:27, God **i** dwell on the earth
2 Chr. 6:18, will God **i** dwell with mankind
John 8:36, you shall be free **i**
Rom. 14:20, All things **i** are clean
1 Tim. 5:5, she who is a widow, **i**

INDEPENDENT 1 Cor. 11:11, woman **i** of man ... man **i** ... woman

INDESTRUCTIBLE—*endless*
Heb. 7:16, power of an **i** life

INDIGNANT Matt. 20:24; Luke 13:14

INDIGNATION—*anger* Jer. 15:17; Nah. 1:6
Ps. 7:11, God who has **i** every day
69:24, Pour out Thine **i** on them
Is. 30:27, lips are filled with **i**

INEXPERIENCED—*tender*
1 Chr. 22:5, My son ... young and **i**

INFECTION—*plague*
Lev. 13:2, becomes an **i** of leprosy

INFERIOR—*base* Is. 3:5, And the **i** against the honorable

INFIRMITIES—*sickness, weakness*
Matt. 8:17, HIMSELF TOOK OUR I

INFLICT Job 5:18, He **i-s** pain, and gives relief

INFORM—*speak* Ruth 4:4; 2 Sam. 15:28; Ezra 4:16
Job 17:5, who **i-s** against friends

INHABITANTS Gen. 34:30; Num. 13:32; Ps. 49:1; Joel 2:1

INHABITED—*habitation* Ps. 107:7,36, an **i** city

INHERIT—*possess, possession* Ex. 32:13, they shall **i** *it*
Ps. 37:11, humble will **i** the land
Prov. 3:35, The wise will **i** honor
14:18, The naive **i** folly
Matt. 5:5, gentle ... **i** the earth
19:29, shall **i** eternal life
25:34, **i** the kingdom prepared
Luke 10:25, do to **i** eternal life
1 Cor. 6:9, shall not **i** the kingdom
15:50, perishable **i** the imperishable
Rev. 21:7, who overcomes shall **i** these things

INHERITANCE—*possession* Judg. 11:2; Ps. 28:9
Ps. 2:8, give the nations as Thine **i**
94:14, Nor will He forsake His **i**
Jer. 3:19, most beautiful **i** of the nations
Mark 12:7, the **i** will be ours
Acts 7:5, He gave him no **i**
Eph. 1:11, also we have obtained an **i**
1 Pet. 1:4, an **i** which is imperishable
Prov. 13:22; Eccles. 7:11; Jer. 12:7,8,9,15; Joel 2:17; Mic. 2:2; Mal. 1:3

INIQUITY—*injustice* Lev. 16:22; Job 4:8; 13:26
Deut. 5:9, visiting the **i** of the fathers
Ps. 25:11, Pardon my **i**, for it is great
51:9, blot out all my **i-es**
Is. 53:5, He was crushed for our **i-es**
James 3:6, tongue is ... world of **i**
Ps. 32:5; 51:5; 79:8; Prov. 22:8; Is. 1:4; 31:2; Jer. 31:30; Ezek. 18:30; 33:8

INJUNCTION—*decree* Dan. 6:7,8

INJURE—*wrong* Acts 7:26, why do you **i** one

INJUSTICE—*iniquity* Lev. 19:15, do no **i**
Deut. 32:4, A God of faithfulness without **i**

INNER—*inward* Matt. 6:6, GO INTO YOUR I ROOM
2 Cor. 4:16, **i** man is being renewed day by day

INNERMOST—*inward*
Job 38:36, wisdom in the **i** being

INNKEEPER—*host* Luke 10:35, denarii ... gave them to the **i**

INNOCENT—*blameless, righteous* Ex. 23:7
Is. 59:7, hasten to shed **i** blood
Matt. 27:4, have sinned by betraying **i** blood
27:24, I am **i** of this Man's blood
Luke 23:47, this man was **i**
Phil. 2:15, blameless and **i**, children of God
Heb. 7:26, holy, **i**, undefiled
2 Sam. 3:28; Job 4:7; 22:19; Prov. 6:17; Matt. 10:16; 12:5,7

INQUIRE—*ask* Judg. 18:5, **I** of God
Matt. 2:4, **i** of them where the Christ

INSANE—*mad* 1 Sam. 21:13, acted **i-ly** in their hands
John 10:20, has a demon, and is **i**

INSCRIBE Hab. 2:2, And **i** *it* on tablets

INSCRIPTION Dan. 5:8, could not read the **i**

INSECTS Ex. 8:21, I will send swarms of **i** on you

INSENSITIVE Is. 6:10, Render ... this people **i**

INSIDE—*within* Gen. 9:21, uncovered himself **i** his tent
Matt. 23:26, Pharisee ... clean the **i** of the cup
Acts 5:23, we found no one **i**
Rev. 5:1, throne a book written **i**

INSIGNIFICANT—*mean, small* 2 Sam. 7:19, **i** in Thine eyes
Job 8:7, your beginning was **i**
40:4, Behold, I am **i**; what can
Acts 21:39, citizen of no **i** city

INSOLENCE—*pride* 1 Sam. 17:28, I know your **i**

INSPIRE—*spiritual* Hos. 9:7, **i-d** man is demented

INSTANT—*moment* Num. 16:21, consume **i-ly**

INSTITUTION 1 Pet. 2:13, Submit ... to every human **i**

INSTRUCT—*discipline*
Neh. 9:20, Thy good Spirit to **i**
Ps. 32:8, I will **i** you and teach you

INSTRUCT *(Continued)*
Matt. 10:5, twelve Jesus sent . . . **i-ing** them
Rom. 2:18, being **i-ed** out of the Law
INSTRUCTION—*admonition*
Job 36:10, He opens . . . ear to **i**
Matt. 11:1, **i-s** to His twelve disciples
Rom. 15:4, was written for our **i**
1 Cor. 7:10, **i-s**, not I, but the Lord
10:11, written for our **i**
Eph. 6:4, discipline and **i** of the Lord
1 Tim. 1:5, goal of our **i** is love
Heb. 6:2, of **i** about washing and laying on of hands
INSTRUMENT—*object, vessel*
Acts 9:15, he is a chosen **i**
Rom. 6:13, as **i-s** of unrighteousness
2 Sam. 12:31; 1 Chr. 20:3; Ps. 150:4; Ezek. 33:32
INSULT—*reproach*
Job 19:3, ten times you have **i-ed** me
Luke 6:22, heap **i-s** upon you
INTEGRITY—*upright* Gen. 20:5; Job 2:3; Prov. 19:1
Ps. 15:2, He who walks with **i**
26:1, have walked in my **i**
Prov. 10:9, who walks in **i** walks securely
20:7, righteous man who walks in his **i**
INTELLIGENT—*prudent*
Matt. 11:25, hide . . . wise and **i**
Mark 12:34, Jesus saw that he had . . . **i-ly**
INTENSE 2 Pet. 3:10, destroyed with **i** heat
INTENT Gen. 8:21, **i** of man's heart is evil
Deut. 31:21, for I know their **i**
Acts 1:10, gazing **i-ly** into the sky
INTERCEDE 1 Sam. 2:25, who can **i**
Is. 53:12, **i-d** for the transgressors
Rom. 8:26, the Spirit Himself **i-s** for *us*
INTERCESSION—*petition*
Heb. 7:25, always lives to make **i**
INTEREST—*usury* Ex. 22:25, not charge him **i**
Deut. 23:20, You may charge **i** to a foreigner
Ps. 15:5, not put out his money at **i**
Matt. 25:27, my *money* back with **i**
Luke 19:23, collected it with **i**
INTERMARRY Ezra 9:14, and **i** with the peoples
INTERPRET—*understand*
Gen. 41:8, dreams . . . no one who could **i** them
1 Cor. 12:10, the **i-ation** of tongues
14:27, and let one **i**
2 Pet. 1:20, *a matter* of one's own **i-ation**
INTIMATE—*close* Job 19:14, my **i** friends have forgotten
Prov. 17:9, matter separates **i** friends
INTRODUCTION Rom. 5:2, obtained our **i** by faith
INVALIDATE Matt. 15:6, you **i-d** the word of God
Mark 7:13, *thus* **i-ing** the word of God
INVESTIGATE—*examine*
Ezra 10:16, convened . . . to **i**
INVESTIGATION Acts 25:26, after the **i** has taken place
INVOLVE—*exercise* Ps. 131:1, Nor do I **i** myself
INWARD—*within* Matt. 7:15, **i-ly** are wolves
IRON 2 Kin. 6:6, and made the **i** float
Job 19:24, with an **i** stylus and lead
Ps. 2:9, break them with a rod of **i**
1 Tim. 4:2, seared . . . as with a branding **i**
Gen. 4:22; Deut. 3:11; 8:9; 33:25; Judg. 1:19; Job 40:18; Prov. 27:17; Jer. 11:4
IRREVERENCE
2 Sam. 6:7, struck him down . . . for his **i**
IRRITATE—*fret* 1 Sam. 1:6, provoke . . . to **i** her
IVORY 1 Kin. 10:18; Song 7:4; Amos 6:4

J

JACKAL Job 30:29, a brother to **j-s**
Jer. 9:11, Jerusalem . . . haunt of **j-s**
JAR—*jug, pitcher, vessel* 1 Kin. 17:10, water in **j**
John 19:29, A **j** full of sour wine
Gen. 24:14; 1 Kin. 14:3; 19:6; 2 Kin. 2:20
JAVELIN—*spear* Josh. 8:18, Stretch out the **j**
Job 41:29, at the rattling of the **j**
JEALOUS—*envy, zealous*
Ex. 20:5, LORD your God, am a **j** God
1 Cor. 13:4, love is kind, *and* is not **j**
Gen. 30:1; 37:11; Ex. 34:14; Num. 11:29; 25:11; Josh. 24:19; Is. 11:13; Ezek. 31:9; Nah. 1:2; Acts 7:9; 17:5; Rom. 10:19; 2 Cor. 11:2
JEALOUSY—*envy, jealous* Num. 5:14; Prov. 6:34
Rom. 13:13, not in strife and **j**
1 Cor. 3:3, since there is **j** . . . among you
2 Cor. 12:20, *there may be* strife, **j**
James 3:14, if you have bitter **j**
3:16, where **j** and selfish ambition exist
Prov. 27:4; Song 8:6; Acts 13:45; Rom. 11:14; Gal. 5:20
JEOPARDIZE Ruth 4:6, **j** my own inheritance
JEWEL—*pearl* Prov. 3:15, more precious than **j-s**
Prov. 31:10, her worth is far above **j-s**
JOIN—*couple* Ex. 23:1; 26:6; Is. 5:8
Matt. 19:6, What . . . God has **j-ed** together
1 Cor. 6:17, one who **j-s** himself to the Lord
JOINT—*dislocate* Ps. 22:14, bones are out of **j**
JOURNEY—*walk, way*
Ezra 8:21, seek from Him a safe **j**
Mark 13:34, like a man, away on a **j**
Luke 9:3, Take nothing for your **j**
13:33, must **j** on today and tomorrow
15:13, a **j** into a distant country
Acts 9:3, **j-ed**, he was approaching Damascus
2 Cor. 11:26, I have been on frequent **j-s**
Gen. 33:12; Josh. 9:11; Neh. 2:6; Matt. 10:10; Acts 1:12
JOY Prov. 17:21, father of a fool has no **j**
Matt. 2:10, with great **j**
25:21, enter into the **j** of your master
Luke 15:7, **j** in heaven over one sinner
John 15:11, My **j** may be in you
Rom. 14:17, and **j** in the Holy Spirit
Gal. 5:22, fruit of the Spirit is love, **j**
Phil. 2:2, make my **j** complete
James 1:2, Consider it all **j** . . . encounter . . .
1 John 1:4, our **j** may be made complete
1 Chr. 15:16; Ezra 3:12; Job 29:13; 33:26
JOYFUL—*merry* Ps. 21:6; 66:1; Is. 52:9
Ps. 126:5, sow in tears . . . reap with **j** shouting
Prov. 17:22, **j** heart is good medicine
JUDGE Gen. 18:25, the **J** of all the earth
Matt. 7:1, not **j** lest you be **j-d**
John 3:17, God did not send the Son . . . to **j**
7:24, but **j** with righteous judgment
7:51, Our Law does not **j** a man
12:47, not come to **j** the world
Acts 10:42, **J** of the living and the dead
2 Thess. 2:12, all may be **j-d** who did not believe
Heb. 4:12, word of God . . . able to **j** the thoughts
12:23, God the **J** of all
13:4, adulterers God will **j**
Gen. 16:5; Matt. 7:2
JUDGMENT—*justice, sentence*
Ps. 1:5, wicked will not stand in the **j**
19:9, **j-s** of the LORD are true
Matt. 10:15, Gomorrah in the day of **j**
11:24, Sodom in *the* day of **j**
27:19, he was sitting on the **j**-seat
John 3:19, this is the **j**, that the light is
5:29, resurrection of **j**
5:30, judge; and My **j** is just
1 Cor. 11:29, eats and drinks **j** to himself
Heb. 9:27, after this *comes* **j**
10:27, terrifying expectation of **j**
James 3:1, shall incur a stricter **j**
5:12, may not fall under **j**
2 Pet. 3:7, kept for the day of **j**
1 John 4:17, confidence in the day of **j**
Jude 15, to execute **j** upon all
Rev. 18:20, God has pronounced **j** for you
19:2, HIS J-S ARE TRUE AND RIGHTEOUS
Ex. 12:12; Lev. 18:4; Deut. 1:17; Ezra 7:26; Ps. 112:5; 2 Pet. 2:11; Jude 9

JUG—*bottle, wineskin* 1 Sam. 1:24; 10:3; 16:20; 25:18; 26:16; 2 Sam. 16:1
JUST—*right* Job 25:4, can a man be **j** with God
John 5:30, My judgment is **j**
Heb. 2:2, received a **j** recompense
1 Pet. 3:18, Christ also died . . . *the* **j** for *the* **un-j**
Lev. 19:36; Ps. 17:1; Luke 23:41
JUSTICE—*right, righteousness*
Job 8:3, Does God pervert **j**
Ps. 89:14, Righteousness and **j** are the
Prov. 28:5, Evil men do not understand **j**
Amos 5:24, let **j** roll down like waters
Mic. 6:8, to do **j**, to love kindness
Gen. 18:19; Deut. 16:19; Job 8:3; 36:6; Prov. 21:3; Is. 59:14; Jer. 10:24
JUSTIFY—*clear, vindicate* Gen. 44:16; Ps. 51:4
Luke 10:29, wishing to **j** himself
Rom. 8:33, God is the one who **j-es**

K

KEEP—*hold, guide, preserve* Gen. 18:19
Ex. 20:6, love Me and **k** My commandments
20:8, sabbath day, to **k** it holy
Num. 6:24, Lord bless you, and **k** you
Ps. 17:8, **K** me as the apple of the eye
34:13, **K** your tongue from evil
Matt. 19:17, enter into life, **k** the commandments
Luke 3:8, fruits in **k-ing** with your repentance
John 8:51, if anyone **k-s** My word
12:25, shall **k** it to life eternal
14:23, If anyone loves Me, he will **k** My word
17:15, **k** them from the evil *one*
1 Tim. 1:19, **k-ing** faith and a good conscience
5:14, bear children, **k** house
5:22, **k** yourself free from sin
James 1:27, **k** oneself unstained by the world
Jude 21, **k** yourselves in the love of God
Lev. 23:32; Prov. 1:15; Eccles. 3:6; Matt. 26:18; 1 Cor. 14:28; 1 Tim. 6:12
KEEPER—*guard* Gen. 4:9, Am I my brother's **k**
Ps. 121:5, The LORD is your **k**
KEPT—*observed* Gen. 37:11, his father **k** the saying
Mark 10:20, Teacher I have **k** all these things
Jude 6, He has **k** in eternal bonds
KERNEL—*grain* Amos 9:9, not a **k** will fall to the ground
KEY Matt. 16:19, **k-s** of the kingdom of heaven
Luke 11:52, taken away the **k** of knowledge
Rev. 1:18, I have the **k-s** of death and of Hades
9:1, **k** of the bottomless pit
KIDNAP—*steal* Deut. 24:7, man is caught **k-ing**
KIDNEY Job 16:13, splits my **k-s** open
KILL 1 Sam. 17:50, Philistine and **k-ed** him
Matt. 10:28, **k** the body . . . unable to **k** the soul
Luke 9:22, **k-ed**, and be raised up . . . third day
15:23, bring the fattened calf, **k** it
John 5:18, Jews were seeking . . . to **k** Him
7:19, Why do you seek to **k** Me
10:10, comes only to steal, and **k**
Acts 11:7, Arise, Peter; **k** and eat
2 Cor. 3:6, the letter **k-s** . . . Spirit gives life
Gen. 4:8,14,23; Ex. 13:15; 21:14; Num. 31:8; 2 Kin. 5:7; Job 5:2; Ps. 10:8; Acts 10:13; 1 Tim. 1:9
KIND—*gentle, gracious* Matt. 5:11, say all **k-s** of evil
1 Cor. 13:4, Love is patient, love is **k**
Eph. 4:32, be **k** to one another
2 Tim. 2:24, but be **k** to all
Gen. 1:11; 6:19; 2 Chr. 10:7
KINDLE—*burn* Ex. 35:3; Prov. 26:21; Is. 50:11
KINDNESS—*goodness, loyalty*
Ruth 3:10, your last **k** to be
Prov. 31:26, teaching of **k** is on her tongue
Acts 24:4, grant us, by your **k**
Rom. 11:22, **k** and severity of God
2 Cor. 6:6, in patience, in **k**, in the Holy Spirit
Col. 3:12, put on a heart of compassion, **k**
1 Pet. 2:3, tasted the **k** of the Lord
2 Pet. 1:7, *your* godliness, brotherly **k**
KING 1 Sam. 8:5, appoint a **k** for us to judge us
1 Sam. 10:24, Long live the **k**
Ps. 5:2, my **K** and my God
24:8, Who is the **K** of glory
Jer. 10:7, fear Thee, O **K** of the nations
Matt. 2:2, who has been born **K** of the Jews
2:9, having heard the **k**
10:18, brought before governors and **k-s** for My sake
21:5, BEHOLD YOUR **K** IS COMING TO YOU
27:11, Are You the **K** of the Jews
Luke 23:2, that He Himself is Christ, a **K**
John 12:15, YOUR **K** COMES SITTING ON A . . . COLT
1 Tim. 6:15, **K** of kings and Lord of lords
1 Pet. 2:17, fear God, honor the **k**
Judg. 9:8; 17:6; Job 18:14; Prov. 8:15; 22:29; Eccles. 10:20; Is. 43:15
KINGDOM—*dominion* Ps. 22:28, For the **k** is the LORD'S
Ps. 145:13, Thy **k** is an everlasting **k**
Matt. 3:2, the **k** of heaven is at hand
4:23, the gospel of the **k**
6:10, Thy **k** come, Thy will be done
13:38, these are the sons of the **k**
16:19, give you the keys of the **k**
19:14, **k** of heaven belongs to such as these
26:29, in My Father's **k**
Mark 10:24, hard it is to enter the **k** of God
12:34, not far from the **k** of God
Luke 6:20, for yours is the **k** of God
12:32, to give you the **k**
22:29, as My Father has granted me a **k**
John 3:3, he cannot see the **k** of God
18:36, My **k** is not of this world
Rom. 14:17, the **k** of God is not eating and drinking
Col. 1:13, to the **k** of His beloved Son
2 Tim. 4:18, bring me safely to His heavenly **k**
James 2:5, heirs of the **k** which He promised
Ex. 19:6; Esth. 1:20; Obad. 21
KISS Matt. 26:48, Whomever I shall **k**
Luke 7:45, has not ceased to **k** My feet
15:20, embraced him and **k-ed** him
22:48, betraying the Son of Man with a **k**
Rom. 16:16, Greet one another with a holy **k**
1 Pet. 5:14, Greet one another with a **k** of love
Gen. 29:11; 2 Sam. 20:9; Song 1:2
KNEE Gen. 41:43, Bow the **k**
Rom. 14:11, EVERY **K** SHALL BOW TO ME
Phil. 2:10, at the name of Jesus every **k** should bow
Heb. 12:12, strengthen . . . the **k-s** that are feeble
KNEEL Gen. 24:11, made the camels **k** down
Ps. 95:6, Let us **k** before the LORD
Matt. 27:29, they **k-ed** down before Him
Luke 22:41, He **k-t** down and *began* to pray
KNEW Jer. 1:5, Before I formed you . . . I **k** you
Matt. 7:23, I will declare . . . I never **k** you
Luke 6:8, But He **k** what they were thinking
John 4:10, If you **k** the gift of God
2 Cor. 5:21, made Him who **k** no sin *to be* sin
KNIFE—*sword* Prov. 30:14, jaw teeth *like* **k-s**
KNOCK—*smite* Nah. 2:10, knees **k-ing**
Matt. 7:7, **k** and it shall be opened
Luke 13:25, stand outside and **k** on the door
Acts 12:13, when he **k-ed** at the door
Rev. 3:20, I stand at the door and **k**
KNOW—*discern, recognize, understand*
Ex. 1:8, new king . . . who did not **k** Joseph
Deut. 4:9, **k-n** to your sons and your grandsons
Job 19:25, I **k** that my Redeemer lives
Ps. 1:6, the LORD **k-s** the way of the righteous
46:10, **k** that I am God
56:9, This I **k**, that God is for me
Prov. 27:1, do not **k** what a day may bring
Eccles. 8:5, wise heart **k-s** the proper time
Is. 59:8, They do not **k** the way of peace

KNOW *(Continued)*
Matt. 6:3, left hand **k** what your right hand
7:11, **k** how to give good gifts
7:20, you will **k** them by their fruits
25:12, I do not **k** you
Luke 10:22, no one **k-s** who the Son is
19:42, If you had **k-n** in this day
22:57, Woman, I do not **k** Him
John 8:32, you shall **k** the truth
10:14, I **k** My own, and My own **k** Me
14:7, If you had **k-n** Me ... **k-n** My Father
21:17, You **k** all things; You **k** that I love You
Acts 1:7, not for you to **k** the times
1 Cor. 1:21, did not *come to* **k** God
13:2, and **k** all mysteries
13:9, we **k** in part and we prophesy
13:12, **k** in part, but then I shall **k** fully
2 Cor. 12:2, **k** a man in Christ ... caught up
Eph. 3:19, to **k** the love of Christ
2 Tim. 3:15, **k-n** the sacred writings
1 John 3:2, We **k** that, if He should appear
3 John 12, you **k** that our witness is true
Rev. 2:2, I **k** your deeds
19:12, name written ... no one **k-s** except Himself
Gen. 3:22; 28:16; Deut. 29:4; 1 Sam. 3:7; Job 13:18; Ps. 81:5; Eccles. 9:5; Is. 7:15; Hos. 6:3; Jon. 4:11; Matt. 9:30; 12:33; Mark 1:24; 13:33; Acts 19:15

KNOWLEDGE Gen. 2:9, tree of the **k** of good and evil
Ps. 19:2, night to night reveals **k**
139:6, *Such* **k** is too wonderful for me
Prov. 1:7, fear of the LORD the beginning of **k**
10:14, Wise men store up **k**
17:27, who restrains his words has **k**
Is. 11:9, full of the **k** of the LORD
Acts 24:22, more exact **k** about the Way
Rom. 10:2, but not in accordance with **k**
11:33, wisdom and **k** of God
1 Cor. 8:1, **K** makes arrogant, but love edifies
13:8, if *there is* **k**, it will be done away
15:34, some have no **k** of God
Eph. 3:19, love of Christ which surpasses **k**
Col. 2:3, treasures of wisdom and **k**
1 Tim. 2:4, come to the **k** of the truth
2 Pet. 1:5, in *your* moral excellence, **k**
1:6, in *your* **k**, self-control
3:18, grow in the grace and **k** of our LORD
Deut. 1:39; 1 Sam. 2:3; 2 Chr. 1:10; Job 10:7; 21:22; Eccles. 1:18; Is. 28:9; Hos. 4:6; Luke 11:52

L

LABOR—*fruit, toil, tribute, weary*
Ex. 20:9, Six days you shall **l**
Ps. 127:1, They **l** in vain who build it
Prov. 14:23, In all **l** there is profit
Eccles. 2:22, what does a man get in all his **l**
Is. 42:14, like a woman in **l** I will groan
1 Cor. 15:10, I **l-ed** even more than all of them
Gal. 4:11, perhaps I have **l-ed** over you in vain
4:19, again in **l** until Christ
Eph. 4:28, rather let him **l**, performing
Phil. 1:22, this *will mean* fruitful **l**
1 Thess. 1:3, work of faith and **l** of love
2 Thess. 3:8, with **l** and hardship we *kept*
Rev. 12:2, cried out, being in **l** and in pain
Gen. 49:15; Job 7:1; Ps. 78:46; Prov. 12:24; Eccles. 4:9; 2 Cor. 11:27

LABORER 1 Kin. 9:21, Solomon ... forced **l-s**

LACK—*need, void, want* Deut. 28:48, in the **l** of all things
Deut. 32:28, a nation **l-ing** in counsel
Judg. 18:10, place where there is no **l**
Prov. 7:7, young man **l-ing** sense
10:21, fools die for **l** of understanding
Is. 34:16, None will **l** its mate
Matt. 19:20, what am I still **l-ing**
Mark 10:21, One thing you **l**
James 1:4, **l-ing** in nothing
1:5, if any of you **l-s** wisdom
Deut. 8:9; 1 Kin. 8:25; Prov. 6:32; Eccles. 10:3

LADY 2 John 1, to the chosen **l**

LAGGING Rom. 12:11, not **l** behind in diligence

LAID Mark 6:5, He **l** His hands upon a few sick
Luke 12:19, many goods **l** up for many years
John 11:34, Where have you **l** him
2 Tim. 4:8, **l** up for me the crown of righteousness
1 John 3:16, He **l** down His life for us
1 Kin. 17:19; Job 6:2; 38:6

LAIR Job 38:40, lie in wait in *their* **l**

LAMB Gen. 22:8, God will provide ... the **l**
Is. 40:11, In His arm He will gather the **l-s**
53:7, Like a **l** that is led to slaughter
65:25, wolf and the **l** shall graze together
Hos. 4:16, Like a **l** in a large field
Luke 10:3, send you out as **l-s**
John 1:29, Behold the **L** of God
21:15, Tend My **l-s**
Acts 8:32, AS A **L** BEFORE ITS SHEARER IS SILENT
1 Pet. 1:19, a **l** unblemished and spotless

LAME Job 29:15, feet to the **l**
Matt. 11:5, and *the* **l** walk
Mark 9:45, better for you to enter life **l**
2 Sam. 9:13; Zeph. 3:19; Matt. 15:31; Acts 14:8

LAMENT—*mourn* Luke 8:52; 23:27; Rev. 18:9

LAMP—*light* Ps. 18:28, Thou dost light my **l**
Ps. 119:105, Thy word is a **l** to my feet
Matt. 5:15, light a **l**, and put it under
6:22, **l** of the body is the eye
25:8, our **l-s** are going out
Rev. 22:5, light of **l** nor ... of sun
1 Sam. 3:3; 2 Sam. 22:29; Job 18:6; Prov. 20:27; Zeph. 1:12; Rev. 4:5

LAMPSTAND Ex. 25:31; 1 Kin. 7:49; 2 Kin. 4:10; Luke 8:16

LAND—*country, earth, ground*
Gen. 1:9, let the dry **l** appear
Deut. 6:3, **l** flowing with milk and honey
Ps. 37:29, righteous will inherit the **l**
88:12, in the **l** of forgetfulness
Is. 66:8, Can a **l** be born in one day
Jer. 22:29, O **l**, **l**, **l**, Hear the word of the LORD
Matt. 2:6, AND YOU, BETHLEHEM, **L** OF JUDAH
27:45, darkness fell upon all the **l**
Luke 14:18, have bought a piece of **l**
23:44, darkness fell over the whole **l**
Heb. 11:29, Red Sea as ... through dry **l**
Gen. 15:18; Ex. 1:7; Deut. 8:8; 1 Sam. 6:5; Job 28:13; Ps. 25:13; 37:9,11,22; 60:2; Prov. 25:25; Eccles. 5:9; Is. 2:7; Jer. 15:10; Ezek. 9:9; Mic. 7:2; Mal. 4:6; Acts 4:37

LANGUAGE—*word, voice*
Gen. 10:5, one according to his **l**
11:1, whole earth used the same **l**
Ezek. 3:5,6, unintelligible speech or difficult **l**
Acts 2:6, hearing them speak in his own **l**
1 Cor. 14:10, many kinds of **l-s**

LANGUISH—*faint* Ps. 119:81, My soul **l-es** for Thy salvation

LAPIS LAZULI—*sapphire* Ezek. 28:13, The **l**, the turquoise

LARGE—*vast* Ps. 31:8; Matt. 28:12; Luke 22:12; Gal. 6:11

LASHES Luke 12:47, shall receive many **l**

LAST—*utmost* Ps. 30:5, weeping may **l** for the night
Is. 44:6, I am the first and I am the **l**
Matt. 5:26, have paid up the **l** cent
12:45, the **l** state of that man
19:30, first will be **l**; and *the* **l**, first
John 6:39, raise it up on the **l** day
1 Cor. 15:45, The **l** Adam *became* a life-giving spirit
15:52, at the **l** trumpet
1 Pet. 1:5, revealed in the **l** time
Rev. 1:17, I am the first and the **l**
Is. 7:9; Luke 11:26

LATER—*afterward* John 13:36, you shall follow **l**

LATTICE—*window*
Is. 60:8, like the doves to their **l-s**

LAUGH—*mock* Gen. 18:13, Why did Sarah l
Job 8:21, fill your mouth with **l-ter**
Prov. 14:13, Even in **l-ter** the heart ... in pain
Eccles. 3:4, time to weep, and a time to l
Matt. 9:24, they were **l-ing** at Him
Luke 6:25, Woe *to you* who l now
James 4:9, let your **l-ter** be turned
LAUGHINGSTOCK—*derision*
Jer. 20:7, a l all day long
LAUNDERER—*fuller* Mark 9:3, no l ... can whiten them
LAW—*teaching* Ps. 19:7, l of the LORD is perfect
Prov. 29:18, happy is he who keeps the l
Matt. 5:17, came to abolish the **L**
7:12, this is the **L** and the Prophets
12:2, disciples do what is not **l-ful**
12:4, bread ... not **l-ful** for him to eat
John 7:51, Our **L** does not judge a man
Rom. 13:10, love ... fulfillment of *the* l
Gal. 3:24, **L** has become our tutor
5:23, against such things there is no l
6:2, thus fulfill the l of Christ
Heb. 7:19, **L** made nothing perfect
James 1:25, the perfect l, the *l* of liberty
Ex. 12:49; Josh. 1:8; 2 Kin. 22:8; Prov. 28:7; John 19:7; Rom. 2:14; 4:15; 1 Cor. 6:2,7; Titus 3:9
LAWLESS—*wicked* 2 Thess. 2:8, l one will be revealed
LAWLESSNESS—*iniquity*
Matt. 24:12, because l is increased
2 Cor. 6:14, righteousness and l
1 John 3:4, and sin is l
LAY Ps. 3:5, I l down and slept
Matt. 6:19, Do not l up for yourselves treasures
John 10:11, good shepherd **l-s** down His life
10:15, I l down My life for the sheep
Rom. 13:12, l aside the deeds of darkness
LAZY—*idle, slothful* Ex. 5:8,17
Matt. 25:26, You wicked, l slave
Titus 1:12, evil beasts, l gluttons
LEAD—*guide* 2 Chr. 23:13; Ps. 25:9; 27:11; Is. 40:11
Ex. 13:21, cloud by day to l them on the way
Ps. 23:2, He **l-s** me beside quiet waters
25:5, **L** me in Thy truth
Is. 11:6, a little boy will l them
Matt. 6:13, do not l us into temptation
John 10:3, calls his own sheep ... **l-s** them out
1 Tim. 2:2, may l a tranquil and quiet life
LEADER—*first, head* Num. 16:2; Luke 22:26
Matt. 2:6, AMONG THE L-S OF JUDAH
LEAK—*drop* Eccles. 10:18, the house **l-s**
LEARN—*instruction* Deut. 31:13; Is. 1:17
Prov. 1:5, wise man will ... increase in **l-ing**
Is. 2:4, never again will they l war
Matt. 11:29, l from Me
Acts 26:24, great **l-ing** is driving you mad
Eph. 4:20, you did not l Christ
2 Tim. 3:7, always **l-ing**
Heb. 5:8, He **l-ed** obedience
LEAST—*young* 2 Kin. 18:24, l of my master's servants
Matt. 2:6, NO MEANS L AMONG THE LEADERS
5:19, called l in the kingdom of heaven
11:11, he who is l ... is greater
1 Cor. 15:9, I am the l of the apostles
Eph. 3:8, To me, the very l of all saints
LEATHER—*skin* Matt. 3:4, John ... l belt about his waist
Mark 1:6, *wore* a l belt around his waist
LEAVE—*abandon, desert, forsake* Ex. 20:7; Job 9:27
Gen. 2:24, man shall l his father ... mother
Ruth 1:16, Do not urge me to l you
Ps. 49:10, l their wealth to others
Matt. 18:12, does he not l the ninety-nine
19:5, MAN SHALL L HIS FATHER AND MOTHER
John 14:27, Peace I l with you
16:28, I am **l-ing** the world again
Prov. 2:17; 3:3

LEAVEN Ex. 12:19; Lev. 6:17
Matt. 13:33, kingdom of heaven is like l
16:6, beware of the l of the Pharisees
Luke 13:21, It is like l
1 Cor. 5:6, a little l **l-s** the whole lump
5:7, Clean out the old l
LEFT—*remain* Matt. 19:27, l everything and followed You
Matt. 26:56, disciples l Him and fled
Mark 1:18, l the nets and followed Him
Luke 5:11, l everything and followed Him
Heb. 11:27, By faith he l Egypt
Gen. 7:23; Matt. 14:20
LEND—*loan* Deut. 15:6; Neh. 5:10; Luke 11:5
Prov. 22:7, borrower *becomes* the **l-er's** slave
Luke 6:34, Even sinners l to sinners
LENGTH—*long* Prov. 3:2; Ezek. 31:7; Eph. 3:18
LENGTHEN Matt. 23:5, l the tassels of *their garments*
LEOPARD Jer. 13:23, Or the l his spots
Rev. 13:2, beast ... was like a l
Is. 11:6; Hos. 13:7
LEPER Matt. 10:8, cleanse *the* **l-s**
Matt. 11:5, *the* **l-s** are cleansed
Lev. 13:51; 2 Chr. 26:21; Matt. 8:2; Mark 14:3
LEPROUS Lev. 13:51, the mark is a l malignancy
LESS Gen. 1:16, **l-er** light to govern the night
Is. 40:17, regarded by Him as l than nothing
2 Cor. 12:15, am I to be loved the l
LET—*suffer* Matt. 19:14, **L** the children alone, and
LETTER 2 Cor. 3:2, You are our l
2 Cor. 3:3, you are a l of Christ
2 Pet. 3:16, as also in all *his* **l-s**
2 Chr. 2:11; Acts 15:30; Rom. 16:22; 2 Cor. 7:8; Col. 4:16; 2 Thess. 2:15; 3:14
LEVEL—*plain* Ps. 27:11, lead me in a l path
Luke 19:44, will l you to the ground
LEVY—*collection* 2 Chr. 24:6, the l *fixed by* Moses
LIAR Job 24:25; John 8:55
Rom. 3:4, every man ... a l
1 Tim. 4:2, by means of the hypocrisy of **l-s**
1 John 5:10, God has made Him a l
LIBATION—*drink* Gen. 35:14, poured out a l
LIBERTY Ps. 119:45, I will walk at l
Is. 61:1, proclaim l to the captives
2 Cor. 3:17, where the Spirit ... is, *there* is l
Gal. 2:4, to spy out our l
James 1:25, perfect law, the *law* of l
LICK 1 Kin. 21:19; Ps. 72:9; Luke 16:21
LIE—*guile, lay, sleep, vain* Deut. 19:11; 31:16
Ps. 4:8, In peace I will both l down
23:2, makes me l down in green pastures
Rom. 1:25, exchanged the truth of God for a l
Col. 3:9, Do not l to one another
Heb. 6:18, impossible for God to l
Rev. 14:5, no l was found in their mouth
Job 7:21; 34:6; 40:21; Ps. 119:69; Eccles. 4:11; Song 1:7; Jer. 8:8; Acts 5:3
LIFE—*flesh, living, soul* Ex. 21:23; Deut. 30:19
Gen. 2:7, into his nostrils the breath of l
Ps. 16:11, make known to me the path of l
36:9, with Thee is the fountain of l
89:47, Remember what my span of l is
133:3, LORD commanded ... l forever
Prov. 3:16, Long l is in her right hand
8:35, he who finds me finds l
Matt. 6:25, do not be anxious for your l
6:27, cubit to his **l-'s** span
10:39, who has lost his l for My sake
16:25, whoever wishes to save his l
19:16, that I may obtain eternal l
20:28, give His l a ransom for many
Mark 8:35, wishes to save his l shall lose it
10:17, shall I do to inherit eternal l
13:20, no l would have been saved
Luke 12:23, l is more than food
18:30, in the age to come, eternal l
John 4:36, gathering fruit for l eternal
5:21, Son also gives l to whom He wishes

LIFE *(Continued)*
5:24, passed out of death into **l**
6:35, I am the bread of **l**
10:11, shepherd lays down His **l**
11:25, I am the resurrection and the **l**
12:25, who loves his **l** loses it
14:6, the way, the truth, and the **l**
15:13, lay down his **l** for his friends
17:3, this is eternal **l**
20:31, you may have **l** in His name
Acts 3:15, put to death the Prince of **l**
Rom. 6:4, walk in newness of **l**
6:23, gift of God is eternal **l**
8:11, give **l** to your mortal bodies
2 Cor. 3:6, but the Spirit gives **l**
Gal. 6:8, from the Spirit reap eternal **l**
Phil. 2:16, holding fast the word of **l**
4:3, names are in the book of **l**
Col. 3:4, Christ, who is our **l**
1 Tim. 2:2, a tranquil and quiet **l**
Titus 3:7, hope of eternal **l**
James 1:12, receive the crown of **l**
1 John 1:1, concerning the Word of **L**
5:12, who has the Son has **l**
Rev. 2:10, give you the crown of **l**
13:8, not been written . . . book of **l** of the Lamb
Deut. 32:39; Josh. 2:14; 1 Sam. 25:29; Job 10:1; Ps. 22:20; 35:17; Prov. 4:13,23; Jer. 21:8; 31:12; 38:16; Ezek. 18:27; Dan. 12:2; Luke 12:15; 15:24; Titus 3:3; Rev. 7:17

LIFT—*exalt, set, take* Num. 6:26, LORD **l** up . . . countenance
Ps. 3:3, the One who **l-s** my head
24:7, **L** up your heads, O gates
116:13, **l** up the cup of salvation
121:1, **l** up my eyes to the mountains
Is. 2:4, Nation will not **l** up sword
John 3:14, Moses **l-ed** up the serpent
Acts 1:9, He was **l-ed** up
Gen. 13:14; Ex. 14:16; Job 38:34; Ps. 134:2; Is. 5:26; 11:12; 13:2; 40:4; Luke 18:13

LIGHT—*dawn, lamp* Ex. 10:23; Job 18:5; 38:19
Gen. 1:3, Let there be **l**; and there was **l**
Ps. 4:6, **l** of Thy countenance upon us
27:1, my **l** and my salvation
119:105, a **l** to my path
Is. 2:5, let us walk in the **l** of the LORD
60:1, Arise, shine; for your **l** has come
Matt. 5:14, You are the **l** of the world
5:15, Nor do men **l** a lamp
6:22, whole body will be full of **l**
11:30, My load is **l**
Luke 2:32, **L** OF REVELATION TO THE GENTILES
16:8, more shrewd . . . than the sons of **l**
John 1:7, bear witness of the **l**
1:9, There was the true **l**
8:12, I am the **l** of the world
12:35, Walk while you have the **l**
1 Cor. 4:5, bring to **l** the things hidden
2 Cor. 4:4, **l** of the gospel of glory
Eph. 5:8, walk as the children of **l**
1 John 1:7, if we walk in the **l** as He
Prov. 4:18; Eccles. 11:7; Is. 5:20; Jer. 31:35; Mic. 7:9; Matt. 10:27

LIKE—*desire* Luke 20:36,46

LIKENESS—*image* Ex. 20:4; Deut. 4:16; Matt. 22:20
Gen. 1:26, in Our image, according to Our **l**
Rom. 8:3, in the **l** of sinful flesh
Phil. 2:7, made in the **l** of men

LILY Song 2:1, **l** of the valleys
Hos. 14:5, He will blossom like the **l**
Matt. 6:28, Observe how the **l-es** of the field

LIMIT—*short* Num. 11:23, LORD's power **l-ed**
Job 15:8, **l** wisdom to yourself

LINE Joel 2:7, they each march in **l**

LINEN Gen. 41:42; Prov. 31:24; Jer. 13:1; Mark 15:46; John 20:5; Rev. 19:14

LINGER 2 Sam. 1:9; Prov. 23:30

LINTEL Ex. 12:7, on the **l** of the houses

LION
1 Pet. 5:8, devil, prowls about like a roaring **l**
Gen. 49:9; 1 Sam. 17:34; 1 Chr. 11:22; Job 10:16; Ps. 7:2; 57:4; Prov. 28:1; Eccles. 9:4; Rev. 9:8

LISTEN—*hear* Mark 4:3, **L** *to this* . . . sower
Mark 4:24, Take care what you **l** to
John 6:60, who can **l** to it
Eph. 1:13, **l-ing** to the message of truth
Gen. 4:23; Ex. 18:19; 20:19; Deut. 4:30; 11:27; Job 13:17; 35:13; 37:14; Prov. 23:22; 25:12; Eccles. 5:1; Dan. 9:19; Amos 5:23

LIT—*enlighten* Ps. 97:4, His lightnings **l** up the world

LITTLE—*small* Ps. 8:5, a **l** lower than God
Ps. 37:16, Better is the **l** of the righteous
Prov. 6:10, **l** sleep, a **l** slumber, A **l** folding
15:16, a **l** with the fear of the LORD
16:8, Better is a **l** with righteousness
Is. 11:6, a **l** boy will lead them
Matt. 6:30, O men of **l** faith
Luke 7:47, he who is forgiven **l**, loves **l**
12:32, Do not be afraid, **l** flock
John 7:33, For a **l** while longer I am with you
1 Cor. 5:6, a **l** leaven leavens the whole lump
Heb. 2:7, FOR A **L** WHILE LOWER THAN THE
Gen. 18:4; Judg. 4:19; 1 Sam. 2:19; Eccles. 5:12; Song 2:15; Is. 28:10

LIVE—*abide, reside, stay* Gen. 3:22; 42:18; Deut. 4:26
Deut. 8:3, man does not **l** by bread alone
Job 19:25, my Redeemer **l-s**
Prov. 21:9, better to **l** in a corner of a roof
Hab. 2:4, righteous will **l** by his faith
Matt. 4:4, MAN SHALL NOT **L** ON BREAD ALONE
Mark 12:44, put in . . . all she had to **l** on
Luke 10:28, DO THIS, AND YOU WILL **L**
20:38, for all **l** to Him
John 11:25, who believes in Me shall **l** even if he dies
Rom. 1:17, RIGHTEOUS *man* SHALL **L** BY FAITH
8:12, to **l** according to the flesh
14:8, if we **l**, we **l** for the Lord
14:9, Christ died and **l-d** again
2 Cor. 5:15, no longer **l** for themselves
Gal. 2:20, no longer I who **l**, but Christ **l-s** in me
Phil. 1:21, to me, to **l** is Christ
James 4:15, If the Lord wills, we shall **l**
Job 7:16; Ps. 119:175; Is. 55:3; Jer. 49:18; Ezek. 5:11; Matt. 12:45

LIVING Gen. 2:7, man became a **l** being
1 Kin. 3:25, Divide the **l** child in two
Matt. 16:16, Son of the **l** God
John 4:10, He would have given you **l** water
6:51, I am the **l** bread
7:38, rivers of **l** water
Acts 10:42, Judge of the **l** and the dead
Rom. 12:1, your bodies a **l** . . . sacrifice
1 Cor. 15:45, Adam, BECAME A **L** SOUL
2 Cor. 6:16, temple of the **l** God
Heb. 4:12, word of God is **l**
Num. 16:48; Deut. 5:26; Job 28:13; Eccles. 7:2; Dan. 6:26; 2 Pet. 2:8

LOAD—*burden* Matt. 11:30, My **l** is light
Matt. 23:4, they tie up heavy **l-s**

LOAN—*lend*
Deut. 23:19, *or* anything that may be **l-ed**

LOATHE Ps. 95:10; Amos 6:8

LOATHSOME Gen. 46:34, every shepherd is **l** to . . . Egyptians
Job 6:7, are like **l** food to me

LOAVES 1 Sam. 10:3, carrying three **l** of bread
Matt. 14:17, five **l** and two fish
Mark 6:52, the *incident of* the **l**

LOBE Ex. 29:13; Lev. 3:4,10,15

LOCK—*shut* Deut. 33:25; Judg. 16:13; Ezek. 44:20
Acts 5:23, prison-house **l-ed** quite securely

LOCUST—*grasshopper* Ex. 10:13; Lev. 11:22; Judg. 6:5; 1 Kin. 8:37; Job 39:20; Prov. 30:27; Joel 2:25; Nah. 3:17; Matt. 3:4

LODGE Job 19:4; 41:22
Ruth 1:16, where you **l**, I will **l**
LOFTY Is. 10:33, **l** will be abased
LOG—*beam* Eccles. 10:9; Luke 6:42
Matt. 7:5, first take the **l** out of your own eye
LOINS—*waist* Ex. 12:11; 2 Kin. 4:29
Eph. 6:14, GIRDED YOUR L WITH TRUTH
LONELY Ps. 25:16, be gracious ... For I am **l**
LONG—*length* Ex. 2:3; 2 Sam. 3:1; Prov. 3:16
Matt. 23:14, for a pretense you make **l** prayers
1 Cor. 11:14, if a man has **l** hair
Eph. 6:3, LIVE L ON THE EARTH
Rev. 6:10, How **l**, O Lord
LONG (v.)—*desire* Job 3:21; Ps. 84:2
Luke 16:21, **l-ing** to be fed with the *crumbs*
Rom. 8:19, anxious **l-ing** of the creation
2 Cor. 5:2, **l-ing** to be clothed with our dwelling
1 Tim. 6:10, by **l-ing** for it have wandered away
1 Pet. 1:12, things into which angels **l** to look
2:2, like newborn babes, **l** for the pure milk
LOOK—*see* Ex. 3:6, he was afraid to **l** at God
Ps. 84:9, **l** upon the face of Thine anointed
Matt. 11:3, shall we **l** for someone else
14:19, and **l-ing** up toward heaven
Luke 2:38, **l-ing** for the redemption of Jerusalem
2:44, began **l-ing** for Him among their
9:62, hand to the plow and **l-ing** back
John 4:35, **l** on the fields
Acts 3:4, Peter ... said, **L** at us
10:21, I am the one you are **l-ing** for
Gal. 6:1, **l-ing** to yourself, lest you
Phil. 2:4, do not ... **l** out for your ... interests
2 Pet. 3:13, **l-ing** for new heavens
Rev. 14:1, I **l-ed**, and behold, the Lamb
Gen. 19:17; Ex. 3:2; Job 35:5; Ps. 91:8; 114:3; Prov. 23:31; Eccles. 12:3; Is. 17:7; Luke 17:23
LOOM Judg. 16:14, pulled out the pin of the **l**
LOOSE—*release* Job 38:31, **l** the cords of Orion
Ps. 116:16, Thou hast **l-d** my bonds
Matt. 16:19, **l** on earth ... **l-d** in heaven
Luke 15:13, his estate with **l** living
LORD 2 Cor. 1:24, Not that we **l** it over your faith
2 Thess. 2:2, day of the **L** has come
LOSE Joel 2:10, stars **l** their brightness
Matt. 10:39, who has found his life shall **l** it
16:25, save his life shall **l** it
Mark 9:41, he shall not **l** his reward
LOSS—*damage* Dan. 6:2; Acts 27:10
2 Cor. 7:9, you might not suffer **l**
LOST—*perish* Lev. 6:3; Ps. 119:176
Matt. 10:6, go to the **l** sheep of ... Israel
18:11, come to save that which was **l**
Luke 15:24, he was **l** and has been found
John 6:12, fragments that nothing may be **l**
LOT—*portion* Lev. 16:8; Num. 26:55
Ps. 22:18, for my clothing they cast **l-s**
Prov. 1:14, Throw in your **l** with us
Jon. 1:7, cast **l-s** and the **l** fell on Jonah
John 19:24, Let us not tear it, but cast **l-s** for it
Acts 1:26, the **l** fell to Matthias
LOUD—*great* Rev. 21:3, I heard a **l** voice from the throne
LOVE (v.) Ex. 20:6; Neh. 13:26; Ps. 31:23; Zech. 8:17
Lev. 19:18, you shall **l** your neighbor as yourself
Deut. 6:5, **l** the LORD your God with all
Prov. 3:12, whom the LORD **l-s** He reproves
8:17, I **l** those who **l** me
12:1, whoever **l-s** discipline **l-s** knowledge
17:17, friend **l-s** at all times
20:13, Do not **l** sleep
Eccles. 3:8, time to **l**, and a time to hate
Amos 5:15, Hate evil, **l** good
Matt. 5:44, **l** your enemies
6:5, for they **l** to stand
6:24, hate the one and **l** the other
22:39, L YOUR NEIGHBOR AS YOURSELF
Luke 6:27, **l** your enemies
John 3:16, God so **l-d** the world
2 Cor. 9:7, God **l-s** a cheerful giver
Eph. 5:2, walk in **l**, just as Christ **l-d** you
Col. 3:19, Husbands, **l** your wives
Titus 2:4, **l** their husbands, to **l** their children
James 2:8, L YOUR NEIGHBOR AS YOURSELF
1 John 4:7, let us **l** one another ... every one who **l-s**
LOVE (n.) Prov. 10:12, **l** covers all transgressions
Matt. 24:12, most people's **l** will grow cold
John 13:35, if you have **l** for one another
15:13, Greater **l** has no one than this
Rom. 12:9, Let **l** be without hypocrisy
1 Cor. 13:1, do not have **l**
14:1, Pursue **l**
Gal. 5:13, through **l** serve one another
Col. 3:14, beyond ... *put on* **l**
1 Tim. 1:5, our instruction is **l**
6:10, **l** of money is a root of ... evil
2 Tim. 2:22, righteousness, faith, **l**
Heb. 13:1, Let **l** of the brethren continue
1 Pet. 4:8, **l** covers a multitude of sins
2 Pet. 1:7, brotherly kindness, Christian **l**
1 John 4:7, **l** is from God
3 John 6, your **l** before the church
Jude 21, keep yourselves in the **l** of God
Rev. 2:4, you have left your first **l**
Gen. 29:20; 2 Sam. 1:26
LOVELY—*beautiful* Song 1:5, I am black but **l**
Is. 52:7, How **l** on the mountains
LOVINGKINDNESS—*compassion, mercy*
Ezra 3:11, His **l** is upon Israel forever
Ps. 86:15, a God ... abundant in **l**
89:1, I will sing of the **l** of the LORD
117:2, His **l** is great toward us
LOW 1 Sam. 2:7, He brings **l**, He also exalts
Ps. 8:5, hast made him a little **l-er** than God
Jer. 9:10, **l-ing** of the cattle
LOWLIEST Dan. 4:17, And sets it over the **l** of men
LOWLY Job 5:11; Ps. 138:6
Rom. 12:16, associate with the **l**
LOYALTY 2 Sam. 16:17; Prov. 20:6
LUMP—*cake* Rom. 11:16, *dough* be holy, the **l** is also
1 Cor. 5:6, leavens the whole **l** of *dough*
5:7, that you may be a new **l**
LUNCH—*dinner* Luke 11:37, Pharisee asked Him to have **l**
LURK Prov. 7:12, And **l-s** by every corner
LUST—*desire* Matt. 5:28, looks on a woman to **l** for her
Rom. 13:14, no provision ... regard to *its* **l-s**
James 4:2, You **l** and do not have
1 John 2:16, **l** of the flesh ... **l** of the eyes
Jude 16, following after their own **l-s**
LUXURIANT Ps. 37:35; Hos. 10:1
LUXURIOUS James 5:5, lived **l-ly** on the earth
LUXURY Prov. 19:10, **L** is not fitting for a fool
Luke 7:25, live in **l** are *found* in royal palaces
LYING Prov. 6:17, Haughty eyes, a **l** tongue
Prov. 12:22, **L** lips are an abomination
LYRE—*harp* Gen. 4:21; Ps. 57:8; Is. 5:12

M

MAD—*insane* Eccles. 2:2, It is **m-ness**
Acts 26:24, learning is driving you **m**
MADE Gen. 1:7, God **m** the expanse
Ps. 8:5, **m** him a little lower than God
119:73, Thy hands **m** me
Eccles. 7:29, that God **m** men upright
Matt. 9:22, your faith has **m** you well
2 Cor. 5:21, **m** Him who knew no sin *to be* sin
Eph. 3:7, of which I was **m** a minister
Heb. 6:4, **m** partakers of the Holy Spirit
Ex. 4:11; Job 4:14; 17:6
MAGI—*wise* Matt. 2:1, **m** from the east arrived
Matt. 2:7, Herod secretly called the **m**
2:16, been tricked by the **m**
MAGIC Acts 19:19, those who practiced **m**

MAGNIFICENT—*gorgeous*
Ezek. 23:12, **m-ly** dressed, horsemen
MAGNIFY Ps. 34:3, O **m** the LORD with me
Acts 19:17; name ... Jesus was being **m-ed**
Rom. 11:13, I **m** my ministry
2 Sam. 7:26; Job 7:17; Eccles. 1:16
MAGNITUDE—*greatness*
Jer. 13:22, the **m** of your iniquity
MAID Prov. 30:19, way of a man with a **m**
Gen. 16:6; Ruth 2:8; 3:9
MAIDEN Judg. 5:30; Job 41:5; Ps. 68:25
MAINTAIN Rom. 3:28, we **m** that a man is justified
MAJESTIC—*excellent* Ps. 8:1, Lord, How **m** is Thy name
Ps. 16:3; 2 Pet. 1:17
MAJESTY—*dignity, excellence*
Ps. 93:1, He is clothed with **m**
Is. 53:2, no *stately* form or **m**
Heb. 1:3, right hand of the **M** on high
Jude 25, glory, **m**, dominion and authority
Job 37:22; Is. 35:2; 2 Pet. 2:10; Jude 8
MAKE Gen. 1:26, Let Us **m** man in Our image
Gen. 2:18, **m** him a helper suitable for him
Ps. 25:4, **M** me know Thy ways, O LORD
Jer. 18:3, he was, **m-ing** something on the wheel
Matt. 3:3, **M** READY THE WAY OF THE LORD
4:19, I will **m** you fishers of men
5:34, **m** no oath at all
John 1:23, **M** STRAIGHT THE WAY OF THE LORD
James 4:13, engage in business and **m** a profit
2 Pet. 1:10, **m** certain about His calling and
Ex. 20:4,25; Deut. 8:18; Job 17:12; Luke 12:33; Rom. 10:19
MAKER Job 4:17; 35:10; Is. 17:7; 54:5; Jer. 10:16
MALE Gen. 5:2, He created them **m** and female
Matt. 2:16, slew all the **m** children
19:4, MADE THEM **M** AND FEMALE
Gen. 34:25; Deut. 4:16; Gal. 3:28
MALICE—*wickedness*
Matt. 22:18, Jesus perceived their **m**
1 Pet. 2:1, putting aside all **m**
1 Cor. 5:8; Eph. 4:31; Col. 3:8
MALICIOUS—*false* Ex. 23:1, to be a **m** witness
2 Tim. 3:3, **m** gossips, without
MALIGN—*speak* Titus 3:2, to **m** no one
MAN—*fellow, person, self* Gen. 1:26; 4:23
Gen. 3:22, the **m** has become like one of Us
Job 5:7, For **m** is born for trouble
Ps. 1:1, blessed is the **m** who does not walk in the
Matt. 4:4, **M** SHALL NOT LIVE ON BREAD ALONE
8:20, Son of **M** has nowhere to lay
26:61, This **m** stated, I am able to destroy
26:71, This **m** was with Jesus
Mark 2:27, not **m** for the Sabbath
10:25, for a rich **m** to enter
Luke 6:45, The good **m** ... the evil **m**
9:22, The Son of **M** must suffer
22:59, this **m** also was with Him
23:2, found this **m** misleading our nation
John 1:6, a **m**, sent from God
3:4, How can a **m** be born when
19:5, Behold, the **M**
1 Cor. 13:11, when I became a **m**
15:21, by a **m** *came* death
Eph. 4:13, to a mature **m**
James 1:8, a double-minded **m**, unstable in
Lev. 16:21; Num. 12:3; 1 Sam. 16:17; 1 Kin. 2:2; 2 Kin. 5:8; Job 14:1; 25:6; 33:12; Ps. 19:5; 37:37; Prov. 3:4; Eccles. 4:8; Is. 2:22; Matt. 26:2; John 7:12; 9:29; 2 Cor. 12:2
MANAGE—*rule* 1 Tim. 3:5, how to **m** his own household
MANGER Job 39:9; Prov. 14:4; Is. 1:3
MANIFEST—*reveal* John 17:6; Rom. 10:20; Col. 1:26
MANIFOLD—*various* Eph. 3:10, the **m** wisdom of God
1 Pet. 4:10, the **m** grace of God
MANKIND 2 Chr. 6:18; Job 4:17
MANNER Gen. 31:35, **m** of women is upon me
MANTLE—*garment* Heb. 1:12, AS A **M** THOU WILT ROLL THEM UP
1 Kin. 19:19; Is. 59:17
MANURE—*refuse*
Luke 14:35, for the soil or for the **m** pile
MANY—*multitude* Ps. 104:24, how **m** are Thy works
Song 8:7, **M** waters cannot quench love
Jer. 14:7, our apostasies have been **m**
Matt. 7:22, **M** will say to Me on that day
22:14, **m** are called, but few
Luke 7:47, her sins, which are **m**
21:8, **m** will come in My name
John 14:2, house are **m** dwelling places
Acts 2:43, **m** wonders and signs
Rom. 12:4, **m** members in one body
1 Cor. 11:30, **m** ... are weak ... a number sleep
James 3:1, **m** *of you* become teachers
Jude 14, **m** thousands of His holy ones
Rev. 1:15, sound of **m** waters
Gen. 16:10; 1 Kin. 11:1; Job 13:23; Ps. 71:7; Prov. 14:20
MARCH—*walk* Joel 2:8, **m** every one in his path
Nah. 2:5, stumble in their **m**
MARK Ps. 37:37, **M** the blameless
2 Thess. 3:17, a distinguishing **m** in every letter
Rev. 14:9, receives a **m** on his forehead
19:20, **m** of the beast
MARKET PLACES
Matt. 11:16, like children sitting in the **m**
Mark 6:56, laying the sick in the **m**
MARRIAGE Matt. 22:30, marry, are given in **m**
Heb. 13:4, Let **m** *be held* in honor
Rev. 19:7, **m** of the Lamb has come
MARRY Matt. 5:32, whoever **m-es** a divorced woman
Matt. 19:9, **m-es** another commits adultery
19:10, it is better not to **m**
Mark 12:25, they neither **m**, nor
Luke 20:34, sons of this age **m**
1 Cor. 7:9, better to **m** than to burn
1 Tim. 5:11, widows ... want to get **m-ed**
MARVEL—*wonder* Ps. 71:7, I have become a **m** to many
Matt. 8:10, when Jesus heard *this*, He **m-ed**
15:31, the multitude **m-ed**
Mark 5:20, and everyone **m-ed**
John 3:7, Do not **m** that I said to you
1 Pet. 2:9, out of darkness into His **m-ous** light
Rev. 15:3, GREAT AND **M-OUS** ARE THY WORKS
MASSAH—*temptation* Ps. 95:8, in the day of **M**
MASTER—*dominion, teacher* Job 3:19; Eph. 6:5
Matt. 6:24, No one can serve two **m-s**
10:24, nor a slave above his **m**
Rom. 6:9, death no longer is **m** over Him
1 Cor. 3:10, as a wise **m-builder** I laid
MATERIAL Deut. 22:11, not wear a **m** mixed ... together
1 Cor. 9:11, we should reap **m** things
MATTER Gen. 21:17; 30:15; 1 Sam. 11:5; 21:8
MEAN—*thought* Gen. 50:20, **m-t** evil against me
Ex. 34:7, by no **m-s** leave *the guilty* unpunished
Matt. 9:13, go and learn what this **m-s**
Acts 17:20, know ... what these things **m**
1 Cor. 14:11, do not know the **m-ing** of the language
Gal. 5:6, neither circumcision ... **m-s** anything
MEANINGLESS—*vain*
Matt. 6:7, do not use **m** repetition
MEASURE Eph. 4:7, according to the **m** of Christ's gift
Rev. 21:16, **m-d** the city with the rod
Gen. 18:6; Deut. 25:15; 2 Kin. 7:1; Ps. 80:5; Matt. 7:2
MEAT—*flesh* Ex. 16:3; Deut. 12:20
MEDDLER—*busybody*
1 Pet. 4:15, troublesome **m**
MEDIATOR Gal. 3:19, by the agency of a **m**
Gal. 3:20, a **m** is not for one *party*

1 Tim. 2:5, one **m** also between God and men
Heb. 8:6, **m** of a better covenant
12:24, to Jesus the **m** of a new covenant
MEDITATE Gen. 24:63, Isaac went out to **m**
Ps. 1:2, in His law he **m-s** day and night
19:14, **m-ion** of my heart
MEDIUM Lev. 19:31; 1 Sam. 28:7
MEETING—*congregation* Acts 13:43, **m** of the synagogue had
MELODY Is. 51:3, sound of a **m**
Eph. 5:19, making **m** with your heart
MELT—*dissolve* Josh. 2:11; Ps. 46:6; 75:3; 97:5; Is. 14:31
MEMBER Matt. 10:25, how much more the **m-s** ... household
1 Cor. 6:15, your bodies are **m-s** of Christ
12:12, the body ... has many **m-s**
12:14, body is not one **m**, but many
MEMORIAL Ex. 3:15; 17:14; Josh. 4:7; Acts 10:4
MEMORY Prov. 10:7, **m** of the righteous is blessed
Matt. 26:13, spoken of in **m** of her
Job 18:17; Ps. 9:6; 109:15
MEN Ps. 116:11, All **m** are liars
Mark 1:17, I will make you ... fishers of **m**
Luke 20:4, from heaven or from **m**
1 Thess. 2:4, not as pleasing **m** but God
Gen. 6:1; 1 Sam 4:9; Job 11:3; Ps. 26:4; 82:7; Matt. 10:17; Mark 6:21; Acts 17:5
MENTION Ps. 71:16; Is. 63:7; Rom. 1:9,10
MERCHANDISE John 2:16, My Father's house a house of **m**
MERCHANT 1 Kin. 10:28; Hos. 12:7; Rev. 18:3
MERCY—*compassion*
2 Sam. 24:14, for His **m-es** are great
Matt. 5:7, for they shall receive **m**
18:33, I had **m** on you
Rom. 9:15, **M** ON WHOM I HAVE **M**
12:1, by the **m-es** of God
1 Cor. 7:25, as one who by the **m** of the LORD
Eph. 2:4, God, being rich in **m**
James 5:11, full of compassion and *is* **m-ful**
MERRY—*joyful* Eccles. 8:15, drink and be **m**
Luke 12:19, eat, drink *and* be **m**
15:29, might be **m** with my friends
MESSAGE—*tidings, word, report, speech*
Luke 4:32, His **m** was with authority
Acts 20:7, his **m** until midnight
Judg. 3:19,20; Jer. 49:14; Is. 53:1; Luke 4:36
MESSENGER Matt. 11:10, MY **M** BEFORE YOUR FACE
2 Cor. 12:7, a **m** of Satan
2 Kin. 6:32; Hag. 1:13
MESSIAH—*Lord, Christ* John 1:41, found the **M**
MIDDLE Josh. 12:2; Ruth 3:8; Prov. 30:19
MIDNIGHT Ps. 119:6; Matt. 25:6; Acts 16:25; 20:7
MIDST—*middle, within*
Matt. 10:16, sheep in the **m** of
18:20, there I am in their **m**
Luke 17:21, kingdom of God is in your **m**
24:36, He Himself stood in their **m**
John 20:26, Jesus ... stood in their **m**
MIGHT Job 39:19, give the horse *his* **m**
Zech. 4:6, Not by **m** or by power
Acts 19:20, word ... was growing **m-ily**
Eph. 1:19, working of the strength of His **m**
Col. 1:29, which **m-ily** works within me
Gen. 49:3; Deut. 6:5; Judg. 5:31; 2 Sam. 6:14; Eccles. 9:10; Jer. 9:23
MIGHTY 2 Sam. 1:19, How have the **m** fallen
Ps. 24:8, strong and **m** ... **m** in battle
89:13, Thy hand is **m**
Jer. 48:17, How has the **m** scepter been broken
Joel 3:10, weak say, I am a **m** man
Mic. 4:3, decisions for **m**, distant nations
Luke 24:19, prophet **m** in deed and word
Acts 2:11, the **m** deeds of God
18:24, **m** in the Scriptures
2 Cor. 13:3, but **m** in you
1 Pet. 5:6, the **m** hand of God
Gen. 6:4; 10:9; Deut. 10:17; Is. 19:4; 63:1; Jer. 32:18
MILE Luke 24:13; John 11:18; Rev. 14:20
MILK Ex. 3:8, land flowing with **m** and honey
1 Cor. 3:2, I gave you **m** to drink
Heb. 5:12, you have come to need **m**
1 Pet. 2:2, pure **m** of the word
Gen. 49:12; Judg. 4:19; Job 10:10; Prov. 30:33
MIND—*heart* Ps. 7:9, tries the hearts and **m-s**
Mark 5:15, and in his right **m**
Acts 28:6, changed their **m-s**
Rom. 1:28, over to a depraved **m**
8:7, **m** set on the flesh is hostile
1 Cor. 1:10, complete in the same **m**
2 Cor. 13:11, be **like-m-ed**, live in peace
Phil. 2:2, being of the same **m**
2:3, with humility of **m** let each
Col. 3:2, Set your **m** on
James 1:8, a **double-m-ed** man
1 Pet. 1:13, gird your **m-s** for action
Gen. 40:14; Ps. 31:12; Is. 46:8; Jer. 17:10; Dan. 4:16; Rom. 14:5; 1 Tim. 6:5; 2 Pet. 1:15
MINISTER Is. 61:6; Eph. 3:7
MINISTRY—*service* 1 Cor. 12:5; 2 Cor. 9:12
Acts 6:4, to the **m** of the word
2 Cor. 5:18, **m** of reconciliation
Col. 4:17, Take heed to the **m**
2 Tim. 4:5, fulfill your **m**
Heb. 8:6, obtained a more excellent **m**
MIRACLE—*marvel, sign, mighty*
Matt. 11:21, if the **m-s** had occurred in Tyre
Ex. 34:10; Mark 6:5; 1 Cor. 12:10
MIRROR 1 Cor. 13:12, we see in a **m** dimly
James 1:23, his natural face in a **m**
Ex. 38:8; Job 37:18; Is. 3:23
MISCARRIAGE Ex. 21:22, so that she has a **m**
MISCARRY—*young* Ex. 23:26, no one **m-ing**
MISCHIEF Job 15:35, They conceive **m**
MISERY Job 10:15; Rom. 3:16
MISGIVING Acts 10:20, accompany them without **m-s**
MISGUIDE Heb. 5:2, deal gently with the ignorant and **m-d**
MISLEAD Deut. 27:18, **m-s** a blind person
Job 12:16, misled and the **m-er** belong to Him
Matt. 24:24, so as to **m** ... even the elect
MISSILE Eph. 6:16, flaming **m-s** of the evil one
MISTAKE Eccles. 5:6; Matt. 22:29; Mark 12:24
MISTREAT—*wrong* Jer. 22:3, do not **m** *or* do violence
Matt. 22:6; Luke 18:32; Acts 7:19
MIX Deut. 22:11; Prov. 23:30; Dan. 2:41; Rev. 18:6
MOCK Prov. 14:9, Fools **m** at sin
Prov. 20:1, Wine is a **m-er**
Gal. 6:7, God is not **m-ed**
2 Kin. 2:23; Job 21:3; 30:1; Hab. 1:10; Matt. 27:29
MODE Judg. 13:12, shall be the boy's **m** of life
MODEL 2 Thess. 3:9, offer ourselves as a **m**
MOMENT—*instant* Ps. 30:5, His anger is for a **m**
Job 34:20, In a **m** they die
1 Cor. 15:52, in a **m**, in the twinkling of an
MONEY—*gain* Gen. 43:12; Deut. 21:14
Eccles. 5:10, who loves **m** will not be satisfied
10:19, **m** is the answer to everything
Matt. 21:12, tables of the **m-changers**
Mark 6:8, no **m** in their belt
Luke 19:23, why ... not put the **m** ... bank
1 Tim. 3:3, free from the love of **m**
6:10, love of **m** is a root ... of evil
2 Kin. 5:26; Eccles. 7:12; Jer. 32:25; Amos 2:6
MONEYLENDER—*creditor*
Luke 7:41, certain **m** had two
MONGREL Zech. 9:6, a **m** race
MONSTER Gen. 1:21, created the great sea **m-s**
Job 7:12, sea, or the sea **m**
Ezek. 32:2, **m** in the seas
MOON—*crescent* Matt. 24:29, **M** WILL NOT GIVE ITS LIGHT
Luke 21:25, signs in the sun and **m**

MOON *(Continued)*
Gen. 37:9; Josh. 10:12; 1 Sam. 20:5; Job 31:26; Ps. 136:9; Song 6:10; Is. 1:13; Joel 2:31; Acts 2:20
MORALS 1 Cor. 15:33, Bad company corrupts good **m**
MORNING—*early* Job 38:7, **m** stars sang together
2 Pet. 1:19, the **m** star arises in your hearts
Rev. 22:16, the bright **m** star
Gen. 19:15; Ex. 8:20; Deut. 28:67; Ps. 55:17; Eccles. 11:6
MORSEL—*piece* Job 31:17; Prov 17:1
MORTAL Rom. 6:12, sin reign in your **m** body
Rom. 8:11, give life to your **m** bodies
1 Cor. 15:53, **m** ... put on immortality
2 Cor. 4:11, manifested in our **m** flesh
MOST—*many, very* Matt. 24:12, **m** people's love will grow
2 Cor. 11:5, least inferior to the **m** eminent
MOTHER Gen. 2:24, leave his father ... **m**
Ex. 20:12, Honor your father and your **m**
Matt. 1:18, When His **m** Mary ... betrothed
2:11, Child with Mary His **m**
2:13, **m** and flee to Egypt
19:19, HONOR YOUR FATHER AND **M**
John 19:27, the disciple, Behold, your **m**
Heb. 7:3, Without father, without **m**
Gen. 3:20; Ex. 22:30; Lev. 22:27; Deut. 22:6; Job 17:14; Ezek. 16:44; Hos. 2:2; Matt. 12:48
MOTION Ex. 15:16; Acts 12:17
MOTIVES—*thought* 1 Cor. 4:5, **m** of men's hearts
James 2:4, judges with evil **m**
MOUND—*bank* 2 Sam. 20:15, a **m** against the city
MOUNTAINS Ps. 121:1, will lift up my eyes to the **m**
Is. 5:25; Mic. 1:4
MOUNTED Zech. 9:9, **m** on a donkey
Matt. 21:5, GENTLE, AND **M** UPON A DONKEY
MOURN—*weep, wail*
Is. 61:2, To comfort all who **m**
Matt. 2:18, WEEPING AND GREAT **M-ING**
5:4, Blessed are those who **m**
Luke 6:25, for you shall **m** and weep
James 4:9, laughter be turned into **m-ing**
Rev. 1:7, TRIBES ... **M** OVER HIM
Gen. 37:35; Deut. 21:13; Jer. 9:17; 15:5; 2 Cor. 12:21
MOUTH—*speech* Ps. 19:14, the words of my **m**
Ps. 39:1, guard my **m** as with a muzzle
Prov. 13:3, who guards his **m** preserves
Song 4:3, your **m** is lovely
Matt. 4:4, PROCEEDS OUT OF THE **M** OF GOD
13:35, OPEN MY **M** IN PARABLES
Acts 3:21, **m** of His holy prophets
James 3:3, put the bits ... horses' **m-s**
Ex. 4:11; Judg. 7:6; Job 8:21; 15:6; Ps. 8:2; 71:15; Prov. 4:24
MOVE 2 Chr. 16:9, eyes of the LORD **m**
Mark 1:41, **m-d** with compassion, He stretched
Acts 17:28, in Him we live and **m**
2 Pet. 1:21, **m-d** by the Holy Spirit
Gen. 1:2; Deut. 19:14; 1 Sam. 1:13; Jer. 4:24
MUCH Prov. 25:27, not good to eat **m** honey
Prov. 29:1, hardens his neck after **m** reproof
Eccles. 1:18, in **m** wisdom there is **m** grief
Luke 7:47, for she loved **m**
16:10, faithful also in **m**
MULTIPLY Gen. 1:22; Ex. 32:13; Deut. 6:3
MULTITUDE Matt. 14:15, send the **m-s** away
Luke 23:27, following Him a great **m**
James 5:20, cover a **m** of sins
1 Pet. 4:8, love covers a **m** of sins
Gen. 17:4; Ex. 23:2; Deut. 1:10
MURDER Ex. 20:13, You shall not **m**
Rom. 1:29, full of envy, **m**, strife
Matt. 5:21; 19:18
MURDERER Num. 35:16; John 8:44; Acts 28:4; 1 John 3:15
MURMUR Ps. 55:17, I will complain and **m**
MUSIC 1 Sam. 18:6; Luke 15:25
MUST—*ought* Acts 5:29, We **m** obey God
MUZZLE Deut. 25:4, not **m** the ox while
1 Cor. 9:9, 1 Tim. 5:18, NOT **M** THE OX WHILE
MYRRH Matt. 2:11, frankincense and **m**
John 19:39, mixture of **m** and aloes
Gen. 43:11; Ps. 45:8; Song 5:13
MYSTERY—*secret* Dan. 4:9, no **m** baffles you
Matt. 13:11, **m-es** of the kingdom
1 Cor. 2:7, God's wisdom in a **m**
4:1, stewards of the **m-es**
13:2, know all **m-es** ... knowledge
Eph. 3:9, administration of the **m**
6:19, the **m** of the gospel
1 Tim. 3:9, the **m** of the faith
MYTHS—*fables* 1 Tim. 1:4, pay attention to **m**
Titus 1:14, paying attention to Jewish **m**

N

NAILS John 20:25, in His hands the imprint of **n**
Deut. 21:12; Dan. 4:33
NAIVE—*simple* Prov. 14:15, **n** believes everything
NAKED—*bare* Gen. 2:25; Job 1:21; 26:6; Matt. 25:36
NAME—*appoint* Job 1:21, Blessed be the **n** of the LORD
Ps. 8:1, How majestic is Thy **n**
18:49, sing praises to Thy **n**
72:17, his **n** endure forever ... **n** increase
102:15, nations will fear the **n** of the LORD
111:9, Holy and awesome is His **n**
Prov. 22:1, good **n** is to be more desired
Matt. 6:9, Hallowed be Thy **n**
10:2, **n-s** of the twelve apostles are
18:5, one such child in My **n**
Mark 5:9, My **n** is Legion; for we are many
Luke 21:8, many will come in My **n**
John 15:16, you ask of the Father in My **n**
Acts 3:16, on the basis of faith in His **n**
4:12, no other **n** under heaven
Phil. 2:9, **n** which is above every **n**
4:3, whose **n-s** are in the book of life
Gen. 3:20; 30:28; Ex. 20:7; Deut. 29:20; Neh. 9:10; Prov. 30:9; Is. 42:8; 48:2; 57:15; Matt. 10:22; Eph. 1:21; 3 John 14
NARROW—*strait* Matt. 7:13, Enter by the **n** gate
NATION—*generation, Gentile*
Ps. 33:12, Blessed is the **n** whose God
Prov. 14:34, Righteousness exalts a **n**
Is. 2:4, **N** will not lift up sword against **n**
Matt. 24:7, **n** will rise against **n**
28:19, Go ... make disciples of all the **n-s**
Acts 2:5, devout men, from every **n**
Gal. 3:8, ALL THE **N-S** SHALL BE BLESSED
Rev. 5:9, and tongue and people and **n**
Gen. 12:2; 20:4; Ex. 19:6; Lev. 26:33; Ps. 2:1; 102:15; Is. 18:2; 52:15; 66:19; Jer. 51:58; John 11:50; Rev. 11:2
NATIVE Acts 28:2,4
NATURAL Rom. 1:26, exchanged the **n** function
1 Cor. 15:44, it is sown a **n** body
NATURE 1 Cor. 11:14, Does not even **n** itself teach
2 Pet. 1:4, partakers of the divine **n**
NEAR—*close* Ps. 34:18, **n** to the brokenhearted
Ps. 145:18, **n** to all who call upon Him
Mark 13:28, you know that the summer is **n**
Eph. 2:13, brought **n** by the blood of Christ
Phil. 4:5, The Lord is **n**
Heb. 10:22, draw **n** with a sincere heart
James 4:8, Draw **n** to God and He will draw **n**
Ex. 19:22; Deut. 4:7; Ps. 22:11; Prov. 27:10; Joel 3:14
NECESSARY—*need*
Luke 10:42, *only* a few things are **n**
24:26, Was it not **n** for the Christ to suffer
NECK Gen. 27:16; Ex. 13:13; Deut. 28:48; Prov. 3:3; Matt. 18:6
NEED—*want* Prov. 25:16, Eat *only* what you **n**
Matt. 6:8, your Father knows what you **n**
9:12, not ... healthy who **n** a physician
21:3, The Lord has **n** of them

Luke 15:14, he began to be in **n**
Phil. 4:19, God shall supply all your **n-s**
Heb. 4:16, help in time of **n**
1 John 3:17, beholds his brother in **n**
Rev. 3:17, have **n** of nothing
1 Cor. 12:21; 1 Thess. 4:12
NEEDLESS Gal. 2:21, then Christ died **n-ly**
NEEDY Ps. 9:18, **n** will not always be forgotten
Ps. 72:13, compassion on the poor and **n**
Is. 14:30, **n** will lie down in security
Ex. 23:6; Deut. 15:11; Job 29:16; Ps. 40:17; 69:33
NEGLECT—*forget*
Matt. 6:16, they **n** their appearance
Luke 15:29, I have never **n-ed** a command
Heb. 13:2,16
NEGLIGENCE—*error* Dan. 6:4, no **n** or corruption was *to be*
NEGLIGENT Prov. 10:4, works with a **n** hand
NEIGHBOR—*fellow-citizen*
Lev. 19:18, you shall love your **n**
Prov. 3:29, Do not devise harm against your **n**
27:10, Better is a **n** who is near
Hab. 2:15, who make your **n-s** drink
Matt. 5:43, YOU SHALL LOVE YOUR N
Luke 10:29, who is my **n**
NEST—*lodge* Matt. 8:20, birds have **n-s**
Luke 13:19, birds ... **n-ed** in its branches
Num. 24:21; Deut. 32:11; Jer. 49:16; Obad. 4
NET Job 19:6; Ps. 57:6; Is. 51:20; Matt. 13:47
NEVER Matt. 7:23, I **n** knew you
John 4:14, of the water ... shall **n** thirst
7:46, **N** did a man speak the way
8:51, he shall **n** see death
Heb. 13:5, I WILL N DESERT YOU
Deut. 15:11; Job 3:16; Ps. 31:1
NEW Lev. 23:14, roasted grain nor **n** growth
Ps. 33:3, Sing to Him a **n** song
Eccles. 1:9, nothing **n** under the sun
Is. 65:17, create **n** heavens and a **n** earth
Ezek. 11:19, put a **n** spirit within them
John 13:34, A **n** commandment I give to you
2 Cor. 5:17, a **n** creature ... **n** things have come
Eph. 4:24, put on the **n** self
Rev. 21:1, a **n** heaven and a **n** earth
NEWS—*tidings* Gen. 29:13, heard the **n** of Jacob
2 Kin. 7:9, day is a day of good **n**
Is. 52:7, feet of him who brings good **n**
Luke 2:10, good **n** of a great joy
1 Thess. 3:6, good **n** of your faith
Prov. 15:30; Matt. 14:1; Mark 1:28,45
NIGHT Ex. 13:21, a pillar of fire by **n**
Ps. 19:2, **n** to **n** reveals knowledge
91:5, not be afraid of the terror by **n**
Is. 21:11, Watchman, how far gone is the **n**
Luke 2:8, watch over their flock by **n**
John 9:4, **n** is coming, when no man can work
Rom. 13:12, **n** is almost gone
2 Cor. 11:27, through many sleepless **n-s**
1 Thess. 5:2, like a thief in the **n**
Gen. 1:5; Josh. 1:8; Job 17:12
NOBLE Ps. 45:9; Prov. 8:6
NOISE—*sound* Is. 22:2, You who were full of **n**
Jer. 50:22, **n** of the battle is in the land
Acts 2:2, came from heaven a **n**
1 Cor. 13:1, have become a **n-y** gong
NONSENSE Luke 24:11, words appeared ... as **n**
NOSTRIL Ezek. 16:12, put a ring in your **n**
NOTHING Job 26:7, hangs the earth on **n**
Ps. 49:17, he will carry **n** away
Prov. 13:7, pretends to be rich, but has **n**
John 15:5, apart from Me you can do **n**
1 Cor. 4:4, conscious of **n** against myself
Gal. 6:3, thinks he is something when he is **n**
Phil. 4:6, Be anxious for **n**
1 Tim. 4:7, have **n** to do with worldly fables
James 1:4, perfect and complete, lacking in **n**
Ex. 21:11; Lam. 1:12; Luke 6:35
NOTICE—*visit* Jer. 15:15, Remember me, take **n** of me
Matt. 6:1, righteousness ... to be **n-d** by them
Matt. 7:3; Luke 6:41
NOURISH 1 Tim. 4:6, **n-ed** on the words of the faith
NULLIFY Rom. 3:3; 4:14; Gal. 2:21; 3:17
NUMBER—*measure, count* Num. 1:3; Job 14:16; Ps. 139:18; Matt. 10:30; 2 Cor. 11:23
NURSE Gen. 35:8; Ex. 2:7; Num. 11:12; 1 Thess. 2:7

O

OAK 2 Sam. 18:10; Is. 1:30; Amos 2:9
OATH—*vow* Gen. 26:3; Josh. 2:20; Acts 23:12
OBEDIENCE Rom. 16:26, to **o** of faith
2 Cor. 10:5, to the **o** of Christ
Heb. 5:8, He learned **o** from the things
OBEDIENT 2 Cor. 2:9, whether you are **o** in all things
Phil. 2:8, **o** to the point of death
1 Pet. 1:14, As **o** children
OBEY—*follow* Ps. 103:20, **O-ing** the voice of His word
Matt. 8:27, the winds and the sea **o** Him
Acts 5:29, **o** God rather than men
Eph. 6:1, Children, **o** your parents
Heb. 11:8, By faith Abraham ... **o-ed**
13:17, **O** your leaders
1 Pet. 1:2, that you may **o** Jesus Christ
Ex. 19:5; Josh. 1:17; 1 Sam. 15:22; Is. 1:19
OBLIGATE Matt. 23:16, whoever swears by the gold ... **o-d**
OBLIGATION Num. 32:22, be free of **o** toward the LORD
Rom. 1:14, I am under **o** both to Greeks
8:12, we are under **o**, not to the flesh
Gal. 5:3, he is under **o** to keep the whole Law
OBSCURE Prov. 22:29; Luke 23:45
OBSERVE—*keep* Deut. 5:15, to **o** the sabbath day
Prov. 6:6, **O** her ways and be wise
Matt. 6:28, **O** how the lilies of the field
28:20, teaching them to **o** all that I commanded
Luke 11:28, hear the word of God, and **o** it
Rom. 14:6, He who **o-s** the day, **o-s** it for the Lord
Prov. 5:2; 6:20; Jer. 2:10; Gal. 4:10
OBSOLETE Heb. 8:13, He has made the first **o**
OBSTACLE Rom. 14:13, not to put an **o** ... in a brother's
OBTAIN—*purchase* Prov. 8:35, **o-s** favor from the LORD
1 Thess. 5:9, for **o-ing** salvation through our Lord
Heb. 11:35, that they might **o** a better resurrection
Gen. 16:2; Acts 8:20
OCCASION 1 Tim. 5:14, give the enemy no **o** for reproach
ODIOUS Ex. 5:21; 1 Sam. 13:4
OFFEND Ex. 2:13, he said to the **o-er**
Job 34:31, I will not **o** *any more*
OFFENSE—*strange* Job 19:17, breath is **o-ive** to my wife
1 Cor. 10:32, Give no **o**
1 Pet. 2:8, AND A ROCK OF O
Gen. 41:9; Eccles. 10:4; Jer. 23:13
OFFER—*present* Ps. 50:14, **O** to God a sacrifice
Mal. 1:8, Why not **o** it to your governor
Matt. 5:23, presenting your **o-ing** at the altar
5:24, come and present your **o-ing**
Luke 6:29, **o** him the other also
Heb. 9:14, **o-ed** Himself without blemish
OFFICE Judg. 5:14; Ps. 109:8; 1 Tim. 3:1; Heb. 7:5
OFFICER—*governor*
Jer. 20:1, chief **o** in the house ... LORD
OFFICIAL 2 Kin. 20:18; 23:11; Is. 39:7; Dan. 1:9; Matt. 9:18
OFFSPRING Deut. 28:53; Is. 65:9
OFTEN Luke 13:34, How **o** I wanted to gather
1 Cor. 11:26, as **o** as you eat this bread

OIL Matt. 25:8, Give us some of your **o**
Luke 10:34, pouring **o** and wine on them
Rev. 6:6, harm the **o** and the wine
Ex. 25:6; Job 29:6; Ps. 23:5; 45:7; 55:21; 104:15; 133:2; Prov. 5:3; Luke 7:46
OINTMENT Job 41:31; John 12:5
OLD Matt. 9:17, new wine into **o** wineskins
John 3:4, man be born when he is **o**
Rom. 6:6, our **o** self was crucified
1 Cor. 5:7, Clean out the **o** leaven
2 Cor. 3:14, reading of the **o** covenant
5:17, the **o** things passed away
Col. 3:9, laid aside the **o** self
Rev. 12:9, serpent of **o** who is called the devil
Gen. 15:15; 44:20; Ruth 1:12; 1 Sam. 12:2; Job 42:17; Prov. 20:29; Matt. 9:16; Heb. 11:2
OLDER—*aged*
Job 32:4, waited ... because they were ... **o**
Titus 2:2,3, **O** men are to be temperate
ONCE—*soon* 1 Sam. 9:13, you will find him at **o**
Matt. 15:28, daughter was healed at **o**
21:20, did the fig tree wither at **o**
Rom. 6:10, died to sin, **o** for all
Heb. 9:28, offered **o** to bear the sins
Gen. 18:32; Is. 66:8
ONE Matt. 6:24, No **o** can serve two masters
Matt. 19:5, TWO SHALL BECOME **O** FLESH
John 10:30, I and the Father are **O**
17:21, that they may all be **o**
Gal. 6:4, let each **o** examine his own work
Eph. 4:4, **o** body and **o** Spirit ... **o** hope
1 Tim. 2:5, **o** God, *and* **o** mediator
James 4:12, only **o** Lawgiver and Judge
Gen. 1:5; Deut. 6:4; 1 Sam. 21:15; 2 Sam. 6:20; Job 33:23; Mark 8:30; John 19:41
ONLY Gen. 6:5, thoughts of his heart ... **o** evil
Ps. 62:2, He **o** is my rock ... salvation
Luke 24:18, You the **o** one visiting
Rom. 16:27, **o** wise God ... glory forever
Heb. 11:17, his **o** begotten *son*
Jude 25, **o** God ... our Lord, *be* glory
OPEN—*explain, wide*
Matt. 7:7, knock and it shall be **o-ed**
20:33, we want our eyes to be **o-ed**
John 1:51, you shall see the heavens **o-ed**
Rev. 4:1, a door *standing* **o** in heaven
5:2, Who is worthy to **o** the book
Gen. 3:5; Job 29:23; Ps. 5:9; 51:15; Prov. 27:5; Is. 26:2; 42:7; Ezek. 16:63; Luke 13:25
OPENING Prov. 8:3; Song 5:4
OPINION—*counsel* 2 Cor. 8:10, give my **o** in this matter
OPPONENT—*adversary* Matt. 5:25; Luke 18:3; Phil. 1:28
OPPORTUNE Mark 14:11, betray Him at an **o** time
OPPORTUNITY—*occasion*
Gal. 5:13, turn your freedom ... **o**
Eph. 4:27, do not give the devil an **o**
OPPOSE—*resist* Ezra 10:15, Jahzeiah ... **o-d** this
Rom. 13:2, he who resists authority has **o-d**
James 4:6, GOD IS **O-D** TO THE PROUD
OPPOSITION Num. 14:34; Gal. 5:17
OPPRESS—*afflict*
Acts 10:38, healing all who were **o-ed**
James 2:6, Is it not the rich who **o** you
Gen. 15:13; Lev. 19:13; 1 Sam. 1:15; Job 5:4; Hos. 12:7
OPPRESSION—*affliction*
Ps. 62:10, Do not trust in **o**
Eccles. 7:7, **o** makes a wise man mad
Is. 30:20; Ezek. 22:12
ORCHARD—*garden* Song 6:11, down to the **o** of nut trees
ORDAIN Ex. 29:29,35; Ps. 8:3; Acts 7:53
ORDER 2 Kin. 20:1; Ps. 5:3; Mark 5:43; Luke 5:14; Titus 1:5; Philem. 8; Heb. 5:6
ORDINANCE—*statute* Job 38:33; Rom. 13:2; Eph. 2:15
ORPHAN—*fatherless*
Ex. 22:22, not afflict any widow or **o**
James 1:27, visit **o-s** and widows
Deut. 10:18; 14:29; 24:17; Job 31:17; Ps. 10:14; Is. 1:23; 10:2; Jer. 49:11; Hos. 14:3; Mal. 3:5
OTHER Ex. 22:20; Mark 16:13
OUGHT John 4:20, place where men **o** to worship
Heb. 5:12, you **o** to be teachers
James 3:10, these things **o** not to be
OUT Ex. 3:10, bring My people ... **o** of Egypt
Ex. 7:5, when I stretch **o** My hand
Num. 32:23, your sin will find you **o**
Prov. 31:20, she stretches **o** her hands to
Matt. 12:13, Stretch **o** your hand
12:34, **o** of that which fills the heart
13:3, the sower went **o** to sow
Mark 1:41, He stretched **o** His hand and touched
7:26, cast the demon **o** of her daughter
2 Tim. 4:2, in season *and* **o** of season
Gen. 8:7,8,18; 19:10; 24:45; Ex. 3:11; Judg. 20:25; 1 Sam. 30:21; 2 Sam. 19:7; Is. 37:36; Jer. 32:21
OUTBURST—*heat*
Deut. 29:24, Why this great **o** of anger
OUTCOME—*end* Rom. 6:21, the **o** of those things is death
Rom. 6:22, the **o**, eternal life
Heb. 13:7, the **o** of their way of life
James 5:11, seen the **o** of the Lord's dealings
1 Pet. 1:9, obtaining as the **o** of your faith
4:17, what will be the **o**
OUTCRY Gen. 18:21; Ps. 144:14
OUTER—*outward*
2 Cor. 4:16, **o** man is decaying
OUTSIDE—*without* Deut. 32:25, **O** the sword
Rev. 22:15, **O** are the dogs
OUTWARD Rom. 2:28, **o** in the flesh
OVEN Gen. 15:17, smoking **o** and a flaming torch
OVER—*spent* Luke 24:29, day is now nearly **o**
Eph. 4:6, who is **o** all
OVERCOME Luke 9:32, companions had been **o** with sleep
John 16:33, I have **o** the world
Rom. 12:21, Do not be **o** by evil
1 John 2:13, you have **o** the evil one
Jer. 20:7; 23:9
OVEREXTENDING—*stretching*
2 Cor. 10:14, we are not **o**
OVERFLOW 2 Cor. 7:4, I am **o-ing** with joy
Ps. 23:5; Prov. 3:10; Song 8:7
OVERLAID 2 Chr. 3:5, he **o** the main room with cypress
OVERPOWER—*prevail*
Matt. 16:18, gates of Hades shall not **o** it
OVERSEER Phil. 1:1, including the **o-s** and deacons
1 Tim. 3:1, aspires to the office of **o**
Titus 1:7, **o** must be above reproach
OVERTAKE Amos 9:10; 1 Thess. 5:4
OVERTHROW Ex. 23:24; Acts 5:39
OVERWHELM Ex. 17:13, Joshua **o-ed** Amalek
OWE—*due* Matt. 18:28, Pay back what you **o**
18:34, repay all that was **o-d** him
Rom. 13:8, **O** nothing to anyone
Philem. 19, you **o** to me even your own self
OWN Prov. 14:10, heart knows its **o** bitterness
John 1:11, came to His **o** ... **o** did not receive
10:3, calls his **o** sheep by name
Acts 2:6, speak in his **o** language
1 Tim. 5:8, does not provide for his **o**
2 Pet. 3:3, following after their **o** lusts
OX—*cow* Prov. 7:22, as an **o** goes to the slaughter
1 Tim. 5:18, MUZZLE THE **O** WHILE HE IS THRESHING
Lev. 22:28; Job 6:5; Prov. 15:17

P

PACT Is. 28:15, we have made a **p**
PAIN—*sorrow, torment, grief* Gen. 3:16, multiply Your **p**

1 Chr. 4:9, Because I bore *him* with **p**
Job 6:10, I rejoice in unsparing **p**
Ps. 127:2, eat the bread of **p-ful** labors
Eccles. 1:18, knowledge results in increasing **p**
Is. 14:3, gives you rest from your **p**
Jer. 30:15, Your **p** is incurable
Lam. 1:12, any **p** like my **p**
Matt. 8:6, home, suffering great **p**
Job 2:13; 15:20; Ps. 73:4; Lam. 3:51; Rev. 21:4
PAIR Judg. 19:3; Is. 21:7
PALATE—*mouth*
Job 29:10, their tongue stuck to their **p**
PALLET Mark 2:9, take up your **p** and walk
John 5:11; Acts 5:15
PALPITATING Is. 35:4, to those with **p** heart fear not
PANEL Jer. 22:14; Hag. 1:4
PANGS—*sorrow* Mark 13:8, beginning birth **p**
PANIC—*trouble* Is. 22:5, has a day of **p**
PANT Job 7:2, a slave who **p-s** for the shade
PAPYRUS Is. 18:2, in **p** vessels
PARAPET Deut. 22:8, a **p** for your roof
PARCH—*dried* Ps. 69:3; Is. 53:2
PARDON Is. 55:7 He will abundantly **p**
Luke 6:37, **p**, and you will be **p-ed**
Ex. 23:21; 2 Chr. 30:18; Ps. 25:11
PARENTS Matt. 10:21, CHILDREN WILL RISE UP AGAINST P
Luke 2:41, His **p** used to go to Jerusalem
18:29, left house ... or **p**
John 9:2, who sinned, this man, or his **p**
Rom. 1:30, disobedient to **p**
2 Cor. 12:14, for *their* **p**, but **p** for *their* children
Eph. 6:1, Children obey your **p**
2 Tim. 3:2, disobedient to **p**, ungrateful
PART Num. 18:20, nor own any **p** among them
Matt. 5:29, one of the **p-s** of your body perish
Luke 10:42, Mary has chosen the good **p**
John 13:8, you have no **p** with Me
Acts 8:21, You have no **p** or portion
1 Cor. 13:9, we know in **p**
PARTAKERS—*partners* Eph. 5:7, do not be **p** with them
Heb. 3:1, **p** of a heavenly calling
3:14, **p** of Christ
6:4, **p** of the Holy Spirit
2 Pet. 1:4, **p** of *the* divine nature
PARTIAL Prov. 28:21, To show **p-ity** is not good
Matt. 22:16, for You are not **p** to any
Acts 10:34, God is not one to show **p-ity**
Rom. 2:11, no **p-ity** with God
Lev. 19:15; Deut. 1:17
PARTICIPATE Eph. 5:11, do not **p** in the unfruitful deeds
PARTNERS Matt. 23:30, not have been **p** with them
PASS Matt. 26:39, let this cup **p** from Me
John 5:24, **p-ed** out of death into life
2 Cor. 5:17, old things **p-ed** away
Heb. 11:25, enjoy the **p-ing** pleasures of sin
Rev. 21:1, first earth **p-ed** away
Gen. 15:17; Ps. 109:23; Prov. 4:15; Is. 16:8; Acts 7:30
PASSION Prov. 14:30, But **p** is rottenness to the bone
Rom. 1:26, gave them over to degrading **p-s**
Col. 3:5, as dead to ... **p**
1 Thess. 4:5, not in lustful **p**
PASSOVER Ex. 12:11, it is the LORD's **P**
Matt. 26:17, prepare for You to eat the **P**
Luke 22:15, desired to eat this **P**
John 18:39, release someone for you at the **P**
Acts 12:4, intending after the **P**
1 Cor. 5:7, Christ our **P** also has been sacrificed
PAST Song 2:11, the winter is **p**, The rain
Jer. 8:20, Harvest is **p**, summer is ended
PASTOR—*shepherd* Eph. 4:11, some *as* **p-s** and teachers
PASTURE—*feed* Song 1:7; Is. 61:5; Jer. 6:3; Zech. 11:4
PATCH—*piece* Matt. 9:16, puts a **p** of unshrunk cloth
PATH—*way* Job 12:24, makes them wander in a **p-less** waste
Ps. 16:11, make known to me the **p** of life
119:105, a light to my **p**
Prov. 4:18, **p** of the righteous is like the light
Eccles. 11:5, the **p** of the wind
Matt. 3:3, MAKE HIS P-S STRAIGHT
Rom. 3:17, P OF PEACE ... NOT KNOWN
Gen. 49:17; Job 28:7; Ps. 27:11
PATIENCE Matt. 18:26, Have **p** with me
2 Cor. 6:6, in **p**, in kindness
Col. 1:11, steadfastness and **p**
2 Tim. 4:2, with great **p** and instruction
PATIENT—*gentle* 1 Cor. 13:4, Love is **p**, love is kind
James 5:8, You too be **p**
2 Pet. 3:9, is **p** toward you
PATTERN—*example* Phil. 3:17, according to **p**
PAY Matt. 18:28, **P** back what you owe
Gen. 50:15; Ex. 22:7; Deut. 23:21; Job 22:27; Mark 12:15
PEACE Num. 6:26, give you **p**
Ps. 34:14, Seek **p**, and pursue it
37:37, man of **p** will have a posterity
119:165, who love Thy law have great **p**
Eccles. 3:8, time for war, and a time for **p**
Is. 9:6, Eternal Father, Prince of **P**
Matt. 10:13, let your *greeting of* **p**
10:34, I did not come to bring **p**
Mark 9:50, be at **p** with one another
Luke 1:79, guide our feet ... way of **p**
2:14, on earth **p** among men
John 14:27, **P** I leave you; My **p**
20:19, **P** *be* with you
Acts 24:2, we have through you attained **p**
Rom. 15:33, the God of **p** be with you
1 Cor. 7:15, God has called us to **p**
Gal. 5:22, fruit of the Spirit is ... **p**
Eph. 2:14, He Himself is our **p**
Phil. 4:7, **p** of God, which surpasses all
1 Thess. 5:13, Live in **p** with one another
5:23, may the God of **P** ... sanctify
2 Thess. 3:16, Lord of **p** ... grant you **p**
Heb. 12:14, Pursue **p** with all men
James 2:16, Go in **p**
1 Pet. 5:14, **P** be to you all
Gen. 15:15; Lev. 26:6; 2 Kin. 9:17; Job 15:21; Ps. 4:8; 147:14; Prov. 3:17; 16:7; Is. 36:16; 52:7; 57:19; Jer. 6:14
PEARLS—*jewel*
Job 28:18, acquisition of wisdom ... **p**
PECK Matt. 13:33, hid in three **p-s** of meal
PECK-MEASURE Matt. 5:15; Mark 4:21
PEG—*nail* Judg. 4:21; Is. 22:23
PENALTY 2 Thess. 1:9, pay the **p** of eternal destruction
PEOPLE Ps. 100:3, *We are* His **p** and the sheep
Prov. 11:14, no guidance, the **p** fall
29:18, no vision, the **p** are unrestrained
Matt. 1:21, save His **p** from their sins
Mark 7:6, P HONORS ME WITH THEIR LIPS
John 11:50, man should die for the **p**
Jude 16, flattering **p** for ... advantage
Ex. 6:7; Ruth 1:16; Ps. 2:1; Mark 6:5; Acts 5:16
PERCEIVING Mark 2:8, Jesus, **p** in His spirit
PERDITION John 17:12, the son of **p**
PERFECT Deut. 32:4, The Rock! His work is **p**
Ps. 19:7, law of the LORD is **p**
Matt. 5:48, Therefore you are to be **p**
1 Cor. 13:10, but when the **p** comes
2 Cor. 12:9, power is **p-ed** in weakness
Phil. 1:6, **p** it until the day of Christ Jesus
James 1:4, endurance have *its* **p** result
1:25, **p** law, the *law* of liberty
1 John 4:17, love is **p-ed** with us
PERFECTER Heb. 12:2, author and **p** of faith
PERFORM—*wrought* Is. 26:12, **p-ed** for us all our works
Ps. 103:6; Luke 1:8; Rom. 4:21

PERFUME Is. 3:24, instead of sweet **p**
Matt. 26:7; Luke 7:46
PERFUMERS 1 Sam. 8:13, daughters for **p**
PERHAPS Mark 11:13; Acts 17:27; 1 Cor. 15:37
PERISH—*fail* Ps. 1:6, way of the wicked will **p**
Matt. 8:25, Save us, Lord; we are **p-ing**
18:14, one of these little ones **p**
John 6:27, work for the food which **p-s**
1 Cor. 9:25, *do it* to receive a **p-able** wreath
15:42, It is sown a **p-able** body
15:53, this **p-able** must put on
2 Cor. 4:3, veiled to those who are **p-ing**
1 Pet. 1:23, not of seed which is **p-able**
2 Pet. 3:9, not wishing for any to **p**
Num. 17:12; 2 Sam. 1:27; Job 34:15; Prov. 22:8; Ezek. 37:11
PERJURY Zech. 8:17, do not love **p**
PERMISSION Mark 5:13, And He gave them **p**
PERMIT—*suffer* Matt. 3:15, **P** *it* at this time
PERPETUAL Ex. 40:15; Num. 25:13, a **p** priesthood
Heb. 7:3, abides a priest **p-ly**
Ex. 31:16; Ps. 9:6; Jer. 15:18; 51:39; Hab. 3:6
PERSECUTE Matt. 5:11, when *men* revile you, and **p** you
5:44, pray for those who **p** you
10:23, they **p** you in this city, flee
John 15:20, If they **p-d** Me, they will also **p**
Acts 9:4, Saul, why are you **p-ing** Me
1 Cor. 4:12, when we are **p-d,** we endure
2 Cor. 4:9, **p-d**, but not forsaken
Job 19:22; Ps. 143:3
PERSEVERANCE Luke 21:19, By your **p** you will win
Rom. 2:7, by **p** in doing good
5:3, tribulation brings about **p**
15:4, **p** and the encouragement of the Scriptures
2 Thess. 1:4, for your **p** and faith
PERSEVERE Rom. 12:12, hope, **p-ing** in tribulation
James 1:12, Blessed is a man who **p-s** under trial
PERSON—*soul* Lev. 4:2, If a **p** sins unintentionally
Eccles. 12:13, this *applies to* every **p**
Is. 32:6, keep the hungry **p** unsatisfied
Rom. 13:1, Let every **p** be in subjection
Jude 4, certain **p-s** have crept in unnoticed
PERSUADE 2 Kin. 4:8, she **p-d** him to eat food
Prov. 25:15, a ruler may be **p-d**
Acts 26:28, you will **p** me
PERSUASIVE 1 Cor. 2:4, were not in **p** words
Col. 2:4, delude you with **p** argument
PERVERSE Acts 20:30, speaking **p** things
Phil. 2:15, a crooked and **p** generation
Deut. 32:5,20; Ps. 101:4; Prov. 23:33
PERVERSION Lev. 18:23, it is a **p**
PERVERT Deut. 16:19; 2 Sam. 22:27; Job 8:3; Prov. 10:31
PETITION Ps. 20:5, the LORD fulfill all your **p-s**
1 Tim. 2:1, prayers, **p-s** and thanksgivings
1 Sam. 1:17; Dan. 6:7,13
PHYSICIAN Jer. 8:22, Is there no **p** there
Matt. 9:12, not ... healthy who need a **p**
Luke 4:23, **P**, heal yourself
Col. 4:14, Luke, the beloved **p**
PICK Mark 16:18, they will **p** up serpents
Gen. 8:11; Mark 2:23
PIECE Matt. 14:20, left over of the broken **p-s**
Mark 6:43, twelve full baskets of broken **p-s**
Gen. 18:5; Ruth 2:14; 1 Sam. 2:36; Luke 24:42
PIERCE—*wound* Judg. 5:26, shattered and **p-d** his temple
Ps. 22:16, They **p-d** my hands ... feet
Is. 53:5, **p-d** through for our transgressions
Zech. 12:10, on Me whom they have **p-d**
Luke 2:35, **p** even your own soul
John 19:34, soldiers **p-d** His side

PIETY 1 Tim. 5:4, practice **p** in regard
PILES Job 27:16, he **p** up silver like dust
PILLAGE Nah. 3:1, city, ... full of lies *and* **p**
PILLAR Gen. 19:26, she became a **p** of salt
Job 26:11, The **p-s** of heaven tremble
Gal. 2:9, John, who were reputed to be **p-s**
1 Tim. 3:15, **p** and support of the truth
Prov. 9:1; Ezek. 26:11
PILOT James 3:4, inclination of the **p** desires
PIT—*destruction, dungeon*
Gen. 14:10, Siddim ... tar **p-s**
37:20, throw him into one of the **p-s**
Ex. 21:33, a man opens a **p**, or digs a **p**
Job 17:14, I call to the **p**, You are my father
33:18, his soul from the **p**
Ps. 16:10, Holy One to see the **p**
103:4, redeems your life from the **p**
Prov. 23:27, a harlot is a deep **p**
Lam. 3:53, they have silenced me in the **p**
Matt. 15:14, both will fall into a **p**
PITCH Gen. 6:14, cover it ... with **p**
Gen. 33:19, where he had **p-ed** his tent
Ex. 2:3, covered it over with tar and **p**
PITCHER—*bowl, jar*
Judg. 7:16, put trumpets and empty **p-s**
1 Kin. 18:33, fill four **p-s**
Eccles. 12:6, the **p** by the well is shattered
Mark 14:13, man ... carrying a **p** of water
PITY—*compassion* Ex. 2:6; Deut. 7:16; Job 19:21
PLACE—*room* Deut. 33:27, eternal God is a dwelling **p**
Ps. 31:8, set my feet in a large **p**
Prov. 15:3, eyes ... LORD ... in every **p**
Matt. 23:6, love the **p** of honor at banquets
24:51, **p** with the hypocrites
26:36, a **p** called Gethsemane
27:33, a **p** called Golgotha ... **P** of a Skull
28:6, **p** where He was lying
Luke 4:17, **p** where it was written
14:8, do not take the **p** of honor
John 14:2, go to prepare a **p** for you
Acts 13:47, I HAVE **P-D** YOU AS A LIGHT FOR
1 Cor. 14:16, fills the **p** of the ungifted
2 Pet. 1:19, lamp shining in a dark **p**
Rev. 20:11, no **p** was found for them
Gen. 1:9; 30:2; Ex. 3:5; 21:13; Num. 32:14; Deut. 2:23; 34:6; Judg. 18:10; Job 9:6; 16:4; Ps. 24:3; Is. 49:20; Jer. 51:51; Dan. 8:14; Hab. 3:11; Luke 14:9; John 18:2
PLAGUE Gen. 12:17; Rev. 16:21; 21:9
PLAIN—*distinct, clear* Is. 40:4; Mark 7:35; John 16:25
PLAN—*devise* Ps. 36:4, He **p-s** wickedness upon his bed
Prov. 16:9, mind of a man **p-s** his way
19:21, Many are the **p-s** in a man's heart
2 Sam. 14:14; Prov. 15:22; Jer. 18:12
PLANT Gen. 3:18, you shall eat the **p-s** of the field
Ps. 1:3, tree ... **p-ed** by streams
Eccles. 3:2, A time to **p**, and a time to
Matt. 13:32; Mark 4:32, larger than ... the garden **p-s**
15:13, **p** ... Father did not **p**
Mark 12:1, A man **P-ED** A VINEYARD
Luke 17:6, be **p-ed** in the sea
1 Cor. 3:6, I **p-ed**, Apollos watered
Gen. 1:29,30; 2:5,8; 9:3; Ex. 9:22,25; 10:12,15; Deut. 6:11; 2 Kin. 19:29; Job 14:9; Ps. 92:13
PLASTER Ezek. 13:10, **p** it over with whitewash
PLAY Gen. 4:21; Ex. 32:6; 1 Sam. 16:17; 1 Kin. 1:40; Job 41:5; Ps. 33:3; Is. 11:8; Matt. 11:17; 1 Cor. 14:7
PLEAD Gen. 42:21; Deut. 3:23; 1 Sam. 12:7; Ps. 43:1; Is. 1:17
PLEASANT—*smooth, sweet*
Ps. 16:6, lines have fallen ... **p**
133:1, how good and how **p** it is
Eccles. 5:12, sleep of the working man is **p**
2 Sam. 1:23; Prov. 9:17; 16:24; Is. 30:10

PLEASE Matt. 3:17, Son, in whom I am well **p-d**
Rom. 15:1, not *just* **p** ourselves
15:3, Christ did not **p** Himself
1 Cor. 7:33, how he may **p** his wife
7:34, how she may **p** her husband
10:5, God was not well **p-d**
Heb. 13:16, sacrifices God is **p-d**
PLEASING—*acceptable*
Prov. 16:7, man's ways ... **p** ... LORD
Matt. 11:26, it was **well-p** in Thy sight
John 8:29, things that are **p** to Him
2 Cor. 5:9, to be **p** to Him
Eph. 5:10, what is **p** to the Lord
Gen. 2:9; 1 Kin. 3:10
PLEASURE Ps. 16:11, there are **p-s** forever
Ps. 149:4, LORD takes **p** in His people
Luke 8:14, worries and riches and **p-s**
Phil. 2:13, to work for *His* good **p**
Heb. 11:25, the passing **p-s** of sin
Gen. 18:12; Job 36:11; Prov. 21:17; Is. 53:10
PLEDGE Prov. 22:26, among those who give **p-s**
2 Cor. 1:22, the Spirit in our hearts as a **p**
5:5, gave to us the Spirit as a **p**
Eph. 1:14, given as a **p** of our inheritance
1 Tim. 5:12, set aside their previous **p**
PLENTEOUS Is. 30:23, it will be rich and **p**
PLENTIFUL Ps. 68:9, didst shed abroad a **p** rain
Matt. 9:37, harvest is **p**
PLENTY Gen. 33:9; Prov. 3:10; 12:11; Joel 2:26
PLOT Prov. 30:32, if you have **p-ed** evil
Matt. 26:4; Acts 9:23; 23:13
PLOW Is. 2:4, their swords into **p-shares**
Joel 3:10, **p-shares** into swords
Luke 9:62, putting his hand to the **p**
1 Cor. 9:10, to **p** in hope
Deut. 22:10; Job 4:8; Prov. 20:4
PLUCK Ps. 25:15; Ezek. 17:22
PLUMAGE Job 39:13, pinion and **p** of love
PLUNDER (n.)—*booty* Judg. 5:19; Hab. 2:7; Zeph. 1:13
PLUNDER (v.)—*spoil* Matt. 12:29, he will **p** his house
Ex. 3:22; Ps. 76:5; Is. 42:22
PLUNGE 1 Tim. 6:9, desires which **p** men into ruin
POINT Jer. 17:1; Mark 5:23; James 2:10
POISON Ps. 140:3; Jer. 8:14; Amos 6:12; Mark 16:18
POLE—*staff* Num. 13:23, carried it on a **p** between two
POLLUTE—*spot* Num. 35:33; Jer. 16:18; Jude 23
POMP Is. 14:11, Your **p** *and* the music
PONDER Prov. 5:6, **p** the path of life
Luke 2:19, **p-ing** them in her heart
POOR Prov. 13:7, *Another* pretends to be **p**
Prov. 20:13, lest you become **p**
Amos 5:11, impose heavy rent upon the **p**
Matt. 5:3, Blessed are the **p** in
11:5, *the* **P** HAVE THE GOSPEL PREACHED
26:11, **p** you have with you always
Mark 10:21, and give *it* to the **p**
12:42, And a **p** widow came
Luke 4:18, PREACH THE GOSPEL TO THE **P**
19:8, my possessions I will give to the **p**
2 Cor. 8:9, for your sake He became **p**
James 2:5, God choose the **p** of this
1 Sam. 2:8; 2 Sam. 12:4; Prov. 22:22; Is. 3:15; 1 Cor. 13:3
PORPOISE SKINS Ex. 25:5; 26:14
PORTION Deut. 32:9, LORD's **p** is His people
2 Kin. 2:9, double **p** of your spirit
Ps. 119:57, The LORD is my **p**
Gen. 31:14; 2 Chr. 10:16; Eccles. 11:2; Acts 8:21
POSSESS Gen. 15:7; 24:60; Ps. 44:3; Is. 54:3; 2 Cor. 6:10
POSSESSION—*property, treasure* Gen. 17:8
Matt. 24:47, in charge of all his **p-s**
Luke 19:8, half of my **p-s** I will give to the
Ex. 6:8; 19:5; 21:16; 34:9; Deut. 4:20; Ps. 104:24; Acts 2:45
POSSIBLE Matt. 19:26, with God all things **p**
Matt. 26:39, **p**, let this cup pass
Luke 18:27, are **p** with God
Rom. 12:18, If **p**, so far as it depends
POT Ex. 16:3; 2 Kin. 4:40; Job 41:31; Jer. 1:13
POUR Eccles. 11:3, clouds are full, they **p** out rain
Joel 2:28, **p** out My Spirit on all mankind
Matt. 26:7, **p-ed** it upon His head
Luke 22:20, cup which is **p-ed** ... covenant in My blood
John 2:15, **p-ed** out the coins
Acts 10:45, gift of the Holy Spirit ... **p-ed** out
Rom. 5:5, love of God **p-ed** out within our hearts
Phil. 2:17, if I am being **p-ed** out as
Rev. 16:2, **p-ed** out his bowl
1 Sam. 1:15; Job 10:10; 29:6; Is. 44:3; Matt. 9:17
POVERTY Prov. 23:21, glutton will come to **p**
Prov. 30:8, neither **p** nor riches
2 Cor. 8:9, through His **p**
POWER—*authority, strength*
Deut. 8:18, you **p** to make wealth
1 Chr. 29:11, the **p** and the glory
Is. 40:29, *who* lacks might He increases **p**
Matt. 6:13, kingdom, and the **p**, and
Mark 5:30, **p** ... from Him had gone forth
9:1, kingdom of God ... come with **p**
13:26, IN CLOUDS with great **p**
14:62, AT THE RIGHT HAND OF **P**
Luke 1:35, **p** of the Most High will overshadow
4:14, in the **p** of the Spirit
22:69, RIGHT HAND of the **p** OF GOD
Acts 1:8, you shall receive **p** when
8:10, called the Great **P** of God
Rom. 1:4, with **p** to be the Son of God
1:16, the **p** of God for salvation
1 Cor. 1:24, Christ the **p** of God
15:56, the **p** of sin is the law
2 Cor. 12:9, **p** is perfected in weakness
Eph. 1:21, authority and **p** and dominion
2:2, prince of the **p** of the air
Phil. 3:21, exertion of the **p**
Heb. 1:3, by the word of His **p**
11:34, quenched the **p** of fire
Ex. 15:6; Judg. 7:2; Job 40:16; Ps. 49:15; Prov. 3:27; Jer. 18:21; 1 Cor. 5:4; 1 Pet. 3:22
PRACTICE Ps. 28:4, evil of their **p-s**
Matt. 6:1, Beware of **p-ing** your righteousness
Acts 19:18, disclosing their **p-s**
1 Cor. 11:16, we have no other **p**
Col. 3:9, laid aside the old self with its *evil* **p-s**
1 Tim. 5:4, **p** piety in regard to their own family
1 John 1:6, we lie and do not **p** the truth
3:8, the one who **p-s** sin is of the
PRAETORIUM Matt. 27:27, soldiers ... took Jesus into the **P**
Mark 15:16, took Him ... into the palace (that is, the **P**)
John 18:28, led Jesus ... into the **P**
18:33, Pilate ... entered ... into the **P**
PRAISE—*bless, commend*
Ex. 15:11, Awesome in **p-s**
Ps. 89:5, heavens will **p** Thy wonders
Prov. 27:21, man *is tested* by the **p**
Matt. 11:25, I **p** Thee, O Father
Luke 16:8, his master **p-d** the unrighteous steward
Rom. 2:29, his **p** is not from men
Phil. 4:8, if anything worthy of **p**
James 5:13, Let him sing **p-s**
Deut. 10:21; 1 Chr. 16:9; Neh. 12:46; Ps. 22:25; Prov. 12:8; Is. 38:18
PRAY—*ask* Is. 45:20, And **p** to a god who cannot save
Matt. 5:44, **p** for those who persecute
6:5, And when you **p**
6:6, **p** to your Father ... in secret
6:7, **p-ing**, do not use meaningless
14:23, mountain by Himself to **p**
26:41, Keep watching and **p-ing**, that
Mark 11:24, you **p** and ask, believe
Luke 11:1, Lord, teach us to **p** just
18:1, they ought to **p** and not
22:40, **P** that you may not ... temptation

PRAY *(Continued)*
1 Cor. 11:13, for a woman to **p** to God
14:14, if I **p** in a tongue
Col. 1:9, not ceased to **p** for you
1 Thess. 5:17, **p** without ceasing
James 5:13, suffering? Let him **p**
5:16, and **p** for one another
Gen. 20:7; Ex. 33:18; 1 Sam. 7:5; 12:23; Jon. 1:14
PRAYER Ps. 55:1, Give ear to my **p**, O God
Is. 56:7, called a house of **p**
Matt. 17:21, out except by **p** and fasting
21:22, everything ... in **p**, believing
Luke 6:12, whole night in **p**
19:46, A HOUSE OF P
Acts 3:1, the hour of **p**
Rom. 1:10, in my **p-s** making request
12:12, devoted to **p**
1 Cor. 7:5; Col. 4:2, devote yourselves to **p**
1 Pet. 3:7, your **p-s** may not be hindered
1 Kin. 8:45; Neh. 11:17; Ps. 4:1
PREACH—*declare, exhort, proclaim*
Matt. 4:17, that time Jesus began to **p**
10:7, go, **p**, saying ... kingdom ... is at hand
11:1, and **p** in their cities
11:5, POOR ... GOSPEL P-ED to them
Mark 13:10, gospel ... **p-ed** to all the nations
16:15, **p** the gospel to all
Luke 4:43, **p** the kingdom of God
Acts 13:32, we **p** to you the good news of the promise
1 Cor. 1:17, not ... to baptize, but to **p**
1:23, we **p** Christ crucified
2 Cor. 4:5, we do not **p** ourselves
1 Tim. 6:2, Teach and **p** these *principles*
2 Tim. 4:2, **p** the word, be ready
PREACHER Eccles. 1:1, words of the **P**
Rom. 10:14, how shall they hear without a **p**
1 Tim. 2:7, I was appointed a **p**
2 Pet. 2:5, Noah, a **p** of righteousness
PREACHING—*talk, word* Matt. 3:1, John ... **p**
Mark 1:4, **p** a baptism of repentance
1:39, **p** and casting out the demons
Acts 5:42, teaching and **p** Jesus
8:4, scattered went about **p** the word
Rom. 16:25, **p** of Jesus Christ
1 Cor. 15:14, then our **p** is vain
PRECEDE 1 Thess. 4:15, **p** those who have fallen asleep
PRECEPT—*statute* Ps. 19:8, **p-s** of the LORD are right
PRECIOUS—*excellent* Ps. 36:7, How **p** is Thy lovingkindness
Ps. 116:15, **P** in the sight of the LORD
Prov. 3:15, more **p** than jewels
Is. 44:9, their **p** things are of no profit
1 Pet. 1:7, more **p** than gold which
1:19, but with **p** blood ... of Christ
PREDETERMINE Acts 2:23, **p-d** plan and foreknowledge of God
PREEMINENT—*excellence*
Gen. 49:3, **P** in dignity and **p** in
PREPARATION—*serve*
Luke 10:40, distracted with all her **p-s**
PREPARE—*fashion, furnish, ready* Gen. 18:6
Ps. 23:5, dost **p** a table before me
78:19, God **p** a table in the
Matt. 11:10, WHO WILL P YOUR WAY
25:34, the kingdom **p-d** for you
John 14:2, I go to **p** a place for you
1 Cor. 2:9, P-D FOR THOSE WHO LOVE HIM
Heb. 11:3, worlds were **p-d** by the word
Lev. 7:9; Job 12:5; Ps. 57:6; Rom. 9:22
PRESCRIBE—*command*
1 Tim. 4:11, **P** and teach these things
PRESENCE Ex. 33:14, My **p** shall go *with you*
Ps. 23:5, **p** of my enemies
44:3, light of Thy **p**
95:2, before His **p** with thanksgiving
Is. 64:2, nations may tremble at Thy **p**
Luke 13:26, ate and drank in Your **p**
Jude 24, **p** of His glory blameless
Rev. 14:10, in the **p** of the Lamb
PRESENT—*offer, yield*
Gen. 43:11, to the man as a **p**
Ps. 46:1, A very **p** help in trouble
Mal. 1:8, **p** the blind ... **p** the lame and
Luke 2:22, to **p** Him to the Lord
Rom. 6:13, **p-ing** the members of your body to sin
12:1, **p** your bodies a living sacrifice
1 Cor. 5:3, but **p** in spirit
Col. 1:22, **p** you before Him holy and blameless
2 Tim. 2:15, **p** yourself approved to God
4:10, loved this **p** world
PRESERVATION—*health*
Acts 27:34, food ... for your **p**
PRESERVE—*guard, keep*
2 Sam. 18:18, no son to **p** my name
Ps. 16:1, **P** me, O God, for I take refuge
86:2, **p** my soul, for I am a godly man
Prov. 14:3, lips of the wise will **p** them
Luke 17:33, loses *his life* shall **p** it
Eph. 4:3, diligent to **p** the unity of the Spirit
1 Thess. 5:23, soul and body be **p-d** complete
PRESS Matt. 27:32, they **p-ed** ... to bear His cross
Luke 6:38, good measure **p-ed** down
Phil. 3:14, I **p** on toward the goal
PRESUME—*dare* Rom. 15:18, I will not **p** to speak
PRESUMPTION Prov. 13:10, Through **p** comes nothing
PRETEND—*disguise* 2 Sam. 14:2, **p** to be a mourner
1 Kin. 14:5,6, **p** to be another woman
Luke 20:20, sent spies who **p-ed** to be righteous
PRETTY Jer. 46:20, Egypt is a **p** heifer
PREVAIL Gen. 7:20, water **p-ed** fifteen cubits higher
1 Sam. 2:9, not by might shall a man **p**
Ps. 65:3; Jer. 20:7
PREVALENT Eccles. 6:1, an evil ... it is **p**
PREVENT Matt. 3:14, John tried to **p** Him,
PREY Ps. 76:4; Ezek. 22:25
PRICE Acts 1:18, field with the **p** of his wickedness
5:2, kept back *some* of the **p**
1 Cor. 6:20, you have been bought with a **p**
Lev. 25:16; Dan. 11:39; Mic. 3:11
PRIDE Prov. 16:18, **P** *goes* before destruction
Mark 7:22, slander, **p** *and* foolishness
1 John 2:16, the boastful **p** of life
Prov. 8:13; Is. 13:19; 60:15; Ezek. 32:12
PRIEST Gen. 14:18, **p** of God Most High
Ex. 19:6, shall be to Me a kingdom of **p-s**
1 Sam. 2:35, raise up for Myself a faithful **p**
Ps. 110:4, **p** forever ... order of Melchizedek
Ezek. 44:21, Nor shall any of the **p-s** drink wine
Matt. 2:4, together all the chief **p-s**
8:4, SHOW YOURSELF TO THE P
Heb. 2:17, faithful high **p**
3:1, High **P** of our confession
5:6, P FOREVER ... ORDER OF MELCHIZEDEK
2 Chr. 15:3; Is. 24:2
PRIME—*flower* 1 Sam. 2:33, will die in the **p** of life
PRINCE—*ruler* Ex. 2:14, Who made you a **p** or a judge
2 Sam. 3:38, **p** and a great man has fallen
Is. 9:6, **P** of Peace
Acts 3:15, put to death the **P** of life
5:31, as a **P** and a Saviour
Eph. 2:2, **p** of the power of the air
PRINCESS—*lady* Judg. 5:29, Her wise **p-es** would answer
PRINCIPALITY Rom. 8:38, nor **p-es** ... nor powers
PRISON Judg. 16:21, he was a grinder in the **p**
Ps. 142:7, Bring my soul out of **p**
Matt. 14:10, had John beheaded in the **p**
Acts 5:19, Lord ... opened the gates of the **p**
16:27, jailer ... had seen the **p** doors opened
1 Kin. 22:27; Rev. 18:2

PRISONER Ps. 102:20, groaning of the **p**
Ps. 146:7, the LORD sets the **p-s** free
Matt. 27:15, release for the multitude *any* one **p**
Rom. 7:23, making me a **p** of the law
Eph. 3:1, Paul, the **p** of Christ Jesus
2 Tim. 1:8, ashamed . . . or of me His **p**
PRIVATION—*adversity, distress*
Is. 30:20, given you bread of **p**
PRIZE Col. 2:18, defrauding you of your **p**
PROCEED Deut. 8:3, everything that **p-s** out of the mouth
Jer. 9:3, **p** from evil to evil
Matt. 4:4, WORD THAT P-S OUT OF THE MOUTH
Mark 7:21, heart of men, **p** the evil thoughts
John 15:26, who **p-s** from the Father
2 Tim. 3:13, imposters will **p** . . . to worse
PROCLAIM—*declare, tell*
Ex. 33:19; Deut. 32:3, **p** the name of the LORD
Is. 61:1, **p** liberty to the captives
61:2, **p** the favorable year of the LORD
Jer. 34:15, **p-ing** release to his neighbor
Matt. 10:27; Luke 12:3, **p-ed** upon the housetops
Acts 17:3, Jesus whom I am **p-ing** to you
17:23, you worship in ignorance, this I **p** to
26:23, **p** light both to the *Jewish* and
1 Pet. 3:19, made **p-ation** to the spirits
1 John 1:3, what we have seen and heard we **p**
PROCONSUL—*deputy* Acts 13:7; 18:12; 19:38
PRODUCE—*yield* Deut. 14:22, tithe all the **p**
Ps. 67:6, the earth has yielded its **p**
2 Tim. 2:23, knowing that they **p** quarrels
James 3:12, Neither can salt water **p** fresh
Lev. 25:19; Hos. 10:1
PRODUCTIVE Luke 12:16, land . . . was **p**
PROFANE—*defile, pollute* Lev. 21:7,23; Ezek. 22:8
Ex. 31:14, Everyone who **p-s** it . . . put to death
Lev. 20:3, to **p** My holy name
Ezek. 23:38, have **p-d** My sabbaths
1 Tim. 1:9, law . . . for the unholy and **p**
PROFESS—*confession* Rom. 1:22, **P-ing** to be wise
Titus 1:16, They **p** to know God
PROFIT Job 15:3, words which are not **p-able**
Prov. 14:23, In all labor there is **p**
15:27, who **p-s** illicitly troubles his own
Matt. 16:26; Luke 9:25, will a man be **p-ed**
John 6:63, the flesh **p-s** nothing
Acts 16:19; hope of **p** was gone
1 Cor. 6:12; 10:23, not all things are **p-able**
13:3, not have love, it **p-s** me nothing
1 Tim. 4:8, bodily discipline is only of little **p**
2 Tim. 3:16, Scripture . . . **p-able** for teaching
James 4:13, engage in business and make a **p**
Gen. 37:26; Prov. 3:14; Is. 48:17; Jer. 16:19
PROGRESS Phil. 1:12, greater **p** of the gospel
PROLONG Prov. 10:27, fear of the Lord **p-s** life
PROMINENCE Acts 13:50, devout women of **p**
PROMINENT Mark 15:43, Joseph . . . **p** member
PROMISCUITY Rom. 13:13, not in sexual **p** and sensuality
PROMISE Acts 2:33, **p** of the Holy Spirit
Acts 26:6, hope of the **p** made by God
Rom. 4:14, **p** is nullified
9:8, children of the **p**
Gal. 3:14, might receive the **p** of the Spirit
Eph. 6:2, first commandment with a **p**
2 Tim. 1:1, **p** of life in Christ Jesus
Titus 1:2, **p-d** long ages ago
Heb. 10:23, for He who **p-d** is faithful
2 Pet. 1:4, His precious and magnificent **p-s**
PROMOTE Esth. 5:11; Ps. 140:8
PRONOUNCE—*utter* Jer. 1:16, I will **p** My judgments
Luke 23:24, Pilate **p-d** sentence
PROOF Acts 17:31, furnished **p** to all men
2 Cor. 8:24, show them the **p** of your love
13:3, **p** of the Christ who speaks in me

PROPER Rom. 13:13, Let us behave **p-ly** as in the day
1 Cor. 11:13, is it **p** for a woman to pray
14:40, let all things be done **p-ly**
Eph. 5:3, as is **p** among saints
1 Thess. 4:12, you may behave **p-ly** toward outsiders
1 Tim. 2:6, testimony *borne* at the **p** time
PROPERTY—*goods*
Gen. 34:10, and acquire **p** in it
Matt. 12:29, carry off his **p**
19:22, one who owned much **p**
Acts 2:45, selling their **p** and possessions
PROPHECY Dan. 9:24, seal up vision and **p**
1 Cor. 13:2, if I have the gift of **p**
2 Pet. 1:21, no **p** was ever made by . . . human will
Rev. 19:10, testimony . . . is the spirit of **p**
PROPHESY 1 Sam. 10:11, he **p-ed** now with the prophets
Is. 30:10, not **p** to us what is right
Matt. 7:22, did we not **p** in Your name
26:68, **P** to us, You Christ
1 Cor. 13:9, know in part, and we **p** in part
1 Chr. 25:3; Jer. 14:14; Ezek. 37:4; Joel 2:28
PROPHET Matt. 1:22, spoken . . . through the **p**
Matt. 2:5, it had been written by the **p**
2:15, through the **p** might be fulfilled
2:17, Jeremiah the **p**
5:12, so they persecuted the **p-s**
10:41, **p** shall receive a **p-'s** reward
11:9, one who is more than a **p**
11:13, all the **p-s** and the Law
13:57, **p** is not without honor
21:11, the **p** Jesus, from Nazareth
Luke 4:24, no **p** is welcome in his home town
6:23, their fathers used to treat the **p-s**
John 1:21, Are you the **P**
4:19, perceive that You are a **p**
7:52, see that no **p** arises out of Galilee
Acts 13:15, reading of the Law and the **P-s**
1 Cor. 14:37, If anyone thinks he is a **p**
Eph. 4:11, some *as* apostles, and some *as* **p-s**
Heb. 1:1, to the fathers in the **p-s**
Gen. 20:7; Deut. 13:1; 18:18; Judg. 4:4; 1 Sam. 9:9; 1 Kin. 20:35; Is. 9:15; Jer. 23:11; Ezek. 13:3; Hos. 12:10; Amos 7:14; Acts 13:6
PROPHETIC 1 Thess. 5:20, do not despise **p** utterances
2 Pet. 1:19, the **p** word made more sure
PROSELYTE Matt. 23:15, make one **p**
Acts 2:10, both Jews and **p-s**
13:43, God-fearing **p-s** followed Paul
PROSPER 1 Sam. 18:14, David was **p-ing**
Ps. 10:5, His ways **p** at all times
Prov. 28:13, his transgressions will not **p**
1 Cor. 16:2, save, as he may **p**
Gen. 39:3; 1 Sam. 18:5
PROSPERITY—*wealth*
Ezra 9:12, never seek . . . their **p**
Job 21:13, spend their days in **p**
Ps. 25:13, His soul will abide in **p**
73:3, saw the **p** of the wicked
Acts 19:25, our **p** depends upon this business
PROSPEROUS
Prov. 11:25, generous man will be **p**
PROSTITUTES
Hos. 4:14, offer sacrifices with temple **p**
PROSTRATE 2 Sam. 9:6, fell on his face and **p-d** himself
Job 14:10, man dies and lies **p**
PROTECT Is. 31:5, He will **p** and deliver it
PROTECTION Num. 14:9, Their **p** has been removed
Eccles. 7:12, wisdom is **p** *just as* money is **p**
PROUD—*arrogant, conceited*
Ps. 94:2, recompense to the **p**
Luke 1:51, **p** in the thoughts of their heart
James 4:6, GOD IS OPPOSED TO THE P
Is. 3:16; 13:11

PROVE—*test* Prov. 30:6; 2 Cor. 8:8
Acts 9:22, **p-ing** that this *Jesus* is the Christ
Rom. 12:2, **p** what the will of God is
PROVERB 1 Kin. 4:32, He also spoke 3,000 **p-s**
1 Kin. 9:7, Israel will become a **p** and a byword
Deut. 28:37; Jer. 24:9; 2 Pet. 2:22
PROVIDE—*gave* Gen. 22:8, God will **p** for Himself the Lamb
Neh. 9:15, didst **p** bread from heaven
1 Tim. 5:8, if any one does not **p** for his own
Lev. 25:24; 1 Sam. 16:17
PROVISION Josh. 9:5, bread of their **p** was dry
Ps. 132:15, abundantly bless her **p**
Rom. 13:14, make no **p** for the flesh
PROVOKE Prov. 20:2, who **p-s** him to anger
1 Cor. 13:5, is not **p-d**
Eph. 6:4, do not **p** your children to anger
2 Chr. 25:19; Job 12:6
PROW Acts 27:41, the **p** stuck fast and remained
PROWL—*walk* Ps. 104:20, beast of the forest **p**
1 Pet. 5:8, devil, **p-s** about like a roaring lion
PRUDENT Prov. 12:16, **p** man conceals dishonor
Prov. 19:14, a **p** wife is from the LORD
Jer. 49:7, good counsel been lost to the **p**
PSALMS Ps. 95:2, shout joyfully to Him with **p**
Luke 20:42, David ... says in the book of **P**
24:44, the **P** must be fulfilled
Eph. 5:19, speaking to one another in **p**
PUGNACIOUS 1 Tim. 3:3, addicted to wine or **p**
PULL Ps. 31:4, **p** me out of the net
Luke 14:5, **p** him out on a Sabbath day
PULVERIZE Mic. 4:13, That you may **p** many peoples
PUNISH—*visit* Lev. 26:18,28, will **p** you seven times
Is. 13:11, **p** the world for its evil
Lam. 4:22, He will **p** your iniquity
2 Cor. 10:6, to **p** all disobedience
Prov. 22:3; Luke 23:16; Acts 26:11
PUNISHMENT Gen. 4:13, **p** is too great to bear
Job 19:29, the **p** of the sword
Matt. 25:46, go away into eternal **p**
2 Cor. 2:6, Sufficient ... is this **p**
1 John 4:18, because fear involves **p**
Jude 7, the **p** of eternal fire
PUPIL Deut. 32:10, **p** of His eye
Luke 6:40, a **p** is not above his teacher
PURCHASE Gen. 49:32, field ... **p-d** from
Acts 20:28, He **p-d** with His own blood
Rev. 5:9, **p** for God with Thy blood
PURE Ps. 12:6, words of the LORD are **p** words
Ps. 19:8, commandment of the LORD is **p**
24:4, clean hands and a **p** heart
Matt. 5:8, Blessed are the **p** in heart
2 Cor. 11:2, present you *as* a **p** virgin
Phil. 4:8, whatever is **p**
1 Tim. 1:5, love from a **p** heart
Titus 1:15, To the **p**, all things are **p**
2:5, *be* sensible, **p**
James 1:27, **p** and undefiled religion
2 Sam. 22:27; Job 4:17; 11:4; 15:15; Song 6:10; Dan. 7:9
PURGE Dan. 12:10, Many will be **p-d**, purified, refined
PURIFY Ps. 51:7, **P** me with hyssop
1 Pet. 1:22, obedience ... **p-ed** your souls
2 Pet. 1:9, **p-cation** from his former sins
2 Kin. 2:21; Dan. 12:10
PURPOSE—*cause, devise, reason*
Jer. 49:20, **p-s** which He has **p-d**
Lam. 2:17, The LORD has done what He **p-d**
Ezek. 22:9, **p** of shedding blood
Luke 7:30, rejected God's **p**
Acts 26:16, for this **p** I have appeared to you
Rom. 8:28, called according to His **p**
Eph. 3:11, in accordance with the eternal **p**
6:22, for this very **p**
Heb. 6:17, unchangeableness of His **p**
1 Pet. 4:6, has for this **p** been preached
PURSE Is. 46:6; Hag. 1:6; Luke 12:33
PURSUE—*follow, persecute, sought* Gen. 31:36
Ps. 34:14, Seek peace, and **p** it
Prov. 21:21, who **p-s** righteousness and loyalty
Heb. 12:14, **P** peace with all men
1 Pet. 3:11, SEEK PEACE AND **P** IT
Lev. 26:17; Judg. 3:28; 2 Sam. 1:6; Job 30:15; Ps. 7:1; Is. 5:11
PUSH—*thrust* Ps. 118:13, **p-ed** me violently
PUT Gen. 3:15, I will **p** enmity Between you and
Ex. 9:15, now I had **p** forth My hand
Ps. 40:3, **p** a new song in my mouth
Matt. 1:19, desired to **p** her away secretly
12:18, I WILL **P** MY SPIRIT UPON HIM
26:52, **P** your sword back into its place
Mark 12:42, widow came ... **p** in two
Luke 9:62, **p-ing** his hand to the plow
John 19:2, crown of thorns ... **p** it on His head
20:27, hand, and **p** it into My side
Rom. 13:14, **p** on the Lord Jesus Christ
1 Cor. 15:53, **p** on the imperishable, **p** on immortality
Eph. 4:24, **p** on the new self
6:11, **P** on the full armor of God
1 Pet. 2:1, **p-ing** aside all malice
Rev. 14:15, **P** in your sickle
Josh. 1:18; 2 Chr. 18:22; Job 31:24; 38:36; Song 8:6; Mark 4:21; John 21:7

Q

QUAKE—*tremble, shake*
Judg. 5:4, The earth **q-d**, the heavens
Judg. 5:5; Ps. 68:8
QUARREL—*contend, war*
Ex. 21:18, if men have a **q**
James 4:1, source of **q-s** and conflicts
Ex. 17:2; Prov. 20:3; 1 Cor. 1:11
QUEEN 1 Kin. 10:1, the **q** of Sheba
Is. 47:5, the **q** of kingdoms
Matt. 12:42, **Q** of *the* South shall rise
Esth. 1:9; Is. 47:7; Jer. 7:18; Acts 8:27
QUENCH 1 Thess. 5:19, Do not **q** the Spirit
Ps. 104:11; Song 8:7
QUESTION 1 Kin. 10:1, test with difficult **q-s**
Mark 11:29, I will ask you one **q**
22:35, a lawyer, asked Him a **q**
Acts 18:15, **q-s** about words and names
1 Cor. 10:25, without asking **q-s** for conscience' sake
1 Tim. 6:4, **q-s** and disputes about words
QUICK—*swift, soon* Acts 7:54, cut to the **q**
Titus 1:7, not **q-tempered**, not addicted to
James 1:19, every one be **q** to hear
Judg. 2:23; John 11:31
QUICKLY—*shortly, suddenly*
Matt. 5:25, Make friends **q** with your opponent
John 13:27, what you do, do **q**
Rom. 9:28, EXECUTE HIS WORD ... **Q**
Rev. 3:11; 22:20, I am coming **q**
Gen. 18:6; Deut. 7:4; Ps. 31:2; Eccles. 4:12; 2 Thess. 2:2
QUICK-TEMPERED Prov. 14:17; 14:29; Titus 1:7
QUIET Job 20:20, he knew no **q** within him
Ps. 23:2, beside **q** waters
1 Thess. 4:11, your ambition to lead a **q** life
1 Tim. 2:2, lead a tranquil and **q** life
Prov. 17:1; Eccles. 9:17; Amos 6:10
QUILT 1 Sam. 19:13, put a **q** of goats' *hair*
QUOTA Ex. 5:18, deliver the **q** of bricks

R

RABBI Matt. 26:25; Mark 9:5
RABBIT Lev. 11:6; Deut. 14:7
RACE Eccles. 9:11, **r** is not to the swift
Nah. 2:4, chariots **r** madly in the streets
1 Cor. 9:24, those who run in a **r** all run
1 Pet. 2:9, A CHOSEN **R**, A ROYAL
RADIANCE Heb. 1:3, **r** of His glory
RADIANT Jer. 31:12, **r** over the bounty of the LORD
RAFTER Hab. 2:11, the **r** will answer it
RAGES—*frets* Prov. 19:3, his heart **r** against

RAID Gen. 49:19, raiders shall **r** him . . . **r** at their heels
RAIMENT—*clothing* Is. 63:3, I stained all My **r**
RAIN Gen. 7:12, **r** fell upon the earth for forty days
Ex. 16:4, will **r** bread from heaven for you
Matt. 5:45, **r** on *the* righteous . . . unrighteous
7:25, and the **r** descended
Heb. 6:7, ground that drinks the **r**
Lev. 26:4; Deut. 32:2; Job 24:8; Prov. 25:14; 25:23; Song 2:11
RAISE Matt. 20:19, third day He . . . **r-d** up
John 2:19, in three days I will **r** it up
6:39, **r** it up on the last day
1 Cor. 15:13, not even Christ . . . **r-d**
15:35, How are the dead **r-d**
15:42, it is **r-d**
15:44, **r-d** a spiritual body
Eph. 2:6, **r-d** us up with Him
Col. 3:1, If . . . been **r-d** up with Christ
Heb. 11:19, God is able to **r** *men* from
Deut. 18:18; Judg. 2:16; Is. 2:2; Dan. 12:7; Hos. 6:2; Mic. 4:1; Luke 3:8
RAISIN 2 Sam. 6:19; Song 2:5; Hos. 3:1
RAMPARTS—*siege works* Ps. 48:13; Is. 26:1
RAN—*fled* Luke 8:34, they **r** away and reported
RANK—*high* Ps. 62:9, men of **r** are a lie
RANSOM Matt. 20:28, give His life a **r** for many
1 Tim. 2:6, gave Himself as a **r** for all
Ex. 30:12; Prov. 6:35
RAPID—*swift* Prov. 6:18, Feet that run **r-ly** to evil
RARE—*precious*
1 Sam. 3:1, word from the LORD was **r**
RASH Job 6:3, my words have been **r**
RATION—*provision* Dan. 1:5; Luke 12:42
RAVAGE Gen. 41:30; 1 Sam. 6:5; Acts 8:3
RAVINE—*valley* Luke 3:5, EVERY **R** SHALL BE
RAYS Hab. 3:4, He has **r** *flashing* from His hand
READ Hab. 2:2, one who **r-s** it may run
Luke 4:16, stood up to **r**
Acts 8:28, was **r-ing** the prophet Isaiah
2 Cor. 3:14, at the **r-ing** of the old covenant
1 Tim. 4:13, give attention to the public **r-ing**
Rev. 1:3, Blessed is he who **r-s**
Ex. 24:7; Is. 34:16; Dan. 5:8
READINESS 2 Cor. 8:12, if the **r** is present
READY 1 Chr. 7:11; Ps. 86:5; Prov. 24:27
REALIZED Prov. 13:19, Desire **r** is sweet
REALLY—*indeed* Luke 24:34, The Lord has **r** risen
REAP—*harvest* Hos. 8:7, they **r** the whirlwind
Matt. 6:26, neither do they **r**, nor
25:26, **r** where I did not sow
Luke 12:24, ravens . . . neither sow nor **r**
2 Cor. 9:6, shall also **r** sparingly
Gal. 6:7, this he will also **r**
6:8, flesh **r** corruption
6:9, in due time we shall **r**
Lev. 19:9; Ps. 126:5; Prov. 22:8; Rev. 14:16
REASON—*thought*
Job 23:7, the upright would **r** with Him
Is. 1:18, let us **r** together
Luke 5:22, Why are you **r-ing** in your hearts
Acts 17:17, he was **r-ing** in the synagogue
1 Cor. 3:20, KNOWS THE **R-INGS** of the wise
1 Tim. 1:16, for this **r** I found mercy
James 3:17, gentle, **r-able**, full of mercy
REBEL Ps. 107:11, **r-ed** against the words of God
Is. 63:10, **r-ed** . . . grieved His Holy Spirit
Num. 14:9; 1 Sam. 12:15; Ezek. 20:21
REBELLION—*transgression* 1 Sam. 24:11; Job 13:23
REBELLIOUS—*disobedient*
1 Tim. 1:9, those who are lawless and **r**
Ex. 23:21; Deut. 9:7; Ps. 66:7; 78:8; Jer. 5:23
REBUILD Is. 58:12, **r** the ancient ruins
REBUKE—*reprove, reproof*
Matt. 8:26, **r-d** the winds and
17:18, Jesus **r-d** him, and the demon
Mark 9:25, **r-d** the unclean spirit
Luke 4:39, He **r-d** the fever, and it left
1 Tim. 5:1, not sharply **r** an older man
Job 26:11; Ps. 38:1; Prov. 27:5; Zech. 3:2
RECEIVE—*accept* Prov. 1:3, **r** instruction in wise
Matt. 10:8, freely you **r-d**, freely give
10:14, whoever does not **r** you
10:40, who **r-s** you **r-s** Me
10:41, who **r-s** a prophet in *the* name of
11:5, BLIND **R** SIGHT
18:5, **r-s** one such child
25:27, **r-d** my money back with interest
Mark 16:19, **r-d** up into heaven
Luke 15:2, This man **r-s** sinners
20:47, **r** greater condemnation
John 1:11, His own did not **r** Him
5:44, **r** glory from one another
14:3, **r** you to Myself
20:22, **R** the Holy Spirit
Acts 20:35, blessed to give than to **r**
Rom. 5:17, **r** the abundance of grace
8:15, **r-d** a spirit of adoption
1 Cor. 3:8, will **r** his own reward
9:24, one **r-s** the prize
Gal. 4:5, **r** the adoption as sons
1 Thess. 1:6, **r-d** the word in much
2 Thess. 2:10, did not **r** the love of the
Heb. 2:2, **r-d** a just recompense
James 1:12, **r** the crown of life
Job 3:12; Is. 40:2
RECEPTION—*feast* Luke 14:13, you give a **r**
RECKLESS 2 Tim. 3:4, treacherous, **r** . . . lovers of pleasure
RECKON—*impute* Rom. 4:4, his wage is not **r-ed**
Rom. 4:6, God **r-s** righteousness
RECLINE—*sat* Matt. 9:10; 26:20, He was **r-ing**
RECOGNIZE—*know* Acts 19:15, I **r** Jesus
Gen. 27:23; 1 Cor. 14:38
RECOMPENSE—*reward*
Ps. 94:2, Render **r** to the proud
Heb. 2:2, received a just **r**
Ps. 28:4; Jer. 51:6
RECONCILE Matt. 5:24, be **r-d** to your brother
1 Cor. 7:11, be **r-d** to her husband
2 Cor. 5:20, be **r-d** to God
Col. 1:20, **r** all things to Himself
RECONCILIATION
Rom. 5:11, we have now received the **r**
RECORD—*write* Hab. 2:2, **R** the vision
RECOVERY—*health* Is. 58:8, your **r** will speedily spring
RED—*dull* Gen. 25:25, first came forth **r**, all over
Ex. 10:19, drove them into the **R** Sea
Prov. 23:31, on the wine when it is **r**
Is. 1:18, they are **r** like crimson
Zech. 1:8, man was riding on a **r** horse
Matt. 16:2, fair weather . . . sky is **r**
Rev. 6:4, another, a **r** horse, went out
REDEEM—*purchase*
Ex. 6:6, **r** you with an outstretched arm
Ps. 26:11, **R** me, and be gracious
49:15, God will **r** my soul
Gal. 3:13, **r-ed** us from the curse
Titus 2:14, **R** US FROM EVERY . . . DEED
Ruth 4:4; 2 Sam. 4:9
REDEEMER Job 19:25, know that my **R** lives
Ps. 19:14, my rock and my **r**
Is. 63:16, our Father, Our **R**
Jer. 50:34, Their **R** is strong
REDEMPTION Ps. 130:7, with Him is abundant **r**
Luke 21:28, your **r** is drawing near
Rom. 3:24, **r** which is in Christ Jesus
Eph. 1:7, **r** through His blood
4:30, sealed for the day of **r**
REDUCE—*diminish* Ex. 5:8, you are not to **r** any of it
REED—*bulrushes, rod*
Ex. 2:3, set it among the **r-s** by
Is. 42:3, bruised **r** He will not break
Matt. 27:30, **r** and *began* to beat Him
27:48, wine, and put it on a **r**
Is. 36:6; Matt. 11:7

REEF Jude 12, hidden **r-s** in your love-feasts
REEL Is. 28:7, these also **r** with wine
REFINE—*purify, try* Ps. 12:6, silver ... **r-d** seven times
Rev. 3:18, gold **r-d** by fire
REFORM Acts 24:2, **r-s** are being carried out
REFRAIN 1 Pet. 3:10, R HIS TONGUE FROM EVIL
Ex. 23:5; Job 30:10; 1 Cor. 9:6; 2 Cor. 12:6
REFRESH—*comfort* 1 Cor. 16:18, **r-ed** my spirit and yours
Gen. 18:5; Ex. 23:12; 31:17; Song 2:5
REFUGE—*defense, strength, trust*
2 Sam. 22:3, God, my rock, in whom I take **r**
Ps. 46:1, God is our **r** and strength
Is. 17:10, remembered the rock of your **r**
33:16, His **r** will be the impregnable rock
Judg. 9:15; Ps. 55:8; Is. 28:17; Jer. 16:19
REFUSE (n.) Ex. 29:14; Judg. 3:22; Is. 57:20
REFUSE (v.) Gen. 23:6, none ... will **r** you his grave
Prov. 21:25, his hands **r** to work
Matt. 2:18, SHE R-D TO BE COMFORTED
Acts 10:47, no one can **r** the water for these
2 Tim. 2:23, **r** foolish and ignorant speculations
Jer. 13:10; Heb. 12:25
REFUTE Job 32:12; Titus 1:9
REGARD Rom. 14:5, **r-s** one day above another
Phil. 2:3, you **r** one another as more important
Gen. 4:4; Job 18:3; 41:27; Prov. 15:5; Is. 17:7; Lam. 4:2; Luke 7:2
REGION Matt. 2:22, he departed for the **r-s** of Galilee
Mark 5:17; Luke 2:8; Acts 27:2
REGISTER—*number, written* Num. 11:26; 2 Sam. 24:4
REGRET 1 Sam. 15:35, the LORD **r-ed** that
2 Cor. 7:10, produces a repentance without **r**
REGULAR Dan. 8:11; 11:31; 12:11, **r** sacrifice
REIGN—*rule* Ex. 15:18, LORD shall **r** forever and
Luke 19:14, not want this man to **r** over
1 Cor. 15:25, must **r** until He has put
2 Tim. 2:12, we shall also **r** with Him
Rev. 20:6, **r** with Him for a thousand years
Gen. 37:8; Judg. 9:8; Prov. 8:15; Is. 32:1
REJECT Prov. 3:11, do not **r** the discipline of the LORD
Prov. 15:5, A fool **r-s** his father's discipline
Matt. 21:42, STONE ... BUILDERS R-ED
Luke 10:16, the one who **r-s** you **r-s** Me
17:25, **r-ed** by this generation
John 12:48, He who **r-s** Me
1 Thess. 4:8, who **r-s** *this* is not **r-ing** man but God
2 Tim. 3:8, **r-ed** as regards the faith
1 Pet. 2:4, **r-ed** by men
2:7; Ps. 118:22, STONE ... BUILDERS R-ED
Num. 11:20; Ps. 53:5; Is. 14:19; 30:12; 33:15; Jer. 6:30; Ezek. 20:13,16; Hos. 4:6; Amos 2:4
REJOICE Prov. 5:18, **r** in the wife of your youth
Matt. 2:10, they **r-d** exceedingly
5:12, **R**, and be glad
John 14:28, loved Me, you would have **r-d**
Rom. 12:15, **R** with those who **r**
1 Cor. 13:6, not **r** in unrighteousness
Phil. 3:1, brethren, **r** in the Lord
4:4, **R** in the Lord always
1 Thess. 5:16, **R** always
1 Pet. 1:8, **r** with joy inexpressible
Job 21:12; Eccles. 11:9; Is. 60:5; Luke 10:21; 1 Thess. 3:9
REJOICING Ps. 19:8, LORD are right, **r** the heart
Ps. 65:12, hills gird themselves with **r**
Joel 1:12, **r** dries up
Acts 5:41, **r** ... been considered worthy
8:39, went on his way **r**
Rom. 12:12, **r** in hope, persevering
2 Cor. 6:10, sorrowful yet always **r**
RELATE Acts 8:33, WHO SHALL R HIS GENERATION
RELATIONSHIP
Matt. 19:10, **r** of the man with his wife
RELATIVE Luke 1:36,58
RELEASE—*deliverance, liberty*
Lev. 25:10, proclaim a **r** through the land
Matt. 27:26, Then he **r-d** Barabbas
Mark 15:9, **r** for you the King ... Jews
Luke 4:18, PROCLAIM R TO THE CAPTIVES
23:20, Pilate, wanting to **r** Jesus
John 19:12, Pilate made efforts to **r** Him
Rom. 7:6, we have been **r-d** from the Law
1 Cor. 7:27, Are you **r-d** from a wife
Heb. 11:35, not accepting their **r**
Rev. 1:5, **r-d** us from our sins
RELIEF Job 32:20, speak that I may get **r**
RELIEVED Ps. 4:1, Thou hast **r** me in my distress
REMAIN—*abide, live, reside*
Gen. 8:22, While the earth **r-s**
Eccles. 1:4, But the earth **r-s** forever
Matt. 2:13, **r** there until I tell
11:23, **r-ed** to this day
26:38, **r** here and keep watch
John 1:32, He **r-ed** upon Him
19:31, not **r** on the cross
21:22, want him to **r** until I come
1 Cor. 3:14, If any man's work ... **r-s**
7:8, they **r** even as I
7:11, let her **r** unmarried
Gal. 2:5, gospel might **r** with you
1 Thess. 4:15, **r** until the coming of
Titus 1:5, set in order what **r-s**
Rev. 3:2, strengthen the things that **r**
Ex. 16:29; Deut. 9:9; 1 Sam. 5:7; 16:11; Job 14:2; 21:34; John 8:35
REMARKABLE—*strange*
Luke 5:26, seen **r** things today
REMEMBER Gen. 9:15, I will **r** My covenant
Ex. 20:8, **R** the sabbath day
Job 7:7, **R** that my life is *but* breath
11:16, As waters ... passed by ... **r** *it*
Ps. 25:7, not **r** the sins of my youth
Eccles. 12:1, **R** also your Creator
Jer. 31:34, their sin I will **r** no more
Matt. 26:75, Peter **r-ed** the word which Jesus
27:63, **r** ... that deceiver said
Luke 17:32, **R** Lot's wife
23:42, **r** me when You come in
John 15:20, **R** the word that I said
Acts 20:35, **r** the words of the Lord
Gal. 2:10, us to **r** the poor
Heb. 13:7, **R** those who led you
Rev. 2:5, **R** ... from where you have fallen
Deut. 5:15; 32:7; 1 Chr. 16:12; Ps. 63:6; 105:42; Is. 46:8; Jer. 15:15; Lam. 3:20; Ezek. 21:32; Acts 10:31; Heb. 13:3
REMEMBRANCE Mal. 3:16, a book of **r** was written
Luke 22:19, do this in **r** of Me
1 Cor. 11:25, drink *it*, in **r** of Me
Eccles. 1:11; Is. 26:14; 43:26
REMNANT Rom. 11:5, **r** according to *God's* gracious choice
Deut. 3:11; Jer. 6:9; 23:3; Mal. 2:15
REMOTE—*utmost* Neh. 1:9, most **r** part of the heavens
REMOVE Gen. 8:13, Noah **r-d** the covering of the ark
Ex. 3:5, **r** your sandals from your feet
1 Kin. 15:12, **r-d** all the idols
2 Kin. 17:23, LORD **r-d** Israel from His sight
Ps. 103:12, **r-d** our transgressions
Is. 29:13, **r** their hearts far from
Ezek. 36:26, **r** the heart of stone
Matt. 3:11, not *even* fit to **r** His sandals
Luke 22:42, **r** this cup from Me
John 11:39, **R** the stone
1 Cor. 13:2, so as to **r** mountains
Ruth 4:8; 2 Kin. 18:4; Job 24:2
REND 1 Kin. 19:11; Is. 64:1; Joel 2:13
RENDER—*repay* Matt. 22:21, **r** to Caesar the things that
Rom. 13:7, **R** to all ... due them
Deut. 32:41; Ps. 94:2; Prov. 24:12

RENEW Ps. 51:10, **r** a steadfast spirit within
Ps. 103:5, youth is **r-ed** like the
Lam. 5:21, **R** our days as of old
Rom. 12:2, **r-ing** of your mind
2 Cor. 4:16, inner man is being **r-ed** day by day
Col. 3:10, **r-ed** to a true knowledge
Titus 3:5, **r-ing** by the Holy Spirit
REPAY—*recompense* Gen. 44:4, **r-d** evil for good
Matt. 6:4,6,18, in secret will **r** you
Luke 10:35, return, I will **r** you
Rom. 12:19, I WILL R, SAYS THE LORD
1 Thess. 5:15, no one **r-s** . . . evil for evil
Philem. 19, own hand, I will **r** it
Heb. 10:30, VENGEANCE IS MINE, I WILL R
Deut. 7:10; 32:6; 2 Sam. 3:39; Jer. 18:20; 51:56; Luke 14:14
REPENT Job 42:6, **r** in dust and ashes
Matt. 3:2, **R**, for the kingdom of
11:21, **r-ed** long ago in sackcloth
Mark 1:15, **r** and believe in the gospel
6:12, preached that *men* should **r**
Luke 13:3, unless you **r**, you will all
15:7, one sinner who **r-s**
Acts 2:38, **R**, and . . . be baptized
3:19, **R** therefore and return
26:20, **r** and turn to God
Num. 23:19; Ezek. 18:30
REPENTANCE Matt. 3:8, fruit . . . with *your* **r**
Matt. 3:11, in water for **r**
Mark 1:4, a baptism of **r**
Luke 24:47, **r** for forgiveness of sins
Acts 26:20, performing deeds . . . to **r**
2 Cor. 7:10, God produces a **r** without regret
Heb. 6:1, laying . . . foundation of **r**
2 Pet. 3:9, all to come to **r**
REPHAIM—*giant*
Deut. 3:13, it is called the land of **R**
REPORT Matt. 2:8, have found *Him*, **r** to me
Matt. 11:4, Go and **r** to John the things
Luke 7:17, this **r** concerning Him
John 12:38, WHO HAS BELIEVED OUR R
REPROACH Jer. 29:18, a hissing and a **r**
Ezek. 5:14, a **r** among the nations
Matt. 11:20, He began to **r** the cities
1 Tim. 3:7, fall into **r** and the snare of
Titus 2:8, speech which is beyond **r**
Heb. 11:26, considering the **r** of Christ
Gen. 30:23; Job 27:6; Ps. 4:2; 44:13; 119:39; Is. 51:7; Jer. 24:9; Hos. 12:14; Rom. 15:3
REPROBATE Ps. 15:4, a **r** is despised
REPROOF Prov. 15:10, who hates **r** will die
2 Tim. 3:16, for teaching, for **r**, for correction
Prov. 1:30; 10:17; 15:5; 29:1,15
REPROVE—*correct*
Job 5:17, the man whom God **r-s**
Prov. 3:12, whom the LORD loves He **r-s**
Matt. 18:15, **r** him in private
2 Tim. 4:2, **r**, rebuke, exhort, with . . . patience
Rev. 3:19, I love, I **r** and discipline
Lev. 19:17; Job 13:10; 40:2; Prov. 9:8; Jer. 2:19
REPUTATION—*report*
Acts 6:3, seven men of good **r**
1 Tim. 5:10, having a **r** for good works
REPUTE—*report* Phil. 4:8, whatever is of good **r**
REQUEST—*desire*
Rom. 1:10, in my prayers making **r**
Phil. 4:6, let your **r-s** be made known
Judg. 8:24; 1 Kin. 2:16; Neh. 2:4; Job 6:8; Mark 15:6
REQUIRE Mic. 6:8, what does the Lord **r** of you
Luke 12:20, night your soul is **r-d** of you
1 Cor. 4:2, it is **r-d** of stewards
Gen. 9:5; Deut. 10:12; Ezra 3:4; Ps. 10:13; Is. 1:12
RESCUE Ps. 144:10; 2 Pet. 2:7
RESERVED 1 Pet. 1:4, **r** in heaven for you
2 Pet. 3:7, are being **r** for fire
Gen. 27:36; Job 21:30
RESIDE Matt. 2:23, **r-d** in a city called Nazareth
Lev. 19:34; Eccles. 7:9; Jer. 49:18

RESIST Matt. 5:39, do not **r** him who is evil
Luke 21:15, opponents will be able to **r** or
Acts 7:51, are always **r-ing** the Holy Spirit
Rom. 13:2, he who **r-s** authority has opposed
Heb. 12:4, not yet **r-ed** to the point of shedding
James 4:7, **R** the devil, and he
RESOLUTELY—*steadfastly*
1 Chr. 28:7, **r** performs My
Luke 9:51, He **r** set His face to go
RESPECT Matt. 21:37, They will **r** my son
Luke 18:2, and did not **r** man
Eph. 5:33, let the wife . . . **r** her husband
1 Pet. 3:2, chaste and **r-ful** behavior
Gen. 34:19; Mal. 1:6; 1 Pet. 2:18
RESPOND Is. 19:22, LORD, and He will **r** to them
Col. 4:6, how you should **r** to each person
RESPONSE 2 Kin. 4:31, was neither sound nor **r**
REST—*stand* Josh. 1:13, God gives you **r**
Josh. 14:15, the land had **r** from war
Ps. 37:7, **R** in the LORD and wait
116:7, Return to your **r**, O my soul
Prov. 14:33, Wisdom **r-s** in the heart
Is. 11:2, Spirit of the LORD will **r** upon Him
11:10, His **r-ing** place will be glorious
Jer. 6:16, find **r** for your souls
Matt. 11:28, and I will give you **r**
11:29, R FOR YOUR SOULS
Luke 11:24, waterless places seeking **r**
1 Cor. 2:5, **r** on the wisdom of men
2 Cor. 2:13, I had no **r** for my spirit
Heb. 3:11, THEY SHALL NOT ENTER MY R
1 Pet. 4:2, live the **r** of the time in
Gen. 5:29; 8:9; 49:15; Ex. 10:5; Deut. 28:65; Ruth 1:9; 2 Sam. 4:5; Job 3:17; 11:18; Prov. 19:20; Eccles. 4:6; Is. 14:3; 38:10; 57:2; Lam. 5:5; Matt. 22:6; Rev. 19:21
RESTED Gen. 2:2, and He **r** on the seventh day
Ex. 24:16, glory of the LORD **r**
Acts 2:3, tongues of fire . . . **r** on each one
RESTITUTION Lev. 6:5; 2 Sam. 12:6
RESTORE—*turn* Ps. 19:7, perfect **r-ing** the soul
Ps. 23:3, He **r-s** my soul; He guides
Matt. 17:11, is coming, and will **r** all things
Mark 3:5, his hand was **r-d**
James 5:15, prayer . . . will **r** the one who is sick
Gen. 20:7; Neh. 3:8; 4:2; Ps. 80:3; Jer. 30:17
RESTRAIN Prov. 10:19, who **r-s** his lips is wise
Acts 14:18, they with difficulty **r-ed** the crowds
2 Cor. 6:12, You are not **r-ed** by us, but
Gen. 8:2; Job 7:11; 11:10; Jer. 31:16; 2 Pet. 2:16
RESTRICT Jer. 36:5, I am **r-ed**; I cannot go
RESULT—*work* Eph. 4:14, As a **r** . . . no longer
James 1:4, endurance have *its* perfect **r**
RESURRECTION Matt. 22:23, say there is no **r**
Matt. 22:30, **r** they neither marry, nor
Luke 14:14, at the **r** of the righteous
20:27, who say that there is no **r**
20:36, being sons of the **r**
John 5:29, **r** of life . . . **r** of judgment
11:25, the **r**, and the life
Acts 24:15, **r** of both the righteous and the
24:21, For the **r** of the dead
1 Cor. 15:13, if there is no **r**
Phil. 3:11, attain to the **r**
Heb. 11:35, might obtain a better **r**
1 Pet. 1:3, living hope through the **r**
Rev. 20:5, This is the first **r**
RETAIN John 20:23, **r** the sins of any . . . **r-ed**
RETIRE Ps. 127:2, To **r** late
RETRIBUTION Hos. 9:7, days of **r** have come
Rom. 11:9, STUMBLING BLOCK . . . A R
RETURN—*turn back*
Gen. 43:18, money . . . **r-ed** in our sacks
Deut. 30:2, **r** to the LORD your God
Eccles. 4:9, a good **r** for their labor
Mal. 3:7, **R** to Me, and I will **r** to you
Matt. 10:13, let your . . . peace **r** to you
Luke 2:39, they **r-ed** to Galilee
4:14, **r-ed** . . . in the power of the Spirit
10:17, the seventy **r-ed** with joy
24:9, **r-ed** from the tomb

RETURN *(Continued)*
Acts 3:19, Repent therefore and **r**
1 Tim. 5:4, make some **r** to their parents
1 Pet. 2:25, now you have **r-ed** to the
3:9, not **r-ing** evil for evil
Gen. 3:19; 32:9; Ex. 14:28; Ruth 1:12; 1 Sam. 7:3; 25:21; 2 Sam. 1:22; 1 Kin. 22:17; Job 1:21; 10:21; 33:25; Eccles. 12:2,7; Is. 10:22; 55:11; Jer. 3:22; 4:1; Ezek. 16:55; Dan. 4:36; Matt. 12:44; Acts 13:34

REVEAL—*manifest* Job 20:27, will **r** his iniquity
Is. 40:5, glory of the LORD will be **r-ed**
53:1, arm of the LORD been **r-ed**
Matt. 11:25, didst **r** them to babes
16:17, blood did not **r** *this* to you
Luke 17:30, the Son of Man is **r-ed**
Rom. 8:18, glory that is to be **r-ed** to us
8:19, **r-ing** of the sons of God
1 Cor. 3:13, it is *to be* **r-ed** with fire
Gal. 1:16, to **r** His Son in me
Eph. 3:5, **r-ed** to His holy apostles
2 Thess. 2:3, man of lawlessness is **r-ed**
2:8, lawless one will be **r-ed**
1 Pet. 1:5, be **r-ed** in the last time
1 Sam. 14:8,11; Job 12:22; Prov. 11:13; 25:9; Is. 26:21; Dan. 2:47

REVEL 2 Pet. 2:13, to **r** in the daytime

REVELATION Rom. 16:25, the **r** of the mystery
1 Cor. 1:7, awaiting eagerly the **r**
14:6, speak ... by way of **r**
Gal. 1:12, through a **r** of Jesus Christ
2:2, because of a **r** that I went up
Eph. 1:17, spirit of wisdom and **r**
Rev. 1:1, The **R** of Jesus Christ

REVENGE Jer. 20:10, take our **r** on him
Rom. 12:19, Never take your own **r**

REVERE Lev. 19:30; Zeph. 3:7

REVERENCE—*fear*
Ps. 2:11, Worship the LORD with **r**
5:7, bow in **r** for Thee
Heb. 11:7, in **r** prepared an ark
12:28, service with **r** and awe
Job 15:4; Is. 29:13

REVILE Ps. 74:10, long, will the adversary **r**
Matt. 5:11, when *men* **r** you
Acts 23:4, Do you **r** God's high priest
1 Cor. 4:12, when we are **r-d**, we bless
1 Pet. 2:23, being **r-d**, He did not **r**
4:14, **r-d** for the name of Christ

REVIVE Ps. 119:88, **R** me ... Thy lovingkindness

REWARD—*recompense*
Job 15:31, emptiness will be his **r**
Ps. 58:11, a **r** for the righteous
Prov. 11:18, righteousness *gets* a true **r**
Is. 62:11, His **r** is with Him
Matt. 5:12, your **r** in heaven is great
6:1, no **r** with your Father who
6:2,5,16, have their **r** in full
10:42, shall not lose his **r**
1 Cor. 3:8, will receive his own **r**
Heb. 11:26, he was looking to the **r**
2 John 8, that you may receive a full **r**
Rev. 22:12, My **r** is with Me
Gen. 15:1; Ruth 2:12; Prov. 11:31; Is. 1:23; 45:13

RICH Gen. 13:2, Abram was very **r** in livestock
Jer. 9:23, **r** man boast of his riches
Matt. 19:23, hard for a **r** man to enter
Luke 1:53, sent away the **r** empty-handed
6:24, woe to you who are **r**
16:1, There was a certain **r** man
16:21, *crumbs* ... falling from the **r** man's table
18:23, for he was extremely **r**
1 Cor. 4:8, filled, you have already become **r**
Eph. 2:4, God, being **r** in mercy
Col. 3:16, word of Christ **r-ly** dwell within
1 Tim. 6:18, to be **r** in good works
James 1:11, **r** man ... will fade away
2:6, Is it not the **r** who oppress you
Rev. 13:16, **r** and the poor, and the free
Gen. 49:20; Ex. 30:15; 1 Sam. 2:7; Ps. 49:2; Prov. 10:4; 18:23; Eccles. 10:20

RICHES—*possessions* Prov. 11:4, **R** do not profit in the day
Prov. 22:1, more desired than great **r**
30:8, neither poverty nor **r**
Matt. 13:22, deceitfulness of **r**
Luke 8:14, choked with worries and **r**
Rom. 10:12, abounding in **r** for all who call
Eph. 1:7, **r** of His grace
3:8, unfathomable **r** of Christ
1 Tim. 6:17, hope on the uncertainty of **r**
James 5:2, Your **r** are rotted
1 Kin. 3:11; Job 20:15; 36:19; Ps. 62:10; Prov. 3:16; Jer. 9:23

RIDE 1 Kin. 1:33; Is. 19:1; Ezek. 23:12

RIGHT—*justice, just*
Judg. 17:6, man did what was **r**
Ps. 19:8, precepts of the LORD are **r**
Prov. 14:12, a way *which seems* **r**
Hos. 14:9, ways of the LORD are **r**
Matt. 5:29, **r** eye makes you stumble
22:44, SIT AT MY **R** HAND
26:64, AT THE **R** HAND OF POWER
Mark 5:15, and in his **r** mind
16:19, SAT DOWN AT THE **R** HAND OF GOD
Luke 22:50, cut off his **r** ear
John 1:12, the **r** to become children of God
Acts 8:21, your heart is not **r**
Rom. 9:21, potter have a **r** over the clay
12:17, **r** in the sight of all men
1 Cor. 9:18, full use of my **r** in the
2 Cor. 13:7, you may do what is **r**
Gal. 2:9, **r** hand of fellowship
Phil. 4:8, whatever is **r**
2 Pet. 2:15, forsaking the **r** way
Rev. 22:14, **r** to the tree of life
Gen. 24:48; Ex. 21:10; Deut. 12:25; 21:17; 2 Kin. 10:15; Job 9:2; 34:6; Prov. 24:26; Is. 41:13; Jer. 40:4; Ezek. 18:25,29; 33:17,20

RIGHTEOUS Gen. 6:9, Noah was a **r** man
Ps. 7:9, establish the **r**
Prov. 10:30, **r** will never be shaken
11:28, **r** will flourish
Jer. 23:5, David a **r** Branch
Hab. 2:4, the **r** will live by his faith
Matt. 5:45, rain on *the* **r** and *the* unrighteous
9:13, not come to call *the* **r**
10:41, a **r** man's reward
13:43, **R** WILL SHINE FORTH
25:46, **r** into eternal life
Luke 15:7, ninety-nine **r** persons
23:50, Joseph ... a good and **r** man
John 7:24, with **r** judgment
Acts 7:52, the coming of the **R** One
Rom. 1:17, THE **R** *man* SHALL LIVE BY FAITH
3:10, NONE **R**, NOT EVEN
1 Tim. 1:9, Law ... for a **r** man
James 5:16, prayer of a **r** man can
1 Pet. 4:18, THAT THE **R** IS SAVED
1 John 1:9, **r** to forgive us our sins
2:1, Jesus Christ the **r**
Gen. 18:23; Ex. 9:27; 23:7; 1 Sam. 24:17; Job 9:20; Ps. 1:5; 11:5; 33:1; 37:16; 55:22; 119:75,137; Prov. 2:20; 3:33; 4:18; 13:5; 16:13; 24:16; 28:1; Eccles. 3:17; 7:16; Is. 26:7; 32:1; 53:11; Jer. 33:15; Ezek. 13:22; Dan. 9:14; Amos 2:6

RIGHTEOUSNESS—*judgment, justice*
Ps. 23:3, in the paths of **r**
96:13, judge the world in **r**
97:6, heavens declare His **r**
111:3, His **r** endures forever
Prov. 14:34, **R** exalts a nation
16:8, Better is a little with **r**
Jer. 22:13, builds his house without **r**
23:6, The LORD our **r**
Dan. 12:3, lead the many to **r**
Matt. 3:15, fitting for us to fulfill all **r**
5:6, hunger and thirst for **r**
5:10, persecuted ... sake of **r**
5:20, your **r** surpasses *that*
6:1, your **r** before men
6:33, seek first ... and His **r**

Luke 1:75, holiness and **r** before Him
Rom. 4:3,22; Gal. 3:6, RECKONED TO HIM AS **R**
5:18, through one act of **r**
8:10, spirit is alive ... **r**
2 Cor. 6:14, what partnership have **r** and
Gal. 2:21, if **r** *comes* through Law
Eph. 4:24, created in **r**
6:14, BREASTPLATE OF **R**
1 Tim. 6:11, pursue **r**
2 Tim. 4:8, the crown of **r**
Heb. 7:2, king of **r**
12:11, peaceful fruit of **r**
James 1:20, anger ... not achieve the **r**
1 Pet. 3:14, for the sake of **r**
1 John 3:10, does not practice **r** is not
Gen. 15:6; 18:19; 1 Sam. 26:23; Job 27:6; 29:14; 36:3; Ps. 17:15; 48:10; Prov. 10:2; 11:19; Is. 45:8; 48:18; 51:5; 59:17; 60:17; Jer. 31:23; Ezek. 18:5; 33:13; Hos. 10:12; Mal. 4:2; Acts 13:10

RIPE Gen. 40:10; Jer. 24:2; Joel 3:13; Rev. 14:15,18

RISE Prov. 31:15, She **r-s** also while
Matt. 24:7, nation ... **r** against nation
27:63, I *am* to **r** again
Mark 12:25, when they **r** from the dead
13:12, children will **r** up against parents
16:6, He has **r-n**, He is not here
Luke 5:23, **R** and walk
11:31, Queen of the South shall **r**
12:54, cloud **r-ing** in the west
22:46, **R** and pray that
24:34, Lord has really **r-n**
1 Thess. 4:16, dead in Christ shall **r**
Gen. 19:2; Lev. 19:32; Num. 24:17; Josh. 12:1; Ps. 35:11; 86:14; 113:3; Is. 32:9; 60:1; Jer. 47:2; Matt. 14:2; Luke 16:31

RIVER—*water* Ps. 46:4, a **r** whose streams make glad
Eccles. 1:7, All the **r-s** flow into the sea
Mark 1:5, baptized by him in the Jordan **R**
John 7:38, shall flow **r-s** of living water
2 Cor. 11:26, in dangers from **r-s**
Rev. 22:1, a **r** of the water of life
Gen. 2:10; Josh. 1:4; 24:2; Job 40:23; Ps. 24:2; 66:6; 137:1; Is. 11:15; Lam. 2:18; Ezek. 47:5

ROAD—*way* Luke 19:36, garments in the **r**
Acts 9:27, seen the Lord on the **r**

ROAM Job 1:7, From **r-ing** about on the earth

ROAR 1 Pet. 5:8, devil prowls about like a **r-ing** lion
2 Pet. 3:10, heavens pass away with a **r**
1 Chr. 16:32; Job 4:10; 37:4; Ps. 96:11; Jer. 25:30

ROAST Lev. 2:14, grain **r-ed** in the fire

ROB Prov. 22:22, Do not **r** the poor
Mal. 3:8, Will a man **r** God
2 Cor. 11:8, I **r-ed** other churches
Judg. 9:25; Prov. 17:12; 28:24; Is. 10:2

ROBBER Jer. 7:11, become a den of **r-s**
Matt. 21:13, making it a **r-s'** den
Mark 15:27, crucified two **r-s** with Him
Luke 10:30, he fell among **r-s**
22:52, come out ... as against a **r**
John 10:1, he is a thief and a **r**
18:40, Now Barabbas was a **r**
Acts 19:37, neither **r-s** of temples

ROBBERY Ps. 62:10, do not vainly hope in **r**
Matt. 23:25, full of **r** and self-indulgence
Luke 11:39, full of **r** and wickedness

ROBE—*garment* Is. 61:10, with a **r** of righteousness
Matt. 27:28, put a scarlet **r** on Him
Mark 12:38, walk around in long **r-s**
16:5, young man ... wearing a white **r**
Luke 15:22, bring out the best **r**
20:46, like to walk around in long **r-s**
John 19:2, arrayed Him in a purple **r**
Rev. 1:13, a **r** reaching to the feet
7:14, have washed their **r-s**
19:16, on His **r** and on His thigh
1 Sam. 24:4; Job 1:20; 29:14

ROCK—*stone, strength* Num. 20:11, struck the **r** twice
Ps. 19:14, LORD, my **r** and my redeemer
31:3, Thou art my **r** and my fortress
Matt. 7:24, built his house upon the **r**
13:5, fell upon the **r-y** places
16:18, upon this **r** I will build My church
Mark 15:46, tomb ... hewn out in the **r**
Luke 8:6, other seed fell on **r-y** *soil*
Rom. 9:33, A **R** OF OFFENSE
1 Cor. 10:4, were drinking from a spiritual **r**
Ex. 17:6; 33:22; Deut. 32:4,13; 1 Sam. 2:2; 2 Sam. 22:2; Job 19:24; 28:2; 29:6; Ps. 18:2; 27:5; Prov. 30:19; Is. 8:14; 26:4; 51:1; Jer. 5:3

ROD Ps. 2:9, break them with a **r** of iron
Ps. 23:4, Thy **r** and Thy staff, they comfort
Prov. 13:24, spares his **r** hates his son
2 Cor. 11:25, Three times ... beaten with **r-s**
Heb. 9:4, Aaron's **r** which budded
Rev. 19:15, rule them with a **r** of iron
Gen. 30:37; Num. 17:8; 2 Sam. 7:14; Prov. 26:3; Is. 10:5; Ezek. 20:37; 40:5; 41:8

ROGUE Is. 32:5, **r** be spoken of *as* generous

ROLL Is. 34:4, sky will be **r-ed** up
Matt. 27:60, he **r-ed** a large stone against
28:2, came and **r-ed** away the stone
Is. 22:18; Mark 16:3; Heb. 1:12

ROOF Gen. 19:8; Josh. 2:6; 2 Sam. 11:2; Matt. 8:8; Mark 2:4

ROOM Jer. 22:14, build myself a **r-y** house
Matt. 6:6, GO INTO YOUR INNER **R**
Mark 14:15, large upper **r** furnished
Luke 2:7, no **r** for them in the inn
Acts 1:13, went up to the upper **r**
Gen. 6:14; Judg. 3:24; Prov. 18:16; Matt. 24:26; Rom. 12:19

ROOT Matt. 3:10, axe ... laid at the **r** of the trees
Mark 4:6, it had no **r**, it withered
Rom. 11:16, if the **r** be holy
Eph. 3:17, being **r-ed** and grounded in love
1 Tim. 6:10, money is a **r** of all sorts of evil
Deut. 29:18; Job 5:3; Ps. 80:9; Is. 5:24; 53:2; Jer. 12:2

ROPE Is. 3:24, Instead of a belt, a **r**

ROSE (n.) Song 2:1, I am the **r** of Sharon

ROSE (v.) Josh. 3:16, waters ... **r** up in one heap

ROT—*wither* Is. 19:6, reeds and rushes will **r**
Zech. 14:12, tongue will **r** in their mouth
James 5:2, Your riches have **r-ed**

ROTTEN Matt. 7:17, **r** tree bears bad fruit

ROUND Lev. 19:27, not **r** off the side-growth

ROUGH Prov. 18:23; Is. 40:4

ROUT Judg. 4:15; 8:12; 2 Sam. 22:15; Ps. 18:14

RUBBISH Phil. 3:8, count them but **r**

RUIN—*destruction*
Ex. 9:31, flax ... barley were **r-ed**
Prov. 10:15, **r** of the poor is their poverty
18:7, fool's mouth is his **r**
26:28, flattering mouth works **r**
Song 2:15, foxes that are **r-ing** the vineyards
Luke 6:49, **r** of that house was great
Acts 15:16, WILL REBUILD ITS **R-S**
Job 2:3; Ps. 74:3; Prov. 10:14,29; 14:28; Is. 23:13; 61:4; Lam. 2:13

RULE Judg. 8:22, **R** over us
Job 34:30, godless men should not **r**
Rom. 15:12, TO **R** OVER THE GENTILES
Gal. 6:16, will walk by this **r**
Eph. 1:21, far above all **r** and authority
Col. 3:15, peace of Christ **r** in your hearts
Rev. 2:27, **R** THEM WITH A ROD OF IRON
Gen. 1:26; Ps. 8:6; 49:14; Prov. 8:16; 16:32; Is. 3:12; 26:13

RULER Ex. 22:28, nor curse a **r** of your people
Matt. 2:6, SHALL COME FORTH A **R**, WHO WILL SHEPHERD
9:34, **r** of the demons
Mark 10:42, **r-s** of the Gentiles
John 3:1, Nicodemus, a **r** of the Jews
12:31, **r** of this world shall be cast out

RULER *(Continued)*
Acts 7:27, WHO MADE YOU A R AND JUDGE
Eph. 6:12, struggle is ... against the **r-s**
Titus 3:1, Remind them to be subject to **r-s**
Gen. 42:6; Ps. 2:2; Prov. 6:7; 29:12; Is. 22:3
RUMOR Matt. 24:6, wars and **r-s** of wars
Ex. 23:1; Ezek. 7:26
RUN Prov. 1:16, their feet **r** to evil
Is. 40:31, **r** and not get tired
1 Cor. 9:24, those who **r** in a race all **r**
Gal. 5:7, You were **r-ing** well
Heb. 12:1, let us **r** with endurance the race
Gen. 49:22; Lev. 15:13; 2 Kin. 4:22; Ps. 18:29; 19:5; Prov. 6:18; Ezek. 32:14; Gal. 2:2
RUSH Matt. 8:32, herd **r-ed** down the steep
Rev. 9:9, many horses **r-ing** to battle
RUSHES—*reeds* Job 8:11; Is. 19:6
RUST Matt. 6:19, moth and **r** destroy
James 5:3, Your gold and your silver have **r-ed**
RUTHLESS—*terrible*
Ezek. 28:7, most **r** of the nations

S

SABBATH Ex. 20:8, Remember the **s** day
Lev. 25:8, count off seven **s-s** of years
Matt. 12:8, is Lord of the **S**
28:1, Now late on the **S**
Mark 2:27, **S** was made for man
3:4, on the **S** to do good
John 19:31, that **S** was a high *day*
Acts 1:12, a **S** day's journey away
Ex. 16:26; 20:11; 31:15; 35:3; Lev. 26:2; Num. 15:32; Deut. 5:12; 2 Kin. 4:23
SACKCLOTH Matt. 11:21, repented ... in **s**
Rev. 6:12, sun became black as **s** *made* of hair
Esth. 4:1; Job 16:15; Dan. 9:3
SACRED 2 Kin. 12:18, Joash ... took all the **s** things
2 Tim. 3:15, have known the **s** writings
SACRIFICE Ps. 51:17, **s-s** of God are a broken
Matt. 9:13, COMPASSION, AND NOT **S**
Rom. 12:1, bodies a living and holy **s**
1 Cor. 8:1, things **s-d** to idols
10:20, they **s** to demons
Phil. 4:18, an acceptable **s**, well pleasing
Heb. 9:26, put away sin by the **s** of
11:4, a better **s** than Cain
13:16, such **s-s** God is pleased
Gen. 31:54; Ex. 12:27; Prov. 15:8; Is. 43:23; Dan. 11:31; Hos. 6:6; Acts 7:41
SAD—*sore* Prov. 15:13, when the heart is **s**
Is. 59:11, And moan **s-ly** like doves
Neh. 2:2; Luke 24:17
SADDLE Gen. 31:34, the camel's **s**
SAFE Job 21:9, houses are **s** from fear
Luke 15:27, received him back **s** and sound
Acts 27:43, centurion ... bring Paul **s-ly**
Phil. 3:1, it is a **s-guard** for you
SAFETY Ezek. 39:6, inhabit the coastlands in **s**
SAIL Acts 28:13, from there we **s-ed** around
SAINT Matt. 27:52, bodies of the **s-s** ... were raised
Acts 26:10, lock up ... **s-s** in prisons
Rom. 1:7, called *as* **s-s**
8:27, He intercedes for the **s-s**
1 Cor. 6:2, **s-s** will judge the world
Eph. 2:19, fellow-citizens with the **s-s**
Phil. 1:1, all the **s-s** in Christ Jesus
1 Thess. 3:13, Lord Jesus with all His **s-s**
Rev. 14:12, perseverance of the **s-s**
20:9, the camp of the **s-s**
SAKE Ps. 23:3, For His name's **s**
Ps. 44:22, for Thy **s** we are killed
Is. 42:21, for His righteousness' **s**
Matt. 16:25, loses his life for My **s**
Mark 13:20, for the **s** of the elect
Luke 6:22, the **s** of the Son of Man
18:29, for the **s** of the kingdom of God
Rom. 8:36, THY **S** WE ARE ... PUT TO DEATH
13:5, for conscience' **s**
1 Cor. 9:23, for the **s** of the gospel
2 Cor. 8:9, for your **s** He became poor
Phil. 1:29, for Christ's **s** ... suffer for his **s**
1 Tim. 5:23, wine for the **s** of your stomach
Titus 1:11, for the **s** of sordid gain
2 John 2, for the **s** of the truth
SALT Gen. 19:26, became a pillar of **s**
Matt. 5:13, You are the **s** of the earth
Mark 9:50, **S** is good
Col. 4:6, seasoned, *as it were,* with **s**
James 3:12, *can* **s** water produce fresh
Judg. 9:45; Job 6:6
SALVATION Ps. 3:8, **S** belongs to the LORD
Ps. 27:1, LORD is my light and my **s**
62:1, From Him is my **s**
85:9, **s** is near to those who fear Him
98:3, seen the **s** of our God
Is. 59:17, helmet of **s** on His head
Luke 1:71, **S** FROM OUR ENEMIES
2:30, mine eyes have seen Thy **s**
3:6, FLESH SHALL SEE THE **S** OF GOD
19:9, **s** has come to this house
Acts 4:12, is **s** in no one else
13:26, word of this **s** is sent out
16:17, proclaiming to you the way of **s**
Rom. 1:16, power of God for **s**
11:11, **s** *has come* to the Gentiles
2 Cor. 6:2, ON THE DAY OF **S**
7:10, repentance ... *leading* to **s**
Eph. 6:17, take the helmet of **s**
Phil. 2:12, work out your **s** with fear
1 Thess. 5:9, obtaining **s** through our Lord
2 Tim. 3:15, wisdom that leads to **s**
Titus 2:11, grace of God ... bringing **s**
Heb. 1:14, who will inherit **s**
2:3, if we neglect so great a **s**
9:28, not to bear sin ... for **s**
1 Pet. 1:5, through faith for a **s**
2 Pet. 3:15, patience of our Lord *to be* **s**
Rev. 7:10, **S** to our God who sits
12:10, Now the **s**, and the power
Gen. 49:18; Ex. 15:2; Deut. 32:15; Job 13:16; Ps. 116:13; 119:155; Is. 12:3; 33:2; 49:6; 51:6; 52:7; 56:1; Jon. 2:9; Zech. 9:9
SAME Ps. 102:27, But Thou art the **s**
Matt. 5:46, even the tax gatherers do the **s**
Luke 2:8, in the **s** region ... shepherds
23:40, under the **s** sentence of
Rom. 10:12, **s** *Lord* is Lord of all
1 Cor. 12:4, of gifts, but the **s** Spirit
Heb. 13:8, Christ ... **s** yesterday and today
SANCTIFY Lev. 22:32, I am the LORD who **s-es**
John 10:36, whom the Father **s-ed**
17:17, **S** them in the truth
Rom. 15:16, **s-ed** by the Holy Spirit
1 Cor. 6:11, washed, but you were **s-ed**
7:14, wife is **s-ed** ... believing husband
1 Thess. 5:23, God of peace ... **s** you entirely
Heb. 2:11, who **s-es** and those who are **s-ed**
Gen. 2:3; Ex. 13:2; Is. 29:23; Ezek. 20:20; 44:24
SANCTITY 1 Tim. 2:15, faith and love and **s**
SANCTUARY Ps. 150:1, Praise God in His **s**
Is. 60:13, beautify the place of My **s**
Heb. 8:2, a minister in the **s**
Ex. 25:8; Lev. 19:30; Ps. 73:17; Amos 7:13
SAND Gen. 32:12, descendants as the **s** of the sea
Matt. 7:26, built his house upon the **s**
Heb. 11:12, **S** ... BY THE SEASHORE
Deut. 33:19; Job 29:18; Prov. 27:3
SANDAL Matt. 3:11, fit to remove His **s-s**
Matt. 10:10, tunics, or **s-s**, or
Ex. 12:11; Deut. 29:5; Amos 2:6; Mark 1:7; Acts 7:33
SANK Gen. 42:28, their hearts **s**
SAPPHIRE—*lapis lazuli* Ex. 28:18; Song 5:14; Rev. 21:19
SASH Ex. 28:40; 29:9
SAT Mark 16:19, **S** DOWN AT THE RIGHT HAND OF GOD
Luke 7:15, the dead man **s** up
Ex. 2:15; 16:3; Jon. 4:5; Mark 11:2

SATAN Matt. 4:10, Begone, **S**
Matt. 12:26, **S** casts out **S**
16:23, Get behind Me, **S**
Mark 1:13, forty days being tempted by **S**
Luke 10:18, watching **S** fall from heaven
22:3, **S** entered into Judas
Acts 5:3, why has **S** filled your heart
Rom. 16:20, crush **S** under your feet
2 Cor. 2:11, no advantage . . . of us by **S**
1 Thess. 2:18, *yet* **S** thwarted us
1 Tim. 1:20, I have delivered over to **S**
Rev. 3:9, *those* of the synagogue of **S**
12:9, called the Devil and **S**
20:7, **S** . . . released from his prison
Job 1:6; Zech. 3:2
SATIATE Is. 34:5, My sword is **s-d**
SATISFY Ps. 22:26, afflicted shall eat and be **s-ed**
Ps. 91:16, with long life I will **s** him
Mark 8:4, **s** these men with bread
Gen. 25:8; Lev. 26:26; Esth. 5:13; Job 21:23; 27:14; 38:27; Ps. 78:30; Prov. 6:30; 27:20; Is. 29:8; Joel 2:26; Mark 15:15
SATYR—*demon* 2 Chr. 11:15, he set up priests . . . for the **s-s**
SAVE—*deliver, escape, except*
Ps. 6:4, **S** me because of Thy lovingkindness
86:2, **s** Thy servant who trusts in Thee
Is. 35:4, God will come . . . He will **s** you
45:22, Turn to Me, and be **s-d**
63:1, mighty to **s**
Jer. 8:20, summer is ended . . . we are not **s-d**
Matt. 1:21, **s** His people from their sins
10:22, who has endured . . . will be **s-d**
16:25, **s** his life shall lose it
18:11, come to **s** that which is lost
19:25, Then who can be **s-d**
Mark 3:4, to **s** a life or to kill
13:13, one who has endured . . . will be **s-d**
16:16, been baptized shall be **s-d**
Luke 7:50, Your faith has **s-d** you; go in peace
23:35, let Him **s** Himself if . . . the Christ
John 3:17, world should be **s-d** through Him
10:9, enters through Me, he shall be **s-d**
12:27, Father, **s** Me from this hour
Acts 4:12, by which we must be **s-d**
16:30, what must I do to be **s-d**
Rom. 5:10, we shall be **s-d** by His life
8:24, in hope we have been **s-d**
1 Cor. 7:16, **s** your husband . . . **s** your wife
16:2, each . . . put aside and **s**
Eph. 2:5, by grace you have been **s-d**
1 Tim. 1:15, into the world to **s** sinners
2 Tim. 1:9, who has **s-d** us, and called us
James 1:21, able to **s** your souls
4:12, able to **s** and to destroy
1 Pet. 4:18, WITH DIFFICULTY . . . RIGHTEOUS **S-D**
Deut. 28:29; 33:29; 1 Sam. 14:6; Job 22:29; Ps. 28:9; 44:7; 60:5; Prov. 20:22; Jer. 30:10; 42:11; Ezek. 18:27; Amos 2:14; Acts 28:4
SAVIOR 2 Sam. 22:3, My **s**, Thou dost save me
Ps. 106:21, forgot God their **S**
Is. 19:20, He will send them a **S**
43:11, there is no **s** besides Me
45:21, a righteous God and a **S**
49:26, know that I, the LORD, am your **S**
Luke 2:11, a **S**, who is Christ the Lord
John 4:42, One is indeed the **S** of the world
Acts 5:31, as a Prince and a **S**
Eph. 5:23, He Himself *being* the **S** of the body
1 Tim. 4:10, God, who is the **S** of all men
2 Tim. 1:10, appearing of our **S** Christ Jesus
Titus 2:13, God and **S**, Christ Jesus
2 Pet. 1:11, our Lord and **S** Jesus Christ
1 John 4:14, sent the Son *to be* the **S**
SAW Gen. 1:4, God **s** that the light was good
Matt. 2:2, **s** His star in the east
2:11, **s** the Child with Mary
Mark 1:10, **s** the heavens opening
John 1:48, under the fig tree, I **s** you
Num. 22:23; Job 29:11; Eccles. 2:13; Is. 59:16; Dan. 4:5

SAY—*speak* Ps. 106:48, let all the people **s**,
Matt. 7:22, Many will **s** to Me on that day
16:13, Who do people **s** . . . Son of Man is
Luke 7:40, Simon, I have something to **s** to you
17:21, nor will they **s**, Look, here *it is*
1 John 1:8, If we **s** that we have no sin
Rev. 22:17, Spirit and the bride **s**, Come
Gen. 20:13; Ex. 3:13; Deut. 9:4; Job 33:32; 37:19; Prov. 3:28; 30:15; Is.58:9
SAYING Gen. 37:11; Ps. 78:2; Luke 18:34
SCALE Prov. 20:23, a false **s** is not good
Is. 40:15, as a speck of dust on the **s-s**
Amos 8:5, to cheat with dishonest **s-s**
Mic. 6:11, Can I justify wicked **s-s**
Rev. 6:5, a pair of **s-s** in his hand
Job 31:6; Is. 40:12; 46:6; Jer. 32:10
SCALE-ARMOR Jer. 46:4; 51:3
SCARCE—*want*
Ezek. 4:17, bread and water will be **s**
Is. 13:12; Luke 9:39
SCARLET Is. 1:18, Though your sins are as **s**
Matt. 27:28, put a **s** robe on Him
Rev. 17:3, woman sitting on a **s** beast
Gen. 38:28; Ex. 25:4; Josh. 2:18; Song 4:3; Jer. 4:30; Nah. 2:3
SCATTER
Ps. 92:9, All who do iniquity will be **s-ed**
Matt. 21:44, it will **s** him like dust
26:31, the flock shall be **s-ed**
Lev. 26:33; Job 18:15; 38:24; Ps. 141:7; Prov. 11:24; Is. 41:16; Jer. 23:1
SCENT Job 39:25, he **s-s** the battle from afar
SCHEME Esth. 8:3; Job 5:5; Ps. 37:7; Dan. 11:24,25; Mic. 2:1; 2 Cor. 2:11
SCOFF Ps. 2:4, The Lord **s-s** at them
Luke 16:14, the Pharisees . . . were **s-ing** at Him
SCOFFER Acts 13:41, BEHOLD, YOU **S-S**, AND MARVEL
SCORCH Jer. 4:11, A **s-ing** wind from the bare heights
SCORN Deut. 32:15; Prov. 30:17; Ezek. 25:6,15; 36:5
SCOURGE Job 5:21, hidden from the **s** of the tongue
Matt. 10:17, **s** you in their synagogues
20:19, mock and **s** and crucify Him
27:26, but Jesus he **s-d**
John 2:15, He made a **s** of cords
Heb. 12:6, **S-S** EVERY SON WHOM HE RECEIVES
SCRIBE Matt. 2:4, chief priests and **s-s** of the people
Matt. 23:13, Woe to you, **s-s** and Pharisees
Mark 1:22, authority, and not as **s-s**
12:38, Beware of the **s-s**
1 Cor. 1:20, Where is the **s**
Neh. 8:4; Jer. 8:8
SCRIPTURE(S), *writing*
Matt. 21:42, Did you never read in the **S-s**
22:29, not understanding the **S-s**
Mark 14:49, that the **S-s** might be fulfilled
Luke 4:21, Today this **S** has been fulfilled
24:32, He was explaining the **S-s** to us
John 5:39, You search the **S-s**
10:35, the **S** cannot be broken
20:9, they did not understand the **S**
Acts 18:24, he was mighty in the **S-s**
Rom. 4:3, For what does the **S** say
15:4, encouragement of the **S-s**
2 Tim. 3:16, All **S** is inspired by God
SCROLL—*roll* Jer. 36:2, Take a **s** and write
Ezek. 3:1, eat this **s**, and go
Zech. 5:1, behold, *there was* a flying **s**
SEA Gen. 1:10, He called **s-s**
Gen. 1:26, rule over the fish of the **s**
Ex. 10:19, drove them into the Red **S**
Ps. 24:2, founded it upon the **s-s**
107:23, down to the **s** in ships
146:6, The **s** and all that is in them
Is. 57:20, wicked are like the tossing **s**
Matt. 8:26, rebuked the winds and the **s**
14:26, saw Him walking on the **s**

SEA *(Continued)*
Rev. 4:6, **s** of glass like crystal
21:1, There is no longer *any* **s**
2 Sam. 17:11; Job 7:12; 38:8; Ps. 65:5; Is. 11:9; Jer. 25:22; Nah. 1:4; 2 Cor. 11:26
SEAL—*shut* Dan. 12:4, **s** up the book ... end of time
Rom. 4:11, **s** of the righteous of the faith
2 Cor. 1:22, who also **s-ed** us
Eph. 1:13, **s-ed** in Him with the Holy Spirit
Rev. 5:1, **s-ed** up with seven **s-s**
9:4, **s** of God on their foreheads
1 Kin. 21:8; Job 14:17; Song 4:12; 8:6; Is. 29:11; Jer. 32:10; Dan. 9:24; 12:4
SEA MONSTER Ps. 148:7; Matt. 12:40
SEARCH 1 Chr. 28:9, LORD **s-es** all hearts
Job 28:3, to the farthest limit he **s-es** out
Ps. 139:23, **S** me ... know my heart
Prov. 20:27, **S-ing** all the innermost parts
Jer. 17:10, I, the LORD, **s** the heart
Matt. 2:8, make careful **s** for the Child
2:13, Herod is going to **s**
John 5:39, You **s** the Scriptures, because
7:52, **S**, and see that no prophet arises
2 Tim. 1:17, he eagerly **s-ed** for me
Judg. 5:16; 1 Sam. 26:20; 1 Kin. 1:3
SEASON—*times* Ps. 1:3, yields its fruit in its **s**
Ps. 104:27, their food in due **s**
Luke 14:34, with what will it be **s-ed**
Gal. 4:10, observe days ... **s-s** and years
Col. 4:6, with grace, **s-ed**, *as it were,* with salt
2 Tim. 4:2, ready in **s** *and* out of **s**
Gen. 1:14; Lev. 26:4; Job 5:26
SEAT—*sat* Ps. 1:1, Nor sit in the **s** of the scoffers
Matt. 23:6, chief **s-s** in the synagogues
27:19, sitting on the judgment **s**
Luke 10:39, Mary ... **s-ed** at His feet
Rom. 14:10, the judgment **s** of God
Ex. 25:17; 1 Sam. 4:18; Ezek. 28:2
SECOND Matt. 22:39, And a **s** is like it
1 Cor. 15:47, the **s** man is from heaven
Rev. 2:11, not be hurt by the **s** death
Gen. 1:8; Ezek. 10:14
SECRET Ps. 44:21, knows the **s-s** of the heart
Prov. 9:17, bread *eaten* in **s** is pleasant
21:14, gift in **s** subdues anger
Matt. 6:4, your alms may be in **s**
6:6,18, your Father who is in **s**
Rom. 2:16, God will judge the **s-s**
16:25, kept **s** for long ages past
Deut. 27:15; Job 11:6; 15:8; Song 2:14; Is. 45:3,19; Hab. 3:14
SECRETLY Josh. 2:1, two men as spies **s**
Judg. 4:21, went **s** to him
Matt. 1:19, Joseph ... put her away **s**
2:7, Then Herod **s** called the
John 11:28, called Mary her sister, saying **s**
Deut. 13:6; Job 13:10; 31:27
SECURE—*sure* Prov. 3:23, walk in your way **s-ly**
Matt. 27:66, made the grave **s**
Acts 16:23, the jailer to guard them **s-ly**
Lev. 26:5; Ezek. 34:27
SECURITY Judg. 18:7, living in **s**
SEDUCES—*entice* Ex. 22:16, if a man **s** a virgin
SEE—*perceive* Ex. 33:20, no man can **s** Me and live
Job 19:26, without my flesh I shall **s** God
Ps. 16:10, allow Thy Holy One to **s** the pit
34:8, **s** that the LORD is good
66:5, Come and **s** the works of God
115:5, eyes, but they cannot **s**
Is. 35:2, **s** the glory of the LORD
62:2, nations will **s** your righteousness
Joel 2:28, young men will **s** visions
Matt. 5:16, may **s** your good works
11:8, what did you go out to **s**
16:28, **s** the Son of Man coming
Luke 2:26, would not **s** death before
8:10, **S-ING THEY MAY NOT S**
John 4:29, **s** a man who told me
7:52, Search, and **s** that no prophet
12:19, **s** that you are not doing any good
16:16, little while, and you will **s** Me
1 Cor. 13:12, now we **s** in a mirror dimly
Heb. 12:14, no one will **s** the Lord
1 John 3:2, we shall **s** Him just as He is
Ex. 10:23; Num 14:23; 24:17; Job 6:28; 9:11; 24:15; 34:32; Ps. 36:9; 49:19; Eccles. 6:9; Song 7:12; Is. 29:18; Ezek. 12:2
SEED—*descendant, offspring*
Gen. 8:22, **S-time** and harvest
Matt. 13:22, **s** was sown among the thorns
13:31, heaven is like a mustard **s**
Luke 8:5, sower went out to sow his **s**
8:11, the **s** is the word of God
1 Pet. 1:23, not of **s** which is perishable
Gen. 1:11; Lev. 19:19; 26:16; Eccles. 11:6; Is. 55:10; Hag. 2:19
SEEK—*desire, search* 2 Chr. 7:14, pray, and **s** My face
Ps. 24:6, generation of those who **s** Him
34:14, **S** peace and pursue it
63:1, I shall **s** Thee earnestly
119:2, **s** Him with all *their* heart
Prov. 8:17, who diligently **s** me will find me
Is. 55:6, **S** the LORD while He may be found
Jer. 29:13, you will **s** Me and find *Me*
Amos 5:4, **S** Me that you may live
Matt. 6:33, **s** first His kingdom
7:7, **s**, and you shall find
12:46, His brothers were ... **s-ing** to speak
Mark 8:12, this generation **s** for a sign
Luke 11:10, he who **s-s** finds
John 1:38, What do you **s**
5:30, I do not **s** My own will
8:50, One who **s-s** and judges
1 Cor. 10:24, Let no one **s** his own *good*
13:5, it does not **s** its own
Phil. 4:17, Not that I **s** the gift ... I **s** for the profit
Col. 3:1, keep **s-ing** the things above
Deut. 4:29; 2 Chr. 16:12; Job 7:21; Eccles. 7:25; Is. 34:16; Ezek. 7:25; 34:16; Dan. 9:3; Hos. 10:12; Amos 5:14; Gal. 1:10
SEEM—*appear* Gen. 29:20; Prov. 14:12
SEEN—*appeared* Gen. 9:14, bow shall be **s** in the cloud
Is. 6:5, my eyes have **s** the King
Luke 2:30, eyes have **s** Thy salvation
John 1:18, no man has **s** God at any time
Rom. 8:24, hope that is not **s** is not hope
1 Cor. 2:9, EYE HAS NOT **S**
Heb. 11:1, conviction of things not **s**
Gen. 32:30; Job 5:3; 38:22
SEIZE—*take* John 7:30, seeking ... to **s** Him
Jer. 50:24; Mic. 2:2
SELECT Acts 6:3, **s** from among you ... seven men
SELF Rom. 6:6, our old **s** was crucified
Col. 3:9, laid aside the old **s**
SELF-ABASEMENT Col. 2:18, delighting in **s**
Col. 2:23, wisdom in self-made religion and **s**
SELF-CONTROL Acts 24:25, righteousness, **s**, and the judgment
Gal. 5:23, gentleness, **s**
SELFISH Phil. 2:3, do nothing from **s-ness**
James 3:14,16, jealousy and **s** ambition
SELL Prov. 23:23, Buy truth, and do not **s** *it*
Matt. 19:21, go *and* **s** your possessions
Gen. 25:31; Lev. 25:29; Deut. 2:28; 2 Kin. 4:7
SEND—*cast* Is. 6:8, Whom shall I **s** ... Here
Matt. 5:45, **s-s** rain on *the* righteous
9:38, **s** out workers into His harvest
1 Cor. 7:13, let her not **s** her husband away
16:11, **s** him on his way in peace
2 Thess. 2:11, **s** ... a deluding influence
Gen. 7:4; 24:7; Num. 13:2; Job 5:10; 38:35
SENSELESS—*stupid* Ps. 49:10, stupid and the **s** alike perish
Ps. 92:6, **s** man has no knowledge
SENSIBLE Tit. 2:5, *to be* **s**, pure, workers at home
SENSUAL Ezek. 33:32, like a **s** song
SENSUALITY Eph. 4:19, given ... over to **s**
Rev. 18:3, rich by the wealth of her **s**

SENSUOUS Rev. 18:7, she ... lived **s-ly**
SENT Is. 61:1, He has **s** me to bind up the broken-hearted
Matt. 10:5, These twelve Jesus **s** out after
Luke 4:18, He has **s** Me to proclaim release
Acts 13:4, So, being **s** out by the Holy Spirit
Gal. 4:4, God **s** forth His Son
1 Pet. 1:12, Holy Spirit **s** from heaven
1 John 4:9, that God has **s** His only begotten
Gen. 8:7,8; Is. 48:16
SENTENCE—*condemnation*
Matt. 23:33, escape the **s** of hell
SEPARATE—*divide* Gen. 1:4, God **s-d** the light
Prov. 16:28, a slanderer **s-s** intimate friends
Matt. 19:6, let no man **s**
25:32, He will **s** them from one another
Rom. 8:35, Who shall **s** us from the love
Gen. 13:9; Lev. 20:24; Job 41:17; Ps. 22:7
SERIOUS Acts 25:7, **s** charges against him
SERPENT Gen. 3:1, Now the **s** was more crafty
Num. 21:9, Moses made a bronze **s**
Ps. 58:4, venom of a **s**
Matt. 10:16, be shrewd as **s-s**
Mark 16:18, they will pick up **s-s**
John 3:14, Moses lifted up the **s** in the wilderness
2 Cor. 11:3, lest as the **s** deceived Eve
Rev. 12:9, the **s** of old who is called the devil
Gen. 49:17; Ex. 7:12; Deut. 32:33; Ps. 91:13; Prov. 23:32; Is. 30:6; Jer. 8:17
SERVANT—*minister* Job 1:8, have you considered My **s** Job
Ps. 31:16, face to shine upon Thy **s**
Matt. 20:26, shall be your **s**
Luke 1:2, and **s-s** of the Word
2 Cor. 3:6, **s-s** of a new covenant
11:23, Are they **s-s** of Christ
1 Tim. 4:6, be a good **s** of Christ Jesus
Gen. 9:25; Ex. 14:31; Ruth 2:9; 1 Sam. 3:9; Ezra 7:24; Job 4:18; Prov. 11:29; Joel 2:29
SERVE—*worship, minister*
Ps. 100:2, **S** the LORD with gladness
Matt. 4:10, GOD, AND **S** HIM ONLY
6:24, No one can **s** two masters
20:28, not come to be **s-d**, but to **s**
John 12:26, If any one **s-s** Me, let him
Acts 24:14, I do **s** the God of our fathers
Rom. 7:6, so that we **s** in newness of the Spirit
12:11, fervent in spirit, **s-ing** the Lord
Gal. 5:13, through love **s** one another
1 Tim. 3:10, let them **s** as deacons
Josh. 22:5; 1 Chr. 6:10; 24:2; Jer. 5:19
SERVICE—*ministry*
Rom. 12:1, *which* is your spiritual **s**
Eph. 4:12, for the work of **s**
Phil. 2:30, was deficient in your **s** to me
Heb. 12:28, offer to God an acceptable **s**
Is. 32:17; Jer. 22:13
SET Gen. 9:13, I **s** my bow in the cloud
Ex. 2:3, she ... **s** it among the reeds
Deut. 30:19, I have **s** before you life and death
Ps. 40:2, He **s** my feet upon a rock
Matt. 5:14, A city **s** on a hill cannot
Col. 3:2, **S** your mind on the things above
James 3:6, and is **s** on fire by hell
Lev. 17:10; Prov. 9:2; Eccles. 10:6; Is. 3:24; 38:1; Jer. 5:26; Ezek. 2:2
SETTING Prov. 25:11, apples of gold in **s-s** of silver
SETTLE—*reckon* Matt. 25:19, came and **s-d** accounts with them
Deut. 21:5; Nah. 3:17
SEVEN Gen. 29:20, Jacob served **s** years for Rachel
Ps. 119:164, **S** times a day I praise Thee
Is. 4:1, For **s** women will take hold of one man
Matt. 12:45, along with it **s** other spirits
18:21, forgive him? Up to **s** times
Acts 6:3, **s** men of good reputation
Rev. 1:4, John to the **s** churches
1:12, I saw **s** golden lampstands
3:1, He who has the **s** Spirits of God
15:1, **s** angels who had **s** plagues
Gen. 21:29; Prov. 9:1; Eccles. 11:2; Dan. 9:25; Zech. 4:2
SEVERE—*great* Matt. 28:2, a **s** earthquake
Song 8:6; Ezek. 34:4
SHACK Is. 24:20, it totters like a **s**
SHACKLES Mark 5:4, the **s** broken in pieces
SHADOW 2 Kin. 20:11, **s** on the stairway back ten steps
Ps. 17:8, Hide me in the **s** of Thy wings
23:4, valley of the **s** of death
91:1, abide in the **s** of the Almighty
Col. 2:17, a *mere* **s** of what is to come
Heb. 8:5, copy and **s** of the heavenly things
James 1:17, no variation, or shifting **s**
1 Chr. 29:15; Song 2:17
SHAKE—*tremble*
Prov. 10:30, righteous ... never be **s-n**
Is. 13:13, earth ... **s-n** from its place
Matt. 10:14, **s** off the dust of your feet
11:7, A reed **s-n** by the wind
Luke 6:38, pressed down, **s-n** together
Job 4:14; 16:4; Ps. 109:23
SHAME Acts 5:41, worthy to suffer **s**
2 Cor. 4:2, things hidden because of **s**
Phil. 3:19, glory is in their **s**
1 John 2:28, not shrink ... Him in **s**
Prov. 19:26; Is. 54:4; Zeph. 3:5
SHARE—*portion* Luke 15:12, **s** of the estate
1 Cor. 10:16, a **s-ing** in the blood of Christ
10:20, to become **s-rs** in demons
Gal. 6:6, **s** ... with him who teaches
1 Tim. 6:18, ready to **s**
Heb. 13:16, doing good and **s-ing**
SHARP Deut. 32:41, **s-en** My flashing sword
Ps. 57:4, tongue a **s** sword
64:3, **s-ened** their tongue
Prov. 5:4, **S** as a two-edged sword
27:17, Iron **s-ens** iron
Eccles. 10:10, does not **s-en** *its* edge
Heb. 4:12, **s-er** than any two-edged sword
SHATTER Ex. 15:6; Ps. 2:9
SHAVE Gen. 41:14; Judg. 16:19; 2 Sam. 10:4; Is. 7:20; 1 Cor. 11:6
SHEAR Deut. 18:4, first **s-ing** of your sheep
SHED—*pour* Matt. 26:28, My blood ... **s** on behalf of many
Rom. 3:15, feet are swift to **s** blood
Gen. 9:6; Prov. 1:16
SHEEP—*flock* Ps. 44:22, a **s** to be slaughtered
Ps. 100:3, the **s** of his pasture
119:176, astray like a lost **s**
Is. 53:6, All of us like **s** have gone astray
53:7, **s** ... silent before its shearers
Matt. 9:36, **s** without a shepherd
10:16, I send you out as **s**
15:24, lost **s** of the house of Israel
25:32, separates the **s** from the goats
26:31, **s** of the flock ... scattered
Luke 15:6, found my **s** which was lost
John 10:3, calls his own **s** by name
10:7, I am the door of the **s**
10:27, My **s** hear My voice
21:16, Shepherd My **s**
Heb. 13:20, great Shepherd of the **s**
1 Pet. 2:25, straying like **s**
Gen. 29:9; Num. 27:17; 1 Sam. 15:14; Job 31:20; Jer. 12:3; 50:6
SHEKELS—*piece* Gen. 23:16; Zech. 11:12
SHELTER Ps. 5:11, mayest Thou **s** them
Ps. 61:4, refuge in the **s** of Thy wings
Gen. 19:8; Is. 1:8; 4:6; 32:2; Jon. 4:5
SHEOL Deut. 32:22, burns to the lowest ... of **S**
Job 17:13, look for **S** as my home
26:6, Naked is **S** before Him
Ps. 16:10, not abandon my soul to **S**
30:3, brought up my soul from **S**
49:15, redeem ... from the power of **S**
86:13, my soul from the depths of **S**
139:8, If I make my bed in **S**

SHEOL *(Continued)*
Prov. 5:5, Her steps lay hold of **S**
Ezek. 32:21, speak ... from the midst of **S**
Amos 9:2, Though they dig into **S**
Jon. 2:2, help from the depth of **S**
2 Sam. 22:6; Prov. 27:20; Song 8:6; Hab. 2:5
SHEPHERD (n.)—*pastor*
Ps. 23:1, The LORD is my **s**
28:9, Be their **s** also
Is. 40:11, Like a **s** He will tend His flock
Jer. 3:15, I will give you **s-s**
23:1, **s-s** who are destroying ... the sheep
Zech. 11:16, I am going to raise up a **s**
Matt. 9:36, like sheep without a **s**
26:31, I will strike down the **s**
Luke 2:8, **s-s** staying out in the fields
John 10:11, I am the good **s**
Heb. 13:20, the great **S** of the sheep
1 Pet. 2:25, returned to the **S** and Guardian
5:4, when the Chief **S** appears
Rev. 7:17, the Lamb ... shall be their **s**
Gen. 46:34; 48:15; Num. 27:17; 1 Sam. 17:40; Jer. 10:21; Ezek. 34:5; 37:24; Zeph. 2:6
SHEPHERD (v.)—*fed* Ps. 78:72, David **s-ed**
Matt. 2:6, WHO WILL **S** MY PEOPLE
John 21:16, **S** My sheep
Acts 20:28, to **s** the church of God
1 Pet. 5:2, **s** the flock of God
SHIELD Ps. 18:2, My **s** and the horn of my salvation
Ps. 28:7, my strength and my **s**
91:4, His faithfulness is a **s**
Eph. 6:16, taking up the **s** of faith
Gen. 15:1; 2 Sam. 22:3,31; Ps. 7:10; 89:18; Prov. 2:7
SHINE Num. 6:25, make His face **s** on you
Job 9:7, sun not to **s**
41:32, Behind him ... a wake to **s**
Prov. 4:18, **s-s** brighter and brighter
Is. 60:1, Arise, **s**; for your light has come
Matt. 5:16, Let your light **s** before men
13:43, RIGHTEOUS WILL **S** FORTH
John 1:5, light **s-s** in the darkness
2 Pet. 1:19, a lamp **s-ing** in a dark place
1 John 2:8, true light is already **s-ing**
SHOCK Deut. 1:29, Do not be **s-ed**, nor fear them
SHONE Luke 2:9, glory of the Lord **s** around
Ex. 34:29; 2 Kin. 3:22
SHOOK Neh. 5:13, also **s** out ... my garment
Acts 28:5, he **s** the creature off
Heb. 12:26, His voice **s** the earth
SHOOT Is. 11:1, a **s** will spring from ... Jesse
Is. 53:2, grew up ... like a tender **s**
1 Sam. 20:20; Ps. 11:2; 64:4
SHORT Rom. 3:23, fall **s** of the glory of God
1 Cor. 7:29, time has been **s-ened**
SHOT 1 Sam. 20:20, as though I **s** at a target
SHOULD Matt. 23:23, these ... things you **s** have done
SHOUT Josh. 6:16, Joshua said ... **S**
Ps. 47:5, God has ascended with a **s**
66:1, **S** joyfully to God
Matt. 25:6, at midnight ... a **s**
1 Thess. 4:16, descend from heaven with a **s**
SHOW—*demonstrate*
Matt. 22:19, **S** Me the coin
John 14:8, Lord, **s** us the Father
1 Cor. 3:13, for the day will **s** it
Gal. 6:12, make a good **s-ing** in the flesh
Gen. 12:1; Ex. 33:18; Deut. 5:10; 2 Sam. 10:12; 1 Chr. 19:13; Job 11:6
SHOWER 1 Kin. 18:41; Ps. 65:10; Jer. 14:22; Luke 12:54
SHREWD—*wise*
Job 5:13, wise by their own **s-ness**
Matt. 10:16, be **s** as serpents
SHRINE Ezek. 16:24,31,39
SHRINK—*draw* Heb. 10:38, IF HE **S-S** BACK, MY SOUL HAS NO PLEASURE
SHUDDER Jer. 2:12, and **s**, be very desolate
James 2:19, demons also believe, and **s**
SHUN—*refrain* Eccles. 3:5, time to **s** embracing
SHUT—*close* Matt. 6:6, WHEN YOU HAVE **S** YOUR DOOR
Matt. 23:13, **s** off the kingdom of heaven
Gal. 3:23, being **s** up to the faith
Job 5:16; Prov. 21:13; Dan. 6:22
SICK Prov. 13:12, Hope ... *makes* the heart **s**
Matt. 10:8, Heal *the* **s**, raise
25:36, I was **s**, and you visited Me
Mark 1:30, Simon's mother-in-law ... lying **s**
2:17, physician, but those who are **s**
Luke 7:2, and **s** and about to die
John 11:2, brother Lazarus was **s**
James 5:14, Is anyone among you **s**
5:15, prayer ... restore the one who is **s**
Ps. 41:3; Song 2:5
SICKLE Deut. 16:9, put the **s** to the standing grain
Joel 3:13, Put in the **s** ... harvest is ripe
Rev. 14:15, Put in your **s** and reap
SICKLINESS Is. 17:11, a day of **s** and incurable pain
SICKNESS Matt. 4:23, healing every kind of **s**
Matt. 10:1, authority ... to heal ... **s**
Luke 13:12, are freed from your **s**
John 5:5, thirty-eight years in his **s**
11:4, This **s** is not unto death
Deut. 7:15; 2 Kin. 1:2; 8:8,9
SIDE Ezek. 36:3, crushed you from every **s**
John 19:34, pierced His **s** with a spear
20:20, showed ... His hands and His **s**
SIEGEWORKS Deut. 20:20; Eccles. 9:14
SIGHT Ps. 19:14, acceptable in Thy **s**
Ps. 90:4, thousand years in Thy **s**
Matt. 11:5, BLIND RECEIVE **S**
20:34, they received their **s**
Luke 4:18, RECOVERY OF **S** TO THE BLIND
Acts 9:9, three days without **s**
22:13, Saul, receive your **s**
2 Cor. 5:7, walk by faith, not by **s**
Gen. 2:9; 18:3; Ruth 2:13; Job 19:15
SIGN—*signal, witness, wonder*
Gen. 9:12, the **s** of the covenant
Ex. 3:12, this shall be a **s** to you
12:13, blood shall be a **s** ... on the houses
Ps. 86:17, Show me a **s** for good
Matt. 12:38, we want a **s** from You
16:3, cannot *discern* the **s-s** of the times
24:3, *will be* the **s** of Your coming
Mark 13:22, show **s-s** and wonders
16:20, confirmed the word by the **s-s**
Luke 1:22, he kept making **s-s** to them
21:25, will be **s-s** in sun
23:8, hoping to see some **s** performed
John 2:11, beginning of *His* **s-s** Jesus did
10:41, John performed no **s**
11:47, this man is performing many **s-s**
Acts 5:12, many **s-s** and wonders were taking place
1 Cor. 1:22, Jews ask for **s-s**
Phil. 1:28, a **s** of destruction
2 Thess. 2:9, all power and **s-s**
Rev. 12:1, a great **s** appeared in heaven
15:1, saw another **s** in heaven
Gen. 4:15; Ex. 31:13; Is. 7:11,14; 55:13; Ezek. 14:8
SIGNAL Mark 14:44, had given them a **s**
Is. 11:10; 30:17
SILENCE Ps. 62:1, My soul *waits* in **s** for God
Titus 1:11, who must be **s-d**
Rev. 8:1, there was **s** in heaven
SILENT Eccles. 3:7, A time to be **s**
Matt. 26:63, But Jesus kept **s**
Luke 1:20, you shall be **s** and unable to speak
9:36, they kept **s**, and reported to no one
Acts 18:9, go on speaking ... not be **s**
1 Cor. 14:28, keep **s** in the church
14:34, Let the women keep **s**
Judg. 18:19; Esth. 7:4; Job 6:24; 13:13
SILVER Matt. 10:9, Do not acquire gold, or **s**
Matt. 26:15, thirty pieces of **s**

Acts 3:6, I do not possess **s** and gold
8:20, May your **s** perish with you
20:33, coveted no one's **s**
James 5:3, gold and **s** have rusted
Gen. 13:2; Job 27:16; Prov. 16:16; 25:11; Is. 1:22; 39:2; Jer. 6:30; Zech. 11:12
SIMPLE—*naive* Ps. 19:7, making wise the **s**
Ps. 116:6, LORD preserves the **s**
SIN—*transgression* Ps. 25:7, remember the **s-s**
Ps. 51:3, my **s** is ever before me
Prov. 14:9, Fools mock at **s**
Is. 1:18, your **s-s** are as scarlet
Matt. 1:21, save His people from their **s-s**
3:6, as they confessed their **s-s**
12:31, **s** and blasphemy ... forgiven men
18:15, if your brother **s-s**
18:21, brother **s** against me
26:28, for forgiveness of **s-s**
Mark 2:7, forgive **s-s** but God alone
Luke 11:4, forgive us our **s-s**
John 1:29, Lamb ... takes away **s** of the world
8:7, He who is without **s**
8:11, go your way ... **s** no more
15:22, they have no excuse for their **s**
16:8, convict the world concerning **s**
Acts 22:16, wash away your **s-s**
26:18, receive forgiveness of **s-s**
Rom. 5:12, **s** entered into the world
6:23, wages of **s** is death
14:23, whatever is not from faith is **s**
1 Cor. 15:3, Christ died for our **s-s**
15:56, sting of death is **s**
2 Cor. 5:21, Him who knew no **s** *to be* **s** on our behalf
Heb. 9:7, for the **s-s** of the people
11:25, enjoy the ... pleasures of **s**
James 5:16, confess your **s-s** to one another
5:20, cover a multitude of **s-s**
1 Pet. 2:22, WHO COMMITTED NO **S**
1 John 1:8, If we say we have no **s**
1:9, If we confess our **s-s**
2:1, If anyone **s-s**, we have an Advocate
3:4, **s** is lawlessness
5:16, there is a **s** leading to death
5:17, All unrighteousness is **s**
Rev. 1:5, released us from our **s-s**
Gen. 4:7; 18:20; Ex. 10:17; 32:30; Job 1:22; 2:10; Ps. 51:2; 79:9; Is. 30:1; Mic. 6:7
SINCE Matt. 18:25, **s** he did not have *the means* to repay
1 Cor. 11:7, **s** he is the image and glory
Heb. 2:14, **S** then the children share
Gen. 41:39; Deut. 12:12
SINFUL Mark 8:38, **s** generation
Luke 5:8, I am a **s** man, O Lord
Rom. 8:3, the likeness of **s** flesh
Num. 32:14; Is. 1:4
SING—*shout, utter* Ps. 5:11, Let them ever **s** for joy
Ps. 33:3, **S** to Him a new song
100:2, Come before Him with joyful **s-ing**
1 Cor. 14:15, I shall **s** with the spirit
Col. 3:16, **s-ing** with thankfulness
James 5:13, cheerful? Let him **s** praises
Ex. 15:1; Judg. 5:12; 2 Sam. 22:50; 1 Chr. 16:23; 2 Chr. 23:13; Job 29:13; Prov. 29:6; Is. 5:1; Rev. 5:9
SINK Prov. 2:18, her house **s-s** down to death
SINNED Ps. 41:4, I have **s** against Thee
Ps. 51:4, Thee only, I have **s**
Luke 15:18, **s** against heaven
Rom. 3:23, **s**, and fall short of the glory
5:12, spread to all men, because all **s**
1 John 1:10, If we say that we have not **s**
Lev. 5:16; Deut. 1:41; Dan. 9:15
SINNER Ps. 1:1, stand in the path of **s-s**
Matt. 9:10, tax-gatherers and **s-s**
9:13, call *the* righteous, but **s-s**
11:19, a friend of ... **s-s**
Mark 2:17, to call *the* righteous, but **s-s**
14:41, into the hands of **s-s**
Luke 6:34, Even **s-s** lend to **s-s**
15:7, *more* joy in heaven over one **s**
18:13, be merciful to me, the **s**
John 9:31, God does not hear **s-s**
Rom. 5:8, while we were yet **s-s**
1 Tim. 1:15, Jesus came ... to save **s-s**
James 4:8, Cleanse your hands, you **s-s**
Prov. 1:10; 13:21; 23:17; Eccles. 9:18
SISTER Job 17:14, my mother, and my **s**
Matt. 12:50, is My brother and **s**
Luke 10:39, had a **s** called Mary
Gen. 12:13; Prov. 7:4; Song 8:8; Rom. 16:1
SIT Ps. 1:1, **S** in the seat of scoffers
Ps. 26:4, not **s** with deceitful men
110:1, **S** at My right hand
Matt. 4:16, WERE **S-ING** IN DARKNESS
9:9, Matthew, **s-ing** in the tax office
26:36, **S** here while I go
27:61, Mary, **s-ing** opposite the grave
Luke 2:46, temple, **s-ing** ... midst of the teachers
8:35, **s-ing** down at the feet of Jesus
John 12:15, **S-ING** ON A DONKEY'S COLT
Acts 8:28, **s-ing** in his chariot
Gen. 18:1; 1 Kin. 22:19; Job 2:8; Ezek. 28:2
SITUATE Ps. 144:15, people who are so **s-d**
SIZE—*stature* Num. 13:32, are men of *great* **s**
SKILL Ps. 137:5, my right hand forget her **s**
SKILLFUL Gen. 25:27; Ex. 28:8; 1 Sam. 16:16; Ps. 139:15; Is. 3:3
SKIN Ex. 34:29, the **s** of his face shone
Job 2:4, **S** for **s**
10:11, Clothe me with **s** and flesh
Jer. 13:23, Ethiopian change his **s**
Job 19:20; 30:30
SKIP Job 21:11, children **s** about
SKULL Judg. 9:53, Abimelech's head, crushing his **s**
Matt. 27:33, which means Place of a **S**
SKY Ps. 36:5, faithfulness *reaches* to the **s-s**
Matt. 16:2,3, for the **s** is red
Luke 12:56, analyze the appearance ... the **s**
Gen. 1:26,28; Deut. 4:17; 2 Sam. 21:10; Job 37:18; Prov. 30:19; James 5:18
SLACK Prov. 18:9, who is **s** in his work
SLAIN 1 Sam. 18:7; 29:5, Saul has **s** his thousands
Rev. 5:12, Worthy ... Lamb that was **s**
SLANDER Ps. 15:3, He does not **s**
Prov. 30:10, Do not **s** a slave to his master
1 Cor. 4:13, when we are **s-ed**, we try to conciliate
2 Cor. 12:20, disputes, **s-s**, gossip
Eph. 4:31, and **s** be put away from you
SLANDERER—*whisperer*
Prov. 16:28, **s** separates ... friends
Rom. 1:30, **s-s**, haters of God
SLAP Job 16:10, **s-ed** me on the cheek
Matt. 5:39, **s-s** you on your right cheek
SLAUGHTER—*sacrifice*
Ps. 44:22, as sheep to be **s-ed**
Is. 53:7, lamb that is led to **s**
Rom. 8:36, AS SHEEP TO BE **S-ED**
James 5:5, in a day of **s**
Prov. 7:22; Jer. 46:10
SLAVE Prov. 22:7, borrower becomes the lender's **s**
Matt. 25:21, Well done ... faithful **s**
1 Cor. 7:21, Were you called while a **s**
9:27, body and make it my **s**
Gal. 4:7, no longer a **s**, but a son
Ex. 23:12; Lev. 19:20; 25:39,44; Deut. 15:15; 16:12; 24:18; Col. 3:22
SLAVERY—*bondage* Rom. 8:15, a spirit of **s**
Gal. 5:1, subject again to a yoke of **s**
Heb. 2:15, subject to **s** all their lives
SLAY—*destroy* Job 5:2, vexation **s-s** the foolish man
Job 13:15, Though He **s** me, I will hope
Ps. 34:21, Evil shall **s** the wicked
2 Thess. 2:8, the Lord will **s** with the breath of
SLEDGE Is. 41:15, a new, sharp threshing **s**

SLEEP Gen. 2:21, deep **s** to fall upon the man
Ps. 13:3, **s** the *sleep of* death
Prov. 6:10, A little **s**, a little slumber
Eccles. 5:12, **s** of the working man
Matt. 1:24, Joseph arose from his **s**
26:40,43, found them **s-ing**
26:45, Are you still **s-ing** and taking
Acts 20:9, sinking into a deep **s**
1 Cor. 15:51, we shall not all **s**
1 Thess. 5:7, those who **s** do their **s-ing** at night
Ps. 76:6; Prov. 3:24; 20:13; Jer. 31:26; Mark 14:40
SLEW Matt. 2:16, **s** all the male children
SLING 1 Sam. 17:40, his **s** was in his hand
Judg. 20:16; 1 Sam. 25:29
SLOTHFUL Prov. 12:27, **s** man does not roast
SLOW Ex. 4:10, **s** of speech and **s** of tongue
Ps. 103:8, **S** to anger and abounding
Prov. 16:32, He who is **s** to anger
Luke 24:25, foolish men and **s** of heart
James 1:19, **s** to speak *and* **s** to anger
2 Pet. 3:9, The Lord is not **s**
SLUGGISH Heb. 6:12, that you may not be **s**
SLUMBER Ps. 121:3, who keeps you will not **s**
Prov. 6:10, A little sleep, a little **s**
Job 33:15; Ps. 132:4; Is. 5:27; 56:10
SMALL—*little* Prov. 30:24, Four things are **s** on the earth
Mark 8:7, They also had a few **s** fish
James 3:4, directed by a very **s** rudder
3:5, tongue is a **s** part of the body
Num. 26:56; 35:8; Deut. 25:13; Is. 10:19
SMEAR Ezek. 22:28, prophets have **s-ed** whitewash
SMELL Gen. 27:27; Deut. 4:28; Ps. 115:6
SMELT Is. 1:25, **s** away your dross with lye
SMOKE Gen. 15:17; Job 41:20; Ps. 102:3; Prov. 10:26; Is. 6:4
SMOLDERING Matt. 12:20, S WICK HE WILL
SMOOTH Ps. 55:21, speech was **s-er** than butter
Prov. 5:3, **s-er** than oil is her speech
Is. 45:13, I will make all his ways **s**
Luke 3:5, THE ROUGH ROADS S
Gen. 27:11,16; 1 Sam. 17:40; Prov. 6:24; 11:5; Is. 40:3
SNAKE Matt. 7:10, he will not . . . a **s**, will he
SNARE—*web* Prov. 7:23, bird hastens to the **s**
Rom. 11:9, THEIR TABLE BECOME A S
2 Tim. 2:26, *escape* from the **s** of the devil
Ex. 10:7; Job 34:30; Ps. 91:3; Eccles. 7:26
SNATCH—*pluck* John 10:12, the wolf **s-es** them
John 10:28, **s** them out of My hand
Jude 23, **s-ing** them out of the fire
SNEER—*scoff* Luke 23:35, the rulers were **s-ing**
SNOW Ps. 51:7, I shall be whiter than **s**
Prov. 26:1, Like **s** in summer
Is. 1:18, scarlet . . . be as white as **s**
Matt. 28:3, his garment as white as **s**
Rev. 1:14, white like white wool, like **s**
Num. 12:10; Job 9:30; 38:22; Prov. 25:13
SOBER—*watch* Acts 26:25, utter words of **s** truth
1 Thess. 5:6, let us be alert and **s**
2 Tim. 4:5, be **s** in all things
1 Pet. 4:7, **s** *spirit* . . . purpose of prayer
5:8, Be of **s** *spirit*
SOFT Matt. 11:8, who wear **s** *clothing* are in
Ps. 65:10; Prov. 25:15
SOIL—*earth, ground*
Ezek. 17:5, planted it in fertile **s**
Matt. 13:5; Mark 4:5, did not have much **s**
13:8, others fell on the good **s**
James 5:7, the precious produce of the **s**
Rev. 3:4, few . . . who have not **s-ed** their garments
SOJOURN Gen. 26:3; Ex. 12:48
SOJOURNER—*foreigner, alien* Ex. 2:22; 12:45; 18:3; 20:10
SOLD Gen. 25:33, **s** his birthright
Gen. 45:4, brother Joseph, whom you **s** into
Matt. 10:29, two sparrows **s** for a cent
13:46, went and **s** all that he had
Acts 5:1, his wife Sapphira, **s** a piece of
Rom. 7:14, of flesh, **s** into bondage to sin
Lev. 25:23; 1 Kin. 21:20; Joel 3:3
SOLDIER Mark 15:16, the **s-s** took Him away
Luke 23:36, the **s-s** also mocked Him
John 19:23, four parts, a part to every **s**
Acts 28:16, with the **s** who was guarding
2 Tim. 2:3, as a good **s** of Christ Jesus
SOLVE—*dissolve*
Dan. 5:12, **s-ing** of difficult problems
5:16, give interpretations and **s** difficult
SOMEBODY Acts 5:36, Theudas rose up, claiming to be **s**
SOMEONE Luke 8:46, **S** did touch Me
SOMETHING—*this* 1 Kin. 2:14, have **s** *to say* to you
Hab. 1:5, *I* am doing **s** in your days
Luke 7:40, I have **s** to say to you
Acts 25:26, I may have **s** to write
SON 2 Sam. 13:37, *David* mourned for his **s**
Ps. 2:7, Thou art My **S**
8:4, **s** of man, that Thou dost care
Prov. 10:1, A wise **s** makes a father glad
17:25, A foolish **s** is a grief
Is. 7:14, a virgin will . . . bear a **s**
14:12, O star of the morning . . . **s** of
60:4, Your **s-s** will come from afar
Dan. 7:13, One like a **S** of Man
Hos. 11:1, out of Egypt I called My **s**
Matt. 1:25, virgin until she gave birth to a **S**
2:15, OUT OF EGYPT . . . CALL MY S
3:17, This is My beloved **S**
11:27, No one knows the **S**
13:55, Is not this the carpenter's **s**
16:16, the **S** of the living God
22:42, Christ, whose **s** is He
26:63, are the Christ, the **S** of God
27:43, I am the **S** of God
Mark 5:7, Jesus, **S** of the Most High God
12:6, one more *to send,* a . . . **s**
14:61, the **S** of the Blessed *One*
Luke 1:31, bear a **s**, and you shall name
2:7, birth to her first-born **s**
4:22, Is this not Joseph's **s**
15:11, A certain man had two **s-s**
15:24, this **s** of mine was dead
John 4:50, Go your way, your **s** lives
5:21, the **S** also gives life
6:42, this Jesus, the **s** of Joseph
12:36, may become **s-s** of light
14:13, may be glorified in the **S**
19:26, Woman, behold, your **s**
Acts 4:36, translated . . . **S** of Encouragement
Rom. 8:32, did not spare His own **S**
Gal. 4:7, but a **s**; and if a **s**
2 Thess. 2:3, revealed, the **s** of destruction
Heb. 6:6, again crucify . . . the **S** of God
1 John 2:22, denies the Father and the **S**
Rev. 21:7, be his God . . . will be My **s**
Gen. 6:2; 22:2; 37:33; Ex. 20:10; Deut. 8:5; 2 Kin. 2:3; Job 5:4; Eccles. 4:8; Is. 30:9; Ezek. 2:1; Mal. 3:17
SONG—*music, taunt*
Ex. 15:2, LORD is my strength and **s**
Judg. 5:12, Awake, awake, sing a **s**
Job 35:10, gives **s-s** in the night
Ps. 33:3, Sing to Him a new **s**
137:4, How . . . sing the LORD's **s**
Prov. 25:20, Sings **s-s** to a troubled heart
Eccles. 12:4, the daughters of **s**
Song 1:1, The **S** of **S-s**
Eph. 5:19, hymns and spiritual **s-s**
Is. 5:1; 23:16; 24:9; Ezek. 33:32
SOON—*shortly* Ex. 2:18, you come *back* so **s**
Job 32:22, Maker would **s** take me away
Heb. 13:23, if he comes **s**
SOOT Lam. 4:8, appearance is blacker than **s**
SOOTHE Gen. 8:21, LORD smelled a **s-ing** aroma
SORDID Titus 1:11, for the sake of **s** gain
SORE Luke 16:21, dogs . . . licking his **s-s**

SORROW Gen. 42:38, bring ... down ... in **s**
Ps. 31:10, my life is spent with **s**
Eccles. 7:3, **S** is better than laughter
Is. 35:10, **s** and sighing will flee away
53:3, A man of **s-s**
Jer. 8:18, My **s** is beyond healing
John 16:20, be **s-ful**, but your **s**
2 Cor. 2:2, For if I cause you **s**
2:5, he has caused **s** not to me
2:7, overwhelmed by excessive **s**
7:9, made **s-ful** according to *the will* of God
7:10, **s** ... produces a repentance
Jer. 45:3; Luke 22:45
SORRY Gen. 6:6, the LORD was **s** ... made man
Jer. 13:14, I will not show pity nor be **s**
SOUGHT—*seek, visit* Is. 26:16, they **s** Thee in distress
Matt. 2:20, who **s** the Child's life
21:46, they **s** to seize Him
Gal. 4:18, to be eagerly **s**
Ex. 33:7; Eccles. 7:29
SOUL—*life, person*
Deut. 4:29, with all your heart ... **s**
1 Sam. 1:26, As your **s** lives
Job 33:30, bring back his **s** from the pit
Ps. 16:10, not abandon my **s** to Sheol
19:7, LORD is perfect, restoring the **s**
23:3, He restores my **s**
24:4, not lifted up his **s** to falsehood
42:1, So my **s** pants for Thee
62:1, My **s** *waits* in silence for God
63:1, My **s** thirsts for Thee
103:1, Bless the LORD, O my **s**
107:9, satisfied the thirsty **s**
Prov. 24:12, who keeps your **s**
25:25, cold water to a weary **s**
Ezek. 18:4, **s** who sins will die
Matt. 10:28, unable to kill the **s**
11:29, FIND REST FOR YOUR **S-S**
16:26, world, and forfeits his **s**
26:38, My **s** is deeply grieved
Luke 1:46, My **s** exalts the Lord
12:19, say to my **s**, **S** you have many
John 12:27, My **s** has become troubled
Acts 4:32, were of one heart and **s**
1 Thess. 5:23, your spirit and **s** and body
Heb. 4:12, division of **s** and spirit
6:19, as an anchor of the **s**
10:39, to the preserving of the **s**
James 1:21, is able to save your **s-s**
5:20, save his **s** from death
1 Pet. 2:11, which wage war against the **s**
2 Pet. 2:14, enticing unstable **s-s**
Deut. 4:9; Judg. 16:16; 1 Sam. 18:1; Job 3:20; 10:1
SOUND—*roar, shout, voice* Ex. 32:17; Lev. 26:36
Gen. 3:8, heard the **s** of the LORD God
Prov. 3:21, Keep **s** wisdom
Luke 15:27, received him back safe and **s**
1 Tim. 1:10, contrary to **s** teaching
2 Tim. 1:13, Retain ... standard of **s** words
Titus 1:13, may be **s** in the faith
Rev. 1:15, **s** of many waters
8:7, And the first **s-ed**
Judg. 4:21; 1 Kin. 18:41; 19:12; Job 15:21; 33:15; Prov. 2:7; Eccles. 12:4; Jer. 25:10; Joel 2:1
SOUR Jer. 31:29, fathers have eaten **s** grapes
SOURCE Heb. 5:9, the **s** of eternal salvation
SOUTH Matt. 12:42, Queen of *the* **S**
Luke 12:55, *see* a **s** wind blowing
Acts 27:13, when a moderate **s** wind came up
Job 37:9,17; Eccles. 11:3
SOW Job 4:8, those who **s** trouble harvest it
Ps. 126:5, **s** in tears shall reap
Prov. 22:8, who **s-s** iniquity ... reap vanity
Is. 55:10, furnishing seed to the **s-er**
Matt. 6:26, birds ... they do not **s**
13:3, **s-er** went out to **s**
Luke 12:24, neither **s** nor reap
19:21, reap what you did not **s**
John 4:36, he who **s-s** and he who reaps
1 Cor. 9:11, **s-ed** spiritual things in you
15:42, **s-n** a perishable body
15:44, **s-n** a natural body
2 Cor. 9:6, he who **s-s** sparingly
Gal. 6:7, whatever a man **s-s**
James 3:18, is **s-n** in peace
Gen. 47:23; Lev. 26:16; Deut. 22:9; Job 31:8; Eccles. 11:4,6; Is. 32:20; Jer. 4:3; Hos. 8:7
SPACE—*time* Lev. 25:30, the **s** of a full year
SPACIOUS—*large* Ex. 3:8, to a good and **s** land
SPARE Ps. 78:50, **s** their soul from death
Prov. 13:24, **s-s** his rod hates his son
Acts 20:29, not **s-ing** the flock
Rom. 8:32, did not **s** His own Son
11:21, not **s** the natural branches
2 Cor. 9:6, who sows **s-ingly**
13:2, I come again, I will not **s**
2 Pet. 2:4, God did not **s** angels
Is. 9:19; Jer. 50:14; Mal. 3:17
SPARKLE Prov. 23:31, When it **s-s** in the cup
SPEAK—*tell, utter* Ps. 135:16, but they do not **s**
Prov. 23:9, Do not **s** ... hearing of a fool
Eccles. 3:7, silent, and a time to **s**
Is. 32:4, stammerers will hasten to **s** clearly
Matt. 10:19, how or what you will **s**
10:20, Spirit of your Father who **s-s**
Mark 16:17, will **s** with new tongues
Luke 1:20, silent and unable to **s**
6:26, all men **s** well of you
John 3:11, we **s** that which we know
7:46, Never did a man **s** ... this man **s-s**
8:45, because I **s** the truth
16:13, not **s** on His own initiative
Acts 2:4, began to **s** with other tongues
18:9, not be afraid ... but go on **s-ing**
19:6, they began **s-ing** with tongues
Rom. 3:5, I am **s-ing** in human terms
1 Cor. 2:7, we **s** God's wisdom
13:1, I **s** with the tongues of men
13:11, I used to **s** as a child
2 Cor. 12:4, a man is not permitted to **s**
Eph. 5:19, **s-ing** to one another
6:20, **s** boldly, as I ought to **s**
Titus 3:8, I want you to **s** confidently
James 1:19, slow to **s** *and* slow to anger
2:12, so **s** and so act
4:11, not **s** against one another
1 Pet. 4:11, Whoever **s-s**, *let him s*
2 Pet. 2:18, **s-ing** out arrogant *words*
Gen. 18:32; Ex. 4:14; Lev. 1:2; Num. 22:35; Deut. 5:24; 1 Kin. 12:7; Job 2:13; 11:5; 33:14; 41:3; Ps. 28:3; 41:5; 101:7; Is. 29:4; 40:2; Mark 13:11; John 12:49; 2 Cor. 12:6
SPEAR 1 Sam. 26:7, his **s** stuck in the ground
2 Sam. 1:6, Saul was leaning on his **s**
Ps. 46:9, cuts the **s** in two
Is. 2:4, their **s-s** into pruning hooks
Joel 3:10, pruning hooks into **s-s**
John 19:34, pierced His side with a **s**
SPECIFICALLY 1 Sam. 20:21, If I **s** say to the lad
SPECULATIONS—*question*
Rom. 1:21, futile in their **s**
2 Cor. 10:5, *We are* destroying **s**
2 Tim. 2:23, foolish and ignorant **s**
SPED—*fly* Ps. 18:10, He **s** upon the wings of the wind
SPEECH—*message, word* Ex. 4:10, slow of **s**
Rom. 16:18, by their smooth and flattering **s**
1 Cor. 1:17, not in cleverness of **s**
2 Cor. 11:6, even if I am unskilled in **s**
Col. 4:6, **s** always be with grace
Deut. 32:2; Job 13:17; Prov. 17:7; Is. 33:19; Ezek. 3:5
SPEED—*quickly* Is. 5:19, Let Him make **s**
Luke 18:8, bring about justice ... **s-ily**
SPELT Ezek. 4:9, beans, lentils, millet and **s**
SPEND Is. 55:2, Why do you **s** money
2 Cor. 12:15, I will most gladly **s** and
Gen. 19:2; Num. 22:8; Job 21:13
SPENT Gen. 47:15, money was all **s**
Ps. 31:10, my life is **s** with sorrow
Mark 5:26, **s** all that she had

SPICE Ex. 35:28; Song 8:2; Ezek. 24:10; John 19:40
SPIES Gen. 42:9, You are **s**
Josh. 6:23, young men who were **s**
Luke 20:20, sent **s** who pretended
Heb. 11:31, she had welcomed the **s**
SPIRIT Gen. 1:2, the **S** of God was moving
Ps. 31:5, Into Thy hand I commit my **s**
51:10, renew a steadfast **s** within me
Eccles. 12:7, the **s** will return to God
Is. 11:2, **s** of wisdom ... understanding
32:15, Until the **S** is poured
61:1, **S** of the Lord God is upon
Joel 2:28, pour out My **S** on all mankind
Matt. 1:18, with child by the Holy **S**
3:16, **S** of God descending
5:3, Blessed are the poor in **s**
10:1, authority over unclean **s-s**
10:20, **S** of your Father who speaks
12:18, PUT MY **S** UPON HIM
12:31, blasphemy against the **S**
12:45, seven other **s-s** more
27:50, cried ... yielded up *His* **s**
28:19, Son and the Holy **S**
Mark 1:8, baptize you with the Holy **S**
1:10, **S** like a dove descending
14:38, **s** is willing, but
Luke 1:15, be filled with the Holy **S**
4:18, **S** OF THE LORD IS UPON ME
11:13, give the Holy **S** to those
24:37, thought ... seeing a **s**
24:39, **s** does not have flesh
John 3:5, is born of water ... **s**
4:24, God is **s**
14:17, *that is* the **S** of truth
Acts 2:4, all filled with the Holy **S**
18:25, being fervent in **s**
Rom. 2:29, by the **S**, not by
8:6, mind set on the **S** is life
15:19, in the power of the **S**
1 Cor. 2:10, the **S** searches all things
2:13, taught by the **S**
3:16, **S** of God dwells in you
5:3, absent ... present in **s**
12:4, gifts, but the same **S**
14:15, I shall pray with the **s**
2 Cor. 3:6, of the letter, but of the **S**
13:14, fellowship of the Holy **S**
Gal. 4:6, sent forth the **S** of His Son
5:16, walk by the **S**
5:22, fruit of the **S** is love
Eph. 1:13, with the Holy **S** of promise
2:18, access in one **S** to
4:4, body and one **S**
4:30, not grieve the Holy **S** of
Phil. 1:27, standing firm in one **s**
1 Thess. 5:19, Do not quench the **S**
Heb. 4:12, division of soul and **s**
James 2:26, body without *the* **s** is dead
1 Pet. 4:6, in the **s** according ... *will of* God
1 John 4:1, not believe every **s**
5:7, **S** who bears witness
5:8, the **S** and the water ... blood
Rev. 1:10, in the **S** on the Lord's
14:13, Yes, says the **S**
22:17, **S** and the bride say
Ex. 31:3; Judg. 9:23; 2 Kin. 2:9; Eccles. 7:8; Is. 42:1; 57:15; Ezek. 11:19; Acts 2:17
SPIRITIST Lev. 20:27; 2 Kin. 23:24
SPIRITUAL Rom. 15:27, shared in their **s** things
1 Cor. 10:3, ate the same **s** food
14:1, desire ... **s** *gifts*
15:44, raised a **s** body
Eph. 1:3, blessed us ... every **s** blessing
5:19, hymns and **s** songs
1 Pet. 2:5, built up as a **s** house
SPIT Job 30:10, refrain from **s-ing** ... face
Matt. 26:67, they **s** in His face
27:30, they **s** on Him
Mark 8:23, after **s-ing** on his eyes
14:65, some began to **s** at Him
John 9:6, made clay of the **s-tle**

SPLENDID—*gorgeous* Luke 7:25, who are **s-ly** clothed
SPLENDOR—*glory, honor*
Ps. 8:1, hast displayed Thy **s**
96:6, **S** and majesty are before Him
SPLIT Lev. 11:3,7,26
SPOIL—*plunder* Gen. 49:27; Prov. 16:19; Is. 10:2; Ezek. 25:7
SPOKE—*declared, told* Gen. 8:15, God **s** to Noah
Ps. 33:9, He **s**, and it was done
40:10, I have **s-n** of Thy faithfulness
62:11, Once God has **s-n**
78:19, they **s** against God
87:3, Glorious things are **s-n** of you
Prov. 25:11, word **s-n** in right circumstances
Matt. 13:34, Jesus **s** ... in parables
Mark 14:9, be **s-n** of in memory
Rom. 14:16, thing be **s-n** of as evil
1 Cor. 14:5, that you all **s** in tongues
Heb. 1:2, last days has **s-n** to us
2 Pet. 1:21, men ... **s** from God
Mal. 3:16; Mark 7:32
SPOT—*blemish, defect*
Gen. 30:32, speckled and **s-ed** sheep
Jer. 13:23, Or the leopard his **s-s**
Eph. 5:27, having no **s** or wrinkle
1 Pet. 1:19, lamb unblemished and **s-less**
SPREAD—*disperse*
Prov. 15:7, lips ... wise **s** knowledge
Matt. 21:8, multitude **s** their garments
Ex. 1:12; 9:29; Job 29:19; 37:18; Prov. 7:16; 29:5; Is. 19:8; 33:23; Ezek. 12:15; 16:8; Joel 2:2; Luke 19:36
SPRING—*well* Ps. 85:11, Truth **s-s** from the earth
Is. 45:8, righteousness **s** up with it
58:11, like a **s** of water
John 4:14, well of water **s-ing** up
Heb. 12:15, root of bitterness **s-ing**
Rev. 7:17, **s-s** of the water of life
21:6, thirsts from the **s** of the water
Gen. 16:7; 2 Kin. 3:19; Prov. 5:16; 25:26; Song 4:12; Is. 11:1
SPROUT—*grow* Gen. 1:11; Ex. 10:5; Ps. 90:5; 92:7; Is. 61:11
SPURNED—*despised* Ps. 10:13; 107:11; Prov. 1:30; 5:12
SPY Judg. 1:23, house of Joseph **s-ed** out Bethel
SQUANDERED—*wasted* Luke 15:13, **s** his estate
SQUARE Gen. 19:2; Ex. 27:1; Judg. 19:20; Rev. 21:16
STABILITY Col. 2:5, **s** of your faith
STAFF Gen. 38:18, your **s** that is in your hand
Ex. 7:12, Aaron's **s** swallowed up
Ps. 23:4, Thy rod and Thy **s**
Matt. 10:10, sandals, or a **s**
Ex. 4:4; Judg. 6:21; 2 Kin. 4:29; Is. 14:5; Ezek. 4:16; Zech. 11:10; Mark 6:8
STAIN 1 Tim. 6:14, commandment without **s**
2 Pet. 2:13, They are **s-s** and blemishes
STAIRWAY
2 Kin. 20:11, brought the shadow on the **s** back
Is. 38:8, shadow on the **s** ... sun on the **s** of
STAND—*arise, form, rest, stood* Gen. 18:2
Ps. 1:5, will not **s** in the judgment
130:3, O Lord, who could **s**
Is. 40:8, word of our God **s-s** forever
Matt. 6:5, love to **s** and pray
12:25, house divided ... shall not **s**
20:3, **s-ing** idle in the market place
Mark 11:25, whenever you **s** praying forgive
John 1:26, among you **s-s** One
19:25, were **s-ing** by the cross
20:11, Mary was **s-ing** outside
Acts 1:11, why do you **s** looking into
7:33, PLACE ON WHICH YOU ARE **S-ING** IS HOLY
21:40, Paul, **s-ing** on the stairs
Rom. 5:2, this grace in which we **s**
14:4, Lord is able to make him **s**
1 Cor. 16:13, **s** firm in the faith
2 Cor. 1:24, in your faith you are **s-ing** firm

Eph. 6:14, **S** firm ... HAVING GIRDED YOUR LOINS
1 Tim. 3:13, obtain ... a high **s-ing**
2 Tim. 2:19, foundation of God **s-s**
Rev. 3:20, Behold I **s** at the door
5:6, Lamb **s-ing**, as if slain
20:12, dead **s-ing** before the throne
Ex. 14:13; Num. 22:22; Josh. 10:12; Job 8:15; Prov. 22:29; 27:4; Is. 50:8; Jer. 6:16; 35:19; Ezek. 2:1; 13:5; Amos 7:7; Nah. 1:6

STANDARD—*banner*
Ps. 74:4, set up their own **s-s** for signs
Is. 13:2, Lift up a **s**
1 Chr. 17:17; Is. 5:26; 18:3; 31:9

STAR Gen. 1:16, *He made* the **s-s** also
Num. 24:17, A **s** shall come forth ... Jacob
Job 38:7, morning **s-s** sang together
Ps. 147:4, counts the number of the **s-s**
Matt. 2:2, saw His **s** in the east
2:7, ascertained ... time the **s** appeared
2:10, when they saw the **s**
24:29, **S-S** WILL FALL from the sky
1 Cor. 15:41, for **s** differs from **s**
2 Pet. 1:19, **s** arises in your hearts
Jude 13, wandering **s-s**, for whom
Rev. 1:16, right hand He held seven **s-s**
8:10, great **s** fell from heaven
8:11, **s** is called Wormwood
22:16, the bright morning **s**
Job 22:12; Ps. 136:9; Jer. 31:35

STARE Song 1:6, Do not **s** at me

STARVE Zeph. 2:11, He will **s** all the gods

STATE—*declare* Josh. 20:4; Luke 1:48

STATEMENT Matt. 5:37, your **s** be, Yes, yes
John 6:60, This is a difficult **s**
1 Tim. 1:15, It is a trustworthy **s**

STATURE—*size* 1 Sam. 16:7, the height of his **s**
Luke 2:52, increasing in wisdom and **s**
19:3, he was small in **s**

STATUTE—*precept*
Ps. 119:12, Teach me Thy **s-s**
Mal. 3:7, turned aside from My **s-s**
Gen. 26:5; Ex. 29:9; Lev. 18:5; Num. 35:29, Is. 10:1; Ezek. 5:7

STAY—*lodge, remain* Luke 2:8, shepherds **s-ing**
Luke 19:5, today I must **s** at your house
24:29, **S** with us ... over. And ... **s** with them
John 1:38, Rabbi ... where are you **s-ing**
2:12, there they **s-ed** a few days
Acts 10:6, **s-ing** with a ... tanner *named* Simon
1 Pet. 1:17, time of your **s** *upon earth*
Gen. 19:17; Ruth 2:8; 1 Sam. 20:38; 22:23; Ps. 18:18; Hos. 3:3; Luke 1:56; John 1:39; Acts 18:3

STEADFAST—*resolute*
Job 11:15, you would be **s**
Ps. 51:10, renew a **s** spirit within me
57:7, My heart is **s**, O God, my
112:7, His heart is **s**, trusting
1 Cor. 15:58, brethren, be **s**
Col. 1:11, all **s-ness** and patience
2 Thess. 3:5, into the **s-ness** of Christ

STEAL—*deceive* Matt. 6:19, break in and **s**
Matt. 19:18, YOU SHALL NOT **S**
Ex. 20:15; Lev. 19:11; Deut. 5:19; 2 Sam. 19:3; Prov. 30:9; Mark 10:19; Eph. 4:28

STEALTH—*craft* Mark 14:1, to seize Him by **s**

STEED 1 Kin. 4:28; Esth. 8:10

STEP Job 18:8, he **s-s** on the webbing
Rom. 4:12, follow in the **s-s** of the faith
1 Pet. 2:21, you to follow in His **s-s**
1 Kin. 10:19; Job 14:16; 29:6; Prov. 5:5

STERN Eccles. 8:1, causes his **s** face to beam

STEWARD Gen. 43:19, near to Joseph's house **s**
Luke 12:42, faithful and sensible **s**
1 Cor. 4:1, **s-s** of the mysteries of God
4:2, it is required of **s-s**

STEWARDSHIP Luke 16:2, an account of your **s**
1 Cor. 9:17, I have a **s** entrusted to me
Eph. 3:2, the **s** of God's grace
Col. 1:25, according to the **s** from God

STICK Prov. 18:24, friend who **s-s**
Num. 22:27; 2 Kin. 6:6; Job 33:21; 38:38; Ezek. 37:16,19

STILL Lev. 5:17, **s** he is guilty
Judg. 7:4, people are **s** too many
Dan. 11:35, **s** *to come* ... appointed time
Matt. 19:20, what am I **s** lacking
Luke 24:44, while I was **s** with you
Rom. 5:6, while we were **s** helpless
Josh. 10:12; Ps. 65:7; 107:29; Jer. 8:14; Mark 4:39

STING 1 Cor. 15:55, O DEATH ... YOUR **S**
1 Cor. 15:56, **s** of death is sin
Prov. 23:32; Rev. 9:10

STINKWEED Job 31:40, And **s** instead of barley

STIR Deut. 32:11, eagle that **s-s** up its nest
Ps. 35:23, **S** up Thyself, and awake
Prov. 10:12, Hatred **s-s** up strife
15:1, harsh word **s-s** up anger
28:25, arrogant man **s-s** up strife
29:22, angry man **s-s** up strife
Acts 14:2, Jews who disbelieved **s-ed** up
2 Pet. 3:1, I am **s-ing** up your

STOCKS Job 13:27; Acts 16:24

STOLE Gen. 31:19; 2 Sam. 15:6; Prov. 9:17

STOMACH Mark 7:19, but into his **s**

STONE Ex. 34:1, Cut out ... two **s** tablets
Deut. 9:9, the tablets of **s**
1 Sam. 17:49, from it a **s** and slung
Ps. 118:22, **s** which the builders rejected
Ezek. 20:32, serving wood and **s**
Dan. 2:34, a **s** was cut out without
Matt. 3:9, God is able from these **s-s**
4:3, command ... **s-s** become bread
4:6, YOUR FOOT AGAINST A **S**
7:9, will give him a **s**
21:42, **S** WHICH THE BUILDERS REJECTED
27:60, large **s** against the entrance
28:2, rolled away the **s** and sat
Luke 19:44, one **s** upon another
John 2:6, six **s** waterpots
8:7, first to throw a **s** at her
11:39, Jesus said, Remove the **s**
Acts 7:59, went on **s-ing** Stephen
2 Cor. 3:3, not on tablets of **s**
1 Pet. 2:5, also, as living **s-s**
2:8, **S** OF STUMBLING
Gen. 11:3; 29:3; Ex. 15:16; 20:25; Lev. 20:2; Num. 15:35; Deut. 8:9; 2 Sam. 17:13; 1 Kin. 6:18; 2 Kin. 12:12; 2 Chr. 34:11; Job 14:19; 41:24; Ps. 18:12; 91:12; Prov. 26:27; 27:3; Is. 28:16; 54:11; 57:6; Ezek. 11:19; Amos 5:11; Hab. 2:11; Luke 22:41; Rev. 2:17

STOOD Deut. 31:15, pillar of cloud **s** at
Josh. 10:13, So the sun **s** still
Matt. 2:9, came and **s** over where
4:5, devil ... **s** Him on the pinnacle
Luke 4:16, and **s** up to read
24:36, He Himself **s** in their midst
John 21:4, Jesus **s** on the beach
Rev. 13:1, he **s** on the sand

STOP 1 Kin. 18:44; Ps. 63:11; 2 Cor. 11:10

STORE Prov. 10:14, Wise men **s** up knowledge
Luke 12:17, I have no place to **s** my crops
1 Tim. 6:19, **s-ing** up treasure
James 5:3, have **s-d** up your treasure

STOREHOUSE—*treasure* Deut. 28:12; Job 38:22

STORM—*tempest, whirlwind* Jon. 1:4, a great **s**
Jon. 1:12, this great **s** *has come* upon you
Matt. 16:3, *There will be* a **s** today
Acts 27:18, we were being violently **s-tossed**
2 Pet. 2:17, mists driven by a **s**
Job 21:18; 37:9; Ps. 55:8; 107:25; Is. 25:4; Ezek. 38:9

STRAIGHT—*equity* Matt. 3:3, MAKE PATHS **S**
Luke 3:5, CROOKED SHALL BECOME **S**
John 1:23, MAKE **S** THE WAY OF THE LORD
Acts 9:11, street called **S**
Heb. 12:13, make **s** paths for your feet
1 Sam. 6:12, Ps. 5:8; Eccles. 1:15; Mic. 3:9

STRAIGHTFORWARD Gal. 2:14, not **s** about the truth
STRAIT—*narrow* 1 Sam. 13:6, they were in a **s**
STRANGE Heb. 13:9, varied and **s** teachings
1 Pet. 4:12, some **s** thing were happening
Jude 7, went after **s** flesh
STRANGER—*alien, sojourner*
Gen. 23:4, I am a **s** and
Matt. 25:35, I was a **s**, and you invited
27:7, Potter's Field ... for **s-s**
John 10:5, do not know the voice of **s-s**
Eph. 2:19, you are no longer **s-s** and aliens
Heb. 13:2, show hospitality to **s-s**
Gen. 15:13; Ex. 22:21; Is. 1:7; Jer. 22:3
STRATEGIC Mark 6:21, a **s** day came when Herod
STRAW Gen. 24:25; Ex. 5:7; 1 Kin. 4:28; Job 41:27; Is. 11:7
STRAY Prov. 7:25, not **s** into her paths
James 5:19, any among you **s-s** from the truth
1 Pet. 2:25, **s-ing** like sheep
STREAM—*river* Ps. 1:3, planted by the **s-s** of water
Is. 32:2, **s-s** of water in a dry country
STREET—*square*
Prov. 1:20, Wisdom shouts in the **s**
Is. 59:14, truth has stumbled in the **s**
Matt. 6:2, **s-s**, that they may be honored
6:5, pray ... on the **s** corners
Acts 9:11, **s** called Straight
Rev. 21:21, **s** of the city was pure gold
2 Sam. 1:20; 22:43; Jer. 37:21; Nah. 2:4
STRENGTH Ex. 15:2, the LORD is my **s** and song
Ps. 28:7, LORD is my **s** and my shield
46:1, God is our refuge and **s**
Prov. 20:29, glory of young men ... **s**
Is. 40:29, He gives **s** to the weary
Mark 12:30, MIND, AND WITH ALL YOUR **S**
1 Pet. 4:11, by the **s** which God supplies
Rev. 1:16, sun shining in its **s**
Gen. 4:12; Judg. 6:14; 8:21; 16:6; 1 Sam. 28:20; Job 6:12; 21:23; Ps. 84:7; Prov. 31:3; Eccles. 9:16; Is. 41:1; Hab. 3:19
STRENGTHEN—*fortify* 1 Sam. 30:6, David **s-ed**
Is. 35:3, **s** the feeble
Luke 22:32, **s** your brothers
Col. 1:11, **s-ed** with all power
2 Thess. 2:17, **s** your hearts in every
1 Tim. 1:12, who has **s-ed** me
Heb. 13:9, heart to be **s-ed** by grace
James 5:8, **s** your hearts, for the coming
1 Pet. 5:10, confirm, **s** *and* establish you
Deut. 3:28; Judg. 16:28; 2 Chr. 11:11; Job 4:3; Is. 35:3; Ezek. 34:16; Nah. 3:14
STRETCH Ps. 68:31, **s** out her hands to God
Ps. 104:2, **s-ing** out heaven like
Is. 28:20, too short ... to **s** out
Job 30:24; 38:5; Jer. 10:12
STRETCHER
Luke 5:19, let him down ... with his **s**
STRICKEN Is. 53:4, we ... esteemed Him **s**
Is. 1:5; Jer. 14:19
STRICT Acts 26:5, the **s-est** sect of our religion
STRIFE—*quarrel*
Prov. 16:28, perverse man spreads **s**
18:6, fool's lips bring **s**
Rom. 13:13, not in **s** and jealousy
1 Cor. 3:3, jealousy and **s** among you
Gal. 5:20, enmities, **s**, jealousy
Titus 3:9, foolish controversies ... and **s**
Gen. 13:7; Prov. 6:14,19; 10:12; 13:10; 20:3; Is. 58:4
STRIKE Ex. 7:17, I will **s** the water
Ex. 12:12, **s** down all the first-born
Ps. 91:12; Matt. 4:6; Luke 4:11, **s** your foot
Matt. 26:31, I WILL **S** DOWN THE SHEPHERD
Acts 23:3, God is going to **s** you
Gen. 4:23; Prov. 17:26; 19:25; Is. 49:10; Jer. 18:18
STRING Ps. 11:2; 33:2; Hab. 3:19
STRIP Ps. 29:9, **s-s** the forests bare

STRIPES Deut. 25:3, beat him with **s**
STRIVE Gen. 6:3, Spirit shall not **s** with man
Ps. 103:9, not always **s** *with us*
Luke 13:24, **S** to enter by the narrow door
STRONG—*courage* 2 Sam. 22:33, God is my **s** fortress
Ps. 24:8, the LORD **s** and mighty
Prov. 20:1, **s** drink a brawler
Jer. 50:34, Their Redeemer is **s**
Luke 2:40, Child ... grow and become **s**
1 Cor. 4:10, we are weak, but you are **s**
2 Cor. 12:10, when I am weak, then I am **s**
Eph. 6:10, be **s** in the Lord
Heb. 11:34, from weakness were made **s**
James 3:4, ships ... driven by **s** winds
Gen. 49:14; Ex. 10:19; 14:21; Lev. 10:9; Deut. 31:6; Judg. 14:18; Job 17:9; Ps. 19:5; Prov. 31:6; Song 8:6; Is. 5:11; 41:6; Ezek. 30:21; Luke 14:31
STRONGHOLD—*fortress, refuge*
Ps. 9:9, **s** in times of trouble
59:9,17, For God is my **s**
94:22, the LORD has been my **s**
2 Sam. 5:9; 22:3; 1 Chr. 11:5,7; Ps. 62:2; Prov. 10:29; Ezek. 33:27
STRUCK—*touched*
Job 19:21, hand of God has **s** me
Ex. 7:20; Num. 20:11; 22:23; Acts 12:23
STRUGGLE Col. 2:1, how great a **s** I have
STUBBORN Rom. 2:5, **s-ness** and unrepentant heart
Jer. 3:17; Hos. 4:16
STUMBLE—*fall*
Matt. 5:29, right eye makes you **s**
11:6, blessed ... keeps from **s-ing** over
Luke 17:2, cause one of these ... to **s**
James 3:2, For we all **s** in many *ways*
1 Pet. 2:8, **s** because they are disobedient
2 Pet. 1:10, you will never **s**
Prov. 3:23; Is. 8:14; 40:30; Jer. 50:32; Dan. 11:19
STUMBLING BLOCK—*ruin*
Ezek. 18:30, not become a **s**
Matt. 16:23, Satan! You are a **s** to Me
18:7, Woe ... because of its **s-s**
Gal. 5:11, the **s** of the cross
STUPID—*senseless* Ps. 49:10; Prov. 30:2; Jer. 10:8,21
STUPOR Rom. 11:8, gave them a spirit of **s**
SUBJECT Luke 2:51, He continued in **s-ion** to them
Rom. 8:20, was **s-ed** to futility
Eph. 5:24, church is **s** to Christ
Titus 2:5, **s** to their own husbands
Heb. 2:8, PUT ALL THINGS IN **S-ION** UNDER
12:9, **s** to the Father
1 Pet. 3:22, and powers had been **s-ed** to Him
5:5, be **s** to your elders
SUBMISSIVE 1 Tim. 2:11, instruction with ... **s-ness**
1 Pet. 2:18, be **s** to your masters
3:1, be **s** to your own husbands
SUBSIDED Judg. 8:3, their anger ... **s**
SUBSTANCE Deut. 33:11, O LORD, bless his **s**
SUCCESS Gen. 24:12, grant me **s** today
SUDDENLY Mark 13:36, come **s** and find
Luke 21:34, come on you **s** like a trap
Acts 2:2, **s** there came from heaven
Job 21:13; Is. 29:5
SUFFER Job 3:20, light given to him who **s-s**
Ps. 34:10, lions do lack and **s** hunger
Mark 8:31, Son of Man must **s** many
Luke 24:46, Christ should **s** and rise again
Acts 28:5, into the fire and **s-ed** no harm
2 Tim. 2:3, **S** hardship with *me*
James 5:13, Is anyone among you **s-ing**
1 Pet. 2:21, Christ also **s-ed** for you
4:13, you share the **s-ings** of Christ
SUFFICIENT Ex. 36:7, material they had was **s**
Lev. 25:47, means of a stranger ... becomes **s**
John 6:7, denarii worth of bread is not **s**
2 Cor. 12:9, My grace is **s** for you

SUIT Gen. 2:18; 2 Sam. 15:2
SULLEN 1 Kin. 21:5, your spirit is so **s**
SUM 1 Pet. 3:8, To **s** up, let all be harmonious
SUMMER Jer. 8:20, past, **s** is ended
Matt. 24:32, you know that **s** is near
Gen. 8:22; Ps. 74:17; Prov. 26:1; Zech. 14:8
SUMMON—*call* Num. 10:2, use them for **s-ing**
Job 9:19, who can **s** Him
SUN Eccles. 1:9, nothing new under the **s**
Is. 38:8 **s-'s** shadow went back ten steps
Matt. 5:45, causes His **s** to rise
13:43, RIGHTEOUS . . . SHINE FORTH AS THE **S**
Luke 21:25, will be signs in **s**
1 Cor. 15:41, There is one glory of the **s**
Eph. 4:26, **s** go down on your anger
Rev. 12:1, woman clothed with the **s**
22:5, nor the light of the **s**
Gen. 15:12; Ex. 16:21; Lev. 22:7; Josh. 10:12; Ps. 72:5; 84:11; 104:19; 121:6; Song. 6:10; Is. 60:19; Ezek. 32:7; Amos 8:9
SUNK Ps. 38:2, Thine arrows have **s** deep
SUNRISE Luke 1:78, the **S** from on high shall visit us
SUNSHINE 2 Sam. 23:4, Through **s** after rain
SUPERIORITY 1 Cor. 2:1, not come with **s** of speech
SUPPER John 13:4, rose from **s** and laid aside
1 Cor. 11:20, not to eat the Lord's **S**
Rev. 19:9, marriage **s** of the Lamb
SUPPLANTS Prov. 30:23, maidservant . . . **s** her mistress
SUPPLICATION Ex. 9:28, Make **s** to the LORD
Ps. 28:2, Hear the voice of my **s-s**
Dan. 9:3, seek *Him by* prayer and **s-s**
SUPPLY Is. 3:1, **s** of bread . . . **s** of water
SUPPORT Matt. 10:10, worker is worthy of his **s**
Ex. 17:12; 2 Tim. 4:16
SURE—*trust* Num. 32:23, be **s** your sin will find you out
Ps. 19:7, testimony of the LORD is **s**
Heb. 13:18, **s** that we have a good conscience
2 Pet. 1:19, prophetic word made more **s**
SURELY Gen. 2:17, eat from it you shall **s** die
Gen. 28:16, **S** the LORD is in this place
Deut. 14:22, **s** tithe all the produce
Ps. 23:6, **S** goodness and lovingkindness
Is. 53:4, **S** our griefs He . . . bore
Mark 14:70 **S** you are *one* of them
Heb. 6:14, **S** BLESS YOU . . . **S** MULTIPLY YOU
Ex. 31:13; 2 Sam. 17:11; Job 35:13; Jer. 23:39
SURFACE Gen. 1:2; 7:18; Job 38:30
SURMISE Acts 27:27, sailors *began* to **s**
SURPASS 2 Chr. 9:6, You **s** the report I heard
Eph. 1:19, the **s-ing** greatness of His power
2:7, the **s-ing** riches of His grace
SURPLUS Mark 12:44, put in out of their **s**
SURPRISE 1 Pet. 4:12, do not be **s-d** . . . fiery ordeal
SURROUND Ps. 18:5, cords of Sheol **s-ed** me
Luke 19:43, your enemies . . . and **s** you
SUSTAIN Gen. 13:6; 36:7; Song 2:5
SWALLOW Matt. 23:24, gnat and **s** a camel
1 Cor. 15:54, DEATH IS **S-ED** UP IN VICTORY
Gen. 41:7,24; Num. 16:34; Job 20:15; Is. 25:8; Jon. 1:17; Hab. 1:13
SWEAR Gen. 50:5; Lev. 19:12; Is. 45:23; Zech. 5:3; Matt. 23:18; 26:74; Mark 14:71; James 5:12
SWEET 2 Sam. 23:1, the **s** psalmist of Israel
Ps. 55:14, had **s** fellowship together
Prov. 3:24, your sleep will be **s**
9:17, Stolen water is **s**
Is. 5:20; 43:24; Jer. 6:20
SWELL—*bulge* Num. 5:21,22; Deut. 8:4
SWIFT Job 7:6, My days are **s-er** than
Eccles. 9:11, race is not to the **s**
Rom. 3:15, FEET ARE **S** TO SHED BLOOD
SWINDLER Luke 18:11, 1 Cor. 5:11, 6:10
SWINE Prov. 11:22, ring of gold in a **s-'s** snout
Matt. 7:6, throw your pearls before **s**
Mark 5:11, big herd of **s** feeding there
Luke 15:15, into his fields to feed **s**
SWOOP Job 9:26, eagle that **s-s** on its prey
SWORD Gen. 3:24, flaming **s** which turned
Gen. 27:40, by your **s** you shall live
Ps. 57:4, their tongue a sharp **s**
64:3, sharpened their tongue like a **s**
Prov. 5:4, Sharp as a two-edged **s**
Is. 2:4; Mic. 4:3, hammer their **s-s** into plowshares
Hos. 2:18, abolish the bow, the **s**, and war
Matt. 10:34, not . . . peace, but a **s**
26:51, drew out his **s** and struck the slave
26:52, take up the **s** shall perish by the **s**
Eph. 6:17, **s** of the Spirit
Rev. 1:16, mouth became a sharp . . . **s**
Ex. 5:3; Deut. 32:25; Judg. 3:16,21,22; 2 Sam. 2:26; Is. 2:4; Jer. 15:2; Hos. 1:7
SYNAGOGUE Matt. 6:2, the **s-s** and in the streets
Matt. 6:5, pray in the **s-s** and on
12:9, He went into their **s**
13:54, teaching them in their **s**
John 16:2, make you outcasts from the **s**
18:20, I always taught in **s-s**
Acts 9:20, proclaim Jesus in the **s-s**
Rev. 2:9, but are a **s** of Satan

T

TABERNACLE Ex. 26:1, **t** with ten curtains
Matt. 17:4, make three **t-s** here
Rev. 21:3, **t** of God is among men
TABLE Is. 21:5, They set the **t**
Matt. 21:12, **t-s** of the money-changers
Mark 7:28, dogs under the **t** feed
John 2:15, overturned their **t-s**
Acts 6:2, word of God . . . to serve **t-s**
1 Cor. 10:21, partake of the **t** of the Lord
Lev. 24:6; Judg. 1:7; 2 Kin. 4:10; Ps. 23:5
TABLET Ex. 24:12, give you the stone **t-s**
Ex. 31:18, two **t-s** of the testimony
Luke 1:63, asked for a **t**
2 Cor. 3:3, on **t-s** of human hearts
Is. 8:1; Jer. 17:1
TAKE Ex. 20:7, not **t** the name of the LORD
Ex. 34:9, **t** us as Thine own possession
Prov. 4:13, **T** hold of instruction
Is. 4:1, seven women will **t** hold of
Matt. 5:40, **t** your shirt
7:5, first **t** the log out . . . eye
11:29, **T** My yoke upon you
26:26, **T**, eat; this is My body
Mark 2:9, Arise, and **t** up your pallet
13:33, **T** heed, keep on the alert
Luke 9:3, **T** nothing for your journey
John 1:29, **t-s** away the sin of the world
20:2, have **t-n** away the Lord
Acts 1:20, HIS OFFICE LET ANOTHER MAN **T**
Eph. 6:16, **t-ing** up the shield of faith
Rev. 10:9, **T** it, and eat it
Gen. 3:22; 12:19; 22:2; Num. 30:2; Judg. 21:22; 1 Sam. 4:3; Ezek. 18:17; 37:19; Hos. 1:2; Mic. 2:4; Matt. 21:21; 1 Cor. 13:5
TALE 2 Pet. 1:16, cleverly devised **t-s**
TALK Acts 20:9, as Paul kept on **t-ing**
Eph. 5:4, *no* filthiness and silly **t**
Titus 1:10, empty **t-ers** and deceivers
Job 11:2; 15:3; Prov. 24:2; Luke 1:65
TARGET—*mark* 1 Sam. 20:20; Lam. 3:12
TASK Eccles. 2:26, sinner He has given the **t**
TASTE Ex. 16:31, **t** was like wafers
Ps. 34:8, **t** and see that the LORD is good
Matt. 16:28, shall not **t** death
Acts 23:14, **t** nothing until we have killed Paul
Heb. 2:9, **t** death for every one
6:4, **t-d** of the heavenly gift
Job 6:6; 34:3; Prov. 24:13; Dan. 10:3
TAUGHT Ps. 71:17, hast **t** me from my youth
Is. 54:13, sons will be **t** of the LORD
John 8:28, I speak . . . as the Father **t** Me
Gal. 1:12, nor was I **t** it
1 Thess. 4:9, **t** by God to love one another

TAUNT Deut. 28:37; Job 30:9
TAX—*tribute* Num. 31:28, levy a **t** for the LORD
Matt. 17:24, teacher not pay the ... **t**
22:19, coin *used* for the **poll-t**
Luke 20:22, pay **t-es** to Caesar
Rom. 13:7, **t** to whom **t** is *due*
2 Kin. 23:35; Matt. 9:9
TAX-GATHERER Matt. 5:46, even the **t-s** do the same
Matt. 10:3, Matthew the **t**
Luke 18:13, **t**, standing some distance away
TEACH Ps. 25:4, **T** me Thy paths
Ps. 27:11, **T** me Thy way, O LORD
143:10, **T** me to do Thy will
Prov. 1:8, do not forsake your mother's **t-ing**
Matt. 7:29, **t-ing** them as *one* having authority
11:1, **t** and preach in their cities
15:9, **T-ING** AS THEIR DOCTRINES
Mark 1:22, they were amazed at His **t-ing**
4:2, **t-ing** them ... in parables
Luke 11:1, Lord, **t** us to pray
19:47, **t-ing** daily in the temple
John 7:16, My **t-ing** is not Mine, but His
14:26, He will **t** you all things
Acts 1:1, Jesus began to do and **t**
2:42, devoting ... to the apostles' **t-ing**
15:35, **t-ing** and preaching
Rom. 2:21, **t** another, do you not **t** yourself
16:17, contrary to the **t-ing** which you learned
1 Cor. 11:14, nature itself **t** you
Col. 2:22, commandments and **t-ings** of men
3:16, **t-ing** and admonishing
1 Tim. 1:3, not to **t** strange doctrines
2:12, do not allow a woman to **t**
2 Tim. 3:10, you followed my **t-ing**
Titus 2:3, **t-ing** what is good
Heb. 8:11, NOT **T** EVERY ONE HIS FELLOW
Rev. 2:20, **t-es** and leads my bond-servants
2:24, the rest ... who do not hold this **t-ing**
Ex. 4:12; Deut. 32:2; 1 Kin. 8:36; Job 11:4; 15:5; 21:22; 37:19; Prov. 4:2; Is. 28:9
TEACHER Matt. 8:19, **T**, I will follow You
Matt. 10:24, disciple is not above his **t**
17:24, Does your **t** not pay
23:8, for One is your **T**
Mark 5:35, why trouble the **T** any more
Luke 2:46, in the midst of the **t-s**
5:17, Pharisees and **t-s** of the law
John 3:2, come from God *as* a **t**
3:10, Are you the **t** of Israel
13:13, You call Me **T** and Lord
Acts 5:34, Gamaliel, a **t** of the Law
Rom. 2:20, a **t** of the immature
1 Cor. 12:29, All are not **t-s**
Eph. 4:11, some *as* pastors and **t-s**
1 Tim. 2:7, **t** of the Gentiles in faith
2 Tim. 4:3, accumulate for themselves **t-s**
James 3:1, Let not many *of you* become **t-s**
2 Pet. 2:1, be false **t-s** among you
1 Chr. 25:8; Prov. 5:13
TEAR—*rend* Eccles. 3:7, time to **t** apart
Matt. 5:29, makes you stumble, **t** it out
7:6, turn and **t** you to pieces
Luke 12:18, I will **t** down my barns
John 19:24, Let us not **t** it, but cast
Lev. 10:6; Job 18:4; Ps. 7:2; Prov. 14:1; Ezek. 13:20
TEAR—*weep* Ps. 80:5, fed them ... bread of **t-s**
Ps. 126:5, sow in **t-s** shall reap with joyful shouting
Is. 25:8, God will wipe **t-s** away
Luke 7:38, wet His feet with her **t-s**
2 Tim. 1:4, even as I recall your **t-s**
Rev. 7:17, God shall wipe away every **t**
21:4, He shall wipe away every **t**
2 Kin. 20:5; Ps. 56:8; Eccles. 4:1; Is. 16:9; Jer. 9:1; Lam. 1:2; 2:18
TEETH Gen. 49:12; Job 13:14; 19:20; 41:14; Ps. 57:4; Prov. 10:26; Jer. 31:29; Amos 4:6; Matt. 8:12

TELL 1 Chr. 16:24; Ps. 96:3, **T** of His glory among
Ps. 19:1, heavens are **t-ing** of the glory of God
66:16, I will **t** of what He has done for my soul
118:17, **t** of the works of the LORD
Matt. 8:4, See that you **t** no one
26:63, **t** us whether You are the Christ
Luke 13:32, Go and **t** that fox
John 18:34, did others **t** you about Me
Ex. 19:3; Lev. 5:1; Judg. 14:14; Ps. 2:7; Eccles. 10:14; Dan. 2:2,36; Joel 1:3; Zeph. 3:13
TEMPER Prov. 29:11, A fool ... loses his **t**
TEMPERATE Titus 2:2, Older men are to be **t**
TEMPEST Job 9:17; Ps. 55:8; Is. 28:2; Amos 1:14
TEMPLE—*house* 2 Sam. 22:7, from His **t** He heard my voice
Ps. 11:4, LORD is in His holy **t**
Is. 6:4, **t** was filling with smoke
Jer. 7:4, **t** of the LORD, the **t** of the LORD
Matt. 4:5, pinnacle of the **t**
12:6, something greater than the **t**
Mark 14:58, destroy this **t** made with hands
Luke 23:45, veil of the **t** was torn
John 2:19, Destroy this **t** ... I will raise it
2:21, speaking of the **t** of His body
1 Cor. 3:17, **t** of God is holy ... what you are
2 Cor. 6:16, we are the **t** of the living God
2 Thess. 2:4, takes his seat in the **t** of God
Rev. 21:22, God ... and the Lamb are its **t**
1 Sam. 1:9; 1 Chr. 29:1; Neh. 6:11
TEMPT—*test* Matt. 4:1, Jesus ... **t-ed** by the devil
Matt. 4:3, **t-er** came and said to Him
Luke 4:2, forty days while **t-ed** by the devil
1 Cor. 10:13, not allow you to be **t-ed**
1 Thess. 3:5, tempter might have **t-ed** you
Heb. 4:15, **t-ed** in all things as *we are*
James 1:13, God cannot be **t-ed** by evil
TEMPTATION—*trial*
Matt. 6:13, do not lead us into **t**
26:41, you may not enter into **t**
Luke 8:13, time of **t** fall away
1 Cor. 10:13, No **t** has overtaken you
2 Pet. 2:9, rescue the godly from **t**
TEN Deut. 10:4, the **T** Commandments
Ps. 91:7, **t** thousand at your right hand
Matt. 25:1, comparable to **t** virgins
Luke 15:8, if she has **t** silver coins
17:17, Were there not **t** cleansed
Gen. 31:7; Num. 14:22; Job 19:3; Ps. 33:2; Song 5:10; Is. 38:8; Ezek. 45:14; Dan. 1:14; 7:7
TEND John 21:15,17
TENDER Is. 53:2, He grew up ... like a **t** shoot
Matt. 24:32, branch has already become **t**
Luke 1:78, **t** mercy of our God
Eph. 4:32, **t-hearted**, forgiving each other
Gen. 18:7; 2 Sam. 23:4; 2 Kin. 22:19
TENT—*tabernacle* 1 Kin. 12:16, To your **t-s**, O Israel
Ps. 15:1, who may abide in Thy **t**
61:4, dwell in Thy **t** forever
84:10, in the **t-s** of wickedness
Is. 38:12, Like a shepherd's **t**
Gen. 4:20; 18:1; 24:67; 25:27; Num. 24:5; Job 12:6; Song 1:8; Jer. 10:20
TENTH—*tithe* Gen. 14:20, he gave him a **t** of all
Heb. 7:2, Abraham apportioned a **t** part
7:5, to collect a **t** from the people
Rev. 11:13, a **t** of the city fell
TERMS Gal. 3:15, Speak in **t** of human relations
TERRIBLE—*dread*
Deut. 8:15, great and **t** wilderness
Mal. 4:5, the great and **t** day of the LORD
Mark 9:26, throwing him into **t** convulsions
TERRIFYING Is. 21:1, wilderness, from a **t** land
Heb. 10:27, **t** expectation of judgment
10:31, **t** thing to fall into the hands of
TERROR—*fear, dread* Ps. 91:5, afraid of the **t** by night
Luke 21:11, **t-s** and great signs

Lev. 26:16; Deut. 32:25; Job 15:21; 24:17; 41:14;
Ps. 116:3; Eccles. 12:5; Is. 33:18

TEST—*try* Gen. 22:1, God **t-ed** Abraham
Ex. 17:2, Why do you **t** the LORD
Deut. 6:16, shall not put the LORD . . . to the **t**
2 Sam. 22:31, word of the LORD is **t-ed**
Job 12:11, Does not the ear **t** words
Ps. 26:2, **T** my mind and my heart
Prov. 30:5, Every word of God is **t-ed**
Is. 28:16, a **t-ed** stone . . . costly
Matt. 22:18, Why are you **t-ing** Me
Acts 5:9, put the Spirit . . . to the **t**
1 Cor. 3:13, fire itself will **t** . . . man's work
2 Cor. 13:5, **T** yourselves *to see* if you are
James 1:3, **t-ing** of your faith
1 Pet. 1:7, even though **t-ed** by fire
4:12, fiery ordeal . . . for your **t-ing**
1 John 4:1, **t** the spirits to see
Ex. 20:20; 1 Kin. 10:1

TESTIFY
Acts 2:40, many other words he . . . **t-ed**
20:24, to **t** solemnly of the gospel
26:22, **t-ing** both to small and great
Gal. 5:3, **t** again to every man
1 Pet. 5:12, **t-ing** that this is the true
Ex. 23:2; 2 Sam. 1:16; 1 Kin. 21:10; Job 15:6;
Is. 59:12

TESTIMONY—*witness* Ps. 19:7, **t** of the LORD is sure
Ps. 119:46, speak of Thy **t-s** before kings
Matt. 8:4, the offering . . . for a **t**
Luke 22:71, need do we have of **t**
John 8:17, the **t** of two men is true
1 Cor. 1:6, **t** concerning Christ was confirmed
2 Tim. 1:8, ashamed of the **t** of our Lord
Titus 1:13, This **t** is true
Rev. 19:10, **t** of Jesus is the spirit
Ex. 16:34; 25:16; 31:18; Lev. 16:13; Num. 35:30;
Is. 8:16

THANK 1 Chr. 16:7, to give **t-s** to the LORD
1 Chr. 16:34, O give **t-s** to the LORD
Ps. 92:1, good to give **t-s** to the LORD
100:4, Give **t-s** to Him
Matt. 15:36, giving **t-s**, He broke *them*
26:27, took a cup and gave **t-s**
Luke 18:11, God, I **t** Thee that I am not
22:19, when He had given **t-s**, He broke
Rom. 6:17, But **t-s** be to God
14:6, he gives **t-s** to God
1 Cor. 14:16, Amen at your giving of **t-s**
15:57, but **t-s** be to God
Eph. 1:16, do not cease giving **t-s** for you
5:20, always giving **t-s** for all things
1 Thess. 3:9, what **t-s** can we render to God
5:18, in everything give **t-s**
2 Thess. 1:3, always to give **t-s** to God

THANKSGIVING—*gratitude*
Ps. 26:7, with the voice of **t**
95:2, before His presence with **t**
100:4, Enter His gates with **t**
Phil. 4:6, supplication with **t**
Rev. 7:12, and **t** and honor and power
Lev. 7:12; Neh. 11:17

THEIR Gen. 15:13, a land that is not **t-s**
Matt. 5:3, **t-s** is the kingdom of heaven
1 Cor. 1:2, Christ, **t** *Lord* and ours

THEN—*therefore* Gen. 4:26, **T** *men* began to call
Ex. 15:1, **T** Moses . . . sang this song
Matt. 6:9, Pray, **t**, in this way
24:14, **t** the end shall come
Mark 4:28, first the blade, **t** the head
13:26, T THEY SHALL SEE THE SON
Luke 20:25, **T** render to Caesar
Rom. 3:9, What **t**? Are we better
1 Cor. 13:12, but **t** face to face
2 Cor. 12:10, **t** I am strong

THERE Gen. 1:3, Let **t** be light; and **t** was
Lev. 7:7, **t** is one law for them
Matt. 2:13, remain **t** until I tell you
24:23, Behold, here is Christ or **t** *He is*
Luke 8:32, **t** was a herd of many swine
Rev. 21:25, **t** shall be no night **t**

THEREFORE 1 Pet. 4:1, **T**, since Christ has suffered
1 Pet. 4:7, **t**, be of sound judgment

THICK Ex. 10:22; Deut. 32:15; Joel 2:2

THIEF Matt. 6:19, **t-s** break in and steal
John 10:10, **t** comes only to steal
1 Cor. 6:10, nor **t-s**, nor covetous
1 Thess. 5:2, just like a **t** in the night
Deut. 24:7; Job 24:14; Ps. 50:18; Prov. 29:24;
Is. 1:23; Joel 2:9

THINE Luke 22:42, not My will, but **T** be done
John 17:10, Mine are **T**, and **T** are Mine

THING Ps. 8:6, put all **t-s** under his feet
Eccles. 3:1, appointed time for **every-t**
Matt. 19:20, All these **t-s** I have kept
19:26, with God all **t-s** are possible
21:24, I will ask you one **t**
Mark 9:23, All **t-s** are possible to him
10:21, One **t** you lack
Luke 2:19, Mary treasured . . . these **t-s**
10:42, *only* a few **t-s** are necessary
John 14:14, ask Me **any-t** in My name
Acts 2:44, had all **t-s** in common
Phil. 3:13, but one **t** *I do*
4:8, let your mind dwell on these **t-s**
1 Tim. 4:15, Take pains with these **t-s**
James 3:10, **t-s** ought not to be this way
Rev. 16:3, every living **t** in the sea died
Gen. 7:23; 15:1; Ex. 20:17; Job 42:2; Ps. 2:1;
Eccles. 9:5; Is. 7:13; 12:5; Ezek. 8:17

THINK—*esteem, thought* Prov. 23:7, as he **t-s**
Matt. 5:17, not **t** that I came to abolish
22:42, do you **t** about the Christ
John 5:39, you **t** that in them . . . life
Rom. 12:3, but to **t** so as . . . sound
14:14, to him who **t-s** anything to be unclean
1 Cor. 13:11, child, **t** as a child
14:20, do not be children in your **t-ing**
2 Cor. 11:16, no one **t** me foolish
Gal. 6:3, anyone **t-s** he is something
James 1:26, **t-s** himself to be religious

THIRD Ex. 20:5, **t** and fourth *generations*
Matt. 16:21, raised up on the **t** day
Luke 24:21, is the **t** day since
John 21:17, said to him the **t** time
1 Cor. 15:4, raised on the **t** day
2 Cor. 12:2, caught up to the **t** heaven

THIRST Ps. 42:2, My soul **t-s** for God
Matt. 5:6, **t** for righteousness
25:35, I was **t-y**, and you gave
John 4:13, drinks of this water shall **t**
6:35, believes . . . shall never **t**
19:28, said, I am **t-y**
Rom. 12:20, IF HE IS T-Y, GIVE HIM
2 Cor. 11:27, in hunger and **t**
Ex. 17:3; Judg. 15:18; Job 24:11; Ps. 69:21;
104:11; Is. 29:8; 41:17; 49:10; 65:13; Lam.
4:4

THIRTY Matt. 26:15, to him **t** pieces of silver
Ex. 21:32; Num. 20:29; Judg. 10:4; 12:9; 14:12;
Zech. 11:12; Luke 3:23

THIRTY-NINE
2 Cor. 11:24, received . . . **t** *lashes*

THIS—*something* Rev. 2:4, I have **t** against you

THISTLE Is. 34:13, Nettles and **t-s** in its fortified cities

THORN—*hook* Prov. 15:19, as a hedge of **t-s**
Prov. 26:9, *Like* a **t** . . . into the hand of
Is. 55:13, Instead of the **t** bush the cypress
Jer. 4:3, not sow among **t-s**
12:13, sown wheat . . . reaped **t-s**
Matt. 7:16, Grapes . . . from **t** bushes
13:7, others fell among the **t-s**
27:29, weaving a crown of **t-s**
John 19:5, wearing the crown of **t-s**
2 Cor. 12:7, a **t** in the flesh
Gen. 3:18; Num. 33:55; Judg. 8:7; Eccles. 7:6;
Song 2:2

THOROUGH—*diligent*
Deut. 19:18, judges shall investigate **t-ly**

THOUGHT—*reason, motive, plot*
Gen. 6:5, **t-s** of his heart
1 Chr. 28:9, every intent of the **t-s**
Job 21:27, I know your **t-s**
Ps. 94:11, know the **t-s** of man
Is. 55:8, My **t-s** are not your **t-s**
Matt. 9:4, Jesus knowing their **t-s**
15:19, heart come evil **t-s**
THOUSAND—*countless, clan*
1 Sam. 18:7, slain his **t-s** ... David his ten **t-s**
Job 9:3, answer Him ... a **t** *times*
Ps. 84:10, a day in Thy ... better than ... **t**
91:7, **t** may fall ... ten **t** at your right
Eccles. 7:28, found one man among a **t**
Mark 6:44, five **t** men who ate
8:9, about four **t** were *there*
1 Cor. 14:19, ten **t** words in a tongue
2 Pet. 3:8, **t** years as one day
Jude 14, came with many **t-s** of His
Lev. 26:8; Eccles. 6:6
Song 4:4; Is. 30:17; Jer. 32:18; Dan. 7:10; Rev. 5:11
THRASH Judg. 8:7, **t** your bodies with the thorns
THREE Job 2:11, Job's **t** friends heard
Prov. 30:15, **t** things ... not be satisfied
30:18, **t** things ... too wonderful
30:21, **t** things ... earth quakes
30:29, **t** things ... are stately
Dan. 6:10, knees **t** times a day
Jon. 1:17, fish **t** days and **t** nights
Matt. 12:40, JONAH WAS T DAYS AND T NIGHTS
17:4, make **t** tabernacles here
18:20, two or **t** have gathered
26:34, deny Me **t** times
27:63, After **t** days I *am*
Luke 2:46, after **t** days they found Him
10:36, Which of these **t** ... a neighbor
John 2:19, in **t** days I will raise it
Acts 2:41, about **t** thousand souls
9:9, **t** days without sight
1 Cor. 13:13, faith, hope, love, these **t**
Gen. 6:10; Ex. 34:23; Eccles. 4:12; Luke 12:52; 2 Cor. 11:25; 12:8
THRESH—*tread, beat, trample*
Deut. 25:4; 2 Sam. 24:21; 1 Chr. 21:20; Is. 21:10; 1 Tim. 5:18
THRESHING FLOOR
Matt. 3:12, thoroughly clean His **t**
THRESHOLD—*door* Ps. 84:10, stand at the **t** of the house
THREW—*toss, put*
2 Sam. 16:13, cast stones and **t** dust
2 Kin. 9:33, So they **t** her down
Luke 9:42, **t** him ... convulsion
19:35, they **t** their garments on the colt
THRIVE Job 8:16, He **t-s** before the sun
THROAT Ps. 69:3, crying; my **t** is parched
Rom. 3:13, T IS AN OPEN GRAVE
Ps. 5:9; 115:7; Prov. 23:2
THRONE Ps. 11:4, LORD's **t** is in heaven
Ps. 93:2, **t** is established from of old
Is. 66:1, Heaven is My **t**
Matt. 5:34, for it is THE T OF GOD
19:28, sit upon twelve **t-s**
Acts 7:49, HEAVEN IS MY T
Heb. 1:8, THY T ... IS FOREVER AND EVER
4:16, with confidence to the **t** of grace
Rev. 4:2, **t** was standing in heaven
20:11, I saw a great white **t**
Gen. 41:40; Ex. 11:5; 1 Kin. 22:19
THRONG Ps. 55:14, in the house of God in the **t**
THROUGH Is. 43:2, **t** the waters ... **t** the fire
Matt. 19:24, camel ... **t** the eye of a needle
Luke 6:1, passing **t** *some* grainfields
John 3:17, world should be saved **t** Him
Acts 10:43, bear witness that **t** His name
Rom. 1:8, thank my God **t** Jesus Christ
Gal. 4:7, then an heir **t** God
Eph. 2:8, you have been saved **t** faith
Phil. 4:13, do all things **t** Him
1 John 4:9, we might live **t** Him
Gen. 12:6; Ex. 14:16; Eccles. 10:18; Is. 62:10
THROW Gen. 37:20, **t** him into one of the pits
Eccles. 3:6, time to keep ... time to **t** away
Luke 9:39, **t-s** him into a convulsion
THRUSH Jer. 8:7, the swift and the **t**
THRUST—*cast, push* Josh. 23:5; Prov. 12:18; 18:5
THUNDER Mark 3:17, Boanerges ... Sons of **T**
John 12:29, multitude ... saying that it had **t-ed**
Rev. 14:2, voice ... like the sound of loud **t**
Ex. 9:23; 1 Sam. 2:10; 2 Sam. 22:14; Job 26:14; Ps. 81:7; Is. 29:6
THWART 2 Sam. 15:34; 17:14; 1 Thess. 2:18
TIDINGS—*message, news*
Ps. 112:7, He will not fear evil **t**
Rom. 10:15, BRING GLAD T OF GOOD THINGS
TILL—*cultivate* Jer. 27:11; Heb. 6:7
TIMBER—*wood*
2 Chr. 2:16, cut whatever **t** you need
TIME—*season, day, hour* Gen. 4:3; Judg. 15:1; Prov. 25:13
Job 22:16, snatched away before their **t**
Eccles. 3:1–8, appointed **t** for everything
9:12, man does not know his **t**
Is. 25:8, will swallow up death for all **t**
Dan. 12:7, for a **t**, **t-s**, and half a **t**
Hos. 10:12, it is **t** to seek the LORD
Matt. 2:7, ascertained from them the **t**
24:45, give them their food ... proper **t**
26:18, My **t** is at hand
John 7:6, My **t** is not yet at hand
1 Cor. 7:29, the **t** has been shortened
Gal. 6:9, in due **t** we shall reap
1 Tim. 2:6, testimony *borne* at the proper **t**
Jude 18, In the last **t** there shall be mockers
Rev. 1:3, for the **t** is near
2:21, I gave her **t** to repent
Eccles. 7:17; Song 2:12; Amos 5:13; Hag. 1:2; Zech. 14:7; Matt. 13:30; 24:43; Acts 5:34
TIMELY Prov. 15:23, how delightful is a **t** word
TIMES—*season*
1 Chr. 12:32, men who understood the **t**
Job 24:1, **t** not stored up by the Almighty
Ps. 9:9, stronghold in **t** of trouble
31:15, My **t** are in Thy hand
Dan. 2:21, changes the **t** and epochs
Matt. 16:3, *discern* the signs of the **t**
Acts 1:7, not for you to know **t**
Rev. 12:14, time and **t** and half a time
TIMID—*fearful* Matt. 8:26; Mark 4:40
TINGLE 1 Sam. 3:11; 2 Kin. 21:12; Jer. 19:3
TIP Job 38:37, Or **t** the water jars of the heavens
TIRED Gen. 27:46, I am **t** of living
TITHE—*tenth* Lev. 27:30, all the **t** of the land
Num. 18:26, take from ... Israel the **t**
18:28, offering to the LORD from your **t-s**
Deut. 12:17, the **t** of your grain
14:22, **t** all the produce
Matt. 23:23, you **t** mint and dill
Luke 18:12, pay **t-s** of all that I get
Heb. 7:8, mortal men receive **t-s**
TODAY—*age, day, life* Gen. 41:9, mention **t** of my own offenses
Ps. 2:7, **T** I have begotten Thee
Luke 23:43, **t** you shall be with Me in Paradise
Acts 13:33; Heb. 1:5, T I HAVE BEGOTTEN THEE
Heb. 13:8, Jesus Christ *is* the same ... **t**
TOIL—*labor, work, trouble*
Gen. 5:29, the **t** of our hands
31:42, and the **t** of my hands
Job 9:29, Why then should I **t** in vain
Matt. 6:28, do not **t** nor do they spin
1 Cor. 15:58, knowing that your **t** is not *in* vain
TOLD Matt. 24:25, I have **t** you in advance
Mark 3:9, He **t** His disciples
Luke 2:18, **t** them by the shepherds
John 4:39, **t** me all the things that I *have* done
14:2, not so, I would have **t** you
TOMB—*grave, place*
Is. 22:16, you have hewn a **t** for
Matt. 23:27, like whitewashed **t-s**
27:52, the **t-s** were opened

John 11:17, been in the **t** four days
12:17, Lazarus out of the **t**
19:41, in the garden a new **t**, in which
20:11, standing outside the **t** weeping
Rev. 11:9, bodies to be laid in a **t**
TOMORROW Prov. 27:1, Do not boast about **t**
Is. 22:13, drink, for **t** we may die
Matt. 6:34, do not be anxious for **t**
James 4:14, not know ... life will be like **t**
TONE—*voice* Gal. 4:20, and to change my **t**
TONGUE—*language*
Ex. 4:10, speech and slow of **t**
Job 5:21, hidden from the scourge of the **t**
Ps. 5:9, They flatter with their **t**
34:13, keep your **t** from evil
57:4, their **t** a sharp sword
64:3, sharpened their **t** like a sword
140:3, sharpen their **t-s** as a serpent
Prov. 12:18, **t** of the wise brings healing
15:4, soothing **t** is a tree of life
25:15, soft **t** breaks the bone
Is. 30:27, His **t** is like a consuming fire
Mark 7:35, impediment of his **t** was removed
16:17, they will speak with new **t-s**
Luke 16:24, in water and cool off my **t**
Acts 2:4, began to speak with other **t-s**
Rom. 14:11, EVERY T SHALL GIVE PRAISE
1 Cor. 13:1, with the **t-s** of men and of
14:4, who speaks in a **t** edifies himself
14:5, that you all spoke in **t-s**
14:14, if I pray in a **t**
14:39, do not forbid to speak in **t-s**
Phil. 2:11, every **t** should confess ... Jesus
James 3:5, **t** is a small part
3:8, no one can tame the **t**
1 Pet. 3:10, REFRAIN HIS T FROM EVIL
Rev. 5:9, *men* from every tribe and **t**
Job 6:30; 20:12; 29:10; Prov. 6:17; Is. 50:4; Jer. 9:8
TOOK Gen. 8:9, **t** her, and brought her into the ark
Ex. 4:7, **t** it out of his bosom
TOOTH Ex. 21:24; Lev. 24:20
Deut. 19:21, eye, **t** for **t**
Prov. 25:19, like a bad **t**
Matt. 5:38, EYE FOR AN EYE, AND A T FOR A T
TOP Gen. 28:12, **t** reaching to heaven
Ex. 19:20, to the **t** of the mountain
2 Kin. 19:26, as grass on the house **t-s**
Matt. 27:51, veil ... torn ... from **t** to bottom
Heb. 11:21, leaning on the **t** of his staff
TORCH Gen. 15:17, a flaming **t** which passed
Judg. 15:5, set fire to the **t-es**
Dan. 10:6, his eyes were like flaming **t-es**
TORE Matt. 26:65, high priest **t** his robes
2 Sam. 13:19; 1 Kin. 11:30; Job 1:20
TORMENT Job 19:2, How long will you **t** me
Luke 8:28, do not **t** me
16:23, Hades ... being in **t**
16:28, to this place of **t**
2 Pet. 2:8, felt *his* righteous soul **t-ed**
Rev. 9:5, **t** was like the **t** of a scorpion
TORN Gen. 37:33, Joseph ... been **t** to pieces
Josh. 9:4, wineskins, worn-out and **t**
Job 18:14, is **t** from the security
Matt. 27:51, veil of the temple was **t**
TOSS—*shake* Job 7:4, I am continually **t-ing**
Is. 54:11, **storm-t-ed**, and not comforted
Acts 22:23, **t-ing** dust into the air
Eph. 4:14, **t-ed** here and there by waves
James 1:6, driven and **t-ed** by the wind
TOTTER Is. 24:20; 28:7
TOUCH—*handle* Gen. 3:3, not eat from it or **t** it
Ps. 105:15, Do not **t** My anointed ones
Matt. 9:21, If I only **t** His garment
Mark 5:30, Who **t-ed** My garments
Luke 24:39, it is I Myself; **t** Me and see
1 Cor. 7:1, not to **t** a woman
Col. 2:21, do not taste, do not **t**
Ex. 19:12; Lev. 5:2; Job 5:19
TOWARD—*against* Rom. 8:7, is hostile **t** God
TOWER—*stronghold*
Prov. 18:10, name ... is a strong **t**
Matt. 21:33, AND BUILT A T
Gen. 11:4; Ps. 48:12; Mic. 4:8
TRADE—*craft* Acts 18:3, he was of the same **t**
Acts 19:25, with the workmen of similar **t-s**
TRADER 2 Chr. 9:14, the **t-s** and merchants
TRAIN—*fit, instruct* 1 Chr. 12:8, men **t-ed** for war
2 Tim. 3:16, for **t-ing** in righteousness
Heb. 5:14, senses **t-ed** to discern good and evil
12:11, to those who have been **t-ed**
TRAMPLE Job 9:8, **t-s** down the waves
Prov. 25:26, *Like* a **t-d** spring
Hab. 3:12, didst **t** the nations
TRANSCRIBE
Prov. 25:1, proverbs ... king of Judah, **t-d**
TRANSFORM—*change*
Rom. 12:2, **t-ed** by the renewing of
Phil. 3:21, who will **t** the body
TRANSGRESS Num. 14:41; Josh. 7:11; Jer. 2:8
TRANSGRESSION—*trespass, sin*
Job 14:17, My **t** is sealed up
33:9, pure without **t**
Ps. 32:1, he whose **t** is forgiven
39:8, Deliver me from all my **t-s**
51:3, I know my **t-s**
103:12, removed our **t-s** from us
Matt. 6:14, forgive men for their **t-s**
Col. 2:13, forgiven us all our **t-s**
Gen. 31:36; Ex. 34:7; Num. 14:18; Josh. 24:19; Prov. 10:12; 29:6; Is. 53:5; Ezek. 18:30; Matt. 6:15
TRANSGRESSOR
Ps. 37:38, **t-s** will be ... destroyed
51:13, I will teach **t-s** Thy ways
Is. 53:12, numbered with the **t-s**
Mark 15:28, reckoned with **t-s**
James 2:11, become a **t** of the law
TRANSLATE Ezra 4:18, has been **t-d** and read
John 1:42, which **t-d** means Peter
TRAP—*entangle*
Matt. 22:15, how they might **t**
Mark 12:13, to **t** Him in a statement
TREACHEROUS
Prov. 2:22, the **t** will be uprooted
13:15, way of the **t** is hard
2 Sam. 18:13; Prov. 22:12; Is. 21:2; 24:16; Jer. 3:20; Lam. 1:2; Hos. 5:7; Mal. 2:10
TREAD—*trample* Luke 10:19, **t** upon serpents
Rev. 19:15, **t-s** the wine press
Job 24:11; Is. 16:10; 41:25; Jer. 25:30
TREASURE—*possession, gain*
Gen. 43:23, given you **t** in your
Is. 33:6, fear of the LORD is his **t**
Matt. 2:11, opening their **t-s** they presented
6:21, where your **t** is, there will
12:35, out of his good **t** brings
13:44, **t** hidden in the field
19:21, you shall have **t** in heaven
Col. 2:3, hidden all the **t-s** of wisdom
James 5:3, stored up your **t**
Deut. 33:19; Job 3:21; 23:12; Prov. 21:20
TREAT Mark 12:4, **t-ed** him shamefully
Luke 2:48, why have You **t-ed** us this way
TREE—*grove, cross* Gen. 1:11, fruit **t-s** bearing
Gen. 2:9, **t** of life ... knowledge
3:8, God among the **t-s**
Ps. 1:3, **t** firmly planted by streams
37:35, like a luxuriant **t**
104:16, **t-s** of the LORD drink their fill
Prov. 3:18, She is a **t** of life
Is. 55:12, **t-s** ... will clap *their* hands
Matt. 3:10, every **t** ... not bear good fruit
7:17, good **t** bears good fruit
12:33, **t** is known by its fruit
Mark 8:24, see men ... like **t-s**
Luke 19:4, climbed up into a sycamore **t**
John 1:50, saw you under the fig **t**
Jude 12, autumn **t-s** without fruit
Rev. 2:7, eat of the **t** of life

TREE *(Continued)*
Gen. 18:4; 21:33; Deut. 20:19; 21:22; Judg. 9:8; Prov. 27:18; Song 8:5; Is. 40:20; Mic. 4:4
TREMBLE—*fear*
1 Chr. 16:30; Ps. 96:9, **T** before Him ... earth
Job 26:11, pillars of heaven **t**
Ps. 4:4, **T**, and do not sin
Is. 13:13, make the heavens **t**, and the earth
Mark 5:33, woman fearing and **t-ing**
Phil. 2:12, with fear and **t-ing**
2 Pet. 2:10, do not **t** when they revile
Lev. 26:6; Deut. 20:3; Ps. 2:11
TRENCH 2 Kin. 3:16, valley full of **t-es**
TRESPASS—*fault*
Gal. 6:1, if a man is caught in any **t**
Eph. 2:1, dead in your **t-s** and sins
TRIAL Deut. 7:19, great **t-s** which your eyes saw
Acts 4:9, if we are on **t** today
Gal. 4:14, a **t** to you in my bodily condition
James 1:12, a man who perseveres under **t**
TRIBE Gen. 49:28, these are the twelve **t-s**
Num. 1:4, a man of each **t**
Ps. 122:4, even the **t-s** of the LORD
Matt. 24:30, all the **t-s** of the earth
Luke 22:30, judging the twelve **t-s**
TRIBULATION—*affliction*
Matt. 24:21, will be a great **t**
John 16:33, world you have **t**
Rom. 5:3, **t** brings about perseverance
12:12, persevering in **t**
Eph. 3:13, not to lose heart at my **t-s**
TRIBUNAL—*judgment*
Acts 25:10, standing before Caesar's **t**
TRIBUTE—*tax* Ezra 7:24, impose tax, **t** or toll
TRICK—*craftiness* Matt. 2:16, Herod ... **t-ed** by the magi
Luke 20:23, He detected their **t-ery**
TRIED Ex. 2:15, Pharaoh ... **t** to kill Moses
Ps. 12:6, As silver **t** in a furnace
TRIM Ex. 30:7, when he **t-s** the lamps
TRIUMPH Ex. 32:18, sound of the cry of **t**
TROUBLE—*distress, affliction, pain*
1 Kin. 20:7, see how this man is looking for **t**
Job 4:8, plow iniquity ... who sow **t** harvest it
5:6, does **t** sprout from the ground
5:7, man is born for **t**
Ps. 9:9, A stronghold in times of **t**
25:18, my affliction and my **t**
27:5, day of **t** He will conceal
41:1, deliver him in a day of **t**
Prov. 10:10, who winks the eye causes **t**
25:20, sings songs to a **t-d** heart
31:7, remember his **t** no more
Eccles. 8:6, a man's **t** is heavy
Matt. 2:3, Herod ... heard it, he was **t-d**
Luke 6:18, **t-d** with unclean spirits
24:38, Why are you **t-d**
John 12:27, My soul has become **t-d**
Acts 20:10, Do not be **t-d**
1 Pet. 3:14, DO NOT BE **T-D**
Gen. 41:51; Ps. 77:4; 138:7; Is. 65:16; Ezek. 32:9
TRUE—*sure*
Prov. 11:18, sows righteousness ... **t** reward
Luke 16:11, entrust the **t** *riches*
John 1:9, There was the **t** light
6:32, gives you the **t** bread
6:55, My flesh is **t** food ... is **t** drink
7:28, He who sent Me is **t**
8:17, testimony of two men is **t**
Rom. 3:4, let God be found **t**
Phil. 4:8, whatever is **t**
Titus 1:13, This testimony is **t**
1 Pet. 5:12, the **t** grace of God
Rev. 3:14, faithful and **t** Witness
TRULY—*indeed* Josh. 7:20, **T**, I have sinned
Is. 45:15, **T**, Thou art a God who
Matt. 5:18, For **t** I say to you
John 1:51, **T**, **t**, I say to you
Gen. 24:49; 2 Sam. 14:5
TRUMPET—*horn* Is. 27:13, great **t** will be blown
Matt. 6:2, alms, do not sound a **t**
Ex. 19:16; Judg. 7:16
TRUST—*faith, confidence*
2 Chr. 20:20, **t** in the LORD ... **t**
Job 8:14, whose **t** a spider's web
Ps. 4:5, And **t** in the LORD
118:8, Than to **t** in man
Prov. 11:28, **t-s** in his riches will fall
31:11, husband **t-s** in her
Is. 26:4, **T** in the LORD forever
Jer. 7:4, Do not **t** in deceptive words
20:10, All my **t-ed** friends
Mic. 7:5, Do not **t** in a neighbor
2 Cor. 1:9, should not **t** in ourselves
Heb. 2:13, I WILL PUT MY **T** IN HIM
TRUSTWORTHY—*true*
Prov. 20:6, who can find a **t** man
1 Tim. 3:1; 4:9, It is a **t** statement
TRUTH 1 Kin. 2:4, walk before Me in **t**
Ps. 15:2, speaks **t** in his heart
119:160, Thy word is **t**
Prov. 3:3, not let kindness and **t** leave you
23:23, Buy **t**, and do not sell *it*
Matt. 22:16, we know that You are **t-ful**
Luke 4:25, But I say to you in **t**
John 1:14, full of grace and **t**
8:32, **t** shall make you free
14:6, way, and the **t**, and the life
Rom. 1:25, **t** of God for a lie
Gal. 2:5, **t** of the gospel might remain
Phil. 1:18, in pretense or in **t**
1 Tim. 3:15, pillar and support of the **t**
2 Tim. 2:15, handling ... the word of **t**
1 John 1:8, the **t** is not in us
Gen. 42:16; 1 Kin. 22:16; Is. 39:8; Zech. 8:16
TRY—*prove* Luke 14:19, oxen ... going to **t** them
Luke 19:3, **t-ing** to see who Jesus was
Deut. 4:34; Is. 22:4; Acts 9:26
TUNIC—*garment, coat* Gen. 37:3; Lev. 16:4; Matt. 10:10; Luke 9:3
TURBAN—*diadem* Job 29:14; Ezek. 21:26
TURMOIL—*trouble* Prov. 15:16; Jer. 50:34
TURN 2 Kin. 20:10, shadow **t** backward ten steps
2 Chr. 34:2, did not **t** aside to the right or to the left
Job 23:11, kept His way and not **t-ed** aside
Ps. 119:157, I do not **t** aside from Thy
Prov. 7:25, Do not let your heart **t** aside
Is. 45:22, **T** to Me, and be saved
53:6, Each ... has **t-ed** to his own way
Jer. 26:3, everyone will **t** from his evil way
Hos. 11:7, My people are bent on **t-ing** from Me
Joel 2:31, sun will be **t-ed** into darkness
Matt. 5:39, cheek, **t** to him the other
Acts 1:25, from which Judas **t-ed** aside
1 Tim. 5:15, **t-ed** aside to follow Satan
James 5:20, who **t-s** a sinner from the error
1 Pet. 3:11, **T** AWAY FROM EVIL
Ex. 23:2; Deut. 17:11; Ruth 1:16; 1 Kin. 20:26; 2 Kin. 17:13; Job 1:1; 2:3; 23:13; 36:21; Ps. 80:14; 119:51; Prov. 4:5; Is. 1:4; Jer. 23:20; Joel 2:14
TUTOR—*instruct* 1 Cor. 4:15, have countless **t-s** in Christ
TWELVE Gen. 17:20, become the father of **t** princes
Gen. 35:22, there were **t** sons of Jacob
Matt. 10:1, summoned His **t** disciples
Mark 3:14, He appointed **t**
Luke 2:42, when He became **t**
John 11:9, **t** hours in the day
Rev. 12:1, a crown of **t** stars
TWICE—*doubly*
Gen. 41:32, repeating ... dream to Pharaoh **t**
Num. 20:11, struck the rock **t**
1 Sam. 18:11, David escaped ... **t**
Mark 14:30, before a cock crows **t**
Luke 18:12, I fast **t** a week
TWITTER Is. 38:14, *like* a crane, so I **t**
TWO—*both* Gen. 1:16, God made the **t** great lights
Ex. 31:18, **t** tablets of the testimony

Matt. 2:16, children ... **t** years old
5:41, one mile, go with him **t**
6:24, No one can serve **t** masters
18:19, **t** of you agree on earth
19:5, T SHALL BECOME ONE FLESH
Luke 17:35, **t** women grinding
1 Cor. 6:16, T WILL BECOME ONE FLESH
Gal. 4:24, these *women* are **t** covenants
Eph. 2:15, make the **t** into one new man
Lev. 8:2; Eccles. 4:9

U

UGLY—*bad* Gen. 41:3, **u** and gaunt
UMPIRE Job 9:33, There is no **u** between us
UNAPPROACHABLE
1 Tim. 6:16, dwells in **u** light
UNAPPROVED
2 Cor. 13:7, though we ... appear **u**
UNAWARE Rom. 1:13, do not want you to be **u**
UNBELIEF Mark 9:24, help *me in* my **u**
Rom. 11:23, continue in their **u**
Heb. 3:12, an evil, **u-ing** heart
UNBELIEVERS Luke 12:46, a place with the **u**
1 Cor. 14:23, ungifted men or **u**
2 Cor. 6:14, bound together with **u**
UNBLEMISHED 1 Pet. 1:19, **u** and spotless
UNCEASING Rom. 9:2, sorrow and **u** grief
UNCLEAN Lev. 5:2, person touches any **u** thing
2 Chr. 29:5, **u-ness** out from the holy place
Job 14:4, make the clean out of the **u**
Ps. 106:39, became **u** in their practices
Is. 6:5, man of **u** lips
Ezek. 4:13, eat their bread **u**
Matt. 10:1, authority over **u** spirits
Mark 5:13, **u** spirits entered the swine
9:25, He rebuked the **u** spirit
Luke 9:42, Jesus rebuked the **u** spirit
Acts 10:14, eaten anything unholy and **u**
Rom. 14:14, nothing is **u** in itself
Rev. 16:13, three **u** spirits like frogs
18:2, prison of every **u** spirit
21:27, nothing **u** ... shall ever come into it
UNCOVER Ezek. 21:24; Hos. 7:1
UNDEFILED Heb. 7:26, holy, innocent, **u**
Heb. 13:4, *marriage* bed *be* **u**
James 1:27, pure and **u** religion
UNDER Ex. 23:5, lying *helpless* **u** its load
Matt. 5:15, put it **u** the peck-measure
John 1:50, saw you **u** the fig tree
Rom. 3:9, Jews and Greeks are all **u** sin
Eph. 1:22, all things ... **u** His feet
1 Pet. 5:6, **u** the mighty hand of God
UNDERGARMENTS Lev. 6:10; 16:4; Ezek. 44:18
UNDERSTAND—*know, perceive* 1 Chr. 28:19
Gen. 11:7, not **u** one another's speech
Jer. 17:9, the heart ... Who can **u** it
Matt. 15:17, Do you not **u**
Luke 24:45, opened ... to **u** the Scriptures
John 8:43, Why do you not **u** what I am saying
Acts 10:34, **u** *now* that God is not one
2 Pet. 3:16, some things hard to **u**
Prov. 1:6; Is. 6:9; Dan. 8:17; Matt. 15:10
UNDERSTANDING—*comprehending*
Prov. 2:2, Incline your heart to **u**
Jer. 10:12, by His **u** He has stretched
Matt. 15:16, Are you also still without **u**
Eph. 4:18, being darkened in their **u**
2 Tim. 2:7, Lord will give you **u**
Ex. 36:1; Job 17:4; Ps. 32:9
UNDISCIPLINED 2 Thess. 3:7, not act in an **u** manner
2 Thess. 3:11, leading an **u** life
UNDISTURBED Judg. 8:28, land was **u** for forty years
2 Chr. 14:1, land was **u** for ten years
UNEDUCATED Acts 4:13, that they were **u** and untrained
UNFAITHFUL Ezra 10:2, **u** to our God
UNFATHOMABLE Rom. 11:33, How ... **u** His ways
UNFEELING Ps. 17:10, closed their **u** heart
UNFOLDING Ps. 119:130, **u** of Thy words gives light
UNFRUITFUL—*barren*
2 Kin. 2:19, water is bad, and the land is **u**
Matt. 13:22; Mark 4:19, and it becomes **u**
1 Cor. 14:14, my mind is **u**
Eph. 5:11, **u** deeds of darkness
2 Pet. 1:8, neither useless nor **u** in the true knowledge
UNGIFTED—*uneducated*
1 Cor. 14:16, the **u** say the Amen
UNGODLY—*wicked, worthless*
Rom. 5:6, Christ died for the **u**
Titus 2:12, to deny **u-ness**
Jude 18, after their own **u** lusts
UNHOLY—*common*
Acts 10:15, no *longer* consider **u**
UNIMPRESSIVE—*weak*
2 Cor. 10:10, personal presence is **u**
UNINTENTIONALLY Lev. 4:2; 5:15; Num. 15:27
UNITE Phil. 2:2, same love, **u-d** in spirit
Heb. 4:2, not **u-d** by faith
UNJUST—*unrighteous*
Prov. 29:27, **u** man is abominable
Jer. 17:11, makes a fortune, but **u-ly**
Heb. 6:10, God is not **u** so as to forget
1 Pet. 3:18, *the* just for *the* **u**
UNKNOWN Acts 17:23, TO AN U GOD
2 Cor. 6:9, as **u** yet well-known
Gal. 1:22, I was still **u** by sight
UNLESS—*except* Gen. 32:26, **u** you bless me
Ps. 127:1, U the LORD builds the house
Matt. 5:20, **u** your righteousness surpasses
18:3, **u** you are converted
24:22, **u** those days had been cut short
Mark 13:20, **u** the Lord had shortened *those* days
Luke 13:3, **u** you repent, you will ... perish
John 3:2, **u** God is with him
3:3, **u** one is born again
4:48, U you *people* see signs
6:53, **u** you eat the flesh
20:25, U I shall see ... imprint of the nails
Rom. 10:15, shall they preach **u** they are sent
1 Cor. 15:36, does not come to life **u** it dies
2 Tim. 2:5, **u** he competes according to the rules
Deut. 32:30; Is. 1:9; Amos 3:3
UNLOVING Rom. 1:31, untrustworthy, **u**
2 Tim. 3:3, **u**, irreconcilable
UNOCCUPIED Matt. 12:44, finds it **u**
UNPLEASANT—*evil*
Gen. 47:9, few and **u** have been the years
UNPROFITABLE Titus 3:9, they are **u** and worthless
Heb. 13:17, this would be **u** for you
UNPUNISHED Ex. 21:19; 1 Kin. 2:9
Ex. 20:7, LORD will not leave him **u**
UNQUENCHABLE
Matt. 3:12, burn ... chaff with **u** fire
Mark 9:43, into the **u** fire
UNREASONING 2 Pet. 2:12, like **u** animals
UNRESTRAIN
Prov. 29:18, no vision, people are **u-ed**
UNRIGHTEOUS—*unjust*
Is. 55:7, the **u** man his thoughts
Matt. 5:45, rain on *the* righteous and *the* **u**
Luke 16:10, **u** in ... little thing is **u** also in much
16:11, faithful in the *use of* **u** Mammon
Rom. 3:5, God who inflicts wrath is not **u**
1 Cor. 6:9, **u** shall not inherit the kingdom
2 Pet. 2:9, keep the **u** under punishment
UNRIGHTEOUSNESS
1 Cor. 13:6, not rejoice in **u**
1 John 5:17, All **u** is sin
UNRULY 1 Thess. 5:14, admonish the **u**
2 Thess. 3:6, who leads an **u** life
UNSETTLING Acts 15:24, **u** your souls
UNSTEADY Prov. 25:19, and an **u** foot
UNSUSPECTING Rom. 16:18, hearts of the **u**
UNTAUGHT—*uneducated*
2 Pet. 3:16, **u** and unstable distort

UNTIE Luke 19:30, a colt ... **u** it and bring it
UNTIL John 5:17, My Father is working **u** now
UNTIMELY 1 Cor. 15:8, to one **u** born
UNTRAINED Acts 4:13, uneducated and **u** men
UNWISE Deut. 32:6, O foolish and **u** people
Eph. 5:15, walk, not as **u** men
UNWORTHY
Gen. 32:10, **u** of all the lovingkindness
Luke 17:10, We are **u** slaves
UP Ex. 15:8, flowing waters stood **u** like a heap
UPHOLD Ps. 119:117, **U** me that I may be safe
Is. 41:13, God, who **u-s** your right hand
UPPER 2 Sam. 11:21, woman throw an **u** millstone
Luke 22:12, large, furnished, **u** room
Acts 1:13, they went up to the **u** room
19:1, Paul ... passed through the **u** country
UPRIGHT Deut. 32:4, Righteous and **u** is He
Prov. 4:11, led you in **u** paths
Eccles. 7:29, God made men **u**
Mic. 7:2, is no **u** person among men
Acts 14:10, Stand **u** on your feet
1 Thess. 2:10, devoutly and **u-ly** and blamelessly
Num. 23:10; Job 1:8; 4:7
UPRIGHTNESS Prov. 17:26; Is. 59:14; Mal. 2:6
UPROAR 1 Kin. 1:41, city making such an **u**
Ps. 2:1, Why are the nations in an **u**
UPROOT Job 19:10, has **u-ed** my hope
Luke 17:6, Be **u-ed** and be planted
UPSET—*turn* 2 Sam. 6:6, oxen nearly **u** *it*
Acts 17:6, men ... **u** the world have come here
2 Tim. 2:18, **u** the faith of some
Titus 1:11, **u-ing** whole families
UPWARD Phil. 3:14, prize of the **u** call
URGE—*constrain* Ruth 1:16, Do not **u** me to leave you
Prov. 16:26, his hunger **u-s** him *on*
Luke 24:29, And they **u-d** Him, saying
Rom. 12:1, I **u** you therefore, brethren
URGENT 1 Sam. 21:8, king's matter was **u**
USE Gen. 21:15; Deut. 32:23
1 Chr. 12:2, **u-ing** both the right hand and
2 Cor. 3:12, **u** great boldness in *our* speech
1 Tim. 5:23, **u** a little wine for the sake
USELESS Lev. 26:16, sow your seed **u-ly**
Rom. 3:12, TOGETHER THEY HAVE BECOME U
USURIOUS Lev. 25:36, not take **u** interest from him
USURY—*interest* Neh. 5:10, leave off this **u**
Prov. 28:8, increases his wealth by ... **u**
UTENSILS Ex. 31:8, the table also and its **u**
UTMOST—*remote*
1 Thess. 2:16, wrath has come ... to the **u**
UTTER—*speak* Ps. 119:171, Let my lips **u** praise
Acts 26:25, I **u** words of sober truth
1 Cor. 14:9, **u** by the tongue speech
UTTERANCE Luke 21:15, give you **u** and wisdom
Acts 2:4, Spirit was giving them **u**
2 Cor. 8:7, in faith and **u** and knowledge
Eph. 6:19, **u** may be given to me
UTTERLY—*greatly* Is. 42:17, be **u** put to shame
Rom. 7:13, sin might become **u** sinful

V

VAGRANT Gen. 4:12, a **v** and a wanderer
VAIN—*empty, futile* Ps. 2:1, peoples devising a **v** thing
Prov. 12:11, he who pursues **v** *things*
1 Cor. 15:14, then our preaching is **v**
VALLEY—*ravine*
Ps. 23:4, through the **v** of the shadow
Song 2:1, The lily of the **v-s**
Jer. 31:40, the whole **v** of the dead bodies
Ezek. 37:1, **v**; and it was full of bones
Joel 3:14, the **v** of decision
Gen. 14:17; 19:17; Josh. 10:12; 2 Sam. 18:18; 1 Kin. 20:28; 2 Kin. 3:16
VALUATION Lev. 5:15, according to your **v** in silver
Lev. 27:25, Every **v** of yours
Num. 18:16, redeem them, by your **v**
VALUE—*price* Matt. 10:31, you are of more **v** than
Matt. 12:12, how much more **v** is a man than a sheep
13:46, one pearl of great **v**
VANITY—*breath, emptiness, futility*
Prov. 22:8, sows iniquity will reap **v**
Eccles. 1:2, **V** of **v-es**! All is **v**
2 Pet. 2:18, arrogant *words* of **v**
VARICOLORED—*colored*
Gen. 37:3, made him a **v** tunic
Gen. 37:23,32
VARIETY 1 Cor. 12:4, there are **v-es** of gifts
VARIOUS—*manifold*
Matt. 4:24, taken with **v** diseases
24:7, in **v** places there will be famines
2 Tim. 3:6, led on by **v** impulses
James 1:2, when you encounter **v** trials
1 Pet. 1:6, distressed by **v** trials
VAST—*large* Is. 22:18, *To be cast* into a **v**
VAULT Job 22:14, walks on the **v** of heaven
VEGETABLES Deut. 11:10; 1 Kin. 21:2
Prov. 15:17, better is a dish of **v** where love is
Rom. 14:2, he who is weak eats **v** *only*
VEGETATION—*grass* Gen. 1:11, earth sprout **v**
Ps. 104:14, **v** for the labor of man
Gen. 1:12; Ps. 105:35; Is. 42:15; Jer. 12:4
VEIL Is. 25:7, **v** ... stretched over all nations
Matt. 27:51, **v** of the temple was torn
2 Cor. 3:13, put a **v** over his face
Heb. 6:19, which enters within the **v**
9:3, behind the second **v**
Gen. 24:65; Ex. 34:33; Lev. 4:6; Song 4:1; Is. 47:2
VENGEANCE—*revenge*
Lev. 19:18, You shall not take **v**
Deut. 32:35, **V** is Mine
Ps. 94:1, O LORD, God of **v**
Is. 34:8, the LORD has a day of **v**
Heb. 10:30, **V** IS MINE
Gen. 4:15; 2 Sam. 22:48; Ps. 18:47; Jer. 15:15; Nah. 1:2
VENOM—*poison*
Deut. 32:24, **v** of crawling things
32:33, wine is the **v** of serpents
Job 20:14, the **v** of cobras
VENTURE Job 4:2, one **v-s** a word with you
VERY Gen. 1:31, behold, it was **v** good
Num. 12:3, Moses was **v** humble
Judg. 3:17, Eglon was a **v** fat man
1 Sam. 5:11, hand of God was **v** heavy
Ps. 46:1, A **v** present help in trouble
Matt. 17:15, an epileptic, and is **v** ill
Mark 16:2, **v** early on the first day
Luke 12:7, the **v** hairs of your head
Ex. 14:10; Mark 6:26
VESSEL Num. 5:17, holy water in ... **v**
Ps. 31:12, I am like a broken **v**
Rom. 9:22, **v-s** of wrath
2 Cor. 4:7, treasure in earthen **v-s**
2 Tim. 2:21, will be a **v** for honor
1 Pet. 3:7, as with a weaker **v**
Rev. 2:27, AS THE V-S OF THE POTTER
Ex. 7:19; 2 Kin. 4:3; Is. 22:24; Jer. 48:11
VEXATION—*wrath* Prov. 12:16, fool's **v** is known
VICTORIOUS Rev. 15:2, come off **v** from the beast
VICTORY—*deliverance*
2 Sam. 23:10, LORD brought ... great **v**
2 Kin. 5:1, had given **v** to Syria
1 Chr. 11:14, the LORD saved them by a great **v**
29:11, the glory and the **v**
Ps. 98:1, holy arm have gained the **v**
Matt. 12:20, HE LEADS JUSTICE TO V
1 Cor. 15:54, DEATH IS SWALLOWED UP IN V
15:55, DEATH, WHERE IS YOUR V
1 John 5:4, **v** that has overcome the world
VIGOR Deut. 34:7, Moses ... nor his **v** abated

VINDICATE Ps. 82:3, **V** the weak and fatherless
Matt. 11:19, wisdom is **v-d** by her deeds
VINE Matt. 26:29, drink ... fruit of the **v**
John 15:1, I am the true **v**
Gen. 40:9; Judg. 9:12; 1 Kin. 4:25; Ps. 128:3; Song 2:13; Is. 36:16; Jer. 2:21; Ezek. 19:10; Joel 1:12; Mal. 3:11
VINEGAR Ruth 2:14; Ps. 69:21; Prov. 10:26
VINEYARD 1 Cor. 9:7, Who plants a **v**, and does not eat
Gen. 9:20; Lev. 19:10; 1 Kin. 21:1; Song 1:6; 2:15; Is. 1:8; Jer. 12:10; Matt. 20:4
VIOLATE 2 Sam. 13:12, do not **v** me
Rom. 4:15, law, neither is there **v-ion**
VIOLENCE Gen. 6:11, earth was filled with **v**
Ps. 55:9, **v** and strife in the city
Prov. 4:17, drink the wine of **v**
16:29, man of **v** entices his neighbor
Is. 53:9, He had done no **v**
Matt. 11:12, kingdom of heaven suffers **v**
Gen. 49:5; Job 5:21; Ps. 27:12; Prov. 26:6; Is. 60:18; Jer. 22:3
VIOLENT Ps. 18:48, rescue me from the **v** man
Ps. 37:35, seen a **v**, wicked man
Prov. 11:16, **v** men attain riches
Matt. 8:28, so exceedingly **v** that no one
VIPER—*adder, serpent* Job 20:16, **v-'s** tongue
Matt. 3:7, You brood of **v-s**
Acts 28:3, a **v** came out because of the heat
Is. 11:8; 14:29; 30:6
VIRGIN—*maid, maiden*
Matt. 1:23, **V** SHALL BE WITH CHILD
1:25, kept her a **v**
25:1, comparable to ten **v-s**
Luke 1:27, **v-'s** name was Mary
1 Cor. 7:28, if a **v** should marry
2 Cor. 11:2, to Christ ... a pure **v**
Gen. 24:16; Ex. 22:16,17; Judg. 19:24; Job 31:1; Ps. 148:12; Jer. 2:32; 31:13
VISIBLE Eph. 5:13, **v** when ... exposed by the light
VISION Prov. 29:18, Where there is no **v**
Is. 22:1, concerning the valley of **v**
Joel 2:28, young men will see **v-s**
Hab. 2:2, Record the **v** And inscribe *it*
Matt. 17:9, Tell the **v** to no one
Acts 2:17, YOUNG MEN SHALL SEE **V-S**
2 Cor. 12:1, to **v-s** and revelations
Gen. 15:1; 1 Sam. 3:1; Job 20:8; Lam. 2:9; Dan. 2:19
VISIT Ex. 20:5, **v-ing** the iniquity of
Matt. 25:36, sick, and you **v-ed** Me
Luke 1:68, **v-ed** us ... redemption for His people
James 1:27, **v** orphans and widows
VOICE—*sound* Ps. 19:3, Their **v** is not heard
Prov. 5:13, the **v** of my teachers
Eccles. 5:3, the **v** of a fool
Song 2:12, **v** of the turtledove
Is. 28:23, Give ear and hear my **v**
Matt. 2:18, **V** WAS HEARD IN RAMAH
3:3, **V** OF ONE CRYING
3:17, behold, a **v** out of the heavens
Mark 9:7, **v** came out of the cloud
Luke 3:4, **v** of one crying ... wilderness
John 5:25, **v** of the Son of God
Acts 10:13, **v** came to him, Arise, Peter
Rom. 10:18, **V** HAS GONE OUT INTO ALL
1 Thess. 4:16, **v** of *the* archangel
Heb. 12:26, His **v** shook the earth
2 Pet. 2:16, dumb donkey ... **v** of a man
Rev. 3:20, if any one hears My **v**
5:11, heard the **v** of many angels
Deut. 4:30; Josh. 6:10; 2 Sam. 19:35; Job 4:10; Is. 40:3; Jer. 7:34; Dan. 4:31; Rev. 6:1
VOID—*empty*
Gen. 1:2, earth was formless and **v**
Jer. 19:7, make **v** the counsel
Rom. 4:14, faith is made **v**
VOLUNTARILY—*willing* 1 Cor. 9:17, I do this **v**
VOLUNTEER Judg. 5:2, That the people **v-ed**
VOMIT Job 20:15, will **v** them up
Prov. 26:11, dog that returns to its **v**
Is. 19:14, staggers in his **v**
Jon. 2:10, fish ... **v-ed** Jonah up
2 Pet. 2:22, DOG RETURNS TO ITS OWN **V**
VOTIVE—*vow* Lev. 7:16, his offering is a **v**
VOW—*oath, votive* Gen. 28:20, Jacob made a **v**
Deut. 23:22, if you refrain from **v-ing**
Judg. 11:30, Jephthah made a **v**
2 Sam. 15:7, let me go and pay my **v**
Ps. 22:25, I shall pay my **v-s**
Eccles. 5:5, not **v** ... **v** and not pay
Matt. 5:33, MAKE FALSE **V-S** ... FULFILL YOUR **V-S**
Acts 18:18, he was keeping a **v**
VULTURES Matt. 24:28, the **v** will gather
Luke 17:37, will the **v** be gathered

W

WAGED—*fought*
Rev. 12:7, dragon and his angels **w** war
WAGES—*hire* Gen. 30:18, God has given me **w**
Deut. 23:18, the **w** of a dog
Job 7:2, hired man ... waits for his **w**
Luke 3:14, be content with your **w**
10:7; 1 Tim. 5:18, laborer is worthy ... **w**
John 4:36, who reaps is receiving **w**
2 Pet. 2:13, **w** of doing wrong
2:15, **w** of unrighteousness
Gen. 29:15; Ex. 2:9; Lev. 19:13; Deut. 24:15; Prov. 11:18; Jer. 22:13; Hag. 1:6; Zech. 8:10; 11:12; Mal. 3:5
WAIL—*mourn, weep* Jer. 9:19, voice of **w-ing** is heard
Mark 5:38, loudly weeping and **w-ing**
Esth. 4:3; Mic. 1:8
WAIST Matt. 3:4, leather belt about his **w**
WAISTBAND Jer. 13:1, Go and buy ... a linen **w**
WAIT Gen. 49:18, For Thy salvation I **w**
Ps. 25:5, For Thee I **w** all day
27:14; 37:34, **W** for the LORD
119:81, I **w** for Thy word
Prov. 1:18, **w** for their own blood
Is. 26:8, have **w-ed** for Thee eagerly
30:18, He **w-s** on high
Mark 15:43, **w-ing** for the kingdom
Luke 12:36, men who are **w-ing**
Rom. 8:23, **w-ing** eagerly for *our* adoption
Gal. 5:5, **w-ing** for the hope of
Phil. 3:20, we ... **w** for a Savior
Ruth 3:18; 2 Kin. 5:2; Job 14:14; Lam. 3:10; Dan. 12:12; Hos. 6:9; Mic. 7:2; Hab. 2:3; 3:16
WALK—*follow, journey* Gen. 3:8, God **w-ing** in the garden
Gen. 5:24, Enoch **w-ed** with God
Ex. 14:29, Israel **w-ed** on dry land
Lev. 26:3, If you **w** in My statutes
Josh. 18:8, Go and **w** through the land
1 Sam. 2:30, **w** before Me forever
Job 22:14, **w-s** on the vault of
Ps. 1:1, not **w** in the counsel of
15:2, He who **w-s** with integrity
23:4, **w** through the valley of
26:3, have **w-ed** in Thy truth
39:6, man **w-s** about as a phantom
Prov. 10:9, **w-s** in integrity **w-s** securely
Eccles. 2:14, fool **w-s** in darkness
Is. 2:3, we may **w** in His paths
2:5, **w** in the light of the LORD
3:16, **w** with heads held high
9:2, people who **w** in darkness
Amos 3:3, Do two men **w** together unless
Mic. 6:8, **w** humbly with your God
Matt. 9:5, Rise, and **w**
14:29, Peter ... **w-ed** on the water
John 6:19, Jesus **w-ing** on the sea
Acts 3:6, name of Jesus ... **w**
14:8, lame ... who had never **w-ed**
Rom. 6:4, **w** in newness of life
1 Cor. 3:3, fleshly ... not **w-ing** like mere men
2 Cor. 4:2, not **w-ing** in craftiness
5:7, **w** by faith, not by sight

WALK *(Continued)*
Gal. 5:16, **w** by the Spirit
6:16, **w** by this rule
Eph. 4:1, **w** in a manner worthy of
5:2, **w** in love, just as Christ also
5:8, **w** as children of light
Col. 2:6, so **w** in Him
1 Thess. 2:12, **w** in a manner worthy
1 John 2:6, **w** in the same manner as He **w-ed**
Rev. 3:4, will **w** with Me in white
21:24, nations shall **w** by its light
Deut. 33:25; 1 Kin. 2:4; Job 1:7; Eccles. 10:7; Jer. 2:5; 9:14; Ezek. 36:12; Hos. 11:10; Zeph. 1:17; Mal. 2:6; John 7:1
WALL Ex. 14:22, waters *were like* a **w**
Josh. 2:15, she was living on the **w**
2 Kin. 20:2, turned his face to the **w**
Neh. 4:6, So we built the **w**
Acts 9:25, **w**, lowering him in a basket
23:3, strike you, you white-washed **w**
Eph. 2:14, barrier of the dividing **w**
Heb. 11:30, **w-s** of Jericho fell
Rev. 21:12, had a great and high **w**
Gen. 49:22; 1 Kin. 20:30; Job 24:11; Ps. 18:29; Prov. 18:11; Is. 25:4; Jer. 52:4; Ezek. 4:2; 8:7; 12:5; Joel 2:9; Amos 7:7; Hab. 2:11
WANDER—*flee* Gen. 21:14, **w-ed** about in the wilderness
Ps. 55:7, I would **w** far away
119:21, Who **w** from Thy commandments
Prov. 27:8, bird ... **w-s** from her nest
1 Tim. 6:10, **w-ed** away from the faith
Jude 13, **w-ing** stars, for whom
Job 15:23; Is. 35:8; Lam. 4:14; Hos. 9:17
WANT—*lack, need*
Job 30:3, From **w** and famine they are
Ps. 23:1, shepherd, I shall not **w**
Prov. 28:27, who gives to the poor never **w**
Mark 9:35, If any one **w-s** to be first
Luke 23:8, Herod ... had **w-ed** to see Him
Gal. 4:21, you who **w** to be under law
WAR—*fight, quarrel, battle* Gen. 14:2; Ex. 13:17
Josh. 11:23, the land had rest from **w**
Ps. 46:9, makes **w-s** to cease
55:21, his heart was **w**
76:3, weapons of **w**
Eccles. 3:8, A time for **w**
Is. 2:4, never ... will they learn **w**
Dan. 9:26, to the end there will be **w**
Matt. 24:6, hearing of **w-s** and rumors of **w-s**
Rom. 7:23, waging **w** against the law of my
2 Cor. 10:3, do not **w** according to the flesh
James 4:1, wage **w** in your members
1 Pet. 2:11, which wage **w** against the soul
Rev. 12:7, there was **w** in heaven
19:11, He judges and wages **w**
Num. 21:14; Prov. 20:18; Mic. 2:8; Rev. 2:16
WAR-CLUB Jer. 51:20, You are My **w**
WARD Dan. 4:35, no one can **w** off His hand
WARFARE 2 Sam. 17:8, father is an expert in **w**
2 Cor. 10:4, weapons of our **w** are not
WARM Eccles. 4:11, two lie down ... keep **w**
Mark 14:54, **w-ing** himself at the fire
John 18:25, Peter was standing and **w-ing** himself
James 2:16, be **w-ed** and be filled
1 Kin. 1:1; 2 Kin. 4:34; Job 31:20; Is. 47:14; Hag. 1:6
WARN Ezek. 33:8, speak to **w** the wicked
Matt. 2:12, having been **w-ed** *by God*
2:22, **w-ed** *by God* in a dream
3:7, vipers, who **w-ed** you to flee
Titus 3:10, after a first and second **w-ing**
Heb. 8:5, Moses was **w-ed** by God
11:7, being **w-ed** *by God*
2 Kin. 6:10; Eccles. 12:12
WARRIOR Job 16:14; Eccles. 9:11
WASH—*bathe, cleanse* 2 Kin. 5:10, Go ... **w** in the Jordan
Ps. 26:6, **w** my hands in innocence
51:2, **W** me ... from my iniquity
Is. 1:16, **W** yourselves, make yourselves clean
Matt. 6:17, **w** your face
15:2, not **w** their hands when
Luke 11:38, first ... **w-ed** before the meal
John 9:7, Go, **w** in the pool of Siloam
Acts 22:16, **w** away your sins
1 Cor. 6:11, you were **w-ed** ... sanctified
1 Tim. 5:10, she has **w-ed** the saints' feet
Heb. 6:2, instruction about **w-ings**
9:10, drink and various **w-ings**
10:22; bodies **w-ed** with pure water
Gen. 18:4; Ex. 19:10; 1 Kin. 22:38; Job 9:30; Jer. 4:14; Ezek. 16:9
WASTE Prov. 23:8, And **w** your compliments
Matt. 12:25; Luke 11:17, kingdom ... laid **w**
26:8, What is the point of this **w**
Rev. 18:19, in one hour she has been laid **w**
Lev. 26:31; Ps. 79:7; Is. 5:6; 45:18; Jer. 33:12; Ezek. 6:6; Joel 1:7
WATCH—*observe, guard* Gen. 31:49, Lord **w**
Ps. 63:6, in the night **w-es**
Prov. 4:23, **W** over your heart with all diligence
8:34, **W-ing** daily at my gates
Eccles. 11:4, He who **w-es** the wind will not sow
Matt. 26:40, could not keep **w** with Me
Luke 2:8, keeping **w** over their flock
Heb. 13:17, they keep **w** over your souls
Ex. 14:24; 2 Kin. 11:5; Job 7:20; Prov. 4:26; Zech. 11:11
WATCHMAN Is. 21:11, **W**, how far gone is the night
2 Kin. 9:17; Song 3:3; Hos. 9:8
WATER Gen. 1:2, over the surface of the **w-s**
Ex. 2:10, drew him out of the **w**
15:8, The flowing **w-s** stood up
2 Sam. 14:14, like **w** spilled on the ground
Job 14:19, **W** wears away stones
Ps. 1:3, planted by streams of **w**
23:2, beside quiet **w-s**
106:32, wrath at the **w-s** of Meribah
Prov. 9:17, Stolen **w** is sweet
Eccles. 11:1, your bread on the ... **w-s**
Is. 1:30, garden that has no **w**
11:9, As the **w-s** cover the sea
Jer. 2:13, fountain of living **w-s**
Matt. 3:11, baptize you in **w**
10:42, little ones even a cup of cold **w**
Mark 14:13, man ... carrying a pitcher of **w**
Luke 7:44, gave Me no **w** for My feet
John 3:5, unless one is born of **w**
4:10, given you living **w**
Acts 1:5, John baptized with **w**
8:36, Look! **W**! What prevents
1 Cor. 3:6, I planted, Apollos **w-ed**
Eph. 5:26, washing of **w** with the word
1 Tim. 5:23, No longer drink **w** *exclusively*
James 3:11, fresh and bitter **w**
1 Pet. 3:20, eight persons ... through *the* **w**
1 John 5:6, who came by **w** and blood
Rev. 22:17, take the **w** of life without cost
Gen. 24:43; Ex. 20:4; Deut. 8:7; Josh. 7:5; Judg. 5:4; 6:38; 1 Kin. 13:22; 2 Kin. 3:11; Neh. 9:11; Job 8:11; 11:16; Ps. 22:14; 46:3; Prov. 5:15; 20:5; Song 5:12; Is. 19:5; 32:2; Jer. 8:14; Lam. 1:16; Ezek. 4:11; 7:17; Dan. 1:12; 2 Pet. 3:5
WATERLESS Matt. 12:43, unclean spirit ... passes through **w**
WAVE Ps. 42:7, Thy **w-s** have rolled over me
Is. 48:18, righteousness like the **w-s**
Matt. 8:24, covered with the **w-s**
Mark 4:37, **w-s** were breaking over the boat
Jude 13, wild **w-s** of the sea
2 Sam. 22:5; Job 9:8; Zech. 2:9
WAX Ps. 22:14, My heart is like **w**
WAY—*journey, manner, path, road*
Gen. 3:24, **w** to the tree of life
Josh. 23:14, the **w** of all the earth
Job 3:23, a man whose **w** is hidden

Ps. 1:6, the **w** of the righteous
18:30, His **w** is blameless
25:8, instructs sinners in the **w**
Is. 30:21, This is the **w**, walk in it
Jer. 12:1, **w** of the wicked prospered
Ezek. 3:18, wicked from his wicked **w**
Matt. 2:12, departed ... by another **w**
3:3, READY THE **W** OF THE LORD
6:9, Pray, then, in this **w**
7:13, the **w** is broad
15:32, lest they faint on the **w**
Mark 1:3, MAKE READY THE **W** OF THE LORD
9:33, What were you discussing on the **w**
Luke 1:79, into the **w** of peace
John 1:23, STRAIGHT THE **W** OF THE LORD
14:6, I am the **w**, and the truth, and
Acts 9:2, found any belonging to the **W**
1 Cor. 12:31, a still more excellent **w**
2 Cor. 4:8, afflicted in every **w**
Heb. 10:20, by a new and living **w**
James 5:20, from the error of his **w**
2 Pet. 2:2, **w** of the truth will be maligned
2:15, forsaking the right **w**
Jude 11, gone the **w** of Cain
1 Sam. 12:23; 2 Sam. 22:33; Neh. 9:19; Ps. 50:23; Prov. 7:27; 12:15; Is. 26:7; 40:3; Jer. 2:36; 6:16; Nah. 1:3; Mal. 3:1

WAYS Deut. 8:6, to walk in His **w**
2 Kin. 17:13, Turn from your evil **w**
Prov. 6:6, ant ... Observe her **w**
Is. 2:3, teach us concerning His **w**
Hab. 3:6, His **w** are everlasting
Rom. 11:33, unfathomable His **w**
1 Cor. 4:17, **w** which are in Christ
James 1:8, unstable in all his **w**
Judg. 5:6; Prov. 3:17; Lam. 3:40; Ezek. 7:3

WEAK—*unimpressive*
Matt. 26:41; Mark 14:38, but the flesh is **w**
Acts 20:35, you must help the **w**
Rom. 4:19, without becoming **w** in faith
1 Cor. 1:27, **w** things of the world
4:10, we are **w**, but you are strong
1 Thess. 5:14, help the **w**
Num. 13:18; Judg. 16:17; Is. 14:10; Joel 3:10

WEAKNESS—*infirmity*
Rom. 15:1, bear the **w-es** of those
1 Cor. 1:25, **w** of God is stronger than
2:3, with you in **w** and in fear
15:43, it is sown in **w**
2 Cor. 12:9, power is perfected in **w**
13:4, crucified because of **w**
Heb. 4:15, sympathize with our **w-es**
11:34, from **w** were made strong

WEALTH—*substance, prosperity* Gen. 31:1
Deut. 8:18, giving you power to make **w**
2 Chr. 1:11, not ask for riches, **w**
Job 5:5, schemer is eager for their **w**
Ps. 49:6, those who trust in their **w**
Prov. 3:9, Honor the LORD from your **w**
13:7, poor, but has great **w**
13:11, **W** *obtained* by fraud
Eccles. 5:19, given riches and **w**
Is. 45:3, hidden **w** of secret places
Hag. 2:7, come with the **w** of all nations
2 Cor. 8:2, **w** of their liberality
Rev. 3:17, rich, and have become **w-y**
18:19, became rich by her **w**
Ruth 2:1; Job 20:10; Prov. 23:4; Is. 5:17

WEAPONS—*armor*
Eccles. 9:18, Wisdom is better than **w**
Jer. 21:4, turn back the **w** of war
Ezek. 32:27, down to Sheol with their **w**
2 Cor. 6:7, **w** of righteousness
10:4, **w** of our warfare
Deut. 1:41; 1 Sam. 31:9; 2 Chr. 23:10; Neh. 4:17; Job 20:24

WEAR Deut. 22:5, woman shall not **w** man's clothing
Job 14:19, Water **w-s** away stones
John 19:5, Jesus ... **w-ing** the crown of
James 2:3, who is **w-ing** the fine clothes
1 Pet. 3:3, and **w-ing** gold jewelry
Ex. 18:18; Deut. 8:4; Is. 50:9; Dan. 7:25; Matt. 11:8

WEARY—*faint, exhaust*
Job 3:17, there the **w** are at rest
Prov. 23:4, Do not **w** yourself to gain riches
25:25, cold water to a **w** soul
Eccles. 12:12, **w-ing** to the body
Is. 5:27, No one in it is **w** or stumbles
40:29, strength to the **w**
40:31, They will walk and not become **w**
50:4, sustain the **w** one with a word
Hab. 2:13, nations grow **w** for nothing
Matt. 11:28, Come to Me, all who are **w**
John 4:6, **w-ed** from His journey
Gal. 6:9, if we do not grow **w**
2 Sam. 17:2; Ps. 69:3; Prov. 25:17; Jer. 6:11

WEATHER—*day* Matt. 16:2, *will be* fair **w**

WEAVE—*embroider* Ex. 28:39; 38:23

WEB Job 18:8, he steps on the **w-ing**

WEDDING—*marriage* Song 3:11, day of his **w**
John 2:1, there was a **w** in Cana

WEEK Gen. 29:27, Complete the bridal **w**
Ex. 34:22, celebrate the Feast of **W-s**
Dan. 9:24, Seventy **w-s** have been decreed
Matt. 28:1, first *day* of the **w**
Luke 18:12, I fast twice a **w**

WEEP 1 Sam. 1:8, Hannah, why do you **w**
Neh. 8:9, do not mourn or **w**
Job 16:16, face is flushed from **w-ing**
16:20, My eye **w-s** to God
Eccles. 3:4, A time to **w**, and a time to laugh
Matt. 2:18, RACHEL **W-ING** FOR HER
13:42, **w-ing** and gnashing of
Mark 5:39, Why make a commotion and **w**
Luke 6:21, Blessed *are* you who **w** now
7:32, you did not **w**
John 11:31, to the tomb to **w** there
Acts 9:39, widows stood beside him **w-ing**
Rom. 12:15, who rejoice, and **w** with
James 4:9, miserable and mourn and **w**
Rev. 5:4, I *began* to **w** greatly
5:5, Stop **w-ing**; behold, the Lion
Gen. 43:30; Num. 11:13; Deut. 34:8; Judg. 11:37; Ps. 6:8; Is. 22:4; Jer. 9:1; Joel 1:5

WEIGH Prov. 16:2, the LORD **w-s** the motives
Dan. 5:27, you have been **w-ed** on the scales
Gen. 23:16; 24:22; 1 Sam. 2:3; Job 6:2; Ps. 58:2

WEIGHT Lev. 19:36, just balances, just **w-s**
Prov. 11:1, a just **w** is His delight
Ezek. 4:16, will eat bread by **w**
2 Cor. 4:17, eternal **w** of glory
Deut. 25:15; Job 28:25; Mic. 6:11

WELFARE 1 Sam. 17:18, the **w** of your brothers

WELL—*health, whole* Gen. 43:28, father is **w**
Deut. 4:40, that it may go **w** with you
1 Sam. 9:10, **W** said; come
2 Sam. 18:29, Is it **w** with the young man
Eccles. 12:6, pitcher by the **w** is shattered
Matt. 3:17, whom I am **w** pleased
Mark 7:37, has done all things **w**
Luke 5:31, not ... **w** who need a physician
6:26, men speak **w** of you
John 4:6, Jacob's **w** was there
5:6, Do you wish to get **w**
Gal. 5:7, You were running **w**
1 Tim. 3:4, his own household **w**
Gen. 4:7; Lev. 24:16; 2 Sam. 17:21; 20:9; 1 Chr. 11:17; Prov. 5:15; Eccles. 8:13; Song 4:15; Acts 15:29

WENT Is. 38:8, sun's *shadow* **w** back ten steps
Mark 1:28, news about Him **w** out
Jude 7, **w** after strange flesh

WEPT—*weep* Gen. 50:17, Joseph **w** when they
Matt. 26:75, went out and **w** bitterly
Luke 19:41, city and **w** over it
John 11:35, Jesus **w**

WEST Gen. 12:8, with Bethel on the **w**
Ex. 10:19, a very strong **w** wind
Ps. 107:3, east and from the **w**
Dan. 8:4, saw the ram butting **w-ward**

WET—*drench* Job 24:8, **w** with the mountain rains
Luke 7:44, **w** My feet with her tears
WHATEVER—*all* Ps. 1:3, in **w** he does, he prospers
Eccles. 9:10, **W** your hand finds to do
Matt. 7:12, **w** you want others to do for you
Luke 12:3, **w** you have said in the dark
John 11:22, **w** You ask of God
Rom. 14:23, **w** is not from faith is sin
1 Cor. 10:31, eat or drink or **w** you do
Gal. 6:7, for **w** a man sows
Eph. 6:8, **w** good things each one does
Phil. 4:8, **w** is true, **w** is honorable
Col. 3:17, **w** you do in word or deed
Gen. 31:16; Job 37:12
WHEAT—*kernel* Matt. 3:12, gather His **w** into the barn
Luke 22:31, to sift you like **w**
John 12:24, unless a grain of **w** falls
Rev. 6:6, quart of **w** for a denarius
Gen. 30:14; Ex. 34:22; Deut. 8:8; Judg. 6:11; 1 Sam. 12:17; Job 31:40
WHEEL—*whirl* Eccles. 12:6, **w** at the cistern is crushed
Is. 5:28, **w-s** like a whirlwind
Ezek. 1:16, one **w** were within another
1 Kin. 7:33; Prov. 20:26; Dan. 7:9; Nah. 3:2
WHELP Gen. 49:9; Deut. 33:22
WHERE Gen. 3:9, **W** are you
Ruth 1:17, **W** you die, I will die
Job 28:12, **w** can wisdom be found
Ps. 42:3, **W** is your God
139:7, **W** can I go from Thy Spirit
Prov. 29:18, **W** there is no vision
Is. 19:12, **w** are your wise men
Matt. 2:2, **W** is He who has been born
Luke 8:25, **W** is your faith
John 8:19, **W** is Your Father
8:21, **w** I am going, you cannot come
11:34, **W** have you laid him
Rom. 4:15, **w** there is no law
Gen. 28:15; 1 Sam. 27:10; 1 Cor. 1:20
WHILE—*moment* Is. 26:20, Hide for a little **w**
John 5:35, willing to rejoice for a **w**
WHIP 1 Kin. 12:11, disciplined you with **w-s**
Prov. 26:3, A **w** is for the horse
Nah. 3:2, The noise of the **w**
WHIRL Ps. 83:13, God, make them ... **w-ing** dust
WHIRLWIND—*storm, wind*
2 Kin. 2:1, Elijah by a **w** to
Ps. 58:9, sweep them away with a **w**
Prov. 1:27, calamity comes on ... **w**
Jer. 4:13; Hos. 8:7
WHISPER Ps. 41:7, hate me **w** together
WHITE Gen. 49:12, teeth **w** from milk
Ps. 51:7, I shall be **w-r** than snow
Is. 1:18, They will be as **w** as snow
Matt. 5:36, make one hair **w** or black
Luke 9:29, clothing *became* **w** *and* gleaming
John 4:35, they are **w** for harvest
Acts 23:3, you **w-washed** wall
Rev. 6:2, and behold, a **w** horse
Num. 12:10; Job 6:6; Dan. 7:9
WHOLE Gen. 2:6, water the **w** surface
Matt. 6:22, **w** body will be full of light
1 Cor. 5:6, leavens the **w** lump
1 John 2:2, *those of* the **w** world
WICK—*flax* Matt. 12:20, SMOLDERING **W** HE WILL NOT PUT OUT
WICKED—*evil, lawless, ungodly* Ex. 23:1
Ps. 1:1, not walk in the counsel of the **w**
Prov. 4:19, way of the **w** is like darkness
10:30, **w** will not dwell in the land
11:7, When a **w** man dies
13:9, lamp of the **w** goes out
Is. 53:9, His grave ... with **w** men
Acts 17:5, taking along some **w** men from the
24:15, both the righteous and the **w**
Job 8:22; 10:15; 11:20; Ps. 10:13; 12:8; 17:13; Eccles. 7:17; Ezek. 3:18; Dan. 12:10
WICKEDNESS—*evil* Gen. 6:5, the **w** of man was great
Ps. 10:7, Under his tongue is ... **w**
Prov. 4:17, they eat the bread of **w**
Is. 9:18, **w** burns like a fire
32:6, his heart inclines toward **w**
Acts 8:22, repent of this **w** of yours
Eph. 6:12, spiritual *forces* of **w** in the heavenly
Judg. 20:3; Jer. 14:20; Ezek. 3:19; Hos. 10:13
WIDE Nah. 3:13, gates of your land are opened **w**
Matt. 7:13, for the gate is **w**
28:15, story was **w-ly** spread
WIDOW Matt. 23:14, you devour **w-s** houses
Mark 12:43, **w** put in more than all
Luke 18:5, this **w** bothers me
1 Tim. 5:3, Honor **w-s** who are **w-s** indeed
Gen. 38:11; Ex. 22:22; Lev. 21:14; 2 Sam. 14:5; Job 22:9; Ps. 68:5; Is. 1:17
WIELD Judg. 5:14, those who **w** the staff of office
WIFE Gen. 2:24, shall cleave to his **w**
Ex. 20:17, not covet your neighbor's **w**
Prov. 12:4, excellent **w** ... crown of her husband
18:22, finds a **w** finds a good thing
Matt. 5:31, WHOEVER DIVORCES HIS **W**
Luke 17:32, Remember Lot's **w**
1 Cor. 7:2, each man have his own **w**
Eph. 5:23, husband ... head of the **w**
1 Tim. 3:2, husband of one **w**
Lev. 18:15; Job 31:10; Ps. 128:3
WILD Gen. 37:20,33, **w** beast devoured him
Mark 1:6, John ... diet was locusts and **w** honey
Gen. 16:12; Job 11:12; Ps. 104:11
WILDERNESS—*desert*
Deut. 29:5, forty years in the **w**
Is. 35:6, waters will break forth in the **w**
40:3, Clear the way ... LORD in the **w**
43:19, make a roadway in the **w**
Matt. 3:1, preaching ... **w** of Judea
3:3, VOICE ... CRYING IN THE **W**
4:1, led ... into the **w** to be tempted
24:26, Behold, He is in the **w**
Mark 1:13, He was in the **w** forty days
John 6:31, Our fathers ate manna in the **w**
1 Cor. 10:5, laid low in the **w**
Heb. 3:8, DAY OF TRIAL IN THE **W**
Rev. 12:6, woman fled into the **w**
Gen. 16:7; Ex. 5:3; 14:11; 19:2; Lev. 7:38; Ps. 65:12; 102:6; Is. 51:3; Jer. 2:6; 17:6
WILL Ps. 40:8, delight to do Thy **w**
Matt. 6:10, Thy **w** be done
7:21, who does the **w** of My Father
Mark 3:35, whoever does the **w** of God
Luke 22:42, not My **w**, but Thine be done
John 1:13, **w** of the flesh ... **w** of man
4:34, **w** of Him who sent Me
Acts 21:14, **w** of the Lord be done
Rom. 12:2, may prove what the **w** of God is
1 Cor. 4:19, if the Lord **w-s**
Eph. 5:17, what the **w** of the Lord is
Phil. 2:13, both to **w** and to work
Heb. 10:9, HAVE COME TO DO THY **W**
James 4:15, If the Lord **w-s**, we shall live
WILLING Ps. 51:12, with a **w** spirit
Matt. 26:41, spirit is **w** ... flesh is weak
Luke 22:42, Father, if Thou art **w**
Gen. 24:5; Ex. 35:5; 1 Chr. 28:9
WIN—*gain* Prov. 11:30, he who is wise **w-s** souls
Matt. 28:14, we will **w** him over and keep
Luke 21:19, perseverance you will **w** ... souls
1 Cor. 9:20, that I might **w** the Jews
9:24, Run in such a way that you may **w**
WIND—*breath, whirlwind*
Job 16:3, no limit to **w-y** words
Ps. 1:4, chaff which the **w** drives
Is. 17:13, like the chaff ... before the **w**
Matt. 7:25, floods came, and the **w-s** blew
11:7, reed shaken by the **w**
Mark 4:41, **w** and the sea obey Him

Luke 8:24, He rebuked the **w**
John 3:8, **w** blows where it wishes
Acts 2:2, noise like a violent, rushing **w**
Eph. 4:14, every **w** of doctrine
Heb. 1:7, MAKES HIS ANGELS **W-S**
James 3:4, are driven by strong **w-s**
Jude 12, carried along by **w-s**
Gen. 8:1; 1 Kin. 19:11; 2 Kin. 3:17; Prov. 11:29; Eccles. 5:16; Song 4:16; Is. 7:2; Jer. 22:22; Ezek. 37:9; Hos. 8:7; Rev. 6:13
WINDOW Josh. 2:15, by a rope through the **w**
Acts 20:9, sitting on the **w-sill**
2 Cor. 11:33, through a **w** in the wall
Judg. 5:28; 2 Kin. 7:2; Jer. 9:21; Joel 2:9
WINE—*vinegar* Lev. 10:9, Do not drink **w**
Ps. 60:3, Thou hast given us **w** to drink
Jer. 35:6, We will not drink **w**
Matt. 9:17, new **w** into old wineskins
27:48, sponge, he filled it with sour **w**
Mark 15:23, give Him **w** mixed with myrrh
Luke 10:34, pouring oil and **w** on *them*
John 2:3, when the **w** gave out
2:9, water which had become **w**
19:29, A jar full of sour **w**
Acts 2:13, are full of sweet **w**
Eph. 5:18, do not get drunk with **w**
1 Tim. 3:3, not addicted to **w**
Rev. 6:6, not harm the oil and the **w**
Gen. 9:24; 1 Sam. 1:14; 2 Sam. 13:28; Prov. 3:10; Eccles. 9:7; Song 1:2; Is. 5:22
WINESKIN—*jug* Job 32:19, Like new **w-s** it is
Ps. 119:83, like a **w** in the smoke
Matt. 9:17; Mark 2:22, new wine ... fresh **w-s**
Josh. 9:13; Luke 5:37
WINGS—*feathers* Job 39:13, ostriches' **w** flap
Ps. 17:8, in the shadow of Thy **w**
91:4, under His **w** you may seek refuge
Prov. 23:5, *wealth* certainly makes itself **w**
Mal. 4:2, with healing in its **w**
Matt. 23:37, chicks under her **w**
Luke 13:34, her brood under her **w**
Ex. 19:4; Lev. 1:17; Deut. 32:11; Ruth 2:12; 2 Sam. 22:11; Is. 6:2; Jer. 48:9; Ezek. 1:6; Zech. 5:9
WINK Ps. 35:19; Prov. 6:13
WINNOW Is. 30:24; 41:16; Matt. 3:12
WINTER Gen. 8:22; Song 2:11; 1 Cor. 16:6
WIPE—*blot, erase* Is. 25:8, God will **w** tears
Is. 44:22, **w-d** out your transgressions
John 11:2, **w-d** His feet with her hair
Acts 3:19, Repent ... sins may be **w-ed** away
Rev. 21:4, He shall **w** away every tear
WISDOM Ex. 28:3, endowed with the spirit of **w**
1 Kin. 2:6, act according to your **w**
2 Chr. 1:10, Give me now **w**
Job 12:2, with you **w** will die
Ps. 51:6, make me know **w**
Prov. 1:7, Fools despise **w** and instruction
4:5, Acquire **w**! Acquire understanding
24:3, By **w** a house is built
Eccles. 1:18, in much **w** there is much grief
7:12, **w** preserves the lives
Jer. 9:23, wise man boast of his **w**
Mic. 6:9, it is sound **w** to fear Thy name
Matt. 11:19, **w** is vindicated by her deeds
Luke 2:52, Jesus kept increasing in **w** and stature
21:15, give you utterance and **w**
2 Cor. 1:12, not in fleshly **w**
2 Tim. 3:15, **w** that leads to salvation
James 1:5, if any of you lacks **w**
Rev. 13:18, Here is **w**
WISE—*shrewd* Gen. 3:6, tree ... to make one **w**
Job 17:10, I do not find a **w** man
Ps. 19:7, making **w** the simple
Prov. 3:7, not be **w** in your own eyes
Luke 10:21, hide these things from *the* **w**
Rom. 1:14, the **w** and to the foolish
1 Cor. 1:19, DESTROY THE WISDOM OF THE **W**
3:18, that he may become **w**
Eph. 5:15, not as unwise men, but as **w**
James 3:13, Who ... is **w** and understanding
Is. 19:12; Hos. 13:13
WISH—*desire*
Luke 5:39, drinking old *wine* **w-es** for new
Luke 8:20, brothers are ... **w-ing**
10:24, prophets and kings **w-ed** to see
John 16:19, Jesus knew they **w-ed** to question
1 Cor. 10:27, If one ... invites you, and you **w**
2 Pet. 3:9, not **w-ing** for any to perish
WITHDRAW Josh. 8:26; 1 Sam. 14:19
WITHER Ps. 1:3, leaf does not **w**
Ps. 37:2, **w** quickly like the grass
102:11, I **w** away like grass
Is. 34:4, As a leaf **w-s** from the vine
64:6, **w** like a leaf
Jer. 8:13, the leaf shall **w**
Zech. 11:17, His arm will be totally **w-ed**
Matt. 13:6, had no root, they **w-ed**
Mark 3:1, man ... with a **w-ed** hand
11:20, fig tree **w-ed** from the roots up
James 1:11, **w-s** the grass
WITHHELD Job 22:7, from the hungry you ... **w** bread
Hag. 1:10, sky has **w** its dew
WITHHOLD Prov. 11:24,26
WITHIN Ps. 51:10, renew a steadfast spirit **w** me
Jer. 31:33, put My law **w** them
Mark 7:23, evil things proceed from **w**
1 Cor. 5:12, not judge those who are **w** *the church*
2 Cor. 7:5, conflicts without, fears **w**
Prov. 22:18; Ezek. 11:19
WITHOUT 2 Chr. 15:3, Israel was **w** the true God
Is. 52:3, redeemed **w** money
Matt. 13:57, prophet is not **w** honor
Mark 14:58, made **w** hands
John 8:7, He who is **w** sin
Rom. 12:9, love be **w** hypocrisy
2 Cor. 7:5, conflicts **w**, fears within
Eph. 2:12, no hope and **w** God in the world
1 Thess. 5:17, pray **w** ceasing
1 Tim. 6:14, commandment **w** stain
Heb. 7:3, **W** father, **w** mother, **w** genealogy
13:2, entertained angels **w** knowing it
James 2:20, faith **w** works is useless
2 Pet. 2:17, are springs **w** water
Jude 12, **w** fear ... **w** water ... **w** fruit
Job 5:9; 8:11; Hos. 7:11; Col. 2:11
WITNESS—*advocate, testimony*
Ex. 4:8, **w** of the last sign
20:16, shall not bear false **w**
Judg. 11:10, LORD is **w** between us
Job 21:29, do you not recognize their **w**
Ps. 89:37, **w** in the sky is faithful
Matt. 19:18; Mark 10:19, NOT BEAR FALSE **W**
John 1:7, he might bear **w** of the light
1:32, John bore **w** saying, I have
3:11, bear **w** ... do not receive our **w**
5:39, these that bear **w** of Me
8:14, **w** of Myself, My **w** is true
21:24, we know his **w** is true
1 Cor. 15:15, found *to be* false **w-es** of God
2 Cor. 1:23, God as **w** to my soul
Phil. 1:8, For God is my **w**
Heb. 10:15, Holy Spirit also bears **w**
1 John 5:8, three that bear **w**
5:9, If we receive the **w** of men
Rev. 1:5, Christ, the faithful **w**
Gen. 31:48; Deut. 4:26; Job 16:19; Prov. 6:19; Is. 19:20
WIVES Deut. 17:17, Neither shall he multiply **w**
Eph. 5:22, **W** *be subject* to ... husbands
1 Pet. 3:1, you **w**, be submissive
3:7, husbands, live with your **w**
WOE Prov. 23:29, Who has **w**?
Mark 14:21, **w** to that man by whom
Rev. 8:13, **W**, **w**, **w** ... who dwell on the earth
18:10,16,19, **W**, **w**, the great city
Num. 21:29; Job 10:15; Ps. 120:5; Is. 6:5; Jer. 4:13; 44:11; Matt. 11:21
WOLF Is. 65:25, **w** and the lamb shall graze
Matt. 7:15, inwardly are ravenous **w-s**
10:16, sheep in the midst of **w-s**
Gen. 49:27; Jer. 5:6

WOMAN Gen. 2:23, She shall be called **W**
Ex. 2:9, **w** took the child
Deut. 22:5, **w** shall not wear man's clothing
Ruth 2:5, Whose young **w** is this
3:11, you are a **w** of excellence
Job 14:1, Man, who is born of **w**
Prov. 11:16, gracious **w** attains honor
Is. 49:15, **w** forget her nursing child
Matt. 5:28, looks on a **w** to lust for her
15:28, O **w**, your faith is great
Luke 7:44, said to Simon, Do you see this **w**
10:38, a **w** named Martha
John 4:7, **w** of Samaria to draw water
8:4, **w** has been caught in adultery
Acts 9:36, **w** abounding with deeds of kindness
1 Cor. 7:1, a man not to touch a **w**
7:2, each **w** have her own husband
14:35, a **w** to speak in church
Gal. 4:4, His Son, born of a **w**
1 Tim. 2:11, Let a **w** quietly receive instruction
Rev. 12:1, **w** clothed with the sun
Judg. 11:2; 1 Sam. 1:15; Eccles. 9:9
WOMB Gen. 25:23, Two nations are in your **w**
Ex. 13:2, first offspring of every **w**
Job 1:21, Naked ... from my mother's **w**
Luke 1:41, baby leaped in her **w**
John 3:4, enter ... into his mother's **w**
Acts 3:2, lame from his mother's **w**
Num. 12:12; Deut. 7:13; Ruth 1:11; Ps. 110:3; Prov. 30:16; Is. 44:2
WOMEN 2 Sam. 1:26, Than the love of **w**
1 Kin. 11:1, loved many foreign **w**
Ezra 10:2, have married foreign **w**
Prov. 31:3, not your strength to **w**
Is. 4:1, seven **w** will take hold of one man
Matt. 24:41, Two **w** *will be* grinding
Mark 15:40, *some* **w** looking on from afar
Acts 17:4, and a number of the leading **w**
1 Tim. 2:9, **w** to adorn themselves in proper
4:7, fables fit only for old **w**
2 Tim. 3:6, weak **w** weighed down with sins
Titus 2:4, young **w** to love their husbands
1 Pet. 3:5, the holy **w** also
Gen. 31:35; Judg. 5:24; Song 1:8; Jer. 50:37
WON Matt. 18:15, you have **w** your brother
WONDER—*marvel, sign*
1 Chr. 16:9, Speak of all His **w-s**
Job 37:14, consider the **w-s** of God
Ps. 9:1, I will tell of all Thy **w-s**
72:18, Who alone works **w-s**
78:12, He wrought **w-s** before their fathers
Is. 9:6, name will be called **W-ful** Counselor
Joel 2:30, display **w-s** in the sky
Rom. 15:19, power of signs and **w-s**
2 Thess. 2:9, signs and false **w-s**
Deut. 4:34; Dan. 6:27
WONDROUS—*marvelous* Job 9:10, **w** works
Job 37:5, God thunders ... **w-ly**
Ps. 17:7, **W-ly** show Thy lovingkindness
71:17, I still declare Thy **w** deeds
Joel 2:26, dealt **w-ly** with you
WOOD Gen. 6:14, an ark of gopher **w**
1 Cor. 3:12, stones, **w**, hay, straw
Rev. 18:12, *made* from very costly **w**
Deut. 19:5; 2 Kin. 2:24; 2 Chr. 27:4; Neh. 8:4; Job 41:27; Prov. 26:20; Jer. 7:18; Lam. 5:4; Ezek. 24:10
WOOL Ps. 147:16, He gives snow like **w**
Is. 1:18, They will be like **w**
Heb. 9:19, scarlet **w** and hyssop
Rev. 1:14, His hair ... white like white **w**
Deut. 22:11; Judg. 6:37; Ezek. 44:17; Dan. 7:9
WORD—*edict, message, speech* Gen. 15:1
Gen. 11:1, same language ... same **w-s**
Ps. 12:6, **w-s** of the Lord are pure **w-s**
19:3, There is no speech, nor are there **w-s**
19:14, Let the **w-s** of my mouth
Prov. 15:1, a harsh **w** stirs up anger
15:23, how delightful is a timely **w**
Is. 5:24, despised the **w** of the Holy One
29:11, **w-s** of a sealed book
Matt. 4:4, on every **w** that proceeds
6:7, for their many **w-s**
7:24, every one who hears these **w-s**
8:8, but just say the **w**
10:14, nor heed your **w-s**
12:36, every careless **w** that men ... speak
Mark 4:14, The sower sows the **w**
4:18, ones who have heard the **w**
7:13, invalidating the **w** of God
Luke 1:2, eyewitnesses and servants of the **W**
John 1:1, the beginning was the **W**
1:14, the **W** became flesh
6:68, **w-s** of eternal life
8:51, if anyone keeps My **w**
Acts 2:41, received his **w** were baptized
6:7, **w** of God kept on spreading
Rom. 10:8, **W** IS NEAR YOU ... **w** of faith
1 Cor. 1:17, kingdom of God ... in **w-s**
1:18, the **w** of the cross is to those
2 Cor. 4:2, not ... adulterating the **w** of God
Gal. 5:14, Law is fulfilled in one **w**
Eph. 4:29, Let no unwholesome **w** proceed ... mouth
5:6, deceive you with empty **w-s**
Phil. 2:16, holding fast the **w** of life
Col. 3:16, Let the **w** of Christ ... dwell within you
4:3, open up to us a door for the **w**
1 Thess. 1:5, gospel did not come ... in **w** only
2 Thess. 2:17, in every good work and **w**
1 Tim. 4:5, sanctified by the **w** of God
2 Tim. 2:15, handling accurately the **w** of truth
Titus 1:9, holding fast the faithful **w**
Heb. 2:2, **w** spoken through angels
4:12, **w** of God is living
James 1:21, receive the **w** implanted
1:22, prove yourselves doers of the **w**
1 Pet. 1:23, living and abiding **w** of God
2 Pet. 1:19, prophetic **w** *made* more sure
1 John 1:1, concerning the **W** of life
Rev. 19:13, name is called The **W** of God
Gen. 30:34; Ex. 20:1; Lev. 10:7; Num. 30:2; Deut. 5:5; Josh. 24:26; Judg. 13:12; 1 Sam. 3:1; 2 Kin. 9:5; 18:36; 1 Chr. 21:19; 2 Chr. 6:17; Job 2:13; 6:25; 12:11; Ps. 49:13; 55:21; Eccles. 5:2; Jer. 5:13; Mal. 1:1
WORK—*deed, labor, toil*
Gen. 2:2, God completed His **w**
Ex. 20:9, Six days ... do all your **w**
30:25, the **w** of a perfumer
Lev. 23:3, For six days **w** may be done
1 Sam. 14:45, he has **w-ed** with God this day
Neh. 4:6, the people had a mind to **w**
Ps. 19:1, declaring the **w** of His hands
62:12, a man according to his **w**
Prov. 16:3, Commit your **w-s** to the LORD
Eccles. 5:12, sleep of the **w-ing** man
7:13, Consider the **w** of God
10:12, LORD has completed all His **w**
Matt. 5:16, may see your good **w-s**
11:2, John ... heard of the **w-s** of Christ
20:12, last men have **w-ed** *only* one hour
Mark 16:20, the Lord **w-ed** with them
Luke 5:5, we **w-ed** hard all night
13:14, six days in which **w** should be
John 5:17, **w-ing** until now, and I
6:27, Do not **w** for the food which
6:28, may **w** the **w-s** of God
9:4, **w** the **w-s** of Him who sent Me
Acts 18:3, they were **w-ing**
Rom. 2:15, show the **w** of the Law
3:20, by the **w-s** of the Law no flesh
3:28, justified by faith apart from **w-s** of the Law
8:28, all things to **w** together for good
16:12, who has **w-ed** hard in the Lord
1 Cor. 3:13, man's **w** will become evident
3:14, If any man's **w** ... remains
4:12, **w-ing** with our own hands

2 Cor. 6:1, **w-ing** together *with Him*
Gal. 2:8, effectually **w-ed** for Peter
Eph. 2:9, not as a result of **w-s**
4:12, saints for the **w** of service
Phil. 2:12, **w** out your salvation
2:13, both to will and to **w**
Col. 1:10, bearing fruit in every good **w**
2 Thess. 3:8, labor and hardship we *kept* **w-ing**
3:10, If anyone will not **w**
1 Tim. 6:18, be rich in good **w-s**
2 Tim. 4:5, do the **w** of an evangelist
Heb. 6:1, repentance from dead **w-s**
James 2:18, show you my faith by my **w-s**
1 John 3:8, destroy the **w-s** of the devil
Deut. 4:28; 1 Sam. 14:6; 1 Chr. 23:4; 2 Chr. 15:7; Is. 5:19; Ezek. 46:1
WORKER Ps. 52:2, O **w** of deceit
Prov. 10:29, **w-s** of iniquity
Matt. 10:10, **w** is worthy of his support
1 Cor. 12:29, are not **w-s** of miracles
Phil. 3:2, beware of the evil **w-s**
Titus 2:5, sensible, pure, **w-s** at home
WORKMAN Eph. 2:10, For we are His **w-ship**
Ex. 38:23; 2 Kin. 22:5
WORLD—*age* 2 Sam. 22:16, foundations of **w**
2 Chr. 16:30, **w** is firmly established
Job 34:13, laid *on Him* the whole **w**
Ps. 17:14, From men of the **w**
Prov. 8:26, first dust of the **w**
Is. 14:21, fill ... the **w** with cities
Matt. 5:14, You are the light of the **w**
13:38, the field is the **w**
Mark 10:30, **w** to come, eternal life
John 1:10, **w** was made through Him
3:16, God so loved the **w**
4:42, Savior of the **w**
6:33, gives light to the **w**
7:7, **w** cannot hate you
8:12, I am the light of the **w**
Acts 17:6, men who have upset the **w**
Rom. 5:12, sin entered into the **w**
1 Cor. 1:28, base things of the **w**
2:12, not the spirit of the **w**
2 Cor. 7:10, sorrow of the **w** produces death
1 Tim. 6:17, rich in this present **w**
James 1:27, unstained by the **w**
2 Pet. 2:5, did not spare the ancient **w**
1 John 2:15, Do not love the **w**
2:17, the **w** is passing away
WORLDLY—*profane* 1 Tim. 4:7, **w** fables fit only for old
2 Tim. 2:16, avoid **w** *and* empty chatter
WORM Ex. 16:20, it bred **w-s** and became foul
Job 7:5, My flesh is clothed with **w-s**
Ps. 22:6, But I am a **w**
Is. 14:11, And **w-s** are your covering
Mark 9:48, where THEIR **W** DOES NOT DIE
Acts 12:23, he was eaten by **w-s**
Job 24:20; Jon. 4:7
WORMWOOD
Deut. 29:18, poisonous fruit and **w**
Prov. 5:4, she is bitter as **w**
Jer. 23:15, feed them **w**
Amos 5:7, turn justice into **w**
Rev. 8:11, star is called **W**
WORN—*old* Deut. 29:5, sandal has not **w** out
WORRY Luke 8:14, choked with **w-es** and riches
Luke 10:41, you are **w-ed** and bothered
12:29, do not keep **w-ing**
WORSE Matt. 9:16, a **w** tear results
John 5:14, nothing **w** may befall you
1 Cor. 11:17, better but for the **w**
2 Tim. 3:13, proceed *from bad* to **w**
WORSHIP—*bow, serve*
Ex. 34:14, shall not **w** any other
Ps. 2:11, **W** the LORD with reverence
29:2, **W** the LORD in holy array
Matt. 2:2, and have come to **w** Him
2:8, come and **w** Him
2:11, fell down and **w-ed** Him
4:10, SHALL **W** THE LORD YOUR GOD
John 4:20, place where men ought to **w**
4:22, we **w** that which we know
Phil. 3:3, **w** in the Spirit of God
Heb. 9:6, performing the divine **w**
Rev. 4:10, **w** Him who lives forever
Gen. 22:5; Deut. 6:13; 2 Chr. 29:28
WORTH—*price* Prov. 31:10, her **w** is far above jewels
WORTHLESS—*ungodly* Prov. 16:27, A **w** man
Matt. 25:30, cast out the **w** slave
Gal. 4:9, **w** elemental things
Titus 1:16, **w** for any good deed
James 1:26, this man's religion is **w**
Judg. 9:4; Is. 5:2
WORTHY—*befit, deserving, fit*
1 Kin. 1:52, If he will be a **w** man
Matt. 10:10, worker is **w** of his support
10:11, enter, inquire who is **w** in it
10:13, if the house is **w**
10:37, who loves father more ... not **w** of Me
Luke 10:7, laborer is **w** of his wages
Rom. 16:2, a manner **w** of the saints
Phil. 1:27, a manner **w** of the gospel
Eph. 4:1, manner **w** of the calling
1 Thess. 2:12, walk in a manner **w** of God
Heb. 11:38, the world was not **w**
Rev. 5:2, Who is **w** to open the book
WOUND—*bruise, pierce*
Luke 10:34, bandaged up his **w-s**
Acts 19:16, fled ... naked and **w-ed**
1 Pet. 2:24, by His **w-s** you were healed
Gen. 4:23; Ex. 21:25; Deut. 32:39; Job 34:6; Ps. 147:3; Prov. 23:29; Jer. 30:12,17; Nah. 3:19; Mark 12:4
WRANGLE 2 Tim. 2:14, not to **w** about words
WRAPPED Matt. 27:59, **w** it in a clean linen
Mark 15:46, **w** Him in the linen sheet
Luke 2:7, she **w** Him in cloths
Gen. 38:14; 1 Kin. 19:13; Job 26:8; Is. 59:17; Ezek. 16:10; 21:15
WRAPPINGS—*cloth* John 11:44; 20:7
WRATH—*anger, indignation* Deut. 29:28
Ps. 6:1, Nor chasten me in Thy **w**
Matt. 3:7, flee from the **w** to come
John 3:36, **w** of God abides on him
Rom. 2:5, **w** for yourself in the day of **w**
3:5, God who inflicts **w** is not unrighteous
Eph. 2:3, by nature children of **w**
Col. 3:6, **w** of God will come
1 Thess. 5:9, has not destined us for **w**
Heb. 3:11, I swore in My **w**
Rev. 6:16, from the **w** of the Lamb
Ps. 37:8; 89:38; Is. 27:4; Jer. 4:4; 6:11; 30:23; Ezek. 5:13; 23:25; Mic. 5:15; Nah. 1:2
WREATH—*crown*
1 Cor. 9:25, to receive a perishable **w**
WRITE—*record* Ex. 17:14; Is. 8:1
Prov. 3:3, **w** them on the tablet of your heart
Mark 10:4, **w** a certificate of divorce
John 19:21, Do not **w**, The King of the Jews
Rom. 16:22, I, Tertius, who **w** this letter
Heb. 10:16, UPON THEIR MIND I WILL **W** THEM
2 John 12, **w** ... not ... with paper and ink
Rev. 14:13, **W**, Blessed are the dead
WRITING—*inscription, letter*
Eccles. 12:12, the **w** of many books is endless
John 5:47, if you do not believe his **w-s**
1 Tim. 3:14, I am **w** these things to you
2 Tim. 3:15, you have known the sacred **w-s**
Philem. 19, **w** this with my own hand
1 John 2:8, **w** a new commandment
2 John 5, **w** ... a new commandment
Ex. 32:16; 1 Chr. 28:19; Dan. 10:21
WRITTEN Ex. 31:18, **w** by the finger of God
Job 19:23, that my words were **w**
Mal. 3:16, book of remembrance was **w**
Matt. 2:5, been **w** by the prophet
4:4, It is **w**, MAN SHALL NOT LIVE
4:6, for it is **w**, HE WILL GIVE
11:10, one about whom it was **w**
John 19:22, What I have **w** I have **w**

WRITTEN *(Continued)*
Acts 1:20, **w** in the book of Psalms
Rom. 2:15, Law **w** in their hearts
Rev. 13:8, not been **w** ... in the book of life
17:5, forehead a name *was* **w**
WRONG—*defraud, wicked* Ex. 22:21, not **w** a stranger
Lev. 25:14, you shall not **w** one another
2 Sam. 24:17, I who have done **w**
Matt. 20:13, Friend, I am doing you no **w**
John 18:23, If I have spoken **w-ly**
Rom. 13:10, Love does no **w**
1 Cor. 6:7, Why not rather be **w-ed**
2 Cor. 7:2, we **w-ed** no one
Rev. 22:11, Let the one who does **w**, still do **w**
Gen. 16:5; 1 Chr. 12:17; Esth. 1:16
WRONGDOER—*unrighteous* Ps. 71:4, the **w** and
WROTE Ex. 24:4, Moses **w** down all the words
Jer. 36:18, **w** them with ink on the
Mark 12:19, Teacher, Moses **w**
Luke 1:63, he asked for a tablet and **w**
John 8:6, finger **w** on the ground
3 John 9, I **w** something to the church
WROUGHT—*accomplished* John 3:21, been **w** in

X, Y, Z

YEAR—*annual* Gen. 1:14, for seasons ... **y-s**
Ps. 90:4, thousand **y-s** in Thy sight
90:9, finished our **y-s** like a sigh
Prov. 4:10, **y-s** of your life will be many
Is. 61:2, favorable **y** of the LORD
Luke 3:23, was about thirty **y-s** of age
Gal. 4:10, months and season and **y-s**
Rev. 9:15, day and month and **y**
Gen. 7:11; Ex. 13:10; Lev. 16:34; Num. 14:34; 2 Sam. 14:26; 1 Kin. 17:1; 2 Chr. 14:6; Job 10:5; Jer. 11:23; Joel 2:25; Matt. 2:16
YEARN—*faint* Ps. 84:2, longed and even **y-ed**
YESTERDAY Ex. 5:14, **y** or today in making brick
Job 8:9, For we are *only* of **y**
Ps. 90:4, in Thy sight Are like **y**
Acts 7:28, KILLED THE EGYPTIAN Y
Heb. 13:8, the same **y** and today
YET—*still* Ps. 37:10, **Y** a little while
John 2:4, My hour has not **y** come
Heb. 11:7, things not **y** seen
1 John 3:2, appeared as **y** what we shall be
Deut. 9:29; Jon. 3:4
YIELD—*bear, produce* Ps. 1:3, Which **y-s** its fruit in
Ps. 67:6, earth has **y-ed** its produce
Heb. 12:11, **y-s** the peaceful fruit
YIELDING—*bearing* Gen. 1:11,29; Mark 4:8
YOKE Matt. 11:29, Take My **y** upon you
Matt. 11:30, For My **y** is easy
Gal. 5:1, to a **y** of slavery
1 Tim. 6:1, under the **y** as slaves
Gen. 27:40; Lev. 26:13; Deut. 28:48; 1 Kin. 12:4; Is. 9:4; Jer. 27:2; Lam. 1:14
YOUNG Ps. 37:25, been **y**, and now I am old
Prov. 20:29, glory of **y** men is their
Eccles. 11:9, Rejoice, **y** man, during your
Is. 11:7, Their **y** will lie down together
Acts 2:17, Y MEN SHALL SEE VISIONS
Titus 2:4, **y** women to love ... husbands
1 John 2:13, I am writing ... **y** men
Deut. 32:11; Judg. 6:15; 1 Sam. 8:16; Job 19:18; Ezek. 17:4
YOUNGER Luke 15:13, **y** son gathered
John 21:18, when you were **y**
1 Tim. 5:11, refuse *to put* **y** widows
1 Pet. 5:5, You **y** men, likewise
Gen. 25:23; Judg. 15:2
YOUR—*Thine* Gen. 22:2, **y** son, **y** only son
Ex. 4:4, Stretch out **y** hand and grasp *it*
2 Chr. 20:15, battle is not **y-s** but God's
Luke 6:20, **y-s** is the kingdom of God
15:31, all that is mine is **y-s**
John 15:20, they will keep **y-s** also
2 Cor. 12:14, I do not seek what is **y-s**
Gen. 45:20; Josh. 2:14; 1 Kin. 20:4; Jer. 5:19
YOURSELVES
Matt. 6:19, Do not lay ... **y** treasures
Mark 9:50, Have salt in **y**
Luke 12:33, make **y** purses
Rom. 6:13, present **y** to God
2 Cor. 13:5, recognize ... **y**
1 John 5:21, guard **y** from idols
Jude 21, keep **y** in the love of God
Gen. 18:4; Lev. 11:44; Deut. 4:16; Josh. 24:22; 2 Chr. 29:31; Jer. 37:9
YOUTH—*childhood* Acts 26:4, life from my **y** up
1 Tim. 4:12, look down on your **y-fulness**
2 Tim. 2:22, flee from **y-ful** lusts
Gen. 8:21; Num. 30:16; Judg. 8:20; Job 33:25; Ps. 25:7; Prov. 5:18; Is. 40:30; Jer. 3:4; 31:19
ZEAL—*concern* 2 Kin. 10:16, see my **z** for the LORD
Ps. 119:139, My **z** has consumed me
John 2:17, Z FOR THY HOUSE WILL
Rom. 10:2, have a **z** for God
2 Cor. 7:7, your **z** for me
7:11, what longing, what **z**
Phil. 3:6, as to **z**
2 Sam. 21:2; Eccles. 9:6; Is. 26:11; 59:17
ZEALOUS—*eager* 1 Kin. 19:10, very **z** for the LORD
Acts 21:20, all **z** for the law
1 Cor. 14:12, **z** of spiritual *gifts*
Titus 2:14, **z** for good deeds
Rev. 3:19, be **z** therefore, and repent

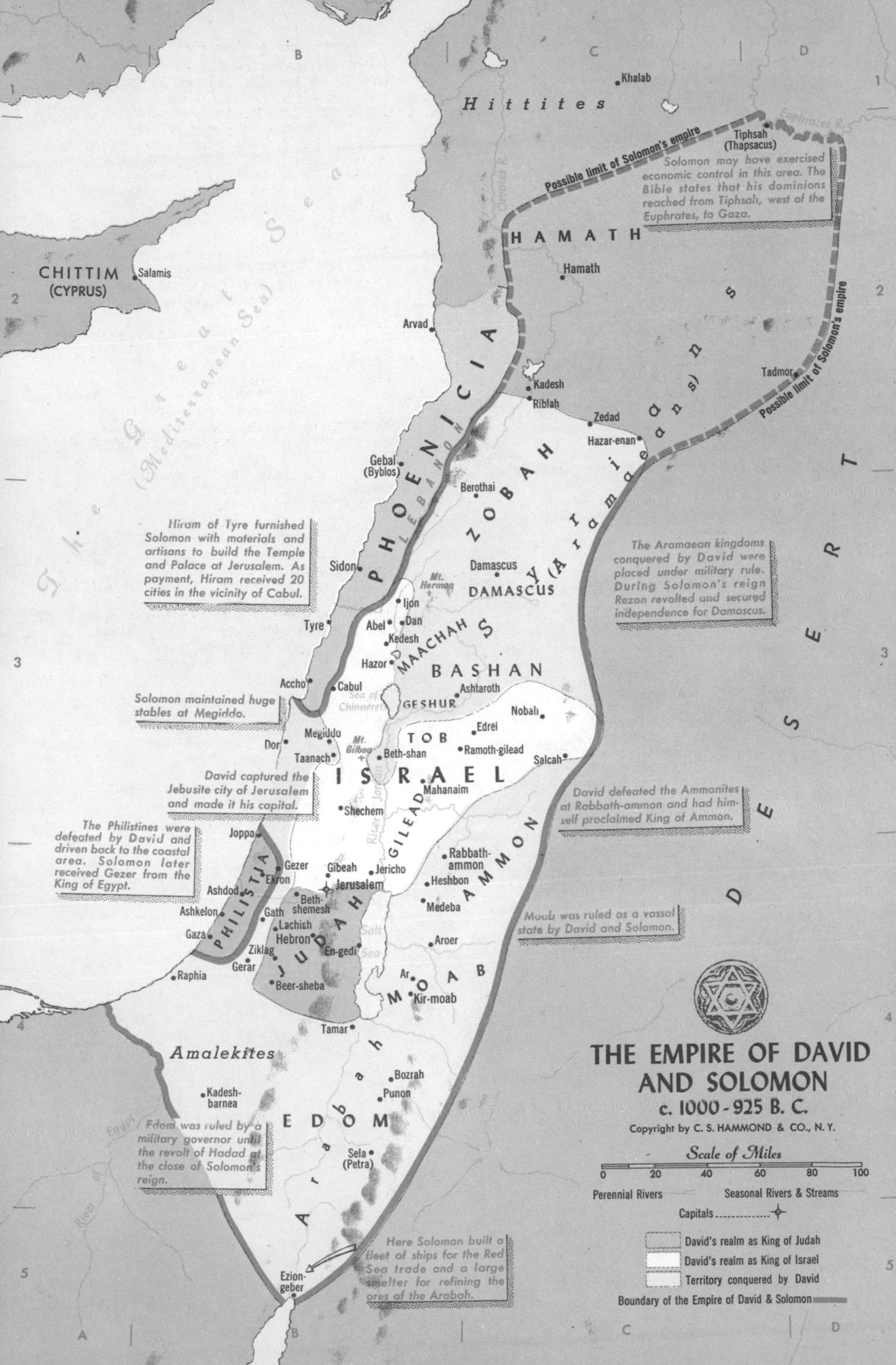

THE EMPIRE OF DAVID AND SOLOMON
c. 1000 - 925 B. C.
Copyright by C. S. HAMMOND & CO., N. Y.
Scale of Miles
0 20 40 60 80 100
Perennial Rivers
Seasonal Rivers & Streams
Capitals
David's realm as King of Judah
David's realm as King of Israel
Territory conquered by David
Boundary of the Empire of David & Solomon
Hittites
Khalab
Tiphsah (Thapsacus)
Euphrates R.
Possible limit of Solomon's empire
Solomon may have exercised economic control in this area. The Bible states that his dominions reached from Tiphsah, west of the Euphrates, to Gaza.
HAMATH
Hamath
CHITTIM (CYPRUS)
Salamis
The Great Sea (Mediterranean Sea)
Arvad
PHOENICIA
Kadesh
Riblah
Zedad
Hazar-enan
Tadmor
ZOBAH
Syria (Arameans)
Gebal (Byblos)
LEBANON
Berothai
Hiram of Tyre furnished Solomon with materials and artisans to build the Temple and Palace at Jerusalem. As payment, Hiram received 20 cities in the vicinity of Cabul.
Sidon
Damascus
Mt. Hermon
DAMASCUS
The Aramaean kingdoms conquered by David were placed under military rule. During Solomon's reign Rezon revolted and secured independence for Damascus.
Ijon
Dan
Abel
Kedesh
Tyre
MAACHAH
Hazor
BASHAN
Accho
Cabul
Ashtaroth
Sea of Chinnereth
GESHUR
Solomon maintained huge stables at Megiddo.
Nobah
Edrei
Megiddo
TOB
Dor
Mt. Gilboa
Beth-shan
Ramoth-gilead
Taanach
Salcah
ISRAEL
David captured the Jebusite city of Jerusalem and made it his capital.
Mahanaim
David defeated the Ammonites at Rabbath-ammon and had himself proclaimed King of Ammon.
Shechem
River Jordan
GILEAD
The Philistines were defeated by David and driven back to the coastal area. Solomon later received Gezer from the King of Egypt.
Joppa
Rabbath-ammon
Gezer
Gibeah
Jericho
Ekron
Heshbon
AMMON
Ashdod
Jerusalem
Beth-shemesh
Ashkelon
Medeba
Gath
PHILISTIA
Lachish
Moab was ruled as a vassal state by David and Solomon.
Gaza
Hebron
Salt Sea
Aroer
JUDAH
Ziklag
En-gedi
Gerar
Raphia
Ar
Beer-sheba
MOAB
Kir-moab
Tamar
Amalekites
Arabah
Bozrah
Kadesh-barnea
Punon
EDOM
Edom was ruled by a military governor until the revolt of Hadad at the close of Solomon's reign.
Sela (Petra)
River of Egypt
DESERT
Here Solomon built a fleet of ships for the Red Sea trade and a large smelter for refining the ores of the Arabah.
Ezion-geber

THE KINGDOMS OF ISRAEL AND JUDAH
c. 925-842 B. C.
Copyright by C. S. HAMMOND & CO., N. Y.
Scale of Miles
0 5 10 20 30 40
Perennial Rivers
Seasonal Rivers & Streams
Capitals
Egyptian & Syrian Attacks
Elijah took refuge in Zarephath and brought back to life the widow's son.
In the reign of Baasha the cities of northern Israel were raided by the King of Damascus in league with Asa, King of Judah.
Aram waged almost constant war against Israel. The Syrians were held in check by Ahab until his death in battle at Ramoth-gilead.
Elijah challenged the prophets of Baal at Mt. Carmel.
The introduction of Phoenician cults following the marriage of Ahab with Jezebel caused violent reactions in Israel that eventually wiped out the house of Omri.
Samaria, fortress capital of Israel was built by Omri c. 870 B. C.
Moab was ruled as a vassal kingdom during the Omri dynasty. The Dibon stele commemorates the victory of Mesha, King of Moab, over Israel and the return of Moabite independence.
Shishak (Sheshonk), Egyptian Pharaoh, raided the divided kingdoms, plundering Jerusalem c. 925 B. C.
During the reign of Jehosophat Judah regained control over Edom.
The Great Sea
(Mediterranean Sea)
PHOENICIA
MOUNT LEBANON
MT. HERMON
ARAM
Syrians
GESHUR
Bashan
Havoth-jair
ISRAEL
GILEAD
AMMON
MOAB
JUDAH
PHILISTIA
EDOM
Plain of Sharon
Plain of Jezreel
Wilderness of Judah
Valley of Salt
Sea of Chinnereth
Salt Sea (Dead Sea)
River Jordan
MT. CARMEL
Kishon
Mt. Tabor
Mt. Ebal
Mt. Gerizim
Mt. Nebo
Yarmuk R.
Jabbok R.
Abana R.
Sidon
Zarephath
Tyre
Damascus
Ijon
Dan
Abel-beth-maachah
Kedesh
Hazor
Accho
Cabul
Chinnereth
Karnaim
Ashtaroth
Aphek
Hammath
Edrei
Dor
Shunem
Megiddo
Jezreel
Ramoth-gilead
Taanach
Beth-shan
Dothan
Ibleam
Jabesh-gilead
Tishbe
Mahanaim
Sochoh
Abel-meholah
Samaria
Tirzah
Shechem
Penuel
Janohah
Aphek
Joppa
Shiloh
Jeshanah
Lod
Zemaraim
Rabbath-ammon
Beth-horon
Bethel
Jabneel
Gezer
Aijalon
Mizpeh
Geba
Jericho
Ekron
Gibbethon
Ramah
Gilgal
Elealeh
Heshbon
Ashdod
Timnah
Zorah
Jerusalem
Beth-shemesh
Azekah
Bethlehem
Medeba
Ashkelon
Shoco
Etam
Baal-meon
Libnah
Adullam
Tekoa
Jahaz
Gath
Mareshah
Beth-zur
Lachish
Ataroth
Gaza
Hebron
Adoraim
Dibon
Debir
Ziph
Aroer
En-gedi
Gerar
Ziklag
Raphia
Ar
Beer-sheba
Kir-moab (Kir-hareseth)

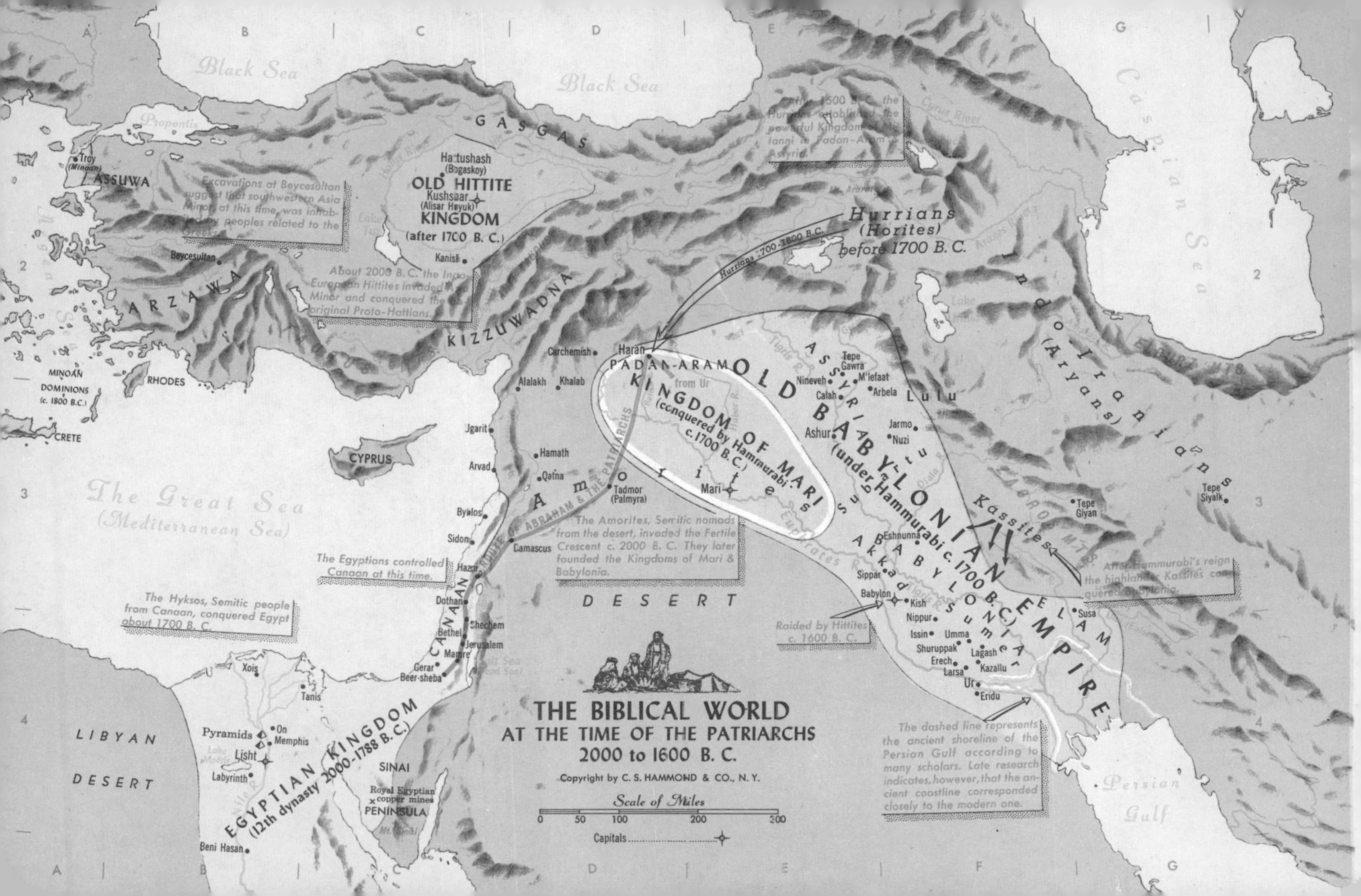
THE BIBLICAL WORLD
AT THE TIME OF THE PATRIARCHS
2000 to 1600 B. C.
Copyright by C. S. HAMMOND & CO., N. Y.
Scale of Miles
0 50 100 200 300
Capitals
Black Sea
Black Sea
Caspian Sea
The Great Sea
(Mediterranean Sea)
Persian Gulf
Propontis
GASGAS
Hattushash
(Bogaskoy)
OLD HITTITE
Kushsaar
(Alisar Huyuk)
KINGDOM
(after 1700 B. C.)
Kanish
Troy
(Minoan)
ASSUWA
Beycesultan
ARZAWA
KIZZUWADNA
MINOAN
DOMINIONS
(c. 1800 B.C.)
RHODES
CRETE
CYPRUS
Excavations at Beycesultan suggest that southwestern Asia Minor at this time was inhabited by peoples related to the Greeks.
About 2000 B. C. the Indo-European Hittites invaded Asia Minor and conquered the original Proto-Hattians.
Hurrians
(Horites)
before 1700 B. C.
Hurrians 1700-1600 B.C.
Indo-Iranians
(Aryans)
Cyrus River
Carchemish
Haran
PADAN-ARAM
OLD BABYLONIAN EMPIRE
(under Hammurabi c. 1700 B.C.)
KINGDOM OF MARI
(conquered by Hammurabi c.1700 B.C.)
from Ur
Habor R.
Tigris R.
Euphrates R.
Diala R.
ASSYRIA
Tepe Gawra
Nineveh
M'lefaat
Calah
Arbela
Lulu
Ashur
Jarmo
Nuzi
Alalakh
Khalab
Ugarit
Hamath
Arvad
Qatna
Byblos
Sidon
Damascus
Tadmor
(Palmyra)
Mari
Amorites
ROUTE OF ABRAHAM & THE PATRIARCHS
The Amorites, Semitic nomads from the desert, invaded the Fertile Crescent c. 2000 B. C. They later founded the Kingdoms of Mari & Babylonia.
DESERT
Eshnunna
BABYLONIA
Akkad
Sumer
Sippar
Babylon
Kish
Nippur
Issin
Umma
Shuruppak
Lagash
Erech
Larsa
Kazallu
Ur
Eridu
Raided by Hittites c. 1600 B. C.
Kassites
ZAGROS MTS.
ELAM
Susa
Tepe Giyan
Tepe Siyalk
After Hammurabi's reign the highlander Kassites conquered Babylonia.
The dashed line represents the ancient shoreline of the Persian Gulf according to many scholars. Late research indicates, however, that the ancient coastline corresponded closely to the modern one.
The Egyptians controlled Canaan at this time.
Hazor
Dothan
CANAAN
Shechem
Bethel
Jerusalem
Mamre
Gerar
Beer-sheba
Salt Sea
(Dead Sea)
The Hyksos, Semitic people from Canaan, conquered Egypt about 1700 B. C.
Xois
Tanis
Pyramids
On
Memphis
Lisht
Labyrinth
Beni Hasan
Nile R.
LIBYAN
DESERT
EGYPTIAN KINGDOM
(12th dynasty 2000-1788 B. C.)
SINAI
Royal Egyptian copper mines
PENINSULA
Mt. Sinai

CANAAN AS DIVIDED AMONG THE TWELVE TRIBES
c. 1200-1020 B. C.
Copyright by C. S. HAMMOND & CO., N. Y.
Scale of Miles
0 5 10 20 30 40
Perennial Rivers
Seasonal Rivers & Streams
The tribal divisions marked on this map are only approximate since boundary lists are incomplete.
Part of the tribe of Dan, unable to secure its inheritance, migrated north and captured Laish, renaming it Dan.
Although all of Bashan was assigned to the half tribe of Manasseh, it is doubtful that settlement reached beyond the Yarmuk Valley.
The Israelites were unable to capture the fortified towns of the plains during the early period of settlement.
The Israelites were under constant attack from Philistine invaders who occupied the coastal area at about this time.
During the period of Judges, invading Ammonites, Moabites and Midianites were repulsed by the Israelites.
The cities assigned to Simeon were also a part of the inheritance of Judah. Simeon as a tribe was later absorbed by Judah.
The priestly tribe of Levi did not receive a definite territory but instead was allotted 48 cities distributed over the tribal areas.
The Great Sea
(Mediterranean Sea)
Sidonians (Phoenicians)
MOUNT LEBANON
MT. HERMON
Sidon
Zarephath
Damascus
Tyre
Abel-beth-maachah
DAN
Laish or Leshem (Dan)
Kanah
ASHER
NAPHTALI
Hammon
Misrephoth-maim
En-hazor
Iron
Kedesh
Bashan
Achzib
Abdon
Hazor
Beth-emek
MANASSEH
Accho
Cabul
Achshaph
Ramah
Hukkok
Chinnereth
Karnaim
Aphek
Madon
Geshur
Ashtaroth
Argob
Rimmon
Sea of Chinnereth
Golan
Hannathon
Aphek
MT. CARMEL
Kishon
ZEBULUN
Shimron
Gath-hepher
Hammath
Harosheth
Chesulloth
Tabor
Jabneel
Jokneam
Sarid
En-dor
Yarmuk R.
Dor
Plain of Jezreel
Shunem
Ophrah
Havoth-jair
Edrei
Megiddo
ISSACHAR
Camon
Jezreel
Harod
Ramoth-gilead
Taanach
MT. Gilboa
Beth-shan
Ibleam
Pella
GAD
Dothan
Jabesh-gilead
Gilead
Plain of Sharon
Bezek
Mahanaim
MANASSEH
Abel-meholah
Tirzah
Thebez
AMMON
Mt. Ebal
Zaphon
Shechem
Succoth
Pirathon
Mt. Gerizim
Taanath-shiloh
Penuel
Kanah
Mizpeh
Janohah
Gath-rimmon
Aphek
Tappuah
Adam
Joppa (Japho)
Bene-berak
Shiloh
Lebonah
Ataroth
Ono
EPHRAIM
Timnath-serah
Jogbehah
Jazer
Rabbath-ammon
Lod
Ajalon
Betonim
Bethel
Naarath
Ai
Beth-horon
Mizpeh
Beth-nimrah
Jabneel
Ekron
Gezer
Gibeon
Geba
Jericho
Gilgal
Mephaath
Gibbethon
Kirjath-jearim
BENJAMIN
Abel-shittim
Elealeh
Beth-hoglah
Heshbon
Eltekeh
DAN
Beth-jeshimoth
Zorah
Chesalon
Ashdod
Timnah
Jerusalem (Jebus)
Mt. Nebo
Beth-shemesh
Makkedah
Medeba
Jarmuth
Azekah
Etam
Bethlehem
Baal-meon
Libnah
Adullam
Jahaz
Ashkelon
Tekoa
REUBEN
Gath
Mareshah
Keilah
Beth-zur
Philistines
JUDAH
Zareth-shahar
Eglon
Lachish
Ataroth
Kiriathaim
Gaza
Hebron
Salt Sea (Dead Sea)
Dibon
Debir
Caleb
Ziph
Aroer
En-gedi
Juttah
Carmel
Gerar
Eshtemoh
Ziklag
Anab
Maon
Madmannah
Raphia
Jattir
Sharuhen
Arad
Cherethites
Kenites
Ar
Beer-sheba
Moladah
MOAB
Hormah
Kir-moab (Kir-hareseth)
Beth-palet
Aroer
SIMEON
Rehoboth
Ascent of Akrabbim
Wilderness of Zin
EDOM
A B C D E
1 2 3 4 5 6 7

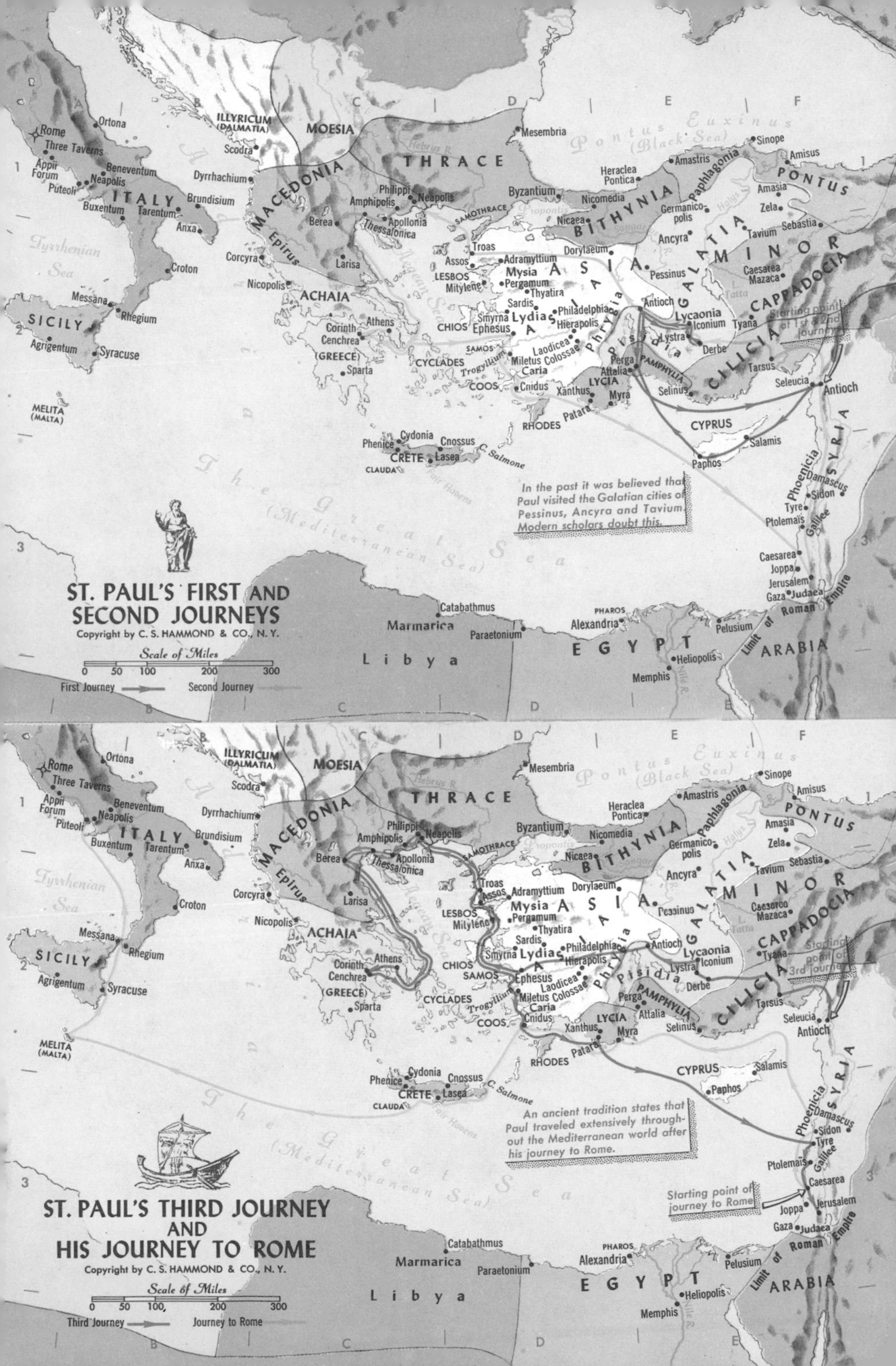
ST. PAUL'S FIRST AND SECOND JOURNEYS
Copyright by C. S. HAMMOND & CO., N. Y.
Scale of Miles
0 50 100 200 300
First Journey
Second Journey
In the past it was believed that Paul visited the Galatian cities of Pessinus, Ancyra and Tavium. Modern scholars doubt this.
Starting point of 1st & 2nd journeys
Rome
Ortona
Three Taverns
Appii Forum
Puteoli
Neapolis
Beneventum
ITALY
Brundisium
Buxentum
Tarentum
Anxa
Tyrrhenian Sea
Croton
Messana
Rhegium
SICILY
Agrigentum
Syracuse
MELITA (MALTA)
ILLYRICUM (DALMATIA)
Scodra
Dyrrhachium
MOESIA
THRACE
Hebrus R.
Mesembria
MACEDONIA
Philippi
Neapolis
Amphipolis
Apollonia
Thessalonica
Berea
SAMOTHRACE
Epirus
Larisa
Corcyra
Nicopolis
ACHAIA
Athens
Corinth
Cenchrea
(GREECE)
Sparta
Aegean Sea
CYCLADES
Pontus Euxinus (Black Sea)
Sinope
Amisus
Amastris
Paphlagonia
Heraclea Pontica
PONTUS
Amasia
Zela
Byzantium
Propontis
Nicomedia
BITHYNIA
Nicaea
Germanicopolis
Halys R.
Sangarius R.
GALATIA
Ancyra
Tavium
Sebastia
Troas
Assos
Adramyttium
Dorylaeum
ASIA
MINOR
LESBOS
Mitylene
Mysia
Pergamum
Thyatira
Pessinus
Caesarea Mazaca
CAPPADOCIA
L. Tatta
Sardis
Lydia
Philadelphia
Antioch
Lycaonia
Iconium
Tyana
CHIOS
Smyrna
Ephesus
Hierapolis
Phrygia
Pisidia
Lystra
Derbe
SAMOS
Laodicea
Colossae
Trogyllium
Miletus
Caria
Perga
Attalia
PAMPHYLIA
CILICIA
Tarsus
COOS
Cnidus
LYCIA
Xanthus
Myra
Selinus
Seleucia
Antioch
Patara
RHODES
CYPRUS
Salamis
Paphos
SYRIA
Phenice
Cydonia
Cnossus
CRETE
Lasea
C. Salmone
CLAUDA
Fair Havens
The Great Sea (Mediterranean Sea)
Phoenicia
Damascus
Sidon
Tyre
Ptolemais
Galilee
Caesarea
Joppa
Jerusalem
Gaza
Judaea
Limit of Roman Empire
Catabathmus
Marmarica
Paraetonium
Libya
PHAROS
Alexandria
Pelusium
EGYPT
Heliopolis
Memphis
Nile R.
ARABIA
ST. PAUL'S THIRD JOURNEY AND HIS JOURNEY TO ROME
Copyright by C. S. HAMMOND & CO., N. Y.
Scale of Miles
0 50 100 200 300
Third Journey
Journey to Rome
An ancient tradition states that Paul traveled extensively throughout the Mediterranean world after his journey to Rome.
Starting point of 3rd journey
Starting point of journey to Rome

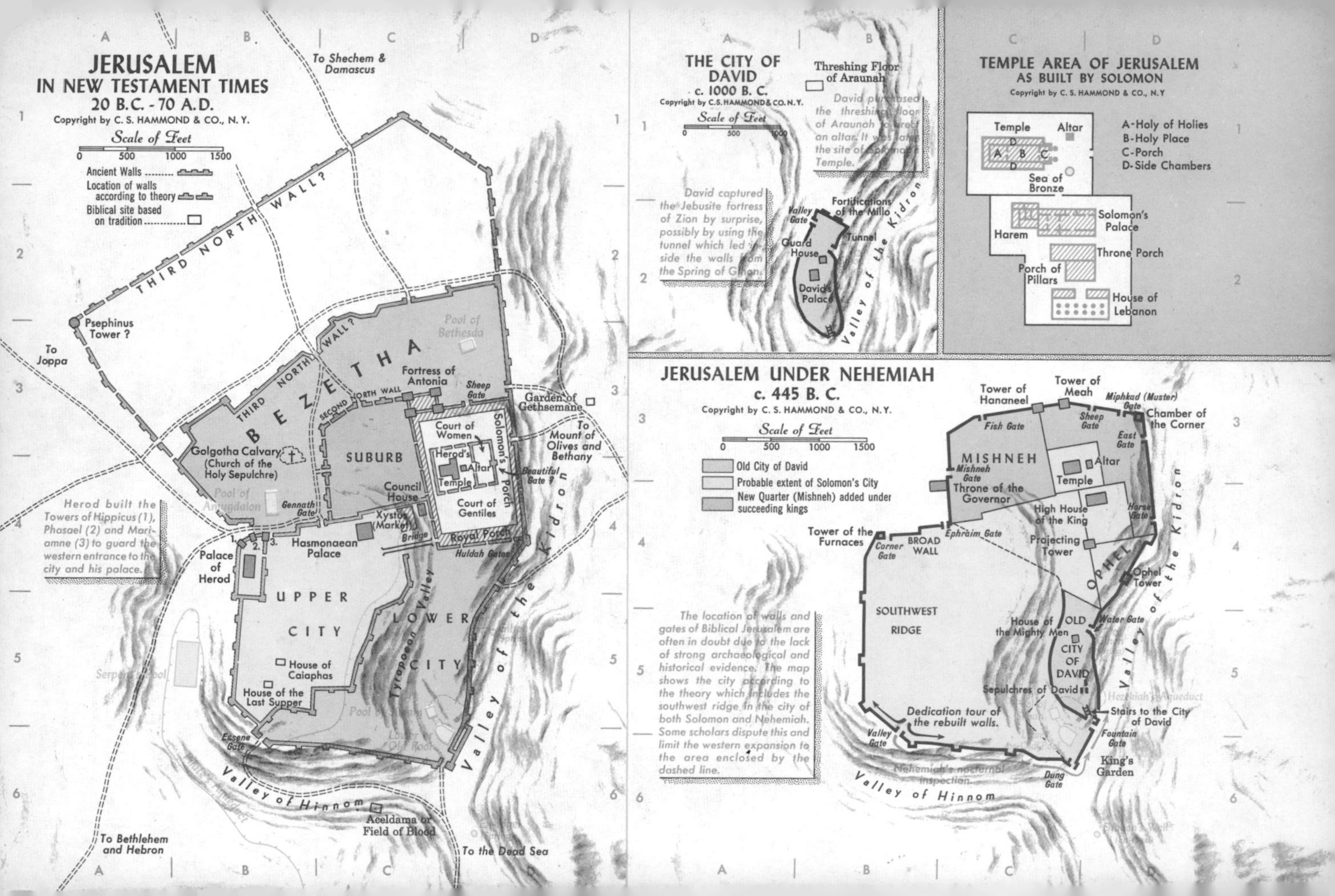
JERUSALEM
IN NEW TESTAMENT TIMES
20 B.C. - 70 A.D.
Copyright by C. S. HAMMOND & CO., N. Y.
Scale of Feet
0 500 1000 1500
Ancient Walls
Location of walls according to theory
Biblical site based on tradition
To Shechem & Damascus
THIRD NORTH WALL?
Psephinus Tower ?
To Joppa
WALL?
THIRD NORTH
SECOND NORTH WALL
BEZETHA
Pool of Bethesda
Fortress of Antonia
Sheep Gate
Garden of Gethsemane
To Mount of Olives and Bethany
Golgotha Calvary (Church of the Holy Sepulchre)
SUBURB
Court of Women
Herod's
Altar
Temple
Solomon's Porch
Beautiful Gate ?
Council House
Court of Gentiles
Pool of Amygdalon
Gennath Gate
Xystus (Market)
Bridge
Royal Porch
Huldah Gates
Herod built the Towers of Hippicus (1), Phasael (2) and Mariamne (3) to guard the western entrance to the city and his palace.
Palace of Herod
Hasmonaean Palace
UPPER CITY
LOWER CITY
Tyropoeon Valley
Valley of the Kidron
House of Caiaphas
House of the Last Supper
Essene Gate
Valley of Hinnom
Aceldama or Field of Blood
To Bethlehem and Hebron
To the Dead Sea
THE CITY OF DAVID
c. 1000 B. C.
Copyright by C.S.HAMMOND & CO.N.Y.
Scale of Feet
0 500 1000
Threshing Floor of Araunah
David purchased the threshing floor of Araunah to erect an altar. It was later the site of Solomon's Temple.
David captured the Jebusite fortress of Zion by surprise, possibly by using the tunnel which led inside the walls from the Spring of Gihon.
Valley Gate
Fortifications of the Millo
Guard House
Tunnel
David's Palace
Valley of the Kidron
TEMPLE AREA OF JERUSALEM
AS BUILT BY SOLOMON
Copyright by C. S. HAMMOND & CO., N.Y
Temple
Altar
A-Holy of Holies
B-Holy Place
C-Porch
D-Side Chambers
Sea of Bronze
Solomon's Palace
Harem
Throne Porch
Porch of Pillars
House of Lebanon
JERUSALEM UNDER NEHEMIAH
c. 445 B. C.
Copyright by C. S. HAMMOND & CO., N. Y.
Scale of Feet
0 500 1000 1500
Old City of David
Probable extent of Solomon's City
New Quarter (Mishneh) added under succeeding kings
Tower of Hananeel
Tower of Meah
Miphkad (Muster) Gate
Chamber of the Corner
Fish Gate
Sheep Gate
East Gate
MISHNEH
Mishneh Gate
Altar
Temple
Throne of the Governor
High House of the King
Horse Gate
Tower of the Furnaces
Corner Gate
BROAD WALL
Ephraim Gate
Projecting Tower
OPHEL
Ophel Tower
SOUTHWEST RIDGE
House of the Mighty Men
OLD CITY OF DAVID
Water Gate
Valley of the Kidron
The location of walls and gates of Biblical Jerusalem are often in doubt due to the lack of strong archaeological and historical evidence. The map shows the city according to the theory which includes the southwest ridge in the city of both Solomon and Nehemiah. Some scholars dispute this and limit the western expansion to the area enclosed by the dashed line.
Sepulchres of David
Hezekiah's Aqueduct
Stairs to the City of David
Dedication tour of the rebuilt walls.
Valley Gate
Fountain Gate
Nehemiah's nocturnal inspection
King's Garden
Dung Gate
Valley of Hinnom

GREAT EMPIRES OF THE SIXTH CENTURY B. C.
Copyright by C. S. HAMMOND & CO., N. Y.
Scale of Miles
0 100 200 300 400 500
Capitals
Limits of the Persian Empire c. 500 B.C.
Persian Royal Road
Red Sea-Nile Canal Built by Darius I
Darius I extended the Persian Empire into Europe. Attempts to subjugate Greece by Darius and Xerxes I failed as the Greeks won at Marathon and Salamis.
The Persians under Cyrus the Great overthrew the Medes, conquered Lydia and Babylonia to fulfill the prophecy of Daniel.
Pharaoh Necho defeated Josiah of Judah but was later driven out of Palestine after being defeated by Nebuchadnezzar at Carchemish (605 B. C.).
The rise of the New Babylonian (Chaldaean) Empire brought an end to the Kingdom of Judah and exile of her people.
The Edict of Cyrus (538 B.C.) allowed the Jews to return to their homeland.
Egypt came under Persian rule after Cambyses defeated Psamtik III at Pelusium in 525 B. C.
Scythians
Massagetae
Sakas (Scythians)
ILLYRIA
EPIRUS
MACEDONIA
THRACE
GREECE
Thermopylae
Marathon
Athens
SALAMIS
Sparta
CRETE
RHODES
LYCIA
Miletus
Ephesus
Sardis
PISIDIA
KINGDOM OF LYDIA (670-546 B.C.)
Byzantium
Chalcedon
BITHYNIA
PAPHLAGONIA
Sinope
Apollonia
Olbia
Chersonesus
Panticapaeum
Black Sea (Pontus Euxinus)
Phasis
COLCHIS
Trapezus
Pteria
Ancyra
CAPPADOCIA
Halys R.
ARMENIA
MEDIAN EMPIRE (625-550 B.C.)
CILICIA
Tarsus
Carchemish
Haran
ASSYRIA
Thapsacus
Tadmor
NEW BABYLONIAN EMPIRE (625-539 B.C.)
CYPRUS
Mediterranean Sea
Arvad
Byblos
Sidon
Tyre
Damascus
Megiddo
Jerusalem
JUDAH
Gaza
ARABIA
Cyrene
Barca
Libyans
Naucratis
Sais
Pelusium
Tahpanhes
On
Memphis (Noph)
Ammonium
KINGDOM OF EGYPT (26th DYNASTY 663-525 B.C.)
Thebes (No)
Pathros
Syene (Elephantine I.)
Nile River
ETHIOPIA (CUSH)
Red Sea
Elath
Mt. Sinai
Arbela
Tigris R.
Ecbatana (Achmetha)
Behistun
Cadusii
Amardi
Rhagae
Sippar
Cois
Babylon
Nippur
Erech
ELAM (SUSIANA)
Susa (Shushan)
Aspadana
Caspian Sea (Mare Hyrcanium)
HYRCANIA
Dahae
Aral Sea
Jaxartes R.
CHORASMIA
MARGIANA
Bagae
Oxus R.
Maracanda (Samarkand)
SOGDIANA
Bactra
BACTRIA
PARTHIA
ARIA
PERSIAN EMPIRE
Sagartians
DRANGIANA
Sarangians
ARACHOSIA
Pactyans
Taxila
GANDARA
INDIA
Pasargadae
Persepolis
PERSIS
Persian Gulf
CARMANIA
Utians
Paricanians
GEDROSIA (MAKA)
Pattala
Present shoreline
Arabian Sea
A B C D E F G
1 2 3

PALESTINE IN THE TIME OF CHRIST
Copyright by C. S. HAMMOND & CO., N. Y.
Scale of Miles
0 5 10 20 30 40
Perennial Rivers
Capitals
Seasonal Rivers & Streams
Roads & Trade Routes
Tetrarchy of Lysanias
Areas tributary to Salome
Tetrarchy of Philip
Decapolis*
Tetrarchy of Herod Antipas
Independent*
Territory under Roman procurator
Roman province of Syria
Cities of the Decapolis
* The Decapolis and Ascalon retained their independence under the Roman governor of the province of Syria.
The Great Sea
(Mediterranean Sea)
Residence of Roman procurators.
Archelaus, upon Herod's death, became ruler of Judaea, Samaria and Idumaea. His reign lasted until 6 A. D. when he was removed and exiled. His territory then was placed under a Roman procurator.
Salome, Herod's sister, was given Jamnia, Azotus and Phasaelis. They, in turn, passed to Livia, wife of Augustus and then to Emperor Tiberius.
Horns of Hattin (Kurûn Hattin) is a possible site of the Sermon on the Mount.
The Dead Sea Scrolls were found in a cave here; also the ruins of an Essene monastery.
Here John the Baptist was imprisoned and beheaded by order of Herod Antipas.
PHOENICIA
SYRIA
ITURAEA
ABILENE
MOUNT LEBANON
MT. HERMON
PANIAS
ULATHA
TRACHONITIS
GAULANITIS
BATANAEA
BASHAN
AURANITIS
GALILEE
SAMARIA
DECAPOLIS
GILEAD
PERAEA
JUDAEA
IDUMAEA
AMMON
NABATAEA
ARABIA
NABATAEANS
Abila
Damascus
Sidon
Sarepta (Zarephath)
Tyre
Dan
Caesarea Philippi
Ladder of Tyre
Cadasa (Kedesh)
Lake Semechonitis
Gischala
Seleucia
Raphana
Ptolemais (Accho)
Chorazin
Bethsaida (Julias)
Capernaum
Magdala (Dalmanutha)
Tabigha
Jotapata
Cana
Horns of Hattin
Gergesa
Gamala
Sea of Galilee
Tiberias
MT. CARMEL
Sepphoris
Hippos
Dion
Nazareth
Philoteria
Yarmuk R.
Mt. Tabor
Abila
Plain of Esdraelon
Gadara
Dora
Nain
Capitolias
Edrei
Bethabara
Caesarea
En-gannim (Ginaea)
Scythopolis (Beth-shan)
Pella
Plain of Sharon
Jordan River
Samaria (Sebaste)
Mt. Ebal
Gerasa
Apollonia
Shechem
Sychar
Jacob's Well
Mt. Gerizim
Amathus
Jabbok R.
Antipatris
Joppa
Arimathaea (Ramathaim)
Phasaelis
Lydda (Diospolis)
Gophna
Archelais
Bethel
Ephraim
Beth-nimrah
Philadelphia (Rabbath-ammon)
Jamnia
Gezer (Gazara)
Ramah
Jericho
Ekron
Nicopolis (Emmaus)
Emmaus
Mt. of Olives
Julias (Livias, Beth-haram)
Heshbon
Jerusalem
Khirbet Qumran
Bethany
Azotus (Ashdod)
Bethlehem
Herodium
Ascalon
Wilderness of Judah
Callirhoe
Mareshah (Marisa)
Machaerus
Hebron
Gaza
Dibon
Ziph
Juttah
En-gedi
Dead Sea
Salt Sea
(L. Asphaltitis)
Gerar
Carmel
Masada
Raphia
Rabbath Moab (Areopolis, Rabba)
Beersheba
Kir-moab (Kir-hareseth)
A B C D E
1 2 3 4 5 6 7